Lloyd's Register of Ships

2014-2015

S-Z

LLOYD'S REGISTER
FOUNDED 1760

Lloyd's Register of Ships

2014-2015

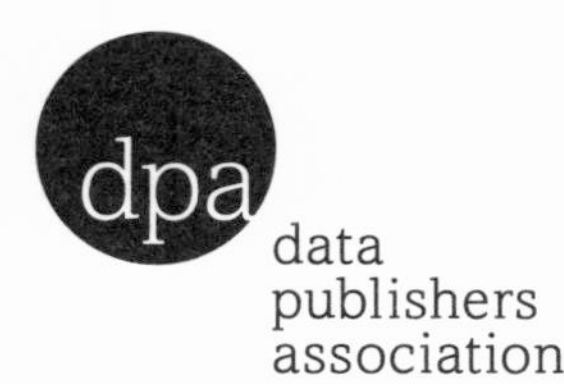

Enquiries should be addressed to:
IHS
Customer Care
Willoughby Road
Bracknell
RG12 8FB
United Kingdom
Telephone: +44 (0)1344 328300
Fax: +44 (0)1344 328005
Email: customer.support@ihs.com
Website: www.ihs.com

Published by:
IHS Maritime
Sentinel House
163 Brighton Road
Coulsdon
Surrey
CR5 2YH
United Kingdom
Telephone: +44 (0)20 3253 2100
Fax: +44 (0)20 3253 2103

Printed by:
Polestar Wheatons Ltd
Hennock Road
Marsh Barton
Exeter
Devon
EX2 8RP
United Kingdom

ISBN 978-1-906313-76-0

British Library
Cataloguing-in-Publication Data.
A catalogue record for this book is available from the British Library.

Foreword

First published in 1764, Lloyd's Register of Ships continues to be the authoritative source of information on the world fleet. Listing all self-propelled, sea-going merchant ships of 100 GT and above, the 2014-2015 edition contains details of over 107,000 ships.

Lloyd's Register of Ships includes a Shipbuilder and Existing Ships Index, which can be located in the fifth volume.

The information published in the Register has been obtained from sources believed to be reliable, but IHS Maritime is unable to guarantee the accuracy of the details. To obtain up-to-date information please be sure to consult Shipfinder Online, our web based update service designed to provide subscribers with the very latest information on key fields.

CONTENTS

Notes

Alphabetical order of ships

Ships' names commencing with an abbreviation of a word (e.g. DR – DOCTOR, ST – SAINT) are listed in strict alphabetical order immediately before other ships whose names commence with the letters DRA or STA respectively.

Ships' names commencing with a Roman numeral are listed under the letter of the numeral e.g. XXX Aniversario appears under letter X.

The registered Ship Name is recorded to existing IHS Maritime publishing guidelines for sort order purposes. However, certain certificates and other sources include the use of prefix of "M/Y", "M.T.", "M.V." or similar before the actual ship name and these are not recorded.

Deletion of ships

IHS Maritime reserves the right to delete a ship's entry from Lloyd's Register of Ships on sufficient grounds that no supporting evidence is available to substantiate the accuracy and continued existence of that entry. Such measures are only undertaken following exhaustive enquiries to authoritative sources.

Key to the Lloyd's Register of Ships 2014-15

1 Registration

LR/IMO NUMBER

A unique seven digit number printed in **bold type** which is used for data processing purposes, and which remains unchanged during the life of the ship.

The IMO (International Maritime Organization) identification number was adopted on 19th November 1987 in IMO Resolution A.600(15) and remains constant in the event of rebuilding or shiptype conversion. This unique number is assigned to the total or greater portion of the hull enclosing the machinery space and is the determining factor should additional hull sections be added. The LR/IMO Number is never reassigned to another vessel. This number is also utilised in respect of SOLAS XI 1/3 and 1/5.

IHS Maritime is the sole authority for identifying and assigning an LR/IMO number.

IMO Resolution A.600(15)

IMO Resolution A.600(15) applies to seagoing ships of 100 Gross Tonnage and above, with the exception of the following:-

- Vessels solely engaged in fishing;
- Ships without mechanical means of propulsion;
- Pleasure yachts;
- Ships engaged on special service (e.g. lightships, floating radio stations, search & rescue vessels);
- Hopper barges;
- Hydrofoils, hovercraft;
- Floating docks and structures classified in a similar manner;
- Ships of war and troop ships;
- Wooden ships in general.

CALL SIGN

Signal letters or radio call sign assigned by the relevant national authority. This is shown in italics. A dash (-) will be displayed where confirmation is awaited.

FISHING NUMBER

The identification number assigned by the relevant national authority to ships engaged in the fishing industry. The number is displayed, on the vessel's hull, for permanent identification.

A dash (-) will be displayed for ships other than fishing vessels or where the information is awaiting confirmation.

2 Names and owners

SHIP'S NAME

The current ship's name is displayed in **bold type**. Ships are listed in the Register in alphabetical order and are subject to IHS Maritime internal name style punctuation, with numeric entries appearing after the end of the letter 'Z'.

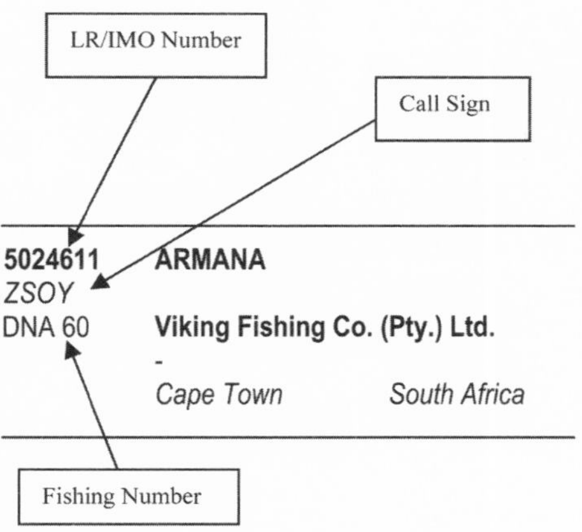

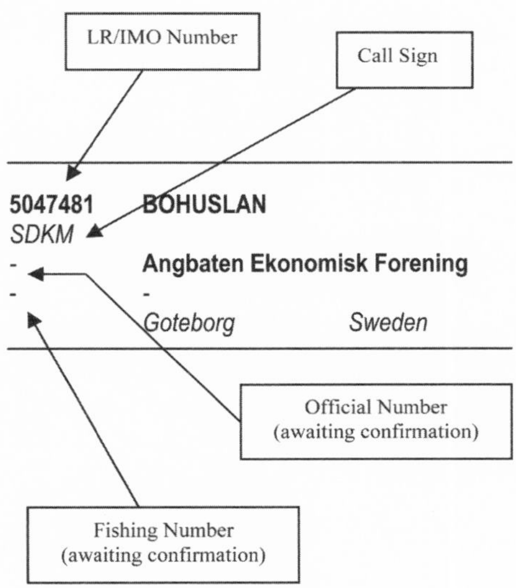

Radio Communications & Safety of Navigation

Subscribers seeking information should in the first instance refer to SOLAS chapters IV and V. Chapter IV was revised in 1988 to incorporate amendments to introduce the Global Maritime Distress and Safety System (GMDSS) and details requirements for all passenger ships and all cargo ships of 300GT and upwards engaged on international voyages to carry equipment such as Satellite Emergency Positioning Indicating Radio Beacons (EPIRBs) and Search and Rescue Transponders (SARTs).

Chapter V references, inter alia, the carriage of Voyage Data Recorders (VDRs) and Automatic Ship Identification Systems (AIS) for certain ships.

FORMER NAMES

The figures following the former name of a ship indicate the year, where known, in which the change of name occurred and are listed in chronological order. The year of change is displayed in italics and is preceded by a dash (-).

(In the absence of date changes being advised, an estimated date has been included). Entries where no date is published denotes unknown date of name change.

Where a name changes prior to the ship being commissioned, a 'Launched as' or 'Completed as' entry will be displayed.

OWNERS

The registered owners are recorded in **bold type**. The underlined letter in each owner's name indicates the sort letter under which the entry appears in the List of Shipowners. A dash (-) will be displayed where confirmation of registered owners is awaited.

This field represents the legal owner of the ship and the name that appears on the ship's papers. It may be an owner/manager or a wholly-owned subsidiary in a larger shipping group or a company created on paper to legally own a ship or ships and limit liability for the real owners. This may be a legal requirement of the flag state with which it is registered.

MANAGERS

The managers are recorded in normal type. The underlined letter in each manager's name indicates the letter under which the entry appears in the **List of Shipowners**.

A dash (-) will be displayed where confirmation of the manager is awaited or is not applicable.

The company is responsible for the commercial decisions concerning the operation of a ship.

PORT OF REGISTRY

The port of registry shown is that which is displayed on the ship and is published in italics.

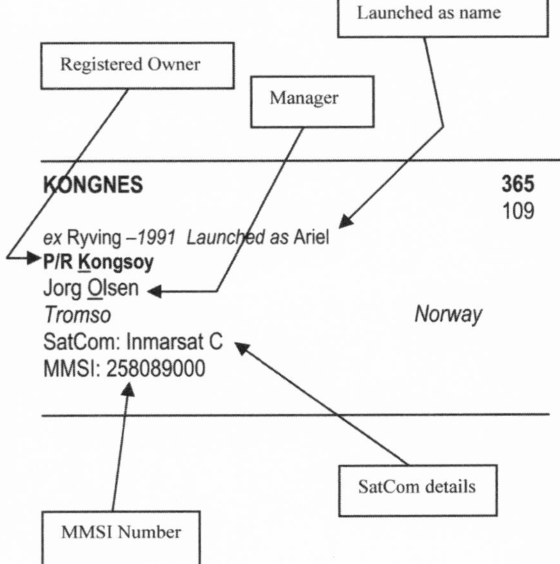

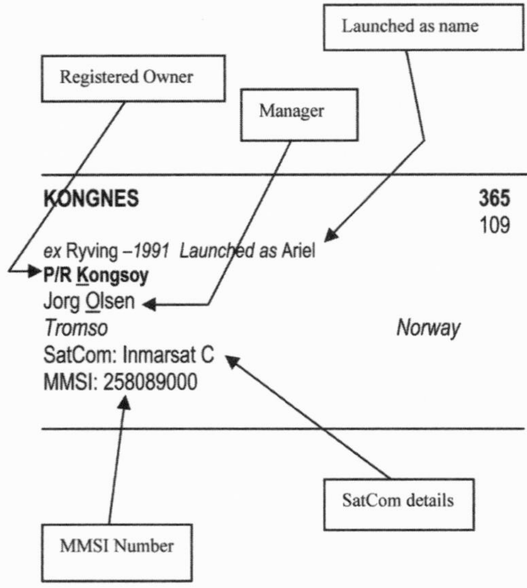

FLAG

This indicates the flag registry under which the ship normally operates and is displayed in italics.

A considerable number of ships now operate under Parallel Registry, which can result in confused identification of a ship. IHS policy is to publish the Registry (flag and port), following verification, which is painted on the ship's stern.

SATELLITE COMMUNICATION DATA

Details of the service provider and the types of receiver are listed. The various types are as follows:-

- Inmarsat-A (Analogue system, supports voice, telex, fax and data)
- Inmarsat-B (Digital system, supports voice, fax, data & telex)
- Inmarsat-M (Digital system, capable of voice, fax & data)
- Inmarsat-Mini-M (Digital system, supports voice, fax, data and email)
- Inmarsat-C (Store & forward data, telex system)

MMSI NUMBER

The Maritime Mobile Service Identity (MMSI) is displayed where known. These identifiers are supplied by National Authorities under the auspices of the International Telecommunications Union (ITU), which is based in Geneva.

The ITU is an international organisation within the United Nations System, where governments and the private sector co-ordinate global telecommunication networks and services.
(web site address www.itu.org)

Each number is unique and used to identify an individual vessel (or shore-based) radio installation. It is used within GMDSS as a vessel code.

OFFICIAL NUMBER

The identification number assigned by the national registration authority.

3 Tonnage

GROSS TONNAGE

The Gross Tonnage printed in **bold type** indicates that the ship has been measured in accordance with the requirements of the 1969 International Convention on Tonnage Measurement of Ships. The Gross Tonnage generally comprises the moulded volume of all enclosed spaces of the ship, to which a formula is then applied in accordance with the Convention requirements. Accordingly, no unit of measurement is assigned and the figure attained is simply referred to as the ship's "Gross Tonnage" (GT). A dash (-) will be displayed where confirmation of the gross tonnage is awaited.

The Gross Tonnage printed in italic type indicates that the ship has been measured in accordance with tonnage regulations adopted prior to the 18th July 1982, when the 1969 Convention came into force. This tonnage is referred to as "Gross Registered Tonnage" (GRT).

NET TONNAGE

The Net Tonnage in normal ship types is derived in accordance with the requirements of the 1969 International Convention on Tonnage Measurement of Ships. The Net Tonnage generally comprises the moulded volume of all cargo spaces on board, to which a formula is then applied in accordance with the Convention requirements. The formula for Net Tonnage also takes account of the varying factors such as ships depth, draught, number of passengers but notwithstanding the above, will never be less than GT x 0.3. Accordingly, no unit of measurement is assigned and the figure attained is simply referred to as the ship's "Net Tonnage" (NT).

The Net Tonnage printed in italic type indicates that the ship has been measured in accordance with tonnage regulations adopted prior to the 18th July 1982, when the 1969 Convention came into force. This tonnage is referred to as "Net Registered Tonnage" (NRT).

The Net Registered Tonnage is derived by deducting spaces used for the accommodation of the master, officers, crew, navigation, and propelling machinery.

A dash (-) will be displayed where confirmation of the net tonnage is awaited.

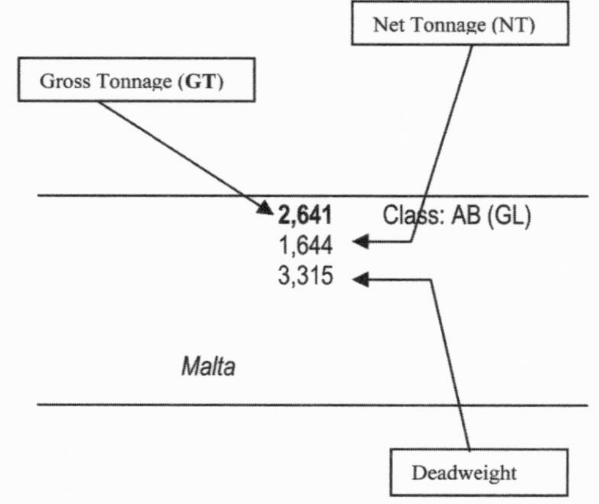

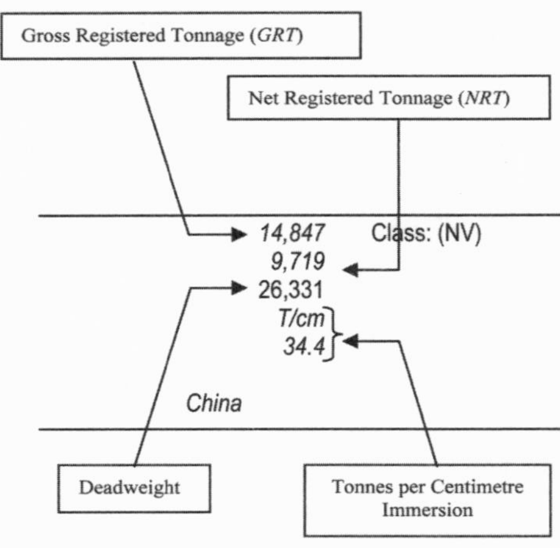

DEADWEIGHT

The Deadweight is the weight in tonnes (1,000 kg) of cargo, stores, fuel, passengers and crew carried by the ship when loaded to the maximum summer loadline. In the case of vessels with more than 1 load line measurement, IHS Maritime record the higher deadweight and corresponding draught only.
A dash (-) will be displayed where confirmation of the deadweight is awaited.

TONNES PER CENTIMETRE IMMERSION

The Tonnes per Centimetre Immersion (T/cm), displayed in italic type, is the weight in tonnes (1,000 kg) required to immerse the hull of the ship by one centimetre at a particular draught. The value shown is that corresponding to the maximum summer draught.

4 Classification

GENERAL CLASS DETAILS

If a ship is currently classed, the initial letters of the Society are recorded. In the event that a ship is disclassed the initial letters of the Society will be recorded in parentheses. Previous class history is recorded in sequence order.

Where a ship has applied for class which has not been confirmed '(Class Contemplated)' will be displayed immediately after the initials of the Society.

LLOYD'S REGISTER – CLASS SYMBOLS (HULL & EQUIPMENT)

In the event that a ship is currently classed with Lloyd's Register (LR) then the following hull and equipment symbols may be displayed.

The Maltese Cross denotes that the ship was constructed under LR's Special Survey in compliance with their Rules. This will be displayed in **bold** if applicable.

100 This character figure is assigned to ships considered suitable for sea-going service. This will be displayed in bold if applicable. (Prior to 1948 this figure was not included in the class notation of ships intended for limited sea-going service.

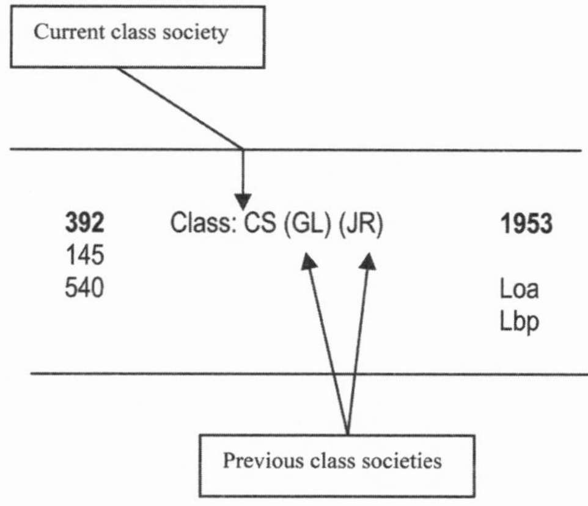

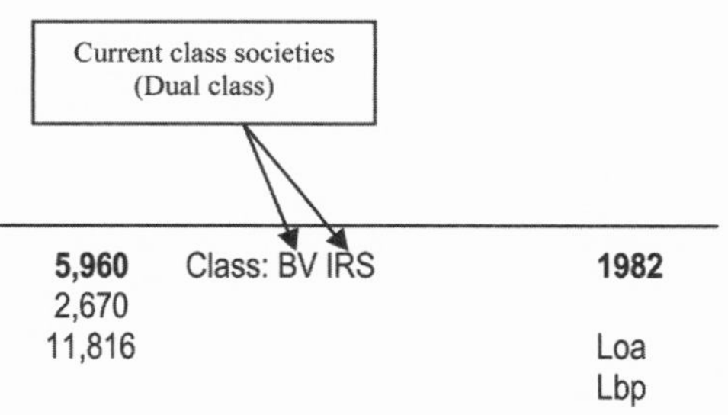

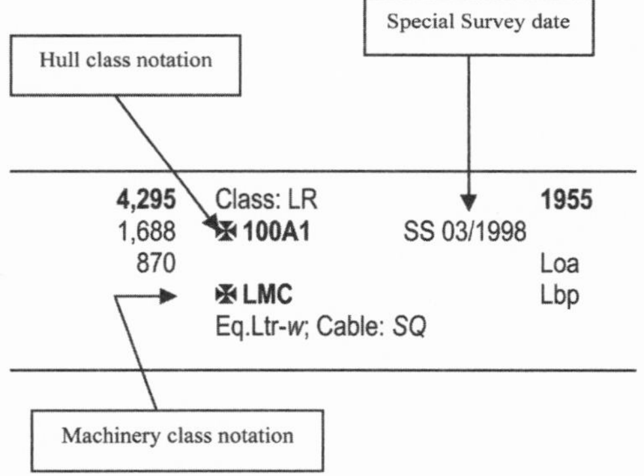

A The character letter is assigned to ships which have been constructed or accepted into class in accordance with LR's Rules and Regulations and which are maintained in good and efficient condition. This will be displayed in **bold** if applicable.

1 This character figure is assigned to:-
(a) Ships having on board, in good and efficient condition, anchoring and/or mooring equipment in accordance with the Rules.
(b) Ships classed for special service, for which no specific anchoring and mooring Rules have been published, having on board, in good and efficient condition, anchoring and/or mooring equipment considered suitable and sufficient by LR for the particular service.
This will be displayed in **bold** if applicable.

- This character symbol, in the position usually occupied by the figure 1, is assigned to ships when the anchoring and mooring equipment is not in accordance with the requirements of the Rules, but is considered to be acceptable for the particular service. This symbol is no longer assigned.

N This character letter is assigned to ships on which anchoring and mooring equipment need not be fitted in view of their particular service. This will be displayed in **bold** if applicable.

T This character letter is assigned to ships which are intended to perform their primary designed service function only while they are anchored, moored, towed or linked and which have in good and efficient condition, adequately attached anchoring, mooring, towing or linking equipment which has been approved as suitable and sufficient for the intended service. This will be displayed in **bold** if applicable.

OU/OI These character letters are assigned to offshore units classed with LR and can be assigned to self-propelled or non-propelled offshore units other than ships. This will be displayed in **bold** if applicable.

* Denotes that the ship was built under the supervision of the surveyors in accordance with the Rules of the British Corporation (BS).

BS Denotes that the hull and equipment of iron and steel ships classed in accordance to British Corporation Rules.

LLOYD'S REGISTER – CLASS NOTATIONS (SERVICE RESTRICTIONS)

Service restriction notations will generally be assigned in one of the following forms but this does not preclude special consideration for other forms in unusual cases.

Protected Waters Service – Service in sheltered water adjacent to sand banks, reefs, breakwaters or other coastal features, and in sheltered water between islands.

Extended Protected Waters Service – Service in protected waters and also for distances (generally less than 15 nautical miles) beyond protected waters in reasonable weather. Reasonable weather is defined as Wind strengths of force 6 or less in the Beaufort scale, associated with sea states sufficiently moderate to ensure that green water is taken on board the ship's deck at infrequent intervals only or not at all.

Service restriction notation

205 Class: LR (IRS) 1956
61 **100A1** SS08/2000
292 coastal service west coast of Africa extending from Namibia to Sierra Leone including Nigeria. Loa Lbp
LMC
Eq.Ltr-*(c)*

Machinery class notation

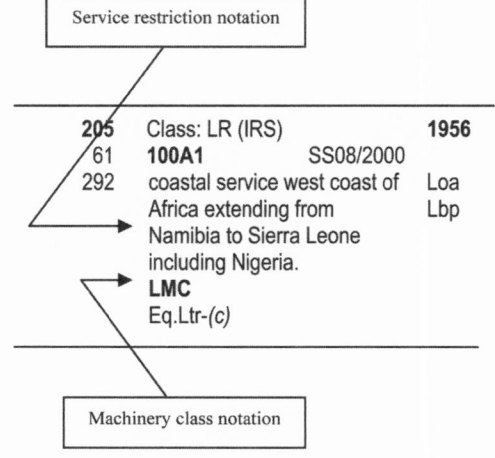

'Fetch', 'sheltered water' and 'reasonable weather' are defined in LR's Rules and Regulations

Specified Coastal Service – Service along a coast, and for a distance out to sea not exceeding 21 nautical miles, unless some other distance is specified for "coastal service" by the Administration with which the ship is registered, or by the Administration of the coast off which it is operating, as applicable.

Specified Route Service – This notation means that the ship is intended for service between two or more ports, or other geographical features which are indicated.

Specified Operating Area Service – This notation means that the ship is intended for service within one or more geographical areas as indicated.

Short International Voyage – This expression means an international voyage in the course of which a ship is not more than 200 nautical miles from a port or place in which the passengers and crew could be placed in safety, and which does not exceed 600 nautical miles in length between the last port of call in the country in which the voyage begins and the final port of destination. This notation is no longer assigned.

LLOYD'S REGISTER – CLASS NOTATIONS (HULL STRENGTHENING)

Heavy Cargoes – When the scantlings and arrangements have been approved for the carriage of such cargoes a class notation 'Strengthened for heavy cargoes' is assigned.

As from January 1978 this notation is assigned to general cargo ships and bulk carriers, where applicable, but in the case of ore or oil carriers the class notation 'ore carrier' or 'ore or oil carrier' will be assigned.

'Strengthened for regular discharge by heavy grabs' is assigned at the owner's option where cargoes are regularly discharged by heavy grabs, and the thickness of the plating of the hold inner bottom, hopper and tranverse bulkhead bottom stool is increased in accordance with the requirements of the Rules.

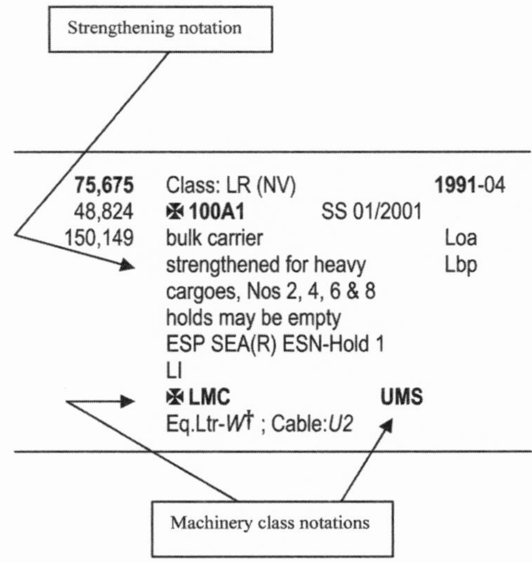

Ice Strengthening – Ice classification notations and degrees of strengthening for navigation in ice are displayed within the class notation. Where a ship was previously assigned ice classification by the British Corporation this will be displayed as 'Ice strengthening'.

The abbreviations and their descriptions can be found in the section 'Abbreviations used in the Register'

LLOYD'S REGISTER – SHIPRIGHT NOTATION

Structural Design Assessment (SDA), Fatigue Design Assessment (FDA) and Construction Monitoring (CM) are notations assigned where a ship complies with the procedure for the Design, Construction and Lifetime Care of Ships.

The abbreviations and their descriptions can be found in the section 'Abbreviations used in the Register'

LLOYD'S REGISTER – CLASS NOTATIONS (SPECIAL SURVEYS)

SS-with date	Special Survey of the hull.
CS-with date	Continuous Survey of the hull
Lake SS	Periodical Survey of ship classed for Great Lakes service.

LLOYD'S REGISTER – CLASS NOTATIONS (MACHINERY)

¸LMC Notation assigned when the propelling and essential auxiliary machinery has been constructed, installed and tested under LR's Special Survey and in accordance with the requirements of the Rules.

¯LMC Notation assigned when the propelling and essential auxiliary machinery has been constructed under the survey of a recognised authority in accordance with the Rules and Regulations equivalent to those of LR and, in addition, the whole of the machinery has been installed and tested under LR's Special Survey in accordance with LR's Rules.

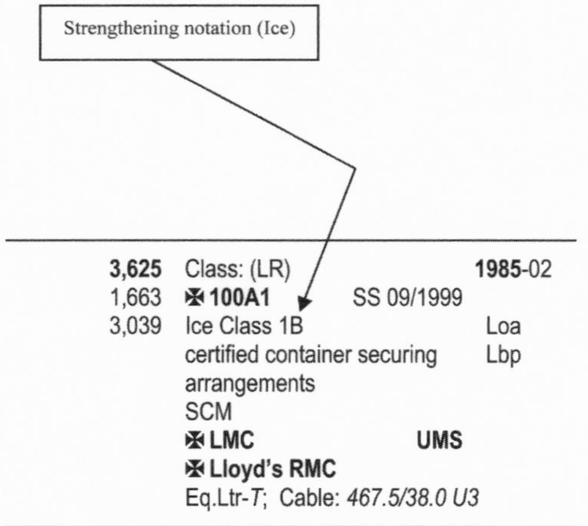

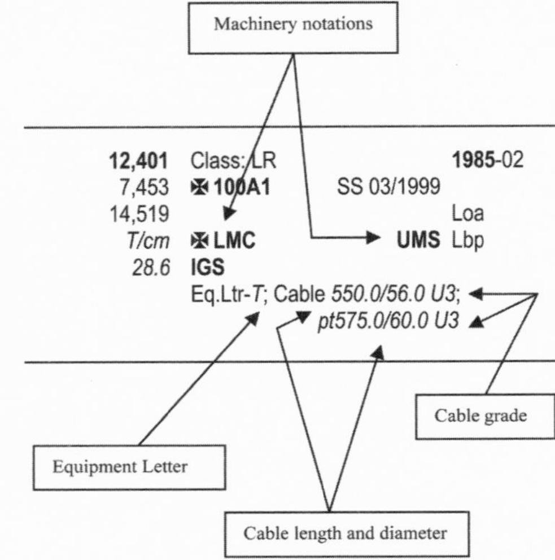

LMC Notation assigned when the propelling and essential auxiliary machinery has neither been constructed nor installed under LR's Special Survey but the existing machinery, its installation and arrangement, have been tested and found to be acceptable by LR.

¸OMC Notation

OMC MBS* Denotes that the machinery was built and installed under the supervision of the surveyors to the Rules of the British Corporation or of LR respectively.

UMS This notation may be assigned to a ship classed with LR which can be operated with the machinery spaces unattended and that the control equipment has been arranged, installed and tested in accordance with LR's Rules.

CCS This notation may be assigned to a ship classed with LR which can be operated with the machinery spaces under continuous supervision from a centralised control station and that the control engineering equipment has been arranged, installed and tested in accordance with LR's Rules.

¸Lloyd's RMC Denotes that the refrigerated cargo installation of a ship classed with LR and has been constructed, installed and tested under LR's Special Survey in accordance with the relevant requirements of the Rules.

Lloyd's RMC Denotes that the refrigerated cargo installation of a ship is classed with LR and that the installation has been found to be equivalent to the requirements of the Rules and has been tested in accordance with the relevant requirements of the Rules.

¸Lloyd's RMC (LG) This notation is assigned to a liquefied gas carrier or tanker classed with LR in which reliquefaction or refrigeration equipment is approved and fitted for cargo temperature and pressure control, where the equipment has been constructed, installed and tested in accordance with the relevant requirements of the Rules.

Lloyd's RMC (LG) This notation is assigned to a liquefied gas carrier or tanker classed with LR in which reliquefaction or refrigeration equipment is fitted for cargo temperature and pressure control, where the equipment has been found to be equivalent to the requirements of the Rules and tested in accordance with the relevant requirements of the Rules.

IGS This notation will be assigned to a ship classed with LR when the ships is intended for the carriage of oil in bulk, or for the carriage of liquid chemicals in bulk and is fitted with an approved system for producing gas and for inerting the cargo tanks in accordance with the requirements of LR's Rules.

In all instances where the notation is shown in parentheses it denotes that the class has been temporarily suspended

LLOYD'S REGISTER – CLASS NOTATIONS (EQUIPMENT LETTER, CABLE DETAILS)

The Equipment Letter (A, A†, B*, etc.), determined by LR's Rules, is displayed in italics prefixed by 'Eq.Ltr'. This is followed by the length (metres) and diameter (millimetres) of the chain cable, prefixed by 'Cable' and then the grade of chain cable. The dimensions and grade of cable are also displayed in italics. If the chain cable is made up of more than one part the dimension sets are displayed with a 'pt' separator.

When shown in parentheses the Equipment Letter denotes that the actual equipment number permitted by the Rules differs from the calculated equipment number.

The character symbols U1, U2, U3 and U4 denote the grades of chain cable (other than wrought iron or mild steel fire-welded) as defined in LR's Rules.

LLOYD'S REGISTER – CLASS WITHDRAWAL

When a ship becomes disclassed, either at owner's request or withdrawn by LR, the general class field will display LR in parentheses. All LR class related details will be deleted and in their place the notation '¸Classed LR until –date' or 'Classed LR until –date' will be displayed.

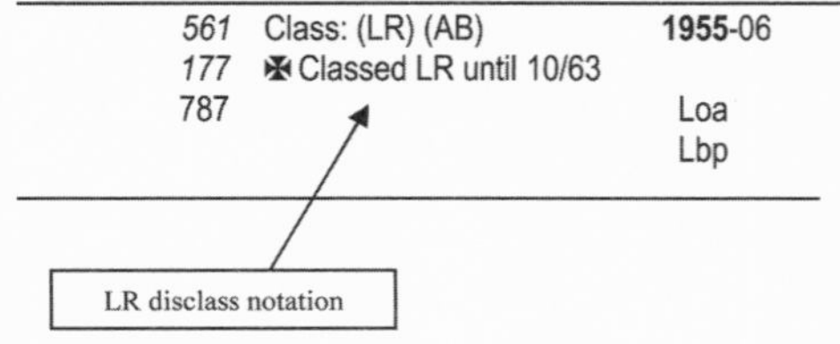

5 Hull

DATE OF BUILD

The date of build is displayed in **bold** and reflects the actual completion date or an estimate in the absence of confirmed data.

(In the absence of date changes being advised, an estimated date has been included).

In the event that there has been a significant interval between the launching and the completion and/or commissioning of the ship, dates may be recorded in parentheses after the shipbuilder prefixed by one of the following; 'launched', 'completed', 'commissioned', 'lengthened & completed', 'reassembled' 're-erected', ' assembled' or 're-built'.

SHIPBUILDER

The shipbuilder and place of build are displayed in bold type after the date of build. The underlined letter in each shipbuilder's name indicates the sort letter under which the entry appears in the Shipbuilder and Existing Ships Index. This normally records where the hull of the ship was built. Where a ship has major hull sections constructed by other builders, the date of build, shipbuilder and place of build, hull section, construction date detail and yard number are recorded.

IACS Procedural Requirements 1996 – No.11
It should be noted that where modifications, possibly extensive, have been carried out, the original 'Date of Build' shall remain assigned to the ship. Where a complete replacement or addition of a major portion of the ship (e.g. forward section, after section, main cargo section) is involved then the 'Date of Build' associated with each major portion of the ship shall be indicated.

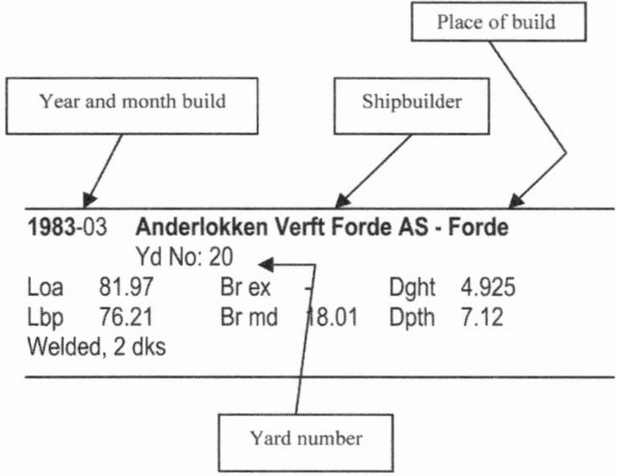

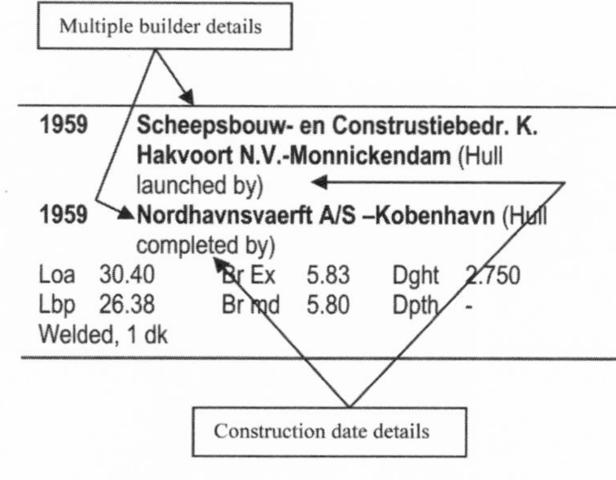

When the shipbuilder is unknown '…' is displayed. In the event that only the place, region or country is known this will be displayed prefixed by either 'in', 'at' or 'on'.

YARD NUMBER

The shipbuilder's number, known as yard or hull number, is displayed for the hull section, prefixed by 'Yd No:'. Where construction may involve more than one hull section or builder each shipbuilder's number is recorded.

CONVERSIONS

Details of ship conversions are recorded, listing the previous shiptype and date, prefixed by 'Converted from:'. Where a ship has been converted more than once the conversions will be recorded in reverse chronological order.

(In the absence of date changes being advised, an estimated date has been included).

ALTERATIONS

Details of alterations (lengthened etc.) are recorded, listing the type of alteration and date. Where more than one alteration takes place at the same time these will be grouped together.

(In the absence of date changes being advised, an estimated date has been included).

LENGTH OVERALL / REGISTERED LENGTH

The extreme length of the ship, recorded in metres to two decimal places, is displayed, prefixed by 'Loa'. A dash (-) will be displayed where confirmation of the length overall is awaited. Where the length overall is followed by the notation 'BB' this indicates that the ship has a bulbous bow. In these instance the recorded measurement includes any protrusion of that bow.

If the length overall is not available, the registered length, as given on the ship's certificates, may be recorded, prefixed by 'L reg'.

LENGTH BETWEEN PERPENDICULARS

The length between perpendiculars, recorded in metres to two decimal places, is displayed, prefixed by 'Lbp'. A dash (-) will be displayed where confirmation of the length between perpendiculars is awaited. This is the distance on the summer load waterline from the fore side of the stem to the after side of the rudder post, or to the centre of the rudder stock if there is no rudder post.

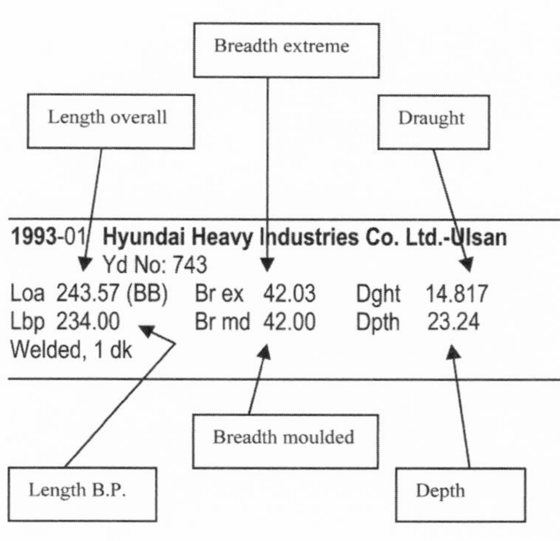

EXTREME BREADTH

The extreme breadth, recorded in metres to two decimal places, is displayed, prefixed by 'Br ex'. A dash (-) will be displayed where confirmation of the extreme breadth is awaited. This is the maximum breadth to the outside of the ship's structure.

MOULDED BREADTH

The moulded breadth, recorded in metres to two decimal places, is displayed, prefixed by 'Br md'. A dash (-) will be displayed where confirmation of the moulded breadth is awaited. This is the greatest breadth at amidships from heel of frame to heel of frame.

MAXIMUM DRAUGHT

The maximum draught, recorded in metres to three decimal places, is displayed, prefixed by 'Dght'. A dash (-) will be displayed where confirmation of the maximum draught is awaited. In most cases this is the maximum draught amidships, but in some ships of special construction the maximum draught is measured at the deepest point of the hull or any fixed appendages, and this measurement is recorded, where defined.

MOULDED DEPTH

The moulded depth, recorded in metres to two decimal places, is displayed, prefixed by 'Dpth'. A dash (-) will be displayed where confirmation of the moulded depth is awaited. This is the vertical distance at amidships from the top of the keel to the top of the upper deck beam at side.

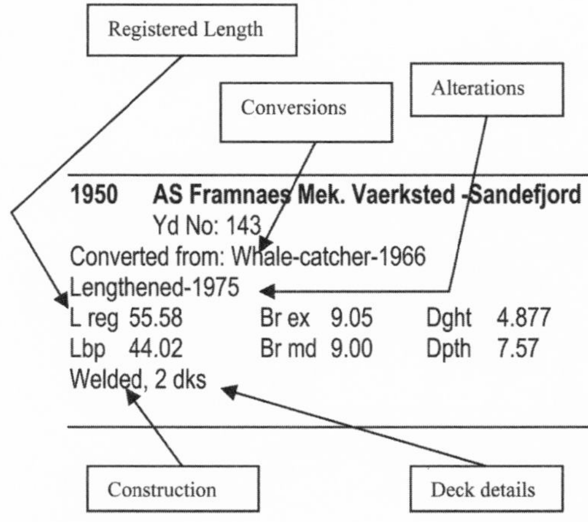

CONSTRUCTION
The construction of the ship is displayed and is recorded as one of the following:-

Welded
Riveted
Riveted/Welded
Bonded

DECKS
Details on the number and type of decks are displayed after the construction information.

The abbreviations and their descriptions can be found in the section 'Abbreviations used in the Register'

6 Shiptype/cargo facilities

SHIPTYPE
The description of the ship is displayed in bold type and indicates the basic type of the ship (i.e. tanker, tug, general cargo ship). It should be noted that these are not classification notations.

HULL MATERIAL
Hull material is displayed, prefixed by 'Hull material:', when a ship is constructed from a material other than steel. Unless otherwise stated, ships are of steel construction.

HULL TYPE
Details of specialised hull types are recorded where applicable. For instance 'Triple Hull' 'Split Hull'.

SHIP SUBTYPES
The ship subtypes are displayed, where applicable, and indicate in more detail the known specific function of the ship.

DOUBLE HULL
Where ships have been constructed with double skin sides and double bottoms, the description 'Double Hull' will be displayed. For tankers where it is known that these comply with the requirements of IMO the description 'Double Hull (MARPOL)' will be displayed.

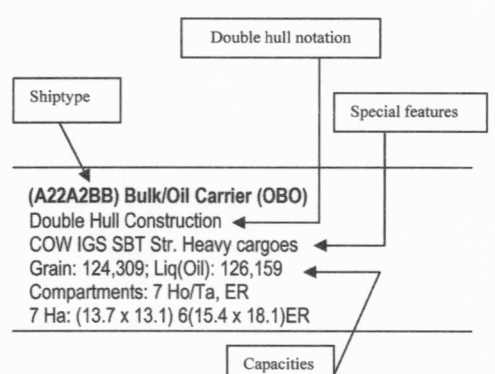

Double hull notation
Shiptype
Special features
(A22A2BB) Bulk/Oil Carrier (OBO)
Double Hull Construction
COW IGS SBT Str. Heavy cargoes
Grain: 124,309; Liq(Oil): 126,159
Compartments: 7 Ho/Ta, ER
7 Ha: (13.7 x 13.1) 6(15.4 x 18.1)ER
Capacities

SPECIAL FEATURES
Special feature notations are displayed for ships with specific shiptype facilities or strengthening. For example 'F-S Ice Rules Notation', 'pt higher tensile steel', 'Str. Heavy cargoes', 'DB' (Double bottom), 'SBT' (Segregated ballast tanks), etc.

In addition Lloyd's Register ShipRight notations are displayed where a ship complies on a voluntary basis with the applicable requirements of the Procedures for the Design, Construction and Lifetime Care of Ships.

The abbreviations and their descriptions can be found in the section 'Abbreviations used in the Register'

PASSENGERS
Details of the number of passengers a ship is licensed to carry are recorded, prefixed by 'Passengers:' and are defined by 'deck', 'unberthed' and 'berths'. Where confirmation of individual categories is awaited the total number of passengers is given.

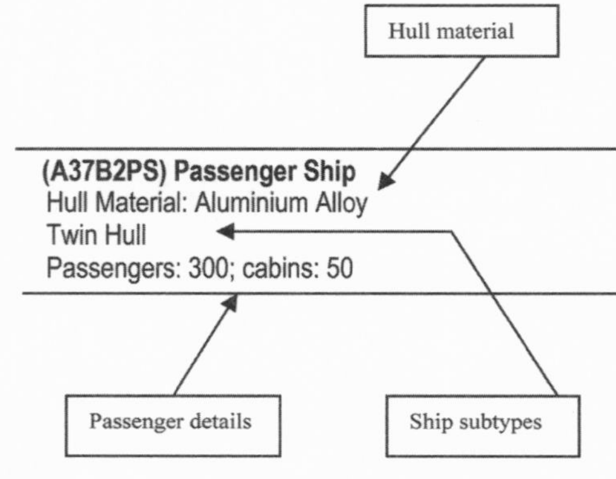

RO/RO FACILITIES
Details of ramps, lanes, vehicle counts are recorded for ships with Ro/Ro facilities.

Ramps – The number and type of ramps, position, length, width and safe working load are displayed where known. The dimensions for length, width and safe working load are prefixed with 'Len', 'Wid' and 'Swl' respectively. In the event that a ship has ramps with different dimensions these will be displayed sequentially.

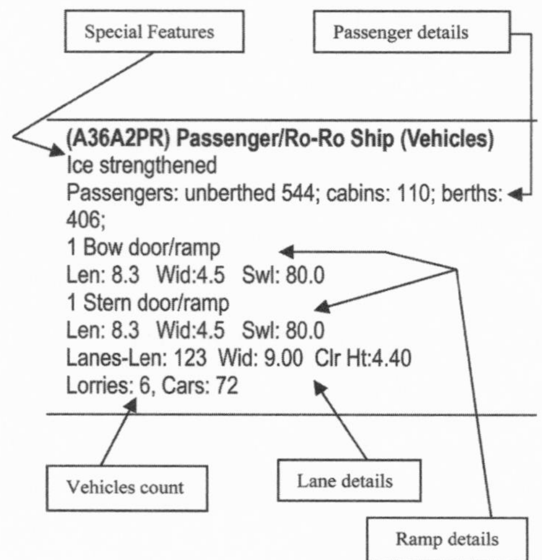

Lanes – The total maximum linear lane length, the maximum width of ro-ro lane and the maximum deck head clearance between adjacent fixed or movable decks are displayed, in metres, where known. The dimensions for length, width and clear height are prefixed with 'Len', 'Wid' and 'Clr Ht' respectively

Vehicle Counts – The details of vehicle counts are displayed, prefixed by the types of vehicle. For example 'Cars', 'Lorries', 'Trailers', 'Rail wagons' etc.

CAPACITIES
Details of cargo capacities are recorded, prefixed by the appropriate types. The key definitions are as follows:-

Grain: The capacity of cargo spaces, measured to outside of frames, to top of ceiling and to top of beams, including hatchways. This does not include insulated spaces or spaces allocated to containers. Grain capacity is measured in cubic metres.

Bale: The capacity of cargo spaces, measure to inside of cargo battens, to top of ceiling and to underside of beams, including hatchways. This does not include spaces allocated to containers. Bale capacity is measured in cubic metres.

For insulated (Ins), liquid (Liq), liquid gas (Liq(Gas)), liquid oil (Liq(Oil)), asphalt (asphalt), ore (ore) and hopper (hopper) the capacities are also measured in cubic metres. Imperial equivalents are given to reflect industry standards, where appropriate.

Liquid and liquid oil capacities are recorded, where known as 98% of the total volume of the cargo carrying capacity, allowing 2% for expansion.

Where known information on cargo heating coils is recorded.

CONTAINER DETAILS
For a container ship (fully cellular) or part container ship container details expressed in TEU (twenty foot equivalent units), are displayed as follows:-

C. Total carrying capacity in TEU. This information is only recorded when the separate number of laden containers carried in holds and those on deck is awaited.

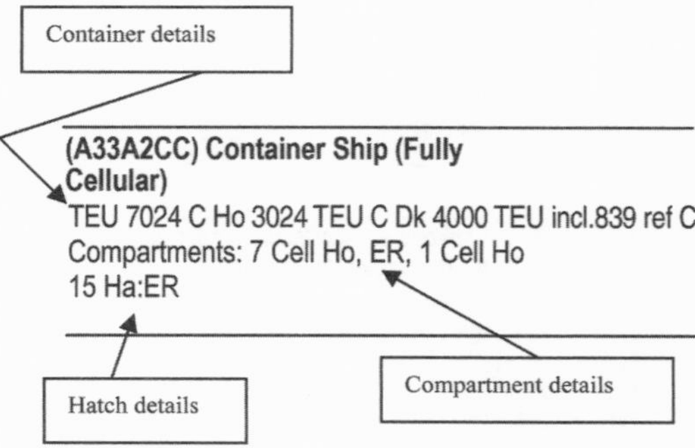

C.Dk. Carrying capacity in TEU on weather deck.
C.Ho. Carrying capacity in TEU in holds.
Cell.Ho. Holds fitted with fixed cellguides for the carriage of laden containers.
C.Ro-Ro Dk. Carrying capacity in TEU containers on internal decks accessed by doors and ramps.

In all instances the values are inclusive of any refrigerated units.

COMPARTMENTS (HOLDS)
Details of the number and types of compartment are recorded, together with specific material where appropriate. Within the sequence of hold information 'ER' indicates the position of the engine room. Hold information is displayed prefixed by 'Compartment'.

The abbreviations and their descriptions can be found in the section 'Abbreviations used in the Register'

COMPARTMENTS (TANKS)
Details of the number, type, design, material, shape and alignment are recorded. Within the sequence of tank information 'ER' indicates the position of the engine room. Tank information is displayed prefixed by 'Compartment'.

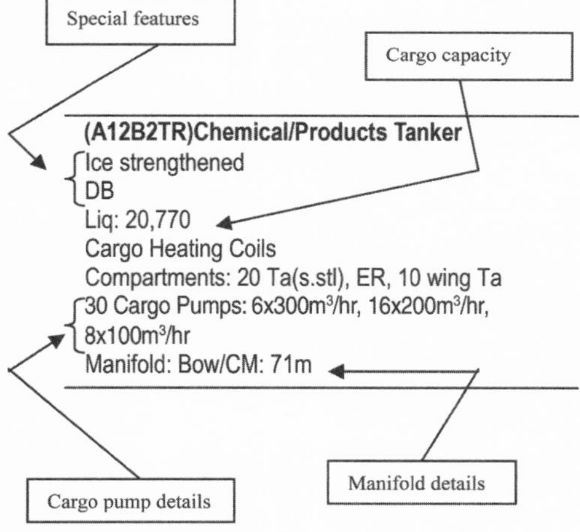

The abbreviations and their descriptions can be found in the section 'Abbreviations used in the Register'

HATCHES
Details of the number, position and dimensions of hatches are recorded. The hatches are given in order, commencing at No.1 from forward and are grouped by centreline (Ha) and wing (Wing Ha) and dimensions.

For tapered hatchways only the narrower breadth is recorded. Hatch dimensions are not recorded under 2 metres. For partial measurements the dimension under 2 metres is represented by '-'. Within the sequence of hatch information 'ER' indicates the position of the engine room

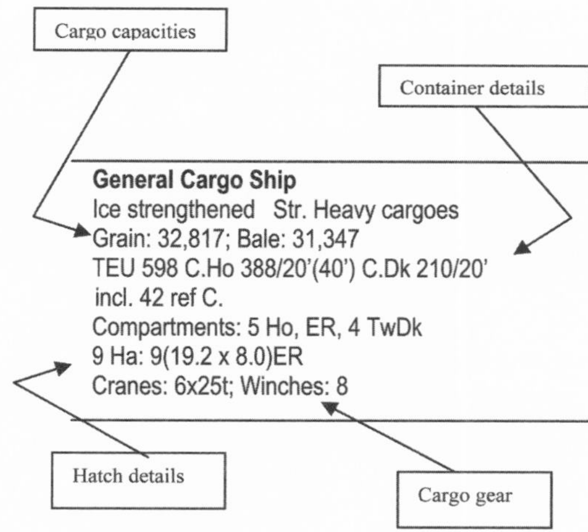

CARGO GEAR
Details of the number and lifting capacity (SWL) of a ship's cargo gear are displayed, prefixed by the type (i.e cranes, derricks, etc.). The number of winches is also displayed.

CARGO PUMPS
Details of the number and output of a ship's cargo pumps are displayed, grouped by output and prefixed by 'Cargo Pumps'. The output is recorded in 'm³/hr'.

MANIFOLD
The distance between the bow and the centre manifold is recorded in metres, prefixed by 'Manifold: Bow/CM'.

7 Machinery

SUMMARY
A summary, listing the number and prime mover type (in bold), gearing information, number of shafts and the number and propeller type, is displayed. For diesel electric installations the number of main generators and electric motors are recorded. Main generator output for each unit is displayed in kilowatts (kW). The total electric motor output is displayed in shaft horsepower (shp) and kilowatts (kW).

TOTAL PRIME MOVER POWER
The total output of the prime movers is displayed in kilowatts (kW) and horsepower (hp), prefixed by 'Total Power'.

SPEED
The ship's service speed is displayed to the right of the total power and is defined as the speed that the ship is capable of maintaining at sea in normal weather and at normal service draught.

PRIME MOVER DESIGN
The design of each prime mover is displayed. Ships with more than one prime mover of the same design and designation will be grouped together, unless manufactured or fitted at different times. Where a ship has prime movers of different designs these will be recorded individually.

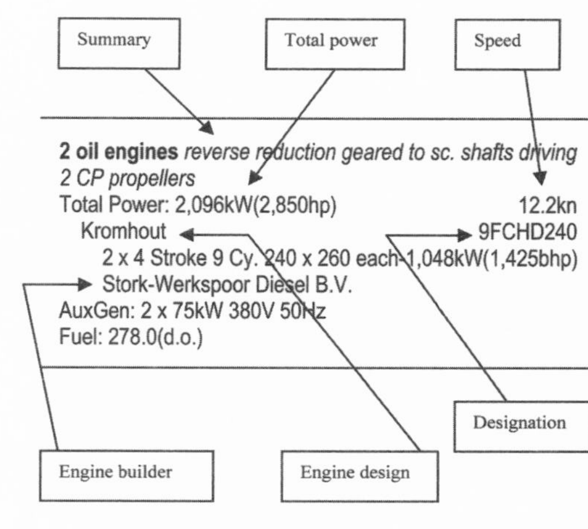

PRIME MOVER DESIGNATION
The designation of the prime mover is displayed to the right of the main engine design.

PRIME MOVER DETAILS
Oil Engines – For each main engine group the number, configuration (if vee), stroke cycle, number of cylinders, bore and stroke dimensions, are displayed. In the event that the engine was manufactured significantly earlier than the ship then the date of manufacture is recorded. Similarly if the engine is replaced or re-conditioned dates of manufacture and fitting are recorded, where known.

(In the absence of date changes being advised, an estimated date has been included)

The output of each engine is recorded in kilowatts (kW) and brake horsepower (bhp).

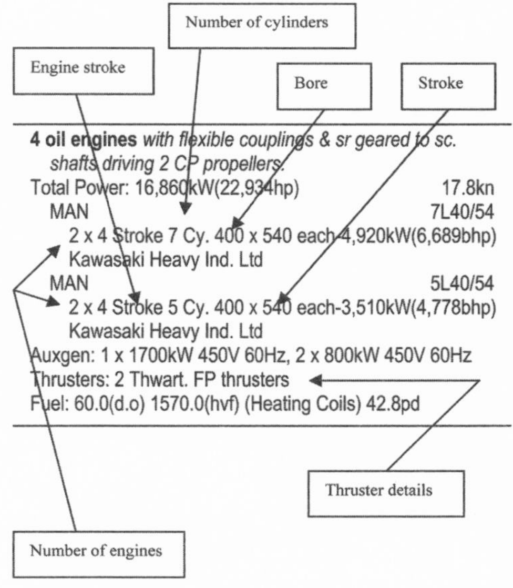

Gas Turbines – The number of gas turbines and relative outputs, recorded in kilowatts (kW) and shaft horsepower (shp), are displayed. In the event that the gas turbine was manufactured significantly earlier than the ship then the date of manufacture is recorded.

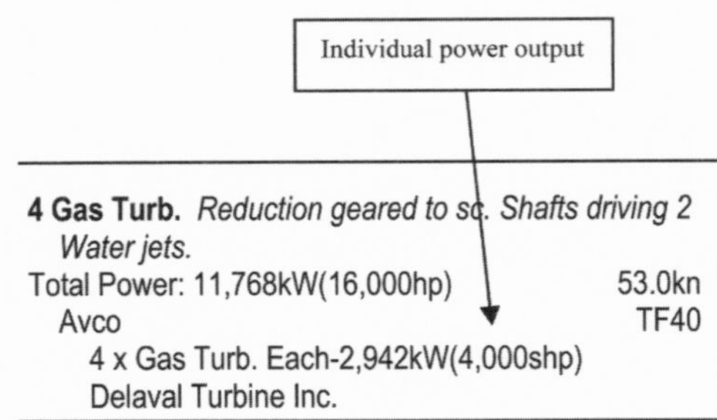

Individual power output
4 Gas Turb. Reduction geared to sc. Shafts driving 2 Water jets.
Total Power: 11,768kW(16,000hp) 53.0kn
Avco TF40
4 x Gas Turb. Each-2,942kW(4,000shp)
Delaval Turbine Inc.

Similarly if the gas turbine is replaced or re-conditioned dates of manufacture and fitting are recorded, where known.

(In the absence of date changes being advised, an estimated date has been included).

Steam Turbines – The number of steam turbines and relative outputs, recorded in kilowatts (kW) and shaft horsepower (shp), are displayed. In the event that the steam turbine was manufactured significantly earlier than the ship then the date of manufacture is recorded. Similarly if the steam turbine is replaced or re-conditioned dates of manufacture and fitting are recorded, where known.
(In the absence of date changes being advised, an estimated date has been included).

Steam Reciprocating Engines - For each steam reciprocating engine group the number, type, configuration, number of cylinders, bore of each cylinder (High, Intermediate and Low Pressure) and stroke dimension, are displayed. In the event that the engine was manufactured significantly earlier than the ship then the date of manufacture is recorded. Similarly if the engine is replaced or re-conditioned dates of manufacture and fitting are recorded, where known.

(In the absence of date changes being advised, an estimated date has been included).

The output of each engine is recorded in kilowatts (kW) and indicated horsepower (ihp)

ENGINE MANUFACTURER

The manufacturer of each engine group is displayed.

AUXILIARY GENERATORS

The number, rated power output and voltage for each auxiliary generator group is displayed. For 'a.c.' installations the frequency is recorded in hertz (Hz). Auxiliary generator details are prefixed by 'AuxGen:'. Emergency sources of power and sets used solely for harbour purposes are not recorded.

BOILERS

Information on boilers is only recorded for vessels currently classed with Lloyd's Register and details are prefixed by 'Boilers:' For each boiler group the number, type, firing type, receiver (rcv) and heater (htr) details, pressures, superheater temperature and pressure details, and heating surface area (m²) are recorded. In the event that the boiler was manufactured significantly earlier than the ship then the date of manufacture is recorded. Similarly if the boiler is replaced or reconditioned dates of manufacture and fitting are recorded.

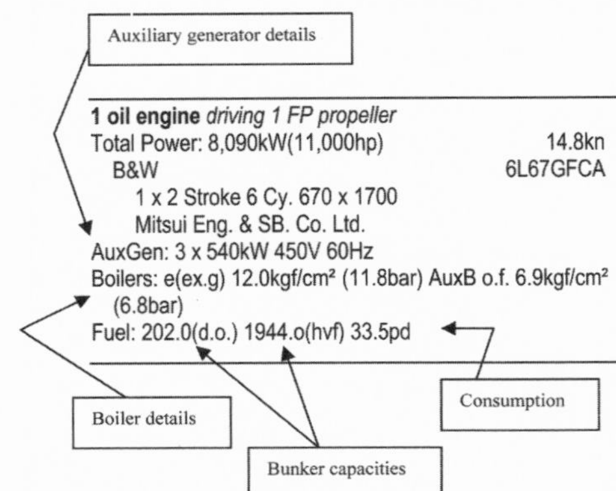

Auxiliary generator details
1 oil engine driving 1 FP propeller
Total Power: 8,090kW(11,000hp) 14.8kn
B&W 6L67GFCA
1 x 2 Stroke 6 Cy. 670 x 1700
Mitsui Eng. & SB. Co. Ltd.
AuxGen: 3 x 540kW 450V 60Hz
Boilers: e(ex.g) 12.0kgf/cm² (11.8bar) AuxB o.f. 6.9kgf/cm² (6.8bar)
Fuel: 202.0(d.o.) 1944.o(hvf) 33.5pd
Consumption
Boiler details
Bunker capacities

Where details of boilers are recorded in parentheses this indicates that the boiler is temporarily out of use.

The abbreviations and their descriptions can be found in the section 'Abbreviations used in the Register'

THRUSTERS

Details of special positioning units are recorded prefixed by 'Thrusters:'. For each type the number, type and position are displayed.

BUNKERS

Bunker capacities, together with the daily fuel consumption, are recorded in tonnes, prefixed by 'Fuel'. Where a ship has heating coils fitted for bunker fuel these will be recorded after the fuel type.

Abbreviations used in the Lloyd's Register of Ships

Abbreviation	Column	Explanation
,	4 & 7	LR class character symbol (See Key for full explanation)
100	4	LR class character figure (See Key for full explanation)
_	4	LR class character symbol (See Key for full explanation)
A	4	LR class character letter (See Key for full explanation)
1	4	LR class character figure (See Key for full explanation)
–	4	LR class character symbol (See Key for full explanation)
N	4	LR class character letter (See Key for full explanation)
T	4	LR class character letter (See Key for full explanation)
*	4 & 7	British Corporation class character symbol (See Key for full explanation)
A, A¬, B*, (A), (A¬), (B*) etc.	4	Equipment Letters (See Key for full explanation)
a or (a)	4, 5, 6 & 7	aft
a.c.	7	Alternating current
AB	2 & 5	Alberta
AB	4	American Bureau of Shipping
AC	4	Sociedad Andina de Certificacion
ACT	2 & 5	Australian Capital Territory
AD	4	Arados Bureau for Sea Services (ABSS)
AH	5	Anhui
AI	5	Aichi
AK	2 & 5	Alaska
AK	5	Akita
AL	2 & 5	Alabama
AL	4	Albanian Register of Shipping
(alu)	6	Aluminium
AO	5	Aomori
AR	2 & 5	Arkansas
AR	4	American Register of Shipping
(Arg)	5	Argentina
AS	4	Asia Classification Society
aux	4, 5 & 7	Auxiliary
AuxB	7	Auxiliary Boiler(s) (LR) (See Key for full explanation)
AuxGen	7	Auxiliary generators
AZ	2 & 5	Arizona
B	4	Bridge
BB	5	Bulbous bow
BC	2 & 5	British Columbia
BC	4	British Corporation (LR)
bhp	7	Brake horsepower (See Key for full explanation)
BJ	5	Beijing
Bow/CM	6	Distance from bow to centre manifold
BR	4	Bulgarski Koraben Registar
Br ex	5	Breadth extreme
Br md	5	Breadth moulded
BS	4	Black Sea Bureau of Shipping
BS	4	British Corporation class character letters – (LR) (See Key for full explanation)
btm	4 & 6	Bottom
BV	4	Bureau Veritas
BWMP	6	Balla st Water Management Plan (LR)
BZ	4	Belize Maritime Bureau
C	4	Diameter of wrought iron cable in sixteenths of an inch (BC Rules)
C	7	Compound expansion engine
C.	6	Total carrying capacity of containers
C. Dk	6	Containers carried on deck
C. Ho	6	Containers carried in hold(s)
C.Ro/Ro	6	Containers carried on internal decks
C.Ro/RoDk	6	Containers carried on internal decks
(CA)	4	Controlled Atmosphere denotes one or more cargo chambers enclosed in an air-tight envelope. (LR)
CA	4	Where ship is provided with a Controlled Atmosphere system which will maintain specified ranges of oxygen and carbon dioxide levels. (LR)
CA	2 & 5	California
CA	4	Columbus American Register
CAC	4	Crew Accommodation Comfort (LR)
CASPPR	4	Canadian Arctic Shipping Pollution Prevention Regulations
CBT	6	Clean Ballast arrangements
CC	4	China Classification Society
CCS or (CCS)	4	Centralised Control System (LR) – (See Key for full explanation)
ccy	6	Conical cylindrical
Cell.Ho.	6	Cellular hold fitted with fixed cellguides
CG	4	Cargo gear on ships (LR)
CH	5	Chiba
Clr Ht	6	Clear height (RoRo ramps & lanes)
CM	4 & 6	Construction Monitoring (LR)
CN	4	CNRIN
CO	2 & 5	Colorado
(Col)	5	Colombia
Comb. or comb.	5 & 6	Combined
COW or COW(LR)	6	Crude Oil Washing
CP	7	Controllable pitch (propellers or thrusters)
CQ	5	Chongqing
CR	4	Cargo ramps (LR)
CR	4	China Corporation Register
CR	4	Corrosion Resistant material (LR)
CS	4	Continuous Survey of the Hull (LR)
CS	4	Hrvatski Registar Brodova
CSD	6	Closed Shelter Deck Ship
CT	2 & 5	Connecticut
CY	4	Cyprus Bureau of Shipping
Cy	7	Cylinders (engine)
cyl	6	Cylindrical
d.c.	7	Direct current
d.o.	7	Diesel oil
db	7	Domestic boiler
DB	5 & 6	Double bottom
DC	2 & 5	District of Columbia
dcc	6	Double cylindrical conical
dcy	6	Double-lobe cylindrical
DD	6	Double deck
DE	2 & 5	Delaware
Dght	5	Draught
Diam.	6	Diameter of manifold
Disch.	6	Discharge
dk or dks	4, 5 & 6	Deck(s)
DP	4	R J Del Pan
DP (AA)	4	Dynamic Positioning with fully redundant automatic control system (LR)
DP (AAA)	4	Dynamic Positioning with fully redundant automatic control system and emergency automatic control system (LR)
DP (AM)	4	Dynamic Positioning with automatic and centralised remote manual control system (LR)
DP (CM)	4	Dynamic Positioning with centralised remote manual control system (LR)
Dp Ta	6	Deep tank
Dpth	5	Moulded depth
dr	7	Double reduction (gearing)
DR	4	Dromon Bureau of Shipping
DS	4	Deutsche Schiffs-Revision und -Klassifikation
DSS	6	Double skin sides
DT or DTs or DTa	4, 5 & 6	Deep tank(s)
DTf	4, 5 & 6	Deep tank forward
DTm	4, 5 & 6	Deep tank midship
DTma	4, 5 & 6	Deep tank aft midship
DTmf	4, 5 & 6	Deep tank forward midship
dwt	6	Deadweight
econ	7	Economiser (Boilers – LR)
e(ex.g)	7	Exhaust gas economiser (Boilers – LR)
EH	5	Ehime
elec.	7	Electric
EP	4 & 6	Environmental Protection (LR)
Eq.Ltr	4	Equipment Letter (LR)
ER	5 & 6	Engine room
ES	4 & 6	Enhanced Scantlings (LR)
ESN	4	Enhanced Survivability Notation (LR)
ESN-Hold 1	4	Notation assigned to a ship that has been assessed for flooding No.1 hold and complies with or has been strengthened to comply with the requirements of the relevant LR Rules
ESN- Hold 1 with Loading Restrictions	4	Notation assigned to a ship that has been assessed for flooding No.1 hold and complies with the requirements of the relevant LR Rules by virtue of imposed loading restrictions.
ESN-All Holds		Notation assigned to a ship that has been assessed for flooding of all holds and complies with or has been strengthened to comply with the requirements of the relevant LR Rules
ESN-All Holds with Loading Restrictions in Hold(s) No....		Notation assigned to a ship that has been assessed for flooding of all holds and complies with the requirements of the relevant LR Rules by virtue of imposed loading restrictions.
ESP	4	Enhanced Survey Programme (LR)
Est.	5	Estimated
ETA	6	Emergency Towing Arrangements (LR)
(ex.g)	7	Exhaust gas (boilers)
exp	7	Expansion
f or (f)	4, 5, 6 & 7	Forward
F-S	6	Finnish-Swedish Ice Rules notation
fcsa	6	Freight container securing arrangements (LR)
FDA	4 & 6	Fatigue Design Assessment (LR)
FEU	6	Forty Foot Equivalent Units (containers)
FI	5	Fukui
FJ	5	Fujian
FL	2 & 5	Florida
FO	5	Fukuoka
FP	4	Flash point (in degrees Celsius) (LR)
FP	7	Fixed pitch (propeller or thruster)
FS	5	Fukushima
FSWR	4	Flexible Steel Wire Ropes (LR)
FV	4	Filipino Vessels Classificat'n System

Abbreviation	Column	Explanation
		Association Inc
fwd	4, 5 & 7	Forward
G1 –G5	4	Service Limits (LR)
GA	2 & 5	Georgia
GC	4	Global Shipping Class
GD	5	Guangdong
Gen or gen	7	Generators
GL	4	Germanischer Lloyd
GM	5	Gunma
GM	4	Global Marine Bureau
GS	4	Global Shipping Bureau
GS	5	Gansu
GX	5	Guangxi
GZ	5	Guizhou
HA	5	Henan
Ha	6	Hatchways
HB	5	Hubei
HCM	6	Hull Condition Monitoring (LR)
HE	5	Hebei
HG	5	Hyogo
HI	2	Hainan
HI	2 & 5	Hawaii
HK	5	Hokkaido
HL	5	Heilongjiang
HM	4	Honduras Maritime Inspection (HMI)
HN	5	Hunan
Ho	6	Dry cargo hold
Ho/Ta	6	Hold/Tank(s)
Ho(comb)	6	Combined hold
hp	7	Horsepower
HP	7	High Pressure
HR	4	Hellenic Register of Shipping
HRS Level 1SS	6	Hull Renovation Scheme (LR)
HRS Level 2SS	6	Hull Renovation Scheme (LR)
hs	7	Heating surface (boilers)
HS	5	Hiroshima
HSC	4	High Speed Craft
htr	7	Heater (boiler details)
hvf	7	High viscosity fuel
HWH	7	Hot Water Heater
Hz	7	Hertz
HZ	4	HORINSIB
*I.W.S.	4	Ship arranged for In Water Survey (LR)
i.f.o.	7	Intermediate fuel oil
IA	2 & 5	Iowa
IB	5	Ibaraki
IB	4	Isthmus Bureau of Shipping
IBS	4	Integrated Bridge Navigation System (LR)
IC	4	INCLAMAR
ICC	4	Integrated Computer Control (LR)
Ice Class 1*, 1, 2 & 3	4	Ice Class Notations for general service (LR)
Ice Class 1AS, A, B, C & D	4	Ice Class Notations for general service (LR)
Ice Class AC1, AC1-5, AC2 & AC3	4	Ice Class Notations for Arctic and Antarctic Service (LR)
ID	2 & 5	Idaho
IFP	4	Integrated Fire Protection (LR)
IGS or IGS (LR)	6	Inert Gas System
IGS or (IGS)	4	Inert Gas System (See Key for full explanation)
ihp	7	Indicated horsepower
IK	4	Intertek Maritime Bureau
IL	2 & 5	Illinois
IM	4	Isthmus Maritime Classification Society
IN	2 & 5	Indiana
IN	4	Iranian Classification Society
incl.	5, 6 & 7	Including
(Ind)	5	India
Inmarsat-A	2	(See Key for full explanation)
Inmarsat-B	2	(See Key for full explanation)
Inmarsat-M	2	(See Key for full explanation)
Inmarsat-Mini-M	2	(See Key for full explanation)
Inmarsat-C	2	(See Key for full explanation)
Ins	6	Insulated cargo capacity
IO	4	Icons Marine Services
IP	4	Integrated Propulsion (LR)
IP	7	Intermediate Pressure
IR	4	Indian Register of Shipping
IS	5	Ishikawa
IS	4	International Register of Shipping
IT	4	Intermarine Certification Services
IU	4	International Maritime Bureau
IV	4	International Naval Surveys Bureau
IZ	4	International Ship Classification
IW	5	Iwate
JL	5	Jilin
JR	4	Jugoslavenski Registar Brodova
JS	5	Jiangsu
JX	5	Jiangxi
KC	5	Kochi
KC	4	Korea Classification Society
KG	5	Kagawa
KI	4	Biro Klasifikasi Indonesia
KM	5	Kumamoto
kn	7	Knots
KN	5	Kanagawa
KR	4	Korean Register of Shipping
KS	5	Kagoshima
KS	2 & 5	Kansas
KT	4	Korea Ship Safety Technology
kW	4 & 7	Kilowatts
KY	2 & 5	Kentucky
KY	5	Kyoto
L reg	5	Registered length
L.S.'O'.	4	Loading Sequence Accelerated (LR)
L.S.'T'.	4	Loading Sequence Normal (LR)
LA	4	Lifting Appliance (LR)
LA	2 & 5	Louisiana
Lake SS	4	Periodical Survey of ship classed for Great Lakes Service (LR)
Lbp	5	Length between perpendiculars
LDC	4	Light Displacement Craft
Len	6	Length (RoRo ramps & lanes)
LI	4 & 6	Loading Instrument (LR)
Liq	6	Liquid cargo capacity
Liq(Gas)	6	Liquid gas capacity
Liq(Oil)	6	Liquid oil capacity
Lloyd's RMC or (Lloyd's RMC)	4	Refrigerated Cargo Installation Class (LR) – (See Key for full explanation)
Lloyd's RMC (LG) or ((Lloyd's RMC (LG))	4	Class for refrigerating equipment for dealing with boil-off gas on a liquefied gas carrier (LR) – (See Key for full explanation)
LMA	4 & 6	Lloyd's Manoeuvring Assessment (LR)
LMC or (LMC)	4	Machinery Class (LR) – (See Key for full explanation)
LN	5	Liaoning
LNG		Liquefied Natural Gas
Loa	5	Length overall
LP	7	Low Pressure
LPG	5 & 6	Liquefied Petroleum Gas
LR	4 & 6	Lloyd's Register of Shipping
Lwr or lwr	5 & 6	Lower
m	4, 5 & 6	Midship
m^3/hr	6	Cubic metres per hour
MA	2 & 5	Massachusetts
MB	4	Maritime Bureau of Shipping
MB	2 & 5	Manitoba
MC	4	Macosnar Corp
Mchy or mchy	5, 6 & 7	Machinery
MD	2 & 5	Maryland
ME	2 & 5	Maine
ME	5	Mie
(Mex)	5	Mexico
MG	4	Maritime Lloyd Georgia
MG	5	Miyagi
MI	2 & 5	Michigan
MN	2 & 5	Minnesota
MO	2 & 5	Missouri
MS	2 & 5	Mississippi
MT	4	Maritime Technical Systems & Services
MY	4	Ships Classification Malaysia
MZ	5	Miyazaki
N	4	Equipment not required (LR)
NA	4	National Shipping Adjuster
NAV	4	Lloyd's Navigation Certificate (LR)
NAV1	4	Lloyd's Navigation Certificate for periodic One Man Watch (LR)
NauxB	7	New Auxiliary Boilers (LR)
NB	2 & 5	New Brunswick
NC	4	Naval Classification Bureau
NC	2 & 5	North Carolina
ND	2 & 5	North Dakota
NE	2 & 5	Nebraska
NG	4	DNV-GL
NH	2 & 5	New Hampshire
NI	5	Niigata
Ni.stl	6	Nickel Steel
NJ	2 & 5	New Jersey
NK	4	Nippon Kaiji Kyokai
NL	2 & 5	Newfoundland & Labrador
NM	2 & 5	Nei Menggu (Inner Mongolia)
NM	2 & 5	New Mexico
NN	5	Nagano
NR	5	Nara
NR	7	Nuclear Reactor
NS	5	Nagasaki
NS	2 & 5	Nova Scotia
NSW	2 & 5	New South Wales
NT	2 & 5	Northern Territory
NT	2 & 5	Northwest Territories
NU	2 & 5	Nunavut
NV	2 & 5	Nevada
NV	4	Det Norske Veritas
NX	5	Ningxia
NY	2 & 5	New York State
(NZ)	5	New Zealand
o.f.	7	Oil fuel or oil-fired boilers
OBO	5	Ore/Bulk/Oil
OH	2 & 5	Ohio
OK	2 & 5	Oklahoma
OM	4	Overseas Marine Certification Service

Abbreviations used in the Lloyd's Register of Ships 2014-15

Abbreviation	Column	Explanation
ON	5	Okinawa
ON	2 & 5	Ontario
OR	6	Oregon
OS	5	Osaka
OSD	6	Open Shelter Deck Ship
OSD/CSD	6	Open & Closed Shelter Deck Ship
OT	5	Oita
OU/OI	4	LR class character letters (See Key for full explanation)
OY	5	Okayama
p	4, 5, 6 & 7	Port
PA	2 & 5	Pennsylvania
PA	4	Pacific Register of Ships
PAC	4	Passenger Accommodation Comfort (LR)
PB	4	Panama Bureau of Shipping
PC	4	Panama Register
PCR	4	Performance Capability Rating (LR)
PCWBT	6	Protective Coatings in Water Ballast Tanks (LR)
pd	7	Per day (fuel consumption)
PD	4	Panama Maritime Documentation Services
PE	2 & 5	Prince Edward Island
PM	4	Panama Marine Survey & Certification Services
Pmp rm	6	Pump room
PMS	6	Approved Planned Maintenance Scheme (LR)
PMS(CM)	6	Approved Planned Maintenance Scheme based on machinery condition monitoring (LR)
PP	4	Philippine Register of Ships
PR	4	Polski Rejestr Statkow
pri	7	Prismatic
PS	4	Panama Shipping Registrar
PSMR	4	Propulsion and Steering Machinery Redundancy (LR)
PSMR*	4	Propulsion and Steering Machinery Redundancy Located in Separate Machinery Spaces(LR)
pt	4, 5 & 6	Part
pv	4	Pressure/vacuum relief valves for cargo tanks with positive setting where greater than 0.2 bar
PV	4	Panama Maritime Surveyors Bureau
PX	4	Phoenix Register of Shipping
QC	2 & 5	Province of Quebec
QH	2 & 5	Qinghai
QLD	2 & 5	Queensland
RB	4	Registro Brasileiro de Navios e Aero-naves
RC	4	Registro Cubano de Buques
rcv	7	Receiver (boiler details)
rec	6	Rectangular
Recip.	7	Reciprocating engine
ref	6	Ships fitted with refrigerated cargo installation
Ref C.	6	Refrigerated containers
Retract.	7	Retractable
RI	4	Registro Italiano Navale
RI	2 & 5	Rhode Island
RN	4	Registrul Naval Roman
RoRo	6	Roll on Roll off
RP	4	Rinave Portuguesa
rpm	4	Revolutions per minute
RR	4	Russian River Register
RS	4	Russian Maritime Register of Shipping
s	4, 5 & 7	Starboard
SA	2 & 5	South Australia
S.dk	5	Shelter deck (s.stl) or s.stl 6 Stainless steel
SB	7	Single-ended Main Boiler (LR)
SBP	6	Steady Bollard Pull (LR)
SBT or SBT (LR)	6	Segregated Ballast Tanks
SBT/PL or SBT/PL(LR)	6	Segregated Ballast Tanks
SC	4	Service Craft
SC	4	SingClass International
SC	5	Sichuan
SC	2 & 5	South Carolina
sc. shaft(s)	7	Screw shaft(s)
SCM	4 & 6	Screwshaft Condition Monitoring (LR)
SD	5	Shandong
SD	2 & 5	South Dakota
SDA	4 & 6	Structural Design Assessment (LR)
SDS or SDS(LR)	6	SOLAS Damage Stability
SEA	6	Ship Event Analysis (LR)
SEA (HSS)	6	Ship Event Analysis (Hull Surveillance System) (LR)
SEA(R)	6	Ship Event Analysis with Continuous Data Recording Capability (LR)
SEA(VDR)	6	Ship Event Analysis (Voyage Data Recorder System) (LR)
SERS or SERS(LR)	6	Ship Emergency Response Service
SG	5	Saga
SG	4, 6 & 7	Specific gravity
SH	5	Shanghai
SH	5	Shiga
shp	7	Shaft horsepower
Ship Type	4	Notations assigned to chemical tankers which comply with relevant requirements of LR's Rules. (LR)
Ship Type 1*, 2* & 3*	4	Notations assigned to chemical tankers which comply with relevant requirements of LR's Rules, where the International certificate of fitness is to be issued by an authority other than LR. (LR)
SK	2 & 5	Saskatchewan
SL	4	Sing-Lloyd
Slop Ta	6	Slop tank
SM	5	Shimane
SMR or SMR*	4	Steering Machinery Redundancy (LR)
SN	5	Shaanxi
(Sp)	5	Spain
sph	6	Spherical
SPM	4	Single Point Mooring
spt	7	Superheater (boilers) (LR)
SQ	4	Special Quality Steel Cable
sr	7	Single reduction (gearing)
SS	4	Special Survey (LR)
SSC	4	Special Service Craft
ST	5	Saitama
St or STs	6	Side Tank(s)
stbd	4, 5, 6 & 7	Starboard
(stl) or stl	5 & 6	Steel
str	6	Strengthened
Swl	6	Safe working load (RoRo ramps)
SWATH	4 & 6	Small waterplane area twin-hull
SX	5	Shanxi
SZ	5	Shizuoka
T	6 & 7	Tonnes (1000kg)
T/cm	3	Tonnes per centimetre immersion
T/hr	6	Tonnes per hour
T/m³	4	Tonnes per cubic metre
Ta	4 & 6	Cargo tank
Ta-Cln	6	Clean ballast tank
Ta-Seg	6	Segregated ballast tank
TAS	2 & 5	Tasmania
TC	4	Temperature Control (LR)
TCM	6	Main steam Turbine Condition Monitoring (LR)
TEU	6	Twenty Foot Equivalent Units
TJ	5	Tianjin
TK	5	Tokyo
TL	4	Turk Loydu
TM	4	Tsunami Marine Ltd (TML)
TN	4	Emirates Classification Tasneef
TN	2 & 5	Tennessee
TOC	4	Transfer of Class
TOH	7	Thermal Oil Heater
Top Ho.	6	Dry cargo hold topside
Topside Ta	6	Cargo tank topside
tr	7	Triple reduction (gearing)
TS	5	Tokushima
TT	5	Tottori
turb.	7	Turbine
Twd	4 & 5	'Tween Deck Tank(s)
Twd	6	'Tween Deck Space
TX	2 & 5	Texas
TY	5	Toyama
Type A, B & C	4	Notations refer to chemical cargoes for the carriage for which the ship has been approved (LR)
U1, U2, U3 or U4	4	Grades of chain cable (LR)
U dk	5	Upper deck
UA	4	Ukraine Shipping Register
UB	4	Union Bureau of Shipping
UC	4	Union Marine Classification
(UK)	6	United Kingdom
UM	4	Universal Maritime Bureau
UMS or (UMS)	4	Unattended Machinery Space (LR) – (See Key for full explanation)
UN	4	Universal Marine Classification
Upr. or upr	5 & 6	Upper
UT	2 & 5	Utah
UV	4	Universal Shipping Bureau
V	7	Volts
VA	2 & 5	Virginia
VIC	2 & 5	Victoria
VR	4	Vietnam Register
VT	2 & 5	Vermont
VZ	4	Venezuelan Register
WA	2 & 5	Washington State
WA	2 & 5	Western Australia
WI	2 & 5	Wisconsin
WI	4	Wrought Iron cable
Wid	6	Width (RoRo ramps & lanes)
Wing Ha	6	Wing hatches
WK	5	Wakayama
WTAuxB	7	Water Tube Auxiliary Boiler (LR)
WTB	7	Water Tube Main Boiler (LR)
Wtdb	7	Water tube domestic boiler (LR)
WV	2 & 5	West Virginia
WY	2 & 5	Wyoming
XJ	5	Xinjiang
XZ	5	Xizang (Tibet)
YC	5	Yamaguchi
Yd No	5	Shipbuilder yard number
YN	5	Yunnan
YT	5	Yamagata
YT	2 & 5	Yukon Territory
ZC	4	Zianlian Chuen
ZH	4	Joson Classification Society
ZJ	5	Zhejiang

IHS Maritime

IHS Maritime holds the largest maritime database in the world, evolved from The Lloyd's Register of Ships which has been continuously published since 1764.

With IHS Maritime you can:

- Track live ship positions with unrivalled AIS coverage
- Identify every merchant and military ship
- Contact 240,000 ship owners, operators and managers
- Receive insights for profitable, efficient and safe shipping
- Plan a port call with ease

With extensive ship, movement, casualty, company, port and news databases, as well as research, forecasting and consultancy services, IHS Maritime has developed a range of high quality products and services that are unique to the industry.

As the sole originating authority for assigning and validating IMO Ship and Company numbers, IHS Maritime databases are able to guarantee a level of comprehensiveness no-one else can.

AISLive

AISLive was the first global Automatic Identification System (AIS) network providing access to real-time ship movements through an online application. It displays the position of every AIS-equipped ship within the areas of shore-based coverage, and is updated every three minutes, 24/7.

Today, this award-winning service provides coverage of up to 127,000 vessels every day across five continents. It is relied upon by charterers, civil authorities, port authorities, ship agents, brokers, and owners for timely and accurate information.

Click on a ship to view details such as IMO number, MMSI, ship details, ownership, technical manager and commercial operator, images, position (Lat/Long), course, speed, nearest ports, next port of call, last four port callings and a ship track for the last 24 hours. Ships are tracked right to the berth.

Greater visibility of your fleets' deep sea and offshore movements
Latest version enhancements:
- 25% increase in AIS terrestrial network coverage
- 18% growth in satellite AIS in terms of vessels seen
- 11% growth in hourly positions recorded
- Enhanced ship track with animation. Ability to select date range and draught threshold
- Increased ship track history
- 197 filters including: All ships –destination port, destination country, ETA, draught, speed and hazardous cargo, last seen.

Verified ships - DWT, GT , flag, operator, technical manager, last port of call and last country of call
- Export the WatchList into EXCEL
- Dynamic real time intelligence reporting
- New measuring tool to approximate distances on the map
- Ability to add notes to a ship in the WatchList

User Interface Updates
- Set ship symbols color to indicate ship type or speed/recency
- Tanker and dry cargo berths shown on map
- Clearly identify high/low areas of traffic density
- Improved process for adding ships to zones

These enhancements are included in all versions of AISLive.

Features include
- Coverage of up to 127,000 vessels every day
- The latest positions of over 100,000 ships
- Over 2,500 ports, terminals and anchorages covered
- Trigger zone and ship tracking email Alerts
- Tile-based chart application with 16 levels of zoom
- Links to ship characteristics database
- 25 million positions a day.

Alerts
When a ship of your choice enters your selected trigger area you will receive an email Alert advising its current AIS position. This can be used for many purposes, for instance to alert a harbour master that an awaited ship is about to enter port.

Antennas
If your port is not on AISLive already, we can supply the installation kit necessary to connect to the network. Please note that a permanent internet connection is required. Prices include a subscription to AISLive.

App
You can track live ship positions whilst on the move with the AISLive mobile app, available for Android (OS2.2 and above), iPhone, iPad and Blackberry.

25% more coverage
We have a dedicated team tasked with growing the network and the quality of the service. In the last year our network has grown by 25%. We are adding more antenna stations all the time.

AIS Data
A range of tailored data supply services are available on request. Deep ocean coverage received by satellite as well as historical movement information can also be provided.

AISLive Premium
AISLive Premium, combining all the great features of AISLive Standard & AISLive Plus but with an added dimension, **the inclusion of satellite data for the complete coverage of ship movements.**
AISLive Premium gives you greater visibility of your fleets' deep sea and offshore movements. By combining all the great features of IHS Maritime AISLive Standard and AISLive Plus services, the new AISLive Premium service includes satellite data, giving you complete coverage. You will get live coverage of ship positions and movements along the world's critical maritime trading routes for asset tracking or risk assessment.

Advertising
Put your message across one of the most visited sites in shipping, in a cost effective way. With 10,000 visits a day, and 5,000,000 page views a month, you will consistently reach a wide global audience.

Distance Tables Module
This module provides online distance tables supplied by Vesson Nautical, and offer a convenient tool to access millions of routes for voyage estimation and comparison. The tool enables users to calculate an accurate time of arrival to verify that provided in the AIS message (inputted by the crew).

ShipWatch Services (Alerts & Watchlist)
Use the AISLive dynamic ShipWatch service to monitor vessels current positions and be automatically emailed when a vessel has entered a zone. Using itinerary alerts, be notified immediately when a ship has changed its destination or estimated time of arrival, now with greater function and quotas.

Bespoke Data Solutions

With over 20 databases to select from and close to 600 fields of information the possibilities are virtually unlimited, giving you the opportunity to select the precise records and all of the related information that you require.

Customised extracts and data analysis from the databases can be supplied and updated in a variety of formats to allow you to build or use existing in-house business applications, linking your own information with ours. Databases include ships, companies, ports, movements, news and images.

Examples of organisations already benefiting:
• Banking • Chartering • Engine manufacturers, repairers and spare part suppliers • Government agencies and regulatory authorities • Insurance • Lawyers, solicitors and legal consultants • Marine consultants • Paint and coatings manufacturers • Port authorities • Product manufacturers • Brokers • Shipbuilders • Shipowners, operators and managers • Ship repairers • Ship vetting • Suppliers of bunkers and lubricants • VTS

Full details of our tailored data services, together with an electronic spreadsheet of all our data fields is available on request.

Movements Plus
Movements Plus is an analytical tool that combines the power of IHS expertise with IHS Maritime's AIS data, to create 6 unique product offerings supporting strategic decision making. Movements Plus offers unique insight into your area of interest:
- Bespoke reports to meet individual needs
- Reports are available in PDF and PPT formats
- Alongside the reports data will be provided in XML, KML, EXCEL

Sea-web

***Sea*-web**™ – The Lloyd's Register of Ships online - is the ultimate maritime reference tool. It contains up to 600 fields of information on over 197,000 ships, with more than 240,000 company records, in a single application.

***Sea*-web**™ is the ultimate maritime reference tool that helps you to: Sea-web™ combines extensive ships, owners, shipbuilders, ship movements, fixtures and casualty information integrated with Sea-web Ports, Sea-web Insight & News (maritime news and analysis), and Sea-web Directory (comprehensive search tool). To enhance your service, there are additional modules to choose from, covering real-time ship positions and historic port callings, credit reports, fixtures, casualties, and the ability to create WatchLists and Alerts to notify you of changes. It's an easy-to-use service that provides a range of search capabilities, from simple look-ups through to complex database queries.

Latest version enhancements:

• Translation of Sea-web fields and menus now available for twelve additional languages: Russian, Chinese,
Turkish, Italian, Greek Japanese, German, Spanish, French, Dutch, Portuguese and Korean
• Insight & News
• Ship Performance Benchmark demo – sample of the data set, insight into what is in the module
• Movements module – new voyage search function added –This helps to identify trends – vessel routes, identify all movements within date range, port of call, country of call, destination port

It's an easy-to-use service that provides a range of search capabilities, from simple look-ups through to complex database queries.

- Details of over 197,000 ships
- Up to 600 fields of information
- 179,000 ship photographs
- 240,000 company records
- 7 levels of ownership
- Reporting and exporting facilities
- Powerful analytical grid tool
- 24 hour online access
- Mobile app
- Additional modules available

***Sea*-web™ Modules**

Enhance your ***Sea*-web™** subscription by selecting any of the following modules.

Sea-web Insight

Sea-web Insight with IHS Maritime Fairplay and IHS Technology is the trusted source for maritime information around the globe. This module brings you daily breaking maritime news and insight for profitable, safe and efficient shipping. Available across web, email, digital and print.

It covers a full spectrum of shipping and port-related issues appealing to the entire maritime community, and pays particular attention to: Shipping markets, trade and commerce, shipping logistics and supply chain, technological solutions to commercial problems comprehensive data on newbuildings orders of 100 GT and above, maritime safety and regulations, dredging and port construction and best practices in port operations.

Sea-web Insight presents you with a customisable screen so that you can put the range of news content in any order
you wish. News articles are published online as soon as they have been written and verified. Content comes from the same editorial desks that create IHS Maritime Fairplay magazine, IHS Safety at Sea and IHS Dredging and Port Construction,
ensuring that you have access to the most complete maritime news source available.

There are two elements to this service:

• NEWS • ANALYSIS

Daily & Weekly News email newsletters– the day's top stories and breaking news delivered direct to your inbox with a with a weekly compilation delivered each Wednesday. IHS Maritime Fairplay (weekly) & IHS Maritime Technology (monthly) Digital Magazines. Published and ready to view ahead of the print version and using state-of-the-art technology, the digital version of the magazine has user-friendly search functionality and is accessible via most wireless media platforms, including PC, MAC, and Apple and Android devices. Login to view each issue, search your archive or download PDF.

Print

IHS Maritime Fairplay (weekly) & IHS Technology (monthly) delivered to your doorstep

Formats: Daily email, Weekly 7 Day roundup, Daily coverage from our global editors, digital and print magazines, Newbuildings online. All content delivered in real-time.

Sea-News:
IHS Safety at Sea

Sea-web News Module with Safety at Sea is the only information service dedicated to global maritime safety IHS Safety at Sea is the no. 1 choice for shipowners and managers looking to improve the safety and security of their vessels, crews and cargoes.

IHS Sea-web News Module

Daily breaking maritime news from the IHS Sea-web News Module. Compiled and delivered by our expert editorial
teams and covering the full spectrum of shipping and port related issues, this service from IHS Sea-web, the ultimate
maritime reference tool, ensures that you will always be up-to-date with the latest news from your industry.

Daily and weekly email newsletters

IHS Safety at Sea Daily & Weekly News email – the day's top stories and breaking news delivered direct to your inbox with
a with a weekly compilation delivered each Wednesday.

Print

IHS Safety at Sea print magazine (12 issues per year)

IHS Safety at Sea Digital Magazine

Published and ready to view ahead of the print version and using state-of-the-art technology, the digital version of
the magazine has user-friendly search functionality and is accessible via most wireless media platforms, including PC,
MAC, and Apple and Android devices. Login to view each issue, search your archive or download PDF.

Subscription package at a glance:

Online: IHS Sea-web News Module
Daily & weekly email newsletters
Print & Digital IHS Safety at Sea digital magazine - (12 issues per year)

Sea-web News:
IHS Dredging and Port Construction

At the heart of global marine civil engineering IHS Dredging and Port Construction is the only international title focusing on port construction, development and dredging campaigns of all types and is dedicated to keeping its readers up-to-date with marine civil engineering projects as they happen around
the world.

IHS *Sea*-web™ News Module

The official magazine for major industry organisations including CEDA (Central Dredging Association) and EADA
(Eastern Dredging Association), IHS Dredging and Port Construction is also the official voice of CHIDA (China Dredging Association) and an associate member of IAPH (International Association of Ports & Harbors).

Daily breaking maritime news from the IHS Sea-web™ News Module. Compiled and delivered by our expert editorial teams and covering the full spectrum of shipping and port-related issues, this service from IHS Sea-web™, the ultimate maritime reference tool, ensures that you will always be up to date with the latest news from your industry.

Print

IHS Dredging and Port Construction (Monthly) delivered to your doorstep.

IHS Dredging and Port Construction Digital Magazine

Published and ready to view ahead of the print version and using state-of-the-art technology, the digital version of
the magazine has user-friendly search functionality and is accessible via most wireless media platforms, including PC,
MAC, and Apple and Android devices. Login to view each issue, search your archive or download PDF.

Subscription package at a glance:

Online: **IHS *Sea*-web**™ News Module
IHS Dredging and Port Construction digital magazine - (12 issues per year)
Print: IHS Dredging and Port Construction print magazine - (12 issues per year)

Movements

View a ship's current position or last reported position, as well as the fleet position of a particular owner, manager or operator. Access historic movements and port callings as recorded on AISLive. Search by ship name or LR/IMO No, or search movements by port and country, movement type, date ranges and a number of key ship fields. You can also plot a ship's most recent port callings on a map.

Ports

This module provides comprehensive details of over 13,000 ports & terminals, including a complete description of the port and relevant facilities, pre-arrival and navigation details, berths and cargo, tanker berths, over 4,000 plans and mooring diagrams, contact details of port service providers and agents (over 26,600 in total), port photographs, as well as local weather conditions.

Security

Bringing together the resources of IHS Maritime and IHS Janes, and updated every working day, this online service provides you with up-to-date coverage of global events affecting the security of your ships such as piracy and security related issues.

The archive of news and events affecting port conditions is linked by port, country, region and subject. An executive summary provides a quick reference to the risk pointers affecting each country, and a history of recent events affecting internal and external affairs.

Any changes to the risk evaluation information are highlighted in a daily email update

Distance Tables
Supplied by Veson Nautical, distance tables offer a convenient tool to access millions of routes for voyage estimation and comparison.
Routing can be edited to reflect seasonal constraints and user specific requirements. Optional functionality includes point to port and point to point distance and route retrieval.

AutoWatch
Create WatchLists of ships or companies and set up email Alerts to receive notification of when key fields of data change. You can also make use of pre-defined WatchLists such as OFAC SDN* listed ships, ships in casualty, ships coming off fixture and ship detentions. If taken with the Movements Module you can also watch ship positions, port arrivals and departures, updated ETAs and the passing of key global transit points.

Casualty
View a ship's casualty history or search for an incident by a number of combined criteria. Search through 121,000 non-serious and serious casualties, as well as total losses and demolitions.

Fixtures
Access details on dry and wet ships engaged in international charter markets, supplied by Maritime Research Inc. It includes an extensive search facility, providing ship and fixture details, voyage and cargo details and fixture dates. Information is supplied on the charterer and commodity; charter party tonnage, terms, dates & commodity; load area & port; discharge area & port; date on & off fixture; and fixture history.

Credit Reports
This module offers summary company credit reports, provided by Ocean Intelligence Pte Limited.2,700 up-to-date credit analysis summaries are available, linking 4,500 ship owning, operating and management companies. Each report contains a summary of Reputation and Payment Performance, indicators for Credit and Payment Performance Ratings together with the report date.

Enhanced Credit Reports
Download full company credit reports and gain access to in-depth, accurate and timely information and analysis on organisations working in the maritime trading sector. The information is supplied by Ocean Intelligence Pte Ltd and is subject to their company report terms and conditions.

World Register of Ships

Tactical Maritime Surveillance Support on the Bridge or in a Command Centre.

World Register of Ships is the single most authoritative database on global merchant and military ships.

Whilst patrolling an operational area, World Register of Ships gives you the capability to quickly locate all relevant data on a ship you are about to board or assist. At the same time, you can retrieve all you need to know about an unfamiliar warship that's emerging over the horizon.
The search engine is intuitive and user friendly, providing instant information and imagery – just type in the IMO number or ship name.

World Register of Ships allows you to:
- Recognise and identify ships at sea
- Classify encountered ships
- Assess maritime risk factors
- Inform the Recognised Maritime Picture
- Stay up to date with the latest warship capabilities
- Watch for programme changes and emerging requirements
- Make informed decisions when evaluating new technology and systems.

Standard:
- Up to 300 data fields on every ship over 100 GT in service or under construction
- Information on 190,000 ships including capacities, class, tonnage, cargo type, gear and machinery
- Information on 12,000 warships from 164 countries including capabilities and weapon systems
- An extensive library of ship photographs, searchable by attribute or class
- Line drawings and silhouettes of warships
- Virtually unlimited searching, sorting, reporting and exporting capabilities

Enhanced:
- As above + commercial fixtures, detentions and casualty modules

Commercial:
- The Commercial version contains all merchant ships over 100 GT, including ships on order and under construction, together with extensive ownership information. A complete database of marine company records is also provided.

Format:
- Mailed to you on a new and freshly updated external hard drive every month, ideal for secure environments.

LNGLive

LNGLive brings together the resources of IHS Maritime and energy trading software specialist Innovez Ltd to provide a state-of-the-art daily reporting service on the global flow of LNG.

Plus:
Monday – Eighteen month, by country stacked total regas and liquefaction graphs
Tuesday – By region, trailing three month source of gas report (includes pie charts). Also, analysis of developments within the LNG market, provided by IHS Global Insight.
Wednesday – By region, trailing three month destination of gas report (includes pie charts)
Thursday – By region, 2011, 2012 & 2013 year on year regas comparison charts
Friday – By region, 2011, 2012 & 2013 year on year liquefaction comparison charts

LNGLive offers a groundbreaking solution for LNG analysts and traders alike. It provides information on gas flows between countries, daily changes in destination, port calling history and movement analysis for the LNG fleet, including terminal type and ship capacity.

Advanced predictive algorithms are used to determine port callings that occur even when a ship's AIS transponder is not switched on, and improve the accuracy of crew entered data.

In addition, the package includes:
- Every trip for every ship from January 2010 to date, including algorithm-based predicted callings
- Interactive by country, monthly regas and liquefaction cross tabulation, to include numerical details whereby users can exclude predicted callings
- Interactive source of gas report (time period specific)
- Interactive destination of gas report (time period specific)
- First Monday of the month: by region, trailing twelve month destination of gas and source of gas reports for baseline figures (includes pie charts).

Daily Newbuildings News

Features include
- Daily rumours and market intelligence section
- Newbuilding activity of ships of 100 GT and above
- Daily summary with technical specifications for each ship
- Contact details for shipyard and operator

Access the latest information on shipbuilding activity for propelled sea-going merchant ships of 100 GT and above, including rumours, contracts and negotiations.

Daily Newbuildings News is an email service compiled by an experienced team of editors.

Each report includes a news summary, highlighting the very latest newbuilding rumours, as well as all confirmed orders. These are listed by builder and operator and include full address and communication details. The ship information includes yard number, delivery date, order status, IMO number, shiptype, GT, Dwt, capacity, dimensions, main machinery and reported newbuilding price.

Subscribers also have access to the Newbuilding News Search, a fully searchable online archive of all newbuilding stories published since its launch in 1997.

World Shipping Encylopaedia

Updated quarterly, this DVD provides expanded fleet criteria (all ships of 100 GT and above) as well as companies and ports data to give you a complete marine information system.

Features include
- Details of over 119,000 ships of 100 GT and above
- Over 167,000 maritime related companies
- Over 13,000 ports and terminals
- Distance tables
- Export facility

Ships
With details of all ships of 100 GT and above including newbuildings, the Encyclopaedia is a powerful database giving access to up to 200 fields of information. Vessel images are also provided through photofinder.
Companies

Covering every aspect of the industry, the database allows you to quickly identify the company, contact details, personnel, industry sector, products and services of over 167,000 maritime companies.

Ports and terminals
Full details including port descriptions, restrictions, location, port plans, atlas and service providers are given on over 11,000 ports and terminals worldwide.

Distance tables
With 3,000 locations and route selections, the distance tables supplied by Veson Nautical provide the fastest and most accurate method to calculate the distances and voyage times between major ports and terminals.

User notes
Users can add notes to each ship, company and port record, all of which are searchable and automatically updated with each new release of the Encyclopaedia.

Reports and exports
A comprehensive range of reporting and exporting functions are provided. You can export up to 2,500 records, up to 12 fields at a time.

Ports & Terminals Guide CD-ROM

Features include
- Details on more than 13,000 ports
- Over 26,600 port service providers
- Worldwide distance table
- Tanker berth information
- Country overviews
- Full colour plans
- Photographs
- Provision to add user notes and links
- Report generator
- SPS details and contact information

Comprehensive details are provided on over 13,000 ports and terminals including a complete description of the port and all of the relevant facilities, plans and mooring diagrams (nearly 4,000 in total), contact details of port service providers and agents, maritime atlas, port photographs and a worldwide distance table.

User notes can be added to each port and can be categorised by user, date, subject and content. The flexible report generator allows for customised reporting.

Designed for use onboard the ship and within the vessel operations department, the Ports & Terminals Guide CD-ROM is more than a simple replacement for printed guides. It provides the very best port information in a format that is both clear and easy to access.

Location: Port or terminal name, position, time zone, UNLOCODE

Country information: Flag, time zones, national holidays, government departments, currency, national regulations, ISPS designated authority

Port description: Location, general overview, load line zone, maximum vessel size

Pre arrival information: ETAs, documentation required, sample documents, communications, health, customs regulations, immigration, standard messages, flags, notice of readiness, regulations and general notices, agency

Navigation: Port limits, sea buoys, fairways and channels, pilotage, anchorage, tides, dock density, weather, navigation aids, charts and publications, traffic schemes, restrictions, tugs, coast guard, mooring information

Berths and cargo: Berths, names/nos, facilities, storage cargo, barges, ballast and slops, security, safety requirements

General: Repairs, docking, bunkers, water and stores, medical facilities, transport, crew change, consuls, holidays, working hours, developments, surveyors, seaman's missions, garbage removal, officials and visitors, fumigation, pollution control

Tanker berths: Berth restrictions, mooring arrangement, connections, cargoes, largest vessel

Address and contacts: Chandlers, civilian authorities, pilotage authorities, port authorities, port operators, port agents, stevedores, ship repairers, port bunkerers, towage companies, seaman's missions, Port Security Officers

Plans, mooring diagrams, photographs and maps: Colour port location atlas, colour port plans and mooring diagrams

Distance Tables: Comprehensive distance tables, ETA speed calculator, bunker consumption, total voyage costs

Ports & Terminals Guide 2015-2016

This latest edition of the Guide includes up-to-date information on more than 13,000 ports and terminals worldwide.

The subscription package includes both the four volume printed set and CD-ROM version. With over 7,000 pages of information the Guide includes contact details of over 26,600 port service providers such as agents, bunker suppliers, stevedores, chandlers, towage and repair companies; and nearly 4,000 ports plans, mooring diagrams and photographs.

The CD-ROM combines comprehensive information with a powerful database offering excellent functionality. Electronic distance tables, tanker berth details, photographs and plans make this an unrivalled source of information for use both in the office and onboard ship.

Location: Port or terminal name, position, time zone, UNLOCODE

Country information: Flag•, time zones, national holidays, government departments, currency, national regulations, ISPS designated authority

Port description: Location, general overview, load line zone, maximum vessel size

Pre arrival information: ETAs, documentation required, sample documents•, communications, health, customs regulations, immigration, standard messages, flags, notice of readiness, regulations and general notices, agency

Navigation: Port limits, sea buoys, fairways and channels, pilotage, anchorage, tides, dock density, weather, navigation aids, charts and publications, traffic schemes, restrictions, tugs, coast guard, mooring information

Berths and cargo: Berths, names/nos, facilities, storage cargo, barges, ballast and slops, security, safety requirements

General: Repairs, docking, bunkers, water and stores, medical facilities, transport, crew change, consuls, banks, holidays, working hours, developments, surveyors, seaman's missions, garbage removal, officials and visitors, fumigation, pollution control

•Tanker berths: Berth restrictions, mooring arrangement, connections, cargoes, largest vessel

Address and contacts: Chandlers, civilian authorities, pilotage authorities, port authorities, port operators, port agents, stevedores, ship repairers, port bunkerers, towage companies, seaman's missions, Port Security Officers

Plans, mooring diagrams, photographs • and maps: Colour port location atlas, colour port plans and mooring diagrams (mono in printed version)

•Distance Tables: Comprehensive distance tables, ETA speed calculator, bunker consumption, total voyage costs

Key: •CD-ROM only

List of Shipowners & Managers 2014-2015

A single hardback volume, the List of Shipowners & Managers contains over 1,000 pages of ownership and ship information.

A team of editorial experts verifies every entry before adding the information to the List of Shipowners & Managers, giving you the assurance that you are using a directory from the world's leading authority.

Companies are listed alphabetically within the main publication and a geographic index is provided to assist users when searching for companies by country and town. Information includes postal addresses, telephone, fax and email. Each vessel that makes up a fleet is named and its ship type, flag, IMO number, year of build and GT provided.

The List of Shipowners & Managers complements The Lloyd's Register of Ships by providing details of shipowners and the fleets they manage.

Shipowners Online
The web service provides subscribers with the latest address and contact details of the companies appearing in the printed edition. Subscribers will have access up to July 2015.

World Shipbuilding Statistics 2014

A quarterly summary of the shipbuilding activity for all self-propelled, seagoing merchant ships of 100 GT and above.

The World Shipbuilding Statistics provides details of all ships that are on order or under construction, together with their intended registration.

Information is gathered from shipbuilding yards before being submitted to our specialist new construction team for analysis.

Once verified, it is added to our maritime information database, the largest and most comprehensive of its type in the world.

Subscribers are kept up-to-date with changes that occur within the shipbuilding industry during each of the shipbuilding quarters.

World Fleet Statistics 2013

This annual publication shows the composition of the current self-propelled, seagoing merchant fleet of 100 GT and above, as at 31 December 2012.

It contains tables and notes about vessels completed within the year, together with total losses and disposals. In addition the World Fleet Statistics summarises the previous five years' merchant fleet and completions by country of build, registration, nationality and ship type, together with ships lost or broken up.

World Casualty Statistics 2013

Produced annually, this publication lists all ships for 2010 removed from the propelled seagoing merchant fleet, as total losses or disposals.

Total losses are analysed and disposals are categorised. Details include the ship name, flag, GT, year of build, location and a complete summary of the casualty incident, including the fate of the ship and crew.

Docking Handbook

This comprehensive manual is an ideal tool from which to prepare for a ship's docking and to monitor the performance of the work.

- New and improved checklists
- Extensive details of repairs carried out in China (steel, delays, workforce, time, contract and payment)
- Advice on how to avoid unnecessary expense
- Up-to-date database of repairers and marine equipment suppliers

With over 470 pages of standard forms and checklists, the handbook provides all of the documentation needed for planning, pre-arrival, during and after docking to improve efficiency and control. All the documents and checklists contained within the publication can be downloaded from the CD-ROM onto your PC, enabling you to complete and send them electronically and archive them for future reference.

The CD-ROM also contains a fully searchable database of ship repairers and marine equipment companies worldwide, simplifying the task of finding suitable suppliers.

Superintendent's Handbook

This publication provides marine superintendents with guidelines for carrying out day-to-day business both in the office and when visiting a vessel.

With over 410 pages the publication focuses on best practice rather than theory. Both experienced superintendents and those new to the role will benefit from this comprehensive reference. Keeping vessels trading on time and within budget, while ensuring compliance with ever increasing regulations, is the role of the superintendent. This publication will assist in virtually every aspect of that task.

All of the documents and checklist contained within the publication can be downloaded from the CD-ROM onto your PC. Similar to the Docking Handbook the CD-ROM also contains a fully searchable database of ship repairers and marine equipment suppliers worldwide, simplifying the task of finding suitable suppliers. suitable suppliers.

Pollution Prevention Handbook

The purpose of this handbook is to provide vessel operators and ship crew with operational guidelines for pollution prevention.
Studies sponsored by the Department of Transport some years ago identified that only 40% of the oily water separators installed on ships worked within the limits set out by the marine pollution convention.

This handbook provides a framework for reasonable solutions, covering systems, procedures and regulations, and describes the fundamentals of pollution prevention measures in simple language and with many practical checklists.

Technical departments will be able to use the handbook to highlight deficiencies where improvements can be made, and to ensure that they comply with MARPOL regulations and avoid costly fines and ship detentions.

All of the documents and checklists contained within the book can be downloaded from the accompanying CD-ROM.

Ship Repair & Maintenance Handbook

Shipboard maintenance is still an area of weakness for many companies, with repair costs featuring heavily on budgets. There is no point in creating an expensive, computer-based maintenance system if onboard equipment/machinery is poorly maintained. Ships' staff must always observe manufacturers' instructions for maintenance.

The Ship Repair and Maintenance Handbook aims to assist technical and safety staff by providing practical advice about onboard maintenance, enabling them to interpret any changes in equipment performance and avoid expensive breakdowns or marine casualties.

This handbook looks at the practical side of repair and maintenance, rather than reliance on computer-based instruction, to assist onboard and shore-based personnel in minimising problems and expensive repairs. It also emphasises the importance of investment in education, spare parts and regular inspection by superintendents.

Safety & Environmental Handbook

The introduction of the ISM code highlighted the need to improve awareness and understanding of safety and environmental issues.

Due to reduced manning levels, standards of training and communication problems between crew members from various countries, onboard safety is generally an area where improvements can be made.

The Safety and Environmental Handbook will help officers and crew to quickly increase their knowledge of systems, procedures and regulations relating to safety and environmental issues.

The handbook describes the fundamentals of basic safety requirements and environmental subjects in simple language and includes many practical checklists.

One of the sections includes the development and conception of a ship-specific ISPS manual, including a working example. Security officers will be able to refer to the handbook for help when drawing up their own manual, as required by the ISPS Code.

Classification & Statutory Surveys Handbook

The Classification and Statutory Surveys Handbook written by the Classification experts of Lloyd's Register, explains the how and why of Classification. It reveals in an easy-to-read and absorbing style the details behind the Classification process and explains the role of the modern Classification Society in certifying compliance with statutory legislation.

With over 200 pages of interesting text, photographs, diagrams, flow charts and checklists, the handbook provides the most comprehensive guide to surveys available. It also describes the links and differences between Class, SOLAS, MARPOL, STCW, ISM and ISPS in an easy-to-read format.

This comprehensive handbook is a must for any professional in the marine industry. Superintendents, shipbuilders, ship owners, ship's officers, ship repairers, surveyors, lawyers, financiers, insurers and students will all benefit from the wealth of detail in this invaluable reference work. Containing a variety of checklists and flowcharts, the latest changes in International Maritime legislation are explained in a logical and easy to follow manner.

Port Security Handbook

The International Ship and Port facility Security (ISPS) Code – Port Security Handbook written by Lloyd's Register in its role as a Recognised Security

Organisation, explains the intricacies of this new and important piece of international maritime legislation.

With over 200 pages of interesting text, full colour photographs, diagrams, flow charts and checklists, the handbook provides the most comprehensive guide to the ISPS Code. The handbook describes the roles and responsibilities of the Port Facility Security Officer and describes the practical steps needed to ensure the most rapid and efficient compliance with code requirements.

This comprehensive handbook is a must for all designated Port Facility Security Officers, Port Operators and Managers, Shippers, Subcontractors, Transport and Security professionals in the ports industry. Packed with a wealth of detail, this invaluable reference work will prove to be an essential working guide to meeting the ongoing challenge of implementing and maintaining port security.

DPA Handbook

This is a practical guide to the role and responsibilities of the Designated Person Ashore (DPA), under the ISM Code, whose influence should significantly affect the development and implementation of a safety culture within a Company.
This book contains safety management guidance and comprehensive coverage of many vital topics such as regulations, auditing, management systems, self-protection, accident and Near-Miss analysis and Port State Control. It includes many practical case studies and check lists. The author (Mick Caulkin) and his colleagues at Regs4ships are experienced Merchant Navy officers, Port State Control Inspectors, flag State surveyors and auditors. The author was also a founding member of the Enforcement Unit in the UK Maritime and Coastguard Agency and has seen at first hand the value of a Safety Management System that protects individuals and Companies; and how the lack of a system makes their defence to allegations of breaking the law very difficult.

So that this book does not date, it is presented in loose-leaf format to facilitate quarterly updates for those wishing to receive them. An Insight section in each update will cover new law cases, accidents and matters of concern or interest.

LLOYD'S REGISTER
FOUNDED 1760

Register of Ships S-Z

8938655 **S 07**
-
-
ex Rising Sun *-2007*
Seacraft Shipyard LLC
-
Morgan City, LA *United States of America*
Official number: 1022677

138
41
-

1994 Master Boat Builders, Inc. — Coden, Al
Yd No: 178
L reg 24.11 Br ex - Dght -
Lbp - Br md 7.32 Dpth 3.81
Welded, 1 dk

(B11B2FV) Fishing Vessel

1 oil engine driving 1 FP propeller

1008499 **S-100-1**
-
-
CMI Yachts
-

500
300
-

2006-02 Guangzhou Huangpu Shipbuilding Co Ltd — Guangzhou GD Yd No: Y-1
Loa 30.60 Br ex - Dght 2.130
Lbp - Br md 7.62 Dpth -
Welded, 1 dk

(X11A2YP) Yacht

2 oil engines geared to sc. shafts driving 2 Propellers
Total Power: 662kW (900hp) 12.0kn
Caterpillar 3406E
2 x 4 Stroke 6 Cy. 137 x 165 each-331kW (450bhp)
Caterpillar Inc-USA

1008762 **S-100-2**
-
-
CMI Yachts
-

500
300
-

2006-10 Guangzhou Huangpu Shipbuilding Co Ltd — Guangzhou GD Yd No: Y-2
Loa 30.60 Br ex - Dght 2.130
Lbp - Br md 7.62 Dpth -
Welded, 1 dk

(X11A2YP) Yacht

2 oil engines geared to sc. shafts driving 2 Propellers
Total Power: 662kW (900hp)
Caterpillar 3406E
2 x 4 Stroke 6 Cy. 137 x 165 each-331kW (450bhp)
Caterpillar Inc-USA

8745149 **S 201**
FGD6467
-
Mayotte - Conseil General
Service des Transports Maritimes de Mayotte (STM)
Dzaoudzi *France*
Official number: 925771

196
-
-

1999 Hydroland — Nantes
Loa 34.10 Br ex - Dght -
Lbp - Br md 9.80 Dpth -
Welded, 1 dk

(A36A2PR) Passenger/Ro-Ro Ship (Vehicles)

2 oil engines reduction geared to sc. shafts driving 2 Propellers
Total Power: 532kW (724hp)
Iveco Aifo 8210M
2 x 4 Stroke 6 Cy. 137 x 156 each-266kW (362bhp)
IVECO AIFO S.p.A.-Pregnana Milanese

7628136 **S. A. AGULHAS**
ZSAF
-
Government of The Republic of South Africa (South African Maritime Safety Authority (SAMSA))
Smit Amandla Marine Pty Ltd
SatCom: Inmarsat C 460100011
Cape Town *South Africa*
MMSI: 601048000
Official number: 350810

6,122
1,836
3,246

Class: LR
✠ **100A1** SS 03/2013
DTm - oil cargoes FP 60~C and above
Ice Class 1*
✠ **LMC**
Eq.Ltr: X; Cable: 495.0/50.0 U2

1978-01 Mitsubishi Heavy Industries Ltd. — Shimonoseki Yd No: 789
Loa 111.45 Br ex 18.04 Dght 6.058
Lbp 100.72 Br md 18.00 Dpth 10.11
Welded, 2 dks

(B31A2SR) Research Survey Vessel
Passengers: berths: 98
Grain: 1,776; Bale: 1,712; Ins: 111; Liq: 497
Compartments: 3 Ho, 2 Wing Ta, ER
3 Ha: (2.3 x 4.2) (7.9 x 6.0) (10.6 x 6.0)ER
Cranes: 1x25t,1x5t
Ice Capable

2 oil engines sr geared to sc. shaft driving 1 CP propeller
Total Power: 4,414kW (6,002hp)
Mirrlees KMR-6
2 x 4 Stroke 6 Cy. 381 x 457 each-2207kW (3001bhp)
Mirrlees Blackstone (Stockport)Ltd.-Stockport
AuxGen: 3 x 700kW 390V 50Hz a.c
Boilers: 2 e (ex.g.) (New boiler: 1978) 4.1kgf/cm² (4.0bar), 2 TOH (o.f.) 8.0kgf/cm² (7.8bar)
Thrusters: 2 Thwart. FP thruster (f); 2 Tunnel thruster (a)
Fuel: 697.0

9577135 **S. A. AGULHAS II**
ZSNO
-
Government of The Republic of South Africa (Department of Environmental Affairs)
Smit Amandla Marine Pty Ltd
Cape Town *South Africa*
MMSI: 601986000
Official number: 11205

12,897
3,870
4,780

Class: NV

2012-04 STX Finland Oy — Rauma Yd No: 1369
Loa 134.20 Br ex 22.00 Dght 7.650
Lbp 121.25 Br md 21.70 Dpth 10.55
Welded, 1 dk

(B31A2SR) Research Survey Vessel
Passengers: 100; cabins: 46
Grain: 4,000
Cranes: 1

4 diesel electric oil engines driving 4 gen. each 3000kW a.c Connecting to 2 elec. motors each (4500kW) driving 2 CP propellers
Total Power: 12,000kW (16,316hp) 14.0kn
Wartsila 6L32
4 x 4 Stroke 6 Cy. 320 x 400 each-3000kW (4079bhp)
Wartsila Finland Oy-Finland
Thrusters: 2 Thwart. FP thruster (f); 1 Thwart. FP thruster (a)
Fuel: 3650.0 (d.f.)

7385241 **S. A. KUSWAG I**
-
-
-
-

170
51

Class: (AB)

1974-01 Sandock-Austral Ltd. — Durban
Yd No: 57
Loa 28.96 Br ex 6.43 Dght 3.163
Lbp 26.67 Br md 6.41 Dpth 3.36
Welded, 1 dk

(B34G2SE) Pollution Control Vessel

1 oil engine driving 1 CP propeller
Total Power: 588kW (799hp) 11.0kn
Alpha 408-26VO
1 x 2 Stroke 8 Cy. 260 x 400 588kW (799bhp)
Alpha Diesel A/S-Denmark
AuxGen: 2 x 28kW

8912273 **S ACE**
DSNP8
-
ex BJ Ace *-2008* *ex* Isabela *-2004*
ex Shine Star *-1997* *ex* Engi Ace *-1994*
KEB Capital Inc
Seorae Holdings Corp
Jeju *South Korea*
MMSI: 440058000
Official number: JJR-049462

5,898
2,644
8,124

Class: KR (NK)

1990-03 Murakami Hide Zosen K.K. — Imabari
Yd No: 312
Loa 106.50 (BB) Br ex - Dght 7.723
Lbp 97.00 Br md 18.20 Dpth 8.35
Welded, 1 dk

(A31A2GX) General Cargo Ship
Grain: 13,222; Bale: 12,001
Compartments: 2 Ho, ER
2 Ha: (25.2 x 9.0) (28.0 x 9.0)ER
Cranes: 2x25t; Derricks: 2x15t

1 oil engine driving 1 FP propeller
Total Power: 2,795kW (3,800hp) 12.0kn
B&W 5L35MC
1 x 2 Stroke 5 Cy. 350 x 1050 2795kW (3800bhp)
Makita Diesel Co Ltd-Japan
AuxGen: 3 x 144kW a.c

7928976 **S. ANDREA**
IVQF
-
Azienda del Consorzio Trasporti Veneziano (ACTV)
Venice *Italy*
MMSI: 247290800
Official number: 7884

174
90
50

Class: RI

1981-02 Cant. Nav. Dante Castracani Srl — Ancona Yd No: 130
Loa 38.41 Br ex 7.78 Dght 2.045
Lbp 33.51 Br md 7.76 Dpth 2.87
Welded, 1 dk

(A37B2PS) Passenger Ship

2 oil engines geared to sc. shafts driving 2 FP propellers
Total Power: 294kW (400hp)
Isotta Fraschini ID36N8V
2 x Vee 4 Stroke 8 Cy. 170 x 170 each-147kW (200bhp)
Isotta Fraschini SpA-Italy

9185968 **S B M 1**
-
-
Sabang Marine Services Pte Ltd
-

123
37
-

Class: (BV)

1997-01 Tuong Aik (Sarawak) Sdn Bhd — Sibu
Yd No: 9701
Loa 23.26 Br ex - Dght 2.220
Lbp 22.96 Br md 7.00 Dpth 2.90
Welded, 1 dk

(B32A2ST) Tug

2 oil engines geared to sc. shafts driving 2 FP propellers
Total Power: 780kW (1,060hp) 10.8kn
Yanmar 6LAA-UTE
2 x 4 Stroke 6 Cy. 148 x 165 each-390kW (530bhp)
Yanmar Diesel Engine Co Ltd-Japan
AuxGen: 2 x 40kW 415V 50Hz a.c

9585352 **S BERNARDO**
2DHH7
-
Banco Espirito Santo SA
Pelagos Yachts Ltd
Ramsey *Isle of Man (British)*
MMSI: 235078989
Official number: 741799

458
137
-

Class: AB

2010-06 Heesen Shipyards B.V. — Oss
Yd No: 15044
Loa 44.17 Br ex 9.00 Dght 2.500
Lbp 38.00 Br md 8.50 Dpth 3.92
Welded, 1 dk

(X11A2YP) Yacht
Hull Material: Aluminium Alloy

2 oil engines reverse reduction geared to sc. shafts driving 2 FP propellers
Total Power: 5,444kW (7,402hp) 23.5kn
M.T.U. 16V4000M90
2 x Vee 4 Stroke 16 Cy. 165 x 190 each-2722kW (3701bhp)
MTU Friedrichshafen GmbH-Friedrichshafen
AuxGen: 2 x 65kW a.c
Fuel: 69.0 (d.f.)

8025185 **S. C. 32**
HSB2983
-
ex Matsukaze *-2003*
SC Management Co Ltd
-
Bangkok *Thailand*
Official number: 460000828

270
81
-

1980-12 Nagasaki Zosen K.K. — Nagasaki
Yd No: 753
Loa 35.56 Br ex - Dght 2.501
Lbp 33.84 Br md 8.62 Dpth 3.61
Welded, 1 dk

(B34G2SE) Pollution Control Vessel

1 oil engine driving 1 FP propeller
Total Power: 405kW (551hp)
Yanmar S185L-UT
1 x 4 Stroke 6 Cy. 185 x 230 405kW (551bhp)
Yanmar Diesel Engine Co Ltd-Japan

7402922 **S. C. LANCER**
3ETH8
-
ex Ben Ocean Lancer *-1990*
Turasoria SA
Schahin Engenharia SA
SatCom: Inmarsat A 1550453
Panama *Panama*
MMSI: 355226000
Official number: 2005492G

10,848
3,254
9,193

Class: BV (LR)
✠ Classed LR until 11/11/99

1977-03 Scotts' SB. Co. Ltd. — Greenock
Yd No: 744
Loa 153.68 Br ex 23.53 Dght 8.002
Lbp 137.32 Br md 23.46 Dpth 12.48
Welded, 2 dks

(B22B20D) Drilling Ship
Cranes: 1x40t,1x25t
Ice Capable

6 diesel electric oil engines driving 1 gen. of 2000kW 6600V 5 gen. each 2850kW 6600V Connecting to 2 elec. motors each (2206kW) driving 2 CP propellers
Total Power: 17,125kW (23,283hp) 12.0kn
EMD (Electro-Motive) 16-645-E9
1 x Vee 2 Stroke 16 Cy. 230 x 254 2205kW (2998bhp)
(Re-engined , Reconditioned & fitted 1997)
General Motors Corp.Electro-Motive Div.-La Grange
EMD (Electro-Motive) 20-645-E9
5 x Vee 2 Stroke 20 Cy. 230 x 254 each-2984kW (4057bhp)
(Re-engined , Reconditioned & fitted 1997)
General Motors Corp.Electro-Motive Div.-La Grange
Thrusters: 3 Thwart. FP thruster (f); 2 Tunnel thruster (a)

8307088 **S. CHAMP**
DSND4
-
ex C. Champ *-2008* *ex* Ken Pleiades *-2003*
ex New Pleiades *-1994* *ex* New Princesa *-1992*
ex Sanko Princesa *-1986*
KEB Capital Inc
Hanaro Shipping Co Ltd
Jeju *South Korea*
MMSI: 441305000
Official number: JJR-038882

19,757
11,551
33,326
T/cm
42.3

Class: KR (NK)

1984-07 Kanda Zosensho K.K. — Kawajiri
Yd No: 281
Loa 179.51 (BB) Br ex 27.64 Dght 10.767
Lbp 170.01 Br md 27.60 Dpth 15.12
Welded, 1 dk

(A21A2BC) Bulk Carrier
Grain: 42,820; Bale: 41,185
Compartments: 5 Ho, ER
5 Ha: (16.8 x 11.9)4 (19.2 x 14.4)ER
Cranes: 4x25t

1 oil engine driving 1 FP propeller
Total Power: 5,686kW (7,731hp) 14.0kn
Mitsubishi 6UEC52LA
1 x 2 Stroke 6 Cy. 520 x 1600 5686kW (7731bhp)
Kobe Hatsudoki KK (Akasaka Tekkosho KK (Akasaka DieselLtd)-Japan
AuxGen: 3 x 370kW 450V 60Hz a.c
Fuel: 115.0 (d.f.) (Heating Coils) 1585.5 (r.f.) 22.0pd

9118795 **S CHINA**
DSPX4
-
ex Bright MSN *-2009* *ex* Apollo Tujuh *-2008*
KEB Capital Inc
Seorae Holdings Corp
Jeju *South Korea*
MMSI: 441479000
Official number: JJR-089486

6,364
2,865
8,142

Class: KR (NK)

1995-04 Higaki Zosen K.K. — Imabari Yd No: 450
Loa 100.72 (BB) Br ex - Dght 7.928
Lbp 92.80 Br md 18.60 Dpth 8.50
Welded, 1 dk

(A31A2GX) General Cargo Ship
Grain: 14,442; Bale: 12,893
Compartments: 2 Ho, ER
2 Ha: (21.0 x 12.6) (27.3 x 12.6)ER
Cranes: 2x25t; Derricks: 1x30t

1 oil engine driving 1 FP propeller
Total Power: 3,089kW (4,200hp) 11.5kn
Mitsubishi 6UEC37LA
1 x 2 Stroke 6 Cy. 370 x 880 3089kW (4200bhp)
Kobe Hatsudoki KK-Japan

9151735 *5NTC* -	**S. D. GUMEL** **Nigerian Ports Authority (NPA)** - *Lagos* *Nigeria* Official number: 376973	**2,761** 828 3,707	Class: (LR) ✠ Classed LR until 27/8/03	**1998-01 Rijnwaal Shipyards B.V. — Hardinxveld-Giessendam** Yd No: 711 Loa 89.30 Br ex 15.88 Dght 4.600 Lbp 82.67 Br md 15.50 Dpth 6.00 Welded, 1 dk	**(B33B2DT) Trailing Suction Hopper Dredger** Hopper: 2,500	**2 oil engines** geared to sc. shafts driving 2 FP propellers Total Power: 1,770kW (2,406hp) Deutz TBD620BV8 2 x Vee 4 Stroke 8 Cy. 170 x 195 each-885kW (1203bhp) Motoren Werke Mannheim AG (MWM)-Mannheim AuxGen: 2 x 108kW 415V 50Hz a.c Thrusters: 1 Thwart. FP thruster (f)
8873609 - -	**S D R** **PT Sejahtera Swadaya** - *Samarinda* *Indonesia*	**136** 81 -	Class: (KI)	**1992-07 C.V. Lima Pandawa — Samarinda** L reg 25.50 Br ex - Dght 2.800 Lbp 22.60 Br md 7.50 Dpth 3.50 Welded, 1 dk	**(B32A2ST) Tug**	**2 oil engines** reduction geared to sc. shafts driving 2 FP propellers Total Power: 1,176kW (1,598hp) 9.3kn Cummins KT-38-M 2 x Vee 4 Stroke 12 Cy. 159 x 159 each-588kW (799bhp) (made 1991) Cummins Engine Co Inc-USA AuxGen: 1 x 54kW 230/400V a.c
6522634 *A9D2708* -	**S. D. SEVERN** **Gulf Dragon Trading Co WLL** - *Bahrain* *Bahrain* MMSI: 408310000 Official number: BN 3011	**1,235** 370 -	Class: BV (LR) ✠ Classed LR until 26/1/05	**1966-03 Charles Hill & Sons Ltd. — Bristol** Yd No: 452 Loa 64.70 Br ex 13.54 Dght 4.547 Lbp 60.97 Br md 13.11 Dpth 5.49 Welded, 1 dk	**(B33B2DT) Trailing Suction Hopper Dredger** Hopper: 1,100	**2 oil engines** with flexible couplings & sr reverse geared to sc. shafts driving 2 FP propellers Total Power: 1,544kW (2,100hp) 10.0kn Ruston 8VEBCM 2 x 4 Stroke 8 Cy. 260 x 368 each-772kW (1050bhp) Ruston & Hornsby Ltd.-Lincoln Thrusters: 1 Thwart. FP thruster (f)
9212539 *IFIK* -	**S. ERASMO** **Azienda del Consorzio Trasporti Veneziano (ACTV)** - *Venice* *Italy*	**129** 84 50	Class: RI	**2000-04 Cant. Nav. S.M.E.B. S.p.A. — Messina** Yd No: 181 Loa 30.40 Br ex - Dght - Lbp 27.50 Br md 5.56 Dpth 2.30 Welded, 1 dk	**(A37B2PS) Passenger Ship**	**2 oil engines** reduction geared to sc. shafts driving 2 FP propellers Total Power: 324kW (440hp) Fiat 821M 2 x 4 Stroke 6 Cy. 137 x 156 each-162kW (220bhp) Fiat OM Applicazioni Industriali-Milano
7607845 *XCZJ* -	**S. FLORIANA** *ex* Smit Floriana *ex* Smit Falcon *-1987* *ex* F 32 *-1985* **Naviera Armamex SA de CV** - *Dos Bocas* *Mexico* MMSI: 345050004	**336** 100 -	Class: GL (AB)	**1976-06 K.K. Imai Seisakusho — Kamijima** (Hull) Yd No: 157 **1976-06 Mitsui Ocean Development & Eng. Co. Ltd. — Japan** Yd No: S-071 Loa 34.80 Br ex 9.22 Dght 3.988 Lbp 34.02 Br md 9.21 Dpth 4.25 Welded, 1 dk	**(B32A2ST) Tug**	**2 oil engines** reverse reduction geared to sc. shafts driving 2 FP propellers Total Power: 1,838kW (2,498hp) Niigata 6MG25BX 2 x 4 Stroke 6 Cy. 250 x 320 each-919kW (1249bhp) Niigata Engineering Co Ltd-Japan AuxGen: 2 x 144kW a.c, 1 x 24kW a.c
9580936 *YDA4954* -	**S G PEACE** **PT Bintang Dunia Marina** - *Tanjung Priok* *Indonesia*	**157** 48 132	Class: NK	**2011-09 Far East Shipyard Co Sdn Bhd — Sibu** Yd No: 59 Loa 23.50 Br ex - Dght 2.710 Lbp 21.32 Br md 7.32 Dpth 3.20 Welded, 1 dk	**(B32A2ST) Tug**	**2 oil engines** reduction geared to sc. shafts driving 2 FP propellers Total Power: 970kW (1,318hp) Yanmar 6AYM-STE 2 x 4 Stroke 6 Cy. 155 x 180 each-485kW (659bhp) Yanmar Diesel Engine Co Ltd-Japan Fuel: 90.0 (d.f.)
9290347 *3ETA9* -	**S GLORY** *ex* Ardenne Venture *-2014* **Gulf Glory SA** Sinokor Merchant Marine Co Ltd *Panama* *Panama* MMSI: 356869000 Official number: 45525PEXT	**161,045** 109,921 318,000 T/cm 180.8	Class: KR (BV)	**2004-08 Hyundai Heavy Industries Co Ltd — Ulsan** Yd No: 1553 Loa 333.00 (BB) Br ex - Dght 22.500 Lbp 319.00 Br md 60.00 Dpth 30.40 Welded, 1 dk	**(A13A2TV) Crude Oil Tanker** Double Hull (13F) Liq: 352,000; Liq (Oil): 352,000 Compartments: 5 Ta, 10 Wing Ta, 2 Wing Slop Ta, ER 3 Cargo Pump (s): 3x5000m^3/hr Manifold: Bow/CM: 166m	**1 oil engine** driving 1 FP propeller Total Power: 28,926kW (39,328hp) 14.4kn B&W 6S90MC-C 1 x 2 Stroke 6 Cy. 900 x 3188 28926kW (39328bhp) Hyundai Heavy Industries Co Ltd-South Korea AuxGen: 3 x 1100kW 440/220V 60Hz a.c Fuel: 400.0 (d.f.) 7536.0 (r.f.)
9359909 *AQAD* -	**S. H. B. AHAD** *ex* Xijiang 05101 *-2007* **Karachi Port Trust** - *Karachi* *Pakistan* MMSI: 463033103 Official number: 1034-M	**1,044** 313 1,204	Class: (LR) ✠ Classed LR until 9/3/11	**2007-02 Xijiang Shipyard — Liuzhou GX** Yd No: 05101 Loa 60.78 Br ex 12.34 Dght 3.800 Lbp 57.50 Br md 11.80 Dpth 4.95 Welded, 1 dk	**(B34A2SH) Hopper, Motor**	**2 oil engines** with clutches, flexible couplings & sr reverse geared to sc. shafts driving 2 FP propellers Total Power: 1,200kW (1,632hp) MAN 6L20/27 2 x 4 Stroke 6 Cy. 200 x 270 each-600kW (816bhp) Shanghai Xinzhong Power MachinePlant-China AuxGen: 2 x 140kW 400V 50Hz a.c
9359911 - -	**S. H. B. AHSAN** **Karachi Port Trust** - *Karachi* *Pakistan* MMSI: 463033104 Official number: 1035-M	**1,044** 313 1,460	Class: (LR) ✠ Classed LR until 9/3/11	**2007-02 Xijiang Shipyard — Liuzhou GX** Yd No: 05102 Loa 60.78 Br ex 12.35 Dght 3.800 Lbp 57.52 Br md 11.80 Dpth 4.95 Welded, 1 dk	**(B34A2SH) Hopper, Motor**	**2 oil engines** with clutches, flexible couplings & sr reverse geared to sc. shafts driving 2 FP propellers Total Power: 1,200kW (1,632hp) MAN 6L20/27 2 x 4 Stroke 6 Cy. 200 x 270 each-600kW (816bhp) Shanghai Xinzhong Power MachinePlant-China AuxGen: 2 x 140kW 400V 50Hz a.c
9085223 - -	**S. H. B. BHIT SHAH** **Karachi Port Trust** - *Karachi* *Pakistan* Official number: 886-M	**963** 288 1,250 T/cm 3.6	Class: (LR) ✠ Classed LR until 22/3/04	**1999-03 Karachi Shipyard & Engineering Works Ltd. — Karachi** Yd No: 225 Loa 61.50 Br ex 11.68 Dght 3.850 Lbp 58.00 Br md 11.60 Dpth 4.64 Welded, 1 dk	**(B34A2SH) Hopper, Motor** Hopper: 800 Compartments: 1 Ho, ER 1 Ha: ER	**2 oil engines** with clutches, flexible couplings & reverse reduction geared to sc. shafts driving 2 FP propellers Total Power: 1,140kW (1,550hp) MAN 6L20/27 2 x 4 Stroke 6 Cy. 200 x 270 each-570kW (775bhp) MAN B&W Diesel AG-Augsburg AuxGen: 3 x 40kW 400V 50Hz a.c
5303823 - -	**S. H. B. SEAHORSE** **Associated British Ports Holdings Plc** -	*156* 45 -	Class: (LR) ✠ Classed LR until 1/76	**1958-11 J. Pollock, Sons & Co. Ltd. — Faversham** Yd No: 2108 Loa 27.56 Br ex 8.28 Dght - Lbp 23.53 Br md 7.93 Dpth 3.05 Riveted	**(B34Q2QB) Buoy Tender** Derricks: 1x7t	**2 oil engines** sr reverse geared to sc. shafts driving 2 FP propellers Total Power: 224kW (304hp) Gardner 8L3B 2 x 4 Stroke 8 Cy. 140 x 197 each-112kW (152bhp) L. Gardner & Sons Ltd.-Manchester AuxGen: 1 x 72kW 220V d.c, 1 x 70kW 220V d.c, 1 x 2kW 220V d.c
9085235 - -	**S. H. B. SEHWAN** **Karachi Port Trust** - *Karachi* *Pakistan* MMSI: 463033105 Official number: 887-M	**963** 288 1,250	**✠100AN** SS 09/2010 spilt hopper barge for service at Karachi Port **✠LMC** Eq.Ltr: K; Cable: 357.5/28.0 U2 (a)	**1999-03 Karachi Shipyard & Engineering Works Ltd. — Karachi** Yd No: 226 Loa 61.50 Br ex 11.68 Dght 3.850 Lbp 58.00 Br md 11.60 Dpth 4.64 Welded, 1 dk	**(B34A2SH) Hopper, Motor** Hopper: 800 Compartments: 1 Ho, ER 1 Ha: ER	**2 oil engines** with clutches, flexible couplings & reverse reduction geared to sc. shafts driving 2 FP propellers Total Power: 1,140kW (1,550hp) MAN 6L20/27 2 x 4 Stroke 6 Cy. 200 x 270 each-570kW (775bhp) MAN B&W Diesel AG-Augsburg AuxGen: 3 x 40kW 400V 50Hz a.c
7318937 *6YRR8* -	**S H KING** *ex* Hermes *-2013* **Portside Towing Ltd** - *Jamaica* MMSI: 339300800	*194* 131 -		**1973 Burton Shipyard Co., Inc. — Port Arthur, Tx** Yd No: 501 Loa - Br ex 9.20 Dght 3.966 Lbp 29.55 Br md 9.15 Dpth 4.58 Welded, 1 dk	**(B32A2ST) Tug**	**2 oil engines** geared to sc. shafts driving 2 FP propellers Total Power: 1,766kW (2,402hp) EMD (Electro-Motive) 12-645-E6 2 x Vee 2 Stroke 12 Cy. 230 x 254 each-883kW (1201bhp) General Motors Corp-USA AuxGen: 2 x 60kW 120V 60Hz a.c
8222783 *H04955* -	**S HACIBEKIROGLU** *ex* Dong Yuan *-2006* *ex* Fengshun Union *-2004* *ex* Arktis Pearl *-2001* **Sibtus Shipping & Trading Ltd** Ibrahim Denizcilik ve Ticaret AS *Panama* *Panama* MMSI: 353335000 Official number: 3486009	**1,557** 790 2,300	Class: IV (LR) (CC) (BV) ✠ Classed LR until 12/93	**1984-08 A/S Nordsovaerftet — Ringkobing** Yd No: 171 Loa 74.33 Br ex 11.36 Dght 4.620 Lbp 70.16 Br md 11.21 Dpth 6.71 Welded, 2 dks	**(A31A2GX) General Cargo Ship** Grain: 3,355; Bale: 3,014 TEU 54 C.Ho 36/20' (40') C.Dk 18/20' (40') Compartments: 1 Ho, ER, 1 Tw Dk 2 Ha: 2 (18.7 x 8.0)ER Derricks: 2x22t; Winches: 2 Ice Capable	**1 oil engine** with clutches, flexible couplings & sr geared to sc. shaft driving 1 CP propeller Total Power: 810kW (1,101hp) 9.0kn Alpha 6T23L-KVO 1 x 4 Stroke 6 Cy. 225 x 300 810kW (1101bhp) MAN B&W Diesel A/S-Denmark AuxGen: 3 x 84kW 380V 50Hz a.c, 1 x 40kW 380V 50Hz a.c Fuel: 38.0 (d.f.) 151.0 (r.f.) 4.0pd
8714786 *VB5112* -	**S.J. MAGALIE** **Robert F Hache** - *Caraquet, NB* *Canada* MMSI: 316003348 Official number: 809217	*104* 47 94		**1987-09 L'Industrie Marine de Caraquet Ltee — Caraquet NB** Loa 19.79 Br ex 6.81 Dght 3.201 Lbp 17.38 Br md 6.71 Dpth 3.66 Welded	**(B11B2FV) Fishing Vessel**	**1 oil engine** sr geared to sc. shaft driving 1 FP propeller Total Power: 397kW (540hp) Caterpillar 3412TA 1 x Vee 4 Stroke 12 Cy. 137 x 152 397kW (540bhp) Caterpillar Inc-USA Thrusters: 1 Thwart. FP thruster (f)
8737817 *YD7018* -	**S J P 01** **PT Sinar Haluan Samudra** - *Samarinda* *Indonesia*	**149** 89 -	Class: KI	**2001-12 PT Menumbar Kaltim — Samarinda** Loa 23.88 Br ex - Dght 2.400 Lbp 22.03 Br md 6.06 Dpth 3.20 Welded, 1 dk	**(B32A2ST) Tug**	**2 oil engines** driving 2 Propellers Total Power: 544kW (740hp) Nissan RE10 2 x Vee 4 Stroke 10 Cy. 135 x 132 each-272kW (370bhp) Nissan Diesel Motor Co. Ltd.-Ageo

8991231 **S JOAO** | 226 | 67 | -
PS5462
- **SAGA Rebocadores & Servicos Maritimos Ltda**
Camorim Servicos Maritimos Ltda
Salvador *Brazil*

Class: (BV)

2003-09 Estaleiros Rio Negro Ltda (ERIN) — Manaus Yd No: 1365
Loa 26.00 Br ex - Dght 3.600
Lbp 24.07 Br md 8.90 Dpth 4.50
Welded, 1 dk

(B32A2ST) Tug

2 oil engines geared to sc. shafts driving 2 Directional propellers
Total Power: 2,758kW (3,750hp) 11.7kn
Caterpillar 3512B
2 x Vee 4 Stroke 12 Cy. 170 x 215 each-1379kW (1875bhp)
Caterpillar Inc-USA
AuxGen: 2 x 64kW 220V 60Hz a.c

9155779 **S. JULIAO** | 445 | 176 | 63
CSKW
- **Transtejo-Transportes Tejo EP**
-
Lisbon *Portugal*
MMSI: 263700002
Official number: LX-3179-TL

Class: LR
✠ **100A1** SS 10/2012
HSC passenger catamaran ferry, group 2,
estuary of the River Tejo
✠ **LMC** **CCS**
Eq.Ltr: F; Cable: 13.5/19.0 U1

1997-10 FBM Marine Ltd. — Cowes Yd No: 1440
Loa 48.13 Br ex 12.20 Dght 1.340
Lbp 44.25 Br md 11.80 Dpth 2.90
Welded, 1 dk

(A37B2PS) Passenger Ship
Hull Material: Aluminium Alloy
Passengers: unberthed: 496

2 oil engines with clutches, flexible couplings & sr geared to sc. shafts driving 2 Water jets
Total Power: 2,480kW (3,372hp) 20.0kn
M.T.U. 12V396TE74
2 x Vee 4 Stroke 12 Cy. 165 x 185 each-1240kW (1686bhp)
MTU Friedrichshafen GmbH-Friedrichshafen
AuxGen: 2 x 46kW 380V 50Hz a.c
Fuel: 19.6 (d.f.)

9432103 **S. K LINE 3** | 217 | 65 | 103
9WGY5
- **SK Marine Sdn Bhd**
-
Kuching *Malaysia*
MMSI: 533000546
Official number: 330833

Class: NK (LR)
✠ Classed LR until 19/10/12

2007-10 Nam Cheong Dockyard Sdn Bhd — Miri Yd No: 535
Loa 34.00 Br ex 8.23 Dght 1.860
Lbp 31.00 Br md 8.00 Dpth 3.31
Welded, 1 dk

(B22G2OY) Standby Safety Vessel

2 oil engines with clutches, flexible couplings & reverse reduction geared to sc. shafts driving 2 FP propellers
Total Power: 1,074kW (1,460hp) 12.0kn
Caterpillar 3412C
2 x Vee 4 Stroke 12 Cy. 137 x 152 each-537kW (730bhp)
Caterpillar Inc-USA
AuxGen: 2 x 84kW 416V 50Hz a.c
Thrusters: 1 Thwart. FP thruster (f)
Fuel: 60.0 (d.f.)

9432098 **S. K LINE 4** | 217 | 65 | 103
9WGY4
- **SK Marine Sdn Bhd**
-
Kuching *Malaysia*
MMSI: 533000541
Official number: 330834

Class: LR
✠ **100A1** SS 07/2012
✠ **LMC**
Eq.Ltr: D†;
Cable: 275.0/17.0 U2 (a)

2007-07 Nam Cheong Dockyard Sdn Bhd — Miri Yd No: 534
Loa 34.00 Br ex 8.23 Dght 1.850
Lbp 32.30 Br md 8.00 Dpth 3.30
Welded, 1 dk

(B22G2OY) Standby Safety Vessel

2 oil engines with clutches, flexible couplings & sr reverse geared to sc. shafts driving 2 FP propellers
Total Power: 1,074kW (1,460hp) 12.0kn
Caterpillar 3412C
2 x Vee 4 Stroke 12 Cy. 137 x 152 each-537kW (730bhp)
Caterpillar Inc-USA
AuxGen: 2 x 84kW 416V 50Hz a.c
Thrusters: 1 Thwart. FP thruster (f)

9466075 **S. K LINE 9** | 217 | 65 | 103
9WHG9
- **Nam Cheong Dockyard Sdn Bhd**
-
Kuching *Malaysia*
MMSI: 533000697
Official number: 330941

Class: LR
✠ **100A1** SS 01/2013
✠ **LMC**
Eq.Ltr: D;
Cable: 330.0/17.5 U2 (a)

2008-01 Nam Cheong Dockyard Sdn Bhd — Miri Yd No: 550
Loa 34.00 Br ex 8.23 Dght 1.880
Lbp 32.30 Br md 8.00 Dpth 3.31
Welded, 1 dk

(B22G2OY) Standby Safety Vessel

2 oil engines with clutches, flexible couplings & reverse reduction geared to sc shafts driving 2 FP propellers
Total Power: 1,074kW (1,460hp)
Caterpillar 3412TA
2 x Vee 4 Stroke 12 Cy. 137 x 152 each-537kW (730bhp)
Caterpillar Inc-USA
AuxGen: 2 x 84kW 416V 50Hz a.c
Thrusters: 1 Thwart. FP thruster (f)

9210359 **S KUZNETSOV** | 6,204 | 2,900 | 7,625
UBLK7 *ex* Atlantic Steamer *-2013* *ex* BBC Spain *-2011*
- **Joint Stock Northern Shipping Co (A/O 'Severnoye Morskoye Parokhodstvo') (NSC ARKHANGELSK)**
-
Arkhangelsk *Russia*
MMSI: 273336180
Official number: 05-26-307

Class: GL

2001-04 Stocznia Gdanska - Grupa Stoczni Gdynia SA — Gdansk Yd No: 8203/12
Loa 107.75 Br ex - Dght 7.500
Lbp 102.10 Br md 18.20 Dpth 10.10
Welded, 1 dk

(A31A2GX) General Cargo Ship
Grain: 9,904; Bale: 9,904
TEU 377 C Ho 201 TEU C Dk 176 TEU
Compartments: 2 Ho, ER
2 Ha: (20.0 x 15.9) (44.5 x 15.9)ER
Cranes: 2x80t
Ice Capable

1 oil engine reduction geared to sc. shaft driving 1 CP propeller
Total Power: 3,840kW (5,221hp) 14.3kn
MAN 8L32/40
1 x 4 Stroke 8 Cy. 320 x 400 3840kW (5221bhp)
H Cegielski Poznan SA-Poland
AuxGen: 1 x 424kW 220/380V 50Hz a.c, 2 x 312kW 220/380V 50Hz a.c
Thrusters: 1 Tunnel thruster (f)

8987503 **S L K** | 931 | 442
- *ex* Jin Ping *-2005* *ex* Tong Da *-2000*
-
-
-

1981-08 Weihai Shipyard — Weihai SD Yd No: 8012
Loa 65.23 Br ex - Dght 4.400
Lbp 59.23 Br md 10.80 Dpth 5.35
Welded, 1 dk

(A31A2GX) General Cargo Ship

1 oil engine driving 1 Propeller
Total Power: 662kW (900hp)

9544853 **S. LEADER** | 3,375 | 1,013 | 4,931
9V9829
- **Ocean Glory Pte Ltd**
MosesTide Pte Ltd
SatCom: Inmarsat C 456640410
Singapore *Singapore*
MMSI: 566404000
Official number: 397637

Class: KR (NK)

2010-11 Kurinoura Dockyard Co Ltd — Yawatahama EH Yd No: 405
Converted From: Asphalt Tanker-2010
Loa 100.00 (BB) Br ex - Dght 6.350
Lbp 93.50 Br md 15.80 Dpth 8.00
Welded, 1 dk

(A12A2LP) Molten Sulphur Tanker
Double Hull (13F)
Asphalt: 2,700

1 oil engine driving 1 FP propeller
Total Power: 3,089kW (4,200hp) 13.0kn
Mitsubishi 6UEC37LA
1 x 2 Stroke 6 Cy. 370 x 880 3089kW (4200bhp)
Akasaka Tekkosho KK (Akasaka DieselLtd)-Japan

8803501 **S. M. RIGEL** | 482 | - | 176
-
- **SCT**
-
Mexico

Class: (AB)

1991-08 Astilleros Unidos de Guaymas S.A. de C.V. (AUGUSA) — Guaymas Yd No: 170
Loa - Br ex - Dght 2.000
Lbp 33.60 Br md 10.00 Dpth 3.00
Welded

(B34Q2QB) Buoy Tender

2 oil engines driving 2 FP propellers
Total Power: 607kW (825hp) 13.0kn
Deutz SBA6M816
1 x 4 Stroke 6 Cy. 142 x 160 303kW (412bhp) (made 1990)
Motoren Werke Mannheim AG (MWM)-Mannheim
Deutz SBA6M816
1 x 4 Stroke 6 Cy. 142 x 160 304kW (413bhp)
Motoren Werke Mannheim AG (MWM)-Mannheim

8959441 **S. MARCO** | *1,150* | 1,090 | 100
IUCH
- **Grandi Lavori Fincosit SpA**
-
Taranto *Italy*
MMSI: 247244200
Official number: 4475

Class: RI

1990-01 Cantiere Navale Visentini di Visentini F e C SAS — Porto Viro Yd No: 159
Loa 44.02 Br ex - Dght -
Lbp 44.00 Br md 21.98 Dpth 3.80
Welded, 1 dk

(B34B2SC) Crane Vessel
Cranes: 1x150t

2 oil engines geared to sc. shafts driving 2 Directional propellers
Total Power: 882kW (1,200hp) 6.8kn
MAN D2842LE
2 x Vee 4 Stroke 12 Cy. 128 x 142 each-441kW (600bhp)
MAN Nutzfahrzeuge AG-Nuernberg
AuxGen: 1 x 15kW 220/380V 50Hz a.c, 1 x 12kW 220/380V 50Hz a.c

---

8959025 **S. MARIA** | *746* | 464 | -
IVOG *ex* Mara *-2000*
- **Igeco Srl**
-
Gallipoli *Italy*
Official number: 3802

Class: RI

1979 CA-EM S.r.l. — Malcontenta
Loa 55.00 Br ex - Dght 2.571
Lbp 53.35 Br md 11.98 Dpth 3.50
Welded, 1 dk

(B34B2SC) Crane Vessel

2 oil engines driving 2 FP propellers
Total Power: 648kW (882hp)
Iveco Aifo 8281 SRM
2 x Vee 4 Stroke 8 Cy. 145 x 130 each-324kW (441bhp) (new engine 1988)
IVECO AIFO S.p.A.-Pregnana Milanese
AuxGen: 1 x 140kW 220/380V 50Hz a.c, 1 x 24kW 220/380V a.c
Thrusters: 1 Thwart. FP thruster (f)

6818320 **S. NAM No. 1** | *194* | 73 | -
- *ex* Tokai Maru No. 11 *-1996*
-
-
-

1968 Hayashikane Shipbuilding & Engineering Co Ltd — Nagasaki NS Yd No: 663
Loa 38.97 Br ex 7.32 Dght 2.947
Lbp 33.58 Br md 7.29 Dpth 3.41
Welded, 1 dk

(B11B2FV) Fishing Vessel

1 oil engine driving 1 FP propeller
Total Power: 515kW (700hp)
Daihatsu 6PSTCM-26D
1 x 4 Stroke 6 Cy. 260 x 320 515kW (700bhp)
Daihatsu Kogyo-Japan

6818332 **S. NAM No. 2** | *192* | 73 | -
- *ex* Tokai Maru No. 12 *-1996*
-
-
-

1968 Hayashikane Shipbuilding & Engineering Co Ltd — Nagasaki NS Yd No: 665
Loa 38.97 Br ex 7.32 Dght 2.947
Lbp 33.58 Br md 7.29 Dpth 3.41
Welded, 1 dk

(B11B2FV) Fishing Vessel

1 oil engine driving 1 FP propeller
Total Power: 515kW (700hp)
Daihatsu 6PSTCM-26D
1 x 4 Stroke 6 Cy. 260 x 320 515kW (700bhp)
Daihatsu Kogyo-Japan

6821456 **S. NAM No. 3** | *194* | 72 | -
- *ex* Tokai Maru No. 13 *-1996*
-
-
-

1968 Hayashikane Shipbuilding & Engineering Co Ltd — Nagasaki NS Yd No: 666
Loa 38.89 Br ex 7.32 Dght 2.947
Lbp 33.58 Br md 7.29 Dpth 3.41
Welded, 1 dk

(B11B2FV) Fishing Vessel

1 oil engine driving 1 FP propeller
Total Power: 515kW (700hp)
Daihatsu 6PSTCM-26D
1 x 4 Stroke 6 Cy. 260 x 320 515kW (700bhp)
Daihatsu Kogyo-Japan

8006335 **S. OCEAN SKIPPER** | *1,065* | 319 | -
- *ex* Lydia L *-2004* *ex* Murman Pride *-2000*
- *ex* Cape Brier *-1999*
Wiriya Sirichai-Ekawat
Sirichai Fisheries Co Ltd (Sirichai Fisheries Group)

Class: (LR)
✠ Classed LR until 30/3/05

1981-07 Halifax Industries Ltd — Halifax NS Yd No: 69
Loa 49.92 (BB) Br ex 11.92 Dght 4.201
Lbp 42.02 Br md 11.80 Dpth 6.89
Welded, 2 dks

(B11A2FS) Stern Trawler
Ins: 426

1 oil engine with flexible couplings & sr gearedto sc. shaft driving 1 CP propeller
Total Power: 2,940kW (3,997hp) 13.5kn
MaK 8M453AK
1 x 4 Stroke 8 Cy. 320 x 420 2940kW (3997bhp)
Krupp MaK Maschinenbau GmbH-Kiel
AuxGen: 1 x 760kW 450V 60Hz a.c, 1 x 148kW 450V 60Hz a.c
Fuel: 208.5 (d.f.) 7.0pd

IMO / Call sign	Name / Owner / Port	Tonnage	Class	Builder / Dimensions	Type	Machinery
8882492 - -	**S. P.** - **Pattani Dern Rua Thai Ltd** - *San Lorenzo* *Honduras* Official number: L-1323075	*158* 105 -		**1984 Mits Decisions Co., Ltd. — Samut Sakhon** Loa - Br ex - Dght 2.380 Lbp 34.88 Br md 6.50 Dpth 2.80 Welded, 1 dk	**(A13B2TU) Tanker (unspecified)**	**1 oil engine** driving 1 FP propeller 7.0kn General Motors 1 x 6 Cy. General Motors Corp-USA
7648631 *HSB2023* -	**S. P. P.** *ex* Choke Navee 1 *-1988* *ex* Ryosei Maru *-1978* **Cosmo Oil Co Ltd (Thailand)** - *Bangkok* *Thailand* Official number: 210822391	*499* 297 1,008		**1967**-03 **Murakami Hide Zosen K.K. — Imabari** Yd No: 42 Loa 53.62 Br ex - Dght 4.201 Lbp 49.00 Br md 8.81 Dpth 4.40 Welded, 1dk	**(A13B2TU) Tanker (unspecified)** Liq: 1,450; Liq (Oil): 1,450 Compartments: 4 Ta, ER	**1 oil engine** driving 1 FP propeller Total Power: 625kW (850hp) 10.0kn Mitsubishi 1 x 625kW (850bhp) Kobe Hatsudoki KK-Japan
7719246 *A9KH* -	**S.P. SPLIT - I** *ex* Test *-2012* *ex* W. D. Test *-2001* *ex* DB 308 *-1990* *ex* GC 308 *-1987* **Al Jazeera Shipping Co WLL (AJS)** - *Manama* *Bahrain* MMSI: 408854000 Official number: BN 6083	**1,543** 462 2,807	Class: BV (Class contemplated) LR ✠ **100A1** SS 04/2012 hopper barge ✠ **LMC** Eq.Ltr: N; Cable: 412.5/34.0 U2	**1978**-07 **A. Vuijk & Zonen's Scheepswerven B.V. — Capelle a/d IJssel** Yd No: 884 Loa 72.94 Br ex 13.29 Dght 4.600 Lbp 69.13 Br md 13.20 Dpth 5.65 Welded, 1 dk	**(B34A2SH) Hopper, Motor**	**2 oil engines** sr geared to sc. shafts driving 2 FP propellers Total Power: 1,214kW (1,650hp) 10.0kn Blackstone ESL6MK2 2 x 4 Stroke 6 Cy. 222 x 292 each-607kW (825bhp) Mirrlees Blackstone (Stamford)Ltd.-Stamford AuxGen: 2 x 360kW 380V 50Hz a.c, 2 x 118kW 380V 50Hz a.c Thrusters: 1 Thwart. CP thruster (f); 1 Tunnel thruster (a)
7721055 *A9KJ* -	**S.P. SPLIT - II** *ex* Itchen *-2012* *ex* W. D. Itchen *-2001* *ex* DB 307 *-1990* *ex* GC 307 *-1987* **Al Jazeera Shipping Co WLL (AJS)** - *Manama* *Bahrain* MMSI: 408855000 Official number: BN 6084	**1,543** 462 2,807	Class: BV (Class contemplated) LR ✠ **100A1** SS 04/2012 hopper barge ✠ **LMC** Eq.Ltr: N; Cable: 412.5/34.0 U2	**1978**-05 **Scheepswerf "De Waal" B.V. — Zaltbommel** Yd No: 712 Loa 72.94 Br ex 13.29 Dght 4.600 Lbp 69.13 Br md 13.20 Dpth 5.65 Welded, 1 dk	**(B34A2SH) Hopper, Motor**	**2 oil engines** sr reverse geared to sc. shafts driving 2 FP propellers Total Power: 1,214kW (1,650hp) 10.0kn Blackstone ESL6MK2 2 x 4 Stroke 6 Cy. 222 x 292 each-607kW (825bhp) Mirrlees Blackstone (Stamford)Ltd.-Stamford AuxGen: 2 x 360kW 380V 50Hz a.c, 2 x 118kW 380V 50Hz a.c Thrusters: 1 Thwart. CP thruster (f); 1 Tunnel thruster (a)
7720972 - -	**S.P. SPLIT - III** *ex* Avon *-2012* *ex* DB 306 *-1990* *ex* GC 306 *-1987* **Al Jazeera Shipping Co WLL (AJS)** - *Manama* *Bahrain* MMSI: 408856000 Official number: BN 6085	**1,543** 462 2,807	Class: BV (Class contemplated) LR ✠ **100A1** SS 02/2011 hopper barge ✠ **LMC** Eq.Ltr: N; Cable: 412.5/34.0 U2	**1978**-05 **Scheepsw. en Mfbk."De Biesbosch-Dordrecht" B.V. — Dordrecht** Yd No: 690 Loa 72.94 Br ex 13.29 Dght 4.600 Lbp 69.13 Br md 13.20 Dpth 5.65 Welded, 1 dk	**(B34A2SH) Hopper, Motor**	**2 oil engines** sr geared to sc. shafts driving 2 FP propellers Total Power: 1,214kW (1,650hp) 10.0kn Blackstone ESL6MK2 2 x 4 Stroke 6 Cy. 222 x 292 each-607kW (825bhp) Mirrlees Blackstone (Stamford)Ltd.-Stamford AuxGen: 2 x 360kW 380V 50Hz a.c, 2 x 118kW 380V 50Hz a.c Thrusters: 1 Thwart. CP thruster (f); 1 Tunnel thruster (a)
7434418 *IRDC* -	**S. PANAGIA** - **Augustea Imprese Marittime e di Salvataggi SpA** - *Augusta* *Italy* MMSI: 247224400 Official number: 39	*215* 25 160	Class: RI	**1977**-03 **Bacino di Carenaggio S.p.A. — Trapani** Yd No: 8 Loa 31.02 Br ex 8.62 Dght 3.802 Lbp 28.02 Br md 8.60 Dpth 4.25 Welded, 1 dk	**(B32A2ST) Tug**	**1 oil engine** geared to sc. shaft driving 1 CP propeller Total Power: 1,442kW (1,961hp) MAN G8V30/45ATL 1 x 4 Stroke 8 Cy. 300 x 450 1442kW (1961bhp) Maschinenbau Augsburg Nuernberg (MAN)-Augsburg
5303976 *PPBI* -	**S. PAULO** - **Companhia Docas do Estado de Sao Paulo (CODESP)** - *Santos* *Brazil* Official number: 3810511641	*226* 67 -	Class: (LR) ✠ Classed LR until 9/65	**1930**-05 **Henry Robb Ltd. — Leith** Yd No: 155 Loa 35.59 Br ex 9.05 Dght 4.115 Lbp 33.53 Br md 9.00 Dpth - Riveted, 1 dk	**(B32A2ST) Tug** Compartments: 1 Ho, ER Winches: 1	**2 Steam Recips** driving 2 FP propellers 10.0kn MacColl & Pollock Ltd.-Sunderland Fuel: 71.0 (r.f.)
8991243 *PS6552* -	**S. PAULO** - **SAGA Rebocadores & Servicos Maritimos Ltda** - *Rio de Janeiro* *Brazil*	**226** 67 -	Class: (BV)	**2004**-01 **Estaleiros Rio Negro Ltda (ERIN) — Manaus** Yd No: 1366 Loa 26.00 Br ex - Dght 3.600 Lbp 24.07 Br md 8.90 Dpth 4.50 Welded, 1 dk	**(B32A2ST) Tug**	**2 oil engines** geared to sc. shafts driving 2 Directional propellers Total Power: 2,758kW (3,750hp) 12.0kn Caterpillar 3512B 2 x Vee 4 Stroke 12 Cy. 170 x 215 each-1379kW (1875bhp) Caterpillar Inc-USA AuxGen: 2 x 64kW 220V 60Hz a.c
7309986 *WY2350* -	**S. PEDRO** *ex* Gazela *-1987* *ex* Wendy C *-1975* **S P R Fishing Corp** - *New Bedford, MA* *United States of America* Official number: 511681	*135* 92 -		**1967 Master Marine, Inc. — Bayou La Batre, Al** L reg 22.13 Br ex 6.79 Dght - Lbp - Br md - Dpth 3.51 Welded	**(B11B2FV) Fishing Vessel**	**1 oil engine** driving 1 FP propeller Total Power: 279kW (379hp)
9005118 *DSRF2* -	**S PEGASUS** *ex* Aisha 2 *-2011* *ex* Aisha *-2009* **Shinhan Capital Co Ltd** SC Shipping Co Ltd SatCom: Inmarsat C 444080810 *Jeju* *South Korea* MMSI: 441808000 Official number: JJR-111058	**3,387** 1,017 4,319 T/cm 11.7	Class: KR (NV) (NK)	**1991**-02 **Shinhama Dockyard Co. Ltd. — Anan** Yd No: 806 Loa 99.60 (BB) Br ex - Dght 5.765 Lbp 92.00 Br md 15.80 Dpth 7.30 Welded, 1 dk	**(A11B2TG) LPG Tanker** Double Bottom Entire Compartment Length Liq (Gas): 3,208 2 x Gas Tank (s); 2 independent horizontal 2 Cargo Pump (s): 2x300m³/hr Manifold: Bow/CM: 47.4m	**1 oil engine** driving 1 FP propeller Total Power: 2,427kW (3,300hp) 13.0kn Mitsubishi 6UEC37LA 1 x 2 Stroke 6 Cy. 370 x 880 2427kW (3300bhp) Akasaka Tekkosho KK (Akasaka DieselLtd)-Japan AuxGen: 2 x 240kW 440V 60Hz a.c Fuel: 82.0 (d.f.) 445.0 (r.f.)
9118628 *KAWM* -	**S/R AMERICAN PROGRESS** *ex* American Progress *-2000* **SeaRiver Maritime Inc** - SatCom: Inmarsat Mini-M 761117222 *Norfolk, VA* *United States of America* MMSI: 366505000 Official number: 1053997	**30,415** 11,125 46,103 T/cm 52.4	Class: AB	**1997**-09 **Newport News Shipbuilding — Newport News, Va** Yd No: 647C Loa 183.00 (BB) Br ex 32.20 Dght 12.216 Lbp 174.30 Br md 32.20 Dpth 19.15 Welded, 1 dk	**(A13A2TW) Crude/Oil Products Tanker** Double Hull (13F) Liq: 52,787; Liq (Oil): 52,787 Compartments: 14 Wing Ta, 2 Wing Slop Ta, ER 3 Cargo Pump (s): 3x1400m³/hr Manifold: Bow/CM: 93.1m	**1 oil engine** driving 1 FP propeller Total Power: 7,944kW (10,801hp) 14.5kn B&W 6L60MC 1 x 2 Stroke 6 Cy. 600 x 1944 7944kW (10801bhp) Kawasaki Heavy Industries Ltd-Japan AuxGen: 1 x 850kW 450V 60Hz a.c, 2 x 600kW 450V 60Hz a.c Fuel: 237.0 (d.f.) (Heating Coils) 1466.4 (r.f.) 36.0pd
9196931 *V2FP6* -	**S. RAFAEL** *ex* Amrum *-2001* **Briese Schiffahrts GmbH & Co KG ms 'Wiesede'** Briese Schiffahrts GmbH & Co KG *Saint John's* *Antigua & Barbuda* MMSI: 305750000 Official number: 4894	**4,454** 2,141 5,539 T/cm 14.5	Class: GL	**2000**-06 **Qingshan Shipyard — Wuhan HB** Yd No: KS960303 Loa 100.60 (BB) Br ex 19.11 Dght 6.654 Lbp 95.80 Br md 18.80 Dpth 8.40 Welded, 1 dk	**(A33A2CC) Container Ship (Fully Cellular)** Grain: 7,177 TEU 501 C Ho 141 TEU C Dk 360 TEU incl 84 ref C. Compartments: 3 Cell Ho, ER 3 Ha: (6.5 x 7.8)2 (25.2 x 15.7)ER Cranes: 2x40t	**1 oil engine** with clutches, flexible couplings & sr geared to sc. shaft driving 1 CP propeller Total Power: 4,320kW (5,873hp) 15.0kn MAN 9L32/40 1 x 4 Stroke 9 Cy. 320 x 400 4320kW (5873bhp) MAN B&W Diesel AG-Augsburg AuxGen: 1 x 700kW 440V 60Hz a.c, 2 x 384kW 440V 60Hz a.c Thrusters: 1 Thwart. FP thruster (f) Fuel: 88.0 (d.f.) 540.0 (r.f.) 40.0pd
7351123 *INJU* -	**S. RAFFAELE** - **Societa Cooperativa Pescatori Srl San Raffaele** - *Palermo* *Italy* Official number: 571	*211* 63 -	Class: (RI)	**1974**-06 **Cant. Nav. Ugo Codecasa S.p.A. — Viareggio** Yd No: 23 Lengthened-1998 Loa - Br ex 7.55 Dght 2.972 Lbp 35.90 Br md 7.52 Dpth 3.66 Welded, 1 dk	**(B11B2FV) Fishing Vessel**	**1 oil engine** driving 1 FP propeller Total Power: 915kW (1,244hp) MWM TBD604BV12 1 x Vee 4 Stroke 12 Cy. 170 x 195 915kW (1244bhp) (new engine 1987) Kloeckner Humboldt Deutz AG-West Germany AuxGen: 2 x 120kW 220/380V 50Hz a.c
9550541 - -	**S. RUANGCHAI** - **Somchai Klongpramong** -	**212** 144 -		**2008**-05 **Mahachai Dockyard Co., Ltd. — Samut Sakhon** Loa 31.00 Br ex - Dght - Lbp 29.70 Br md 6.45 Dpth 3.45 Welded, 1 dk	**(A34A2GR) Refrigerated Cargo Ship**	**1 oil engine** reduction geared to sc. shaft driving 1 FP propeller Total Power: 380kW (517hp) Cummins KT-19-M 1 x 4 Stroke 6 Cy. 159 x 159 380kW (517bhp) Cummins Engine Co Inc-USA
8320016 *9WFT* -	**S. S. DARLING** *ex* Asie III *-1992* **Multimarket Sdn Bhd** - *Labuan* *Malaysia* Official number: 324935	**257** 85 -	Class: (NV)	**1984**-03 **AS Fjellstrand Aluminium Yachts — Omastrand** Yd No: 1562 Loa 31.53 Br ex - Dght 1.677 Lbp 30.03 Br md 9.42 Dpth 3.51 Welded, 1 dk	**(B21A2OC) Crew/Supply Vessel** Hull Material: Aluminium Alloy	**2 oil engines** sr geared to sc. shafts driving 2 CP propellers Total Power: 2,942kW (4,000hp) 30.0kn M.T.U. 16V396TE74 2 x Vee 4 Stroke 16 Cy. 165 x 185 each-1471kW (2000bhp) MTU Friedrichshafen GmbH-Friedrichshafen AuxGen: 2 x 40kW 440V 60Hz a.c Thrusters: 1 Thwart. FP thruster (f) Fuel: 30.0 (d.f.) 19.0pd

8963703 *WBR4896* -	**S.S. LEGACY** *ex* Safari Legacy *-2013* *ex* Spirit of '98 *-2011* *ex* Victorian Empress *-1993* *ex* Colonial Explorer *-1988* *ex* Pilgrim Belle *-1988* **Innersea Discoveries LLC (Un-Cruise Adventures)** - *Sitka, AK* *United States of America* MMSI: 367578110 Official number: 677464	**1,472** 512 -	Class: (AB)	**1984-11 Bender Shipbuilding & Repair Co Inc — Mobile AL** Yd No: 140 Loa 58.52 Br ex Dght 2.890 Lbp 58.52 Br md 12.19 Dpth 3.86 Welded, 1 dk	**(A37A2PC) Passenger/Cruise** Passengers: cabins: 49; berths: 104	**2 oil engines** driving 2 FP propellers Total Power: 1,544kW (2,100hp) 13.0kn
7804651 *PMBA* -	**S. T. I. 3** *ex* Shan Furyu *-2008* *ex* Furyu Maru *-1990* **PT Sumatra Timur Indonesia** - *Tanjung Priok* *Indonesia* MMSI: 525019375	**1,222** 806 1,620	Class: KI	**1978-04 Mategata Zosen K.K. — Namikata** Yd No: 152 Loa 68.90 Br ex - Dght 4.250 Lbp 64.01 Br md 11.51 Dpth 6.30 Riveted\Welded, 1 dk	**(A31A2GX) General Cargo Ship**	**1 oil engine** driving 1 FP propeller Total Power: 1,103kW (1,500hp) Makita KNLH630 1 x 4 Stroke 6 Cy. 300 x 480 1103kW (1500bhp) Makita Diesel Co Ltd-Japan
9253363 - -	**S. T. W. 2** - **STW Marine Co Ltd** -	**247** 168 -		**2001 Mits Decisions Co., Ltd. — Samut Sakhon** Loa 34.00 Br ex 7.50 Dght - Lbp - Br md - Dpth 4.30 Welded, 1 dk	**(B11B2FV) Fishing Vessel**	**1 oil engine** geared to sc. shaft driving 1 FP propeller Total Power: 634kW (862hp) Cummins KTA-38-M 1 x Vee 4 Stroke 12 Cy. 159 x 159 634kW (862bhp) Cummins Engine Co Inc-USA
7220219 - -	**S. TERENZIO** *ex* Mazarpesca Terzo *-1990* **Mateco Co Ltd** -	*199* 90 -		**1972 Cant. Nav. M. Morini & C. — Ancona** Yd No: 133 Loa 32.64 Br ex 7.04 Dght 3.099 Lbp - Br md 7.01 Dpth 3.66 Welded, 1 dk	**(B11A2FT) Trawler**	**1 oil engine** driving 1 FP propeller Total Power: 441kW (600hp) Deutz SBV6M545 1 x 4 Stroke 6 Cy. 320 x 450 441kW (600bhp) Kloeckner Humboldt Deutz AG-West Germany
9107241 *DSPQ8* -	**S THAI** *ex* Bright Winner *-2009* *ex* Apollo Lima *-2007* **Seorae Sea Merchant Corp** Hanaro Shipping Co Ltd *Jeju* *South Korea* MMSI: 441423000 Official number: JJR-072122	**6,655** 2,346 8,629	Class: KR (NK)	**1994-12 Shin Kurushima Dockyard Co. Ltd. — Akitsu** Yd No: 2837 Loa 100.61 (BB) Br ex - Dght 8.200 Lbp 93.50 Br md 18.80 Dpth 13.60 Welded, 2 dks	**(A31A2GX) General Cargo Ship** Grain: 15,212; Bale: 13,574 Compartments: 2 Ho, ER 2 Ha: (27.0 x 12.6) (21.0 x 12.6)ER Cranes: 1x30t,2x20t	**1 oil engine** driving 1 FP propeller Total Power: 3,089kW (4,200hp) 12.6kn B&W 5L35MC 1 x 2 Stroke 5 Cy. 350 x 1050 3089kW (4200bhp) Makita Corp-Japan AuxGen: 3 x a.c Fuel: 695.0
9421362 *YD3892* -	**S VICTORY 15** *ex* Bina Ocean 8a *-2012* **PT Pelarayan Samudera Victory Shipping** - *Tanjungpinang* *Indonesia*	**119** 36 94	Class: KI (GL)	**2007-01 PT Marcopolo Shipyard — Batam** Yd No: H008 Loa 23.17 Br ex - Dght 2.405 Lbp - Br md 7.00 Dpth 2.90 Welded, 1 dk	**(B32A2ST) Tug**	**2 oil engines** reduction geared to sc. shafts driving 2 Propellers Total Power: 896kW (1,218hp) 10.0kn Caterpillar 3412C 2 x Vee 4 Stroke 12 Cy. 137 x 152 each-448kW (609bhp) Caterpillar Inc-USA AuxGen: 2 x 50kW 400V a.c
9304409 - -	**S. VIGILIO** *ex* San Vigilio *-2005* **Government of The Republic of Italy (Ministero dei Trasporti e della Navigazione - Unita' Gestione Infrastrutture)** - *Italy* Official number: 0027 BS N	**549** 247 170	Class: (RI)	**2005-03 Cant. Nav. Rosetti — Ravenna** Yd No: 75 Loa 46.30 Br ex - Dght 2.315 Lbp - Br md 9.60 Dpth 3.65 Welded, 1 dk	**(A36A2PR) Passenger/Ro-Ro Ship (Vehicles)** Passengers: unberthed: 300	**2 oil engines** geared to sc. shafts driving 2 Propellers Total Power: 1,096kW (1,490hp) 12.0kn M.T.U. 12V2000M60 2 x Vee 4 Stroke 12 Cy. 130 x 150 each-548kW (745bhp) MTU Friedrichshafen GmbH-Friedrichshafen AuxGen: 2 x 125kW 220/24V 50Hz a.c
9132624 *DSPE8* -	**S VINA** *ex* Bright Ace *-2009* *ex* Lucky Emblem *-2007* **KEB Capital Inc** Hanaro Shipping Co Ltd *Jeju* *South Korea* MMSI: 440878000 Official number: JJR-079464	**6,049** 2,766 10,304	Class: KR (NK)	**1995-10 Higaki Zosen K.K. — Imabari** Yd No: 462 Loa 100.48 (BB) Br ex 18.62 Dght 7.892 Lbp 92.80 Br md 18.60 Dpth 13.10 Welded, 1 dk	**(A31A2GX) General Cargo Ship** Grain: 14,604; Bale: 13,564 Compartments: 2 Ho, ER 2 Ha: (21.0 x 11.2) (25.2 x 11.2)ER Derricks: 2x30t,2x25t	**1 oil engine** driving 1 FP propeller Total Power: 3,089kW (4,200hp) 12.3kn Mitsubishi 6UEC37LA 1 x 2 Stroke 6 Cy. 370 x 880 3089kW (4200bhp) Kobe Hatsudoki KK-Japan Fuel: 387.0 (r.f.) 11.0pd
5304085 *ISXY* -	**S. VITALE** - **Ecolmare Gargano Srl** - *Manfredonia* *Italy* Official number: 246	*164* 47 -	Class: RI	**1962 Cantieri Navali Apuania SpA — Carrara** Yd No: 66 Loa 27.41 Br ex 7.60 Dght 3.252 Lbp 24.95 Br md 7.55 Dpth 3.92 Riveted\Welded, 1 dk	**(B32A2ST) Tug**	**1 oil engine** driving 1 CP propeller Total Power: 706kW (960hp) 11.9kn Alpha 498-VO 1 x 2 Stroke 8 Cy. 290 x 490 706kW (960bhp) Alpha Diesel A/S-Denmark
7650660 *3FHZ4* -	**SA 8** *ex* Sunny King *-1999* *ex* Creator *-1995* *ex* Lien Ta *-1993* *ex* Mitsu Maru No. 8 *-1990* *ex* Ryusho Maru *-1985* **Stardust Navigation SA** - *Panama* *Panama* MMSI: 355622000 Official number: 19933PEXT8	**1,107** 529 1,489		**1974-11 K.K. Kakimoto Zosensho — Hinase** Yd No: 220 Loa 65.51 (BB) Br ex - Dght 4.201 Lbp 61.02 Br md 11.51 Dpth 6.00 Welded, 1 dk	**(A31A2GX) General Cargo Ship**	**1 oil engine** driving 1 FP propeller Total Power: 1,324kW (1,800hp) 13.0kn Hanshin 6LU35 1 x 4 Stroke 6 Cy. 350 x 550 1324kW (1800bhp) The Hanshin Diesel Works Ltd-Japan
9221205 *C6RS4* -	**SA ALTIUS** - **Abacus Maritime Inc** Enterprises Shipping & Trading SA SatCom: Inmarsat C 431116510 *Nassau* *Bahamas* MMSI: 311165000 Official number: 8000289	**87,542** 56,714 171,480 T/cm 120.3	Class: BV	**2001-03 Hyundai Heavy Industries Co Ltd — Ulsan** Yd No: 1329 Loa 288.87 (BB) Br ex - Dght 17.720 Lbp 275.91 Br md 45.00 Dpth 24.10 Welded, 1 dk	**(A21A2BC) Bulk Carrier** Grain: 191,400 Compartments: 9 Ho 9 Ha: 7 (15.5 x 20.6)2 (15.5 x 17.2)	**1 oil engine** driving 1 FP propeller Total Power: 16,859kW (22,921hp) 14.5kn B&W 6S70MC 1 x 2 Stroke 6 Cy. 700 x 2674 16859kW (22921bhp) Hyundai Heavy Industries Co Ltd-South Korea Fuel: 240.4 (d.f.) 3686.0 (r.f.) 55.0pd
9355783 *D8BX* -	**SA ARAON** *ex* Kwangmyoung No. 1 *-2013* *ex* Tazawako *-2012* **ASTK Co Ltd** Sung Kyung Maritime Co Ltd (SK Maritime) *Jeju* *South Korea* MMSI: 441971000 Official number: JJR-131030	**2,030** 1,284 3,375	Class: KR (BV) (CC)	**2005-11 Huangdao Shipyard of Qingdao Ocean Shipping Co — Qingdao SD** Yd No: HDZ-006 Loa 81.00 Br ex - Dght 5.500 Lbp 76.00 Br md 13.60 Dpth 6.80 Welded, 1 dk	**(A31A2GX) General Cargo Ship** Ice Capable	**1 oil engine** geared to sc. shaft driving 1 FP propeller Total Power: 1,323kW (1,799hp) 11.8kn Chinese Std. Type G6300ZC 1 x 4 Stroke 6 Cy. 300 x 380 1323kW (1799bhp) Wuxi Antai Power Machinery Co Ltd-China
7729071 *J8B2039* -	**SA EXPLORER** *ex* Sakawe Explorer *-2013* *ex* Seaspan *-2003* *ex* Strong Cajun *-2000* *ex* Bigorange X *-1993* *ex* Big Orange X *-1992* **Global Mineral Holdings Ltd** ARGO Ship Management & Services Srl *Kingstown* *St Vincent & The Grenadines* MMSI: 375445000 Official number: 8511	**2,632** 870 2,133	Class: (BV) (AB)	**1979-03 Burton Shipyard Co., Inc. — Port Arthur, Tx** Yd No: 526 Converted From: Deck Cargo Vessel-2004 Converted From: Production Testing Vessel-1993 Lengthened & Widened-1993 Loa 83.67 Br ex - Dght 3.990 Lbp 79.53 Br md 19.63 Dpth 4.88 Welded, 1 dk	**(B35C2SM) Mining Vessel** TEU 160 C. 160/20' Cranes: 1x25t	**3 diesel electric oil engines** driving 3 gen. each 2650kW a.c Connecting to 2 elec. motors each (1103kW) driving 2 Azimuth electric drive units Total Power: 8,385kW (11,400hp) 12.0kn General Electric 7FDS16-A2 3 x Vee 4 Stroke 16 Cy. 229 x 267 each-2795kW (3800bhp) General Electric Co.-Lynn, Ma AuxGen: 2 x 250kW 480V 60Hz a.c, 1 x 1700kW a.c Thrusters: 1 Thwart. FP thruster (f) Fuel: 418.0 (d.f.)
9221217 *C6RT5* -	**SA FORTIUS** - **Braverus Maritime Inc** Enterprises Shipping & Trading SA SatCom: Inmarsat C 431118210 *Nassau* *Bahamas* MMSI: 311182000 Official number: 8000302	**87,542** 56,714 171,509 T/cm 120.3	Class: BV	**2001-06 Hyundai Heavy Industries Co Ltd — Ulsan** Yd No: 1330 Loa 288.87 (BB) Br ex - Dght 17.720 Lbp 275.91 Br md 45.00 Dpth 24.10 Welded, 1 dk	**(A21A2BC) Bulk Carrier** Grain: 191,424 Compartments: 9 Ho 9 Ha: 7 (15.5 x 20.6)2 (15.5 x 17.2)	**1 oil engine** driving 1 FP propeller Total Power: 16,859kW (22,921hp) 14.5kn B&W 6S70MC 1 x 2 Stroke 6 Cy. 700 x 2674 16859kW (22921bhp) Hyundai Heavy Industries Co Ltd-South Korea AuxGen: 3 x 2100kW 440/220V 60Hz a.c Fuel: 240.4 (d.f.) 3686.0 (r.f.) 55.0pd
8824220 *HMYX7* -	**SA HYANG SAN** *ex* Hong Yuan *-2009* *ex* Koei Maru No. 18 *-2007* *ex* Tenjin Maru No. 68 *-1995* **Rason Kangsong Trading Corp** - *Rajin* *North Korea* MMSI: 445277000 Official number: 3901418	**2,506** 1,664 4,192	Class: KC	**1989-05 Nagashima Zosen KK — Kihoku ME** Converted From: Grab Dredger-2008 Lengthened & Deepened-2008 Loa 90.38 Br ex - Dght 5.600 Lbp 84.10 Br md 13.40 Dpth 7.30 Welded, 1 dk	**(A31A2GX) General Cargo Ship**	**1 oil engine** reverse geared to sc. shaft driving 1 FP propeller Total Power: 736kW (1,001hp) Akasaka A31R 1 x 4 Stroke 6 Cy. 310 x 600 736kW (1001bhp) Akasaka Tekkosho KK (Akasaka DieselLtd)-Japan

IMO / Call sign	Name / Owner	Tonnage	Class	Build / Dimensions	Type	Machinery
8826046 *P5DP* -	**SA JA BONG** *ex* Kan Baek San *-2013* *ex* Gan Baek San *-2010* *ex* Ryong Nam San *-2003* **Kimchaek Fishery Co** - *Chongjin* *North Korea* MMSI: 445368000 Official number: 3001672	*6,399* 3,024 9,073	Class: KC	**1985 Wonsan Shipyard — Wonsan** Loa 127.30 Br ex - Dght 5.700 Lbp - Br md 18.42 Dpth - Welded, 1 dk	**(A31A2GX) General Cargo Ship**	**1 oil engine** driving 1 FP propeller 11.5kn
8612483 - -	**SAA** **Pescamar S Lda** Pescanova SA *Mozambique*	**217** 65 108	Class: BV	**1991-12 Polyships S.A. — Vigo** Yd No: 90008 Loa 27.70 Br ex 8.30 Dght 3.100 Lbp 23.60 Br md 8.00 Dpth 4.20 Bonded, 1 dk	**(B11A2FT) Trawler** Hull Material: Reinforced Plastic Ins: 139	**1 oil engine** with clutches, flexible couplings & sr geared to sc. shaft driving 1 CP propeller Total Power: 419kW (570hp) 10.0kn Baudouin 12P15.2S 1 x Vee 4 Stroke 12 Cy. 150 x 150 419kW (570bhp) Societe des Moteurs Baudouin SA-France
9297010 *9KDI* -	**SAAD** **Government of The State of Kuwait (Coast Guard)** - *Kuwait* MMSI: 447114000	**185** 55 14	Class: (LR) ✠ 27/4/05	**2004-01 OCEA SA — St-Nazaire** Yd No: 310 Loa 35.20 Br ex 7.17 Dght 1.230 Lbp 29.85 Br md 6.80 Dpth 3.80 Welded, 1 dk	**(B34H2SQ) Patrol Vessel** Hull Material: Aluminium Alloy	**2 oil engines** with clutches, flexible couplings & sr reverse geared to sc. shafts driving 2 Water jets Total Power: 3,480kW (4,732hp) M.T.U. 12V4000M70 2 x Vee 4 Stroke 12 Cy. 165 x 190 each-1740kW (2366bhp) MTU Friedrichshafen GmbH-Friedrichshafen AuxGen: 2 x 78kW 415V 50Hz a.c
8899548 *HO2197* -	**SA'AD I** *ex* Gemilang Samudera *-2006* **Adil Sa'eed Abdal Kareem** - *Panama* *Panama* Official number: 3325607A	**204** 62 91	Class: IS (KI) (GL)	**1995-07 C.V. Karya Lestari Industri — Samarinda** Yd No: 005 Loa 28.20 Br ex - Dght 2.100 Lbp 25.30 Br md 7.95 Dpth 2.90 Welded, 1 dk	**(B32A2ST) Tug**	**2 oil engines** geared to sc. shafts driving 2 FP propellers Total Power: 1,838kW (2,498hp) 10.0kn Caterpillar D399TA 2 x Vee 4 Stroke 16 Cy. 159 x 203 each-919kW (1249bhp) Caterpillar Inc-USA
9070503 *9HCJ9* -	**SAADET** *ex* Alexander *-2008* *ex* Epsilon Mikaella *-2002* *ex* Settam *-2000* *ex* Setta *-2000* *ex* Andreea *-1999* *ex* Aktau *-1995* **Eurasia North Shipping Ltd** Unimarin Denizcilik Sanayi ve Ticaret Ltd Sti *Valletta* *Malta* MMSI: 256781000 Official number: 9070503	**2,598** 1,122 3,050	Class: BV (Class contemplated) RS (GL)	**1993-08 Societatea Comerciala Severnav S.A. — Drobeta-Turnu Severin** Yd No: 007 Loa 86.40 (BB) Br ex 14.54 Dght 5.550 Lbp 79.84 Br md 14.50 Dpth 6.70 Welded, 1 dk	**(A31A2GX) General Cargo Ship** Grain: 4,122; Bale: 4,038 TEU 96 C. 96/20' Compartments: 2 Ho, ER 2 Ha: 2 (19.0 x 10.2)ER Cranes: 2x5t	**1 oil engine** driving 1 FP propeller Total Power: 1,802kW (2,450hp) 13.0kn B&W 4L35MCE 1 x 2 Stroke 4 Cy. 350 x 1050 1802kW (2450bhp) Hudong Shipyard-China AuxGen: 2 x 330kW 220V 50Hz a.c Fuel: 220.0 (d.f.)
8719580 - -	**SAADIA S** - *Lagos* *Nigeria*	*150* - -		**1987 Master Marine, Inc. — Bayou La Batre, Al** Yd No: 280 Loa 25.30 Br ex - Dght - Lbp - Br md - Dpth - Welded	**(B11B2FV) Fishing Vessel**	**1 oil engine** geared to sc. shaft driving 1 FP propeller Total Power: 530kW (721hp) Caterpillar 3412T 1 x Vee 4 Stroke 12 Cy. 137 x 152 530kW (721bhp) Caterpillar Inc-USA
8730027 - -	**SAAK** *ex* Grigoriy Kotovskiy *-2005* -	**768** 230 332	Class: (RS)	**1989-09 Volgogradskiy Sudostroitelnyy Zavod — Volgograd** Yd No: 255 Loa 53.75 Br ex 10.72 Dght 4.041 Lbp 47.93 Br md - Dpth 6.02 Welded, 1 dk	**(B11A2FS) Stern Trawler** Ins: 218	**1 oil engine** driving 1 CP propeller Total Power: 969kW (1,317hp) 12.7kn S.K.L. 8NVD48A-2U 1 x 4 Stroke 8 Cy. 320 x 480 969kW (1317bhp) VEB Schwermaschinenbau "KarlLiebknecht" (SKL)-Magdeburg AuxGen: 1 x 300kW a.c, 3 x 160kW a.c
9144213 *CB5707* -	**SAAM** **Sudamericana Agencias Aereas y Maritimas SA (SAAM)** - *Valparaiso* *Chile* MMSI: 725000336 Official number: 2882	**223** 66 -	Class: AB	**1996-01 President Marine Pte Ltd — Singapore** Yd No: 207 Loa 29.00 Br ex - Dght 3.710 Lbp 26.49 Br md 8.60 Dpth 4.08 Welded, 1 dk	**(B32A2ST) Tug**	**2 oil engines** driving 2 FP propellers Total Power: 2,060kW (2,800hp) Yanmar T240A-ET 2 x 4 Stroke 6 Cy. 240 x 310 each-1030kW (1400bhp) Yanmar Diesel Engine Co Ltd-Japan
9655872 *XCTV9* -	**SAAM ANAHUAC** **Inversiones Habsburgo SA** SAAM Remolques SA de CV *Lazaro Cardenas* *Mexico* MMSI: 345160700 Official number: 1601155332-3	**462** 138 200	Class: AB	**2012-06 Shunde Huaxing Shipyard — Foshan GD** (Hull) Yd No: HY-2184 **2012-06 Bonny Fair Development Ltd — Hong Kong** Yd No: HY-2184 Loa 31.00 Br ex 11.40 Dght 4.600 Lbp 27.70 Br md 11.00 Dpth 5.60 Welded, 1 dk	**(B32A2ST) Tug**	**2 oil engines** reduction geared to sc. shafts driving 2 Propellers Total Power: 3,650kW (4,962hp) Caterpillar 3516C-HD 2 x Vee 4 Stroke 16 Cy. 170 x 215 each-1825kW (2481bhp) Caterpillar Inc-USA AuxGen: 2 x 155kW a.c Fuel: 200.0 (d.f.)
9234604 *XCZZ* -	**SAAM AZTECA** **SAAM Remolques SA de CV** - *Altamira* *Mexico* MMSI: 345070038 Official number: 2805062625-2	**332** 99 200	Class: AB (Class contemplated) (NV) (BV)	**2000-09 Detroit Chile SA — Puerto Montt** Yd No: 48 Loa 29.50 Br ex 10.10 Dght 4.000 Lbp 27.00 Br md 10.00 Dpth 4.80 Welded, 2 dks	**(B32A2ST) Tug**	**2 oil engines** with flexible couplings & dr gearedto sc. shafts driving 2 FP propellers Total Power: 3,428kW (4,660hp) M.T.U. 12V4000M60 2 x Vee 4 Stroke 12 Cy. 165 x 190 each-1714kW (2330bhp) Detroit Diesel Corporation-Detroit, Mi
9580792 - -	**SAAM AZTLAN** *completed as* Bonny Fair (HY2174) *-2010* **SAAM Remolques SA de CV** - *Lazaro Cardenas* *Mexico* Official number: 16011447325	**277** 83 109	Class: AB	**2010-10 Guangzhou Panyu Lingnan Shipbuilding Co Ltd — Guangzhou GD** (Hull) **2010-10 Bonny Fair Development Ltd — Hong Kong** Yd No: HY2174 Loa 26.00 Br ex - Dght 3.500 Lbp 25.13 Br md 9.80 Dpth 4.50 Welded, 1 dk	**(B32A2ST) Tug**	**2 oil engines** reduction geared to sc. shafts driving 2 Z propellers Total Power: 3,282kW (4,462hp) Caterpillar 3516B-TA 2 x Vee 4 Stroke 16 Cy. 170 x 190 each-1641kW (2231bhp) Caterpillar Inc-USA AuxGen: 2 x 86kW 50Hz a.c
9282302 *XCAV4* -	**SAAM CHICHIMECA** **SAAM Remolques SA de CV** - *Veracruz* *Mexico* MMSI: 345030043	**332** 99 187	Class: NV (BV)	**2002-12 Detroit Chile SA — Puerto Montt** Yd No: 43 Loa 29.50 Br ex 10.10 Dght 4.320 Lbp 27.70 Br md 10.00 Dpth 4.80 Welded, 1 dk	**(B32A2ST) Tug**	**2 oil engines** geared to sc. shafts driving 2 FP propellers Total Power: 3,428kW (4,660hp) 12.0kn M.T.U. 12V4000M60 2 x Vee 4 Stroke 12 Cy. 165 x 190 each-1714kW (2330bhp) Detroit Diesel Corporation-Detroit, Mi
9680384 *XCAE7* -	**SAAM CITLALI** **Inversiones Habsburgo SA** SAAM Remolques SA de CV *Veracruz* *Mexico* Official number: 30027296329	**496** 149 299	Class: AB	**2013-07 Shunde Huaxing Shipyard — Foshan GD** (Hull) Yd No: HY2198 **2013-07 Bonny Fair Development Ltd — Hong Kong** Yd No: HY2198 Loa 32.60 Br ex - Dght 4.600 Lbp 28.28 Br md 12.50 Dpth 5.80 Welded, 1 dk	**(B32A2ST) Tug**	**2 oil engines** reduction geared to sc. shafts driving 2 Propellers Total Power: 4,920kW (6,690hp) Caterpillar C280-8 2 x 4 Stroke 8 Cy. 280 x 300 each-2460kW (3345bhp) Caterpillar Inc-USA AuxGen: 3 x 150kW a.c Fuel: 250.0
9561318 *XCNL8* -	**SAAM CORA** **Sudamericana Agencias Aereas y Maritimas SA (SAAM)** - *Altamira* *Mexico* MMSI: 345010064 Official number: 2805075932-8	**453** 136 218	Class: AB	**2009-11 Guangzhou Panyu Lingnan Shipbuilding Co Ltd — Guangzhou GD** (Hull) **2009-11 Bonny Fair Development Ltd — Hong Kong** Yd No: HY2161 Loa 30.50 Br ex - Dght 4.300 Lbp 28.63 Br md 11.00 Dpth 5.60 Welded, 1 dk	**(B32A2ST) Tug**	**2 oil engines** geared to sc. shafts driving 2 Z propellers Total Power: 3,650kW (4,962hp) Caterpillar 3516B-HD 2 x Vee 4 Stroke 16 Cy. 170 x 215 each-1825kW (2481bhp) Caterpillar Inc-USA AuxGen: 2 x 99kW a.c Fuel: 224.0
9061318 *XCPX* -	**SAAM HUASTECA** *ex* Puertos Mexicanos 1 *-1999* **SAAM Remolques SA de CV** - *Veracruz* *Mexico* MMSI: 345030045 Official number: 3002022525-2	*331* 99 -	Class: AB (NV)	**1991-10 Astilleros Unidos de Mazatlan S.A. de C.V. (AUMAZ) — Mazatlan** Yd No: 022 Loa 32.10 Br ex - Dght 3.750 Lbp 30.52 Br md 9.00 Dpth 4.75 Welded, 1 dk	**(B32A2ST) Tug**	**2 oil engines** reverse reduction geared to sc. shafts driving 2 FP propellers Total Power: 3,200kW (4,350hp) 12.5kn Deutz SBV8M628 1 x 4 Stroke 8 Cy. 240 x 280 1600kW (2175bhp) Kloeckner Humboldt Deutz AG-Germany Deutz SBV8M628 1 x 4 Stroke 8 Cy. 240 x 280 1600kW (2175bhp) Motoren Werke Mannheim AG (MWM)-Mannheim AuxGen: 2 x 64kW a.c Fuel: 154.4 (d.f.)

IMO / Call sign	Name / Owner / Manager / Port / Flag	Tonnage	Class	Builder / Dimensions	Type	Machinery
9561320 *XCNP3* -	**SAAM HUICHOL** **Inversiones Habsburgo SA** SAAM Remolques SA de CV *Lazaro Cardenas* *Mexico* MMSI: 345160014 Official number: 16011396328	**453** 136 200	Class: AB	**2009-12 Guangzhou Panyu Lingnan Shipbuilding Co Ltd — Guangzhou GD** (Hull) **2009-12 Bonny Fair Development Ltd — Hong Kong** Yd No: HY2162 Loa 30.50 Br ex - Dght 4.300 Lbp 28.68 Br md 11.00 Dpth 5.60 Welded, 1 dk	**(B32A2ST) Tug**	**2 oil engines** geared to sc. shafts driving 2 Z propellers Total Power: 3,946kW (5,364hp) Caterpillar 3516B 2 x Vee 4 Stroke 16 Cy. 170 x 190 each-1973kW (2682bhp) Caterpillar Inc-USA
9620920 *XCSU6* -	**SAAM ITZA** **SAAM Remolques SA de CV** - *Veracruz* *Mexico* MMSI: 345030077	**453** 136 199	Class: AB	**2011-11 Shunde Huaxing Shipyard — Foshan GD** (Hull) Yd No: (HY2182) **2011-11 Bonny Fair Development Ltd — Hong Kong** Yd No: HY2182 Loa 30.50 Br ex 11.30 Dght 4.650 Lbp 28.62 Br md 11.00 Dpth 5.60 Welded, 1 dk	**(B32A2ST) Tug**	**2 oil engines** reduction geared to sc. shafts driving 2 Z propellers Total Power: 3,840kW (5,220hp) Caterpillar 3516B-HD 2 x Vee 4 Stroke 16 Cy. 170 x 215 each-1920kW (2610bhp) Caterpillar Inc-USA AuxGen: 2 x 99kW a.c Fuel: 245.0
9309394 *XCEC8* -	**SAAM IXCATECA** *ex* Fardela III *-2004* **SAAM Remolques SA de CV** - *Altamira* *Mexico* MMSI: 345010041 Official number: 2805067735-3	**333** 100 203	Class: (AB) (NV) (BV)	**2004-02 Detroit Chile SA — Puerto Montt** Yd No: 71 Loa 29.50 Br ex 10.32 Dght 4.190 Lbp 27.00 Br md 10.00 Dpth 4.80 Welded, 1 dk	**(B32A2ST) Tug**	**2 oil engines** geared to sc. shafts driving 2 Directional propellers Total Power: 3,520kW (4,786hp) M.T.U. 16V4000M60 2 x Vee 4 Stroke 16 Cy. 165 x 190 each-1760kW (2393bhp) MTU Friedrichshafen GmbH-Friedrichshafen AuxGen: 2 x 70kW a.c
9316622 *XCFD8* -	**SAAM JAROCHO** **Inversiones Alaria SA** SAAM Remolques SA de CV *Veracruz* *Mexico* MMSI: 345030046	**460** 138 277	Class: AB (LR) (NV) ✠ Classed LR until 17/3/06	**2005-01 Guangdong Hope Yue Shipbuilding Industry Ltd — Guangzhou GD** Yd No: 2130 Loa 30.50 Br ex 11.52 Dght 4.600 Lbp 27.30 Br md 11.00 Dpth 5.60 Welded, 1 dk	**(B32A2ST) Tug**	**2 oil engines** gearing integral to driving 2 Z propellers Total Power: 3,840kW (5,220hp) 12.0kn Caterpillar 3516B-TA 2 x Vee 4 Stroke 16 Cy. 170 x 190 each-1920kW (2610bhp) Caterpillar Inc-USA AuxGen: 2 x 99kW 440V 60Hz a.c
9488504 *XCJZ8* -	**SAAM KABAH** **SAAM Remolques SA de CV** SAAM Remolcadores SA de CV *Altamira* *Mexico* MMSI: 345010054 Official number: 2805072639-9	**453** 136 224	Class: AB	**2008-04 Guangzhou Southern Shipbuilding Co Ltd — Guangzhou GD** (Hull) **2008-04 Guangdong Hope Yue Shipbuilding Industry Ltd — Guangzhou GD** Yd No: 2146 Loa 30.00 Br ex - Dght 4.650 Lbp 27.50 Br md 11.00 Dpth 5.60 Welded, 1 dk	**(B32A2ST) Tug**	**2 oil engines** geared to sc. shafts driving 2 Directional propellers Total Power: 4,690kW (6,376hp) Caterpillar 3516C 2 x Vee 4 Stroke 16 Cy. 170 x 215 each-2345kW (3188bhp) Caterpillar Inc-USA AuxGen: 2 x 99kW 440V 60Hz a.c Fuel: 135.0 (d.f.)
9488516 *XCLB9* -	**SAAM MAYA** **SAAM Remolques SA de CV** - *Lazaro Cardenas* *Mexico* MMSI: 345160010 Official number: 160113179	**454** 136 279	Class: AB	**2008-12 Guangzhou Southern Shipbuilding Co Ltd — Guangzhou GD** (Hull) **2008-12 Guangdong Hope Yue Shipbuilding Industry Ltd — Guangzhou GD** Yd No: 2147 Loa 30.50 Br ex - Dght 4.600 Lbp 28.68 Br md 11.00 Dpth 5.60 Welded, 1 dk	**(B32A2ST) Tug**	**2 oil engines** geared to sc. shafts driving 2 Propellers Total Power: 5,050kW (6,866hp) Caterpillar 3516C 2 x Vee 4 Stroke 16 Cy. 170 x 215 each-2525kW (3433bhp) Caterpillar Inc-USA AuxGen: 2 x 99kW a.c
9066629 *HP5329* -	**SAAM MEXICA** **SAAM Remolcadores SA de CV** - *Panama* *Panama* Official number: 4459113	**213** 64 -	Class: AB (LR) (NV) ✠ Classed LR until 8/8/99	**1997-11 Stocznia Tczew Sp z oo — Tczew** (Hull) **1997-11 B.V. Scheepswerf Damen — Gorinchem** Yd No: 3186 Loa 30.50 Br ex 8.42 Dght 3.430 Lbp 27.05 Br md 7.80 Dpth 4.05 Welded, 1 dk	**(B32A2ST) Tug**	**2 oil engines** with clutches, flexible couplings & sr reverse geared to sc. shafts driving 2 FP propellers Total Power: 3,132kW (4,258hp) 13.7kn Caterpillar 3516B-TA 2 x Vee 4 Stroke 16 Cy. 170 x 190 each-1566kW (2129bhp) Caterpillar Inc-USA Fuel: 100.0 (d.f.)
9488528 *XCKP6* -	**SAAM MIXTECO** **SAAM Remolques SA de CV** - *Altamira* *Mexico* MMSI: 345010033 Official number: 2805073539-9	**454** 136 286	Class: AB	**2008-09 Guangzhou Southern Shipbuilding Co Ltd — Guangzhou GD** (Hull) **2008-09 Guangdong Hope Yue Shipbuilding Industry Ltd — Guangzhou GD** Yd No: 2148 Loa 30.50 Br ex - Dght 4.760 Lbp 28.68 Br md 11.00 Dpth 5.60 Welded, 1 dk	**(B32A2ST) Tug**	**2 oil engines** reduction geared to sc. shafts driving 2 Propellers Total Power: 4,700kW (6,390hp) Caterpillar 3516C-HD 2 x Vee 4 Stroke 16 Cy. 170 x 215 each-2350kW (3195bhp) Caterpillar Inc-USA
8906145 *XCSP3* -	**SAAM OLMECA** *ex* SPTA-3 *-1999* **SAAM Remolques SA de CV** - *Tampico* *Mexico*	*331* 99 330	Class: AB (NV)	**1989-11 Astilleros Unidos de Mazatlan S.A. de C.V. (AUMAZ) — Mazatlan** (Assembled by) Yd No: 010 **1989-11 B.V. Scheepswerf Damen — Gorinchem** (Parts for assembly by) Yd No: 4706 Loa 32.10 Br ex - Dght 4.750 Lbp 30.52 Br md 9.00 Dpth - Welded, 1 dk	**(B32A2ST) Tug**	**2 oil engines** reverse reduction geared to sc. shafts driving 2 FP propellers Total Power: 2,354kW (3,200hp) 12.5kn Deutz SBV6M628 2 x 4 Stroke 6 Cy. 240 x 280 each-1177kW (1600bhp) Kloeckner Humboldt Deutz AG-West Germany AuxGen: 2 x 63kW a.c Fuel: 157.5 (d.f.)
9253648 *XCCE3* -	**SAAM OTOMI** *ex* Fardela *-2004* **SAAM Remolques SA de CV** - *Altamira* *Mexico* MMSI: 345010027 Official number: 2805066535-3	**316** 94 179	Class: AB (LR) (NV) ✠ Classed LR until 26/6/03	**2002-03 Yuexin Shipbuilding Co Ltd — Guangzhou GD** Yd No: XY-2111 Loa 30.50 Br ex 10.30 Dght 3.500 Lbp 29.75 Br md 9.80 Dpth 4.50 Welded, 1 dk	**(B32A2ST) Tug**	**2 oil engines** gearing integral to driving 2 Z propellers Total Power: 2,984kW (4,058hp) 11.5kn Caterpillar 3512B-HD 2 x Vee 4 Stroke 12 Cy. 170 x 215 each-1492kW (2029bhp) Caterpillar Inc-USA AuxGen: 2 x 85kW 380V 50Hz a.c Fuel: 130.0 (r.f.)
9332468 *XCGD7* -	**SAAM PUREPECHA** **SAAM Remolques SA de CV** - *Lazaro Cardenas* *Mexico* MMSI: 345160007	**460** 138 261	Class: NV (LR) ✠ Classed LR until 12/10/06	**2005-09 Guangdong Hope Yue Shipbuilding Industry Ltd — Guangzhou GD** Yd No: 2133 Loa 30.50 Br ex 11.52 Dght 4.600 Lbp 27.30 Br md 11.00 Dpth 5.60 Welded, 1 dk	**(B32A2ST) Tug**	**2 oil engines** gearing integral to driving 2 Z propellers Total Power: 4,118kW (5,598hp) 12.0kn Caterpillar 3606 2 x 4 Stroke 6 Cy. 280 x 300 each-2059kW (2799bhp) Caterpillar Inc-USA AuxGen: 2 x 99kW 440V 60Hz a.c, 1 x 40kW 440V 60Hz a.c
9680396 - -	**SAAM QUETZAL** **Inversiones Habsburgo SA** SAAM Remolques SA de CV *Dos Bocas* *Mexico* Official number: 27013538325	**496** 149 299	Class: AB	**2013-07 Shunde Huaxing Shipyard — Foshan GD** (Hull) Yd No: HY2199 **2013-07 Bonny Fair Development Ltd — Hong Kong** Yd No: HY2199 Loa 32.60 Br ex - Dght 4.600 Lbp 28.28 Br md 12.50 Dpth 5.80 Welded, 1 dk	**(B32A2ST) Tug**	**2 oil engines** reduction geared to sc. shafts driving 2 Propellers Total Power: 4,920kW (6,690hp) Caterpillar C280-8 2 x 4 Stroke 8 Cy. 280 x 300 each-2460kW (3345bhp) Caterpillar Inc-USA AuxGen: 3 x 150kW a.c Fuel: 250.0
9229099 *XCTM* -	**SAAM TACUATE** **SAAM Remolques SA de CV** - *Veracruz* *Mexico* MMSI: 345030044	**201** 60 61	Class: NV (BV)	**2000-06 Detroit Chile SA — Puerto Montt** Yd No: 55 Loa 24.39 Br ex 9.47 Dght 4.500 Lbp 22.90 Br md 9.15 Dpth - Welded, 1 dk	**(B32A2ST) Tug**	**2 oil engines** geared to sc. shafts driving 2 Directional propellers Total Power: 2,800kW (3,806hp) 12.0kn M.T.U. 12V4000M70 2 x Vee 4 Stroke 12 Cy. 165 x 190 each-1400kW (1903bhp) Detroit Diesel Corporation-Detroit, Mi AuxGen: 2 x 57kW a.c
9316634 *XCFA5* -	**SAAM TAJIN** **SAAM Remolques SA de CV** - *Lazaro Cardenas* *Mexico* MMSI: 345160006	**460** 138 277	Class: AB (LR) (NV) ✠ Classed LR until 10/2/06	**2005-01 Guangdong Hope Yue Shipbuilding Industry Ltd — Guangzhou GD** Yd No: 2131 Loa 30.50 Br ex 11.52 Dght 4.600 Lbp 27.30 Br md 11.00 Dpth 5.60 Welded, 1 dk	**(B32A2ST) Tug**	**2 oil engines** gearing integral to driving 2 Z propellers Total Power: 3,840kW (5,220hp) 12.0kn Caterpillar 3516B-TA 2 x Vee 4 Stroke 16 Cy. 170 x 190 each-1920kW (2610bhp) Caterpillar Inc-USA AuxGen: 2 x 99kW 440V 60Hz a.c
8519045 *XCSM* -	**SAAM TARASCO** *ex* Tarasco II *-2004* **SAAM Remolques SA de CV** - *Lazaro Cardenas* *Mexico* MMSI: 345160004 Official number: 8519045	*342* 102 -	Class: AB (NV)	**1988-11 Astilleros Unidos de Mazatlan S.A. de C.V. (AUMAZ) — Mazatlan** Yd No: 006 Loa - Br ex - Dght - Lbp 30.53 Br md 9.00 Dpth 4.75 Welded	**(B32A2ST) Tug**	**2 oil engines** reverse reduction geared to sc. shafts driving 2 FP propellers Total Power: 3,202kW (4,354hp) 10.0kn Deutz SBV8M628 2 x 4 Stroke 8 Cy. 240 x 280 each-1601kW (2177bhp) Kloeckner Humboldt Deutz AG-West Germany AuxGen: 2 x 100kW a.c Fuel: 150.4 (d.f.)

9580807 *XCQZ1* - **SAAM TEPEYAC**
Inversiones Habsburgo SA
SAAM Remolques SA de CV
Lazaro Cardenas *Mexico*
Official number: 16011457327
277 83 105
Class: AB
2010-11 Guangzhou Panyu Lingnan Shipbuilding Co Ltd — Guangzhou GD (Hull)
2010-11 Bonny Fair Development Ltd — Hong Kong Yd No: HY2175
Loa 26.00 Br ex - Dght 3.500
Lbp 25.13 Br md 9.80 Dpth 4.50
Welded, 1 dk
(B32A2ST) Tug
2 oil engines reduction geared to sc. shafts driving 2 Z propellers
Total Power: 3,282kW (4,462hp)
Caterpillar 3516B-TA
2 x Vee 4 Stroke 16 Cy. 170 x 190 each-1641kW (2231bhp)
Caterpillar Inc-USA
AuxGen: 2 x 86kW a.c

9154921 *XCIE6* - **SAAM TLALOC**
ex Cormoran I *-2007* *ex* Taechong *-2007*
SAAM Remolques SA de CV
-
Lazaro Cardenas *Mexico*
MMSI: 345160008
Official number: 1601110735-6
375 112 153
Class: AB (BV) (KR)
1996-09 Kyeong-In Engineering & Shipbuilding Co Ltd — Incheon Yd No: 152
Loa 34.85 Br ex - Dght 3.300
Lbp 32.54 Br md 10.00 Dpth 4.50
Welded, 1 dk
(B32A2ST) Tug
2 oil engines with clutches, flexible couplings & reduction geared to sc. shafts driving 2 FP propellers
Total Power: 3,178kW (4,320hp) 14.0kn
Pielstick 8PA5L
2 x 4 Stroke 8 Cy. 255 x 270 each-1589kW (2160bhp)
Ssangyong Heavy Industries Co Ltd-South Korea

9214238 *XCNO* - **SAAM TOTONACA**
SAAM Remolques SA de CV
-
Tampico *Mexico*
MMSI: 345030041
332 99 210
Class: AB (NV) (BV)
1999-09 Detroit Chile SA — Puerto Montt Yd No: 42
Loa 30.40 Br ex - Dght 3.780
Lbp 27.44 Br md 10.00 Dpth 4.80
Welded, 1 dk
(B32A2ST) Tug
2 oil engines with clutches, flexible couplings & dr geared to sc. shafts driving 2 FP propellers
Total Power: 3,428kW (4,660hp) 12.0kn
M.T.U. 12V4000M70
2 x Vee 4 Stroke 12 Cy. 165 x 190 each-1714kW (2330bhp)
Detroit Diesel Corporation-Detroit, Mi

9561291 *XCMD1* - **SAAM TULUM**
ex Saam 1 *-2009*
Sudamericana Agencias Aereas y Maritimas SA (SAAM)
-
Veracruz *Mexico*
MMSI: 345030067
Official number: 30021939359
277 83 136
Class: AB
2009-07 Guangzhou Panyu Lingnan Shipbuilding Co Ltd — Guangzhou GD (Hull)
2009-07 Bonny Fair Development Ltd — Hong Kong Yd No: HY2159
Loa 26.00 Br ex - Dght 3.500
Lbp 25.13 Br md 9.80 Dpth 4.50
Welded, 1 dk
(B32A2ST) Tug
2 oil engines reduction geared to sc. shafts driving 2 Z propellers
Total Power: 3,132kW (4,258hp)
Caterpillar 3516B-TA
2 x Vee 4 Stroke 16 Cy. 170 x 190 each-1566kW (2129bhp)
Caterpillar Inc-USA
AuxGen: 2 x 86kW a.c
Fuel: 100.0 (d.f.)

9561306 *XCMQ5* - **SAAM UXMAL**
SAAM Remolques SA de CV
Sudamericana Agencias Aereas y Maritimas SA (SAAM)
Lazaro Cardenas *Mexico*
MMSI: 345160012
Official number: 16011374
277 83 134
Class: AB
2009-08 Guangzhou Panyu Lingnan Shipbuilding Co Ltd — Guangzhou GD (Hull)
2009-08 Bonny Fair Development Ltd — Hong Kong Yd No: HY2160
Loa 26.00 Br ex - Dght 3.500
Lbp 25.13 Br md 9.80 Dpth 4.50
Welded, 1 dk
(B32A2ST) Tug
2 oil engines geared to sc. shafts driving 2 Z propellers
Total Power: 3,090kW (4,202hp)
Caterpillar 3516B
2 x Vee 4 Stroke 16 Cy. 170 x 190 each-1545kW (2101bhp)
Caterpillar Inc-USA
AuxGen: 2 x 86kW a.c

9121223 *HP9050* - **SAAM XALAPA**
ex SAAM Tuxpan *-2005* *ex* Maju 3 *-2005*
Inversiones Habsburgo SA
Tugbrasil Apoio Portuario SA
Panama *Panama*
Official number: 4511713
322 97 132
Class: NK
1994-10 Donghai Shipyard — Shanghai Yd No: 93327
Loa 32.81 Br ex 9.50 Dght 3.404
Lbp 30.05 Br md - Dpth 4.30
Welded, 1 dk
(B32A2ST) Tug
2 oil engines reduction geared to sc. shafts driving 2 FP propellers
Total Power: 2,354kW (3,200hp) 12.7kn
Daihatsu 6DLM-26
2 x 4 Stroke 6 Cy. 260 x 340 each-1177kW (1600bhp)
Daihatsu Diesel Manufacturing Co Lt-Japan
AuxGen: 2 x 75kW a.c
Fuel: 48.0 (d.f.)

9620918 *XCST5* - **SAAM YAQUI**
SAAM Remolques SA de CV
-
Veracruz *Mexico*
MMSI: 345030700
Official number: 3002720232-6
453 136 184
Class: AB
2011-11 Shunde Huaxing Shipyard — Foshan GD (Hull) Yd No: (HY2181)
2011-11 Bonny Fair Development Ltd — Hong Kong Yd No: HY2181
Loa 30.50 Br ex 11.30 Dght 4.650
Lbp 28.62 Br md 11.00 Dpth 5.60
Welded, 1 dk
(B32A2ST) Tug
2 oil engines reduction geared to sc. shafts driving 2 Z propellers
Total Power: 3,840kW (5,220hp)
Caterpillar 3516B-HD
2 x Vee 4 Stroke 16 Cy. 170 x 215 each-1920kW (2610bhp)
Caterpillar Inc-USA
AuxGen: 2 x 99kW a.c
Fuel: 245.0

9289233 *XCCV2* - **SAAM ZAPOTECA**
ex Fardela *-2005*
SAAM Remolques SA de CV
-
Lazaro Cardenas *Mexico*
MMSI: 345160005
Official number: 1601085735-4
313 93 -
Class: AB (LR) (NV)
✠ Classed LR until 5/12/05
2003-11 Yuexin Shipbuilding Co Ltd — Guangzhou GD Yd No: XY-2117
Loa 30.50 Br ex 10.30 Dght 3.500
Lbp 27.20 Br md 9.80 Dpth 4.50
Welded, 1 dk
(B32A2ST) Tug
2 oil engines geared to sc. shafts driving 2 Directional propellers
Total Power: 3,132kW (4,258hp)
Caterpillar 3516B
2 x Vee 4 Stroke 16 Cy. 170 x 190 each-1566kW (2129bhp)
Caterpillar Inc-USA
AuxGen: 2 x 99kW 440V 60Hz a.c

9126285 *2DJK2* - **SAAMIS ADVENTURER**
Kiwi Shipping SA
Mitsui OSK Lines Ltd (MOL)
Douglas *Isle of Man (British)*
MMSI: 235079504
Official number: 741947
20,597 7,644 30,938 T/cm 41.4
Class: NK
1996-05 Minaminippon Shipbuilding Co Ltd — Usuki OT Yd No: 639
Loa 175.00 (BB) Br ex 27.73 Dght 10.016
Lbp 166.00 Br md 27.00 Dpth 16.00
Welded, 1 dk
(A12B2TR) Chemical/Products Tanker
Double Hull (13F)
Liq: 36,923; Liq (Oil): 36,923
Compartments: 12 Wing Ta, ER
14 Cargo Pump (s): 14x300m³/hr
Manifold: Bow/CM: 89m
1 oil engine driving 1 FP propeller
Total Power: 7,944kW (10,801hp) 15.0kn
Mitsubishi 6UEC52LS
1 x 2 Stroke 6 Cy. 520 x 1850 7944kW (10801bhp)
Kobe Hatsudoki KK-Japan
AuxGen: 4 x 720kW 450V 60Hz a.c
Fuel: 163.7 (d.f.) (Heating Coils) 2191.6 (r.f.) 31.0pd

9041356 - - **SAAR II**
Ashdod Port Co Ltd
-
Ashdod *Israel*
Official number: MS.333
267 80 80
Class: LR
✠ **100A1** SS 05/2013
tug
Eastern Mediterranean and Red Sea service
✠ **LMC** **UMS**
Eq.Ltr: G; Cable: 305.8/20.5 U2
1993-05 Israel Shipyards Ltd. — Haifa Yd No: 1070
Loa 28.70 Br ex 9.24 Dght -
Lbp 27.00 Br md 9.20 Dpth 3.70
Welded, 1 dk
(B32A2ST) Tug
2 oil engines gearing integral to driving 2 Voith-Schneider propellers
Total Power: 2,116kW (2,876hp)
Deutz SBV6M628
2 x 4 Stroke 6 Cy. 240 x 280 each-1058kW (1438bhp)
Motoren Werke Mannheim AG (MWM)-Mannheim
AuxGen: 2 x 90kW 380V 50Hz a.c
Fuel: 64.5 (d.f.)

9474072 *ESJQ* - **SAAREMAA**
Saaremaa Ferry Erste Beteiligungs Gmbh & Co KG
Saaremaa Shipping Co Ltd (AS Saaremaa Laevakompanii)
Roomassaare *Estonia*
MMSI: 276788000
Official number: 5P10F02
5,233 1,849 940
Class: NV
2010-06 UAB Vakaru Laivu Remontas (JSC Western Shiprepair) — Klaipeda (Hull) Yd No: (64)
2010-06 Fiskerstrand Verft AS — Fiskarstrand Yd No: 64
Loa 97.90 Br ex 18.50 Dght 4.000
Lbp 92.46 Br md 18.00 Dpth 8.70
Welded, 2 dks
(A36A2PR) Passenger/Ro-Ro Ship (Vehicles)
Single Hull
Passengers: unberthed: 690
Bow door (centre)
Len: - Wid: 9.50 Swl: -
Stern door (centre)
Len: - Wid: 9.50 Swl: -
Lane-clr ht: 5.00
Cars: 150
Ice Capable
4 diesel electric oil engines driving 2 gen. each 1500kW a.c 2 gen. each 960kW a.c reduction geared to sc. shafts driving 2 Azimuth electric drive units Contra-Rotating propellers
Total Power: 5,600kW (7,614hp) 15.0kn
Wartsila 6L20
2 x 4 Stroke 6 Cy. 200 x 280 each-1200kW (1632bhp)
Wartsila Finland Oy-Finland
Wartsila 8L20
2 x 4 Stroke 8 Cy. 200 x 280 each-1600kW (2175bhp)
Wartsila Finland Oy-Finland
Fuel: 105.0 (d.f.) 10.0pd

9135781 *A8LO7* - **SAARGAS**
Chemgas Schiffahrts GmbH & Co mt 'Gaschem Saar' KG
Hartmann Schiffahrts GmbH & Co KG (Hartmann Reederei)
Monrovia *Liberia*
MMSI: 636091285
Official number: 91285
3,932 1,180 3,442 T/cm 12.7
Class: GL
2001-08 Societatea Comerciala Severnav S.A. — Drobeta-Turnu Severin Yd No: 010
Loa 96.90 (BB) Br ex 15.63 Dght 5.500
Lbp 89.45 Br md 15.60 Dpth 8.80
Welded, 1 dk
(A11B2TG) LPG Tanker
Double Bottom Entire Compartment Length
Liq (Gas): 3,424
2 x Gas Tank (s); 2 independent (stl) cyl horizontal
2 Cargo Pump (s): 2x250m³/hr
Manifold: Bow/CM: 41.5m
Ice Capable
1 oil engine driving 1 FP propeller
Total Power: 2,400kW (3,263hp) 13.0kn
B&W 4L35MC
1 x 2 Stroke 4 Cy. 350 x 1050 2400kW (3263bhp)
U.C.M. Resita S.A.-Resita
AuxGen: 3 x 229kW 380/220V 60Hz a.c
Thrusters: 1 Tunnel thruster (f)
Fuel: 94.0 (d.f.) 402.0 (r.f.)

6417308 *4JEK* - **SAATLY**
Azerbaijan State Caspian Shipping Co (ASCSS)
Meridian Shipping & Management LLC
Baku *Azerbaijan*
MMSI: 423057100
Official number: DGR-0069
3,363 1,400 4,286 T/cm 13.0
Class: (RS)
1962-12 Navashinskiy Sudostroitelnyy Zavod 'Oka' — Navashino Yd No: 948
Loa 120.00 Br ex 15.02 Dght 4.401
Lbp 111.99 Br md 14.97 Dpth 6.53
Welded, 1 dk
(A31A2GX) General Cargo Ship
Grain: 5,485; Bale: 5,174
Compartments: 4 Ho, ER
4 Ha: (11.8 x 8.0)3 (13.7 x 8.0)ER
Cranes: 2x5t
Ice Capable
2 oil engines driving 2 FP propellers
Total Power: 1,176kW (1,598hp) 11.5kn
Russkiy 8DR30/50
2 x 2 Stroke 8 Cy. 300 x 500 each-588kW (799bhp) (new engine 1976)
Mashinostroitelnyy Zavod"Russkiy-Dizel"-Leningrad
AuxGen: 3 x 100kW
Fuel: 75.0 (r.f.)

9644067 *DLJU* - **SAATSEE**
Government of The Federal Republic of Germany (Wasser- und Schiffahrtsdirektion Kiel)
-
Rendsburg *Germany*
MMSI: 211570140
221 66 276
Class: GL
2012-09 Fr Fassmer GmbH & Co KG — Berne Yd No: 10/1/5020
Loa 25.61 Br ex 9.00 Dght 2.700
Lbp 21.80 Br md 8.60 Dpth 3.80
Welded, 1 dk
(B32A2ST) Tug
Ice Capable
2 oil engines reduction geared to sc. shafts driving 2 Directional propellers
Total Power: 1,618kW (2,200hp)
MAN D2842LE
2 x Vee 4 Stroke 12 Cy. 128 x 142 each-809kW (1100bhp)
MAN B&W Diesel AG-Augsburg
AuxGen: 1 x 182kW a.c, 1 x 95kW a.c
Thrusters: 1 Tunnel thruster (f)

7637060 **SAAXIL**
-
- **Somali Ports Authority (Wakaaladda Dekedaha Soomaliyeed)**
-
Berbera *Somalia*

157
-
60

Class: (BV)

1979-04 Staalin B.V. — 's-Gravenhage (Hull)
1979-04 B.V. Scheepswerf Damen — Gorinchem
Yd No: 2708
Loa 19.31 Br ex - Dght -
Lbp - Br md 6.80 Dpth 3.43
Welded, 1 dk

(B32A2ST) Tug

2 oil engines geared to sc. shafts driving 2 FP propellers
Total Power: 842kW (1,144hp)
Caterpillar D379SCAC
2 x Vee 4 Stroke 8 Cy. 159 x 203 each-421kW (572bhp)
Caterpillar Tractor Co-USA

7237444 **SABA**
J8B4795 *ex* Mario *-1999* *ex* Rutana I *-1999*
- *ex* GCSB-II *-1999* *ex* Saba *-1999*
ex Gulf Fleet No. 7 *-1990*
Tariq Star Shipping & Trading Ltd
Seawaves Shipping Co LLC
Kingstown *St Vincent & The Grenadines*
MMSI: 375808000
Official number: 11268

497
150
844

Class: GL (HR) (AB)

1972 Zigler Shipyards Inc — Jennings LA
Yd No: 227
Loa 53.60 Br ex - Dght 3.603
Lbp 47.85 Br md 11.60 Dpth 4.26
Welded, 1 dk

(B21A20S) Platform Supply Ship

2 oil engines dr reverse geared to sc. shafts driving 2 FP propellers
Total Power: 1,654kW (2,248hp) 13.0kn
Kromhout 8FBHD240
2 x 4 Stroke 8 Cy. 240 x 260 each-827kW (1124bhp) (new engine 1981)
Stork Werkspoor Diesel BV-Netherlands
AuxGen: 2 x 60kW 440V a.c
Thrusters: 1 Thwart. FP thruster (f)
Fuel: 206.5 (d.f.)

8871792 **SABA**
V3GX2 *ex* Oil Clarion *-2010* *ex* King of Kings *-2010*
- **Blackrock Shipping SA**
Belize City *Belize*
MMSI: 312160000
Official number: 019811255

159
47
-

Class: AB (GL)

1981 Breaux Bay Craft, Inc. — Loreauville, La
Yd No: 1501
L reg 31.97 Br ex - Dght -
Lbp - Br md 7.32 Dpth 2.71
Welded, 1 dk

(B21A20C) Crew/Supply Vessel

4 oil engines reverse reduction geared to sc. shafts driving 4 FP propellers
Total Power: 1,988kW (2,704hp) 16.0kn
G.M. (Detroit Diesel) 12V-71-TI
4 x Vee 2 Stroke 12 Cy. 108 x 127 each-497kW (676bhp)
General Motors Detroit DieselAllison Divn-USA
AuxGen: 2 x 24kW 110/220V a.c

9550797 **SABA 12**
HP7285 *ex* Swissco Supplier II *-2011*
- **Global Epic Roads Sdn Bhd**
-
Panama *Panama*
MMSI: 356432000
Official number: 4399212A

1,139
341
1,102

Class: (BV)

2009-09 Guangzhou Panyu Lingshan Shipyard Ltd — Guangzhou GD Yd No: 163
Loa 55.00 Br ex 13.84 Dght 4.300
Lbp 53.50 Br md 13.80 Dpth 5.50
Welded, 1 dk

(B21B20A) Anchor Handling Tug Supply

2 oil engines reduction geared to sc. shafts driving 2 Z propellers
Total Power: 3,090kW (4,202hp) 12.0kn
Caterpillar 3516B
2 x Vee 4 Stroke 16 Cy. 170 x 190 each-1545kW (2101bhp)
Caterpillar Inc-USA
AuxGen: 3 x 245kW 415V 50Hz a.c
Thrusters: 1 Tunnel thruster (f)
Fuel: 420.0 (d.f.)

9024164 **SABA LAUT**
YD4822 *ex* Fire Style No. 23 *-2002*
- **PT Samudera Mas Jaya**
-
Cirebon *Indonesia*
MMSI: 525016248

111
66
-

Class: KI

1988-01 in Hong Kong
Loa 21.20 Br ex - Dght -
Lbp 20.30 Br md 6.30 Dpth 1.10
Welded, 1 dk

(B32A2ST) Tug

2 oil engines geared to sc. shafts driving 2 Propellers
Total Power: 918kW (1,248hp)
Caterpillar 3412
2 x Vee 4 Stroke 12 Cy. 137 x 152 each-459kW (624bhp)
Caterpillar Inc-USA
AuxGen: 2 x 30kW 400V a.c

8622024 **SABA NIAGA**
YHYR *ex* Myojin Maru No. 3 *-1988*
- *ex* Saiwa Maru No. 16 *-1988*
PT Fresco Line Samudera
-
Tanjung Priok *Indonesia*

471
-
700

Class: KI

1984-05 Y.K. Takasago Zosensho — Naruto
Yd No: 135
Loa 53.19 Br ex - Dght 3.010
Lbp 48.01 Br md 11.00 Dpth 5.14
Welded, 1 dk

(B33A2DS) Suction Dredger

1 oil engine driving 1 FP propeller
Total Power: 515kW (700hp) 10.0kn
Matsui MS25GSC-3
1 x 4 Stroke 6 Cy. 250 x 470 515kW (700bhp)
Matsui Iron Works Co Ltd-Japan

7388578 **SABADO SANTO**
LW6048
- **Pesquera Santa Cruz SA**
-
Puerto Deseado *Argentina*
MMSI: 701006002
Official number: 0669

241
141
-

Class: (BV)

1975-04 Construcciones Navales Santodomingo SA — Vigo Yd No: 506
Loa 29.19 Br ex 7.55 Dght 3.379
Lbp 25.48 Br md 7.50 Dpth 5.39
Welded, 1 dk

(B11A2FS) Stern Trawler
Grain: 180
Compartments: 1 Ho, ER

1 oil engine driving 1 FP propeller
Total Power: 588kW (799hp) 11.0kn
Stork DR0218K
1 x 4 Stroke 8 Cy. 210 x 300 588kW (799bhp) (made 1972, fitted 1975)
Naval Stork Werkspoor SA-Spain
Fuel: 115.0 (d.f.)

7030585 **SABAH**
9KHD
- **Government of The State of Kuwait (Agriculture Affairs Fish Resources Authority)**
-
Kuwait *Kuwait*
Official number: KT1063

192
11
242

Class: (LR)
✠ Classed LR until 19/3/97

1970-11 Scheepswerf & Machinefabriek Fa A van Bennekum NV — Sliedrecht Yd No: 84
Loa 30.21 Br ex 7.47 Dght -
Lbp 25.61 Br md 7.37 Dpth 3.81
Welded, 1 dk

(B11A2FT) Trawler
Ins: 2,295

1 oil engine sr reverse geared to sc. shaft driving 1 FP propeller
Total Power: 372kW (506hp) 10.5kn
Caterpillar D379TA
1 x Vee 4 Stroke 8 Cy. 159 x 203 372kW (506bhp)
Caterpillar Tractor Co-USA
AuxGen: 2 x 26kW 220V 50Hz a.c
Fuel: 32.5 (d.f.)

9370525 **SABAHAT SONAY**
TCSL8
- **AY Denizcilik AS**
Sonay Denizcilik Ltd Sti (Sonay Shipping Co Ltd)
Istanbul *Turkey*
MMSI: 271000918

9,490
4,535
13,000

Class: BV

2007-01 Celiktekne Sanayii ve Ticaret A.S. — Tuzla, Istanbul Yd No: 66
Loa 143.41 Br ex - Dght 8.243
Lbp 134.00 Br md 21.70 Dpth 11.10
Welded, 1 dk

(A31A2GX) General Cargo Ship
Grain: 16,306

1 oil engine driving 1 FP propeller
Total Power: 4,440kW (6,037hp) 14.0kn
MAN-B&W 6S35MC
1 x 2 Stroke 6 Cy. 350 x 1400 4440kW (6037bhp)
AuxGen: 3 x 345kW a.c

8111831 **SABAHAT TELLI**
TCSQ6 *ex* Bonaire *-2007*
- **Gemiciler Denizcilik Sanayi ve Ticaret Ltd Sti**
-
Istanbul *Turkey*
MMSI: 271000961

3,253
1,465
4,557
T/cm
13.3

Class: GL

1982-01 Ernst Menzer-Werft — Geesthacht
Yd No: 513
Loa 98.89 (BB) Br ex 15.52 Dght 6.011
Lbp 92.00 Br md 15.51 Dpth 7.01
Welded, 1 dk

(A12A2TC) Chemical Tanker
Double Bottom Entire Compartment Length
Liq: 5,225
Cargo Heating Coils
Compartments: 9 Ta (s.stl), 16 Wing Ta, ER
19 Cargo Pump (s): 19x80m³/hr
Manifold: Bow/CM: 44m
Ice Capable

1 oil engine driving 1 CP propeller
Total Power: 2,868kW (3,899hp) 14.0kn
Mitsubishi 6UEC37/88H
1 x 2 Stroke 6 Cy. 370 x 880 2868kW (3899bhp)
Kobe Hatsudoki KK-Japan
AuxGen: 1 x 224kW 440V 60Hz a.c, 2 x 212kW 440V 60Hz a.c
Thrusters: 1 Thwart. FP thruster (f)
Fuel: 65.0 (d.f.) 320.0 (r.f.)

8906183 **SABAHI**
9KNE
- **Kuwait Oil Co KSC**
-
Kuwait *Kuwait*
MMSI: 447007000
Official number: KT1538

548
164
280
T/cm
3.7

Class: LR
✠ **100A1** SS 01/2010
tug
Arabian Gulf service
✠ **LMC**
Eq.Ltr: F; Cable: 302.5/19.0 U2

1990-01 Scheepsbouw Alblas B.V. — Hendrik-Ido-Ambacht (Hull)
1990-01 B.V. Scheepswerf Damen — Gorinchem
Yd No: 8670
Loa 39.65 Br ex 11.63 Dght 4.502
Lbp 35.85 Br md 11.00 Dpth 5.90
Welded, 1 dk

(B32A2ST) Tug

2 oil engines with clutches, flexible couplings & sr geared to sc. shafts driving 2 CP propellers
Total Power: 4,180kW (5,684hp)
Caterpillar 3608TA
2 x 4 Stroke 8 Cy. 280 x 300 each-2090kW (2842bhp)
Caterpillar Inc-USA
AuxGen: 3 x 53kW 440V 50Hz a.c
Fuel: 280.0 (d.f.)

9082972 **SABAHTUG No. 5**
-
- **Tug Boat (Sabah) Sdn Bhd**
-

134
-
94

Class: (NK)

1993-05 Bengkel Bombalai — Tawau Yd No: 8
Loa - Br ex - Dght 2.297
Lbp 21.42 Br md 7.52 Dpth 2.94
Welded, 1 dk

(B32A2ST) Tug

2 oil engines geared to sc. shafts driving 2 FP propellers
Total Power: 700kW (952hp) 9.5kn
Caterpillar 3408TA
2 x Vee 4 Stroke 8 Cy. 137 x 152 each-350kW (476bhp)
Caterpillar Inc-USA

9127722 **SABAHTUG No. 6**
-
- **Tug Boat (Sabah) Sdn Bhd**
-

134
9
95

Class: (NK)

1995-03 Bengkel Bombalai — Tawau Yd No: 17
L reg 21.42 Br ex - Dght 2.297
Lbp 21.42 Br md 7.52 Dpth 2.94
Welded, 1 dk

(B32A2ST) Tug

2 oil engines reduction geared to sc. shafts driving 2 FP propellers
Total Power: 692kW (940hp) 9.5kn
Caterpillar 3408TA
2 x Vee 4 Stroke 8 Cy. 137 x 152 each-346kW (470bhp)
Caterpillar Inc-USA

8931669 **SABAHTUG No. 11**
- *ex* Singtel 1 *-2001* *ex* Ocean India *-1997*
- **Cowie Marine Transportation Sdn Bhd**
-
Labuan *Malaysia*

144
44
103

Class: (GL)

1996 PT Nanindah Mutiara Shipyard — Batam
Yd No: T41
Loa 23.40 Br ex - Dght 2.500
Lbp - Br md 7.50 Dpth 3.10
Welded, 1 dk

(B32A2ST) Tug

2 oil engines reduction geared to sc. shafts driving 2 FP propellers
Total Power: 940kW (1,278hp) 10.0kn
Yanmar 6LAHM-STE
2 x 4 Stroke 6 Cy. 150 x 165 each-470kW (639bhp)
Yanmar Diesel Engine Co Ltd-Japan
AuxGen: 2 x 32kW 220/380V a.c
Fuel: 91.0 (d.f.)

9077496 **SABAHTUG NO. 12**
9WEP8 *ex* Ocean Emerald *-2004*
- **Cowie Marine Transportation Sdn Bhd**
-
Labuan *Malaysia*

144
44
155

Class: (GL)

1993 Borneo Shipping & Timber Agencies Sdn Ltd — Bintulu Yd No: 9
Loa 25.30 Br ex - Dght 2.998
Lbp - Br md 7.30 Dpth 3.50
Welded, 1 dk

(B32A2ST) Tug

2 oil engines reverse reduction geared to sc. shafts driving 2 FP propellers
Total Power: 808kW (1,098hp)
Yanmar 6LAAM-UTE
2 x 4 Stroke 6 Cy. 148 x 165 each-404kW (549bhp)
Yanmar Diesel Engine Co Ltd-Japan
AuxGen: 2 x 12kW 220V a.c

IMO / Call sign / Flag	Name / Owner / Port	Tonnage	Class	Build / Dimensions	Type	Machinery
8860250 *TC4289* -	**SABAN KAPTAN** **Haci Saban Zorer Denizcilik Nakliyat ve Ticaret Ltd Sti** - *Istanbul* *Turkey* Official number: 4013	*296* 188 567		**1970 Gemi-is Kolleketif Sirketi — Fener, Istanbul** Loa 48.00 Br ex - Dght 3.150 Lbp 44.22 Br md 7.25 Dpth 3.97 Welded, 1 dk	**(A31A2GX) General Cargo Ship** Compartments: 1 Ho, ER 1 Ha: (11.6 x 4.3)ER Cranes: 2x3t	**1 oil engine** driving 1 FP propeller Total Power: 223kW (303hp) 8.0kn Russkiy 1 x 4 Stroke 223kW (303bhp) Mashinostroitelnyy Zavod"Russkiy-Dizel"-Leningrad
9494307 *YJQR4* -	**SABANDO TIDE** *ex* Posh Veritas *-2010* **Aqua Fleet Ltd** Tidewater Marine International Inc *Port Vila* *Vanuatu* MMSI: 576002000 Official number: 1990	**2,538** 761 2,623	Class: AB	**2008-06 Yuexin Shipbuilding Co Ltd — Guangzhou GD** Yd No: 3081 Loa 69.90 Br ex - Dght 5.900 Lbp 61.20 Br md 16.60 Dpth 7.20 Welded, 1 dk	**(B21B20A) Anchor Handling Tug Supply**	**2 oil engines** reduction geared to sc. shafts driving 2 CP propellers Total Power: 5,844kW (7,946hp) 12.5kn MAN-B&W 8L27/38 2 x 4 Stroke 8 Cy. 270 x 380 each-2922kW (3973bhp) (new engine 2008) MAN Diesel A/S-Denmark AuxGen: 2 x 1200kW 440V 60Hz a.c, 2 x 370kW 440V 60Hz a.c Thrusters: 2 Tunnel thruster (f); 1 Tunnel thruster (a) Fuel: 833.0 (d.f.)
7647106 *YD4661* -	**SABANG 8** *ex* Sabang Agung 8 *-2008* *ex* Sabang VIII *-2001* *ex* Aspa Power 8 *-1990* *ex* Assets 2602 *-1990* **PT Sabang Raya Indah** - *Palembang* *Indonesia*	*148* 45 -	Class: KI (GL) (AB)	**1976-10 Sing Koon Seng Pte Ltd — Singapore** Yd No: SKS363 L reg 24.28 Br ex 7.62 Dght 2.520 Lbp 21.98 Br md 7.46 Dpth 3.54 Welded, 1 dk	**(B32A2ST) Tug**	**2 oil engines** reverse reduction geared to sc. shafts driving 2 FP propellers Total Power: 832kW (1,132hp) 10.0kn Caterpillar D379SCAC 2 x Vee 4 Stroke 8 Cy. 159 x 203 each-416kW (566bhp) Caterpillar Tractor Co-USA AuxGen: 2 x 40kW 220V a.c
9024176 - -	**SABANG 9** **PT Prima Sarana Lestari** - *Jambi* *Indonesia*	**102** 61 -	Class: KI	**1992-05 P.T. Sabang Raya Indah — Jambi** Loa 23.90 Br ex - Dght 2.240 Lbp 22.28 Br md 6.50 Dpth 2.85 Welded, 1 dk	**(B32A2ST) Tug**	**2 oil engines** geared to sc. shafts driving 2 Propellers Total Power: 918kW (1,248hp) Caterpillar 3412TA 2 x Vee 4 Stroke 12 Cy. 137 x 152 each-459kW (624bhp) Caterpillar Inc-USA AuxGen: 2 x 12kW 220V a.c
8892617 - -	**SABANG 21** **PT Pelayaran Nasional Fajar Marindo Raya** - *Jambi* *Indonesia*	*150* 45 -	Class: KI	**1995-04 P.T. Sabang Raya Indah — Jambi** Loa 26.00 Br ex - Dght - Lbp 23.65 Br md 7.00 Dpth 3.50 Welded, 1 dk	**(B32A2ST) Tug**	**2 oil engines** driving 2 FP propellers Total Power: 810kW (1,102hp) Yanmar S165L-ST 2 x 4 Stroke 6 Cy. 165 x 210 each-405kW (551bhp) Yanmar Diesel Engine Co Ltd-Japan
9024188 - -	**SABANG 25** **PT Pelayaran Nasional Fajar Marindo Raya** - *Jambi* *Indonesia*	**153** 46 -	Class: KI	**1996-06 P.T. Sabang Raya Indah — Jambi** Loa 26.00 Br ex - Dght 2.990 Lbp 23.65 Br md 7.00 Dpth 3.50 Welded, 1 dk	**(B32A2ST) Tug**	**2 oil engines** geared to sc. shafts driving 2 Propellers Total Power: 918kW (1,248hp) 10.5kn Caterpillar 3412TA 2 x Vee 4 Stroke 12 Cy. 137 x 152 each-459kW (624bhp) (made 1996) Caterpillar Inc-USA AuxGen: 2 x 80kW 380/220V a.c
9024205 *YD4543* -	**SABANG 29** **PT Sabang Raya Indah** - *Jambi* *Indonesia*	**149** 45 -	Class: KI	**1997-08 P.T. Sabang Raya Indah — Jambi** Loa 26.00 Br ex - Dght 2.850 Lbp 23.65 Br md 7.00 Dpth 3.50 Welded, 1 dk	**(B32A2ST) Tug**	**2 oil engines** geared to sc. shafts driving 2 Propellers Total Power: 956kW (1,300hp) 10.0kn Caterpillar 3412 2 x Vee 4 Stroke 12 Cy. 137 x 152 each-478kW (650bhp) (made 1996) Caterpillar Inc-USA AuxGen: 2 x 300kW 400V a.c
9024217 *YD4554* -	**SABANG 31** **PT Pelayaran Nasional Fajar Marindo Raya** - *Jambi* *Indonesia*	**149** 45 -	Class: KI	**1997-11 P.T. Sabang Raya Indah — Jambi** Loa 26.00 Br ex - Dght 2.850 Lbp 24.32 Br md 7.00 Dpth 3.50 Welded, 1 dk	**(B32A2ST) Tug**	**2 oil engines** geared to sc. shafts driving 2 Propellers Total Power: 956kW (1,300hp) 10.0kn Caterpillar 3412 2 x Vee 4 Stroke 12 Cy. 137 x 152 each-478kW (650bhp) (made 1996) Caterpillar Inc-USA AuxGen: 2 x 32kW 400/240V a.c
9024229 - -	**SABANG 35** - **PT Sabang Raya Indah** - *Jambi* *Indonesia*	**156** 93 -	Class: KI	**2001-04 P.T. Sabang Raya Indah — Jambi** Loa 23.00 Br ex - Dght 3.120 Lbp 21.31 Br md 7.50 Dpth 3.50 Welded, 1 dk	**(B32A2ST) Tug**	**2 oil engines** geared to sc. shafts driving 2 Propellers Total Power: 1,250kW (1,700hp) 10.0kn Caterpillar D398B 2 x Vee 4 Stroke 12 Cy. 153 x 203 each-625kW (850bhp) Caterpillar Inc-USA AuxGen: 2 x 60kW 400V a.c
9024231 - -	**SABANG 37** **PT Indonesia Marine Transportation** - *Jambi* *Indonesia*	**156** 93 -	Class: KI	**2003-05 P.T. Sabang Raya Indah — Jambi** Loa 23.00 Br ex - Dght 2.990 Lbp 21.31 Br md 7.50 Dpth 3.50 Welded, 1 dk	**(B32A2ST) Tug**	**2 oil engines** geared to sc. shafts driving 2 Propellers Total Power: 920kW (1,250hp) 10.0kn Caterpillar 3412 2 x Vee 4 Stroke 12 Cy. 137 x 152 each-460kW (625bhp) (made 2002) Caterpillar Inc-USA AuxGen: 2 x 74kW 400V a.c
8730649 *YDA4271* -	**SABANG 39** **PT Sabang Raya Indah** - *Jambi* *Indonesia*	**157** 48 -	Class: KI	**2007-05 P.T. Sabang Raya Indah — Jambi** Loa 25.00 Br ex - Dght 2.910 Lbp 24.06 Br md 7.50 Dpth 3.50 Welded, 1 dk	**(B32A2ST) Tug**	**2 oil engines** reduction geared to sc. shafts driving 2 Propellers Total Power: 956kW (1,300hp) Mitsubishi S6A3-MPTK2 2 x 4 Stroke 6 Cy. 150 x 175 each-478kW (650bhp) Mitsubishi Heavy Industries Ltd-Japan
8730651 *YDA4306*	**SABANG 51** **PT Sabang Raya Indah** - *Jambi* *Indonesia*	**157** 48 -	Class: KI	**2007-08 P.T. Sabang Raya Indah — Jambi** L reg 25.00 Br ex - Dght 2.890 Lbp 23.61 Br md 7.50 Dpth 3.50 Welded, 1 dk	**(B32A2ST) Tug**	**2 oil engines** reduction geared to sc. shafts driving 2 Propellers Total Power: 956kW (1,300hp) Mitsubishi S6A3-MPTK2 2 x 4 Stroke 6 Cy. 150 x 175 each-478kW (650bhp) Mitsubishi Heavy Industries Ltd-Japan
8735625 *YDA4447* -	**SABANG 53** **PT Citra Borneo Samudra** - *Jambi* *Indonesia*	**157** 48 -	Class: KI	**2008-12 P.T. Sabang Raya Indah — Jambi** Loa 25.00 Br ex - Dght 2.890 Lbp 23.52 Br md 7.50 Dpth 3.50 Welded, 1 dk	**(B32A2ST) Tug**	**2 oil engines** driving 2 Propellers Total Power: 1,516kW (2,062hp) Mitsubishi S6R2-MTK3L 2 x 4 Stroke 6 Cy. 170 x 220 each-758kW (1031bhp) Mitsubishi Heavy Industries Ltd-Japan
8738770 *YDA4480* -	**SABANG 55** **PT Sabang Raya Indah** - *Jambi* *Indonesia*	**163** 49 -	Class: KI	**2008-12 PT Pahala Harapan Lestari — Pangkalpinang** Loa 25.00 Br ex - Dght 2.880 Lbp 23.22 Br md 7.50 Dpth 3.40 Welded, 1 dk	**(B32A2ST) Tug**	**2 oil engines** driving 2 Propellers Total Power: 956kW (1,300hp) Mitsubishi S6A3-MPTK2 2 x 4 Stroke 6 Cy. 150 x 175 each-478kW (650bhp) Mitsubishi Heavy Industries Ltd-Japan
8740577 - -	**SABANG 57** **PT Sabang Raya Indah** - *Jambi* *Indonesia*	**163** 49 -	Class: KI	**2009-06 PT Pahala Harapan Lestari — Pangkalpinang** Loa 25.00 Br ex - Dght - Lbp 23.22 Br md 7.50 Dpth 3.40 Welded, 1 dk	**(B32A2ST) Tug**	**2 oil engines** driving 2 Propellers Total Power: 1,220kW (1,658hp) Yanmar 6AYM-ETE 2 x 4 Stroke 6 Cy. 155 x 180 each-610kW (829bhp) Yanmar Diesel Engine Co Ltd-Japan
9025376 *YD4827* -	**SABANG 388** *ex* SDS 26 *-2008* **PT Indonesia Marine Transportation** - *Jakarta* *Indonesia*	**177** 54 -	Class: KI	**2002-01 P.T. Mariana Bahagia — Palembang** L reg 25.20 Br ex - Dght - Lbp 23.64 Br md 8.00 Dpth 3.00 Welded, 1 dk	**(B32A2ST) Tug**	**2 oil engines** geared to sc. shafts driving 2 Propellers Total Power: 1,204kW (1,636hp) 8.0kn Mitsubishi S6R2-MPTK 2 x 4 Stroke 6 Cy. 170 x 220 each-602kW (818bhp) (made 2001) Mitsubishi Heavy Industries Ltd-Japan
8984680 *YB3377* -	**SABANG MARINDO II** **PT Pelayaran Nasional Fajar Marindo Raya** - *Batam* *Indonesia* MMSI: 525011017	**136** 41 36	Class: (KI)	**1998-03 P.T. Sekip Hilir Shipyard — Batam** Yd No: 0320098 Loa 30.00 Br ex 5.42 Dght - Lbp 27.07 Br md 5.40 Dpth 2.77 Welded, 1 dk	**(A37B2PS) Passenger Ship** Hull Material: Aluminium Alloy	**3 oil engines** geared to sc. shafts driving 3 Propellers Total Power: 2,427kW (3,300hp) 25.0kn Caterpillar 3412E-TA 1 x Vee 4 Stroke 12 Cy. 137 x 152 809kW (1100bhp) Caterpillar Inc-USA Yanmar 12LAKM-STE 2 x Vee 4 Stroke 12 Cy. 150 x 165 each-809kW (1100bhp) Yanmar Diesel Engine Co Ltd-Japan AuxGen: 2 x 60kW a.c

Ship / Owner	Tonnage	Class	Builder / Dimensions	Type	Machinery
9537575 **SABANG MARINDO VIII** *YB3533* - **PT Pelayaran Nasional Fajar Marindo Raya** - *Batam* *Indonesia*	**143** 43 -	Class: KI	**2008-06 P.T. Batam Expressindo Shipyard — Batam** Yd No: 815 Loa 27.20 Br ex - Dght 1.230 Lbp 23.00 Br md 6.00 Dpth 2.80 Welded, 1 dk	**(A37B2PS) Passenger Ship** Hull Material: Aluminium Alloy	**2 oil engines** geared to sc. shafts driving 2 Propellers Total Power: 1,618kW (2,200hp) Caterpillar 3412E 2 x Vee 4 Stroke 12 Cy. 137 x 152 each-809kW (1100bhp) Caterpillar Inc-USA
7649154 **SABANG PUTRA** *YHBT* *ex* Dunia Bintang *-2004* *ex* Star Progress *-1999* - *ex* Orion *-1994* *ex* Capella *-1992* *ex* Navi Star *-1990* *ex* Star III *-1989* *ex* Kyosei Maru *-1988* *ex* Koshin Maru *-1985* **PT Fajar Putra Sabang Line** - *Sabang* *Indonesia*	**890** 586 1,450	Class: KI (NK)	**1974-03 Suzuki Shipyard Co. Ltd. — Yokkaichi** Loa 63.40 Br ex - Dght 4.090 Lbp 59.50 Br md 11.00 Dpth 5.03 Welded, 1 dk	**(A12A2TC) Chemical Tanker** Liq: 2,170 Compartments: 3 Ta, ER	**1 oil engine** driving 1 FP propeller Total Power: 956kW (1,300hp) 10.0kn Niigata 6L25BX 1 x 4 Stroke 6 Cy. 250 x 320 956kW (1300bhp) Niigata Tekkosho-Japan
6905575 **SABAR** *TC4484* *ex* Huseyin Aga *-2000* *ex* Isikurt *-1986* - *ex* Dacka *-1986* **Karden Denizcilik Nakliyat ve Ticaret Ltd Sti** - *Istanbul* *Turkey* MMSI: 271010169 Official number: 3917	**294** 218 629	Class: (AB)	**1969-06 Gesan Tersanesi — Sutluce, Istanbul** Yd No: 10 Loa 38.99 Br ex 7.22 Dght 2.590 Lbp 35.51 Br md 7.21 Dpth 2.93 Welded, 1 dk	**(A13B2TU) Tanker (unspecified)** Compartments: 8 Ta, ER	**1 oil engine** reverse reduction geared to sc. shaft driving 1 FP propeller Total Power: 147kW (200hp) 10.0kn Stork 1 x 4 Stroke 5 Cy. 150 x 225 147kW (200bhp) Koninklijke Machinefabriek GebrStork & Co NV-Netherlands Fuel: 6.0
8823898 **SABAR** *YB5225* *ex* Sahid *-2008* *ex* Eiwa Maru No. 38 *-2002* - **PT Jasa Bahtera Lestari Mulia (Pelayaran Nasional)** - *Surabaya* *Indonesia*	*799* 319 745	Class: KI	**1988-09 K.K. Yoshida Zosen Kogyo — Arida** Loa 56.70 Br ex - Dght 3.520 Lbp 49.92 Br md 11.60 Dpth 5.50 Welded, 1 dk	**(A31A2GX) General Cargo Ship**	**1 oil engine** driving 1 FP propeller Total Power: 662kW (900hp) Niigata 6M28BGT 1 x 4 Stroke 6 Cy. 280 x 480 662kW (900bhp) Niigata Engineering Co Ltd-Japan AuxGen: 2 x 74kW 220V a.c
9014432 **SABARIMALA GAS** *H8NM* *ex* Temse *-2014* *ex* BW Helga *-2011* - *ex* Helga *-2009* **Green Spanker Shipping SA** Synergy Maritime Pvt Ltd *Panama* *Panama* MMSI: 351590000	**22,521** 8,624 30,761 T/cm 39.1	Class: NV	**1994-03 Kawasaki Heavy Industries Ltd — Kobe HG** Yd No: 1434 Loa 170.00 (BB) Br ex 27.39 Dght 11.350 Lbp 161.29 Br md 27.36 Dpth 18.20 Welded, 1 dk	**(A11B2TG) LPG Tanker** Double Bottom Entire Compartment Length Liq (Gas): 34,754 3 x Gas Tank (s); 3 independent (C.mn.stl) pri horizontal 6 Cargo Pump (s): 6x440m³/hr Manifold: Bow/CM: 89m	**1 oil engine** driving 1 FP propeller Total Power: 10,800kW (14,684hp) 16.0kn B&W 5S60MC 1 x 2 Stroke 5 Cy. 600 x 2292 10800kW (14684bhp) Kawasaki Heavy Industries Ltd-Japan AuxGen: 3 x 820kW 440V 60Hz a.c Thrusters: 1 Thwart. CP thruster (f) Fuel: 320.0 (d.f.) 1963.0 (r.f.)
7395997 **SABARY** - *ex* Diamissa No. 5 *-1988* - *ex* Koryo Maru No. 108 *-1988* **Daerim Fishery Co Ltd** - *Busan* *South Korea* Official number: 9702003-6260004	**217** - 507	Class: (KR) (BV)	**1974-09 Niigata Engineering Co Ltd — Niigata NI** Yd No: 1321 Loa 55.07 Br ex 9.02 Dght 3.271 Lbp 49.69 Br md 9.00 Dpth 5.69 Welded, 2 dks	**(B11A2FS) Stern Trawler**	**1 oil engine** driving 1 FP propeller Total Power: 1,471kW (2,000hp) 13.3kn Niigata 6M40EX 1 x 4 Stroke 6 Cy. 400 x 600 1471kW (2000bhp) Niigata Engineering Co Ltd-Japan
8938069 **SABATIS M** - *ex* Pescarus 4 *-2004* - **Elter SA Construction & Holding Co**	**111** 33 -	Class: (RN)	**1982 Santierul Naval Drobeta-Turnu Severin S.A. — Drobeta-Turnu S.** Yd No: 11434003 Loa 23.39 Br ex - Dght 2.350 Lbp 20.61 Br md 6.96 Dpth 3.30 Welded, 1 dk	**(B32A2ST) Tug**	**2 oil engines** driving 2 FP propellers Total Power: 410kW (558hp) 10.8kn Maybach MB836BB 2 x 4 Stroke 8 Cy. 175 x 205 each-205kW (279bhp) Uzina 23 August Bucuresti-Bucuresti AuxGen: 2 x 35kW 400V 50Hz a.c Fuel: 9.4 (d.f.)
9277137 **SABAWANGSA NO. 1601** *9WEF4* *ex* Bonggaya 91 *-2006* - **Sabawangsa Sdn Bhd** - *Kota Kinabalu* *Malaysia* MMSI: 533002380 Official number: 329798	*192* 58 161	Class: NV (NK)	**2002-09 Super-Light Shipbuilding Contractor — Sibu** Yd No: 50 Loa 25.00 Br ex - Dght 3.012 Lbp 23.33 Br md 8.00 Dpth 3.90 Welded, 1 dk	**(B32A2ST) Tug**	**2 oil engines** geared to sc. shafts driving 2 FP propellers Total Power: 1,204kW (1,636hp) 11.0kn Mitsubishi S6R2-MPTK 2 x 4 Stroke 6 Cy. 170 x 220 each-602kW (818bhp) Mitsubishi Heavy Industries Ltd-Japan
9281255 **SABAWANGSA NO. 1602** *9WEF5* *ex* Bonggaya 92 *-2006* - **Sabawangsa Sdn Bhd** - *Kota Kinabalu* *Malaysia* MMSI: 533002390 Official number: 329799	**160** 26 158	Class: NV (NK)	**2002-12 Rajang Maju Shipbuilding Sdn Bhd — Sibu** Yd No: 45 Loa 25.00 (BB) Br ex - Dght 2.712 Lbp 22.39 Br md 7.32 Dpth 3.35 Welded, 1 dk	**(B32A2ST) Tug**	**2 oil engines** geared to sc. shafts driving 2 Propellers Total Power: 1,204kW (1,636hp) 11.0kn Mitsubishi S6R2-MPTK 2 x 4 Stroke 6 Cy. 170 x 220 each-602kW (818bhp) Mitsubishi Heavy Industries Ltd-Japan AuxGen: 2 x 41kW a.c Fuel: 110.0 (d.f.) 6.0pd
8842349 **SABAWANGSA NO. 1603** *9WTF* *ex* Boo Hin No. 88 *-1998* *ex* Marina Jaya *-1998* - **Sabawangsa Sdn Bhd** - *Kota Kinabalu* *Malaysia* Official number: 325627	**190** 57 157	Class: (NK) (AB)	**1989-11 Zarah Sdn Bhd — Tawau** Yd No: 009 Loa 26.00 Br ex - Dght 2.730 Lbp 24.52 Br md 8.60 Dpth 3.74 Welded, 1 dk	**(B32A2ST) Tug**	**2 oil engines** reverse reduction geared to sc. shafts driving 2 FP propellers Total Power: 740kW (1,006hp) 10.0kn Caterpillar 3412T 2 x Vee 4 Stroke 12 Cy. 137 x 152 each-370kW (503bhp) Caterpillar Inc-USA AuxGen: 2 x 49kW a.c
8746911 **SABIK** *9MHT9* - **Government of Malaysia (Director of Marine & Ministry of Transport)** - *Port Klang* *Malaysia* Official number: 333805	**140** 42 25		**2008-03 Kay Marine Sdn Bhd — Kuala Terengganu** (Assembled by) Yd No: J104-5 **0000* Inform Marine Technology — Fremantle WA** (Parts for assembly by) Loa 26.00 Br ex - Dght 1.200 Lbp - Br md 9.20 Dpth 2.55 Welded, 1 dk	**(A37B2PS) Passenger Ship** Hull Material: Aluminium Alloy	**2 oil engines** reduction geared to sc. shafts driving 2 Propellers Total Power: 2,206kW (3,000hp) M.T.U. 12V2000M91 2 x Vee 4 Stroke 12 Cy. 130 x 150 each-1103kW (1500bhp) MTU Friedrichshafen GmbH-Friedrichshafen
7633399 **SABIN** *5IM404* *ex* Dalhem *-2010* *ex* Vento Di Ponente *-2008* - *ex* Dalhem *-2006* *ex* Sabine D *-1996* *ex* Gustav Behrmann *-1989* *ex* Contship Two *-1979* *ex* Gustav Behrmann *-1977* **MBM Shipping Co SA** - *Zanzibar* *Tanzania (Zanzibar)* MMSI: 677030400 Official number: 300154	**2,581** 1,321 2,937	Class: (GL)	**1977-06 KG Norderwerft GmbH & Co. — Hamburg** (Hull) **1977-06 J.J. Sietas Schiffswerft — Hamburg** Yd No: 805 Loa 88.40 (BB) Br ex 15.78 Dght 4.848 Lbp 81.21 Br md 15.45 Dpth 6.91 Welded, 2 dks	**(A31A2GX) General Cargo Ship** Grain: 4,445; Bale: 4,151 TEU 220 C Ho 72 TEU C Dk 148 TEU Compartments: 1 Ho, ER 1 Ha: (50.0 x 12.5)ER Ice Capable	**1 oil engine** sr geared to sc. shaft driving 1 CP propeller Total Power: 1,949kW (2,650hp) 13.3kn MaK 8M453AK 1 x 4 Stroke 8 Cy. 320 x 420 1949kW (2650bhp) MaK Maschinenbau GmbH-Kiel AuxGen: 1 x 368kW 220/380V 50Hz a.c, 2 x 160kW 220/380V 50Hz a.c Thrusters: 1 Thwart. FP thruster (f) Fuel: 350.0 (d.f.) 10.0pd
6917243 **SABIN S** - - **Industria Pesquera Hondurena** - *Roatan* *Honduras*	*109* 54 55	Class: (BV)	**1969 Ast. Celaya — Bilbao** Yd No: 97 Loa 26.42 Br ex 6.89 Dght 2.744 Lbp 22.56 Br md 6.86 Dpth 3.20 Welded, 1 dk	**(B11A2FT) Trawler** Grain: 117 Compartments: 1 Ho, ER 1 Ha: (1.9 x 1.9)	**1 oil engine** driving 1 FP propeller Total Power: 276kW (375hp) 9.0kn Caterpillar D353SCAC 1 x 4 Stroke 6 Cy. 159 x 203 276kW (375bhp) Caterpillar Tractor Co-USA
8616635 **SABINA** *OJMJ* *ex* Atula *-2006* *ex* RMS Mercator *-1996* - *ex* Atula *-1994* **Helmer Lundstrom AB Oy** - *Vastanfjard* *Finland* MMSI: 230989850 Official number: 12416	**2,006** 1,096 2,722	Class: GL	**1986-12 Heinrich Brand Schiffswerft GmbH & Co. KG — Oldenburg** Yd No: 227 Loa 81.87 Br ex 12.65 Dght 4.520 Lbp 78.47 Br md 12.62 Dpth 4.70 Welded, 2 dks	**(A31A2GX) General Cargo Ship** Grain: 3,697; Bale: 3,692 TEU 104 C. 104/20' (40') Compartments: 1 Ho, ER 1 Ha: (51.3 x 10.1)ER Ice Capable	**1 oil engine** with flexible couplings & sr reverse geared to sc. shaft driving 1 FP propeller Total Power: 1,185kW (1,611hp) 11.0kn Deutz SBV6M628 1 x 4 Stroke 6 Cy. 240 x 280 1185kW (1611bhp) Kloeckner Humboldt Deutz AG-West Germany AuxGen: 2 x 150kW 380V 50Hz a.c, 1 x 94kW 380V 50Hz a.c Thrusters: 1 Thwart. FP thruster (f)
8842973 **SABINA** - - **Seokang Co Ltd** - *Busan* *South Korea* Official number: 9407070-6210009	*358* 151 875	Class: (KR)	**1990-04 Pesca Altura Alteanas S.A. — Spain** Loa 57.80 Br ex - Dght - Lbp 49.00 Br md 11.20 Dpth 4.60 Welded, 2 dks	**(B11A2FS) Stern Trawler** Ins: 1,250	**1 oil engine** driving 1 FP propeller Total Power: 1,618kW (2,200hp) 12.0kn Wartsila 6R32 1 x 4 Stroke 6 Cy. 320 x 350 1618kW (2200bhp) Construcciones Echevarria SA-Spain AuxGen: 4 x 220kW 380V a.c

9205718 *HBEB* -
SABINA
mv Sabina AG
Enzian Ship Management AG
Basel *Switzerland*
MMSI: 269052000
Official number: 157
5,968 3,422 9,231
Class: LR
✠ **100A1** SS 06/2010
strengthened for heavy cargoes, container cargoes in holds and on upper deck hatch covers
✠ **LMC** **UMS**
Eq.Ltr: 0†;
Cable: 498.6/46.0 U3 (a)
2000-06 B.V. Scheepswerf Damen Hoogezand — Foxhol Yd No: 804
2000-06 Santierul Naval Damen Galati S.A. — Galati (Hull) Yd No: 927
Loa 127.87 (BB) Br ex 15.97 Dght 7.450
Lbp 121.66 Br md 15.85 Dpth 9.75
Welded, 1 dk
(A31A2GX) General Cargo Ship
Grain: 12,528
TEU 434 C.Ho 256/20' C.Dk 178/20'
Compartments: 2 Ho, ER
2 Ha: (38.2 x 13.2) (51.3 x 13.2)ER
Cranes: 1x60t
1 oil engine with flexible couplings & sr gearedto sc. shaft driving 1 CP propeller
Total Power: 4,320kW (5,873hp) 14.5kn
MaK 9M32
1 x 4 Stroke 9 Cy. 320 x 480 4320kW (5873bhp)
MaK Motoren GmbH & Co. KG-Kiel
AuxGen: 1 x 440kW 400V 50Hz a.c, 2 x 280kW 400V 50Hz a.c
Boilers: TOH (o.f.) 10.2kgf/cm^2 (10.0bar), TOH (ex.g.) 10.2kgf/cm^2 (10.0bar)
Thrusters: 1 Thwart. CP thruster (f)
Fuel: 50.9 (d.f.) 519.8 (r.f.) 18.0pd

8121379 *J8MG* -
SABINA A
ex Inishfree -2000 ex Lenneborg -1997
Anral Lines Ltd
Ocean Management Inc
SatCom: Inmarsat C 437540110
Kingstown *St Vincent & The Grenadines*
MMSI: 375401000
3,222 1,743 5,350
Class: (BV)
1983-05 Nieuwe Noord Nederlandse Scheepswerven B.V. — Groningen Yd No: 404
Loa 82.38 (BB) Br ex 15.83 Dght 7.460
Lbp 74.97 Br md 15.41 Dpth 9.00
Welded, 2 dks
(A31A2GX) General Cargo Ship
Grain: 5,889
TEU 146 C. 146/20' (40')
Compartments: 1 Ho, ER, 1 Tw Dk
1 Ha: (49.2 x 12.7)ER
Cranes: 2x16t
Ice Capable
1 oil engine sr geared to sc. shaft driving 1 CP propeller
Total Power: 2,045kW (2,780hp) 11.5kn
Wartsila 6R32
1 x 4 Stroke 6 Cy. 320 x 350 2045kW (2780bhp)
Oy Wartsila Ab-Finland
Thrusters: 1 Thwart. FP thruster (f)

7101891 *UALB* -
SABINE
ex Sormovskiy-19 -2000
Transintershipping Co Ltd
-
St Petersburg *Russia*
MMSI: 273320100
2,478 999 3,355
Class: RS
1970-11 Sudostroitelnyy Zavod "Krasnoye Sormovo" — Gorkiy Yd No: 25
Loa 114.20 Br ex 13.21 Dght 3.810
Lbp 110.15 Br md 13.00 Dpth 5.52
Welded, 1 dk
(A31A2GX) General Cargo Ship
Bale: 4,297
Compartments: 4 Ho, ER
4 Ha: (17.6 x 9.3)3 (18.1 x 9.3)ER
Ice Capable
2 oil engines driving 2 FP propellers
Total Power: 1,132kW (1,540hp) 10.7kn
S.K.L. 6NVD48A-2U
2 x 4 Stroke 6 Cy. 320 x 480 each-566kW (770bhp) (new engine 1983)
VEB Schwermaschinenbau "KarlLiebknecht" (SKL)-Magdeburg
AuxGen: 3 x 50kW
Fuel: 84.0 (d.f.)

9397391 *WDD7182* -
SABINE
Seabulk Towing Inc
-
Port Arthur, TX *United States of America*
MMSI: 367182980
Official number: 1190056
281 84 214
Class: AB
2007-09 Eastern Shipbuilding Group — Panama City, Fl Yd No: 897
Loa 29.87 Br ex - Dght 3.660
Lbp 25.15 Br md 10.98 Dpth 4.54
Welded, 1 dk
(B32A2ST) Tug
2 oil engines reduction geared to sc. shafts driving 2 Z propellers
Total Power: 3,525kW (4,792hp)
Caterpillar 3516B-HD
2 x Vee 4 Stroke 16 Cy. 170 x 215 each-1686kW (2292bhp)
Caterpillar Inc-USA
AuxGen: 2 x 99kW 60Hz a.c
Fuel: 95.4 (d.f.)

9594755 *V7UU6* -
SABINE
DSS C LLC
Diamond S Management LLC
SatCom: Inmarsat C 453837765
Majuro *Marshall Islands*
MMSI: 538004033
Official number: 4033
81,341 51,270 158,493 T/cm 119.6
Class: AB
2012-07 Samsung Heavy Industries Co Ltd — Geoje Yd No: 1954
Loa 274.39 (BB) Br ex 48.04 Dght 17.000
Lbp 264.00 Br md 48.00 Dpth 23.20
Welded, 1 dk
(A13A2TV) Crude Oil Tanker
Double Hull (13F)
Liq: 167,400; Liq (Oil): 167,400
Cargo Heating Coils
Compartments: 12 Wing Ta, 2 Wing Slop Ta, ER
3 Cargo Pump (s): 3x4000m^3/hr
Manifold: Bow/CM: 137m
1 oil engine driving 1 FP propeller
Total Power: 18,215kW (24,765hp) 15.5kn
MAN-B&W 6S70MC-C
1 x 2 Stroke 6 Cy. 700 x 2800 18215kW (24765bhp)
Doosan Engine Co Ltd-South Korea
AuxGen: 3 x 900kW a.c
Fuel: 130.0 (d.f.) 3400.0 (r.f.)

9307554 - -
SABINE VI
ex Majulah -2005
Marine Supply CA
-
La Guaira *Venezuela*
282 85 40
Class: (BV)
2005-01 Yuexin Shipbuilding Co Ltd — Guangzhou GD Yd No: P140
Loa 29.00 Br ex 10.10 Dght 3.500
Lbp 23.50 Br md 9.50 Dpth 4.70
Welded, 1 dk
(B32A2ST) Tug
2 oil engines geared to sc. shafts driving 2 Z propellers
Total Power: 2,648kW (3,600hp)
Niigata 6L22HLX
2 x 4 Stroke 6 Cy. 220 x 300 each-1324kW (1800bhp)
Niigata Engineering Co Ltd-Japan

9183154 *EAQU* 3-VILL-17-
SABINO SEGUNDO
Juan Antonio Perez Vidal
-
Santa Eugenia de Ribeira *Spain*
Official number: 3-7/1997
208 - 123
1997-12 Astilleros Armon Burela SA — Burela Yd No: 93
Loa 28.00 (BB) Br ex - Dght 3.000
Lbp 23.00 Br md 7.50 Dpth 3.30
Welded, 1 dk
(B11A2FS) Stern Trawler
Ins: 132
1 oil engine with flexible couplings & reverse reduction geared to sc. shaft driving 1 FP propeller
Total Power: 221kW (300hp) 9.0kn
GUASCOR F360TA-SP
1 x Vee 4 Stroke 12 Cy. 152 x 165 221kW (300bhp)
Gutierrez Ascunce Corp (GUASCOR)-Spain

8726985 - -
SABIR BABAYEV
ex Aslan -2001 ex Titan -2001
Baku International Sea Trade Port
-
Baku *Azerbaijan*
MMSI: 423310100
Official number: DGR-0235
182 54 57
Class: RS
1987-09 Gorokhovetskiy Sudostroitelnyy Zavod — Gorokhovets Yd No: 227
Loa 29.30 Br ex 8.60 Dght 3.400
Lbp 27.00 Br md 8.30 Dpth 4.30
Welded, 1 dk
(B32A2ST) Tug
Ice Capable
2 oil engines driving 2 CP propellers
Total Power: 1,180kW (1,604hp) 11.5kn
Pervomaysk 8CHNP25/34
2 x 4 Stroke 8 Cy. 250 x 340 each-590kW (802bhp)
Pervomaydizelmash (PDM)-Pervomaysk

8128171 *4JDE* -
SABIT ORUJOV
Specialized Sea Oil Fleet Organisation, Caspian Sea Oil Fleet, State Oil Co of the Republic of Azerbaijan
-
Baku *Azerbaijan*
MMSI: 423086100
Official number: DGR-0099
2,621 786 549
Class: RS
1983-09 Oy Wartsila Ab — Helsinki Yd No: 462
Loa 73.92 Br ex 14.82 Dght 3.601
Lbp 66.22 Br md 14.81 Dpth 8.06
Welded, 2 dks
(A37B2PS) Passenger Ship
Passengers: unberthed: 577
2 oil engines driving 2 Directional propellers
Total Power: 1,766kW (2,402hp)
Wartsila 6R22
2 x 4 Stroke 6 Cy. 220 x 240 each-883kW (1201bhp)
Oy Wartsila Ab-Finland
AuxGen: 2 x 590kW
Thrusters: 1 Thwart. FP thruster (f)
Fuel: 294.0 (d.f.)

9636022 *YJTH8* -
SABLE
4K+3GP
Edison Chouest Offshore LLC
Port Vila *Vanuatu*
MMSI: 577159000
Official number: 2222
3,806 1,780 5,462
Class: AB
2013-07 Remontowa Shipbuilding SA — Gdansk (Hull) Yd No: (B851/3)
2013-07 Gdanska Stocznia 'Remontowa' SA — Gdansk Yd No: B851/13
Loa 92.65 (BB) Br ex - Dght 6.050
Lbp 86.60 Br md 18.80 Dpth 7.40
Welded, 1 dk
(B21A2OS) Platform Supply Ship
Cranes: 1x3t
4 diesel electric oil engines driving 4 gen. Connecting to 2 elec. motors each (2000kW) driving 2 Azimuth electric drive units
Total Power: 7,060kW (9,600hp) 12.0kn
Caterpillar 3512C
2 x Vee 4 Stroke 12 Cy. 170 x 215 each-1765kW (2400bhp)
Caterpillar Inc-USA
Fuel: 275.0

5304384 - -
SABOO
-
-
169 - -
Class: (LR)
✠ Classed LR until 10/64
1953-04 L Smit & Zoon's Scheeps- & Werktuigbouw NV — Kinderdijk Yd No: C0256
Loa 32.01 Br ex 7.50 Dght 2.223
Lbp 30.00 Br md 7.47 Dpth 3.05
Welded, 1 dk
(B32A2ST) Tug
Compartments: 1 Ho, ER
1 Ha: (1.8 x -)
2 oil engines driving 2 FP propellers
10.0kn
Crossley HRN6
2 x 2 Stroke 6 Cy. 267 x 343
Crossley Bros. Ltd.-Manchester
Fuel: 35.5

9413389 *9BJQ* -
SABOOR 1
Government of The Islamic Republic of Iran (Ports & Maritime Organisation)
-
Bandar Imam Khomeini *Iran*
MMSI: 422557000
260 99 126
Class: (BV)
2007-07 Penglai Bohai Shipyard Co Ltd — Penglai SD Yd No: PBZ05-52
Loa 31.54 Br ex - Dght 3.600
Lbp 28.34 Br md 9.60 Dpth 4.50
Welded, 1 dk
(B32A2ST) Tug
2 oil engines reduction geared to sc. shafts driving 2 Z propellers
Total Power: 2,400kW (3,264hp) 12.0kn
MaK 6M20
2 x 4 Stroke 6 Cy. 200 x 300 each-1200kW (1632bhp)
Caterpillar Motoren GmbH & Co. KG-Germany

9507635 *9BRA* -
SABOOR 2
Government of The Islamic Republic of Iran (Ports & Maritime Organisation)
-
Bandar Imam Khomeini *Iran*
MMSI: 422752000
416 125 240
Class: (BV)
2009-10 Penglai Bohai Shipyard Co Ltd — Penglai SD Yd No: PBZ07-82
Loa 31.00 Br ex 11.66 Dght 3.800
Lbp 27.70 Br md 11.00 Dpth 4.70
Welded, 1 dk
(B32A2ST) Tug
2 oil engines reduction geared to sc. shafts driving 2 Z propellers
Total Power: 3,236kW (4,400hp)
Wartsila 9L20
2 x 4 Stroke 9 Cy. 200 x 280 each-1618kW (2200bhp)
Wartsila Finland Oy-Finland
AuxGen: 2 x 150kW 50Hz a.c

9134050 - -
SABORA
Alexandria Port Authority
-
Egypt
120 - -
2007-01 Port Said Engineering Works — Port Said Yd No: 661
Loa 80.00 Br ex - Dght -
Lbp - Br md 14.75 Dpth 4.35
Welded, 1 dk
(B34G2SE) Pollution Control Vessel
1 oil engine geared to sc. shaft driving 1 Propeller
Total Power: 597kW (812hp)
Cummins KTA-38-M0
1 x Vee 4 Stroke 12 Cy. 159 x 159 597kW (812bhp)

8871106 - -
SABORA 2
Alexandria Port Authority
-
Alexandria *Egypt*
101 - 225
Class: (GL)
1992-12 Port Said Engineering Works — Port Said
L reg 30.90 Br ex - Dght 2.003
Lbp - Br md 6.60 Dpth 2.75
Welded, 1 dk
(B34E2SW) Waste Disposal Vessel
Liq: 255; Liq (Oil): 255
2 oil engines reverse reduction geared to sc. shafts driving 2 FP propellers
Total Power: 428kW (582hp) 7.0kn
M.T.U. 10V183AA61
2 x Vee 4 Stroke 10 Cy. 128 x 142 each-214kW (291bhp)
MTU Friedrichshafen GmbH-Friedrichshafen
AuxGen: 1 x 24kW 220/380V a.c

8805951 **SABRATAH**
-
- **Government of Libya (Socialist Ports Co)**
-
Libya

208 62 -

Class: (LR)
✠ Classed LR until 11/9/96

1991-11 Tczewska Stocznia Rzeczna — Tczew (Hull) Yd No: HP2600L5
1991-11 B.V. Scheepswerf Damen — Gorinchem Yd No: 3171
Loa 30.02 Br ex 8.07 Dght 3.430
Lbp 27.06 Br md 7.80 Dpth 4.05
Welded, 1 dk

(B32A2ST) Tug

2 oil engines with clutches, flexible couplings & sr reverse geared to sc. shafts driving 2 FP propellers
Total Power: 2,400kW (3,264hp)
Deutz SBV6M628
2 x 4 Stroke 6 Cy. 240 x 280 each-1200kW (1632bhp)
Kloeckner Humboldt Deutz AG-Germany
AuxGen: 2 x 68kW 380V 50Hz a.c, 1 x 38kW 380V 50Hz a.c

9054456 *PR7569* - **SABRE**
Saveiros Camuyrano - Servicos Maritimos SA
-
Santos *Brazil*
Official number: 11594

154 46 91

Class: LR
✠ **100A1** SS 06/2013
tug
Brazilian coastal service
LMC Cable: 247.5/16.0 U1 (a)

1993-06 Wilson, Sons SA — Guaruja Yd No: 018
Loa 26.55 Br ex 7.85 Dght 3.100
Lbp 24.91 Br md 7.80 Dpth 3.80
Welded, 1 dk

(B32A2ST) Tug

2 oil engines with clutches, flexible couplings & sr reverse geared to sc. shafts driving 2 FP propellers
Total Power: 1,486kW (2,020hp) 9.0kn
Kromhout 6FGHD240
2 x 4 Stroke 6 Cy. 240 x 260 each-743kW (1010bhp)
Motores Stork Werkspoor-Argentina
AuxGen: 2 x 60kW 440V 60Hz a.c

8107919 *HO3188* - **SABRE SPIRIT**
ex Sabre Service -2007
ex K Marine No. IV -1990
Ferrols Trucking Services Inc
Water Spirit Freight Services Inc
Panama *Panama*
MMSI: 372977000
Official number: 3356408A

684 205 1,200

Class: (AB)

1982-03 McDermott Shipyards Inc — New Iberia LA Yd No: 143
Loa 58.53 Br ex - Dght 3.601
Lbp 53.95 Br md 12.20 Dpth 4.27
Welded, 1 dk

(B21A2OS) Platform Supply Ship

2 oil engines reverse reduction geared to sc. shafts driving 2 FP propellers
Total Power: 2,206kW (3,000hp) 12.0kn
EMD (Electro-Motive) 12-645-E6
2 x Vee 2 Stroke 12 Cy. 230 x 254 each-1103kW (1500bhp)
General Motors Corp.Electro-Motive Div.-La Grange
AuxGen: 2 x 99kW
Thrusters: 1 Thwart. FP thruster (f)

9278624 *HPTN* - **SABREWING**
New Glory Shipping SA
Bernhard Schulte Shipmanagement (Singapore) Pte Ltd
Panama *Panama*
MMSI: 355470000
Official number: 2962004B

29,647 13,428 49,323 T/cm 52.8

Class: AB

2004-01 Naikai Zosen Corp — Onomichi HS (Setoda Shipyard) Yd No: 678
Loa 186.00 (BB) Br ex - Dght 11.600
Lbp 178.00 Br md 32.20 Dpth 18.40
Welded, 1 Dk.

(A12B2TR) Chemical/Products Tanker
Double Hull (13F)
Liq: 57,400; Liq (Oil): 57,400
Compartments: 20 Ta, ER
20 Cargo Pump (s): 20x500m³/hr
Manifold: Bow/CM: 93m

1 oil engine driving 1 FP propeller
Total Power: 9,488kW (12,900hp) 14.6kn
B&W 6S50MC-C
1 x 2 Stroke 6 Cy. 500 x 2000 9488kW (12900bhp)
Hitachi Zosen Corp-Japan
AuxGen: 3 x 600kW a.c
Fuel: 170.0 (d.f.) 2636.0 (r.f.)

9585247 *9BQE* - **SABRIN**
Bank Mellat
-
Iran
MMSI: 422728000

488 317 1,000

2013-08 Moosavi Shipyard — Khorramshahr Yd No: 621
Loa 44.90 Br ex - Dght 3.240
Lbp - Br md 9.55 Dpth 4.00
Welded, 1 dk

(A31A2GX) General Cargo Ship

2 oil engines reduction geared to sc. shafts driving 2 Propellers
Total Power: 1,002kW (1,362hp)
Yanmar 6LAH-STE3
2 x 4 Stroke 6 Cy. 150 x 165 each-501kW (681bhp)
Yanmar Diesel Engine Co Ltd-Japan

9414735 *A8KJ6* - **SABRINA**
ex St. Valentina -2013 ex Lidia -2007
Sabrina Marine Ltd
INTRESCO GmbH
Monrovia *Liberia*
MMSI: 636013067
Official number: 13067

6,278 3,687 10,975

Class: RS

2006-10 Yueqing Jinchuan Shipbuilding Co Ltd — Yueqing ZJ Yd No: 1
Loa 128.00 (BB) Br ex - Dght 7.320
Lbp 116.73 Br md 18.60 Dpth 9.70
Welded, 1 dk

(A31A2GX) General Cargo Ship
Grain: 11,371
Compartments: 3 Ho, ER
3 Ha: 2 (24.7 x 13.0)ER (15.0 x 13.0)

1 oil engine reduction geared to sc. shaft driving 1 FP propeller
Total Power: 2,500kW (3,399hp) 11.0kn
Daihatsu 8DKM-28
1 x 4 Stroke 8 Cy. 280 x 390 2500kW (3399bhp)
Shaanxi Diesel Heavy Industry Co Lt-China
AuxGen: 3 x 150kW a.c
Fuel: 349.0

9448841 *VREN2* - **SABRINA**
ex Elisabeth -2008
Farnwick Shipping Ltd
Exmar Marine NV
Hong Kong *Hong Kong*
MMSI: 477144500
Official number: HK-2256

4,484 1,346 5,359 T/cm 16.5

Class: NK

2008-11 Shitanoe Shipbuilding Co Ltd — Usuki OT Yd No: 7036
Loa 106.00 (BB) Br ex 17.63 Dght 5.964
Lbp 100.00 Br md 17.60 Dpth 8.10
Welded, 1 dk

(A11B2TG) LPG Tanker
Double Hull (13F)
Liq (Gas): 5,000
2 x Gas Tank (s); 2 independent (C.mn.stl) cyl horizontal
2 Cargo Pump (s): 2x300m³/hr
Manifold: Bow/CM: 49.8m

1 oil engine driving 1 FP propeller
Total Power: 3,120kW (4,242hp) 13.5kn
Mitsubishi 6UEC33LSII
1 x 2 Stroke 6 Cy. 330 x 1050 3120kW (4242bhp)
Akasaka Tekkosho KK (Akasaka DieselLtd)-Japan
AuxGen: 2 x 450kW a.c
Fuel: 123.0 (d.f.) 556.0 (r.f.)

9240471 *V2OI2* - **SABRINA**
ex SCM Olympic -2005 ex Sabrina -2004
ex MSC Rades -2004 ex Sabrina -2002
ms 'Sabrina' Conship GmbH & Co Reederei KG
Intersee Schiffahrtsgesellschaft mbH & Co KG
Saint John's *Antigua & Barbuda*
MMSI: 304365000
Official number: 3788

7,406 3,859 10,643 T/cm 21.0

Class: GL (LR)
✠ Classed LR until 19/11/10

2002-05 B.V. Scheepswerf Damen Hoogezand — Foxhol Yd No: 820
2002-05 OAO Damen Shipyards Okean — Nikolayev (Hull)
Loa 142.69 (BB) Br ex 18.29 Dght 7.330
Lbp 136.71 Br md 18.25 Dpth 10.15
Welded, 1 dk

(A31A2GX) General Cargo Ship
Grain: 14,695
TEU 668 C Ho 291 TEU C Dk 377 TEU incl 60 ref C.
Cranes: 3x60t

1 oil engine with flexible couplings & sr geared to sc. shaft driving 1 CP propeller
Total Power: 4,320kW (5,873hp) 14.8kn
MaK 9M32
1 x 4 Stroke 9 Cy. 320 x 480 4320kW (5873bhp)
Caterpillar Motoren GmbH & Co. KG-Germany
AuxGen: 1 x 680kW 400V 50Hz a.c, 3 x 350kW 400V 50Hz a.c
Boilers: TOH (ex.g.) 10.2kgf/cm² (10.0bar), TOH (o.f.) 10.2kgf/cm² (10.0bar)

8215742 *EPBN* - **SABRINA**
ex Iran Basheer -2010 ex Uranos -1989
Khazar Sea Shipping Lines
-
SatCom: Inmarsat C 442210810
Bandar Anzali *Iran*
MMSI: 422108000

2,563 959 2,885

Class: (GL)

1982-12 Schiffs. Hugo Peters Wewelsfleth Peters & Co. GmbH — Wewelsfleth Yd No: 594
Loa 93.63 Br ex 13.47 Dght 4.406
Lbp 85.20 Br md 13.40 Dpth 6.61
Welded, 2 dks

(A31A2GX) General Cargo Ship
Grain: 4,219; Bale: 4,217
TEU 141 C.Ho 96/20' (40') C.Dk 45/20' (40')
Compartments: 1 Ho, ER
1 Ha: (50.3 x 10.2)ER
Cranes: 2x5t
Ice Capable

1 oil engine with flexible couplings & sr reverse geared to sc. shaft driving 1 FP propeller
Total Power: 735kW (999hp) 10.5kn
Deutz SBV8M628
1 x 4 Stroke 8 Cy. 240 x 280 735kW (999bhp)
Kloeckner Humboldt Deutz AG-West Germany
AuxGen: 1 x 232kW 380V 50Hz a.c, 1 x 115kW 380V 50Hz a.c, 1 x 60kW 380V 50Hz a.c
Thrusters: 1 Thwart. FP thruster (f)

7907336 *IBUY* - **SABRINA**
ex Rugalson -2001 ex Baltic Sprinter -1999
ex Oparis -1996 ex Global Oparis -1992
ex Oparis -1991 ex Obotrita -1987
ex Ville de Syrte -1983 ex Obotrita -1981
Logbrin Shipping Srl
-
Brindisi *Italy*
MMSI: 247015900
Official number: 002

4,257 1,277 3,560

Class: (RI) (GL)

1980-03 Howaldtswerke-Deutsche Werft AG (HDW) — Hamburg Yd No: 166
Loa 92.08 (BB) Br ex 18.42 Dght 4.550
Lbp 80.02 Br md 18.01 Dpth 8.62
Welded, 2 dks

(A35A2RR) Ro-Ro Cargo Ship
Stern door/ramp (centre)
Len: 10.00 Wid: 7.60 Swl: 195
Lane-Len: 896
Lane-Wid: 1.87
Lane-clr ht: 3.55
Grain: 6,174; Bale: 5,847
TEU 333 C.Ho 132/20' (40') C.Dk 201/20' (40') incl. 20 ref C.
Compartments: 1 Ho, ER
1 Ha: (68.2 x 15.0)ER
Cranes: 2x38t
Ice Capable

2 oil engines geared to sc. shafts driving 2 FP propellers
Total Power: 2,700kW (3,670hp) 11.5kn
Deutz SBV12M628
2 x Vee 4 Stroke 12 Cy. 240 x 280 each-1350kW (1835bhp) (new engine 1996)
Deutz AG-Koeln
AuxGen: 3 x 184kW 440V 60Hz a.c
Thrusters: 1 Thwart. FP thruster (f)
Fuel: 76.0 (d.f.) 335.5 (r.f.)

7652357 *S2QM* - **SABRINA**
ex Shinsei Maru No. 8 -1982
ex Nisshu Maru -1978 ex Heiyo Maru -1978
Sabrina Shipping Ltd
-
Chittagong *Bangladesh*
Official number: 384912

499 254 803

Class: (NK)

1964 K.K. Uwajima Zosensho — Uwajima Yd No: 252
Loa 53.60 Br ex - Dght 3.823
Lbp 48.01 Br md 8.50 Dpth 4.30
Welded, 1 dk

(A31A2GX) General Cargo Ship
Grain: 1,027; Bale: 919
Compartments: 1 Ho, ER
1 Ha: (25.8 x 5.3)ER

1 oil engine driving 1 FP propeller
Total Power: 736kW (1,001hp) 11.8kn
Kubota M6D26BHCS
1 x 4 Stroke 6 Cy. 260 x 320 736kW (1001bhp)
Kubota Tekkosho-Japan

9183946 *PNIS* - **SABRINA**
PT Segara Gloria Anugrah Marine
-
Jakarta *Indonesia*
MMSI: 525010557
Official number: 2359 / PPM

1,499 542 2,500

Class: (AB)

1997-12 PT Nanindah Mutiara Shipyard — Batam Yd No: T38
Loa 60.44 Br ex - Dght 3.500
Lbp 60.44 Br md 15.00 Dpth 5.20
Welded, 1 dk

(A13A2TV) Crude Oil Tanker
Double Hull

2 oil engines driving 2 FP propellers
Total Power: 1,176kW (1,598hp)
Yanmar 6N165-EN
2 x 4 Stroke 6 Cy. 165 x 232 each-588kW (799bhp)
Yanmar Diesel Engine Co Ltd-Japan
AuxGen: 3 x 240kW a.c
Fuel: 187.0 (d.f.)

9172052 *5IQY26* - **SABRINA**
ex Magnolia -2013 ex Sarvestan -2012
ex Iran Sarvestan -2008
Magnolia Shipping Co Ltd
NITC
Zanzibar *Tanzania (Zanzibar)*
MMSI: 677002500

81,479 50,676 159,711 T/cm 117.5

Class: (GL) (NV)

2000-01 Daewoo Heavy Industries Ltd — Geoje Yd No: 5133
Loa 274.00 (BB) Br ex 48.04 Dght 17.020
Lbp 264.00 Br md 48.00 Dpth 23.20
Welded, 1 dk

(A13A2TV) Crude Oil Tanker
Double Hull (13F)
Liq: 166,683; Liq (Oil): 163,386
Compartments: 12 Wing Ta, ER, 2 Wing Slop Ta
3 Cargo Pump (s): 3x3500m³/hr
Manifold: Bow/CM: 129m

1 oil engine driving 1 FP propeller
Total Power: 16,859kW (22,921hp) 15.0kn
B&W 6S70MC
1 x 2 Stroke 6 Cy. 700 x 2674 16859kW (22921bhp)
HSD Engine Co Ltd-South Korea
AuxGen: 3 x 1008kW 440V 60Hz a.c
Fuel: 282.0 (d.f.) (Heating Coils) 4491.0 (r.f.) 59.4pd

7405766 *DUA6109* - **SABRINA D. R. 5**
ex James -2002 ex Yamasen Maru No. 23 -1987
ex Suwa Maru No. 33 -1982
Fortune Star Marine Resources Inc
-
Manila *Philippines*
Official number: MNLD003492

127 82 -

1974-06 Nagasaki Zosen K.K. — Nagasaki Yd No: 386
Loa 34.27 Br ex 6.02 Dght 2.363
Lbp 28.99 Br md 6.00 Dpth 2.70
Welded, 1 dk

(B11B2FV) Fishing Vessel

1 oil engine driving 1 FP propeller
Total Power: 544kW (740hp)
Niigata 6L25BX
1 x 4 Stroke 6 Cy. 250 x 320 544kW (740bhp)
Niigata Engineering Co Ltd-Japan

6415312 *DVJW* -
SABRINA D.R. 11
ex Miguelita D. R. *-2010*
ex Konpira Maru No. 28 *-1980*
Fortune Star Marine Resources Inc
-
Manila *Philippines*
Official number: MNLD000897
357 174 -

1964 Niigata Engineering Co Ltd — Niigata NI Yd No: 570
Loa 42.65 Br ex 7.65 Dght -
Lbp 37.50 Br md 7.60 Dpth 3.36
Welded, 1 dk

(B11B2FV) Fishing Vessel

1 oil engine driving 1 FP propeller
Total Power: 515kW (700hp) 10.3kn
Niigata M6F31HS
1 x 4 Stroke 6 Cy. 310 x 440 515kW (700bhp)
Niigata Engineering Co Ltd-Japan

7114630 *HQRF6* -
SABRINA I
ex Gulf Splendour *-1995*
ex Gulf Esplendour *-1992* *ex* Ioanna A *-1990*
ex Meli *-1989* *ex* Iwonicz Zdroj *-1986*
Sabrina Investment Corp
-
San Lorenzo *Honduras*
Official number: L-0336165
1,585 797 1,911
Class: (BV) (PR)

1971 Santierul Naval Drobeta-Turnu Severin S.A. — Drobeta-Turnu S. Yd No: 3932
Loa 89.92 Br ex 12.40 Dght 5.100
Lbp 82.33 Br md 12.35 Dpth 7.07
Welded, 2 dks

(A31A2GX) General Cargo Ship
Grain: 3,275; Bale: 3,069; Ins: 393
Compartments: 3 Ho, ER
3 Ha: (11.5 x 5.0) (14.1 x 5.0) (10.2 x 5.0)ER
Derricks: 8x5t; Winches: 8
Ice Capable

1 oil engine driving 1 FP propeller
Total Power: 1,655kW (2,250hp) 14.0kn
Sulzer 6TAD48
1 x 2 Stroke 6 Cy. 480 x 700 1655kW (2250bhp)
Zaklady Urzadzen Technicznych'Zgoda' SA-Poland
AuxGen: 3 x 120kW 400V 50Hz a.c
Thrusters: 1 Thwart. FP thruster (f)
Fuel: 120.0 (d.f.) 7.0pd

9274927 *HPZW* -
SABRINA I
-
Pro Shipping Inc
Portline - Transportes Maritimos Internacionais SA
Panama *Panama*
MMSI: 356917000
Official number: 3040905B
30,064 17,927 52,501 T/cm 55.5
Class: AB

2005-01 Tsuneishi Heavy Industries (Cebu) Inc — Balamban Yd No: SC-047
Loa 189.99 (BB) Br ex - Dght 12.000
Lbp 182.00 Br md 32.26 Dpth 17.00
Welded, 1 dk

(A21A2BC) Bulk Carrier
Grain: 67,500; Bale: 65,601
Compartments: 5 Ho, ER
5 Ha: ER
Cranes: 4x30t

1 oil engine driving 1 FP propeller
Total Power: 7,800kW (10,605hp) 14.3kn
MAN-B&W 6S50MC
1 x 2 Stroke 6 Cy. 500 x 1910 7800kW (10605bhp)
Mitsui Engineering & Shipbuilding CLtd-Japan
AuxGen: 3 x 480kW 220/440V 60Hz a.c
Fuel: 183.0 (d.f.) 2386.0 (r.f.)

8983478 *WDA7965* -
SABRINA MARIE
-
Sabrina Marie Inc
-
Port Lavaca, TX *United States of America*
MMSI: 366849150
Official number: 1124505
140 42 -

2002 in the United States of America Yd No: 171
L reg 24.14 Br ex - Dght -
Lbp - Br md 7.31 Dpth 3.65
Welded, 1 dk

(B11B2FV) Fishing Vessel

1 oil engine driving 1 Propeller

9482500 *VRGW8* -
SABRINA VENTURE
-
Chainhurst Ltd
Wah Kwong Ship Management (Hong Kong) Ltd
SatCom: Inmarsat C 447703179
Hong Kong *Hong Kong*
MMSI: 477961400
Official number: HK-2751
32,591 17,787 53,456 T/cm 57.3
Class: BV

2010-11 Chengxi Shipyard Co Ltd — Jiangyin JS Yd No: CX4252
Loa 189.90 (BB) Br ex - Dght 12.540
Lbp 183.25 Br md 32.26 Dpth 17.50
Welded, 1 dk

(A21A2BC) Bulk Carrier
Grain: 65,753; Bale: 64,837
Compartments: 5 Ho, ER
5 Ha: 4 (21.6 x 22.4)ER (19.2 x 20.8)
Cranes: 4x36t

1 oil engine driving 1 FP propeller
Total Power: 9,480kW (12,889hp) 14.2kn
MAN-B&W 6S50MC-C
1 x 2 Stroke 6 Cy. 500 x 2000 9480kW (12889bhp)
Hudong Heavy Machinery Co Ltd-China
AuxGen: 3 x 680kW a.c
Fuel: 2210.0 (r.f.)

9106338 *HZBN* -
SABS 1
ex San Nicola *-2001* *ex* Orient Tiger *-2001*
Yusuf Bin Ahmed Kanoo
Saudi Arabian Bunkering Services (SABS)
Dammam *Saudi Arabia*
MMSI: 403514000
Official number: 1075
4,228 1,926 6,506 T/cm 14.5
Class: NK (BV)

1995-02 Fukuoka Shipbuilding Co Ltd — Fukuoka FO Yd No: 1183
Loa 110.00 (BB) Br ex - Dght 6.764
Lbp 102.20 Br md 16.06 Dpth 9.30
Welded, 1 dk

(A12B2TR) Chemical/Products Tanker
Double Hull (13F)
Liq: 6,891; Liq (Oil): 6,891
Cargo Heating Coils
Compartments: 10 Wing Ta, 2 Wing Slop Ta, ER
4 Cargo Pump (s): 2x500m³/hr, 2x200m³/hr
Manifold: Bow/CM: 55m

1 oil engine driving 1 FP propeller
Total Power: 2,405kW (3,270hp) 12.2kn
MAN-B&W 6S26MC
1 x 2 Stroke 6 Cy. 260 x 980 2405kW (3270bhp)
Makita Corp-Japan
AuxGen: 3 x 240kW 440/100V 60Hz a.c
Fuel: 35.0 (d.f.) 340.0 (r.f.) 9.8pd

8026232 *9WFN* -
SABUILD SATU
-
Sabah Shipyard Sdn Bhd
-
Labuan *Malaysia*
Official number: 324957
245 73 137
Class: (LR)
✠ Classed LR until 24/3/10

1984-02 Sabah Shipyard Sdn Bhd — Labuan Yd No: 116
Loa 28.81 Br ex 8.79 Dght 3.341
Lbp 27.21 Br md 8.50 Dpth 4.42
Welded, 1 dk

(B32A2ST) Tug

2 oil engines with clutches & sr geared to sc. shafts driving 2 CP propellers
Total Power: 1,148kW (1,560hp) 12.5kn
Alpha 5T23L-KVO
2 x 4 Stroke 5 Cy. 225 x 300 each-574kW (780bhp)
B&W Alpha Diesel A/S-Denmark
AuxGen: 2 x 69kW 415V 50Hz a.c
Fuel: 47.0 (d.f.)

9618458 *PNXL* -
SABUK NUSANTARA 27
-
Government of The Republic of Indonesia (Direktorat Jenderal Perhubungan Laut - Ministry of Sea Communications)
-
Banyuwangi *Indonesia*
784 236 497
Class: KI

2011-02 P.T. Daya Radar Utama — Jakarta Yd No: 146
Loa 51.80 Br ex - Dght 2.850
Lbp 46.84 Br md 10.40 Dpth 4.20
Welded, 1 dk

(A32A2GF) General Cargo/Passenger Ship

2 oil engines reduction geared to sc. shafts driving 2 Propellers
Total Power: 980kW (1,332hp) 11.0kn
Mitsubishi S6A3-MPTK
2 x 4 Stroke 6 Cy. 150 x 175 each-490kW (666bhp)
Mitsubishi Heavy Industries Ltd-Japan

9618460 *PNQX* -
SABUK NUSANTARA 28
-
Government of The Republic of Indonesia (Direktorat Jenderal Perhubungan Laut - Ministry of Sea Communications)
-
Merauke *Indonesia*
1,158 348 642
Class: KI

2011-03 P.T. Daya Radar Utama — Jakarta Yd No: 147
Loa 58.50 Br ex - Dght 2.750
Lbp 53.76 Br md 12.00 Dpth 4.50
Welded, 1 dk

(A32A2GF) General Cargo/Passenger Ship

2 oil engines reduction geared to sc. shafts driving 2 Propellers
Total Power: 980kW (1,332hp) 11.0kn
Mitsubishi S6A3-MPTK
2 x 4 Stroke 6 Cy. 150 x 175 each-490kW (666bhp)
Mitsubishi Heavy Industries Ltd-Japan
AuxGen: 2 x 120kW a.c

9647136 *POFW* -
SABUK NUSANTARA 29
-
Government of The Republic of Indonesia (Direktorat Jenderal Perhubungan Darat - Ministry of Land Communications)
-
Jakarta *Indonesia*
MMSI: 525019595
Official number: 1275/dda
811 244 -
Class: KI

2012-02 P.T. Mariana Bahagia — Palembang Yd No: 60
Loa 51.80 Br ex - Dght 2.850
Lbp 46.56 Br md 10.40 Dpth 4.20
Welded, 1 dk

(A32A2GF) General Cargo/Passenger Ship

2 oil engines reduction geared to sc. shafts driving 2 Propellers
Total Power: 956kW (1,300hp) 10.0kn
Mitsubishi S6A3-MTK2
2 x 4 Stroke 6 Cy. 150 x 175 each-478kW (650bhp)
Mitsubishi Heavy Industries Ltd-Japan

9642746 *POGO* -
SABUK NUSANTARA 30
-
Government of The Republic of Indonesia (Direktorat Jenderal Perhubungan Laut - Ministry of Sea Communications)
-
Jakarta *Indonesia*
MMSI: 525016704
1,202 361 446
Class: KI

2011-11 P.T. Daya Radar Utama — Jakarta Yd No: 153
Loa 63.00 Br ex - Dght 2.700
Lbp 57.90 Br md 12.00 Dpth 4.00
Welded, 1 dk

(A32A2GF) General Cargo/Passenger Ship

2 oil engines reduction geared to sc. shaft (s) driving 2 Propellers
Total Power: 1,516kW (2,062hp)
Mitsubishi S6R2-MPTK
2 x 4 Stroke 6 Cy. 170 x 220 each-758kW (1031bhp)
Mitsubishi Heavy Industries Ltd-Japan
AuxGen: 3 x 130kW 380V a.c

9642758 *POFR* -
SABUK NUSANTARA 31
-
Government of The Republic of Indonesia (Direktorat Jenderal Perhubungan Laut - Ministry of Sea Communications)
-
Jakarta *Indonesia*
MMSI: 525016702
1,202 361 446
Class: KI

2011-11 P.T. Daya Radar Utama — Jakarta Yd No: 155
Loa 62.80 Br ex - Dght 2.700
Lbp 57.90 Br md 12.00 Dpth 4.00
Welded, 1 dk

(A32A2GF) General Cargo/Passenger Ship

2 oil engines reduction geared to sc. shaft (s) driving 2 Propellers
Total Power: 1,516kW (2,062hp)
Mitsubishi S6R2-MPTK
2 x 4 Stroke 6 Cy. 170 x 220 each-758kW (1031bhp)
Mitsubishi Heavy Industries Ltd-Japan
AuxGen: 3 x 130kW 380V a.c

9642760 *POHI* -
SABUK NUSANTARA 32
-
Government of The Republic of Indonesia (Direktorat Jenderal Perhubungan Laut - Ministry of Sea Communications)
-
Sorong *Indonesia*
MMSI: 525016705
1,202 361 446
Class: KI

2011-11 P.T. Daya Radar Utama — Jakarta Yd No: 156
Loa 62.80 Br ex - Dght 2.700
Lbp 57.36 Br md 12.00 Dpth 4.00
Welded, 1 dk

(A32A2GF) General Cargo/Passenger Ship

2 oil engines reduction geared to sc. shaft (s) driving 2 Propellers
Total Power: 1,516kW (2,062hp)
Mitsubishi S6R2-MPTK
2 x 4 Stroke 6 Cy. 170 x 220 each-758kW (1031bhp)
Mitsubishi Heavy Industries Ltd-Japan
AuxGen: 3 x 130kW 380V a.c

9675028 *POXS* -
SABUK NUSANTARA 33
-
Government of The Republic of Indonesia (Direktorat Jenderal Perhubungan Laut - Ministry of Sea Communications)
-
Jakarta *Indonesia*
MMSI: 525001075
1,202 361 446
Class: KI

2013-02 P.T. Daya Radar Utama — Jakarta Yd No: 188
Loa 62.80 Br ex - Dght 2.700
Lbp 59.00 Br md 12.00 Dpth 4.00
Welded, 1 dk

(A32A2GF) General Cargo/Passenger Ship

2 oil engines reduction geared to sc. shafts driving 2 Propellers
Total Power: 1,220kW (1,658hp)
Mitsubishi S6R2-MPTK
2 x 4 Stroke 6 Cy. 170 x 220 each-610kW (829bhp)
Mitsubishi Heavy Industries Ltd-Japan
AuxGen: 3 x 132kW 400V a.c

IMO / Call sign	Name / Owner	Tonnage	Class	Build	Type	Machinery
9675016 *POXT* -	**SABUK NUSANTARA 34** **Government of The Republic of Indonesia (Direktorat Jenderal Perhubungan Laut - Ministry of Sea Communications)** - *Jakarta* *Indonesia*	**1,202** 361 446	Class: KI	**2013-02 P.T. Daya Radar Utama — Jakarta** Yd No: 187 Loa 62.80 Br ex - Dght 2.700 Lbp 57.36 Br md 12.00 Dpth 4.00 Welded, 1 dk	**(A32A2GF) General Cargo/Passenger Ship**	**2 oil engines** reduction geared to sc. shafts driving 2 Propellers Total Power: 1,220kW (1,658hp) Mitsubishi S6R2-MPTK 2 x 4 Stroke 6 Cy. 170 x 220 each-610kW (829bhp) Mitsubishi Heavy Industries Ltd-Japan AuxGen: 3 x 132kW 400V a.c
9691694 - -	**SABUK NUSANTARA 35** **Government of The Republic of Indonesia (Direktorat Jenderal Perhubungan Darat - Ministry of Land Communications)** PT ASDP Indonesia Ferry (Persero) - Angkutan Sungai Danau & Penyeberangan *Tanjung Priok* *Indonesia*	**1,161** 349 750	Class: KI	**2012-12 P.T. Adiluhung Sarana Segara Industri — Bangkalan** Yd No: A.032 Loa 53.50 Br ex 12.20 Dght 2.750 Lbp 52.30 Br md 12.00 Dpth 4.50 Welded, 1 dk	**(A36A2PR) Passenger/Ro-Ro Ship (Vehicles)**	**2 oil engines** reduction geared to sc. shafts driving 2 Propellers Total Power: 1,220kW (1,658hp) Yanmar 6AYM-WET 2 x 4 Stroke 6 Cy. 155 x 180 each-610kW (829bhp) Yanmar Diesel Engine Co Ltd-Japan
9734044 - -	**SABUK NUSANTARA 43** **Government of The Republic of Indonesia (Direktorat Jenderal Perhubungan Laut - Ministry of Sea Communications)** - *Ambon* *Indonesia*	**2,004** 581 595	Class: KI (Class contemplated)	**2014-01 P.T. Daya Radar Utama — Jakarta** Yd No: 262 Loa 68.50 Br ex - Dght 2.900 Lbp 63.00 Br md 14.00 Dpth 6.20 Welded, 1 dk	**(A32A2GF) General Cargo/Passenger Ship**	**2 oil engines** reduction geared to sc. shafts driving 2 Propellers Total Power: 2,420kW (3,290hp) Mitsubishi S12R-MPTK 2 x Vee 4 Stroke 12 Cy. 170 x 180 each-1210kW (1645bhp) Mitsubishi Heavy Industries Ltd-Japan
9734056 - -	**SABUK NUSANTARA 44** **Government of The Republic of Indonesia (Direktorat Jenderal Perhubungan Laut - Ministry of Sea Communications)** - *Ambon* *Indonesia*	**2,004** 581 595	Class: KI (Class contemplated)	**2014-01 P.T. Daya Radar Utama — Jakarta** Yd No: 263 Loa 68.50 Br ex - Dght 2.900 Lbp 63.00 Br md 14.00 Dpth 6.20 Welded, 1 dk	**(A32A2GF) General Cargo/Passenger Ship**	**2 oil engines** reduction geared to sc. shafts driving 2 Propellers Total Power: 2,420kW (3,290hp) Mitsubishi S12R-MPTK 2 x Vee 4 Stroke 12 Cy. 170 x 180 each-1210kW (1645bhp) Mitsubishi Heavy Industries Ltd-Japan
7517284 *H02509* -	**SABUL** *ex* Man To *-2007* *ex* Lak *-2005* *ex* Reutovo *-2005* **Oriental Shipping Co Ltd Inc** Sun Glory Shipping Co Ltd *Panama* *Panama* MMSI: 372540000 Official number: 35417PEXT	**617** 185 304	Class: (RS)	**1975 Khabarovskiy Sudostroitelnyy Zavod im Kirova — Khabarovsk** Yd No: 249 Loa 54.84 Br ex 9.38 Dght 3.810 Lbp 49.99 Br md - Dpth 4.73 Welded, 1 dk	**(B11A2FT) Trawler** Bale: 284 Compartments: 2 Ho, ER 2 Ha: 2 (1.5 x 1.6) Derricks: 1x3t Ice Capable	**1 oil engine** driving 1 FP propeller Total Power: 588kW (799hp) 11.8kn S.K.L. 8NVD48-2U 1 x 4 Stroke 8 Cy. 320 x 480 588kW (799bhp) VEB Schwermaschinenbau "KarlLiebknecht" (SKL)-Magdeburg
7741342 - -	**SABURSK** **LLC Trading House Palladium** -	**739** 221 332	Class: (RS)	**1979-04 Zavod "Leninskaya Kuznitsa" — Kiyev** Yd No: 240 Loa 53.73 (BB) Br ex 10.72 Dght 4.290 Lbp 47.92 Br md - Dpth 6.00 Welded, 1 dk	**(B11A2FS) Stern Trawler** Ins: 220 Compartments: 1 Ho, ER 2 Ha: 2 (1.6 x 1.6) Derricks: 2x3.3t Ice Capable	**1 oil engine** driving 1 CP propeller Total Power: 971kW (1,320hp) 12.5kn S.K.L. 8NVD48A-2U 1 x 4 Stroke 8 Cy. 320 x 480 971kW (1320bhp) VEB Schwermaschinenbau "KarlLiebknecht" (SKL)-Magdeburg Thrusters: 1 Thwart. FP thruster (f); 1 Tunnel thruster (a)
8134742 - -	**SABYA** **Yusuf Bin Ahmed Kanoo WLL** - *Jeddah* *Saudi Arabia*	*176* - -	Class: (BV)	**1976 Deltawerf BV — Sliedrecht** Loa - Br ex - Dght 1.601 Lbp 15.75 Br md 4.86 Dpth 2.32 Welded, 1 dk	**(B35X2XX) Vessel (function unknown)**	**2 oil engines** geared to sc. shafts driving 2 FP propellers Total Power: 500kW (680hp) 10.0kn G.M. (Detroit Diesel) 12V-71 2 x Vee 2 Stroke 12 Cy. 108 x 127 each-250kW (340bhp) General Motors Detroit DieselAllison Divn-USA
9154529 *HZWQ* -	**SABYA** *ex* Al-Sabahia *-2013* **United Arab Shipping Co (UASC)** - *Dammam* *Saudi Arabia* MMSI: 403524001 Official number: SA1173	**48,154** 26,721 49,848 T/cm 75.2	Class: LR ✠ **100A1** SS 03/2013 container ship CCSA *IWS LI ✠ **LMC** **UMS** Eq.Ltr: R†; Cable: 690.4/84.0 U3	**1998-03 Mitsui Eng. & SB. Co. Ltd., Chiba Works — Ichihara** Yd No: 1441 Loa 276.50 (BB) Br ex 32.30 Dght 12.521 Lbp 259.90 Br md 32.20 Dpth 21.20 Welded, 1 dk	**(A33A2CC) Container Ship (Fully Cellular)** TEU 3802 C Ho 2068 TEU C Dk 1734 TEU incl 360 ref C. Compartments: ER, 8 Cell Ho 16 Ha: (6.4 x 18.4) (13.2 x 18.4)Tappered (12.6 x 23.6)Tappered ER 13 (12.6 x 28.7)	**1 oil engine** driving 1 FP propeller Total Power: 34,348kW (46,700hp) 24.0kn B&W 10L80MC 1 x 2 Stroke 10 Cy. 800 x 2592 34348kW (46700bhp) Mitsui Engineering & Shipbuilding CLtd-Japan AuxGen: 3 x 2280kW 450V 60Hz a.c Boilers: e (ex.g.) 11.9kgf/cm² (11.7bar), AuxB (o.f.) 8.0kgf/cm² (7.8bar) Thrusters: 1 Thwart. CP thruster (f) Fuel: 440.0 (d.f.) (Heating Coils) 5390.0 (r.f.) 139.0pd
9269049 - -	**SACHAL** **Port Qasim Authority** - *Karachi* *Pakistan*	**360** 108 261	Class: LR ✠ **100A1** SS 03/2010 tug ✠ **LMC** Eq.Ltr: G; Cable: 302.5/20.5 U2 (a)	**2005-03 Karachi Shipyard & Engineering Works Ltd. — Karachi** Yd No: 247 Loa 32.00 Br ex 9.70 Dght 3.750 Lbp 29.97 Br md 9.50 Dpth 4.70 Welded, 1 dk	**(B32A2ST) Tug**	**2 oil engines** with clutches, flexible couplings & sr reverse geared to sc. shafts driving 2 FP propellers Total Power: 2,640kW (3,590hp) 12.0kn M.T.U. 12V4000M60 2 x Vee 4 Stroke 12 Cy. 165 x 190 each-1320kW (1795bhp) MTU Friedrichshafen GmbH-Friedrichshafen AuxGen: 2 x 90kW 380V 50Hz a.c
9371232 *JD2203* -	**SACHI MARU** **Nipponkai Eisen KK** - *Niigata, Niigata* *Japan* Official number: 140274	*159* - -		**2006-03 Niigata Shipbuilding & Repair Inc — Niigata NI** Yd No: 0013 Loa 31.02 Br ex - Dght 2.750 Lbp 27.00 Br md 8.80 Dpth 3.48 Welded, 1 dk	**(B32A2ST) Tug**	**2 oil engines** reduction geared to sc. shafts driving 2 Propellers Total Power: 2,354kW (3,200hp) 12.5kn Niigata 6L26HLX 2 x 4 Stroke 6 Cy. 260 x 350 each-1177kW (1600bhp) Niigata Engineering Co Ltd-Japan
9046318 *JD2418* -	**SACHI MARU** **Kushiro Tug Boat KK** - *Kushiro, Hokkaido* *Japan* Official number: 128554	*153* - -		**1991-11 Kushiro Jukogyo K.K. — Kushiro** Yd No: 133 Loa 30.70 Br ex 9.20 Dght 2.700 Lbp 27.00 Br md 9.00 Dpth 3.65 Welded, 1 dk	**(B32A2ST) Tug**	**2 oil engines** Geared Integral to driving 1 Propeller , 1 Z propeller Total Power: 2,428kW (3,302hp) 12.5kn Niigata 6L25HX 2 x 4 Stroke 6 Cy. 250 x 350 each-1214kW (1651bhp) Niigata Engineering Co Ltd-Japan
8961731 *JL5697* -	**SACHI MARU NO. 1** *ex* Shinpo Maru *-2008* - - *Kochi, Kochi* *Japan* Official number: 129970	*199* - -		**1990-05 Daio Zoki K.K. — Japan** Loa 47.00 Br ex - Dght - Lbp 45.00 Br md 11.00 Dpth 5.20 Welded, 1 dk	**(B35X2XX) Vessel (function unknown)**	**1 oil engine** driving 1 FP propeller
8708115 *JJ3573* -	**SACHI MARU No. 11** *ex* Sansha Maru No. 11 *-1999* **Kiyoe Mitsuuchi** - *Kochi, Kochi* *Japan* Official number: 130787	*198* - 643		**1988-02 K.K. Murakami Zosensho — Naruto** Yd No: 176 Loa 49.92 (BB) Br ex 10.52 Dght 3.220 Lbp 46.21 Br md 10.51 Dpth 5.31 Welded, 2 dks	**(B33A2DG) Grab Dredger** Grain: 494 Compartments: 1 Ho, ER 1 Ha: ER Cranes: 1	**1 oil engine** with clutches, flexible couplings & reverse reduction geared to sc. shaft driving 1 FP propeller Total Power: 588kW (799hp) Daihatsu 6DLM-24FS 1 x 4 Stroke 6 Cy. 240 x 320 588kW (799bhp) Daihatsu Diesel Manufacturing Co Lt-Japan
7855351 - -	**SACHI MARU No. 18** - -	*259* - -		**1973-04 Edogawa Shipbuilding Co. Ltd. — Tokyo** Loa 28.50 Br ex 11.02 Dght 1.701 Lbp 26.50 Br md 11.00 Dpth 2.60 Welded, 1 dk	**(B34B2SC) Crane Vessel**	**2 oil engines** driving 2 FP propellers Total Power: 442kW (600hp) 8.0kn Yanmar 2 x 4 Stroke each-221kW (300bhp) Yanmar Diesel Engine Co Ltd-Japan
8850384 - -	**SACHI MARU No. 58** - -	*199* 113 -		**1977 Suzuki Zosen — Ishinomaki** L reg 33.90 Br ex - Dght - Lbp - Br md 7.20 Dpth 3.10 Welded, 1 dk	**(B11B2FV) Fishing Vessel**	**1 oil engine** driving 1 FP propeller Niigata 1 x 4 Stroke Niigata Engineering Co Ltd-Japan
9539511 *JD2934* -	**SACHIHISA MARU** **Hisamoto Kisen Co Ltd (Hisamoto Kisen KK)** - *Bizen, Okayama* *Japan* Official number: 141049	*498* - 1,250		**2009-08 KK Ura Kyodo Zosensho — Awaji HG** Yd No: 336 Loa 64.46 Br ex - Dght 4.200 Lbp 60.00 Br md 10.00 Dpth 4.50 Welded, 1 dk	**(A12A2TC) Chemical Tanker** Double Hull (13F) Liq: 1,231 Compartments: 8 Wing Ta, ER 2 Cargo Pump (s): 2x300m³/hr	**1 oil engine** driving 1 FP propeller Total Power: 736kW (1,001hp) 11.5kn Hanshin LH28G 1 x 4 Stroke 6 Cy. 280 x 460 736kW (1001bhp) The Hanshin Diesel Works Ltd-Japan

IMO / Call sign	Name / Owner	Tonnage	Class	Build / Dimensions	Type	Machinery
9194799 *AUMT* -	**SACHINAM** *ex* Sarwaguna Limabelas *-2006* **Shiv Vani Oil & Gas Exploration Services Ltd** Modest Maritime Services Pvt Ltd *Mumbai* *India* MMSI: 419063500 Official number: 3228	**174** 104 24	Class: IR (KI) (AB)	**1998**-06 **Penguin Boat International Ltd — Singapore** Yd No: 115 Loa 25.00 Br ex - Dght 1.250 Lbp 22.40 Br md 6.00 Dpth 3.00 Welded, 1 dk	**(B21A2OC) Crew/Supply Vessel**	**2 oil engines** reverse reduction geared to sc. shafts driving 2 FP propellers Total Power: 1,472kW (2,002hp) 12.0kn MAN D2842LE 2 x Vee 4 Stroke 12 Cy. 128 x 142 each-736kW (1001bhp) MAN Nutzfahrzeuge AG-Nuernberg AuxGen: 2 x 72kW 380V 50Hz a.c Fuel: 14.0 (d.f.)
7923043 - - -	**SACHINAMI** - - -	*111* - -		**1979**-06 **Mitsubishi Heavy Industries Ltd. — Nagasaki** Yd No: 13006 Loa 22.00 Br ex - Dght 2.150 Lbp 20.00 Br md 11.40 Dpth 3.00 Welded, 1 dk	**(B34G2SE) Pollution Control Vessel**	**2 oil engines** driving 2 FP propellers Total Power: 552kW (750hp) Mitsubishi S6A-T 2 x 4 Stroke 6 Cy. 145 x 160 each-276kW (375bhp) Mitsubishi Heavy Industries Ltd-Japan
9630884 *CSGB2* -	**SACOR II** **Sacor Maritima SA** - *Lisbon* *Portugal* MMSI: 263702340 Official number: LX3207TL	**1,615** 692 2,500		**2012**-02 **Estaleiros Navais de Peniche SA (ENP) — Peniche** Yd No: C-978 Loa 74.37 Br ex - Dght 4.500 Lbp 68.82 Br md 14.00 Dpth 5.60 Welded, 1 dk	**(A13B2TP) Products Tanker** Double Hull (13F)	**2 oil engines** reduction geared to sc. shafts driving 1 Propeller Total Power: 2,280kW (3,100hp) M.T.U. 12V4000M61 2 x Vee 4 Stroke 12 Cy. 165 x 190 each-1140kW (1550bhp) MTU Friedrichshafen GmbH-Friedrichshafen
9257773 *FOOD* BL 899838	**SACRE COEUR DE JESUS** **Ludovic Caloin** - *Boulogne* *France* MMSI: 227144600 Official number: 899838	**103** 54 -		**2001**-08 **SOCARENAM — Boulogne** Yd No: 183 Loa - Br ex - Dght - Lbp - Br md - Dpth - Welded, 1 dk	**(B11B2FV) Fishing Vessel**	**1 oil engine** reduction geared to sc. shaft driving 1 FP propeller A.B.C. 6MDXC 1 x 4 Stroke 6 Cy. 242 x 320 Anglo Belgian Corp NV (ABC)-Belgium
7926710 - -	**SACRED HEART** **Three Friends Vessels Corp** - *Gloucester, MA* *United States of America* Official number: 617233	*165* 112 -		**1980**-02 **Quality Marine, Inc. — Bayou La Batre, Al** Yd No: 131 L reg 24.88 Br ex - Dght - Lbp - Br md 7.32 Dpth 3.87 Welded, 1 dk	**(B11A2FS) Stern Trawler**	**1 oil engine** driving 1 FP propeller Total Power: 625kW (850hp) Caterpillar D398SCAC 1 x Vee 4 Stroke 12 Cy. 159 x 203 625kW (850bhp) Caterpillar Tractor Co-USA
7900467 *DUH2186* -	**SACRED STARS** *ex* Filipinas Surigao *-2006* *ex* Ferry Seishin *-1994* **Roble Shipping Lines Inc** - *Cebu* *Philippines* Official number: CEB1000103	*509* 215 220	Class: (BV)	**1979**-04 **Kanda Zosensho K.K. — Japan** Yd No: 238 Loa 49.00 (BB) Br ex - Dght 3.093 Lbp 43.21 Br md 10.22 Dpth 3.81 Welded, 2 dks	**(A36A2PR) Passenger/Ro-Ro Ship (Vehicles)** Passengers: unberthed: 322	**2 oil engines** reduction geared to sc. shafts driving 2 FP propellers Total Power: 1,472kW (2,002hp) Daihatsu 6DSM-22 2 x 4 Stroke 6 Cy. 220 x 280 each-736kW (1001bhp) Daihatsu Diesel Manufacturing Co Lt-Japan Thrusters: 1 Tunnel thruster (f)
7438115 *9HNF8* -	**SACRO CUOR I** *ex* Siddisen *-2006* *ex* Borgtank *-1996* *ex* Smerek *-1995* **Diane Holdings Ltd** Cassar Fuel Ltd *Valletta* *Malta* MMSI: 256175000 Official number: 7438115	**341** 131 419	Class: (GL) (PR)	**1974 Wroclawska Stocznia Rzeczna — Wroclaw** Yd No: ZB400/C1 Loa 43.39 Br ex - Dght 3.001 Lbp 39.50 Br md 8.11 Dpth 3.41 Welded, 1 dk	**(A13B2TU) Tanker (unspecified)** Liq: 458; Liq (Oil): 458 Compartments: 10 Ta, ER Ice Capable	**1 oil engine** reduction geared to sc. shaft driving 1 FP propeller Total Power: 428kW (582hp) 10.0kn S.K.L. 6NVD36A-1U 1 x 4 Stroke 6 Cy. 240 x 360 428kW (582bhp) VEB Schwermaschinenbau "KarlLiebknecht" (SKL)-Magdeburg AuxGen: 2 x 38kW 400V a.c
9218935 *JJ3952* -	**SADA MARU NO. 20** *ex* Yoshishige Maru No. 18 *-2004* **Seitoku Kaiun Kensetsu KK** - *Toba, Mie* *Japan* Official number: 134207	*498* - 1,500		**1999**-03 **Nagashima Zosen KK — Kihoku ME** Yd No: 517 Loa 70.63 Br ex - Dght - Lbp 62.60 Br md 13.50 Dpth 7.00 Welded, 1 dk	**(A31A2GX) General Cargo Ship**	**1 oil engine** driving 1 FP propeller Total Power: 1,471kW (2,000hp) 12.5kn Hanshin LH36LG 1 x 4 Stroke 6 Cy. 360 x 670 1471kW (2000bhp) The Hanshin Diesel Works Ltd-Japan
8870516 *JH3302* -	**SADA MARU No. 36** **Seitoku Kaiun Kensetsu KK** - *Toba, Mie* *Japan* Official number: 133208	*499* - 800		**1993**-09 **Nagashima Zosen KK — Kihoku ME** L reg 67.00 Br ex - Dght - Lbp - Br md 13.50 Dpth 6.90 Welded, 1 dk	**(A24D2BA) Aggregates Carrier**	**1 oil engine** driving 1 FP propeller Total Power: 736kW (1,001hp) 12.4kn Akasaka A37 1 x 4 Stroke 6 Cy. 370 x 720 736kW (1001bhp) Akasaka Tekkosho KK (Akasaka DieselLtd)-Japan
9699385 *JD3568* -	**SADA MARU NO. 37** **Seitoku Kaiun Kensetsu KK** - *Japan* MMSI: 431005101	*749* - 2,400	Class: FA	**2013**-12 **Kegoya Dock K.K. — Kure** Yd No: 1152 Loa 77.70 Br ex - Dght 4.720 Lbp - Br md 14.50 Dpth - Welded, 1 dk	**(A31A2GX) General Cargo Ship** Grain: 2,100	**1 oil engine** reduction geared to sc. shaft driving 1 Propeller Total Power: 2,060kW (2,801hp) Akasaka A38R 1 x 4 Stroke 6 Cy. 380 x 740 2060kW (2801bhp) Akasaka Tekkosho KK (Akasaka DieselLtd)-Japan
9180475 *JH3415* -	**SADA MARU No. 38** **Seitoku Kaiun Kensetsu KK** - *Toba, Mie* *Japan* Official number: 134458	*492* - -		**1997**-03 **Nagashima Zosen KK — Kihoku ME** Loa 70.63 Br ex - Dght - Lbp 62.60 Br md 13.50 Dpth 7.07 Welded, 1 dk	**(A24D2BA) Aggregates Carrier**	**1 oil engine** driving 1 FP propeller Total Power: 1,471kW (2,000hp) 12.5kn Akasaka A37 1 x 4 Stroke 6 Cy. 370 x 720 1471kW (2000bhp) Akasaka Tekkosho KK (Akasaka DieselLtd)-Japan
8961901 *JI3678* -	**SADA MARU No. 68** **Seitoku Kaiun Kensetsu KK** - *Toba, Mie* *Japan* Official number: 136806	*141* - -		**2000**-07 **Hangzhou Dongfeng Shipbuilding Co Ltd — Hangzhou ZJ** Loa 21.95 Br ex - Dght - Lbp 19.95 Br md 8.00 Dpth 3.79 Welded, 1 dk	**(B32B2SP) Pusher Tug**	**2 oil engines** geared to sc. shaft driving 2 FP propellers Total Power: 1,838kW (2,498hp) 11.1kn Akasaka 6U28AK 2 x 4 Stroke 6 Cy. 280 x 380 each-919kW (1249bhp) Akasaka Tekkosho KK (Akasaka DieselLtd)-Japan Fuel: 30.0 (d.f.)
9415521 *TCTG8* -	**SADABAT** **Istanbul Deniz Otobusleri Sanayi ve Ticaret AS (IDO)** - *Istanbul* *Turkey* MMSI: 271002615	**1,065** 608 250	Class: TL	**2008**-08 **Ceksan Tersanesi — Turkey** Yd No: 44 Loa 73.20 Br ex - Dght 2.600 Lbp 71.10 Br md 18.00 Dpth 4.40 Welded, 1 dk	**(A36A2PR) Passenger/Ro-Ro Ship (Vehicles)** Bow ramp (f) Stern ramp (a)	**4 oil engines** reduction geared to sc. shafts driving 2 Voith-Schneider propellers 2 propellers aft, 2 fwd. Total Power: 2,440kW (3,316hp) Mitsubishi S6R2-MPTA 4 x 4 Stroke 6 Cy. 170 x 220 each-610kW (829bhp) Mitsubishi Heavy Industries Ltd-Japan AuxGen: 1 x 71kW a.c, 1 x 62kW a.c
5201300 *A6E2124* -	**SADAF** *ex* Mushrif *-1988* *ex* Geena *-1980* *ex* Abota *-1973* *ex* Labotas *-1972* **NAL Scrap & Old Ships Trading Co** - *Dubai* *United Arab Emirates*	*499* 222 905	Class: (LR) ✠ Classed LR until 3/3/82	**1958**-03 **N.V. Scheepswerf "Westerbroek" v/h J.G. Broerken — Westerbroek** Yd No: 153 Loa 64.85 Br ex 9.91 Dght 3.703 Lbp 59.75 Br md 9.81 Dpth 5.80 Riveted\Welded, 2 dks	**(A31A2GX) General Cargo Ship** Bale: 1,744 Compartments: 2 Ho, ER 2 Ha: (8.0 x 4.0) (12.1 x 4.0)ER Derricks: 2x6t,4x3t; Winches: 6 Ice Capable	**1 oil engine** driving 1 FP propeller Total Power: 552kW (750hp) 10.8kn Werkspoor 1 x 4 Stroke 6 Cy. 390 x 680 552kW (750bhp) NV Werkspoor-Netherlands AuxGen: 3 x 25kW 110V d.c Fuel: 226.5 (d.f.)
8860107 - -	**SADAF BALUCHESTAN** *ex* Ayad *-1972* *ex* Serah *-2002* *ex* Palakaria *-1998* *ex* Malka *-1995* **Brahim Zehi** - *Chabahar* *Iran* Official number: 801	**190** 57 76	Class: AS (BR) (RS)	**1992**-03 **OAO Astrakhanskaya Sudoverf — Astrakhan** Yd No: 93 Loa 31.35 Br ex 7.08 Dght 2.100 Lbp 28.60 Br md 6.90 Dpth 3.15 Welded, 1 dk	**(B12B2FC) Fish Carrier** Ins: 100	**1 oil engine** geared to sc. shaft driving 1 FP propeller Total Power: 232kW (315hp) 10.3kn Daldizel 6CHSPN2A18-315 1 x 4 Stroke 6 Cy. 180 x 220 232kW (315bhp) Daldizel-Khabarovsk AuxGen: 2 x 25kW a.c Fuel: 14.0 (d.f.)
8422084 *EQKQ* -	**SADAF POSHTIBAN** *ex* Iran Hormuz 26 *-2009* **Darya Fan Qeshm Industries Co (SADAF)** - SatCom: Inmarsat C 442216510 *Bandar Abbas* *Iran* MMSI: 422165000 Official number: 59258	**2,024** 607 738	Class: (LR) ✠ Classed LR until 2/12/09	**1986**-03 **Inchon Engineering & Shipbuilding Corp — Incheon** Yd No: 118 Converted From: Ferry (Passenger/Vehicle)-2009 Loa 73.06 Br ex 14.23 Dght 2.501 Lbp 68.00 Br md 14.01 Dpth 4.02 Welded, 1 dk	**(A35A2RR) Ro-Ro Cargo Ship** Passengers: unberthed: 300 Bow door/ramp Len: 4.50 Wid: 5.40 Swl: 18 Stern door/ramp Len: 4.50 Wid: 5.40 Swl: 18 Lane-Len: 68 Lane-Wid: 10.00 Lane-clr ht: 4.50 Lorries: 11, Cars: 50 TEU 24 C. 24/20' (40') incl. 11 ref C.	**2 oil engines** with clutches, flexible couplings & dr reverse geared to sc. shafts driving 2 FP propellers Total Power: 2,206kW (3,000hp) 12.0kn Daihatsu 6DLM-26S 2 x 4 Stroke 6 Cy. 260 x 340 each-1103kW (1500bhp) Daihatsu Diesel Manufacturing Co Lt-Japan AuxGen: 3 x 150kW 380V 50Hz a.c Thrusters: 1 Thwart. FP thruster (f) Fuel: 305.0 (d.f.) 7.0pd

9237149 *TCRB* -	**SADAN BAYRAKTAR** *ex* CMA CGM Alger *-2002* *ex* Sadan Bayraktar *-2001* **Say Denizcilik Sanayi ve Ticaret AS** Bayraktar Gemi Isletmeciligi ve Kiralama AS (Bayraktar Shipmanagement & Chartering SA) *Istanbul* *Turkey* MMSI: 271000653 Official number: 7878	**5,886** 2,701 8,080	Class: AB	**2001-10 Torgem Gemi Insaat Sanayii ve Ticaret a.s. — Tuzla, Istanbul** Yd No: 65 Loa 118.40 (BB) Br ex - Dght 7.500 Lbp 105.50 Br md 18.40 Dpth 9.50 Welded, 1 dk	**(A33A2CC) Container Ship (Fully Cellular)** TEU 657 incl 80 ref C. Compartments: 3 Cell Ho, ER 3 Ha: ER Cranes: 2x40t	**1 oil engine** driving 1 CP propeller Total Power: 5,180kW (7,043hp) 15.0kn B&W 7S35MC 1 x 2 Stroke 7 Cy. 350 x 1400 5180kW (7043bhp) MAN B&W Diesel A/S-Denmark AuxGen: 3 x 400kW 380V 50Hz a.c, 1 x 788kW 380V 50Hz a.c Thrusters: 1 Thwart. FP thruster (f) Fuel: 50.0 (d.f.) (Heating Coils) 515.0 (r.f.) 16.0pd
9483499 *V7TK7* -	**SADAN K** *ex* Sadan *-2010* **Queen Maritime Ltd** Haci Ismail Kaptanoglu Shipmanagement & Trading Ltd *Majuro* *Marshall Islands* MMSI: 538003821 Official number: 3821	**43,834** 26,694 80,306 T/cm 71.9	Class: LR ✠ **100A1** SS 03/2010 bulk carrier BC-A GRAB (20) Nos. 2, 4 & 6 holds may be empty ESP **ShipRight** (ACS (B), CM) *IWS LI EP (B) ✠ **LMC** **UMS** Eq.Ltr: Q†; Cable: 687.5/81.0 U3 (a)	**2010-03 STX Offshore & Shipbuilding Co Ltd — Changwon (Jinhae Shipyard)** Yd No: 2081 Loa 229.00 (BB) Br ex 32.28 Dght 14.500 Lbp 222.00 Br md 32.24 Dpth 20.10 Welded, 1 dk	**(A21A2BC) Bulk Carrier** Grain: 95,172 Compartments: 7 Ho, ER 7 Ha: ER	**1 oil engine** driving 1 FP propeller Total Power: 11,060kW (15,037hp) 14.4kn MAN-B&W 7S50MC-C 1 x 2 Stroke 7 Cy. 500 x 2000 11060kW (15037bhp) Hyundai Heavy Industries Co Ltd-South Korea AuxGen: 3 x 620kW 440V 60Hz a.c Boilers: AuxB (Comp) 9.0kgf/cm² (8.8bar)
8512188 *5ITW* -	**SADANI** - **Government of The United Republic of Tanzania** - *Dar es Salaam* *Tanzania*	*148* 47 141	Class: (NK)	**1986-01 Hayashikane Shipbuilding & Engineering Co Ltd — Shimonoseki YC** Yd No: 1292 Loa 28.30 Br ex - Dght 2.923 Lbp 25.20 Br md 7.21 Dpth 3.03 Welded, 1 dk	**(B11A2FT) Trawler** Ins: 81	**1 oil engine** driving 1 FP propeller Total Power: 331kW (450hp) 8.5kn Yanmar S165L-UT 1 x 4 Stroke 6 Cy. 165 x 210 331kW (450bhp) Yanmar Diesel Engine Co Ltd-Japan AuxGen: 2 x 72kW a.c
8823109 - -	**SADAQA** - **Yemen Fishing Corp** - *Aden* *Yemen*	*635* 198 405	Class: (RS)	**1980-04 Zavod "Leninskaya Kuznitsa" — Kiyev** Yd No: 1475 Loa 54.82 Br ex 9.95 Dght 4.140 Lbp 50.29 Br md - Dpth 5.00 Welded, 1 dk	**(B11A2FS) Stern Trawler** Ice Capable	**1 oil engine** driving 1 CP propeller Total Power: 736kW (1,001hp) 12.0kn S.K.L. 8NVD48AU 1 x 4 Stroke 8 Cy. 320 x 480 736kW (1001bhp) VEB Schwermaschinenbau "KarlLiebknecht" (SKL)-Magdeburg
8328367 - -	**SADAR INDAH** - **PT Pelayaran Lautan Kumala** - *Jakarta* *Indonesia*	*174* 103 250	Class: KI	**1977 P.N. Alir Menjaya — Palembang** Loa 39.43 Br ex - Dght - Lbp 37.01 Br md 7.03 Dpth 2.37 Welded, 1 dk	**(A31A2GX) General Cargo Ship** Compartments: 1 Ho, ER 1 Ha: ER	**1 oil engine** driving 1 FP propeller Total Power: 257kW (349hp) Otsuka SODHS6S24 1 x 4 Stroke 6 Cy. 240 x 390 257kW (349bhp) KK Otsuka Diesel-Japan
8328379 - -	**SADAR JAYA** *ex* Kiki V *-2010* **PT Pelayaran Lautan Kumala** - *Palembang* *Indonesia*	**164** - -	Class: (KI)	**1978 C.V. Uni — Jakarta** Loa 31.60 Br ex - Dght 1.801 Lbp 30.00 Br md 6.00 Dpth 2.49 Welded, 1 dk	**(A31A2GX) General Cargo Ship** Compartments: 1 Ho, ER 1 Ha: (12.0 x 3.9)ER	**1 oil engine** driving 1 FP propeller Total Power: 150kW (204hp) 6.0kn Ruston 6VCBM 1 x 4 Stroke 6 Cy. 203 x 273 150kW (204bhp) Ruston Diesels Ltd.-Newton-le-Willows
7601463 *SUBZ* -	**SADAT** - **Compagnie Orientale des Petroles d'Egypte** - *Suez* *Egypt* Official number: 1348	*496* - 645	Class: LR ✠ **100A1** SS 03/2010 tug ✠ **LMC** Eq.Ltr: (l) ; Cable: U2	**1976-12 K.K. Imai Seisakusho — Kamijima** (Hull) Yd No: 158 **1976-12 Mitsui Ocean Development & Eng. Co. Ltd. — Japan** Yd No: S-067 Loa 42.22 Br ex 10.04 Dght 3.401 Lbp 38.36 Br md 9.81 Dpth 4.60 Welded, 1 dk	**(B32A2ST) Tug**	**2 oil engines** reverse reduction geared to sc. shafts driving 2 FP propellers Total Power: 1,656kW (2,252hp) Caterpillar D399SCAC 2 x Vee 4 Stroke 16 Cy. 159 x 203 each-828kW (1126bhp) Caterpillar Tractor Co-USA AuxGen: 2 x 210kW 380V 50Hz a.c
9029396 *YD6852* -	**SADEWA** - **PT Hacienda Offshore** - *Samarinda* *Indonesia* MMSI: 525010126	**253** 76 -	Class: KI	**2005-07 PT Menumbar Kaltim — Samarinda** Loa 30.60 Br ex - Dght 3.500 Lbp 28.00 Br md 8.60 Dpth 4.11 Welded, 1 dk	**(B32A2ST) Tug**	**2 oil engines** driving 2 Propellers Total Power: 2,500kW (3,400hp) Pielstick 6PA5LX 2 x 4 Stroke 6 Cy. 255 x 270 each-1250kW (1700bhp) Niigata Engineering Co Ltd-Japan AuxGen: 2 x 108kW 380V a.c
6729696 - -	**SADIA II** *ex* Queen Haya *-2010* *ex* Lady Maya *-2008* *ex* Mers El Hadjadj *-2006* *ex* Nelly S *-1993* *ex* Giannis *-1985* *ex* Punch *-1981* *ex* Lady Caroline *-1979* *ex* Atlantic Proctor *-1976* *ex* Vibeke Theilgaard *-1974* - - *Algeria* MMSI: 605246121	**971** 482 1,117	Class: (BV)	**1968 E.J. Smit & Zoon's Scheepswerven N.V. — Westerbroek** Yd No: 786 Loa 65.64 Br ex 10.34 Dght 3.709 Lbp 59.64 Br md 10.32 Dpth 6.13 Welded, 1 dk	**(A31A2GX) General Cargo Ship** Grain: 1,769; Bale: 1,614 Compartments: 1 Ho, ER 2 Ha: (10.2 x 5.0) (20.4 x 6.0)ER Derricks: 3x3t; Winches: 3 Ice Capable	**1 oil engine** driving 1 FP propeller Total Power: 588kW (799hp) 11.0kn MaK 6M451AK 1 x 4 Stroke 6 Cy. 320 x 450 588kW (799bhp) Atlas MaK Maschinenbau GmbH-Kiel AuxGen: 2 x 250kW 220V d.c Fuel: 118.0 (d.f.) 3.5pd
8663559 - -	**SADIA ONIK 2** *ex* Savimex 02 *-2013* **Sadia Enterprise** Viet An Shipping Co Ltd *Ho Chi Minh City* *Vietnam* Official number: SG5671	**662** 465 1,220	Class: VR (Class contemplated)	**2010-07 An Phu Works — Ho Chi Minh City** Yd No: 1200-03-13HC Loa 55.90 Br ex - Dght 3.600 Lbp - Br md 10.70 Dpth 5.14 Welded, 1 dk	**(A13B2TP) Products Tanker**	**2 oil engines** reduction geared to sc. shafts driving 2 FP propellers Total Power: 514kW (698hp) Cummins NTA-855-M 2 x 4 Stroke 6 Cy. 140 x 152 each-257kW (349bhp) Cummins Engine Co Ltd-United Kingdom
8839524 *POOE* -	**SADIRA** *ex* Daiyu *-2013* *ex* Daiyu Maru No. 8 *-2012* *ex* Hoseizan Maru *-2007* **PT Pelayaran Kalao-Lao** - *Tanjung Priok* *Indonesia* MMSI: 525007104	**837** 315 627	Class: KI	**1989-10 Y.K. Okajima Zosensho — Matsuyama** Loa 54.42 Br ex - Dght 3.600 Lbp 49.50 Br md 9.10 Dpth 5.87 Welded, 1 dk	**(A31A2GX) General Cargo Ship** Grain: 1,131; Bale: 1,055 Compartments: 1 Ho 1 Ha: (28.5 x 6.8)ER	**1 oil engine** driving 1 FP propeller Total Power: 588kW (799hp) 10.0kn Niigata 6M26BGT 1 x 4 Stroke 6 Cy. 260 x 460 588kW (799bhp) Niigata Engineering Co Ltd-Japan AuxGen: 1 x 74kW 225V a.c Fuel: 22.0 (d.f.)
8928698 - -	**SADKO** *ex* BK-1211G *-1976* **Russ-Olimp Ltd** - *Magadan* *Russia* Official number: 743318	*187* - 46	Class: RS	**1975-04 Gorokhovetskiy Sudostroitelnyy Zavod — Gorokhovets** Yd No: 327 Loa 29.30 Br ex 8.49 Dght 3.090 Lbp 27.00 Br md 8.30 Dpth 4.35 Welded, 1 dk	**(B32A2ST) Tug** Ice Capable	**2 oil engines** driving 2 CP propellers Total Power: 882kW (1,200hp) 11.4kn Russkiy 6D30/50-4-2 2 x 2 Stroke 6 Cy. 300 x 500 each-441kW (600bhp) Mashinostroitelnyy Zavod"Russkiy-Dizel"-Leningrad AuxGen: 2 x 30kW a.c Fuel: 36.0 (d.f.)
7329209 *UBRS* -	**SADKO** - **Shiprepair Centre 'Zvyozdochka' JSC (OAO Tsentr Sudoremonta 'Zvyozdochka')** - *Arkhangelsk* *Russia* MMSI: 273430350 Official number: 620895	**609** 182 214	Class: RS	**1962 "Petrozavod" — Leningrad** Yd No: 624 Loa 47.60 Br ex 10.29 Dght 4.211 Lbp 43.00 Br md 10.00 Dpth 5.49 Welded, 1 dk	**(B32A2ST) Tug** Ice Capable	**2 diesel electric oil engines** driving 2 gen. Connecting to 1 elec. Motor of (1400kW) driving 1 FP propeller Total Power: 1,472kW (2,002hp) 13.0kn Penza 6CHN31.8/33 2 x 4 Stroke 6 Cy. 318 x 330 each-736kW (1001bhp) (new engine 1974) Penzdizelmash-Penza AuxGen: 2 x 100kW, 2 x 50kW Fuel: 108.0 (d.f.)
9521239 *UBWF5* -	**SADKO** - **Future Link Shipping Co** JSC Rosnefteflot SatCom: Inmarsat C 427311331 *St Petersburg* *Russia* MMSI: 273336330	**294** 88 131	Class: RS (LR) ✠ Classed LR until 1/6/09	**2009-05 Damen Shipyards Gdynia SA — Gdynia** (Hull) Yd No: (511562) **2009-05 B.V. Scheepswerf Damen — Gorinchem** Yd No: 511562 Loa 28.67 Br ex 10.43 Dght 3.700 Lbp 25.78 Br md 9.80 Dpth 4.60 Welded, 1 dk	**(B32A2ST) Tug** Ice Capable	**2 oil engines** reduction geared to sc. shafts driving 2 Z propellers Total Power: 3,132kW (4,258hp) Caterpillar 3516B-TA 2 x Vee 4 Stroke 16 Cy. 170 x 190 each-1566kW (2129bhp) Caterpillar Inc-USA AuxGen: 2 x 85kW 400V 50Hz a.c
9063615 *JF2153* -	**SADO MARU** - - - *Nanao, Ishikawa* *Japan* Official number: 120103	*147* - -		**1993-01 Sagami Zosen Tekko K.K. — Yokosuka** Yd No: 256 Loa 31.20 Br ex 8.82 Dght - Lbp 27.00 Br md 8.80 Dpth 3.50 Welded, 1 dk	**(B32A2ST) Tug**	**2 oil engines** Geared Integral to driving 2 Z propellers Total Power: 2,280kW (3,100hp) 12.5kn Pielstick 6PA5 2 x 4 Stroke 6 Cy. 255 x 270 each-1140kW (1550bhp) Niigata Engineering Co Ltd-Japan

IMO / Call sign	Name / Owner / Port	Tonnage	Class	Builder / Dimensions	Type	Machinery
7828700 *UGEL* -	**SADOVSK** **Dalmoreprodukt Holding Co (Kholdingovaya Kompaniya 'Dalmoreprodukt')** - *Vladivostok* *Russia* MMSI: 273812600 Official number: 781273	**739** 221 332	Class: RS	**1979-09 Zavod "Leninskaya Kuznitsa" — Kiyev** Yd No: 242 Loa 53.75 (BB) Br ex 10.72 Dght 4.290 Lbp 47.92 Br md 10.50 Dpth 6.00 Welded, 1 dk	**(B11A2FS) Stern Trawler** Ins: 218 Compartments: 1 Ho, ER 1 Ha: (1.6 x 1.6) Derricks: 2x3.3t Ice Capable	**1 oil engine** driving 1 CP propeller Total Power: 971kW (1,320hp) 12.8kn S.K.L. 8NVD48A-2U 1 x 4 Stroke 8 Cy. 320 x 480 971kW (1320bhp) VEB Schwermaschinenbau "KarlLiebknecht" (SKL)-Magdeburg AuxGen: 1 x 300kW, 3 x 160kW Fuel: 185.0 (d.f.)
9049085 - -	**SADP XXV** **PT Sinar Alam Duta Perdana** - *Banjarmasin* *Indonesia*	**190** 57 -	Class: KI	**2001-01 CV Sumber Jaya — Banjarmasin** Loa 25.00 Br ex - Dght - Lbp 24.00 Br md 7.50 Dpth 3.50 Welded, 1 dk	**(B32A2ST) Tug**	**2 oil engines** geared to sc. shafts driving 2 Propellers Total Power: 1,250kW (1,700hp) 9.0kn Caterpillar D398B 2 x Vee 4 Stroke 12 Cy. 153 x 203 each-625kW (850bhp) Caterpillar Inc-USA AuxGen: 2 x 90kW 380/220V a.c
9029102 - -	**SADP XXX** **PT Lintas Samudra Borneo Line** - *Banjarmasin* *Indonesia*	**136** 81 -	Class: KI	**2003-07 P.T. Permata Barito — Marabahan** Loa 25.30 Br ex - Dght - Lbp 23.85 Br md 7.35 Dpth 3.10 Welded, 1 dk	**(B32A2ST) Tug**	**2 oil engines** geared to sc. shafts driving 2 Propellers Total Power: 1,250kW (1,700hp) 8.5kn Caterpillar D398 2 x Vee 4 Stroke 12 Cy. 159 x 203 each-625kW (850bhp) Caterpillar Inc-USA AuxGen: 2 x 48kW 380V a.c
9046954 *CNRZ* -	**SADR** **Societe Atlantique d'Exploitation Maritime (SAETMA)** - SatCom: Inmarsat C 424241210 *Tan-Tan* *Morocco*	**392** 118 -	Class: (BV)	**1992-01 Construcciones Navales P Freire SA — Vigo** Yd No: 388 Loa - Br ex - Dght 3.850 Lbp 31.50 Br md 8.50 Dpth 6.20 Welded, 1 dk	**(B11A2FS) Stern Trawler** Ins: 315	**1 oil engine** sr reverse geared to sc. shaft driving 1 FP propeller Total Power: 853kW (1,160hp) 11.6kn Deutz SBA8M528 1 x 4 Stroke 8 Cy. 220 x 280 853kW (1160bhp) Kloeckner Humboldt Deutz AG-Germany AuxGen: 2 x 140kW 220/380V a.c
8746923 *9MHU9* -	**SADR** **Government of Malaysia (Director of Marine & Ministry of Transport)** - *Port Klang* *Malaysia* Official number: 333806	**140** 42 25		**2008-05 Kay Marine Sdn Bhd — Kuala Terengganu** (Assembled by) Yd No: J104-6 **0000* Inform Marine Technology — Fremantle WA** (Parts for assembly by) Loa 26.00 Br ex - Dght 1.200 Lbp - Br md 9.20 Dpth 2.55 Welded, 1 dk	**(A37B2PS) Passenger Ship** Hull Material: Aluminium Alloy	**2 oil engines** reduction geared to sc. shafts driving 2 Propellers Total Power: 2,206kW (3,000hp) M.T.U. 12V2000M91 2 x Vee 4 Stroke 12 Cy. 130 x 150 each-1103kW (1500bhp) MTU Friedrichshafen GmbH-Friedrichshafen
8741674 *5IM275* -	**SADRA** *ex* Feiry 1 *-2013* *ex* Fiery 1 *-2013* *ex* Noor Alhuda *-2009* **Withstand Shipping & Oil Product Inc** Middle East Petroleum Inc *Zanzibar* *Tanzania (Zanzibar)* MMSI: 677017500 Official number: 300033	**258** 123 -		**2003-08 UR-Dock — Basrah** Yd No: 302 Loa 30.20 Br ex - Dght 1.500 Lbp - Br md 8.00 Dpth 3.25 Welded, 1 dk	**(B21B20T) Offshore Tug/Supply Ship**	**2 oil engines** reduction geared to sc. shafts driving 2 Propellers Total Power: 810kW (1,102hp) Caterpillar 2 x Vee 4 Stroke 12 Cy. each-405kW (551bhp) Caterpillar Inc-USA
8905153 - -	**SADRA HOMA** **Iran Marine Industrial Co (IMICO) Sherkate Sanati Daryai Iran (SADRA)** - *Bushehr* *Iran*	*274* 82 -	Class: (LR) ✠ Classed LR until 1/5/96	**1993-01 Iran Marine Ind. Co. (IMICO) — Bushehr** Yd No: 6675 Loa 33.50 Br ex 8.69 Dght - Lbp 30.50 Br md 8.45 Dpth 4.25 Welded, 1 dk	**(B32A2ST) Tug**	**2 oil engines** with clutches, flexible couplings & sr reverse geared to sc. shafts driving 2 FP propellers Total Power: 2,400kW (3,264hp) MWM TBD440-8K 2 x 4 Stroke 8 Cy. 230 x 270 each-1200kW (1632bhp) Motoren Werke Mannheim AG (MWM)-Mannheim AuxGen: 2 x 50kW 380V 50Hz a.c
8983387 - -	**SADRA KHAZAR** - - *Now Shahr* *Iran*	**114** 45 295		**1993 Sadra International — Bandar Abbas** Loa 26.30 Br ex - Dght 3.000 Lbp - Br md 8.70 Dpth 3.87 Welded, 1 dk	**(B32A2ST) Tug**	**2 oil engines** geared to sc. shafts driving 2 Propellers Total Power: 1,030kW (1,400hp) MWM TBD234V12 2 x Vee 4 Stroke 12 Cy. 128 x 140 each-515kW (700bhp)
9048433 - -	**SADRA NEDA** **Iran Marine Industrial Co (IMICO) Sherkate Sanati Daryai Iran (SADRA)** - *Bushehr* *Iran* Official number: 16516	**170** 51 -	Class: AS	**1994-12 Iran Marine Ind. Co. (IMICO) — Bushehr** Yd No: 2278 Loa 27.00 Br ex - Dght 3.150 Lbp 23.50 Br md 7.00 Dpth 3.71 Welded, 1 dk	**(B32A2ST) Tug**	**1 oil engine** reduction geared to sc. shaft driving 1 CP propeller Total Power: 1,177kW (1,600hp) Deutz SBV8M628 1 x 4 Stroke 8 Cy. 240 x 280 1177kW (1600bhp) Motoren Werke Mannheim AG (MWM)-Mannheim
9153721 - -	**SADRA NEKA 1** **Iran Marine Industrial Co (IMICO) Sherkate Sanati Daryai Iran (SADRA)** - *Bushehr* *Iran* Official number: 17522	**140** 42 -	Class: AS	**2003-03 Iran Marine Ind. Co. (IMICO) — Bushehr** Yd No: 2312 Loa 26.32 Br ex - Dght 3.000 Lbp 24.16 Br md 8.07 Dpth 3.87 Welded, 1 dk	**(B32A2ST) Tug**	**2 oil engines** geared to sc. shafts driving 2 FP propellers Total Power: 1,000kW (1,360hp) 12.0kn MWM TBD234V12 2 x Vee 4 Stroke 12 Cy. 128 x 140 each-500kW (680bhp) Motoren Werke Mannheim AG (MWM)-Mannheim
8409666 - -	**SADRA TALASH** *ex* Talash *-1993* **Iran Marine Industrial Co (IMICO) Sherkate Sanati Daryai Iran (SADRA)** - *Bushehr* *Iran*	**103** 31 28	Class: (LR) ✠ Classed LR until 14/6/95	**1985-01 Sumidagawa Zosen K.K. — Tokyo** Yd No: N58-33 Loa 27.11 Br ex 5.31 Dght 1.250 Lbp 24.52 Br md 5.21 Dpth 2.70 Welded, 1 dk	**(B34H2SQ) Patrol Vessel**	**2 oil engines** reverse reduction geared to sc. shafts driving 2 FP propellers Total Power: 2,044kW (2,780hp) M.T.U. 12V396TE64 2 x Vee 4 Stroke 12 Cy. 165 x 185 each-1022kW (1390bhp) MTU Friedrichshafen GmbH-Friedrichshafen AuxGen: 2 x 72kW 380V 50Hz a.c
8132562 - -	**SAE CHANG No. 1** *ex* Nam Bong *-1991* *ex* Sam Han *-1987* - -	**348** - 596	Class: (KR)	**1981 Keumchang Shipyard — Geoje** Loa 54.62 Br ex - Dght 3.412 Lbp 49.00 Br md 8.40 Dpth 3.81 Welded, 1 dk	**(A31A2GX) General Cargo Ship** Bale: 492 1 Ha: (18.6 x 5.4) Derricks: 1x1t	**1 oil engine** driving 1 FP propeller Total Power: 405kW (551hp) 9.5kn Daihatsu 6DSM-18A 1 x 4 Stroke 6 Cy. 180 x 230 405kW (551bhp) Daihatsu Diesel Manufacturing Co Lt-Japan AuxGen: 2 x 38kW 225V a.c
9102368 - -	**SAE GYOUNG HO** *ex* Hae Sung No. 3 *-1987* **Sae Gyoung Shipping Co Ltd** - *Yeosu* *South Korea* Official number: YSR-934352	**209** - 568	Class: KR	**1993-02 Hanryu Shipbuilding Co Ltd — Tongyeong** Yd No: 103 Loa 39.00 Br ex - Dght 3.511 Lbp 34.00 Br md 7.50 Dpth 4.00 Welded, 1 dk	**(A13B2TP) Products Tanker**	**1 oil engine** geared to s.c. shaft driving 1 FP propeller Total Power: 500kW (680hp) 11.9kn Caterpillar 3412TA 1 x Vee 4 Stroke 12 Cy. 137 x 152 500kW (680bhp) Caterpillar Inc-USA
9022453 *DSOT4* -	**SAE HAN NO. 1** *ex* Dae Jin No. 211 *-1987* *ex* Hae Sung No. 201 *-1987* **Dae Kyung Shipping Co Ltd** - *Busan* *South Korea* MMSI: 440312000 Official number: BSR-914380	**161** 48 -	Class: KT	**1991-03 Busan Shipbuilding Co Ltd — Busan** Yd No: 99 Loa 35.15 Br ex - Dght 2.700 Lbp 30.60 Br md 7.00 Dpth 3.50 Welded, 1 dk	**(B32A2ST) Tug**	**1 oil engine** driving 1 Propeller Total Power: 1,655kW (2,250hp) Daihatsu 6DSM-32 1 x 4 Stroke 6 Cy. 320 x 380 1655kW (2250bhp) Daihatsu Diesel Manufacturing Co Lt-Japan
7103485 *D8VC* -	**SAE HWA No. 1** *ex* Keo Yang No. 1 *-1995* *ex* Kum Jung No. 15 *-1991* *ex* Je Won No. 7 *-1986* *ex* Orient Garnet *-1984* *ex* Sanpo Maru *-1981* **Dong Cheon Shipping** - *Yeosu* *South Korea* Official number: YSR-705876	*508* 247 997	Class: (KR)	**1970 Kishimoto Zosen — Osakikamijima** Yd No: 363 Loa 55.96 Br ex 9.02 Dght 4.050 Lbp 51.72 Br md 9.00 Dpth 4.50 Welded, 1 dk	**(A12A2TC) Chemical Tanker** Liq: 970	**1 oil engine** driving 1 FP propeller Total Power: 736kW (1,001hp) 10.4kn Hanshin 6LU28 1 x 4 Stroke 6 Cy. 280 x 440 736kW (1001bhp) Hanshin Nainenki Kogyo-Japan AuxGen: 1 x 40kW 225V a.c
7311939 - -	**SAE JO YANG** **Kim Chun Saeng** - *Mokpo* *South Korea* Official number: MM4888	*131* 53 -		**1972 Hyangdo Shipbuilding Co Ltd — Pohang** Loa 32.57 Br ex 5.34 Dght - Lbp 29.01 Br md 5.19 Dpth 2.39 Welded, 2 dks	**(A31A2GX) General Cargo Ship**	**1 oil engine** driving 1 FP propeller Total Power: 382kW (519hp) Matsue Z-23L 1 x 4 Stroke 6 Cy. 230 x 380 382kW (519bhp) Matsue Diesel KK-Japan

IMO / Call sign / Fishing no.	Name / Former names / Owner / Manager / Port / Flag	Tonnage	Class	Builder / Dimensions	Type	Machinery
9138020 - -	**SAE JONG FERRY** - **Han Heung Ferry Ltd** - *Mokpo* *South Korea* Official number: MPR-954523	*200* - 125	Class: (KR)	**1995-11 Han-Il Shipbuilding & Engineering Co Ltd — Mokpo** Yd No: 95-01 Loa 49.50 Br ex - Dght 1.611 Lbp 42.43 Br md 8.20 Dpth 2.30 Welded, 1 dk	**(A37B2PS) Passenger Ship**	**2 oil engines** geared to sc. shaft driving 1 FP propeller Total Power: 824kW (1,120hp) M.T.U. 12V183 2 x Vee 4 Stroke 12 Cy. 128 x 142 each-412kW (560bhp) Daewoo Heavy Industries Ltd-South Korea
8123614 *D9DB* -	**SAE KYUNG GI** - **Korea Development Leasing Corp** Sunjoo Shipping Co Ltd *Incheon* *South Korea* Official number: ICR-810018	*492* 257 294	Class: (KR)	**1981-04 Korea Tacoma Marine Industries Ltd — Changwon** Yd No: 10154 Loa 55.50 Br ex - Dght 2.062 Lbp 52.00 Br md 8.60 Dpth 3.26 Welded, 1 dk	**(A37B2PS) Passenger Ship** Grain: 194; Bale: 155 2 Ha: (3.6 x 3.1) (2.3 x 2.4)	**2 oil engines** driving 2 FP propellers Total Power: 2,354kW (3,200hp) 17.8kn Niigata 8MG25BX 2 x 4 Stroke 8 Cy. 250 x 320 each-1177kW (1600bhp) Ssangyong Heavy Industries Co Ltd-South Korea
8031562 *D8FG* -	**SAE MA EUL** - **Semo Marine Co Ltd** - *Yeocheon* *South Korea* Official number: YSR-804963	*199* 115 44	Class: (KR)	**1980 Chungmu Shipbuilding Co Inc — Tongyeong** Loa 40.70 Br ex - Dght - Lbp 37.01 Br md 6.00 Dpth 2.80 Welded, 1 dk	**(A37B2PS) Passenger Ship**	**1 oil engine** driving 1 FP propeller Total Power: 956kW (1,300hp) 16.0kn Makita KNLH6275 1 x 4 Stroke 6 Cy. 275 x 450 956kW (1300bhp) Makita Diesel Co Ltd-Japan AuxGen: 1 x 24kW 225V a.c
7720623 *D7PP* -	**SAE SU HYUP** - **National Federation of Fisheries Cooperatives** - *Busan* *South Korea* Official number: BM43413	*136* 44 -	Class: (KR)	**1977-09 Dae Sun Shipbuilding & Engineering Co Ltd — Busan** Yd No: 197 Loa 28.91 Br ex 6.43 Dght - Lbp 25.20 Br md 6.30 Dpth 2.60 Welded, 1 dk	**(B34U2QH) Hospital Vessel**	**1 oil engine** driving 1 FP propeller Total Power: 405kW (551hp) 10.5kn Daihatsu 6DSM-18A 1 x 4 Stroke 6 Cy. 180 x 230 405kW (551bhp) Daihatsu Diesel Manufacturing Co Lt-Japan AuxGen: 2 x 40kW 220V a.c
6808894 *6LVL* -	**SAE WOON NO. 7** *ex* O Yang No. 1 *-1989* *ex* Waka Maru No. 18 *-1976* *ex* Ryotei Maru No. 1 *-1976* **Jun Young-Pyo** - *Busan* *South Korea* Official number: BS02-A1853	*135* 42 138	Class: (KR)	**1968 Nichiro Zosen K.K. — Hakodate** Yd No: 246 Loa 35.23 Br ex 6.53 Dght 2.682 Lbp 31.60 Br md 6.51 Dpth 2.80 Welded, 1 dk	**(B11A2FS) Stern Trawler** Ins: 91 1 Ha: (7.2 x 1.9)ER	**1 oil engine** driving 1 FP propeller Total Power: 625kW (850hp) 11.3kn Niigata 6M28KHS 1 x 4 Stroke 6 Cy. 280 x 440 625kW (850bhp) Niigata Engineering Co Ltd-Japan AuxGen: 2 x 28kW 225V a.c
9033804 *D8WX* -	**SAE YU DAL** - **Government of The Republic of South Korea (Ministry of Education)** Mokpo National Maritime University (MMU) SatCom: Inmarsat C 444085017 *Mokpo* *South Korea* MMSI: 440100016 Official number: MPR-934483	**3,644** 1,093 1,914	Class: KR	**1993-10 Daedong Shipbuilding Co Ltd — Busan** Yd No: 369 Loa 102.70 (BB) Br ex - Dght 5.214 Lbp 93.00 Br md 14.50 Dpth 9.50 Welded, 2 dks	**(B34K2QT) Training Ship**	**1 oil engine** driving 1 FP propeller Total Power: 2,920kW (3,970hp) 15.2kn B&W 8S26MC 1 x 2 Stroke 8 Cy. 260 x 980 2920kW (3970bhp) Ssangyong Heavy Industries Co Ltd-South Korea AuxGen: 3 x 400kW 450V a.c
9415387 *J8B4019* -	**SAEB** - **Leonardo Marine Services Ltd** Whitesea Shipping & Supply (LLC) *Kingstown* *St Vincent & The Grenadines* MMSI: 375708000 Official number: 10492	**1,579** 473 1,500	Class: BV	**2009-09 Keppel Nantong Shipyard Co Ltd — Nantong JS** (Hull) Yd No: 014 **2009-09 Keppel Singmarine Pte Ltd — Singapore** Yd No: 333 Loa 62.20 Br ex - Dght 4.900 Lbp 59.06 Br md 15.00 Dpth 6.00 Welded, 1 dk	**(B21B20A) Anchor Handling Tug Supply** Cranes: 1x10t	**2 oil engines** reduction geared to sc. shafts driving 2 Directional propellers Total Power: 4,080kW (5,548hp) 12.5kn Wartsila 6L26A 2 x 4 Stroke 6 Cy. 260 x 320 each-2040kW (2774bhp) Wartsila Finland Oy-Finland AuxGen: 2 x 1200kW 380V 50Hz a.c, 2 x 280kW 380V 50Hz a.c Thrusters: 2 Tunnel thruster (f)
9256688 *DTBG5* -	**SAEBADA** - **Government of The Republic of South Korea (Ministry of Education & Human Resources Development)** Kyungsang National University *Tongyeong* *South Korea* MMSI: 441117000 Official number: 0107016-6482208	**1,358** 407 912	Class: KR	**2001-08 Dae Sun Shipbuilding & Engineering Co Ltd — Busan** Yd No: 436 Loa 70.57 Br ex 12.32 Dght 4.500 Lbp 60.60 Br md 12.30 Dpth 7.40 Welded, 1 dk	**(B34K2QT) Training Ship**	**1 oil engine** geared to sc. shaft driving 1 FP propeller Total Power: 2,427kW (3,300hp) 15.0kn Niigata 6MG34HX 1 x 4 Stroke 6 Cy. 340 x 450 2427kW (3300bhp) Niigata Engineering Co Ltd-Japan
6622745 *6LSK* -	**SAEBADA** *ex* Shinsei Maru No. 2 *-2000* **Government of The Republic of South Korea (Ministry of Education)** Kyungsang National University SatCom: Inmarsat B 344024010 *Donghae, Gangwon-do* *South Korea* Official number: 9503458-6482205	*2,275* 1,119 1,404	Class: (KR) (NK)	**1966-11 Usuki Iron Works Co Ltd — Saiki OT** Yd No: 1077 Converted From: Stern Trawler-1979 Loa 87.91 Br ex 13.64 Dght 5.160 Lbp 79.30 Br md 13.62 Dpth 6.68 Welded, 2 dks	**(B11A2FG) Factory Stern Trawler** Ins: 2,381 2 Ha: (2.5 x 4.8) (2.0 x 2.8)ER Derricks: 2x3t,2x1t	**2 oil engines** geared to sc. shafts driving 2 FP propellers Total Power: 2,648kW (3,600hp) 13.0kn MAN V8V-22/30ATL 2 x Vee 4 Stroke 16 Cy. 220 x 300 each-1324kW (1800bhp) Kawasaki Dockyard Co Ltd-Japan AuxGen: 3 x 440kW 445V 60Hz a.c Fuel: 1062.0
7012492 *TFTR* HF 224	**SAEBERG** *ex* Gestur *-1997* *ex* Stjornutindur *-1993* *ex* Lytingur *-1988* *ex* Gissur *-1985* *ex* Torjo *-1971* **Ocean Direct Ehf** - *Hafnarfjordur* *Iceland* MMSI: 251273110 Official number: 1143	**146** 44 -	Class: (NV)	**1966-01 Langsten Slip & Baatbyggeri AS — Tomrefjord** Yd No: 30 Lengthened-1969 Loa 31.02 Br ex 6.53 Dght - Lbp - Br md 6.48 Dpth 2.95 Welded, 1 dk	**(B11B2FV) Fishing Vessel**	**1 oil engine** geared to sc. shaft driving 1 FP propeller Total Power: 552kW (750hp) Grenaa 6FR24TK 1 x 4 Stroke 6 Cy. 240 x 300 552kW (750bhp) (new engine 1982) A/S Grenaa Motorfabrik-Denmark AuxGen: 1 x 31kW 220V 50Hz a.c, 1 x 28kW 220V 50Hz a.c
7382938 *TFBP* -	**SAEBJORG** *ex* Akraborg *-1998* *ex* Betancuria *-1982* *ex* Benchijigua *-1980* **Slysavarnafelagid Landsbjorg** - *Reykjavik* *Iceland* MMSI: 251005110 Official number: 1627	**1,774** 1,129 482	Class: (NV)	**1974-06 AS Trondhjems Mekaniske Verksted — Trondheim** Yd No: 712 Converted From: Ferry (Passenger/Vehicle)-1998 Loa 68.79 Br ex 11.51 Dght 3.450 Lbp 63.15 Br md 11.49 Dpth 4.50 Welded, 2 dks	**(B34K2QT) Training Ship**	**2 oil engines** driving 2 CP propellers Total Power: 1,700kW (2,312hp) 12.0kn Polar SF16RS-F 2 x 4 Stroke 6 Cy. 250 x 300 each-850kW (1156bhp) AB NOHAB-Sweden AuxGen: 3 x 99kW 220V 50Hz a.c Thrusters: 1 Thwart. FP thruster (f) Fuel: 35.5 (d.f.) 6.5pd
9126596 *LIFA* M-27-VD	**SAEBJORN** - **A/S Saebjorn** - *Aalesund* *Norway* MMSI: 259374000	**1,742** 591 1,000	Class: NV	**1996-09 Stocznia Remontowa 'Nauta' SA — Gdynia** (Hull launched by) Yd No: TN65/7 **1996-09 Eidsvik Skipsbyggeri AS — Uskedalen** (Hull completed by) Yd No: 52 Loa 65.70 Br ex - Dght 5.800 Lbp 57.60 Br md 12.60 Dpth 8.40 Welded, 1 dk	**(B11B2FV) Fishing Vessel** Ice Capable	**1 oil engine** geared to sc. shaft driving 1 CP propeller Total Power: 3,972kW (5,400hp) 17.5kn Wichmann 12V28B 1 x Vee 2 Stroke 12 Cy. 280 x 360 3972kW (5400bhp) Wartsila Propulsion AS-Norway Thrusters: 1 Thwart. FP thruster (f); 1 Tunnel thruster (a)
5427710 - -	**SAEBORG** *ex* Asver *-1977* *ex* Jorundur III *-1973* - -	**255** 77 -	Class: (LR) ✠ Classed LR until 9/5/80	**1964-04 Cochrane & Sons Ltd. — Selby** Yd No: 1494 Loa 36.45 Br ex 7.65 Dght 3.480 Lbp 31.93 Br md 7.62 Dpth 3.66 Welded	**(B11A2FT) Trawler** Ice Capable	**1 oil engine** sr geared to sc. shaft driving 1 CP propeller Total Power: 588kW (799hp) Blackstone ESS8 1 x 4 Stroke 8 Cy. 222 x 292 588kW (799bhp) Lister Blackstone Marine Ltd.-Dursley
9535292 *OZ2076* -	**SAEBORG** - **P/F 6 September 2006** P/F Skansi Offshore *Leirvik* *Faeroes (FAS)* MMSI: 231850000	**3,260** 1,373 4,300	Class: NV	**2011-09 Cemre Muhendislik Gemi Insaat Sanayi ve Ticaret Ltd Sti — Altinova** (Hull) Yd No: (102) **2011-09 Havyard Leirvik AS — Leirvik i Sogn** Yd No: 102 Loa 86.00 (BB) Br ex 18.30 Dght 6.387 Lbp 74.40 Br md 17.60 Dpth 7.70 Welded, 1 dk	**(B21A20S) Platform Supply Ship** Cranes: 1x100t	**4 diesel electric oil engines** driving 4 gen. each 1560kW a.c Connecting to 2 elec. motors each (1600kW) driving 2 Azimuth electric drive units Total Power: 6,240kW (8,484hp) 14.5kn M.T.U. 12V4000M33S 4 x Vee 4 Stroke 12 Cy. 170 x 210 each-1560kW (2121bhp) MTU Friedrichshafen GmbH-Friedrichshafen Thrusters: 2 Tunnel thruster (f)
9318577 *A6E3018* -	**SAEED** *ex* Danum 19 *-2005* **Liwa Marine Services LLC** - *Abu Dhabi* *United Arab Emirates* MMSI: 470857000 Official number: 5114	**297** 89 232	Class: BV	**2005-01 Shin Yang Shipyard Sdn Bhd — Miri** Yd No: 182 Loa 31.00 Br ex - Dght 3.048 Lbp 28.25 Br md 9.50 Dpth 3.80 Welded, 1 dk	**(B21A20S) Platform Supply Ship**	**2 oil engines** geared to sc. shafts driving 2 FP propellers Total Power: 1,516kW (2,062hp) Mitsubishi S6R2-MPTK2 2 x 4 Stroke 6 Cy. 170 x 220 each-758kW (1031bhp) Mitsubishi Heavy Industries Ltd-Japan

IMO / Call sign	Name / Owners	Tonnage	Class	Builder / Dimensions	Type	Machinery
8872318 *H06034* -	**SAEED 7** *ex* Yellow Gold *-2011* *ex* Al Samha I *-2011* *ex* Sea Mate *-2009* *ex* Samara *-2009* *ex* Angel I *-2007* *ex* Barry *-2006* *ex* Gulf Breeze *-2000* *ex* Sea Breeze *-1992* *ex* Labby *-1976* **Universal Gas Trading & Shipping Inc** IPC Marine Services LLC *Panama* *Panama* MMSI: 351640000 Official number: 4363412	*177* 122 850	Class: (HR)	**1976 American Marine Corp. — New Orleans, La** Loa 50.29 Br ex 10.97 Dght 3.160 Lbp 49.23 Br md 10.96 Dpth 3.81 Welded, 1 dk	**(B21B20T) Offshore Tug/Supply Ship**	**2 oil engines** reduction geared to sc. shafts driving 2 FP propellers Total Power: 1,230kW (1,672hp) 10.0kn Caterpillar D398SCAC 2 x Vee 4 Stroke 12 Cy. 159 x 203 each-615kW (836bhp) Caterpillar Tractor Co-USA AuxGen: 1 x 85kW 220/440V a.c, 2 x 75kW 220/440V a.c
9113343 *HP5051* -	**SAEED 14** *ex* Shelela *-2011* **Kamal Marei** Marei Transportation Co *Panama* *Panama* Official number: 42226PEXT	**250** 80 250	Class: (GL)	**1995 Port Said Engineering Works — Port Said** Yd No: 659 Converted From: Pollution Control Vessel-2011 Loa 25.00 Br ex 6.50 Dght 1.800 Lbp 21.50 Br md 6.00 Dpth 2.75 Welded, 1 dk	**(B34R2QY) Supply Tender**	**2 oil engines** with clutches & sr reverse geared to sc. shafts driving 2 FP propellers Total Power: 682kW (928hp) M.T.U. 10V183AA61 2 x Vee 4 Stroke 10 Cy. 128 x 142 each-341kW (464bhp) MTU Friedrichshafen GmbH-Friedrichshafen
9041277 *TFOG* -	**SAEFARI** *ex* Oileain Arann *-2008* **Rikissjodur Island** Samskip hf *Grimsey* *Iceland* MMSI: 251521110 Official number: 2691	**507** 128 225	Class: LR ✠ **100A1** SS 04/2013 cargo/passenger ferry ✠ **LMC** Eq.Ltr: H; Cable: 302.5/22.0 U2 (a)	**1992-12 McTay Marine — Bromborough** (Hull) **1992-12 James N. Miller & Sons Ltd. — St. Monans** Yd No: 1047 Loa 39.74 (BB) Br ex 10.28 Dght 2.505 Lbp 35.50 Br md 9.97 Dpth 3.69 Welded, 1 dk	**(A32A2GF) General Cargo/Passenger Ship** Passengers: unberthed: 200 Compartments: 1 Ho, ER	**2 oil engines** with clutches, flexible couplings & sr reverse geared to sc. shafts driving 2 FP propellers Total Power: 2,040kW (2,774hp) Caterpillar 3512TA 2 x Vee 4 Stroke 12 Cy. 170 x 190 each-1020kW (1387bhp) Caterpillar Inc-USA AuxGen: 2 x 100kW 380V 50Hz a.c Thrusters: 1 Thwart. FP thruster (f)
8909056 *TFHT* AR 170	**SAEFARI** *ex* Grundfirdingur *-2008* *ex* Fanney *-2008* *ex* Joi a Nesi *-1990* **Hafnarnes VER hf** - *Thorlakshofn* *Iceland* MMSI: 251247110 Official number: 1964	*159* 58 -		**1988 Stocznia 'Wisla' — Gdansk** Yd No: KB21/04 Loa 27.49 Br ex - Dght 2.612 Lbp 23.07 Br md 6.01 Dpth 3.03 Welded	**(B11A2FT) Trawler**	**1 oil engine** geared to sc. shaft driving 1 FP propeller Total Power: 465kW (632hp) Caterpillar 1 x 4 Stroke 465kW (632bhp) Caterpillar Inc-USA
9141962 *3FNH6* -	**SAEHAN AURORA** *ex* Global Express No. 2 *-2011* **SMG Aurora SA** Saehan Marine (Operation) Co Ltd SatCom: Inmarsat C 435680910 *Panama* *Panama* MMSI: 356809000 Official number: 2340897CH	**3,516** 1,055 4,252 T/cm 13.5	Class: KR (NK)	**1996-09 Honda Zosen — Saiki** Yd No: 1000 Loa 99.82 (BB) Br ex - Dght 5.623 Lbp 92.00 Br md 16.40 Dpth 7.10 Welded, 1 dk	**(A11B2TG) LPG Tanker** Double Bottom Entire Compartment Length Liq (Gas): 3,441 2 x Gas Tank (s); 2 independent cyl 2 Cargo Pump (s): 2x360m³/hr Manifold: Bow/CM: 46.4m	**1 oil engine** driving 1 FP propeller Total Power: 3,089kW (4,200hp) 13.5kn Mitsubishi 6UEC37LA 1 x 2 Stroke 6 Cy. 370 x 880 3089kW (4200bhp) Akasaka Tekkosho KK (Akasaka DieselLtd)-Japan AuxGen: 2 x 240kW a.c Fuel: 108.0 (d.f.) 488.0 (r.f.) 12.4pd
9157557 *DSMT2* -	**SAEHAN CAPELLA** *ex* Gas Natalie *-2010* *ex* Fountain Gas *-2007* *ex* Venus Gas *-2005* **Saehan Marine Gas Co Ltd** SM Management Co Ltd *Jeju* *South Korea* MMSI: 441931000 Official number: JJR-108872	**3,050** 915 3,175 T/cm 11.6	Class: KR (AB) (NK)	**1997-03 Shitanoe Shipbuilding Co Ltd — Usuki OT** Yd No: 1186 Loa 96.00 Br ex 15.03 Dght 5.214 Lbp 89.50 Br md 15.00 Dpth 7.00 Welded, 1 dk	**(A11B2TG) LPG Tanker** Double Bottom Entire Compartment Length Liq (Gas): 3,150 2 x Gas Tank (s); 2 independent (stl) pri 3 Cargo Pump (s): 3x300m³/hr Manifold: Bow/CM: 44.1m	**1 oil engine** driving 1 FP propeller Total Power: 2,427kW (3,300hp) 13.0kn Akasaka A41 1 x 4 Stroke 6 Cy. 410 x 800 2427kW (3300bhp) Akasaka Tekkosho KK (Akasaka DieselLtd)-Japan Fuel: 61.0 (d.f.) 337.0 (r.f.)
9058517 *DSQC6* -	**SAEHAN CHEMSTAR** *ex* Southern Tiger *-2008* *ex* Ryushin *-2001* **Saehan Marine Co Ltd** Saehan Marine Service Co Ltd *Jeju* *South Korea* MMSI: 441528000 Official number: JJR-088698	**4,969** 1,733 9,325 T/cm 17.4	Class: KR (NK)	**1992-12 Hayashikane Dockyard Co Ltd — Nagasaki NS** Yd No: 1000 Loa 113.95 (BB) Br ex 18.40 Dght 7.914 Lbp 108.00 Br md 18.40 Dpth 9.80 Welded, 1 dk	**(A12B2TR) Chemical/Products Tanker** Double Hull (13F) Liq: 6,502; Liq (Oil): 13,004 Cargo Heating Coils Compartments: 4 Ta, ER 4 Cargo Pump (s): 4x300m³/hr Manifold: Bow/CM: 58.6m	**1 oil engine** driving 1 FP propeller Total Power: 3,354kW (4,560hp) 13.0kn B&W 6L35MC 1 x 2 Stroke 6 Cy. 350 x 1050 3354kW (4560bhp) Hitachi Zosen Corp-Japan AuxGen: 3 x 360kW 445V a.c Fuel: 86.0 (d.f.) 540.0 (r.f.)
9012173 *DSQR2* -	**SAEHAN DREAMSTAR** *ex* Osm Encore *-2010* *ex* Sun Geranium *-2009* *ex* Sun Asia *-2007* *ex* Sun Melody *-2003* *ex* Fukushin *-2003* **Saehan Marine Co Ltd** SM Management Co Ltd *Jeju* *South Korea* MMSI: 441676000 Official number: JJR-101845	**4,976** 2,929 8,789 T/cm 17.4	Class: KR (NK)	**1991-04 Hayashikane Dockyard Co Ltd — Nagasaki NS** Yd No: 985 Loa 113.95 (BB) Br ex 18.80 Dght 7.914 Lbp 108.00 Br md 18.40 Dpth 9.80 Welded, 1 dk	**(A12A2TC) Chemical Tanker** Double Hull (13F) Liq: 8,051 Cargo Heating Coils Compartments: 8 Ta, 12 Wing Ta 20 Cargo Pump (s): 8x300m³/hr, 12x150m³/hr Manifold: Bow/CM: 60.8m	**1 oil engine** driving 1 FP propeller Total Power: 3,354kW (4,560hp) 13.0kn B&W 6L35MC 1 x 2 Stroke 6 Cy. 350 x 1050 3354kW (4560bhp) Hitachi Zosen Corp-Japan Fuel: 100.0 (d.f.) 572.0 (r.f.)
9203332 *3FEU4* -	**SAEHAN ESTRELLA** *ex* Hermia *-2012* **SMC Estrella SA** SM Management Co Ltd *Panama* *Panama* MMSI: 373424000 Official number: 4415412	**7,375** 3,632 11,914 T/cm 21.2	Class: KR (NK)	**1999-03 Miyoshi Shipbuilding Co Ltd — Uwajima EH** Yd No: 350 Loa 131.00 (BB) Br ex 19.63 Dght 8.651 Lbp 122.00 Br md 19.60 Dpth 11.00 Welded, 1 dk	**(A12B2TR) Chemical/Products Tanker** Double Hull (13F) Liq: 11,699; Liq (Oil): 12,441 Cargo Heating Coils Compartments: 22 Wing Ta (s.stl), 2 Wing Slop Ta (s.stl), ER 22 Cargo Pump (s): 22x200m³/hr Manifold: Bow/CM: 66m	**1 oil engine** driving 1 FP propeller Total Power: 4,891kW (6,650hp) 14.2kn B&W 7S35MC 1 x 2 Stroke 7 Cy. 350 x 1400 4891kW (6650bhp) Makita Corp-Japan AuxGen: 3 x 360kW 450V 60Hz a.c Thrusters: 1 Tunnel thruster (f) Fuel: 96.0 (d.f.) 829.0 (r.f.)
9246944 *H9UK* -	**SAEHAN FREESIA** *ex* Eastern Honesty *-2013* **SMC Freesia SA** Saehan Marine (Operation) Co Ltd *Panama* *Panama* MMSI: 354154000 Official number: 30160PEXT3	**5,372** 2,621 8,719 T/cm 17.5	Class: KR (NK)	**2002-02 Shin Kurushima Dockyard Co. Ltd. — Hashihama, Imabari** Yd No: 5151 Loa 113.98 (BB) Br ex 18.20 Dght 7.478 Lbp 108.50 Br md 18.20 Dpth 9.65 Welded, 1 dk	**(A12B2TR) Chemical/Products Tanker** Double Hull (13F) Liq: 8,568; Liq (Oil): 9,173 Compartments: 18 Ta (s.stl), ER 18 Cargo Pump (s): 18x200m³/hr Manifold: Bow/CM: 57.5m	**1 oil engine** driving 1 FP propeller Total Power: 3,901kW (5,304hp) 13.7kn B&W 6L35MC 1 x 2 Stroke 6 Cy. 350 x 1050 3901kW (5304bhp) Makita Corp-Japan AuxGen: 2 x 450kW Thrusters: 1 Tunnel thruster (f) Fuel: 92.0 (d.f.) 463.0 (r.f.)
8915316 *DSNE4* -	**SAEHAN GALAXY** *ex* Eka Pratama *-2003* *ex* Neo Avante *-1995* **Saehan Marine Gas Co Ltd** SM Management Co Ltd *Jeju* *South Korea* MMSI: 441315000 Official number: JJR-038903	**2,810** 845 3,336 T/cm 11.1	Class: KR (NK)	**1990-01 Shin Kurushima Dockyard Co. Ltd. — Akitsu** Yd No: 2662 Loa 91.90 (BB) Br ex - Dght 5.300 Lbp 85.08 Br md 15.40 Dpth 7.00 Welded, 1 dk	**(A11B2TG) LPG Tanker** Double Bottom Entire Compartment Length Liq (Gas): 2,656 2 x Gas Tank (s); 2 Cargo Pump (s): 2x300m³/hr Manifold: Bow/CM: 42.2m	**1 oil engine** driving 1 FP propeller Total Power: 2,205kW (2,998hp) 13.3kn Hanshin 6EL40 1 x 4 Stroke 6 Cy. 400 x 800 2205kW (2998bhp) The Hanshin Diesel Works Ltd-Japan Fuel: 121.0 (d.f.) 417.0 (r.f.)
9175731 *3FYK9* -	**SAEHAN GLORIA** *ex* Southern Mermaid *-2014* **SMC Gloria SA** Saehan Marine (Operation) Co Ltd *Panama* *Panama* Official number: 45516PEXT	**5,999** 3,306 10,588 T/cm 19.1	Class: KR (NK)	**1997-12 Asakawa Zosen K.K. — Imabari** Yd No: 401 Loa 118.00 (BB) Br ex 19.22 Dght 8.255 Lbp 110.00 Br md 19.20 Dpth 10.40 Welded, 1 dk	**(A12B2TR) Chemical/Products Tanker** Double Hull (13F) Liq: 11,424; Liq (Oil): 10,109 Cargo Heating Coils Compartments: 4 Ta, 16 Wing Ta, ER, 2 Wing Slop Ta 20 Cargo Pump (s): 12x200m³/hr, 8x150m³/hr Manifold: Bow/CM: 53.8m	**1 oil engine** driving 1 FP propeller Total Power: 4,193kW (5,701hp) 13.8kn MAN-B&W 6S35MC 1 x 2 Stroke 6 Cy. 350 x 1400 4193kW (5701bhp) Hitachi Zosen Corp-Japan AuxGen: 3 x 441kW 450V 60Hz a.c Thrusters: 1 Thwart. CP thruster (f) Fuel: 90.0 (d.f.) (Heating Coils) 662.0 (r.f.) 15.2pd
9016698 *DSML2* -	**SAEHAN STELLAR** *ex* Gas Orchis *-2009* *ex* Gas East *-2000* **Saehan Marine Gas Co Ltd** SM Management Co Ltd *Jeju* *South Korea* MMSI: 441723000 Official number: JJR-092201	**3,615** 1,085 3,866 T/cm 13.2	Class: KR (NK)	**1991-06 Shin Kochi Jyuko K.K. — Kochi** Yd No: 7013 Loa 103.02 (BB) Br ex 16.02 Dght 5.318 Lbp 96.00 Br md 16.00 Dpth 7.60 Welded, 1 dk	**(A11B2TG) LPG Tanker** Single Hull Liq (Gas): 3,518 2 x Gas Tank (s); 2 independent (s.stl) cyl horizontal 2 Cargo Pump (s): 2x300m³/hr Manifold: Bow/CM: 47.6m	**1 oil engine** driving 1 FP propeller Total Power: 2,425kW (3,297hp) 13.3kn Hanshin 6EL40 1 x 4 Stroke 6 Cy. 400 x 800 2425kW (3297bhp) The Hanshin Diesel Works Ltd-Japan AuxGen: 2 x 240kW 440V 60Hz a.c Fuel: 128.0 (d.f.) 560.0 (r.f.) 10.5pd
9003627 *DSOI9* -	**SAEHAN SULPHUR** *ex* Yamabishi Maru No. 5 *-2000* **Ocean Rex Korea Co Ltd** SM Management Co Ltd *Incheon* *South Korea* MMSI: 440740000 Official number: ICR-052662	**1,340** 402 1,605	Class: KR (NK)	**1990-06 Imamura Zosen — Kure** Yd No: 311 Loa 72.95 (BB) Br ex - Dght 4.527 Lbp 68.00 Br md 12.00 Dpth 5.60 Welded, 1 dk	**(A12A2LP) Molten Sulphur Tanker** Double Hull Liq: 770 Compartments: 6 Wing Ta, ER 2 Cargo Pump (s): 2x90m³/hr Manifold: Bow/CM: 36.3m	**1 oil engine** driving 1 FP propeller Total Power: 1,471kW (2,000hp) 12.4kn Hanshin 6EL35 1 x 4 Stroke 6 Cy. 350 x 700 1471kW (2000bhp) The Hanshin Diesel Works Ltd-Japan Fuel: 8.0 (d.f.) 170.0

7350636 *9GJC* -	**SAELJON** *ex* Sligo *-2000* **Quaman Co Ltd** - *Takoradi* *Ghana* MMSI: 627030000 Official number: GSR 0030	**224** 67 -		**1974-10 Slippstodin h/f — Akureyri** Yd No: 54 Loa 31.15 Br ex 6.70 Dght - Lbp 28.19 Br md 6.66 Dpth 5.60 Welded, 1 dk	**(B11B2FV) Fishing Vessel**	**1 oil engine** geared to sc. shaft driving 1 FP propeller Total Power: 416kW (566hp) 11.0kn Caterpillar D398TA 1 x Vee 4 Stroke 12 Cy. 159 x 203 416kW (566bhp) Caterpillar Tractor Co-USA
8962266 *TFRH* GK 004	**SAEMUNDUR** *ex* Magnus *-2004* *ex* Steinunn *-2004* *ex* Klaus Hillesoy *-1973* *ex* Myrebuen *-1973* **Stakkavik Ehf** - *Grindavik* *Iceland* MMSI: 251328110 Official number: 1264	**147** 44 -	Class: (NV)	**1968 Rolf Rekdal AS — Tomrefjord** Yd No: 67 Loa 27.86 Br ex - Dght - Lbp - Br md 6.20 Dpth 5.30 Welded, 1 dk	**(B11B2FV) Fishing Vessel**	**1 oil engine** driving 1 FP propeller Total Power: 313kW (426hp) Caterpillar 1 x 4 Stroke 313kW (426bhp) (new engine 1982) Caterpillar Tractor Co-USA
7737030 *D7GA* -	**SAENG MYUNG** *ex* Mugunghwa *-1991* **The Juridical Person of The General Assembly of Presbyterian Church** - *Mokpo* *South Korea* Official number: MPR-772197	*128* 51 -	Class: (KR)	**1977-01 ShinA Shipbuilding Co Ltd — Tongyeong** Loa 29.60 Br ex - Dght - Lbp 26.98 Br md 5.99 Dpth 2.60 Welded, 1 dk	**(B34U2QH) Hospital Vessel**	**1 oil engine** driving 1 FP propeller Total Power: 268kW (364hp) 10.5kn Caterpillar 3408TA 1 x Vee 4 Stroke 8 Cy. 137 x 152 268kW (364bhp) Caterpillar Tractor Co-USA AuxGen: 2 x 16kW 225V a.c
8738902 *DSBJ8* -	**SAENURI** *ex* Dae Won *-2013* *ex* Hua Dan Tuo 2 *-2009* **Rho Jae-Cheong** - *Incheon* *South Korea* MMSI: 440102730 Official number: ICR073066	**497** 149 -		**1999-03 Guangdong New China Shipyard Co Ltd — Dongguan GD** Loa 40.60 Br ex - Dght 3.000 Lbp 37.40 Br md 10.00 Dpth 4.60 Welded, 1 dk	**(B32A2ST) Tug**	**2 oil engines** reduction geared to sc. shafts driving 2 Propellers Total Power: 1,940kW (2,638hp) S.K.L. 8NVD48A-2U 2 x 4 Stroke 8 Cy. 320 x 480 each-970kW (1319bhp) SKL Motoren u. Systemtechnik AG-Magdeburg
9288643 *D8QS* -	**SAENURI** **Government of The Republic of South Korea (Ministry of Education & Human Resources Development)** Mokpo National Maritime University (MMU) *Mokpo* *South Korea* MMSI: 440135000 Official number: MPR-034863	**4,701** 1,410 1,806	Class: KR	**2003-04 Hyundai Heavy Industries Co Ltd — Ulsan** Yd No: P098 Loa 102.74 Br ex 15.62 Dght 5.400 Lbp 94.00 Br md 15.60 Dpth 9.90 Welded	**(B34K2QT) Training Ship**	**1 oil engine** driving 1 FP propeller Total Power: 4,440kW (6,037hp) 16.8kn B&W 6S35MC 1 x 2 Stroke 6 Cy. 350 x 1400 4440kW (6037bhp) Hyundai Heavy Industries Co Ltd-South Korea AuxGen: 4 x 600kW 450V a.c
7713034 *TFPA* -	**SAERUN** *ex* La Reina *-2000* *ex* Hornoy *-1998* **Seatours Ltd (Saeferdir Ehf)** - *Stykkisholmur* *Iceland* MMSI: 251435110 Official number: 2427	**194** - 30	Class: (NV)	**1978-07 Westermoen Hydrofoil AS — Mandal** Yd No: 66 Rebuilt & Lengthened-2000 Loa 28.15 Br ex 9.02 Dght - Lbp 26.12 Br md 9.00 Dpth 2.48 Welded, 1 dk	**(A37B2PS) Passenger Ship** Hull Material: Aluminium Alloy Passengers: unberthed: 150	**2 oil engines** geared to sc. shafts driving 2 FP propellers Total Power: 1,912kW (2,600hp) 26.0kn M.T.U. 12V493TY70 2 x Vee 4 Stroke 12 Cy. 175 x 205 each-956kW (1300bhp) MTU Friedrichshafen GmbH-Friedrichshafen
9384069 *SVAO6* -	**SAETTA** **Nautica Shipmanagement SA** TMS Tankers Ltd *Piraeus* *Greece* MMSI: 240865000 Official number: 11844	**58,418** 32,391 107,023 T/cm 92.0	Class: AB	**2009-02 Shanghai Waigaoqiao Shipbuilding Co Ltd — Shanghai** Yd No: 1083 Loa 243.80 (BB) Br ex 42.34 Dght 15.100 Lbp 233.00 Br md 42.00 Dpth 21.40 Welded, 1 dk	**(A13A2TW) Crude/Oil Products Tanker** Double Hull (13F) Liq: 113,656; Liq (Oil): 118,075 Cargo Heating Coils Compartments: 12 Wing Ta, 2 Wing Slop Ta, ER 3 Cargo Pump (s): 3x2800m³/hr Manifold: Bow/CM: 121.7m	**1 oil engine** driving 1 FP propeller Total Power: 13,560kW (18,436hp) 15.0kn MAN-B&W 6S60MC-C 1 x 2 Stroke 6 Cy. 600 x 2400 13560kW (18436bhp) Hudong Heavy Machinery Co Ltd-China AuxGen: 3 x 800kW a.c Fuel: 230.0 (d.f.) 2740.0 (r.f.)
8653657 - -	**SAETTIA** **Government of The Republic of Italy (Comando Generale del Corpo della Capitaneria di Porto)** - *Italy*	**550** 302 -		**1985-12 Fincantieri-Cant. Nav. Italiani S.p.A. — La Spezia** Converted From: Attack Vessel, Naval-1999 Loa 53.05 Br ex - Dght - Lbp 47.20 Br md 8.10 Dpth 5.40 Welded, 1 dk	**(B34H2SQ) Patrol Vessel**	**4 oil engines** reduction geared to sc. shafts driving 4 CP propellers M.T.U. 16V538TB93 4 x Vee 4 Stroke 16 Cy. 185 x 200 MTU Friedrichshafen GmbH-Friedrichshafen
9207950 *TFHM* -	**SAEVAR** **Government of The Republic of Iceland (The Icelandic Directorate of Roads) (Vegagerdin)** Eyfar Ehf *Hrisey* *Iceland* MMSI: 251006110 Official number: 2378	*149* 45 139	Class: (LR) ✠ Classed LR until 8/1/10	**2001-04 'Crist' Sp z oo — Gdansk** (Hull) **2001-04 Stalsmidjan h/f — Reykjavik** Yd No: 10 Loa 22.70 Br ex - Dght 1.800 Lbp 20.00 Br md 6.70 Dpth 2.40 Welded	**(A37B2PS) Passenger Ship**	**2 oil engines** reduction geared to sc. shafts driving 2 Directional propellers Total Power: 596kW (810hp) 11.0kn Cummins N14-M 2 x 4 Stroke 6 Cy. 140 x 152 each-298kW (405bhp) Cummins Engine Co Inc-USA AuxGen: 2 x 52kW 230V 50Hz a.c Thrusters: 1 Thwart. FP thruster (f)
7383035 *TFQN* SF 107	**SAEVIK** *ex* Hafursey *-2013* *ex* Steinunn *-2012* *ex* Arney *-2012* *ex* Asborg *-1993* *ex* Skardsvik *-1992* **Thorus Ehf** - *Grindavik* *Iceland* MMSI: 251295110 Official number: 1416	**475** 142 406	Class: (NV)	**1975-03 Batservice Verft AS — Mandal** Yd No: 619 Loa 43.57 Br ex 8.31 Dght - Lbp 37.62 Br md 8.21 Dpth 6.07 Welded, 2 dks	**(B11A2FT) Trawler** Ice Capable	**1 oil engine** driving 1 FP propeller Total Power: 919kW (1,249hp) Wichmann 5AXA 1 x 2 Stroke 5 Cy. 300 x 450 919kW (1249bhp) Wichmann Motorfabrikk AS-Norway AuxGen: 1 x 200kW 380V 50Hz a.c, 1 x 104kW 380V 50Hz a.c Thrusters: 1 Thwart. FP thruster (f); 1 Tunnel thruster (a)
9227431 *LCFI* M-72-HO	**SAEVIKSON** *ex* Saevikson 1 *-2010* *ex* Stromnes *-2008* *ex* Senior *-2004* **Saevikson AS** - SatCom: Inmarsat C 425809510 *Fosnavaag* *Norway* MMSI: 258095000	**1,211** 363 -	Class: NV	**2000-06 RO Brodogradiliste Novi Sad — Novi Sad** (Hull) **2000-06 Fitjar Mek. Verksted AS — Fitjar** Yd No: 16 Loa 61.75 Br ex - Dght 6.000 Lbp 55.00 Br md 11.60 Dpth 7.00 Welded, 1 dk	**(B11B2FV) Fishing Vessel** Ins: 1,050	**1 oil engine** geared to sc. shaft driving 1 FP propeller Total Power: 2,940kW (3,997hp) MAN-B&W 12V28/32A 1 x Vee 4 Stroke 12 Cy. 280 x 320 2940kW (3997bhp) MAN B&W Diesel A/S-Denmark AuxGen: 1 x 435kW a.c Thrusters: 1 Thwart. FP thruster (f); 1 Tunnel thruster (a)
7830076 *D8YL* -	**SAEYANG No. 7** *ex* Taeyang *-1993* *ex* Dae Myung *-1987* *ex* Chemicarry No. 16 *-1982* *ex* Koka Maru *-1976* **Shin Yong Mun & One Other** - *Busan* *South Korea* Official number: BSR-675655	*433* 195 570	Class: (KR)	**1967 Daiko Dockyard Co. Ltd. — Osaka** Yd No: 53 Loa 49.31 Br ex - Dght 3.591 Lbp 45.01 Br md 8.01 Dpth 3.81 Welded, 1 dk	**(A12A2TC) Chemical Tanker** Liq: 301	**1 oil engine** driving 1 FP propeller Total Power: 552kW (750hp) 9.5kn Niigata 6MG25AX 1 x 4 Stroke 6 Cy. 250 x 320 552kW (750bhp) Niigata Engineering Co Ltd-Japan AuxGen: 2 x 50kW
8888161 - -	**SAFA** *ex* Al Aber *-2008* *ex* Belait Kingfisher *-2005* *ex* Sanergy Jentayu *-2000* *ex* Tarsisia *-1997* **Island Pearl Shipping & Cargo LLC**	**368** 110 740		**1995-07 Wonsan Shipyard — Wonsan** L reg 56.60 Br ex - Dght - Lbp - Br md 10.80 Dpth 2.60 Welded, 1 dk	**(B34L2QU) Utility Vessel**	**2 oil engines** driving 2 FP propellers Total Power: 464kW (630hp) 10.0kn Russkiy 2 x each-232kW (315bhp) Mashinostroitelnyy Zavod"Russkiy-Dizel"-Sankt-Peterburg
5252567 - -	**SAFA 1** *ex* Gal Oya *-2009* *ex* Nilwala *-2006* **Alco Shipping Services LLC** -	**405** 139 610	Class: (LR) ✠ Classed LR until 18/3/08	**1958-10 Clelands (Successors) Ltd. — Wallsend** Yd No: 233 Converted From: Water Tanker-2007 Converted From: Oil Tanker-2006 Loa 45.52 Br ex 8.97 Dght 3.734 Lbp 42.83 Br md 8.54 Dpth 4.27 Welded, 1 dk	**(A13B2TU) Tanker (unspecified)** Compartments: 6 Ta, ER 2 Cargo Pump (s): 2x130m³/hr Manifold: Bow/CM: 21m	**2 oil engines** sr reverse geared to sc. shafts driving 2 FP propellers Total Power: 354kW (482hp) G.M. (Detroit Diesel) 8V-71 2 x Vee 2 Stroke 8 Cy. 108 x 127 each-177kW (241bhp) (new engine 1985) General Motors Corp-USA AuxGen: 2 x 30kW 110V d.c
9387401 - -	**SAFA 1** *ex* Safa *-2006* **Government of The Arab Republic of Egypt (Ministry of Maritime Transport - Ports & Lighthouses Administration)** - *Suez* *Egypt*	*318* 173 304	Class: (AB)	**2006-03 Moss Point Marine, Inc. — Escatawpa, Ms** Yd No: 1959 Loa - Br ex - Dght 5.180 Lbp 29.26 Br md 10.97 Dpth 4.03 Welded, 1 dk	**(B32A2ST) Tug**	**2 oil engines** reduction geared to sc. shafts driving 2 Voith-Schneider propellers Total Power: 3,300kW (4,486hp) 12.5kn Wartsila 9L20C 2 x 4 Stroke 9 Cy. 200 x 280 each-1650kW (2243bhp) Wartsila Finland Oy-Finland AuxGen: 2 x 75kW a.c

IMO / Call sign	Name / Owner	Tonnage	Class	Build / Dimensions	Type	Machinery
7004732 *CUJV* -	**SAFADO** *ex* Monte Da Luz **Lutamar-Prestacao de Servicos a Navegacao Lda** - *Lisbon* *Portugal* Official number: LX-101-RL	*123* 13 24	Class: (LR) ✠ Classed LR until 15/4/76	**1969**-12 **Soc. Argibay de Const. Navais e Mecanicas S.A.R.L. — Alverca** Yd No: 124 Loa 25.76 Br ex 7.42 Dght - Lbp 25.00 Br md 7.19 Dpth 3.00 Welded, 1 dk	**(B32A2ST) Tug**	**2 oil engines** driving 2 Voith-Schneider propellers Total Power: 1,192kW (1,620hp) 11.5kn Deutz RBA8M528 2 x 4 Stroke 8 Cy. 220 x 280 each-596kW (810bhp) Kloeckner Humboldt Deutz AG-West Germany AuxGen: 2 x 26kW 380V 50Hz a.c, 1 x 8kW 380V 50Hz a.c Fuel: 17.5 (d.f.)
7529445 *HZG5547* -	**SAFANIYA 3** **Saudi Arabian Oil Co (SAUDI ARAMCO)** - *Dammam* *Saudi Arabia* MMSI: 403700610 Official number: 223/402	*768* 358 836	Class: AB	**1976**-11 **Vosper Thornycroft Pte Ltd — Singapore** Yd No: B.970 Loa 56.11 Br ex 11.61 Dght 3.074 Lbp 52.61 Br md 11.43 Dpth 3.43 Welded, 1 dk	**(B22D2OZ) Production Testing Vessel**	**2 oil engines** reverse reduction geared to sc. shafts driving 2 FP propellers Total Power: 1,214kW (1,650hp) 11.5kn Caterpillar D398SCAC 2 x Vee 4 Stroke 12 Cy. 159 x 203 each-607kW (825bhp) Caterpillar Tractor Co-USA AuxGen: 2 x 210kW a.c, 1 x 40kW a.c
7625366 *HZG5565* -	**SAFANIYA 4** **Saudi Arabian Oil Co (SAUDI ARAMCO)** - *Dammam* *Saudi Arabia* MMSI: 403700710 Official number: 224/402	*773* 426 836	Class: AB	**1977**-05 **B.V. Scheepswerven v/h H.H. Bodewes — Millingen a/d Rijn** Yd No: 737 Loa 56.82 Br ex - Dght 2.671 Lbp 53.40 Br md 11.43 Dpth 3.36 Welded, 1 dk	**(B22D2OZ) Production Testing Vessel**	**2 oil engines** reverse reduction geared to sc. shafts driving 2 FP propellers Total Power: 1,250kW (1,700hp) Caterpillar D398SCAC 2 x Vee 4 Stroke 12 Cy. 159 x 203 each-625kW (850bhp) Caterpillar Tractor Co-USA AuxGen: 2 x 204kW a.c, 1 x 55kW a.c Thrusters: 1 Thwart. FP thruster (f)
8023797 *HZG5560* -	**SAFANIYA 5** **Saudi Arabian Oil Co (SAUDI ARAMCO)** - *Dammam* *Saudi Arabia* MMSI: 403700810 Official number: 829/404	*448* 141 965	Class: AB	**1981**-08 **Halter Marine, Inc. — New Orleans, La** Yd No: 946 Loa 55.00 Br ex 12.40 Dght 3.664 Lbp 54.87 Br md 12.20 Dpth 4.27 Welded, 1 dk	**(B34L2QU) Utility Vessel**	**2 oil engines** with clutches & sr reverse geared to sc. shafts driving 2 FP propellers Total Power: 1,654kW (2,248hp) 12.0kn Caterpillar D399SCAC 2 x Vee 4 Stroke 16 Cy. 159 x 203 each-827kW (1124bhp) Caterpillar Tractor Co-USA AuxGen: 2 x 300kW 440V 60Hz a.c Thrusters: 1 Thwart. FP thruster (f) Fuel: 328.5 (d.f.) 11.0pd
8205395 *HZG5552* -	**SAFANIYA 6** **Saudi Arabian Oil Co (SAUDI ARAMCO)** - *Dammam* *Saudi Arabia* MMSI: 403700910 Official number: 631/403	*1,301* 390 1,500	Class: AB	**1983**-06 **B.V. Scheepswerf Jonker & Stans — Hendrik-Ido-Ambacht** Yd No: 362 Loa 61.19 Br ex 13.80 Dght 3.950 Lbp 57.99 Br md 13.50 Dpth 4.60 Welded, 1 dk	**(B22A2OR) Offshore Support Vessel**	**2 oil engines** with clutches, flexible couplings & sr reverse geared to sc. shafts driving 2 FP propellers Total Power: 2,060kW (2,800hp) 12.0kn EMD (Electro-Motive) 12-645-E6 2 x Vee 2 Stroke 12 Cy. 230 x 254 each-1030kW (1400bhp) General Motors Corp.Electro-Motive Div.-La Grange AuxGen: 3 x 300kW 480V 60Hz a.c Thrusters: 1 Thwart. CP thruster (f) Fuel: 170.0 (d.f.)
9102277 *C6OO2* -	**SAFANIYAH** **The National Shipping Company of Saudi Arabia (BAHRI)** Mideast Ship Management Ltd SatCom: Inmarsat Mini-M 764631849 *Nassau* *Bahamas* MMSI: 309774000 Official number: 729582	**163,882** 97,415 300,361 T/cm 171.9	Class: LR ✠ **100A1** SS 01/2012 Double Hull oil tanker ESP *IWS SPM **ShipRight** (SDA, FDA, CM) ✠ **LMC** **UMS IGS** Eq.Ltr: F*; Cable: 770.0/122.0 U3 (a)	**1997**-01 **Mitsubishi Heavy Industries Ltd. — Nagasaki** Yd No: 2097 Loa 340.00 (BB) Br ex 56.05 Dght 22.528 Lbp 328.89 Br md 56.00 Dpth 31.80 Welded, 1 dk	**(A13A2TV) Crude Oil Tanker** Double Hull (13F) Liq: 333,213; Liq (Oil): 333,213 Compartments: 5 Ta, 10 Wing Ta, ER, 2 Wing Slop Ta 4 Cargo Pump (s): 3x5000m³/hr, 1x2750m³/hr Manifold: Bow/CM: 168.5m	**1 oil engine** driving 1 FP propeller Total Power: 24,713kW (33,600hp) 15.0kn Mitsubishi 7UEC85LSII 1 x 2 Stroke 7 Cy. 850 x 3150 24713kW (33600bhp) Mitsubishi Heavy Industries Ltd-Japan AuxGen: 1 x 1000kW 450V a.c, 3 x 1050kW 450V a.c Boilers: 2 AuxB (o.f.) 21.9kgf/cm² (21.5bar), AuxB (ex.g.) 12.0kgf/cm² (11.8bar) Fuel: 356.0 (d.f.) (Heating Coils) 6840.4 (r.f.) 95.0pd
8874859 *UBTT* -	**SAFAR** *ex* Feniks *-2005* *ex* Modisk 5 *-2004* *ex* El Saged *-2003* *ex* Nin *-2001* *ex* Yekaterinburg *-2000* *ex* Kazym *-2000* **Primol Shipping International Corp** Astrakhan Shipping Agency Ltd (ASA Ltd) SatCom: Inmarsat C 427352087 *Astrakhan* *Russia* MMSI: 273447720	**1,696** 715 2,187	Class: (RS)	**1979**-06 **VEB Elbewerften Boizenburg/Rosslau — Rosslau** Yd No: 3422 Loa 82.00 Br ex 11.82 Dght 3.350 Lbp 78.11 Br md 11.61 Dpth 4.00 Welded, 1 dk	**(A31A2GX) General Cargo Ship** TEU 70 C.Ho 34/20' C.Dk 36/20' Compartments: 2 Ho, ER 2 Ha: ER	**2 oil engines** geared to sc. shafts driving 2 FP propellers Total Power: 882kW (1,200hp) S.K.L. 8VD36/24A-1 2 x 4 Stroke 8 Cy. 240 x 360 each-441kW (600bhp) VEB Schwermaschinenbau "KarlLiebknecht" (SKL)-Magdeburg
5151050 - -	**SAFARI** *ex* Fast Ferry I *-1998* *ex* Hinnoy *-1993* **Africa Shipping Corp** - *Tanzania*	*384* 124 -	Class: (BV) (NV)	**1960 Bodo Skipsverft & Mek. Verksted AS — Bodo** Yd No: 29 Loa 47.81 Br ex 9.73 Dght 3.750 Lbp 42.02 Br md - Dpth 4.09 Welded, 1 dk	**(A36A2PR) Passenger/Ro-Ro Ship (Vehicles)** Passengers: unberthed: 234 Bow door/ramp Cars: 30, Trailers: 2 Compartments: 1 Ho, ER 1 Ha: (1.8 x 1.9) Derricks: 1x2t; Winches: 1	**1 oil engine** driving 1 FP propeller Total Power: 706kW (960hp) 12.0kn Alpha 498R 1 x 2 Stroke 8 Cy. 290 x 490 706kW (960bhp) Alpha Diesel A/S-Denmark AuxGen: 2 x 20kW 220V a.c Fuel: 30.5 (d.f.) 4.0pd
9093402 *YD6934* -	**SAFARI 01** **PT Safari Samudra Raya** - *Samarinda* *Indonesia*	**164** 50 -	Class: KI	**2006**-01 **C.V. Karya Lestari Industri — Samarinda** Loa 26.50 Br ex - Dght - Lbp 22.94 Br md 9.00 Dpth 4.25 Welded, 1 dk	**(B32A2ST) Tug**	**2 oil engines** geared to sc. shafts driving 2 Propellers Total Power: 889kW (1,209hp) Caterpillar 3412C 2 x Vee 4 Stroke 12 Cy. 137 x 152 each-441kW (600bhp) Caterpillar Inc-USA
8737207 *YDA6160* -	**SAFARI 02** **PT Safari Samudra Raya** - *Banjarmasin* *Indonesia*	**141** 43 -	Class: KI	**2008**-09 **PT Muji Rahayu Shipyard — Tenggarong** Loa 24.00 Br ex - Dght 3.200 Lbp 22.00 Br md 7.00 Dpth 3.20 Welded, 1 dk	**(B32A2ST) Tug**	**2 oil engines** driving 2 Propellers Total Power: 970kW (1,318hp) Yanmar 6AYM-STE 2 x 4 Stroke 6 Cy. 155 x 180 each-485kW (659bhp) Yanmar Diesel Engine Co Ltd-Japan
9558505 *YDA6298* -	**SAFARI 03** *ex* Sapor S15/2007 *-2009* **PT Safari Samudra Raya** - *Banjarmasin* *Indonesia*	**154** 47 -	Class: KI (BV)	**2009**-03 **Sapor Shipbuilding Industries Sdn Bhd — Sibu** Yd No: S15/2007 Loa 23.90 Br ex - Dght 3.500 Lbp 22.50 Br md 7.30 Dpth 3.50 Welded, 1 dk	**(B32A2ST) Tug**	**2 oil engines** reduction geared to sc. shaft driving 2 FP propellers Total Power: 970kW (1,318hp) Yanmar 6AYM-STE 2 x 4 Stroke 6 Cy. 155 x 180 each-485kW (659bhp) Yanmar Diesel Engine Co Ltd-Japan AuxGen: 2 x 26kW 50Hz a.c Fuel: 90.0 (d.f.)
9593737 *YDA6564* -	**SAFARI 05** **PT Safari Samudra Raya** - *Banjarmasin* *Indonesia*	**294** 93 313	Class: KI (BV)	**2010**-08 **Sapor Shipbuilding Industries Sdn Bhd — Sibu** Yd No: SAPOR 32 Loa 31.20 Br ex - Dght 3.800 Lbp 29.76 Br md 9.00 Dpth 4.60 Welded, 1 dk	**(B32A2ST) Tug**	**2 oil engines** geared to sc. shafts driving 2 FP propellers Total Power: 1,472kW (2,002hp) Yanmar 6RY17P-GV 2 x 4 Stroke 6 Cy. 165 x 219 each-736kW (1001bhp) Yanmar Diesel Engine Co Ltd-Japan AuxGen: 2 x 80kW a.c
8963698 *WDG2742* -	**SAFARI ENDEAVOUR** *ex* Spirit of Endeavour *-2011* *ex* Seaspirit *-1992* *ex* Newport Clipper *-1992* **Sea Lodge IV LLC** Innersea Discoveries LLC (Un-Cruise Adventures) *Juneau, AK* *United States of America* MMSI: 338423000 Official number: 661485	**1,425** 511 -	Class: (AB)	**1983**-09 **Jeffboat, Inc. — Jeffersonville, In** Yd No: 82-2542 Loa 66.14 (BB) Br ex - Dght 2.560 Lbp 56.17 Br md 11.27 Dpth 3.50 Welded, 1 dk	**(A37A2PC) Passenger/Cruise** Passengers: cabins: 51; berths: 107	**2 oil engines** reverse reduction geared to sc. shafts driving 2 FP propellers Total Power: 2,206kW (3,000hp) 13.0kn Caterpillar 3512B-HD 2 x Vee 4 Stroke 12 Cy. 170 x 215 each-1103kW (1500bhp) Caterpillar Tractor Co-USA AuxGen: 2 x 350kW a.c Fuel: 115.0 (d.f.)
8964654 *WCY5674* -	**SAFARI EXPLORER** *ex* Rapture *-2009* **Safari Explorer Charters LLC** Innersea Discoveries LLC (Un-Cruise Adventures) *Juneau, AK* *United States of America* MMSI: 366339000 Official number: 1069513	**695** 213 -		**1998**-08 **Freeport Shipbuilding & Marine Repair, Inc. — Freeport, Fl** Yd No: 151 Converted From: Research Vessel-1998 Loa 38.70 Br ex - Dght - Lbp 38.60 Br md 10.97 Dpth 2.13 Welded, 1 dk	**(A37B2PS) Passenger Ship**	**2 oil engines** driving 2 FP propellers Total Power: 1,030kW (1,400hp) Lugger 2 x 4 Stroke each-515kW (700bhp)
8963753 *HKJC6* -	**SAFARI VOYAGER** *ex* Sea Voyager *-2013* *ex* Temptress Voyager *-2002* *ex* America *-2002* **Mukilteo Maritime Contractors LLC** Innersea Discoveries LLC (Un-Cruise Adventures) *Cartagena de Indias* *Colombia* MMSI: 730151012	**1,195** 762 -		**1982 Chesapeake Marine Railway Co. — Baltimore, Md** Yd No: 32 Loa 51.87 Br ex - Dght - Lbp 51.87 Br md 10.97 Dpth 3.64 Welded, 1 dk	**(A37A2PC) Passenger/Cruise** Passengers: cabins: 33; berths: 60	**2 oil engines** reduction geared to sc. shaft (s) driving 2 FP propellers Total Power: 698kW (950hp) 12.0kn Caterpillar 3408TA 2 x Vee 4 Stroke 8 Cy. 137 x 152 each-349kW (475bhp) Caterpillar Tractor Co-USA

Ship	Tonnage	Class	Build	Type	Machinery
8758823 **SAFE BRITANNIA** *9VKB7* *ex* Safe Concordia *-1987* - **Prosafe Rigs Pte Ltd** Prosafe Offshore Pte Ltd *Singapore* *Singapore* MMSI: 565082000 Official number: 391891	**23,684** 7,106 -	Class: NV	**1980-01 Gotaverken Arendal AB — Goteborg** Yd No: 911 Loa 120.80 Br ex 73.65 Dght 11.900 Lbp - Br md - Dpth 33.80 Welded, 1 dk	**(Z11C3ZA) Accommodation Platform, semi submersible** Passengers: berths: 748 Cranes: 1x50t,1x40t	**1 oil engine** driving 1 Propeller
8664333 **SAFE CAT** *VWKU* - **Marine Traders Pvt Ltd** - *Mumbai* *India* MMSI: 419017400 Official number: 2818	**195** 59 -		**2000-11 Alang Marine Ltd — Bhavnagar** Yd No: 516 Loa 22.35 Br ex - Dght - Lbp - Br md 12.00 Dpth 3.00 Welded, 1 dk	**(A37B2PS) Passenger Ship**	**2 oil engines** reduction geared to sc. shafts driving 2 Propellers Total Power: 242kW (330hp) Cummins N-743-M 2 x 4 Stroke 6 Cy. 130 x 152 each-121kW (165bhp) Cummins India Ltd-India
8768127 **SAFE CONCORDIA** *9VMH2* - **Prosafe Rigs Pte Ltd** Prosafe Offshore Pte Ltd *Singapore* *Singapore* MMSI: 565295000 Official number: 392509	**16,700** 5,010 -	Class: AB	**2005-03 Keppel FELS Ltd — Singapore** Yd No: B261 Loa 99.97 Br ex 45.11 Dght 5.940 Lbp - Br md - Dpth 20.11 Welded, 1 dk	**(Z11C3ZA) Accommodation Platform, semi submersible** Cranes: 1x120t,1x40t	**5 diesel electric oil engines** driving 5 gen. each 3610kW 6300V a.c Connecting to 4 elec. motors each (2500kW) driving 4 Directional propellers Total Power: 18,600kW (25,290hp) Wartsila 12V26 5 x Vee 4 Stroke 12 Cy. 260 x 320 each-3720kW (5058bhp) Wartsila France SA-France
1003592 **SAFE CONDUCT** - - **Ritco Ltd** -	*137* 96 -	Class: (LR) ✠ Classed LR until 17/6/98	**1987-11 Cant. Nav. Picchiotti SpA — Viareggio** Loa 22.35 Br ex 5.80 Dght 2.100 Lbp 19.00 Br md - Dpth 3.30 Welded, 1 dk	**(X11A2YP) Yacht**	**2 oil engines** geared to sc. shafts driving 2 FP propellers Total Power: 250kW (340hp) Gardner 8LXB 2 x 4 Stroke 8 Cy. 121 x 152 each-125kW (170bhp) L. Gardner & Sons Ltd.-Manchester
9189859 **SAFE GAS** *D7LI* *ex* Buena Estela *-2013* **Myung Shin Shipping Co Ltd** - *Ulsan* *South Korea* MMSI: 440145900 Official number: USR-134805	**2,954** 950 3,192 T/cm 11.2	Class: KR (NK)	**1998-11 Kanrei Zosen K.K. — Naruto** Yd No: 382 Loa 96.00 (BB) Br ex 15.00 Dght 5.513 Lbp 89.50 Br md 15.00 Dpth 7.00 Welded, 1 dk	**(A11B2TG) LPG Tanker** Double Bottom Entire, Double Sides Partial Liq (Gas): 3,513 2 x Gas Tank (s); independent 4 Cargo Pump (s): 4x190m³/hr Manifold: Bow/CM: 44.7m	**1 oil engine** driving 1 FP propeller Total Power: 2,405kW (3,270hp) 13.2kn B&W 6S26MC 1 x 2 Stroke 6 Cy. 260 x 980 2405kW (3270bhp) Makita Corp-Japan Fuel: 100.0 (d.f.) 376.0 (r.f.)
8759176 **SAFE HIBERNIA** *V7IS8* *ex* Polyconcord *-2002* *ex* Treasure Finder *-1991* - **Prosafe Rigs Pte Ltd** Cotemar SA de CV *Majuro* *Marshall Islands* MMSI: 538002445 Official number: 2445	**15,719** 4,716 9,142	Class: NV	**1977-01 Rauma-Repola Oy — Pori** Yd No: 9 Converted From: Drilling Rig, Semi-submersible-1979 Loa 108.20 Br ex 67.36 Dght 21.340 Lbp - Br md - Dpth 36.58 Welded, 1 dk	**(Z11C3ZA) Accommodation Platform, semi submersible** Cranes: 1x40t,1x25t	**4 diesel electric oil engines** driving 4 gen. each 1600kW 600V a.c 1 gen. of 400kW 440V a.c Connecting to 4 elec. motors each (1250kW) driving 2 FP propellers Bergens KVGB-12 4 x Vee 4 Stroke 12 Cy. 250 x 300 AS Bergens Mek Verksteder-Norway
8218328 **SAFE LANCIA** *9VKB9* - **Prosafe Rigs Pte Ltd** Prosafe Offshore Pte Ltd *Singapore* *Singapore* MMSI: 565084000 Official number: 391893	**13,002** 3,900 -	Class: LR ✠ **OU100A1** SS 03/2012 Survival condition- Max. wave heigh t 30 m , Max. draught 15.8 m, Max. wind speed 51.5 m/sec, Current 1 m/ sec Operating condition- Max. wave heig ht 17 m, Max. draught 19.4 m, Max. wind speed 23.3 m/sec, Current 0.77 m/sec Transit condition- Max. wave height 8 m, Max. draught 10.7 m, Max. win d speed 21 m/sec, Current 1 m/sec (Draughts measured from underside of thrusters) Min. air temperature -1 5 degree C OIWS ✠ **LMC** **UMS**	**1984-01 Gotaverken Arendal AB — Goteborg** Yd No: 935 Loa 92.37 Br ex 65.40 Dght - Lbp - Br md - Dpth - Welded, 1 dk	**(Z11C3ZA) Accommodation Platform, semi submersible** Cranes: 1x50t,1x25t	**5 diesel electric oil engines** driving 2 gen. each 3200kW 6300V a.c 1 gen. of 2100kW 450V a.c 2 gen. each 2900kW 6300V a.c driving 4 Directional propellers Total Power: 14,300kW (19,443hp) Nohab F312V 1 x Vee 4 Stroke 12 Cy. 250 x 300 2100kW (2855bhp) Nohab Diesel AB-Sweden Nohab F316A 2 x Vee 4 Stroke 16 Cy. 250 x 300 each-2900kW (3943bhp) Nohab Diesel AB-Sweden Nohab F316V 2 x Vee 4 Stroke 16 Cy. 250 x 300 each-3200kW (4351bhp) Nohab Diesel AB-Sweden AuxGen: 1 x 2100kW 450V a.c, 2 x 2800kW 6300V a.c, 1 x 200kW 440V a.c Thrusters: 4 Directional thruster (centre) Fuel: 1580.0
8898386 **SAFE OCEAN** *H05583* *ex* Wei Hai Wei *-2008* - **Weihai Safe Ocean Co Ltd** - *Panama* *Panama* MMSI: 370599000 Official number: 37920PEXTF1	**1,528** 895 2,419	Class: CC	**1995-05 Shandong Weihai Shipyard — Weihai SD** Loa 73.80 Br ex - Dght 5.110 Lbp 68.00 Br md 12.80 Dpth 6.20 Welded, 1 dk	**(A31A2GX) General Cargo Ship**	**1 oil engine** reduction geared to sc. shaft driving 1 FP propeller Total Power: 509kW (692hp) 10.0kn Chinese Std. Type LB6250ZLC 1 x 4 Stroke 6 Cy. 250 x 320 509kW (692bhp) Zibo Diesel Engine Factory-China AuxGen: 2 x 90kW 400V a.c
8408090 **SAFE SAILING** *XUEV3* *ex* Ocean Focus *-2008* *ex* Zhongri No. 1 *-2004* - *ex* Ai Feng Hua *-2004* *ex* Double Glory *-2002* *ex* Calbee Potato Maru *-1999* **Tian Hong Shipping Co Ltd** Yantai Shunsheng International Shipping Management Co Ltd *Phnom Penh* *Cambodia* MMSI: 515663000 Official number: 0484163	**1,458** 778 1,491	Class: (NK)	**1984-10 K.K. Miura Zosensho — Saiki** Yd No: 716 Loa 78.01 (BB) Br ex - Dght 3.622 Lbp 71.00 Br md 13.01 Dpth 6.51 Welded, 2 dks	**(A31A2GX) General Cargo Ship** Grain: 2,859; Bale: 2,825 Compartments: 1 Ho, ER 1 Ha: (40.8 x 10.5)ER	**1 oil engine** driving 1 FP propeller Total Power: 1,177kW (1,600hp) 11.5kn Niigata 6M31AFTE 1 x 4 Stroke 6 Cy. 310 x 530 1177kW (1600bhp) Niigata Engineering Co Ltd-Japan
8011835 **SAFE SUPPORTER 1** *MLFC3* *ex* Shannon *-2012* *ex* Eldergarth *-1999* - **Equinity Investments Ltd** - *Lowestoft* *United Kingdom* MMSI: 235032612 Official number: 911225	**402** 120 173	Class: LR ✠ **100A1** SS 10/2009 tug ✠ **LMC** Eq.Ltr: G; Cable: 275.0/30.0 U2 (a)	**1981-10 McTay Marine Ltd. — Bromborough** Yd No: 40 Converted From: Tug-2009 Loa 34.27 Br ex 10.06 Dght 3.850 Lbp 30.00 Br md 9.50 Dpth 4.70 Welded, 1 dk	**(B31A2SR) Research Survey Vessel** A-frames: 1	**2 oil engines** gearing integral to driving 2 Z propellers Total Power: 2,354kW (3,200hp) 12.8kn Niigata 8L25BX 2 x 4 Stroke 8 Cy. 250 x 320 each-1177kW (1600bhp) Niigata Engineering Co Ltd-Japan AuxGen: 3 x 80kW 440V 50Hz a.c Fuel: 75.0 (d.f.) 11.0pd
9442718 **SAFE VOYAGER** *3EMI4* - **Chijin Shipping SA** Nippon Yusen Kabushiki Kaisha (NYK Line) *Panama* *Panama* MMSI: 352147000 Official number: 3337208B	**43,158** 27,291 82,514 T/cm 70.2	Class: NV (NK)	**2007-08 Tsuneishi Holdings Corp Tsuneishi Shipbuilding Co — Fukuyama HS** Yd No: 1399 Loa 228.99 Br ex - Dght 14.430 Lbp 222.00 Br md 32.26 Dpth 20.03 Welded, 1 dk	**(A21A2BC) Bulk Carrier** Grain: 97,186 Compartments: 7 Ho, ER 7 Ha: ER	**1 oil engine** driving 1 FP propeller Total Power: 9,800kW (13,324hp) 14.5kn MAN-B&W 7S50MC-C 1 x 2 Stroke 7 Cy. 500 x 2000 9800kW (13324bhp) Mitsui Engineering & Shipbuilding CLtd-Japan AuxGen: 3 x a.c Fuel: 2870.0
8655796 **SAFEER AL HUSEIN** *HP4533* *ex* Al Husine *-2011* - **Abdul Zahra Abdul Hussein Matoori** - *Panama* *Panama* MMSI: 373692000 Official number: 43569PEXT	**486** 240 -		**2006-07 UR-Dock — Basrah** Yd No: 43 Loa 46.00 Br ex 12.60 Dght - Lbp 44.30 Br md 12.40 Dpth 6.45 Welded, 1 dk	**(A31A2GX) General Cargo Ship**	**2 oil engines** reduction geared to sc. shafts driving 2 Propellers Total Power: 710kW (966hp) 9.0kn Yanmar 2 x each-355kW (483bhp) Yanmar Diesel Engine Co Ltd-Japan
9324887 **SAFFARI DJEMA** *FGD5243* - **Mayotte - Conseil General** Service des Transports Maritimes de Mayotte (STM) *Dzaoudzi* *France* MMSI: 660000420 Official number: 909642	**335** 100 50	Class: BV	**2004-07 Societe des Etablissemnets Merre (SEEM) — Nort-sur-Erdre** Yd No: 2007 Loa 49.00 Br ex - Dght 1.700 Lbp 39.50 Br md 10.80 Dpth 3.00 Welded, 1 dk	**(A36A2PR) Passenger/Ro-Ro Ship (Vehicles)** Passengers: unberthed: 110 Cars: 27	**3 diesel electric oil engines** driving 3 gen. each 326kW a.c Connecting to 4 elec. motors each (166kW) driving 4 Water jets 2 propellers aft, 2 fwd. Total Power: 993kW (1,350hp) 9.0kn Baudouin 6M26SR 3 x 4 Stroke 6 Cy. 150 x 150 each-331kW (450bhp) Societe des Moteurs Baudouin SA-France

8417118 *TCUZ* -	**SAFFET BEY** *ex* UND Saffet Bey *-2003* *ex* N. D. S. Atlantic *-1995* *ex* Caracas *-1989* *launched as* Mercandian Pacific II *-1987* **Ulusoy Lojistik Tasimacilik ve Konteyner Hizmetleri AS (Ulusoy Logistic Transportation & Container Services SA)** Ulusoy Ro/Ro Isletmeleri AS (Ulusoy Ro/Ro Management SA) SatCom: Inmarsat C 427111213 *Istanbul* *Turkey* MMSI: 271000419 Official number: 6761	**19,689** 9,257 14,107	Class: LR (NV) **100A1** SS 06/2012 roll on - roll off cargo ship *IWS **LMC** **UMS** Eq.Ltr: H†; Cable: 605.0/62.0 U3 (a)	**1987-06 Danyard A/S — Frederikshavn** Yd No: 421 Loa 163.81 (BB) Br ex - Dght 8.816 Lbp 148.62 Br md 23.51 Dpth 14.20 Welded, 3 dks	**(A35A2RR) Ro-Ro Cargo Ship** Passengers: cabins: 6; driver berths: 12 Stern door/ramp (p. a.) Len: 18.50 Wid: 7.30 Swl: 45 Stern door/ramp (s. a.) Len: 18.50 Wid: 7.30 Swl: 45 Side door/ramp (s) Len: 18.50 Wid: 7.30 Swl: 45 Lane-Len: 2760 Lane-Wid: 7.30 Lane-clr ht: 6.30 Trailers: 197 TEU 765 incl 72 ref C.	**1 oil engine** with flexible couplings & sr gearedto sc. shaft driving 1 CP propeller Total Power: 6,610kW (8,987hp) 17.5kn MaK 6M601AK 1 x 4 Stroke 6 Cy. 580 x 600 6610kW (8987bhp) Krupp MaK Maschinenbau GmbH-Kiel AuxGen: 1 x 1100kW 440V 60Hz a.c, 1 x 745kW 440V 60Hz a.c, 1 x 228kW 440V 60Hz a.c Boilers: AuxB 4.1kgf/cm^2 (4.0bar) Thrusters: 1 Thwart. CP thruster (f); 1 Tunnel thruster (a) Fuel: 28.0 (r.f.)
9293416 *TCCU7* -	**SAFFET ULUSOY** **UN Ro-Ro Isletmeleri AS (UN Ro-Ro Management Inc)** Bluewater Ship Management Ltd *Istanbul* *Turkey* MMSI: 271000747	**29,004** 8,702 11,400	Class: NV	**2005-03 Flensburger Schiffbau-Ges. mbH & Co. KG — Flensburg** Yd No: 726 Loa 193.00 (BB) Br ex 26.04 Dght 6.450 Lbp 182.39 Br md 26.00 Dpth 16.70 Welded, 3 dks	**(A35A2RR) Ro-Ro Cargo Ship** Passengers: driver berths: 12 Stern door/ramp (centre) Len: 15.00 Wid: 17.00 Swl: 120 Lane-Len: 3726 Trailers: 255	**2 oil engines** reduction geared to sc. shafts driving 2 CP propellers Total Power: 16,200kW (22,026hp) 21.5kn MaK 9M43 2 x 4 Stroke 9 Cy. 430 x 610 each-8100kW (11013bhp) Caterpillar Motoren GmbH & Co. KG-Germany AuxGen: 2 x 900kW a.c, 2 x 1600kW a.c Thrusters: 1 Tunnel thruster (f)
9357511 *PHOM* -	**SAFFIER** **Saffier BV** De Bock Maritiem BV *Alkmaar* *Netherlands* MMSI: 245184000 Official number: 51788	**3,970** 2,066 5,800	Class: BV	**2008-04 Barkmeijer Stroobos B.V. — Stroobos** Yd No: 315 Loa 99.99 (BB) Br ex - Dght 6.600 Lbp 94.75 Br md 15.20 Dpth 8.35 Welded, 1 dk	**(A31A2GX) General Cargo Ship** Grain: 7,447 TEU 213 Compartments: 1 Ho, ER 1 Ha: ER (66.2 x 13.0)	**1 oil engine** geared to sc. shaft driving 1 CP propeller Total Power: 2,720kW (3,698hp) 14.0kn MAN-B&W 8L27/38 1 x 4 Stroke 8 Cy. 270 x 380 2720kW (3698bhp) MAN Diesel A/S-Denmark Thrusters: 1 Tunnel thruster (f)
9374428 *A8MI5* -	**SAFFO** **Benton Shipping BV** Marwave Shipmanagement BV *Monrovia* *Liberia* MMSI: 636013345 Official number: 13345	**24,112** 11,118 38,396 T/cm 46.5	Class: RI (AB)	**2008-01 Guangzhou Shipyard International Co Ltd — Guangzhou GD** Yd No: 05130003 Loa 182.86 (BB) Br ex - Dght 11.610 Lbp 174.50 Br md 27.40 Dpth 16.80 Welded, 1 dk	**(A12B2TR) Chemical/Products Tanker** Double Hull (13F) Liq: 37,963; Liq (Oil): 37,963 Cargo Heating Coils Compartments: 10 Wing Ta, 2 Wing Slop Ta, ER 10 Cargo Pump (s): 10x540m^3/hr Manifold: Bow/CM: 89.8m	**1 oil engine** driving 1 FP propeller Total Power: 9,480kW (12,889hp) 14.2kn MAN-B&W 6S50MC-C 1 x 2 Stroke 6 Cy. 500 x 2000 9480kW (12889bhp) Dalian Marine Diesel Works-China AuxGen: 3 x 910kW a.c Thrusters: 1 Tunnel thruster (f)
7108899 *5VBW7* -	**SAFI** *ex* Josefine *-1999* *ex* Mathilde *-1999* *ex* Anden *-1988* *ex* Traverway Spirit *-1986* *ex* Masa *-1986* *ex* Tainio *-1984* *ex* Anna Knuppel *-1981* **Manessa Maritime SA** Global Management & Trading Co Ltd *Lome* *Togo* MMSI: 671327000 Official number: TG-00392L	**2,526** 1,104 2,410	Class: IV (NV) (GL)	**1971-06 Husumer Schiffswerft — Husum** Yd No: 1295 Loa 92.79 Br ex 13.44 Dght 4.909 Lbp 83.22 Br md 13.21 Dpth 7.50 Welded, 2 dks	**(A31A2GX) General Cargo Ship** Grain: 5,009; Bale: 4,738 TEU 178 C. 178/20' incl. 20 ref C. Compartments: 1 Ho, ER 1 Ha: ER (50.0 x 10.2) Ice Capable	**1 oil engine** driving 1 FP propeller Total Power: 1,912kW (2,600hp) 14.0kn MAN G8V40/60 1 x 4 Stroke 8 Cy. 400 x 600 1912kW (2600bhp) Maschinenbau Augsburg Nuernberg (MAN)-Augsburg
9313357 *CNA254* -	**SAFI IV** **Finance Company of Souss SA (Fishing Port Agadir Morocco) SOFINAS SA** - *Agadir* *Morocco*	**316** 94 200	Class: BV	**2004-03 Francisco Cardama, SA — Vigo** Yd No: 212 Loa 32.00 Br ex - Dght - Lbp 27.00 Br md 8.20 Dpth 5.80 Welded, 1 dk	**(B11A2FS) Stern Trawler**	**1 oil engine** geared to sc. shaft driving 1 FP propeller Total Power: 662kW (900hp) GUASCOR F360TA-SP 1 x Vee 4 Stroke 12 Cy. 152 x 165 662kW (900bhp) Gutierrez Ascunce Corp (GUASCOR)-Spain
5304920 - -	**SAFINATUL HASSAN** **Bangladesh Wapda** - *Narayanganj* *Bangladesh*	*422* 125	Class: (LR) ✠ Classed LR until 10/58	**1953-07 NV Scheepsbouwwerf & Machinefabriek 'De Klop' — Sliedrecht** Yd No: 599 Loa 47.66 Br ex 10.04 Dght - Lbp 45.52 Br md 9.99 Dpth 3.05 Riveted\Welded, 1 dk	**(B33A2DC) Cutter Suction Dredger**	**1 Steam Recip** driving 1 FP propeller NV Scheepsbouwwerf & Machinefabriek'De Klop'-Netherlands
8414128 *OW2354* KG 339	**SAFIR** *ex* Fostuvardi *-2002* **P/F J F K Trol** - *Klaksvik* *Faeroe Islands (Danish)* MMSI: 231190000 Official number: D2915	**305** 138 -	Class: NV	**1984-07 p/f Torshavnar Skipasmidja — Torshavn** Yd No: 25 Loa 32.42 Br ex 8.02 Dght 4.000 Lbp 28.71 Br md 8.00 Dpth 6.15 Welded, 2 dks	**(B11A2FS) Stern Trawler**	**1 oil engine** geared to sc. shaft driving 1 FP propeller Total Power: 869kW (1,181hp) MWM TBD440-6 1 x 4 Stroke 6 Cy. 230 x 270 869kW (1181bhp) Motoren Werke Mannheim AG (MWM)-West Germany AuxGen: 2 x 75kW 380V 50Hz a.c
8112689 *LLOU* -	**SAFIR** *ex* Vaernes *-2002* *ex* With Junior *-1998* *ex* Austborg *-1988* **Sjotransport Rotsund AS** - *Tromso* *Norway* MMSI: 257302500 Official number: 19793	**1,175** 352 840	Class: NV	**1982-10 Vaagland Baatbyggeri AS — Vaagland** Yd No: 102 Loa 55.94 Br ex - Dght 4.010 Lbp 49.61 Br md 12.07 Dpth 7.70 Welded, 2 dks	**(A31A2GX) General Cargo Ship** Stern door/ramp Side doors (p) Bale: 1,860 Compartments: 1 Ho, ER 1 Ha: (22.6 x 6.1) Cranes: 1x20t Ice Capable	**1 oil engine** driving 1 FP propeller Total Power: 780kW (1,060hp) Caterpillar 3512TA 1 x Vee 4 Stroke 12 Cy. 170 x 190 780kW (1060bhp) (new engine 1988) Caterpillar Inc-USA AuxGen: 1 x a.c, 1 x a.c Thrusters: 1 Thwart. FP thruster (f)
6800177 *EPUC* -	**SAFIR 10** *ex* Mahnaz Karoon *-1988* *ex* Bugsier 11 *-1976* *ex* Bugsier 3 *-1976* **Sholinajad F** - *Bandar Imam Khomeini* *Iran* Official number: 20502	*133* 40 -	Class: AS (GL)	**1953-01 F Schichau AG — Bremerhaven** Yd No: 1648 Widened-1967 L reg 24.45 Br ex 7.73 Dght - Lbp - Br md - Dpth 2.98 Welded, 1 dk	**(B32A2ST) Tug**	**1 oil engine** driving 1 FP propeller Total Power: 625kW (850hp) 11.0kn Deutz RBV8M545 1 x 4 Stroke 8 Cy. 320 x 450 625kW (850bhp) Kloeckner Humboldt Deutz AG-West Germany Fuel: 23.5 (d.f.)
9577173 *EPAJ5* -	**SAFIR KISH 1** **Kish Acme Tower Co** - *Bandar Abbas* *Iran* MMSI: 422895000 Official number: 955	**226** 67 -	Class: (BV)	**2010-01 NGV Tech Sdn Bhd — Telok Panglima Garang** Yd No: 1122 Loa 34.00 Br ex 8.80 Dght 1.500 Lbp 31.67 Br md 7.85 Dpth 3.30 Welded, 1 dk	**(B34J2SD) Crew Boat** Hull Material: Aluminium Alloy	**3 oil engines** reduction geared to sc. shafts driving 3 FP propellers Total Power: 3,198kW (4,347hp) 25.0kn Caterpillar C32 3 x Vee 4 Stroke 12 Cy. 145 x 162 each-1066kW (1449bhp) Caterpillar Inc-USA AuxGen: 2 x 85kW 50Hz a.c
9577161 *EPAJ6* -	**SAFIR KISH 2** **Kish Acme Tower Co** - *Bandar Abbas* *Iran* MMSI: 422896000 Official number: 956	**226** 67 -	Class: (BV)	**2010-01 NGV Tech Sdn Bhd — Telok Panglima Garang** Yd No: 1121 Loa 34.00 Br ex 8.80 Dght 1.500 Lbp 31.67 Br md 7.85 Dpth 3.30 Welded, 1 dk	**(B34J2SD) Crew Boat** Hull Material: Aluminium Alloy	**3 oil engines** reduction geared to sc. shafts driving 3 FP propellers Total Power: 3,198kW (4,347hp) 25.0kn Caterpillar C32 3 x Vee 4 Stroke 12 Cy. 145 x 162 each-1066kW (1449bhp) Caterpillar Inc-USA AuxGen: 2 x 85kW 50Hz a.c
9559078 *EPAP6* -	**SAFIR KISH 3** *ex* Borcos Fasihah 1 *-2011* **Kish Acme Tower Co** - *Bandar Abbas* *Iran*	**499** 149 380	Class: (BV)	**2011-03 NGV Tech Sdn Bhd — Telok Panglima Garang** Yd No: 1159 Loa 52.00 Br ex - Dght 2.500 Lbp 48.35 Br md 10.00 Dpth 4.00 Welded, 1 dk	**(B21A20C) Crew/Supply Vessel** Hull Material: Aluminium Alloy	**3 oil engines** reduction geared to sc. shafts driving 3 FP propellers Total Power: 6,861kW (9,327hp) 25.5kn M.T.U. 16V4000M70 3 x Vee 4 Stroke 16 Cy. 165 x 190 each-2287kW (3109bhp) MTU Friedrichshafen GmbH-Friedrichshafen AuxGen: 2 x 162kW 50Hz a.c
9670456 *ZGBU4* -	**SAFIRA** **Tyneside Yachts Ltd** - *George Town* *Cayman Islands (British)* MMSI: 319576000 Official number: 743600	**425** 127 -	Class: AB	**2013-02 Newcastle Shipyards LLC — Palatka FL** Yd No: 1004 Loa 39.26 Br ex 8.74 Dght 2.800 Lbp 31.36 Br md 8.55 Dpth 4.55 Welded, 1 dk	**(X11A2YP) Yacht**	**2 oil engines** driving 2 Propellers Caterpillar 2 x 4 Stroke Caterpillar Inc-USA

8829115 **SAFIRA**
SPRL
\-
ex Kaszubski Brzeg *-2009*
YBM Sp zoo (YBM Ltd)
\-
Gdansk *Poland*
MMSI: 261001970

165
49
\-

Class: (PR)

1956 Stocznia Polnocna (Northern Shipyard) — Gdansk Yd No: B11/PR12/4
Converted From: Research Vessel-2009
Loa 32.57 Br ex - Dght 2.860
Lbp - Br md 6.74 Dpth 3.35
Welded, 1 dk

(X11A2YP) Yacht

1 oil engine driving 1 FP propeller
Total Power: 221kW (300hp)
Buckau R8DV136
1 x 4 Stroke 8 Cy. 240 x 360 221kW (300bhp)
VEB Schwermaschinenbau "KarlLiebknecht" (SKL)-Magdeburg
AuxGen: 1 x 50kW 230V a.c, 1 x 40kW 115V a.c

7332660 **SAFIRA NUSANTARA**
YHHN
\-
ex Morning Star 10 *-2003*
ex Seikan Maru No. 7 *-1993*
PT Prima Eksekutif
PT Jembatan Nusantara
Surabaya *Indonesia*
MMSI: 525002086

6,345
2,552
1,500

Class: KI

1973-10 Naikai Shipbuilding & Engineering Co Ltd — Onomichi HS (Setoda Shipyard)
Yd No: 373
Loa 120.54 Br ex 16.82 Dght 5.410
Lbp 110.01 Br md 16.79 Dpth 6.61
Riveted\Welded, 2 dks

(A36A2PR) Passenger/Ro-Ro Ship (Vehicles)
Passengers: unberthed: 700

2 oil engines reduction geared to sc. shafts driving 2 FP propellers
Total Power: 10,298kW (14,002hp) 20.0kn
Pielstick 14PC2-2V-400
2 x Vee 4 Stroke 14 Cy. 400 x 460 each-5149kW (7001bhp)
Nippon Kokan KK (NKK Corp)-Japan
AuxGen: 2 x 750kW 445V 60Hz a.c
Fuel: 94.5 (d.f.) 190.5 (r.f.) 22.0pd

9319947 **SAFIYE ANA**
TCCW9
\-
Capa Denizcilik Nakliyat Sanayi ve Ticaret Ltd Sti (Capa Shipping & Trading Co Ltd)
\-
Istanbul *Turkey*
MMSI: 271000770

2,313
1,329
3,536

Class: TL

2004-10 Arkadas Denizcilik Insaat Sanayi Ticaret Ltd Sti — Istanbul (Tuzla) Yd No: 2
Loa 87.20 (BB) Br ex - Dght 5.730
Lbp 80.00 Br md 12.80 Dpth 7.00
Welded, 1 dk

(A31A2GX) General Cargo Ship

1 oil engine driving 1 FP propeller
Total Power: 853kW (1,160hp)
S.K.L. 8NVD48A-2U
1 x 4 Stroke 8 Cy. 320 x 480 853kW (1160bhp) (made 1988)
The Hanshin Diesel Works Ltd-Japan
Thrusters: 1 Tunnel thruster (f)

9412830 **SAFMARINE BANDAMA**
3ELD5
\-
Los Halillos Shipping Co SA
New Century Overseas Management Inc
Panama *Panama*
MMSI: 372922000
Official number: 3302707

17,294
7,814
21,470

Class: NK

2007-07 Imabari Shipbuilding Co Ltd — Imabari EH (Imabari Shipyard) Yd No: 657
Loa 171.99 (BB) Br ex - Dght 9.517
Lbp 160.00 Br md 27.60 Dpth 14.00
Welded, 1 dk

(A33A2CC) Container Ship (Fully Cellular)
TEU 1700 incl 192 ref C.
Compartments: 5 Cell Ho, ER
Cranes: 3x40t

1 oil engine driving 1 FP propeller
Total Power: 15,820kW (21,509hp) 19.7kn
MAN-B&W 7S60MC-C
1 x 2 Stroke 7 Cy. 600 x 2400 15820kW (21509bhp)
Mitsui Engineering & Shipbuilding CLtd-Japan
AuxGen: 3 x a.c
Thrusters: 1 Tunnel thruster (f)
Fuel: 2179.0

9355355 **SAFMARINE BAYETE**
VRKZ9
\-
launched as Maersk Besar *-2009*
Maersk Shipping Hong Kong Ltd
A P Moller - Maersk A/S
Hong Kong *Hong Kong*
MMSI: 477211100
Official number: HK-3606

35,835
17,687
43,197

Class: AB (LR)
✠ Classed LR until 27/4/09

2009-02 Hanjin Heavy Industries & Construction Co Ltd — Busan Yd No: 189
Loa 223.30 (BB) Br ex 32.20 Dght 10.800
Lbp 212.00 Br md 32.20 Dpth 19.30
Welded, 1 dk

(A33A2CC) Container Ship (Fully Cellular)
TEU 2787 C Ho 1229 TEU C Dk 1558 TEU incl 813 ref C
Compartments: 6 Cell Ho, ER
6 Ha: ER

1 oil engine driving 1 FP propeller
Total Power: 28,880kW (39,265hp) 22.0kn
MAN-B&W 8K80ME-C
1 x 2 Stroke 8 Cy. 800 x 2300 28880kW (39265bhp)
Hyundai Heavy Industries Co Ltd-South Korea
AuxGen: 1 x 1595kW 450V 60Hz a.c, 3 x 2055kW 450V 60Hz a.c
Boilers: AuxB (o.f.) 9.2kgf/cm² (9.0bar), AuxB (ex.g.) 9.2kgf/cm² (9.0bar)
Thrusters: 1 Thwart. CP thruster (f)

9355367 **SAFMARINE BENGUELA**
VRLA3
\-
launched as Maersk Bukom *-2009*
Maersk Shipping Hong Kong Ltd
A P Moller - Maersk A/S
Hong Kong *Hong Kong*
MMSI: 477552400
Official number: HK-3608

35,835
17,687
43,083

Class: AB (LR)
✠ Classed LR until 24/5/09

2009-04 Hanjin Heavy Industries & Construction Co Ltd — Busan Yd No: 190
Loa 223.30 (BB) Br ex 32.20 Dght 10.800
Lbp 212.00 Br md 32.20 Dpth 19.30
Welded, 1 dk

(A33A2CC) Container Ship (Fully Cellular)
TEU 2787 C Ho 1229 TEU C Dk 1558 TEU incl 813 ref C
Compartments: 6 Cell Ho, ER
6 Ha: ER

1 oil engine driving 1 FP propeller
Total Power: 28,880kW (39,265hp) 22.0kn
MAN-B&W 8K80ME-C
1 x 2 Stroke 8 Cy. 800 x 2300 28880kW (39265bhp)
Hyundai Heavy Industries Co Ltd-South Korea
AuxGen: 3 x 2055kW 450V 60Hz a.c, 1 x 1595kW 450V 60Hz a.c
Boilers: AuxB (o.f.) 9.2kgf/cm² (9.0bar), AuxB (ex.g.) 9.2kgf/cm² (9.0bar)
Thrusters: 1 Thwart. CP thruster (f)

9289180 **SAFMARINE CAMEROUN**
9V9863
\-
A P Moller Singapore Pte Ltd
\-
Singapore *Singapore*
MMSI: 566415000
Official number: 397673

24,488
10,441
28,936

Class: AB (LR)
✠ Classed LR until 15/8/09

2004-05 Volkswerft Stralsund GmbH — Stralsund Yd No: 449
Loa 195.50 (BB) Br ex 32.26 Dght 10.970
Lbp 183.72 Br md 32.24 Dpth 16.90
Welded, 1 dk

(A33A2CC) Container Ship (Fully Cellular)
TEU 2096 C Ho 868 TEU C Dk 1228 TEU incl 340 ref C
Compartments: 5 Cell Ho, ER
Cranes: 3x48t

1 oil engine driving 1 FP propeller
Total Power: 21,240kW (28,878hp) 21.5kn
Sulzer 9RT-flex60C
1 x 2 Stroke 9 Cy. 600 x 2250 21240kW (28878bhp)
Doosan Engine Co Ltd-South Korea
AuxGen: 4 x 1320kW 450V 60Hz a.c
Boilers: e (ex.g.) 9.5kgf/cm² (9.3bar), WTAuxB (o.f.) 9.5kgf/cm² (9.3bar)
Thrusters: 1 Thwart. CP thruster (f); 1 Thwart. CP thruster (a)

9525388 **SAFMARINE CHACHAI**
VRJT6
\-
Maersk Shipping Hong Kong Ltd
A P Moller - Maersk A/S
SatCom: Inmarsat C 447704277
Hong Kong *Hong Kong*
MMSI: 477174900
Official number: HK-3344

50,869
29,691
61,614

Class: AB

2012-05 Hyundai Heavy Industries Co Ltd — Ulsan Yd No: 2348
Loa 249.12 (BB) Br ex - Dght 13.500
Lbp 235.00 Br md 37.40 Dpth 22.10
Welded, 1 dk

(A33A2CC) Container Ship (Fully Cellular)
TEU 4,496 incl 700 ref C
Cranes: 4x50t

1 oil engine driving 1 FP propeller
Total Power: 2,300kW (3,127hp) 21.3kn
MAN-B&W 6S80ME-C9
1 x 2 Stroke 6 Cy. 800 x 3450 2300kW (3127bhp)
Hyundai Heavy Industries Co Ltd-South Korea
AuxGen: 1 x 3100kW a.c, 2 x 2250kW a.c, 1 x 1650kW a.c
Thrusters: 1 Tunnel thruster (f)
Fuel: 279.0 (d.f.) 5068.0 (r.f.)

9525376 **SAFMARINE CHAMBAL**
VRJT5
\-
Maersk Shipping Hong Kong Ltd
A P Moller Singapore Pte Ltd
Hong Kong *Hong Kong*
MMSI: 477083800
Official number: HK-3343

50,869
29,691
61,614

Class: AB

2012-03 Hyundai Heavy Industries Co Ltd — Ulsan Yd No: 2347
Loa 249.12 (BB) Br ex - Dght 13.500
Lbp 235.00 Br md 37.40 Dpth 22.10
Welded, 1 dk

(A33A2CC) Container Ship (Fully Cellular)
TEU 4,496 incl 700 ref C
Compartments: 6 Cell Ho, ER
Cranes: 4x50t

1 oil engine driving 1 FP propeller
Total Power: 23,000kW (31,271hp) 21.3kn
MAN-B&W 6S80ME-C9
1 x 2 Stroke 6 Cy. 800 x 3450 23000kW (31271bhp)
Hyundai Heavy Industries Co Ltd-South Korea
AuxGen: 1 x 3100kW a.c, 2 x 2250kW a.c, 1 x 1650kW a.c
Thrusters: 1 Tunnel thruster (f)
Fuel: 270.0 (d.f.) 5060.0 (r.f.)

9525364 **SAFMARINE CHILKA**
VRJT4
\-
Maersk Shipping Hong Kong Ltd
A P Moller - Maersk A/S
Hong Kong *Hong Kong*
MMSI: 477083700
Official number: HK-3342

50,869
29,691
61,614

Class: AB

2012-02 Hyundai Heavy Industries Co Ltd — Ulsan Yd No: 2346
Loa 249.12 (BB) Br ex - Dght 13.500
Lbp 235.00 Br md 37.40 Dpth 22.10
Welded, 1 dk

(A33A2CC) Container Ship (Fully Cellular)
TEU 4,496 incl 700 ref C
Compartments: 6 Cell Ho, ER
Cranes: 4x50t

1 oil engine driving 1 FP propeller
Total Power: 23,000kW (31,271hp) 21.3kn
MAN-B&W 6S80ME-C9
1 x 2 Stroke 6 Cy. 800 x 3450 23000kW (31271bhp)
Hyundai Heavy Industries Co Ltd-South Korea
AuxGen: 1 x 3100kW a.c, 2 x 2250kW a.c, 1 x 1650kW a.c
Thrusters: 1 Tunnel thruster (f)
Fuel: 270.0 (d.f.) 5060.0 (r.f.)

9289207 **SAFMARINE KURAMO**
9V9864
\-
A P Moller Singapore Pte Ltd
\-
Singapore *Singapore*
MMSI: 566416000
Official number: 397674

24,488
10,441
28,844

Class: AB (LR)
✠ Classed LR until 28/11/09

2004-11 Volkswerft Stralsund GmbH — Stralsund Yd No: 451
Loa 195.50 (BB) Br ex 32.26 Dght 10.970
Lbp 183.72 Br md 32.24 Dpth 16.90
Welded, 1 dk

(A33A2CC) Container Ship (Fully Cellular)
TEU 2096 C Ho 868 TEU C Dk 1228 TEU incl 340 ref C
Compartments: 5 Cell Ho, ER
Cranes: 3x48t

1 oil engine driving 1 FP propeller
Total Power: 21,240kW (28,878hp) 20.8kn
Sulzer 9RT-flex60C
1 x 2 Stroke 9 Cy. 600 x 2250 21240kW (28878bhp)
Doosan Engine Co Ltd-South Korea
AuxGen: 4 x 1320kW 450V 60Hz a.c
Boilers: e (ex.g.) 9.3kgf/cm² (9.1bar), WTAuxB (o.f.) 9.3kgf/cm² (9.1bar)
Thrusters: 1 Thwart. FP thruster (f); 1 Thwart. CP thruster (a)

9500065 **SAFMARINE LIMPOPO**
4RBK
\-
ex Senta Friederich *-2010*
ms 'Senta Friederich' Schifffahrtsges mbH & Co KG
Reederei Eugen Friederich GmbH & Co KG
Colombo *Sri Lanka*
MMSI: 417222324
Official number: 113335

9,772
4,384
12,337

Class: GL

2010-03 Tongfang Jiangxin Shipbuilding Co Ltd — Hukou County JX Yd No: JX602
Loa 139.99 (BB) Br ex 21.77 Dght 8.200
Lbp 133.00 Br md 21.50 Dpth 11.40
Welded, 1 dk

(A31A2GX) General Cargo Ship
Grain: 15,900
TEU 712
Cranes: 2x80t,1x45t
Ice Capable

1 oil engine driving 1 FP propeller
Total Power: 7,860kW (10,686hp) 16.5kn
MAN-B&W 6S46MC-C
1 x 2 Stroke 6 Cy. 460 x 1932 7860kW (10686bhp)
Hyundai Heavy Industries Co Ltd-South Korea
AuxGen: 3 x 800kW 450V a.c
Thrusters: 1 Tunnel thruster (f)

9500089 **SAFMARINE LINYATI**
4RBS
\-
ex Stella Friederich *-2010*
ms 'Stella Friederich' Schifffahrtsgesellschaft mbH & Co KG
Mercantile Marine Management Ltd
Colombo *Sri Lanka*
MMSI: 417222332

9,772
4,384
12,325

Class: GL

2010-12 Tongfang Jiangxin Shipbuilding Co Ltd — Hukou County JX Yd No: JX604
Loa 139.99 (BB) Br ex 21.77 Dght 8.200
Lbp 133.00 Br md 21.50 Dpth 11.40
Welded, 1 dk

(A31A2GX) General Cargo Ship
Grain: 15,900
TEU 712
Cranes: 2x80t,1x45t
Ice Capable

1 oil engine driving 1 FP propeller
Total Power: 7,860kW (10,686hp) 16.5kn
MAN-B&W 6S46MC-C
1 x 2 Stroke 6 Cy. 460 x 1932 7860kW (10686bhp)
Hyundai Heavy Industries Co Ltd-South Korea
AuxGen: 3 x 800kW 450V a.c
Thrusters: 1 Tunnel thruster (f)

9500077 **SAFMARINE LONGA**
4RBQ
\-
ex Sonja Friederich *-2010*
ms 'Sonja Friederich' Schifffahrtsges mbH & Co KG
Reederei Eugen Friederich GmbH & Co KG
Colombo *Sri Lanka*
MMSI: 417222330

9,772
4,384
12,349

Class: GL

2010-09 Tongfang Jiangxin Shipbuilding Co Ltd — Hukou County JX Yd No: JX603
Loa 140.07 Br ex 21.77 Dght 8.200
Lbp 133.00 Br md 21.50 Dpth 11.40
Welded, 1 dk

(A31A2GX) General Cargo Ship
Grain: 19,500
TEU 712
Cranes: 3x40t
Ice Capable

1 oil engine driving 1 FP propeller
Total Power: 7,860kW (10,686hp) 16.5kn
MAN-B&W 6S46MC-C
1 x 2 Stroke 6 Cy. 460 x 1932 7860kW (10686bhp)
Hyundai Heavy Industries Co Ltd-South Korea
AuxGen: 3 x 780kW 450V a.c
Thrusters: 1 Tunnel thruster (f)

ID	Name / Owner	Tonnage	Class	Builder / Dimensions	Type / Capacity	Machinery
9500053 *4RBI* -	**SAFMARINE LUALABA** *launched as* Sarah Friederich *-2009* **ms 'Sarah Friederich' Schifffahrtsges mbH & Co KG** Reederei Eugen Friederich GmbH & Co KG *Colombo* *Sri Lanka* MMSI: 417222322	**9,772** 5,594 12,342	Class: GL	**2009-10 Tongfang Jiangxin Shipbuilding Co Ltd — Hukou County JX** Yd No: JX601 Loa 139.86 (BB) Br ex 21.77 Dght 8.200 Lbp 133.00 Br md 21.50 Dpth 11.40 Welded, 1 dk	**(A31A2GX) General Cargo Ship** Grain: 15,900 TEU 712 Cranes: 2x80t,1x45t Ice Capable	**1 oil engine** driving 1 FP propeller Total Power: 7,860kW (10,686hp) 16.5kn MAN-B&W 6S46MC-C 1 x 2 Stroke 6 Cy. 460 x 1932 7860kW (10686bhp) Hyundai Heavy Industries Co Ltd-South Korea AuxGen: 3 x 800kW 450V a.c Thrusters: 1 Tunnel thruster (f)
9314210 *9VBB3* -	**SAFMARINE MAFADI** **A P Moller Singapore Pte Ltd** - *Singapore* *Singapore* MMSI: 566627000 Official number: 398080	**50,686** 29,491 61,433 T/cm 78.7	Class: LR ✠**100A1** SS 05/2012 container ship **ShipRight** (SDA, FDA, CM) *IWS LI ✠**LMC** **UMS** Eq.Ltr: S†; Cable: 719.5/87.0 U3 (a)	**2007-05 Hyundai Heavy Industries Co Ltd — Ulsan** Yd No: 1701 Loa 292.08 (BB) Br ex 32.30 Dght 13.500 Lbp 277.00 Br md 32.25 Dpth 21.70 Welded, 1 dk	**(A33A2CC) Container Ship (Fully Cellular)** TEU 4154 C Ho 1948 TEU C Dk 2206 TEU incl 700 ref C. Compartments: 8 Cell Ho, ER	**1 oil engine** driving 1 FP propeller Total Power: 45,760kW (62,215hp) 24.0kn Wartsila 8RT-flex96C 1 x 2 Stroke 8 Cy. 960 x 2500 45760kW (62215bhp) Hyundai Heavy Industries Co Ltd-South Korea AuxGen: 4 x 2030kW 450V 60Hz a.c Boilers: e (ex.g.) 8.2kgf/cm² (8.0bar), WTAuxB (o.f.) 8.2kgf/cm² (8.0bar) Thrusters: 1 Thwart. CP thruster (f); 1 Thwart. CP thruster (a) Fuel: 339.7 (d.f.) 5075.5 (r.f.)
9318319 *9V6784* -	**SAFMARINE MAKUTU** **A P Moller Singapore Pte Ltd** - *Singapore* *Singapore* MMSI: 566625000 Official number: 398081	**50,686** 29,491 61,407 T/cm 78.7	Class: LR ✠**100A1** SS 09/2012 container ship **ShipRight** (SDA, FDA, CM) *IWS LI ✠**LMC** **UMS** Eq.Ltr: S†; Cable: 719.5/87.0 U3 (a)	**2007-09 Hyundai Heavy Industries Co Ltd — Ulsan** Yd No: 1733 Loa 292.08 (BB) Br ex 32.30 Dght 13.500 Lbp 277.00 Br md 32.25 Dpth 21.70 Welded, 1 dk	**(A33A2CC) Container Ship (Fully Cellular)** TEU 4154 C Ho 1948 TEU C Dk 2206 TEU incl 700 ref C. Compartments: 8 Cell Ho, ER 8 Ha: ER	**1 oil engine** driving 1 FP propeller Total Power: 45,760kW (62,215hp) 24.0kn Wartsila 8RT-flex96C 1 x 2 Stroke 8 Cy. 960 x 2500 45760kW (62215bhp) Hyundai Heavy Industries Co Ltd-South Korea AuxGen: 4 x 2030kW 450V 60Hz a.c Boilers: e (ex.g.) 8.0kgf/cm² (7.8bar), WTAuxB (o.f.) 8.2kgf/cm² (8.0bar) Thrusters: 1 Thwart. CP thruster (f); 1 Thwart. CP thruster (a)
9311696 *9V6535* -	**SAFMARINE MERU** **A P Moller Singapore Pte Ltd** - *Singapore* *Singapore* MMSI: 566624000 Official number: 398078	**50,686** 29,491 61,392 T/cm 78.7	Class: LR ✠**100A1** SS 12/2011 container ship *IWS LI **ShipRight** (SDA, FDA, CM) ✠**LMC** **UMS** Eq.Ltr: S†; Cable: 719.5/87.0 U3 (a)	**2006-12 Hyundai Heavy Industries Co Ltd — Ulsan** Yd No: 1699 Loa 292.08 (BB) Br ex 32.35 Dght 13.500 Lbp 277.00 Br md 32.25 Dpth 21.70 Welded, 1 dk	**(A33A2CC) Container Ship (Fully Cellular)** TEU 4154 C Ho 1948 TEU C Dk 2206 TEU incl. 700 ref C. Compartments: ER, 8 Cell Ho	**1 oil engine** driving 1 FP propeller Total Power: 45,760kW (62,215hp) 24.5kn Sulzer 8RT-flex96C 1 x 2 Stroke 8 Cy. 960 x 2500 45760kW (62215bhp) Hyundai Heavy Industries Co Ltd-South Korea AuxGen: 4 x 2030kW 450V 60Hz a.c Boilers: e (ex.g.) 8.2kgf/cm² (8.0bar), WTAuxB (o.f.) 8.2kgf/cm² (8.0bar) Thrusters: 1 Thwart. CP thruster (f); 1 Thwart. CP thruster (a) Fuel: 339.7 (d.f.) 5075.5 (r.f.)
9311701 *9VJR8* -	**SAFMARINE MULANJE** **A P Moller Singapore Pte Ltd** A P Moller *Singapore* *Singapore* MMSI: 566622000 Official number: 398079	**50,686** 29,491 61,447 T/cm 78.7	Class: LR ✠**100A1** SS 02/2012 container ship **ShipRight** (SDA, FDA, CM) *IWS LI ✠**LMC** **UMS** Eq.Ltr: S†; Cable: 687.5/87.0 U3 (a)	**2007-02 Hyundai Heavy Industries Co Ltd — Ulsan** Yd No: 1700 Loa 292.08 (BB) Br ex 32.35 Dght 13.500 Lbp 277.49 Br md 32.25 Dpth 21.70 Welded, 1 dk	**(A33A2CC) Container Ship (Fully Cellular)** TEU 4154 C Ho 1948 TEU C Dk 2206 TEU incl 700 ref C. Compartments: ER, 8 Cell Ho	**1 oil engine** driving 1 FP propeller Total Power: 45,760kW (62,215hp) 24.5kn Wartsila 8RT-flex96C 1 x 2 Stroke 8 Cy. 960 x 2500 45760kW (62215bhp) Hyundai Heavy Industries Co Ltd-South Korea AuxGen: 4 x 2030kW 450V 60Hz a.c Boilers: e (ex.g.) 8.0kgf/cm² (7.8bar), WTAuxB (o.f.) 8.2kgf/cm² (8.0bar) Thrusters: 1 Thwart. CP thruster (f); 1 Thwart. CP thruster (a) Fuel: 339.7 (d.f.) 5075.5 (r.f.)
9356103 *VRKZ8* -	**SAFMARINE NAKURU** **Maersk Shipping Hong Kong Ltd** A P Moller - Maersk A/S *Hong Kong* *Hong Kong* MMSI: 477552900 Official number: HK-3605	**25,904** 12,668 35,137 T/cm 45.0	Class: AB (LR) **CCS** ✠ Classed LR until 25/10/08	**2008-07 Volkswerft Stralsund GmbH — Stralsund** Yd No: 469 Loa 210.54 (BB) Br ex 29.88 Dght 11.400 Lbp 198.74 Br md 29.80 Dpth 16.40 Welded, 1 dk	**(A33A2CC) Container Ship (Fully Cellular)** TEU 2478 C Ho 992 TEU C Dk 1486 TEU incl 488 ref C. Compartments: 5 Cell Ho, ER	**1 oil engine** driving 1 FP propeller Total Power: 21,770kW (29,598hp) 21.5kn MAN-B&W 7L70ME-C 1 x 2 Stroke 7 Cy. 700 x 2360 21770kW (29598bhp) Doosan Engine Co Ltd-South Korea AuxGen: 2 x 1944kW 450V 60Hz a.c, 1 x 1296kW 450V 60Hz a.c Boilers: e (ex.g.) 9.3kgf/cm² (9.1bar), AuxB (o.f.) 9.3kgf/cm² (9.1bar) Thrusters: 1 Thwart. CP thruster (f)
9356074 *9V9862* -	**SAFMARINE NGAMI** **A P Moller Singapore Pte Ltd** - *Singapore* *Singapore* MMSI: 566414000 Official number: 397672	**25,904** 12,668 35,119 T/cm 45.0	Class: AB (LR) ✠ Classed LR until 15/11/08	**2008-02 Volkswerft Stralsund GmbH — Stralsund** Yd No: 466 Loa 210.40 (BB) Br ex 29.88 Dght 11.400 Lbp 198.74 Br md 29.83 Dpth 16.40 Welded, 1 dk	**(A33A2CC) Container Ship (Fully Cellular)** TEU 2478 C Ho 992 TEU C Dk 1486 TEU incl 488 ref C. Compartments: 5 Cell Ho, ER 9 Ha: 8 (12.6 x 25.5)ER (12.6 x 20.4)	**1 oil engine** driving 1 FP propeller Total Power: 21,770kW (29,598hp) 21.5kn MAN-B&W 7L70ME-C 1 x 2 Stroke 7 Cy. 700 x 2360 21770kW (29598bhp) Doosan Engine Co Ltd-South Korea AuxGen: 1 x 1296kW 450V 60Hz a.c, 2 x 1944kW 450V 60Hz a.c Boilers: e (ex.g.) 9.3kgf/cm² (9.1bar), AuxB (o.f.) 9.3kgf/cm² (9.1bar) Thrusters: 1 Thwart. CP thruster (f)
9356098 *VRKZ6* -	**SAFMARINE NILE** **Maersk Shipping Hong Kong Ltd** A P Moller - Maersk A/S *Hong Kong* *Hong Kong* MMSI: 477552700 Official number: HK-3603	**25,904** 12,668 35,181 T/cm 45.0	Class: AB (LR) **CCS** ✠ Classed LR until 8/11/08	**2008-05 Volkswerft Stralsund GmbH — Stralsund** Yd No: 468 Loa 210.54 (BB) Br ex 29.88 Dght 11.400 Lbp 198.74 Br md 29.80 Dpth 16.40 Welded, 1 dk	**(A33A2CC) Container Ship (Fully Cellular)** TEU 2478 C Ho 992 TEU C Dk 1486 TEU incl 488 ref C. Compartments: 5 Cell Ho, ER	**1 oil engine** driving 1 FP propeller Total Power: 21,770kW (29,598hp) 21.5kn MAN-B&W 7L70ME-C 1 x 2 Stroke 7 Cy. 700 x 2360 21770kW (29598bhp) Doosan Engine Co Ltd-South Korea AuxGen: 2 x 1944kW 450V 60Hz a.c, 1 x 1296kW 450V 60Hz a.c Boilers: e (ex.g.) 9.3kgf/cm² (9.1bar), AuxB (o.f.) 9.3kgf/cm² (9.1bar) Thrusters: 1 Thwart. CP thruster (f)
9289192 *9V9861* -	**SAFMARINE NIMBA** **A P Moller Singapore Pte Ltd** A P Moller - Maersk A/S SatCom: Inmarsat C 456641310 *Singapore* *Singapore* MMSI: 566413000 Official number: 397671	**24,488** 10,441 28,897	Class: AB (LR) ✠ Classed LR until 29/8/09	**2004-08 Volkswerft Stralsund GmbH — Stralsund** Yd No: 450 Loa 195.50 (BB) Br ex 32.26 Dght 10.970 Lbp 183.72 Br md 32.24 Dpth 16.90 Welded, 1 dk	**(A33A2CC) Container Ship (Fully Cellular)** TEU 2096 C Ho 868 TEU C Dk 1228 TEU incl 340 ref C Compartments: 5 Cell Ho, ER Cranes: 3x48t	**1 oil engine** driving 1 FP propeller Total Power: 21,240kW (28,878hp) 21.5kn Sulzer 9RT-flex60C 1 x 2 Stroke 9 Cy. 600 x 2250 21240kW (28878bhp) Doosan Engine Co Ltd-South Korea AuxGen: 4 x 1320kW 450V 60Hz a.c Boilers: AuxB (ex.g.) 9.5kgf/cm² (9.3bar), WTAuxB (o.f.) 9.5kgf/cm² (9.3bar) Thrusters: 1 Thwart. CP thruster (f); 1 Thwart. CP thruster (a)
9294393 *VRLA4* -	**SAFMARINE NOKWANDA** **Safmarine Container Lines NV (SCL)** A P Moller - Maersk A/S *Hong Kong* *Hong Kong* MMSI: 477552200 Official number: HK3609	**50,657** 26,654 63,150	Class: LR ✠**100A1** CS 01/2010 container ship LI *IWS **ShipRight** (SDA, FDA, CM) ✠**LMC** **UMS** Eq.Ltr: U†; Cable: 715.0/92.0 U3 (a)	**2005-01 Odense Staalskibsvaerft A/S — Munkebo (Lindo Shipyard)** Yd No: 195 Loa 265.84 (BB) Br ex 37.40 Dght 14.025 Lbp 252.40 Br md 37.30 Dpth 21.35 Welded, 1 dk	**(A33A2CC) Container Ship (Fully Cellular)** TEU 4045 C Ho 1635 TEU C Dk 2410 TEU incl 1109 ref C Compartments: 6 Cell Ho, ER	**1 oil engine** driving 1 FP propeller Total Power: 45,760kW (62,215hp) 24.0kn Sulzer 8RT-Flex96C 1 x 2 Stroke 8 Cy. 960 x 2500 45760kW (62215bhp) Doosan Engine Co Ltd-South Korea AuxGen: 3 x 2749kW 6600V 60Hz a.c, 1 x 3665kW 6600V 60Hz a.c Boilers: AuxB (ex.g.) 8.2kgf/cm² (8.0bar), WTAuxB (o.f.) 8.2kgf/cm² (8.0bar) Thrusters: 1 Thwart. CP thruster (f); 1 Thwart. CP thruster (a)
9294381 *VRKZ7* -	**SAFMARINE NOMAZWE** **Maersk Shipping Hong Kong Ltd** Safmarine Pty Ltd *Hong Kong* *Hong Kong* MMSI: 477552800 Official number: HK3604	**50,657** 26,654 62,994	Class: LR ✠**100A1** CS 12/2009 container ship LI *IWS **ShipRight** (SDA, FDA, CM) ✠**LMC** **UMS** Eq.Ltr: U†; Cable: 715.0/92.0 U3 (a)	**2004-12 Odense Staalskibsvaerft A/S — Munkebo (Lindo Shipyard)** Yd No: 194 Loa 265.84 (BB) Br ex 37.40 Dght 14.025 Lbp 252.40 Br md 37.30 Dpth 21.35 Welded, 1 dk	**(A33A2CC) Container Ship (Fully Cellular)** TEU 4045 C Ho 1635 TEU C Dk 2410 TEU incl 1109 ref C Compartments: 6 Cell Ho, ER 6 Ha: ER	**1 oil engine** driving 1 FP propeller Total Power: 45,760kW (62,215hp) 24.0kn Sulzer 8RT-flex96C 1 x 2 Stroke 8 Cy. 960 x 2500 45760kW (62215bhp) Doosan Engine Co Ltd-South Korea AuxGen: 1 x 3665kW 6600V 60Hz a.c, 3 x 2749kW 6600V 50Hz a.c Boilers: AuxB (ex.g.) 8.2kgf/cm² (8.0bar), WTAuxB (o.f.) 8.2kgf/cm² (8.0bar) Thrusters: 1 Thwart. CP thruster (f); 1 Thwart. CP thruster (a)

9356115 *VRLA5* -	**SAFMARINE NUBA** **Maersk Shipping Hong Kong Ltd** A P Moller - Maersk A/S *Hong Kong* *Hong Kong* MMSI: 477552100 Official number: HK-3610	**25,904** 12,668 35,144 T/cm 45.0	Class: AB (LR) ✠ Classed LR until 6/11/08	**2008-08 Volkswerft Stralsund GmbH — Stralsund** Yd No: 470 Loa 210.54 (BB) Br ex 29.88 Dght 11.400 Lbp 198.74 Br md 29.80 Dpth 16.40 Welded, 1 dk	**(A33A2CC) Container Ship (Fully Cellular)** TEU 2478 C Ho 992 TEU C Dk 1486 TEU incl 488 ref C. Compartments: 5 Cell Ho, ER	**1 oil engine** driving 1 FP propeller Total Power: 21,770kW (29,598hp) 21.5kn MAN-B&W 7L70ME-C 1 x 2 Stroke 7 Cy. 700 x 2360 21770kW (29598bhp) Doosan Engine Co Ltd-South Korea AuxGen: 2 x 1944kW 450V 60Hz a.c, 1 x 1296kW 450V 60Hz a.c Boilers: e (ex.g.) 9.3kgf/cm^2 (9.1bar), AuxB (o.f.) 9.3kgf/cm^2 (9.1bar) Thrusters: 1 Thwart. CP thruster (f)
9356086 *VRLA2* -	**SAFMARINE NYASSA** **Maersk Shipping Hong Kong Ltd** A P Moller - Maersk A/S *Hong Kong* *Hong Kong* MMSI: 477552300 Official number: HK-3607	**25,904** 12,668 35,292 T/cm 45.0	Class: AB (LR) ✠ Classed LR until 29/11/08	**2008-04 Volkswerft Stralsund GmbH — Stralsund** Yd No: 467 Loa 210.54 (BB) Br ex 29.88 Dght 11.400 Lbp 198.74 Br md 29.80 Dpth 16.40 Welded, 1 dk	**(A33A2CC) Container Ship (Fully Cellular)** TEU 2478 C Ho 992 TEU C Dk 1486 TEU incl 488 ref C. Compartments: 5 Cell Ho, ER	**1 oil engine** driving 1 FP propeller Total Power: 21,770kW (29,598hp) 21.5kn MAN-B&W 7L70ME-C 1 x 2 Stroke 7 Cy. 700 x 2360 21770kW (29598bhp) Doosan Engine Co Ltd-South Korea AuxGen: 2 x 1944kW 450V 60Hz a.c, 1 x 1296kW 450V 60Hz a.c Boilers: e (ex.g.) 9.2kgf/cm^2 (9.0bar), AuxB (o.f.) 9.2kgf/cm^2 (9.0bar) Thrusters: 1 Thwart. CP thruster (f)
9538880 *2EUL6* -	**SAFMARINE SAHARA** **Safmarine Container Lines NV (SCL)** Enzian Ship Management AG *Liverpool* *United Kingdom* MMSI: 235088254 Official number: 917708	**14,859** 6,300 17,884	Class: LR ✠ **100A1** SS 08/2011 strengthened for heavy cargoes, any holds may be empty, container cargoes in all holds and on all hatch covers *IWS LI ✠ **LMC** **UMS** Eq.Ltr: I†; Cable: 605.0/62.0 U3 (a)	**2011-08 Wuhu Xinlian Shipbuilding Co Ltd — Wuhu AH** Yd No: W0821 Loa 161.50 (BB) Br ex - Dght 8.600 Lbp 153.50 Br md 25.20 Dpth 12.40 Welded, 1 dk	**(A31A2GX) General Cargo Ship** Grain: 25,500; Bale: 25,500 TEU 1054 C Ho 426 TEU C Dk 628 TEU incl 101 ref C Compartments: 3 Ho, ER 3 Ha: ER Cranes: 3x80t	**1 oil engine** driving 1 FP propeller Total Power: 9,960kW (13,542hp) 17.0kn MAN-B&W 6S50MC-C 1 x 2 Stroke 6 Cy. 500 x 2000 9960kW (13542bhp) Doosan Engine Co Ltd-South Korea AuxGen: 3 x 960kW 450V 60Hz a.c Boilers: AuxB (Comp) 9.0kgf/cm^2 (8.8bar) Thrusters: 1 Tunnel thruster (f) Fuel: 180.0 (d.f.) 1700.0 (r.f.)
9539365 *VRIP4* -	**SAFMARINE SAHEL** **Safmarine Container Lines NV (SCL)** Enzian Ship Management AG SatCom: Inmarsat C 447703849 *Hong Kong* *Hong Kong* MMSI: 477196900 Official number: HK-3110	**14,859** 6,299 17,954	Class: LR ✠ **100A1** SS 11/2011 strengthened for heavy cargoes, container cargoes in all holds and on upper deck and on all hatch covers *IWS LI ✠ **LMC** **UMS** Eq.Ltr: I†; Cable: 605.0/62.0 U3 (a)	**2011-11 Wuhu Xinlian Shipbuilding Co Ltd — Wuhu AH** Yd No: W0822 Loa 161.50 (BB) Br ex - Dght 8.600 Lbp 153.50 Br md 25.20 Dpth 12.40 Welded, 1 dk	**(A31A2GX) General Cargo Ship** Grain: 25,500; Bale: 25,500 TEU 1054 C Ho 426 TEU C Dk 628 TEU incl 145 ref C Compartments: 3 Ho, ER 3 Ha: ER Cranes: 3x80t	**1 oil engine** driving 1 FP propeller Total Power: 9,960kW (13,542hp) 17.0kn MAN-B&W 6S50MC-C 1 x 2 Stroke 6 Cy. 500 x 2000 9960kW (13542bhp) (new engine 2011) Doosan Engine Co Ltd-South Korea AuxGen: 3 x 960kW 450V 60Hz a.c Boilers: AuxB (Comp) 9.0kgf/cm^2 (8.8bar) Thrusters: 1 Tunnel thruster (f) Fuel: 180.0 (d.f.) 1700.0 (r.f.)
9412842 *3EMH6* -	**SAFMARINE SANAGA** **Misuga SA** Misuga Kaiun Co Ltd *Panama* *Panama* MMSI: 357573000 Official number: 3333307A	**17,294** 7,814 21,436	Class: NK	**2007-09 Imabari Shipbuilding Co Ltd — Imabari EH (Imabari Shipyard)** Yd No: 658 Loa 171.99 (BB) Br ex - Dght 9.517 Lbp 160.00 Br md 27.60 Dpth 14.00 Welded, 1 dk	**(A33A2CC) Container Ship (Fully Cellular)** TEU 1700 incl 192 ref C Cranes: 3x40t	**1 oil engine** driving 1 FP propeller Total Power: 15,820kW (21,509hp) 19.7kn MAN-B&W 7S60MC-C 1 x 2 Stroke 7 Cy. 600 x 2400 15820kW (21509bhp) Mitsui Engineering & Shipbuilding CLtd-Japan AuxGen: 3 x a.c Thrusters: 1 Tunnel thruster (f) Fuel: 2180.0
9430222 *VRIP5* -	**SAFMARINE SHABA** - Enzian Ship Management AG *Hong Kong* *Hong Kong* MMSI: 477167200 Official number: HK-3111	**14,859** 6,307 18,010	Class: LR ✠ **100A1** SS 02/2012 strengthened for heavy cargoes container cargoes in all holds and on upper deck and on all hatch covers LI ✠ **LMC** **UMS** Eq.Ltr: H†; Cable: 605.0/62.0 U3 (a)	**2012-02 Jiangsu Sugang Shipbuilding Co Ltd — Yizheng JS** Yd No: 18000-2 Loa 161.50 (BB) Br ex 25.26 Dght 8.600 Lbp 153.50 Br md 25.23 Dpth 12.43 Welded, 1 dk	**(A31A2GX) General Cargo Ship** Grain: 25,500; Bale: 25,500 TEU 1048 incl 152 ref C Compartments: 3 Ho, ER 3 Ha: ER Cranes: 3x80t	**1 oil engine** driving 1 FP propeller Total Power: 9,960kW (13,542hp) 14.0kn MAN-B&W 6S50MC-C 1 x 2 Stroke 6 Cy. 500 x 2000 9960kW (13542bhp) STX Engine Co Ltd-South Korea AuxGen: 3 x 900kW 450V 60Hz a.c Boilers: AuxB (Comp) 8.8kgf/cm^2 (8.6bar) Thrusters: 1 Thwart. CP thruster (f)
9539389 *VRIP2* -	**SAFMARINE SUGUTA** **Safmarine Container Lines NV (SCL)** Enzian Ship Management AG *Hong Kong* *Hong Kong* MMSI: 477902400 Official number: HK-3108	**14,859** 6,315 17,907	Class: LR ✠ **100A1** SS 03/2012 strengthened for heavy cargoes, container cargoes in all holds and on upper deck and on all hatch covers **ShipRight** ACS (B) *IWS LI ✠ **LMC** **UMS** Eq.Ltr: I†; Cable: 605.0/62.0 U3 (a)	**2012-03 Wuhu Xinlian Shipbuilding Co Ltd — Wuhu AH** Yd No: W0824 Loa 161.50 (BB) Br ex 25.20 Dght 8.600 Lbp 153.50 Br md 25.20 Dpth 12.40 Welded, 1 dk	**(A31A2GX) General Cargo Ship** Grain: 25,500; Bale: 25,500 TEU 1054 C Ho 426 TEU C Dk 628 incl 145 ref C Compartments: 3 Ho, ER 3 Ha: ER Cranes: 3x80t	**1 oil engine** driving 1 FP propeller Total Power: 9,960kW (13,542hp) 17.0kn MAN-B&W 6S50MC-C 1 x 2 Stroke 6 Cy. 500 x 2000 9960kW (13542bhp) Doosan Engine Co Ltd-South Korea AuxGen: 3 x 960kW 450V 60Hz a.c Boilers: AuxB (Comp) 9.2kgf/cm^2 (9.0bar) Thrusters: 1 Thwart. CP thruster (f) Fuel: 180.0 (d.f.) 1700.0 (r.f.)
9423516 *VRHH2* -	**SAFMARINE SUMBA** **Safmarine MPV NV** Enzian Ship Management AG *Hong Kong* *Hong Kong* MMSI: 477852800 Official number: HK-2833	**14,859** 6,278 18,019	Class: LR ✠ **100A1** SS 10/2010 strengthened for heavy cargoes, container cargoes in all holds and on upper deck and on all hatch covers LI ✠ **LMC** **UMS** Eq.Ltr: H†; Cable: 605.0/62.0 U3 (a)	**2010-10 Jiangsu Sugang Shipbuilding Co Ltd — Yizheng JS** Yd No: 18000-1 Loa 161.50 (BB) Br ex 25.26 Dght 8.600 Lbp 153.50 Br md 25.23 Dpth 12.43 Welded, 1 dk	**(A31A2GX) General Cargo Ship** Grain: 25,500; Bale: 25,500 TEU 1048 incl 152 ref C Compartments: 3 Ho, ER 3 Ha: ER Cranes: 3x80t	**1 oil engine** reduction geared to sc. shaft driving 1 FP propeller Total Power: 9,960kW (13,542hp) 14.0kn MAN-B&W 6S50MC-C 1 x 2 Stroke 6 Cy. 500 x 2000 9960kW (13542bhp) STX Engine Co Ltd-South Korea AuxGen: 3 x 900kW 450V 60Hz a.c Boilers: AuxB (Comp) 8.8kgf/cm^2 (8.6bar) Thrusters: 1 Thwart. CP thruster (f)
9445019 *3ERU* -	**SAFMARINE TARABA** **Misuga SA** Misuga Kaiun (HK) Ltd *Panama* *Panama* MMSI: 370169000 Official number: 3405508A	**17,294** 7,814 21,464	Class: NK	**2008-06 Imabari Shipbuilding Co Ltd — Imabari EH (Imabari Shipyard)** Yd No: 663 Loa 171.99 (BB) Br ex - Dght 9.517 Lbp 160.00 Br md 27.60 Dpth 14.00 Welded, 1 dk	**(A33A2CC) Container Ship (Fully Cellular)** TEU 1577 incl 192 ref c Cranes: 3x40t	**1 oil engine** driving 1 FP propeller Total Power: 15,820kW (21,509hp) 19.7kn MAN-B&W 7S60MC-C 1 x 2 Stroke 7 Cy. 600 x 2400 15820kW (21509bhp) Mitsui Engineering & Shipbuilding CLtd-Japan AuxGen: 3 x a.c Thrusters: 1 Tunnel thruster (f) Fuel: 2420.0 (r.f.)
7832385 *UGEJ* -	**SAFONOVO** **Deepsea Global Co Ltd (OOO Dipsi Global)** - *Vladivostok* *Russia* MMSI: 273810600	**739** 221 327	Class: (RS)	**1980 Volgogradskiy Sudostroitelnyy Zavod — Volgograd** Yd No: 889 Loa 53.74 (BB) Br ex 10.71 Dght 4.290 Lbp 47.92 Br md - Dpth 6.02 Welded, 1 dk	**(B11A2FS) Stern Trawler** Ins: 218 1 Ha: (1.6 x 1.6) Derricks: 2x1.5t Ice Capable	**1 oil engine** driving 1 FP propeller Total Power: 971kW (1,320hp) 12.8kn S.K.L. 8NVD48A-2U 1 x 4 Stroke 8 Cy. 320 x 480 971kW (1320bhp) VEB Schwermaschinenbau "KarlLiebknecht" (SKL)-Magdeburg
6615950 *HO2619* -	**SAFRA** *ex Medregal -2001* **Espama Fishing Co Ltd** - *Panama* *Panama* MMSI: 351944000 Official number: 29914PEXT	**524** 232 659	Class: RC (BV)	**1966 Ast. del Cadagua W. E. Gonzalez S.A. — Bilbao** Yd No: 69 Loa 55.25 Br ex 9.02 Dght 3.753 Lbp 49.61 Br md 9.00 Dpth 4.25 Welded, 2 dks	**(B11B2FV) Fishing Vessel** Ins: 555 Compartments: 3 Ho, ER 3 Ha: 3 (1.6 x 1.6)ER Derricks: 3x1t	**1 oil engine** driving 1 FP propeller Total Power: 956kW (1,300hp) 10.0kn MAN G9V30/45ATL 1 x 4 Stroke 9 Cy. 300 x 450 956kW (1300bhp) Maschinenbau Augsburg Nuernberg (MAN)-Augsburg Fuel: 291.0 (d.f.)
9041124 *TCVF* -	**SAFRAN 1** *ex Ahmet Fatoglu -2004* **MB Denizcilik Tasimacilik Ltd Sti** Manta Denizcilik Nakliyat ve Ticaret Ltd Sti SatCom: Inmarsat C 427120280 *Istanbul* *Turkey* MMSI: 271000359 Official number: 110	**2,805** 1,714 4,495	Class: NK (BV)	**1991-07 Gemyat A.S. — Tuzla** Loa 95.70 (BB) Br ex - Dght 6.250 Lbp 84.70 Br md 14.50 Dpth 7.50 Welded	**(A31A2GX) General Cargo Ship** Grain: 5,983; Bale: 5,739 Compartments: 2 Ho, ER 2 Ha: 2 (25.1 x 10.2)ER Derricks: 4x3t	**1 oil engine** reduction geared to sc. shaft driving 1 FP propeller Total Power: 1,486kW (2,020hp) 12.0kn Blackstone ESL9MK2 1 x 4 Stroke 9 Cy. 222 x 292 1486kW (2020bhp) Mirrlees Blackstone (Stamford)Ltd.-Stamford AuxGen: 4 x 395kW 220/380V 50Hz a.c

IMO / Call sign	Name / Owner / Registry	Tonnage	Class	Builder / Dimensions	Type / Cargo	Machinery
9223887 *C6SD6* -	**SAFWA** **The National Shipping Company of Saudi Arabia (BAHRI)** Mideast Ship Management Ltd SatCom: Inmarsat C 431128610 *Nassau* *Bahamas* MMSI: 311286000 Official number: 8000393	**159,990** 109,408 303,138 T/cm 173.4	Class: AB	**2002-06 Samsung Heavy Industries Co Ltd — Geoje** Yd No: 1339 Loa 333.28 (BB) Br ex 58.00 Dght 22.532 Lbp 318.00 Br md 56.00 Dpth 31.25 Welded, 1 dk	**(A13A2TV) Crude Oil Tanker** Double Hull (13F) Liq: 332,222; Liq (Oil): 332,222 Compartments: 5 Ta, ER, 10 Wing Ta, 2 Wing Slop Ta 3 Cargo Pump (s): 3x5000m³/hr Manifold: Bow/CM: 169.4m	**1 oil engine** driving 1 FP propeller Total Power: 32,833kW (44,640hp) 17.1kn Sulzer 7RTA84T-D 1 x 2 Stroke 7 Cy. 840 x 3150 32833kW (44640bhp) Doosan Engine Co Ltd-South Korea AuxGen: 3 x 1360kW 440/220V 60Hz a.c Fuel: 480.0 (d.f.) 10220.0 (r.f.) 125.0pd
8741090 *WBN2075* -	**SAG RIVER** **Puget Sound Tug & Barge Co** - *Seattle, WA* *United States of America* MMSI: 366889350 Official number: 564493	*105* 50 -		**1975-01 Colberg Boat Works — Stockton, Ca** Yd No: 75-1 Loa - Br ex - Dght - Lbp 19.51 Br md 8.23 Dpth 1.83 Welded, 1 dk	**(B32A2ST) Tug**	**3 oil engines** reduction geared to sc. shafts driving 3 Propellers Total Power: 804kW (1,092hp) Caterpillar D343 3 x 4 Stroke 6 Cy. 137 x 165 each-268kW (364bhp) Caterpillar Tractor Co-USA
9225794 *V7KV5* -	**SAG WESTFALEN** *ex* CMA CGM Esmeraldas *-2011* *ex* Kaedi *-2006* *ex* Irma Delmas *-2003* **SAG Unternehmensbeteiligungsgesellschaft ms 'Westfalen' mbH & Co KG** - *Majuro* *Marshall Islands* MMSI: 538090257 Official number: 90257	**26,061** 10,209 30,453 T/cm 49.4	Class: GL (BV)	**2003-06 China Shipbuilding Corp — Keelung** Yd No: 778 Loa 195.60 (BB) Br ex - Dght 11.010 Lbp 185.50 Br md 30.20 Dpth 16.60 Welded, 1 dk	**(A33A2CC) Container Ship (Fully Cellular)** TEU 2207 C Ho 870 TEU C Dk 1337 TEU incl 350 ref C. Compartments: 5 Cell Ho, ER 9 Ha: ER Cranes: 3x45t	**1 oil engine** driving 1 FP propeller Total Power: 24,824kW (33,751hp) 21.5kn MAN-B&W 8S70MC-C 1 x 2 Stroke 8 Cy. 700 x 2800 24824kW (33751bhp) Hyundai Heavy Industries Co Ltd-South Korea AuxGen: 4 x 1200kW 440/220V 60Hz a.c Thrusters: 1 Thwart. CP thruster (f)
9345752 *CB8841* -	**SAGA** - - *Valparaiso* *Chile* MMSI: 725003720 Official number: 3136	**729** 219 846		**2005-10 Detroit Chile SA — Puerto Montt** Yd No: 87 Loa 51.80 (BB) Br ex - Dght 3.200 Lbp 46.20 Br md 12.00 Dpth 4.30 Welded, 1 dk	**(A31A2GX) General Cargo Ship**	**2 oil engines** geared to sc. shafts driving 2 Propellers Total Power: 1,200kW (1,632hp) 12.7kn Chinese Std. Type CW6200ZC 2 x 4 Stroke 6 Cy. 200 x 270 each-600kW (816bhp) in China Thrusters: 1 Tunnel thruster (f)
9425100 *HKCG2* -	**SAGA** *ex* Zenon Spirit *-2008* **International Tugs SA (INTERTUG)** - *Santa Marta* *Colombia* Official number: MC-04-029	**279** 83 270	Class: LR (BV) **100A1** SS 02/2012 tug **LMC** Cable: 302.0/22.0	**2007-02 Rushan Shipbuilding Co Ltd — Rushan SD** Yd No: SRC06-02 Loa 32.00 Br ex - Dght 3.800 Lbp 29.92 Br md 9.20 Dpth 4.50 Welded, 1 dk	**(B32A2ST) Tug**	**2 oil engines** with clutches, flexible couplings & dr geared to sc. shafts driving 2 FP propellers Total Power: 2,388kW (3,246hp) 12.0kn Cummins KTA-50-M2 2 x Vee 4 Stroke 16 Cy. 159 x 159 each-1194kW (1623bhp) Cummins Engine Co Ltd-United Kingdom AuxGen: 2 x 115kW 400V 50Hz a.c Fuel: 230.0 (d.f.)
9528031 *9HA2591* -	**SAGA** **Olympian Zeus Owners Inc** TMS Tankers Ltd SatCom: Inmarsat Mini-M 765059297 *Valletta* *Malta* MMSI: 248964000 Official number: 9528031	**61,332** 35,877 115,738 T/cm 99.1	Class: AB	**2011-01 Samsung Heavy Industries Co Ltd — Geoje** Yd No: 1833 Loa 249.97 (BB) Br ex 43.84 Dght 15.000 Lbp 239.00 Br md 43.80 Dpth 21.00 Welded, 1 dk	**(A13A2TW) Crude/Oil Products Tanker** Double Hull (13F) Liq: 123,650; Liq (Oil): 123,650 Cargo Heating Coils Compartments: 12 Wing Ta, 2 Wing Slop Ta, ER 3 Cargo Pump (s): 3x2800m³/hr Manifold: Bow/CM: 123.7m	**1 oil engine** driving 1 FP propeller Total Power: 14,400kW (19,578hp) 15.3kn MAN-B&W 7S60MC-C 1 x 2 Stroke 7 Cy. 600 x 2400 14400kW (19578bhp) Hyundai Heavy Industries Co Ltd-South Korea AuxGen: 3 x 800kW a.c Fuel: 220.0 (d.f.) 2900.0 (r.f.)
6616746 *HMVJ6* -	**SAGA** *ex* Sunko *-2005* *ex* Korni *-1984* *ex* Silco *-1978* **Roza General Trading LLC** - *Wonsan* *North Korea* MMSI: 445849000 Official number: 1601503	**698** 312 821	Class: (NV)	**1966-07 Orens Mek. Verksted — Trondheim** Yd No: 35 Loa 55.00 Br ex 9.33 Dght 3.506 Lbp 50.02 Br md 9.30 Dpth 3.56 Welded, 2 dks	**(A31A2GX) General Cargo Ship** Grain: 1,578; Bale: 1,419 Compartments: 1 Ho, ER 2 Ha: 2 (13.3 x 6.0)ER Derricks: 2x2.5t; Winches: 2 Ice Capable	**1 oil engine** sr geared to sc. shaft driving 1 CP propeller Total Power: 625kW (850hp) 10.5kn Normo LDMCB-6 1 x 4 Stroke 6 Cy. 250 x 300 625kW (850bhp) AS Bergens Mek Verksteder-Norway AuxGen: 2 x 21kW 220V 50Hz a.c, 1 x 8kW 220V 50Hz a.c Fuel: 40.5 (d.f.) 3.0pd
7423433 *LW6319* -	**SAGA** *ex* Aquamarine 504 *-1986* **NATE Navegacion y Tecnologia Maritima SA (NATE SA)** - SatCom: Inmarsat C 470181669 *Buenos Aires* *Argentina* MMSI: 701006105 Official number: 02511	*608* 224 850	Class: AB (RI)	**1978-08 South Texas Shipyard, Inc. — Corpus Christi, Tx** Yd No: 104 Loa 56.39 Br ex - Dght 3.982 Lbp 49.99 Br md 12.20 Dpth 4.55 Welded, 1 dk	**(B21B20T) Offshore Tug/Supply Ship**	**3 oil engines** reverse reduction geared to sc. shafts driving 3 FP propellers Total Power: 3,618kW (4,920hp) 13.0kn EMD (Electro-Motive) 16-645-E2 3 x Vee 2 Stroke 16 Cy. 230 x 254 each-1206kW (1640bhp) (Re-engined ,made 1951, Reconditioned & fitted 1978) General Motors Corp.Electro-Motive Div.-La Grange AuxGen: 2 x 150kW
7933579 *WBY7391* -	**SAGA** **FV Saga LLC** - *Homer, AK* *United States of America* MMSI: 366993150 Official number: 606800	*198* 134 -		**1979 Bender Welding & Machine Co Inc — Mobile AL** Yd No: 755 L reg 28.75 Br ex 9.15 Dght - Lbp - Br md - Dpth 3.38 Welded, 1 dk	**(B11B2FV) Fishing Vessel**	**2 oil engines** geared to sc. shafts driving 2 FP propellers Total Power: 912kW (1,240hp) Caterpillar 3412TA 2 x Vee 4 Stroke 12 Cy. 137 x 152 each-456kW (620bhp) Caterpillar Tractor Co-USA
8407979 *AUUD* -	**SAGA** *ex* Senor D *-2007* *ex* Suhaili 5201 *-2005* **Epsom Shipping (I) Pvt Ltd** ABS Marine Services Pvt Ltd *Mumbai* *India* MMSI: 419697000 Official number: 3418	**923** 277 1,025	Class: IR (BV) (AB)	**1986-07 Sing Koon Seng Pte Ltd — Singapore** Yd No: 623 Loa 52.20 Br ex - Dght 3.763 Lbp 49.03 Br md 15.00 Dpth 4.22 Welded, 1 dk	**(B34L2QU) Utility Vessel** Cranes: 1x20t	**2 oil engines** reverse reduction geared to sc. shafts driving 2 FP propellers Total Power: 1,486kW (2,020hp) 13.0kn Caterpillar 3512TA 2 x Vee 4 Stroke 12 Cy. 170 x 190 each-743kW (1010bhp) Caterpillar Tractor Co-USA AuxGen: 2 x 190kW 415/220V 50Hz a.c Thrusters: 1 Thwart. FP thruster (f) Fuel: 269.0 (d.f.)
8607191 *V4YC2* -	**SAGA** *ex* Eva *-2013* *ex* Blue Wave *-2013* *ex* Alta *-2007* *ex* White Shark *-2007* *ex* Vasiliy Filippov *-2001* **Saga Seafood Ltd** - *St Kitts & Nevis* MMSI: 341190000 Official number: SKN 1002660	**7,765** 2,329 3,372	Class: NV (RS)	**1988-12 VEB Volkswerft Stralsund — Stralsund** Yd No: 810 Loa 120.43 Br ex 19.03 Dght 6.630 Lbp 108.12 Br md 19.02 Dpth 12.22 Welded, 3 dks	**(B11A2FG) Factory Stern Trawler** Ins: 3,900 Ice Capable	**2 oil engines** with clutches, flexible couplings & reduction geared to sc. shaft driving 1 CP propeller Total Power: 5,298kW (7,204hp) 14.9kn S.K.L. 6VDS48/42AL-2 2 x 4 Stroke 6 Cy. 420 x 480 each-2649kW (3602bhp) VEB Schwermaschinenbau "KarlLiebknecht" (SKL)-Magdeburg AuxGen: 2 x 1500kW a.c, 2 x 760kW a.c
9317406 *VRBL4* -	**SAGA ADVENTURE** **Saga Shipholding (Norway) AS** Saga Forest Carriers International AS *Hong Kong* *Hong Kong* MMSI: 477076500 Official number: HK-1616	**29,758** 14,440 46,627 T/cm 53.5	Class: NV	**2005-11 Oshima Shipbuilding Co Ltd — Saikai NS** Yd No: 10427 Loa 199.20 (BB) Br ex 30.59 Dght 11.800 Lbp 194.70 Br md 30.50 Dpth 16.40 Welded, 1 dk	**(A31A2GO) Open Hatch Cargo Ship** Double Hull Grain: 53,232 TEU 760 C Hold 360 TEU C Dk 400 TEU Compartments: 10 Ho, ER 10 Ha: ER 10 (13.2 x 25.3) Gantry cranes: 2x40t	**1 oil engine** driving 1 FP propeller Total Power: 9,510kW (12,930hp) 14.5kn Sulzer 7RTA52 1 x 2 Stroke 7 Cy. 520 x 1800 9510kW (12930bhp) Diesel United Ltd.-Aioi AuxGen: 3 x a.c Thrusters: 1 Tunnel thruster (f)
9197002 *VRMV6* -	**SAGA ANDORINHA** *ex* Andorinha *-2001* **Saga Shipholding (Norway) AS** Saga Forest Carriers International AS *Hong Kong* *Hong Kong* MMSI: 477686700 Official number: HK-3989	**29,729** 14,528 47,027 T/cm 53.5	Class: NV	**1998-09 Oshima Shipbuilding Co Ltd — Saikai NS** Yd No: 10249 Loa 199.20 (BB) Br ex - Dght 11.823 Lbp 190.00 Br md 30.50 Dpth 16.40 Welded, 1 dk	**(A31A2GO) Open Hatch Cargo Ship** Grain: 53,232 TEU 400 Compartments: 10 Ho, ER 10 Ha: 10 (13.2 x 25.3)ER Gantry cranes: 2x40t	**1 oil engine** driving 1 FP propeller Total Power: 8,952kW (12,171hp) 14.5kn Sulzer 7RTA52 1 x 2 Stroke 7 Cy. 520 x 1800 8952kW (12171bhp) Diesel United Ltd.-Aioi AuxGen: 3 x 700kW 100/450V 60Hz a.c Fuel: 139.2 (d.f.) (Heating Coils) 2726.0 (r.f.) 33.1pd
9160798 *VRVN8* -	**SAGA BEIJA-FLOR** *ex* Beija-Flor *-2003* **Saga Shipholding (Norway) AS** Saga Forest Carriers International AS SatCom: Inmarsat B 347755410 *Hong Kong* *Hong Kong* MMSI: 477554000 Official number: HK-0373	**29,729** 14,528 46,990 T/cm 53.5	Class: NV	**1997-11 Oshima Shipbuilding Co Ltd — Saikai NS** Yd No: 10235 Loa 199.20 (BB) Br ex - Dght 11.823 Lbp 190.00 Br md 30.50 Dpth 16.40 Welded, 1 dk	**(A31A2GO) Open Hatch Cargo Ship** Double Hull Grain: 53,232 Compartments: 10 Ho, ER 10 Ha: 10 (13.2 x 25.3)ER Gantry cranes: 2x40t	**1 oil engine** driving 1 FP propeller Total Power: 8,952kW (12,171hp) 14.5kn Sulzer 7RTA52 1 x 2 Stroke 7 Cy. 520 x 1800 8952kW (12171bhp) Diesel United Ltd.-Aioi AuxGen: 3 x 700kW 100/450V 60Hz a.c

IMO / Call sign	Name / Owner / Manager / Flag	Tonnage	Classification	Builder / Dimensions	Type / Cargo	Machinery
9014066 *VRWR7* -	**SAGA CREST** **JYS Shipping SA** Saga Forest Carriers International AS SatCom: Inmarsat A 1315512 *Hong Kong* *Hong Kong* MMSI: 477818000 Official number: HK-0625	**29,381** 14,155 47,069 T/cm 53.5	Class: LR (NV) **100A1** SS 03/2009 LI **LMC** **UMS** Eq.Ltr: M†; Cable: 632.5/73.0 U3	**1994**-03 **Oshima Shipbuilding Co Ltd — Saikai NS** Yd No: 10164 Loa 199.20 (BB) Br ex - Dght 11.823 Lbp 190.00 Br md 30.50 Dpth 16.40 Welded, 1 dk	**(A31A2GO) Open Hatch Cargo Ship** Grain: 51,946 Compartments: 10 Ho, ER 10 Ha: 10 (13.2 x 25.3)ER Gantry cranes: 2x40t	**1 oil engine** driving 1 FP propeller Total Power: 8,951kW (12,170hp) 14.5kn Sulzer 7RTA52 1 x 2 Stroke 7 Cy. 520 x 1800 8951kW (12170bhp) Diesel United Ltd.-Aioi AuxGen: 3 x 600kW 450V 60Hz a.c Boilers: AuxB (Comp) 7.0kgf/cm² (6.9bar)
9317418 *VRBR8* -	**SAGA DISCOVERY** **Saga Shipholding (Norway) AS** Saga Forest Carriers International AS *Hong Kong* *Hong Kong* MMSI: 477105200 Official number: HK-1668	**29,758** 14,440 46,618 T/cm 53.5	Class: NV	**2006**-04 **Oshima Shipbuilding Co Ltd — Saikai NS** Yd No: 10429 Loa 199.20 (BB) Br ex 30.59 Dght 11.800 Lbp 194.70 Br md 30.50 Dpth 16.40 Welded, 1 dk	**(A31A2GO) Open Hatch Cargo Ship** Double Hull Grain: 53,232 TEU 760 C Hold 360 TEU C Dk 400 TEU Compartments: 10 Ho, ER 5 Ha: ER 5 (13.2 x 25.3) Gantry cranes: 2x40t	**1 oil engine** driving 1 FP propeller Total Power: 11,200kW (15,228hp) 14.5kn Sulzer 7RTA52U 1 x 2 Stroke 7 Cy. 520 x 1800 11200kW (15228bhp) Diesel United Ltd.-Aioi AuxGen: 3 x a.c Thrusters: 1 Tunnel thruster (f)
9343481 *VRCC8* -	**SAGA ENTERPRISE** **NST Enterprise SA** Saga Forest Carriers International AS *Hong Kong* *Hong Kong* MMSI: 477282600 Official number: HK-1757	**29,758** 14,440 46,550 T/cm 53.5	Class: NV	**2006**-09 **Oshima Shipbuilding Co Ltd — Saikai NS** Yd No: 10470 Loa 199.20 (BB) Br ex 30.56 Dght 11.800 Lbp 194.70 Br md 30.50 Dpth 16.40 Welded, 1 dk	**(A31A2GO) Open Hatch Cargo Ship** Double Hull Grain: 53,232 TEU 760 C Hold 360 TEU C Dk 400 TEU Compartments: 10 Ho, ER 5 Ha: ER 5 (13.2 x 25.3) Gantry cranes: 2x40t	**1 oil engine** driving 1 FP propeller Total Power: 9,510kW (12,930hp) 14.5kn Sulzer 7RTA52 1 x 2 Stroke 7 Cy. 520 x 1800 9510kW (12930bhp) Diesel United Ltd.-Aioi AuxGen: 3 x a.c Thrusters: 1 Tunnel thruster (f)
9343493 *VRCI8* -	**SAGA EXPLORER** **Navire Shipping Co Ltd** Saga Forest Carriers International AS SatCom: Inmarsat C 447760760 *Hong Kong* *Hong Kong* MMSI: 477607600 Official number: HK-1805	**29,758** 14,440 46,589 T/cm 53.5	Class: NV	**2006**-12 **Oshima Shipbuilding Co Ltd — Saikai NS** Yd No: 10471 Loa 199.20 (BB) Br ex 30.59 Dght 11.800 Lbp 194.70 Br md 30.50 Dpth 16.40 Welded, 1 dk	**(A31A2GO) Open Hatch Cargo Ship** Double Hull Grain: 53,232 TEU 760 C Hold 360 TEU C Dk 400 TEU Compartments: 10 Ho, ER 5 Ha: ER 5 (13.2 x 25.3) Gantry cranes: 2x40t	**1 oil engine** driving 1 FP propeller Total Power: 9,510kW (12,930hp) 14.5kn Sulzer 7RTA52 1 x 2 Stroke 7 Cy. 520 x 1800 9510kW (12930bhp) Diesel United Ltd.-Aioi AuxGen: 3 x a.c Thrusters: 1 Tunnel thruster (f)
9613848 *VRKX7* -	**SAGA FALCON** **Saga Shipholding (Norway) AS** Saga Forest Carriers International AS *Hong Kong* *Hong Kong* MMSI: 477914600 Official number: HK-3588	**37,499** 15,791 55,596	Class: NV	**2012**-11 **Daewoo Shipbuilding & Marine Engineering Co Ltd — Geoje** Yd No: 1219 Loa 199.90 (BB) Br ex 32.29 Dght 13.316 Lbp 191.20 Br md 32.26 Dpth 19.50 Welded, 1 dk	**(A31A2GO) Open Hatch Cargo Ship** Grain: 64,458 TEU 2022 C Ho 1376 TEU C Dk 646 TEU Compartments: 10 Ho, ER 10 Ha: (13.2 x 23.0)8 (13.2 x 27.7)ER (13.2 x 17.4) Gantry cranes: 2x42t	**1 oil engine** driving 1 FP propeller Total Power: 9,560kW (12,998hp) 14.5kn MAN-B&W 5S60ME-C8 1 x 2 Stroke 5 Cy. 600 x 2400 9560kW (12998bhp) STX Engine Co Ltd-South Korea AuxGen: 2 x 1562kW a.c, 1 x 937kW a.c Thrusters: 1 Tunnel thruster (f) Fuel: 260.0 (d.f.) 2220.0 (r.f.)
9658953 *VRLT9* -	**SAGA FANTASY** **Saga Shipholding (Norway) AS** Saga Forest Carriers International AS *Hong Kong* *Hong Kong* MMSI: 477486300 Official number: HK3767	**37,441** 15,805 55,973	Class: NV	**2013**-04 **Oshima Shipbuilding Co Ltd — Saikai NS** Yd No: 10708 Loa 199.90 (BB) Br ex 32.27 Dght 13.300 Lbp 194.02 Br md 32.26 Dpth 19.50 Welded, 1 dk	**(A31A2GO) Open Hatch Cargo Ship** Double Hull Grain: 64,300 TEU 2030 C Ho 1384 TEU C Dk 646 TEU Compartments: 10 Ho, ER 10 Ha: (13.2 x 23.0)8 (13.2 x 27.7)ER (13.2 x 17.4) Gantry cranes: 2x42t	**1 oil engine** driving 1 FP propeller Total Power: 10,470kW (14,235hp) 13.5kn Wartsila 6RT-flex50 1 x 2 Stroke 6 Cy. 500 x 2050 10470kW (14235bhp) Diesel United Ltd.-Aioi Thrusters: 1 Tunnel thruster (f)
9613862 *VRLL2* -	**SAGA FJORD** **Saga Shipholding (Norway) AS** Saga Forest Carriers International AS *Hong Kong* *Hong Kong* MMSI: 477319400 Official number: HK-3696	**37,499** 15,791 55,596	Class: NV	**2013**-03 **Daewoo Shipbuilding & Marine Engineering Co Ltd — Geoje** Yd No: 1221 Loa 199.90 (BB) Br ex 32.29 Dght 13.323 Lbp 191.20 Br md 32.26 Dpth 19.50 Welded, 1 dk	**(A31A2GO) Open Hatch Cargo Ship** Grain: 64,385 TEU 2030 C Ho 1384 TEU C Dk 646 TEU Compartments: 10 Ho, ER 10 Ha: (13.2 x 23.0)8 (13.2 x 27.7)ER (13.2 x 17.4) Gantry cranes: 2x42t	**1 oil engine** driving 1 FP propeller Total Power: 9,560kW (12,998hp) 14.5kn MAN-B&W 5S60ME-C8 1 x 2 Stroke 5 Cy. 600 x 2400 9560kW (12998bhp) STX Engine Co Ltd-South Korea AuxGen: 1 x a.c, 2 x a.c Thrusters: 1 Tunnel thruster (f)
9644524 *VRLF8* -	**SAGA FORTUNE** **Saga Shipholding (Norway) AS** Saga Forest Carriers International AS *Hong Kong* *Hong Kong* MMSI: 477001300 Official number: HK-3654	**37,441** 15,805 56,023	Class: NV	**2012**-11 **Oshima Shipbuilding Co Ltd — Saikai NS** Yd No: 10707 Loa 199.80 (BB) Br ex 32.26 Dght 13.323 Lbp 194.02 Br md 32.26 Dpth 19.50 Welded, 1 dk	**(A31A2GO) Open Hatch Cargo Ship** Grain: 64,300 TEU 2002 C Ho 1384 TEU C Dk 618 TEU Compartments: 10 Ho, ER 10 Ha: ER 10 (13.5 x 27.9) Gantry cranes: 2x42t	**1 oil engine** driving 1 FP propeller Total Power: 9,474kW (12,881hp) 13.5kn Wartsila 6RT-flex50 1 x 2 Stroke 6 Cy. 500 x 2050 9474kW (12881bhp) Diesel United Ltd.-Aioi AuxGen: 2 x 1100kW a.c, 1 x 720kW a.c Thrusters: 1 Tunnel thruster (f) Fuel: 257.0 (d.f.) 3188.0 (r.f.)
9613874 *VRLL3* -	**SAGA FRAM** **Saga Shipholding (Norway) AS** Saga Forest Carriers International AS *Hong Kong* *Hong Kong* MMSI: 477224800 Official number: HK-3697	**37,499** 15,791 54,930	Class: NV	**2013**-04 **Daewoo Shipbuilding & Marine Engineering Co Ltd — Geoje** Yd No: 1222 Loa 199.90 (BB) Br ex - Dght 13.300 Lbp 191.20 Br md 32.26 Dpth 19.50 Welded, 1 dk	**(A31A2GO) Open Hatch Cargo Ship** Double Hull Grain: 64,385 TEU 2030 C Ho 1384 TEU C Dk 646 TEU Compartments: 10 Ho, ER 10 Ha: (13.2 x 23.0)8 (13.2 x 27.7)ER (13.2 x 17.4) Gantry cranes: 2x42t	**1 oil engine** driving 1 FP propeller Total Power: 11,900kW (16,179hp) 15.0kn MAN-B&W 5S60ME-C8 1 x 2 Stroke 5 Cy. 600 x 2400 11900kW (16179bhp) STX Engine Co Ltd-South Korea AuxGen: 2 x a.c, 1 x a.c Thrusters: 1 Tunnel thruster (f)
9613850 *VRLK7* -	**SAGA FRIGG** **Saga Shipholding (Norway) AS** Saga Forest Carriers International AS *Hong Kong* *Hong Kong* MMSI: 477444500 Official number: HK-3693	**37,499** 15,791 55,596	Class: NV	**2013**-01 **Daewoo Shipbuilding & Marine Engineering Co Ltd — Geoje** Yd No: 1220 Loa 199.90 (BB) Br ex 32.29 Dght 13.300 Lbp 191.20 Br md 32.26 Dpth 19.50 Welded, 1 dk	**(A31A2GO) Open Hatch Cargo Ship** Grain: 64,458 TEU 2022 C Ho 1376 TEU C Dk 646 TEU Compartments: 10 Ho, ER 10 Ha: ER 10 (13.5 x 28.1) Gantry cranes: 2x42t	**1 oil engine** driving 1 FP propeller Total Power: 9,560kW (12,998hp) 14.5kn MAN-B&W 5S60ME-C8 1 x 2 Stroke 5 Cy. 600 x 2400 9560kW (12998bhp) STX Engine Co Ltd-South Korea AuxGen: 1 x 937kW a.c, 2 x 1562kW a.c Thrusters: 1 Tunnel thruster (f) Fuel: 260.0 (d.f.) 2220.0 (r.f.)
9343510 *VRCP2* -	**SAGA FRONTIER** **Saga Shipholding (Norway) AS** Saga Forest Carriers International AS *Hong Kong* *Hong Kong* MMSI: 477657600 Official number: HK-1855	**29,758** 14,440 46,500 T/cm 53.5	Class: NV	**2007**-04 **Oshima Shipbuilding Co Ltd — Saikai NS** Yd No: 10473 Loa 199.20 (BB) Br ex 30.59 Dght 11.800 Lbp 190.00 Br md 30.50 Dpth 16.40 Welded, 1 dk	**(A31A2GO) Open Hatch Cargo Ship** Double Hull Grain: 53,232 TEU 760 C Hold 360 TEU C Dk 400 TEU Compartments: 10 Ho, ER Gantry cranes: 2x40t	**1 oil engine** driving 1 FP propeller Total Power: 9,510kW (12,930hp) 14.9kn Sulzer 7RTA52 1 x 2 Stroke 7 Cy. 520 x 1800 9510kW (12930bhp) Diesel United Ltd.-Aioi AuxGen: 3 x a.c Thrusters: 1 Tunnel thruster (f)
9609457 *VRMS3* -	**SAGA FUJI** **Pudding Shipholding SA** Nippon Yusen Kabushiki Kaisha (NYK Line) *Hong Kong* *Hong Kong* MMSI: 477050700 Official number: HK-3962	**37,441** 15,805 56,023 T/cm 61.0	Class: NV	**2013**-11 **Oshima Shipbuilding Co Ltd — Saikai NS** Yd No: 10661 Loa 199.90 (BB) Br ex 32.27 Dght 13.323 Lbp 194.03 Br md 32.26 Dpth 19.50 Welded, 1 dk	**(A31A2GO) Open Hatch Cargo Ship** Grain: 64,300 TEU 2002 C Ho 1384 TEU C Dk 618 TEU Compartments: 10 Ho, ER 10 Ha: ER 10 (13.5 x 27.9) Gantry cranes: 2x42t	**1 oil engine** driving 1 FP propeller Total Power: 9,474kW (12,881hp) 13.5kn Wartsila 6RT-flex50 1 x 2 Stroke 6 Cy. 500 x 2050 9474kW (12881bhp) Diesel United Ltd.-Aioi AuxGen: 2 x 1100kW a.c, 1 x 720kW a.c Thrusters: 1 Tunnel thruster (f) Fuel: 280.0 (d.f.) 3540.0 (r.f.)
9613836 *VRKX8* -	**SAGA FUTURE** **Saga Shipholding (Norway) AS** Saga Forest Carriers International AS *Hong Kong* *Hong Kong* MMSI: 477914700 Official number: HK-3589	**37,499** 15,791 55,596	Class: NV	**2012**-10 **Daewoo Shipbuilding & Marine Engineering Co Ltd — Geoje** Yd No: 1218 Loa 199.90 (BB) Br ex 32.29 Dght 13.316 Lbp 191.20 Br md 32.26 Dpth 19.50 Welded, 1 dk	**(A31A2GO) Open Hatch Cargo Ship** Grain: 64,458 TEU 2022 C Ho 1376 TEU C Dk 646 TEU Compartments: 10 Ho, ER 10 Ha: 8 (13.5 x 28.1)ER 2 (13.5 x 23.4) Gantry cranes: 2x42t	**1 oil engine** driving 1 FP propeller Total Power: 9,560kW (12,998hp) 14.5kn MAN-B&W 5S60ME-C8 1 x 2 Stroke 5 Cy. 600 x 2400 9560kW (12998bhp) STX Engine Co Ltd-South Korea AuxGen: 2 x 1562kW a.c, 1 x 937kW a.c Thrusters: 1 Tunnel thruster (f) Fuel: 260.0 (d.f.) 220.0 (r.f.)
9121297 *VRUZ9* -	**SAGA HORIZON** **Saga Shipholding (Norway) AS** Saga Forest Carriers International AS SatCom: Inmarsat C 447737910 *Hong Kong* *Hong Kong* MMSI: 477379000 Official number: HK-0288	**29,381** 14,155 47,016 T/cm 48.8	Class: NV	**1995**-11 **Oshima Shipbuilding Co Ltd — Saikai NS** Yd No: 10196 Loa 199.20 (BB) Br ex - Dght 11.823 Lbp 190.00 Br md 30.50 Dpth 16.40 Welded, 1 dk	**(A31A2GO) Open Hatch Cargo Ship** Grain: 51,946 Compartments: 10 Ho, ER 10 Ha: 10 (13.2 x 25.3)ER Gantry cranes: 2x40t	**1 oil engine** driving 1 FP propeller Total Power: 8,952kW (12,171hp) 14.5kn Sulzer 7RTA52 1 x 2 Stroke 7 Cy. 520 x 1800 8952kW (12171bhp) Diesel United Ltd.-Aioi AuxGen: 3 x 700kW 450V 60Hz a.c Fuel: 140.0 (d.f.) (Heating Coils) 2823.0 (r.f.) 36.5pd

9200421 *VRYO9* -	**SAGA JANDAIA** *ex Jandaia -2001* **Saga Shipholding (Norway) AS** Saga Forest Carriers International AS *Hong Kong* *Hong Kong* MMSI: 477398000 Official number: HK-1023	**29,729** 14,528 47,027 T/cm 53.5	Class: NV	**1998-12 Oshima Shipbuilding Co Ltd — Saikai NS** Yd No: 10255 Loa 199.20 (BB) Br ex - Dght 11.823 Lbp 190.00 Br md 30.50 Dpth 16.40 Welded, 1 dk	**(A31A2GO) Open Hatch Cargo Ship** Double Bottom Entire Compartment Length Grain: 53,232 Compartments: 10 Ho, ER 10 Ha: 10 (13.2 x 25.3)ER Gantry cranes: 2x40t	**1 oil engine** driving 1 FP propeller Total Power: 8,952kW (12,171hp) 14.5kn Sulzer 7RTA52 1 x 2 Stroke 7 Cy. 520 x 1800 8952kW (12171bhp) Diesel United Ltd.-Aioi AuxGen: 3 x 700kW 100/450V 60Hz a.c Fuel: 154.1 (d.f.) (Heating Coils) 2710.3 (r.f.) 32.5pd
9363637 *VRCY8* -	**SAGA JOURNEY** **Saga Shipholding (Norway) AS** Saga Forest Carriers International AS SatCom: Inmarsat C 447700677 *Hong Kong* *Hong Kong* MMSI: 477883200 Official number: HK-1933	**29,758** 14,440 46,652 T/cm 53.5	Class: NV	**2007-07 Oshima Shipbuilding Co Ltd — Saikai NS** Yd No: 10474 Loa 199.20 (BB) Br ex 30.59 Dght 11.800 Lbp 190.00 Br md 30.50 Dpth 16.40 Welded, 1 dk	**(A31A2GO) Open Hatch Cargo Ship** Double Hull Grain: 53,232 TEU 760 C Hold 360 TEU C Dk 400 TEU Compartments: 10 Ho, ER 10 Ha: ER 10 (13.2 x 25.3) Gantry cranes: 2x40t	**1 oil engine** driving 1 FP propeller Total Power: 10,920kW (14,847hp) 14.9kn Sulzer 7RTA52U 1 x 2 Stroke 7 Cy. 520 x 1800 10920kW (14847bhp) Diesel United Ltd.-Aioi AuxGen: 3 x a.c Thrusters: 1 Tunnel thruster (f)
6913376 *SBZY* -	**SAGA LEJON** *ex Amadeus -2004 ex Seemowe II -1999* *ex Malmo -1976* **Royal Stockholm Cruise Line AB** - *Mem* *Sweden* MMSI: 265528920	**1,178** 353 174	Class: (BV) (GL)	**1969-04 Husumer Schiffswerft — Husum** Yd No: 1270 Loa 58.93 Br ex 11.74 Dght 2.910 Lbp 51.01 Br md 11.71 Dpth 3.94 Welded, 2 dks	**(A37B2PS) Passenger Ship** Passengers: unberthed: 700 Ice Capable	**2 oil engines** driving 2 CP propellers Total Power: 1,324kW (1,800hp) 15.0kn MaK 6MU451A 2 x 4 Stroke 6 Cy. 320 x 450 each-662kW (900bhp) Atlas MaK Maschinenbau GmbH-Kiel AuxGen: 3 x 152kW 380V 50Hz a.c Fuel: 45.5 (d.f.) 7.0pd
8865107 *JM6171* -	**SAGA MARU No. 5** **Saga Kisen YK** - *Karatsu, Saga* *Japan* Official number: 133479	*199* - 699		**1992-07 YK Furumoto Tekko Zosensho — Osakikamijima** Yd No: 601 Loa 58.24 Br ex - Dght 3.280 Lbp 53.00 Br md 9.40 Dpth 5.55 Welded, 2 dks	**(A31A2GX) General Cargo Ship** Compartments: 1 Ho, ER	**1 oil engine** reverse geared to sc. shaft driving 1 FP propeller Total Power: 662kW (900hp) Matsui ML627GSC 1 x 4 Stroke 6 Cy. 270 x 480 662kW (900bhp) Matsui Iron Works Co Ltd-Japan
9291860 *YDA4364* -	**SAGA MAS 1600** *ex LM Pacific -2008* **PT Saga Mas Asia** - *Cirebon* *Indonesia*	**222** 67 144	Class: KI (NK)	**2003-07 C E Ling Shipbuilding Sdn Bhd — Miri** Yd No: 3302 Loa 26.50 Br ex - Dght 2.790 Lbp 24.44 Br md 8.23 Dpth 3.60 Welded, 1 dk	**(B32B2SP) Pusher Tug**	**2 oil engines** geared to sc. shafts driving 2 FP propellers Total Power: 1,204kW (1,636hp) Mitsubishi S6R2-MPTK 2 x 4 Stroke 6 Cy. 170 x 220 each-602kW (818bhp) Mitsubishi Heavy Industries Ltd-Japan AuxGen: 1 x 68kW 415V a.c, 1 x 27kW 415V a.c
9117739 *VRZQ9* -	**SAGA MONAL** *ex Hoegh Monal -2004* *ex Saga Challenger -2002* **Attic Forest AS** Saga Forest Carriers International AS SatCom: Inmarsat C 447787810 *Hong Kong* *Hong Kong* MMSI: 477878000 Official number: HK-1246	**36,463** 16,961 56,816	Class: NV	**1996-12 Mitsui Eng. & SB. Co. Ltd. — Tamano** Yd No: 1429 Loa 199.90 (BB) Br ex - Dght 13.519 Lbp 190.00 Br md 32.20 Dpth 19.50 Welded, 1 dk	**(A31A2GO) Open Hatch Cargo Ship** Grain: 67,354 TEU 2247 Compartments: 11 Ho, ER 11 Ha: ER Gantry cranes: 2x40t Ice Capable	**1 oil engine** driving 1 FP propeller Total Power: 12,130kW (16,492hp) 16.4kn B&W 6S60MC 1 x 2 Stroke 6 Cy. 600 x 2292 12130kW (16492bhp) Mitsui Engineering & Shipbuilding CLtd-Japan AuxGen: 3 x 980kW 220/440V 60Hz a.c Thrusters: 1 Thwart. FP thruster (f)
6500387 - -	**SAGA MOON** *ex Sun XXVI -1997* **Saint Vincent Tugs & Salvage Ltd** - *Kingstown* *St Vincent & The Grenadines* Official number: 400433	**248** 74 -	Class: (LR) ✠ Classed LR until 30/1/02	**1965-03 Charles D. Holmes & Co. Ltd. — Beverley** Yd No: 992 Loa 35.39 Br ex 8.67 Dght 3.607 Lbp 32.01 Br md 8.54 Dpth 3.97 Riveted\Welded, 1 dk	**(B32A2ST) Tug**	**1 oil engine** sr reverse geared to sc. shaft driving 1 FP propeller Total Power: 1,331kW (1,810hp) 12.0kn Mirrlees KLSSDM-6 1 x 4 Stroke 6 Cy. 381 x 508 1331kW (1810bhp) Mirrlees National Ltd.-Stockport AuxGen: 1 x 250kW 440V 60Hz a.c, 2 x 50kW 440V 60Hz a.c
9117741 *VRZQ8* -	**SAGA MORUS** *ex Hoegh Morus -2004* **Attic Forest AS** Saga Forest Carriers International AS SatCom: Inmarsat C 447728330 *Hong Kong* *Hong Kong* MMSI: 477283000 Official number: HK-1245	**36,463** 16,961 56,816	Class: NV	**1997-09 Mitsui Eng. & SB. Co. Ltd. — Tamano** Yd No: 1430 Loa 199.90 (BB) Br ex - Dght 13.519 Lbp 190.00 Br md 32.20 Dpth 19.50 Welded, 1 dk	**(A31A2GO) Open Hatch Cargo Ship** Grain: 67,354 TEU 2247 Compartments: 11 Ho, ER 11 Ha: ER Gantry cranes: 2x40t Ice Capable	**1 oil engine** driving 1 FP propeller Total Power: 12,130kW (16,492hp) 16.4kn B&W 6S60MC 1 x 2 Stroke 6 Cy. 600 x 2292 12130kW (16492bhp) Mitsui Engineering & Shipbuilding CLtd-Japan AuxGen: 3 x 980kW 220/440V 60Hz a.c Thrusters: 1 Thwart. FP thruster (f)
8954489 *JL6402* -	**SAGA MYOJIN MARU No. 123** **KK Shoei Maru** - *Kuroshio, Kochi* *Japan* MMSI: 431459000 Official number: 136498	*224* - -		**1999-11 Y.K. Kobayashi Zosensho — Yunotsu** Loa 48.05 (BB) Br ex - Dght - Lbp 37.80 Br md 6.60 Dpth 3.09 Welded, 1 dk	**(B11B2FV) Fishing Vessel** Hull Material: Aluminium Alloy	**1 oil engine** reduction geared to sc. shaft driving 1 FP propeller Total Power: 2,650kW (3,603hp) Niigata 16V26FX 1 x Vee 4 Stroke 16 Cy. 260 x 275 2650kW (3603bhp) Niigata Engineering Co Ltd-Japan AuxGen: 2 x 280kW 225V a.c Thrusters: 1 Thwart. FP thruster (f)
9371062 *VRDA4* -	**SAGA NAVIGATOR** **Saga Shipholding (Norway) AS** Saga Forest Carriers International AS *Hong Kong* *Hong Kong* MMSI: 477897700 Official number: HK-1946	**29,758** 14,440 46,573 T/cm 53.5	Class: NV	**2007-10 Oshima Shipbuilding Co Ltd — Saikai NS** Yd No: 10477 Loa 199.20 (BB) Br ex - Dght 11.800 Lbp 190.00 Br md 30.50 Dpth 16.40 Welded, 1 dk	**(A31A2GO) Open Hatch Cargo Ship** Double Hull Grain: 53,232 TEU 760 C Hold 360 TEU C Dk 400 TEU Compartments: 10 Ho, ER 10 Ha: ER 10 (13.2 x 25.3) Gantry cranes: 2x40t	**1 oil engine** driving 1 FP propeller Total Power: 10,920kW (14,847hp) 14.5kn Sulzer 7RTA52 1 x 2 Stroke 7 Cy. 520 x 1800 10920kW (14847bhp) Diesel United Ltd.-Aioi AuxGen: 3 x a.c Thrusters: 1 Tunnel thruster (f)
9401788 *VRDU9* -	**SAGA ODYSSEY** **Saga Shipholding (Norway) AS** Saga Forest Carriers International AS *Hong Kong* *Hong Kong* MMSI: 477058200 Official number: HK-2111	**29,758** 14,440 46,500 T/cm 53.5	Class: NV	**2008-05 Oshima Shipbuilding Co Ltd — Saikai NS** Yd No: 10480 Loa 199.20 (BB) Br ex - Dght 11.800 Lbp 190.00 Br md 30.50 Dpth 16.40 Welded, 1 dk	**(A31A2GO) Open Hatch Cargo Ship** Grain: 53,232 TEU 760 C Hold 360 TEU C Dk 400 TEU Compartments: 10 Ho, ER 10 Ha: ER 10 (13.2 x 25.3) Gantry cranes: 2x40t	**1 oil engine** driving 1 FP propeller Total Power: 9,510kW (12,930hp) 14.9kn Sulzer 7RTA52 1 x 2 Stroke 7 Cy. 520 x 1800 9510kW (12930bhp) Diesel United Ltd.-Aioi AuxGen: 3 x a.c Thrusters: 1 Tunnel thruster (f)
8000214 *9HA2950* -	**SAGA PEARL II** *ex Quest For Adventure -2013* *ex Saga Pearl II -2012 ex Astoria -2010* *ex Arkona -2002 ex Astor -1985* **Acromas Shipping Ltd** Saga Cruises Ltd *Valletta* *Malta* MMSI: 256878000 Official number: 8000214	**18,627** 6,267 3,245	Class: GL (DS)	**1981-12 Howaldtswerke-Deutsche Werft AG (HDW) — Hamburg** Yd No: 165 Loa 164.35 (BB) Br ex 22.89 Dght 6.101 Lbp 140.01 Br md 22.61 Dpth 16.06 Welded, 5 dks	**(A37A2PC) Passenger/Cruise** Passengers: cabins: 304; berths: 602 Ice Capable	**4 oil engines** dr geared to sc. shafts driving 2 CP propellers Total Power: 9,708kW (13,200hp) 18.0kn MAN 6L40/45 4 x 4 Stroke 6 Cy. 400 x 450 each-2427kW (3300bhp) Maschinenbau Augsburg Nuernberg (MAN)-Augsburg AuxGen: 1 x 2800kW 220/440V 60Hz a.c, 3 x 1400kW 220/440V 60Hz a.c, 1 x 240kW 220/440V 60Hz a.c Thrusters: 1 Thwart. FP thruster (f) Fuel: 55.0 (d.f.) 914.5 (r.f.) 58.0pd
9380764 *VRED4* -	**SAGA PIONEER** **Saga Shipholding (Norway) AS** Saga Forest Carriers International AS *Hong Kong* *Hong Kong* MMSI: 477102200 Official number: HK-2178	**29,758** 14,440 46,559 T/cm 53.5	Class: NV	**2008-08 Oshima Shipbuilding Co Ltd — Saikai NS** Yd No: 10486 Loa 199.20 (BB) Br ex 30.57 Dght 11.800 Lbp 194.70 Br md 30.50 Dpth 16.40 Welded, 1 dk	**(A31A2GO) Open Hatch Cargo Ship** Double Bottom Entire Compartment Length Grain: 53,232 TEU 760 C Hold 360 TEU C Dk 400 TEU Compartments: 10 Ho, ER 10 Ha: ER 10 (13.2 x 25.3) Gantry cranes: 2x40t	**1 oil engine** driving 1 FP propeller Total Power: 9,510kW (12,930hp) 14.9kn Sulzer 7RTA52 1 x 2 Stroke 7 Cy. 520 x 1800 9510kW (12930bhp) Diesel United Ltd.-Aioi AuxGen: 3 x a.c Thrusters: 1 Tunnel thruster (f)
9317054 - -	**SAGA QUEEN** - -	**624** 187 175		**2004-10 AS Rigas Kugu Buvetava (Riga Shipyard) — Riga** (Hull) Yd No: RKB-010/1 **2004-10 A/S Hvide Sande Skibs- og Baadebyggeri — Hvide Sande** Yd No: 100 Loa 49.70 Br ex 11.30 Dght 2.000 Lbp 44.10 Br md 11.00 Dpth 3.50 Welded, 1 dk	**(A37B2PS) Passenger Ship** Passengers: unberthed: 212	**1 oil engine** reduction geared to sc. shaft driving 1 Propeller Total Power: 537kW (730hp) 10.0kn Mitsubishi S12A2-MPTA 1 x Vee 4 Stroke 12 Cy. 150 x 160 537kW (730bhp) Mitsubishi Heavy Industries Ltd-Japan AuxGen: 2 x 180kW a.c Thrusters: 2 Tunnel thruster (f)
7434509 *PP3096* -	**SAGA RONCADOR** *ex Astro Roncador -2013 ex Rubim -2013* **SAGA Rebocadores & Servicos Maritimos Ltda** - *Rio de Janeiro* *Brazil* MMSI: 710999973 Official number: 3810248631	*869* 377 1,209	Class: AB	**1976-12 Atlantic Marine — Jacksonville, Fl** Yd No: 140 Loa 56.47 Br ex 11.61 Dght 4.206 Lbp 51.77 Br md 11.59 Dpth 4.91 Welded, 1 dk	**(B21B20T) Offshore Tug/Supply Ship**	**2 oil engines** reverse reduction geared to sc. shafts driving 2 FP propellers Total Power: 4,230kW (5,752hp) 15.0kn EMD (Electro-Motive) 16-645-E7 2 x Vee 2 Stroke 16 Cy. 230 x 254 each-2115kW (2876bhp) General Motors Corp-USA AuxGen: 2 x 125kW 440V 60Hz a.c Thrusters: 1 Thwart. FP thruster (f) Fuel: 374.0 (d.f.)

7822457 *9HOF8* -	**SAGA SAPPHIRE** *ex* Bleu De France *-2012* *ex* Holiday Dream *-2008* *ex* Superstar Aries *-2004* *ex* Superstar Europe *-1999* *ex* Europa *-1999* **Acromas Shipping Ltd** - *Valletta* *Malta* MMSI: 256208000 Official number: 7822457	**37,049** 13,555 5,168	Class: GL (NV)	**1981-12 Bremer Vulkan AG Schiffbau u. Maschinenfabrik — Bremen** Yd No: 1001 Loa 199.63 (BB) Br ex 28.55 Dght 8.421 Lbp 175.19 Br md 28.50 Dpth 12.98 Welded, 6 dks	**(A37A2PC) Passenger/Cruise** Passengers: cabins: 374; berths: 752 Ice Capable	**2 oil engines** driving 2 FP propellers Total Power: 21,270kW (28,918hp) 21.0kn MAN K7SZ70/125B 2 x 2 Stroke 7 Cy. 700 x 1250 each-10635kW (14459bhp) Bremer Vulkan AG Schiffbau u.Maschinenfabrik-Bremen AuxGen: 2 x 1920kW 440V 60Hz a.c, 5 x 1700kW 440V 60Hz a.c Thrusters: 1 Thwart. FP thruster (f)
7390416 *LNSK* N-301-W	**SAGA SEA** *ex* Kamchatka *-2005* *ex* Saga Sea *-2003* *ex* Alexandre *-1990* *ex* Bruse *-1980* *ex* Sea Bruse *-1980* **Aker Biomarine Antarctic AS** - SatCom: Inmarsat C 425953910 *Svolvaer* *Norway* MMSI: 259539000	**4,848** 1,513 877	Class: NV (BV) (AB)	**1974-11 Mangone Shipbuilding Co. — Houston, Tx** Yd No: 114 **1990-06 Soviknes Verft AS — Sovik** (Additional cargo section) Yd No: 103 Converted From: Offshore Supply Ship-1990 Lengthened & Rebuilt-1990 Loa 92.00 (BB) Br ex 16.53 Dght 7.950 Lbp 86.05 Br md 16.50 Dpth 8.50 Welded, 2 dks	**(B11A2FG) Factory Stern Trawler** Ins: 3,740 Ice Capable	**1 oil engine** reduction geared to sc. shaft driving 1 CP propeller Total Power: 4,437kW (6,033hp) 15.5kn Wartsila 12V32 1 x Vee 4 Stroke 12 Cy. 320 x 350 4437kW (6033bhp) (new engine 1990) Wartsila Diesel Oy-Finland AuxGen: 1 x 2000kW 440V 60Hz a.c, 2 x 1070kW 440V 60Hz a.c Thrusters: 1 Retract. directional thruster (f) Fuel: 169.5 (d.f.) 14.0pd
9144354 *VRYB8* -	**SAGA SKY** **Saga Shipholding (Norway) AS** Saga Forest Carriers International AS SatCom: Inmarsat C 447719810 *Hong Kong* *Hong Kong* MMSI: 477198000 Official number: HK-0917	**29,381** 14,155 47,053 T/cm 53.5	Class: NV	**1996-03 Oshima Shipbuilding Co Ltd — Saikai NS** Yd No: 10197 Loa 199.20 (BB) Br ex 30.57 Dght 11.823 Lbp 190.00 Br md 30.50 Dpth 16.40 Welded, 1 dk	**(A31A2GO) Open Hatch Cargo Ship** Grain: 51,946 TEU 1688 Compartments: 10 Ho, ER 10 Ha: 10 (13.2 x 25.3)ER Gantry cranes: 2x40t	**1 oil engine** driving 1 FP propeller Total Power: 8,951kW (12,170hp) 14.5kn Sulzer 7RTA52 1 x 2 Stroke 7 Cy. 520 x 1800 8951kW (12170bhp) Diesel United Ltd.-Aioi AuxGen: 3 x 700kW 450V 60Hz a.c Fuel: 140.0 (d.f.) (Heating Coils) 2823.0 (r.f.) 32.8pd
9014078 *VRWW5* -	**SAGA SPRAY** **Attic Forest AS** Saga Forest Carriers International AS SatCom: Inmarsat C 447785710 *Hong Kong* *Hong Kong* MMSI: 477857000 Official number: HK-0663	**29,381** 14,155 47,029 T/cm 53.5	Class: NV	**1994-04 Oshima Shipbuilding Co Ltd — Saikai NS** Yd No: 10165 Loa 199.20 (BB) Br ex - Dght 11.823 Lbp 190.00 Br md 30.50 Dpth 16.40 Welded, 1 dk	**(A31A2GO) Open Hatch Cargo Ship** Grain: 51,946 TEU 1688 Compartments: 10 Ho, ER 10 Ha: (13.2 x 12.3)9 (13.2 x 25.3)ER Gantry cranes: 2x40t	**1 oil engine** driving 1 FP propeller Total Power: 8,952kW (12,171hp) 14.5kn Sulzer 7RTA52 1 x 2 Stroke 7 Cy. 520 x 1800 8952kW (12171bhp) Diesel United Ltd.-Aioi AuxGen: 3 x 700kW 450V 60Hz a.c Fuel: 120.0 (d.f.) 2690.0 (r.f.) 34.9pd
6822254 - -	**SAGA SUN** *ex* Sun XXVII *-1997* **Mariners Haven Ltd** - *Kingstown* *St Vincent & The Grenadines*	**249** 74 -	Class: (LR) ✠ Classed LR until 7/2/01	**1968-12 J. Pollock, Sons & Co. Ltd. — Faversham** Yd No: 2144 Loa 35.44 Br ex 8.69 Dght 3.607 Lbp 32.01 Br md 8.54 Dpth 4.04 Riveted\Welded, 1 dk	**(B32A2ST) Tug** Derricks: 1x1.5t	**1 oil engine** sr reverse geared to sc. shaft driving 1 FP propeller Total Power: 1,331kW (1,810hp) 12.5kn Mirrlees KLSSGMR6 1 x 4 Stroke 6 Cy. 381 x 508 1331kW (1810bhp) Mirrlees National Ltd.-Stockport AuxGen: 1 x 250kW 440V 60Hz a.c, 2 x 42kW 440V 60Hz a.c Fuel: 61.0 (d.f.)
8918277 *VRYO8* -	**SAGA TIDE** **Saga Shipholding (Norway) AS** Saga Forest Carriers International AS SatCom: Inmarsat C 447732310 *Hong Kong* *Hong Kong* MMSI: 477323000 Official number: HK-1022	**29,235** 14,088 47,029 T/cm 53.5	Class: LR (NV) (NK) **100A1** SS 09/2011 LI **LMC** **UMS** Eq.Ltr: M†; Cable: 632.5/73.0 U3	**1991-09 Oshima Shipbuilding Co Ltd — Saikai NS** Yd No: 10137 Loa 199.20 (BB) Br ex 30.57 Dght 11.800 Lbp 191.09 Br md 30.50 Dpth 16.40 Welded, 1 dk	**(A31A2GO) Open Hatch Cargo Ship** Grain: 51,946 TEU 1688 C Ho 1128 TEU C Dk 560 TEU incl 50 ref C. Compartments: 10 Ho, ER 10 Ha: 10 (13.2 x 25.5)ER Gantry cranes: 2x40t	**1 oil engine** driving 1 FP propeller Total Power: 8,951kW (12,170hp) 14.5kn Sulzer 7RTA52 1 x 2 Stroke 7 Cy. 520 x 1800 8951kW (12170bhp) Diesel United Ltd.-Aioi AuxGen: 3 x 600kW 450V 60Hz a.c Boilers: AuxB (Comp) 7.0kgf/cm² (6.9bar) Fuel: 138.0 (d.f.) 2777.0 (r.f.) 34.9pd
9160803 *VRVP2* -	**SAGA TUCANO** *ex* Tucano *-2001* **Saga Shipholding (Norway) AS** Saga Forest Carriers International AS SatCom: Inmarsat C 447758710 *Hong Kong* *Hong Kong* MMSI: 477587000 Official number: HK-0385	**29,729** 14,528 46,990 T/cm 53.5	Class: NV	**1998-01 Oshima Shipbuilding Co Ltd — Saikai NS** Yd No: 10236 Loa 199.20 (BB) Br ex - Dght 11.823 Lbp 190.00 Br md 30.50 Dpth 16.40 Welded, 1 dk	**(A31A2GO) Open Hatch Cargo Ship** Double Hull Grain: 53,232 Compartments: 10 Ho, ER 10 Ha: 10 (13.2 x 25.3)ER Gantry cranes: 2x40t	**1 oil engine** driving 1 FP propeller Total Power: 8,952kW (12,171hp) 14.5kn Sulzer 7RTA52 1 x 2 Stroke 7 Cy. 520 x 1800 8952kW (12171bhp) Diesel United Ltd.-Aioi AuxGen: 3 x 700kW 100/450V 60Hz a.c Fuel: 158.0 (d.f.) (Heating Coils) 2765.0 (r.f.) 33.0pd
9233466 *VRXO6* -	**SAGA VIKING** **JYS Shipping SA** Saga Forest Carriers International AS *Hong Kong* *Hong Kong* MMSI: 477018000 Official number: HK-0805	**29,867** 14,529 46,901 T/cm 53.5	Class: NV	**2002-02 Oshima Shipbuilding Co Ltd — Saikai NS** Yd No: 10308 Loa 199.20 (BB) Br ex - Dght 11.800 Lbp 190.00 Br md 30.50 Dpth 16.40 Welded, 1 dk	**(A31A2GO) Open Hatch Cargo Ship** Grain: 53,232 TEU 760 C Hold 360 TEU C Dk 400 TEU Compartments: 10 Ho, ER 10 Ha: ER 10 (13.2 x 25.3) Gantry cranes: 2x40t	**1 oil engine** driving 1 FP propeller Total Power: 9,511kW (12,931hp) 14.9kn Sulzer 7RTA52 1 x 2 Stroke 7 Cy. 520 x 1800 9511kW (12931bhp) Diesel United Ltd.-Aioi
9233454 *VRXL8* -	**SAGA VOYAGER** **Navire Shipping Co Ltd** Saga Forest Carriers International AS SatCom: Inmarsat C 447797330 *Hong Kong* *Hong Kong* MMSI: 477973000 Official number: HK-0788	**29,867** 14,529 46,882 T/cm 53.5	Class: NV	**2001-12 Oshima Shipbuilding Co Ltd — Saikai NS** Yd No: 10307 Loa 199.20 (BB) Br ex - Dght 11.820 Lbp 190.00 Br md 30.50 Dpth 16.40 Welded, 1 dk	**(A31A2GO) Open Hatch Cargo Ship** Grain: 53,232 TEU 760 C Hold 360 TEU C Dk 400 TEU Compartments: 10 Ho, ER 10 Ha: ER 10 (13.2 x 25.3) Gantry cranes: 2x40t	**1 oil engine** driving 1 FP propeller Total Power: 9,511kW (12,931hp) 14.9kn Sulzer 7RTA52 1 x 2 Stroke 7 Cy. 520 x 1800 9511kW (12931bhp) Diesel United Ltd.-Aioi
8918289 *VRYO7* -	**SAGA WAVE** **Saga Shipholding (Norway) AS** Saga Forest Carriers International AS *Hong Kong* *Hong Kong* MMSI: 477322000 Official number: HK-1021	**29,235** 14,088 47,062 T/cm 53.5	Class: LR (NV) (NK) **100A1** SS 11/2011 **LMC** **UMS** Eq.Ltr: M†; Cable: 632.5/73.0 U3	**1991-11 Oshima Shipbuilding Co Ltd — Saikai NS** Yd No: 10138 Loa 199.20 (BB) Br ex 30.57 Dght 11.800 Lbp 191.09 Br md 30.50 Dpth 16.40 Welded, 1 dk	**(A31A2GO) Open Hatch Cargo Ship** Grain: 51,946 TEU 1688 C Ho 1128 TEU C Dk 560 TEU incl 50 ref C. Compartments: 10 Ho, ER 10 Ha: 10 (13.2 x 25.5)ER Gantry cranes: 2x40t	**1 oil engine** driving 1 FP propeller Total Power: 8,951kW (12,170hp) 14.5kn Sulzer 7RTA52 1 x 2 Stroke 7 Cy. 520 x 1800 8951kW (12170bhp) Diesel United Ltd.-Aioi AuxGen: 3 x 600kW 450V 60Hz a.c Boilers: AuxB (Comp) 7.0kgf/cm² (6.9bar) Fuel: 138.0 (d.f.) 2777.0 (r.f.) 34.9pd
9074078 *VRUR7* -	**SAGA WIND** **Saga Shipholding (Norway) AS** Saga Forest Carriers International AS SatCom: Inmarsat C 447728710 *Hong Kong* *Hong Kong* MMSI: 477287000 Official number: HK-0217	**29,381** 14,155 47,053 T/cm 53.5	Class: NV	**1994-11 Oshima Shipbuilding Co Ltd — Saikai NS** Yd No: 10173 Loa 199.20 (BB) Br ex - Dght 11.823 Lbp 190.00 Br md 30.50 Dpth 16.40 Welded, 1 dk	**(A31A2GO) Open Hatch Cargo Ship** Grain: 51,946 TEU 1688 Compartments: 10 Ho, ER 10 Ha: 10 (13.2 x 25.3)ER Gantry cranes: 2x40t	**1 oil engine** driving 1 FP propeller Total Power: 8,952kW (12,171hp) 14.5kn Sulzer 7RTA52 1 x 2 Stroke 7 Cy. 520 x 1800 8952kW (12171bhp) Diesel United Ltd.-Aioi AuxGen: 3 x 700kW 450V 60Hz a.c Fuel: 107.0 (d.f.) 2396.0 (r.f.)
7943079 *OXYZ* -	**SAGAFJORD** *ex* Party *-2000* *ex* Deepsea Inspector *-1987* *ex* Strilborg *-1984* *ex* Halsnoy *-1981* **Rita & Eric Hansen** Rederiet Sagafjord *Roskilde* *Denmark* MMSI: 219001185 Official number: B299	**305** 95 -	Class: (NV)	**1957 Holmens Verft — Risor** Yd No: 85 Converted From: Diving Support Vessel-1989 Converted From: Ferry (Passenger/Vehicle)-1984 Loa 38.74 Br ex 6.96 Dght - Lbp - Br md - Dpth 3.10 Welded, 1 dk	**(A37B2PS) Passenger Ship** Passengers: unberthed: 150	**2 oil engines** driving 2 FP propellers Total Power: 308kW (418hp) 11.0kn Deutz RA6M428 2 x 4 Stroke 6 Cy. 220 x 280 each-154kW (209bhp) Kloeckner Humboldt Deutz AG-West Germany
8406793 *XYNS* -	**SAGAING** **Myanma Five Star Line** - *Yangon* *Myanmar* MMSI: 506061000 Official number: 1877	**9,990** 5,588 13,055	Class: LR ✠ **100A1** SS 05/2010 strengthened for heavy cargoes, certified container securing arrangements on deck ✠ **LMC** **UMS** Eq.Ltr: F†; Cable: 577.5/58.0 U3	**1985-05 Seebeckwerft AG — Bremerhaven** Yd No: 1048 Loa 148.80 (BB) Br ex 22.66 Dght 8.202 Lbp 140.01 Br md 22.41 Dpth 10.75 Welded, 2 dks	**(A31A2GX) General Cargo Ship** Double Sides Entire Compartment Length Grain: 18,829; Bale: 17,060 TEU 383 C Ho 215 TEU C Dk 168 TEU incl 24 ref C. Compartments: 4 Ho, ER, 4 Tw Dk 4 Ha: (12.6 x 8.0)2 (25.5 x 13.5) (12.7 x 13.5)ER Cranes: 5x25t	**1 oil engine** driving 1 FP propeller Total Power: 6,649kW (9,040hp) 15.5kn B&W 5L60MCE 1 x 2 Stroke 5 Cy. 600 x 1944 6649kW (9040bhp) Mitsui Engineering & Shipbuilding CLtd-Japan AuxGen: 3 x 480kW 450V 60Hz a.c Boilers: e 7.1kgf/cm² (7.0bar), AuxB (o.f.) 7.1kgf/cm² (7.0bar) Fuel: 227.0 (d.f.) 1131.5 (r.f.)

8952390 *JL6401* -	**SAGAKATSU MARU No. 63** **YK Sagakatsu Maru** - *Kuroshio, Kochi* *Japan* MMSI: 431346000 Official number: 136497	*122* - -		**1999-01 Higashi Kyushu Shipbuilding Co Ltd — Usuki OT** Yd No: 828 L reg 29.70 Br ex - Dght - Lbp - Br md 5.69 Dpth 2.48 Bonded, 1 dk	**(B11B2FV) Fishing Vessel** Hull Material: Reinforced Plastic	**1 oil engine** driving 1 FP propeller Total Power: 1,839kW (2,500hp) Yanmar 6N280-EN 1 x 4 Stroke 6 Cy. 280 x 380 1839kW (2500bhp) Yanmar Diesel Engine Co Ltd-Japan
1007304 *ZCYC5* -	**SAGAMAR** *ex* Saga *-2008* *ex* Midnight Saga *-2004* **Sagamar Marine Ltd** Moran Yacht Management Inc *George Town* *Cayman Islands (British)* MMSI: 319001200 Official number: 741361	**271** 81 65	Class: LR ✠ **100A1** SS 09/2012 SSC Yacht, mono, G6 **LMC** Cable: 385.0/19.0 U2 (a)	**2002-09 Scheepswerf Made B.V. — Made** (Hull) **2002-09 Scheepsbouw en Machinefabriek Hakvoort B.V. — Monnickendam** Yd No: 234 Loa 33.70 Br ex 8.40 Dght 2.380 Lbp 28.13 Br md 8.10 Dpth 3.90 Welded, 1 dk	**(X11A2YP) Yacht**	**2 oil engines** with clutches, flexible couplings & sr reverse geared to sc. shafts driving 2 FP propellers Total Power: 708kW (962hp) 13.0kn Caterpillar 3406E 2 x 4 Stroke 6 Cy. 137 x 165 each-354kW (481bhp) Caterpillar Inc-USA AuxGen: 2 x 80kW 400V 50Hz a.c Thrusters: 1 Thwart. FP thruster (f)
9710842 *JD3595* -	**SAGAMI** - **Imoto Lines Ltd** - *Kobe, Hyogo* *Japan* Official number: 142041	*2,446* - 3,853	Class: NK	**2013-11 Koike Zosen Kaiun KK — Osakikamijima** Yd No: 557 Loa 110.72 (BB) Br ex - Dght 5.045 Lbp 101.00 Br md 17.40 Dpth 8.20 Welded, 1 dk	**(A33A2CC) Container Ship (Fully Cellular)** TEU 382	**1 oil engine** reduction geared to sc. shaft driving 1 Propeller Total Power: 3,309kW (4,499hp) Hanshin LH46LA 1 x 4 Stroke 6 Cy. 460 x 880 3309kW (4499bhp) The Hanshin Diesel Works Ltd-Japan AuxGen: 2 x 370kW a.c Fuel: 230.0
9597886 *JD3126* -	**SAGAMI MARU** - **Tokyo Kisen KK** - *Yokohama, Kanagawa* *Japan* Official number: 141345	*198* - -		**2010-11 Kanagawa Zosen — Kobe** Yd No: 618 Loa 40.00 Br ex - Dght - Lbp 35.25 Br md 9.20 Dpth 3.79 Welded, 1 dk	**(B32A2ST) Tug**	**2 oil engines** reduction geared to sc. shafts driving 2 Z propellers Total Power: 3,676kW (4,998hp) Niigata 6L28HX 2 x 4 Stroke 6 Cy. 280 x 370 each-1838kW (2499bhp) Niigata Engineering Co Ltd-Japan
8614285 *JG4669* -	**SAGAMI MARU** - - - *Kitakyushu, Fukuoka* *Japan* Official number: 129727	*182* - -		**1986-11 Kanagawa Zosen — Kobe** Yd No: 290 Loa 35.01 Br ex - Dght 2.701 Lbp 30.99 Br md 8.60 Dpth 3.61 Welded, 1 dk	**(B32A2ST) Tug**	**2 oil engines** Geared Integral to driving 2 Z propellers Total Power: 2,206kW (3,000hp) 12.5kn Niigata 6L25CXE 2 x 4 Stroke 6 Cy. 250 x 320 each-1103kW (1500bhp) Niigata Engineering Co Ltd-Japan
9005077 *9LY2129* -	**SAGAMIKO** *ex* Senyo Maru *-2005* *ex* Eifuku Maru *-2004* **Best Union International Shipping Co Ltd** Dalian Ningyang International Ship Management Co Ltd *Freetown* *Sierra Leone* MMSI: 667830000 Official number: SL100830	**1,554** 870 1,599	Class: OM	**1990-10 K.K. Murakami Zosensho — Naruto** Yd No: 188 Loa 75.42 (BB) Br ex - Dght 4.073 Lbp 70.00 Br md 12.00 Dpth 7.00 Welded	**(A31A2GX) General Cargo Ship** Grain: 2,412; Bale: 2,191 Compartments: 1 Ho, ER 1 Ha: ER	**1 oil engine** with clutches, flexible couplings & dr reverse geared to sc. shaft driving 1 FP propeller Total Power: 541kW (736hp) Niigata 6M30FT 1 x 4 Stroke 6 Cy. 300 x 530 541kW (736bhp) Niigata Engineering Co Ltd-Japan
9127863 *WDA2040* -	**SAGAMORE** *ex* Mint Arrow *-2000* *ex* Fas Red Sea II *-1997* *ex* Mint Arrow *-1996* **Sagamore Shipping LLC** Sealift Inc SatCom: Inmarsat M 630960720 *Dover, DE* *United States of America* MMSI: 338279000 Official number: 1101282	**3,838** 2,035 5,151	Class: AB	**1996-07 Yardimci Tersanesi A.S. — Tuzla** Yd No: 003 Loa 100.71 (BB) Br ex - Dght 6.125 Lbp 93.90 Br md 17.10 Dpth 7.95 Welded, 1 dk	**(A31A2GX) General Cargo Ship** Grain: 6,800; Bale: 6,739 TEU 364 C.Ho 144/40' C.Dk 220/20' incl. 45 ref C. Compartments: 1 Ho, ER 1 Ha: ER Cranes: 2x40t	**1 oil engine** with clutches, flexible couplings & sr geared to sc. shaft driving 1 CP propeller Total Power: 3,280kW (4,459hp) 14.0kn Wartsila 8R32E 1 x 4 Stroke 8 Cy. 320 x 350 3280kW (4459bhp) Wartsila Diesel Oy-Finland AuxGen: 1 x 700kW a.c, 2 x 400kW a.c Thrusters: 1 Thwart. CP thruster (f)
8656829 *PQ5425* -	**SAGAMORIM II** - **Camorim Offshore Servicos Maritimos Ltda** - *Rio de Janeiro* *Brazil* MMSI: 710009870 Official number: 3813884228	**418** 125 420	Class: RB (Class contemplated)	**2011-11 SRD Offshore SA — Angra dos Reis** Yd No: SS-001-014 Loa 32.00 Br ex Dght Lbp - Br md 11.00 Dpth 5.00 Welded, 1 dk	**(B32A2ST) Tug**	**3 oil engines** reduction geared to sc. shafts driving 3 Propellers Total Power: 2,277kW (3,096hp) Mitsubishi S6R2-MTK3L 3 x 4 Stroke 6 Cy. 170 x 220 each-759kW (1032bhp) Mitsubishi Heavy Industries Ltd-Japan
6513138 - -	**SAGAMYOJI MARU NO. 31** *ex* Kaiho Maru No. 7 *-1996* **Shinyo Suisan** - *South Korea*	*192* 65		**1965 Miho Zosensho K.K. — Shimizu** Yd No: 533 Loa 41.51 Br ex 6.61 Dght - Lbp 34.09 Br md 6.58 Dpth 3.20 Welded, 1 dk	**(B11B2FV) Fishing Vessel** Compartments: 4 Ho, ER 4 Ha: 4 (1.2 x 1.2)	**1 oil engine** driving 1 FP propeller Total Power: 515kW (700hp) Niigata 6L28BX 1 x 4 Stroke 6 Cy. 280 x 320 515kW (700bhp) Niigata Engineering Co Ltd-Japan AuxGen: 1 x 48kW 225V 60Hz a.c
8876998 *JL6227* -	**SAGAMYOJIN MARU No. 63** - **Myojin Suisan KK** - *Kuroshio, Kochi* *Japan* MMSI: 431389000 Official number: 133887	*168* - -		**1994-02 Higashi Kyushu Shipbuilding Co Ltd — Usuki OT** L reg 34.90 Br ex - Dght - Lbp - Br md 6.07 Dpth 2.86 Bonded, 1 dk	**(B11B2FV) Fishing Vessel** Hull Material: Reinforced Plastic	**1 oil engine** driving 1 FP propeller Total Power: 471kW (640hp) Niigata 1 x 4 Stroke 471kW (640bhp) Niigata Engineering Co Ltd-Japan
9176890 *JH3456* -	**SAGAMYOJIN MARU NO. 83** *ex* Sumiyoshi Maru *-2009* **Myojin Suisan KK** - *Kuroshio, Kochi* *Japan* Official number: 134459	*149* - -		**1997-03 Higashi Kyushu Shipbuilding Co Ltd — Usuki OT** L reg 33.20 Br ex - Dght - Lbp - Br md 5.89 Dpth 2.70 Bonded, 1 dk	**(B11B2FV) Fishing Vessel** Hull Material: Reinforced Plastic	**1 oil engine** geared to sc. shaft driving 1 FP propeller Yanmar 1 x 4 Stroke Yanmar Diesel Engine Co Ltd-Japan
9140205 *JL6399* -	**SAGAMYOJIN MARU NO. 183** *ex* Sagamyojin Maru No. 83 *-2009* **Myojin Suisan KK** - *Kuroshio, Kochi* *Japan* MMSI: 431826000 Official number: 135105	*190* - 207		**1996-03 Miho Zosensho K.K. — Shimizu** Yd No: 1468 Loa 45.00 (BB) Br ex - Dght 2.600 Lbp 35.00 Br md 6.00 Dpth - Bonded, 1 dk	**(B11B2FV) Fishing Vessel** Hull Material: Reinforced Plastic	**1 oil engine** with flexible couplings & sr gearedto sc. shaft driving 1 FP propeller Total Power: 853kW (1,160hp) Daihatsu 6DKM-28 1 x 4 Stroke 6 Cy. 280 x 390 853kW (1160bhp) Daihatsu Diesel Manufacturing Co Lt-Japan
9184043 *9LY2567* -	**SAGAN** *ex* Jembawati *-2012* **Global Eminence Ltd** Ocean Grow International Shipmanagement Consultant Corp *Freetown* *Sierra Leone* MMSI: 667003370	**5,404** 1,808 6,685 T/cm 17.5	Class: (NK)	**1999-05 K.K. Tachibana Senpaku Tekko — Anan** Yd No: 868 Loa 107.90 (BB) Br ex 19.22 Dght 6.013 Lbp 103.00 Br md 19.20 Dpth 9.30 Welded, 1 dk	**(A12B2TR) Chemical/Products Tanker** Double Hull (13F) Liq: 8,250; Liq (Oil): 8,670 Cargo Heating Coils Compartments: 12 Wing Ta, 2 Wing Slop Ta, ER 4 Cargo Pump (s): 4x500m³/hr Manifold: Bow/CM: 58.4m	**1 oil engine** driving 1 FP propeller Total Power: 3,310kW (4,500hp) 13.0kn B&W 6L35MC 1 x 2 Stroke 6 Cy. 350 x 1050 3310kW (4500bhp) The Hanshin Diesel Works Ltd-Japan AuxGen: 3 x a.c Fuel: 430.0 (r.f.) 90.0 (d.f.)
5422306 *VWTY* -	**SAGAR** - **Kolkata Port Trust** - *Kolkata* *India* Official number: 1100	*1,993* 522 929	Class: (LR) (IR) ✠ Classed LR until 26/1/79	**1964-05 Blyth Dry Docks & SB. Co. Ltd. — Blyth** Yd No: 384 Loa 83.62 Br ex 13.31 Dght 4.744 Lbp 76.21 Br md 13.26 Dpth 7.17 Riveted\Welded, 1 dk, 2nd dk except in mchy. space 3rd dk in fwd hold	**(B34N2QP) Pilot Vessel**	**2 oil engines** sr reverse geared to sc. shafts driving 2 FP propellers Total Power: 1,236kW (1,680hp) MAN G9V30/45ATL 2 x 4 Stroke 9 Cy. 300 x 450 each-618kW (840bhp) Maschinenbau Augsburg Nuernberg (MAN)-Augsburg AuxGen: 3 x 175kW 220V d.c
9213052 - -	**SAGAR** - **Government of The Republic of India (Coast Guard)** - *India*	**1,888** 566 417	Class: (LR) (IR) ✠ 17/10/03	**2003-09 Goa Shipyard Ltd. — Goa** Yd No: 1180 Loa 102.00 Br ex 11.56 Dght - Lbp 94.10 Br md 11.50 Dpth 6.00 Welded, 2 dks	**(B34H2SQ) Patrol Vessel**	**2 oil engines** with clutches, flexible couplings & sr geared to sc. shafts driving 2 CP propellers Total Power: 9,130kW (12,414hp) Pielstick 16PA6V280 2 x Vee 4 Stroke 16 Cy. 280 x 290 each-4565kW (6207bhp) Kirloskar Oil Engines Ltd-India AuxGen: 4 x 400kW 415V 50Hz a.c

IMO / Call sign	Name / Owner	Tonnage	Class	Build / Dimensions	Type	Machinery
8308484 *VWRF* -	**SAGAR 4** *ex* SCI-04 *-2013* **SS Offshore Pte Ltd** Amba Shipping & Logistics Pvt Ltd *Mumbai* *India* MMSI: 419258000 Official number: 2041	**1,310** 393 1,812	Class: IR (NV)	**1984-12 Robin Shipyard Pte Ltd — Singapore** Yd No: 337 Loa 58.60 Br ex 13.01 Dght 5.936 Lbp 51.62 Br md 12.98 Dpth 6.76 Welded, 2 dks	**(B21B20A) Anchor Handling Tug Supply**	**4 oil engines** with clutches, flexible couplings & sr geared to sc. shafts driving 2 CP propellers Total Power: 3,972kW (5,400hp) Daihatsu 6DSM-26A 4 x 4 Stroke 6 Cy. 260 x 300 each-993kW (1350bhp) Daihatsu Diesel Manufacturing Co Lt-Japan AuxGen: 2 x 680kW 380V 50Hz a.c, 2 x 245kW 380V 50Hz a.c Thrusters: 1 Thwart. CP thruster (f)
8407266 *VVGF* -	**SAGAR BHUSHAN** **Oil & Natural Gas Corp Ltd** Luminus Energy Pvt Ltd SatCom: Inmarsat C 441956210 *Mumbai* *India* MMSI: 419383000 Official number: 2126	**11,103** 3,331 9,113	Class: AB IR	**1987-05 Hindustan Shipyard Ltd — Visakhapatnam** Yd No: 1181 Loa 157.46 Br ex 24.54 Dght 6.701 Lbp 136.81 Br md 24.50 Dpth 11.21 Welded, 1 dk	**(B22B20D) Drilling Ship** Cranes: 1x60t,1x40t	**4 diesel electric oil engines** driving 4 gen. each 1750kW 600V a.c Connecting to 4 elec. motors driving 2 FP propellers Total Power: 7,648kW (10,400hp) 10.0kn Daihatsu 6DV-26A 4 x Vee 4 Stroke 12 Cy. 260 x 300 each-1912kW (2600bhp) Daihatsu Diesel Manufacturing Co Lt-Japan AuxGen: 1 x 700kW 480V 60Hz a.c, 1 x 560kW 480V 60Hz a.c
8821034 *VWSI* -	**SAGAR DEEP II** **Government of The Republic of India (Directorate General of Lighthouses & Lightships)** Tradex Shipping Co Pvt Ltd (Tradex India) *Mumbai* *India* MMSI: 419030800 Official number: 2849	**2,466** 740 1,357 T/cm 9.2	Class: IR (LR) ✠ Classed LR until 4/11/03	**2002-08 Hooghly Dock & Port Engineers Ltd. — Haora** Yd No: 464 Loa 82.60 Br ex 14.02 Dght 4.250 Lbp 75.00 Br md 14.00 Dpth 6.00 Welded, 1 dk	**(B34Q2QX) Lighthouse Tender**	**2 oil engines** with clutches, flexible couplings & sr geared to sc. shafts driving 2 CP propellers Total Power: 1,980kW (2,692hp) 12.0kn Bergens KRMB-6 2 x 4 Stroke 6 Cy. 250 x 300 each-990kW (1346bhp) Rolls Royce Marine AS-Norway AuxGen: 3 x 480kW 415V 50Hz a.c Thrusters: 1 Thwart. FP thruster (f) Fuel: 157.0 (d.f.)
7603356 *AUQU* -	**SAGAR I** *ex* Tong Lian *-2007* *ex* Shinnihon Maru No. 2 *-1982* **S S Offshore Pvt Ltd** - *Mumbai* *India* MMSI: 419069500 Official number: 3331	**303** 91 264	Class: IR (NK)	**1976-03 Usuki Iron Works Co Ltd — Usuki OT** Yd No: 951 Loa 35.60 Br ex 8.51 Dght 3.237 Lbp 31.31 Br md 8.49 Dpth 3.61 Welded, 1 dk	**(B32A2ST) Tug**	**2 oil engines** geared to sc. shafts driving 2 FP propellers Total Power: 1,766kW (2,402hp) 11.0kn Yanmar 6GA-ET 2 x 4 Stroke 6 Cy. 240 x 290 each-883kW (1201bhp) Yanmar Diesel Engine Co Ltd-Japan AuxGen: 2 x 60kW 225V 60Hz a.c Fuel: 190.0 (d.f.)
9086150 *AVCG* -	**SAGAR III** *ex* Greenville 11 *-2009* *ex* TPC 3 *-1994* **S S Offshore Pvt Ltd** - *Mumbai* *India* MMSI: 419090800 Official number: 3627	**161** 49 150	Class: IR (NK)	**1993-09 Nam Cheong Dockyard Sdn Bhd — Miri** Yd No: 383 Loa 25.00 Br ex - Dght 2.810 Lbp 23.17 Br md 7.60 Dpth 3.50 Welded, 1 dk	**(B32A2ST) Tug**	**2 oil engines** reduction geared to sc. shafts driving 2 FP propellers Total Power: 1,176kW (1,598hp) Cummins KT-38-M 2 x Vee 4 Stroke 12 Cy. 159 x 159 each-588kW (799bhp) Cummins Engine Co Inc-USA AuxGen: 2 x 28kW a.c Fuel: 110.0 (d.f.)
9520962 *3FYM3* -	**SAGAR JYOTI** **Pavo Maritime SA** Tata NYK Shipping Pte Ltd SatCom: Inmarsat C 437117712 *Panama* *Panama* MMSI: 371177000 Official number: 4298911	**32,305** 19,458 58,110 T/cm 57.4	Class: NK	**2011-09 Tsuneishi Group (Zhoushan) Shipbuilding Inc — Daishan County ZJ** Yd No: SS-075 Loa 189.99 (BB) Br ex - Dght 12.824 Lbp 185.60 Br md 32.26 Dpth 18.00 Welded, 1 dk	**(A21A2BC) Bulk Carrier** Grain: 72,689; Bale: 70,122 Compartments: 5 Ho, ER 5 Ha: ER Cranes: 4x30t	**1 oil engine** driving 1 FP propeller Total Power: 8,400kW (11,421hp) 14.5kn MAN-B&W 6S50MC-C 1 x 2 Stroke 6 Cy. 500 x 2000 8400kW (11421bhp) Mitsui Engineering & Shipbuilding CLtd-Japan Fuel: 2380.0
9533440 *9V2049* -	**SAGAR KANTA** **Tata NYK Shipping Pte Ltd** Nippon Yusen Kabushiki Kaisha (NYK Line) *Singapore* *Singapore* MMSI: 566877000 Official number: 398542	**33,990** 19,965 60,835 T/cm 60.0	Class: NK	**2013-03 Oshima Shipbuilding Co Ltd — Saikai NS** Yd No: 10658 Loa 199.98 (BB) Br ex - Dght 12.840 Lbp 196.00 Br md 32.26 Dpth 18.33 Welded, 1 dk	**(A21A2BC) Bulk Carrier** Grain: 76,912; Bale: 75,311 Compartments: 5 Ho, ER 5 Ha: (21.4 x 18.6)2 (23.3 x 18.6) (22.3 x 18.6)ER (17.7 x 18.6) Cranes: 4x30t	**1 oil engine** driving 1 FP propeller Total Power: 8,201kW (11,150hp) 14.5kn MAN-B&W 6S50MC-C 1 x 2 Stroke 6 Cy. 500 x 2000 8201kW (11150bhp) Kawasaki Heavy Industries Ltd-Japan AuxGen: 3 x a.c Fuel: 1987.0
9679139 *3FRK7* -	**SAGAR KANYA** **TN-Hyuga Shipping SA** Fleet Ship Management Pte Ltd *Panama* *Panama* MMSI: 370953000 Official number: 45306KJ	**33,192** 19,143 58,609 T/cm 59.5	Class: NK	**2013-11 Nantong COSCO KHI Ship Engineering Co Ltd (NACKS) — Nantong JS** Yd No: 145 Loa 197.00 (BB) Br ex - Dght 12.676 Lbp 194.00 Br md 32.26 Dpth 18.10 Welded, 1 dk	**(A21A2BC) Bulk Carrier** Grain: 73,679; Bale: 70,963 Compartments: 5 Ho, ER 5 Ha: ER Cranes: 4x30.5t	**1 oil engine** driving 1 FP propeller Total Power: 8,630kW (11,733hp) 14.5kn MAN-B&W 6S50ME-C8 1 x 2 Stroke 6 Cy. 500 x 2000 8630kW (11733bhp) Hudong Heavy Machinery Co Ltd-China Fuel: 2200.0
8123183 *VTJR* -	**SAGAR KANYA** **Government of The Republic of India (Department of Ocean Development)** The Shipping Corporation of India Ltd (SCI) SatCom: Inmarsat C 441958110 *Mumbai* *India* MMSI: 419320000 Official number: 1976	*4,888* 1,466 1,554	Class: IR (LR) ✠ Classed LR until 8/91	**1983-03 Schlichting-Werft GmbH — Luebeck** Yd No: 1452 Loa 100.51 Br ex 16.39 Dght 5.601 Lbp 89.01 Br md 16.31 Dpth 9.81 Welded, 2 dks	**(B31A2SR) Research Survey Vessel**	**5 diesel electric oil engines** driving 5 gen. each 896kW 660V a.c Connecting to 4 elec. motors driving 2 FP propellers Total Power: 6,000kW (8,160hp) 14.3kn Wartsila 6L20 5 x 4 Stroke 6 Cy. 200 x 280 each-1200kW (1632bhp) (new engine 2005) Wartsila Finland Oy-Finland Thrusters: 1 Thwart. FP thruster (f) Fuel: 781.0 (d.f.)
9342920 *AUKJ* -	**SAGAR MANJUSHA** **Government of The Republic of India (National Institute of Ocean Technology)** Seaport Shipping Pvt Ltd *Chennai* *India* MMSI: 419063100 Official number: 3173	**1,065** 320 407	Class: IR	**2006-06 Hindustan Shipyard Ltd — Visakhapatnam** Yd No: 11119 Loa 59.90 Br ex 11.00 Dght 3.012 Lbp 52.80 Br md 10.98 Dpth 5.00 Welded, 1 dk	**(B31A2SR) Research Survey Vessel** A-frames: 1; Cranes: 2	**2 oil engines** geared to sc. shafts driving 2 FP propellers Total Power: 1,156kW (1,572hp) 11.5kn Caterpillar 3508B 2 x Vee 4 Stroke 8 Cy. 170 x 190 each-578kW (786bhp) Caterpillar Inc-USA AuxGen: 3 x 215kW 415V 50Hz a.c Thrusters: 1 Tunnel thruster (f) Fuel: 138.0 (d.f.)
9165073 *YHYO* -	**SAGAR MANTHAN** **PT Van Oord Indonesia** Van Oord Ship Management BV *Jakarta* *Indonesia* MMSI: 525015072	**534** 160 182	Class: BV (KI)	**1997-02 Southern Ocean Shipbuilding Co Pte Ltd — Singapore (Hull)** Yd No: 212 **1997-02 Tille Scheepsbouw Kootstertille B.V. — Kootstertille** Yd No: 319 Loa 46.50 Br ex 11.28 Dght 2.500 Lbp 40.56 Br md 11.20 Dpth 4.00 Welded, 1 dk	**(B33A2DS) Suction Dredger**	**2 oil engines** with clutches, flexible couplings & sr reverse geared to sc. shafts driving 2 FP propellers Total Power: 746kW (1,014hp) 8.5kn Cummins KTA-19-M 2 x 4 Stroke 6 Cy. 159 x 159 each-373kW (507bhp) Cummins Engine Co Inc-USA AuxGen: 2 x 91kW 220/380V 50Hz a.c Thrusters: 1 Water jet (f) Fuel: 125.0 (d.f.)
7627572 *ATST* -	**SAGAR MEXICANA I** **Chowgule & Co Pvt Ltd** Chowgule Steamships Ltd *Mormugao* *India*	*198* - -	Class: (BV)	**1978 Chowgule & Co Pvt Ltd — Goa** Yd No: 73 Loa 23.75 Br ex 7.50 Dght 2.901 Lbp 21.21 Br md 7.48 Dpth 3.43 Welded, 1 dk	**(B11A2FT) Trawler**	**1 oil engine** reverse reduction geared to sc. shaft driving 1 FP propeller Total Power: 268kW (364hp) 8.5kn Caterpillar D353TA 1 x 4 Stroke 6 Cy. 159 x 203 268kW (364bhp) Caterpillar Tractor Co-USA Fuel: 34.0 (d.f.)
7627584 *ATSW* -	**SAGAR MEXICANA II** **Chowgule & Co Pvt Ltd** - *Mormugao* *India*	*198* - -	Class: IR (BV)	**1979-04 Chowgule & Co Pvt Ltd — Goa** Yd No: 74 Loa 23.70 Br ex - Dght 2.901 Lbp 21.21 Br md 7.48 Dpth 3.43 Welded, 1 dk	**(B11A2FT) Trawler**	**1 oil engine** reverse reduction geared to sc. shaft driving 1 FP propeller Total Power: 268kW (364hp) Caterpillar D353TA 1 x 4 Stroke 6 Cy. 159 x 203 268kW (364bhp) Caterpillar Tractor Co-USA
7802859 *ATUP* -	**SAGAR MEXICANA III** **Chowgule & Co Pvt Ltd** Chowgule Steamships Ltd *Mormugao* *India* Official number: 1820	*130* 71 75	Class: (NV)	**1980-02 Chowgule & Co Pvt Ltd — Goa** Yd No: 75 Loa 23.75 Br ex - Dght 2.552 Lbp 20.65 Br md 7.48 Dpth 3.64 Welded, 1 dk	**(B11A2FT) Trawler**	**1 oil engine** driving 1 FP propeller Total Power: 257kW (349hp) Caterpillar D353TA 1 x 4 Stroke 6 Cy. 159 x 203 257kW (349bhp) Caterpillar Tractor Co-USA AuxGen: 2 x 72kW 415V 50Hz a.c

IMO / Call sign	Name / Owner / Manager / Port / Numbers	Tonnage	Class	Build / Dimensions	Type	Machinery
7802823 *ATUR* -	**SAGAR MEXICANA IV** **Chowgule & Co Pvt Ltd** - *Mormugao* *India* Official number: 1821	*130* 71 75	Class: IR (NV)	**1980-05 Chowgule & Co Pvt Ltd — Goa** Yd No: 76 Loa 23.78 Br ex - Dght 2.552 Lbp 20.65 Br md 7.48 Dpth 3.64 Welded, 1 dk	**(B11A2FT) Trawler**	**1 oil engine** driving 1 FP propeller Total Power: 257kW (349hp) Caterpillar D353TA 1 x 4 Stroke 6 Cy. 159 x 203 257kW (349bhp) Caterpillar Tractor Co-USA AuxGen: 2 x 72kW 415V 50Hz a.c
9583146 *3FLZ3* -	**SAGAR MOTI** **Lyra Maritime SA** Fleet Ship Management Pte Ltd *Panama* *Panama* MMSI: 356799000 Official number: 4450313	**32,305** 19,458 58,097 T/cm 57.4	Class: NK	**2012-12 Tsuneishi Group (Zhoushan) Shipbuilding Inc — Daishan County ZJ** Yd No: SS-098 Loa 189.99 Br ex 32.29 Dght 12.826 Lbp 185.60 Br md 32.26 Dpth 18.00 Welded, 1 dk	**(A21A2BC) Bulk Carrier** Grain: 72,689; Bale: 70,122 Compartments: 5 Ho, ER 5 Ha: ER Cranes: 4x30t	**1 oil engine** driving 1 FP propeller Total Power: 8,400kW (11,421hp) 14.5kn MAN-B&W 6S50MC-C 1 x 2 Stroke 6 Cy. 500 x 2000 8400kW (11421bhp) Mitsui Engineering & Shipbuilding CLtd-Japan Fuel: 2380.0
9384485 *AUCE* -	**SAGAR NIDHI** **Government of The Republic of India (National Institute of Ocean Technology)** ABS Marine Services Pvt Ltd *Chennai* *India* MMSI: 419683000 Official number: 3016	**5,050** 1,459 3,250	Class: IR NV	**2007-12 Fincantieri-Cant. Nav. Italiani S.p.A. — La Spezia** Yd No: 6147 Loa 103.60 (BB) Br ex 18.03 Dght 5.200 Lbp 87.60 Br md 18.00 Dpth 7.80 Welded, 1 dk	**(B31A2SR) Research Survey Vessel** Ice Capable	**4 diesel electric oil engines** driving 4 gen. Connecting to 2 elec. motors driving 2 Azimuth electric drive units Total Power: 5,680kW (7,724hp) 14.6kn Wartsila 8L20 4 x 4 Stroke 8 Cy. 200 x 280 each-1420kW (1931bhp) Wartsila Finland Oy-Finland Thrusters: 1 Tunnel thruster (f); 1 Tunnel thruster (a)
8928313 *VTTK* -	**SAGAR PASCHIMI** **Government of The Republic of India (Department of Ocean Development)** Seaport Shipping Pvt Ltd SatCom: Inmarsat M 641902610 *Mumbai* *India* MMSI: 419004200 Official number: 2661	**188** 56 50	Class: IR	**1996 Alcock Ashdown (Gujarat) Ltd. — Bhavnagar** Yd No: 205 Loa 30.15 Br ex 6.68 Dght 1.880 Lbp 27.20 Br md 6.51 Dpth 4.10 Welded, 1 dk	**(B31A2SR) Research Survey Vessel**	**2 oil engines** sr geared to sc. shafts driving 2 CP propellers Total Power: 216kW (294hp) 8.0kn Cummins NT-495-M 2 x 4 Stroke 4 Cy. 130 x 152 each-108kW (147bhp) Kirloskar Cummins Ltd-India AuxGen: 2 x 80kW 415V 50Hz a.c Fuel: 16.0 (d.f.)
9183441 *AVCT* -	**SAGAR PRINCE** *ex* MLC Nancy 3 *-2009* *ex* Ocean Silver 8 *-2002* **SS Offshore Pte Ltd** - *Mumbai* *India* MMSI: 419092600 Official number: 3640	**250** 75 195	Class: IR (AB)	**1997-11 Jiangdong Shipyard — Wuhu AH** Yd No: XT-03 Loa 27.01 Br ex - Dght 3.950 Lbp - Br md 9.00 Dpth 4.25 Welded, 1 dk	**(B32A2ST) Tug**	**2 oil engines** reduction geared to sc. shafts driving 2 FP propellers Total Power: 1,766kW (2,402hp) 11.2kn Yanmar M220-EN 2 x 4 Stroke 6 Cy. 220 x 300 each-883kW (1201bhp) Yanmar Diesel Engine Co Ltd-Japan AuxGen: 2 x 70kW a.c
9123829 *VWFQ* -	**SAGAR PURVI** **Government of The Republic of India (Department of Ocean Development)** Seaport Shipping Pvt Ltd SatCom: Inmarsat A 1641212 *Kolkata* *India* MMSI: 419062000 Official number: 2662	**187** 56 50	Class: IR	**1996-12 Corporated Consultancy & Eng Enterprise Pvt Ltd — Haora** Yd No: 230 Loa 30.15 Br ex 6.51 Dght 1.950 Lbp 27.20 Br md 6.50 Dpth 4.10 Welded, 1 dk	**(B31A2SR) Research Survey Vessel**	**2 oil engines** sr geared to sc. shafts driving 2 CP propellers Total Power: 200kW (272hp) 8.6kn Cummins N-495-M 2 x 4 Stroke 4 Cy. 130 x 152 each-100kW (136bhp) Kirloskar Cummins Ltd-India AuxGen: 2 x 80kW 415V 50Hz a.c Fuel: 15.0 (d.f.)
9533438 *9V8842* -	**SAGAR RATAN** **Tata NYK Shipping Pte Ltd** - *Singapore* *Singapore* MMSI: 564372000 Official number: 396304	**33,910** 19,965 61,664 T/cm 60.0	Class: NK	**2010-08 Oshima Shipbuilding Co Ltd — Saikai NS** Yd No: 10551 Loa 199.98 (BB) Br ex - Dght 12.850 Lbp 196.00 Br md 32.26 Dpth 18.33 Welded, 1 dk	**(A21A2BC) Bulk Carrier** Grain: 76,913; Bale: 75,312 Compartments: 5 Ho, ER 5 Ha: (21.4 x 18.6)2 (23.3 x 18.6) (22.3 x 18.6)ER (17.7 x 18.6) Cranes: 4x30t	**1 oil engine** driving 1 FP propeller Total Power: 8,201kW (11,150hp) 14.5kn MAN-B&W 6S50MC-C 1 x 2 Stroke 6 Cy. 500 x 2000 8201kW (11150bhp) Kawasaki Heavy Industries Ltd-Japan Fuel: 2045.0 (r.f.)
8300080 *VWXS* -	**SAGAR SAMPADA** **Government of The Republic of India (Department of Ocean Development)** The Shipping Corporation of India Ltd (SCI) SatCom: Inmarsat C 441958210 *Mumbai* *India* MMSI: 419323000 Official number: 2064	**2,661** 798 1,140	Class: IR (NV)	**1984-11 Dannebrog Vaerft A/S — Aarhus** Yd No: 186 Loa 71.51 Br ex 16.59 Dght 5.601 Lbp 63.02 Br md 16.41 Dpth 9.00 Welded, 2 dks	**(B12D2FR) Fishery Research Vessel** Ice Capable	**1 oil engine** with clutches, flexible couplings & sr geared to sc. shaft driving 1 CP propeller Total Power: 1,681kW (2,285hp) 13.5kn Alpha 8SL28L-VO 1 x 4 Stroke 8 Cy. 280 x 320 1681kW (2285bhp) B&W Alpha Diesel A/S-Denmark AuxGen: 2 x 517kW 415V 50Hz a.c, 2 x 307kW 415V 50Hz a.c Thrusters: 1 Thwart. CP thruster (f)
8754750 *ATIL* -	**SAGAR SAMRAT** **Oil & Natural Gas Corp Ltd** - *Mumbai* *India* Official number: 1504	**6,821** 2,045 3,105	Class: AB (IR)	**1973-03 Mitsubishi Heavy Industries Ltd. — Hiroshima** Yd No: 241003 Loa 77.41 Br ex 39.62 Dght 5.340 Lbp - Br md - Dpth 6.70 Welded, 1 dk	**(Z11C4ZD) Drilling Rig, jack up** Passengers: berths: 72 Cranes: 2x50t	**4 diesel electric oil engines** driving 4 gen. Connecting to 4 elec. motors driving 2 Propellers Total Power: 6,532kW (8,880hp) 8.0kn Alco 12V251C 4 x Vee 4 Stroke 12 Cy. 229 x 267 each-1633kW (2220bhp) White Industrial Power Inc-USA
7229681 *VTQN* -	**SAGAR SEVAK** *ex* Ferdinandtor *-1986* **Safe & Sure Marine Services Pvt Ltd** - *Mumbai* *India* MMSI: 419412000 Official number: 2342	*490* 230 826	Class: (IR) (AB) (GL)	**1972 JG Hitzler Schiffswerft und Masch GmbH & Co KG — Lauenburg** Yd No: 732 Loa 52.86 Br ex 11.33 Dght 3.442 Lbp 49.20 Br md 11.00 Dpth 3.97 Welded, 1 dk	**(B21A2OS) Platform Supply Ship** Ice Capable	**2 oil engines** reverse reduction geared to sc. shafts driving 2 FP propellers Total Power: 1,398kW (1,900hp) 12.5kn MWM TBD440-8 2 x 4 Stroke 8 Cy. 230 x 270 each-699kW (950bhp) Motoren Werke Mannheim AG (MWM)-West Germany AuxGen: 3 x 112kW 220/380V 50Hz a.c Thrusters: 1 Thwart. FP thruster (f) Fuel: 304.0 (d.f.)
9583122 *9V9913* -	**SAGAR SHAKTI** **Tata NYK Shipping Pte Ltd** Fleet Ship Management Pte Ltd SatCom: Inmarsat C 456647610 *Singapore* *Singapore* MMSI: 566476000 Official number: 397741	**32,305** 19,458 58,097 T/cm 57.4	Class: NK	**2012-04 Tsuneishi Group (Zhoushan) Shipbuilding Inc — Daishan County ZJ** Yd No: SS-096 Loa 190.00 (BB) Br ex 32.29 Dght 12.830 Lbp 185.60 Br md 32.26 Dpth 18.00 Welded, 1 dk	**(A21A2BC) Bulk Carrier** Grain: 72,689; Bale: 70,122 Compartments: 5 Ho, ER 5 Ha: ER Cranes: 4x30t	**1 oil engine** driving 1 FP propeller Total Power: 8,400kW (11,421hp) 14.5kn MAN-B&W 6S50MC-C 1 x 2 Stroke 6 Cy. 500 x 2000 8400kW (11421bhp) Mitsui Engineering & Shipbuilding CLtd-Japan Fuel: 2380.0
8605571 *VWGE* -	**SAGAR SUKTI** *ex* Kavita *-2004* **Government of The Republic of India (National Institute of Oceanography)** Seaport Shipping Pvt Ltd *Mormugao* *India* Official number: 2802	*151* 45 51	Class: (IR)	**1989-12 Hooghly Dock & Port Engineers Ltd. — Haora** Yd No: 447 Loa 23.50 Br ex 6.51 Dght 2.890 Lbp 21.00 Br md 6.50 Dpth 3.40 Welded, 1 dk	**(B12D2FR) Fishery Research Vessel**	**1 oil engine** geared to sc. shaft driving 1 FP propeller Total Power: 405kW (551hp) 9.4kn Caterpillar 3408TA 1 x Vee 4 Stroke 8 Cy. 137 x 152 405kW (551bhp) Caterpillar Inc-USA AuxGen: 2 x 26kW 450V 50Hz a.c Fuel: 26.0 (d.f.)
6513358 *ATMY* -	**SAGAR TARANI** *ex* Mini *-1975* *ex* Finnmini *-1971* *ex* Pinocchio *-1969* **Sagar Lines (India) Pvt Ltd** - *Kolkata* *India* Official number: 1635	*497* 178 712	Class: IR (NV)	**1965 Valmet Oy — Turku** Yd No: 285 Loa 60.00 Br ex 8.54 Dght 3.449 Lbp 53.70 Br md 8.49 Dpth 3.71 Welded, 1 dk	**(A13B2TU) Tanker (unspecified)** Liq: 947; Liq (Oil): 947 Compartments: 6 Ta, ER	**1 oil engine** driving 1 FP propeller Total Power: 375kW (510hp) 10.0kn Alpha 406-24VO 1 x 2 Stroke 6 Cy. 240 x 400 375kW (510bhp) Alpha Diesel A/S-Denmark AuxGen: 1 x 52kW 380V 50Hz a.c, 1 x 40kW 380V 50Hz a.c, 1 x 24kW 380V 50Hz a.c
8401183 *ATEI* -	**SAGAR VIJAY** **Oil & Natural Gas Corp Ltd** Luminus Energy Pvt Ltd SatCom: Inmarsat C 441956010 *Mumbai* *India* MMSI: 419382000 Official number: 2091	*11,104* 3,331 9,239	Class: AB IR	**1985-02 Hitachi Zosen Corp — Sakai OS** Yd No: K1052 Loa 145.85 Br ex - Dght 6.720 Lbp 136.80 Br md 24.50 Dpth 11.20 Welded	**(B22B2OD) Drilling Ship** Cranes: 1x60t,1x45t	**4 diesel electric oil engines** driving 4 gen. each 1750kW 600V a.c Connecting to 4 elec. motors driving 2 FP propellers Total Power: 6,912kW (9,396hp) 10.0kn Daihatsu 6DV-26A 4 x Vee 4 Stroke 12 Cy. 260 x 300 each-1728kW (2349bhp) Daihatsu Diesel Manufacturing Co Lt-Japan AuxGen: 1 x 700kW 480V 60Hz a.c, 1 x 500kW 480V 60Hz a.c
7903952 *DUSZ* -	**SAGARA BABYLYN** *ex* Zuiho Maru No. 28 *-1999* **Trans-Pacific Journey Fishing Corp** - *Manila* *Philippines* Official number: MNLD010271	*498* 326 -		**1979-08 Niigata Engineering Co Ltd — Niigata NI** Yd No: 1628 Loa 61.42 Br ex - Dght 4.161 Lbp 54.21 Br md 10.22 Dpth 6.33 Welded	**(B11B2FV) Fishing Vessel**	**1 oil engine** driving 1 FP propeller Total Power: 2,207kW (3,001hp) Niigata 6M40X 1 x 4 Stroke 6 Cy. 400 x 600 2207kW (3001bhp) Niigata Engineering Co Ltd-Japan

8835798 - -	**SAGARA RANI** **Government of The Republic of India (Port Department of Kerala)** - *Kochi* *India*	*126* 46 16	Class: IR	**1990-05 Cochin Shipyard Ltd — Ernakulam** Yd No: BY-11 Loa 26.00 Br ex 6.68 Dght 1.250 Lbp 23.25 Br md 6.38 Dpth 2.30 Welded, 1 dk	**(A37B2PS) Passenger Ship** Passengers: unberthed: 60	**2 oil engines** driving 2 FP propellers Total Power: 218kW (296hp) 8.0kn Leyland ALM 680 2 x 4 Stroke 6 Cy. 127 x 146 each-109kW (148bhp) Ashok Leyland Ltd-India AuxGen: 2 x 12kW 415V 50Hz a.c Fuel: 4.0 (d.f.)
8941573 - -	**SAGARIA 1** *ex* Sagaria A *-2012* *ex* Transpacific 1 *-2009* *ex* Tropical 1 *-2004* *ex* Transpacific 1 *-2004* *ex* Merit Metro No. 1 *-1998* **Leesin Sdn Bhd** *Kuching* *Malaysia* Official number: 334783	**186** 55 -	Class: BV	**1997-03 Nga Chai Shipyard Sdn Bhd — Sibu** Yd No: 9604 Loa 26.00 Br ex - Dght 3.000 Lbp 24.36 Br md 7.92 Dpth 3.65 Welded, 1 dk	**(B32A2ST) Tug**	**2 oil engines** driving 2 FP propellers Total Power: 1,204kW (1,636hp) Mitsubishi S6R2-MPTA 2 x 4 Stroke 6 Cy. 170 x 220 each-602kW (818bhp) Mitsubishi Heavy Industries Ltd-Japan AuxGen: 2 x 64kW 415V a.c
9078799 *VTLX* -	**SAGARIKA** **Government of The Republic of India (Ministry of Agriculture & Cooperation)** - *Kochi* *India*	*189* 56 -	Class: IR (NK)	**1993-12 Niigata Engineering Co Ltd — Niigata NI** Yd No: 2261 Loa 28.80 Br ex - Dght - Lbp 24.80 Br md 7.30 Dpth 3.25 Welded, 1 dk	**(B12D2FR) Fishery Research Vessel** Ins: 121	**1 oil engine** with clutches & sr geared to sc. shaft driving 1 CP propeller Total Power: 478kW (650hp) 9.0kn Niigata 6NSD-M 1 x 4 Stroke 6 Cy. 160 x 210 478kW (650bhp) Niigata Engineering Co Ltd-Japan AuxGen: 2 x 64kW a.c
9507776 *9V8070* -	**SAGARJEET** **Tata NYK Shipping Pte Ltd** Fleet Ship Management Pte Ltd SatCom: Inmarsat C 456389510 *Singapore* *Singapore* MMSI: 563895000 Official number: 395257	**32,343** 19,458 58,079 T/cm 57.4	Class: NK	**2009-05 Tsuneishi Group (Zhoushan) Shipbuilding Inc — Daishan County ZJ** Yd No: SS-109 Loa 189.99 (BB) Br ex - Dght 12.826 Lbp 185.60 Br md 32.26 Dpth 18.00 Welded, 1 dk	**(A21A2BC) Bulk Carrier** Grain: 72,689; Bale: 70,122 Compartments: 5 Ho, ER 5 Ha: ER Cranes: 4x30t	**1 oil engine** driving 1 FP propeller Total Power: 8,400kW (11,421hp) 14.5kn MAN-B&W 6S50MC-C 1 x 2 Stroke 6 Cy. 500 x 2000 8400kW (11421bhp) Mitsui Engineering & Shipbuilding CLtd-Japan AuxGen: 3 x 480kW a.c Fuel: 2150.0
9369655 *PCGU* -	**SAGASBANK** **Bankship IV BV** Pot Scheepvaart BV SatCom: Inmarsat C 424606111 *Delfzijl* *Netherlands* MMSI: 246061000 Official number: 47194	**2,999** 1,662 4,500	Class: BV	**2010-11 Brodogradiliste Apatin AD — Apatin** (Hull) Yd No: (737) **2010-11 Bijlsma Shipyard BV — Lemmer** Yd No: 737 Loa 89.95 (BB) Br ex - Dght 5.830 Lbp 81.98 Br md 14.40 Dpth 7.35 Welded, 1 dk	**(A31A2GX) General Cargo Ship** Grain: 6,032 Compartments: 1 Ho, ER 1 Ha: ER	**1 oil engine** reduction geared to sc. shaft driving 1 CP propeller Total Power: 1,860kW (2,529hp) 11.5kn Wartsila 6L26 1 x 4 Stroke 6 Cy. 260 x 320 1860kW (2529bhp) Wartsila Italia SpA-Italy AuxGen: 1 x 312kW 400V 50Hz a.c, 2 x 188kW 400V 50Hz a.c Thrusters: 1 Tunnel thruster (f)
8915495 *CB4404* -	**SAGASCA** **Pesquera Indo SA** - *Valparaiso* *Chile* MMSI: 725000111 Official number: 2700	*545* 163 605	Class: (BV)	**1990-11 Ast. y Maestranzas de la Armada (ASMAR Chile) — Talcahuano** Yd No: 41 Loa 48.00 (BB) Br ex - Dght 4.500 Lbp 42.80 Br md 10.00 Dpth 5.00 Welded	**(B11B2FV) Fishing Vessel** Ins: 650	**1 oil engine** geared to sc. shaft driving 1 CP propeller Total Power: 1,779kW (2,419hp) 14.0kn Deutz SBV8M628 1 x 4 Stroke 8 Cy. 240 x 280 1779kW (2419bhp) Kloeckner Humboldt Deutz AG-West Germany AuxGen: 2 x 64kW 220/380V d.c
8633152 *LLMD* -	**SAGASUND** *ex* Saga Lejon *-2001* *ex* Malarsund *-1993* *ex* Tyrihans *-1989* **ms Turisten Tore Nybro Hansen & Co & DA Aslakstrom Gard** Tore Nybro Hansen *Halden* *Norway* MMSI: 258279000	**257** 82 -	Class: (NV)	**1964-12 Hjorungavaag Verksted AS — Hjorungavaag** (Hull) **1964-12 Ulstein Mek. Verksted AS — Ulsteinvik** Yd No: 28 Loa 35.16 Br ex 7.43 Dght 2.068 Lbp - Br md 7.22 Dpth - Welded, 1 dk	**(A37A2PC) Passenger/Cruise** Passengers: 292	**1 oil engine** driving 1 FP propeller Total Power: 485kW (659hp) MWM 1 x 4 Stroke 485kW (659bhp) Motoren Werke Mannheim AG (MWM)-West Germany
7039103 *6VOC* DAK 44	**SAGATTA** *ex* Rubyan IV *-1977* **Armement Frigorifique Senegalais** - *Dakar* *Senegal*	*130* 63 -	Class: (BV)	**1970 Soc Nouvelle des Ats et Chs de La Rochelle-Pallice — La Rochelle** Yd No: 00153 Loa 25.20 Br ex 6.86 Dght 2.515 Lbp 22.59 Br md 6.71 Dpth 3.51 Welded, 1 dk	**(B11A2FT) Trawler** Ins: 148 Compartments: 1 Ho, ER 1 Ha: (1.1 x 1.6)	**1 oil engine** driving 1 FP propeller Total Power: 291kW (396hp) 9.0kn Caterpillar D353SCAC 1 x 4 Stroke 6 Cy. 159 x 203 291kW (396bhp) Caterpillar Tractor Co-USA Fuel: 48.5 (d.f.)
8988466 *WDB8034* -	**SAGE LAB** *ex* Miss Callie P. *-2006* **Rexmere Crewboats LLC** Laborde Marine LLC *New Orleans, LA* *United States of America* Official number: 1151506	**341** 102 411		**2004-03 Breaux Bay Craft, Inc. — Loreauville, La** Yd No: 1727 Loa - Br ex - Dght - Lbp 45.14 Br md 9.00 Dpth 3.65 Welded, 1 dk	**(B21A20C) Crew/Supply Vessel** Hull Material: Aluminium Alloy Passengers: unberthed: 72	**4 oil engines** reduction geared to sc. shafts driving 4 FP propellers Total Power: 4,632kW (6,296hp) Caterpillar 3512B 4 x Vee 4 Stroke 12 Cy. 170 x 190 each-1158kW (1574bhp) Caterpillar Inc-USA Thrusters: 1 Thwart. FP thruster (f)
9233545 *H9AV* -	**SAGE SAGITTARIUS** **Hesperus Maritime SA** Hachiuma Steamship Co Ltd (Hachiuma Kisen KK) SatCom: Inmarsat C 435537610 *Panama* *Panama* MMSI: 355376000 Official number: 2790301C	**73,427** 24,641 105,708	Class: NK	**2001-03 Imabari Shipbuilding Co Ltd — Marugame KG (Marugame Shipyard)** Yd No: 1351 Loa 234.93 (BB) Br ex - Dght 15.268 Lbp 226.00 Br md 43.00 Dpth 25.40 Welded, 1 dk	**(A21A2BC) Bulk Carrier** Double Hull Grain: 126,189 Compartments: 6 Ho, ER 6 Ha: 6 (26.4 x 28.8)ER Gantry cranes: 2x49t	**1 oil engine** driving 1 FP propeller Total Power: 15,300kW (20,802hp) 15.0kn Mitsubishi 8UEC60LSII 1 x 2 Stroke 8 Cy. 600 x 2300 15300kW (20802bhp) Mitsubishi Heavy Industries Ltd-Japan AuxGen: 4 x 1190kW 450V 60Hz a.c Fuel: 293.0 (d.f.) (Heating Coils) 4232.0 (r.f.) 59.0pd
8509076 *EPBX* -	**SAGHA 1** **Government of The Islamic Republic of Iran (Ports & Maritime Organisation)** - *Bandar Abbas* *Iran* Official number: 582	**458** 165 750	Class: AS	**1987-12 Iran Marine Ind. Co. (IMICO) — Bushehr** Yd No: 13024 Loa 49.92 Br ex 10.29 Dght 1.950 Lbp 47.96 Br md 9.95 Dpth 2.98 Welded, 1 dk	**(A35D2RL) Landing Craft** Bow door/ramp	**2 oil engines** with clutches & reverse reduction geared to sc. shafts driving 2 FP propellers Total Power: 900kW (1,224hp) MWM TBD234V12 2 x Vee 4 Stroke 12 Cy. 128 x 140 each-450kW (612bhp) Motoren Werke Mannheim AG (MWM)-West Germany
8512176 *EPBL* -	**SAGHA 2** **Parsian Offshore Engineering & Installation Co** - *Bandar Imam Khomeini* *Iran* Official number: 555	**515** 162 750	Class: AS	**1988 Iran Marine Ind. Co. (IMICO) — Bushehr** Yd No: 12865 L reg 41.20 Br ex - Dght 1.701 Lbp 39.20 Br md 12.20 Dpth 3.87 Welded, 1 dk	**(A35D2RL) Landing Craft**	**2 oil engines** geared to sc. shafts driving 2 FP propellers Total Power: 432kW (588hp) MWM TD232V12 2 x Vee 4 Stroke 12 Cy. 120 x 130 each-216kW (294bhp) Motoren Werke Mannheim AG (MWM)-West Germany
7807184 *EQHC* -	**SAGHAR** *ex* Bahregan 8 *-2008* *ex* Iran Ghadr *-2006* *ex* Arya Dokht *-1980* **Mr S B Darbaudi & Mr S A Heydaryan** Sam Langar Shipping & Marine Services Ltd *Bandar Abbas* *Iran* MMSI: 422091000	**1,485** 727 1,662	Class: AS (LR) (AB) Classed LR until 14/11/99	**1978-09 Teraoka Shipyard Co Ltd — Minamiawaji HG** Yd No: 176 Loa 53.65 Br ex 11.25 Dght 5.001 Lbp 49.89 Br md 10.81 Dpth 5.80 Welded, 1 dk	**(A35D2RL) Landing Craft** Bow door/ramp (centre) Lane-Len: 138 Lane-Wid: 4.98 Lane-clr ht: 4.00 Grain: 1,452; Bale: 1,435 TEU 10 C.Ho 6/20' C.Dk 4/20' Compartments: 1 Ho, ER 1 Ha: (19.8 x 7.0)ER	**2 oil engines** reverse reduction geared to sc. shafts driving 2 FP propellers Total Power: 1,618kW (2,200hp) 12.5kn Yanmar 6GL-ST 2 x 4 Stroke 6 Cy. 240 x 290 each-809kW (1100bhp) Yanmar Diesel Engine Co Ltd-Japan AuxGen: 2 x 40kW 225V 60Hz a.c
5173876 *VF2560* -	**SAGINAW** *ex* John J. Boland *-1999* **Lower Lakes Towing Ltd** *Port Dover, ON* *Canada* MMSI: 316004950 Official number: 822418	**14,066** 5,412 19,390 T/cm 37.6	Class: AB	**1953-10 Manitowoc Shipbuilding Inc — Manitowoc WI** Yd No: 417 Loa 195.00 Br ex 22.00 Dght 7.800 Lbp 189.90 Br md 21.95 Dpth 11.00 Welded, 1 dk	**(A23A2BK) Bulk Carrier, Self-discharging, Laker** Compartments: 6 Ho, ER 30 Ha: 30 (3.6 x 13.9)ER	**1 oil engine** reduction geared to sc. shaft driving 1 FP propeller Total Power: 6,000kW (8,158hp) 14.0kn MaK 6M43C 1 x 4 Stroke 6 Cy. 430 x 610 6000kW (8158bhp) (new engine 2008) Caterpillar Motoren GmbH & Co. KG-Germany AuxGen: 1 x 1550kW 60Hz a.c, 1 x 1290kW 60Hz a.c Thrusters: 1 Thwart. FP thruster (f) Fuel: 396.5 (r.f.)
9205237 - -	**SAGITARIO** **Government of The Republic of Portugal (Ministerio do Marinha)** - *Portugal*	**150** - 68		**2001-01 Estaleiros Navais do Mondego S.A. — Figueira da Foz** Yd No: 242 Loa 28.40 Br ex - Dght - Lbp - Br md 5.95 Dpth 3.48 Welded, 1 dk	**(B34H2SQ) Patrol Vessel** Hull Material: Aluminium Alloy	**1 oil engine** geared to sc. shaft driving 1 FP propeller Cummins KTA-50-M2 1 x Vee 4 Stroke 16 Cy. 159 x 159 Cummins Engine Co Ltd-United Kingdom

9605827 - -	**SAGITARIO** **Government of Mexico (Secretaria de Comunicaciones y Transportes, Sub-Secretaria de Operacion, Direccion General de Marina Mercante, Direccion de Senalamiento Maritimo)** - *Mexico* Official number: 115991	**313** 79 -	Class: GL	**2010-12 Servicios Navales e Industriales SA de CV (SENI) — Mazatlan** Yd No: 009 Loa 35.06 Br ex - Dght - Lbp 33.50 Br md 10.50 Dpth - Welded, 1 dk	**(B34Q2QB) Buoy Tender**	**2 oil engines** driving 2 FP propellers Total Power: 1,066kW (1,450hp) Caterpillar C18 2 x 4 Stroke 6 Cy. 145 x 183 each-533kW (725bhp) Caterpillar Inc-USA
7328499 - -	**SAGITT** *ex* Tongga *-2007* *ex* Razdan *-2007* **Ocean Shipping Co Ltd SA** -	**498** 149 304	Class: (RS)	**1973-06 Khabarovskiy Sudostroitelnyy Zavod im Kirova — Khabarovsk** Yd No: 232 Loa 54.84 Br ex 9.38 Dght 3.810 Lbp 49.99 Br md - Dpth 4.73 Welded, 1 dk	**(B11A2FT) Trawler** Ins: 284 Compartments: 2 Ho, ER 2 Ha: 2 (1.5 x 1.6) Derricks: 1x3t; Winches: 1 Ice Capable	**1 oil engine** driving 1 CP propeller Total Power: 588kW (799hp) 11.8kn S.K.L. 8NVD48-2U 1 x 4 Stroke 8 Cy. 320 x 480 588kW (799bhp) VEB Schwermaschinenbau "KarlLiebknecht" (SKL)-Magdeburg
1007299 *ELXW8* -	**SAGITTA** **Radius Shipping Co Ltd** - *Monrovia* *Liberia* MMSI: 636011247 Official number: 11247	**826** 247 160	Class: LR ✠ **100A1** SS 05/2011 SSC Yacht mono HSC LDC G6 service area **LMC** **UMS** Eq.Ltr: I; Cable: 330.0/22.0 U2	**2001-06 Oceanfast Pty Ltd — Fremantle WA** Yd No: 74 Loa 57.27 Br ex 10.76 Dght 2.710 Lbp 49.54 Br md 10.52 Dpth 5.30 Welded, 2 dks	**(X11A2YP) Yacht**	**2 oil engines** with clutches, flexible couplings & sr reverse geared to sc. shafts driving 2 FP propellers Total Power: 4,944kW (6,722hp) 23.0kn M.T.U. 16V4000M70 2 x Vee 4 Stroke 16 Cy. 165 x 190 each-2472kW (3361bhp) MTU Friedrichshafen GmbH-Friedrichshafen AuxGen: 2 x 185kW 380V 50Hz a.c Thrusters: 1 Thwart. FP thruster (f)
8979049 *V4PH2* -	**SAGITTA** *ex* El Nino *-2007* **Island Windjammers Inc** - *Basseterre* *St Kitts & Nevis* MMSI: 341387000 Official number: SKN 1002410	**254** 75 -		**1961 Falkenbergs Varv AB — Falkenberg** Loa 36.50 Br ex - Dght 3.350 Lbp 31.69 Br md 6.70 Dpth - Welded, 1 dk	**(A37A2PC) Passenger/Cruise** Passengers: cabins: 10; berths: 16; driver berths: 5	**2 oil engines** driving 2 Propellers Total Power: 272kW (370hp) 8.5kn Scania 2 x 4 Stroke each-136kW (185bhp) AB Scania Vabis-Sweden AuxGen: 2 x 40kW 120/240V 60Hz a.c
9370109 *V2DG3* -	**SAGITTA** **ms 'Marpessa' Schiffahrtsgesellschaft mbH & Co KG** Peter Doehle Schiffahrts-KG *Saint John's* *Antigua & Barbuda* MMSI: 305204000 Official number: 4429	**9,556** 4,404 13,464	Class: GL	**2008-02 Jiangsu Yangzijiang Shipbuilding Co Ltd — Jiangyin JS** Yd No: 2004-694C Loa 138.07 Br ex - Dght 8.000 Lbp 130.00 Br md 21.00 Dpth 11.00 Welded, 1 dk	**(A31A2GX) General Cargo Ship** Grain: 16,230 Compartments: 3 Ho, ER 3 Ha: ER Cranes: 2x35t	**1 oil engine** driving 1 FP propeller Total Power: 5,180kW (7,043hp) 10.5kn MAN-B&W 7S35MC 1 x 2 Stroke 7 Cy. 350 x 1400 5180kW (7043bhp) MAN Diesel A/S-Denmark AuxGen: 3 x 400kW 450V a.c, 1 x 700kW 450V a.c Thrusters: 1 Tunnel thruster (f)
9401166 *V7UO5* -	**SAGITTA** *launched as* Frisia Brussel *-2010* **Likiep Shipping Co Inc** Unitized Ocean Transport Ltd *Majuro* *Marshall Islands* MMSI: 538003988 Official number: 3988	**36,087** 15,774 42,614	Class: GL	**2010-06 Nordseewerke GmbH — Emden** Yd No: 558 Loa 228.50 (BB) Br ex - Dght 12.000 Lbp 218.22 Br md 32.20 Dpth 18.55 Welded, 1 dk	**(A33A2CC) Container Ship (Fully Cellular)** TEU 3414 C Ho 1384 TEU C Dk 2030 TEU incl 500 ref C Compartments: 6 Cell Ho, ER	**1 oil engine** driving 1 FP propeller Total Power: 28,880kW (39,265hp) 23.5kn MAN-B&W 8K80MC-C 1 x 2 Stroke 8 Cy. 800 x 2300 28880kW (39265bhp) Hyundai Heavy Industries Co Ltd-South Korea AuxGen: 2 x 2200kW 450V a.c, 1 x 1720kW 450V a.c Thrusters: 1 Tunnel thruster (f)
8918033 *FGEX* SB 764603	**SAGITTAIRE** **Armement Dahouetin** - SatCom: Inmarsat C 422755310 *Saint-Brieuc* *France* MMSI: 227553000 Official number: 764603	*170* - -		**1990-06 SOCARENAM — Boulogne** Yd No: 139 Loa 23.60 Br ex 7.21 Dght 3.400 Lbp 20.28 Br md 7.20 Dpth 3.80 Welded	**(B11A2FS) Stern Trawler** Ins: 90	**1 oil engine** with clutches, flexible couplings & dr geared to sc. shaft driving 1 CP propeller Total Power: 441kW (600hp) Cummins KT-38-M 1 x Vee 4 Stroke 12 Cy. 159 x 159 441kW (600bhp) Cummins Engine Co Inc-USA Thrusters: 1 Thwart. FP thruster (f)
7329417 *IQNR* -	**SAGITTARIO** **Matteo Giordana** - *Cetara* *Italy* Official number: 562	*197* 100 -		**1973 Cant. Nav. Fratelli Maccioni — Viareggio** Yd No: 6 Loa 37.67 Br ex 7.14 Dght 1.931 Lbp 28.05 Br md 7.12 Dpth 3.81 Welded, 1 dk	**(B11A2FT) Trawler**	**1 oil engine** geared to sc. shaft driving 1 FP propeller Total Power: 809kW (1,100hp) MAN G8V30/45ATL 1 x 4 Stroke 8 Cy. 300 x 450 809kW (1100bhp) Maschinenbau Augsburg Nuernberg (MAN)-Augsburg
9122473 *A8OG2* -	**SAGITTARIUS** *ex* CMA CGM Ipanema *-2008* *ex* DAL Madagascar *-2007* *ex* Sagittarius *-2003* **Scio Sea Maritime SA** MCC Transport Singapore Pte Ltd *Monrovia* *Liberia* MMSI: 636013618 Official number: 13618	**16,803** 8,648 23,051 T/cm 37.1	Class: NK (LR) (GL) Classed LR until 3/4/11	**2001-04 Stocznia Szczecinska Porta Holding SA — Szczecin** Yd No: B170/I/21 Loa 184.10 (BB) Br ex - Dght 9.850 Lbp 171.94 Br md 25.30 Dpth 13.50 Welded, 1 dk	**(A33A2CC) Container Ship (Fully Cellular)** Grain: 29,816; Bale: 29,668 TEU 1730 C Ho 634 TEU C Dk 1096 TEU incl 200 ref C. Compartments: 4 Cell Ho, ER 9 Ha: (12.5 x 13.0)8 (12.5 x 20.6)ER Cranes: 3x40t	**1 oil engine** driving 1 FP propeller Total Power: 13,320kW (18,110hp) 19.7kn Sulzer 6RTA62 1 x 2 Stroke 6 Cy. 620 x 2150 13320kW (18110bhp) H Cegielski Poznan SA-Poland AuxGen: 3 x 1192kW 450V 60Hz a.c Boilers: e (ex.g.) 9.2kgf/cm² (9.0bar), AuxB (o.f.) 9.2kgf/cm² (9.0bar) Thrusters: 1 Thwart. FP thruster (f) Fuel: 165.9 (d.f.) 2229.6 (r.f.) 54.0pd
9096870 *CUFD9* A-3636-C	**SAGITTARIUS** **Testa y Cunhas SA** - *Aveiro* *Portugal*	**256** 77 396	Class: BV	**2004-02 Astilleros Armon SA — Navia** Yd No: 591 Loa 28.50 Br ex - Dght 3.410 Lbp 25.29 Br md 8.00 Dpth 5.70 Welded, 2 dks	**(B11A2FS) Stern Trawler**	**1 oil engine** reduction geared to sc. shaft driving 1 CP propeller Total Power: 596kW (810hp) 10.5kn A.B.C. 6DXC 1 x 4 Stroke 6 Cy. 242 x 320 596kW (810bhp) Anglo Belgian Corp NV (ABC)-Belgium AuxGen: 1 x 108kW 380/220V 50Hz a.c, 1 x 78kW 380/220V 50Hz a.c
8963258 - -	**SAGITTARIUS-II** *ex* Sumiyoshi Maru No. 53 *-2001* **Dalko International Ltd** -	**149** 44 -		**1981-01 Daikyo Zosen K.K. — Japan** L reg 23.83 Br ex - Dght - Lbp - Br md 5.38 Dpth 2.00 Welded, 1 dk	**(B11B2FV) Fishing Vessel**	**1 oil engine** driving 1 FP propeller Total Power: 221kW (300hp) Matsui 1 x 4 Stroke 221kW (300bhp) Matsui Iron Works Co Ltd-Japan
9283887 *3EAB7* -	**SAGITTARIUS LEADER** **Sagittarius Maritima SA** Wilhelmsen Ship Management Sdn Bhd SatCom: Inmarsat C 435441010 *Panama* *Panama* MMSI: 354410000 Official number: 3063205B	**61,804** 18,542 20,098 T/cm 55.6	Class: NK	**2005-03 Imabari Shipbuilding Co Ltd — Marugame KG (Marugame Shipyard)** Yd No: 1424 Loa 199.94 (BB) Br ex - Dght 10.016 Lbp 190.00 Br md 32.26 Dpth 34.80 Welded, 12 dks	**(A35B2RV) Vehicles Carrier** Side door/ramp (s) Len: 20.00 Wid: 4.20 Swl: 15 Quarter stern door/ramp (s. a.) Len: 35.00 Wid: 8.00 Swl: 80 Cars: 5,415	**1 oil engine** driving 1 FP propeller Total Power: 15,540kW (21,128hp) 20.0kn Mitsubishi 8UEC60LSII 1 x 2 Stroke 8 Cy. 600 x 2300 15540kW (21128bhp) Kobe Hatsudoki KK-Japan AuxGen: 4 x 1070kW 440/220V 60Hz a.c Thrusters: 1 Tunnel thruster (f) Fuel: 3280.0
9194725 *A4DD6* -	**SAGLA** **Bahwan Lamnalco LLC** - *Port Sultan Qaboos* *Oman* MMSI: 461000006 Official number: 848	**191** 57 -	Class: BV	**1999-06 Stocznia Tczew Sp z oo — Tczew** (Hull) **1999-06 B.V. Scheepswerf Damen — Gorinchem** Yd No: 7005 Loa 26.15 Br ex 7.95 Dght 3.220 Lbp 25.22 Br md 7.90 Dpth 4.05 Welded, 1 dk	**(B32A2ST) Tug**	**2 oil engines** with clutches, flexible couplings & sr reverse geared to sc. shafts driving 2 FP propellers Total Power: 2,028kW (2,758hp) 13.0kn Caterpillar 3512B-HD 2 x Vee 4 Stroke 12 Cy. 170 x 215 each-1014kW (1379bhp) Caterpillar Inc-USA AuxGen: 2 x 48kW 230/400V 50Hz a.c Fuel: 72.2 (d.f.) 4.5pd
8701997 - -	**SAGRADO CORAZON** **Pennisi, Bonaccorso y Malvica SRL** -	*100* - -		**1987-12 SANYM S.A. — Buenos Aires** Yd No: 80 Loa 23.50 Br ex - Dght 3.001 Lbp 20.91 Br md 6.51 Dpth 3.31 Welded, 1 dk	**(B11A2FS) Stern Trawler** Ins: 115	**1 oil engine** geared to sc. shaft driving 1 FP propeller Total Power: 313kW (426hp) Caterpillar D353SCAC 1 x 4 Stroke 6 Cy. 159 x 203 313kW (426bhp) Caterpillar Inc-USA
7367809 - -	**SAGRES** *ex* Concordia *-1993* *ex* Hermina *-1984* *ex* Willem *-1984* *ex* Lodewijk Cornelis *-1978* **NV Tasda Fish** - *Paramaribo* *Suriname* Official number: SA-99	**230** 69 -		**1973 J.E. Verharen, Scheepswerf "De Rietpol" — Spaarndam** Yd No: 50 Loa 34.02 Br ex 7.55 Dght - Lbp - Br md - Dpth 3.61 Welded, 1 dk	**(B11A2FT) Trawler**	**1 oil engine** driving 1 FP propeller Total Power: 993kW (1,350hp) 11.5kn Bolnes 8DNL170/600 1 x 2 Stroke 8 Cy. 190 x 350 993kW (1350bhp) 'Bolnes' Motorenfabriek BV-Netherlands Fuel: 41.5 (d.f.)

5115771 **SAGVAG**
LANA *ex* Fjaerlandsfjord *-1977* *ex* Gula *-1954*
- *ex* Wischhafen *-1952*
Bergsvag Husbat AS
-
Bergen *Norway*

291 87 -

1943 in Germany (Aft section)
1951 Harttermann & Krooss — Wischhafen (Fwd section) Yd No: N
Converted From: Oil Tanker, Inland Waterways-1951
Joined-1951
Loa 29.27 Br ex 8.16 Dght -
Lbp - Br md 8.13 Dpth -
Welded, 1 dk

(A36A2PR) Passenger/Ro-Ro Ship (Vehicles)
Passengers: unberthed: 100
Cars: 22

1 oil engine driving 1 FP propeller
Total Power: 177kW (241hp)
Wichmann 3ACA
1 x 2 Stroke 3 Cy. 280 x 420 177kW (241bhp) (new engine 1959)
Wichmann Motorfabrikk AS-Norway

7602821 **SAHAB**
A9D2953 *ex* Sea Diamond IV *-2007*
- *ex* Stevin Sha'm *-2001* *ex* F 30 *-1978*
Bahrain Bulk Trade WLL
-
Bahrain *Bahrain*
MMSI: 408323000
Official number: BN 4092

410 123 -
Class: BV (AB)

1976-03 K.K. Imai Seisakusho — Kamijima (Hull) Yd No: 155
1976-03 Mitsui Ocean Development & Eng. Co. Ltd. — Japan Yd No: S-066
L reg 38.00 Br ex 9.22 Dght 3.988
Lbp 34.02 Br md 9.21 Dpth 4.25
Welded, 1 dk

(B32A2ST) Tug

2 oil engines reverse reduction geared to sc. shafts driving 2 FP propellers
Total Power: 1,838kW (2,498hp) 11.5kn
Niigata 6MG25BX
2 x 4 Stroke 6 Cy. 250 x 320 each-919kW (1249bhp)
Niigata Engineering Co Ltd-Japan
AuxGen: 2 x 96kW
Thrusters: 1 Thwart. FP thruster (f)

1005423 **SAHAB IV**
ZCMD8
- **Sahab Marine Ltd**
Golden Union Shipping Co SA
George Town *Cayman Islands (British)*
MMSI: 319255000
Official number: 729066

621 186 -
Class: LR
✠**100A1** SS 02/2012
Yacht
✠**LMC** Cable: 330.0/22.0 U2 (a)

1997-02 Italam '86 Srl. — Ancona Yd No: 112
Loa 49.95 Br ex - Dght 2.250
Lbp 40.80 Br md 9.20 Dpth 4.90
Welded, 2 dks

(X11A2YP) Yacht

2 oil engines with clutches, flexible couplings & sr geared to sc. shafts driving 2 Directional propellers
Total Power: 3,042kW (4,136hp) 16.0kn
Deutz TBD620BV12
2 x Vee 4 Stroke 12 Cy. 170 x 195 each-1521kW (2068bhp)
Motoren Werke Mannheim AG (MWM)-Mannheim
AuxGen: 2 x 170kW 380V 50Hz a.c
Thrusters: 1 Thwart. FP thruster (f)

7034402 **SAHABAT LESTARI**
YFCU *ex* Perita Jaya *-2010* *ex* Kinyu Maru *-1988*
- **PT Mandiri Sejahtera Abadi Line**
-
Jakarta *Indonesia*

1,585 955 2,584
Class: KI

1970-07 Kishimoto Zosen — Osakikamijima Yd No: 380
Loa 73.16 Br ex 11.54 Dght 5.703
Lbp 68.03 Br md 11.51 Dpth 5.80
Welded, 1 dk

(A31A2GX) General Cargo Ship
Grain: 3,524; Bale: 3,309
Compartments: 1 Ho, ER
1 Ha: (35.9 x 8.0)ER

1 oil engine driving 1 FP propeller
Total Power: 1,471kW (2,000hp) 11.0kn
Makita ESHC640
1 x 4 Stroke 6 Cy. 400 x 600 1471kW (2000bhp)
Makita Tekkosho-Japan
AuxGen: 2 x 64kW 445V a.c
Fuel: 7.0

8204042 **SAHABAT PRIMA 8**
YEEA *ex* Bosowa Ii *-2012* *ex* Petta Ponggawa *-2004*
- *ex* Petta *-1999* *ex* Koharuzan Maru *-1988*
Honggo Wijaya
-
Jakarta *Indonesia*
MMSI: 525014117

2,620 1,492 4,109
Class: KI (NK)

1982-10 Kinoura Zosen K.K. — Imabari Yd No: 85
Loa 86.34 Br ex 14.03 Dght 6.128
Lbp 80.02 Br md 14.01 Dpth 6.40
Welded, 1 dk

(A31A2GX) General Cargo Ship
Grain: 6,143; Bale: 5,618
Compartments: 2 Ho, ER
2 Ha: (14.0 x 8.4) (25.9 x 8.4)ER
Derricks: 3x15t

1 oil engine driving 1 FP propeller
Total Power: 1,618kW (2,200hp) 11.5kn
Akasaka A34
1 x 4 Stroke 6 Cy. 340 x 660 1618kW (2200bhp)
Akasaka Tekkosho KK (Akasaka DieselLtd)-Japan
AuxGen: 2 x 96kW 445V 60Hz a.c
Fuel: 28.0 (d.f.) 240.0 (r.f.) 6.0pd

7434597 **SAHABAT SEJATI**
YCHV *ex* Melodi *-2004* *ex* Niaga XIX *-1990*
- *ex* Komodo VI *-1978*
ex Kansei Maru No. 1 *-1978*
PT Sejati
-
Surabaya *Indonesia*
Official number: 3628

1,209 627 2,044
Class: KI (KR) (NK)

1974-12 Goko Zosen K.K. — Kitakyushu Yd No: 1010
Loa 70.01 Br ex 11.23 Dght 5.563
Lbp 65.69 Br md 11.21 Dpth 5.72
Welded, 1 dk

(A31A2GX) General Cargo Ship
Grain: 2,230; Bale: 1,934
2 Ha: (12.0 x 6.0) (15.4 x 6.0)ER
Derricks: 2x10t

1 oil engine driving 1 FP propeller
Total Power: 1,214kW (1,651hp) 13.0kn
Fuji 6S32FH
1 x 4 Stroke 6 Cy. 320 x 500 1214kW (1651bhp)
Fuji Diesel Co Ltd-Japan

8950134 **SAHABE**
5RSK
- **Refrige Peche Establishment**
-
Toamasina *Madagascar*
Official number: 97001

133 - -

1998-06 Chantiers Piriou — Concarneau Yd No: 192
Loa - Br ex - Dght 2.200
Lbp 25.96 Br md 7.04 Dpth 3.35
Welded, 1 dk

(B11A2FS) Stern Trawler

1 oil engine driving 1 FP propeller
Total Power: 316kW (430hp) 11.0kn
Poyaud
1 x 4 Stroke 316kW (430bhp)
Wartsila NSD France SA-France

8808836 **SAHAISANT NAVA**
-
- **Sahaisant Co Ltd**
-

100 - -

1989-02 The Sahaisant Co., Ltd. — Bangkok Yd No: 109
Loa - Br ex - Dght 2.552
Lbp 18.42 Br md 6.81 Dpth 3.03
Welded, 1 dk

(B32A2ST) Tug

2 oil engines driving 2 FP propellers

9375238 **SAHAM**
3FWF2
- **Saham Maritime Transportation Co SA**
Oman Ship Management Co SAOC
SatCom: Inmarsat C 435297810
Panama *Panama*
MMSI: 352978000
Official number: 4257211

156,919 100,233 299,991 T/cm 178.4
Class: AB

2010-10 Universal Shipbuilding Corp — Nagasu KM (Ariake Shipyard) Yd No: 112
Loa 330.00 (BB) Br ex 60.04 Dght 21.669
Lbp 316.00 Br md 60.00 Dpth 29.70
Welded, 1 dk

(A13A2TV) Crude Oil Tanker
Double Hull (13F)
Liq: 324,660; Liq (Oil): 324,700
Compartments: 5 Ta, 10 Wing Ta, 2 Wing Slop Ta, ER
3 Cargo Pump (s): 3x5500m³/hr
Manifold: Bow/CM: 162.1m

1 oil engine driving 1 FP propeller
Total Power: 25,090kW (34,112hp) 15.6kn
MAN-B&W 7S80MC
1 x 2 Stroke 7 Cy. 800 x 3056 25090kW (34112bhp)
Hitachi Zosen Corp-Japan
AuxGen: 3 x 820kW a.c
Fuel: 469.4 (d.f.) 7243.8 (r.f.)

9683221 **SAHAN 18**
9W003
- **Emas Dinamik Sdn Bhd**
-
Kota Kinabalu *Malaysia*
MMSI: 533002610
Official number: 332718

253 76 132
Class: NK

2013-10 Tang Tiew Hee & Sons Sdn Bhd — Sibu Yd No: 68
Loa 35.40 Br ex 8.02 Dght 2.112
Lbp 32.74 Br md 8.00 Dpth 3.50
Welded, 1 dk

(B34L2QU) Utility Vessel

2 oil engines reduction geared to sc. shafts driving 2 FP propellers
Total Power: 1,220kW (1,658hp)
Yanmar 6AYM-WET
1 x 4 Stroke 6 Cy. 155 x 180 610kW (829bhp)
Yanmar Diesel Engine Co Ltd-Japan
Fuel: 69.0

9683233 **SAHAN 19**
9W004
- **Emas Dinamik Sdn Bhd**
-
Kota Kinabalu *Malaysia*
MMSI: 533002620
Official number: 332719

253 76 130
Class: NK

2013-12 Tang Tiew Hee & Sons Sdn Bhd — Sibu Yd No: 69
Loa 35.40 Br ex 8.02 Dght 2.100
Lbp 32.74 Br md 8.00 Dpth 3.50
Welded, 1 dk

(B32A2ST) Tug

2 oil engines reduction geared to sc. shafts driving 2 Propellers
Total Power: 1,220kW (1,658hp)
Yanmar 6AYM-WET
1 x 4 Stroke 6 Cy. 155 x 180 610kW (829bhp)
Yanmar Diesel Engine Co Ltd-Japan

9485679 **SAHAND**
J8B4712 *ex* Nancy 6 *-2013* *ex* Mlc Nancy 6 *-2012*
- **Sahand Shipping & Trading Co Ltd**
Echo Cargo & Shipping LLC
Kingstown *St Vincent & The Grenadines*
MMSI: 376114000
Official number: 11185

273 82 288
Class: AB (NK)

2008-02 Yong Choo Kui Shipyard Sdn Bhd — Sibu Yd No: 26118
Loa 31.20 Br ex 8.62 Dght 3.612
Lbp 29.15 Br md 8.60 Dpth 4.35
Welded, 1 dk

(B32A2ST) Tug

2 oil engines geared to sc. shafts driving 2 Propellers
Total Power: 1,790kW (2,434hp)
Cummins KTA-38-M2
2 x Vee 4 Stroke 12 Cy. 159 x 159 each-895kW (1217bhp)
Cummins Engine Co Inc-USA
AuxGen: 2 x 78kW a.c

9105877 **SAHAND 40**
HP2935 *ex* Tina 1 *-2010* *ex* Atlas *-2009*
- **Amy Shipping SA**
-
Panama *Panama*
Official number: 41000PEXT2

129 39 230
Class: (LR)
✠ 4/5/98

1998-05 Naval Shipyard — Bandar Abbas (Assembled by)
1998-05 Delta Shipyard Sliedrecht BV — Sliedrecht (Parts for assembly by) Yd No: 904
Converted From: Fishing Vessel-2010
Loa 23.95 Br ex - Dght 3.000
Lbp 21.70 Br md 6.60 Dpth 3.40
Welded, 1 dk

(B32A2ST) Tug

1 oil engine with clutches & sr reverse geared to sc. shaft driving 1 FP propeller
Total Power: 375kW (510hp) 10.0kn
Volvo Penta TAMD162C
1 x 4 Stroke 6 Cy. 144 x 165 375kW (510bhp)
AB Volvo Penta-Sweden
AuxGen: 2 x 30kW 380V 50Hz a.c

8313908 **SAHAND 85**
EPAM9 *ex* Zakher Hercules *-2005* *ex* Sea Rex *-2004*
- *ex* Neftegaz-5 *-1997*
Deep Offshore Technology Co
-
Iran
MMSI: 422912000

2,737 821 1,396
Class: (BV) (RS)

1983-11 Stocznia Szczecinska im A Warskiego — Szczecin Yd No: B92/05
Loa 81.16 Br ex 16.30 Dght 4.750
Lbp 71.46 Br md 15.97 Dpth 7.22
Welded, 2 dks

(B21B20A) Anchor Handling Tug Supply
Passengers: berths: 140
Ice Capable

2 oil engines geared to sc. shafts driving 2 FP propellers
Total Power: 5,296kW (7,200hp) 15.2kn
Sulzer 6ZL40/48
2 x 4 Stroke 6 Cy. 400 x 480 each-2648kW (3600bhp)
Zaklady Urzadzen Technicznych'Zgoda' SA-Poland
AuxGen: 3 x 249kW 380/220V 50Hz a.c
Thrusters: 1 Thwart. FP thruster (f)
Fuel: 569.0

9028160 **SAHAR 3**
9BDY
- **Abdol Emam Shabani**
Reza Shamsimehr
Bandar Imam Khomeini *Iran*
Official number: 20546

382 272 800
Class: AS

2004-03 Arshia Sahel Karoun — Khorramshahr Yd No: 1307
Loa 44.05 Br ex - Dght 3.600
Lbp 41.35 Br md 8.00 Dpth 4.05
Welded, 1 dk

(A31A2GX) General Cargo Ship

2 oil engines geared to sc. shafts driving 2 Propellers
Total Power: 588kW (800hp)
Cummins NTA-855-M
2 x 4 Stroke 6 Cy. 140 x 152 each-294kW (400bhp)
Cummins Engine Co Inc-USA

No. / Call sign	Name / Owner	Tonnage	Class	Build / Dimensions	Type / Cargo	Machinery
8614778 *A6E2395* -	**SAHAR FOLK** *ex* LMS Digana *-2011* *ex* Francesco A. *-2009* **Folk Shipping LLC** - *Dubai* *United Arab Emirates* MMSI: 470316000	**4,938** 2,616 8,838 T/cm 17.0	Class: RI	**1988-06 Soc. Esercizio Cant. S.p.A. — Viareggio** Yd No: 767 Conv to DH-2001 Loa 114.92 (BB) Br ex - Dght 7.462 Lbp 108.36 Br md 17.51 Dpth 9.61 Welded, 1 dk	**(A13B2TP) Products Tanker** Double Hull (13F) Liq: 8,825; Liq (Oil): 8,825 Compartments: 12 Ta, ER, 2 Wing Slop Ta 3 Cargo Pump (s): 3x600m³/hr Manifold: Bow/CM: 58m	**2 oil engines** with clutches, flexible couplings & sr geared to sc. shaft driving 1 CP propeller Total Power: 2,250kW (3,060hp) 14.5kn Wartsila 6R32 2 x 4 Stroke 6 Cy. 320 x 350 each-1125kW (1530bhp) Wartsila Diesel Oy-Finland Thrusters: 1 Thwart. CP thruster (f); 1 Thwart. CP thruster (a) Fuel: 315.0 (r.f.) 80.0 (d.f.) 16.0pd
6600826 *9HA2102* -	**SAHARA** *ex* Oceanographer *-2009* **G Shipping Ltd** - SatCom: Inmarsat C 424996110 *Valletta* *Malta* MMSI: 249961000 Official number: 6600826	*3,604* 1,081 1,208	Class: (AB)	**1966-03 Jacksonville Shipyards, Inc. — Jacksonville, Fl** Yd No: 633 Loa 92.36 Br ex 16.06 Dght 6.417 Lbp 82.00 Br md 15.85 Dpth 8.79 Welded, 2 dks	**(B31A2SR) Research Survey Vessel**	**4 diesel electric oil engines** Connecting to 4 elec. motors driving 2 FP propellers Total Power: 4,228kW (5,748hp) 16.0kn Fairbanks, Morse 8-38D8-1/8 4 x 2 Stroke 8 Cy. 207 x 254 each-1057kW (1437bhp) Fairbanks Morse & Co.-New Orleans, La AuxGen: 3 x 400kW 450V 60Hz a.c Thrusters: 1 Thwart. FP thruster (f) Fuel: 1210.0
8905141 - -	**SAHAY** **Visakhapatnam Port Trust** - *Visakhapatnam* *India* Official number: 2477	**392** 118 99	Class: (IR)	**1993-02 Hooghly Dock & Port Engineers Ltd. — Haora** Yd No: 462 Loa 33.50 Br ex 10.42 Dght 5.100 Lbp - Br md 10.00 Dpth 4.20 Welded, 1 dk	**(B32A2ST) Tug**	**2 oil engines** with clutches, flexible couplings & sr geared to sc. shafts driving 2 Directional propellers Total Power: 2,220kW (3,018hp) 11.0kn Sulzer 6ASL25D 2 x 4 Stroke 6 Cy. 250 x 300 each-1110kW (1509bhp) H Cegielski Poznan SA-Poland AuxGen: 1 x 160kW 415V 50Hz a.c Fuel: 55.0 (r.f.)
9388273 *C6XW5* -	**SAHBA** **The National Shipping Company of Saudi Arabia (BAHRI)** Mideast Ship Management Ltd SatCom: Inmarsat Mini-M 764937680 *Nassau* *Bahamas* MMSI: 311024100 Official number: 8001659	**160,782** 109,346 317,563 T/cm 178.0	Class: AB	**2009-09 Hyundai Samho Heavy Industries Co Ltd — Samho** Yd No: S340 Loa 333.04 (BB) Br ex 60.05 Dght 22.522 Lbp 319.00 Br md 60.00 Dpth 30.40 Welded, 1 dk	**(A13A2TV) Crude Oil Tanker** Double Hull (13F) Liq: 336,500; Liq (Oil): 336,500 Compartments: 5 Ta, 10 Wing Ta, 2 Wing Slop Ta, ER 3 Cargo Pump (s): 3x5500m³/hr Manifold: Bow/CM: 165m	**1 oil engine** driving 1 FP propeller Total Power: 30,266kW (41,150hp) 15.5kn Sulzer 8RTA84T-D 1 x 2 Stroke 8 Cy. 840 x 3150 30266kW (41150bhp) Hyundai Heavy Industries Co Ltd-South Korea AuxGen: 3 x 1300kW 50Hz a.c Fuel: 400.0 (d.f.) 8950.0 (r.f.)
9415349 *J8B4015* -	**SAHEB** **Goya Marine Services Ltd** Whitesea Shipping & Supply (LLC) *Kingstown* *St Vincent & The Grenadines* MMSI: 377601000 Official number: 10488	**1,579** 473 1,488	Class: BV	**2009-02 Keppel Nantong Shipyard Co Ltd — Nantong JS** (Hull) Yd No: 009 **2009-02 Keppel Singmarine Pte Ltd — Singapore** Yd No: 329 Loa 62.20 Br ex - Dght 4.900 Lbp 59.06 Br md 15.00 Dpth 6.00 Welded, 1 dk	**(B21B20A) Anchor Handling Tug Supply** Cranes: 1x10t	**2 oil engines** reduction geared to sc. shafts driving 2 Directional propellers Total Power: 4,080kW (5,548hp) 12.5kn Wartsila 6L26 2 x 4 Stroke 6 Cy. 260 x 320 each-2040kW (2774bhp) Wartsila Finland Oy-Finland AuxGen: 2 x 280kW 380V 50Hz a.c, 2 x 1200kW 380V 50Hz a.c Thrusters: 2 Tunnel thruster (f)
9365087 *9BIT* -	**SAHEL KHAMIR** *ex* Sinar Anugrah Perdana *-2005* **Bank Mellat** - *Bandar Abbas* *Iran* MMSI: 422541000 Official number: 844	**412** 124 1,000	Class: AS KI	**2005-07 C.V. Dok & Galangan Kapal Perlun — Samarinda** Yd No: 1000/02 Loa 53.35 Br ex 11.00 Dght 2.250 Lbp 46.60 Br md 10.80 Dpth 3.00 Welded, 1 dk	**(A35D2RL) Landing Craft** Bow ramp (f)	**2 oil engines** reduction geared to sc. shafts driving 2 Propellers Total Power: 588kW (800hp) 8.0kn Caterpillar 3408TA 2 x Vee 4 Stroke 8 Cy. 137 x 152 each-294kW (400bhp) Caterpillar Inc-USA
9071507 *9BJU* -	**SAHEL SAYD 704** **Mahmoud Amini** - *Bandar Abbas* *Iran* Official number: 11347	*181* 54 80	Class: AS	**2003-04 Bahr Shipbuilding — Iran** (Assembled by) **2003-04 Sing Koon Seng Shipyard Pte Ltd — Singapore** (Parts for assembly by) Yd No: 704 L reg 25.80 Br ex - Dght - Lbp 22.70 Br md 7.48 Dpth 4.19 Welded	**(B11A2FS) Stern Trawler**	**1 oil engine** geared to sc. shaft driving 1 FP propeller Total Power: 478kW (650hp) Caterpillar 3412TA 1 x Vee 4 Stroke 12 Cy. 137 x 152 478kW (650bhp) Caterpillar Inc-USA
7829601 - -	**SAHID 1** *ex* YTK Singapore 8 *-1983* *ex* Lady Anne *-1982* **Sahid Sdn Bhd** - *Bandar Seri Begawan* *Brunei* Official number: 0032	*116* 33 156	Class: (NK)	**1979 Ocean Shipyard Co Sdn Bhd — Sibu** Loa 26.83 Br ex 6.13 Dght 1.982 Lbp 24.69 Br md 6.10 Dpth 2.90 Welded, 1 dk	**(B34T2QR) Work/Repair Vessel**	**2 oil engines** driving 2 CP propellers Total Power: 764kW (1,038hp) 13.0kn Caterpillar 3412TA 2 x Vee 4 Stroke 12 Cy. 137 x 152 each-382kW (519bhp) Caterpillar Tractor Co-USA AuxGen: 2 x 49kW
9415507 *TCTB2* -	**SAHILBENT** **Istanbul Deniz Otobusleri Sanayi ve Ticaret AS (IDO)** - *Istanbul* *Turkey* MMSI: 271001039	**1,065** 608 250	Class: TL	**2008-03 Ceksan Tersanesi — Turkey** Yd No: 42 Loa 73.20 Br ex - Dght 2.600 Lbp 70.10 Br md 18.00 Dpth 4.40 Welded, 1 dk	**(A36A2PR) Passenger/Ro-Ro Ship (Vehicles)** Passengers: 600 Cars: 80	**4 oil engines** reduction geared to sc. shafts driving 2 Voith-Schneider propellers 2 propellers aft, 2 fwd. Total Power: 2,440kW (3,316hp) 12.5kn Mitsubishi S6R2-MPTA 4 x 4 Stroke 6 Cy. 170 x 220 each-610kW (829bhp) Mitsubishi Heavy Industries Ltd-Japan AuxGen: 1 x 71kW a.c, 1 x 62kW a.c
7946473 *TC3475* -	**SAHIN UZMEZ-1** *ex* Tuzun Ekmekcioglu *-1995* *ex* Aksoy Ufuk *-1995* *ex* Halic 16 *-1995* **Keziban Guldogan & Mehmet Yumak** - *Istanbul* *Turkey* Official number: 4212	*254* 128 425		**1920 in the Netherlands** Loa 42.85 Br ex - Dght 2.690 Lbp 40.11 Br md 6.30 Dpth 3.20 Welded, 1 dk	**(A31A2GX) General Cargo Ship**	**1 oil engine** driving 1 FP propeller Total Power: 331kW (450hp) 6.0kn B&W 1 x 4 Cy. 331kW (450bhp) Holeby Dieselmotor Fabrik A/S-Denmark
8813037 *DYCC* -	**SAHIWAL EXPRESS** *ex* Lis E *-2004* *ex* Elisabeth *-1997* *ex* Elsborg *-1993* *ex* Elisabeth *-1992* **Sahiwal Express BV** Livestock Express BV SatCom: Inmarsat C 454869230 *Manila* *Philippines* MMSI: 548692000 Official number: MNLA000623	**2,725** 818 2,177	Class: BV (LR) (GL) ✠ Classed LR until 18/8/93	**1990-03 Orskov Christensens Staalskibsvaerft A/S — Frederikshavn** Yd No: 170 Converted From: General Cargo Ship (with Ro-Ro Facility)-1999 Loa 91.50 (BB) Br ex 16.83 Dght 4.250 Lbp 84.98 Br md 16.20 Dpth 6.90 Welded, 1 dk	**(A38A2GL) Livestock Carrier** Bale: 3,800 Compartments: 5 Ho, ER 5 Ha: 4 (12.4 x 7.6)ER (6.3 x 7.4) Cranes: 1x40t,1x27t Ice Capable	**2 oil engines** with clutches, flexible couplings & sr geared to sc. shafts driving 2 CP propellers Total Power: 2,400kW (3,264hp) 12.0kn MaK 6M332C 2 x 4 Stroke 6 Cy. 240 x 330 each-1200kW (1632bhp) Krupp MaK Maschinenbau GmbH-Kiel AuxGen: 2 x 600kW 380V 50Hz a.c, 2 x 400kW 380/220V 50Hz a.c Thrusters: 1 Thwart. CP thruster (f)
8710390 *CNZC* -	**SAHM** **Al Amine Securities Co** Dounia Peche SA SatCom: Inmarsat C 424231010 *Tan-Tan* *Morocco*	**336** 114 318	Class: BV	**1989-04 SA Juliana Constructora Gijonesa — Gijon** Yd No: 329 Loa 39.40 (BB) Br ex - Dght 4.101 Lbp 33.02 Br md 9.01 Dpth 6.15 Welded, 1 dk	**(B11A2FS) Stern Trawler** Ins: 365	**1 oil engine** with clutches, flexible couplings & reduction geared to sc. shaft driving 1 FP propeller Total Power: 883kW (1,201hp) 12.2kn Yanmar M220-EN 1 x 4 Stroke 6 Cy. 220 x 300 883kW (1201bhp) Yanmar Diesel Engine Co Ltd-Japan AuxGen: 2 x 360kW 380V a.c Fuel: 190.0 (d.f.)
8903789 - -	**SAHM** **Canal Naval Construction Co Ltd** - *Port Said* *Egypt*	*180* - - T/cm 0.9		**1990-10 Canal Naval Construction Co. — Port Said (Port Fuad)** Yd No: 418 Loa 21.60 Br ex 5.90 Dght 2.200 Lbp 19.60 Br md 5.70 Dpth 2.90 Welded, 1 dk	**(B32A2ST) Tug**	**1 oil engine** sr geared to sc. shaft driving 1 FP propeller Total Power: 552kW (750hp) S.K.L. 6VD26/20AL-2 1 x 4 Stroke 6 Cy. 200 x 260 552kW (750bhp) VEB Schwermaschinenbau "KarlLiebknecht" (SKL)-Magdeburg AuxGen: 2 x 23kW 380V 50Hz a.c Fuel: 20.0 (d.f.)
7118234 - -	**SAHMY** *ex* Sahel I *-2007* *ex* Hodo *-2000* *ex* Marim *-1998* *ex* Sunflower B *-1996* *ex* Bensol 1 *-1996* *ex* Minol 13 *-1995* **Doraleh Shipping FZCO** -	**765** 465 732	Class: (DS) (GL)	**1971-06 Wroclawska Stocznia Rzeczna — Wroclaw** Yd No: ZB700/05 Loa 57.33 Br ex 9.02 Dght 3.350 Lbp 54.62 Br md 9.00 Dpth 3.76 Welded, 1 dk	**(A13B2TU) Tanker (unspecified)** Liq: 882; Liq (Oil): 882 Compartments: 8 Ta, ER Ice Capable	**1 oil engine** sr geared to sc. shaft driving 1 CP propeller Total Power: 295kW (401hp) 10.0kn Sulzer 8BAH22 1 x 2 Stroke 8 Cy. 220 x 320 295kW (401bhp) Zaklady Przemyslu Metalowego 'HCegielski' SA-Poznan AuxGen: 3 x 120kW 220/380V 50Hz a.c Fuel: 22.0 (d.f.) (Heating Coils)

8654144 - -	**SAHOYA** **PT Sinar Alam Duta Perdana** - *Banjarmasin* *Indonesia*	**2,539** 1,210 -	Class: KI	**2011-02 PT Karya Teknik Utama — Batam** Loa 82.29 Br ex - Dght - Lbp 79.00 Br md 21.33 Dpth 5.48 Welded, 1 dk	**(A13B2TP) Products Tanker** Double Hull (13F)	**2 oil engines** reduction geared to sc. shafts driving 2 Propellers 11.5kn AuxGen: 2 x 30kW 400V a.c
8651972 *YDA6595* -	**SAHOYA 02** **PT Sinar Alam Duta Perdana** - *Banjarmasin* *Indonesia* Official number: GT207NO2638/PPM	**207** 63 164	Class: KI	**2010-11 PT Karya Teknik Utama — Batam** Yd No: 13361 Loa 27.00 Br ex - Dght 2.990 Lbp 24.67 Br md 8.20 Dpth 4.00 Welded, 1 dk	**(B32A2ST) Tug**	**2 oil engines** reduction geared to sc. shafts driving 2 Propellers Total Power: 1,618kW (2,200hp) Yanmar 12LAK (M)-STE2 2 x Vee 4 Stroke 12 Cy. 150 x 165 each-809kW (1100bhp) Yanmar Diesel Engine Co Ltd-Japan AuxGen: 2 x 50kW 400V a.c
8663406 - -	**SAI DEEP** **Adani Enterprises Ltd** - *Panaji* *India* Official number: PNJ 529	**1,290** 1,122 2,178	Class: IR	**2010-11 Dempo Engineering Works Ltd. — Goa** Yd No: 436 Loa 69.80 Br ex 13.42 Dght 3.300 Lbp 67.20 Br md 13.40 Dpth 4.35 Welded, 1 dk	**(A31A2GX) General Cargo Ship** Compartments: 1 Ho, ER 1 Ha: ER	**2 oil engines** reduction geared to sc. shafts driving 2 Propellers Total Power: 536kW (728hp) Cummins NT-855-M 2 x 4 Stroke 6 Cy. 140 x 152 each-268kW (364bhp) Cummins India Ltd-India
9143130 *XVOV* -	**SAI GON GAS** *ex* Gas Prophet *-2010* *ex* Ming Long *-2009* *ex* Gas Prophet *-2006* *ex* Bente Kosan *-2004* *ex* Isle Spirit *-2004* **International Gas Products Shipping JSC (Gas Shipping JSC)** - SatCom: Inmarsat C 457464210 *Saigon* *Vietnam* MMSI: 574642000 Official number: VNSG-2011-TG	**3,556** 1,067 2,999 T/cm 12.6	Class: NV VR (LR) (CC) (NK) Classed LR until 3/4/10	**1996-07 Watanabe Zosen KK — Imabari EH** Yd No: 296 Loa 95.50 (BB) Br ex 16.64 Dght 4.500 Lbp 88.50 Br md 16.60 Dpth 7.10 Welded, 1 dk	**(A11B2TG) LPG Tanker** Liq (Gas): 3,515 2 x Gas Tank (s); 2 independent cyl horizontal 2 Cargo Pump (s) Manifold: Bow/CM: 40.7m	**1 oil engine** driving 1 FP propeller Total Power: 2,438kW (3,315hp) 13.0kn B&W 6S26MC 1 x 2 Stroke 6 Cy. 260 x 980 2438kW (3315bhp) The Hanshin Diesel Works Ltd-Japan AuxGen: 2 x 240kW 445V 60Hz a.c Boilers: WTAuxB (Comp) 7.1kgf/cm² (7.0bar)
8749262 *HMVV7* -	**SAI NAL** **Ocean Victory Int'l Holdings Ltd** Korea Kunhae Co Ltd *Nampho* *North Korea* MMSI: 445688000 Official number: 5903181	**2,982** 1,669 5,078	Class: KC	**2009-07 Nampo Shipyard — Nampo** Yd No: 970-5 Loa 97.00 Br ex - Dght 5.900 Lbp 92.62 Br md 15.80 Dpth 7.40 Welded, 1 dk	**(A31A2GX) General Cargo Ship**	**1 oil engine** reduction geared to sc. shaft driving 1 FP propeller Total Power: 1,768kW (2,404hp) 11.0kn Chinese Std. Type G8300ZC 1 x 4 Stroke 8 Cy. 300 x 380 1768kW (2404bhp) Wuxi Antai Power Machinery Co Ltd-China
8651398 *HMKT* -	**SAI NAL 2** *ex* Xin Sheng Gang *-2009* **Dalian Port Heizuizi Shipping Co Ltd** Korea Kunhae Co Ltd *Nampho* *North Korea* MMSI: 445012000 Official number: 5907551	**2,981** 1,669 5,297	Class: KC	**2009-07 Nanjing Hongying Shipbuilding Co Ltd — Nanjing JS** Yd No: BY20071130 Loa 97.00 Br ex - Dght 5.900 Lbp 92.62 Br md 15.80 Dpth 7.40 Welded, 1 dk	**(A31A2GX) General Cargo Ship**	**1 oil engine** reduction geared to sc. shaft driving 1 FP propeller Total Power: 2,000kW (2,719hp) 11.0kn Chinese Std. Type G8300ZC 1 x 4 Stroke 8 Cy. 300 x 380 2000kW (2719bhp) Wuxi Antai Power Machinery Co Ltd-China
9098206 *HMKS* -	**SAI NAL 3** *ex* Silvery Ocean *-2012* *ex* Zhuo Chen Hao *-2011* *ex* Fu Lin 88 *-2008* *ex* Xin Yuan 503 *-2000* **Grandtex Shipping Co Ltd** Korea Kunhae Co Ltd *Nampho* *North Korea* MMSI: 445017000 Official number: 4005460	**1,998** 1,099 3,200	Class: KC (UB)	**1990-11 Jiangxi Jiujiang Shipyard — Hukou County JX** Loa 85.16 Br ex - Dght 5.700 Lbp 79.80 Br md 12.00 Dpth 7.46 Welded, 1 dk	**(A31A2GX) General Cargo Ship**	**1 oil engine** driving 1 Propeller Total Power: 1,545kW (2,101hp) Chinese Std. Type 1 x 4 Stroke 1545kW (2101bhp) Ningbo Engine Factory-China
1007586 *MLYN5* -	**SAI RAM** **Sairam Marine Ltd** Camper & Nicholsons France SARL *London* *United Kingdom* MMSI: 235010870 Official number: 911161	**812** 243 183	Class: LR ✠ **100A1** SS 12/2013 SSC Yacht, mono, G6 **LMC** Cable: 440.0/20.5 U3 (a)	**2003-12 Azimut-Benetti SpA — Viareggio** Yd No: FB229 Loa 51.80 Br ex 10.63 Dght 2.800 Lbp 44.80 Br md 10.40 Dpth 5.45 Welded, 3 dks	**(X11A2YP) Yacht**	**2 oil engines** with clutches, flexible couplings & sr reverse geared to sc. shafts driving 2 FP propellers Total Power: 2,760kW (3,752hp) 16.0kn Caterpillar 3512B 2 x Vee 4 Stroke 12 Cy. 170 x 190 each-1380kW (1876bhp) (made 2003) Caterpillar Inc-USA AuxGen: 2 x 155kW 380V 50Hz a.c Thrusters: 1 Thwart. FP thruster (f)
8909355 *3FTB2* -	**SAI SUNRISE** *ex* Rousse *-2010* *ex* Nedlloyd Musi *-1997* *ex* Watergids *-1991* *ex* Kariba *-1991* *ex* Watergids *-1991* *ex* CMB Effort *-1990* *completed as* Watergids *-1989* **Sunrise Maritime Pte Ltd** Sai Maritime & Management Pvt Ltd (SMMPL) *Panama* *Panama* MMSI: 356363000 Official number: 4233211	**11,982** 5,568 14,101	Class: GL (BR)	**1989-06 VEB Mathias-Thesen-Werft — Wismar** Yd No: 175 Loa 156.85 (BB) Br ex - Dght 8.600 Lbp 145.33 Br md 22.86 Dpth 11.20 Welded, 1 dk	**(A31A2GX) General Cargo Ship** Grain: 18,687; Bale: 18,500 TEU 1034 C Ho 364 TEU C Dk 670 TEU incl 60 ref C. Compartments: 3 Ho, ER 3 Ha: (25.2 x 13.2)Tappered (38.0 x 18.8) (25.1 x 18.8)ER Cranes: 1x40t,2x25t Ice Capable	**1 oil engine** driving 1 FP propeller Total Power: 7,950kW (10,809hp) 16.0kn Sulzer 5RTA58 1 x 2 Stroke 5 Cy. 580 x 1700 7950kW (10809bhp) Zaklady Przemyslu Metalowego 'HCegielski' SA-Poznan AuxGen: 1 x 800kW 440V 60Hz a.c, 3 x 480kW 440V 60Hz a.c Thrusters: 1 Thwart. FP thruster (f) Fuel: 101.6 (d.f.) 929.7 (r.f.) 50.8pd
7341996 *SLAK* LL1248	**SAIBON AV KUNGSHAMN** *ex* Kenty *-2010* *ex* Hallo *-2003* *ex* Diligent *-1999* *ex* Linarolynn *-1989* *ex* Coronella *-1979* **Dolf Olle Larsson** - *Kungshamn* *Sweden* MMSI: 265804000	*184* - 242		**1977-09 George Brown & Co. (Marine) Ltd. — Greenock** (Hull launched by) Yd No: 279 **1977-09 J. & G. Forbes & Co. — Sandhaven** (Hull completed by) Lengthened-1984 Loa 32.11 Br ex 7.09 Dght 4.331 Lbp 29.37 Br md 7.01 Dpth - Welded, 1 dk	**(B11A2FT) Trawler** Ins: 209	**1 oil engine** reverse reduction geared to sc. shaft driving 1 FP propeller Total Power: 552kW (750hp) Blackstone ESL6MK2 1 x 4 Stroke 6 Cy. 222 x 292 552kW (750bhp) Mirrlees Blackstone Ltd-Dursley
7641126 *CNA2424* -	**SAID** *ex* Layyah *-1989* **SOMAGEC (Soc Marocaine de Genie Civil)** - *Casablanca* *Morocco* MMSI: 242083100 Official number: 6-141	*268* 113 278	Class: (LR) (AB) Classed LR until 11/5/09	**1977-03 Narasaki Senpaku Kogyo K.K. — Muroran** Yd No: 114 Loa 35.00 Br ex 8.74 Dght 3.241 Lbp 31.00 Br md 8.50 Dpth 3.60 Welded, 1 dk	**(B32A2ST) Tug**	**2 oil engines** dr geared to sc. shaft driving 1 CP propeller Total Power: 1,706kW (2,320hp) 12.0kn Deutz SBA8M528 2 x 4 Stroke 8 Cy. 220 x 280 each-853kW (1160bhp) Kloeckner Humboldt Deutz AG-West Germany AuxGen: 2 x 80kW 225V 60Hz a.c Fuel: 160.5 (d.f.)
8724731 *UDHI* -	**SAID AFANDI** *ex* Master *-2001* *ex* Geroy Volkov *-1999* **Said Afandi Shipping Ltd** State Enterprise Makhachkala International Sea Commercial Port *Makhachkala* *Russia* MMSI: 273423660	**4,178** 1,416 6,179 T/cm 19.1	Class: (RS)	**1987-06 Volgogradskiy Sudostroitelnyy Zavod — Volgograd** Yd No: 33 Loa 125.06 (BB) Br ex 16.63 Dght 4.830 Lbp 121.12 Br md 16.60 Dpth 6.90 Welded, 1dk	**(A13B2TP) Products Tanker** Liq: 5,904; Liq (Oil): 5,904 Compartments: 6 Ta, ER Ice Capable	**2 oil engines** driving 2 FP propellers Total Power: 2,296kW (3,122hp) 11.3kn Dvigatel Revolyutsii 6CHRNP36/45 2 x 4 Stroke 6 Cy. 360 x 450 each-1148kW (1561bhp) Zavod "Dvigatel Revolyutsii"-Gorkiy AuxGen: 4 x 160kW a.c Thrusters: 1 Thwart. FP thruster (f) Fuel: 253.0 (d.f.)
7237858 *HP8387* -	**SAIF** *ex* Redwood *-1995* *ex* Myosho Maru No. 8 *-1993* **Saif Shipping SA** - *Panama* *Panama* MMSI: 355729000 Official number: 24593PEXT	**688** 435 1,464	Class: (GL)	**1972-03 Matsuura Tekko Zosen K.K. — Osakikamijima** Yd No: 223 Loa 52.02 Br ex 11.03 Dght 3.950 Lbp 48.52 Br md 11.00 Dpth 4.02 Welded, 1 dk	**(A13B2TP) Products Tanker** Liq: 1,654; Liq (Oil): 1,654 Compartments: 8 Ta, ER	**2 oil engines** driving 2 Directional propellers Total Power: 808kW (1,098hp) 10.0kn Daihatsu 6PSHTCM-20F 2 x 4 Stroke 6 Cy. 200 x 250 each-404kW (549bhp) Daihatsu Diesel Manufacturing Co Lt-Japan AuxGen: 2 x 48kW 220V a.c
5265992 - -	**SAIGON 240** *ex* Osceola *-1973* *ex* Pvt. Lewis A. Reihm *-1962* *ex* LT-61 *-1962* **Government of The Socialist Republic of Vietnam (Saigon Port Authority)** - *Saigon* *Vietnam*	*392* 182 -	Class: (VR) (AB)	**1944-03 Calumet Shipyard & Dry Dock Co. — Chicago, Il** Yd No: 157 L reg 35.36 Br ex 9.20 Dght 4.598 Lbp 35.06 Br md 9.15 Dpth 5.49 Welded, 1 dk	**(B32A2ST) Tug**	**1 oil engine** driving 1 FP propeller Total Power: 1,765kW (2,400hp) Alco 16V251E 1 x Vee 4 Stroke 16 Cy. 229 x 267 1765kW (2400bhp) (new engine 1963) Alco Products Inc-USA AuxGen: 2 x 80kW 115V d.c Fuel: 183.0 (d.f.)

IMO / Call sign	Name / Owner	Tonnage	Class	Builder / Dimensions	Type	Machinery
9444998 *3EPF8* -	**SAIGON BRIDGE** **Bamboo Shipping Co** Sugahara Kisen KK *Panama* *Panama* MMSI: 351540000 Official number: 3364608A	**17,211** 7,875 21,980	Class: NK	**2008**-03 **Imabari Shipbuilding Co Ltd — Imabari EH (Imabari Shipyard)** Yd No: 661 Loa 171.99 (BB) Br ex 27.60 Dght 9.517 Lbp 160.00 Br md 27.60 Dpth 14.00 Welded, 1 dk	**(A33A2CC) Container Ship (Fully Cellular)** TEU 1708 C Ho 610 TEU C Dk 1098 incl 290 ref C	**1 oil engine** driving 1 FP propeller Total Power: 15,820kW (21,509hp) 19.7kn MAN-B&W 7S60MC-C 1 x 2 Stroke 7 Cy. 600 x 2400 15820kW (21509bhp) Kawasaki Heavy Industries Ltd-Japan AuxGen: 3 x a.c Thrusters: 1 Tunnel thruster (f) Fuel: 2180.0
9301809 *VRBT7* -	**SAIGON EXPRESS** *completed as* CP Jasper *-2006* **Seaspan Corp** Hapag-Lloyd AG *Hong Kong* *Hong Kong* MMSI: 477106800 Official number: HK-1684	**39,941** 24,458 50,869 T/cm 70.4	Class: LR ✠ **100A1** SS 04/2011 container ship *IWS LI **ShipRight** (SDA, FDA, CM) ✠ **LMC** **UMS** Eq.Ltr: St; Cable: 687.5/87.0 U3 (a)	**2006**-04 **Samsung Heavy Industries Co Ltd — Geoje** Yd No: 1542 Loa 260.10 (BB) Br ex 32.35 Dght 12.728 Lbp 244.80 Br md 32.25 Dpth 19.30 Welded, 1 dk	**(A33A2CC) Container Ship (Fully Cellular)** TEU 4253 C Ho 1584 TEU C Dk 2669 TEU incl 400 ref C. Compartments: 7 Cell Ho, ER 7 Ha: ER	**1 oil engine** driving 1 FP propeller Total Power: 36,560kW (49,707hp) 23.3kn MAN-B&W 8K90MC-C 1 x 2 Stroke 8 Cy. 900 x 2300 36560kW (49707bhp) Hyundai Heavy Industries Co Ltd-South Korea AuxGen: 4 x 1700kW 450V 60Hz a.c Boilers: AuxB (Comp) 8.0kgf/cm² (7.8bar) Thrusters: 1 Thwart. CP thruster (f)
9562960 *XVXD* -	**SAIGON PRINCESS** **Saigon Shipping JSC (SAIGONSHIP) (Cong Ty Co Phan Van Tai Bien Saigon)** - SatCom: Inmarsat C 457493010 *Saigon* *Vietnam* MMSI: 574930000 Official number: VNSG-1985-TH	**4,332** 2,615 6,829	Class: VR	**2009**-11 **in Vietnam** Yd No: SSC01 Loa 103.17 Br ex 17.03 Dght 7.200 Lbp 94.50 Br md 17.00 Dpth 9.10 Welded, 1 dk	**(A21A2BC) Bulk Carrier** Grain: 9,100; Bale: 8,677 Compartments: 2 Ho, ER 2 Ha: (25.9 x 9.9)ER (23.3 x 9.9) Derricks: 4x25t	**1 oil engine** driving 1 FP propeller Total Power: 2,648kW (3,600hp) 12.5kn Hanshin LH41LA 1 x 4 Stroke 6 Cy. 410 x 800 2648kW (3600bhp) The Hanshin Diesel Works Ltd-Japan AuxGen: 2 x 240kW a.c Fuel: 400.0
8428856 - -	**SAIHUT** **Yemen Fishing Corp** - *Aden* *Yemen*	**286** 84 -		**1976 Guangzhou Fishing Vessel Shipyard — Guangzhou GD** Loa 44.82 Br ex 7.60 Dght 2.200 Lbp - Br md - Dpth 2.70 Welded, 1 dk	**(B11B2FV) Fishing Vessel**	**1 oil engine** geared to sc. shaft driving 1 FP propeller Total Power: 441kW (600hp) Chinese Std. Type 6300 1 x 4 Stroke 6 Cy. 300 x 380 441kW (600bhp) Guangzhou Diesel Engine Factory CoLtd-China
9446087 *3FYT6* -	**SAIKO** **Picer Marine SA** World Marine Co Ltd SatCom: Inmarsat C 435633510 *Panama* *Panama* MMSI: 356335000 Official number: 4172310	**90,105** 59,287 180,178 T/cm 121.0	Class: NK	**2010**-05 **Imabari Shipbuilding Co Ltd — Saijo EH (Saijo Shipyard)** Yd No: 8078 Loa 288.93 (BB) Br ex - Dght 18.170 Lbp 280.80 Br md 45.00 Dpth 24.70 Welded, 1 dk	**(A21A2BC) Bulk Carrier** Grain: 199,724 Compartments: 9 Ho, ER 9 Ha: ER	**1 oil engine** driving 1 FP propeller Total Power: 18,660kW (25,370hp) 14.5kn MAN-B&W 6S70MC-C 1 x 2 Stroke 6 Cy. 700 x 2800 18660kW (25370bhp) Mitsui Engineering & Shipbuilding CLtd-Japan Fuel: 5984.0 (r.f.)
9355525 *YJRM9* -	**SAIKO MAJESTY** *ex* Sanko Majesty *-2012* **Stevens Line Co Ltd** Sato Steamship Co Ltd (Sato Kisen KK) *Port Vila* *Vanuatu* MMSI: 577056000 Official number: 2122	**30,488** 15,289 50,790	Class: NK	**2009**-02 **Oshima Shipbuilding Co Ltd — Saikai NS** Yd No: 10505 Loa 189.99 (BB) Br ex - Dght 12.260 Lbp 186.00 Br md 32.26 Dpth 17.31 Welded, 1 dk	**(A31A2GO) Open Hatch Cargo Ship** Double Hull Grain: 57,886; Bale: 57,782 TEU 306 Compartments: 8 Ho, ER 8 Ha: ER Cranes: 4x40t	**1 oil engine** driving 1 FP propeller Total Power: 10,187kW (13,850hp) 14.0kn MAN-B&W 5S60MC-C 1 x 2 Stroke 5 Cy. 600 x 2400 10187kW (13850bhp) Kawasaki Heavy Industries Ltd-Japan AuxGen: 3 x 525kW a.c Fuel: 2350.0
9478602 *3WTM* -	**SAIL 36** **Linh Trung Shipping Co Ltd** - SatCom: Inmarsat C 457408410 *Saigon* *Vietnam* MMSI: 574084000	**2,551** 1,497 4,373	Class: VR	**2007**-12 **Dai Duong Shipbuilding Co Ltd — Haiphong** Yd No: HP703-02 Loa 90.72 Br ex 13.00 Dght 6.160 Lbp 84.90 Br md 12.98 Dpth 7.60 Welded, 1 dk	**(A31A2GX) General Cargo Ship** Grain: 4,850	**1 oil engine** reduction geared to sc. shaft driving 1 Propeller Total Power: 1,500kW (2,039hp) 11.0kn Chinese Std. Type G8300ZC 1 x 4 Stroke 8 Cy. 300 x 380 1500kW (2039bhp) Wuxi Antai Power Machinery Co Ltd-China
8827703 - -	**SAIL No. 102** **Sail Marine Sightseeing Co Ltd** *South Korea* Official number: SGR-879718	*109* - -	Class: (KR)	**1987**-06 **Dae Sun Shipbuilding & Engineering Co Ltd — Busan** Loa 25.15 Br ex - Dght 2.364 Lbp 23.00 Br md 8.50 Dpth 2.80 Welded, 1 dk	**(A37B2PS) Passenger Ship**	**2 oil engines** reduction geared to sc. shafts driving 2 FP propellers Total Power: 264kW (358hp) 8.6kn MAN D2156ME 2 x 4 Stroke 6 Cy. 121 x 150 each-132kW (179bhp) Daewoo Heavy Industries Ltd-South Korea AuxGen: 1 x 14kW 225V a.c
9245512 *A7D6421* -	**SAILAIN** **Qatar Shipping Co (Q Ship) SPC** - *Doha* *Qatar* Official number: 168/2001	**448** 134 297	Class: AB	**2001**-03 **Bharati Shipyard Ltd — Ratnagiri** Yd No: 279 Loa 33.00 Br ex 10.90 Dght 4.500 Lbp 31.65 Br md 10.70 Dpth 5.50 Welded, 1 dk	**(B32A2ST) Tug**	**2 oil engines** with clutches, flexible couplings & sr geared to sc. shafts driving 2 Directional propellers Total Power: 3,380kW (4,596hp) 12.0kn Wartsila 9L20 2 x 4 Stroke 9 Cy. 200 x 280 each-1690kW (2298bhp) Wartsila Finland Oy-Finland AuxGen: 1 x 245kW a.c, 2 x 145kW a.c Thrusters: 1 Thwart. FP thruster (f) Fuel: 155.0 (d.f.)
9655664 *A7GM* -	**SAILAIN II** **Qatar Navigation QSC (Milaha)** - *Doha* *Qatar* MMSI: 466110000	**294** - -	Class: LR (Class contemplated) **100A1** 02/2014	**2014**-02 **Nakilat Damen Shipyards Qatar Ltd — Ras Laffan** (Hull) Yd No: (511591) **2014**-02 **B.V. Scheepswerf Damen — Gorinchem** Yd No: 511591 Loa 28.67 Br ex - Dght - Lbp - Br md 9.80 Dpth 4.60 Welded, 1 dk	**(B32A2ST) Tug**	**2 oil engines** reduction geared to sc. shaft (s) driving 2 Directional propellers Caterpillar 2 x Vee 4 Stroke
8867040 *UBKG4* -	**SAILBARON** *ex* Omskiy-139 *-2008* **Sailbaron Maritime Ltd** Sailtrade Denizcilik ve Ticaret Ltd Sti *Taganrog* *Russia* MMSI: 273352800	**2,570** 967 2,957	Class: RS	**1989**-02 **Santierul Naval Oltenita S.A. — Oltenita** Yd No: 451 Loa 108.40 Br ex 14.80 Dght 3.290 Lbp 102.53 Br md - Dpth 5.00 Welded, 1 dk	**(A31A2GX) General Cargo Ship** Grain: 4,315 Ice Capable	**2 oil engines** driving 2 FP propellers Total Power: 1,030kW (1,400hp) 10.0kn S.K.L. 6NVD48A-2U 2 x 4 Stroke 6 Cy. 320 x 480 each-515kW (700bhp) VEB Schwermaschinenbau "KarlLiebknecht" (SKL)-Magdeburg AuxGen: 3 x 50kW a.c Fuel: 171.0 (d.f.)
8846761 *UBFF5* -	**SAILBEAUTY** *ex* Midland 201 *-2007* *ex* Rezekne *-2002* *ex* Omskiy-136 *-1991* **Sailbeauty Maritime Ltd** Sailtrade Denizcilik ve Ticaret Ltd Sti *Taganrog* *Russia* MMSI: 273335410	**2,554** 971 3,104	Class: RS	**1988**-07 **Santierul Naval Oltenita S.A. — Oltenita** Yd No: 276 Loa 108.40 Br ex 15.03 Dght 3.260 Lbp 102.00 Br md 14.80 Dpth 5.00 Welded, 1 dk	**(A31A2GX) General Cargo Ship** Grain: 4,340 Compartments: 4 Ho, ER 4 Ha: 4 (15.6 x 10.9)ER Ice Capable	**2 oil engines** driving 2 FP propellers Total Power: 1,030kW (1,400hp) S.K.L. 6NVD48A-2U 2 x 4 Stroke 6 Cy. 320 x 480 each-515kW (700bhp) VEB Schwermaschinenbau "KarlLiebknecht" (SKL)-Magdeburg
8936798 *UBCF4* -	**SAILCOUNTESS** *ex* Davenport *-2007* *ex* Rigel *-2005* *ex* Tayshet *-2004* **Sailcountess Maritime Ltd** Sailtrade Denizcilik ve Ticaret Ltd Sti *Taganrog* *Russia* MMSI: 273337010	**2,454** 969 3,201	Class: RS	**1986**-05 **Santierul Naval Oltenita S.A. — Oltenita** Yd No: 261 Loa 108.40 Br ex 15.00 Dght 3.260 Lbp 103.54 Br md 14.80 Dpth 5.00 Welded, 1 dk	**(A31A2GX) General Cargo Ship** Grain: 4,678 TEU 96 C. 96/20' Compartments: 4 Ho, ER 4 Ha: 4 (15.6 x 10.5)ER	**2 oil engines** driving 2 FP propellers Total Power: 1,030kW (1,400hp) 10.5kn S.K.L. 8NVD48A-2U 2 x 4 Stroke 8 Cy. 320 x 480 each-515kW (700bhp) VEB Schwermaschinenbau "KarlLiebknecht" (SKL)-Magdeburg AuxGen: 4 x 50kW Fuel: 89.0 (d.f.)
8884957 *UBNF3* -	**SAILDAISY** *ex* Yorkville *-2007* *ex* Spika *-2005* *ex* Omsk *-2004* **Saildaisy Maritime Ltd** SailTrade Ltd *Taganrog* *Russia* MMSI: 273331320	**2,360** 910 3,284	Class: RS	**1989**-06 **Krasnoyarskiy Sudostroitelnyy Zavod — Krasnoyarsk** Yd No: 45 Loa 108.40 Br ex 14.80 Dght 3.260 Lbp 102.23 Br md 14.80 Dpth 5.00 Welded, 1 dk	**(A31A2GX) General Cargo Ship** Compartments: 4 Ho, ER 4 Ha: 4 (15.5 x 11.0)ER	**2 oil engines** driving 2 FP propellers Total Power: 1,030kW (1,400hp) 10.0kn S.K.L. 6NVDS48A-2U 2 x 4 Stroke 6 Cy. 320 x 480 each-515kW (700bhp) VEB Schwermaschinenbau "KarlLiebknecht" (SKL)-Magdeburg AuxGen: 3 x 84kW a.c Fuel: 84.0 (d.f.)

8899988 *UBFF2* -	**SAILDUKE** *ex* Dufferin *-2007* *ex* Mintaka *-2005* *ex* Salekhard *-2005* **Sailduke Maritime Ltd** Sailtrade Denizcilik ve Ticaret Ltd Sti *Taganrog* *Russia* MMSI: 273332410	**2,451** 969 3,197	Class: RS (RR)	**1987**-04 **Krasnoyarskiy Sudostroitelnyy Zavod — Krasnoyarsk** Loa 108.40 Br ex 15.00 Dght 3.260 Lbp 101.80 Br md 14.80 Dpth 5.00 Welded, 1 dk	**(A31A2GX) General Cargo Ship** Grain: 4,340 TEU 100 Compartments: 4 Ho 4 Ha: 4 (15.5 x 10.9)	**2 oil engines** driving 2 FP propellers Total Power: 1,030kW (1,400hp) 10.0kn S.K.L. 6NVD48A-2U 2 x 4 Stroke 6 Cy. 320 x 480 each-515kW (700bhp) VEB Schwermaschinenbau "KarlLiebknecht" (SKL)-Magdeburg AuxGen: 3 x 50kW a.c Fuel: 70.0 (d.f.)
6614190 *WX5011* -	**SAILELE** *ex* Momi *-2009* *ex* Joe Sevier *-2005* **Government of American Samoa** - *Pago Pago, AS* *United States of America* MMSI: 366823020 Official number: 500799	*163* 86 -	Class: (AB)	**1965 Fellows & Stewart Inc. — Terminal Island, Ca** Yd No: 55 Loa 24.39 Br ex 7.37 Dght 3.518 Lbp 23.25 Br md 7.32 Dpth 3.87 Welded, 1 dk	**(B32A2ST) Tug**	**2 oil engines** sr geared to sc. shafts driving 2 FP propellers Total Power: 1,126kW (1,530hp) Caterpillar D398TA 2 x Vee 4 Stroke 12 Cy. 159 x 203 each-563kW (765bhp) Caterpillar Tractor Co-USA AuxGen: 2 x 40kW Fuel: 62.0
8763074 *WDC6574* -	**SAILFISH** *ex* Superior Synergy *-2005* *ex* Gulf Island III *-2005* *ex* Atlantic IV *-2005* **All Coast LLC** - *New Orleans, LA* *United States of America* MMSI: 367058050 Official number: 650777	*179* 122 -		**1987 Crown Point Industries — Marrero, La** Yd No: 107 L reg 22.22 Br ex - Dght 1.520 Lbp - Br md 10.97 Dpth 2.13 Welded, 1 dk	**(B22A2ZM) Offshore Construction Vessel, jack up** Cranes: 1x70t	**2 oil engines** geared to sc. shafts driving 2 Propellers G.M. (Detroit Diesel) 8V-71 2 x Vee 2 Stroke 8 Cy. 108 x 127 Detroit Diesel Corporation-Detroit, Mi
9421348 *XCTJ5* -	**SAILFISH** *launched as* Rigdon Sailfish *-2007* **Facileasing SA de CV** Naviera Petrolera Integral SA de CV *Isla del Carmen* *Mexico* MMSI: 345070294 Official number: 04001357227-5	**444** 133 316	Class: AB	**2007**-05 **Midship Marine, Inc. — New Orleans, La** Yd No: 314 Loa 53.37 Br ex - Dght 2.130 Lbp 48.78 Br md 9.76 Dpth 3.96 Welded, 1 dk	**(B21A20C) Crew/Supply Vessel** Hull Material: Aluminium Alloy	**4 oil engines** reduction geared to sc. shafts driving 4 Water jets Total Power: 5,296kW (7,200hp) 20.0kn Cummins KTA-50-M2 4 x Vee 4 Stroke 16 Cy. 159 x 159 each-1324kW (1800bhp) Cummins Engine Co Inc-USA AuxGen: 2 x 148kW a.c Thrusters: 1 Tunnel thruster (f) Fuel: 139.5 (d.f.)
8962981 *FW9426* PV 916455	**SAILFORT** - **Armement Porcher SAS** - *Port-Vendres* *France* MMSI: 227315560 Official number: 916455	**157** 47 -	Class: (BV)	**2000**-08 **SOCARENAM — Boulogne** Yd No: 172 Loa 23.40 Br ex - Dght 3.273 Lbp 20.00 Br md 7.20 Dpth 3.80 Welded, 1 dk	**(B11B2FV) Fishing Vessel** Compartments: 1 Ho 2 Ha:	**1 oil engine** with clutches, flexible couplings & sr geared to sc. shaft driving 1 CP propeller Total Power: 316kW (430hp) Baudouin 12M26SR 1 x Vee 4 Stroke 12 Cy. 150 x 150 316kW (430bhp) Societe des Moteurs Baudouin SA-France Thrusters: 1 Thwart. FP thruster (f)
7368645 *LNWW* R-112-ES	**SAILOR** *ex* Vikingbank *-2003* *ex* Lingbank *-2001* **Rune/Peder Fishing AS** - *Egersund* *Norway* MMSI: 257888500	**223** 66 -		**1974**-07 **Eidsvik Skipsbyggeri AS — Uskedalen** Yd No: 31 Loa 28.05 Br ex 7.04 Dght - Lbp 25.00 Br md 7.01 Dpth 3.71 Welded, 1 dk	**(B11B2FV) Fishing Vessel**	**1 oil engine** driving 1 CP propeller Total Power: 515kW (700hp) Alpha 407-26VO 1 x 2 Stroke 7 Cy. 260 x 400 515kW (700bhp) Alpha Diesel A/S-Denmark
8857681 *UBKG2* -	**SAILPRIDE** *ex* Omskiy-138 *-2008* **Sailpride Maritime Ltd** SailTrade Ltd *Taganrog* *Russia* MMSI: 273356700	**2,583** 967 2,955	Class: RS	**1989**-03 **Santierul Naval Oltenita S.A. — Oltenita** Yd No: 278 Loa 108.36 Br ex 15.03 Dght 3.290 Lbp 105.00 Br md 14.80 Dpth 5.00 Welded, 1 dk	**(A31A2GX) General Cargo Ship** Grain: 4,315 Ice Capable	**2 oil engines** driving 2 FP propellers Total Power: 1,030kW (1,400hp) 10.2kn S.K.L. 6NVD48A-2U 2 x 4 Stroke 6 Cy. 320 x 480 each-515kW (700bhp) VEB Schwermaschinenbau "KarlLiebknecht" (SKL)-Magdeburg AuxGen: 3 x 50kW a.c Fuel: 171.0 (d.f.)
8846802 *UBCF8* -	**SAILPRINCE** *ex* Midland 203 *-2007* *ex* Cesis *-2002* *ex* Tsesis *-1991* **Sailprince Maritime Ltd** SailTrade Ltd *Taganrog* *Russia* MMSI: 273334110	**2,554** 971 3,020	Class: RS	**1990**-09 **Santierul Naval Oltenita S.A. — Oltenita** Yd No: 458 Loa 108.40 Br ex 15.03 Dght 3.120 Lbp 102.00 Br md 14.80 Dpth 5.00 Welded, 1 dk	**(A31A2GX) General Cargo Ship** Grain: 4,340 4 Ha: 4 (15.6 x 10.9)ER Ice Capable	**2 oil engines** driving 2 FP propellers Total Power: 1,030kW (1,400hp) S.K.L. 6NVD48A-2U 2 x 4 Stroke 6 Cy. 320 x 480 each-515kW (700bhp) VEB Schwermaschinenbau "KarlLiebknecht" (SKL)-Magdeburg
8876182 *UBMF9* -	**SAILPRINCESS** *ex* Finch *-2007* *ex* Dana *-2005* *ex* Aleksandr Gorbachevskiy *-2004* **Sailprincess Maritime Ltd** SailTrade Ltd *Taganrog* *Russia* MMSI: 273330320	**2,594** 859 3,054	Class: RS	**1990**-08 **Krasnoyarskiy Sudostroitelnyy Zavod — Krasnoyarsk** Yd No: 02 Loa 113.30 Br ex 14.80 Dght 3.160 Lbp 107.28 Br md - Dpth 5.00 Welded, 1 dk	**(A31A2GX) General Cargo Ship**	**2 oil engines** driving 2 FP propellers Total Power: 1,030kW (1,400hp) 10.0kn S.K.L. 6NVD48A-2U 2 x 4 Stroke 6 Cy. 320 x 480 each-515kW (700bhp) VEB Schwermaschinenbau "KarlLiebknecht" (SKL)-Magdeburg AuxGen: 3 x 50kW a.c Fuel: 115.0 (d.f.)
8884933 *UBDF2* -	**SAILQUEEN** *ex* Bloor *-2007* *ex* Altair *-2006* *ex* Aleksandr Kerosinskiy *-2004* **Sailqueen Maritime Ltd** Sailtrade Denizcilik ve Ticaret Ltd Sti *Taganrog* *Russia* MMSI: 273336110	**2,692** 923 3,058	Class: RS	**1991**-08 **Krasnoyarskiy Sudostroitelnyy Zavod — Krasnoyarsk** Yd No: 03 Loa 113.37 Br ex 15.00 Dght 3.160 Lbp 106.40 Br md 14.80 Dpth 5.00 Welded, 1 dk	**(A31A2GX) General Cargo Ship** Grain: 4,370 Compartments: 4 Ho, ER 4 Ha: 4 (15.5 x 11.0)ER	**2 oil engines** driving 2 FP propellers Total Power: 1,030kW (1,400hp) 10.2kn S.K.L. 6NVDS48A-2U 2 x 4 Stroke 6 Cy. 320 x 480 each-515kW (700bhp) SKL Motoren u. Systemtechnik AG-Magdeburg AuxGen: 3 x 84kW a.c Fuel: 84.0 (d.f.)
8876170 *UBMF8* -	**SAILROSE** *ex* Pemberton *-2007* *ex* Vega *-2006* *ex* Inzhener Dmitriyev *-2004* **Sailrose Maritime Ltd** SailTrade Ltd *Taganrog* *Russia* MMSI: 273339220	**2,594** 859 3,046	Class: RS	**1989**-08 **Krasnoyarskiy Sudostroitelnyy Zavod — Krasnoyarsk** Yd No: 0001 Loa 113.30 Br ex 14.80 Dght 3.160 Lbp 107.28 Br md - Dpth 5.00 Welded, 1 dk	**(A31A2GX) General Cargo Ship** Grain: 4,370 TEU 104 C. 104/20' Compartments: 4 Ho, ER 4 Ha: 4 (15.5 x 10.9)ER Cranes: 2x8t	**2 oil engines** driving 2 FP propellers Total Power: 1,030kW (1,400hp) 10.0kn S.K.L. 6NVDS48A-2U 2 x 4 Stroke 6 Cy. 320 x 480 each-515kW (700bhp) VEB Schwermaschinenbau "KarlLiebknecht" (SKL)-Magdeburg AuxGen: 3 x 50kW a.c Fuel: 115.0 (d.f.)
8932297 *9LC2088* -	**SAILSTAR** *ex* Hilda *-2007* *ex* Regul *-2006* *ex* Tula *-2004* **Lybra Logistics LLP** Nord Shipping Ltd *Freetown* *Sierra Leone* MMSI: 667509000	**2,456** 969 3,128	Class: RS	**1980**-08 **Santierul Naval Oltenita S.A. — Oltenita** Yd No: 118 Loa 108.40 Br ex 15.00 Dght 3.260 Lbp 102.50 Br md 14.80 Dpth 5.00 Welded, 1 dk	**(A31A2GX) General Cargo Ship** Grain: 4,737 TEU 96 C. 96/20' Compartments: 4 Ho	**2 oil engines** driving 2 FP propellers Total Power: 1,030kW (1,400hp) 10.5kn S.K.L. 6NVD48A-2U 2 x 4 Stroke 6 Cy. 320 x 480 each-515kW (700bhp) VEB Schwermaschinenbau "KarlLiebknecht" (SKL)-Magdeburg AuxGen: 3 x 50kW Fuel: 89.0 (d.f.)
9288069 *PHCQ* -	**SAIMAAGRACHT** - **Rederij Saimaagracht** Spliethoff's Bevrachtingskantoor BV *Amsterdam* *Netherlands* MMSI: 246293000 Official number: 42281	**18,321** 7,647 23,660	Class: LR ✠ **100A1** SS 03/2010 strengthened for heavy cargoes, container cargoes in holds, on upper deck and upper deck hatch covers, timber deck cargoes, tanktop suitable for discharge by grabs LI *IWS Ice Class 1A FS at draught of 10.832m Max/min draught aft 11.47/6.60m Max/min draught fwd 10.47/4.22m Power required 4492kw, installed 12060kw ✠ **LMC** **UMS** Eq.Ltr: I†; Cable: 605.0/64.0 U3 (a)	**2005**-03 **Stocznia Szczecinska Nowa Sp z oo — Szczecin** Yd No: B587/IV/7 Loa 185.40 (BB) Br ex 25.66 Dght 10.600 Lbp 173.50 Br md 25.30 Dpth 14.60 Welded, 1 dk	**(A31A2GX) General Cargo Ship** Grain: 27,600 TEU 1291 C Ho 555 TEU C Dk 736 TEU incl 120 ref C. Compartments: 3 Ho, ER 3 Ha: ER Cranes: 3x120t Ice Capable	**1 oil engine** with flexible couplings & sr geared to sc. shaft driving 1 CP propeller Total Power: 12,060kW (16,397hp) 19.1kn Wartsila 6L64 1 x 4 Stroke 6 Cy. 640 x 900 12060kW (16397bhp) Wartsila Italia SpA-Italy AuxGen: 3 x 450kW 445V 60Hz a.c, 1 x 1000kW 445V 60Hz a.c Boilers: TOH (o.f.) 10.2kgf/cm² (10.0bar), TOH (ex.g.) 10.2kgf/cm² (10.0bar) Thrusters: 1 Thwart. CP thruster (f) Fuel: 265.0 (d.f.) 1775.0 (r.f.)

7728833 **SAINA** 199 / - / 127
- / - / **Alexandria Port Authority** / - / *Alexandria* *Egypt*
Class: (LR) ✠ Classed LR until 31/12/80
1978-11 Towa Zosen K.K. — Shimonoseki Yd No: 510
Loa 30.00 Br ex 8.77 Dght 2.915
Lbp 27.01 Br md 6.88 Dpth 3.61
Welded, 1 dk
(B32A2ST) Tug
2 oil engines reverse reduction geared to sc. shafts driving 2 FP propellers
Total Power: 1,176kW (1,598hp) 12.0kn
Yanmar 6GL-DT
2 x 4 Stroke 6 Cy. 240 x 290 each-588kW (799bhp)
Yanmar Diesel Engine Co Ltd-Japan
AuxGen: 2 x 52kW 380/220V 50Hz a.c

9305817 *FMAO* PV 916346 **SAINT ANTOINE MARIE II** **350** / - / -
Thon de Roussillon / - / *Port-Vendres* *France*
MMSI: 228189900
Official number: 916346
Class: (BV)
2004-04 Chantiers Piriou — Concarneau Yd No: 257
Loa 43.42 Br ex - Dght -
Lbp - Br md 9.50 Dpth -
Welded, 1 dk
(B11B2FV) Fishing Vessel
2 oil engines geared to sc. shafts driving 2 Propellers
Total Power: 800kW (1,088hp)
Wartsila
2 x 4 Stroke each-400kW (544bhp)
Wartsila France SA-France

7434092 *CA3115* - **SAINT BRANDAN** **1,017** / 485 / 1,394
Maritima Transaustral Ltd / - / *Chile*
MMSI: 725000755
Class: (LR) ✠ Classed LR until 1/6/09
1976-12 J. W. Cook & Co. (Wivenhoe) Ltd. — Wivenhoe Yd No: 1451
Loa 63.81 Br ex 10.77 Dght 4.115
Lbp 59.44 Br md 10.52 Dpth 4.88
Welded, 1 dk
(A31A2GA) General Cargo Ship (with Ro-Ro facility)
Bow ramp
Len: 3.75 Wid: 5.72 Swl: 60
Lane-Len: 42
Lane-Wid: 6.50
Grain: 1,842; Bale: 1,750
Compartments: 1 Ho, ER
1 Ha: (32.7 x 7.4)ER
1 oil engine reverse reduction geared to sc. shaft driving 1 FP propeller
Total Power: 971kW (1,320hp) 10.0kn
Ruston 6RKCM
1 x 4 Stroke 6 Cy. 254 x 305 971kW (1320bhp)
Ruston Paxman Diesels Ltd.-Colchester
AuxGen: 2 x 26kW 240/415V 50Hz a.c, 1 x 17kW 240/415V 50Hz a.c
Fuel: 76.0 (d.f.) 4.5pd

7641009 *9GSN* - **SAINT BRENDAN** *154* / 43 / 166
ex Yaa Asantewaa *-2011*
PW Ghana Ltd / - / *Takoradi* *Ghana*
Class: (LR) ✠ Classed LR until 29/4/98
1977-10 Asia-Pacific Shipyard Pte Ltd — Singapore Yd No: 337
Loa 26.09 Br ex 7.90 Dght 3.264
Lbp 23.80 Br md 7.62 Dpth 3.81
Welded, 1 dk
(B32A2ST) Tug
2 oil engines reverse reduction geared to sc. shafts driving 2 FP propellers
Total Power: 912kW (1,240hp)
Blackstone ESL8MK2
2 x 4 Stroke 8 Cy. 222 x 292 each-456kW (620bhp)
Mirrlees Blackstone (Stamford)Ltd.-Stamford
AuxGen: 2 x 40kW 415V 50Hz a.c

8806773 *EINQ3* - **SAINT CLAIR** **182** / 65 / -
ex Kamizaze II *-2004* *ex* Douric II *-2001*
- / *Sligo* *Irish Republic*
MMSI: 250002776
1987-04 Chantiers Piriou — Concarneau
Loa 24.41 Br ex - Dght -
Lbp 20.81 Br md 7.21 Dpth 3.87
Welded, 1 dk
(B11A2FS) Stern Trawler
Ins: 100
1 oil engine sr geared to sc. shaft driving 1 CP propeller
Total Power: 500kW (680hp) 11.5kn
Poyaud A12150SRHM
1 x Vee 4 Stroke 12 Cy. 150 x 180 500kW (680bhp)
Poyaud S.S.C.M.-Surgeres

8992924 *WDE4798* - **SAINT CRISPIN** *137* / 93 / -
ex Mannie Cenac *-2005* *ex* Carol Fenn *-2005*
Kirby Inland Marine LP / - / *Houston, TX* *United States of America*
MMSI: 367479650
Official number: 627224
1980-01 Louis G. Ortis Boat Co., Inc. — Krotz Springs, La Yd No: 90
L reg 19.20 Br ex - Dght -
Lbp - Br md 7.35 Dpth 3.05
Welded, 1 dk
(B32B2SP) Pusher Tug
2 oil engines driving 2 FP propellers
Total Power: 1,268kW (1,724hp)
Cummins KTA-38-M0
2 x Vee 4 Stroke 12 Cy. 159 x 159 each-634kW (862bhp) (new engine 1980)
Cummins Engine Co Inc-USA

8617342 *FHFO* - **SAINT DENIS** **221** / 78 / 74
Boluda France SAS
Boluda Nantes Saint Nazaire
St-Nazaire *France*
MMSI: 228051000
Class: BV
1986-10 Chantiers Breheret Leroux et Lotz — Ingrandes Yd No: 1276
Loa 28.86 Br ex - Dght 3.031
Lbp 27.01 Br md 9.52 Dpth 3.71
Welded, 1 dk
(B32A2ST) Tug
2 oil engines sr geared to sc. shafts driving 2 Directional propellers
Total Power: 1,800kW (2,448hp)
MWM TBD440-6K
2 x 4 Stroke 6 Cy. 230 x 270 each-900kW (1224bhp)
Motoren Werke Mannheim AG (MWM)-West Germany

9486398 *V7XD9* - **SAINT DIMITRIOS** **23,322** / 11,202 / 33,788
launched as Triton *-2011*
Zefxis Maritime Corp
Transman Shipmanagers SA
Majuro *Marshall Islands*
MMSI: 538004456
Official number: 4456
Class: AB
2011-09 21st Century Shipbuilding Co Ltd — Tongyeong Yd No: 1003
Loa 181.10 (BB) Br ex - Dght 9.900
Lbp 172.00 Br md 30.00 Dpth 14.80
Welded, 1 dk
(A21A2BC) Bulk Carrier
Grain: 47,558; Bale: 45,180
Compartments: 5 Ho, ER
5 Ha: ER
Cranes: 4x30.7t
1 oil engine driving 1 FP propeller
Total Power: 6,480kW (8,810hp) 14.5kn
MAN-B&W 6S42MC7
1 x 2 Stroke 6 Cy. 420 x 1764 6480kW (8810bhp)
Hyundai Heavy Industries Co Ltd-South Korea
AuxGen: 3 x 570kW a.c
Fuel: 132.0 (d.f.) 1608.0 (r.f.)

6918986 *9GSL* - **SAINT FINBAR** *150* / 41 / -
ex Yendi *-2011*
P W Ghana Ltd / - / *Takoradi* *Ghana*
Official number: 316585
Class: (LR) ✠ Classed LR until 27/3/85
1969-05 C Cassens Schiffswerft — Emden (Hull) Yd No: 96
1969-05 Schiffs- u. Yachtwerft Abeking & Rasmussen GmbH & Co. — Lemwerder Yd No: 6319
Loa 29.32 Br ex 8.06 Dght 2.896
Lbp 26.45 Br md 7.62 Dpth 3.81
Welded, 1 dk
(B32A2ST) Tug
2 oil engines reverse reduction geared to sc. shafts driving 2 FP propellers
Total Power: 984kW (1,338hp)
Blackstone ERS8
2 x 4 Stroke 8 Cy. 222 x 292 each-492kW (669bhp)
Lister Blackstone Marine Ltd.-Dursley
AuxGen: 2 x 36kW 231/400V 50Hz a.c, 1 x 20kW 231/400V 50Hz a.c
Fuel: 34.5 (d.f.)

5406546 *TUN2158* AN 800 **SAINT FRANCOIS** *197* / 64 / 541
ex Le Martinet *-1972* *ex* Boston Swallow *-1963*
Societe de Peche Abidjanaise (SOPA) / - / *Abidjan* *Cote d'Ivoire*
Class: (LR) (BV) ✠ Classed LR until 11/68
1958-01 Richards Iron Works Ltd — Lowestoft Yd No: 439
Loa 35.01 Br ex 7.12 Dght 3.004
Lbp 31.70 Br md 7.01 Dpth 3.92
Riveted\Welded, 1 dk
(B11A2FT) Trawler
3 Ha: (0.7 x 1.1)2 (1.1 x 1.0)
1 oil engine driving 1 FP propeller
Total Power: 405kW (551hp) 10.0kn
Widdop GMB5
1 x 4 Stroke 5 Cy. 318 x 470 405kW (551bhp)
H. Widdop & Co. Ltd.-Keighley
Fuel: 31.0 (d.f.)

9452323 *5BDY3* - **SAINT GEORGE** **6,680** / 3,190 / 8,500
ex Clipper Maria *-2013* *ex* Nunukas *-2011*
ex Lehmann Forester *-2010*
ex Onego Forester *-2009* *ex* Hyfour *-2008*
Great Options Investments Ltd
Pacific & Atlantic (Shipmanagers) Inc
Limassol *Cyprus*
MMSI: 209152000
Class: LR (GL) (CC)
100A1 SS 03/2013
container ship
container cargoes on upper deck and on all hatch covers
LI
LMC
2008-03 Fujian New Shenghai Ship Co Ltd — Longhai FJ Yd No: 0509001
Loa 131.55 (BB) Br ex - Dght 6.940
Lbp 122.00 Br md 18.80 Dpth 9.40
Welded, 1 dk
(A31A2GX) General Cargo Ship
Grain: 10,928; Bale: 10,928
TEU 468 C Ho 216 TEU C Dk 252 TEU.
Compartments: 3 Ho, ER
3 Ha: (31.1 x 15.0)ER 2 (25.2 x 15.0)
Cranes: 2x35t
Ice Capable
1 oil engine reduction geared to sc. shaft driving 1 CP propeller
Total Power: 3,824kW (5,199hp) 14.3kn
Pielstick 8PC2-5L
1 x 4 Stroke 8 Cy. 400 x 460 3824kW (5199bhp)
Thrusters: 1 Tunnel thruster (f)
Fuel: 47.0 (d.f.) 324.0 (r.f.)

8811534 *FHVG* CC 683638 **SAINT GOTHARD** **273** / 73 / -
Saint Gothard SNC
Armement Dhellemmes SA
SatCom: Inmarsat C 422737810
Concarneau *France*
MMSI: 227378000
Official number: 683638
Class: BV
1989-09 Chantiers Piriou — Concarneau Yd No: 145
Loa 32.28 Br ex - Dght 3.820
Lbp 29.18 Br md 8.20 Dpth 6.53
Welded, 1 dk
(B11A2FS) Stern Trawler
Ins: 170
1 oil engine with clutches & sr geared to sc. shaft driving 1 CP propeller
Total Power: 587kW (798hp) 11.5kn
Deutz SBV6M628
1 x 4 Stroke 6 Cy. 240 x 280 587kW (798bhp)
Kloeckner Humboldt Deutz AG-West Germany
AuxGen: 2 x 67kW 380/220V a.c

7387495 - - **SAINT GREGORY** **263** / 78 / -
ex Marineda *-1997* *ex* Jomar *-1992*
- / - / -
Class: (BV)
1974-09 Astilleros Gondan SA — Castropol Yd No: 103
Loa 34.70 Br ex 7.04 Dght 3.499
Lbp 30.00 Br md 7.01 Dpth 3.97
Welded, 1 dk
(B11A2FT) Trawler
Grain: 200
Compartments: 1 Ho, ER
1 oil engine driving 1 FP propeller
Total Power: 721kW (980hp) 10.5kn
Skoda 6L350IIPN
1 x 4 Stroke 6 Cy. 350 x 500 721kW (980bhp)
CKD Praha-Praha
Fuel: 100.0 (d.f.)

7119501 *FM4674* - **SAINT HERMELAND** *252* / 179 / 140
Government of The Republic of France (Departement de la Loire-Atlantique)
Compagnie Des Bacs de Loire
Nantes *France*
Official number: 293196
Class: (BV)
1970 Soc. des At. Francais de l'Ouest — St. Nazaire Yd No: BA1
Loa 63.51 Br ex 12.58 Dght 1.632
Lbp 42.75 Br md 12.25 Dpth 2.32
Welded, 1 dk
(A37B2PS) Passenger Ship
Passengers: 300
2 oil engines geared to sc. shafts driving 2 CP propellers
Total Power: 662kW (900hp) 7.0kn
Crepelle 8SN1
2 x 4 Stroke 8 Cy. 260 x 280 each-331kW (450bhp)
Crepelle et Cie-France
AuxGen: 2 x 24kW 220V 50Hz a.c
Fuel: 38.0 (d.f.)

9199866 *FOOJ* BL 914059 **SAINT JACQUES II** **153** / 46 / -
Loic & Jacques Margolle / - / *Boulogne* *France*
Official number: 914059
1998-09 SOCARENAM — Boulogne Yd No: 168
Loa 22.50 Br ex 7.26 Dght -
Lbp 19.70 Br md 7.20 Dpth 3.60
Welded, 1 dk
(B11A2FS) Stern Trawler
1 oil engine with clutches, flexible couplings & sr geared to sc. shaft driving 1 Directional propeller
Total Power: 1,020kW (1,387hp)
A.B.C. 6MDXS
1 x 4 Stroke 6 Cy. 242 x 320 1020kW (1387bhp)
Anglo Belgian Corp NV (ABC)-Belgium
Thrusters: 1 Thwart. FP thruster (f)

5168417 *TUN2111* AN 695 **SAINT JEAN** *211* / 69 / -
ex Jalene *-1970*
Societe de Peche Abidjanaise (SOPA) / - / *Abidjan* *Cote d'Ivoire*
Class: (BV)
1961 Soc Industrielle et Commerciale de Consts Navales (SICCNa) — St-Malo Yd No: 45
Loa 35.01 Br ex 7.60 Dght -
Lbp 30.48 Br md 7.52 Dpth 3.87
Riveted\Welded, 1 dk
(B11A2FT) Trawler
4 Ha: 3 (1.1 x 1.1) (0.9 x 1.0)
Derricks: 1x2t,1x1t
1 oil engine driving 1 FP propeller
Total Power: 552kW (750hp) 13.0kn
Deutz RBV6M545
1 x 4 Stroke 6 Cy. 320 x 450 552kW (750bhp)
Kloeckner Humboldt Deutz AG-West Germany
Fuel: 53.5 (d.f.)

Identity / Owner	Tonnage / Class	Builder / Dimensions	Type / Cargo	Machinery
9257785 **SAINT JEAN PRIEZ POUR NOUS** *FPZI* *ex* Socarenam Boulogne 184 BL 899847 **Patrick Margolle & Philippe Becquelin** - *Boulogne* *France* MMSI: 227146400 Official number: 899847	**136** 54 -	**2001-12 SOCARENAM — Boulogne** Yd No: 184 Loa 21.00 Br ex - Dght - Lbp 17.76 Br md 7.20 Dpth 3.60 Welded, 1 dk	**(B11A2FS) Stern Trawler**	**1 oil engine** with clutches, flexible couplings & sr geared to sc. shaft driving 1 CP propeller Total Power: 316kW (430hp) A.B.C. 6MDXC 1 x 4 Stroke 6 Cy. 242 x 320 316kW (430bhp) Anglo Belgian Corp NV (ABC)-Belgium Thrusters: 1 Thwart. FP thruster (f)
7019828 **SAINT JEREMY** *CBSJ* *ex* Araki *-1999* *ex* New Iris *-1996* - *ex* Mas Rose *-1994* *ex* Ibn Korra *-1992* *ex* Atlan Rubi *-1975* **Transportes Miramar SA** - *Valparaiso* *Chile* MMSI: 725002100 Official number: 2960	*1,179* Class: (LR) 771 ✠ Classed LR until 26/8/98 1,727	**1970-06 Sociedad Metalurgica Duro Felguera — Gijon** Yd No: 57 Loa 72.70 Br ex 11.54 Dght 5.195 Lbp 64.01 Br md 11.51 Dpth 6.10 Welded, 2 dks	**(A31A2GX) General Cargo Ship** Grain: 2,266; Bale: 2,112 Compartments: 3 Ho, ER, 3 Tw Dk 3 Ha: (14.5 x 5.2)2 (5.5 x 5.2)ER Derricks: 2x20t,4x5t,4x3t	**1 oil engine** driving 1 FP propeller Total Power: 1,103kW (1,500hp) 15.0kn Deutz RBV6M358 1 x 4 Stroke 6 Cy. 400 x 580 1103kW (1500bhp) Hijos de J Barreras SA-Spain AuxGen: 2 x 125kW 380V 50Hz a.c
7050042 **SAINT JOSEPH** *WBQ7171* - **Lockland V Jones** Angove Accounting Service *Morro Bay, CA* *United States of America* MMSI: 366398920 Official number: 515433	*131* 89 -	**1968 Bender Welding & Machine Co Inc — Mobile AL** Yd No: 656 L reg 22.16 Br ex 6.84 Dght - Lbp - Br md - Dpth 3.54 Welded	**(B11B2FV) Fishing Vessel**	**1 oil engine** driving 1 FP propeller Total Power: 257kW (349hp)
5336442 **SAINT JOSEPH II** - *ex* Roland Express *-1991* *ex* Micado Maru *-1988* - *ex* Kanaloa *-1982* *ex* Veslevik *-1978* *ex* Larki *-1974* *ex* Specht *-1973* - -	*299* Class: (GL) 137 503	**1961 Adler Werft GmbH — Bremen** Yd No: 23 Loa 50.96 Br ex 7.95 Dght 2.591 Lbp 47.05 Br md 7.93 Dpth 2.85 Welded, 1 dk	**(A31A2GX) General Cargo Ship** Grain: 868; Bale: 820 Compartments: 2 Ho, ER 2 Ha: (10.0 x 4.4) (10.5 x 4.4)ER Derricks: 2x2t; Winches: 2	**2 oil engines** reverse reduction geared to sc. shafts driving 2 FP propellers Total Power: 338kW (460hp) 10.3kn Deutz SBA6M528 2 x 4 Stroke 6 Cy. 220 x 280 each-169kW (230bhp) Kloeckner Humboldt Deutz AG-West Germany Fuel: 20.5 (d.f.) 2.0pd
8847208 **SAINT JOSSE** - *ex* Saint Josse III *-2000* WD 2 **Brian White & Brendan, John, Denis & Seamus O'Flaherty** - *Wexford* *Irish Republic* Official number: 403534	**165** 65 -	**1988-03 Chantiers Piriou — Concarneau** Yd No: 116 Loa 24.40 Br ex - Dght 3.465 Lbp 22.14 Br md 7.20 Dpth 3.87 Welded, 1 dk	**(B11A2FT) Trawler**	**1 oil engine** geared to sc. shaft driving 1 FP propeller Total Power: 441kW (600hp) 10.0kn Caterpillar 3508TA 1 x Vee 4 Stroke 8 Cy. 170 x 190 441kW (600bhp) Caterpillar Inc-USA
9228679 **SAINT JOSSE IV** *FUOM* BL 914099 **Emmanuel Fournier** - *Boulogne* *France* MMSI: 227143700 Official number: 914099	**120** Class: (BV) - -	**2001-02 Chantiers Piriou — Concarneau** Yd No: 225 L reg 24.00 Br ex - Dght - Lbp - Br md 8.00 Dpth 4.15 Welded, 1 dk	**(B11B2FV) Fishing Vessel**	**1 oil engine** driving 1 FP propeller Total Power: 588kW (799hp) 11.5kn
7334424 **SAINT JUDE** - - **Societe des Peches Maritimes de Guinee Sarl (SOPEMAGUI)** - *Conakry* *Guinea*	*582* Class: (BV) 234 411	**1973 Stocznia im Komuny Paryskiej — Gdynia** Yd No: B423/18 Loa 54.26 Br ex 11.03 Dght 4.601 Lbp 46.21 Br md 11.00 Dpth 5.19 Welded, 2 dks	**(B11A2FS) Stern Trawler** Ins: 517 Compartments: 1 Ho, ER	**1 oil engine** geared to sc. shaft driving 1 CP propeller Total Power: 1,471kW (2,000hp) 14.5kn Crepelle 12PSN 1 x Vee 4 Stroke 12 Cy. 260 x 280 1471kW (2000bhp) Crepelle et Cie-France AuxGen: 2 x 197kW 380V 50Hz a.c, 1 x 144kW 380V 50Hz a.c Fuel: 202.0 (d.f.)
7926655 **SAINT JUDE** *WDD2068* *ex* Sea Fisher 4 *-1991* - **Iljin USA Inc** - *New Bedford, MA* *United States of America* MMSI: 367110480 Official number: 617393	*135* 92 -	**1980 Quality Marine, Inc. — Bayou La Batre, Al** Yd No: 123 Loa 25.33 Br ex - Dght - Lbp - Br md 7.01 Dpth 3.69 Welded, 1 dk	**(B11A2FS) Stern Trawler**	**1 oil engine** driving 1 FP propeller Total Power: 382kW (519hp) Caterpillar 3412TA 1 x Vee 4 Stroke 12 Cy. 137 x 152 382kW (519bhp) Caterpillar Tractor Co-USA
6917762 **SAINT KEVIN** - *ex* Anloga *-1991* *ex* Awunaga *-1991* - **P W Ghana Ltd** - *Takoradi* *Ghana* Official number: 316586	*150* Class: (LR) 41 ✠ Classed LR until 5/3/97 -	**1969-06 C Cassens Schiffswerft — Emden** (Hull) Yd No: 97 **1969-06 Schiffs- u. Yachtwerft Abeking & Rasmussen GmbH & Co. — Lemwerder** Yd No: 6320 Loa 29.32 Br ex 8.06 Dght 2.896 Lbp 26.45 Br md 7.62 Dpth 3.79 Welded, 1 dk	**(B32A2ST) Tug**	**2 oil engines** reverse reduction geared to sc. shafts driving 2 FP propellers Total Power: 970kW (1,318hp) 10.5kn Blackstone ERS8M 2 x 4 Stroke 8 Cy. 222 x 292 each-485kW (659bhp) Lister Blackstone MirrleesMarine Ltd.-Dursley AuxGen: 2 x 36kW 400V 50Hz a.c, 1 x 20kW 400V 50Hz a.c Fuel: 34.5 (d.f.)
7017222 **SAINT LOUIS** - *ex* Shinko Maru No. 3 *-1985* - **Esco Fisheries SA** - *Kingstown* *St Vincent & The Grenadines*	*423* Class: (KR) 210 567	**1970 Narasaki Zosen KK — Muroran HK** Yd No: 721 Loa 57.46 Br ex - Dght - Lbp 49.00 Br md 9.01 Dpth 4.09 Welded, 1 dk	**(B11B2FV) Fishing Vessel**	**1 oil engine** driving 1 FP propeller Total Power: 1,103kW (1,500hp) 12.8kn Akasaka AH30 1 x 4 Stroke 6 Cy. 300 x 480 1103kW (1500bhp) Akasaka Tekkosho KK (Akasaka DieselLtd)-Japan AuxGen: 2 x 128kW 220V a.c
6823387 **SAINT LOUIS II** - *ex* Calomex No. 81 *-1987* - *ex* Duk Soo No. 81 *-1983* *ex* Kaiun Maru No. 38 *-1976* **Esco Fisheries SA** - *Kingstown* *St Vincent & The Grenadines*	*407* Class: (RI) (KR) 226 349	**1968 Narasaki Zosen KK — Muroran HK** Yd No: 629 Loa 50.53 Br ex 8.72 Dght 3.455 Lbp 45.32 Br md 8.60 Dpth 5.90 Welded, 2 dks	**(B11A2FS) Stern Trawler** Ins: 478 2 Ha: 2 (1.7 x 1.7)	**1 oil engine** driving 1 FP propeller Total Power: 1,214kW (1,651hp) 12.8kn Fuji 6SD37BH 1 x 4 Stroke 6 Cy. 370 x 550 1214kW (1651bhp) Fuji Diesel Co Ltd-Japan AuxGen: 2 x 128kW 225V a.c
5258121 **SAINT MARC** *TUN2133* *ex* Notre Dame de Boulogne *-1969* - **Societe de Peche Abidjanaise (SOPA)** - *Abidjan* *Cote d'Ivoire*	*283* Class: (BV) 99 -	**1962 N.V. Scheepsbouw. "De Dageraad" v/h Wed. J. Boot — Woubrugge** Yd No: 505 Loa 41.00 Br ex 7.70 Dght 3.645 Lbp 36.00 Br md 7.65 Dpth 4.12 Welded, 1 dk	**(B11A2FT) Trawler** Derricks: 1x4t	**1 oil engine** driving 1 FP propeller Total Power: 625kW (850hp) 12.0kn Deutz RBV6M545 1 x 4 Stroke 6 Cy. 320 x 450 625kW (850bhp) Kloeckner Humboldt Deutz AG-West Germany AuxGen: 2 x 40kW 110V
7822330 **SAINT MARY** - *ex* Dane Swan *-2011* *ex* Lotus *-1999* - *ex* Beckenham *-1995* **Macchalis International Co Ltd** -	**840** Class: (LR) 386 ✠ Classed LR until 17/10/12 1,165 T/cm 6.1	**1980-01 A/S Nordsovaerftet — Ringkobing** Yd No: 138 Loa 64.17 Br ex 11.51 Dght 3.263 Lbp 60.51 Br md 11.19 Dpth 4.12 Welded, 1 dk	**(A13B2TP) Products Tanker** Double Bottom Entire Compartment Length Liq: 1,379; Liq (Oil): 1,379 Compartments: 14 Wing Ta, ER 2 Cargo Pump (s)	**1 oil engine** sr geared to sc. shaft driving 1 CP propeller Total Power: 912kW (1,240hp) 11.0kn Alpha 8V23L-VO 1 x Vee 4 Stroke 8 Cy. 225 x 300 912kW (1240bhp) B&W Alpha Diesel A/S-Denmark AuxGen: 2 x 42kW 415V 50Hz a.c Thrusters: 1 Thwart. FP thruster (f)
9229362 **SAINT NICHOLAS** *9HFZ7* - **Global Maritime Ltd** Thenamaris (Ships Management) Inc *Valletta* *Malta* MMSI: 215202000 Official number: 7657	**57,301** Class: LR 32,526 ✠ **100A1** SS 06/2012 105,541 Double Hull oil tanker T/cm ESP 92.0 *IWS LI SPM **ShipRight** (SDA, FDA, CM) ✠ **LMC** **UMS IGS** Eq.Ltr: T†; Cable: 715.0/87.0 U3 (a)	**2002-06 Samho Heavy Industries Co Ltd — Samho** Yd No: 134 Loa 244.00 (BB) Br ex 42.03 Dght 14.900 Lbp 234.00 Br md 42.00 Dpth 21.00 Welded, 1 dk	**(A13A2TV) Crude Oil Tanker** Double Hull (13F) Liq: 117,963; Liq (Oil): 118,084 Cargo Heating Coils Compartments: 12 Wing Ta, 2 Wing Slop Ta, ER 3 Cargo Pump (s): 3x3000m³/hr Manifold: Bow/CM: 122.8m	**1 oil engine** driving 1 FP propeller Total Power: 11,327kW (15,400hp) 14.5kn MAN-B&W 6S60MC 1 x 2 Stroke 6 Cy. 600 x 2292 11327kW (15400bhp) Hyundai Heavy Industries Co Ltd-South Korea AuxGen: 3 x 730kW 450V 60Hz a.c Boilers: WTAuxB (o.f.) 18.0kgf/cm² (17.7bar), WTAuxB (o.f.) 8.1kgf/cm² (7.9bar) Fuel: 195.0 (d.f.) 2417.0 (r.f.)
1008918 **SAINT NICOLAS** *ZCPZ3* *launched as* Nemo *-2007* - **Nemo Shipping Ltd** Nigel Burgess Ltd (BURGESS) *George Town* *Cayman Islands (British)* MMSI: 319762000 Official number: 739789	**1,938** Class: LR 581 ✠ **100A1** SS 05/2012 252 SSC Yacht (P), mono, G6 ✠ **LMC** **UMS** Cable: 192.5/28.0 U3 (a)	**2007-05 Kroeger Werft GmbH & Co. KG — Schacht-Audorf** Yd No: 13643 Loa 70.20 Br ex 13.11 Dght 3.650 Lbp 56.86 Br md 12.80 Dpth 6.75 Welded, 2 dks	**(X11A2YP) Yacht**	**2 oil engines** with clutches, flexible couplings & sr reverse geared to sc. shafts driving 2 FP propellers Total Power: 3,000kW (4,078hp) 15.5kn Caterpillar 3512B-TA 2 x Vee 4 Stroke 12 Cy. 170 x 190 each-1500kW (2039bhp) Caterpillar Inc-USA AuxGen: 3 x 280kW 400V 50Hz a.c Thrusters: 1 Thwart. CP thruster (f)

5373701 *A3CF8* -
SAINT NICOLAS
ex Sotirios *-2001* *ex* Peng *-1999*
ex Elena J *-1999* *ex* Penelope *-1997*
ex Sotirios *-1994* *ex* Stella Mavra *-1982*
ex La Perla *-1979* *ex* Unterweser *-1972*
-
-
Nuku'alofa *Tonga*
Official number: 1088
494 223 690 Class: (GL)
1957-04 **C. Luehring — Brake** Yd No: 5603
Lengthened-1965
Loa 57.31 Br ex 8.54 Dght 3.090
Lbp 51.95 Br md 8.51 Dpth 3.46
Riveted\Welded, 1 dk
(A31A2GX) General Cargo Ship
Grain: 970; Bale: 912
Compartments: 1 Ho, ER
2 Ha: (14.5 x 5.0) (12.9 x 5.0)ER
Derricks: 3x2t
1 oil engine driving 1 FP propeller
Total Power: 221kW (300hp) 9.5kn
MaK MAU423
1 x 4 Stroke 8 Cy. 290 x 420 221kW (300bhp)
Maschinenbau Kiel AG (MaK)-Kiel

9304734 *V7CQ4* -
SAINT NIKOLAOS
ex Rio Alster *-2013* *ex* MCC Shanghai *-2013*
ex Rio Alster *-2010* *ex* Maersk Naples *-2009*
Brand Marine SA
Transman Shipmanagers SA
Majuro *Marshall Islands*
MMSI: 538005306
Official number: 5306
27,059 12,221 34,355 Class: GL
2004-11 **Howaldtswerke-Deutsche Werft AG (HDW) — Kiel** (Aft & pt cargo sections)
Yd No: 379
2004-11 **SSW Schichau Seebeck Shipyard GmbH — Bremerhaven** (Fwd & pt cargo sections)
Loa 211.85 (BB) Br ex - Dght 11.400
Lbp 199.95 Br md 29.80 Dpth 16.70
Welded, 1 dk
(A33A2CC) Container Ship (Fully Cellular)
TEU 2490 C Ho 958 TEU C Dk 1532 TEU incl 566 ref C.
Cranes: 3x45t
1 oil engine driving 1 FP propeller
Total Power: 15,857kW (21,559hp) 22.0kn
Sulzer 7RTA72U-B
1 x 2 Stroke 7 Cy. 720 x 2500 15857kW (21559bhp)
Hyundai Heavy Industries Co Ltd-South Korea
AuxGen: 3 x 2225kW 450/230V 60Hz a.c
Thrusters: 1 Thwart. CP thruster (f)

9551272 *WDE4831* -
SAINT PAUL
-
Saint Paul LLC
-
St Paul, AK *United States of America*
MMSI: 367358360
Official number: 1211672
131 105 -
2008-05 **Fred Wahl Marine Construction Inc — Reedsport, Or** Yd No: 08-58-22
L reg 17.67 (BB) Br ex - Dght -
Lbp - Br md 7.92 Dpth 4.20
Welded, 1 dk
(B11B2FV) Fishing Vessel
1 oil engine reduction geared to sc. shaft driving 1 Propeller
Total Power: 380kW (517hp)
Cummins KT-19-M
1 x 4 Stroke 6 Cy. 159 x 159 380kW (517bhp)
Cummins Engine Co Inc-USA

9653707 *WDF9560* -
SAINT PETER
-
Saint Peter LLC
-
St Paul, AK *United States of America*
MMSI: 367506420
Official number: 1235623
131 105 -
2011-10 **Fred Wahl Marine Construction Inc — Reedsport, Or** Yd No: 11-58-33
L reg 17.67 Br ex - Dght -
Lbp - Br md 7.92 Dpth 3.96
Welded, 1 dk
(B11B2FV) Fishing Vessel
1 oil engine reduction geared to sc. shaft driving 1 Propeller
Total Power: 597kW (812hp)
Cummins QSK19-M
1 x 4 Stroke 6 Cy. 159 x 159 597kW (812bhp)
Cummins Engine Co Inc-USA

1001518 *MMGF6* -
SAINT PETER
ex Aphaea *-2008* *ex* Ego II *-2001*
Swansea Marine Ltd
-
London *United Kingdom*
MMSI: 232683000
Official number: 718325
128 - - Class: (LR)
✠ Classed LR until 9/3/11
1990-09 **at Istanbul**
Loa 25.00 Br ex 6.01 Dght 2.000
Lbp 21.60 Br md 6.00 Dpth 3.29
Welded, 1 dk
(X11A2YP) Yacht
2 oil engines geared to sc. shafts driving 2 FP propellers
Total Power: 538kW (732hp)
Cummins NT-855-M
2 x 4 Stroke 6 Cy. 140 x 152 each-269kW (366bhp)
Cummins Engine Co Ltd-United Kingdom

7515640 *WDA5502* -
SAINT PETER
ex Jimmy Dian *-2001*
De Nguyen
-
Biloxi, MS *United States of America*
MMSI: 366820790
Official number: 550775
119 81 -
1973 **Toche Enterprises, Inc. — Ocean Springs, Ms** Yd No: 1058
L reg 21.34 Br ex 6.71 Dght -
Lbp - Br md - Dpth 3.28
Welded, 1 dk
(B11A2FT) Trawler
1 oil engine driving 1 FP propeller
Total Power: 335kW (455hp)

5129813 - AN 799
SAINT PIERRE
ex Felix Valton *-2001*
ex Germaine Anne Marie *-1966*
Societe de Peche Abidjanaise (SOPA)
-
Abidjan *Cote d'Ivoire*
134 43 - Class: (BV)
1959 **Chantiers et Ateliers de La Perriere — Lorient**
Loa 29.01 Br ex 6.91 Dght -
Lbp - Br md - Dpth -
Welded, 1 dk
(B11A2FT) Trawler
Ins: 133
Compartments: 1 Ho, ER
2 Ha: 2 (0.9 x 0.9)
Derricks: 1x2.5t; Winches: 1
1 oil engine driving 1 FP propeller
Total Power: 309kW (420hp) 9.5kn
Duvant 6VHK
1 x 4 Stroke 6 Cy. 230 x 330 309kW (420bhp)
Moteurs Duvant-France
Fuel: 40.5 (d.f.)

8717453 *CB7575* -
SAINT PIERRE
-
Pesca Chile SA
-
Valparaiso *Chile*
MMSI: 725012800
Official number: 3059
1,295 388 600 Class: BV
1989-03 **Societe Nouvelle des Ateliers et Chantiers du Havre — Le Havre**
Yd No: 275
Loa 49.98 Br ex 13.27 Dght 5.512
Lbp 43.50 Br md 13.00 Dpth 8.10
Welded, 1 dk
(B11A2FS) Stern Trawler
Ins: 600
Ice Capable
2 oil engines with flexible couplings & sr geared to sc. shaft driving 1 CP propeller
Total Power: 2,208kW (3,002hp) 13.5kn
Caterpillar 3606TA
2 x 4 Stroke 6 Cy. 280 x 300 each-1104kW (1501bhp)
Caterpillar Inc-USA
AuxGen: 1 x 420kW 380V a.c
Fuel: 440.0 (d.f.)

9209714 *MZBQ8* -
SAINT PIRAN
-
Cornwall County Council
Cornwall Sea Fisheries
Penzance *United Kingdom*
MMSI: 232612000
Official number: 903190
117 - - Class: (LR)
✠ Classed LR until 16/8/01
2000-05 **ALU International Shipyard Sp z oo — Gdansk** (Hull)
2000-05 **B.V. Scheepswerf Damen — Gorinchem**
Yd No: 505648
Loa 27.17 Br ex 6.75 Dght 1.626
Lbp 23.99 Br md 6.48 Dpth 3.40
Welded, 1 dk
(B34H2SQ) Patrol Vessel
Hull Material: Aluminium Alloy
2 oil engines with clutches, flexible couplings & sr reverse geared to sc. shafts driving 2 FP propellers
Total Power: 1,940kW (2,638hp) 20.0kn
Cummins KTA-38-M2
2 x Vee 4 Stroke 12 Cy. 159 x 159 each-970kW (1319bhp)
Cummins Engine Co Ltd-United Kingdom
AuxGen: 2 x 48kW 230/400V 50Hz a.c
Thrusters: 1 Thwart. FP thruster (f)
Fuel: 9.7 (d.f.)

8321204 - -
SAINT RAPHAEL
ex Ajax *-2004* *ex* Azores *-2000*
ex Akmeya *-1997*
Saint Raphael Fishing SA
-
San Lorenzo *Honduras*
Official number: L-1528067
249 74 80 Class: (BV) (RS)
1986-05 **Stocznia Ustka SA — Ustka**
Yd No: B275/15
Loa 29.80 Br ex 8.19 Dght 3.280
Lbp 26.37 Br md 8.01 Dpth 4.00
Welded, 1 dk
(B11A2FS) Stern Trawler
1 oil engine geared to sc. shaft driving 1 CP propeller
Total Power: 552kW (750hp) 10.7kn
Sulzer 6AL20/24
1 x 4 Stroke 6 Cy. 200 x 240 552kW (750bhp)
Zaklady Przemyslu Metalowego 'HCegielski' SA-Poznan
AuxGen: 2 x 100kW
Fuel: 51.0 (d.f.)

7724306 *C6NS4* -
SAINT ROCH
ex Hoegh Belle *-1981*
CMA CGM SA (The French Line)
Midocean (IOM) Ltd
Nassau *Bahamas*
MMSI: 309507000
Official number: 727503
31,007 9,302 24,282 Class: BV (NV)
1980-12 **Stocznia im Komuny Paryskiej — Gdynia**
Yd No: B484/02
Loa 186.60 (BB) Br ex 32.29 Dght 10.648
Lbp 170.69 Br md 32.28 Dpth 12.30
Welded, 3 dks
(A35A2RR) Ro-Ro Cargo Ship
Quarter stern door/ramp (s)
Len: 49.70 Wid: 12.00 Swl: 350
Lane-Len: 3308
Lane-Wid: 12.00
Lane-clr ht: 6.30
Lorries: 150, Cars: 320
Bale: 44,780; Ins: 509
TEU 1187 C Ho 619 TEU C Dk 568 TEU incl 50 ref C.
Cranes: 1x40t
Ice Capable
1 oil engine driving 1 FP propeller
Total Power: 12,798kW (17,400hp) 18.0kn
Sulzer 6RND90
1 x 2 Stroke 6 Cy. 900 x 1550 12798kW (17400bhp)
Zaklady Przemyslu Metalowego 'HCegielski' SA-Poznan
AuxGen: 1 x 1335kW 440V 60Hz a.c, 4 x 960kW 440V 60Hz a.c
Thrusters: 1 Thwart. FP thruster (f); 1 Tunnel thruster (a)
Fuel: 501.5 (d.f.) 2495.0 (r.f.) 61.5pd

9251470 *FPCT* ST 859076
SAINT SOPHIE FRANCOIS II
-
Nicolas Giordano
-
Sete *France*
MMSI: 227145600
Official number: 859076
210 63 181
2002-01 **Astilleros Armon SA — Navia** Yd No: 544
Loa 32.00 Br ex - Dght 2.210
Lbp 31.70 Br md 8.25 Dpth 3.45
Welded, 1 dk
(B11B2FV) Fishing Vessel
Bale: 140
2 oil engines reduction geared to sc. shafts driving 2 FP propellers
Total Power: 1,854kW (2,520hp)
Volvo Penta D49A MT
2 x Vee 4 Stroke 12 Cy. 170 x 180 each-927kW (1260bhp)
AB Volvo Penta-Sweden

9264415 *FQCB* ST 923752
SAINT SOPHIE FRANCOIS III
-
Francisco Javier Giordano
-
Sete *France*
MMSI: 228141800
Official number: 923752
150 - - Class: (BV)
2002-04 **Astilleros Armon SA — Navia** Yd No: 575
Loa 32.00 Br ex - Dght 3.450
Lbp 31.70 Br md 8.25 Dpth 3.52
Welded, 1 dk
(B11B2FV) Fishing Vessel
Bale: 128
2 oil engines geared to sc. shafts driving 2 FP propellers
Total Power: 516kW (702hp)
Volvo Penta D49A MT
2 x Vee 4 Stroke 12 Cy. 170 x 180 each-258kW (351bhp)
AB Volvo Penta-Sweden

8403519 *FH2387* -
SAINT TUDY
-
Conseil General du Morbihan
Compagnie Oceane
Lorient *France*
MMSI: 227001450
Official number: 614592
437 163 200 Class: BV
1985-06 **Chantiers et Ateliers de La Perriere — Lorient** Yd No: 346
Loa 44.51 Br ex - Dght 2.401
Lbp 40.52 Br md 11.02 Dpth 3.61
Welded, 1 dk
(A36A2PR) Passenger/Ro-Ro Ship (Vehicles)
Passengers: unberthed: 319
Stern door/ramp (centre)
Len: 4.50 Wid: 6.00 Swl: 30
Angled side door/ramp (p. f.)
Len: 4.50 Wid: 6.00 Swl: 30
2 oil engines sr geared to sc. shafts driving 2 CP propellers
Total Power: 920kW (1,250hp)
Crepelle 4SN3
2 x 4 Stroke 4 Cy. 260 x 280 each-460kW (625bhp)
Moteurs Duvant Crepelle-France
Thrusters: 1 Thwart. FP thruster (f)

9486403 *V7YE3* -	**SAINT VASSILIOS** *launched as* Poseidon *-2012* **Fyglia Marine Inc** Transman Shipmanagers SA SatCom: Inmarsat C 453837344 *Majuro* *Marshall Islands* MMSI: 538004639 Official number: 4639	**23,322** 11,202 33,889	Class: AB	**2012-04 21st Century Shipbuilding Co Ltd — Tongyeong** Yd No: 1004 Loa 181.10 (BB) Br ex Dght 9.900 Lbp 172.00 Br md 30.00 Dpth 14.80 Welded, 1 dk	**(A21A2BC) Bulk Carrier** Grain: 47,558; Bale: 45,180 Compartments: 5 Ho, ER 5 Ha: ER Cranes: 4x30.7t	**1 oil engine** driving 1 FP propeller Total Power: 6,480kW (8,810hp) 14.5kn MAN-B&W 6S42MC 1 x 2 Stroke 6 Cy. 420 x 1764 6480kW (8810bhp) Hyundai Heavy Industries Co Ltd-South Korea AuxGen: 3 x 570kW a.c Fuel: 132.0 (d.f.) 1609.0 (r.f.)
9095321 *FMJM* BL 925506	**SAINTE CATHERINE LABOURE** **Armement L M Perrault** - *Boulogne* *France* MMSI: 228242700 Official number: 925606	**186** 55 -		**2006-07 Astilleros Armon SA — Navia** Yd No: 634 Loa 24.40 (BB) Br ex Dght - Lbp 22.10 Br md 8.00 Dpth 3.95 Welded, 1 dk	**(B11A2FS) Stern Trawler** Ins: 94	**1 oil engine** geared to sc. shaft driving 1 Propeller Total Power: 970kW (1,319hp) Caterpillar 3512B 1 x Vee 4 Stroke 12 Cy. 170 x 190 970kW (1319bhp) Caterpillar Inc-USA Thrusters: 1 Thwart. FP thruster (f)
9010759 *FQGH* BL 735100	**SAINTE MARIE DE LA MER** **Sainte-Marie-de-la-Mer** - *Boulogne* *France* MMSI: 227106100 Official number: 735100	*102* 34 34		**1991-03 Forges Caloin — Etaples** Yd No: 58 Loa 24.60 Br ex - Dght - Lbp 24.00 Br md 6.80 Dpth 3.60 Welded	**(B11A2FS) Stern Trawler** Ins: 100	**1 oil engine** with clutches, flexible couplings & sr geared to sc. shaft driving 1 CP propeller Total Power: 526kW (715hp) Caterpillar 3508TA 1 x Vee 4 Stroke 8 Cy. 170 x 190 526kW (715bhp) Caterpillar Inc-USA
9154995 - -	**SAINTPAULIA** **Chuwa Bussan Co Ltd** - *China*	*106* - -		**1996-03 K.K. Izumiotsu Zosensho — Japan** Yd No: 249 Loa 28.00 Br ex - Dght 2.030 Lbp 24.80 Br md 8.00 Dpth 3.00 Welded, 1 dk	**(B32A2ST) Tug**	**2 oil engines** driving 2 FP propellers Total Power: 810kW (1,102hp) 9.8kn Niigata 6NSDL-M 2 x 4 Stroke 6 Cy. 160 x 235 each-405kW (551bhp) Niigata Engineering Co Ltd-Japan
9640164 - -	**SAINTY GALAXY** **Sainty Marine (S) Pte Ltd** Tongbao (Singapore) Shipping Pte Ltd	**5,770** 1,731 10,500	Class: BV	**2012-06 Sainty Shipbuilding (Jiangdu) Corp Ltd — Yangzhou JS** Yd No: SAM10030B Loa 106.20 Br ex - Dght 5.900 Lbp 101.60 Br md 25.00 Dpth 8.60 Welded, 1 dk	**(A31C2GD) Deck Cargo Ship**	**2 oil engines** reduction geared to sc. shafts driving 2 FP propellers Total Power: 2,942kW (4,000hp) 10.0kn Chinese Std. Type LB8250ZLC 2 x 4 Stroke 8 Cy. 250 x 320 each-1471kW (2000bhp) Qingdao Zichai Boyang Diesel EngineCo Ltd-China Fuel: 210.0
9640152 *YHYW* -	**SAINTY GENERAL** **PT Surya Indo Bahari** - *Tanjung Priok* *Indonesia* MMSI: 525007179	**5,770** 1,731 10,500	Class: BV	**2012-06 Sainty Shipbuilding (Jiangdu) Corp Ltd — Yangzhou JS** Yd No: SAM10029B Loa 106.02 Br ex - Dght 5.900 Lbp 101.60 Br md 25.00 Dpth 8.60 Welded, 1 dk	**(A31C2GD) Deck Cargo Ship**	**2 oil engines** reduction geared to sc. shafts driving 2 FP propellers Total Power: 2,942kW (4,000hp) 10.0kn Chinese Std. Type LB8250ZLC 2 x 4 Stroke 8 Cy. 250 x 320 each-1471kW (2000bhp) Qingdao Zichai Boyang Diesel EngineCo Ltd-China AuxGen: 2 x 200kW 50Hz a.c Fuel: 210.0
9631589 *YCVO* -	**SAINTY GIANT** **PT Surya Indo Bahari** - *Tanjung Priok* *Indonesia* MMSI: 525007177	**5,770** 1,731 10,000	Class: BV	**2012-06 Sainty Shipbuilding (Jiangdu) Corp Ltd — Yangzhou JS** Yd No: SAM10020B Loa 106.02 Br ex - Dght 5.900 Lbp 101.60 Br md 25.00 Dpth 8.00 Welded, 1 dk	**(A31C2GD) Deck Cargo Ship**	**2 oil engines** reduction geared to sc. shafts driving 2 FP propellers Total Power: 2,940kW (3,998hp) 10.0kn Chinese Std. Type LB8250ZLC 2 x 4 Stroke 8 Cy. 250 x 320 each-1470kW (1999bhp) Zibo Diesel Engine Factory-China AuxGen: 2 x 240kW 50Hz a.c Fuel: 250.0
9640176 - -	**SAINTY GLOBE** **Sainty Marine (S) Pte Ltd** Tongbao (Singapore) Shipping Pte Ltd	**5,770** 1,731 10,500	Class: BV	**2012-06 Sainty Shipbuilding (Jiangdu) Corp Ltd — Yangzhou JS** Yd No: SAM10031B Loa 106.02 Br ex - Dght 5.900 Lbp 101.60 Br md 25.00 Dpth 8.60 Welded, 1 dk	**(A31C2GD) Deck Cargo Ship**	**2 oil engines** reduction geared to sc. shafts driving 1 FP propeller Total Power: 2,942kW (4,000hp) 10.0kn Chinese Std. Type LB8250ZLC 2 x 4 Stroke 8 Cy. 250 x 320 each-1471kW (2000bhp) Qingdao Zichai Boyang Diesel EngineCo Ltd-China AuxGen: 2 x 240kW 50Hz a.c Fuel: 210.0
9633305 *YHYZ* -	**SAINTY GOVERNOR** **PT Surya Indo Bahari** - *Tanjung Priok* *Indonesia* MMSI: 525007178	**5,770** 1,731 10,500	Class: BV	**2012-06 Sainty Shipbuilding (Jiangdu) Corp Ltd — Yangzhou JS** Yd No: SAM10021B Loa 106.02 Br ex - Dght 5.900 Lbp 101.60 Br md 25.00 Dpth 8.00 Welded, 1 dk	**(A31C2GD) Deck Cargo Ship**	**2 oil engines** reduction geared to sc. shafts driving 2 FP propellers Total Power: 2,322kW (3,156hp) 10.0kn Chinese Std. Type LB8250ZLC 2 x 4 Stroke 8 Cy. 250 x 320 each-1161kW (1578bhp) Zibo Diesel Engine Factory-China Fuel: 250.0
9633317 - -	**SAINTY GUIDER** **Sainty Marine (S) Pte Ltd** Tongbao (Singapore) Shipping Pte Ltd	**5,770** 1,731 10,500	Class: BV	**2012-06 Sainty Shipbuilding (Jiangdu) Corp Ltd — Yangzhou JS** Yd No: SAM10028B Loa 106.02 Br ex - Dght 5.900 Lbp 101.60 Br md 25.00 Dpth 8.60 Welded, 1 dk	**(A31C2GD) Deck Cargo Ship**	**2 oil engines** reduction geared to sc. shafts driving 2 FP propellers Total Power: 2,942kW (4,000hp) 10.0kn Chinese Std. Type LB8250ZLC 2 x 4 Stroke 8 Cy. 250 x 320 each-1471kW (2000bhp) Zibo Diesel Engine Factory-China Fuel: 210.0
9660578 *VRLJ5* -	**SAINTY VANGUARD** **Shiny Shipping Ltd** Graig Ship Management Ltd *Hong Kong* *Hong Kong* MMSI: 477030300 Official number: HK-3683	**43,974** 27,688 82,000	Class: BV	**2013-05 Sainty Shipbuilding (Yangzhou) Corp Ltd — Yizheng JS** Yd No: SAM 10063B Loa 229.00 (BB) Br ex 32.66 Dght 14.450 Lbp 225.50 Br md 32.26 Dpth 20.05 Welded, 1 dk	**(A21A2BC) Bulk Carrier** Grain: 97,000 Compartments: 7 Ho, ER 7 Ha: ER	**1 oil engine** driving 1 FP propeller Total Power: 11,900kW (16,179hp) 14.1kn MAN-B&W 5S60MC-C8 1 x 2 Stroke 5 Cy. 600 x 2400 11900kW (16179bhp) Doosan Engine Co Ltd-South Korea
9607112 *VRMX3* -	**SAINTY VELOCITY** *launched as* Theresa Guangxi *-2014* **Symbol Shipping Ltd** Huahai Ship Management (Jiangsu) Co Ltd *Hong Kong* *Hong Kong* MMSI: 477771100 Official number: HK-4002	**43,974** 27,688 82,000	Class: BV	**2014-01 Sainty Shipbuilding (Yangzhou) Corp Ltd — Yizheng JS** Yd No: SAM 10016B Loa 229.00 (BB) Br ex 32.60 Dght 14.580 Lbp 225.50 Br md 32.26 Dpth 20.05 Welded, 1 dk	**(A21A2BC) Bulk Carrier** Grain: 97,000 Compartments: 7 Ho, ER 7 Ha: ER	**1 oil engine** driving 1 FP propeller Total Power: 11,300kW (15,363hp) 14.1kn MAN-B&W 5S60MC-C 1 x 2 Stroke 5 Cy. 600 x 2400 11300kW (15363bhp) Doosan Engine Co Ltd-South Korea
9683491 *V7DV3* -	**SAINTY VIGOUR** *ex* Sainty Yangzhou Sam11050t *-2014* **Sophie Shipping Ltd** Sainty Marine Corp Ltd *Majuro* *Marshall Islands* MMSI: 538005437 Official number: 5437	**11,716** 4,884 13,800	Class: GL	**2014-03 Sainty Shipbuilding (Yangzhou) Corp Ltd — Yizheng JS** Yd No: SAM11050T Loa 158.37 (BB) Br ex - Dght 8.050 Lbp 147.70 Br md 24.00 Dpth 11.60 Welded, 1 dk	**(A33A2CC) Container Ship (Fully Cellular)** TEU 1072 C Ho 354 teu Dk 718 TEU incl 180 ref C Cranes: 1x45t,1x40t	**1 oil engine** reduction geared to sc. shaft driving 1 CP propeller Total Power: 9,600kW (13,052hp) 18.3kn MAN-B&W 8L48/60CR 1 x 4 Stroke 8 Cy. 480 x 600 9600kW (13052bhp) MAN B&W Diesel AG-Augsburg
9660566 *VRLJ6* -	**SAINTY VISIONARY** *launched as* Spring *-2013* **Sandy Shipping Ltd** Graig Ship Management Ltd *Hong Kong* *Hong Kong* MMSI: 477222300 Official number: HK-3684	**43,974** 27,688 82,000	Class: BV	**2013-01 Sainty Shipbuilding (Yangzhou) Corp Ltd — Yizheng JS** Yd No: SAM 10062B Loa 229.00 (BB) Br ex 32.66 Dght 14.450 Lbp 225.50 Br md 32.26 Dpth 20.05 Welded, 1 dk	**(A21A2BC) Bulk Carrier** Grain: 97,000 Compartments: 7 Ho, ER 7 Ha: ER	**1 oil engine** driving 1 FP propeller Total Power: 9,800kW (13,324hp) 14.1kn MAN-B&W 5S60MC-C8 1 x 2 Stroke 5 Cy. 600 x 2400 9800kW (13324bhp) Doosan Engine Co Ltd-South Korea AuxGen: 3 x 600kW 60Hz a.c Fuel: 2750.0
9603996 *VRMX4* -	**SAINTY VITALITY** *launched as* Theresa Fujian *-2014* **Symbol Shipping Ltd** Huahai Ship Management (Jiangsu) Co Ltd *Hong Kong* *Hong Kong* MMSI: 477776600 Official number: HK-4003	**43,974** 27,688 82,000	Class: BV LR (Class contemplated) **100A1** 01/2014 Class contemplated	**2014-01 Sainty Shipbuilding (Yangzhou) Corp Ltd — Yizheng JS** Yd No: SAM 10015B Loa 229.00 (BB) Br ex 32.60 Dght 14.580 Lbp 225.50 Br md 32.26 Dpth 20.05 Welded, 1 dk	**(A21A2BC) Bulk Carrier** Grain: 97,000 Compartments: 7 Ho, ER 7 Ha: ER	**1 oil engine** driving 1 FP propeller Total Power: 9,800kW (13,324hp) 14.1kn MAN-B&W 5S60MC-C8 1 x 2 Stroke 5 Cy. 600 x 2400 9800kW (13324bhp) Doosan Engine Co Ltd-South Korea AuxGen: 3 x 550kW 60Hz a.c

9683477 *V7CK6* -	**SAINTY VOGUE** **Stefan Shipping Ltd** Graig Ship Management Ltd *Majuro* *Marshall Islands* MMSI: 538005276 Official number: 5276	**11,716** 4,884 13,800	Class: GL	**2013-10 Sainty Shipbuilding (Yangzhou) Corp Ltd — Yizheng JS** Yd No: SAM11049T Loa 158.39 (BB) Br ex Dght 8.050 Lbp 147.70 Br md 23.99 Dpth 11.60 Welded, 1 dk	**(A33A2CC) Container Ship (Fully Cellular)** TEU 1072 C Ho 354 teu Dk 718 TEU incl 180 ref C Cranes: 1x45t,1x40t Ice Capable	**1 oil engine** reduction geared to sc. shaft. driving 1 CP propeller Total Power: 9,600kW (13,052hp) 18.3kn MAN-B&W 8L48/60CR 1 x 4 Stroke 8 Cy. 480 x 600 9600kW (13052bhp) MAN B&W Diesel AG-Augsburg
8309165 *C6SW6* -	**SAIPEM 3000** *ex* Maxita *-2003* *ex* Ugland Maxita *-1992* *ex* Snimos King *-1991* **SAIPEM (Portugal) Comercio Maritima Sociedade Unipessoal Lda** Equipment Rental & Services BV (ERS) *Nassau* *Bahamas* MMSI: 311516000 Official number: 8000617	**20,639** 6,192 15,761	Class: AB (NV) (NK)	**1984-06 Mitsubishi Heavy Industries Ltd. — Nagasaki** Yd No: 1951 Converted From: Pipelayer-2003 Converted From: Heavy Load Carrier-1992 Loa 162.00 (BB) Br ex 38.05 Dght 6.371 Lbp 152.63 Br md 38.02 Dpth 9.02 Welded, 1 dk	**(B34B2SC) Crane Vessel** Passengers: berths: 85 Cranes: 1x2400t,1x210t,1x15t	**2 diesel electric oil engines** driving 2 gen. each 5500kW a.c Connecting to 2 elec. motors each (4500kW) driving 2 Directional propellers Total Power: 12,000kW (16,316hp) 10.0kn MaK 12M32C 2 x Vee 4 Stroke 12 Cy. 320 x 420 each-6000kW (8158bhp) (new engine 2003, added 2003) Caterpillar Motoren GmbH & Co. KG-Germany AuxGen: 2 x 3200kW 440V 60Hz a.c, 2 x 2250kW 440V 60Hz a.c Thrusters: 2 Retract. directional thruster (f); 1 Tunnel thruster (f); 1 Retract. directional thruster (a) Fuel: 280.0 (d.f.) 2760.0 (r.f.) 27.5pd
8501567 *C6NO5* -	**SAIPEM 7000** *ex* Micoperi 7000 *-1995* **SAIPEM Offshore Norway AS** Equipment Rental & Services BV (ERS) *Nassau* *Bahamas* MMSI: 309461000 Official number: 727472	**117,812** 35,343 -	Class: AB RI (LR) ✠ Classed LR until 1/1/13	**1987-10 Fincantieri-Cant. Nav. Italiani S.p.A. — Monfalcone** Yd No: 5824 Loa 197.95 Br ex 87.03 Dght 10.500 Lbp 165.00 Br md 87.00 Dpth 43.50 Welded, 1 dk	**(Z11C3ZK) Pipe layer Platform, semi submersible** Cranes: 2x7000t	**12 diesel electric oil engines** driving 12 gen. each 5600kW a.c Connecting to 4 elec. motors each (4500kW) driving 4 Directional propellers Total Power: 71,600kW (97,348hp) GMT A420.12V 8 x Vee 4 Stroke 12 Cy. 420 x 500 each-5990kW (8144bhp) Fincantieri Cantieri Navalilitaliani SpA-Italy Wartsila 16V32 4 x Vee 4 Stroke 16 Cy. 320 x 350 each-5920kW (8049bhp) Wartsila Diesel Oy-Finland Thrusters: 2 Thwart. FP thruster (f); 2 Retract. directional thruster (f); 4 Retract. directional thruster (f)
9187605 *C6RC9* -	**SAIPEM 10000** **SAIPEM (Portugal) Comercio Maritima Sociedade Unipessoal Lda** SAIPEM Maritime Asset Management Luxembourg Sarl *Nassau* *Bahamas* MMSI: 308728000 Official number: 8000101	**59,221** 17,786 61,118	Class: AB	**2000-03 Samsung Heavy Industries Co Ltd — Geoje** Yd No: 1273 Loa 227.81 Br ex - Dght 12.000 Lbp 219.40 Br md 42.00 Dpth 19.00 Welded, 1 dk	**(B22B2OD) Drilling Ship** Cranes: 1x350t,4x85t	**6 diesel electric oil engines** driving 6 gen. each 7000kW Connecting to 6 elec. motors each (4000kW) driving 2 Directional propellers Total Power: 42,000kW (57,102hp) 12.0kn Wartsila 18V32 6 x Vee 4 Stroke 18 Cy. 320 x 350 each-7000kW (9517bhp) Wartsila NSD Finland Oy-Finland Thrusters: 2 Retract. directional thruster (f); 2 Retract. directional thruster (a)
9437359 *C6YF4* -	**SAIPEM 12000** **SAIPEM (Portugal) Comercio Maritima Sociedade Unipessoal Lda** SAIPEM SpA (Societa Azionaria Italiana Perforazioni e Montaggi SpA) *Nassau* *Bahamas* MMSI: 311030700 Official number: 8001717	**60,538** 18,161 59,116	Class: AB	**2010-04 Samsung Heavy Industries Co Ltd — Geoje** Yd No: 1702 Loa 228.00 Br ex - Dght 13.000 Lbp 219.40 Br md 42.00 Dpth 19.00 Welded, 1 dk	**(B22B2OD) Drilling Ship** Passengers: berths: 200 Cranes: 4x85t	**6 diesel electric oil engines** driving 6 gen. each 7400kW 1100V a.c Connecting to 3 elec. motors each (4500kW) driving 3 Azimuth electric drive units Total Power: 48,000kW (65,262hp) 12.0kn MAN-B&W 16V32/40 6 x Vee 4 Stroke 16 Cy. 320 x 400 each-8000kW (10877bhp) STX Engine Co Ltd-South Korea Thrusters: 3 Thwart. FP thruster (f)
5307051 *IUGP* -	**SAIPEM APE** **SAIPEM SpA (Societa Azionaria Italiana Perforazioni e Montaggi SpA)** SNAM SpA *Genoa* *Italy* Official number: 3249	*392* 186 542 T/cm 0.3	Class: (RI)	**1961 Cantiere Navale M & B Benetti — Viareggio** Yd No: 51 Loa 47.17 Br ex 9.83 Dght 2.614 Lbp 42.02 Br md 9.78 Dpth 3.05 Riveted\Welded, 1 dk	**(A13B2TP) Products Tanker** Liq: 479; Liq (Oil): 479 Compartments: 12 Ta, ER	**2 oil engines** driving 2 FP propellers Total Power: 860kW (1,170hp) 11.0kn Deutz RBA8M528 2 x 4 Stroke 8 Cy. 220 x 280 each-430kW (585bhp) (, fitted 1961) Kloeckner Humboldt Deutz AG-West Germany
9210749 *C6RK6* -	**SAIPEM FDS** *ex* Saibos Fds *-2006* **SAIPEM Offshore Norway AS** Equipment Rental & Services BV (ERS) *Nassau* *Bahamas* MMSI: 311066000 Official number: 8000219	**20,988** 6,251 11,000	Class: NV	**2000-11 Samsung Heavy Industries Co Ltd — Geoje** Yd No: 1311 Loa 163.46 Br ex 30.04 Dght 8.000 Lbp 152.00 Br md 30.00 Dpth 12.50 Welded, 1 dk	**(B22C2OQ) Pipe Layer Crane Vessel** Passengers: berths: 235 Cranes: 1x600t,2x50t Ice Capable	**6 diesel electric oil engines** driving 6 gen. Connecting to 2 elec. motors each (4400kW) driving 2 Azimuth electric drive units Total Power: 26,000kW (35,350hp) 13.3kn Wartsila 16V26 4 x Vee 4 Stroke 16 Cy. 260 x 320 each-5200kW (7070bhp) Wartsila Nederland BV-Netherlands Wartsila 8L26 2 x 4 Stroke 8 Cy. 260 x 320 each-2600kW (3535bhp) Wartsila Nederland BV-Netherlands Thrusters: 2 Retract. directional thruster (f); 2 Tunnel thruster (f)
9542362 *C6YW3* -	**SAIPEM FDS 2** **SAIPEM (Portugal) Comercio Maritima Sociedade Unipessoal Lda** SAIPEM SpA (Societa Azionaria Italiana Perforazioni e Montaggi SpA) *Nassau* *Bahamas* MMSI: 311047300 Official number: 8001841	**33,622** 10,086 18,018	Class: AB	**2011-03 Samsung Heavy Industries Co Ltd — Geoje** Yd No: 1861 Loa 183.60 Br ex - Dght 11.100 Lbp 171.00 Br md 32.20 Dpth 14.50 Welded, 1 dk	**(B34B2SC) Crane Vessel** Cranes: 1x1000t,2x50t,2x20t Ice Capable	**6 diesel electric oil engines** driving 6 gen. each 6000kW Connecting to 2 elec. motors each (5000kW) driving 2 Azimuth electric drive units Total Power: 36,000kW (48,948hp) 10.0kn MAN-B&W 12V32/40 6 x Vee 4 Stroke 12 Cy. 320 x 400 each-6000kW (8158bhp) Thrusters: 2 Tunnel thruster (f); 1 Retract. directional thruster ; 1 Retract. directional thruster ; 1 Retract. directional thruster Fuel: 3970.0 (d.f.)
8746935 *9MHV9* -	**SAIPH** **Government of Malaysia (Director of Marine & Ministry of Transport)** - *Port Klang* *Malaysia* Official number: 333807	**140** 42 25		**2008-06 Kay Marine Sdn Bhd — Kuala Terengganu** (Assembled by) Yd No: J104-7 **0000* Inform Marine Technology — Fremantle WA** (Parts for assembly by) Loa 26.00 Br ex - Dght 1.200 Lbp - Br md 9.20 Dpth 2.55 Welded, 1 dk	**(A37B2PS) Passenger Ship** Hull Material: Aluminium Alloy	**2 oil engines** reduction geared to sc. shafts driving 2 Propellers Total Power: 2,206kW (3,000hp) M.T.U. 12V2000M91 2 x Vee 4 Stroke 12 Cy. 130 x 150 each-1103kW (1500bhp) MTU Friedrichshafen GmbH-Friedrichshafen
9384239 *A8NB3* -	**SAIPH STAR** **Vela International Marine Ltd** - SatCom: Inmarsat C 463704416 *Monrovia* *Liberia* MMSI: 636013451 Official number: 13451	**162,252** 111,896 319,410 T/cm 179.0	Class: LR ✠ **100A1** SS 03/2014 Double Hull oil tanker ESP **ShipRight** (SDA, FDA plus, CM) *IWS LI SPM ✠ **LMC** **UMS IGS** Eq.Ltr: E*; Cable: 770.0/117.0 U3 (a)	**2009-03 Daewoo Shipbuilding & Marine Engineering Co Ltd — Geoje** Yd No: 5306 Loa 333.00 (BB) Br ex 60.04 Dght 22.500 Lbp 320.00 Br md 60.00 Dpth 30.50 Welded, 1 dk	**(A13A2TV) Crude Oil Tanker** Double Hull (13F) Liq: 340,989; Liq (Oil): 340,989 Compartments: 5 Ta, 10 Wing Ta, 2 Wing Slop Ta, ER 3 Cargo Pump (s): 3x5500m³/hr Manifold: Bow/CM: 167m	**1 oil engine** driving 1 FP propeller Total Power: 29,340kW (39,891hp) 15.3kn MAN-B&W 6S90MC-C 1 x 2 Stroke 6 Cy. 900 x 3188 29340kW (39891bhp) Doosan Engine Co Ltd-South Korea AuxGen: 2 x 1600kW 450V 60Hz a.c, 1 x 1400kW 450V 60Hz a.c Boilers: e (ex.g.) 27.5kgf/cm² (27.0bar), WTAuxB (o.f.) 21.9kgf/cm² (21.5bar) Fuel: 340.0 (d.f.) 6100.0 (r.f.)
9406166 *3EZD4* -	**SAIQ** **Saiq Maritime Transportation Co SA** Oman Shipping Co SAOC SatCom: Inmarsat C 435570511 *Panama* *Panama* MMSI: 355705000 Official number: 4298111	**156,935** 100,308 299,999 T/cm 178.2	Class: LR ✠ **100A1** SS 04/2011 Double Hull oil tanker ESP **ShipRight** (SDA,FDA,CM) LI ✠ **LMC** **UMS IGS** Eq.Ltr: C*; Cable: 770.0/111.0 U3 (a)	**2011-04 Universal Shipbuilding Corp — Nagasu KM (Ariake Shipyard)** Yd No: 126 Loa 330.00 (BB) Br ex 60.04 Dght 21.500 Lbp 316.00 Br md 60.00 Dpth 29.70 Welded, 1 dk	**(A13A2TV) Crude Oil Tanker** Double Hull (13F) Liq: 324,700; Liq (Oil): 324,700 Compartments: 5 Ta, 10 Wing Ta, 2 Wing Slop Ta, ER 3 Cargo Pump (s): 3x5500m³/hr Manifold: Bow/CM: 161m	**1 oil engine** driving 1 FP propeller Total Power: 25,090kW (34,112hp) 16.0kn MAN-B&W 7S80MC 1 x 2 Stroke 7 Cy. 800 x 3056 25090kW (34112bhp) Hitachi Zosen Corp-Japan AuxGen: 3 x 816kW 450V 60Hz a.c Boilers: e (ex.g.) 26.8kgf/cm² (26.3bar)669°C , WTAuxB (o.f.) 21.9kgf/cm² (21.5bar) Fuel: 490.0 (d.f.) 7200.0 (r.f.)
8712714 - -	**SAIRYO MARU** - **-** - *South Korea*	*198* - 510		**1987-09 K.K. Mukai Zosensho — Nagasaki** Yd No: 578 Loa 47.96 Br ex 7.83 Dght 3.300 Lbp 44.12 Br md 7.80 Dpth 3.51 Welded, 1 dk	**(A13B2TP) Products Tanker** Liq: 579; Liq (Oil): 579 Compartments: 6 Ta, ER	**1 oil engine** with clutches & reverse reduction geared to sc. shaft driving 1 FP propeller Total Power: 588kW (799hp) Hanshin 6LU26G 1 x 4 Stroke 6 Cy. 260 x 440 588kW (799bhp) Hanshin Nainenki Kogyo-Japan

8604369 *3EOY2* -
SAISABAN
ex Maria A *-2012* *ex* African Cobra *-2008*
ex Nerano *-2005* *ex* Emerald 10 *-1997*
ex Emerald Sea *-1993* *ex* Nerano *-1988*
Sealion Shipping & Trading SA
Mallah Ship Management Co Ltd
Panama *Panama*
MMSI: 356813000
Official number: 3447808A
15,847 8,996 26,648 T/cm 31.6
Class: NK (BV) (NV)
1986-09 Kurushima Dockyard Co. Ltd. — Onishi Yd No: 2483
Loa 167.20 (BB) Br ex - Dght 9.541
Lbp 160.03 Br md 26.00 Dpth 13.30
Welded, 1 dk
(A21A2BC) Bulk Carrier
Grain: 33,903; Bale: 32,733
Compartments: 5 Ho, ER
5 Ha: (13.9 x 13.1)4 (19.3 x 13.1)ER
Cranes: 4x30t
1 oil engine driving 1 FP propeller
Total Power: 5,075kW (6,900hp) 14.0kn
B&W 6L50MCE
1 x 2 Stroke 6 Cy. 500 x 1620 5075kW (6900bhp)
Hitachi Zosen Corp-Japan
AuxGen: 2 x 400kW 440V 60Hz a.c
Fuel: 1360.0

8916310 *JG4928* -
SAISEI MARU
-
Saisei Kai Hospital
-
Tokyo *Japan*
Official number: 131957
166 - 50
1990-02 Teraoka Shipyard Co Ltd — Minamiawaji HG Yd No: 287
L reg 29.40 Br ex - Dght 2.500
Lbp - Br md 7.00 Dpth 3.00
Welded
(B34U2QH) Hospital Vessel
2 oil engines driving 2 FP propellers
Total Power: 736kW (1,000hp)
Yanmar S165L-ST
2 x 4 Stroke 6 Cy. 165 x 210 each-368kW (500bhp)
Yanmar Diesel Engine Co Ltd-Japan

9691199 - -
SAISEI MARU
-
Social Welfare Organization Saiseikai Imperial Gift Foundation Inc
-
Japan
180 - -
Class: FA
2013-12 Kanagawa Zosen — Kobe Yd No: 647
Loa 33.00 Br ex - Dght 3.300
Lbp - Br md 7.00 Dpth -
Welded, 1 dk
(B34U2QH) Hospital Vessel
2 oil engines reduction geared to sc. shafts driving 2 Propellers
Total Power: 736kW (1,000hp)
Yanmar 6RY17W
2 x 4 Stroke 6 Cy. 165 x 219 each-368kW (500bhp)
Yanmar Diesel Engine Co Ltd-Japan

9643544 *5BBA4* -
SAITA I
-
Halcyon Shipping Inc
Efnav Co Ltd
Cyprus
43,400 27,700 81,600 T/cm 70.2
Class: NK (Class contemplated)
2014-04 Tsuneishi Group (Zhoushan) Shipbuilding Inc — Daishan County ZJ Yd No: SS-132
Loa 229.00 (BB) Br ex - Dght 14.400
Lbp 225.10 Br md 32.26 Dpth 20.03
Welded, 1 dk
(A21A2BC) Bulk Carrier
Grain: 97,000
Compartments: 7 Ho, ER
7 Ha: ER
1 oil engine driving 1 FP propeller
Total Power: 13,560kW (18,436hp) 14.5kn
MAN-B&W 6S60MC-C
1 x 2 Stroke 6 Cy. 600 x 2400 13560kW (18436bhp)

8840585 *JH3140* -
SAITA MARU
-
Masahiko Kitano
-
Hiroshima, Hiroshima *Japan*
Official number: 128485
495 - 447
1989-06 Y.K. Okajima Zosensho — Matsuyama
Loa 49.86 Br ex - Dght 3.420
Lbp 43.00 Br md 11.00 Dpth 3.50
Welded, 1 dk
(A24D2BA) Aggregates Carrier
Compartments: 1 Ho, ER
1 Ha: ER
1 oil engine driving 1 FP propeller
Total Power: 736kW (1,001hp)
Yanmar MF28-ST
1 x 4 Stroke 6 Cy. 280 x 450 736kW (1001bhp)
Matsue Diesel KK-Japan

7936416 - - -
SAIWAI
ex Saiwai Maru No. 5 *-1999*
-
-
194 - 425
1980-02 Y.K. Kaneko Zosensho — Hojo Yd No: 135
L reg 39.02 Br ex - Dght 3.110
Lbp - Br md 7.80 Dpth 4.91
Welded, 1 dk
(A31A2GX) General Cargo Ship
1 oil engine driving 1 FP propeller
Total Power: 353kW (480hp)
Yanmar MF24-HT
1 x 4 Stroke 6 Cy. 240 x 420 353kW (480bhp)
Yanmar Diesel Engine Co Ltd-Japan

9103465 *JL6147* -
SAIWAI MARU
ex New Shoshin *-2005*
YK Saiwai Kisen
-
Kure, Hiroshima *Japan*
MMSI: 431400237
Official number: 133875
184 - 364
1993-11 Hongawara Zosen K.K. — Fukuyama Yd No: 397
Loa 42.80 Br ex - Dght 3.100
Lbp 38.50 Br md 7.50 Dpth 3.20
Welded, 1 dk
(A12A2LP) Molten Sulphur Tanker
Liq: 173
1 oil engine geared to sc. shaft driving 1 FP propeller
Total Power: 478kW (650hp) 10.0kn
Hanshin 6LC26G
1 x 4 Stroke 6 Cy. 260 x 440 478kW (650bhp)
The Hanshin Diesel Works Ltd-Japan

7735680 - -
SAIWAI MARU No. 1
-
-
199 - 500
1970 Yano Zosen K.K. — Imabari Yd No: 46
Loa - Br ex - Dght 3.200
Lbp 35.31 Br md 8.01 Dpth 3.51
Welded, 1 dk
(A24D2BA) Aggregates Carrier
1 oil engine driving 1 FP propeller

9124940 *JL6362* -
SAIWAI MARU No. 3
-
YK Youmei Kaiun
-
Matsuyama, Ehime *Japan*
Official number: 133985
199 - 540
1995-08 Shirahama Zosen K.K. — Honai Yd No: 171
Loa 48.25 Br ex - Dght 3.050
Lbp 44.00 Br md 8.00 Dpth 3.45
Welded, 1 dk
(A12A2TC) Chemical Tanker
Compartments: 6 Ta, ER
2 Cargo Pump (s): 2x150m³/hr
1 oil engine driving 1 FP propeller
Total Power: 736kW (1,001hp)
Hanshin LH26G
1 x 4 Stroke 6 Cy. 260 x 440 736kW (1001bhp)
The Hanshin Diesel Works Ltd-Japan

8974697 *JL6589* -
SAIWAI MARU NO. 15
-
YK Shimamoto Kaiun
-
Matsuyama, Ehime *Japan*
Official number: 136561
199 - 644
2001-08 Y.K. Okajima Zosensho — Matsuyama Yd No: 257
Loa 59.46 Br ex - Dght 3.600
Lbp 52.00 Br md 9.30 Dpth 5.47
Welded, 1 dk
(A31A2GX) General Cargo Ship
1 oil engine driving 1 Propeller
Total Power: 736kW (1,001hp) 11.0kn
Hanshin LH26G
1 x 4 Stroke 6 Cy. 260 x 440 736kW (1001bhp)
The Hanshin Diesel Works Ltd-Japan

9568225 *A8ZS9* -
SAIYO
-
Seno Kisen Co Ltd & Estrella Navigation SA
Toyo Sangyo Co Ltd (Toyo Sangyo KK)
SatCom: Inmarsat C 463710290
Monrovia *Liberia*
MMSI: 636015291
Official number: 15291
50,927 29,849 92,014
Class: NK
2011-07 Namura Shipbuilding Co Ltd — Imari SG Yd No: 336
Loa 234.88 (BB) Br ex - Dght 14.228
Lbp 226.00 Br md 38.00 Dpth 20.00
Welded, 1 dk
(A21A2BC) Bulk Carrier
Double Hull
Grain: 110,413
Compartments: 6 Ho, ER
6 Ha: ER
1 oil engine driving 1 FP propeller
Total Power: 12,240kW (16,642hp) 14.7kn
MAN-B&W 6S60MC-C
1 x 2 Stroke 6 Cy. 600 x 2400 12240kW (16642bhp)
Mitsui Engineering & Shipbuilding CLtd-Japan
Fuel: 3620.0

9603570 *JD3067* HG1-88
SAIZEN MARU
-
Mamoru Nishimura
-
Kami, Hyogo *Japan*
Official number: 141244
125 - -
2010-07 Fukushima Zosen Ltd. — Matsue
Loa 37.80 (BB) Br ex - Dght -
Lbp - Br md 6.25 Dpth 2.58
Welded, 1 dk
(B11B2FV) Fishing Vessel
1 oil engine reduction geared to sc. shaft driving 1 Propeller
Total Power: 1,323kW (1,799hp)
Niigata 6MG22HLX
1 x 4 Stroke 6 Cy. 220 x 300 1323kW (1799bhp)
Niigata Engineering Co Ltd-Japan

9551571 *HP6351* -
SAJALICES
-
Panama Canal Authority
-
SatCom: Inmarsat C 437076312
Panama *Panama*
Official number: 4324211
359 107 138
Class: (LR)
✠ Classed LR until 27/4/12
2011-01 Hin Lee (Zhuhai) Shipyard Co Ltd — Zhuhai GD (Hull) Yd No: 203
2011-01 Cheoy Lee Shipyards Ltd — Hong Kong Yd No: 4991
Loa 27.40 Br ex 12.20 Dght 3.700
Lbp 25.20 Br md 12.20 Dpth 5.05
Welded, 1 dk
(B32A2ST) Tug
2 oil engines gearing integral to driving 2 Z propellers
Total Power: 3,924kW (5,336hp)
GE Marine 12V228
2 x Vee 4 Stroke 12 Cy. 229 x 267 each-1962kW (2668bhp)
General Electric Co.-Lynn, Ma
AuxGen: 2 x 103kW 208V 60Hz a.c
Fuel: 110.0 (d.f.)

7001302 - -
SAJAMBRE
ex Iesus *-2003* *ex* Sajambre *-2003*
ex Duc de Praslin *-1993* *ex* Via Foehn *-1991*
ex Toubab Dialaw *-1990*
ex President Henri Polo *-1983*
Empropesca SA
-
Manta *Ecuador*
945 - 676
Class: (BV)
1969 Ateliers et Chantiers de La Manche — Dieppe Yd No: 1212
Loa 47.00 Br ex 10.90 Dght 5.100
Lbp 41.00 Br md 10.60 Dpth 5.11
Welded, 2 dks
(B11B2FV) Fishing Vessel
Ins: 500; Liq: 510
Derricks: 1x10t,2x5t,2x1t
1 oil engine reduction geared to sc. shaft driving 1 FP propeller
Total Power: 1,324kW (1,800hp) 13.2kn
AGO 240G12VS
1 x Vee 4 Stroke 12 Cy. 240 x 220 1324kW (1800bhp)
Societe Alsacienne de ConstructionsMecaniques (SACM)-France
AuxGen: 2 x 206kW 380V 50Hz a.c
Fuel: 149.5 (d.f.)

7814632 *UBTQ* -
SAJANY
ex Olskiy Rybak *-2013* *ex* Ataman *-2001*
ex Jacquelyn R *-1997*
ex Clipper Cat Island *-1987*
-
SatCom: Inmarsat A 1504154
Petropavlovsk-Kamchatskiy *Russia*
MMSI: 273846120
Official number: 794254
604 181 768
Class: RS (AB)
1979-10 Houma Fabricators Inc — Houma LA Yd No: 63
Converted From: Offshore Supply Ship-1987
Loa 48.12 Br ex 11.63 Dght 3.753
Lbp 45.90 Br md 11.60 Dpth 4.35
Welded, 1 dk
(B11B2FV) Fishing Vessel
Ins: 397
2 oil engines reverse reduction geared to sc. shafts driving 2 FP propellers
Total Power: 1,368kW (1,860hp) 10.5kn
G.M. (Detroit Diesel) 16V-149
2 x Vee 2 Stroke 16 Cy. 146 x 146 each-684kW (930bhp)
General Motors Detroit DieselAllison Divn-USA
AuxGen: 2 x 350kW a.c, 1 x 75kW
Thrusters: 1 Thwart. FP thruster (f)
Fuel: 317.0 (d.f.)

8223074 *V3SZ2* -
SAJDA
ex Lenglo *-2013* *ex* Celtic Pride *-2009*
ex Normannia *-2005* *ex* Baursberg *-1997*
Dartija Group Ltd
Ingeri Shipping OU
Belize City *Belize*
MMSI: 312725000
1,946 885 2,904
Class: IV (Class contemplated) (LR) (BV) (GL)
Classed LR until 10/1/06
1983-07 J.J. Sietas KG Schiffswerft GmbH & Co. — Hamburg Yd No: 909
Loa 87.97 (BB) Br ex 11.54 Dght 4.680
Lbp 85.32 Br md 11.30 Dpth 6.75
Welded, 2 dks
(A31A2GX) General Cargo Ship
Grain: 3,777; Bale: 3,752
TEU 90 C.Ho 54/20' (40') C.Dk 36/20' (40')
Compartments: 1 Ho, ER
1 Ha: (55.9 x 9.3)ER
1 oil engine with clutches, flexible couplings & sr geared to sc. shaft driving 1 FP propeller
Total Power: 441kW (600hp) 11.5kn
Deutz SBV6M628
1 x 4 Stroke 6 Cy. 240 x 280 441kW (600bhp)
Kloeckner Humboldt Deutz AG-West Germany
AuxGen: 1 x 152kW 380V 50Hz a.c, 1 x 60kW 380V 50Hz a.c, 1 x 32kW 380V 50Hz a.c
Thrusters: 1 Thwart. CP thruster (f)
Fuel: 44.0 (d.f.) 153.0 (r.f.) 5.5pd

8424135 - -	**SAJE COMMANDER** *ex* Marine Commander *-2007* *ex* Challenge (ATA-201) *-2007* *ex* Challenge (ATR-128) *-1944* **Ivaline Group SA** - *San Lorenzo* *Honduras* MMSI: 334632000 Official number: L-3828250	**477** 143 -		**1944-11 Gulfport Boiler & Welding Works, Inc. — Port Arthur, Tx** Yd No: 246 Loa - Br ex - Dght 4.190 Lbp 41.20 Br md 10.06 Dpth 5.19 Welded, 1 dk	**(B34L2QU) Utility Vessel**	**1 oil engine** driving 1 FP propeller Total Power: 1,103kW (1,500hp)
8520264 *JBUI* HK1-974	**SAJI MARU No. 3** *ex* Taisei Maru No. 3 *-1998* **KK Moritan** - *Monbetsu, Hokkaido* *Japan* Official number: 127099	*160* - -		**1985-12 Niigata Engineering Co Ltd — Niigata NI** Yd No: 1873 Loa 37.80 (BB) Br ex 7.42 Dght 3.369 Lbp 30.99 Br md 7.41 Dpth 4.65 Welded, 2 dks	**(B11A2FS) Stern Trawler**	**1 oil engine** with clutches, flexible couplings & sr geared to sc. shaft driving 1 CP propeller Total Power: 1,030kW (1,400hp) Niigata 6MG28BXF 1 x 4 Stroke 6 Cy. 280 x 350 1030kW (1400bhp) Niigata Engineering Co Ltd-Japan
9683635 *6KCC7* -	**SAJO ALEXANDRIA** - **Sajo Industries Co Ltd** - *Busan* *South Korea* Official number: 1401001-6261403	**2,177** 653 2,000	Class: KR	**2014-01 Sungdong Shipbuilding & Marine Engineering Co Ltd — Tongyeong** Yd No: 8004 Loa 79.56 (BB) Br ex - Dght 8.450 Lbp 70.00 Br md 14.50 Dpth 8.45 Welded, 1 dk	**(B11B2FV) Fishing Vessel**	**1 oil engine** reduction geared to sc. shaft driving 1 Propeller Total Power: 3,530kW (4,799hp) Niigata 8MG34HX 1 x 4 Stroke 8 Cy. 340 x 450 3530kW (4799bhp) Niigata Engineering Co Ltd-Japan
9618379 - -	**SAJO COLUMBIA** - **Sajo Industries Co Ltd** - *South Korea*	**2,116** - 1,900		**2012-08 Sungdong Shipbuilding & Marine Engineering Co Ltd — Tongyeong** Yd No: 8001 Loa 79.60 Br ex - Dght 5.850 Lbp - Br md 14.50 Dpth - Welded, 1 dk	**(B11B2FV) Fishing Vessel**	**1 oil engine** reduction geared to sc. shaft driving 1 Propeller Total Power: 3,530kW (4,799hp) Niigata 8MG34HX 1 x 4 Stroke 8 Cy. 340 x 450 3530kW (4799bhp) Niigata Engineering Co Ltd-Japan
9619323 *6KCA3* -	**SAJO FAMILIA** - **Sajo Industries Co Ltd** - *South Korea* MMSI: 441853000	**2,116** - 1,900	Class: KT	**2012-12 Sungdong Shipbuilding & Marine Engineering Co Ltd — Tongyeong** Yd No: 8002 Loa 79.60 Br ex - Dght 5.850 Lbp - Br md 14.50 Dpth - Welded, 1 dk	**(B11B2FV) Fishing Vessel**	**1 oil engine** reduction geared to sc. shaft driving 1 Propeller Total Power: 3,530kW (4,799hp) Niigata 8MG34HX 1 x 4 Stroke 8 Cy. 340 x 450 3530kW (4799bhp) Niigata Engineering Co Ltd-Japan
8102921 *6LCU* -	**SAJO OLYMPIA** *ex* Ocean Pearl *-1988* **Sajo Industries Co Ltd** - SatCom: Inmarsat C 444044114 *Busan* *South Korea* MMSI: 440671000 Official number: 9506100-6210002	*972* 431 1,530	Class: KR	**1981-12 Campbell Industries — San Diego, Ca** Yd No: 134 Loa 67.52 Br ex 12.55 Dght 6.044 Lbp 59.67 Br md 12.26 Dpth 8.21 Welded, 2 dks	**(B11B2FV) Fishing Vessel** Ins: 1,189 Compartments: 15 Ta, ER	**1 oil engine** sr reverse geared to sc. shaft driving 1 FP propeller Total Power: 2,648kW (3,600hp) 14.3kn EMD (Electro-Motive) 20-645-E7 1 x Vee 2 Stroke 20 Cy. 230 x 254 2648kW (3600bhp) General Motors Corp.Electro-Motive Div.-La Grange Thrusters: 1 Thwart. FP thruster (f)
9683623 *6KCC5* -	**SAJO POSEDONIA** - **Oyang Corp** Sajo Industries Co Ltd *Busan* *South Korea* MMSI: 441930000	**2,177** 653 1,718	Class: KR	**2013-12 Sungdong Shipbuilding & Marine Engineering Co Ltd — Tongyeong** Yd No: 8003 Loa 79.56 (BB) Br ex - Dght 8.450 Lbp 70.76 Br md 14.50 Dpth 8.45 Welded, 1 dk	**(B11B2FV) Fishing Vessel**	**1 oil engine** reduction geared to sc. shaft driving 1 Propeller Total Power: 3,309kW (4,499hp) 16.0kn Niigata 8MG34HX 1 x 4 Stroke 8 Cy. 340 x 450 3309kW (4499bhp) Niigata Engineering Co Ltd-Japan
9587063 *DTBX6* -	**SAJO POTENTIA** - **Sajo Industries Co Ltd** - *Busan* *South Korea* MMSI: 441675000 Official number: 1002001-6261105	**1,061** 546 2,172		**2010-03 Jong Shyn Shipbuilding Co., Ltd. — Kaohsiung** Yd No: 189 Loa 70.75 Br ex - Dght 4.750 Lbp 61.94 Br md 12.30 Dpth 7.25 Welded, 1 dk	**(B11B2FV) Fishing Vessel**	**1 oil engine** reduction geared to sc. shaft driving 1 FP propeller Total Power: 2,647kW (3,599hp) Akasaka DM41AK 1 x 4 Stroke 6 Cy. 410 x 640 2647kW (3599bhp) Akasaka Tekkosho KK (Akasaka DieselLtd)-Japan
8660442 *DTBV2* -	**SAJOMELITA** *ex* Tahir Kaptan 1 *-2010* **Sajo Industries Co Ltd** Melita Blu Sea Ltd *Busan* *South Korea* MMSI: 441501000 Official number: 1104001-6261403	**105** - -		**2006-06 Basaran Gemi Sanayi — Trabzon** Yd No: 83 Loa 26.50 (BB) Br ex - Dght - Lbp - Br md 9.20 Dpth 2.83 Welded, 1 dk	**(B11B2FV) Fishing Vessel**	**2 oil engines** reduction geared to sc. shafts driving 2 Propellers 11.0kn
9118812 *JM6355* -	**SAKAE MARU** - **YK Hiramatsu Shokai** - *Sasebo, Nagasaki* *Japan* MMSI: 431600375 Official number: 133637	*692* - 1,855		**1995-04 Honda Zosen — Saiki** Yd No: 873 Loa 81.00 Br ex - Dght 4.270 Lbp 75.00 Br md 14.50 Dpth 7.45 Welded, 1 dk	**(A31A2GX) General Cargo Ship**	**1 oil engine** driving 1 FP propeller Total Power: 1,471kW (2,000hp) Niigata 6M38GT 1 x 4 Stroke 6 Cy. 380 x 720 1471kW (2000bhp) Niigata Engineering Co Ltd-Japan
8630681 - -	**SAKAE MARU** - - - *South Korea*	*118* - -		**1987-02 Kushiro Jukogyo K.K. — Kushiro** Yd No: 118 Loa 28.00 Br ex 8.22 Dght 2.500 Lbp 24.00 Br md 8.20 Dpth 3.39 Welded, 1 dk	**(B32B2SP) Pusher Tug**	**1 oil engine** driving 1 FP propeller Total Power: 1,250kW (1,700hp) Yanmar 1 x 4 Stroke 1250kW (1700bhp) Yanmar Diesel Engine Co Ltd-Japan
8626240 *JM5417* -	**SAKAE MARU** *ex* Hoyo Maru *-1988* **YK Eiriki Kaiun** - *Karatsu, Saga* *Japan* Official number: 127773	*199* - 699		**1984-11 Sokooshi Zosen K.K. — Osakikamijima** Loa 53.97 Br ex - Dght 3.340 Lbp 49.50 Br md 9.00 Dpth 5.30 Welded, 1 dk	**(A31A2GX) General Cargo Ship** Grain: 1,275; Bale: 1,136	**1 oil engine** driving 1 FP propeller Total Power: 368kW (500hp) 9.0kn Hanshin 1 x 4 Stroke 368kW (500bhp) The Hanshin Diesel Works Ltd-Japan
7506273 *JH2634* -	**SAKAE MARU** - **Kambara Logistics Co Ltd** - *Fukuyama, Hiroshima* *Japan* Official number: 118344	*260* - -		**1975-07 Kanagawa Zosen — Kobe** Yd No: 155 Loa 33.00 Br ex 9.22 Dght 3.201 Lbp 28.99 Br md 9.20 Dpth 4.20 Welded, 1 dk	**(B32A2ST) Tug**	**2 oil engines** Geared Integral to driving 2 Z propellers Total Power: 2,354kW (3,200hp) Niigata 8L25BX 2 x 4 Stroke 8 Cy. 250 x 320 each-1177kW (1600bhp) Niigata Engineering Co Ltd-Japan
7396501 - -	**SAKAE MARU** *ex* Shinriki Maru No. 5 *-1985* **Bright Star Marine SA** -	*199* 123 699		**1974-02 Sasaki Shipbuilding Co Ltd — Osakikamijima HS** Yd No: 243 Loa - Br ex 8.41 Dght 3.302 Lbp 48.01 Br md 8.39 Dpth 3.38 Welded, 1 dk	**(A31A2GX) General Cargo Ship**	**1 oil engine** driving 1 FP propeller Total Power: 552kW (750hp) Usuki 1 x 4 Stroke 552kW (750bhp) Usuki Tekkosho-Usuki
9674414 *JD3450* -	**SAKAE MARU** - **Nagoya Kisen KK (Nagoya Kisen Kaisha Ltd)** - *Nagoya, Aichi* *Japan* Official number: 141817	*176* - -		**2013-02 Kanagawa Zosen — Kobe** Yd No: 650 Loa 32.50 Br ex - Dght 4.000 Lbp - Br md 8.80 Dpth - Welded, 1 dk	**(B32A2ST) Tug**	**2 oil engines** reduction geared to sc. shafts driving 2 Propellers Total Power: 2,942kW (4,000hp) Niigata 6L26HLX 2 x 4 Stroke 6 Cy. 260 x 350 each-1471kW (2000bhp) Niigata Engineering Co Ltd-Japan
9142069 *JK5463* -	**SAKAE MARU 2** - **Eikichi Kaiun KK** - *Tamano, Okayama* *Japan* Official number: 134779	*132* - -		**1996-06 Kanagawa Zosen — Kobe** Yd No: 427 Loa 30.00 Br ex - Dght 3.100 Lbp 25.50 Br md 8.00 Dpth 3.59 Welded, 1 dk	**(B32A2ST) Tug**	**2 oil engines** driving 2 FP propellers Total Power: 3,824kW (5,200hp) 13.0kn Yanmar 6HAL-TN 2 x 4 Stroke 6 Cy. 130 x 150 each-1912kW (2600bhp) Yanmar Diesel Engine Co Ltd-Japan
9030931 - -	**SAKAE MARU No. 1** - - -	*147* - -		**1990-08 Kesennuma Tekko — Kesennuma** Yd No: 275 L reg 31.60 (BB) Br ex - Dght - Lbp 31.50 Br md 6.40 Dpth 2.70 Welded, 1 dk	**(B11B2FV) Fishing Vessel** Ins: 138	**1 oil engine** with clutches, flexible couplings & geared to sc. shaft driving 1 CP propeller Total Power: 669kW (910hp) Pielstick 6PA5LX 1 x 4 Stroke 6 Cy. 255 x 270 669kW (910bhp) Niigata Engineering Co Ltd-Japan Thrusters: 1 Thwart. FP thruster (f); 1 Thwart. FP thruster (a)

8980373 *JJ4043* -	**SAKAE MARU NO. 16** *ex* Kasuga Maru *-2006* **Muneta Zosen KK (Muneta Shipbuilding Co Ltd)** - *Hachinohe, Aomori* *Japan* Official number: 135991	*149* - -		**2002-06 Muneta Zosen K.K. — Akashi** Yd No: 1125 Loa 28.37 Br ex - Dght 2.900 Lbp 26.00 Br md 8.00 Dpth 3.19 Welded, 1 dk	**(B32A2ST) Tug**	**2 oil engines** reduction geared to sc. shafts driving 2 Propellers Total Power: 1,472kW (2,002hp) Yanmar 6RY17P-GV 2 x 4 Stroke 6 Cy. 165 x 219 each-736kW (1001bhp) Yanmar Diesel Engine Co Ltd-Japan
8963466 *JH2410* -	**SAKAEI MARU** **Matsuo Inayoshi** - *Gamagori, Aichi* *Japan* Official number: 111193	*174* - 350		**1970-12 Kozo Suzuki — Japan** Loa 32.50 Br ex - Dght 2.800 Lbp 31.40 Br md 6.77 Dpth 2.98 Welded, 1 dk	**(A31A2GX) General Cargo Ship** Compartments: 1 Ho, 1 Ta 1 Ha: (22.0 x 5.2)ER	**1 oil engine** driving 1 FP propeller Total Power: 257kW (349hp) 6.0kn Yanmar 1 x 4 Stroke 257kW (349bhp) Yanmar Diesel Engine Co Ltd-Japan
9124756 *JH3358* -	**SAKAEMARU** *ex* Settsu Maru No. 1 *-2014* *ex* Fujiharu *-2009* **Settsu Kaiun KK** - *Kobe, Hyogo* *Japan* MMSI: 431200121 Official number: 133268	*499* - 1,600	Class: NK	**1995-10 Honda Zosen — Saiki** Yd No: 881 Loa 75.53 Br ex - Dght 4.171 Lbp 70.00 Br md 12.20 Dpth 7.15 Welded, 1 dk	**(A31A2GX) General Cargo Ship** 1 Ha: (40.2 x 10.0)	**1 oil engine** reduction geared to sc. shaft driving 1 FP propeller Total Power: 736kW (1,001hp) 10.0kn Daihatsu 6DKM-28 1 x 4 Stroke 6 Cy. 280 x 390 736kW (1001bhp) Daihatsu Diesel Manufacturing Co Lt-Japan Fuel: 75.0 (d.f.)
9119218 *JI3579* -	**SAKAI MARU** **Tsukiboshi Kaiun KK** - *Osaka, Osaka* *Japan* MMSI: 431300271 Official number: 135022	**749** - 2,100		**1995-05 K.K. Tachibana Senpaku Tekko — Anan** Yd No: 841 Loa 84.19 Br ex - Dght 4.610 Lbp 78.00 Br md 13.00 Dpth 7.85 Welded, 1 dk	**(A31A2GX) General Cargo Ship**	**1 oil engine** driving 1 FP propeller Total Power: 1,618kW (2,200hp) 12.0kn Niigata 6M34AGT 1 x 4 Stroke 6 Cy. 340 x 620 1618kW (2200bhp) Niigata Engineering Co Ltd-Japan
9384928 *3EYR6* -	**SAKAIDE MARU** **Eastern Cross Shipping SA** Toyo Kaiun Co Ltd SatCom: Inmarsat C 435489810 *Panama* *Panama* MMSI: 354898000 Official number: 4112010	**58,135** 33,658 106,349 T/cm 98.0	Class: BV (NK)	**2010-01 Oshima Shipbuilding Co Ltd — Saikai NS** Yd No: 10449 Loa 254.62 (BB) Br ex - Dght 13.470 Lbp 249.62 Br md 43.00 Dpth 19.43 Welded, 1 dk	**(A21A2BC) Bulk Carrier** Grain: 130,151 Compartments: 7 Ho, ER 7 Ha: ER	**1 oil engine** driving 1 FP propeller Total Power: 12,268kW (16,680hp) 14.3kn MAN-B&W 6S60MC 1 x 2 Stroke 6 Cy. 600 x 2292 12268kW (16680bhp) Kawasaki Heavy Industries Ltd-Japan AuxGen: 4 x 420kW 60Hz a.c Fuel: 3997.6
9152258 *HZEO* -	**SAKAKA** *ex* Abu Dhabi *-2013* **United Arab Shipping Co (UASC)** - *Dammam* *Saudi Arabia* MMSI: 403522001 Official number: SA1169	**48,154** 26,721 49,844 T/cm 75.2	Class: LR ✠ **100A1** SS 03/2013 container ship CCSA *IWS LI ✠ **LMC** **UMS** Eq.Ltr: R†; Cable: 691.3/84.0 U3	**1998-03 Mitsubishi Heavy Industries Ltd. — Nagasaki** Yd No: 2131 Loa 276.50 (BB) Br ex 32.30 Dght 12.500 Lbp 259.90 Br md 32.20 Dpth 21.20 Welded, 1 dk	**(A33A2CC) Container Ship (Fully Cellular)** TEU 3802 C Ho 2068 TEU C Dk 1734 TEU incl 360 ref C. Compartments: ER, 8 Cell Ho 16 Ha: (6.4 x 18.4) (13.2 x 18.4)Tappered (12.6 x 23.6)Tappered ER 13 (12.6 x 28.7)	**1 oil engine** driving 1 FP propeller Total Power: 34,348kW (46,700hp) 24.4kn B&W 10L80MC 1 x 2 Stroke 10 Cy. 800 x 2592 34348kW (46700bhp) Kawasaki Heavy Industries Ltd-Japan AuxGen: 3 x 2280kW 450V 60Hz a.c Boilers: e (ex.g.) 11.9kgf/cm² (11.7bar), AuxB (o.f.) 8.0kgf/cm² (7.8bar) Thrusters: 1 Thwart. CP thruster (f) Fuel: 5707.0 (r.f.) 116.5pd
7039608 *6VOB* DAK 455	**SAKAL** *ex* Shemahi II *-1977* **Armement Frigorifique Senegalais** - *Dakar* *Senegal*	*130* 63 -	Class: (BV)	**1970 Soc Nouvelle des Ats et Chs de La Rochelle-Pallice — La Rochelle** Yd No: 00157 Loa 25.20 Br ex 6.86 Dght 2.515 Lbp 22.59 Br md 6.71 Dpth 3.51 Welded, 1 dk	**(B11A2FT) Trawler** Ins: 141 Compartments: 1 Ho, ER 1 Ha: (1.2 x 1.6)	**1 oil engine** driving 1 FP propeller Total Power: 291kW (396hp) 9.0kn Caterpillar D353SCAC 1 x 4 Stroke 6 Cy. 159 x 203 291kW (396bhp) Caterpillar Tractor Co-USA Fuel: 48.5 (d.f.)
9104811 *9HTC4* -	**SAKAR** **Sakar Maritime Ltd** Navigation Maritime Bulgare SatCom: Inmarsat C 424939810 *Valletta* *Malta* MMSI: 249398000 Official number: 4590	**13,957** 7,249 21,583 T/cm 36.0	Class: GL (BR)	**1995-07 Varna Shipyard AD — Varna** Yd No: 454 Loa 168.57 Br ex 25.00 Dght 8.498 Lbp 159.00 Br md 25.00 Dpth 11.50 Welded, 1 dk	**(A21A2BC) Bulk Carrier** Grain: 24,948; Bale: 24,650 TEU 226 Compartments: 5 Ho, ER 5 Ha: (9.1 x 13.0)4 (18.6 x 14.3)ER Ice Capable	**1 oil engine** driving 1 FP propeller Total Power: 5,884kW (8,000hp) 13.5kn B&W 8L42MC 1 x 2 Stroke 8 Cy. 420 x 1360 5884kW (8000bhp) AO Bryanskiy MashinostroitelnyyZavod (BMZ)-Bryansk AuxGen: 3 x 384kW 400V 50Hz a.c Fuel: 276.7 (d.f.) (Part Heating Coils) 1355.0 (r.f.) 25.7pd
1003633 - -	**SAKARA** *ex* Dodi *-1977* *ex* Kyra *-1977* *ex* Primavera *-1977* *ex* Kirin *-1977* *ex* Magdalene *-1977* *ex* Kirin *-1977* **Dodi Ltd** Agenzia Sicumare Marittima SatCom: Inmarsat M 623225210 *Jersey* *Jersey* Official number: 359924	*135* 98 -	Class: LR ✠ **100A1** SS 06/2009 Yacht **LMC**	**1913-01 George Lawley & Son Corp. — Boston, Ma** Loa 34.16 Br ex 7.01 Dght 4.420 Lbp 26.80 Br md - Dpth 4.48 Welded, 1 dk	**(X11A2YS) Yacht (Sailing)**	**1 oil engine** driving 1 FP propeller Total Power: 213kW (290hp) Volvo Penta 1 x 4 Stroke 6 Cy. 213kW (290bhp) Skofde Gjuteri & Mekaniska Verkstad-Sweden
6726711 *URK* -	**SAKARYA** *ex* Sikker Havn *-2008* *ex* Flornes *-1992* *ex* Trillingen *-1971* **Valana Investment Co** Enka Insaat ve Sanayi AS *Aqtau* *Kazakhstan* MMSI: 436000115	**732** 233 130	Class: RS (BV)	**1967-10 Cant. Nav. Felszegi — Trieste** Yd No: 87 Converted From: General Cargo Ship-2004 Lengthened-2004 Loa 49.93 Br ex 9.53 Dght 3.322 Lbp 44.50 Br md 9.50 Dpth 5.72 Welded, 2 dks	**(B22A2ZA) Accommodation Ship** Passengers: cabins: 28; berths: 60 Ice Capable	**1 oil engine** driving 1 FP propeller Total Power: 588kW (799hp) 10.0kn MaK 6MU451AK 1 x 4 Stroke 6 Cy. 320 x 450 588kW (799bhp) Atlas MaK Maschinenbau GmbH-Kiel Thrusters: 1 Thwart. CP thruster (f) Fuel: 70.0 (d.f.) 3.0pd
9257199 *TCVU3* -	**SAKARYA** *ex* Eternal Confidence *-2012* **MB Denizcilik Tasimacilik Ltd Sti** Manta Denizcilik Nakliyat ve Ticaret Ltd Sti *Istanbul* *Turkey* MMSI: 271043415	**17,953** 10,748 29,905 T/cm 40.5	Class: NK	**2002-09 Shikoku Dockyard Co. Ltd. — Takamatsu** Yd No: 1004 Loa 170.70 Br ex - Dght 9.720 Lbp 163.50 Br md 27.00 Dpth 13.80 Welded, 1 dk	**(A21A2BC) Bulk Carrier** Grain: 40,031; Bale: 38,422 Compartments: 5 Ho, ER 5 Ha: 4 (20.0 x 17.8) (12.8 x 16.2)ER Cranes: 4x30t	**1 oil engine** driving 1 FP propeller Total Power: 6,487kW (8,820hp) 14.3kn B&W 6S42MC 1 x 2 Stroke 6 Cy. 420 x 1764 6487kW (8820bhp) Mitsui Engineering & Shipbuilding CLtd-Japan Fuel: 1670.0
9425356 *9HLY9* -	**SAKARYA** **Marine Unity Co Ltd** CSM Denizcilik Ltd Sti (Chemfleet) *Valletta* *Malta* MMSI: 249150000 Official number: 9425356	**7,321** 3,582 11,258 T/cm 22.6	Class: BV	**2008-05 Dearsan Gemi Insaat ve Sanayii Koll. Sti. — Tuzla** Yd No: 2045 Loa 129.50 (BB) Br ex - Dght 8.150 Lbp 122.10 Br md 19.80 Dpth 10.40 Welded, 1 dk	**(A12B2TR) Chemical/Products Tanker** Double Hull (13F) Liq: 12,186; Liq (Oil): 12,186 Cargo Heating Coils Compartments: 12 Wing Ta, 2 Wing Slop Ta, Wing ER 12 Cargo Pump (s): 12x250m³/hr Manifold: Bow/CM: 62.3m Ice Capable	**1 oil engine** reduction geared to sc. shaft driving 1 CP propeller Total Power: 4,500kW (6,118hp) 14.5kn MAN-B&W 9L32/40 1 x 4 Stroke 9 Cy. 320 x 400 4500kW (6118bhp) MAN B&W Diesel AG-Augsburg AuxGen: 3 x 620kW 450V 60Hz a.c, 1 x 1400kW 450V 60Hz a.c Thrusters: 1 Tunnel thruster (f) Fuel: 92.0 (d.f.) 579.0 (r.f.)
8630954 *YB5228* -	**SAKATA** *ex* Konpira I *-2004* *ex* Konpira Maru *-2002* **PT Dharma Ichtiar Indo Lines** - *Surabaya* *Indonesia*	**497** 218 461	Class: KI	**1987-07 Y.K. Okajima Zosensho — Matsuyama** Loa 50.57 Br ex 8.22 Dght 3.250 Lbp 45.00 Br md 8.20 Dpth 5.00 Welded, 1 dk	**(A31A2GX) General Cargo Ship**	**1 oil engine** driving 1 FP propeller Total Power: 434kW (590hp) 11.0kn Yanmar MF24-UT 1 x 4 Stroke 6 Cy. 240 x 420 434kW (590bhp) Matsue Diesel KK-Japan
8894847 *YD4679* -	**SAKATA MAJU No. 11** *ex* Sakata Maru No. 1 *-2000* **PT Aneka Atlanticindo Nidyatama** - *Palembang* *Indonesia*	**125** 38 -	Class: KI	**1980-09 K.K. Murakami Zosensho — Naruto** Loa 26.87 Br ex - Dght 2.500 Lbp 24.50 Br md 6.30 Dpth 2.99 Welded, 1 dk	**(B32A2ST) Tug**	**1 oil engine** driving 1 FP propeller Total Power: 883kW (1,201hp) 10.0kn Yanmar MF28-UT 1 x 4 Stroke 6 Cy. 280 x 450 883kW (1201bhp) Yanmar Diesel Engine Co Ltd-Japan
6816657 - -	**SAKATA MARU** *ex* Narita Maru *-1984* - - *South Korea*	*194* - -		**1967 Geibi Zosen Kogyo — Kure** Yd No: 196 Loa 28.99 Br ex 8.62 Dght 2.896 Lbp 26.01 Br md 8.59 Dpth 3.79 Welded, 1 dk	**(B32A2ST) Tug**	**2 oil engines** driving 2 FP propellers Total Power: 1,516kW (2,062hp) Fuji 6SD32H 2 x 4 Stroke 6 Cy. 320 x 500 each-758kW (1031bhp) Fuji Diesel Co Ltd-Japan AuxGen: 2 x 30kW 225V a.c
8884517 *V5JN* -	**SAKAWE SURVEYOR** *ex* Jaya Noura *-2003* *ex* Atco Noura *-1995* *ex* Natco 5 *-1995* **Samicor Diamond Mining Pty Ltd** - *Luderitz* *Namibia*	*199* 59 -	Class: (NV) (AB)	**1981 Scully Bros. Boat Building, Inc. — Morgan City, La** Yd No: 138 Loa 35.35 Br ex - Dght 2.290 Lbp - Br md 7.92 Dpth 3.20 Welded, 1 dk	**(B21A20S) Platform Supply Ship**	**2 oil engines** reverse reduction geared to sc. shafts driving 2 FP propellers Total Power: 882kW (1,200hp) G.M. (Detroit Diesel) 16V-92 2 x Vee 2 Stroke 16 Cy. 123 x 127 each-441kW (600bhp) General Motors Detroit DieselAllison Divn-USA AuxGen: 2 x 40kW a.c

8207745 V3IU3 - **SAKHALIN** ex Ziemia Zamojska -2012 **Emerald Shipping Ltd** Sadent Shipping Ltd Belize City, Belize MMSI: 312792000 Official number: 291330155
16,694 8,911 26,700 T/cm 36.8 Class: PR (NV)
1984-08 **Astilleros Alianza S.A. — Avellaneda** Yd No: 44
Loa 180.25 (BB) Br ex 23.14 Dght 9.840
Lbp 172.02 Br md 23.11 Dpth 13.92
Welded, 1 dk
(A21A2BC) Bulk Carrier
Grain: 34,850; Bale: 33,563
Compartments: 5 Ho, ER
5 Ha: (16.8 x 11.4) (12.8 x 13.1)3 (19.2 x 13.1)ER
Ice Capable
1 oil engine driving 1 FP propeller
Total Power: 5,766kW (7,839hp) 14.5kn
B&W 4L67GFCA
1 x 2 Stroke 4 Cy. 670 x 1700 5766kW (7839bhp)
Zaklady Przemyslu Metalowego 'HCegielski' SA-Poznan
AuxGen: 3 x 488kW 440V 60Hz a.c
Fuel: 146.0 (d.f.) 1070.0 (r.f.) 28.0pd

8330516 UERK - **SAKHALIN-8** **JSC Marine Ferry Lines Vanino-Sakhalin** Sakhalin Shipping Co (SASCO) Vanino, Russia MMSI: 273187000 Official number: 810349
9,420 3,491 2,240 Class: RS
1985-07 **Pribaltiyskiy Sudostroitelnyy Zavod "Yantar" — Kaliningrad** Yd No: S-147
Loa 127.30 Br ex 20.32 Dght 6.600
Lbp 112.91 Br md 19.80 Dpth 8.80
Welded, 2 dks
(A36A2PT) Passenger/Ro-Ro Ship (Vehicles/Rail)
Passengers: 72; cabins: 90
Lane-Len: 413
Lane-Wid: 3.25
Lane-clr ht: 6.20
Rail Wagons: 26
Ice Capable
6 diesel electric oil engines driving 6 gen. each 1912kW Connecting to 2 elec. motors each (5640kW) driving 2 Propellers 1 fwd and 1 aft
Total Power: 11,472kW (15,600hp) 16.8kn
Fairbanks, Morse 10-38D8-1/8
6 x 2 Stroke 10 Cy. 207 x 254 each-1912kW (2600bhp) in the U.S.S.R.
AuxGen: 4 x 550kW a.c, 1 x 320kW a.c
Fuel: 284.0 (d.f.)

8728543 UCEE - **SAKHALIN-9** **JSC Marine Ferry Lines Vanino-Sakhalin** - Vanino, Russia MMSI: 273185600 Official number: 841296
9,346 3,234 2,400 Class: RS
1986-12 **Pribaltiyskiy Sudostroitelnyy Zavod "Yantar" — Kaliningrad** Yd No: S-148
Loa 127.30 Br ex 20.32 Dght 6.600
Lbp 112.91 Br md 19.80 Dpth 8.80
Welded, 2 dk
(A36A2PT) Passenger/Ro-Ro Ship (Vehicles/Rail)
Passengers: 72
Stern door/ramp
Lane-Len: 413
Ice Capable
6 diesel electric oil engines driving 6 gen. each 1912kW Connecting to 2 elec. motors each (5640kW) driving 2 FP propellers 1 fwd and 1 aft
Total Power: 11,472kW (15,600hp) 16.8kn
Fairbanks, Morse 10-38D8-1/8
6 x 2 Stroke 10 Cy. 207 x 254 each-1912kW (2600bhp) in the U.S.S.R.
AuxGen: 4 x 550kW a.c, 1 x 320kW a.c
Fuel: 283.0 (d.f.)

8857667 UCDL - **SAKHALIN-10** **Sakhalin Shipping Co (SASCO)** - Kholmsk, Russia MMSI: 273186400 Official number: 890108
9,419 3,409 2,820 Class: RS
1992-09 **AO Pribaltiyskiy Sudostroitelnyy Zavod "Yantar" — Kaliningrad** Yd No: 149
Loa 127.00 Br ex 20.30 Dght 6.600
Lbp 112.91 Br md 19.80 Dpth 8.80
Welded, 1 dk
(A36A2PT) Passenger/Ro-Ro Ship (Vehicles/Rail)
Passengers: 72
Stern door/ramp
Lane-Len: 350
Ice Capable
6 diesel electric oil engines driving 6 gen. each 1912kW Connecting to 2 elec. motors each (5640kW) driving 2 Propellers 1 fwd and 1 aft
Total Power: 11,472kW (15,600hp) 16.8kn
Fairbanks, Morse 10-38D8-1/8
6 x 2 Stroke 10 Cy. 207 x 254 each-1912kW (2600bhp) (made 1986) in the U.S.S.R.
AuxGen: 4 x 550kW a.c, 1 x 320kW a.c
Fuel: 283.0 (d.f.)

9249128 P3TV9 - **SAKHALIN ISLAND** **Brava Lines Shipmanagement Ltd** SCF Unicom Singapore Pte Ltd SatCom: Inmarsat C 421075010 Limassol, Cyprus MMSI: 210750000 Official number: 9249128
58,918 34,228 108,078 T/cm 94.4 Class: NV
2004-05 **Brodosplit - Brodogradiliste doo — Split** Yd No: 439
Loa 247.24 (BB) Br ex 42.03 Dght 14.919
Lbp 236.00 Br md 42.00 Dpth 20.99
Welded, 1 dk
(A13A2TW) Crude/Oil Products Tanker
Double Hull (13F)
Liq: 120,932; Liq (Oil): 120,932
Cargo Heating Coils
Compartments: 12 Wing Ta, 2 Wing Slop Ta, ER
4 Cargo Pump (s): 4x3000m³/hr
Manifold: Bow/CM: 122.2m
Ice Capable
1 oil engine driving 1 FP propeller
Total Power: 14,130kW (19,211hp) 15.0kn
MAN-B&W 7S60MC-C
1 x 2 Stroke 7 Cy. 600 x 2400 14130kW (19211bhp)
Brodosplit Tvornica Dizel Motoradoo-Croatia
AuxGen: 3 x 910kW 440/220V 60Hz a.c
Fuel: 137.5 (d.f.) 2681.1 (r.f.) 58.0pd

9076650 UHKZ - **SAKHALINETS** **FRK 'Haron-Holding'** - Sovetskaya Gavan, Russia MMSI: 273895500 Official number: 920197
117 35 30 Class: RS
1992-08 **Sosnovskiy Sudostroitelnyy Zavod — Sosnovka** Yd No: 823
Loa 25.50 Br ex 7.00 Dght 2.390
Lbp 22.00 Br md 6.80 Dpth 3.30
Welded, 1 dk
(B11A2FS) Stern Trawler
Ice Capable
1 oil engine driving 1 FP propeller
Total Power: 220kW (299hp) 9.5kn
S.K.L. 6NVD26A-2
1 x 4 Stroke 6 Cy. 180 x 260 220kW (299bhp)
SKL Motoren u. Systemtechnik AG-Magdeburg
Fuel: 15.0 (d.f.)

6914588 UBXN - **SAKHALINNEFT** ex MB-7004 -1969 **Morport Co Ltd** - Nikolayevsk-na-Amure, Russia
231 69 91 Class: RS
1968-12 **VEB Schiffswerft "Edgar Andre" — Magdeburg** Yd No: 7004
Loa 34.78 Br ex 8.51 Dght 2.861
Lbp 30.41 Br md 8.21 Dpth 3.71
Welded, 1 dk
(B32A2ST) Tug
Ice Capable
1 oil engine driving 1 CP propeller
Total Power: 552kW (750hp) 11.3kn
S.K.L. 6NVD48A-2U
1 x 4 Stroke 6 Cy. 320 x 480 552kW (750bhp)
VEB Schwermaschinenbau "KarlLiebknecht" (SKL)-Magdeburg

9400382 3FAB7 - **SAKHARA LOTUS** **Shintoku Panama SA** Mitsui OSK Lines Ltd (MOL) SatCom: Inmarsat C 437253010 Panama, Panama MMSI: 372530000 Official number: 4066109
19,572 9,141 32,107 T/cm 40.6 Class: NK
2009-08 **Kitanihon Zosen K.K. — Hachinohe** Yd No: 387
Loa 170.00 (BB) Br ex - Dght 10.916
Lbp 162.00 Br md 26.60 Dpth 16.00
Welded, 1 dk
(A12B2TR) Chemical/Products Tanker
Double Hull (13F)
Liq: 32,723; Liq (Oil): 37,700
Compartments: 10 Wing Ta, 2 Wing Slop Ta, ER
10 Cargo Pump (s): 10x330m³/hr
Manifold: Bow/CM: 87m
1 oil engine driving 1 FP propeller
Total Power: 8,670kW (11,788hp) 14.7kn
Mitsubishi 6UEC50LSII
1 x 2 Stroke 6 Cy. 500 x 1950 8670kW (11788bhp)
Akasaka Tekkosho KK (Akasaka DieselLtd)-Japan
AuxGen: 3 x 950kW 450V 60Hz a.c
Fuel: 126.0 (d.f.) 1708.0 (r.f.)

8622115 XUCL8 - **SAKHISLAND** ex Matsushima -2008 ex Matsushima Maru No. 18 -1996 **Sakhisland Shipping Co Ltd** - Phnom Penh, Cambodia MMSI: 515538000 Official number: 0483018
498 170 700
1983 **Shitanoe Shipbuilding Co Ltd — Usuki OT** Yd No: 1032
Loa 55.38 Br ex - Dght 3.290
Lbp 52.00 Br md 9.50 Dpth 5.57
Welded, 1 dk
(A31A2GX) General Cargo Ship
1 oil engine driving 1 FP propeller
Total Power: 662kW (900hp) 11.0kn
Niigata
1 x 4 Stroke 662kW (900bhp)
Niigata Engineering Co Ltd-Japan

7636652 UIEH - **SAKHOIL** ex MYS Kodosh -2012 **JSC 'Nakhodkatanker'** - Nakhodka, Russia MMSI: 273832000 Official number: 792225
5,105 1,834 4,995 Class: RS
1980-05 **Rauma-Repola Oy — Rauma** Yd No: 257
Loa 115.50 Br ex 17.05 Dght 6.410
Lbp 105.01 Br md 17.00 Dpth 8.51
Welded, 1 dk
(A13B2TP) Products Tanker
Single Hull
Bale: 203; Liq: 6,420; Liq (Oil): 6,420
Part Cargo Heating Coils
Compartments: 1 Ho, 8 Ta, ER
1 Ha: (2.5 x 3.2)ER
2 Cargo Pump (s): 2x100m³/hr
Ice Capable
1 oil engine driving 1 FP propeller
Total Power: 2,465kW (3,351hp) 14.0kn
B&W 5DKRN50/110-2
1 x 2 Stroke 5 Cy. 500 x 1100 2465kW (3351bhp)
Bryanskiy Mashinostroitelnyy Zavod (BMZ)-Bryansk
AuxGen: 3 x 264kW 380V 50Hz a.c
Fuel: 88.0 (d.f.) (Part Heating Coils) 400.0 (r.f.) 16.5pd

9463968 HSB3901 - **SAKHON WISAI** **Government of The Kingdom of Thailand (Marine Department)** - Thailand MMSI: 567348000 Official number: 540000150
4,396 1,319 1,499 Class: NK
2010-11 **Italthai Marine Co., Ltd. — Samut Prakan** Yd No: 154
Loa 90.00 (BB) Br ex - Dght 5.200
Lbp 82.00 Br md 16.80 Dpth 9.30
Welded, 1 dk
(B34K2QT) Training Ship
Teu 24 C Ho 16 C Dk 8
Cranes: 1x18t
1 oil engine reduction geared to sc. shaft driving 1 CP propeller
Total Power: 3,500kW (4,759hp)
MAN-B&W 7L32/40
1 x 4 Stroke 7 Cy. 320 x 400 3500kW (4759bhp)
MAN B&W Diesel AG-Augsburg
AuxGen: 3 x 450kW
Thrusters: 1 Tunnel thruster (f)
Fuel: 60.0 (d.f.) 285.0 (r.f.)

8842997 UEKI - **SAKHRYBA** ex Nadezhdinskiy -2011 **Sakhryba-1 Co Ltd** - SatCom: Inmarsat A 1407356 Kholmsk, Russia MMSI: 273829410 Official number: 900348
683 233 529 Class: RS
1991-05 **Khabarovskiy Sudostroitelnyy Zavod im Kirova — Khabarovsk** Yd No: 881
Loa 54.99 Br ex 9.49 Dght 4.340
Lbp 50.04 Br md 9.30 Dpth 5.16
Welded, 1 dk
(B12B2FC) Fish Carrier
Ins: 632
1 oil engine driving 1 FP propeller
Total Power: 588kW (799hp) 11.3kn
S.K.L. 6NVD48A-2U
1 x 4 Stroke 6 Cy. 320 x 480 588kW (799bhp)
SKL Motoren u. Systemtechnik AG-Magdeburg
AuxGen: 3 x 160kW a.c

8727721 LYKP - **SAKIAI** ex Yasenyevo -1992 **Authority of Klaipeda State Seaport (Klaipedos Valstybinio Juru Uosto Direkcija)** - SatCom: Inmarsat M 627707810 Klaipeda, Lithuania MMSI: 277078000
774 232 390 Class: (RS)
1987-10 **Yaroslavskiy Sudostroitelnyy Zavod — Yaroslavl** Yd No: 369
Converted From: Stern Trawler-1999
Loa 56.40 (BB) Br ex 10.71 Dght 4.650
Lbp 46.20 Br md 10.50 Dpth 6.00
Welded, 1 dk
(B34P2QV) Salvage Ship
Ice Capable
1 oil engine driving 1 CP propeller
Total Power: 970kW (1,319hp) 12.6kn
S.K.L. 8NVD48A-2U
1 x 4 Stroke 8 Cy. 320 x 480 970kW (1319bhp)
VEB Schwermaschinenbau "KarlLiebknecht" (SKL)-Magdeburg
AuxGen: 3 x 300kW a.c, 3 x 150kW a.c
Fuel: 143.0 (d.f.)

7856329 JM3770 - **SAKIBE MARU** **Sasebo Jyukogyo KK** - Sasebo, Nagasaki, Japan MMSI: 431600991 Official number: 118048
199 74 -
1975-05 **Nitchitsu Co. Ltd. — Matsuura**
Loa 32.11 Br ex - Dght 2.871
Lbp 28.50 Br md 8.81 Dpth 3.87
Welded, 1 dk
(B32A2ST) Tug
2 oil engines Geared Integral to driving 2 Z propellers
Total Power: 2,354kW (3,200hp) 12.3kn
Niigata
2 x 4 Stroke each-1177kW (1600bhp)
Niigata Engineering Co Ltd-Japan

IMO / Call sign	Name / Owner	Tonnage	Class	Builder / Dimensions	Type	Machinery
9019482 - -	**SAKICHI MARU NO. 8** *ex* Choshin Maru No. 18 *-2002* - - *Indonesia* MMSI: 525235888	*119* - -		**1990-07 Kesennuma Tekko — Kesennuma** Yd No: 273 L reg 31.60 (BB) Br ex - Dght - Lbp 31.50 Br md 6.40 Dpth 2.80 Welded	**(B11B2FV) Fishing Vessel**	**1 oil engine** with clutches, flexible couplings & sr geared to sc. shaft driving 1 CP propeller Total Power: 592kW (805hp) Niigata 6M26AFTE 1 x 4 Stroke 6 Cy. 260 x 460 592kW (805bhp) Niigata Engineering Co Ltd-Japan
9062233 *JG5173* -	**SAKIMORI NO. 1** *ex* Natsume *-2003* **KK Daito Corp** - *Tokyo* *Japan* Official number: 133816	*173* - 25		**1992-10 Hanasaki Zosensho K.K. — Yokosuka** Yd No: 230 L reg 29.00 Br ex - Dght 2.900 Lbp 27.80 Br md 8.80 Dpth 3.90 Welded, 1 dk	**(B32A2ST) Tug**	**2 oil engines** with clutches, flexible couplings & reduction geared to sc. shafts driving 2 Z propellers Total Power: 2,280kW (3,100hp) Niigata 6L25HX 2 x 4 Stroke 6 Cy. 250 x 350 each-1140kW (1550bhp) Niigata Engineering Co Ltd-Japan
6811152 *HP4483* -	**SAKIS P** *ex* Cemenmar Uno *-2010* **Thestia Shipping SA** Gremex Shipping SA de CV *Panama* *Panama* MMSI: 370266000 Official number: 4176210	**1,550** 703 2,497	Class: (LR) ✠ Classed LR until 2/2/12	**1968-04 Maritima del Musel S.A. — Gijon** Yd No: 93 Loa 81.44 Br ex 12.53 Dght 5.138 Lbp 73.51 Br md 12.49 Dpth 5.90 Welded, 1 dk	**(A24A2BT) Cement Carrier** Grain: 2,620 Compartments: 2 Ho, ER	**1 oil engine** driving 1 FP propeller Total Power: 1,140kW (1,550hp) 11.0kn Werkspoor TMABS396 1 x 4 Stroke 6 Cy. 390 x 680 1140kW (1550bhp) Naval Stork Werkspoor SA-Spain AuxGen: 3 x 158kW 380V 50Hz a.c Fuel: 68.0 (d.f.)
9380245 *JD2350* -	**SAKISHIMA** **Government of Japan (Okinawa Customs Office)** - *Naha, Okinawa* *Japan* Official number: 140461	*115* - 135		**2007-03 Universal Shipbuilding Corp — Yokohama KN (Keihin Shipyard)** Yd No: 0030 L reg 31.14 Br ex - Dght - Lbp - Br md 6.50 Dpth 3.13 Welded, 1 dk	**(B34H2SQ) Patrol Vessel** Hull Material: Aluminium Alloy	**2 oil engines** reduction geared to sc. shafts driving 2 Propellers Total Power: 4,640kW (6,308hp) M.T.U. 16V4000M70 2 x Vee 4 Stroke 16 Cy. 165 x 190 each-2320kW (3154bhp) MTU Friedrichshafen GmbH-Friedrichshafen
8909109 *UDZD* -	**SAKITI MARU NO. 1** *ex* Zenpo Maru No. 23 *-2005* **OOO 'Tsentr Pribrezhnogo Rybolovstva Ostrovnoy' (LLC Center of Offshore Fisheries 'Ostrovnoy')** - *Nevelsk* *Russia* MMSI: 273314370 Official number: 887266	**202** 63 135	Class: RS	**1988-09 Kesennuma Tekko — Kesennuma** Yd No: 270 Loa 38.10 (BB) Br ex - Dght 2.500 Lbp 33.22 Br md 6.40 Dpth 2.80 Welded, 1 dk	**(B11B2FV) Fishing Vessel**	**1 oil engine** driving 1 CP propeller Total Power: 592kW (805hp) 12.0kn Niigata 6M26AFTE 1 x 4 Stroke 6 Cy. 260 x 460 592kW (805bhp) Niigata Engineering Co Ltd-Japan
9656400 *3FKU2* -	**SAKIZAYA ACE** **Sakizaya Marine SA** Wisdom Marine Lines SA *Panama* *Panama* MMSI: 354048000 Official number: 4493913	**40,350** 24,954 74,936 T/cm 67.3	Class: NK	**2013-04 Sasebo Heavy Industries Co. Ltd. — Sasebo Yard, Sasebo** Yd No: 810 Loa 225.00 (BB) Br ex 32.25 Dght 14.140 Lbp 218.00 Br md 32.20 Dpth 19.80 Welded, 1 dk	**(A21A2BC) Bulk Carrier** Double Hull Grain: 90,771; Bale: 88,783 Compartments: 7 Ho, ER 7 Ha: 6 (17.0 x 14.4)ER (15.3 x 12.9)	**1 oil engine** driving 1 FP propeller Total Power: 9,210kW (12,522hp) 14.5kn MAN-B&W 7S50MC-C8 1 x 2 Stroke 7 Cy. 500 x 2000 9210kW (12522bhp) Mitsui Engineering & Shipbuilding CLtd-Japan AuxGen: 3 x 430kW a.c Fuel: 2730.0
9656412 *3FIE7* -	**SAKIZAYA BRAVE** *ex* Sakizaya Wisdom Iii *-2013* **Sakizaya Line SA** Wisdom Marine Lines SA *Panama* *Panama* MMSI: 351170000 Official number: 4512913	**40,350** 24,954 74,940 T/cm 67.3	Class: NK	**2013-06 Sasebo Heavy Industries Co. Ltd. — Sasebo Yard, Sasebo** Yd No: 811 Loa 225.00 (BB) Br ex 32.25 Dght 14.140 Lbp 218.00 Br md 32.20 Dpth 19.80 Welded, 1 dk	**(A21A2BC) Bulk Carrier** Double Hull Grain: 90,771; Bale: 88,783 Compartments: 7 Ho, ER 7 Ha: ER	**1 oil engine** driving 1 FP propeller Total Power: 9,210kW (12,522hp) 14.5kn MAN-B&W 7S50MC-C8 1 x 2 Stroke 7 Cy. 500 x 2000 9210kW (12522bhp) Mitsui Engineering & Shipbuilding CLtd-Japan AuxGen: 3 x a.c Fuel: 2732.0
9680360 *3FYU2* -	**SAKIZAYA CHAMPION** **Sakizaya Navigation SA** Wisdom Marine Lines SA *Panama* *Panama* MMSI: 351647000 Official number: 45700TT	**41,766** 26,057 78,080	Class: NK	**2014-04 Sasebo Heavy Industries Co. Ltd. — Sasebo Yard, Sasebo** Yd No: 820 Loa 225.00 (BB) Br ex 32.25 Dght 14.429 Lbp 221.75 Br md 32.20 Dpth 20.00 Welded, 1 dk	**(A21A2BC) Bulk Carrier** Grain: 90,911; Bale: 88,950 Compartments: 7 Ho, ER 7 Ha: ER	**1 oil engine** driving 1 FP propeller Total Power: 9,660kW (13,134hp) 14.5kn MAN-B&W 6S60ME-C8 1 x 2 Stroke 6 Cy. 600 x 2400 9660kW (13134bhp) Mitsui Engineering & Shipbuilding CLtd-Japan AuxGen: 4 x 2000kW a.c
9460590 *3FAJ4* -	**SAKIZAYA WISDOM** **Sakizaya Wisdom SA** Wisdom Marine Lines SA SatCom: Inmarsat C 435586010 *Panama* *Panama* MMSI: 355860000 Official number: 4324411	**40,034** 25,279 76,457 T/cm 67.1	Class: BV (NK)	**2011-09 Oshima Shipbuilding Co Ltd — Saikai NS** Yd No: 10560 Loa 225.00 (BB) Br ex - Dght 14.120 Lbp 220.00 Br md 32.26 Dpth 19.39 Welded, 1 dk	**(A21A2BC) Bulk Carrier** Grain: 87,706; Bale: 85,726 Compartments: 7 Ho, ER 7 Ha: ER	**1 oil engine** driving 1 FP propeller Total Power: 9,319kW (12,670hp) 14.5kn MAN-B&W 5S60MC-C 1 x 2 Stroke 5 Cy. 600 x 2400 9319kW (12670bhp) Kawasaki Heavy Industries Ltd-Japan AuxGen: 3 x 420kW 60Hz a.c Fuel: 2200.0
7910591 - -	**SAKKR 1** **Misr Petroleum Co** *Port Said* *Egypt*	*100* - 20	Class: (LR) ✠	**1981-07 Governmental Irrigation Workshops — Cairo** Yd No: 1021 Loa 24.36 Br ex 4.70 Dght 0.951 Lbp 23.09 Br md 4.50 Dpth 1.50 Welded, 1 dk	**(A31A2GX) General Cargo Ship**	**1 oil engine** with clutches & sr reverse geared to sc. shaft driving 1 FP propeller Total Power: 200kW (272hp) Deutz SBA6M816 1 x 4 Stroke 6 Cy. 142 x 160 200kW (272bhp) Kloeckner Humboldt Deutz AG-West Germany AuxGen: 1 x 10kW 380V 50Hz a.c
7910606 - -	**SAKKR 2** **Misr Petroleum Co** *Port Said* *Egypt*	*100* - 20	Class: (LR) ✠	**1981-11 Governmental Irrigation Workshops — Cairo** Yd No: 1022 Loa 24.36 Br ex 4.70 Dght 0.951 Lbp 23.09 Br md 4.50 Dpth 1.50 Welded, 1 dk	**(A31A2GX) General Cargo Ship** Compartments: 1 Ho, ER 1 Ha: ER	**1 oil engine** reverse reduction geared to sc. shaft driving 1 FP propeller Total Power: 200kW (272hp) Deutz SBA6M816 1 x 4 Stroke 6 Cy. 142 x 160 200kW (272bhp) Kloeckner Humboldt Deutz AG-West Germany AuxGen: 1 x 10kW 380V 50Hz a.c
7942934 - -	**SAKMARA** **OOO 'Interrybflot'** -	**962** 288 332	Class: RS	**1981 Zavod "Leninskaya Kuznitsa" — Kiyev** Yd No: 249 Loa 53.75 (BB) Br ex 10.72 Dght 4.290 Lbp 47.92 Br md - Dpth 6.02 Welded, 1 dk	**(B11A2FS) Stern Trawler** Ins: 218 Compartments: 1 Ho, ER 1 Ha: (1.6 x 1.6) Derricks: 2x1.5t Ice Capable	**1 oil engine** driving 1 FP propeller Total Power: 971kW (1,320hp) 12.8kn S.K.L. 8NVD48A-2U 1 x 4 Stroke 8 Cy. 320 x 480 971kW (1320bhp) VEB Schwermaschinenbau "KarlLiebknecht" (SKL)-Magdeburg Fuel: 185.0 (d.f.)
5011157 - -	**SAKOBA** *ex* Alicante *-1996* *ex* Ciudad de Alicante *-1954* - - *Kenya*	**270** 81 -	Class: (RI) (BV)	**1950 Hijos de J. Barreras S.A. — Vigo** Yd No: 1022 L reg 37.16 Br ex 6.71 Dght 3.665 Lbp - Br md - Dpth - Welded, 1 dk	**(B11A2FT) Trawler** 2 Ha: 2 (0.9 x 0.9)	**1 oil engine** geared to sc. shaft driving 1 FP propeller Total Power: 705kW (959hp) 11.0kn Deutz SBA8M528 1 x 4 Stroke 8 Cy. 220 x 280 705kW (959bhp) (new engine 1972) Kloeckner Humboldt Deutz AG-West Germany AuxGen: 3 x 93kW 220/380V 50Hz a.c Fuel: 65.0
5307336 - -	**SAKR** *ex* Empire Warlock *-1947* **Government of The Arab Republic of Egypt (Ministry of Maritime Transport - Ports & Lighthouses Administration)** - *Alexandria* *Egypt*	*253* 2 -	Class: (LR) ✠ Classed LR until 12/47	**1942-09 Ferguson Bros (Port Glasgow) Ltd — Port Glasgow** Yd No: 361 Loa 35.34 Br ex 8.26 Dght 3.302 Lbp - Br md - Dpth - Welded, 1 dk	**(B32A2ST) Tug**	**1 Steam Recip** driving 1 FP propeller Total Power: 738kW (1,003hp) 1 x Steam Recip. 738kW (1003ihp) Ferguson Bros (Port Glasgow) Ltd-United Kingdom
9085778 *9LY2464* -	**SAKRA TRANSPORTER** **Penguin International Ltd** Pelican Ship Management Services Pte Ltd *Freetown* *Sierra Leone* MMSI: 667003267 Official number: SL103267	*487* 146 381	Class: AB	**1994-02 Southern Ocean Shipbuilding Co Pte Ltd — Singapore** Yd No: 197 Converted From: Ferry (Passenger only)-2009 Loa 52.80 Br ex - Dght 1.804 Lbp - Br md 14.00 Dpth 2.50 Welded, 1 dk	**(B21A2OC) Crew/Supply Vessel**	**2 oil engines** geared to sc. shaft driving 2 Voith-Schneider propellers Total Power: 600kW (816hp) 8.0kn Caterpillar 3408TA 2 x Vee 4 Stroke 8 Cy. 137 x 152 each-300kW (408bhp) Caterpillar Inc-USA AuxGen: 2 x 40kW a.c

IMO / Call sign	Name / Owners	Tonnage	Class	Builder / Dimensions	Type / Cargo	Machinery
7530004 *OW2317* FD 125	**SAKSABERG** *ex* Research *-1996* *ex* Kings Cross *-1987* **P/F Desin** - *Faeroe Islands (Danish)* MMSI: 231047000	**670** 391 -	Class: NV	**1975-**02 **Volda Mek. Verksted AS — Volda** Yd No: 11 Loa 42.82 Br ex 8.62 Dght 5.003 Lbp 38.19 Br md 8.59 Dpth 6.48 Welded, 2 dks	**(B11B2FV) Fishing Vessel** Compartments: 6 Ta, ER Ice Capable	**1 oil engine** driving 1 CP propeller Total Power: 1,214kW (1,651hp) Wichmann 6AXA 1 x 2 Stroke 6 Cy. 300 x 450 1214kW (1651bhp) Wichmann Motorfabrikk AS-Norway AuxGen: 2 x 115kW 380V 50Hz a.c, 1 x 28kW 380V 50Hz a.c Thrusters: 1 Thwart. FP thruster (f); 1 Tunnel thruster (a)
8100117 *AUQX* -	**SAKTHI** *ex* Vamsee *-2011* *ex* Sea Rose *-2007* *ex* Emilie K *-1999* *ex* Arktis Star *-1995* **Sakthi Shipping Services (India) Pvt Ltd** - *Chennai* *India* MMSI: 419068400 Official number: 3334	**1,510** 770 2,164	Class: IR (LR) (BV) ✠ Classed LR until 10/7/02	**1982-**07 **A/S Nordsovaerftet — Ringkobing** Yd No: 156 Loa 72.45 Br ex 11.36 Dght 4.540 Lbp 70.08 Br md 11.21 Dpth 6.70 Welded, 2 dks	**(A31A2GX) General Cargo Ship** Grain: 3,403; Bale: 3,048 TEU 54 C. 54/20' (40') Compartments: 1 Ho, 1 Tw Dk, ER 2 Ha: 2 (18.7 x 8.0)ER Derricks: 2x15t; Winches: 2 Ice Capable	**1 oil engine** with clutches, flexible couplings & sr geared to sc. shaft driving 1 CP propeller Total Power: 800kW (1,088hp) 10.0kn Alpha 7T23L-KVO 1 x 4 Stroke 7 Cy. 225 x 300 800kW (1088bhp) B&W Alpha Diesel A/S-Denmark AuxGen: 2 x 105kW 380V 50Hz a.c, 1 x 72kW 380V 50Hz a.c, 1 x 40kW 380V 50Hz a.c Fuel: 130.0 (d.f.) 4.0pd
8032140 *V4FD* -	**SAKTHI** *ex* Cana *-2005* *ex* May *-1997* *ex* Radius *-1997* *ex* Sea Sources *-1997* *ex* Shinsei Maru No. 2 *-1994* **Radius Maritime SA** Golden Star Marine Pte Ltd *Basseterre* *St Kitts & Nevis* MMSI: 341132000 Official number: SKN 1001132	**438** 179 700	Class: IS (GL)	**1980-**01 **YK Furumoto Tekko Zosensho — Osakikamijima** Yd No: 506 Loa 46.95 Br ex - Dght 3.544 Lbp 46.11 Br md 8.50 Dpth 4.00 Welded, 1 dk	**(A13B2TU) Tanker (unspecified)**	**1 oil engine** driving 1 FP propeller
5307348 *VTJP* -	**SAKTI** *ex* Empire Samson *-1948* **Government of The Republic of India** - *Chennai* *India* Official number: 169086	*261* - -	Class: (LR) *Classed BC until 6/48	**1943 Goole SB. & Repairing Co. Ltd. — Goole** Yd No: 397 L reg 32.25 Br ex 9.17 Dght 3.810 Lbp - Br md 9.12 Dpth - Welded, 1 dk	**(B32A2ST) Tug**	**1 Steam Recip** driving 1 FP propeller Total Power: 930kW (1,264hp) 9.0kn 1 x Steam Recip. 930kW (1264ihp) Amos & Smith Ltd.-Hull
8717685 *PNSL* -	**SAKTI** *ex* Kiyooki Maru *-2010* **PT Indobaruna Bulk Transport** - *Jakarta* *Indonesia* MMSI: 525019570 Official number: 2010 PST NO. 6595/L	**4,322** 1,297 6,294	Class: KI NK	**1988-**06 **Shinhama Dockyard Co. Ltd. — Anan** Yd No: 778 Loa 111.67 Br ex - Dght 6.664 Lbp 105.01 Br md 16.00 Dpth 8.50 Welded, 1 dk	**(A24A2BT) Cement Carrier** Grain: 5,024	**1 oil engine** with clutches, flexible couplings & sr geared to sc. shaft driving 1 CP propeller Total Power: 2,398kW (3,260hp) 13.0kn MaK 8M453B 1 x 4 Stroke 8 Cy. 320 x 420 2398kW (3260bhp) Ube Industries Ltd-Japan Thrusters: 1 Thwart. FP thruster (f); 1 Tunnel thruster (a) Fuel: 165.0 (r.f.)
7344558 - -	**SAKTIMAN** *launched as* Kattabomman *-1984* **Kolkata Port Trust** - *Kolkata* *India* Official number: 1766	*342* 103 103	Class: (IR)	**1984-**09 **Central Inland Water Transport Corp. Ltd. — Kolkata** Yd No: 357 Loa 33.02 Br ex - Dght 3.301 Lbp 29.95 Br md 9.01 Dpth 3.41 Welded, 1 dk	**(B32A2ST) Tug**	**2 oil engines** with clutches, flexible couplings & sr reverse geared to sc. shafts driving 2 FP propellers Total Power: 1,250kW (1,700hp) MAN G5V30/45ATL 2 x 4 Stroke 5 Cy. 300 x 450 each-625kW (850bhp) Garden Reach Shipbuilders &Engineers Ltd-India
9213686 *9GRP* -	**SAKUMO LAGOON** - **Government of The Republic of Ghana (Ports & Harbours Authority)** - *Takoradi* *Ghana* MMSI: 627330100 Official number: GSR 0015	**269** 80 200	**✠ 100A1** SS 10/2010 tug **LMC** Eq.Ltr: F; Cable: 275.0/17.5 U2 (a)	**2005-**10 **Stal-Rem SA — Gdansk** (Hull) Yd No: (511607) **2005-**10 **B.V. Scheepswerf Damen — Gorinchem** Yd No: 511607 Loa 29.75 Br ex 9.95 Dght 3.558 Lbp 26.63 Br md 9.95 Dpth 4.40 Welded, 1 dk	**(B32A2ST) Tug**	**2 oil engines** with clutches, flexible couplings & sr reverse geared to sc. shafts driving 2 FP propellers Total Power: 3,542kW (4,816hp) Caterpillar 3516B-TA 2 x Vee 4 Stroke 16 Cy. 170 x 190 each-1771kW (2408bhp) Caterpillar Inc-USA AuxGen: 2 x 78kW 400V 50Hz a.c
9199218 *JL6539* -	**SAKURA** - **Uwajima Unyu KK** - *Yawatahama, Ehime* *Japan* MMSI: 431500784 Official number: 135557	*2,334* - 1,529		**1998-**01 **Naikai Zosen Corp — Onomichi HS (Setoda Shipyard)** Yd No: 633 Loa 114.34 Br ex - Dght 4.565 Lbp 105.00 Br md 16.00 Dpth 10.60 Welded, 2 dks	**(A35A2RR) Ro-Ro Cargo Ship** Bow door/ramp Len: 6.70 Wid: 4.30 Swl: - Stern door/ramp Len: 4.80 Wid: 5.00 Swl: - Cars: 25, Trailers: 35	**2 oil engines** reduction geared to sc. shafts driving 2 FP propellers Total Power: 6,620kW (9,000hp) 20.2kn Daihatsu 6DLM-40 2 x 4 Stroke 6 Cy. 400 x 480 each-3310kW (4500bhp) Daihatsu Diesel Manufacturing Co Lt-Japan Thrusters: 1 Thwart. FP thruster (f)
9410430 *3FGY5* -	**SAKURA** - **Kei Field Maritime SA** Kitaura Kaiun KK SatCom: Inmarsat C 435642413 *Panama* *Panama* MMSI: 356424000 Official number: 4131410	**113,928** 43,997 229,069	Class: NK	**2010-**02 **Namura Shipbuilding Co Ltd — Imari SG** Yd No: 295 Loa 319.58 (BB) Br ex - Dght 18.127 Lbp 308.00 Br md 54.00 Dpth 24.30 Welded, 1 dk	**(A21B2BO) Ore Carrier** Grain: 146,958 Compartments: 5 Ho, ER 9 Ha: ER	**1 oil engine** driving 1 FP propeller Total Power: 22,432kW (30,499hp) 15.1kn Mitsubishi 6UEC85LSII 1 x 2 Stroke 6 Cy. 850 x 3150 22432kW (30499bhp) Mitsubishi Heavy Industries Ltd-Japan Fuel: 6410.0
7312799 - -	**SAKURA** *ex* Toko Maru *-2006* *ex* Nagato *-1993* *ex* Atago Maru *-1986* **ACG Joy Express Liner** - *Manila* *Philippines* Official number: 00-0001305	*184* - 194		**1973-**02 **Oshima Dock KK — Imabari EH** Yd No: 508 Loa 27.80 Br ex 8.64 Dght 3.277 Lbp 23.50 Br md 8.62 Dpth 3.79 Riveted\Welded, 1 dk	**(B32A2ST) Tug**	**2 oil engines** geared integral to driving 2 Z propellers Total Power: 1,766kW (2,402hp) 12.5kn Niigata 6L25BX 2 x 4 Stroke 6 Cy. 250 x 320 each-883kW (1201bhp) Niigata Engineering Co Ltd-Japan AuxGen: 2 x 48kW 225V
5307439 - -	**SAKURA** *ex* Sakura Maru *-1992* - -	*147* 49 -		**1962 Iino Jukogyo KK — Maizuru KY** Yd No: 66 Loa 24.91 Br ex 7.55 Dght 2.240 Lbp 24.00 Br md 7.50 Dpth 3.25 Riveted\Welded, 1 dk	**(B32A2ST) Tug**	**2 oil engines** driving 2 FP propellers Total Power: 736kW (1,000hp) 10.5kn Fuji 6SD30 2 x 4 Stroke 6 Cy. 300 x 430 each-368kW (500bhp) Fuji Diesel Co Ltd-Japan Fuel: 15.0
9057862 *JG5141* -	**SAKURA** - **Toko Service KK** - *Tokyo* *Japan* Official number: 133795	*181* - -		**1992-**07 **Kanagawa Zosen — Kobe** Yd No: 377 Loa 33.20 Br ex - Dght 2.900 Lbp 29.00 Br md 8.80 Dpth 3.80 Welded, 1 dk	**(B32A2ST) Tug**	**2 oil engines** driving 2 FP propellers Total Power: 2,280kW (3,100hp) Niigata 6L25HX 2 x 4 Stroke 6 Cy. 250 x 350 each-1140kW (1550bhp) Niigata Engineering Co Ltd-Japan
8986482 *JG5711* -	**SAKURA** - **KK Daito Corp** - *Tokyo* *Japan* Official number: 137191	*178* - -		**2003-**12 **Hanasaki Zosensho K.K. — Yokosuka** Yd No: 272 Loa 32.25 Br ex - Dght 2.900 Lbp - Br md 8.80 Dpth 3.88 Welded, 1 dk	**(B32A2ST) Tug**	**2 oil engines** geared to sc. shafts driving 2 Z propellers Total Power: 2,942kW (4,000hp) Niigata 6L26HLX 2 x 4 Stroke 6 Cy. 260 x 350 each-1471kW (2000bhp) Niigata Engineering Co Ltd-Japan
9104328 *PNFE* -	**SAKURA 9** *ex* Kisho Maru *-2012* **PT Suntraco Intim Transport Inc** - *Surabaya* *Indonesia*	**1,428** 485 1,185	Class: KI	**1994-**09 **K.K. Miura Zosensho — Saiki** Yd No: 1108 Loa 74.90 Br ex - Dght - Lbp 70.00 Br md 11.50 Dpth 6.90 Welded, 1 dk	**(A31A2GX) General Cargo Ship**	**1 oil engine** driving 1 FP propeller Total Power: 736kW (1,001hp) Niigata 6M30BGT 1 x 4 Stroke 6 Cy. 300 x 530 736kW (1001bhp) Niigata Engineering Co Ltd-Japan
9650858 *3FCN6* -	**SAKURA DREAM** - **Shunzan Kaiun Co Ltd & Primavera Montana SA** Shunzan Kaiun KK (Shunzan Kaiun Co Ltd) *Panama* *Panama* MMSI: 351357000 Official number: 44505KJ	**23,264** 12,134 38,213 T/cm 48.6	Class: NK	**2013-**04 **Imabari Shipbuilding Co Ltd — Imabari EH (Imabari Shipyard)** Yd No: 780 Loa 179.97 (BB) Br ex - Dght 10.538 Lbp 173.00 Br md 29.80 Dpth 15.00 Welded, 1 dk	**(A21A2BC) Bulk Carrier** Grain: 47,125; Bale: 45,369 Compartments: 5 Ho, ER 5 Ha: 4 (20.0 x 20.0)ER (15.9 x 17.2) Cranes: 4x30.5t	**1 oil engine** driving 1 FP propeller Total Power: 7,860kW (10,686hp) 14.7kn MAN-B&W 6S46MC-C 1 x 2 Stroke 6 Cy. 460 x 1932 7860kW (10686bhp) Makita Corp-Japan AuxGen: 3 x 450kW a.c Fuel: 1940.0
9302865 *VRIW3* -	**SAKURA EXPRESS** - **World Star Shipping Ltd** Island Navigation Corp International Ltd SatCom: Inmarsat C 447703844 *Hong Kong* *Hong Kong* MMSI: 477434900 Official number: HK-3166	**27,994** 12,193 45,718 T/cm 49.9	Class: AB (Class contemplated) (NK)	**2004-**03 **Minaminippon Shipbuilding Co Ltd — Usuki OT** Yd No: 679 Loa 179.80 (BB) Br ex 32.49 Dght 12.116 Lbp 171.00 Br md 32.20 Dpth 18.80 Welded, 1 dk	**(A13B2TP) Products Tanker** Double Hull (13F) Liq: 55,000; Liq (Oil): 55,000 Cargo Heating Coils Compartments: 12 Wing Ta, 2 Wing Slop Ta, ER 4 Cargo Pump (s): 4x950m³/hr Manifold: Bow/CM: 92m	**1 oil engine** driving 1 FP propeller Total Power: 8,580kW (11,665hp) 14.5kn B&W 6S50MC 1 x 2 Stroke 6 Cy. 500 x 1910 8580kW (11665bhp) Mitsui Engineering & Shipbuilding CLtd-Japan AuxGen: 3 x Fuel: 162.9 (d.f.) 2442.1 (r.f.)

IMO / Call sign	Name / Owner	Tonnage	Class	Built / Dimensions	Type / Capacity	Machinery
9079767 *POMD* -	**SAKURA EXPRESS** *ex* Sakura *-2012* *ex* Hanil Carferry No. 2 *-2012* *ex* Shimanto *-2004* **PT Bukit Merapin Nusantara Lines** - *Tanjung Priok* *Indonesia*	**3,610** 1,471 602	Class: KI (KR)	**1994**-03 **Usuki Shipyard Co Ltd — Usuki OT** Yd No: 1625 Loa 89.00 (BB) Br ex - Dght 4.100 Lbp 82.50 Br md 14.20 Dpth 9.51 Welded	**(A36A2PR) Passenger/Ro-Ro Ship (Vehicles)** Passengers: unberthed: 484 Bow ramp Len: 6.00 Wid: 4.50 Swl: - Stern ramp Len: 5.00 Wid: 4.50 Swl: - Cars: 56	**2 oil engines** reduction geared to sc. shafts driving 2 FP propellers Total Power: 4,412kW (5,998hp) 19.0kn Daihatsu 8DLM-32 2 x 4 Stroke 8 Cy. 320 x 400 each-2206kW (2999bhp) Daihatsu Diesel Manufacturing Co Lt-Japan Thrusters: 1 Thwart. FP thruster (f) Fuel: 128.0 (d.f.)
9629873 *3FVK9* -	**SAKURA GAS** **LPG Sunshine Panama SA** Iino Marine Service Co Ltd *Panama* *Panama* MMSI: 354957000 Official number: 4451713	**47,964** 14,390 55,214 T/cm 71.3	Class: NK	**2013**-01 **Mitsubishi Heavy Industries Ltd. — Nagasaki** Yd No: 2286 Loa 230.00 (BB) Br ex - Dght 11.575 Lbp 219.00 Br md 36.60 Dpth 21.65 Welded, 1 dk	**(A11B2TG) LPG Tanker** Liq (Gas): 83,385 4 x Gas Tank (s); 4 independent (C.mn.stl) pri horizontal	**1 oil engine** driving 1 FP propeller Total Power: 13,000kW (17,675hp) 16.7kn Mitsubishi 7UEC60LSII 1 x 2 Stroke 7 Cy. 600 x 2300 13000kW (17675bhp) Mitsubishi Heavy Industries Ltd-Japan AuxGen: 3 x 980kW a.c Fuel: 3700.0
9609237 *3FII4* -	**SAKURA GLORY** **Leeward Navigation SA** Tokai Shipping Co Ltd (Tokai Shosen KK) SatCom: Inmarsat C 437328110 *Panama* *Panama* MMSI: 373281000 Official number: 4388312	**32,714** 19,015 58,163	Class: NK	**2012**-05 **Shin Kurushima Dockyard Co. Ltd. — Onishi** Yd No: 5667 Loa 189.93 (BB) Br ex - Dght 12.925 Lbp 185.50 Br md 32.26 Dpth 18.40 Welded, 1 dk	**(A21A2BC) Bulk Carrier** Grain: 73,142; Bale: 70,183 Compartments: 5 Ho, ER 5 Ha: ER Cranes: 4x30.5t	**1 oil engine** driving 1 FP propeller Total Power: 8,100kW (11,013hp) 14.2kn MAN-B&W 6S50MC-C 1 x 2 Stroke 6 Cy. 500 x 2000 8100kW (11013bhp) Fuel: 2280.0
9473688 *H8QN* -	**SAKURA KOBE** **Nitta Kisen Kaisha Ltd & Azalea Shipping SA** Nitta Kisen Kaisha Ltd SatCom: Inmarsat C 435456110 *Panama* *Panama* MMSI: 354561000 Official number: 4307411	**21,192** 11,615 33,735	Class: NK	**2011**-09 **Shin Kochi Jyuko K.K. — Kochi** Yd No: 7255 Loa 179.99 (BB) Br ex - Dght 10.100 Lbp 172.00 Br md 28.20 Dpth 14.30 Welded, 1 dk	**(A21A2BC) Bulk Carrier** Double Hull Grain: 44,038; Bale: 43,164 Compartments: 5 Ho, ER 5 Ha: 3 (20.8 x 23.8) (19.2 x 23.8)ER (16.8 x 17.2) Cranes: 4x30t	**1 oil engine** driving 1 FP propeller Total Power: 6,250kW (8,498hp) 14.3kn Mitsubishi 6UEC45LSE 1 x 2 Stroke 6 Cy. 450 x 1840 6250kW (8498bhp) Kobe Hatsudoki KK-Japan Fuel: 1620.0
9041734 *JJ3707* -	**SAKURA MARU** **Miura Kaiun KK** - *Kobe, Hyogo* *Japan* Official number: 132352	*198* - -		**1992**-01 **K.K. Odo Zosen Tekko — Shimonoseki** Yd No: 502 Loa 34.00 Br ex 9.66 Dght 3.000 Lbp 29.00 Br md 9.20 Dpth 4.20 Welded, 1 dk	**(B32A2ST) Tug**	**2 oil engines** with clutches, flexible couplings & dr geared to sc. shafts driving 2 FP propellers Total Power: 2,648kW (3,600hp) Yanmar 6Z280-EN 2 x 4 Stroke 6 Cy. 280 x 360 each-1324kW (1800bhp) Yanmar Diesel Engine Co Ltd-Japan
9136802 *JG5244* -	**SAKURA MARU** **Corporation for Advanced Transport & Technology & Uyeno Transtech Co Ltd** Uyeno Transtech Co Ltd *Yokohama, Kanagawa* *Japan* MMSI: 431100221 Official number: 134952	*2,997* - 4,999	Class: NK	**1996**-03 **Naikai Zosen Corp — Onomichi HS (Setoda Shipyard)** Yd No: 612 Loa 104.80 (BB) Br ex 15.22 Dght 6.515 Lbp 97.60 Br md 15.20 Dpth 7.50 Welded, 1 dk	**(A13B2TP) Products Tanker** Single Hull Liq: 5,120; Liq (Oil): 5,120 Compartments: 10 Ta, ER 2 Cargo Pump (s): 2x1300m³/hr	**1 oil engine** driving 1 FP propeller Total Power: 3,354kW (4,560hp) 13.4kn B&W 6L35MC 1 x 2 Stroke 6 Cy. 350 x 1050 3354kW (4560bhp) The Hanshin Diesel Works Ltd-Japan AuxGen: 2 x 400kW a.c Thrusters: 1 Thwart. CP thruster (f) Fuel: 187.0 (d.f.) 13.3pd
8806230 *JI3329* -	**SAKURA MARU** *ex* Masuei Maru No. 23 *-2010* **Masuei Sangyo KK** - *Kochi, Kochi* *Japan* Official number: 128733	*160* - -		**1988**-03 **Oshima Shipbuilding Co Ltd — Saikai NS** Yd No: 10110 Loa 30.30 Br ex 8.82 Dght 2.601 Lbp 26.01 Br md 8.81 Dpth 3.69 Welded, 1 dk	**(B32A2ST) Tug**	**2 oil engines** geared integral to driving 2 Z propellers Total Power: 2,206kW (3,000hp) 12.5kn Niigata 6L25CXE 2 x 4 Stroke 6 Cy. 250 x 320 each-1103kW (1500bhp) Niigata Engineering Co Ltd-Japan
8618528 *JH3089* -	**SAKURA MARU** **Nagoya Kisen KK (Nagoya Kisen Kaisha Ltd)** *Nagoya, Aichi* *Japan* Official number: 128459	*160* - -		**1987**-05 **Kanagawa Zosen — Kobe** Yd No: 295 Loa 32.47 Br ex - Dght 2.701 Lbp 27.11 Br md 8.62 Dpth 3.81 Welded, 1 dk	**(B32A2ST) Tug**	**2 oil engines** Geared Integral to driving 2 Z propellers Total Power: 1,912kW (2,600hp) Niigata 6L25CXE 2 x 4 Stroke 6 Cy. 250 x 320 each-956kW (1300bhp) Niigata Engineering Co Ltd-Japan
6607147 - -	**SAKURA MARU No. 8** *ex* Naburi Maru No. 7 *-2010* **Shinyo Suisan** - *South Korea*	*192* 73 -		**1965 Niigata Engineering Co Ltd — Niigata NI** Yd No: 628 Loa 41.81 Br ex 6.63 Dght - Lbp 34.40 Br md 6.61 Dpth 3.20 Welded, 1 dk	**(B11B2FV) Fishing Vessel**	**1 oil engine** driving 1 FP propeller Total Power: 515kW (700hp) Niigata 1 x 4 Stroke 6 Cy. 280 x 440 515kW (700bhp) Niigata Engineering Co Ltd-Japan
8865236 *JK5197* -	**SAKURA No. 2** *ex* Nanakuni *-2001* - *Kure, Hiroshima* *Japan* Official number: 133699	*268* - 104		**1992**-10 **Kanbara Zosen K.K. — Onomichi** Yd No: 432 Loa 44.80 Br ex - Dght 2.300 Lbp 35.90 Br md 10.40 Dpth 3.20 Welded, 1 dk	**(A36A2PR) Passenger/Ro-Ro Ship (Vehicles)**	**2 oil engines** with clutches, flexible couplings & reduction geared to sc. shafts driving 2 Propellers 1 fwd and 1 aft Total Power: 882kW (1,200hp) Daihatsu 6DLM-24FS 2 x 4 Stroke 6 Cy. 240 x 320 each-441kW (600bhp) Daihatsu Diesel Manufacturing Co Lt-Japan
9599822 *3FRC8* -	**SAKURA OCEAN** **Shunzan Kaiun Co Ltd & Primavera Montana SA** Shunzan Kaiun KK (Shunzan Kaiun Co Ltd) *Panama* *Panama* MMSI: 354708000 Official number: 4275711	**23,268** 12,134 38,239 T/cm 48.6	Class: NK	**2011**-06 **Imabari Shipbuilding Co Ltd — Imabari EH (Imabari Shipyard)** Yd No: 769 Loa 179.97 (BB) Br ex - Dght 10.536 Lbp 173.00 Br md 29.80 Dpth 15.00 Welded, 1 dk	**(A21A2BC) Bulk Carrier** Double Hull Grain: 47,125; Bale: 45,369 Compartments: 5 Ho, ER 5 Ha: ER Cranes: 4x30.5t	**1 oil engine** driving 1 FP propeller Total Power: 7,860kW (10,686hp) 14.7kn MAN-B&W 6S46MC-C 1 x 2 Stroke 6 Cy. 460 x 1932 7860kW (10686bhp) Fuel: 1900.0
9358541 *D5BI8* -	**SAKURA PRINCESS** **Universal Reserve SA** Tsakos Columbia Shipmanagement (TCM) SA *Monrovia* *Liberia* MMSI: 636015526 Official number: 15526	**55,909** 29,810 105,365 T/cm 88.9	Class: LR ✠ **100A1** SS 06/2012 Double Hull oil tanker ESP **ShipRight** (SDA, FDA, CM) *IWS LI EP (B,P,S,Vc,Vp) ✠ **LMC** **UMS IGS** Eq.Ltr: R†; Cable: 689.6/84.0 U3 (a)	**2007**-06 **Sumitomo Heavy Industries Marine & Engineering Co., Ltd. — Yokosuka** Yd No: 1334 Loa 228.60 (BB) Br ex 42.04 Dght 14.780 Lbp 217.80 Br md 42.00 Dpth 21.50 Welded, 1 dk	**(A13A2TV) Crude Oil Tanker** Double Hull (13F) Liq: 98,688; Liq (Oil): 98,688 Compartments: 10 Wing Ta, 2 Wing Slop Ta, ER, 1 Slop Ta 3 Cargo Pump (s): 3x2500m³/hr Manifold: Bow/CM: 116.6m	**1 oil engine** driving 1 FP propeller Total Power: 12,350kW (16,791hp) 14.8kn MAN-B&W 6S60MC-C 1 x 2 Stroke 6 Cy. 600 x 2400 12350kW (16791bhp) Mitsui Engineering & Shipbuilding CLtd-Japan AuxGen: 3 x 800kW 450V 60Hz a.c Boilers: e (ex.g.) 21.4kgf/cm² (21.0bar), WTAuxB (o.f.) 18.3kgf/cm² (17.9bar)
9447378 *3ESB4* -	**SAKURA SYMPHONY** **Manama Pride Inc** Stealth Maritime Corp SA *Panama* *Panama* MMSI: 370249000 Official number: 3399408B	**2,997** 948 3,161 T/cm 11.4	Class: NK	**2008**-06 **K.K. Miura Zosensho — Saiki** Yd No: 1323 Loa 95.88 (BB) Br ex - Dght 5.513 Lbp 89.50 Br md 15.00 Dpth 7.00 Welded, 1 dk	**(A11B2TG) LPG Tanker** Double Bottom Entire Compartment Length Liq (Gas): 3,514 2 x Gas Tank (s); 2 independent (C.mn.stl) cyl 2 Cargo Pump (s): 2x300m³/hr Manifold: Bow/CM: 44.7m	**1 oil engine** driving 1 FP propeller Total Power: 2,647kW (3,599hp) 15.8kn Hanshin LH41LA 1 x 4 Stroke 6 Cy. 410 x 800 2647kW (3599bhp) The Hanshin Diesel Works Ltd-Japan AuxGen: 2 x 250kW a.c Thrusters: 1 Tunnel thruster (f) Fuel: 102.0 (d.f.) 378.0 (r.f.)
9554183 *3FAK3* -	**SAKURA WAVE** **Lotus Land Shipping SA** NS United Kaiun Kaisha Ltd *Panama* *Panama* MMSI: 370107000 Official number: 4155410	**48,022** 26,714 88,299 T/cm 79.7	Class: NK	**2010**-04 **Imabari Shipbuilding Co Ltd — Marugame KG (Marugame Shipyard)** Yd No: 1492 Loa 229.93 (BB) Br ex - Dght 13.820 Lbp 220.00 Br md 38.00 Dpth 19.90 Welded, 1 dk	**(A21A2BC) Bulk Carrier** Grain: 101,695 Compartments: 5 Ho, ER 5 Ha: ER	**1 oil engine** driving 1 FP propeller Total Power: 12,240kW (16,642hp) 14.7kn MAN-B&W 6S60MC 1 x 2 Stroke 6 Cy. 600 x 2292 12240kW (16642bhp) Mitsui Engineering & Shipbuilding CLtd-Japan Fuel: 2880.0 (r.f.)
9391751 *7JFL* -	**SAKURAGAWA** **Jasmine Ship Holding LLC** Kawasaki Kisen Kaisha Ltd (Kawasaki Kisen KK) ('K' Line) SatCom: Inmarsat C 443270710 *Kobe, Hyogo* *Japan* MMSI: 432707000 Official number: 141042	**160,068** 95,829 315,000 T/cm 185.0	Class: NK	**2009**-06 **Kawasaki Shipbuilding Corp — Sakaide KG** Yd No: 1612 Loa 332.93 (BB) Br ex - Dght 21.080 Lbp 324.00 Br md 60.00 Dpth 29.00 Welded, 1 dk	**(A13A2TV) Crude Oil Tanker** Double Hull (13F) Liq: 337,210; Liq (Oil): 344,576 Compartments: 5 Ta, 10 Wing Ta, 2 Wing Slop Ta, ER 3 Cargo Pump (s): 3x5500m³/hr Manifold: Bow/CM: 166.5m	**1 oil engine** driving 1 FP propeller Total Power: 25,480kW (34,643hp) 15.6kn MAN-B&W 7S80MC-C 1 x 2 Stroke 7 Cy. 800 x 3200 25480kW (34643bhp) Kawasaki Heavy Industries Ltd-Japan AuxGen: 3 x 1060kW a.c Fuel: 500.0 (d.f.) 6500.0 (r.f.)

Ship	Tonnage	Class	Built / Dimensions	Type	Machinery
9566198 **SAKURAJIMA MARU** *JD3136* - **Kagoshima Prefecture, Toshima-Mura** *Kagoshima, Kagoshima* Japan Official number: 141356	*1,330* - 380		**2011-02 Nakatani Shipyard Co. Ltd. — Etajima** Yd No: 622 Loa 57.36 Br ex - Dght 3.100 Lbp 47.30 Br md 13.50 Dpth 4.50 Welded, 1 dk	**(A36A2PR) Passenger/Ro-Ro Ship (Vehicles)** Passengers: unberthed: 657 Cars: 41	**2 oil engines** reduction geared to sc. shafts driving 2 Directional propellers contra-rotating Total Power: 1,600kW (2,176hp) Yanmar 6N21L-EV 2 x 4 Stroke 6 Cy. 210 x 290 each-800kW (1088bhp) Yanmar Diesel Engine Co Ltd-Japan
8920737 **SAKURAJIMA MARU No. 5** *JM5963* - - - *Kagoshima, Kagoshima* Japan MMSI: 431000491 Official number: 131362	*600* - 200		**1990-03 Hayashikane Dockyard Co Ltd — Nagasaki NS** Yd No: 981 Loa - Br ex - Dght - Lbp 49.03 Br md 13.01 Dpth 3.51 Welded, 1 dk	**(A36A2PR) Passenger/Ro-Ro Ship (Vehicles)**	**4 oil engines** geared to sc. shafts driving 2 FP propellers Total Power: 2,060kW (2,800hp) Hanshin 6LB26G 4 x 4 Stroke 6 Cy. 260 x 440 each-515kW (700bhp) The Hanshin Diesel Works Ltd-Japan
9038218 **SAKURAJIMA MARU No. 13** *JM6031* - - - *Kagoshima, Kagoshima* Japan MMSI: 431000652 Official number: 132650	*731* - 340		**1992-01 Sanuki Shipbuilding & Iron Works Co Ltd — Mitoyo KG** Yd No: 1222 Loa 53.00 Br ex - Dght 2.600 Lbp 46.50 Br md 13.00 Dpth 3.60 Welded, 1 dk	**(A36A2PR) Passenger/Ro-Ro Ship (Vehicles)** Passengers: unberthed: 488 Cars: 30	**2 oil engines** geared to sc. shafts driving 2 FP propellers Total Power: 1,472kW (2,002hp) Hanshin LH26G 2 x 4 Stroke 6 Cy. 260 x 440 each-736kW (1001bhp) The Hanshin Diesel Works Ltd-Japan
9115016 **SAKURAJIMA MARU No. 15** *JM6299* - - - *Kagoshima, Kagoshima* Japan MMSI: 431000651 Official number: 133578	*1,134* - 365		**1995-01 Hayashikane Dockyard Co Ltd — Nagasaki NS** Yd No: 1012 Loa 50.01 Br ex - Dght 2.800 Lbp 49.00 Br md 13.50 Dpth 3.80 Welded, 1 dk	**(A36A2PR) Passenger/Ro-Ro Ship (Vehicles)**	**2 oil engines** with clutches & reverse geared to sc. shafts driving 4 Propellers 2 fwd and 2 aft Total Power: 2,060kW (2,800hp) Hanshin LH28G 2 x 4 Stroke 6 Cy. 280 x 460 each-1030kW (1400bhp) The Hanshin Diesel Works Ltd-Japan
9194438 **SAKURAJIMA MARU NO. 16** *JM6565* - - - *Kagoshima, Kagoshima* Japan Official number: 136413	*997* - 365		**1999-01 Sanuki Shipbuilding & Iron Works Co Ltd — Mitoyo KG** Yd No: 1286 Loa 50.00 Br ex - Dght 2.800 Lbp - Br md 13.40 Dpth 3.80 Welded	**(A37B2PS) Passenger Ship**	**2 oil engines** driving 2 FP propellers Total Power: 1,766kW (2,402hp) Hanshin LH26G 2 x 4 Stroke 6 Cy. 260 x 440 each-883kW (1201bhp) The Hanshin Diesel Works Ltd-Japan
8979623 **SAKURAJIMA MARU NO. 18** *JM6743* - - - *Kagoshima, Kagoshima* Japan Official number: 136836	*1,279* - -		**2003-02 Evergreen Shipyard Corp — Nagasaki NS** Yd No: 1057 Loa 56.10 Br ex - Dght - Lbp - Br md 13.50 Dpth 3.80 Welded, 1 dk	**(A36A2PR) Passenger/Ro-Ro Ship (Vehicles)**	**2 oil engines** driving 2 Propellers Hanshin LH28G 2 x 4 Stroke 6 Cy. 280 x 460 The Hanshin Diesel Works Ltd-Japan
7344120 **SAL** - - **Mormugao Port Trust** *Mormugao* India Official number: 1702	*441* 185 482	Class: (LR) (IR) ✠ Classed LR until 24/9/91	**1976-05 Chowgule & Co Pvt Ltd — Goa** Yd No: 61 Loa 40.01 Br ex 10.32 Dght 3.010 Lbp 37.50 Br md 10.01 Dpth 3.99 Welded, 1 dk	**(B33B2DG) Grab Hopper Dredger** Hopper: 250	**2 oil engines** reverse reduction geared to sc. shafts driving 2 FP propellers Total Power: 548kW (746hp) 9.5kn MAN W8V175/22A 2 x 4 Stroke 8 Cy. 175 x 220 each-274kW (373bhp) Kirloskar Oil Engines Ltd-India AuxGen: 2 x 86kW 415V 50Hz a.c, 1 x 28kW 415V 50Hz a.c
7513707 **SAL 17** - *ex* Kiku Maru No. 7 *-1992* - **Sal Fishing Corp** - *Iloilo* Philippines Official number: ILO3002031	*129* 63 -		**1975-09 Nagasaki Zosen K.K. — Nagasaki** Yd No: 531 Loa 35.97 Br ex 6.33 Dght 2.388 Lbp 30.18 Br md 6.30 Dpth 2.80 Welded, 1 dk	**(B11B2FV) Fishing Vessel**	**1 oil engine** driving 1 FP propeller Total Power: 515kW (700hp) Niigata 6L25BX 1 x 4 Stroke 6 Cy. 250 x 320 515kW (700bhp) Niigata Engineering Co Ltd-Japan
7740013 **SAL 23** - *ex* Shinsei Maru No. 12 *-1996* - *ex* Fujishima Maru *-1984* **Sal Fishing Corp** - *Iloilo* Philippines Official number: ILO3000463	*211* 130 360		**1978-03 Sokooshi Zosen K.K. — Osakikamijima** Yd No: 250 Loa 39.50 Br ex - Dght 3.069 Lbp 35.51 Br md 7.10 Dpth 4.60 Welded, 2 dks	**(A31A2GX) General Cargo Ship**	**1 oil engine** driving 1 FP propeller Total Power: 552kW (750hp) Niigata 6M26ZG 1 x 4 Stroke 6 Cy. 260 x 400 552kW (750bhp) Niigata Engineering Co Ltd-Japan
7735422 **SAL 27** *DUG6305* *ex* Katoku Maru No. 38 *-1994* - *ex* Hoyo Maru No. 83 *-1985* **Sal Fishing Corp** - *Iloilo* Philippines Official number: ILO3000642	*245* 139 -		**1978-07 Maebata Zosen Tekko K.K. — Sasebo** Yd No: 130 Loa - Br ex - Dght - Lbp 41.80 Br md 7.70 Dpth 3.60 Welded	**(B11B2FV) Fishing Vessel**	**1 oil engine** driving 1 FP propeller
8623676 **SAL CATORSE** *DUG6006* *ex* Chotoku Maru No. 18 *-1992* - *ex* Marufuku Maru No. 31 *-1990* **Sal Fishing Corp** - *Iloilo* Philippines Official number: ILO3002033	*142* 63 -		**1976 in Japan** L reg 33.21 Br ex - Dght - Lbp 33.20 Br md 6.61 Dpth 3.00 Welded	**(B11B2FV) Fishing Vessel**	**1 oil engine** driving 1 FP propeller
8029143 **SAL DIECESEIS** - *ex* Shotoku Maru No. 21 *-1992* - **Sal Fishing Corp** - *Iloilo* Philippines Official number: ILO3001507	*193* 80 -		**1981-01 Nagasaki Zosen K.K. — Nagasaki** Yd No: 755 Loa 37.85 Br ex 7.40 Dght 2.350 Lbp 31.04 Br md 7.00 Dpth 2.77 Welded, 1 dk	**(B11B2FV) Fishing Vessel**	**1 oil engine** reduction geared to sc. shaft driving 1 FP propeller Total Power: 883kW (1,201hp) Niigata 6MG28BX 1 x 4 Stroke 6 Cy. 280 x 320 883kW (1201bhp) Niigata Engineering Co Ltd-Japan
7709825 **SAL DIECINUEVE** *DUG6255* *ex* Sano Maru No. 28 *-1992* - **Sal Fishing Corp** - *Iloilo* Philippines Official number: ILO3000597	*245* 154 358		**1977-06 Yamanishi Shipbuilding Co Ltd — Ishinomaki MG** Yd No: 826 Loa 49.66 Br ex - Dght 3.236 Lbp 42.96 Br md 8.21 Dpth 3.56 Welded	**(B11B2FV) Fishing Vessel**	**1 oil engine** driving 1 FP propeller Total Power: 736kW (1,001hp) Niigata 6L28X 1 x 4 Stroke 6 Cy. 280 x 440 736kW (1001bhp) Niigata Engineering Co Ltd-Japan
7513719 **SAL DIECIOCHO** - *ex* Kiku Maru No. 8 *-1992* - **Sal Fishing Corp** - *Iloilo* Philippines Official number: ILO3003034	*183* 63 154		**1975-09 Nagasaki Zosen K.K. — Nagasaki** Yd No: 532 Loa 35.97 Br ex 6.33 Dght 2.388 Lbp 30.18 Br md 6.30 Dpth 2.80 Welded, 1 dk	**(B11B2FV) Fishing Vessel**	**1 oil engine** driving 1 FP propeller Total Power: 515kW (700hp) Niigata 6L25BX 1 x 4 Stroke 6 Cy. 250 x 320 515kW (700bhp) Niigata Engineering Co Ltd-Japan
7608186 **SAL DIEZ** *DUG6003* *ex* Ebisu Maru No. 3 *-1994* - **Sal Fishing Corp** - *Iloilo* Philippines Official number: ILO3000599	*183* 41 -		**1976-05 Nagasaki Zosen K.K. — Nagasaki** Yd No: 565 Loa 35.56 Br ex 6.33 Dght 2.394 Lbp 29.29 Br md 6.30 Dpth 2.80 Welded, 1 dk	**(B11B2FV) Fishing Vessel**	**1 oil engine** driving 1 FP propeller Total Power: 515kW (700hp) Niigata 6L25BX 1 x 4 Stroke 6 Cy. 250 x 320 515kW (700bhp) Niigata Engineering Co Ltd-Japan
7709746 **SAL IV** - *ex* Koyo Maru No. 58 *-1990* - *ex* Koyo Maru No. 15 *-1989* - *ex* Iyo Maru No. 3 *-1987* **Sal Fishing Corp** - *Iloilo* Philippines Official number: ILO3001895	*134* 56 -		**1977-07 Tokushima Zosen K.K. — Fukuoka** Yd No: 1250 Loa 38.05 (BB) Br ex 6.96 Dght 2.450 Lbp 31.40 Br md 6.95 Dpth 2.75 Welded, 1 dk	**(B11B2FV) Fishing Vessel**	**1 oil engine** driving 1 FP propeller Total Power: 809kW (1,100hp) Niigata 6L25BX 1 x 4 Stroke 6 Cy. 250 x 320 809kW (1100bhp) Niigata Engineering Co Ltd-Japan

7823700 - -	**SAL NUEVE** *ex* Koyo Maru No. 11 *-1991* *ex* Koyo Maru No. 15 *-1990* *ex* Koyo Maru No. 18 *-1989* *ex* Koyo Maru No. 8 *-1984* **Sal Fishing Corp** - *Iloilo* *Philippines* Official number: ILO3001380	*134* 56 -		**1978-12 Sanuki Shipbuilding & Iron Works Co Ltd — Mitoyo KG** Yd No: 1007 Loa - Br ex - Dght - Lbp 31.58 Br md 6.95 Dpth 2.77 Riveted\Welded, 1 dk	**(B11B2FV) Fishing Vessel**	**1 oil engine** driving 1 FP propeller Total Power: 883kW (1,201hp) Niigata 6L28BX 1 x 4 Stroke 6 Cy. 280 x 320 883kW (1201bhp) Niigata Engineering Co Ltd-Japan
7608198 *DUG6004* -	**SAL ONSE** *ex* Ebisu Maru No. 5 *-1994* **Sal Fishing Corp** - *Iloilo* *Philippines* Official number: ILO3002032	*136* 41 -		**1976-05 Nagasaki Zosen K.K. — Nagasaki** Yd No: 566 Loa 35.56 Br ex 6.33 Dght 2.401 Lbp 29.29 Br md 6.30 Dpth 2.80 Welded, 1 dk	**(B11B2FV) Fishing Vessel**	**1 oil engine** driving 1 FP propeller Total Power: 515kW (700hp) Niigata 6L25BX 1 x 4 Stroke 6 Cy. 250 x 320 515kW (700bhp) Niigata Engineering Co Ltd-Japan
8029117 - -	**SAL QUINCE** *ex* Myojin Maru No. 71 *-1992* **Euthynnus Venture Corp** - *Iloilo* *Philippines* Official number: ILO3000977	*200* 72 -		**1981-03 K.K. Murakami Zosensho — Ishinomaki** Yd No: 1065 L reg 31.30 Br ex - Dght - Lbp 30.66 Br md 7.04 Dpth 2.80 Welded, 1 dk	**(B11B2FV) Fishing Vessel**	**1 oil engine** driving 1 FP propeller Total Power: 754kW (1,025hp) Yanmar 6ZL-DT 1 x 4 Stroke 6 Cy. 280 x 340 754kW (1025bhp) Yanmar Diesel Engine Co Ltd-Japan
6908826 *D4FJ* -	**SAL-REI** *ex* Dugvan *-2006* *ex* Schleswig Holstein *-1985* **Sociedad de Transportes Maritimos Ltda (STM)** - *Sao Vicente* *Cape Verde* MMSI: 617053000 Official number: 617053000	**1,581** 474 244	Class: (LR) (GL) Classed LR until 6/6/07	**1969-04 D.W. Kremer Sohn — Elmshorn** Yd No: 1136 Loa 61.73 Br ex 11.54 Dght 4.020 Lbp 54.00 Br md 11.50 Dpth 9.90 Welded, 1 dk	**(A36A2PR) Passenger/Ro-Ro Ship (Vehicles)** Passengers: unberthed: 400 Bow door & ramp	**2 oil engines** dr geared to sc. shafts driving 2 CP propellers Total Power: 1,988kW (2,702hp) 15.0kn MaK 8M331AK 2 x 4 Stroke 8 Cy. 240 x 330 each-994kW (1351bhp) Atlas MaK Maschinenbau GmbH-Kiel AuxGen: 2 x 175kW 280V 50Hz a.c Thrusters: 1 Thwart. FP thruster (f)
9092575 *DUG6264* -	**SAL VIENTE CUATRO** *ex* Kyoei Maru No. 38 *-1993* **Sal Fishing Corp** - *Iloilo* *Philippines* Official number: ILO3000596	**185** 101 -		**1973-07 in Japan** L reg 33.01 Br ex - Dght - Lbp - Br md 6.60 Dpth 3.20 Welded, 1 dk	**(B11B2FV) Fishing Vessel**	**1 oil engine** driving 1 Propeller
7735290 - -	**SAL VIENTE DOS** *ex* Shinko Maru No. 28 *-1993* *ex* Nomura Maru No. 28 *-1989* **Sal Fishing Corp** - *Iloilo* *Philippines* Official number: ILO3000593	*155* 87 -		**1978-09 K.K. Izutsu Zosensho — Nagasaki** Yd No: 786 Loa 38.10 Br ex 7.80 Dght - Lbp 30.84 Br md 7.00 Dpth 2.82 Welded, 1 dk	**(B11B2FV) Fishing Vessel**	**1 oil engine** reduction geared to sc. shaft driving 1 FP propeller Total Power: 772kW (1,050hp) Yanmar 6Z-DT 1 x 4 Stroke 6 Cy. 280 x 340 772kW (1050bhp) Yanmar Diesel Engine Co Ltd-Japan
7706110 *DUG6285* -	**SAL VIENTE SEIS** *ex* Ebisu Maru No. 27 *-1993* **Sal Fishing Corp** - *Iloilo* *Philippines* Official number: ILO3000594	*143* 67 -		**1977-06 Nagasaki Zosen K.K. — Nagasaki** Yd No: 608 Loa 35.56 Br ex 6.35 Dght 2.401 Lbp 29.32 Br md 6.32 Dpth 2.82 Welded, 1 dk	**(B11B2FV) Fishing Vessel**	**1 oil engine** geared to sc. shaft driving 1 FP propeller Total Power: 515kW (700hp) Niigata 6L25BX 1 x 4 Stroke 6 Cy. 250 x 320 515kW (700bhp) Niigata Engineering Co Ltd-Japan
7380174 *DUG6306* -	**SAL VIII** *ex* Kotobuki Maru No. 28 *-1986* *ex* Kotobuki Maru No. 37 *-1983* **Sal Fishing Corp** - *Iloilo* *Philippines* Official number: ILO3000976	*142* 49 -		**1974-03 Niigata Engineering Co Ltd — Niigata NI** Yd No: 1275 Loa 37.01 Br ex 6.94 Dght 2.363 Lbp 30.79 Br md 6.91 Dpth 2.80 Welded, 1 dk	**(B11B2FV) Fishing Vessel**	**1 oil engine** driving 1 FP propeller Total Power: 838kW (1,139hp) Niigata 8L25BX 1 x 4 Stroke 8 Cy. 250 x 320 838kW (1139bhp) Niigata Engineering Co Ltd-Japan
7038044 - -	**SALACA** *ex* Stepan Kozak *-1991* - -	**666** 205 310	Class: (RS)	**1968 Zavod "Leninskaya Kuznitsa" — Kiyev** Yd No: 1294 Loa 54.23 Br ex 9.38 Dght 4.200 Lbp 49.99 Br md 9.30 Dpth 4.75 Welded, 1 dk	**(B11A2FT) Trawler** Ins: 290 Compartments: 2 Ho, ER 2 Ha: 2 (1.5 x 1.6) Derricks: 1x2t,1x1.5t; Winches: 2 Ice Capable	**1 oil engine** driving 1 CP propeller Total Power: 588kW (799hp) 12.0kn S.K.L. 8NVD48AU 1 x 4 Stroke 8 Cy. 320 x 480 588kW (799bhp) VEB Schwermaschinenbau "KarlLiebknecht" (SKL)-Magdeburg AuxGen: 3 x 88kW Fuel: 163.0 (d.f.)
6601806 *TC5460* -	**SALACAK** **Izmir Buyuksehir Belediye Baskanligi** Izmir Deniz Isletmeciligi Nakliye ve Turizm Ticaret AS (Izdeniz AS) *Izmir* *Turkey* MMSI: 271001245 Official number: 3665	*900* 265 -	Class: (LR) (TL) ✠ Classed LR until 5/1/79	**1966-07 Denizcilik Bankasi T.A.O. — Camialti, Istanbul** Yd No: 138 Loa 58.20 Br ex 17.00 Dght 3.000 Lbp 53.00 Br md 14.52 Dpth 4.23 Welded, 1 dk	**(A36A2PR) Passenger/Ro-Ro Ship (Vehicles)**	**2 oil engines** sr geared to sc. shaft driving 2 Propellers aft, 1 fwd Total Power: 764kW (1,038hp) 9.0kn Fiat B300.6L 2 x 4 Stroke 6 Cy. 300 x 450 each-382kW (519bhp) (made 1957, fitted 1966) SA Fiat SGM-Torino AuxGen: 3 x 30kW 220V d.c
9055931 *3FBM4* -	**SALACAK** *ex* Philipos *-2011* *ex* SCM Alexander *-2005* *ex* SCM Tocoma *-2002* *ex* Marcorsar *-2002* *ex* Torben *-2001* *ex* Zim Venezuela I *-1998* *ex* Torben *-1998* **Salacak Shipping Inc** Statu Gemi Kiralama ve Ticaret Ltd Sti (Statu Chartering & Shipping Agency Ltd) *Panama* *Panama* MMSI: 373532000 Official number: 4429012	**7,708** 3,571 9,457 T/cm 20.0	Class: BV (LR) (GL) ✠ Classed LR until 24/2/99	**1993-11 Varna Shipyard AD — Varna** Yd No: 276 Loa 126.08 (BB) Br ex 20.04 Dght 8.080 Lbp 114.45 Br md 20.00 Dpth 10.40 Welded, 1 dk	**(A31A2GX) General Cargo Ship** Grain: 11,960; Bale: 11,220 TEU 518 incl 30 ref C. Compartments: 3 Ho, ER 3 Ha: (12.8 x 9.0)2 (25.5 x 15.5)ER Cranes: 2x40t Ice Capable	**1 oil engine** driving 1 FP propeller Total Power: 4,480kW (6,091hp) 13.8kn B&W 8L35MC 1 x 2 Stroke 8 Cy. 350 x 1050 4480kW (6091bhp) H Cegielski Poznan SA-Poland AuxGen: 1 x 520kW 220/440V 50Hz a.c, 2 x 400kW 220/440V 50Hz a.c
9323390 *V7LO6* -	**SALACGRIVA** **Straupe Navigation Inc** Latvian Shipping Co (Latvijas Kugnieciba) *Majuro* *Marshall Islands* MMSI: 538002778 Official number: 2778	**30,641** 15,320 52,620 T/cm 56.8	Class: LR (NV) **100A1** SS 07/2013 Double Hull oil and chemical tanker, Ship Type 2 ESP LI *IWS SPM Ice Class 1B at a maximum draught of 12.798m Max/min draughts fwd 12.798/5.918m Max/min draughts aft 13.088/7.588m Minimum power required 8716kw, installed power 9650kw **LMC** **UMS IGS**	**2008-07 '3 Maj' Brodogradiliste dd — Rijeka** Yd No: 703 Loa 195.17 (BB) Br ex 32.24 Dght 12.518 Lbp 187.30 Br md 32.20 Dpth 17.80 Welded, 1 dk	**(A12B2TR) Chemical/Products Tanker** Double Hull (13F) Liq: 56,190; Liq (Oil): 57,330 Compartments: 12 Wing Ta, 2 Wing Slop Ta, ER 12 Cargo Pump (s): 12x550m³/hr Manifold: Bow/CM: 97.1m Ice Capable	**1 oil engine** driving 1 FP propeller Total Power: 9,650kW (13,120hp) 14.0kn Wartsila 7RTA48T 1 x 2 Stroke 7 Cy. 480 x 2000 9650kW (13120bhp) '3 Maj' Motori i Dizalice dd-Croatia AuxGen: 3 x 960kW 450V 60Hz a.c Fuel: 190.0 (d.f.) 1590.0 (r.f.)
7731414 *3VJA* -	**SALACTA** **Direction des Peches** - *Mahdia* *Tunisia*	*193* 67 -	Class: (NV)	**1977 Egyptian Shipbuilding & Repairs Co. — Alexandria** Yd No: 1/75 Loa 25.02 Br ex 7.01 Dght - Lbp 21.52 Br md - Dpth 3.51 Welded, 1 dk	**(B11B2FV) Fishing Vessel**	**1 oil engine** driving 1 FP propeller Total Power: 441kW (600hp) Baudouin DVX12 1 x Vee 4 Stroke 12 Cy. 185 x 200 441kW (600bhp) Societe des Moteurs Baudouin SA-France
8301474 *5AOU* -	**SALADIN** **Zueitina Oil Co** - *Tripoli* *Libya*	*504* 36 516	Class: (LR) (GL) ✠ Classed LR until 30/11/96	**1983-08 Matsuura Tekko Zosen K.K. — Osakikamijima** Yd No: 296 Loa 43.52 Br ex 10.75 Dght 4.645 Lbp 37.01 Br md 10.51 Dpth 5.01 Welded, 1 dk	**(B32A2ST) Tug**	**2 oil engines** with clutches, flexible couplings & dr reverse geared to sc. shafts driving 2 FP propellers Total Power: 3,384kW (4,600hp) Daihatsu 8DSM-26 2 x 4 Stroke 8 Cy. 260 x 320 each-1692kW (2300bhp) Daihatsu Diesel Manufacturing Co Lt-Japan AuxGen: 2 x 144kW 445V 60Hz a.c Thrusters: 1 Thwart. FP thruster (f) Fuel: 315.0 (d.f.)

7639616 *9LD2150* -	**SALAH ALDEEN 2** *ex* Captain Joy *-2012* *ex* Porthos *-2007* *ex* Thor *-1996* *ex* Flensburger Flagge *-1995* *ex* Bremer Flagge *-1995* *ex* Schwinge *-1977* **Alsali Livestock Co** Mina Group Shipping Ltd *Freetown* *Sierra Leone* MMSI: 667651000 Official number: SL100651	**2,351** 925 2,378	Class: DR (RS) (GL)	**1977-09 Nitchitsu Co. Ltd. — Matsuura** Yd No: 013 Loa 86.52 (BB) Br ex 13.03 Dght 4.860 Lbp 77.02 Br md 13.01 Dpth 4.98 Welded, 2 dks	**(A31A2GX) General Cargo Ship** Grain: 4,750; Bale: 4,623 TEU 140 C. 140/20' incl. 15 ref C. Compartments: 1 Ho, ER 1 Ha: (50.3 x 10.2)ER Ice Capable	**1 oil engine** reduction geared to sc. shaft driving 1 FP propeller Total Power: 1,545kW (2,101hp) 12.5kn MaK 6M453AK 1 x 4 Stroke 6 Cy. 320 x 420 1545kW (2101bhp) MaK Maschinenbau GmbH-Kiel AuxGen: 1 x 220kW Thrusters: 1 Tunnel thruster (f)
9163908 - -	**SALAH EDDINE** **Lattakia General Port Co** - *Syria*	**135** 40 68	Class: (LR) ✠ Classed LR until 25/09//04	**2003-06 DD Brodogradiliste Brodotehnika — Belgrade** (Hull) **2003-06 B.V. Scheepswerf Damen — Gorinchem** Yd No: 506538 Loa 22.58 Br ex 7.45 Dght 3.180 Lbp 19.82 Br md 7.20 Dpth 3.74 Welded, 1 dk	**(B32A2ST) Tug**	**2 oil engines** with clutches, flexible couplings & sr reverse geared to sc. shafts driving 2 FP propellers Total Power: 1,566kW (2,130hp) 10.0kn Caterpillar 3508B 2 x Vee 4 Stroke 8 Cy. 170 x 190 each-783kW (1065bhp) Caterpillar Inc-USA AuxGen: 2 x 50kW 380V 50Hz a.c Fuel: 30.0 (d.f.)
7530925 *SUZX* -	**SALAH ELDEAN EL AYOBY** **Suez Canal Authority** *Port Said* *Egypt* MMSI: 622123210	*7,689* 4,164 10,953	Class: BV	**1977-03 Mitsubishi Heavy Industries Ltd. — Hiroshima** Yd No: 280 Loa 119.92 Br ex 19.64 Dght 7.902 Lbp 113.01 Br md 19.61 Dpth 10.52 Welded, 1 dk	**(B33B2DT) Trailing Suction Hopper Dredger** Hopper: 6,328	**2 oil engines** geared to sc. shafts driving 2 CP propellers Total Power: 7,356kW (10,002hp) 14.0kn Pielstick 12PC2-2V-400 2 x Vee 4 Stroke 12 Cy. 400 x 460 each-3678kW (5001bhp) Niigata Engineering Co Ltd-Japan AuxGen: 3 x 595kW, 1 x 250kW Thrusters: 1 Thwart. FP thruster (f)
7943249 - -	**SALAIR** **OOO 'Samotlor-Ryba'** -	**739** 221 332	Class: (RS)	**1981-07 Zavod "Leninskaya Kuznitsa" — Kiyev** Yd No: 250 Loa 53.75 (BB) Br ex 10.72 Dght 4.290 Lbp 47.92 Br md - Dpth 6.00 Welded, 1 dk	**(B11A2FS) Stern Trawler** Ins: 218 Compartments: 1 Ho, ER 1 Ha: (1.6 x 1.6) Derricks: 2x1.5t Ice Capable	**1 oil engine** driving 1 CP propeller Total Power: 971kW (1,320hp) 12.6kn S.K.L. 8NVD48A-2U 1 x 4 Stroke 8 Cy. 320 x 480 971kW (1320bhp) VEB Schwermaschinenbau "KarlLiebknecht" (SKL)-Magdeburg AuxGen: 1 x 300kW, 3 x 160kW Fuel: 168.0 (d.f.)
9321079 *A4DG6* -	**SALALAH** **Salalah Port Services** - *Salalah* *Oman*	**246** 73 90	Class: LR ✠ **100A1** SS 03/2010 tug *IWS ✠ **LMC** Eq.Ltr: E; Cable: 330.0/22.0 U2 (a)	**2005-03 Keppel Batangas Shipyard Inc — Bauan** Yd No: H80 Loa 27.90 Br ex 9.58 Dght 3.800 Lbp 23.33 Br md 9.00 Dpth 4.70 Welded, 1 dk	**(B32A2ST) Tug**	**2 oil engines** gearing integral to driving 2 Z propellers Total Power: 2,646kW (3,598hp) 12.0kn Niigata 6L25HX 2 x 4 Stroke 6 Cy. 250 x 350 each-1323kW (1799bhp) Niigata Engineering Co Ltd-Japan AuxGen: 2 x 95kW 380V 50Hz a.c
9300817 *3EDE9* -	**SALALAH LNG** **Tiwi LNG Carrier SA** Oman Ship Management Co SAOC SatCom: Inmarsat C 437156110 *Panama* *Panama* MMSI: 371561000 Official number: 3155106A	**96,671** 29,001 81,034	Class: NK (AB)	**2005-12 Samsung Heavy Industries Co Ltd — Geoje** Yd No: 1536 Loa 285.10 (BB) Br ex - Dght 12.120 Lbp 272.04 Br md 43.40 Dpth 26.00 Welded, 1 dk	**(A11A2TN) LNG Tanker** Liq (Gas): 148,174 5 x Gas Tank (s); 4 membrane (s.stl) pri horizontal, ER 8 Cargo Pump (s): 8x1750m³/hr	**1 Steam Turb** reduction geared to sc. shaft driving 1 FP propeller Total Power: 27,066kW (36,799hp) 19.5kn Kawasaki UA-400 1 x steam Turb 27066kW (36799shp) Kawasaki Heavy Industries Ltd-Japan AuxGen: 2 x 3750kW 6600/220V 60Hz a.c, 1 x 3750kW 6600/220V 60Hz a.c Thrusters: 1 Tunnel thruster (f) Fuel: 8060.0
9569645 *5IXP01* -	**SALALEH** *ex* Songbird *-2013* **NITC** - *Zanzibar* *Tanzania (Zanzibar)* MMSI: 677010000	**164,680** 108,000 318,000 T/cm 181.2	Class: (LR) ✠ Classed LR until 23/4/13	**2013-04 Shanghai Waigaoqiao Shipbuilding Co Ltd — Shanghai** Yd No: 1224 Loa 333.00 (BB) Br ex 60.05 Dght 22.640 Lbp 320.00 Br md 60.00 Dpth 30.50 Welded, 1 dk	**(A13A2TV) Crude Oil Tanker** Double Hull (13F) Liq: 334,900; Liq (Oil): 334,900 Cargo Heating Coils Compartments: 5 Ta, 10 Wing Ta, ER, 2 Wing Slop Ta 3 Cargo Pump (s): 3x5500m³/hr Manifold: Bow/CM: 165.2m	**1 oil engine** driving 1 FP propeller Total Power: 31,640kW (43,018hp) 16.1kn Wartsila 7RT-flex82T 1 x 2 Stroke 7 Cy. 820 x 3375 31640kW (43018bhp) Fuel: 480.0 (d.f.) 8440.0 (r.f.)
7105110 *E3BA* -	**SALAM** *ex* West *-1990* *ex* Westfjord *-1988* **Eritrean Shipping Lines** - *Massawa* *Eritrea* MMSI: 625012000 Official number: M0002	**1,742** 1,077 2,910	Class: (HR) (GL) (NV)	**1971-05 Aukra Bruk AS — Aukra** Yd No: 38 Lengthened-1978 Loa 89.11 (BB) Br ex 13.03 Dght 4.731 Lbp 83.80 Br md 13.00 Dpth 5.69 Welded, 1 dk	**(A31A2GX) General Cargo Ship** Grain: 3,805; Bale: 3,393 Compartments: 2 Ho, ER 2 Ha: (27.6 x 7.0) (22.8 x 8.0)ER Derricks: 4x5t; Winches: 4	**1 oil engine** driving 1 FP propeller Total Power: 1,397kW (1,899hp) 12.5kn MaK 8M452AK 1 x 4 Stroke 8 Cy. 320 x 450 1397kW (1899bhp) Atlas MaK Maschinenbau GmbH-Kiel AuxGen: 1 x 195kW 220/380V a.c
7711933 - -	**SALAM 1** **Suez Canal Authority** - *Port Said* *Egypt*	*387* - 136	Class: LR ✠ **100A1** SS 12/2007 tug ✠ **LMC** Eq.Ltr: I; Cable: 330.0/24.0 U2	**1978-06 B.V. Scheepswerven v/h H.H. Bodewes — Millingen a/d Rijn** Yd No: 738 Loa 35.41 Br ex 11.64 Dght 4.998 Lbp 33.63 Br md 11.00 Dpth 4.02 Welded, 1 dk	**(B32A2ST) Tug**	**2 oil engines** gearing integral to driving 2 Voith-Schneider propellers Total Power: 2,942kW (4,000hp) M.T.U. 16V652TB61 1 x Vee 4 Stroke 16 Cy. 190 x 230 1471kW (2000bhp) MTU Friedrichshafen GmbH-Friedrichshafen M.T.U. 16V652TB61 1 x Vee 4 Stroke 16 Cy. 190 x 230 1471kW (2000bhp) (new engine 2005, fitted 2005) MTU Friedrichshafen GmbH-Friedrichshafen AuxGen: 3 x 147kW 400V 50Hz a.c
7711945 - -	**SALAM 2** **Suez Canal Authority** - *Port Said* *Egypt*	*387* - 136	Class: LR ✠ **100A1** SS 10/2009 tug ✠ **LMC** Eq.Ltr: I; Cable: 330.0/24.0 U2	**1978-07 B.V. Scheepswerven v/h H.H. Bodewes — Millingen a/d Rijn** Yd No: 739 Loa 35.41 Br ex 11.64 Dght 4.998 Lbp 33.63 Br md 11.02 Dpth 4.04 Welded, 1 dk	**(B32A2ST) Tug**	**2 oil engines** gearing integral to driving 2 Voith-Schneider propellers Total Power: 2,942kW (4,000hp) M.T.U. 16V652TB61 2 x Vee 4 Stroke 16 Cy. 190 x 230 each-1471kW (2000bhp) MTU Friedrichshafen GmbH-Friedrichshafen AuxGen: 3 x 147kW 400V 50Hz a.c
7712200 - -	**SALAM 3** **Suez Canal Authority** - *Ismailia* *Egypt*	*387* 136 136	Class: LR ✠ **100A1** SS 03/2010 tug ✠ **LMC** Eq.Ltr: I; Cable: 330.0/24.0 U2	**1980-03 Timsah SB. Co. — Ismailia** Yd No: 380 Loa 35.41 Br ex - Dght 2.923 Lbp 33.63 Br md 10.99 Dpth 4.04 Welded, 1 dk	**(B32A2ST) Tug**	**2 oil engines** with flexible couplings & sr geared to sc. shafts driving 2 Voith-Schneider propellers Total Power: 2,942kW (4,000hp) M.T.U. 16V652TB61 2 x Vee 4 Stroke 16 Cy. 190 x 230 each-1471kW (2000bhp) MTU Friedrichshafen GmbH-Friedrichshafen AuxGen: 3 x 147kW 400V 50Hz a.c
7712212 - -	**SALAM 4** **Suez Canal Authority** - *Ismailia* *Egypt*	*387* 136 136	Class: (LR) ✠ Classed LR until 3/7/13	**1980-06 Timsah SB. Co. — Abu Qir, Alexandria** Yd No: 381 Loa 35.41 Br ex 11.54 Dght 2.923 Lbp 33.63 Br md 10.99 Dpth 3.99 Welded, 1 dk	**(B32A2ST) Tug**	**2 oil engines** with flexible couplings & sr gearedto sc. shafts driving 2 Voith-Schneider propellers Total Power: 2,942kW (4,000hp) M.T.U. 16V652TB61 2 x Vee 4 Stroke 16 Cy. 190 x 230 each-1471kW (2000bhp) MTU Friedrichshafen GmbH-Friedrichshafen AuxGen: 3 x 147kW 400V 50Hz a.c
9047805 *SSIP* -	**SALAM 5** **Suez Canal Authority** - *Port Said* *Egypt* MMSI: 622123208	**379** 119 136	Class: GL	**1994-04 Timsah SB. Co. — Ismailia** Yd No: 915 Loa 35.40 Br ex 11.54 Dght 3.377 Lbp 33.60 Br md 10.99 Dpth 3.99 Welded, 1 dk	**(B32A2ST) Tug**	**2 oil engines** gearing integral to driving 2 Voith-Schneider propellers Total Power: 3,676kW (4,998hp) Daihatsu 6DLM-32 2 x 4 Stroke 6 Cy. 320 x 400 each-1838kW (2499bhp) Daihatsu Diesel Manufacturing Co Lt-Japan AuxGen: 3 x 160kW a.c
9218349 *6AFJ* -	**SALAM 6** **Suez Canal Authority** - *Port Said* *Egypt* MMSI: 622123243	**459** - 450	Class: GL	**2007-06 Suez Canal Authority — Port Said** Yd No: 206 Loa 35.00 Br ex - Dght 3.780 Lbp 33.50 Br md 11.00 Dpth 4.50 Welded, 1 dk	**(B32A2ST) Tug**	**2 oil engines** geared to sc. shafts driving 2 CP propellers Total Power: 3,678kW (5,000hp) Daihatsu 8DKM-28 2 x 4 Stroke 8 Cy. 280 x 390 each-1839kW (2500bhp)

IMO / Call sign / Flag	Name / Owner / Port	GT / NT / DWT	Class	Built / Dimensions	Type	Machinery
9429390 - -	**SALAM 7** - **Suez Canal Authority** - *Port Said* *Egypt*	**459** - 450	Class: (GL)	**2009-06 Suez Canal Authority — Port Said** Yd No: 213 Loa 35.00 Br ex - Dght 3.780 Lbp 33.50 Br md 11.00 Dpth 4.50 Welded, 1 dk	**(B32A2ST) Tug**	**2 oil engines** reduction geared to sc. shafts driving 2 Voith-Schneider propellers Total Power: 3,840kW (5,220hp) Yanmar 6EY26 2 x 4 Stroke 6 Cy. 260 x 385 each-1920kW (2610bhp) Yanmar Diesel Engine Co Ltd-Japan
9429405 *6AFM* -	**SALAM 8** - **Suez Canal Authority** - *Port Said* *Egypt*	**459** - 450	Class: (GL)	**2009-07 Suez Canal Authority — Port Said** Yd No: 216 Loa 35.00 Br ex - Dght 3.780 Lbp 33.50 Br md 11.00 Dpth 4.50 Welded, 1 dk	**(B32A2ST) Tug**	**2 oil engines** reduction geared to sc. shafts driving 2 Voith-Schneider propellers Total Power: 3,032kW (4,122hp) Niigata 8L28HLX 2 x 4 Stroke 8 Cy. 280 x 400 each-1516kW (2061bhp) Niigata Engineering Co Ltd-Japan
9429417 - -	**SALAM 9** - **Suez Canal Authority** - *Port Said* *Egypt* MMSI: 622123000	**459** - 450	Class: (GL)	**2010-02 Suez Canal Authority — Port Said** Yd No: 217 Loa 35.00 Br ex - Dght 3.780 Lbp 33.50 Br md 11.00 Dpth 4.50 Welded, 1 dk	**(B32A2ST) Tug**	**2 oil engines** reduction geared to sc. shafts driving 2 Voith-Schneider propellers Total Power: 3,680kW (5,004hp) Yanmar 6EY26 2 x 4 Stroke 6 Cy. 260 x 385 each-1840kW (2502bhp) Yanmar Diesel Engine Co Ltd-Japan
8022236 *A6E2283* -	**SALAM GLORY** *ex* Arab Pearl *-2011* *ex* Union Pearl *-1990* **Gulf Glory Marine Services (LLC)** Whitesea Shipping & Supply (LLC) *Abu Dhabi* *United Arab Emirates* MMSI: 470433000 Official number: 772	*906* 272 946	Class: NK	**1981-04 Yokohama Zosen — Chiba** Yd No: 1391 Loa 54.50 Br ex 12.25 Dght 3.989 Lbp 51.24 Br md 12.01 Dpth 4.60 Welded, 1 dk	**(B21B20T) Offshore Tug/Supply Ship** Grain: 113 Cranes: 1x10t	**2 oil engines** reduction geared to sc. shafts driving 2 FP propellers Total Power: 2,648kW (3,600hp) 13.0kn Fuji 6L27.5G 2 x 4 Stroke 6 Cy. 275 x 320 each-1324kW (1800bhp) Fuji Diesel Co Ltd-Japan Fuel: 255.0 (d.f.)
8102012 *YHSJ* -	**SALAM MAS** *ex* City of Dubai *-2004* *ex* Azrou *-2002* *ex* Mercandian Diplomat *-1989* *ex* Diplomat *-1985* *ex* Mercandian Diplomat *-1985* **PT Roro Samudera Putra Harmonimas** - *Tanjung Priok* *Indonesia* MMSI: 525015030 Official number: 49	**7,956** 2,655 7,194	Class: KI (BV) (NV)	**1983-09 Frederikshavn Vaerft A/S — Frederikshavn** Yd No: 404 Loa 131.71 (BB) Br ex 20.12 Dght 6.163 Lbp 126.02 Br md 19.38 Dpth 11.61 Welded, 2 dks	**(A35A2RR) Ro-Ro Cargo Ship** Stern door/ramp (centre) Len: 15.85 Wid: 7.70 Swl: 80 Side door/ramp (s. a.) Len: 12.05 Wid: 4.00 Swl: 60 Lane-Len: 1497 Trailers: 111 Bale: 14,661 TEU 414 incl 50 ref C.	**1 oil engine** with clutches, flexible couplings & sr geared to sc. shaft driving 1 CP propeller Total Power: 3,509kW (4,771hp) 15.5kn MaK 12M453AK 1 x Vee 4 Stroke 12 Cy. 320 x 420 3509kW (4771bhp) Krupp MaK Maschinenbau GmbH-Kiel AuxGen: 3 x 280kW 440V 60Hz a.c Thrusters: 1 Thwart. FP thruster (f)
9353943 *9MHR5* -	**SALAM MESRA** *ex* Kota Daya *-2008* **Malaysia Shipping Corp Sdn Bhd** Pacific International Lines (Pte) Ltd *Port Klang* *Malaysia* MMSI: 533016600 Official number: 332469	**6,245** 2,656 8,150	Class: LR ✠ **100A1** SS 10/2012 container ship LI ✠ **LMC** Cable: 550.0/50.0 U3 (a)	**2007-10 Penglai Bohai Shipyard Co Ltd — Penglai SD** Yd No: PBZ05-45 Loa 115.38 (BB) Br ex 21.40 Dght 7.000 Lbp 109.03 Br md 20.82 Dpth 9.21 Welded, 1 dk	**(A33A2CC) Container Ship (Fully Cellular)** TEU 606 C Ho 174 TEU C Dk 432 TEU incl. 60 ref C. Compartments: 3 Cell Ho, ER Cranes: 2x45t	**1 oil engine** with clutches, flexible couplings & reverse reduction geared to sc. shaft driving 1 FP propeller Total Power: 3,310kW (4,500hp) 14.0kn Yanmar 8N330-EN 1 x 4 Stroke 8 Cy. 330 x 440 3310kW (4500bhp) Yanmar Diesel Engine Co Ltd-Japan AuxGen: 3 x 450kW 450V 60Hz a.c Boilers: e (ex.g.) 11.7kgf/cm² (11.5bar), AuxB (o.f.) 8.0kgf/cm² (7.8bar) Thrusters: 1 Thwart. FP thruster (f)
8745060 - -	**SALAMA 3** - **Merna Marine Supplier Co** - *Port Said* *Egypt* Official number: 1388/B	**265** - -		**1996 Port Said Marine Shipyard — Port Said** Loa 37.35 Br ex 7.55 Dght 2.600 Lbp 34.65 Br md 7.50 Dpth 2.90 Welded, 1 dk	**(B22A2OR) Offshore Support Vessel**	**2 oil engines** reduction geared to sc. shafts driving 2 Propellers Total Power: 626kW (852hp) 9.0kn Caterpillar 2 x 4 Stroke each-313kW (426bhp) Caterpillar Inc-USA
8745113 *FI2280* -	**SALAMA DJEMA** - **Mayotte - Conseil General** Service des Transports Maritimes de Mayotte (STM) *Dzaoudzi* *France* Official number: 7505MAY	**187** - -	Class: BV	**1987-06 IMC — Tonnay-Charente** Loa 35.70 Br ex - Dght - Lbp - Br md 8.70 Dpth - Welded, 1 dk	**(A37B2PS) Passenger Ship**	**2 oil engines** reduction geared to sc. shafts driving 2 Propellers Total Power: 662kW (900hp) Baudouin 6M26SR 2 x 4 Stroke 6 Cy. 150 x 150 each-331kW (450bhp) Societe des Moteurs Baudouin SA-France
9058438 - -	**SALAMA DJEMA II** - - -	**265** 108 50	Class: BV	**1992-05 Chantiers Piriou — Concarneau** Yd No: 161 Loa 34.80 Br ex - Dght 1.700 Lbp 31.40 Br md 9.80 Dpth 2.35 Welded, 1 dk	**(A36B2PL) Passenger/Landing Craft**	**2 oil engines** sr geared to sc. shaft driving 2 Directional propellers Total Power: 662kW (900hp) 8.8kn Baudouin 6PT52 2 x 4 Stroke 6 Cy. 150 x 150 each-331kW (450bhp) Societe des Moteurs Baudouin SA-France
9113355 *FN9792* -	**SALAMA DJEMA III** - **Mayotte - Conseil General** Service des Transports Maritimes de Mayotte (STM) *Dzaoudzi* *France* MMSI: 227001300 Official number: 899054	**265** 108 138	Class: BV	**1995-06 Chantiers Piriou — Concarneau** Yd No: 174 Loa 34.80 Br ex - Dght 1.500 Lbp 30.80 Br md 9.80 Dpth 2.35 Welded, 1 dk	**(A36B2PL) Passenger/Landing Craft** Passengers: unberthed: 597 Lane-Len: 36 Lane-Wid: 2.50 Cars: 11	**2 oil engines** reduction geared to sc. shafts driving 2 Directional propellers Total Power: 662kW (900hp) 8.0kn Baudouin 6M26SR 2 x 4 Stroke 6 Cy. 150 x 150 each-331kW (450bhp) Societe des Moteurs Baudouin SA-France Fuel: 14.7 (d.f.) 0.5pd
9210127 *FW9788* -	**SALAMA DJEMA IV** - **Mayotte - Conseil General** Service des Transports Maritimes de Mayotte (STM) *Dzaoudzi* *France* MMSI: 228132900 Official number: 911301	**265** 108 30	Class: BV	**1999-09 Chantiers Piriou — Concarneau** Yd No: 202 Loa 34.80 Br ex - Dght 1.600 Lbp 31.40 Br md 9.80 Dpth 2.35 Welded, 1 dk	**(A36B2PL) Passenger/Landing Craft** Passengers: unberthed: 329	**2 oil engines** reduction geared to sc. shafts driving 2 Directional propellers Total Power: 662kW (900hp) 8.5kn Baudouin 6M26SR 2 x 4 Stroke 6 Cy. 150 x 150 each-331kW (450bhp) Societe des Moteurs Baudouin SA-France AuxGen: 2 x 5kW 24V d.c
8204494 *9V5763* -	**SALAMAH** *ex* Sansha Maru No. 1 *-1999* **Sirius Maritime Pte Ltd** Sirius Marine Pte Ltd *Singapore* *Singapore* MMSI: 563005190 Official number: 388517	**458** 178 690	Class: GL	**1983-03 K.K. Odo Zosen Tekko — Shimonoseki** Yd No: 288 Loa 52.91 Br ex - Dght 3.431 Lbp 48.52 Br md 9.40 Dpth 3.51 Welded, 1 dk	**(A13B2TP) Products Tanker** Double Bottom Entire Compartment Length Liq: 694; Liq (Oil): 694 Compartments: 8 Ta, ER	**1 oil engine** reverse reduction geared to sc. shaft driving 1 FP propeller Total Power: 736kW (1,001hp) 10.0kn Niigata 6M26AGT 1 x 4 Stroke 6 Cy. 260 x 460 736kW (1001bhp) Niigata Engineering Co Ltd-Japan AuxGen: 1 x 64kW a.c
8981767 *XUCZ8* -	**SALAMANDRA** *ex* Erdemler III *-2004* **Comvilla Corp** - *Phnom Penh* *Cambodia* MMSI: 515574000 Official number: 0499063	**190** 57 -		**1999-01 Ustaoglu Yat ve Gemi Sanayi Ticaret Ltd Sti — Karadeniz Eregli** Loa 29.15 Br ex - Dght - Lbp 26.85 Br md 7.50 Dpth 2.25 Welded, 1 dk	**(A37B2PS) Passenger Ship**	**2 oil engines** geared to sc. shafts driving 2 Propellers Total Power: 588kW (800hp) Iveco Aifo 8280-38 2 x Vee 4 Stroke 8 Cy. 145 x 130 each-294kW (400bhp) IVECO AIFO S.p.A.-Pregnana Milanese
9546875 *D6EW5* -	**SALAMANDRA** - **Intracoastal Trading Services SA** - *Moroni* *Union of Comoros* MMSI: 616753000 Official number: 1200880	**2,800** 1,400 1,000		**2009-06 Linhai Hangchang Shipbuilding Co Ltd — Linhai ZJ** Yd No: HC0703 Loa 91.45 Br ex - Dght 3.700 Lbp 78.72 Br md 14.70 Dpth 8.80 Welded, 1 dk	**(A35A2RR) Ro-Ro Cargo Ship** Stern door/ramp (centre)	**2 oil engines** reduction geared to sc. shafts driving 2 Propellers Total Power: 3,372kW (4,584hp) Caterpillar 3516B-HD 2 x Vee 4 Stroke 16 Cy. 170 x 215 each-1686kW (2292bhp) Caterpillar Inc-USA
6908814 - -	**SALAMANZA** - **Companhia de Pesca e Congelacao de Cabo Verde Lda** -	*361* 167 335	Class: (GL)	**1968 AG Weser, Werk Seebeck — Bremerhaven** Yd No: 931 Loa 38.79 Br ex 9.35 Dght 4.198 Lbp 34.24 Br md 9.30 Dpth 4.40 Welded, 1 dk	**(B11B2FV) Fishing Vessel** Compartments: 4 Ho, ER 4 Ha: Derricks: 1x10t,1x2t	**1 oil engine** driving 1 FP propeller Total Power: 736kW (1,001hp) 11.5kn Deutz RBV6M545 1 x 4 Stroke 6 Cy. 320 x 450 736kW (1001bhp) Kloeckner Humboldt Deutz AG-West Germany

Ship	Tonnage	Classification	Build / Dimensions	Type / Cargo	Machinery
9382968 **SALAMINA** *A8RM7* *launched as* Salamis *-2009* - **Dorsett Shipping Corp** Tsakos Columbia Shipmanagement (TCM) SA *Monrovia* *Liberia* MMSI: 636014128 Official number: 14128	**41,676** 21,792 74,251 T/cm 67.2	Class: AB	**2009**-02 **Sungdong Shipbuilding & Marine Engineering Co Ltd — Tongyeong** Yd No: 3016 Loa 228.00 (BB) Br ex 32.56 Dght 14.317 Lbp 219.00 Br md 32.24 Dpth 20.60 Welded, 1 dk	**(A13A2TW) Crude/Oil Products Tanker** Double Hull (13F) Liq: 78,928; Liq (Oil): 83,104 Cargo Heating Coils Compartments: 12 Wing Ta, 2 Wing Slop Ta, ER 3 Cargo Pump (s): 3x2000m³/hr Manifold: Bow/CM: 113.1m	**1 oil engine** driving 1 FP propeller Total Power: 12,240kW (16,642hp) 15.3kn MAN-B&W 6S60MC 1 x 2 Stroke 6 Cy. 600 x 2292 12240kW (16642bhp) STX Engine Co Ltd-South Korea AuxGen: 3 x 680kW a.c Fuel: 122.0 (d.f.) 2138.0 (r.f.)
9567245 **SALAMINA 1** *H9QB* *ex* Salamina *-2013* - **Baupres Shipping Lda** Navesco SA *Panama* *Panama* MMSI: 356701000 Official number: 44307PEXT	**4,951** 2,384 7,850	Class: BV	**2010**-10 **Astilleros de Murueta S.A. — Gernika-Lumo** Yd No: 288 Loa 118.79 (BB) Br ex - Dght 7.060 Lbp 112.45 Br md 15.30 Dpth 9.85 Welded, 1 dk	**(A31A2GX) General Cargo Ship** Grain: 9,342 TEU 270 C Ho 153 TEU C Dk 117 TEU Compartments: 2 Ho, ER 2 Ha: (54.0 x 12.7)ER (27.8 x 12.7) Cranes: 2x40t	**1 oil engine** reduction geared to sc. shaft driving 1 CP propeller Total Power: 4,000kW (5,438hp) 12.5kn Wartsila 8L32 1 x 4 Stroke 8 Cy. 320 x 400 4000kW (5438bhp) Wartsila Diesel S.A.-Bermeo AuxGen: 3 x 256kW 400V a.c, 1 x 348kW 400V a.c Thrusters: 1 Tunnel thruster (f) Fuel: 90.0 (d.f.) 550.0 (r.f.)
9233399 **SALAMINIA** *C6WU7* *ex* Maine *-2008* *ex* Lake Maine *-2008* - **Salaminia Shipping Inc** Petrofin Ship Management Inc *Nassau* *Bahamas* MMSI: 311577000 Official number: 8001465	**29,963** 18,486 53,531	Class: NK	**2001**-04 **Imabari Shipbuilding Co Ltd — Marugame KG (Marugame Shipyard)** Yd No: 1355 Loa 189.94 (BB) Br ex - Dght 12.300 Lbp 182.00 Br md 32.26 Dpth 17.30 Welded, 1 dk	**(A21A2BC) Bulk Carrier** Double Bottom Entire Compartment Length Grain: 68,927 Cargo Heating Coils Compartments: 5 Ho, ER 5 Ha: 5 (21.1 x 17.6)ER Cranes: 4x30.5t	**1 oil engine** driving 1 FP propeller Total Power: 9,481kW (12,890hp) 15.0kn B&W 6S50MC-C 1 x 2 Stroke 6 Cy. 500 x 2000 9481kW (12890bhp) Mitsui Engineering & Shipbuilding CLtd-Japan AuxGen: 3 x 440kW 110/440V 60Hz a.c Fuel: 147.5 (d.f.) (Heating Coils) 2041.9 (r.f.) 35.0pd
8998916 **SALAMINIA II** - - - -	**941** 489 942		**2004**-07 **in Greece** Loa 88.40 Br ex - Dght 2.400 Lbp 77.06 Br md 17.50 Dpth 3.40 Welded, 1 dk	**(A36A2PR) Passenger/Ro-Ro Ship (Vehicles)** Passengers: unberthed: 1264 Bow door/ramp (f) Stern door/ramp (a) Lane-clr ht: 5.05 Cars: 125	**4 oil engines** reduction geared to sc. shafts driving 4 FP propellers Total Power: 1,796kW (2,440hp) 12.0kn Caterpillar 3412 4 x Vee 4 Stroke 12 Cy. 137 x 152 each-449kW (610bhp) Caterpillar Inc-USA
8647804 **SALAMINOMACHOS** *SVA2209* - **Kyxreas Shipping Co** Koinopraxia Epivatochimatagogon Salaminos *Piraeus* *Greece* MMSI: 239414100 Official number: 11593	**996** 639 -		**2008 in Greece** Loa 100.60 Br ex - Dght - Lbp - Br md 18.80 Dpth - Welded, 1 dk	**(A36A2PR) Passenger/Ro-Ro Ship (Vehicles)**	**4 oil engines** reduction geared to sc. shafts driving 4 Propellers
9165281 **SALAMIS** *C6XD2* *ex* Overseas Aquamar *-2008* *ex* Aquamar *-2005* - *ex* Alam Berkat *-2002* **Salamis Trading SA** World Tankers Management Pte Ltd *Nassau* *Bahamas* MMSI: 311005100 Official number: 8001511	**28,400** 12,385 47,236 T/cm 50.3	Class: AB	**1998**-03 **Onomichi Dockyard Co Ltd — Onomichi HS** Yd No: 428 Loa 182.50 (BB) Br ex 32.23 Dght 12.666 Lbp 172.00 Br md 32.20 Dpth 19.10 Welded, 1 dk	**(A13B2TP) Products Tanker** Double Hull (13F) Liq: 50,335; Liq (Oil): 50,335 Cargo Heating Coils Compartments: 2 Ta, 12 Wing Ta, 2 Wing Slop Ta, ER 4 Cargo Pump (s): 4x1000m³/hr Manifold: Bow/CM: 92.9m	**1 oil engine** driving 1 FP propeller Total Power: 8,562kW (11,641hp) 15.3kn MAN-B&W 6S50MC 1 x 2 Stroke 6 Cy. 500 x 1910 8562kW (11641bhp) Mitsui Engineering & Shipbuilding CLtd-Japan AuxGen: 3 x 420kW 450V 60Hz a.c Fuel: 111.8 (d.f.) (Heating Coils) 1409.6 (r.f.) 48.0pd
9188776 **SALAMIS** *A8QS5* *ex* Vinashin Energy *-2008* *ex* Isere *-2006* - **Lavender Maritime Co** Mantinia Shipping Co SA *Monrovia* *Liberia* MMSI: 636013993 Official number: 13993	**22,848** 9,242 35,437 T/cm 43.8	Class: NV	**1999**-09 **Daewoo Heavy Industries Ltd — Geoje** Yd No: 5144 Converted From: Chemical/Products Tanker-1999 Loa 184.60 (BB) Br ex 27.48 Dght 11.016 Lbp 176.00 Br md 27.40 Dpth 17.00 Welded, 1 dk	**(A13B2TP) Products Tanker** Double Hull (13F) Liq: 40,330; Liq (Oil): 40,330 Part Cargo Heating Coils Compartments: 12 Wing Ta, 2 Wing Slop Ta, ER 14 Cargo Pump (s): 12x550m³/hr, 2x300m³/hr Manifold: Bow/CM: 88.2m	**1 oil engine** driving 1 FP propeller Total Power: 8,562kW (11,641hp) 15.0kn MAN-B&W 6S50MC 1 x 2 Stroke 6 Cy. 500 x 1910 8562kW (11641bhp) Korea Heavy Industries & ConstrCo Ltd (HANJUNG)-South Korea AuxGen: 3 x 800kW 440V 60Hz a.c Fuel: 86.0 (d.f.) 1114.0 (r.f.)
7359400 **SALAMIS FILOXENIA** *5BUY2* *ex* Van Gogh *-2009* *ex* Club 1 *-1999* - *ex* Club Cruise I *-1999* *ex* Odessa Sky *-1998* *ex* Gruziya *-1995* **Mana Shipping Co Ltd** Salamis Lines Ltd *Limassol* *Cyprus* MMSI: 209167000	**15,402** 6,057 3,000	Class: NV (RS)	**1975**-06 **Oy Wartsila Ab — Turku** Yd No: 1213 Converted From: Ferry (Passenger/Vehicle)-1992 Loa 156.27 (BB) Br ex 22.05 Dght 5.920 Lbp 134.02 Br md 22.00 Dpth 16.31 Welded, 3 dks	**(A37A2PC) Passenger/Cruise** Passengers: cabins: 250; berths: 795 Ice Capable	**2 oil engines** driving 2 CP propellers Total Power: 13,240kW (18,002hp) 22.0kn Pielstick 18PC2-2V-400 2 x Vee 4 Stroke 18 Cy. 400 x 460 each-6620kW (9001bhp) Oy Wartsila Ab-Finland AuxGen: 4 x 912kW 400V 50Hz a.c, 1 x 168kW 400V 50Hz a.c Thrusters: 1 Thwart. FP thruster (f)
7742138 **SALAMMBO** - *ex* De Steiguer *-1992* - **Government of The Republic of Tunisia** *Tunisia*	*1,143* 397 255	Class: (AB)	**1969**-03 **Northwest Marine Iron Works — Portland, Or** Yd No: 53 Loa 63.51 Br ex 11.89 Dght 4.966 Lbp 58.32 Br md 11.36 Dpth 6.58 Welded, 1 dk	**(B31A2SR) Research Survey Vessel**	**2 diesel electric oil engines** driving 1 FP propeller Total Power: 978kW (1,330hp) 10.0kn Caterpillar D398TA 2 x Vee 4 Stroke 12 Cy. 159 x 203 each-489kW (665bhp) Caterpillar Tractor Co-USA AuxGen: 3 x 200kW Thrusters: 1 Thwart. FP thruster (f)
9142461 **SALAMMBO 7** *TSMS* - **Compagnie Tunisienne de Navigation SA (COTUNAV)** - SatCom: Inmarsat B 367224710 *La Goulette* *Tunisia* MMSI: 672247000 Official number: TG846	**17,907** 5,372 5,914 T/cm 32.6	Class: BV	**1997**-09 **SSW Faehr- und Spezialschiffbau GmbH — Bremerhaven** Yd No: 1094 Loa 161.43 (BB) Br ex 25.82 Dght 6.018 Lbp 146.11 Br md 25.80 Dpth 14.20 Welded, 3 dks, incl. 1 hoistable dk.	**(A36A2PR) Passenger/Ro-Ro Ship (Vehicles)** Passengers: cabins: 50; berths: 100; driver berths: 100 Stern door/ramp Len: 12.00 Wid: 11.60 Swl: 132 Lane-Len: 1950 Trailers: 150 Ice Capable	**4 oil engines** with clutches, flexible couplings & sr geared to sc. shafts driving 2 CP propellers Total Power: 14,000kW (19,036hp) 20.0kn Sulzer 6ZAL40S 4 x 4 Stroke 6 Cy. 400 x 560 each-3500kW (4759bhp) Zaklady Urzadzen Technicznych'Zgoda' SA-Poland AuxGen: 2 x 650kW 230/400V 50Hz a.c, 2 x 1248kW 230/400V 50Hz a.c Thrusters: 2 Thwart. CP thruster (f) Fuel: 247.6 (d.f.) (Heating Coils) 997.2 (r.f.) 56.0pd
9185786 **SALANDI** *3FEB9* *ex* World Rye *-2004* - **Sailing Cruise Inc** Capital Management Services SA (CMS) SatCom: Inmarsat C 435725210 *Panama* *Panama* MMSI: 357252000 Official number: 2616299CH	**38,852** 24,517 74,502 T/cm 67.0	Class: LR (NK) **100A1** SS 03/2009 bulk carrier strengthened for heavy cargoes, Nos. 2, 4 & 6 holds may be empty ESP ESN-Hold 1 **LMC** **UMS** Eq.Ltr: P†; Cable: 660.0/78.0 U3 (a)	**1999**-03 **Sasebo Heavy Industries Co. Ltd. — Sasebo Yard, Sasebo** Yd No: 448 Loa 225.00 (BB) Br ex - Dght 13.821 Lbp 218.00 Br md 32.20 Dpth 19.20 Welded, 1 dk	**(A21A2BC) Bulk Carrier** Grain: 87,590 Compartments: 7 Ho, ER 7 Ha: (15.3 x 12.8)6 (17.0 x 14.4)ER	**1 oil engine** driving 1 FP propeller Total Power: 8,826kW (12,000hp) 14.5kn B&W 6S60MC 1 x 2 Stroke 6 Cy. 600 x 2292 8826kW (12000bhp) Mitsui Engineering & Shipbuilding CLtd-Japan AuxGen: 3 x 400kW 440V a.c, 1 x 100kW 440V a.c Boilers: AuxB (Comp) 7.1kgf/cm² (7.0bar)
7222310 **SALANGEN** *LGXC* *ex* Goalsevarre *-2004* - **Torghatten Nord AS** *Tromso* *Norway* MMSI: 257266400	**652** 197 -	Class: (NV)	**1972 AS Tromso Skipsverft & Mek. Verksted — Tromso** Yd No: 40 Loa 44.71 Br ex 10.80 Dght 2.890 Lbp 40.52 Br md 10.62 Dpth 4.22 Welded, 1 dk	**(A36A2PR) Passenger/Ro-Ro Ship (Vehicles)** Passengers: 250	**1 oil engine** driving 1 FP propeller Total Power: 728kW (990hp) 13.0kn Wichmann 6ACA 1 x 2 Stroke 6 Cy. 280 x 420 728kW (990bhp) Wichmann Motorfabrikk AS-Norway AuxGen: 2 x 64kW 220V 50Hz a.c Thrusters: 1 Thwart. FP thruster (f)
7824572 **SALANGO** *HC4417* *ex* Stapafell *-2001* - **Ecuanave CA** Negocios Navieros y de Transporte Transneg SA SatCom: Inmarsat C 425112110 *Guayaquil* *Ecuador* MMSI: 735057593 Official number: TN-00-0432	**1,619** 742 2,038 T/cm 7.5	Class: LR (GL) **100A1** SS 06/2011 oil tanker ESP **LMC UMS** Cable: 440.0/40.0 U2	**1979**-10 **JG Hitzler Schiffswerft und Masch GmbH & Co KG — Lauenburg** Yd No: 763 Loa 75.75 Br ex 13.56 Dght 4.790 Lbp 70.03 Br md 13.20 Dpth 5.00 Welded, 1 dk	**(A13B2TP) Products Tanker** Double Hull Liq: 2,562; Liq (Oil): 2,562 Compartments: 10 Wing Ta, 2 Slop Ta, ER 2 Cargo Pump (s): 2x300m³/hr	**1 oil engine** reduction geared to sc. shaft driving 1 CP propeller Total Power: 2,280kW (3,100hp) 13.5kn Deutz SBV6M540 1 x 4 Stroke 6 Cy. 370 x 400 2280kW (3100bhp) Kloeckner Humboldt Deutz AG-West Germany AuxGen: 3 x 253kW 380/220V 50Hz a.c Boilers: AuxB (o.f.) 10.0kgf/cm² (9.8bar) Thrusters: 1 Thwart. FP thruster (f) Fuel: 22.8 (d.f.) 233.8 (r.f.)

IMO / Call sign	Name / Owner / Manager / Port	GT / NT / DWT	Class	Builder / Dimensions	Type	Machinery
7048283 - -	**SALARA 1** *ex* Carla J *-2006* *ex* Rudolph Charles *-1995* *ex* Pathfinder *-1991* **Farkad Sami Al Jader** -	*156* 106 -		**1968 American Marine Corp. — New Orleans, La** Yd No: 1006 Loa 40.24 Br ex 8.95 Dght 3.293 Lbp 36.89 Br md 8.54 Dpth 3.74 Welded, 1 dk	**(B21A20S) Platform Supply Ship**	**2 oil engines** geared to sc. shafts driving 2 FP propellers Total Power: 1,250kW (1,700hp) 13.0kn Caterpillar D398TA 2 x Vee 4 Stroke 12 Cy. 159 x 203 each-625kW (850bhp) Caterpillar Tractor Co-USA AuxGen: 2 x 60kW 220V 60Hz a.c
7902233 *VCQL* -	**SALARIUM** *ex* Nanticoke *-2009* **The CSL Group Inc (Canada Steamship Lines)** CSL Americas SatCom: Inmarsat A 1560355 *Toronto, ON* *Canada* MMSI: 316043000 Official number: 383534	**21,870** 8,618 35,686 T/cm 50.8	Class: LR ✠**100A1** Lake SS 04/2012 Great Lakes and St. Lawrence River service, also Strait of Belle Isle South of 52 degree North latitude and coasting South from St. John's, Newfoundland to the Eastern seaboard of Canada ✠**LMC** Cable: 330.0/52.5 U3	**1980-06 Collingwood Shipyards Ltd — Collingwood ON** Yd No: 218 Loa 222.46 (BB) Br ex 23.22 Dght 9.800 Lbp 216.90 Br md 23.14 Dpth 14.18 Welded, 1 dk	**(A23A2BK) Bulk Carrier, Self-discharging, Laker** Grain: 34,355 Compartments: 5 Ho, ER 22 Ha: 22 (3.3 x 14.6)ER	**2 oil engines** sr geared to sc. shaft driving 1 CP propeller Total Power: 7,870kW (10,700hp) 13.0kn Pielstick 10PC2-2V-400 2 x Vee 4 Stroke 10 Cy. 400 x 460 each-3935kW (5350bhp) A.P.E. Allen Ltd.-Bedford AuxGen: 3 x 880kW 575V 60Hz a.c Boilers: e (ex.g.) 8.4kgf/cm² (8.2bar), AuxB (o.f.) 7.0kgf/cm² (6.9bar) Thrusters: 1 Thwart. FP thruster (f)
8730302 *UGXE* M-0393	**SALATSGRIVA** *ex* Salacgriva *-1998* *ex* Salatsgriva *-1992* **North-West Fishing Company-Murmansk Co Ltd (OOO 'Severo-Zapadnaya Rybopromyshlennaya Kompaniya-Murmansk')** - *Murmansk* *Russia* MMSI: 273412090	**814** 244 414	Class: RS	**1989-10 Zavod "Leninskaya Kuznitsa" — Kiyev** Yd No: 1617 Loa 54.84 Br ex 10.15 Dght 4.141 Lbp 50.32 Br md 9.80 Dpth 5.00 Welded	**(B11A2FS) Stern Trawler** Ins: 412 Ice Capable	**1 oil engine** driving 1 CP propeller Total Power: 852kW (1,158hp) 12.0kn S.K.L. 8NVD48A-2U 1 x 4 Stroke 8 Cy. 320 x 480 852kW (1158bhp) VEB Schwermaschinenbau "KarlLiebknecht" (SKL)-Magdeburg AuxGen: 4 x 160kW a.c
8898489 *UFMD* -	**SALAVAT** *ex* ST-1359 *-1999* **Bashkirian River Shipping Co** Neva-Hugen Ltd *Taganrog* *Russia* MMSI: 273315510	**1,456** 504 1,533	Class: RR	**1988 Sudostroitelnyy Zavod im. "40-aya Godovshchina Oktyabrya"-Bor** Yd No: 311 Shortened Loa 82.00 Br ex 12.30 Dght 2.500 Lbp 80.85 Br md 12.00 Dpth 3.50 Welded, 1 dk	**(A31A2GX) General Cargo Ship** Grain: 2,230 Compartments: 1 Ho, ER 2 Ha: 2 (19.8 x 9.0)ER	**2 oil engines** driving 2 FP propellers Total Power: 884kW (1,202hp) 10.0kn S.K.L. 8VDS36/24A-1 2 x 4 Stroke 8 Cy. 240 x 360 each-442kW (601bhp) (made 1980) VEB Schwermaschinenbau "KarlLiebknecht" (SKL)-Magdeburg
9268992 *9HFM9* -	**SALDANHA** *ex* Shinyo Brilliance *-2007* **Team-Up Owning Co Ltd** TMS Bulkers Ltd *Valletta* *Malta* MMSI: 256913000 Official number: 9268992	**38,886** 25,208 75,707 T/cm 65.8	Class: NK	**2004-01 Sanoyas Hishino Meisho Corp — Kurashiki OY** Yd No: 1215 Loa 225.00 (BB) Br ex 32.30 Dght 13.994 Lbp 217.00 Br md 32.26 Dpth 19.30 Welded, 1 dk	**(A21A2BC) Bulk Carrier** Double Bottom Entire Compartment Length Grain: 89,250 Compartments: 7 Ho, ER 7 Ha: (16.3 x 13.4)6 (17.1 x 15.0)ER	**1 oil engine** driving 1 FP propeller Total Power: 8,974kW (12,201hp) 14.0kn B&W 7S50MC-C 1 x 2 Stroke 7 Cy. 500 x 2000 8974kW (12201bhp) Mitsui Engineering & Shipbuilding CLtd-Japan AuxGen: 3 x 400kW 450V 60Hz a.c Fuel: 151.0 (d.f.) (Heating Coils) 2691.0 (r.f.) 30.5pd
7104300 *6VOA* DAK 457	**SALDE** *ex* Shemahi IV *-1977* **Armement Frigorifique Senegalais** - *Dakar* *Senegal*	*130* 63 -	Class: (BV)	**1971 Ch. Normands Reunis — Courseulles-sur-Mer** Yd No: 22 Loa 25.20 Br ex 6.81 Dght 2.490 Lbp 21.72 Br md 6.71 Dpth 3.51 Welded, 1 dk	**(B11A2FT) Trawler** Ins: 142 Compartments: 1 Ho, ER 1 Ha: (1.2 x 1.6)	**1 oil engine** driving 1 FP propeller Total Power: 279kW (379hp) 9.0kn Caterpillar D353SCAC 1 x 4 Stroke 6 Cy. 159 x 203 279kW (379bhp) Caterpillar Tractor Co-USA Fuel: 48.5 (d.f.)
8652952 *LCQF* -	**SALEE** *ex* Circus I *-2004* *ex* Gulfstreamer II *-2004* *ex* Golden Greek II *-2004* *ex* Georgie Boy *-2004* **Risoy Eiendom AS** - *Haugesund* *Norway*	**209** 62 -		**1981 Cantiere Navale Fratelli Benetti — Viareggio** Yd No: 132 Loa 34.80 Br ex 6.95 Dght 2.960 Lbp 28.42 Br md - Dpth 3.95 Welded, 1 dk	**(X11A2YP) Yacht**	**2 oil engines** reduction geared to sc. shafts driving 2 Propellers Total Power: 552kW (750hp) 12.0kn Caterpillar 3408TA 2 x Vee 4 Stroke 8 Cy. 137 x 152 each-276kW (375bhp) Caterpillar Inc-USA
9415351 *J8B4016* -	**SALEH** **Ingres Marine Services Ltd** Whitesea Shipping & Supply (LLC) *Kingstown* *St Vincent & The Grenadines* MMSI: 376784000 Official number: 10489	**1,579** 473 1,500	Class: BV	**2009-03 Keppel Nantong Shipyard Co Ltd — Nantong JS** (Hull) Yd No: 010 **2009-03 Keppel Singmarine Pte Ltd — Singapore** Yd No: 330 Loa 62.20 Br ex - Dght 4.900 Lbp 59.60 Br md 15.00 Dpth 6.00 Welded, 1 dk	**(B21B20A) Anchor Handling Tug Supply** Cranes: 1x10t	**2 oil engines** reduction geared to sc. shafts driving 2 Directional propellers Total Power: 4,080kW (5,548hp) 12.5kn Wartsila 6L26 2 x 4 Stroke 6 Cy. 260 x 320 each-2040kW (2774bhp) Wartsila Finland Oy-Finland AuxGen: 2 x 280kW 380V 50Hz a.c, 2 x 1200kW 380V 50Hz a.c Thrusters: 2 Tunnel thruster (f)
5402863 *ZDDP3* -	**SALEM** *ex* Cumulus *-1998* **Silver Patina Ltd** - *Gibraltar* *Gibraltar (British)* MMSI: 236044000 Official number: 730173	*2,083* 624 587	Class: BV	**1963 N.V. Scheepswerf Gebr. van der Werf — Deest** Yd No: 296 Converted From: Research Vessel-1998 Loa 74.00 Br ex 12.83 Dght 4.850 Lbp 65.79 Br md 12.50 Dpth 9.25 Welded, 3 dks	**(X11A2YP) Yacht**	**1 oil engine** reduction geared to sc. shaft driving 1 FP propeller Total Power: 2,939kW (3,996hp) 15.0kn MAN-B&W 12V28/32A 1 x Vee 4 Stroke 12 Cy. 280 x 320 2939kW (3996bhp) (new engine 1998) MAN B&W Diesel AG-Augsburg AuxGen: 3 x 160kW 380V 50Hz a.c Fuel: 223.5 (d.f.)
7617838 *HZSM* -	**SALEM** *ex* Tyrving *-1989* *ex* Draupner *-1987* **Bin Mahfooz Shipping Agencies** - *Jeddah* *Saudi Arabia* Official number: SA1634	*248* 141 40	Class: (NV)	**1977-04 Westermoen Hydrofoil AS — Mandal** Yd No: 51 Loa 29.13 Br ex 9.02 Dght 2.620 Lbp - Br md - Dpth 2.90 Welded, 1 dk	**(A37B2PS) Passenger Ship** Hull Material: Aluminium Alloy Passengers: unberthed: 178	**2 oil engines** geared to sc. shafts driving 2 FP propellers Total Power: 2,648kW (3,600hp) 30.0kn AGO 195V12CSHR 2 x Vee 4 Stroke 12 Cy. 195 x 180 each-1324kW (1800bhp) Societe Alsacienne de ConstructionsMecaniques (SACM)-France AuxGen: 2 x 25kW 230V 50Hz a.c
8734322 *9BTY* -	**SALEM 1** *ex* Altamimi *-2008* **Hassan Nasari** - *Khorramshahr* *Iran* MMSI: 422838000 Official number: 921	**496** 328 970		**2006-07 UR-Dock — Basrah** Loa 46.00 Br ex 11.00 Dght 5.000 Lbp 43.47 Br md 10.98 Dpth 6.00 Welded, 1 dk	**(A31A2GX) General Cargo Ship**	**3 oil engines** reduction geared to sc. shafts driving 3 Propellers Total Power: 2,177kW (2,960hp) Caterpillar 2 x Vee 4 Stroke 6 Cy. each-353kW (480bhp) Caterpillar Inc-USA Niigata 6L26HLX 1 x 4 Stroke 6 Cy. 260 x 350 1471kW (2000bhp) Niigata Engineering Co Ltd-Japan
9017563 *IRZA* -	**SALERNO JET** *ex* Marconi *-2006* **Navigazione Libera del Golfo Srl** - *Naples* *Italy* MMSI: 247343000 Official number: 756	*391* 149 -	Class: RI	**1992-01 Rodriquez Cantieri Navali SpA — Messina** Yd No: 253 Loa 46.90 Br ex - Dght 1.340 Lbp 37.09 Br md 7.60 Dpth 3.90 Welded	**(A37B2PS) Passenger Ship** Hull Material: Aluminium Alloy Passengers: unberthed: 400	**2 oil engines** with clutches, flexible couplings & sr geared to sc. shafts driving 2 FP propellers Total Power: 4,000kW (5,438hp) 34.0kn M.T.U. 16V396TE74L 2 x Vee 4 Stroke 16 Cy. 165 x 185 each-2000kW (2719bhp) MTU Friedrichshafen GmbH-Friedrichshafen AuxGen: 2 x 150kW 220V 50Hz a.c
9142289 *3FYM4* -	**SALGIR** *ex* Reifu *-2007* *ex* Baystars II *-2003* **Salgir Shipping Ltd** JSC 'Yugreftransflot' *Panama* *Panama* MMSI: 355199000 Official number: 4309411	**3,767** 1,568 4,241	Class: RS (NK)	**1996-05 Shin Kurushima Dockyard Co. Ltd. — Hashihama, Imabari** Yd No: 2886 Loa 100.72 (BB) Br ex 16.62 Dght 6.620 Lbp 93.00 Br md 16.60 Dpth 9.90 Welded, 1 dk	**(A34A2GR) Refrigerated Cargo Ship** Ins: 4,766 Compartments: 4 Ho, ER 4 Ha: ER Derricks: 8x5t	**1 oil engine** driving 1 FP propeller Total Power: 3,089kW (4,200hp) 15.1kn B&W 5L35MC 1 x 2 Stroke 5 Cy. 350 x 1050 3089kW (4200bhp) Makita Corp-Japan AuxGen: 2 x 600kW a.c Thrusters: 1 Thwart. FP thruster (f) Fuel: 880.0 (r.f.) 12.2pd
7407374 *C9QB* -	**SALIA** *ex* Ifcor V *-1978* **Empresa Mocambicana de Pesca EE (EMOPESCA)** - *Maputo* *Mozambique*	*109* 74 -	Class: (AB)	**1975-03 Sandock-Austral Ltd. — Durban** Yd No: 66 Loa 22.89 Br ex 6.48 Dght 2.464 Lbp 20.73 Br md 6.38 Dpth 3.33 Welded, 1 dk	**(B11A2FS) Stern Trawler**	**1 oil engine** driving 1 FP propeller Total Power: 313kW (426hp) 8.5kn Caterpillar D353SCAC 1 x 4 Stroke 6 Cy. 159 x 203 313kW (426bhp) Caterpillar Tractor Co-USA AuxGen: 2 x 20kW a.c Fuel: 26.5 (d.f.)

9238703 *EBTL* -	**SALICA FRIGO** **Albafrigo Canarias SA** - SatCom: Inmarsat C 422412410 *Las Palmas* *Spain (CSR)* MMSI: 224124000 Official number: 7/2001	**7,207** 2,441 7,748	Class: BV	**2001**-12 **Hijos de J. Barreras S.A. — Vigo** Yd No: 1586 Loa 132.90 (BB) Br ex - Dght 8.080 Lbp 120.00 Br md 18.80 Dpth 13.08 Welded, 1 dk	**(A34A2GR) Refrigerated Cargo Ship** Ins: 9,111 TEU 18 incl 18 ref C Compartments: 4 Ho, ER 4 Ha: 3 (10.0 x 8.8)ER (8.1 x 4.9) Cranes: 4x6t	**1 oil engine** with flexible couplings & reduction geared to sc. shaft driving 1 CP propeller Total Power: 6,304kW (8,571hp) 17.0kn Wartsila 6L46C 1 x 4 Stroke 6 Cy. 460 x 580 6304kW (8571bhp) Wartsila Diesel S.A.-Bermeo AuxGen: 2 x 920kW 380/220V 50Hz a.c, 1 x 560kW 380/220V 50Hz a.c, 1 x 1500kW 380/220V 50Hz a.c Thrusters: 1 Thwart. CP thruster (f) Fuel: 475.0 (d.f.) 1180.0 (r.f.)
7811642 - -	**SALIF** - **Hodeidah Port Authority** - *Hodeidah* *Yemen*	*260* - -		**1979**-05 **van der Werf Staalbouw B.V. — Papendrecht** Yd No: 2202 Loa 23.09 Br ex 6.89 Dght 3.417 Lbp 21.19 Br md - Dpth 2.49 Welded, 1 dk	**(B32A2ST) Tug**	**2 oil engines** reverse reduction geared to sc. shafts driving 2 FP propellers Total Power: 1,704kW (2,316hp) G.M. (Detroit Diesel) 16V-149-T 2 x Vee 2 Stroke 16 Cy. 146 x 146 each-852kW (1158bhp) General Motors Detroit DieselAllison Divn-USA
9378096 *TCSR4* -	**SALIH REIS-4** **Istanbul Deniz Otobusleri Sanayi ve Ticaret AS (IDO)** - *Istanbul* *Turkey* MMSI: 271002465	**644** 220 50	Class: TL (BV)	**2007**-02 **Damen Shipyards Singapore Pte Ltd — Singapore** (Hull) Yd No: 90 **2007**-02 **B.V. Scheepswerf Damen — Gorinchem** Yd No: 538722 Loa 43.00 (BB) Br ex - Dght 1.550 Lbp 41.86 Br md 12.40 Dpth 3.80 Welded, 1 dk	**(A37B2PS) Passenger Ship** Hull Material: Aluminium Alloy Passengers: unberthed: 449	**4 oil engines** reduction geared to sc. shafts driving 2 CP propellers Total Power: 4,264kW (5,796hp) 32.4kn Caterpillar C32 ACERT 4 x Vee 4 Stroke 12 Cy. 145 x 162 each-1066kW (1449bhp) Caterpillar Inc-USA AuxGen: 2 x 200kW 380/220V 50Hz a.c
9012185 *PNDG* -	**SALILA** *ex* Yaizu *-2009* **PT Yatra Pratama Oreint** - *Jakarta* *Indonesia* MMSI: 525016556	**707** 213 -	Class: KI	**1991**-03 **KK Kanasashi Zosen — Shizuoka SZ** Yd No: 3251 Loa 48.70 (BB) Br ex 9.02 Dght 3.401 Lbp 48.35 Br md 9.00 Dpth 3.80 Welded	**(B11A2FS) Stern Trawler** Ins: 90	**1 oil engine** sr geared to sc. shaft driving 1 CP propeller Total Power: 1,324kW (1,800hp) Akasaka K31FD 1 x 4 Stroke 6 Cy. 310 x 530 1324kW (1800bhp) Akasaka Tekkosho KK (Akasaka DieselLtd)-Japan AuxGen: 2 x 400kW 450V a.c Thrusters: 1 Thwart. CP thruster (f)
8106238 *CNVE* -	**SALIM I** **La Societe de Navigation d'Armement et de Peche (SONARP)** - SatCom: Inmarsat C 424243310 *Agadir* *Morocco* MMSI: 242433000 Official number: 8-570	*502* 222 625	Class: (NK) (KR)	**1981**-07 **Narasaki Zosen KK — Muroran HK** Yd No: 1004 Loa 55.86 Br ex 9.53 Dght 4.096 Lbp 50.40 Br md 9.50 Dpth 6.05 Welded, 2 dks	**(B11A2FS) Stern Trawler** Ins: 441 Compartments: 2 Ho, ER 2 Ha: (2.6 x 2.6) (1.3 x 2.0) Derricks: 2x1.3t	**1 oil engine** driving 1 CP propeller Total Power: 1,618kW (2,200hp) 12.0kn Akasaka A34 1 x 4 Stroke 6 Cy. 340 x 660 1618kW (2200bhp) Akasaka Tekkosho KK (Akasaka DieselLtd)-Japan AuxGen: 2 x 220kW 440V 60Hz a.c Thrusters: 1 Thwart. CP thruster (f) Fuel: 440.0 (d.f.) 5.5pd
8106240 *CNVF* -	**SALIM II** **La Societe de Navigation d'Armement et de Peche (SONARP)** - SatCom: Inmarsat C 424243710 *Agadir* *Morocco* MMSI: 242437000 Official number: 8-616	*503* 222 636	Class: (BV) (NK) (KR)	**1981**-08 **Narasaki Zosen KK — Muroran HK** Yd No: 1006 Loa 55.86 Br ex 9.53 Dght 4.096 Lbp 50.40 Br md 9.50 Dpth 6.05 Welded, 2 dks	**(B11A2FS) Stern Trawler** Ins: 441 Compartments: 2 Ho, ER 2 Ha: (2.6 x 2.6) (1.3 x 2.0) Derricks: 2x1.3t	**1 oil engine** driving 1 CP propeller Total Power: 1,618kW (2,200hp) 12.0kn Akasaka A34 1 x 4 Stroke 6 Cy. 340 x 660 1618kW (2200bhp) Akasaka Tekkosho KK (Akasaka DieselLtd)-Japan AuxGen: 2 x 220kW 440V 60Hz a.c Thrusters: 1 Thwart. CP thruster (f) Fuel: 440.0 (d.f.) 5.5pd
8106252 *CNVG* -	**SALIM III** **La Societe de Navigation d'Armement et de Peche (SONARP)** - SatCom: Inmarsat C 424243810 *Agadir* *Morocco* MMSI: 242438000 Official number: 8-575	*502* 222 627	Class: (BV) (NK) (KR)	**1981**-10 **Narasaki Zosen KK — Muroran HK** Yd No: 1007 Loa 55.86 Br ex 9.53 Dght 4.082 Lbp 50.40 Br md 9.50 Dpth 4.09 Welded, 2 dks	**(B11A2FS) Stern Trawler** Ins: 441 Compartments: 2 Ho, ER 2 Ha: (2.6 x 2.6) (1.3 x 2.0) Derricks: 2x1.3t	**1 oil engine** driving 1 CP propeller Total Power: 1,618kW (2,200hp) 12.0kn Akasaka A34 1 x 4 Stroke 6 Cy. 340 x 660 1618kW (2200bhp) Akasaka Tekkosho KK (Akasaka DieselLtd)-Japan AuxGen: 2 x 220kW 440V 60Hz a.c Thrusters: 1 Thwart. CP thruster (f) Fuel: 440.0 (d.f.) 5.5pd
8734592 *PMTC* -	**SALIM MUJUR 1** *ex* Ren He 1 *-2010* *ex* Chang Shun Da 16 *-2009* **PT Salim Mujur** - *Bitung* *Indonesia*	**1,638** 582 2,500	Class: KI	**1995**-11 **Zhangshu Shipping Transportation Co Shipyard — Zhangshu JX** Loa 78.96 Br ex - Dght - Lbp 72.30 Br md 12.00 Dpth 6.70 Welded, 1 dk	**(A31A2GX) General Cargo Ship**	**1 oil engine** driving 1 Propeller Total Power: 735kW (999hp) Hanshin 1 x 735kW (999bhp) The Hanshin Diesel Works Ltd-Japan
8122713 *CNVI* -	**SALIM V** **La Societe de Navigation d'Armement et de Peche (SONARP)** - SatCom: Inmarsat C 424243910 *Agadir* *Morocco* MMSI: 242439000 Official number: 8-574	*502* 222 626	Class: (BV) (NK) (KR)	**1981**-12 **Narasaki Zosen KK — Muroran HK** Yd No: 1008 Loa 55.86 Br ex 9.53 Dght 4.082 Lbp 50.40 Br md 9.50 Dpth 6.05 Welded, 2 dks	**(B11A2FS) Stern Trawler** Ins: 441 Compartments: 2 Ho, ER 2 Ha: (2.6 x 2.6) (1.3 x 2.0) Derricks: 2x1.3t	**1 oil engine** driving 1 CP propeller Total Power: 1,618kW (2,200hp) 12.0kn Akasaka A34 1 x 4 Stroke 6 Cy. 340 x 660 1618kW (2200bhp) Akasaka Tekkosho KK (Akasaka DieselLtd)-Japan AuxGen: 2 x 220kW 440V 60Hz a.c Thrusters: 1 Thwart. CP thruster (f) Fuel: 440.0 (d.f.) 5.5pd
8122725 *CNVJ* -	**SALIM VI** **La Societe de Navigation d'Armement et de Peche (SONARP)** - SatCom: Inmarsat C 424244010 *Agadir* *Morocco* MMSI: 242440000	*502* 222 635	Class: (BV) (NK) (KR)	**1982**-01 **Narasaki Zosen KK — Muroran HK** Yd No: 1009 Loa 55.86 Br ex 9.53 Dght 4.082 Lbp 50.40 Br md 9.50 Dpth 6.05 Welded, 2 dks	**(B11A2FS) Stern Trawler** Ins: 441 Compartments: 2 Ho, ER 2 Ha: (2.6 x 2.6) (1.3 x 2.0) Derricks: 2x1.3t	**1 oil engine** driving 1 CP propeller Total Power: 1,618kW (2,200hp) 12.0kn Akasaka A34 1 x 4 Stroke 6 Cy. 340 x 660 1618kW (2200bhp) Akasaka Tekkosho KK (Akasaka DieselLtd)-Japan AuxGen: 2 x 220kW 440V 60Hz a.c Thrusters: 1 Thwart. CP thruster (f) Fuel: 440.0 (d.f.) 5.5pd
8122737 *CNVK* -	**SALIM VII** **La Societe de Navigation d'Armement et de Peche (SONARP)** - SatCom: Inmarsat C 424244110 *Agadir* *Morocco* MMSI: 242441000	*502* 222 635	Class: (BV) (NK) (KR)	**1982**-01 **Narasaki Zosen KK — Muroran HK** Yd No: 1010 Loa 55.86 Br ex 9.53 Dght 4.082 Lbp 50.40 Br md 9.50 Dpth 6.05 Welded, 2 dks	**(B11A2FS) Stern Trawler** Ins: 441 Compartments: 2 Ho, ER 2 Ha: (2.6 x 2.6) (1.3 x 2.0) Derricks: 2x1.3t	**1 oil engine** driving 1 CP propeller Total Power: 1,618kW (2,200hp) 12.0kn Akasaka A34 1 x 4 Stroke 6 Cy. 340 x 660 1618kW (2200bhp) Akasaka Tekkosho KK (Akasaka DieselLtd)-Japan AuxGen: 2 x 220kW 440V 60Hz a.c Thrusters: 1 Thwart. CP thruster (f) Fuel: 440.0 (d.f.) 5.5pd
8122749 *CNVL* -	**SALIM VIII** **La Societe de Navigation d'Armement et de Peche (SONARP)** - SatCom: Inmarsat C 424244210 *Agadir* *Morocco* MMSI: 242442000 Official number: 8-599	*503* 222 636	Class: (BV) (NK) (KR)	**1982**-03 **Narasaki Zosen KK — Muroran HK** Yd No: 1011 Loa 55.86 Br ex 9.53 Dght 4.082 Lbp 50.40 Br md 9.50 Dpth 6.05 Welded, 2 dks	**(B11A2FS) Stern Trawler** Ins: 441 Compartments: 2 Ho, ER 2 Ha: (2.6 x 2.6) (1.3 x 2.0) Derricks: 2x1.3t	**1 oil engine** driving 1 CP propeller Total Power: 1,618kW (2,200hp) 12.0kn Akasaka A34 1 x 4 Stroke 6 Cy. 340 x 660 1618kW (2200bhp) Akasaka Tekkosho KK (Akasaka DieselLtd)-Japan AuxGen: 2 x 220kW 440V 60Hz a.c Thrusters: 1 Thwart. CP thruster (f) Fuel: 440.0 (d.f.) 5.5pd
8130588 *CNVN* -	**SALIM X** **La Societe de Navigation d'Armement et de Peche (SONARP)** - SatCom: Inmarsat C 424243410 *Agadir* *Morocco* MMSI: 242434000 Official number: 8-609	*503* 222 624	Class: (NK) (KR)	**1982**-05 **Narasaki Zosen KK — Muroran HK** Yd No: 1012 Loa 55.86 Br ex 9.53 Dght 4.082 Lbp 50.40 Br md 9.50 Dpth 6.05 Welded, 2 dks	**(B11A2FS) Stern Trawler** Ins: 441 Compartments: 2 Ho, ER 2 Ha: (2.5 x 2.5) (1.3 x 2.0) Derricks: 2x1.3t	**1 oil engine** driving 1 CP propeller Total Power: 1,618kW (2,200hp) 12.0kn Akasaka A34 1 x 4 Stroke 6 Cy. 340 x 660 1618kW (2200bhp) Akasaka Tekkosho KK (Akasaka DieselLtd)-Japan AuxGen: 2 x 220kW 440V 60Hz a.c Thrusters: 1 Thwart. CP thruster (f) Fuel: 440.0 (d.f.) 5.5pd
8130590 *CNVH* -	**SALIM XI** **La Societe de Navigation d'Armement et de Peche (SONARP)** - SatCom: Inmarsat A 1140103 *Agadir* *Morocco* Official number: 8-616	*502* 220 636	Class: (BV) (NK) (KR)	**1982**-07 **Narasaki Zosen KK — Muroran HK** Yd No: 1013 Loa 55.86 Br ex 9.53 Dght 4.082 Lbp 50.40 Br md 9.50 Dpth 5.08 Welded, 2 dks	**(B11A2FS) Stern Trawler** Ins: 442 Derricks: 2x1.3t	**1 oil engine** driving 1 CP propeller Total Power: 1,618kW (2,200hp) 12.0kn Akasaka A34 1 x 4 Stroke 6 Cy. 340 x 660 1618kW (2200bhp) Akasaka Tekkosho KK (Akasaka DieselLtd)-Japan AuxGen: 2 x 220kW 440V 60Hz a.c Thrusters: 1 Thwart. CP thruster (f) Fuel: 440.0 (d.f.) 5.5pd

IMO / Call sign	Name / Owner	Tonnage	Class	Builder / Dimensions	Type	Machinery
8130605 *CNVM* -	**SALIM XII** **La Societe de Navigation d'Armement et de Peche (SONARP)** - SatCom: Inmarsat C 424243510 *Agadir* *Morocco* MMSI: 242435000 Official number: 8-629	*503* 220 631	Class: (BV) (NK) (KR)	**1982-07 Narasaki Zosen KK — Muroran HK** Yd No: 1014 Loa 55.86 Br ex 9.53 Dght 4.096 Lbp 50.40 Br md 9.50 Dpth 5.08 Welded, 2 dks	**(B11A2FS) Stern Trawler** Ins: 442 Compartments: 2 Ho, ER 2 Ha: (2.5 x 2.5) (1.3 x 2.0) Derricks: 2x1.3t	**1 oil engine** driving 1 CP propeller Total Power: 1,618kW (2,200hp) 12.0kn Akasaka A34 1 x 4 Stroke 6 Cy. 340 x 660 1618kW (2200bhp) Akasaka Tekkosho KK (Akasaka DieselLtd)-Japan AuxGen: 2 x 220kW 440V 60Hz a.c Thrusters: 1 Thwart. CP thruster (f) Fuel: 440.0 (d.f.) 5.5pd
8816716 *CNA2477* -	**SALIMA** **Fishelect SA** - *Casablanca* *Morocco*	**393** 118 300	Class: (BV)	**1989-06 Construcciones Navales P Freire SA — Vigo** Yd No: 365 Loa 37.17 Br ex 8.52 Dght 4.050 Lbp 31.50 Br md 8.51 Dpth 6.20 Welded, 2 dks	**(B11A2FS) Stern Trawler** Ins: 315	**1 oil engine** with flexible couplings & sr geared to sc. shaft driving 1 FP propeller Total Power: 772kW (1,050hp) 11.0kn Wartsila 6R22 1 x 4 Stroke 6 Cy. 220 x 240 772kW (1050bhp) Construcciones Echevarria SA-Spain
8994439 - -	**SALIMA K** *ex* Mary Lynn Lytal *-2005* **Esskay Construction Services** - *Port of Spain* *Trinidad & Tobago* Official number: TT030036	**132** 39 -		**1980-03 Offshore Trawlers, Inc. — Bayou La Batre, Al** Yd No: 91 L reg 25.45 Br ex - Dght - Lbp - Br md 7.31 Dpth 2.13 Welded, 1 dk	**(B34L2QU) Utility Vessel**	**1 oil engine** driving 1 Propeller
8013118 *9HVP8* -	**SALINA BAY** *ex* Arduity *-2007* *ex* Asprella *-1999* *ex* Shell Seafarer *-1993* **Salina Bay Maritime Ltd** Tankship Management Ltd *Valletta* *Malta* MMSI: 256487000 Official number: 8013118	**1,676** 792 3,027 T/cm 8.8	Class: LR ✠ **100A1** SS 02/2010 Double Hull oil tanker MARPOL 21.1.2. (FP above 60 degress C) (cc) ESP ✠ **LMC** **UMS** Eq.Ltr: Q; Cable: 440.0/38.0 U2	**1981-11 Goole SB. & Repairing Co. Ltd. — Goole** Yd No: 599 Converted From: Products Tanker-2007 Conv to DH-2008 Loa 79.25 Br ex 13.19 Dght 5.529 Lbp 74.70 Br md 13.10 Dpth 6.50 Welded, 1 dk	**(A13B2TP) Products Tanker** Double Hull (13F) Liq: 3,436; Liq (Oil): 3,436 Cargo Heating Coils Compartments: 10 Wing Ta, ER, 1 Slop Ta 5 Cargo Pump (s): 5x250m³/hr Manifold: Bow/CM: 33m	**1 oil engine** with flexible couplings & sr gearedto sc. shaft driving 1 CP propeller Total Power: 2,207kW (3,001hp) 11.5kn Mirrlees KMR-6 1 x 4 Stroke 6 Cy. 381 x 457 2207kW (3001bhp) Mirrlees Blackstone (Stockport)Ltd.-Stockport AuxGen: 3 x 230kW 415V 50Hz a.c Thrusters: 1 Thwart. FP thruster (f) Fuel: 30.8 (d.f.) (Part Heating Coils) 69.1 (r.f.) 13.0pd
5364279 *HP8925* -	**SALINA II** *ex* Salina *-1997* *ex* Karla *-1992* *ex* Mebeto *-1971* *ex* Tommelise *-1965* **Robert Thorne** - *Panama* *Panama* Official number: 26041PEXT1	**212** 112 371	Class: (NV)	**1962 Salthammer Baatbyggeri AS — Vestnes** Yd No: 87 Loa 35.41 Br ex 7.45 Dght 3.201 Lbp 31.60 Br md 7.42 Dpth 3.41 Welded, 1 dk	**(A31A2GX) General Cargo Ship** Grain: 453; Bale: 396 Compartments: 1 Ho, ER 1 Ha: (18.1 x 4.5)ER Derricks: 2x3t; Winches: 2 Ice Capable	**1 oil engine** driving 1 FP propeller Total Power: 276kW (375hp) 9.0kn Caterpillar 3408TA 1 x Vee 4 Stroke 8 Cy. 137 x 152 276kW (375bhp) (new engine 1980) Caterpillar Tractor Co-USA
9340910 *IBCL* -	**SALINA M** *ex* Aruba Trader *-2013* *ex* Clipper Klara *-2013* **Augusta Due Srl** - *Catania* *Italy* MMSI: 247324900 Official number: 46	**7,687** 3,266 11,283 T/cm 20.7	Class: RI (AB)	**2007-07 STX Shipbuilding Co Ltd — Busan** Yd No: 5012 Loa 116.50 (BB) Br ex 20.03 Dght 8.400 Lbp 109.00 Br md 20.00 Dpth 11.70 Welded, 1 dk	**(A12B2TR) Chemical/Products Tanker** Double Hull (13F) Liq: 12,268; Liq (Oil): 11,597 Cargo Heating Coils Compartments: 10 Wing Ta, ER, 2 Wing Slop Ta 10 Cargo Pump (s): 10x300m³/hr Manifold: Bow/CM: 52.7m	**1 oil engine** driving 1 FP propeller Total Power: 4,457kW (6,060hp) 13.6kn MAN-B&W 6S35MC 1 x 2 Stroke 6 Cy. 350 x 1400 4457kW (6060bhp) STX Engine Co Ltd-South Korea AuxGen: 3 x 450kW a.c Thrusters: 1 Thwart. FP thruster (f) Fuel: 93.0 (d.f.) 812.0 (r.f.)
7640029 *YFOV* -	**SALINDO MUTIARA I** *ex* Tamarii Moorea VIII *-1999* *ex* Kurihama Maru *-1986* **PT Gerbang Samudra Sarana** - *Jakarta* *Indonesia* MMSI: 525010053	*1,002* 301 459	Class: KI (BV)	**1977-04 Shimoda Dockyard Co. Ltd. — Shimoda** Yd No: 277 Loa 67.37 Br ex 13.82 Dght 3.314 Lbp 64.01 Br md 13.81 Dpth 4.63 Welded	**(A36A2PR) Passenger/Ro-Ro Ship (Vehicles)** Passengers: unberthed: 590 Bow door/ramp Cars: 80	**2 oil engines** driving 2 FP propellers Total Power: 2,206kW (3,000hp) 13.3kn Niigata 6M31X 2 x 4 Stroke 6 Cy. 310 x 460 each-1103kW (1500bhp) Niigata Engineering Co Ltd-Japan
7324443 *YD4296* -	**SALINDO PUTRA SETYA II** *ex* Sea Service *-1991* *ex* Anidah *-1991* *ex* Kristina *-1984* **PT Pelayaran Sulkatim** - *Jakarta* *Indonesia*	**170** 51 -	Class: (LR) (KI) (GL) (AB) Classed LR until 12/89	**1973-12 Promet Pte Ltd — Singapore** Yd No: 34 Loa 30.48 Br ex 7.50 Dght 2.833 Lbp 28.28 Br md 3.61 Dpth 3.54 Welded, 1 dk	**(B21A20S) Platform Supply Ship**	**2 oil engines** with clutches, flexible couplings & dr reverse geared to sc. shafts driving 2 FP propellers Total Power: 1,030kW (1,400hp) 10.0kn G.M. (Detroit Diesel) 12V-149 2 x Vee 2 Stroke 12 Cy. 146 x 146 each-515kW (700bhp) General Motors Detroit DieselAllison Divn-USA AuxGen: 1 x 30kW 220/380V 50Hz a.c, 1 x 22kW 220/380V 50Hz a.c
5307843 - -	**SALIPAZARI** **Government of The Republic of Turkey (Turkiye Cumhuriyeti Devlet Demir Yollari - Mersin Liman Isletmesi) (Turkish Republic State Railways - Mersin Harbour Management)** - *Mersin* *Turkey* Official number: 121	*108* 29 -	Class: (TL) (GL)	**1961 D.W. Kremer Sohn — Elmshorn** Yd No: 1078 Loa 26.17 Br ex 6.76 Dght 2.631 Lbp 24.49 Br md 6.73 Dpth 3.46 Riveted\Welded, 1 dk	**(B32A2ST) Tug**	**1 oil engine** reverse reduction geared to sc. shaft driving 1 FP propeller Total Power: 588kW (799hp) 11.5kn Deutz SBV8M536 1 x 4 Stroke 8 Cy. 270 x 360 588kW (799bhp) Kloeckner Humboldt Deutz AG-West Germany
8703672 *YDA4295* -	**SALIRA** *ex* Joyo Maru No. 21 *-2007* **PT Buana Jaya Pratama** - *Jakarta* *Indonesia*	**262** 79 -	Class: KI	**1987-05 Osaka Shipbuilding Co Ltd — Osaka OS** Yd No: 446 Loa 27.80 Br ex - Dght 3.201 Lbp 26.68 Br md 8.50 Dpth 4.10 Welded, 1 dk	**(B32A2ST) Tug**	**2 oil engines** reverse reduction geared to sc. shafts driving 2 FP propellers Total Power: 1,766kW (2,402hp) Hanshin 6LU28G 2 x 4 Stroke 6 Cy. 280 x 440 each-883kW (1201bhp) The Hanshin Diesel Works Ltd-Japan
9618329 *WDF6992*	**SALISH** **State of Washington (Department of Transportation)** - *Seattle, WA* *United States of America* MMSI: 367480010 Official number: 1229903	**4,623** 1,883 1,400		**2011-05 Todd Pacific Shipyards Corp. — Seattle, Wa** Yd No: 100 Loa 83.39 Br ex - Dght 3.230 Lbp 72.54 Br md 19.50 Dpth 3.35 Welded, 1 dk	**(A36A2PR) Passenger/Ro-Ro Ship (Vehicles)** Passengers: unberthed: 750 Bow door (centre) Stern door (centre) Cars: 64	**2 oil engines** reduction geared to sc. shafts driving 2 CP propellers Total Power: 4,412kW (5,998hp) 16.0kn EMD (Electro-Motive) 12-710-G7C 2 x Vee 2 Stroke 12 Cy. 230 x 279 each-2206kW (2999bhp) General Motors Corp.Electro-Motive Div.-La Grange
7398573 *WUT4384* -	**SALISHAN** *ex* Taroze Vizier *-1988* **Sause Bros Inc** - *Portland, OR* *United States of America* MMSI: 367007920 Official number: 552788	**387** 116 -		**1973 American Gulf Shipbuilding Corp. — Larose, La** Yd No: 5 Loa - Br ex - Dght 4.420 Lbp 35.03 Br md 9.73 Dpth 4.98 Welded, 1 dk	**(B32A2ST) Tug**	**2 oil engines** geared to sc. shafts driving 2 FP propellers Total Power: 2,648kW (3,600hp) EMD (Electro-Motive) 16-567-BC 2 x Vee 2 Stroke 16 Cy. 216 x 254 each-1324kW (1800bhp) General Motors Corp.Electro-Motive Div.-La Grange
8135198 *YGZV* -	**SALIT** *ex* Horyu Maru *-2003* **PT Samudera Lintas Indonesia Timur** - *Surabaya* *Indonesia*	*444* 266 541	Class: KI	**1982-07 K.K. Kamishima Zosensho — Osakikamijima** Yd No: 127 Loa 47.00 Br ex - Dght 3.400 Lbp 42.00 Br md 8.01 Dpth 5.01 Welded, 1 dk	**(A31A2GX) General Cargo Ship** Grain: 984; Bale: 902 Compartments: 1 Ho, ER 1 Ha: (24.8 x 6.0)ER	**1 oil engine** driving 1 FP propeller Total Power: 441kW (600hp) 9.5kn Matsui 1 x 4 Stroke 441kW (600bhp) Matsui Iron Works Co Ltd-Japan
8520446 *E5U2647* -	**SALIX** *ex* Viseu *-2006* *ex* Bargstedt *-1996* **Kayali Shipping Ltd Co** Wakes & Co Ltd *Aitutaki* *Cook Islands* MMSI: 518700000 Official number: 1736	**2,120** 1,092 3,020	Class: NK (LR) (RS) (GL) Classed LR until 31/1/11	**1986-02 J.J. Sietas KG Schiffswerft GmbH & Co. — Hamburg** Yd No: 987 Loa 92.18 (BB) Br ex 11.54 Dght 5.190 Lbp 89.21 Br md 11.31 Dpth 6.91 Welded, 2 dks	**(A31A2GX) General Cargo Ship** Grain: 4,060; Bale: 4,039 TEU 100 C. 100/20' (40') incl. 12 ref C. Compartments: 1 Ho, ER 1 Ha: (61.7 x 9.3)ER	**1 oil engine** with flexible couplings & sr reverse geared to sc. shaft driving 1 FP propeller Total Power: 599kW (814hp) 9.0kn Deutz SBV6M628 1 x 4 Stroke 6 Cy. 240 x 280 599kW (814bhp) Kloeckner Humboldt Deutz AG-West Germany AuxGen: 2 x 84kW 380V 50Hz a.c Thrusters: 1 Thwart. FP thruster (f) Fuel: 190.0 (d.f.) 3.0pd
7810648 *D9RY* -	**SALKO T-26** *ex* Dongbang No. 3 *-2012* *ex* Cho Kwang No. 3 *-2011* *ex* Zuiho *-1989* **Salko Co Ltd** - *Busan* *South Korea* MMSI: 440135390 Official number: MSR-887725	**158** 78 74	Class: KR	**1978-09 Osaka Shipbuilding Co Ltd — Osaka OS** Yd No: 389 Loa - Br ex - Dght 2.801 Lbp 30.82 Br md 8.81 Dpth 3.92 Riveted\Welded, 1 dk	**(B32A2ST) Tug**	**2 oil engines** driving 2 FP propellers Total Power: 1,912kW (2,600hp) Niigata 6L25BX 2 x 4 Stroke 6 Cy. 250 x 320 each-956kW (1300bhp) Niigata Engineering Co Ltd-Japan

9194737 *A4DD5* -	**SALL** **Bahwan Lamnalco LLC** - *Port Sultan Qaboos* *Oman* MMSI: 461000005 Official number: 847	**191** 57 -	Class: BV	**1999-04 Stocznia Tczew Sp z oo — Tczew** (Hull) **1999-04 B.V. Scheepswerf Damen — Gorinchem** Yd No: 7006 Loa 26.15 Br ex 7.95 Dght 3.210 Lbp 23.96 Br md 7.80 Dpth 4.05 Welded, 1 dk	**(B32A2ST) Tug**	**2 oil engines** with clutches, flexible couplings & sr reverse geared to sc. shafts driving 2 FP propellers Total Power: 2,028kW (2,758hp) 11.0kn Caterpillar 3512B-HD 2 x Vee 4 Stroke 12 Cy. 170 x 215 each-1014kW (1379bhp) Caterpillar Inc-USA AuxGen: 2 x 48kW 400V 50Hz a.c Fuel: 75.0 (d.f.)
9169627 *MDSK3* -	**SALLIE KNUTSEN** *ex Knock Sallie -2003* **Luky KS** Knutsen OAS Shipping AS SatCom: Inmarsat B 323537218 *Douglas* *Isle of Man (British)* MMSI: 235809000 Official number: 737093	**87,827** 44,535 153,617 T/cm 125.0	Class: NV	**1999-04 Hyundai Heavy Industries Co Ltd — Ulsan** Yd No: 1126 Converted From: Crude Oil Tanker-1999 Loa 276.65 (BB) Br ex 50.03 Dght 16.020 Lbp 264.00 Br md 50.00 Dpth 23.30 Welded, 1 dk	**(A13A2TS) Shuttle Tanker** Double Hull (13F) Liq: 165,111; Liq (Oil): 165,111 Compartments: 12 Wing Ta, 2 Wing Slop Ta, ER 3 Cargo Pump (s): 3x4500m³/hr Manifold: Bow/CM: 139m	**2 oil engines** driving 2 CP propellers Total Power: 17,810kW (24,214hp) 14.7kn B&W 6S60MC 2 x 2 Stroke 6 Cy. 600 x 2292 each-8905kW (12107bhp) Hyundai Heavy Industries Co Ltd-South Korea AuxGen: 4 x 2500kW 220/440V 60Hz a.c, 2 x 1000kW 220/440V 60Hz a.c Thrusters: 3 Thwart. CP thruster (f); 1 Retract. directional thruster (f); 2 Tunnel thruster (a) Fuel: 234.3 (d.f.) (Heating Coils) 4642.6 (r.f.) 65.0pd
7431571 *OUIG2* E 180	**SALLING** *ex Pernille-Vibeke -2007 ex Skagerak -1983* **Karl Cecilius Knudsen** North Sea Ship Agency *Esbjerg* *Denmark (DIS)* MMSI: 219338000 Official number: H638	**396** 118 175		**1974-01 A/S Bogense Skibsvaerft — Bogense** Yd No: 216 Loa 37.90 Br ex 7.19 Dght - Lbp 34.50 Br md 7.17 Dpth 3.46 Welded, 1 dk	**(B11B2FV) Fishing Vessel**	**1 oil engine** reduction geared to sc. shaft driving 1 CP propeller Total Power: 786kW (1,069hp) Alpha 6L23/30 1 x 4 Stroke 6 Cy. 225 x 300 786kW (1069bhp) Alpha Diesel A/S-Denmark
6711962 - -	**SALLING** *ex Simmelholm -1997* *ex Anne Lundgaard -1986 ex Laila Morup -1981* *ex Helene Jacobsen -1970* **Jorgen Dahl Madsen** -	*149* 73 178	Class: (BV)	**1967 VEB Rosslauer Schiffswerft — Rosslau** Loa 33.58 Br ex 6.61 Dght 2.699 Lbp 29.57 Br md 6.58 Dpth 3.31 Welded, 1 dk	**(B11A2FT) Trawler** Compartments: 2 Ho, ER 2 Ha: 2 (1.5 x 1.2)ER Derricks: 1x0.5t; Winches: 1	**1 oil engine** driving 1 CP propeller Total Power: 412kW (560hp) 11.0kn Callesen 6-427-FS 1 x 4 Stroke 6 Cy. 270 x 400 412kW (560bhp) (new engine 1973) Aabenraa Motorfabrik, HeinrichCallesen A/S-Denmark AuxGen: 2 x 16kW 220V d.c Fuel: 17.5 (d.f.)
8117457 *5VAH6* -	**SALLY** *ex Beveland -2003 ex Elan -1996* *ex Vlieland -1993* **SAS Magnani Italo & C** - *Lome* *Togo* MMSI: 671063000	**1,054** 633 1,495	Class: (BV)	**1982-04 Scheepswerf Bijlsma BV — Wartena** Yd No: 616 Loa 78.92 Br ex - Dght 3.150 Lbp 74.91 Br md 9.96 Dpth 4.22 Welded, 1 dk	**(A31A2GX) General Cargo Ship** Grain: 2,231; Bale: 2,157 Compartments: 3 Ho, ER 3 Ha: 3 (17.0 x 7.6)ER	**1 oil engine** with clutches, flexible couplings & sr reverse geared to sc. shaft driving 1 FP propeller Total Power: 870kW (1,183hp) 9.5kn Waukesha L5792DSIM 1 x Vee 4 Stroke 12 Cy. 216 x 216 870kW (1183bhp) Waukesha Engine Div. DresserIndustries Inc.-Waukesha, Wi AuxGen: 3 x 42kW 220/380V 50Hz a.c Thrusters: 1 Thwart. FP thruster (f) Fuel: 46.6 (d.f.) 3.5pd
8973019 *WDC3701* -	**SALLY** **Wilmington Tug Inc** - *New Castle, DE* *United States of America* MMSI: 367012660 Official number: 919715	*180* 144 -		**1987 Gladding-Hearn SB. Duclos Corp. — Somerset, Ma** Yd No: T-264 Loa 21.30 Br ex - Dght - Lbp - Br md 9.10 Dpth 3.90 Welded, 1 dk	**(B32A2ST) Tug**	**2 oil engines** gearing integral to driving 2 Z propellers Total Power: 1,766kW (2,402hp) G.M. (Detroit Diesel) 12V-149-TI 2 x Vee 2 Stroke 12 Cy. 146 x 146 each-883kW (1201bhp) General Motors Detroit DieselAllison Divn-USA
9338151 *MPXF5* -	**SALLY ANN C** **Yaoki Shipping SA** Carisbrooke Shipping Ltd *Cowes* *United Kingdom* MMSI: 232977000 Official number: 3236207A	**9,177** 4,751 13,538 T/cm 24.1	Class: LR (BV) **100A1** SS 01/2012 *IWS LI strengthened for heavy cargoes **LMC** **UMS** Cable: U3 (a)	**2007-01 Kyokuyo Shipyard Corp — Shimonoseki YC** Yd No: 468 Loa 136.43 (BB) Br ex - Dght 8.350 Lbp 126.40 Br md 21.20 Dpth 11.30 Welded, 1 dk	**(A31A2GX) General Cargo Ship** Double Sides Entire Compartment Length Grain: 17,000; Bale: 16,870 Compartments: 4 Ho, ER 4 Ha: (24.9 x 17.6) (24.8 x 17.6) (15.8 x 17.6)ER (16.1 x 12.6) Cranes: 2x30t	**1 oil engine** driving 1 FP propeller Total Power: 5,180kW (7,043hp) 14.0kn MAN-B&W 7S35MC 1 x 2 Stroke 7 Cy. 350 x 1400 5180kW (7043bhp) Mitsui Engineering & Shipbuilding CLtd-Japan AuxGen: 3 x 400kW 450V 60Hz a.c Boilers: TOH (o.f.) 10.0kgf/cm² (9.8bar), TOH 10.0kgf/cm² (9.8bar) Thrusters: 1 Tunnel thruster (f) Fuel: 90.0 (d.f.) 1000.0 (r.f.)
8718756 *TRFI* -	**SALLY BELL** **Smit International (Gabon) SA** - *Port-Gentil* *Gabon* MMSI: 626040000 Official number: PG3777	**436** 250 500	Class: BV (AB)	**1988-05 Scheepswerf Bijlholt B.V. — Foxhol** (Hull) Yd No: 650 **1988-05 B.V. Scheepswerf Damen — Gorinchem** Yd No: 8618 Loa 50.02 Br ex 11.99 Dght 2.271 Lbp - Br md - Dpth 3.00 Welded, 1 dk	**(A35D2RL) Landing Craft** Bow door/ramp	**2 oil engines** with clutches, flexible couplings & sr reverse geared to sc. shafts driving 2 FP propellers Total Power: 740kW (1,006hp) 9.5kn Caterpillar 3412TA 2 x Vee 4 Stroke 12 Cy. 137 x 152 each-370kW (503bhp) Caterpillar Inc-USA AuxGen: 2 x 90kW a.c Fuel: 180.0 (d.f.)
8980000 *WDA8541* -	**SALLY KIM IV** **Tommy Nguyen** - *Biloxi, MS* *United States of America* MMSI: 366855470 Official number: 1126659	*173* 51 -		**2002-01 La Force Shipyard Inc — Coden AL** Yd No: 128 L reg 26.18 Br ex - Dght - Lbp - Br md 7.62 Dpth 3.65 Welded, 1 dk	**(B11B2FV) Fishing Vessel**	**1 oil engine** driving 1 Propeller
9152844 *3FFE8* -	**SALLY M** *ex Sb Noble -2012 ex Hai Sung -2012* *ex Brother Royal -2007* **Gulf International Co Ltd** - *Panama* *Panama* MMSI: 370998000 Official number: 45211PEXT1	**4,569** 2,871 7,435	Class: RI (Class contemplated) (KR) (NK)	**1997-06 Chungmu Shipbuilding Co Inc — Tongyeong** Yd No: 247 Loa 100.80 (BB) Br ex - Dght 7.514 Lbp 93.00 Br md 18.00 Dpth 9.50 Welded, 1 dk	**(A21A2BC) Bulk Carrier** Grain: 10,367; Bale: 9,632 Compartments: 2 Ho, ER 2 Ha: (22.8 x 10.6) (29.3 x 10.6)ER Derricks: 2x30t,2x25t	**1 oil engine** driving 1 FP propeller Total Power: 2,574kW (3,500hp) 12.5kn Hanshin LH41LA 1 x 4 Stroke 6 Cy. 410 x 800 2574kW (3500bhp) The Hanshin Diesel Works Ltd-Japan
9120865 *OZHS2*	**SALLY MAERSK** **A P Moller - Maersk A/S** A P Moller SatCom: Inmarsat B 321932420 *Gilleleje* *Denmark (DIS)* MMSI: 219324000 Official number: D3622	**92,198** 53,625 110,387 T/cm 124.0	Class: AB (LR) ✠ Classed LR until 28/12/08	**1998-03 Odense Staalskibsvaerft A/S — Munkebo (Lindo Shipyard)** Yd No: 162 Loa 346.98 (BB) Br ex 42.92 Dght 14.941 Lbp 331.54 Br md 42.80 Dpth 24.10 Welded, 1 dk	**(A33A2CC) Container Ship (Fully Cellular)** TEU 9578 incl 817 ref C Compartments: ER, 20 Cell Ho 20 Ha: ER	**1 oil engine** driving 1 FP propeller Total Power: 54,840kW (74,560hp) 24.6kn B&W 12K90MC 1 x 2 Stroke 12 Cy. 900 x 2550 54840kW (74560bhp) Mitsui Engineering & Shipbuilding CLtd-Japan AuxGen: 5 x 3000kW 6600V 60Hz a.c Boilers: AuxB (o.f.) 10.2kgf/cm² (10.0bar), AuxB (ex.g.) 10.2kgf/cm² (10.0bar) Thrusters: 1 Thwart. FP thruster (f); 2 Tunnel thruster (a)
8738536 *YDA6269* -	**SALMA** **PT Masada Jaya Lines** - *Banjarmasin* *Indonesia* MMSI: 525016415	**209** 63 164	Class: KI	**2009-04 PT Karya Teknik Utama — Batam** Loa 27.00 Br ex - Dght 3.000 Lbp 24.50 Br md 8.20 Dpth 4.00 Welded, 1 dk	**(B32A2ST) Tug**	**2 oil engines** driving 2 Propellers Total Power: 1,472kW (2,002hp) Caterpillar C32 ACERT 2 x Vee 4 Stroke 12 Cy. 145 x 162 each-736kW (1001bhp) Caterpillar Inc-USA
7945728 *UEIA* -	**SALMA** **Novyy Mir Fishing Collective (Rybolovetskiy Kolkhoz 'Novyy Mir')** - *Nakhodka* *Russia* MMSI: 273823300 Official number: 802164	**779** 233 326	Class: RS	**1981 Zavod "Leninskaya Kuznitsa" — Kiyev** Yd No: 251 Loa 53.75 (BB) Br ex 10.72 Dght 4.290 Lbp 47.92 Br md 10.50 Dpth 6.02 Welded, 1 dk	**(B11A2FS) Stern Trawler** Ins: 218 Compartments: 1 Ho, ER 1 Ha: (1.6 x 1.6) Derricks: 2x1.5t Ice Capable	**1 oil engine** driving 1 FP propeller Total Power: 971kW (1,320hp) 12.8kn S.K.L. 8NVD48A-2U 1 x 4 Stroke 8 Cy. 320 x 480 971kW (1320bhp) VEB Schwermaschinenbau "KarlLiebknecht" (SKL)-Magdeburg Fuel: 184.0 (d.f.)
9382425 *A6E3040* -	**SALMA** **Liwa Marine Services LLC** - *Abu Dhabi* *United Arab Emirates* MMSI: 470882000 Official number: 5178	**481** 144 558	Class: BV	**2006-05 Piasau Slipways Sdn Bhd — Miri** Yd No: 219 Loa 47.00 Br ex - Dght 2.500 Lbp 43.21 Br md 11.00 Dpth 3.20 Welded, 1 dk	**(A35D2RL) Landing Craft**	**2 oil engines** reduction geared to sc. shafts driving 2 FP propellers Total Power: 942kW (1,280hp) 10.0kn Cummins KTA-19-M3 2 x 4 Stroke 6 Cy. 159 x 159 each-471kW (640bhp) Cummins Engine Co Inc-USA

8630760 *YHAB* -	**SALMADRISANA** *ex* Spontan *-2012* *ex* K. K. 34 *-2006* *ex* Bisan Maru No. 8 *-2001* **PT Bayumas Jaya Mandiri Lines** - *Cirebon* *Indonesia*	**935** 610 759	Class: KI	**1987-02 Y.K. Takasago Zosensho — Naruto** Converted From: Suction Dredger-2001 Loa 48.65 Br ex 10.00 Dght 4.460 Lbp 44.20 Br md 9.98 Dpth 5.30 Welded, 1 dk	**(A31A2GX) General Cargo Ship**	**1 oil engine** driving 1 FP propeller Total Power: 736kW (1,001hp) 10.0kn Yanmar MF26-HT 1 x 4 Stroke 6 Cy. 260 x 500 736kW (1001bhp) Yanmar Diesel Engine Co Ltd-Japan AuxGen: 1 x 75kW 225/130V a.c
7431337 *ES2408* EK-9905	**SALME** *ex* Neshamar *-1999* *ex* Arnasteinur *-1999* *ex* Dana Bank *-1999* **Tallinna Tehnikaulikool** - *Tallinn* *Estonia* MMSI: 276329000 Official number: 399FC10	**223** 67 262		**1974 Carl B Hoffmanns Maskinfabrik A/S — Esbjerg** Yd No: 9 Converted From: Fishing Vessel-2009 Loa 31.30 Br ex 7.22 Dght 3.400 Lbp 26.87 Br md 7.19 Dpth 3.46 Welded, 1 dk	**(B31A2SR) Research Survey Vessel**	**1 oil engine** driving 1 CP propeller Total Power: 485kW (659hp) Alpha 406-26VO 1 x 2 Stroke 6 Cy. 260 x 400 485kW (659bhp) Alpha Diesel A/S-Denmark
9099016 - -	**SALMEEN** - - -	**480** 144 1,200		**2005-01 UR-Dock — Basrah** Yd No: 35 Loa 46.00 Br ex - Dght 4.750 Lbp - Br md 10.85 Dpth 5.75 Welded, 1 dk	**(A31A2GX) General Cargo Ship**	**3 oil engines** Reduction geared to sc. shafts driving 3 Propellers Total Power: 1,825kW (2,482hp)
7320758 - -	**SALMI** - **Konsul-M JSC (A/O 'Konsul-M')** -	**745** 223 395	Class: (RS)	**1973 Zavod "Leninskaya Kuznitsa" — Kiyev** Yd No: 1370 Loa 54.82 Br ex 9.96 Dght 4.111 Lbp 50.29 Br md 9.80 Dpth 5.03 Welded, 1 dk	**(B11A2FS) Stern Trawler** Ins: 400 Compartments: 2 Ho, ER 3 Ha: 3 (1.5 x 1.6) Derricks: 2x1.3t; Winches: 2 Ice Capable	**1 oil engine** driving 1 CP propeller Total Power: 736kW (1,001hp) 12.0kn S.K.L. 8NVD48-2U 1 x 4 Stroke 8 Cy. 320 x 480 736kW (1001bhp) VEB Schwermaschinenbau "KarlLiebknecht" (SKL)-Magdeburg AuxGen: 2 x 150kW a.c, 2 x 100kW a.c Fuel: 197.0 (d.f.)
8730314 - -	**SALMISTU** - - -	**117** 35 30	Class: (RS)	**1977-12 Sosnovskiy Sudostroitelnyy Zavod — Sosnovka** Loa 25.50 Br ex 7.00 Dght 2.390 Lbp 22.00 Br md - Dpth 3.30 Welded, 1 dk	**(B11A2FS) Stern Trawler** Ins: 64	**1 oil engine** driving 1 CP propeller Total Power: 221kW (300hp) 9.5kn S.K.L. 6NVD26A-2 1 x 4 Stroke 6 Cy. 180 x 260 221kW (300bhp) VEB Schwermaschinenbau "KarlLiebknecht" (SKL)-Magdeburg
7616858 *8PAK5* -	**SALMO** - **Wilson Shipowning AS** Bergen Shipping Chartering AS *Bridgetown* *Barbados* MMSI: 314421000	**2,171** 1,389 3,225	Class: BV (NV)	**1979-05 Robb Caledon Shipbuilders Ltd. — Dundee** Yd No: 571 Lengthened-1983 Loa 91.56 Br ex 14.08 Dght 5.100 Lbp 85.95 Br md 13.42 Dpth 6.51 Welded, 1 dk	**(A31A2GX) General Cargo Ship** Grain: 4,544; Bale: 4,389 Compartments: 1 Ho, ER 1 Ha: (53.9 x 9.7)ER Gantry cranes: 1x10t Ice Capable	**1 oil engine** driving 1 CP propeller Total Power: 1,287kW (1,750hp) 11.0kn Wichmann 7AXA 1 x 2 Stroke 7 Cy. 300 x 450 1287kW (1750bhp) Wichmann Motorfabrikk AS-Norway AuxGen: 2 x 96kW 380V 50Hz a.c, 1 x 88kW 380V 50Hz a.c Thrusters: 1 Thwart. FP thruster (f)
6704919 *MDDH8* -	**SALMO SALAR** *ex* Strilkyst *-1983* *ex* Lostar *-1982* *ex* Stalskjell *-1981* **Ellenborough Investments Ltd** - *Lerwick* *United Kingdom* MMSI: 235007010 Official number: 908283	**206** 61 224 T/cm 1.8	Class: (NV)	**1967 AS Haugesunds Slip — Haugesund** Yd No: 8 Converted From: Products Tanker-1983 Loa 35.08 Br ex 7.01 Dght 2.655 Lbp 31.22 Br md 6.86 Dpth 2.87 Welded, 1 dk	**(B12C2FL) Live Fish Carrier (Well Boat)** Liq: 268; Liq (Oil): 268 Compartments: 4 Ho, 4 Ta, ER 4 Ha: 2 (3.4 x 1.8)2 (2.4 x 1.8) Manifold: Bow/CM: 18m Ice Capable	**1 oil engine** driving 1 CP propeller Total Power: 276kW (375hp) 10.0kn Wichmann 5DCT 1 x 2 Stroke 5 Cy. 200 x 300 276kW (375bhp) Wichmann Motorfabrikk AS-Norway AuxGen: 1 x 40kW 220V 50Hz a.c, 1 x 25kW 220V 50Hz a.c Fuel: 10.0 (d.f.) 1.5pd
9168178 - -	**SALMO VEST** - - -	**467** 161 -		**1997-10 Sletta Baatbyggeri AS — Mjosundet** Yd No: 85 Loa 40.30 Br ex - Dght - Lbp 36.50 Br md 9.50 Dpth 5.00 Welded, 1 dk	**(B12C2FL) Live Fish Carrier (Well Boat)**	**1 oil engine** driving 1 FP propeller Total Power: 1,118kW (1,520hp) 11.0kn Caterpillar 3512B-HD 1 x Vee 4 Stroke 12 Cy. 170 x 215 1118kW (1520bhp) Caterpillar Inc-USA Thrusters: 1 Thwart. FP thruster (f)
8803331 *CB4149* -	**SALMON** - **South Pacific Korp SA (SPK)** - *Valparaiso* *Chile* MMSI: 725000192 Official number: 2613	*500* 147 -	Class: (BV)	**1989-08 Astilleros Marco Chilena Ltda. — Iquique** Yd No: 188 Loa 44.50 (BB) Br ex - Dght - Lbp 40.70 Br md 10.10 Dpth 5.31 Welded	**(B11B2FV) Fishing Vessel** Ins: 500	**1 oil engine** geared to sc. shaft driving 1 FP propeller Total Power: 1,037kW (1,410hp) 13.4kn Caterpillar 3516TA 1 x Vee 4 Stroke 16 Cy. 170 x 190 1037kW (1410bhp) Caterpillar Inc-USA AuxGen: 2 x 32kW 380V a.c Thrusters: 1 Thwart. FP thruster (f); 1 Tunnel thruster (a)
8907840 - -	**SALMON** *launched as* Caroline *-1990* **Aqua Products Peru SA** - *Peru* Official number: CE-12517-PM	**274** 118 381	Class: (LR) ✠ Classed LR until 21/2/96	**1989-12 Mawei Shipyard — Fuzhou FJ** Yd No: 806A-3 Loa 38.50 Br ex - Dght 3.600 Lbp 34.00 Br md 8.20 Dpth 4.20 Welded, 1 dk	**(B11B2FV) Fishing Vessel**	**1 oil engine** reverse reduction geared to sc. shaft driving 1 FP propeller Total Power: 1,118kW (1,520hp) Caterpillar 3512TA 1 x Vee 4 Stroke 12 Cy. 170 x 190 1118kW (1520bhp) Caterpillar Inc-USA AuxGen: 2 x 40kW 400V 50Hz a.c
8306187 - -	**SALMON** - **Purnandan Barclay** - *Georgetown* *Guyana* Official number: 708097	*108* 48 98		**1983-09 Bender Shipbuilding & Repair Co Inc — Mobile AL** Yd No: 191 Loa - Br ex - Dght 2.590 Lbp 21.95 Br md 6.11 Dpth 3.28 Welded, 1 dk	**(B11A2FT) Trawler**	**1 oil engine** sr geared to sc. shaft driving 1 FP propeller Total Power: 268kW (364hp) 9.3kn Caterpillar 3408TA 1 x Vee 4 Stroke 8 Cy. 137 x 152 268kW (364bhp) Caterpillar Tractor Co-USA AuxGen: 2 x 3kW 32V d.c Fuel: 43.5 (d.f.) 1.0pd
5169758 *HP8264* -	**SALMON KING** *ex* Jane *-1995* **Pesquera Best Salmon Ltd** - SatCom: Inmarsat C 435533210 *Panama* *Panama* Official number: 24317RH	**421** 202 574	Class: (GL)	**1956-12 Gebr. Schuerenstedt KG Schiffs- u. Bootswerft — Berne** Yd No: 1047 Lengthened-1963 Loa 50.97 Br ex 8.54 Dght 2.947 Lbp 44.94 Br md 8.41 Dpth 3.51 Riveted\Welded, 1 dk	**(A31A2GX) General Cargo Ship** Grain: 760; Bale: 704 Compartments: 1 Ho, ER 2 Ha: (10.6 x 5.0) (14.5 x 5.0)ER Ice Capable	**1 oil engine** driving 1 FP propeller Total Power: 287kW (390hp) 9.0kn MaK MSU423 1 x 4 Stroke 6 Cy. 290 x 420 287kW (390bhp) Maschinenbau Kiel AG (MaK)-Kiel AuxGen: 1 x 5kW 24V d.c, 1 x 3kW 24V d.c Fuel: 32.5 (d.f.)
5035816 *VGTF* -	**SALMON SEEKER** *ex* Banksland Surveyor *-1993* *ex* Banksland *-1981* *ex* Auriga *-1956* **Oak Bay Marina Ltd** - *Victoria, BC* *Canada* MMSI: 316004442 Official number: 188246	*634* 190 332	Class: (LR) Classed LR until 16/4/93	**1953-12 Scheepswerf "De Waal" N.V. — Zaltbommel** Yd No: 647 Converted From: Research Vessel-1993 Converted From: General Cargo Ship Loa 50.60 Br ex 8.31 Dght 2.750 Lbp 48.34 Br md 8.26 Dpth 3.64 Riveted\Welded, 1 dk	**(X11A2YP) Yacht** Passengers: berths: 28	**1 oil engine** sr reverse geared to sc. shaft driving 1 FP propeller Total Power: 736kW (1,001hp) 10.0kn Caterpillar D399TA 1 x Vee 4 Stroke 16 Cy. 159 x 203 736kW (1001bhp) (new engine ,made 1973, fitted 1981) Caterpillar Tractor Co-USA AuxGen: 2 x 250kW 480V 60Hz a.c Thrusters: 1 Water jet (f) Fuel: 30.5 (d.f.)
8745254 - -	**SALMON TRANSPORTER** *ex* Porte Dauphine (YNG 186) *-1996* **Marine Harvest Canada Inc** - *Vancouver, BC* *Canada* Official number: 313111	**315** 94 -		**1952-12 Pictou Foundry & Machine Co — Pictou NS** Converted From: Boom-defence Vessel-1997 L reg 35.60 Br ex - Dght - Lbp - Br md 7.84 Dpth 4.34 Welded, 1 dk	**(B12C2FL) Live Fish Carrier (Well Boat)**	**1 oil engine** reduction geared to sc. shaft driving 1 Propeller Total Power: 552kW (750hp) 11.0kn
8725711 - -	**SALNYY** - **Ecosoyuz Co Ltd** - *Murmansk* *Russia* MMSI: 273133900	**204** 83 264	Class: RS	**1986-12 Sudoremontnyy Zavod "Yakor" — Sovetskaya Gavan** Yd No: 815 Loa 36.01 Br ex 7.65 Dght 2.500 Lbp 35.50 Br md 7.42 Dpth 3.10 Welded, 1 dk	**(B35E2TF) Bunkering Tanker** Liq: 253; Liq (Oil): 253 Compartments: 6 Ta, ER Ice Capable	**1 oil engine** geared to sc. shaft driving 1 FP propeller Total Power: 166kW (226hp) 7.0kn Daldizel 6CHNSP18/22 1 x 4 Stroke 6 Cy. 180 x 220 166kW (226bhp) Daldizel-Khabarovsk AuxGen: 1 x 30kW Fuel: 7.0 (d.f.)
8650447 *PP8637* -	**SALOBO** - **Vale SA** - *Rio de Janeiro* *Brazil* Official number: 3813876454	**232** - -		**2011-07 H. Dantas Construcoes e Reparos Navais Ltda. — Aracaju** Loa - Br ex - Dght - Lbp - Br md - Dpth - Welded, 1 dk	**(B32A2ST) Tug**	**1 oil engine** driving 1 Propeller

IMO / Call sign	Name, owner, manager, port	Tonnage	Class	Builder, dimensions	Type, capacity	Machinery
8623016 *DUA2572* -	**SALOMAGUE** *ex* Inari Maru No. 73 *-1982* **J & C Deep Sea Fishing Corp** - *Manila* *Philippines* Official number: MNLD000310	*130* 104 -		**1966 Tokushima Zosen K.K. — Fukuoka** Loa 33.99 Br ex 6.33 Dght 2.601 Lbp 29.49 Br md 6.30 Dpth 3.00 Welded, 1 dk	**(B11A2FT) Trawler**	**1 oil engine** driving 1 FP propeller Total Power: 397kW (540hp) Niigata 1 x 4 Stroke 6 Cy. 397kW (540bhp) Niigata Engineering Co Ltd-Japan
9515412 *9V9112* -	**SALOME** **Mark V Shipping Pte Ltd** Wallenius Marine Singapore Pte Ltd SatCom: Inmarsat C 456608610 *Singapore* *Singapore* MMSI: 566086000 Official number: 396643	**75,251** 27,215 43,878	Class: NV	**2012-06 Mitsubishi Heavy Industries Ltd. — Nagasaki** Yd No: 2265 Loa 265.00 (BB) Br ex 33.27 Dght 12.300 Lbp 250.00 Br md 32.26 Dpth 33.22 Welded, 9 dks incl. 6 hoistable dks.	**(A35B2RV) Vehicles Carrier** Angled stern door/ramp (s. a.) Len: 44.30 Wid: 12.50 Swl: 505 Cars: 5,990 Bale: 138,000	**1 oil engine** driving 1 FP propeller Total Power: 21,770kW (29,598hp) 20.3kn MAN-B&W 7L70ME-C8 1 x 2 Stroke 7 Cy. 700 x 2360 21770kW (29598bhp) Kawasaki Heavy Industries Ltd-Japan AuxGen: 1 x 1100kW a.c, 3 x 2360kW a.c Thrusters: 1 Tunnel thruster (f); 1 Tunnel thruster (a) Fuel: 637.0 (d.f.) 5390.0 (r.f.)
9013012 *J8B4719* -	**SALONA** *ex* Elizabeth F *-2012* *ex* Derk *-2005* *ex* Skylge *-2001* *ex* Sea Loire *-1999* *ex* Skylge *-1997* **Solinska Plovidba doo** - SatCom: Inmarsat C 437609910 *Kingstown* *St Vincent & The Grenadines* MMSI: 376099000 Official number: 11192	**1,276** 672 1,686	Class: CS (BV)	**1991-07 Scheepswerf- en Reparatiebedrijf "Harlingen" B.V. — Harlingen** Yd No: 94 Loa 79.10 Br ex - Dght 3.850 Lbp 74.31 Br md 10.50 Dpth 4.75 Welded, 1 dk	**(A31A2GX) General Cargo Ship** Compartments: 1 Ho, ER 1 Ha: ER (53.4 x 8.3) Ice Capable	**1 oil engine** reduction geared to sc. shaft driving 1 FP propeller Total Power: 944kW (1,283hp) 10.0kn A.B.C. 6MDZC 1 x 4 Stroke 6 Cy. 256 x 310 944kW (1283bhp) Anglo Belgian Corp NV (ABC)-Belgium
8303185 *HPUS* -	**SALOOS** *ex* Industrial Achiever *-2011* *ex* Ostara *-2004* *ex* Callisto *-1994* *ex* Jumbo Callisto *-1994* *ex* Tiger Creek *-1990* *ex* Callisto *-1990* *ex* Jumbo Callisto *-1989* *ex* Callisto *-1988* **Navang Shipping SA** Jade SA *Panama* *Panama* MMSI: 371933000 Official number: 4312311	**6,950** 2,085 4,403	Class: (GL)	**1983-12 Husumer Schiffswerft Inh. Gebr. Kroeger GmbH & Co. KG — Husum** Yd No: 1489 Loa 106.25 (BB) Br ex 19.94 Dght 4.971 Lbp 95.61 Br md 19.61 Dpth 10.95 Welded, 2 dks	**(A35A2RR) Ro-Ro Cargo Ship** Stern door/ramp Len: 15.00 Wid: 11.50 Swl: - Lane-Len: 430 Trailers: 35 Grain: 10,618; Bale: 10,571 TEU 438 incl 20 ref C Compartments: 1 Ho, ER, 1 Tw Dk 1 Ha: (86.6 x 15.0)ER Cranes: 2x35t Ice Capable	**2 oil engines** sr reverse geared to sc. shafts driving 2 CP propellers Total Power: 2,942kW (4,000hp) 12.0kn MaK 6M453AK 2 x 4 Stroke 6 Cy. 320 x 420 each-1471kW (2000bhp) Krupp MaK Maschinenbau GmbH-Kiel AuxGen: 1 x 350kW 220/380V 50Hz a.c, 2 x 318kW 220/380V 50Hz a.c, 1 x 206kW 220/380V 50Hz a.c Thrusters: 1 Thwart. FP thruster (f) Fuel: 51.8 (d.f.) 466.4 (r.f.) 14.8pd
1011393 *ZCYN4* -	**SALPERTON** **Primero Maritime Ltd** - *George Town* *Cayman Islands (British)* MMSI: 319608000 Official number: 741450	**221** 66 46	Class: LR ✠ **100A1** SS 06/2009 SSC Yacht, mono G6 Cable: 140.0/17.5 U2 (a)	**2009-06 Fitzroy Yachts Ltd — New Plymouth** Yd No: 11 Loa 45.07 Br ex 9.34 Dght 4.750 Lbp 40.29 Br md 9.30 Dpth 3.68 Welded, 1 dk	**(X11A2YS) Yacht (Sailing)** Hull Material: Aluminium Alloy	**1 oil engine** with clutches, flexible couplings & sr geared to sc. shaft driving 1 CP propeller Total Power: 641kW (872hp) 14.0kn Caterpillar 3406E-TA 1 x 4 Stroke 6 Cy. 137 x 165 641kW (872bhp) Caterpillar Inc-USA AuxGen: 2 x 90kW 400V 50Hz a.c Thrusters: 1 Thwart. FP thruster (f); 1 Thwart. FP thruster (f)
7939080 *S2QL* -	**SALSABIL** **MHK Enterprise Ltd** - *Chittagong* *Bangladesh* Official number: 384884	*126* 41 -	Class: (NK)	**1980-12 ShinA Shipbuilding Co Ltd — Tongyeong** Yd No: 251 Loa 24.16 Br ex 6.43 Dght 2.941 Lbp 21.04 Br md 6.41 Dpth 3.51 Welded, 1 dk	**(B11B2FV) Fishing Vessel** Ins: 72	**1 oil engine** geared to sc. shaft driving 1 FP propeller Total Power: 294kW (400hp) 9.0kn Yanmar S165L-ST 1 x 4 Stroke 6 Cy. 165 x 210 294kW (400bhp) Yanmar Diesel Engine Co Ltd-Japan AuxGen: 2 x 52kW
8815138 *SSDL* -	**SALSABIL** **Government of The Arab Republic of Egypt (Ministry of Agriculture- Agriculture Guidance Project Code 8004)** Government of The Arab Republic of Egypt (Ministry of Scientific Research National Institute of Oceanography & Fisheries) *Alexandria* *Egypt* MMSI: 622122237 Official number: 3207	**193** 58 178	Class: NK	**1989-01 Niigata Engineering Co Ltd — Niigata NI** Yd No: 2110 Loa 30.71 Br ex - Dght 3.193 Lbp 26.00 Br md 7.41 Dpth 3.15 Welded, 1 dk	**(B12D2FR) Fishery Research Vessel** Ins: 50	**1 oil engine** with clutches, flexible couplings & sr geared to sc. shaft driving 1 CP propeller Total Power: 662kW (900hp) 10.0kn Niigata 6NSC-M 1 x 4 Stroke 6 Cy. 190 x 260 662kW (900bhp) Niigata Engineering Co Ltd-Japan AuxGen: 2 x 80kW a.c Fuel: 70.0 (d.f.)
9505015 *2HGF3* -	**SALT ISLAND** *ex* Ak Tue *-2014* *launched as* Dulas Island *-2008* **Holyhead Towing Co Ltd** - *Beaumaris* *United Kingdom* Official number: 9505015	**213** 63 -	Class: LR (BV) **100A1** SS 05/2013 SSC workboat G5 **LMC** Cable: 192.5/20.5 U2 (a)	**2008-05 Neptune Shipyards BV — Aalst (Nl)** Yd No: 326 Loa 25.10 Br ex - Dght 2.390 Lbp 23.61 Br md 9.90 Dpth 3.50 Welded, 1 dk	**(B34L2QU) Utility Vessel**	**2 oil engines** reverse reduction geared to sc. shafts driving 2 FP propellers Total Power: 1,940kW (2,638hp) Cummins KTA-38-M2 2 x Vee 4 Stroke 12 Cy. 159 x 159 each-970kW (1319bhp) Cummins Engine Co Inc-USA AuxGen: 2 x 120kW a.c
9314129 *C4DS2* -	**SALT LAKE CITY** *ex* Thalassini Niki *-2007* **Marfort Navigation Co Ltd** Diana Shipping Services SA SatCom: Inmarsat C 421076110 *Limassol* *Cyprus* MMSI: 210761000 Official number: 9314129	**89,076** 56,303 171,810	Class: BV	**2005-08 Daewoo Shipbuilding & Marine Engineering Co Ltd — Geoje** Yd No: 1160 Loa 289.00 (BB) Br ex - Dght 17.920 Lbp 279.00 Br md 45.00 Dpth 24.20 Welded, 1 dk	**(A21A2BC) Bulk Carrier** Double Hull Grain: 187,606 Compartments: 9 Ho, ER 9 Ha: 7 (14.7 x 21.0)ER 2 (14.7 x 15.3)	**1 oil engine** driving 1 FP propeller Total Power: 18,660kW (25,370hp) 15.1kn B&W 6S70MC-C 1 x 2 Stroke 6 Cy. 700 x 2800 18660kW (25370bhp) Doosan Engine Co Ltd-South Korea AuxGen: 3 x 800kW 450/220V 60Hz a.c Fuel: 232.0 (d.f.) 4457.0 (r.f.) 51.0pd
7320617 - -	**SALT RIVER** *ex* Nelson *-1988* **Blaslov Fishing Pty Ltd** - *Fremantle, WA* *Australia* Official number: 355150	*352* 247 -	Class: (NV)	**1973 Ocean Shipyards & Offshore Eng Services Pty Ltd — Fremantle WA** Yd No: 109 Loa 25.73 Br ex 7.93 Dght 2.972 Lbp 24.62 Br md 7.78 Dpth 3.74 Welded, 1 dk	**(B11A2FT) Trawler**	**1 oil engine** driving 1 FP propeller Total Power: 405kW (551hp) 10.0kn Cummins VT-28-M1 1 x Vee 4 Stroke 12 Cy. 140 x 152 405kW (551bhp) Cummins Engine Co Inc-USA AuxGen: 1 x 148kW 415V 50Hz a.c, 1 x 110kW 415V 50Hz a.c
9419242 *A8WC6* -	**SALTA** *ex* Aphrodite *-2011* *ex* Botany Sea *-2011* *ex* Aphrodite *-2010* *ex* Alcmene *-2009* *launched as* Botany Sea *-2009* **ms 'Botany Sea' Schifffahrtsgesellschaft mbH & Co KG** NSC Shipping GmbH & Cie KG *Monrovia* *Liberia* MMSI: 636092067 Official number: 92067	**35,240** 16,425 52,998	Class: GL (NV)	**2009-12 Zhoushan Wuzhou Ship Repairing & Building Co Ltd — Zhoushan ZJ** Yd No: WZ0050603 Loa 196.21 (BB) Br ex - Dght 13.250 Lbp 186.80 Br md 32.25 Dpth 19.50 Welded, 1 dk	**(A31A2GO) Open Hatch Cargo Ship** Grain: 64,231 TEU 2033 C Ho 1298 TEU C Dk 735 TEU Compartments: 8 Ho, ER 8 Ha: ER Cranes: 4x45t	**1 oil engine** driving 1 FP propeller Total Power: 11,060kW (15,037hp) 15.0kn MAN-B&W 7S50MC-C 1 x 2 Stroke 7 Cy. 500 x 2000 11060kW (15037bhp) STX Engine Co Ltd-South Korea AuxGen: 3 x 910kW a.c
7367720 *EIVS* WD 38	**SALTEES QUEST** *ex* Jacob *-2002* *ex* Liliane J *-1999* *ex* Liliane *-1984* *ex* Jozina *-1981* **Brendan, John, Denis & James O'Flaherty** - SatCom: Inmarsat C 425048910 *Wexford* *Irish Republic* MMSI: 250489000 Official number: 403801	**227** 68 -		**1974-07 Scheepsbouw- en Constructiebedr. K. Hakvoort N.V. — Monnickendam** Yd No: 139 Loa 35.01 Br ex 7.52 Dght 2.850 Lbp 30.68 Br md 7.50 Dpth 3.80 Welded	**(B11A2FT) Trawler**	**1 oil engine** driving 1 FP propeller Total Power: 883kW (1,201hp) A.B.C. 6MDZC 1 x 4 Stroke 6 Cy. 256 x 310 883kW (1201bhp) (new engine 1991) Anglo Belgian Corp NV (ABC)-Belgium
9281061 *LMFM* -	**SALTEN** **Torghatten Nord AS** - *Narvik* *Norway* MMSI: 259387000	**539** 162 46	Class: (NV)	**2003-04 Image Marine Pty Ltd — Fremantle WA** Yd No: 242 Loa 41.30 Br ex 11.90 Dght 1.450 Lbp 36.20 Br md 11.60 Dpth 4.30 Welded	**(A37B2PS) Passenger Ship** Hull Material: Aluminium Alloy Passengers: unberthed: 216	**2 oil engines** geared to sc. shafts driving 2 Water jets Total Power: 4,596kW (6,248hp) 33.0kn M.T.U. 16V4000M70 2 x Vee 4 Stroke 16 Cy. 165 x 190 each-2298kW (3124bhp) MTU Friedrichshafen GmbH-Friedrichshafen
8708385 - -	**SALTEN II** *ex* Salten *-1997* - -	**340** 109 50	Class: (NV)	**1988-05 AB Nya Oskarshamns Varv — Oskarshamn** Yd No: 508 Loa 36.50 Br ex 9.80 Dght 1.701 Lbp 31.10 Br md 9.50 Dpth 3.69 Welded, 1 dk	**(A37B2PS) Passenger Ship** Hull Material: Aluminium Alloy Passengers: unberthed: 186 Bale: 60 Compartments: 1 Ho, ER	**2 oil engines** with flexible couplings & sr gearedto sc. shafts driving 2 Water jets Total Power: 4,076kW (5,542hp) 40.5kn M.T.U. 16V396TB84 2 x Vee 4 Stroke 16 Cy. 165 x 185 each-2038kW (2771bhp) (made 1988) MTU Friedrichshafen GmbH-Friedrichshafen AuxGen: 2 x 56kW 220V 50Hz a.c

9492933 *9HRM9* -
SALTINA *ex* Universe 4 *-2008*
Massatlantic (Malta) Ltd
Massoel Ltd
Valletta *Malta*
MMSI: 249416000
Official number: 9492933
5,087 2,625 7,300
Class: BV
2008-09 Universe Shipbuilding (Yangzhou) Co Ltd — Yizheng JS Yd No: 06-004
Loa 112.80 Br ex - Dght 6.900
Lbp 106.00 Br md 17.20 Dpth 9.10
Welded, 1 dk
(A21A2BC) Bulk Carrier
Grain: 9,394
Compartments: 3 Ho, ER
3 Ha: ER
Cranes: 2x25t
1 oil engine reduction geared to sc. shaft driving 1 FP propeller
Total Power: 2,500kW (3,399hp) 11.0kn
Daihatsu 8DKM-28
1 x 4 Stroke 8 Cy. 280 x 390 2500kW (3399bhp)
Shaanxi Diesel Heavy Industry Co Lt-China
AuxGen: 3 x 250kW 50Hz a.c

8603121 *D7MG* -
SALTLAKE *ex* Katah *-1990*
Saltlake Maritime Ltd
Ji Sung Shipping Co Ltd
Jeju *South Korea*
MMSI: 440116000
Official number: JJR-131060
3,437 1,751 4,269
Class: KR (NK)
1986-03 Kochi Jyuko (Eiho Zosen) K.K. — Kochi Yd No: 1885
Loa 96.78 (BB) Br ex - Dght 6.524
Lbp 89.55 Br md 16.20 Dpth 6.85
Welded, 3 dks
(A34A2GR) Refrigerated Cargo Ship
Ins: 5,149
Compartments: 3 Ho, ER
3 Ha: 3 (5.0 x 5.0)ER
Derricks: 6x5t
1 oil engine driving 1 FP propeller
Total Power: 2,979kW (4,050hp) 14.8kn
Mitsubishi 6UEC37LA
1 x 2 Stroke 6 Cy. 370 x 880 2979kW (4050bhp)
Akasaka Tekkosho KK (Akasaka DieselLtd)-Japan
AuxGen: 2 x 560kW a.c

5308108 - -
SALTO *ex* Ganguil I *-1945*
Fluvial Trans-Salto SRL
-
Argentina
Official number: 0526
492 221 -
1902 Fa A F Smulders — Schiedam
Loa 52.10 Br ex 9.05 Dght 3.455
Lbp - Br md 9.00 Dpth -
Riveted, 1 dk
(A31A2GX) General Cargo Ship
Grain: 742; Bale: 694
Winches: 2
1 Steam Recip driving 1 FP propeller 8.5kn

8825535 - -
SALTO *ex* Tinny *-1992*
Ole Pedersen
-
Argentina
107 32 -
1987 AB Hasse Wester Mekaniska Verkstad — Uddevalla
Loa 18.75 Br ex 6.06 Dght -
Lbp - Br md - Dpth -
Welded
(B11B2FV) Fishing Vessel
1 oil engine driving 1 FP propeller

7922130 *UBMG5* -
SALTSTRAUM
OOO 'KD Bunker'
-
SatCom: Inmarsat C 427303991
Russia
MMSI: 273359900
1,881 640 2,533 T/cm 8.5
Class: (NV)
1980-12 Bolsones Verft AS — Molde Yd No: 269
Loa 80.16 (BB) Br ex 13.02 Dght 5.184
Lbp 75.50 Br md 13.01 Dpth 7.35
Welded, 1 dk.
(A12B2TR) Chemical/Products Tanker
Liq: 2,562; Liq (Oil): 2,562
Cargo Heating Coils
Compartments: 5 Ta (s.stl), 1 Ta, 8 Wing Ta, 2 Wing Slop Ta, ER
14 Cargo Pump (s): 14x175m³/hr
Manifold: Bow/CM: 40.5m
Ice Capable
1 oil engine reduction geared to sc. shaft driving 1 CP propeller
Total Power: 1,655kW (2,250hp) 13.0kn
Normo KVM-12
1 x Vee 4 Stroke 12 Cy. 250 x 300 1655kW (2250bhp)
AS Bergens Mek Verksteder-Norway
AuxGen: 3 x 132kW 380V 50Hz a.c
Thrusters: 1 Tunnel thruster (f)
Fuel: 36.0 (d.f.) 126.0 (r.f.)

8962905 *SIMB* FG-47
SALTVIK *ex* Vastvag *-1987*
Benny Anders Karlsson
-
Glommen *Sweden*
MMSI: 266056000
109 32 -
1979 Marinvarvet — Farosund
Loa 19.61 Br ex 7.20 Dght 2.210
Lbp - Br md - Dpth -
Welded, 1 dk
(B11B2FV) Fishing Vessel
2 oil engines driving 2 FP propellers
Total Power: 530kW (720hp)
Volvo Penta TAMD120B
2 x 4 Stroke 6 Cy. 130 x 150 each-265kW (360bhp)
AB Volvo Penta-Sweden

8975706 - -
SALTY DOG *ex* C Smith *-2013* *ex* Captain Linton *-2009*
Dragnet Seafood LLC
-
Chauvin, LA *United States of America*
Official number: 1118259
101 80 -
2001-01 Gulfbound LLC — Chauvin, La
L reg 22.25 Br ex - Dght -
Lbp - Br md 7.00 Dpth 2.74
Welded, 1 dk
(B11B2FV) Fishing Vessel
1 oil engine driving 1 Propeller

7908055 - -
SALTY II
-
Hadden Salt
-
United States of America
185 - -
1978-12 Eastern Marine, Inc. — Panama City, Fl Yd No: 7
Loa - Br ex - Dght 2.291
Lbp 28.68 Br md 7.33 Dpth 3.20
Welded, 1 dk
(B11B2FV) Fishing Vessel
1 oil engine geared to sc. shaft driving 1 FP propeller
Total Power: 386kW (525hp) 10.0kn
G.M. (Detroit Diesel) 12V-71-TI
1 x Vee 2 Stroke 12 Cy. 108 x 127 386kW (525bhp)
General Motors Detroit DieselAllison Divn-USA
AuxGen: 1 x 75kW, 1 x 40kW

9522805 *2AQA8* -
SALU
Deep Blue Yacht Charters Ltd
-
Douglas *Isle of Man (British)*
MMSI: 235062013
Official number: 739386
193 57 30
Class: AB
2008-06 Azimut-Benetti SpA — Fano Yd No: 19
Loa 30.20 Br ex - Dght 1.880
Lbp 25.66 Br md 7.15 Dpth 3.54
Bonded, 1 dk
(X11A2YP) Yacht
Hull Material: Reinforced Plastic
2 oil engines reduction geared to sc. shafts driving 2 Propellers
Total Power: 1,490kW (2,026hp) 12.5kn
Caterpillar C18
2 x 4 Stroke 6 Cy. 145 x 183 each-745kW (1013bhp)
Caterpillar Inc-USA
AuxGen: 2 x 50kW a.c

8976449 *YB4365* -
SALUANG
Primo Peningkatan Angkutan Penyeberangan
PT ASDP Indonesia Ferry (Persero) - Angkutan Sungai Danau & Penyeberangan
Semarang *Indonesia*
114 34 -
Class: KI
2000 P.T. Sanur Marindo Shipyard — Tegal
Loa 30.50 Br ex - Dght -
Lbp 27.00 Br md 8.15 Dpth 2.45
Welded, 1 dk
(A37B2PS) Passenger Ship
1 oil engine geared to sc. shaft driving 1 Propeller
Total Power: 177kW (241hp)
Yanmar 6HA-DTE
1 x 4 Stroke 6 Cy. 130 x 150 177kW (241bhp)
Yanmar Diesel Engine Co Ltd-Japan
AuxGen: 1 x 60kW 380/220V a.c

9129378 *DSQZ3* -
SALUS *ex* Emmanuela *-2010* *ex* Selendang Kasa *-2010*
KDB Capital Corp
Neo Field Shipping Co Ltd
Jeju *South Korea*
MMSI: 441761000
Official number: JJR-106295
18,507 10,098 28,410 T/cm 39.3
Class: KR (LR)
✠ Classed LR until 1/10/10
1997-03 Hudong Shipbuilding Group — Shanghai Yd No: H1234A
Loa 174.76 (BB) Br ex 26.52 Dght 10.119
Lbp 165.00 Br md 26.40 Dpth 14.21
Welded, 1 dk
(A21A2BC) Bulk Carrier
Grain: 37,996; Bale: 37,037
Compartments: 5 Ho, ER
5 Ha: (14.4 x 12.8)4 (19.2 x 14.4)ER
Cranes: 4x30t
1 oil engine driving 1 FP propeller
Total Power: 6,460kW (8,783hp) 13.5kn
B&W 5L50MC
1 x 2 Stroke 5 Cy. 500 x 1620 6460kW (8783bhp)
Hudong Shipyard-China
AuxGen: 3 x 490kW 450V 60Hz a.c
Boilers: AuxB (Comp) 8.4kgf/cm² (8.2bar)

7517052 *HO8578* -
SALUS *ex* Balau *-2001*
Newport Shipping Ltd
-
Panama *Panama*
MMSI: 373749000
Official number: 42823PEXT1
260 78 -
✠ 100A1 SS 03/2008
tug
✠ LMC
Eq.Ltr: H; Cable: U2
1976-10 B.V. Scheepswerf "De Hoop" — Hardinxveld-Giessendam Yd No: 739
Loa 31.02 Br ex 9.63 Dght 3.804
Lbp 27.21 Br md 9.01 Dpth 4.45
Welded, 1 dk
(B32A2ST) Tug
2 oil engines sr geared to sc. shafts driving 2 CP propellers
Total Power: 1,816kW (2,470hp) 11.0kn
Kromhout 8FHD240
2 x 4 Stroke 8 Cy. 240 x 260 each-908kW (1235bhp)
Stork Werkspoor Diesel BV-Netherlands
AuxGen: 2 x 96kW 390V 50Hz a.c

9503392 *PA3064* -
SALUTE
Salute Malta Ltd
-
's-Hertogenbosch *Netherlands*
MMSI: 245002000
Official number: 23417 Z 2012
473 141 97
Class: AB
2008-04 Perini Navi SpA (Divisione Picchiotti) — Viareggio Yd No: 2095
Loa 55.90 Br ex - Dght 2.290
Lbp 40.06 Br md 11.28 Dpth 3.90
Welded, 1 dk
(X11A2YS) Yacht (Sailing)
Hull Material: Aluminium Alloy
2 oil engines reduction geared to sc. shafts driving 2 Propellers
Total Power: 1,440kW (1,958hp)
M.T.U. 8V2000M72
2 x Vee 4 Stroke 8 Cy. 135 x 156 each-720kW (979bhp)
MTU Friedrichshafen GmbH-Friedrichshafen
AuxGen: 3 x 90kW a.c
Fuel: 54.4 (d.f.)

9267522 *9HA3080* -
SALUZI *ex* Tia Moana *-2011*
Falkenberg Investments Ltd
Societe Maritime Cote d'Azur SAS
Valletta *Malta*
MMSI: 229113000
Official number: 9267522
1,739 548 78
Class: BV
2003-04 Austal Ships Pty Ltd — Fremantle WA Yd No: 173
Loa 69.10 Br ex - Dght 2.100
Lbp 59.40 Br md 13.80 Dpth 4.80
Welded
(A37A2PC) Passenger/Cruise
Hull Material: Aluminium Alloy
Passengers: cabins: 37; berths: 40
2 oil engines geared to sc. shafts driving 2 FP propellers
Total Power: 1,600kW (2,176hp) 14.0kn
M.T.U. 16V2000M60
2 x Vee 4 Stroke 16 Cy. 130 x 150 each-800kW (1088bhp)
MTU Friedrichshafen GmbH-Friedrichshafen
Thrusters: 1 Tunnel thruster (f)

8858805 *HP7247* -
SALVA INDAH *ex* Salvation *-1993* *ex* Ikoma Maru No. 2 *-1992*
Supernat Shipping SA
PT Pelayaran Taruna Kusan Explosive (TAREXSHIP)
Panama *Panama*
Official number: 2132594
108 27 -
1962 Shin Yamamoto Shipbuilding & Engineering Co Ltd — Kochi KC
Loa 26.00 Br ex - Dght 2.300
Lbp 22.00 Br md 6.50 Dpth 2.90
Welded, 1 dk
(B32A2ST) Tug
1 oil engine driving 1 FP propeller
Total Power: 441kW (600hp) 6.5kn
Fuji 6SD26D
1 x 4 Stroke 6 Cy. 260 x 400 441kW (600bhp)
Fuji Diesel Co Ltd-Japan

8426171 *DUI2008* -
SALVACION 3 *ex* Fortunata *-1987*
Josefina Balena
-
Tacloban *Philippines*
Official number: CEB1001324
175 115 -
1981 at Mandaue
Loa 34.84 Br ex 6.13 Dght -
Lbp 27.21 Br md 6.10 Dpth 2.75
Welded, 1 dk
(A32A2GF) General Cargo/Passenger Ship
Passengers: 345
1 oil engine driving 1 FP propeller
Total Power: 162kW (220hp)

8944666 - -
SALVACION 5 *ex* Sanvic - 2 *-1987*
J B & Sons Shipping Corp
-
Tacloban *Philippines*
Official number: CEB1001537
366 230 -
1987 at Cebu
L reg 57.05 Br ex - Dght -
Lbp - Br md 8.54 Dpth 3.45
Welded, 1 dk
(A31A2GX) General Cargo Ship
1 oil engine driving 1 FP propeller
Total Power: 530kW (721hp)
Isuzu
1 x 4 Stroke 530kW (721bhp)
Isuzu Marine Engine Inc-Japan

IMO No. / Call sign	Name / Owner	Tonnage	Class	Builder / Dimensions	Type	Machinery
8032542 *DUH1424* -	**SALVACION VI** *ex* Sumiho Maru No. 18 *-1996* **J B & Sons Shipping Corp** - *Cebu* *Philippines* Official number: CEB1004410	*248* 174 699		**1980-09 Shin Nippon Jukogyo K.K. — Osakikamijima** Yd No: 165 Loa 54.50 Br ex - Dght 3.250 Lbp 50.81 Br md 9.01 Dpth 5.11 Welded, 1 dk	**(A31A2GX) General Cargo Ship** Grain: 1,392; Bale: 1,303 Compartments: 1 Ho, ER 1 Ha: (28.2 x 6.6)ER	**1 oil engine** driving 1 FP propeller Total Power: 588kW (799hp) 11.0kn Niigata 6M28AGT 1 x 4 Stroke 6 Cy. 280 x 480 588kW (799bhp) Niigata Engineering Co Ltd-Japan
7125603 - -	**SALVADOR** - - -	*787* 386 1,829	Class: (LR) ✠ Classed LR until 31/8/05	**1971-12 Appledore Shipbuilders Ltd — Bideford** Yd No: A.S. 79 Loa 57.76 Br ex 11.92 Dght 3.887 Lbp 53.35 Br md 11.59 Dpth 4.50 Welded, 1 dk	**(B34A2SH) Hopper, Motor**	**1 oil engine** sr geared to sc. shaft driving 1 CP propeller Total Power: 971kW (1,320hp) 10.0kn English Electric 6RK3CM 1 x 4 Stroke 6 Cy. 254 x 305 971kW (1320bhp) English Electric Diesels Ltd.-Glasgow AuxGen: 2 x 84kW 440V 60Hz a.c
9048407 *HKBE2* -	**SALVADOR** *ex* Svitzer Orinoco *-2011* *ex* Tito Neri *-2004* - - *Cartagena de Indias* *Colombia* MMSI: 730080000 Official number: MC-05-620	**347** 104 160	Class: (RI)	**1992-12 Deutsche Industrie-Werke GmbH — Berlin (Hull)** Yd No: 169 **1992-12 Detlef Hegemann Rolandwerft GmbH & Co. KG — Berne** Yd No: 169 Loa 31.50 Br ex 9.90 Dght 4.668 Lbp 27.00 Br md 9.50 Dpth 5.20 Welded, 1 dk	**(B32A2ST) Tug**	**2 oil engines** gearing integral to driving 2 Z propellers Total Power: 2,970kW (4,038hp) 12.5kn Deutz SBV8M628 2 x 4 Stroke 8 Cy. 240 x 280 each-1470kW (1999bhp) Kloeckner Humboldt Deutz AG-Germany AuxGen: 3 x 109kW 380V 50Hz a.c Thrusters: 1 Thwart. FP thruster (f)
9328950 *EATX* -	**SALVADOR DALI** - **Remolques y Servicios Maritimos SL (REYSER)** SAR Remolcadores SL *Barcelona* *Spain* MMSI: 224063980 Official number: 1-2/2005	**324** 97 96	Class: LR ✠ **100A1** SS 07/2010 tug fire fighting Ship 1 (2400m3/hr) with water spray EP (A,G,O) *IWS ✠ **LMC** **UMS CCS** Eq.Ltr: G; Cable: 550.0/20.5 U2 (a)	**2005-07 Astilleros Zamakona SA — Santurtzi** Yd No: 611 Loa 27.55 Br ex 16.12 Dght 1.500 Lbp 26.84 Br md 15.25 Dpth 3.30 Welded, 1 dk	**(B32A2ST) Tug**	**2 oil engines** gearing integral to driving 2 Z propellers Total Power: 3,730kW (5,072hp) 12.0kn Caterpillar 3516B 2 x Vee 4 Stroke 16 Cy. 170 x 215 each-1865kW (2536bhp) Caterpillar Inc-USA AuxGen: 2 x 98kW 400V 50Hz a.c
8886838 *WY8719* -	**SALVADOR R** *ex* Jesus G *-2005* *ex* Teresa *-2005* **Rios Trawler Corp** - *Brownsville, TX* *United States of America* Official number: 524866	*130* 89 -		**1970 Southern Shipbuilding Co. — Brownsville, Tx** Yd No: 17 L reg 21.90 Br ex - Dght - Lbp - Br md 6.76 Dpth 3.65 Welded, 1 dk	**(B11B2FV) Fishing Vessel**	**1 oil engine** driving 1 FP propeller
8747745 - -	**SALVADOR R** - **Urbipez SA** - *Argentina* Official number: 02755	*138* - -		**2010-05 Ast. Naval Federico Contessi y Cia. S.A. — Mar del Plata** Loa 25.70 Br ex - Dght - Lbp - Br md 7.20 Dpth 3.72 Welded, 1 dk	**(B11B2FV) Fishing Vessel**	**1 oil engine** driving 1 Propeller
8841981 - -	**SALVAGE 1** *ex* Rosa M *-2000* *ex* Rosa M. *-2000* *ex* Daryl C *-1988* *ex* Daryl C. Hannah *-1984* *ex* Taboga (ATF-172) *-1975* *ex* Taboga (ATR-99) *-1943* **Gulf & Caribbean Tug Service Ltd**	*461* 138 -		**1943 Gulfport Boiler & Welding Works, Inc. — Port Arthur, Tx** Yd No: 226 Loa - Br ex - Dght 4.181 Lbp 41.00 Br md 10.09 Dpth 5.18 Welded, 1 dk	**(B32A2ST) Tug**	**1 oil engine** driving 1 FP propeller Total Power: 2,207kW (3,001hp)
7626841 *J8VJ8* -	**SALVAGE ACE** *ex* Sable Cape *-2010* *ex* Hyundai T No. 1001 *-1998* *ex* Chung Ryong No. 1 *-1984* *ex* Hyundai No. 109 *-1984* *ex* Hoko Maru No. 6 *-1984* **Asian Towage Development Ltd** Asian Marine Co Ltd SatCom: Inmarsat C 437651310 *Kingstown* *St Vincent & The Grenadines* MMSI: 376513000 Official number: 7902	**1,714** 514 1,741	Class: AB (KR) (NK)	**1976-12 Miyoshi Shipbuilding Co Ltd — Uwajima EH** Yd No: 230 Loa 72.40 Br ex - Dght 5.391 Lbp 64.80 Br md 13.01 Dpth 6.00 Welded, 1 dk	**(B32A2ST) Tug**	**2 oil engines** driving 2 FP propellers Total Power: 6,620kW (9,000hp) 13.8kn Hanshin 6LU54 2 x 4 Stroke 6 Cy. 540 x 860 each-3310kW (4500bhp) Hanshin Nainenki Kogyo-Japan AuxGen: 2 x 280kW 445V a.c Thrusters: 1 Tunnel thruster (f)
7640263 *J8KV7* -	**SALVAGE CHALLENGER** *ex* Hyundai T No. 1003 *-1995* *ex* Chung Ryong No. 3 *-1984* *ex* Hyundai No. 111 *-1984* **Asian Salvage Ltd** Asian Marine Co Ltd SatCom: Inmarsat C 437600370 *Kingstown* *St Vincent & The Grenadines* MMSI: 376115000 Official number: 6541	**1,695** 508 1,805	Class: KR (AB)	**1977-04 Hyundai Shipbuilding & Heavy Industries Co Ltd — Ulsan** Yd No: H38 Loa 71.02 Br ex 13.59 Dght 5.669 Lbp 65.00 Br md 13.01 Dpth 6.30 Welded, 1 dk	**(B32A2ST) Tug**	**2 oil engines** reverse reduction geared to sc. shafts driving 2 FP propellers Total Power: 8,826kW (12,000hp) 14.0kn Pielstick 12PC2-2V-400 2 x Vee 4 Stroke 12 Cy. 400 x 460 each-4413kW (6000bhp) Niigata Engineering Co Ltd-Japan AuxGen: 3 x 264kW 445V a.c
7530444 *J8B2604* -	**SALVAGE CHAMPION** *ex* CRI Supreme *-2002* *ex* Pacific Tide No. 3 *-1993* *ex* Ocean Tiger *-1990* *ex* Ocean Tiger No. 1 *-1988* *ex* Ocean Tiger *-1987* *ex* Nippon Maru *-1983* **Asian Maritime Ltd** Asian Marine Co Ltd SatCom: Inmarsat C 437722310 *Kingstown* *St Vincent & The Grenadines* MMSI: 377223000 Official number: 9076	**1,830** 549 1,737	Class: AB (NK)	**1976-06 Miyoshi Shipbuilding Co Ltd — Uwajima EH** Yd No: 227 Loa 72.40 Br ex 13.06 Dght 5.381 Lbp 64.83 Br md 13.00 Dpth 5.90 Welded, 1 dk	**(B34P2QV) Salvage Ship** Grain: 326; Bale: 284 1 Ha: (3.5 x 4.5)ER	**2 oil engines** driving 2 FP propellers Total Power: 6,620kW (9,000hp) 12.0kn Hanshin 6LU54 2 x 4 Stroke 6 Cy. 540 x 860 each-3310kW (4500bhp) Hanshin Nainenki Kogyo-Japan AuxGen: 3 x 584kW Thrusters: 1 Tunnel thruster (f)
5308251 *WKGY* -	**SALVAGE CHIEF** *ex* LSM 380 *-1983* **The Marine Salvage Consortium Inc** Fred Devine Diving & Salvage Co *Portland, OR* *United States of America* MMSI: 366766530 Official number: 258699	**490** 389 -		**1945-03 Brown Shipbuilding Co. — Houston, Tx** Yd No: 257 Loa 61.57 Br ex 10.42 Dght 2.909 Lbp 57.99 Br md 10.37 Dpth 3.41 Welded, 1 dk	**(B34P2QV) Salvage Ship**	**2 oil engines** driving 2 FP propellers Total Power: 2,648kW (3,600hp) Fairbanks, Morse 10-38D8-1/8 2 x 2 Stroke 10 Cy. 207 x 254 each-1324kW (1800bhp) Fairbanks Morse & Co.-New Orleans, La AuxGen: 5 x 250kW 440V 60Hz a.c Fuel: 256.0
7902788 *J8B3672* -	**SALVAGE DUKE** *ex* Strong Deliverer *-2007* *ex* Haedong Star No. 99 *-2004* *ex* Nissho Maru No. 1 *-1998* *ex* Nissho Maru *-1997* *ex* Shinei Maru *-1987* **Asian Merchant Marine Ltd** Asian Marine Co Ltd SatCom: Inmarsat C 437661910 *Kingstown* *St Vincent & The Grenadines* MMSI: 376619000 Official number: 10145	**1,059** 317 808	Class: RS (KR) (NK)	**1979-06 Kochi Jyuko (Eiho Zosen) K.K. — Kochi** Yd No: 1317 Loa 55.07 Br ex - Dght 4.881 Lbp 49.66 Br md 11.61 Dpth 5.31 Welded, 1 dk	**(B32A2ST) Tug**	**2 oil engines** driving 2 FP propellers Total Power: 5,296kW (7,200hp) 13.0kn Hanshin 6LU46A 2 x 4 Stroke 6 Cy. 460 x 740 each-2648kW (3600bhp) The Hanshin Diesel Works Ltd-Japan AuxGen: 2 x 240kW Fuel: 793.0 (r.f.)
7021546 - -	**SALVAGE KING** *ex* Chinghwa I *-1989* *ex* Khalifa *-1986* *ex* Achille *-1981* *ex* Lady Laurie *-1974* **Asian Marine & Supply Ltd** Asian Marine Co Ltd	**550** 165 698	Class: (LR) ✠ Classed LR until 31/7/12	**1970-07 Carrington Slipways Pty Ltd — Newcastle NSW** Yd No: 52 Loa 49.28 Br ex 10.39 Dght 3.550 Lbp 44.28 Br md 10.06 Dpth 4.12 Welded, 1 dk	**(B21B2OT) Offshore Tug/Supply Ship**	**2 oil engines** geared to sc. shafts driving 2 FP propellers Total Power: 2,354kW (3,200hp) 12.5kn Ruston 8RKCM 2 x Vee 4 Stroke 8 Cy. 254 x 305 each-1177kW (1600bhp) English Electric Diesels Ltd.-Glasgow AuxGen: 3 x 180kW 415V 50Hz a.c Thrusters: 1 Thwart. FP thruster (f)

Ship	Tonnage	Class	Build / Dimensions	Type	Machinery
7510468 **SALVAGE LEADER** *J8VE4* *ex* Tambau *-1998* - **Asian Marine Services Co Ltd** Asian Marine Co Ltd SatCom: Inmarsat C 437662510 *Kingstown* *St Vincent & The Grenadines* MMSI: 376625000 Official number: 7858	**907** 272 1,920	Class: AB	**1976-04 Mitsui SB. & Eng. Co. Ltd. — Tamano** Yd No: F438 Loa 86.01 Br ex 14.64 Dght 6.001 Lbp 79.02 Br md 14.61 Dpth 7.22 Welded, 1 dk	**(B32A2ST) Tug** Derricks: 2x5t	**2 oil engines** reverse reduction geared to sc. shafts driving 2 CP propellers Total Power: 8,826kW (12,000hp) 14.0kn Pielstick 12PC2-2V-400 2 x Vee 4 Stroke 12 Cy. 400 x 460 each-4413kW (6000bhp) Niigata Engineering Co Ltd-Japan AuxGen: 2 x 500kW a.c, 1 x 240kW a.c Thrusters: 1 Thwart. FP thruster (f) Fuel: 1998.0 (d.f.)
5308275 **SALVAGE MONARCH** *VC3439* - **Heritage Harbour Marine Ltd** - *Montreal, QC* *Canada* Official number: 310514	*219* 6 -	Class: (LR) ✠ Classed LR until 13/1/78	**1959-10 P K Harris & Sons Ltd — Bideford** Yd No: 125 Loa 29.77 Br ex 9.00 Dght 3.995 Lbp 27.23 Br md 8.54 Dpth 4.42 Welded, 1 dk	**(B32A2ST) Tug** Ice Capable	**2 oil engines** sr reverse geared to sc. shaft driving 1 FP propeller Total Power: 970kW (1,318hp) Blackstone ERS8M 2 x 4 Stroke 8 Cy. 222 x 292 each-485kW (659bhp) Lister Blackstone Marine Ltd.-Dursley
9276664 **SALVANGUARD** *9V6418* - **Posh Terasea (I) Pte Ltd** Posh Fleet Services Pte Ltd *Singapore* *Singapore* MMSI: 564533000 Official number: 390204	**3,342** 1,002 3,197	Class: LR ✠ **100A1** SS 01/2014 tug fire fighting Ship 1 (2400 cubic m/hr) with water spray *IWS ✠ **LMC** Eq.Ltr: T; Cable: 660.0/38.0 U3 (a)	**2004-01 President Marine Pte Ltd — Singapore** Yd No: 314 Loa 75.00 Br ex 18.07 Dght 6.400 Lbp 66.60 Br md 18.00 Dpth 8.00 Welded, 1 dk	**(B32A2ST) Tug**	**4 oil engines** driving 2 gen. each 350kW with clutches, flexible couplings & sr geared to sc. shafts driving 2 CP propellers Total Power: 9,840kW (13,380hp) 14.0kn Wartsila 6R32 4 x 4 Stroke 6 Cy. 320 x 350 each-2460kW (3345bhp) Wartsila Finland Oy-Finland AuxGen: 2 x 1200kW 415V 50Hz a.c, 2 x 350kW 415V 50Hz a.c Boilers: TOH (o.f.) 10.2kgf/cm² (10.0bar) Thrusters: 1 Thwart. CP thruster (f); 1 Thwart. CP thruster (a) Fuel: 170.0 (d.f.) 1980.0 (r.f.)
7723510 **SALVANITA** *A9D2280* *ex* Progress Pride *-1980* - **Gulf Dragon Trading Co WLL** - *Bahrain* *Bahrain* MMSI: 408728000	*657* 191 191	Class: BV (NV) (AB)	**1977-04 Promet Pte Ltd — Singapore** Yd No: 87 Loa 44.00 Br ex - Dght 5.042 Lbp 39.96 Br md 10.61 Dpth 5.80 Welded, 1 dk	**(B32A2ST) Tug**	**2 oil engines** reverse reduction geared to sc. shafts driving 2 FP propellers Total Power: 2,280kW (3,100hp) 12.0kn Fuji 6S30B 2 x 4 Stroke 6 Cy. 300 x 450 each-1140kW (1550bhp) Fuji Diesel Co Ltd-Japan AuxGen: 2 x 132kW 400V 50Hz a.c
9133692 **SALVANITY** *D6DK6* *ex* Greenville 20 *-1997* - **Homay General Trading Co LLC** Seaport International Shipping Co LLC *Moroni* *Union of Comoros* MMSI: 616474000 Official number: 1200550	**401** 120 -	Class: BV	**1995-07 Yantai Promet Shipbuilding Co Ltd — Yantai SD** Yd No: 88 Loa 32.10 Br ex - Dght 4.200 Lbp 28.60 Br md 9.50 Dpth 5.20 Welded, 1 dk	**(B32A2ST) Tug**	**2 oil engines** geared to sc. shafts driving 2 Z propellers Total Power: 3,088kW (4,198hp) 9.5kn Nohab 6R25 2 x 4 Stroke 6 Cy. 250 x 300 each-1544kW (2099bhp) Wartsila Diesel AB-Sweden AuxGen: 2 x 90kW 400V 50Hz a.c Fuel: 140.7
9206360 **SALVAREE** *9V5827* - **Semco Salvage (V) Pte Ltd** Posh Fleet Services Pte Ltd *Singapore* *Singapore* MMSI: 563544000 Official number: 388687	**874** 282 838	Class: BV	**2000-03 President Marine Pte Ltd — Singapore** Yd No: 303 Loa 48.00 Br ex 13.02 Dght 4.800 Lbp 43.20 Br md 13.00 Dpth 5.80 Welded, 1 dk	**(B21B20A) Anchor Handling Tug Supply** Passengers: berths: 32	**2 oil engines** with clutches, flexible couplings & sr geared to sc. shafts driving 2 CP propellers Total Power: 2,972kW (4,040hp) 12.5kn Wartsila 9L20 2 x 4 Stroke 9 Cy. 200 x 280 each-1486kW (2020bhp) Wartsila NSD Finland Oy-Finland AuxGen: 2 x 350kW 415/240V 50Hz a.c, 1 x 250kW 415V 50Hz a.c Thrusters: 1 Thwart. CP thruster (f) Fuel: 155.0 (d.f.) 12.2pd
5308316 **SALVATIERRA** - - -	*220* 95 91		**1949 Hijos de J. Barreras S.A. — Vigo** Yd No: 1013 Loa 34.65 Br ex 6.71 Dght 3.353 Lbp - Br md 6.66 Dpth - Welded	**(B11A2FT) Trawler** Compartments: 1 Ho, ER Derricks: 1x1t; Winches: 1	**1 oil engine** driving 1 FP propeller 9.0kn Werkspoor 1 x 4 Stroke 6 Cy. 270 x 500 NV Werkspoor-Netherlands
7223285 **SALVATOR II** *HP8288* *ex* Aladin *-1995* *ex* Alad *-1988* *ex* Aladin *-1987* - *ex* Tender Trout *-1978* **Billiard Corp SA** International Boat Services Ltd SatCom: Inmarsat C 435540310 *Panama* *Panama* MMSI: 355403000 Official number: 2514398B	**726** 218 833	Class: (GL) (BV) (AB)	**1972-09 Mangone Shipbuilding Co. — Houston, Tx** Yd No: 105 Loa 56.39 Br ex 11.61 Dght 4.131 Lbp 51.80 Br md 11.59 Dpth 4.88 Welded, 1 dk	**(B21B20A) Anchor Handling Tug Supply**	**2 oil engines** driving 2 CP propellers Total Power: 2,942kW (4,000hp) 12.0kn EMD (Electro-Motive) 16-645-E2 2 x Vee 2 Stroke 16 Cy. 230 x 254 each-1471kW (2000bhp) General Motors Corp.Electro-Motive Div.-La Grange AuxGen: 1 x 150kW 440V 60Hz a.c, 2 x 125kW 440V 60Hz a.c Thrusters: 1 Thwart. FP thruster (f) Fuel: 413.5 (d.f.)
9454060 **SALVATORE** *HKJI* - **Sundrive Ltd** Augustea Ship Management Srl *Barranquilla* *Colombia* MMSI: 730053000 Official number: MC-03-0114	**407** 122 174	Class: AB	**2007-04 Yiu Lian Dockyards Ltd — Hong Kong** Yd No: 5-04T Loa 36.80 Br ex - Dght 3.400 Lbp 34.43 Br md 10.00 Dpth 4.40 Welded, 1 dk	**(B32A2ST) Tug**	**2 oil engines** reverse geared to sc. shafts driving 2 Directional propellers Total Power: 2,206kW (3,000hp) Niigata 6L26HLX 2 x 4 Stroke 6 Cy. 260 x 350 each-1103kW (1500bhp) Niigata Engineering Co Ltd-Japan AuxGen: 2 x 100kW 400V a.c
9183221 **SALVATORE CAFIERO** *IBTW* - **Augustea Atlantica SpA** - *Naples* *Italy* MMSI: 247015700	**40,115** 25,125 75,668 T/cm 66.7	Class: GL (RI) (AB)	**2001-03 Mitsui Eng. & SB. Co. Ltd., Chiba Works — Ichihara** Yd No: 1484 Loa 225.00 (BB) Br ex - Dght 13.928 Lbp 216.00 Br md 32.26 Dpth 19.25 Welded, 1 dk	**(A21A2BC) Bulk Carrier** Double Bottom Entire Compartment Length Grain: 87,856 Cargo Heating Coils Compartments: 7 Ho, ER 7 Ha: (17.6 x 12.8)6 (16.8 x 16.0)ER	**1 oil engine** driving 1 FP propeller Total Power: 9,121kW (12,401hp) 14.0kn B&W 7S50MC-C 1 x 2 Stroke 7 Cy. 500 x 2000 9121kW (12401bhp) Mitsui Engineering & Shipbuilding CLtd-Japan AuxGen: 3 x 450kW 450V 60Hz a.c Fuel: 209.0 (d.f.) (Heating Coils) 2469.0 (r.f.) 34.0pd
7233008 **SALVATORE GANCITANO** - *ex* Sarinella Rustico *-1978* - **Neptune Fishing Co Ltd** -	*199* 73 -		**1972 P. Stampa — Trapani** Yd No: 2 Loa 33.10 Br ex 7.14 Dght - Lbp 25.13 Br md 7.12 Dpth 3.56 Welded	**(B11A2FT) Trawler**	**1 oil engine** driving 1 FP propeller Total Power: 368kW (500hp) Deutz SBV6M545 1 x 4 Stroke 6 Cy. 320 x 450 368kW (500bhp) Kloeckner Humboldt Deutz AG-West Germany
5422356 **SALVATORE GIACALONE** *IUGT* *ex* Velia *-1963* - **Oceanpesca Srl di Giuseppe Quinci** - *Mazara del Vallo* *Italy* Official number: 127	*324* 117 -	Class: (LR) (RI) ✠ Classed LR until 12/65	**1952-10 Cook, Welton & Gemmell Ltd. — Beverley** Yd No: 839 Lengthened-1960 Loa 45.12 Br ex 8.11 Dght - Lbp 39.93 Br md 8.08 Dpth 3.97 Riveted\Welded, 1 dk	**(B11A2FT) Trawler**	**1 oil engine** driving 1 FP propeller Total Power: 574kW (780hp) 11.0kn Mirrlees KSSDM-7 1 x 4 Stroke 7 Cy. 381 x 457 574kW (780bhp) Mirrlees, Bickerton & Day-Stockport Fuel: 67.0
7941461 **SALVATORE MARRONE** *IREL* - **Matteo Marrone** - *Mazara del Vallo* *Italy* Official number: 66	*147* 54 -		**1967 Cant. Marino Campana — Mazara del Vallo** Loa 31.81 Br ex 6.96 Dght 3.631 Lbp 24.21 Br md 6.80 Dpth 3.59 Welded, 1 dk	**(B11B2FV) Fishing Vessel**	**1 oil engine** driving 1 FP propeller Total Power: 368kW (500hp) MaK 6M351AK 1 x 4 Stroke 6 Cy. 240 x 350 368kW (500bhp) Atlas MaK Maschinenbau GmbH-Kiel
7329390 **SALVATORE PADRE** *IRMU* - **Tommaso Spadaro** - *Isola delle Femmine* *Italy* Official number: 1008	*195* 83 -		**1973 Cant. Nav. Ugo Codecasa S.p.A. — Viareggio** Yd No: 18 Loa 35.54 Br ex 7.14 Dght 1.829 Lbp 28.02 Br md 7.12 Dpth 3.51 Welded, 1 dk	**(B11A2FT) Trawler**	**1 oil engine** driving 1 FP propeller Total Power: 809kW (1,100hp) MaK 8M282AK 1 x 4 Stroke 8 Cy. 240 x 280 809kW (1100bhp) MaK Maschinenbau GmbH-Kiel
7938933 **SALVATORE PRIMO** *IPZP* - **Italfish Srl** - SatCom: Inmarsat C 424799511 *Naples* *Italy* MMSI: 247110330 Official number: 1886	**695** 231 -	Class: RI	**1979 Cant. Nav. Ugo Codecasa S.p.A. — Viareggio** Yd No: 34 Loa 55.61 Br ex 10.04 Dght 3.860 Lbp 46.00 Br md 10.00 Dpth 4.75 Welded, 1 dk	**(B11B2FV) Fishing Vessel**	**1 oil engine** driving 1 CP propeller Total Power: 1,839kW (2,500hp) Nohab F212V 1 x Vee 4 Stroke 12 Cy. 250 x 300 1839kW (2500bhp) Nohab Diesel AB-Sweden

6711534 *ILRL* -	**SALVATORE SECONDO** *ex* Nesna *-1985* **Procida Lines 2000 Srl** - *Naples* *Italy* Official number: 1512	*222* 130 79	Class: (RI) (NV)	**1967**-02 **Aukra Bruk AS — Aukra** Yd No: 29 Loa 33.66 Br ex 8.54 Dght 2.747 Lbp 29.60 Br md 8.49 Dpth 3.46 Welded, 1 dk	**(A36A2PR) Passenger/Ro-Ro Ship (Vehicles)** Passengers: 200 Derricks: 1x5t,1x2.5t	**1 oil engine** geared to sc. shaft driving 1 CP propeller Total Power: 441kW (600hp) 12.0kn GUASCOR E318TA-SP 1 x Vee 4 Stroke 12 Cy. 150 x 150 441kW (600bhp) (new engine 1985) Gutierrez Ascunce Corp (GUASCOR)-Spain AuxGen: 2 x 60kW 220V 50Hz a.c Fuel: 20.5 (d.f.) 2.0pd
7521560 *9H8798* -	**SALVE REGINA** - **Marech Co Ltd** - *Valletta* *Malta* MMSI: 256000325 Official number: 7521560	*139* - 150		**1977**-09 **Scheepswerf "De Amstel" B.V. — Ouderkerk a/d Amstel** Yd No: 150H Loa 27.41 Br ex 7.32 Dght 3.607 Lbp 24.13 Br md 7.31 Dpth 3.74 Welded, 1 dk	**(B11A2FS) Stern Trawler**	**1 oil engine** driving 1 FP propeller Total Power: 699kW (950hp) 12.0kn Kromhout 6F/SW240 1 x 4 Stroke 6 Cy. 240 x 260 699kW (950bhp) Stork Werkspoor Diesel BV-Netherlands
9351828 *S6HA5* -	**SALVERITAS** - **Posh Terasea (I) Pte Ltd** Posh Fleet Services Pte Ltd *Singapore* *Singapore* MMSI: 565336000 Official number: 392059	**2,658** 797 2,804	Class: AB	**2007**-01 **Universal Shipbuilding Corp — Yokohama KN (Keihin Shipyard)** Yd No: 0025 Loa 68.00 Br ex - Dght 6.000 Lbp 60.00 Br md 16.40 Dpth 7.20 Welded, 1 dk	**(B32A2ST) Tug** Cranes: 1x5t	**2 oil engines** reduction geared to sc. shafts driving 2 CP propellers Total Power: 9,000kW (12,236hp) 14.2kn Wartsila 9L32 2 x 4 Stroke 9 Cy. 320 x 400 each-4500kW (6118bhp) Wartsila Finland Oy-Finland AuxGen: 2 x 330kW 415/220V 50Hz a.c, 2 x 1200kW 415/220V 50Hz a.c Thrusters: 1 Tunnel thruster (f); 1 Tunnel thruster (a) Fuel: 170.0 (d.f.) 2042.5 (r.f.)
8888549 *D6DK7* -	**SALVERITY** *ex* Greenville 30 *-2000* **Homay General Trading Co LLC** Seaport International Shipping Co LLC *Moroni* *Union of Comoros* MMSI: 616475000 Official number: 1200551	**401** 120 -	Class: BV	**1995**-06 **Yantai Promet Shipbuilding Co Ltd — Yantai SD** Yd No: 89 Loa 32.10 Br ex - Dght 4.200 Lbp 28.60 Br md 9.50 Dpth 5.20 Welded, 1 dk	**(B32A2ST) Tug**	**2 oil engines** geared to sc. shafts driving 2 Z propellers Total Power: 3,090kW (4,202hp) 9.5kn Nohab 6R25 2 x 4 Stroke 6 Cy. 250 x 300 each-1545kW (2101bhp) Wartsila Diesel AB-Sweden AuxGen: 2 x 90kW 380V 50Hz a.c
8614261 *PMOX* -	**SALVIA** - **PT Bukit Merapin Nusantara Lines** - *Jakarta* *Indonesia* MMSI: 525015359	**2,439** 1,096 609	Class: KI	**1987**-06 **Hayashikane Shipbuilding & Engineering Co Ltd — Nagasaki NS** Yd No: 939 Loa 80.16 Br ex 13.62 Dght 3.601 Lbp 70.01 Br md 13.61 Dpth 4.53 Welded, 1 dk	**(A36A2PR) Passenger/Ro-Ro Ship (Vehicles)** Passengers: unberthed: 450 Cars: 4, Trailers: 20	**2 oil engines** sr geared to sc. shafts driving 2 FP propellers Total Power: 2,800kW (3,806hp) 19.0kn Daihatsu 6DLM-32 2 x 4 Stroke 6 Cy. 320 x 400 each-1400kW (1903bhp) Daihatsu Diesel Manufacturing Co Lt-Japan
9338876 *ZCXR* -	**SALVIA ACE** - **Polar Express SA** MOL Ship Management Singapore Pte Ltd SatCom: Inmarsat C 431990410 *George Town* *Cayman Islands (British)* MMSI: 319904000 Official number: 740752	**42,401** 12,721 15,013	Class: NK	**2008**-07 **Shin Kurushima Dockyard Co. Ltd. — Onishi** Yd No: 5501 Loa 186.03 Br ex - Dght 8.524 Lbp 181.00 Br md 28.20 Dpth 12.45 Welded, 9 dks plus 2 movable dks	**(A35B2RV) Vehicles Carrier** Side door/ramp (s) Quarter stern door/ramp (s. a.) Cars: 4,216	**1 oil engine** driving 1 FP propeller Total Power: 11,441kW (15,555hp) 19.2kn MAN-B&W 8S50MC 1 x 2 Stroke 8 Cy. 500 x 1910 11441kW (15555bhp) Mitsui Engineering & Shipbuilding CLtd-Japan AuxGen: 3 x a.c Thrusters: 1 Tunnel thruster (f) Fuel: 2291.0
7331006 - -	**SALVIA-L** *ex* Eastern No. 108 *-1995* *ex* Neptune 108 *-1995* *ex* Nankai Maru No. 28 *-1989* *ex* Rokunoshima Maru No. 18 *-1985* **Infitco Ltd** - *Conakry* *Guinea* Official number: 011P/6DI	*299* 154 416	Class: (RI)	**1973**-09 **KK Kanasashi Zosen — Shizuoka SZ** Yd No: 1131 Loa 49.10 Br ex 8.34 Dght 3.296 Lbp 43.39 Br md 8.31 Dpth 3.66 Welded, 1 dk	**(B11B2FV) Fishing Vessel**	**1 oil engine** driving 1 FP propeller Total Power: 883kW (1,201hp) Niigata 6L28X 1 x 4 Stroke 6 Cy. 280 x 440 883kW (1201bhp) Niigata Engineering Co Ltd-Japan
9054080 *JG5174* -	**SALVIA MARU** *ex* Salvia Maru No. 2 *-1998* **Tokai Kisen Co Ltd** - *Tokyo* *Japan* MMSI: 431100403 Official number: 133817	*4,992* 1,236 1,236		**1992**-12 **Mitsubishi Heavy Industries Ltd. — Shimonoseki** Yd No: 971 Loa 120.54 (BB) Br ex 15.22 Dght 5.400 Lbp 108.00 Br md 15.20 Dpth 8.75 Welded, 3 dks	**(A32A2GF) General Cargo/Passenger Ship** Grain: 436; Bale: 436 TEU 32 C. 32/20' Cranes: 1x10t	**2 oil engines** driving 2 CP propellers Total Power: 8,238kW (11,200hp) 20.3kn Mitsubishi 8UEC37LA 2 x 2 Stroke 8 Cy. 370 x 880 each-4119kW (5600bhp) Kobe Hatsudoki KK-Japan Thrusters: 1 Thwart. CP thruster (f)
9351830 *S6HA6* -	**SALVICEROY** - **Posh Terasea (I) Pte Ltd** Posh Fleet Services Pte Ltd *Singapore* *Singapore* MMSI: 565337000 Official number: 392060	**2,658** 797 2,804	Class: AB	**2007**-03 **Universal Shipbuilding Corp — Yokohama KN (Keihin Shipyard)** Yd No: 0026 Loa 68.00 Br ex - Dght 6.000 Lbp 60.00 Br md 16.40 Dpth 7.20 Welded, 1 dk	**(B32A2ST) Tug**	**2 oil engines** reduction geared to sc. shafts driving 2 CP propellers Total Power: 9,000kW (12,236hp) 14.2kn Wartsila 9L32 2 x 4 Stroke 9 Cy. 320 x 400 each-4500kW (6118bhp) Wartsila Finland Oy-Finland AuxGen: 2 x 350kW 415V 50Hz a.c, 2 x 1200kW 415V 50Hz a.c Thrusters: 1 Tunnel thruster (f); 1 Tunnel thruster (a) Fuel: 200.0 (d.f.) 2150.0 (r.f.)
9351842 *S6HA7* -	**SALVIGILANT** - **Posh Terasea (I) Pte Ltd** Posh Fleet Services Pte Ltd *Singapore* *Singapore* MMSI: 565338000 Official number: 392061	**2,658** 797 2,809	Class: AB	**2007**-07 **Universal Shipbuilding Corp — Yokohama KN (Keihin Shipyard)** Yd No: 0032 Loa 68.00 Br ex - Dght 6.400 Lbp 60.00 Br md 16.40 Dpth 7.20 Welded, 1 dk	**(B32A2ST) Tug**	**2 oil engines** reduction geared to sc. shafts driving 2 CP propellers Total Power: 9,000kW (12,236hp) 14.2kn Wartsila 9L32 2 x 4 Stroke 9 Cy. 320 x 400 each-4500kW (6118bhp) Wartsila Finland Oy-Finland AuxGen: 2 x 360kW 415V 50Hz a.c, 2 x 1200kW 415V 50Hz a.c Thrusters: 1 Tunnel thruster (f); 1 Tunnel thruster (a) Fuel: 170.0 (d.f.) 2042.5 (r.f.)
9495961 *9V2491* -	**SALVIN DIAMOND** *ex* Arifah Adni *-2013* *ex* PS Diamond *-2009* **Sal Maritime Pte Ltd** - *Singapore* *Singapore* MMSI: 564044000 Official number: 399089	**580** 174 432	Class: AB	**2008**-12 **Jiangsu Wuxi Shipyard Co Ltd — Wuxi JS** (Hull) Yd No: (1302) **2008**-12 **Pacific Ocean Engineering & Trading Pte Ltd (POET) — Singapore** Yd No: 1302 Loa 41.80 Br ex 10.48 Dght 3.200 Lbp 37.40 Br md 10.00 Dpth 4.20 Welded, 1 dk	**(B22G2OY) Standby Safety Vessel**	**2 oil engines** reduction geared to sc. shafts driving 2 Propellers Total Power: 1,472kW (2,002hp) 11.0kn Yanmar 6RY17P-GV 2 x 4 Stroke 6 Cy. 165 x 219 each-736kW (1001bhp) Yanmar Diesel Engine Co Ltd-Japan AuxGen: 3 x a.c
9676412 *9MQC5* -	**SALVIN RUBY** - **Salvin Far East (M) Sdn Bhd** - *Port Klang* *Malaysia* MMSI: 533130944 Official number: 334501	**493** 148 400	Class: BV	**2012**-12 **Guangzhou Panyu Lingshan Shipyard Ltd — Guangzhou GD** Yd No: 183 Loa 40.62 Br ex 10.26 Dght 3.100 Lbp 36.80 Br md 10.00 Dpth 3.70 Welded, 1 dk	**(B32A2ST) Tug**	**2 oil engines** reduction geared to sc. shafts driving 2 FP propellers Total Power: 1,302kW (1,770hp) Caterpillar 3412D 2 x Vee 4 Stroke 12 Cy. 145 x 162 each-651kW (885bhp) (made 2008) Caterpillar Inc-USA Fuel: 220.0
9676424 *9MQC6* -	**SALVIN TOPAZ** - **Salvin Far East (M) Sdn Bhd** - *Port Klang* *Malaysia* MMSI: 533130943 Official number: 334502	**493** 148 400	Class: BV	**2012**-12 **Guangzhou Panyu Lingshan Shipyard Ltd — Guangzhou GD** Yd No: 184 Loa 40.62 Br ex 10.26 Dght 3.100 Lbp 36.80 Br md 10.00 Dpth 3.70 Welded, 1 dk	**(B32A2ST) Tug**	**2 oil engines** reduction geared to sc. shafts driving 2 FP propellers Total Power: 1,302kW (1,770hp) Caterpillar 3412D 2 x Vee 4 Stroke 12 Cy. 145 x 162 each-651kW (885bhp) Caterpillar Inc-USA Fuel: 220.0 (d.f.)
9419084 *A8KK8* -	**SALVINIA** *ex* St. Zoya *-2013* *ex* Laneia *-2007* **Salvinia Shipping Ltd** INTRESCO GmbH *Monrovia* *Liberia* MMSI: 636013076 Official number: 13076	**6,619** 3,901 10,407	Class: RS	**2006**-11 **Yueqing Jinchuan Shipbuilding Co Ltd — Yueqing ZJ** Yd No: 2 Loa 131.32 Br ex - Dght 7.460 Lbp 119.87 Br md 18.00 Dpth 9.70 Welded, 1 dk	**(A31A2GX) General Cargo Ship** Grain: 12,916 Compartments: 3 Ho, ER 3 Ha: 2 (25.4 x 13.0)ER (15.0 x 13.0)	**1 oil engine** reduction geared to sc. shaft driving 1 FP propeller Total Power: 2,868kW (3,899hp) 11.5kn Pielstick 6PC2-5L 1 x 4 Stroke 6 Cy. 400 x 460 2868kW (3899bhp) Shaanxi Diesel Heavy Industry Co Lt-China AuxGen: 3 x 200kW a.c Fuel: 327.0

IMO / Call sign / Flag	Name / Former names / Owner	Tonnage	Class	Builder / Dimensions	Type	Machinery
7612890 - - -	**SALVIOLA** *ex* Asiatic Gala *-1982* - -	*239* 69 -	Class: (NK)	**1976**-09 **Hamamoto Zosensho K.K. — Tokushima** Yd No: 590 Loa 33.51 Br ex 8.41 Dght 3.207 Lbp 30.84 Br md 8.01 Dpth 3.51 Welded, 1 dk	**(B32A2ST) Tug**	**2 oil engines** sr geared to sc. shafts driving 2 FP propellers Total Power: 1,472kW (2,002hp) 11.5kn Yanmar 6G-ST 2 x 4 Stroke 6 Cy. 240 x 290 each-736kW (1001bhp) Yanmar Diesel Engine Co Ltd-Japan AuxGen: 2 x 40kW
9363338 *9V6779* -	**SALVIRILE** **Semco Salvage (I) Pte Ltd** Horizon Marine Services Pte Ltd *Singapore* *Singapore* MMSI: 563922000 Official number: 391602	**951** 285 892	Class: AB	**2005**-11 **Guangxi Guijiang Shipyard — Wuzhou GX** Yd No: 01-2004-03 Loa 49.95 Br ex - Dght 4.500 Lbp 43.60 Br md 12.60 Dpth 5.75 Welded, 1 dk	**(B32A2ST) Tug**	**2 oil engines** reduction geared to sc. shafts driving 2 CP propellers Total Power: 3,840kW (5,220hp) Yanmar 6EY26 2 x 4 Stroke 6 Cy. 260 x 385 each-1920kW (2610bhp) Yanmar Diesel Engine Co Ltd-Japan AuxGen: 3 x 300kW 415/220V 50Hz a.c Thrusters: 1 Thwart. CP thruster (f) Fuel: 430.0 (d.f.) 12.0pd
9276676 *9V6419* -	**SALVISCOUNT** **Posh Terasea (I) Pte Ltd** Posh Fleet Services Pte Ltd *Singapore* *Singapore* MMSI: 563600000 Official number: 390205	**3,342** 1,002 3,197	Class: LR ✠ **100A1** SS 02/2014 tug fire fighting Ship 1 (2400 cubic m/hr) with water spray *IWS ✠ **LMC** Eq.Ltr: T; Cable: 660.0/38.0 U3 (a)	**2004**-02 **President Marine Pte Ltd — Singapore** Yd No: 315 Loa 75.00 Br ex 18.07 Dght 6.416 Lbp 66.60 Br md 18.00 Dpth 8.00 Welded, 1 dk	**(B32A2ST) Tug**	**4 oil engines** driving 2 gen. each 350kW with clutches, flexible couplings & sr geared to sc. shafts driving 2 CP propellers Total Power: 9,840kW (13,380hp) 14.0kn Wartsila 6R32 4 x 4 Stroke 6 Cy. 320 x 350 each-2460kW (3345bhp) Wartsila Finland Oy-Finland AuxGen: 2 x 350kW 415/220V 50Hz a.c, 2 x 1200kW 415/220V 50Hz a.c Boilers: TOH (o.f.) 10.2kgf/cm² (10.0bar) Thrusters: 1 Thwart. CP thruster (f); 1 Thwart. CP thruster (a) Fuel: 170.0 (d.f.) 1980.0 (r.f.) 44.0pd
9363340 *9V6780* -	**SALVISION** **Semco Salvage (IV) Pte Ltd** Horizon Marine Services Pte Ltd *Singapore* *Singapore* MMSI: 563926000 Official number: 391603	**951** 285 892	Class: AB	**2005**-12 **Guangxi Guijiang Shipyard — Wuzhou GX** Yd No: 01-2004-04 Loa 49.95 Br ex - Dght 4.800 Lbp 43.60 Br md 12.60 Dpth 5.75 Welded, 1 dk	**(B32A2ST) Tug**	**2 oil engines** reduction geared to sc. shafts driving 2 CP propellers Total Power: 3,840kW (5,220hp) 12.0kn Yanmar 6EY26 2 x 4 Stroke 6 Cy. 260 x 385 each-1920kW (2610bhp) Yanmar Diesel Engine Co Ltd-Japan AuxGen: 3 x 300kW 415/220V 50Hz a.c Thrusters: 1 Tunnel thruster (f) Fuel: 430.0 (d.f.) 12.0pd
8941781 *9V5903* -	**SALVIXEN** *ex* Mohammad Express *-1998* **Semco Salvage (V) Pte Ltd** POSH Semco Pte Ltd *Singapore* *Singapore* Official number: 388907	**212** 63 -	Class: AB	**1982**-01 **Master Boat Builders, Inc. — Coden, Al** Yd No: 47 Loa 34.00 Br ex - Dght 2.908 Lbp 33.52 Br md 7.92 Dpth 3.20 Welded, 1 dk	**(B21A20S) Platform Supply Ship**	**2 oil engines** reduction geared to sc. shafts driving 2 FP propellers Total Power: 882kW (1,200hp) 12.0kn G.M. (Detroit Diesel) 16V-92 2 x Vee 2 Stroke 16 Cy. 123 x 127 each-441kW (600bhp) General Motors Detroit DieselAllison Divn-USA AuxGen: 2 x 45kW 220V 60Hz a.c Fuel: 68.7 (d.f.)
7304778 *DUA2216* -	**SALVOR** *ex* Kwai Chung *-1989* *ex* Kitakyushu Maru *-1972* **Malayan Towage & Salvage Corp (SALVTUG)** - *Manila* *Philippines* Official number: MNLD001335	*207* 63 -	Class: (BV)	**1969 Kanagawa Zosen — Kobe** Yd No: 93 L reg 27.89 Br ex 8.44 Dght - Lbp - Br md - Dpth 4.02 Welded, 1 dk	**(B32A2ST) Tug**	**2 oil engines** driving 2 FP propellers Total Power: 2,206kW (3,000hp) 12.0kn Nippon Hatsudoki HS6NVA38 2 x 4 Stroke 6 Cy. 380 x 540 each-1103kW (1500bhp) Nippon Hatsudoki-Japan
5427019 - -	**SALVOR** *ex* Esther Moran *-2000* **McKeil Work Boats Ltd** McKeil Marine Ltd *Hamilton, ON* *Canada* MMSI: 316001327 Official number: 822510	*407* 122 -	Class: (AB)	**1963**-07 **Jakobson Shipyard, Inc. — Oyster Bay, NY** Yd No: 417 Loa 36.58 Br ex 9.99 Dght 5.154 Lbp 34.14 Br md 9.61 Dpth 5.72 Welded, 1 dk	**(B32A2ST) Tug**	**2 oil engines** reverse reduction geared to sc. shafts driving 2 FP propellers Total Power: 4,230kW (5,752hp) 12.0kn EMD (Electro-Motive) 16-645 2 x Vee 2 Stroke 16 Cy. 230 x 254 each-2115kW (2876bhp) (new engine 1969) General Motors Corp-USA AuxGen: 2 x 75kW Fuel: 336.5 (d.f.)
6522919 *HIOY* -	**SALVOR MASTER** *ex* Progreso II *-1985* *ex* G. O. R. Fleet No. 3 *-1984* *ex* Friesland *-1981* **Oil Transport Co SA** - *Santo Domingo* *Dominican Rep.*	*584* 128 -	Class: (LR) ✠ Classed LR until 23/2/94	**1965**-12 **Handel en Scheepsbouw Mij. Kramer & Booy N.V. — Kootstertille** Yd No: 139 Loa 48.29 Br ex 10.39 Dght 4.090 Lbp 43.67 Br md 10.06 Dpth 5.19 Welded, 1 dk	**(B32A2ST) Tug**	**2 oil engines** dr geared to sc. shaft driving 1 CP propeller Total Power: 2,322kW (3,156hp) MaK 6M452AK 2 x 4 Stroke 6 Cy. 320 x 450 each-1161kW (1578bhp) (new engine 1975) MaK Maschinenbau GmbH-Kiel
6505648 *LDQV* R-12-K	**SALVOY** *ex* Kvalstein *-2011* *ex* Gisund *-1974* **Bommelfisk AS** - *Haugesund* *Norway* MMSI: 259122000	**375** 157 -		**1965 Kleven Mek Verksted AS — Ulsteinvik** Yd No: 9 Lengthened-1997 Loa 41.18 Br ex 7.14 Dght - Lbp - Br md 7.12 Dpth 3.81 Welded, 1 dk	**(B11B2FV) Fishing Vessel**	**1 oil engine** driving 1 FP propeller Total Power: 1,492kW (2,029hp) 13.2kn Caterpillar 3516B 1 x Vee 4 Stroke 16 Cy. 170 x 190 1492kW (2029bhp) (new engine 1997) Caterpillar Inc-USA Thrusters: 1 Thwart. FP thruster (f)
6501587 *SUMP* -	**SALWA** *ex* Jacqueline *-1982* *ex* Jacqueline Broere *-1982* **Hassan Sado & Co** Hassan Sado *Suez* *Egypt* MMSI: 622123101 Official number: 2150	*638* 369 1,260	Class: (LR) ✠ Classed LR until 12/4/09	**1965**-02 **A. Vuijk & Zonen's Scheepswerven N.V. — Capelle a/d IJssel** Yd No: 788 Lengthened-1970 Loa 70.74 Br ex 9.66 Dght 3.850 Lbp 64.55 Br md 9.40 Dpth 4.27 Welded, 1 dk	**(A13B2TP) Products Tanker** Liq: 2,333; Liq (Oil): 2,333 Cargo Heating Coils Compartments: 12 Ta, ER	**1 oil engine** driving 1 FP propeller Total Power: 736kW (1,001hp) 11.0kn Deutz RBV8M545 1 x 4 Stroke 8 Cy. 320 x 450 736kW (1001bhp) Kloeckner Humboldt Deutz AG-West Germany AuxGen: 2 x 24kW 220V 50Hz a.c, 1 x 7kW 220V 50Hz a.c Boilers: db 10.8kgf/cm² (10.6bar) Fuel: 74.0 3.0pd
8710651 *CNZT* -	**SALWA** **Omnium Marocaine de Peche** - SatCom: Inmarsat C 424240410 *Tan-Tan* *Morocco*	**336** 114 300	Class: BV	**1989**-06 **Astilleros de Santander SA (ASTANDER) — El Astillero** Yd No: 176 Loa 31.60 Br ex - Dght 3.852 Lbp 31.60 Br md 8.31 Dpth 6.13 Welded	**(B11A2FS) Stern Trawler**	**1 oil engine** geared to sc. shaft driving 1 FP propeller Total Power: 883kW (1,201hp) 11.5kn Yanmar M220-EN 1 x 4 Stroke 6 Cy. 220 x 300 883kW (1201bhp) Yanmar Diesel Engine Co Ltd-Japan
6511910 *SUXB* -	**SALWA 2** *ex* Tamin 5 *-1989* *ex* Bellan To *-1981* *ex* Kathe Mac *-1977* *ex* Nicola *-1967* **Pharonic Oil Service Co** - *Suez* *Egypt*	*499* 323 1,084	Class: (LR) (GL) Classed LR until 17/9/97	**1964**-12 **Bayerische Schiffbaug. mbH vorm. A. Schellenberger — Erlenbach** Yd No: 977 Loa 63.68 Br ex 10.00 Dght 3.100 Lbp 59.00 Br md 9.90 Dpth 4.10 Welded, 1 dk	**(A13B2TU) Tanker (unspecified)** Liq: 1,359; Liq (Oil): 1,359 Compartments: 10 Ta, ER	**1 oil engine** driving 1 FP propeller Total Power: 600kW (816hp) 12.0kn MaK 6MU451A 1 x 4 Stroke 6 Cy. 320 x 450 600kW (816bhp) Maschinenbau Kiel AG (MaK)-Kiel AuxGen: 3 x 175kW 220/380V 50Hz a.c, 1 x 44kW 380V 50Hz a.c Fuel: 76.0 (d.f.) 3.5pd
7001601 *A6E2898* -	**SALWAN** *ex* Mac Tide 26 *-1997* *ex* Jaramac XXVI *-1993* *ex* Nusa Ende *-1992* *ex* Jaramac XXVI *-1985* **Al Qamarain Shipping Co LLC** - *Dubai* *United Arab Emirates* MMSI: 470700000	**369** 110 220	Class: (AB) (KI)	**1969**-11 **Tokushima Zosen Sangyo K.K. — Komatsushima** Yd No: 300 Loa 34.93 Br ex 9.76 Dght 3.330 Lbp 31.78 Br md 9.58 Dpth 4.81 Riveted\Welded, 1 dk	**(B32A2ST) Tug**	**2 oil engines** reverse reduction geared to sc. shafts driving 2 FP propellers Total Power: 1,872kW (2,546hp) Enterprise DMG-38 2 x 4 Stroke 8 Cy. 305 x 381 each-936kW (1273bhp) Delaval Turbine Inc (Enterprise Div.)-USA AuxGen: 2 x 150kW Fuel: 197.0
9569621 - -	**SALWEEN** *ex* Atlantis *-2013* *launched as* Strength *-2012* **Seaboard Investment Holding Ltd** NITC *Zanzibar* *Tanzania (Zanzibar)*	**164,796** 108,699 317,473 T/cm 181.2	Class: (LR) ✠ Classed LR until 27/12/12	**2012**-12 **Shanghai Waigaoqiao Shipbuilding Co Ltd — Shanghai** Yd No: 1222 Loa 333.00 (BB) Br ex 60.05 Dght 22.640 Lbp 320.00 Br md 60.00 Dpth 30.50 Welded, 1 dk	**(A13A2TV) Crude Oil Tanker** Double Hull (13F) Liq: 334,900; Liq (Oil): 334,900 Cargo Heating Coils Compartments: 5 Ta, 10 Wing Ta, ER, 2 Wing Slop Ta 3 Cargo Pump (s): 3x5500m³/hr Manifold: Bow/CM: 165.2m	**1 oil engine** driving 1 FP propeller Total Power: 31,640kW (43,018hp) 16.1kn Wartsila 7RT-flex82T 1 x 2 Stroke 7 Cy. 820 x 3375 31640kW (43018bhp) CSSC MES Diesel Co Ltd-China AuxGen: 3 x 1600kW 450V 60Hz a.c Boilers: e (ex.g.) 26.5kgf/cm² (26.0bar), WTAuxB (o.f.) 21.9kgf/cm² (21.5bar) Fuel: 480.0 (d.f.) 8440.0 (r.f.)

8105363 - -
SALY
ex Rosy *-1990*
Societa Rifi
-
Ancona *Italy*
Official number: 767
151 68 -
Class: (RI)
1982-01 Cant. Nav. M. Morini & C. — Ancona
Yd No: 182
Loa 29.11 Br ex 6.63 Dght 2.371
Lbp 22.46 Br md 6.61 Dpth 3.20
Welded, 1 dk
(B11A2FS) Stern Trawler
Ins: 100
Compartments: 1 Ho, ER
1 oil engine sr reverse geared to sc. shaft driving 1 FP propeller
Total Power: 588kW (799hp)
MaK 6M332AK
1 x 4 Stroke 6 Cy. 240 x 330 588kW (799bhp)
Krupp MaK Maschinenbau GmbH-Kiel

7813925 *D6EU2* -
SALY REEFER
ex Fenland *-2007* *ex* Norbrit Vries *-1988*
ex Boston Sea Lance *-1983*
Fishing & Cargo Services SA
West Coast Frozen Fish SA
Moroni *Union of Comoros*
MMSI: 616735000
Official number: 1200859
2,004 638 1,815
Class: IV (LR) (BV)
✠ Classed LR until 9/89
1979-10 Cochrane Shipbuilders Ltd. — Selby
Yd No: 108
Lengthened-1985
Loa 90.79 (BB) Br ex 12.10 Dght 5.214
Lbp 84.84 Br md 12.01 Dpth 7.12
Welded, 2 dks, 2nd dk light cargoes only
(A34A2GR) Refrigerated Cargo Ship
Grain: 2,253; Ins: 3,193
Compartments: 4 Ho, ER, 4 Tw Dk
5 Ha: 5 (7.2 x 7.0)ER
Derricks: 2x6t,6x3t
Ice Capable
1 oil engine sr geared to sc. shaft driving 1 CP propeller
Total Power: 2,207kW (3,001hp) 13.5kn
Mirrlees KMR-6
1 x 4 Stroke 6 Cy. 381 x 457 2207kW (3001bhp)
Mirrlees Blackstone (Stockport)Ltd.-Stockport
AuxGen: 1 x 450kW 415V 60Hz a.c, 2 x 200kW 415V 60Hz a.c
Thrusters: 1 Thwart. FP thruster (f)
Fuel: 408.0 (d.f.)

8728787 - -
SALYUT
Specialized Sea Oil Fleet Organisation, Caspian Sea Oil Fleet, State Oil Co of the Republic of Azerbaijan
-
Baku *Azerbaijan*
MMSI: 423192100
Official number: DGR-0119
136 49 81
Class: RS
1972-07 Astrakhan. SSZ im 10-iy God Oktyabrskoy Revolyutsii — Astrakhan
Yd No: 17
Loa 28.20 Br ex 7.30 Dght 2.770
Lbp 26.00 Br md 7.00 Dpth 3.75
Welded, 1 dk
(B21B20T) Offshore Tug/Supply Ship
Ice Capable
2 oil engines driving 2 FP propellers
Total Power: 440kW (598hp) 10.2kn
Pervomaysk 6CHRP25/34
2 x 4 Stroke 6 Cy. 250 x 340 each-220kW (299bhp)
Pervomaydizelmash (PDM)-Pervomaysk
AuxGen: 2 x 60kW
Fuel: 11.0 (d.f.)

8928686 - -
SALYUT
-
Turkmen Shipping Co (Turkmenistanyn Denyiz Paroxodjylygy)
-
Turkmenbashy *Turkmenistan*
Official number: 742599
187 - 46
Class: (RS)
1974 Gorokhovetskiy Sudostroitelnyy Zavod — Gorokhovets Yd No: 320
Loa 29.30 Br ex 8.49 Dght 3.090
Lbp 27.00 Br md - Dpth 4.30
Welded, 1 dk
(B32A2ST) Tug
Ice Capable
2 oil engines driving 2 CP propellers
Total Power: 882kW (1,200hp) 11.4kn
Russkiy 6D30/50-4-2
2 x 2 Stroke 6 Cy. 300 x 500 each-441kW (600bhp)
Mashinostroitelnyy Zavod"Russkiy-Dizel"-Leningrad
AuxGen: 2 x 30kW a.c
Fuel: 36.0 (d.f.)

8508917 *3FAN6* -
SALZGITTER
ex Freccia *-2000* *ex* Kassel *-1996*
Pureza Ships SA
Wilhelmsen Ship Management Sdn Bhd
SatCom: Inmarsat C 435617210
Panama *Panama*
MMSI: 356172000
Official number: 2288196D
34,960 10,488 12,077
Class: NV
1987-06 Brodogradiliste 'Uljanik' — Pula
Yd No: 371
Loa 172.52 (BB) Br ex 29.41 Dght 9.020
Lbp 160.61 Br md 29.37 Dpth 11.00
Welded, 8 dks
(A35B2RV) Vehicles Carrier
Side door/ramp (s)
Len: 17.00 Wid: 4.50 Swl: 10
Quarter stern door/ramp (s)
Len: 31.00 Wid: 7.50 Swl: 70
Lane-Len: 1740
Cars: 3,555
Ice Capable
1 oil engine driving 1 FP propeller
Total Power: 7,921kW (10,769hp) 17.5kn
B&W 6L60MCE
1 x 2 Stroke 6 Cy. 600 x 1944 7921kW (10769bhp)
Tvornica Dizel Motora 'Uljanik'-Yugoslavia
AuxGen: 1 x 960kW 440V 60Hz a.c, 1 x 800kW 440V 60Hz a.c, 1 x 728kW 440V 60Hz a.c
Thrusters: 1 Thwart. CP thruster (f); 1 Tunnel thruster (a)
Fuel: 96.0 (d.f.) 1432.5 (r.f.) 30.0pd

7916454 *5VAL5* -
SAM
ex Adi Ii *-2013* *ex* North Star *-2009*
ex Walili *-2007*
Wendy Maritime Ltd
Sigma Grains Ltd
SatCom: Inmarsat C 467109210
Lome *Togo*
MMSI: 671092000
3,801 1,213 4,300
Class: BR (BV)
1980-08 Miho Zosensho K.K. — Shimizu
Yd No: 1152
Loa 91.39 Br ex 15.83 Dght 5.501
Lbp 83.90 Br md 15.80 Dpth 6.58
Welded, 1 dk
(A34A2GR) Refrigerated Cargo Ship
Ins: 6,088
1 oil engine driving 1 FP propeller
Total Power: 2,824kW (3,840hp) 15.3kn
Hanshin 6LUS46
1 x 4 Stroke 6 Cy. 460 x 740 2824kW (3840bhp)
Hanshin Nainenki Kogyo-Japan

8110643 *ERMC* -
SAM
ex Sesam *-2011*
Yamab Ltd
Tomini Trading Srl
Giurgiulesti *Moldova*
MMSI: 214181303
1,499 597 1,768
Class: MB (BV) (GL)
1981-09 Schiffs. Hugo Peters Wewelsfleth Peters & Co. GmbH — Wewelsfleth Yd No: 586
Loa 82.48 Br ex 11.33 Dght 3.534
Lbp 76.82 Br md 11.31 Dpth 5.41
Welded, 2 dks
(A31A2GX) General Cargo Ship
Grain: 2,914; Bale: 2,909
TEU 48 C. 48/20'
Compartments: 1 Ho, ER
1 Ha: (49.8 x 9.0)ER
Ice Capable
1 oil engine reverse reduction geared to sc. shaft driving 1 FP propeller
Total Power: 441kW (600hp) 10.5kn
Deutz SBA8M528
1 x 4 Stroke 8 Cy. 220 x 280 441kW (600bhp)
Kloeckner Humboldt Deutz AG-West Germany
AuxGen: 2 x 92kW 220/380V 50Hz a.c, 1 x 41kW 220/380V 50Hz a.c
Thrusters: 1 Thwart. FP thruster (f)

7602168 *OW2146* -
SAM
ex Sam II *-1977*
Foroyar Landsstyri
Strandfaraskip Landsins
Vestmanna *Faeroe Islands (Danish)*
MMSI: 231096009
Official number: A340
217 73 30
Class: NV
1975-12 Blaalid Slip & Mek Verksted AS — Raudeberg Yd No: 29
Loa 33.16 Br ex 9.61 Dght 2.812
Lbp 30.10 Br md 9.40 Dpth 4.00
Welded, 1 dk
(A37B2PS) Passenger Ship
Stern door/ramp (centre)
2 oil engines geared to sc. shafts driving 2 CP propellers
Total Power: 486kW (660hp)
Grenaa 6F24
2 x 4 Stroke 6 Cy. 240 x 300 each-243kW (330bhp) (new engine 1981)
A/S Grenaa Motorfabrik-Denmark
AuxGen: 1 x 220V 50Hz a.c, 1 x a.c
Thrusters: 1 Thwart. FP thruster (f)

8913629 *V7TC4* -
SAM
ex Regent *-2009* *ex* Relentless *-2009*
ex Polyanka *-2004*
Sam Shipping Corp
Oil Marketing & Trading International FZC
Majuro *Marshall Islands*
MMSI: 538003778
Official number: 3778
28,223 13,568 47,071 T/cm 51.6
Class: GL (NV)
1992-07 Halla Engineering & Heavy Industries Ltd — Incheon Yd No: 177
Loa 183.20 (BB) Br ex 32.23 Dght 12.205
Lbp 174.00 Br md 32.20 Dpth 18.00
Welded, 1 dk
(A13A2TW) Crude/Oil Products Tanker
Double Hull (13F)
Liq: 54,079; Liq (Oil): 54,079
Compartments: 8 Ta, 2 Wing Slop Ta, ER
8 Cargo Pump (s): 8x850m³/hr
Manifold: Bow/CM: 90.3m
Ice Capable
1 oil engine driving 1 FP propeller
Total Power: 7,466kW (10,151hp) 14.5kn
B&W 6S50MC
1 x 2 Stroke 6 Cy. 500 x 1910 7466kW (10151bhp)
Hyundai Heavy Industries Co Ltd-South Korea
AuxGen: 3 x 600kW 440V 60Hz a.c
Fuel: 182.0 (d.f.) (Heating Coils) 1404.8 (r.f.)

9092355 *9BNN* -
SAM 2
ex Matso *-2007* *ex* Matipuno *-2000*
ex Cargolift Czar *-1995*
International Tug Boat Service Co
-
Bandar Abbas *Iran*
Official number: 862
148 44 -
Class: AS
1991-01 Tito Peralta — Zambales
Loa 34.60 Br ex - Dght 2.200
Lbp 31.20 Br md 6.50 Dpth 2.63
Welded, 1 dk
(B32A2ST) Tug
1 oil engine driving 1 Propeller
Total Power: 713kW (969hp)
Daihatsu 6D3M26FS
1 x 4 Stroke 6 Cy. 260 x 380 713kW (969bhp)
Daihatsu Diesel Manufacturing Co Lt-Japan

8944654 *9BNM* -
SAM 3
ex Antonio Miguel *-2007* *ex* Mariejoy 7 *-1996*
International Tug Boat Service Co
-
Bandar Abbas *Iran*
MMSI: 422654000
Official number: 863
855 431 -
Class: AS
1989-01 Cebu Shipyard & Engineering Works Inc — Lapu-Lapu
L reg 63.50 Br ex - Dght -
Lbp - Br md 9.70 Dpth 4.60
Welded, 1 dk
(A31A2GX) General Cargo Ship
1 oil engine driving 1 FP propeller
Total Power: 809kW (1,100hp)
Kinoshita
1 x 4 Stroke 809kW (1100bhp)
Kinoshita Tekkosho-Japan

9176175 *BR3431* -
SAM BO LUN
ex Shoju Maru *-2010*
Far Ocean Marine Transport Corp
-
Chinese Taipei
199 - 635
1997-10 K.K. Miura Zosensho — Saiki Yd No: 1187
Loa - Br ex - Dght -
Lbp 54.45 Br md 9.60 Dpth 5.40
Welded, 1 dk
(A31A2GX) General Cargo Ship
1 oil engine geared to sc. shaft driving 1 FP propeller
Total Power: 736kW (1,001hp)
Hanshin LH28LG
1 x 4 Stroke 6 Cy. 280 x 530 736kW (1001bhp)
The Hanshin Diesel Works Ltd-Japan

7220867 *6LKT* -
SAM BO No. 305
ex Jinam No. 203 *-1990*
Kim Sung-Yool
-
Busan *South Korea*
Official number: BS02-A403
235 113 290
Class: (KR)
1968 Korea Shipbuilding & Engineering Corp — Busan
Loa 45.86 Br ex - Dght 3.238
Lbp 41.23 Br md 7.29 Dpth 3.36
Welded, 1 dk
(B11B2FV) Fishing Vessel
Ins: 260
3 Ha: 3 (1.5 x 1.5)
Derricks: 4x2t
1 oil engine driving 1 FP propeller
Total Power: 478kW (650hp) 11.5kn
Hanshin Z76
1 x 4 Stroke 6 Cy. 270 x 400 478kW (650bhp)
Hanshin Nainenki Kogyo-Japan
AuxGen: 2 x 64kW 230V a.c

8031574 *D7PD* -
SAM BU No. 11
-
Sambu Shipping Co Ltd
-
Busan *South Korea*
Official number: BSR-806401
1,133 663 1,599
Class: (KR)
1980-04 ShinA Shipbuilding Co Ltd — Tongyeong
Yd No: 189
Loa 69.40 Br ex - Dght 4.400
Lbp 63.00 Br md 10.51 Dpth 5.26
Welded, 1 dk
(A13B2TP) Products Tanker
Liq: 2,270; Liq (Oil): 2,270
1 oil engine driving 1 FP propeller
Total Power: 1,177kW (1,600hp) 13.0kn
Hanshin 6LUN28
1 x 4 Stroke 6 Cy. 280 x 480 1177kW (1600bhp)
The Hanshin Diesel Works Ltd-Japan
AuxGen: 2 x 60kW 225V a.c

5190769 *6MIH* -
SAM CHANG No. 7
ex Nam Chang No. 2 *-1995*
ex Dai Ho No. 9 *-1986*
ex Kochi Maru No. 3 *-1972*
Sam Kwang Shipping Co Ltd
-
Mokpo *South Korea*
Official number: JS4345-A2435
281 - 434
Class: (KR)
1961 Miho Zosensho K.K. — Shimizu Yd No: 296
Loa 50.70 Br ex 8.13 Dght -
Lbp 45.06 Br md 8.08 Dpth 3.89
Welded, 1 dk
(B11B2FV) Fishing Vessel
Ins: 100
1 oil engine driving 1 FP propeller
Total Power: 552kW (750hp) 11.7kn
Niigata M6DR
1 x 4 Stroke 6 Cy. 370 x 520 552kW (750bhp)
Niigata Tekkosho-Japan
AuxGen: 3 x 70kW 230V a.c

IMO / Call sign	Name / Owner / Manager / Port	Tonnage	Class	Builder / Dimensions	Type / Cargo	Machinery
8226038 *DTBO* -	**SAM CHANG No. 101** - **Kim Ea-Kyung** - *Busan* *South Korea* Official number: BS-A-1773	*142* 60 -	Class: (KR)	**1979 Cheunggu Marine Industry Co Ltd — Ulsan** Loa 35.08 Br ex - Dght - Lbp 30.00 Br md 6.41 Dpth 2.85 Welded, 1 dk	**(B11A2FS) Stern Trawler** 4 Ha: 2 (1.0 x 0.9) (1.2 x 1.2) (1.0 x 1.2)	**1 oil engine** driving 1 FP propeller Total Power: 588kW (799hp) 11.8kn Akasaka 6MH25SSR 1 x 4 Stroke 6 Cy. 250 x 400 588kW (799bhp) Akasaka Tekkosho KK (Akasaka DieselLtd)-Japan AuxGen: 1 x 80kW 225V a.c
9711781 - -	**SAM CHEOK 1** - **Samcheok Tug Co Ltd** - *Samcheok* *South Korea* MMSI: 440601090 Official number: DHR-145301	**281** - 119	Class: KR	**2014-03 Samkwang Shipbuilding & Engineering Co Ltd — Incheon** Yd No: SKSB216 Loa 36.50 Br ex 10.02 Dght 3.312 Lbp 31.15 Br md 10.00 Dpth 4.50 Welded, 1 dk	**(B32A2ST) Tug**	**2 oil engines** reduction geared to sc. shafts driving 2 Propellers Total Power: 3,676kW (4,998hp) Niigata 6L28HX 2 x 4 Stroke 6 Cy. 280 x 370 each-1838kW (2499bhp) Niigata Engineering Co Ltd-Japan
9711793 - -	**SAM CHEOK 3** - **Samcheok Tug Co Ltd** - *Samcheok* *South Korea* Official number: DHR-145302	**281** - 113	Class: KR	**2014-03 Samkwang Shipbuilding & Engineering Co Ltd — Incheon** Yd No: SKSB217 Loa 36.50 Br ex 10.02 Dght 3.312 Lbp 31.15 Br md 10.00 Dpth 4.50 Welded, 1 dk	**(B32A2ST) Tug**	**2 oil engines** reduction geared to sc. shafts driving 2 Propellers Total Power: 3,676kW (4,998hp) Niigata 6L28HX 2 x 4 Stroke 6 Cy. 280 x 370 each-1838kW (2499bhp) Niigata Engineering Co Ltd-Japan
9129029 *VRIA6* -	**SAM DRAGON** *ex* Pretty Flourish *-2009* **Lasting Asset Ltd** Univan Ship Management Ltd *Hong Kong* *Hong Kong* MMSI: 477351800 Official number: HK-2991	**27,792** 15,379 46,841 T/cm 51.8	Class: BV (KR)	**1997-02 Daedong Shipbuilding Co Ltd — Changwon (Jinhae Shipyard)** Yd No: 1001 Loa 190.00 (BB) Br ex - Dght 11.617 Lbp 179.24 Br md 32.00 Dpth 16.50 Welded, 1 dk	**(A21A2BC) Bulk Carrier** Grain: 58,687; Bale: 55,494 Compartments: 5 Ho, ER 5 Ha: (17.6 x 16.0)4 (19.2 x 16.0)ER Cranes: 4x25t	**1 oil engine** driving 1 FP propeller Total Power: 8,562kW (11,641hp) 14.5kn B&W 6S50MC 1 x 2 Stroke 6 Cy. 500 x 1910 8562kW (11641bhp) Hyundai Heavy Industries Co Ltd-South Korea AuxGen: 3 x 500kW 450V a.c Fuel: 1910.0 (r.f.)
9559676 *VRFY3* -	**SAM EAGLE** *launched as* Shinyo Progress *-2010* **SPV SAM Eagle Inc** Univan Ship Management Ltd *Hong Kong* *Hong Kong* MMSI: 477634200 Official number: HK-2550	**20,846** 11,985 32,581	Class: AB	**2010-01 Jiangsu Zhenjiang Shipyard Co Ltd — Zhenjiang JS** Yd No: VZJ432-0601 Loa 179.90 (BB) Br ex 28.43 Dght 10.150 Lbp 171.50 Br md 28.40 Dpth 14.10 Welded, 1 dk	**(A21A2BC) Bulk Carrier** Grain: 43,964 Compartments: 5 Ho, ER 5 Ha: ER Cranes: 4x30.5t	**1 oil engine** driving 1 FP propeller Total Power: 7,150kW (9,721hp) 14.0kn MAN-B&W 5S50MC 1 x 2 Stroke 5 Cy. 500 x 1910 7150kW (9721bhp) Hyundai Heavy Industries Co Ltd-South Korea AuxGen: 3 x 440kW a.c Fuel: 136.0 (d.f.) 1460.0 (r.f.)
7220594 *D7WN* -	**SAM EUN** *ex* Heung A No. 5 *-1989* **Dong Kwang Marine Bunkering Co Ltd** - *Busan* *South Korea* Official number: BSR-675662	*323* - 792	Class: (KR)	**1967-01 Daehan Shipbuilding & Iron Works — Busan** Converted From: General Cargo Ship-1992 Loa 52.51 Br ex 8.62 Dght 4.011 Lbp 47.99 Br md 8.59 Dpth 4.25 Welded, 1 dk	**(B35E2TF) Bunkering Tanker** Liq: 1,033; Liq (Oil): 1,033	**1 oil engine** driving 1 FP propeller Total Power: 515kW (700hp) 10.0kn AuxGen: 2 x 16kW 220V a.c
9586710 *VRHX4* -	**SAM FALCON** - **SPV SAM Falcon Inc** Univan Ship Management Ltd SatCom: Inmarsat C 447703333 *Hong Kong* *Hong Kong* MMSI: 477051700 Official number: HK2965	**22,137** 11,328 33,500 T/cm 44.4	Class: BV	**2011-01 Zhejiang Jingang Shipbuilding Co Ltd — Wenling ZJ** Yd No: 025 Loa 179.50 (BB) Br ex - Dght 10.650 Lbp 172.98 Br md 28.00 Dpth 15.20 Welded, 1 dk	**(A21A2BC) Bulk Carrier** Grain: 44,075 Compartments: 5 Ho, ER 5 Ha: ER Cranes: 4x30t	**1 oil engine** driving 1 FP propeller Total Power: 6,480kW (8,810hp) 14.0kn MAN-B&W 6S42MC 1 x 2 Stroke 6 Cy. 420 x 1764 6480kW (8810bhp) Hyundai Heavy Industries Co Ltd-South Korea AuxGen: 3 x 520kW 60Hz a.c Fuel: 1477.0
7213876 *BVVO* -	**SAM FUH** - **Hae Fah Fisheries Co Ltd** - *Kaohsiung* *Chinese Taipei*	*253* 161 -	Class: (CR)	**1969 Sen Koh Shipbuilding Corp — Kaohsiung** Loa 36.81 Br ex 6.63 Dght 2.642 Lbp 32.01 Br md 6.61 Dpth 3.03 Welded, 1 dk	**(B11B2FV) Fishing Vessel** Compartments: 3 Ho, ER 4 Ha: 2 (1.0 x 0.9)2 (1.0 x 1.1)ER	**1 oil engine** driving 1 FP propeller Total Power: 405kW (551hp) 10.5kn Matsue 6MZ-28 1 x 4 Stroke 6 Cy. 280 x 420 405kW (551bhp) Matsue Diesel KK-Japan AuxGen: 2 x 64kW
7020657 *V3LT3* -	**SAM GLORY 9** *ex* Yashiro Maru *-2009* **Jicore Group Inc M Sdn Bhd** - *Belize City* *Belize* MMSI: 312093000 Official number: 130810785	*190* 57 -		**1970-02 Akitsu Dock K.K. — Akitsu** Yd No: 371 Loa 26.74 Br ex 8.82 Dght - Lbp 26.01 Br md 8.79 Dpth 3.80 Welded, 1 dk	**(B32A2ST) Tug**	**2 oil engines** geared to sc. shaft driving 1 FP propeller Total Power: 1,692kW (2,300hp) 11.0kn Hanshin 6LUS28G 2 x 4 Stroke 6 Cy. 280 x 440 each-846kW (1150bhp) Hanshin Nainenki Kogyo-Japan
6715528 *6NVN* -	**SAM HAE No. 101** *ex* Koyo Maru No. 28 *-2009* **Seong Jin Colombia Corp** - *Busan* *South Korea* Official number: BS02-A790	*237* 115 246	Class: (KR)	**1967 Miho Zosensho K.K. — Shimizu** Yd No: 614 Loa 43.59 Br ex 7.55 Dght 3.070 Lbp 38.10 Br md 7.52 Dpth 3.33 Welded, 1 dk	**(B11B2FV) Fishing Vessel**	**1 oil engine** driving 1 FP propeller Total Power: 603kW (820hp) 11.5kn Akasaka TM6SSI 1 x 4 Stroke 6 Cy. 300 x 440 603kW (820bhp) Akasaka Tekkosho KK (Akasaka DieselLtd)-Japan AuxGen: 2 x 104kW 230V a.c
9637416 *VRLP5* -	**SAM HAWK** - **SPV SAM Hawk Inc** Shipping Asset Management (SAM) SA SatCom: Inmarsat C 447704954 *Hong Kong* *Hong Kong* MMSI: 477222500 Official number: HK3731	**31,760** 19,043 57,200 T/cm 57.3	Class: BV	**2013-01 STX Offshore & Shipbuilding Co Ltd — Changwon (Jinhae Shipyard)** Yd No: 1510 Loa 190.00 (BB) Br ex - Dght 13.000 Lbp 183.30 Br md 32.26 Dpth 18.50 Welded, 1 dk	**(A21A2BC) Bulk Carrier** Grain: 71,354 Compartments: 5 Ho, ER 5 Ha: 4 (19.7 x 18.3)ER (18.0 x 18.3) Cranes: 4x30t	**1 oil engine** driving 1 FP propeller Total Power: 9,480kW (12,889hp) 14.5kn MAN-B&W 6S50MC-C 1 x 2 Stroke 6 Cy. 500 x 2000 9480kW (12889bhp) STX Engine Co Ltd-South Korea AuxGen: 3 x 625kW 60Hz a.c Fuel: 2120.0
7238785 *P7AO* -	**SAM HUNG 3** *ex* Teru Maru No. 53 *-1988* *ex* Choko Maru No. 5 *-1984* **Korea Amrokgang Co** - *Sinuiju* *North Korea* Official number: 2301001	*295* 85 267	Class: KC	**1972 Sanuki Shipbuilding & Iron Works Co Ltd — Mitoyo KG** Yd No: 668 Loa - Br ex 7.35 Dght 2.600 Lbp 34.02 Br md 7.32 Dpth 2.90 Riveted\Welded, 1 dk	**(B11B2FV) Fishing Vessel**	**1 oil engine** driving 1 FP propeller Total Power: 552kW (750hp) Hanshin 6L26BGSH 1 x 4 Stroke 6 Cy. 260 x 400 552kW (750bhp) Hanshin Nainenki Kogyo-Japan
8403636 *YGNR* -	**SAM I** *ex* Selamat *-2003* *ex* Paco *-2001* *ex* Asahi Maru No. 8 *-1996* **PT Mulia Kawan Sejati** - *Surabaya* *Indonesia*	*612* 348 693	Class: KI	**1984-03 Hakata Zosen K.K. — Imabari** Yd No: 301 Loa 53.83 Br ex 9.02 Dght 3.350 Lbp 49.51 Br md 9.01 Dpth 5.31 Welded, 1 dk	**(A31A2GX) General Cargo Ship** Grain: 1,299; Bale: 1,198 Compartments: 1 Ho, ER 1 Ha: ER	**1 oil engine** with clutches, flexible couplings & reverse reduction geared to sc. shaft driving 1 FP propeller Total Power: 500kW (680hp) 10.0kn Matsui 6M26KGHS 1 x 4 Stroke 6 Cy. 260 x 400 500kW (680bhp) Matsui Iron Works Co Ltd-Japan
8017138 - -	**SAM I** - **Productos Pesqueros Mexicanos SA de CV** - *Ciudad del Carmen* *Mexico*	*130* 43 69	Class: (PR)	**1981-06 Stocznia Ustka SA — Ustka** Yd No: B273/01 Loa 25.68 Br ex - Dght 2.961 Lbp 23.02 Br md 7.21 Dpth 3.51 Welded, 1 dk	**(B11A2FS) Stern Trawler**	**1 oil engine** geared to sc. shaft driving 1 FP propeller Total Power: 419kW (570hp) 11.5kn Sulzer 6AL20/24 1 x 4 Stroke 6 Cy. 200 x 240 419kW (570bhp) Zaklady Przemyslu Metalowego 'HCegielski' SA-Poznan AuxGen: 1 x 40kW 400V a.c, 1 x 36kW 400V a.c
8107335 - -	**SAM II** - **Productos Pesqueros Mexicanos SA de CV** - *Ciudad del Carmen* *Mexico*	*130* 43 70	Class: (PR)	**1982-03 Stocznia Ustka SA — Ustka** Yd No: B273/02 Loa 25.71 Br ex - Dght 2.991 Lbp 24.41 Br md 7.23 Dpth 3.51 Welded, 1 dk	**(B11A2FS) Stern Trawler**	**1 oil engine** sr geared to sc. shaft driving 1 FP propeller Total Power: 419kW (570hp) 11.5kn Sulzer 6AL20/24 1 x 4 Stroke 6 Cy. 200 x 240 419kW (570bhp) Zaklady Przemyslu Metalowego 'HCegielski' SA-Poznan AuxGen: 1 x 36kW 400V 50Hz a.c
8623779 - -	**SAM IL** - **-** -	**302** - 788	Class: (KR)	**1981 Mokpo Shipbuilding & Engineering Co Ltd — Mokpo** Loa 50.81 Br ex - Dght 3.512 Lbp 46.31 Br md 8.40 Dpth 3.92 Welded, 1 dk	**(A31A2GX) General Cargo Ship** Grain: 932 Compartments: 1 Ho, ER 1 Ha: (24.7 x 5.5)ER Derricks: 2x1t	**1 oil engine** driving 1 FP propeller Total Power: 313kW (426hp) 8.0kn Niigata 6MG16X 1 x 4 Stroke 6 Cy. 160 x 200 313kW (426bhp) Niigata Tekkosho-Japan AuxGen: 2 x 5kW 32V d.c
8413564 *6MQW* -	**SAM IL No. 105** - **Lim Hak-Jin** - *Ulleung* *South Korea* Official number: KN7166-A460	*120* 42 -		**1983-06 Chungmu Shipbuilding Co Inc — Tongyeong** Yd No: 123 Loa 35.51 (BB) Br ex 6.91 Dght 2.301 Lbp 29.77 Br md 5.91 Dpth 2.82 Welded, 1 dk	**(B11B2FV) Fishing Vessel** Ins: 93	**1 oil engine** with clutches, flexible couplings & sr reverse geared to sc. shaft driving 1 FP propeller Total Power: 331kW (450hp) Niigata 6L16XB-B 1 x 4 Stroke 6 Cy. 160 x 200 331kW (450bhp) Ssangyong Heavy Industries Co Ltd-South Korea

9637428 **SAM JAGUAR** **31,760** Class: BV
VRMI2 19,300
\- **SPV SAM Jaguar Inc** 57,200
Univan Ship Management Ltd T/cm
Hong Kong *Hong Kong* 57.3
MMSI: 477592900

2013-09 **STX Offshore & Shipbuilding Co Ltd — Changwon (Jinhae Shipyard)** Yd No: 1511
Loa 190.00 (BB) Br ex - Dght 13.000
Lbp 183.30 Br md 32.26 Dpth 18.50
Welded, 1 dk

(A21A2BC) Bulk Carrier
Grain: 71,313
Compartments: 5 Ho, ER
5 Ha: 4 (19.7 x 18.3)ER (18.0 x 18.3)
Cranes: 4x30t

1 oil engine driving 1 FP propeller
Total Power: 9,480kW (12,889hp) 14.5kn
MAN-B&W 6S50MC-C
1 x 2 Stroke 6 Cy. 500 x 2000 9480kW (12889bhp)
STX Engine Co Ltd-South Korea
AuxGen: 3 x 625kW 60Hz a.c
Fuel: 2140.0

7334498 **SAM JIN No. 5** *976* Class: (KR) (NK)
D9IQ *ex* Sae Han No. 5 *ex* Kyokuryu Maru No. 1 *-1982* 584
\- **Sam Hyun Co Ltd** 861
\-
Busan *South Korea*
MMSI: 440102920
Official number: BSR-730052

1961 **Nakamura Shipbuilding & Engine Works Co. Ltd. — Matsue** Yd No: 116
Loa 62.41 Br ex 10.52 Dght 4.200
Lbp 56.09 Br md 10.49 Dpth 4.81
Welded, 1 dk

(A11B2TG) LPG Tanker
Liq (Gas): 1,247
2 x Gas Tank (s);

1 oil engine driving 1 FP propeller
Total Power: 1,471kW (2,000hp) 13.0kn
Hanshin 6LUD35
1 x 4 Stroke 6 Cy. 350 x 550 1471kW (2000bhp)
Hanshin Nainenki Kogyo-Japan
AuxGen: 2 x 160kW
Fuel: 110.5 6.5pd

8002195 **SAM JIN No. 7** **2,045** Class: KR (NK)
DSFQ6 *ex* Filipinas Gas *-2001* *ex* Coral Gas *-1994* 610
\- **SJ Tanker Co Ltd** 2,524
\- T/cm
Busan *South Korea* 8.5
MMSI: 441130000
Official number: BSR-010917

1980-06 **Teraoka Shipyard Co Ltd — Minamiawaji HG** Yd No: 194
Loa 83.50 (BB) Br ex - Dght 5.385
Lbp 77.05 Br md 13.50 Dpth 6.40
Welded, 1 dk

(A11B2TG) LPG Tanker
Liq (Gas): 1,871
2 x Gas Tank (s); 2 independent (C.mn.stl) cyl horizontal
2 Cargo Pump (s): 2x250m³/hr
Manifold: Bow/CM: 38.5m

1 oil engine driving 1 FP propeller
Total Power: 1,912kW (2,600hp) 12.0kn
Hanshin 6LU40
1 x 4 Stroke 6 Cy. 400 x 640 1912kW (2600bhp)
The Hanshin Diesel Works Ltd-Japan
AuxGen: 2 x 200kW 450V 60Hz a.c
Fuel: 96.0 (d.f.) (Part Heating Coils) 250.0 (r.f.) 8.0pd

8429214 **SAM KWANG** *127* Class: (KR)
6KYS *ex* O Dae Yang No. 71 *-1994* 35
\- **Keum Young Fisheries Co Ltd** 133
Busan *South Korea*
Official number: 9505086-6210003

1978-12 **Koo-Il Industries Co Ltd — Busan**
Loa 38.82 Br ex 7.04 Dght -
Lbp 32.52 Br md 7.01 Dpth 2.80
Welded, 1 dk

(B11B2FV) Fishing Vessel

1 oil engine driving 1 FP propeller
Total Power: 147kW (200hp) 11.3kn
Daihatsu
1 x 4 Stroke 6 Cy. 260 x 320 147kW (200bhp)
Daihatsu Diesel Manufacturing Co Lt-Japan
AuxGen: 1 x 72kW 220V a.c

6423096 **SAM KYUNG** *234* Class: (KR)
6NFL *ex* Heung Young No. 5 *-1988* 119
\- *ex* Tae Chang No. 2 *-1981* 300
ex Shinei Maru No. 3 *-1976*
Shin Yang Shipping Co Ltd
\-
Busan *South Korea*
Official number: BS02-A891

1964 **KK Kanasashi Zosen — Shizuoka SZ** Yd No: 597
Loa 43.21 Br ex 7.57 Dght 3.160
Lbp 37.98 Br md 7.50 Dpth 3.38
Welded, 1 dk

(B11B2FV) Fishing Vessel
Ins: 341
3 Ha: (1.0 x 0.9)2 (1.2 x 1.3)ER
Derricks: 1x1t

1 oil engine driving 1 FP propeller
Total Power: 515kW (700hp) 10.8kn
Fuji 6SD30
1 x 4 Stroke 6 Cy. 300 x 430 515kW (700bhp)
Fuji Diesel Co Ltd-Japan
AuxGen: 2 x 64kW 230V a.c

7390210 **SAM LAUD** *11,619* Class: AB
WZC7602 8,036
\- **American Steamship Co** 23,857
\- T/cm
Philadelphia, PA *United States of America* 38.0
MMSI: 366938760
Official number: 564002

1975-01 **Bay Shipbuilding Co — Sturgeon Bay WI** Yd No: 712
Loa 193.53 Br ex 20.73 Dght 8.332
Lbp 188.07 Br md 20.68 Dpth 12.20
Welded, 1 dk

(A23A2BK) Bulk Carrier, Self-discharging, Laker
Grain: 17,310
Compartments: 5 Ho, ER
20 Ha: 20 (3.3 x 12.1)ER

2 oil engines sr geared to sc. shaft driving 1 CP propeller
Total Power: 5,296kW (7,200hp) 14.0kn
EMD (Electro-Motive) 20-645-E7
2 x Vee 2 Stroke 20 Cy. 230 x 254 each-2648kW (3600bhp)
General Motors Corp.Electro-Motive Div.-La Grange
AuxGen: 3 x 670kW
Thrusters: 1 Thwart. FP thruster (f); 1 Tunnel thruster (a)
Fuel: 279.5 (d.f.)

9620164 **SAM LION** **31,760** Class: BV
VRKP7 19,043
\- **SPV SAM Lion Inc** 57,200
Univan Ship Management Ltd T/cm
Hong Kong *Hong Kong* 57.3
MMSI: 477813900
Official number: HK-3522

2012-07 **STX Offshore & Shipbuilding Co Ltd — Changwon (Jinhae Shipyard)** Yd No: 1506
Loa 190.00 (BB) Br ex - Dght 13.000
Lbp 184.28 Br md 32.26 Dpth 18.50
Welded, 1 dk

(A21A2BC) Bulk Carrier
Grain: 71,354
Compartments: 5 Ho, ER
5 Ha: ER
Cranes: 4x30t

1 oil engine driving 1 FP propeller
Total Power: 9,480kW (12,889hp) 14.5kn
MAN-B&W 6S50MC-C
1 x 2 Stroke 6 Cy. 500 x 2000 9480kW (12889bhp)
STX Engine Co Ltd-South Korea
AuxGen: 3 x 625kW a.c
Fuel: 2100.0

8988698 **SAM M. TAALAK** **481**
WDE4074 144
\- **Qayaq Marine Transportation LLC** 450
Sea Coast Transportation LLC
Barrow, AK *United States of America*
Official number: 1051807

1997-05 **Diversified Marine, Inc. — Portland, Or** Yd No: 1
Loa - Br ex - Dght 1.580
Lbp 45.72 Br md 15.24 Dpth 2.43
Welded, 1 dk

(A35D2RL) Landing Craft
Bow ramp (f)
Len: 8.50 Wid: 7.60 Swl: -

3 oil engines geared to sc. shafts driving 3 Propellers
Total Power: 1,125kW (1,530hp)
Caterpillar 3412
3 x Vee 4 Stroke 12 Cy. 137 x 152 each-375kW (510bhp)
Caterpillar Inc-USA

8021579 **SAM MA** *418* Class: KC
HMCR *ex* Ok Ryu *-2001* *ex* Ok Ryu Ho *-2001* 200
\- *ex* Taiyo Maru No. 3 *-2001* 949
Korea Samma Shipping Co
\-
Pyongyang *North Korea*
MMSI: 445219000
Official number: 3105260

1981-03 **Maeno Zosen KK — Sanyoonoda YC** Yd No: 65
Loa 58.63 Br ex - Dght 3.923
Lbp 53.01 Br md 10.01 Dpth 6.02
Welded, 2 dks

(A31A2GX) General Cargo Ship

1 oil engine driving 1 FP propeller
Total Power: 809kW (1,100hp)
Yanmar MF28-DT
1 x 4 Stroke 6 Cy. 280 x 450 809kW (1100bhp)
Yanmar Diesel Engine Co Ltd-Japan

8106496 **SAM MA 2** **962** Class: KC (NK)
HMY05 *ex* Myong Sin *-2001* *ex* Ali *-2001* 573
\- *ex* Cleanseas Coral *-2000* 1,731
ex Wakatsuru Maru No. 6 *-1995*
Korea Samma Shipping Co
\-
SatCom: Inmarsat C 4445220000
Wonsan *North Korea*
MMSI: 445220000
Official number: 3104019

1981-12 **Suzuki Shipyard Co. Ltd. — Yokkaichi** Yd No: 360
Loa 70.00 Br ex - Dght 4.387
Lbp 65.11 Br md 11.00 Dpth 5.01
Welded, 1 dk

(A13B2TP) Products Tanker
Liq: 2,150; Liq (Oil): 2,150
Compartments: 2 Ho, 10 Ta, ER
2 Ha: ER

1 oil engine sr geared to sc. shaft driving 1 FP propeller
Total Power: 1,177kW (1,600hp) 10.0kn
Hanshin 6LU32
1 x 4 Stroke 6 Cy. 320 x 510 1177kW (1600bhp)
The Hanshin Diesel Works Ltd-Japan

8848305 **SAM O'CAT** *323* Class: RS (AB)
\- *ex* Soll Dunga *-2013* *ex* Umuda Maju *-2002* 107
\- *ex* Armada Maju *-1999* 347
Nikesto Investments Ltd
CJSC 'Perspective Technologies Agency'
Novorossiysk *Russia*
MMSI: 273443260

1991 **Kian Juan Dockyard Sdn Bhd — Miri**
Loa 38.85 Br ex 9.00 Dght 2.210
Lbp 36.10 Br md - Dpth 2.70
Welded, 1 dk

(A35D2RL) Landing Craft
Bow door/ramp

2 oil engines reverse geared to sc. shafts driving 2 FP propellers
Total Power: 626kW (852hp) 10.0kn
Cummins KT-19-M
2 x 4 Stroke 6 Cy. 159 x 159 each-313kW (426bhp)
Cummins Engine Co Inc-USA
AuxGen: 2 x 32kW a.c
Fuel: 43.0 (d.f.)

8973679 **SAM OF YEMEN** **3,621** Class: (PR)
7OSG *ex* 0139 *-2002* 1,086
\- **Yemen Economical Corp (YECO)** 2,500
\-
Aden *Yemen*
MMSI: 473111125
Official number: 0104

1978 **Stocznia Polnocna im Bohaterow Westerplatte — Gdansk** Yd No: B775/11
Converted From: Tank Landing Craft-2002
Loa 112.60 Br ex 15.10 Dght 5.050
Lbp 105.00 Br md 15.00 Dpth 7.00
Welded, 1 dk

(A35A2RR) Ro-Ro Cargo Ship

2 diesel electric oil engines driving 2 gen. Connecting to 2 elec. motors driving 2 FP propellers
Total Power: 10,380kW (14,112hp) 12.0kn
Sulzer 16ZV40/48
2 x Vee 2 Stroke 16 Cy. 400 x 480 each-5190kW (7056bhp)
Zaklady Urzadzen Technicznych'Zgoda' SA-Poland

9467952 **SAM PANTHER** **21,650** Class: KR
VRHS9 *ex* Jin Glory *-2010* 11,208
\- **SPV SAM Panther Inc** 33,395
Univan Ship Management Ltd
SatCom: Inmarsat C 447703120
Hong Kong *Hong Kong*
MMSI: 477986100
Official number: HK-2929

2010-11 **Orient Shipyard Co Ltd — Busan** Yd No: 1002
Loa 178.90 (BB) Br ex - Dght 9.818
Lbp 171.30 Br md 28.80 Dpth 14.20
Welded, 1 dk

(A21A2BC) Bulk Carrier
Grain: 43,538
Compartments: 5 Ho, ER
5 Ha: 4 (20.0 x 20.0)ER (13.6 x 15.4)
Cranes: 4x30t

1 oil engine driving 1 FP propeller
Total Power: 6,480kW (8,810hp) 13.5kn
MAN-B&W 6S42MC
1 x 2 Stroke 6 Cy. 420 x 1764 6480kW (8810bhp)
STX Engine Co Ltd-South Korea

9588407 **SAM PHOENIX** **22,137** Class: BV
VRIS7 11,328
\- **Shinyo Wisdom Ltd** 33,859
Shipping Asset Management (SAM) SA T/cm
Hong Kong *Hong Kong* 44.4
MMSI: 477899900
Official number: HK-3138

2011-07 **Zhejiang Jingang Shipbuilding Co Ltd — Wenling ZJ** Yd No: 027
Loa 179.50 (BB) Br ex - Dght 10.650
Lbp 172.00 Br md 28.00 Dpth 15.20
Welded, 1 dk

(A21A2BC) Bulk Carrier
Grain: 43,939; Bale: 43,060
Compartments: 5 Ho, ER
5 Ha: 3 (19.6 x 20.8) (19.6 x 20.0)ER (14.0 x 20.0)
Cranes: 4x30t

1 oil engine driving 1 FP propeller
Total Power: 6,480kW (8,810hp) 14.0kn
MAN-B&W 6S42MC7
1 x 2 Stroke 6 Cy. 420 x 1764 6480kW (8810bhp)
Hyundai Heavy Industries Co Ltd-South Korea
AuxGen: 3 x 520kW 60Hz a.c
Fuel: 111.0 (d.f.) 1346.0 (r.f.) 27.0pd

8032023 **SAM POONG** *519* Class: (KR)
D8RO *ex* Su Jin No. 77 *-1991* 312
\- **Shinsung Shipping Co Ltd** 929
\-
Busan *South Korea*
Official number: BSR-808653

1980 **Hyangdo Shipbuilding Co Ltd — Pohang**
Loa 56.90 Br ex - Dght 3.462
Lbp 52.00 Br md 8.81 Dpth 3.76
Welded, 1 dk

(A31A2GX) General Cargo Ship
Bale: 540
1 Ha: (18.7 x 5.7)
Derricks: 2x3t

1 oil engine driving 1 FP propeller
Total Power: 552kW (750hp) 9.3kn
Akasaka 6DH27SS
1 x 4 Stroke 6 Cy. 270 x 420 552kW (750bhp)
Akasaka Tekkosho KK (Akasaka DieselLtd)-Japan
AuxGen: 1 x 80kW 220V a.c

7103411 *6LZU* -	**SAM POONG No. 7** *ex* Chil Bo San No. 3 *-1995* **Sam Poong Shipping Co Ltd** - *Busan* South Korea Official number: BS02-A65	*1,651* 880 2,516	Class: (KR) (NK)	**1971-01 Hayashikane Shipbuilding & Engineering Co Ltd — Nagasaki NS** Yd No: 755 Loa 88.45 Br ex 12.63 Dght 5.462 Lbp 82.00 Br md 12.60 Dpth 6.30 Welded, 1 dk	**(A34A2GR) Refrigerated Cargo Ship** Ins: 2,510 Compartments: 3 Ho, ER 3 Ha: 3 (3.2 x 3.0)ER Derricks: 6x3t	**1 oil engine** driving 1 FP propeller Total Power: 1,912kW (2,600hp) 13.3kn Akasaka 6DH46SS 1 x 4 Stroke 6 Cy. 460 x 720 1912kW (2600bhp) Akasaka Tekkosho KK (Akasaka DieselLtd)-Japan AuxGen: 2 x 220kW 445V a.c
9578282 *PNKY* -	**SAM PROSPER I** - **PT Pelayaran Sumatra Wahana Perkasa** - *Jakarta* Indonesia MMSI: 525015768	**302** 91 215	Class: BV KI	**2010-08 PT Dok dan Perkapalan Surabaya (Persero) — Surabaya** Yd No: 08036 Loa 34.00 Br ex 9.02 Dght 2.800 Lbp 31.00 Br md 9.00 Dpth 3.60 Welded, 1 dk	**(B34L2QU) Utility Vessel**	**2 oil engines** reduction geared to sc. shafts driving 2 Propellers Total Power: 2,238kW (3,042hp) Cummins KTA-38-M2 2 x Vee 4 Stroke 12 Cy. 159 x 159 each-1119kW (1521bhp) Cummins Engine Co Inc-USA
9151981 *YCTJ* -	**SAM RATULANGI PB 1600** - **Government of The Republic of Indonesia (Direktorat Jenderal Perhubungan Laut - Ministry of Sea Communications)** PT Djakarta Lloyd (Persero) *Jakarta* Indonesia MMSI: 525003026	**18,247** 9,903 26,510	Class: (GL) (KI)	**2001-01 P.T. PAL Indonesia — Surabaya** Yd No: 156 Loa 177.35 (BB) Br ex 27.91 Dght 9.700 Lbp 167.74 Br md 27.50 Dpth 14.30 Welded, 1 dk	**(A33A2CC) Container Ship (Fully Cellular)** TEU 1644 incl 200 ref C. 9 Ha: Ice Capable	**1 oil engine** driving 1 FP propeller Total Power: 13,440kW (18,273hp) 19.0kn B&W 7L60MC 1 x 2 Stroke 7 Cy. 600 x 1944 13440kW (18273bhp) Hitachi Zosen Corp-Japan AuxGen: 3 x 880kW 440/220V a.c Thrusters: 1 Tunnel thruster (f) Fuel: 2154.0 (r.f.)
9031519 *3EXH9* -	**SAM RUSS** *ex* Co-Op Akebono *-2013* **East & West Shipping Inc** Penta Ocean Ship Management & Operation LLC *Panama* Panama MMSI: 351315000 Official number: 44672PEXT	**42,539** 15,519 49,242 T/cm 66.9	Class: NK	**1993-02 Kawasaki Heavy Industries Ltd — Sakaide KG** Yd No: 1430 Loa 224.05 (BB) Br ex 36.02 Dght 11.021 Lbp 212.47 Br md 36.00 Dpth 20.70 Welded, 1 dk	**(A11B2TG) LPG Tanker** Double Bottom Entire Compartment Length Liq (Gas): 73,882 4 x Gas Tank (s); 4 independent (C.mn.stl) pri horizontal 8 Cargo Pump (s): 8x600m³/hr Manifold: Bow/CM: 108.1m	**1 oil engine** driving 1 FP propeller Total Power: 9,121kW (12,401hp) 15.3kn B&W 5S70MCE 1 x 2 Stroke 5 Cy. 700 x 2674 9121kW (12401bhp) Kawasaki Heavy Industries Ltd-Japan AuxGen: 3 x 1040kW 450V 60Hz a.c Fuel: 600.0 (d.f.) 2090.0 (r.f.)
9173678 *YJUC4* -	**SAM S ALLGOOD** *ex* Monarch Bay *-2003* **Orange Fleet Ltd** Tidewater Marine Australia Pty Ltd SatCom: Inmarsat B 331023659 *Port Vila* Vanuatu MMSI: 576899000 Official number: 1534	**1,969** 845 3,107	Class: AB (NV)	**1998-09 Brattvaag Skipsverft AS — Brattvaag** (Hull launched by) Yd No: 72 **1998-09 Brevik Construction AS — Brevik** (Hull completed by) Yd No: 12 Loa 67.00 Br ex - Dght 6.000 Lbp 61.80 Br md 16.00 Dpth 7.00 Welded, 1 dk	**(B21A20S) Platform Supply Ship**	**2 oil engines** reduction geared to sc. shafts driving 2 CP propellers Total Power: 4,010kW (5,452hp) 12.0kn Normo KRMB-9 2 x 4 Stroke 9 Cy. 250 x 300 each-2005kW (2726bhp) Ulstein Bergen AS-Norway AuxGen: 2 x 1280kW 440V 60Hz a.c, 2 x 248kW 440V 60Hz a.c Thrusters: 1 Thwart. FP thruster (a); 1 Thwart. FP thruster (f); 1 Retract. directional thruster (f) Fuel: 734.0 (d.f.)
8031598 *D8RS* -	**SAM SHIN No. 1** - **Hae Man Co Ltd** - *Masan* South Korea Official number: MSR-808692	*497* 245 707	Class: (KR)	**1980 Hyupsung Shipbuilding Co — Pohang** Loa 48.32 Br ex - Dght 3.582 Lbp 43.01 Br md 8.60 Dpth 4.02 Welded, 1 dk	**(A31A2GX) General Cargo Ship** 1 Ha: (18.6 x 4.8)	**1 oil engine** driving 1 FP propeller Total Power: 478kW (650hp) 9.8kn Matsui MU623CHS 1 x 4 Stroke 6 Cy. 230 x 380 478kW (650bhp) Matsui Iron Works Co Ltd-Japan AuxGen: 2 x 20kW 225V a.c
9053452 *PA6615* -	**SAM SIMON** *ex* New Atlantis *-2012* *ex* Kaiko Maru No. 8 *-2012* *ex* Seifu Maru *-2010* **New Atlantis Ventures LLC** Sea Shepherd Conservation Society Netherlands MMSI: 244810415	*484* - 323		**1993-01 Ishikawajima-Harima Heavy Industries Co Ltd (IHI) — Tokyo** Yd No: 3035 Loa 55.50 (BB) Br ex - Dght 3.500 Lbp 50.00 Br md 9.80 Dpth 4.30 Welded, 1 dk	**(B31A2SR) Research Survey Vessel**	**1 oil engine** driving 1 CP propeller Total Power: 1,324kW (1,800hp) 12.0kn Akasaka A31 1 x 4 Stroke 6 Cy. 310 x 600 1324kW (1800bhp) Akasaka Tekkosho KK (Akasaka DieselLtd)-Japan Thrusters: 1 Thwart. CP thruster (f)
8893130 - -	**SAM SON 16** - **Thang Dong Transport Co-operative (Hop Tac Xa Thanh Dong Thanh Hoa)** - *Haiphong* Vietnam	**166** 86 200	Class: (VR)	**1988 at Thanh Hoa** Loa 36.35 Br ex - Dght 1.950 Lbp 33.50 Br md 7.00 Dpth 2.50 Welded, 1 dk	**(A31A2GX) General Cargo Ship** Grain: 375 2 Ha: 2 (6.5 x 4.5)ER	**1 oil engine** reduction geared to sc. shaft driving 1 FP propeller Total Power: 103kW (140hp) 8.0kn Yanmar 5KDGGE 1 x 4 Stroke 5 Cy. 145 x 170 103kW (140bhp) (made 1977) Yanmar Diesel Engine Co Ltd-Japan
8839108 *XVCJ* -	**SAM SON 17** *ex* Tien Phong *-1994* **Cong Thanh Sea Transport Co (Cong Ty Van Tai Bien Cong Thanh)** - *Saigon* Vietnam	*190* 108 200	Class: (VR)	**1985 Dong Tien Shipyard — Ho Chi Minh City** Loa 33.20 Br ex - Dght 3.000 Lbp - Br md 6.80 Dpth 4.00 Welded, 1 dk	**(A31A2GX) General Cargo Ship**	**1 oil engine** geared to sc. shaft driving 1 FP propeller Total Power: 515kW (700hp) Cummins KT-38-M 1 x Vee 4 Stroke 12 Cy. 159 x 159 515kW (700bhp) Cummins Engine Co Inc-USA
8893831 - -	**SAM SON 24** - **Thang Dong Transport Co-operative (Hop Tac Xa Thanh Dong Thanh Hoa)** - *Haiphong* Vietnam	**155** 62 200	Class: (VR)	**1993 at Haiphong** Loa 35.00 Br ex - Dght 2.200 Lbp - Br md 6.20 Dpth 2.90 Welded, 1 dk	**(A31A2GX) General Cargo Ship**	**1 oil engine** reduction geared to sc. shaft driving 1 FP propeller Total Power: 99kW (135hp) Skoda 6L160 1 x 4 Stroke 6 Cy. 160 x 225 99kW (135bhp) CKD Praha-Praha AuxGen: 1 x 12kW a.c
8868082 - -	**SAM SON 27** *ex* Ngoai Thuong-06 *-1998* **Thanh Dong Transport Co-operative (Hop Tac Xa Thanh Dong Thanh Hoa)** - *Haiphong* Vietnam Official number: VN-1231-VT	**154** 73 200	Class: (VR)	**1989 at Haiphong** Loa 36.50 Br ex - Dght 1.950 Lbp - Br md 7.00 Dpth 2.50 Welded, 1 dk	**(A31A2GX) General Cargo Ship** Grain: 375 Compartments: 2 Ho, ER 2 Ha: 2 (7.0 x 4.0)ER	**1 oil engine** reduction geared to sc. shaft driving 1 FP propeller Total Power: 103kW (140hp) 8.0kn Yanmar 5KDGGE 1 x 4 Stroke 5 Cy. 145 x 170 103kW (140bhp) (made 1977) Yanmar Diesel Engine Co Ltd-Japan
8868836 *XVWP* -	**SAM SON 36** *ex* Song Sinh 09 *-1996* *ex* Song Uong 01 *-1994* **Thang Dong Transport Co-operative (Hop Tac Xa Thanh Dong Thanh Hoa)** - *Quang Ninh* Vietnam	**155** 73 150	Class: (VR)	**1989 at Thanh Hoa** Loa 36.55 Br ex - Dght 1.700 Lbp - Br md 7.20 Dpth 2.50 Welded, 1 dk	**(A31A2GX) General Cargo Ship** Grain: 311 Compartments: 2 Ho, ER 2 Ha: 2 (7.0 x 4.0)ER	**1 oil engine** reduction geared to sc. shaft driving 1 FP propeller Total Power: 103kW (140hp) 10.0kn Yanmar 5KDGGE 1 x 4 Stroke 5 Cy. 145 x 170 103kW (140bhp) (made 1987) Yanmar Diesel Engine Co Ltd-Japan AuxGen: 1 x 5kW a.c
8893788 - -	**SAM SON 42** - **Tien Hung Transport Co (Xi Nghiep Van Tai Bien Tien Hung Thanh Hoa)** - *Haiphong* Vietnam	**166** 86 200	Class: (VR)	**1986 at Haiphong** Loa 36.50 Br ex - Dght 1.950 Lbp 33.50 Br md 7.00 Dpth 2.50 Welded, 1 dk	**(A31A2GX) General Cargo Ship** Compartments: 2 Ho, ER 2 Ha: 2 (6.5 x 4.0)ER	**1 oil engine** reduction geared to sc. shaft driving 1 FP propeller Total Power: 99kW (135hp) Skoda 6L160 1 x 4 Stroke 6 Cy. 160 x 225 99kW (135bhp) (made 1980) CKD Praha-Praha
7355612 *6MTK* -	**SAM SONG No. 23** - **Sam Song Industrial Co Ltd** - *Busan* South Korea Official number: BS-A-778	*221* 109 -	Class: (KR)	**1974 Busan Shipbuilding Co Ltd — Busan** Yd No: 123 Loa 42.37 Br ex 6.94 Dght - Lbp 37.75 Br md 6.91 Dpth 3.20 Welded, 1 dk	**(B11B2FV) Fishing Vessel** Ins: 315 4 Ha: 2 (1.1 x 0.9)2 (1.1 x 1.3)	**1 oil engine** driving 1 FP propeller Total Power: 552kW (750hp) 11.0kn Yanmar 6MHL-UT 1 x 4 Stroke 6 Cy. 200 x 240 552kW (750bhp) Yanmar Diesel Engine Co Ltd-Japan AuxGen: 2 x 80kW 225V a.c
6418041 *6LWG* -	**SAM SONG No. 71** *ex* Yoshi Maru No. 23 *-1970* **Sam Song Industrial Co Ltd** - *Busan* South Korea Official number: BS-A-18	*232* 114 -	Class: (KR)	**1963 Uchida Zosen — Ise** Yd No: 585 Loa 37.80 Br ex 7.45 Dght 2.947 Lbp - Br md 7.40 Dpth 3.46 Riveted\Welded, 1 dk	**(B11B2FV) Fishing Vessel**	**1 oil engine** driving 1 FP propeller Total Power: 478kW (650hp) 11.0kn Niigata 6M28DHS 1 x 4 Stroke 6 Cy. 280 x 440 478kW (650bhp) Niigata Engineering Co Ltd-Japan AuxGen: 2 x 64kW 230V a.c
6413429 - -	**SAM SONG No. 73** *ex* Kinsei Maru No. 26 *-1970* **Trio Pines Panama SA** Sam Song Industrial Co Ltd *Panama* Panama Official number: 942679	*226* 118 -	Class: (KR)	**1963 KK Kanasashi Zosen — Shizuoka SZ** Yd No: 550 Loa 43.69 Br ex 7.57 Dght 2.896 Lbp 38.54 Br md 7.50 Dpth 3.31 Welded, 1 dk	**(B11B2FV) Fishing Vessel**	**1 oil engine** driving 1 FP propeller Total Power: 478kW (650hp) 11.0kn Niigata 6M28DHS 1 x 4 Stroke 6 Cy. 280 x 440 478kW (650bhp) Niigata Engineering Co Ltd-Japan AuxGen: 2 x 82kW 230V a.c

IMO / Call sign / Flag	Name / Owner / Manager	Tonnage	Class	Builder / Dimensions	Type / Capacities	Machinery
6402432 - -	**SAM SONG No. 75** *ex* Tatsumi Maru No. 15 **Trio Pines Panama SA** Sam Song Industrial Co Ltd	227 118 -	Class: (KR)	**1963 KK Kanasashi Zosen — Shizuoka SZ** Yd No: 533 Loa 42.88 Br ex 7.35 Dght - Lbp 37.62 Br md 7.31 Dpth 3.41 Welded, 1 dk	**(B11B2FV) Fishing Vessel**	**1 oil engine** driving 1 FP propeller Total Power: 515kW (700hp) 10.5kn Fuji 6SD30 1 x 4 Stroke 6 Cy. 300 x 430 515kW (700bhp) Fuji Diesel Co Ltd-Japan AuxGen: 2 x 60kW 230V a.c
6401062 *6LZX* -	**SAM SONG No. 76** *ex* Tatsumi Maru No. 8 *-1970* **Sam Song Industrial Co Ltd** - *Busan* *South Korea* Official number: BS-A-122	235 107 -	Class: (KR)	**1963 Miho Zosensho K.K. — Shimizu** Yd No: 378 Loa 43.59 Br ex 7.57 Dght - Lbp 38.59 Br md 7.50 Dpth 3.36 Welded, 1 dk	**(B11B2FV) Fishing Vessel** 4 Ha: 2 (0.9 x 1.3)2 (1.5 x 1.3)	**1 oil engine** driving 1 FP propeller Total Power: 515kW (700hp) 11.0kn Akasaka MK6SS 1 x 4 Stroke 6 Cy. 300 x 420 515kW (700bhp) Akasaka Tekkosho KK (Akasaka DieselLtd)-Japan AuxGen: 2 x 64kW 225V a.c
7312244 *6MBK* -	**SAM SONG No. 77** *ex* Fumi Maru No. 2 *-1970* **Sam Song Industrial Co Ltd** - *Busan* *South Korea* Official number: BF35531	231 112 -	Class: (KR)	**1964 Kochiken Zosen — Kochi** Loa 42.80 Br ex - Dght - Lbp 38.10 Br md 7.40 Dpth 3.41 Welded, 1 dk	**(B11B2FV) Fishing Vessel**	**1 oil engine** driving 1 FP propeller Total Power: 515kW (700hp) 11.3kn Hanshin 1 x 4 Stroke 6 Cy. 320 x 420 515kW (700bhp) Hanshin Nainenki Kogyo-Japan
7355648 *6MPC* -	**SAM SONG No. 301** - **Sam Song Industrial Co Ltd** - *Busan* *South Korea* Official number: BS-A-729	396 255 -	Class: (KR)	**1974 Daedong Shipbuilding Co Ltd — Busan** Yd No: 107 Loa 52.63 Br ex - Dght 3.565 Lbp 47.30 Br md 8.39 Dpth 3.81 Welded, 1 dk	**(B11B2FV) Fishing Vessel** Ins: 737 Compartments: 3 Ho, ER 3 Ha: (0.9 x 0.9)2 (1.6 x 1.6) Derricks: 1x1t	**1 oil engine** driving 1 FP propeller Total Power: 736kW (1,001hp) 11.5kn Hanshin 6LUD26G 1 x 4 Stroke 6 Cy. 260 x 440 736kW (1001bhp) Hanshin Nainenki Kogyo-Japan AuxGen: 2 x 176kW 225V a.c
7355650 *6MPD* -	**SAM SONG No. 302** - **Sam Song Industrial Co Ltd** Han Ryoong Co-operated Co *Busan* *South Korea* Official number: BS-A-731	395 254 -	Class: (KR)	**1974 Daedong Shipbuilding Co Ltd — Busan** Yd No: 108 Loa 52.63 Br ex - Dght 3.565 Lbp 47.30 Br md 8.39 Dpth 3.81 Welded, 1 dk	**(B11B2FV) Fishing Vessel** Compartments: 3 Ho, ER 3 Ha: (0.9 x 0.9)2 (1.6 x 1.6) Derricks: 1x1t	**1 oil engine** driving 1 FP propeller Total Power: 736kW (1,001hp) 11.5kn Hanshin 6LUD26G 1 x 4 Stroke 6 Cy. 260 x 440 736kW (1001bhp) Hanshin Nainenki Kogyo-Japan AuxGen: 2 x 176kW 225V d.c Fuel: 366.0 (d.f.)
7739739 *6KWK* -	**SAM SONG No. 502** - **Sam Song Industrial Co Ltd** Eoryong Industrial Co Ltd *Busan* *South Korea* Official number: BS-A-2063	448 283 516	Class: (KR)	**1978 Daedong Shipbuilding Co Ltd — Busan** Loa 55.15 Br ex 8.62 Dght 3.611 Lbp 49.00 Br md 8.60 Dpth 3.99 Welded, 1 dk	**(B11B2FV) Fishing Vessel** Ins: 542	**1 oil engine** driving 1 FP propeller Total Power: 956kW (1,300hp) 13.0kn Niigata 6M28X 1 x 4 Stroke 6 Cy. 280 x 440 956kW (1300bhp) Niigata Engineering Co Ltd-Japan AuxGen: 2 x 200kW 225V a.c
9140035 - -	**SAM SUNG No. 2** *ex* Iyo Maru *-2013* - - *South Korea* MMSI: 440113620	698 - 2,100		**1996-03 Hitachi Zosen Mukaishima Marine Co Ltd — Onomichi HS** Yd No: 106 Loa - Br ex - Dght 4.830 Lbp 69.00 Br md 14.50 Dpth 8.09 Welded, 1 dk	**(A31A2GX) General Cargo Ship**	**1 oil engine** geared to sc. shaft driving 1 FP propeller Total Power: 1,471kW (2,000hp) Hanshin 6EL38G 1 x 4 Stroke 6 Cy. 380 x 760 1471kW (2000bhp) The Hanshin Diesel Works Ltd-Japan
9136981 - -	**SAM SUNG NO. 5** *ex* Juzan Maru No. 11 *-2009* **Sam Sung Shipping Co Ltd** - *South Korea*	748 - 2,099		**1996-01 K.K. Watanabe Zosensho — Nagasaki** Yd No: 037 Loa 83.02 (BB) Br ex - Dght 4.250 Lbp 76.00 Br md 14.00 Dpth 7.44 Welded, 2 dks	**(A31A2GX) General Cargo Ship** Compartments: 1 Ho, ER 1 Ha: ER	**1 oil engine** driving 1 FP propeller Total Power: 1,471kW (2,000hp) Niigata 6M38GT 1 x 4 Stroke 6 Cy. 380 x 720 1471kW (2000bhp) Niigata Engineering Co Ltd-Japan Thrusters: 1 Thwart. FP thruster (f)
8413722 *6MQD* -	**SAM SUNG No. 32** - **Jung Yang-Yon** - *Ulleung* *South Korea* Official number: KN7166-A360	180 - -		**1982-08 Sungpo Shipyard Co — Geoje** Yd No: 69 Loa 37.11 Br ex 6.91 Dght 2.401 Lbp 31.63 Br md 5.91 Dpth 2.82 Welded, 1 dk	**(B11B2FV) Fishing Vessel** Ins: 155	**1 oil engine** with clutches, flexible couplings & sr reverse geared to sc. shaft driving 1 FP propeller Total Power: 441kW (600hp) Niigata 6MG18CX 1 x 4 Stroke 6 Cy. 180 x 240 441kW (600bhp) Ssangyong Heavy Industries Co Ltd-South Korea
9254513 *VREV3* -	**SAM TIGER** *ex* Jin Kang *-2009* *ex* Canton Trader *-2009* **SPV SAM Tiger Inc** Univan Ship Management Ltd *Hong Kong* *Hong Kong* MMSI: 477192300 Official number: HK-2320	**30,011** 17,843 52,454 T/cm 55.5	Class: BV	**2003-04 Tsuneishi Heavy Industries (Cebu) Inc — Balamban** Yd No: SC-036 Loa 189.90 Br ex - Dght 12.020 Lbp 182.00 Br md 32.26 Dpth 17.00 Welded, 1 dk	**(A21A2BC) Bulk Carrier** Grain: 67,500; Bale: 65,600 Compartments: 6 Ho, ER 6 Ha: 5 (21.0 x 18.4)ER (20.4 x 18.4) Cranes: 4x30t	**1 oil engine** driving 1 FP propeller Total Power: 7,796kW (10,599hp) 14.5kn B&W 6S50MC 1 x 2 Stroke 6 Cy. 500 x 1910 7796kW (10599bhp) Mitsui Engineering & Shipbuilding CLtd-Japan
9620176 *VRLH8* -	**SAM WOLF** - **SPV SAM Wolf Inc** Univan Ship Management Ltd *Hong Kong* *Hong Kong* MMSI: 477305700	**31,760** 19,043 57,200 T/cm 57.3	Class: BV	**2012-10 STX Offshore & Shipbuilding Co Ltd — Changwon (Jinhae Shipyard)** Yd No: 1507 Loa 190.00 (BB) Br ex - Dght 13.000 Lbp 183.30 Br md 32.26 Dpth 18.50 Welded, 1 dk	**(A21A2BC) Bulk Carrier** Grain: 71,354 Compartments: 5 Ho, ER 5 Ha: ER Cranes: 4x30t	**1 oil engine** driving 1 FP propeller Total Power: 9,480kW (12,889hp) 14.5kn MAN-B&W 6S50MC-C 1 x 2 Stroke 6 Cy. 500 x 2000 9480kW (12889bhp) STX Engine Co Ltd-South Korea AuxGen: 3 x 625kW 60Hz a.c
6711053 *6KCZ* -	**SAM WON** *ex* Peonia *-1982* *ex* Okuni Maru *-1981* **Sam Won Fisheries Co Ltd** - *Busan* *South Korea* Official number: BS-A-1957	1,502 715 1,577	Class: (KR) (NK)	**1967 Shikoku Dockyard Co. Ltd. — Takamatsu** Yd No: 720 Loa 75.39 Br ex 12.22 Dght 5.031 Lbp 69.12 Br md 12.20 Dpth 5.72 Riveted\Welded, 2 dks	**(B11A2FS) Stern Trawler** Ins: 1,392 2 Ha: (2.2 x 2.2) (2.2 x 3.8) Derricks: 2x3t,2x1.5t	**1 oil engine** driving 1 FP propeller Total Power: 1,942kW (2,640hp) 13.0kn B&W 8-35VBF-62 1 x 2 Stroke 8 Cy. 350 x 620 1942kW (2640bhp) Hitachi Zosen Corp-Japan AuxGen: 2 x 360kW 445V a.c Fuel: 575.0
9084279 - -	**SAM WON** *ex* Rebun Maru No. 1 *-2013* **Sam Won Shipping Co Ltd** - *South Korea* MMSI: 440106310	699 - 1,609	Class: KR (Class contemplated) (NK)	**1993-12 Shin Kochi Jyuko K.K. — Kochi** Yd No: 7040 Loa 75.02 (BB) Br ex - Dght 4.251 Lbp 70.00 Br md 11.20 Dpth 5.10 Welded, 1 dk	**(A13B2TP) Products Tanker** Liq: 2,197; Liq (Oil): 2,197 Compartments: 10 Ta, ER	**1 oil engine** driving 1 FP propeller Total Power: 1,471kW (2,000hp) 12.7kn Hanshin LH32LG 1 x 4 Stroke 6 Cy. 320 x 640 1471kW (2000bhp) The Hanshin Diesel Works Ltd-Japan AuxGen: 3 x 116kW a.c Fuel: 70.0 (d.f.)
6413388 *6MBE* -	**SAM WON No. 11** *ex* Iwakuni Maru No. 2 *-1971* **Sam Won Fisheries Co Ltd** - *Busan* *South Korea* Official number: BF35533	225 110 -	Class: (KR)	**1963 KK Kanasashi Zosen — Shizuoka SZ** Yd No: 555 Loa 43.72 Br ex 7.57 Dght 2.896 Lbp 38.54 Br md 7.50 Dpth 3.31 Welded, 1 dk	**(B11B2FV) Fishing Vessel**	**1 oil engine** driving 1 FP propeller Total Power: 515kW (700hp) 11.5kn Akasaka MK6SS 1 x 4 Stroke 6 Cy. 300 x 420 515kW (700bhp) Akasaka Tekkosho KK (Akasaka DieselLtd)-Japan
9327607 *HO4660* -	**SAM WOO** - **S K Lines SA** Meta Tugboat Co Ltd *Panama* *Panama* MMSI: 354714000 Official number: 3238807	**191** 57 -	Class: KR	**2004-07 Yeunsoo Shipbuilding Co Ltd — Janghang** Yd No: 17 Loa 28.50 Br ex - Dght 2.400 Lbp 24.00 Br md 7.80 Dpth 3.40 Welded, 1 dk	**(B32A2ST) Tug**	**2 oil engines** geared to sc. shafts driving 2 Propellers Total Power: 1,492kW (2,028hp) Cummins KTA-38-M1 2 x Vee 4 Stroke 12 Cy. 159 x 159 each-746kW (1014bhp) Cummins Engine Co Ltd-United Kingdom
7829560 *D7EW* -	**SAM WOO HAN DONG** *ex* Yuriwang No. 8 *-1991* **Han Dong Co Ltd** - *Incheon* *South Korea* Official number: ICR-780027	393 220 611	Class: (KR)	**1978 Inchon Engineering & Shipbuilding Corp — Incheon** Yd No: 7801 Loa 47.00 Br ex - Dght 3.112 Lbp 43.01 Br md 8.60 Dpth 3.61 Welded, 1 dk	**(A31A2GX) General Cargo Ship** Grain: 709 2 Ha: 2 (3.2 x 1.7)	**1 oil engine** driving 1 FP propeller Total Power: 368kW (500hp) 10.5kn Sumiyoshi S6UDTSS 1 x 4 Stroke 6 Cy. 260 x 400 368kW (500bhp) Sumiyoshi Marine Diesel Co Ltd-Japan AuxGen: 1 x 29kW 225V a.c
5394078 *6MTW* -	**SAM YANG No. 501** *ex* Dong Sung No. 123 *-1988* *ex* Anei Maru No. 18 *-1988* *ex* Yachiyo Maru No. 15 *-1988* **Hai Mi Co Ltd** - *Busan* *South Korea* Official number: BS02-A720	268 145 -	Class: (KR)	**1962 KK Kanasashi Zosen — Shizuoka SZ** Yd No: 492 Loa 46.18 Br ex 7.55 Dght 3.300 Lbp 40.54 Br md 7.50 Dpth 3.61 Welded, 1 dk	**(B11B2FV) Fishing Vessel** Ins: 447 4 Ha: 4 (1.2 x 1.2)	**1 oil engine** driving 1 FP propeller Total Power: 552kW (750hp) 11.3kn Akasaka TR6SS 1 x 4 Stroke 6 Cy. 326 x 460 552kW (750bhp) Akasaka Tekkosho KK (Akasaka DieselLtd)-Japan AuxGen: 2 x 94kW 230V a.c

IMO / Call sign	Name / Owner / Port	Tonnage	Class	Builder / Dimensions	Type	Machinery
8413588 *6KYA* -	**SAM YANG No. 803** - **Song Yung-Woo** - *Busan* South Korea Official number: BS-A2112	*120* 42 -		**1983-11 Chungmu Shipbuilding Co Inc — Tongyeong** Yd No: 125 Loa 35.51 (BB) Br ex 6.91 Dght 2.301 Lbp 29.77 Br md 5.91 Dpth 2.82 Welded, 1 dk	**(B11B2FV) Fishing Vessel** Ins: 93	**1 oil engine** with clutches, flexible couplings & sr reverse geared to sc. shaft driving 1 FP propeller Total Power: 331kW (450hp) Niigata 6L16XB-B 1 x 4 Stroke 6 Cy. 160 x 200 331kW (450bhp) Ssangyong Heavy Industries Co Ltd-South Korea
8816273 - -	**SAM YOUNG** *ex* Koshin Maru *-2003* **C& Merchant Marine Co Ltd** - *Busan* South Korea MMSI: 440106950 Official number: BSR-030356	*699* - 1,957	Class: KR (NK)	**1989-02 Hakata Zosen K.K. — Imabari** Yd No: 386 Loa 69.98 (BB) Br ex - Dght 4.851 Lbp 66.00 Br md 12.00 Dpth 5.30 Welded, 1 dk	**(A13B2TP) Products Tanker** Liq: 2,198; Liq (Oil): 2,198 Compartments: 10 Ta, ER	**1 oil engine** driving 1 CP propeller Total Power: 1,324kW (1,800hp) 11.5kn Hanshin LH31G 1 x 4 Stroke 6 Cy. 310 x 530 1324kW (1800bhp) The Hanshin Diesel Works Ltd-Japan AuxGen: 3 x 93kW a.c
7115206 *6MDH* -	**SAM YOUNG NO. 77** *ex* Tae Jin No. 77 *-1990* *ex* Kwang Shin No. 99 *-1990* *ex* Kwang Myung No. 99 *-1987* **Sam Young Fisheries Co Ltd** - *Busan* South Korea MMSI: 440789000 Official number: 9512093-6260009	*467* 237 417	Class: (KR)	**1971-05 Dae Sun Shipbuilding & Engineering Co Ltd — Busan** Loa 57.05 Br ex 9.02 Dght 3.612 Lbp 51.49 Br md 9.00 Dpth 3.99 Welded, 1 dk	**(B11B2FV) Fishing Vessel** Ins: 468 3 Ha: 2 (1.0 x 1.3) (1.6 x 1.6)ER	**1 oil engine** driving 1 FP propeller Total Power: 1,103kW (1,500hp) 13.0kn Niigata 6M37AHS 1 x 4 Stroke 6 Cy. 370 x 540 1103kW (1500bhp) Niigata Engineering Co Ltd-Japan AuxGen: 2 x 200kW 225V a.c
8413760 *6MQU* -	**SAM YOUNG No. 101** - **Kim In-Do** - *Guryongpo* South Korea Official number: KN6865-A1365	*105* - -		**1982-12 Sungpo Shipyard Co — Geoje** Yd No: 84 Loa 32.82 Br ex 6.10 Dght 2.201 Lbp 27.61 Br md 5.71 Dpth 2.72 Welded, 1 dk	**(B11B2FV) Fishing Vessel** Ins: 55	**1 oil engine** with clutches, flexible couplings & sr reverse geared to sc. shaft driving 1 FP propeller Total Power: 441kW (600hp) Niigata 6MG18CX 1 x 4 Stroke 6 Cy. 180 x 240 441kW (600bhp) Ssangyong Heavy Industries Co Ltd-South Korea
8827583 *6MOR* -	**SAM YOUNG NO. 101** *ex* Dong Won No. 312 *-2004* **Sam Young Fisheries Co Ltd** - SatCom: Inmarsat A 1660133 *Busan* South Korea MMSI: 440684000 Official number: 9510065-6260007	**661** - 672	Class: (KR)	**1988-10 Shin Tien Erh Shipbuilding Co, Ltd — Kaohsiung** Loa 62.50 Br ex - Dght 4.105 Lbp 54.20 Br md 9.60 Dpth 4.35 Welded, 1 dk	**(B11B2FV) Fishing Vessel**	**1 oil engine** driving 1 FP propeller Total Power: 1,103kW (1,500hp) 12.2kn Matsui 1 x 4 Stroke 6 Cy. 280 x 520 1103kW (1500bhp) (made 1988) Matsui Iron Works Co Ltd-Japan AuxGen: 3 x 1168kW 225V a.c
6414667 *DTBV9* -	**SAM YOUNG NO. 601** *ex* Chang Jin No. 601 *-2008* *ex* Duk Soo No. 15 *-2005* *ex* Satsu Maru No. 17 *-1976* *ex* Tenshin Maru *-1976* **S & H Co Ltd** - *Busan* South Korea MMSI: 441565000	**747** 339 945	Class: (KR)	**1964-02 Nippon Kokan KK (NKK Corp) — Shizuoka SZ** Yd No: 227 Loa 55.65 Br ex 9.78 Dght 3.700 Lbp 50.00 Br md 9.75 Dpth 4.20 Riveted\Welded, 1 dk	**(B11B2FV) Fishing Vessel**	**1 oil engine** driving 1 FP propeller Total Power: 1,030kW (1,400hp) 11.5kn Niigata M6F43CHS 1 x 4 Stroke 6 Cy. 430 x 620 1030kW (1400bhp) Niigata Engineering Co Ltd-Japan Fuel: 308.0
7311941 *6LMN* -	**SAM YUNG** - **Oh Jun Dong** - *Mokpo* South Korea Official number: MM5230	*171* 93 -		**1972-01 Dongyang Shipbuilding Industrial Co Ltd — Busan** Loa 36.38 Br ex 6.23 Dght - Lbp 32.19 Br md 6.20 Dpth 2.70 Welded, 2 dks	**(A37B2PS) Passenger Ship**	**1 oil engine** driving 1 FP propeller Total Power: 441kW (600hp) Makita 1 x 4 Stroke 6 Cy. 275 x 400 441kW (600bhp) Makita Tekkosho-Japan
7434391 *D6DM5* -	**SAMA** *ex* Morning Star *-2009* *ex* Ali 1 *-2006* *ex* Olympic Glory *-2005* *ex* Glory A *-2000* *ex* Lampis *-1999* *ex* Khalifah *-1996* *ex* Lamnalco 15 *-1995* *ex* Lamnalco Tern *-1982* **Sama Marine Shipping Inc** Pacific Light Operation & Ship Management LLC *Moroni* Union of Comoros MMSI: 616488000 Official number: 1200565	**203** 60 338	Class: (LR) (BV) ✠ Classed LR until 1/3/87	**1975-07 Kip Plaisance Contractors, Inc. — Golden Meadow, La** Yd No: 5 Loa 35.56 Br ex 8.13 Dght 2.640 Lbp 32.01 Br md 7.93 Dpth 3.51 Welded, 1 dk	**(B21A20C) Crew/Supply Vessel** Cranes: 1x7t	**2 oil engines** reverse reduction geared to sc. shafts driving 2 FP propellers Total Power: 1,030kW (1,400hp) 10.0kn G.M. (Detroit Diesel) 16V-71-N 2 x Vee 2 Stroke 16 Cy. 108 x 127 each-515kW (700bhp) General Motors Detroit DieselAllison Divn-USA AuxGen: 2 x 30kW 120/208V 60Hz a.c
7642584 *3FTX6* -	**SAMA** *ex* Arktouros *-1996* *ex* Sunstar *-1996* *ex* Tegesos *-1995* *ex* Tervete *-1995* *ex* Maldis Skreya *-1995* **Success Shipping Co** El Moez Maritime Co *Panama* Panama MMSI: 351003000 Official number: 4307711	**2,136** 997 2,180 T/cm 8.3	Class: (LR) (RS) Classed LR until 9/4/11	**1977-03 Santierul Naval Drobeta-Turnu Severin S.A. — Drobeta-Turnu S.** Yd No: 31018 Loa 88.75 Br ex 12.85 Dght 5.387 Lbp 80.40 Br md 12.81 Dpth 6.71 Welded, 2 dks	**(A31A2GX) General Cargo Ship** Grain: 3,575; Bale: 3,240 TEU 57 C.Ho 38/20' C.Dk 19/20' Compartments: 3 Ho, ER, 3 Tw Dk 3 Ha: (7.7 x 8.8)2 (12.9 x 10.2)ER Derricks: 1x20t,2x10t; Winches: 9	**1 oil engine** driving 1 FP propeller Total Power: 1,530kW (2,080hp) 10.0kn Sulzer 8TAD36 1 x 2 Stroke 8 Cy. 360 x 600 1530kW (2080bhp) Zaklady Przemyslu Metalowego 'HCegielski' SA-Poznan AuxGen: 3 x 220V 50Hz a.c Boilers: AuxB (o.f.) 5.0kgf/cm² (4.9bar), AuxB (ex.g.) 5.0kgf/cm² (4.9bar) Fuel: 44.5 (d.f.) 133.0 (r.f.) 7.0pd
9127758 *6AHH* -	**SAMA-1** *ex* Makkah *-2011* *ex* Tanger Jet *-2011* *ex* Solidor 3 *-2001* **Fortune Maritime for Fast Ferries** United Company for Marine Lines *Hurghada* Egypt MMSI: 622111301 Official number: 355	**2,165** 649 110	Class: GL (BV) (NV)	**1996-06 Kvaerner Fjellstrand AS — Omastrand** Yd No: 1630 Loa 60.00 (BB) Br ex - Dght 2.150 Lbp 54.00 Br md 16.50 Dpth 5.73 Welded, 1 dk	**(A36A2PR) Passenger/Ro-Ro Ship (Vehicles)** Passengers: unberthed: 572 Stern door/ramp Len: 3.80 Wid: 6.00 Swl: - Lane-Len: 230 Cars: 58	**2 oil engines** with flexible couplings & reductiongeared to sc. shafts driving 2 Water jets Total Power: 10,800kW (14,684hp) 33.0kn M.T.U. 20V1163TB73 2 x Vee 4 Stroke 20 Cy. 230 x 280 each-5400kW (7342bhp) MTU Friedrichshafen GmbH-Friedrichshafen AuxGen: 2 x 230kW 230/400V 50Hz a.c Thrusters: 2 Thwart. FP thruster (f) Fuel: 48.0 (d.f.) 26.3pd
8211954 *9BOU* -	**SAMAD 21** *ex* Abdul Samad *-2007* *ex* HMT-103 *-2006* *ex* Yukon Power *-1999* **Mallahi M** - *Bandar Abbas* Iran MMSI: 422689000 Official number: 11527	*126* 38 -	Class: AS (KR) (AB)	**1983-01 Heng Huat Shipbuilding & Construction Pte Ltd — Singapore** Yd No: T6 Loa 23.50 Br ex - Dght 2.509 Lbp 21.50 Br md 7.50 Dpth 3.15 Welded, 1 dk	**(B32A2ST) Tug**	**2 oil engines** reduction geared to sc. shafts driving 2 FP propellers Total Power: 1,268kW (1,724hp) 9.0kn Caterpillar 3056 1 x 4 Stroke 6 Cy. 100 x 127 634kW (862bhp) Caterpillar Tractor Co-USA Caterpillar 3056 1 x 4 Stroke 6 Cy. 100 x 127 634kW (862bhp) (new engine 1983) Caterpillar Tractor Co-USA AuxGen: 2 x 22kW a.c
1008671 *ZCOY9* -	**SAMADHI** *ex* April Fool *-2013* **Big Dog Marine Ltd** Vessel Safety Management LLC *George Town* Cayman Islands (British) MMSI: 319420000 Official number: 738557	**1,036** 310 220	Class: LR ✠ **100A1** SS 06/2011 SSC Yacht (P), mono, G6 **LMC** **UMS** Cable: 389.8/26.0 U2 (a)	**2006-06 Eltink's Scheeps- en Jachtwerf B.V. — Katwijk a/d Maas (Hull)** Yd No: (792) **2006-06 Jacht- en Scheepswerf C. van Lent & Zonen B.V. — Kaag** Yd No: 792 Loa 60.96 Br ex 10.90 Dght 3.450 Lbp 51.92 Br md 10.50 Dpth 5.55 Welded, 1 dk	**(X11A2YP) Yacht**	**2 oil engines** with clutches, flexible couplings & sr reverse geared to sc. shafts driving 2 FP propellers Total Power: 2,984kW (4,058hp) Caterpillar 3516B-TA 2 x Vee 4 Stroke 16 Cy. 170 x 190 each-1492kW (2029bhp) Caterpillar Inc-USA AuxGen: 2 x 200kW 400V 50Hz a.c, 1 x 150kW 400V 50Hz a.c Thrusters: 1 Thwart. FP thruster (f)
9503237 *HOJV* -	**SAMAIL** - **Samail Maritime Transportation Co SA** Oman Ship Management Co SAOC *Panama* Panama MMSI: 357867000 Official number: 4357612	**156,836** 101,675 302,845 T/cm 179.4	Class: AB	**2011-07 Universal Shipbuilding Corp — Nagasu KM (Ariake Shipyard)** Yd No: 138 Loa 330.00 (BB) Br ex 60.04 Dght 21.635 Lbp 318.00 Br md 60.00 Dpth 29.50 Welded, 1 dk	**(A13A2TV) Crude Oil Tanker** Double Hull (13F) Liq: 326,627; Liq (Oil): 324,700 Compartments: 5 Ta, 10 Wing Ta, 2 Wing Slop Ta, ER 3 Cargo Pump (s): 3x5500m³/hr Manifold: Bow/CM: 162m	**1 oil engine** driving 1 FP propeller Total Power: 25,130kW (34,167hp) 16.0kn MAN-B&W 7S80ME-C8 1 x 2 Stroke 7 Cy. 800 x 3200 25130kW (34167bhp) Hitachi Zosen Corp-Japan AuxGen: 3 x 950kW a.c Fuel: 548.0 (d.f.) 7601.0 (r.f.)
9330446 *DUA3121* -	**SAMAL ISLAND** *ex* Sunny Kitty *-2010* *ex* Seongho Ace *-2006* **Islas Tankers Shipping Corp** Magsaysay Maritime Corp *Manila* Philippines MMSI: 548538200 Official number: 00-0000375	**3,694** 1,777 5,555 T/cm 13.8	Class: NK (KR)	**2005-10 Ilheung Shipbuilding & Engineering Co Ltd — Mokpo** Yd No: 04-127 Loa 101.00 (BB) Br ex - Dght 6.613 Lbp 94.00 Br md 16.00 Dpth 8.50 Welded, 1 dk	**(A12B2TR) Chemical/Products Tanker** Double Hull (13F) Liq: 6,085; Liq (Oil): 6,085 Compartments: 10 Wing Ta, ER, 2 Wing Slop Ta 10 Cargo Pump (s): 10x200m³/hr Manifold: Bow/CM: 55.5m	**1 oil engine** driving 1 Propeller Total Power: 2,647kW (3,599hp) 14.5kn Hanshin LH41LA 1 x 4 Stroke 6 Cy. 410 x 800 2647kW (3599bhp) The Hanshin Diesel Works Ltd-Japan Fuel: 90.0 (d.f.) 460.0 (r.f.)

9654892 *9WKR2* -	**SAMALAJU JAYA** **Jaya Coastal Marine Logistic Sdn Bhd** - *Kuching Malaysia* Official number: 333267	**299** 89 -	Class: BV	**2012-05 Sing Kiong Hong Dockyard Sdn Bhd — Sibu** Yd No: 5016 Loa 28.00 Br ex - Dght 4.000 Lbp 26.58 Br md 10.00 Dpth 4.80 Welded, 1 dk	**(B32A2ST) Tug**	**2 oil engines** reduction geared to sc. shafts driving 2 Directional propellers Total Power: 1,766kW (2,402hp) Yanmar 2 x 4 Stroke each-883kW (1201bhp) Yanmar Diesel Engine Co Ltd-Japan Fuel: 110.0
9168166 *EPAB9* -	**SAMAN** *ex* Victoria I *-2009* **Golden Sea Shipping Co Ltd** Parsian Golden Sea Shipping Co *Bandar Anzali Iran* MMSI: 422861000 Official number: 930	**4,955** 1,781 5,885 T/cm 20.0	Class: AS (RS)	**1997-05 Sudostroitelnyy Zavod "Krasnoye Sormovo" — Nizhniy Novgorod** Yd No: 19610/40 Loa 139.93 Br ex 16.65 Dght 4.680 Lbp 134.00 Br md 16.40 Dpth 6.70 Welded, 1 dk	**(A31A2GX) General Cargo Ship** Grain: 6,843; Bale: 6,785 TEU 140 C.Ho 92/20' C.Dk 48/20' Compartments: 4 Ho, ER 4 Ha: 4 (18.7 x 11.8)ER	**2 oil engines** driving 2 FP propellers Total Power: 1,426kW (1,938hp) 9.5kn S.K.L. 8NVDS48A-3U 2 x 4 Stroke 8 Cy. 320 x 480 each-713kW (969bhp) SKL Motoren u. Systemtechnik AG-Magdeburg AuxGen: 3 x 160kW 380V 50Hz a.c Thrusters: 1 Thwart. CP thruster (f) Fuel: 171.0 (d.f.) 196.0 (r.f.) 7.8pd
9177129 - -	**SAMANALA DEVI** - **Scandia Trading (S) Pte Ltd** - *Sri Lanka*	**105** - 235		**1998-03 P.T. Batamas Jala Nusantara — Batam** Yd No: 24 Loa 28.70 Br ex - Dght 2.150 Lbp 27.61 Br md 6.50 Dpth 2.40 Welded, 1 dk	**(B34A2SH) Hopper, Motor**	**1 oil engine** gearing integral to driving 1 Z propeller Total Power: 132kW (179hp) 7.0kn Cummins 6BT5.9-M 1 x 4 Stroke 6 Cy. 102 x 120 132kW (179bhp) Cummins Engine Co Inc-USA
9177131 - -	**SAMANALA KURAMI** - **Scandia Trading (S) Pte Ltd** - *Sri Lanka*	**105** - 235		**1998-03 P.T. Batamas Jala Nusantara — Batam** Yd No: 25 Loa 28.70 Br ex - Dght 2.150 Lbp 27.61 Br md 6.50 Dpth 2.40 Welded, 1 dk	**(B34A2SH) Hopper, Motor**	**1 oil engine** gearing integral to driving 1 Z propeller Total Power: 132kW (179hp) 7.0kn Cummins 6BT5.9-M 1 x 4 Stroke 6 Cy. 102 x 120 132kW (179bhp) Cummins Engine Co Inc-USA
7415151 - -	**SAMANCO** *ex* Ultramar III *-2002* **Petrolera Transoceanica SA** - *Peru*	*205* 12 -	Class: (LR) (GL) Classed LR until 21/1/09	**1974-12 Werftunion GmbH & Co, Zweigniederlassung Emden — Emden** Yd No: 116 Loa 31.15 Br ex 8.79 Dght 4.080 Lbp 27.01 Br md 8.23 Dpth 4.60 Welded, 1 dk	**(B32A2ST) Tug**	**1 oil engine** driving 1 FP propeller Total Power: 956kW (1,300hp) 11.0kn MWM TBD501-6 1 x 4 Stroke 6 Cy. 360 x 450 956kW (1300bhp) Motoren Werke Mannheim AG (MWM)-West Germany Fuel: 53.0 (d.f.)
8818350 - -	**SAMANCO 1** - **Envasadora Chimbote Export SA** Enrique Silva Nano *Pisco Peru* Official number: CE-004501-PM	*328* 130 -	Class: (GL)	**1989-12 Andina de Desarrollo S.A. — Callao** Yd No: 098 Loa 37.50 Br ex - Dght 3.486 Lbp 32.20 Br md 8.18 Dpth 3.91 Welded, 1 dk	**(B11B2FV) Fishing Vessel**	**1 oil engine** with clutches & sr reverse geared to sc. shaft driving 1 FP propeller Total Power: 662kW (900hp) 12.0kn Caterpillar 3512TA 1 x Vee 4 Stroke 12 Cy. 170 x 190 662kW (900bhp) Caterpillar Inc-USA AuxGen: 2 x 6kW 24V d.c
8818374 - -	**SAMANCO 3** - **Envasadora Chimbote Export SA** Enrique Silva Nano *Pisco Peru* Official number: CE-004503-PM	*328* 130 -	Class: (GL)	**1990-01 Andina de Desarrollo S.A. — Callao** Yd No: 100 Loa 37.50 Br ex - Dght 3.486 Lbp 32.20 Br md 8.18 Dpth 3.91 Welded, 1 dk	**(B11B2FV) Fishing Vessel**	**1 oil engine** with clutches & sr reverse geared to sc. shaft driving 1 FP propeller Total Power: 662kW (900hp) 12.0kn Caterpillar 3512TA 1 x Vee 4 Stroke 12 Cy. 170 x 190 662kW (900bhp) Caterpillar Inc-USA AuxGen: 2 x 6kW 24V d.c
9073816 - -	**SAMANCO 5** - **Envasadora Chimbote Export SA** Enrique Silva Nano *Chimbote Peru* Official number: CE-010500-PM	*378* 174 433	Class: (GL)	**1993-12 Andina de Desarrollo S.A. — Callao** Yd No: 118 L reg 38.75 Br ex - Dght 3.725 Lbp - Br md 8.30 Dpth 4.15 Welded	**(B11B2FV) Fishing Vessel** Ins: 420	**1 oil engine** reduction geared to sc. shaft driving 1 FP propeller Total Power: 780kW (1,060hp) 12.0kn Caterpillar 3512TA 1 x Vee 4 Stroke 12 Cy. 170 x 190 780kW (1060bhp) Caterpillar Inc-USA AuxGen: 2 x 12kW a.c
9073828 - -	**SAMANCO 6** - **Envasadora Chimbote Export SA** Enrique Silva Nano *Chimbote Peru* Official number: CE-010501-PM	*378* 174 433	Class: (GL)	**1994-02 Andina de Desarrollo S.A. — Callao** Yd No: 119 L reg 38.75 Br ex - Dght 3.725 Lbp - Br md 8.30 Dpth 4.15 Welded	**(B11B2FV) Fishing Vessel** Ins: 420	**1 oil engine** reduction geared to sc. shaft driving 1 FP propeller Total Power: 780kW (1,060hp) 12.0kn Caterpillar 3512TA 1 x Vee 4 Stroke 12 Cy. 170 x 190 780kW (1060bhp) Caterpillar Inc-USA AuxGen: 2 x 12kW a.c
8035350 - -	**SAMAND** *ex* Gulriz *-2002* *ex* Nader *-1993* *ex* Sea Rock *-1989* *ex* Gulf Dealer *-1989* *ex* New Park Sunflower *-1981* *ex* Miss Julie *-1981* **A Azarmi Bejand** - *Bandar Abbas Iran* Official number: 10962	*110* 75 -	Class: AS (GL) (HR)	**1966 Service Machine & Shipbuilding Co — Amelia LA** Loa 19.80 Br ex 6.74 Dght - Lbp 19.75 Br md 6.55 Dpth 2.86 Welded, 1 dk	**(B32A2ST) Tug**	**2 oil engines** reverse reduction geared to sc. shaft driving 2 FP propellers Total Power: 986kW (1,340hp) 10.0kn G.M. (Detroit Diesel) 16V-71-N 2 x Vee 2 Stroke 16 Cy. 108 x 127 each-493kW (670bhp) General Motors Detroit DieselAllison Divn-USA
9312547 *J8B3042* -	**SAMAND** *ex* Green *-2009* *launched as* Pac-Orient *-2004* **Oscar Shipping & Trading Co Ltd** Echo Cargo & Shipping LLC *Kingstown St Vincent & The Grenadines* MMSI: 377755000 Official number: 9514	**252** 75 133	Class: BV (AB)	**2004-01 Pacific Ocean Engineering & Trading Pte Ltd (POET) — Singapore** Yd No: 1149 Loa 29.50 Br ex - Dght 3.500 Lbp 27.49 Br md 9.00 Dpth 4.16 Welded, 1 dk	**(B32A2ST) Tug**	**2 oil engines** geared to sc. shafts driving 2 FP propellers Total Power: 2,060kW (2,800hp) Yanmar 8N21A-UN 2 x 4 Stroke 8 Cy. 210 x 290 each-1030kW (1400bhp) Yanmar Diesel Engine Co Ltd-Japan AuxGen: 2 x 135kW a.c
9099169 *9BCM* -	**SAMAND I** - **Babak Katani Zadeh** - *Bandar Imam Khomeini Iran* MMSI: 422382000 Official number: 20540	**470** 223 -	Class: AS	**2003-05 Shenavaran Ziba Shipbuilding Co — Khorramshahr** Loa 45.10 Br ex - Dght - Lbp - Br md 11.42 Dpth 3.00 Welded, 1 dk	**(A31A2GX) General Cargo Ship**	**1 oil engine** driving 1 Propeller Total Power: 662kW (900hp) Caterpillar D348 1 x Vee 4 Stroke 12 Cy. 137 x 165 662kW (900bhp) Caterpillar Inc-USA
9364241 *YDBL* -	**SAMANDAR** - **Government of The Republic of Indonesia (Direktorat Jenderal Perhubungan Darat - Ministry of Land Communications)** - *Palembang Indonesia*	**468** 140 -	Class: KI	**2005-07 P.T. Mariana Bahagia — Palembang** Yd No: 041 Loa 40.00 Br ex - Dght 2.000 Lbp 34.50 Br md 10.50 Dpth 2.80 Welded, 1 dk	**(A36A2PR) Passenger/Ro-Ro Ship (Vehicles)**	**2 oil engines** reduction geared to sc. shafts driving 2 Propellers Total Power: 810kW (1,102hp) Yanmar 6KH-STE 2 x 4 Stroke 6 Cy. 135 x 160 each-405kW (551bhp) (made 2004) Yanmar Diesel Engine Co Ltd-Japan AuxGen: 2 x 58kW 380V a.c
7715264 *EQHH* -	**SAMANGAN** - **Government of The Islamic Republic of Iran (Ports & Maritime Organisation)** - *Khorramshahr Iran*	*331* 94 189	Class: (LR) ✠ Classed LR until 19/11/82	**1978-08 Yokohama Yacht Co Ltd — Yokohama KN** Yd No: 739-2 Loa 35.62 Br ex 8.82 Dght 3.309 Lbp 32.16 Br md 8.51 Dpth 4.32 Welded, 1 dk	**(B34F2SF) Fire Fighting Vessel**	**2 oil engines** reverse reduction geared to sc. shafts driving 2 FP propellers Total Power: 1,898kW (2,580hp) MWM TBD602V16K 2 x Vee 4 Stroke 16 Cy. 160 x 165 each-949kW (1290bhp) Motoren Werke Mannheim AG (MWM)-West Germany AuxGen: 2 x 188kW 231V 50Hz a.c, 1 x 72kW 231V 50Hz a.c
8035439 *7LQJ* -	**SAMANI MARU** - **KK Minamigumi** - *Samani, Hokkaido Japan* MMSI: 431800346 Official number: 118617	*469* - -		**1981-05 Muneta Zosen K.K. — Akashi** L reg 40.12 Br ex - Dght - Lbp - Br md 15.00 Dpth 3.00 Welded, 1 dk	**(B34B2SC) Crane Vessel**	**2 oil engines** driving 2 FP propellers
9000297 *A8PL4* -	**SAMANTA** *ex* Alam Selaras *-2008* **Samanta Shipping Ltd** IPC Marine Services LLC *Monrovia Liberia* MMSI: 636013792 Official number: 13792	**21,941** 12,531 39,110 T/cm 47.2	Class: RS (LR) ✠ Classed LR until 9/4/08	**1992-02 Ishikawajima-Harima Heavy Industries Co Ltd (IHI) — Tokyo** Yd No: 3010 Loa 180.80 (BB) Br ex 30.54 Dght 10.900 Lbp 171.00 Br md 30.50 Dpth 15.30 Welded, 1 dk	**(A21A2BC) Bulk Carrier** Grain: 46,112; Bale: 44,492 Compartments: 5 Ho, ER 5 Ha: (15.2 x 12.8)4 (19.2 x 15.2)ER Cranes: 4x25t	**1 oil engine** driving 1 FP propeller Total Power: 5,808kW (7,897hp) 14.5kn Sulzer 6RTA52 1 x 2 Stroke 6 Cy. 520 x 1800 5808kW (7897bhp) Diesel United Ltd.-Aioi AuxGen: 3 x 450kW 450V 60Hz a.c Boilers: e (ex.g.) 11.4kgf/cm² (11.2bar), AuxB (o.f.) 8.1kgf/cm² (7.9bar)

IMO / Call sign / Flag	Name / Owner / Port	Tonnage	Class	Builder / Dimensions	Type	Machinery
8728775 - -	**SAMANTA SMIT** **State Enterprise 'Yalta Sea Trade Port'** - *Yalta* *Ukraine* Official number: 850702	**176** 53 31	Class: (RS)	**1986-05 Ilyichyovskiy Sudoremontnyy Zavod im. "50-letiya SSSR" — Ilyichyovsk** Yd No: 5 Loa 38.10 Br ex 7.21 Dght 1.620 Lbp 32.64 Br md - Dpth 2.90 Welded, 1 dk	**(A37B2PS) Passenger Ship** Passengers: unberthed: 294	**3 oil engines** reduction geared to sc. shafts driving 3 FP propellers Total Power: 960kW (1,306hp) 17.0kn Barnaultransmash 3D6C 2 x 4 Stroke 6 Cy. 150 x 180 each-110kW (150bhp) Barnaultransmash-Barnaul Zvezda M412 1 x Vee 4 Stroke 12 Cy. 180 x 200 740kW (1006bhp) "Zvezda"-Leningrad AuxGen: 2 x 16kW Fuel: 6.0 (d.f.)
6717485 *J8AQ6* -	**SAMANTHA** *ex* Oceans Free Ride *-2012* *ex* Olympiakos *-2010* *ex* Artico *-2010* *ex* Artic *-2005* *ex* Clara *-2004* *ex* Le Compagnon *-2003* *ex* Arctic Viking *-2002* *ex* Baltic Viking *-1981* **Mystic Alhambra Corp** - *St Vincent & The Grenadines* MMSI: 377971000	*1,522* 493 2,073	Class: (LR) ✠ Classed LR until 6/2/02	**1967-06 Kroegerwerft GmbH & Co. KG — Schacht-Audorf** Yd No: 1343 Loa 74.53 Br ex 12.58 Dght 5.176 Lbp 70.62 Br md 12.45 Dpth 6.96 Welded, 2 dks	**(A31A2GX) General Cargo Ship** Grain: 3,689; Bale: 3,502 Compartments: 1 Ho, ER 2 Ha: (17.0 x 7.0) (17.0 x 8.2)ER Cranes: 2x5t; Derricks: 2x20t Ice Capable	**1 oil engine** driving 1 FP propeller Total Power: 1,618kW (2,200hp) 12.0kn MWM RHS345AU 1 x 4 Stroke 8 Cy. 360 x 450 1618kW (2200bhp) Motoren Werke Mannheim AG (MWM)-West Germany AuxGen: 3 x 112kW 450V 60Hz a.c Fuel: 236.5 (d.f.)
9592587 *VMQ9903* -	**SAMANTHA** **Darwin Offshore Pty Ltd** - SatCom: Inmarsat C 450303994 *Brisbane, Qld* *Australia* MMSI: 503540300 Official number: 859922	**196** 59 -	Class: NV (NK)	**2011-04 YCK Shipbuilding Sdn Bhd — Sibu** Yd No: 29010 Loa 26.00 Br ex - Dght 3.000 Lbp 23.86 Br md 8.00 Dpth 3.65 Welded, 1 dk	**(B32A2ST) Tug**	**2 oil engines** reduction geared to sc. shafts driving 2 FP propellers Total Power: 1,220kW (1,658hp) Yanmar 6AYM-ETE 2 x 4 Stroke 6 Cy. 155 x 180 each-610kW (829bhp) Yanmar Diesel Engine Co Ltd-Japan Fuel: 140.0
9078995 *YD2073* -	**SAMANTHA I** *ex* Hiu II *-2005* *ex* Shinyoshin Maru *-2005* **PT Pelayaran Pandupasifik Karismaraya** - *Belawan* *Indonesia*	*200* 60 -	Class: KI	**1993-05 K.K. Watanabe Zosensho — Nagasaki** Yd No: 1222 Converted From: Work/Repair Vessel-2005 Loa 27.01 Br ex - Dght 2.390 Lbp 25.00 Br md 9.00 Dpth 3.10 Welded, 1 dk	**(B32A2ST) Tug**	**2 oil engines** driving 2 FP propellers Total Power: 1,324kW (1,800hp) 9.0kn Matsui ML624GHS 2 x 4 Stroke 6 Cy. 240 x 400 each-662kW (900bhp) Matsui Iron Works Co Ltd-Japan
9007324 *VTNN* -	**SAMAR** **Government of The Republic of India (Coast Guard)** - *India*	**1,888** 566 417	Class: (LR) (IR) ✠ Classed LR until 17/12/96	**1995-09 Goa Shipyard Ltd. — Goa** Yd No: 1151 Loa 101.95 Br ex 11.52 Dght 3.580 Lbp 94.10 Br md 11.50 Dpth 6.00 Welded, 2 dks	**(B34H2SQ) Patrol Vessel**	**2 oil engines** with clutches, flexible couplings & sr geared to sc. shafts driving 2 CP propellers Total Power: 9,130kW (12,414hp) Pielstick 16PA6V280 2 x Vee 4 Stroke 16 Cy. 280 x 290 each-4565kW (6207bhp) Kirloskar Oil Engines Ltd-India AuxGen: 4 x 400kW 415V 50Hz a.c
1008190 *ZCPC8* -	**SAMAR** *launched as* Lana *-2006* **Caumsett Ltd** Fraser Worldwide SAM *George Town* *Cayman Islands (British)* MMSI: 319771000 Official number: 739096	**2,159** 647 317	Class: LR ✠ **100A1** SS 05/2011 SSC Yacht (P), mono, G6 ✠ **LMC** **UMS** Cable: 192.5/32.0 U2 (a)	**2006-05 Appledore Shipbuilders (2004) Ltd — Bideford (Hull)** Yd No: A.S.191 **2006-05 Devonport Engineering Consortium Ltd — Plymouth** Yd No: 053 Loa 75.88 Br ex 13.30 Dght 3.400 Lbp 69.00 Br md 12.80 Dpth 6.97 Welded, 1 dk	**(X11A2YP) Yacht**	**3 diesel electric oil engines** driving 3 gen. each 1360kW 440V a.c Connecting to 2 elec. motors each (1800kW) driving 2 FP propellers Total Power: 4,590kW (6,240hp) 16.5kn Wartsila 9L20 3 x 4 Stroke 9 Cy. 200 x 280 each-1530kW (2080bhp) Wartsila Finland Oy-Finland Thrusters: 2 Thwart. FP thruster
6817089 *DUNK2* -	**SAMAR STAR** *ex* Asaka *-1995* *ex* Samar Queen *-1994* *ex* Asaka Maru *-1980* **Maypalad Shipping Lines Inc** - *Cebu* *Philippines* Official number: CEB1003311	*233* 127 203		**1968-07 Wakamatsu Zosen K.K. — Kitakyushu** Yd No: 177 Loa 56.60 Br ex 9.07 Dght 3.480 Lbp 55.00 Br md 9.05 Dpth 5.57 Welded, 1 dk	**(A36A2PR) Passenger/Ro-Ro Ship (Vehicles)** Passengers: 280 Compartments: 4 Ho, ER	**1 oil engine** driving 1 FP propeller Total Power: 956kW (1,300hp) 11.0kn Nippon Hatsudoki HS6NV138 1 x 4 Stroke 6 Cy. 380 x 540 956kW (1300bhp) Nippon Hatsudoki-Japan
9637351 *PKSD* -	**SAMARA** *ex* New Morin *-2013* **PT Pelayaran Athalla Putra Cipunagara** - *Cirebon* *Indonesia* MMSI: 525019637 Official number: 5119/L	**1,222** - 2,500	Class: RI	**2013-07 PT Citra Bahari Shipyard — Tegal** Yd No: N007 Loa 76.77 Br ex - Dght - Lbp 74.50 Br md 15.24 Dpth 3.80 Welded, 1 dk	**(A13B2TP) Products Tanker** Double Hull (13F)	**2 oil engines** reduction geared to sc. shafts driving 2 FP propellers Total Power: 1,118kW (1,520hp) 7.0kn Caterpillar C32 2 x Vee 4 Stroke 12 Cy. 145 x 162 each-559kW (760bhp) Caterpillar Inc-USA AuxGen: 2 x 93kW 400V 50Hz a.c
8711966 *UBSS* -	**SAMARA CITY** **Shipping Co 'Rosmortrans' Ltd** Oil Marine Group *Astrakhan* *Russia* MMSI: 273342900	**4,407** 1,353 5,857	Class: RS	**1993-04 Rousse Shipyard Ltd — Rousse** Yd No: 106 Loa 138.00 Br ex 17.00 Dght 4.090 Lbp 130.24 Br md 16.50 Dpth 6.40 Welded, 1 dk	**(A13B2TP) Products Tanker** Double Hull (13F) Liq: 6,487; Liq (Oil): 6,487 Cargo Heating Coils Compartments: 12 Ta, ER Ice Capable	**2 oil engines** driving 2 FP propellers Total Power: 1,766kW (2,402hp) 10.8kn S.K.L. 8NVD48A-2U 2 x 4 Stroke 8 Cy. 320 x 480 each-883kW (1201bhp) SKL Motoren u. Systemtechnik AG-Magdeburg AuxGen: 3 x 150kW 380V 50Hz a.c Thrusters: 1 Thwart. CP thruster (f)
8853831 - -	**SAMARA I** *ex* Successor *-1995* *ex* Clipper Two *-1990* - -	*100* 40 -		**1980 Camcraft, Inc. — Crown Point, La** Loa 38.49 Br ex - Dght - Lbp - Br md 6.72 Dpth 2.62 Welded, 1 dk	**(A37B2PS) Passenger Ship**	**3 oil engines** geared to sc. shafts driving 3 FP propellers Total Power: 1,146kW (1,557hp) 20.0kn G.M. (Detroit Diesel) 12V-71 3 x Vee 2 Stroke 12 Cy. 108 x 127 each-382kW (519bhp) General Motors Corp-USA
7713917 *V4FC* -	**SAMARAI** *ex* Elizabeth *-2011* *ex* Transjaya *-2008* *ex* Kilkilun *-2005* *ex* Pusaka 2 *-2002* *ex* Toyopower *-2002* *ex* Allwell Proceed *-1999* *ex* Toyo Maru No. 72 *-1991* **Toyopower Marine SA** Canter Singapore Pte Ltd *Basseterre* *St Kitts & Nevis* MMSI: 341131000 Official number: SKN 1001131	**656** 357 1,117	Class: IS (GL)	**1977-09 Imamura Zosen — Kure** Yd No: 231 Loa 56.27 Br ex - Dght 4.252 Lbp 52.02 Br md 10.01 Dpth 4.58 Welded, 1 dk	**(A13B2TP) Products Tanker** Liq: 1,304; Liq (Oil): 1,304	**1 oil engine** driving 1 FP propeller Total Power: 956kW (1,300hp) 10.0kn Hanshin 6LU32 1 x 4 Stroke 6 Cy. 320 x 510 956kW (1300bhp) The Hanshin Diesel Works Ltd-Japan AuxGen: 2 x 112kW a.c
8749858 - -	**SAMARAI MURUA** **PT Masindo Mitra Papua** - *Samarinda* *Indonesia*	**216** 65 -	Class: (KI)	**2010-06 C.V. Karya Lestari Industri — Samarinda** Loa 41.20 Br ex - Dght 1.720 Lbp - Br md 8.00 Dpth 2.40 Welded, 1 dk	**(A35D2RL) Landing Craft**	**2 oil engines** reduction geared to sc. shafts driving 2 Propellers
8501402 *XUFL6* -	**SAMARGA** *ex* Wajd *-2011* *ex* Jabal Ali 7 *-2011* *ex* QC Pintail *-2007* *ex* Vento di Tramontana *-1996* *ex* Transport Maas *-1993* *ex* C. U. R. Caroline *-1989* *ex* L. Craeybeckx *-1988* **Inderton Ltd SA** Acrex Corp *Phnom Penh* *Cambodia* MMSI: 514497000 Official number: 1287068	**5,608** 3,088 7,130	Class: GM (IB) (GL)	**1987-02 N.V. Boelwerf S.A. — Temse** Yd No: 1523 Loa 116.85 (BB) Br ex 19.64 Dght 6.133 Lbp 106.86 Br md 19.61 Dpth 8.01 Welded, 1 dk	**(A31A2GA) General Cargo Ship (with Ro-Ro facility)** Stern door/ramp (centre) Len: 11.00 Wid: 6.50 Swl: - Grain: 9,150 TEU 574 C.Ho 206/20' C.Dk 368/20' incl. 30 ref C. Compartments: 1 Ho, ER 1 Ha: (76.5 x 15.2)ER Cranes: 2x35t Ice Capable	**1 oil engine** with flexible couplings & sr gearedto sc. shaft driving 1 CP propeller Total Power: 3,199kW (4,349hp) 13.0kn MaK 6M551AK 1 x 4 Stroke 6 Cy. 450 x 550 3199kW (4349bhp) Krupp MaK Maschinenbau GmbH-Kiel AuxGen: 2 x 320kW 440V 60Hz a.c Thrusters: 1 Thwart. FP thruster (f)
9182643 *5BYR3* -	**SAMARIA** *ex* Calapadria *-2008* *ex* Samaria *-2004* *ex* P&O Nedlloyd Samaria *-2003* *ex* Samaria *-2000* **ms 'Samaria' Schiffahrtsgesellschaft mbH & Co KG** Nordic Hamburg Shipmanagement GmbH & Co KG *Limassol* *Cyprus* MMSI: 212194000 Official number: 9182643	**19,131** 10,095 25,450	Class: GL	**2000-11 Hudong Shipbuilding Group — Shanghai** Yd No: H1256A Loa 188.55 (BB) Br ex - Dght 10.500 Lbp 176.42 Br md 26.50 Dpth 14.20 Welded, 1 dk	**(A33A2CC) Container Ship (Fully Cellular)** TEU 1716 C Ho 708 TEU C Dk 1008 TEU incl 250 ref C. Compartments: 6 Cell Ho, ER 9 Ha: ER Cranes: 3x45t	**1 oil engine** driving 1 FP propeller Total Power: 16,969kW (23,071hp) 20.4kn B&W 6L70MC 1 x 2 Stroke 6 Cy. 700 x 2268 16969kW (23071bhp) Hudong Heavy Machinery Co Ltd-China AuxGen: 1 x 1200kW 220/440V a.c, 2 x 900kW 220/440V a.c Thrusters: 1 Thwart. FP thruster (f) Fuel: 86.3 (d.f.) (Heating Coils) 1656.0 (r.f.) 65.0pd

8834354 *SW2709* -	**SAMARIA I** - **Anonymos Naftiliaki Eteria Notioditikis Kritis (ANENDYK)** - *Chania* *Greece* MMSI: 237030900 Official number: 16	**445** 230 115	Class: RI (RS) (HR)	**1986 Karageorgis — Piraeus** Loa 45.98 Br ex - Dght 2.200 Lbp 44.45 Br md 12.00 Dpth 3.00 Welded, 1 dk	**(A36A2PR) Passenger/Ro-Ro Ship (Vehicles)** Bow ramp (centre)	**2 oil engines** driving 2 FP propellers Total Power: 736kW (1,000hp) 14.0kn A.B.C. 6MDX 2 x 4 Stroke 6 Cy. 242 x 320 each-368kW (500bhp) Anglo Belgian Corp NV (ABC)-Belgium AuxGen: 2 x 48kW 400V a.c
8888379 *YFSK* -	**SAMARINDA EXPRES 1** - **PT Perusahaan Pelayaran Rusianto Bersaudara** - *Samarinda* *Indonesia* Official number: 1419/II K	**1,022** 307 -	Class: (AB) (KI)	**1995-07 Zhenjiang Sumec Shipbuilding & Engineering Co — Zhenjiang JS** Yd No: 2-1991 Loa 60.00 Br ex - Dght 3.009 Lbp 53.18 Br md 10.97 Dpth 4.48 Welded, 1 dk	**(A37B2PS) Passenger Ship**	**2 oil engines** geared to sc. shafts driving 2 FP propellers Total Power: 2,126kW (2,890hp) 16.0kn Caterpillar 3512TA 2 x Vee 4 Stroke 12 Cy. 170 x 190 each-1063kW (1445bhp) Caterpillar Inc-USA
8032085 - -	**SAMARINDA RAYA** *ex* Motoura Maru No. 27 *-2000* *ex* Koyo Maru *-1990* **PT Pelayaran Laut Baru** - *Indonesia*	*812* 244 -		**1980-12 Azumi Zosen Kensetsu K.K. — Himeji** Yd No: 83 Loa - Br ex - Dght - Lbp 49.00 Br md 17.01 Dpth 3.51 Welded, 1 dk	**(B21A2OS) Platform Supply Ship**	**1 oil engine** driving 1 FP propeller Total Power: 736kW (1,001hp) Yanmar MF28-HT 1 x 4 Stroke 6 Cy. 280 x 450 736kW (1001bhp) Yanmar Diesel Engine Co Ltd-Japan
8206105 *JVWV4* -	**SAMARITAN** *ex* Mutawa Seven *-2006* **Trinity Marine Services Inc** Midgulf Offshore Ship Chartering LLC *Ulaanbaatar* *Mongolia* MMSI: 457641000 Official number: 31541282	*422* 126 -	Class: BV (AB)	**1982-08 Maroil Engineers & Shipbuilders Pte Ltd — Singapore** Yd No: 18 Loa 38.00 Br ex 9.52 Dght 3.461 Lbp 35.41 Br md 9.50 Dpth 3.71 Welded, 1 dk	**(B34L2QU) Utility Vessel**	**2 oil engines** reverse reduction geared to sc. shafts driving 2 FP propellers Total Power: 1,030kW (1,400hp) 11.0kn G.M. (Detroit Diesel) 12V-149-NA 2 x Vee 2 Stroke 12 Cy. 146 x 146 each-515kW (700bhp) General Motors Detroit DieselAllison Divn-USA AuxGen: 1 x 135kW a.c, 2 x 99kW a.c Thrusters: 1 Thwart. FP thruster (f)
7357153 - -	**SAMARITAN** - - -	*400* 131 -	Class: (AB)	**1975-01 Robin Shipyard Pte Ltd — Singapore** Yd No: 141 Loa - Br ex - Dght 3.960 Lbp 37.34 Br md 9.01 Dpth 4.50 Welded, 1 dk	**(B32A2ST) Tug**	**2 oil engines** reverse reduction geared to sc. shafts driving 2 FP propellers Total Power: 2,354kW (3,200hp) 12.5kn Niigata 16V25X 2 x Vee 4 Stroke 16 Cy. 250 x 320 each-1177kW (1600bhp) Niigata Engineering Co Ltd-Japan AuxGen: 2 x 80kW a.c
9236171 *9HCX9* -	**SAMATAN** *ex* Trans Atlantic *-2007* *ex* Yong Ler *-2005* **Boone Star Owners Inc** TMS Bulkers Ltd *Valletta* *Malta* MMSI: 256804000 Official number: 9236171	**40,437** 25,855 74,823 T/cm 67.0	Class: AB (CC)	**2001-01 Hudong Shipbuilding Group — Shanghai** Yd No: H1282A Loa 225.00 (BB) Br ex - Dght 14.250 Lbp 217.00 Br md 32.26 Dpth 19.60 Welded, 1 dk	**(A21A2BC) Bulk Carrier** Grain: 91,718; Bale: 89,882 Compartments: 7 Ho, ER 7 Ha: (14.6 x 13.2)6 (14.6 x 15.0)ER	**1 oil engine** driving 1 FP propeller Total Power: 10,224kW (13,901hp) 14.5kn MAN-B&W 5S60MC 1 x 2 Stroke 5 Cy. 600 x 2292 10224kW (13901bhp) Hudong Heavy Machinery Co Ltd-China AuxGen: 3 x 530kW 450V a.c
9065637 - -	**SAMATUG No. 1** *ex* TQ Super *-1995* - -	**106** 32 91	Class: (NK)	**1992-05 Fong Syn Shipyard Sdn Bhd — Sibu** Yd No: 6691 Loa 23.00 Br ex - Dght 2.132 Lbp 21.40 Br md 6.70 Dpth 2.85 Welded, 1 dk	**(B32A2ST) Tug**	**2 oil engines** reduction geared to sc. shafts driving 2 FP propellers Total Power: 670kW (910hp) 10.0kn Caterpillar 3408TA 2 x Vee 4 Stroke 8 Cy. 137 x 152 each-335kW (455bhp) Caterpillar Inc-USA AuxGen: 2 x 20kW a.c
1005071 *ZGAP* -	**SAMAX** *ex* Sammax *-2001* *ex* Tits *-2000* **Samax Holdings Ltd** YCO SAM *George Town* *Cayman Islands (British)* MMSI: 319915000 Official number: 904102	**881** 264 -	Class: LR ✠ **100A1** SS 06/2011 Yacht ✠ **LMC** **UMS** Cable: 336.1/26.0 U2	**1996-06 Eltink's Scheeps- en Jachtwerf B.V. — Katwijk a/d Maas** (Hull) Yd No: 152 **1996-06 Jacht- en Scheepswerf C. van Lent & Zonen B.V. — Kaag** Yd No: 775 Loa 55.00 Br ex 10.32 Dght 3.200 Lbp 47.50 Br md 10.00 Dpth 5.30 Welded, 1 dk	**(X11A2YP) Yacht**	**2 oil engines** with clutches, hydraulic couplings & sr reverse geared to sc. shafts driving 2 FP propellers Total Power: 3,878kW (5,272hp) 18.0kn Caterpillar 3516TA 2 x Vee 4 Stroke 16 Cy. 170 x 190 each-1939kW (2636bhp) Caterpillar Inc-USA AuxGen: 3 x 125kW 400V 50Hz a.c Thrusters: 1 Thwart. FP thruster (f)
8503175 *YCZG* -	**SAMB 01** *ex* Kishi Maru No. 8 *-2012* **PT Surya Anugrah Maju Bersama** - *Surabaya* *Indonesia*	**542** 163 732	Class: KI (NK)	**1985-08 K.K. Miura Zosensho — Saiki** Yd No: 723 Loa 57.99 Br ex - Dght 3.510 Lbp 52.02 Br md 9.21 Dpth 4.12 Welded, 1 dk	**(A12B2TR) Chemical/Products Tanker** Liq: 618; Liq (Oil): 618	**1 oil engine** geared to sc. shaft driving 1 FP propeller Total Power: 883kW (1,201hp) 11.0kn Daihatsu 6DLM-26 1 x 4 Stroke 6 Cy. 260 x 340 883kW (1201bhp) Daihatsu Diesel Manufacturing Co Lt-Japan AuxGen: 2 x 72kW a.c
6715334 *LMAN* -	**SAMBA** *ex* Samband *-1998* **Samba AS** - *Bergen* *Norway* MMSI: 257072700	**180** 54 -	Class: (NV)	**1967 AS Haugesunds Slip — Haugesund** Yd No: 9 Loa 31.12 Br ex 9.56 Dght 2.661 Lbp 28.81 Br md 9.50 Dpth 3.51 Welded, 1 dk	**(A36A2PR) Passenger/Ro-Ro Ship (Vehicles)** Passengers: unberthed: 200 Bow door & ramp Stern door & ramp Cars: 20	**1 oil engine** driving 1 FP propeller Total Power: 294kW (400hp) 10.0kn Wichmann 4ACA 1 x 2 Stroke 4 Cy. 280 x 420 294kW (400bhp) Wichmann Motorfabrikk AS-Norway Fuel: 18.5 (d.f.) 1.5pd
8979051 *HC2098* -	**SAMBA** *ex* Zamba *-1998* **Martin Schreyer Goerlitz** Angermeyer Cruises SA *Puerto Ayora* *Ecuador* Official number: TN-00-0109	*134* 60		**1966 Spaanderman V.o.f. Visserijbedrijf — Vlissingen** Converted From: Yacht Loa 23.77 Br ex - Dght - Lbp - Br md 5.48 Dpth - Welded, 1 dk	**(A37A2PC) Passenger/Cruise** Passengers: cabins: 6; berths: 12	**2 oil engines** driving 2 Propellers Total Power: 162kW (220hp) Daf 2 x 4 Stroke each-81kW (110bhp) van Doorne's Automobielfabriek (DAF)-Eindhoven AuxGen: 2 x 21kW 110/220V 60Hz a.c
9428205 *V2FE3* -	**SAMBA** *ex* Ice Sun *-2012* **W Bockstiegel GmbH & Co Reederei KG ms 'Pacifc Island'** W Bockstiegel Reederei GmbH & Co KG *Saint John's* *Antigua & Barbuda* MMSI: 305649000 Official number: 4802	**7,584** 3,165 8,199	Class: GL	**2007-11 Sainty Shipbuilding (Yangzhou) Corp Ltd — Yizheng JS** Yd No: 05STIG013 Loa 129.65 (BB) Br ex - Dght 7.400 Lbp 120.34 Br md 20.60 Dpth 10.80 Welded, 1 dk	**(A33A2CC) Container Ship (Fully Cellular)** Double Bottom Entire Compartment Length Grain: 12,643; Bale: 12,643 TEU 698 C Ho 226 TEU C Dk 472 TEU incl 120 ref C Compartments: 4 Cell Ho, ER 4 Ha: (12.5 x 15.8)2 (25.4 x 15.8)ER (6.4 x 10.7) Ice Capable	**1 oil engine** reduction geared to sc. shaft driving 1 CP propeller Total Power: 7,200kW (9,789hp) 16.0kn MaK 8M43C 1 x 4 Stroke 8 Cy. 430 x 610 7200kW (9789bhp) Caterpillar Motoren GmbH & Co. KG-Germany AuxGen: 3 x 550kW 450V a.c, 1 x 1000kW 450V a.c Thrusters: 1 Tunnel thruster (f)
9423803 *6WIV* -	**SAMBA LAOBE FALL** *launched as* Baliseur Senegal *-2008* **Government of The Republic of Senegal** - *Dakar* *Senegal*	**393** 118 -	Class: BV	**2008-01 OCEA SA — Les Sables-d'Olonne** Yd No: 05-02001 Loa 44.60 Br ex - Dght 2.400 Lbp 44.50 Br md 9.60 Dpth 3.30 Welded, 1 dk	**(B34Q2QB) Buoy Tender** Hull Material: Aluminium Alloy	**2 oil engines** geared to sc. shafts driving 2 CP propellers Total Power: 892kW (1,212hp) 13.0kn Baudouin 2 x 4 Stroke each-446kW (606bhp) Societe des Moteurs Baudouin SA-France
9637686 *C6AN4* -	**SAMBA SPIRIT** - **Samba Spirit LLC** Teekay Shipping Ltd *Nassau* *Bahamas* MMSI: 311000095 Official number: 7000535	**83,882** 48,528 154,107	Class: AB	**2013-05 Samsung Heavy Industries Co Ltd — Geoje** Yd No: 2037 Loa 282.00 (BB) Br ex - Dght - Lbp 267.00 Br md 49.00 Dpth 23.60 Welded, 1 dk	**(A13A2TS) Shuttle Tanker** Double Hull (13F) Liq: 158,350; Liq (Oil): 158,350 Compartments: 6 Wing Ta, 6 Wing Ta, 1 Wing Slop Ta, 1 Wing Slop Ta, ER 3 Cargo Pump (s): 3x3500m³/hr	**1 oil engine** driving 1 FP propeller Total Power: 14,270kW (19,401hp) 15.0kn MAN-B&W 6S70ME-C8 1 x 2 Stroke 6 Cy. 700 x 2800 14270kW (19401bhp) Doosan Engine Co Ltd-South Korea AuxGen: 2 x 4300kW a.c, 2 x 2300kW a.c Fuel: 559.0 (d.f.) 3231.0 (r.f.)
7103095 *YBNQ* -	**SAMBAS** - **PT PERTAMINA (PERSERO)** - *Jakarta* *Indonesia* Official number: 4306+BA	*140* 9 94	Class: (KI) (AB)	**1971-02 Robin Shipyard Pte Ltd — Singapore** Yd No: 42 Loa 29.11 Br ex 7.62 Dght 2.430 Lbp 26.83 Br md 7.42 Dpth 3.75 Welded, 1 dk	**(B32A2ST) Tug**	**2 oil engines** reverse reduction geared to sc. shafts driving 2 FP propellers Total Power: 860kW (1,170hp) 11.0kn Daihatsu 6PSHTCM-26D 2 x 4 Stroke 6 Cy. 260 x 320 each-430kW (585bhp) Daihatsu Diesel Manufacturing Co Lt-Japan AuxGen: 1 x 24kW, 1 x 12kW Fuel: 65.0 (d.f.)
6610302 *6VRM* -	**SAMBEL** *ex* Genkai Maru No. 77 *-1981* **Societe Senegalaise pour l'Expansion de la Peche, Surgelation et Conditionnement des Aliments (SENEPESCA)** - *Dakar* *Senegal*	*172* 60 -	Class: (BV)	**1966 Hayashikane Shipbuilding & Engineering Co Ltd — Nagasaki NS** Yd No: 583 Loa 33.30 Br ex 6.84 Dght 2.896 Lbp 30.31 Br md 6.81 Dpth 3.31 Welded, 1 dk	**(B11B2FV) Fishing Vessel**	**1 oil engine** driving 1 FP propeller Total Power: 478kW (650hp) 11.5kn Daihatsu 6PSTCM-26E 1 x 4 Stroke 6 Cy. 260 x 320 478kW (650bhp) Daihatsu Kogyo-Japan

7344376 **SAMBHAVI** *337* Class: (LR) (IR)
- 130 ✠ Classed LR until 31/5/85
- **Visakhapatnam Port Trust** 120
-
Chennai *India*

1979-03 Hooghly Docking & Engineering Co. Ltd. — Haora Yd No: 419
Loa 36.33 Br ex 9.22 Dght 3.612
Lbp 32.03 Br md 8.50 Dpth 5.01
Welded, 1 dk

(B32A2ST) Tug

2 oil engines reverse reduction geared to sc. shafts driving 2 FP propellers
Total Power: 1,876kW (2,550hp)
MAN G6V30/45ATL
2 x 4 Stroke 6 Cy. 300 x 450 each-938kW (1275bhp)
Garden Reach Shipbuilders &Engineers Ltd-India
AuxGen: 2 x 128kW 415V 50Hz a.c

8515051 **SAMBI HO** *198*
- *ex* Wooyang 101 *-2007* -
- *ex* Taisei Maru No. 17 *-1995* 445
Kamchatfleetbunker
-
Ulsan *South Korea*
Official number: 051212D

1985-12 Suzuki Shipyard Co. Ltd. — Yokkaichi Yd No: 521
Loa - Br ex - Dght 3.250
Lbp 42.02 Br md 7.80 Dpth 3.41
Welded, 1 dk

(A12A2TC) Chemical Tanker
Liq: 245
Compartments: 6 Ta, ER

1 oil engine driving 1 FP propeller
Total Power: 515kW (700hp)
Yanmar MF24-DT
1 x 4 Stroke 6 Cy. 240 x 420 515kW (700bhp)
Yanmar Diesel Engine Co Ltd-Japan

9090943 **SAMBONG** *106* Class: (KR)
- *ex* Fuki 5 *-2004* -
- **Dokdo Shipping Ltd** 33
-
Pohang *South Korea*

1988-06 Suzuki Shipyard Co. Ltd. — Yokkaichi Yd No: 627/3
Loa 31.30 Br ex - Dght 1.129
Lbp 26.85 Br md 6.50 Dpth 2.60
Welded, 1 dk

(A37B2PS) Passenger Ship
Hull Material: Aluminium Alloy
Passengers: unberthed: 210

2 oil engines geared to sc. shafts driving 2 Propellers
Total Power: 1,470kW (1,998hp) 24.0kn
Yanmar 12LAK-ST1
2 x Vee 4 Stroke 12 Cy. 150 x 165 each-735kW (999bhp)
Yanmar Diesel Engine Co Ltd-Japan

7629659 **SAMBU** **996** Class: (NK)
YCHU *ex* Taiyo Maru No. 3 *-1978* 629
- **PT PERTAMINA (PERSERO)** 2,005
-
Jakarta *Indonesia*

1969-12 Murakami Hide Zosen K.K. — Imabari Yd No: 73
Loa 70.44 Br ex 11.43 Dght 5.015
Lbp 65.00 Br md 11.41 Dpth 5.85
Welded, 1 dk

(A13B2TP) Products Tanker
Liq: 2,600; Liq (Oil): 2,600
Compartments: 4 Ta, ER

1 oil engine driving 1 FP propeller
Total Power: 1,324kW (1,800hp) 10.8kn
Akasaka 6DH38SS
1 x 4 Stroke 6 Cy. 380 x 560 1324kW (1800bhp)
Akasaka Tekkosho KK (Akasaka DieselLtd)-Japan
AuxGen: 2 x 48kW 225V a.c

9508732 **SAMBU** **24,167** Class: KI NV
YFQE 7,253
- **PT PERTAMINA (PERSERO)** 29,756
-
Jakarta *Indonesia*
MMSI: 525008065

2011-04 Zhejiang Chenye Shipbuilding Co Ltd — Daishan County ZJ Yd No: 0801
Loa 180.03 (BB) Br ex 30.53 Dght 9.000
Lbp 173.00 Br md 30.50 Dpth 15.91
Welded, 1 dk

(A13B2TP) Products Tanker
Double Hull (13F)
Liq: 33,000; Liq (Oil): 33,000

1 oil engine driving 1 FP propeller
Total Power: 6,480kW (8,810hp) 14.0kn
MAN-B&W 6S42MC
1 x 2 Stroke 6 Cy. 420 x 1764 6480kW (8810bhp)
Hyundai Heavy Industries Co Ltd-South Korea
AuxGen: 3 x a.c

8602842 **SAMBUIA** **167** Class: (BV)
- 50
- **Sociedade Metropolitana de Construcoes SA (Somec)** -
-
Bissau *Guinea-Bissau*

1985-06 B.V. Scheepswerf Damen — Gorinchem Yd No: 3701
Loa 30.05 Br ex - Dght 1.442
Lbp 29.04 Br md 8.01 Dpth 2.62
Welded, 1 dk

(B34Q2QB) Buoy Tender

2 oil engines driving 2 FP propellers
Total Power: 604kW (822hp) 9.0kn
Volvo Penta TMD100A
2 x 4 Stroke 6 Cy. 121 x 140 each-302kW (411bhp)
AB Volvo Penta-Sweden

9735426 **SAMCHEOK 5** **288** Class: KR
- *completed as* Sam Cheok5 *-2014* -
- **Samcheok Tug Co Ltd** 233
-
Samcheok *South Korea*
Official number: DHR-145303

2014-03 Geumgang Shipbuilding Co Ltd — Janghang Yd No: GGS-17
Loa 38.00 Br ex 10.20 Dght 3.659
Lbp 34.78 Br md 10.00 Dpth 4.50
Welded, 1 dk

(B32A2ST) Tug

2 oil engines reduction geared to sc. shaft (s) driving 2 Propellers
Total Power: 3,676kW (4,998hp)
Niigata 6L28HX
2 x 4 Stroke 6 Cy. 280 x 370 each-1838kW (2499bhp)
Niigata Engineering Co Ltd-Japan

9735440 **SAMCHEOK 7** **288** Class: KR
- *completed as* Sam Cheok7 *-2014* -
- **Samcheok Tug Co Ltd** 233
-
Samcheok *South Korea*
Official number: DHR-145304

2014-03 Geumgang Shipbuilding Co Ltd — Janghang Yd No: GGS-18
Loa 38.00 Br ex 10.20 Dght 3.659
Lbp 34.78 Br md 10.00 Dpth 4.50
Welded, 1 dk

(B32A2ST) Tug

2 oil engines reduction geared to sc. shaft (s) driving 2 Propellers
Total Power: 3,676kW (4,998hp)
Niigata 6L28HX
2 x 4 Stroke 6 Cy. 280 x 370 each-1838kW (2499bhp)
Niigata Engineering Co Ltd-Japan

9528794 **SAMCO AMAZON** **160,928** Class: NV (AB)
FIED 110,502
- **Samco Eta Ltd** 318,129
Samco Shipholding Pte Ltd T/cm
Marseille *France (FIS)* 178.0
MMSI: 228026700

2011-08 Hyundai Samho Heavy Industries Co Ltd — Samho Yd No: S501
Loa 333.04 (BB) Br ex 60.05 Dght 22.522
Lbp 319.00 Br md 60.00 Dpth 30.40
Welded, 1 dk

(A13A2TV) Crude Oil Tanker
Double Hull (13F)
Liq: 339,325; Liq (Oil): 336,520
Compartments: 5 Ta, 10 Wing Ta, ER, 2 Wing Slop Ta
3 Cargo Pump (s): 3x5500m³/hr
Manifold: Bow/CM: 165m

1 oil engine driving 1 FP propeller
Total Power: 31,640kW (43,018hp) 15.5kn
Wartsila 7RTA82T
1 x 2 Stroke 7 Cy. 820 x 3375 31640kW (43018bhp)
Wartsila Switzerland Ltd-Switzerland
Fuel: 405.0 (d.f.) 8900.0 (r.f.)

9315161 **SAMCO CHINA** **160,882** Class: NV (AB)
FIFE 109,809
- **Samco Epsilon Ltd** 317,794
Samco Shipholding Pte Ltd T/cm
Marseille *France (FIS)* 180.0
MMSI: 228031600
Official number: RI931256K

2007-05 Hyundai Samho Heavy Industries Co Ltd — Samho Yd No: S275
Loa 332.99 (BB) Br ex - Dght 22.520
Lbp 319.00 Br md 60.00 Dpth 30.40
Welded, 1 dk

(A13A2TV) Crude Oil Tanker
Double Hull (13F)
Liq: 333,858; Liq (Oil): 338,786
Compartments: 5 Ta, 10 Wing Ta, 2 Wing Slop Ta, ER
3 Cargo Pump (s): 3x5000m³/hr
Manifold: Bow/CM: 165.2m

1 oil engine driving 1 FP propeller
Total Power: 29,346kW (39,899hp) 15.5kn
MAN-B&W 6S90MC-C
1 x 2 Stroke 6 Cy. 900 x 3188 29346kW (39899bhp)
Hyundai Heavy Industries Co Ltd-South Korea
AuxGen: 3 x 1150kW a.c
Fuel: 329.0 (d.f.) 7750.0 (r.f.) 114.0pd

9315159 **SAMCO EUROPE** **160,882** Class: NV (AB)
V7KC8 109,809
- **Samco Delta Ltd** 317,713
Nova Tankers A/S T/cm
Majuro *Marshall Islands* 180.1
MMSI: 538002606
Official number: 2606

2007-04 Hyundai Samho Heavy Industries Co Ltd — Samho Yd No: S274
Loa 332.99 (BB) Br ex 60.04 Dght 22.520
Lbp 319.00 Br md 60.00 Dpth 30.40
Welded, 1 dk

(A13A2TV) Crude Oil Tanker
Double Hull (13F)
Liq: 333,858; Liq (Oil): 339,052
Compartments: 5 Ta, 10 Wing Ta, 2 Wing Slop Ta, ER
3 Cargo Pump (s): 3x5000m³/hr
Manifold: Bow/CM: 165.2m

1 oil engine driving 1 FP propeller
Total Power: 29,730kW (40,421hp) 15.5kn
MAN-B&W 6S90MC-C
1 x 2 Stroke 6 Cy. 900 x 3188 29730kW (40421bhp)
Hyundai Heavy Industries Co Ltd-South Korea
AuxGen: 3 x 1150kW 440V 60Hz a.c
Fuel: 390.0 (d.f.) 12910.0 (r.f.) 114.0pd

9528940 **SAMCO REDWOOD** **160,928** Class: NV (AB)
FICW 110,502
- **Samco Kappa Ltd** 318,129
Samco Shipholding Pte Ltd T/cm
SatCom: Inmarsat C 422801891 178.1
Marseille *France (FIS)*
MMSI: 228019800

2011-10 Hyundai Samho Heavy Industries Co Ltd — Samho Yd No: S502
Loa 333.08 (BB) Br ex 60.05 Dght 22.625
Lbp 319.00 Br md 60.00 Dpth 30.40
Welded, 1 dk

(A13A2TV) Crude Oil Tanker
Double Hull (13F)
Liq: 338,536; Liq (Oil): 336,520
Compartments: 5 Ta, 10 Wing Ta, ER, 2 Wing Slop Ta
3 Cargo Pump (s): 3x5000m³/hr
Manifold: Bow/CM: 167m

1 oil engine driving 1 FP propeller
Total Power: 31,640kW (43,018hp) 15.5kn
Wartsila 7RTA82T
1 x 2 Stroke 7 Cy. 820 x 3375 31640kW (43018bhp)
Hyundai Heavy Industries Co Ltd-South Korea
AuxGen: 1 x 1500kW a.c, 2 x 1130kW a.c
Fuel: 1481.0 (d.f.) 7159.0 (r.f.)

9315147 **SAMCO SCANDINAVIA** **160,882** Class: AB
V7KC7 109,809
- **Samco Gamma Ltd** 317,826
Nova Tankers A/S T/cm
SatCom: Inmarsat C 453800431 180.3
Majuro *Marshall Islands*
MMSI: 538002605
Official number: 2605

2006-11 Hyundai Samho Heavy Industries Co Ltd — Samho Yd No: S273
Loa 333.00 (BB) Br ex - Dght 22.525
Lbp 319.00 Br md 60.00 Dpth 30.40
Welded, 1 dk

(A13A2TV) Crude Oil Tanker
Double Hull (13F)
Liq: 339,055; Liq (Oil): 339,055
Compartments: 5 Ta, 10 Wing Ta, 2 Wing Slop Ta, ER
3 Cargo Pump (s): 3x5000m³/hr
Manifold: Bow/CM: 165.2m

1 oil engine driving 1 FP propeller
Total Power: 29,346kW (39,899hp) 15.5kn
MAN-B&W 6S90MC-C
1 x 2 Stroke 6 Cy. 900 x 3188 29346kW (39899bhp)
Hyundai Heavy Industries Co Ltd-South Korea
AuxGen: 3 x 1150kW a.c
Fuel: 349.3 (d.f.) 12748.8 (r.f.) 114.0pd

9590876 **SAMCO SUNDARBANS** **160,928** Class: AB
V7XT6 110,502
- **Samco Theta Ltd** 318,000
Samco Shipholding Pte Ltd T/cm
Majuro *Marshall Islands* 178.0
MMSI: 538004567
Official number: 4567

2012-05 Hyundai Samho Heavy Industries Co Ltd — Samho Yd No: S556
Loa 333.04 (BB) Br ex 60.05 Dght 22.520
Lbp 319.00 Br md 60.00 Dpth 30.40
Welded, 1 dk

(A13A2TV) Crude Oil Tanker
Double Hull (13F)
Liq: 336,520; Liq (Oil): 336,520
Compartments: 5 Ta, 10 Wing Ta, ER, 2 Wing Slop Ta
3 Cargo Pump (s): 3x5500m³/hr
Manifold: Bow/CM: 165m

1 oil engine driving 1 FP propeller
Total Power: 31,640kW (43,018hp) 15.5kn
Wartsila 7RT-flex82T
1 x 2 Stroke 7 Cy. 820 x 3375 31640kW (43018bhp)
Hyundai Heavy Industries Co Ltd-South Korea
AuxGen: 1 x 1500kW a.c, 2 x 1130kW a.c, 1 x 530kW a.c
Fuel: 405.0 (d.f.) 8900.0 (r.f.)

9590888 **SAMCO TAIGA** **160,928** Class: AB
V7XT7 110,502
- **Samco Iota Ltd** 317,788
Samco Shipholding Pte Ltd T/cm
Majuro *Marshall Islands* 178.0
MMSI: 538004568
Official number: 4568

2012-09 Hyundai Samho Heavy Industries Co Ltd — Samho Yd No: S557
Loa 333.00 (BB) Br ex 60.05 Dght 22.610
Lbp 319.00 Br md 60.00 Dpth 30.40
Welded, 1 dk

(A13A2TV) Crude Oil Tanker
Double Hull (13F)
Liq: 336,520; Liq (Oil): 336,520
Compartments: 5 Ta, 10 Wing Ta, ER, 2 Wing Slop Ta
3 Cargo Pump (s): 3x5500m³/hr
Manifold: Bow/CM: 165m

1 oil engine driving 1 FP propeller
Total Power: 31,640kW (43,018hp) 15.5kn
Wartsila 7RT-flex82T
1 x 2 Stroke 7 Cy. 820 x 3375 31640kW (43018bhp)
Hyundai Heavy Industries Co Ltd-South Korea
AuxGen: 1 x 1500kW a.c, 2 x 1130kW a.c, 1 x 530kW a.c
Fuel: 1511.0 (d.f.) 7346.0 (r.f.)

9415375 **SAMED** **1,579** Class: BV
J8B4018 473
- **Munch Marine Services Ltd** 1,500
Whitesea Shipping & Supply (LLC)
SatCom: Inmarsat C 437700081
Kingstown *St Vincent & The Grenadines*
MMSI: 377417000
Official number: 10491

2009-07 Keppel Nantong Shipyard Co Ltd — Nantong JS (Hull) Yd No: 012
2009-07 Keppel Singmarine Pte Ltd — Singapore Yd No: 332
Loa 62.20 Br ex - Dght 4.900
Lbp 59.60 Br md 15.00 Dpth 6.00
Welded, 1 dk

(B21B20A) Anchor Handling Tug Supply

2 oil engines reduction geared to sc. shafts driving 2 Directional propellers
Total Power: 4,046kW (5,500hp) 12.5kn
Wartsila 6L26A
2 x 4 Stroke 6 Cy. 260 x 320 each-2023kW (2750bhp)
Wartsila Finland Oy-Finland
AuxGen: 2 x 280kW 380V 50Hz a.c, 2 x 1200kW 380V 50Hz a.c
Thrusters: 2 Tunnel thruster (f)

IMO / Call sign	Ship / Owner / Flag	Tonnage	Class	Built / Dimensions	Type / Cargo	Machinery
9477177 *3FFT9* -	**SAMEER 1** *ex* Onsys Century I *-2014* *ex* Qaseh *-2011* *ex* Nepline 1 *-2009* **Astoria International Group Inc** Sameer Ships Pte Ltd *Panama* *Panama* MMSI: 370602000 Official number: 45378PEXT	**5,036** 2,272 7,119 T/cm 17.6	Class: BV	**2008**-03 **Zhejiang Zhenxing Shiprepair & Building Co Ltd — Wenling ZJ** Yd No: 2006/005 Loa 118.00 (BB) Br ex - Dght 6.600 Lbp 110.00 Br md 17.60 Dpth 9.00 Welded, 1 dk	**(A13B2TP) Products Tanker** Double Hull (13F) Liq: 8,063; Liq (Oil): 8,063 Cargo Heating Coils Compartments: 10 Wing Ta, ER, 2 Wing Slop Ta 2 Cargo Pump (s): 2x750m³/hr Manifold: Bow/CM: 58.2m	**1 oil engine** reduction geared to sc. shaft driving 1 CP propeller Total Power: 2,970kW (4,038hp) 12.0kn MaK 9M25 1 x 4 Stroke 9 Cy. 255 x 400 2970kW (4038bhp) Caterpillar Motoren GmbH & Co. KG-Germany Fuel: 50.0 (d.f.) 348.0 (r.f.)
8917936 - -	**SAMEERA 1** - **Sagarika Sea Crafts Ltd** - *India*	*120* - -		**1989 EMS Holdings Pty Ltd — Fremantle WA** Yd No: 100 L reg 21.20 Br ex - Dght 3.050 Lbp 23.00 Br md 6.40 Dpth - Welded, 1 dk	**(B11A2FT) Trawler** Ins: 92	**1 oil engine** driving 1 FP propeller
8832954 *4LGO* -	**SAMEGRELO** - **Redut-Kale Co-operative Enterprises** - *Poti* *Georgia* Official number: C-01594	**104** 31 61	Class: MG (RS)	**1990**-05 **Yeyskiy Sudostroitelnyy Zavod — Yeysk** Yd No: 2016 Loa 26.50 Br ex 6.60 Dght 2.340 Lbp 22.90 Br md - Dpth 3.08 Welded, 1dk	**(B11A2FS) Stern Trawler** Ins: 66	**1 oil engine** geared to sc. shaft driving 1 FP propeller Total Power: 165kW (224hp) 9.3kn Daldizel 6CHSPN2A18-225 1 x 4 Stroke 6 Cy. 180 x 220 165kW (224bhp) Daldizel-Khabarovsk AuxGen: 2 x 30kW a.c Fuel: 10.0 (d.f.)
9572422 *9BOK* -	**SAMEN** - **Bank Mellat** - *Khorramshahr* *Iran* MMSI: 422678000 Official number: 20737	**481** 268 1,000	Class: AS	**2010**-01 **Moosavi Shipyard — Khorramshahr** Yd No: 619 Loa 42.52 Br ex - Dght - Lbp - Br md 9.55 Dpth 4.00 Welded, 1 dk	**(A31A2GX) General Cargo Ship**	**2 oil engines** reduction geared to sc. shafts driving 2 Propellers Total Power: 1,002kW (1,362hp) Yanmar 6LAH-STE3 2 x 4 Stroke 6 Cy. 150 x 165 each-501kW (681bhp) Yanmar Diesel Engine Co Ltd-Japan
8320389 *HP7901* -	**SAMENR** *ex* Khader *-2013* *ex* Gulf Glory *-2009* *ex* Hae Kup No. 6 *-2007* *ex* Deug Yong *-1987* **Sun Land Shipping Trading Co Ltd Inc** - *Panama* *Panama* Official number: 43623PEXT1	**803** 632 1,474	Class: (KR)	**1983**-12 **Banguhjin Engineering & Shipbuilding Co Ltd — Ulsan** Yd No: 29 Loa 65.36 Br ex - Dght 4.311 Lbp 51.44 Br md 9.12 Dpth 4.65 Welded, 1 dk	**(A13B2TP) Products Tanker** Liq: 1,161; Liq (Oil): 1,161 Compartments: 4 Ta, ER	**1 oil engine** with clutches & reverse reduction geared to sc. shaft driving 1 FP propeller Total Power: 552kW (750hp) 9.0kn Hanshin 6L26BGSH 1 x 4 Stroke 6 Cy. 260 x 400 552kW (750bhp) Ssangyong Heavy Industries Co Ltd-South Korea AuxGen: 2 x 38kW 225V a.c
7201079 *EPAE5* -	**SAMER** *ex* Qaem 12 *-2010* *ex* Dusty Dawn *-1980* **Ahmad Pour Sameri** - *Bandar Imam Khomeini* *Iran*	*165* 81 -	Class: AS	**1967**-01 **Bollinger Machine Shop & Shipyard, Inc. — Lockport, La** Converted From: Fishing Vessel-1990 L reg 24.45 Br ex 7.32 Dght - Lbp - Br md - Dpth 3.48 Welded, 1 dk	**(B34L2QU) Utility Vessel**	**1 oil engine** reduction geared to sc. shaft driving 1 FP propeller Total Power: 670kW (911hp) 6.0kn Deutz SBA6M528 1 x 4 Stroke 6 Cy. 220 x 280 670kW (911bhp) (new engine ,made 1967) Deutz AG-Koeln
8844763 *9BHM* -	**SAMER 1** *ex* Kiho Maru No. 6 *-2005* **MZ Rostaei** - *Bushehr* *Iran* MMSI: 422521000 Official number: 835	**392** 118 477	Class: AS	**1990**-10 **Higo Zosen — Kumamoto** Loa 45.00 Br ex - Dght 3.400 Lbp 40.00 Br md 10.00 Dpth 4.50 Welded, 1 dk	**(B33A2DG) Grab Dredger**	**1 oil engine** driving 1 FP propeller Total Power: 625kW (850hp) Niigata 6M26ZE 1 x 4 Stroke 6 Cy. 260 x 400 625kW (850bhp) Niigata Engineering Co Ltd-Japan
6616928 *ERAF* -	**SAMER M** *ex* Lady F *-2010* *ex* Lady Farida *-2010* *ex* Nour Elaslam *-1999* *ex* Gertje *-1994* *ex* Inka Dede *-1985* *ex* Aros Trent *-1977* *ex* Inka Dede *-1976* *ex* Klaus *-1974* **Mandour Shipping Corp** Kenmar Shipping Agencies *Moldova* MMSI: 214180106	*399* 224 1,177	Class: DR KC (GL)	**1966 J.J. Sietas Schiffswerft — Hamburg** Yd No: 576 Loa 68.36 Br ex 10.55 Dght 3.957 Lbp 62.11 Br md 10.51 Dpth 6.25 Welded, 2 dks	**(A31A2GX) General Cargo Ship** Grain: 2,451; Bale: 2,259 TEU 39 C. 39/20' Compartments: 2 Ho, ER 2 Ha: (11.9 x 6.4) (21.5 x 7.9)ER Cranes: 3x3t Ice Capable	**1 oil engine** driving 1 FP propeller Total Power: 809kW (1,100hp) 11.0kn Deutz RBV6M545 1 x 4 Stroke 6 Cy. 320 x 450 809kW (1100bhp) Kloeckner Humboldt Deutz AG-West Germany Fuel: 71.0 (d.f.)
9324368 *A6E2967* -	**SAMHA** - **Liwa Marine Services LLC** Khalid Faraj Marine Shipping *Abu Dhabi* *United Arab Emirates* MMSI: 470777000	**456** 137 -	Class: BV	**2004**-09 **Piasau Slipways Sdn Bhd — Miri** Yd No: 189 Loa 47.00 Br ex - Dght 2.438 Lbp 42.67 Br md 11.00 Dpth 3.20 Welded, 1 dk	**(A35D2RL) Landing Craft** Bow door/ramp (f)	**2 oil engines** geared to sc. shafts driving 2 Propellers Total Power: 716kW (974hp) 10.0kn Caterpillar 3408 2 x Vee 4 Stroke 8 Cy. 137 x 152 each-358kW (487bhp) Caterpillar Inc-USA
9081174 *V7FU6* -	**SAMHO CROWN** *ex* Overseas Crown *-2007* *ex* Crown Unity *-2006* **SY Tankers Ltd** - SatCom: Inmarsat C 453845955 *Majuro* *Marshall Islands* MMSI: 538002025 Official number: 2025	**156,852** 107,698 300,482 T/cm 168.2	Class: (LR) ✠ Classed LR until 17/4/12	**1996**-01 **Hyundai Heavy Industries Co Ltd — Ulsan** Yd No: 905 Loa 330.27 (BB) Br ex 58.04 Dght 22.222 Lbp 314.00 Br md 58.00 Dpth 31.00 Welded, 1 dk, sunken dk aft 31.6m	**(A13A2TV) Crude Oil Tanker** Double Hull (13F) Liq: 331,538; Liq (Oil): 331,538 Compartments: 5 Ta, 10 Wing Ta, 2 Wing Slop Ta, ER 3 Cargo Pump (s): 3x5000m³/hr Manifold: Bow/CM: 164m	**1 oil engine** driving 1 FP propeller Total Power: 24,468kW (33,267hp) 14.7kn B&W 7S80MC 1 x 2 Stroke 7 Cy. 800 x 3056 24468kW (33267bhp) Hyundai Heavy Industries Co Ltd-South Korea AuxGen: 3 x 850kW 450V 60Hz a.c Boilers: 2 AuxB (o.f.) 18.1kgf/cm² (17.8bar), e (ex.g.) 23.1kgf/cm² (22.7bar) Fuel: 409.0 (d.f.) (Heating Coils) 7625.0 (r.f.) 105.5pd
8801759 - -	**SAMHO MARINER** *ex* Nammyung *-2003* *ex* Hoki Maru *-2001* **Jin Yang Tanker Co Ltd** Korea Oil Tanker Co Ltd *Ulsan* *South Korea* MMSI: 440104690 Official number: USR-011189	*1,515* - 3,080	Class: KR (NK)	**1987**-12 **Sasaki Shipbuilding Co Ltd — Osakikamijima HS** Yd No: 513 Loa 88.96 Br ex - Dght 5.700 Lbp 82.30 Br md 12.60 Dpth 6.41 Welded, 1 dk	**(A13A2TV) Crude Oil Tanker** Liq: 3,399; Liq (Oil): 3,399 Compartments: 8 Ta, ER	**1 oil engine** with clutches, flexible couplings & reduction geared to sc. shaft driving 1 FP propeller Total Power: 1,912kW (2,600hp) 13.6kn Makita LS38L 1 x 4 Stroke 6 Cy. 380 x 740 1912kW (2600bhp) Makita Diesel Co Ltd-Japan AuxGen: 3 x 116kW
9137387 *DSBB850* -	**SAMHO No. 101** *ex* Halla Tugboat No. 1 *-2000* **Hyundai Samho Heavy Industries Co Ltd** - *Mokpo* *South Korea* Official number: MPR-954495	**177** - 86	Class: KR	**1995**-11 **Seohae Shipbuilding & Engineering Co Ltd — Incheon** Yd No: 94-06 Loa 32.00 Br ex - Dght 2.673 Lbp 27.00 Br md 8.70 Dpth 3.80 Welded, 1 dk	**(B32A2ST) Tug**	**2 oil engines** reduction geared to sc. shafts driving 2 FP propellers Total Power: 2,354kW (3,200hp) Pielstick 6PA5L255 2 x 4 Stroke 6 Cy. 255 x 270 each-1177kW (1600bhp) Ssangyong Heavy Industries Co Ltd-South Korea
9140906 - -	**SAMHO No. 102** *ex* Halla Tugboat No. 2 *-2000* **Hyundai Samho Heavy Industries Co Ltd** - *Mokpo* *South Korea* MMSI: 440304900 Official number: MPR-954509	**177** - 86	Class: KR	**1995**-12 **Seohae Shipbuilding & Engineering Co Ltd — Incheon** Yd No: 94-07 Loa 32.00 Br ex - Dght 2.673 Lbp 27.00 Br md 8.70 Dpth 3.80 Welded, 1 dk	**(B32A2ST) Tug**	**2 oil engines** sr geared to sc. shafts driving 2 FP propellers Total Power: 2,354kW (3,200hp) Pielstick 6PA5L255 2 x 4 Stroke 6 Cy. 255 x 270 each-1177kW (1600bhp) Ssangyong Heavy Industries Co Ltd-South Korea
9139660 - -	**SAMHO No. 103** *ex* Halla Tugboat No. 3 *-2000* **Hyundai Samho Heavy Industries Co Ltd** - *Mokpo* *South Korea* Official number: MPR-954516	*177* - 86	Class: KR	**1996**-01 **Seohae Shipbuilding & Engineering Co Ltd — Incheon** Yd No: 94-08 Loa 32.00 Br ex - Dght 2.673 Lbp 27.00 Br md 8.70 Dpth 3.80 Welded, 1 dk	**(B32A2ST) Tug**	**2 oil engines** sr geared to sc. shafts driving 2 FP propellers Total Power: 2,354kW (3,200hp) Pielstick 6PA5L255 2 x 4 Stroke 6 Cy. 255 x 270 each-1177kW (1600bhp) Ssangyong Heavy Industries Co Ltd-South Korea
9121340 *DSAV7* -	**SAMHO T-1** *ex* Bu Lim No. 507 *-2005* **Samho Industry & Development Co Ltd** - *Busan* *South Korea* Official number: BSR-942214	*133* - 59	Class: KR	**1994**-04 **Samkwang Shipbuilding & Engineering Co Ltd — Incheon** Yd No: 93-10 Loa 32.30 Br ex - Dght 2.136 Lbp 30.00 Br md 8.40 Dpth 2.80 Welded, 1 dk	**(B32A2ST) Tug**	**2 oil engines** with clutches, flexible couplings & sr geared to sc. shafts driving 2 FP propellers Total Power: 1,898kW (2,580hp) 13.2kn Caterpillar 3512TA 2 x Vee 4 Stroke 12 Cy. 170 x 190 each-949kW (1290bhp) Caterpillar Inc-USA AuxGen: 2 x 55kW 225V a.c Fuel: 40.0
9486128 - -	**SAMHO T-7** - **Korin Marine Co Ltd** - *Busan* *South Korea* Official number: BSR-071401	**213** - -	Class: KR	**2007**-11 **Yeunsoo Shipbuilding Co Ltd — Janghang** Yd No: 129 Loa 33.80 Br ex 9.40 Dght 3.100 Lbp 28.50 Br md 9.40 Dpth 4.15 Welded, 1 dk	**(B32A2ST) Tug**	**2 oil engines** gearing integral to driving 2 Z propellers Total Power: 2,644kW (3,594hp) 13.5kn Niigata 6L25HX 2 x 4 Stroke 6 Cy. 250 x 350 each-1322kW (1797bhp) Niigata Engineering Co Ltd-Japan AuxGen: 3 x 56kW 220V a.c

IMO / Call sign	Name / Owner / Manager / Port	Tonnage	Class	Build / Dimensions	Type / Capacity	Machinery
9618434 *DSQZ7* -	**SAMHO T-9** **KDB Capital Corp** Myung Jin Shipping Co Ltd *Busan* *South Korea* MMSI: 441768000 Official number: BSR-110007	**446** 133 235	Class: KR	**2011-02 Namyang Shipbuilding Co Ltd — Yeosu** Yd No: 1093 Loa 38.00 Br ex - Dght 3.735 Lbp 31.80 Br md 10.00 Dpth 4.50 Welded, 1 dk	**(B32A2ST) Tug**	**2 oil engines** reduction geared to sc. shafts driving 2 Propellers Total Power: 3,310kW (4,500hp) Niigata 6L28HX 2 x 4 Stroke 6 Cy. 280 x 370 each-1655kW (2250bhp) Niigata Engineering Co Ltd-Japan
9627813 *DSRD8* -	**SAMHO T-10** **Kwangseong Development Ltd** Samho Industry & Development Co Ltd *Busan* *South Korea* MMSI: 441787000 Official number: BSR-110044	**446** 133 235	Class: KR	**2011-05 Namyang Shipbuilding Co Ltd — Yeosu** Yd No: 1094 Loa 38.00 Br ex - Dght 3.735 Lbp 31.80 Br md 10.00 Dpth 4.50 Welded, 1 dk	**(B32A2ST) Tug**	**2 oil engines** reduction geared to sc. shafts driving 2 Propellers Total Power: 3,308kW (4,498hp) Niigata 6L28HX 2 x 4 Stroke 6 Cy. 280 x 370 each-1654kW (2249bhp) Niigata Engineering Co Ltd-Japan AuxGen: 2 x 148kW 225V a.c Fuel: 143.0 (d.f.)
7419729 - -	**SAMI I** *ex* Kyoyo Maru No. 1 *-1987* **Maypalad Shipping Lines Inc** - *Cebu* *Philippines*	*235* 143 415		**1974-09 Miho Zosensho K.K. — Shimizu** Yd No: 937 Loa 51.06 Br ex 9.30 Dght 3.328 Lbp 42.98 Br md 7.98 Dpth 3.69 Welded, 1 dk	**(B11B2FV) Fishing Vessel**	**1 oil engine** driving 1 FP propeller Total Power: 1,103kW (1,500hp) Hanshin 6LUD32 1 x 4 Stroke 6 Cy. 320 x 510 1103kW (1500bhp) Hanshin Nainenki Kogyo-Japan
7509794 - -	**SAMIA** - **Bangladesh Inland Water Transport Authority** - *Chittagong* *Bangladesh*	*127* 34 163	Class: (NK)	**1975-10 Ishimura Zosen — Kimaishi** Yd No: 119 Loa 30.00 Br ex - Dght 1.448 Lbp 27.61 Br md 5.80 Dpth 2.75 Welded, 1 dk	**(B31A2SR) Research Survey Vessel**	**2 oil engines** geared to sc. shafts driving 2 FP propellers Total Power: 442kW (600hp) 10.8kn Daihatsu 6PKT-16 2 x 4 Stroke 6 Cy. 160 x 210 each-221kW (300bhp) Daihatsu Diesel Manufacturing Co Lt-Japan
9088665 *S2CJ* -	**SAMIA-1** *ex* Kotoku Escort *-2012* *ex* Keifuku Maru *-2005* *ex* New Katsuragi *-2002* **Birds Bangladesh Agencies Ltd** - *Chittagong* *Bangladesh* Official number: C-1777	**488** 242 1,015	Class: RI (NK)	**1994-02 Shinosaki Zosen — Kumamoto** Yd No: 108 Loa 60.65 (BB) Br ex 10.42 Dght 3.894 Lbp 55.65 Br md 10.40 Dpth 4.30 Welded, 1 dk	**(A12A2TC) Chemical Tanker** Double Hull (13F) Liq: 893 Cargo Heating Coils Compartments: 6 Wing Ta, 2 Wing Slop Ta, ER 2 Cargo Pump (s): 2x200m³/hr Manifold: Bow/CM: 29.3m	**1 oil engine** reverse geared to sc. shaft driving 1 CP propeller Total Power: 736kW (1,001hp) 10.0kn Akasaka K26SR 1 x 4 Stroke 6 Cy. 260 x 480 736kW (1001bhp) Akasaka Tekkosho KK (Akasaka DieselLtd)-Japan AuxGen: 2 x 100kW 450V 60Hz a.c Fuel: 52.0 (d.f.)
8351302 *S2ET* -	**SAMIA-2** *ex* Nichiasu Maru No. 2 *-1995* **Ebadee Petro Carriers (Pvt) Ltd** - *Chittagong* *Bangladesh* Official number: C.1129	**749** 557 1,250	Class: RI (NK)	**1983 Kinoura Zosen K.K. — Imabari** Yd No: 101 Loa 67.90 Br ex - Dght 3.701 Lbp 56.01 Br md 10.20 Dpth 4.30 Welded, 1 dk	**(A13C2LA) Asphalt/Bitumen Tanker** Asphalt: 1,494	**1 oil engine** driving 1 FP propeller Total Power: 1,324kW (1,800hp) 14.3kn Hanshin 6EL30 1 x 4 Stroke 6 Cy. 300 x 600 1324kW (1800bhp) The Hanshin Diesel Works Ltd-Japan Fuel: 25.0 (d.f.)
8810281 - -	**SAMIL NO. 501** *ex* Kinei Maru No. 8 *-2001* *ex* Sekijyu Maru No. 72 *-2001* **Tea Yang Shipping Co Ltd** - *Busan* *South Korea* MMSI: 440105630 Official number: BSR-020631	**1,482** - 3,371	Class: (KR)	**1989-02 Honda Zosen — Saiki** Yd No: 786 Loa 75.18 (BB) Br ex - Dght 4.252 Lbp 63.00 Br md 13.00 Dpth 7.00 Welded, 1 dk	**(A24D2BA) Aggregates Carrier** Compartments: 1 Ho, ER 1 Ha: ER	**1 oil engine** with clutches & reverse geared to sc. shaft driving 1 FP propeller Total Power: 1,471kW (2,000hp) Niigata 6M34AGT 1 x 4 Stroke 6 Cy. 340 x 620 1471kW (2000bhp) Niigata Engineering Co Ltd-Japan Thrusters: 1 Thwart. FP thruster (f)
8422228 *4JAF* -	**SAMIR GULIYEV** *ex* Neftegaz-18 *-1993* **Specialized Sea Oil Fleet Organisation, Caspian Sea Oil Fleet, State Oil Co of the Republic of Azerbaijan** - SatCom: Inmarsat C 442312110 *Baku* *Azerbaijan* MMSI: 423121100 Official number: DGR-0184	**2,737** 821 1,329	Class: RS	**1985-06 Stocznia Szczecinska im A Warskiego — Szczecin** Yd No: B92/18 Loa 81.16 Br ex 16.30 Dght 4.900 Lbp 71.45 Br md 15.97 Dpth 7.22 Welded, 2 dks	**(B21B20T) Offshore Tug/Supply Ship** 20 TEU C. Derricks: 1x12.5t Ice Capable	**2 oil engines** reduction geared to sc. shafts driving 2 CP propellers Total Power: 5,296kW (7,200hp) 15.3kn Sulzer 6ZL40/48 2 x 4 Stroke 6 Cy. 400 x 480 each-2648kW (3600bhp) Zaklady Urzadzen Technicznych'Zgoda' SA-Poland AuxGen: 3 x 384kW 400V 50Hz a.c Thrusters: 1 Thwart. FP thruster (f) Fuel: 399.0 (r.f.)
8731966 *MNDV5* -	**SAMIRA** *ex* Sealyon *-2011* *ex* Oscar 2 *-2007* **Arena Leisure Ltd** - *Douglas* *Isle of Man (British)* MMSI: 235037307 Official number: 737823	**167** 50 -	Class: BV	**2006-06 Overmarine SpA — Viareggio** Yd No: 105/26 Loa 31.46 Br ex - Dght 1.100 Lbp 27.85 Br md 6.90 Dpth 3.70 Bonded, 1 dk	**(X11A2YP) Yacht** Hull Material: Reinforced Plastic	**2 oil engines** geared to sc. shafts driving 2 Water jets Total Power: 3,358kW (4,566hp) 35.0kn M.T.U. 16V2000M93 2 x Vee 4 Stroke 16 Cy. 135 x 156 each-1679kW (2283bhp) MTU Friedrichshafen GmbH-Friedrichshafen AuxGen: 2 x 31kW
9240744 *PCCG* -	**SAMIRA** *launched as* Hansa London *-2004* **Toucan Maritime** - *Heerhugowaard* *Netherlands* MMSI: 245015000 Official number: 40127	**1,435** 718 1,700	Class: BV	**2004-07 Leda doo — Korcula** (Hull) **2004-07 Scheepswerf Peters B.V. — Kampen** Yd No: 501 Loa 79.99 Br ex - Dght 3.400 Lbp 78.80 Br md 10.40 Dpth 4.80 Welded, 1 dk	**(A31A2GX) General Cargo Ship** Grain: 2,691 TEU 72 C.Ho 48/20' C.Dk 24/20' Compartments: 1 Ho, ER 1 Ha: ER (53.4 x 8.4)	**1 oil engine** reduction geared to sc. shaft driving 1 FP propeller Total Power: 1,118kW (1,520hp) 9.5kn Caterpillar 3512TA 1 x Vee 4 Stroke 12 Cy. 170 x 190 1118kW (1520bhp) Caterpillar Inc-USA AuxGen: 2 x 280kW 340V 50Hz a.c, 1 x 60kW 340V 50Hz a.c Thrusters: 1 Tunnel thruster (f)
8631025 *DSFC5* -	**SAMJIN LUCKY** *ex* Hokoku Maru *-2000* **Sam Jin Co Ltd** - *Seogwipo* *South Korea* MMSI: 440104630 Official number: SGR-998923	**1,102** - 1,986	Class: KR	**1987-04 Honda Zosen — Saiki** Yd No: 752 L reg 76.20 Br ex 12.52 Dght 4.312 Lbp 76.00 Br md 12.50 Dpth 6.50 Welded, 1 dk	**(A31A2GX) General Cargo Ship**	**1 oil engine** driving 1 FP propeller Total Power: 1,324kW (1,800hp) Fuji 6S32G2 1 x 4 Stroke 6 Cy. 320 x 610 1324kW (1800bhp) Fuji Diesel Co Ltd-Japan
8708878 - -	**SAMJIN LUCKY 3** *ex* Seiyu Maru No. 18 *-2001* - -	*499* - 1,229	Class: KR	**1987-09 K.K. Matsuura Zosensho — Osakikamijima** Yd No: 338 Loa 66.10 (BB) Br ex 13.03 Dght 4.330 Lbp 60.00 Br md 13.01 Dpth 7.01 Welded, 2 dks	**(A24D2BA) Aggregates Carrier** Grain: 780 Compartments: 1 Ho, ER 1 Ha: ER	**1 oil engine** with clutches, flexible couplings & reverse reduction geared to sc. shaft driving 1 FP propeller Total Power: 736kW (1,001hp) 11.4kn Hanshin 6LU35G 1 x 4 Stroke 6 Cy. 350 x 550 736kW (1001bhp) The Hanshin Diesel Works Ltd-Japan Thrusters: 1 Thwart. FP thruster (f)
9124237 - -	**SAMJIN NO. 1** *ex* Bo Kwang No. 7 *-2010* *ex* Sam Woo *-2010* *ex* Kiyo Maru No. 3 *-2010* *ex* Senkai Maru *-2002* **Wonjin Co Ltd** - *Busan* *South Korea* MMSI: 440134750 Official number: BSR-091321	*890* - 2,064	Class: KR (NK)	**1995-09 Sasaki Shipbuilding Co Ltd — Osakikamijima HS** Yd No: 598 Lengthened & Conv to DH-2010 Loa 84.27 Br ex - Dght 4.512 Lbp 79.44 Br md 11.50 Dpth 5.25 Welded, 1 dk	**(A13B2TP) Products Tanker** Double Hull (13F) Liq: 2,300; Liq (Oil): 2,148	**1 oil engine** driving 1 FP propeller Total Power: 1,618kW (2,200hp) 12.2kn Akasaka A34C 1 x 4 Stroke 6 Cy. 340 x 620 1618kW (2200bhp) Akasaka Tekkosho KK (Akasaka DieselLtd)-Japan Fuel: 70.0 (d.f.)
9149017 *SYKT* -	**SAMJOHN AMITY** **Krios Shipping Co Special Maritime Enterprise (ENE)** Golden Flame Shipping SA SatCom: Inmarsat B 323952810 *Piraeus* *Greece* MMSI: 239528000 Official number: 10521	**38,846** 24,517 74,744 T/cm 67.0	Class: LR ✠**100A1** SS 01/2013 bulk carrier strengthened for heavy cargoes, Nos. 2, 4 & 6 holds may be empty ESP LI **ShipRight** (SDA, FDA, CM) ESN-Hold 1 ✠**LMC** **UMS** Eq.Ltr: O†; Cable: 660.0/78.0 U3	**1998-01 Nippon Kokan KK (NKK Corp) — Tsu ME** Yd No: 169 Loa 225.00 (BB) Br ex 32.30 Dght 13.767 Lbp 217.00 Br md 32.26 Dpth 19.10 Welded, 1 dk	**(A21A2BC) Bulk Carrier** Grain: 87,667 Compartments: 7 Ho, ER 7 Ha: (16.1 x 13.3)6 (17.1 x 15.0)ER	**1 oil engine** driving 1 FP propeller Total Power: 8,826kW (12,000hp) 14.6kn Sulzer 7RTA48T 1 x 2 Stroke 7 Cy. 480 x 2000 8826kW (12000bhp) Diesel United Ltd.-Aioi AuxGen: 3 x 400kW 450V 60Hz a.c Boilers: AuxB (Comp) 7.0kgf/cm² (6.9bar) Fuel: 2449.0 (r.f.) 32.0pd

IMO / Call sign	Name / Owner / Manager	Tonnage	Class	Builder / Dimensions	Type / Capacity	Machinery
9612064 *SVBI3* -	**SAMJOHN DREAM** **Marine Dream Special Maritime Enterprise (ENE)** Golden Flame Shipping SA *Piraeus* *Greece* MMSI: 241129000 Official number: 12106	**107,198** 68,025 206,610	Class: LR **✠100A1** SS 03/2012 bulk carrier CSR BC-A GRAB (30) Nos. 2, 4 and 6 holds may be empty ESP **ShipRight** (CM, ACS (B)) *IWS LI **✠LMC** **UMS** Eq.Ltr: B*; Cable: 742.5/107.0 U3 (a)	**2012**-03 **Daehan Shipbuilding Co Ltd — Hwawon (Haenam Shipyard)** Yd No: 1051 Loa 300.00 (BB) Br ex 50.05 Dght 18.590 Lbp 290.00 Br md 50.00 Dpth 25.10 Welded, 1 dk	**(A21A2BC) Bulk Carrier** Grain: 223,000 Compartments: 9 Ho, ER 9 Ha: 7 (16.3 x 22.9) (15.4 x 16.4)ER (14.4 x 16.4)	**1 oil engine** driving 1 FP propeller Total Power: 19,620kW (26,675hp) 15.4kn MAN-B&W 6S70ME-C8 1 x 2 Stroke 6 Cy. 700 x 2800 19620kW (26675bhp) STX Engine Co Ltd-South Korea AuxGen: 3 x 900kW 450V 60Hz a.c Boilers: e (ex.g.) 12.2kgf/cm² (12.0bar), AuxB (o.f.) 9.2kgf/cm² (9.0bar) Fuel: 370.0 (d.f.) 5800.0 (r.f.)
9434436 *SVBA5* -	**SAMJOHN LEGACY** **Fasoli Shipping Co Special Maritime Enterprise (ENE)** Golden Flame Shipping SA SatCom: Inmarsat C 424101910 *Piraeus* *Greece* MMSI: 241019000 Official number: 12012	**94,995** 59,477 180,736 T/cm 124.0	Class: LR **✠100A1** SS 08/2010 bulk carrier CSR BC-A GRAB (30) Nos. 2, 4 6 & 8 holds may be empty ESP **ShipRight** (ACS (B), CM) *IWS LI **✠LMC** **UMS** Eq.Ltr: B*; Cable: 742.5/107.0 U3 (a)	**2010**-08 **STX Offshore & Shipbuilding Co Ltd — Changwon (Jinhae Shipyard)** Yd No: 1315 Loa 292.00 (BB) Br ex 45.05 Dght 18.200 Lbp 283.00 Br md 45.00 Dpth 24.80 Welded, 1 dk	**(A21A2BC) Bulk Carrier** Double Bottom Entire Compartment Length Grain: 199,000 Compartments: 9 Ho, ER 9 Ha: 7 (15.8 x 20.4)ER 2 (15.8 x 15.3)	**1 oil engine** driving 1 FP propeller Total Power: 18,660kW (25,370hp) 14.3kn MAN-B&W 6S70MC-C 1 x 2 Stroke 6 Cy. 700 x 2800 18660kW (25370bhp) STX Engine Co Ltd-South Korea AuxGen: 3 x 900kW 450V 60Hz a.c Boilers: AuxB (Comp) 9.2kgf/cm² (9.0bar)
9149029 *SVLE* -	**SAMJOHN LIBERTY** **Brave Shipping Co Special Maritime Enterprise (ENE)** Golden Flame Shipping SA SatCom: Inmarsat B 323952710 *Piraeus* *Greece* MMSI: 239527000 Official number: 10523	**38,846** 24,517 74,761 T/cm 67.0	Class: LR **✠100A1** SS 01/2013 bulk carrier strengthened for heavy cargoes, Nos. 2, 4 & 6 holds may be empty ESP LI **ShipRight** (SDA, FDA, CM) ESN-Hold 1 **✠LMC** **UMS** Eq.Ltr: O†; Cable: 660.0/78.0 U3	**1998**-01 **Nippon Kokan KK (NKK Corp) — Tsu ME** Yd No: 170 Loa 225.00 (BB) Br ex 32.30 Dght 13.767 Lbp 217.00 Br md 32.26 Dpth 19.10 Welded, 1 dk	**(A21A2BC) Bulk Carrier** Grain: 87,667 Compartments: 7 Ho, ER 7 Ha: (16.1 x 13.3)6 (17.1 x 15.0)ER	**1 oil engine** driving 1 FP propeller Total Power: 8,826kW (12,000hp) 15.6kn Sulzer 7RTA48T 1 x 2 Stroke 7 Cy. 480 x 2000 8826kW (12000bhp) Diesel United Ltd.-Aioi AuxGen: 3 x 400kW 450V 60Hz a.c Boilers: AuxB (Comp) 7.0kgf/cm² (6.9bar)
9074688 *SWFM* -	**SAMJOHN LIGHT** **Aegokeros Shipping Co Special Maritime Enterprise (ENE)** Golden Flame Shipping SA SatCom: Inmarsat A 1132207 *Piraeus* *Greece* MMSI: 239300000 Official number: 10214	**38,077** 24,124 71,756 T/cm 65.8	Class: AB	**1994**-08 **Hitachi Zosen Corp — Maizuru KY** Yd No: 4874 Loa 223.70 (BB) Br ex - Dght 13.461 Lbp 215.00 Br md 32.20 Dpth 18.60 Welded, 1 dk	**(A21A2BC) Bulk Carrier** Grain: 85,107; Bale: 82,337 Compartments: 7 Ho, ER 7 Ha: (16.2 x 13.0)6 (17.9 x 14.6)ER	**1 oil engine** driving 1 FP propeller Total Power: 9,003kW (12,240hp) 14.0kn B&W 6S60MCE 1 x 2 Stroke 6 Cy. 600 x 2292 9003kW (12240bhp) Hitachi Zosen Corp-Japan AuxGen: 3 x 400kW a.c
9434424 *SVBA4* -	**SAMJOHN SOLIDARITY** **Arrowstone Shipping Co Special Maritime Enterprise (ENE)** Golden Flame Shipping SA SatCom: Inmarsat C 424101810 *Piraeus* *Greece* MMSI: 241018000 Official number: 12007	**94,995** 59,477 180,702 T/cm 124.0	Class: LR **✠100A1** SS 07/2010 bulk carrier CSR BC-A GRAB (20) Nos. 2, 4, 6 & 8 holds may be empty ESP **ShipRight** (ACS (B), CM) *IWS LI **✠LMC** **UMS** Eq.Ltr: B*; Cable: 741.4/107.0 U3 (a)	**2010**-07 **STX Offshore & Shipbuilding Co Ltd — Changwon (Jinhae Shipyard)** Yd No: 1310 Loa 292.00 (BB) Br ex 45.05 Dght 18.200 Lbp 283.00 Br md 45.00 Dpth 24.80 Welded, 1 dk	**(A21A2BC) Bulk Carrier** Double Bottom Entire Compartment Length Grain: 199,000 Compartments: 9 Ho, ER 9 Ha: 7 (15.8 x 20.4)ER 2 (15.8 x 15.3)	**1 oil engine** driving 1 FP propeller Total Power: 18,660kW (25,370hp) 14.3kn MAN-B&W 6S70MC-C 1 x 2 Stroke 6 Cy. 700 x 2800 18660kW (25370bhp) STX Engine Co Ltd-South Korea AuxGen: 3 x 900kW 450V 60Hz a.c Boilers: AuxB (Comp) 9.2kgf/cm² (9.0bar)
9074676 *SVCJ* -	**SAMJOHN SPIRIT** **Toxotis Shipping Co Special Maritime Enterprise (ENE)** Golden Flame Shipping SA SatCom: Inmarsat C 423928210 *Piraeus* *Greece* MMSI: 239282000 Official number: 10200	**38,077** 24,124 71,730 T/cm 65.8	Class: AB	**1994**-05 **Hitachi Zosen Corp — Maizuru KY** Yd No: 4873 Loa 223.70 (BB) Br ex - Dght 13.461 Lbp 215.00 Br md 32.00 Dpth 18.60 Welded, 1 dk	**(A21A2BC) Bulk Carrier** Grain: 85,108; Bale: 82,337 Compartments: 7 Ho, ER 7 Ha: (16.2 x 13.0)6 (17.9 x 14.6)ER	**1 oil engine** driving 1 FP propeller Total Power: 9,003kW (12,240hp) 14.5kn B&W 6S60MCE 1 x 2 Stroke 6 Cy. 600 x 2292 9003kW (12240bhp) Hitachi Zosen Corp-Japan AuxGen: 3 x 480kW a.c
9612076 *SVBI4* -	**SAMJOHN VISION** **Marine Vision Special Maritime Enterprise (ENE)** Golden Flame Shipping SA SatCom: Inmarsat C 424112810 *Piraeus* *Greece* MMSI: 241128000 Official number: 12116	**107,198** 68,025 206,562	Class: LR **✠100A1** SS 05/2012 bulk carrier CSR BC-A GRAB (30) Nos. 2, 4, 6 & 8 holds may be empty ESP **ShipRight** (CM,ACS (B)) *IWS LI **✠LMC** **UMS** Eq.Ltr: B*; Cable: 770.0/111.0 U3 (a)	**2012**-05 **Daehan Shipbuilding Co Ltd — Hwawon (Haenam Shipyard)** Yd No: 1052 Loa 300.00 (BB) Br ex 50.05 Dght 18.570 Lbp 290.00 Br md 50.00 Dpth 25.10 Welded, 1 dk	**(A21A2BC) Bulk Carrier** Grain: 223,000 Compartments: 9 Ho, ER 9 Ha: 7 (16.3 x 22.9) (15.4 x 16.4)ER (14.4 x 16.4)	**1 oil engine** driving 1 FP propeller Total Power: 19,620kW (26,675hp) 15.4kn MAN-B&W 6S70ME-C8 1 x 2 Stroke 6 Cy. 700 x 2800 19620kW (26675bhp) STX Engine Co Ltd-South Korea AuxGen: 3 x 900kW 450V 60Hz a.c Boilers: e (ex.g.) 12.2kgf/cm² (12.0bar), AuxB (o.f.) 9.2kgf/cm² (9.0bar) Fuel: 370.0 (d.f.) 5800.0 (r.f.)
5308794 *OXWI2* -	**SAMKA** **Museumsforeningen til bevarelse af ms Samka** Marstal Sofartsmuseum *Marstal* *Denmark (DIS)* MMSI: 219001218 Official number: E521	**148** 81 240	Class: BV	**1956 H C Christensens Staalskibsvaerft af 1949 — Marstal** Yd No: 69 Loa 33.51 Br ex 6.51 Dght 3.023 Lbp 30.48 Br md 6.48 Dpth - Riveted\Welded, 1 dk	**(A31A2GX) General Cargo Ship** 1 Ha: (12.8 x 4.0) Derricks: 2x2t; Winches: 2 Ice Capable	**1 oil engine** driving 1 FP propeller Total Power: 250kW (340hp) 10.0kn Alpha 404-24VO 1 x 2 Stroke 4 Cy. 240 x 400 250kW (340bhp) Alpha Diesel A/S-Denmark Fuel: 8.0 (d.f.)
7022655 - -	**SAMLEI** **Paradip Port Trust** - *Kolkata* *India* Official number: 1347	*261* 78 381	Class: (LR) (IR) ✠ Classed LR until 22/12/82	**1974**-03 **East Bengal Engineering Works — Kolkata** Loa 33.53 Br ex 8.59 Dght 3.506 Lbp 30.48 Br md 8.39 Dpth 4.27 Welded, 1 dk	**(B32A2ST) Tug**	**1 oil engine** reverse reduction geared to sc. shaft driving 1 FP propeller Total Power: 982kW (1,335hp) MAN G9V30/45ATL 1 x 4 Stroke 9 Cy. 300 x 450 982kW (1335bhp) Dok en Werf Mij. Wilton FijenoordB.V.-Schiedam AuxGen: 2 x 56kW 230V d.c
9582491 *3ETS7* -	**SAMMY** **Nikko Kisen Co Ltd & Sun Lanes Shipping SA** Cleanseas Shipmanagement Inc *Panama* *Panama* MMSI: 373842000 Official number: 4415212	**43,013** 27,239 82,167 T/cm 70.2	Class: NK	**2012**-09 **Tsuneishi Shipbuilding Co Ltd — Tadotsu KG** Yd No: 1478 Loa 228.99 (BB) Br ex - Dght 14.430 Lbp 222.00 Br md 32.26 Dpth 20.05 Welded, 1 dk	**(A21A2BC) Bulk Carrier** Grain: 97,381 Compartments: 7 Ho, ER 7 Ha: ER	**1 oil engine** driving 1 FP propeller Total Power: 9,710kW (13,202hp) 14.5kn MAN-B&W 6S60MC-C 1 x 2 Stroke 6 Cy. 600 x 2400 9710kW (13202bhp) Mitsui Engineering & Shipbuilding CLtd-Japan Fuel: 3180.0

7947611 *WDC3615* -	**SAMMYJO** *ex* Lutador *-2005* *ex* Our Lady of the Sea *-2001* **Sammyjo Fishing LLC** - *Boston, MA* *United States of America* Official number: 609865	*166* 113 -		**1979 Quality Marine, Inc. — Theodore, Al** Yd No: 114 L reg 24.88 Br ex 7.32 Dght - Lbp - Br md - Dpth 3.84 Welded, 1 dk	**(B11B2FV) Fishing Vessel**	**1 oil engine** driving 1 FP propeller Total Power: 401kW (545hp)
9136163 *C5AG1* -	**SAMO** **Government of The Republic of Gambia (Ports Authority)** - *Banjul* *Gambia*	**369** 110 415	Class: (LR) ✠ Classed LR until 29/8/01	**1997-01 Brodogradiliste Beograd — Belgrade** (Hull) Yd No: 1169 **1997-01 IHC Holland NV Beaver Dredgers — Sliedrecht** Yd No: 9390 Loa 38.40 Br ex 10.70 Dght 2.675 Lbp 35.00 Br md 10.00 Dpth 3.00 Welded, 1 dk	**(B33B2DG) Grab Hopper Dredger** Hopper: 250	**1 oil engine** with clutches, flexible couplings & sr reverse geared to sc. shaft driving 1 FP propeller Total Power: 625kW (850hp) 8.0kn Alpha 5L23/30 1 x 4 Stroke 5 Cy. 225 x 300 625kW (850bhp) MAN B&W Diesel A/S-Denmark AuxGen: 2 x 101kW 400V 50Hz a.c
8618891 *3ESB7* -	**SAMO C** *ex* Samothraki *-2008* **Samo Navigation Ltd** Caroil Transport Marine Ltd *Panama* *Panama* MMSI: 370253000 Official number: 3443408	**27,793** 13,451 46,538 T/cm 51.2	Class: LR (GL) **100A1** SS 01/2009 Double Hull oil tanker MARPOL 20.1.3. ESP SPM LI **LMC** **UMS IGS** Eq.Ltr: L†; Cable: 632.5/70.0 U3	**1989-01 Korea Shipbuilding & Engineering Corp — Busan** Yd No: 3035 Loa 183.20 (BB) Br ex 32.23 Dght 12.198 Lbp 174.00 Br md 32.20 Dpth 18.00 Welded, 1 dk	**(A13A2TW) Crude/Oil Products Tanker** Double Hull Liq: 53,587; Liq (Oil): 53,587 Cargo Heating Coils Compartments: 4 Wing Ta, 6 Ta, 2 Wing Slop Ta, ER 4 Cargo Pump (s): 3x1000m³/hr, 1x500m³/hr Manifold: Bow/CM: 91m	**1 oil engine** driving 1 FP propeller Total Power: 6,581kW (8,948hp) 14.6kn B&W 6L60MC 1 x 2 Stroke 6 Cy. 600 x 1944 6581kW (8948bhp) Korea Heavy Industries & ConstrCo Ltd (HANJUNG)-South Korea AuxGen: 2 x 800kW 440V 60Hz a.c, 2 x 600kW 440V 60Hz a.c, 1 x 100kW 440V 60Hz a.c Boilers: 2 TOH (o.f.) 10.1kgf/cm² (9.9bar), e (ex.g.) 7.0kgf/cm² (6.9bar), AuxB (o.f.) 8.2kgf/cm² (8.0bar) Fuel: 154.3 (d.f.) 1052.4 (r.f.) 25.0pd
9082269 - -	**SAMOA** **La Riviera SA** - *Pisco* *Peru* Official number: PS-010415-PM	*266* 107 130		**1993-10 Remesa Astilleros S.A. — Callao** Yd No: 045 Loa - Br ex - Dght - Lbp - Br md - Dpth - Welded	**(B11B2FV) Fishing Vessel**	**1 oil engine** geared to sc. shaft driving 1 FP propeller Total Power: 372kW (506hp) Caterpillar D379TA 1 x Vee 4 Stroke 8 Cy. 159 x 203 372kW (506bhp) Caterpillar Inc-USA
9473157 *9HA2205* -	**SAMOA** **Netfor Ltd** Sea Traders SA *Valletta* *Malta* MMSI: 248147000 Official number: 9473157	**41,342** 25,325 75,506 T/cm 68.2	Class: BV	**2010-01 Jiangnan Shipyard (Group) Co Ltd — Shanghai** Yd No: H2451 Loa 225.00 (BB) Br ex - Dght 14.200 Lbp 217.00 Br md 32.26 Dpth 19.60 Welded, 1 dk	**(A21A2BC) Bulk Carrier** Grain: 90,100 Compartments: 7 Ho, ER 7 Ha: 6 (15.5 x 14.4)ER (14.6 x 13.2)	**1 oil engine** driving 1 FP propeller Total Power: 10,200kW (13,868hp) 14.5kn MAN-B&W 5S60MC 1 x 2 Stroke 5 Cy. 600 x 2292 10200kW (13868bhp) Hudong Heavy Machinery Co Ltd-China AuxGen: 3 x 560kW 60Hz a.c
8897021 *5WCB* -	**SAMOA EXPRESS** *ex* Barge Express *-2001* *ex* Kingfisher Baru *-2000* **Samoa Shipping Corp Ltd** - SatCom: Inmarsat C 456100013 *Apia* *Samoa* MMSI: 561002000 Official number: 0050	**340** 130 416	Class: (LR) (BV) Classed LR until 30/9/09	**1995 Kian Juan Dockyard Sdn Bhd — Miri** Yd No: 83 Loa 42.00 Br ex - Dght 2.200 Lbp 38.72 Br md 9.75 Dpth 2.74 Welded, 1 dk	**(A35D2RL) Landing Craft** Passengers: 60 Bow ramp (centre)	**2 oil engines** reverse reduction geared to sc. shafts driving 2 FP propellers Total Power: 810kW (1,102hp) 9.0kn Caterpillar 3408TA 2 x Vee 4 Stroke 8 Cy. 137 x 152 each-405kW (551bhp) Caterpillar Inc-USA AuxGen: 2 x 48kW 230/415V 50Hz a.c
7115751 *UCQL* -	**SAMOBYTNYY** **Tomarinskiy Port Enterprise** - *Nevelsk* *Russia* Official number: 701194	**172** 40 94	Class: (RS)	**1971 Zavod 'Nikolayevsk-na-Amure' — Nikolayevsk-na-Amure** Yd No: 44 Loa 33.96 Br ex 7.09 Dght 2.899 Lbp - Br md - Dpth 3.69 Welded, 1 dk	**(B11B2FV) Fishing Vessel** Bale: 115 Compartments: 1 Ho, ER 1 Ha: (1.3 x 1.6) Derricks: 2x2t; Winches: 2 Ice Capable	**1 oil engine** driving 1 FP propeller Total Power: 224kW (305hp) 9.5kn S.K.L. 8NVD36-1U 1 x 4 Stroke 8 Cy. 240 x 360 224kW (305bhp) VEB Schwermaschinenbau "KarlLiebknecht" (SKL)-Magdeburg
7936868 *YBZA* -	**SAMODRA 01** **PT Perikanan Samodra Besar** - *Jakarta* *Indonesia*	*111* 45 -		**1973-02 Nichiro Zosen K.K. — Ishinomaki** Yd No: 311 Loa 27.82 Br ex - Dght - Lbp 24.01 Br md 5.91 Dpth 2.54 Welded, 1 dk	**(B11B2FV) Fishing Vessel**	**1 oil engine** driving 1 FP propeller Total Power: 272kW (370hp) Yanmar 6ML-T 1 x 4 Stroke 6 Cy. 200 x 240 272kW (370bhp) Yanmar Diesel Engine Co Ltd-Japan
9486934 *C6YO4* -	**SAMOS** **Hibiya Maritime SA** Samos Steamship Co *Nassau* *Bahamas* MMSI: 311040100 Official number: 8001773	**56,326** 29,819 104,649 T/cm 89.0	Class: LR ✠ **100A1** SS 09/2010 Double Hull oil tanker CSR ESP **ShipRight** (CM) *IWS LI DSPM4 ✠ **LMC** **UMS IGS** Eq.Ltr: T†; Cable: 724.4/87.0 U3 (a)	**2010-09 Sumitomo Heavy Industries Marine & Engineering Co., Ltd. — Yokosuka** Yd No: 1362 Loa 228.60 (BB) Br ex 42.04 Dght 14.800 Lbp 217.80 Br md 42.00 Dpth 21.50 Welded, 1 dk	**(A13A2TW) Crude/Oil Products Tanker** Double Hull (13F) Liq: 98,695; Liq (Oil): 98,695 Cargo Heating Coils Compartments: 10 Wing Ta, 2 Wing Slop Ta, 1 Slop Ta, ER 3 Cargo Pump (s): 3x2500m³/hr Manifold: Bow/CM: 116.6m	**1 oil engine** driving 1 FP propeller Total Power: 12,350kW (16,791hp) 14.8kn MAN-B&W 6S60MC-C 1 x 2 Stroke 6 Cy. 600 x 2400 12350kW (16791bhp) Mitsui Engineering & Shipbuilding CLtd-Japan AuxGen: 3 x 800kW 450V 60Hz a.c Boilers: e (ex.g.) 22.3kgf/cm² (21.9bar), WTAuxB (o.f.) 18.6kgf/cm² (18.2bar) Fuel: 250.0 (d.f.) 2170.0 (r.f.)
7831771 *SW7764* -	**SAMOS FLYING DOLPHIN I** *ex* Delfini III *-1996* *ex* Delfini XX *-1996* *ex* Kometa-46 *-1991* **Arion VD Naftiki Eteria** - *Samos* *Greece* MMSI: 237019900 Official number: 54	**142** 93 14	Class: (HR) (BV) (RS)	**1980 Feodosiyskoye Sudostroitelnoye Obyedineniye "More" — Feodosiya** Loa 35.11 Br ex 9.56 Dght 1.140 Lbp 30.36 Br md 6.00 Dpth 1.81 Welded, 1 dk	**(A37B2PS) Passenger Ship** Hull Material: Aluminium Alloy Passengers: unberthed: 100	**2 oil engines** geared to sc. shafts driving 2 FP propellers Total Power: 1,472kW (2,002hp) 35.0kn Zvezda M401A-1 2 x Vee 4 Stroke 12 Cy. 180 x 200 each-736kW (1001bhp) "Zvezda"-Leningrad
7832335 *SX6726* -	**SAMOS FLYING DOLPHIN III** *ex* Kometa-1 *-1998* **Kos Sea Lines Co** Samos Hydrofoils *Piraeus* *Greece* MMSI: 237026800 Official number: 11233	*142* 92 14	Class: (BV) (RS)	**1980 Zavod im. "Ordzhonikidze" — Poti** Yd No: 874 Loa 35.11 Br ex 11.00 Dght 1.140 Lbp 30.36 Br md 6.00 Dpth 1.81 Welded, 1 dk	**(A37B2PS) Passenger Ship** Hull Material: Aluminium Alloy	**2 oil engines** geared to sc. shafts driving 2 Contra-rotating propellers Total Power: 1,472kW (2,002hp) 31.0kn Zvezda M401A-1 2 x Vee 4 Stroke 12 Cy. 180 x 200 each-736kW (1001bhp) "Zvezda"-Leningrad AuxGen: 2 x 3kW 24V d.c, 1 x 5kW 24V d.c Fuel: 4.0 (d.f.)
9105891 *A8VV2* -	**SAMOS LEGEND** *ex* Peoria *-2010* **Blue Dream Marine Corp** Samos (Island) Maritime Co Ltd *Monrovia* *Liberia* MMSI: 636014673 Official number: 14673	**36,615** 23,344 70,231 T/cm 64.0	Class: NK (NV) (AB)	**1996-01 Sanoyas Hishino Meisho Corp — Kurashiki OY** Yd No: 1129 Loa 225.00 (BB) Br ex - Dght 13.294 Lbp 217.00 Br md 32.26 Dpth 18.30 Welded, 1 dk	**(A21A2BC) Bulk Carrier** Grain: 81,839; Bale: 78,529 Compartments: 7 Ho, ER 7 Ha: (16.7 x 13.4)6 (16.7 x 15.3)ER	**1 oil engine** driving 1 FP propeller Total Power: 7,834kW (10,651hp) 14.0kn Sulzer 7RTA52U 1 x 2 Stroke 7 Cy. 520 x 1800 7834kW (10651bhp) Diesel United Ltd.-Aioi AuxGen: 3 x 420kW 440/220V 60Hz a.c Fuel: 2950.0 29.2pd
8012748 *SY4635* -	**SAMOS SPIRIT** *ex* Holt *-2004* *ex* Anholt *-2003* **Aegean Navigation Maritime Co** - *Samos* *Greece* MMSI: 240166000 Official number: 57	**546** 205 80	Class: (BV)	**1981-05 Dannebrog Vaerft A/S — Aarhus** Yd No: 177 Loa 41.03 Br ex - Dght 2.452 Lbp 36.33 Br md 8.91 Dpth 5.90 Welded, 1 dk	**(A37B2PS) Passenger Ship** Ice Capable	**2 oil engines** geared to sc. shafts driving 2 CP propellers Total Power: 484kW (658hp) 10.8kn Grenaa 6F24 2 x 4 Stroke 6 Cy. 240 x 300 each-242kW (329bhp) A/S Grenaa Motorfabrik-Denmark AuxGen: 2 x 208kW 380/220V 50Hz a.c
8869270 *SW9247* -	**SAMOS STAR** *ex* Saronic Star *-1999* **Fournoi-Ormos Marathikampou Shipping Co** - *Samos* *Greece* MMSI: 237007300 Official number: 55	**245** 110 -	Class: RS	**1993 Derzhavne Vyrobnyche Obednannya Illichivskyi SRZ — Illichivsk** Loa 40.10 Br ex - Dght 1.900 Lbp 35.91 Br md 6.90 Dpth 2.90 Welded, 1 dk	**(A37B2PS) Passenger Ship** Passengers: unberthed: 287	**3 oil engines** geared to sc. shafts driving 3 FP propellers Total Power: 1,266kW (1,721hp) 14.0kn Daewoo 3 x 4 Stroke each-265kW (360bhp) (new engine 1993) Daewoo Heavy Industries & MachineryCo Ltd-South Korea AuxGen: 2 x 52kW a.c Fuel: 9.0
8999556 - -	**SAMOS SUN** *ex* Gramvousa Express *-2004* *ex* Nadya *-1996* **Premier Commuter Services SA** -	**107** 35 -	Class: (HR)	**1978-01 Ilyichyovskiy Sudoremontnyy Zavod im. "50-letiya SSSR" — Ilyichyovsk** Loa 34.10 Br ex 5.30 Dght - Lbp 30.00 Br md - Dpth 2.30 Welded, 1 dk	**(A37B2PS) Passenger Ship**	**2 oil engines** reduction geared to sc. shafts driving 2 FP propellers Total Power: 530kW (720hp) Daewoo L126TIH 2 x 4 Stroke 6 Cy. 123 x 155 each-265kW (360bhp) (new engine 2004) Daewoo Heavy Industries Ltd-South Korea

IMO / Call sign	Name / Owner / Manager / Flag	Tonnage	Class	Builder / Dimensions	Type / Capacity	Machinery
9551727 *7JQQ* -	**SAMPAGUITA DREAM** **Mitsui OSK Lines Ltd (MOL)** Bernhard Schulte Shipmanagement (India) Pvt Ltd *Tokyo* *Japan* MMSI: 432963000 Official number: 142091	**92,155** - 180,694	Class: NK	**2014-02 Tsuneishi Heavy Industries (Cebu) Inc — Balamban** Yd No: SC-181 Loa 291.90 Br ex - Dght 18.068 Lbp 286.90 Br md 45.00 Dpth 24.50 Welded, 1 dk	**(A21A2BC) Bulk Carrier** Grain: 200,998 Compartments: 9 Ho, ER 9 Ha: ER	**1 oil engine** driving 1 FP propeller Total Power: 20,090kW (27,314hp) 14.5kn MAN-B&W 7S65ME-C 1 x 2 Stroke 7 Cy. 650 x 2730 20090kW (27314bhp) Mitsui Engineering & Shipbuilding CLtd-Japan
7391410 *DYET* -	**SAMPAGUITA FERRY 2** *ex* Delsan IV *-1997* *ex* Mariya Savina *-1997* **Sampaguita Shipping Corp** - SatCom: Inmarsat C 454854810 *Zamboanga* *Philippines* MMSI: 548548000 Official number: ZAM2D00343	**4,251** 1,439 1,465	Class: (RS)	**1975-06 Brodogradiliste 'Titovo' — Kraljevica** Yd No: 407 Loa 100.01 (BB) Br ex 16.24 Dght 4.650 Lbp 90.00 Br md 16.21 Dpth 7.01 Welded, 2 dks	**(A37A2PC) Passenger/Cruise** Passengers: unberthed: 56; cabins: 52; berths: 206 Bale: 750 Compartments: 1 Ho, ER 1 Ha: (5.6 x 3.9) Cranes: 1x3.3t Ice Capable	**2 oil engines** driving 2 FP propellers Total Power: 3,884kW (5,280hp) 17.0kn B&W 8-35VF-62 2 x 2 Stroke 8 Cy. 350 x 620 each-1942kW (2640bhp) Tvornica Dizel Motora 'Uljanik'-Yugoslavia
8404874 *ELEH5* -	**SAMPAN** *ex* Tribuno *-2000* **Crown Finance Co** Compania Latinoamericana de Navegacion SA (CLAN SA) SatCom: Inmarsat A 1240163 *Monrovia* *Liberia* MMSI: 636007690 Official number: 7690	**23,609** 14,104 38,476 T/cm 46.1	Class: RI (LR) ✠ Classed LR until 29/2/08	**1985-01 'Georgi Dimitrov' Shipyard — Varna** Yd No: 077 Loa 198.56 (BB) Br ex 27.87 Dght 11.199 Lbp 187.71 Br md 27.81 Dpth 15.60 Welded, 1 dk	**(A21A2BC) Bulk Carrier** Grain: 46,066; Bale: 42,481 Compartments: 7 Ho, ER 7 Ha: (12.8 x 11.2)6 (12.8 x 12.5)ER Cranes: 4x25t Ice Capable	**1 oil engine** driving 1 FP propeller Total Power: 8,504kW (11,562hp) 13.0kn Sulzer 6RND68M 1 x 2 Stroke 6 Cy. 680 x 1250 8504kW (11562bhp) Zaklady Przemyslu Metalowego 'HCegielski' SA-Poznan AuxGen: 3 x 504kW 400V 50Hz a.c Boilers: e 6.9kgf/cm² (6.8bar), AuxB (o.f.) 6.9kgf/cm² (6.8bar) Fuel: 350.0 (d.f.) 1749.5 (r.f.)
8904941 *3EQZ7* -	**SAMPAQUITA** *ex* White Castle *-2003* **Sasanqua Shipping SA** Santoku Senpaku Co Ltd SatCom: Inmarsat A 1333107 *Panama* *Panama* MMSI: 356616000 Official number: 1864389E	**6,557** 3,204 7,129	Class: NK	**1989-10 Shikoku Dockyard Co. Ltd. — Takamatsu** Yd No: 853 Loa 146.02 (BB) Br ex - Dght 7.130 Lbp 138.00 Br md 18.50 Dpth 10.65 Welded, 2 dks	**(A34A2GR) Refrigerated Cargo Ship** Ins: 9,440 TEU 12 incl 12 ref C 4 Ha: 4 (9.1 x 7.5)ER Derricks: 8x5t	**1 oil engine** driving 1 FP propeller Total Power: 6,841kW (9,301hp) 18.2kn B&W 6L50MC 1 x 2 Stroke 6 Cy. 500 x 1620 6841kW (9301bhp) Mitsui Engineering & Shipbuilding CLtd-Japan AuxGen: 3 x 560kW 450V 60Hz a.c Fuel: 970.0 (r.f.)
9405772 *D5DJ8* -	**SAMPATIKI** *ex* Golden Emerald *-2011* *ex* Eugenia *-2008* **Cassiel Maritime SA** Avin International SA *Monrovia* *Liberia* MMSI: 636015901 Official number: 15901	**5,031** 1,681 6,436 T/cm 16.1	Class: AB	**2008-01 Zhenjiang Sopo Shiprepair & Building Co Ltd — Zhenjiang JS** Yd No: SP0504 Loa 100.12 (BB) Br ex - Dght 6.500 Lbp 94.00 Br md 18.00 Dpth 9.60 Welded, 1 dk	**(A12B2TR) Chemical/Products Tanker** Double Hull (13F) Liq: 7,300; Liq (Oil): 7,300 Compartments: 12 Wing Ta, 2 Wing Slop Ta, ER 12 Cargo Pump (s): 12x300m³/hr	**1 oil engine** reduction geared to sc. shaft driving 1 CP propeller Total Power: 2,970kW (4,038hp) 12.0kn MaK 9M25 1 x 4 Stroke 9 Cy. 255 x 400 2970kW (4038bhp) Caterpillar Motoren GmbH & Co. KG-Germany AuxGen: 3 x 500kW a.c Thrusters: 1 Tunnel thruster (f) Fuel: 99.0 (d.f.) 291.0 (r.f.)
5308938 *OIWK* -	**SAMPO** **Kemin Kaupunki (City of Kemi)** - *Kemi* *Finland* MMSI: 230990040 Official number: 10300	**2,630** 789 3,597		**1961-01 Wartsila-Koncernen, Ab Sandvikens Skeppsdocka & MV — Helsinki** Yd No: 368 Converted From: Icebreaker-1988 Loa 74.68 Br ex 17.40 Dght 6.211 Lbp 69.12 Br md 17.38 Dpth - Welded, 2 dks	**(A37B2PS) Passenger Ship** Passengers: unberthed: 150 Ice Capable	**4 diesel electric oil engines** Connecting to 2 elec. motors driving 2 Propellers , 2 fwd Total Power: 5,516kW (7,500hp) Sulzer 5MH51 4 x 2 Stroke 5 Cy. 510 x 550 each-1379kW (1875bhp) Wartsila Koncernen, Ab SandvikensSkeppsdocka & MV-Finland Fuel: 474.5 (d.f.) 29.5pd
9069504 *YD8011* -	**SAMPOERNA 88** *ex* Malindo No. 1 *-2007* **PT Sinar Jaya Wijaya** - *Bitung* *Indonesia*	**193** 58 -	Class: KI	**2000-01 Nga Chai Shipyard Sdn Bhd — Sibu** Loa 26.00 Br ex - Dght 3.090 Lbp 23.30 Br md 8.00 Dpth 3.90 Welded, 1 dk	**(B32A2ST) Tug**	**2 oil engines** driving 2 Propellers Total Power: 1,204kW (1,636hp) Mitsubishi S6R2-MPTK 2 x 4 Stroke 6 Cy. 170 x 220 each-602kW (818bhp) Mitsubishi Heavy Industries Ltd-Japan
9288071 *PHDL* -	**SAMPOGRACHT** **CV Scheepvaartonderneming Kuipersgracht, CV Scheepvaartonderneming Poolgracht & CV Scheepvaartondeneming Parkgracht** Spliethoff's Bevrachtingskantoor BV *Amsterdam* *Netherlands* MMSI: 246396000 Official number: 42280	**18,321** 7,647 23,688	Class: LR ✠ **100A1** SS 07/2010 strengthened for heavy cargoes, container cargoes in holds and on upper deck hatch covers timber deck cargoes, *IWS LI Ice Class 1A FS at draught of 10.832m Max/min draught fwd 11.47/4.22m Max/min draught aft 11.47/6.60m Power required 4492kw, installed 12060kw ✠ **LMC** **UMS** Eq.Ltr: I†; Cable: 616.4/64.0 U3 (a)	**2005-07 Stocznia Szczecinska Nowa Sp z oo — Szczecin** Yd No: B587/IV/8 Loa 185.40 (BB) Br ex 25.66 Dght 10.600 Lbp 173.50 Br md 25.30 Dpth 14.60 Welded, 1 dk	**(A31A2GX) General Cargo Ship** Grain: 27,600 TEU 1291 C Ho 555 TEU C Dk 736 TEU incl 120 ref C. Compartments: 3 Ho, ER 3 Ha: ER Cranes: 3x120t Ice Capable	**1 oil engine** with flexible couplings & sr geared to sc. shaft driving 1 CP propeller Total Power: 12,060kW (16,397hp) 19.1kn Wartsila 6L64 1 x 4 Stroke 6 Cy. 640 x 900 12060kW (16397bhp) Wartsila Italia SpA-Italy AuxGen: 3 x 450kW 445V 60Hz a.c, 1 x 1000kW 445V 60Hz a.c Boilers: TOH (o.f.) 10.2kgf/cm² (10.0bar), TOH (ex.g.) 10.2kgf/cm² (10.0bar) Thrusters: 1 Thwart. CP thruster (f)
9429455 *HP6245* -	**SAMPSON** **CVI Global Lux Oil & Gas 4 Sarl** Coastline Maritime Pte Ltd *Panama* *Panama* MMSI: 353376000 Official number: 4170610B	**28,632** 8,589 20,971	Class: AB	**2010-06 PT Drydocks World Pertama — Batam** Yd No: 191 Loa 180.00 (BB) Br ex - Dght 7.500 Lbp 168.00 Br md 32.00 Dpth 12.00 Welded, 1 dk	**(B22A2OR) Offshore Support Vessel** Cranes: 1x1600t,1x100t	**8 oil engines** driving 3 Directional propellers Total Power: 20,200kW (27,464hp) 12.0kn Caterpillar 3516C 8 x Vee 4 Stroke 16 Cy. 170 x 215 each-2525kW (3433bhp) Caterpillar Inc-USA Thrusters: 2 Tunnel thruster (f); 2 Retract. directional thruster (f) Fuel: 4259.0 (r.f.)
9176656 *VVFI* -	**SAMPURNA SWARAJYA** **The Shipping Corporation of India Ltd (SCI)** - SatCom: Inmarsat B 341904610 *Mumbai* *India* MMSI: 419213000 Official number: 2739	**21,827** 8,330 32,950 T/cm 40.0	Class: IR (BV)	**1999-01 Hyundai Heavy Industries Co Ltd — Ulsan** Yd No: 1104 Loa 172.95 (BB) Br ex 25.90 Dght 11.300 Lbp 166.40 Br md 25.87 Dpth 17.50 Welded, 1 dk	**(A13B2TP) Products Tanker** Double Hull (13F) Liq: 37,706; Liq (Oil): 37,706 Cargo Heating Coils Compartments: 12 Wing Ta, 2 Wing Slop Ta, ER	**1 oil engine** driving 1 FP propeller Total Power: 6,634kW (9,020hp) 14.0kn MAN-B&W 5S50MC 1 x 2 Stroke 5 Cy. 500 x 1910 6634kW (9020bhp) Hyundai Heavy Industries Co Ltd-South Korea AuxGen: 3 x 650kW 450V 60Hz a.c Fuel: 219.0 (d.f.) 1075.0 (r.f.)
9331141 *5AXG* -	**SAMRAA ALKHALEEJ** *ex* Spike *-2009* **Philadelphia Navigation Ltd** Executive Ship Management Pte Ltd SatCom: Inmarsat Mini-M 764945685 *Misratah* *Libya* MMSI: 642122021	**61,348** 35,445 114,858 T/cm 99.0	Class: NV	**2006-07 Samsung Heavy Industries Co Ltd — Geoje** Yd No: 1592 Loa 248.99 (BB) Br ex 43.84 Dght 14.940 Lbp 240.70 Br md 43.80 Dpth 21.30 Welded, 1 dk	**(A13A2TV) Crude Oil Tanker** Double Hull (13F) Liq: 123,859; Liq (Oil): 123,970 Cargo Heating Coils Compartments: 12 Wing Ta, 2 Wing Slop Ta, ER 3 Cargo Pump (s): 3x2800m³/hr Manifold: Bow/CM: 125.3m Ice Capable	**1 oil engine** driving 1 FP propeller Total Power: 15,820kW (21,509hp) 14.6kn MAN-B&W 7S60MC-C 1 x 2 Stroke 7 Cy. 600 x 2400 15820kW (21509bhp) Doosan Engine Co Ltd-South Korea AuxGen: 3 x a.c Fuel: 270.0 (d.f.) 3400.0 (r.f.)
8001127 - -	**SAMRIYAH** *ex* Al-Mojil XXII *-1995* *ex* Samriyah *-1994* **Marine Fleets Inc** Midgulf Offshore Ship Chartering LLC	**320** 96 290	Class: (LR) ✠ Classed LR until 20/6/09	**1980-08 Sing Koon Seng Pte Ltd — Singapore** Yd No: SKS539 Loa 34.40 Br ex 9.78 Dght 3.201 Lbp 31.15 Br md 9.00 Dpth 3.61 Welded, 1 dk	**(B34L2QU) Utility Vessel** Cranes: 1x7t	**2 oil engines** reverse reduction geared to sc. shafts driving 2 FP propellers Total Power: 764kW (1,038hp) Kelvin TBSC8 2 x 4 Stroke 8 Cy. 165 x 184 each-382kW (519bhp) GEC Diesels Ltd.Kelvin Marine Div.-Glasgow AuxGen: 2 x 56kW 380V 50Hz a.c Fuel: 150.0
7911777 *J8B4883* -	**SAMRIYAH** *ex* AOS Venus *-2013* *ex* Al Mojil Xxxi *-2013* *ex* Astro Mero *-1993* **MGM Offshore Ltd** Midgulf Offshore Ship Chartering LLC *Kingstown* *St Vincent & The Grenadines* MMSI: 376987000 Official number: 11356	**808** 242 550	Class: BV (AB)	**1983-07 Maclaren IC Estaleiros e Servicos S.A. — Niteroi** Yd No: 259 Loa 54.87 Br ex - Dght 4.003 Lbp 51.99 Br md 11.61 Dpth 4.63 Welded, 1 dk	**(B21A2OS) Platform Supply Ship**	**2 oil engines** reverse reduction geared to sc. shafts driving 2 FP propellers Total Power: 1,824kW (2,480hp) 12.0kn Alpha 8V23LU 2 x Vee 4 Stroke 8 Cy. 225 x 300 each-912kW (1240bhp) Equipamentos Villares SA-Brazil AuxGen: 2 x 128kW Thrusters: 1 Thwart. FP thruster (f)

IMO / Call sign	Name / Owner / Manager / Flag	Tonnage	Class	Build / Dimensions	Type / Capacity	Machinery
9271963 *5BYT3* -	**SAMSKIP AKRAFELL** *ex Asian Carrier -2013 ex Asian Favour -2008* **Naveco BV** Q-Shipping BV *Limassol* *Cyprus* MMSI: 212201000	**4,450** 2,141 5,565	Class: GL	**2003-09 Jinling Shipyard — Nanjing JS** Yd No: 98-0106 Loa 99.95 (BB) Br ex - Dght 6.654 Lbp 95.80 Br md 18.80 Dpth 8.40 Welded, 1 dk	**(A31A2GX) General Cargo Ship** Double Bottom Entire Compartment Length Grain: 7,177 TEU 511 C Ho 117 TEU C Dk 394 TEU incl 84 ref C Cranes: 2x40t Ice Capable	**1 oil engine** geared to sc. shaft driving 1 CP propeller Total Power: 4,320kW (5,873hp) 15.5kn MAN 9L32/40 1 x 4 Stroke 9 Cy. 320 x 400 4320kW (5873bhp) MAN B&W Diesel AG-Augsburg AuxGen: 2 x 570kW 440/220V a.c, 1 x 700kW 440/220V a.c Thrusters: 1 Tunnel thruster (f)
9322578 *V2BT6* -	**SAMSKIP COURIER** **ms 'Swipall' J Kahrs Schiffahrts GmbH & Co KG** J Kahrs Bereederungs GmbH & Co KG SatCom: Inmarsat C 430492310 *Saint John's* *Antigua & Barbuda* MMSI: 304923000 Official number: 4119	**7,852** 3,363 9,340 T/cm 24.6	Class: BV (GL)	**2006-05 B.V. Scheepswerf Damen Hoogezand — Foxhol** Yd No: 857 **2006-05 Santierul Naval Damen Galati S.A. — Galati** (Hull) Yd No: 1065 Loa 140.64 (BB) Br ex 22.00 Dght 7.327 Lbp 130.00 Br md 21.80 Dpth 9.50 Welded, 1 dk	**(A33A2CC) Container Ship (Fully Cellular)** TEU 804 C Ho 206 TEU C Dk 598 TEU incl 180 ref C. Ice Capable	**1 oil engine** geared to sc. shaft driving 1 CP propeller Total Power: 8,400kW (11,421hp) 18.0kn MaK 9M43 1 x 4 Stroke 9 Cy. 430 x 610 8400kW (11421bhp) Caterpillar Motoren GmbH & Co. KG-Germany AuxGen: 2 x 424kW 60Hz a.c, 1 x 1600kW 60Hz a.c Thrusters: 1 Tunnel thruster (f); 1 Tunnel thruster (a)
9436290 *5BEY3* -	**SAMSKIP ENDEAVOUR** *ex Jens M -2011* **Samskip Endeavour BV** Q-Shipping BV SatCom: Inmarsat C 420938010 *Limassol* *Cyprus* MMSI: 209380000 Official number: 9436290	**7,852** 3,363 9,315 T/cm 24.6	Class: GL	**2011-02 Santierul Naval Damen Galati S.A. — Galati** (Hull) Yd No: 1150 **2011-02 B.V. Scheepswerf Damen — Gorinchem** Yd No: 568308 Loa 140.62 (BB) Br ex - Dght 7.335 Lbp 130.00 Br md 21.80 Dpth 9.50 Welded, 1 dk	**(A33A2CC) Container Ship (Fully Cellular)** TEU 812 C Ho 206 TEU C Dk 606 TEU incl 210 ref C. Ice Capable	**1 oil engine** reduction geared to sc. shaft driving 1 CP propeller Total Power: 8,400kW (11,421hp) 18.0kn MaK 9M43C 1 x 4 Stroke 9 Cy. 430 x 610 8400kW (11421bhp) Caterpillar Motoren GmbH & Co. KG-Germany AuxGen: 1 x 1600kW 440V a.c, 2 x 432kW 440V a.c Thrusters: 1 Tunnel thruster (f); 1 Tunnel thruster (a)
9323479 *V2BZ8* -	**SAMSKIP EXPRESS** **ms 'Skyndir' J Kahrs Schiffahrts GmbH & Co KG** J Kahrs Bereederungs GmbH & Co KG SatCom: Inmarsat C 430495510 *Saint John's* *Antigua & Barbuda* MMSI: 304965000	**7,852** 3,363 9,313 T/cm 24.6	Class: BV (GL)	**2006-08 B.V. Scheepswerf Damen Hoogezand — Foxhol** Yd No: 859 **2006-08 Santierul Naval Damen Galati S.A. — Galati** (Hull) Yd No: 1071 Loa 140.64 (BB) Br ex 22.00 Dght 7.330 Lbp 130.00 Br md 21.80 Dpth 9.50 Welded, 1 dk	**(A33A2CC) Container Ship (Fully Cellular)** Double Bottom Entire Compartment Length TEU 803 C Ho 206 TEU C Dk 597 TEU incl 180 ref C. Ice Capable	**1 oil engine** geared to sc. shaft driving 1 CP propeller Total Power: 8,400kW (11,421hp) 18.0kn MaK 9M43C 1 x 4 Stroke 9 Cy. 430 x 610 8400kW (11421bhp) Caterpillar Motoren GmbH & Co. KG-Germany AuxGen: 1 x 1600kW 440/230V 60Hz a.c, 2 x 424kW 440/230V 60Hz a.c Thrusters: 1 Thwart. CP thruster (f); 1 Thwart. CP thruster (a) Fuel: 105.0 (d.f.) 880.0 (r.f.)
9436214 *5BEX3* -	**SAMSKIP INNOVATOR** *launched as Marita M -2011* **Samskip Innovator BV** Meyering Bereederungs GmbH & Co KG SatCom: Inmarsat C 420936110 *Limassol* *Cyprus* MMSI: 209361000 Official number: 9436214	**7,852** 3,285 9,350 T/cm 24.6	Class: GL	**2011-01 Santierul Naval Damen Galati S.A. — Galati** (Hull) Yd No: 1149 **2011-01 B.V. Scheepswerf Damen — Gorinchem** Yd No: 568307 Loa 140.61 (BB) Br ex - Dght 7.335 Lbp 130.00 Br md 21.80 Dpth 9.50 Welded, 1 dk	**(A33A2CC) Container Ship (Fully Cellular)** TEU 803 C Ho 206 TEU C Dk 597 TEU incl 210 ref C. Ice Capable	**1 oil engine** reduction geared to sc. shaft driving 1 CP propeller Total Power: 8,400kW (11,421hp) 18.0kn MaK 9M43C 1 x 4 Stroke 9 Cy. 430 x 610 8400kW (11421bhp) Caterpillar Motoren GmbH & Co. KG-Germany AuxGen: 1 x 1600kW 440V a.c, 2 x 430kW 440V a.c Thrusters: 1 Tunnel thruster (f); 1 Tunnel thruster (a)
9652686 - -	**SAMSON** **Tuapse Commercial Sea Port (A/O 'Tuapsinskiy Morskoy Torgovyy Port')** - *Tuapse* *Russia* MMSI: 273359670	**186** 52 94	Class: RS (BV)	**2012-07 Song Cam Shipyard — Haiphong** (Hull) Yd No: (509849) **2012-07 B.V. Scheepswerf Damen — Gorinchem** Yd No: 509849 Loa 26.16 Br ex 8.54 Dght 3.200 Lbp 25.52 Br md 7.94 Dpth 4.07 Welded, 1 dk	**(B32A2ST) Tug**	**2 oil engines** reduction geared to sc. shafts driving 2 FP propellers Total Power: 3,530kW (4,800hp) Caterpillar 3512C 2 x Vee 4 Stroke 12 Cy. 170 x 215 each-1765kW (2400bhp) Caterpillar Inc-USA AuxGen: 2 x 51kW a.c Fuel: 63.0 (d.f.)
7827172 *WCW5544* -	**SAMSON** *ex H. O. S. Samson -2011* *ex Point Samson -1990* **Point Marine LLC** Tidewater Marine LLC *New Orleans, LA* *United States of America* Official number: 613844	*293* 199 1,200	Class: AB	**1979-10 Halter Marine, Inc. — Moss Point, Ms** Yd No: 810 Loa - Br ex - Dght 3.664 Lbp 54.89 Br md 12.20 Dpth 4.27 Welded, 1 dk	**(B21B20A) Anchor Handling Tug Supply** Ice Capable	**2 oil engines** reverse reduction geared to sc. shafts driving 2 FP propellers Total Power: 2,942kW (4,000hp) 12.0kn EMD (Electro-Motive) 16-645-E6 2 x Vee 2 Stroke 16 Cy. 230 x 254 each-1471kW (2000bhp) (Re-engined ,made 1971, Reconditioned & fitted 1979) General Motors Corp.Electro-Motive Div.-La Grange AuxGen: 2 x 98kW Thrusters: 1 Thwart. FP thruster (f)
8100129 *CB9975* -	**SAMSON** *ex Susan K -2005 ex Nautilus -1994* *ex Svea Atlantic -1993 ex Herborg -1988* *ex Carimed Sea -1987 ex Naz -1985* *ex Herborg -1985* **Danvi Ship SA** - *Valparaiso* *Chile* MMSI: 725004360 Official number: 3219	**1,510** 796 2,166	Class: (LR) (RS) (BV) ✠ Classed LR until 28/4/02	**1982-11 A/S Nordsovaerftet — Ringkobing** Yd No: 158 Loa 72.45 Br ex 11.36 Dght 4.530 Lbp 68.28 Br md 11.21 Dpth 6.71 Welded, 2 dks	**(A31A2GX) General Cargo Ship** Grain: 3,403; Bale: 3,048 TEU 54 C. 54/20' (40') Compartments: 2 Ho, ER, 2 Tw Dk 2 Ha: 2 (18.7 x 8.0)ER Derricks: 2x15t; Winches: 2 Ice Capable	**1 oil engine** with clutches, flexible couplings & sr geared to sc. shaft driving 1 CP propeller Total Power: 800kW (1,088hp) 11.0kn Alpha 7T23L-KVO 1 x 4 Stroke 7 Cy. 225 x 300 800kW (1088bhp) B&W Alpha Diesel A/S-Denmark AuxGen: 2 x 84kW 380V 50Hz a.c, 1 x 72kW 380V 50Hz a.c, 1 x 40kW 380V 50Hz a.c Fuel: 26.5 (d.f.) 4.0pd
8227525 *WDD7155* -	**SAMSON** **Seabulk Towing Services Inc** Seabulk Towing Inc *Houston, TX* *United States of America* MMSI: 367182630 Official number: 630017	*182* 124 -		**1980 Delta Shipyard — Houma, La** Yd No: 128 Loa - Br ex - Dght 3.582 Lbp 31.40 Br md 9.15 Dpth 4.47 Welded, 1 dk	**(B32A2ST) Tug**	**2 oil engines** reduction geared to sc. shafts driving 2 FP propellers Total Power: 2,868kW (3,900hp) EMD (Electro-Motive) 16-645-E2 2 x Vee 2 Stroke 16 Cy. 230 x 254 each-1434kW (1950bhp) in the United States of America
7636901 *A9D2568* -	**SAMSON** *ex Evelynn -1998 ex Swaabie -1996* **Al Jazeera Shipping Co** Al Jazeera Shipping Co WLL (AJS) *Bahrain* *Bahrain* MMSI: 408718000 Official number: BN 2086	**439** 131 213	Class: BV (LR) ✠ Classed LR until 5/7/03	**1978-09 Hall, Russell & Co. Ltd. — Aberdeen** Yd No: 977 Loa 37.98 Br ex 10.55 Dght 4.230 Lbp 32.92 Br md 10.01 Dpth 5.24 Welded, 1 dk	**(B32A2ST) Tug**	**2 oil engines** sr geared to sc. shafts driving 2 CP propellers Total Power: 2,794kW (3,798hp) Ruston 12RKCM 2 x Vee 4 Stroke 12 Cy. 254 x 305 each-1397kW (1899bhp) Ruston Diesels Ltd.-Newton-le-Willows AuxGen: 2 x 80kW 440V 50Hz a.c, 1 x 78kW 440V 50Hz a.c Thrusters: 1 Thwart. FP thruster (f) Fuel: 130.0 (d.f.)
9550955 *9V1253* -	**SAMSON 7** *ex Zumaia Septimo -2012 ex Armada 42 -2009* **Samson Maritime Pte Ltd** Samson Maritime Holdings Pty Ltd (Samson Express Offshore) *Singapore* *Singapore* MMSI: 566568000 Official number: 397874	**290** 87 150	Class: BV (RI)	**2009-09 Astilleros y Varaderos Armada SA — Vigo** Yd No: 42 Loa 25.99 Br ex - Dght 2.570 Lbp 24.00 Br md 11.50 Dpth 3.50 Welded, 1 dk	**(B32A2ST) Tug** Cranes: 1x13.7t,1x10t	**3 oil engines** reduction geared to sc. shafts driving 3 FP propellers Total Power: 1,830kW (2,487hp) Yanmar 6AYM-ETE 3 x 4 Stroke 6 Cy. 155 x 180 each-610kW (829bhp) Yanmar Diesel Engine Co Ltd-Japan AuxGen: 2 x 100kW 400/230V 50Hz a.c Thrusters: 1 Water jet (f) Fuel: 120.0 (d.f.)
9375094 *HP4783* -	**SAMSON 101** *ex Swissco 101 -2009* **Stardazz Pte Ltd** - *Panama* *Panama* Official number: 4428112	**218** 66 -	Class: GL	**2005-11 Singapore Marine Logistic Pte Ltd — Singapore** Yd No: 55 Loa 26.00 Br ex - Dght 2.377 Lbp - Br md 11.00 Dpth 3.25 Welded, 1 dk	**(B34T2QR) Work/Repair Vessel** Cranes: 1x9.5t	**2 oil engines** reduction geared to sc. shafts driving 2 FP propellers Total Power: 1,060kW (1,442hp) Caterpillar 3412C 2 x Vee 4 Stroke 12 Cy. 137 x 152 each-530kW (721bhp) Caterpillar Inc-USA AuxGen: 2 x 69kW 415V 50Hz a.c Fuel: 150.0 (d.f.)
8322325 *VNW5532* -	**SAMSON EXPLORER** *ex Philanderer III -1999* **DSL Marine Holdings Pty Ltd** Bhagwan Marine Pty Ltd *Dampier, WA* *Australia* MMSI: 503096000 Official number: 851556	*341* 110 100	Class: AB	**1984-12 Eglo Engineering Pty Ltd — Port Adelaide SA** Yd No: EG01 Converted From: Ferry (Passenger/Vehicle)-2004 Loa 35.01 Br ex 13.21 Dght 1.866 Lbp 33.86 Br md 13.01 Dpth 3.81 Welded, 1 dk	**(B34L2QU) Utility Vessel**	**2 oil engines** reduction geared to sc. shafts driving 2 FP propellers Total Power: 882kW (1,200hp) Cummins KT-19-M3 1 x 4 Stroke 6 Cy. 159 x 159 441kW (600bhp) (new engine 2004) Cummins Engine Co Inc-USA Cummins KTA-19-M3 1 x 4 Stroke 6 Cy. 159 x 159 441kW (600bhp) (new engine 2004) Cummins Engine Co Inc-USA AuxGen: 2 x 212kW a.c Thrusters: 1 Tunnel thruster (f)

7042851 *WCN3586* -	**SAMSON MARINER** *ex* Allie B *-1990* *ex* Mister B. *-1989* *ex* Captain Carl *-1988* **Samson Tug & Barge Co Inc** - *Sitka, AK* *United States of America* MMSI: 303496000 Official number: 527248	*158* 107 -		**1970 Halter Marine Services, Inc. — Lockport, La** Yd No: 245 Loa 30.48 Br ex 8.92 Dght 3.737 Lbp 28.61 Br md 8.77 Dpth 4.40 Welded, 1 dk	**(B32A2ST) Tug**	**2 oil engines** driving 2 FP propellers Total Power: 1,250kW (1,700hp) Caterpillar D398B 2 x Vee 4 Stroke 12 Cy. 153 x 203 each-625kW (850bhp) Caterpillar Tractor Co-USA AuxGen: 2 x 60kW 480V 60Hz a.c
9087001 *HP4485* -	**SAMSON MARINER** *ex* Marineco Rakshaa *-2008* *ex* Smit Bison *-2004* *ex* D. H. Alpha *-2003* **Stardazz Pte Ltd** - *Panama* *Panama* MMSI: 373512000 Official number: 4427712	**158** 48 100	Class: BV GL	**1994-01 B.V. Scheepswerf Damen Bergum — Bergum** Yd No: 9930 Loa 23.30 Br ex - Dght 2.300 Lbp 21.79 Br md 9.65 Dpth 2.75 Welded, 1 dk	**(B32A2ST) Tug** Cranes: 1x6.5t	**2 oil engines** with flexible couplings & sr reverse geared to sc. shafts driving 2 FP propellers Total Power: 864kW (1,174hp) 8.8kn Cummins KTA-19-M 2 x 4 Stroke 6 Cy. 159 x 159 each-432kW (587bhp) Cummins Engine Co Inc-USA AuxGen: 2 x 48kW 380/220V a.c Fuel: 61.0 (d.f.)
9541227 *HO7966* -	**SAMSON SUPPLIER** - **Stardazz Pte Ltd** - SatCom: Inmarsat C 450303714 *Panama* *Panama* MMSI: 355127000 Official number: 4201510B	**273** 71 82	Class: BV (AB)	**2009-12 Strategic Marine (S) Pte Ltd — Singapore** Yd No: H160 Loa 40.36 Br ex - Dght 1.580 Lbp 36.38 Br md 7.50 Dpth 3.23 Welded, 1 dk	**(B21A2OC) Crew/Supply Vessel** Hull Material: Aluminium Alloy Passengers: 50	**3 oil engines** reduction geared to sc. shafts driving 3 FP propellers Total Power: 3,354kW (4,561hp) 26.0kn Cummins KTA-38-M2 2 x Vee 4 Stroke 12 Cy. 159 x 159 each-1006kW (1368bhp) Cummins Engine Co Inc-USA Cummins KTA-50-M2 1 x Vee 4 Stroke 16 Cy. 159 x 159 1342kW (1825bhp) Cummins Engine Co Inc-USA AuxGen: 2 x 80kW 60Hz a.c Thrusters: 2 Tunnel thruster (f) Fuel: 44.0 (d.f.)
9541215 *HO7802* -	**SAMSON SUPPORTER** - **Stardazz Pte Ltd** - *Panama* *Panama* MMSI: 357998000 Official number: 4200710B	**237** 71 83	Class: BV (AB)	**2009-07 Strategic Marine (S) Pte Ltd — Singapore** Yd No: H159 Loa 40.37 Br ex - Dght 1.548 Lbp 36.38 Br md 7.50 Dpth 3.23 Welded, 1 dk	**(B21A2OC) Crew/Supply Vessel** Hull Material: Aluminium Alloy Passengers: 50	**3 oil engines** reduction geared to sc. shafts driving 3 FP propellers Total Power: 3,354kW (4,561hp) 26.0kn Cummins KTA-38-M2 2 x Vee 4 Stroke 12 Cy. 159 x 159 each-1006kW (1368bhp) Cummins Engine Co Inc-USA Cummins KTA-50-M2 1 x Vee 4 Stroke 16 Cy. 159 x 159 1342kW (1825bhp) Cummins Engine Co Inc-USA AuxGen: 2 x 80kW 60Hz a.c Thrusters: 2 Tunnel thruster (f) Fuel: 43.0 (d.f.)
9452878 *HP5018* -	**SAMSON VI** *ex* Zumaia Sexto *-2011* **Stardazz Pte Ltd** Miclyn Express Offshore Pte Ltd *Panama* *Panama* MMSI: 373536000 Official number: 4427512	**248** 74 -	Class: GL (RI)	**2008-04 Astilleros y Varaderos Armada SA — Vigo** Yd No: 39 Loa 24.99 Br ex - Dght 2.520 Lbp 23.83 Br md 11.50 Dpth 3.50 Welded, 1 dk	**(B32A2ST) Tug** Cranes: 1x10t,1x6t	**3 oil engines** reduction geared to sc. shafts driving 3 FP propellers Total Power: 1,653kW (2,247hp) Iveco Aifo VECTOR 750 3 x Vee 4 Stroke 8 Cy. 145 x 152 each-551kW (749bhp) Iveco Pegaso-Madrid AuxGen: 2 x 100kW 400/230V 50Hz a.c Thrusters: 1 Tunnel thruster (f) Fuel: 120.0 (d.f.)
9657777 *9HA3158* -	**SAMSUN** *ex* Yangzhou Dayang Dy4035 *-2013* **Samsun Maritime Ltd** Ciner Gemi Acente Isletmeleri Sanayi ve Ticaret AS (Ciner Ship Management) *Valletta* *Malta* MMSI: 229220000 Official number: 9657777	**35,812** 21,224 63,500 T/cm 62.1	Class: AB (BV)	**2013-05 Yangzhou Dayang Shipbuilding Co Ltd — Yangzhou JS** Yd No: DY4035 Loa 199.99 (BB) Br ex - Dght 13.300 Lbp 193.74 Br md 32.26 Dpth 18.50 Welded, 1 dk	**(A21A2BC) Bulk Carrier** Grain: 77,493; Bale: 75,555 Compartments: 5 Ho, ER 5 Ha: 4 (22.1 x 18.6)ER (14.8 x 17.0) Cranes: 4x36t	**1 oil engine** driving 1 FP propeller Total Power: 8,300kW (11,285hp) 14.5kn MAN-B&W 5S60ME-C8 1 x 2 Stroke 5 Cy. 600 x 2400 8300kW (11285bhp) Doosan Engine Co Ltd-South Korea AuxGen: 3 x 610kW a.c Fuel: 210.0 (d.f.) 2130.0 (r.f.)
7615684 *TCSL* -	**SAMSUN** - **Denizciler Turizm ve Denizcilik AS** - *Istanbul* *Turkey* MMSI: 271000160 Official number: 5376	**10,870** 4,100 1,788	Class: NV	**1985-06 Stocznia Szczecinska im A Warskiego — Szczecin** Yd No: B490/04 Loa 127.59 (BB) Br ex 19.46 Dght 5.420 Lbp 120.02 Br md 19.41 Dpth 7.29 Welded, 5 dks	**(A36A2PR) Passenger/Ro-Ro Ship (Vehicles)** Passengers: unberthed: 122; cabins: 137; berths: 388 Bow door & ramp Stern door/ramp Side door/ramp (p) Side door/ramp (s) Lane-Len: 470 Cars: 214 Ice Capable	**4 oil engines** sr geared to sc. shafts driving 2 CP propellers Total Power: 12,356kW (16,800hp) 17.0kn Sulzer 6ZL40/48 4 x 4 Stroke 6 Cy. 400 x 480 each-3089kW (4200bhp) Zaklady Urzadzen Technicznych'Zgoda' SA-Poland AuxGen: 4 x 1000kW 380V 50Hz a.c, 2 x 880kW 380V 50Hz a.c Thrusters: 2 Thwart. CP thruster (f) Fuel: 80.0 (d.f.) 449.0 (r.f.) 60.0pd
8031500 *D7UA* -	**SAMSUNG NO. 1** *ex* Dae Yong No. 91 *-2000* *ex* Do Nam No. 11 *-1991* *ex* Lucky Star *-1987* *ex* Nam Jung No. 1 *-1981* - - *South Korea* MMSI: 440112500	*1,996* 1,202 3,217	Class: (KR)	**1980-10 ShinA Shipbuilding Co Ltd — Tongyeong** Yd No: 233 Loa 88.19 Br ex - Dght 5.334 Lbp 81.51 Br md 13.01 Dpth 6.51 Welded, 1 dk	**(A31A2GX) General Cargo Ship** Grain: 4,055; Bale: 3,971 3 Ha: (16.5 x 8.0)2 (26.5 x 8.0) Derricks: 1x20t,2x15t	**1 oil engine** driving 1 FP propeller Total Power: 1,692kW (2,300hp) 13.8kn Hanshin 6LUS38 1 x 4 Stroke 6 Cy. 380 x 580 1692kW (2300bhp) Ssangyong Heavy Industries Co Ltd-South Korea AuxGen: 2 x 120kW 445V a.c
7831264 *D8FA* -	**SAMSUNG T-1** *ex* Tristar *-2005* **Samsung Heavy Industries Co Ltd** - *Geoje* *South Korea* Official number: JPR-784987	*198* 43 56	Class: KR	**1978-12 Samsung Shipbuilding Co Ltd — Geoje** Yd No: FS01 Loa 31.73 Br ex - Dght - Lbp 26.50 Br md 8.60 Dpth 3.51 Welded, 1 dk	**(B32A2ST) Tug**	**2 oil engines** driving 2 FP propellers Total Power: 1,912kW (2,600hp) 13.0kn Daihatsu 6DSM-26 2 x 4 Stroke 6 Cy. 260 x 320 each-956kW (1300bhp) Daihatsu Diesel Manufacturing Co Lt-Japan AuxGen: 3 x 34kW 445V a.c
8877411 - -	**SAMSUNG T-2** - **Samsung Heavy Industries Co Ltd** - *Geoje* *South Korea* MMSI: 440101368 Official number: JPR-947160	**167** - 95	Class: KR	**1994-10 Dae Sun Shipbuilding & Engineering Co Ltd — Busan** Yd No: 410 Loa 31.98 Br ex - Dght - Lbp 26.91 Br md 8.80 Dpth 3.80 Welded, 1 dk	**(B32A2ST) Tug**	**2 oil engines** reduction geared to sc. shafts driving 2 FP propellers Total Power: 2,354kW (3,200hp) 12.7kn Pielstick 6PA5L255 2 x 4 Stroke 6 Cy. 255 x 270 each-1177kW (1600bhp) Ssangyong Heavy Industries Co Ltd-South Korea AuxGen: 2 x 104kW 445V a.c Fuel: 42.0
9108714 *DSDQ* -	**SAMSUNG T-3** - **Samsung Heavy Industries Co Ltd** - *Geoje* *South Korea* Official number: JPR-947184	**167** - 83	Class: KR	**1994-12 ShinA Shipbuilding Co Ltd — Tongyeong** Yd No: 373 Loa - Br ex - Dght - Lbp - Br md - Dpth - Welded, 1 dk	**(B32A2ST) Tug**	**2 oil engines** driving 2 FP propellers Total Power: 2,354kW (3,200hp) Pielstick 6PA5L255 2 x 4 Stroke 6 Cy. 255 x 270 each-1177kW (1600bhp) Ssangyong Heavy Industries Co Ltd-South Korea
9140889 *DSEE7* -	**SAMSUNG T-5** - **Samsung C & T Corp** Samsung Heavy Industries Co Ltd *Geoje* *South Korea* Official number: JPR-957174	**453** 135 311	Class: KR	**1995-12 Dae Sun Shipbuilding & Engineering Co Ltd — Busan** Yd No: 420 Loa 39.62 Br ex - Dght 4.012 Lbp 33.50 Br md 10.00 Dpth 4.60 Welded, 1 dk	**(B32A2ST) Tug**	**2 oil engines** driving 2 FP propellers Total Power: 3,530kW (4,800hp) Pielstick 8PA5L 2 x 4 Stroke 8 Cy. 255 x 270 each-1765kW (2400bhp) Ssangyong Heavy Industries Co Ltd-South Korea
9307683 - -	**SAMSUNG T-6** - **Samsung Heavy Industries Co Ltd** - *Geoje* *South Korea* Official number: JPR-037641	**250** - -	Class: KR	**2003-11 Samkwang Shipbuilding & Engineering Co Ltd — Incheon** Yd No: 02-10 Loa 36.00 Br ex - Dght 3.300 Lbp 30.00 Br md 10.00 Dpth 4.50 Welded, 1 dk	**(B32A2ST) Tug**	**2 oil engines** geared to sc. shafts driving 2 Propellers Total Power: 3,090kW (4,202hp) Yanmar 6N260M-GV 2 x 4 Stroke 6 Cy. 260 x 360 each-1545kW (2101bhp) Yanmar Diesel Engine Co Ltd-Japan
9310173 - -	**SAMSUNG T-7** - **Samsung Heavy Industries Co Ltd** - *Geoje* *South Korea* Official number: JPR-037659	**199** - -	Class: KR	**2003-12 Samkwang Shipbuilding & Engineering Co Ltd — Incheon** Yd No: 02-11 Loa 34.00 Br ex - Dght 3.100 Lbp 28.50 Br md 9.40 Dpth 4.20 Welded, 1 dk	**(B32A2ST) Tug**	**2 oil engines** geared to sc. shafts driving 2 Propellers Total Power: 2,648kW (3,600hp) Yanmar 6N260M-GV 2 x 4 Stroke 6 Cy. 260 x 360 each-1324kW (1800bhp) Yanmar Diesel Engine Co Ltd-Japan

IMO / Call sign	Name / Owner / Flag	Tonnage	Class	Builder / Dimensions	Type	Machinery
5309059 *YBDA* -	**SAMUDERA** - **PT Amas Internasional Line** - *Jakarta* *Indonesia*	*191* 74 -	Class: (LR) (KI) ✠ Classed LR until 9/58	**1952-08 NV Ferus Smit v/h Fa J Smit & Zoon — Westerbroek** Yd No: 113 Loa 36.05 Br ex 6.53 Dght - Lbp 35.01 Br md 6.51 Dpth 2.95 Riveted\Welded, 1 dk	**(B12D2FR) Fishery Research Vessel**	**1 oil engine** driving 1 FP propeller Total Power: 316kW (430hp) Werkspoor TMAS276 1 x 4 Stroke 6 Cy. 270 x 500 316kW (430bhp) NV Werkspoor-Netherlands AuxGen: 1 x 30kW 110V d.c
9004724 *YB5316* -	**SAMUDERA 01** *ex* Aso *-2008* **PT Karya Jaya Samudera** - *Surabaya* *Indonesia*	*190* 57 -	Class: KI	**1990-07 Sumidagawa Zosen K.K. — Tokyo** Yd No: N1-22 Converted From: Fishery Patrol Vessel-2008 Loa 36.60 Br ex - Dght 1.300 Lbp 34.70 Br md 6.60 Dpth 3.31 Welded	**(B34J2SD) Crew Boat**	**2 oil engines** geared to sc. shaft driving 1 FP propeller Total Power: 3,016kW (4,100hp) M.T.U. 16V396TB93 2 x Vee 4 Stroke 16 Cy. 165 x 185 each-1508kW (2050bhp) MTU Friedrichshafen GmbH-Friedrichshafen AuxGen: 2 x 60kW 225V a.c
8010025 *PNYG* -	**SAMUDERA 02** *ex* White River *-2011* *ex* Marsea Three *-1991* **PT Karya Jaya Samudera** - *Surabaya* *Indonesia*	**701** 210 1,200	Class: KI (AB)	**1980-10 Halter Marine, Inc. — Moss Point, Ms** Yd No: 939 Loa 54.86 Br ex 12.22 Dght 3.664 Lbp 50.70 Br md 12.20 Dpth 4.27 Welded, 1 dk	**(B21A20S) Platform Supply Ship**	**2 oil engines** reverse reduction geared to sc. shafts driving 2 FP propellers Total Power: 1,882kW (2,558hp) 12.0kn G.M. (Detroit Diesel) 16V-149-TI 2 x Vee 2 Stroke 16 Cy. 146 x 146 each-941kW (1279bhp) General Motors Detroit DieselAllison Divn-USA AuxGen: 2 x 125kW Thrusters: 1 Thwart. FP thruster (f)
9735684 - -	**SAMUDERA-03** - **PT Karya Jaya Samudera** - *Surabaya* *Indonesia* Official number: GT.262.NO.4921/Pst	**262** 79 -	Class: KI (Class contemplated)	**2013-10 Gimhwak Shipyard Sdn Bhd — Sibu** Yd No: GSY-025 Loa 32.00 Br ex - Dght - Lbp - Br md 9.14 Dpth 4.20 Welded, 1 dk	**(B34L2QU) Utility Vessel**	**2 oil engines** reduction geared to sc. shafts driving 2 Propellers Total Power: 2,238kW (3,042hp) Cummins KTA-38-M2 2 x Vee 4 Stroke 12 Cy. 159 x 159 each-1119kW (1521bhp) Cummins Engine Co Inc-USA
8329373 - -	**SAMUDERA 5** - **PT Pelayaran Hesti Kencana Utama Lloyd** - *Semarang* *Indonesia*	*140* 104 -	Class: (KI)	**1967 P.T. Menara — Tegal** Loa 31.75 Br ex 6.02 Dght - Lbp - Br md - Dpth 2.26 Welded, 1 dk	**(A13B2TU) Tanker (unspecified)**	**1 oil engine** driving 1 FP propeller Total Power: 184kW (250hp) MWM TD232V8 1 x Vee 4 Stroke 8 Cy. 120 x 130 184kW (250bhp) Motoren Werke Mannheim AG (MWM)-West Germany
9159517 *9V9104* -	**SAMUDERA BANGSA** *ex* Mercury K *-2011* **Trada Samudera Bangsa Pte Ltd** PT Trada Maritime *Singapore* *Singapore* MMSI: 563185000 Official number: 396635	**37,846** 23,677 72,421 T/cm 66.9	Class: NK	**1997-03 Sasebo Heavy Industries Co. Ltd. — Sasebo Yard, Sasebo** Yd No: 420 Loa 225.00 (BB) Br ex - Dght 13.521 Lbp 218.00 Br md 32.20 Dpth 18.70 Welded, 1 dk	**(A21A2BC) Bulk Carrier** Grain: 84,790 Compartments: 7 Ho, ER 7 Ha: (15.3 x 12.8)6 (17.0 x 14.4)ER	**1 oil engine** driving 1 FP propeller Total Power: 9,754kW (13,262hp) 14.5kn B&W 6S60MC 1 x 2 Stroke 6 Cy. 600 x 2292 9754kW (13262bhp) Mitsui Engineering & Shipbuilding CLtd-Japan Fuel: 2430.0
8033405 *HQRF9* -	**SAMUDERA I** *ex* Raja I *-2011* *ex* Damo *-2011* *ex* Pan-United 33 *-1982* *ex* Choyo Maru No. 25 *-1982* *ex* Hoei Maru No. 81 *-1979* **Hilman Gunadi** Coastal Engineering Services Pte Ltd *San Lorenzo* *Honduras* Official number: L-1726179	**184** 56 90	Class: (NK)	**1973-07 Ieshima Dock K.K. — Himeji** Loa 31.00 Br ex - Dght 2.700 Lbp 28.00 Br md 8.01 Dpth 3.38 Welded, 1 dk	**(B32A2ST) Tug**	**1 oil engine** driving 1 FP propeller Total Power: 1,471kW (2,000hp) 12.0kn Hanshin 6LUD35 1 x 4 Stroke 6 Cy. 350 x 550 1471kW (2000bhp) The Hanshin Diesel Works Ltd-Japan AuxGen: 2 x 22kW
7652694 *YFLE* -	**SAMUDERA I** *ex* Smooth Ocean *-1994* *ex* Jorge I *-1994* *ex* Princess Anne *-1992* *ex* Shinyo Maru No. 11 *-1992* **PT Pelayaran Armada Bandar Bangun Persada** - *Surabaya* *Indonesia*	**755** 393 800	Class: KI	**1973-10 Shin Nippon Jukogyo K.K. — Osakikamijima** Converted From: Bulk Aggregates Carrier-1998 Loa 53.50 Br ex - Dght 2.990 Lbp 49.00 Br md 11.00 Dpth 5.52 Welded, 2dks	**(A31A2GX) General Cargo Ship** Grain: 550 Compartments: 1 Ho, ER 1 Ha: ER	**1 oil engine** geared to sc. shaft driving 1 FP propeller Total Power: 1,177kW (1,600hp) 12.0kn Yanmar 6Z-ST 1 x 4 Stroke 6 Cy. 280 x 340 1177kW (1600bhp) Yanmar Diesel Engine Co Ltd-Japan AuxGen: 2 x 46kW a.c
9664495 - -	**SAMUDERA INDONESIA** - **PT Surya Samudra Indonesia** - *Samarinda* *Indonesia*	**562** 169 -	Class: KI	**2012-03 PT Bunga Nusa Mahakam — Samarinda** Yd No: 026 Loa 58.59 Br ex - Dght 2.500 Lbp 52.19 Br md 11.00 Dpth 3.35 Welded, 1 dk	**(A35D2RL) Landing Craft** Bow ramp (centre)	**2 oil engines** reduction geared to sc. shafts driving 2 Propellers Total Power: 736kW (1,000hp) Mitsubishi 2 x each-368kW (500bhp) Mitsubishi Heavy Industries Ltd-Japan AuxGen: 2 x 44kW 400V a.c
8992053 *V3GV3* -	**SAMUDERA JAYA** *ex* Kantang *-1999* **Orient Global Shipping & Services Sdn Bhd** - *Belize City* *Belize* MMSI: 312875000 Official number: 130610739	**134** 62 -		**1999-07 Deltamarine Boat Industries Sdn Bhd — Sibu** L reg 36.00 Br ex - Dght - Lbp - Br md 5.50 Dpth 2.83 Welded, 1 dk	**(A31A2GX) General Cargo Ship**	**2 oil engines** driving 2 Propellers Total Power: 956kW (1,300hp) 10.0kn Cummins 2 x 4 Stroke each-478kW (650bhp) Cummins Engine Co Inc-USA
8999453 - -	**SAMUDERA JAYA 6** - **PT Surya Indah Jaya** - *Tanjungpinang* *Indonesia*	**122** 37 -	Class: (KI)	**1996-09 P.T. Ocean Ship — Tanjungpinang** L reg 30.50 Br ex - Dght 0.990 Lbp 28.10 Br md 5.00 Dpth 2.20 Bonded, 1 dk	**(A37B2PS) Passenger Ship** Hull Material: Reinforced Plastic	**3 oil engines** geared to sc. shafts driving 3 Propellers Total Power: 2,538kW (3,450hp) 30.0kn M.T.U. 12V183TE93 3 x Vee 4 Stroke 12 Cy. 128 x 142 each-846kW (1150bhp) Motoren Werke Mannheim AG (MWM)-Mannheim
9049188 - -	**SAMUDERA MAKMUR** - **PT Makhota Samudera Makmur** - *Banjarmasin* *Indonesia*	**154** 92 -	Class: KI	**2005-01 PT Sumber Mahkota Penghidupan — Banjarmasin** Loa 24.15 Br ex - Dght 2.540 Lbp 22.21 Br md 7.25 Dpth 3.00 Welded, 1 dk	**(B32A2ST) Tug**	**2 oil engines** geared to sc. shafts driving 2 Propellers Total Power: 1,000kW (1,360hp) 10.0kn Cummins KTA-19-M2 2 x 4 Stroke 6 Cy. 159 x 159 each-500kW (680bhp) (made 1995, fitted 2005) Cummins Engine Co Inc-USA AuxGen: 2 x 18kW 380V a.c
8749731 *YDA6286* -	**SAMUDERA MAKMUR 02** - **PT Makhota Samudera Makmur** - *Banjarmasin* *Indonesia*	**197** 60 306	Class: KI	**2009 PT Sumber Mahkota Penghidupan — Banjarmasin** Loa 27.25 Br ex - Dght 2.890 Lbp 25.48 Br md 7.75 Dpth 3.50 Welded, 1 dk	**(B32A2ST) Tug**	**2 oil engines** reduction geared to sc. shafts driving 2 FP propellers Total Power: 1,864kW (2,534hp) Caterpillar 3512TA 2 x Vee 4 Stroke 12 Cy. 170 x 190 each-932kW (1267bhp) Caterpillar Inc-USA AuxGen: 2 x 21kW 380V a.c
9069944 *PKGW* -	**SAMUDERA MAS** *ex* Xing Ning 16 *-2007* **PT Pelayaran Tempuran Emas Tbk (TEMAS Line)** - *Jakarta* *Indonesia* MMSI: 525019362	**2,993** 1,971 5,252	Class: KI	**2005-01 Zhejiang Hongguan Ship Industry Co Ltd — Linhai ZJ** Loa 96.50 (BB) Br ex - Dght 5.950 Lbp 90.80 Br md 15.80 Dpth 7.40 Welded, 1 dk	**(A33A2CC) Container Ship (Fully Cellular)** TEU 266	**1 oil engine** geared to sc. shaft driving 1 Propeller Total Power: 1,765kW (2,400hp) 11.0kn Chinese Std. Type G8300ZC 1 x 4 Stroke 8 Cy. 300 x 380 1765kW (2400bhp) Wuxi Antai Power Machinery Co Ltd-China
8021294 *JZJN* -	**SAMUDERA PASE** *ex* Lily Glory *-2013* *ex* Asian Breeze *-2010* *ex* Hyakuyo Maru *-2004* **PT Pasai Jaya** - *Jakarta* *Indonesia* MMSI: 525023209	**5,607** 1,873 7,867	Class: NK	**1981-11 Honda Zosen — Saiki** Yd No: 693 Loa 125.28 Br ex - Dght 7.080 Lbp 117.00 Br md 18.20 Dpth 9.00 Welded, 1 dk	**(A24A2BT) Cement Carrier** Grain: 6,772	**1 oil engine** driving 1 CP propeller Total Power: 5,737kW (7,800hp) 12.0kn Pielstick 12PC2-5V-400 1 x Vee 4 Stroke 12 Cy. 400 x 460 5737kW (7800bhp) Niigata Engineering Co Ltd-Japan AuxGen: 1 x 960kW 450V 60Hz a.c, 1 x 800kW 450V 60Hz a.c, 1 x 400kW 450V 60Hz a.c Fuel: 60.5 (d.f.) 292.0 (r.f.) 16.5pd
7921162 - -	**SAMUDERA PASIFIC NO. 8** *ex* Hakko Maru No. 18 *-2012* **-** - *Zanzibar* *Tanzania*	**498** 151 377		**1980-01 Niigata Engineering Co Ltd — Niigata NI** Yd No: 1667 Loa 49.92 (BB) Br ex - Dght 3.472 Lbp 44.02 Br md 8.62 Dpth 3.66 Welded, 1 dk	**(B11B2FV) Fishing Vessel**	**1 oil engine** geared to sc. shaft driving 1 FP propeller Total Power: 736kW (1,001hp) Niigata 6M28AFT 1 x 4 Stroke 6 Cy. 280 x 480 736kW (1001bhp) Niigata Engineering Co Ltd-Japan

8936114 *YD4524* -	**SAMUDERA PERMATA** *ex* Pelangi Delta *-2008* *ex* Auskerry *-2008* *ex* Cougar *-2008* **PT Haluan Samudra Abadi** - *Jakarta* *Indonesia*	**110** 33 -	Class: KI	**1969 Breaux Bay Craft, Inc. — Loreauville, La** Loa 30.49 Br ex - Dght - Lbp 29.05 Br md 6.10 Dpth 3.05 Welded, 1 dk	**(B21A2OC) Crew/Supply Vessel** Hull Material: Aluminium Alloy	**2 oil engines** geared to sc. shafts driving 2 FP propellers Total Power: 1,030kW (1,400hp) 19.0kn G.M. (Detroit Diesel) 12V-149 2 x Vee 2 Stroke 12 Cy. 146 x 146 each-515kW (700bhp) General Motors Detroit DieselAllison Divn-USA
8340561 *YCUT* -	**SAMUDERA RAYA** **PT Pelayaran Pupan Sejahtera Pertana** - *Pontianak* *Indonesia*	*411* 198 -	Class: (KI)	**1980 P.T. Tunas Samudera — Ketapang** Loa 42.68 Br ex - Dght 2.440 Lbp 39.78 Br md 9.15 Dpth 3.36 Welded, 1 dk	**(A31A2GX) General Cargo Ship**	**1 oil engine** geared to sc. shaft driving 1 FP propeller Total Power: 537kW (730hp) Cummins KT-1150-M 1 x 4 Stroke 6 Cy. 159 x 159 537kW (730bhp) Cummins Engine Co Ltd-United Kingdom
9739616 - -	**SAMUDERA UTAMA** **PT Bunga Nusa Mahakam** - *Samarinda* *Indonesia*	**1,058** 318 -	Class: KI (Class contemplated)	**2013-10 PT Bunga Nusa Mahakam — Samarinda** Yd No: 58 Loa 70.47 Br ex - Dght 2.737 Lbp 64.77 Br md 14.60 Dpth 3.65 Welded, 1 dk	**(A35D2RL) Landing Craft**	**2 oil engines** reduction geared to sc. shafts driving 2 Propellers Total Power: 1,210kW (1,646hp) Mitsubishi 2 x each-605kW (823bhp) Mitsubishi Heavy Industries Ltd-Japan
6402298 *VWTZ* -	**SAMUDRA** **Kolkata Port Trust** - *Kolkata* *India* Official number: 1101	*1,993* 522 929	Class: (LR) (IR) ✠ Classed LR until 23/2/79	**1964-06 Blyth Dry Docks & SB. Co. Ltd. — Blyth** Yd No: 385 Loa 83.62 Br ex 13.31 Dght 4.744 Lbp 76.21 Br md 13.26 Dpth 7.17 Riveted\Welded, 1 dk, 2nd dk except in mchy. space,3rd dk in fwd hold	**(B34N2QP) Pilot Vessel**	**2 oil engines** with flexible couplings & sr reverse geared to sc. shafts driving 2 FP propellers Total Power: 1,236kW (1,680hp) MAN G9V30/45ATL 2 x 4 Stroke 9 Cy. 300 x 450 each-618kW (840bhp) Maschinenbau Augsburg Nuernberg (MAN)-Augsburg AuxGen: 3 x 175kW 220V d.c Fuel: 211.5 (d.f.)
8740333 *YDA4452* -	**SAMUDRA** **Hendri Wahyudi** - *Pontianak* *Indonesia*	**237** 72 -	Class: (KI)	**2003 CV Sarana Kapuas — Pontianak** Loa 27.95 Br ex - Dght - Lbp 26.50 Br md 8.20 Dpth 3.90 Welded, 1 dk	**(B32A2ST) Tug**	**2 oil engines** driving 2 Propellers Total Power: 1,716kW (2,334hp) Mitsubishi S12A2-MPTK 2 x Vee 4 Stroke 12 Cy. 150 x 160 each-858kW (1167bhp) Mitsubishi Heavy Industries Ltd-Japan
8730807 *YFCH* -	**SAMUDRA ABADI VIII** *ex* Eikyu Maru No. 8 *-2001* **PT Sumba Harapan** - *Surabaya* *Indonesia*	*198* 118 698	Class: KI	**1977-11 Shin Nippon Jukogyo K.K. — Osakikamijima** Loa 52.20 Br ex - Dght 3.300 Lbp 49.00 Br md 8.40 Dpth 5.00 Welded, 1 dk	**(A31A2GX) General Cargo Ship** 1 Ha: ER (28.0 x 6.5)	**1 oil engine** driving 1 Propeller Total Power: 736kW (1,001hp) 9.5kn Matsue Z-30US 1 x 4 Stroke 6 Cy. 300 x 430 736kW (1001bhp) Matsue Nainenki Kogyo-Japan
9666584 - -	**SAMUDRA AGUNG 189** **PT Pelayaran Samudra Agung** - *Batam* *Indonesia*	**147** 45 -	Class: KI	**2013-02 PT Marindo Jaya Samudera — Batam** Yd No: 046 Loa 23.50 Br ex 7.32 Dght 2.400 Lbp 21.50 Br md 7.00 Dpth 3.30 Welded, 1 dk	**(B32A2ST) Tug**	**2 oil engines** reduction geared to sc. shafts driving 2 Propellers Total Power: 516kW (702hp) Weifang X6170ZC 2 x 4 Stroke 6 Cy. 170 x 200 each-258kW (351bhp) Weichai Power Co Ltd-China
8749755 *YB6205* -	**SAMUDRA BERLIAN** *ex* Niaga Jaya VII *-2010* **PT Samudra Abadi Jaya** - *Samarinda* *Indonesia*	**230** 69 -	Class: KI	**1999-01 PT Bahari Harapan Permai — Samarinda** Loa 38.10 Br ex - Dght 1.790 Lbp 37.20 Br md 9.76 Dpth 2.38 Welded, 1 dk	**(A35D2RL) Landing Craft**	**2 oil engines** reduction geared to sc. shafts driving 2 Propellers Total Power: 440kW (598hp) Caterpillar 3306PCTA 2 x 4 Stroke 6 Cy. 121 x 152 each-220kW (299bhp) Caterpillar Tractor Co-USA AuxGen: 2 x 34kW 380/220V a.c
8749406 - -	**SAMUDRA BINTAN 88** **Su Meng Liang** - *Batam* *Indonesia*	**105** 32 -	Class: KI	**2009-01 PT Alima Usaha Samudera — Tanjungpinang** Loa 21.00 Br ex - Dght 2.290 Lbp 19.58 Br md 6.50 Dpth 2.75 Welded, 1 dk	**(B32A2ST) Tug**	**2 oil engines** reduction geared to sc. shafts driving 2 Propellers Total Power: 760kW (1,034hp) Cummins KT-19-M 2 x 4 Stroke 6 Cy. 159 x 159 each-380kW (517bhp) Cummins Engine Co Inc-USA AuxGen: 2 x 26kW 380V a.c
8659376 - -	**SAMUDRA BINTAN 89** **Su Meng Liang** - *Batam* *Indonesia*	**105** 32 -	Class: KI	**2011-08 PT Alima Usaha Samudera — Tanjungpinang** Loa 28.05 Br ex - Dght 3.350 Lbp 19.58 Br md 8.60 Dpth 4.30 Welded, 1 dk	**(B32A2ST) Tug**	**2 oil engines** reduction geared to sc. shafts driving 2 FP propellers Total Power: 596kW (810hp) Cummins NTA-855-M 2 x 4 Stroke 6 Cy. 140 x 152 each-298kW (405bhp) Chongqing Cummins Engine Co Ltd-China AuxGen: 2 x 58kW 380V a.c
9421350 *YD3978* -	**SAMUDRA BINTAN 90** *ex* Bina Ocean 15 *-2012* **PT Angkutan Laut Samudra Bintan** - *Tanjungpinang* *Indonesia*	**123** 37 94	Class: KI (GL)	**2006-11 PT Marcopolo Shipyard — Batam** Yd No: H002 Loa 23.17 Br ex - Dght 2.400 Lbp 21.74 Br md 7.00 Dpth 2.90 Welded, 1 dk	**(B32A2ST) Tug**	**2 oil engines** reverse reduction geared to sc. shafts driving 2 FP propellers Total Power: 884kW (1,202hp) Caterpillar 3412C 2 x Vee 4 Stroke 12 Cy. 137 x 152 each-442kW (601bhp) Caterpillar Inc-USA AuxGen: 2 x 30kW 400V a.c
7235771 *ATKY* -	**SAMUDRA DEVI** *launched as* Norad *-1973* **Government of The Republic of India (National Institute of Fisheries Post Harvest Technology & Training)** - *Kochi* *India* Official number: 1563	*194* 78 -	Class: IR (NV)	**1973-06 Sigbjorn Iversen — Flekkefjord** Yd No: 22 Loa 27.28 Br ex 8.06 Dght 4.134 Lbp 23.98 Br md 8.03 Dpth - Welded, 1 dk	**(B11A2FS) Stern Trawler** Compartments: 1 Ho, ER 1 Ha: (3.5 x 2.5)ER	**1 oil engine** geared to sc. shaft driving 1 FP propeller Total Power: 552kW (750hp) Caterpillar D398TA 1 x Vee 4 Stroke 12 Cy. 159 x 203 552kW (750bhp) Caterpillar Tractor Co-USA AuxGen: 1 x 76kW 220V 50Hz a.c Thrusters: 1 Thwart. FP thruster (f)
8114807 *YGXV* -	**SAMUDRA EXPRESS** *ex* Yoshiga Maru No. 18 *-2001* *ex* Seifuku Maru No. 18 *-1995* **PT Sumba Harapan** - *Surabaya* *Indonesia*	**620** 274 697	Class: KI	**1981-06 K.K. Saidaiji Zosensho — Okayama** Yd No: 80 Loa 53.01 Br ex - Dght 3.201 Lbp 52.00 Br md 9.01 Dpth 4.91 Welded, 1 dk	**(A31A2GX) General Cargo Ship**	**1 oil engine** driving 1 FP propeller Total Power: 736kW (1,001hp) Hanshin 6LU28 1 x 4 Stroke 6 Cy. 280 x 440 736kW (1001bhp) Hanshin Nainenki Kogyo-Japan
8743488 *YDA4588* -	**SAMUDRA I** **PT Pelayaran Rimba Megah Armada** - *Pontianak* *Indonesia* Official number: 3304/HHA	**239** 72 -	Class: KI (Class contemplated)	**2006-07 CV Sarana Kapuas — Pontianak** Yd No: 2201 Loa 29.90 Br ex - Dght - Lbp - Br md 8.50 Dpth 3.90 Welded, 1 dk	**(B32A2ST) Tug**	**2 oil engines** reduction geared to sc. shafts driving 2 Propellers Total Power: 1,618kW (2,200hp) Yanmar 2 x 4 Stroke each-809kW (1100bhp) Yanmar Diesel Engine Co Ltd-Japan
8826060 - -	**SAMUDRA INDAH** **PT Garutama Putra Maluku** - *Pontianak* *Indonesia*	**171** 110 -	Class: KI	**1983 P.T. Tunas Samudera — Ketapang** Loa 34.20 Br ex 6.60 Dght - Lbp 29.50 Br md - Dpth 2.40 Welded, 1 dk	**(A31A2GX) General Cargo Ship** Grain: 175 Compartments: 1 Ho, ER 1 Ha: (15.4 x 4.5)ER	**2 oil engines** geared to sc. shafts driving 2 FP propellers Total Power: 198kW (270hp) 8.0kn Chinese Std. Type 6135 2 x 4 Stroke 6 Cy. 135 x 140 each-99kW (135bhp) in China AuxGen: 1 x 12kW 400V a.c
9024633 - -	**SAMUDRA INDAH** **PT Samudera Indah** - *Samarinda* *Indonesia*	**178** 69 -	Class: (KI)	**2002-04 P.T. Kaltim Shipyard — Samarinda** Loa 34.20 Br ex - Dght 1.990 Lbp 29.50 Br md 6.60 Dpth 2.40 Welded, 1 dk	**(B32A2ST) Tug**	**2 oil engines** reduction geared to sc. shafts driving 2 Propellers Total Power: 692kW (940hp) Caterpillar 3408TA 2 x Vee 4 Stroke 8 Cy. 137 x 152 each-346kW (470bhp) Caterpillar Inc-USA AuxGen: 1 x 12kW 400V a.c
9532238 *9WHS2* -	**SAMUDRA JAYA 1** **First Everway Sdn Bhd** - *Kuching* *Malaysia* MMSI: 533000739 Official number: 332962	**299** 90 203	Class: NK	**2008-08 Celtug Service Shipyard Sdn Bhd — Sibu** Yd No: 0610 Loa 31.00 Br ex 9.02 Dght 3.200 Lbp 28.43 Br md 9.00 Dpth 4.00 Welded, 1 dk	**(B32A2ST) Tug**	**2 oil engines** reduction geared to sc. shafts driving 2 Propellers Total Power: 1,472kW (2,002hp) Yanmar 6RY17P-GV 2 x 4 Stroke 6 Cy. 165 x 219 each-736kW (1001bhp) Yanmar Diesel Engine Co Ltd-Japan Fuel: 200.0

9024645 - -	**SAMUDRA JAYA 2** - **PT Bangun Putra Remaja** - *Tanjungpinang* *Indonesia* Official number: YB3176	**121** 37 -	Class: KI	**1993**-07 **P.T. Ocean Ship — Tanjungpinang** Loa 33.20 Br ex - Dght 1.270 Lbp 29.95 Br md 5.20 Dpth 2.17 Welded, 1 dk	**(A37B2PS) Passenger Ship** Hull Material: Reinforced Plastic	**3 oil engines** geared to sc. shafts driving 3 Propellers Total Power: 2,208kW (3,003hp) M.T.U. 12V183TE92 3 x Vee 4 Stroke 12 Cy. 128 x 142 each-736kW (1001bhp) (made 1993) MTU Friedrichshafen GmbH-Friedrichshafen AuxGen: 2 x 68kW 380/220V a.c
8826072 - -	**SAMUDRA JAYA VI** *ex* Nila Kandi V **PT Pelayaran Madju Nusa** - *Palembang* *Indonesia*	*171* 74 -	Class: (KI)	**1970 P.T. Nila Kandi — Palembang** Loa 37.47 Br ex 6.07 Dght 1.670 Lbp 34.56 Br md - Dpth 2.25 Welded, 1 dk	**(A31A2GX) General Cargo Ship**	**2 oil engines** driving 2 FP propellers Total Power: 354kW (482hp) Caterpillar 2 x 4 Stroke 6 Cy. each-177kW (241bhp) Caterpillar Tractor Co-USA AuxGen: 5 x 220V a.c
8316778 *VWSM* -	**SAMUDRA KAUSTUBH** **Government of The Republic of India (Ministry of Steel)** The Shipping Corporation of India Ltd (SCI) SatCom: Inmarsat C 441958010 *Mumbai* *India* MMSI: 419321000 Official number: 2047	*284* 85 -	Class: IR (LR) ✠ Classed LR until 26/9/86	**1984**-08 **Scheepswerf Bijlsma BV — Wartena** Yd No: 624 Loa 35.08 Br ex 8.41 Dght 1.609 Lbp 32.75 Br md 8.26 Dpth 2.80 Welded, 1 dk	**(B31A2SR) Research Survey Vessel**	**2 oil engines** with clutches, flexible couplings & sr reverse geared to sc. shafts driving 2 FP propellers Total Power: 544kW (740hp) Cummins KT-1150-M 2 x 4 Stroke 6 Cy. 159 x 159 each-272kW (370bhp) Cummins Engine Co Inc-USA AuxGen: 2 x 200kW 380V 50Hz a.c, 1 x 68kW 380V 50Hz a.c Thrusters: 1 Thwart. FP thruster (f) Fuel: 42.5 (d.f.)
5304401 *ATCR* -	**SAMUDRA MANTHAN** *ex* Vishva Vinay *-1983* *ex* Sabratha *-1968* **Government of The Republic of India (Geological Survey of India)** The Shipping Corporation of India Ltd (SCI) SatCom: Inmarsat C 441957810 *Mumbai* *India* MMSI: 419314000 Official number: 1295	*2,373* 1,272 1,825	Class: IR (GL)	**1958**-04 **AG Weser, Werk Seebeck — Bremerhaven** Yd No: 845 Converted From: General Cargo Ship-1983 Loa 88.80 Br ex 12.96 Dght 5.058 Lbp 80.02 Br md 12.90 Dpth 7.50 Riveted\Welded, 2 dks	**(B31A2SR) Research Survey Vessel** Derricks: 8x5t	**2 oil engines** dr geared to sc. shaft driving 1 FP propeller Total Power: 1,574kW (2,140hp) 6.0kn MAN G9V30/45 2 x 4 Stroke 9 Cy. 300 x 450 each-787kW (1070bhp) Maschinenbau Augsburg Nuernberg (MAN)-Augsburg AuxGen: 2 x 300kW 415V 50Hz a.c, 2 x 100kW 220V d.c Fuel: 277.0 (d.f.)
8350308 *YFGP* -	**SAMUDRA MAS** *ex* Shojyu Maru No. 5 *-2001* *ex* Hojuzan Maru *-1988* **PT Sumba Harapan** - *Surabaya* *Indonesia*	*613* 259 750	Class: KI	**1975**-10 **Y.K. Hashimoto Zosensho — Amakusa** Loa 53.01 Br ex - Dght 3.350 Lbp 49.00 Br md 9.01 Dpth 5.21 Welded, 1 dk	**(A31A2GX) General Cargo Ship**	**1 oil engine** driving 1 FP propeller Total Power: 588kW (799hp) 10.0kn Hanshin 1 x 4 Stroke 588kW (799bhp) The Hanshin Diesel Works Ltd-Japan
8503333 *VVGN* -	**SAMUDRA NIDHI** **Oil & Natural Gas Corp Ltd** The Shipping Corporation of India Ltd (SCI) SatCom: Inmarsat C 441953210 *Mumbai* *India* MMSI: 419384000 Official number: 2136	**2,995** 898 2,189	Class: IR NV (KR)	**1986**-03 **Daewoo Shipbuilding & Heavy Machinery Ltd — Geoje** Yd No: 7905 Loa 82.00 Br ex 18.04 Dght 5.014 Lbp 72.01 Br md 18.00 Dpth 7.01 Welded, 2 dks	**(B22F20W) Well Stimulation Vessel**	**4 diesel electric oil engines** driving 4 gen. each 1600kW 690V a.c Connecting to 2 elec. motors driving 2 CP propellers Total Power: 5,796kW (7,880hp) Wartsila 12V22 4 x Vee 4 Stroke 12 Cy. 220 x 240 each-1449kW (1970bhp) Wartsila Power Singapore Pte Ltd-Singapore AuxGen: 1 x 144kW 390V 50Hz a.c Thrusters: 2 Thwart. CP thruster (f)
7814931 - -	**SAMUDRA No. 2** *ex* Sagami Maru *-1994* - -	*240* 67 187		**1978**-11 **Hayashikane Shipbuilding & Engineering Co Ltd — Yokosuka KN** Yd No: 747 Loa 38.51 Br ex 8.79 Dght 2.901 Lbp 32.21 Br md 7.31 Dpth 3.18 Welded	**(B12D2FR) Fishery Research Vessel**	**1 oil engine** driving 1 FP propeller Total Power: 736kW (1,001hp) 12.4kn Niigata 6L25BX 1 x 4 Stroke 6 Cy. 250 x 320 736kW (1001bhp) Niigata Engineering Co Ltd-Japan
9341225 *AVDV* -	**SAMUDRA PAHEREDAR** **Government of The Republic of India (Coast Guard)** - *India* MMSI: 419096200	**3,178** 954 1,500	Class: (NV)	**2012**-07 **ABG Shipyard Ltd — Surat** Yd No: 222 Loa 95.05 (BB) Br ex - Dght 3.800 Lbp 86.15 Br md 15.50 Dpth 6.50 Welded, 1 dk	**(B34G2SE) Pollution Control Vessel**	**2 oil engines** geared to sc. shafts driving 2 CP propellers Total Power: 6,000kW (8,158hp) 20.0kn Bergens B32: 40L6P 2 x 4 Stroke 6 Cy. 320 x 400 each-3000kW (4079bhp) Rolls Royce Marine AS-Norway Thrusters: 1 Retract. directional thruster (f)
8875396 *YDA4095* -	**SAMUDRA PERKASA I** *ex* Gasindo 9 *-2001* **PT Armada Arung Samudra Perkasa** - *Jakarta* *Indonesia*	**224** 68 -	Class: KI (AB)	**1994**-09 **President Marine Pte Ltd — Singapore** Yd No: 179 Loa 29.00 Br ex - Dght 3.720 Lbp 28.40 Br md 8.60 Dpth 4.11 Welded, 1 dk	**(B32A2ST) Tug**	**2 oil engines** geared to sc. shafts driving 2 FP propellers Total Power: 1,790kW (2,434hp) Yanmar M220-EN 2 x 4 Stroke 6 Cy. 220 x 300 each-895kW (1217bhp) Yanmar Diesel Engine Co Ltd-Japan
8875401 *YDA4096* -	**SAMUDRA PERKASA II** *ex* Gasindo 12 *-2000* **PT Armada Arung Samudra Perkasa** - *Jakarta* *Indonesia*	**224** 68 -	Class: KI (AB)	**1994**-09 **President Marine Pte Ltd — Singapore** Yd No: 180 Loa 29.00 Br ex - Dght 3.500 Lbp 28.00 Br md 8.60 Dpth 4.11 Welded, 1 dk	**(B32A2ST) Tug**	**2 oil engines** geared to sc. shafts driving 2 FP propellers Total Power: 1,766kW (2,402hp) 10.0kn Yanmar M220-EN 2 x 4 Stroke 6 Cy. 220 x 300 each-883kW (1201bhp) Yanmar Diesel Engine Co Ltd-Japan AuxGen: 2 x 60kW 415V a.c
9050761 *YDA4097* -	**SAMUDRA PERKASA III** *ex* Gasindo 7 *-2000* *ex* Genindo C. I. 1 *-1996* *ex* Marine Diamond *-1993* **PT Armada Arung Samudra Perkasa** - *Jakarta* *Indonesia* MMSI: 525016580 Official number: 154/AB	**178** 54 126	Class: KI (LR) (AB) ✠ Classed LR until 14/12/02	**1992**-12 **Xinle Shipyard — Ningbo ZJ** Yd No: 91-1 Loa 26.00 Br ex 8.22 Dght 2.400 Lbp 23.52 Br md 8.00 Dpth 3.00 Welded, 1 dk	**(B32A2ST) Tug**	**2 oil engines** with clutches, flexible couplings & sr reverse geared to sc. shafts driving 2 FP propellers Total Power: 1,350kW (1,836hp) Caterpillar 3508 2 x Vee 4 Stroke 8 Cy. 170 x 190 each-675kW (918bhp) Caterpillar Inc-USA AuxGen: 2 x 80kW 50Hz a.c
8514095 *YD4829* -	**SAMUDRA PERKASA IV** *ex* Sumisei Maru No. 21 *-2001* **PT Armada Arung Samudra Perkasa** - *Samarinda* *Indonesia*	*275* 83 -	Class: KI	**1985**-09 **Masui Zosensho K.K. — Nandan** Yd No: 183 Loa 32.25 Br ex - Dght 3.101 Lbp 29.01 Br md 8.72 Dpth 3.92 Welded, 1 dk	**(B32A2ST) Tug**	**2 oil engines** sr geared to sc. shafts driving 2 FP propellers Total Power: 1,472kW (2,002hp) Yanmar 6G-ST 2 x 4 Stroke 6 Cy. 240 x 290 each-736kW (1001bhp) Yanmar Diesel Engine Co Ltd-Japan
8892590 - -	**SAMUDRA PERKASA V** *ex* Sabang XVII *-2000* **PT Armada Arung Samudra Perkasa** - *Jambi* *Indonesia*	*217* 65 -	Class: KI	**1994**-08 **P.T. Sabang Raya Indah — Jambi** L reg 29.00 Br ex - Dght - Lbp 28.00 Br md 8.60 Dpth 4.11 Welded, 1 dk	**(B32A2ST) Tug**	**2 oil engines** geared to sc. shafts driving 2 FP propellers Total Power: 1,766kW (2,402hp) Yanmar M220-EN 2 x 4 Stroke 6 Cy. 220 x 300 each-883kW (1201bhp) (made 1992) Yanmar Diesel Engine Co Ltd-Japan
8821228 *YD6507* -	**SAMUDRA PERKASA VII** *ex* Kokudo Maru No. 2 *-2004* **PT Armada Arung Samudra Perkasa** - *Samarinda* *Indonesia*	*153* 46 -	Class: (KI)	**1989**-05 **Kanrei Zosen K.K. — Naruto** Yd No: 333 L reg 28.02 Br ex - Dght 2.620 Lbp 26.00 Br md 9.00 Dpth 3.50 Welded, 1 dk	**(B32A2ST) Tug**	**2 oil engines** geared to sc. shafts driving 2 FP propellers Total Power: 1,472kW (2,002hp) 10.0kn Yanmar M220-UN 2 x 4 Stroke 6 Cy. 220 x 300 each-736kW (1001bhp) Yanmar Diesel Engine Co Ltd-Japan
8826084 - -	**SAMUDRA PERMAI** - **PT Dharma Samudera Fishing Industry** - *Pontianak* *Indonesia*	*406* 222 -	Class: KI	**1984**-02 **P.T. Tunas Samudera — Ketapang** Loa 38.10 Br ex 8.55 Dght 2.440 Lbp 36.00 Br md - Dpth 3.05 Welded, 1 dk	**(A31A2GX) General Cargo Ship** Compartments: 1 Ho, ER 2 Ha: ER	**2 oil engines** driving 2 FP propellers Total Power: 354kW (482hp) Yanmar 6HAL-HTE 2 x 4 Stroke 6 Cy. 130 x 150 each-177kW (241bhp) Yanmar Diesel Engine Co Ltd-Japan AuxGen: 1 x 13kW 400V a.c
8512085 *VVJL* -	**SAMUDRA PRABHA** **Oil & Natural Gas Corp Ltd** The Shipping Corporation of India Ltd (SCI) SatCom: Inmarsat C 441953310 *Mumbai* *India* MMSI: 419393000 Official number: 2153	**4,018** 1,205 2,121	Class: IR LR ✠ **100A1** SS 07/2011 offshore supply ship/diving support ship firefighting ship 2 (7200cub.m/hr) with water spray, helicopter deck ✠ **LMC** **UMS** Eq.Ltr: (U) ;	**1986**-12 **Hyundai Heavy Industries Co Ltd — Ulsan** Yd No: P034 Loa 91.50 Br ex 17.43 Dght 5.166 Lbp 78.01 Br md 17.40 Dpth 7.78 Welded, 2 dks	**(B21A20S) Platform Supply Ship**	**4 diesel electric oil engines** driving 4 gen. each 2000kW 6600V a.c Connecting to 2 elec. motors each (1560kW) driving 2 Directional propellers Total Power: 8,600kW (11,692hp) 12.0kn Bergens KVGB-12 4 x Vee 4 Stroke 12 Cy. 250 x 300 each-2150kW (2923bhp) AS Bergens Mek Verksteder-Norway Thrusters: 2 Thwart. CP thruster (f)

9341213 *AVDU* -	**SAMUDRA PRAHARI** **Government of The Republic of India (Coast Guard)** - *India*	**3,178** 954 500	Class: (NV)	**2010-09 ABG Shipyard Ltd — Surat** Yd No: 221 Loa 94.00 (BB) Br ex - Dght 3.800 Lbp 86.10 Br md 15.60 Dpth 6.51 Welded, 1 dk	**(B34G2SE) Pollution Control Vessel**	**2 oil engines** reduction geared to sc. shafts driving 2 CP propellers Total Power: 6,000kW (8,158hp) 20.0kn Bergens B32: 40L6P 2 x 4 Stroke 6 Cy. 320 x 400 each-3000kW (4079bhp) Rolls Royce Marine AS-Norway AuxGen: 2 x a.c, 4 x 1200kW a.c Thrusters: 1 Retract. directional thruster (f)
7209899 *YFMD* -	**SAMUDRA PRATAMA** *ex* Sandy I *-1996* *ex* Anabas *-1992* *ex* Ageshio Maru *-1989* **PT Sinar Samudra Tripratama** - *Jakarta* *Indonesia* MMSI: 525707077	*1,035* 646 1,568	Class: KI	**1971-07 Sasaki Shipbuilding Co Ltd — Osakikamijima HS** Yd No: 153 Loa 63.91 Br ex 11.03 Dght 4.249 Lbp 60.00 Br md 11.00 Dpth 4.35 Welded, 2 dks	**(A31A2GX) General Cargo Ship** Grain: 1,915; Bale: 1,746 Compartments: 1 Ho, ER 1 Ha: (33.0 x 7.4)	**1 oil engine** driving 1 FP propeller Total Power: 1,214kW (1,651hp) 12.0kn Hanshin 6LU35 1 x 4 Stroke 6 Cy. 350 x 550 1214kW (1651bhp) Hanshin Nainenki Kogyo-Japan AuxGen: 2 x 60kW 220V a.c
8910732 *PMBN* -	**SAMUDRA PRIMA I** *ex* Perkasa *-2011* *ex* Yosei Maru *-2007* **Albinus Ho** - *Surabaya* *Indonesia*	**1,486** 529 1,600	Class: KI	**1989-12 K.K. Miura Zosensho — Saiki** Yd No: 863 Loa 75.50 Br ex - Dght 4.101 Lbp 72.14 Br md 12.51 Dpth 7.01 Welded	**(A31A2GX) General Cargo Ship** Compartments: 1 Ho, ER 1 Ha: ER	**1 oil engine** driving 1 FP propeller Total Power: 1,324kW (1,800hp) Niigata 6M31AFTE 1 x 4 Stroke 6 Cy. 310 x 530 1324kW (1800bhp) Niigata Engineering Co Ltd-Japan
9639581 *AVWP* -	**SAMUDRA RATNAKAR** **Geological Survey of India (GSI)/Ministry of Mines** - *Mumbai* *India* MMSI: 419000633 Official number: 4051	**6,551** 1,965 2,700	Class: IR NV	**2013-09 Hyundai Heavy Industries Co Ltd — Ulsan** Yd No: P136 Loa 103.60 Br ex - Dght 6.200 Lbp 93.60 Br md 19.20 Dpth 8.50 Welded, 1 dk	**(B31A2SR) Research Survey Vessel**	**4 diesel electric oil engines** driving 4 gen. Connecting to 2 elec. motors driving 2 Azimuth electric drive units Total Power: 9,240kW (12,564hp) Hyundai Himsen 7H25/33P 4 x 4 Stroke 7 Cy. 250 x 330 each-2310kW (3141bhp) Hyundai Heavy Industries Co Ltd-South Korea Thrusters: 1 Tunnel thruster (f); 1 Tunnel thruster (a)
9268227 *9WGE2* -	**SAMUDRA RAYA 1** *ex* Majumaya 1 *-2004* **First Everway Sdn Bhd** - *Kuching* *Malaysia* MMSI: 533000887 Official number: 329558	**217** 66 238	Class: NK (KI)	**2002-03 C E Ling Shipbuilding Sdn Bhd — Miri** Yd No: 031 Loa 26.07 Br ex - Dght 3.312 Lbp 23.20 Br md 8.23 Dpth 4.00 Welded, 1 dk	**(B32A2ST) Tug**	**2 oil engines** reduction geared to sc. shafts driving 2 FP propellers Total Power: 1,204kW (1,636hp) 11.0kn Mitsubishi S6R2-MTK 2 x 4 Stroke 6 Cy. 170 x 220 each-602kW (818bhp) (made 2001) Mitsubishi Heavy Industries Ltd-Japan Fuel: 195.0 (d.f.)
8418851 *VVJK* -	**SAMUDRA SARVEKSHAK** **Oil & Natural Gas Corp Ltd** The Shipping Corporation of India Ltd (SCI) SatCom: Inmarsat C 441953110 *Mumbai* *India* MMSI: 419385000 Official number: 2152	**3,444** 1,033 538	Class: IR NV (BV)	**1986-12 Soc Nouvelle des Ats et Chs de La Rochelle-Pallice — La Rochelle** Yd No: 1239 Loa 83.47 Br ex 16.95 Dght 4.001 Lbp 77.53 Br md 16.91 Dpth 8.21 Welded, 2 dks	**(B22A2OR) Offshore Support Vessel**	**2 oil engines** dr geared to sc. shafts driving 2 Directional propellers Total Power: 3,002kW (4,082hp) 11.5kn Pielstick 6PA6L280 2 x 4 Stroke 6 Cy. 280 x 290 each-1501kW (2041bhp) Alsthom Atlantique-France AuxGen: 1 x 1300kW 380V 50Hz a.c, 1 x 600kW 380V 50Hz a.c, 1 x 360kW 380V 50Hz a.c Thrusters: 2 Directional thruster (f)
7356965 - -	**SAMUDRA SATU** **Samudra Transportation Co** -	*120* - 199		**1974 Hiap Tye Shipbuilding Industry Sdn Bhd — Sibu** Loa - Br ex - Dght 1.651 Lbp 30.46 Br md 6.71 Dpth - Welded, 1 dk	**(A13B2TU) Tanker (unspecified)**	**1 oil engine** driving 1 FP propeller Kubota 1 x 4 Stroke Kubota Tekkosho-Japan
8318453 *VWFN* -	**SAMUDRA SEVAK** **Oil & Natural Gas Corp Ltd** The Shipping Corporation of India Ltd (SCI) SatCom: Inmarsat C 441953510 *Mumbai* *India* MMSI: 419395000 Official number: 2025	**5,455** 1,637 4,000	Class: NV (IR)	**1988-08 Mazagon Dock Ltd. — Mumbai** Yd No: 741 Loa 101.80 Br ex - Dght 6.200 Lbp 91.00 Br md 19.50 Dpth 8.70 Welded, 2 dks	**(B21A2OS) Platform Supply Ship** Passengers: berths: 93 Cranes: 1x120t	**5 diesel electric oil engines** driving 4 gen. each 2800kW 6600V 1 gen. of 2100kW 6600V a.c Connecting to 3 elec. motors driving 2 Azimuth electric drive units , 1 CP propeller Total Power: 13,300kW (18,083hp) 13.0kn Bergens KVGB-12 1 x Vee 4 Stroke 12 Cy. 250 x 300 2100kW (2855bhp) AS Bergens Mek Verksteder-Norway Bergens KVGB-16 4 x Vee 4 Stroke 16 Cy. 250 x 300 each-2800kW (3807bhp) AS Bergens Mek Verksteder-Norway Thrusters: 2 Thwart. CP thruster (f)
8316766 *VWSK* -	**SAMUDRA SHAUDHIKAMA** **Government of The Republic of India (Ministry of Steel)** The Shipping Corporation of India Ltd (SCI) SatCom: Inmarsat C 441957910 *Mumbai* *India* MMSI: 419322000 Official number: 2048	*284* 85 -	Class: IR (LR) ✠ Classed LR until 26/9/86	**1984-08 Scheepsbouw en Machinefabriek De Greuns B.V. — Leeuwarden** Yd No: 700 Loa 35.08 Br ex 8.41 Dght 1.609 Lbp 32.75 Br md 8.26 Dpth 2.80 Welded, 1 dk	**(B31A2SR) Research Survey Vessel**	**2 oil engines** with clutches, flexible couplings & sr reverse geared to sc. shafts driving 2 FP propellers Total Power: 544kW (740hp) Cummins KT-1150-M 2 x 4 Stroke 6 Cy. 159 x 159 each-272kW (370bhp) Cummins Engine Co Inc-USA AuxGen: 2 x 200kW 380V 50Hz a.c, 1 x 68kW 380V 50Hz a.c Thrusters: 1 Thwart. FP thruster (f) Fuel: 42.5 (d.f.)
9024657 - -	**SAMUDRA SINDO** **PT Usda Seroja Jaya** - *Dumai* *Indonesia*	**103** 63 -	Class: KI	**1997-01 PT Usda Seroja Jaya — Rengat** Loa 24.73 Br ex - Dght - Lbp 22.00 Br md 5.50 Dpth 2.80 Welded, 1 dk	**(B32A2ST) Tug**	**1 oil engine** driving 1 Propeller Total Power: 956kW (1,300hp) 10.9kn Niigata 6L25BX 1 x 4 Stroke 6 Cy. 250 x 320 956kW (1300bhp) Niigata Engineering Co Ltd-Japan AuxGen: 3 x 16kW 400V a.c
7823607 *YD3533* -	**SAMUDRA SINDO 28** *ex* Tomiei Maru No. 6 *-2009* **PT Samudra Sindo** - *Dumai* *Indonesia*	*125* 38 -	Class: KI	**1979-01 Masui Zosensho K.K. — Nandan** Yd No: 152 Loa 25.80 Br ex - Dght 3.100 Lbp 23.61 Br md 7.50 Dpth 3.18 Riveted\Welded, 1 dk	**(B32A2ST) Tug**	**2 oil engines** driving 2 FP propellers Total Power: 1,104kW (1,500hp) Niigata 6MG20AX 2 x 4 Stroke 6 Cy. 200 x 260 each-552kW (750bhp) Niigata Engineering Co Ltd-Japan
8910342 *PNQK* -	**SAMUDRA SINDO 38** *ex* Kisaragi Maru No. 8 *-2010* **PT Samudra Sindo** - *Dumai* *Indonesia* MMSI: 525021217	**1,002** 610 2,095	Class: KI (NK)	**1990-01 Hakata Zosen K.K. — Imabari** Yd No: 503 Loa 75.83 (BB) Br ex - Dght 4.789 Lbp 72.00 Br md 11.50 Dpth 5.35 Welded, 1 dk	**(A13B2TP) Products Tanker** Liq: 2,190; Liq (Oil): 2,190 Compartments: 10 Ta, ER	**1 oil engine** driving 1 CP propeller Total Power: 1,324kW (1,800hp) 11.8kn Hanshin 6EL30 1 x 4 Stroke 6 Cy. 300 x 600 1324kW (1800bhp) The Hanshin Diesel Works Ltd-Japan AuxGen: 2 x 160kW 500V a.c Fuel: 95.0 (r.f.)
9078701 *POAN* -	**SAMUDRA SINDO 168** *ex* Takawa Maru *-2011* **PT Samudra Sindo** - *Pontianak* *Indonesia* MMSI: 525010147	**2,014** 856 3,321	Class: KI (NK)	**1993-12 K.K. Miura Zosensho — Saiki** Yd No: 1081 Loa 92.80 Br ex - Dght 5.823 Lbp 85.00 Br md 13.00 Dpth 6.40 Welded, 1 dk	**(A13B2TP) Products Tanker** Liq: 3,349; Liq (Oil): 3,349	**1 oil engine** driving 1 CP propeller Total Power: 2,000kW (2,719hp) 12.5kn Hanshin 6EL38 1 x 4 Stroke 6 Cy. 380 x 760 2000kW (2719bhp) The Hanshin Diesel Works Ltd-Japan AuxGen: 1 x 400kW a.c, 1 x 224kW a.c Fuel: 150.0 (r.f.)
9024669 - -	**SAMUDRA SINDO I** **PT Usda Seroja Jaya** - *Dumai* *Indonesia*	**107** 64 -	Class: KI	**1997-04 PT Usda Seroja Jaya — Rengat** Loa 24.73 Br ex - Dght - Lbp 22.00 Br md 5.50 Dpth 2.80 Welded, 1 dk	**(B32A2ST) Tug**	**1 oil engine** driving 1 Propeller Total Power: 956kW (1,300hp) 10.1kn Niigata 6L25BX 1 x 4 Stroke 6 Cy. 250 x 320 956kW (1300bhp) Niigata Engineering Co Ltd-Japan AuxGen: 2 x 56kW 400V a.c
9024671 - -	**SAMUDRA SINDO II** **PT Usda Seroja Jaya** - *Dumai* *Indonesia*	**107** 64 -	Class: KI	**1997-12 PT Usda Seroja Jaya — Rengat** Loa 24.73 Br ex - Dght - Lbp 22.00 Br md 5.50 Dpth 2.80 Welded, 1 dk	**(B32A2ST) Tug**	**1 oil engine** driving 1 Propeller Total Power: 1,048kW (1,425hp) 10.7kn Niigata 6L31AX 1 x 4 Stroke 6 Cy. 310 x 380 1048kW (1425bhp) (Re-engined ,made 1978, refitted 1997) Niigata Engineering Co Ltd-Japan AuxGen: 2 x 25kW 400V a.c
7123813 *YD3883* -	**SAMUDRA SINDO III** *ex* Shoki *-1998* *ex* Shinko Maru No. 11 *-1983* **PT Usda Seroja Jaya** - *Batam* *Indonesia*	*168* 51 61	Class: KI	**1971-10 Sanyo Zosen K.K. — Onomichi** Yd No: 608 Loa - Br ex 7.04 Dght 2.801 Lbp 26.50 Br md 7.01 Dpth 3.31 Riveted\Welded, 1 dk	**(B32A2ST) Tug**	**1 oil engine** driving 1 FP propeller Total Power: 993kW (1,350hp) Hanshin 6LU32 1 x 4 Stroke 6 Cy. 320 x 510 993kW (1350bhp) Hanshin Nainenki Kogyo-Japan

7512662 *YD4638* -	**SAMUDRA SINDO V** *ex* Chitose Maru No. 11 *-1999* *ex* Shoichi Maru No. 21 *-1991* *ex* Yamasan Maru No. 1 *-1987* **PT Usda Seroja Jaya** - *Palembang* *Indonesia*	**177** 54 -	Class: (KI)	**1975-08 Kochi Jyuko K.K. — Kochi** Yd No: 1205 Converted From: Fishing Vessel-1999 Loa - Br ex 7.01 Dght 2.337 Lbp 30.94 Br md 6.99 Dpth 2.70 Riveted\Welded, 1 dk	**(B32A2ST) Tug**	**1 oil engine** geared to sc. shaft driving 1 FP propeller Total Power: 883kW (1,201hp) Daihatsu 8DSM-26 1 x 4 Stroke 8 Cy. 260 x 320 883kW (1201bhp) Daihatsu Diesel Manufacturing Co Lt-Japan
8932417 *YD4657* -	**SAMUDRA SINDO VI** *ex* Kinyu *-2000* *ex* Aki Maru *-1999* **PT Usda Seroja Jaya** - *Palembang* *Indonesia*	**175** 53 -	Class: KI	**1970-05 Fukae Zosen K.K. — Etajima** Yd No: 126 Loa 30.00 Br ex - Dght 2.600 Lbp 27.20 Br md 7.00 Dpth 3.50 Welded, 1 dk	**(B32A2ST) Tug**	**1 oil engine** driving 1 FP propeller Total Power: 883kW (1,201hp) 12.0kn Sumiyoshi 1 x 4 Stroke 883kW (1201bhp) Sumiyoshi Marine Diesel Co Ltd-Japan
7527746 *YD4691* -	**SAMUDRA SINDO VII** *ex* Nhe 1 *-1998* *ex* Tsukasa Go *-1997* *ex* Toku Maru No. 5 *-1996* *ex* Kamone *-1991* **PT Usda Seroja Jaya** - *Palembang* *Indonesia*	**195** 59 -	Class: KI	**1975-12 Usuki Iron Works Co Ltd — Usuki OT** Yd No: 946 Loa 31.73 Br ex 7.93 Dght 2.490 Lbp 29.60 Br md 7.90 Dpth 3.38 Welded, 1 dk	**(B32A2ST) Tug**	**2 oil engines** geared to sc. shafts driving 2 FP propellers Total Power: 1,472kW (2,002hp) 10.0kn Daihatsu 8PSHTCM-26D 2 x 4 Stroke 8 Cy. 260 x 320 each-736kW (1001bhp) (new engine 1980) Daihatsu Diesel Manufacturing Co Lt-Japan AuxGen: 1 x 100kW 225/130V a.c
8954518 *YD3144* -	**SAMUDRA SINDO VIII** *ex* Wakamiyo Maru *-2002* *ex* Ryochu Maru *-2000* *ex* Shinkai Chosa Maru *-2000* *ex* Saiko Maru No. 1 *-2000* **PT Usda Seroja Jaya** - *Dumai* *Indonesia*	**157** 48 -	Class: KI	**1980-12 Mikami Zosen K.K. — Japan** Converted From: Fishing Vessel-2002 Loa 34.60 Br ex - Dght - Lbp - Br md 6.68 Dpth 2.48 Welded, 1 dk	**(B32A2ST) Tug**	**1 oil engine** driving 1 FP propeller Total Power: 736kW (1,001hp) Akasaka DM28A 1 x 4 Stroke 6 Cy. 280 x 460 736kW (1001bhp) Akasaka Tekkosho KK (Akasaka DieselLtd)-Japan
9049102 - -	**SAMUDRA SINDO XI** - **PT Samudra Sindo** - *Dumai* *Indonesia*	**245** 74 -	Class: KI	**2004-08 PT Usda Seroja Jaya — Rengat** Loa 30.00 Br ex - Dght 2.810 Lbp 26.00 Br md 9.00 Dpth 3.40 Welded, 1 dk	**(B32A2ST) Tug**	**2 oil engines** geared to sc. shafts driving 2 Propellers Total Power: 1,176kW (1,598hp) 8.0kn Matsui 6M26KGHS 2 x 4 Stroke 6 Cy. 260 x 400 each-588kW (799bhp) Matsui Iron Works Co Ltd-Japan AuxGen: 2 x 26kW 380/220V a.c
9028110 *YD3178* -	**SAMUDRA SINDO XII** *ex* Maruhama Maru No. 26 *-2002* **PT Usda Seroja Jaya** - *Dumai* *Indonesia*	**154** 92 69	Class: KI	**1989-11 Okumura Zosen Kogyo K.K. — Himeji** Loa 24.50 Br ex - Dght 2.490 Lbp 22.00 Br md 7.60 Dpth 2.98 Welded, 1 dk	**(B32A2ST) Tug**	**1 oil engine** geared to sc. shaft driving 1 Propeller Total Power: 736kW (1,001hp) 8.0kn Hanshin 6LU35G 1 x 4 Stroke 6 Cy. 350 x 550 736kW (1001bhp) The Hanshin Diesel Works Ltd-Japan AuxGen: 2 x 46kW 225/130V a.c
9078787 *VTLY* -	**SAMUDRIKA** **Government of The Republic of India (Ministry of Agriculture & Cooperation)** - *Kochi* *India* Official number: F-CHN-010	*189* 56 112	Class: (NK)	**1993-12 Niigata Engineering Co Ltd — Niigata NI** Yd No: 2260 Loa 28.00 Br ex - Dght - Lbp 24.80 Br md 7.30 Dpth 3.25 Welded, 1 dk	**(B12D2FR) Fishery Research Vessel** Ins: 94	**1 oil engine** with clutches & sr geared to sc. shaft driving 1 CP propeller Total Power: 478kW (650hp) 9.0kn Niigata 6NSD-M 1 x 4 Stroke 6 Cy. 160 x 210 478kW (650bhp) Niigata Engineering Co Ltd-Japan AuxGen: 2 x 64kW a.c
8311687 *VVFC* -	**SAMUDRIKA-1** - **Oil & Natural Gas Corp Ltd** The Shipping Corporation of India Ltd (SCI) SatCom: Inmarsat C 441953710 *Mumbai* *India* MMSI: 419396000 Official number: 2097	**951** 285 1,248	Class: IR (NV)	**1986-02 Goa Shipyard Ltd. — Goa** Yd No: 1112 Loa 55.33 Br ex 12.86 Dght 5.098 Lbp 47.99 Br md 12.51 Dpth 5.82 Welded, 1 dk	**(B21B20A) Anchor Handling Tug Supply**	**2 oil engines** sr geared to sc. shafts driving 2 CP propellers Total Power: 2,354kW (3,200hp) 13.0kn Normo LDMB-8 2 x 4 Stroke 8 Cy. 250 x 300 each-1177kW (1600bhp) AS Bergens Mek Verksteder-Norway AuxGen: 2 x 448kW 415V 50Hz a.c, 2 x 224kW 415V 50Hz a.c Thrusters: 1 Thwart. CP thruster (f) Fuel: 392.0 (d.f.)
8311699 *VVFD* -	**SAMUDRIKA-2** - **Oil & Natural Gas Corp Ltd** Sical Logistics Ltd SatCom: Inmarsat C 441953810 *Mumbai* *India* MMSI: 419397000 Official number: 2098	**951** 285 1,248	Class: IR (NV)	**1986-04 Goa Shipyard Ltd. — Goa** Yd No: 1113 Loa 55.31 Br ex 12.86 Dght 5.097 Lbp 48.01 Br md 12.51 Dpth 5.82 Welded, 2 dks	**(B21B20A) Anchor Handling Tug Supply**	**2 oil engines** geared to sc. shafts driving 2 CP propellers Total Power: 2,354kW (3,200hp) 12.0kn Normo LDMB-8 2 x 4 Stroke 8 Cy. 250 x 300 each-1177kW (1600bhp) AS Bergens Mek Verksteder-Norway AuxGen: 2 x 448kW 415V 50Hz a.c, 2 x 224kW 415V 50Hz a.c Thrusters: 1 Thwart. CP thruster (f) Fuel: 392.0 (d.f.)
8311704 *VVFF* -	**SAMUDRIKA-3** *ex* Sam 3 *-2007* *ex* Samudrika-3 *-2007* **Oil & Natural Gas Corp Ltd** The Shipping Corporation of India Ltd (SCI) SatCom: Inmarsat C 441951710 *Mumbai* *India* MMSI: 419398000 Official number: 2099	**951** 285 1,248	Class: IR (NV)	**1986-09 Goa Shipyard Ltd. — Goa** Yd No: 1114 Loa 55.43 Br ex 12.81 Dght 5.100 Lbp 48.01 Br md 12.51 Dpth 5.82 Welded, 1 dk	**(B21B20A) Anchor Handling Tug Supply**	**2 oil engines** sr geared to sc. shafts driving 2 CP propellers Total Power: 2,354kW (3,200hp) 12.0kn Normo LDMB-8 2 x 4 Stroke 8 Cy. 250 x 300 each-1177kW (1600bhp) Garden Reach Shipbuilders &Engineers Ltd-India AuxGen: 2 x 448kW 415V 50Hz a.c, 2 x 224kW 415V 50Hz a.c Thrusters: 1 Thwart. CP thruster (f) Fuel: 392.0 (d.f.)
8311728 *VTKM* -	**SAMUDRIKA-4** - **Oil & Natural Gas Corp Ltd** The Shipping Corporation of India Ltd (SCI) SatCom: Inmarsat C 441953910 *Mumbai* *India* MMSI: 419399000 Official number: 2085	**951** 285 1,231	Class: IR (NV)	**1985-12 Hindustan Shipyard Ltd — Visakhapatnam** Yd No: 1151 Loa 55.35 Br ex 12.53 Dght 5.090 Lbp 47.96 Br md 12.50 Dpth 5.80 Welded, 1 dk	**(B21B20A) Anchor Handling Tug Supply**	**2 oil engines** sr geared to sc. shafts driving 2 CP propellers Total Power: 2,354kW (3,200hp) 13.0kn Normo LDMB-8 2 x 4 Stroke 8 Cy. 250 x 300 each-1177kW (1600bhp) AS Bergens Mek Verksteder-Norway AuxGen: 2 x 448kW 415V 50Hz a.c, 2 x 216kW 415V 50Hz a.c Thrusters: 1 Thwart. CP thruster (f) Fuel: 392.0 (d.f.)
8311730 *VVFG* -	**SAMUDRIKA-5** - **Oil & Natural Gas Corp Ltd** The Shipping Corporation of India Ltd (SCI) SatCom: Inmarsat C 441954010 *Mumbai* *India* MMSI: 419400000 Official number: 2100	**951** 285 1,239	Class: IR (NV)	**1986-03 Hindustan Shipyard Ltd — Visakhapatnam** Yd No: 1152 Loa 55.28 Br ex 12.53 Dght 5.090 Lbp 48.21 Br md 12.50 Dpth 8.89 Welded, 1 dk	**(B21B20A) Anchor Handling Tug Supply**	**2 oil engines** sr geared to sc. shafts driving 2 CP propellers Total Power: 2,354kW (3,200hp) 13.0kn Normo LDMB-8 2 x 4 Stroke 8 Cy. 250 x 300 each-1177kW (1600bhp) AS Bergens Mek Verksteder-Norway AuxGen: 2 x 448kW 415V 50Hz a.c, 2 x 224kW 415V 50Hz a.c Thrusters: 1 Thwart. CP thruster (f) Fuel: 392.0 (d.f.)
8311742 *VVFJ* -	**SAMUDRIKA-6** - **Oil & Natural Gas Corp Ltd** Sical Logistics Ltd SatCom: Inmarsat C 441951810 *Mumbai* *India* MMSI: 419401000 Official number: 2101	**951** 285 1,237	Class: IR (NV)	**1986-09 Hindustan Shipyard Ltd — Visakhapatnam** Yd No: 1153 Loa 55.43 Br ex 12.86 Dght 5.090 Lbp 48.32 Br md 12.51 Dpth 5.82 Welded, 1 dk	**(B21B20A) Anchor Handling Tug Supply**	**2 oil engines** sr geared to sc. shafts driving 2 CP propellers Total Power: 2,354kW (3,200hp) 13.0kn Normo LDMB-8 2 x 4 Stroke 8 Cy. 250 x 300 each-1177kW (1600bhp) AS Bergens Mek Verksteder-Norway AuxGen: 2 x 448kW 415V 50Hz a.c, 2 x 224kW 415V 50Hz a.c Thrusters: 1 Thwart. CP thruster (f) Fuel: 392.0 (d.f.)
8311613 *VVFW* -	**SAMUDRIKA-8** - **Oil & Natural Gas Corp Ltd** The Shipping Corporation of India Ltd (SCI) SatCom: Inmarsat C 441954110 *Mumbai* *India* MMSI: 419403000 Official number: 2117	**951** 285 1,150	Class: IR (NV)	**1986-02 Garden Reach Shipbuilders & Engineers Ltd. — Kolkata** Yd No: 2024 Loa 55.00 Br ex 12.83 Dght 4.901 Lbp 48.01 Br md 12.51 Dpth 5.82 Welded, 1 dk	**(B21B20A) Anchor Handling Tug Supply**	**2 oil engines** with clutches, flexible couplings & sr geared to sc. shafts driving 2 CP propellers Total Power: 2,354kW (3,200hp) 13.0kn Normo LDMB-8 2 x 4 Stroke 8 Cy. 250 x 300 each-1177kW (1600bhp) AS Bergens Mek Verksteder-Norway AuxGen: 2 x 448kW 415V 50Hz a.c, 2 x 224kW 390V 50Hz a.c Thrusters: 1 Thwart. CP thruster (f) Fuel: 392.0 (d.f.)
8311766 *VVFS* -	**SAMUDRIKA-11** - **Oil & Natural Gas Corp Ltd** The Shipping Corporation of India Ltd (SCI) SatCom: Inmarsat C 441952010 *Mumbai* *India* MMSI: 419387000 Official number: 2114	**950** 285 1,167	Class: IR (NV)	**1986-03 Hooghly Dock & Port Engineers Ltd. — Haora** Yd No: 438 Loa 55.12 Br ex 12.50 Dght 4.901 Lbp 47.83 Br md 12.45 Dpth 5.82 Welded, 1 dk	**(B21B20A) Anchor Handling Tug Supply**	**2 oil engines** sr geared to sc. shafts driving 2 CP propellers Total Power: 2,354kW (3,200hp) 13.0kn Normo LDMB-8 2 x 4 Stroke 8 Cy. 250 x 300 each-1177kW (1600bhp) AS Bergens Mek Verksteder-Norway AuxGen: 2 x 448kW 415V 50Hz a.c, 2 x 224kW 415V 50Hz a.c Thrusters: 1 Thwart. CP thruster (f) Fuel: 427.0 (d.f.)

8413801 *VWNT* -	**SAMUDRIKA-15** **Oil & Natural Gas Corp Ltd** Sical Logistics Ltd SatCom: Inmarsat C 441955110 *Mumbai* *India* MMSI: 419389000 Official number: 2087	**954** 319 1,500	Class: IR (NV)	**1985**-06 **Southern Ocean Shipbuilding Co Pte Ltd — Singapore** Yd No: 157 Loa 51.36 Br ex 12.50 Dght 5.060 Lbp 48.01 Br md 12.48 Dpth 5.80 Welded, 1 dk	**(B21B20A) Anchor Handling Tug Supply**	**2 oil engines** with clutches, flexible couplings & sr geared to sc. shafts driving 2 CP propellers Total Power: 2,354kW (3,200hp) Daihatsu 6DSM-28FS 2 x 4 Stroke 6 Cy. 280 x 340 each-1177kW (1600bhp) Daihatsu Diesel Manufacturing Co Lt-Japan AuxGen: 2 x 448kW 415V 50Hz a.c, 2 x 224kW 390V 50Hz a.c Thrusters: 1 Thwart. CP thruster (f)
8413813 *VWFJ* -	**SAMUDRIKA-16** **Oil & Natural Gas Corp Ltd** The Shipping Corporation of India Ltd (SCI) SatCom: Inmarsat C 441952210 *Mumbai* *India* MMSI: 419390000 Official number: 2088	**954** 319 1,500	Class: IR (NV)	**1985**-03 **Southern Ocean Shipbuilding Co Pte Ltd — Singapore** Yd No: 158 Loa 51.36 Br ex 12.50 Dght 5.060 Lbp 48.01 Br md 12.48 Dpth 5.80 Welded, 1 dk	**(B21B20A) Anchor Handling Tug Supply**	**2 oil engines** with clutches, flexible couplings & sr geared to sc. shafts driving 2 CP propellers Total Power: 2,354kW (3,200hp) Daihatsu 6DSM-28FS 2 x 4 Stroke 6 Cy. 280 x 340 each-1177kW (1600bhp) Daihatsu Diesel Manufacturing Co Lt-Japan AuxGen: 2 x 448kW 415V 50Hz a.c, 2 x 224kW 390V 50Hz a.c Thrusters: 1 Thwart. CP thruster (f)
8413837 *VWGX* -	**SAMUDRIKA-18** **Oil & Natural Gas Corp Ltd** The Shipping Corporation of India Ltd (SCI) SatCom: Inmarsat C 441955710 *Mumbai* *India* MMSI: 419419000 Official number: 2090	**954** 319 1,500	Class: IR (NV)	**1985**-03 **Southern Ocean Shipbuilding Co Pte Ltd — Singapore** Yd No: 160 Loa 51.36 Br ex 12.50 Dght 5.060 Lbp 48.01 Br md 12.48 Dpth 5.80 Welded, 1 dk	**(B21B20A) Anchor Handling Tug Supply**	**2 oil engines** with clutches, flexible couplings & sr geared to sc. shafts driving 2 CP propellers Total Power: 2,354kW (3,200hp) Daihatsu 6DSM-28FS 2 x 4 Stroke 6 Cy. 280 x 340 each-1177kW (1600bhp) Daihatsu Diesel Manufacturing Co Lt-Japan AuxGen: 2 x 448kW 415V 50Hz a.c, 2 x 224kW 390V 50Hz a.c Thrusters: 1 Thwart. CP thruster (f)
7929748 *YFHU* -	**SAMUDRO ENDAH** *ex* Argo Makmur *-2005* *ex* Lestari Makmur *-2004* *ex* Rubby *-1996* *ex* Tagonoura No. 3 *-1995* *ex* Seiryu Maru *-1988* **PT Lintas Kumala Abadi** - *Palembang* *Indonesia*	**926** 545 1,850	Class: KI	**1980**-04 **K.K. Miura Zosensho — Saiki** Yd No: 603 Loa - Br ex - Dght 3.341 Lbp 59.52 Br md 10.51 Dpth 5.31 Welded, 1 dk	**(A31A2GX) General Cargo Ship**	**1 oil engine** driving 1 FP propeller Total Power: 883kW (1,201hp) Hanshin 6LU28G 1 x 4 Stroke 6 Cy. 280 x 440 883kW (1201bhp) Hanshin Nainenki Kogyo-Japan
5309085 *GRAM* -	**SAMUEL ARMSTRONG** **Western Towage & Salvage Co** - *Ipswich* *United Kingdom* Official number: 185842	*364* 161 427	Class: (LR) ✠ Classed LR until 2/2/98	**1956**-03 **Henry Robb Ltd. — Leith** Yd No: 441 Loa 41.56 Br ex 9.25 Dght 3.220 Lbp 39.17 Br md 8.69 Dpth 3.66 Riveted\Welded, 1 dk	**(B33B2DG) Grab Hopper Dredger** Hopper: 278 Cranes: 1x5t	**1 oil engine** driving 1 FP propeller Total Power: 515kW (700hp) 10.0kn Crossley HSN8 1 x 2 Stroke 8 Cy. 267 x 343 515kW (700bhp) Crossley Bros. Ltd.-Manchester AuxGen: 2 x 25kW 110V d.c Fuel: 28.5 (d.f.)
7433799 *WDC8307* -	**SAMUEL DE CHAMPLAIN** *ex* Norfolk *-2005* *ex* Vortice *-1999* *ex* Margarita *-1983* *ex* Tender Panther *-1979* *ex* Musketeer Fury *-1978* **American Transport Leasing Inc** Andrie Inc *Cleveland, OH* *United States of America* MMSI: 367084930 Official number: 1077852	**876** 262 -	Class: AB (RI)	**1976**-11 **Mangone Shipbuilding Co. — Houston, Tx** Yd No: 120 Converted From: Tug-2006 Loa 45.65 Br ex 11.94 Dght 3.814 Lbp 41.92 Br md 11.89 Dpth 6.18 Welded, 1 dk	**(B32B2SA) Articulated Pusher Tug** Ice Capable	**2 oil engines** sr geared to sc. shafts driving 2 CP propellers Total Power: 5,296kW (7,200hp) 15.0kn EMD (Electro-Motive) 20-645-E5 2 x Vee 2 Stroke 20 Cy. 230 x 254 each-2648kW (3600bhp) General Motors Corp.Electro-Motive Div.-La Grange AuxGen: 2 x 125kW Thrusters: 1 Thwart. FP thruster (f) Fuel: 468.5 (d.f.)
9234408 *FQCF* -	**SAMUEL DE CHAMPLAIN** **GIE Dragages-Ports** - *Rouen* *France* MMSI: 228160900 Official number: 920574	**8,072** 2,421 12,150	Class: BV	**2002**-10 **IZAR Construcciones Navales SA — Gijon** Yd No: 366 Loa 117.00 (BB) Br ex - Dght 8.000 Lbp 110.00 Br md 24.00 Dpth 10.00 Welded, 1 dk	**(B33B2DT) Trailing Suction Hopper Dredger** Hopper: 8,500	**3 diesel electric oil engines** driving 2 gen. each 3088kW 6600V 1 gen. of 2312kW 6600V a.c Connecting to 2 elec. motors each (2550kW) driving 2 FP propellers Total Power: 8,800kW (11,965hp) 13.0kn Wartsila 12V200 1 x Vee 4 Stroke 12 Cy. 200 x 240 2400kW (3263bhp) Wartsila France SA-France Wartsila 16V200 2 x Vee 4 Stroke 16 Cy. 200 x 240 each-3200kW (4351bhp) Wartsila France SA-France AuxGen: 1 x 531kW 220V 50Hz a.c Thrusters: 1 Tunnel thruster (f)
5415949 - - -	**SAMUEL F** *ex* Hornby *-1984* *ex* J. H. Lamey *-1970* - -	**205** 61 -	Class: (LR) ✠ Classed LR until 3/68	**1964**-03 **Cochrane & Sons Ltd. — Selby** Yd No: 1492 Loa 32.72 Br ex 8.56 Dght - Lbp 29.27 Br md 8.08 Dpth 4.12 Riveted\Welded, 1 dk	**(B32A2ST) Tug**	**1 oil engine** with flexible couplings & sr geared to sc. shaft driving 1 FP propeller Total Power: 956kW (1,300hp) 12.0kn MWM RH348AU 1 x 4 Stroke 8 Cy. 320 x 480 956kW (1300bhp) Motoren Werke Mannheim AG (MWM)-West Germany AuxGen: 2 x 25kW 220V d.c
8322442 *CG2960* -	**SAMUEL RISLEY** **Government of Canada (Canadian Coast Guard)** - *Ottawa, ON* *Canada* MMSI: 316001890 Official number: 805575	*1,967* 649 1,186	Class: (LR) ✠ Classed LR until 19/9/86	**1985**-06 **Vito Steel Boat & Barge Construction Ltd — Delta BC** Yd No: 161 Loa 69.73 Br ex 14.36 Dght 5.811 Lbp 59.01 Br md 13.71 Dpth 6.71 Welded, 1 dk	**(B34Q2QB) Buoy Tender** Ice Capable	**4 oil engines** with clutches, flexible couplings & sr geared to sc. shafts driving 2 CP propellers Total Power: 6,356kW (8,640hp) 14.5kn Wartsila 12V22 4 x Vee 4 Stroke 12 Cy. 220 x 240 each-1589kW (2160bhp) Oy Wartsila Ab-Finland AuxGen: 2 x 1000kW 600V 60Hz a.c, 2 x 395kW 600V 60Hz a.c Thrusters: 1 Water jet (f); 1 Water jet (a) Fuel: 692.5 (d.f.)
8625002 *PNRG* -	**SAMUGARA 9** *ex* Daebo No. 2 *-2011* *ex* Keihin Maru No. 5 *-2010* **PT Samugara Artajaya** - *Pontianak* *Indonesia*	**356** 178 566	Class: KI	**1985**-03 **Iisaku Zosen K.K. — Nishi-Izu** Yd No: 85121 Loa 43.00 Br ex - Dght 2.680 Lbp 40.00 Br md 9.00 Dpth 3.20 Welded, 1 dk	**(A13B2TP) Products Tanker** Liq: 699; Liq (Oil): 699	**1 oil engine** driving 1 FP propeller Total Power: 368kW (500hp) 8.5kn Matsui 1 x 4 Stroke 368kW (500bhp) Matsui Iron Works Co Ltd-Japan
8734554 *YB4658* -	**SAMUGARA I** **PT Samugara Artajaya** - *Tanjung Priok* *Indonesia*	**297** 145 -	Class: KI	**2008**-09 **P.T. Inggom Shipyard — Jakarta** Loa 40.50 Br ex - Dght - Lbp 39.00 Br md 9.00 Dpth 2.60 Welded, 1 dk	**(B35E2TF) Bunkering Tanker**	**2 oil engines** driving 2 Propellers Total Power: 272kW (370hp) Mitsubishi S6B-MPTK 2 x 4 Stroke 6 Cy. 150 x 160 each-136kW (185bhp) Mitsubishi Heavy Industries Ltd-Japan
8876003 *YDZL* -	**SAMUGARA II** *ex* Merry *-2009* *ex* Jun Jin *-2009* *ex* Saemangeum No. 2 *-2005* *ex* Su Hyup Ho No. 2 *-2005* **Eridman Tascha** - *Bitung* *Indonesia*	**160** 60 225	Class: KI (KR)	**1994**-02 **Kyungnam Shipbuilding Co Ltd — Busan** Yd No: 93-3 Loa 33.70 Br ex - Dght 2.850 Lbp 30.00 Br md 6.00 Dpth 3.00 Welded, 1 dk	**(A13B2TU) Tanker (unspecified)** Liq: 273; Liq (Oil): 273	**1 oil engine** driving 1 FP propeller Total Power: 419kW (570hp) 10.5kn Yanmar 6LAH-STE3 1 x 4 Stroke 6 Cy. 150 x 165 419kW (570bhp) Kwangyang Diesel Engine Co Ltd-South Korea AuxGen: 2 x 78kW 445V a.c Fuel: 7.0 (d.f.)
9116371 *HP8442* -	**SAMUNDRA I** *ex* Bolero *-2013* *ex* Bolero I *-2001* **Samundra I Shipping Inc** Auburn Shipmanagement JLT *Panama* *Panama* MMSI: 352424000 Official number: 4528013	**28,414** 12,646 44,999 T/cm 51.0	Class: NV	**1996**-06 **Halla Engineering & Heavy Industries Ltd — Incheon** Yd No: 225 Loa 183.20 (BB) Br ex 32.20 Dght 10.970 Lbp 173.98 Br md 32.20 Dpth 18.00 Welded, 1 dk	**(A12B2TR) Chemical/Products Tanker** Double Hull (13F) Liq: 51,878; Liq (Oil): 51,878 Cargo Heating Coils Compartments: 8 Ta, 2 Wing Slop Ta, ER 8 Cargo Pump (s): 8x850m³/hr Manifold: Bow/CM: 92m	**1 oil engine** driving 1 FP propeller Total Power: 8,422kW (11,451hp) 14.5kn B&W 6S50MC 1 x 2 Stroke 6 Cy. 500 x 1910 8422kW (11451bhp) Hyundai Heavy Industries Co Ltd-South Korea AuxGen: 1 x 700kW 220/450V 60Hz a.c, 3 x 950kW 220/450V 60Hz a.c
7601683 *4JBH* -	**SAMUR** **Azerbaijan State Caspian Shipping Co (ASCSS)** - *Baku* *Azerbaijan* Official number: 762889	*498* 215 1,060	Class: (RS)	**1977**-05 **Ulstein Hatlo AS — Ulsteinvik** Yd No: 146 Loa 64.39 Br ex - Dght 3.799 Lbp 56.39 Br md 13.80 Dpth 6.91 Welded, 1 dk	**(B21B20A) Anchor Handling Tug Supply**	**2 oil engines** reduction geared to sc. shafts driving 2 CP propellers Total Power: 5,178kW (7,040hp) 15.0kn Nohab F216V 2 x Vee 4 Stroke 16 Cy. 250 x 300 each-2589kW (3520bhp) AB Bofors NOHAB-Sweden Thrusters: 1 Thwart. FP thruster (f)

IMO / Call sign	Name / Owner	Tonnage	Class	Builder / Dimensions	Type	Machinery
8867430 *UIFE* -	**SAMUR 3** *ex* Samur-3 *-2003* *ex* Ruza-2 *-2001* *ex* ST-1312 *-2001* **Trans-Nord Ltd** - *Arkhangelsk* *Russia* MMSI: 273426650	**1,839** 552 2,755	Class: RS	**1986-03 Sudostroitelnyy Zavod im Volodarskogo — Rybinsk** Yd No: 04906 Loa 88.90 Br ex 12.30 Dght 4.100 Lbp 83.60 Br md 12.00 Dpth 6.00 Welded, 1 dk	**(A31A2GX) General Cargo Ship** Grain: 2,230 TEU 54 C.Ho 36/20' C.Dk 18/20' Compartments: 1 Ho, ER 2 Ha: 2 (19.8 x 9.0)ER Ice Capable	**2 oil engines** driving 2 FP propellers Total Power: 1,030kW (1,400hp) S.K.L. 6NVDS48A-2U 2 x 4 Stroke 6 Cy. 320 x 480 each-515kW (700bhp) VEB Schwermaschinenbau "KarlLiebknecht" (SKL)-Magdeburg
9378876 *A8PX7* -	**SAMURAI** - **Palmdale Investments Inc** Dynacom Tankers Management Ltd SatCom: Inmarsat C 463703868 *Monrovia* *Liberia* MMSI: 636013852 Official number: 13852	**78,845** 47,229 149,993 T/cm 118.0	Class: LR ✠ **100A1** SS 02/2009 Double Hull oil tanker ESP **ShipRight** (SDA, FDA plus, CM) *IWS LI SPM ✠ **LMC** **UMS IGS** Eq.Ltr: X†; Cable: 742.5/97.0 U3 (a)	**2009-02 Universal Shipbuilding Corp — Tsu ME** Yd No: 113 Loa 274.20 (BB) Br ex 48.04 Dght 15.990 Lbp 263.00 Br md 48.00 Dpth 22.40 Welded, 1 dk	**(A13A2TV) Crude Oil Tanker** Double Hull (13F) Liq: 160,636; Liq (Oil): 160,636 Cargo Heating Coils Compartments: 12 Wing Ta, 2 Wing Slop Ta, ER 3 Cargo Pump (s): 3x3500m³/hr Manifold: Bow/CM: 133.8m	**1 oil engine** driving 1 FP propeller Total Power: 16,440kW (22,352hp) 15.4kn Wartsila 6RTA72U 1 x 2 Stroke 6 Cy. 720 x 2500 16440kW (22352bhp) Diesel United Ltd.-Aioi AuxGen: 3 x 800kW 450V 60Hz a.c Boilers: e (ex.g.) 22.9kgf/cm² (22.5bar), WTAuxB (o.f.) 17.8kgf/cm² (17.5bar) Fuel: 259.0 (d.f.) 3486.0 (r.f.)
9401312 *9HA2333* -	**SAMUS SWAN** *ex* Kardemir *-2014* **Istanbul Celik Enerji Tersane ve Ulasim Sanayi AS (ICDAS)** North Sea Tankers BV *Valletta* *Malta* MMSI: 248363000 Official number: 9401312	**4,001** 1,837 5,717 T/cm 15.0	Class: BV (NK) (RI)	**2009-08 Icdas Celik Enerji Tersane ve Ulasim Sanayi AS — Biga** Yd No: 12 Loa 105.50 (BB) Br ex - Dght 6.290 Lbp 99.35 Br md 16.80 Dpth 7.40 Welded, 1 dk	**(A12B2TR) Chemical/Products Tanker** Double Hull (13F) Liq: 6,291; Liq (Oil): 6,585 Cargo Heating Coils Compartments: 10 Wing Ta, 2 Wing Slop Ta, ER 10 Cargo Pump (s): 10x200m³/hr Manifold: Bow/CM: 45.6m Ice Capable	**1 oil engine** reduction geared to sc. shaft driving 1 CP propeller Total Power: 2,720kW (3,698hp) 13.0kn MAN-B&W 8L27/38 1 x 4 Stroke 8 Cy. 270 x 380 2720kW (3698bhp) MAN B&W Diesel AG-Augsburg AuxGen: 3 x 400kW 380/220V 50Hz a.c, 1 x 800kW 380/220V 50Hz a.c Thrusters: 1 Tunnel thruster (f) Fuel: 64.0 (d.f.) 253.0 (r.f.)
9503328 *9V7615* -	**SAMWOH COURAGE** *ex* SG 26 *-2009* **Samwoh Shipping Pte Ltd** - *Singapore* *Singapore* MMSI: 563011450 Official number: 394514	**137** 42 107	Class: GL	**2008-09 Hung Seng Shipbuilding Sdn Bhd — Sibu** Yd No: 05 Loa 23.50 Br ex - Dght 2.430 Lbp 21.38 Br md 7.32 Dpth 3.10 Welded, 1 dk	**(B32A2ST) Tug**	**2 oil engines** reverse reduction geared to sc. shafts driving 2 FP propellers Total Power: 893kW (1,214hp) Cummins KTA-19-M3 2 x 4 Stroke 6 Cy. 159 x 159 each-446kW (606bhp) Cummins Engine Co Inc-USA AuxGen: 2 x 28kW 415V a.c
9545962 *9V8326* -	**SAMWOH INFINITY** *ex* Fordeco 93 *-2009* **Samwoh Shipping Pte Ltd** - *Singapore* *Singapore* MMSI: 563014320 Official number: 395618	**158** 48 167	Class: GL (NK)	**2009-10 Sapangar Shipyard Sdn Bhd — Lahad Datu** Yd No: SS015 Loa 24.45 Br ex - Dght 3.050 Lbp 22.49 Br md 7.32 Dpth 3.55 Welded, 1 dk	**(B32A2ST) Tug**	**2 oil engines** geared to sc. shafts driving 2 FP propellers Total Power: 894kW (1,216hp) Cummins KTA-19-M3 2 x 4 Stroke 6 Cy. 159 x 159 each-447kW (608bhp) Cummins Engine Co Inc-USA Fuel: 105.0 (d.f.)
9433248 *9V7055* -	**SAMWOH PRIDE** *launched as* Bestwin 148 *-2007* **Samwoh Marine Pte Ltd** - *Singapore* *Singapore* MMSI: 563009570 Official number: 392706	**141** 43 109	Class: GL (NK)	**2007-09 in Indonesia** Yd No: 179 Loa 23.50 Br ex 7.32 Dght 2.710 Lbp 21.07 Br md 7.32 Dpth 3.20 Welded, 1 dk	**(B32A2ST) Tug**	**2 oil engines** reduction geared to sc. shafts driving 2 FP propellers Total Power: 954kW (1,298hp) Cummins KTA-19-M3 2 x 4 Stroke 6 Cy. 159 x 159 each-477kW (649bhp) Cummins Engine Co Ltd-United Kingdom AuxGen: 2 x 31kW a.c Fuel: 93.0 (d.f.)
9263851 - -	**SAMWOO HO** - **Seongbo Shipping Co Ltd** - *Seosan* *South Korea* MMSI: 440200144 Official number: DSR-029015	**115** - -	Class: KR	**2002-01 Yeunsoo Shipbuilding Co Ltd — Janghang** Yd No: 6 Loa 28.50 Br ex 7.90 Dght 2.400 Lbp 25.86 Br md 7.80 Dpth 3.40 Welded, 1 dk	**(B32A2ST) Tug**	**2 oil engines** reduction geared to sc. shafts driving 2 FP propellers Total Power: 1,472kW (2,002hp) Cummins KTA-38-M1 2 x Vee 4 Stroke 12 Cy. 159 x 159 each-736kW (1001bhp) Cummins Engine Co Inc-USA
6512263 *DSOB2* -	**SAMYANG NO. 1** *ex* Sang Yang No. 1 *-2008* *ex* Sung Woo No. 7 *-2008* *ex* Kono Maru No. 58 *-2004* *ex* Kono Maru No. 7 *-2004* *ex* Kanda Maru *-1988* *ex* Yawata Maru No. 2 *-1988* **Samyang Shipping Co Ltd** - *Busan* *South Korea* MMSI: 440124440 Official number: BSR-041548	**137** - -		**1965-03 Hitachi Zosen Corp — Osaka OS** Yd No: 4080 Loa 29.90 Br ex - Dght 2.700 Lbp 27.22 Br md 8.20 Dpth 3.72 Welded, 1 dk	**(B32A2ST) Tug**	**1 oil engine** Total Power: 736kW (1,001hp) Hanshin 1 x 4 Stroke 6 Cy. 320 x 380 736kW (1001bhp) (made 1980) The Hanshin Diesel Works Ltd-Japan
8623145 *HLLN* -	**SAMYOUNG No. 301** *ex* Kwang Sung No. 301 *-1996* *ex* Jeong Chang No. 1 *-1993* **Sam Young Fisheries Co Ltd** - SatCom: Inmarsat A 1660523 *Busan* *South Korea* MMSI: 440076000 Official number: 9512317-6260008	**454** - 350	Class: KR	**1986-10 Sungkwang Shipbuilding Co Ltd — Tongyeong** Yd No: 172 Loa 57.70 (BB) Br ex - Dght 3.820 Lbp 49.50 Br md 9.00 Dpth - Welded, 1 dk	**(B11B2FV) Fishing Vessel**	**1 oil engine** driving 1 FP propeller Total Power: 883kW (1,201hp) 12.5kn Hanshin 6LUN28 1 x 4 Stroke 6 Cy. 280 x 480 883kW (1201bhp) Ssangyong Heavy Industries Co Ltd-South Korea AuxGen: 4 x 345kW 220V a.c
8810578 *9LF7082* -	**SAMZIN 8** *ex* Hongrun *-2013* *ex* Hai Xing No. 8 *-2008* *ex* Hakuyo Maru *-2007* **Samzin Shipping Co Ltd** East Grand Shipping Co Ltd *Freetown* *Sierra Leone* MMSI: 667007082 Official number: SL107082	**2,980** 1,918 -	Class: UM	**1989-03 Suzuki Shipyard Co. Ltd. — Yokkaichi** Yd No: 555 Converted From: Grab Dredger-2008 Lengthened & Deepened-2008 Loa 85.00 (BB) Br ex - Dght - Lbp 80.00 Br md 13.50 Dpth 8.10 Welded, 1 dk	**(A31A2GX) General Cargo Ship** Bale: 1,016 Compartments: 1 Wing Ho	**1 oil engine** driving 1 FP propeller Total Power: 1,471kW (2,000hp) Akasaka DM36KFD 1 x 4 Stroke 6 Cy. 360 x 540 1471kW (2000bhp) Akasaka Tekkosho KK (Akasaka DieselLtd)-Japan
9521851 *A8ZR2* -	**SAN** - **Hermione Six Maritime Ltd** Polska Zegluga Morska PP (POLSTEAM) *Monrovia* *Liberia* MMSI: 636015277 Official number: 15277	**13,579** 5,247 16,620	Class: AB PR	**2012-06 Taizhou Sanfu Ship Engineering Co Ltd — Taizhou JS** Yd No: SF080106 Loa 149.96 (BB) Br ex - Dght 8.250 Lbp 140.80 Br md 23.60 Dpth 12.50 Welded, 1 dk	**(A21A2BC) Bulk Carrier** Grain: 23,800 Compartments: 5 Ho, ER 5 Ha: ER Cranes: 3x30t Ice Capable	**1 oil engine** driving 1 CP propeller Total Power: 6,570kW (8,933hp) 14.0kn MAN-B&W 5S50MC-C 1 x 2 Stroke 5 Cy. 500 x 2000 6570kW (8933bhp) STX (Dalian) Engine Co Ltd-China AuxGen: 1 x 645kW a.c, 2 x 520kW a.c Thrusters: 1 Tunnel thruster (f)
9347279 *A8PC8* -	**SAN ADRIANO** *ex* Ibn Qutaibah *-2009* *launched as* San Adriano *-2008* **KG Zweite ms 'San Adriano' Offen Reederei GmbH & Co** Reederei Claus-Peter Offen GmbH & Co KG *Monrovia* *Liberia* MMSI: 636091533 Official number: 91533	**22,914** 9,277 28,147	Class: GL	**2008-03 Hyundai Mipo Dockyard Co Ltd — Ulsan** Yd No: 4010 Loa 186.35 (BB) Br ex - Dght 11.300 Lbp 175.00 Br md 27.60 Dpth 17.10 Welded, 1 dk	**(A33A2CC) Container Ship (Fully Cellular)** TEU 1819 C Ho 736 TEU C Dk 1083 TEU incl 462 ref C. Compartments: 4 Cell Ho, ER Cranes: 3x35t	**1 oil engine** driving 1 FP propeller Total Power: 19,620kW (26,675hp) 21.0kn MAN-B&W 6L70MC-C 1 x 2 Stroke 6 Cy. 700 x 2360 19620kW (26675bhp) Hyundai Heavy Industries Co Ltd-South Korea AuxGen: 4 x 1570kW 450V a.c Thrusters: 1 Tunnel thruster (f) Fuel: 200.0 (d.f.) 2180.0 (r.f.)
7020774 - -	**SAN AGUSTIN REYES** *ex* Ehime No. 8 *-1994* **Viva Shipping Lines Co Inc** - *Batangas* *Philippines* Official number: BAT5001085	*253* 116 66		**1969 Yoshiura Zosen — Kure** Yd No: 210 Loa 32.21 Br ex 8.01 Dght 2.032 Lbp 28.50 Br md 7.40 Dpth 2.90 Welded, 1 dk	**(A37B2PS) Passenger Ship** Passengers: 148	**1 oil engine** driving 1 FP propeller Total Power: 441kW (600hp) 11.5kn Daihatsu 6PST6M-26D 1 x 4 Stroke 6 Cy. 260 x 320 441kW (600bhp) Daihatsu Kogyo-Japan AuxGen: 1 x 15kW 225V a.c

8415160 *DUTU5* -	**SAN AGUSTIN UNO** *ex* Irbe Gauja *-2008* *ex* Santa Maria *-2006* **Caprotec Corp** Negros Navigation Co Inc *Manila* *Philippines* MMSI: 548299100 Official number: 00-0001419	**3,062** 1,413 3,885	Class: GL	**1985-10 Schiffswerft und Maschinenfabrik Cassens GmbH — Emden** Yd No: 167 Loa 99.31 (BB) Br ex 14.03 Dght 5.070 Lbp 94.21 Br md 14.01 Dpth 7.15 Welded, 2 dks	**(A31A2GX) General Cargo Ship** Grain: 5,423; Bale: 5,380 TEU 198 C.Ho 117/20' (40') C.Dk 81/20' (40') incl. 9 ref C. Compartments: 1 Ho, ER, 1 Tw Dk 1 Ha: (62.2 x 11.1)ER Cranes: 2x25t Ice Capable	**1 oil engine** with flexible couplings & sr gearedto sc. shaft driving 1 CP propeller Total Power: 1,662kW (2,260hp) 12.0kn MWM TBD510-6 1 x 4 Stroke 6 Cy. 330 x 360 1662kW (2260bhp) Motoren Werke Mannheim AG (MWM)-West Germany AuxGen: 3 x 196kW a.c Thrusters: 1 Thwart. FP thruster (f) Fuel: 31.0 (d.f.) 180.0 (r.f.)
9347293 *A8PG8* -	**SAN ALESSIO** **KG Zweite ms 'San Alessio' Offen Reederei GmbH & Co** Reederei Claus-Peter Offen GmbH & Co KG *Monrovia* *Liberia* MMSI: 636091546 Official number: 91546	**22,914** 9,277 28,142	Class: GL	**2008-04 Hyundai Mipo Dockyard Co Ltd — Ulsan** Yd No: 4012 Loa 186.37 (BB) Br ex - Dght 11.300 Lbp 175.00 Br md 27.60 Dpth 17.10 Welded, 1 dk	**(A33A2CC) Container Ship (Fully Cellular)** TEU 1819 C Ho 736 TEU C Dk 1083 TEU incl 462 ref C. Compartments: 4 Cell Ho, ER Cranes: 3x45t	**1 oil engine** driving 1 FP propeller Total Power: 19,620kW (26,675hp) 21.0kn MAN-B&W 6L70MC-C 1 x 2 Stroke 6 Cy. 700 x 2360 19620kW (26675bhp) Hyundai Heavy Industries Co Ltd-South Korea AuxGen: 4 x 1570kW a.c Thrusters: 1 Tunnel thruster (f) Fuel: 220.0 (d.f.) 2180.0 (r.f.)
9344693 *A8OK6* -	**SAN AMERIGO** **KG ms 'San Amerigo' Offen Reederei GmbH & Co** Reederei Claus-Peter Offen GmbH & Co KG *Monrovia* *Liberia* MMSI: 636091490 Official number: 91490	**22,914** 9,277 28,186	Class: GL	**2008-01 Hyundai Mipo Dockyard Co Ltd — Ulsan** Yd No: 4007 Loa 186.34 (BB) Br ex - Dght 11.300 Lbp 175.00 Br md 27.60 Dpth 17.10 Welded, 1 dk	**(A33A2CC) Container Ship (Fully Cellular)** TEU 1819 C.Ho 736 TEU C.Dk 1083 TEU incl 462 ref C. Compartments: 4 Cell Ho, ER Cranes: 3x45t	**1 oil engine** driving 1 FP propeller Total Power: 19,620kW (26,675hp) 21.0kn MAN-B&W 6L70MC-C 1 x 2 Stroke 6 Cy. 700 x 2360 19620kW (26675bhp) Hyundai Heavy Industries Co Ltd-South Korea AuxGen: 4 x 1570kW a.c Thrusters: 1 Tunnel thruster (f) Fuel: 220.0 (d.f.) 2180.0 (r.f.) 71.0pd
9347255 *A8OK7* -	**SAN ANDRES** **KG ms 'San Andres' Offen Reederei GmbH & Co** Reederei Claus-Peter Offen GmbH & Co KG *Monrovia* *Liberia* MMSI: 636091491 Official number: 91491	**22,914** 9,277 28,156	Class: GL	**2008-01 Hyundai Mipo Dockyard Co Ltd — Ulsan** Yd No: 4008 Loa 186.34 (BB) Br ex - Dght 11.300 Lbp 175.00 Br md 27.60 Dpth 17.10 Welded, 1 dk	**(A33A2CC) Container Ship (Fully Cellular)** TEU 1819 C Ho 736 TEU C Dk 1083 TEU incl 462 ref C Compartments: 4 Cell Ho, ER Cranes: 3x45t	**1 oil engine** driving 1 FP propeller Total Power: 19,620kW (26,675hp) 21.0kn MAN-B&W 6L70MC-C 1 x 2 Stroke 6 Cy. 700 x 2360 19620kW (26675bhp) Hyundai Heavy Industries Co Ltd-South Korea AuxGen: 4 x 1570kW a.c Thrusters: 1 Tunnel thruster (f) Fuel: 220.0 (d.f.) 2180.0 (r.f.) 71.0pd
8327985 - -	**SAN ANDRES** - **Cannavo SA** - *Cumana* *Venezuela* Official number: 3369	*109* 65 -	Class: (RI)	**1973 Astillero Paraguana — Punto Fijo** Loa 22.51 Br ex 6.10 Dght - Lbp - Br md - Dpth 3.05 Riveted\Welded, 1 dk	**(B11B2FV) Fishing Vessel**	**1 oil engine** driving 1 FP propeller Total Power: 313kW (426hp) Caterpillar D379TA 1 x Vee 4 Stroke 8 Cy. 159 x 203 313kW (426bhp) Caterpillar Tractor Co-USA
8909252 *HC4154* -	**SAN ANDRES** *ex* Isabel Tuna *-1998* **Conservas Isabel Ecuatoriana SA** Conservas Garavilla SA SatCom: Inmarsat A 1101122 *Manta* *Ecuador* MMSI: 735565000 Official number: P-04-0596	**2,193** 658 1,800	Class: BV	**1991-09 Astilleros de Murueta S.A. — Gernika-Lumo** Yd No: 179 Loa 78.00 (BB) Br ex - Dght 6.000 Lbp 68.16 Br md 14.00 Dpth 8.00 Welded, 2 dks	**(B11B2FV) Fishing Vessel** Ins: 1,862	**1 oil engine** with flexible couplings & reduction geared to sc. shaft driving 1 FP propeller Total Power: 3,448kW (4,688hp) 13.5kn MaK 6M551AK 1 x 4 Stroke 6 Cy. 450 x 550 3448kW (4688bhp) Krupp MaK Maschinenbau GmbH-Kiel AuxGen: 3 x 675kW 380V 50Hz a.c Thrusters: 1 Thwart. CP thruster (f) Fuel: 843.0 (d.f.)
8319768 *DYUV* -	**SAN ANDRES 179** *ex* Shin Asahi *-1996* *ex* Shinasahi Maru *-1990* **TSP Livestock & Development Corp** - SatCom: Inmarsat C 454879310 *General Santos* *Philippines* MMSI: 548793000 Official number: DAV4003514	**499** 226 1,454	Class: (NK)	**1983-05 Yamanaka Zosen K.K. — Imabari** Yd No: 268 Loa 73.70 (BB) Br ex - Dght 4.232 Lbp 69.01 Br md 11.70 Dpth 4.26 Welded, 2 dks	**(A34A2GR) Refrigerated Cargo Ship** Ins: 1,749 Compartments: 2 Ho, ER 2 Ha: 2 (6.0 x 5.0)ER Derricks: 4x3t; Winches: 4	**1 oil engine** driving 1 FP propeller Total Power: 1,618kW (2,200hp) 12.0kn Makita GSHL637 1 x 4 Stroke 6 Cy. 370 x 590 1618kW (2200bhp) Makita Diesel Co Ltd-Japan AuxGen: 3 x 200kW a.c
8621379 - -	**SAN ANDRES APOSTOL** *ex* Hotaka Maru *-2003* *ex* Sur Este No. 701 *-2003* *ex* Hotaka Maru *-1992* *ex* Hokko Maru No. 77 *-1987* **Antonio Baldino E Hijos SA** -	**550** 240 512	Class: (KR) (NK)	**1976 Narasaki Senpaku Kogyo K.K. — Muroran** Yd No: 113 Loa 57.51 Br ex - Dght 3.490 Lbp 51.01 Br md 9.01 Dpth 3.84 Welded, 2 dks	**(B11B2FV) Fishing Vessel** Ins: 408	**1 oil engine** driving 1 FP propeller Total Power: 1,692kW (2,300hp) 12.8kn Hanshin 6LU40 1 x 4 Stroke 6 Cy. 400 x 640 1692kW (2300bhp) The Hanshin Diesel Works Ltd-Japan AuxGen: 2 x 264kW 445V a.c
8129450 *HKMS* -	**SAN ANDRES II** *ex* Ellen *-2008* *ex* Ellen Theresa *-2007* *ex* Cheyenne *-2000* *ex* Cisca *-1986* *ex* Regina *-1983* **Transpetrol Ltda** - *Cartagena de Indias* *Colombia* MMSI: 730060000 Official number: MC-05-0606	**1,734** 740 2,593 T/cm 9.9	Class: LR (GL) **100A1** SS 06/2013 oil tanker ESP Ice Class 1D coastal service between Cartagena de Indias and San Andres Islas, Colombia **LMC** **UMS** Cable: 440.0/36.0 U2 (a)	**1983-06 Meltem Beykoz Tersanesi — Beykoz** Yd No: 40 Converted From: Edible Oil Tanker-2011 Loa 84.99 Br ex 13.03 Dght 4.750 Lbp 78.92 Br md 13.01 Dpth 6.02 Welded, 1 dk.	**(A13B2TP) Products Tanker** Double Bottom Entire Compartment Length Liq: 2,218; Liq (Oil): 2,218 Cargo Heating Coils Compartments: 10 Wing Ta, ER 4 Cargo Pump (s): 2x250m^3/hr, 1x165m^3/hr, 1x78m^3/hr Manifold: Bow/CM: 41.3m Ice Capable	**1 oil engine** with flexible couplings & sr geared to sc. shaft driving 1 CP propeller Total Power: 1,320kW (1,795hp) 12.0kn MaK 6M452AK 1 x 4 Stroke 6 Cy. 320 x 450 1320kW (1795bhp) Krupp MaK Maschinenbau GmbH-Kiel AuxGen: 1 x 307kW 400V 50Hz a.c, 2 x 202kW 400V 50Hz a.c Boilers: AuxB (o.f.) 14.3kgf/cm^2 (14.0bar) Thrusters: 1 Thwart. FP thruster (f)
7943885 *HO9618* -	**SAN ANTONIO** *ex* Geminis *-2005* *ex* Quepos *-1988* **Geminis Fishing Inc** - *Panama* *Panama* Official number: 0835977E	*246* 82 -	Class: (GL)	**1976 Intermar S.A. — Callao** Yd No: 04 Loa 34.55 Br ex 7.95 Dght - Lbp 30.48 Br md 7.93 Dpth 4.30 Welded, 1 dk	**(B11B2FV) Fishing Vessel**	**1 oil engine** reverse reduction geared to sc. shaft driving 1 FP propeller Total Power: 992kW (1,349hp) 13.5kn Caterpillar 3512TA 1 x Vee 4 Stroke 12 Cy. 170 x 190 992kW (1349bhp) (new engine 1988) Caterpillar Inc-USA AuxGen: 2 x 54kW 220V a.c, 1 x 24kW 220V a.c
8959300 *ITDS* -	**SAN ANTONIO** **Societa Italiana per Condotte d'Acqua SpA** Servizio Gestione e Armamento Mezzi Marittimi *Rome* *Italy* Official number: 7634	**1,185** 355 824	Class: RI (AB)	**1974-10 Cant. Nav. Sgorbini — La Spezia** Yd No: 93 Loa 46.32 Br ex - Dght - Lbp 45.98 Br md 23.00 Dpth 3.81 Welded, 1 dk	**(B34B2SC) Crane Vessel**	**2 oil engines** driving 2 FP propellers Total Power: 276kW (376hp) 3.0kn Deutz F10L413 2 x Vee 4 Stroke 10 Cy. 120 x 125 each-138kW (188bhp) (, fitted 1974) Kloeckner Humboldt Deutz AG-West Germany AuxGen: 1 x 160kW 380V 50Hz a.c, 1 x 32kW 380V 50Hz a.c
9347267 *A8PC7* -	**SAN ANTONIO** *ex* Ibn Rushd *-2009* *completed as* San Antonio *-2008* **KG ms 'San Antonio' Offen Reederei GmbH & Co** Reederei Claus-Peter Offen GmbH & Co KG *Monrovia* *Liberia* MMSI: 636091532 Official number: 91532	**22,914** 9,277 28,196	Class: GL	**2008-02 Hyundai Mipo Dockyard Co Ltd — Ulsan** Yd No: 4009 Loa 186.33 (BB) Br ex - Dght 11.300 Lbp 175.00 Br md 27.60 Dpth 17.10 Welded, 1 dk	**(A33A2CC) Container Ship (Fully Cellular)** Double Bottom Entire Compartment Length TEU 1819 C Ho 736 TEU C Dk 1083 TEU incl 462 ref C Compartments: 4 Cell Ho, ER Cranes: 3x45t	**1 oil engine** driving 1 FP propeller Total Power: 19,620kW (26,675hp) 21.0kn MAN-B&W 6L70MC-C 1 x 2 Stroke 6 Cy. 700 x 2360 19620kW (26675bhp) Hyundai Heavy Industries Co Ltd-South Korea AuxGen: 4 x 1675kW 450V 60Hz a.c Thrusters: 1 Tunnel thruster (f)
9514066 *VRKG4* -	**SAN ANTONIO** **Challenger Inc** AM Nomikos Transworld Maritime Agencies SA *Hong Kong* *Hong Kong* MMSI: 477413100 Official number: HK-3446	**31,540** 18,765 55,768 T/cm 56.9	Class: NK	**2012-03 IHI Marine United Inc — Yokohama KN** Yd No: 3296 Loa 190.00 (BB) Br ex - Dght 12.735 Lbp 185.00 Br md 32.26 Dpth 18.10 Welded, 1 dk	**(A21A2BC) Bulk Carrier** Grain: 72,062; Bale: 67,062 Compartments: 5 Ho, ER 5 Ha: ER Cranes: 4x30t	**1 oil engine** driving 1 FP propeller Total Power: 8,890kW (12,087hp) 14.5kn Wartsila 6RT-flex50 1 x 2 Stroke 6 Cy. 500 x 2050 8890kW (12087bhp) Diesel United Ltd.-Aioi Fuel: 2470.0
8740022 *EBXO* 3-SS-15-01	**SAN ANTONIO BERRIA** - **Victor Manuel Dorronsoro Potularrumbe y otros** - *Orio* *Spain* Official number: 3-5/2001	**179** 54 -		**2002-07 Constructora Metalica — Zumaya** Loa 34.80 Br ex - Dght - Lbp 29.00 Br md - Dpth - Welded, 1 dk	**(B11B2FV) Fishing Vessel**	**1 oil engine** driving 1 Propeller Total Power: 441kW (600hp)

9410052 **SAN ANTONIO III** **300**
-
- **Pesquera Santa Rosa SA** -
-
Peru
Official number: CE-10474-PM

2006-09 SIMA Serv. Ind. de la Marina Chimbote (SIMACH) — Chimbote Yd No: 507
Loa - Br ex - Dght -
Lbp 39.50 Br md 7.80 Dpth 4.00
Welded, 1 dk

(B11B2FV) Fishing Vessel

1 oil engine driving 1 Propeller

9383041 **SAN ANTONIO V** **250**
- -
- - -
-

2005-10 SIMA Serv. Ind. de la Marina Chimbote (SIMACH) — Chimbote Yd No: 501
Loa - Br ex - Dght -
Lbp 30.23 Br md 7.67 Dpth 3.42
Welded, 1 dk

(B11B2FV) Fishing Vessel

1 oil engine driving 1 Propeller

9383065 **SAN ANTONIO VI** **200**
- -
- - -
-

2005-10 SIMA Serv. Ind. de la Marina Chimbote (SIMACH) — Chimbote Yd No: 503
Loa - Br ex - Dght -
Lbp 27.74 Br md 7.06 Dpth 3.42
Welded, 1 dk

(B11B2FV) Fishing Vessel

1 oil engine driving 1 Propeller

6816891 **SAN ANTONIO VI** *200* Class: (GL)
- *ex* Macabi 7 *ex* PH 26 *-1976* 89
CE8370 **Pesquera Santa Rosa SA** -
-
Chimbote *Peru*
Official number: CE-004022-PM

1968 Ast. Picsa S.A. — Callao Yd No: 222
L reg 26.83 Br ex 7.07 Dght -
Lbp - Br md 7.04 Dpth 3.46
Welded, 1 dk

(B11B2FV) Fishing Vessel

1 oil engine geared to sc. shaft driving 1 FP propeller
Total Power: 279kW (379hp)
Caterpillar D353SCAC
1 x 4 Stroke 6 Cy. 159 x 203 279kW (379bhp)
Caterpillar Tractor Co-USA

9057111 **SAN AOTEA II** **1,079** Class: NV
ZM2534 *ex* Camo *-1998* *ex* Kapitan Samoylenko *-1998* 323
- **Sanford Ltd** 496
-
SatCom: Inmarsat B 327319810
Auckland *New Zealand*
MMSI: 512008000
Official number: 876305

1993-06 Soviknes Verft AS — Sovik Yd No: 111
Loa 46.50 (BB) Br ex - Dght 4.900
Lbp - Br md 10.80 Dpth 5.40
Welded, 2 dks

(B11B2FV) Fishing Vessel
Ins: 415
Ice Capable

1 oil engine reduction geared to sc. shaft driving 1 FP propeller
Total Power: 791kW (1,075hp)
Caterpillar 3512TA
1 x Vee 4 Stroke 12 Cy. 170 x 190 791kW (1075bhp)
Caterpillar Inc-USA
AuxGen: 2 x 400kW 230/380V 50Hz a.c

8608224 **SAN ARAWA II** *1,265* Class: NV
LW4990 *ex* Polar Storm *-1992* *ex* Polarfarid *-1989* 608
- *ex* Radhamar *-1988* 1,235
completed as Gullak Gullaksen *-1987*
San Arawa SA
-
SatCom: Inmarsat C 470100723
Ushuaia *Argentina*
MMSI: 701000880
Official number: 02098

1987-02 Soviknes Verft AS — Sovik Yd No: 100
Loa 61.40 Br ex - Dght 6.500
Lbp 51.62 Br md 14.01 Dpth 8.01
Welded, 1 dk

(B11A2FG) Factory Stern Trawler
Ins: 1,000
Ice Capable

1 oil engine reduction geared to sc. shaft driving 1 CP propeller
Total Power: 3,089kW (4,200hp) 14.5kn
MWM TBD510-8
1 x 4 Stroke 8 Cy. 330 x 360 3089kW (4200bhp)
Motoren Werke Mannheim AG (MWM)-West Germany
AuxGen: 1 x 1280kW 440V 60Hz a.c, 2 x 416kW 440V 60Hz a.c, 1 x 46kW 440V 60Hz a.c

---

9226528 **SAN ASPIRING** **1,508** Class: NV (LR)
ZMGO *ex* Gudni Olafsson *-2004* 452 ✠ Classed LR until 17/9/04
- **Sanford Ltd** 200
-
Auckland *New Zealand*
MMSI: 512027000
Official number: 876371

2001-11 Guangzhou Huangpu Shipyard — Guangzhou GD Yd No: FV-4
Loa 51.30 (BB) Br ex 12.23 Dght 5.400
Lbp 44.70 Br md 12.00 Dpth 10.60
Welded, 1 dk

(B11B2FV) Fishing Vessel
Ice Capable

1 oil engine with clutches, flexible couplings & sr geared to sc. shaft driving 1 CP propeller
Total Power: 1,730kW (2,352hp) 14.5kn
Caterpillar 3606TA
1 x 4 Stroke 6 Cy. 280 x 300 1730kW (2352bhp)
Caterpillar Inc-USA
AuxGen: 1 x 600kW 440V 60Hz a.c, 1 x 620kW 440V 60Hz a.c
Thrusters: 1 Tunnel thruster (f)

9347281 **SAN AURELIO** **22,914** Class: GL
A8PC9 9,277
- **KG Zweite ms 'San Aurelio' Offen Reederei GmbH & Co** 28,170
Reederei Claus-Peter Offen GmbH & Co KG
Monrovia *Liberia*
MMSI: 636091534
Official number: 91534

2008-03 Hyundai Mipo Dockyard Co Ltd — Ulsan Yd No: 4011
Loa 186.35 (BB) Br ex - Dght 11.300
Lbp 175.00 Br md 27.60 Dpth 17.10
Welded, 1 dk

(A33A2CC) Container Ship (Fully Cellular)
TEU 1819 C Ho 736 TEU C Dk 1083 TEU incl 462 ref C
Compartments: 4 Cell Ho, ER
Cranes: 3x45t

1 oil engine driving 1 FP propeller
Total Power: 19,620kW (26,675hp) 21.0kn
MAN-B&W 6L70MC-C
1 x 2 Stroke 6 Cy. 700 x 2360 19620kW (26675bhp)
Hyundai Heavy Industries Co Ltd-South Korea
AuxGen: 4 x 1570kW 450V a.c
Thrusters: 1 Tunnel thruster (f)
Fuel: 220.0 (d.f.) 2180.0 (r.f.) 71.0pd

9531765 **SAN BEATO** **5,832** Class: BV
HBLC *ex* CF Paris *-2010* 1,749
San Beato Schiffahrt AG 6,603
ABC Maritime AG T/cm
Basel *Switzerland* 17.1
MMSI: 269032000

2010-05 Geo Marine Engineering & Shipbuilding Co — Changwon Yd No: 110
Loa 110.20 (BB) Br ex - Dght 6.713
Lbp 102.00 Br md 18.20 Dpth 10.00
Welded, 1 dk

(A13C2LA) Asphalt/Bitumen Tanker
Double Hull (13F)
Asphalt: 6,091
Compartments: 8 Wing Ta, ER
2 Cargo Pump (s): 2x400m³/hr
Manifold: Bow/CM: 50m

1 oil engine reduction geared to sc. shaft driving 1 CP propeller
Total Power: 2,620kW (3,562hp) 12.6kn
Hyundai Himsen 9H25/33P
1 x 4 Stroke 9 Cy. 250 x 330 2620kW (3562bhp)
Hyundai Heavy Industries Co Ltd-South Korea
AuxGen: 2 x 535kW 60Hz a.c
Thrusters: 1 Tunnel thruster (f)
Fuel: 77.0 (d.f.) 533.0 (r.f.)

8015491 **SAN BENIGNO** **199** Class: RI
IOJM 72
- **Rimorchiatori Napoletani Srl** 124
-
Naples *Italy*
Official number: 1397

1982-02 Cantiere Navale di Pesaro SpA (CNP) — Pesaro Yd No: 51
Loa 33.53 Br ex 9.28 Dght 3.757
Lbp 28.99 Br md 8.60 Dpth 4.25
Welded, 1 dk

(B32A2ST) Tug

1 oil engine sr reverse geared to sc. shaft driving 1 FP propeller
Total Power: 1,622kW (2,205hp) 13.0kn
MAN G9V30/45ATL
1 x 4 Stroke 9 Cy. 300 x 450 1622kW (2205bhp)
Maschinenbau Augsburg Nuernberg (MAN)-Augsburg

9272565 **SAN BENJAMINO** **4,064** Class: BV
9HA2525 *launched as* Bitumen Star *-2005* 1,219
ex Cap Farina *-2002* 4,500
San Benjamino Schiffahrt AG T/cm
ABC Maritime AG 13.6
Valletta *Malta*
MMSI: 248816000
Official number: 9272565

2003-08 Zhejiang Shipbuilding Co Ltd — Ningbo ZJ Yd No: 01-104
Loa 106.00 Br ex - Dght 6.300
Lbp 98.72 Br md 15.80 Dpth 9.75
Welded, 1 dk

(A12B2TR) Chemical/Products Tanker
Double Hull (13F)
Liq: 4,218; Liq (Oil): 4,218; Asphalt: 4,218
Compartments: 8 Wing Ta, ER
2 Cargo Pump (s): 2x450m³/hr
Manifold: Bow/CM: 53m
Ice Capable

1 oil engine geared to sc. shaft driving 1 CP propeller
Total Power: 2,880kW (3,916hp) 14.0kn
MaK 6M32C
1 x 4 Stroke 6 Cy. 320 x 480 2880kW (3916bhp)
Caterpillar Motoren GmbH & Co. KG-Germany
AuxGen: 3 x 368kW 440/220V 60Hz a.c, 1 x 352kW 440/220V 60Hz a.c
Thrusters: 1 Tunnel thruster (f)
Fuel: 55.0 (d.f.) 340.0 (r.f.) 14.0pd

9264116 **SAN BERNARDINO** **3,977** Class: BV
HBLV *ex* Artha *-2005* 1,193
San Bernardino Schiffahrt AG 4,232
ABC Maritime AG T/cm
Basel *Switzerland* 13.3
MMSI: 269087000
Official number: 174

2002-10 Zhejiang Shipyard — Ningbo ZJ Yd No: 00-093
Loa 106.00 Br ex - Dght 6.012
Lbp 98.50 Br md 15.80 Dpth 9.40
Welded, 1 dk

(A12B2TR) Chemical/Products Tanker
Double Hull (13F)
Liq: 3,998; Liq (Oil): 3,998; Asphalt: 3,998
Cargo Heating Coils
Compartments: 8 Wing Ta, ER
2 Cargo Pump (s): 2x450m³/hr
Manifold: Bow/CM: 51.1m
Ice Capable

1 oil engine geared to sc. shaft driving 1 CP propeller
Total Power: 2,880kW (3,916hp) 13.0kn
MaK 6M32
1 x 4 Stroke 6 Cy. 320 x 480 2880kW (3916bhp)
Caterpillar Motoren GmbH & Co. KG-Germany
AuxGen: 3 x 360kW 460/220V 60Hz a.c, 1 x 350kW 460/220V 60Hz a.c
Thrusters: 1 Thwart. FP thruster (f)
Fuel: 70.0 (d.f.) (Heating Coils) 335.0 (r.f.) 12.0pd

8816223 **SAN BOSCO** **525** Class: (LR)
CB4128 170 ✠ Classed LR until 12/1/90
- **South Pacific Korp SA (SPK)** 550
-
Valparaiso *Chile*
MMSI: 725000209
Official number: 2687

1990-01 Ast. y Maestranzas de la Armada (ASMAR Chile) — Talcahuano Yd No: 38
Loa 42.15 (BB) Br ex 9.52 Dght 5.210
Lbp 36.35 Br md 9.50 Dpth 6.80
Welded, 2 dks

(B11B2FV) Fishing Vessel
Ins: 550

1 oil engine with clutches, flexible couplings & sr geared to sc. shaft driving 1 CP propeller
Total Power: 1,303kW (1,772hp) 12.5kn
Deutz SBV6M628
1 x 4 Stroke 6 Cy. 240 x 280 1303kW (1772bhp)
Kloeckner Humboldt Deutz AG-West Germany
AuxGen: 1 x 192kW 380V 50Hz a.c, 1 x 54kW 380V 50Hz a.c
Thrusters: 1 Thwart. FP thruster (f); 1 Thwart. FP thruster (a)

7945194 **SAN CARLO** *441* Class: (RI)
- *ex* Daniela Prima *-2010* *ex* Gioconda *-1991* 246
- **Emarine Ltd** 246

1979 Szczecinska Stocznia Remontowa 'Gryfia' SA — Szczecin
Loa 59.24 Br ex 9.50 Dght 1.628
Lbp 58.15 Br md 9.20 Dpth 3.36

(B34A2SH) Hopper, Motor
Hopper: 660

2 oil engines driving 2 FP propellers
Total Power: 464kW (630hp)
Scania DSI1440M
2 x Vee 4 Stroke 8 Cy. 127 x 140 each-232kW (315bhp)
Saab Scania AB-Sweden

8214786 **SAN CARLOS NO. 3** **587**
DUTK4 *ex* Sea Dog *-2006* *ex* Hoshin Maru No. 55 *-2004* 208
OHLL-01614 **Sun Warm Tuna Corp** 383
-
Manila *Philippines*
Official number: 00-0002460

1982-12 Niigata Engineering Co Ltd — Niigata NI Yd No: 1766
Loa 49.94 (BB) Br ex 8.62 Dght 3.570
Lbp 44.02 Br md 8.60 Dpth 3.66
Welded, 1 dk

(B11B2FV) Fishing Vessel
Compartments: 4 Ho, ER
4 Ha: ER

1 oil engine with clutches, flexible couplings & sr geared to sc. shaft driving 1 CP propeller
Total Power: 883kW (1,201hp)
Niigata 6M28AFT
1 x 4 Stroke 6 Cy. 280 x 480 883kW (1201bhp)
Niigata Engineering Co Ltd-Japan

Ship	Tonnage / Class	Construction	Type / Cargo	Machinery
8504337 *IJSL* - **SAN CATALDO** **Rimorchiatori Napoletani Srl** - SatCom: Inmarsat C 424756020 *Taranto* *Italy* MMSI: 247012400 Official number: 147	**274** Class: RI 82 121 T/cm 2.3	**1986**-07 **Cantiere Navale di Pesaro SpA (CNP) — Pesaro** Yd No: 60 Loa 32.42 Br ex - Dght 3.990 Lbp 29.01 Br md 8.58 Dpth 4.27 Welded, 1 dk	**(B32A2ST) Tug**	**1 oil engine** with flexible couplings & sr gearedto sc. shaft driving 1 CP propeller Total Power: 2,270kW (3,086hp) 13.5kn Nohab F312V 1 x Vee 4 Stroke 12 Cy. 250 x 300 2270kW (3086bhp) Wartsila Diesel AB-Sweden AuxGen: 3 x 112kW 220/380V 50Hz a.c Thrusters: 1 Thwart. FP thruster (f) Fuel: 95.0 (d.f.) 11.0pd
6525210 *LW4289* - **SAN CAYETANO I** **Patagonian Celeiro SA** - *San Antonio Oeste* *Argentina* MMSI: 701000731 Official number: 01022	*104* 77 202	**1965**-01 **S.L. Ardeag — Bilbao** Yd No: 27 Loa 27.01 Br ex 6.33 Dght 2.553 Lbp 23.02 Br md 6.30 Dpth 3.15 Riveted\Welded, 1 dk	**(B11B2FV) Fishing Vessel**	**1 oil engine** driving 1 FP propeller Total Power: 221kW (300hp) 10.0kn
8868343 *HP7616* - **SAN CHENG** *ex* Kakusui Maru *-1993* **Suo Yang Shipping SA** Tokyo Aki International Ltd *Panama* *Panama* Official number: D8441789PEXT	*193* 101 330	**1968 Oka Zosen Tekko K.K. — Ushimado** L reg 33.15 Br ex - Dght 3.100 Lbp - Br md 7.20 Dpth 3.20 Welded, 1 dk	**(A13B2TU) Tanker (unspecified)** Liq: 452; Liq (Oil): 452 Cargo Heating Coils	**1 oil engine** driving 1 FP propeller Total Power: 221kW (300hp) 9.0kn Mitsubishi 1 x 221kW (300bhp) Mitsubishi Heavy Industries Ltd-Japan
8746349 *YD3608* - **SAN CHUAN MARINE 18** *ex* Kaiyo Maru No. 23 *-2009* *ex* Shuho Maru No. 5 *-2009* **PT Puma Pratama** - *Dumai* *Indonesia*	**102** Class: KI 31 -	**1983**-05 **Muneta Zosen K.K. — Akashi** Loa 24.50 Br ex - Dght 2.150 Lbp 22.71 Br md 6.20 Dpth 2.69 Welded, 1 dk	**(B32A2ST) Tug**	**1 oil engine** reduction geared to sc. shaft driving 1 Propeller Total Power: 882kW (1,199hp) 10.0kn Niigata 6M26AGTE 1 x 4 Stroke 6 Cy. 260 x 460 882kW (1199bhp) Niigata Engineering Co Ltd-Japan AuxGen: 1 x 62kW 230/225V a.c, 1 x 20kW 230/225V a.c
7737896 *BEVY* - **SAN CHUAN No. 1** **San Ta Fishery Co Ltd** - *Kaohsiung* *Chinese Taipei* Official number: 4477	*329* Class: (CR) 156 86	**1973 Kaohsiung Prov. Junior College of Marine Tech. SY — Kaohsiung** Loa 40.95 Br ex 7.68 Dght 3.110 Lbp 35.01 Br md 7.60 Dpth 3.61 Welded, 1 dk	**(B11B2FV) Fishing Vessel** Ins: 346 Compartments: 3 Ho, ER	**1 oil engine** driving 1 FP propeller Total Power: 809kW (1,100hp) 10.8kn Sumiyoshi S6YGTSS 1 x 4 Stroke 6 Cy. 280 x 450 809kW (1100bhp) Sumiyoshi Marine Diesel Co Ltd-Japan AuxGen: 2 x 80kW 220V a.c
9229219 *IZOR* - **SAN CIRIACO** **Societa Termolese Esercizio Rimorchi e Salvataggi (STERS) Srl** Gesmar Srl (Gestioni Marittime) SatCom: Inmarsat C 424702892 *Ravenna* *Italy* MMSI: 247077800 Official number: RA 179	**312** Class: RI (LR) 93 ✠ Classed LR until 5/12/02 -	**2002**-11 **PO SevMash Predpriyatiye — Severodvinsk** (Hull) **2002**-11 **B.V. Scheepswerf Damen — Gorinchem** Yd No: 511706 Loa 30.82 Br ex 10.20 Dght 3.760 Lbp 28.03 Br md 9.40 Dpth 4.80 Welded, 1 dk	**(B32A2ST) Tug**	**2 oil engines** reduction geared to sc. shafts driving 2 Directional propellers Total Power: 3,374kW (4,588hp) 12.5kn Caterpillar 3516B-HD 2 x Vee 4 Stroke 16 Cy. 170 x 215 each-1687kW (2294bhp) Caterpillar Inc-USA AuxGen: 2 x 85kW 400V 50Hz a.c
8201167 *ZMA2925* - **SAN COLUMBIA** **Sanford Ltd** - *Auckland* *New Zealand* MMSI: 512143000 Official number: 394810	**205** 62 204	**1981**-12 **Marine Construction & Design Co. (MARCO) — Seattle, Wa** Yd No: 429 Loa 32.95 Br ex 8.82 Dght 3.914 Lbp 29.27 Br md 8.58 Dpth 3.96 Welded, 1 dk	**(B11B2FV) Fishing Vessel** Ins: 8,844 Compartments: 6 Ho, ER 6 Ha:	**1 oil engine** dr reverse geared to sc. shaft driving 1 FP propeller Total Power: 631kW (858hp) 11.5kn Caterpillar D398TA 1 x Vee 4 Stroke 12 Cy. 159 x 203 631kW (858bhp) Caterpillar Tractor Co-USA AuxGen: 1 x 75kW 110/220V 60Hz a.c, 1 x 40kW 110/220V 60Hz a.c Fuel: 72.5 (d.f.)
6621296 *HC4426* - **SAN CRISTOBAL** *ex* San Cristobal I *-1990* *ex* Athina S *-1990* *ex* Kathe Dancoast *-1988* *ex* Grit *-1974* *ex* Dagmar Stenhoj *-1970* **Galapagos Cargo SA (Galacargo)** Cap Gerardo Aguilera Jimenez *Guayaquil* *Ecuador* Official number: TN-00-0319	**893** Class: BV 476 1,209	**1966 Husumer Schiffswerft — Husum** Yd No: 1234 Loa 67.09 Br ex 10.44 Dght 3.941 Lbp 60.10 Br md 10.42 Dpth 6.05 Welded, 1 dk & S dk	**(A31A2GX) General Cargo Ship** Grain: 2,388; Bale: 2,199 Compartments: 1 Ho, ER 2 Ha: (19.8 x 6.3) (11.3 x 6.3)ER Derricks: 1x10t,4x3t; Winches: 5 Ice Capable	**1 oil engine** driving 1 FP propeller Total Power: 588kW (799hp) 12.5kn Deutz RBV8M545 1 x 4 Stroke 8 Cy. 320 x 450 588kW (799bhp) Kloeckner Humboldt Deutz AG-West Germany AuxGen: 4 x 16kW 220V a.c Fuel: 63.0 (d.f.)
5309578 - - **SAN DIEGAN** **Galaxie Marine Service CA** - *Venezuela* Official number: AJZL-26218	*186* 88 -	**1953**-01 **Pacific Coast Eng. Co. — Alameda, Ca** Yd No: 155 L reg 33.53 Br ex 7.93 Dght 3.699 Lbp 30.74 Br md 7.90 Dpth 4.20 Welded, 1 dk	**(B32A2ST) Tug**	**2 oil engines** driving 2 FP propellers Total Power: 1,250kW (1,700hp) Caterpillar 2 x 4 Stroke each-625kW (850bhp) (new engine 1967) Caterpillar Tractor Co-USA
8421200 *UBCI2* - **SAN DIEGO** *ex* Motovskiy Zaliv *-2004* **Euphrates Co Ltd** - *St Petersburg* *Russia* MMSI: 273352840	**12,383** Class: BV (NV) (RS) 3,776 9,360	**1984**-06 **VEB Mathias-Thesen-Werft — Wismar** Yd No: 227 Converted From: Fish Carrier-2009 Loa 152.94 Br ex - Dght 8.300 Lbp 142.02 Br md 22.22 Dpth 13.62 Welded, 1 dk, 2nd & 3rd dk in holds only	**(A34A2GR) Refrigerated Cargo Ship** Ins: 13,184 Compartments: 4 Ho, ER 4 Ha: 4 (6.0 x 4.0)ER Derricks: 8x5t Ice Capable	**1 oil engine** driving 1 FP propeller Total Power: 7,600kW (10,333hp) 12.5kn MAN K5SZ70/125 1 x 2 Stroke 5 Cy. 700 x 1250 7600kW (10333bhp) VEB Dieselmotorenwerk Rostock-Rostock AuxGen: 4 x 588kW 390V 50Hz a.c Fuel: 322.0 (d.f.) 3276.0 (r.f.)
9006954 *SNNE* - **SAN DIEGO** *ex* Juan Diego *-2013* *ex* Sandwater *-2003* *ex* Oxelosund *-1996* *ex* Sandwater *-1995* **Zegluga Gdanska Sp z oo (Marine Services Enterprise)** - *Gdansk* *Poland* MMSI: 261517000 Official number: RO/S-G-1303	**1,960** Class: GL (NV) 979 3,036	**1993**-07 **Astilleros Unidos de Veracruz S.A. de C.V. (AUVER) — Veracruz** (Hull) Yd No: 122 **1993**-07 **B.V. Scheepswerf Damen — Gorinchem** Yd No: 8216 Loa 88.30 Br ex - Dght 4.642 Lbp 84.13 Br md 12.50 Dpth 6.50 Welded, 1 dk	**(A31A2GX) General Cargo Ship** Grain: 4,006 TEU 154 C.Ho 78/20' C.Dk 76/20' Compartments: 1 Ho, ER 1 Ha: (62.7 x 10.1)ER Ice Capable	**1 oil engine** with flexible couplings & reverse reduction geared to sc. shaft driving 1 FP propeller Total Power: 1,500kW (2,039hp) 11.6kn Deutz SBV8M628 1 x 4 Stroke 8 Cy. 240 x 280 1500kW (2039bhp) Motoren Werke Mannheim AG (MWM)-Mannheim AuxGen: 2 x 80kW 220/380V 50Hz a.c Thrusters: 1 Thwart. FP thruster (f) Fuel: 189.9 (d.f.) 5.0pd
9560376 *3FTY6* - **SAN DIEGO BRIDGE** **Cypress Maritime (Panama) SA & Koyo Shosen Kaisha Ltd** Shoei Kisen Kaisha Ltd SatCom: Inmarsat C 435754710 *Panama* *Panama* MMSI: 357547000 Official number: 4191510	**71,787** Class: NK 26,914 72,912 T/cm 95.3	**2010**-07 **Koyo Dockyard Co Ltd — Mihara HS** Yd No: 2292 Loa 293.18 (BB) Br ex - Dght 14.021 Lbp 276.00 Br md 40.00 Dpth 24.30 Welded, 1 dk	**(A33A2CC) Container Ship (Fully Cellular)** TEU 6350 C Ho 2912 TEU C Dk 3438 TEU incl 500 ref C.	**1 oil engine** driving 1 FP propeller Total Power: 62,920kW (85,546hp) 25.0kn MAN-B&W 11K98MC 1 x 2 Stroke 11 Cy. 980 x 2660 62920kW (85546bhp) Mitsui Engineering & Shipbuilding CLtd-Japan AuxGen: 5 x a.c Thrusters: 1 Tunnel thruster (f) Fuel: 10240.0 (r.f.)
9636084 *BRYV* - **SAN DING CHANG CHUN** **Shenzhen Tri-Dynas Oil & Shipping Co Ltd** - SatCom: Inmarsat C 441253611 *Shenzhen, Guangdong* *China* MMSI: 412536000	**43,718** Class: CC 21,966 75,507 T/cm 68.0	**2012**-06 **Dalian Shipbuilding Industry Co Ltd — Dalian LN (No 1 Yard)** Yd No: PC760-23 Loa 228.60 (BB) Br ex 32.30 Dght 14.700 Lbp 220.00 Br md 32.26 Dpth 21.20 Welded, 1 dk	**(A13B2TP) Products Tanker** Double Hull (13F) Liq: 80,430; Liq (Oil): 80,430 Compartments: 6 Wing Ta, 6 Wing Ta, 1 Wing Slop Ta, 1 Wing Slop Ta, ER Ice Capable	**1 oil engine** driving 1 FP propeller Total Power: 12,240kW (16,642hp) 15.4kn MAN-B&W 6S60MC 1 x 2 Stroke 6 Cy. 600 x 2292 12240kW (16642bhp) Dalian Marine Diesel Co Ltd-China AuxGen: 3 x 740kW 450V a.c
9617571 *BRYQ* - **SAN DING CHANG LE** **Shenzhen Tri-Dynas Oil & Shipping Co Ltd** - *Shenzhen, Guangdong* *China* MMSI: 412066000	**43,718** Class: CC 21,966 75,461 T/cm 68.0	**2013**-04 **Dalian Shipbuilding Industry Co Ltd — Dalian LN (No 1 Yard)** Yd No: PC760-28 Loa 228.60 (BB) Br ex 32.30 Dght 14.700 Lbp 220.00 Br md 32.26 Dpth 21.20 Welded, 1 dk	**(A13B2TP) Products Tanker** Double Hull (13F) Liq: 80,430; Liq (Oil): 80,430 Compartments: 6 Wing Ta, 6 Wing Ta, 1 Wing Slop Ta, 1 Wing Slop Ta, 1 Slop Ta, ER Ice Capable	**1 oil engine** driving 1 FP propeller Total Power: 12,240kW (16,642hp) 15.4kn MAN-B&W 6S60MC 1 x 2 Stroke 6 Cy. 600 x 2292 12240kW (16642bhp) Dalian Marine Diesel Co Ltd-China AuxGen: 3 x 740kW 450V a.c

8901523 *ZMA2601* -	**SAN DISCOVERY** *ex* Angie *-1996* *ex* Mys Lamanon *-1996* **Sanford Ltd** - SatCom: Inmarsat A 1663402 *Auckland* *New Zealand* MMSI: 512000125 Official number: 876197	**1,899** 592 1,283	Class: NV	**1992-04 Sterkoder AS — Kristiansund** Yd No: 130 Loa 64.00 Br ex - Dght 6.435 Lbp 55.55 Br md 13.00 Dpth 8.85 Welded, 2 dks	**(B11A2FG) Factory Stern Trawler** Ins: 950 Ice Capable	**1 oil engine** reduction geared to sc. shaft driving 1 FP propeller Total Power: 2,458kW (3,342hp) Wartsila 6R32E 1 x 4 Stroke 6 Cy. 320 x 350 2458kW (3342bhp) Wartsila Diesel Oy-Finland AuxGen: 1 x 1304kW 380V 50Hz a.c, 2 x 336kW 380V 50Hz a.c Thrusters: 1 Thwart. FP thruster (f)
8807129 *AVKL* -	**SAN DOMINO** - **Creative Gaming Solutions Pvt Ltd** - *Mumbai* *India* Official number: 3811	*2,544* 763 273	Class: RI	**1989-03 Cant. Nav. de Poli S.p.A. — Pellestrina** Yd No: 127 Loa 68.49 (BB) Br ex 11.82 Dght 2.872 Lbp 59.50 Br md 11.80 Dpth 3.90 Welded, 1 dk	**(A36A2PR) Passenger/Ro-Ro Ship (Vehicles)**	**2 oil engines** sr geared to sc. shafts driving 2 FP propellers Total Power: 2,920kW (3,970hp) GMT BL230.8V 2 x Vee 4 Stroke 8 Cy. 230 x 310 each-1460kW (1985bhp) Fincantieri Cantieri Navalitaliani SpA-Italy Thrusters: 1 Thwart. CP thruster (f)
9608752 *VRIP6* -	**SAN DU AO** - **Xin Yuan Ocean Shipping (HK) Group Ltd** COSCO Southern Asphalt Shipping Co Ltd *Hong Kong* *Hong Kong* MMSI: 477229900 Official number: HK-3112	**9,963** 3,197 12,780 T/cm 27.7	Class: BV	**2011-08 No 4807 Shipyard of PLA — Fu'an FJ** Yd No: SL801 Loa 146.00 (BB) Br ex - Dght 7.900 Lbp 137.20 Br md 22.00 Dpth 10.80 Welded, 1 dk	**(A13C2LA) Asphalt/Bitumen Tanker** Double Hull (13F) Liq: 11,578; Liq (Oil): 11,578 Cargo Heating Coils Compartments: 8 Ta, ER 3 Cargo Pump (s): 3x250m³/hr Manifold: Bow/CM: 50.5m	**1 oil engine** driving 1 FP propeller Total Power: 4,440kW (6,037hp) 13.0kn MAN-B&W 6S35MC 1 x 2 Stroke 6 Cy. 350 x 1400 4440kW (6037bhp) Yichang Marine Diesel Engine Co Ltd-China AuxGen: 3 x 500kW 450V 50Hz a.c Thrusters: 1 Tunnel thruster (f) Fuel: 106.0 (d.f.) 807.0 (r.f.)
8901420 *ZMR3161* -	**SAN ENTERPRISE** *ex* Navarin *-1999* **Sanford Ltd** - SatCom: Inmarsat A 1401322 *Auckland* *New Zealand* MMSI: 512000122 Official number: 876315	**1,899** 592 1,258	Class: NV	**1990-02 Sterkoder Mek. Verksted AS — Kristiansund** Yd No: 120 Loa 64.00 (BB) Br ex - Dght 6.435 Lbp 55.55 Br md 13.00 Dpth 5.97 Welded	**(B11A2FG) Factory Stern Trawler** Grain: 130; Ins: 930 Ice Capable	**1 oil engine** reduction geared to sc. shaft driving 1 CP propeller Total Power: 2,458kW (3,342hp) 14.4kn Wartsila 6R32E 1 x 4 Stroke 6 Cy. 320 x 350 2458kW (3342bhp) Wartsila Diesel Oy-Finland AuxGen: 1 x 1304kW 380V 50Hz a.c, 2 x 336kW 380V 50Hz a.c Thrusters: 1 Thwart. FP thruster (f)
9416434 *9HA2811* -	**SAN FELICE** - **Lavant Shipping Co Ltd** SeaFlag Srl *Valletta* *Malta* MMSI: 256054000 Official number: 9416434	**23,985** 10,652 34,053	Class: NV	**2010-02 Pha Rung Shipyard Co. — Haiphong** Yd No: HR-34-PR01 Loa 180.00 (BB) Br ex - Dght 9.850 Lbp 176.75 Br md 30.00 Dpth 14.70 Welded, 1 dk	**(A21A2BC) Bulk Carrier** Grain: 45,517 Compartments: 5 Ho, ER 5 Ha: 4 (19.2 x 20.3)ER (16.0 x 18.7) Cranes: 4x30t	**1 oil engine** driving 1 FP propeller Total Power: 7,860kW (10,686hp) 14.0kn MAN-B&W 6S46MC-C 1 x 2 Stroke 6 Cy. 460 x 1932 7860kW (10686bhp) STX Engine Co Ltd-South Korea AuxGen: 3 x 600kW a.c Fuel: 200.0 (d.f.) 1700.0 (r.f.) 28.6pd
9317614 *EBVW* 3-SS-16-03	**SAN FERMIN BERRIA** - **Carlos Eizaguirre Elizazu & others** - *Fuenterrabia* *Spain* Official number: 3-6/2003	**148** 44 -		**2004-07 Astilleros Ria de Aviles SL — Nieva** Yd No: 96 Loa - Br ex - Dght - Lbp - Br md - Dpth - Welded, 1 dk	**(B11B2FV) Fishing Vessel**	**1 oil engine** geared to sc. shaft driving 1 FP propeller Total Power: 441kW (600hp) Caterpillar 3512TA 1 x Vee 4 Stroke 12 Cy. 170 x 190 441kW (600bhp) Caterpillar Inc-USA
9322384 *2CYD8* -	**SAN FERNANDO** - **Leopard Tankers SA** Mitsui OSK Lines Ltd (MOL) *Douglas* *Isle of Man (British)* MMSI: 235076731 Official number: 741948	**29,654** 12,904 48,315 T/cm 49.9	Class: NK	**2005-03 Minaminippon Shipbuilding Co Ltd — Usuki OT** Yd No: 684 Loa 186.00 (BB) Br ex 32.23 Dght 12.116 Lbp 177.20 Br md 32.20 Dpth 18.80 Welded, 1 dk	**(A12A2TC) Chemical Tanker** Double Hull (13F) Liq: 54,937 Compartments: 12 Wing Ta, ER, 2 Wing Slop Ta 14 Cargo Pump (s): 14x470m³/hr Manifold: Bow/CM: 92.9m	**1 oil engine** driving 1 FP propeller Total Power: 10,010kW (13,610hp) 15.2kn B&W 7S50MC 1 x 2 Stroke 7 Cy. 500 x 1910 10010kW (13610bhp) Mitsui Engineering & Shipbuilding CLtd-Japan AuxGen: 4 x 800kW 440/100V 60Hz a.c Fuel: 137.7 (d.f.) 2374.0 (r.f.)
9157844 - -	**SAN FERNANDO** - **Grupo de Negocios SA** - *Callao* *Peru* Official number: CO-16401-PM	**379** 121 -	Class: (GL)	**1997-05 Factoria Naval S.A. — Callao** Yd No: 027 Loa - Br ex - Dght 4.080 Lbp 40.50 Br md 8.90 Dpth 4.55 Welded, 1 dk	**(B11A2FG) Factory Stern Trawler**	**1 oil engine** reduction geared to sc. shaft driving 1 CP propeller Total Power: 960kW (1,305hp) 13.2kn Alpha 6L23/30A 1 x 4 Stroke 6 Cy. 225 x 300 960kW (1305bhp) MAN B&W Diesel A/S-Denmark AuxGen: 2 x 130kW 220V a.c
7852634 - -	**SAN FERNANDO** *ex* Ganne No. 8 *-1994* *ex* Oshima Maru No. 8 *-1978* **Sto Domingo Shipping Lines** - *Batangas* *Philippines* Official number: MNLD001118	*327* 192 -		**1972 Binan Senpaku Kogyo K.K. — Onomichi** Loa 40.01 Br ex - Dght 2.801 Lbp 35.01 Br md 9.50 Dpth 3.10 Welded, 1 dk	**(A36A2PR) Passenger/Ro-Ro Ship (Vehicles)** Passengers: 500	**1 oil engine** driving 1 FP propeller Total Power: 736kW (1,001hp) 12.0kn Yanmar 6G-ST 1 x 4 Stroke 6 Cy. 240 x 290 736kW (1001bhp) Yanmar Diesel Engine Co Ltd-Japan
9226023 *EA4702* 3-VILL-12-	**SAN FIDEL** - **Nicolasin SL** - *Santa Eugenia de Ribeira* *Spain* Official number: 3-2/2000	**136** 40 -		**2000-11 Astilleros Villavieja (Gestinaval SL) — Ribadeo** Yd No: 22 Loa 23.00 Br ex - Dght 2.300 Lbp 18.50 Br md 6.40 Dpth 2.70 Welded, 1 dk	**(B11B2FV) Fishing Vessel** Bale: 94	**1 oil engine** geared to sc. shaft driving 1 FP propeller Total Power: 293kW (398hp) Mitsubishi 1 x 4 Stroke 293kW (398bhp) Mitsubishi Heavy Industries Ltd-Japan
9448918 *ICHM* -	**SAN FRANCESCO** - **Petrolmar Trasporti e Servizi Marittimi SpA** - *Genoa* *Italy* MMSI: 247270900	**1,393** 907 2,358	Class: RI	**2009-05 Off. Mecc. Nav. e Fond. San Giorgio del Porto — Genoa** Yd No: 113 Loa 74.70 Br ex - Dght 4.440 Lbp 68.80 Br md 13.48 Dpth 5.50 Welded, 1 dk	**(A13B2TP) Products Tanker** Double Hull (13F)	**2 oil engines** reduction geared to sc. shafts driving 2 Directional propellers Total Power: 1,220kW (1,658hp) 9.0kn Yanmar 6AYM-ETE 2 x 4 Stroke 6 Cy. 155 x 180 each-610kW (829bhp) Yanmar Diesel Engine Co Ltd-Japan
9477476 *IINU2* -	**SAN FRANCESCO AT** - **Adriatic Towage Srl** - *Venice* *Italy* MMSI: 247255500	**467** 140 276	Class: BV	**2008-12 Ge-Ta Corp. — Istanbul** Yd No: 009 Loa 32.50 Br ex - Dght 4.290 Lbp 27.60 Br md 11.70 Dpth 5.60 Welded, 1 dk	**(B32A2ST) Tug**	**2 oil engines** geared to sc. shafts driving 2 Directional propellers Total Power: 3,282kW (4,462hp) 13.0kn Caterpillar 3516B-TA 2 x Vee 4 Stroke 16 Cy. 170 x 190 each-1641kW (2231bhp) Caterpillar Inc-USA AuxGen: 2 x 108kW 50Hz a.c
9245469 *WDA3425* -	**SAN FRANCISCO** - **San Francisco Bar Pilots** - *San Francisco, CA* *United States of America* MMSI: 366798310 Official number: 1105895	**224** 152 -		**2000-12 MARCO Shipyard, Inc. — Seattle, Wa** Yd No: 486 Loa 31.70 Br ex - Dght - Lbp - Br md 9.00 Dpth 3.80 Welded, 1 dk	**(B34N2QP) Pilot Vessel**	**2 oil engines** geared to sc. shafts driving 2 FP propellers Total Power: 1,618kW (2,200hp) 14.0kn Caterpillar 3508B 2 x Vee 4 Stroke 8 Cy. 170 x 190 each-809kW (1100bhp) Caterpillar Inc-USA
7909695 *CXAL* -	**SAN FRANCISCO** *ex* Biezelinge *-1997* **Riovia SA** - *Montevideo* *Uruguay* MMSI: 770576060 Official number: P692	**188** 48 -	Class: BV	**1979-10 Appingedam Niestern Delfzijl B.V. — Delfzijl** Yd No: W499 Loa 25.80 Br ex 9.07 Dght 1.100 Lbp 22.77 Br md 9.00 Dpth 2.52 Welded, 1 dk	**(B22B20D) Drilling Ship**	**2 oil engines** driving 2 FP propellers Total Power: 302kW (410hp) 12.5kn G.M. (Detroit Diesel) 6V-71-N 2 x Vee 2 Stroke 6 Cy. 108 x 127 each-151kW (205bhp) Detroit Diesel Corporation-Detroit, Mi
8123286 - -	**SAN FRANCISCO** - **Multipesca SA de CV** - *La Union* *El Salvador*	*144* 97 -	Class: (AB)	**1982-06 Bayou Marine Builders, Inc. — Bayou La Batre, Al** Yd No: M4 Loa - Br ex - Dght - Lbp 23.50 Br md 7.32 Dpth 3.66 Welded, 1 dk	**(B11A2FT) Trawler** Compartments: 1 Ho, ER 1 Ha: (1.8 x 1.8)	**1 oil engine** reverse reduction geared to sc. shaft driving 1 FP propeller Total Power: 382kW (519hp) 11.5kn Caterpillar 3412PCTA 1 x Vee 4 Stroke 12 Cy. 137 x 152 382kW (519bhp) Caterpillar Tractor Co-USA AuxGen: 1 x 30kW

IMO / Call sign	Name / Owners / Port	Tonnage	Class	Build / Dimensions	Type / Cargo	Machinery
7716610 *HP7389* -	**SAN FRANCISCO** - - - *Panama* *Panama* Official number: 22630PEXT2	**1,218** 365 1,592	Class: (BV) (NV)	**1979**-11 **Sandnessjoen Slip & Mek. Verksted — Sandnessjoen** Yd No: 42 Loa 71.46 Br ex 17.30 Dght 3.433 Lbp 64.95 Br md 17.00 Dpth 4.50 Welded, 1 dk	**(A35D2RL) Landing Craft** Bow door/ramp (f) Len: 6.00 Wid: 4.50 Swl: - Lane-Len: 52 Lane-Wid: 4.50 Lorries: 30, Cars: 50, Trailers: 24 TEU 148 C. 148/20'	**1 oil engine** driving 1 CP propeller Total Power: 1,324kW (1,800hp) 10.5kn Wichmann 6AXA 1 x 2 Stroke 6 Cy. 300 x 450 1324kW (1800bhp) Wichmann Motorfabrikk AS-Norway AuxGen: 2 x 100kW 440V 60Hz a.c Thrusters: 1 Thwart. FP thruster (f) Fuel: 132.0 (d.f.) 7.0pd
9560364 *3FPV6* -	**SAN FRANCISCO BRIDGE** - **Primavera Montana SA** 'K' Line Ship Management Co Ltd (KLSM) SatCom: Inmarsat C 435540010 *Panama* *Panama* MMSI: 355400000 Official number: 4174910	**71,787** 26,914 72,890 T/cm 95.3	Class: NK	**2010**-06 **Koyo Dockyard Co Ltd — Mihara HS** Yd No: 2287 Loa 293.18 (BB) Br ex - Dght 14.021 Lbp 276.00 Br md 40.00 Dpth 24.30 Welded, 1 dk	**(A33A2CC) Container Ship (Fully Cellular)** TEU 6350 C Ho 2912 TEU C Dk 3438 TEU incl 500 ref C.	**1 oil engine** driving 1 FP propeller Total Power: 62,920kW (85,546hp) 25.0kn MAN-B&W 11K98MC 1 x 2 Stroke 11 Cy. 980 x 2660 62920kW (85546bhp) Mitsui Engineering & Shipbuilding CLtd-Japan AuxGen: 5 x a.c Thrusters: 1 Tunnel thruster (f) Fuel: 10240.0 (r.f.)
9241542 *YYNH* -	**SAN FRANCISCO DEASIS** *ex* Federico Garcia Lorca *-2013* **Bolivaria de Puertos SA** Balearia Eurolineas Maritimas SA *Pampatar* *Venezuela* MMSI: 775514000 Official number: ARSH-14796	**5,637** 1,691 2,000	Class: RI	**2001**-06 **Rodriquez Cantieri Navali SpA — Pietra Ligure** Yd No: 278 Loa 115.25 Br ex - Dght 5.000 Lbp 96.20 Br md 17.00 Dpth 11.00 Welded	**(A36A2PR) Passenger/Ro-Ro Ship (Vehicles)** Hull Material: Aluminium Alloy Passengers: unberthed: 884 Stern door/ramp (p) Stern door/ramp (s) Lane-Len: 300 Cars: 210	**4 oil engines** reduction geared to sc. shafts driving 4 Water jets Total Power: 28,800kW (39,156hp) 40.0kn Caterpillar 3618 4 x Vee 4 Stroke 18 Cy. 280 x 300 each-7200kW (9789bhp) Caterpillar Inc-USA AuxGen: 4 x 320kW a.c
9252565 *DCPP2* -	**SAN FRANCISCO EXPRESS** *launched as* Northern Majestic *-2004* **Beteiligungs KG ms 'Northern Majestic' Schiffahrtsges mbH & Co** Norddeutsche Reederei H Schuldt GmbH & Co KG SatCom: Inmarsat C 421177910 *Hamburg* *Germany* MMSI: 211779000 Official number: 20446	**75,590** 42,233 85,400 T/cm 102.3	Class: GL	**2004**-02 **Daewoo Shipbuilding & Marine Engineering Co Ltd — Geoje** Yd No: 4094 Loa 300.00 (BB) Br ex - Dght 14.500 Lbp 286.56 Br md 40.00 Dpth 24.20 Welded, 1 dk	**(A33A2CC) Container Ship (Fully Cellular)** Double Bottom Entire Compartment Length TEU 6732 C Ho 3174 TEU C Dk 3558 TEU incl 550 ref C. Compartments: ER, 7 Cell Ho	**1 oil engine** driving 1 FP propeller Total Power: 57,075kW (77,599hp) 25.6kn B&W 10K98MC-C 1 x 2 Stroke 10 Cy. 980 x 2400 57075kW (77599bhp) Doosan Engine Co Ltd-South Korea AuxGen: 2 x 2400kW 440/220V 60Hz a.c, 2 x 2700kW 440/220V 60Hz a.c Thrusters: 1 Thwart. CP thruster (f) Fuel: 295.0 (d.f.) 7538.0 (r.f.) 213.0pd
8621800 *YBVN* -	**SAN FRANSISCO** *ex* Expres *-2009* *ex* Hoyoshi Maru No. 11 *-2006* **PT Samudra Intim Perkasa** - *Surabaya* *Indonesia*	*470* 228 600	Class: KI	**1984**-03 **Tokuoka Zosen K.K. — Naruto** Yd No: 121 Loa 47.58 Br ex - Dght 3.780 Lbp 43.20 Br md 8.21 Dpth 4.91 Welded, 1 dk	**(A31A2GX) General Cargo Ship**	**1 oil engine** driving 1 FP propeller Total Power: 478kW (650hp) 10.0kn Hanshin 6LU26G 1 x 4 Stroke 6 Cy. 260 x 440 478kW (650bhp) The Hanshin Diesel Works Ltd-Japan
8616271 - -	**SAN GALLAN** *ex* Fulgor *-1997* *ex* Lady Dulcie *-1990* **Petrolera Transoceanica SA** - *Callao* *Peru* Official number: CO-16601-EM	**157** 89 89	Class: (LR) (RI) ✠ Classed LR until 24/7/13	**1988**-08 **Cochrane Shipbuilders Ltd. — Selby** Yd No: 139 Loa 24.34 Br ex 7.73 Dght 3.187 Lbp 22.03 Br md 7.31 Dpth 3.81 Welded, 1 dk	**(B32A2ST) Tug**	**2 oil engines** with clutches, flexible couplings & sr reverse geared to sc. shafts driving 2 FP propellers Total Power: 1,416kW (1,926hp) 10.5kn Ruston 6AP230M 2 x 4 Stroke 6 Cy. 230 x 273 each-708kW (963bhp) Ruston Diesels Ltd.-Newton-le-Willows AuxGen: 2 x 80kW 415V 50Hz a.c Fuel: 33.5 (d.f.)
6905185 - -	**SAN GALLAN 6** *ex* Mar de Arabia *-1976* - -	*158* 72 -	Class: (AB) (GL)	**1966 Promecan Ingenieros S.A. — Callao** Yd No: 47 Loa - Br ex 6.79 Dght - Lbp 21.49 Br md 6.71 Dpth 3.81 Welded, 1 dk	**(B11B2FV) Fishing Vessel** Compartments: 1 Ho, ER 1 Ha: (1.9 x 3.3)	**1 oil engine** reduction geared to sc. shaft driving 1 CP propeller Total Power: 221kW (300hp) 10.0kn Normo Z4 1 x 2 Stroke 4 Cy. 300 x 360 221kW (300bhp) AS Bergens Mek Verksteder-Norway Fuel: 9.0
6905161 - -	**SAN GALLAN 7** *ex* Mar Adriatico *-1976* **Empresa Manumar SA** - *Callao* *Peru* Official number: CO-006659-PM	*145* 67 -	Class: (AB) (GL)	**1966 Promecan Ingenieros S.A. — Callao** Yd No: 52 Loa - Br ex 6.79 Dght - Lbp 21.49 Br md 6.71 Dpth 3.81 Welded, 1 dk	**(B11B2FV) Fishing Vessel** Compartments: 1 Ho, ER 1 Ha: (1.9 x 3.3)	**1 oil engine** reduction geared to sc. shaft driving 1 CP propeller Total Power: 221kW (300hp) 10.0kn Normo Z4 1 x 2 Stroke 4 Cy. 300 x 360 221kW (300bhp) AS Bergens Mek Verksteder-Norway Fuel: 9.0
6905202 - -	**SAN GALLAN 8** *ex* Mar de Celebes *-1976* - -	*158* 72 -	Class: (AB) (GL)	**1966 Promecan Ingenieros S.A. — Callao** Yd No: 49 Loa - Br ex 6.79 Dght - Lbp 21.49 Br md 6.71 Dpth 3.81 Welded, 1 dk	**(B11B2FV) Fishing Vessel** Compartments: 1 Ho, ER 1 Ha: (1.9 x 3.3)	**1 oil engine** reduction geared to sc. shaft driving 1 CP propeller Total Power: 221kW (300hp) 10.0kn Normo Z4 1 x 2 Stroke 4 Cy. 300 x 360 221kW (300bhp) AS Bergens Mek Verksteder-Norway Fuel: 9.0
6905214 - -	**SAN GALLAN 9** *ex* Mar Jonico *-1976* **Pesquera Marbella SA** - *Chimbote* *Peru* Official number: CE-000235-PM	*200* 67 -	Class: (AB)	**1966 Promecan Ingenieros S.A. — Callao** Yd No: 48 Loa - Br ex 6.79 Dght - Lbp 21.49 Br md 6.71 Dpth 3.51 Welded, 1 dk	**(B11B2FV) Fishing Vessel** Compartments: 1 Ho, ER 1 Ha: (1.9 x 3.3)	**1 oil engine** driving 1 CP propeller Total Power: 221kW (300hp) Normo Z4 1 x 2 Stroke 4 Cy. 300 x 360 221kW (300bhp) AS Bergens Mek Verksteder-Norway Fuel: 9.0
7346142 - -	**SAN GENARO** - **Transmaru Cooperative Transport** - *Montevideo* *Uruguay*	*110* - -		**1976**-08 **Astillero Anibal Vanoli y Cia. S. en C. — Quequen** Yd No: 24 Loa 27.01 Br ex - Dght - Lbp 24.11 Br md 6.09 Dpth 3.13 Welded, 1 dk	**(B11A2FT) Trawler**	**1 oil engine** driving 1 FP propeller Total Power: 313kW (426hp) Caterpillar D353SCAC 1 x 4 Stroke 6 Cy. 159 x 203 313kW (426bhp) Caterpillar Tractor Co-USA
9043586 *LW8674* -	**SAN GENARO** - **Le Saumon Sociedad Anonima** - *Mar del Plata* *Argentina* MMSI: 701055000 Official number: 0763	**110** 78 130		**1992**-12 **SANYM S.A. — Buenos Aires** Yd No: 88 Loa 26.50 Br ex - Dght 2.890 Lbp 23.90 Br md 6.50 Dpth 3.30 Welded, 1 dk	**(B11A2FS) Stern Trawler** Ins: 165	**1 oil engine** geared to sc. shaft driving 1 FP propeller Total Power: 397kW (540hp) 10.0kn Caterpillar 3412TA 1 x Vee 4 Stroke 12 Cy. 137 x 152 397kW (540bhp) Caterpillar Inc-USA
6410829 *IUHW* -	**SAN GENNARO** - **SBS Leasing SpA** - *Naples* *Italy* Official number: 942	*240* 55 49	Class: RI	**1964 Cantiere Navale M & B Benetti — Viareggio** Yd No: 60 Loa 29.39 Br ex 7.73 Dght 3.560 Lbp 25.86 Br md 7.70 Dpth 4.02 Riveted\Welded, 1 dk	**(B32A2ST) Tug**	**1 oil engine** geared to sc. shaft driving 1 FP propeller Total Power: 772kW (1,050hp) 12.0kn MAN G8V30/45ATL 1 x 4 Stroke 8 Cy. 300 x 450 772kW (1050bhp) Maschinenbau Augsburg Nuernberg (MAN)-Augsburg AuxGen: 1 x 20kW 220V d.c, 1 x 15kW 220V d.c
9438987 *IIOT2* -	**SAN GENNARO** - **Rimorchiatori Napoletani Srl** - *Naples* *Italy* MMSI: 247295700	**441** 132 -	Class: RI	**2010**-12 **Cantieri San Marco Srl — La Spezia** Yd No: 22 Loa 26.89 Br ex 14.05 Dght 3.916 Lbp 25.10 Br md 13.28 Dpth 5.00 Welded, 1 dk	**(B32A2ST) Tug**	**2 oil engines** geared to sc. shafts driving 2 Directional propellers Total Power: 3,900kW (5,302hp) Wartsila 6L26 2 x 4 Stroke 6 Cy. 260 x 320 each-1950kW (2651bhp) Wartsila Italia SpA-Italy
8959295 *ITTS* -	**SAN GENNARO PRIMO** - **Societa Italiana per Condotte d'Acqua SpA** Servizio Gestione e Armamento Mezzi Marittimi *Rome* *Italy* MMSI: 247317800 Official number: 7633	**1,148** 344 -	Class: RI	**1974**-08 **Cant. Nav. Sgorbini — La Spezia** Yd No: 92 Loa 46.32 Br ex - Dght - Lbp 45.90 Br md 23.00 Dpth 3.81 Welded, 1 dk	**(B34B2SC) Crane Vessel**	**2 oil engines** geared to sc. shafts driving 2 FP propellers Total Power: 930kW (1,264hp) 3.0kn Caterpillar 3412TA 2 x Vee 4 Stroke 12 Cy. 137 x 152 each-465kW (632bhp) (new engine 1992) Caterpillar Inc-USA AuxGen: 1 x 160kW 380V 50Hz a.c, 1 x 32kW 380V 50Hz a.c
6821793 *INDK* -	**SAN GIACOMO** *ex* Neptunia Seconda *-2003* **Rimorchiatori Salerno Srl** - *Genoa* *Italy* MMSI: 247036900 Official number: 1205	*392* 336 791	Class: RI	**1968 Cant. Nav. Sgorbini — La Spezia** Yd No: 80 Loa 45.50 Br ex 8.01 Dght 1.988 Lbp 43.01 Br md 7.98 Dpth 3.20 Welded, 1 dk	**(A14A2LO) Water Tanker** Grain: 63; Liq: 790 Compartments: 1 Ho, 6 Ta, ER	**1 oil engine** driving 1 Directional propeller Total Power: 184kW (250hp) Deutz F12L714 1 x Vee 4 Stroke 12 Cy. 120 x 140 184kW (250bhp) Kloeckner Humboldt Deutz AG-West Germany AuxGen: 2 x 9kW 380V 50Hz a.c

IMO / Call sign	Name / Owner	Tonnage	Class	Builder / Dimensions	Type	Machinery
9625918 *9HA3306* -	**SAN GIORGIO** **Sonnet Shipping Ltd** Eastern Mediterranean Maritime Ltd *Valletta* *Malta* MMSI: 229404000 Official number: 9625918	**20,239** 7,688 24,157	Class: BV GL	**2013-05 SPP Shipbuilding Co Ltd — Sacheon** Yd No: H4077 Loa 170.06 (BB) Br ex - Dght 8.500 Lbp 160.00 Br md 29.80 Dpth 14.50 Welded, 1 dk	**(A33A2CC) Container Ship (Fully Cellular)** TEU 1756 incl 350 ref C Cranes: 3x40t	**1 oil engine** driving 1 FP propeller Total Power: 14,280kW (19,415hp) 20.0kn MAN-B&W 6S60ME-B8 1 x 2 Stroke 6 Cy. 600 x 2400 14280kW (19415bhp) Thrusters: 1 Tunnel thruster (f)
9529449 *IIOK2* -	**SAN GIORGIO AT** **Adriatic Towage Srl** - *Venice* *Italy* MMSI: 247278900	**478** 143 -	Class: RI	**2009-12 Cantieri San Marco Srl — La Spezia** Yd No: 24 Loa 32.51 Br ex 11.90 Dght 4.440 Lbp 30.28 Br md 11.70 Dpth 5.60 Welded, 1 dk	**(B32A2ST) Tug**	**2 oil engines** reduction geared to sc. shafts driving 2 Directional propellers Total Power: 4,202kW (5,714hp) Caterpillar 3516B 2 x Vee 4 Stroke 16 Cy. 170 x 190 each-2101kW (2857bhp) Caterpillar Inc-USA
7510755 *IOZT* -	**SAN GIOVANNI** **Societa Italiana per Condotte d'Acqua SpA** - SatCom: Inmarsat C 424703351 *Rome* *Italy* MMSI: 247006300 Official number: 749	**1,046** 313 1,982	Class: RI	**1974-06 Hilgers AG — Rheinbrohl** Yd No: 723-903 Loa 60.10 Br ex 12.73 Dght 4.039 Lbp 58.76 Br md 12.40 Dpth 5.01 Welded, 1 dk	**(B34A2SH) Hopper, Motor** Hopper: 1,000 Compartments: 1 Ho, ER	**2 oil engines** driving 2 Directional propellers Total Power: 750kW (1,020hp) Deutz BF12M716 2 x Vee 4 Stroke 12 Cy. 135 x 160 each-375kW (510bhp) Kloeckner Humboldt Deutz AG-West Germany
8959386 *IVXV* -	**SAN GIUSEPPE PRIMO** *ex* San Giuseppe *-2000* **Societa Italiana per Condotte d'Acqua SpA** Servizio Gestione e Armamento Mezzi Marittimi *Rome* *Italy* MMSI: 247235900 Official number: 7679	**455** 136 100	Class: RI	**1976 Lisnave - Estaleiros Navais de Lisboa SARL — Lisbon** Loa 35.32 Br ex - Dght - Lbp 35.00 Br md 16.00 Dpth 3.00 Welded, 1 dk	**(B34B2SC) Crane Vessel**	**2 oil engines** driving 2 FP propellers Total Power: 276kW (376hp) Deutz F10L413 2 x Vee 4 Stroke 10 Cy. 120 x 125 each-138kW (188bhp) Kloeckner Humboldt Deutz AG-West Germany AuxGen: 1 x 100kW 380V 50Hz a.c
9698927 *IJGU2* -	**SAN GIUSTO** **Ocean Srl** - *Trieste* *Italy* MMSI: 247334200 Official number: 549	**172** 55 -	Class: RI	**2013-09 Nuovo Arsenale Cartubi Srl — Trieste** Yd No: 15/2012 Loa 28.10 Br ex - Dght 2.750 Lbp 26.20 Br md 7.50 Dpth 3.30 Welded, 1 dk	**(B32A2ST) Tug**	**2 oil engines** reduction geared to sc. shafts driving 2 FP propellers Total Power: 1,790kW (2,434hp) Caterpillar C32 2 x Vee 4 Stroke 12 Cy. 145 x 162 each-895kW (1217bhp) Caterpillar Inc-USA AuxGen: 2 x 320kW 220V 50Hz a.c
7636080 *XCAR9* -	**SAN GUILLERMO** *ex* Marino *-2002* *ex* Picasso *-2001* *ex* Poker *-1995* *ex* Beaverdale *-1991* *ex* Wuppertal *-1987* *ex* Canaima *-1979* *ex* Wuppertal *-1978* **Transportacion Maritima de California SA de CV** - *La Paz* *Mexico* MMSI: 345040013	**5,369** 1,700 2,840	Class: NV (RI) (GL)	**1977-11 Rickmers Rhederei GmbH Rickmers Werft — Bremerhaven** Yd No: 375 Loa 115.12 (BB) Br ex 17.45 Dght 5.320 Lbp 103.41 Br md 17.42 Dpth 10.83 Welded, 2 dks	**(A35A2RR) Ro-Ro Cargo Ship** Passengers: driver berths: 12 Stern door/ramp (centre) Len: 9.72 Wid: 7.40 Swl: - Lane-Len: 796 Lane-clr ht: 4.37 Cars: 60, Trailers: 65 Bale: 9,758 TEU 130 Ice Capable	**2 oil engines** driving 2 CP propellers Total Power: 5,002kW (6,800hp) 17.0kn MaK 8M551AK 2 x 4 Stroke 8 Cy. 450 x 550 each-2501kW (3400bhp) MaK Maschinenbau GmbH-Kiel AuxGen: 3 x 380kW 220/440V 60Hz a.c Thrusters: 1 Thwart. FP thruster (f) Fuel: 406.5 (d.f.) 25.5pd
9234006 *9HYT6* -	**SAN GWANN** **Majorca Maritime Ltd** Virtu Ferries Ltd *Valletta* *Malta* MMSI: 248984000 Official number: 7233	**992** 306 89	Class: NV	**2001-05 Fjellstrand AS — Omastrand** Yd No: 1658 Loa 49.00 Br ex 12.03 Dght 2.150 Lbp 46.03 Br md 12.00 Dpth 4.75 Welded, 1 dk	**(A36A2PR) Passenger/Ro-Ro Ship (Vehicles)** Passengers: unberthed: 427 Cars: 21	**4 oil engines** reduction geared to sc. shafts driving 4 Water jets Total Power: 7,040kW (9,572hp) 38.0kn M.T.U. 16V4000M70 4 x Vee 4 Stroke 16 Cy. 165 x 190 each-1760kW (2393bhp) MTU Friedrichshafen GmbH-Friedrichshafen
8858295 *HP7000* -	**SAN HANG PAO 3** **CCCC Third Harbor Engineering Co Ltd** - *Panama* *Panama* Official number: 45512PEXT	*485* 145 639		**1987-04 Jiangnan Shipyard — Shanghai** Loa 49.50 Br ex - Dght 2.430 Lbp 46.70 Br md 11.15 Dpth 3.70 Welded, 1 dk	**(B34A2SS) Stone Carrier**	**2 oil engines** geared to sc. shafts driving 2 FP propellers Total Power: 596kW (810hp) Cummins NTA-855-M 2 x 4 Stroke 6 Cy. 140 x 152 each-298kW (405bhp) Cummins Engine Co Inc-USA
8603676 *HP9720* -	**SAN HANG PAO 4** **CCCC Third Harbor Engineering Co Ltd** - *Panama* *Panama* Official number: 45513PEXT	*498* 149 1,109	Class: (CC)	**1987-01 Ishii Zosen K.K. — Futtsu** Yd No: 201 Loa 53.62 Br ex 11.99 Dght 3.001 Lbp 51.00 Br md 11.50 Dpth 4.10 Welded, 1 dk	**(B34A2SS) Stone Carrier** Grain: 500	**2 oil engines** with clutches & dr geared to sc. shafts driving 2 FP propellers Total Power: 588kW (800hp) 7.8kn Niigata 8NSAK-Z 2 x 4 Stroke 8 Cy. 133 x 160 each-294kW (400bhp) Niigata Engineering Co Ltd-Japan AuxGen: 1 x 40kW 380V 50Hz a.c
8858300 *BSXC* -	**SAN HANG PAO YI HAO** **Government of The People's Republic of China (Ministry of Transport)** - *Lianyungang, Jiangsu* *China*	**607** 182 612	Class: (CC)	**1987 in Syria** Loa 49.90 Br ex - Dght 2.680 Lbp 47.30 Br md 11.40 Dpth 4.00 Welded, 1 dk	**(B34A2SS) Stone Carrier**	**2 oil engines** geared to sc. shafts driving 2 FP propellers Cummins NTA-855-M 2 x 4 Stroke 6 Cy. 140 x 152 Cummins Engine Co Inc-USA
8666460 - -	**SAN HANG QI 15** **CCCC Third Harbor Engineering Co Ltd** - *Shanghai* *China*	**1,617** 485 -		**2006-09 Jingjiang Hailing Shipyard Ltd — Jingjiang JS** Loa 56.70 Br ex - Dght 2.200 Lbp 55.30 Br md 20.80 Dpth 4.20 Welded, 1 dk	**(B34B2SC) Crane Vessel**	**2 oil engines** driving 2 Propellers Total Power: 370kW (504hp)
8707147 - -	**SAN HANG QIJIU** **Government of The People's Republic of China** - *China* MMSI: 412043280	**1,219** 365 1,392		**1987-09 Teraoka Shipyard Co Ltd — Minamiawaji HG** Yd No: 261 Loa - Br ex - Dght 2.812 Lbp 43.01 Br md 20.01 Dpth 4.02 Welded	**(B34B2SC) Crane Vessel**	**1 oil engine** driving 1 FP propeller Total Power: 610kW (829hp) Yanmar 1 x 4 Stroke 610kW (829bhp) Yanmar Diesel Engine Co Ltd-Japan
8858283 - -	**SAN HANG TUO 910** **Government of The People's Republic of China (Third Navigation Engineering Bureau Construction Shipping Co Ltd)** - *Shanghai* *China*	**185** 55 -	Class: (CC)	**1980 Shanghai Shipyard — Shanghai** Loa 29.50 Br ex - Dght - Lbp 27.00 Br md 8.00 Dpth 3.80 Welded, 1 dk	**(B32A2ST) Tug**	**1 oil engine** driving 1 FP propeller Total Power: 721kW (980hp) Skoda 6L350PN 1 x 4 Stroke 6 Cy. 350 x 500 721kW (980bhp) CKD Praha-Praha AuxGen: 2 x 56kW 400V a.c
8870695 - -	**SAN HANG TUO 1002** **Government of The People's Republic of China (Third Navigation Engineering Bureau Construction Shipping Co Ltd)** - *Shanghai* *China*	*237* 71 -	Class: (CC)	**1991 Jian Shipyard — Shanghai** Loa 31.50 Br ex - Dght 2.700 Lbp 28.50 Br md 8.60 Dpth 3.80 Welded, 1 dk	**(B32A2ST) Tug**	**1 oil engine** reduction geared to sc. shaft driving 1 FP propeller Total Power: 808kW (1,099hp) 12.0kn Daihatsu 6DSM-22 1 x 4 Stroke 6 Cy. 220 x 280 808kW (1099bhp) Shaanxi Diesel Engine Factory-China AuxGen: 2 x 64kW 400V a.c
8870700 *BSWR* -	**SAN HANG TUO 1003** **Government of The People's Republic of China (Third Navigation Engineering Bureau Construction Shipping Co Ltd)** - *Shanghai* *China*	*223* 66 -	Class: (CC)	**1979 Tianjin Xingang Shipyard — Tianjin** Loa 32.56 Br ex - Dght 3.040 Lbp 29.70 Br md 8.20 Dpth 4.20 Welded, 1 dk	**(B32A2ST) Tug**	**1 oil engine** driving 1 FP propeller Total Power: 1,228kW (1,670hp) Skoda 9TSR35/50-2 1 x 4 Stroke 9 Cy. 350 x 500 1228kW (1670bhp) Skoda-Praha AuxGen: 2 x 90kW 400V a.c
8649785 *HP4948* -	**SAN HANG TUO 1007** **No 3 Engineering Co Ltd** CCCC Third Harbor Engineering Co Ltd *Panama* *Panama* Official number: 4361212	**222** 67 -	Class: ZC	**1979 Tianjin Xingang Shipyard — Tianjin** Loa 32.56 Br ex - Dght 3.000 Lbp - Br md 8.20 Dpth 4.20 Welded, 1 dk	**(B32A2ST) Tug**	**1 oil engine** driving 1 Propeller Total Power: 1,228kW (1,670hp) 13.0kn Skoda 9TSR35/50-2 1 x 4 Stroke 9 Cy. 350 x 500 1228kW (1670bhp) CKD Praha-Praha

8830425 *BSWU* -	**SAN HANG TUO 2001** **Government of The People's Republic of China (Third Navigation Engineering Bureau Construction Shipping Co Ltd)** - *Shanghai* *China* MMSI: 412043010	**984** 284 -	Class: CC	**1977 Guangzhou Wenchong Shipyard — Guangzhou GD** Loa 60.98 Br ex - Dght 4.400 Lbp 54.00 Br md 16.00 Dpth 5.70 Welded, 1 dk	**(B32A2ST) Tug**	**2 oil engines** driving 2 FP propellers Total Power: 1,942kW (2,640hp) 13.0kn S.K.L. 8NVD48A-2U 2 x 4 Stroke 8 Cy. 320 x 480 each-971kW (1320bhp) VEB Schwermaschinenbau "KarlLiebknecht" (SKL)-Magdeburg AuxGen: 3 x 90kW 400V a.c
8830413 *HP4629* -	**SAN HANG TUO 2002** **Pingjiang International Shipping Co Ltd** CCCG Third Navigation Engineering Bureau Construction Shipping Co Ltd *Panama* *Panama* MMSI: 373513000 Official number: 43419PEXT	*848* 254 -	Class: (CC)	**1978-11 Guangzhou Wenchong Shipyard — Guangzhou GD** Loa 60.22 Br ex - Dght 4.300 Lbp 54.00 Br md 11.60 Dpth 5.70 Welded, 1 dk	**(B32A2ST) Tug**	**2 oil engines** driving 1 FP propeller Total Power: 1,940kW (2,638hp) 12.0kn S.K.L. 8NVD48A-2U 1 x 4 Stroke 8 Cy. 320 x 480 970kW (1319bhp) VEB Schwermaschinenbau "KarlLiebknecht" (SKL)-Magdeburg AuxGen: 3 x 90kW 400V a.c
8830401 *BSWW* -	**SAN HANG TUO 2003** **Government of The People's Republic of China (Ministry of Transport)** - *Xiamen, Fujian* *China*	*386* 115 -	Class: (CC)	**1988 Jiangnan Shipyard — Shanghai** Loa 37.70 Br ex - Dght 3.360 Lbp 32.00 Br md 10.00 Dpth 4.50 Welded, 1 dk	**(B32A2ST) Tug**	**2 oil engines** driving 2 FP propellers Total Power: 1,472kW (2,002hp) Daihatsu 6DLM-22 2 x 4 Stroke 6 Cy. 220 x 300 each-736kW (1001bhp) Daihatsu Diesel Manufacturing Co Lt-Japan AuxGen: 2 x 80kW 380V a.c, 1 x 40kW 380V a.c
8865298 - -	**SAN HANG TUO 2007** *ex Aki Maru -2005* **CCCC Third Harbor Engineering Co Ltd** - *Shanghai* *China*	**272** 81 -		**1992 Hongawara Zosen K.K. — Fukuyama** Loa 31.52 Br ex - Dght 2.980 Lbp 28.00 Br md 8.20 Dpth 3.60 Welded, 1 dk	**(B32A2ST) Tug**	**2 oil engines** reduction geared to sc. shafts driving 2 FP propellers Total Power: 1,104kW (1,500hp) Yanmar MF26-ST 2 x 4 Stroke 6 Cy. 260 x 500 each-552kW (750bhp) Yanmar Diesel Engine Co Ltd-Japan
7850002 *HP3777* -	**SAN HANG TUO 3001** *ex Sanuki Maru -1979* **CCCC Third Harbor Engineering Co Ltd** - *Panama* *Panama* Official number: 45515PEXT	*301* 90 -		**1977 Sagami Zosen Tekko K.K. — Yokosuka** Loa 32.90 Br ex - Dght 2.401 Lbp 28.60 Br md 9.63 Dpth 4.18 Welded, 1 dk	**(B32A2ST) Tug**	**2 oil engines** geared to sc. shafts driving 2 FP propellers Total Power: 2,354kW (3,200hp) 10.2kn Daihatsu 8DSM-26 2 x 4 Stroke 8 Cy. 260 x 320 each-1177kW (1600bhp) Daihatsu Diesel Manufacturing Co Lt-Japan AuxGen: 2 x 75kW 445V 60Hz a.c
9547556 *BSXR* -	**SAN HANG TUO 3005** **Government of The People's Republic of China (Third Navigation Engineering Bureau Construction Shipping Co Ltd)** - SatCom: Inmarsat C 441216663 *Shanghai* *China* MMSI: 412043780	**973** 291 -	Class: CC	**2008-12 Qingdao Shipyard — Qingdao SD** Yd No: QDZ452 Loa 49.98 Br ex - Dght 4.200 Lbp 45.60 Br md 12.50 Dpth 5.20 Welded, 1 dk	**(B32A2ST) Tug**	**2 oil engines** reduction geared to sc. shafts driving 2 Propellers Total Power: 2,600kW (3,534hp) Niigata 6MG26HLX 2 x 4 Stroke 6 Cy. 260 x 350 each-1300kW (1767bhp) Niigata Engineering Co Ltd-Japan AuxGen: 2 x 140kW 400V a.c
9445760 *BSXS* -	**SAN HANG TUO 6001** **CCCG Third Navigation Engineering Bureau Construction Shipping Co Ltd** - *Shanghai* *China* MMSI: 413043030	**1,841** 552 1,281	Class: CC	**2007-10 Qingdao Shipyard — Qingdao SD** Yd No: QDZ449 Loa 61.30 Br ex - Dght 4.900 Lbp 55.80 Br md 13.80 Dpth 6.40 Welded, 1 dk	**(B32A2ST) Tug**	**2 oil engines** reduction geared to sc. shafts driving 2 Propellers Total Power: 4,412kW (5,998hp) Niigata 6MG28HLX 2 x 4 Stroke 6 Cy. 280 x 400 each-2206kW (2999bhp) Niigata Engineering Co Ltd-Japan AuxGen: 3 x 200kW 400V a.c
7824120 *ZMA2709* -	**SAN HAURAKI** **Sanford Ltd** - *Auckland* *New Zealand* Official number: 380247	**243** 72 183	Class: (LR) ✠	**1979-03 Kanmon Zosen K.K. — Shimonoseki** Yd No: 343 Loa 29.01 Br ex 8.08 Dght 3.328 Lbp 25.51 Br md 8.07 Dpth 3.95 Welded, 1 dk	**(B11A2FS) Stern Trawler**	**1 oil engine** reduction geared to sc. shaft driving 1 FP propeller Total Power: 552kW (750hp) 10.0kn Daihatsu 6PSHTCM-26E 1 x 4 Stroke 6 Cy. 260 x 320 552kW (750bhp) Daihatsu Diesel Manufacturing Co Lt-Japan AuxGen: 2 x 48kW 405V 50Hz a.c
9275804 *ZMT9911* -	**SAN HIKURANGI** *ex Gorm -2009 ex Gasholmur -2007* *ex Gashovdi -2006* **Sanford Ltd** - *Auckland* *New Zealand*	**113** 40 60	Class: (NV)	**2003-06 'Crist' Sp z oo — Gdansk** (Hull) Yd No: B22/1 **2003-06 Osey hf — Hafnarfjordur** Yd No: B11 Loa 21.95 Br ex 6.66 Dght 2.800 Lbp 20.50 Br md 6.50 Dpth 3.30 Welded, 1 dk	**(B11B2FV) Fishing Vessel**	**1 oil engine** geared to sc. shaft driving 1 FP propeller Total Power: 367kW (499hp) Caterpillar 3412TA 1 x Vee 4 Stroke 12 Cy. 137 x 152 367kW (499bhp) Caterpillar Inc-USA
8874005 - -	**SAN I No. 23** **Pesquera Ensenada de Barragan** -	**475** 249 -		**1989 Lien Ho Shipbuilding Co, Ltd — Kaohsiung** L reg 51.00 Br ex - Dght - Lbp - Br md 9.00 Dpth 4.30 Welded, 1 dk	**(B11B2FV) Fishing Vessel**	**2 oil engines** driving 2 FP propellers Total Power: 810kW (1,102hp) 12.0kn Akasaka 2 x 4 Stroke each-405kW (551bhp) Akasaka Tekkosho KK (Akasaka DieselLtd)-Japan
8882741 *DUG6329* -	**SAN IGNACIO 4** *ex Shinko Maru No. 88 -2006* *ex Hama Maru No. 21 -2006* *ex Yusei Maru No. 83 -2006* **Martin Agro-Industrial Corp** *Iloilo* *Philippines* Official number: ILO3001012	*153* 89 -		**1976 Minami-Nippon Zosen KK — Ichikikushikino KS** L reg 29.51 Br ex - Dght - Lbp - Br md 5.95 Dpth 2.70 Welded, 1 dk	**(B11A2FS) Stern Trawler**	**1 oil engine** driving 1 FP propeller Yanmar 1 x 4 Stroke Yanmar Diesel Engine Co Ltd-Japan
8842454 *WDC3248* -	**SAN JOAQUIN RIVER** **Foss Maritime Co** - *San Francisco, CA* *United States of America* MMSI: 367004670 Official number: 295630	*140* 73 -		**1964 Colberg Boat Works — Stockton, Ca** Yd No: 1163-2 Loa - Br ex - Dght - Lbp 19.57 Br md 7.96 Dpth 2.44 Welded, 1 dk	**(B32A2ST) Tug**	**1 oil engine** driving 1 FP propeller Total Power: 736kW (1,001hp)
6525882 *LW4305* -	**SAN JORGE MARTIR** *ex Cecilia -2003 ex Le Matelot -1976* **Compania Frigocen SAIC** - *Mar del Plata* *Argentina* Official number: 02152	**694** 531 376	Class: (BV)	**1966 Beliard-Murdoch S.A. — Oostende** Yd No: 193 Loa 58.22 Br ex 10.19 Dght 4.395 Lbp 50.60 Br md 10.09 Dpth 6.13 Welded, 1 dk	**(B11A2FS) Stern Trawler** Ins: 325 Compartments: 2 Ho, ER 4 Ha: 4 (1.5 x 0.9) Cranes: 1x6t	**1 oil engine** driving 1 FP propeller Total Power: 1,048kW (1,425hp) 14.0kn MAN G9V30/45ATL 1 x 4 Stroke 9 Cy. 300 x 450 1048kW (1425bhp) Maschinenbau Augsburg Nuernberg (MAN)-Augsburg Fuel: 142.0 (d.f.)
9276121 *EBWX* 3-HU-39-01	**SAN JORGE R** **Mariscos Rodriguez SA** - *Huelva* *Spain* MMSI: 224060000 Official number: 3-9/2001	**273** 81 421	Class: BV	**2001-11 Astilleros La Parrilla S.A. — San Esteban de Pravia** Yd No: 175 Loa - Br ex - Dght - Lbp - Br md - Dpth - Welded, 1 dk	**(B11B2FV) Fishing Vessel**	**1 oil engine** reduction geared to sc. shaft driving 1 FP propeller Total Power: 397kW (540hp) Caterpillar 3512TA 1 x Vee 4 Stroke 12 Cy. 170 x 190 397kW (540bhp) Caterpillar Inc-USA
8979063 *HC2017* -	**SAN JOSE** **Marchena Tour SA (MARTOUR)** - *Puerto Baquerizo Moreno* *Ecuador* Official number: TN-01-0904	*304* 91 -		**1996 Ing. Jose Mendieta — Ecuador** L reg 34.00 Br ex - Dght - Lbp - Br md 8.00 Dpth - Welded, 1 dk	**(A37A2PC) Passenger/Cruise** Passengers: cabins: 8; berths: 16	**2 oil engines** geared to sc. shafts driving 2 Propellers Total Power: 678kW (922hp) 10.0kn G.M. (Detroit Diesel) 16V-71 2 x Vee 2 Stroke 16 Cy. 108 x 127 each-339kW (461bhp) Detroit Diesel Corporation-Detroit, Mi
9184407 *CBJS* -	**SAN JOSE** *ex Murman-2 -2006* **Pesquera San Jose SA** - *Valparaiso* *Chile* MMSI: 725003670 Official number: 3140	**2,005** 603 1,850	Class: LR (NV) **100A1** SS 07/2013 fishing vessel **LMC** Eq.Ltr: O; Cable: 412.5/34.0 U2 (a)	**1998-07 Astilleros y Servicios Navales S.A. (ASENAV) — Valdivia** Yd No: 121 Loa 74.50 (BB) Br ex - Dght 5.700 Lbp 66.00 Br md 12.60 Dpth 8.20 Welded, 1 dk	**(B11B2FV) Fishing Vessel** Ins: 1,800	**1 oil engine** reduction geared to sc. shaft driving 1 CP propeller Total Power: 4,500kW (6,118hp) 17.0kn MaK 9M32C 1 x 4 Stroke 9 Cy. 320 x 480 4500kW (6118bhp) (new engine 2008, fitted 2008) Caterpillar Motoren GmbH & Co. KG-Germany AuxGen: 1 x 1420kW a.c, 1 x 1150kW a.c Thrusters: 1 Thwart. CP thruster (f); 1 Thwart. CP thruster (a)

7653806 *DVEN* -	**SAN JOSE D. R.** *ex* Maria Bella D. R. *-2007* *ex* Maria Cristina RJL *-2007* *ex* Seizan Maru No. 58 *-1987* **Philmariner Aqua Ventures Corp** - *Manila* *Philippines* Official number: MNLD000857	*247* 79 -		**1972 Fujiwara Zosensho — Imabari** Yd No: 31 L reg 35.40 Br ex - Dght - Lbp 34.50 Br md 6.80 Dpth 3.55 Welded, 1 dk	**(B11B2FV) Fishing Vessel**	**1 oil engine** driving 1 FP propeller Total Power: 736kW (1,001hp) Niigata 1 x 4 Stroke 736kW (1001bhp) Niigata Engineering Co Ltd-Japan
8034514 - -	**SAN JOSE I** *ex* Waterspout *-1987* **Ana Maria Montemayor Cavazos** - *Tampico* *Mexico*	*105* 72 -		**1982-09 Steiner Shipyard, Inc. — Bayou La Batre, Al** Yd No: 135 Loa 22.81 Br ex - Dght 2.401 Lbp 20.12 Br md 6.71 Dpth 3.36 Welded, 1 dk	**(B11A2FT) Trawler**	**1 oil engine** geared to sc. shaft driving 1 FP propeller Total Power: 268kW (364hp) Cummins KT-1150-M 1 x 4 Stroke 6 Cy. 159 x 159 268kW (364bhp) Cummins Engine Co Inc-USA
8034538 - -	**SAN JOSE II** *ex* Capt. Dooley *-1987* **Ana Maria Montemayor Cavazos** - *Tampico* *Mexico*	*105* 72 -		**1982-10 Steiner Shipyard, Inc. — Bayou La Batre, Al** Yd No: 137 Loa 22.81 Br ex - Dght 2.401 Lbp 20.12 Br md 6.71 Dpth 3.36 Welded, 1 dk	**(B11A2FT) Trawler**	**1 oil engine** geared to sc. shaft driving 1 FP propeller Total Power: 268kW (364hp) Cummins KT-1150-M 1 x 4 Stroke 6 Cy. 159 x 159 268kW (364bhp) Cummins Engine Co Inc-USA
8642622 *DYDV* -	**SAN JUAN** **Government of The Republic of The Philippines (Ministry of Transportation & Communications)** - SatCom: Inmarsat C 454856210 *Philippines* MMSI: 548562000	*807* - -		**2000-07 Tenix Shipbuilding WA — Fremantle WA** Loa - Br ex 10.55 Dght 5.400 Lbp - Br md - Dpth - Welded, 1 dk	**(B34M2QS) Search & Rescue Vessel**	**1 oil engine** driving 1 Propeller
8305365 - -	**SAN JUAN** **Compania Pesquera Vikingos de Colombia SA** - *Cartagena de Indias* *Colombia* Official number: MC-05-389	*130* 24 22		**1982 Desco Marine — Saint Augustine, Fl** Loa 22.86 Br ex 6.71 Dght 0.920 Lbp 19.99 Br md 6.51 Dpth 4.09 Bonded, 1 dk	**(B11A2FT) Trawler** Hull Material: Reinforced Plastic Ins: 67 Compartments: 1 Ho, ER 1 Ha:	**1 oil engine** with clutches & sr geared to sc. shaft driving 1 FP propeller Total Power: 331kW (450hp) Caterpillar 3412T 1 x Vee 4 Stroke 12 Cy. 137 x 152 331kW (450bhp) Caterpillar Tractor Co-USA
5060720 - -	**SAN JUAN I** *ex* Cap Saint Jean *-1977* **Vieira Argentina SA** -	**440** 225 350	Class: (BV)	**1959 AG Weser, Werk Seebeck — Bremerhaven** Yd No: 867 Loa 54.31 Br ex 8.92 Dght 4.390 Lbp 48.90 Br md 8.89 Dpth 4.65 Riveted, 1 dk	**(B11A2FT) Trawler** Ins: 427 4 Ha: 4 (0.9 x 0.9) Derricks: 1x3t,1x2t; Winches: 2	**1 oil engine** with hydraulic coupling driving 1 FP propeller Total Power: 1,103kW (1,500hp) 15.0kn Deutz SBV6M358 1 x 4 Stroke 6 Cy. 400 x 580 1103kW (1500bhp) Kloeckner Humboldt Deutz AG-West Germany AuxGen: 3 x 60kW 220V d.c Fuel: 147.0 (d.f.)
9253765 *LW4200* -	**SAN JULIAN** *ex* Cabo Froward *-2003* **Antares Naviera SA** - *Buenos Aires* *Argentina* MMSI: 701080000 Official number: 02206	**40,456** 20,334 69,554 T/cm 67.5	Class: LR ✠ **100A1** SS 01/2013 Double Hull oil tanker ESP *IWS LI **ShipRight** (SDA, FDA, CM) ✠ **LMC** **UMS IGS** Eq.Ltr: 0†; Cable: 660.0/78.0 U3 (a)	**2003-01 Daewoo Shipbuilding & Marine Engineering Co Ltd — Geoje** Yd No: 5226 Loa 228.00 (BB) Br ex 32.23 Dght 12.200 Lbp 219.00 Br md 32.20 Dpth 19.80 Welded, 1 dk	**(A13B2TP) Products Tanker** Double Hull (13F) Liq: 77,630; Liq (Oil): 79,214 Compartments: 12 Wing Ta, 2 Wing Slop Ta, ER 12 Cargo Pump (s): 12x900m³/hr Manifold: Bow/CM: 112.8m	**1 oil engine** driving 1 FP propeller Total Power: 11,282kW (15,339hp) 14.6kn MAN-B&W 5S60MC-C 1 x 2 Stroke 5 Cy. 600 x 2400 11282kW (15339bhp) Doosan Engine Co Ltd-South Korea AuxGen: 3 x 850kW 450V 60Hz a.c Boilers: AuxB (Comp) 9.2kgf/cm² (9.0bar), WTAuxB (o.f.) 11.7kgf/cm² (11.5bar) Fuel: 185.0 (d.f.) (Heating Coils) 2087.0 (r.f.)
8972900 *ZAPQ* -	**SAN LORENCO** *ex* Demir Milaqi *-2003* **Bardh Spahiu** - *Durres* *Albania* Official number: M-691	**112** 79 120		**1977 Kantieri Detar "Durres" — Durres** Loa 25.00 Br ex - Dght 2.540 Lbp - Br md 6.20 Dpth 3.00 Welded, 1 dk	**(A31A2GX) General Cargo Ship**	**1 oil engine** geared to sc. shaft driving 1 FP propeller Total Power: 425kW (578hp) S.K.L. 8NVD36A-1U 1 x 4 Stroke 8 Cy. 240 x 360 425kW (578bhp) VEB Schwermaschinenbau "KarlLiebknecht" (SKL)-Magdeburg
9123453 - - -	**SAN LORENZO** *ex* QS Forward *-1995* - -	*143* 43 -	Class: (GL) (AB)	**1994 Pacific Ocean Engineering & Trading Pte Ltd (POET) — Singapore** Yd No: 1045 Loa 23.00 Br ex - Dght 2.700 Lbp 21.78 Br md 7.50 Dpth 3.23 Welded, 1 dk	**(B32A2ST) Tug**	**2 oil engines** reduction geared to sc. shafts driving 2 FP propellers Total Power: 882kW (1,200hp) Cummins KTA-19-M3 2 x 4 Stroke 6 Cy. 159 x 159 each-441kW (600bhp) Cummins Engine Co Inc-USA AuxGen: 2 x 60kW a.c Fuel: 70.0 (d.f.)
9439163 *IBUQ* -	**SAN LORENZO** **Petrolmar Trasporti e Servizi Marittimi SpA** - SatCom: Inmarsat C 424702798 *Genoa* *Italy* MMSI: 247276200	**6,296** 2,152 8,962 T/cm 17.5	Class: BV RI	**2009-12 Brodogradiliste Kraljevica dd — Kraljevica** Yd No: 547 Loa 108.50 (BB) Br ex - Dght 8.260 Lbp 99.90 Br md 18.60 Dpth 10.60 Welded, 1 dk	**(A12B2TR) Chemical/Products Tanker** Double Hull (13F) Liq: 7,593; Liq (Oil): 7,593 Compartments: 4 Wing Ta, 4 Ta, ER, 2 Wing Slop Ta 2 Cargo Pump (s): 2x400m³/hr Manifold: Bow/CM: 56.9m	**1 oil engine** geared to sc. shaft driving 1 CP propeller Total Power: 4,000kW (5,438hp) 13.7kn Wartsila 8L32 1 x 4 Stroke 8 Cy. 320 x 400 4000kW (5438bhp) Wartsila Finland Oy-Finland AuxGen: 2 x 1100kW 60Hz a.c Thrusters: 1 Thwart. FP thruster (f) Fuel: 76.5 (d.f.) 433.0 (r.f.)
6728800 - PS8271	**SAN LORENZO 1** *ex* Independencia *-1975* **AMG Embarcaciones SA** - *Chimbote* *Peru* Official number: CE-000257-PM	*200* 89 -	Class: (GL)	**1967 Ast. Picsa S.A. — Callao** Yd No: 196 L reg 26.83 Br ex 26.62 Dght - Lbp - Br md 7.04 Dpth 3.46 Welded, 1 dk	**(B11A2FT) Trawler**	**1 oil engine** sr reverse geared to sc. shaft driving 1 FP propeller Total Power: 279kW (379hp) Caterpillar D353TA 1 x 4 Stroke 6 Cy. 159 x 203 279kW (379bhp) Caterpillar Tractor Co-USA
6916055 - -	**SAN LORENZO 2** *ex* Moquegua *-1979* **Pesquera Neptuno SA** - *Chimbote* *Peru* Official number: CE-6577-PM	*190* 118 333	Class: (BV)	**1968 Maestranza y Astillero Delta S.A. — Callao** L reg 27.59 Br ex 7.60 Dght 3.315 Lbp - Br md 7.57 Dpth 3.69 Welded, 1 dk	**(B11A2FT) Trawler** Grain: 335 Compartments: 2 Ho, ER 2 Ha: (2.5 x 2.1) (1.4 x 2.1) Derricks: 1x0.5t; Winches: 1	**1 oil engine** driving 1 FP propeller Total Power: 515kW (700hp) 10.0kn G.M. (Detroit Diesel) 16V-71 1 x Vee 2 Stroke 16 Cy. 108 x 127 515kW (700bhp) General Motors Corp-USA
6726761 - -	**SAN LORENZO 3** *ex* Dorado IV *-1976* - -	*200* 89 -	Class: (GL)	**1967 Ast. Picsa S.A. — Callao** L reg 26.83 Br ex 7.07 Dght - Lbp - Br md 7.04 Dpth 3.46 Welded, 1 dk	**(B11A2FT) Trawler**	**1 oil engine** sr reverse geared to sc. shaft driving 1 FP propeller Total Power: 279kW (379hp) Caterpillar D353SCAC 1 x 4 Stroke 6 Cy. 159 x 203 279kW (379bhp) Caterpillar Tractor Co-USA
6902638 - -	**SAN LORENZO 4** *ex* Don John *-1975* - -	*200* 89 -	Class: (GL)	**1968 Ast. Picsa S.A. — Callao** Yd No: 235 L reg 26.83 Br ex 7.07 Dght - Lbp - Br md 7.04 Dpth 3.46 Welded, 1 dk	**(B11B2FV) Fishing Vessel**	**1 oil engine** sr reverse geared to sc. shaft driving 1 FP propeller Total Power: 279kW (379hp) Caterpillar D353TA 1 x 4 Stroke 6 Cy. 159 x 203 279kW (379bhp) Caterpillar Tractor Co-USA
6800206 - PS8266	**SAN LORENZO 5** *ex* Dona Carmen *-1975* **Herain Soto Giraldo** - *Pisco* *Peru* Official number: PS-003633-PM	*200* 89 -	Class: (GL)	**1967 Ast. Picsa S.A. — Callao** L reg 26.83 Br ex 7.37 Dght - Lbp 23.78 Br md 7.32 Dpth 3.46 Welded, 1 dk	**(B11B2FV) Fishing Vessel**	**1 oil engine** sr reverse geared to sc. shaft driving 1 FP propeller Total Power: 279kW (379hp) Caterpillar D353TA 1 x 4 Stroke 6 Cy. 159 x 203 279kW (379bhp) Caterpillar Tractor Co-USA AuxGen: 2 x 40kW
6726759 - - -	**SAN LORENZO 6** *ex* Dona Juanita *-1975* - -	*200* 89 -	Class: (GL)	**1967 Ast. Picsa S.A. — Callao** Yd No: 203 L reg 26.83 Br ex 7.07 Dght - Lbp - Br md - Dpth 3.46 Welded, 1 dk	**(B11B2FV) Fishing Vessel**	**1 oil engine** sr reverse geared to sc. shaft driving 1 FP propeller Total Power: 279kW (379hp) Caterpillar D353TA 1 x 4 Stroke 6 Cy. 159 x 203 279kW (379bhp) Caterpillar Tractor Co-USA

IMO / Call sign / Flag	Name / Former names / Owner / Port	Tonnage	Class	Build / Dimensions	Type / Capacity	Machinery
6728678 - -	**SAN LORENZO 7** *ex* Anpesa 1 *-1976* - -	*200* 89 -	Class: (GL)	**1967 Ast. Picsa S.A. — Callao** Yd No: 200 L reg 26.83 Br ex 7.07 Dght - Lbp - Br md 7.04 Dpth 3.48 Welded, 1 dk	**(B11A2FT) Trawler**	**1 oil engine** sr reverse geared to sc. shaft driving 1 FP propeller Total Power: 279kW (379hp) Caterpillar D353SCAC 1 x 4 Stroke 6 Cy. 159 x 203 279kW (379bhp) Caterpillar Tractor Co-USA
6906488 - -	**SAN LORENZO 10** *ex* Meche *-1976* - -	*199* 92 -	Class: (LR) (GL) ✠ Classed LR until 28/7/82	**1969-02 Fabricaciones Metallicas E.P.S. (FABRIMET) — Callao** Yd No: 371 Loa 28.02 Br ex 7.78 Dght 3.709 Lbp 22.46 Br md 7.62 Dpth 3.71 Welded, 1 dk	**(B11B2FV) Fishing Vessel**	**1 oil engine** reverse reduction geared to sc. shaft driving 1 FP propeller Total Power: 515kW (700hp) G.M. (Detroit Diesel) 16V-71 1 x Vee 2 Stroke 16 Cy. 108 x 127 515kW (700bhp) General Motors Corp-USA AuxGen: 1 x 1kW 24V d.c
7119862 - -	**SAN LORENZO RUIZ** *ex* Sweet Faith *-1989* *ex* Hakodate Maru No. 11 *-1987* **Sto Domingo Shipping Lines** - *Batangas* *Philippines* Official number: BAT5000382	*1,492* 499 1,014		**1971-06 Narasaki Zosen KK — Muroran HK** (Hull) Yd No: 755 **1971-06 The Hakodate Dock Co Ltd — Japan** Yd No: 525 Loa 82.81 Br ex 16.18 Dght 4.242 Lbp 76.23 Br md 14.03 Dpth 5.11 Welded, 1 dk	**(A36A2PR) Passenger/Ro-Ro Ship (Vehicles)** Passengers: unberthed: 400	**4 oil engines** geared to sc. shafts driving 2 FP propellers Total Power: 3,912kW (5,320hp) 15.5kn Niigata 8MG25BX 4 x 4 Stroke 8 Cy. 250 x 320 each-978kW (1330bhp) Niigata Engineering Co Ltd-Japan AuxGen: 3 x 104kW 445V 60Hz a.c Fuel: 132.0 (d.f.) 14.0pd
7647546 *IOZQ* -	**SAN LUCA PRIMO** - **Fratelli Scuttari di Scuttari Benito en C** - *Rome* *Italy* MMSI: 247153900 Official number: 748	**1,046** 313 1,982	Class: RI	**1974-01 Deggendorfer Werft u. Eisenbau GmbH — Deggendorf** Yd No: 481 Loa 60.09 Br ex 12.73 Dght 4.039 Lbp 58.76 Br md 12.40 Dpth 5.01 Welded, 1 dk	**(B34A2SH) Hopper, Motor** Hopper: 1,000 Compartments: 1 Ho, ER	**2 oil engines** geared to sc. shafts driving 2 Directional propellers Total Power: 750kW (1,020hp) Deutz SBF12M716 2 x Vee 4 Stroke 12 Cy. 135 x 160 each-375kW (510bhp) Kloeckner Humboldt Deutz AG-West Germany
7018812 *LW8506* -	**SAN LUCAS I** *ex* Frumar I *-1997* *ex* Fukuju Maru No. 87 *-1991* *ex* Yusho Maru No. 3 *-1984* **Frutos Marinos SA (FRUMAR)** - *Buenos Aires* *Argentina* MMSI: 701000506 Official number: 076	**365** 109 351	Class: (NK) (KR)	**1969 Miho Zosensho K.K. — Shimizu** Yd No: 721 Loa 54.30 Br ex 8.41 Dght 3.476 Lbp 49.10 Br md 8.39 Dpth 3.87 Welded, 1 dk	**(B11B2FV) Fishing Vessel** Ins: 553	**1 oil engine** driving 1 FP propeller Total Power: 1,103kW (1,500hp) Akasaka AH30 1 x 4 Stroke 6 Cy. 300 x 480 1103kW (1500bhp) Akasaka Tekkosho KK (Akasaka DieselLtd)-Japan
8842519 *TEF34* -	**SAN LUCAS II** *ex* Frisia VIII *-2003* **Coonatramar RL** - *Puntarenas* *Costa Rica*	**1,058** 449 255	Class: (GL)	**1962-03 Jos L Meyer — Papenburg** Yd No: 514 Lengthened-1986 Lengthened & Deepened-1974 Lengthened-1969 Loa 63.70 Br ex - Dght 1.700 Lbp 61.20 Br md 12.00 Dpth 2.90 Welded, 1 dk	**(A36A2PR) Passenger/Ro-Ro Ship (Vehicles)** Passengers: unberthed: 800 Bow door (centre) Stern ramp (centre) Cars: 52 Ice Capable	**3 oil engines** reduction geared to sc. shafts driving 2 Directional propellers Total Power: 1,113kW (1,512hp) 12.5kn Deutz SBA12M816 3 x Vee 4 Stroke 12 Cy. 142 x 160 each-371kW (504bhp) (new engine 1982) Kloeckner Humboldt Deutz AG-West Germany AuxGen: 2 x 76kW 220/380V 50Hz a.c
8959245 *ISXC* -	**SAN MARCO** - **Azienda del Consorzio Trasporti Veneziano (ACTV)** - *Venice* *Italy* MMSI: 247291100 Official number: 2611	*483* 300 100	Class: RI	**1961-02 Cant. Nav. Breda S.p.A. — Venezia** Yd No: 219 Loa 53.05 Br ex - Dght 2.460 Lbp 49.76 Br md 11.50 Dpth 3.00 Welded, 1 dk	**(A36A2PR) Passenger/Ro-Ro Ship (Vehicles)**	**2 oil engines** driving 2 FP propellers Total Power: 706kW (960hp) 11.5kn Fiat L230.6S 2 x 4 Stroke 6 Cy. 230 x 350 each-353kW (480bhp) (new engine 1971) SA Fiat SGM-Torino AuxGen: 2 x 100kW 220V 50Hz a.c Thrusters: 1 Thwart. FP thruster (f)
9529437 *IIOJ2* -	**SAN MARCO AT** - **Adriatic Towage Srl** - *Venice* *Italy* MMSI: 247277200	**478** 243 -	Class: RI	**2009-10 Cantieri San Marco Srl — La Spezia** Yd No: 23 Loa 32.51 Br ex 11.90 Dght 4.440 Lbp 30.28 Br md 11.70 Dpth 5.60 Welded, 1 dk	**(B32A2ST) Tug**	**2 oil engines** reduction geared to sc. shafts driving 2 Directional propellers Total Power: 4,202kW (5,714hp) 13.0kn Caterpillar 3516B 2 x Vee 4 Stroke 16 Cy. 170 x 190 each-2101kW (2857bhp) Caterpillar Inc-USA
7510731 *IOZR* -	**SAN MARCO SECONDO** - **Impresa Pietro Cidonio SpA** - *Rome* *Italy* MMSI: 247062300 Official number: 750	**1,046** 313 1,982	Class: RI	**1974-06 Hilgers AG — Rheinbrohl** Yd No: 723-901 Loa 60.10 Br ex 12.73 Dght 4.039 Lbp 58.76 Br md 12.40 Dpth 5.01 Welded, 1 dk	**(B34A2SH) Hopper, Motor** Hopper: 1,000 Compartments: 1 Ho, ER	**2 oil engines** driving 2 Directional propellers Total Power: 750kW (1,020hp) Deutz BF12M716 2 x Vee 4 Stroke 12 Cy. 135 x 160 each-375kW (510bhp) Kloeckner Humboldt Deutz AG-West Germany
8625430 *H4SM* -	**SAN MARCOS** *ex* Nikkai Maru No. 2 *-2010* **Lauru Shipping Ltd** - *Honiara* *Solomon Islands*	*156* - 316		**1986-02 Towa Zosen K.K. — Shimonoseki** Yd No: 313 Loa 41.97 Br ex - Dght 2.850 Lbp 35.01 Br md 7.21 Dpth 3.20 Welded, 1 dk	**(A31A2GX) General Cargo Ship**	**1 oil engine** driving 1 FP propeller Total Power: 478kW (650hp) Daihatsu 6DLM-22S 1 x 4 Stroke 6 Cy. 220 x 300 478kW (650bhp) Daihatsu Diesel Manufacturing Co Lt-Japan
9509621 *A8UR2* -	**SAN MARINO TRADER** *launched as* Medbagira *-2010* **ms 'San Marino Trader' Schiffahrts UG (haftungsbeschrankt) & Co KG** Hermann Buss GmbH & Cie KG SatCom: Inmarsat C 463707080 *Monrovia* *Liberia* MMSI: 636091935 Official number: 91935	**22,863** 10,602 33,217	Class: GL (BV)	**2010-02 Zhejiang Ouhua Shipbuilding Co Ltd — Zhoushan ZJ** Yd No: 553 Loa 179.44 (BB) Br ex 28.23 Dght 10.800 Lbp 168.95 Br md 28.00 Dpth 15.10 Welded, 1 dk	**(A31A2GX) General Cargo Ship** Grain: 39,927; Bale: 37,490 TEU 1158 C Ho 484 TEU C Dk 674 incl 30 ref C. Compartments: 5 Ho, ER 5 Ha: 3 (25.6 x 24.4) (12.8 x 24.4)ER (12.6 x 20.4) Cranes: 4x60t	**1 oil engine** driving 1 FP propeller Total Power: 8,800kW (11,964hp) 15.0kn MAN-B&W 6S50MC-C 1 x 2 Stroke 6 Cy. 500 x 2000 8800kW (11964bhp) STX Engine Co Ltd-South Korea AuxGen: 2 x 500kW 400V 60Hz a.c, 1 x 400kW 400V 60Hz a.c Fuel: 120.0 (d.f.) 2040.0 (r.f.)
7303334 - -	**SAN MARTIN 6** *ex* Chimu III *-1979* - -	*310* - -		**1973 Ast. Jorge Labarthe S.A. — Callao** Yd No: F131 Loa - Br ex - Dght - Lbp - Br md - Dpth - Welded, 1 dk	**(B11B2FV) Fishing Vessel**	**1 oil engine** geared to sc. shaft driving 1 FP propeller Caterpillar 1 x 4 Stroke Caterpillar Tractor Co-USA
7014969 - -	**SAN MARTIN 7** *ex* Arcopunco *-1976* **Peruana de Pesca SA (PEPESCA)** -	*150* - -	Class: (AB)	**1970 Metal Empresa S.A. — Callao** Yd No: L-12 Loa - Br ex 6.76 Dght - Lbp 21.47 Br md 6.71 Dpth 3.51 Welded, 1 dk	**(B11B2FV) Fishing Vessel** Compartments: 1 Ho, ER 1 Ha:	**1 oil engine** geared to sc. shaft driving 1 FP propeller Total Power: 386kW (525hp) G.M. (Detroit Diesel) 12V-71 1 x Vee 2 Stroke 12 Cy. 108 x 127 386kW (525bhp) General Motors Detroit DieselAllison Divn-USA Fuel: 5.0 (d.f.)
6911029 - -	**SAN MARTIN 8** *ex* Isla San Martin 8 *-1976* *ex* Angela *-1975* **Pesquera Maria Milagros SRL** - *Ilo* *Peru* Official number: IO-000226-PM	*199* 92 -	Class: (LR) ✠ Classed LR until 24/11/82	**1969-04 Fabricaciones Metallicas E.P.S. (FABRIMET) — Callao** Yd No: 377 Loa 27.67 Br ex 7.78 Dght 3.709 Lbp 23.88 Br md 7.62 Dpth 3.71 Welded	**(B11B2FV) Fishing Vessel**	**1 oil engine** reverse reduction geared to sc. shaft driving 1 FP propeller Total Power: 515kW (700hp) G.M. (Detroit Diesel) 16V-71 1 x Vee 2 Stroke 16 Cy. 108 x 127 515kW (700bhp) General Motors Corp-USA AuxGen: 1 x 1kW 24V d.c
6911146 - -	**SAN MARTIN 9** *ex* Isla San Martin 9 *-1976* *ex* Diego Puertas *-1976* - -	*150* - -	Class: (LR) ✠ Classed LR until 26/6/81	**1969-03 Fabricaciones Metallicas E.P.S. (FABRIMET) — Callao** Yd No: 370 Loa 27.67 Br ex 7.78 Dght 3.709 Lbp 23.88 Br md 7.62 Dpth 3.71 Welded	**(B11B2FV) Fishing Vessel**	**1 oil engine** reverse reduction geared to sc. shaft driving 1 FP propeller Total Power: 515kW (700hp) G.M. (Detroit Diesel) 16V-71 1 x Vee 2 Stroke 16 Cy. 108 x 127 515kW (700bhp) General Motors Corp-USA AuxGen: 2 x 3kW 240V 60Hz a.c
6915099 - -	**SAN MARTIN 10** *ex* Ivanka *-1976* **Juan Ramirez Zavala** - *Ilo* *Peru* Official number: CE-0228-PM	*150* - -	Class: (LR) ✠ Classed LR until 23/7/82	**1969-04 Fabricaciones Metallicas E.P.S. (FABRIMET) — Callao** Yd No: 378 Loa 27.67 Br ex 7.78 Dght - Lbp 23.88 Br md 7.62 Dpth 3.71 Welded	**(B11B2FV) Fishing Vessel**	**1 oil engine** reverse reduction geared to sc. shaft driving 1 FP propeller Total Power: 515kW (700hp) G.M. (Detroit Diesel) 16V-71 1 x Vee 2 Stroke 16 Cy. 108 x 127 515kW (700bhp) General Motors Corp-USA AuxGen: 1 x 1kW 24V d.c

8897162 **SAN MARTIN I** **825** **1973 Jeffboat, Inc. — Jeffersonville, In** **(B32A2ST) Tug**
ZPPC *ex* San Martin *-2000* *ex* Soledad *-2000*
247
\- **Oceanpar SA**
\-
Paraguay
L reg 42.27 Br ex - Dght -
Lbp - Br md 14.63 Dpth 3.26
Welded, 1 dk
3 oil engines reduction geared to sc. shafts driving 3 FP propellers
Total Power: 4,515kW (6,138hp) 10.0kn
MAN-B&W 7L21/31
3 x 4 Stroke 7 Cy. 210 x 310 each-1505kW (2046bhp)
STX Engine Co Ltd-South Korea

8742575 **SAN MARTINO** **343** Class: (BV)
IKXV2 219
\- **Cooperativa San Martino Srl** -
\-
Venice *Italy*
MMSI: 247225600
Official number: VE9145
2008-03 CoRiNa Srl — Venice Yd No: 043/06
Loa 40.00 Br ex - Dght 2.060
Lbp 39.76 Br md 12.90 Dpth 2.15
Welded, 1 dk
(B33A2DH) Backhoe Dredger
2 oil engines reduction geared to sc. shafts driving 2 Directional propellers
Total Power: 412kW (560hp)
Cummins KT-19-M
2 x 4 Stroke 6 Cy. 159 x 159 each-206kW (280bhp)
Cummins Engine Co Inc-USA

8725620 **SAN MATEO** **397** Class: (KR)
LW8966 *ex* Chang Bo Go II *-1998* 126
\- *ex* Sam Kyung No. 18 *-1994* 641
ex Han Young No. 105 *-1993*
ex Sam Kyung No. 72 *-1991*
ex Oriental Star No. 2 *-1990*
ex Jeong Chang No. 3 *-1990*
IBERCONSA de Argentina SA
\-
SatCom: Inmarsat C 470144810
Mar del Plata *Argentina*
MMSI: 701000597
Official number: 070
1987-12 Hyangdo Shipbuilding Co Ltd — Pohang Yd No: 57
Loa 57.70 Br ex - Dght 3.660
Lbp 49.50 Br md 9.00 Dpth 3.80
Welded, 1 dk
(B11B2FV) Fishing Vessel
Ins: 635
1 oil engine geared to sc. shaft driving 1 FP propeller
Total Power: 919kW (1,249hp) 12.3kn
Cummins KTA-50-M
1 x Vee 4 Stroke 16 Cy. 159 x 159 919kW (1249bhp)
Ssangyong Heavy Industries Co Ltd-South Korea
AuxGen: 2 x 280kW 225V a.c

9298789 **SAN MATIAS I** **40,027** Class: LR
LW9727 *ex* Cabo San Vicente *-2005* 20,360 ✠ **100A1** SS 05/2010
\- *completed as* San Matias *-2005* 69,648 Double Hull oil tanker
Sociedad Anonima de Navegacion Petrolera (SONAP) T/cm ESP
Antares Naviera SA 67.5 *IWS
SatCom: Inmarsat B 370108238 LI
Buenos Aires *Argentina* **ShipRight** (SDA, FDA, CM)
MMSI: 701051000 ✠ **LMC** **UMS IGS**
Official number: 02440 Eq.Ltr: 0†;
Cable: 660.0/78.0 U3 (a)
2005-05 Daewoo Shipbuilding & Marine Engineering Co Ltd — Geoje Yd No: 5281
Loa 228.00 (BB) Br ex 32.23 Dght 12.200
Lbp 219.00 Br md 32.20 Dpth 19.80
Welded, 1 dk
(A13B2TP) Products Tanker
Double Hull
Liq: 78,400; Liq (Oil): 78,400
Compartments: 12 Wing Ta, 2 Wing Slop Ta, ER
14 Cargo Pump (s)
Manifold: Bow/CM: 112m
1 oil engine driving 1 FP propeller
Total Power: 11,282kW (15,339hp) 15.6kn
MAN-B&W 5S60MC-C
1 x 2 Stroke 5 Cy. 600 x 2400 11282kW (15339bhp)
Doosan Engine Co Ltd-South Korea
AuxGen: 3 x 850kW 450V 60Hz a.c
Boilers: AuxB (Comp) 9.1kgf/cm² (8.9bar), WTAuxB (o.f.) 11.5kgf/cm² (11.3bar)
Fuel: 162.0 (d.f.) 2371.2 (r.f.)

9286437 **SAN MATTEO** **3,500** Class: BV RI
IBHW *ex* Bitumiera *-2004* 1,513
\- **Petrolmar Trasporti e Servizi Marittimi SpA** 5,765
T/cm
Genoa *Italy* 17.0
MMSI: 247103700
Official number: 050
2004-06 Madenci Gemi Sanayii Ltd. Sti. — Karadeniz Eregli Yd No: 22
Loa 110.00 Br ex - Dght 6.000
Lbp 103.50 Br md 17.80 Dpth 8.60
Welded, 1 dk
(A13B2TP) Products Tanker
Double Hull (13F)
Liq: 5,451; Liq (Gas): 5,000; Liq (Oil): 5,451
Cargo Heating Coils
Compartments: 2 Ta, ER
2 Cargo Pump (s): 2x500m³/hr
Manifold: Bow/CM: 49m
1 oil engine geared to sc. shaft driving 1 CP propeller
Total Power: 3,840kW (5,221hp) 14.0kn
MaK 8M32
1 x 4 Stroke 8 Cy. 320 x 480 3840kW (5221bhp)
Caterpillar Motoren GmbH & Co. KG-Germany
AuxGen: 1 x 800kW 440/220V 60Hz a.c, 3 x 590kW 440/220V 60Hz a.c

---

7510743 **SAN MATTEO PRIMO** **1,046** Class: RI
IOZS 313
\- **Societa Italiana per Condotte d'Acqua SpA** 1,982
Rome *Italy*
MMSI: 247145000
Official number: 751
1974-06 Hilgers AG — Rheinbrohl Yd No: 723-902
Loa 60.10 Br ex 12.73 Dght 4.039
Lbp 58.76 Br md 12.40 Dpth 5.00
Welded, 1 dk
(B34A2SH) Hopper, Motor
Hopper: 1,000
Compartments: 1 Ho, ER
2 oil engines driving 2 Directional propellers
Total Power: 750kW (1,020hp)
Deutz BF12M716
2 x Vee 4 Stroke 12 Cy. 135 x 160 each-375kW (510bhp)
Kloeckner Humboldt Deutz AG-West Germany
AuxGen: 2 x 3kW 24V d.c

7642857 **SAN MIGUEL** *600* Class: (BV)
3CABD *ex* Cleveland *-2004* 446
\- **Grupo Martinez Hermanos SL** 250
Equatorial Guinea
1976 Papastefanou — Piraeus
Loa 62.01 Br ex 12.76 Dght 2.452
Lbp 52.23 Br md 11.00 Dpth 3.00
Welded, 1 dk
(A36A2PR) Passenger/Ro-Ro Ship (Vehicles)
2 oil engines driving 2 FP propellers
Total Power: 558kW (758hp)
Caterpillar D343TA
2 x 4 Stroke 6 Cy. 137 x 165 each-279kW (379bhp)
Caterpillar Tractor Co-USA

9192155 **SAN MIGUEL** **3,821** Class: GL
D5BN8 *ex* Fockeburg *-2012* *ex* Tracy Scan *-2011* 1,992
\- *ex* BBC Venezuela *-2010* *ex* Global Africa *-2001* 5,218
ex Fockeburg *-2000*
Notos Marine Inc
NSC Shipping GmbH & Cie KG
Monrovia *Liberia*
MMSI: 636015566
Official number: 15566
1999-12 Marmara Tersanesi — Yarimca Yd No: 58
Loa 99.98 Br ex - Dght 6.281
Lbp 94.00 Br md 15.82 Dpth 8.10
Welded, 1 dk
(A31A2GX) General Cargo Ship
Grain: 6,650
TEU 375 C. 375/20'
Compartments: 1 Ho, ER
1 Ha: (58.3 x 12.9)ER
Cranes: 2x65t
Ice Capable
1 oil engine reduction geared to sc. shaft driving 1 CP propeller
Total Power: 3,840kW (5,221hp) 14.5kn
MaK 8M32
1 x 4 Stroke 8 Cy. 320 x 480 3840kW (5221bhp)
MaK Motoren GmbH & Co. KG-Kiel
AuxGen: 1 x 720kW 220/380V a.c, 2 x 344kW 220/380V a.c
Fuel: 337.0 (d.f.)

9209075 **SAN MIGUEL** **1,004** Class: AB
WDA9648 301
\- **Banc of America Leasing & Capital LLC** 1,059
SEACOR Marine LLC
Port Hueneme, CA *United States of America*
MMSI: 338359000
Official number: 1075884
1999-03 Eastern Shipbuilding Group — Panama City, Fl Yd No: 634
Loa 62.75 Br ex - Dght 4.137
Lbp 57.91 Br md 13.41 Dpth 4.88
Welded, 1 dk
(B21B20A) Anchor Handling Tug Supply
Passengers: 10
2 oil engines reduction geared to sc. shafts driving 2 FP propellers
Total Power: 2,984kW (4,058hp) 11.0kn
Caterpillar 3516B
2 x Vee 4 Stroke 16 Cy. 170 x 190 each-1492kW (2029bhp)
Caterpillar Inc-USA
AuxGen: 2 x 175kW a.c
Thrusters: 1 Thwart. FP thruster (f)
Fuel: 240.0

8102866 **SAN NANUMEA** **1,678**
ZMSN *ex* Chloe *-2001* *ex* Chloe Z *-1998* 419
\- *ex* El Audaz *-1989* -
Sanford Ltd
\-
Auckland *New Zealand*
MMSI: 512000089
Official number: 876342
1982-12 Bender Shipbuilding & Repair Co Inc — Mobile AL Yd No: 1163
Loa 77.20 (BB) Br ex 12.61 Dght 5.366
Lbp - Br md 12.50 Dpth 5.80
Welded, 1 dk
(B11B2FV) Fishing Vessel
Compartments: 2 Ho, ER
2 Ha:
1 oil engine geared to sc. shaft driving 1 FP propeller
Total Power: 2,648kW (3,600hp)
EMD (Electro-Motive) 20-645-E7
1 x Vee 2 Stroke 20 Cy. 230 x 254 2648kW (3600bhp)
General Motors Corp.Electro-Motive Div.-La Grange

8961183 **SAN NICOLA** **368** Class: RI
IRSH 110
\- **Societa Italiana per Condotte d'Acqua SpA** 100
Servizio Gestione e Armamento Mezzi Marittimi
Rome *Italy*
Official number: 7800
1979-12 Cantiere Navale Visentini di Visentini F e C SAS — Porto Viro Yd No: 142
Loa 35.24 Br ex - Dght -
Lbp 35.00 Br md 14.00 Dpth 2.75
Welded, 1 dk
(B34B2SC) Crane Vessel
2 oil engines driving 2 FP propellers
Total Power: 382kW (520hp)
Deutz BF12L714
2 x Vee 4 Stroke 12 Cy. 120 x 140 each-191kW (260bhp)
Kloeckner Humboldt Deutz AG-West Germany
AuxGen: 1 x 100kW 220/380V 50Hz a.c

9477464 **SAN NICOLA AT** **467** Class: BV
IINT2 *launched as* Bogazici 3 *-2008* 140
\- **Adriatic Towage Srl** -
\-
Venice *Italy*
MMSI: 247246500
2008-08 Ge-Ta Corp. — Istanbul Yd No: 008
Loa 32.50 Br ex - Dght 4.300
Lbp 27.60 Br md 11.70 Dpth 5.60
Welded, 1 dk
(B32A2ST) Tug
2 oil engines geared to sc. shafts driving 2 CP propellers
Total Power: 4,200kW (5,710hp) 13.0kn
Caterpillar 3516B-TA
2 x Vee 4 Stroke 16 Cy. 170 x 190 each-2100kW (2855bhp)
Caterpillar Inc-USA
AuxGen: 2 x 108kW a.c

9221475 **SAN NICOLAS** **4,028** Class: GL (BV)
D5BC7 *ex* List *-2011* *ex* Delmas Mauritius *-2006* 2,218
\- *ex* Jolly Arancione *-2003* *ex* Marcape *-2002* 5,099
ms 'Tamara' Schifffahrtsgesellschaft mbH & Co KG
NSC Shipping GmbH & Cie KG
SatCom: Inmarsat C 463711573
Monrovia *Liberia*
MMSI: 636092367
Official number: 92367
2000-01 Jinling Shipyard — Nanjing JS Yd No: 98-0111
Loa 100.55 (BB) Br ex - Dght 6.470
Lbp 95.40 Br md 18.50 Dpth 8.25
Welded, 1 dk
(A31A2GX) General Cargo Ship
Grain: 7,646
TEU 519 C.Ho 143/20' (40') C.Dk 376/20' (40') incl. 60 ref C.
Compartments: 3 Ho, ER
3 Ha: (6.8 x 13.3) (25.9 x 15.9) (25.5 x 15.9)ER
Cranes: 2x40t
Ice Capable
1 oil engine geared to sc. shaft driving 1 CP propeller
Total Power: 3,960kW (5,384hp) 16.0kn
MaK 9M32
1 x 4 Stroke 9 Cy. 320 x 480 3960kW (5384bhp)
MaK Motoren GmbH & Co. KG-Kiel
AuxGen: 1 x 624kW 380V 50Hz a.c, 3 x 340kW 380V 50Hz a.c
Thrusters: 1 Thwart. FP thruster (f)

9198422 **SAN NICOLO** **630** Class: RI
IFXO 240
\- **Azienda del Consorzio Trasporti Veneziano (ACTV)** 500
\-
Venice *Italy*
MMSI: 247290100
1998 Cantiere Navale Visentini Srl — Porto Viro Yd No: 189
Loa 57.85 Br ex - Dght -
Lbp 54.08 Br md 13.10 Dpth 3.63
Welded, 1 dk
(A36A2PR) Passenger/Ro-Ro Ship (Vehicles)
2 oil engines reduction geared to sc. shafts driving 2 FP propellers
Total Power: 1,274kW (1,732hp)
Caterpillar 3508TA
2 x Vee 4 Stroke 8 Cy. 170 x 190 each-637kW (866bhp)
Caterpillar Inc-USA
Thrusters: 1 Thwart. FP thruster (f)

8932091 *SY2969* - **SAN NIKOLAS** *ex* Mimosa *-2002* *ex* Admiral II *-1996* **Sunrise Line Ltd** - *Chios* *Greece* MMSI: 237579900 Official number: 256 | **103** 49 - | Class: RS
1980 Khersonskiy Sudostroitelnyy Zavod — Kherson Loa 30.00 Br ex - Dght 1.540 Lbp - Br md 5.10 Dpth 2.55 Welded, 1 dk
(A37B2PS) Passenger Ship
2 oil engines driving 2 FP propellers Total Power: 440kW (598hp) Barnaultransmash 3D12A 2 x Vee 4 Stroke 12 Cy. 150 x 180 each-220kW (299bhp) Barnaultransmash-Barnaul

9139971 *3FOZ6* - **SAN NIKOLAS** *ex* Marine Bulker *-2013* *ex* Marine Island *-2006* **Star Dominion SA** Athenian Shipping SA SatCom: Inmarsat C 435688111 *Panama* *Panama* MMSI: 356881000 Official number: 2324596D | **17,542** 10,264 28,322 T/cm 40.1 | Class: NK
1996-09 The Hakodate Dock Co Ltd — Hakodate HK Yd No: 763 Loa 177.46 (BB) Br ex - Dght 9.672 Lbp 170.01 Br md 26.00 Dpth 13.60 Welded, 1 dk
(A21A2BC) Bulk Carrier Grain: 37,993; Bale: 36,553 Compartments: 5 Ho, ER 5 Ha: (16.2 x 13.1)4 (20.0 x 18.0)ER Cranes: 4x30.5t
1 oil engine driving 1 FP propeller Total Power: 6,157kW (8,371hp) 14.1kn B&W 6S42MC 1 x 2 Stroke 6 Cy. 420 x 1764 6157kW (8371bhp) Mitsui Engineering & Shipbuilding CLtd-Japan Fuel: 1140.0 (r.f.)

8131441 *ZMNK* - **SAN NIKUNAU** *ex* Stella Maris *-2001* *ex* Pacific Freedom *-1995* *launched as* Amy Rose *-1991* **Sanford Ltd** - *Auckland* *New Zealand* MMSI: 512085000 Official number: 876339 | **1,957** 587 2,080 | Class: (NV)
1991-07 INMA SpA — La Spezia (Hull launched by) Yd No: 119 **1991-07 Nuovi Cantieri Liguri SpA — Pietra Ligure** (Hull completed by) **1991-07 Baatbygg AS — Raudeberg** Loa 84.13 (BB) Br ex - Dght - Lbp 73.85 Br md 12.88 Dpth 8.31 Welded, 2 dks
(B11A2FT) Trawler
1 oil engine geared to sc. shaft driving 1 FP propeller Total Power: 2,998kW (4,076hp) 12.0kn Nohab F316V 1 x Vee 4 Stroke 16 Cy. 250 x 300 2998kW (4076bhp) (made 1982) Nohab Diesel AB-Sweden AuxGen: 2 x 610kW 440V 60Hz a.c Thrusters: 1 Tunnel thruster (f)

5423063 *LW6967* - **SAN PABLO** *ex* Wilhelmina Maria *-1974* **San Pablo SA** - SatCom: Inmarsat C 470154710 *Mar del Plata* *Argentina* MMSI: 701007010 Official number: 0759 | **278** 139 -
1963 N.V. Scheepswerf Gebr. Pot — Bolnes Yd No: 949 Loa 48.47 Br ex 7.60 Dght - Lbp 42.40 Br md 7.50 Dpth 4.02 Welded
(B11A2FT) Trawler
1 oil engine driving 1 FP propeller Deutz RBV8M545 1 x 4 Stroke 8 Cy. 320 x 450 Kloeckner Humboldt Deutz AG-West Germany

9235361 *A8VJ4* - **SAN PABLO** *ex* Cape Delfaro *-2012* **ms 'San Pablo' Schiffahrtsges mbH & Co KG** NSC Schiffahrtsgesellschaft mbH & Cie KG *Monrovia* *Liberia* MMSI: 636092010 Official number: 92010 | **23,132** 9,375 30,343 T/cm 46.7 | Class: GL
2004-03 Dalian Shipyard Co Ltd — Dalian LN Yd No: MC300-6 Loa 192.90 (BB) Br ex - Dght 11.200 Lbp 182.00 Br md 27.80 Dpth 15.50 Welded, 1 dk
(A31A2GX) General Cargo Ship Grain: 34,773 TEU 1842 C Ho 786 TEU C Dk 1056 TEU incl 150 ref C. Compartments: 5 Ho, ER, 5 Tw Dk 9 Ha: Cranes: 2x100t,2x50t Ice Capable
1 oil engine driving 1 FP propeller Total Power: 15,789kW (21,467hp) 19.4kn B&W 7S60MC-C 1 x 2 Stroke 7 Cy. 600 x 2400 15789kW (21467bhp) Dalian Marine Diesel Works-China Thrusters: 1 Thwart. FP thruster (f)

5136892 - - **SAN PABLO APOSTOL** *ex* Grzywacz *-1973* **Yamari SA** - | **167** 113 110 | Class: (PR)
1956 Stocznia Polnocna (Northern Shipyard) — Gdansk Yd No: B17/14 Loa 34.45 Br ex 6.79 Dght 2.629 Lbp 30.33 Br md 6.70 Dpth 3.61 Riveted\Welded, 1 dk
(B11B2FV) Fishing Vessel
1 oil engine driving 1 FP propeller Total Power: 221kW (300hp) 9.0kn Buckau R8DV136 1 x 4 Stroke 8 Cy. 240 x 360 221kW (300bhp) Maschinenfabrik Buckau R. Wolf AGWerk Kiel-Kiel AuxGen: 1 x 66kW 110/330V d.c, 1 x 18kW 110/330V d.c, 1 x 6kW 110/330V d.c

9610339 *HBFI* - **SAN PADRE PIO** *ex* Beaufort *-2013* **San Padre Pio Schiffahrt AG** ABC Maritime AG *Basel* *Switzerland* MMSI: 269305000 | **5,422** 2,444 7,616 | Class: BV
2012-06 Taixing Ganghua Ship Industry Co Ltd — Taixing JS Yd No: GHCY 7500-07 Loa 112.70 (BB) Br ex - Dght 7.200 Lbp 106.00 Br md 17.60 Dpth 9.40 Welded, 1 dk
(A12B2TR) Chemical/Products Tanker Double Hull (13F) Liq: 8,449; Liq (Oil): 8,449 Compartments: 6 Wing Ta, 6 Wing Ta, 1 Wing Slop Ta, 1 Wing Slop Ta, ER Ice Capable
2 oil engines reduction geared to sc. shafts driving 2 CP propellers Total Power: 3,440kW (4,678hp) 14.0kn MAN-B&W 8L21/31 2 x 4 Stroke 8 Cy. 210 x 310 each-1720kW (2339bhp) Shanghai Xinzhong Power MachinePlant-China AuxGen: 3 x 400kW 60Hz a.c, 2 x 500kW 60Hz a.c Fuel: 330.0

9082506 *LW9297* - **SAN PASCUAL** **Baldimar SA** - SatCom: Inmarsat C 470113910 *Argentina* MMSI: 701006057 Official number: 0367 | **110** 80 110
1993-10 SANYM S.A. — Buenos Aires Yd No: 98 Loa - Br ex - Dght 3.000 Lbp 26.50 Br md 6.50 Dpth 3.30 Welded
(B11A2FS) Stern Trawler Ins: 165
1 oil engine geared to sc. shaft driving 1 FP propeller Total Power: 397kW (540hp) 10.0kn Caterpillar 3412TA 1 x Vee 4 Stroke 12 Cy. 137 x 152 397kW (540bhp) Caterpillar Inc-USA

7049251 *TUN2140* - **SAN PEDRO** **Union des Remorqueurs D'Abidjan (UAR)** *Abidjan* *Cote d'Ivoire* Official number: 735 | *209* 65 106 | Class: (BV)
1971 Muetzelfeldtwerft GmbH — Cuxhaven Yd No: 183 Loa 29.60 Br ex 8.49 Dght 2.998 Lbp 25.99 Br md 8.11 Dpth 3.76 Welded, 1 dk
(B32A2ST) Tug
1 oil engine driving 1 FP propeller Total Power: 978kW (1,330hp) 12.0kn Crepelle 8PSN3 1 x 4 Stroke 8 Cy. 260 x 280 978kW (1330bhp) Crepelle et Cie-France Fuel: 70.0 (d.f.)

9231145 *A8VI9* - **SAN PEDRO** *ex* Anhui *-2013* *ex* Cape Darnley *-2011* **ms 'San Pedro' Schiffahrtsges mbH & Co KG** NSC Schiffahrtsgesellschaft mbH & Cie KG *Monrovia* *Liberia* MMSI: 636092007 Official number: 92007 | **23,132** 9,375 30,345 T/cm 46.7 | Class: GL
2003-04 Dalian Shipyard Co Ltd — Dalian LN Yd No: MC300-4 Loa 192.90 (BB) Br ex - Dght 11.200 Lbp 182.00 Br md 27.80 Dpth 15.50 Welded, 1 dk
(A31A2GX) General Cargo Ship Grain: 34,773 TEU 1842 C Ho 786 TEU C Dk 1056 TEU incl 150 ref C. Compartments: 5 Ho, ER, 5 Tw Dk 9 Ha: Cranes: 2x100t,2x50t Ice Capable
1 oil engine driving 1 FP propeller Total Power: 15,806kW (21,490hp) 19.4kn B&W 7S60MC-C 1 x 2 Stroke 7 Cy. 600 x 2400 15806kW (21490bhp) Dalian Marine Diesel Works-China Thrusters: 1 Thwart. FP thruster (f)

6509876 - - **SAN PEDRO BAY** - *Fremantle, WA* *Australia* Official number: 317464 | *101* 55 65
1964 Stannard Bros Slipway & Engineering Pty Ltd — Sydney NSW L reg 19.51 Br ex 5.85 Dght - Lbp - Br md - Dpth - Welded, 1 dk
(B11B2FV) Fishing Vessel Compartments: 1 Ho, ER Derricks: 1x1t
1 oil engine driving 1 FP propeller Total Power: 515kW (700hp) G.M. (Detroit Diesel) 16V-71 1 x Vee 2 Stroke 16 Cy. 108 x 127 515kW (700bhp) General Motors Corp-USA AuxGen: 2 x 25kW 240/415V 50Hz a.c Thrusters: 1 Thwart. FP thruster (f)

9162095 *DUE2650* - **SAN PEDRO CALUNGSOD** *ex* Aegir *-2013* **Caprotec Corp** Negros Navigation Co Inc *Batangas* *Philippines* Official number: 04-0002607 | **6,393** 3,278 8,350 | Class: GL
1997-10 Detlef Hegemann Rolandwerft GmbH & Co. KG — Berne Yd No: 180 Loa 132.38 (BB) Br ex - Dght 7.338 Lbp 125.50 Br md 19.40 Dpth 9.45 Welded, 1 dk
(A33A2CC) Container Ship (Fully Cellular) TEU 698 C Ho 204 TEU C Dk 494 TEU incl 80 ref C. Compartments: 3 Cell Ho, ER 3 Ha: (25.6 x 13.2)2 (25.6 x 15.8)ER Cranes: 2x40t
1 oil engine driving 1 CP propeller Total Power: 4,891kW (6,650hp) 17.0kn B&W 7S35MC 1 x 2 Stroke 7 Cy. 350 x 1400 4891kW (6650bhp) MAN B&W Diesel A/S-Denmark AuxGen: 1 x 600kW 450V a.c, 2 x 360kW 450V a.c Thrusters: 1 Thwart. FP thruster (f) Fuel: 138.0 (d.f.) (Heating Coils) 519.0 (r.f.) 26.2pd

7513410 *WCW8349* - **SAN PEDRO PRIDE** *ex* Cape Devine *-2001* *ex* Vonnie Marie *-1991* *ex* Vessel of Faith *-1980* *ex* Vessel of Honor *-1977* **Ercole Joe Terzoli** - *San Pedro, CA* *United States of America* MMSI: 366724330 Official number: 549506 | *163* 123 -
1973 Toche Enterprises, Inc. — Ocean Springs, Ms L reg 24.27 Br ex 7.47 Dght - Lbp - Br md - Dpth 3.74 Welded, 1 dk
(B11A2FT) Trawler
1 oil engine driving 1 FP propeller Total Power: 324kW (441hp)

8427931 - - **SAN PEDRO SAN PABLO** **Interisland Lighterage Corp** - *Cebu* *Philippines* Official number: 220318 | *102* 30 -
1972 at Davao Loa - Br ex 6.10 Dght - Lbp 26.27 Br md 6.10 Dpth 3.05 Welded, 1 dk
(B32A2ST) Tug
1 oil engine driving 1 FP propeller Total Power: 441kW (600hp)

9610341 *HBGM* -	**SAN PIETRO** *ex* Bering *-2013* **San Pietro Schifffahrt AG** ABC Maritime AG *Basel* *Switzerland* MMSI: 269013000	**5,422** 2,444 7,530	Class: BV	**2012-11 Taixing Ganghua Ship Industry Co Ltd — Taixing JS** Yd No: GHCY 7500-08 Loa 112.70 Br ex 17.63 Dght 7.200 Lbp 106.00 Br md 17.60 Dpth 9.40 Welded, 1 dk	**(A12B2TR) Chemical/Products Tanker** Double Hull (13F) Liq: 8,448; Liq (Oil): 8,448 Compartments: 6 Wing Ta, 6 Wing Ta, 1 Wing Slop Ta, 1 Wing Slop Ta, ER Ice Capable	**2 oil engines** reduction geared to sc. shafts driving 2 CP propellers Total Power: 3,440kW (4,678hp) 14.0kn MAN-B&W 8L21/31 2 x 4 Stroke 8 Cy. 210 x 310 each-1720kW (2339bhp) Zhenjiang Marine Diesel Works-China AuxGen: 2 x 500kW 60Hz a.c, 3 x 400kW 60Hz a.c Fuel: 339.6
7110256 - -	**SAN PIETRO UNO** *ex* San Pietro *-2001* **Cooperativa Pescatori Srl San Pietro Apostolo** - *Cetara* *Italy* Official number: 547	*197* 101 -		**1971 Cant. Nav. Ugo Codecasa S.p.A. — Viareggio** Yd No: 15 Loa - Br ex 7.04 Dght 2.794 Lbp 31.54 Br md 7.01 Dpth 3.51 Welded, 1 dk	**(B11A2FT) Trawler**	**1 oil engine** driving 1 FP propeller Total Power: 860kW (1,169hp) MWM TBD604BV12 1 x Vee 4 Stroke 12 Cy. 170 x 195 860kW (1169bhp) (new engine 1986) Motoren Werke Mannheim AG (MWM)-West Germany
7125809 *IUSV* -	**SAN PIO** *ex* Capo S. Vito *-2011* **Societa Armamento Gestione Navi Agenzia Marittima Srl (SARGENAVI)** - *Naples* *Italy* MMSI: 247119900 Official number: 1146	*198* 44 -	Class: (RI)	**1972 Cant. dell 'alto Adriatico — Trieste** Yd No: 180 Loa 30.82 Br ex 8.62 Dght 3.660 Lbp 28.00 Br md 8.60 Dpth 4.27 Welded, 1 dk	**(B32A2ST) Tug**	**1 oil engine** driving 1 FP propeller Total Power: 1,405kW (1,910hp) 12.0kn MAN G9V30/45ATL 1 x 4 Stroke 9 Cy. 300 x 450 1405kW (1910bhp) Maschinenbau Augsburg Nuernberg (MAN)-Augsburg
7506297 *DXEZ* -	**SAN PIO** *ex* Monalinda 87 *-2003* *ex* Shotoku Maru No. 78 *-1994* *ex* Shotoku Maru No. 72 *-1989* *ex* Jinkyu Maru No. 18 *-1988* **Prime A Fishing Corp** - *Manila* *Philippines* Official number: MNLD002026	*360* 207 -		**1975-09 KK Kanasashi Zosen — Shizuoka SZ** Yd No: 1196 Loa 49.28 Br ex 8.31 Dght 3.302 Lbp 43.57 Br md 8.28 Dpth 3.66 Welded, 1 dk	**(B11B2FV) Fishing Vessel**	**1 oil engine** driving 1 FP propeller Total Power: 883kW (1,201hp) Niigata 6M31X 1 x 4 Stroke 6 Cy. 310 x 460 883kW (1201bhp) Niigata Engineering Co Ltd-Japan
9587805 *ILFZ2* -	**SAN POLO** *completed as* P Cinquantuno *-2010* **Petromar Srl** - *Venice* *Italy* MMSI: 247280900 Official number: VE777	**990** 400 2,000		**2010-03 Shiptech Srl — Venice** Yd No: 46/08 Loa 65.80 Br ex - Dght - Lbp - Br md 11.60 Dpth 4.00 Welded, 1 dk	**(A13B2TP) Products Tanker** Double Hull (13F)	**2 oil engines** reduction geared to sc. shafts driving 2 Propellers Total Power: 772kW (1,050hp) MAN-B&W 2 x each-386kW (525bhp)
9181948 *EAUY* 3-SS-33-98	**SAN PRUDENTZIO BERRIA** **Aguirrezabalaga/Iribar/Olaskoaga/Aldalur** - *Getaria* *Spain* Official number: 3-3/1998	**224** 67 -		**1999-02 Astilleros de Pasaia SA — Pasaia** Yd No: 300 Loa 36.00 Br ex - Dght 3.350 Lbp 30.00 Br md 7.40 Dpth 4.00 Welded, 1 dk	**(B11B2FV) Fishing Vessel** Bale: 114; Liq: 94	**1 oil engine** geared to sc. shaft driving 1 FP propeller Total Power: 883kW (1,201hp) GUASCOR 1 x 4 Stroke 883kW (1201bhp) Gutierrez Ascunce Corp (GUASCOR)-Spain
9231133 *A8VJ2* -	**SAN RAFAEL** *ex* Cape Donington *-2012* *ex* Golden Isle *-2004* *ex* Cape Donington *-2003* **ms 'San Rafael' Schiffahrtsges mbH & Co KG** NSC Schifffahrtsgesellschaft mbH & Cie KG *Monrovia* *Liberia* MMSI: 636092008 Official number: 92008	**23,132** 9,375 30,490 T/cm 46.7	Class: GL	**2003-02 Dalian Shipyard Co Ltd — Dalian LN** Yd No: MC300-3 Loa 192.90 (BB) Br ex - Dght 11.200 Lbp 182.00 Br md 27.80 Dpth 15.50 Welded, 1 dk	**(A31A2GX) General Cargo Ship** Grain: 34,773 TEU 1842 C Ho 786 TEU C Dk 1056 TEU incl 150 ref C. Compartments: 5 Ho, ER, 5 Tw Dk 9 Ha: Cranes: 2x100t,2x50t Ice Capable	**1 oil engine** driving 1 FP propeller Total Power: 15,785kW (21,461hp) 19.4kn B&W 7S60MC-C 1 x 2 Stroke 7 Cy. 600 x 2400 15785kW (21461bhp) Dalian Marine Diesel Works-China AuxGen: 1 x 1060kW 440/220V a.c, 2 x 910kW 440/220V a.c Thrusters: 1 Thwart. FP thruster (f)
9232436 *XCRN* -	**SAN RAFAEL** **Naviera Bourbon Tamaulipas SA de CV** - *Tampico* *Mexico* MMSI: 345010016 Official number: 2804301432-8	**1,054** 316 1,624	Class: AB	**2000-07 Eastern Shipbuilding Group — Panama City, Fl** Yd No: 687 Loa 62.18 Br ex 13.41 Dght 4.110 Lbp 58.20 Br md 13.40 Dpth 4.90 Welded, 1 dk	**(B21A20S) Platform Supply Ship**	**2 oil engines** reduction geared to sc. shafts driving 2 FP propellers Total Power: 2,942kW (4,000hp) 12.0kn Caterpillar 3516B 2 x Vee 4 Stroke 16 Cy. 170 x 190 each-1471kW (2000bhp) Caterpillar Inc-USA AuxGen: 2 x 170kW a.c Thrusters: 1 Retract. directional thruster (f)
8513417 *4DED2* -	**SAN RAFAEL DOS** *ex* Kyowa Salvia *-2009* *ex* Kyowa Violet *-2003* **Caprotec Corp** Negros Navigation Co Inc *Cebu* *Philippines* MMSI: 548324100 Official number: CEB1008123	**7,337** 2,848 8,038	Class: (NK)	**1985-06 Taihei Kogyo K.K. — Hashihama, Imabari** Yd No: 1793 Loa 117.97 (BB) Br ex - Dght 7.355 Lbp 107.40 Br md 19.21 Dpth 8.01 Welded, 2 dks	**(A35A2RR) Ro-Ro Cargo Ship** Grain: 15,972; Bale: 14,927 TEU 292 Compartments: 2 Ho, ER 2 Ha: 2 (25.2 x 10.2)ER Derricks: 1x30t,2x25t	**1 oil engine** driving 1 FP propeller Total Power: 3,501kW (4,760hp) 13.8kn B&W 7L35MC 1 x 2 Stroke 7 Cy. 350 x 1050 3501kW (4760bhp) Hitachi Zosen Corp-Japan AuxGen: 2 x 320kW a.c Fuel: 800.0 (r.f.)
8902838 *DUE2656* -	**SAN RAFAEL UNO** *ex* Kyowa Mermaid *-2009* *ex* Ocean Leo *-2005* *ex* Cosmic Pioneer *-1996* **Negros Navigation Co Inc** - *Cebu* *Philippines* MMSI: 548554300 Official number: CEB1008130	**7,624** 2,843 8,212	Class: NK	**1989-09 Shin Kurushima Dockyard Co. Ltd. — Hashihama, Imabari** Yd No: 2622 Loa 115.02 (BB) Br ex - Dght 7.368 Lbp 104.00 Br md 19.20 Dpth 13.40 Welded, 2 dks	**(A31A2GA) General Cargo Ship (with Ro-Ro facility)** Quarter stern ramp (s. a.) Grain: 18,281; Bale: 17,156 2 Ha: 2 (30.1 x 11.0)ER Cranes: 2x40t; Derricks: 2x20t	**1 oil engine** driving 1 FP propeller Total Power: 4,300kW (5,846hp) 13.8kn B&W 8L35MC 1 x 2 Stroke 8 Cy. 350 x 1050 4300kW (5846bhp) Hitachi Zosen Corp-Japan AuxGen: 2 x 280kW 450V a.c Fuel: 126.0 (d.f.) 472.0 (r.f.) 16.1pd
9149926 *ZMA3228* -	**SAN RAKAIA** **Sanford Ltd** - *Auckland* *New Zealand* Official number: 876202	**498** 149 -	Class: (BV)	**1997-03 Astilleros Armon SA — Navia** Yd No: 421 Loa 32.00 Br ex - Dght 4.000 Lbp 26.80 Br md 10.00 Dpth 4.20 Welded, 1 dk	**(B11A2FS) Stern Trawler** Ins: 250	**1 oil engine** reduction geared to sc. shaft driving 1 CP propeller Total Power: 1,037kW (1,410hp) 10.5kn Caterpillar 3516TA 1 x Vee 4 Stroke 16 Cy. 170 x 190 1037kW (1410bhp) Caterpillar Inc-USA AuxGen: 2 x 160kW a.c Fuel: 87.2 (d.f.)
7722530 - -	**SAN RAKINO** - -	**227** 68 178	Class: (LR) ✠ Classed LR until 8/6/79	**1978-01 Kanmon Zosen K.K. — Shimonoseki** Yd No: 337 Loa 29.01 Br ex 8.08 Dght 3.652 Lbp 25.51 Br md 8.07 Dpth 3.95 Welded, 1 dk	**(B11A2FS) Stern Trawler**	**1 oil engine** reverse reduction geared to sc. shaft driving 1 FP propeller Total Power: 552kW (750hp) 10.5kn Daihatsu 6PSHTCM-26E 1 x 4 Stroke 6 Cy. 260 x 320 552kW (750bhp) Daihatsu Diesel Manufacturing Co Lt-Japan AuxGen: 2 x 48kW 405V 50Hz a.c
5176816 - -	**SAN RAMON** *ex* Jules Verne *-1976* **Chubut SAIP** -	*241* 178 -	Class: (BV)	**1957 Anciens Chantiers Mougin — St-Malo** Yd No: 26 L reg 35.45 Br ex 7.83 Dght - Lbp - Br md 7.82 Dpth 4.20 Welded, 1 dk	**(B11A2FT) Trawler** 3 Ha: 3 (1.3 x 1.3)ER Derricks: 1x2t	**4 oil engines** geared to sc. shaft driving 1 CP propeller Total Power: 816kW (1,110hp) 12.0kn Baudouin 2 x 4 Stroke 6 Cy. 185 x 200 Societe des Moteurs Baudouin SA-France Poyaud 2 x 4 Stroke 6 Cy. 150 x 180 each-408kW (555bhp) Societe Surgerienne de ConstructionMecaniques-France Fuel: 68.0 (d.f.)
6507983 *J8B2632* -	**SAN REMO** *ex* Saxen *-1989* **Sonata Shipping Co Ltd** Lubecker Schifffahrtsgesellschaft mbH SatCom: Inmarsat C 437725512 *Kingstown* *St Vincent & The Grenadines* MMSI: 377255000 Official number: 9104	**1,283** 490 1,225	Class: BV (GL)	**1965-04 Kroegerwerft GmbH & Co. KG — Schacht-Audorf** Yd No: 1191 Loa 72.07 Br ex 11.31 Dght 3.680 Lbp 66.63 Br md 11.28 Dpth 6.51 Welded, 1 dk & S dk	**(A31A2GX) General Cargo Ship** Grain: 2,998; Bale: 2,643 Compartments: 1 Ho, ER 2 Ha: 2 (17.3 x 6.4)ER Derricks: 4x3t; Winches: 4 Ice Capable	**1 oil engine** driving 1 FP propeller Total Power: 971kW (1,320hp) 12.3kn Deutz RBV8M545 1 x 4 Stroke 8 Cy. 320 x 450 971kW (1320bhp) Kloeckner Humboldt Deutz AG-West Germany Thrusters: 1 Thwart. FP thruster (f) Fuel: 97.5 (d.f.) 5.0pd

9146053 **SAN REMO II**
D5FP6 *ex* Panos G *-2008* *ex* Ayutthaya Ruby *-2006*
\- **Arcadia Navigation Co Ltd**
NAF Shipping Inc
Monrovia *Liberia*
MMSI: 636016332
Official number: 16332

6,001 3,541 10,100
Class: NK

1996-12 **Shin Kochi Jyuko K.K. — Kochi** Yd No: 7088
Loa 113.33 (BB) Br ex - Dght 8.023
Lbp 107.00 Br md 19.40 Dpth 10.40
Welded, 1 dk

(A21A2BC) Bulk Carrier
Grain: 12,175; Bale: 11,703
Compartments: 3 Ho, ER
3 Ha: (15.0 x 10.7)2 (20.0 x 12.5)ER
Cranes: 2x30t; Derricks: 1x25t

1 oil engine driving 1 FP propeller
Total Power: 3,883kW (5,279hp) 13.6kn
B&W 6L35MC
1 x 2 Stroke 6 Cy. 350 x 1050 3883kW (5279bhp)
Makita Corp-Japan
AuxGen: 2 x 280kW 450V 60Hz a.c
Fuel: 65.0 (d.f.) (Heating Coils) 501.0 (r.f.) 20.4pd

6801808 **SAN ROQUE**
EFDK
\- **Compania Iberica de Remolcadores del Estrecho SA (CIRESA)**
\-
Santander *Spain*
Official number: 1-1/1996

212 4 -
Class: (LR)
✠ Classed LR until 18/7/94

1967-09 **Astilleros de Santander SA (ASTANDER) — El Astillero** Yd No: 43
Loa 32.42 Br ex 9.02 Dght 3.252
Lbp 28.50 Br md 8.60 Dpth 4.09
Welded, 1 dk

(B32A2ST) Tug

2 oil engines reduction geared to sc. shaft driving 1 CP propeller
Total Power: 1,104kW (1,500hp) 12.0kn
Deutz RBA8M528
2 x 4 Stroke 8 Cy. 220 x 280 each-552kW (750bhp)
Kloeckner Humboldt Deutz AG-West Germany
AuxGen: 2 x 40kW 220V 50Hz a.c

9188063 **SAN ROQUE DIVINO**
EA3317
3-ST-23-98 **Echevarria/Valle**
Laredo *Spain*
Official number: 3-3/1998

133 40 130

1998-04 **Astilleros Armon SA — Navia** Yd No: 410
Loa 29.00 Br ex - Dght 2.640
Lbp 24.00 Br md 6.80 Dpth 3.35
Welded, 1 dk

(B11B2FV) Fishing Vessel

1 oil engine driving 1 FP propeller
Total Power: 235kW (320hp) 10.0kn
Baudouin
1 x 4 Stroke 235kW (320bhp)
Societe des Moteurs Baudouin SA-France

9593426 **SAN SABA**
V7UT8
\- **DSS 1 LLC**
Diamond S Management LLC
SatCom: Inmarsat C 453837261
Majuro *Marshall Islands*
MMSI: 538004027
Official number: 4027

81,346 52,264 159,018 T/cm 118.3
Class: AB

2012-06 **Hyundai Heavy Industries Co Ltd — Ulsan** Yd No: 2440
Loa 274.34 (BB) Br ex 48.05 Dght 17.160
Lbp 264.00 Br md 48.00 Dpth 23.10
Welded, 1 dk

(A13A2TV) Crude Oil Tanker
Double Hull (13F)
Liq: 166,850; Liq (Oil): 167,500
Cargo Heating Coils
Compartments: 12 Wing Ta, ER, 2 Wing Slop Ta
3 Cargo Pump (s): 3x4000m³/hr
Manifold: Bow/CM: 138m

1 oil engine driving 1 FP propeller
Total Power: 19,620kW (26,675hp) 15.7kn
MAN-B&W 6S70MC-C8
1 x 2 Stroke 6 Cy. 700 x 2800 19620kW (26675bhp)
Hyundai Heavy Industries Co Ltd-South Korea
AuxGen: 3 x 860kW a.c
Fuel: 380.7 (d.f.) 4377.9 (r.f.)

8980828 **SAN SAN**
6YRB *ex* Regina *-2006*
\- **Yacht Leasing Ltd**
Watersports Enterprises Ltd
Montego Bay *Jamaica*
Official number: JMR04003

116 34 -

1983 Lydia Yachts — Stuart, Fl
Loa 25.66 Br ex 6.38 Dght -
Lbp - Br md - Dpth 2.82
Welded, 1 dk

(X11A2YP) Yacht
Passengers: 80

2 oil engines geared to sc. shafts driving 2 Propellers
Total Power: 416kW (566hp)
Cummins
2 x 4 Stroke each-208kW (283bhp)
Cummins Engine Co Inc-USA

9502439 **SAN SAN H**
A8SP2 *ex* Jiujiang *-2011*
\- **Palette Maritime Ltd**
Compania Naviera Horamar SA
Monrovia *Liberia*
MMSI: 636014262
Official number: 14262

11,253 4,992 16,880 T/cm 28.0
Class: BV

2010-04 **Jiujiang Yinxing Shipbuilding Co Ltd — Xingzi County JX** Yd No: YX009
Loa 144.71 (BB) Br ex - Dght 8.800
Lbp 135.60 Br md 23.00 Dpth 12.50
Welded, 1 dk

(A12B2TR) Chemical/Products Tanker
Double Hull (13F)
Liq: 19,052; Liq (Oil): 19,052
Cargo Heating Coils
Compartments: 12 Wing Ta, 2 Wing Slop Ta, ER
4 Cargo Pump (s): 4x500m³/hr
Manifold: Bow/CM: 74m

1 oil engine driving 1 FP propeller
Total Power: 5,180kW (7,043hp) 13.5kn
MAN-B&W 7S35MC
1 x 2 Stroke 7 Cy. 350 x 1400 5180kW (7043bhp)
STX Engine Co Ltd-South Korea
AuxGen: 3 x 560kW 60Hz a.c
Thrusters: 1 Tunnel thruster (f)
Fuel: 740.0 (r.f.)

7112670 **SAN SEBASTIAN DE URABA**
HKPZ *ex* India Catalina *-1988* *ex* Anamar *-1987*
\- *ex* India Catalina *-1986* *ex* Anamar *-1986*
ex Don Alfonso *-1986* *ex* Eastern Pearl *-1986*
ex Golden Hill *-1975* *ex* Fukuzaki Maru *-1973*
Pizano SA
\-
Isla de San Andres *Colombia*
MMSI: 730039000
Official number: MC-07-097

6,748 3,614 9,425
Class: (LR) (AB) (NK)
Classed LR until 22/11/98

1971-08 **Tsuneishi Shipbuilding Co Ltd — Fukuyama HS** Yd No: 255
Loa 127.97 Br ex 18.34 Dght 7.532
Lbp 119.00 Br md 18.29 Dpth 9.50
Riveted\Welded, 1 dk

(A31A2GX) General Cargo Ship
Grain: 12,365; Bale: 11,789
Compartments: 3 Ho, ER
3 Ha: (14.7 x 9.0) (31.5 x 9.0) (18.4 x 9.0)ER
Derricks: 4x15t

1 oil engine driving 1 FP propeller
Total Power: 3,972kW (5,400hp) 14.5kn
Mitsubishi 6UEC52/105C
1 x 2 Stroke 6 Cy. 520 x 1050 3972kW (5400bhp)
Kobe Hatsudoki Seizosho-Japan
AuxGen: 2 x 255kW 440V 60Hz a.c
Fuel: 843.5 17.5pd

8222501 **SAN TANGAROA**
VL6354 *ex* Admiralty Pearl *-2008*
\- **Sanford Australia Pty Ltd (Racovolis Amalgamated Fish Agents)**
\-
Portland, Vic *Australia*
Official number: 851179

202 61 144
Class: (NV)

1984-07 **North Arm Slipway Pty Ltd — Port Adelaide SA** Yd No: 14
Loa 25.96 Br ex 8.31 Dght 3.850
Lbp 23.50 Br md 8.11 Dpth -
Welded, 1 dk

(B11A2FT) Trawler
Compartments: 1 Ho, ER
1 Ha:

1 oil engine driving 1 CP propeller
Total Power: 423kW (575hp)
Callesen 5-427-EOT
1 x 4 Stroke 5 Cy. 270 x 400 423kW (575bhp)
Aabenraa Motorfabrik, HeinrichCallesen A/S-Denmark
AuxGen: 2 x 104kW 415V 50Hz a.c
Fuel: 62.0 (d.f.) 2.5pd

8316584 **SAN TEODORO**
8PWM *ex* Yarmouth *-2009* *ex* Federal Oslo *-2000*
\- *ex* Paolo Pittaluga *-1991*
Linden Marine SA
G Bulk Corp
Bridgetown *Barbados*
MMSI: 314314000

17,730 9,971 29,462
Class: BV (LR) (NV)
✠ Classed LR until 16/2/96

1985-03 **Usuki Iron Works Co Ltd — Saiki OT** Yd No: 1319
Loa 183.01 (BB) Br ex 23.17 Dght 10.610
Lbp 172.02 Br md 23.11 Dpth 14.91
Welded, 1 dk

(A21A2BC) Bulk Carrier
Grain: 37,812; Bale: 35,540
Compartments: 5 Ho, ER
5 Ha: (13.6 x 11.6)4 (18.4 x 11.6)ER
Cranes: 4x25t

1 oil engine driving 1 FP propeller
Total Power: 6,170kW (8,389hp) 14.0kn
B&W 6L60MCE
1 x 2 Stroke 6 Cy. 600 x 1944 6170kW (8389bhp)
Mitsui Engineering & Shipbuilding CLtd-Japan
AuxGen: 3 x 400kW 445V 60Hz a.c
Fuel: 182.5 (d.f.) 1252.5 (r.f.)

7204758 **SAN TIYAGO**
DUTS3 *ex* Unity Galaxy *-2008* *ex* Dona Victoria B *-2008*
\- *ex* Daiyu Maru No. 8 *-1980*
Ovinal Lim Salvame
Manila *Philippines*
Official number: ZAM2F00085

322 153 -

1971 K.K. Ichikawa Zosensho — Ise Yd No: 1297
Loa - Br ex 7.73 Dght 3.271
Lbp 44.58 Br md 7.70 Dpth 3.66
Riveted\Welded, 1 dk

(B11B2FV) Fishing Vessel

1 oil engine driving 2 FP propellers
Total Power: 1,103kW (1,500hp)
Hanshin 6LU35
1 x 4 Stroke 6 Cy. 350 x 550 1103kW (1500bhp)
Hanshin Nainenki Kogyo-Japan

6410831 **SAN TOMMASO**
IUMD
\- **Istituto Tecnico Nautico Statale Leone Acciaiuoli**
\-
Pescara *Italy*
MMSI: 247152900
Official number: 305

169 24 -
Class: RI

1964 Cantiere Navale di Pesaro SpA (CNP) — Pesaro Yd No: 6
Loa 37.58 Br ex 6.00 Dght 2.521
Lbp 32.36 Br md 5.97 Dpth 2.80
Welded, 1 dk

(B34K2QT) Training Ship

1 oil engine driving 1 Directional propeller
Total Power: 375kW (510hp) 10.8kn
Ansaldo 196/RS
1 x 4 Stroke 6 Cy. 190 x 240 375kW (510bhp) (new engine 1969)
SA Ansaldo Stabilimento Meccaniche-Italy
AuxGen: 1 x 17kW 220V d.c, 1 x 11kW 220V d.c

8981339 **SAN TONG 6**
\- *ex* Zhe Zhou Yu Leng 236 *-2004*
\-
\-

498 290 -

1979-09 **Hudong Shipyard — Shanghai**
Loa 59.20 Br ex - Dght 3.420
Lbp 53.00 Br md 9.60 Dpth 5.70
Welded, 1 dk

(A34A2GR) Refrigerated Cargo Ship

1 oil engine driving 1 Propeller
Total Power: 662kW (900hp)
Chinese Std. Type 6350
1 x 4 Stroke 6 Cy. 350 x 500 662kW (900bhp)
Hongwei Machinery Factory-China

9149914 **SAN TONGARIRO**
ZMA3180
\- **Sanford Ltd**
Auckland *New Zealand*
Official number: 876201

498 149 282
Class: (BV)

1997-01 **Astilleros Armon SA — Navia** Yd No: 420
Loa 32.00 (BB) Br ex - Dght 4.000
Lbp 26.80 Br md 10.00 Dpth 4.20
Welded, 1 dk

(B11A2FS) Stern Trawler
Ins: 250

1 oil engine reduction geared to sc. shaft driving 1 CP propeller
Total Power: 1,037kW (1,410hp) 10.5kn
Caterpillar 3516TA
1 x Vee 4 Stroke 16 Cy. 170 x 190 1037kW (1410bhp)
Caterpillar Inc-USA
AuxGen: 2 x 160kW a.c

7922336 **SAN TORTUGAS**
ZM2248 *ex* Tortugas *-1988*
\- **Sanford Ltd**
Auckland *New Zealand*
Official number: 875432

206 62 300

1980-05 **Vaagland Baatbyggeri AS — Vaagland** Yd No: 99
Loa 32.92 Br ex 8.62 Dght 3.601
Lbp 30.51 Br md 8.58 Dpth 3.96
Welded, 1 dk

(B11B2FV) Fishing Vessel

1 oil engine reverse reduction geared to sc. shaft driving 1 FP propeller
Total Power: 662kW (900hp)
G.M. (Detroit Diesel) 16V-149
1 x Vee 2 Stroke 16 Cy. 146 x 146 662kW (900bhp)
General Motors Detroit DieselAllison Divn-USA

9113159 **SAN VALENTIN**
3ERH7 *ex* Almudaina *-2008*
\- **Marcia Shipholding Ltd**
Servicios Maritimos Portuarios (SEMAPORT)
SatCom: Inmarsat C 437005310
Panama *Panama*
MMSI: 370053000
Official number: 37273PEXT

3,265 979 198
Class: (BV) (NV)

1996-05 **EN Bazan de Construcciones Navales Militares SA — San Fernando (Sp)** Yd No: 325
Loa 96.20 Br ex 14.60 Dght 2.133
Lbp 81.48 Br md 11.82 Dpth 8.90
Welded, 2 dks

(A36A2PR) Passenger/Ro-Ro Ship (Vehicles)
Hull Material: Aluminium Alloy
Passengers: unberthed: 450
Stern ramp
Len: 12.50 Wid: 6.00 Swl: -
Side door/ramp (p. f.)
Len: 9.50 Wid: 4.50 Swl: -
Cars: 84

4 oil engines sr geared to sc. shafts driving 4 Water jets
Total Power: 20,000kW (27,192hp) 37.3kn
Caterpillar 3616TA
4 x Vee 4 Stroke 16 Cy. 280 x 300 each-5000kW (6798bhp)
Caterpillar Inc-USA
Thrusters: 1 Thwart. FP thruster (f)

IMO / Call sign	Name / Owner	Tonnage	Class	Builder / Dimensions	Type	Machinery
9190418 *IFJP* -	**SAN VENERIO** **Rimorchiatori Riuniti Spezzini-Imprese Marittime e Salvataggi Srl** - *La Spezia* *Italy* MMSI: 247841000 Official number: 245	**307** 91 -	Class: RI	**2000-12 PO SevMash Predpriyatiye — Severodvinsk** (Hull) **2000-12 B.V. Scheepswerf Damen — Gorinchem** Yd No: 7939 Loa 30.16 Br ex - Dght 3.770 Lbp 29.80 Br md 9.40 Dpth 4.80 Welded, 1 dk	**(B32A2ST) Tug**	**2 oil engines** reduction geared to sc. shafts driving 2 Directional propellers Total Power: 3,720kW (5,058hp) 14.3kn Wartsila 6L26 2 x 4 Stroke 6 Cy. 260 x 320 each-1860kW (2529bhp) Wartsila NSD Nederland BV-Netherlands AuxGen: 2 x 100kW 380/220V 50Hz a.c
5031676 *CSME* -	**SAN VICENTE** *ex* Galito *-1999* *ex* Tiverton *-1990* *ex* Avongarth *-1989* - - *Barreiro* *Portugal*	*156* - -	Class: (LR) ✠ Classed LR until 21/7/93	**1960-06 W. J. Yarwood & Sons Ltd. — Northwich** Yd No: 920 Loa 29.37 Br ex 7.60 Dght 3.264 Lbp 26.22 Br md 7.17 Dpth 3.66 Riveted\Welded	**(B32A2ST) Tug**	**1 oil engine** with flexible couplings & sr reverse geared to sc. shaft driving 1 FP propeller Total Power: 706kW (960hp) 10.0kn Ruston 8VGBXM 1 x 4 Stroke 8 Cy. 318 x 381 706kW (960bhp) Ruston & Hornsby Ltd.-Lincoln AuxGen: 2 x 40kW 220V d.c Fuel: 36.5 (d.f.)
8226571 *IVQC* -	**SAN VITO** *ex* Stella Lucente Terza *-1989* *ex* Inge *-1997* **Giovanni Giacalone** - *Palermo* *Italy* Official number: 1294	**120** 39 -	Class: (RI)	**1982 Cant. Nav. Catasta — San Benedetto del Tronto** Yd No: 27 Loa 29.49 Br ex 6.74 Dght 3.130 Lbr 23.88 Br md 6.66 Dpth 3.51 Welded, 1 dk	**(B11B2FV) Fishing Vessel**	**1 oil engine** driving 1 FP propeller Total Power: 485kW (659hp) S.K.L. 6NVD48-2U 1 x 4 Stroke 6 Cy. 320 x 480 485kW (659bhp) VEB Schwermaschinenbau "KarlLiebknecht" (SKL)-Magdeburg
8901468 *ZM3175* -	**SAN WAITAKI** *ex* Novik *-1999* **Sanford Ltd** - SatCom: Inmarsat A 1402203 *Auckland* *New Zealand* MMSI: 512000126 Official number: 876314	**1,899** 592 -	Class: NV	**1991-01 Sterkoder Mek. Verksted AS — Kristiansund** Yd No: 124 Loa 64.05 Br ex - Dght 6.500 Lbp 55.55 Br md 13.00 Dpth 8.85 Welded, 1 dk	**(B11A2FG) Factory Stern Trawler** Ice Capable	**1 oil engine** reduction geared to sc. shaft driving 1 FP propeller Total Power: 2,458kW (3,342hp) Wartsila 6R32 1 x 4 Stroke 6 Cy. 320 x 350 2458kW (3342bhp) Wartsila Diesel Oy-Finland AuxGen: 1 x 1304kW 380V 50Hz a.c, 2 x 336kW 380V 50Hz a.c Thrusters: 1 Thwart. FP thruster (f)
7737901 *BYPM* -	**SAN YI No. 1** **San Yi Oceanic Enterprise Co Ltd** - *Kaohsiung* *Chinese Taipei* Official number: 5620	*328* 218 -	Class: (CR)	**1975 San Yang Shipbuilding Co., Ltd. — Kaohsiung** Loa 42.14 Br ex 7.27 Dght 2.801 Lbp 36.00 Br md 7.21 Dpth 3.20 Welded, 1 dk	**(B11B2FV) Fishing Vessel** Ins: 330 Compartments: 3 Ho, ER 3 Ha: (1.2 x 1.3) (2.5 x 2.3) (1.0 x 1.3)ER	**1 oil engine** driving 1 FP propeller Total Power: 772kW (1,050hp) 10.8kn Akasaka 6MH25SSR 1 x 4 Stroke 6 Cy. 250 x 400 772kW (1050bhp) Akasaka Tekkosho KK (Akasaka DieselLtd)-Japan AuxGen: 1 x 180kW 230V a.c, 2 x 64kW 220V a.c
8649773 *BG3683* CT5-001683	**SAN ZAI FA NO. 12** **Chi-Teng Chi** Ocean Bountiful Ltd *Kaohsiung* *Chinese Taipei* MMSI: 416003955 Official number: 014999	**180** 54 -		**2009-11 Shing Sheng Fa Boat Building Co — Kaohsiung** Loa 30.20 Br ex - Dght - Lbp - Br md 6.20 Dpth 2.60 Bonded, 1 dk	**(B11B2FV) Fishing Vessel** Hull Material: Reinforced Plastic	**1 oil engine** reduction geared to sc. shaft driving 1 FP propeller Total Power: 759kW (1,032hp) Mitsubishi S6R2-MTK3L 1 x 4 Stroke 6 Cy. 170 x 220 759kW (1032bhp) Mitsubishi Heavy Industries Ltd-Japan
9209336 *EPBQ6* -	**SANA** *ex* Gabriela *-2012* *ex* Rosemary *-2012* *ex* Dandelion *-2011* *ex* New State *-2008* *ex* Iran Tehran *-2008* **Kish Roaring Ocean Shipping Co PJS** Rahbaran Omid Darya Ship Management Co *Qeshm Island* *Iran* MMSI: 422031100 Official number: 1067	**36,014** 19,431 41,937	Class: (GL)	**2000-07 Hyundai Heavy Industries Co Ltd — Ulsan** Yd No: 1245 Loa 240.22 (BB) Br ex 32.20 Dght 11.700 Lbp 225.20 Br md 32.20 Dpth 19.20 Welded, 1 dk	**(A33A2CC) Container Ship (Fully Cellular)** TEU 3280 incl 300 ref C. 13 Ha: Ice Capable	**1 oil engine** driving 1 FP propeller Total Power: 24,184kW (32,881hp) 22.0kn B&W 8S70MC-C 1 x 2 Stroke 8 Cy. 700 x 2800 24184kW (32881bhp) Hyundai Heavy Industries Co Ltd-South Korea AuxGen: 4 x 1475kW 220/440V a.c Thrusters: 1 Thwart. FP thruster (f)
7226110 *3FVT6* -	**SANA 1** *ex* Volgo-Balt 32 *-1996* **Thrivetrade Ltd Inc** - *Panama* *Panama* Official number: 25737BE	**2,421** 984 2,818	Class: (RS)	**1967 Astrakhanskaya Sudoverf im. "Kirova" — Astrakhan** Yd No: 2726 Loa 114.12 Br ex 13.22 Dght 3.690 Lbp 110.15 Br md - Dpth 5.50 Welded, 1 dk	**(A31A2GX) General Cargo Ship** Grain: 4,510 Compartments: 4 Ho, ER 4 Ha: 4 (16.5 x 9.3)ER Ice Capable	**2 oil engines** driving 2 FP propellers Total Power: 970kW (1,318hp) 10.5kn S.K.L. 6NVD48-2U 2 x 4 Stroke 6 Cy. 320 x 480 each-485kW (659bhp) VEB Schwermaschinenbau "KarlLiebknecht" (SKL)-Magdeburg
7825526 - -	**SANAA** **Hodeidah Port Authority** - *Hodeidah* *Yemen*	*260* - -		**1979-10 van der Werf Staalbouw B.V. — Papendrecht** (Hull) Yd No: 2203 **1979-10 B.V. Scheepswerf Damen — Gorinchem** Yd No: 967 Loa 23.19 Br ex 7.17 Dght 2.601 Lbp 21.06 Br md - Dpth 3.43 Welded, 1 dk	**(B32A2ST) Tug**	**2 oil engines** reverse reduction geared to sc. shafts driving 2 FP propellers Total Power: 1,704kW (2,316hp) G.M. (Detroit Diesel) 16V-149-T 2 x Vee 2 Stroke 16 Cy. 146 x 146 each-852kW (1158bhp) General Motors Detroit DieselAllison Divn-USA
8134730 - -	**SANAA** **Yemen Gulf Trading & Contracting Co** - *Yemen*	*112* - -	Class: (BV)	**1976 Deltawerf BV — Sliedrecht** Loa - Br ex - Dght 1.501 Lbp 14.00 Br md 4.01 Dpth 2.01 Welded, 1 dk	**(B35X2XX) Vessel (function unknown)**	**1 oil engine** geared to sc. shaft driving 1 FP propeller Total Power: 250kW (340hp) G.M. (Detroit Diesel) 12V-71 1 x Vee 2 Stroke 12 Cy. 108 x 127 250kW (340bhp) General Motors Detroit DieselAllison Divn-USA
9621522 *PCOT* -	**SANABORG** **Noordereems BV** Wagenborg Kazakhstan BV *Delfzijl* *Netherlands* MMSI: 244885000	**1,520** 456 867	Class: BV	**2012-08 Niestern Sander B.V. — Delfzijl** Yd No: 844 Loa 68.20 Br ex 14.30 Dght 3.150 Lbp 64.90 Br md 14.00 Dpth - Welded, 1 dk	**(B21B20T) Offshore Tug/Supply Ship** Ice Capable	**2 diesel electric oil engines** driving 2 gen. each 1750kW 690V a.c Connecting to 2 elec. motors each (1750kW) driving 2 Azimuth electric drive units Total Power: 4,000kW (5,438hp) 12.0kn Caterpillar 3516C 2 x Vee 4 Stroke 16 Cy. 170 x 215 each-2000kW (2719bhp) Thrusters: 1 Tunnel thruster (f)
9182552 *A9KO* -	**SANAD** *ex* Celtic King *-2013* *ex* Emily Borchard *-2007* *ex* Celtic King *-2003* **Tylos Shipping & Marine Services** - *Bahrain* *Bahrain* MMSI: 408541000	**4,015** 1,974 6,250	Class: RI (LR) ✠ Classed LR until 9/10/13	**1999-02 Madenci Gemi Sanayii Ltd. Sti. — Karadeniz Eregli** Yd No: 12 Loa 99.80 (BB) Br ex 17.20 Dght 6.355 Lbp 94.25 Br md 17.00 Dpth 8.20 Welded, 1 dk	**(A31A2GX) General Cargo Ship** Grain: 7,079 TEU 467 C. 467/20' Compartments: 2 Ho, ER 1 Ha: (64.8 x 13.2)ER	**1 oil engine** driving 1 CP propeller Total Power: 4,900kW (6,662hp) 15.5kn B&W 7S35MC 1 x 2 Stroke 7 Cy. 350 x 1400 4900kW (6662bhp) MAN B&W Diesel A/S-Denmark AuxGen: 1 x 828kW 380V 50Hz a.c, 2 x 359kW 380V 50Hz a.c Boilers: TOH (o.f.) 10.2kgf/cm² (10.0bar), TOH (ex.g.) 10.2kgf/cm² (10.0bar) Thrusters: 1 Thwart. CP thruster (f)
9170652 *A8CD4* -	**SANAGA** *ex* Paclogger *-1998* **First Ocean Bulk Ltd** John T Essberger GmbH & Co KG *Monrovia* *Liberia* MMSI: 636090631 Official number: 90631	**17,784** 9,924 28,215 T/cm 39.5	Class: LR (AB) **100A1** SS 10/2010 bulk carrier strengthened for heavy cargoes Nos. 2 & 4 holds may be empty ESP ESN-Hold No. 1 LI **LMC** **UMS**	**1997-12 Bohai Shipyard — Huludao LN** Yd No: 407-1 Loa 169.00 (BB) Br ex - Dght 9.692 Lbp 160.30 Br md 27.20 Dpth 13.60 Welded, 1 dk	**(A21A2BC) Bulk Carrier** Grain: 37,407; Bale: 35,850 Compartments: 5 Ho, ER 5 Ha: (13.6 x 16.0)4 (17.6 x 20.0)ER Cranes: 4x30t	**1 oil engine** driving 1 FP propeller Total Power: 7,003kW (9,521hp) 14.4kn Sulzer 5RTA52 1 x 2 Stroke 5 Cy. 520 x 1800 7003kW (9521bhp) Shanghai Shipyard-China AuxGen: 3 x 500kW a.c
8033211 *UDON* -	**SANAGA** **JSC Close Type Fish Industrial Corp 'Starodubskoe' (AOZT RPK 'Starodubskoe')** - *Petropavlovsk-Kamchatskiy* *Russia* MMSI: 273894700 Official number: 810423	**735** 221 332	Class: (RS)	**1981-12 Zavod "Leninskaya Kuznitsa" — Kiyev** Yd No: 252 Loa 53.75 (BB) Br ex 10.72 Dght 4.290 Lbp 47.92 Br md - Dpth 6.02 Welded, 1 dk	**(B11A2FS) Stern Trawler** Ins: 218 Compartments: 1 Ho, ER 1 Ha: (1.6 x 1.6) Derricks: 2x1.5t Ice Capable	**1 oil engine** driving 1 FP propeller Total Power: 971kW (1,320hp) 12.8kn S.K.L. 8NVD48-2U 1 x 4 Stroke 8 Cy. 320 x 480 971kW (1320bhp) VEB Schwermaschinenbau "KarlLiebknecht" (SKL)-Magdeburg
9174854 *TJPA0* -	**SANAGA I** **Societe Camerounaise de Leasing Maritime** - *Kribi* *Cameroon* Official number: K-79	**135** - -		**1998-07 Construcciones Navales Santodomingo SA — Vigo** Yd No: 623 Loa 27.50 Br ex - Dght 3.000 Lbp 22.50 Br md 7.20 Dpth 5.45 Welded, 1 dk	**(B11A2FS) Stern Trawler** Ins: 110 Compartments: 1 Ho 1 Ha:	**1 oil engine** with flexible couplings & sr gearedto sc. shaft driving 1 FP propeller Total Power: 519kW (706hp) 9.7kn Caterpillar 3508TA 1 x Vee 4 Stroke 8 Cy. 170 x 190 519kW (706bhp) Caterpillar Inc-USA

IMO / Call sign / Official no.	Name / Former names / Owner / Port	Tonnage (GT / NT / DWT)	Class	Builder / Dimensions	Type / Cargo	Machinery
9174866 *TJPAP* -	**SANAGA II** **Societe Camerounaise de Leasing Maritime** - *Kribi* *Cameroon* Official number: K-80	**135** - -		**1998-07 Construcciones Navales Santodomingo SA — Vigo** Yd No: 624 Loa 27.50 Br ex - Dght 3.000 Lbp 22.50 Br md 7.20 Dpth 5.45 Welded, 1 dk	**(B11A2FS) Stern Trawler** Ins: 110 Compartments: 1 Ho 1 Ha:	**1 oil engine** with flexible couplings & sr gearedto sc. shaft driving 1 FP propeller Total Power: 519kW (706hp) 9.7kn Caterpillar 3508TA 1 x Vee 4 Stroke 8 Cy. 170 x 190 519kW (706bhp) Caterpillar Inc-USA
9174892 - -	**SANAGA V** **Societe Camerounaise de Leasing Maritime** - *Kribi* *Cameroon*	**135** - -		**1998-07 Construcciones Navales P Freire SA — Vigo** (Hull) **1998-07 Construcciones Navales Santodomingo SA — Vigo** Yd No: 630 Loa 27.50 Br ex - Dght 3.000 Lbp 22.50 Br md 7.20 Dpth 3.35 Welded, 1 dk	**(B11A2FS) Stern Trawler** Ins: 110	**1 oil engine** geared to sc. shaft driving 1 FP propeller Total Power: 519kW (706hp) 9.7kn Caterpillar 3508TA 1 x Vee 4 Stroke 8 Cy. 170 x 190 519kW (706bhp) Caterpillar Inc-USA
9107992 *2AGI5* TN 44	**SANAMEDIO** **Denmuir Ltd** - *Fleetwood* *United Kingdom* MMSI: 235059379 Official number: C19165	**317** 95 152	Class: BV	**1995-03 Construcciones Navales P Freire SA — Vigo** Yd No: 477 Loa 36.00 Br ex 7.72 Dght 3.850 Lbp 32.74 Br md 7.70 Dpth 5.60 Welded, 1 dk	**(B11A2FS) Stern Trawler** Ins: 125	**1 oil engine** geared to sc. shaft driving 1 FP propeller Total Power: 681kW (926hp) MAN 8L20/27 1 x 4 Stroke 8 Cy. 200 x 270 681kW (926bhp) EN Bazan de Construcciones NavalesMilitares SA-Spain
9332389 *UEQK* -	**SANAR-1** *ex* Alkor *-2012* **Rosewood Shipping LLC** LLC 'Shipping Agency Yug Rusi' *Taganrog* *Russia* MMSI: 273438670	**4,207** 1,288 5,404	Class: RS	**2004-12 AO Sudostroitelnyy Zavod "3rd International" — Astrakhan** (Hull) Yd No: 481003 **2004-12 OAO Volgogradskiy Sudostroitelnyy Zavod — Volgograd** Yd No: 341 Loa 136.11 Br ex 16.74 Dght 3.850 Lbp 131.90 Br md 16.60 Dpth 6.10 Welded, 1 dk	**(A12B2TR) Chemical/Products Tanker** Double Hull (13F) Ice Capable	**2 oil engines** reduction geared to sc. shafts driving 2 FP propellers Total Power: 1,860kW (2,528hp) 10.0kn Wartsila 6L20 2 x 4 Stroke 6 Cy. 200 x 280 each-930kW (1264bhp) Wartsila Finland Oy-Finland
9328663 *UEZV* -	**SANAR-2** *ex* Alshar *-2012* **Rosewood Shipping LLC** LLC 'Shipping Agency Yug Rusi' *Taganrog* *Russia* MMSI: 273433590	**4,207** 1,288 5,404	Class: RS	**2005-06 OAO Volgogradskiy Sudostroitelnyy Zavod — Volgograd** Yd No: 342 Loa 136.11 Br ex 16.74 Dght 3.850 Lbp 130.12 Br md 16.60 Dpth 6.10 Welded, 1 dk	**(A12B2TR) Chemical/Products Tanker** Double Hull (13F) Liq: 6,374; Liq (Oil): 6,374 Compartments: 12 Wing Ta, 1 Slop Ta, ER Ice Capable	**2 oil engines** reduction geared to sc. shafts driving 2 FP propellers Total Power: 1,860kW (2,528hp) 10.0kn Wartsila 6L20C 2 x 4 Stroke 6 Cy. 200 x 280 each-930kW (1264bhp) Wartsila Finland Oy-Finland AuxGen: 3 x 211kW Fuel: 230.0 (d.f.)
9457804 *UBPI2* -	**SANAR-3** *ex* AET Gala *-2012* *launched as* Aet Hazar *-2010* *ex* Eagle Hazar *-2010* **Rosewood Shipping LLC** - *Taganrog* *Russia* MMSI: 273358760	**4,740** 1,577 6,670	Class: RS (BV)	**2010-05 OAO Okskaya Sudoverf — Navashino** Yd No: 1216 Loa 139.93 (BB) Br ex - Dght 4.060 Lbp 138.50 Br md 16.70 Dpth 6.40 Welded, 1 dk	**(A12B2TR) Chemical/Products Tanker** Double Hull (13F) Liq: 7,607; Liq (Oil): 7,920 Compartments: 6 Ta, ER Ice Capable	**2 oil engines** reduction geared to sc. shafts driving 2 Directional propellers Total Power: 2,984kW (4,058hp) 10.5kn Cummins KTA-50-M2 2 x Vee 4 Stroke 16 Cy. 159 x 159 each-1492kW (2029bhp) Cummins Engine Co Ltd-United Kingdom AuxGen: 2 x 390kW 50Hz a.c Thrusters: 1 Tunnel thruster (f) Fuel: 180.0 (r.f.)
9476771 *UBPI3* -	**SANAR-4** *ex* Aet Sanjar *-2012* *launched as* Aet Astana *-2010* *ex* Eagle Astana *-2009* **Rosewood Shipping LLC** - *Taganrog* *Russia* MMSI: 273359760	**4,740** 1,577 6,670	Class: RS (BV)	**2010-05 OAO Okskaya Sudoverf — Navashino** Yd No: 1217 Loa 139.93 (BB) Br ex - Dght 4.060 Lbp 138.50 Br md 16.70 Dpth 6.40 Welded, 1 dk	**(A12B2TR) Chemical/Products Tanker** Double Hull (13F) Liq: 7,607; Liq (Oil): 7,920 Compartments: 6 Ta, ER Ice Capable	**2 oil engines** reduction geared to sc. shafts driving 2 Directional propellers Total Power: 2,984kW (4,058hp) 10.5kn Cummins KTA-50-M2 2 x Vee 4 Stroke 16 Cy. 159 x 159 each-1492kW (2029bhp) Cummins Engine Co Ltd-United Kingdom AuxGen: 2 x 390kW 50Hz a.c Thrusters: 1 Tunnel thruster (f) Fuel: 180.0 (r.f.)
9476783 *UBPI4* -	**SANAR-5** *ex* Aet Nissa *-2012* *ex* Aet Sanjar *-2010* *ex* Eagle Sanjar *-2010* **Rosewood Shipping LLC** - *Taganrog* *Russia* MMSI: 273350860	**4,740** 1,577 6,670	Class: RS (BV)	**2010-07 OAO Okskaya Sudoverf — Navashino** Yd No: 1218 Loa 139.93 (BB) Br ex 16.77 Dght 4.060 Lbp 138.50 Br md 16.70 Dpth 6.40 Welded, 1 dk	**(A12B2TR) Chemical/Products Tanker** Double Hull (13F) Liq: 7,607; Liq (Oil): 7,920 Compartments: 6 Ta, ER Ice Capable	**2 oil engines** reduction geared to sc. shafts driving 2 Directional propellers Total Power: 2,386kW (3,244hp) 10.5kn Cummins KTA-50-M2 2 x Vee 4 Stroke 16 Cy. 159 x 159 each-1193kW (1622bhp) Cummins Engine Co Ltd-United Kingdom AuxGen: 2 x 390kW 50Hz a.c, 1 x 150kW 50Hz a.c Fuel: 180.0 (d.f.)
9211999 *9HA3369* -	**SANAR-7** *ex* Valbruna *-2013* **Sunor Ltd** Rosewood Shipping LLC *Valletta* *Malta* MMSI: 229483000 Official number: 9211999	**62,569** 33,027 113,424 T/cm 99.0	Class: RS (RI) (BV) (AB)	**2000-05 Samsung Heavy Industries Co Ltd — Geoje** Yd No: 1297 Loa 249.20 (BB) Br ex 44.04 Dght 14.620 Lbp 238.00 Br md 44.00 Dpth 21.20 Welded, 1 dk	**(A13A2TW) Crude/Oil Products Tanker** Double Hull (13F) Liq: 122,686; Liq (Oil): 126,414 Cargo Heating Coils Compartments: 12 Wing Ta, ER, 2 Wing Slop Ta 3 Cargo Pump (s): 3x2800m³/hr Manifold: Bow/CM: 117.9m	**1 oil engine** driving 1 FP propeller Total Power: 13,549kW (18,421hp) 15.0kn B&W 6S60MC-C 1 x 2 Stroke 6 Cy. 600 x 2400 13549kW (18421bhp) HSD Engine Co Ltd-South Korea AuxGen: 3 x 700kW 440V 60Hz a.c Fuel: 175.8 (d.f.) (Heating Coils) 3218.6 (r.f.) 56.0pd
9212008 *9HA3350* -	**SANAR-8** *ex* Vallombrosa *-2013* **Sunor Ltd** Rosewood Shipping LLC *Valletta* *Malta* MMSI: 229461000 Official number: 9212008	**62,569** 33,027 113,424 T/cm 99.0	Class: RS (RI) (BV) (AB)	**2000-07 Samsung Heavy Industries Co Ltd — Geoje** Yd No: 1298 Loa 249.00 (BB) Br ex 44.04 Dght 14.620 Lbp 238.00 Br md 44.00 Dpth 21.20 Welded, 1 dk	**(A13A2TW) Crude/Oil Products Tanker** Double Hull (13F) Liq: 122,686; Liq (Oil): 126,414 Cargo Heating Coils Compartments: 12 Wing Ta, ER, 2 Wing Slop Ta 3 Cargo Pump (s): 3x2800m³/hr Manifold: Bow/CM: 117.9m	**1 oil engine** driving 1 FP propeller Total Power: 13,549kW (18,421hp) 15.0kn B&W 6S60MC-C 1 x 2 Stroke 6 Cy. 600 x 2400 13549kW (18421bhp) HSD Engine Co Ltd-South Korea Fuel: 175.8 (d.f.) (Heating Coils) 3218.6 (r.f.) 53.6pd
7434511 - -	**SANATARIA IX** **Pesqueria Santaria SA** - *Mexico*	*125* - -		**1975-03 Desco Marine — Saint Augustine, Fl** Yd No: 194-F Loa 22.84 Br ex - Dght - Lbp - Br md 6.68 Dpth - Bonded	**(B11B2FV) Fishing Vessel** Hull Material: Reinforced Plastic	**1 oil engine** driving 1 FP propeller Total Power: 268kW (364hp) Caterpillar D343SCAC 1 x 4 Stroke 6 Cy. 137 x 165 268kW (364bhp) Caterpillar Tractor Co-USA
7434523 - -	**SANATARIA XI** **Pesqueria Santaria SA** - *Mexico*	*125* - -		**1975-03 Desco Marine — Saint Augustine, Fl** Yd No: 195-F Loa 22.84 Br ex - Dght - Lbp - Br md 6.68 Dpth - Bonded	**(B11B2FV) Fishing Vessel** Hull Material: Reinforced Plastic	**1 oil engine** driving 1 FP propeller Total Power: 268kW (364hp) Caterpillar D343SCAC 1 x 4 Stroke 6 Cy. 137 x 165 268kW (364bhp) Caterpillar Tractor Co-USA
9152064 *JG5483* -	**SANBE** **Government of Japan (Ministry of Land, Infrastructure & Transport) (The Coastguard)** - *Tokyo* *Japan* Official number: 135849	*198* - -		**1997-01 Hitachi Zosen Corp — Kawasaki KN** Yd No: 117106 Loa 46.00 Br ex - Dght - Lbp 43.00 Br md 7.50 Dpth 4.09 Welded, 1 dk	**(B34H2SQ) Patrol Vessel**	**3 oil engines** with clutches, flexible couplings & sr reverse geared to sc. shafts driving 2 FP propellers , 1 Water jet Total Power: 7,922kW (10,770hp) 35.0kn Pielstick 12PA4V200VGA 1 x Vee 4 Stroke 12 Cy. 200 x 210 2720kW (3698bhp) Niigata Engineering Co Ltd-Japan Pielstick 16PA4V200VGA 2 x Vee 4 Stroke 16 Cy. 200 x 210 each-2601kW (3536bhp) Niigata Engineering Co Ltd-Japan
6523535 *HO9323* -	**SANBLAS FERRY** *ex* Grand Manan *-2013* *ex* Grand Manan IV *-1993* *ex* Grand Manan *-1991* **Fritz the Cat SA** - *Panama* *Panama* Official number: 45106PEXT1	*1,443* 896 213	Class: (LR) ✠ Classed LR until 28/7/13	**1965-09 Saint John Shipbuilding & Dry Dock Co Ltd — Saint John NB** Yd No: 1076 Loa 52.68 Br ex 12.86 Dght 3.061 Lbp 47.25 Br md 12.20 Dpth 8.39 Welded, 2 dks	**(A37B2PS) Passenger Ship** Passengers: unberthed: 100 1 Ha: (6.1 x 3.3) Derricks: 1x3t	**2 oil engines** with clutches & reverse geared to sc. shafts driving 2 FP propellers Total Power: 2,236kW (3,040hp) 11.0kn Caterpillar 3512TA 2 x Vee 4 Stroke 12 Cy. 170 x 190 each-1118kW (1520bhp) (new engine 1991) Caterpillar Inc-USA AuxGen: 2 x 100kW 440V 60Hz a.c Boilers: db 3.5kgf/cm² (3.4bar) Fuel: 45.5 (d.f.)

IMO / Call sign	Name / Former names / Owner / Port	Tonnage / Class	Builder / Dimensions	Type	Machinery
8960907 - -	**SANBRENDORE** *ex* I. V .Y *-2013* **Les Pecheries HJES Inc** - *Cap-aux-Meules, QC* *Canada* MMSI: 316007310 Official number: 821717	*114* 85 -	**2000 Chantier Naval Matane Inc — Matane QC** Loa - Br ex - Dght - Lbp 18.50 Br md 7.30 Dpth 3.90 Welded, 1 dk	**(B11B2FV) Fishing Vessel**	**1 oil engine** driving 1 FP propeller Total Power: 492kW (669hp) 10.0kn
9356608 *5ISL41* -	**SANCHI** *ex* Seahorse *-2013* *ex* Gardenia *-2012* *ex* Sepid *-2012* *ex* Saman *-2008* **NITC** - *Zanzibar* *Tanzania (Zanzibar)* MMSI: 677004000	**85,462** Class: (BV) (NV) 53,441 164,154	**2008-04 Hyundai Samho Heavy Industries Co Ltd — Samho** Yd No: S316 Loa 274.18 (BB) Br ex 50.04 Dght 17.000 Lbp 265.07 Br md 50.00 Dpth 23.10 Welded, 1 dk	**(A13A2TV) Crude Oil Tanker** Double Hull (13F) Liq: 169,000; Liq (Oil): 180,890 Cargo Heating Coils Compartments: 12 Wing Ta, 2 Wing Slop Ta 3 Cargo Pump (s): 3x4000m³/hr	**1 oil engine** driving 1 FP propeller Total Power: 18,660kW (25,370hp) 15.4kn MAN-B&W 6S70MC-C 1 x 2 Stroke 6 Cy. 700 x 2800 18660kW (25370bhp) Hyundai Heavy Industries Co Ltd-South Korea AuxGen: 3 x 1050kW 60Hz a.c Fuel: 155.0 (d.f.) 4076.0 (r.f.)
9029425 *YD3183* -	**SANCHUAN NO. 2** *ex* Hakuryu Maju *-2006* *ex* Hakuryu Maru No. 8 *-2002* **PT Samudra Sindo** - *Dumai* *Indonesia*	**102** Class: KI 31 41	**1974-02 Nichiro Zosen K.K. — Hakodate** Loa 29.20 Br ex - Dght 1.980 Lbp 24.20 Br md 5.90 Dpth 2.50 Welded, 1 dk	**(B32A2ST) Tug**	**1 oil engine** driving 1 Propeller Total Power: 434kW (590hp) 8.0kn Niigata 6MG25BXB 1 x 4 Stroke 6 Cy. 250 x 320 434kW (590bhp) Niigata Engineering Co Ltd-Japan AuxGen: 1 x 70kW 225V a.c, 1 x 10kW 225V a.c
9250206 *ZDHH3* -	**SANCO CHASER** **Sanco Holding AS** Sanco Shipping AS *Gibraltar* *Gibraltar (British)* MMSI: 236317000	**1,346** Class: NV 404 1,230	**2002-05 Societatea Comerciala Severnav S.A. — Drobeta-Turnu Severin** (Hull) Yd No: 38 **2002-05 Larsnes Mek. Verksted AS — Larsnes** Yd No: 38 Loa 51.30 (BB) Br ex 12.03 Dght 5.500 Lbp 43.80 Br md 12.00 Dpth 6.20 Welded, 1 dk	**(B31A2SR) Research Survey Vessel** Cranes: 1x10t	**2 oil engines** reduction geared to sc. shafts driving 2 CP propellers Total Power: 2,648kW (3,600hp) 11.0kn A.B.C. 6DZC 2 x 4 Stroke 6 Cy. 256 x 310 each-1324kW (1800bhp) Anglo Belgian Corp NV (ABC)-Belgium AuxGen: 1 x 170kW 440/220V 60Hz a.c, 2 x 1000kW 440/220V 60Hz a.c Thrusters: 1 Tunnel thruster (f); 1 Tunnel thruster (a) Fuel: 1100.0 (d.f.) 5.0pd
9204295 *ZDHF4* -	**SANCO SEA** **Sanco Holding AS** Sanco Shipping AS *Gibraltar* *Gibraltar (British)* MMSI: 236310000	**1,129** Class: NV 339 806	**1999-11 Societatea Comerciala Severnav S.A. — Drobeta-Turnu Severin** (Hull) Yd No: 290001 **1999-11 Voldnes Skipsverft AS — Fosnavaag** Yd No: 57 Loa 51.30 (BB) Br ex - Dght 5.200 Lbp 43.80 Br md 12.00 Dpth 6.20 Welded, 1 dk	**(B31A2SR) Research Survey Vessel** Cranes: 1x8t	**2 oil engines** reduction geared to sc. shafts driving 2 CP propellers Total Power: 2,650kW (3,602hp) 11.0kn A.B.C. 6DZC 2 x 4 Stroke 6 Cy. 256 x 310 each-1325kW (1801bhp) Anglo Belgian Corp NV (ABC)-Belgium AuxGen: 2 x 700kW 440/230V 60Hz a.c, 1 x 170kW 440/230V 60Hz a.c Thrusters: 1 Thwart. FP thruster (f) Fuel: 1030.0
9349033 *ZDHW8* -	**SANCO SKY** **Sanco Holding AS** Sanco Shipping AS *Gibraltar* *Gibraltar (British)* MMSI: 236384000	**2,250** Class: NV 675 2,750	**2007-04 AS Rigas Kugu Buvetava (Riga Shipyard) — Riga** (Hull) **2007-04 Aas Mek. Verksted AS — Vestnes** Yd No: 176 Loa 72.40 (BB) Br ex 13.27 Dght 6.100 Lbp 66.13 Br md 13.20 Dpth 7.50 Welded, 1 dk	**(B31A2SR) Research Survey Vessel** Cranes: 1x7.5t Ice Capable	**2 oil engines** reduction geared to sc. shafts driving 2 CP propellers Total Power: 2,648kW (3,600hp) 11.0kn A.B.C. 6DZC 2 x 4 Stroke 6 Cy. 256 x 310 each-1324kW (1800bhp) Anglo Belgian Corp NV (ABC)-Belgium AuxGen: 2 x 1000kW 440/230V 60Hz a.c, 1 x 170kW 440/230V 60Hz a.c Thrusters: 1 Tunnel thruster (f); 1 Tunnel thruster (a) Fuel: 550.0 (d.f.) 2200.0 (r.f.) 12.0pd
9429936 *ZDJN3* -	**SANCO SPIRIT** **Sanco Holding AS** Sanco Shipping AS *Gibraltar* *Gibraltar (British)* MMSI: 236538000 Official number: 9429936	**4,396** Class: NV 1,319 2,550	**2009-10 Helgeland Sveiseindustri — Nesna** (Hull) **2009-10 Vaagland Baatbyggeri AS — Vaagland** Yd No: 141 Loa 86.50 (BB) Br ex - Dght 5.750 Lbp 82.95 Br md 16.00 Dpth 6.50 Welded, 1 dk	**(B31A2SR) Research Survey Vessel** Cranes: 1x5t Ice Capable	**4 diesel electric oil engines** driving 4 gen. each 2400kW 690V a.c Connecting to 2 elec. motors each (2500kW) driving 2 CP propellers Total Power: 7,072kW (9,616hp) 13.0kn A.B.C. 8DZC 1 x 4 Stroke 8 Cy. 256 x 310 1768kW (2404bhp) Anglo Belgian Corp NV (ABC)-Belgium A.B.C. 8DZC 3 x 4 Stroke 8 Cy. 256 x 310 each-1768kW (2404bhp) Anglo Belgian Corp NV (ABC)-Belgium Thrusters: 1 Retract. directional thruster amid; 1 Tunnel thruster (f); 1 Tunnel thruster (a) Fuel: 1100.0 (d.f.)
9410313 *ZDIT8* -	**SANCO STAR** **Sanco Holding AS** Sanco Shipping AS SatCom: Inmarsat C 423648310 *Gibraltar* *Gibraltar (British)* MMSI: 236483000	**3,953** Class: NV 1,186 2,150	**2008-11 Helgeland Sveiseindustri — Nesna** (Hull) **2008-11 Vaagland Baatbyggeri AS — Vaagland** Yd No: 140 Loa 80.50 (BB) Br ex - Dght 6.100 Lbp 76.95 Br md 16.00 Dpth 11.70 Welded	**(B31A2SR) Research Survey Vessel** Ice Capable	**3 diesel electric oil engines** driving 3 gen. each 1500kW 690V a.c Connecting to 2 elec. motors each (2500kW) driving 2 CP propellers Total Power: 4,779kW (6,498hp) A.B.C. 8DZC 3 x 4 Stroke 8 Cy. 256 x 310 each-1593kW (2166bhp) Anglo Belgian Corp NV (ABC)-Belgium Thrusters: 1 Tunnel thruster (f); 1 Retract. directional thruster (f); 1 Tunnel thruster (a) Fuel: 1100.0 (d.f.)
9630494 *ZDKY8* -	**SANCO SWIFT** **Sanco Holding AS** Sanco Shipping AS *Gibraltar* *Gibraltar (British)* MMSI: 236111851	**8,772** Class: NV 2,632 3,250	**2013-07 'Crist' SA — Gdansk** (Hull) **2013-07 Myklebust Mek. Verksted AS — Gursken** Yd No: 355 Loa 96.15 (BB) Br ex 23.00 Dght 7.000 Lbp 84.60 Br md 21.50 Dpth 8.80 Welded, 1 dk	**(B31A2SR) Research Survey Vessel** Cranes: 2x16t Ice Capable	**4 diesel electric oil engines** driving 4 gen. each 2600kW 690V a.c Connecting to 2 elec. motors driving 2 CP propellers Total Power: 16,000kW (21,752hp) 14.0kn MAN-B&W 8L32/40 4 x 4 Stroke 8 Cy. 320 x 400 each-4000kW (5438bhp) MAN B&W Diesel AG-Augsburg Thrusters: 1 Retract. directional thruster (f); 1 Tunnel thruster (a) Fuel: 400.0 (d.f.) 1750.0 (r.f.)
9662100 *ZDNE7* -	**SANCO SWORD** **Sanco Holding AS** Sanco Shipping AS *Gibraltar* *Gibraltar (British)* MMSI: 236111902	**8,772** Class: NV 2,632 2,900	**2014-03 'Crist' SA — Gdansk** (Hull) Yd No: (358) **2014-03 Myklebust Mek. Verksted AS — Gursken** Yd No: 358 Loa 96.15 (BB) Br ex 23.00 Dght 7.000 Lbp 84.60 Br md 21.50 Dpth - Welded, 1 dk	**(B31A2SR) Research Survey Vessel**	**4 diesel electric oil engines** driving 4 gen. Connecting to 2 elec. motors driving 2 CP propellers Total Power: 16,000kW (21,752hp) 14.0kn MAN-B&W 8L32/40 4 x 4 Stroke 8 Cy. 320 x 400 each-4000kW (5438bhp) MAN B&W Diesel AG-Augsburg Thrusters: 1 Retract. directional thruster (f); 1 Tunnel thruster (a) Fuel: 400.0 (d.f.) 1700.0 (r.f.)
7926681 *WCT7532* -	**SANCOR** *ex* Sea Fisher 7 *-1989* **C & B Fishing Corp** - *New Bedford, MA* *United States of America* MMSI: 367055040 Official number: 620731	*134* 99 -	**1980 Quality Marine, Inc. — Bayou La Batre, Al** Yd No: 134 Loa 25.33 Br ex - Dght - Lbp - Br md 7.01 Dpth 3.69 Welded, 1 dk	**(B11A2FS) Stern Trawler**	**1 oil engine** driving 1 FP propeller Total Power: 382kW (519hp) Caterpillar 3412TA 1 x Vee 4 Stroke 12 Cy. 137 x 152 382kW (519bhp) Caterpillar Tractor Co-USA
7524287 *H9MX* -	**SANCRIS** *ex* Ocean Line 1 *-2000* *ex* Busteni *-1997* **Naval Heritage Maritime SA** Transocean Services Srl *Panama* *Panama* MMSI: 351576000 Official number: 2863902A	**5,983** Class: IS (RN) 3,531 8,750	**1975-07 Santierul Naval Galati S.A. — Galati** Yd No: 654 Loa 130.78 Br ex - Dght 8.100 Lbp 121.21 Br md 17.70 Dpth 10.20 Welded, 1 dk & S dk	**(A31A2GX) General Cargo Ship** Grain: 11,980; Bale: 11,067 Compartments: 4 Ho, ER 4 Ha: (11.9 x 5.9)3 (13.6 x 9.9)ER Cranes: 4x5t Ice Capable	**1 oil engine** driving 1 FP propeller Total Power: 4,487kW (6,101hp) 13.0kn Sulzer 5RD68 1 x 2 Stroke 5 Cy. 680 x 1250 4487kW (6101bhp) Zaklady Przemyslu Metalowego 'HCegielski' SA-Poznan AuxGen: 3 x 200kW 400V 50Hz a.c Fuel: 1149.0
8962993 *FOXY* BL 899837	**SANCTA MARIA** **Jean-Michel Cousin** - *Boulogne* *France* Official number: 899837	**144** Class: (BV) 43 -	**2000-08 SOCARENAM — Boulogne** Yd No: 173 Loa 22.50 Br ex - Dght 3.016 Lbp 19.70 Br md 6.90 Dpth 3.60 Welded, 1 dk	**(B11B2FV) Fishing Vessel** Compartments: 1 Ho 2 Ha:	**1 oil engine** with clutches, flexible couplings & sr geared to sc. shaft driving 1 CP propeller Total Power: 442kW (601hp) A.B.C. 6MDXC 1 x 4 Stroke 6 Cy. 242 x 320 442kW (601bhp) Anglo Belgian Corp NV (ABC)-Belgium Thrusters: 1 Thwart. FP thruster (f)

IMO / Call sign / Fishing no.	Name / Owner / Port	Tonnage	Classification	Builder / Dimensions	Type	Machinery
8662141 *2FOV7* N 29	**SANCTA MARIA** *ex* Sancta Maria 1 *-2001* *ex* Caroline Marie *-1992* *ex* Glorieuse Vierge Marie Ii *-1989* **Mr D Harding & Mr RH James** - *Newry* *United Kingdom* Official number: C20118	**106** 51 -		**1979 C.E.R.N.A.T. — Nantes** Loa 20.37 Br ex - Dght - Lbp - Br md 6.00 Dpth - Welded, 1 dk	**(B11B2FV) Fishing Vessel**	**1 oil engine** reduction geared to sc. shaft driving 1 Propeller Total Power: 330kW (449hp)
9387487 *JWOJ* -	**SAND** - **Norled AS** - *Stavanger* *Norway* MMSI: 257109000	**879** 263 500	Class: (NV)	**2007-03 UAB Vakaru Laivu Remontas (JSC Western Shiprepair) — Klaipeda** (Hull) Yd No: 026/05-N **2007-03 Fiskerstrand Verft AS — Fiskarstrand** Yd No: 57 Loa 64.20 Br ex - Dght 3.150 Lbp 62.90 Br md 13.70 Dpth 4.80 Welded, 1 dk	**(A36A2PR) Passenger/Ro-Ro Ship (Vehicles)** Passengers: unberthed: 255 Bow ramp (centre) Stern ramp (centre) Cars: 50	**4 oil engines** reduction geared to sc. shafts driving 4 Directional propellers Total Power: 1,764kW (2,400hp) 11.0kn Scania DI16 43M 4 x Vee 4 Stroke 8 Cy. 127 x 154 each-441kW (600bhp) Scania AB-Sweden
8034526 - -	**SAND BAR** - **Cesar Chala Perlaza** -	**127** 90 -		**1982 Steiner Shipyard, Inc. — Bayou La Batre, Al** Yd No: 136 Loa 22.81 Br ex - Dght 2.401 Lbp 20.12 Br md 6.71 Dpth 3.45 Welded, 1 dk	**(B11A2FT) Trawler**	**1 oil engine** geared to sc. shaft driving 1 FP propeller Total Power: 268kW (364hp) Cummins KT-1150-M 1 x 4 Stroke 6 Cy. 159 x 159 268kW (364bhp) Cummins Engine Co Inc-USA
8031603 *D7UT* -	**SAND CARRY 5** *ex* Se Won *-1995* **Ban Byung-Kun** - *Busan* *South Korea* Official number: BSR-806111	*397* 237 750	Class: (KR)	**1980-01 ShinA Shipbuilding Co Ltd — Tongyeong** Loa 56.01 Br ex - Dght 3.001 Lbp 50.53 Br md 10.51 Dpth 3.51 Welded, 1 dk	**(A31A2GX) General Cargo Ship** Grain: 772; Bale: 757 1 Ha: (19.9 x 7.4) Cranes: 1x5t	**1 oil engine** driving 1 FP propeller Total Power: 552kW (750hp) 10.5kn Hanshin 6L26BGSH 1 x 4 Stroke 6 Cy. 260 x 400 552kW (750bhp) Ssangyong Heavy Industries Co Ltd-South Korea AuxGen: 2 x 32kW 445V a.c
9151553 *MXAW7* -	**SAND FALCON** - **CEMEX UK Marine Ltd** - *Southampton* *United Kingdom* MMSI: 232215000 Official number: 900972	**6,534** 1,960 9,154	Class: BV (LR) ✠ Classed LR until 24/2/03	**1998-04 Merwede Shipyard BV — Hardinxveld** Yd No: 674 Lengthened-2003 Loa 120.20 Br ex 19.69 Dght 7.781 Lbp - Br md 19.50 Dpth 10.00 Welded, 1 dk	**(B33B2DT) Trailing Suction Hopper Dredger** Hopper: 5,022	**2 oil engines** with clutches, flexible couplings & sr geared to sc. shafts driving 2 CP propellers Total Power: 4,920kW (6,690hp) 12.5kn Wartsila 6R32E 2 x 4 Stroke 6 Cy. 320 x 350 each-2460kW (3345bhp) Wartsila NSD Finland Oy-Finland AuxGen: 2 x 1856kW 600V 50Hz a.c, 2 x 284kW 220/220V 50Hz a.c Thrusters: 1 Thwart. FP thruster (f) Fuel: 60.0 (d.f.)
8801498 *HO2914* -	**SAND FORTUNE** *ex* Tatsumi Maru No. 12 *-2002* *ex* Shoei Maru No. 18 *-1998* *ex* Manei Maru No. 8 *-1997* **Sand Fortune Enterprises Inc** - *Panama* *Panama* MMSI: 355296000 Official number: 3493109	**676** 203 933		**1988-03 Imamura Zosen — Kure** Yd No: 328 Loa 55.00 (BB) Br ex 11.71 Dght 4.020 Lbp 50.02 Br md 11.51 Dpth 4.14 Welded, 1 dk	**(A31A2GX) General Cargo Ship** Grain: 764 Compartments: 1 Ho, ER 1 Ha: ER	**1 oil engine** with clutches & reverse reduction geared to sc. shaft driving 1 FP propeller Total Power: 1,177kW (1,600hp) Yanmar MF33-DT 1 x 4 Stroke 6 Cy. 330 x 620 1177kW (1600bhp) Matsue Nainenki Kogyo-Japan Thrusters: 1 Thwart. FP thruster (f)
9174127 *MYTP4* -	**SAND FULMAR** - **British Dredging Ltd** CEMEX UK Marine Ltd *Cardiff* *United Kingdom* MMSI: 232003580 Official number: 901502	**5,307** 1,592 9,153	Class: LR ✠ **100A1** SS 09/2013 hopper dredger near continental trading area including Baltic Sea (20 degrees E, 57 degrees N) in ice free conditions at a draught of 7.78 metres service ✠ **LMC** **UMS** Eq.Ltr: Y; Cable: 522.5/48.0 U3	**1998-09 Merwede Shipyard BV — Hardinxveld** Yd No: 675 Loa 99.90 Br ex 19.60 Dght 7.780 Lbp 94.87 Br md 19.50 Dpth 10.00 Welded, 1 dk	**(B33B2DT) Trailing Suction Hopper Dredger** Hopper: 4,000	**2 oil engines** with clutches, flexible couplings & sr geared to sc. shafts driving 2 FP propellers Total Power: 4,920kW (6,690hp) 12.3kn Wartsila 6R32E 2 x 4 Stroke 6 Cy. 320 x 350 each-2460kW (3345bhp) Wartsila NSD Finland Oy-Finland AuxGen: 2 x 1972kW 690V 50Hz a.c, 2 x 250kW 400V 50Hz a.c Thrusters: 1 Thwart. FP thruster (f)
8900713 *MMVV5* -	**SAND HARRIER** - **CEMEX UK Marine Ltd** - SatCom: Inmarsat C 423200048 *Southampton* *United Kingdom* MMSI: 232704000 Official number: 719485	**3,751** 1,125 5,916 T/cm 14.3	Class: BV (LR) ✠ Classed LR until 26/1/99	**1990-11 BV Scheepswerf & Mfbk 'De Merwede' v/h van Vliet & Co — Hardinxveld** Yd No: 656 Loa 99.00 (BB) Br ex 16.50 Dght 6.560 Lbp 94.50 Br md 16.30 Dpth 8.60 Welded, 1 dk	**(B33B2DT) Trailing Suction Hopper Dredger** Hopper: 2,500	**1 oil engine** with flexible couplings & sr geared to sc. shaft driving 1 CP propeller Total Power: 3,879kW (5,274hp) 11.5kn Mirrlees KMR8MK3 1 x 4 Stroke 8 Cy. 400 x 457 3879kW (5274bhp) Mirrlees Blackstone (Stockport)Ltd.-Stockport AuxGen: 1 x 3200kW 660V 50Hz a.c, 1 x 625kW 415V 50Hz a.c, 1 x 110kW 415V 50Hz a.c Thrusters: 1 Thwart. FP thruster (f) Fuel: 236.0 (d.f.) 14.2pd
8900701 *MLSA4* -	**SAND HERON** - **CEMEX UK Marine Ltd** - SatCom: Inmarsat C 423200033 *Southampton* *United Kingdom* MMSI: 232626000 Official number: 719215	**3,751** 1,125 5,916 T/cm 14.3	Class: LR ✠ **100A1** SS 05/2010 hopper dredger near continental trading area including Baltic Sea (20 degrees E, 57 degrees N) in ice free conditions at a draught of 6.56 metres limited to 15 nm from land at a draught of 7.02 metres service ✠ **LMC** **UMS** Eq.Ltr: V; Cable: 496.0/42.0 U3	**1990-05 BV Scheepswerf & Mfbk 'De Merwede' v/h van Vliet & Co — Hardinxveld** Yd No: 655 Loa 99.00 Br ex 16.50 Dght 6.540 Lbp 94.50 Br md 16.30 Dpth 8.60 Welded, 1 dk	**(B33B2DT) Trailing Suction Hopper Dredger** Hopper: 2,500	**1 oil engine** with flexible couplings & sr geared to sc. shaft driving 1 CP propeller Total Power: 3,875kW (5,268hp) 11.5kn Mirrlees KMR8MK3 1 x 4 Stroke 8 Cy. 400 x 457 3875kW (5268bhp) Mirrlees Blackstone (Stockport)Ltd.-Stockport AuxGen: 1 x 3200kW 660V 50Hz a.c, 1 x 624kW 415V 50Hz a.c, 1 x 110kW 415V 50Hz a.c Thrusters: 1 Thwart. FP thruster (f) Fuel: 236.0 (d.f.) 14.2pd
7307251 *WY2625* -	**SAND ISLAND** *ex* First Captain Kim *-2001* *ex* Mr. Kiffe *-2001* **Boat Mr Kiffe Inc** - *Houma, LA* *United States of America* Official number: 507164	*135* 92 -		**1967 Duet Marine Service — Galliano, La** L reg 21.58 Br ex 6.86 Dght - Lbp - Br md - Dpth 3.51 Welded, 1 dk	**(B11B2FV) Fishing Vessel**	**1 oil engine** driving 1 FP propeller Total Power: 279kW (379hp)
7216426 *HQVO3* -	**SAND ISLAND II** *ex* Four Point X *-1997* *ex* Ocean Diver I *-1981* *ex* Rio Service *-1977* **Adendy Transportation S de RL** - *Roatan* *Honduras* Official number: U-0326771	*392* 240 -		**1968 Burton Shipyard Co., Inc. — Port Arthur, Tx** Yd No: 427 Converted From: Offshore Supply Ship Loa 50.30 Br ex 11.61 Dght 3.406 Lbp 47.33 Br md 11.59 Dpth 3.97 Welded, 1 dk	**(B11B2FV) Fishing Vessel**	**2 oil engines** driving 2 FP propellers Total Power: 1,250kW (1,700hp) 11.0kn Caterpillar D398B 2 x Vee 4 Stroke 12 Cy. 153 x 203 each-625kW (850bhp) Caterpillar Tractor Co-USA
8744987 - -	**SAND LAUNCE** - **S & M Enterprises Ltd** - *St John's, NL* *Canada* Official number: 348705	**144** 108 -		**1975-01 Marystown Shipping Enterprises Ltd — Marystown NL** L reg 18.64 Br ex - Dght - Lbp - Br md 6.71 Dpth 3.35 Welded, 1 dk	**(B11B2FV) Fishing Vessel**	**1 oil engine** reduction geared to sc. shaft driving 1 Propeller Total Power: 515kW (700hp) 10.0kn
9197246 *JM6595* -	**SAND No. 1** - **Sand Kogyo KK** - *Iki, Nagasaki* *Japan* Official number: 135477	*1,599* - 3,500		**1998-06 K.K. Watanabe Zosensho — Nagasaki** Yd No: 065 Loa 83.27 (BB) Br ex - Dght 5.500 Lbp 75.00 Br md 17.20 Dpth 7.80 Welded, 1 dk	**(B33A2DU) Dredger (unspecified)** Grain: 2,204 Compartments: 1 Ho, ER 1 Ha: (26.7 x 10.0)ER	**2 oil engines** driving 2 FP propellers Total Power: 2,206kW (3,000hp) 11.8kn Mitsubishi S6U-MTK 2 x 4 Stroke 6 Cy. 240 x 260 each-1103kW (1500bhp) Mitsubishi Heavy Industries Ltd-Japan AuxGen: 1 x 1040kW a.c, 1 x 160kW a.c, 1 x 80kW a.c Fuel: 68.0 (d.f.) 10.2pd
9351440 *V7DA7* -	**SAND SHINER** *ex* Hellespont Prosperity *-2014* **Sand Shiner Solutions Inc** Hellespont Ship Management GmbH & Co KG *Majuro* *Marshall Islands* MMSI: 538005358 Official number: 5358	**42,010** 22,444 73,715 T/cm 67.1	Class: AB	**2006-12 New Century Shipbuilding Co Ltd — Jingjiang JS** Yd No: 0307336 Loa 228.60 (BB) Br ex 32.29 Dght 14.520 Lbp 219.70 Br md 32.26 Dpth 20.80 Welded, 1 dk	**(A13B2TP) Products Tanker** Double Hull (13F) Liq: 81,300; Liq (Oil): 81,300 Cargo Heating Coils Compartments: 12 Wing Ta, ER, 2 Wing Slop Ta 3 Cargo Pump (s): 3x2300m³/hr Manifold: Bow/CM: 113.5m	**1 oil engine** driving 1 FP propeller Total Power: 11,300kW (15,363hp) 14.0kn MAN-B&W 5S60MC-C 1 x 2 Stroke 5 Cy. 600 x 2400 11300kW (15363bhp) Hudong Heavy Machinery Co Ltd-China AuxGen: 3 x 900kW a.c Fuel: 205.7 (d.f.) 1749.3 (r.f.) 50.6pd

5310709 *GHTK* -	**SAND SNIPE** - **D G W Sand Co Ltd** - *Southampton* *United Kingdom* Official number: 303366	*517* 176 691	Class: (LR) ✠ Classed LR until 28/4/93	**1961**-10 **J. Bolson & Son Ltd. — Poole** Yd No: 538 Loa 52.89 Br ex 9.25 Dght 3.512 Lbp 48.67 Br md 9.14 Dpth 3.97 Riveted\Welded, 1 dk	**(B33A2DS) Suction Dredger** Hopper: 350	**1 oil engine** driving 1 FP propeller Total Power: 434kW (590hp) Crossley HGN6 1 x 2 Stroke 6 Cy. 267 x 343 434kW (590bhp) Crossley Bros. Ltd.-Manchester
6913510 *LYTH* -	**SAND SWAN** - - - *Klaipeda* *Lithuania* MMSI: 277434000 Official number: 834	**1,204** 361 1,944	Class: (LR) ✠ Classed LR until 26/2/10	**1970**-03 **J. Bolson & Son Ltd. — Poole** Yd No: 565 Loa 66.60 Br ex 12.53 Dght 4.401 Lbp 62.79 Br md 12.19 Dpth 5.11 Welded, 1 dk	**(B33A2DS) Suction Dredger** Grain: 775; Hopper: 773	**1 oil engine** sr geared to sc. shaft driving 1 FP propeller Total Power: 861kW (1,171hp) 10.0kn Paxman 8YLCM 1 x Vee 4 Stroke 8 Cy. 248 x 267 861kW (1171bhp) Davey, Paxman & Co. Ltd.-Colchester AuxGen: 2 x 128kW 440V 50Hz a.c
8326981 *HP9219* -	**SAND TROOPER** *ex* Pertuis *-1998* **Cantabrian Shipping Inc** Salveg Savare *Panama* *Panama* MMSI: 355834000 Official number: 2629999A	**995** 298 1,669	Class: (BV)	**1983 IMC — Tonnay-Charente** Yd No: 300 Loa 62.11 Br ex - Dght 3.920 Lbp 58.50 Br md 13.01 Dpth 5.11 Welded, 1 dk	**(B33B2DS) Suction Hopper Dredger** Hopper: 720	**2 oil engines** reduction geared to sc. shafts driving 2 FP propellers Total Power: 970kW (1,318hp) 11.0kn Poyaud A12150SRHM 2 x Vee 4 Stroke 12 Cy. 150 x 180 each-485kW (659bhp) Societe Surgerienne de ConstructionMecaniques-France
7340899 *A9D3239* -	**SAND WEAVER** - **Sea Shore & Services SPC** - *Bahrain* *Bahrain* MMSI: 408564000 Official number: BN7007	**3,497** 1,049 5,271	Class: BV (Class contemplated) LR ✠ **100A1** SS 10/2008 sand carrier near Continental trading area ✠ **LMC** **UMS** Eq.Ltr: T; Cable: U2	**1975**-05 **Ferguson Bros (Port Glasgow) Ltd — Port Glasgow** Yd No: 468 Loa 96.40 Br ex 16.74 Dght 6.109 Lbp 91.50 Br md 16.30 Dpth 7.80 Welded, 1 dk	**(B33A2DS) Suction Dredger** Hopper: 2,300	**1 oil engine** sr geared to sc. shaft driving 1 CP propeller Total Power: 3,530kW (4,799hp) 12.0kn Mirrlees KMR-8 1 x 4 Stroke 8 Cy. 381 x 457 3530kW (4799bhp) Mirrlees Blackstone (Stockport)Ltd.-Stockport AuxGen: 1 x 284kW 440V 50Hz a.c Thrusters: 1 Thwart. FP thruster (f)
8630356 *HO2421* -	**SAND WIND** *ex* Tamayoshi Maru No. 8 *-2003* **Sand Wind Enterprise SA** - *Panama* *Panama* Official number: 3496910	**573** 172 698		**1986**-09 **K.K. Saidaiji Zosensho — Okayama** Loa 48.20 Br ex 10.00 Dght 3.670 Lbp 44.80 Br md 9.98 Dpth 3.75 Welded, 1 dk	**(B33A2DG) Grab Dredger**	**1 oil engine** driving 1 FP propeller Total Power: 662kW (900hp) 10.0kn Hanshin 6LU28G 1 x 4 Stroke 6 Cy. 280 x 440 662kW (900bhp) The Hanshin Diesel Works Ltd-Japan
9083201 *UBFK* -	**SANDAL** - **CJSC 'Armator'** CJSC 'Onegoship' *St Petersburg* *Russia* MMSI: 273418060	**1,596** 831 2,300	Class: RS	**1993**-10 **TOO Onega Arminius Shipbuilders — Petrozavodsk** Yd No: 10523/001 Loa 81.20 Br ex 11.40 Dght 4.250 Lbp 77.40 Br md 11.30 Dpth 5.40 Welded, 1 dk	**(A31A2GX) General Cargo Ship** Grain: 2,945 TEU 72 C.Ho 48/20' C/Dk 24/20' Compartments: 1 Ho, ER 1 Ha: (50.4 x 9.0)ER	**1 oil engine** reduction geared to sc. shaft driving 1 FP propeller Total Power: 1,000kW (1,360hp) 11.0kn MaK 6M332C 1 x 4 Stroke 6 Cy. 240 x 330 1000kW (1360bhp) Krupp MaK Maschinenbau GmbH-Kiel AuxGen: 2 x 322kW 380V 50Hz a.c Thrusters: 1 Thwart. FP thruster (f) Fuel: 93.0 (d.f.) 4.6pd
8948868 - -	**SANDAL 1** *ex* Liao Yu 847 *-1992* - -	**198** 70 -		**1988 Dalian Fishing Vessel Co — Dalian LN** L reg 38.56 Br ex - Dght - Lbp - Br md 7.60 Dpth 3.80 Welded, 1 dk	**(B11B2FV) Fishing Vessel**	**1 oil engine** geared to sc. shaft driving 1 FP propeller Total Power: 441kW (600hp) 11.7kn Chinese Std. Type 8300 1 x 4 Stroke 8 Cy. 300 x 380 441kW (600bhp) Dalian Fishing Vessel Co-China
8948870 - -	**SANDAL 2** *ex* Liao Yu 848 *-1992* - -	**198** 70 -		**1988 Dalian Fishing Vessel Co — Dalian LN** L reg 38.56 Br ex - Dght - Lbp - Br md 7.60 Dpth 3.80 Welded, 1 dk	**(B11B2FV) Fishing Vessel**	**1 oil engine** geared to sc. shaft driving 1 FP propeller Total Power: 441kW (600hp) 11.7kn Chinese Std. Type 8300 1 x 4 Stroke 8 Cy. 300 x 380 441kW (600bhp) Dalian Fishing Vessel Co-China
8948882 - -	**SANDAL 3** *ex* Liao Yu 849 *-1992* - -	**198** 70 -		**1991 Dalian Fishing Vessel Co — Dalian LN** L reg 38.56 Br ex - Dght - Lbp - Br md 7.60 Dpth 3.80 Welded, 1 dk	**(B11B2FV) Fishing Vessel**	**1 oil engine** geared to sc. shaft driving 1 FP propeller Total Power: 441kW (600hp) 11.7kn Chinese Std. Type 8300 1 x 4 Stroke 8 Cy. 300 x 380 441kW (600bhp) Dalian Fishing Vessel Co-China
8948894 - -	**SANDAL 4** *ex* Liao Yu 850 *-1992* - -	**198** 70 -		**1991 Dalian Fishing Vessel Co — Dalian LN** L reg 38.56 Br ex - Dght - Lbp - Br md 7.60 Dpth 3.80 Welded, 1 dk	**(B11B2FV) Fishing Vessel**	**1 oil engine** geared to sc. shaft driving 1 FP propeller Total Power: 441kW (600hp) 11.7kn Chinese Std. Type 8300 1 x 4 Stroke 8 Cy. 300 x 380 441kW (600bhp) Dalian Fishing Vessel Co-China
7853688 - -	**SANDD MARINE NO. 9** *ex* Metrikurnia *-1998* *ex* Tuck Lee Hang No. 2 *-1998* *ex* SPHB 501 *-1997* *ex* Doun Maru No. 501 *-1997* **Sand Marine International Pte Ltd** - *San Lorenzo* *Honduras* Official number: L-0326307	**288** 108 500		**1962 Shikoku Dockyard Co. Ltd. — Takamatsu** Yd No: 620 Loa 44.00 Br ex - Dght 3.301 Lbp 40.01 Br md 8.01 Dpth 4.02 Welded, 1 dk	**(A24D2BA) Aggregates Carrier**	**1 oil engine** driving 1 FP propeller Total Power: 368kW (500hp) 8.0kn
7411818 *DVDU* -	**SANDECOR** - **Aras-Asan Timber Co** - *Cebu* *Philippines* Official number: S0019	*697* 388 1,400		**1975**-12 **Sandoval Shipyards Inc. — Consolacion** Yd No: 1 Loa 53.01 Br ex 10.65 Dght 4.201 Lbp 50.27 Br md 10.43 Dpth 5.03 Welded, 1 dk	**(A31A2GX) General Cargo Ship**	**2 oil engines** reverse reduction geared to sc. shafts driving 2 FP propellers Total Power: 354kW (482hp) Yanmar 6KDAL-T 2 x 4 Stroke 6 Cy. 145 x 170 each-177kW (241bhp) Yanmar Diesel Engine Co Ltd-Japan
8667347 *SLVJ* GG-781	**SANDEFJORD** - **Sandefjord Fiske AB** - *Foto* *Sweden* MMSI: 266150000	**155** 46 -		**2000 O-varvet AB — Ockero** Yd No: 112 Loa 21.96 Br ex - Dght - Lbp - Br md 6.67 Dpth - Welded, 1 dk	**(B11B2FV) Fishing Vessel**	**1 oil engine** driving 1 Propeller
8747109 *OZGZ2* -	**SANDER 2** *ex* Bremerhaven *-2011* **CT Offshore AS** - *Klintebjerg* *Denmark (DIS)* MMSI: 219015793 Official number: D4533	**258** 77 58	Class: GL	**1983**-12 **Fr Schweers Schiffs- und Bootswerft GmbH & Co KG — Berne** Yd No: 6458 Converted From: Patrol Vessel-2011 Loa 38.40 Br ex - Dght 1.950 Lbp 34.58 Br md 7.80 Dpth 3.90 Welded, 1 dk	**(B31A2SR) Research Survey Vessel** Hull Material: Aluminium Alloy A-frames: 1x4t	**3 oil engines** reduction geared to sc. shaft driving 2 Water jets Total Power: 2,649kW (3,603hp) 14.5kn MWM TBD604BV12 3 x Vee 4 Stroke 12 Cy. 170 x 195 each-883kW (1201bhp) Motoren Werke Mannheim AG (MWM)-West Germany Thrusters: 1 Tunnel thruster (f)
9176539 *LJBC* M-66-HO	**SANDER ANDRE** *ex* Vestbas *-2013* **Mirsel AS** - *Svolvaer* *Norway* MMSI: 259478000	**467** 177 -	Class: NV	**1997**-12 **Voldnes Skipsverft AS — Fosnavaag** Yd No: 55 Lengthened-2009 Loa 33.47 (BB) Br ex - Dght 4.325 Lbp 30.25 Br md 9.00 Dpth 4.50 Welded, 1 dk	**(B11B2FV) Fishing Vessel**	**1 oil engine** reduction geared to sc. shaft driving 1 CP propeller Total Power: 1,104kW (1,501hp) 11.5kn Caterpillar 3512TA 1 x Vee 4 Stroke 12 Cy. 170 x 190 1104kW (1501bhp) Caterpillar Inc-USA AuxGen: 1 x 500kW 220/380V 50Hz a.c, 1 x 400kW 220/380V 50Hz a.c Thrusters: 1 Thwart. FP thruster (f); 1 Tunnel thruster (a)
8514514 *LNYZ* T-251-T	**SANDER ANDRE II** *ex* Tjeldoy *-2013* *ex* Solvaerskjaer 2 *-2009* *ex* Solvaerskjaer *-2009* *ex* Einar Erlend *-2001* **Mirsel AS** - *Svolvaer* *Norway* MMSI: 257435500	**278** 111 -		**1985**-04 **Herfjord Slip & Verksted AS — Revsnes i Fosna** (Hull) **1985**-04 **Solstrand Slip & Baatbyggeri AS — Tomrefjord** Yd No: 40 Loa 27.75 Br ex - Dght - Lbp - Br md 8.60 Dpth - Welded, 1 dk	**(B11B2FV) Fishing Vessel**	**1 oil engine** geared to sc. shaft driving 1 FP propeller Total Power: 397kW (540hp) 10.0kn Caterpillar 3412TA 1 x Vee 4 Stroke 12 Cy. 137 x 152 397kW (540bhp) Caterpillar Tractor Co-USA Thrusters: 1 Thwart. FP thruster (f); 1 Tunnel thruster (a)

IMO No. / Call sign	Ship / Owner	Tonnage	Class	Builder / Dimensions	Type	Machinery
9409481 *ZCTI7* -	**SANDERLING ACE** **FGL Lotus (Cayman) Ltd** MOL Ship Management Singapore Pte Ltd *George Town* *Cayman Islands (British)* MMSI: 319913000 Official number: 740067	**58,685** 18,167 18,865	Class: NK	**2007**-06 **Minaminippon Shipbuilding Co Ltd — Usuki OT** Yd No: 705 Loa 199.95 (BB) Br ex - Dght 9.816 Lbp 190.00 Br md 32.26 Dpth 14.70 Welded, 12 dks	**(A35B2RV) Vehicles Carrier** Side door/ramp (s) Quarter stern door/ramp (s. a.) Cars: 6,237	**1 oil engine** driving 1 FP propeller Total Power: 15,130kW (20,571hp) 20.7kn MAN-B&W 7S60MC-C 1 x 2 Stroke 7 Cy. 600 x 2400 15130kW (20571bhp) Mitsui Engineering & Shipbuilding CLtd-Japan AuxGen: 4 x 975kW a.c Thrusters: 1 Tunnel thruster (f) Fuel: 2660.0
6829795 *3BQF* -	**SANDERUS** **Codralux SA** - *Port Louis* *Mauritius* MMSI: 645273000	**4,970** 1,422 5,080	Class: BV	**1968**-06 **NV Scheepsbouwwerf & Machinefabriek 'De Klop' — Sliedrecht** Yd No: C0585 Loa 103.00 Br ex 18.32 Dght 7.751 Lbp 95.00 Br md - Dpth 10.01 Welded, 1 dk	**(B33B2DT) Trailing Suction Hopper Dredger** Hopper: 5,300	**2 oil engines** driving 2 FP propellers Total Power: 4,222kW (5,740hp) 12.5kn MAN 2 x 4 Stroke 9 Cy. 450 x 660 each-2111kW (2870bhp) Smit Kinderdijk Vof-Netherlands Fuel: 604.0 (d.f.)
8012085 *FKHI* FC 716999	**SANDETTIE** *ex Johanna Maria -1994* **Jaczon BV** - SatCom: Inmarsat C 422730311 *Fecamp* *France* MMSI: 227303000 Official number: 716999	**2,068** 830 1,890	Class: NV (LR) ✠ Classed LR until 3/6/13	**1981**-07 **Scheepswerf en Mfbk. Ysselwerf B.V. — Capelle a/d IJssel** Yd No: 200 Lengthened-1994 Loa 86.25 (BB) Br ex 12.73 Dght 5.230 Lbp 78.76 Br md 12.51 Dpth 8.01 Welded, 2 dks	**(B11A2FS) Stern Trawler** Compartments: 1 Ho, ER 1 Ha: ER	**1 oil engine** sr geared to sc. shaft driving 1 CP propeller Total Power: 2,940kW (3,997hp) 13.5kn MaK 8M453AK 1 x 4 Stroke 8 Cy. 320 x 420 2940kW (3997bhp) Krupp MaK Maschinenbau GmbH-Kiel AuxGen: 1 x 380V 50Hz a.c, 1 x 380V 50Hz a.c, 1 x 380V 50Hz a.c Boilers: TOH (o.f.) 10.2kgf/cm² (10.0bar), TOH (ex.g.) 10.2kgf/cm² (10.0bar) Fuel: 112.0 (d.f.) 345.5 (r.f.) 10.0pd
9214018 *PCCJ* -	**SANDETTIE** **CV Scheepvaartonderneming Sandettie** Wagenborg Shipping BV *Harlingen* *Netherlands* MMSI: 244054000 Official number: 37879	**2,088** 1,168 2,934	Class: BV	**2004**-08 **Ceskoslovenska Plavba Labska a.s. (CSPL) — Decin (Hull)** **2004**-08 **Scheepswerf Peters B.V. — Kampen** Yd No: 474 Loa 88.95 Br ex - Dght 4.340 Lbp 86.34 Br md 12.50 Dpth 5.65 Welded, 1 dk	**(A31A2GX) General Cargo Ship** Grain: 4,559 TEU 102 Compartments: 1 Ho, ER 1 Ha: ER (62.4 x 10.2) Ice Capable	**1 oil engine** geared to sc. shaft driving 1 FP propeller Total Power: 1,440kW (1,958hp) Wartsila 8L20 1 x 4 Stroke 8 Cy. 200 x 280 1440kW (1958bhp) Wartsila Nederland BV-Netherlands
6602496 *OZ2012* -	**SANDFRAKT** *ex Floyen -1988 ex Torshammer -1979* **P/F Sandgrevstur** - *Fuglafjordur* *Faeroes (FAS)* MMSI: 231059000 Official number: D3211	**299** 132 575	Class: BV	**1966** **Sonderborg Skibsvaerft A/S — Sonderborg** Yd No: 47 Loa 47.12 Br ex 8.82 Dght 3.412 Lbp 42.14 Br md 8.81 Dpth - Welded, 1 dk	**(A31A2GX) General Cargo Ship** Grain: 669; Bale: 592 Compartments: 1 Ho, ER 1 Ha: (21.0 x 5.0)ER Derricks: 2x3t; Winches: 2 Ice Capable	**1 oil engine** driving 1 CP propeller Total Power: 368kW (500hp) 10.0kn Alpha 405-26VO 1 x 2 Stroke 5 Cy. 260 x 400 368kW (500bhp) (new engine 1970) Alpha Diesel A/S-Denmark Fuel: 48.0 (d.f.)
9309186 *SGEF* -	**SANDHAMN** **Waxholms Angfartygs AB** - *Vaxholm* *Sweden* MMSI: 265547830 Official number: 181204	**686** 218 68		**2004**-12 **Moen Slip AS — Kolvereid** Yd No: 60 Loa 39.80 Br ex 10.46 Dght 2.850 Lbp 37.20 Br md 10.30 Dpth 4.40 Welded, 1 dk	**(A37B2PS) Passenger Ship** Passengers: unberthed: 350 Ice Capable	**4 oil engines** belt drive & geared to sc. shafts driving 2 Directional propellers twin propellers Total Power: 1,324kW (1,800hp) 12.0kn Volvo Penta D12 4 x 4 Stroke 6 Cy. 131 x 150 each-331kW (450bhp) AB Volvo Penta-Sweden AuxGen: 2 x 225kW 400/230V 50Hz a.c Thrusters: 1 Thwart. FP thruster (f) Fuel: 25.0 (d.f.)
6815976 *OWTH* -	**SANDHOLM** *ex Inger Sten -2006 ex Aluk -2006* *ex Stevns Hoj -1986 ex Rigger Stevns -1984* *ex Argonaut R -1980 ex Bredgrund -1976* **Flintholm Sten & Grus ApS** JMB Bjerrum & Jensen ApS *Svendborg* *Denmark* MMSI: 219002493 Official number: H1658	**349** 104 500	Class: (BV)	**1968** **Scheepswerf Vooruit B.V. — Zaandam** Yd No: 319 Loa 44.61 Br ex - Dght 3.302 Lbp 41.61 Br md 8.60 Dpth 3.51 Welded, 1 dk	**(B33A2DS) Suction Dredger** Hopper: 325 Compartments: 1 Ho, ER 1 Ha: (12.1 x 8.5)ER Derricks: 1x3.5t; Winches: 1 Ice Capable	**1 oil engine** driving 1 CP propeller Total Power: 441kW (600hp) 9.7kn Alpha 406-26VO 1 x 2 Stroke 6 Cy. 260 x 400 441kW (600bhp) (new engine 1990) MAN B&W Diesel A/S-Denmark AuxGen: 1 x 110V d.c Thrusters: 1 Thwart. FP thruster (f)
8740242 *PMLS* -	**SANDI PERKASA** **PT Sandi Adi Perkasa** - *Pontianak* *Indonesia*	**396** 174 -	Class: KI	**2008** **CV Sarana Kapuas — Pontianak** Loa 42.00 Br ex - Dght 3.090 Lbp 41.00 Br md 9.00 Dpth 3.90 Welded, 1 dk	**(A13B2TU) Tanker (unspecified)**	**2 oil engines** driving 2 Propellers Total Power: 596kW (810hp) Cummins NTA-855-M 2 x 4 Stroke 6 Cy. 140 x 152 each-298kW (405bhp) Cummins Engine Co Inc-USA
9024683 *YD3130* -	**SANDIA II** *ex Yokota Maru No. 18 -2001* *ex Tsuru Maru No. 18 -2001* **PT Buana Sandia Lestari** - *Dumai* *Indonesia*	**115** 69 -	Class: KI	**1972**-08 **Higo Zosen — Kumamoto** Loa 26.80 Br ex - Dght - Lbp 24.00 Br md 6.80 Dpth 2.80 Welded, 1 dk	**(B32A2ST) Tug**	**1 oil engine** geared to sc. shaft driving 1 Propeller Total Power: 883kW (1,201hp) Niigata 6MG25BX 1 x 4 Stroke 6 Cy. 250 x 320 883kW (1201bhp) Niigata Engineering Co Ltd-Japan AuxGen: 2 x 12kW 110V a.c
9024695 *YD3137* -	**SANDIA III** *ex Kaiko Maru No. 18 -2001* **PT Buana Sandia Lestari** - *Dumai* *Indonesia*	**126** 75 -	Class: KI	**1977**-08 **Kumamoto Dock K.K. — Yatsushiro** Loa 26.00 Br ex - Dght - Lbp 23.15 Br md 7.00 Dpth 3.00 Welded, 1 dk	**(B32A2ST) Tug**	**1 oil engine** driving 1 Propeller Total Power: 736kW (1,001hp) Hanshin 6LUD26G 1 x 4 Stroke 6 Cy. 260 x 440 736kW (1001bhp) The Hanshin Diesel Works Ltd-Japan AuxGen: 2 x 56kW 225V a.c
6823375 *YD3165* -	**SANDIA IV** *ex Dokai Maru No. 5 -2002 ex Dokai -1985* *ex Junei Maru No. 2 -1985* **PT Buana Sandia Lestari** - *Dumai* *Indonesia*	*155* 47 -	Class: KI	**1968**-07 **Kanmon Zosen K.K. — Shimonoseki** Yd No: 283 Loa 26.80 Br ex 7.62 Dght 2.591 Lbp 24.21 Br md 7.60 Dpth 3.41 Welded, 1 dk	**(B32A2ST) Tug**	**2 oil engines** geared to sc. shafts driving 2 FP propellers Total Power: 1,206kW (1,640hp) 8.3kn Daihatsu 6PSHTM-26D 2 x 4 Stroke 6 Cy. 260 x 320 each-603kW (820bhp) (made 1967) Daihatsu Kogyo-Japan AuxGen: 2 x 20kW 225V a.c
7300019 *YD4818* -	**SANDIDEWA 5** *ex Kuala Raja I -2001 ex Chuan Light -1984* *ex Waka Maru No. 12 -1980* **PT Pelayaran Sandidewa Samudera** - *Jakarta* *Indonesia*	**160** 48 -	Class: (KI) (GL) (NK)	**1971**-07 **Asahi Zosen K.K. — Sumoto** Yd No: 108 L reg 30.50 Br ex 7.01 Dght 2.848 Lbp 29.00 Br md 7.00 Dpth 3.40 Welded, 1 dk	**(B32A2ST) Tug**	**1 oil engine** driving 1 FP propeller Total Power: 956kW (1,300hp) 10.0kn Otsuka SODHS6A30 1 x 4 Stroke 6 Cy. 300 x 460 956kW (1300bhp) KK Otsuka Diesel-Japan AuxGen: 1 x 17kW 220V a.c Fuel: 51.0
7428366 *YD4819* -	**SANDIDEWA 7** *ex Bali I -2001 ex Kay Chuan XI -1984* *ex Sunlight Alice -1976* **PT Pelayaran Indonesia Sejahtera** - *Jakarta* *Indonesia*	**110** 66 -	Class: (KI) (AB)	**1974**-01 **Sing Koon Seng Pte Ltd — Singapore** Yd No: LY154 Loa 22.56 Br ex 6.41 Dght 2.720 Lbp 21.34 Br md 6.40 Dpth 3.78 Welded, 1 dk	**(B32A2ST) Tug**	**2 oil engines** reverse reduction geared to sc. shafts driving 2 FP propellers Total Power: 588kW (800hp) Deutz BF8M716 2 x 4 Stroke 6 Cy. 135 x 160 each-294kW (400bhp) Kloeckner Humboldt Deutz AG-West Germany AuxGen: 2 x 20kW Fuel: 60.0 (d.f.)
7742188 *YCLE* -	**SANDIDEWA 11** *ex Mutiara V -1988 ex Kay Chuan V -1978* *ex Poly Bay -1978* **PT Pelayaran Sandidewa Samudera** - *Jakarta* *Indonesia*	**157** 48 236	Class: KI (NK)	**1945** **Tampa Marine Corp — Tampa FL** Loa 26.65 Br ex 7.05 Dght 2.472 Lbp 23.59 Br md 6.98 Dpth 2.95 Welded, 1 dk	**(B32A2ST) Tug**	**1 oil engine** geared to sc. shaft driving 1 FP propeller Total Power: 883kW (1,201hp) 10.0kn Yanmar 6GA-ET 1 x 4 Stroke 6 Cy. 240 x 290 883kW (1201bhp) (, fitted 1978) Yanmar Diesel Engine Co Ltd-Japan
8848616 *YD4491* -	**SANDIDEWA 13** *ex STU III -1997* **PT Pelayaran Sandidewa Samudera** - *Jambi* *Indonesia*	**113** 67 -	Class: KI (GL)	**1989**-04 **Guangdong Jiangmen Shipyard — Jiangmen GD** L reg 22.13 Br ex - Dght 3.020 Lbp 21.98 Br md 6.80 Dpth 3.60 Welded, 1 dk	**(B32A2ST) Tug**	**1 oil engine** sr reverse geared to sc. shaft driving 1 FP propeller Total Power: 941kW (1,279hp) 9.0kn Caterpillar 3512TA 1 x Vee 4 Stroke 12 Cy. 170 x 190 941kW (1279bhp) (made 1987) Caterpillar Inc-USA AuxGen: 1 x 20kW 220/380V a.c

IMO / Call sign	Name / Former names / Owner / Port	Tonnage	Class	Builder / Dimensions	Type / Cargo	Machinery
9040027 *YD4490* -	**SANDIDEWA 15** *ex* STU I *-1996* *ex* Wah Hong 2 *-1990* **PT Pelayaran Sandidewa Samudera** - *Jambi* *Indonesia*	**142** 85 -	Class: KI (GL)	**1990-12 Guangdong New China Shipyard Co Ltd — Dongguan GD** L reg 25.20 Br ex - Dght 2.899 Lbp 23.88 Br md 6.80 Dpth 3.81 Welded, 1 dk	**(B32A2ST) Tug**	**1 oil engine** reverse reduction geared to sc. shaft driving 1 FP propeller Total Power: 691kW (939hp) 11.5kn Cummins KTA-38-M 1 x Vee 4 Stroke 12 Cy. 159 x 159 691kW (939bhp) Cummins Engine Co Inc-USA
8935500 *YD4495* -	**SANDIDEWA 17** *ex* STU VII *-1997* *ex* Java Seahawk *-1997* *ex* TS 23-2 *-1991* **PT Pelayaran Sandidewa Samudera** - *Jambi* *Indonesia*	*179* 107 -	Class: KI (BV)	**1991 Hangzhou Dongfeng Shipyard — Hangzhou ZJ** Yd No: 191 Loa 23.00 Br ex - Dght 3.250 Lbp 21.12 Br md 7.00 Dpth 3.55 Welded, 1 dk	**(B32A2ST) Tug**	**2 oil engines** geared to sc. shafts driving 2 FP propellers Total Power: 736kW (1,000hp) 10.0kn Caterpillar 3412TA 2 x Vee 4 Stroke 12 Cy. 137 x 152 each-368kW (500bhp) Caterpillar Inc-USA AuxGen: 2 x 64kW 220V 50Hz a.c
9052018 *YD4496* -	**SANDIDEWA 19** *ex* STU IX *-1997* *ex* TS 23-4 *-1991* **PT Pelayaran Sandidewa Samudera** - *Jambi* *Indonesia*	*123* 73 -	Class: KI (BV)	**1992-01 Hangzhou Dongfeng Shipyard — Hangzhou ZJ** Yd No: 199 L reg 23.45 Br ex - Dght 3.340 Lbp 21.12 Br md 7.00 Dpth 3.55 Welded	**(B32A2ST) Tug**	**2 oil engines** geared to sc. shafts driving 2 FP propellers Total Power: 740kW (1,006hp) 10.0kn Caterpillar 3412TA 2 x Vee 4 Stroke 12 Cy. 137 x 152 each-370kW (503bhp) Caterpillar Inc-USA Fuel: 95.0 (d.f.)
8924630 *YD4574* -	**SANDIDEWA 21** *ex* Luwi 1 *-2001* **PT Pelayaran Sandidewa Samudera** - *Jakarta* *Indonesia*	**137** 82 103	Class: KI (GL)	**1997-01 PT Nanindah Mutiara Shipyard — Batam** Yd No: T36 Loa 23.50 Br ex - Dght - Lbp 21.31 Br md 7.50 Dpth 3.10 Welded, 1 dk	**(B32A2ST) Tug**	**2 oil engines** reduction geared to sc. shafts driving 2 FP propellers Total Power: 956kW (1,300hp) 10.0kn Caterpillar 3412TA 2 x Vee 4 Stroke 12 Cy. 137 x 152 each-478kW (650bhp) Caterpillar Inc-USA AuxGen: 2 x 48kW 415V a.c Fuel: 92.0 (d.f.)
8924501 *YD4575* -	**SANDIDEWA 23** *ex* Luwi 3 *-2002* **PT Pelayaran Sandidewa Samudera** - *Jakarta* *Indonesia*	**137** 82 -	Class: KI (GL)	**1997-03 PT Nanindah Mutiara Shipyard — Batam** Yd No: T37 L reg 23.50 Br ex - Dght - Lbp 21.44 Br md 7.50 Dpth 3.10 Welded, 1 dk	**(B32A2ST) Tug**	**2 oil engines** reduction geared to sc. shafts driving 2 FP propellers Total Power: 956kW (1,300hp) 10.0kn Caterpillar 3412TA 2 x Vee 4 Stroke 12 Cy. 137 x 152 each-478kW (650bhp) Caterpillar Inc-USA
8933538 *YD4820* -	**SANDIDEWA 25** *ex* Luwi 5 *-2001* **PT Pelayaran Sandidewa Samudera** - *Jakarta* *Indonesia*	**137** 82 103	Class: KI (GL)	**1997-11 PT Nanindah Mutiara Shipyard — Batam** Yd No: T42 Loa 23.50 Br ex - Dght 2.490 Lbp 21.44 Br md 7.50 Dpth 3.10 Welded, 1 dk	**(B32A2ST) Tug**	**2 oil engines** reduction geared to sc. shafts driving 2 FP propellers Total Power: 956kW (1,300hp) 10.0kn Caterpillar 3412TA 2 x Vee 4 Stroke 12 Cy. 137 x 152 each-478kW (650bhp) (made 1996) Caterpillar Inc-USA AuxGen: 2 x 32kW 415V a.c Fuel: 92.0 (d.f.)
9680061 - -	**SANDIDEWA 27** - **PT Pelayaran Sandidewa Samudera** - *Jakarta* *Indonesia*	**256** 77 193	Class: NK	**2012-12 PT Palma Progress Shipyard — Batam** Yd No: 504 Loa 28.05 Br ex - Dght 3.312 Lbp 25.77 Br md 8.60 Dpth 4.30 Welded, 1 dk	**(B32A2ST) Tug**	**2 oil engines** reduction geared to sc. shaft (s) driving 2 FP propellers Total Power: 1,518kW (2,064hp) Mitsubishi S6R2-MTK3L 2 x 4 Stroke 6 Cy. 170 x 220 each-759kW (1032bhp) Mitsubishi Heavy Industries Ltd-Japan Fuel: 220.0
7123136 *HP8659* -	**SANDIE** *ex* Takenaka Maru No. 1 *-1994* **Sand Carrers Inc** - *Panama* *Panama* Official number: 25282PEXT	*260* 74 -		**1971 Shimoda Dockyard Co. Ltd. — Shimoda** Yd No: 190 L reg 29.00 Br ex 8.51 Dght 2.801 Lbp 26.50 Br md 8.49 Dpth 3.92 Welded, 2 dks	**(B32A2ST) Tug**	**2 oil engines** driving 2 FP propellers Total Power: 2,354kW (3,200hp) 14.0kn Hanshin 6LU35 2 x 4 Stroke 6 Cy. 350 x 550 each-1177kW (1600bhp) Hanshin Nainenki Kogyo-Japan
7392622 *YHHB* -	**SANDIKA** *ex* Essberger Pioneer *-2002* *ex* Alpha Lady *-1992* *ex* Ellen Essberger *-1986* *ex* Solvent Venturer *-1981* *ex* Essberger Pioneer *-1977* **PT Bahtera Kencana Adinusa** - *Jakarta* *Indonesia* MMSI: 525002048	**1,641** 754 2,456 T/cm 6.9	Class: (KI) (GL)	**1975-01 JG Hitzler Schiffswerft und Masch GmbH & Co KG — Lauenburg** Yd No: 745 Loa 77.12 Br ex 12.53 Dght 5.204 Lbp 72.01 Br md 12.50 Dpth 7.01 Welded, 1 dk.	**(A12A2TC) Chemical Tanker** Double Bottom Entire Compartment Length Liq: 2,731 Cargo Heating Coils Compartments: 12 Ta, ER 12 Cargo Pump (s): 12x77m³/hr Manifold: Bow/CM: 49m Ice Capable	**1 oil engine** driving 1 CP propeller Total Power: 1,324kW (1,800hp) 12.0kn MaK 6M452AK 1 x 4 Stroke 6 Cy. 320 x 450 1324kW (1800bhp) MaK Maschinenbau GmbH-Kiel AuxGen: 3 x 112kW 380V 60Hz a.c Fuel: 58.0 (d.f.) (Heating Coils) 175.5 (r.f.) 4.5pd
8947589 *YFKW* -	**SANDIKA KARYA** *ex* Shinko Maru *-1999* *ex* Nita I *-1993* *ex* Shotoku Maru *-1992* **PT Sapta Sandika Krida** - *Pontianak* *Indonesia*	*399* 247 644	Class: (KI)	**1975-09 Mategata Zosen K.K. — Namikata** Loa 54.00 Br ex - Dght 3.300 Lbp 49.00 Br md 9.00 Dpth 5.20 Welded, 1 dk	**(A31A2GX) General Cargo Ship** Grain: 1,305; Bale: 1,143 Compartments: 1 Ho, ER 1 Ha: (27.0 x 6.5)ER	**1 oil engine** driving 1 FP propeller Total Power: 552kW (750hp) 10.0kn Daihatsu 1 x 4 Stroke 552kW (750bhp) Daihatsu Diesel Manufacturing Co Lt-Japan
7008805 *ZR9411* -	**SANDILE** *ex* De Giosa T. *-2005* **Blue Continent Products Pty Ltd** - *Cape Town* *South Africa* Official number: 10410	**1,345** 403 874	Class: (RI) (GL)	**1970-03 Soc. Esercizio Cant. S.p.A. — Viareggio** Yd No: 569 Loa 73.18 Br ex 12.04 Dght 5.925 Lbp 62.82 Br md 12.02 Dpth 7.90 Welded, 2 dks	**(B11A2FS) Stern Trawler** Ins: 1,398 Compartments: 3 Ho, ER Cranes: 3x1.5t	**1 oil engine** driving 1 FP propeller Total Power: 2,133kW (2,900hp) 12.5kn MaK 8MU551AK 1 x 4 Stroke 8 Cy. 450 x 550 2133kW (2900bhp) Atlas MaK Maschinenbau GmbH-Kiel AuxGen: 3 x 264kW 220/380V 50Hz a.c
9441178 *H09773* -	**SANDINO** *ex* Cape Taura *-2009* **Tovase Development Corp** Caroil Transport Marine Ltd *Panama* *Panama* MMSI: 370921000 Official number: 4077609	**42,006** 22,454 73,719 T/cm 67.1	Class: LR (AB) **100A1** SS 03/2014 Double Hull oil tanker ESP *IWS LI **LMC** **UMS IGS**	**2009-03 New Times Shipbuilding Co Ltd — Jingjiang JS** Yd No: 0307354 Loa 228.60 (BB) Br ex 32.30 Dght 14.518 Lbp 219.70 Br md 32.26 Dpth 20.80 Welded, 1 dk	**(A12B2TR) Chemical/Products Tanker** Double Hull (13F) Liq: 78,168; Liq (Oil): 81,311 Compartments: 12 Wing Ta, 2 Wing Slop Ta, ER 3 Cargo Pump (s): 3x2300m³/hr Manifold: Bow/CM: 114.1m	**1 oil engine** driving 1 FP propeller Total Power: 11,300kW (15,363hp) 14.7kn MAN-B&W 5S60MC-C 1 x 2 Stroke 5 Cy. 600 x 2400 11300kW (15363bhp) Hudong Heavy Machinery Co Ltd-China AuxGen: 3 x 900kW a.c Fuel: 283.2 (d.f.) 2110.0 (r.f.)
9306029 *V2CJ4* -	**SANDNES** - **Partenreederei Hans-Jurgen Hartmann ms 'Sandnes'** HJH Shipmanagement GmbH & Co KG SatCom: Inmarsat C 430478310 *Saint John's* *Antigua & Barbuda* MMSI: 304783000 Official number: 4521	**17,357** 5,748 27,711	Class: GL	**2005-04 Daewoo-Mangalia Heavy Industries S.A. — Mangalia** (Hull) Yd No: 1044 **2005-04 J.J. Sietas KG Schiffswerft GmbH & Co. — Hamburg** Yd No: 1219 Loa 166.70 (BB) Br ex 24.75 Dght 10.500 Lbp 160.58 Br md 24.50 Dpth 14.00 Welded, 1 dk	**(A23A2BD) Bulk Carrier, Self-discharging** Double Bottom Entire Compartment Length Grain: 20,046 Compartments: 7 Ho, ER 7 Ha: (13.3 x 14.0)5 (14.7 x 14.0)ER (12.6 x 14.0)	**1 oil engine** reduction geared to sc. shaft driving 1 CP propeller Total Power: 7,300kW (9,925hp) 14.1kn MaK 8M43 1 x 4 Stroke 8 Cy. 430 x 610 7300kW (9925bhp) Caterpillar Motoren GmbH & Co. KG-Germany AuxGen: 1 x 1800kW 450/230V 60Hz a.c, 3 x 640kW 450/230V a.c Thrusters: 1 Tunnel thruster (f); 1 Thwart. CP thruster (a) Fuel: 233.0 (d.f.) 1022.0 (r.f.) 28.0pd
5310905 *LCFB* -	**SANDNES** *ex* Sjokurs *-2007* *ex* Gann *-1995* *ex* Vikingfjord *-1978* *ex* Sandnes *-1974* **Ryfylke Dampskibsselskab AS** - *Sandnes* *Norway* MMSI: 258126000	**1,432** 663 721	Class: (NV)	**1950-03 Nylands Verksted — Oslo** Yd No: 374 Converted From: General Cargo/Passenger Ship-2007 Loa 72.54 Br ex 11.00 Dght 4.801 Lbp 67.58 Br md 10.95 Dpth 6.96 Riveted\Welded, 2 dks, 3rd dk fwd	**(B34K2QT) Training Ship** Passengers: 550 Grain: 736; Bale: 696 Compartments: 2 Ho, ER 2 Ha: (6.0 x 2.9) (4.0 x 2.9) Derricks: 2x5t,2x3t; Winches: 4	**1 oil engine** driving 1 CP propeller Total Power: 1,324kW (1,800hp) 16.0kn Polar M66T 1 x 2 Stroke 6 Cy. 500 x 700 1324kW (1800bhp) Atlas Diesel AB-Sweden AuxGen: 2 x 120kW 220V d.c Fuel: 71.0 (d.f.) 6.0pd
8816194 *HSTA2* -	**SANDON 7** - **Port Authority of Thailand (Marine Department)** - *Bangkok* *Thailand* MMSI: 567035800 Official number: 331000086	*2,100* 1,995 3,510	Class: (BV)	**1989-12 Italthai Marine Co., Ltd. — Samut Prakan** Yd No: 75 Loa 77.00 Br ex 14.92 Dght 6.400 Lbp 70.93 Br md 14.60 Dpth 7.40 Welded, 1 dk	**(B33B2DT) Trailing Suction Hopper Dredger** Hopper: 2,500	**2 oil engines** geared to sc. shafts driving 2 FP propellers Total Power: 2,200kW (2,992hp) 11.0kn Yanmar T220L-ET 2 x 4 Stroke 6 Cy. 220 x 280 each-1100kW (1496bhp) Yanmar Diesel Engine Co Ltd-Japan Thrusters: 1 Tunnel thruster (f)
9107825 *HSTE* -	**SANDON 8** - **Port Authority of Thailand (Marine Department)** - *Bangkok* *Thailand* MMSI: 567000340 Official number: 361005448	**2,738** 821 3,250		**1993-06 Italthai Marine Co., Ltd. — Samut Prakan** Yd No: 119 Loa 77.00 Br ex 14.92 Dght 6.400 Lbp 71.00 Br md 14.60 Dpth 7.40 Welded, 1 dk	**(B33B2DT) Trailing Suction Hopper Dredger** Hopper: 2,500	**2 oil engines** driving 2 FP propellers Total Power: 2,200kW (2,992hp) 11.0kn Yanmar T220L-ET 2 x 4 Stroke 6 Cy. 220 x 280 each-1100kW (1496bhp) Yanmar Diesel Engine Co Ltd-Japan AuxGen: 3 x 480kW a.c Thrusters: 1 Tunnel thruster (f)

9173123 *HSTI* -	**SANDON 9** **Port Authority of Thailand (Marine Department)** - *Bangkok* *Thailand* MMSI: 567004400 Official number: 411001314	**3,182** 954 3,578	Class: (GL)	**1998-12 Italthai Marine Co., Ltd. — Samut Prakan** Yd No: 129 Loa 90.60 Br ex 14.95 Dght 5.500 Lbp 84.65 Br md 14.60 Dpth 7.40 Welded, 1 dk	**(B33B2DT) Trailing Suction Hopper Dredger**	**2 oil engines** with clutches, flexible couplings & sr reverse geared to sc. shafts driving 2 CP propellers Total Power: 2,206kW (3,000hp) 11.0kn Yanmar T260-ET 2 x 4 Stroke 6 Cy. 260 x 330 each-1103kW (1500bhp) Yanmar Diesel Engine Co Ltd-Japan AuxGen: 3 x 485kW 380V 50Hz a.c Thrusters: 1 Thwart. FP thruster (f) Fuel: 318.9 (d.f.) 6.2pd
8960414 *LJSU* M-17-AE	**SANDOY JUNIOR** *ex* Engdal Junior *-2011* *ex* Gangstad *-2005* *ex* Krystad *-2001* *ex* Skjoldevaering *-1995* *ex* Mollavaering *-1991* *ex* Lind Junior *-1988* *ex* Sivertsen Junior *-1985* **BJ Senior AS** - *Molde* *Norway* MMSI: 257500600	**126** 50 67		**1981 Johan Drage AS — Rognan** Yd No: 381 Loa 22.15 Br ex - Dght 3.700 Lbp - Br md 5.60 Dpth - Welded, 1 dk	**(B11B2FV) Fishing Vessel**	**1 oil engine** driving 1 FP propeller Total Power: 441kW (600hp) 9.0kn Volvo Penta 1 x 4 Stroke 441kW (600bhp) (new engine 1998) AB Volvo Penta-Sweden Thrusters: 1 Thwart. FP thruster (f)
9623831 *5BQD3* -	**SANDPIPER** **Access Shipping Ltd** - SatCom: Inmarsat C 421005410 *Limassol* *Cyprus* MMSI: 210054000 Official number: 9623831	**32,839** 19,559 58,000 T/cm 59.2	Class: LR (BV) **100A1** SS 05/2012 bulk carrier CSR BC-A Nos. 2 & 4 holds may be empty GRAB (20) **ShipRight** (ACS (B)) ESP LI *IWS **LMC** **UMS**	**2012-05 Yangzhou Dayang Shipbuilding Co Ltd — Yangzhou JS** Yd No: DY144 Loa 189.99 (BB) Br ex - Dght 12.950 Lbp 185.00 Br md 32.26 Dpth 18.00 Welded, 1 dk	**(A21A2BC) Bulk Carrier** Grain: 71,549; Bale: 69,760 Compartments: 5 Ho, ER 5 Ha: ER Cranes: 4x35t	**1 oil engine** driving 1 FP propeller Total Power: 8,700kW (11,829hp) 14.3kn MAN-B&W 6S50MC-C 1 x 2 Stroke 6 Cy. 500 x 2000 8700kW (11829bhp) Doosan Engine Co Ltd-South Korea AuxGen: 3 x 620kW a.c
9441427 *V7WM8* -	**SANDPIPER BULKER** **Sandpiper Shipping LLC** Eagle Shipping International (USA) LLC *Majuro* *Marshall Islands* MMSI: 538004341 Official number: 4341	**33,045** 20,115 57,809 T/cm 59.2	Class: LR ✠**100A1** SS 10/2011 bulk carrier CSR BC-A GRAB (28) Hold Nos. 2 & 4 may be empty ESP **ShipRight** (CM,ACS (B)) *IWS LI ✠**LMC** **UMS** Eq.Ltr: M†; Cable: 632.5/73.0 U3 (a)	**2011-10 Yangzhou Dayang Shipbuilding Co Ltd — Yangzhou JS** Yd No: DY3047 Loa 188.58 (BB) Br ex 32.30 Dght 12.950 Lbp 185.00 Br md 32.26 Dpth 18.00 Welded, 1 dk	**(A21A2BC) Bulk Carrier** Grain: 71,549; Bale: 69,760 Compartments: 5 Ho, ER 5 Ha: ER Cranes: 4x35t	**1 oil engine** driving 1 FP propeller Total Power: 9,480kW (12,889hp) 14.3kn MAN-B&W 6S50MC-C 1 x 2 Stroke 6 Cy. 500 x 2000 9480kW (12889bhp) Doosan Engine Co Ltd-South Korea AuxGen: 3 x 600kW 450V 60Hz a.c Boilers: AuxB (Comp) 8.9kgf/cm² (8.7bar)
9479890 *V7QQ4* -	**SANDRA** **Sandra Shipco LLC** Maryville Maritime Inc SatCom: Inmarsat C 453833726 *Majuro* *Marshall Islands* MMSI: 538003419 Official number: 3419	**90,095** 59,287 180,274 T/cm 121.0	Class: NK	**2008-12 Koyo Dockyard Co Ltd — Mihara HS** Yd No: 2288 Loa 288.93 (BB) Br ex - Dght 18.171 Lbp 280.80 Br md 45.00 Dpth 24.70 Welded, 1 dk	**(A21A2BC) Bulk Carrier** Grain: 199,724 Compartments: 9 Ho, ER 9 Ha: ER	**1 oil engine** driving 1 FP propeller Total Power: 18,660kW (25,370hp) 14.5kn MAN-B&W 6S70MC-C 1 x 2 Stroke 6 Cy. 700 x 2800 18660kW (25370bhp) Mitsui Engineering & Shipbuilding CLtd-Japan AuxGen: 3 x a.c Fuel: 5390.0
9510371 *A8PP2* -	**SANDRA** **Sandra Marine Ltd** INTRESCO GmbH SatCom: Inmarsat C 463711578 *Monrovia* *Liberia* MMSI: 636013805 Official number: 13805	**32,305** 19,458 58,110 T/cm 57.4	Class: NK	**2012-01 Tsuneishi Group (Zhoushan) Shipbuilding Inc — Daishan County ZJ** Yd No: SS-077 Loa 189.99 (BB) Br ex - Dght 12.830 Lbp 185.60 Br md 32.26 Dpth 18.00 Welded, 1 dk	**(A21A2BC) Bulk Carrier** Grain: 72,689; Bale: 70,122 Compartments: 5 Ho, ER 5 Ha: ER Cranes: 4x30t	**1 oil engine** driving 1 FP propeller Total Power: 8,400kW (11,421hp) 14.5kn MAN-B&W 6S50MC-C 1 x 2 Stroke 6 Cy. 500 x 2000 8400kW (11421bhp) Mitsui Engineering & Shipbuilding CLtd-Japan Fuel: 2380.0
5412777 - DAK 630	**SANDRA** *ex* Notre Dame de Pitie *-1985* **Sotipeche** - *Dakar* *Senegal*	*157* 52 -	Class: (BV)	**1963 Ateliers & Chantiers de La Rochelle-Pallice — La Rochelle** Yd No: 5079 Loa 27.13 Br ex 6.76 Dght 2.660 Lbp 25.30 Br md 6.71 Dpth 3.61 Welded, 1 dk	**(B11A2FT) Trawler** Ins: 97 3 Ha: 2 (0.9 x 1.0) (0.9 x 0.9)	**1 oil engine** driving 1 FP propeller Total Power: 331kW (450hp) 11.0kn Deutz RBV6M536 1 x 4 Stroke 6 Cy. 270 x 360 331kW (450bhp) Kloeckner Humboldt Deutz AG-West Germany AuxGen: 2 x 20kW 110V d.c Fuel: 30.0 (d.f.)
8001828 *DUH2344* -	**SANDRA** *ex* Yamato Maru No. 7 *-1996* **Amparo Shipping Corp** - *Cebu* *Philippines* Official number: CEB1002290	*498* 340 1,237		**1980-07 K.K. Miura Zosensho — Saiki** Yd No: 602 Loa - Br ex - Dght 3.901 Lbp 61.22 Br md 10.51 Dpth 6.02 Welded, 1 dk	**(A31A2GX) General Cargo Ship**	**1 oil engine** driving 1 FP propeller Total Power: 956kW (1,300hp) Akasaka DM28A 1 x 4 Stroke 6 Cy. 280 x 460 956kW (1300bhp) Akasaka Tekkosho KK (Akasaka DieselLtd)-Japan
8333582 *OPDK* O 89	**SANDRA** **Rederij De Zeebries BVBA** - *Ostend* *Belgium* MMSI: 205278000 Official number: 01 00270 1996	**233** 69 -		**1982 N.V. Scheepswerven L. de Graeve — Zeebrugge** Loa 33.53 Br ex - Dght - Lbp - Br md 7.58 Dpth - Welded, 1 dk	**(B11A2FT) Trawler**	**1 oil engine** driving 1 FP propeller Total Power: 736kW (1,001hp) A.B.C. 1 x 4 Stroke 736kW (1001bhp) Anglo Belgian Corp NV (ABC)-Belgium
6708305 *9GDP* -	**SANDRA A** *ex* Berry Palmer *-1991* *ex* Shahzad 2 *-1987* *ex* Hurghada *-1987* **Kiku Co Ltd** - *Takoradi* *Ghana* Official number: 316782	*1,406* 647 1,417	Class: (LR) ✠ Classed LR until 11/4/90	**1967-08 Astilleros Construcciones SA — Meira** Yd No: 67 Loa 76.99 Br ex 12.05 Dght 4.769 Lbp 67.01 Br md 12.01 Dpth 7.29 Riveted\Welded, 2 dks	**(B11A2FS) Stern Trawler** Ins: 1,412	**1 oil engine** driving 1 FP propeller Total Power: 1,471kW (2,000hp) Werkspoor TMABS398 1 x 4 Stroke 8 Cy. 390 x 680 1471kW (2000bhp) Naval Stork Werkspoor SA-Spain AuxGen: 3 x 280kW 380V 50Hz a.c
7940455 - -	**SANDRA ANITA** **Sandra Anita Inc**	*131* 89		**1978 Desco Marine — Saint Augustine, Fl** L reg 20.94 Br ex 6.74 Dght - Lbp - Br md - Dpth 3.74 Bonded, 1 dk	**(B11A2FT) Trawler** Hull Material: Reinforced Plastic	**1 oil engine** geared to sc. shaft driving 1 FP propeller Total Power: 268kW (364hp) Cummins KT-1150-M 1 x 4 Stroke 6 Cy. 159 x 159 268kW (364bhp) Cummins Engine Co Inc-USA
7366659 - -	**SANDRA C** **Pescatun de Colombia SA** SatCom: Inmarsat A 1502617 *Cartagena de Indias* *Colombia* Official number: MC-05-490	**990** 469 1,200		**1973-12 Campbell Industries — San Diego, Ca** Yd No: 93 L reg 59.87 Br ex 12.20 Dght 4.979 Lbp - Br md 12.12 Dpth 7.50 Welded, 1 dk	**(B11B2FV) Fishing Vessel**	**1 oil engine** driving 1 FP propeller Total Power: 2,648kW (3,600hp) 17.0kn EMD (Electro-Motive) 20-645-E7B 1 x Vee 2 Stroke 20 Cy. 230 x 254 2648kW (3600bhp) General Motors Corp-USA AuxGen: 3 x 300kW
8958667 *WCY5597* -	**SANDRA FIVE** **Heuker Bros Inc** - *Warrendale, OR* *United States of America* MMSI: 366752970 Official number: 1068196	**299** 89 -		**1998 Fred Wahl Marine Construction Inc — Reedsport, Or** Yd No: 98-113-9 Loa 34.57 Br ex - Dght - Lbp - Br md 9.44 Dpth 3.35 Welded, 1 dk	**(B11B2FV) Fishing Vessel**	**2 oil engines** reduction geared to sc. shafts driving 2 FP propellers Total Power: 736kW (1,000hp) Cummins KTA-19-M 2 x 4 Stroke 6 Cy. 159 x 159 each-368kW (500bhp) Cummins Engine Co Inc-USA
7502576 *WYL4908* -	**SANDRA FOSS** **Foss Maritime Co** - *Seattle, WA* *United States of America* MMSI: 366934290 Official number: 571854	**364** 109 -	Class: (AB)	**1976-11 Fairhaven Shipyard, Inc. — Bellingham, Wa** Yd No: 48 Loa 33.99 Br ex 10.39 Dght 4.122 Lbp 32.36 Br md 10.37 Dpth 4.83 Welded, 1 dk	**(B32A2ST) Tug**	**2 oil engines** reverse reduction geared to sc. shafts driving 2 FP propellers Total Power: 2,132kW (2,898hp) 13.0kn EMD (Electro-Motive) 8-645-E7 2 x Vee 2 Stroke 8 Cy. 230 x 254 each-1066kW (1449bhp) General Motors Corp.Electro-Motive Div.-La Grange AuxGen: 2 x 115kW Fuel: 324.0 (d.f.)

8940579 - -	**SANDRA G** **Joseph Garcia** - *Port Lavaca, TX* *United States of America* Official number: 1044431	*132* 105 -		**1996 Rodriguez Boat Builders, Inc. — Coden, Al** Yd No: 149 L reg 23.77 Br ex - Dght - Lbp - Br md 6.71 Dpth 3.51 Welded, 1 dk	**(B11B2FV) Fishing Vessel**	**1 oil engine** driving 1 FP propeller
9369227 *WDD9019* -	**SANDRA HUGH** **Amnav Maritime Corp (Amnav Maritime Services)** - *San Francisco, CA* *United States of America* MMSI: 367305920 Official number: 1202954	*144* 98 -		**2007-08 Foss Maritime Shipyard — Rainier, Or** Yd No: 008 Loa 23.80 Br ex - Dght - Lbp - Br md 10.40 Dpth 4.27 Welded, 1 dk	**(B32A2ST) Tug**	**2 oil engines** reduction geared to sc. shafts driving 2 Directional propellers Total Power: 3,736kW (5,080hp) Caterpillar 3512B-HD 2 x Vee 4 Stroke 12 Cy. 170 x 215 each-1868kW (2540bhp) Caterpillar Inc-USA
8975378 *WDF3432* -	**SANDRA J BANTA** *ex* Miss Jennifer Ann *-2010* *ex* Compass Watch *-1988* *ex* Bailey Thomas *-1988* **M/V Sandy B LLC** Chem Carriers LLC *Baton Rouge, LA* *United States of America* MMSI: 366913020 Official number: 641607	*154* 104 -		**1981 Balehi Marine Corp. — Lacombe, La** Yd No: 43 L reg 18.37 Br ex - Dght - Lbp - Br md 7.62 Dpth 3.05 Welded, 1 dk	**(B32A2ST) Tug**	**1 oil engine** driving 1 Propeller
8719475 *WTE2819* -	**SANDRA JANE** **J & M Fishing Inc** - *Boston, MA* *United States of America* MMSI: 367327960 Official number: 925518	*199* 135 -		**1987-12 Atlantic Marine — Jacksonville, Fl** Loa 28.96 Br ex - Dght - Lbp 25.76 Br md 7.62 Dpth 4.08 Welded, 1 dk	**(B11B2FV) Fishing Vessel**	**1 oil engine** geared to sc. shaft driving 1 FP propeller Total Power: 1,118kW (1,520hp) Caterpillar 3512TA 1 x Vee 4 Stroke 12 Cy. 170 x 190 1118kW (1520bhp) Caterpillar Inc-USA
8953150 *YYV2594* -	**SANDRA KAY** *ex* Jeanette Belcher *-1982* **Constructora Camsa CA** - *Maracaibo* *Venezuela* Official number: AJZL - 27.042	*168* 50 -		**1971-04 American Marine Corp. — New Orleans, La** Yd No: 1070 L reg 25.94 Br ex - Dght 3.350 Lbp - Br md 8.53 Dpth 3.66 Welded, 1 dk	**(B32A2ST) Tug**	**2 oil engines** driving 2 FP propellers Total Power: 1,324kW (1,800hp) 12.0kn General Motors 2 x each-662kW (900bhp) General Motors Detroit DieselAllison Divn-USA
8981963 *WDA7188* -	**SANDRA KAY** **Keith Howard Wallis** - *Port Lavaca, TX* *United States of America* MMSI: 366840630 Official number: 1123050	**126** 101 -		**2002 Williams Boat Works, Inc. — Coden, Al** Yd No: 47 L reg 23.77 Br ex - Dght - Lbp - Br md 6.70 Dpth 3.35 Welded, 1 dk	**(B11B2FV) Fishing Vessel**	**1 oil engine** driving 1 Propeller
9286750 *YJVC7* -	**SANDRA TIDE** **Green Fleet Ltd** Tidex Nigeria Ltd *Port Vila* *Vanuatu* MMSI: 576263000 Official number: 1730	**341** 102 -	Class: AB	**2002-11 Breaux Bay Craft, Inc. — Loreauville, La** Yd No: 1726 Loa 49.38 Br ex - Dght 2.530 Lbp 45.15 Br md 8.13 Dpth 3.57 Welded, 1 dk	**(B21A20C) Crew/Supply Vessel** Hull Material: Aluminium Alloy	**4 oil engines** geared to sc. shafts driving 4 FP propellers Total Power: 4,206kW (5,718hp) Caterpillar 3512B 4 x Vee 4 Stroke 12 Cy. 170 x 190 each-1051kW (1429bhp) Caterpillar Inc-USA AuxGen: 2 x 75kW a.c
9212527 *ITSD* -	**SANDRA Z** **Azienda del Consorzio Trasporti Veneziano (ACTV)** - *Venice* *Italy*	*293* 178 110	Class: (RI)	**2000-01 Cant. Nav. S.M.E.B. S.p.A. — Messina** Yd No: 180 Loa 40.05 Br ex 8.08 Dght 2.130 Lbp 37.80 Br md 7.50 Dpth 2.87 Welded, 1 dk	**(A37B2PS) Passenger Ship**	**2 oil engines** geared to sc. shafts driving 2 Directional propellers Total Power: 618kW (840hp) Fiat 8291M 2 x Vee 4 Stroke 12 Cy. 145 x 130 each-309kW (420bhp) IVECO AIFO S.p.A.-Pregnana Milanese
8112811 *EZCJ* -	**SANDRAH** **GAC Marine LLC** GAC Marine SA *Turkmenbashy* *Turkmenistan* MMSI: 434112400	**504** 151 480	Class: BV	**1982-03 Southern Ocean Shipbuilding Co Pte Ltd — Singapore** Yd No: 123 Loa 38.00 Br ex 11.03 Dght 3.301 Lbp 36.50 Br md 11.00 Dpth 4.50 Welded, 1 dk	**(B21B20A) Anchor Handling Tug Supply** Passengers: berths: 10	**2 oil engines** sr geared to sc. shaft driving 2 FP propellers Total Power: 2,368kW (3,220hp) 11.0kn Wartsila 8R22 2 x 4 Stroke 8 Cy. 220 x 240 each-1184kW (1610bhp) Oy Wartsila Ab-Finland AuxGen: 2 x 145kW 380/220V 50Hz a.c, 1 x 60kW 380/220V 50Hz a.c Thrusters: 1 Thwart. FP thruster (f) Fuel: 277.5 (d.f.) 6.5pd
7413153 *CUZF* -	**SANDRO CUNHA** *ex* Cidade de Lagos *-1984* **Farinhas e Oleos de Peixe Lda (FRAPEC)** - SatCom: Inmarsat C 426350610 *Olhao* *Portugal*	*288* 127 250	Class: (LR) ✠ Classed LR until 6/88	**1982-08 Est. Navais da Figueira da Foz Lda. (FOZNAVE) — Figueira da Foz** Yd No: 013 Loa 36.50 Br ex 8.59 Dght 3.501 Lbp 31.50 Br md 8.41 Dpth 4.12 Welded, 1 dk	**(B11A2FS) Stern Trawler**	**1 oil engine** with clutches, flexible couplings & reverse reduction geared to sc. shaft driving 1 CP propeller Total Power: 809kW (1,100hp) MaK 8M281AK 1 x 4 Stroke 8 Cy. 240 x 280 809kW (1100bhp) Krupp MaK Maschinenbau GmbH-Kiel AuxGen: 1 x 160kW 380V 50Hz a.c, 1 x 65kW
7013202 - -	**SANDSEND** *ex* Wels *-1993* - - -	**321** 96 -	Class: (DS)	**1957 VEB Elbewerft — Boizenburg** Loa 47.96 Br ex 8.34 Dght 2.699 Lbp 46.72 Br md 8.00 Dpth 3.00 Welded, 1 dk	**(B34A2SH) Hopper, Motor**	**1 oil engine** driving 1 FP propeller Total Power: 159kW (216hp) 8.0kn S.K.L. 1 x 4 Stroke 6 Cy. 240 x 360 159kW (216bhp) VEB Schwermaschinenbau "KarlLiebknecht" (SKL)-Magdeburg AuxGen: 1 x 12kW 230V 50Hz a.c, 1 x 3kW 230V 50Hz a.c
8995861 *MCPR4* -	**SANDSEND** *ex* B. 33 *-2003* **Scarborough Borough Council** - *Whitby* *United Kingdom* MMSI: 235013567 Official number: 907924	**268** 82 -		**2000-08 Ganz Danubius, Shipyard & Crane Factory plc — Budapest** Converted From: Hopper-2003 Loa 44.82 Br ex 8.00 Dght 2.740 Lbp - Br md 7.95 Dpth - Welded, 1 dk	**(B34A2SH) Hopper, Motor** Hopper: 330	**2 oil engines** geared to sc. shafts driving 2 Directional propellers Total Power: 294kW (400hp) Caterpillar 2 x 4 Stroke each-147kW (200bhp) (new engine 2003, added 2003) Caterpillar Inc-USA Thrusters: 1 Thwart. FP thruster (f)
8891065 *GNQE* -	**SANDSFOOT CASTLE** *ex* Dalmatian *-2003* **Portland Port Ltd** - *Portland* *United Kingdom* MMSI: 232002877 Official number: 909308	**149** 44 -	Class: (LR) ✠ Classed LR until 31/1/05	**1965-07 J. S. Doig (Grimsby) Ltd. — Grimsby** Yd No: 84 Loa 28.66 Br ex 7.72 Dght 2.740 Lbp 25.91 Br md 7.39 Dpth 3.66 Welded, 1 dk	**(B32A2ST) Tug**	**2 oil engines** sr reverse geared to sc. shafts driving 2 FP propellers Total Power: 970kW (1,318hp) 12.0kn Blackstone ERS8 2 x 4 Stroke 8 Cy. 222 x 292 each-485kW (659bhp) Blackstone & Co. Ltd.-Stamford AuxGen: 2 x 40kW 220V d.c
8763775 *WDC4891* -	**SANDSHARK** *ex* Mr. Jim *-2003* **All Coast LLC** - *New Orleans, LA* *United States of America* MMSI: 367032420 Official number: 645540	*196* 133 -		**1982 Blue Streak Industries, Inc. — Chalmette, La** Yd No: BLU JB 57 Loa 28.43 Br ex - Dght - Lbp - Br md 11.58 Dpth 2.43 Welded, 1 dk	**(B22A2ZM) Offshore Construction Vessel, jack up**	**2 oil engines** geared to sc. shafts driving 2 Propellers G.M. (Detroit Diesel) 12V-71 2 x Vee 2 Stroke 12 Cy. 108 x 127 Detroit Diesel Corporation-Detroit, Mi
8802428 *OW2435* FD 588	**SANDSHAVID** *ex* Fugltugvan *-2011* **P/F Torvanes** Johan David Joensen *Eidi* *Faeroe Islands (Danish)* MMSI: 231004000 Official number: D3171	**335** 100 -	Class: NV	**1988-03 Strandby Skibsvaerft I/S — Strandby** Yd No: 88 Lengthened-2006 Loa 34.05 Br ex 7.50 Dght 6.050 Lbp 30.20 Br md - Dpth 6.09 Welded, 2 dks	**(B11B2FV) Fishing Vessel** Ice Capable	**1 oil engine** driving 1 FP propeller Total Power: 423kW (575hp) Callesen 5-427-EOT 1 x 4 Stroke 5 Cy. 270 x 400 423kW (575bhp) Aabenraa Motorfabrik, HeinrichCallesen A/S-Denmark AuxGen: 1 x 96kW 380V 50Hz a.c

5149760 **SANDSHORN**
DCNY *ex* Gerlene *-2007* *ex* Hertraud *-1988*
- **Jan Christiansen Frachtschifffahrt**
-
Wyk auf Foehr *Germany*
MMSI: 211223310
Official number: 12603

217 / 136 / 372 — Class: GL

1962-01 **Julius Diedrich Schiffswerft GmbH & Co KG — Moormerland** Yd No: 88
Loa 40.77 Br ex 7.14 Dght 2.185
Lbp 39.20 Br md 7.12 Dpth 2.49
Welded, 1 dk

(A31A2GX) General Cargo Ship
2 Ha: (10.0 x 5.0)
Cranes: 1x6t

1 oil engine geared to sc. shaft driving 1 FP propeller
Total Power: 147kW (200hp) 7.0kn
Deutz RA6M428
1 x 4 Stroke 6 Cy. 220 x 280 147kW (200bhp)
Kloeckner Humboldt Deutz AG-West Germany

7207683 **SANDSOY JUNIOR**
- *ex* Bjornoybuen *-2000* *ex* Sirafisk *-1986*
- *ex* Ny Argo *-1979* *ex* Barmnes Jr. *-1971*
ex Vikstrom *-1971*
-
-

191 / 58 / -

1964 **Kr.K. Frostad & Sonner — Tomrefjord**
Yd No: 17
Lengthened-1968
Loa 28.35 Br ex 6.20 Dght -
Lbp - Br md 6.18 Dpth -
Welded, 1 dk

(B11B2FV) Fishing Vessel

1 oil engine driving 1 FP propeller
Total Power: 368kW (500hp) 9.0kn
Wichmann 4ACA
1 x 2 Stroke 4 Cy. 280 x 420 368kW (500bhp) (new engine 1971)
Wichmann Motorfabrikk AS-Norway

6525064 **SANDSTRAND**
LIDD *ex* Vitin *-2002* *ex* Helle Tholstrup *-1984*
- **Boston AS**
-
Kopervik *Norway*
MMSI: 259351000

300 / 167 / 354 — Class: BV

1965 **A/S Svendborg Skibsvaerft — Svendborg**
Yd No: 112
Converted From: LPG Tanker-1985
Loa 46.92 Br ex 8.13 Dght 2.693
Lbp 42.02 Br md 8.11 Dpth 3.03
Welded, 1 dk

(B33A2DS) Suction Dredger
Hopper: 240
Ice Capable

1 oil engine geared to sc. shaft driving 1 CP propeller
Total Power: 368kW (500hp) 10.0kn
Grenaa 6F24
1 x 4 Stroke 6 Cy. 240 x 300 368kW (500bhp) (new engine 1974)
A/S Grenaa Motorfabrik-Denmark

6721113 **SANDSUND**
LEIM *ex* Paul Barsoe *-1977*
- **R/E Bulkmegling AS**
-
Bergen *Norway*
MMSI: 258451000

616 / 257 / 990 — Class: (BV)

1967-07 **Sonderborg Skibsvaerft A/S — Sonderborg** Yd No: 54
Lengthened-1989
Loa 60.10 Br ex 9.80 Dght -
Lbp 55.00 Br md 9.78 Dpth 3.79
Welded, 1 dk

(A31A2GX) General Cargo Ship
Grain: 998; Bale: 840
Compartments: 1 Ho, ER
1 Ha: (28.6 x 5.1)ER

1 oil engine driving 1 CP propeller
Total Power: 507kW (689hp) 10.5kn
Callesen 6-427-FOT
1 x 4 Stroke 6 Cy. 270 x 400 507kW (689bhp)
Aabenraa Motorfabrik, HeinrichCallesen A/S-Denmark
Fuel: 37.5 (d.f.) 2.0pd

7500293 **SANDTOR**
-
- **VTG Supply Boat Liberia Inc**
Tidewater Marine North Sea Ltd

863 / 259 / 854 — Class: (GL)

1976-12 **JG Hitzler Schiffswerft und Masch GmbH & Co KG — Lauenburg** Yd No: 755
Loa 57.51 Br ex 12.12 Dght 4.502
Lbp 50.63 Br md 11.70 Dpth 5.62
Welded, 1 dk

(B21B20A) Anchor Handling Tug Supply
Ice Capable

2 oil engines reduction geared to sc. shafts driving 2 FP propellers
Total Power: 3,384kW (4,600hp) 13.0kn
MAN V8V-22/30ATL
2 x Vee 4 Stroke 16 Cy. 220 x 300 each-1692kW (2300bhp)
Maschinenbau Augsburg Nuernberg (MAN)-Augsburg

5311088 **SANDVIK**
SGYQ
- **Ove Wetterberg**
Wetecon AB
Stockholm *Sweden*

128 / 38 / -

1928 **Bergsunds Mekaniska Verkstads AB — Stockholm** Yd No: 401
Loa 25.35 Br ex 6.53 Dght 3.501
Lbp - Br md 6.51 Dpth -
Riveted, 1 dk

(B32A2ST) Tug

1 oil engine driving 1 FP propeller
9.0kn
Fuel: 25.5 (d.f.)

9264764 **SANDWIG**
V2BF6 *ex* MCC Chalice *-2011*
- *ex* Maersk Edinburgh *-2007*
completed as Sandwig *-2003*
ms 'Sandwig' Schiffahrtsgesellschaft mbH & Co KG
Brise Schiffahrts GmbH
Saint John's *Antigua & Barbuda*
MMSI: 304568000
Official number: 2699

6,704 / 3,557 / 8,015 / T/cm 20.7 — Class: GL

2003-11 **Zhejiang Yangfan Ship Group Co Ltd — Zhoushan ZJ** Yd No: 2009
Loa 132.60 (BB) Br ex - Dght 7.218
Lbp 123.40 Br md 19.20 Dpth 9.20
Welded, 1 dk

(A33A2CC) Container Ship (Fully Cellular)
Double Bottom Entire Compartment Length
TEU 657 C Ho 228 TEU C Dk 429 TEU incl 116 ref C.
Cranes: 2x50t

1 oil engine geared to sc. shaft driving 1 CP propeller
Total Power: 6,300kW (8,565hp) 17.0kn
MaK 7M43
1 x 4 Stroke 7 Cy. 430 x 610 6300kW (8565bhp)
Caterpillar Motoren GmbH & Co. KG-Germany
AuxGen: 2 x 370kW 380/220V a.c, 1 x 1200kW 380/220V a.c
Thrusters: 1 Tunnel thruster (f)

6602680 **SANDY**
-
- -
-

105 / - / - — Class: (LR) ✠ Classed LR until 5/74

1965-11 **Fabricaciones Metallicas E.P.S. (FABRIMET) — Callao** Yd No: 304
Loa 22.36 Br ex 6.76 Dght -
Lbp 19.13 Br md 6.63 Dpth 3.18
Welded

(B11B2FV) Fishing Vessel

1 oil engine reverse reduction geared to sc. shaft driving 1 FP propeller
Total Power: 386kW (525hp)
G.M. (Detroit Diesel) 12V-71
1 x Vee 2 Stroke 12 Cy. 108 x 127 386kW (525bhp)
General Motors Corp-USA

5385730 **SANDY**
- *ex* Waterdale *-1988* *ex* Walter Richter *-1972*
- **Harry Franklin**
-
Saint John's *Antigua & Barbuda*
Official number: 1278

235 / 108 / 650 — Class: (GL)

1957 **Heinrich Brand KG Schiffswerft — Oldenburg** Yd No: 139
Loa 53.01 Br ex 8.74 Dght 3.506
Lbp 46.49 Br md 8.69 Dpth 3.66
Riveted\Welded, 1 dk

(A31A2GX) General Cargo Ship
Grain: 852; Bale: 766
Compartments: 1 Ho, ER
2 Ha: (9.3 x 5.4) (12.6 x 5.4)ER

1 oil engine driving 1 FP propeller
Total Power: 221kW (300hp) 9.0kn
MaK MSU423
1 x 4 Stroke 6 Cy. 290 x 420 221kW (300bhp)
Maschinenbau Kiel AG (MaK)-Kiel
AuxGen: 1 x 8kW 24V d.c
Fuel: 25.5 (d.f.)

7742786 **SANDY J**
- *ex* Robin Lee *-2001* *ex* Prayer Warrior *-2001*
- *ex* Capt. Johnny *-2001*
Rampersaud Sookdeo
-
Georgetown *Guyana*
Official number: 0000159

121 / 82 / -

1978 **Rodriguez Boat Builders, Inc. — Coden, Al**
L reg 21.98 Br ex 6.76 Dght -
Lbp - Br md - Dpth 3.38
Welded, 1 dk

(B11B2FV) Fishing Vessel

1 oil engine driving 1 FP propeller
Total Power: 416kW (566hp)

9640774 **SANDY M**
2FFC5
- **Gareloch Support Services (Plant) Ltd**
-
Greenock *United Kingdom*
MMSI: 235090733

135 / 40 / - — Class: BV

2012-02 **Neptune Shipyards BV — Aalst (Nl)**
Yd No: 407
Loa 23.95 Br ex - Dght 2.100
Lbp 22.00 Br md 9.54 Dpth 3.10
Welded, 1 dk

(B34L2QU) Utility Vessel

2 oil engines reduction geared to sc. shafts driving 2 FP propellers
Total Power: 1,640kW (2,230hp) 9.0kn
Caterpillar C32
2 x Vee 4 Stroke 12 Cy. 145 x 162 each-820kW (1115bhp)
Caterpillar Inc-USA

7626853 **SANDY PEARL**
3EJH2 *ex* Sandy Cape *-2007*
- *ex* Hyundai T No. 1002 *-1998*
ex Chung Ryong No. 2 *-1984*
ex Hyundai No. 110 *-1979*
ex Hoko Maru No. 7 *-1979*
Yoshida Trading Corp
YTC Co Ltd
Panama *Panama*
MMSI: 372517000
Official number: 3282407A

1,819 / 547 / 1,825 — Class: IR (AB) (KR) (NK)

1977-02 **Miyoshi Shipbuilding Co Ltd — Uwajima EH** Yd No: 233
Loa 72.40 Br ex - Dght 5.388
Lbp 65.26 Br md 13.01 Dpth 6.00
Welded, 1 dk

(B32A2ST) Tug

2 oil engines driving 2 FP propellers
Total Power: 5,884kW (8,000hp) 13.5kn
Niigata 8MG40X
2 x 4 Stroke 8 Cy. 400 x 520 each-2942kW (4000bhp)
Niigata Engineering Co Ltd-Japan
AuxGen: 2 x 280kW 445V a.c

8991085 **SANDY POINT**
WDB8067
- **Higman Barge Lines Inc**
-
Houston, TX *United States of America*
MMSI: 366952360
Official number: 1163278

232 / 157 / -

2004 **in the United States of America** Yd No: 3571
L reg 22.56 Br ex - Dght -
Lbp - Br md 9.75 Dpth 3.05
Welded, 1 dk

(B32A2ST) Tug

2 oil engines driving 1 Propeller
Total Power: 736kW (1,001hp)

9220079 **SANDY RICKMERS**
V7DJ6 *ex* OOCL Moscow *-2009*
- *ex* Sandy Rickmers *-2007*
Peel Navigation Ltd
Rickmers Shipmanagement (Singapore) Pte Ltd
Majuro *Marshall Islands*
MMSI: 538001652
Official number: 1652

14,290 / 4,914 / 14,901 / T/cm 31.7 — Class: GL

2002-01 **Hanjin Heavy Industries & Construction Co Ltd — Ulsan** Yd No: 651
Loa 158.75 (BB) Br ex - Dght 9.200
Lbp 150.00 Br md 25.60 Dpth 13.76
Welded, 1 dk

(A33A2CC) Container Ship (Fully Cellular)
TEU 1216 C Ho 398 TEU C Dk 818 TEU incl 200 ref C.
Ice Capable

1 oil engine driving 1 CP propeller
Total Power: 17,771kW (24,161hp) 22.0kn
Sulzer 8RTA62U
1 x 2 Stroke 8 Cy. 620 x 2150 17771kW (24161bhp)
Hyundai Heavy Industries Co Ltd-South Korea
AuxGen: 3 x 1050kW 440/220V 60Hz a.c
Thrusters: 1 Thwart. CP thruster (f)
Fuel: 132.9 (d.f.) 1564.0 (r.f.) 69.0pd

8108640 **SANE MENTERENG**
C5N
- **Government of The Republic of Gambia (Ministry of Agriculture & Natural Resourses)**
-
Banjul *Gambia*
Official number: 100015

128 / 35 / 106 — Class: (LR) ✠ Classed LR until 2/3/84

1982-04 **Carl B Hoffmanns Maskinfabrik A/S — Esbjerg** (Hull) Yd No: 44
1982-04 **Soren Larsen & Sonners Skibsvaerft A/S — Nykobing Mors** Yd No: 151
Loa 24.62 Br ex 6.76 Dght 3.056
Lbp 21.21 Br md 6.71 Dpth 3.31
Welded, 1 dk

(B11A2FS) Stern Trawler

1 oil engine reverse reduction geared to sc. shaft driving 1 CP propeller
Total Power: 345kW (469hp)
Alpha 405-26VO
1 x 2 Stroke 5 Cy. 260 x 400 345kW (469bhp)
B&W Alpha Diesel A/S-Denmark
AuxGen: 2 x 36kW 380V 50Hz a.c

8824397 **SANEI**
- *ex* Sanei Maru No. 8 *-2013*
- **PT Indo Shipping Operator**
-

433 / - / 1,087 — Class: IZ

1989-06 **Tokuoka Zosen K.K. — Naruto**
Loa 58.00 (BB) Br ex - Dght 4.550
Lbp 50.00 Br md 12.00 Dpth 6.15
Welded, 1 dk

(B33A2DG) Grab Dredger

1 oil engine driving 1 FP propeller
Total Power: 736kW (1,001hp) 10.5kn
Niigata 6M30GT
1 x 4 Stroke 6 Cy. 300 x 530 736kW (1001bhp)
Niigata Engineering Co Ltd-Japan
Fuel: 40.0

7850868 - -	**SANEI MARU** **Yuchang** - *China*	*299* - 570		**1966 K.K. Fujishiro Zosen — Chiba** Loa 41.51 Br ex - Dght 3.201 Lbp 37.24 Br md 7.98 Dpth 3.31 Welded, 1 dk	**(A13B2TU) Tanker (unspecified)**	**1 oil engine** driving 1 FP propeller Total Power: 294kW (400hp) 10.0kn Yanmar 1 x 4 Stroke 294kW (400bhp) Yanmar Diesel Engine Co Ltd-Japan
8604436 - -	**SANEI MARU** **Sung Woo Shipping Co** - *South Korea*	*268* - 704		**1986-05 Murakami Hide Zosen K.K. — Imabari** Yd No: 250 Loa 54.01 Br ex 8.51 Dght 3.250 Lbp 50.02 Br md - Dpth 3.61 Welded, 1 dk	**(A12A2TC) Chemical Tanker** Liq: 629 Compartments: 6 Ta, ER	**1 oil engine** with clutches & reverse reduction geared to sc. shaft driving 1 FP propeller Total Power: 662kW (900hp) Hanshin 6LUD24G 1 x 4 Stroke 6 Cy. 240 x 410 662kW (900bhp) The Hanshin Diesel Works Ltd-Japan
8821280 *7LVR* KG1-112	**SANEI MARU No. 1** **Kyoei Suisan YK** - *Ichikikushikino, Kagoshima* *Japan* MMSI: 431300000 Official number: 131215	*379* - 465		**1989-03 Miho Zosensho K.K. — Shimizu** Yd No: 1343 Loa 54.80 (BB) Br ex 8.62 Dght 3.405 Lbp 48.00 Br md 8.60 Dpth 3.75 Welded, 1 dk	**(B11B2FV) Fishing Vessel** Ins: 620	**1 oil engine** with clutches & sr reverse geared to sc. shaft driving 1 FP propeller Total Power: 736kW (1,001hp) Hanshin LH28G 1 x 4 Stroke 6 Cy. 280 x 460 736kW (1001bhp) The Hanshin Diesel Works Ltd-Japan
9119957 *JDMY* KG1-233	**SANEI MARU No. 8** **Kyoei Suisan KK** - SatCom: Inmarsat C 443175010 *Ichikikushikino, Kagoshima* *Japan* MMSI: 431750000 Official number: 134536	*379* - 466		**1995-06 Miho Zosensho K.K. — Shimizu** Yd No: 1456 Loa 56.00 (BB) Br ex - Dght - Lbp 49.00 Br md 8.00 Dpth 3.00 Welded	**(B11B2FV) Fishing Vessel** Ins: 524	**1 oil engine** sr geared to sc. shaft driving 1 FP propeller Total Power: 736kW (1,001hp) Hanshin LH28LG 1 x 4 Stroke 6 Cy. 280 x 530 736kW (1001bhp) The Hanshin Diesel Works Ltd-Japan
9202912 *JG5010* -	**SANEI MARU No. 8** **Sanei Kaiun KK** - *Kisaradu, Chiba* *Japan* Official number: 132789	*129* - -		**1998-01 Takao Zosen Kogyo K.K. — Tateyama** Yd No: 126 Loa 35.46 Br ex - Dght - Lbp 33.00 Br md 8.00 Dpth 3.00 Welded, 1 dk	**(A24D2BA) Aggregates Carrier**	**1 oil engine** driving 1 FP propeller Total Power: 257kW (349hp) 9.0kn Yanmar MF24-HT 1 x 4 Stroke 6 Cy. 240 x 420 257kW (349bhp) Yanmar Diesel Engine Co Ltd-Japan
8821101 *JG4849* -	**SANEI MARU No. 21** **Norimichi Matsuda** Sanei Koun KK *Kisaradu, Chiba* *Japan* Official number: 130281	*426* - 405		**1989-06 Ishii Zosen K.K. — Futtsu** Yd No: 251 Loa 47.00 Br ex - Dght 3.073 Lbp 40.00 Br md 10.60 Dpth 3.10 Welded, 1 dk	**(A24D2BA) Aggregates Carrier** Grain: 650 Compartments: 1 Ho, ER 1 Ha: ER	**1 oil engine** driving 1 FP propeller Total Power: 736kW (1,001hp) Yanmar MF26-HT 1 x 4 Stroke 6 Cy. 260 x 500 736kW (1001bhp) Matsue Diesel KK-Japan
9038244 *JG4989* -	**SANEI MARU No. 28** **Norimichi Matsuda** Sanei Koun KK *Kisaradu, Chiba* *Japan* Official number: 132043	*477* - 410		**1992-02 Shitanoe Shipbuilding Co Ltd — Usuki OT** Yd No: 1128 Loa 46.32 Br ex - Dght 3.000 Lbp - Br md 11.00 Dpth 3.20 Welded	**(B33A2DG) Grab Dredger** Cranes: 1	**1 oil engine** driving 1 FP propeller Total Power: 390kW (530hp) 10.5kn Yanmar MF28-UT 1 x 4 Stroke 6 Cy. 280 x 450 390kW (530bhp) Yanmar Diesel Engine Co Ltd-Japan
9311921 *JGCF* -	**SANEI MARU NO. 51** **Kotoshiro Gyogyo KK** - *Ichikikushikino, Kagoshima* *Japan* MMSI: 432444000 Official number: 137201	*439* 241 -		**2004-03 Miho Zosensho K.K. — Shimizu** Yd No: 1505 Loa 56.77 Br ex - Dght 3.530 Lbp 49.50 Br md 9.00 Dpth 3.90 Welded, 1 dk	**(B11B2FV) Fishing Vessel**	**1 oil engine** geared to sc. shaft driving 1 FP propeller Total Power: 736kW (1,001hp) Hanshin LH28G 1 x 4 Stroke 6 Cy. 280 x 460 736kW (1001bhp) The Hanshin Diesel Works Ltd-Japan
8305456 *VTJF* -	**SANFOOD I** **Sancheti Food Products Ltd** - *Kolkata* *India* Official number: 1988	*144* 115 50	Class: (IR)	**1982-12 Desco Marine — Saint Augustine, Fl** Yd No: 328-F Loa 22.69 Br ex - Dght 3.010 Lbp - Br md 6.71 Dpth 4.27 Bonded, 1 dk	**(B11A2FT) Trawler** Hull Material: Reinforced Plastic Compartments: 1 Ho, ER 1 Ha:	**1 oil engine** sr reverse geared to sc. shaft driving 1 FP propeller Total Power: 268kW (364hp) 8.5kn Caterpillar 3408TA 1 x Vee 4 Stroke 8 Cy. 137 x 152 268kW (364bhp) Caterpillar Tractor Co-USA Fuel: 30.0 (d.f.)
8305468 *VTJN* -	**SANFOOD II** **Sancheti Food Products Ltd** - *Kolkata* *India* Official number: 1987	*144* 115 50	Class: (IR)	**1982-12 Desco Marine — Saint Augustine, Fl** Yd No: 329-F Loa 22.86 Br ex - Dght 3.010 Lbp 20.81 Br md 6.71 Dpth 4.27 Bonded, 1 dk	**(B11A2FT) Trawler** Hull Material: Reinforced Plastic Ins: 84 Compartments: 1 Ho, ER 1 Ha:	**1 oil engine** sr reverse geared to sc. shaft driving 1 FP propeller Total Power: 268kW (364hp) 8.5kn Caterpillar 3408TA 1 x Vee 4 Stroke 8 Cy. 137 x 152 268kW (364bhp) Caterpillar Tractor Co-USA Fuel: 30.0 (d.f.)
9094224 *JD2143* -	**SANFUJI** **Yuko Furunaka** - *Kure, Hiroshima* *Japan* Official number: 140201	*199* - 695		**2005-07 Taiyo Shipbuilding Co Ltd — Sanyoonoda YC** Yd No: 307 Loa 55.63 Br ex - Dght 3.290 Lbp 51.00 Br md 9.50 Dpth 5.45 Welded, 1 dk	**(A31A2GX) General Cargo Ship** 1 Ha: ER (30.0 x 7.5)	**1 oil engine** geared to sc. shaft driving 1 Propeller Total Power: 736kW (1,001hp) 11.5kn Hanshin LH26G 1 x 4 Stroke 6 Cy. 260 x 440 736kW (1001bhp) The Hanshin Diesel Works Ltd-Japan
7713905 *9WBY3* -	**SANG BEAGLE** *ex* Sea Beagle *-1993* *ex* Ryuko Maru *-1992* *ex* Futami Maru *-1991* **Sang Muara Sdn Bhd** *Labuan* *Malaysia* Official number: 326267	**229** 69 -	Class: (BV)	**1978-01 Imamura Zosen — Kure** Yd No: 228 Loa 28.50 Br ex 8.62 Dght 2.950 Lbp 26.52 Br md 8.60 Dpth 3.50 Welded, 1 dk	**(B32A2ST) Tug**	**2 oil engines** geared to sc. shafts driving 2 FP propellers Total Power: 1,912kW (2,600hp) Yanmar G250-ET 2 x 4 Stroke 6 Cy. 250 x 290 each-956kW (1300bhp) Yanmar Diesel Engine Co Ltd-Japan
7701081 - -	**SANG COLLIE** *ex* Sea Collie *-1996* *ex* Taka Maru *-1992* **Sang Muara Sdn Bhd** PSA Marine Pte Ltd	**228** 69 -	Class: (BV)	**1977-05 Kegoya Dock K.K. — Kure** Yd No: 753 Loa 31.73 Br ex 8.62 Dght 2.947 Lbp 26.52 Br md 8.60 Dpth 3.51 Welded, 1 dk	**(B32A2ST) Tug**	**2 oil engines** driving 1 FP propeller Total Power: 1,912kW (2,600hp) 12.5kn Yanmar G250-ET 2 x 4 Stroke 6 Cy. 250 x 290 each-956kW (1300bhp) Yanmar Diesel Engine Co Ltd-Japan
5229388 *6MBG* -	**SANG JI No. 71** *ex* Han Gil No. 11 *-1995* *ex* Kum Bong No. 11 *-1976* *ex* Seishu Maru No. 31 *-1971* *ex* Matsusei Maru No. 15 *-1971* **Sang Ji Fisheries Co Ltd** *Busan* *South Korea* Official number: 9501017-6210004	**232** 111 214	Class: (KR)	**1962 KK Kanasashi Zosen — Shizuoka SZ** Yd No: 453 Loa 46.85 Br ex 7.35 Dght 3.333 Lbp 41.60 Br md 7.31 Dpth 3.41 Welded, 1 dk	**(B11B2FV) Fishing Vessel** Ins: 269 3 Ha:	**1 oil engine** driving 1 FP propeller Total Power: 515kW (700hp) 11.0kn Akasaka MK6SS 1 x 4 Stroke 6 Cy. 300 x 420 515kW (700bhp) Akasaka Tekkosho KK (Akasaka DieselLtd)-Japan AuxGen: 2 x 72kW 230V a.c
7606334 *6MGJ* -	**SANG SENG** - - *Busan* *South Korea* Official number: BSR-769315	*133* 45 64	Class: (KR)	**1976-02 Daedong Shipbuilding Co Ltd — Busan** Yd No: 159 Loa 27.72 Br ex - Dght 2.450 Lbp 24.52 Br md 7.51 Dpth 3.26 Welded, 1 dk	**(B32A2ST) Tug**	**1 oil engine** driving 1 FP propeller Total Power: 883kW (1,201hp) 12.5kn Makita GNLH6275 1 x 4 Stroke 6 Cy. 275 x 450 883kW (1201bhp) Makita Diesel Co Ltd-Japan AuxGen: 2 x 18kW 225V a.c
7326491 - -	**SANG UTAMA** *ex* Sea Mastiff *-1992* - -	*264* 84 -	Class: (BV)	**1973 Matsuura Tekko Zosen K.K. — Osakikamijima** Yd No: 232 Loa 31.50 Br ex 8.67 Dght 3.506 Lbp 27.51 Br md 8.51 Dpth 4.40 Welded, 1 dk	**(B32A2ST) Tug**	**2 oil engines** geared to sc. shafts driving 2 FP propellers Total Power: 2,354kW (3,200hp) 12.5kn Fuji 6M27.5FH 2 x 4 Stroke 6 Cy. 275 x 320 each-1177kW (1600bhp) Fuji Diesel Co Ltd-Japan
7734818 *6KVQ* -	**SANG WON No. 101** *ex* Dae Kyung No. 301 *-1988* *ex* Dong In No. 51 *-1982* *ex* Ocean Bear No. 15 *-1982* *ex* Ocean Glory No. 2 *-1982* **Hyo Song Mool San Co Ltd** *Busan* *South Korea* Official number: 9505022-6210009	*291* 158 380	Class: (KR)	**1962 Fukuoka Shipbuilding Co Ltd — Fukuoka FO** Loa 40.52 Br ex - Dght 3.409 Lbp 40.01 Br md 7.60 Dpth 3.71 Welded, 1 dk	**(B11B2FV) Fishing Vessel**	**1 oil engine** driving 1 FP propeller Total Power: 662kW (900hp) 9.0kn Niigata M6DHS 1 x 4 Stroke 6 Cy. 370 x 520 662kW (900bhp) Niigata Engineering Co Ltd-Japan AuxGen: 2 x 80kW 110V a.c

8117093 **SANGA-SANGA/PERTAMINA 3009**
YDXZ
\- **PT PERTAMINA (PERSERO)**
\-
Jakarta *Indonesia*
MMSI: 525008026

21,747
7,524
29,944
T/cm
46.6

Class: KI (LR)
✠ Classed LR until 14/12/07

1983-04 **Onomichi Dockyard Co Ltd — Onomichi HS** Yd No: 307
Loa 180.02 (BB) Br ex 30.03 Dght 9.102
Lbp 171.00 Br md 30.00 Dpth 15.02
Welded, 1 dk

(A13B2TP) Products Tanker
Single Hull
Liq: 39,302; Liq (Oil): 39,302
Compartments: 10 Ta, ER
4 Cargo Pump (s): 4x1000m³/hr
Manifold: Bow/CM: 90m

1 oil engine driving 1 FP propeller
Total Power: 9,731kW (13,230hp) 15.0kn
Sulzer 6RLB66
1 x 2 Stroke 6 Cy. 660 x 1400 9731kW (13230bhp)
Ishikawajima Harima Heavy IndustrieCo Ltd (IHI)-Japan
AuxGen: 3 x 680kW 450V 60Hz a.c
Boilers: e 22.5kgf/cm² (22.1bar), AuxB (o.f.) 17.9kgf/cm² (17.6bar)
Fuel: 213.0 (d.f.) (Part Heating Coils) 930.0 (r.f.) 39.0pd

7941693 **SANGAN**
UGER *ex Surskoye -2002*
\- **Nirey LLC**
\-
Nevelsk *Russia*
MMSI: 273818600
Official number: 801208

815
221
332

Class: RS

1980-12 **Yaroslavskiy Sudostroitelnyy Zavod — Yaroslavl** Yd No: 344
Loa 53.73 (BB) Br ex 10.72 Dght 4.290
Lbp 47.92 Br md 10.50 Dpth 6.00
Welded, 1 dk

(B11A2FS) Stern Trawler
Ins: 218
Compartments: 1 Ho, ER
2 Ha: 2 (1.6 x 1.6)
Derricks: 2x3.3t
Ice Capable

1 oil engine driving 1 CP propeller
Total Power: 971kW (1,320hp) 12.8kn
S.K.L. 8NVD48A-2U
1 x 4 Stroke 8 Cy. 320 x 480 971kW (1320bhp)
VEB Schwermaschinenbau "KarlLiebknecht" (SKL)-Magdeburg
Thrusters: 1 Thwart. FP thruster (f); 1 Tunnel thruster (a)
Fuel: 185.0 (d.f.)

8340028 **SANGATTA**
\-
\- **PT PERTAMINA (PERSERO)**
\-
Balikpapan *Indonesia*

223
137
\-

Class: (KI)

1973 **Asia-Pacific Shipyard Pte Ltd — Singapore**
Loa 32.39 Br ex - Dght -
Lbp - Br md 10.71 Dpth 1.68
Welded, 1 dk

(A31A2GX) General Cargo Ship

2 oil engines geared to sc. shafts driving 2 FP propellers
Total Power: 536kW (728hp)
Cummins NTA-855-M
2 x 4 Stroke 6 Cy. 140 x 152 each-268kW (364bhp)
Cummins Engine Co Inc-USA

9615200 **SANGEET**
7JMG
\- **GL Liberty Leasing Ltd & Breeze Leasing Co Ltd**
Taiyo Nippon Kisen Co Ltd
SatCom: Inmarsat C 443286410
Kobe, Hyogo *Japan*
MMSI: 432864000
Official number: 141699

50,624
31,541
95,655

Class: NK

2012-06 **Imabari Shipbuilding Co Ltd — Marugame KG (Marugame Shipyard)**
Yd No: 1581
Loa 234.98 (BB) Br ex - Dght 14.468
Lbp 227.00 Br md 38.00 Dpth 19.90
Welded, 1 dk

(A21A2BC) Bulk Carrier
Grain: 109,477
Compartments: 7 Ho, ER
7 Ha: ER

1 oil engine driving 1 FP propeller
Total Power: 12,950kW (17,607hp) 14.5kn
MAN-B&W 6S60MC-C
1 x 2 Stroke 6 Cy. 600 x 2400 12950kW (17607bhp)
Mitsui Engineering & Shipbuilding CLtd-Japan
Fuel: 3990.0

9323601 **SANGEN MARU**
JL5229
\- **Sanko Unyu KK (Sanko Unyu Co Ltd)**
\-
Matsuyama, Ehime *Japan*
MMSI: 431501792
Official number: 140006

749
\-
1,906

Class: NK

2004-07 **Murakami Hide Zosen K.K. — Imabari**
Yd No: 540
Loa 72.02 Br ex - Dght 4.786
Lbp 68.60 Br md 12.00 Dpth 5.25
Welded, 1 dk

(A12B2TR) Chemical/Products Tanker
Double Hull (13F)
Liq: 1,880; Liq (Oil): 1,880
Compartments: 5 Ta, ER

1 oil engine driving 1 FP propeller
Total Power: 1,618kW (2,200hp) 12.2kn
Hanshin LH34LG
1 x 4 Stroke 6 Cy. 340 x 640 1618kW (2200bhp)
The Hanshin Diesel Works Ltd-Japan
Fuel: 55.0

7905792 **SANGHA**
\-
\- **Government of The Republic of Congo**
\-
Pointe Noire *Congo*
Official number: PN121

119
39
\-

Class: (BV)

1982-06 **Empresa Brasileira de Construcao Naval S.A. (EBRASA) — Itajai** Yd No: 078
Loa 27.77 Br ex 7.07 Dght 2.971
Lbp 25.46 Br md 7.01 Dpth 3.74
Welded, 2 dks

(B11A2FS) Stern Trawler

1 oil engine geared to sc. shaft driving 1 FP propeller
Total Power: 368kW (500hp)
Caterpillar D379TA
1 x Vee 4 Stroke 8 Cy. 159 x 203 368kW (500bhp)
Caterpillar Tractor Co-USA

9157208 **SANGIANG**
YFSQ
\- **Government of The Republic of Indonesia (Direktorat Jenderal Perhubungan Laut - Ministry of Sea Communications)**
PT Pelayaran Nasional Indonesia (PELNI)
Benoa *Indonesia*
MMSI: 525005037

2,620
786
400

Class: KI (GL)

1999-03 **P.T. PAL Indonesia — Surabaya** (Assembled by) Yd No: 122
1999-03 **Jos L Meyer GmbH — Papenburg** (Parts for assembly by)
Loa 74.00 Br ex - Dght 2.850
Lbp 68.00 Br md 15.20 Dpth 6.00
Welded, 3 dks

(A37B2PS) Passenger Ship
Passengers: unberthed: 510; berths: 44

2 oil engines reduction geared to sc. shafts driving 2 FP propellers
Total Power: 1,766kW (2,402hp) 14.0kn
MaK 8M20
2 x 4 Stroke 8 Cy. 200 x 300 each-883kW (1201bhp)
MaK Motoren GmbH & Co. KG-Kiel

9119086 **SANGITA**
V3TR4 *ex KEN Sho -2013*
\- **Sangita Shipping SA**
Alma Shipmanagement & Trading SA
Belize City *Belize*
MMSI: 312983000
Official number: 701330040

14,704
7,883
23,581
T/cm
34.2

Class: NK

1995-10 **Saiki Heavy Industries Co Ltd — Saiki OT** (Hull) Yd No: 1055
1995-10 **Onomichi Dockyard Co Ltd — Onomichi HS** Yd No: 394
Loa 154.50 (BB) Br ex - Dght 9.518
Lbp 146.00 Br md 26.00 Dpth 13.35
Welded, 1 dk

(A21A2BC) Bulk Carrier
Grain: 30,716; Bale: 29,963
Compartments: 4 Ho, ER
4 Ha: (19.2 x 12.7)2 (20.5 x 17.5) (20.8 x 17.5)ER
Cranes: 4x30t

1 oil engine driving 1 FP propeller
Total Power: 4,891kW (6,650hp) 13.0kn
B&W 7S35MC
1 x 2 Stroke 7 Cy. 350 x 1400 4891kW (6650bhp)
Mitsui Engineering & Shipbuilding CLtd-Japan
Fuel: 278.0 (d.f.) 974.0 (r.f.)

9080900 **SANGITA**
VWTO *ex Sanergy Sembilan -2000*
\- **Gol Offshore Ltd**
\-
Mumbai *India*
MMSI: 419004400
Official number: 2855

398
119
218

Class: AB IR

1994-01 **President Marine Pte Ltd — Singapore**
Yd No: 161
Loa 34.00 Br ex 10.82 Dght 4.000
Lbp 32.00 Br md 10.60 Dpth 4.96
Welded, 1 dk

(B32A2ST) Tug
Passengers: berths: 181

2 oil engines sr geared to sc. shafts driving 2 Z propellers
Total Power: 2,898kW (3,940hp) 10.5kn
Nohab 6R25
2 x 4 Stroke 6 Cy. 250 x 300 each-1449kW (1970bhp)
Wartsila Diesel AB-Sweden
AuxGen: 2 x 120kW 415/220V 50Hz a.c
Fuel: 170.0 (d.f.)

8738419 **SANGKE PALANGGA**
YCEM
\- **Government of The Republic of Indonesia (Direktorat Jenderal Perhubungan Darat - Ministry of Land Communications)**
\-
Jakarta *Indonesia*

556
168
\-

Class: KI

2007-03 **P.T. Daya Radar Utama — Jakarta**
Loa 45.50 Br ex - Dght 2.140
Lbp 40.15 Br md 12.00 Dpth 3.20
Welded, 1 dk

(A36A2PR) Passenger/Ro-Ro Ship (Vehicles)
Bow ramp (centre)
Stern ramp (centre)

2 oil engines driving 2 Propellers
Total Power: 1,220kW (1,658hp)
Yanmar 6AYM-ETE
2 x 4 Stroke 6 Cy. 155 x 180 each-610kW (829bhp)
Yanmar Diesel Engine Co Ltd-Japan

9136632 **SANGO TAN**
3FZG5 *ex Adoracion -2011*
\- **Iwaship SA**
Iwasaki Kisen KK (Iwasaki Kisen Co Ltd)
SatCom: Inmarsat C 435611310
Panama *Panama*
MMSI: 356113000
Official number: 2288396CH

1,899
570
2,297

Class: NK

1996-03 **Kegoya Dock K.K. — Kure** Yd No: 980
Loa 82.45 (BB) Br ex 12.82 Dght 4.920
Lbp 78.00 Br md 12.80 Dpth 5.80
Welded, 1 dk

(A12A2TC) Chemical Tanker
Liq: 1,650
Compartments: 3 Ta, ER
2 Cargo Pump (s): 2x320m³/hr

1 oil engine driving 1 FP propeller
Total Power: 1,603kW (2,179hp) 12.0kn
B&W 4S26MC
1 x 2 Stroke 4 Cy. 260 x 980 1603kW (2179bhp)
The Hanshin Diesel Works Ltd-Japan
AuxGen: 2 x 240kW a.c
Fuel: 194.0 (d.f.) 7.5pd

9007336 **SANGRAM**
VTNP
\- **Government of The Republic of India (Coast Guard)**
\-
India

1,888
566
417

Class: (LR) (IR)
✠

1997-04 **Goa Shipyard Ltd. — Goa** Yd No: 1152
Loa 102.00 Br ex 11.56 Dght 3.400
Lbp 94.10 Br md 11.50 Dpth 8.48
Welded, 1 dk

(B34H2SQ) Patrol Vessel

2 oil engines with clutches, flexible couplings & sr geared to sc. shafts driving 2 CP propellers
Total Power: 9,130kW (12,414hp)
Pielstick 16PA6V280
2 x Vee 4 Stroke 16 Cy. 280 x 290 each-4565kW (6207bhp)
Kirloskar Oil Engines Ltd-India

9684055 **SANGROK 7**
\-
\- **Haeyang Shipping Co Ltd**
\-
Seosan *South Korea*
MMSI: 440213620
Official number: DSR-127820

324
81
329

Class: KR (Class contemplated)

2012-12 **Geumgang Shipbuilding Co Ltd — Janghang** Yd No: GGS-10
Loa 39.80 Br ex 10.62 Dght 3.550
Lbp - Br md 10.60 Dpth 4.70
Welded, 1 dk

(B32A2ST) Tug

2 oil engines reduction geared to sc. shafts driving 2 Propellers
Total Power: 4,760kW (6,472hp)
MAN-B&W 7L27/38
2 x 4 Stroke 7 Cy. 270 x 380 each-2380kW (3236bhp)
STX Engine Co Ltd-South Korea

9691058 **SANGROK 8**
\-
\- **Haeyang Shipping Co Ltd**
\-
Seosan *South Korea*
MMSI: 440213660
Official number: DSR-137801

287
111
246

2013-02 **Geumgang Shipbuilding Co Ltd — Janghang** Yd No: GGS-14
Loa 38.00 Br ex 10.02 Dght 3.450
Lbp 34.78 Br md 10.00 Dpth 4.50
Welded, 1 dk

(B32A2ST) Tug

2 oil engines reduction geared to sc. shafts driving 2 Propellers
Total Power: 3,680kW (5,004hp)
Yanmar 6EY26
2 x 4 Stroke 6 Cy. 260 x 385 each-1840kW (2502bhp)
Yanmar Diesel Engine Co Ltd-Japan

8123793 **SANGU**
S2WW
\- **Bangladesh Inland Water Transport Corp**
\-
Chittagong *Bangladesh*
Official number: C.334

1,150
802
1,707

Class: (LR)
✠ Classed LR until 23/10/96

1983-02 **Carl B Hoffmanns Maskinfabrik A/S — Esbjerg** (Hull) Yd No: 46
1983-02 **Assens Skibsvaerft A/S — Assens**
Yd No: 308
Loa 63.45 Br ex 12.30 Dght 3.671
Lbp 59.42 Br md 12.21 Dpth 4.73
Welded, 1 dk

(A31A2GX) General Cargo Ship
Grain: 2,432; Bale: 2,357
Compartments: 2 Ho, ER
2 Ha: (15.6 x 8.2) (15.6 x 8.9)ER
Cranes: 1

1 oil engine with clutches, flexible couplings & sr geared to sc. shaft driving 1 CP propeller
Total Power: 800kW (1,088hp)
Alpha 7V23LU
1 x 4 Stroke 7 Cy. 225 x 300 800kW (1088bhp)
B&W Alpha Diesel A/S-Denmark
AuxGen: 3 x 48kW 380V 50Hz a.c
Fuel: 68.5 (d.f.)

Ship	Tonnage / Class	Builder / Dimensions	Type	Machinery
7534593 **SANGUAN SIN PLA PON** *HSLZ* *ex* Sang Thai 3 *-1994* - *ex* Yamato Maru No. 12 *-1976* *ex* Meitoku Maru No. 15 *-1976* **Sanguansin Fish Meal Partnership Ltd** - *Bangkok* *Thailand* Official number: 191011388	*827* Class: (NK) 467 1,515	**1967 Watanabe Zosen KK — Imabari EH** Yd No: 86 Converted From: General Cargo Ship-1994 Loa 69.02 Br ex 10.04 Dght 4.514 Lbp 61.40 Br md 10.01 Dpth 5.11 Welded, 1 dk	**(B12A2FF) Fish Factory Ship** Grain: 1,750; Bale: 1,650	**1 oil engine** driving 1 FP propeller Total Power: 978kW (1,330hp) 12.0kn Daihatsu 8PSTM-30 1 x 4 Stroke 8 Cy. 300 x 380 978kW (1330bhp) Daihatsu Diesel Manufacturing Co Lt-Japan AuxGen: 2 x 160kW
6701802 **SANGUIL** *6VMY* *ex* Akashi Maru No. 12 *-1976* DAK 411 **Societe Senegalaise pour l'Expansion de la Peche, Surgelation et Conditionnement des Aliments (SENEPESCA)** - *Dakar* *Senegal*	*213* Class: (BV) 69 -	**1966 Hayashikane Shipbuilding & Engineering Co Ltd — Shimonoseki YC** Yd No: 1071 Loa 40.06 Br ex 7.62 Dght 3.320 Lbp 35.62 Br md 7.60 Dpth 3.76 Welded, 1 dk	**(B11B2FV) Fishing Vessel**	**1 oil engine** driving 1 FP propeller Total Power: 736kW (1,001hp) 13.3kn Daihatsu 8PSHT-26D 1 x 4 Stroke 8 Cy. 260 x 320 736kW (1001bhp) Daihatsu Kogyo-Japan
9367994 **SANIA** *9BOR* *ex* Iran Nowshahr *-2010* - **Khazar Sea Shipping Lines** - *Bandar Anzali* *Iran* MMSI: 422684000	**5,676** Class: IN (LR) (RS) 3,334 ✠ Classed LR until 1/8/11 7,004 T/cm 22.0	**2007-05 OAO Volgogradskiy Sudostroitelnyy Zavod — Volgograd** Yd No: 242 Loa 139.95 (BB) Br ex 16.70 Dght 4.600 Lbp 135.69 Br md 16.50 Dpth 6.00 Welded, 1 dk	**(A31A2GX) General Cargo Ship** Grain: 10,956 TEU 274 C Ho 204 TEU C Dk 70 TEU Compartments: 4 Ho, ER 4 Ha: ER	**2 oil engines** with flexible couplings & reduction geared to sc. shafts driving 2 FP propellers Total Power: 2,400kW (3,264hp) 10.5kn Wartsila 6L20 2 x 4 Stroke 6 Cy. 200 x 280 each-1200kW (1632bhp) Wartsila Finland Oy-Finland AuxGen: 3 x 240kW 400V 50Hz a.c Boilers: 2 WTAuxB (ex.g.) 7.1kgf/cm² (7.0bar), WTAuxB (o.f.) 7.1kgf/cm² (7.0bar) Thrusters: 1 Thwart. FP thruster (f)
8929056 **SANITAR-1** - - **Tuapse Commercial Sea Port (A/O 'Tuapsinskiy Morskoy Torgovyy Port')** - *Tuapse* *Russia*	*205* Class: RS 77 326	**1974 Bakinskiy Sudostroitelnyy Zavod im Vano Sturua — Baku** Yd No: 300 Loa 29.17 Br ex 8.01 Dght 3.120 Lbp 28.50 Br md 7.58 Dpth 3.60 Welded, 1 dk	**(B34G2SE) Pollution Control Vessel** Liq: 336; Liq (Oil): 336 Compartments: 8 Ta Ice Capable	**1 oil engine** geared to sc. shaft driving 1 FP propeller Total Power: 166kW (226hp) 7.5kn Daldizel 6CHNSP18/22 1 x 4 Stroke 6 Cy. 180 x 220 166kW (226bhp) Daldizel-Khabarovsk AuxGen: 1 x 50kW a.c, 1 x 30kW a.c Fuel: 11.0 (d.f.)
7914468 **SANJAR** *EZDP* *ex* C. M. Cormorant *-2013* - *ex* Seabulk Cormorant *-2010* *ex* Red Cormorant *-1999* *ex* Rem Contest *-1997* *ex* Scout Fish *-1997* *ex* Maersk Helper *-1992* *ex* Smit-Lloyd 118 *-1982* *launched as* Atlas Hartog *-1980* **Goldfish Star AHTS Tug & Salvage Services Shipping & Trading Inc** Ilk Insaat Taahhut Sanayi ve Ticaret AS *Turkmenbashy* *Turkmenistan* MMSI: 434115600	**1,398** Class: BV (NV) 419 1,939	**1980-09 Samsung Shipbuilding Co Ltd — Geoje** Yd No: 1002 Loa 64.42 Br ex - Dght 6.010 Lbp 56.42 Br md 13.81 Dpth 6.91 Welded, 1 dk	**(B21B20A) Anchor Handling Tug Supply**	**2 oil engines** geared to sc. shafts driving 2 CP propellers Total Power: 5,178kW (7,040hp) 16.0kn Nohab F216V 2 x Vee 4 Stroke 16 Cy. 250 x 300 each-2589kW (3520bhp) Nohab Diesel AB-Sweden AuxGen: 3 x 200kW 415V 50Hz a.c, 1 x 125kW 415V 50Hz a.c Thrusters: 1 Thwart. FP thruster (f)
8658865 **SANJAYA 01** *PNWU* - **H Syahran** - *Samarinda* *Indonesia* Official number: GT 1106 NO.5353/IIK	**1,106** Class: KI 528 -	**2010-12 PT Syandi Perdana — Samarinda** Yd No: 5353 Loa - Br ex - Dght - Lbp 68.00 Br md 9.00 Dpth 2.93 Welded, 1 dk	**(A35D2RL) Landing Craft** Bow ramp (f)	**2 oil engines** reduction geared to sc. shafts driving 2 Propellers Total Power: 1,544kW (2,100hp) Mitsubishi S12A2-MPTK 2 x Vee 4 Stroke 12 Cy. 150 x 160 each-772kW (1050bhp) Mitsubishi Heavy Industries Ltd-Japan AuxGen: 2 x 88kW 400V a.c
9569487 **SANJIR** *J8Y4258* - **Sanakthe Holdings Ltd** Corpag Management (BVI) Ltd *Kingstown* *St Vincent & The Grenadines* MMSI: 377387000 Official number: 40728	**261** Class: (AB) 78 27	**2009-07 Cantieri di Pisa — Pisa** Yd No: 678 Loa 38.70 Br ex 7.50 Dght 1.850 Lbp 31.80 Br md 7.30 Dpth 3.70 Bonded, 1 dk	**(X11A2YP) Yacht** Hull Material: Reinforced Plastic	**2 oil engines** reverse reduction geared to sc. shafts driving 2 FP propellers Total Power: 4,080kW (5,548hp) M.T.U. 12V4000M90 2 x Vee 4 Stroke 12 Cy. 165 x 190 each-2040kW (2774bhp) MTU Friedrichshafen GmbH-Friedrichshafen AuxGen: 2 x 55kW a.c
8905634 **SANKAMAP** *P2V4688* - **Government of Papua New Guinea (North Solomons Provincial Government)** - *Kieta* *Papua New Guinea*	**406** Class: (LR) 125 ✠ Classed LR until 27/5/97 245	**1989-08 Siong Huat Shipyard Pte Ltd — Singapore** Yd No: 254 Loa 38.00 Br ex 8.63 Dght 2.500 Lbp 33.50 Br md 8.40 Dpth 3.30 Welded, 1 dk	**(A32A2GF) General Cargo/Passenger Ship** Passengers: unberthed: 106; cabins: 2; berths: 8 Grain: 180; Ins: 28 Compartments: 1 Ho, ER	**2 oil engines** with clutches & sr reverse geared to sc. shafts driving 2 FP propellers Total Power: 640kW (870hp) Caterpillar 3406TA 2 x 4 Stroke 6 Cy. 137 x 165 each-320kW (435bhp) Caterpillar Inc-USA AuxGen: 2 x 99kW 415V 50Hz a.c
8108030 **SANKATY** *WCE6015* *ex* Insignia *-2001* - **Woods Hole, Martha's Vineyard & Nantucket Steamship Authority** - *Woods Hole, MA* *United States of America* MMSI: 366917530 Official number: 640565	*351* Class: (AB) 239 1,200	**1981-09 RYSCO Shipyard Inc. — Blountstown, Fl** Yd No: 53 Converted From: Offshore Tug/Supply Ship-1994 Lengthened & Widened-2006 Loa 71.63 Br ex 15.85 Dght 3.709 Lbp - Br md 15.85 Dpth 4.27 Welded, 1 dk	**(A36A2PR) Passenger/Ro-Ro Ship (Vehicles)** Passengers: unberthed: 300	**2 oil engines** reverse reduction geared to sc. shafts driving 2 FP propellers Total Power: 1,854kW (2,520hp) 12.0kn EMD (Electro-Motive) 12-645-E2 2 x Vee 2 Stroke 12 Cy. 230 x 254 each-927kW (1260bhp) (Re-engined ,made 1980, Reconditioned & fitted 1981) General Motors Corp.Electro-Motive Div.-La Grange AuxGen: 2 x 99kW Thrusters: 1 Thwart. FP thruster (f)
9132911 **SANKEI MARU** *JL6365* - **Sanko Tanker Co Ltd** Sanko Unyu KK (Sanko Unyu Co Ltd) *Matsuyama, Ehime* *Japan* MMSI: 431500398 Official number: 133988	*747* Class: NK - 2,051	**1995-11 Shirahama Zosen K.K. — Honai** Yd No: 172 Loa 74.50 (BB) Br ex - Dght 4.836 Lbp 70.00 Br md 11.20 Dpth 5.40 Welded, 1 dk	**(A13A2TW) Crude/Oil Products Tanker** Liq: 2,200; Liq (Oil): 2,200 Compartments: 10 Ta, ER	**1 oil engine** with clutches & reverse geared to sc. shaft driving 1 FP propeller Total Power: 736kW (1,001hp) 10.5kn Hanshin LH32LG 1 x 4 Stroke 6 Cy. 320 x 640 736kW (1001bhp) The Hanshin Diesel Works Ltd-Japan Fuel: 60.0 (d.f.)
8850358 **SANKICHI MARU No. 1** - - - - -	*138* - -	**1977 K.K. Otsuchi Kogyo — Otsuchi** L reg 30.30 Br ex - Dght - Lbp - Br md 6.30 Dpth 2.80 Welded, 1 dk	**(B11B2FV) Fishing Vessel**	**1 oil engine** driving 1 FP propeller Total Power: 346kW (470hp) Niigata 6M26ZG 1 x 4 Stroke 6 Cy. 260 x 400 346kW (470bhp) Niigata Engineering Co Ltd-Japan
8967761 **SANKITI MARU NO. 5** *UEYP* *ex* Sankichi Maru No. 5 *-2001* - **OOO 'Soyuzokean'** - *Kholmsk* *Russia* MMSI: 273453070	*119* Class: RS 35 80	**1980-02 K.K. Otsuchi Kogyo — Otsuchi** Loa 24.94 Br ex - Dght 2.150 Lbp 23.94 Br md 5.37 Dpth 2.38 Welded, 1 dk	**(B11B2FV) Fishing Vessel**	**1 oil engine** driving 1 FP propeller Total Power: 255kW (347hp) Niigata 6MG20AX 1 x 4 Stroke 6 Cy. 200 x 260 255kW (347bhp) Niigata Engineering Co Ltd-Japan
9156670 **SANKO 2** *JM6538* - **Sanko Kaiun YK** - *Kamiamakusa, Kumamoto* *Japan* Official number: 134653	*198* - 515	**1996-12 Koa Sangyo KK — Takamatsu KG** Yd No: 598 Loa 48.90 Br ex - Dght 3.200 Lbp 45.00 Br md 7.80 Dpth 3.40 Welded, 1 dk	**(A12A2TC) Chemical Tanker** 2 Cargo Pump (s): 2x150m³/hr	**1 oil engine** driving 1 FP propeller Total Power: 736kW (1,001hp) 11.0kn Hanshin LH26G 1 x 4 Stroke 6 Cy. 260 x 440 736kW (1001bhp) The Hanshin Diesel Works Ltd-Japan
8975328 **SANKO 68** *JL6258* - **Sanei Tanker KK** - *Osaka, Osaka* *Japan* Official number: 134837	*103* - -	**1994-05 Y.K. Yoshida Zosensho — Iyo-Mishima** L reg 29.90 Br ex - Dght - Lbp - Br md 7.00 Dpth 3.00 Welded, 1 dk	**(A13B2TP) Products Tanker**	**1 oil engine** driving 1 Propeller Total Power: 294kW (400hp) Yanmar 6M-HTS 1 x 4 Stroke 6 Cy. 200 x 240 294kW (400bhp) Yanmar Diesel Engine Co Ltd-Japan
8975988 **SANKO 71** *JI3706* - **Sanko Kaiun KK** - *Osaka, Osaka* *Japan* Official number: 135589	*106* - -	**1997-11 Tokuoka Zosen K.K. — Naruto** L reg 29.84 Br ex - Dght 2.870 Lbp - Br md 7.20 Dpth 3.27 Welded, 1 dk	**(A13B2TP) Products Tanker**	**1 oil engine** driving 1 Propeller Total Power: 368kW (500hp) Yanmar MF24-HT 1 x 4 Stroke 6 Cy. 240 x 420 368kW (500bhp) Yanmar Diesel Engine Co Ltd-Japan

9427744 *A8SP6* -	**SANKO BARON** **Far East Offshore AS** Sanko Ship Management Co Ltd SatCom: Inmarsat C 436705299 *Monrovia* *Liberia* MMSI: 636014265 Official number: 14265	**2,428** 799 2,547	Class: AB	**2009-07 Universal Shipbuilding Corp — Yokohama KN (Keihin Shipyard)** Yd No: 0040 Loa 68.00 Br ex - Dght 6.000 Lbp 61.45 Br md 16.39 Dpth 7.20 Welded, 1 dk	**(B21B20A) Anchor Handling Tug Supply**	**2 oil engines** reduction geared to sc. shafts driving 2 CP propellers Total Power: 9,000kW (12,236hp) Wartsila 9L32 2 x 4 Stroke 9 Cy. 320 x 400 each-4500kW (6118bhp) Wartsila Finland Oy-Finland AuxGen: 2 x 320kW 440V 60Hz a.c, 2 x 1800kW 440V 60Hz a.c Thrusters: 2 Thwart. FP thruster (f); 1 Thwart. CP thruster (a) Fuel: 828.0 (r.f.)
9307152 *3ECZ3* -	**SANKO BREEZE** **South Stability Shipping Inc** Sanko Ship Management Co Ltd SatCom: Inmarsat C 437149910 *Panama* *Panama* MMSI: 371499000 Official number: 3106505A	**56,172** 32,082 105,712 T/cm 88.8	Class: LR ✠ **100A1** SS 10/2010 Double Hull oil tanker ESP LI **ShipRight** (SDA, FDA, CM) ✠ **LMC UMS IGS** Eq.Ltr: R†; Cable: 690.4/84.0 U3 (a)	**2005-10 Sumitomo Heavy Industries Marine & Engineering Co., Ltd. — Yokosuka** Yd No: 1314 Loa 239.00 (BB) Br ex 42.03 Dght 14.850 Lbp 229.00 Br md 42.00 Dpth 21.30 Welded, 1 dk	**(A13A2TV) Crude Oil Tanker** Double Hull (13F) Liq: 122,000; Liq (Oil): 122,000 Cargo Heating Coils Compartments: 12 Wing Ta, 2 Wing Slop Ta, ER 3 Cargo Pump (s): 3x2500m³/hr Manifold: Bow/CM: 116.4m	**1 oil engine** driving 1 FP propeller Total Power: 12,000kW (16,315hp) 15.3kn Sulzer 6RTA58T 1 x 2 Stroke 6 Cy. 580 x 2416 12000kW (16315bhp) Diesel United Ltd.-Aioi AuxGen: 3 x 650kW 450V 60Hz a.c Boilers: e (ex.g.) 21.4kgf/cm² (21.0bar), WTAuxB (o.f.) 17.9kgf/cm² (17.6bar) Fuel: 285.0 (d.f.) 2791.3 (r.f.)
9427756 *A8SP7* -	**SANKO BRILLIANCE** **Far East Offshore AS** Sanko Ship Management Co Ltd SatCom: Inmarsat C 463705784 *Monrovia* *Liberia* MMSI: 636014266 Official number: 14266	**2,428** 799 2,554	Class: AB	**2009-09 Universal Shipbuilding Corp — Yokohama KN (Keihin Shipyard)** Yd No: 0041 Loa 68.00 Br ex - Dght 6.000 Lbp 60.00 Br md 16.39 Dpth 7.20 Welded, 1 dk	**(B21B20A) Anchor Handling Tug Supply**	**2 oil engines** reduction geared to sc. shafts driving 2 CP propellers Total Power: 9,000kW (12,236hp) Wartsila 9L32 2 x 4 Stroke 9 Cy. 320 x 400 each-4500kW (6118bhp) Wartsila Finland Oy-Finland AuxGen: 2 x 320kW 440V 60Hz a.c, 2 x 1800kW 440V 60Hz a.c Thrusters: 2 Thwart. CP thruster (f); 1 Thwart. CP thruster (a) Fuel: 828.0 (r.f.)
9545780 *A8YA9* -	**SANKO ENERGY** **Energy Offshore Ltd** The Sanko Steamship Co Ltd (Sanko Kisen KK) *Monrovia* *Liberia* MMSI: 636015010 Official number: 15010	**3,260** 978 3,170	Class: AB	**2011-09 Universal Shipbuilding Corp — Yokohama KN (Keihin Shipyard)** Yd No: 0059 Loa 75.27 (BB) Br ex - Dght 6.600 Lbp 65.00 Br md 18.00 Dpth 8.10 Welded, 1 dk	**(B21B20A) Anchor Handling Tug Supply**	**2 oil engines** reduction geared to sc. shafts driving 2 CP propellers Total Power: 12,000kW (16,316hp) 11.0kn Wartsila 12V32 2 x Vee 4 Stroke 12 Cy. 320 x 400 each-6000kW (8158bhp) (new engine 2011) Wartsila Finland Oy-Finland AuxGen: 2 x 444kW a.c, 2 x 425kW a.c Thrusters: 2 Tunnel thruster (f); 2 Tunnel thruster (a) Fuel: 950.0
9532202 *D5AR7* -	**SANKO FORTUNE** **Fortune Bulkship Ltd** Sanko Ship Management Co Ltd *Monrovia* *Liberia* MMSI: 636015431 Official number: 15431	**40,325** 24,902 74,940 T/cm 67.3	Class: AB	**2012-01 Sasebo Heavy Industries Co. Ltd. — Sasebo Yard, Sasebo** Yd No: 796 Loa 225.00 (BB) Br ex - Dght 14.110 Lbp 218.00 Br md 32.20 Dpth 19.80 Welded, 1 dk	**(A21A2BC) Bulk Carrier** Grain: 90,771; Bale: 88,783 Compartments: 7 Ho, ER 7 Ha: ER	**1 oil engine** driving 1 FP propeller Total Power: 9,230kW (12,549hp) 14.5kn MAN-B&W 7S50MC-C 1 x 2 Stroke 7 Cy. 500 x 2000 9230kW (12549bhp) Mitsui Engineering & Shipbuilding CLtd-Japan AuxGen: 3 x 400kW a.c Fuel: 154.0 (d.f.) 2625.0 (r.f.)
9369760 *A8QJ9* -	**SANKO INDEPENDENCE** **Independence Gas Shipping Inc** Sanko Ship Management Co Ltd *Monrovia* *Liberia* MMSI: 636013946 Official number: 13946	**23,032** 6,909 26,466 T/cm 41.5	Class: LR ✠ **100A1** SS 08/2013 liquefied gas carrier, Ship Type 2G Propane, butane, butylenes, propylene, anhydrous ammonia and butadiene in independent tanks Type A, maximum SG 0.70, partial loading vinyl chloride monomer with maximum SG 0.97, maximum vapour pressure 0.25 bar (0.45 bar in harbour), minmum cargo temperature minus 48 degree C LI *IWS **ShipRight** (SDA) ✠ **LMC UMS +Lloyd's RMC (LG) IGS** Eq.Ltr: K†; Cable: 632.5/68.0 U3 (a)	**2008-08 Hyundai Heavy Industries Co Ltd — Ulsan** Yd No: 1897 Loa 174.20 (BB) Br ex 28.02 Dght 10.400 Lbp 165.00 Br md 28.00 Dpth 17.80 Welded, 1 dk	**(A11B2TG) LPG Tanker** Double Bottom Entire Compartment Length Liq (Gas): 34,483 3 x Gas Tank (s); 3 independent (C.mn.stl) pri horizontal 6 Cargo Pump (s): 6x400m³/hr Manifold: Bow/CM: 88.2m	**1 oil engine** driving 1 FP propeller Total Power: 9,480kW (12,889hp) 16.5kn MAN-B&W 6S50MC-C 1 x 2 Stroke 6 Cy. 500 x 2000 9480kW (12889bhp) Hyundai Heavy Industries Co Ltd-South Korea AuxGen: 4 x 615kW 450V 60Hz a.c Boilers: AuxB (Comp) 8.2kgf/cm² (8.0bar) Fuel: 233.0 (d.f.) 1826.0 (r.f.)
9369772 *A8QK2* -	**SANKO INNOVATOR** **Innovator Gas Shipping Inc** Sanko Ship Management Co Ltd *Monrovia* *Liberia* MMSI: 636013947 Official number: 13947	**23,032** 6,909 26,471 T/cm 41.5	Class: LR ✠ **100A1** SS 08/2013 liquefied gas carrier, Ship Type 2G Propane, butane, butylene, propylene, anhydrous ammonia and butadiene in independent tanks Type A, maximum SG 0.70, partial loading vinyl chloride monomer with maximum SG 0.97, maximum vapour pressure 0.25 bar (0.45 bar in harbour), minimum cargo temperture 48 degree C LI *IWS **ShipRight** (SDA) ✠ **LMC UMS +Lloyd's RMC (LG)** Eq.Ltr: K†; Cable: 632.5/68.0 U3 (a)	**2008-08 Hyundai Heavy Industries Co Ltd — Ulsan** Yd No: 1898 Loa 174.20 (BB) Br ex 28.02 Dght 10.400 Lbp 165.00 Br md 28.00 Dpth 17.80 Welded, 1 dk	**(A11B2TG) LPG Tanker** Liq (Gas): 34,483 3 x Gas Tank (s); 3 independent (C.mn.stl) pri horizontal 6 Cargo Pump (s): 6x400m³/hr Manifold: Bow/CM: 88.2m	**1 oil engine** driving 1 FP propeller Total Power: 9,480kW (12,889hp) 16.5kn MAN-B&W 6S50MC-C 1 x 2 Stroke 6 Cy. 500 x 2000 9480kW (12889bhp) Hyundai Heavy Industries Co Ltd-South Korea AuxGen: 4 x 615kW 450V 60Hz a.c Boilers: AuxB (Comp) 8.2kgf/cm² (8.0bar) Fuel: 233.0 (d.f.) 1826.0 (r.f.)
9294654 *JI3709* -	**SANKO KAIRYU** **Sanko Kaiun KK** - *Osaka, Osaka* *Japan* Official number: 137234	*194* - 370		**2003-02 Tokuoka Zosen K.K. — Naruto** Yd No: 271 Loa 42.39 Br ex 8.12 Dght 3.080 Lbp 38.00 Br md 8.10 Dpth 3.45 Welded, 1 dk	**(A13B2TP) Products Tanker**	**1 oil engine** geared to sc. shaft driving 1 FP propeller Total Power: 441kW (600hp) Yanmar 1 x 4 Stroke 441kW (600bhp) Yanmar Diesel Engine Co Ltd-Japan
8730637 *JD2610* -	**SANKO KINEI** **YK Kinei Kaiun** - *Nagoya, Aichi* *Japan* Official number: 140193	*101* - -		**2005-05 K.K. Nanpei Zosensho — Ise** L reg 29.86 Br ex - Dght - Lbp - Br md 7.60 Dpth 3.00 Welded, 1 dk	**(A13B2TP) Products Tanker** Double Hull (13F)	**1 oil engine** driving 1 Propeller Total Power: 603kW (820hp) Mitsubishi S6R2F-MTK 1 x 4 Stroke 6 Cy. 170 x 220 603kW (820bhp) Mitsubishi Heavy Industries Ltd-Japan
8907644 - - -	**SANKO MARU** - - *South Korea*	*198* - 535		**1989-11 Suzuki Shipyard Co. Ltd. — Yokkaichi** Yd No: 571 Loa 47.60 Br ex - Dght 3.202 Lbp 44.00 Br md 7.90 Dpth 3.40 Welded, 1 dk	**(A12A2TC) Chemical Tanker** Liq: 334	**1 oil engine** driving 1 FP propeller Total Power: 588kW (799hp) Yanmar MF24-UT 1 x 4 Stroke 6 Cy. 240 x 420 588kW (799bhp) Matsue Diesel KK-Japan

Ship / Owner	Tonnage	Class	Builder / Dimensions	Type / Cargo	Machinery
9110078 **SANKO MARU** *JG5227* - **Japan Railway Construction, Transport & Technology Agency & Sanko Unyu Co Ltd** Sanko Unyu KK (Sanko Unyu Co Ltd) *Yokohama, Kanagawa* *Japan* MMSI: 431100146 Official number: 134028	*2,946* - 4,906	Class: NK	**1994-10 Kurinoura Dockyard Co Ltd — Yawatahama EH** Yd No: 325 Loa 103.98 (BB) Br ex 15.23 Dght 6.426 Lbp 97.00 Br md 15.20 Dpth 7.50 Welded, 1 dk	**(A12B2TR) Chemical/Products Tanker** Liq: 5,384; Liq (Oil): 5,384 Cargo Heating Coils Compartments: 10 Ta, ER 5 Cargo Pump (s): 3x750m^3/hr, 2x600m^3/hr Manifold: Bow/CM: 56m	**1 oil engine** driving 1 CP propeller Total Power: 3,310kW (4,500hp) 14.1kn Akasaka A45S 1 x 4 Stroke 6 Cy. 450 x 880 3310kW (4500bhp) Akasaka Tekkosho KK (Akasaka DieselLtd)-Japan AuxGen: 2 x 240kW 440V 60Hz a.c Thrusters: 1 Thwart. CP thruster (f) Fuel: 106.3 (d.f.) (Part Heating Coils) 233.8 (r.f.) 13.5pd
9199309 **SANKO MARU** *JH3458* - **Yoshikazu Ishikura** - *Kihoku, Mie* *Japan* MMSI: 431545000 Official number: 135639	*153* - -		**1998-03 Higashi Kyushu Shipbuilding Co Ltd — Usuki OT** L reg 33.20 Br ex - Dght - Lbp - Br md 5.89 Dpth 2.70 Bonded, 1 dk	**(B11B2FV) Fishing Vessel** Hull Material: Reinforced Plastic	**1 oil engine** geared to sc. shaft driving 1 FP propeller Total Power: 839kW (1,141hp) Daihatsu 6DKM-28 1 x 4 Stroke 6 Cy. 280 x 390 839kW (1141bhp) Daihatsu Diesel Manufacturing Co Lt-Japan
7927192 **SANKO MARU No. 2** - - - - *China*	*494* - 995		**1980-02 Kyoei Zosen KK — Mihara HS** Yd No: 101 Loa 59.95 Br ex 9.83 Dght 4.101 Lbp 55.02 Br md 9.81 Dpth 4.32 Welded, 1 dk	**(A12A2TC) Chemical Tanker**	**1 oil engine** driving 1 FP propeller Total Power: 956kW (1,300hp) Makita KNLH6275 1 x 4 Stroke 6 Cy. 275 x 450 956kW (1300bhp) Makita Diesel Co Ltd-Japan
7933074 **SANKO MARU No. 5** - - **Myung Po Bunkering Co Ltd** - *South Korea*	*175* - 320		**1979 Kominato Zosen K.K. — Amatsu-Kominato** Yd No: 757 Loa 35.51 Br ex - Dght 2.350 Lbp 33.51 Br md 7.80 Dpth 2.60 Welded, 1 dk	**(A13B2TU) Tanker (unspecified)**	**1 oil engine** driving 1 FP propeller Total Power: 243kW (330hp) Sumiyoshi S6UCTE 1 x 4 Stroke 6 Cy. 260 x 400 243kW (330bhp) Sumiyoshi Marine Diesel Co Ltd-Japan
8608755 **SANKO MARU No. 6** *JK4711* *ex* Kyoshin Maru No. 3 *-1999* - **Tokyo Sekiyu KK** - *Kawasaki, Kanagawa* *Japan* Official number: 128033	*199* - 484		**1986-11 Koa Sangyo KK — Takamatsu KG** Yd No: 526 Loa 48.60 Br ex - Dght 3.100 Lbp 45.00 Br md 7.80 Dpth 3.30 Welded, 1 dk	**(A12A2TC) Chemical Tanker** Liq: 393 Compartments: 6 Ta, ER 2 Cargo Pump (s): 2x150m^3/hr	**1 oil engine** driving 1 FP propeller Total Power: 552kW (750hp) Niigata 6M26BGT 1 x 4 Stroke 6 Cy. 260 x 460 552kW (750bhp) Niigata Engineering Co Ltd-Japan
6926971 **SANKO MARU No. 6** *HP4840* *ex* Shibaura Maru No. 5 *-1999* - **Sankyo Navegacion Inc** - *Panama* *Panama* Official number: 1763788A	*135* 37 -	Class: (NK)	**1969 Matsuura Tekko Zosen K.K. — Osakikamijima** Yd No: 200 Loa 26.32 Br ex 7.62 Dght 2.286 Lbp 24.01 Br md 7.60 Dpth 3.00 Welded, 1 dk	**(B32A2ST) Tug**	**1 oil engine** driving 1 FP propeller Total Power: 883kW (1,201hp) 10.8kn Fuji F6S27.5FH4C 1 x 4 Stroke 6 Cy. 275 x 450 883kW (1201bhp) Fuji Diesel Co Ltd-Japan AuxGen: 2 x 12kW
9094559 **SANKO MARU NO. 13** *JD2200* - **Sanko Kaiun YK** - *Tokushima, Tokushima* *Japan* Official number: 140270	*498* - 1,800		**2006-01 Tokuoka Zosen K.K. — Naruto** Yd No: 287 Loa 74.99 Br ex - Dght 4.430 Lbp 69.00 Br md 11.80 Dpth 7.50 Welded, 1 dk	**(A31A2GX) General Cargo Ship** Grain: 2,762; Bale: 2,537 1 Ha: ER (40.0 x 9.5)	**1 oil engine** driving 1 Propeller Total Power: 1,618kW (2,200hp) 11.6kn Hanshin LH34LA 1 x 4 Stroke 6 Cy. 340 x 640 1618kW (2200bhp) The Hanshin Diesel Works Ltd-Japan
8858910 **SANKO MARU No. 18** *JL5942* - **YK Sanko Kaiun** - *Anan, Tokushima* *Japan* Official number: 131511	*402* - 1,000		**1991-07 K.K. Yoshida Zosen Kogyo — Arida** Loa 71.45 Br ex - Dght 3.470 Lbp 66.00 Br md 11.00 Dpth 6.10 Welded, 1 dk	**(A31A2GX) General Cargo Ship** Grain: 1,971 1 Ha: (36.6 x 8.6)ER	**1 oil engine** driving 1 FP propeller Total Power: 736kW (1,001hp) 10.5kn Niigata 6M28BGT 1 x 4 Stroke 6 Cy. 280 x 480 736kW (1001bhp) Niigata Engineering Co Ltd-Japan
9033270 **SANKO MARU NO. 23** *JL6059* - **Shirakawa Kisen KK** - *Tokushima, Tokushima* *Japan* Official number: 132148	*499* - 1,567		**1992-01 K.K. Matsuura Zosensho — Osakikamijima** Yd No: 382 Loa 75.85 (BB) Br ex 12.52 Dght 4.060 Lbp 70.00 Br md 12.50 Dpth 7.00 Welded, 2 dks	**(A31A2GX) General Cargo Ship** Grain: 2,518 Compartments: 1 Ho, ER 1 Ha: ER	**1 oil engine** sr reverse geared to sc. shaft driving 1 FP propeller Total Power: 736kW (1,001hp) Hanshin LH31G 1 x 4 Stroke 6 Cy. 310 x 530 736kW (1001bhp) The Hanshin Diesel Works Ltd-Japan Thrusters: 1 Thwart. FP thruster (f)
9103673 **SANKO MARU No. 28** *JL6256* - **YK Sanko Kaiun** - *Anan, Tokushima* *Japan* Official number: 134835	*419* - 1,600		**1994-04 K.K. Yoshida Zosen Kogyo — Arida** Yd No: 491 Loa - Br ex - Dght - Lbp 69.30 Br md 11.40 Dpth 6.30 Welded, 1 dk	**(A31A2GX) General Cargo Ship** Compartments: 1 Ho 1 Ha: (38.8 x 9.0)	**1 oil engine** driving 1 FP propeller Total Power: 736kW (1,001hp) 10.0kn Hanshin LH28LG 1 x 4 Stroke 6 Cy. 280 x 530 736kW (1001bhp) The Hanshin Diesel Works Ltd-Japan
9535917 **SANKO MARU NO. 35** *JD2661* - **Sanko Kaiun YK** - *Tokushima, Tokushima* *Japan* MMSI: 431000563 Official number: 140762	*498* - 1,830		**2008-04 Tokuoka Zosen K.K. — Naruto** Yd No: 310 Loa 74.98 Br ex - Dght - Lbp 69.00 Br md 11.80 Dpth 7.52 Welded, 1 dk	**(A31A2GX) General Cargo Ship**	**1 oil engine** driving 1 Propeller Total Power: 1,618kW (2,200hp) Niigata 6M34BGT 1 x 4 Stroke 6 Cy. 340 x 620 1618kW (2200bhp) Niigata Engineering Co Ltd-Japan
9648116 **SANKO MARU NO. 38** *JD3318* - **Sanko Kaiun YK** - *Tokushima, Tokushima* *Japan* Official number: 141623	*499* - 1,765		**2012-02 Tokuoka Zosen K.K. — Naruto** Yd No: 333 Loa 75.27 (BB) Br ex - Dght 4.280 Lbp 69.60 Br md 12.00 Dpth 7.28 Welded, 1 dk	**(A31A2GX) General Cargo Ship** Compartments: 1 Ho, ER 1 Ha: ER	**1 oil engine** reduction geared to sc. shaft driving 1 FP propeller Total Power: 1,618kW (2,200hp) 11.5kn Niigata 6M34BGT 1 x 4 Stroke 6 Cy. 340 x 620 1618kW (2200bhp) Niigata Engineering Co Ltd-Japan Thrusters: 1 Thwart. FP thruster (f)
9401910 **SANKO MERMAID** *A8TF7* - **Mermaid Bulkship Ltd** The Sanko Steamship Co Ltd (Sanko Kisen KK) SatCom: Inmarsat C 463705186 *Monrovia* *Liberia* MMSI: 636014341 Official number: 14341	**30,488** 15,289 50,779	Class: NK	**2009-07 Oshima Shipbuilding Co Ltd — Saikai NS** Yd No: 10525 Loa 189.99 (BB) Br ex - Dght 12.200 Lbp 186.00 Br md 32.26 Dpth 17.31 Welded, 1 dk	**(A31A2GO) Open Hatch Cargo Ship** Double Hull Grain: 57,886; Bale: 57,782 TEU 306 Compartments: 8 Ho, ER 8 Ha: ER Cranes: 4x40t	**1 oil engine** driving 1 FP propeller Total Power: 10,187kW (13,850hp) 15.5kn MAN-B&W 5S60MC-C 1 x 2 Stroke 5 Cy. 600 x 2400 10187kW (13850bhp) Kawasaki Heavy Industries Ltd-Japan Fuel: 2350.0
9355513 **SANKO MINERAL** *7JDH* - **The Sanko Steamship Co Ltd (Sanko Kisen KK)** - *Tokyo* *Japan* MMSI: 432649000 Official number: 140774	**30,360** 15,170 50,757	Class: NK	**2008-06 Oshima Shipbuilding Co Ltd — Saikai NS** Yd No: 10494 Loa 189.99 (BB) Br ex - Dght 12.257 Lbp 186.00 Br md 32.26 Dpth 17.31 Welded, 1 dk	**(A31A2GO) Open Hatch Cargo Ship** Double Hull Grain: 57,886; Bale: 57,782 TEU 306 Compartments: 1 Dp Ta, 7 Ho, ER 8 Ha: ER Cranes: 4x40t	**1 oil engine** driving 1 FP propeller Total Power: 11,300kW (15,363hp) 15.5kn MAN-B&W 5S60MC-C 1 x 2 Stroke 5 Cy. 600 x 2400 11300kW (15363bhp) Kawasaki Heavy Industries Ltd-Japan AuxGen: 3 x 525kW a.c Fuel: 2350.0
9562843 **SANKO SHOMA** *JD2932* - **Sanko Kaiun KK** - *Osaka, Osaka* *Japan* Official number: 141044	*119* - 230		**2009-05 Tokuoka Zosen K.K. — Naruto** Yd No: 317 Loa 32.96 Br ex - Dght 2.750 Lbp 29.85 Br md 7.60 Dpth 2.96 Welded, 1 dk	**(A13B2TP) Products Tanker** Double Hull (13F) Liq: 190; Liq (Oil): 190	**1 oil engine** driving 1 FP propeller Total Power: 405kW (551hp) Yanmar 6NY16-ST 1 x 4 Stroke 6 Cy. 160 x 200 405kW (551bhp) Yanmar Diesel Engine Co Ltd-Japan
9189926 **SANKO SINCERE** *JNAV* - **Sun Light Shipping Co Ltd** The Sanko Steamship Co Ltd (Sanko Kisen KK) SatCom: Inmarsat B 343121110 *Tokyo* *Japan* MMSI: 431211000 Official number: 136646	**29,688** 15,595 50,655	Class: NK	**1998-10 Namura Shipbuilding Co Ltd — Imari SG** Yd No: 968 Loa 194.94 (BB) Br ex 32.24 Dght 12.225 Lbp 187.00 Br md 32.20 Dpth 16.80 Welded, 1 dk	**(A31A2GO) Open Hatch Cargo Ship** Double Hull Grain: 52,864; Bale: 52,533 Compartments: 8 Ho, ER 8 Ha: (12.6 x 12.9)2 (13.4 x 27.4)4 (14.3 x 27.4) (16.8 x 16.1)ER Cranes: 4x30t	**1 oil engine** driving 1 FP propeller Total Power: 10,474kW (14,240hp) 15.6kn Mitsubishi 6UEC60LSII 1 x 2 Stroke 6 Cy. 600 x 2300 10474kW (14240bhp) Mitsubishi Heavy Industries Ltd-Japan AuxGen: 3 x 615kW 450V 60Hz a.c Fuel: 213.9 (d.f.) (Part Heating Coils) 2492.4 (r.f.) 39.0pd
8975316 **SANKO TSUBASA** *JI3708* - **Sanko Kaiun KK** - *Osaka, Osaka* *Japan* Official number: 137078	*107* - -		**2001-06 Tokuoka Zosen K.K. — Naruto** L reg 29.86 Br ex - Dght 2.500 Lbp - Br md 7.60 Dpth 2.85 Welded, 1 dk	**(A13B2TP) Products Tanker**	**1 oil engine** driving 1 Propeller Total Power: 405kW (551hp) Yanmar S165-ST 1 x 4 Stroke 6 Cy. 165 x 210 405kW (551bhp) Yanmar Diesel Engine Co Ltd-Japan

7620990 *5VAQ9* -	**SANKOFA** *ex Adamas -2010 ex April -2009* *ex Artemis -2005 ex Pablito 1 -2003* *ex Cordouan -1997 ex Dior -1995* *ex Phisika -1994 ex Nortank Fighter -1990* *ex Turid Cob -1987 ex Tofuku Maru -1987* **Magrat Shipping Ltd** Morgan Energy Ltd *Lome* *Togo* MMSI: 671131000	**7,240** 3,860 11,969 T/cm 22.0	Class: (BV) (NV) (NK)	**1977-06 Kyokuyo Shipbuilding & Iron Works Co Ltd — Shimonoseki YC** Yd No: 291 Loa 135.52 (BB) Br ex 19.44 Dght 8.321 Lbp 125.02 Br md 19.41 Dpth 10.11 Welded, 1 dk	**(A13B2TP) Products Tanker** Single Hull Liq: 14,154; Liq (Oil): 14,154 Cargo Heating Coils 4 Cargo Pump (s) Manifold: Bow/CM: 62m	**1 oil engine** driving 1 FP propeller Total Power: 3,751kW (5,100hp) 12.5kn Mitsubishi 6UET52/90D 1 x 2 Stroke 6 Cy. 520 x 900 3751kW (5100bhp) Kobe Hatsudoki KK-Japan AuxGen: 4 x 320kW 450V 60Hz a.c
9597446 *JD3145* -	**SANKOU MARU** *ex Yamanaka 806 -2010* **Japan Railway Construction, Transport & Technology Agency & Yamanaka Zosen** Yamanaka Zousen KK (Yamanaka Shipbuilding Corp) *Imabari, Ehime* *Japan* Official number: 141372	*498* - 1,710		**2010-11 Yamanaka Zosen K.K. — Imabari** Yd No: 806 Loa 75.24 Br ex - Dght 4.170 Lbp 69.00 Br md 12.00 Dpth 7.12 Welded, 1 dk	**(A31A2GX) General Cargo Ship** Grain: 2,936; Bale: 2,852 Compartments: 1 Ho, ER 1 Ha: ER (40.0 x 9.5)	**1 oil engine** reduction geared to sc. shaft driving 1 Propeller Total Power: 1,323kW (1,799hp) Hanshin LA28G 1 x 4 Stroke 6 Cy. 280 x 590 1323kW (1799bhp) The Hanshin Diesel Works Ltd-Japan
8736411 *JD2465* -	**SANKOUSHIN** - **Koizumi Kisen KK** - *Anan, Tokushima* *Japan* Official number: 140592	*499* - 1,830		**2007-07 Tokuoka Zosen K.K. — Naruto** Yd No: 306 Loa 74.95 Br ex - Dght 4.370 Lbp 69.00 Br md 11.80 Dpth 7.41 Welded, 1 dk	**(A31A2GX) General Cargo Ship** Compartments: 1 Ho, ER 1 Ha: ER (40.0 x 9.3)	**1 oil engine** driving 1 Propeller Total Power: 1,618kW (2,200hp) 11.5kn Niigata 6M34BGT 1 x 4 Stroke 6 Cy. 340 x 620 1618kW (2200bhp) Niigata Engineering Co Ltd-Japan
8860614 *UHYA* -	**SANKT-PETERBURG** - **Soyuz Ltd** - *Murmansk* *Russia* MMSI: 273293400	**741** 222 414	Class: RS	**1992-07 ATVT Zavod "Leninska Kuznya" — Kyyiv** Yd No: 1653 Loa 54.82 Br ex 10.15 Dght 4.140 Lbp 50.30 Br md 9.80 Dpth 5.00 Welded, 1 dk	**(B11A2FS) Stern Trawler** Ice Capable	**1 oil engine** driving 1 FP propeller Total Power: 852kW (1,158hp) 12.0kn S.K.L. 8NVD48-2U 1 x 4 Stroke 8 Cy. 320 x 480 852kW (1158bhp) SKL Motoren u. Systemtechnik AG-Magdeburg
8929044 *UAMI* -	**SANKT-PETERBURG** - **Federal State Unitary Enterprise Rosmorport** - *St Petersburg* *Russia* MMSI: 273436530	**959** 287 260	Class: RS	**1979 Bakinskiy Sudostroitelnyy Zavod im Vano Sturua — Baku** Yd No: 340 Loa 59.20 Br ex 10.55 Dght 3.750 Lbp 53.40 Br md - Dpth 5.40 Welded, 1 dk	**(B34N2QP) Pilot Vessel** Ice Capable	**2 oil engines** driving 2 FP propellers Total Power: 1,280kW (1,740hp) 13.6kn S.K.L. 6NVD48A-2U 2 x 4 Stroke 6 Cy. 320 x 480 each-640kW (870bhp) (made 1973) VEB Schwermaschinenbau "KarlLiebknecht" (SKL)-Magdeburg AuxGen: 2 x 100kW a.c Fuel: 161.0 (d.f.)
9326586 *UBHF6* -	**SANKT-PETERBURG** - **Federal State Unitary Enterprise Rosmorport** - *St Petersburg* *Russia* MMSI: 273334710	**9,460** 2,840 6,430	Class: RS	**2009-07 AO Baltiyskiy Zavod — Sankt-Peterburg** Yd No: 05602 Loa 114.00 Br ex - Dght 8.500 Lbp 97.20 Br md 22.50 Dpth 12.40 Welded, 1 dk	**(B34C2SI) Icebreaker** Ice Capable	**2 diesel electric oil engines** driving 2 gen. Connecting to 2 elec. motors each (8200kW) driving 2 Azimuth electric drive units Total Power: 12,000kW (16,316hp) 17.0kn Wartsila 12V32 2 x Vee 4 Stroke 12 Cy. 320 x 400 each-6000kW (8158bhp) Wartsila Finland Oy-Finland Thrusters: 1 Tunnel thruster (f)
9288980 *UFZC* -	**SANKT-PETERBURG** - **OOO Sudokhodnaya Kompaniya 'Astronavt' (Astronaut Shipping Co Ltd)** Navigator LLC *Astrakhan* *Russia* MMSI: 273443330	**4,378** 1,313 5,600 T/cm 22.0	Class: RS	**2003-06 Sudostroitelnyy Zavod "Krasnoye Sormovo" — Nizhniy Novgorod** Yd No: 19614/2 Loa 141.00 Br ex 16.90 Dght 3.740 Lbp 134.88 Br md 16.80 Dpth 6.10 Welded, 1 dk	**(A13B2TP) Products Tanker** Double Hull (13F) Liq: 6,587; Liq (Oil): 6,721 Compartments: 1 Slop Ta, 12 Wing Ta, ER 2 Cargo Pump (s): 2x250m³/hr Manifold: Bow/CM: 70m Ice Capable	**2 oil engines** reduction geared to sc. shafts driving 2 FP propellers Total Power: 10,230kW (13,908hp) 10.0kn Wartsila 6L20 2 x 4 Stroke 6 Cy. 200 x 280 each-930kW (1264bhp) Wartsila Finland Oy-Finland AuxGen: 3 x 160kW 380/220V 50Hz a.c Thrusters: 1 Thwart. FP thruster (f) Fuel: 32.0 (d.f.) (Heating Coils) 105.0 (r.f.) 13.6pd
9671307 - -	**SANKT-PETERBURG** - - - *Vladivostok* *Russia* Official number: 100779	**257** 92 -	Class: RS (Class contemplated)	**2012-08 OAO Vostochnaya Verf — Vladivostok** Yd No: CD342 Loa 26.56 Br ex - Dght - Lbp - Br md 8.10 Dpth 3.00 Bonded, 1 dk	**(A37B2PS) Passenger Ship** Hull Material: Reinforced Plastic	**2 oil engines** driving 1 Propeller
9660188 *JD3465* -	**SANKYO MARU NO. 2** - **Kyokai Kaiun KK (Kyokai Shipping Co Ltd)** - *Matsuyama, Ehime* *Japan* MMSI: 431004181 Official number: 141839	*748* - 1,581		**2013-02 Hakata Zosen K.K. — Imabari** Yd No: 751 Loa 69.90 Br ex - Dght 4.500 Lbp - Br md 10.60 Dpth - Welded, 1 dk	**(A12A2TC) Chemical Tanker** Double Hull (13F) Liq: 1,250	**1 oil engine** reduction geared to sc. shaft driving 1 Propeller Total Power: 1,370kW (1,863hp) Yanmar 6EY22 1 x 4 Stroke 6 Cy. 220 x 320 1370kW (1863bhp) Yanmar Diesel Engine Co Ltd-Japan
9646168 *JD3047* -	**SANKYO MARU NO. 77** - **Sankyo Sangyo KK** - *Osaka, Osaka* *Japan* Official number: 141219	*158* - -		**2010-09 Sakamoto Zosensho — Nandan** Loa 28.00 Br ex - Dght 2.900 Lbp 25.50 Br md 8.80 Dpth 3.25 Welded, 1 dk	**(B32B2SP) Pusher Tug**	**2 oil engines** reduction geared to sc. shafts driving 2 FP propellers Total Power: 1,472kW (2,002hp) Matsui ML627GSC 2 x 4 Stroke 6 Cy. 270 x 480 each-736kW (1001bhp) Matsui Iron Works Co Ltd-Japan
8742587 *JD2818* -	**SANKYO MARU NO. 88** - **Sankyo Sangyo KK** - *Osaka, Osaka* *Japan* Official number: 140869	*147* - -		**2009-01 Fukae Zosen K.K. — Etajima** Loa 28.00 Br ex - Dght 2.700 Lbp 25.50 Br md 8.00 Dpth 3.25 Welded, 1 dk	**(B32B2SP) Pusher Tug**	**2 oil engines** reduction geared to sc. shafts driving 2 Propellers Total Power: 1,472kW (2,002hp) Matsui 2 x 4 Stroke each-736kW (1001bhp) Matsui Iron Works Co Ltd-Japan
8894809 *YDA4026* -	**SANLE 1** *ex Amanda 2 -2007* **PT Pelayaran Sanle Makmur** - *Tanjung Priok* *Indonesia*	**133** 79 -	Class: KI (BV)	**1995-01 Zhuhai Xiangzhou Shipyard — Zhuhai GD** Yd No: 1-363 Loa 25.50 Br ex 6.80 Dght 2.520 Lbp 22.25 Br md 6.70 Dpth 3.85 Welded, 1 dk	**(B32A2ST) Tug**	**1 oil engine** reduction geared to screwshaft driving 1 FP propeller Total Power: 926kW (1,259hp) 11.8kn Caterpillar 3512TA 1 x Vee 4 Stroke 12 Cy. 170 x 190 926kW (1259bhp) Caterpillar Inc-USA AuxGen: 2 x 44kW 380V a.c Fuel: 30.2 (d.f.)
7204552 *YDA4152* -	**SANLE 5** *ex Ocean Silver V -2008 ex Miyashio -1997* **PT Ocean Buana Lines** - *Tanjung Priok* *Indonesia*	**209** 63 -	Class: KI	**1971-09 Ishikawajima Ship & Chemical Plant Co Ltd — Tokyo** Yd No: 422 Loa 28.40 Br ex 8.64 Dght 2.528 Lbp 25.00 Br md 8.62 Dpth 3.51 Welded, 2 dks	**(B32A2ST) Tug**	**2 oil engines** driving 2 FP propellers Total Power: 1,472kW (2,002hp) Daihatsu 8PSHTCM-26D 2 x 4 Stroke 8 Cy. 260 x 320 each-736kW (1001bhp) Daihatsu Diesel Manufacturing Co Lt-Japan
8137433 - -	**SANLE 7** *ex Aso VIII -2000 ex Hamaei 11 -1996* *ex Hamaei Maru No. 11 -1995* *ex Heian Maru No. 3 -1983* **PT Pelayaran Sanle Makmur** - *Indonesia*	**119** 36 -		**1961 Matsuura Tekko Zosen K.K. — Osakikamijima** Loa 26.00 Br ex - Dght 2.500 Lbp 23.00 Br md 6.50 Dpth 2.90 Welded, 1 dk	**(B32A2ST) Tug**	**2 oil engines** driving 2 FP propellers Total Power: 1,402kW (1,906hp)
7052002 - -	**SANLE 8** *ex Perpetual -2007 ex Tsuru Maru No. 2 -2005* **PT Pelayaran Sanle Makmur** - *Indonesia*	**263** 80 -		**1970-10 Shimoda Dockyard Co. Ltd. — Shimoda** Yd No: 181 Loa 29.01 Br ex 8.56 Dght 2.794 Lbp 26.52 Br md 8.50 Dpth 3.89 Welded, 1 dk	**(B32B2SP) Pusher Tug**	**2 oil engines** geared to sc. shafts driving 2 FP propellers Total Power: 1,956kW (2,660hp) 8.3kn Daihatsu 8PSTCM-30 2 x 4 Stroke 8 Cy. 300 x 380 each-978kW (1330bhp) Daihatsu Diesel Manufacturing Co Lt-Japan AuxGen: 2 x 56kW 205V a.c Fuel: 81.5 4.0pd

9581071 *YDA4520* -	**SANLE 18** **PT Pelayaran Sanle Makmur** - *Jakarta* *Indonesia* Official number: 2009pstha5885/L	**297** 90 -	Class: (KI)	**2009-09 Tanoto Shipyard Pte Ltd — Singapore** Yd No: TSY-S18-F09 Loa 38.12 Br ex - Dght 3.200 Lbp 34.65 Br md 9.00 Dpth 4.00 Welded, 1 dk	**(B32A2ST) Tug**	**2 oil engines** reduction geared to sc. shafts driving 2 Propellers Total Power: 2,722kW (3,700hp) Fuji 2 x 4 Stroke each-1361kW (1850bhp) Fuji Diesel Co Ltd-Japan
9581083 *YDA4547* -	**SANLE 20** **PT Pelayaran Sanle Makmur** - *Jakarta* *Indonesia*	**166** 50 -	Class: (KI)	**2009-11 Tanoto Shipyard Pte Ltd — Singapore** Yd No: TSY-S20-F09 Loa 25.20 Br ex - Dght 2.430 Lbp 23.52 Br md 8.00 Dpth 3.00 Welded, 1 dk	**(B32A2ST) Tug**	**2 oil engines** reduction geared to sc. shafts driving 2 Propellers Total Power: 1,176kW (1,598hp) Yanmar 2 x 4 Stroke each-588kW (799bhp) Yanmar Diesel Engine Co Ltd-Japan
9708136 *YDB4222* -	**SANLE 22** **PT WHS Global Mandiri** - *Tanjung Priok* *Indonesia* Official number: 2013 BA NO.3298/L	**146** 44 -	Class: KI	**2013-01 PT Alima Usaha Samudera — Tanjungpinang** Yd No: 027 Loa 23.50 Br ex - Dght 2.700 Lbp 21.50 Br md 7.32 Dpth 3.20 Welded, 1 dk	**(B32A2ST) Tug**	**2 oil engines** reduction geared to sc. shafts driving 2 FP propellers Total Power: 662kW (900hp) Mitsubishi S6A-MTK 2 x 4 Stroke 6 Cy. each-331kW (450bhp) (made 1984, fitted 2013) Mitsubishi Heavy Industries Ltd-Japan AuxGen: 2 x 40kW a.c
9602370 *YDA4700* -	**SANLE 25** **PT WHS Global Mandiri** - *Tanjung Priok* *Indonesia* Official number: 2010 BA NO. 1953/L	**256** 77 -	Class: KI	**2010-08 PT Alima Usaha Samudera — Tanjungpinang** Yd No: AUS2509 Loa 29.00 Br ex - Dght 4.250 Lbp 26.68 Br md 9.00 Dpth 4.25 Welded, 1 dk	**(B32A2ST) Tug**	**2 oil engines** geared to sc. shafts driving 2 Propellers Total Power: 1,472kW (2,002hp) 10.0kn Caterpillar 2 x 4 Stroke each-736kW (1001bhp) Caterpillar Inc-USA
9570034 *9V8307* -	**SANLE 26** **Tanoto Shipyard Pte Ltd** - *Singapore* *Singapore* Official number: 395591	**266** 80 265	Class: NK	**2009-10 Tuong Aik Shipyard Sdn Bhd — Sibu** Yd No: 2819 Loa 29.00 Br ex - Dght 3.612 Lbp 26.78 Br md 8.60 Dpth 4.20 Welded, 1 dk	**(B32A2ST) Tug**	**2 oil engines** reduction geared to sc. shafts driving 2 Propellers Total Power: 1,518kW (2,064hp) Mitsubishi S6R2-MTK3L 2 x 4 Stroke 6 Cy. 170 x 220 each-759kW (1032bhp) Mitsubishi Heavy Industries Ltd-Japan Fuel: 174.0 (d.f.)
9580687 *YDB4227* -	**SANLE 27** **PT WHS Global Mandiri** - *Tanjung Priok* *Indonesia*	**254** 77 279	Class: NK	**2012-11 Forward Marine Enterprise Sdn Bhd — Sibu** Yd No: FM-77 Loa 30.00 Br ex 8.62 Dght 3.510 Lbp 28.04 Br md 8.60 Dpth 4.12 Welded, 1 dk	**(B32A2ST) Tug**	**2 oil engines** reduction geared to sc. shafts driving 2 FP propellers Total Power: 1,472kW (2,002hp) Yanmar 6RY17P-GV 2 x 4 Stroke 6 Cy. 165 x 219 each-736kW (1001bhp) Yanmar Diesel Engine Co Ltd-Japan Fuel: 210.0
9576284 - -	**SANLE 28** **PT Pelayaran Sanle Makmur** - *Jakarta* *Indonesia*	**196** 59 -	Class: (AB) (KI)	**2009-12 Tanoto Shipyard Pte Ltd — Singapore** Yd No: TSY-S29-F09 Loa 29.00 Br ex - Dght 3.300 Lbp 26.02 Br md 8.50 Dpth 3.80 Welded, 1 dk	**(B32A2ST) Tug**	**2 oil engines** reduction geared to sc. shafts driving 2 Propellers Total Power: 2,060kW (2,800hp) Mitsubishi 2 x 4 Stroke each-1030kW (1400bhp) Mitsubishi Heavy Industries Ltd-Japan
9580601 *YDB4229* -	**SANLE 29** **PT WHS Global Mandiri** - *Tanjung Priok* *Indonesia*	**267** 81 277	Class: NK	**2012-10 Forward Marine Enterprise Sdn Bhd — Sibu** Yd No: FM-64 Loa 30.00 Br ex 8.62 Dght 3.460 Lbp 27.73 Br md 8.60 Dpth 4.12 Welded, 1 dk	**(B32A2ST) Tug**	**2 oil engines** reduction geared to sc. shafts driving 2 FP propellers Total Power: 1,472kW (2,002hp) Yanmar 6RY17P-GV 2 x 4 Stroke 6 Cy. 165 x 219 each-736kW (1001bhp) Yanmar Diesel Engine Co Ltd-Japan Fuel: 210.0 (d.f.)
9677961 *YDB4230* -	**SANLE 30** **PT WHS Global Mandiri** - *Tanjung Priok* *Indonesia*	**117** 35 -	Class: RI	**2012-10 Tai Tung Hing Shipyard Sdn Bhd — Sibu** Yd No: 54 Loa 22.12 Br ex - Dght 2.400 Lbp 20.04 Br md 6.71 Dpth 2.89 Welded, 1 dk	**(B32A2ST) Tug**	**2 oil engines** reduction geared to sc. shafts driving 2 Propellers Total Power: 736kW (1,000hp) Yanmar 6HYM-WET 2 x 4 Stroke 6 Cy. 133 x 165 each-368kW (500bhp) Yanmar Diesel Engine Co Ltd-Japan
9641182 *YDA4931* -	**SANLE 31** **PT WHS Global Mandiri** - *Tanjung Priok* *Indonesia* Official number: 334667	**117** 35 -	Class: RI	**2011-12 Tai Tung Hing Shipyard Sdn Bhd — Sibu** Yd No: 36 Loa 22.12 Br ex - Dght 2.400 Lbp 20.04 Br md 6.71 Dpth 2.90 Welded, 1 dk	**(B32A2ST) Tug**	**2 oil engines** reduction geared to sc. shafts driving 2 FP propellers Total Power: 736kW (1,000hp) Yanmar 6HYM-WET 2 x 4 Stroke 6 Cy. 133 x 165 each-368kW (500bhp) Yanmar Diesel Engine Co Ltd-Japan
9641194 *YDA4932* -	**SANLE 32** **PT WHS Global Mandiri** - *Tanjung Priok* *Indonesia* Official number: 334667	**117** 35 -	Class: RI	**2011-12 Tai Tung Hing Shipyard Sdn Bhd — Sibu** Yd No: 37 Loa 22.12 Br ex - Dght 2.400 Lbp 20.04 Br md 6.71 Dpth 2.90 Welded, 1 dk	**(B32A2ST) Tug**	**2 oil engines** reduction geared to sc. shafts driving 2 FP propellers Total Power: 736kW (1,000hp) Yanmar 6HYM-WET 2 x 4 Stroke 6 Cy. 133 x 165 each-368kW (500bhp) Yanmar Diesel Engine Co Ltd-Japan
9677985 *YDB4235* -	**SANLE 35** **PT WHS Global Mandiri** - *Tanjung Priok* *Indonesia*	**117** 35 -	Class: RI	**2013-02 Tai Tung Hing Shipyard Sdn Bhd — Sibu** Yd No: 56 Loa 22.12 Br ex - Dght 2.400 Lbp 20.72 Br md 6.71 Dpth 2.89 Welded, 1 dk	**(B32A2ST) Tug**	**2 oil engines** reduction geared to sc. shafts driving 2 FP propellers Total Power: 736kW (1,000hp) 10.0kn Yanmar 6HYM-WET 2 x 4 Stroke 6 Cy. 133 x 165 each-368kW (500bhp) Yanmar Diesel Engine Co Ltd-Japan AuxGen: 2 x 16kW 50Hz a.c
9677997 *YDB4236* -	**SANLE 36** **PT WHS Global Mandiri** - *Tanjung Priok* *Indonesia*	**117** 35 -	Class: RI	**2013-04 Tai Tung Hing Shipyard Sdn Bhd — Sibu** Yd No: 57 Loa 22.12 Br ex - Dght 2.400 Lbp 20.72 Br md 6.71 Dpth 2.90 Welded, 1 dk	**(B32A2ST) Tug**	**2 oil engines** reduction geared to sc. shafts driving 2 Propellers Total Power: 736kW (1,000hp) 10.0kn Yanmar 6HYM-WET 2 x 4 Stroke 6 Cy. 133 x 165 each-368kW (500bhp) Yanmar Diesel Engine Co Ltd-Japan
9677973 *YDB4237* -	**SANLE 37** **PT WHS Global Mandiri** - *Tanjung Priok* *Indonesia*	**117** 35 -	Class: RI	**2013-01 Tai Tung Hing Shipyard Sdn Bhd — Sibu** Yd No: 55 Loa 22.12 Br ex - Dght 2.400 Lbp 20.72 Br md 6.71 Dpth 2.89 Welded, 1 dk	**(B32A2ST) Tug**	**2 oil engines** reduction geared to sc. shafts driving 2 FP propellers Total Power: 736kW (1,000hp) 10.0kn Yanmar 6HYM-WET 2 x 4 Stroke 6 Cy. 133 x 165 each-368kW (500bhp) Yanmar Diesel Engine Co Ltd-Japan AuxGen: 2 x 16kW 50Hz a.c
8746595 *YDA6374* -	**SANLIM II** **PT Sanlim Samudra Jaya** - *Samarinda* *Indonesia*	**163** 49 -	Class: KI	**2009 P.T. Galangan Teluk Bajau Kaltim — Samarinda** Loa 25.00 Br ex - Dght 2.890 Lbp 23.41 Br md 7.50 Dpth 3.40 Welded, 1 dk	**(B32A2ST) Tug**	**2 oil engines** reduction geared to sc. shafts driving 2 Propellers Total Power: 980kW (1,332hp) Mitsubishi S6A3-MPTK 2 x 4 Stroke 6 Cy. 150 x 175 each-490kW (666bhp) Mitsubishi Heavy Industries Ltd-Japan AuxGen: 2 x 88kW 400V a.c
8746600 *YDA6375* -	**SANLIM III** **PT Sanlim Samudra Jaya** - *Samarinda* *Indonesia*	**151** 46 -	Class: KI	**2009-12 P.T. Galangan Teluk Bajau Kaltim — Samarinda** Loa - Br ex - Dght 2.720 Lbp 23.80 Br md 7.30 Dpth 3.20 Welded, 1 dk	**(B32A2ST) Tug**	**2 oil engines** reduction geared to sc. shafts driving 2 Propellers Total Power: 980kW (1,332hp) Mitsubishi S6A3-MPTK 2 x 4 Stroke 6 Cy. 150 x 175 each-490kW (666bhp) Mitsubishi Heavy Industries Ltd-Japan AuxGen: 2 x 88kW 400V a.c
9681455 *JD3503* -	**SANMANYOSHI** **YK Sanmanyoshi** - *Kasaoka, Okayama* *Japan* Official number: 141904	*267* - 800		**2013-04 Yano Zosen K.K. — Imabari** Yd No: 272 Loa 61.00 Br ex - Dght 3.440 Lbp - Br md 9.80 Dpth 6.00 Welded, 1 dk	**(A31A2GX) General Cargo Ship** Double Hull Grain: 1,452; Bale: 1,403	**1 oil engine** reduction geared to sc. shaft driving 1 Propeller Total Power: 1,029kW (1,399hp) Niigata 6M28BGT 1 x 4 Stroke 6 Cy. 280 x 480 1029kW (1399bhp) Niigata Engineering Co Ltd-Japan

IMO / Call sign / Flag	Name / Former names / Owner / Port	Tonnage	Class	Builder / Dimensions	Type / Cargo	Machinery
8926391 *JK5470* -	**SANMANYOSHI 3** *ex* Showa Maru *-2007* **YK Sanmanyoshi** - *Bizen, Okayama* Japan Official number: 135306	*199* - 700		**1996**-12 **Shinwa Sangyo K.K. — Osakikamijima** Yd No: 553 Loa 57.77 Br ex - Dght - Lbp 53.00 Br md 9.40 Dpth 5.40 Welded, 1 dk	**(A31A2GX) General Cargo Ship** Bale: 1,155	**1 oil engine** driving 1 FP propeller Total Power: 736kW (1,001hp) 12.0kn Matsui ML627GSC 1 x 4 Stroke 6 Cy. 270 x 480 736kW (1001bhp) Matsui Iron Works Co Ltd-Japan
9608013 *JD3207* -	**SANMANYOSHI 5** - **YK Sanmanyoshi** - *Kasaoka, Okayama* Japan MMSI: 431002518 Official number: 141456	*267* - 800		**2011**-05 **Yano Zosen K.K. — Imabari** Yd No: 231 Loa 61.00 (BB) Br ex - Dght 3.428 Lbp 55.40 Br md 9.80 Dpth 6.00 Welded, 1 dk	**(A31A2GX) General Cargo Ship** Double Hull Grain: 1,371; Bale: 1,328 1 Ha: ER (31.0 x 7.5)	**1 oil engine** reduction geared to sc. shaft driving 1 Propeller Total Power: 1,029kW (1,399hp) Niigata 6M28BGT 1 x 4 Stroke 6 Cy. 280 x 480 1029kW (1399bhp) Niigata Engineering Co Ltd-Japan
9705392 - -	**SANMANYOSHI 16** - **YK Sanmanyoshi** - Japan	*499* - 1,730		**2013**-07 **Koike Zosen Kaiun KK — Osakikamijima** Yd No: 556 Loa - Br ex - Dght - Lbp - Br md - Dpth - Welded, 1 dk	**(A31A2GX) General Cargo Ship**	**1 oil engine** reduction geared to sc. shaft driving 1 Propeller
9055058 *UNV* -	**SANMAR-2** *ex* Sanmar II *-2001* **BUE Bulkers Ltd** BUE Kazakhstan Ltd *Aqtau* Kazakhstan MMSI: 436000022	**354** 106 124	Class: RS (TL)	**1992**-09 **Cicek Tersanesi — Tuzla** Loa 36.75 Br ex - Dght 4.000 Lbp 32.80 Br md 9.10 Dpth 4.80 Welded, 1 dk	**(B32A2ST) Tug**	**1 oil engine** reduction geared to sc. shaft driving 1 FP propeller Total Power: 2,028kW (2,757hp) Caterpillar 3606TA 1 x 4 Stroke 6 Cy. 280 x 300 2028kW (2757bhp) Caterpillar Inc-USA
8850578 *UNU* -	**SANMAR I** - **BUE Bulkers Ltd** BUE Kazakhstan Ltd *Aqtau* Kazakhstan MMSI: 436000021 Official number: 896663	*132* 40 36	Class: RS (TL)	**1990**-01 **Gemak Sanayi ve Ticaret Koll. Sti. — Tuzla** Loa 27.10 Br ex - Dght 2.700 Lbp 24.57 Br md 7.20 Dpth 3.20 Welded, 1 dk	**(B32A2ST) Tug**	**1 oil engine** driving 1 FP propeller Total Power: 898kW (1,221hp) MWM TBD440-6K 1 x 4 Stroke 6 Cy. 230 x 270 898kW (1221bhp) Motoren Werke Mannheim AG (MWM)-West Germany
9116242 *AUJQ* -	**SANMAR MAJESTY** *ex* Cristal *-2005* *ex* Panam Cristal *-2002* **Sanmar Shipping Ltd** - *Mumbai* India MMSI: 419559000 Official number: 3159	**5,973** 3,253 10,314 T/cm 19.6	Class: IR NK	**1996**-01 **Asakawa Zosen K.K. — Imabari** Yd No: 390 Loa 125.00 (BB) Br ex 18.82 Dght 7.764 Lbp 117.00 Br md 18.80 Dpth 9.90 Welded, 1 dk	**(A12B2TR) Chemical/Products Tanker** Double Hull (13F) Liq: 11,564; Liq (Oil): 11,564 Compartments: 21 Ta, ER 21 Cargo Pump (s): 7x300m³/hr, 14x150m³/hr Manifold: Bow/CM: 62.2m	**1 oil engine** driving 1 FP propeller Total Power: 3,884kW (5,281hp) 13.5kn B&W 6L35MC 1 x 2 Stroke 6 Cy. 350 x 1050 3884kW (5281bhp) Hitachi Zosen Corp-Japan AuxGen: 2 x 400kW 450V 60Hz a.c Thrusters: 1 Thwart. FP thruster (f) Fuel: 90.0 (d.f.) 562.0 (r.f.) 15.5pd
9112325 *AUQB* -	**SANMAR PARAGON** *ex* Avalon *-2007* **Sanmar Shipping Ltd** - *Mumbai* India MMSI: 419648000 Official number: 3312	**38,560** 24,567 73,080 T/cm 64.3	Class: IR LR ✠ **100A1** SS 06/2011 bulk carrier strengthened for heavy cargoes, Nos. 2, 4 & 6 holds may be empty ESP *IWS ESN-Hold 1 ✠ **LMC** **UMS** Eq.Ltr: O†; Cable: 660.0/78.0 U3	**1996**-06 **Samsung Heavy Industries Co Ltd — Geoje** Yd No: 1151 Loa 224.95 (BB) Br ex 32.28 Dght 13.896 Lbp 216.00 Br md 32.24 Dpth 19.10 Welded, 1 dk	**(A21A2BC) Bulk Carrier** Grain: 85,606 Compartments: 7 Ho, ER 7 Ha: (16.6 x 11.1)6 (16.6 x 14.1)ER	**1 oil engine** driving 1 FP propeller Total Power: 8,680kW (11,801hp) 13.5kn B&W 6S60MC 1 x 2 Stroke 6 Cy. 600 x 2292 8680kW (11801bhp) Samsung Heavy Industries Co Ltd-South Korea AuxGen: 3 x 500kW 450V 60Hz a.c Boilers: AuxB (Comp) 8.0kgf/cm² (7.8bar) Fuel: 152.5 (d.f.) (Heating Coils) 2341.0 (r.f.) 32.5pd
8320523 *ATVG* -	**SANMAR PHOENIX** *ex* Sanmar Symphony *-2009* *ex* Torm Thyra *-1996* **Sanmar Shipping Ltd** - SatCom: Inmarsat A 1641171 *Mumbai* India MMSI: 419196000 Official number: 2681	**33,285** 17,343 54,747	Class: IR RI (LR) ✠ Classed LR until 9/1/09	**1985**-10 **Odense Staalskibsvaerft A/S — Munkebo (Lindo Shipyard)** (Aft section) Yd No: 108 **2009**-01 **COSCO (Nantong) Shipyard Co Ltd — Nantong JS** (Fwd & cargo sections) Converted From: Crude Oil/Products Tanker-2009 Lengthened & New forept-2009 Loa 199.40 (BB) Br ex 32.24 Dght 12.700 Lbp 195.90 Br md 32.20 Dpth 17.81 Welded, 1 dk	**(A21A2BC) Bulk Carrier** Double Hull Grain: 66,000 Compartments: 5 Ho, ER 5 Ha: 4 (21.6 x 20.8)ER (15.8 x 20.8) Cranes: 4x36t	**1 oil engine** driving 1 FP propeller Total Power: 7,950kW (10,809hp) 14.0kn B&W 5L70MCE 1 x 2 Stroke 5 Cy. 700 x 2268 7950kW (10809bhp) Mitsui Engineering & Shipbuilding CLtd-Japan AuxGen: 3 x 800kW 450V 60Hz a.c Boilers: AuxB (Comp) 10.1kgf/cm² (9.9bar), AuxB (o.f.) 15.2kgf/cm² (14.9bar) Fuel: 180.0 (d.f.) (Heating Coils) 1638.0 (r.f.) 30.0pd
9015357 *AUEZ* -	**SANMAR SERENADE** *ex* Garnet Lady *-2004* *ex* Garnet River *-2000* **Sanmar Shipping Ltd** - *Mumbai* India MMSI: 419512000 Official number: 3082	**25,877** 12,610 45,696 T/cm 47.6	Class: IR LR (NK) **100A1** SS 08/2012 oil tanker ESP **LMC** **IGS** Eq.Ltr: K†; Cable: 632.5/68.0 U3 (a)	**1992**-08 **Tsuneishi Shipbuilding Co Ltd — Fukuyama HS** Yd No: 658 Loa 181.00 (BB) Br ex 30.03 Dght 12.522 Lbp 172.00 Br md 30.00 Dpth 18.20 Welded, 1 dk	**(A13A2TW) Crude/Oil Products Tanker** Double Hull (13F) Liq: 47,259; Liq (Oil): 47,259 Cargo Heating Coils Compartments: 7 Ta, 2 Wing Slop Ta, ER 4 Cargo Pump (s): 4x1250m³/hr Manifold: Bow/CM: 88m	**1 oil engine** driving 1 FP propeller Total Power: 6,550kW (8,905hp) 14.0kn B&W 6L60MCE 1 x 2 Stroke 6 Cy. 600 x 1944 6550kW (8905bhp) Mitsui Engineering & Shipbuilding CLtd-Japan AuxGen: 3 x 550kW 450V 60Hz a.c, 1 x 100kW 450V 60Hz a.c Boilers: e (ex.g.) 21.9kgf/cm² (21.5bar), AuxB (o.f.) 17.9kgf/cm² (17.6bar) Fuel: 200.0 (d.f.) 1689.0 (r.f.)
9152832 *AVDS* -	**SANMAR SONNET** *ex* River Spring *-2009* **Sanmar Shipping Ltd** - *Mumbai* India MMSI: 419094800 Official number: 3658	**56,854** 22,758 99,999 T/cm 88.3	Class: IR NK	**1997**-04 **Namura Shipbuilding Co Ltd — Imari SG** Yd No: 954 Loa 240.99 (BB) Br ex 42.03 Dght 14.339 Lbp 232.00 Br md 42.00 Dpth 21.20 Welded, 1 dk	**(A13B2TP) Products Tanker** Double Hull (13F) Liq: 109,602; Liq (Oil): 119,601 Cargo Heating Coils Compartments: 12 Wing Ta, 2 Wing Slop Ta, ER 3 Cargo Pump (s): 3x2600m³/hr Manifold: Bow/CM: 120.5m	**1 oil engine** driving 1 FP propeller Total Power: 12,791kW (17,391hp) 15.0kn Sulzer 7RTA62 1 x 2 Stroke 7 Cy. 620 x 2150 12791kW (17391bhp) Mitsubishi Heavy Industries Ltd-Japan AuxGen: 3 x 520kW a.c Fuel: 110.0 (d.f.) 2500.0 (r.f.)
9174488 *AVIR* -	**SANMAR STANZA** *ex* Freja Spring *-2010* **Sanmar Shipping Ltd** - *Mumbai* India MMSI: 419000204 Official number: 3774	**28,546** 12,369 47,110 T/cm 50.2	Class: IR LR (NK) **100A1** SS 04/2009 Double Hull oil tanker ESP *IWS LI **LMC** **UMS IGS**	**1999**-04 **Onomichi Dockyard Co Ltd — Onomichi HS** Yd No: 436 Loa 182.50 (BB) Br ex 32.23 Dght 12.667 Lbp 172.00 Br md 32.20 Dpth 19.10 Welded, 1 dk	**(A13B2TP) Products Tanker** Double Hull (13F) Liq: 51,431; Liq (Oil): 51,431 Cargo Heating Coils Compartments: 2 Ta, 12 Wing Ta, 2 Wing Slop Ta, ER 4 Cargo Pump (s): 4x1000m³/hr Manifold: Bow/CM: 91.7m	**1 oil engine** driving 1 FP propeller Total Power: 8,562kW (11,641hp) 14.5kn B&W 6S50MC 1 x 2 Stroke 6 Cy. 500 x 1910 8562kW (11641bhp) Mitsui Engineering & Shipbuilding CLtd-Japan AuxGen: 3 x 420kW a.c Fuel: 111.0 (d.f.) 1520.0 (r.f.) 33.4pd
9418470 *ICHN* -	**SANMARI** *ex* Bodrum-C *-2007* **Rimorchiatori Laziali Impresa di Salvataggio e Rimorchi SpA** Cafiservice SpA *Naples* Italy MMSI: 247219300	**3,050** 1,397 4,500	Class: BV (RI)	**2007**-09 **Arkadas Denizcilik Insaat Sanayi Ticaret Ltd Sti — Istanbul (Tuzla)** Yd No: 02 Loa 80.10 (BB) Br ex - Dght 5.850 Lbp 77.31 Br md 15.00 Dpth 7.20 Welded, 1 dk	**(A31A2GX) General Cargo Ship** Cranes: 2	**1 oil engine** reduction geared to sc. shafts driving 1 FP propeller Total Power: 1,980kW (2,692hp) 13.0kn MaK 6M25 1 x 4 Stroke 6 Cy. 255 x 400 1980kW (2692bhp) Caterpillar Motoren GmbH & Co. KG-Germany AuxGen: 2 x 443kW a.c Thrusters: 1 Tunnel thruster (f)
9606065 *OZEK* -	**SANNA** - **Gronlands Naturinstitut (Greenland Institute of Natural Resources)** - *Nuuk* Denmark MMSI: 331394000 Official number: H1707	**399** 137 200		**2012**-03 **'Crist' SA — Gdansk** (Hull) **2012**-03 **Karstensens Skibsvaerft A/S — Skagen** Yd No: 416 Loa 32.35 (BB) Br ex - Dght - Lbp - Br md 10.00 Dpth - Welded, 1 dk	**(B31A2SR) Research Survey Vessel** A-frames: 1x4t	**1 oil engine** reduction geared to sc. shaft driving 1 Propeller Total Power: 634kW (862hp) Cummins KTA-38-M0 1 x Vee 4 Stroke 12 Cy. 159 x 159 634kW (862bhp) Cummins Engine Co Inc-USA Thrusters: 1 Tunnel thruster (f)
8655954 - -	**SANNE** *ex* Munsterberg *-2006* *ex* Maintank 18 *-2006* **Aeolus Marine Inc** -	**862** 663 2,072		**1971** **Bayerische Schiffbaug. mbH vorm. A. Schellenberger — Erlenbach** Loa 105.00 Br ex 9.05 Dght 2.900 Lbp 102.00 Br md 9.00 Dpth 4.85 Welded, 1 dk	**(A13B2TP) Products Tanker**	**1 oil engine** reduction geared to sc. shafts driving 1 Propeller Total Power: 1,250kW (1,700hp) Deutz 1 x 1250kW (1700bhp)
8749602 *OYFG2* -	**SANNE A** *ex* Dino *-2007* *ex* Peldosais Celtinis LM-PK60 *-2005* *ex* DP-ZPGDY-5 *-2000* **Jens Alfastsen Rederiet** - *Horsens* Denmark (DIS) Official number: M 982	**683** 204 161	Class: (BV)	**1973**-12 **IHC Verschure BV — Amsterdam** Yd No: 822 Loa 36.00 Br ex - Dght 2.500 Lbp - Br md 20.40 Dpth 3.60 Welded, 1 dk	**(B34B2SC) Crane Vessel** Cranes: 1x60t	**2 oil engines** driving 2 Directional propellers Total Power: 536kW (728hp) Deutz BF12M716 1 x Vee 4 Stroke 12 Cy. 135 x 160 268kW (364bhp) Kloeckner Humboldt Deutz AG-West Germany AuxGen: 1 x 250kW 400V 50Hz a.c

Number / Call sign	Name / Owner / Port	Tonnage	Class	Build / Dimensions	Type	Machinery
9087922 *JM6347* -	**SANNO NO. 1** *ex* Kashii Maru *-2012* - - *Hiroshima, Hiroshima* *Japan* MMSI: 431600217 Official number: 134468	*699* - 2,022		**1994-04 K.K. Matsuura Zosensho — Osakikamijima** Yd No: 506 Loa 81.22 (BB) Br ex 12.63 Dght 4.647 Lbp 75.00 Br md 12.60 Dpth 7.50 Welded, 2 dks	**(A31A2GX) General Cargo Ship** Compartments: 1 Ho, ER	**1 oil engine** driving 1 FP propeller Total Power: 1,618kW (2,200hp) Akasaka A34 1 x 4 Stroke 6 Cy. 340 x 660 1618kW (2200bhp) Akasaka Tekkosho KK (Akasaka DieselLtd)-Japan Thrusters: 1 Thwart. FP thruster (f)
9146259 *JM6530* -	**SANNOU** *ex* Kinwa Maru *-2011* - - *Hiroshima, Hiroshima* *Japan* Official number: 134634	*497* - 1,485		**1996-06 K.K. Yoshida Zosen Kogyo — Arida** Yd No: 501 Loa 76.50 Br ex - Dght 3.970 Lbp 70.00 Br md 12.00 Dpth 7.00 Welded, 1 dk	**(A31A2GX) General Cargo Ship**	**1 oil engine** driving 1 FP propeller Total Power: 1,471kW (2,000hp) Hanshin LH34LAG 1 x 4 Stroke 6 Cy. 340 x 640 1471kW (2000bhp) The Hanshin Diesel Works Ltd-Japan
9601766 *JD3198* -	**SANNOU NO. 2** - **YK Yaegaki Senpaku Shokai** - *Hiroshima, Hiroshima* *Japan* MMSI: 431002504 Official number: 141444	*229* - 780		**2011-04 Taiyo Shipbuilding Co Ltd — Sanyoonoda YC** Yd No: 326 Loa 60.02 Br ex - Dght 3.250 Lbp 55.00 Br md 9.50 Dpth 5.45 Welded, 1 dk	**(A31A2GX) General Cargo Ship** Single Hull Grain: 1,216; Bale: 1,211 1 Ha: ER (31.0 x 7.5)	**1 oil engine** reduction geared to sc. shaft driving 1 Propeller Total Power: 1,030kW (1,400hp) 12.5kn Hanshin LH28G 1 x 4 Stroke 6 Cy. 280 x 460 1030kW (1400bhp) The Hanshin Diesel Works Ltd-Japan
9094987 *ZCTG4* -	**SANOO** *ex* XS Of London *-2008* **Windsor Investment Services Ltd** - *George Town* *Cayman Islands (British)* MMSI: 319340000 Official number: 909862	**328** 98 33	Class: RI	**2005-01 C.R.N. Cant. Nav. Ancona S.r.l. — Ancona** Yd No: 128/02 Loa 39.56 Br ex 7.53 Dght 2.780 Lbp - Br md 7.50 Dpth 3.71 Bonded, 1 dk	**(X11A2YP) Yacht** Hull Material: Reinforced Plastic Passengers: cabins: 5; berths: 10	**2 oil engines** geared to sc. shafts driving 2 Propellers Total Power: 4,080kW (5,548hp) 23.0kn M.T.U. 12V4000M90 2 x Vee 4 Stroke 12 Cy. 165 x 190 each-2040kW (2774bhp) MTU Friedrichshafen GmbH-Friedrichshafen Thrusters: 1 Thwart. FP thruster (f)
5365247 *9BFD* -	**SANOOBAR** *ex* Salwa 1 *-2008* *ex* Lyngsaa *-1980* *ex* Rafi *-1975* *ex* Torosand *-1972* **Mohmad Reza Jarrahi** Tohid Hamidey *Bandar Imam Khomeini* *Iran* MMSI: 422455000 Official number: 20459	*389* 199 610	Class: AS (GL)	**1952 Flensburger Maschinenbau-Anstalt Johannsen & Soerensen — Flensburg** Yd No: 112 Lengthened-1956 Loa 48.72 Br ex 7.52 Dght 3.252 Lbp 44.60 Br md 7.47 Dpth 3.79 Riveted\Welded, 1 dk	**(A31A2GX) General Cargo Ship** Grain: 850; Bale: 801 Compartments: 1 Ho, ER 2 Ha: (11.5 x 5.0) (11.9 x 5.0)ER Derricks: 2x2t; Winches: 2	**1 oil engine** reduction geared to sc. shaft driving 1 FP propeller Total Power: 609kW (828hp) Yanmar 6LX-ET 1 x 4 Stroke 6 Cy. 150 x 165 609kW (828bhp) Yanmar Diesel Engine Co Ltd-Japan Fuel: 17.5 (d.f.)
1004716 *ZHGE* -	**SANORA** *ex* Xanthia B *-1997* *ex* Rora V *-1996* **Sanora Marine Ltd** Sete Yacht Management SA *George Town* *Cayman Islands (British)* Official number: 725080	**453** 135 -	Class: LR ✠ **100A1** SS 02/2009 Yacht **LMC** Cable: 266.7/19.0 U2	**1994-02 de Vries Scheepsbouw B.V. — Aalsmeer** Yd No: 648 Loa 44.00 Br ex 8.75 Dght 2.900 Lbp 38.80 Br md 8.40 Dpth 4.80 Welded, 1 dk	**(X11A2YP) Yacht**	**2 oil engines** with clutches, flexible couplings & sr reverse geared to sc. shafts driving 2 FP propellers Total Power: 1,156kW (1,572hp) Caterpillar 3508TA 2 x Vee 4 Stroke 8 Cy. 170 x 190 each-578kW (786bhp) Caterpillar Inc-USA AuxGen: 2 x 84kW 380V 50Hz a.c Thrusters: 1 Thwart. FP thruster (f)
8738641 - -	**SANPAI** - **Government of The Republic of Indonesia (Dinas Perhubungan Propinsi Papua - Papua Province Communications Service)** - *Jayapura* *Indonesia*	**200** 77 -	Class: KI	**2007-11 P.T. Mariana Bahagia — Palembang** Loa 32.00 Br ex - Dght 2.400 Lbp 27.50 Br md 8.00 Dpth 2.80 Welded, 1 dk	**(A35D2RL) Landing Craft**	**2 oil engines** driving 2 Propellers Total Power: 376kW (512hp) Yanmar 6CH-UTE 2 x 4 Stroke 6 Cy. 105 x 125 each-188kW (256bhp) Yanmar Diesel Engine Co Ltd-Japan
8740034 *EBZE* 3-VILL-14-	**SANPER** - **Campo Eder SL** - *Santa Eugenia de Ribeira* *Spain* Official number: 3-4/2001	**175** 52 -		**2002-03 Astilleros y Talleres Ferrolanos S.A. (ASTAFERSA) — Ferrol** Loa 20.60 Br ex - Dght - Lbp - Br md 7.50 Dpth 3.30 Welded, 1 dk	**(B11A2FS) Stern Trawler**	**1 oil engine** driving 1 Propeller Total Power: 242kW (329hp) 0.8kn
7815090 - -	**SANPO MARU** - **Puerto Naviera SA** -	**739** 339 1,250		**1978-10 Kochi Jyuko K.K. — Kochi** Yd No: 1276 Loa - Br ex - Dght 4.252 Lbp 59.01 Br md 10.01 Dpth 4.53 Riveted\Welded, 1 dk	**(A13B2TP) Products Tanker**	**1 oil engine** driving 1 FP propeller Total Power: 883kW (1,201hp) Hanshin 6LU28G 1 x 4 Stroke 6 Cy. 280 x 440 883kW (1201bhp) Hanshin Nainenki Kogyo-Japan
9213234 *JM6698* -	**SANPO MARU** - **Nishi Nippon Kaiun KK** - *Kitakyushu, Fukuoka* *Japan* Official number: 136447	*198* - -		**1999-10 K.K. Odo Zosen Tekko — Shimonoseki** Yd No: 581 Loa 34.00 Br ex - Dght 3.100 Lbp 29.00 Br md 9.20 Dpth 4.15 Welded, 1 dk	**(B32A2ST) Tug**	**2 oil engines** Geared Integral to driving 2 Z propellers Total Power: 2,942kW (4,000hp) 13.0kn Niigata 6L28HX 2 x 4 Stroke 6 Cy. 280 x 370 each-1471kW (2000bhp) Niigata Engineering Co Ltd-Japan
9066100 *JL6219* -	**SANPO MARU No. 2** - **Corporation for Advanced Transport & Technology & Sanpo Kisen KK** Sanpo Kisen KK *Imabari, Ehime* *Japan* MMSI: 431500116 Official number: 133944	*1,499* - 2,999	Class: NK	**1993-08 Asakawa Zosen K.K. — Imabari** Yd No: 376 Loa 84.97 (BB) Br ex - Dght 5.812 Lbp 79.00 Br md 12.80 Dpth 6.50 Welded, 1 dk	**(A13B2TP) Products Tanker** Liq: 3,310; Liq (Oil): 3,310 Compartments: 10 Ta, ER	**1 oil engine** driving 1 FP propeller Total Power: 2,060kW (2,801hp) 13.0kn Hanshin 6EL38 1 x 4 Stroke 6 Cy. 380 x 760 2060kW (2801bhp) The Hanshin Diesel Works Ltd-Japan Thrusters: 1 Thwart. CP thruster (f) Fuel: 180.0 (r.f.)
9114971 *JL6343* -	**SANPO MARU No. 5** - **Sanpo Kisen KK** - *Imabari, Ehime* *Japan* MMSI: 431500283 Official number: 134913	*749* - 1,911	Class: NK	**1994-12 Asakawa Zosen K.K. — Imabari** Yd No: 383 Loa 70.95 Br ex - Dght 4.711 Lbp 68.00 Br md 12.00 Dpth 5.20 Welded, 1 dk	**(A13B2TP) Products Tanker** Liq: 2,199; Liq (Oil): 2,199	**1 oil engine** driving 1 FP propeller Total Power: 1,471kW (2,000hp) 12.4kn Hanshin LH32LG 1 x 4 Stroke 6 Cy. 320 x 640 1471kW (2000bhp) The Hanshin Diesel Works Ltd-Japan AuxGen: 3 x a.c Fuel: 70.0 (d.f.)
8625703 - -	**SANPO MARU No. 8** - - - *South Korea*	*165* - 402		**1985-12 Y.K. Matsubara Koki Zosen — Onomichi** Loa 43.90 (BB) Br ex - Dght 3.261 Lbp 40.01 Br md 9.50 Dpth 5.01 Welded, 1 dk	**(B33A2DG) Grab Dredger**	**1 oil engine** geared to sc. shaft driving 1 FP propeller Total Power: 478kW (650hp) 10.8kn Daihatsu 6PSHTCM-26H 1 x 4 Stroke 6 Cy. 260 x 320 478kW (650bhp) Daihatsu Diesel Manufacturing Co Lt-Japan
8706894 - -	**SANPO MARU No. 10** - - - *South Korea*	*469* - 592		**1987-07 Matsuura Tekko Zosen K.K. — Osakikamijima** Yd No: 331 Loa 50.65 (BB) Br ex 10.57 Dght 3.210 Lbp 45.01 Br md 10.51 Dpth 5.31 Welded, 2 dks	**(A24D2BA) Aggregates Carrier** Grain: 380 Compartments: 1 Ho, ER 1 Ha: ER	**1 oil engine** with clutches & sr reverse geared to sc. shaft driving 1 FP propeller Total Power: 552kW (750hp) Daihatsu 6DLM-24FS 1 x 4 Stroke 6 Cy. 240 x 320 552kW (750bhp) Daihatsu Diesel Manufacturing Co Lt-Japan
9658381 *7JKE* -	**SANREI** - **Government of Japan (Ministry of Land, Infrastructure & Transport) (The Coastguard)** - *Tokyo* *Japan* Official number: 141531	*209* - 40		**2012-03 Mitsubishi Heavy Industries Ltd. — Shimonoseki** Loa 46.00 Br ex - Dght 1.500 Lbp - Br md 7.80 Dpth 4.13 Welded, 1 dk	**(B34H2SQ) Patrol Vessel** Hull Material: Aluminium Alloy	**3 oil engines** reduction geared to sc. shafts driving 3 Water jets 35.0kn
8633061 - -	**SANRI** *ex* Huger *-2010* *ex* Ocean No. 7 *-2009* *ex* Wind *-2008* *ex* Tikano *-2007* *ex* Chigori *-2006* *ex* Sea Spaces *-2003* *ex* Meisho Maru No. 81 *-2000* **United Marine Tramp SA** -	**203** 61 -		**1981-07 Sasaki Shipbuilding Co Ltd — Osakikamijima HS** L reg 28.20 Br ex - Dght 2.200 Lbp 30.33 Br md 5.60 Dpth 2.70 Welded, 1 dk	**(B11B2FV) Fishing Vessel**	**1 oil engine** driving 1 FP propeller Total Power: 324kW (441hp) Sumiyoshi 1 x 4 Stroke 324kW (441bhp) Sumiyoshi Tekkosho-Japan

IMO / Call sign / Flag	Name / Owner / Port	Tonnage	Class	Build / Dimensions	Type	Machinery
5311545 - LBV 1029	**SANS PEUR** - **Armement Even** - *Libreville* *Gabon*	*117* 18 50	Class: (BV)	**1957 Ateliers et Chantiers de La Manche — Dieppe** Yd No: 1143 Loa 27.01 Br ex 6.18 Dght 3.449 Lbp 22.51 Br md 6.08 Dpth 3.66 Riveted, 1 dk	**(B11A2FT) Trawler** Compartments: 1 Ho, ER 2 Ha: 2 (0.9 x 0.9) Cranes: 1x2t	**1 oil engine** driving 1 FP propeller Total Power: 276kW (375hp) 11.0kn Sulzer 6BAH22 1 x 4 Stroke 6 Cy. 220 x 320 276kW (375bhp) Cie de Constructions Mecaniques (CCM), procede Sulzer-France AuxGen: 1 x 10kW 24V d.c Fuel: 50.0 (d.f.)
5311557 - -	**SANS REPROCHE** - **Armement Even** - *Libreville* *Gabon*	*117* 17 50	Class: (BV)	**1958 Ateliers et Chantiers de La Manche — Dieppe** Yd No: 1148 Loa 27.51 Br ex 6.38 Dght 3.449 Lbp 22.51 Br md 6.08 Dpth 3.66 Riveted, 1 dk	**(B11A2FT) Trawler** Compartments: 1 Ho, ER 2 Ha: 2 (0.9 x 0.9) Cranes: 1x2t	**1 oil engine** driving 1 FP propeller Total Power: 276kW (375hp) 11.0kn Sulzer 6BAH22 1 x 4 Stroke 6 Cy. 220 x 320 276kW (375bhp) Cie de Constructions Mecaniques (CCM), procede Sulzer-France AuxGen: 1 x 10kW 24V d.c Fuel: 41.5 (d.f.)
9079731 *JM6316* -	**SANSEI MARU** - **GK Koyo Kisen** - *Kamiamakusa, Kumamoto* *Japan* Official number: 133596	*497* - 1,312		**1993-12 Y.K. Takasago Zosensho — Naruto** Yd No: 201 Loa 74.84 (BB) Br ex - Dght 4.100 Lbp 68.00 Br md 11.60 Dpth 7.00 Welded, 2 dks	**(A31A2GX) General Cargo Ship** Compartments: 1 Ho, ER 1 Ha: ER	**1 oil engine** driving 1 FP propeller Total Power: 736kW (1,001hp) Niigata 6M34AGT 1 x 4 Stroke 6 Cy. 340 x 620 736kW (1001bhp) Niigata Engineering Co Ltd-Japan
9140176 *JK5420* -	**SANSHA MARU** - **Sansha Kisen KK** - *Kure, Hiroshima* *Japan* Official number: 134718	*498* - 1,510		**1996-04 Matsuura Tekko Zosen K.K. — Osakikamijima** Yd No: 393 Loa 76.00 (BB) Br ex - Dght 4.100 Lbp 71.00 Br md 11.80 Dpth 7.10 Welded, 1 dk	**(A31A2GX) General Cargo Ship** Grain: 2,942; Bale: 2,501 Compartments: 1 Ho, ER 1 Ha: ER	**1 oil engine** reverse geared to sc. shaft driving 1 FP propeller Total Power: 736kW (1,001hp) Hanshin LH32LG 1 x 4 Stroke 6 Cy. 320 x 640 736kW (1001bhp) The Hanshin Diesel Works Ltd-Japan Thrusters: 1 Thwart. FP thruster (f)
9200615 *JM6679* -	**SANSHA MARU NO. 1** - **Yoshitake Kaiun KK** - *Okawa, Fukuoka* *Japan* Official number: 136425	*332* - 1,200		**1999-03 K.K. Odo Zosen Tekko — Shimonoseki** Yd No: 575 Loa 58.50 (BB) Br ex - Dght 2.150 Lbp 52.80 Br md 9.00 Dpth 3.50 Welded, 1 dk	**(A13B2TP) Products Tanker** Double Hull Liq: 709; Liq (Oil): 709	**1 oil engine** driving 1 FP propeller Total Power: 736kW (1,001hp) 12.0kn Niigata 6M28BGT 1 x 4 Stroke 6 Cy. 280 x 480 736kW (1001bhp) Niigata Engineering Co Ltd-Japan
8803862 - -	**SANSHA MARU NO. 18** *ex Katsu Maru No. 33 -1997* **Shanghai JiuHe Ship Import & Export Co Ltd** - *China*	*467* - 1,383		**1988-10 Hamamoto Zosensho K.K. — Tokushima** Yd No: 715 Loa 62.65 (BB) Br ex - Dght 4.522 Lbp 55.00 Br md 12.50 Dpth 6.50 Welded, 1 dk	**(B33A2DG) Grab Dredger** Compartments: 1 Ta, ER	**1 oil engine** driving 1 FP propeller Total Power: 736kW (1,001hp) Hanshin 6LU32G 1 x 4 Stroke 6 Cy. 320 x 510 736kW (1001bhp) The Hanshin Diesel Works Ltd-Japan
9145944 *JM6525* -	**SANSHA MARU No. 21** - **Yoshitake Kaiun KK** - *Okawa, Fukuoka* *Japan* Official number: 135400	*196* - 550		**1996-07 K.K. Odo Zosen Tekko — Shimonoseki** Yd No: 556 Loa 45.10 (BB) Br ex 7.22 Dght 3.250 Lbp 40.35 Br md 7.20 Dpth 3.50 Welded, 1 dk	**(A13B2TP) Products Tanker** Liq: 460; Liq (Oil): 460 Compartments: 6 Ta, ER	**1 oil engine** with clutches & reverse geared to sc. shaft driving 1 FP propeller Total Power: 735kW (999hp) Yanmar MF26-SD 1 x 4 Stroke 6 Cy. 260 x 500 735kW (999bhp) Yanmar Diesel Engine Co Ltd-Japan
7354096 - -	**SANSHA MARU No. 28** - **Liaoning Metals & Minerals Import & Export Corp** -	*255* 140 491		**1973 Tokushima Zosen K.K. — Fukuoka** Yd No: 1126 Loa 46.36 Br ex 7.24 Dght 3.010 Lbp 39.02 Br md 7.22 Dpth 3.31 Welded, 1 dk	**(B34E2SW) Waste Disposal Vessel**	**1 oil engine** driving 1 FP propeller Total Power: 441kW (600hp) Hanshin 6L26AGSH 1 x 4 Stroke 6 Cy. 260 x 400 441kW (600bhp) Hanshin Nainenki Kogyo-Japan
8630655 - -	**SANSHA MARU No. 28** - - - *China*	*419* - 1,032		**1987-02 K.K. Yoshida Zosen Kogyo — Arida** Loa 61.20 Br ex 13.22 Dght 3.680 Lbp 55.00 Br md 13.20 Dpth 5.70 Welded, 1 dk	**(B33A2DG) Grab Dredger**	**1 oil engine** driving 1 FP propeller Total Power: 736kW (1,001hp) 10.5kn Hanshin 6LUN30AG 1 x 4 Stroke 6 Cy. 300 x 480 736kW (1001bhp) The Hanshin Diesel Works Ltd-Japan
9166912 *JJ3940* -	**SANSHA MARU No. 45** - **Akiyama Zosen YK** - *Himeji, Hyogo* *Japan* Official number: 134195	*496* - 1,600		**1997-06 Shitanoe Shipbuilding Co Ltd — Usuki OT** Yd No: 1191 Loa 69.02 Br ex - Dght - Lbp 61.00 Br md 13.00 Dpth 7.60 Welded, 1 dk	**(A24D2BA) Aggregates Carrier**	**1 oil engine** driving 1 FP propeller Total Power: 736kW (1,001hp) 11.0kn Daihatsu 6DLM-32 1 x 4 Stroke 6 Cy. 320 x 400 736kW (1001bhp) Daihatsu Diesel Manufacturing Co Lt-Japan
9140255 *JM6523* -	**SANSHA MARU No. 81** - **Yoshitake Kaiun KK** - *Okawa, Fukuoka* *Japan* Official number: 134646	*499* - 1,578		**1996-04 K.K. Miura Zosensho — Saiki** Yd No: 1156 Loa - Br ex - Dght - Lbp 70.00 Br md 12.30 Dpth 6.87 Welded, 1 dk	**(A31A2GX) General Cargo Ship**	**1 oil engine** driving 1 FP propeller Total Power: 1,471kW (2,000hp) 11.7kn Hanshin LH34LAG 1 x 4 Stroke 6 Cy. 340 x 640 1471kW (2000bhp) The Hanshin Diesel Works Ltd-Japan
8632847 *UDZE* -	**SANSHIRO MARU** *ex Vek -2006 ex Kaiun Maru No. 21 -2006* *ex Hatsue Maru No. 32 -1997* *ex Tenyu Maru No. 31 -1990* **Atlantica Co Ltd** - *Kholmsk* *Russia*	**214** 108 135	Class: RS	**1984-03 Kyowa Zosen — Kesennuma** Yd No: 207 Loa 38.97 Br ex 7.42 Dght 2.730 Lbp 33.73 Br md 6.20 Dpth 2.90 Welded, 1 dk	**(B11B2FV) Fishing Vessel**	**1 oil engine** driving 1 FP propeller Total Power: 596kW (810hp) 10.0kn Niigata 6M26AFT 1 x 4 Stroke 6 Cy. 260 x 460 596kW (810bhp) Niigata Engineering Co Ltd-Japan
9624043 *3FKP6* -	**SANSHO** - **Pana Star Line SA** Daiichi Chuo Kisen Kaisha SatCom: Inmarsat C 437366910 *Panama* *Panama* MMSI: 373669000 Official number: 4401312	**31,538** 18,765 55,848 T/cm 56.9	Class: NK	**2012-07 IHI Marine United Inc — Kure HS** Yd No: 3330 Loa 190.00 (BB) Br ex - Dght 12.735 Lbp 185.00 Br md 32.26 Dpth 18.10 Welded, 1 dk	**(A21A2BC) Bulk Carrier** Grain: 72,062; Bale: 67,062 Compartments: 5 Ho, ER 5 Ha: ER Cranes: 4x30t	**1 oil engine** driving 1 FP propeller Total Power: 8,890kW (12,087hp) 14.5kn Wartsila 6RT-flex50 1 x 2 Stroke 6 Cy. 500 x 2050 8890kW (12087bhp) Diesel United Ltd.-Aioi Fuel: 2490.0
7852921 *HP7621* -	**SANSHO MARU** - **Sinkobe Enterprise** - *Panama* *Panama* Official number: D8461789PEXT	*406* 245 1,171		**1975 Kogushi Zosen K.K. — Okayama** Loa 52.86 Br ex - Dght 3.101 Lbp 48.11 Br md 9.01 Dpth 3.81 Welded, 1 dk	**(A12A2TC) Chemical Tanker**	**1 oil engine** driving 1 FP propeller Total Power: 809kW (1,100hp) 10.0kn Hanshin 1 x 4 Stroke 809kW (1100bhp) The Hanshin Diesel Works Ltd-Japan
9114062 *JH3343* -	**SANSHO MARU** - **Meisei Kisen KK** - *Toyohashi, Aichi* *Japan* Official number: 133256	*170* - 1,260		**1995-05 Suzuki Shipyard Co. Ltd. — Yokkaichi** Yd No: 620 Loa 39.00 (BB) Br ex - Dght 3.217 Lbp 35.00 Br md 8.00 Dpth 3.50 Welded, 1 dk	**(A13B2TP) Products Tanker** Liq: 439; Liq (Oil): 439 Compartments: 6 Ta, ER	**1 oil engine** reduction geared to sc. shaft driving 1 FP propeller Total Power: 588kW (799hp) Yanmar 6N165-EN 1 x 4 Stroke 6 Cy. 165 x 232 588kW (799bhp) Yanmar Diesel Engine Co Ltd-Japan
8998435 *JD2097* -	**SANSHU** - **Sanyo Kaiji Co Ltd** - *Nagoya, Aichi* *Japan* Official number: 140156	*154* - -		**2005-04 Hatayama Zosen KK — Yura WK** Yd No: 245 L reg 29.18 Br ex - Dght - Lbp - Br md 8.60 Dpth 3.50 Welded, 1 dk	**(B32A2ST) Tug**	**2 oil engines** Geared Integral to driving 2 Z propellers Total Power: 1,766kW (2,402hp) 13.4kn Yanmar 6N21A-SV 2 x 4 Stroke 6 Cy. 210 x 290 each-883kW (1201bhp) Yanmar Diesel Engine Co Ltd-Japan
9067192 *JM6233* -	**SANSHU MARU** - **Kimura Kaiun KK** - *Nagasaki, Nagasaki* *Japan* Official number: 133518	*498* - 1,168	Class: NK	**1993-12 Shitanoe Shipbuilding Co Ltd — Usuki OT** Yd No: 1146 Loa 64.85 Br ex - Dght 4.111 Lbp 61.00 Br md 10.30 Dpth 4.50 Welded, 1 dk	**(A12A2TC) Chemical Tanker** Liq: 1,230 Cargo Heating Coils 2 Cargo Pump (s): 2x300m³/hr	**1 oil engine** driving 1 FP propeller Total Power: 736kW (1,001hp) 11.0kn Hanshin LH28G 1 x 4 Stroke 6 Cy. 280 x 460 736kW (1001bhp) The Hanshin Diesel Works Ltd-Japan AuxGen: 3 x 112kW a.c Fuel: 45.0 (d.f.)

IMO / Call sign	Name / Owner / Port	Tonnage	Class	Builder / Dimensions	Type / Capacity	Machinery
8743282 *JD2889* -	**SANSHU MARU** **Sanko Unyu KK** - *Matsuyama, Ehime* *Japan* MMSI: 431000879 Official number: 140983	*499* - 1,830		**2009-03 Yano Zosen K.K. — Imabari** Yd No: 222 Loa 74.50 (BB) Br ex - Dght 4.440 Lbp 68.30 Br md 12.00 Dpth 7.50 Welded, 1 dk	**(A31A2GX) General Cargo Ship** Grain: 2,484; Bale: 2,494 Compartments: 1 Ho, ER 1 Ha: ER (40.0 x 9.5)	**1 oil engine** driving 1 FP propeller Total Power: 1,620kW (2,203hp) 12.0kn Akasaka A34C 1 x 4 Stroke 6 Cy. 340 x 620 1620kW (2203bhp) Akasaka Tekkosho KK (Akasaka DieselLtd)-Japan Thrusters: 1 Tunnel thruster (f)
8919996 *JNZJ* -	**SANSHU MARU** **Nippon Yusen Kabushiki Kaisha (NYK Line)** Hachiuma Steamship Co Ltd (Hachiuma Kisen KK) SatCom: Inmarsat A 1204521 *Tokyo* *Japan* MMSI: 431294000 Official number: 132831	**55,130** 24,202 88,495	Class: NK	**1991-05 Mitsubishi Heavy Industries Ltd. — Nagasaki** Yd No: 2048 Loa 249.90 (BB) Br ex - Dght 11.878 Lbp 240.00 Br md 43.00 Dpth 18.70 Welded, 1 dk	**(A21A2BC) Bulk Carrier** Grain: 110,455 Compartments: 7 Ho, ER 7 Ha: (15.6 x 16.0) (15.6 x 20.1) (18.2 x 20.1)4 (18.2 x 20.1)ER	**1 oil engine** driving 1 FP propeller Total Power: 9,489kW (12,901hp) 14.0kn Mitsubishi 6UEC60LS 1 x 2 Stroke 6 Cy. 600 x 2200 9489kW (12901bhp) Mitsubishi Heavy Industries Ltd-Japan Fuel: 2880.0 (r.f.)
9370501 *JD2266* -	**SANSHUN MARU** **Daiichi Marine Co Ltd** Daiichi Tanker Co Ltd *Tokyo* *Japan* MMSI: 431101145 Official number: 140337	*498* - 1,197		**2006-06 KK Ura Kyodo Zosensho — Awaji HG** Yd No: 326 Loa 64.46 Br ex - Dght 4.200 Lbp 60.00 Br md 10.00 Dpth 4.50 Welded, 1 dk	**(A13B2TP) Products Tanker** Double Hull (13F) Liq: 1,250; Liq (Oil): 1,250 2 Cargo Pump (s): 2x750m³/hr	**1 oil engine** reverse geared to sc. shaft driving 1 FP propeller Total Power: 1,177kW (1,600hp) 11.5kn Akasaka K28S 1 x 4 Stroke 6 Cy. 280 x 500 1177kW (1600bhp) Akasaka Tekkosho KK (Akasaka DieselLtd)-Japan
9504267 *V2DT6* -	**SANSIBAR** *ex* BBC Thailand *-2012* *ex* Sansibar *-2008* *ex* Heng Yuan 7 *-2008* **ms 'Sansibar' GmbH & Co KG** Freese Shipping GmbH & Co KG *Saint John's* *Antigua & Barbuda* MMSI: 305333000	**6,478** 2,721 7,966	Class: BV	**2008-10 in the People's Republic of China** Yd No: HY061201 Loa 116.23 (BB) Br ex - Dght 7.000 Lbp 110.00 Br md 18.00 Dpth 10.40 Welded, 1 dk	**(A31A2GX) General Cargo Ship** Grain: 11,309; Bale: 11,309 TEU 354 Compartments: 2 Ho, 2 Tw Dk, ER 2 Ha: (32.2 x 15.0)ER (29.4 x 15.0)Tappered Cranes: 2x35t Ice Capable	**1 oil engine** reduction geared to sc. shaft driving 1 FP propeller Total Power: 2,970kW (4,038hp) 12.2kn MaK 9M25 1 x 4 Stroke 9 Cy. 255 x 400 2970kW (4038bhp) Caterpillar Motoren GmbH & Co. KG-Germany Thrusters: 1 Thwart. CP thruster (f) Fuel: 90.0 (d.f.) 340.0 (r.f.) 11.0pd
5036420 *XCSG* -	**SANSON** *ex* Barbara George *-2008* **Naval Mexicana SA de CV** - *Tampico* *Mexico* Official number: 2804022335-5	*205* 62 -	Class: (AB)	**1957 Gulfport Shipbuilding Corp. — Port Arthur, Tx** Yd No: 505 Loa 32.47 Br ex 8.51 Dght 3.871 Lbp 30.56 Br md 8.26 Dpth 4.27 Welded, 1 dk	**(B32A2ST) Tug**	**1 oil engine** driving 1 FP propeller Total Power: 1,250kW (1,700hp) General Motors 16-278-A 1 x Vee 2 Stroke 16 Cy. 222 x 267 1250kW (1700bhp) (made 1942, fitted 1957) General Motors Corp-USA AuxGen: 2 x 60kW 110/220V d.c, 1 x 20kW 110/220V d.c Fuel: 84.5 (d.f.)
6923137 - -	**SANSON** - -	*193* 115 -		**1969 Maestranza y Astillero Delta S.A. — Callao** L reg 27.89 Br ex 7.68 Dght 3.582 Lbp - Br md 7.65 Dpth 3.97 Welded, 1 dk	**(B11B2FV) Fishing Vessel** Ins: 328 Compartments: 2 Ho, ER 2 Ha: (2.5 x 2.1) (1.5 x 2.1) Derricks: 1x0.5t	**1 oil engine** driving 1 FP propeller Total Power: 515kW (700hp) 10.0kn G.M. (Detroit Diesel) 16V-71 1 x Vee 2 Stroke 16 Cy. 108 x 127 515kW (700bhp) General Motors Corp-USA
5311662 *IUBX* -	**SANSONE** **Rimorchiatori Riuniti Spezzini-Imprese Marittime e Salvataggi Srl** - *Siracusa* *Italy* Official number: 180	*169* 53 203	Class: (RI)	**1954 Cant. Nav. L. Accinelli — La Spezia** Yd No: 13 Loa 27.84 Br ex 7.60 Dght 3.601 Lbp 24.80 Br md 7.35 Dpth 4.14 Welded, 1 dk	**(B32A2ST) Tug**	**1 oil engine** driving 1 FP propeller Total Power: 1,361kW (1,850hp) 10.0kn Fiat 1 x 2 Stroke 7 Cy. 400 x 480 1361kW (1850bhp) SA Fiat SGM-Torino AuxGen: 2 x 60kW 220V d.c, 1 x 5kW 220V d.c Fuel: 203.0 (d.f.)
8105064 *V3SG5* -	**SANSSOUCI STAR** **Hays Maritime DK ApS** Tonmar Shipping Ltd *Belize City* *Belize* MMSI: 312339000 Official number: 581310015	**453** 136 132	Class: GL	**1982-03 Husumer Schiffswerft Inh. Gebr. Kroeger GmbH & Co. KG — Husum** Yd No: 1473 Converted From: Ferry (Passenger only)-2006 Converted From: Patrol Vessel-1984 Lengthened-1992 Lengthened-1984 Loa 53.53 (BB) Br ex - Dght 2.550 Lbp 43.92 Br md 7.70 Dpth 3.84 Welded, 1 dk	**(A31A2GX) General Cargo Ship** Passengers: berths: 12	**2 oil engines** reverse reduction geared to sc. shafts driving 2 FP propellers Total Power: 1,890kW (2,570hp) 13.5kn M.T.U. 12V396TC62 2 x Vee 4 Stroke 12 Cy. 165 x 185 each-945kW (1285bhp) MTU Friedrichshafen GmbH-Friedrichshafen Thrusters: 1 Thwart. FP thruster (f); 1 Water jet (a)
9105487 *DSQX2* -	**SANSTAR DREAM** *ex* Miyarabi *-2010* **Star Link Co Ltd** Panstar Tree Co Ltd *Jeju* *South Korea* MMSI: 441743000 Official number: JJR-101280	**11,820** - 5,690	Class: KR (NK)	**1995-01 Onomichi Dockyard Co Ltd — Onomichi HS** Yd No: 387 Loa 149.57 (BB) Br ex - Dght 6.700 Lbp 138.00 Br md 23.00 Dpth 15.45 Welded, 2 dks	**(A35A2RR) Ro-Ro Cargo Ship** Quarter bow door/ramp (s) Len: 15.00 Wid: 7.00 Swl: - Quarter stern door/ramp (s) Len: 15.00 Wid: 7.50 Swl: - Lane-Len: 288 Lorries: 5, Cars: 136, Trailers: 24 Bale: 19,109 TEU 258	**1 oil engine** with flexible couplings & reduction geared to sc. shaft driving 1 CP propeller Total Power: 12,505kW (17,002hp) 20.4kn Pielstick 12PC4-2V-570 1 x Vee 4 Stroke 12 Cy. 570 x 620 12505kW (17002bhp) Nippon Kokan KK (NKK Corp)-Japan AuxGen: 3 x 880kW 450V 60Hz a.c Thrusters: 1 Thwart. CP thruster (f); 1 Tunnel thruster (a) Fuel: 600.0 (r.f.) 46.0pd
9183881 - -	**SANSU T-1** *ex* Hakuho Maru *-2011* **Sansu Marine** - *South Korea*	*128* - 100		**1998-01 K.K. Watanabe Zosensho — Nagasaki** (Hull) Yd No: 062 **1998-01 K.K. Miura Zosensho — Saiki** Yd No: 1201 Loa - Br ex - Dght 4.010 Lbp 24.00 Br md 9.20 Dpth 6.10 Welded, 1 dk	**(B32A2ST) Tug**	**2 oil engines** driving 2 FP propellers Total Power: 2,354kW (3,200hp) Hanshin LH28LG 2 x 4 Stroke 6 Cy. 280 x 530 each-1177kW (1600bhp) The Hanshin Diesel Works Ltd-Japan
8738067 *JD2579* -	**SANSUMIFUKU** **Mifuku Kaiun YK** - *Shodoshima, Kagawa* *Japan* Official number: 140702	*499* - 1,830		**2008-01 Tokuoka Zosen K.K. — Naruto** Yd No: 308 Loa 74.95 Br ex - Dght 4.370 Lbp 69.00 Br md 11.80 Dpth 7.41 Welded, 1 dk	**(A31A2GX) General Cargo Ship** Grain: 2,596; Bale: 2,596 1 Ha: ER (40.0 x 9.3)	**1 oil engine** driving 1 Propeller Total Power: 1,618kW (2,200hp) 12.0kn Niigata 6M34BGT 1 x 4 Stroke 6 Cy. 340 x 620 1618kW (2200bhp) Niigata Engineering Co Ltd-Japan
7120201 *HC2977* -	**SANSUN RANGER** *ex* Sun Ranger *-1998* *ex* Samsun Ranger *-1995* *ex* Woo Jin No. 7 *-1986* *ex* Mary Lucille *-1982* *ex* City of Lisbon *-1978* **Jose Ramon Paladines Bazurto** Paladines Hermanos *Manta* *Ecuador* Official number: P-04-00522	**1,576** 553 853	Class: (KR)	**1971-07 San Diego Mar. Co. — San Diego, Ca** Yd No: 171 Loa 65.33 Br ex 11.03 Dght 4.952 Lbp 59.26 Br md 10.98 Dpth 5.34 Welded, 1 dk	**(B11B2FV) Fishing Vessel** Ins: 1,033	**1 oil engine** driving 1 FP propeller Total Power: 2,648kW (3,600hp) 14.0kn EMD (Electro-Motive) 20-645-E5 1 x Vee 2 Stroke 20 Cy. 230 x 254 2648kW (3600bhp) General Motors Corp.Electro-Motive Div.-La Grange AuxGen: 3 x 265kW 460V a.c Fuel: 305.0 (d.f.)
8020850 - -	**SANT ANNA** **Societa Cooperativa Siculpesca** - *Mazara del Vallo* *Italy*	*197* - -		**1981-08 Cant. Nav. A. Stabile — Trapani** Yd No: 55 Loa - Br ex - Dght - Lbp - Br md - Dpth - Welded, 1 dk	**(B11A2FS) Stern Trawler**	**1 oil engine** geared to sc. shaft driving 1 FP propeller Total Power: 744kW (1,012hp) MaK 1 x 4 Stroke 6 Cy. 744kW (1012bhp) Krupp MaK Maschinenbau GmbH-Kiel
7363841 *CXQE* -	**SANT BULT** *ex* San Bull *-1992* *ex* Palancia *-1991* *ex* Boluda Cuarto *-1976* **Remolcadores y Lanchas SA** - *Montevideo* *Uruguay*	**106** 17 71	Class: (LR) (GL) ✠ Classed LR until 17/10/80	**1975-10 Ast. Neptuno — Valencia** Yd No: 54 Loa 23.63 Br ex 7.45 Dght 3.277 Lbp 20.05 Br md 6.90 Dpth 4.12 Welded, 1 dk	**(B32A2ST) Tug**	**1 oil engine** reverse reduction geared to sc. shaft driving 1 FP propeller Total Power: 839kW (1,141hp) 11.0kn Caterpillar D399SCAC 1 x Vee 4 Stroke 16 Cy. 159 x 203 839kW (1141bhp) Caterpillar Tractor Co-USA AuxGen: 2 x 32kW 220V 50Hz a.c
9070060 *IPQN* -	**SANT' ELMO** **Rimorchiatori Napoletani Srl** - *Naples* *Italy* MMSI: 247034700 Official number: 1873	*319* 95 248	Class: RI	**1993-06 Cooperativa Ing G Tommasi Cantiere Navale Srl — Ancona** Yd No: 67 Loa 30.28 Br ex 10.65 Dght 4.012 Lbp 26.30 Br md 10.00 Dpth 5.00 Welded, 1 dk	**(B32A2ST) Tug**	**2 oil engines** with clutches & sr geared to sc. shafts driving 2 Directional propellers Total Power: 2,760kW (3,752hp) 12.0kn Nohab 6R25 2 x 4 Stroke 6 Cy. 250 x 300 each-1380kW (1876bhp) Wartsila Diesel AB-Sweden AuxGen: 2 x 100kW 380V 50Hz a.c Fuel: 102.0 (d.f.) 12.5pd

Identity	Name / Owner	Tonnage	Class	Builder / Dimensions	Type	Machinery
8739750 *EA4551* 3-CP-12-00	**SANT JOAN B** - **Juan Baptista & Miguel Angel Borja Ibanez** - *Burriana* *Spain* Official number: 3-2/2000	**103** - -		**2000**-05 **Asfibe S.A. — Benicarlo** Loa 25.06 Br ex - Dght 2.610 Lbp 21.50 Br md 6.13 Dpth 3.61 Bonded, 1 dk	**(B11A2FS) Stern Trawler** Hull Material: Reinforced Plastic	**1 oil engine** driving 1 Propeller Total Power: 300kW (408hp) 10.0kn
8919427 *TGSY3* -	**SANT YAGO TRES** *ex* Cap Coz *-2014* *ex* Thai Union 1 *-2011* *ex* Success 1 *-2007* *ex* Prosperous *-2007* *ex* Amazon Victory *-2006* *ex* TS Excellence *-2005* *ex* Pinna *-1997* - - *Puerto Quetzal* *Guatemala* MMSI: 332001001	**2,109** 633 1,650	Class: BV (RS)	**1991**-09 **Ast. de Huelva S.A. — Huelva** Yd No: 463 Loa 79.80 Br ex - Dght 6.250 Lbp 69.20 Br md 13.50 Dpth 8.90 Welded, 2 dks	**(B11B2FV) Fishing Vessel** Ins: 1,935	**1 oil engine** with flexible couplings & sr geared to sc. shaft driving 1 FP propeller Total Power: 3,646kW (4,957hp) 15.0kn Wartsila 9R32E 1 x 4 Stroke 9 Cy. 320 x 350 3646kW (4957bhp) Construcciones Echevarria SA-Spain AuxGen: 4 x 400kW 220/380V 60Hz a.c Thrusters: 1 Thwart. CP thruster (f); 1 Thwart. CP thruster (a) Fuel: 137.0 (d.f.)
8919439 *TGQU* -	**SANT YAGO UNO** *ex* Sant Yago I *-2003* *ex* Dourveil *-1997* *ex* Purpura *-1996* **Atunera Sant Yago SA** Jealsa Rianxeira SA *Puerto Quetzal* *Guatemala*	**2,109** 633 1,897	Class: BV	**1991**-11 **Ast. de Huelva S.A. — Huelva** Yd No: 464 Loa 79.80 Br ex - Dght 6.250 Lbp 69.20 Br md 13.50 Dpth 8.90 Welded, 2 dks	**(B11B2FV) Fishing Vessel** Ins: 1,935	**1 oil engine** with flexible couplings & sr geared to sc. shaft driving 1 FP propeller Total Power: 3,646kW (4,957hp) 15.0kn Wartsila 9R32E 1 x 4 Stroke 9 Cy. 320 x 350 3646kW (4957bhp) Construcciones Echevarria SA-Spain AuxGen: 4 x 400kW 220/380V 60Hz a.c Thrusters: 1 Thwart. CP thruster (f); 1 Tunnel thruster (a)
9089750 *FVQL* GV 730415	**SANT YANN II** - **Christian Bourhis** - *Guilvinec* *France* MMSI: 228339000 Official number: 730415	**145** -		**1988**-01 **Chantiers Piriou — Concarneau** Loa 22.40 Br ex - Dght - Lbp 19.66 Br md 6.75 Dpth - Welded, 1 dk	**(B11A2FS) Stern Trawler**	**1 oil engine** driving 1 Propeller Total Power: 392kW (533hp)
8721791 *UBIJ* -	**SANTA** *ex* Vidzeme *-1992* **Belomor Fishing Collective (Rybolovetskiy Kolkhoz 'Belomor')** - SatCom: Inmarsat C 427300895 *Murmansk* *Russia* MMSI: 273211800 Official number: 872379	**739** 222 414	Class: RS	**1988**-04 **Zavod "Leninskaya Kuznitsa" — Kiyev** Yd No: 1591 Loa 54.82 Br ex 10.15 Dght 4.140 Lbp 50.30 Br md - Dpth 5.00 Welded, 1 dk	**(B11A2FS) Stern Trawler** Ice Capable	**1 oil engine** driving 1 CP propeller Total Power: 852kW (1,158hp) 12.0kn S.K.L. 8NVD48A-2U 1 x 4 Stroke 8 Cy. 320 x 480 852kW (1158bhp) VEB Schwermaschinenbau "KarlLiebknecht" (SKL)-Magdeburg AuxGen: 4 x 160kW a.c
8132043 *ZADP2* -	**SANTA** *ex* Flying Dolphin Xv *-2011* **Ionian Cruises ShPK** - *Durres* *Albania* MMSI: 201100141	*142* 93 16	Class: (RI) (BV)	**1981 Zavod im. "Ordzhonikidze" — Poti** Yd No: 711 Loa 35.21 Br ex 9.56 Dght 3.601 Lbp 30.00 Br md 6.00 Dpth 1.81 Welded, 1 dk	**(A37B2PS) Passenger Ship** Hull Material: Aluminium Alloy Passengers: unberthed: 116	**2 oil engines** driving 2 FP propellers Total Power: 1,540kW (2,094hp) 32.0kn M.T.U. 8V396TB83 2 x Vee 4 Stroke 8 Cy. 165 x 185 each-770kW (1047bhp) (new engine 1989) MTU Friedrichshafen GmbH-Friedrichshafen
9378747 *YLCU* -	**SANTA** - **Freeport of Riga Fleet (Rigas Brivostas Flote)** Freeport of Riga Authority (Rigas Brivostas Parvalde) *Riga* *Latvia* MMSI: 275347000	**445** 140 176	Class: (BV)	**2008**-04 **AS Rigas Kugu Buvetava (Riga Shipyard) — Riga** Yd No: 1501 Loa 34.20 Br ex - Dght 3.900 Lbp 30.39 Br md 12.10 Dpth 5.63 Welded, 1 dk	**(B32A2ST) Tug** Ice Capable	**2 oil engines** reduction geared to sc. shafts driving 2 Propellers Total Power: 3,310kW (4,500hp) 13.5kn Caterpillar 3516B 2 x Vee 4 Stroke 16 Cy. 170 x 190 each-1655kW (2250bhp) Caterpillar Inc-USA
6710279 - -	**SANTA 1** *ex* Rio Santa 1 *-1976* *ex* Atlanta 3 *-1976* - -	*120* -	Class: (LR) ✠ Classed LR until 28/7/82	**1967**-03 **Fabricaciones Metallicas E.P.S. (FABRIMET) — Callao** Yd No: 350 Loa 25.20 Br ex 7.14 Dght 3.175 Lbp 21.49 Br md 7.01 Dpth 3.46 Welded, 1 dk	**(B11B2FV) Fishing Vessel**	**1 oil engine** reverse reduction geared to sc. shaft driving 1 FP propeller Total Power: 399kW (542hp) Caterpillar D353SCAC 1 x 4 Stroke 6 Cy. 159 x 203 399kW (542bhp) Caterpillar Tractor Co-USA
6710281 - -	**SANTA 2** *ex* Rio Santa 2 *-1976* *ex* Atlanta 4 *-1976* - -	*120* -	Class: (LR) ✠ Classed LR until 28/7/82	**1967**-03 **Fabricaciones Metallicas E.P.S. (FABRIMET) — Callao** Yd No: 352 Loa 25.20 Br ex 7.14 Dght 3.175 Lbp 21.49 Br md 7.01 Dpth 3.46 Welded, 1 dk	**(B11B2FV) Fishing Vessel**	**1 oil engine** reverse reduction geared to sc. shaft driving 1 FP propeller Total Power: 399kW (542hp) Caterpillar D353SCAC 1 x 4 Stroke 6 Cy. 159 x 203 399kW (542bhp) Caterpillar Tractor Co-USA
7109738 - -	**SANTA 3** *ex* Em VII *-1976* - -	*105* - -	Class: (AB)	**1967 Promecan Ingenieros S.A. — Callao** Yd No: 88 Loa - Br ex 6.74 Dght - Lbp 21.49 Br md 6.71 Dpth 3.51 Welded, 1 dk	**(B11A2FT) Trawler** Compartments: 1 Ho, ER 1 Ha: (1.9 x 3.3)	**1 oil engine** driving 1 FP propeller Total Power: 279kW (379hp) Caterpillar D353SCAC 1 x 4 Stroke 6 Cy. 159 x 203 279kW (379bhp) Caterpillar Tractor Co-USA Fuel: 5.0 (d.f.)
6618548 - -	**SANTA 4** *ex* Galicia *-1976* - -	*120* -	Class: (LR) ✠ Classed LR until 28/7/82	**1966**-09 **Fabricaciones Metallicas E.P.S. (FABRIMET) — Callao** Yd No: 317 Loa 25.20 Br ex 7.14 Dght 2.693 Lbp 21.49 Br md 7.01 Dpth 3.46 Welded, 1 dk	**(B11B2FV) Fishing Vessel**	**1 oil engine** reverse reduction geared to sc. shaft driving 1 FP propeller Total Power: 399kW (542hp) Caterpillar D353SCAC 1 x 4 Stroke 6 Cy. 159 x 203 399kW (542bhp) Caterpillar Tractor Co-USA
6915996 - -	**SANTA 5** *ex* Don Quijote *-1976* - -	*145* 67 -	Class: (AB) (GL)	**1966 Promecan Ingenieros S.A. — Callao** Yd No: 46 Loa 25.05 Br ex 6.74 Dght - Lbp 19.87 Br md 6.71 Dpth 3.51 Welded, 1 dk	**(B11A2FT) Trawler** Compartments: 1 Ho, ER 1 Ha: (1.9 x 0.3)	**1 oil engine** driving 1 FP propeller Total Power: 279kW (379hp) Caterpillar D353TA 1 x 4 Stroke 6 Cy. 159 x 203 279kW (379bhp) Caterpillar Tractor Co-USA
7008063 - -	**SANTA 6** *ex* Sama 5 *-1976* - -	*150* -	Class: (AB)	**1968 Metal Empresa S.A. — Callao** Yd No: L-2 Br ex 6.79 Dght - Lbp 21.49 Br md 6.71 Dpth 3.51 Welded, 1 dk	**(B11B2FV) Fishing Vessel** Compartments: 1 Ho, ER 1 Ha: (1.9 x 3.3)	**1 oil engine** driving 1 FP propeller Total Power: 279kW (379hp) Caterpillar D353SCAC 1 x 4 Stroke 6 Cy. 159 x 203 279kW (379bhp) Caterpillar Tractor Co-USA Fuel: 5.0
7508984 - -	**SANTA 7** *ex* Propicia *-1976* - -	*105* - -	Class: (AB)	**1965 Promecan Ingenieros S.A. — Callao** Yd No: 35 Loa - Br ex - Dght - Lbp 24.39 Br md 6.41 Dpth 3.28 Welded, 1 dk	**(B11A2FT) Trawler** Compartments: 1 Ho, ER 1 Ha: (1.9 x 3.3)	**1 oil engine** driving 1 FP propeller Total Power: 279kW (379hp) Caterpillar D353SCAC 1 x 4 Stroke 6 Cy. 159 x 203 279kW (379bhp) Caterpillar Tractor Co-USA Fuel: 5.0 (d.f.)
7109752 - -	**SANTA 8** *ex* Prolija *-1976* - -	*105* - -	Class: (AB)	**1965 Promecan Ingenieros S.A. — Callao** Yd No: 36 Loa - Br ex 6.74 Dght - Lbp 21.49 Br md 6.71 Dpth 3.51 Welded, 1 dk	**(B11A2FT) Trawler** Compartments: 1 Ho, ER 1 Ha: (1.9 x 3.3)	**1 oil engine** driving 1 FP propeller Total Power: 279kW (379hp) Caterpillar D353SCAC 1 x 4 Stroke 6 Cy. 159 x 203 279kW (379bhp) Caterpillar Tractor Co-USA Fuel: 5.0 (d.f.)
6615223 - -	**SANTA 9** *ex* Proeza *-1976* **PEEA Pesquera Inti SCR Ltda** - *Supe* *Peru* Official number: SE-000829-PM	*145* 67 -	Class: (AB)	**1965 Promecan Ingenieros S.A. — Callao** Yd No: 33 Loa - Br ex - Dght - Lbp 21.49 Br md 6.71 Dpth 3.51 Welded, 1 dk	**(B11B2FV) Fishing Vessel** Compartments: 1 Ho, ER 1 Ha: (1.9 x 3.3)	**1 oil engine** driving 1 FP propeller Total Power: 279kW (379hp) Caterpillar D353SCAC 1 x 4 Stroke 6 Cy. 159 x 203 279kW (379bhp) Caterpillar Tractor Co-USA Fuel: 5.0
6615211 - -	**SANTA 10** *ex* Prodigio *-1977* **Pelicano SCR Ltda** - *Callao* *Peru* Official number: CO-011974-PM	*148* 73 -	Class: (AB)	**1965 Promecan Ingenieros S.A. — Callao** Yd No: 32 Loa - Br ex - Dght - Lbp 21.49 Br md 6.71 Dpth 3.51 Welded, 1 dk	**(B11B2FV) Fishing Vessel** Compartments: 1 Ho, ER 1 Ha: (1.9 x 3.3)	**1 oil engine** driving 1 FP propeller Total Power: 279kW (379hp) Caterpillar D353SCAC 1 x 4 Stroke 6 Cy. 159 x 203 279kW (379bhp) Caterpillar Tractor Co-USA Fuel: 5.0

9652545 *3EWN* -	**SANTA ADRIANA** **Compania Flor de Vapores SA** Mitsubishi Ore Transport Co Ltd (Mitsubishi Koseki Yuso KK) *Panama* *Panama* MMSI: 372791000 Official number: 44449PEXT1	**40,962** 25,965 77,040 T/cm 67.1	Class: AB NK (Class contemplated)	**2013-06 Oshima Shipbuilding Co Ltd — Saikai NS** Yd No: 10716 Loa 225.00 (BB) Br ex - Dght 14.000 Lbp 220.00 Br md 32.26 Dpth 19.79 Welded, 1 dk	**(A21A2BC) Bulk Carrier** Grain: 89,449; Bale: 87,463 Compartments: 7 Ho, ER 7 Ha: 6 (16.9 x 15.9)ER (16.0 x 14.1)	**1 oil engine** driving 1 FP propeller Total Power: 9,318kW (12,669hp) 14.5kn MAN-B&W 5S60MC-C 1 x 2 Stroke 5 Cy. 600 x 2400 9318kW (12669bhp) Mitsui Engineering & Shipbuilding CLtd-Japan AuxGen: 3 x 440kW a.c Fuel: 290.0 (d.f.) 2530.0 (r.f.)
7420558 *YVY2054* -	**SANTA ANA** *ex* Lagoven Santa Ana *-1994* **PDV Marina SA** - SatCom: Inmarsat A 1565144 *Maracaibo* *Venezuela* Official number: AJZL-11050	*259* 105 -	Class: (AB)	**1979-06 Vadelca — Maracaibo** Yd No: VA-046 Loa 28.50 Br ex 8.51 Dght 3.810 Lbp 26.85 Br md 8.35 Dpth 4.42 Welded, 1 dk	**(B32A2ST) Tug**	**1 oil engine** geared to sc. shaft driving 1 CP propeller Total Power: 1,699kW (2,310hp) Nohab F312V 1 x Vee 4 Stroke 12 Cy. 250 x 300 1699kW (2310bhp) AB Bofors NOHAB-Sweden
5251381 - -	**SANTA ANGELA** *ex* Nicolas Appert *-1994* - -	*587* 220 472	Class: (BV)	**1957 Beliard, Crichton & Cie. S.A. — Oostende** Yd No: 164 L reg 55.39 Br ex 9.40 Dght 5.322 Lbp 52.10 Br md 9.38 Dpth - Riveted\Welded, 1 dk	**(B11A2FT) Trawler** 4 Ha: 4 (1.0 x 1.0) Derricks: 1x3t,2x2t	**1 oil engine** driving 1 FP propeller Total Power: 919kW (1,249hp) 14.5kn Werkspoor 1 x 4 Stroke 8 Cy. 330 x 600 919kW (1249bhp) NV Werkspoor-Netherlands
8882959 - -	**SANTA ANITA** *ex* 312 Rio Barca Grande *-1994* **RM Maritima SA** - *Argentina* Official number: 02516	**144** 52 -		**1962 Talleres de Reparaciones Navales (TARENA) — Buenos Aires** L reg 28.30 Br ex - Dght - Lbp - Br md 8.75 Dpth 2.90 Welded, 1 dk	**(B32A2ST) Tug**	**2 oil engines** driving 2 FP propellers Total Power: 662kW (900hp) 6.0kn
9331232 *3EIC2* -	**SANTA ANNA** **Royal Bulkship SA** Rudolf A Oetker KG *Panama* *Panama* MMSI: 372071000 Official number: 3222906A	**31,247** 18,504 56,019 T/cm 55.8	Class: NK	**2006-11 Mitsui Eng. & SB. Co. Ltd. — Tamano** Yd No: 1628 Loa 189.99 (BB) Br ex - Dght 12.575 Lbp 182.00 Br md 32.26 Dpth 17.90 Welded, 1 dk	**(A21A2BC) Bulk Carrier** Grain: 70,811; Bale: 68,084 Compartments: 5 Ho, ER 5 Ha: 4 (21.1 x 18.9)ER (17.6 x 18.9) Cranes: 4x30.5t	**1 oil engine** driving 1 FP propeller Total Power: 9,480kW (12,889hp) 14.5kn MAN-B&W 6S50MC-C 1 x 2 Stroke 6 Cy. 500 x 2000 9480kW (12889bhp) Mitsui Engineering & Shipbuilding CLtd-Japan Fuel: 2260.0
9673044 *2FKB2* -	**SANTA ANNA B** **UniCredit Leasing SpA** - *London* *United Kingdom* MMSI: 235091932 Official number: 918077	**308** 92 39	Class: RI	**2011-07 Cant. Nav. San Lorenzo SpA — Viareggio** Yd No: 122/19 Loa 37.44 Br ex - Dght 2.700 Lbp 31.59 Br md 8.00 Dpth - Bonded, 1 dk	**(X11A2YP) Yacht** Hull Material: Reinforced Plastic	**2 oil engines** reduction geared to sc. shafts driving 2 Propellers Total Power: 1,492kW (2,028hp) 11.0kn Caterpillar C32 ACERT 2 x Vee 4 Stroke 12 Cy. 145 x 162 each-746kW (1014bhp) Caterpillar Inc-USA
7310715 *YGQH* -	**SANTA BAHARI** *ex* Capitaine la Perouse *-1997* *ex* Capitaine la Perouse III *-1996* *ex* Range *-1987* *ex* Verge *-1980* **PT Santa Bahtera** - *Jakarta* *Indonesia*	**4,873** 3,025 7,410	Class: KI (BV) (GL)	**1973-07 Dorman Long (Africa) Ltd. — Durban** Yd No: N.1800 Loa 116.41 (BB) Br ex 17.30 Dght 7.500 Lbp 107.98 Br md 17.28 Dpth 9.91 Welded, 2 dks	**(A31A2GX) General Cargo Ship** Grain: 10,675; Bale: 10,028 TEU 160 Compartments: 3 Ho, ER 3 Ha: (12.9 x 7.7)2 (19.5 x 10.5)ER Derricks: 1x30t,1x22t,3x10t; Winches: 5 Ice Capable	**1 oil engine** reduction geared to sc. shaft driving 1 FP propeller Total Power: 2,944kW (4,003hp) 15.0kn MaK 8M551AK 1 x 4 Stroke 8 Cy. 450 x 550 2944kW (4003bhp) MaK Maschinenbau GmbH-Kiel AuxGen: 3 x 218kW 380V a.c Fuel: 482.4
9330513 *A8JZ4* -	**SANTA BALBINA** *ex* Maersk Jackson *-2011* *completed as* Santa Balbina *-2006* **KG ms 'Santa Balbina' Offen Reederei GmbH & Co** Reederei Claus-Peter Offen GmbH & Co KG *Monrovia* *Liberia* MMSI: 636091163 Official number: 91163	**28,616** 14,769 39,359 T/cm 56.7	Class: GL	**2006-09 Hyundai Mipo Dockyard Co Ltd — Ulsan** Yd No: 0431 Loa 222.11 (BB) Br ex - Dght 12.000 Lbp 210.00 Br md 30.00 Dpth 16.80 Welded, 1 dk	**(A33A2CC) Container Ship (Fully Cellular)** TEU 2824 C Ho 1026 TEU C Dk 1798 TEU incl 586 ref C.	**1 oil engine** driving 1 FP propeller Total Power: 25,228kW (34,300hp) 23.0kn MAN-B&W 7K80MC-C 1 x 2 Stroke 7 Cy. 800 x 2300 25228kW (34300bhp) Hyundai Heavy Industries Co Ltd-South Korea AuxGen: 4 x 1600kW 450/230V 60Hz a.c Thrusters: 1 Tunnel thruster (f) Fuel: 215.0 (d.f.) 3241.0 (r.f.)
9354868 *V7KK3* -	**SANTA BARBARA** *ex* Bulk Eight *-2006* **Santa Barbara Shipco LLC** Maryville Maritime Inc *Majuro* *Marshall Islands* MMSI: 538002632 Official number: 2632	**43,189** 27,291 82,266 T/cm 70.2	Class: NV (NK)	**2006-03 Tsuneishi Corp — Fukuyama HS** Yd No: 1382 Loa 228.99 Br ex 32.29 Dght 14.429 Lbp 222.00 Br md 32.26 Dpth 20.03 Welded, 1 dk	**(A21A2BC) Bulk Carrier** Grain: 95,064 Compartments: 7 Ho, ER 7 Ha: 6 (17.8 x 15.4)ER (13.2 x 13.8)	**1 oil engine** driving 1 FP propeller Total Power: 11,060kW (15,037hp) 14.5kn MAN-B&W 7S50MC-C 1 x 2 Stroke 7 Cy. 500 x 2000 11060kW (15037bhp) Mitsui Engineering & Shipbuilding CLtd-Japan AuxGen: 3 x a.c
9476953 *3FWW8* -	**SANTA BARBARA** *ex* Torm Ocean *-2012* **Compania Flor de Vapores SA** Mitsubishi Ore Transport Co Ltd (Mitsubishi Koseki Yuso KK) SatCom: Inmarsat C 437223010 *Panama* *Panama* MMSI: 372230000 Official number: 4298411A	**40,077** 25,302 76,361 T/cm 67.1	Class: NK	**2011-09 Oshima Shipbuilding Co Ltd — Saikai NS** Yd No: 10564 Loa 225.00 (BB) Br ex - Dght 14.000 Lbp 220.00 Br md 32.26 Dpth 19.39 Welded, 1 dk	**(A21A2BC) Bulk Carrier** Grain: 89,957; Bale: 87,978 Compartments: 7 Ho, ER 7 Ha: ER	**1 oil engine** driving 1 FP propeller Total Power: 9,319kW (12,670hp) 14.5kn MAN-B&W 5S60MC-C 1 x 2 Stroke 5 Cy. 600 x 2400 9319kW (12670bhp) Mitsui Engineering & Shipbuilding CLtd-Japan AuxGen: 3 x a.c Fuel: 2690.0
9430399 *DIXP2* -	**SANTA BARBARA** **Containerschiffsreederei ms Santa Barbara GmbH & Co KG** Columbus Shipmanagement GmbH SatCom: Inmarsat C 421853810 *Hamburg* *Germany* MMSI: 218538000 Official number: 23369	**86,601** 42,501 92,915	Class: GL	**2012-05 Daewoo Shipbuilding & Marine Engineering Co Ltd — Geoje** Yd No: 4234 Loa 299.95 (BB) Br ex - Dght 13.500 Lbp 286.80 Br md 42.80 Dpth 24.20 Welded, 1 dk	**(A33A2CC) Container Ship (Fully Cellular)** TEU 7100 incl 1365 ref C	**1 oil engine** driving 1 FP propeller Total Power: 41,184kW (55,994hp) 22.2kn Wartsila 8RT-flex96C 1 x 2 Stroke 8 Cy. 960 x 2500 41184kW (55994bhp) Doosan Engine Co Ltd-South Korea AuxGen: 4 x 4686kW 6600/450V a.c Thrusters: 1 Tunnel thruster (f); 1 Tunnel thruster (a)
9633006 *9V9962* -	**SANTA BARBARA** **Konlink Shipping Pte Ltd** Philippe Barko Management Inc *Singapore* *Singapore* MMSI: 566801000 Official number: 397795	**34,830** 20,238 61,381 T/cm 61.4	Class: AB	**2013-01 Iwagi Zosen Co Ltd — Kamijima EH** Yd No: 350 Loa 199.98 (BB) Br ex - Dght 13.000 Lbp 195.00 Br md 32.24 Dpth 18.60 Welded, 1 dk	**(A21A2BC) Bulk Carrier** Grain: 77,674; Bale: 73,552 Compartments: 5 Ho, ER 5 Ha: 4 (23.5 x 19.0)ER (18.7 x 19.0) Cranes: 4x30.7t	**1 oil engine** driving 1 FP propeller Total Power: 8,450kW (11,489hp) 14.5kn MAN-B&W 6S50MC-C8 1 x 2 Stroke 6 Cy. 500 x 2000 8450kW (11489bhp) Hitachi Zosen Corp-Japan AuxGen: 3 x 480kW a.c Fuel: 200.0 (d.f.) 2430.0 (r.f.)
7314864 *SX6659* -	**SANTA BARBARA** *ex* City of Portsmouth *-1999* *ex* Chichester Star *-1990* **Perko Marine Services Maritime Co** - *Piraeus* *Greece* MMSI: 237007100 Official number: 10529	**1,046** 313 1,708	Class: (LR) (BV) ✠ Classed LR until 30/3/84	**1973-07 Goole SB. & Repairing Co. Ltd. — Goole** Yd No: 577 Loa 59.75 Br ex 11.97 Dght 4.382 Lbp 56.39 Br md 11.89 Dpth 4.96 Welded, 1 dk	**(B33A2DS) Suction Dredger** Hopper: 784	**1 oil engine** reverse reduction geared to sc. shaft driving 1 FP propeller Total Power: 919kW (1,249hp) 10.0kn Blackstone EZSL8 1 x 4 Stroke 8 Cy. 222 x 292 919kW (1249bhp) Mirrlees Blackstone (Stamford)Ltd.-Stamford AuxGen: 2 x 70kW 415V 50Hz a.c
6916562 *LW5156* -	**SANTA BARBARA** *ex* Shetland *-1984* **Pesca Costera SA** - *Mar del Plata* *Argentina* Official number: 01885	**884** 657 646	Class: (BV)	**1969 Stocznia im Komuny Paryskiej — Gdynia** Yd No: B411/01 Loa 60.00 Br ex 11.64 Dght 4.255 Lbp 52.02 Br md 11.61 Dpth 6.35 Welded, 1 dk	**(B11A2FS) Stern Trawler** Ins: 540 Compartments: 2 Ho, ER 7 Ha: 2 (0.9 x 0.7) (1.4 x 0.9)4 (1.3 x 0.9)	**1 oil engine** geared to sc. shaft driving 1 FP propeller Total Power: 1,250kW (1,700hp) 14.0kn MAN G8V30/45ATL 1 x 4 Stroke 8 Cy. 300 x 450 1250kW (1700bhp) Maschinenbau Augsburg Nuernberg (MAN)-Augsburg AuxGen: 1 x 290kW 220V d.c, 2 x 144kW 220V d.c Fuel: 249.5 (d.f.)
8109010 *8PAG4* -	**SANTA BARBARA** *ex* Parnassos *-2011* *ex* Pandias *-1999* *ex* Kepbay *-1985* **Marvel Oceanway SA** G Bulk Corp *Bridgetown* *Barbados* MMSI: 314389000 Official number: 733653	**24,844** 13,104 40,907 T/cm 48.6	Class: NV	**1984-04 Mitsui Eng. & SB. Co. Ltd., Chiba Works — Ichihara** Yd No: 1267 Loa 182.81 (BB) Br ex - Dght 11.021 Lbp 174.02 Br md 30.60 Dpth 15.78 Welded, 1 dk	**(A21A2BC) Bulk Carrier** Grain: 49,970; Bale: 48,863 Compartments: 5 Ho, ER 5 Ha: (13.6 x 15.6)4 (16.8 x 15.6)ER Cranes: 4x25t	**1 oil engine** driving 1 FP propeller Total Power: 8,091kW (11,001hp) 14.8kn B&W 6L67GFCA 1 x 2 Stroke 6 Cy. 670 x 1700 8091kW (11001bhp) Mitsui Engineering & Shipbuilding CLtd-Japan AuxGen: 3 x 497kW 450V 60Hz a.c Fuel: 202.0 (d.f.) 1944.0 (r.f.) 33.5pd

7832220 *WUU9211* -	**SANTA BARBARA** *ex* Lori & Sandra *-1993* *ex* Christina & Sandra II *-1993* **Christina & Sandra Fishing Corp** - *New Bedford, MA* *United States of America* Official number: 596283	*199* 135 -		**1978 Master Marine, Inc. — Bayou La Batre, Al** Yd No: 202 L reg 25.76 Br ex 7.32 Dght - Lbp - Br md - Dpth 3.54 Welded, 1dk	**(B11B2FV) Fishing Vessel**	**1 oil engine** driving 1 FP propeller Total Power: 662kW (900hp) G.M. (Detroit Diesel) 16V-149 1 x Vee 2 Stroke 16 Cy. 146 x 146 662kW (900bhp) General Motors Detroit DieselAllison Divn-USA
9330525 *A8JZ3* -	**SANTA BELINA** *ex* Maersk Jamestown *-2011* *completed as* Santa Belina *-2006* **KG ms 'Santa Belina' Offen Reederei GmbH & Co** Reederei Claus-Peter Offen GmbH & Co KG *Monrovia* *Liberia* MMSI: 636091162 Official number: 91162	**28,616** 14,769 39,358 T/cm 56.7	Class: GL	**2006-10 Hyundai Mipo Dockyard Co Ltd — Ulsan** Yd No: 0432 Loa 222.14 (BB) Br ex - Dght 12.000 Lbp 210.00 Br md 30.00 Dpth 16.80 Welded, 1 dk	**(A33A2CC) Container Ship (Fully Cellular)** TEU 2824 C Ho 1026 TEU C Dk 1798 TEU incl 586 ref C.	**1 oil engine** driving 1 FP propeller Total Power: 25,228kW (34,300hp) 23.0kn MAN-B&W 7K80MC-C 1 x 2 Stroke 7 Cy. 800 x 2300 25228kW (34300bhp) Hyundai Heavy Industries Co Ltd-South Korea AuxGen: 4 x 1600kW 450/230V 60Hz a.c Thrusters: 1 Tunnel thruster (f) Fuel: 215.0 (d.f.) 3241.0 (r.f.)
7411791 *DUH2236* -	**SANTA BERNARDITA 2** *ex* Puzon Iii *-1996* **Cebu Clan Investment Management Inc** - *Cebu* *Philippines* Official number: CEB1000076	*796* 529 1,400		**1976-01 Sandoval Shipyards Inc. — Consolacion** Yd No: 2 Loa 53.01 Br ex 10.44 Dght 4.201 Lbp 50.02 Br md 10.41 Dpth 5.01 Welded, 1 dk	**(A31A2GX) General Cargo Ship**	**2 oil engines** reverse reduction geared to sc. shafts driving 2 FP propellers Total Power: 486kW (660hp) Yanmar 2 x 4 Stroke 6 Cy. 145 x 170 each-243kW (330bhp) Yanmar Diesel Engine Co Ltd-Japan
9338084 *A8NQ5* -	**SANTA BETTINA** *ex* Cap Byron *-2011* *launched as* Santa Bettina *-2007* **KG ms 'Santa Bettina' Offen Reederei GmbH & Co** Reederei Claus-Peter Offen GmbH & Co KG *Monrovia* *Liberia* MMSI: 636091432 Official number: 91432	**28,616** 14,769 39,276 T/cm 56.7	Class: GL	**2007-10 Hyundai Mipo Dockyard Co Ltd — Ulsan** Yd No: 0458 Loa 222.14 (BB) Br ex - Dght 12.000 Lbp 210.03 Br md 30.00 Dpth 16.80 Welded, 1 dk	**(A33A2CC) Container Ship (Fully Cellular)** TEU 2824 C Ho 1026 TEU C Dk 1798 TEU incl 586 ref C	**1 oil engine** driving 1 FP propeller Total Power: 25,228kW (34,300hp) 23.0kn MAN-B&W 7K80MC-C 1 x 2 Stroke 7 Cy. 800 x 2300 25228kW (34300bhp) Hyundai Heavy Industries Co Ltd-South Korea AuxGen: 4 x 1600kW 450/230V 60Hz a.c Thrusters: 1 Tunnel thruster (f) Fuel: 215.0 (d.f.) 3241.0 (r.f.)
9341122 *A8PG7* -	**SANTA BRUNELLA** *ex* Cap Beaufort *-2012* *launched as* Santa Brunella *-2008* **KG ms 'Santa Brunella' Offen Reederei GmbH & Co** Reederei Claus-Peter Offen GmbH & Co KG *Monrovia* *Liberia* MMSI: 636091545 Official number: 91545	**28,616** 14,769 39,337 T/cm 56.7	Class: GL	**2008-03 Hyundai Mipo Dockyard Co Ltd — Ulsan** Yd No: 0466 Loa 222.11 (BB) Br ex - Dght 12.000 Lbp 210.00 Br md 30.00 Dpth 16.80 Welded, 1 dk	**(A33A2CC) Container Ship (Fully Cellular)** TEU 2824 C Ho 1026 TEU C Dk 1798 TEU incl 586 ref C	**1 oil engine** driving 1 FP propeller Total Power: 25,270kW (34,357hp) 23.0kn MAN-B&W 7K80MC-C 1 x 2 Stroke 7 Cy. 800 x 2300 25270kW (34357bhp) Hyundai Heavy Industries Co Ltd-South Korea AuxGen: 4 x 1600kW 450/230V 60Hz a.c Thrusters: 1 Tunnel thruster (f) Fuel: 215.0 (d.f.) 3241.0 (r.f.)
7306439 - -	**SANTA CATALINA IV** *ex* Propemex A-36 *-2008* **Pesquera Santa Catalina SA de CV** - *Mazatlan* *Mexico*	*110* 52 -	Class: (LR) ✠ Classed LR until 30/1/76	**1973-03 Construcciones Navales y Hidraulicas S.A. — Mazatlan** Yd No: 3 Loa 21.95 Br ex 6.18 Dght 2.560 Lbp 19.51 Br md 6.05 Dpth 3.41 Welded, 1 dk	**(B11B2FV) Fishing Vessel** Compartments: 1 Ho, ER 1 Ha: (2.7 x 1.8)	**1 oil engine** reverse reduction geared to sc. shaft driving 1 FP propeller Total Power: 252kW (343hp) Rolls Royce C8TFLM 1 x 4 Stroke 8 Cy. 130 x 152 252kW (343bhp) Rolls Royce Ltd.-Shrewsbury AuxGen: 1 x 5kW 32V d.c, 1 x 1kW 32V d.c
7385045 - -	**SANTA CATARINA** - **ALGARPESCA - Armadores de Pesca Lda Armadores de Pesca Lda** - *Portimao* *Portugal*	*184* 54 -		**1975-07 Estaleiros Navais do Mondego S.A. — Figueira da Foz** Yd No: 172 Loa 32.80 Br ex 7.42 Dght 2.928 Lbp 27.08 Br md 7.21 Dpth 3.41 Welded, 1 dk	**(B11A2FS) Stern Trawler**	**1 oil engine** driving 1 FP propeller Total Power: 772kW (1,050hp) Polar SF16RS-F 1 x 4 Stroke 6 Cy. 250 x 300 772kW (1050bhp) (made 1973, fitted 1975) AB NOHAB-Sweden AuxGen: 1 x 1000kW 440/220V 60Hz a.c, 2 x 700kW 440/220V 60Hz a.c
9444730 *A8YJ9* -	**SANTA CATARINA** *ex* Santa Clio *-2011* **Containerschiffsreederei ms 'Santa Catarina' GmbH & Co KG** Hamburg Sudamerikanische Dampfschifffahrts Gesellschaft KG SatCom: Inmarsat C 463709432 *Monrovia* *Liberia* MMSI: 636092199 Official number: 92199	**85,676** 42,501 93,591	Class: GL	**2011-03 Daewoo Shipbuilding & Marine Engineering Co Ltd — Geoje** Yd No: 4150 Loa 299.95 (BB) Br ex - Dght 13.500 Lbp 286.80 Br md 42.80 Dpth 24.20 Welded, 1 dk	**(A33A2CC) Container Ship (Fully Cellular)** TEU 7100 incl 1365 ref C	**1 oil engine** driving 1 FP propeller Total Power: 45,760kW (62,215hp) 22.2kn Wartsila 8RT-flex96C 1 x 2 Stroke 8 Cy. 960 x 2500 45760kW (62215bhp) Doosan Engine Co Ltd-South Korea AuxGen: 4 x 4685kW 6600/450V a.c Thrusters: 1 Tunnel thruster (f); 1 Tunnel thruster (a)
9213777 *C6RL4* -	**SANTA CATHARINA** - **Disko Bay Shipping Co Ltd** Seatrade Groningen BV *Nassau* *Bahamas* MMSI: 311091000 Official number: 8000190	**8,597** 4,734 9,566	Class: BV	**2000-10 Kitanihon Zosen K.K. — Hachinohe** Yd No: 328 Loa 143.00 (BB) Br ex - Dght 9.260 Lbp 133.61 Br md 21.80 Dpth 13.00 Welded, 4 dks	**(A34A2GR) Refrigerated Cargo Ship** Ins: 12,410 TEU 227 incl 135 ref C Compartments: 4 Ho, ER, 12 Tw Dk 4 Ha: (7.4 x 8.4)3 (13.0 x 8.4)ER Cranes: 2x40t,2x8t Ice Capable	**1 oil engine** driving 1 FP propeller Total Power: 11,010kW (14,969hp) 19.8kn Mitsubishi 8UEC50LSII 1 x 2 Stroke 8 Cy. 500 x 1950 11010kW (14969bhp) Akasaka Tekkosho KK (Akasaka DieselLtd)-Japan AuxGen: 3 x 1000kW 225/440V 60Hz a.c Thrusters: 1 Tunnel thruster (f) Fuel: 115.0 (d.f.) 1285.0 (r.f.) 42.0pd
9444716 *DAJT* -	**SANTA CLARA** - **Containerschiffsreederei MS Santa Clara GmbH & Co KG** Hamburg Sudamerikanische Dampfschifffahrts Gesellschaft KG SatCom: Inmarsat C 421843210 *Hamburg* *Germany* MMSI: 218432000 Official number: 22753	**85,676** 42,501 93,551	Class: GL	**2010-10 Daewoo Shipbuilding & Marine Engineering Co Ltd — Geoje** Yd No: 4148 Loa 299.95 (BB) Br ex - Dght 13.500 Lbp 286.80 Br md 42.80 Dpth 24.20 Welded, 1 dk	**(A33A2CC) Container Ship (Fully Cellular)** TEU 7100 incl 1365 ref C	**1 oil engine** driving 1 FP propeller Total Power: 45,760kW (62,215hp) 22.2kn Wartsila 8RT-flex96C 1 x 2 Stroke 8 Cy. 960 x 2500 45760kW (62215bhp) Doosan Engine Co Ltd-South Korea AuxGen: 4 x 4686kW 6600/450V a.c Thrusters: 1 Tunnel thruster (f); 1 Tunnel thruster (a) Fuel: 8700.0 (r.f.)
7036656 - -	**SANTA CLARA** - **Santa Clara SA**	**132** 95 -		**1970 Empec S.A. — Tigre** Yd No: 24 Loa 26.83 Br ex 6.99 Dght 2.998 Lbp 24.80 Br md - Dpth 3.51 Welded, 1 dk	**(B11A2FT) Trawler**	**1 oil engine** driving 1 FP propeller Total Power: 276kW (375hp) Caterpillar D353TA 1 x 4 Stroke 6 Cy. 159 x 203 276kW (375bhp) Caterpillar Tractor Co-USA
8417261 *OA2012* -	**SANTA CLARA B** *ex* Santa Clara *-2010* **Santa Clara Marine Corp** Transgas Shipping Lines SAC *Callao* *Peru* MMSI: 760001220	**7,581** 2,274 7,850 T/cm 21.1	Class: GL	**1985-10 Schiffswerft u. Masch. Paul Lindenau GmbH & Co. KG — Kiel** Yd No: 221 Loa 136.25 (BB) Br ex 19.00 Dght 6.754 Lbp 127.00 Br md 18.97 Dpth 10.55 Welded, 1 dk	**(A11B2TG) LPG Tanker** Double Bottom Entire Compartment Length Liq (Gas): 7,278 5 x Gas Tank (s); 5 independent (9% Ni.stl) cyl horizontal 5 Cargo Pump (s): 5x160m³/hr Manifold: Bow/CM: 59.4m Ice Capable	**1 oil engine** reduction geared to sc. shaft driving 1 CP propeller Total Power: 4,650kW (6,322hp) 14.0kn MAN 6L52/55B 1 x 4 Stroke 6 Cy. 520 x 550 4650kW (6322bhp) MAN B&W Diesel GmbH-Augsburg AuxGen: 1 x 1000kW 220/440V 60Hz a.c, 3 x 500kW 220/440V 60Hz a.c Thrusters: 1 Thwart. FP thruster (f) Fuel: 453.0 (d.f.) 1051.0 (r.f.) 18.5pd
6608309 *CUFE* A-1827-N	**SANTA CRISTINA** - **Empresa de Pesca de Aveiro Sarl** - *Aveiro* *Portugal* MMSI: 263531000	**1,919** 575 804	Class: RP (LR) ✠ Classed LR until 31/12/97	**1966-10 Estaleiros Sao Jacinto S.A. — Aveiro** Yd No: 71 Loa 80.32 Br ex 12.55 Dght 6.200 Lbp 70.01 Br md 12.50 Dpth 8.62 Riveted\Welded, 2 dks	**(B11A2FS) Stern Trawler** Ice Capable	**2 oil engines** sr geared to sc. shaft driving 1 CP propeller Total Power: 1,854kW (2,520hp) 15.0kn Werkspoor TEBF296 2 x 2 Stroke 6 Cy. 290 x 400 each-927kW (1260bhp) NV Werkspoor-Netherlands AuxGen: 1 x 250kW 400V 50Hz a.c, 2 x 140kW 230V d.c, 2 x 127kW 400V 50Hz a.c, 1 x 112kW 400V 50Hz a.c
7736268 - -	**SANTA CRUZ** - -	*121* 82 -		**1977 Marine Mart, Inc. — Port Isabel, Tx** L reg 19.39 Br ex - Dght - Lbp - Br md 6.13 Dpth 3.92 Welded, 1 dk	**(B11B2FV) Fishing Vessel**	**1 oil engine** driving 1 FP propeller Total Power: 268kW (364hp)

No.	Name / Owner	Tonnage	Class	Builder / Dimensions	Type	Machinery
7907075 - -	**SANTA CRUZ** **Arenera Iguazu SA** -	*280* - 450		**1979-07 Astilleros Carrara Hermanos y Cia. — Tigre** Yd No: 16 Loa - Br ex - Dght - Lbp 38.51 Br md 9.21 Dpth 2.42 Welded, 1 dk	**(A24D2BA) Aggregates Carrier**	**1 oil engine** driving 1 FP propeller Total Power: 257kW (349hp)
7811721 *HCSZ* -	**SANTA CRUZ** **Empresa Turistica Internacional CA (ETICA)** - SatCom: Inmarsat B 373505910 *Guayaquil* *Ecuador* MMSI: 735059022 Official number: TN-00-0136	*1,602* 944 420	Class: AB	**1979-11 Ast. y Talleres Celaya S.A. — Bilbao** Yd No: 178 Loa 69.60 Br ex 12.12 Dght 3.152 Lbp 63.61 Br md 11.84 Dpth 3.99 Welded, 3 dks	**(A37A2PC) Passenger/Cruise** Passengers: cabins: 47; berths: 96	**2 oil engines** reverse reduction geared to sc. shafts driving 2 FP propellers Total Power: 2,384kW (3,242hp) 15.0kn Sulzer 6ASL25/30 2 x 4 Stroke 6 Cy. 250 x 300 each-1192kW (1621bhp) Astilleros Espanoles SA (AESA)-Spain AuxGen: 2 x 425kW a.c, 1 x 268kW a.c Fuel: 241.0 (d.f.) 12.0pd
9444742 *LXCA* -	**SANTA CRUZ** **Containerschiffsreederei ms Santa Cruz GmbH & Co KG** Columbus Shipmanagement GmbH *Luxembourg* *Luxembourg* MMSI: 253011000	**85,676** 42,501 93,423	Class: GL	**2011-05 Daewoo Shipbuilding & Marine Engineering Co Ltd — Geoje** Yd No: 4151 Loa 299.95 (BB) Br ex - Dght 13.500 Lbp 286.78 Br md 42.80 Dpth 24.20 Welded, 1 dk	**(A33A2CC) Container Ship (Fully Cellular)** TEU 7100 incl 1365 ref C	**1 oil engine** driving 1 FP propeller Total Power: 45,760kW (62,215hp) 22.2kn Wartsila 8RT-flex96C 1 x 2 Stroke 8 Cy. 960 x 2500 45760kW (62215bhp) Doosan Engine Co Ltd-South Korea AuxGen: 4 x 4696kW 6600/450V a.c Thrusters: 1 Tunnel thruster (f); 1 Tunnel thruster (a)
9442495 *3FRS3* -	**SANTA CRUZ** *ex* Torm Atlantic *-2012* **Compania Flor de Vapores SA** Mitsubishi Ore Transport Co Ltd (Mitsubishi Koseki Yuso KK) *Panama* *Panama* MMSI: 355821000 Official number: 4283511A	**44,366** 27,201 83,456 T/cm 71.0	Class: NK	**2011-06 Sanoyas Hishino Meisho Corp — Kurashiki OY** Yd No: 1296 Loa 229.00 (BB) Br ex - Dght 14.598 Lbp 224.00 Br md 32.24 Dpth 20.20 Welded, 1 dk	**(A21A2BC) Bulk Carrier** Grain: 96,078 Compartments: 7 Ho, ER 7 Ha: ER	**1 oil engine** driving 1 FP propeller Total Power: 10,740kW (14,602hp) 14.0kn MAN-B&W 6S60MC-C 1 x 2 Stroke 6 Cy. 600 x 2400 10740kW (14602bhp) Mitsui Engineering & Shipbuilding CLtd-Japan Fuel: 3190.0
9207948 *WDA9649* -	**SANTA CRUZ** **Banc of America Leasing & Capital LLC** SEACOR Marine LLC *Port Hueneme, CA* *United States of America* MMSI: 367891000 Official number: 1075883	**1,004** 301 1,059	Class: AB	**1999-01 Eastern Shipbuilding Group — Panama City, Fl** Yd No: 629 Loa 57.91 Br ex - Dght 4.137 Lbp 53.90 Br md 13.41 Dpth 4.88 Welded, 1 dk	**(B21B20A) Anchor Handling Tug Supply** Passengers: 10	**2 oil engines** reduction geared to sc. shafts driving 2 FP propellers Total Power: 2,984kW (4,058hp) 11.0kn Caterpillar 3516B 2 x Vee 4 Stroke 16 Cy. 170 x 190 each-1492kW (2029bhp) Caterpillar Inc-USA AuxGen: 2 x 175kW a.c Thrusters: 1 Thwart. FP thruster (f) Fuel: 245.0
7713591 *LRGQ* -	**SANTA CRUZ 260-C** **Government of The Argentine Republic (Direccion Nacional de Construcciones Portuarias y Vias Navegables)** - *Mar del Plata* *Argentina* Official number: 0120-F	**3,256** 2,648 3,100	Class: (LR) ✠ Classed LR until 9/3/84	**1979-06 Astilleros Espanoles SA (AESA) — Sestao** Yd No: 219 Loa 116.52 Br ex 19.46 Dght 3.941 Lbp 110.60 Br md 18.90 Dpth 5.95 Welded, 1 dk	**(B33B2DT) Trailing Suction Hopper Dredger** Hopper: 2,483 Compartments: 1 Ho, ER Cranes: 1x8t	**3 diesel electric oil engines** driving 3 gen. each 2260kW 660V a.c Connecting to 4 elec. motors driving 2 FP propellers Total Power: 7,149kW (9,720hp) Sulzer 12ASV25/30 3 x Vee 4 Stroke 12 Cy. 250 x 300 each-2383kW (3240bhp) Astilleros Espanoles SA (AESA)-Spain AuxGen: 1 x 260kW 400V 50Hz a.c Thrusters: 1 Thwart. FP thruster (f)
9041447 *D5BP8* -	**SANTA CRUZ I** *ex* Frankopan *-2012* **Nephele Marine Inc** Avin International SA *Monrovia* *Liberia* MMSI: 636015578 Official number: 15578	**55,743** 28,317 101,605 T/cm 88.8	Class: BV CS (LR) ✠ Classed LR until 18/3/00	**1995-08 Brodosplit - Brodogradiliste doo — Split** Yd No: 377 Loa 244.30 (BB) Br ex 39.44 Dght 14.669 Lbp 236.00 Br md 39.40 Dpth 21.30 Welded, 1 dk	**(A13A2TV) Crude Oil Tanker** Double Hull (13F) Liq: 104,690; Liq (Oil): 104,690 Cargo Heating Coils Compartments: 7 Ta, ER 3 Cargo Pump (s): 3x2300m³/hr	**1 oil engine** driving 1 FP propeller Total Power: 10,440kW (14,194hp) 13.7kn B&W 6L60MC 1 x 2 Stroke 6 Cy. 600 x 1944 10440kW (14194bhp) Brodosplit Tvornica Dizel Motoradoo-Croatia AuxGen: 1 x 880kW 440V 60Hz a.c, 2 x 600kW 440V 60Hz a.c Fuel: 319.0 (d.f.) (Heating Coils) 2803.0 (r.f.) 39.4pd
6722064 - -	**SANTA CRUZ III** *ex* Arlene E. Mellon *-1993* *ex* Unifox *-1969* - -	*651* 322 391	Class: (LR) ✠ Classed LR until 10/69	**1967-09 Marine Industries Ltee (MIL) — Sorel QC** Yd No: 375 Loa 50.75 Br ex 9.28 Dght 4.395 Lbp 43.01 Br md 9.24 Dpth 6.76 Welded, 2 dks	**(B11A2FS) Stern Trawler** Compartments: 1 Ho, ER 3 Ha: 2 (1.5 x 1.0) (1.9 x 1.3)ER	**1 oil engine** sr geared to sc. shaft driving 1 CP propeller Total Power: 1,125kW (1,530hp) 15.0kn Deutz RBV8M545 1 x 4 Stroke 8 Cy. 320 x 450 1125kW (1530bhp) Kloeckner Humboldt Deutz AG-West Germany AuxGen: 2 x 80kW 230V 60Hz a.c
6710190 *HC2368* -	**SANTA ELENA** *ex* Coopermartir 3 *-1979* *ex* Mercedes 3 *-1973* **Pescamar SA** - *Guayaquil* *Ecuador* Official number: P-00-0558	*153* 40 -	Class: (GL) (AB)	**1966 Promecan Ingenieros S.A. — Callao** Yd No: 70 Loa 25.28 Br ex 6.74 Dght - Lbp 21.49 Br md 6.71 Dpth 3.81 Welded, 1 dk	**(B11B2FV) Fishing Vessel** Compartments: 1 Ho, ER 1 Ha: (1.9 x 3.3)	**1 oil engine** reverse reduction geared to sc. shaft driving 1 CP propeller Total Power: 357kW (485hp) 10.0kn G.M. (Detroit Diesel) 16V-71-N 1 x Vee 2 Stroke 16 Cy. 108 x 127 357kW (485bhp) (new engine 1982) General Motors Detroit DieselAllison Divn-USA AuxGen: 1 x 12kW 110V Fuel: 12.0
8125600 *9HWG5* -	**SANTA ELENA** *ex* Vemaoil VI *-2004* *ex* Mawar *-1998* *ex* Cendana *-1994* *ex* Neptank I *-1993* *ex* Golden Fortune Maru *-1990* *ex* Golden Fortune *-1983* **SL Elena Shipping Ltd** Falzon Service Station Ltd *Valletta* *Malta* MMSI: 248230000 Official number: 6048	**1,847** 721 2,825 T/cm 9.3	Class: NV (NK)	**1982-06 Iwagi Zosen Co Ltd — Kamijima EH** Yd No: 28 Loa 81.32 Br ex - Dght 5.012 Lbp 74.80 Br md 13.00 Dpth 6.00 Welded, 1 dk	**(A13B2TP) Products Tanker** Double Bottom Entire Compartment Length Liq: 3,509; Liq (Oil): 3,509 Compartments: 8 Ta, ER 2 Cargo Pump (s)	**2 oil engines** sr geared to sc. shafts driving 2 FP propellers Total Power: 1,324kW (1,800hp) 10.0kn Yanmar T220-ST 2 x 4 Stroke 6 Cy. 220 x 280 each-662kW (900bhp) Yanmar Diesel Engine Co Ltd-Japan AuxGen: 2 x 96kW 440V 60Hz a.c
8872617 *D6GI6* -	**SANTA ELENA** *ex* Virginia *-2011* *ex* Cheyenne *-1999* *ex* Volgo-Balt 163 *-1993* **Feru Shipping Co Ltd** - SatCom: Inmarsat C 461600099 *Moroni* *Union of Comoros* MMSI: 616999063 Official number: 1201221	**2,576** 1,065 3,286	Class: UA (RS)	**1972-07 Zavody Tazkeho Strojarstva (ZTS) — Komarno** Yd No: 1363 Loa 114.00 Br ex 13.20 Dght 3.640 Lbp 110.00 Br md 13.00 Dpth 5.50 Welded, 1 dk	**(A31A2GX) General Cargo Ship**	**2 oil engines** driving 2 FP propellers Total Power: 1,030kW (1,400hp) 11.0kn Skoda 6L275IIIPN 2 x 4 Stroke 6 Cy. 275 x 350 each-515kW (700bhp) CKD Praha-Praha AuxGen: 2 x 80kW a.c, 1 x 58kW a.c Fuel: 110.0 (d.f.)
9329837 *9V8977* -	**SANTA ELENA** **OMC Shipping Pte Ltd (OMCS)** Fairmont Shipping (Canada) Ltd *Singapore* *Singapore* MMSI: 564476000 Official number: 396456	**31,247** 18,504 56,011 T/cm 55.8	Class: NK	**2005-08 Mitsui Eng. & SB. Co. Ltd. — Tamano** Yd No: 1618 Loa 189.99 (BB) Br ex - Dght 12.575 Lbp 182.00 Br md 32.26 Dpth 17.90 Welded, 1 dk	**(A21A2BC) Bulk Carrier** Grain: 70,811; Bale: 68,044 Compartments: 5 Ho, ER 5 Ha: 4 (21.1 x 18.9)ER (17.6 x 18.9) Cranes: 4x30.5t	**1 oil engine** driving 1 FP propeller Total Power: 9,480kW (12,889hp) 14.5kn MAN-B&W 6S50MC-C 1 x 2 Stroke 6 Cy. 500 x 2000 9480kW (12889bhp) Mitsui Engineering & Shipbuilding CLtd-Japan Fuel: 2260.0
6902676 - -	**SANTA ELENA IV** - -	*104* 53 -	Class: (GL)	**1964 Promotora Comercial SA — Lima** L reg 24.66 Br ex 5.97 Dght - Lbp - Br md 5.95 Dpth 3.20 Welded, 1 dk	**(B11B2FV) Fishing Vessel**	**1 oil engine** reverse reduction geared to sc. shaft driving 1 FP propeller Total Power: 177kW (241hp) MAN R6V16/18TL 1 x Vee 4 Stroke 6 Cy. 160 x 180 177kW (241bhp) Maschinenbau Augsburg Nuernberg (MAN)-Augsburg
6902688 - -	**SANTA ELENA V** - -	*104* 53 -	Class: (GL)	**1964 Promotora Comercial SA — Lima** L reg 24.66 Br ex 5.97 Dght - Lbp - Br md 5.95 Dpth 3.20 Welded, 1 dk	**(B11B2FV) Fishing Vessel**	**1 oil engine** reverse reduction geared to sc. shaft driving 1 FP propeller Total Power: 177kW (241hp) MAN R6V16/18TL 1 x Vee 4 Stroke 6 Cy. 160 x 180 177kW (241bhp) Maschinenbau Augsburg Nuernberg (MAN)-Augsburg
6902690 - -	**SANTA ELENA VI** - -	*104* 53 -	Class: (GL)	**1964 Consorcio Ballenero S.A. — Pisco** L reg 24.66 Br ex 5.97 Dght - Lbp - Br md 5.95 Dpth 3.20 Welded, 1 dk	**(B11B2FV) Fishing Vessel**	**1 oil engine** reverse reduction geared to sc. shaft driving 1 FP propeller Total Power: 177kW (241hp) MAN R6V16/18TL 1 x Vee 4 Stroke 6 Cy. 160 x 180 177kW (241bhp) Maschinenbau Augsburg Nuernberg (MAN)-Augsburg

7015042 - -	**SANTA ELENA XIX** **Peruana de Pesca SA (PEPESCA)** - *Callao* *Peru* Official number: CO-011577-PM	*158* 72 -	Class: (AB)	**1970 Metal Empresa S.A. — Callao** Yd No: L-20 Loa - Br ex - Dght - Lbp 21.49 Br md 6.71 Dpth 3.51 Welded, 1 dk	**(B11A2FT) Trawler** Compartments: 1 Ho, ER 1 Ha: (1.9 x 3.3)	**1 oil engine** reverse reduction geared to sc. shaft driving 1 FP propeller Total Power: 313kW (426hp) Caterpillar D353SCAC 1 x 4 Stroke 6 Cy. 159 x 203 313kW (426bhp) Caterpillar Tractor Co-USA Fuel: 5.0 (d.f.)
7015030 - -	**SANTA ELENA XVIII** **Government of The Republic of Peru (Empresa Publica de Servicios Pesqueros)** - *Callao* *Peru* Official number: CO-011578-PM	*158* 72 -	Class: (AB)	**1970 Metal Empresa S.A. — Callao** Yd No: L-19 Loa - Br ex - Dght - Lbp 21.47 Br md 6.71 Dpth 3.51 Welded, 1 dk	**(B11A2FT) Trawler** Compartments: 1 Ho, ER 1 Ha: (1.9 x 3.3)	**1 oil engine** sr geared to sc. shaft driving 1 FP propeller Total Power: 313kW (426hp) Caterpillar D353SCAC 1 x 4 Stroke 6 Cy. 159 x 203 313kW (426bhp) Caterpillar Tractor Co-USA AuxGen: 2 x 9kW Fuel: 5.0 (d.f.)
7237303 - -	**SANTA ELENA XXXI** -	*307* 137 -		**1972 Metal Empresa S.A. — Callao** Yd No: L-49 Loa - Br ex - Dght - Lbp - Br md - Dpth - Welded, 1 dk	**(B11B2FV) Fishing Vessel**	**1 oil engine** geared to sc. shaft driving 1 FP propeller
7019696 *DZQH* -	**SANTA EMILIA** *ex* Mikado Maru *-1977* **Loadstar Shipping Co Inc** - SatCom: Inmarsat C 454810710 *Manila* *Philippines* Official number: MNLD000125	*4,871* 1,375 8,685	Class: (NK)	**1970-03 Kasado Dockyard Co Ltd — Kudamatsu YC** Yd No: 257 Loa 115.02 Br ex 17.48 Dght 7.595 Lbp 107.04 Br md 17.43 Dpth 9.61 Welded, 1 dk	**(A21B2BO) Ore Carrier** Grain: 4,769; Bale: 4,715 Compartments: 3 Ho, ER 3 Ha: (14.0 x 7.0)2 (16.0 x 7.0)ER Derricks: 6x5t	**1 oil engine** driving 1 FP propeller Total Power: 3,678kW (5,001hp) 13.0kn Mitsubishi 6UET52/90 1 x 2 Stroke 6 Cy. 520 x 900 3678kW (5001bhp) Akasaka Tekkosho KK (Akasaka DieselLtd)-Japan AuxGen: 2 x 184kW 440V 60Hz a.c Fuel: 754.0 16.5pd
9609524 *H9XP* -	**SANTA EMILIA** **Compania Flor de Vapores SA** Mitsubishi Ore Transport Co Ltd (Mitsubishi Koseki Yuso KK) *Panama* *Panama* MMSI: 354227000	**41,400** - 77,134 T/cm 67.1	Class: AB NK (Class contemplated)	**2014-03 Oshima Shipbuilding Co Ltd — Saikai NS** Yd No: 10693 Loa 225.00 (BB) Br ex - Dght 14.000 Lbp 220.00 Br md 32.26 Dpth 19.79 Welded, 1 dk	**(A21A2BC) Bulk Carrier** Grain: 89,449; Bale: 87,463 Compartments: 7 Ho, ER 7 Ha: 6 (16.9 x 15.9)ER (16.0 x 14.1) Ice Capable	**1 oil engine** driving 1 FP propeller Total Power: 8,565kW (11,645hp) 14.5kn MAN-B&W 5S60MC-C 1 x 2 Stroke 5 Cy. 600 x 2400 8565kW (11645bhp) Mitsui Engineering & Shipbuilding CLtd-Japan AuxGen: 3 x 440kW a.c Fuel: 290.0 (d.f.) 2520.0 (r.f.)
9144861 - -	**SANTA EMMA** -	**1,000** - 1,450		**2000-05 SIMA Serv. Ind. de la Marina Callao (SIMAC) — Callao** Yd No: 58 Loa - Br ex - Dght - Lbp 44.50 Br md 10.30 Dpth 5.00 Welded, 1 dk	**(B11A2FT) Trawler**	**1 oil engine** geared to sc. shaft driving 1 FP propeller Total Power: 1,067kW (1,451hp) Crepelle 6R26L 1 x 4 Stroke 6 Cy. 260 x 320 1067kW (1451bhp) Moteurs Duvant Crepelle-France
7948110 *WDA8862* -	**SANTA FE** *ex* Campechana Cruz *-2004* **Santa Fe Cruz LLC** - *Port Isabel, TX* *United States of America* MMSI: 366858840 Official number: 614724	*103* 70 -		**1979 Marine Mart, Inc. — Port Isabel, Tx** Yd No: 197 L reg 19.69 Br ex 6.13 Dght - Lbp - Br md - Dpth 3.43 Welded, 1 dk	**(B11B2FV) Fishing Vessel**	**1 oil engine** driving 1 FP propeller Total Power: 305kW (415hp) Caterpillar 3412TA 1 x Vee 4 Stroke 12 Cy. 137 x 152 305kW (415bhp) Caterpillar Tractor Co-USA
9423566 *A8UQ8* -	**SANTA FE** *ex* Asteria *-2012* *launched as* Biscay Sea *-2010* **ms 'Biscay Sea' Schifffahrtsgesellschaft mbH & Co KG** NSC Schiffahrtsgesellschaft mbH & Cie KG *Monrovia* *Liberia* MMSI: 636091933 Official number: 91933	**35,240** 16,425 52,928	Class: GL (NV)	**2010-06 Zhoushan Wuzhou Ship Repairing & Building Co Ltd — Zhoushan ZJ** Yd No: WZ0070605 Loa 196.22 (BB) Br ex - Dght 13.250 Lbp 186.80 Br md 32.25 Dpth 19.50 Welded, 1 dk	**(A31A2GO) Open Hatch Cargo Ship** Grain: 64,231 TEU 2033 C.Ho 1298/20' C.Dk 735/20' Compartments: 8 Ho, ER 8 Ha: ER Cranes: 4x45t	**1 oil engine** driving 1 FP propeller Total Power: 11,060kW (15,037hp) 15.0kn MAN-B&W 7S50MC-C 1 x 2 Stroke 7 Cy. 500 x 2000 11060kW (15037bhp) STX Engine Co Ltd-South Korea AuxGen: 3 x 910kW 450V 60Hz a.c
7713577 *LW3774* -	**SANTA FE 258-C** **Government of The Argentine Republic (Direccion Nacional de Construcciones Portuarias y Vias Navegables)** - *Buenos Aires* *Argentina* Official number: 0107-F	**2,620** 1,255 3,100	Class: (LR) ✠ Classed LR until 21/9/83	**1979-03 Astilleros Espanoles SA (AESA) — Sestao** Yd No: 217 Loa 116.52 Br ex 19.44 Dght 3.941 Lbp 110.62 Br md 18.92 Dpth 5.97 Welded, 1 dk	**(B33B2DT) Trailing Suction Hopper Dredger** Hopper: 2,483 Compartments: 1 Ho, ER Cranes: 1x8t	**3 diesel electric oil engines** driving 3 gen. each 2260kW 660V a.c Connecting to 4 elec. motors driving 2 FP propellers Total Power: 7,149kW (9,720hp) Sulzer 12ASV25/30 3 x Vee 4 Stroke 12 Cy. 250 x 300 each-2383kW (3240bhp) Astilleros Espanoles SA (AESA)-Spain AuxGen: 1 x 260kW 400V 50Hz a.c Thrusters: 1 Thwart. FP thruster (f)
9162277 *A8IQ2* -	**SANTA FELICITA** *ex* P&O Nedlloyd Seoul *-2002* **KG ms 'Santa Felicita' Offen Reederei GmbH & Co** Reederei Claus-Peter Offen GmbH & Co KG *Monrovia* *Liberia* MMSI: 636091021 Official number: 91021	**21,583** 11,807 30,135 T/cm 45.4	Class: GL	**1999-03 Flender Werft AG — Luebeck** Yd No: 670 Loa 183.71 (BB) Br ex - Dght 11.540 Lbp 172.71 Br md 29.80 Dpth 15.60 Welded, 1 dk	**(A33A2CC) Container Ship (Fully Cellular)** TEU 2169 C Ho 866 TEU C Dk 1303 TEU incl 420 ref C Compartments: ER, 5 Cell Ho 9 Ha: (12.7 x 15.4) (12.7 x 20.4)ER 7 (12.7 x 25.4) Cranes: 2x45t,2x35t	**1 oil engine** driving 1 FP propeller Total Power: 12,240kW (16,642hp) 20.0kn B&W 6S60MC 1 x 2 Stroke 6 Cy. 600 x 2292 12240kW (16642bhp) Hyundai Heavy Industries Co Ltd-South Korea AuxGen: 4 x 960kW a.c Thrusters: 1 Thwart. CP thruster (f) Fuel: 174.3 (d.f.) (Heating Coils) 1548.3 (r.f.) 47.6pd
9188219 *DGSR* -	**SANTA FRANCESCA** *ex* CMA CGM Volta *-2009* *ex* Santa Francesca *-2007* *ex* P&O Nedlloyd Sao Paulo *-2002* *launched as* Santa Francesca *-1998* **KG ms 'Santa Francesca' Offen Reederei GmbH & Co** Reederei Claus-Peter Offen GmbH & Co KG *Hamburg* *Germany* MMSI: 211529000 Official number: 18533	**21,583** 11,807 30,029 T/cm 45.4	Class: GL	**1998-11 Flender Werft AG — Luebeck** Yd No: 669 Loa 183.63 (BB) Br ex - Dght 11.541 Lbp 172.71 Br md 29.80 Dpth 15.60 Welded, 1 dk	**(A33A2CC) Container Ship (Fully Cellular)** TEU 2169 C Ho 866 TEU C Dk 1303 TEU incl 420 ref C Compartments: 5 Cell Ho, ER 9 Ha: (12.7 x 15.4) (12.7 x 20.4)7 (12.7 x 25.4)ER Cranes: 2x45t,2x35t	**1 oil engine** driving 1 FP propeller Total Power: 12,240kW (16,642hp) 20.0kn B&W 6S60MC 1 x 2 Stroke 6 Cy. 600 x 2292 12240kW (16642bhp) Mitsui Engineering & Shipbuilding CLtd-Japan AuxGen: 3 x 1040kW a.c, 1 x 780kW a.c Thrusters: 1 Thwart. CP thruster (f) Fuel: 174.6 (d.f.) 1548.3 (r.f.) 43.8pd
9248198 *H9DE* -	**SANTA FRANCISCA** **Santa Monica Navigation SA** Nissho Odyssey Ship Management Pte Ltd *Panama* *Panama* MMSI: 356697000 Official number: 2791201B	**16,941** 10,498 28,494	Class: NK	**2001-04 Imabari Shipbuilding Co Ltd — Imabari EH (Imabari Shipyard)** Yd No: 566 Loa 169.26 (BB) Br ex - Dght 9.778 Lbp 160.40 Br md 27.20 Dpth 13.60 Welded, 1 dk	**(A21A2BC) Bulk Carrier** Grain: 37,523; Bale: 35,762 Compartments: 5 Ho, ER 5 Ha: (13.6 x 16.0)4 (19.2 x 17.6)ER Cranes: 4x30.5t	**1 oil engine** driving 1 FP propeller Total Power: 5,848kW (7,951hp) 14.0kn B&W 6S42MC 1 x 2 Stroke 6 Cy. 420 x 1764 5848kW (7951bhp) Hitachi Zosen Corp-Japan Fuel: 1250.0
9141780 *A8IP8* -	**SANTA GIANNINA** *ex* Cala Palamos *-2008* *ex* P&O Nedlloyd Salsa *-2005* *ex* Santa Giannina *-2003* *ex* P&O Nedlloyd Kingston *-2002* *launched as* Santa Giannina *-1997* **KG ms 'Santa Giannina' Offen Reederei GmbH & Co** Reederei Claus-Peter Offen GmbH & Co KG *Monrovia* *Liberia* MMSI: 636091019 Official number: 91019	**21,531** 11,839 29,700 T/cm 45.3	Class: GL	**1997-07 Flender Werft AG — Luebeck** Yd No: 666 Loa 182.03 (BB) Br ex - Dght 11.550 Lbp 172.71 Br md 29.80 Dpth 15.60 Welded, 1 dk	**(A33A2CC) Container Ship (Fully Cellular)** TEU 2061 C Ho 866 TEU C Dk 1195 TEU incl 150 ref C. Compartments: 5 Cell Ho, ER 9 Ha: (12.7 x 15.4) (12.7 x 20.4)7 (12.7 x 25.4)ER Cranes: 2x40t,1x25t,1x10t	**1 oil engine** driving 1 CP propeller Total Power: 12,240kW (16,642hp) 19.0kn B&W 6S60MC 1 x 2 Stroke 6 Cy. 600 x 2292 12240kW (16642bhp) Dieselmotorenwerk Vulkan GmbH-Rostock AuxGen: 1 x 1300kW 220/440V a.c, 2 x 720kW 220/440V a.c Thrusters: 1 Thwart. CP thruster (f) Fuel: 315.0 (d.f.) 1556.0 (r.f.) 50.7pd
9141792 *A8IP9* -	**SANTA GIORGINA** *ex* CMA CGM Lagos *-2009* *ex* Canmar Promise *-2006* *ex* Santa Giorgina *-2003* *ex* P&O Nedlloyd Rio Grande *-2002* *launched as* Santa Giorgina *-1997* **KG ms 'Santa Giorgina' Offen Reederei GmbH & Co** Reederei Claus-Peter Offen GmbH & Co KG *Monrovia* *Liberia* MMSI: 636091020 Official number: 91020	**21,531** 11,839 30,188 T/cm 45.3	Class: GL	**1997-11 Flender Werft AG — Luebeck** Yd No: 667 Loa 181.92 (BB) Br ex 29.94 Dght 11.550 Lbp 172.71 Br md 29.80 Dpth 15.60 Welded, 1 dk	**(A33A2CC) Container Ship (Fully Cellular)** TEU 2061 C Ho 866 TEU C Dk 1195 TEU incl 150 ref C. Compartments: 5 Cell Ho, ER 9 Ha: (12.7 x 15.4) (12.7 x 20.4)7 (12.7 x 25.4)ER Cranes: 2x40t,1x25t,1x10t	**1 oil engine** driving 1 CP propeller Total Power: 12,240kW (16,642hp) 19.0kn B&W 6S60MC 1 x 2 Stroke 6 Cy. 600 x 2292 12240kW (16642bhp) Dieselmotorenwerk Vulkan GmbH-Rostock AuxGen: 1 x 1300kW 220/440V a.c, 2 x 720kW 220/440V a.c Thrusters: 1 Thwart. CP thruster (f) Fuel: 314.3 (d.f.) 1556.0 (r.f.) 50.7pd

9126479 **SANTA GIOVANNA** **21,531** Class: GL
DGGH *ex* CMA CGM Tema *-2009* 11,839
\- *ex* Santa Giovanna *-2006* 30,201
ex P&O Nedlloyd Amazonas *-2001* T/cm
ex Santa Giovanna *-2001* 45.3
ex P&O Nedlloyd Amazonas *-2001*
ex Nedlloyd Amazonas *-1999*
ex Santa Giovanna *-1996*
KG ms 'Santa Giovanna' Offen Reederei GmbH & Co
Reederei Claus-Peter Offen GmbH & Co KG
Hamburg *Germany*
MMSI: 211651000
Official number: 17940

1996-06 Flender Werft AG — Luebeck Yd No: 661
Loa 182.02 (BB) Br ex 29.94 Dght 11.550
Lbp 172.71 Br md 29.80 Dpth 15.60
Welded, 1 dk

(A33A2CC) Container Ship (Fully Cellular)
TEU 2061 C Ho 866 TEU C Dk 1195 TEU incl 150 ref C.
Compartments: 5 Cell Ho, ER
9 Ha: (12.7 x 15.4) (12.7 x 20.4)7 (12.7 x 25.4)ER
Cranes: 2x40t,1x25t,1x10t

1 oil engine driving 1 CP propeller
Total Power: 12,240kW (16,642hp) 19.0kn
B&W 6S60MC
1 x 2 Stroke 6 Cy. 600 x 2292 12240kW (16642bhp)
Dieselmotorenwerk Vulkan GmbH-Rostock
AuxGen: 1 x 1300kW a.c, 2 x 720kW a.c
Thrusters: 1 Thwart. CP thruster (f)
Fuel: 315.0 (d.f.) 1521.0 (r.f.) 50.7pd

8830669 **SANTA GIULIA** *492* Class: RI
IJCD 385
\- **Petrolmar Trasporti e Servizi Marittimi SpA** 1,388
\- T/cm
Genoa *Italy* 6.0
MMSI: 247174800
Official number: 3504

1972 Cantiere Navale Visentini di Visentini F e C SAS — Porto Viro
Loa 60.86 Br ex 10.38 Dght 3.311
Lbp 59.50 Br md 9.53 Dpth 3.60
Welded, 1 dk

(B35E2TF) Bunkering Tanker
Single Hull
Liq: 1,615; Liq (Oil): 1,615
Cargo Heating Coils
Compartments: 9 Wing Ta, 9 Wing Ta, ER
3 Cargo Pump (s): 2x350m³/hr, 1x50m³/hr

2 oil engines driving 2 FP propellers
Total Power: 382kW (520hp) 7.0kn
Deutz BF12L714
2 x Vee 4 Stroke 12 Cy. 120 x 140 each-191kW (260bhp)
Kloeckner Humboldt Deutz AG-West Germany

9126481 **SANTA GIULIANA** **21,531** Class: GL
ELYR2 *ex* Delmas Bouake *-2009* *ex* Clan Tangun *-2008* 11,839
\- *ex* Santa Giuliana *-2005* 30,095
ex P&O Nedlloyd Orinoco *-2001* T/cm
ex Nedlloyd Orinoco *-1999* 45.3
completed as Santa Giuliana *-1996*
KG ms 'Santa Giuliana' Offen Reederei GmbH & Co
Reederei Claus-Peter Offen GmbH & Co KG
SatCom: Inmarsat B 321816410
Monrovia *Liberia*
MMSI: 636090443
Official number: 90443

1996-10 Flender Werft AG — Luebeck Yd No: 662
Loa 182.09 (BB) Br ex 29.94 Dght 11.550
Lbp 172.71 Br md 29.80 Dpth 15.60
Welded, 1 dk

(A33A2CC) Container Ship (Fully Cellular)
TEU 2061 C Ho 866 TEU C Dk 1195 TEU incl 150 ref C.
Compartments: 5 Cell Ho, ER
9 Ha: (12.7 x 15.4) (12.7 x 20.4)7 (12.7 x 25.4)ER
Cranes: 2x40t,1x25t,1x10t

1 oil engine driving 1 CP propeller
Total Power: 12,240kW (16,642hp) 19.0kn
B&W 6S60MC
1 x 2 Stroke 6 Cy. 600 x 2292 12240kW (16642bhp)
Dieselmotorenwerk Vulkan GmbH-Rostock
AuxGen: 1 x 1300kW 440V 60Hz a.c, 2 x 720kW 440V 60Hz a.c
Thrusters: 1 Thwart. CP thruster (f)
Fuel: 314.0 (d.f.) 1556.0 (r.f.) 41.5pd

9141778 **SANTA GIULIETTA** **21,531** Class: GL
DGGE *ex* Delmas Abuja *-2009* *ex* Santa Giulietta *-2007* 11,839
\- *ex* P&O Nedlloyd Parana *-2002* 30,202
launched as Santa Giulietta *-1997* T/cm
KG ms 'Santa Giulietta' Offen Reederei GmbH & Co 45.3
Reederei Claus-Peter Offen GmbH & Co KG
Hamburg *Germany*
MMSI: 211638000
Official number: 18135

1997-03 Flender Werft AG — Luebeck Yd No: 665
Loa 182.09 (BB) Br ex 29.94 Dght 11.550
Lbp 172.71 Br md 29.80 Dpth 15.60
Welded, 1 dk

(A33A2CC) Container Ship (Fully Cellular)
TEU 2061 C Ho 866 TEU C Dk 1195 TEU incl 150 ref C.
Compartments: 5 Cell Ho, ER
9 Ha: (12.7 x 15.4) (12.7 x 20.4)7 (12.7 x 25.4)ER
Cranes: 2x40t,1x25t,1x10t

1 oil engine driving 1 CP propeller
Total Power: 12,240kW (16,642hp) 19.0kn
B&W 6S60MC
1 x 2 Stroke 6 Cy. 600 x 2292 12240kW (16642bhp)
Dieselmotorenwerk Vulkan GmbH-Rostock
AuxGen: 1 x 1300kW a.c, 2 x 720kW a.c
Thrusters: 1 Thwart. CP thruster (f)
Fuel: 314.3 (d.f.) 1556.0 (r.f.) 50.7pd

9518103 **SANTA GRACIELA** **43,025** Class: NK
3EVL7 27,210
\- **Compania Flor de Vapores SA** 82,149
Mitsubishi Ore Transport Co Ltd (Mitsubishi Koseki Yuso KK) T/cm
Panama *Panama* 70.2
MMSI: 373500000
Official number: 4466313

2013-03 Tsuneishi Shipbuilding Co Ltd — Fukuyama HS Yd No: 1503
Loa 228.99 Br ex - Dght 14.429
Lbp 222.00 Br md 32.26 Dpth 20.05
Welded, 1 dk

(A21A2BC) Bulk Carrier
Grain: 97,294
Compartments: 7 Ho, ER
7 Ha: ER

1 oil engine driving 1 FP propeller
Total Power: 9,710kW (13,202hp) 14.5kn
MAN-B&W 6S60MC-C
1 x 2 Stroke 6 Cy. 600 x 2400 9710kW (13202bhp)
Mitsui Engineering & Shipbuilding CLtd-Japan
Fuel: 3180.0

9527415 **SANTA HELENA** **32,714** Class: NK
3EWK6 19,015
\- **M Ship SA** 58,215
Onward Marine Service Co Ltd
Panama *Panama*
MMSI: 373864000
Official number: 4421012

2012-09 Shin Kurushima Dockyard Co. Ltd. — Onishi Yd No: 5651
Loa 189.93 (BB) Br ex - Dght 12.925
Lbp 185.50 Br md 32.26 Dpth 18.40
Welded, 1 dk

(A21A2BC) Bulk Carrier
Grain: 73,142; Bale: 70,183
Compartments: 5 Ho, ER
5 Ha: ER
Cranes: 4x30.5t

1 oil engine driving 1 FP propeller
Total Power: 8,100kW (11,013hp) 14.2kn
MAN-B&W 6S50MC-C
1 x 2 Stroke 6 Cy. 500 x 2000 8100kW (11013bhp)
Mitsui Engineering & Shipbuilding CLtd-Japan
Fuel: 2280.0

7942130 **SANTA III** *142* Class: AL (HR) (RS)
ZADL8 *ex* Kometa-49 *-1993* 49
\- **Albkorfuz ShPK** 14
\-
Durres *Albania*
MMSI: 201100138

1981 Zavod im. "Ordzhonikidze" — Poti Yd No: 885
Loa 35.13 Br ex 11.00 Dght 1.140
Lbp 30.38 Br md 6.01 Dpth 1.80
Welded, 1 dk

(A37B2PS) Passenger Ship
Hull Material: Aluminium Alloy
Passengers: unberthed: 100

2 oil engines geared to sc. shafts driving 2 FP propellers
Total Power: 1,472kW (2,002hp) 31.0kn
Zvezda M401A-1
2 x Vee 4 Stroke 12 Cy. 180 x 200 each-736kW (1001bhp)
"Zvezda"-Leningrad

8328056 **SANTA INES** *104* Class: (RI)
\- 59
\- **Cannavo SA** -
\-
Cumana *Venezuela*
Official number: 3091

1973 Astillero Marino — Cumana
Loa 21.95 Br ex 6.20 Dght -
Lbp 21.01 Br md 6.10 Dpth 3.20
Riveted\Welded, 1 dk

(B11B2FV) Fishing Vessel

1 oil engine driving 1 FP propeller
Total Power: 405kW (551hp)
Caterpillar D379TA
1 x Vee 4 Stroke 8 Cy. 159 x 203 405kW (551bhp)
Caterpillar Tractor Co-USA

9444845 **SANTA INES** **86,601** Class: GL
D5CL4 42,501
\- **Containerschiffsreederei ms Santa Ines GmbH & Co KG** 92,910
Hamburg Sudamerikanische Dampfschifffahrts Gesellschaft KG
SatCom: Inmarsat C 463712655
Monrovia *Liberia*
MMSI: 636092432
Official number: 92432

2012-06 Daewoo Shipbuilding & Marine Engineering Co Ltd — Geoje Yd No: 4235
Loa 299.95 (BB) Br ex - Dght 13.500
Lbp 285.20 Br md 42.80 Dpth 24.20
Welded, 1 dk

(A33A2CC) Container Ship (Fully Cellular)
TEU 7100 incl 1365 ref C

1 oil engine driving 1 FP propeller
Total Power: 41,184kW (55,994hp) 22.2kn
Wartsila 8RT-flex96C
1 x 2 Stroke 8 Cy. 960 x 2500 41184kW (55994bhp)
Thrusters: 1 Tunnel thruster (f); 1 Tunnel thruster (a)

6617805 **SANTA IRENE** *416* Class: (LR) (NV)
CB2501 *ex* Hillero *-1978* 224 Classed LR until 24/10/83
\- **Alimentos Marinos SA (ALIMAR)** 610
\-
Valparaiso *Chile*
MMSI: 725000350
Official number: 2382

1966-06 AS Hommelvik Mek. Verksted — Hommelvik Yd No: 102
Lengthened-1971
Loa 46.94 Br ex 8.26 Dght 4.839
Lbp 42.52 Br md 8.23 Dpth 4.70
Welded, 1 dk

(B11B2FV) Fishing Vessel
Compartments: 3 Ho, ER
3 Ha: (3.5 x 3.2) (2.9 x 6.0) (2.5 x 3.2)ER
Derricks: 1x3t; Winches: 1
Ice Capable

1 oil engine sr geared to sc. shaft driving 1 CP propeller
Total Power: 1,140kW (1,550hp) 12.5kn
Alpha 10V23L-VO
1 x Vee 4 Stroke 10 Cy. 225 x 300 1140kW (1550bhp) (new engine 1976)
Alpha Diesel A/S-Denmark
AuxGen: 1 x 51kW 220V 50Hz a.c, 1 x 40kW 220V 50Hz a.c
Thrusters: 1 Thwart. FP thruster (f); 1 Tunnel thruster (a)

9249972 **SANTA IRIA** **110**
\- -
\- **Mareoocidental Transportes Maritimos** 30
\-
Horta *Portugal*

2002-02 Francisco Cardama, SA — Vigo Yd No: 207
Loa 22.70 Br ex - Dght -
Lbp 20.16 Br md 6.20 Dpth 2.90
Welded, 1 dk

(A32A2GF) General Cargo/Passenger Ship
Passengers: unberthed: 12
Bale: 110

1 oil engine geared to sc. shaft driving 1 FP propeller
Total Power: 441kW (600hp) 11.0kn
Cummins KTA-19-M3
1 x 4 Stroke 6 Cy. 159 x 159 441kW (600bhp)
Cummins Engine Co Inc-USA

7224540 **SANTA ISABEL** **2,251** Class: RP (LR)
CUEG 675 ✠ Classed LR until 28/2/98
\- **Traz Peixe - Sociedade de Pescas Lda** 2,040
\-
Ponta Delgada *Portugal*
MMSI: 204820000
Official number: PD454N

1972-12 Estaleiros Navais de Viana do Castelo S.A. — Viana do Castelo Yd No: 91
Loa 84.79 (BB) Br ex 14.03 Dght 5.817
Lbp 75.01 Br md 14.00 Dpth 8.92
Riveted\Welded, 2 dks

(B11A2FS) Stern Trawler
Ice Capable

2 oil engines sr geared to sc. shaft driving 1 CP propeller
Total Power: 2,648kW (3,600hp)
Fairbanks, Morse 9-38D8-1/8
2 x 2 Stroke 9 Cy. 207 x 254 each-1324kW (1800bhp)
Fairbanks Morse & Co.-New Orleans, La
AuxGen: 1 x 500kW 380V 50Hz a.c, 3 x 200kW 380V 50Hz a.c

8819811 **SANTA ISABEL** *196*
WDA7748 *ex* Alpha & Omega II *-1978* 133
\- **Santa Isabel Fishing Corp** -
\-
Boston, MA *United States of America*
MMSI: 366846750
Official number: 944084

1989-02 Master Marine, Inc. — Bayou La Batre, Al Yd No: 291
Loa 30.48 Br ex - Dght -
Lbp 25.91 Br md 8.22 Dpth 4.11
Bonded

(B11A2FS) Stern Trawler
Hull Material: Reinforced Plastic

1 oil engine geared to sc. shaft driving 1 FP propeller
Total Power: 942kW (1,281hp)
Caterpillar 3512TA
1 x Vee 4 Stroke 12 Cy. 170 x 190 942kW (1281bhp)
Caterpillar Inc-USA

9316816 *3EES8* -	**SANTA ISABELLA** **Forever Shipping SA** Hisafuku Kisen KK *Panama* *Panama* MMSI: 371806000 Official number: 3144406A	**30,822** 18,258 55,862 T/cm 56.1	Class: NK	**2006-02 Kawasaki Shipbuilding Corp — Kobe HG** Yd No: 1564 Loa 189.90 (BB) Br ex 32.26 Dght 12.522 Lbp 185.00 Br md 32.26 Dpth 17.80 Welded, 1 dk	**(A21A2BC) Bulk Carrier** Grain: 69,450; Bale: 66,368 Compartments: 5 Ho, ER 5 Ha: 4 (20.5 x 18.6)ER (17.8 x 18.6) Cranes: 4x30.5t	**1 oil engine** driving 1 FP propeller Total Power: 8,201kW (11,150hp) 14.6kn MAN-B&W 6S50MC-C 1 x 2 Stroke 6 Cy. 500 x 2000 8201kW (11150bhp) Kawasaki Heavy Industries Ltd-Japan AuxGen: 3 x a.c Fuel: 1790.0
6923424 - - -	**SANTA JOANA** *ex Sydero -1984* - -	*836* 407 646	Class: (BV)	**1969 Stocznia im Komuny Paryskiej — Gdynia** Yd No: B411/02 Loa 60.00 Br ex 11.64 Dght 5.160 Lbp 53.95 Br md 11.61 Dpth 6.35 Welded, 1 dk	**(B11A2FS) Stern Trawler** Ins: 540 Compartments: 2 Ho, ER 7 Ha: 3 (1.4 x 1.2)2 (1.2 x 1.2) (0.6 x 0.6) (0.9 x 0.9)	**1 oil engine** geared to sc. shaft driving 1 FP propeller Total Power: 1,250kW (1,700hp) 14.0kn MAN G8V30/45ATL 1 x 4 Stroke 8 Cy. 300 x 450 1250kW (1700bhp) Maschinenbau Augsburg Nuernberg (MAN)-Augsburg AuxGen: 1 x 290kW, 1 x 144kW, 2 x 120kW Fuel: 249.5 (r.f.)
9425930 *3EVE8* -	**SANTA KATARINA** **Asian Shipping SA** Meiho Kaiun KK (Meiho Kaiun Co Ltd) SatCom: Inmarsat C 435268010 *Panama* *Panama* MMSI: 352680000 Official number: 4214710	**32,287** 19,458 58,096 T/cm 57.4	Class: NK	**2010-11 Tsuneishi Heavy Industries (Cebu) Inc — Balamban** Yd No: SC-126 Loa 189.99 Br ex - Dght 12.826 Lbp 185.60 Br md 32.26 Dpth 18.00 Welded, 1 dk	**(A21A2BC) Bulk Carrier** Grain: 72,689; Bale: 70,122 Compartments: 5 Ho, ER 5 Ha: ER Cranes: 4x30t	**1 oil engine** driving 1 FP propeller Total Power: 8,450kW (11,489hp) 14.5kn MAN-B&W 6S50MC-C 1 x 2 Stroke 6 Cy. 500 x 2000 8450kW (11489bhp) Mitsui Engineering & Shipbuilding CLtd-Japan
9143609 *3FUT5* -	**SANTA KATERINA I** *ex Antonella -2013 ex Lukandi -2008* *ex Mologa -2001* **Ance Maritime Corp** Nova Komenco Ltd *Panama* *Panama* MMSI: 373391000 Official number: 45302PEXT	**2,914** 1,311 4,237	Class: RI (GL) (RS)	**1996-06 Sudostroitelnyy Zavod "Krasnoye Sormovo" — Nizhniy Novgorod** Yd No: 17310/03 Loa 96.30 Br ex 13.60 Dght 5.490 Lbp 92.15 Br md - Dpth 6.70 Welded, 1 dk	**(A31A2GX) General Cargo Ship** TEU 122 C. 122/20' Compartments: 2 Ho, ER 2 Ha: ER Ice Capable	**1 oil engine** geared to sc. shaft driving 1 FP propeller Total Power: 1,740kW (2,366hp) 11.5kn Wartsila 12V22HF 1 x Vee 4 Stroke 12 Cy. 220 x 240 1740kW (2366bhp) Wartsila Diesel Oy-Finland AuxGen: 2 x 160kW a.c, 1 x 50kW a.c Thrusters: 1 Thwart. FP thruster (f) Fuel: 190.0 (d.f.)
8884919 *CXFU* -	**SANTA LUCIA** *ex Akela -2005 ex Marineco Akela -2004* *ex Akela -2002 ex Waabs -2001* **Invital SA** - *Uruguay* MMSI: 770576172	**104** 31 45	Class: (GL)	**1985 Gustav W. Rogge GmbH & Co. — Bremerhaven** Yd No: 1192 L reg 18.58 Br ex - Dght 1.806 Lbp - Br md 6.50 Dpth 2.50 Welded, 1 dk	**(B34R2QY) Supply Tender**	**2 oil engines** reduction geared to sc. shafts driving 2 FP propellers Total Power: 442kW (600hp) 9.5kn Deutz SBA6M816 2 x 4 Stroke 6 Cy. 142 x 160 each-221kW (300bhp) Kloeckner Humboldt Deutz AG-West Germany AuxGen: 2 x 20kW 220/380V 50Hz a.c Fuel: 10.0 (d.f.)
9336024 *3EGG4* -	**SANTA LUCIA** **Compania Flor de Vapores SA** Mitsubishi Ore Transport Co Ltd (Mitsubishi Koseki Yuso KK) SatCom: Inmarsat C 437106510 *Panama* *Panama* MMSI: 371065000 Official number: 3196706A	**89,726** 58,779 176,760 T/cm 121.7	Class: NK	**2006-08 Namura Shipbuilding Co Ltd — Imari SG** Yd No: 269 Loa 288.97 (BB) Br ex 45.00 Dght 17.955 Lbp 279.00 Br md 45.00 Dpth 24.40 Welded, 1 dk	**(A21A2BC) Bulk Carrier** Grain: 198,738; Bale: 195,968 Compartments: 9 Ho, ER 9 Ha: 3 (16.3 x 20.2)4 (16.3 x 20.2) (16.3 x 15.1)ER (16.3 x 16.8)	**1 oil engine** driving 1 FP propeller Total Power: 16,860kW (22,923hp) 14.5kn MAN-B&W 6S70MC 1 x 2 Stroke 6 Cy. 700 x 2674 16860kW (22923bhp) Mitsui Engineering & Shipbuilding CLtd-Japan AuxGen: 3 x a.c Fuel: 4225.0
9194921 *A8IP5* -	**SANTA LUCIA** *launched as Santa Lucia II -1999* **'Santa Lucia' Schiffahrts GmbH & Co KG** Triton Schiffahrts GmbH *Monrovia* *Liberia* MMSI: 636091017 Official number: 91017	**8,507** 4,734 9,566	Class: BV	**1999-03 Kitanihon Zosen K.K. — Hachinohe** Yd No: 313 Loa 143.00 (BB) Br ex - Dght 9.260 Lbp 133.00 Br md 21.80 Dpth 13.00 Welded, 4 dks	**(A34A2GR) Refrigerated Cargo Ship** Ins: 12,410 TEU 236 incl 135 ref C Compartments: 4 Ho, ER, 12 Tw Dk 4 Ha: (7.4 x 8.4)3 (13.0 x 8.4)ER Cranes: 2x40t,2x8t Ice Capable	**1 oil engine** driving 1 FP propeller Total Power: 11,003kW (14,960hp) 20.0kn Mitsubishi 8UEC50LSII 1 x 2 Stroke 8 Cy. 500 x 1950 11003kW (14960bhp) Akasaka Tekkosho KK (Akasaka DieselLtd)-Japan AuxGen: 3 x 1000kW 450V 60Hz a.c Thrusters: 1 Thwart. CP thruster (f) Fuel: 150.0 (d.f.) (Heating Coils) 1350.0 (r.f.) 46.5pd
9181950 *EAUX* 3-SS-34-98	**SANTA LUZIA HIRU** **Emeterio Urresti Isasti & others** - *Zumaia* *Spain* Official number: 3-4/1998	**194** 58 -		**1999-03 Astilleros de Pasaia SA — Pasaia** Yd No: 301 Loa 31.20 Br ex - Dght 3.300 Lbp 28.00 Br md 7.20 Dpth 3.82 Welded, 1 dk	**(B11B2FV) Fishing Vessel** Bale: 84; Liq: 69	**1 oil engine** geared to sc. shaft driving 1 FP propeller Total Power: 883kW (1,201hp) GUASCOR 1 x 4 Stroke 883kW (1201bhp) Gutierrez Ascunce Corp (GUASCOR)-Spain
9010228 *CUQJ* -	**SANTA MAE LAURA** **Sociedade de Pesca Brasilia Lda** - SatCom: Inmarsat C 426343210 *Nazare* *Portugal* Official number: N2463C	**171** 57 73	Class: (BV) (RP)	**1991-06 Estaleiros Sao Jacinto S.A. — Aveiro** Yd No: 183 Loa 24.00 Br ex - Dght 2.943 Lbp 20.97 Br md 7.43 Dpth 3.50 Welded, 1 dk	**(B11A2FS) Stern Trawler** Ins: 80	**1 oil engine** sr geared to sc. shaft driving 1 CP propeller Total Power: 403kW (548hp) 10.0kn Yanmar S165L-ST 1 x 4 Stroke 6 Cy. 165 x 210 403kW (548bhp) Yanmar Diesel Engine Co Ltd-Japan AuxGen: 1 x 70kW 220/380V 50Hz a.c
6805268 *CUFH* A-1940-N	**SANTA MAFALDA** **Empresa de Pesca de Aveiro Sarl** - SatCom: Inmarsat C 426352810 *Aveiro* *Portugal* MMSI: 263528000	**1,944** 583 1,718	Class: RP (LR) ✠ Classed LR until 28/2/98	**1968-04 Lisnave - Estaleiros Navais de Lisboa SARL — Lisbon** Yd No: 223 Loa 80.32 Br ex 12.53 Dght 6.211 Lbp 70.21 Br md 12.50 Dpth 8.72 Riveted\Welded, 2 dks	**(B11A2FS) Stern Trawler** Ice Capable	**2 oil engines** dr geared to sc. shaft driving 1 CP propeller Total Power: 2,178kW (2,962hp) MAN G7V30/45ATL 2 x 4 Stroke 7 Cy. 300 x 450 each-1089kW (1481bhp) (new engine ,made 1979, fitted 1982) Maschinenbau Augsburg Nuernberg (MAN)-Augsburg AuxGen: 2 x 250kW 380V 50Hz a.c, 1 x 127kW 380V 50Hz a.c
8411267 *XCNH4* -	**SANTA MARCELA** *ex Saga Moon -2010 ex Lidartindur -1986* **Transportacion Maritima de California SA de CV** - *La Paz* *Mexico* MMSI: 345040022	**7,746** 2,324 4,011	Class: NV (GL)	**1984-10 Schlichting-Werft GmbH — Luebeck** Yd No: 2021 Lengthened-1995 Loa 134.80 (BB) Br ex 17.90 Dght 5.222 Lbp 119.30 Br md 17.51 Dpth 12.02 Welded, 2 dks	**(A35A2RR) Ro-Ro Cargo Ship** Passengers: driver berths: 12 Stern door/ramp (a) Len: 15.00 Wid: 13.00 Swl: 100 Lane-Len: 948 Lane-clr ht: 6.00 Trailers: 72 Ice Capable	**2 oil engines** with flexible couplings & sr geared to sc. shafts driving 2 CP propellers Total Power: 5,400kW (7,342hp) 15.5kn MaK 9M453AK 2 x 4 Stroke 9 Cy. 320 x 420 each-2700kW (3671bhp) Krupp MaK Maschinenbau GmbH-Kiel AuxGen: 1 x 800kW 440V 60Hz a.c, 3 x 540kW 440V 60Hz a.c Thrusters: 1 Thwart. FP thruster (f) Fuel: 111.0 (d.f.) 331.8 (r.f.) 18.0pd
6825610 - - -	**SANTA MARGARITA I** *ex Zermatt -1993* - -	*652* 318 391	Class: (LR) ✠ Classed LR until 10/69	**1968-10 Marine Industries Ltee (MIL) — Sorel QC** Yd No: 379 Loa 50.70 Br ex 9.25 Dght 4.395 Lbp 42.98 Br md 9.22 Dpth 6.74 Welded, 2 dks	**(B11A2FS) Stern Trawler**	**1 oil engine** sr geared to sc. shaft driving 1 CP propeller Total Power: 1,125kW (1,530hp) 12.0kn Deutz RBV8M545 1 x 4 Stroke 8 Cy. 320 x 450 1125kW (1530bhp) Kloeckner Humboldt Deutz AG-West Germany AuxGen: 2 x 68kW 230V 60Hz a.c
6912322 - - -	**SANTA MARIA** *ex Sven Germa -1993 ex Vita Fish -1993* - -	*295* 141 1,006		**1956 Ateliers et Chantiers Duchesne et Bossiere — Le Havre** Yd No: 112 L reg 53.99 Br ex - Dght - Lbp - Br md - Dpth - Welded, 1 dk	**(A31A2GX) General Cargo Ship** 2 Ha: 2 (10.3 x 4.7) Derricks: 4x2.5t	**1 oil engine** driving 1 FP propeller Total Power: 559kW (760hp) 12.0kn MaK MAU423A 1 x 4 Stroke 8 Cy. 290 x 420 559kW (760bhp) Maschinenbau Kiel AG (MaK)-Kiel Fuel: 55.0
7037466 - -	**SANTA MARIA** *ex PSK-20 -2001 ex STR-20 -1970* **Kaspmornefteflot** -	*208* - 21	Class: (RS)	**1965 Stocznia 'Wisla' — Gdansk** Yd No: 20 Loa 28.67 Br ex 6.51 Dght 1.880 Lbp 24.69 Br md - Dpth 3.02 Welded, 1 dk	**(A37B2PS) Passenger Ship** Passengers: unberthed: 70 Bale: 18 Compartments: 1 Ho, ER 1 Ha: (1.2 x 1.2)	**2 oil engines** driving 2 FP propellers Total Power: 220kW (300hp) 11.0kn Barnaultransmash 3D6C 2 x 4 Stroke 6 Cy. 150 x 180 each-110kW (150bhp) (new engine 1988) Barnaultransmash-Barnaul AuxGen: 2 x 13kW a.c Fuel: 10.0 (d.f.)
7315466 *SQPJ* -	**SANTA MARIA** *ex KOL-168 -1996* **Maria Nowakowska & Irena Towarnicka** - *Kolobrzeg* *Poland*	*105* - -	Class: PR	**1973 Stocznia Ustka SA — Ustka** Yd No: B25s/A16 Converted From: Fishing Vessel-1996 Loa 24.52 Br ex 6.58 Dght 2.420 Lbp 21.85 Br md 6.56 Dpth 3.38 Welded, 1 dk	**(A37B2PS) Passenger Ship** Passengers: unberthed: 186	**1 oil engine** driving 1 CP propeller Total Power: 257kW (349hp) 10.0kn Wola 22H12A 1 x Vee 4 Stroke 12 Cy. 135 x 155 257kW (349bhp) Zaklady Mechaniczne 'PZL Wola' im MNowotki-Poalnd AuxGen: 1 x 4kW 30V d.c, 1 x 3kW 30V d.c

7332165 - - -	**SANTA MARIA** - - -	*250* - 191		**1973 Ast. de Huelva S.A. — Huelva** Loa 36.40 Br ex - Dght 3.252 Lbp 31.50 Br md 7.29 Dpth 3.89 Welded, 1 dk	**(B11A2FT) Trawler**	**2 oil engines** geared to sc. shaft driving 1 FP propeller Total Power: 626kW (852hp) Caterpillar D398TA 2 x Vee 4 Stroke 12 Cy. 159 x 203 each-313kW (426bhp) Caterpillar Tractor Co-USA
7423732 *9HLQ8* -	**SANTA MARIA** *ex* Ditte Theresa *-2006* *ex* Bravado *-1996* **SL Maria Navigation Ltd** SL Ship Management Co Ltd *Valletta* *Malta* MMSI: 256128000 Official number: 9952	**2,813** 1,334 4,501 T/cm 10.1	Class: LR (AB) (NV) **100A1** SS 12/2011 Double Hull oil tanker SG 1.2 centre tanks 1 to 4 ESP occasional oil recovery duty **LMC** **UMS** Eq.Ltr: R;	**1977-08 Fosen Mek. Verksteder AS — Rissa** Yd No: 16 Converted From: Chemical/Products Tanker-1977 Conv to DH-2009 Loa 92.82 Br ex 14.69 Dght 6.828 Lbp 84.21 Br md 14.51 Dpth 9.10 Welded, 1 dk.	**(A13B2TP) Products Tanker** Double Hull (13F) Liq: 4,494; Liq (Oil): 4,500 Cargo Heating Coils Compartments: 4 Ta, 18 Wing Ta, ER 7 Cargo Pump (s): 3x120m³/hr, 4x100m³/hr Manifold: Bow/CM: 51m	**1 oil engine** reduction geared to sc. shaft driving 1 CP propeller Total Power: 2,940kW (3,997hp) 13.0kn MaK 8M453AK 1 x 4 Stroke 8 Cy. 320 x 420 2940kW (3997bhp) MaK Maschinenbau GmbH-Kiel AuxGen: 3 x 133kW 220V 50Hz a.c Boilers: sg 8.2kgf/cm² (8.0bar), WTAuxB (o.f.) Thrusters: 1 Thwart. FP thruster (f) Fuel: 250.0 (d.f.) 10.0pd
7634745 *C4SK* -	**SANTA MARIA** *ex* Fenna *-1996* **Astreos & Koukias** - *Limassol* *Cyprus* Official number: 374217	**105** 60 -		**1961 Scheepswerf Metz B.V. — Urk** Loa - Br ex 6.00 Dght - Lbp 23.47 Br md - Dpth - Welded, 1 dk	**(B11A2FT) Trawler**	**2 oil engines** driving 2 FP propellers Total Power: 220kW (300hp) 10.0kn Brons 5GB 2 x 2 Stroke 5 Cy. 220 x 380 each-110kW (150bhp) Brons Industrie NV-Netherlands
7523910 *VRVI7* -	**SANTA MARIA** - **Polycross International Ltd** Shun Tak-China Travel Ship Management Ltd (TurboJET) *Hong Kong* *Hong Kong* MMSI: 477032000 Official number: 356536	**267** 97 -	Class: AB	**1975-06 Boeing Marine Systems — Seattle, Wa** Yd No: 0005 Loa 30.10 Br ex 9.50 Dght 1.505 Lbp 23.93 Br md 8.54 Dpth 2.60 Welded, 2 dks	**(A37B2PS) Passenger Ship** Hull Material: Aluminium Alloy Passengers: unberthed: 236	**2 Gas Turbs** dr geared to sc. shafts driving 2 Water jets Total Power: 5,442kW (7,398hp) 43.0kn Allison 501-K20A 2 x Gas Turb each-2721kW (3699shp) General Motors Detroit DieselAllison Divn-USA AuxGen: 2 x 50kW 440V 60Hz a.c Thrusters: 1 Thwart. FP thruster (f)
9004011 *JI3409* -	**SANTA MARIA** - **Osaka Suijyo Bus KK** - *Osaka, Osaka* *Japan* MMSI: 431000619 Official number: 131640	*566* - 103		**1990-03 Naikai Shipbuilding & Engineering Co Ltd — Onomichi HS (Taguma Shipyard)** Yd No: 552 Loa 49.59 Br ex - Dght 2.609 Lbp 39.00 Br md 12.40 Dpth 5.30 Welded, 1 dk	**(A37B2PS) Passenger Ship**	**2 oil engines** reduction geared to sc. shafts driving 2 FP propellers Total Power: 1,472kW (2,002hp) 12.7kn Niigata 6L22HX 2 x 4 Stroke 6 Cy. 220 x 280 each-736kW (1001bhp) Niigata Engineering Co Ltd-Japan AuxGen: 2 x 200kW 60Hz a.c Thrusters: 1 Thwart. CP thruster (f)
8961327 *WDD3199* -	**SANTA MARIA** - **Trawler Santa Maria Inc** - *Port Lavaca, TX* *United States of America* MMSI: 367127250 Official number: 1103906	**113** 33 -		**2000 T.M. Jemison Construction Co., Inc. — Bayou La Batre, Al** Yd No: 148 L reg 22.25 Br ex - Dght - Lbp - Br md 6.70 Dpth 3.59 Welded, 1 dk	**(B11B2FV) Fishing Vessel**	**1 oil engine** driving 1 FP propeller
8843159 *WUY7705* -	**SANTA MARIA** - **Santa Maria Fishing Corp** - *Boston, MA* *United States of America* MMSI: 366210110 Official number: 933995	*198* 134 -		**1988 Horton Boats, Inc. — Bayou La Batre, Al** Yd No: 251 Loa - Br ex - Dght - Lbp 26.67 Br md 7.68 Dpth 3.66 Welded, 1 dk	**(B11B2FV) Fishing Vessel**	**1 oil engine** driving 1 FP propeller
8719748 - -	**SANTA MARIA** - **Keith L Breaux** - *New Orleans, LA* *United States of America* Official number: 910757	*152* 103 -		**1987-05 Rodriguez Boat Builders, Inc. — Coden, Al** Yd No: 59 Loa 26.83 Br ex - Dght - Lbp 23.50 Br md 7.32 Dpth 3.78 Welded, 1 dk	**(B11A2FT) Trawler**	**1 oil engine** geared to sc. shaft driving 1 FP propeller Total Power: 530kW (721hp) Caterpillar 3412T 1 x Vee 4 Stroke 12 Cy. 137 x 152 530kW (721bhp) Caterpillar Inc-USA
9194957 *A8IN7* -	**SANTA MARIA** *launched as* Santa Marie III *-1999* **'Santa Maria' Schiffahrtsgesellschaft mbH & Co KG** Triton Schiffahrts GmbH *Monrovia* *Liberia* MMSI: 636091004 Official number: 91004	**8,507** 4,734 9,566	Class: BV	**1999-05 Kitanihon Zosen K.K. — Hachinohe** Yd No: 323 Loa 143.00 (BB) Br ex 21.82 Dght 9.268 Lbp 133.61 Br md 21.80 Dpth 13.00 Welded, 4 dks	**(A34A2GR) Refrigerated Cargo Ship** Ins: 12,410 TEU 236 incl 135 ref C Compartments: 4 Ho, ER, 12 Tw Dk 4 Ha: (7.8 x 8.4)3 (13.0 x 8.4)ER Cranes: 2x40t,2x8t Ice Capable	**1 oil engine** driving 1 FP propeller Total Power: 11,004kW (14,961hp) 19.8kn Mitsubishi 8UEC50LSII 1 x 2 Stroke 8 Cy. 500 x 1950 11004kW (14961bhp) Akasaka Tekkosho KK (Akasaka DieselLtd)-Japan AuxGen: 3 x 1000kW 440V 60Hz a.c Thrusters: 1 Thwart. CP thruster (f) Fuel: 130.6 (d.f.) (Heating Coils) 1427.0 (r.f.)
9675779 *9V2430* -	**SANTA MARIA** - **Konlink Shipping Pte Ltd** Phelippe Barko Management Inc *Singapore* *Singapore* MMSI: 564118000 Official number: 399009	**34,802** 20,098 61,000 T/cm 61.4	Class: BV	**2014-02 Iwagi Zosen Co Ltd — Kamijima EH** Yd No: 336 Loa 199.98 (BB) Br ex - Dght 13.000 Lbp 195.00 Br md 32.24 Dpth 18.60 Welded, 1 dk	**(A21A2BC) Bulk Carrier** Grain: 77,674; Bale: 73,552 Compartments: 5 Ho, ER 5 Ha: 4 (23.5 x 19.0)ER (18.7 x 19.0) Cranes: 4x30.7t	**1 oil engine** driving 1 FP propeller Total Power: 8,260kW (11,230hp) 14.5kn MAN-B&W 6S50MC-C8 1 x 2 Stroke 6 Cy. 500 x 2000 8260kW (11230bhp) Hitachi Zosen Corp-Japan AuxGen: 3 x 480kW 60Hz a.c Fuel: 2570.0
8215041 *EHFN* -	**SANTA MARIA DE ESPANA** - **Cartago Marpol SL** - *Cartagena* *Spain* Official number: 5-1/2003	*131* 67 130	Class: (BV)	**1983-03 Talleres del Puerto Llastarry S.A. — Puerto Llastarry** Yd No: 42 Loa 22.00 Br ex 8.69 Dght 1.650 Lbp 20.30 Br md 8.50 Dpth 2.52 Welded, 1 dk	**(B34A2SH) Hopper, Motor** Grain: 80 Compartments: 1 Ho, ER 1 Ha: ER	**2 oil engines** with clutches, flexible couplings & sr reverse geared to sc. shafts driving 2 FP propellers Total Power: 676kW (920hp) Chrysler BS-36M 2 x 4 Stroke 6 Cy. 130 x 150 each-338kW (460bhp) Pegaso Empresa Nacional deAutocamiones S.A.-Madrid
5312599 *IUCF* -	**SANTA MARIA DEL MARE** *ex* Abril *-1957* *ex* Maoz (K 24) *-1955* *ex* Ben Hecht *-1948* *ex* Satira *-1946* *ex* Abril *-1945* *ex* Cythera (PY 31) *-1945* *ex* Vita *-1942* *ex* Argosy *-1934* **Navigazione Libera del Golfo Srl** - *Naples* *Italy* Official number: 784	*498* 188 -	Class: (LR) (RI) (BV) Classed LR until 00/39	**1931 Fried. Krupp Germaniawerft AG — Kiel** Yd No: 516 Converted From: Ferry (Passenger only)-2010 Converted From: Patrol Vessel-1957 Converted From: Yacht-1942 Loa 62.18 Br ex 9.17 Dght 3.366 Lbp 54.62 Br md 9.12 Dpth 4.86 Riveted, 1 dk	**(X11A2YP) Yacht** Passengers: unberthed: 700 Stern door & ramp Len: 3.20 Wid: 5.10 Swl: - Cars: 14	**2 oil engines** driving 2 FP propellers Total Power: 2,648kW (3,600hp) 17.5kn MaK 8MU452AK 2 x 4 Stroke 8 Cy. 320 x 450 each-1324kW (1800bhp) (new engine 1967) Atlas MaK Maschinenbau GmbH-Kiel
7503099 - -	**SANTA MARIA I** *ex* Cata *-1991* *ex* Algarrobo *-1985* *ex* Isidoro Artaza *-1980* - - *Puerto la Cruz* *Venezuela*	*697* 363 1,196	Class: (HR) (BV)	**1975-12 Astilleros Luzuriaga SA — Pasaia** Yd No: 208 Loa 63.68 Br ex 10.62 Dght 3.988 Lbp 55.71 Br md 10.60 Dpth 4.45 Welded, 1 dk	**(A31A2GX) General Cargo Ship** Grain: 1,515; Bale: 1,370 Compartments: 1 Ho, ER 1 Ha: (25.1 x 7.6)	**1 oil engine** driving 1 FP propeller Total Power: 883kW (1,201hp) 12.0kn Duvant 8VNRS 1 x 4 Stroke 8 Cy. 315 x 480 883kW (1201bhp) Carmelo Unanue-Spain Fuel: 112.0 (d.f.)
7302067 *HP8469* -	**SANTA MARIA I** *ex* Sea Cougar *-1995* *ex* Guilin *-1990* *ex* Sea Cougar *-1987* **Primex Holding Inc** - *Panama* *Panama* MMSI: 355992000 Official number: 24826PEXT3	**322** 96 199	Class: (BV)	**1973 Matsuura Tekko Zosen K.K. — Osakikamijima** Yd No: 228 Loa 31.53 Br ex 8.72 Dght 3.734 Lbp 27.59 Br md 8.49 Dpth 4.40 Welded, 1 dk	**(B32A2ST) Tug**	**2 oil engines** geared to sc. shafts driving 2 FP propellers Total Power: 1,692kW (2,300hp) 12.5kn Fuji 6M27.5FH 2 x 4 Stroke 6 Cy. 275 x 320 each-846kW (1150bhp) Fuji Diesel Co Ltd-Japan
8328006 *YYP2916* -	**SANTA MARIA II** - **Cannavo SA** - *Cumana* *Venezuela* Official number: APNN-4705	*400* 180 -	Class: (RI)	**1981 Mitchel Duane Phares — Los Angeles, La** Loa 28.61 Br ex 9.00 Dght - Lbp 27.31 Br md 8.50 Dpth 4.30 Riveted\Welded, 1 dk	**(B11B2FV) Fishing Vessel**	**1 oil engine** driving 1 FP propeller Total Power: 736kW (1,001hp) Caterpillar D399TA 1 x Vee 4 Stroke 16 Cy. 159 x 203 736kW (1001bhp) Caterpillar Tractor Co-USA

IMO / Call sign	Name / Owner	Tonnage	Class	Built / Dimensions	Type	Machinery
9141584 *CB4122* -	**SANTA MARIA II** **Lota Protein SA** - *Valparaiso* *Chile* MMSI: 725000219	**839** 325 1,126	Class: BV	**1996**-10 **Astilleros Marco Chilena Ltda. — Iquique** Yd No: 213 Loa 53.50 (BB) Br ex - Dght 6.220 Lbp 48.50 Br md 10.40 Dpth 7.30 Welded, 1 dk	**(B11B2FV) Fishing Vessel**	**1 oil engine** reduction geared to sc. shaft driving 1 CP propeller Total Power: 1,824kW (2,480hp) Caterpillar 3606TA 1 x 4 Stroke 6 Cy. 280 x 300 1824kW (2480bhp) Caterpillar Inc-USA Thrusters: 1 Thwart. CP thruster (f); 1 Thwart. CP thruster (a)
5144241 *HQIS8* -	**SANTA MARIA III** *ex* Havmaagen **Philipp Schober Shipping S de RL** Lis Elvang *San Lorenzo* *Honduras* Official number: L-1823422	*207* 62 350		**1944 A/S Nakskov Skibsvaerft — Nakskov** Yd No: 112 Loa 33.70 Br ex 7.04 Dght 2.000 Lbp - Br md 7.00 Dpth 2.50 Welded, 1 dk	**(B34R2QY) Supply Tender**	**2 diesel electric oil engines** Connecting to 2 elec. motors driving 1 FP propeller Total Power: 364kW (494hp) Frichs 2 x 4 Stroke 6 Cy. 185 x 260 each-182kW (247bhp) Frichs A/S-Denmark
8940189 *WDE6116* -	**SANTA MARIA IV** **Santa Maria I Inc** - *Biloxi, MS* *United States of America* Official number: 1043819	**161** 48 -		**1996 Master Boat Builders, Inc. — Coden, Al** Yd No: 227 L reg 25.97 Br ex - Dght - Lbp - Br md 7.62 Dpth 3.81 Welded, 1 dk	**(B11B2FV) Fishing Vessel**	**1 oil engine** driving 1 FP propeller
6719421 - -	**SANTA MARIA IX** *ex* Zeven *-1993* - - -	*649* 316 391	Class: (LR) ✠ Classed LR until 10/69	**1967**-08 **Marine Industries Ltee (MIL) — Sorel QC** Yd No: 358 Loa 50.65 Br ex 9.25 Dght 4.395 Lbp 42.98 Br md 9.22 Dpth 6.76 Welded, 2 dks	**(B11A2FS) Stern Trawler** Ins: 378	**1 oil engine** sr geared to sc. shaft driving 1 CP propeller Total Power: 1,125kW (1,530hp) 12.0kn Deutz RBV8M545 1 x 4 Stroke 8 Cy. 320 x 450 1125kW (1530bhp) Kloeckner Humboldt Deutz AG-West Germany AuxGen: 2 x 68kW 230V 60Hz a.c
5312628 *CSKO* -	**SANTA MARIA MANUELA** **Pascoal & Filhos SA** - SatCom: Inmarsat C 420400490 *Aveiro* *Portugal* MMSI: 263759000 Official number: A201	**607** 182 142	Class: RP (LR) ✠ Classed LR until 4/72	**1937**-06 **Companhia Uniao Fabril — Lisbon** Yd No: 33 **2010**-05 **Factoria Naval de Marin S.A. — Marin** Converted From: Fishing Vessel-2010 Converted From: Fishing Vessel Loa 62.64 Br ex 9.92 Dght 4.480 Lbp 52.68 Br md 9.90 Dpth 5.94 Riveted, 1 dk	**(X11B2QN) Sail Training Ship**	**2 oil engines** with flexible coupling & sr geared to sc. shaft driving 2 FP propellers Total Power: 746kW (1,014hp) 9.0kn Volvo Penta D16C-A 2 x 4 Stroke 6 Cy. 144 x 165 each-373kW (507bhp) (new engine 2010) AB Volvo Penta-Sweden AuxGen: 1 x 139kW
9225835 *EAPA* 3-HU-310-9	**SANTA MARIA R** **Mariscos Rodriguez SA** - *Huelva* *Spain* MMSI: 224935000 Official number: 3-10/1999	**293** 88 -	Class: BV	**2000**-02 **Ast. de Huelva S.A. — Huelva** Yd No: 607 Loa 32.60 Br ex - Dght 3.450 Lbp 27.70 Br md 7.90 Dpth 5.60 Welded, 1 dk	**(B11A2FS) Stern Trawler** Ins: 250	**1 oil engine** geared to sc. shaft driving 1 CP propeller Total Power: 625kW (850hp) Caterpillar 3512TA 1 x Vee 4 Stroke 12 Cy. 170 x 190 625kW (850bhp) Caterpillar Inc-USA
8619675 *EEMX* -	**SANTA MARINA** *ex* Villa de Bueu *-1997* **Pesquera Barra SA** - *Vigo* *Spain* MMSI: 224888000 Official number: 3-10026/	**778** 233 319	Class: BV (LR) ✠ Classed LR until 19/6/08	**1989**-01 **Hijos de J. Barreras S.A. — Vigo** Yd No: 1517 Lengthened-1999 Loa 53.76 Br ex 9.58 Dght 4.247 Lbp 46.77 Br md 9.52 Dpth 6.41 Welded, 2 dks	**(B11A2FS) Stern Trawler** Ins: 400	**1 oil engine** with flexible couplings & sr geared to sc. shaft driving 1 CP propeller Total Power: 1,066kW (1,449hp) 12.0kn Deutz SBV6M628 1 x 4 Stroke 6 Cy. 240 x 280 1066kW (1449bhp) Hijos de J Barreras SA-Spain AuxGen: 2 x 200kW 380V 50Hz a.c, 1 x 200kW 380V 50Hz a.c
8735869 *EA3039* 3-AT-41-97	**SANTA MARTA PRIMER** **Bonmati Blasco R&M, Jose Andres Bonmati Fragoso & Angela Fragoso Molina** - *Villajoyosa* *Spain* Official number: 3-1/1997	**101** - -		**1997**-04 **Asfibe S.A. — Benicarlo** Loa 23.05 Br ex - Dght 2.270 Lbp 19.67 Br md 5.87 Dpth 3.21 Bonded, 1 dk	**(B11A2FS) Stern Trawler** Hull Material: Reinforced Plastic	**1 oil engine** driving 1 Propeller Total Power: 249kW (339hp)
8856429 *WAJ8155* -	**SANTA MONICA** **Santa Monica Inc** - *Port Isabel, TX* *United States of America* MMSI: 367126630 Official number: 663953	*117* 94 -		**1984 Marine Mart, Inc. — Port Isabel, Tx** Yd No: 234 Loa - Br ex - Dght - Lbp 21.34 Br md 6.10 Dpth 3.66 Welded, 1 dk	**(B11B2FV) Fishing Vessel**	**1 oil engine** driving 1 FP propeller
9099195 - -	**SANTA MONICA** *ex* Lori *-2003* *ex* Don Emilio *-1996* **Armando S Advincula** - *Cebu* *Philippines* Official number: CEB1000595	*385* 224 -		**1989**-01 **Republic Drydock Corp. — Danao** L reg 35.00 Br ex - Dght - Lbp - Br md 7.60 Dpth 2.70 Welded, 1 dk	**(A31A2GX) General Cargo Ship**	**1 oil engine** driving 1 Propeller Total Power: 405kW (551hp) Hanshin 1 x 4 Stroke 405kW (551bhp) The Hanshin Diesel Works Ltd-Japan
9679543 *ZR3532* -	**SANTA MONICA** **SA Tuna Exporters (Pty) Ltd** - *Cape Town* *South Africa* Official number: 11215	**176** 52 -		**2012**-10 **Tallie Marine Pty Ltd — St Helena Bay** Yd No: T83/03 Loa 23.50 Br ex - Dght 2.800 Lbp - Br md 7.20 Dpth 4.20 Welded, 1 dk	**(B11B2FV) Fishing Vessel**	**1 oil engine** reduction geared to sc. shaft driving 1 Propeller Total Power: 336kW (457hp) 10.5kn Cummins 1 x 336kW (457bhp) Cummins Engine Co Inc-USA Fuel: 50.0 (d.f.)
8303305 - -	**SANTA MONICA II** *ex* Bremerhaven *-1995* **Industrial Pesquera Santa Monica SA** - *Piura* *Peru* Official number: PT-012866-PM	**226** 67 195	Class: (GL)	**1983**-12 **Sieghold Werft Bremerhaven GmbH & Co. — Bremerhaven** Yd No: 195 Loa 28.12 Br ex 7.90 Dght 3.257 Lbp 24.01 Br md 7.82 Dpth 3.81 Welded, 1 dk	**(B11A2FS) Stern Trawler** Ins: 132 Compartments: 1 Ho, ER 2 Ha: ER	**1 oil engine** with flexible couplings & sr gearedto sc. shaft driving 1 CP propeller Total Power: 599kW (814hp) 12.0kn Deutz SBV6M628 1 x 4 Stroke 6 Cy. 240 x 280 599kW (814bhp) Kloeckner Humboldt Deutz AG-West Germany AuxGen: 1 x 60kW 380V 50Hz a.c, 1 x 40kW 380V 50Hz a.c Thrusters: 1 Thwart. FP thruster (f)
6727624 - -	**SANTA MONICA II** *ex* Zory *-1993* **Blaze International Inc** -	*651* 316 391	Class: (LR) ✠ Classed LR until 10/69	**1967**-11 **Marine Industries Ltee (MIL) — Sorel QC** Yd No: 361 Loa 48.77 Br ex 9.25 Dght - Lbp 34.83 Br md 9.21 Dpth 6.76 Welded, 2 dks	**(B11A2FS) Stern Trawler**	**1 oil engine** sr geared to sc. shaft driving 1 CP propeller Total Power: 1,125kW (1,530hp) 12.0kn Deutz RBV8M545 1 x 4 Stroke 8 Cy. 320 x 450 1125kW (1530bhp) Kloeckner Humboldt Deutz AG-West Germany AuxGen: 2 x 68kW 230V 60Hz a.c
8616661 - -	**SANTA MONICA III** *ex* Finja *-2001* *ex* Santa Monica III *-2000* *ex* Jan van gent *-1998* **Industrial Pesquera Santa Monica SA** - *Peru* Official number: PT-17479-PM	**359** 107 178	Class: (GL)	**1987**-09 **Muetzelfeldtwerft GmbH — Cuxhaven** Yd No: 209 Loa 33.02 Br ex - Dght 3.801 Lbp 27.01 Br md 8.41 Dpth 6.51 Welded, 2 dks	**(B11A2FS) Stern Trawler** Ins: 185	**1 oil engine** with flexible couplings & sr gearedto sc. shaft driving 1 CP propeller Total Power: 1,080kW (1,468hp) 11.0kn Deutz SBV6M628 1 x 4 Stroke 6 Cy. 240 x 280 1080kW (1468bhp) Kloeckner Humboldt Deutz AG-West Germany AuxGen: 2 x 72kW Thrusters: 1 Thwart. FP thruster (f)
9225512 *H3BC* -	**SANTA PACIFIC** *ex* Santa Pacifica *-2012* **S&F Shipping & Transport Co** Vera Denizcilik Ithalat ve Ihracat Ticaret Ltd (Vera Shipping Import & Export Ltd) *Panama* *Panama* MMSI: 351617000 Official number: 2705200C	**16,848** 10,452 28,520 T/cm 34.9	Class: NK	**2000**-03 **Imabari Shipbuilding Co Ltd — Imabari EH (Imabari Shipyard)** Yd No: 552 Loa 169.03 (BB) Br ex 27.24 Dght 9.759 Lbp 160.40 Br md 27.20 Dpth 13.60 Welded, 1 dk	**(A21A2BC) Bulk Carrier** Double Bottom Entire Compartment Length Grain: 37,523; Bale: 35,762 Compartments: 5 Ho, ER 5 Ha: (13.6 x 16.0)4 (19.2 x 17.6)ER Cranes: 4x30.5t	**1 oil engine** driving 1 FP propeller Total Power: 5,847kW (7,950hp) 14.0kn B&W 6S42MC 1 x 2 Stroke 6 Cy. 420 x 1764 5847kW (7950bhp) Hitachi Zosen Corp-Japan AuxGen: 3 x 550kW 450V 60Hz a.c Fuel: 1381.0 (r.f.) 21.7pd
9326782 *A8IX7* -	**SANTA PAMINA** *ex* Maersk Dunedin *-2013* *ex* P&O Nedlloyd Detroit *-2005* *launched as* Santa Pamina *-2005* **KG Zweite ms 'Santa Pamina' Offen Reederei GmbH & Co** Reederei Claus-Peter Offen GmbH & Co KG *Monrovia* *Liberia* MMSI: 636091049 Official number: 91049	**54,809** 34,226 67,247	Class: GL	**2005**-05 **Hyundai Heavy Industries Co Ltd — Ulsan** Yd No: 1746 Loa 294.51 (BB) Br ex - Dght 13.650 Lbp 283.20 Br md 32.20 Dpth 22.10 Welded, 1 dk	**(A33A2CC) Container Ship (Fully Cellular)** TEU 5047 C Ho 2295 TEU C Dk 2752 TEU incl 550 ref C	**1 oil engine** driving 1 FP propeller Total Power: 45,760kW (62,215hp) 25.0kn Sulzer 8RTA96C 1 x 2 Stroke 8 Cy. 960 x 2500 45760kW (62215bhp) Hyundai Heavy Industries Co Ltd-South Korea AuxGen: 2 x 1800kW 450/230V 60Hz a.c, 2 x 2400kW 450/230V 60Hz a.c Thrusters: 1 Tunnel thruster (f)

IMO / Call sign	Name / Owners / Flag	Tonnage	Class	Builder / Dimensions	Type	Machinery
9290402 *A8IY3* -	**SANTA PAOLA** *ex* Maersk Driscoll *-2010* *ex* P&O Nedlloyd Dalian *-2005* **KG ms 'Santa Paola' Offen Reederei GmbH & Co** Reederei Claus-Peter Offen GmbH & Co KG *Monrovia* *Liberia* MMSI: 636091053 Official number: 91053	**54,809** 34,226 67,310	Class: GL	**2005-04 Hyundai Heavy Industries Co Ltd — Ulsan** Yd No: 1566 Loa 294.51 (BB) Br ex - Dght 13.650 Lbp 283.20 Br md 32.20 Dpth 22.10 Welded, 1 dk	**(A33A2CC) Container Ship (Fully Cellular)** TEU 5047 C Ho 2295 TEU C Dk 2752 TEU incl 550 ref C	**1 oil engine** driving 1 FP propeller Total Power: 45,778kW (62,240hp) 25.0kn Sulzer 8RTA96C 1 x 2 Stroke 8 Cy. 960 x 2500 45778kW (62240bhp) Hyundai Heavy Industries Co Ltd-South Korea AuxGen: 2 x 2400kW 450/230V 60Hz a.c, 2 x 1800kW 450/230V 60Hz a.c Thrusters: 1 Thwart. CP thruster (f)
9317456 *3FOG7* -	**SANTA PAULA** *ex* Torm Pacific *-2012* **Compania Flor de Vapores SA** Mitsubishi Ore Transport Co Ltd (Mitsubishi Koseki Yuso KK) *Panama* *Panama* MMSI: 372855000 Official number: 4072309A	**40,017** 25,653 77,171 T/cm 67.1	Class: NK	**2009-09 Oshima Shipbuilding Co Ltd — Saikai NS** Yd No: 10436 Loa 225.00 (BB) Br ex - Dght 14.190 Lbp 220.00 Br md 32.26 Dpth 19.39 Welded, 1 dk	**(A21A2BC) Bulk Carrier** Double Hull Grain: 90,150; Bale: 88,984 Compartments: 7 Ho, ER 7 Ha: ER	**1 oil engine** driving 1 FP propeller Total Power: 9,326kW (12,680hp) 14.5kn MAN-B&W 6S60MC-C 1 x 2 Stroke 6 Cy. 600 x 2400 9326kW (12680bhp) Mitsui Engineering & Shipbuilding CLtd-Japan AuxGen: 3 x a.c Fuel: 2500.0
8812928 *HQXL5* -	**SANTA PAULA** *ex* Flex *-2003* *ex* Multiflex Sprint *-2002* *ex* Mint Sprint *-1999* *ex* Industrial Spirit *-1998* *ex* Baltimar Apollo *-1995* *ex* Vigour Mindanao *-1993* *ex* Baltimar Apollo *-1992* **HL Boulton & Co SA** Venezuela Container Line *Honduras* MMSI: 334901000	**2,854** 1,107 3,194	Class: (LR) ✠ Classed LR until 26/11/09	**1991-04 Donghai Shipyard — Shanghai** Yd No: 8814 Loa 91.17 (BB) Br ex 15.12 Dght 4.990 Lbp 84.00 Br md 14.70 Dpth 7.60 Welded, 2 dks	**(A31A2GX) General Cargo Ship** Grain: 4,755 TEU 256 C.Ho 96/20' (40') C.Dk 160/20' (40') Compartments: 1 Ho, ER 1 Ha: (53.0 x 10.4)ER Cranes: 2x50t Ice Capable	**1 oil engine** driving 1 FP propeller Total Power: 1,692kW (2,300hp) 12.5kn B&W 4L35MCE 1 x 2 Stroke 4 Cy. 350 x 1050 1692kW (2300bhp) Hudong Shipyard-China AuxGen: 3 x 212kW 380V 50Hz a.c Boilers: TOH (o.f.) 10.2kgf/cm² (10.0bar), TOH (ex.g.) 10.2kgf/cm² (10.0bar) Fuel: 52.6 (d.f.) 204.5 (r.f.) 6.5pd
9642203 *3FCZ5* -	**SANTA PAULINA** **Ambitious Line SA** Shikishima Kisen KK *Panama* *Panama* MMSI: 355142000 Official number: 4454113	**34,815** 20,209 61,381 T/cm 61.4	Class: NK	**2013-01 Iwagi Zosen Co Ltd — Kamijima EH** Yd No: 308 Loa 199.98 (BB) Br ex - Dght 13.010 Lbp 195.00 Br md 32.24 Dpth 18.60 Welded, 1 dk	**(A21A2BC) Bulk Carrier** Grain: 77,674; Bale: 73,551 Compartments: 5 Ho, ER 5 Ha: 4 (23.5 x 19.0)ER (18.7 x 19.0) Cranes: 4x30.7t	**1 oil engine** driving 1 FP propeller Total Power: 8,450kW (11,489hp) 14.5kn MAN-B&W 6S50MC-C8 1 x 2 Stroke 6 Cy. 500 x 2000 8450kW (11489bhp) Mitsui Engineering & Shipbuilding CLtd-Japan Fuel: 2560.0
7740099 - -	**SANTA PENAFRANCIA 7** *ex* Habu Maru No. 12 *-1994* **Sto Domingo Shipping Lines** - *Batangas* *Philippines* Official number: BAT5000383	*301* 150 78		**1978 K.K. Kawamoto Zosensho — Osakikamijima** Loa 38.70 Br ex 8.62 Dght 2.200 Lbp 35.50 Br md 8.60 Dpth 3.00 Welded, 2 dks	**(A37B2PS) Passenger Ship** Passengers: 440	**1 oil engine** driving 1 FP propeller Total Power: 588kW (799hp) 11.0kn Yanmar 6GL-HT 1 x 4 Stroke 6 Cy. 240 x 290 588kW (799bhp) Yanmar Diesel Engine Co Ltd-Japan
9290426 *DCDP2* -	**SANTA PHILIPPA** *ex* Cap Stephens *-2012* *ex* Maersk Durham *-2010* *ex* P&O Nedlloyd Dover *-2005* **KG ms 'Santa Philippa' Offen Reederei GmbH & Co** Reederei Claus-Peter Offen GmbH & Co KG *Hamburg* *Germany* MMSI: 211766000 Official number: 20283	**54,809** 34,226 67,273	Class: GL	**2005-07 Hyundai Heavy Industries Co Ltd — Ulsan** Yd No: 1568 Loa 294.51 (BB) Br ex - Dght 13.650 Lbp 283.20 Br md 32.20 Dpth 22.10 Welded, 1 dk	**(A33A2CC) Container Ship (Fully Cellular)** TEU 5047 C Ho 2295 TEU C Dk 2752 TEU incl 550 ref C	**1 oil engine** driving 1 FP propeller Total Power: 45,778kW (62,240hp) 25.0kn Sulzer 8RTA96C 1 x 2 Stroke 8 Cy. 960 x 2500 45778kW (62240bhp) Hyundai Heavy Industries Co Ltd-South Korea AuxGen: 2 x 1800kW 450/230V 60Hz a.c, 2 x 2400kW 450/230V 60Hz a.c Thrusters: 1 Thwart. CP thruster (f) Fuel: 480.0 (d.f.) 7200.0 (r.f.)
6602903 *HO2010* -	**SANTA PHILOMENA** *ex* Offshore Diver *-2000* *ex* Mary Joanne *-1987* **Honduras Marine Group SA** - *Panama* *Panama* Official number: 28835PEXT	*151* 64 -	Class: (LR) ✠ Classed LR until 1/3/71	**1965-12 Les Chantiers Maritimes de Paspebiac Inc — Paspebiac QC** (Hull) Yd No: 14 **1965-12 Marine Industries Ltee (MIL) — Sorel QC** Yd No: 332 Converted From: Trawler-2000 Loa 27.18 Br ex 6.94 Dght 2.896 Lbp 23.98 Br md 6.60 Dpth 3.36 Welded	**(A31A2GX) General Cargo Ship**	**1 oil engine** sr reverse geared to sc. shaft driving 1 FP propeller Total Power: 515kW (700hp) 7.0kn G.M. (Detroit Diesel) 16V-71 1 x Vee 2 Stroke 16 Cy. 108 x 127 515kW (700bhp) General Motors Corp-USA
9324095 *3EFG7* -	**SANTA PHOENIX** **Sanzo Enterprise (Panama) SA** MOL Ship Management Co Ltd (MOLSHIP) *Panama* *Panama* MMSI: 355759000 Official number: 3189206A	**31,234** 18,504 56,045 T/cm 55.8	Class: NK	**2006-06 Mitsui Eng. & SB. Co. Ltd., Chiba Works — Ichihara** Yd No: 1644 Loa 189.99 (BB) Br ex - Dght 12.550 Lbp 182.00 Br md 32.26 Dpth 17.90 Welded, 1 dk	**(A21A2BC) Bulk Carrier** Grain: 70,810; Bale: 68,083 Compartments: 5 Ho, ER 5 Ha: 4 (21.1 x 18.9)ER (17.6 x 18.9) Cranes: 4x30t	**1 oil engine** driving 1 FP propeller Total Power: 9,480kW (12,889hp) 14.5kn MAN-B&W 6S50MC-C 1 x 2 Stroke 6 Cy. 500 x 2000 9480kW (12889bhp) Mitsui Engineering & Shipbuilding CLtd-Japan AuxGen: 3 x 480kW 450V 60Hz a.c Fuel: 2280.0
9326794 *A8IY2* -	**SANTA PLACIDA** *ex* Maersk Dieppe *-2013* *ex* P&O Nedlloyd Doha *-2005* *ex* Santa Placida *-2005* **KG Zweite ms 'Santa Placida' Offen Reederei GmbH & Co** Reederei Claus-Peter Offen GmbH & Co KG *Monrovia* *Liberia* MMSI: 636091052 Official number: 91052	**54,809** 34,226 66,900	Class: GL	**2005-06 Hyundai Heavy Industries Co Ltd — Ulsan** Yd No: 1747 Loa 294.51 (BB) Br ex - Dght 13.650 Lbp 283.20 Br md 32.20 Dpth 22.10 Welded, 1 dk	**(A33A2CC) Container Ship (Fully Cellular)** TEU 5047 C Ho 2295 TEU C Dk 2752 TEU incl 550 ref C	**1 oil engine** driving 1 FP propeller Total Power: 45,760kW (62,215hp) 25.0kn Sulzer 8RTA96C 1 x 2 Stroke 8 Cy. 960 x 2500 45760kW (62215bhp) Hyundai Heavy Industries Co Ltd-South Korea AuxGen: 2 x 1800kW 450/230V 60Hz a.c, 2 x 2400kW 450/230V 60Hz a.c Thrusters: 1 Tunnel thruster (f)
9297474 *A8KN6* -	**SANTA PRISCILLA** *ex* Uasc Dammam *-2012* *ex* Maersk Donegal *-2010* *ex* P&O Nedlloyd Dublin *-2005* **KG ms 'Santa Priscilla' Offen Reederei GmbH & Co** Reederei Claus-Peter Offen GmbH & Co KG *Monrovia* *Liberia* MMSI: 636091198 Official number: 91198	**54,809** 34,226 67,222	Class: GL	**2005-09 Hyundai Heavy Industries Co Ltd — Ulsan** Yd No: 1598 Loa 294.51 (BB) Br ex - Dght 13.650 Lbp 283.20 Br md 32.20 Dpth 22.10 Welded, 1 dk	**(A33A2CC) Container Ship (Fully Cellular)** TEU 5047 C Ho 2295 TEU C Dk 2752 TEU incl 550 ref C	**1 oil engine** driving 1 FP propeller Total Power: 51,480kW (69,992hp) 25.0kn Sulzer 9RTA96C 1 x 2 Stroke 9 Cy. 960 x 2500 51480kW (69992bhp) Hyundai Heavy Industries Co Ltd-South Korea AuxGen: 2 x 1800kW 450/230V 60Hz a.c, 2 x 2400kW 450/230V 60Hz a.c Thrusters: 1 Thwart. CP thruster (f)
9227297 *DPRB* -	**SANTA RAFAELA** *ex* Southampton Express *-2009* *ex* Maersk Denia *-2007* *ex* P&O Nedlloyd Remuera *-2006* *launched as* Santa Rafaela *-2002* **KG ms 'Santa Rafaela' Offen Reederei GmbH & Co** Reederei Claus-Peter Offen GmbH & Co KG SatCom: Inmarsat C 421114310 *Hamburg* *Germany* MMSI: 211143000 Official number: 19318	**45,803** 25,077 53,328	Class: GL	**2002-01 Samsung Heavy Industries Co Ltd — Geoje** Yd No: 1357 Loa 281.03 (BB) Br ex - Dght 12.500 Lbp 268.00 Br md 32.20 Dpth 19.85 Welded, 1 dk	**(A33A2CC) Container Ship (Fully Cellular)** Double Bottom Entire Compartment Length TEU 4112 C Ho 1693 TEU C Dk 2419 TEU incl 1300 ref C.	**1 oil engine** driving 1 FP propeller Total Power: 51,434kW (69,930hp) 25.0kn Sulzer 9RTA96C 1 x 2 Stroke 9 Cy. 960 x 2500 51434kW (69930bhp) Doosan Engine Co Ltd-South Korea AuxGen: 4 x 3060kW a.c, 1 x 2600kW a.c Thrusters: 1 Thwart. FP thruster (f) Fuel: 400.0 (d.f.) 8500.0 (r.f.) 185.0pd
9227302 *DPGZ* -	**SANTA REBECCA** *ex* Maersk Decatur *-2010* *ex* Maersk Dacartur *-2006* *ex* P&O Nedlloyd Encounter *-2006* *launched as* Santa Rebecca *-2002* **KG ms 'Santa Rebecca' Offen Reederei GmbH & Co** Reederei Claus-Peter Offen GmbH & Co KG SatCom: Inmarsat C 421115110 *Hamburg* *Germany* MMSI: 211151000 Official number: 19350	**45,803** 25,077 53,410	Class: GL	**2002-04 Samsung Heavy Industries Co Ltd — Geoje** Yd No: 1358 Loa 281.00 (BB) Br ex - Dght 12.500 Lbp 268.00 Br md 32.20 Dpth 20.00 Welded, 1 dk	**(A33A2CC) Container Ship (Fully Cellular)** Double Bottom Entire Compartment Length TEU 4112 C Ho 1693 TEU C Dk 2419 TEU incl 1300 ref C.	**1 oil engine** driving 1 FP propeller Total Power: 51,434kW (69,930hp) 25.0kn Sulzer 9RTA96C 1 x 2 Stroke 9 Cy. 960 x 2500 51434kW (69930bhp) Doosan Engine Co Ltd-South Korea AuxGen: 1 x 2600kW a.c, 4 x 3060kW a.c Thrusters: 1 Thwart. FP thruster (f) Fuel: 400.0 (d.f.) 8500.0 (r.f.)

8314562 *ZMSR* -	**SANTA REGINA** **Strait Holdings Ltd** Strait Shipping Ltd *Wellington* *New Zealand* MMSI: 512036000 Official number: 876259	**14,588** 4,376 3,750	Class: LR (BV) **100A1** CS 11/2012 roll on - roll off cargo/passenger ship wine cargo in four integral cargo tanks **LMC** **UMS** Eq.Ltr: B†; Cable: 550.0/58.0 U2 (a)	**1985-05 Societe Nouvelle des Ateliers et Chantiers du Havre — Le Havre** Yd No: 266 Loa 136.02 (BB) Br ex 22.56 Dght 6.401 Lbp 125.81 Br md 22.51 Dpth 19.31 Welded, 3 dks	**(A36A2PR) Passenger/Ro-Ro Ship (Vehicles)** Passengers: berths: 110; driver berths: 110 Stern door/ramp (p) Len: 14.50 Wid: 4.50 Swl: 32 Stern door/ramp (s) Len: 14.50 Wid: 10.10 Swl: 50 Lane-Len: 1350 Lane-Wid: 10.00 Lane-clr ht: 4.50 Cars: 48, Trailers: 110	**2 oil engines** with flexible couplings & sr geared to sc. shafts driving 2 CP propellers Total Power: 9,936kW (13,508hp) 18.5kn Pielstick 9PC2-6L-400 2 x 4 Stroke 9 Cy. 400 x 460 each-4968kW (6754bhp) Alsthom Atlantique-France AuxGen: 2 x 780kW 380V 50Hz a.c, 2 x 780kW 380V 50Hz a.c, 1 x 240kW 380V 50Hz a.c Boilers: AuxB (o.f.) 10.2kgf/cm² (10.0bar), WTAuxB (o.f.) 11.2kgf/cm² (11.0bar) Thrusters: 2 Thwart. CP thruster (f) Fuel: 138.1 (d.f.) 369.6 (r.f.) 37.5pd
9227314 *DPJK* -	**SANTA RICARDA** *ex* Cap Ricarda *-2013* *ex* Maersk Dunafare *-2010* *ex* P&O Nedlloyd Botany *-2005* *launched as* Santa Ricarda *-2002* **KG ms 'Santa Ricarda' Offen Reederei GmbH & Co** Reederei Claus-Peter Offen GmbH & Co KG SatCom: Inmarsat C 421113210 *Hamburg* *Germany* MMSI: 211132000 Official number: 19355	**45,803** 25,077 53,452	Class: GL	**2002-05 Samsung Heavy Industries Co Ltd — Geoje** Yd No: 1359 Loa 281.00 (BB) Br ex - Dght 12.500 Lbp 268.00 Br md 32.20 Dpth 20.00 Welded, 1 dk	**(A33A2CC) Container Ship (Fully Cellular)** TEU 4112 C Ho 1693 TEU C Dk 2419 TEU incl 1300 ref C.	**1 oil engine** driving 1 FP propeller Total Power: 51,434kW (69,930hp) 25.0kn Sulzer 9RTA96C 1 x 2 Stroke 9 Cy. 960 x 2500 51434kW (69930bhp) Doosan Engine Co Ltd-South Korea AuxGen: 4 x 3060kW a.c, 1 x 2600kW a.c Thrusters: 1 Thwart. FP thruster (f)
9425382 *DIOY2* -	**SANTA RITA** **Containerschiffsreederei ms Santa Rita GmbH & Co KG** Columbus Shipmanagement GmbH *Hamburg* *Germany* MMSI: 218670000 Official number: 23038	**85,676** 42,501 93,404	Class: GL	**2011-05 Daewoo Shipbuilding & Marine Engineering Co Ltd — Geoje** Yd No: 4230 Loa 299.95 (BB) Br ex - Dght 13.500 Lbp 286.80 Br md 42.80 Dpth 24.20 Welded, 1 dk	**(A33A2CC) Container Ship (Fully Cellular)** TEU 7100 incl 1365 ref C	**1 oil engine** driving 1 FP propeller Total Power: 41,184kW (55,994hp) 22.2kn Wartsila 8RT-flex96C 1 x 2 Stroke 8 Cy. 960 x 2500 41184kW (55994bhp) Doosan Engine Co Ltd-South Korea AuxGen: 4 x 4685kW 6600/450V a.c Thrusters: 1 Tunnel thruster (f); 1 Tunnel thruster (a)
9448906 *ICHL* -	**SANTA RITA** **Petrolmar Trasporti e Servizi Marittimi SpA** - *Genoa* *Italy* MMSI: 247244700 Official number: 3863	*1,394* 907 2,500	Class: RI	**2008-07 Off. Mecc. Nav. e Fond. San Giorgio del Porto — Genoa** Yd No: 112 Loa 74.70 (BB) Br ex - Dght 4.440 Lbp 68.80 Br md 13.48 Dpth 5.50 Welded, 1 dk	**(A13B2TP) Products Tanker** Double Hull (13F)	**2 oil engines** reduction geared to sc. shafts driving 2 Propellers Total Power: 1,220kW (1,658hp) Yanmar 6AYM-ETE 2 x 4 Stroke 6 Cy. 155 x 180 each-610kW (829bhp) Yanmar Diesel Engine Co Ltd-Japan
9478999 *3EVQ9* -	**SANTA RITA** **Batanagar Shipping Corp** Rudolf A Oetker KG SatCom: Inmarsat C 435181113 *Panama* *Panama* MMSI: 351811000 Official number: 4231811	**31,230** 18,516 55,677 T/cm 56.0	Class: NK	**2010-12 Mitsui Eng. & SB. Co. Ltd. — Tamano** Yd No: 1748 Loa 189.99 (BB) Br ex - Dght 12.573 Lbp 182.00 Br md 32.26 Dpth 17.90 Welded, 1 dk	**(A21A2BC) Bulk Carrier** Grain: 70,868; Bale: 68,116 Compartments: 5 Ho, ER 5 Ha: ER Cranes: 4x30t	**1 oil engine** driving 1 FP propeller Total Power: 9,480kW (12,889hp) 14.5kn MAN-B&W 6S50MC-C 1 x 2 Stroke 6 Cy. 500 x 2000 9480kW (12889bhp) Mitsui Engineering & Shipbuilding CLtd-Japan
8328018 *YYP2215* -	**SANTA RITA** **Cannavo SA** - *Cumana* *Venezuela* Official number: APPN-4561	*400* 180	Class: (RI)	**1981 Mitchel Duane Phares — Los Angeles, La** Loa 28.61 Br ex 9.00 Dght - Lbp 27.31 Br md 8.50 Dpth 4.30 Riveted\Welded, 1 dk	**(B11B2FV) Fishing Vessel**	**1 oil engine** driving 1 FP propeller Total Power: 736kW (1,001hp) Caterpillar D399TA 1 x Vee 4 Stroke 16 Cy. 159 x 203 736kW (1001bhp) Caterpillar Tractor Co-USA
5388407 *IURH* -	**SANTA RITA** *ex* Westfalen *-1964* **Amalfi Navigazione Srl di Renato Florio** - *Salerno* *Italy* Official number: 51	*290* 154 -	Class: (RI) (GL)	**1951-07 Jos L Meyer — Papenburg** Yd No: 457 Loa 41.58 Br ex 7.04 Dght 2.185 Lbp 37.29 Br md 6.99 Dpth 3.10 Riveted\Welded, 1 dk	**(A37B2PS) Passenger Ship**	**1 oil engine** driving 1 FP propeller Total Power: 382kW (519hp) MaK MAU423 1 x 4 Stroke 8 Cy. 290 x 420 382kW (519bhp) Maschinenbau Kiel AG (MaK)-Kiel
8639857 *V7QY3* -	**SANTA RITA I** *ex* Tosca IV *-1964* *ex* Deirdre *-2001* **Stanhore Trading International SA** - *Jaluit* *Marshall Islands* MMSI: 538070595 Official number: 70595	*949* 285 -		**1972-06 Verolme Cork Dockyard Ltd — Cobh** Yd No: 819 Converted From: Fishery Patrol Vessel-2009 Loa 62.61 Br ex - Dght 4.350 Lbp 56.20 Br md 10.40 Dpth 6.70 Welded, 1 dk	**(X11A2YP) Yacht**	**2 oil engines** reduction geared to sc. shafts driving 1 Propeller Total Power: 3,090kW (4,202hp) 12.0kn Polar SF112VS-F 2 x Vee 4 Stroke 12 Cy. 250 x 300 each-1545kW (2101bhp) British Polar Engines Ltd.-Glasgow
9227326 *A8IY4* -	**SANTA ROBERTA** *ex* Cap Roberta *-2013* *ex* Maersk Dominica *-2010* *ex* Sydney Express *-2006* *ex* P&O Nedlloyd Pegasus *-2003* *launched as* Santa Roberta *-2002* **SFL Roberta Inc** MSC Mediterranean Shipping Co SA *Monrovia* *Liberia*	**45,803** 25,077 53,462	Class: GL	**2002-08 Samsung Heavy Industries Co Ltd — Geoje** Yd No: 1360 Loa 281.03 (BB) Br ex - Dght 12.500 Lbp 268.00 Br md 32.20 Dpth 20.00 Welded, 1 dk	**(A33A2CC) Container Ship (Fully Cellular)** Double Bottom Entire Compartment Length TEU 4112 C Ho 1693 TEU C Dk 2419 TEU incl 1300 ref C.	**1 oil engine** driving 1 FP propeller Total Power: 51,434kW (69,930hp) 25.0kn Sulzer 9RTA96C 1 x 2 Stroke 9 Cy. 960 x 2500 51434kW (69930bhp) Doosan Engine Co Ltd-South Korea AuxGen: 1 x 2600kW a.c, 4 x 3060kW a.c Thrusters: 1 Thwart. FP thruster (f) Fuel: 400.0 (d.f.) 8500.0 (r.f.)
9430363 *A8ZS7* -	**SANTA ROSA** **Reederei Santa Containerschiffe GmbH & Co KG** Columbus Shipmanagement GmbH SatCom: Inmarsat C 463710434 *Monrovia* *Liberia* MMSI: 636092266 Official number: 92266	**85,676** 42,501 93,398	Class: GL	**2011-07 Daewoo Shipbuilding & Marine Engineering Co Ltd — Geoje** Yd No: 4231 Loa 299.95 (BB) Br ex - Dght 13.500 Lbp 286.80 Br md 42.81 Dpth 24.20 Welded, 1 dk	**(A33A2CC) Container Ship (Fully Cellular)** TEU 7100 incl 1365 ref C	**1 oil engine** driving 1 FP propeller Total Power: 41,184kW (55,994hp) 22.2kn Wartsila 8RT-flex96C 1 x 2 Stroke 8 Cy. 960 x 2500 41184kW (55994bhp) Doosan Engine Co Ltd-South Korea AuxGen: 4 x 4686kW 6600V a.c Thrusters: 1 Tunnel thruster (f); 1 Tunnel thruster (a)
9006514 *S6BB9* -	**SANTA ROSA** *ex* CMA CGM Oubangui *-2008* *ex* Santa Rosa *-2007* *ex* Caribia Express *-2006* *ex* Cap Vilano *-2004* *ex* Libra Brasil *-2003* *ex* P&O Nedlloyd Pinta *-2002* *ex* P&O Nedlloyd Tema *-2000* *ex* Santa Rosa *-1999* *ex* Panatlantic *-1997* *ex* Santa Rosa *-1997* *ex* Nedlloyd van Rees *-1996* *ex* Santa Rosa *-1995* **Virginia Key Pte Ltd** Seachange Maritime (Singapore) Pte Ltd *Singapore* *Singapore* MMSI: 565429000 Official number: 392932	**21,053** 11,796 30,078 T/cm 44.0	Class: NV (GL)	**1992-04 Thyssen Nordseewerke GmbH — Emden** Yd No: 498 Loa 182.24 (BB) Br ex 28.44 Dght 11.550 Lbp 172.00 Br md 28.40 Dpth 15.60 Welded, 1 dk	**(A33A2CC) Container Ship (Fully Cellular)** Grain: 39,796 TEU 1742 C Ho 794 TEU C Dk 948 TEU incl 100 ref C. Compartments: 5 Cell Ho, ER 26 Ha: 2 (12.8 x 5.3)24 (12.8 x 7.9)ER Cranes: 2x40t,1x36t,1x10t Ice Capable	**1 oil engine** driving 1 CP propeller Total Power: 11,550kW (15,703hp) 19.0kn B&W 7L60MC 1 x 2 Stroke 7 Cy. 600 x 1944 11550kW (15703bhp) Mitsui Engineering & Shipbuilding CLtd-Japan AuxGen: 1 x 1300kW 220/440V 60Hz a.c, 2 x 700kW 220/440V 60Hz a.c Thrusters: 1 Tunnel thruster (f) Fuel: 290.0 (d.f.) (Part Heating Coils) 1577.0 (r.f.) 40.0pd
8804713 - -	**SANTA ROSA A** **La Macchia Fisheries Pty Ltd** - *Port Kembla, NSW* *Australia*	*180*		**1989-02 K Shipyard Construction & Repairs Pty Ltd — Port Adelaide SA** Yd No: 8 Loa 24.08 (BB) Br ex 7.12 Dght - Lbp 21.00 Br md 7.02 Dpth 3.32 Welded	**(B11A2FS) Stern Trawler** Ins: 88	**1 oil engine** sr geared to sc. shaft driving 1 FP propeller Total Power: 331kW (450hp) Yanmar S165L-UT 1 x 4 Stroke 6 Cy. 165 x 210 331kW (450bhp) Yanmar Diesel Engine Co Ltd-Japan Thrusters: 1 Thwart. FP thruster (f)
6805696 - -	**SANTA ROSA II** *ex* Zweeloo *-1993* - -	*649* 314 391	Class: (LR) ✠ Classed LR until 6/69	**1968-04 Marine Industries Ltee (MIL) — Sorel QC** Yd No: 358 Loa 50.65 Br ex 9.25 Dght 4.395 Lbp 42.98 Br md 9.22 Dpth 6.76 Welded, 2 dks	**(B11A2FS) Stern Trawler** Ins: 378	**1 oil engine** sr geared to sc. shaft driving 1 CP propeller Total Power: 1,125kW (1,530hp) 12.0kn Deutz RBV8M545 1 x 4 Stroke 8 Cy. 320 x 450 1125kW (1530bhp) Kloeckner Humboldt Deutz AG-West Germany AuxGen: 2 x 68kW 230V 60Hz a.c

7396446 **SANTA ROSALIA**
XCCG5 *ex* Landego *-2003*
\- **Operadora Portuaria del Noroeste SA de CV**
\-
Guaymas *Mexico*

471 / 218 / 50 — Class: (NV)

1975-05 Bodo Skipsverft & Mek. Verksted AS — Bodo Yd No: 39
Loa 37.11 Br ex 9.38 Dght -
Lbp 33.56 Br md 9.35 Dpth 4.22
Welded, 1 dk

(A36A2PR) Passenger/Ro-Ro Ship (Vehicles)
Passengers: unberthed: 175
Bow ramp (centre)
Stern ramp (centre)
Lane-clr ht: 4.20
Cars: 28

1 oil engine driving 2 CP propellers
Total Power: 486kW (661hp)
Wichmann WX28L4
1 x 4 Stroke 4 Cy. 280 x 420 486kW (661bhp)
Wichmann Motorfabrikk AS-Norway
AuxGen: 2 x 52kW 220V 50Hz a.c

9311189 **SANTA ROSALIA**
3EOA8 *ex* Torm Antwerp *-2012*
\- **SMKY Shipping SA**
Mitsubishi Ore Transport Co Ltd (Mitsubishi Koseki Yuso KK)
Panama *Panama*
MMSI: 354632000
Official number: 3351108B

40,033 / 25,920 / 75,886 / T/cm 68.0 — Class: NK

2008-01 Tsuneishi Holdings Corp Tsuneishi Shipbuilding Co — Fukuyama HS Yd No: 1311
Loa 225.00 (BB) Br ex 32.26 Dght 14.028
Lbp 217.00 Br md 32.26 Dpth 19.30
Welded, 1 dk

(A21A2BC) Bulk Carrier
Grain: 91,311
Compartments: 7 Ho, ER
7 Ha: 6 (17.3 x 15.4)ER (15.6 x 12.8)

1 oil engine driving 1 FP propeller
Total Power: 9,010kW (12,250hp) 14.0kn
MAN-B&W 6S60MC
1 x 2 Stroke 6 Cy. 600 x 2292 9010kW (12250bhp)
Mitsui Engineering & Shipbuilding CLtd-Japan
AuxGen: 3 x 450kW 450V 60Hz a.c
Fuel: 3135.0

9244881 **SANTA RUFINA**
A8RL3 *ex* Maersk Denton *-2010*
\- *ex* MSC Marbella *-2009*
ex Maersk Denton *-2008*
ex P&O Nedlloyd Mairangi *-2006*
ex Santa Rufina *-2002*
KG ms 'Santa Rufina' Offen Reederei GmbH & Co
Reederei Claus-Peter Offen GmbH & Co KG
SatCom: Inmarsat C 463704054
Monrovia *Liberia*
MMSI: 636091670
Official number: 91670

45,803 / 25,077 / 53,115 — Class: GL

2002-12 Samsung Heavy Industries Co Ltd — Geoje Yd No: 1363
Loa 281.00 (BB) Br ex - Dght 12.500
Lbp 268.00 Br md 32.20 Dpth 20.00
Welded, 1 dk

(A33A2CC) Container Ship (Fully Cellular)
Double Bottom Entire Compartment Length
TEU 4112 C Ho 1693 TEU C Dk 2419 TEU incl 1300 ref C.

1 oil engine driving 1 FP propeller
Total Power: 51,434kW (69,930hp) 25.0kn
Sulzer 9RTA96C
1 x 2 Stroke 9 Cy. 960 x 2500 51434kW (69930bhp)
Doosan Engine Co Ltd-South Korea
AuxGen: 1 x 2600kW a.c, 4 x 3060kW a.c
Thrusters: 1 Thwart. FP thruster (f)
Fuel: 400.0 (d.f.) 8500.0 (r.f.) 185.2pd

9527934 **SANTA SERENA**
HODK
\- **Ark Shipholding SA**
Nissho Odyssey Ship Management Pte Ltd
SatCom: Inmarsat C 435493210
Panama *Panama*
MMSI: 354932000
Official number: 42244PEXT1

23,857 / 11,814 / 38,238 / T/cm 51.3 — Class: NK

2011-08 Naikai Zosen Corp — Onomichi HS (Setoda Shipyard) Yd No: 743
Loa 184.75 (BB) Br ex - Dght 10.020
Lbp 177.00 Br md 30.60 Dpth 14.50
Welded, 1 dk

(A31A2GO) Open Hatch Cargo Ship
Double Hull
Grain: 47,235; Bale: 46,315
Compartments: 5 Ho, ER
5 Ha: ER
Cranes: 4x30t

1 oil engine driving 1 FP propeller
Total Power: 6,781kW (9,219hp) 14.2kn
MAN-B&W 6S46MC-C
1 x 2 Stroke 6 Cy. 460 x 1932 6781kW (9219bhp)
Hitachi Zosen Corp-Japan
Fuel: 2230.0

6417877 **SANTA SUSANA**
\-
\- **SSM Fishing Company SA**
\-

301 / 90 / 298 — Class: (BV)

1964 Astilleros y Talleres del Noroeste SA (ASTANO) — Fene
Loa 38.83 Br ex 6.86 Dght 3.607
Lbp 33.13 Br md 6.80 Dpth 3.92
Riveted\Welded, 1 dk

(B11A2FT) Trawler
Ins: 257
Compartments: 2 Ho, ER
3 Ha: 3 (0.9 x 0.9)ER
Derricks: 1

1 oil engine driving 1 FP propeller
Total Power: 588kW (799hp) 12.8kn
Deutz RBV6M545
1 x 4 Stroke 6 Cy. 320 x 450 588kW (799bhp)
Kloeckner Humboldt Deutz AG-West Germany

9430375 **SANTA TERESA**
D5AH6
\- **Containerschiffsreederei ms Santa Teresa GmbH & Co KG**
Columbus Shipmanagement GmbH
Monrovia *Liberia*
MMSI: 636092317
Official number: 92317

85,676 / 42,501 / 93,590 — Class: GL

2011-09 Daewoo Shipbuilding & Marine Engineering Co Ltd — Geoje Yd No: 4232
Loa 299.98 (BB) Br ex - Dght 13.500
Lbp 286.80 Br md 42.80 Dpth 24.20
Welded, 1 dk

(A33A2CC) Container Ship (Fully Cellular)
TEU 7100 incl 1365 ref C

1 oil engine driving 1 FP propeller
Total Power: 45,760kW (62,215hp) 22.2kn
Wartsila 8RT-flex96C
1 x 2 Stroke 8 Cy. 960 x 2500 45760kW (62215bhp)
Doosan Engine Co Ltd-South Korea
AuxGen: 4 x 4686kW 6600V a.c
Thrusters: 1 Tunnel thruster (f); 1 Tunnel thruster (a)

9430387 **SANTA URSULA**
DIWN2
\- **Containerschiffsreederei ms Santa Ursula GmbH & Co KG**
Columbus Shipmanagement GmbH
SatCom: Inmarsat C 421159110
Hamburg *Germany*
MMSI: 211591000
Official number: 23319

86,601 / 42,501 / 93,025 — Class: GL

2012-03 Daewoo Shipbuilding & Marine Engineering Co Ltd — Geoje Yd No: 4233
Loa 299.95 (BB) Br ex - Dght 13.500
Lbp 286.80 Br md 42.80 Dpth 24.20
Welded, 1 dk

(A33A2CC) Container Ship (Fully Cellular)
TEU 7100 incl 1365 ref C

1 oil engine driving 1 FP propeller
Total Power: 41,184kW (55,994hp) 22.2kn
Wartsila 8RT-flex96C
1 x 2 Stroke 8 Cy. 960 x 2500 41184kW (55994bhp)
Doosan Engine Co Ltd-South Korea
AuxGen: 4 x 4710kW 6600V a.c
Thrusters: 1 Tunnel thruster (f); 1 Tunnel thruster (a)

9640059 **SANTA URSULA**
3FDB8
\- **Anne Navigation SA**
\-
SatCom: Inmarsat C 437353410
Panama *Panama*
MMSI: 373534000
Official number: 4408712

34,794 / 20,209 / 61,453 / T/cm 61.4 — Class: NK

2012-06 Imabari Shipbuilding Co Ltd — Imabari EH (Imabari Shipyard) Yd No: 745
Loa 199.98 (BB) Br ex - Dght 13.010
Lbp 195.00 Br md 32.24 Dpth 18.60
Welded, 1 dk

(A21A2BC) Bulk Carrier
Grain: 77,674; Bale: 73,552
Compartments: 5 Ho, ER
5 Ha: 4 (23.5 x 19.0)ER (18.7 x 19.0)
Cranes: 4x30.7t

1 oil engine driving 1 FP propeller
Total Power: 8,450kW (11,489hp) 14.5kn
MAN-B&W 6S50MC-C8
1 x 2 Stroke 6 Cy. 500 x 2000 8450kW (11489bhp)
Mitsui Engineering & Shipbuilding CLtd-Japan
Fuel: 2560.0

9527946 **SANTA VISTA**
3EYL6
\- **Daisy Shipping SA**
Nissho Odyssey Ship Management Pte Ltd
SatCom: Inmarsat C 437002410
Panama *Panama*
MMSI: 370024000
Official number: 4344512

23,857 / 11,814 / 38,206 / T/cm 51.3 — Class: NK

2011-10 Naikai Zosen Corp — Onomichi HS (Setoda Shipyard) Yd No: 744
Loa 184.75 (BB) Br ex - Dght 10.020
Lbp 177.00 Br md 30.60 Dpth 14.50
Welded, 1 dk

(A31A2GO) Open Hatch Cargo Ship
Double Hull
Grain: 47,235; Bale: 46,315
Compartments: 5 Ho, ER
5 Ha: ER
Cranes: 4x30t

1 oil engine driving 1 FP propeller
Total Power: 6,781kW (9,219hp) 14.1kn
MAN-B&W 6S46MC-C
1 x 2 Stroke 6 Cy. 460 x 1932 6781kW (9219bhp)
Hitachi Zosen Corp-Japan
Fuel: 2230.0

9605011 **SANTA VITORIA**
3FDV3
\- **Grace Hawk Shipping SA & Eiko Kisen Co Ltd**
Eiko Kisen Co Ltd
SatCom: Inmarsat C 437305910
Panama *Panama*
MMSI: 373059000
Official number: 4358412

34,795 / 20,209 / 61,438 / T/cm 61.4 — Class: NK

2012-02 Iwagi Zosen Co Ltd — Kamijima EH Yd No: 311
Loa 199.98 (BB) Br ex - Dght 13.010
Lbp 195.00 Br md 32.24 Dpth 18.60
Welded, 1 dk

(A21A2BC) Bulk Carrier
Grain: 77,674; Bale: 73,552
Compartments: 5 Ho, ER
5 Ha: 4 (23.5 x 19.0)ER (18.7 x 19.0)
Cranes: 4x30.7t

1 oil engine driving 1 FP propeller
Total Power: 8,450kW (11,489hp) 14.5kn
MAN-B&W 6S50MC-C8
1 x 2 Stroke 6 Cy. 500 x 2000 8450kW (11489bhp)
Mitsui Engineering & Shipbuilding CLtd-Japan
Fuel: 2560.0

9089413 **SANT'AGOSTINO**
ITCS *ex* Crane Barge 1 *-1985*
\- **Societa Italiana per Condotte d'Acqua SpA**
\-
Rome *Italy*
MMSI: 247317300
Official number: 7895

1,539 / 461 / 2,000 — Class: RI (AB)

1976-03 Mitsui Ocean Development & Eng. Co. Ltd. — Japan Yd No: S-062
Loa 60.00 Br ex - Dght -
Lbp - Br md 24.00 Dpth 4.00
Welded, 1 dk

(B34B2SC) Crane Vessel

2 oil engines geared to sc. shafts driving 2 Directional propellers
Total Power: 1,074kW (1,460hp)
Caterpillar 3412E
2 x Vee 4 Stroke 12 Cy. 137 x 152 each-537kW (730bhp) (new engine 2007, added 2007)
Caterpillar Inc-USA
AuxGen: 2 x 108kW 380V 50Hz a.c

9093323 **SANTAI MARU**
JD2112
\- **Kimura Kaiun KK**
\-
Nagasaki, Nagasaki *Japan*
MMSI: 431602305
Official number: 140172

749 / - / 1,879

2005-08 Maebata Zosen Tekko K.K. — Sasebo Yd No: 268
Loa 72.26 Br ex - Dght 4.910
Lbp 68.00 Br md 11.50 Dpth 5.35
Welded, 1 dk

(A12A2TC) Chemical Tanker
Double Hull (13F)

1 oil engine driving 1 Propeller
Total Power: 1,618kW (2,200hp) 12.5kn
Hanshin LH34LG
1 x 4 Stroke 6 Cy. 340 x 640 1618kW (2200bhp)
The Hanshin Diesel Works Ltd-Japan

9022881 **SANTAMAR**
EBXY
3-CO-22-02 **Pesquera Carpa SA**
\-
La Coruna *Spain*
MMSI: 224067000
Official number: 3-2/2002

392 / 118 / 206

2003-03 Astilleros Armon Burela SA — Burela Yd No: 183
Loa 38.80 Br ex - Dght 3.250
Lbp 32.00 Br md 8.40 Dpth 3.85
Welded, 1 dk

(B11A2FS) Stern Trawler
Ins: 232

1 oil engine geared to sc. shaft driving 1 Propeller
Total Power: 646kW (878hp) 11.0kn
A.B.C. 6DZC
1 x 4 Stroke 6 Cy. 256 x 310 646kW (878bhp)
Anglo Belgian Corp NV (ABC)-Belgium

9051337 **SANTANA**
YEXN *ex* Maulana *-2008*
\- **PT Pelayaran Umum Indonesia (Pelumin)**
\-
Jakarta *Indonesia*
MMSI: 525016151

1,439 / 515 / 1,500 — Class: KI

1993-06 P.T. Inggom Shipyard — Jakarta Yd No: 269
Loa 65.00 Br ex - Dght 3.200
Lbp 61.00 Br md 15.00 Dpth 4.50
Welded, 1 dk

(A13B2TP) Products Tanker

2 oil engines driving 2 FP propellers
Total Power: 1,324kW (1,800hp)
Niigata 6MG19HX
2 x 4 Stroke 6 Cy. 190 x 260 each-662kW (900bhp)
Niigata Engineering Co Ltd-Japan

9133408 *UATF* -	**SANTANA** *ex* Santa *-1995* **Piligrim JSC (A/O 'Piligrim')** - SatCom: Inmarsat C 427321035 *Nevelsk* *Russia* MMSI: 273898100 Official number: 940082	**749** 225 414	Class: RS	**1994**-07 **ATVT Zavod "Leninska Kuznya" — Kyyiv** Yd No: 1686 Loa 54.82 Br ex 10.15 Dght 4.140 Lbp 50.30 Br md 9.80 Dpth 5.00 Welded, 1 dk	**(B11A2FS) Stern Trawler**	**1 oil engine** driving 1 CP propeller Total Power: 852kW (1,158hp) 12.0kn S.K.L. 8NVD48A-2U 1 x 4 Stroke 8 Cy. 320 x 480 852kW (1158bhp) SKL Motoren u. Systemtechnik AG-Magdeburg AuxGen: 4 x 160kW a.c Fuel: 155.0 (d.f.)
9449388 *D5FX2* -	**SANTANA** *ex* Owner *-2014* **Santana Maritime Ltd** - *Monrovia* *Liberia* MMSI: 636016381 Official number: 16381	**7,345** 4,208 10,860	Class: RS	**2007**-12 **Zhejiang Donghong Shipbuilding Co Ltd — Xiangshan County ZJ** Yd No: 05 Loa 126.60 Br ex 18.60 Dght 7.680 Lbp 117.50 Br md 18.60 Dpth 10.10 Welded, 1 dk	**(A31A2GX) General Cargo Ship** Grain: 14,111 Compartments: 3 Ho, ER 3 Ha: ER 3 (12.6 x 25.2)	**1 oil engine** reduction geared to sc. shafts driving 1 FP propeller Total Power: 3,310kW (4,500hp) 12.0kn Yanmar 8N330-EN 1 x 4 Stroke 8 Cy. 330 x 440 3310kW (4500bhp) Qingdao Zichai Boyang Diesel EngineCo Ltd-China AuxGen: 3 x 250kW a.c Fuel: 775.0
7123100 - -	**SANTANA 101** *ex* Zenpo Maru No. 81 *-1993* *ex* Ryoun Maru No. 51 *-1988* *ex* Fuki Maru No. 51 *-1987* *ex* Shinnan Maru No. 31 *-1987* - -	**499** 198 -		**1971 KK Kanasashi Zosen — Shizuoka SZ** Yd No: 1047 Loa 49.54 Br ex 8.23 Dght 3.302 Lbp 44.00 Br md 8.21 Dpth 3.64 Welded, 1 dk	**(B11B2FV) Fishing Vessel**	**1 oil engine** driving 1 FP propeller Total Power: 736kW (1,001hp) Hanshin 6LU28 1 x 4 Stroke 6 Cy. 280 x 440 736kW (1001bhp) Hanshin Nainenki Kogyo-Japan
9193173 *EAVI* 3-SS-35-98	**SANTANA BERRIA** - **Azcue/Egana/Iribar/Machael** - *Zumaia* *Spain* Official number: 3-5/1998	**236** 71 190		**1999**-04 **S.A. Balenciaga — Zumaya** Yd No: 391 Loa 36.00 Br ex - Dght 4.000 Lbp 30.00 Br md 7.40 Dpth - Welded, 1 dk	**(B11B2FV) Fishing Vessel**	**1 oil engine** reduction geared to sc. shafts driving 1 FP propeller Total Power: 485kW (659hp) GUASCOR F480TA-SP 1 x Vee 4 Stroke 16 Cy. 152 x 165 485kW (659bhp) Gutierrez Ascunce Corp (GUASCOR)-Spain
5311698 *MWJL2* -	**SANTANDREA** - **Galaxy Lights Ltd** - *London* *United Kingdom* MMSI: 234773000 Official number: 729237	**170** 51 -	Class: (RI)	**1962 Cant. Nav. Solimano — Savona** Yd No: 33 Converted From: Tug-1997 Loa 29.16 Br ex 7.37 Dght 4.035 Lbp 26.01 Br md 7.32 Dpth 4.53 Riveted\Welded, 1 dk	**(X11A2YP) Yacht**	**1 oil engine** driving 1 FP propeller Total Power: 1,169kW (1,589hp) Caterpillar 3516TA 1 x Vee 4 Stroke 16 Cy. 170 x 190 1169kW (1589bhp) (new engine 1987) Caterpillar Inc-USA
9343948 *IFQQ2* -	**SANTANGELO** *ex* Sanmar Eskort III *-2007* **Somat Srl** - *Naples* *Italy* MMSI: 247185800 Official number: 2137	**461** 139 175	Class: RI (AB)	**2006**-11 **Gemsan Gemi Insa ve Gemi Isletmeciligi San. Ltd. — Tuzla** Yd No: 24 Loa 35.60 Br ex 12.20 Dght 4.312 Lbp 26.21 Br md 11.60 Dpth 5.36 Welded, 1 dk	**(B32A2ST) Tug**	**2 oil engines** geared to sc. shafts driving 2 Z propellers Total Power: 4,046kW (5,500hp) 13.0kn Wartsila 6L26 2 x 4 Stroke 6 Cy. 260 x 320 each-2023kW (2750bhp) Wartsila Finland Oy-Finland AuxGen: 2 x 140kW a.c Fuel: 104.0 (d.f.)
8818104 *LW9251* -	**SANT'ANTONIO** - **ABH Pesquera SA** - *Mar del Plata* *Argentina* MMSI: 701007012 Official number: 0974	**110** 82 130		**1990**-08 **SANYM S.A. — Buenos Aires** Yd No: 84 Loa 25.51 Br ex - Dght 3.001 Lbp 22.92 Br md 6.51 Dpth 3.31 Welded	**(B11A2FT) Trawler** Ins: 155	**1 oil engine** geared to sc. shaft driving 1 FP propeller Total Power: 397kW (540hp) 10.0kn Caterpillar 3412T 1 x Vee 4 Stroke 12 Cy. 137 x 152 397kW (540bhp) Caterpillar Inc-USA
9225720 *ILPU* -	**SANTANTONIO PRIMO** - **Augustea Imprese Marittime e di Salvataggi SpA** - SatCom: Inmarsat C 424702720 *Catania* *Italy* MMSI: 247027500 Official number: 03	**470** - -	Class: RI	**2001**-03 **JG Hitzler Schiffswerft u Masch GmbH & Co KG — Lauenburg** Yd No: 820 Loa 34.30 Br ex - Dght 4.250 Lbp - Br md 11.00 Dpth 5.25 Welded, 1 dk	**(B32A2ST) Tug**	**2 oil engines** reduction geared to sc. shafts driving 2 Directional propellers Total Power: 3,720kW (5,058hp) 13.0kn Wartsila 6L26 2 x 4 Stroke 6 Cy. 260 x 320 each-1860kW (2529bhp) Wartsila Nederland BV-Netherlands Thrusters: 1 Thwart. FP thruster (f)
5316868 *IUJR* -	**SANTANTONIO TERZO** *ex* Seaton *-1972* **Societa Armamento Gestione Navi Agenzia Marittima Srl (SARGENAVI)** - *Naples* *Italy* Official number: 1126	*148* 42 -	Class: (LR) (RI) ✠ Classed LR until 11/62	**1959**-01 **P K Harris & Sons Ltd — Bideford** Yd No: 113 Loa 31.40 Br ex 8.21 Dght 2.980 Lbp 28.35 Br md 7.88 Dpth 3.59 Welded, 1 dk	**(B32A2ST) Tug**	**2 oil engines** geared to sc. shafts driving 2 FP propellers Total Power: 882kW (1,200hp) Blackstone ERS8M 2 x 4 Stroke 8 Cy. 222 x 292 each-441kW (600bhp) Lister Blackstone Marine Ltd.-Dursley AuxGen: 2 x 46kW 110V d.c
8748115 *WDC9336* -	**SANTE ALE** *ex* Alex Mcallister *-2011* *ex* Wal-Row *-2011* **Sante Ale Inc** Sante Shipping Lines Inc *Miami, FL* *United States of America* MMSI: 367100880 Official number: 280535	**150** 98 66		**1960 Walker E Rowe — Georgetown SC** Loa 22.93 Br ex - Dght - Lbp - Br md 6.62 Dpth 2.28 Welded, 1 dk	**(B32A2ST) Tug**	**2 oil engines** reduction geared to sc. shafts driving 2 Propellers Total Power: 736kW (1,000hp) G.M. (Detroit Diesel) 2 x 2 Stroke each-368kW (500bhp) Detroit Diesel Corporation-Detroit, Mi
6622329 - -	**SANTE FE II** *ex* Zebulon *-1993* - -	*649* 316 391	Class: (LR) ✠ Classed LR until 6/68	**1966**-12 **Marine Industries Ltee (MIL) — Sorel QC** Yd No: 357 Loa 50.65 Br ex 9.25 Dght 4.395 Lbp 42.98 Br md 9.22 Dpth 6.76 Welded, 2 dks	**(B11A2FS) Stern Trawler** Ins: 378	**1 oil engine** driving 1 CP propeller Total Power: 1,125kW (1,530hp) 12.0kn Deutz RBV8M545 1 x 4 Stroke 8 Cy. 320 x 450 1125kW (1530bhp) Kloeckner Humboldt Deutz AG-West Germany AuxGen: 2 x 68kW 230V 60Hz a.c
7116834 *3EKF6* -	**SANTE MANNA** *ex* Rio Magdalena *-2009* *ex* Argosy *-2007* *ex* Cuyuni *-1992* *ex* Unicorn Express *-1986* *ex* Atlantic Baron *-1982* *ex* Katharina *-1974* **Sante Manna SA** Sante Shipping Lines Inc *Panama* *Panama* MMSI: 372710000 Official number: 3335707B	**2,556** 1,036 2,500	Class: IS (BV) (GL)	**1972**-12 **Schiffswerft Korneuburg A.G. — Korneuburg** Yd No: 698 Loa 90.20 (BB) Br ex 14.76 Dght 6.800 Lbp 82.02 Br md 14.51 Dpth 7.80 Welded, 2 dks	**(A31A2GX) General Cargo Ship** Grain: 5,380; Bale: 4,898 TEU 180 C Ho 93 TEU C Dk 87 TEU Compartments: 1 Ho, ER 1 Ha: (50.4 x 10.3)ER Ice Capable	**1 oil engine** driving 1 FP propeller Total Power: 2,207kW (3,001hp) 14.5kn MWM TBD501-8 1 x 4 Stroke 8 Cy. 360 x 450 2207kW (3001bhp) Motoren Werke Mannheim AG (MWM)-West Germany
8980763 *WDF7000* -	**SANTE TEO** *ex* Carlo Mcallister *-2010* *ex* Hillsborough *-1999* *ex* Gloria St. Philip *-1998* *ex* YTB *-1981* **Sante Teo Inc** Sante Shipping Lines Inc *Miami, FL* *United States of America* MMSI: 367480080 Official number: 632981	*199* 59 -		**1945 Consolidated Shipbuilding Corp. — New York, NY** L reg 28.68 Br ex - Dght - Lbp - Br md 7.60 Dpth 2.74 Welded, 1 dk	**(B32A2ST) Tug**	**1 oil engine** driving 1 Propeller
8977182 *WDF6486* -	**SANTEE** *ex* Annabeth Mccall *-2011* **Starfleet Marine Transportation Inc** - *New Orleans, LA* *United States of America* MMSI: 367474760 Official number: 950236	**390** 117 287		**1989**-07 **Gulf Craft Inc — Patterson LA** Yd No: 337 Loa 48.76 Br ex - Dght 2.130 Lbp 44.37 Br md 9.14 Dpth 3.35 Welded, 1 dk	**(B21A2OC) Crew/Supply Vessel** Hull Material: Aluminium Alloy Passengers: 83; cabins: 3	**6 oil engines** geared to sc. shafts driving 6 FP propellers Total Power: 3,000kW (4,080hp) 22.0kn Cummins KTA-1150-M 6 x 4 Stroke 6 Cy. 159 x 159 each-500kW (680bhp) Cummins Engine Co Inc-USA Fuel: 54.5 (d.f.) 20.0pd
8924977 *VTSY* MRH-006	**SANTHOME** - **Crown Fisheries Pvt Ltd** - *Mormugao* *India* Official number: F-MRH-006	**127** 38 70	Class: (IR)	**1990 Chowgule & Co Pvt Ltd — Goa** Yd No: 104 Loa 24.00 Br ex 7.38 Dght 2.600 Lbp 20.00 Br md 7.20 Dpth 3.40 Welded, 1 dk	**(B11B2FV) Fishing Vessel**	**1 oil engine** reduction geared to sc. shaft driving 1 FP propeller Total Power: 352kW (479hp) 10.0kn Caterpillar 3412TA 1 x Vee 4 Stroke 12 Cy. 137 x 152 352kW (479bhp) Caterpillar Inc-USA AuxGen: 2 x 50kW 415V 50Hz a.c

9174373 *HCSA* -
SANTIAGO
Empresa Publica Flota Petrolera Ecuatoriana (EP FLOPEC)
-
SatCom: Inmarsat C 473503013
Guayaquil *Ecuador*
MMSI: 735057549
Official number: TI-00-00003
27,607 11,947 45,268 T/cm 50.6
Class: AB
1999-08 **Hyundai Heavy Industries Co Ltd — Ulsan** Yd No: 1130
Loa 183.07 (BB) Br ex 32.23 Dght 12.010
Lbp 174.00 Br md 32.20 Dpth 18.00
Welded, 1 dk
(A13B2TP) Products Tanker
Double Hull (13F)
Liq: 48,402; Liq (Oil): 48,402
Compartments: 12 Wing Ta, ER, 2 Wing Slop Ta
3 Cargo Pump (s): 3x1500m³/hr
Manifold: Bow/CM: 91m
1 oil engine driving 1 FP propeller
Total Power: 7,788kW (10,589hp) 14.5kn
B&W 6S50MC
1 x 2 Stroke 6 Cy. 500 x 1910 7788kW (10589bhp)
Hyundai Heavy Industries Co Ltd-South Korea
AuxGen: 3 x 560kW 450V 60Hz a.c
Fuel: 192.1 (d.f.) (Heating Coils) 1292.0 (r.f.)

8137366 *HKQM* -
SANTIAGO
ex Pidder Lung *-1989* *ex* Ernst Sturm *-1989*
Harinas Y Aceites de Pescado de mar SA Harimar
-
Isla de San Andres *Colombia*
Official number: MC-07-0116
171 57 482
Class: (GL)
1954-08 **Schiffswerften Hugo Peters — Wewelsfleth** Yd No: 72/475
Loa 30.13 Br ex 9.12 Dght 1.501
Lbp 27.21 Br md 9.11 Dpth 2.20
Welded, 1 dk
(A36A2PR) Passenger/Ro-Ro Ship (Vehicles)
2 oil engines reverse geared to sc. shafts driving 2 FP propellers
Total Power: 220kW (300hp) 10.0kn
Deutz SA12L614
2 x Vee 4 Stroke 12 Cy. 110 x 140 each-110kW (150bhp) (, fitted 1954)
Kloeckner Humboldt Deutz AG-West Germany
AuxGen: 1 x 3kW 24V d.c

9462641 *LXNT* -
SANTIAGO
Trivisa SA
Jan De Nul Luxembourg SA
Luxembourg *Luxembourg*
MMSI: 253115000
2,392 717 3,400
Class: BV
2010-01 **Tianjin Xinhe Shipbuilding Heavy Industry Co Ltd — Tianjin** Yd No: SB707
Loa 80.00 Br ex - Dght 4.500
Lbp 76.40 Br md 17.20 Dpth 5.90
Welded, 1 dk
(B34A2SH) Hopper, Motor
Hopper: 1,800
2 oil engines reduction geared to sc. shafts driving 2 Z propellers
Total Power: 1,566kW (2,130hp) 11.0kn
Caterpillar 3508B
2 x Vee 4 Stroke 8 Cy. 170 x 190 each-783kW (1065bhp)
Caterpillar Inc-USA
AuxGen: 2 x 245kW 50Hz a.c
Thrusters: 1 Tunnel thruster (f)

6909832 *EHZR* 3-CO-23850
SANTIAGO APOSTOLO
ex Hermanos Fernandez Pino *-1989*
Cofradia de Pescadores Santiago Apostol
-
La Coruna *Spain*
Official number: 1-1/2002
231 86 194
Class: (RI) (BV)
1968 Construcciones Navales Santodomingo SA — Vigo Yd No: 365
Converted From: Trawler-2001
Loa - Br ex 6.86 Dght 3.328
Lbp 27.51 Br md 6.81 Dpth 3.66
Welded, 1 dk
(B12D2FR) Fishery Research Vessel
Grain: 185
Compartments: 1 Ho, ER
2 Ha: 2 (1.0 x 1.0)ER
1 oil engine driving 1 FP propeller
Total Power: 441kW (600hp) 10.0kn
Baudouin DV12M
1 x Vee 4 Stroke 12 Cy. 185 x 200 441kW (600bhp)
Societe des Moteurs Baudouin SA-France
AuxGen: 1 x 24kW 380V 50Hz a.c

9377999 *VREO2* -
SANTIAGO BASIN
Future Sea Ltd
Pacific Basin Shipping (HK) Ltd
Hong Kong *Hong Kong*
MMSI: 477143900
Official number: HK-2264
20,987 11,524 33,171 T/cm 46.1
Class: LR
✠ **100A1** SS 10/2013
bulk carrier
BC-A
strengthened for heavy cargoes, Nos. 2 and holds may be empty
ESP
ShipRight (SDA, FDA, CM)
timber deck cargoes
*IWS
LI
✠ **LMC** **CCS**
Eq.Ltr: I†;
Cable: 605.0/73.0 U2 (a)
2008-10 **Jiangmen Nanyang Ship Engineering Co Ltd — Jiangmen GD** Yd No: 104
Loa 179.90 (BB) Br ex 28.45 Dght 10.200
Lbp 172.41 Br md 28.41 Dpth 14.11
Welded, 1 dk
(A21A2BC) Bulk Carrier
Grain: 42,565; Bale: 40,558
Compartments: 5 Ho, ER
5 Ha: 3 (20.0 x 19.2) (18.4 x 19.2)ER (14.4 x 17.6)
Cranes: 4x30.5t
1 oil engine driving 1 FP propeller
Total Power: 6,480kW (8,810hp) 13.7kn
MAN-B&W 6S42MC
1 x 2 Stroke 6 Cy. 420 x 1764 6480kW (8810bhp)
STX Engine Co Ltd-South Korea
AuxGen: 3 x 440kW 450V 60Hz a.c
Boilers: AuxB (Comp) 7.6kgf/cm² (7.5bar)
Fuel: 100.0 (d.f.) 1400.0 (r.f.) 24.0pd

7854618 - -
SANTIAGO DE BOHOL
ex Noumi No. 8 *-1989*
Sunline Shipping Corp
Lite Shipping Corp
Cebu *Philippines*
250 170 -
1969 Nakatani Shipyard Co. Ltd. — Etajima Yd No: 397
Loa 37.01 Br ex - Dght -
Lbp 33.00 Br md 9.01 Dpth 2.90
Welded, 1 dk
(A37B2PS) Passenger Ship
Passengers: 400
1 oil engine driving 1 FP propeller
Total Power: 736kW (1,001hp) 11.0kn
Daihatsu 8PSHTCM-26D
1 x 4 Stroke 8 Cy. 260 x 320 736kW (1001bhp)
Daihatsu Diesel Manufacturing Co Lt-Japan

7904982 - -
SANTIAGO I
ex Astra 3 *-2004*
-
-
Mar del Plata *Argentina*
240 98 298
Class: (LR) (NV)
Classed LR until 30/11/98
1980-03 **B&W Skibsvaerft A/S — Copenhagen** Yd No: 894
Loa 31.65 (BB) Br ex 8.13 Dght 3.868
Lbp 27.21 Br md 7.90 Dpth 4.09
Welded, 1 dk
(B11A2FS) Stern Trawler
Ins: 270; Liq: 55
1 oil engine driving 1 CP propeller
Total Power: 566kW (770hp) 10.5kn
Alpha 407-26VO
1 x 2 Stroke 7 Cy. 260 x 400 566kW (770bhp)
B&W Alpha Diesel A/S-Denmark
AuxGen: 2 x 50kW 220V 50Hz a.c

8011201 - -
SANTIAGO NO. 10
ex Urago Maru No. 5 *-2008*
ex Eisho Maru No. 22 *-1989*
Manor Fishing Corp
-
Manila *Philippines*
Official number: 00-0000249
180 54 -
1980-07 **Minami-Kyushu Zosen KK — Ichikikushikino KS** Yd No: 352
Loa 40.26 Br ex 7.29 Dght 2.471
Lbp 33.89 Br md 7.01 Dpth 2.82
Welded, 1 dk
(B11B2FV) Fishing Vessel
1 oil engine driving 1 FP propeller
Total Power: 699kW (950hp)
Yanmar G250-ET
1 x 4 Stroke 6 Cy. 250 x 290 699kW (950bhp)
Yanmar Diesel Engine Co Ltd-Japan

8309713 *C6JE4* -
SANTIAGO PEARL
ex Petersfield *-2013*
Santiago Pearl Shipping Co Ltd
SMT Shipping (Cyprus) Ltd
SatCom: Inmarsat C 430800295
Nassau *Bahamas*
MMSI: 308744000
Official number: 708312
27,818 13,185 41,649 T/cm 48.6
Class: NK (LR) (BV)
Classed LR until 26/6/12
1985-03 **Hyundai Heavy Industries Co Ltd — Ulsan** Yd No: 318
Loa 187.51 (BB) Br ex 29.05 Dght 12.320
Lbp 178.90 Br md 29.00 Dpth 16.92
Welded, 1 dk
(A31A2GO) Open Hatch Cargo Ship
Double Sides Entire Compartment Length
Grain: 47,671; Bale: 46,280
TEU 1584 C Ho 1044 TEU C Dk 540 TEU
Compartments: 7 Ho, ER
7 Ha: (12.4 x 17.0)3 (24.6 x 23.0)3 (12.4 x 23.0)ER
Gantry cranes: 2x35t
1 oil engine driving 1 FP propeller
Total Power: 6,055kW (8,232hp) 13.1kn
B&W 6L60MCE
1 x 2 Stroke 6 Cy. 600 x 1944 6055kW (8232bhp)
Hyundai Engine & Machinery Co Ltd-South Korea
AuxGen: 3 x 750kW 450V 60Hz a.c
Boilers: AuxB (Comp) 8.1kgf/cm² (7.9bar)
Thrusters: 1 Thwart. CP thruster (f)
Fuel: 101.0 (d.f.) 2009.5 (r.f.) 23.5pd

7926916 - -
SANTIKA
ex Eiko Maru *-1994*
-
-
197 114 687
1979-10 **Hakata Zosen K.K. — Imabari** Yd No: 223
Loa - Br ex - Dght 3.201
Lbp 51.11 Br md 9.01 Dpth 5.01
Welded, 1 dk
(A31A2GX) General Cargo Ship
1 oil engine driving 1 FP propeller
Total Power: 736kW (1,001hp)
Makita GNLH6275
1 x 4 Stroke 6 Cy. 275 x 450 736kW (1001bhp)
Makita Diesel Co Ltd-Japan

7419303 - -
SANTILLANA DE CABEZA
-
170 70 163
1977-02 **Astilleros de Santander SA (ASTANDER) — El Astillero** Yd No: 121
Loa 30.71 Br ex - Dght 3.101
Lbp 26.01 Br md 6.61 Dpth 3.61
Welded, 1 dk
(B11A2FT) Trawler
2 oil engines reverse reduction geared to sc. shaft driving 1 FP propeller
Total Power: 632kW (860hp) 12.0kn
Baudouin DNP12M
2 x Vee 4 Stroke 12 Cy. 150 x 150 each-316kW (430bhp)
Internacional Diesel S.A.-Zumaya

9203162 *9H8600* -
SANTINA
ex Punta La Gaviota *-2006*
Mare Blu Tuna Farm Ltd
-
Valletta *Malta*
MMSI: 256384000
Official number: 9203162
251 75 308
1999-03 **Rodman Polyships S.A. — Vigo** Yd No: 120001
Loa 36.25 Br ex - Dght 3.500
Lbp 32.30 Br md 8.00 Dpth 4.20
Bonded, 1 dk
(A34A2GR) Refrigerated Cargo Ship
Hull Material: Reinforced Plastic
1 oil engine sr geared to sc. shaft driving 1 FP propeller
Total Power: 702kW (954hp) 12.0kn
Mitsubishi S12A2-MTK
1 x Vee 4 Stroke 12 Cy. 150 x 160 702kW (954bhp)
Mitsubishi Heavy Industries Ltd-Japan
Thrusters: 1 Thwart. FP thruster (f)

8968739 - -
SANTING DU
Santing Shipping SA
-
San Lorenzo *Honduras*
Official number: L-1528087
173 52 -
1998 Ahmet Cinar — Gemlik
Loa 22.98 Br ex - Dght -
Lbp - Br md 6.80 Dpth 3.38
Welded, 1 dk
(B11A2FS) Stern Trawler
1 oil engine reduction geared to sc. shaft driving 1 FP propeller
Total Power: 405kW (551hp) 9.0kn
Baudouin 8M26SR
1 x 4 Stroke 8 Cy. 150 x 150 405kW (551bhp)
Societe des Moteurs Baudouin SA-France

7622077 *D4FM* -
SANTO ANTAO
ex Sea Falcon *-2009* *ex* Sea Trent *-2000*
ex Sea Avon *-1996*
Agrupamento Polar Lda/Vulcao Correia e Correia
Polaris CIA, SA-Companhia Nacional de Navegacao
Sao Vicente *Cape Verde*
MMSI: 617058000
1,475 711 2,273
Class: (LR)
✠ Classed LR until 13/12/06
1977-07 **Kanrei Zosen K.K. — Tokushima** Yd No: 235
Loa 69.02 Br ex 13.54 Dght 4.480
Lbp 65.00 Br md 13.50 Dpth 5.41
Welded, 2 dks
(A31A2GX) General Cargo Ship
Grain: 2,545; Bale: 2,382
Compartments: 1 Ho, ER, 1 Tw Dk
1 Ha: (40.5 x 10.3)ER
1 oil engine reverse reduction geared to sc. shaft driving 1 FP propeller
Total Power: 883kW (1,201hp) 9.0kn
Niigata 6L25BX
1 x 4 Stroke 6 Cy. 250 x 320 883kW (1201bhp)
Niigata Engineering Co Ltd-Japan
AuxGen: 2 x 70kW 230V 50Hz a.c, 1 x 25kW 230V 50Hz a.c
Fuel: 196.0 (d.f.)

9030292 *CUIX* A-3425 C
SANTO ANTERO
Costa E Franco Lda
-
Aveiro *Portugal*
129 42 86
Class: (BV)
1991-05 **Astilleros Armon SA — Navia** Yd No: 172
Loa 24.20 (BB) Br ex - Dght 3.060
Lbp 20.00 Br md 7.49 Dpth 3.50
Welded, 2 dks
(B11B2FV) Fishing Vessel
Ins: 92
1 oil engine reverse geared to sc. shaft driving 1 FP propeller
Total Power: 368kW (500hp) 10.0kn
GUASCOR E318T-SP
1 x Vee 4 Stroke 12 Cy. 150 x 150 368kW (500bhp)
Gutierrez Ascunce Corp (GUASCOR)-Spain

IMO / Call sign / Reg.	Name / Owner / Port	Tonnage	Class	Builder / Dimensions	Type / Cargo	Machinery
7732808 *WYC3742* -	**SANTO ANTONIO** - - *New Bedford, MA* *United States of America* Official number: 584292	*148* 109 -		**1977 Bender Welding & Machine Co Inc — Mobile AL** Yd No: 472 L reg 22.96 Br ex - Dght - Lbp - Br md 6.71 Dpth 3.38 Welded, 1 dk	**(B11B2FV) Fishing Vessel**	**1 oil engine** driving 1 FP propeller Total Power: 382kW (519hp)
9329174 *ECFA* 3-GC-11-04	**SANTO DO MAR** **Pesquera Derime SL** - *Las Palmas de Gran Canaria* *Spain* Official number: 3-1/2004	**453** 135 -	Class: BV	**2004-05 Montajes Cies S.L. — Vigo** Yd No: 79 Loa 39.50 Br ex - Dght - Lbp 31.50 Br md 8.80 Dpth 3.85 Welded, 1 dk	**(B11A2FS) Stern Trawler**	**1 oil engine** geared to sc. shaft driving 1 FP propeller Total Power: 1,080kW (1,468hp) Wartsila 6L20 1 x 4 Stroke 6 Cy. 200 x 280 1080kW (1468bhp) Wartsila Diesel S.A.-Bermeo
8879615 *JL6321* -	**SANTO MARU** - **Santo Kaiun KK** - *Ikeda, Kagawa* *Japan* MMSI: 431500257 Official number: 134896	*181* - -		**1994-10 Yano Zosen K.K. — Imabari** Yd No: 153 Loa 41.60 Br ex - Dght - Lbp 37.00 Br md 7.60 Dpth 3.00 Welded, 1 dk	**(A13B2TU) Tanker (unspecified)** 1 Cargo Pump (s): 1x400m³/hr	**1 oil engine** driving 1 FP propeller Total Power: 441kW (600hp) 9.0kn Yanmar MF24-HT 1 x 4 Stroke 6 Cy. 240 x 420 441kW (600bhp) Yanmar Diesel Engine Co Ltd-Japan
7117424 *V3RU7* -	**SANTO MUHONGO III** *ex* Oradana *-2013* *ex* Scarlino Primo *-1989* **Organizacaos Antmuhongo - Comercio Geral Importacao E Exportacao Limitada** - *Belize City* *Belize* MMSI: 312690000 Official number: 351320080	**1,639** 556 2,520 T/cm 8.0	Class: NV (RI)	**1971-10 C.L.E.M.N.A. — La Spezia** Yd No: 11 Converted From: Chemical Tanker-1971 Loa 76.00 Br ex 11.52 Dght 4.760 Lbp 71.51 Br md 11.50 Dpth 5.50 Welded, 1 dk	**(A12D2LV) Vegetable Oil Tanker** Ins: 2,206; Liq: 2,206 Compartments: 7 Ta, ER 2 Cargo Pump (s): 2x700m³/hr Manifold: Bow/CM: 33m	**2 oil engines** sr geared to sc. shafts driving 2 FP propellers Total Power: 1,920kW (2,610hp) 11.0kn MAN-B&W 6L23/30A 2 x 4 Stroke 6 Cy. 225 x 300 each-960kW (1305bhp) (new engine 2013) MAN B&W Diesel AG-Augsburg AuxGen: 2 x 380V 50Hz a.c Fuel: 180.9 (d.f.)
8733811 *EALD* 3-AL-24-98	**SANTO NINO** **Pescados Ramon e Hijos SL** - *Santa Cruz de Tenerife* *Spain* Official number: 3-4/1998	**138** 41 -		**1998 Astilleros La Parrilla S.A. — San Esteban de Pravia** Loa 29.85 Br ex - Dght - Lbp 24.00 Br md 6.80 Dpth 3.45 Welded, 1 dk	**(B11B2FV) Fishing Vessel**	**1 oil engine** driving 1 Propeller Total Power: 309kW (420hp)
8989977 *DUA2162* -	**SANTO NINO DE PRAGA** *ex* Prince Valiant I *-1989* **Yu HT** - *Batangas* *Philippines* Official number: MNLD000303	**431** 263 -		**1987 at Manila** L reg 48.72 Br ex - Dght - Lbp - Br md 7.32 Dpth 3.50 Welded, 1 dk	**(A31A2GX) General Cargo Ship**	**1 oil engine** driving 1 Propeller Total Power: 265kW (360hp) Isuzu 1 x Vee 4 Stroke 12 Cy. 265kW (360bhp) Isuzu Marine Engine Inc-Japan
8402826 - -	**SANTO ROCCO DI BAGNARA** **Giuseppe Maiorana** - *Sydney, NSW* *Australia* Official number: 851211	*156* 47 80		**1984-07 K Shipyard Construction & Repairs Pty Ltd — Port Adelaide SA** Yd No: 4 Loa 27.51 Br ex 7.57 Dght - Lbp 25.30 Br md 7.41 Dpth 3.81 Welded, 1 dk	**(B11A2FS) Stern Trawler**	**1 oil engine** geared to sc. shaft driving 1 CP propeller Total Power: 441kW (600hp) Grenaa 6F24T 1 x 4 Stroke 6 Cy. 240 x 300 441kW (600bhp) A/S Grenaa Motorfabrik-Denmark Thrusters: 1 Thwart. FP thruster (f)
9163879 *TGST001* -	**SANTO TOMAS I** **Empresa Portuaria Nacional** - *Santo Tomas de Castilla* *Guatemala* MMSI: 332999993 Official number: ST-217-R99	**122** 43 -	Class: (LR) ✠ Classed LR until 20/5/04	**1999-05 Brodogradiliste 'Brodotehnika' Beograd — Belgrade (Hull)** **1999-05 B.V. Scheepswerf Damen — Gorinchem** Yd No: 6535 Loa 22.58 Br ex 7.45 Dght 3.180 Lbp 19.82 Br md 7.20 Dpth 3.74 Welded, 1 dk	**(B32A2ST) Tug**	**2 oil engines** with clutches, flexible couplings & sr reverse geared to sc. shafts driving 2 FP propellers Total Power: 2,028kW (2,758hp) 11.7kn Caterpillar 3512TA 2 x Vee 4 Stroke 12 Cy. 170 x 190 each-1014kW (1379bhp) Caterpillar Inc-USA AuxGen: 2 x 50kW 380V 50Hz a.c
9093309 *JD2107* -	**SANTOKU MARU** - **Santoku Kaiun YK** - *Anan, Tokushima* *Japan* Official number: 140167	*262* - 750		**2005-11 Hangzhou Dongfeng Shipbuilding Co Ltd — Hangzhou ZJ** Loa 60.95 Br ex - Dght 3.320 Lbp 56.00 Br md 10.00 Dpth 5.50 Welded, 1 dk	**(A31A2GX) General Cargo Ship**	**1 oil engine** driving 1 Propeller Total Power: 735kW (999hp) 11.0kn Hanshin LH28G 1 x 4 Stroke 6 Cy. 280 x 460 735kW (999bhp) The Hanshin Diesel Works Ltd-Japan
8922864 *JL6398* -	**SANTOKU MARU** - **Santoku Sangyo YK** - *Kochi, Kochi* *Japan* Official number: 135103	*495* - 1,634		**1996-02 YK Nakanoshima Zosensho — Kochi KC** Yd No: 160 Loa 67.02 Br ex - Dght 4.370 Lbp 62.00 Br md 13.20 Dpth 6.90 Welded, 1 dk	**(A24D2BA) Aggregates Carrier** Grain: 1,138; Bale: 1,077	**1 oil engine** driving 1 FP propeller Total Power: 736kW (1,001hp) 9.0kn Niigata 6M34AGT 1 x 4 Stroke 6 Cy. 340 x 620 736kW (1001bhp) Niigata Engineering Co Ltd-Japan
8810267 *JM5787* -	**SANTOKU MARU No. 2** - **Marua Sangyo KK** - *Fukuoka, Fukuoka* *Japan* Official number: 130420	*100* - 194		**1988-09 Honda Zosen — Saiki** Yd No: 781 Loa 27.00 Br ex 9.22 Dght 3.550 Lbp 24.00 Br md 9.20 Dpth 5.60 Welded, 1 dk	**(B32B2SP) Pusher Tug**	**2 oil engines** with clutches & reverse reduction geared to sc. shafts driving 2 FP propellers Total Power: 1,472kW (2,002hp) Yanmar T260-ET 2 x 4 Stroke 6 Cy. 260 x 330 each-736kW (1001bhp) Yanmar Diesel Engine Co Ltd-Japan
9172466 *JM6592* -	**SANTOKU MARU No. 5** - **Marua Sangyo KK** - *Fukuoka, Fukuoka* *Japan* Official number: 135472	*136* - -		**1997-12 Sanuki Shipbuilding & Iron Works Co Ltd — Mitoyo KG** Yd No: 1278 Loa - Br ex - Dght 3.900 Lbp 26.00 Br md 14.00 Dpth 6.00 Welded, 1 dk	**(B32B2SP) Pusher Tug**	**2 oil engines** driving 2 FP propellers Total Power: 4,414kW (6,002hp) Yanmar 6N330-UN 2 x 4 Stroke 6 Cy. 330 x 440 each-2207kW (3001bhp) Yanmar Diesel Engine Co Ltd-Japan
9371311 *ZDJE9* -	**SANTORINI** - **Santorini I Maritime Ltd** Aegean Bunkering Services Inc *Gibraltar* *Gibraltar (British)* MMSI: 236518000 Official number: 9371311	**3,220** 1,327 4,629	Class: AB	**2008-09 Fujian Southeast Shipyard — Fuzhou FJ** Yd No: 3500-8 Loa 90.22 (BB) Br ex - Dght 6.000 Lbp 85.00 Br md 15.60 Dpth 7.80 Welded, 1 dk	**(A13B2TP) Products Tanker** Double Hull (13F) Liq: 4,471; Liq (Oil): 4,471 Cargo Heating Coils Compartments: 8 Wing Ta, 2 Wing Slop Ta, ER 3 Cargo Pump (s): 2x500m³/hr, 1x300m³/hr	**1 oil engine** reduction geared to sc. shaft driving 1 FP propeller Total Power: 2,480kW (3,372hp) Wartsila 8L26 1 x 4 Stroke 8 Cy. 260 x 320 2480kW (3372bhp) Wartsila Finland Oy-Finland AuxGen: 3 x 250kW a.c Fuel: 62.0 (d.f.) 290.0 (r.f.)
9609122 *9HA3201*	**SANTORINI** *launched as* Danio *-2013* **Nomar Ltd** Sea Traders SA *Valletta* *Malta* MMSI: 229283000 Official number: 9609122	**44,025** 27,690 81,086 T/cm 71.9	Class: LR ✠ **100A1** SS 01/2013 bulk carrier CSR BC-A GRAB (20) Nos. 2, 4 & 6 holds may be empty ESP **ShipRight** (CM, ACS (B)) *IWS LI EP (R) ✠ **LMC** **UMS** Eq.Ltr: Q†; Cable: 700.0/81.0 U3 (a)	**2013-01 New Century Shipbuilding Co Ltd — Jingjiang JS** Yd No: 0108205 Loa 229.00 (BB) Br ex 32.30 Dght 14.450 Lbp 225.50 Br md 32.26 Dpth 20.05 Welded, 1 dk	**(A21A2BC) Bulk Carrier** Grain: 97,000; Bale: 90,784 Compartments: 7 Ho, ER 7 Ha: ER	**1 oil engine** driving 1 FP propeller Total Power: 11,900kW (16,179hp) 14.1kn MAN-B&W 5S60MC-C 1 x 2 Stroke 5 Cy. 600 x 2400 11900kW (16179bhp) H Cegielski Poznan SA-Poland AuxGen: 3 x 710kW 440V 60Hz a.c Boilers: AuxB (Comp) 8.6kgf/cm² (8.4bar)
7950462 - -	**SANTOS** *ex* Santosu Go *-1993* *ex* Hosei Maru No. 85 *-1993* *ex* Hoyu Maru No. 88 *-1990* *ex* Hokutatsu Maru No. 88 *-1986* *ex* Shinyu Maru No. 8 *-1982* **Trilakes Maritime S de RL** - *San Lorenzo* *Honduras* Official number: L-2624940	*237* 109 -		**1970 Kochiken Zosen — Kochi** Yd No: 401 L reg 38.41 Br ex - Dght - Lbp - Br md 7.60 Dpth 3.31 Welded, 1 dk	**(B11B2FV) Fishing Vessel**	**1 oil engine** driving 1 FP propeller Total Power: 478kW (650hp) Hanshin 1 x 4 Stroke 478kW (650bhp) The Hanshin Diesel Works Ltd-Japan

IMO / Call sign	Name / Owner	Tonnage	Class	Builder / Dimensions	Type	Machinery
7036814 *9WTC* -	**SANTOS** *ex* Asean Mariner *-1988* *ex* Hokunan Maru *-1988* *ex* Sumise Maru No. 6 *-1986* *ex* Hokunan Maru *-1978* **Syarikat Perkapalan Santos Venture Sdn Bhd** - *Labuan* *Malaysia* MMSI: 533483000 Official number: 325625	**1,886** 865 3,014	Class: (NK)	**1970-08 Imabari Shipbuilding Co Ltd — Imabari EH (Imabari Shipyard)** Yd No: 239 Converted From: Bulk Cement Carrier-1985 Loa 82.00 Br ex 12.53 Dght 5.460 Lbp 77.02 Br md 12.50 Dpth 7.60 Riveted\Welded, 1 dk	**(A31A2GX) General Cargo Ship** Grain: 4,630; Bale: 3,289 Compartments: 2 Ho, ER 2 Ha: 2 (22.7 x 7.0)ER	**1 oil engine** driving 1 FP propeller Total Power: 1,471kW (2,000hp) 11.5kn Makita ESHC640 1 x 4 Stroke 6 Cy. 400 x 600 1471kW (2000bhp) Makita Corp-Japan AuxGen: 2 x 40kW 445V 60Hz a.c Fuel: 209.5 7.0pd
7705075 *SJET* GG-361	**SANTOS** *ex* Rita *-1997* *ex* Agbodo *-1994* **Tor Rederi AB** - *Ockero* *Sweden* MMSI: 265719000	**402** 120 390	Class: (LR) ✠ Classed LR until 18/11/97	**1980-09 Tomren Verft AS — Tomrefjord** (Hull) **1980-09 Soviknes Verft AS — Sovik** Yd No: 89 Loa 38.10 Br ex 9.53 Dght 3.352 Lbp 33.61 Br md 9.50 Dpth 4.02 Welded, 1 dk	**(B11B2FV) Fishing Vessel** Ins: 200 Compartments: 4 Wing Ho, 2 Ho, ER 6 Ha: 6 (2.2 x 1.5)ER	**1 oil engine** sr geared to sc. shaft driving 1 CP propeller Total Power: 890kW (1,210hp) Deutz SBA8M528 1 x 4 Stroke 8 Cy. 220 x 280 890kW (1210bhp) Kloeckner Humboldt Deutz AG-West Germany AuxGen: 3 x 240kW 440V 60Hz a.c Thrusters: 1 Thwart. FP thruster (f); 1 Tunnel thruster (a) Fuel: 112.0 (d.f.)
7624386 *PPNG* -	**SANTOS DUMONT** - **Chaval-Navegacao Ltda** - *Rio de Janeiro* *Brazil* MMSI: 710174000 Official number: 3810290041	*4,626* 3,219 7,679	Class: (AB) (GL)	**1979-10 Estaleiros EBIN/So SA — Niteroi** Yd No: 98 Loa 107.50 Br ex 16.44 Dght 7.541 Lbp 100.72 Br md 16.41 Dpth 9.61 Welded, 2 dks	**(A31A2GX) General Cargo Ship** Grain: 9,443; Bale: 8,818 TEU 116 C.Ho 88/20' C.Dk 28/20' Compartments: 3 Ho, ER, 3 Tw Dk 3 Ha: (14.1 x 8.0)2 (15.3 x 10.3)ER Derricks: 2x12t,4x5t	**1 oil engine** geared to sc. shaft driving 1 FP propeller Total Power: 2,207kW (3,001hp) 11.5kn Pielstick 6PC2-2L-400 1 x 4 Stroke 6 Cy. 400 x 460 2207kW (3001bhp) Ishikawajima do Brasil Estaleiros S (ISHIBRAS)-Brazil AuxGen: 1 x 690kW 440V a.c Fuel: 87.0 (d.f.) 367.5 (r.f.) 11.0pd
9301835 *VRCF6* -	**SANTOS EXPRESS** - **Seaspan Corp** Hapag-Lloyd AG *Hong Kong* *Hong Kong* MMSI: 477581400 Official number: HK-1779	**39,941** 24,458 50,869 T/cm 70.4	Class: LR ✠ **100A1** SS 11/2011 container ship **ShipRight** (SDA, FDA, CM) *IWS LI ✠ **LMC** **UMS** Eq.Ltr: S†; Cable: 687.5/87.0 U3 (a)	**2006-11 Samsung Heavy Industries Co Ltd — Geoje** Yd No: 1550 Loa 260.10 (BB) Br ex 32.35 Dght 12.700 Lbp 244.80 Br md 32.25 Dpth 19.30 Welded, 1 dk	**(A33A2CC) Container Ship (Fully Cellular)** TEU 4248 C Ho 1584 TEU C Dk 2664 TEU incl 400 ref C. Compartments: 7 Cell Ho, ER 7 Ha: ER	**1 oil engine** driving 1 FP propeller Total Power: 36,560kW (49,707hp) 23.3kn MAN-B&W 8K90MC-C 1 x 2 Stroke 8 Cy. 900 x 2300 36560kW (49707bhp) Doosan Engine Co Ltd-South Korea AuxGen: 4 x 1700kW 450V 60Hz a.c Boilers: AuxB (Comp) 8.0kgf/cm² (7.8bar) Thrusters: 1 Thwart. CP thruster (f)
8514916 - -	**SANTOS NO. 102** *ex* Yuh Fa No. 102 *-2005* *ex* Sanwa Maru *-2003* *ex* Mito Maru *-2003* **Pole Star Ocean Trading Inc** -	*289* 86 224		**1986-03 K.K. Murakami Zosensho — Ishinomaki** Yd No: 1190 Loa 45.57 (BB) Br ex - Dght - Lbp 37.70 Br md 7.60 Dpth 3.31 Welded, 1 dk	**(B11A2FS) Stern Trawler**	**1 oil engine** with clutches & sr geared to sc. shaft driving 1 CP propeller Total Power: 1,030kW (1,400hp) Niigata 6MG25CXE 1 x 4 Stroke 6 Cy. 250 x 320 1030kW (1400bhp) Niigata Engineering Co Ltd-Japan
9530072 *PPYI* -	**SANTOS SAILOR** - **Bram Offshore Transportes Maritimos Ltda** Opmar Servicos Maritimos Ltda SatCom: Inmarsat C 471011129 *Itajai* *Brazil* MMSI: 710001930 Official number: 4430474168	**2,999** 1,434 4,764	Class: AB	**2009-10 Estaleiro Navship Ltda — Navegantes** Yd No: 114 Loa 84.73 Br ex - Dght 6.240 Lbp 81.68 Br md 18.29 Dpth 7.32 Welded, 1 dk	**(B21B20T) Offshore Tug/Supply Ship**	**2 oil engines** reduction geared to sc. shafts driving 2 Propellers Total Power: 4,920kW (6,690hp) Caterpillar C280-8 2 x 4 Stroke 8 Cy. 280 x 300 each-2460kW (3345bhp) Caterpillar Inc-USA AuxGen: 2 x 910kW a.c, 2 x 2050kW a.c
9530187 *PPYQ* -	**SANTOS SCOUT** - **Bram Offshore Transportes Maritimos Ltda** Opmar Servicos Maritimos Ltda *Itajai* *Brazil* MMSI: 710004180 Official number: 4430475521	**2,999** 1,432 4,735	Class: AB	**2010-06 Estaleiro Navship Ltda — Navegantes** Yd No: 116 Loa 85.34 Br ex - Dght 6.240 Lbp 82.32 Br md 18.29 Dpth 7.32 Welded, 1 dk	**(B21B20T) Offshore Tug/Supply Ship**	**2 oil engines** reduction geared to sc. shafts driving 2 CP propellers Total Power: 4,920kW (6,690hp) Caterpillar C280-8 2 x 4 Stroke 8 Cy. 280 x 300 each-2460kW (3345bhp) Caterpillar Inc-USA AuxGen: 2 x 2050kW a.c, 2 x 910kW a.c Thrusters: 1 Tunnel thruster (f); 1 Retract. directional thruster (f) Fuel: 1200.0 (d.f.)
9530199 *PPYK* -	**SANTOS SERVICE** - **Bram Offshore Transportes Maritimos Ltda** Opmar Servicos Maritimos Ltda SatCom: Inmarsat C 471011188 *Itajai* *Brazil* MMSI: 710002880 Official number: 4430474834	**2,999** 1,432 4,727	Class: AB	**2010-03 Estaleiro Navship Ltda — Navegantes** Yd No: 117 Loa 85.34 Br ex - Dght 6.240 Lbp 82.32 Br md 18.28 Dpth 7.31 Welded, 1 dk	**(B21B20T) Offshore Tug/Supply Ship**	**2 oil engines** reduction geared to sc. shafts driving 2 Propellers Total Power: 5,420kW (7,370hp) Caterpillar C280-8 2 x 4 Stroke 8 Cy. 280 x 300 each-2710kW (3685bhp) Caterpillar Inc-USA AuxGen: 2 x 2050kW a.c, 2 x 910kW a.c
9530204 *PPYL* -	**SANTOS SOLUTION** - **Bram Offshore Transportes Maritimos Ltda** - *Itajai* *Brazil* MMSI: 710002920 Official number: 4430475008	**2,999** 1,432 4,500	Class: AB	**2010-04 Estaleiro Navship Ltda — Navegantes** Yd No: 118 Loa 85.34 Br ex - Dght 6.240 Lbp 82.32 Br md 18.29 Dpth 7.31 Welded, 1 dk	**(B21B20T) Offshore Tug/Supply Ship**	**2 oil engines** geared to sc. shafts driving 2 Propellers Total Power: 5,420kW (7,370hp) Caterpillar C280-8 2 x 4 Stroke 8 Cy. 280 x 300 each-2710kW (3685bhp) Caterpillar Inc-USA Thrusters: 2 Tunnel thruster (f)
9497139 *PPTS* -	**SANTOS SUPPLIER** - **Bram Offshore Transportes Maritimos Ltda** - SatCom: Inmarsat C 471000493 *Itajai* *Brazil* MMSI: 710001010 Official number: 4430473404	**2,999** 1,429 4,820	Class: AB	**2009-05 Estaleiro Navship Ltda — Navegantes** Yd No: 110 Loa 84.37 Br ex - Dght 6.240 Lbp 81.68 Br md 18.29 Dpth 7.31 Welded, 1 dk	**(B21A20S) Platform Supply Ship**	**2 oil engines** geared to sc. shafts driving 2 Propellers Total Power: 5,420kW (7,370hp) Caterpillar C280-8 2 x 4 Stroke 8 Cy. 280 x 300 each-2710kW (3685bhp) Caterpillar Inc-USA
9530175 *PPYJ* -	**SANTOS SUPPORTER** - **Bram Offshore Transportes Maritimos Ltda** Opmar Servicos Maritimos Ltda SatCom: Inmarsat C 471011168 *Itajai* *Brazil* MMSI: 710002450 Official number: 4430474559	**2,999** 1,432 4,759	Class: AB	**2009-12 Estaleiro Navship Ltda — Navegantes** Yd No: 115 Loa 84.73 Br ex - Dght 6.240 Lbp 81.68 Br md 18.29 Dpth 7.31 Welded, 1 dk	**(B21B20T) Offshore Tug/Supply Ship**	**2 oil engines** geared to sc. shafts driving 2 Propellers Total Power: 4,920kW (6,690hp) Caterpillar C280-8 2 x 4 Stroke 8 Cy. 280 x 300 each-2460kW (3345bhp) Caterpillar Inc-USA AuxGen: 2 x 910kW a.c, 2 x 2050kW a.c
8035489 *YFSP* -	**SANTOSA** *ex* Mochizuki Maru *-1997* *ex* Sumiei Maru No. 8 *-1990* **PT Dunia Baru Lestari Indah** - *Surabaya* *Indonesia*	**443** 277 580	Class: KI	**1981-06 Ishida Zosen Kogyo YK — Onomichi HS** Yd No: 145 L reg 47.40 Br ex - Dght 3.200 Lbp 43.90 Br md 8.21 Dpth 4.81 Welded, 1 dk	**(A31A2GX) General Cargo Ship**	**1 oil engine** geared to sc. shaft driving 1 FP propeller Total Power: 368kW (500hp) 8.5kn Yanmar 1 x 4 Stroke 6 Cy. 368kW (500bhp) Yanmar Diesel Engine Co Ltd-Japan
9024750 - -	**SANTOSO 2** - **PT Genta Multiperdana** - *Samarinda* *Indonesia*	**164** 50 -	Class: KI	**1997-11 P.T. Karya Mulyo Teknik — Samarinda** Loa 26.00 Br ex - Dght - Lbp 24.95 Br md 7.00 Dpth 3.55 Welded, 1 dk	**(B32A2ST) Tug**	**2 oil engines** driving 2 Propellers Total Power: 810kW (1,102hp) 12.0kn Yanmar 6UA-UT 2 x 4 Stroke 6 Cy. 200 x 240 each-405kW (551bhp) (made 1981, fitted 1997) Yanmar Diesel Engine Co Ltd-Japan AuxGen: 2 x 64kW 400/120V a.c
9024841 - -	**SANTOSO 3** - **PT Pelayaran Mulyono Santoso** - *Samarinda* *Indonesia*	**135** 41 -	Class: KI	**2002-07 P.T. Karya Mulyo Teknik — Samarinda** Loa 32.80 Br ex - Dght 1.870 Lbp 30.00 Br md 7.60 Dpth 2.30 Welded, 1 dk	**(A35D2RL) Landing Craft** Bow ramp (centre)	**2 oil engines** geared to sc. shafts driving 2 Propellers Total Power: 442kW (600hp) 7.5kn Nissan RD8 2 x Vee 4 Stroke 8 Cy. 135 x 125 each-221kW (300bhp) (made 1995, fitted 2002) Nissan Diesel Motor Co. Ltd.-Ageo AuxGen: 2 x 56kW 380/220V a.c

IMO / Call sign / Flag	Name / Owner / Port	Tonnage	Class	Builder / Dimensions	Type	Machinery
9028407 - -	**SANTOSO 5** - **PT Pelayaran Mulyono Santoso** - *Samarinda* *Indonesia*	**288** 87 -	Class: KI	**2004**-07 **PT Karya Teknik Utama — Batam** Yd No: 26 Loa 32.05 Br ex - Dght - Lbp 29.04 Br md 8.30 Dpth 3.65 Welded, 1 dk	**(B32A2ST) Tug**	**2 oil engines** geared to sc. shafts driving 2 Propellers Total Power: 1,766kW (2,402hp) Niigata 6MG25BX 2 x 4 Stroke 6 Cy. 250 x 320 each-883kW (1201bhp) Niigata Engineering Co Ltd-Japan AuxGen: 2 x 88kW 380/220V a.c
9069592 - -	**SANTOSO 16** - **PT Pelayaran Mulyono Santoso** - *Samarinda* *Indonesia*	**230** 69 -	Class: KI	**2006**-06 **PT Karya Teknik Utama — Batam** Loa 27.00 Br ex - Dght 3.000 Lbp 25.70 Br md 8.20 Dpth 4.00 Welded, 1 dk	**(B32A2ST) Tug**	**2 oil engines** geared to sc. shafts driving 1 Propeller Total Power: 1,618kW (2,200hp) Yanmar 12LAK (M)-STE2 2 x Vee 4 Stroke 12 Cy. 150 x 165 each-809kW (1100bhp) (made 2005) Yanmar Diesel Engine Co Ltd-Japan
8658516 - -	**SANTOSO 19** - **PT Pelayaran Mulyono Santoso** - *Samarinda* *Indonesia*	**128** 39 -	Class: KI	**2009**-12 **P.T. Karya Mulyo Teknik — Samarinda** Loa - Br ex - Dght - Lbp 22.56 Br md 7.00 Dpth 3.30 Welded, 1 dk	**(B32A2ST) Tug**	**2 oil engines** reduction geared to sc. shafts driving 2 FP propellers AuxGen: 2 x 24kW 415/230V a.c
8738586 - -	**SANTOSO 21** - **PT Pelayaran Mulyono Santoso** - *Samarinda* *Indonesia*	**210** 63 -	Class: KI	**2009**-05 **P.T. Karya Mulyo Teknik — Samarinda** Loa 28.00 Br ex - Dght - Lbp 25.92 Br md 8.00 Dpth 3.60 Welded, 1 dk	**(B32A2ST) Tug**	**2 oil engines** driving 2 Propellers Total Power: 1,716kW (2,334hp) Mitsubishi S12A2-MPTK 2 x Vee 4 Stroke 12 Cy. 150 x 160 each-858kW (1167bhp) Mitsubishi Heavy Industries Ltd-Japan
8654053 - -	**SANTOSO 25** - **PT Pelayaran Mulyono Santoso** - *Samarinda* *Indonesia*	**210** 63 -	Class: KI	**2010**-08 **P.T. Karya Mulyo Teknik — Samarinda** Loa 28.50 Br ex - Dght - Lbp 26.11 Br md 8.00 Dpth 3.60 Welded, 1 dk	**(B32A2ST) Tug**	**2 oil engines** reduction geared to sc. shafts driving 2 FP propellers AuxGen: 2 x 60kW 400V a.c
8651623 - -	**SANTOSO 26** - **PT Pelayaran Mulyono Santoso** - *Samarinda* *Indonesia*	**197** 60 -	Class: KI	**2010**-08 **P.T. Karya Mulyo Teknik — Samarinda** Loa 28.00 Br ex - Dght 2.690 Lbp 26.11 Br md 8.00 Dpth 3.60 Welded, 1 dk	**(B32A2ST) Tug**	**2 oil engines** reduction geared to sc. shafts driving 2 Propellers AuxGen: 2 x 66kW 400V a.c
8658645 - -	**SANTOSO 28** - **PT Pelayaran Mulyono Santoso** - *Samarinda* *Indonesia*	**128** 39 -	Class: KI	**2011**-04 **P.T. Karya Mulyo Teknik — Samarinda** Loa 24.50 Br ex - Dght 2.490 Lbp 22.99 Br md 7.50 Dpth 3.30 Welded, 1 dk	**(B32A2ST) Tug**	**2 oil engines** reduction geared to sc. shafts driving 2 Propellers
8659508 - -	**SANTOSO 30** - **PT Pelayaran Mulyono Santoso** - *Samarinda* *Indonesia*	**200** 60 -	Class: KI	**2011**-09 **P.T. Karya Mulyo Teknik — Samarinda** Loa 28.00 Br ex - Dght 2.990 Lbp 26.16 Br md 8.00 Dpth 3.60 Welded, 1 dk	**(B32A2ST) Tug**	**2 oil engines** reduction geared to sc. shafts driving 2 FP propellers AuxGen: 2 x 24kW 400V a.c
9030591 *3FZN9* -	**SANTRINA** *ex* Isola Magenta *-2011* *ex* Four Rivers *-1997* *ex* Carlotta *-1996* **Centrist Holdings Ltd** Norstar Ship Management Pte Ltd *Panama* *Panama* MMSI: 357285000 Official number: 4331911	**20,200** 10,443 36,457 T/cm 43.7	Class: LR (RI) (AB) **100A1** SS 09/2009 Double Hull oil tanker ESP LI **LMC** **UMS IGS**	**1994**-09 **Sestri Cant. Nav. SpA — Genova** Yd No: 5919 Loa 178.78 (BB) Br ex - Dght 10.915 Lbp 168.56 Br md 28.00 Dpth 14.90 Welded, 1 dk	**(A13B2TP) Products Tanker** Double Hull (13F) Liq: 36,052; Liq (Oil): 36,052 Compartments: 4 Wing Ta, 6 Ta, 2 Wing Slop Ta, ER 3 Cargo Pump (s): 3x800m³/hr Manifold: Bow/CM: 92.5m	**1 oil engine** driving 1 FP propeller Total Power: 7,202kW (9,792hp) 14.5kn Sulzer 5RTA52 1 x 2 Stroke 5 Cy. 520 x 1800 7202kW (9792bhp) Fincantieri Cantieri Navalitaliani SpA-Italy AuxGen: 2 x 440kW 220V 60Hz a.c, 1 x a.c Fuel: 207.2 (d.f.) 1213.5 (r.f.)
7942726 *WYC9155* -	**SANTRINA** - **Miss Santrina Inc** - *New Orleans, LA* *United States of America* Official number: 604553	*143* 97 -		**1979 Marine Builders, Inc. — Mobile, Al** Yd No: 116 L reg 23.47 Br ex 6.81 Dght - Lbp - Br md - Dpth 3.41 Welded, 1 dk	**(B11B2FV) Fishing Vessel**	**1 oil engine** driving 1 FP propeller Total Power: 441kW (600hp)
6517158 - -	**SANTUARIO** *ex* Subro Vesta *-1990* *ex* Simbo Vesta *-1990* *ex* Subro Vesta *-1985* *ex* Edward Stone *-1978* **Eugenio Antonio Chassaigne Mejia** - *Sierra Leone*	*196* 120 300		**1965 J. W. Cook & Co. (Wivenhoe) Ltd. — Wivenhoe** Yd No: 1289 Loa 33.46 Br ex 6.68 Dght 2.540 Lbp 31.25 Br md 6.56 Dpth 2.90 Welded, 1 dk	**(A31A2GX) General Cargo Ship**	**1 oil engine** driving 1 FP propeller Total Power: 132kW (179hp) Kelvin T6 1 x 4 Stroke 6 Cy. 165 x 184 132kW (179bhp) Bergius Kelvin Co. Ltd.-Glasgow
9188075 *EARU* 3-GI-43-98	**SANTUARIO BARQUERENO** - **De la Cruz e Hijos** - *Gijon* *Spain* Official number: 3-3/1998	**155** 46 175		**1998**-04 **Astilleros Armon SA — Navia** Yd No: 445 Loa 30.00 Br ex - Dght 3.000 Lbp 24.58 Br md 7.00 Dpth 3.50 Welded, 1 dk	**(B11B2FV) Fishing Vessel**	**1 oil engine** driving 1 FP propeller Total Power: 309kW (420hp) GUASCOR F360TA-SF 1 x Vee 4 Stroke 12 Cy. 152 x 165 309kW (420bhp) Gutierrez Ascunce Corp (GUASCOR)-Spain
9146065 *9VBW2* -	**SANUKI** *ex* Brasil Express *-2006* *ex* Sanuki *-2005* **Meditrina Shipping Pte Ltd** NYK Shipmanagement Pte Ltd *Singapore* *Singapore* MMSI: 565355000 Official number: 392728	**13,448** 5,857 17,182 T/cm 31.5	Class: NK	**1997**-02 **Shin Kochi Jyuko K.K. — Kochi** Yd No: 7090 Loa 159.53 (BB) Br ex - Dght 8.718 Lbp 150.00 Br md 25.00 Dpth 12.80 Welded, 1 dk	**(A33A2CC) Container Ship (Fully Cellular)** TEU 1157 incl 120 ref C. Compartments: 5 Cell Ho, ER 15 Ha: ER Cranes: 2x40t	**1 oil engine** driving 1 FP propeller Total Power: 9,628kW (13,090hp) 18.0kn Mitsubishi 7UEC50LSII 1 x 2 Stroke 7 Cy. 500 x 1950 9628kW (13090bhp) Kobe Hatsudoki KK-Japan AuxGen: 4 x 438kW 440/100V 60Hz a.c Thrusters: 1 Thwart. CP thruster (f) Fuel: 173.0 (d.f.) (Heating Coils) 1810.0 (r.f.) 38.9pd
9021291 - -	**SANUKI** *ex* Nichiwa Maru *-2009* *ex* Nichiyo Maru *-2006* *ex* Nissei Maru No. 3 *-2001* *ex* Taisho Maru *-1995* - -	*328* - 761		**1991**-08 **Mukaishima Zoki Co. Ltd. — Onomichi** Yd No: 271 Loa 52.73 Br ex 9.20 Dght 3.740 Lbp 48.00 Br md 9.00 Dpth 3.90 Welded, 1 dk	**(A12A2TC) Chemical Tanker** Liq: 695 Compartments: 6 Ta, ER	**1 oil engine** with clutches & reverse geared to sc. shaft driving 1 FP propeller Total Power: 736kW (1,001hp) 10.5kn Hanshin LH26G 1 x 4 Stroke 6 Cy. 260 x 440 736kW (1001bhp) The Hanshin Diesel Works Ltd-Japan
8971243 *JJ4034* -	**SANUKI MARU** - **Sanyo Kaiji Co Ltd** - *Amagasaki, Hyogo* *Japan* Official number: 135980	*198* - -		**2001**-10 **Hatayama Zosen KK — Yura WK** Yd No: 237 Loa 32.82 Br ex - Dght 3.100 Lbp 26.50 Br md 9.50 Dpth 4.29 Welded, 1 dk	**(B32A2ST) Tug**	**2 oil engines** Geared Integral to driving 2 Z propellers Total Power: 2,648kW (3,600hp) Yanmar 6N280-UN 2 x 4 Stroke 6 Cy. 280 x 380 each-1324kW (1800bhp) Yanmar Diesel Engine Co Ltd-Japan
8020903 - - -	**SANUKI MARU** - - -	*198* 65 58		**1980**-12 **Hikari Kogyo K.K. — Yokosuka** Yd No: 311 Loa 31.73 Br ex - Dght 2.671 Lbp 26.50 Br md 8.60 Dpth 3.51 Welded, 1 dk	**(B32A2ST) Tug**	**2 oil engines** driving 2 FP propellers Daihatsu 6DSM-26 2 x 4 Stroke 6 Cy. 260 x 320 Daihatsu Diesel Manufacturing Co Lt-Japan
9207742 *AWCP* -	**SANVI** *ex* Brave Star *-2013* *ex* Blumenau *-2010* **Global United Shipping India Pvt Ltd** - *Mumbai* *India* MMSI: 419000789 Official number: 4090	**38,530** 25,069 73,992 T/cm 66.1	Class: IR (NK)	**2000**-03 **Tsuneishi Shipbuilding Co Ltd — Fukuyama HS** Yd No: 1146 Loa 225.00 Br ex - Dght 13.870 Lbp 216.00 Br md 32.26 Dpth 19.10 Welded, 1 dk	**(A21A2BC) Bulk Carrier** Grain: 88,364 Compartments: 7 Ho, ER 7 Ha: (15.3 x 12.8)6 (17.0 x 15.4)ER	**1 oil engine** driving 1 FP propeller Total Power: 8,900kW (12,100hp) 13.8kn MAN-B&W 6S60MC 1 x 2 Stroke 6 Cy. 600 x 2292 8900kW (12100bhp) Mitsui Engineering & Shipbuilding CLtd-Japan AuxGen: 3 x 440kW a.c Fuel: 2200.0
8944719 - -	**SANVIC IV** - **Vicente T Poraque** - *Tacloban* *Philippines* Official number: TAC8000487	*363* 307 -		**1991 at Cebu** L reg 52.96 Br ex - Dght - Lbp - Br md 9.75 Dpth 4.60 Welded, 1 dk	**(A31A2GX) General Cargo Ship**	**1 oil engine** driving 1 FP propeller Total Power: 530kW (721hp) Isuzu 1 x 4 Stroke 530kW (721bhp) Isuzu Marine Engine Inc-Japan
8226193 *YB5201* -	**SANWA** *ex* Shin Showa Maru *-2000* **PT Dharma Ichtiar Indo Lines** - *Surabaya* *Indonesia*	**402** 180 650	Class: KI	**1982**-11 **Hayashi Zosen — Osakikamijima** Yd No: 131 Loa 42.95 Br ex 8.02 Dght 3.800 Lbp 38.00 Br md 8.00 Dpth 4.90 Welded	**(A31A2GX) General Cargo Ship**	**1 oil engine** driving 1 FP propeller Total Power: 331kW (450hp) 11.0kn Matsui MU623CHS 1 x 4 Stroke 6 Cy. 230 x 380 331kW (450bhp) Matsui Iron Works Co Ltd-Japan

8204121 *3FMK4* - | **SANWA FONTAINE** | **Sealand Trading Corp** | Dongwon Industries Co Ltd | SatCom: Inmarsat A 1347321 | *Panama* *Panama* | MMSI: 353937000 | Official number: 2200295D | **3,260** 1,582 3,917 | Class: KR (NK)

1982-09 Kochi Jyuko (Eiho Zosen) K.K. — Kochi Yd No: 1540
Loa 92.21 Br ex - Dght 6.568
Lbp 84.99 Br md 16.21 Dpth 6.86
Welded, 3 dks

(A34A2GR) Refrigerated Cargo Ship
Ins: 4,344
Compartments: 3 Ho, ER
3 Ha: 3 (5.0 x 5.0)ER
Derricks: 6x4t

1 oil engine driving 1 FP propeller
Total Power: 3,310kW (4,500hp) 14.4kn
Hanshin 6ELS44
1 x 4 Stroke 6 Cy. 440 x 880 3310kW (4500bhp)
The Hanshin Diesel Works Ltd-Japan
AuxGen: 2 x 560kW 450V 60Hz a.c
Fuel: 140.0 (d.f.) 640.0 (r.f.)

9093684 *JD2136* - | **SANWA MARU** | **Taiho Unyu KK (Taiho Shipping Co Ltd)** | *Osaka, Osaka* *Japan* | Official number: 140195 | *364* - 882

2005-07 Hongawara Zosen K.K. — Fukuyama Yd No: 576
Loa 53.33 Br ex - Dght 3.850
Lbp 48.50 Br md 9.20 Dpth 4.10
Welded, 1 dk

(A12A2TC) Chemical Tanker
Double Hull (13F)
Liq: 599
Compartments: 3 Ta, ER

1 oil engine driving 1 Propeller
Total Power: 736kW (1,001hp)
Yanmar DY26-SN
1 x 4 Stroke 6 Cy. 260 x 440 736kW (1001bhp)
Yanmar Diesel Engine Co Ltd-Japan

9405124 *JD2298* - | **SANWA MARU** | **Japan Railway Construction, Transport & Technology Agency & Marukyo Kaiun KK** | Marukyo Kaiun KK | *Saiki, Oita* *Japan* | MMSI: 431602345 | Official number: 140379 | *818* - 1,888 | Class: NK

2006-08 Suzuki Shipyard Co. Ltd. — Yokkaichi Yd No: 707
Loa 70.42 Br ex - Dght 4.812
Lbp 66.00 Br md 12.00 Dpth 5.20
Welded, 1 dk

(A13B2TP) Products Tanker
Double Hull (13F)
Liq: 2,174; Liq (Oil): 2,218

1 oil engine reduction geared to sc. shaft driving 1 FP propeller
Total Power: 1,618kW (2,200hp) 12.8kn
Niigata 6M34BGT
1 x 4 Stroke 6 Cy. 340 x 620 1618kW (2200bhp)
Niigata Engineering Co Ltd-Japan
AuxGen: 3 x 615kW a.c
Fuel: 50.0

8922096 *JJ3666* - | **SANWA MARU NO. 8** | *ex* Hokusei Maru *-2006* | **KK Sanwa Dock** | - | *Innoshima, Hiroshima* *Japan* | Official number: 129248 | *117* - -

1990-01 Kanagawa Zosen — Kobe Yd No: 335
Loa 27.00 Br ex - Dght 2.600
Lbp 23.10 Br md 8.00 Dpth 3.58
Welded, 1 dk

(B32A2ST) Tug

2 oil engines driving 2 FP propellers
Total Power: 1,398kW (1,900hp)
Yanmar M220-SN
2 x 4 Stroke 6 Cy. 220 x 300 each-699kW (950bhp)
Yanmar Diesel Engine Co Ltd-Japan

8967228 *JI3687* - | **SANWA MARU No. 38** | **Sanwa Senpaku Kaiun YK** | *Osaka, Osaka* *Japan* | Official number: 137067 | *167* - -

2001-02 Maekawa Zosensho — Japan Yd No: 358
Loa 29.52 Br ex - Dght -
Lbp - Br md 8.00 Dpth 3.50
Welded, 1 dk

(B32A2ST) Tug

2 oil engines reverse geared to sc. shaft driving 2 FP propellers
Total Power: 1,472kW (2,002hp) 10.0kn
Akasaka T26SKR
2 x 4 Stroke 6 Cy. 260 x 440 each-736kW (1001bhp)
Akasaka Tekkosho KK (Akasaka DieselLtd)-Japan

9178393 *9V7726* - | **SANYA** | *ex* Bar'zan *-2008* *ex* Sinar Surya *-2004* | *ex* OOCL Affinity *-2001* *ex* Sinar Surya *-2000* | **Virginia Key Pte Ltd** | Seachange Maritime (Singapore) Pte Ltd | *Singapore* *Singapore* | MMSI: 563630000 | Official number: 394734 | **16,705** 9,118 24,327 T/cm 40.9 | Class: NK

1999-01 Imabari Shipbuilding Co Ltd — Marugame KG (Marugame Shipyard) Yd No: 1299
Loa 183.21 (BB) Br ex - Dght 10.116
Lbp 172.00 Br md 27.60 Dpth 14.00
Welded, 1 dk

(A33A2CC) Container Ship (Fully Cellular)
TEU 1560 incl 200 ref C.
9 Ha: ER

1 oil engine driving 1 FP propeller
Total Power: 12,269kW (16,681hp) 19.1kn
B&W 6S60MC
1 x 2 Stroke 6 Cy. 600 x 2292 12269kW (16681bhp)
Mitsui Engineering & Shipbuilding CLtd-Japan
AuxGen: 3 x 720kW 450V 60Hz a.c
Thrusters: 1 Thwart. FP thruster (f)
Fuel: 2732.0 (r.f.) 45.7pd

7950761 *HQLE6* - | **SANYO LINER** | *ex* Sanyo Maru No. 7 *-2000* | *ex* Yuki Maru No. 11 *-1987* | **Sanyo Shipping S de RL** | - | *San Lorenzo* *Honduras* | Official number: L-2614616 | *119* 34 -

1977-04 K.K. Tago Zosensho — Nishi-Izu Yd No: 151
L reg 31.49 Br ex - Dght -
Lbp - Br md 6.00 Dpth 2.80
Welded, 1 dk

(B11B2FV) Fishing Vessel

1 oil engine driving 1 FP propeller
Total Power: 684kW (930hp)
Daihatsu
1 x 4 Stroke 684kW (930bhp)
Daihatsu Diesel Manufacturing Co Lt-Japan

9072630 *JG5246* - | **SANYO MARU** | *ex* Toho Maru *-2006* | **Kyodo Kisen YK** | Nissen Kisen KK | *Onomichi, Hiroshima* *Japan* | Official number: 133999 | *499* - 1,173

1993-07 Maebata Zosen Tekko K.K. — Sasebo Yd No: 206
Loa 63.98 Br ex - Dght 4.050
Lbp 59.00 Br md 10.00 Dpth 4.50
Welded, 1 dk

(A12A2TC) Chemical Tanker
2 Cargo Pump (s): 2x300m³/hr

1 oil engine driving 1 FP propeller
Total Power: 736kW (1,001hp)
Niigata 6M28BGT
1 x 4 Stroke 6 Cy. 280 x 480 736kW (1001bhp)
Niigata Engineering Co Ltd-Japan

8949020 *JK5567* - | **SANYO MARU** | **Etajima Kaiun KK** | - | *Hiroshima, Hiroshima* *Japan* | Official number: 136147 | *279* - -

1998-11 Kanbara Zosen K.K. — Onomichi Yd No: 506
Loa 38.02 Br ex - Dght -
Lbp 33.00 Br md 9.60 Dpth 4.19
Welded, 1 dk

(B32A2ST) Tug

2 oil engines Geared Integral to driving 2 Z propellers
Total Power: 3,090kW (4,202hp) 13.0kn
Niigata 6L28HX
2 x 4 Stroke 6 Cy. 280 x 370 each-1545kW (2101bhp)
Niigata Engineering Co Ltd-Japan

8879029 *JK5230* - | **SANYO MARU No. 2** | **Sanyo Kensetsu KK** | - | *Mihara, Hiroshima* *Japan* | Official number: 133082 | *176* - -

1994-08 Hongawara Zosen K.K. — Fukuyama Yd No: 420
Loa 33.40 Br ex - Dght 2.500
Lbp 29.00 Br md 8.20 Dpth 3.48
Welded, 1 dk

(B32A2ST) Tug

2 oil engines driving 2 FP propellers
Total Power: 1,766kW (2,402hp)
Niigata
2 x 4 Stroke each-883kW (1201bhp)
Niigata Engineering Co Ltd-Japan

6920989 - - | **SANYO MARU No. 5** | *ex* Kimiichi Maru *-1987* | *ex* Hokko Maru No. 38 *-1983* | *ex* Soryu Maru No. 38 *-1981* | - | - | *317* - -

1969 Niigata Engineering Co Ltd — Niigata NI Yd No: 828
Loa 49.15 Br ex 8.34 Dght -
Lbp 43.59 Br md 8.31 Dpth 3.64
Welded, 1 dk

(B11B2FV) Fishing Vessel

1 oil engine driving 1 FP propeller
Total Power: 699kW (950hp)
Niigata
1 x 4 Stroke 6 Cy. 280 x 440 699kW (950bhp)
Niigata Engineering Co Ltd-Japan

8932390 - - | **SANYO MARU No. 6** | *ex* Shunei Maru No. 21 *-1981* | - | - | *South Korea* | *199* - 480

1971 Y.K. Tokai Zosensho — Tsukumi
Loa 26.00 Br ex 8.00 Dght 2.700
Lbp 22.40 Br md - Dpth 3.80
Welded, 1 dk

(B32A2ST) Tug

1 oil engine driving 1 FP propeller
Total Power: 1,103kW (1,500hp) 10.0kn
Otsuka
1 x 4 Stroke 1103kW (1500bhp)
KK Otsuka Diesel-Japan

8808484 - - | **SANYO MARU No. 8** | - | - | *491* - 1,405

1988-08 Yamanaka Zosen K.K. — Imabari Yd No: 370
Loa 61.95 (BB) Br ex - Dght 4.326
Lbp 57.00 Br md 14.00 Dpth 6.60
Welded, 1 dk

(A24D2BA) Aggregates Carrier
Compartments: 1 Ho, ER

1 oil engine driving 1 FP propeller
Total Power: 1,324kW (1,800hp)
Hanshin 6LU32G
1 x 4 Stroke 6 Cy. 320 x 510 1324kW (1800bhp)
The Hanshin Diesel Works Ltd-Japan
Thrusters: 1 Tunnel thruster (f)

8823393 *JK4754* - | **SANYO MARU No. 15** | **Sanyo Kensetsu KK** | - | *Mihara, Hiroshima* *Japan* | Official number: 130992 | *166* - -

1988-09 Hongawara Zosen K.K. — Fukuyama
Loa 32.20 Br ex - Dght 2.500
Lbp 28.00 Br md 7.60 Dpth 3.48
Welded, 1 dk

(B32B2SP) Pusher Tug

2 oil engines driving 2 FP propellers
Total Power: 1,766kW (2,402hp) 12.6kn
Niigata
2 x 4 Stroke each-883kW (1201bhp)
Niigata Engineering Co Ltd-Japan

8967292 *JVAH4* - | **SANYO MARU No. 18** | **China Harbour Engineering Co Ltd** | - | *Ulaanbaatar* *Mongolia* | MMSI: 457255000 | Official number: 27311001 | *154* - -

2001-06 Hongawara Zosen K.K. — Fukuyama Yd No: 531
Loa 33.25 Br ex - Dght -
Lbp 31.10 Br md 9.00 Dpth 4.50
Welded, 1 dk

(B32B2SP) Pusher Tug

2 oil engines driving 2 FP propellers
Total Power: 2,942kW (4,000hp) 12.3kn
Niigata 6M34BGT
2 x 4 Stroke 6 Cy. 340 x 620 each-1471kW (2000bhp)
Niigata Engineering Co Ltd-Japan

7914004 - - | **SANYO MARU No. 22** | **China Marine Bunker Supply Co (Guangzhou Branch)** | - | *China* | *499* 287 1,150

1979-12 Suzuki Shipyard Co. Ltd. — Yokkaichi Yd No: 318
Loa - Br ex - Dght 4.252
Lbp 56.01 Br md 10.01 Dpth 4.53
Welded, 1 dk

(A13B2TU) Tanker (unspecified)

1 oil engine driving 1 FP propeller
Total Power: 1,030kW (1,400hp)
Yanmar 6ZL-DT
1 x 4 Stroke 6 Cy. 280 x 340 1030kW (1400bhp)
Yanmar Diesel Engine Co Ltd-Japan

9119244 *JL6350* - | **SANYO MARU NO. 37** | *ex* Fuji Maru *-2004* | **Sanyo Kaiun Shokai Co Ltd (KK Sanyo Kaiun Shokai)** | - | *Kainan, Tokushima* *Japan* | Official number: 134920 | *498* - 1,232 | Class: (NK)

1995-01 Watanabe Zosen KK — Imabari EH Yd No: 283
Loa 64.52 (BB) Br ex 10.02 Dght 4.184
Lbp 60.00 Br md 10.00 Dpth 4.45
Welded, 1 dk

(A13B2TP) Products Tanker
Liq: 1,150; Liq (Oil): 1,150

1 oil engine with clutches & reverse geared to sc. shaft driving 1 FP propeller
Total Power: 736kW (1,001hp) 10.5kn
Akasaka K28BR
1 x 4 Stroke 6 Cy. 280 x 480 736kW (1001bhp)
Akasaka Tekkosho KK (Akasaka DieselLtd)-Japan

IMO / Call sign	Name / Owner / Port	Tonnage	Class	Build / Dimensions	Type	Machinery
9241516 *JI3682* -	**SANYO MARU No. 38** - Sanyo Kaiun Shokai Co Ltd (KK Sanyo Kaiun Shokai) - *Osaka, Osaka* *Japan* MMSI: 431301542 Official number: 137062	*749* - 2,098	Class: NK	**2000-12 Hitachi Zosen Mukaishima Marine Co Ltd — Onomichi HS** Yd No: 152 Loa 74.46 Br ex - Dght 4.961 Lbp 69.00 Br md 11.40 Dpth 5.60 Welded, 1 dk	**(A13B2TP) Products Tanker** Liq: 2,229; Liq (Oil): 2,274	**1 oil engine** driving 1 FP propeller Total Power: 1,471kW (2,000hp) 12.4kn Hanshin LH32LG 1 x 4 Stroke 6 Cy. 320 x 640 1471kW (2000bhp) The Hanshin Diesel Works Ltd-Japan Fuel: 69.0
9442031 *JD2488* -	**SANYO MARU NO. 51** - Sanyo Kaiun Shokai Co Ltd (KK Sanyo Kaiun Shokai) - *Osaka, Osaka* *Japan* MMSI: 431000304 Official number: 140617	*748* - 1,937		**2007-09 Miho Zosensho K.K. — Shimizu** Yd No: 1524 Loa 71.57 Br ex - Dght 3.190 Lbp 67.20 Br md 12.00 Dpth 5.20 Welded, 1 dk	**(A13B2TP) Products Tanker** Double Hull (13F)	**1 oil engine** driving 1 FP propeller Total Power: 1,471kW (2,000hp) Hanshin LH34LG 1 x 4 Stroke 6 Cy. 340 x 640 1471kW (2000bhp) The Hanshin Diesel Works Ltd-Japan
9474149 *JD2646* -	**SANYO MARU NO. 56** - Sanyo Kaiun Shokai Co Ltd (KK Sanyo Kaiun Shokai) - *Osaka, Osaka* *Japan* MMSI: 431000568 Official number: 140753	*748* - 1,943		**2008-06 Miho Zosensho K.K. — Shimizu** Yd No: 1525 Loa 71.57 Br ex - Dght 4.700 Lbp 67.20 Br md 12.00 Dpth 5.20 Welded, 1 dk	**(A13B2TP) Products Tanker** Double Hull (13F) Liq: 2,199; Liq (Oil): 2,199	**1 oil engine** driving 1 FP propeller Total Power: 1,471kW (2,000hp) 11.9kn Hanshin LH34LG 1 x 4 Stroke 6 Cy. 340 x 640 1471kW (2000bhp) The Hanshin Diesel Works Ltd-Japan
9084322 *JL6251* -	**SANYO NO. 3** *ex* Yahata Maru No. 18 *-2009* - - *Matsuyama, Ehime* *Japan* Official number: 133929	*499* - 1,500		**1994-02 Shinhama Dockyard Co. Ltd. — Anan** Yd No: 832 Loa - Br ex - Dght - Lbp 72.40 Br md 11.70 Dpth 7.10 Welded, 1 dk	**(A31A2GX) General Cargo Ship**	**1 oil engine** driving 1 FP propeller Total Power: 736kW (1,001hp) Hanshin LH30LG 1 x 4 Stroke 6 Cy. 300 x 600 736kW (1001bhp) The Hanshin Diesel Works Ltd-Japan
9084932 *JL6244* -	**SANYO No. 5** *ex* Omishima No. 2 *-1999* Sanyo Shosen KK - *Takehara, Hiroshima* *Japan* Official number: 134817	*291* - 137		**1994-03 Naikai Zosen Corp — Onomichi HS (Setoda Shipyard)** Yd No: 591 Loa 49.90 Br ex 10.42 Dght 2.620 Lbp 37.25 Br md 10.40 Dpth 3.60 Welded, 1 dk	**(A36A2PR) Passenger/Ro-Ro Ship (Vehicles)** Passengers: unberthed: 250 Bow ramp Stern ramp	**1 oil engine** with clutches, flexible couplings & sr reverse geared to sc. shaft driving 2 FP propellers 1 fwd and 1 aft Total Power: 1,030kW (1,400hp) Daihatsu 6DLM-26FSL 1 x 4 Stroke 6 Cy. 260 x 340 1030kW (1400bhp) Daihatsu Diesel Manufacturing Co Lt-Japan
9181716 *JK5446* -	**SANYO No. 7** - Sanyo Shosen KK - *Takehara, Hiroshima* *Japan* Official number: 135280	*318* - 144		**1997-09 Naikai Zosen Corp — Onomichi HS (Setoda Shipyard)** Yd No: 629 Loa 49.90 Br ex - Dght 2.650 Lbp 38.90 Br md 11.00 Dpth 3.58 Welded, 1 dk	**(A36A2PR) Passenger/Ro-Ro Ship (Vehicles)** Passengers: unberthed: 250 Bow ramp Stern ramp Cars: 10, Vehicles: 4	**1 oil engine** reduction geared to sc. shafts driving 2 Propellers 1 fwd and 1 aft Total Power: 1,177kW (1,600hp) 11.5kn Daihatsu 6DLM-26FSL 1 x 4 Stroke 6 Cy. 260 x 340 1177kW (1600bhp) Daihatsu Diesel Manufacturing Co Lt-Japan AuxGen: 2 x 80kW a.c Fuel: 31.0 (d.f.) 5.4pd
9161625 *JL6561* -	**SANYU MARU** - Fukunaga Kaiun YK - *Anan, Tokushima* *Japan* Official number: 135581	*499* - 1,382		**1997-05 Narasaki Zosen KK — Muroran HK** Yd No: 1161 Loa 75.00 (BB) Br ex - Dght 3.988 Lbp 70.00 Br md 12.00 Dpth 6.00 Welded, 2 dks	**(A31A2GX) General Cargo Ship** Grain: 2,600 Compartments: 1 Ho, ER 1 Ha: ER	**1 oil engine** with clutches & reverse geared to sc. shaft driving 1 FP propeller Total Power: 736kW (1,001hp) Hanshin LH30LG 1 x 4 Stroke 6 Cy. 300 x 600 736kW (1001bhp) The Hanshin Diesel Works Ltd-Japan Thrusters: 1 Thwart. FP thruster (f)
9078866 *JJ3869* -	**SANYU MARU** *ex* Kasuga Maru No. 8 *-2008* Taketani Kaiun KK - *Shodoshima, Kagawa* *Japan* Official number: 132400	*499* - 1,239		**1993-10 Sanuki Shipbuilding & Iron Works Co Ltd — Mitoyo KG** Yd No: 1237 Loa 64.00 (BB) Br ex - Dght 4.202 Lbp 58.00 Br md 10.00 Dpth 4.50 Welded, 1 dk	**(A13B2TP) Products Tanker** Liq: 1,228; Liq (Oil): 1,228	**1 oil engine** reverse geared to sc. shaft driving 1 FP propeller Total Power: 736kW (1,001hp) Hanshin LH28G 1 x 4 Stroke 6 Cy. 280 x 460 736kW (1001bhp) The Hanshin Diesel Works Ltd-Japan
9135327 *JL6436* -	**SANYU MARU No. 2** - - - *Kasaoka, Okayama* *Japan* Official number: 135140	*499* - 1,459		**1995-12 K.K. Miura Zosensho — Saiki** Yd No: 1137 Loa 75.88 Br ex 12.30 Dght 3.980 Lbp 70.00 Br md 12.00 Dpth 7.05 Welded, 1 dk	**(A31A2GX) General Cargo Ship** Bale: 2,551 Compartments: 1 Ho 1 Ha: (40.2 x 9.5)	**1 oil engine** driving 1 FP propeller Total Power: 736kW (1,001hp) 12.5kn Hanshin LH30LG 1 x 4 Stroke 6 Cy. 300 x 600 736kW (1001bhp) The Hanshin Diesel Works Ltd-Japan
7046649 *XVIK* -	**SAO BIEN** *ex* Wakashio Maru *-1996* Vietnam Maritime University (Truong Dai Hoc Hang Hai Vietnam) Flying Dragon Co SA *Haiphong* *Vietnam* Official number: VN-1109-VT	**299** 90 118	Class: VR	**1970 Usuki Iron Works Co Ltd — Usuki OT** Yd No: 752 Loa 42.58 Br ex 7.82 Dght 2.693 Lbp 36.99 Br md 7.80 Dpth 3.71 Welded, 1 dk	**(B11B2FV) Fishing Vessel**	**1 oil engine** driving 1 FP propeller Total Power: 515kW (700hp) Hanshin Z76 1 x 4 Stroke 6 Cy. 270 x 400 515kW (700bhp) Hanshin Nainenki Kogyo-Japan
8829488 - -	**SAO CRISTOVAO** - Camara Municipal de Vila Nova de Cerveira - *Caminha* *Portugal* Official number: C-30-TL	*148* 95 40	Class: RP	**1985-10 Estaleiros Sao Jacinto S.A. — Aveiro** Yd No: 159 L reg 30.00 Br ex 9.50 Dght - Lbp - Br md - Dpth 1.50 Welded, 1 dk	**(A36A2PR) Passenger/Ro-Ro Ship (Vehicles)** Bow ramp Stern ramp	**2 oil engines** reduction geared to sc. shafts driving 2 Propellers 1 fwd and 1 aft Total Power: 224kW (304hp) Cummins 6BT5.9-M 2 x 4 Stroke 6 Cy. 102 x 120 each-112kW (152bhp) Cummins Engine Co Inc-USA Fuel: 9.0 (d.f.) 0.7pd
9492311 *V7ZC8* -	**SAO DOMINGOS SAVIO** - DTB Shipping III LLC Wisby Tankers AB *Majuro* *Marshall Islands* MMSI: 538004792 Official number: 4792	**10,830** 3,612 14,911	Class: BV	**2013-03 '3 Maj' Brodogradiliste dd — Rijeka** Yd No: 717 Loa 133.28 (BB) Br ex 23.03 Dght 8.600 Lbp 128.20 Br md 23.00 Dpth 12.40 Welded, 1 dk	**(A13C2LA) Asphalt/Bitumen Tanker** Double Hull (13F) Liq: 14,599; Liq (Oil): 14,599 Compartments: 6 Wing Ta, 6 Wing Ta, ER	**1 oil engine** driving 1 CP propeller Total Power: 4,500kW (6,118hp) 13.6kn Wartsila 6RT-flex35 1 x 2 Stroke 6 Cy. 350 x 1550 4500kW (6118bhp) '3 Maj' Motori i Dizalice dd-Croatia AuxGen: 1 x 624kW 60Hz a.c, 3 x 680kW 60Hz a.c Fuel: 730.0
5066073 *PVKH* -	**SAO GERALDO** *ex* Catarina *-1977* Sao Geraldo Mini Tour Cargas SA - *Rio de Janeiro* *Brazil* Official number: 3969	*386* 122 526		**1954 Orenstein-Koppel u. Luebecker Maschinenbau AG — Luebeck** Yd No: 485 Loa - Br ex 8.49 Dght - Lbp 38.99 Br md 8.46 Dpth 3.54 Riveted\Welded, 1 dk	**(A31A2GX) General Cargo Ship**	**1 oil engine** driving 1 FP propeller MAN G6V285/42 1 x 4 Stroke 6 Cy. 285 x 420 Maschinenbau Augsburg Nuernberg (MAN)-Augsburg
9179804 *CUVN* A-3484-C	**SAO GONCALINHO** - Pescarias Beira Litoral Sarl - SatCom: Inmarsat C 420424310 *Aveiro* *Portugal*	**249** 76 128		**1998-12 Estaleiros Sao Jacinto S.A. — Aveiro** Yd No: 205 Loa - Br ex - Dght 3.292 Lbp 24.86 Br md 8.00 Dpth 3.50 Welded, 1 dk	**(B11A2FS) Stern Trawler**	**1 oil engine** reduction geared to sc. shaft driving 1 FP propeller Total Power: 588kW (799hp) Cummins KT-38-M 1 x Vee 4 Stroke 12 Cy. 159 x 159 588kW (799bhp) Cummins Engine Co Inc-USA
7385100 *CUVR* -	**SAO JACINTO** - Empresa de Pesca Sao Jacinto SA - *Lisbon* *Portugal* Official number: LX-120-C	**220** 66 102	Class: RP (LR) ✠ Classed LR until 3/11/94	**1975-12 Estaleiros Sao Jacinto S.A. — Aveiro** Yd No: 108 Loa 34.02 (BB) Br ex 7.75 Dght 2.998 Lbp 27.64 Br md 7.50 Dpth 3.41 Welded, 1 dk	**(B11A2FS) Stern Trawler**	**1 oil engine** reverse reduction geared to sc. shaft driving 1 CP propeller Total Power: 662kW (900hp) MaK 6M282AK 1 x 4 Stroke 6 Cy. 240 x 280 662kW (900bhp) MaK Maschinenbau GmbH-Kiel AuxGen: 2 x 64kW 231/400V 50Hz a.c
7933165 *VRDU* -	**SAO JORGE** *ex* Sao Vincente *-1980* *ex* Jet Caribe *-1980* Wideway International Ltd Shun Tak-China Travel Ship Management Ltd (TurboJET) *Hong Kong* *Hong Kong* MMSI: 477033000 Official number: 384765	**267** 97 -	Class: AB	**1976-03 Boeing Marine Systems — Seattle, Wa** Yd No: 0006 Loa 30.10 Br ex 9.50 Dght 5.301 Lbp 23.93 Br md 8.54 Dpth 2.60 Welded, 2 dks	**(A37B2PS) Passenger Ship** Hull Material: Aluminium Alloy Passengers: unberthed: 236	**2 Gas Turbs** dr geared to sc. shafts driving 2 Water jets Total Power: 5,442kW (7,398hp) 43.0kn Allison 501-K20A 2 x Gas Turb each-2721kW (3699shp) General Motors Detroit DieselAllison Divn-USA AuxGen: 2 x 50kW 440V 60Hz a.c Thrusters: 1 Thwart. FP thruster (f)

8005226 **SAO JOSE**
PQ3225 *ex* Duden *-2011* *ex* Alikrator *-1993*
\- *ex* Armenistis *-1993*
Lyra Navegacao Maritima Ltda
\-
Rio de Janeiro *Brazil*
MMSI: 710008280
Official number: 381.3881814

16,211 / 10,598 / 26,975

Class: RB
✠ **100A1** SS 11/2006
bulk carrier
strengthened for heavy cargoes,
No. 3 cargo hold may be e mpty
ESP
LI
ESN-Hold 1
✠ **LMC**
Eq.Ltr: G†; Cable: U3 (a)

1981-12 **Naikai Shipbuilding & Engineering Co Ltd — Onomichi HS (Setoda Shipyard)**
Yd No: 461
Loa 173.01 (BB) Br ex 22.84 Dght 10.626
Lbp 164.01 Br md 22.80 Dpth 14.75
Welded, 1 dk

(A21A2BC) Bulk Carrier
Grain: 37,652; Bale: 32,961
Compartments: 5 Ho, ER
5 Ha: (14.0 x 11.4) (8.7 x 11.4)2 (19.2 x 11.4) (19.6 x 11.4)ER
Cranes: 2x25t,2x15t

1 oil engine driving 1 FP propeller
Total Power: 7,355kW (10,000hp) 15.0kn
B&W 6L67GFCA
1 x 2 Stroke 6 Cy. 670 x 1700 7355kW (10000bhp)
Hitachi Zosen Corp-Japan
AuxGen: 3 x 440kW 450V 60Hz a.c
Fuel: 125.0 (d.f.) (Heating Coils) 1365.0 (r.f.) 30.0pd

9020015 **SAO KIM**
3WIR *ex* Jupiter Ace *-2010*
\- **Vietnam Maritime University (Truong Dai Hoc Hang Hai Vietnam)**
Flight Dragon Shipping Co (Cong Ty Van Tai Bien Thang Long)
Haiphong *Vietnam*
MMSI: 574275000
Official number: VN-3130-VT

5,470 / 2,315 / 6,881

Class: VR (NK)

1991-05 **Higaki Zosen K.K. — Imabari** Yd No: 396
Loa 98.18 (BB) Br ex 18.82 Dght 7.542
Lbp 89.95 Br md 18.00 Dpth 8.00
Welded, 2 dks

(A31A2GX) General Cargo Ship
Grain: 13,493; Bale: 12,483
Compartments: 2 Ho, ER
2 Ha: (22.3 x 9.8) (23.4 x 9.8)ER
Derricks: 4x25t

1 oil engine driving 1 FP propeller
Total Power: 2,427kW (3,300hp) 12.0kn
Hanshin 6EL40
1 x 4 Stroke 6 Cy. 400 x 800 2427kW (3300bhp)
The Hanshin Diesel Works Ltd-Japan
Fuel: 400.0 (r.f.)

8716239 **SAO LUIS**
\- *ex* Sao Luiz *-2003*
\- -
\-

357 / 107 / 248

Class: AB (NV)

1991-12 **Maclaren BA Est. e Servicos Maritimos S.A. — Rio de Janeiro** Yd No: 330
Loa 29.30 Br ex 9.80 Dght 4.100
Lbp 26.20 Br md - Dpth 5.00
Welded, 1 dk

(B32A2ST) Tug

2 oil engines with clutches, flexible couplings & sr geared to sc. shafts driving 2 Directional propellers
Total Power: 2,398kW (3,260hp)
MAN 12V20/27
2 x Vee 4 Stroke 12 Cy. 200 x 270 each-1199kW (1630bhp)
Mecanica Pesada SA-Brazil
AuxGen: 2 x 144kW 450V 60Hz a.c

9055113 **SAO LUIZ**
PPSR *ex* Alianca Sao Luiz *-2008* *ex* Sao Luiz *-2007*
\- **Navegacao Mansur SA**
Posidonia Servicos Maritimos Ltda (Posidonia Shipping)
SatCom: Inmarsat C 471011289
Rio de Janeiro *Brazil*
MMSI: 710070000
Official number: 3810474525

25,039 / 14,743 / 42,815

Class: BV (NV) (AB)

1994-08 **Industrias Reunidas Caneco SA — Rio de Janeiro** Yd No: 336
Loa 200.00 (BB) Br ex - Dght 10.650
Lbp 190.00 Br md 30.00 Dpth 15.10
Welded, 1 dk

(A21A2BC) Bulk Carrier
Grain: 54,427; Bale: 52,794
Compartments: 5 Ho, ER
5 Ha: ER
Cranes: 4

1 oil engine driving 1 FP propeller
Total Power: 7,134kW (9,699hp) 14.0kn
B&W 5S50MC
1 x 2 Stroke 5 Cy. 500 x 1910 7134kW (9699bhp)
Mecanica Pesada SA-Brazil

9492139 **SAO LUIZ**
C6ZT4
\- **Viken Shuttle AS**
Viken Shipping AS
Nassau *Bahamas*
MMSI: 311065600
Official number: 8002005

62,753 / 29,157 / 105,213

Class: AB (NV)

2013-01 **Samsung Heavy Industries Co Ltd — Geoje** Yd No: 1970
Loa 248.00 (BB) Br ex 42.36 Dght 15.100
Lbp 233.00 Br md 42.00 Dpth 22.50
Welded, 1 dk

(A13A2TS) Shuttle Tanker
Double Hull (13F)
Liq: 116,450; Liq (Oil): 116,450
Cargo Heating Coils
Compartments: 12 Wing Ta, 2 Wing Slop Ta, ER
4 Cargo Pump (s): 4x3000m³/hr
Manifold: Bow/CM: 126.3m

1 oil engine driving 1 CP propeller
Total Power: 14,280kW (19,415hp) 14.6kn
MAN-B&W 6S60ME-C8
1 x 2 Stroke 6 Cy. 600 x 2400 14280kW (19415bhp)
Doosan Engine Co Ltd-South Korea
AuxGen: 2 x 4500kW a.c, 2 x 3000kW a.c
Fuel: 510.0 (d.f.) 2780.0 (r.f.)

8008553 **SAO MAI 01**
3WJA *ex* Runde Supplier *-1991*
\- *ex* Maersk Runde *-1987* *ex* Huacai *-1986*
ex Balder Runde *-1984*
Marine Transport & Diving Service Division VIETSOVPETRO Vietnam Soviet Joint Venture Corp
\-
SatCom: Inmarsat C 457407810
Saigon *Vietnam*
MMSI: 574078068
Official number: VNSG-1235M-TK

1,276 / 383 / 1,050

Class: (NV) (VR)

1981-09 **Ulstein Hatlo AS — Ulsteinvik** (Aft section) Yd No: 172
1981-09 **Molde Verft AS — Hjelset** (Fwd section) Yd No: (172)
Loa 64.67 Br ex 14.13 Dght 4.719
Lbp 55.12 Br md 13.81 Dpth 6.91
Welded, 2 dks

(B21B20A) Anchor Handling Tug Supply
Grain: 170
Compartments: 4 Ta, ER

2 oil engines sr geared to sc. shafts driving 2 CP propellers
Total Power: 6,002kW (8,160hp) 16.0kn
Nohab F316V
2 x Vee 4 Stroke 16 Cy. 250 x 300 each-3001kW (4080bhp)
Nohab Diesel AB-Sweden
AuxGen: 2 x 664kW 230/440V 60Hz a.c, 2 x 245kW 230/440V 60Hz a.c
Thrusters: 1 Thwart. CP thruster (f)
Fuel: 794.0 (d.f.) 30.0pd

8017114 **SAO MAI 02**
XVSG *ex* Poronay *-1993*
\- **Marine Transport & Diving Service Division VIETSOVPETRO Vietnam Soviet Joint Venture Corp**
\-
SatCom: Inmarsat C 457410210
Saigon *Vietnam*
MMSI: 574102092
Official number: VNSG-1270N-TK

1,226 / 369 / 1,080

Class: VR (RS)

1981-05 **Ulstein Hatlo AS — Ulsteinvik** (Aft section) Yd No: 174
1981-05 **Molde Verft AS — Hjelset** (Fwd section) Yd No: (174)
Loa 64.39 Br ex 14.30 Dght 4.700
Lbp 56.39 Br md 13.80 Dpth 6.91
Welded, 2 dks

(B21A20S) Platform Supply Ship

2 oil engines reduction geared to sc. shafts driving 2 CP propellers
Total Power: 5,178kW (7,040hp) 13.0kn
Nohab F216V
2 x Vee 4 Stroke 16 Cy. 250 x 300 each-2589kW (3520bhp)
Nohab Diesel AB-Sweden
AuxGen: 2 x 640kW a.c, 2 x 245kW a.c

7601671 **SAO MAI 03**
3WJB *ex* Araks *-1993*
\- **Marine Transport & Diving Service Division VIETSOVPETRO Vietnam Soviet Joint Venture Corp**
\-
SatCom: Inmarsat C 457411910
Saigon *Vietnam*
MMSI: 574119109
Official number: VNSG-1247N-TK

1,226 / 369 / 1,190

Class: VR (RS)

1977-03 **Ulstein Hatlo AS — Ulsteinvik** Yd No: 145
Loa 64.39 Br ex 14.32 Dght 4.750
Lbp 56.39 Br md 13.80 Dpth 6.91
Welded, 1 dk

(B21B20A) Anchor Handling Tug Supply

2 oil engines reduction geared to sc. shafts driving 2 CP propellers
Total Power: 5,178kW (7,040hp) 13.0kn
Nohab F216V
2 x Vee 4 Stroke 16 Cy. 250 x 300 each-2589kW (3520bhp)
AB Bofors NOHAB-Sweden
AuxGen: 2 x 640kW a.c, 2 x 245kW a.c
Thrusters: 1 Thwart. FP thruster (f)

9329617 **SAO MAI 125**
3WHN
\- **Sao Mai Co Ltd (Cong Ty Trach Nhiem Huu Han Sao Mai)**
\-
SatCom: Inmarsat C 457472710
Haiphong *Vietnam*
MMSI: 574727000

498 / 287 / 899

Class: VR

2004-08 **Vinacoal Shipbuilding Co — Ha Long** Yd No: TKC-52-01
Loa 55.57 Br ex 9.02 Dght 3.300
Lbp 51.50 Br md 9.00 Dpth 4.10
Welded, 1 dk

(A31A2GX) General Cargo Ship

1 oil engine geared to sc. shaft driving 1 FP propeller
Total Power: 330kW (449hp) 9.5kn
Weifang X6170ZC
1 x 4 Stroke 6 Cy. 170 x 200 330kW (449bhp) (new engine 2006)
Weifang Diesel Engine Factory-China

8982292 **SAO MAI 126**
\- *ex* Long Thanh 36 *-2003*
\- **Agriculture Leasing Co I**
Sao Mai Co Ltd (Cong Ty Trach Nhiem Huu Han Sao Mai)
SatCom: Inmarsat C 457473710
Haiphong *Vietnam*
MMSI: 574737000
Official number: VN-1609-VT

499 / 339 / 932

Class: VR

2003 **Trung Hai Private Enterprise — Haiphong**
Loa 55.66 Br ex 9.02 Dght 3.320
Lbp 51.50 Br md 9.00 Dpth 4.10
Welded, 1 dk

(A31A2GX) General Cargo Ship

1 oil engine reduction geared to sc. shaft driving 1 FP propeller
Total Power: 330kW (449hp) 10.0kn
Weifang X6170ZC
1 x 4 Stroke 6 Cy. 170 x 200 330kW (449bhp) (new engine 2008)
Weifang Diesel Engine Factory-China

8998033 **SAO MAI 135**
XVMG *ex* Dai Phat 27 *-2006*
\- **Sao Mai Co Ltd (Cong Ty Trach Nhiem Huu Han Sao Mai)**
\-
SatCom: Inmarsat C 457474610
Haiphong *Vietnam*
MMSI: 574746000
Official number: VN-1827-VT

499 / 345 / 936

Class: VR

2004-06 **Haiphong Mechanical & Trading Co. — Haiphong**
Loa 55.20 Br ex 9.12 Dght 3.260
Lbp 51.50 Br md 9.10 Dpth 4.01
Welded, 1 dk

(A31A2GX) General Cargo Ship

1 oil engine driving 1 Propeller
Total Power: 405kW (551hp)
Niigata 6MGL16XC
1 x 4 Stroke 6 Cy. 250 x 320 405kW (551bhp)
Niigata Engineering Co Ltd-Japan

9023938 **SAO MAI 136**
\- *ex* Quang Vinh 07 *-2007*
\- **Sao Mai Co Ltd (Cong Ty Trach Nhiem Huu Han Sao Mai)**
\-
SatCom: Inmarsat C 457497310
Haiphong *Vietnam*
MMSI: 574999518
Official number: VN-1419-VT

499 / 274 / 1,046

Class: VR

2001-07 **Trung Hai Private Enterprise — Haiphong**
Loa 58.10 Br ex 9.02 Dght 3.600
Lbp 53.90 Br md 9.00 Dpth 4.40
Welded, 1 dk

(A31A2GX) General Cargo Ship

1 oil engine reduction geared to sc. shaft driving 1 FP propeller
Total Power: 330kW (449hp) 10.0kn
Weifang X6170ZC
1 x 4 Stroke 6 Cy. 170 x 200 330kW (449bhp) (new engine 2006)
Weifang Diesel Engine Factory-China

8867519 *3WAE* -	**SAO MAI 224** *ex* Huan Luyen 405 *-1994* *ex* Phu Hai 01 *-1992* **Sao Mai Co Ltd (Cong Ty Trach Nhiem Huu Han Sao Mai)** - *Haiphong* *Vietnam* MMSI: 574574000 Official number: VN-1096-VT	**243** 140 416	Class: (VR)	**1990 Kien An Shipbuilding Works — Haiphong** Deepened-2001 Lengthened-1997 Loa 40.46 Br ex 7.45 Dght 2.680 Lbp 37.56 Br md 7.23 Dpth 3.25 Welded, 1 dk	**(A31A2GX) General Cargo Ship** Grain: 424 Compartments: 2 Ho, ER 2 Ha: 2 (9.0 x 4.0)ER	**1 oil engine** driving 1 FP propeller Total Power: 160kW (218hp) 10.0kn S.K.L. 6NVD36-1U 1 x 4 Stroke 6 Cy. 240 x 360 160kW (218bhp) VEB Schwermaschinenbau "KarlLiebknecht" (SKL)-Magdeburg
9026033 - -	**SAO MAI 234** *ex* Hong Linh 10 *-2003* **Sao Mai Co Ltd (Cong Ty Trach Nhiem Huu Han Sao Mai)** - SatCom: Inmarsat C 457460610 *Haiphong* *Vietnam* MMSI: 574606000 Official number: VN-1728-VT	**499** 332 982	Class: VR	**2003-12 Thanh Long Co Ltd — Haiphong** Yd No: MH-16 Loa 57.20 Br ex 9.07 Dght 3.330 Lbp 53.10 Br md 9.05 Dpth 3.97 Welded, 1 dk	**(A31A2GX) General Cargo Ship**	**1 oil engine** driving 1 Propeller Total Power: 315kW (428hp) 9.0kn S.K.L. 6NVD36A-1U 1 x 4 Stroke 6 Cy. 240 x 360 315kW (428bhp) SKL Motoren u. Systemtechnik AG-Magdeburg
8036328 - -	**SAO MARCOS** *ex* Eleanor Eileen IX *-2003* **San Marco Inc** - *Boston, MA* *United States of America* Official number: 619891	*147* 100 -		**1980 St Augustine Trawlers, Inc. — Saint Augustine, Fl** L reg 20.85 Br ex 6.53 Dght - Lbp - Br md - Dpth 3.38 Welded, 1 dk	**(B11B2FV) Fishing Vessel**	**1 oil engine** driving 1 FP propeller Total Power: 482kW (655hp) Caterpillar D379SCAC 1 x Vee 4 Stroke 8 Cy. 159 x 203 482kW (655bhp) Caterpillar Tractor Co-USA
7940352 *WDE3910* -	**SAO MARCOS II** *ex* Luso American II *-2001* **Lucinda Fishing Corp** - *New Bedford, MA* *United States of America* Official number: 603986	*169* 115 -		**1979 Quality Marine, Inc. — Bayou La Batre, Al** Yd No: 99 L reg 24.85 Br ex 7.32 Dght - Lbp - Br md - Dpth 3.84 Welded, 1 dk	**(B11B2FV) Fishing Vessel**	**1 oil engine** driving 1 FP propeller Total Power: 401kW (545hp)
7234961 *CSJV* -	**SAO MIGUEL** **Administracao dos Portos das Ilhas de Sao Miguel e Santa Maria SA (ASPM)** - *Ponta Delgada* *Portugal* MMSI: 204600002	*437* - -	Class: LR ✠ **100A1** SS 05/2011 tug ✠ **LMC** Eq.Ltr: H; Cable: U2	**1973-04 Sorefame — Lobito** Yd No: 60 Loa 38.49 Br ex 10.42 Dght 5.252 Lbp 35.46 Br md 10.16 Dpth 6.05 Welded, 1 dk	**(B32A2ST) Tug**	**2 oil engines** sr geared to sc. shaft driving 1 CP propeller Total Power: 2,500kW (3,400hp) Allen 8S37-E 2 x 4 Stroke 8 Cy. 325 x 370 each-1250kW (1700bhp) W. H. Allen, Sons & Co. Ltd.-Bedford AuxGen: 2 x 150kW 400V 50Hz a.c
7731294 *WBA2263* -	**SAO PAULO** **Cura & Borges Fishing Corp** - *New Bedford, MA* *United States of America* MMSI: 366215330 Official number: 581723	*146* 108 -		**1977 Bender Welding & Machine Co Inc — Mobile AL** L reg 22.96 Br ex 6.71 Dght - Lbp - Br md - Dpth 3.38 Welded, 1 dk	**(B11B2FV) Fishing Vessel**	**1 oil engine** driving 1 FP propeller Total Power: 416kW (566hp)
8036689 *VMQ7172* O787	**SAO PEDRO** *ex* Uncle Pops *-1991* **Sao Pedro Fishing Pty Ltd** Mooloolaba Fisheries Pty Ltd SatCom: Inmarsat C 450301474 *Mooloolaba, Qld* *Australia* MMSI: 503586500 Official number: 856028	**176** 132 -		**1980 at Pascagoula, Ms** L reg 25.64 Br ex 7.24 Dght - Lbp - Br md - Dpth 3.51 Welded, 1 dk	**(B11B2FV) Fishing Vessel**	**1 oil engine** driving 1 FP propeller Total Power: 478kW (650hp)
9275622 *CUSR8* O-2152-C	**SAO PEDRO DO MAR** **Jose Ignacio & filhos Lda** - *Olhao* *Portugal*	*199* - -		**2003-04 Navalfoz - Com. E Desenvolvimento de Proj. Navais Lda. — Figueira da Foz** Yd No: 38 Loa 25.00 Br ex - Dght 2.890 Lbp 19.90 Br md 7.40 Dpth 3.40 Welded, 1 dk	**(B11A2FS) Stern Trawler**	**1 oil engine** geared to sc. shaft driving 1 FP propeller Total Power: 441kW (600hp) Mitsubishi S12N-MPT 1 x Vee 4 Stroke 12 Cy. 160 x 180 441kW (600bhp) Mitsubishi Heavy Industries Ltd-Japan
5313696 - -	**SAO RAFAEL** **Linmar Sea Corp Inc SA** Antonio Conde y Companhia Lda	*1,507* 745 1,444	Class: (LR) (RP) ✠ Classed LR until 28/2/98	**1959-03 Estaleiros Navais de Viana do Castelo S.A. — Viana do Castelo** Yd No: 46 Lengthened-1980 Loa 75.04 Br ex 11.08 Dght 5.011 Lbp 72.32 Br md 11.04 Dpth 5.69 Riveted\Welded, 2 dks	**(B11B2FV) Fishing Vessel** Ice Capable	**1 oil engine** driving 1 CP propeller Total Power: 1,986kW (2,700hp) 10.5kn Wichmann 9AXA 1 x 2 Stroke 9 Cy. 300 x 450 1986kW (2700bhp) (new engine ,made 1977, fitted 1980) Wichmann Motorfabrikk AS-Norway AuxGen: 3 x 320kW 380V 50Hz a.c, 1 x 64kW 380V 50Hz a.c Thrusters: 1 Thwart. CP thruster (f)
7505188 *PPVL* -	**SAO SEBASTIAO** **Navegacao Mansur SA** Posidonia Servicos Maritimos Ltda (Posidonia Shipping) SatCom: Inmarsat C 471001910 *Rio de Janeiro* *Brazil* MMSI: 710074008 Official number: 3810358355	**8,729** 6,785 15,786 T/cm 26.0	Class: (NV) (BV)	**1981-08 Industrias Reunidas Caneco SA — Rio de Janeiro** Yd No: 231 Loa 146.01 Br ex 21.24 Dght 8.873 Lbp 136.02 Br md 21.21 Dpth 11.82 Welded, 1 dk	**(A21A2BC) Bulk Carrier** Grain: 20,940; Bale: 18,873 Compartments: 4 Ho, ER 4 Ha: (13.0 x 9.9)3 (17.3 x 9.9)ER Cranes: 2x20t,4x10t	**1 oil engine** driving 1 FP propeller Total Power: 5,186kW (7,051hp) 15.9kn B&W 8K45GF 1 x 2 Stroke 8 Cy. 450 x 900 5186kW (7051bhp) Equipamentos Villares SA-Brazil AuxGen: 3 x 310kW 115/450V 50Hz a.c Fuel: 868.0 (d.f.)
9030278 *CUIY* LX-161-C	**SAO SEBASTIAO** **Costa E Franco Lda** - *Lisbon* *Portugal* MMSI: 204821000	*129* 42 86	Class: (BV)	**1991-04 Astilleros Armon SA — Navia** Yd No: 170 Loa 24.20 (BB) Br ex - Dght 3.060 Lbp 20.00 Br md 7.49 Dpth 3.50 Welded, 2 dks	**(B11B2FV) Fishing Vessel** Ins: 92	**1 oil engine** with flexible couplings & sr reverse geared to sc. shaft driving 1 FP propeller Total Power: 368kW (500hp) 10.0kn GUASCOR E318T-SP 1 x Vee 4 Stroke 12 Cy. 150 x 150 368kW (500bhp) Gutierrez Ascunce Corp (GUASCOR)-Spain AuxGen: 2 x 80kW 220/380V 50Hz a.c
9492127 *C6ZS8* -	**SAO SEBASTIAO** **Viken Shuttle AS** Petroleo Brasileiro SA (PETROBRAS) *Nassau* *Bahamas* MMSI: 311065200 Official number: 8002001	**62,753** 29,157 105,190	Class: AB NV	**2012-11 Samsung Heavy Industries Co Ltd — Geoje** Yd No: 1969 Loa 248.00 (BB) Br ex 42.03 Dght 15.100 Lbp 233.00 Br md 42.00 Dpth 22.50 Welded, 1 dk	**(A13A2TS) Shuttle Tanker** Double Hull (13F) Liq: 114,580; Liq (Oil): 116,450 Cargo Heating Coils Compartments: 12 Wing Ta, 2 Wing Slop Ta, ER 4 Cargo Pump (s): 4x3000m³/hr Manifold: Bow/CM: 126.3m	**1 oil engine** driving 1 CP propeller Total Power: 14,280kW (19,415hp) 14.6kn MAN-B&W 6S60ME-C8 1 x 2 Stroke 6 Cy. 600 x 2400 14280kW (19415bhp) Doosan Engine Co Ltd-South Korea AuxGen: 2 x 3000kW a.c, 2 x 4500kW a.c Thrusters: 1 Retract. directional thruster (f); 2 Tunnel thruster (f); 1 Retract. directional thruster (a); 1 Tunnel thruster (a) Fuel: 510.0 (d.f.) 2780.0 (r.f.)
9030307 *CUIW* -	**SAO TOME** **Costa E Franco Lda** - *Lisbon* *Portugal* MMSI: 204837000 Official number: PD-506-C	**129** 42 86	Class: (BV)	**1991-06 Astilleros Armon SA — Navia** Yd No: 173 Loa 24.20 (BB) Br ex - Dght 3.060 Lbp 20.00 Br md 7.49 Dpth 3.50 Welded, 2 dks	**(B11B2FV) Fishing Vessel** Ins: 92	**1 oil engine** sr reverse geared to sc. shaft driving 1 FP propeller Total Power: 368kW (500hp) 10.0kn GUASCOR E318T-SP 1 x Vee 4 Stroke 12 Cy. 150 x 150 368kW (500bhp) Gutierrez Ascunce Corp (GUASCOR)-Spain AuxGen: 2 x 80kW 220/380V 50Hz a.c
7625407 *HIRD558* -	**SAONA II** *ex* Jaro *-1990* **Remolcadores Dominicanos SA** - *Santo Domingo* *Dominican Rep.* MMSI: 327809000 Official number: R-0015SDG	*162* - 93	Class: (LR) ✠ Classed LR until 16/9/97	**1978-05 Scheepswerf Jac. den Breejen & Zoon B.V. — Hardinxveld-G.** (Hull) **1978-05 B.V. Scheepswerf Damen — Gorinchem** Yd No: 3101 Loa 26.42 Br ex 8.06 Dght 3.258 Lbp 22.92 Br md 7.80 Dpth 4.04 Welded, 1 dk	**(B32A2ST) Tug**	**2 oil engines** reverse reduction geared to sc. shafts driving 2 FP propellers Total Power: 1,678kW (2,282hp) Caterpillar D399SCAC 2 x Vee 4 Stroke 16 Cy. 159 x 203 each-839kW (1141bhp) Caterpillar Tractor Co-USA AuxGen: 2 x 85kW 400V 50Hz a.c
5280667 *WDC6583* -	**SAOOK BAY** *ex* Blue Star *-2011* *ex* Seattle Star *-2005* *ex* Austholm *-1980* *ex* Polar Tral *-1964* *ex* Pan Trades Andros *-1956* **Channel Construction Inc** - SatCom: Inmarsat A 1503334 *Hoonah, AK* *United States of America* Official number: 250464	*187* 120 -	Class: (NV)	**1946 John H. Mathis Co. — Camden, NJ** Yd No: 170 Lengthened-1957 Loa 40.59 Br ex 7.04 Dght - Lbp 38.87 Br md 7.01 Dpth 4.14 Welded, 1 dk	**(B11A2FT) Trawler** Compartments: 1 Ho, 3 Ta, ER 3 Ha: (0.9 x 0.9) (3.0 x 2.9) (3.6 x 2.9)	**1 oil engine** driving 1 FP propeller Total Power: 552kW (750hp) 11.0kn Wichmann 6ACA 1 x 2 Stroke 6 Cy. 280 x 420 552kW (750bhp) (made 1961, fitted 1965) Wichmann Motorfabrikk AS-Norway AuxGen: 1 x 25kW 110V d.c, 1 x 24kW 110V d.c

8860638 *UZFD* -	**SAOR-2** **Rybflot JSC (A/O 'Rybflot')** - *Sevastopol* *Ukraine* Official number: 910439	**104** 31 58	Class: (RS)	**1991-11 Azovskaya Sudoverf — Azov** Yd No: 1051 Loa 26.50 Br ex 6.59 Dght 2.360 Lbp 22.90 Br md - Dpth 3.05 Welded, 1 dk	**(B11A2FS) Stern Trawler** Ins: 48	**1 oil engine** geared to sc. shaft driving 1 FP propeller Total Power: 165kW (224hp) 9.3kn Daldizel 6CHNSP18/22 1 x 4 Stroke 6 Cy. 180 x 220 165kW (224bhp) (made 1991) Daldizel-Khabarovsk AuxGen: 2 x 30kW Fuel: 9.0 (d.f.)
8860640 - -	**SAOR-3** **Rybflot JSC (A/O 'Rybflot')** -	**104** 31 58	Class: (RS)	**1991-12 Azovskaya Sudoverf — Azov** Yd No: 1052 Loa 26.50 Br ex 6.59 Dght 2.360 Lbp 22.90 Br md - Dpth 3.05 Welded, 1 dk	**(B11A2FS) Stern Trawler** Ins: 48	**1 oil engine** geared to sc. shaft driving 1 FP propeller Total Power: 165kW (224hp) 9.3kn Daldizel 6CHNSP18/22 1 x 4 Stroke 6 Cy. 180 x 220 165kW (224bhp) (made 1991) Daldizel-Khabarovsk AuxGen: 2 x 30kW Fuel: 9.0 (d.f.)
8973136 *SWZF* -	**SAOS II** **Anonymos Naftiliaki Eteria Samothrakis SAOS (SAOS ANES)** SAOS ANES Kai Sia Koinopraxia (SAOS Ferries) *Piraeus* *Greece* MMSI: 237352400 Official number: 10599	**2,149** 1,364 913	Class: RS (HR)	**2001-07 Sithironaftiki Ltd. — Greece** Yd No: 01/1998 Loa 84.00 Br ex 14.42 Dght 4.020 Lbp 74.20 Br md 14.40 Dpth 6.00 Welded, 2 dks	**(A36A2PR) Passenger/Ro-Ro Ship (Vehicles)** Passengers: 500 Stern door/ramp (centre) Cars: 100	**2 oil engines** reduction geared to sc. shafts driving 2 Propellers Total Power: 6,402kW (8,704hp) 18.0kn Wartsila 16V200 2 x Vee 4 Stroke 16 Cy. 200 x 240 each-3201kW (4352bhp) Wartsila France SA-France AuxGen: 1 x 136kW 380V, 3 x 342kW 380V
7407738 *3WZO* -	**SAPA** *ex* Pan King *-1993* *ex* Constanza *-1990* *ex* Daysland IV *-1988* *ex* Action King *-1987* *ex* Active King *-1987* **Petroleum Technical Services Corp (PTSC) (Cong Ty Dich Vu Ky Thuat Dau Khi)** PTSC Marine Co Ltd SatCom: Inmarsat C 457407110 *Saigon* *Vietnam* MMSI: 574071061	**1,250** 375 1,169	Class: (NV)	**1975-11 AS Trondhjems Mekaniske Verksted — Trondheim** Yd No: 730 Loa 64.55 Br ex 13.82 Dght 4.719 Lbp 58.04 Br md 13.80 Dpth 6.91 Welded, 2 dks	**(B21B20A) Anchor Handling Tug Supply**	**2 oil engines** sr geared to sc. shafts driving 2 CP propellers Total Power: 5,178kW (7,040hp) 14.5kn Nohab F216V 2 x Vee 4 Stroke 16 Cy. 250 x 300 each-2589kW (3520bhp) AB Bofors NOHAB-Sweden AuxGen: 3 x 133kW 440V 60Hz a.c Thrusters: 1 Thwart. FP thruster (f) Fuel: 731.5 (d.f.) 26.5pd
7829508 *J8AQ3* -	**SAPADOR** *ex* Tunamar 112 *-2004* *ex* Hsiang Jang 112 *-2004* *ex* O Yang No. 108 *-1997* **Sacrosanct International Co Ltd** National Fisheries Co Ltd *Kingstown* *St Vincent & The Grenadines* MMSI: 375920000 Official number: 400374	**627** 255 510	Class: (KR)	**1978 Daedong Shipbuilding Co Ltd — Busan** Loa 55.17 Br ex - Dght - Lbp 49.00 Br md 8.60 Dpth 4.02 Welded, 1 dk	**(B11B2FV) Fishing Vessel** Ins: 550 3 Ha: 2 (1.3 x 0.9) (1.7 x 1.7)	**1 oil engine** driving 1 FP propeller Total Power: 956kW (1,300hp) 13.3kn Niigata 6L28X 1 x 4 Stroke 6 Cy. 280 x 440 956kW (1300bhp) Niigata Engineering Co Ltd-Japan AuxGen: 2 x 200kW 225V a.c
8820729 *3EHE7* -	**SAPAI** **Carlton Navigation SA** Unison Marine Corp *Panama* *Panama* MMSI: 353369000 Official number: 1845789E	**17,590** 10,303 28,860 T/cm 38.9	Class: NK	**1989-05 Shin Kurushima Dockyard Co. Ltd. — Onishi** Yd No: 2617 Loa 170.02 (BB) Br ex - Dght 10.101 Lbp 162.50 Br md 26.50 Dpth 14.20 Welded, 1 dk	**(A31A2GX) General Cargo Ship** Grain: 37,342; Bale: 36,932 Compartments: 5 Ho, ER 5 Ha: (10.1 x 12.3)2 (25.2 x 21.5) (13.3 x 21.5) (21.0 x 21.5)ER Cranes: 4x30.4t	**1 oil engine** driving 1 FP propeller Total Power: 5,665kW (7,702hp) 14.0kn Mitsubishi 5UEC52LS 1 x 2 Stroke 5 Cy. 520 x 1850 5665kW (7702bhp) Kobe Hatsudoki KK-Japan AuxGen: 3 x 400kW a.c Fuel: 224.4 (d.f.) 720.0 (r.f.) 19.7pd
8866395 *EZAW* -	**SAPARMURAT NIYAZOV** **The Turkmen Marine Merchant Fleet Authority** - *Turkmenbashy* *Turkmenistan* MMSI: 434111300 Official number: 922633	**3,086** 925 3,152 T/cm 12.0	Class: (RS)	**1992-07 Slovenske Lodenice a.s. — Komarno** Yd No: 2343 Loa 116.00 Br ex 13.43 Dght 4.000 Lbp 111.20 Br md 13.00 Dpth 6.00 Welded, 1 dk	**(A31A2GX) General Cargo Ship** Grain: 4,064 TEU 102 C.Ho 62/20' (40') C.Dk 40/20' (40') Compartments: 3 Ho, ER 3 Ha: (11.6 x 10.1) (23.0 x 10.1) (24.0 x 10.1)ER	**2 oil engines** driving 2 FP propellers Total Power: 1,030kW (1,400hp) 10.0kn Skoda 6L275A2 2 x 4 Stroke 6 Cy. 275 x 350 each-515kW (700bhp) CKD Praha-Praha
8664412 *MNGH8* -	**SAPELE** **Crown River Cruises Ltd** - *London* *United Kingdom* Official number: 912135	**217** 65 -		**2006 P H Tinnemans & Zn BV — Maasbracht** L reg 31.90 Br ex - Dght - Lbp - Br md 7.00 Dpth - Welded, 1 dk	**(A37B2PS) Passenger Ship**	**2 oil engines** reduction geared to sc. shafts driving 2 Propellers
8852186 - -	**SAPELE SHORE** *ex* Salipa *-1997* *ex* Durango Service *-1997* - -	*300* 203 -		**1978 Burton Shipyard Co., Inc. — Port Arthur, Tx** Yd No: 533 L reg 53.68 Br ex - Dght - Lbp - Br md 12.20 Dpth 5.20 Welded, 1 dk	**(B21A20S) Platform Supply Ship**	**3 oil engines** driving 3 FP propellers Total Power: 2,427kW (3,300hp) 14.0kn Caterpillar 3 x 4 Stroke each-809kW (1100bhp) Caterpillar Tractor Co-USA
7739492 - -	**SAPELO GAL** **Jack D'Antignac** - *Galveston, TX* *United States of America* Official number: 589673	*127* 87 -		**1977 Desco Marine — Saint Augustine, Fl** L reg 20.97 Br ex 6.74 Dght - Lbp - Br md - Dpth 3.79 Bonded, 1 dk	**(B11A2FT) Trawler** Hull Material: Reinforced Plastic	**1 oil engine** driving 1 FP propeller Total Power: 268kW (364hp) Caterpillar 1 x 4 Stroke 268kW (364bhp) Caterpillar Tractor Co-USA
8728531 *EMMO* -	**SAPFIR** **State Enterprise 'Marine Rescue Service' (SE MARS)** - *Odessa* *Ukraine* MMSI: 272256000 Official number: 872330	**1,178** 353 391	Class: (RS)	**1988-06 Yaroslavskiy Sudostroitelnyy Zavod — Yaroslavl** Yd No: 232 Loa 58.55 Br ex 12.67 Dght 4.760 Lbp 51.60 Br md - Dpth 5.90 Welded, 1 dk	**(B32A2ST) Tug** Ice Capable	**2 diesel electric oil engines** driving 2 gen. each 1100kW Connecting to 1 elec. Motor of (1900kW) driving 1 FP propeller Total Power: 2,200kW (2,992hp) 13.5kn Kolomna 6CHN1A30/38 2 x 4 Stroke 6 Cy. 300 x 380 each-1100kW (1496bhp) Kolomenskiy Zavod-Kolomna AuxGen: 2 x 300kW, 2 x 160kW Fuel: 331.0 (d.f.)
7928213 *UFCZ* -	**SAPFIR-1** *ex* Atlantic *-1999* *ex* Ocean Sun *-1997* *ex* Anso Molgaard *-1994* **OOO 'Promflot'** - *Nevelsk* *Russia* MMSI: 273433540	**863** 271 463	Class: RS (NV)	**1984-09 Orskov Christensens Staalskibsvaerft A/S — Frederikshavn** Yd No: 107 Loa 51.09 Br ex 9.50 Dght 4.250 Lbp 46.26 Br md 9.50 Dpth 6.56 Welded, 2 dks	**(B11A2FT) Trawler** Ins: 680 Ice Capable	**1 oil engine** with flexible couplings & sr gearedto sc. shaft driving 1 CP propeller Total Power: 1,324kW (1,800hp) Alpha 6L28/32 1 x 4 Stroke 6 Cy. 280 x 320 1324kW (1800bhp) B&W Alpha Diesel A/S-Denmark AuxGen: 3 x 242kW 380V 50Hz a.c Fuel: 171.5 (d.f.)
8139039 *UBOZ* -	**SAPFIROVYY** **Almaztranstroy Co Ltd** Diamond East Co Ltd *Petropavlovsk-Kamchatskiy* *Russia* MMSI: 273815040	*677* 233 487	Class: (RS)	**1983-07 Khabarovskiy Sudostroitelnyy Zavod im Kirova — Khabarovsk** Yd No: 843 Loa 55.02 Br ex 9.52 Dght 4.340 Lbp 50.66 Br md 9.30 Dpth 5.19 Welded	**(B12B2FC) Fish Carrier** Ins: 632 Ice Capable	**1 oil engine** driving 1 FP propeller Total Power: 588kW (799hp) 11.3kn S.K.L. 6NVD48A-2U 1 x 4 Stroke 6 Cy. 320 x 480 588kW (799bhp) VEB Schwermaschinenbau "KarlLiebknecht" (SKL)-Magdeburg AuxGen: 3 x 150kW Fuel: 114.0 (d.f.)
9045235 *3FRU3* -	**SAPHINA** *ex* Meridian Vega *-2008* **Saphina Tankers SA** Accord Marine Management Pvt Ltd SatCom: Inmarsat C 437087710 *Panama* *Panama* MMSI: 370877000 Official number: 4051909	**3,885** 2,366 6,500 T/cm 14.7	Class: BV	**1992-10 Malaysia Shipyard & Engineering Sdn Bhd — Pasir Gudang** Yd No: 052 Loa 104.30 Br ex 16.80 Dght 6.680 Lbp 98.70 Br md - Dpth 8.30 Welded, 1 dk	**(A13B2TP) Products Tanker** Single Hull Liq: 8,397; Liq (Oil): 8,397 Compartments: 6 Ta, ER 2 Cargo Pump (s): 2x375m³/hr	**1 oil engine** geared to sc. shaft driving 1 FP propeller Total Power: 2,648kW (3,600hp) 11.5kn Blackstone ESL16MK2 1 x Vee 4 Stroke 16 Cy. 222 x 292 2648kW (3600bhp) Mirrlees Blackstone Ltd-Dursley
9469871 *SVAC9* -	**SAPIENTZA** **Aquanova Shipholding Co** Minerva Marine Inc SatCom: Inmarsat C 424079410 *Piraeus* *Greece* MMSI: 240794000 Official number: 11822	**91,373** 58,745 177,736 T/cm 120.6	Class: AB	**2008-11 Shanghai Jiangnan Changxing Shipbuilding Co Ltd — Shanghai** Yd No: 1141 Loa 291.97 (BB) Br ex - Dght 18.300 Lbp 282.00 Br md 45.00 Dpth 24.80 Welded, 1 dk	**(A21A2BC) Bulk Carrier** Grain: 194,486; Bale: 183,425 Compartments: 9 Ho, ER 9 Ha: ER	**1 oil engine** driving 1 FP propeller Total Power: 16,680kW (22,678hp) 14.0kn MAN-B&W 6S70MC 1 x 2 Stroke 6 Cy. 700 x 2674 16680kW (22678bhp) Hudong Heavy Machinery Co Ltd-China AuxGen: 3 x 900kW a.c Fuel: 331.0 (d.f.) 2346.0 (r.f.)

9622007 *VRMY8* -	**SAPPHIRE** *ex* Seaviolet *-2014* **Sapphire Shipping Co Ltd** Univan Ship Management Ltd *Hong Kong* *Hong Kong* MMSI: 477776900 Official number: HK-4015	**47,873** - 59,366	Class: GL	**2014-01 Zhejiang Ouhua Shipbuilding Co Ltd — Zhoushan ZJ** Yd No: 648 Loa 249.93 (BB) Br ex - Dght 12.500 Lbp 238.28 Br md 37.29 Dpth 19.60 Welded, 1 dk	**(A33A2CC) Container Ship (Fully Cellular)** TEU 4834 C Ho 1778 TEU Dk 3056 TEU C incl 600 ref C	**1 oil engine** driving 1 FP propeller Total Power: 27,060kW (36,791hp) 21.0kn MAN-B&W 6S80ME-C9 1 x 2 Stroke 6 Cy. 800 x 3450 27060kW (36791bhp) AuxGen: 4 x 1672kW 450V 60Hz a.c Thrusters: 1 Tunnel thruster (f) Fuel: 300.0 (d.f.) 4000.0 (r.f.)
9560778 *ZCYG5* -	**SAPPHIRE** - **Newill Co Inc** Thetis Shipholding SA SatCom: Inmarsat C 431915181 *The Creek* *Cayman Islands (British)* MMSI: 319023400 Official number: 741394	**1,591** 414 230	Class: GL	**2011-02 Nobiskrug GmbH — Rendsburg** Yd No: 781 Loa 73.51 Br ex 12.60 Dght 3.650 Lbp 58.85 Br md 12.00 Dpth 6.90 Welded, 1 dk	**(X11A2YP) Yacht**	**2 oil engines** reverse reduction geared to sc. shafts driving 2 FP propellers Total Power: 3,520kW (4,786hp) 14.5kn M.T.U. 16V4000M60 2 x Vee 4 Stroke 16 Cy. 165 x 190 each-1760kW (2393bhp) MTU Friedrichshafen GmbH-Friedrichshafen AuxGen: 2 x 292kW 400V a.c Thrusters: 1 Tunnel thruster (f)
9563914 *V7DB5* -	**SAPPHIRE** *ex* Red Sapphire *-2013* **SMP Sapphire Ltd** - *Bikini* *Marshall Islands* MMSI: 538070969 Official number: 70969	**478** 143 136	Class: AB	**2009-11 Trinity Yachts LLC — New Orleans LA** Yd No: 054 Loa 50.29 Br ex 8.53 Dght 2.590 Lbp - Br md 8.48 Dpth 4.21 Welded, 1 dk	**(X11A2YP) Yacht** Hull Material: Aluminium Alloy	**2 oil engines** reduction geared to sc. shafts driving 2 Propellers Total Power: 5,370kW (7,302hp) M.T.U. 16V4000M90 2 x Vee 4 Stroke 16 Cy. 165 x 190 each-2685kW (3651bhp) MTU Friedrichshafen GmbH-Friedrichshafen
9253959 *9V6215* -	**SAPPHIRE** - **PSA Marine Pte Ltd** - *Singapore* *Singapore* MMSI: 563003460 Official number: 389797	**246** 73 166	Class: LR (AB) **100A1** SS 05/2012 TOC contemplated	**2002-05 Keppel Singmarine Pte Ltd — Singapore** Yd No: 241 Loa 26.33 Br ex - Dght 3.750 Lbp 22.50 Br md 9.00 Dpth 4.70 Welded, 1 dk	**(B32A2ST) Tug**	**2 oil engines** driving 2 Directional propellers Total Power: 2,354kW (3,200hp) Yanmar 8N21A-EN 2 x 4 Stroke 8 Cy. 210 x 290 each-1177kW (1600bhp) Yanmar Diesel Engine Co Ltd-Japan
9189861 *V7XH5* -	**SAPPHIRE** *ex* Kavo Sapphire *-2011* **Sapphire Maritime Corp** AM Nomikos Transworld Maritime Agencies SA *Majuro* *Marshall Islands* MMSI: 538004482 Official number: 4482	**38,799** 25,382 75,574 T/cm 66.6	Class: AB	**1999-09 Sanoyas Hishino Meisho Corp — Kurashiki OY** Yd No: 1173 Loa 225.00 (BB) Br ex - Dght 13.997 Lbp 217.00 Br md 32.26 Dpth 19.30 Welded, 1 dk	**(A21A2BC) Bulk Carrier** Double Bottom Entire Compartment Length Grain: 89,250 Compartments: 7 Ho, ER 7 Ha: (16.2 x 13.4)Tappered 6 (17.1 x 15.0)ER	**1 oil engine** driving 1 FP propeller Total Power: 9,342kW (12,701hp) 14.0kn Sulzer 7RTA48T 1 x 2 Stroke 7 Cy. 480 x 2000 9342kW (12701bhp) Diesel United Ltd.-Aioi AuxGen: 3 x 500kW 450V 60Hz a.c Fuel: 146.6 (d.f.) 2751.8 (r.f.) 33.0pd
9114969 *IBOV* -	**SAPPHIRE** *ex* Ocean Pride *-2008* *ex* Sapphire *-2004* **Finbeta SpA** - SatCom: Inmarsat B 323446310 *Ancona* *Italy* MMSI: 247698000	**9,914** 4,599 14,002 T/cm 25.5	Class: RI (LR) (BV) ✠ Classed LR until 1/9/99	**1997-02 Cant. Nav. Mario Morini S.p.A. — Ancona** Yd No: 253 Loa 142.50 (BB) Br ex 22.03 Dght 8.400 Lbp 132.00 Br md 22.00 Dpth 11.00 Welded, 1 dk	**(A12B2TR) Chemical/Products Tanker** Double Hull (13F) Liq: 15,324; Liq (Oil): 15,708 Cargo Heating Coils Compartments: 8 Ta (s.stl), 16 Wing Ta (s.stl), ER (s.stl) 24 Cargo Pump (s): 18x250m³/hr, 6x150m³/hr Manifold: Bow/CM: 72.5m Ice Capable	**1 oil engine** with clutches, flexible couplings & sr geared to sc. shaft driving 1 CP propeller Total Power: 5,939kW (8,075hp) 14.0kn Stork-Wartsila 9SW38 1 x 4 Stroke 9 Cy. 380 x 475 5939kW (8075bhp) Stork Wartsila Diesel BV-Netherlands AuxGen: 1 x 1200kW 450V 60Hz a.c, 3 x 740kW 450V 60Hz a.c Thrusters: 1 Thwart. FP thruster (f) Fuel: 140.0 (d.f.) (Heating Coils) 1105.0 (r.f.) 23.0pd
8871338 *UEAS* -	**SAPPHIRE** *ex* Sapfir *-2008* *ex* Sapphire *-2003* *ex* Sun Light *-2003* *ex* Ulan-Ude *-2001* *ex* Omskiy-119 *-1996* **Delta Streamline Ltd** Blue Wave Shipping Inc *Taganrog* *Russia* MMSI: 273449370	**2,879** 1,358 3,734	Class: RS (RR)	**1984 Santierul Naval Oltenita S.A. — Oltenita** Yd No: 249 Loa 108.36 Br ex 15.00 Dght 3.620 Lbp 105.00 Br md 14.80 Dpth 5.00 Welded, 1 dk	**(A31A2GX) General Cargo Ship** Ice Capable	**2 oil engines** driving 2 FP propellers Total Power: 1,472kW (2,002hp) 10.0kn S.K.L. 6NVD48A-2U 2 x 4 Stroke 6 Cy. 320 x 480 each-736kW (1001bhp) VEB Schwermaschinenbau "KarlLiebknecht" (SKL)-Magdeburg Fuel: 70.0 (d.f.)
8878051 *HP8139* -	**SAPPHIRE** *ex* South Wind II *-1995* *ex* Cricket *-1994* **Emerson Shipholding Inc** - *Panama* *Panama* Official number: 24018PEXT1	*283* 82 -	Class: (LR) ✠	**1970-03 Charles D. Holmes & Co. Ltd. — Beverley** Yd No: 1018 Loa 34.01 Br ex - Dght - Lbp - Br md 8.53 Dpth 2.44 Welded, 1 dk	**(B34R2QY) Supply Tender**	**1 oil engine** geared to sc. shaft driving 1 FP propeller Total Power: 485kW (659hp) 12.0kn Blackstone ERS8M 1 x 4 Stroke 8 Cy. 222 x 292 485kW (659bhp) Lister Blackstone Marine Ltd.-Dursley
8949367 *V3AU2* -	**SAPPHIRE** *ex* Newton *-2005* *ex* Seacountess *-2004* *ex* Kapitan Vasilyev *-1999* *ex* Volgo-Don 5027 *-1999* **Sapphire Maritime Co Ltd** LLC 'Shipping Agency Yug Rusi' *Belize City* *Belize* MMSI: 312814000 Official number: 140520148	**5,096** 2,728 5,230	Class: RS (RR)	**1971-01 Santierul Naval Oltenita S.A. — Oltenita** Yd No: 457 Loa 138.50 Br ex 16.70 Dght 3.520 Lbp 135.00 Br md 16.50 Dpth 5.50 Welded, 1 dk	**(A31A2GX) General Cargo Ship** Grain: 6,400 Compartments: 2 Ho, ER 2 Ha: (44.1 x 13.6) (45.1 x 13.6)ER Ice Capable	**2 oil engines** driving 2 FP propellers Total Power: 1,324kW (1,800hp) 10.8kn Dvigatel Revolyutsii 6CHRNP36/45 2 x 4 Stroke 6 Cy. 360 x 450 each-662kW (900bhp) Zavod "Dvigatel Revolyutsii"-Gorkiy AuxGen: 2 x 100kW a.c, 1 x 50kW a.c Fuel: 162.0 (d.f.)
8314249 - -	**SAPPHIRE** - **Sapphire Fisheries Pvt Ltd** - *Visakhapatnam* *India* Official number: 2067	**110** 33 44	Class: (LR) (IR) ✠ Classed LR until 25/7/86	**1985-03 B.V. Scheepswerf "De Hoop" — Hardinxveld-Giessendam** Yd No: 781 Loa 23.68 Br ex 6.58 Dght 2.909 Lbp 21.24 Br md 6.51 Dpth 3.43 Welded, 1 dk	**(B11A2FT) Trawler** Ins: 70	**1 oil engine** with clutches, flexible couplings & sr reverse geared to sc. shaft driving 1 FP propeller Total Power: 405kW (551hp) 9.5kn Caterpillar 3408TA 1 x Vee 4 Stroke 8 Cy. 137 x 152 405kW (551bhp) Caterpillar Tractor Co-USA AuxGen: 2 x 26kW 380V 50Hz a.c Fuel: 38.5 (d.f.)
7639288 *YFZP* -	**SAPPHIRE** *ex* Ryuyo Maru No. 3 *-1992* **PT Pelayaran Tahta Bahtera** - *Jakarta* *Indonesia*	*983* 592 2,000	Class: (KI)	**1977-02 Omishima Dock K.K. — Imabari** Yd No: 1057 Loa 68.80 Br ex 11.02 Dght - Lbp 65.21 Br md 11.00 Dpth 5.00 Welded, 1 dk	**(A13B2TP) Products Tanker**	**1 oil engine** driving 1 FP propeller Total Power: 1,324kW (1,800hp) Akasaka DM36 1 x 4 Stroke 6 Cy. 360 x 540 1324kW (1800bhp) Akasaka Tekkosho KK (Akasaka DieselLtd)-Japan
9179294 *JI3654* -	**SAPPHIRE 1** *ex* Aoki Maru No. 35 *-2012* **Aoki Marine Co Ltd** - *Kobe, Hyogo* *Japan* Official number: 135951	*142* - -		**1998-04 Hamamoto Zosensho K.K. — Tokushima** Yd No: 818 Loa 30.50 Br ex - Dght - Lbp 28.00 Br md 9.00 Dpth 4.94 Welded, 1 dk	**(B32A2ST) Tug**	**2 oil engines** geared to sc. shafts driving 2 FP propellers Total Power: 2,206kW (3,000hp) 12.2kn Daihatsu 6DLM-26S 2 x 4 Stroke 6 Cy. 260 x 340 each-1103kW (1500bhp) Daihatsu Diesel Manufacturing Co Lt-Japan
9051806 *3FUX3* -	**SAPPHIRE ACE** - **Polar Express SA** Seiwa Navigation Corp Ltd SatCom: Inmarsat A 1341637 *Panama* *Panama* MMSI: 352713000 Official number: 2116094E	**45,796** 13,739 15,204	Class: NK	**1993-12 Minaminippon Shipbuilding Co Ltd — Usuki OT** Yd No: 626 Loa 188.00 (BB) Br ex - Dght 9.020 Lbp 178.00 Br md 31.20 Dpth 11.80 Welded, 1 dk	**(A35B2RV) Vehicles Carrier** Side door/ramp1 (p) 1 (s) Len: - Wid: - Swl: 20 Quarter stern door/ramp (s. a.) Len: - Wid: - Swl: 150 Cars: 4,055	**1 oil engine** driving 1 FP propeller Total Power: 11,475kW (15,601hp) 18.5kn B&W 6L60MC 1 x 2 Stroke 6 Cy. 600 x 1944 11475kW (15601bhp) Mitsui Engineering & Shipbuilding CLtd-Japan AuxGen: 3 x 820kW a.c Thrusters: 1 Tunnel thruster (f) Fuel: 3580.0 (r.f.)
9380075 *H3HS* -	**SAPPHIRE EXPRESS** - **Interasia Shipping (Panama) SA** Executive Ship Management Pte Ltd SatCom: Inmarsat C 437074010 *Panama* *Panama* MMSI: 370740000 Official number: 4051709A	**26,900** 13,660 47,402 T/cm 50.3	Class: NK	**2009-06 Onomichi Dockyard Co Ltd — Onomichi HS** Yd No: 542 Loa 182.50 (BB) Br ex 32.23 Dght 12.617 Lbp 172.00 Br md 32.20 Dpth 18.10 Welded, 1 dk	**(A13B2TP) Products Tanker** Double Hull (13F) Liq: 50,560; Liq (Oil): 50,560 Cargo Heating Coils Compartments: 12 Wing Ta, 2 Wing Slop Ta, ER 4 Cargo Pump (s): 4x1000m³/hr Manifold: Bow/CM: 93.1m	**1 oil engine** driving 1 FP propeller Total Power: 8,580kW (11,665hp) 14.0kn MAN-B&W 6S50MC 1 x 2 Stroke 6 Cy. 500 x 1910 8580kW (11665bhp) Mitsui Engineering & Shipbuilding CLtd-Japan AuxGen: 3 x Fuel: 105.0 (d.f.) 1450.0 (r.f.)

IMO / Call sign	Ship name, former names, owner, manager, port, flag	Tonnage	Class	Build & dimensions	Type & cargo	Machinery
8810188 *HONF* -	**SAPPHIRE I** *ex* Gaz Atmosphere *-2013* *ex* Sigloo Crystal *-2012* *ex* Polar Belgica *-2006* *ex* Eurogas Terza *-1995* *ex* Polar Belgica *-1995* *ex* Eurogas Terza *-1993* **Palermo Maritime Co** Fareast Shipmanagement HongKong Ltd SatCom: Inmarsat C 437353310 *Panama* *Panama* MMSI: 373533000 Official number: 42926PEXT2	**7,949** 3,144 12,240 T/cm 21.9	Class: BV (LR) (RI) ✠ Classed LR until 1/2/12	**1992**-01 **Cantieri Navali Benetti Gecan SpA — Viareggio** Yd No: 133 Loa 131.35 (BB) Br ex 20.04 Dght 9.400 Lbp 121.13 Br md 20.00 Dpth 12.40 Welded, 1 dk	**(A11B2TH) LPG/Chemical Tanker** Double Bottom Entire Compartment Length Liq: 10,293; Liq (Gas): 10,503 Compartments: 8 Wing Ta, ER, 1 Slop Ta 4 x Gas Tank (s); 4 independent (s.stl) dcy horizontal 8 Cargo Pump (s): 8x150m³/hr Manifold: Bow/CM: 72m Ice Capable	**1 oil engine** driving 1 FP propeller Total Power: 5,594kW (7,606hp) 16.0kn B&W 5L50MC 1 x 2 Stroke 5 Cy. 500 x 1620 5594kW (7606bhp) Hyundai Heavy Industries Co Ltd-South Korea AuxGen: 3 x 990kW 440V 60Hz a.c Boilers: 2 AuxB (o.f.) 8.2kgf/cm² (8.0bar) Fuel: 261.0 (d.f.) 646.0 (r.f.)
8702680 *UDHT* -	**SAPPHIRE II** *ex* Havstrand *-2013* **Kalinin Fishing Collective Farm (Rybolovetskiy Kolkhoz imeni Kalinina)** *Murmansk* *Russia* MMSI: 273355290	**2,071** 711 862	Class: RS (NV)	**1987**-12 **FEAB-Marstrandverken — Marstrand** (Hull) Yd No: 179 **1987**-12 **Brattvag Skipsinnredning AS — Brattvaag** Yd No: 47 Loa 65.51 Br ex 13.02 Dght 5.720 Lbp 57.21 Br md 13.00 Dpth 8.32 Welded, 3 dks	**(B11A2FS) Stern Trawler** Ins: 993 Ice Capable	**1 oil engine** geared to sc. shaft driving 1 CP propeller Total Power: 2,638kW (3,587hp) 15.5kn Wichmann 8V28B 1 x Vee 4 Stroke 8 Cy. 280 x 360 2638kW (3587bhp) Wartsila Wichmann Diesel AS-Norway AuxGen: 1 x 1408kW 440V 60Hz a.c, 1 x 480kW 440V 60Hz a.c, 1 x 160kW 440V 60Hz a.c Thrusters: 1 Thwart. FP thruster (f)
8863173 *WDA5693* -	**SAPPHIRE II** *ex* Purple March *-2005* *ex* Sun Flower 1 *-1998* **H-N Fishery Inc** - *Honolulu, HI* *United States of America* Official number: 926208	*123* 98 -		**1987 Dam Tien Corp. — New Orleans, La** Loa - Br ex - Dght - Lbp 23.16 Br md 6.71 Dpth 3.35 Welded, 1 dk	**(B11B2FV) Fishing Vessel**	**1 oil engine** driving 1 FP propeller
8605569 *VVTL* -	**SAPPHIRE II** - **Sapphire Fisheries Pvt Ltd** - *Visakhapatnam* *India* Official number: 2268	**121** 36 47	Class: (IR)	**1989**-12 **Hooghly Dock & Port Engineers Ltd. — Haora** Yd No: 446 Loa 23.42 Br ex 6.49 Dght 2.650 Lbp 21.02 Br md 6.48 Dpth 3.43 Welded, 1 dk	**(B11A2FS) Stern Trawler** Ins: 80	**1 oil engine** with clutches, flexible couplings & sr geared to sc. shaft driving 1 FP propeller Total Power: 296kW (402hp) Caterpillar 3408TA 1 x Vee 4 Stroke 8 Cy. 137 x 152 296kW (402bhp) Caterpillar Inc-USA
8026335 *2GFM7* -	**SAPPHIRE II** *ex* Marijke *-2014* - - *United Kingdom* MMSI: 235096987	**180** 54 -		**1981**-12 **T. van den Beldt Thz., Scheeps. "Voorwaarts" — West-Graftdijk** Yd No: 469 Loa 26.50 Br ex - Dght 2.930 Lbp 23.34 Br md 7.50 Dpth 3.91 Welded, 1 dk	**(B11B2FV) Fishing Vessel**	**1 oil engine** geared to sc. shaft driving 1 FP propeller Total Power: 588kW (799hp) Kromhout 6FEHD240 1 x 4 Stroke 6 Cy. 240 x 260 588kW (799bhp) Stork Werkspoor Diesel BV-Netherlands
8847870 *WDG2008* -	**SAPPHIRE III** *ex* Capt. Millions IV *-2011* **H-N Fishery Inc** - *Honolulu, HI* *United States of America* MMSI: 367086450 Official number: 964929	*120* 36 -		**1990 Russell Portier, Inc. — Chauvin, La** Loa - Br ex - Dght - Lbp 25.39 Br md 7.47 Dpth 3.32 Welded, 1 dk	**(B11B2FV) Fishing Vessel**	**1 oil engine** driving 1 FP propeller
9539468 *3FGF3* -	**SAPPHIRE ISLAND** - **Aries Marine SA** Kobe Shipmanagement Co Ltd SatCom: Inmarsat C 437319910 *Panama* *Panama* MMSI: 373199000 Official number: 4383712	**21,213** 11,615 33,664	Class: NK	**2012**-04 **Shin Kurushima Dockyard Co. Ltd. — Onishi** Yd No: 5728 Loa 179.99 (BB) Br ex - Dght 10.101 Lbp 172.00 Br md 28.20 Dpth 14.30 Welded, 1 dk	**(A21A2BC) Bulk Carrier** Double Hull Grain: 44,038; Bale: 43,164 Compartments: 5 Ho, ER 5 Ha: 3 (20.8 x 23.8) (19.2 x 23.8)ER (16.8 x 17.2) Cranes: 4x30t	**1 oil engine** driving 1 FP propeller Total Power: 6,250kW (8,498hp) 14.2kn Mitsubishi 6UEC45LSE 1 x 2 Stroke 6 Cy. 450 x 1840 6250kW (8498bhp) Kobe Hatsudoki KK-Japan Fuel: 1620.0
9228186 *ZCDG7* -	**SAPPHIRE PRINCESS** *launched as* Diamond Princess *-2004* **Fairline Shipping International Corp Ltd** Princess Cruise Lines Ltd *Hamilton* *Bermuda (British)* MMSI: 310405000	**115,875** 77,745 14,601	Class: LR ✠ **100A1** CS 05/2009 passenger ship *IWS ✠ **LMC** **CCS** Eq.Ltr: A*; Cable: 742.5/111.0 U3 (a)	**2004**-05 **Mitsubishi Heavy Industries Ltd. — Nagasaki** Yd No: 2180 Loa 290.00 (BB) Br ex 37.75 Dght 8.550 Lbp 246.00 Br md 37.50 Dpth 41.30 Welded, 15 dks	**(A37A2PC) Passenger/Cruise** Passengers: cabins: 1339; berths: 3100	**4 diesel electric oil engines & 1 turbo electric Gas Turb** driving 2 gen. each 9150kW 11000V a.c 2 gen. each 8150kW 11000V a.c 1 gen. of 25000kW 11000V Connecting to 2 elec. motors each (20000kW) driving 2 Azimuth electric drive units Total Power: 60,700kW (82,528hp) 23.0kn Wartsila 8L46C 2 x 4 Stroke 8 Cy. 460 x 580 each-8400kW (11421bhp) Wartsila Finland Oy-Finland Wartsila 9L46C 2 x 4 Stroke 9 Cy. 460 x 580 each-9450kW (12848bhp) Wartsila Finland Oy-Finland GE Marine LM2500+ 1 x Gas Turb 25000kW (33990shp) GE Marine Engines-Cincinnati, Oh Boilers: e (ex.g.) 11.5kgf/cm² (11.3bar), e (ex.g.) 14.7kgf/cm² (14.4bar), AuxB (ex.g.) 10.4kgf/cm² (10.2bar), WTAuxB (o.f.) 10.4kgf/cm² (10.2bar) Thrusters: 3 Thwart. CP thruster (f); 3 Thwart. CP thruster (a)
8967668 *WDC6671* -	**SAPPHIRE PRINCESS** *ex* Blue Heaven Two *-2009* *ex* Lady Sarasota *-2005* *ex* Island Girl XIV *-2005* **Sapphire Princess Charters Inc** *Wilmington, DE* *United States of America* MMSI: 303466000 Official number: 1115416	**185** 65 -		**2001 SkipperLiner, Inc. — La Crosse, Wi** Yd No: 989 Loa 29.26 Br ex - Dght - Lbp - Br md 6.00 Dpth 1.82 Welded, 1 dk	**(A37B2PS) Passenger Ship** Passengers: unberthed: 149	**2 oil engines** driving 2 FP propellers Total Power: 464kW (630hp) Caterpillar 3208TA 2 x Vee 4 Stroke 8 Cy. 114 x 127 each-232kW (315bhp) Caterpillar Inc-USA AuxGen: 1 x 70kW a.c
9301146 *A8NJ5* -	**SAPPHIRE SEAS** *ex* Filia Gem *-2007* *ex* Kandy *-2005* **Protea International Inc** Allseas Marine SA *Monrovia* *Liberia* MMSI: 636013497 Official number: 13497	**31,144** 18,346 53,702	Class: GL (LR) ✠ Classed LR until 30/5/06	**2005**-04 **Xiamen Shipbuilding Industry Co Ltd — Xiamen FJ** Yd No: XSI401C Loa 189.99 (BB) Br ex 32.31 Dght 12.490 Lbp 182.00 Br md 32.26 Dpth 17.20 Welded, 1 dk	**(A21A2BC) Bulk Carrier** Double Hull Grain: 65,748; Bale: 63,629 Compartments: 5 Ho, ER 5 Ha: 4 (21.3 x 18.2)ER (18.9 x 18.2) Cranes: 4x30t	**1 oil engine** driving 1 FP propeller Total Power: 9,480kW (12,889hp) 14.0kn B&W 6S50MC-C 1 x 2 Stroke 6 Cy. 500 x 2000 9480kW (12889bhp) STX Engine Co Ltd-South Korea AuxGen: 3 x 600kW 440/220V 60Hz a.c Boilers: AuxB (Comp) 8.1kgf/cm² (7.9bar) Fuel: 150.0 (d.f.) 2095.0 (r.f.)
9432866 *3EQL6* -	**SAPPHIRE-T** - **Carlsburg Maritime Inc** Transal Denizcilik Ticaret AS SatCom: Inmarsat C 435682611 *Panama* *Panama* MMSI: 353826000 Official number: 3419708A	**7,311** 3,589 11,299 T/cm 22.6	Class: NV (BV)	**2008**-03 **Selah Makina Sanayi ve Ticaret A.S. — Tuzla, Istanbul** Yd No: 51 Loa 129.50 (BB) Br ex - Dght 8.150 Lbp 122.00 Br md 19.80 Dpth 10.40 Welded, 1 dk	**(A12B2TR) Chemical/Products Tanker** Double Hull (13F) Liq: 12,470; Liq (Oil): 12,250 Cargo Heating Coils Compartments: 12 Wing Ta, 2 Wing Slop Ta, ER 12 Cargo Pump (s): 12x250m³/hr Manifold: Bow/CM: 66.8m Ice Capable	**1 oil engine** reduction geared to sc. shafts driving 1 CP propeller Total Power: 4,413kW (6,000hp) 14.5kn MaK 9M32C 1 x 4 Stroke 9 Cy. 320 x 480 4413kW (6000bhp) Caterpillar Motoren GmbH & Co. KG-Germany AuxGen: 3 x 620kW a.c, 1 x a.c Thrusters: 1 Tunnel thruster (f) Fuel: 90.0 (d.f.) 567.0 (r.f.)
8816443 *YCCC* -	**SAPPORO** *ex* Mantap *-2010* *ex* Kiku Maru No. 5 *-2006* **PT Akita Putera Lines** - *Surabaya* *Indonesia*	**678** 261 700	Class: KI	**1988**-08 **Sasaki Shipbuilding Co Ltd — Osakikamijima HS** Yd No: 522 L reg 52.50 Br ex - Dght 3.140 Lbp - Br md 9.50 Dpth 5.30 Welded	**(A31A2GX) General Cargo Ship**	**1 oil engine** driving 1 FP propeller Total Power: 588kW (799hp) Yanmar MF26-HT 1 x 4 Stroke 6 Cy. 260 x 500 588kW (799bhp) Yanmar Diesel Engine Co Ltd-Japan
9439199 *SVAX7* -	**SAPPORO PRINCESS** - **Prosperity Faith SA** Tsakos Columbia Shipmanagement (TCM) SA *Piraeus* *Greece* MMSI: 240983000 Official number: 11980	**55,909** 29,810 105,354 T/cm 88.9	Class: LR ✠ **100A1** SS 04/2010 Double Hull oil tanker ESP **ShipRight** (SDA, FDA, CM) *IWS LI EP (B,P,Vc) ✠ **LMC** **UMS IGS** Eq.Ltr: R†; Cable: 691.9/84.0 U3 (a)	**2010**-04 **Sumitomo Heavy Industries Marine & Engineering Co., Ltd. — Yokosuka** Yd No: 1356 Loa 228.60 (BB) Br ex 42.04 Dght 14.810 Lbp 217.80 Br md 42.00 Dpth 21.50 Welded, 1 dk	**(A13A2TV) Crude Oil Tanker** Double Hull (13F) Liq: 98,687; Liq (Oil): 98,687 Cargo Heating Coils Compartments: 10 Wing Ta, 2 Wing Slop Ta, ER 3 Cargo Pump (s): 3x2500m³/hr Manifold: Bow/CM: 116.6m	**1 oil engine** driving 1 FP propeller Total Power: 12,350kW (16,791hp) 14.8kn MAN-B&W 6S60MC-C 1 x 2 Stroke 6 Cy. 600 x 2400 12350kW (16791bhp) Mitsui Engineering & Shipbuilding CLtd-Japan AuxGen: 3 x 800kW 450V 60Hz a.c Boilers: e (ex.g.) 22.2kgf/cm² (21.8bar), WTAuxB (o.f.) 18.4kgf/cm² (18.0bar) Fuel: 210.0 (d.f.) 2100.0 (r.f.)

No.	Name / Owner	Tonnage	Class	Builder / Dimensions	Type	Machinery
7104465 *YBRA* -	**SAPTA JAYA** *ex Cighra -2007 launched as Trikora I -1970* **PT Bintang Jasa Samudra Line** - *Jakarta* *Indonesia* Official number: 4161	**210** 122 279	Class: KI	**1970-07 P.T. Carya — Jakarta** (Hull launched by) Yd No: 188 **1970-07 P.T. Pakin — Jakarta** (Hull completed by) Yd No: 593 Loa 42.02 Br ex - Dght 2.210 Lbp 39.65 Br md 7.00 Dpth 2.72 Welded, 1 dk	**(A32A2GF) General Cargo/Passenger Ship** Passengers: unberthed: 30 Grain: 340; Bale: 303 Compartments: 2 Ho, ER 2 Ha: 2 (8.0 x 3.9)ER Derricks: 1x2.5t,1x1.5t; Winches: 2	**1 oil engine** reduction geared to sc. shaft driving 1 FP propeller Total Power: 257kW (349hp) 9.0kn Deutz BF8M716 1 x 4 Stroke 8 Cy. 135 x 160 257kW (349bhp) Kloeckner Humboldt Deutz AG-West Germany AuxGen: 1 x 3kW 110V 50Hz a.c Fuel: 10.0 (d.f.)
9101431 *PNBE* -	**SAPTA SAMUDRA** **PT Humpuss Transportasi Kimia** PT Humpuss Intermoda Transportasi Tbk *Jakarta* *Indonesia* MMSI: 525014047 Official number: 525014047	**4,725** 2,004 6,864 T/cm 17.1	Class: KI (NV)	**1994-08 Jurong Shipyard Ltd — Singapore** Yd No: 1043 Loa 105.00 (BB) Br ex - Dght 6.000 Lbp 99.00 Br md 18.80 Dpth 8.50 Welded, 1 dk	**(A13B2TP) Products Tanker** Single Hull Liq: 5,899; Liq (Oil): 5,899 Compartments: 5 Ta, 8 Wing Ta, ER, 2 Wing Slop Ta 3 Cargo Pump (s): 3x300m³/hr Manifold: Bow/CM: 54m	**2 oil engines** reduction geared to sc. shafts driving 2 FP propellers Total Power: 2,500kW (3,400hp) 12.8kn Yanmar 6Z280-EN 2 x 4 Stroke 6 Cy. 280 x 360 each-1250kW (1700bhp) Yanmar Diesel Engine Co Ltd-Japan Fuel: 68.0 (d.f.) 305.0 (r.f.)
8826096 - -	**SAPU BAHARI** *ex Sea Navigator II -1970* **PT Berkah Intan Perkasa** - *Jakarta* *Indonesia*	*152* 46 -	Class: (KI)	**1979 Kanagawa Zosen — Kobe** Loa 24.92 Br ex 7.60 Dght 3.260 Lbp - Br md - Dpth 3.63 Welded, 1 dk	**(B32A2ST) Tug**	**2 oil engines** driving 2 FP propellers Total Power: 1,912kW (2,600hp) Nippon Hatsudoki HS6NV325 2 x 4 Stroke 6 Cy. 325 x 460 each-956kW (1300bhp) Nippon Kokan KK (NKK Corp)-Japan AuxGen: 1 x 40kW 210V a.c
8826101 *YD4571* -	**SAPU LAUT** **PT Maxsteer Dyrynusa Perdana** - *Jakarta* *Indonesia*	*155* 47 -	Class: KI	**1979-01 Shimoda Dockyard Co. Ltd. — Shimoda** Loa 25.50 Br ex 7.60 Dght 3.200 Lbp - Br md - Dpth 3.59 Welded, 1 dk	**(B32A2ST) Tug**	**2 oil engines** driving 2 FP propellers Total Power: 1,912kW (2,600hp) Nippon Hatsudoki HS6NV325 2 x 4 Stroke 6 Cy. 325 x 460 each-956kW (1300bhp) AuxGen: 1 x 24kW 210V a.c
9391270 *9WND8* -	**SAPURA 3000** *ex Sembawang H05-1 -2008* **SapuraAcergy Assets Pte Ltd** SapuraAcergy Sdn Bhd *Labuan* *Malaysia* MMSI: 533835000 Official number: 900043	**32,060** 9,618 17,650	Class: AB	**2008-02 Nantong Yahua Shipbuilding Co Ltd — Nantong JS** (Hull) Yd No: 2004-23 **2008-02 Sembawang Shipyard Pte Ltd — Singapore** Yd No: H05-1 Loa 151.20 Br ex - Dght 6.500 Lbp 144.40 Br md 37.80 Dpth 9.10 Welded, 1 dk	**(B22C2OQ) Pipe Layer Crane Vessel** Passengers: berths: 330 Cranes: 1x3000t,2x40t	**6 diesel electric oil engines** driving 6 gen. each 4000kW a.c Connecting to 2 elec. motors each (2400kW) driving 2 Directional propellers Total Power: 24,000kW (32,628hp) 8.0kn Wartsila 8L32 6 x 4 Stroke 8 Cy. 320 x 400 each-4000kW (5438bhp) Wartsila France SA-France Thrusters: 3 Retract. directional thruster (f); 2 Retract. directional thruster (a) Fuel: 2510.0
9651199 *3FPL5* -	**SAPURAKENCANA 1200** **TL Offshore Sdn Bhd** - *Panama* *Panama* MMSI: 370454000 Official number: 44318PEXT	**32,126** 9,638 9,765	Class: AB	**2014-03 COSCO (Nantong) Shipyard Co Ltd — Nantong JS** Yd No: N448 Loa 153.60 (BB) Br ex 35.03 Dght 7.400 Lbp 143.40 Br md 35.00 Dpth 16.80 Welded, 1 dk	**(B22C2OQ) Pipe Layer Crane Vessel** Cranes: 1x1200t,2x50t,2x10t	**2 diesel electric oil engines** driving 2 Azimuth electric drive units 12.7kn Thrusters: 1 Tunnel thruster (f); 3 Retract. directional thruster (f) Fuel: 2689.0 (d.f.)
9392705 *H9YT* -	**SAPURAKENCANA CONSTRUCTOR** *ex Normand Clough -2013* *ex Rem Clough -2009* **Sapuraclough Java Offshore Pte Ltd** Australian Offshore Solutions Pty Ltd *Panama* *Panama* MMSI: 373335000 Official number: 45233PEXT	**8,337** 2,501 7,345	Class: NV	**2008-10 Kleven Verft AS — Ulsteinvik** Yd No: 321 Loa 117.60 (BB) Br ex 22.05 Dght 7.150 Lbp 109.90 Br md 22.00 Dpth 9.00 Welded, 1 dk	**(B22A2OR) Offshore Support Vessel** Passengers: cabins: 71 Cranes: 1x250t,2x5t	**6 diesel electric oil engines** driving 5 gen. each 2028kW 690V a.c 1 gen. of 910kW 690V a.c Connecting to 2 elec. motors each (3000kW) driving 2 Azimuth electric drive units Total Power: 14,390kW (19,565hp) 12.0kn Caterpillar 3512C 1 x Vee 4 Stroke 12 Cy. 170 x 215 1765kW (2400bhp) Caterpillar Inc-USA Caterpillar 3516C-HD 5 x Vee 4 Stroke 16 Cy. 170 x 215 each-2525kW (3433bhp) Caterpillar Inc-USA Thrusters: 2 Tunnel thruster (f); 1 Retract. directional thruster (f)
8516809 *XJAQ* -	**SAPUTI** *ex Kiliutaq -2006 ex Ango -1991* **Qikiqtaaluk Fisheries Corp** Nataaqnaq Fisheries *Iqaluit, NU* *Canada* MMSI: 316013290 Official number: 818888	**2,634** 791 750	Class: NV	**1987-11 Salthammer Baatbyggeri AS — Vestnes** (Hull) **1987-11 Langsten Slip & Baatbyggeri AS — Tomrefjord** Yd No: 116 Loa 75.90 (BB) Br ex - Dght 5.570 Lbp 67.10 Br md 13.00 Dpth 8.12 Welded, 2 dks	**(B11A2FS) Stern Trawler** Ins: 1,200 Ice Capable	**1 oil engine** reduction geared to sc. shaft driving 1 CP propeller Total Power: 2,998kW (4,076hp) 14.5kn Wartsila 8R32 1 x 4 Stroke 8 Cy. 320 x 350 2998kW (4076bhp) Wartsila Diesel Oy-Finland AuxGen: 1 x 1456kW 440V 60Hz a.c, 3 x 338kW 440V 60Hz a.c Thrusters: 1 Thwart. FP thruster (f)
5313892 - -	**SAQQA** **Karachi Port Trust** - *Karachi* *Pakistan*	*209* - 259		**1963 Karachi Shipyard & Engineering Works Ltd. — Karachi** Yd No: 52 Loa 39.91 Br ex 8.28 Dght 2.001 Lbp - Br md - Dpth - Welded, 1 dk	**(A14A2LO) Water Tanker** Compartments: 4 Ta, ER 2 Cargo Pump (s): 2x116m³/hr Manifold: Bow/CM: 22m	**1 oil engine** driving 1 FP propeller 9.0kn MAN G6V235/330ATL 1 x 4 Stroke 6 Cy. 235 x 330 Maschinenbau Augsburg Nuernberg (MAN)-Augsburg Fuel: 22.0 (d.f.)
9023809 *3WAW* -	**SAR 27-01** **Vietnam Maritime Search & Rescue Coordination Centre (VMRCC)** - SatCom: Inmarsat C 457418010 *Da Nang* *Vietnam* MMSI: 574180170 Official number: VNDN-186-CV	**100** 35 -	Class: VR	**2001-01 Song Cam Shipyard — Haiphong** Loa 29.00 Br ex 6.02 Dght 1.350 Lbp 27.20 Br md 6.00 Dpth 3.00 Welded, 1 dk	**(B34M2QS) Search & Rescue Vessel**	**4 oil engines** reduction geared to sc. shafts driving 3 Propellers Total Power: 2,060kW (2,800hp) Scania DI14 M 4 x Vee 4 Stroke 8 Cy. 127 x 140 each-515kW (700bhp) Scania AB-Sweden
9281451 *3WOP* -	**SAR 272** **Vietnam Maritime Search & Rescue Coordination Centre (VMRCC)** - *Saigon* *Vietnam* MMSI: 574741000 Official number: VNSG-1714-CN	**132** 39 18	Class: VR (LR) ✠ Classed LR until 14/5/04	**2004-05 Song Cam Shipyard — Haiphong** (Hull) **2004-05 B.V. Scheepswerf Damen — Gorinchem** Yd No: 549508 Loa 28.90 Br ex 6.20 Dght 1.660 Lbp 25.45 Br md 5.92 Dpth 3.35 Welded, 1 dk	**(B34M2QS) Search & Rescue Vessel**	**2 oil engines** with clutches, flexible couplings & sr reverse geared to sc. shafts driving 2 FP propellers Total Power: 1,760kW (2,392hp) 29.0kn M.T.U. 8V4000M60 2 x Vee 4 Stroke 8 Cy. 165 x 190 each-880kW (1196bhp) MTU Friedrichshafen GmbH-Friedrichshafen AuxGen: 2 x 60kW 450V 60Hz a.c
9281463 *3WOR* -	**SAR 273** **Vietnam National Maritime Bureau (VINAMARINE)** - *Haiphong* *Vietnam* MMSI: 574723000 Official number: VN-1919-CH	*132* 39 -	Class: VR (LR) ✠ 10/7/04	**2004-07 Song Cam Shipyard — Haiphong** (Hull) Yd No: (549509) **2004-07 B.V. Scheepswerf Damen — Gorinchem** Yd No: 549509 Loa 28.90 Br ex 6.20 Dght 1.660 Lbp 25.45 Br md 5.92 Dpth 3.35 Welded, 1 dk	**(B34M2QS) Search & Rescue Vessel**	**2 oil engines** with clutches, flexible couplings & sr reverse geared to sc. shafts driving 2 FP propellers Total Power: 1,760kW (2,392hp) 29.0kn M.T.U. 8V4000M60 2 x Vee 4 Stroke 8 Cy. 165 x 190 each-880kW (1196bhp) MTU Friedrichshafen GmbH-Friedrichshafen AuxGen: 2 x 60kW 450V 60Hz a.c
9281475 *3WOS* -	**SAR 274** **Vietnam National Maritime Bureau (VINAMARINE)** - *Da Nang* *Vietnam* MMSI: 574500000 Official number: VNDN-207-CV	*132* 39 -	Class: VR (LR) ✠ 17/9/04	**2004-09 Song Cam Shipyard — Haiphong** (Hull) Yd No: (549510) **2004-09 B.V. Scheepswerf Damen — Gorinchem** Yd No: 549510 Loa 28.90 Br ex 6.20 Dght 1.660 Lbp 24.23 Br md 5.92 Dpth 3.35 Welded, 1 dk	**(B34M2QS) Search & Rescue Vessel**	**2 oil engines** with clutches, flexible couplings & sr reverse geared to sc. shafts driving 2 FP propellers Total Power: 1,760kW (2,392hp) 19.0kn M.T.U. 8V4000M60 2 x Vee 4 Stroke 8 Cy. 165 x 190 each-880kW (1196bhp) MTU Friedrichshafen GmbH-Friedrichshafen AuxGen: 2 x 60kW 450V 60Hz a.c
9287247 *3WOQ* -	**SAR 411** **Vietnam National Maritime Bureau (VINAMARINE)** - *Da Nang* *Vietnam* MMSI: 574255000 Official number: VN-1920-CH	**262** 78 80	Class: VR (LR) ✠ 14/1/04	**2004-01 Song Cam Shipyard — Haiphong** (Hull) Yd No: (549857) **2004-01 B.V. Scheepswerf Damen — Gorinchem** Yd No: 549857 Loa 43.80 Br ex 7.30 Dght 2.150 Lbp 38.50 Br md 7.00 Dpth 3.77 Welded, 1 dk	**(B34M2QS) Search & Rescue Vessel**	**2 oil engines** with clutches, flexible couplings & sr reverse geared to sc. shafts driving 2 FP propellers Total Power: 4,640kW (6,308hp) 26.0kn M.T.U. 16V4000M70 2 x Vee 4 Stroke 16 Cy. 165 x 190 each-2320kW (3154bhp) MTU Friedrichshafen GmbH-Friedrichshafen AuxGen: 2 x 80kW 400V 50Hz a.c

IMO / Call sign / Flag	Name / Owner / Port	Tonnage	Class	Builder / Dimensions	Type	Machinery
9287259 *3WOT* -	**SAR 412** **Vietnam National Maritime Bureau (VINAMARINE)** - *Da Nang* Vietnam MMSI: 574290000 Official number: VNDN-217-CV	**262** 78 -	Class: VR (LR) ✠ Classed LR until 21/1/05	**2005-01 Song Cam Shipyard — Haiphong** (Hull) Yd No: (549858) **2005-01 B.V. Scheepswerf Damen — Gorinchem** Yd No: 549858 Loa 43.80 Br ex 7.30 Dght 2.150 Lbp 38.50 Br md 7.00 Dpth 3.77 Welded, 1 dk	**(B34M2QS) Search & Rescue Vessel**	**2 oil engines** with clutches, flexible couplings & sr reverse geared to sc. shafts driving 2 FP propellers Total Power: 4,640kW (6,308hp) 26.0kn M.T.U. 16V4000M70 2 x Vee 4 Stroke 16 Cy. 165 x 190 each-2320kW (3154bhp) MTU Friedrichshafen GmbH-Friedrichshafen AuxGen: 2 x 80kW 400V 50Hz a.c
9287261 *3WOU* -	**SAR 413** **Vietnam National Maritime Bureau (VINAMARINE)** - *Saigon* Vietnam MMSI: 574309000	**262** 78 -	Class: VR (LR) ✠ 20/7/05	**2005-07 Song Cam Shipyard — Haiphong** (Hull) Yd No: (549859) **2005-07 B.V. Scheepswerf Damen — Gorinchem** Yd No: 549859 Loa 43.80 Br ex 7.31 Dght 2.150 Lbp 39.00 Br md 7.00 Dpth 3.77 Welded, 1 dk	**(B34M2QS) Search & Rescue Vessel**	**2 oil engines** with clutches, flexible couplings & sr reverse geared to sc. shafts driving 2 FP propellers Total Power: 4,640kW (6,308hp) 16.0kn M.T.U. 16V4000M70 2 x Vee 4 Stroke 16 Cy. 165 x 190 each-2320kW (3154bhp) MTU Friedrichshafen GmbH-Friedrichshafen AuxGen: 2 x 80kW 400/240V 50Hz a.c
8647593 *2EOQ2* -	**SAR FRITZ BEHRENS** *ex* Fritz Behrens *-2012* **Wesel-Datteln-Kanal Hafen-und Lagergesellschaft EWIV** - *Southampton* United Kingdom MMSI: 235086904	**101** 60 -		**1981-01 Fr Schweers Schiffs- und Bootswerft GmbH & Co KG — Berne** Yd No: 6442 Converted From: Search & Rescue Vessel-1981 Loa 23.99 Br ex - Dght 2.100 Lbp 21.58 Br md 5.50 Dpth - Welded, 1 dk	**(B34L2QU) Utility Vessel** Hull Material: Aluminium Alloy	**2 oil engines** reduction geared to sc. shafts driving 2 Propellers Total Power: 1,300kW (1,768hp) 12.0kn M.T.U. 8V331TC92 2 x Vee 4 Stroke 8 Cy. 165 x 155 each-650kW (884bhp) MTU Friedrichshafen GmbH-Friedrichshafen
9525742 *EAED* -	**SAR GAVIA** **Sociedad de Salvamento y Seguridad Maritima (SASEMAR)** Remolques Maritimos SA *Santa Cruz de Tenerife* Spain (CSR)	**907** 272 550	Class: (BV)	**2011-03 Union Naval Valencia SA (UNV) — Valencia** Yd No: 485 Loa 39.70 Br ex - Dght 4.400 Lbp 34.52 Br md 12.50 Dpth 5.50 Welded, 1 dk	**(B32A2ST) Tug**	**2 oil engines** reduction geared to sc. shafts driving 2 Directional propellers Total Power: 3,536kW (4,808hp) A.B.C. 8DZC 2 x 4 Stroke 8 Cy. 256 x 310 each-1768kW (2404bhp) Anglo Belgian Corp NV (ABC)-Belgium AuxGen: 2 x 400kW 400V 50Hz a.c, 2 x 225kW 400V 50Hz a.c Thrusters: 1 Tunnel thruster (f)
9525730 *EACF* -	**SAR MASTELERO** **Sociedad de Salvamento y Seguridad Maritima (SASEMAR)** - SatCom: Inmarsat C 422448510 *Santa Cruz de Tenerife* Spain (CSR) MMSI: 224485000	**907** 272 550	Class: (BV)	**2011-01 Union Naval Valencia SA (UNV) — Valencia** Yd No: 484 Loa 39.70 Br ex - Dght 4.200 Lbp 34.52 Br md 12.50 Dpth 5.50 Welded, 1 dk	**(B32A2ST) Tug**	**2 oil engines** reduction geared to sc. shafts driving 2 Directional propellers Total Power: 3,536kW (4,808hp) A.B.C. 8DZC 2 x 4 Stroke 8 Cy. 256 x 310 each-1768kW (2404bhp) Anglo Belgian Corp NV (ABC)-Belgium AuxGen: 2 x 400kW 400V 50Hz a.c, 2 x 225kW 400V 50Hz a.c Thrusters: 1 Tunnel thruster (f)
9525754 *EBRD* -	**SAR MESANA** **Sociedad de Salvamento y Seguridad Maritima (SASEMAR)** Remolques Maritimos SA *Santa Cruz de Tenerife* Spain (CSR) MMSI: 224483000	**907** 272 550	Class: (BV)	**2011-06 Union Naval Valencia SA (UNV) — Valencia** Yd No: 486 Loa 39.70 Br ex - Dght 4.400 Lbp 34.52 Br md 12.50 Dpth 5.50 Welded, 1 dk	**(B32A2ST) Tug**	**2 oil engines** reduction geared to sc. shafts driving 2 Directional propellers Total Power: 3,536kW (4,808hp) A.B.C. 8DZC 2 x 4 Stroke 8 Cy. 256 x 310 each-1768kW (2404bhp) Anglo Belgian Corp NV (ABC)-Belgium AuxGen: 2 x 400kW 400V 50Hz a.c, 2 x 225kW 400V 50Hz a.c Thrusters: 1 Tunnel thruster (f) Fuel: 340.0
9259020 *PBWL* -	**SARA** *ex* Thekla *-2013 completed as* Suryawati *-2003* **Vertom UCS mv Sara BV** Vertom UCS Holding BV *Rotterdam* Netherlands MMSI: 244810690	**6,301** 3,582 8,567	Class: BV	**2003-03 Bodewes Scheepswerf "Volharding" Foxhol B.V. — Foxhol** Yd No: 350 Loa 132.20 Br ex - Dght 7.160 Lbp 123.04 Br md 15.87 Dpth 9.65 Welded, 1 dk	**(A31A2GX) General Cargo Ship** Grain: 12,855 TEU 552 C. 552/20' incl. 25 ref C. Compartments: 2 Ho, ER Cranes: 2x40t	**1 oil engine** reduction geared to sc. shaft driving 1 CP propeller Total Power: 3,960kW (5,384hp) 14.5kn MaK 8M32C 1 x 4 Stroke 8 Cy. 320 x 480 3960kW (5384bhp) Caterpillar Motoren GmbH & Co. KG-Germany Thrusters: 1 Tunnel thruster (f) Fuel: 69.0 (d.f.) 573.0 (r.f.)
9322243 *V2BP5* -	**SARA** *ex* Sitc Progress *-2011 ex* Sara *-2008* **ms 'Sara' Schiffahrts GmbH & Co KG** Reederei Harmstorf & Co Thomas Meier-Hedde GmbH & Co KG *Saint John's* Antigua & Barbuda MMSI: 304890000 Official number: 4080	**9,590** 4,748 12,814	Class: GL (NK)	**2006-01 Dae Sun Shipbuilding & Engineering Co Ltd — Busan** Yd No: 453 Loa 142.70 (BB) Br ex - Dght 8.214 Lbp 133.50 Br md 22.60 Dpth 11.20 Welded, 1 dk	**(A33A2CC) Container Ship (Fully Cellular)** Double Hull Grain: 17,487 TEU 1043 C Ho 325 TEU C Dk 718 TEU incl 180 ref C 7 Ha: 6 (12.6 x 18.2)ER (12.6 x 12.8)	**1 oil engine** driving 1 FP propeller Total Power: 7,089kW (9,638hp) 18.0kn MAN-B&W 6S46MC-C 1 x 2 Stroke 6 Cy. 460 x 1932 7089kW (9638bhp) STX Engine Co Ltd-South Korea AuxGen: 3 x 615kW 440V a.c Thrusters: 1 Thwart. CP thruster (f)
8327648 - -	**SARA** *ex* Yuh Lih No. 2 *-2001* **Dhaif A Manie** -	*336* 175 -	Class: CR	**1983 San Yang Shipbuilding Co., Ltd. — Kaohsiung** Loa 46.66 Br ex - Dght 3.271 Lbp 41.08 Br md 7.80 Dpth 3.66 Welded, 1 dk	**(B11B2FV) Fishing Vessel** Compartments: 3 Ho, ER	**1 oil engine** driving 1 FP propeller Total Power: 883kW (1,201hp) Hanshin 6LU28G 1 x 4 Stroke 6 Cy. 280 x 440 883kW (1201bhp) The Hanshin Diesel Works Ltd-Japan AuxGen: 2 x 128kW 120/225V a.c
8814861 *9HEN9* -	**SARA** *ex* Sarabelle II *-2003* **Aegean Bunkers at Sea NV** Aegean Bunkering Services Inc *Valletta* Malta MMSI: 256887000 Official number: 8814861	**4,156** 1,947 6,608 T/cm 15.0	Class: BV	**1990-04 Cant. Navale "Ferrari" S.p.A. — La Spezia** Yd No: 80 Loa 111.23 Br ex - Dght 6.001 Lbp 108.01 Br md 16.76 Dpth 8.82 Welded, 1 dk	**(A13B2TP) Products Tanker** Double Hull (13F) Liq: 6,652; Liq (Oil): 6,652 Compartments: 12 Wing Ta, 2 Wing Slop Ta, ER 12 Cargo Pump (s): 12x250m³/hr	**2 oil engines** geared to sc. shafts driving 2 FP propellers Total Power: 3,490kW (4,746hp) 14.0kn Wartsila 6R32 2 x 4 Stroke 6 Cy. 320 x 350 each-1745kW (2373bhp) Wartsila Diesel Oy-Finland Thrusters: 1 Tunnel thruster (f)
9082245 *3EYW8* -	**SARA 1** *ex* Nepline Dangar *-2011* *ex* Nautica Muar *-2005* *ex* Kemboyang Melati *-2003* **Salih Mahsr Tuayen** - *Panama* Panama MMSI: 370323000 Official number: 42517PEXT	**3,097** 1,660 5,121 T/cm 12.2	Class: (BV) (NV)	**1995-09 ASMAR-Ironwoods Shipyard Sdn Bhd — Kuching** Yd No: A.I.250 Loa 89.93 Br ex - Dght 6.400 Lbp 84.58 Br md 15.60 Dpth 8.00 Welded, 1 dk	**(A13B2TP) Products Tanker** Single Hull Liq: 5,744; Liq (Oil): 5,945 Compartments: 10 Wing Ta, ER 3 Cargo Pump (s): 3x500m³/hr Manifold: Bow/CM: 34.4m	**1 oil engine** geared to sc. shaft driving 1 FP propeller Total Power: 1,764kW (2,398hp) 11.0kn Stork-Werkspoor 6SW280 1 x 4 Stroke 6 Cy. 280 x 300 1764kW (2398bhp) Stork Wartsila Diesel BV-Netherlands AuxGen: 3 x 350kW 220/415V 50Hz a.c Fuel: 459.0 (d.f.)
9301615 *9MQD2* -	**SARA 1** *ex* Ilios Ermis *-2012 ex* Alios Hermes *-2010* **Dialog IPS Marine (Labuan) Ltd** Marine & Offshore Solution Sdn Bhd *Port Klang* Malaysia MMSI: 533130946 Official number: 334507	**2,097** 629 1,504	Class: LR ✠ **100A1** SS 05/2009 Double Hull oil and chemical tanker, Ship Type 3 ESP LI ✠ **LMC** **UMS** Eq.Ltr: R; Cable: 447.0/40.0 U2 (a)	**2004-05 K.K. Miura Zosensho — Saiki** Yd No: 1272 Loa 80.00 (BB) Br ex 14.72 Dght 3.412 Lbp 76.00 Br md 14.70 Dpth 5.50 Welded, 1 dk	**(A12B2TR) Chemical/Products Tanker** Double Hull (13F) Liq: 1,885; Liq (Oil): 1,885 Compartments: 6 Wing Ta, 1 Slop Ta, ER	**1 oil engine** with clutches, flexible couplings & sr reverse geared to sc. shaft driving 1 FP propeller Total Power: 1,456kW (1,980hp) 12.8kn Daihatsu 6DKM-26 1 x 4 Stroke 6 Cy. 260 x 380 1456kW (1980bhp) Daihatsu Diesel Manufacturing Co Lt-Japan AuxGen: 3 x 360kW 445V 50Hz a.c Boilers: TOH (o.f.) Thrusters: 1 Thwart. CP thruster (f) Fuel: 29.0 (d.f.) 117.0 (r.f.)
9495832 *9WNF8* -	**SARA 2** *ex* Menara Satu *-2013* **Sea Wave Maritime Sdn Bhd** - *Labuan* Malaysia MMSI: 533869000 Official number: 900059	**5,036** 2,272 7,097 T/cm 17.6	Class: BV	**2008-12 Zhejiang Haicheng Shipbuilding Co Ltd — Yuhuan County ZJ** Yd No: DMY06-001 Loa 118.00 (BB) Br ex - Dght 6.600 Lbp 110.00 Br md 17.60 Dpth 9.00 Welded, 1 dk	**(A13B2TP) Products Tanker** Double Hull (13F) Liq: 8,063; Liq (Oil): 4,106 Cargo Heating Coils Compartments: 10 Wing Ta, 2 Wing Slop Ta, ER 2 Cargo Pump (s): 2x750m³/hr Manifold: Bow/CM: 63.2m	**1 oil engine** reduction geared to sc. shaft driving 1 FP propeller Total Power: 2,576kW (3,502hp) 12.5kn Yanmar 6N330-EN 1 x 4 Stroke 6 Cy. 330 x 440 2576kW (3502bhp) Qingdao Zichai Boyang Diesel EngineCo Ltd-China
7206603 - -	**SARA A** *ex* Al Marwa *-2010 ex* Haydara *-2007* *ex* Mona Lisa-1 *-2004 ex* Obaid *-1999* *ex* Sea Express I *-1999 ex* Lily Maa *-1996* *ex* Sunrise Two *-1990* *ex* Shinryozan Maru *-1987* - -	**570** 380 1,623		**1971 Imamura Zosen — Kure** Yd No: 175 Loa 65.92 Br ex 11.03 Dght 4.249 Lbp 60.00 Br md 11.00 Dpth 4.35 Welded, 1 dk	**(A31A2GX) General Cargo Ship**	**1 oil engine** driving 1 FP propeller Total Power: 1,103kW (1,500hp) Hanshin 6LU35 1 x 4 Stroke 6 Cy. 350 x 550 1103kW (1500bhp) Hanshin Nainenki Kogyo-Japan

IMO / Call sign	Name / Owner	Tonnage	Class	Builder / Dimensions	Type	Machinery
9354399 *V2BY8* -	**SARA BORCHARD** *ex* Buxtehude *-2009* *ex* Rita *-2007* **ms 'Buxtehude' Schiffahrts GmbH & Co KG** Hans-Uwe Meyer Bereederungs GmbH & Co KG *Saint John's* *Antigua & Barbuda* MMSI: 304962000 Official number: 4166	**9,962** 6,006 11,431	Class: GL	**2006**-07 **J.J. Sietas KG Schiffswerft GmbH & Co. — Hamburg** Yd No: 1238 Loa 134.44 (BB) Br ex - Dght 8.710 Lbp 124.41 Br md 22.50 Dpth 11.30 Welded, 1 dk	**(A33A2CC) Container Ship (Fully Cellular)** TEU 868 C Ho 601 TEU C Dk 267 TEU incl 150 ref C Ice Capable	**1 oil engine** reduction geared to sc. shafts driving 1 CP propeller Total Power: 8,399kW (11,419hp) 18.5kn MaK 9M43 1 x 4 Stroke 9 Cy. 430 x 610 8399kW (11419bhp) Caterpillar Motoren GmbH & Co. KG-Germany AuxGen: 2 x 534kW 400V 50Hz a.c, 1 x 1300kW 400V 50Hz a.c Thrusters: 1 Tunnel thruster (f); 1 Tunnel thruster (a)
7398602 *IVID* -	**SARA D** *ex* Cuma *-2000* *ex* Capri *-1978* *ex* Michelangelo Ischia *-1975* **Delcomar SAS** - *Cagliari* *Italy* MMSI: 247051600 Official number: 168	*496* 272 1,016	Class: RI	**1974**-06 **Cantiere Navale Visentini di Visentini F e C SAS — Porto Viro** Yd No: 87 Loa 65.84 (BB) Br ex 12.98 Dght 2.237 Lbp 60.64 Br md 11.69 Dpth 3.00 Welded, 1 dk	**(A36A2PR) Passenger/Ro-Ro Ship (Vehicles)** Passengers: unberthed: 500 Bow door & ramp	**2 oil engines** driving 2 FP propellers Total Power: 2,354kW (3,200hp) 16.0kn MaK 8M452AK 2 x 4 Stroke 8 Cy. 320 x 450 each-1177kW (1600bhp) MaK Maschinenbau GmbH-Kiel AuxGen: 2 x 193kW 380V 50Hz a.c Fuel: 71.0 (d.f.)
8991578 *WTQ9465* -	**SARA D** *ex* Judy D *-1975* **Marine Transportation Services Inc** - *Panama City, FL* *United States of America* MMSI: 366731670 Official number: 596704	**129** 38 -		**1978** **Camcraft, Inc. — Crown Point, La** Yd No: 174 L reg 32.43 Br ex - Dght - Lbp - Br md 6.55 Dpth 1.34 Welded, 1 dk	**(B34J2SD) Crew Boat** Hull Material: Aluminium Alloy	**1 oil engine** driving 1 Propeller
8998100 *WDC4512* -	**SARA DAY FORET** *ex* Sister Mary Roland *-2014* **Delta Marine Offshore Holdings LLC** Delta Marine Logistics LLC *New Orleans, LA* *United States of America* MMSI: 367025840 Official number: 1167071	**447** 134 522		**2005**-04 **Master Boat Builders, Inc. — Coden, Al** Yd No: 367 Loa - Br ex - Dght - Lbp 41.45 Br md 10.97 Dpth 3.65 Welded, 1 dk	**(B21A2OS) Platform Supply Ship**	**2 oil engines** reduction geared to sc. shafts driving 2 Propellers Total Power: 1,250kW (1,700hp) Caterpillar 3508B 2 x Vee 4 Stroke 8 Cy. 170 x 190 each-625kW (850bhp) Caterpillar Inc-USA Thrusters: 1 Thwart. FP thruster (f)
8912118 *3EW06* -	**SARA EXPRESS** *ex* Union Mercury *-1998* *ex* Donon *-1993* **Trans-Sara S de RL** Americas Marine Management Services Inc *Panama* *Panama* MMSI: 371501000 Official number: 40327PEXT2	**2,252** 676 3,085	Class: IT (LR) (BV) Classed BC until 27/12/02	**1991**-02 **Construcciones Navales Santodomingo SA — Vigo** Yd No: 581 Loa 81.50 (BB) Br ex 14.38 Dght 5.301 Lbp 75.00 Br md 14.00 Dpth 6.50 Welded, 1 dk	**(A31A2GX) General Cargo Ship** Grain: 4,000; Bale: 3,900 Compartments: 1 Ho, ER 1 Ha: ER Ice Capable	**1 oil engine** with flexible couplings & sr geared to sc. shaft driving 1 CP propeller Total Power: 2,206kW (2,999hp) 14.0kn MaK 6M453C 1 x 4 Stroke 6 Cy. 320 x 420 2206kW (2999bhp) Krupp MaK Maschinenbau GmbH-Kiel AuxGen: 1 x 120kW 380V 50Hz a.c, 2 x 108kW 380V 50Hz a.c
9224374 *WDB6861* -	**SARA F. MCCALL** **General Electric Capital Corp** SEACOR Marine (International) Ltd *New Orleans, LA* *United States of America* MMSI: 338190000 Official number: 1087451	**462** 138 -	Class: AB	**1999**-12 **Neuville Boat Works, Inc. — New Iberia, La** Yd No: 165-1 Loa 51.82 Br ex - Dght 2.550 Lbp 50.29 Br md 10.36 Dpth 3.91 Welded, 1 dk	**(B21A2OC) Crew/Supply Vessel** Hull Material: Aluminium Alloy Passengers: unberthed: 73	**5 oil engines** with clutches, flexible couplings & sr reverse geared to sc. shafts driving 5 FP propellers Total Power: 4,965kW (6,750hp) 15.0kn Cummins KTA-38-M2 5 x Vee 4 Stroke 12 Cy. 159 x 159 each-993kW (1350bhp) Cummins Engine Co Inc-USA AuxGen: 2 x 75kW 120/208V 60Hz a.c Thrusters: 1 Retract. directional thruster (f) Fuel: 94.0 (d.f.) 27.0pd
9530527 *3EUT6* -	**SARA H** **HS South Inc** Compania Naviera Horamar SA *Panama* *Panama* MMSI: 371241000 Official number: 39959PEXT1	**6,183** 2,905 9,000	Class: BV	**2010**-01 **No 4807 Shipyard of PLA — Fu'an FJ** Yd No: SL22 Loa 117.60 Br ex - Dght 7.500 Lbp 109.60 Br md 19.00 Dpth 10.00 Welded, 1 dk	**(A13B2TP) Products Tanker** Double Hull (13F) Liq: 9,082; Liq (Oil): 9,082 Compartments: 10 Wing Ta, ER	**1 oil engine** reduction geared to sc. shaft driving 1 FP propeller Total Power: 3,309kW (4,499hp) 14.0kn Daihatsu 6DKM-36 1 x 4 Stroke 6 Cy. 360 x 480 3309kW (4499bhp) Daihatsu Diesel Manufacturing Co Lt-Japan AuxGen: 3 x 400kW 50Hz a.c Fuel: 450.0
7811422 *PHHY* -	**SARA MAATJE VII** *ex* Dingenis Jan *-1991* **Coastal Shipping BV** Acta Marine BV *Harlingen* *Netherlands* MMSI: 246010000 Official number: 2097	**170** 51 -	Class: GL	**1978**-08 **Scheepswerf Gebr. Suurmeijer B.V. — Foxhol** Yd No: 241 Converted From: Fishing Vessel Loa 35.38 Br ex - Dght 1.620 Lbp 33.71 Br md 6.60 Dpth 2.54 Welded, 1 dk	**(B21A2OS) Platform Supply Ship**	**2 oil engines** reverse reduction geared to sc. shaft driving 2 FP propellers Total Power: 442kW (600hp) 9.0kn G.M. (Detroit Diesel) 12V-71-N 2 x Vee 2 Stroke 12 Cy. 108 x 127 each-221kW (300bhp) (new engine 1995) Detroit Diesel Corporation-Detroit, Mi AuxGen: 1 x 116kW 380/220V a.c, 1 x 84kW 380/220V a.c Thrusters: 1 Tunnel thruster (f) Fuel: 30.0 (d.f.)
8871625 *PHIO* -	**SARA MAATJE VIII** **Coastal Shipping BV** Acta Marine BV *Harlingen* *Netherlands* MMSI: 244047000 Official number: 27117	**211** 51 221	Class: GL	**1978**-01 **Ceske Lodenice — Melnik** Yd No: RE-11 Lengthened-1994 Loa 35.40 Br ex - Dght 1.670 Lbp 34.17 Br md 8.50 Dpth 2.40 Welded, 1 dk	**(B21B20T) Offshore Tug/Supply Ship**	**2 oil engines** reduction geared to sc. shafts driving 2 FP propellers Total Power: 426kW (580hp) 8.5kn Mitsubishi S6A-MPTK 2 x 4 Stroke 6 Cy. 145 x 160 each-213kW (290bhp) (new engine 1996) Mitsubishi Heavy Industries Ltd-Japan AuxGen: 2 x 48kW 220/380V a.c
7647443 *PEDI* -	**SARA MAATJE X** *ex* De Nachtwacht *-2000* **Coastal Shipping BV** Acta Marine BV *Harlingen* *Netherlands* MMSI: 244351000 Official number: 1596	**159** 47 -	Class: GL	**1978**-03 **Scheepswerf Metz B.V. — Urk** Yd No: 42 Converted From: Fishing Vessel-2001 Shortened-2000 Loa 33.35 Br ex - Dght 1.601 Lbp - Br md 8.02 Dpth 2.25 Welded, 1 dk	**(B21A2OS) Platform Supply Ship**	**2 oil engines** reverse reduction geared to sc. shafts driving 2 FP propellers Total Power: 596kW (810hp) 8.0kn Cummins N14-M 2 x 4 Stroke 6 Cy. 140 x 152 each-298kW (405bhp) (new engine 2004) Cummins Engine Co Inc-USA AuxGen: 2 x 50kW 380/220V a.c Thrusters: 1 Tunnel thruster (f)
9338113 *IBZK* -	**SARA PRIMA** *ex* Maike-C *-2006* **Euroshipping Srl** Eolo Shipping Srl *Naples* *Italy* MMSI: 247173400	**5,581** 2,835 7,601 T/cm 17.8	Class: RI (GL)	**2005**-08 **Jiangsu Yangzijiang Shipbuilding Co Ltd — Jiangyin JS** Yd No: 2004-686C Loa 108.20 (BB) Br ex - Dght 7.010 Lbp 103.90 Br md 18.20 Dpth 9.00 Welded, 1 dk	**(A31A2GX) General Cargo Ship** Grain: 10,255; Bale: 10,255 Compartments: 4 Ho 3 Ha: ER	**1 oil engine** driving 1 CP propeller Total Power: 2,800kW (3,807hp) 12.4kn MAN-B&W 7S26MC 1 x 2 Stroke 7 Cy. 260 x 980 2800kW (3807bhp) STX Engine Co Ltd-South Korea AuxGen: 2 x 280kW 450/230V 60Hz a.c Thrusters: 1 Thwart. CP thruster (f)
9265770 *9VAY7* -	**SARA THERESA** *ex* Pacific Venturer *-2005* **Herning Shipping Asia Pte Ltd** Herning Shipping A/S *Singapore* *Singapore* MMSI: 563241000 Official number: 390095	**2,490** 912 2,954 T/cm 10.0	Class: BV (LR) (NV) Classed LR until 21/3/13	**2003**-05 **Samho Shipbuilding Co Ltd — Tongyeong** Yd No: 1040 Loa 87.50 (BB) Br ex 14.62 Dght 5.310 Lbp 80.04 Br md 14.40 Dpth 7.50 Welded, 1 dk	**(A13B2TP) Products Tanker** Double Hull (13F) Liq: 3,600; Liq (Oil): 4,000 Compartments: 10 Wing Ta, 2 Wing Slop Ta, ER 10 Cargo Pump (s): 10x200m³/hr Manifold: Bow/CM: 44.3m	**1 oil engine** reduction geared to sc. shaft driving 1 CP propeller Total Power: 2,040kW (2,774hp) MAN-B&W 8L27/38 1 x 4 Stroke 8 Cy. 270 x 380 2040kW (2774bhp) STX Corp-South Korea AuxGen: 1 x 640kW 440V 60Hz a.c, 3 x 240kW 440V 60Hz a.c Boilers: TOH (o.f.) 10.0kgf/cm² (9.8bar) Thrusters: 1 Thwart. FP thruster (f) Fuel: 185.0 (d.f.)
9334325 *IBVS* -	**SARACENA** **Mediterranea di Navigazione SpA** - *Ravenna* *Italy* MMSI: 247221100	**14,701** 6,228 20,890 T/cm 34.9	Class: AB RI	**2007**-11 **Celiktekne Sanayii ve Ticaret A.S. — Tuzla, Istanbul** Yd No: 60 Loa 156.20 (BB) Br ex - Dght 8.890 Lbp 144.20 Br md 25.60 Dpth 12.10 Welded, 1 dk	**(A12B2TR) Chemical/Products Tanker** Double Hull (13F) Liq: 21,164; Liq (Oil): 20,496 Compartments: 10 Wing Ta, 2 Wing Slop Ta, ER 10 Cargo Pump (s): 10x385m³/hr Ice Capable	**2 oil engines** reduction geared to sc. shafts driving 2 CP propellers Total Power: 6,000kW (8,158hp) 14.0kn MaK 6M32C 2 x 4 Stroke 6 Cy. 320 x 480 each-3000kW (4079bhp) Caterpillar Motoren GmbH & Co. KG-Germany AuxGen: 2 x 500kW a.c, 2 x 1900kW a.c Thrusters: 1 Tunnel thruster (f) Fuel: 164.9 (d.f.) 971.0 (r.f.)

9004621 *3FSK3* -	**SARADHA 7** *ex* Duta Bangsa *-2013* *ex* Sunny Giant *-2009* **Middle East Fuel Distribution Co LLC** - *Panama* *Panama* MMSI: 351358000 Official number: 44618PEXT	**3,778** 1,987 5,953 T/cm 13.8	Class: KI RI (NK) (KR)	**1990-07 Sanuki Shipbuilding & Iron Works Co Ltd — Mitoyo KG** Yd No: 1212 Loa 105.50 (BB) Br ex 16.03 Dght 6.915 Lbp 96.50 Br md 16.00 Dpth 8.45 Welded, 1 dk	**(A12B2TR) Chemical/Products Tanker** Double Bottom Partial Compartment Length Liq: 6,916; Liq (Oil): 6,916 Cargo Heating Coils Compartments: 10 Ta, ER 2 Cargo Pump (s) Manifold: Bow/CM: 48.3m	**1 oil engine** driving 1 FP propeller Total Power: 2,427kW (3,300hp) 12.0kn Hanshin 6EL40 1 x 4 Stroke 6 Cy. 400 x 800 2427kW (3300bhp) The Hanshin Diesel Works Ltd-Japan AuxGen: 2 x 280kW 445V 60Hz a.c Fuel: 380.0 (r.f.)
9535424 *A6E2874* -	**SARADHA 9** *ex* Pilgrim *-2013* **Sea Bridge Shipping Management LLC** Middle East Fuel Distribution Co LLC *Sharjah* *United Arab Emirates* MMSI: 470673000	**1,263** 378 1,520 T/cm 6.8	Class: BV	**2011-07 Modest Infrastructure Ltd — Bhavnagar** Yd No: 309 Loa 63.76 Br ex 12.02 Dght 4.200 Lbp 60.30 Br md 12.00 Dpth 6.00 Welded, 1 dk	**(B35E2TF) Bunkering Tanker** Double Hull (13F) Liq: 1,431; Liq (Oil): 1,431 Compartments: 5 Wing Ta, 5 Wing Ta, 1 Slop Ta, ER 4 Cargo Pump (s): 2x250m³/hr, 2x150m³/hr	**2 oil engines** reduction geared to sc. shafts driving 2 FP propellers Total Power: 864kW (1,174hp) 8.0kn Caterpillar C18 2 x 4 Stroke 6 Cy. 145 x 183 each-432kW (587bhp) Caterpillar Inc-USA AuxGen: 2 x 275kW 50Hz a.c Thrusters: 1 Tunnel thruster (f) Fuel: 79.0
9306512 *YJS7154* -	**SARAFENUA** - **IFIRA Shipping Agencies Ltd** - *Port Vila* *Vanuatu* Official number: 7154	**482** 144 189	Class: (CC)	**2003-11 Wuhan Nanhua High Speed Ship Engineering Co Ltd — Wuhan HB** Yd No: 443 Loa 40.00 Br ex - Dght - Lbp 36.00 Br md 8.80 Dpth 3.60 Welded, 1 dk	**(A36A2PR) Passenger/Ro-Ro Ship (Vehicles)**	**2 oil engines** geared to sc. shafts driving 2 FP propellers Total Power: 736kW (1,000hp) Cummins KTA-19-M500 2 x 4 Stroke 6 Cy. 159 x 159 each-368kW (500bhp) Cummins Engine Co Inc-USA
1011123 *ZGBK4* -	**SARAFIN** - **Sarafin Ltd** - *George Town* *Cayman Islands (British)* MMSI: 319026500 Official number: 742887	**114** 34 13	Class: LR ✠ **100A1** SS 03/2012 SSC, Yacht, mono, G6 Cable: 113.7/14.0 U2 (a)	**2012-03 R.M.K. Tersanesi — Tuzla** Yd No: 85 Loa 30.18 Br ex 7.57 Dght 1.310 Lbp 27.40 Br md 7.57 Dpth 3.19 Bonded, 1 dk	**(X11A2YS) Yacht (Sailing)** Hull Material: Reinforced Plastic	**1 oil engine** with clutches, flexible couplings & dr reverse geared to sc. shaft driving 1 CP propeller Total Power: 350kW (476hp) Cummins QSM11-M 1 x 4 Stroke 6 Cy. 125 x 147 350kW (476bhp) Cummins Engine Co Inc-USA AuxGen: 2 x 27kW 380V 50Hz a.c Thrusters: 1 Thwart. FP thruster (f); 1 Thwart. FP thruster (a)
1009120 *ZCXH4* -	**SARAFSA** - **Burgundy Sea Ltd & Ansbacher (BVI) Ltd** Royale Oceanic International Yacht Management Ltd *George Town* *Cayman Islands (British)* MMSI: 319460000 Official number: 740672	**3,179** 953 320	Class: LR ✠ **100A1** SS 06/2013 SSC Yacht (P), mono, G6 ✠ **LMC** **UMS** Cable: 220.0/34.0 U3 (a)	**2008-06 Babcock Marine Appledore — Bideford** (Hull) **2008-06 Devonport Engineering Consortium Ltd — Plymouth** Yd No: 054 Loa 82.00 Br ex 15.03 Dght 3.700 Lbp 74.50 Br md 14.80 Dpth 7.10 Welded, 6 dks	**(X11A2YP) Yacht**	**2 oil engines** with clutches, flexible couplings & sr geared to sc. shafts driving 2 CP propellers Total Power: 3,960kW (5,384hp) M.T.U. 16V4000M 2 x Vee 4 Stroke 16 Cy. 165 x 190 each-1980kW (2692bhp) MTU Friedrichshafen GmbH-Friedrichshafen AuxGen: 3 x 450kW 450V 50Hz a.c Thrusters: 2 Thwart. FP thruster (f)
1007407 *ZCGX* -	**SARAH** - **Sarah Cayman Islands Ltd** Ocean Management GmbH *George Town* *Cayman Islands (British)* MMSI: 319775000 Official number: 735519	**1,370** 411 -	Class: LR ✠ **100A1** SS 06/2012 SSC Yacht (P), mono G6 ✠ **LMC** Cable: 357.5/26.0 U2 (a)	**2002-06 C. van de Graaf B.V. — Hardinxveld-Giessendam** (Hull) Yd No: (438) **2002-06 Amels Holland BV — Makkum** Yd No: 438 Loa 62.00 (BB) Br ex 12.51 Dght 3.850 Lbp 53.82 Br md 11.80 Dpth 6.46 Welded, 2 dks	**(X11A2YP) Yacht**	**2 oil engines** with clutches, flexible couplings & sr reverse geared to sc. shafts driving 2 CP propellers Total Power: 3,732kW (5,074hp) 17.0kn Caterpillar 3516B 2 x Vee 4 Stroke 16 Cy. 170 x 190 each-1866kW (2537bhp) Caterpillar Inc-USA AuxGen: 2 x 216kW 400V 50Hz a.c, 1 x 160kW 400V 50Hz a.c Thrusters: 1 Thwart. FP thruster (f)
7430553 *HO3903* -	**SARAH** *ex* Seabulk Sarah *-2005* *ex* Ocean Discoverer *-1997* *ex* Gray Range *-1995* *ex* Nita *-1981* *launched as* Fook Gee Two *-1981* **Al Khair Metal Trading FZC** - *Panama* *Panama* Official number: 3119905A	*451* 129 451	Class: (LR) (CC) (GL) ✠ Classed LR until 22/4/92	**1981-06 Taiwan Machinery Manufacturing Corp. — Kaohsiung** Yd No: 659 Loa 42.68 Br ex 10.37 Dght 3.893 Lbp 38.99 Br md 10.10 Dpth 4.52 Welded, 1 dk	**(B21B20T) Offshore Tug/Supply Ship**	**2 oil engines** geared to sc. shafts driving 2 CP propellers Total Power: 1,324kW (1,800hp) 10.0kn Alpha 409-26VO 2 x 2 Stroke 9 Cy. 260 x 400 each-662kW (900bhp) B&W Alpha Diesel A/S-Denmark AuxGen: 2 x 52kW 220/380V 50Hz a.c Thrusters: 1 Thwart. FP thruster (f) Fuel: 293.0 (d.f.)
7808463 *ODVY* -	**SARAH** *ex* Nordkyn *-2013* **Spiridon Sarl** - *Lebanon* MMSI: 450554000	**2,503** 791 1,600	Class: (BV) (NV)	**1979-10 Fosen Mek. Verksteder AS — Rissa** Yd No: 22 Loa 77.63 (BB) Br ex 14.53 Dght 5.130 Lbp 70.21 Br md 14.40 Dpth 10.01 Welded, 3 dks	**(A31B2GP) Palletised Cargo Ship** Bale: 4,729; Ins: 538 TEU 26 C incl 14 ref C 1 Ha: (9.9 x 6.4)ER Cranes: 1x40t Ice Capable	**1 oil engine** reduction geared to sc. shaft driving 1 FP propeller Total Power: 2,560kW (3,481hp) 14.0kn Wartsila 8R32 1 x 4 Stroke 8 Cy. 320 x 350 2560kW (3481bhp) Oy Wartsila Ab-Finland AuxGen: 1 x 292kW 380V 50Hz a.c, 2 x 180kW 380V 50Hz a.c Thrusters: 1 Thwart. FP thruster (f) Fuel: 292.0 (d.f.) 14.0pd
9126338 - -	**SARAH** - **Waha Oil Co of Libya Inc** - *Es Sider* *Libya*	**487** 146 789	Class: (LR) ✠ Classed LR until 16/1/13	**1995-12 Bodewes Binnenvaart B.V. — Millingen a/d Rijn** (Hull) Yd No: 855 **1995-12 B.V. Scheepswerf Damen — Gorinchem** Yd No: 6775 Loa 35.32 Br ex 16.32 Dght 1.784 Lbp 33.54 Br md 16.00 Dpth 3.00 Welded, 1 dk	**(B34B2SC) Crane Vessel** Cranes: 1	**2 oil engines** reduction geared to sc. shafts driving 2 Directional propellers Total Power: 532kW (724hp) 8.5kn Kelvin TAS8 2 x 4 Stroke 8 Cy. 165 x 184 each-266kW (362bhp) Kelvin Diesels Ltd., GECDiesels-Glasgow AuxGen: 1 x 190kW 440V 60Hz a.c, 1 x 170kW 440V 60Hz a.c
8945610 *DUA2268* -	**SARAH** - **Asian Shipping Corp** - *Manila* *Philippines* Official number: 00-0000400	*1,076* 692 -		**1983-01 at Manila** Loa 74.98 Br ex - Dght - Lbp - Br md 14.63 Dpth 3.04 Welded, 1 dk	**(A35D2RL) Landing Craft** Bow ramp (f)	**1 oil engine** driving 1 FP propeller Total Power: 971kW (1,320hp)
9386897 *A6E2682* -	**SARAH** - **Gulf Piping Co WLL (GPC)** - *Abu Dhabi* *United Arab Emirates* MMSI: 470346000	**486** 146 460	Class: BV	**2006-04 Yantai Salvage Bureau Shipyard — Yantai SD** Yd No: YJLZ05-12 Loa 36.10 Br ex - Dght 4.000 Lbp 32.75 Br md 10.60 Dpth 4.90 Welded, 1 dk	**(B32A2ST) Tug**	**2 oil engines** reduction geared to sc. shafts driving 2 FP propellers Total Power: 2,350kW (3,196hp) Caterpillar 3512B 2 x Vee 4 Stroke 12 Cy. 170 x 190 each-1175kW (1598bhp) Caterpillar Inc-USA
9354129 - -	**SARAH-1** - **Bin Nowiran Establishment** - *Dammam* *Saudi Arabia* MMSI: 403101010	**322** - -	Class: BV	**2006-11 Santierul Naval Damen Galati S.A. — Galati** (Hull) Yd No: 1099 **2006-11 B.V. Scheepswerf Damen — Gorinchem** Yd No: 511612 Loa 35.53 Br ex 8.84 Dght 3.550 Lbp 34.97 Br md 8.80 Dpth 4.40 Welded, 1 dk	**(B32A2ST) Tug**	**2 oil engines** geared to sc. shafts driving 2 FP propellers Total Power: 3,040kW (4,134hp) MaK 8M20 2 x 4 Stroke 8 Cy. 200 x 300 each-1520kW (2067bhp) Caterpillar Motoren GmbH & Co. KG-Germany Thrusters: 1 Tunnel thruster (f)
9237448 *9KWU* -	**SARAH 8** - **Amal Alkhaleej Co for Marine Contracting** - *Kuwait* *Kuwait* MMSI: 447075000 Official number: KT1658	**442** 132 -	Class: BV (AB)	**2000-12 Keppel Singmarine Dockyard Pte Ltd — Singapore** Yd No: 238 Loa 33.48 Br ex - Dght 4.400 Lbp 27.20 Br md 10.80 Dpth 5.64 Welded, 1 dk	**(B32A2ST) Tug**	**2 oil engines** driving 2 Voith-Schneider propellers Total Power: 3,678kW (5,000hp) Niigata 6L28HX 2 x 4 Stroke 6 Cy. 280 x 370 each-1839kW (2500bhp) Niigata Engineering Co Ltd-Japan
9237450 *9KWV* -	**SARAH 9** - **Amal Alkhaleej Co for Marine Contracting** - *Kuwait* *Kuwait* MMSI: 447076000 Official number: KT1659	**442** 132 -	Class: BV (AB)	**2000-12 Keppel Singmarine Dockyard Pte Ltd — Singapore** Yd No: 239 Loa 33.48 Br ex - Dght 4.400 Lbp 27.20 Br md 10.80 Dpth 5.64 Welded, 1 dk	**(B32A2ST) Tug**	**2 oil engines** driving 2 Voith-Schneider propellers Total Power: 3,678kW (5,000hp) Niigata 6L28HX 2 x 4 Stroke 6 Cy. 280 x 370 each-1839kW (2500bhp) Niigata Engineering Co Ltd-Japan
8983117 *WDB4767* -	**SARAH ANN** *ex* June K *-2010* **Donjon Marine Co Inc** - *New York, NY* *United States of America* MMSI: 366902120 Official number: 1126097	*142* 114 -		**2003** Yd No: 309 L reg 23.77 Br ex - Dght - Lbp - Br md 7.92 Dpth 3.35 Welded, 1 dk	**(B32A2ST) Tug**	**2 oil engines** geared to sc. shafts driving 2 Propellers Total Power: 1,986kW (2,700hp) Caterpillar 3512B 2 x Vee 4 Stroke 12 Cy. 170 x 190 each-993kW (1350bhp) Caterpillar Inc-USA

IMO / Call sign / Fishing no.	Name, former names, owner, manager, port, flag	Tonnage	Classification	Builder / Dimensions	Ship type / Cargo	Machinery
7050951 *WDF6607* -	**SARAH BELLE** *ex* Captain Andy *-2012* **Captain Andy Fisheries Inc** - *Newport, OR* *United States of America* MMSI: 367475970 Official number: 517651	*111* 75 -		**1969 Allied Shipyard, Inc. — Larose, La** L reg 21.13 Br ex 6.56 Dght - Lbp - Br md - Dpth 3.23 Welded	**(B11B2FV) Fishing Vessel**	**1 oil engine** driving 1 FP propeller Total Power: 243kW (330hp)
9350367 *WDC7198* -	**SARAH BORDELON** **Bordelon Marine Inc** - *New Orleans, LA* *United States of America* MMSI: 367067840 Official number: 1174839	**498** 163 625		**2005-10 Bollinger Machine Shop & Shipyard, Inc. — Lockport, La** Yd No: 493 Loa 49.70 Br ex - Dght 2.960 Lbp 46.17 Br md 10.97 Dpth 3.51 Welded, 1 dk	**(B21A2OS) Platform Supply Ship**	**2 oil engines** geared to sc. shafts driving 2 FP propellers Total Power: 1,104kW (1,500hp) Cummins KTA-38-M0 2 x Vee 4 Stroke 12 Cy. 159 x 159 each-552kW (750bhp) Cummins Engine Co Inc-USA AuxGen: 2 x 99kW a.c, 2 x a.c Thrusters: 1 Tunnel thruster (f)
7707619 *GYIH* -	**SARAH D** *ex* Cleveland Endeavour *-2001* **Svitzer Marine Ltd** - *Milford Haven* *United Kingdom* Official number: 341875	**105** 105 -	Class: (LR) ✠ Classed LR until 15/12/97	**1978-10 South Ocean Services (Comm. Craft) Ltd. — Portsmouth** Yd No: 260 Converted From: Fire-fighting Vessel-2001 Loa 24.69 Br ex 8.84 Dght 1.839 Lbp 22.05 Br md 8.59 Dpth 3.05 Welded, 1 dk	**(B34T2QR) Work/Repair Vessel**	**2 oil engines** reverse reduction geared to sc. shafts driving 2 FP propellers Total Power: 338kW (460hp) 10.0kn Ford 2704ET 2 x 4 Stroke 6 Cy. 105 x 115 each-169kW (230bhp) Sabre Engines Ltd.-Wimborne AuxGen: 2 x 88kW 415/240V 50Hz a.c Thrusters: 1 Thwart. FP thruster (f)
9285914 *EI7212* S 411	**SARAH DAVID** **Cornelius & David Minehane** - *Skibbereen* *Irish Republic* MMSI: 250101700 Official number: 403757	**447** 141 530	Class: NV	**2003-07 AS Rigas Kugu Buvetava (Riga Shipyard) — Riga** (Hull) Yd No: (131) **2003-07 Tjornvarvet AB Ronnang — Ronnang** Yd No: 131 Loa 37.30 (BB) Br ex 9.02 Dght 5.630 Lbp 33.02 Br md 9.00 Dpth 6.60 Welded, 1 dk	**(B11A2FS) Stern Trawler**	**1 oil engine** reduction geared to sc. shaft driving 1 FP propeller Total Power: 1,103kW (1,500hp) Caterpillar 3606 1 x 4 Stroke 6 Cy. 280 x 300 1103kW (1500bhp) Caterpillar Inc-USA Thrusters: 1 Thwart. FP thruster (f)
9352171 *XJAB* -	**SARAH DESGAGNES** *ex* Besiktas Greenland *-2008* **Transport Desgagnes Inc** - *Quebec, QC* *Canada* MMSI: 316012308 Official number: 832488	**11,711** 6,026 17,998 T/cm 27.4	Class: LR (BV) **100A1** SS 03/2012 Double Hull oil and chemical tanker, Ship Type 2 ESP *IWS LI Ice Class 1A at a draught of 9.696m Max/min draughts fwd 9.696/4.00m Max/min draughts aft 9.696/6.75m Power required 3417kw, power installed 6300kw **LMC** **UMS IGS**	**2007-03 Gisan Gemi Ins. San — Istanbul** Yd No: 38 Loa 147.50 (BB) Br ex - Dght 9.488 Lbp 138.00 Br md 22.40 Dpth 12.60 Welded, 1 dk	**(A12B2TR) Chemical/Products Tanker** Double Hull (13F) Liq: 20,218; Liq (Oil): 21,300 Cargo Heating Coils Compartments: 14 Wing Ta, 2 Wing Slop Ta, ER 14 Cargo Pump (s): 14x380m³/hr Manifold: Bow/CM: 85.3m Ice Capable	**1 oil engine** reduction geared to sc. shaft driving 1 CP propeller Total Power: 7,000kW (9,517hp) 13.0kn MaK 7M43 1 x 4 Stroke 7 Cy. 430 x 610 7000kW (9517bhp) Caterpillar Motoren GmbH & Co. KG-Germany AuxGen: 3 x 750kW a.c, 1 x 1000kW a.c Thrusters: 1 Tunnel thruster (f) Fuel: 173.0 (d.f.) 830.0 (r.f.) 23.0pd
9390886 *9MGZ3* -	**SARAH GOLD** - **Intan Offshore Sdn Bhd** Emas Offshore Pte Ltd *Port Klang* *Malaysia* MMSI: 533009600 Official number: 332316	**238** 71 90	Class: AB	**2006-12 Strategic Marine (S) Pte Ltd — Singapore** Yd No: H149 Loa 40.37 Br ex - Dght 2.300 Lbp 36.00 Br md 7.50 Dpth 3.22 Welded, 1 dk	**(B21A2OC) Crew/Supply Vessel** Hull Material: Aluminium Alloy Passengers: unberthed: 50	**3 oil engines** reduction geared to sc. shafts driving 3 FP propellers Total Power: 3,310kW (4,500hp) Cummins KTA-38-M2 2 x Vee 4 Stroke 12 Cy. 159 x 159 each-993kW (1350bhp) Cummins Engine Co Inc-USA Cummins KTA-50-M2 1 x Vee 4 Stroke 16 Cy. 159 x 159 1324kW (1800bhp) Cummins Engine Co Inc-USA AuxGen: 2 x 70kW a.c
8956437 *ZQQQ5* -	**SARAH GREY** - **Coastal Launch Services Ltd** - *Southampton* *United Kingdom* MMSI: 235000357 Official number: 902932	*106* - -		**1999 Cladar Ltd. — Portchester** Yd No: 02 Loa 25.00 Br ex - Dght 1.850 Lbp - Br md 9.60 Dpth 2.60 Welded, 1 dk	**(B34T2QR) Work/Repair Vessel** Cranes: 1x100t,1x30t	**2 oil engines** with clutches & sr reverse geared to sc. shafts driving 2 FP propellers Total Power: 1,030kW (1,400hp) 10.0kn Cummins KTA-19-M 2 x 4 Stroke 6 Cy. 159 x 159 each-515kW (700bhp) Cummins Engine Co Ltd-United Kingdom AuxGen: 1 x 48kW a.c Fuel: 60.0 (d.f.) 4.5pd
8022951 *5IM221* -	**SARAH I** *ex* Dar *-2010* *ex* Broa *-1990* **Africa Shipping Corp Ltd** Hammy Distributors & Services Ltd *Zanzibar* *Tanzania* MMSI: 677012100 Official number: 10052	**587** 282 502	Class: (NV)	**1981-05 Vaagland Baatbyggeri AS — Vaagland** Yd No: 101 Loa 42.73 Br ex - Dght 3.610 Lbp 38.61 Br md 9.24 Dpth 6.13 Welded, 2 dks	**(A31A2GX) General Cargo Ship** Grain: 1,245; Bale: 1,125 Compartments: 1 Ho, ER, 1 Tw Dk 1 Ha: (22.0 x 7.2)ER Cranes: 2x5t	**1 oil engine** driving 1 CP propeller Total Power: 423kW (575hp) 10.0kn Callesen 5-427-EOT 1 x 4 Stroke 5 Cy. 270 x 400 423kW (575bhp) Aabenraa Motorfabrik, HeinrichCallesen A/S-Denmark AuxGen: 1 x 72kW 230V 50Hz a.c, 1 x 25kW 230V 50Hz a.c Thrusters: 1 Thwart. FP thruster (f) Fuel: 32.0 (d.f.) 2.5pd
5031315 *HO2620* -	**SARAH II** *ex* Rafiki III *-2008* *ex* Snofjell *-2001* *ex* Ava *-1998* **Emmanuel Mayaka Owanga** - *Panama* *Panama* MMSI: 352021000 Official number: 29915PEXT	**448** 180 675	Class: (NV)	**1958-03 AS Westermoen Baatbyggeri & Mekaniske Verksted — Mandal** Yd No: 461 Loa 44.10 Br ex 8.56 Dght 3.721 Lbp 39.63 Br md 8.54 Dpth 5.36 Welded, 1 dk	**(A31A2GX) General Cargo Ship** Grain: 570 Compartments: 1 Ho, ER 1 Ha: (16.2 x 5.0)ER Derricks: 1x8t; Winches: 2 Ice Capable	**1 oil engine** driving 1 FP propeller Total Power: 287kW (390hp) 10.0kn MaK MSU423 1 x 4 Stroke 6 Cy. 290 x 420 287kW (390bhp) Maschinenbau Kiel AG (MaK)-Kiel AuxGen: 2 x 26kW 220V 50Hz a.c
8822014 - -	**SARAH-J** *launched as* Fortuna II *-1990* **Fortuna Fishing Pty Ltd** - *Newcastle, NSW* *Australia* Official number: 852456	*150* - 77		**1989-10 Port Lincoln Ship Construction Pty Ltd — Port Lincoln SA** Yd No: V14 Loa 23.10 Br ex - Dght 2.546 Lbp 21.50 Br md 7.00 Dpth 3.45 Welded	**(B11B2FV) Fishing Vessel** Ins: 90	**1 oil engine** with flexible couplings & sr geared to sc. shaft driving 1 FP propeller Total Power: 233kW (317hp) Cummins KTA-19-M 1 x 4 Stroke 6 Cy. 159 x 159 233kW (317bhp) Cummins Engine Co Inc-USA
9252814 *9MGM4* -	**SARAH JADE** - **Intan Offshore Sdn Bhd** Emas Offshore Pte Ltd *Port Klang* *Malaysia* MMSI: 533001600 Official number: 330459	**179** 53 59	Class: LR ✠**100A1** SS 11/2011 SSC cargo (A), mono HSC G3, South East Asian water service ✠**LMC** Cable: 110.0/16.0 U2 (a)	**2001-11 Asia-Pac Geraldton Pte Ltd — Singapore** Yd No: 18049 Loa 34.30 Br ex 7.51 Dght 1.440 Lbp 30.50 Br md 7.50 Dpth 2.60 Welded, 1 dk	**(B21A2OC) Crew/Supply Vessel** Hull Material: Aluminium Alloy Passengers: unberthed: 80	**3 oil engines** with clutches, flexible couplings & sr reverse geared to sc. shafts driving 3 FP propellers Total Power: 2,400kW (3,264hp) M.T.U. 16V2000M60 3 x Vee 4 Stroke 16 Cy. 130 x 150 each-800kW (1088bhp) MTU Friedrichshafen GmbH-Friedrichshafen AuxGen: 2 x 109kW 415V 50Hz a.c Thrusters: 1 Thwart. FP thruster (f)
9021710 *2FGY3* BM 41	**SARAH LOUISE** *ex* Osterems *-2012* **Langdon & Philip Ltd** - *Brixham* *United Kingdom* Official number: C20130	**164** 88 -	Class: (GL)	**1991-07 Scheepswerf Visser B.V. — Den Helder** Yd No: 133 Loa 24.00 Br ex 6.75 Dght 3.000 Lbp 21.30 Br md 6.70 Dpth 4.00 Welded, 1 dk	**(B11A2FT) Trawler** Ins: 100	**1 oil engine** with flexible couplings & sr reverse geared to sc. shaft driving 1 FP propeller Total Power: 221kW (300hp) 9.0kn MWM TBD604BL6 1 x 4 Stroke 6 Cy. 170 x 195 221kW (300bhp) Motoren Werke Mannheim AG (MWM)-Mannheim AuxGen: 1 x 164kW 220/380V a.c Thrusters: 1 Thwart. FP thruster (f)
8945892 *DXPZ* -	**SARAH MARGARITA** - **Lazaro Enterprises** - *Manila* *Philippines* Official number: 00-0000231	**273** 177 700		**1988 at Manila** L reg 39.55 Br ex - Dght - Lbp 39.33 Br md 9.76 Dpth 2.97 Welded, 1 dk	**(A13B2TU) Tanker (unspecified)**	**1 oil engine** driving 1 FP propeller Total Power: 368kW (500hp) Cummins 1 x 4 Stroke 368kW (500bhp) Cummins Engine Co Inc-USA

No.	Name / Owner	Tonnage	Class	Builder / Dimensions	Type	Machinery
8974374 *H05029* -	**SARAH PEARL** **Sarah Pearl Shipping Pte Ltd** Emas Offshore Pte Ltd *Panama* *Panama* MMSI: 357355000 Official number: 3411208B	**220** 66 -	Class: LR (GL) **100A1** SS 02/2013 SSC cargo (A) HSC mono, G3, South East Asian water service **LMC** Cable: 14.0/55.0 U2 (a)	2002-12 **Strategic Marine Pty Ltd — Fremantle WA** Yd No: H108 Loa 37.29 Br ex 7.51 Dght 1.700 Lbp 35.00 Br md 7.50 Dpth 2.64 Welded, 1 dk	**(B21A2OC) Crew/Supply Vessel** Hull Material: Aluminium Alloy Passengers: unberthed: 70	**3 oil engines** geared to sc. shafts driving 3 FP propellers Total Power: 2,400kW (3,264hp) 22.0kn M.T.U. 16V2000M60 3 x Vee 4 Stroke 16 Cy. 130 x 150 each-800kW (1088bhp) MTU Friedrichshafen GmbH-Friedrichshafen AuxGen: 2 x 109kW 400V 50Hz a.c Thrusters: 1 Thwart. FP thruster (f)
8964991 - 176105	**SARAH PIERRE** **9000-3997 Quebec Inc** - *Gaspe, QC* *Canada* MMSI: 316003708 Official number: 822183	*147* 110 -		2000 **Chantier Naval Forillon Inc — Gaspe QC** L reg 18.60 Br ex - Dght 3.960 Lbp - Br md 7.20 Dpth 4.40 Welded, 1 dk	**(B11A2FS) Stern Trawler**	**1 oil engine** geared to sc. shaft driving 1 FP propeller Total Power: 449kW (610hp) 10.0kn Caterpillar 3412 1 x Vee 4 Stroke 12 Cy. 137 x 152 449kW (610bhp) Caterpillar Inc-USA
9294159 *5BPA3* -	**SARAH SCHULTE** *ex* Ariake *-2010* *launched as* Sarah Schulte *-2005* **ms 'Sarah Schulte' Shipping GmbH & Co KG** Reederei Thomas Schulte GmbH & Co KG *Limassol* *Cyprus* MMSI: 210409000 Official number: 9294159	**28,592** 14,769 39,383 T/cm 56.7	Class: GL	2005-04 **Hyundai Mipo Dockyard Co Ltd — Ulsan** Yd No: 0341 Loa 222.14 (BB) Br ex 30.00 Dght 12.000 Lbp 210.00 Br md 30.00 Dpth 16.80 Welded, 1 dk	**(A33A2CC) Container Ship (Fully Cellular)** TEU 2824 C Ho 1026 TEU C Dk 1798 TEU incl 586 ref C. Compartments: ER, 6 Cell Ho	**1 oil engine** driving 1 FP propeller Total Power: 25,270kW (34,357hp) 22.0kn B&W 7K80MC-C 1 x 2 Stroke 7 Cy. 800 x 2300 25270kW (34357bhp) Hyundai Heavy Industries Co Ltd-South Korea AuxGen: 4 x 1600kW 440/230V 60Hz a.c Thrusters: 1 Thwart. CP thruster (f) Fuel: 220.0 (d.f.) 3307.0 (r.f.)
9010943 *ICWE* -	**SARAH WONSILD** **Marittima Etnea Srl** Nordic Tankers A/S SatCom: Inmarsat A 1151747 *Augusta* *Italy* MMSI: 247006000 Official number: 102	**2,349** 816 2,702 T/cm 10.3	Class: RI (BV)	1993-01 **Cant. Nav. Metalcost SpA — Sarzana** (Hull) 1993-01 **Soc. Esercizio Cant. S.p.A. — Viareggio** Yd No: 786 Loa 89.60 (BB) Br ex 14.00 Dght 5.213 Lbp 80.90 Br md 13.80 Dpth 6.50 Welded, 1 dk	**(A12A2TC) Chemical Tanker** Double Hull (13F) Liq: 2,966 Cargo Heating Coils Compartments: 14 Wing Ta (s.stl), ER 14 Cargo Pump (s): 14x150m³/hr Manifold: Bow/CM: 47m Ice Capable	**1 oil engine** with clutches, flexible couplings & sr geared to sc. shaft driving 1 CP propeller Total Power: 2,206kW (2,999hp) 13.5kn Yanmar 6N330-EN 1 x 4 Stroke 6 Cy. 330 x 440 2206kW (2999bhp) Yanmar Diesel Engine Co Ltd-Japan AuxGen: 2 x 360kW 440/220V 60Hz a.c, 1 x 200kW 440/220V 60Hz a.c, 1 x 440kW 440V a.c Thrusters: 1 Tunnel thruster (f) Fuel: 293.0 (d.f.) (Part Heating Coils) 11.5pd
5288803 - -	**SARAH'S WISH** *ex* Alana Marie *-1995* *ex* Westkust *-1977* *ex* Racken *-1969* - - *Kingstown* *St Vincent & The Grenadines*	*448* 199 793	Class: (BV)	1960 **Karlstads Varv AB — Karlstad** Yd No: 140 Lengthened-1964 Loa 67.67 Br ex 9.43 Dght 3.020 Lbp - Br md 9.40 Dpth 3.05 Welded, 1 dk & S dk	**(A31A2GX) General Cargo Ship** Grain: 1,416; Bale: 1,274 Compartments: 2 Ho, ER 2 Ha: (17.3 x 4.6) (13.7 x 4.6)ER Derricks: 4x3t; Winches: 4	**1 oil engine** driving 1 FP propeller Total Power: 588kW (799hp) 11.5kn MWM 1 x 4 Stroke 6 Cy. 320 x 480 588kW (799bhp) Motoren Werke Mannheim AG (MWM)-West Germany Fuel: 16.5 (d.f.)
7022667 - -	**SARALA** **Paradip Port Trust** - *Kolkata* *India* Official number: 1346	*265* 67 381	Class: (LR) (IR) ✠ Classed LR until 7/80	1971-08 **East Bengal Engineering Works — Kolkata** Loa 33.53 Br ex 8.59 Dght 3.506 Lbp 30.48 Br md 8.39 Dpth 4.27 Welded, 1 dk	**(B32A2ST) Tug**	**1 oil engine** reverse reduction geared to sc. shaft driving 1 FP propeller Total Power: 982kW (1,335hp) MAN G9V30/45ATL 1 x 4 Stroke 9 Cy. 300 x 450 982kW (1335bhp) N.V. Dok en Werf Mij.Wilton-Fijenoord-Schiedam AuxGen: 2 x 56kW 230V d.c
9380300 *EQLF* -	**SARALAH** *ex* Khalij-E-Fars 4 *-2014* **Government of The Islamic Republic of Iran (Ports & Maritime Organisation)** *Bandar Abbas* *Iran* MMSI: 422842000 Official number: 842	**389** 116 146	Class: (BV)	2006-02 **Penglai Bohai Shipyard Co Ltd — Penglai SD** Yd No: PBZ04/35 Loa 33.98 Br ex 10.40 Dght 3.850 Lbp 30.50 Br md 10.00 Dpth 4.50 Welded, 1 dk	**(B32A2ST) Tug**	**2 oil engines** reduction geared to sc. shafts driving 2 Propellers Total Power: 3,236kW (4,400hp) Deutz SBV8M628 2 x 4 Stroke 8 Cy. 240 x 280 each-1618kW (2200bhp) Deutz AG-Koeln
8112093 - -	**SARALLAH** **Government of The Islamic Republic of Iran (Ports & Maritime Organisation)** - *Bandar Imam Khomeini* *Iran*	**206** 62 135	Class: (LR) ✠ Classed LR until 7/1/12	1983-06 **Scheepsbouw Alblas B.V. — Krimpen a/d IJssel** (Hull) 1983-06 **B.V. Scheepswerf Damen — Gorinchem** Yd No: 3129 Loa 30.21 Br ex 8.06 Dght 3.310 Lbp 26.95 Br md 7.80 Dpth 4.04 Welded, 1 dk	**(B32A2ST) Tug**	**2 oil engines** with clutches, flexible couplings & sr reverse geared to sc. shafts driving 2 FP propellers Total Power: 2,140kW (2,910hp) Deutz SBV6M628 2 x 4 Stroke 6 Cy. 240 x 280 each-1070kW (1455bhp) Kloeckner Humboldt Deutz AG-West Germany AuxGen: 2 x 64kW 380V 50Hz a.c Fuel: 68.0 (d.f.)
6802852 - -	**SARAMAR I** *ex* Sara Mar *-1998* *ex* Truitje *-1997* - -	*110* 38 -		1967-06 **N.V. Jacht- en Scheepswerf M. Veldthuis — Groningen** Yd No: 218 Lengthened-1980 Loa 29.90 Br ex - Dght - Lbp - Br md 6.43 Dpth 2.62 Welded, 1 dk	**(B11A2FT) Trawler**	**1 oil engine** driving 1 FP propeller Total Power: 574kW (780hp) Mitsubishi 1 x 574kW (780bhp) (new engine 1987) Mitsubishi Heavy Industries Ltd-Japan
7221677 *6VQG* DAK 506	**SARAN** *ex* Marie Helene *-2011* **Societe Gabonaise de Peche (SOGAPECHE)** - *Dakar* *Senegal*	*106* 34 -	Class: (BV)	1972 **At. & Ch. C. Auroux — Arcachon** Yd No: 298 Loa 22.00 Br ex 6.41 Dght 2.693 Lbp 19.61 Br md - Dpth 3.26 Welded, 1 dk	**(B11A2FT) Trawler**	**1 oil engine** driving 1 FP propeller Total Power: 316kW (430hp) 12.0kn Baudouin DNP12M 1 x Vee 4 Stroke 12 Cy. 150 x 150 316kW (430bhp) Societe des Moteurs Baudouin SA-France
7941253 *UCYF* -	**SARAN** **Primorskaya Fishery Corp Ltd (OOO 'Primorskaya Rybolovnaya Korporatsiya')** - *Vladivostok* *Russia* MMSI: 273842410	**771** 234 332	Class: (RS)	1980-11 **Zavod "Leninskaya Kuznitsa" — Kiyev** Yd No: 247 Loa 53.75 (BB) Br ex 10.72 Dght 4.341 Lbp 47.92 Br md 10.50 Dpth 6.02 Welded, 1 dk	**(B11A2FS) Stern Trawler** Ins: 218 Compartments: 1 Ho, ER 1 Ha: (1.6 x 1.6) Derricks: 2x1.5t Ice Capable	**1 oil engine** driving 1 FP propeller Total Power: 971kW (1,320hp) 12.8kn S.K.L. 8NVD48A-2U 1 x 4 Stroke 8 Cy. 320 x 480 971kW (1320bhp) VEB Schwermaschinenbau "KarlLiebknecht" (SKL)-Magdeburg Fuel: 168.0 (d.f.)
8864775 *9V3660* -	**SARANA 1601** *ex* Planet I *-1997* *ex* Koei Maru *-1993* **Cipta Sarana Marine (Pte) Ltd** - *Singapore* *Singapore*	*137* 42 -	Class: (GL)	1982 **Asahi Zosen K.K. — Sumoto** Yd No: 262 Loa - Br ex 7.20 Dght 2.408 Lbp 20.76 Br md - Dpth 2.80 Welded, 1 dk	**(B32A2ST) Tug**	**2 oil engines** reverse reduction geared to sc. shafts driving 2 FP propellers Total Power: 1,176kW (1,598hp) 12.0kn Matsui 6M26KGHS 2 x 4 Stroke 6 Cy. 260 x 400 each-588kW (799bhp) Matsui Iron Works Co Ltd-Japan AuxGen: 1 x 24kW 220V a.c, 1 x 16kW 220V a.c
8711162 *9V3276* -	**SARANA 1602** *ex* PU 1602 *-1996* **Cipta Sarana Marine (Pte) Ltd** - *Singapore* *Singapore* Official number: 383565	**217** 65 -	Class: (AB)	1987 **Pan-United Shipping Pte Ltd — Singapore** Yd No: SC-02-85 Loa 26.47 Br ex - Dght - Lbp 25.51 Br md 8.11 Dpth 4.02 Welded, 1 dk	**(B32A2ST) Tug**	**1 oil engine** with clutches, flexible couplings & dr reverse geared to sc. shaft driving 1 FP propeller Total Power: 1,177kW (1,600hp) Niigata 8MG25BX 1 x 4 Stroke 8 Cy. 250 x 320 1177kW (1600bhp) Niigata Engineering Co Ltd-Japan AuxGen: 2 x 48kW a.c
8921690 *YBMA* -	**SARANA ANUGRAH** *ex* Katsu Maru No. 8 *-2007* **PT Bomal Wahana Sagara** - *Surabaya* *Indonesia* Official number: 3468	**1,073** 436 2,403	Class: KI	1990-03 **Honda Zosen — Saiki** Yd No: 808 Loa 71.07 (BB) Br ex - Dght 5.000 Lbp 65.00 Br md 10.50 Dpth 6.20 Welded	**(A31A2GX) General Cargo Ship** Compartments: 1 Ho, ER	**1 oil engine** with clutches, flexible couplings & sr geared to sc. shaft driving 1 FP propeller Total Power: 736kW (1,001hp) Akasaka K28FD 1 x 4 Stroke 6 Cy. 280 x 480 736kW (1001bhp) Akasaka Tekkosho KK (Akasaka DieselLtd)-Japan AuxGen: 1 x 120kW 225/130V a.c
9084334 *JZEM* -	**SARANA LINTAS NUSANTARA** *ex* Sarana Sukses *-2013* *ex* Ichikawa Maru *-2013* **PT Bandar Bahari Permai** - *Surabaya* *Indonesia* Official number: 2013 KA NO. 5813/L	**1,970** 626 2,100	Class: KI (Class contemplated)	1994-05 **Shinhama Dockyard Co. Ltd. — Anan** Yd No: 835 Loa 84.15 Br ex - Dght 4.590 Lbp 78.53 Br md 13.00 Dpth 7.65 Welded, 1 dk	**(A31A2GX) General Cargo Ship** Grain: 3,387; Bale: 3,205 Compartments: 1 Ho, ER 1 Ha: (41.6 x 10.2)ER	**1 oil engine** driving 1 FP propeller Total Power: 1,618kW (2,200hp) 11.0kn Niigata 6M34AGT 1 x 4 Stroke 6 Cy. 340 x 620 1618kW (2200bhp) Niigata Engineering Co Ltd-Japan AuxGen: 2 x 144kW 445V a.c

9084009 *PNNF* -	**SARANA LINTAS UTAMA** *ex* Shotoku Maru *-2010* **PT Bandar Bahari Permai** - *Surabaya* *Indonesia* MMSI: 525006049 Official number: 133627	**3,239** 2,084 5,435	Class: KI (NK)	**1994**-04 **Honda Zosen — Saiki** Yd No: 860 Loa 99.52 Br ex - Dght 7.800 Lbp 92.00 Br md 15.70 Dpth 7.80 Welded	**(A31A2GX) General Cargo Ship** Grain: 6,037; Bale: 6,037 Compartments: 2 Ho, ER 2 Ha: 2 (25.2 x 7.5)ER	**1 oil engine** driving 1 FP propeller Total Power: 2,942kW (4,000hp) 12.5kn Hanshin 6LF50 1 x 4 Stroke 6 Cy. 500 x 800 2942kW (4000bhp) The Hanshin Diesel Works Ltd-Japan Fuel: 130.0 (r.f.)
8002121 *YGRW* -	**SARANA PERKASA** *ex* California *-2001* *ex* Kenwa Maru No. 2 *-1995* *ex* Hoshin Maru No. 11 *-1984* **PT Bandar Bahari Permai** - *Surabaya* *Indonesia* MMSI: 525011003 Official number: 2892	*1,239* 683 2,431	Class: KI	**1980**-02 **Sasaki Shipbuilding Co Ltd — Osakikamijima HS** Yd No: 338 Loa 69.40 Br ex 11.54 Dght 4.800 Lbp 65.03 Br md 11.51 Dpth 6.08 Welded, 2 dks	**(A31A2GX) General Cargo Ship**	**1 oil engine** driving 1 FP propeller Total Power: 1,214kW (1,651hp) Hanshin 6LU35 1 x 4 Stroke 6 Cy. 350 x 550 1214kW (1651bhp) The Hanshin Diesel Works Ltd-Japan
9096026 *YB8107* -	**SARANA PETRO I** *ex* Hengda 888 *-2007* **PT Sarana Petro Samudra** - *Bitung* *Indonesia*	**287** 160 -	Class: KI	**1997**-01 **Yueqing Shipyard Co Ltd — Yueqing ZJ** Loa 41.70 Br ex - Dght 3.200 Lbp 39.10 Br md 7.70 Dpth 3.90 Welded, 1 dk	**(A13B2TU) Tanker (unspecified)**	**1 oil engine** driving 1 Propeller Total Power: 294kW (400hp) Niigata 1 x 4 Stroke 6 Cy. 294kW (400bhp) Niigata Engineering Co Ltd-Japan
8827868 *YB4693* -	**SARANA PETRO II** *ex* Mutiara Jaya *-2009* *ex* Tenaga Laut *-2006* *ex* Dae Young No. 7 *-2005* **PT Sarana Petro Samudra** - *Tanjung Priok* *Indonesia*	**299** 167 567	Class: KI (KR)	**1986**-11 **Banguhjin Engineering & Shipbuilding Co Ltd — Ulsan** Loa 47.35 Br ex - Dght 3.168 Lbp 43.00 Br md 7.00 Dpth 3.30 Welded, 1 dk	**(A13B2TU) Tanker (unspecified)** Liq: 618; Liq (Oil): 618	**1 oil engine** driving 1 FP propeller Total Power: 294kW (400hp) 10.6kn Sumiyoshi S623TS 1 x 4 Stroke 6 Cy. 230 x 400 294kW (400bhp) Sumiyoshi Marine Diesel Co Ltd-Japan AuxGen: 2 x 40kW 225V a.c
9049205 - -	**SARANA PRIMA** - **Hanan** - *Palembang* *Indonesia*	**114** 68 -	Class: KI	**2003**-01 **P.T. Triloga Raya — Palembang** Loa 22.50 Br ex - Dght 2.400 Lbp 22.00 Br md 7.00 Dpth 2.90 Welded, 1 dk	**(B32A2ST) Tug**	**2 oil engines** reduction geared to sc. shafts driving 2 Propellers Total Power: 692kW (940hp) Caterpillar 3408 2 x Vee 4 Stroke 8 Cy. 137 x 152 each-346kW (470bhp) Caterpillar Inc-USA AuxGen: 2 x 60kW 380V a.c
9024853 - -	**SARANA SAMUDERA 09** - **PT Sinar Sarana Samudera** - *Banjarmasin* *Indonesia*	**182** 109 -	Class: (KI)	**1997**-04 **PT Kalimantan Banjarnusa — Banjarmasin** L reg 23.00 Br ex Dght - Lbp 21.13 Br md 7.00 Dpth 1.80 Welded, 1 dk	**(B32A2ST) Tug**	**2 oil engines** reduction geared to sc. shafts driving 2 Propellers Total Power: 692kW (940hp) Caterpillar 3408TA 2 x Vee 4 Stroke 8 Cy. 137 x 152 each-346kW (470bhp) Caterpillar Inc-USA
8652469 - -	**SARANA SAMUDERA 17** - **PT Sinar Sarana Samudera** - *Banjarmasin* *Indonesia*	**203** 61 -	Class: KI	**2010**-09 **PT Kalimantan Banjarnusa — Banjarmasin** Loa 27.00 Br ex - Dght 2.940 Lbp 25.48 Br md 8.00 Dpth 3.50 Welded, 1 dk	**(B32A2ST) Tug**	**2 oil engines** reduction geared to sc. shafts driving 2 Propellers Total Power: 1,716kW (2,334hp) Mitsubishi S12A2-MPTK 2 x Vee 4 Stroke 12 Cy. 150 x 160 each-858kW (1167bhp) Mitsubishi Heavy Industries Ltd-Japan
8910885 *PMKQ* -	**SARANA SUKSES** *ex* Tulip *-2008* *ex* Akishio 21 *-2006* *ex* Shoun Maru No. 21 *-2001* **PT Bandar Bahari Permai** - *Surabaya* *Indonesia* MMSI: 525011004 Official number: 3583	**1,353** 705 2,550	Class: KI	**1990**-03 **K.K. Murakami Zosensho — Naruto** Yd No: 186 Loa 75.45 (BB) Br ex - Dght 3.623 Lbp 70.01 Br md 12.00 Dpth 6.50 Welded, 2 dks	**(A31A2GX) General Cargo Ship** Grain: 2,736; Bale: 2,626 Compartments: 1 Ho, ER 1 Ha: ER	**1 oil engine** with clutches, flexible couplings & reduction geared to sc. shaft driving 1 FP propeller Total Power: 736kW (1,001hp) Hanshin LH28G 1 x 4 Stroke 6 Cy. 280 x 460 736kW (1001bhp) The Hanshin Diesel Works Ltd-Japan AuxGen: 1 x 130kW 225V a.c, 1 x 37kW 225V a.c
7825095 *YGOV* -	**SARANA UTAMA** *ex* Shinei Maru *-1996* **PT Bandar Bahari Permai** - *Surabaya* *Indonesia* MMSI: 525011002 Official number: 2777	**1,176** 736 1,575	Class: KI	**1979**-05 **Sasaki Shipbuilding Co Ltd — Osakikamijima HS** Yd No: 329 Loa 65.65 Br ex 11.51 Dght 4.900 Lbp 61.02 Br md 11.20 Dpth 6.20 Welded, 2 dks	**(A31A2GX) General Cargo Ship**	**1 oil engine** driving 1 FP propeller Total Power: 1,177kW (1,600hp) Hanshin 6LU32 1 x 4 Stroke 6 Cy. 320 x 510 1177kW (1600bhp) The Hanshin Diesel Works Ltd-Japan
9024865 - -	**SARANA UTAMA JAYA** - **Yenny** - *Samarinda* *Indonesia*	**199** 109 -	Class: KI	**2000**-07 **C.V. Swadaya Utama — Samarinda** Loa 40.25 Br ex - Dght - Lbp 38.75 Br md 7.80 Dpth 2.10 Welded, 1 dk	**(A35D2RL) Landing Craft** Bow ramp (centre)	**2 oil engines** geared to sc. shafts driving 2 Propellers Total Power: 470kW (640hp) Mitsubishi 8DC90A 2 x Vee 4 Stroke 8 Cy. 135 x 140 each-235kW (320bhp) Mitsubishi Heavy Industries Ltd-Japan AuxGen: 2 x 60kW 400/220V a.c
9007348 - -	**SARANG** - **Government of The Republic of India (Coast Guard)** - *India*	**1,888** 566 417	Class: (LR) (IR) ✠	**1999**-06 **Goa Shipyard Ltd. — Goa** Yd No: 1153 Loa 101.95 Br ex 11.56 Dght 3.580 Lbp 94.10 Br md 11.50 Dpth 6.00 Welded, 2 dks	**(B34H2SQ) Patrol Vessel**	**2 oil engines** with clutches, flexible couplings & sr geared to sc. shafts driving 2 CP propellers Total Power: 9,130kW (12,414hp) Pielstick 16PA6V280 2 x Vee 4 Stroke 16 Cy. 280 x 290 each-4565kW (6207bhp) Kirloskar Oil Engines Ltd-India AuxGen: 4 x 400kW 415V 50Hz a.c
6918106 *DYA2021* -	**SARANGANI** *ex* Hakurei Maru *-1993* **Eastship Fishing Corp** Eastern Shipping Lines Inc *Cebu* *Philippines* Official number: CEB1000200	*220* 132 128		**1968 Usuki Iron Works Co Ltd — Usuki OT** Yd No: 698 Loa 43.95 Br ex 6.63 Dght 2.769 Lbp 38.99 Br md 6.61 Dpth 3.31 Welded, 1 dk	**(B12D2FP) Fishery Patrol Vessel**	**2 oil engines** driving 2 FP propellers Total Power: 1,472kW (2,002hp) Maybach MB820DB 2 x Vee 4 Stroke 12 Cy. 175 x 205 each-736kW (1001bhp) Ikegai Tekkosho-Japan
8122206 *DUM6160* -	**SARANGANI VIII** *ex* Soltai 88 *-2007* *ex* Sumiei Maru No. 1 *-1991* **DFC Tuna Venture Corp** - *General Santos* *Philippines* Official number: COT9001580	*116* 23 -		**1981**-09 **K.K. Izutsu Zosensho — Nagasaki** Yd No: 837 Loa 39.48 Br ex - Dght 2.401 Lbp 31.17 Br md 6.99 Dpth 2.80 Welded, 1 dk	**(B11B2FV) Fishing Vessel**	**1 oil engine** reduction geared to sc. shaft driving 1 FP propeller Total Power: 1,324kW (1,800hp) Yanmar 6ZL-ST 1 x 4 Stroke 6 Cy. 280 x 340 1324kW (1800bhp) Yanmar Diesel Engine Co Ltd-Japan
9020065 *HSDY2* -	**SARANYA NAREE** *ex* Diamond-A *-2004* **Precious Diamonds Ltd** Great Circle Shipping Agency Ltd *Bangkok* *Thailand* MMSI: 567285000 Official number: 470002327	**16,725** 10,435 28,583 T/cm 39.5	Class: NK	**1991**-05 **Imabari Shipbuilding Co Ltd — Imabari EH (Imabari Shipyard)** Yd No: 490 Loa 169.03 (BB) Br ex 27.24 Dght 9.745 Lbp 160.40 Br md 27.20 Dpth 13.60 Welded, 1 dk	**(A21A2BC) Bulk Carrier** Grain: 37,550; Bale: 35,789 Compartments: 5 Ho, ER 5 Ha: (13.3 x 16.0)4 (19.2 x 17.6)ER Cranes: 4x30.5t	**1 oil engine** driving 1 FP propeller Total Power: 5,737kW (7,800hp) 13.7kn B&W 5S50MC 1 x 2 Stroke 5 Cy. 500 x 1910 5737kW (7800bhp) Hitachi Zosen Corp-Japan AuxGen: 2 x 440kW 450V 60Hz a.c Fuel: 120.3 (d.f.) (Part Heating Coils) 1181.5 (r.f.) 22.6pd
9383869 *SVAJ6* -	**SARASOTA** - **Mariner Shipmanagement SA** TMS Tankers Ltd *Piraeus* *Greece* MMSI: 240804000 Official number: 11824	**58,418** 32,391 106,850 T/cm 92.1	Class: AB	**2008**-11 **Shanghai Waigaoqiao Shipbuilding Co Ltd — Shanghai** Yd No: 1082 Loa 243.80 (BB) Br ex 42.03 Dght 14.800 Lbp 233.00 Br md 42.00 Dpth 21.40 Welded, 1 dk	**(A13A2TW) Crude/Oil Products Tanker** Double Hull (13F) Liq: 113,657; Liq (Oil): 118,077 Cargo Heating Coils Compartments: 12 Wing Ta, 2 Wing Slop Ta, ER 3 Cargo Pump (s): 3x2800m³/hr Manifold: Bow/CM: 121.7m	**1 oil engine** driving 1 FP propeller Total Power: 13,560kW (18,436hp) 15.0kn MAN-B&W 6S60MC-C 1 x 2 Stroke 6 Cy. 600 x 2400 13560kW (18436bhp) Hudong Heavy Machinery Co Ltd-China AuxGen: 3 x 800kW a.c Fuel: 247.0 (d.f.) 3000.0 (r.f.)
7802897 *ATVQ* -	**SARASWATI** - **Government of The Republic of India (Central Institute of Fisheries - Madras Unit)** - *Mumbai* *India* Official number: 1875	*311* 151 108	Class: IR (NV)	**1982**-12 **Goa Shipyard Ltd. — Goa** Yd No: 1086 Loa 36.58 Br ex 8.16 Dght 3.652 Lbp 31.12 Br md 8.01 Dpth 4.42 Welded, 1 dk	**(B11A2FT) Trawler** Ins: 40 Compartments: 2 Ho, ER 2 Ha: ER	**1 oil engine** sr geared to sc. shaft driving 1 CP propeller Total Power: 607kW (825hp) Caterpillar D398TA 1 x Vee 4 Stroke 12 Cy. 159 x 203 607kW (825bhp) Caterpillar Tractor Co-USA AuxGen: 2 x 82kW 440V 60Hz a.c, 1 x 42kW 440V 60Hz a.c

7322263 S2VS - **SARATHI**
Government of The People's Republic of Bangladesh (Ministry of Communications, Roads, Highways, Road Transport & Ports)
-
Chittagong *Bangladesh*
Official number: 317522
365 71 151 | Class: (NK)
1973 Yokohama Zosen — Chiba Yd No: 1349
Loa 42.50 Br ex 8.44 Dght 3.201
Lbp 37.27 Br md 8.39 Dpth 3.81
Welded, 1 dk
(B32A2ST) Tug
2 oil engines driving 2 FP propellers
Total Power: 1,472kW (2,002hp) 11.5kn
Daihatsu 8PSHTB-26D
2 x 4 Stroke 8 Cy. 260 x 320 each-736kW (1001bhp)
Daihatsu Diesel Manufacturing Co Lt-Japan
AuxGen: 2 x 32kW

7328566 - - **SARATOGA**
ex Nareau *-1976* *ex* John Williams VII *-1972*
D A Bradshaw & I H Crayford
Saratoga Shipping Co Ltd
Honiara *Solomon Islands*
Official number: 522
185 69 102 | Class: (LR) ✠ Classed LR until 9/72
1962-11 Brooke Marine Ltd. — Lowestoft Yd No: 297
Loa 28.58 Br ex 7.01 Dght 2.286
Lbp 26.83 Br md 6.96 Dpth 3.13
Welded, 1 dk
(B35A2QZ) Mission Ship
Hull Material: Iron & Wood
Bale: 736
Compartments: 1 Ho, ER
1 Ha: (3.0 x 2.4)
Derricks: 2x1.5t; Winches: 1
2 oil engines geared to sc. shafts driving 2 FP propellers
Total Power: 210kW (286hp) 9.5kn
Gardner 6L3B
2 x 4 Stroke 6 Cy. 140 x 197 each-105kW (143bhp)
L. Gardner & Sons Ltd.-Manchester
AuxGen: 1 x 10kW 220V d.c, 2 x 7kW 220V d.c
Fuel: 30.5 (d.f.)

8520173 XUQG7 - **SARATOGA**
ex Salida *-2013* *ex* Sigma *-2010*
ex MYS Omgon *-2008* *ex* Costa Blanka *-2007*
ex Sumiyoshi Maru No. 11 *-2007*
Nevrona Ltd
-
Phnom Penh *Cambodia*
MMSI: 515664000
Official number: 0686537
497 271 594 | Class: IS (RS)
1986-03 Miho Zosensho K.K. — Shimizu Yd No: 1277
Loa 57.76 (BB) Br ex 9.12 Dght 3.779
Lbp 50.75 Br md 9.11 Dpth 4.17
Welded, 1 dk
(B11B2FV) Fishing Vessel
1 oil engine with clutches, flexible couplings & sr geared to sc. shaft driving 1 FP propeller
Total Power: 1,103kW (1,500hp) 13.5kn
Niigata 6M31AFT
1 x 4 Stroke 6 Cy. 310 x 530 1103kW (1500bhp)
Niigata Engineering Co Ltd-Japan
Fuel: 315.0 (d.f.)

7301685 WYZ7306 - **SARATOGA I**
Sea Quest Inc
-
Morgan City, LA *United States of America*
Official number: 538903
146 99 -
1972 St Charles Steel Works Inc — Thibodaux, La
L reg 22.41 Br ex 7.01 Dght -
Lbp - Br md - Dpth 3.76
Welded
(B11B2FV) Fishing Vessel
1 oil engine driving 1 FP propeller
Total Power: 342kW (465hp)

9466879 V7VC6 - **SARATOV**
ex Fesco Saratov *-2013*
Ayaks Maritime Ltd
Far-Eastern Shipping Co (FESCO)
(Dalnevostochnoye Morskoye Parokhodstvo)
Majuro *Marshall Islands*
MMSI: 538004087
Official number: 4087
33,044 19,231 57,000 T/cm 58.8 | Class: BV
2011-07 Qingshan Shipyard — Wuhan HB Yd No: 20060371
Loa 189.99 (BB) Br ex - Dght 12.800
Lbp 185.00 Br md 32.26 Dpth 18.00
Welded, 1 dk
(A21A2BC) Bulk Carrier
Grain: 71,634; Bale: 68,200
Compartments: 5 Ho, ER
5 Ha: ER
Cranes: 4x30t
1 oil engine driving 1 FP propeller
Total Power: 9,480kW (12,889hp) 14.2kn
MAN-B&W 6S50MC-C
1 x 2 Stroke 6 Cy. 500 x 2000 9480kW (12889bhp)
Doosan Engine Co Ltd-South Korea
AuxGen: 3 x 600kW 60Hz a.c

9384265 UNN - **SARBAS**
Circle Maritime Investment LLP
Caspian Offshore Construction LLP
SatCom: Inmarsat C 443600024
Aqtau *Kazakhstan*
MMSI: 436000014
294 88 267 | Class: RS (BV)
2006-12 IHC DeltaShipyard BV — Sliedrecht Yd No: 11019
Loa 30.05 Br ex 10.05 Dght 2.810
Lbp 28.80 Br md 10.00 Dpth 3.45
Welded, 1 dk
(B32B2SP) Pusher Tug
Ice Capable
2 oil engines reduction geared to sc. shafts driving 2 Directional propellers
Total Power: 1,854kW (2,520hp) 10.0kn
Caterpillar 3512B
2 x Vee 4 Stroke 12 Cy. 170 x 190 each-927kW (1260bhp)
Caterpillar Inc-USA
AuxGen: 1 x 162kW 400/220V 50Hz a.c, 1 x 92kW 400/220V 50Hz a.c
Thrusters: 1 Tunnel thruster (f)
Fuel: 75.0 (d.f.)

7942207 UCIN - **SARBAY**
OOO 'Tranzit-DV Group'
-
SatCom: Inmarsat C 427320810
Sovetskaya Gavan *Russia*
MMSI: 273424300
Official number: 801123
835 250 327 | Class: RS
1981-04 Volgogradskiy Sudostroitelnyy Zavod — Volgograd Yd No: 895
Loa 53.75 (BB) Br ex 10.72 Dght 4.290
Lbp 47.92 Br md 10.50 Dpth 6.00
Welded, 1 dk
(B11A2FS) Stern Trawler
Ins: 218
Compartments: 1 Ho, ER
1 Ha: (1.6 x 1.6)
Derricks: 2x1.5t
Ice Capable
1 oil engine driving 1 FP propeller
Total Power: 971kW (1,320hp) 12.8kn
S.K.L. 8NVD48A-2U
1 x 4 Stroke 8 Cy. 320 x 480 971kW (1320bhp)
VEB Schwermaschinenbau "KarlLiebknecht" (SKL)-Magdeburg
Fuel: 191.0 (d.f.)

9189407 VWDH - **SARDAR PATEL**
Visakhapatnam Port Trust
-
Visakhapatnam *India*
Official number: 2791
488 146 186 | Class: (IR)
2000-05 Hindustan Shipyard Ltd — Visakhapatnam Yd No: 1169
Loa 34.50 Br ex 11.26 Dght 5.210
Lbp 32.50 Br md 11.25 Dpth 5.00
Welded, 1 dk
(B32A2ST) Tug
2 oil engines gearing integral to driving 2 Voith-Schneider propellers
Total Power: 4,010kW (5,452hp) 12.5kn
Normo KRMB-9
2 x 4 Stroke 9 Cy. 250 x 300 each-2005kW (2726bhp)
Ulstein Bergen AS-Norway
AuxGen: 2 x 140kW 380V 50Hz a.c
Fuel: 110.0 (d.f.)

8517231 EQKG - **SARDASHT**
NITC
-
Bandar Abbas *Iran*
MMSI: 422142000
Official number: 11219
478 185 640 | Class: AS (NV)
1985-06 Costruz. Riparaz. Nav. Antonini S.p.A. — La Spezia Yd No: 115
Loa 50.73 Br ex - Dght 2.101
Lbp 47.02 Br md 11.51 Dpth 2.80
Welded, 1 dk
(A35D2RL) Landing Craft
Bow door/ramp
Liq: 718; Liq (Oil): 718
Compartments: 8 Ta, ER
2 oil engines with clutches, flexible couplings & sr reverse geared to sc. shafts driving 2 FP propellers
Total Power: 1,184kW (1,610hp)
Deutz SBA12M816
2 x Vee 4 Stroke 12 Cy. 142 x 160 each-592kW (805bhp)
Kloeckner Humboldt Deutz AG-West Germany
AuxGen: 2 x 164kW 380V 50Hz a.c

7804235 - - **SARDINA I**
Productos Pesqueros Mexicanos SA de CV
-
Topolobampo *Mexico*
170 120 - | Class: (AB)
1981-03 Construcciones Navales de Guaymas S.A. (CONAGUSA) — Guaymas Yd No: 602
Loa - Br ex - Dght 3.201
Lbp 22.28 Br md 7.71 Dpth 3.76
Welded, 1 dk
(B11A2FT) Trawler
1 oil engine reverse reduction geared to sc. shaft driving 1 FP propeller
Total Power: 405kW (551hp) 12.0kn
Cummins VT-28-M1
1 x Vee 4 Stroke 12 Cy. 140 x 152 405kW (551bhp)
Cummins Diesel International Ltd-USA
AuxGen: 2 x 100kW

9481518 9AA5395 - **SARDINA I**
Sardina dd
-
Split *Croatia*
MMSI: 238771340
Official number: 5R-292
328 98 - | Class: CS
2008-08 RLE doo — Vranjic Yd No: 119
Loa 40.15 Br ex 8.65 Dght 3.260
Lbp 32.40 Br md 8.64 Dpth 4.20
Welded, 1 dk
(B11B2FV) Fishing Vessel
1 oil engine reduction geared to sc. shaft driving 1 FP propeller
Total Power: 1,653kW (2,247hp) 14.5kn
Mitsubishi S16R-MPTK2
1 x Vee 4 Stroke 16 Cy. 170 x 180 1653kW (2247bhp)
Mitsubishi Heavy Industries Ltd-Japan

9523524 9AA6076 - **SARDINA II**
Sardina dd
-
Split *Croatia*
MMSI: 238880340
Official number: 5R-297
328 98 - | Class: CS
2008-08 RLE doo — Vranjic Yd No: 120
Loa 40.15 Br ex 8.65 Dght 3.260
Lbp 32.40 Br md 8.64 Dpth 4.20
Welded, 1 dk
(B11B2FV) Fishing Vessel
1 oil engine reduction geared to sc. shaft driving 1 FP propeller
Total Power: 1,250kW (1,700hp) 14.0kn
Mitsubishi S16R-MPTK2
1 x Vee 4 Stroke 16 Cy. 170 x 180 1250kW (1700bhp)
Mitsubishi Heavy Industries Ltd-Japan

7804223 - - **SARDINA III**
Productos Pesqueros Mexicanos SA de CV
-
Guaymas *Mexico*
170 120 - | Class: (AB)
1981-03 Construcciones Navales de Guaymas S.A. (CONAGUSA) — Guaymas Yd No: 601
Loa 22.31 Br ex - Dght 3.201
Lbp 22.26 Br md 7.75 Dpth 3.76
Welded, 1 dk
(B11A2FT) Trawler
1 oil engine reverse reduction geared to sc. shaft driving 1 FP propeller
Total Power: 405kW (551hp) 12.0kn
Cummins VT-28-M1
1 x Vee 4 Stroke 12 Cy. 140 x 152 405kW (551bhp)
Cummins Diesel International Ltd-USA
AuxGen: 2 x 100kW

7804259 - - **SARDINA IV**
Productos Pesqueros Mexicanos SA de CV
-
Topolobampo *Mexico*
170 160 - | Class: (AB)
1981 Construcciones Navales de Guaymas S.A. (CONAGUSA) — Guaymas Yd No: 604
Loa 22.31 Br ex - Dght 3.201
Lbp 22.26 Br md 7.75 Dpth 3.76
Welded, 1 dk
(B11A2FT) Trawler
1 oil engine reverse reduction geared to sc. shaft driving 1 FP propeller
Total Power: 405kW (551hp) 12.0kn
Cummins VT-28-M1
1 x Vee 4 Stroke 12 Cy. 140 x 152 405kW (551bhp)
Cummins Diesel International Ltd-USA
AuxGen: 2 x 100kW

7930802 - - **SARDINA IX**
Productos Pesqueros Mexicanos SA de CV
-
Mazatlan *Mexico*
170 160 328 | Class: (AB)
1981-09 Astilleros Rodriguez S.A. — Ensenada (Mex) Yd No: 185
Loa 22.89 Br ex - Dght 3.728
Lbp 22.31 Br md 7.84 Dpth 3.97
Welded, 1 dk
(B11B2FV) Fishing Vessel
1 oil engine reverse reduction geared to sc. shaft driving 1 FP propeller
Total Power: 405kW (551hp) 12.0kn
Cummins VTA-1710-M2
1 x Vee 4 Stroke 12 Cy. 140 x 152 405kW (551bhp)
Cummins Diesel International Ltd-USA
AuxGen: 2 x 100kW

IMO / Call sign / Flag	Name / Owner / Port	Tonnage	Class	Built / Dimensions	Type	Machinery
7930761 - -	**SARDINA V** - **Productos Pesqueros Mexicanos SA de CV** - *Mazatlan* *Mexico*	*170* 160 -	Class: (AB)	**1981**-03 **Astilleros Rodriguez S.A. — Ensenada (Mex)** Yd No: 181 Loa 22.89 Br ex - Dght 3.728 Lbp 22.31 Br md 7.84 Dpth 3.97 Welded, 1 dk	**(B11B2FV) Fishing Vessel**	**1 oil engine** reverse reduction geared to sc. shaft driving 1 FP propeller Total Power: 405kW (551hp) 12.0kn Cummins VTA-1710-M2 1 x Vee 4 Stroke 12 Cy. 140 x 152 405kW (551bhp) Cummins Diesel International Ltd-USA AuxGen: 2 x 100kW
7930773 - -	**SARDINA VI** - **Productos Pesqueros Mexicanos SA de CV** - *Topolobampo* *Mexico*	*170* 160 328	Class: (AB)	**1981**-06 **Astilleros Rodriguez S.A. — Ensenada (Mex)** Yd No: 182 Loa 22.89 Br ex - Dght 3.728 Lbp 22.31 Br md 7.84 Dpth 3.97 Welded, 1 dk	**(B11B2FV) Fishing Vessel**	**1 oil engine** reverse reduction geared to sc. shaft driving 1 FP propeller Total Power: 456kW (620hp) 12.0kn Cummins VTA-1710-M2 1 x Vee 4 Stroke 12 Cy. 140 x 152 456kW (620bhp) Cummins Diesel International Ltd-USA AuxGen: 2 x 100kW
7930785 - -	**SARDINA VII** - **Productos Pesqueros Mexicanos SA de CV** - *Mazatlan* *Mexico*	*170* 160 328	Class: (AB)	**1981**-08 **Astilleros Rodriguez S.A. — Ensenada (Mex)** Yd No: 183 Loa 22.89 Br ex - Dght 3.728 Lbp 22.31 Br md 7.84 Dpth 3.97 Welded, 1 dk	**(B11B2FV) Fishing Vessel**	**1 oil engine** reverse reduction geared to sc. shaft driving 1 FP propeller Total Power: 456kW (620hp) 12.0kn Cummins VTA-1710-M2 1 x Vee 4 Stroke 12 Cy. 140 x 152 456kW (620bhp) Cummins Diesel International Ltd-USA AuxGen: 2 x 100kW
7930797 - -	**SARDINA VIII** - **Productos Pesqueros Mexicanos SA de CV** - *Topolobampo* *Mexico*	*170* 160 328	Class: (AB)	**1981**-08 **Astilleros Rodriguez S.A. — Ensenada (Mex)** Yd No: 184 Loa 22.89 Br ex - Dght 3.728 Lbp 22.31 Br md 7.84 Dpth 3.97 Welded, 1 dk	**(B11B2FV) Fishing Vessel**	**1 oil engine** reverse reduction geared to sc. shaft driving 1 FP propeller Total Power: 456kW (620hp) 12.0kn Cummins VTA-1710-M2 1 x Vee 4 Stroke 12 Cy. 140 x 152 456kW (620bhp) Cummins Diesel International Ltd-USA AuxGen: 2 x 100kW
7930814 - -	**SARDINA X** - **Productos Pesqueros Mexicanos SA de CV** - *Topolobampo* *Mexico*	*170* 160 328	Class: (AB)	**1982 Astilleros Rodriguez S.A. — Ensenada (Mex)** Yd No: 186 Loa 22.89 Br ex - Dght 3.728 Lbp 22.31 Br md 7.84 Dpth 3.97 Welded, 1 dk	**(B11B2FV) Fishing Vessel** Compartments: 4 Ho, ER 1 Ha: (3.2 x 3.0)	**1 oil engine** reverse reduction geared to sc. shaft driving 1 FP propeller Total Power: 456kW (620hp) 12.0kn Cummins VT-28-M2 1 x Vee 4 Stroke 12 Cy. 140 x 152 456kW (620bhp) Cummins Engine Co Inc-USA AuxGen: 2 x 100kW
8101197 - -	**SARDINA XI** - **Productos Pesqueros Mexicanos SA de CV** - *Mexico*	**226** - 219		**1986 Ast. Unidos de Ensenada S.A. de C.V. (AUENSA) — Ensenada (Mex)** Yd No: 203 Loa 27.01 Br ex - Dght 3.401 Lbp 22.86 Br md 7.85 Dpth 3.97 Welded	**(B11B2FV) Fishing Vessel** Ins: 210	**1 oil engine** driving 1 FP propeller Total Power: 456kW (620hp) Cummins VTA-1710-M2 1 x Vee 4 Stroke 12 Cy. 140 x 152 456kW (620bhp) Cummins Engine Co Inc-USA
8101202 - -	**SARDINA XII** - **Productos Pesqueros Mexicanos SA de CV** - *Mexico*	**226** - 219		**1986 Ast. Unidos de Ensenada S.A. de C.V. (AUENSA) — Ensenada (Mex)** Yd No: 204 Loa 27.01 Br ex - Dght 3.401 Lbp 22.86 Br md 7.85 Dpth 3.97 Welded, 1 dk	**(B11B2FV) Fishing Vessel** Ins: 210	**1 oil engine** driving 1 FP propeller Total Power: 456kW (620hp) Cummins VTA-1710-M2 1 x Vee 4 Stroke 12 Cy. 140 x 152 456kW (620bhp) Cummins Engine Co Inc-USA
8101214 - -	**SARDINA XIII** - **Productos Pesqueros Mexicanos SA de CV** - *Mexico*	**226** - 219		**1986 Ast. Unidos de Ensenada S.A. de C.V. (AUENSA) — Ensenada (Mex)** Yd No: 205 Loa 27.01 Br ex - Dght 3.401 Lbp 22.86 Br md 7.85 Dpth 3.97 Welded	**(B11B2FV) Fishing Vessel** Ins: 210	**1 oil engine** driving 1 FP propeller Total Power: 456kW (620hp) Cummins VTA-1710-M2 1 x Vee 4 Stroke 12 Cy. 140 x 152 456kW (620bhp) Cummins Engine Co Inc-USA
8884660 *DBGF* -	**SARDINE** *ex* LCM 13 Sardine **Government of The Federal Republic of Germany (Land Schleswig-Holstein)** - *Brunsbuettel* *Germany* MMSI: 211229460	**100** 30 52	Class: (GL)	**1966 Gutehoffnungshuette Sterkrade AG Rheinwerft Walsum — Duisburg** Yd No: 1021 Loa - Br ex - Dght 1.149 Lbp 22.90 Br md 6.40 Dpth 1.39 Welded, 1 dk	**(B34G2SE) Pollution Control Vessel**	**2 oil engines** reverse reduction geared to sc. shafts driving 2 FP propellers Total Power: 504kW (686hp) 10.0kn MWM TRHS518A 2 x 4 Stroke 8 Cy. 140 x 180 each-252kW (343bhp) MWM AG Lieferwerk MuenchenSueddeutsche Bremsen-Muenchen
9690406 *JZBJ* -	**SARDINELA** - **Government of The Republic of Indonesia (Direktorat Jenderal Perhubungan Darat - Ministry of Land Communications)** PT ASDP Indonesia Ferry (Persero) - Angkutan Sungai Danau & Penyeberangan *Ambon* *Indonesia*	**1,029** 309 301	Class: KI	**2013**-01 **P.T. Adiluhung Sarana Segara Industri — Bangkalan** Yd No: A.033 Loa 56.02 Br ex 14.04 Dght 2.700 Lbp 48.82 Br md 14.00 Dpth 3.80 Welded, 1 dk	**(A36A2PR) Passenger/Ro-Ro Ship (Vehicles)** Bow ramp (centre)	**2 oil engines** reduction geared to sc. shafts driving 2 Propellers Total Power: 1,472kW (2,002hp) Baudouin 12M26SRP 2 x Vee 4 Stroke 12 Cy. 150 x 150 each-736kW (1001bhp) Societe des Moteurs Baudouin SA-France AuxGen: 2 x 91kW a.c
8029210 *DUNH* -	**SARDINELLA** - **University of The Philippines** - *Iloilo* *Philippines* Official number: ILO3001468	*411* 109 384	Class: (NK)	**1981**-03 **Niigata Engineering Co Ltd — Niigata NI** Yd No: 1712 Loa 40.24 Br ex - Dght 3.944 Lbp 34.42 Br md 8.81 Dpth 4.22 Welded, 1 dk	**(B12D2FR) Fishery Research Vessel** Ins: 93 1 Ha: (1.3 x 1.3)ER	**1 oil engine** driving 1 FP propeller Total Power: 883kW (1,201hp) 9.5kn Niigata 6M28AGTE 1 x 4 Stroke 6 Cy. 280 x 480 883kW (1201bhp) Niigata Engineering Co Ltd-Japan AuxGen: 2 x 200kW 225V 60Hz a.c
8113126 *D3R2330* -	**SARDINHA** - **Empresa Nacional de Abastecimiento Tecnico Material a Industria de Pesca (ENATIP)** - *Luanda* *Angola* Official number: C-783	*136* 60 118	Class: (BV)	**1984**-07 **Astilleros Gondan SA — Castropol** Yd No: 220 Loa 26.01 Br ex - Dght 2.701 Lbp 22.51 Br md 6.51 Dpth 3.26 Welded, 1 dk	**(B11B2FV) Fishing Vessel** Ins: 146	**1 oil engine** with clutches, flexible couplings & sr reverse geared to sc. shaft driving 1 FP propeller Total Power: 368kW (500hp) GUASCOR E318T-SP 1 x Vee 4 Stroke 12 Cy. 150 x 150 368kW (500bhp) Gutierrez Ascunce Corp (GUASCOR)-Spain AuxGen: 2 x 32kW 380V 50Hz a.c
7205910 *IBMS* -	**SARDINIA REGINA** *ex* Corsica Regina *-1996* *ex* Corsica Viva II *-1989* *ex* Drotten *-1985* *ex* Visby *-1980* **Medinvest SpA** Tourship Italia SpA SatCom: Inmarsat C 424709110 *Genoa* *Italy* MMSI: 247079000 Official number: 162	**13,004** 5,916 2,649	Class: RI (LR) (BV) ✠ Classed LR until 10/85	**1972**-10 **Brodogradiliste 'Jozo Lozovina-Mosor' (Brodomosor) — Trogir** Yd No: 161 Lengthened-1989 Loa 146.55 (BB) Br ex 20.86 Dght 5.017 Lbp 130.75 Br md 20.48 Dpth 12.22 Welded, 2 dks	**(A36A2PR) Passenger/Ro-Ro Ship (Vehicles)** Passengers: unberthed: 760; cabins: 222; berths: 1040 Bow door & ramp Len: 7.65 Wid: 8.00 Swl: - Stern door/ramp Len: 8.70 Wid: 6.00 Swl: - Lane-Len: 670 Lane-Wid: 2.50 Lane-clr ht: 4.50 Cars: 460 Ice Capable	**6 oil engines** sr geared to sc. shafts driving 2 CP propellers Total Power: 10,590kW (14,400hp) 20.0kn Polar SF116VS-D 6 x Vee 4 Stroke 16 Cy. 250 x 300 each-1765kW (2400bhp) AB NOHAB-Sweden AuxGen: 2 x 1400kW 400V 50Hz a.c, 2 x 1200kW 400V 50Hz a.c Thrusters: 2 Thwart. FP thruster (f) Fuel: 125.0 (d.f.) 619.0 (r.f.) 51.0pd
7360617 *IBWV* -	**SARDINIA VERA** *ex* Corsica Vera *-1987* *ex* Marine Atlantica *-1986* **Forship SpA** Tourship Italia SpA SatCom: Inmarsat C 424732520 *Olbia* *Italy* MMSI: 247392000 Official number: 151	**12,107** 3,742 2,840	Class: RI (NV)	**1975**-05 **Rickmers Rhederei GmbH Rickmers Werft — Bremerhaven** Yd No: 381 Loa 120.78 (BB) Br ex 19.51 Dght 5.765 Lbp 107.02 Br md 19.00 Dpth 12.35 Welded, 3 dks	**(A36A2PR) Passenger/Ro-Ro Ship (Vehicles)** Passengers: unberthed: 1129; cabins: 28; berths: 112 Bow door/ramp Stern door/ramp Lane-Len: 792 Lane-clr ht: 4.70 Cars: 479 Ice Capable	**2 oil engines** driving 2 CP propellers Total Power: 10,356kW (14,080hp) 18.5kn MaK 12M551AK 2 x Vee 4 Stroke 12 Cy. 450 x 550 each-5178kW (7040bhp) MaK Maschinenbau GmbH-Kiel AuxGen: 4 x 520kW 380V 50Hz a.c, 1 x 144kW 380V 50Hz a.c Thrusters: 1 Thwart. FP thruster (f) Fuel: 528.5 (d.f.)
8000147 *OW2305* VA 361	**SARDIS** *ex* Fjalshamar *-2013* *ex* Fjallshamar *-2009* *ex* Dragasund *-2007* *ex* Sardis *-2002* *ex* Dragaberg *-1988* **P/F Thor** - *Sorvagur* *Faeroe Islands (Danish)* MMSI: 231022000 Official number: D2093	**209** - -	Class: BV	**1981**-03 **Forges Caloin — Etaples** Yd No: 25 Lengthened-1983 Loa 30.99 Br ex - Dght 3.501 Lbp 27.51 Br md 6.81 Dpth 5.82 Welded, 1 dk	**(B11A2FS) Stern Trawler**	**1 oil engine** geared to sc. shaft driving 1 CP propeller Total Power: 625kW (850hp) Caterpillar D398SCAC 1 x Vee 4 Stroke 12 Cy. 159 x 203 625kW (850bhp) Caterpillar Tractor Co-USA

9416903 *J8B3817* -	**SARDIS** **Sardis Shipping Ltd** ABC Maritime AG *Kingstown* *St Vincent & The Grenadines* MMSI: 376528000 Official number: 10290	**1,025** 308 800	Class: BV	**2008-02 Gelibolu Gemi Insa Sanayi ve Ticaret AS — Gelibolu** Yd No: 34 Loa 48.00 Br ex - Dght 4.200 Lbp 46.00 Br md 12.60 Dpth 5.20 Welded, 1 dk	**(B21A20S) Platform Supply Ship**	**2 oil engines** reduction geared to sc. shafts driving 2 Propellers Total Power: 2,354kW (3,200hp) 11.5kn Cummins KTA-50-M2 2 x Vee 4 Stroke 16 Cy. 159 x 159 each-1177kW (1600bhp) Cummins Engine Co Inc-USA AuxGen: 3 x 250kW 380V 50Hz a.c Thrusters: 1 Tunnel thruster (f) Fuel: 231.0 (d.f.)
9518256 *PCLD* -	**SARDIUS** **Sardius BV** De Bock Maritiem BV *Alkmaar* *Netherlands* MMSI: 246798000 Official number: 53031	**3,739** 1,491 5,265	Class: LR ✠ **100A1** SS 06/2011 strengthened for heavy cargoes, container cargoes in all holds and on upper deck and on all hatch covers Ice Class 1A FS at a draught of 6.28 m Max/min draughts fwd 6.28/3.20m Max/min draughts aft 6.28/3.70m Power required 2400kw, power installed 1800kw (1800kw + high efficiency nozzle) ✠ **LMC** **UMS** Eq.Ltr: S; Cable: 467.5/36.0 U3 (a)	**2011-06 Leda doo — Korcula** (Hull) **2011-06 Scheepswerf Peters B.V. — Kampen** Yd No: 1103 Loa 99.99 (BB) Br ex 13.43 Dght 6.150 Lbp 92.50 Br md 13.35 Dpth 9.10 Welded, 1 dk	**(A31A2GX) General Cargo Ship** Grain: 6,644 TEU 188 C Ho 108 TEU C Dk 80 TEU Compartments: 1 Ho, ER 1 Ha: ER (61.8 x 11.2) Ice Capable	**1 oil engine** with clutches, flexible couplings & sr geared to sc. shaft driving 1 CP propeller Total Power: 1,800kW (2,447hp) 12.0kn Wartsila 9L20 1 x 4 Stroke 9 Cy. 200 x 280 1800kW (2447bhp) Wartsila Finland Oy-Finland AuxGen: 1 x 348kW 400V 50Hz a.c, 2 x 170kW 400V 50Hz a.c Boilers: HWH (o.f.) 3.6kgf/cm² (3.5bar) Thrusters: 1 Thwart. FP thruster (f)
8957182 *MQUY6* BF 206	**SARDONYX II** **Peter & J Johnstone Ltd, B W & M D L Watt** Peter & J Johnstone Ltd *Banff* *United Kingdom* MMSI: 234311000 Official number: B13709	*119* 43 -		**1997 Hepworth Shipyard Ltd — Hull** Loa 18.38 Br ex - Dght - Lbp - Br md 6.58 Dpth 2.50 Welded, 1 dk	**(B11A2FS) Stern Trawler**	**1 oil engine** driving 1 FP propeller Total Power: 368kW (500hp) Cummins 1 x 4 Stroke 368kW (500bhp) Cummins Engine Co Inc-USA
9415363 *J8B4017* -	**SAREM** **Raphael Marine Services Ltd** Whitesea Shipping & Supply (LLC) *Kingstown* *St Vincent & The Grenadines* MMSI: 376833000 Official number: 10490	**1,579** 473 1,500	Class: BV	**2009-04 Keppel Nantong Shipyard Co Ltd — Nantong JS** (Hull) Yd No: 011 **2009-04 Keppel Singmarine Pte Ltd — Singapore** Yd No: 331 Loa 62.20 Br ex - Dght 4.900 Lbp 59.06 Br md 15.00 Dpth 6.00 Welded, 1 dk	**(B21B20A) Anchor Handling Tug Supply** Cranes: 1x10t	**2 oil engines** reduction geared to sc. shafts driving 2 Directional propellers Total Power: 4,080kW (5,548hp) 12.5kn Wartsila 6L26 2 x 4 Stroke 6 Cy. 260 x 320 each-2040kW (2774bhp) Wartsila Finland Oy-Finland AuxGen: 2 x 1200kW 380V 50Hz a.c, 2 x 280kW 380V 50Hz a.c Thrusters: 2 Tunnel thruster (f)
8913899 *OWDD* -	**SARFAQ ITTUK** **Arctic Umiaq Line AS** - SatCom: Inmarsat Mini-M 761466355 *Nuuk* *Denmark* MMSI: 331037000 Official number: A434	**2,118** 817 163	Class: NV	**1992-03 Orskov Christensens Staalskibsvaerft A/S — Frederikshavn** Yd No: 156 Lengthened-2000 Loa 72.80 (BB) Br ex - Dght 3.665 Lbp 66.77 Br md 10.99 Dpth 7.07 Welded, 2 dks	**(A37B2PS) Passenger Ship** Passengers: unberthed: 24; berths: 246 Ice Capable	**1 oil engine** with flexible couplings & sr geared to sc. shaft driving 1 CP propeller Total Power: 1,470kW (1,999hp) 13.5kn Alpha 6L28/32A 1 x 4 Stroke 6 Cy. 280 x 320 1470kW (1999bhp) MAN B&W Diesel A/S-Denmark AuxGen: 1 x 240kW 380V 50Hz a.c, 2 x 206kW 400V 50Hz a.c Thrusters: 1 Thwart. CP thruster (f); 1 Thwart. FP thruster (a) Fuel: 76.0 (d.f.) 4.2pd
7828748 *UGEM* -	**SARGAL** *ex* Targa *-2004* *ex* Sargal *-2003* *ex* Valdaysk *-2002* **Poisson LLC** AOZT 'Vostoktransservis' Marine Shipping Co *Vladivostok* *Russia* MMSI: 273813600	**782** 234 332	Class: RS	**1979-09 Volgogradskiy Sudostroitelnyy Zavod — Volgograd** Yd No: 884 Loa 53.75 (BB) Br ex 10.72 Dght 4.290 Lbp 47.92 Br md 10.50 Dpth 6.02 Welded, 1 dk	**(B11A2FS) Stern Trawler** Ins: 218 Compartments: 1 Ho, ER 1 Ha: (1.6 x 1.6) Derricks: 2x3.3t	**1 oil engine** driving 1 FP propeller Total Power: 971kW (1,320hp) 12.8kn S.K.L. 8NVD48A-2U 1 x 4 Stroke 8 Cy. 320 x 480 971kW (1320bhp) VEB Schwermaschinenbau "KarlLiebknecht" (SKL)-Magdeburg Fuel: 146.0 (d.f.)
9615195 *7JLX*	**SARGAM** **Kawasaki Kisen Kaisha Ltd (Kawasaki Kisen KK) ('K' Line)** Taiyo Nippon Kisen Co Ltd SatCom: Inmarsat C 443285710 *Kobe, Hyogo* *Japan* MMSI: 432857000 Official number: 141671	**50,624** 31,530 95,671	Class: NK	**2012-05 Imabari Shipbuilding Co Ltd — Marugame KG (Marugame Shipyard)** Yd No: 1580 Loa 234.98 (BB) Br ex - Dght 14.468 Lbp 227.00 Br md 38.00 Dpth 19.90 Welded, 1 dk	**(A21A2BC) Bulk Carrier** Grain: 109,477 Compartments: 7 Ho, ER 7 Ha: ER	**1 oil engine** driving 1 FP propeller Total Power: 12,950kW (17,607hp) 14.5kn MAN-B&W 6S60MC-C 1 x 2 Stroke 6 Cy. 600 x 2400 12950kW (17607bhp) Mitsui Engineering & Shipbuilding CLtd-Japan Fuel: 4090.0
7733711 - -	**SARGAN** **UTRF-Holding JSC (OAO 'UTRF-Holding')** -	**739** 221 350	Class: (RS)	**1978 Volgogradskiy Sudostroitelnyy Zavod — Volgograd** Yd No: 876 Loa 53.73 (BB) Br ex 10.72 Dght 4.330 Lbp 47.92 Br md - Dpth 6.02 Welded, 1 dk	**(B11A2FS) Stern Trawler** Ins: 218 Compartments: 1 Ho, ER 2 Ha: 2 (1.6 x 1.6) Derricks: 2x1.5t Ice Capable	**1 oil engine** driving 1 CP propeller Total Power: 971kW (1,320hp) 12.5kn S.K.L. 8NVD48A-2U 1 x 4 Stroke 8 Cy. 320 x 480 971kW (1320bhp) VEB Schwermaschinenbau "KarlLiebknecht" (SKL)-Magdeburg Thrusters: 1 Thwart. FP thruster (f); 1 Tunnel thruster (a)
8725929 - -	**SARGAN** *ex* Rybak Ochakova *-2002* **Sargan Fishing Co Ltd (RA OOO 'Sargan')** -	**104** 31 58	Class: (RS)	**1987-07 Azovskaya Sudoverf — Azov** Yd No: 1020 Loa 26.50 Br ex 6.59 Dght 2.360 Lbp 22.90 Br md - Dpth 3.05 Welded, 1 dk	**(B11A2FS) Stern Trawler**	**1 oil engine** geared to sc. shaft driving 1 FP propeller Total Power: 165kW (224hp) 9.3kn Daldizel 6CHNSP18/22 1 x 4 Stroke 6 Cy. 180 x 220 165kW (224bhp) Daldizel-Khabarovsk AuxGen: 2 x 30kW Fuel: 9.0 (d.f.)
9101352 *UGOL* -	**SARGAN** *ex* Arion *-2007* *ex* Liman *-2007* **Parma Co Ltd** - *Kholmsk* *Russia* MMSI: 273561800	**683** 233 529	Class: RS	**1993-08 Khabarovskiy Sudostroitelnyy Zavod im Kirova — Khabarovsk** Yd No: 893 Converted From: Fish Carrier-2009 Loa 54.99 Br ex 9.49 Dght 4.460 Lbp 50.04 Br md 9.30 Dpth 5.16 Welded, 1 dk	**(A34A2GR) Refrigerated Cargo Ship** Ins: 632 Compartments: 2 Ho 2 Ha: 2 (3.0 x 3.0) Derricks: 4x3t Ice Capable	**1 oil engine** driving 1 FP propeller Total Power: 589kW (801hp) 11.3kn S.K.L. 6NVD48A-2U 1 x 4 Stroke 6 Cy. 320 x 480 589kW (801bhp) SKL Motoren u. Systemtechnik AG-Magdeburg AuxGen: 3 x 160kW Fuel: 114.0 (d.f.)
7205324 *DUTQ5* -	**SARGAS** *ex* Kagawa Maru *-2007* **Harbor Star Shipping Services Inc** - *Batangas* *Philippines* MMSI: 548259100 Official number: 04-0001637	*200* 70 61		**1972-01 Ishikawajima Ship & Chemical Plant Co Ltd — Tokyo** Yd No: 427 Loa 29.10 Br ex 8.64 Dght 2.477 Lbp 25.00 Br md 8.62 Dpth 3.51 Welded, 1 dk	**(B32A2ST) Tug**	**2 oil engines** gearing integral to driving 2 Z propellers Total Power: 1,544kW (2,100hp) Usuki 2 x 4 Stroke 8 Cy. 260 x 320 each-772kW (1050bhp) Usuki Tekkosho-Usuki
9712058 *WDH2598* -	**SARGASSO** **Adriatic Marine LLC** - *New Orleans, LA* *United States of America* MMSI: 367599260 Official number: 1250740	**879** 340 1,150	Class: AB (Class contemplated)	**2014-02 C&C Boat Works LLC — Belle Chasse LA** Yd No: 180 Loa 59.34 Br ex 12.16 Dght 3.580 Lbp 56.38 Br md 12.10 Dpth 4.26 Welded, 1 dk	**(B21A20S) Platform Supply Ship**	**2 oil engines** reduction geared to sc. shafts driving 2 Propellers Total Power: 1,268kW (1,724hp) 12.0kn Cummins K38-M 2 x Vee 4 Stroke 12 Cy. 159 x 159 each-634kW (862bhp) Cummins Engine Co Inc-USA Thrusters: 2 Tunnel thruster (f); 1 Tunnel thruster (f)
7388633 - -	**SARGO** *ex* Massira IV *-1999* *ex* Panxon Dos *-1999* - -	*280* 134 52	Class: (BV)	**1976-01 Construcciones Navales Santodomingo SA — Vigo** Yd No: 512 Loa 29.19 Br ex 7.55 Dght 3.601 Lbp 26.24 Br md 7.50 Dpth 5.41 Welded, 1 dk	**(B11A2FS) Stern Trawler**	**1 oil engine** driving 1 FP propeller Total Power: 460kW (625hp) 10.4kn MAN R8V16/18TL 1 x 4 Stroke 8 Cy. 160 x 180 460kW (625bhp) (made 1973, fitted 1976) EN Bazan de Construcciones NavalesMilitares SA-Spain AuxGen: 2 x 168kW 380V 50Hz a.c Fuel: 115.0 (d.f.)

8647256 *EPBH9* -	**SARGOL 110** *ex* Chang Hai Tuo 168 *-2011* *ex* Qiongyangpu F8083 *-2008* **Akhtari Majid** - *Iran* MMSI: 422023400	**496** 148 -		**2007-06 in the People's Republic of China** Yd No: 20060417 Loa 39.80 Br ex - Dght - Lbp 36.27 Br md 10.00 Dpth 4.80 Welded, 1 dk	**(B32A2ST) Tug**	**2 oil engines** reduction geared to sc. shafts driving 2 Propellers Total Power: 2,352kW (3,198hp) Guangzhou 2 x 4 Stroke each-1176kW (1599bhp) Guangzhou Diesel Engine Factory CoLtd-China
7640811 *UIUA* -	**SARGUS** - **Proliv JSC (A/O 'Proliv')** - *Sovetskaya Gavan* *Russia* MMSI: 273564500	**816** 244 322	Class: RS	**1976 Yaroslavskiy Sudostroitelnyy Zavod — Yaroslavl** Yd No: 327 Loa 53.73 (BB) Br ex 10.70 Dght 4.292 Lbp 47.92 Br md 10.50 Dpth 6.02 Welded, 1 dk	**(B11A2FS) Stern Trawler** Ins: 218 Compartments: 1 Ho, ER 2 Ha: 2 (1.6 x 1.6) Derricks: 2x1.5t; Winches: 2 Ice Capable	**1 oil engine** driving 1 CP propeller Total Power: 971kW (1,320hp) 12.8kn S.K.L. 8NVD48A-2U 1 x 4 Stroke 8 Cy. 320 x 480 971kW (1320bhp) VEB Schwermaschinenbau "KarlLiebknecht" (SKL)-Magdeburg AuxGen: 1 x 300kW, 3 x 150kW Thrusters: 1 Thwart. FP thruster (f); 1 Tunnel thruster (a) Fuel: 163.0 (d.f.)
9183661 *YD8007* -	**SARI 3** - **PT Surya Labuan Samudra** - *Bitung* *Indonesia*	**123** 73 -	Class: KI (BV)	**1997-09 Tuong Aik (Sarawak) Sdn Bhd — Sibu** Yd No: 9612 Loa 23.26 Br ex - Dght 2.220 Lbp 21.03 Br md 7.00 Dpth 2.90 Welded, 1 dk	**(B32A2ST) Tug**	**2 oil engines** reduction geared to sc. shafts driving 2 FP propellers Total Power: 780kW (1,060hp) 10.8kn Yanmar 6LAAL-DT 2 x 4 Stroke 6 Cy. 148 x 165 each-390kW (530bhp) Yanmar Diesel Engine Co Ltd-Japan AuxGen: 2 x 25kW 415V 50Hz a.c
7353913 *YHEZ* -	**SARI ANDALAS** *ex* Kunisaki Maru *-2002* **PT Kunangan Citra Bahari** - *Tanjung Priok* *Indonesia* MMSI: 525015511 Official number: 2001 PST NO. 2442/L	**1,464** 508 2,337	Class: KI	**1973-12 Honda Zosen — Saiki** Yd No: 616 Loa 77.02 Br ex 12.35 Dght 5.182 Lbp 72.01 Br md 12.32 Dpth 5.80 Welded, 1 dk	**(A24A2BT) Cement Carrier**	**2 oil engines** reduction geared to sc. shaft driving 1 FP propeller Total Power: 1,766kW (2,402hp) 11.5kn Niigata 6MG25BX 2 x 4 Stroke 6 Cy. 250 x 320 each-883kW (1201bhp) Niigata Engineering Co Ltd-Japan AuxGen: 2 x 128kW 445V 60Hz a.c Fuel: 76.5 (d.f.) 6.5pd
9614787 *POEI* -	**SARI ANDALAS V** - **PT Pelayaran Andalas Bahtera Baruna** - *Jakarta* *Indonesia* MMSI: 525012149	**448** 135 197	Class: AB (KI)	**2011-10 PT United Sindo Perkasa — Batam** (Hull) Yd No: H80019 **2011-10 Jetlee Shipbuilding & Engineering Pte Ltd — Singapore** Yd No: (H80019) Loa 31.00 Br ex - Dght 3.750 Lbp 29.68 Br md 10.00 Dpth 5.00 Welded, 1 dk	**(B32B2SP) Pusher Tug**	**2 oil engines** reduction geared to sc. shafts driving 2 Propellers Total Power: 3,680kW (5,004hp) Yanmar 6EY26 2 x 4 Stroke 6 Cy. 260 x 385 each-1840kW (2502bhp) Yanmar Diesel Engine Co Ltd-Japan AuxGen: 2 x 90kW a.c Fuel: 100.0
7354022 *YHHI* -	**SARI BAHTERA** *ex* Ryoyo Maru No. 1 *-2002* **PT Pelayaran Andalas Bahtera Baruna** - *Jakarta* *Indonesia* MMSI: 525015019	*3,847* 1,664 6,694	Class: KI (NK)	**1973-10 Mitsubishi Heavy Industries Ltd. — Shimonoseki** Yd No: 732 Loa 113.06 Br ex 17.56 Dght 6.916 Lbp 104.15 Br md 16.01 Dpth 8.21 Welded, 1 dk	**(A24A2BT) Cement Carrier** Grain: 5,777	**1 oil engine** driving 1 FP propeller Total Power: 2,795kW (3,800hp) 13.0kn Mitsubishi 6UET45/75C 1 x 2 Stroke 6 Cy. 450 x 750 2795kW (3800bhp) Kobe Hatsudoki KK-Japan AuxGen: 3 x 150kW 450V 60Hz a.c Fuel: 16.5 (d.f.) 114.5 (r.f.) 12.0pd
8617902 - -	**SARI I** - **Onome Foods** - *Nigeria*	*120* - -		**1987-01 Bender Shipbuilding & Repair Co Inc — Mobile AL** Yd No: 1026 Loa - Br ex - Dght - Lbp 25.30 Br md 7.32 Dpth 3.81 Welded	**(B11A2FS) Stern Trawler** Ins: 116	**1 oil engine** geared to sc. shaft driving 1 FP propeller Total Power: 459kW (624hp) 10.0kn Caterpillar 3412TA 1 x Vee 4 Stroke 12 Cy. 137 x 152 459kW (624bhp) Caterpillar Inc-USA
8617897 - -	**SARI II** - **Onome Foods** - *Nigeria*	*120* - -		**1987-01 Bender Shipbuilding & Repair Co Inc — Mobile AL** Yd No: 1027 Loa - Br ex - Dght - Lbp 25.30 Br md 7.32 Dpth 3.81 Welded	**(B11A2FS) Stern Trawler** Ins: 116	**1 oil engine** geared to sc. shaft driving 1 FP propeller Total Power: 459kW (624hp) 10.0kn Caterpillar 3412TA 1 x Vee 4 Stroke 12 Cy. 137 x 152 459kW (624bhp) Caterpillar Inc-USA
9624964 *9V2273* -	**SARI INDAH** - **Sari Indah Pte Ltd** MSI Ship Management Pte Ltd *Singapore* *Singapore* MMSI: 563526000 Official number: 398832	**48,065** 27,700 87,193	Class: AB	**2013-10 Hudong-Zhonghua Shipbuilding (Group) Co Ltd — Shanghai** Yd No: H1677A Loa 229.00 (BB) Br ex - Dght 14.250 Lbp 221.00 Br md 36.80 Dpth 19.90 Welded, 1 dk	**(A21A2BC) Bulk Carrier** Grain: 100,097 Compartments: 7 Ho, ER 7 Ha: ER	**1 oil engine** driving 1 FP propeller Total Power: 10,500kW (14,276hp) 14.5kn MAN-B&W 5S60MC-C8 1 x 2 Stroke 5 Cy. 600 x 2400 10500kW (14276bhp) Hudong Heavy Machinery Co Ltd-China AuxGen: 3 x 600kW a.c
6816683 *YGVJ* -	**SARI PACIFIC** *ex* Pacific Honor *-2002* *ex* Leader Honor *-2000* *ex* Oshima *-1988* *ex* Ryoyo Maru No. 8 *-1988* **PT Pelayaran Andalas Bahtera Baruna** - SatCom: Inmarsat C 435336410 *Jakarta* *Indonesia*	**3,948** 2,097 6,189	Class: (KI) (NK)	**1968-06 Mitsubishi Heavy Industries Ltd. — Shimonoseki** Yd No: 659 Loa 112.99 Br ex 16.02 Dght 6.500 Lbp 104.00 Br md 16.00 Dpth 8.20 Welded, 1 dk	**(A24A2BT) Cement Carrier** Grain: 5,756 Compartments: 4 Ho, ER	**1 oil engine** driving 1 FP propeller Total Power: 2,795kW (3,800hp) 11.0kn Mitsubishi 7UD45 1 x 2 Stroke 7 Cy. 450 x 720 2795kW (3800bhp) Mitsubishi Heavy Industries Ltd-Japan AuxGen: 3 x 140kW 450V 60Hz a.c Fuel: 16.5 (d.f.) 107.5 (r.f.)
9130705 *YD8006* -	**SARI PRATAMA** *ex* Alpha *-2007* *ex* Surya I *-2002* **PT Artha Gunung Mas** - *Bitung* *Indonesia*	**112** 34 113	Class: KI (BV) (NK)	**1995-05 Rajang Maju Shipbuilding Sdn Bhd — Sibu** Yd No: 21 L reg 23.17 Br ex - Dght 2.388 Lbp 21.76 Br md 7.00 Dpth 2.90 Welded, 1 dk	**(B32A2ST) Tug**	**2 oil engines** reduction geared to sc. shafts driving 2 FP propellers Total Power: 794kW (1,080hp) 10.0kn Caterpillar 3408TA 2 x Vee 4 Stroke 8 Cy. 137 x 152 each-397kW (540bhp) Caterpillar Inc-USA
7528934 *YBZV* -	**SARI SAMUDERA 51** - **PT Rejeki Abadi Sakti** - *Semarang* *Indonesia*	*111* 43 -	Class: (KI)	**1973 P.T. Menara — Tegal** Loa - Br ex - Dght - Lbp 21.01 Br md 6.20 Dpth 2.95 Welded, 1 dk	**(B11B2FV) Fishing Vessel**	**1 oil engine** driving 1 FP propeller Total Power: 313kW (426hp) Caterpillar D353TA 1 x 4 Stroke 6 Cy. 159 x 203 313kW (426bhp) Caterpillar Tractor Co-USA AuxGen: 1 x 16kW 225V
7528946 *YBZW* -	**SARI SAMUDERA 52** - **PT Rejeki Abadi Sakti** - *Semarang* *Indonesia*	*111* 43 -	Class: (KI)	**1973-09 P.T. Menara — Tegal** Loa - Br ex - Dght - Lbp 21.01 Br md 6.20 Dpth 2.95 Welded, 1 dk	**(B11B2FV) Fishing Vessel**	**1 oil engine** driving 1 FP propeller Total Power: 313kW (426hp) Caterpillar D353TA 1 x 4 Stroke 6 Cy. 159 x 203 313kW (426bhp) Caterpillar Tractor Co-USA AuxGen: 1 x 16kW 225V
7528958 *YBZX* -	**SARI SAMUDERA 53** - **PT Rejeki Abadi Sakti** - *Semarang* *Indonesia*	*111* 43 -	Class: (KI)	**1973-12 P.T. Menara — Tegal** Loa - Br ex - Dght - Lbp 21.01 Br md 6.20 Dpth 2.95 Welded, 1 dk	**(B11B2FV) Fishing Vessel**	**1 oil engine** driving 1 FP propeller Total Power: 313kW (426hp) Caterpillar D353TA 1 x 4 Stroke 6 Cy. 159 x 203 313kW (426bhp) Caterpillar Tractor Co-USA AuxGen: 1 x 16kW 225V
7528960 *YBZY* -	**SARI SAMUDERA 54** - **PT Rejeki Abadi Sakti** - *Semarang* *Indonesia*	*111* 43 -	Class: (KI)	**1974-05 P.T. Menara — Tegal** Loa - Br ex - Dght - Lbp 21.01 Br md 6.20 Dpth 2.95 Welded, 1 dk	**(B11B2FV) Fishing Vessel**	**1 oil engine** driving 1 FP propeller Total Power: 313kW (426hp) Caterpillar D353TA 1 x 4 Stroke 6 Cy. 159 x 203 313kW (426bhp) Caterpillar Tractor Co-USA AuxGen: 1 x 16kW 225V
7528972 *YBZZ* -	**SARI SAMUDERA 55** - **PT Rejeki Abadi Sakti** - *Semarang* *Indonesia*	*111* 43 -	Class: (KI)	**1973 P.T. Menara — Tegal** Loa - Br ex - Dght - Lbp 21.01 Br md 6.20 Dpth 2.95 Welded, 1 dk	**(B11B2FV) Fishing Vessel**	**1 oil engine** driving 1 FP propeller Total Power: 313kW (426hp) Caterpillar D353TA 1 x 4 Stroke 6 Cy. 159 x 203 313kW (426bhp) Caterpillar Tractor Co-USA AuxGen: 1 x 16kW 225V
8340377 *YCOO* -	**SARI SAMUDERA 61** - **PT Sari Samudera** - *Semarang* *Indonesia*	*144* 87 -	Class: (KI)	**1980 P.T. Menara — Tegal** Loa 32.52 Br ex - Dght 2.750 Lbp 28.00 Br md 7.00 Dpth 3.20 Welded, 1 dk	**(B11B2FV) Fishing Vessel**	**1 oil engine** driving 1 FP propeller Total Power: 478kW (650hp) Niigata 6L20CX 1 x 4 Stroke 6 Cy. 200 x 260 478kW (650bhp) Niigata Engineering Co Ltd-Japan

8340389 *YCOP* - **SARI SAMUDERA 62**
PT Sari Samudera
-
Semarang *Indonesia*
144 87 -
Class: (KI)
1980 P.T. Menara — Tegal
Loa 32.52 Br ex - Dght 2.750
Lbp 28.00 Br md 7.00 Dpth 3.20
Welded, 1 dk
(B11B2FV) Fishing Vessel
1 oil engine driving 1 FP propeller
Total Power: 478kW (650hp)
Niigata 6L20CX
1 x 4 Stroke 6 Cy. 200 x 260 478kW (650bhp)
Niigata Engineering Co Ltd-Japan

8340391 *YCOQ* - **SARI SAMUDERA 63**
PT Sari Samudera
-
Semarang *Indonesia*
144 87 -
Class: (KI)
1981 P.T. Menara — Tegal
Loa 32.52 Br ex - Dght 2.750
Lbp 28.00 Br md 7.00 Dpth 3.20
Welded, 1 dk
(B11B2FV) Fishing Vessel
1 oil engine driving 1 FP propeller
Total Power: 478kW (650hp)
Niigata 6L20CX
1 x 4 Stroke 6 Cy. 200 x 260 478kW (650bhp)
Niigata Engineering Co Ltd-Japan

9164043 *YD6518* - **SARI UTAMA**
ex SRO 8 *-2003*
PT Samudra Utama Shipping
-
Banjarmasin *Indonesia*
137 82 128
Class: KI (NK)
1997-01 Super-Light Shipbuilding Contractor — Sibu Yd No: 22
Loa 23.80 Br ex - Dght 2.512
Lbp 22.04 Br md 7.60 Dpth 3.70
Welded, 1 dk
(B32A2ST) Tug
2 oil engines reduction geared to sc. shafts driving 2 FP propellers
Total Power: 736kW (1,000hp) 10.0kn
Cummins KTA-19-M
2 x 4 Stroke 6 Cy. 159 x 159 each-368kW (500bhp)
Cummins Engine Co Inc-USA
AuxGen: 2 x 20kW a.c

7946904 - **SARIBAS I**
Saribaslar Kollektif Sti
-
Istanbul *Turkey*
Official number: 3813
297 158 400
1968 Gemi-is Kolleketif Sirketi — Fener, Istanbul
Loa 43.52 Br ex - Dght 2.850
Lbp 38.33 Br md 7.00 Dpth 3.31
Welded, 1 dk
(A31A2GX) General Cargo Ship
1 oil engine driving 1 FP propeller
Total Power: 588kW (799hp)
MWM
1 x 4 Stroke 6 Cy. 588kW (799bhp)
Motoren Werke Mannheim AG (MWM)-West Germany

8607880 *TCBH4* - **SARICA BEY**
Istanbul Deniz Otobusleri Sanayi ve Ticaret AS (IDO)
-
Istanbul *Turkey*
MMSI: 271002472
Official number: TUGS 611
431 166 125
Class: TL (NV)
1987-08 Fjellstrand AS — Omastrand Yd No: 1581
Loa 38.82 Br ex 9.71 Dght 1.550
Lbp 36.41 Br md 9.47 Dpth 3.92
Welded, 1 dk
(A37B2PS) Passenger Ship
Hull Material: Aluminium Alloy
Passengers: unberthed: 450
2 oil engines sr geared to sc. shafts driving 2 FP propellers
Total Power: 3,020kW (4,106hp) 32.0kn
M.T.U. 16V396TB83
2 x Vee 4 Stroke 16 Cy. 165 x 185 each-1510kW (2053bhp)
MTU Friedrichshafen GmbH-Friedrichshafen
AuxGen: 2 x 68kW 400V 50Hz a.c

8203608 *EPQV* - **SARINA**
ex Iran Sahar *-2010* *ex* Ra-Ees Ali *-2010*
ex Pegasus *-1992* *ex* Hammonia *-1989*
Khazar Sea Shipping Lines
-
Bandar Abbas *Iran*
MMSI: 422089000
Official number: 2319
2,576 934 2,876
Class: IN (NV) (GL)
1982-06 Schiffs. Hugo Peters Wewelsfleth Peters & Co. GmbH — Wewelsfleth Yd No: 584
Loa 93.63 Br ex 13.47 Dght 4.411
Lbp 85.22 Br md 13.42 Dpth 6.61
Welded, 2 dks
(A31A2GX) General Cargo Ship
Grain: 4,219; Bale: 4,217
TEU 141 C.Ho 96/20' C.Dk 45/20'
Compartments: 1 Ho, ER
1 Ha: (50.3 x 10.2)ER
Cranes: 2x5t
Ice Capable
1 oil engine sr reverse geared to sc. shaft driving 1 FP propeller
Total Power: 736kW (1,001hp) 10.5kn
Deutz SBV8M628
1 x 4 Stroke 8 Cy. 240 x 280 736kW (1001bhp)
Kloeckner Humboldt Deutz AG-West Germany
AuxGen: 1 x 232kW 380V 50Hz a.c, 1 x 115kW 380V 50Hz a.c, 1 x 60kW 380V 50Hz a.c
Thrusters: 1 Thwart. FP thruster (f)

7916193 *YHLS* - **SARINA ANDALAS**
ex Hakozaki Maru *-2004*
PT Pelayaran Andalas Bahtera Baruna
-
Padang *Indonesia*
MMSI: 525015106
Official number: 2003 AAA NO 781/L
1,166 485 1,948
Class: KI (NK)
1979-09 Kanda Zosensho K.K. — Japan Yd No: 248
Loa 71.00 Br ex - Dght 4.901
Lbp 65.03 Br md 11.51 Dpth 5.52
Welded, 1 dk
(A24A2BT) Cement Carrier
Grain: 1,577
1 oil engine reverse reduction geared to sc. shaft driving 1 FP propeller
Total Power: 1,324kW (1,800hp) 11.5kn
Daihatsu 6DSM-28
1 x 4 Stroke 6 Cy. 280 x 340 1324kW (1800bhp)
Daihatsu Diesel Manufacturing Co Lt-Japan
AuxGen: 2 x 289kW

9094365 - - **SARINA CRUISE**
Hotel Sarina Ltd
-
Chittagong *Bangladesh*
Official number: C.1619
300 - -
2006-03 Western Marine Shipyard Ltd — Chittagong Yd No: 034
L reg 40.00 Br ex - Dght -
Lbp - Br md 8.00 Dpth 3.00
Welded, 1 dk
(A37B2PS) Passenger Ship
Passengers: unberthed: 310
2 oil engines reduction geared to sc. shafts driving 2 Propellers
Total Power: 530kW (720hp)
Chinese Std. Type 6160ZC
2 x 4 Stroke 6 Cy. 160 x 225 each-265kW (360bhp)
Weifang Diesel Engine Factory-China

9485186 *9HNN9* - **SARINE**
launched as Universe 3 *-2008*
Massatlantic (Malta) Ltd
Massoel Ltd
SatCom: Inmarsat C 424923310
Valletta *Malta*
MMSI: 249233000
Official number: 9485186
5,087 2,625 7,300
Class: (BV)
2008-05 Universe Shipbuilding (Yangzhou) Co Ltd — Yizheng JS Yd No: 06-003
Loa 112.80 Br ex - Dght 6.900
Lbp 106.00 Br md 17.20 Dpth 9.10
Welded, 1 dk
(A21A2BC) Bulk Carrier
Grain: 9,392
Compartments: 3 Ho, ER
3 Ha: ER
Cranes: 2x25t
1 oil engine reduction geared to sc. shaft driving 1 FP propeller
Total Power: 2,500kW (3,399hp) 12.0kn
Daihatsu 8DKM-28
1 x 4 Stroke 8 Cy. 280 x 390 2500kW (3399bhp)
Shaanxi Diesel Heavy Industry Co Lt-China
AuxGen: 3 x 250kW 50Hz a.c

8832930 - - **SARINSKIY RYBAK**
ex RS-300 No. 77 *-2008*
Azerbalyg State Fishing Enterprise (Predpriyatiye Morskogo Peredvizhnogo Loba Ryby Goskontserna 'Azerbalyg')
-
189 57 73
Class: (RS)
1990-07 Astrakhanskaya Sudoverf im. "Kirova" — Astrakhan Yd No: 77
Loa 31.86 Br ex 7.09 Dght 2.101
Lbp 27.80 Br md - Dpth 3.18
Welded, 1dk
(B11B2FV) Fishing Vessel
Ins: 100
1 oil engine geared to sc. shaft driving 1 FP propeller
Total Power: 232kW (315hp) 10.3kn
Daldizel 6CHSPN2A18-315
1 x 4 Stroke 6 Cy. 180 x 220 232kW (315bhp)
Daldizel-Khabarovsk
AuxGen: 2 x 25kW a.c
Fuel: 14.0 (d.f.)

8934714 - - **SARINTO 2**
ex Samlimsan 12 *-2002*
Samlimsan Shipping Sdn Bhd
-
191 58 178
Class: (NK)
1997-07 Nam Cheong Dockyard Sdn Bhd — Miri Yd No: 507
Loa 26.00 Br ex - Dght 3.012
Lbp 24.35 Br md 7.92 Dpth 3.65
Welded, 1 dk
(B32A2ST) Tug
2 oil engines reduction geared to sc. shafts driving 2 FP propellers
Total Power: 1,060kW (1,442hp) 10.0kn
Mitsubishi S6R2-MTK
2 x 4 Stroke 6 Cy. 170 x 220 each-530kW (721bhp)
Mitsubishi Heavy Industries Ltd-Japan

9368003 *9BPX* - **SARIR**
ex Iran Amirabad *-2010*
Khazar Sea Shipping Lines
-
Bandar Anzali *Iran*
MMSI: 422716000
5,676 3,109 7,004 T/cm 22.0
Class: IN (LR) (RS)
Classed LR until 26/10/11
2007-09 OAO Volgogradskiy Sudostroitelnyy Zavod — Volgograd Yd No: 243
Loa 139.95 (BB) Br ex 16.72 Dght 4.600
Lbp 135.69 Br md 16.50 Dpth 6.00
Welded, 1 dk
(A31A2GX) General Cargo Ship
Grain: 10,956
TEU 274 C Ho 204 TEU C Dk 70 TEU
Compartments: 4 Ho, ER
4 Ha: ER
2 oil engines reduction geared to sc. shafts driving 2 FP propellers
Total Power: 2,400kW (3,264hp) 10.5kn
Wartsila 6L20
2 x 4 Stroke 6 Cy. 200 x 280 each-1200kW (1632bhp)
Wartsila Finland Oy-Finland
AuxGen: 3 x 240kW a.c
Thrusters: 1 Tunnel thruster (f)

5064142 *LW8261* - **SARITA GLORIA**
ex Ona Cecilia *-1999* *ex* Carlos Lumb *-1968*
Astelia SA
-
Argentina
Official number: 01088
136 - -
Class: (LR)
✠ Classed LR until 8/29
1928-07 J. Crichton & Co. Ltd. — Saltney, Chester Yd No: 451
L reg 32.32 Br ex 7.04 Dght -
Lbp - Br md - Dpth 3.00
Riveted
(B32A2ST) Tug
2 oil engines driving 2 FP propellers
Total Power: 596kW (810hp) 8.0kn
Crossley
2 x 2 Stroke 265 x 345 each-298kW (405bhp) (new engine 1949)
Crossley Bros. Ltd.-Manchester

8985854 *MSPM8* - **SARITA SI**
ex Sarita U *-2009* *ex* Virginia Alpha *-2009*
ex Bagheera *-2009* *ex* Idell V *-2009*
Glion Rosien Ltd
Fraser Worldwide SAM
London *United Kingdom*
MMSI: 235867000
Official number: 709644
227 68 -
Class: RI
1973 C.R.N. Cant. Nav. Ancona S.r.l. — Ancona Yd No: 100/34
Loa 38.60 Br ex 7.30 Dght 2.810
Lbp 33.10 Br md 7.20 Dpth 3.25
Welded, 1 dk
(X11A2YP) Yacht
Passengers: cabins: 6; berths: 12
2 oil engines geared to sc. shafts driving 2 FP propellers
Total Power: 1,766kW (2,402hp) 12.0kn
Caterpillar 3412TA
2 x Vee 4 Stroke 12 Cy. 137 x 152 each-883kW (1201bhp) (new engine 2004)
Caterpillar Inc-USA

9417787 *A8NW2* - **SARK**
ex Laura *-2012*
Sark Maritime Ltd
-
SatCom: Inmarsat C 463703242
Monrovia *Liberia*
MMSI: 636013572
Official number: 13572
62,789 34,934 113,041 T/cm 99.7
Class: AB
2009-02 New Times Shipbuilding Co Ltd — Jingjiang JS Yd No: 0311506
Loa 249.96 (BB) Br ex 44.04 Dght 14.819
Lbp 240.00 Br md 44.00 Dpth 21.00
Welded, 1 dk
(A13A2TW) Crude/Oil Products Tanker
Double Hull (13F)
Liq: 124,714; Liq (Oil): 127,491
Cargo Heating Coils
Compartments: 12 Wing Ta, 1 Slop Ta, 2 Wing Slop Ta, ER
3 Cargo Pump (s): 3x3000m³/hr
Manifold: Bow/CM: 123.5m
1 oil engine driving 1 FP propeller
Total Power: 15,820kW (21,509hp) 15.0kn
MAN-B&W 7S60MC-C
1 x 2 Stroke 7 Cy. 600 x 2400 15820kW (21509bhp)
Doosan Engine Co Ltd-South Korea
AuxGen: 3 x 900kW a.c
Fuel: 183.0 (d.f.) 2696.0 (r.f.)

8648858 *MPTP7* - **SARK VIKING**
Isle of Sark Shipping Co Ltd
-
Jersey *Jersey*
Official number: 740348
104 - -
2007 Steelkit Ltd. — Borth (Hull launched by)
2007 Appledore Shipbuilders (2004) Ltd — Bideford (Hull completed by)
Loa 21.24 Br ex - Dght -
Lbp - Br md 7.02 Dpth 3.05
Welded, 1 dk
(A31C2GD) Deck Cargo Ship
2 oil engines reduction geared to sc. shafts driving 2 Propellers
Total Power: 662kW (900hp)
Iveco Aifo 8210 SRM45
2 x 4 Stroke 6 Cy. 137 x 156 each-331kW (450bhp)
IVECO AIFO S.p.A.-Pregnana Milanese

IMO / Call sign	Name / Owner	Tonnage	Class	Builder / Dimensions	Type	Machinery
8936645 *9WGI9* -	**SARKU CLEMENTINE** *ex* Miss Clementine *-2005* *ex* CLV-1 *-1998* **Prominent Energy Sdn Bhd** Sarku Engineering Services Sdn Bhd *Kuching* *Malaysia* MMSI: 533776000 Official number: 329750	**3,637** 1,091 2,806	Class: AB	**1996**-12 **President Marine Pte Ltd — Singapore** Yd No: 223 Converted From: Deck-Cargo Pontoon, Non-propelled-1998 Loa 74.90 Br ex - Dght 4.000 Lbp 70.61 Br md 18.29 Dpth 8.27 Welded, 1 dk	**(B34D2SL) Cable Layer** Cranes: 1x60t,1x30t	**4 oil engines** geared to sc. shafts driving 2 Directional propellers Total Power: 3,000kW (4,080hp) 9.0kn Caterpillar 3508TA 4 x Vee 4 Stroke 8 Cy. 170 x 190 each-750kW (1020bhp) Caterpillar Inc-USA AuxGen: 3 x 550kW a.c, 2 x 200kW a.c Thrusters: 2 Retract. directional thruster (f) Fuel: 1000.0 (d.f.) 7.8pd
7397335 *9WYT* -	**SARKU SAMBANG** *ex* Sambang *-2000* **Kah Kii Lau** - *Kuching* *Malaysia* MMSI: 533506000 Official number: 325044	**720** 216 163	Class: LR (NV) ✠**100A1** SS 07/2005 short international voyages ✠**LMC** Eq.Ltr: H; Cable: U1 (b)	**1975**-03 **Vosper Thornycroft Pte Ltd — Singapore** Yd No: B.952 Converted From: Buoy & Lighthouse Tender-2000 Loa 45.50 Br ex 11.79 Dght 2.200 Lbp 41.15 Br md 11.59 Dpth 4.88 Welded, 2 dks	**(B22A20V) Diving Support Vessel** Cranes: 1x12t	**2 oil engines** reverse reduction geared to sc. shafts driving 2 FP propellers Total Power: 1,082kW (1,472hp) 9.0kn Caterpillar D348TA 2 x Vee 4 Stroke 12 Cy. 137 x 165 each-541kW (736bhp) Caterpillar Tractor Co-USA AuxGen: 2 x 100kW 415V 50Hz a.c Thrusters: 1 Tunnel thruster (f)
7803566 *9WF03* -	**SARKU SANTUBONG** *ex* Cable Installer *-2003* *ex* Star Hercules *-1995* **Sarku Marine Sdn Bhd** Sarku Engineering Services Sdn Bhd *Kuching* *Malaysia* MMSI: 533455000 Official number: 329573	**2,999** 899 2,485	Class: LR ✠**100A1** SS 06/2009 offshore supply ship ✠**LMC** Eq.Ltr: (S) ; Cable: 467.5/40.0 U3	**1980**-02 **Appledore Shipbuilders Ltd — Bideford** Yd No: A.S.126 Converted From: Cable-layer-2003 Converted From: Offshore Supply Ship-1995 Loa 89.42 Br ex 17.61 Dght 4.800 Lbp 73.31 Br md 17.25 Dpth 7.00 Welded, 1 dk	**(B21A20S) Platform Supply Ship** Cranes: 1x30t,1x29t	**2 oil engines** sr geared to sc. shafts driving 2 CP propellers Total Power: 4,148kW (5,640hp) 12.0kn Ruston 12RKCM 2 x Vee 4 Stroke 12 Cy. 254 x 305 each-2074kW (2820bhp) Ruston Diesels Ltd.-Newton-le-Willows AuxGen: 3 x 650kW 440V 60Hz a.c, 1 x 300kW 440V 60Hz a.c Thrusters: 2 Thwart. FP thruster (f); 1 Tunnel thruster (a) Fuel: 1800.0 (d.f.) 21.0pd
7349431 *9WDW2* -	**SARKU SEMANTAN** *ex* Sarku Sementa *-2000* *ex* Osa Lerwick *-2000* *ex* Niederntor *-1986* **Sarku Marine Sdn Bhd** Sarku Engineering Services Sdn Bhd *Kuching* *Malaysia* MMSI: 533509000 Official number: 329284	**1,467** 441 1,330	Class: GL	**1974**-02 **Gutehoffnungshuette Sterkrade AG Rheinwerft Walsum — Duisburg** Yd No: 1110 Loa 56.14 Br ex 14.33 Dght 5.138 Lbp 51.01 Br md 14.03 Dpth 7.57 Welded, 1 dk	**(B21A20S) Platform Supply Ship** Cranes: 1x50t	**2 oil engines** driving 2 FP propellers Total Power: 2,574kW (3,500hp) 9.0kn MWM TBD441V12K 2 x Vee 4 Stroke 12 Cy. 230 x 270 each-1287kW (1750bhp) Motoren Werke Mannheim AG (MWM)-West Germany AuxGen: 3 x 112kW 220/380V 50Hz a.c Thrusters: 1 Thwart. FP thruster (f)
7510676 *YLAG* -	**SARMA 1** *ex* Vega *-2011* *ex* Sea Fox *-2005* *ex* Tinka *-2003* *ex* Taras *-1996* *ex* Ikaria *-1986* **Gloria Shipping Inc** Livonia Shipping Co (SIA 'Livonia Shipping Co') *Riga* *Latvia* MMSI: 275254000 Official number: 0431	**2,219** 1,313 2,560	Class: RS (GL)	**1976**-07 **J.J. Sietas Schiffswerft — Hamburg** Yd No: 708 Loa 81.41 (BB) Br ex 13.47 Dght 5.028 Lbp 74.17 Br md 13.42 Dpth 5.19 Welded, 1 dk	**(A31A2GX) General Cargo Ship** Double Bottom Partial Compartment Length Grain: 4,785; Bale: 4,512 TEU 150 C.Ho 86/20' (40') C.Dk 64/20' (40') Compartments: 1 Ho, ER 1 Ha: (50.4 x 10.2)ER Ice Capable	**1 oil engine** sr geared to sc. shaft driving 1 CP propeller Total Power: 1,949kW (2,650hp) 13.0kn MaK 8M453AK 1 x 4 Stroke 8 Cy. 320 x 420 1949kW (2650bhp) MaK Maschinenbau GmbH-Kiel AuxGen: 1 x 210kW 220/380V 50Hz a.c, 2 x 65kW 220/380V 50Hz a.c Thrusters: 1 Thwart. FP thruster (f)
8027133 *UBVK8* -	**SARMAT** *ex* Marss-1 *-2014* *ex* Mars *-1992* **Alliance Co Ltd** LLC 'Alliance' *St Petersburg* *Russia* MMSI: 273325230	**728** 218 290	Class: RS (LR) Classed LR until 20/7/10	**1982**-09 **Hollming Oy — Rauma** Yd No: 241 Loa 40.21 Br ex 12.50 Dght 6.100 Lbp 38.21 Br md 12.00 Dpth 7.00 Welded, 1 dk	**(B32A2ST) Tug** Ice Capable	**2 oil engines** dr geared to sc. shafts driving 2 CP propellers Total Power: 3,700kW (5,030hp) 14.3kn Wartsila 6R32 2 x 4 Stroke 6 Cy. 320 x 350 each-1850kW (2515bhp) Oy Wartsila Ab-Finland AuxGen: 2 x 200kW 400V 50Hz a.c, 2 x 50kW 400V 50Hz a.c Boilers: db (f.f.) 7.1kgf/cm² (7.0bar)
8721387 *UALK* -	**SARMAT** *ex* Amur-2512 *-2012* **Navigator Shipping Co Ltd (A/O 'Navigator')** - *Taganrog* *Russia* MMSI: 273325000	**2,996** 996 3,340	Class: RS (RR)	**1986**-03 **Zavody Tazkeho Strojarstva (ZTS) — Komarno** Yd No: 2312 Loa 115.70 Br ex 13.43 Dght 4.130 Lbp 109.11 Br md 13.00 Dpth 6.00 Welded, 1 dk	**(A31A2GX) General Cargo Ship** Grain: 4,064 TEU 102 C.Ho 62/20' (40') C.Dk 40/20' (40') Compartments: 3 Ho, ER 3 Ha: (11.6 x 10.1) (23.0 x 10.1) (24.0 x 10.1)ER Ice Capable	**2 oil engines** reverse reduction geared to sc. shafts driving 2 FP propellers Total Power: 1,030kW (1,400hp) 10.0kn Skoda 6L275IIIPN 2 x 4 Stroke 6 Cy. 275 x 350 each-515kW (700bhp) CKD Praha-Praha AuxGen: 3 x 138kW 220/380V a.c, 1 x 25kW 220/380V a.c Thrusters: 1 Thwart. FP thruster (f)
9335238 *EAKF* -	**SARMIENTO DE GAMBOA** **Government of Spain (Consejo Superior de Investigaciones Cientificas CSIC)** - *Vigo* *Spain* MMSI: 224713000 Official number: 8-11/2005	**2,754** 826 850	Class: BV	**2007**-10 **Construcciones Navales P Freire SA — Vigo** Yd No: 600 Loa 70.50 (BB) Br ex - Dght 4.600 Lbp 62.00 Br md 15.50 Dpth 7.90 Welded, 1 dk	**(B31A2SR) Research Survey Vessel** A-frames: 1	**3 diesel electric oil engines** driving 3 gen. each 1400kW 690V a.c Connecting to 2 elec. motors each (1200kW) driving 1 FP propeller Total Power: 4,320kW (5,874hp) 14.0kn Wartsila 8L20 3 x 4 Stroke 8 Cy. 200 x 280 each-1440kW (1958bhp) Wartsila Finland Oy-Finland Thrusters: 1 Retract. directional thruster (f); 1 Tunnel thruster (a) Fuel: 573.0 (r.f.)
9322164 *ZDHZ8* -	**SARNIA CHERIE** *ex* Vedrey Tora *-2009* **Jamesco 750 Ltd** James Fisher (Shipping Services) Ltd *Gibraltar* *Gibraltar (British)* MMSI: 236401000 Official number: 9322164	**3,043** 1,055 3,392 T/cm 11.3	Class: NV	**2007**-06 **AO Sudostroitelnyy Zavod "3rd International" — Astrakhan** (Hull launched by) Yd No: 200-1-31 **2007**-06 **Reval Shipbuilding OU — Tallinn** (Hull completed by) Converted From: Chemical/Products Tanker-2010 Loa 79.90 (BB) Br ex 16.00 Dght 5.514 Lbp 75.00 Br md 15.70 Dpth 7.80 Welded, 1 dk	**(A13B2TP) Products Tanker** Double Hull (13F) Liq: 3,916; Liq (Oil): 4,116 Compartments: 10 Wing Ta, 1 Slop Ta, ER 11 Cargo Pump (s): 11x170m³/hr Manifold: Bow/CM: 39m	**1 oil engine** reduction geared to sc. shaft driving 1 CP propeller Total Power: 2,050kW (2,787hp) 11.5kn Wartsila 6L26A 1 x 4 Stroke 6 Cy. 260 x 320 2050kW (2787bhp) Wartsila Italia SpA-Italy AuxGen: 3 x 485kW a.c, 1 x 800kW a.c Thrusters: 1 Tunnel thruster (f) Fuel: 219.1 (d.f.)
9322176 *ZDHZ7* -	**SARNIA LIBERTY** *ex* Vedrey Thor *-2009* **Jamesco 750 Ltd** James Fisher (Shipping Services) Ltd *Gibraltar* *Gibraltar (British)* MMSI: 236399000 Official number: 9322176	**3,017** 1,038 3,515	Class: NV (GL)	**2008**-03 **AO Sudostroitelnyy Zavod "3rd International" — Astrakhan** (Hull launched by) Yd No: 200-1-33 **2008**-03 **Reval Shipbuilding OU — Tallinn** (Hull completed by) Converted From: Chemical/Products Tanker-2010 Loa 79.90 (BB) Br ex 16.00 Dght 5.500 Lbp 75.58 Br md 15.70 Dpth 7.80 Welded, 1 dk	**(A13B2TP) Products Tanker** Double Hull (13F) Liq: 4,200; Liq (Oil): 4,200 Compartments: 1 Ta, 10 Wing Ta, 1 Slop Ta, ER 11 Cargo Pump (s): 11x170m³/hr Manifold: Bow/CM: 39m	**1 oil engine** reduction geared to sc. shaft driving 1 CP propeller Total Power: 2,025kW (2,753hp) 12.5kn Wartsila 6L26 1 x 4 Stroke 6 Cy. 260 x 320 2025kW (2753bhp) Wartsila Italia SpA-Italy AuxGen: 3 x 368kW 440V 60Hz a.c, 1 x 960kW 440V 60Hz a.c Thrusters: 1 Tunnel thruster (f) Fuel: 221.0 (d.f.) 8.0pd
9214422 *VTRJ* -	**SAROJINI** **Kolkata Port Trust** - *Kolkata* *India* MMSI: 419022700 Official number: 2902	**1,126** 338 439	Class: (IR)	**2002**-05 **The Shalimar Works (1980) Ltd — Haora** Yd No: 761 Loa 55.00 Br ex 10.70 Dght 3.000 Lbp 48.53 Br md 10.60 Dpth 6.80 Welded, 1 dk	**(B31A2SR) Research Survey Vessel**	**2 oil engines** driving 2 Directional propellers Total Power: 1,176kW (1,598hp) 12.5kn Cummins KTA-2300-M 2 x Vee 4 Stroke 12 Cy. 159 x 159 each-588kW (799bhp) Cummins India Ltd-India AuxGen: 2 x 160kW 415V 50Hz a.c Fuel: 69.0 (d.f.)
9129835 - -	**SAROJINI** **West Bengal Surface Transport Corp** - *India*	**250** - -	Class: (IR)	**1997**-03 **A C Roy & Co — Haora** Yd No: 12 Loa - Br ex - Dght - Lbp 27.30 Br md 8.00 Dpth 2.50 Welded, 1 dk	**(A37B2PS) Passenger Ship**	**2 oil engines** geared to sc. shafts driving 2 Propellers Cummins N-495-M 2 x 4 Stroke 4 Cy. 130 x 152 Kirloskar Cummins Ltd-India
9292670 *VTBK* -	**SAROJINI NAIDU** **Government of The Republic of India (Coast Guard)** - SatCom: Inmarsat C 441911010 *Mumbai* *India* MMSI: 419110000	**342** 103 -	Class: (AB)	**2003**-04 **Goa Shipyard Ltd. — Goa** Yd No: 1182 Loa 48.14 Br ex - Dght 2.000 Lbp 44.00 Br md 7.50 Dpth 4.00 Welded, 1 dk	**(B34H2SQ) Patrol Vessel**	**3 oil engines** geared to sc. shafts driving 3 Water jets Total Power: 8,160kW (11,094hp) M.T.U. 16V4000M90 3 x Vee 4 Stroke 16 Cy. 165 x 190 each-2720kW (3698bhp) MTU Friedrichshafen GmbH-Friedrichshafen
8903997 *JG4918* -	**SAROMA** **Government of Japan (Ministry of Land, Infrastructure & Transport) (The Coastguard)** - *Tokyo* *Japan* Official number: 131942	*179* - 10		**1989**-11 **Hitachi Zosen Corp — Kawasaki KN** Yd No: 117100 Loa 43.00 Br ex 7.52 Dght 1.572 Lbp 40.00 Br md 7.50 Dpth 4.09 Welded, 1 dk	**(B34H2SQ) Patrol Vessel** Hull Material: Aluminium Alloy	**3 oil engines** with clutches, flexible couplings & sr reverse geared to sc. shafts driving 2 FP propellers , 1 Water jet Total Power: 7,203kW (9,793hp) 35.0kn Pielstick 12PA4V200VGA 1 x Vee 4 Stroke 12 Cy. 200 x 210 2001kW (2721bhp) Fuji Diesel Co Ltd-Japan Pielstick 16PA4V200VGA 2 x Vee 4 Stroke 16 Cy. 200 x 210 each-2601kW (3536bhp) Fuji Diesel Co Ltd-Japan

6710140 *OYJC* S 158	**SARON** *ex* Galeota *-2010* *ex* Karen Nielsen *-2009* *ex* Rikke Westeraa *-1992* *ex* Laila Majbrit *-1989* *ex* Sonja Irene *-1987* *ex* Mican *-1978* *ex* Nikan *-1971* *ex* Rimfors *-1970* **Saron Fiskeri A/S** - SatCom: Inmarsat C 421929410 *Skagen* *Denmark* MMSI: 219294000 Official number: H1705	**269** 80 -	Class: (BV) (DS)	**1966-12 VEB Rosslauer Schiffswerft — Rosslau** Yd No: 3185 Loa 33.63 Br ex 6.61 Dght 2.699 Lbp 29.55 Br md 6.56 Dpth 3.31 Welded, 1 dk	**(B11A2FT) Trawler** Ins: 210 Compartments: 2 Ho, ER 3 Ha: 2 (1.2 x 0.9) (1.3 x 1.3)ER Derricks: 1x0.5t; Winches: 1 Ice Capable	**1 oil engine** driving 1 CP propeller Total Power: 662kW (900hp) 12.0kn Nohab F26R 1 x 4 Stroke 6 Cy. 250 x 300 662kW (900bhp) Nydqvist & Holm AB-Sweden AuxGen: 1 x 16kW 220V d.c, 1 x 15kW 220V d.c Fuel: 28.5 (d.f.)
9041540 *9HA3479* -	**SARONIC BREEZE** *ex* Columbia *-2012* **Seaview Maritime SA** Baltmed Reefer Services Ltd *Valletta* *Malta* MMSI: 229644000 Official number: 9041540	**6,399** 3,981 7,376	Class: NK	**1991-12 Imabari Shipbuilding Co Ltd — Imabari EH (Imabari Shipyard)** Yd No: 491 Loa 137.55 (BB) Br ex - Dght 7.815 Lbp 129.00 Br md 18.00 Dpth 10.50 Welded, 3 dks	**(A34A2GR) Refrigerated Cargo Ship** Ins: 9,513 Compartments: 4 Ho, ER 5 Ha: 2 (10.5 x 7.5)2 (9.0 x 7.5) Derricks: 8x5t	**1 oil engine** driving 1 FP propeller Total Power: 6,326kW (8,601hp) 18.0kn B&W 5S50MC 1 x 2 Stroke 5 Cy. 500 x 1910 6326kW (8601bhp) Mitsui Engineering & Shipbuilding CLtd-Japan AuxGen: 4 x 280kW a.c Fuel: 1030.0 (r.f.)
9081643 *UBYH9* -	**SARONIC BREEZE** **'Bereg Mechty' JSC** - *St Petersburg* *Russia* MMSI: 273354740	**6,964** 3,103 6,712 T/cm 50.0	Class: RS (GL)	**1996-01 DP Sudnobudivnyi Zavod im. "61 Kommunara" — Mykolayiv** Yd No: 1144 Loa 133.81 (BB) Br ex 18.00 Dght 7.279 Lbp 119.84 Br md 17.98 Dpth 10.70 Welded, 3 dks	**(A34A2GR) Refrigerated Cargo Ship** Ins: 7,619 TEU 91 C Ho 48 TEU C Dk 43 TEU incl 41 ref C Compartments: 4 Ho, ER, 8 Tw Dk 4 Ha: 4 (6.5 x 7.8)ER Derricks: 8x5t Ice Capable	**1 oil engine** driving 1 FP propeller Total Power: 5,100kW (6,934hp) 15.0kn B&W 6L42MC 1 x 2 Stroke 6 Cy. 420 x 1360 5100kW (6934bhp) AO Bryanskiy MashinostroitelnyyZavod (BMZ)-Bryansk AuxGen: 3 x 610kW 400V 50Hz a.c Fuel: 166.0 (d.f.) 1252.0 (r.f.) 26.0pd
9453535 *A8XI3* -	**SARONIC TRADER** **Eyot Seaways Ltd** Lavinia Corp *Monrovia* *Liberia* MMSI: 636014899 Official number: 14899	**51,208** 31,213 93,112 T/cm 80.9	Class: LR ✠ **100A1** SS 07/2011 bulk carrier CSR BC-A Nos. 2, 4 & 6 holds may be empty GRAB (20) ESP **ShipRight** (CM) *IWS LI ✠ **LMC** **UMS** Eq.Ltr: St; Cable: 687.5/87.0 U3 (a)	**2011-07 Jiangsu Jinling Ships Co Ltd — Yizheng JS** Yd No: 07-0420 Loa 230.00 (BB) Br ex 38.05 Dght 14.900 Lbp 222.00 Br md 38.00 Dpth 20.70 Welded, 1 dk	**(A21A2BC) Bulk Carrier** Double Bottom Entire Compartment Length Grain: 110,300 Compartments: 7 Ho, ER 7 Ha: ER	**1 oil engine** driving 1 FP propeller Total Power: 12,240kW (16,642hp) 14.1kn MAN-B&W 6S60MC 1 x 2 Stroke 6 Cy. 600 x 2292 12240kW (16642bhp) Doosan Engine Co Ltd-South Korea AuxGen: 3 x 700kW 450V 60Hz a.c Boilers: AuxB (Comp) 7.5kgf/cm² (7.4bar)
7946710 *TC4067* -	**SAROS** **Sokullu Sezan Kollektif Sti** - *Istanbul* *Turkey* Official number: 3412	*199* 105 -		**1962 Denizcilik Bankasi T.A.O. — Halic, Istanbul** Loa 29.29 Br ex - Dght 3.031 Lbp 26.40 Br md 8.21 Dpth 4.04 Welded, 1 dk	**(B34P2QV) Salvage Ship**	**1 oil engine** driving 1 FP propeller Total Power: 228kW (310hp) Alpha 404-24VO 1 x 2 Stroke 4 Cy. 240 x 400 228kW (310bhp) Holeby Dieselmotor Fabrik A/S-Denmark
8423519 *UWPE* -	**SAROS** *ex* Livadiya *-2005* *ex* Lidiya *-2003* *ex* Kekurnyy *-2000* **Private Enterprise 'Ellada' (Chastnoye Predpriyatiye 'Ellada')** - *Sevastopol* *Ukraine* MMSI: 272334000 Official number: 842138	**742** 255 512	Class: (RS)	**1985 Khabarovskiy Sudostroitelnyy Zavod im Kirova — Khabarovsk** Yd No: 852 Converted From: Fishing Vessel-2000 Converted From: Fish Carrier Loa 55.02 Br ex 9.52 Dght 4.630 Lbp 50.04 Br md - Dpth 5.19 Welded, 1 dk	**(A31A2GX) General Cargo Ship** Grain: 948 Compartments: 2 Ho, ER 2 Ha: (5.0 x 7.8) (6.0 x 7.2)ER Cranes: 1x3t	**1 oil engine** driving 1 FP propeller Total Power: 589kW (801hp) 11.3kn S.K.L. 6NVD48A-2U 1 x 4 Stroke 6 Cy. 320 x 480 589kW (801bhp) VEB Schwermaschinenbau "KarlLiebknecht" (SKL)-Magdeburg AuxGen: 3 x 150kW a.c
9537836 *TSNS* -	**SAROST 5** *ex* SK Sea Lion *-2011* **SAROST SA** - *Tunis* *Tunisia* MMSI: 672707000	**1,761** 528 1,738	Class: BV (AB)	**2010-10 Nam Cheong Dockyard Sdn Bhd — Miri** Yd No: 540 Loa 60.00 Br ex - Dght 5.100 Lbp 53.90 Br md 16.00 Dpth 6.00 Welded, 1 dk	**(B21B20A) Anchor Handling Tug Supply**	**2 oil engines** reduction geared to sc. shafts driving 2 CP propellers Total Power: 3,840kW (5,220hp) 15.0kn Yanmar 6EY26 2 x 4 Stroke 6 Cy. 260 x 385 each-1920kW (2610bhp) Yanmar Diesel Engine Co Ltd-Japan AuxGen: 2 x 275kW 415V 50Hz a.c, 2 x 1000kW 415V 50Hz a.c Thrusters: 1 Tunnel thruster (f); 1 Tunnel thruster (a)
9049750 *YHRU* -	**SAROTAMA** **Government of The Republic of Indonesia (Direktorat Jenderal Perhubungan Laut - Ministry of Sea Communications)** - *Jakarta* *Indonesia* MMSI: 525001015	**878** 263 310	Class: (KI)	**2004-07 PT Dumas — Surabaya** Loa 61.80 Br ex - Dght 3.200 Lbp 55.82 Br md 9.70 Dpth 4.70 Welded, 1 dk	**(B34H2SQ) Patrol Vessel**	**2 oil engines** geared to sc. shafts driving 2 Propellers Total Power: 4,640kW (6,308hp) 18.0kn M.T.U. 16V4000M70 2 x Vee 4 Stroke 16 Cy. 165 x 190 each-2320kW (3154bhp) (made 2003) MTU Friedrichshafen GmbH-Friedrichshafen
7531668 *TC4811* -	**SAROZ 1** *ex* Sonduren-11 *-2011* - - *Istanbul* *Turkey* MMSI: 271002401 Official number: 4986	*394* 82 -	Class: (TL) (AB)	**1981-12 Denizcilik Bankasi T.A.O. — Halic, Istanbul** Yd No: 204 Loa 36.45 Br ex - Dght 4.220 Lbp 32.31 Br md 8.91 Dpth 5.11 Welded, 1 dk	**(B32A2ST) Tug**	**1 oil engine** sr geared to sc. shaft driving 1 CP propeller Total Power: 1,824kW (2,480hp) 13.0kn Alpha 16V23L-VO 1 x Vee 4 Stroke 16 Cy. 225 x 300 1824kW (2480bhp) B&W Alpha Diesel A/S-Denmark AuxGen: 2 x 80kW a.c Fuel: 52.0 (d.f.)
9238052 *C6RZ8* -	**SARPEN** **Lundqvist Shipping Co Ltd** Lundqvist Rederierna AB *Nassau* *Bahamas* MMSI: 311261000 Official number: 8000351	**59,719** 31,451 105,656 T/cm 95.4	Class: NV	**2002-07 Daewoo Shipbuilding & Marine Engineering Co Ltd — Geoje** Yd No: 5214 Loa 248.00 (BB) Br ex 43.04 Dght 14.319 Lbp 237.99 Br md 43.00 Dpth 21.00 Welded, 1 dk	**(A13A2TV) Crude Oil Tanker** Double Hull (13F) Liq: 121,022; Liq (Oil): 114,000 Cargo Heating Coils Compartments: 12 Wing Ta, 2 Wing Slop Ta, ER 3 Cargo Pump (s): 3x2500m³/hr Manifold: Bow/CM: 126m	**1 oil engine** driving 1 FP propeller Total Power: 14,049kW (19,101hp) 15.2kn B&W 5S70MC 1 x 2 Stroke 5 Cy. 700 x 2674 14049kW (19101bhp) Doosan Engine Co Ltd-South Korea AuxGen: 3 x a.c Fuel: 202.2 (d.f.) 3627.7 (r.f.)
8810059 *VHS4758* X7R	**SARRIBA** *ex* Lorna Dorn *-2011* **A Raptis & Sons Pty Ltd** - SatCom: Inmarsat C 450300269 *Port Adelaide, SA* *Australia* Official number: 853145	**295** 89 303		**1989-04 Port Lincoln Ship Construction Pty Ltd — Port Lincoln SA** Yd No: V12 Loa 29.64 Br ex 9.16 Dght 4.180 Lbp - Br md 8.93 Dpth 4.53 Welded	**(B11A2FS) Stern Trawler** Ins: 166	**1 oil engine** with clutches, flexible couplings & sr geared to sc. shaft driving 1 CP propeller Total Power: 387kW (526hp) Caterpillar 3508TA 1 x Vee 4 Stroke 8 Cy. 170 x 190 387kW (526bhp) Caterpillar Inc-USA
7018379 *J8B2964* -	**SARSEN** *ex* G. O. Sars *-2003* **Moir Holdings Australia Pty Ltd** Triton Shipping AB *Kingstown* *St Vincent & The Grenadines* MMSI: 377651000 Official number: 9436	**1,658** 497 1,727	Class: NV	**1970-05 AS Mjellem & Karlsen — Bergen** Yd No: 94 Loa 70.01 Br ex 13.06 Dght 5.310 Lbp 62.13 Br md 13.01 Dpth 7.45 Welded, 2 dks	**(B12D2FR) Fishery Research Vessel** Compartments: 1 Ho, ER 1 Ha: (1.8 x 2.4)ER Derricks: 2x3t Ice Capable	**1 oil engine** geared to sc. shaft driving 1 FP propeller Total Power: 1,655kW (2,250hp) Normo KRMB-9 1 x 4 Stroke 9 Cy. 250 x 300 1655kW (2250bhp) (new engine 1986) AS Bergens Mek Verksteder-Norway AuxGen: 2 x a.c, 1 x a.c
9600334 *AWDJ* -	**SARTHI** **Government of The Republic of India (Navy Department)** - *India*	**323** 97 68	Class: IR	**2014-02 Tebma Shipyards Ltd — Udupi** Yd No: 154 Loa 32.48 Br ex 9.50 Dght 2.800 Lbp 31.75 Br md 9.48 Dpth 4.09 Welded, 1 dk	**(B32A2ST) Tug**	**2 oil engines** reduction geared to sc. shafts driving 2 Propellers

9219898 *POSR* -
SARTIKA BARUNA
ex Shin Hsing No. 2 *-2012*
PT Bahtera Adhiguna (Persero)
-
Jakarta *Indonesia*
MMSI: 525012201
11,556 4,506 13,601 T/cm 31.0
Class: BV CR
2000-10 **Tsuneishi Shipbuilding Co Ltd — Fukuyama HS** Yd No: 1210
Loa 141.40 Br ex - Dght 7.020
Lbp 133.00 Br md 24.00 Dpth 12.30
Welded, 1 dk
(A23A2BD) Bulk Carrier, Self-discharging
Double Bottom Entire Compartment Length
Grain: 16,766
Compartments: 2 Ho, ER
2 Ha: 2 (38.0 x 17.0)ER
2 oil engines with clutches, flexible couplings & sr geared to sc. shafts driving 2 FP propellers
Total Power: 2,646kW (3,598hp) 10.7kn
Daihatsu 6DKM-26
2 x 4 Stroke 6 Cy. 260 x 380 each-1323kW (1799bhp)
Daihatsu Diesel Manufacturing Co Lt-Japan
AuxGen: 3 x 560kW 450V 60Hz a.c
Thrusters: 1 Thwart. CP thruster (f)
Fuel: 82.0 (d.f.) (Heating Coils) 222.0 (r.f.) 21.8pd

8201014 *TCT5* -
SARUHAN SERDAR
ex Orse *-2012*
Nesa Denizcilik Yakit Nakliyat Insaat Turizm ve Ticaret Ltd Sti
-
SatCom: Inmarsat C 427120270
Istanbul *Turkey*
MMSI: 271002026
Official number: 164
1,927 1,010 3,250
Class: TL (AB)
1984-09 **Deniz Endustrisi A.S. — Tuzla, Istanbul** Yd No: 3
Loa 84.15 (BB) Br ex 13.03 Dght 6.139
Lbp 74.44 Br md 13.00 Dpth 7.10
Welded, 1 dk
(A12A2TC) Chemical Tanker
Liq: 3,750
Compartments: 8 Ta, ER
1 oil engine driving 1 FP propeller
Total Power: 1,214kW (1,651hp) 10.0kn
Skoda 9L350IIPS
1 x 4 Stroke 9 Cy. 350 x 500 1214kW (1651bhp)
CKD Praha-Praha
AuxGen: 2 x 202kW a.c, 1 x 43kW a.c

8628250 *VVNB* -
SARVASHAKTHI-1
Sarvashakthi Fisheries Ltd
-
Visakhapatnam *India*
Official number: 2223
116 35 73
Class: (IR) (AB)
1987 **Alcock, Ashdown & Co. Ltd. — Bhavnagar** Yd No: 162
Loa 23.50 Br ex - Dght 2.830
Lbp 20.35 Br md 7.31 Dpth 3.41
Welded, 1 dk
(B11A2FT) Trawler
2 oil engines sr geared to sc. shafts driving 2 FP propellers
Total Power: 296kW (402hp) 9.5kn
Caterpillar 3408TA
2 x Vee 4 Stroke 8 Cy. 137 x 152 each-148kW (201bhp)
Caterpillar Inc-USA
AuxGen: 2 x 40kW 440V 50Hz a.c
Fuel: 49.0 (d.f.)

8628262 *VVNC* -
SARVASHAKTHI-2
Sarvashakthi Fisheries Ltd
-
Visakhapatnam *India*
Official number: 2224
116 35 73
Class: (IR) (AB)
1987 **Alcock, Ashdown & Co. Ltd. — Bhavnagar** Yd No: 163
Loa 23.50 Br ex - Dght 2.830
Lbp 19.99 Br md 7.31 Dpth 3.41
Welded, 1 dk
(B11A2FT) Trawler
2 oil engines sr geared to sc. shafts driving 2 FP propellers
Total Power: 296kW (402hp) 9.5kn
Caterpillar 3408TA
2 x Vee 4 Stroke 8 Cy. 137 x 152 each-148kW (201bhp)
Caterpillar Inc-USA
AuxGen: 2 x 40kW 440V 50Hz a.c
Fuel: 49.0 (d.f.)

9129548 - -
SARVEKSHAK
Government of The Republic of India (Navy Department)
-
India
2,100 - 396
Class: LR
✠ **100A1** SS 12/2001
LMC
Eq.Ltr: 0; Cable: 501.2/34.0
2001-12 **Goa Shipyard Ltd. — Goa** Yd No: 1172
Loa 87.75 Br ex 12.83 Dght 3.430
Lbp 78.10 Br md 12.80 Dpth 5.80
Welded, 1 dk
(B31A2SR) Research Survey Vessel
2 oil engines with clutches, flexible couplings & sr reverse geared to sc. shafts driving 2 FP propellers
Total Power: 3,420kW (4,650hp) 16.0kn
Pielstick 6PA6L280
2 x 4 Stroke 6 Cy. 280 x 290 each-1710kW (2325bhp)
Kirloskar Oil Engines Ltd-India
AuxGen: 4 x 350kW 415V 50Hz a.c
Thrusters: 1 Thwart. FP thruster (f)

9209348 *EPBR5* -
SARVIN
ex Sarita *-2012* *ex* Dandle *-2012*
ex Twelfth Ocean *-2008* *ex* Iran Isfahan *-2007*
Oghiaanous Khoroushan Shipping Lines Co of Kish
Rahbaran Omid Darya Ship Management Co
Qeshm Island *Iran*
MMSI: 422031800
Official number: 1068
36,014 19,431 41,971
Class: (GL)
2000-07 **Hyundai Heavy Industries Co Ltd — Ulsan** Yd No: 1246
Loa 240.22 (BB) Br ex 32.20 Dght 11.700
Lbp 225.20 Br md 32.20 Dpth 19.20
Welded, 1 dk
(A33A2CC) Container Ship (Fully Cellular)
TEU 3280 incl 300 ref C.
13 Ha:
Ice Capable
1 oil engine driving 1 FP propeller
Total Power: 24,184kW (32,881hp) 22.0kn
B&W 8S70MC-C
1 x 2 Stroke 8 Cy. 700 x 2800 24184kW (32881bhp)
Hyundai Heavy Industries Co Ltd-South Korea
AuxGen: 4 x 1475kW 220/440V a.c
Thrusters: 1 Thwart. FP thruster (f)

7428897 *PLQW* -
SARWAGUNA LIMA
PT Perusahaan Pelayaran Nusantara (PANURJWAN)
PT Perusahaan Pelayaran Khusus Lepas Pantai 'CUMAWIS'
Jakarta *Indonesia*
Official number: 2671/L
273 129 300
Class: (KI) (NV)
1974-10 **Singapore Shipbuilding & Engineering Pte Ltd — Singapore** Yd No: 72
Loa - Br ex 9.05 Dght 1.778
Lbp 36.00 Br md 9.00 Dpth 2.75
Welded, 1 dk
(A35D2RL) Landing Craft
Bow door/ramp (centre)
2 oil engines reverse reduction geared to sc. shafts driving 2 FP propellers
Total Power: 448kW (610hp)
MAN D2858M
2 x Vee 4 Stroke 8 Cy. 128 x 150 each-224kW (305bhp)
Maschinenbau Augsburg Nuernberg (MAN)-Augsburg
AuxGen: 1 x 32kW 415V a.c

9024877 *YE4195* -
SARWAGUNA SEPULUH
ex Sea Service I *-1991*
PT Bangun Lintas Bahari
-
Jakarta *Indonesia*
237 72 243
Class: (KI)
1987-07 **Pandan Shipyard Pte Ltd — Singapore**
L reg 40.90 Br ex - Dght -
Lbp 39.80 Br md 8.60 Dpth 2.60
Welded, 1 dk
(A35D2RL) Landing Craft
Bow ramp (centre)
2 oil engines geared to sc. shafts driving 2 Propellers
Total Power: 536kW (728hp)
Caterpillar 3408T
2 x Vee 4 Stroke 8 Cy. 137 x 152 each-268kW (364bhp) (made 1984)
Caterpillar Tractor Co-USA

9488669 *A6E3140* -
SARWAN
launched as Tekun 20265 *-2008*
Liwa Marine Services LLC
-
Abu Dhabi *United Arab Emirates*
MMSI: 470986000
Official number: 5713
256 77 247
Class: BV (NK)
2008-07 **Sapor Shipbuilding Industries Sdn Bhd — Sibu** (Hull)
2008-07 **Bonafile Shipbuilders & Repairs Sdn Bhd — Sandakan** Yd No: 06/07
Loa 30.00 Br ex - Dght 3.512
Lbp 28.07 Br md 8.60 Dpth 4.12
Welded, 1 dk
(B32A2ST) Tug
2 oil engines geared to sc. shafts driving 2 Propellers
Total Power: 1,518kW (2,064hp)
Mitsubishi S6R2-MTK3L
2 x 4 Stroke 6 Cy. 170 x 220 each-759kW (1032bhp)
Mitsubishi Heavy Industries Ltd-Japan
Fuel: 190.0 (d.f.)

8307832 *S2DJ* -
SARWAR JAHAN
ex Custodia Athena *-2009*
ex H Hasan Yardim *-2007*
ex Western Village *-1996* *ex* Sea Elfi *-1990*
SR Shipping Ltd
Brave Royal Shipping Ltd
Chittagong *Bangladesh*
MMSI: 405000073
Official number: 204
23,186 13,036 41,084 T/cm 47.7
Class: NK (TL) (AB)
1985-01 **Sanoyas Corp — Kurashiki OY** Yd No: 1064
Loa 182.75 (BB) Br ex - Dght 11.185
Lbp 174.00 Br md 30.01 Dpth 15.83
Welded, 1 dk
(A21A2BC) Bulk Carrier
Grain: 49,580; Bale: 48,007
Compartments: 5 Ho, ER
5 Ha: (15.4 x 11.0)4 (17.9 x 13.0)ER
Cranes: 4x25t
1 oil engine driving 1 FP propeller
Total Power: 6,950kW (9,449hp) 16.3kn
Sulzer 6RTA58
1 x 2 Stroke 6 Cy. 580 x 1700 6950kW (9449bhp)
Sumitomo Heavy Industries Ltd-Japan
AuxGen: 3 x 440kW 450V 60Hz a.c
Fuel: 1600.0 (r.f.)

9639244 - -
SARYANG
Saryang Fisheries Cooperative
-
Tongyeong *South Korea*
Official number: CMR-114409
377 - 279
Class: KR
2011-05 **Moonchang Shipbuilding Dockyard Co Ltd — Mokpo** Yd No: 10-82
Loa 57.60 Br ex - Dght 2.121
Lbp 47.00 Br md 10.60 Dpth 3.10
Welded, 1 dk
(A36A2PR) Passenger/Ro-Ro Ship (Vehicles)
Bow door/ramp (centre)
2 oil engines reverse reduction geared to sc. shafts driving 2 FP propellers
Total Power: 1,938kW (2,634hp) 12.5kn
Caterpillar C32
2 x Vee 4 Stroke 12 Cy. 145 x 162 each-969kW (1317bhp)
Caterpillar Inc-USA

7832066 *UHGK* -
SARYCHEVSK
Komet Co Ltd
-
Sovetskaya Gavan *Russia*
MMSI: 273824500
867 221 392
Class: RS
1980-08 **Zavod "Leninskaya Kuznitsa" — Kiyev** Yd No: 245
Converted From: Stern Trawler-2001
Loa 53.75 (BB) Br ex 10.72 Dght 4.370
Lbp 47.92 Br md 10.50 Dpth 6.00
Welded, 1 dk
(A31A2GX) General Cargo Ship
Compartments: 1 Ho, ER
1 Ha: (1.6 x 1.6)
Derricks: 2x1.5t
Ice Capable
1 oil engine driving 1 CP propeller
Total Power: 971kW (1,320hp) 12.6kn
S.K.L. 8NVD48A-2U
1 x 4 Stroke 8 Cy. 320 x 480 971kW (1320bhp)
VEB Schwermaschinenbau "KarlLiebknecht" (SKL)-Magdeburg
AuxGen: 1 x 300kW a.c, 3 x 160kW a.c
Fuel: 185.0 (d.f.)

8732075 *YHZR* -
SAS 01
ex Hai Jaya II *-2008* *ex* Min Ping Yu F886 *-2008*
PT Sarana Pintu Mas
-
Ambon *Indonesia*
491 268 -
Class: KI
1989-01 **Yueqing Shipyard Co Ltd — Yueqing ZJ**
Loa - Br ex - Dght -
Lbp 56.70 Br md 8.20 Dpth 3.50
Welded, 1 dk
(A13B2TU) Tanker (unspecified)
1 oil engine driving 1 Propeller
Total Power: 441kW (600hp)
Chinese Std. Type
1 x 4 Stroke 6 Cy. 441kW (600bhp)
Guangzhou Diesel Engine Factory CoLtd-China

9049279 - -
SAS 02
PT Pelayaran Syandi Arung Samudera
-
Samarinda *Indonesia*
294 89 -
Class: KI
2004-01 **PT Syandi Perdana — Samarinda**
Loa 46.95 Br ex - Dght 2.120
Lbp 35.52 Br md 9.00 Dpth 2.55
Welded, 1 dk
(A35D2RL) Landing Craft
Bow ramp (centre)
2 oil engines geared to sc. shafts driving 2 Propellers
Total Power: 618kW (840hp)
Nissan RF10
2 x Vee 4 Stroke 10 Cy. 138 x 142 each-309kW (420bhp)
Nissan Diesel Motor Co. Ltd.-Ageo
AuxGen: 2 x 90kW 380/220V a.c

9099963 *PMDL* -
SAS 05
H Syahran
-
Samarinda *Indonesia*
MMSI: 525015471
Official number: 2007 IIK NO.4112/L
523 157 -
Class: KI
2007-06 **PT Syandi Perdana — Samarinda**
L reg 54.00 Br ex - Dght 2.640
Lbp 51.50 Br md 10.80 Dpth 3.30
Welded, 1 dk
(A35D2RL) Landing Craft
Bow ramp (f)
2 oil engines reduction geared to sc. shafts driving 2 Propellers
Total Power: 706kW (960hp)
Mitsubishi 10DC11
2 x Vee 4 Stroke 10 Cy. 141 x 152 each-353kW (480bhp)
Mitsubishi Heavy Industries Ltd-Japan

9196620 *H3YS* -
SASA
ex Sarah Glory *-2013* *ex* Berge Kyoto *-2001*
Sarah Glory Shipping Ltd
Tufton Oceanic Ltd
SatCom: Inmarsat B 335219210
Panama *Panama*
MMSI: 352192000
Official number: 29427PEXT3
159,397 96,607 300,259 T/cm 181.0
Class: NV (AB)
2001-05 Hitachi Zosen Corp — Nagasu KM Yd No: 4970
Loa 332.95 (BB) Br ex 60.00 Dght 21.190
Lbp 321.34 Br md 60.00 Dpth 29.55
Welded, 1 dk
(A13A2TV) Crude Oil Tanker
Double Hull (13F)
Liq: 323,967; Liq (Oil): 323,967
Compartments: 5 Ta, 10 Wing Ta, ER, 2 Wing Slop Ta
3 Cargo Pump (s): 3x5500m³/hr
Manifold: Bow/CM: 167m
1 oil engine driving 1 FP propeller
Total Power: 25,487kW (34,652hp) 15.5kn
MAN-B&W 7S80MC
1 x 2 Stroke 7 Cy. 800 x 3056 25487kW (34652bhp)
Hitachi Zosen Corp-Japan
AuxGen: 3 x 768kW 220/440V 60Hz a.c
Fuel: 483.3 (d.f.) (Heating Coils) 8278.2 (r.f.) 95.0pd

9016038 - -
SASANKA
-
Kolkata Port Trust
-
Kolkata *India*
Official number: WB-1308
383 114 115
Class: (IR)
1993-12 Bharati Shipyard Ltd — Ratnagiri Yd No: 228
Loa 32.00 Br ex 10.72 Dght 2.300
Lbp 29.76 Br md 10.70 Dpth 3.70
Welded, 1 dk
(B32A2ST) Tug
2 oil engines gearing integral to driving 2 Voith-Schneider propellers
Total Power: 2,500kW (3,400hp) 10.0kn
Normo KRMB-6
2 x 4 Stroke 6 Cy. 250 x 300 each-1250kW (1700bhp)
Garden Reach Shipbuilders &Engineers Ltd-India
AuxGen: 3 x 60kW 415V 50Hz a.c
Fuel: 63.2 (d.f.) 7.7pd

8843161 *HQHM6* -
SASANO 1
ex Myojin Maru No. 3 *-1990*
Dynasty Lines SA
-
San Lorenzo *Honduras*
Official number: L-0323664
197 118 450
1970 Takuma Zosen K.K. — Mitoyo
Loa 42.00 Br ex - Dght 3.200
Lbp 37.50 Br md 7.30 Dpth 3.50
Welded, 1 dk
(A31A2GX) General Cargo Ship
Compartments: 1 Ho, ER
1 oil engine driving 1 FP propeller
Yanmar
1 x 4 Stroke
Yanmar Diesel Engine Co Ltd-Japan

8843185 *HQHM5* -
SASANO 2
ex Daio Maru No. 5 *-1990*
Dynasty Lines SA
-
San Lorenzo *Honduras*
Official number: L-0323665
198 120 532
1969 Nakatani Shipyard Co. Ltd. — Etajima
Loa 46.00 Br ex - Dght 3.300
Lbp 41.00 Br md 7.31 Dpth 5.26
Welded, 1 dk
(A31A2GX) General Cargo Ship
Compartments: 1 Ho, ER
1 oil engine driving 1 FP propeller
Hanshin
1 x 4 Stroke
The Hanshin Diesel Works Ltd-Japan

6907937 *HC2400* -
SASANO MARU No. 7
ex Yuko Maru No. 38 *-1985*
ex Fukusei Maru No. 21 *-1985*
Jose Patricio Pachay Delgado
-
Guayaquil *Ecuador*
Official number: P-00-0745
536 181 -
1968 Yamanishi Shipbuilding Co Ltd — Ishinomaki MG Yd No: 591
Loa 52.99 Br ex 8.34 Dght 3.302
Lbp 47.02 Br md 7.09 Dpth 3.76
Welded, 1 dk
(B11B2FV) Fishing Vessel
1 oil engine driving 1 FP propeller
Total Power: 736kW (1,001hp)
Akasaka SR6SS
1 x 4 Stroke 6 Cy. 350 x 500 736kW (1001bhp)
Akasaka Tekkosho KK (Akasaka DieselLtd)-Japan

9061904 *3FFV3* -
SASANQUA
ex Auckland *-2005*
Sasanqua Shipping SA
Santoku Senpaku Co Ltd
SatCom: Inmarsat C 435225610
Panama *Panama*
MMSI: 352256000
Official number: 2075293CH
7,307 4,812 5,388
Class: NK
1993-03 KK Kanasashi — Shizuoka SZ Yd No: 3307
Loa 134.02 (BB) Br ex - Dght 6.223
Lbp 125.00 Br md 20.80 Dpth 10.17
Welded, 1 dk
(A34A2GR) Refrigerated Cargo Ship
Ins: 11,165
Compartments: 4 Ho, ER, 4 Tw Dk
4 Ha: ER
Derricks: 8x5t
1 oil engine driving 1 FP propeller
Total Power: 7,061kW (9,600hp) 18.0kn
Mitsubishi 8UEC45LA
1 x 2 Stroke 8 Cy. 450 x 1350 7061kW (9600bhp)
Akasaka Tekkosho KK (Akasaka DieselLtd)-Japan
AuxGen: 4 x 387kW a.c
Fuel: 890.0 (r.f.)

9202936 - -
SASAYURI
-
Da Fa Marine Co Ltd
-
Chinese Taipei
250 - -
1998-03 Setouchi Craft Co Ltd — Onomichi
Loa 43.00 Br ex - Dght -
Lbp - Br md 7.80 Dpth 3.52
Welded
(A37B2PS) Passenger Ship
Hull Material: Aluminium Alloy
2 oil engines driving 2 FP propellers
Total Power: 2,994kW (4,070hp) 27.6kn
Hanshin
2 x 4 Stroke each-1497kW (2035bhp)
The Hanshin Diesel Works Ltd-Japan

8854988 *WDA3394* -
SASHA LEE
ex Capt. Huey *-2001* *ex* Virgin Steel *-1998*
ex Miss Monica *-1995*
ex Miss Elizabeth III *-1994*
Sasha Lee Inc
-
New Bedford, MA *United States of America*
MMSI: 366797960
Official number: 909149
132 90 -
1987 Tommy Nguyen — New Iberia, La Yd No: 10
Loa - Br ex - Dght -
Lbp 24.38 Br md 7.01 Dpth 2.99
Welded, 1 dk
(B11B2FV) Fishing Vessel
1 oil engine driving 1 FP propeller

8823331 *JG4591* -
SASHIRO
-
Kashima Futo KK
-
Kamisu, Ibaraki *Japan*
Official number: 128944
160 - -
1989-01 Keihin Dock Co Ltd — Yokohama Yd No: 211
Loa 30.00 Br ex - Dght 2.800
Lbp 27.40 Br md 8.80 Dpth 3.57
Welded, 1 dk
(B32B2SP) Pusher Tug
2 oil engines Geared Integral to driving 2 Z propellers
Total Power: 2,206kW (3,000hp) 13.4kn
Pielstick 6PA5
2 x 4 Stroke 6 Cy. 255 x 270 each-1103kW (1500bhp)
Niigata Engineering Co Ltd-Japan

9401714 *YJVP3* -
SASI TIDE
-
Tidewater Properties Ltd
Tidewater Marine International Inc
Port Vila *Vanuatu*
MMSI: 576528000
Official number: 1814
1,690 507 1,362
Class: AB (BV)
2007-01 Fujian Southeast Shipyard — Fuzhou FJ (Hull) Yd No: H864
2007-01 Jaya Shipbuilding & Engineering Pte Ltd — Singapore Yd No: 864
Loa 59.25 Br ex - Dght 4.950
Lbp 52.20 Br md 14.95 Dpth 6.10
Welded, 1 dk
(B21B20A) Anchor Handling Tug Supply
2 oil engines reduction geared to sc. shafts driving 2 CP propellers
Total Power: 3,840kW (5,220hp) 11.0kn
Caterpillar 3516B-HD
2 x Vee 4 Stroke 16 Cy. 170 x 215 each-1920kW (2610bhp)
Caterpillar Inc-USA
AuxGen: 3 x 320kW 415/220V 50Hz a.c
Thrusters: 1 Tunnel thruster (f)
Fuel: 520.0

9705108 *EAJI* -
SASKIA B
-
Zumaia Offshore SL
-
Bilbao *Spain*
MMSI: 225982147
255 76 -
Class: BV
2013-11 Neptune Shipyards BV — Aalst (Nl) Yd No: 430
Loa 26.48 Br ex - Dght 2.630
Lbp 23.65 Br md 11.00 Dpth 3.70
Welded, 1 dk
(B34L2QU) Utility Vessel
Cranes: 2
2 oil engines reduction geared to sc. shafts driving 2 FP propellers
Total Power: 2,060kW (2,800hp) 10.8kn
Cummins QSK38-M
2 x Vee 4 Stroke 12 Cy. 159 x 159 each-1030kW (1400bhp)
Cummins Engine Co Ltd-United Kingdom
AuxGen: 2 x 200kW 50Hz a.c
Thrusters: 1 Water jet (f)
Fuel: 106.0

8982486 - -
SASOMSAP 9
-
Pantipa Tipsongkoh
-
Bangkok *Thailand*
Official number: 466004288
332 142 -
2003 Mahachai Dockyard Co., Ltd. — Samut Sakhon
Loa 39.00 Br ex - Dght -
Lbp 35.75 Br md 8.00 Dpth 4.20
Welded, 1 dk
(B12B2FC) Fish Carrier
1 oil engine driving 1 Propeller
Total Power: 746kW (1,014hp)
Cummins
1 x 4 Stroke 746kW (1014bhp)
Cummins Engine Co Inc-USA

9544243 *WDE5807* -
SASSAFRAS
-
Fifth Third Equipment Finance Co
Vane Line Bunkering Inc
Baltimore, MD *United States of America*
MMSI: 367371850
Official number: 1205658
270 81 212
2008-11 Chesapeake Shipbuilding, Inc. — Salisbury, Md Yd No: 91
Loa 29.16 Br ex - Dght 3.600
Lbp 28.65 Br md 9.75 Dpth 4.10
Welded, 1 dk
(B32B2SP) Pusher Tug
2 oil engines reduction geared to sc. shafts driving 2 FP propellers
Total Power: 3,530kW (4,800hp) 11.5kn
Caterpillar 3512C
2 x 4 Stroke 12 Cy. 170 x 215 each-1765kW (2400bhp)
Caterpillar Inc-USA
AuxGen: 2 x 99kW a.c
Fuel: 226.0

8705383 *DQEJ* -
SASSNITZ
-
Stena RoRo Navigation Ltd
Stena Line GmbH & Co KG
SatCom: Inmarsat C 421118910
Sassnitz *Germany*
MMSI: 211189000
Official number: 3048
21,154 6,346 3,100
Class: LR (GL)
100A1 SS 03/2009
passenger, vehicle and train ferry
North Sea & Baltic service
*IWS
Ice Class 1C
LMC
Eq.Ltr: E†; Cable: 550.0/62.0 U2
1989-03 Danyard A/S — Frederikshavn Yd No: 690
Loa 171.50 Br ex 24.05 Dght 5.818
Lbp 161.59 Br md 23.70 Dpth 8.00
Welded, 1 dk
(A36A2PT) Passenger/Ro-Ro Ship (Vehicles/Rail)
Passengers: unberthed: 819; cabins: 24; berths: 56
Stern door/ramp
Len: 4.85 Wid: 10.00 Swl: -
Side ramp (s)
Lane-Len: 1150
Lane-Wid: 2.50
Lane-clr ht: 4.85
Lorries: 20, Cars: 50, Rail Wagons: 48
Ice Capable
4 oil engines with flexible couplings & sr gearedto sc. shafts driving 2 CP propellers
Total Power: 17,682kW (24,040hp) 17.8kn
MAN 6L40/54
2 x 4 Stroke 6 Cy. 400 x 540 each-3641kW (4950bhp) (new engine 1994)
Maschinenbau Halberstadt GmbH-Halberstadt
MAN 8L40/54
2 x 4 Stroke 8 Cy. 400 x 540 each-5200kW (7070bhp) (new engine 1994)
Maschinenbau Halberstadt GmbH-Halberstadt
AuxGen: 2 x 1432kW 660V 50Hz a.c, 3 x 1050kW 660V 50Hz a.c, 1 x 300kW 660V 50Hz a.c
Boilers: 5 TOH (ex.g.) 10.2kgf/cm² (10.0bar), TOH (o.f.) 10.2kgf/cm² (10.0bar)
Thrusters: 2 Thwart. CP thruster (f)
Fuel: 47.0 (d.f.) 270.0 (r.f.) 49.0pd

8945672 *DUA2033* -	**SASSY** *ex* Petrotrade Ii *ex* Herma 2 *-2000* **Keeper Oil Waste Recovery Service** - *Manila* *Philippines* Official number: 00-0000015	*220* 148 203		**1985 Navotas Industrial Corp — Manila** L reg 39.71 Br ex - Dght - Lbp - Br md 7.93 Dpth 2.34 Welded, 1 dk	**(A13B2TU) Tanker (unspecified)**	**1 oil engine** driving 1 FP propeller Total Power: 294kW (400hp) Isuzu 1 x Vee 4 Stroke 10 Cy. 294kW (400bhp) Isuzu Marine Engine Inc-Japan
8941248 - -	**SASSY CAT** **John M Sherman** - *Bon Secour, AL* *United States of America* Official number: 1051111	**119** 35 -		**1997 Ocean Marine, Inc. — Bayou La Batre, Al** Yd No: 332 L reg 22.68 Br ex - Dght - Lbp - Br md 7.01 Dpth 3.72 Welded, 1 dk	**(B11B2FV) Fishing Vessel**	**1 oil engine** driving 1 FP propeller
7926734 - -	**SASSY GIRL** *ex* Sea Fighter *-2001* *ex* Three C's *-2001* **Fulcher Enterprises Inc** - *New Bern, NC* *United States of America* Official number: 616434	*113* 77 -		**1980-01 Quality Marine, Inc. — Bayou La Batre, Al** Yd No: 129 Loa 24.39 Br ex - Dght - Lbp - Br md 6.72 Dpth 3.38 Welded, 1 dk	**(B11A2FS) Stern Trawler**	**1 oil engine** driving 1 FP propeller Total Power: 331kW (450hp) G.M. (Detroit Diesel) 16V-71-N 1 x Vee 2 Stroke 16 Cy. 108 x 127 331kW (450bhp) General Motors Detroit DieselAllison Divn-USA
8941092 *WDA3082* -	**SASSY SARAH** **Hiwall Inc** - *Wanchese, NC* *United States of America* MMSI: 366794430 Official number: 1049030	**113** 34 -		**1997 Master Boat Builders, Inc. — Coden, Al** Yd No: 239 L reg 22.46 Br ex - Dght - Lbp - Br md 6.71 Dpth 3.69 Welded, 1 dk	**(B11B2FV) Fishing Vessel**	**1 oil engine** driving 1 FP propeller
9550321 *9V7828* -	**SAT BELLATRIX** **Bellatrix Line Pte Ltd** Apex Ship Management Pte Ltd SatCom: Inmarsat C 456484510 *Singapore* *Singapore* MMSI: 564845000 Official number: 394887	**17,018** 10,108 28,467 T/cm 39.7	Class: AB (NK)	**2009-09 Imabari Shipbuilding Co Ltd — Imabari EH (Imabari Shipyard)** Yd No: 684 Loa 169.37 (BB) Br ex 27.24 Dght 9.819 Lbp 160.40 Br md 27.20 Dpth 13.60 Welded, 1 dk	**(A21A2BC) Bulk Carrier** Grain: 37,303; Bale: 35,724 Compartments: 5 Ho, ER 5 Ha: 4 (19.2 x 17.6)ER (13.6 x 16.0) Cranes: 4x30.5t	**1 oil engine** driving 1 FP propeller Total Power: 5,850kW (7,954hp) 14.0kn MAN-B&W 6S42MC 1 x 2 Stroke 6 Cy. 420 x 1764 5850kW (7954bhp) Makita Corp-Japan AuxGen: 3 x 440kW a.c Fuel: 116.0 (d.f.) 1200.0 (r.f.)
9470789 *9V7526* -	**SAT NUNKI** **Nunki Line Pte Ltd** Apex Ship Management Pte Ltd *Singapore* *Singapore* MMSI: 563938000 Official number: 394398	**17,018** 10,104 28,449 T/cm 39.7	Class: AB (NK)	**2008-10 Imabari Shipbuilding Co Ltd — Imabari EH (Imabari Shipyard)** Yd No: 680 Loa 169.37 (BB) Br ex - Dght 9.800 Lbp 160.40 Br md 27.20 Dpth 13.60 Welded, 1 dk	**(A21A2BC) Bulk Carrier** Grain: 37,304; Bale: 35,724 Compartments: 5 Ho, ER 5 Ha: 4 (19.2 x 17.6)ER (13.6 x 16.0) Cranes: 4x30.5t	**1 oil engine** driving 1 FP propeller Total Power: 5,850kW (7,954hp) 14.0kn MAN-B&W 6S42MC 1 x 2 Stroke 6 Cy. 420 x 1764 5850kW (7954bhp) Makita Corp-Japan AuxGen: 3 x 440kW a.c Fuel: 115.0 (d.f.) 1092.0 (r.f.)
7825899 *HO3186* -	**SATE** **Banco Internacional de Panama SA** - *Panama* *Panama* Official number: 1097181D	*119* 41 110		**1979-09 Ast. Picsa S.A. — Callao** Yd No: 430 Loa 21.70 Br ex 6.94 Dght - Lbp 19.61 Br md 6.71 Dpth 2.75 Welded, 1 dk	**(B11B2FV) Fishing Vessel**	**1 oil engine** driving 1 FP propeller Total Power: 202kW (275hp) Caterpillar 3406PCTA 1 x 4 Stroke 6 Cy. 137 x 165 202kW (275bhp) Caterpillar Tractor Co-USA
8130813 *9LY2391* -	**SATELLITE** *ex* Ul Jl Bong 3 *-2011* *ex* Vodoley *-2009* *ex* Vodolei *-2004* *ex* Hualei *-2003* *ex* Continental Partner No. 2 *-1996* *ex* Sam Hae *-1993* *ex* Secil Franca *-1989* *ex* Montauk Kittiwake *-1983* **Poly Advance Development Ltd** - *Freetown* *Sierra Leone* MMSI: 667003194 Official number: SL103194	**2,963** 1,583 5,094	Class: SL (RS) (KR) (NK)	**1982-12 Sanyo Zosen K.K. — Onomichi** Yd No: 836 Loa 92.31 Br ex 15.24 Dght 6.544 Lbp 84.92 Br md 15.21 Dpth 7.90 Welded, 1 dk	**(A31A2GX) General Cargo Ship** Grain: 5,786; Bale: 5,281 Compartments: 2 Ho, ER 2 Ha: (15.6 x 10.0) (26.0 x 10.0)ER Derricks: 1x15t,2x7.5t; Winches: 3	**1 oil engine** reverse reduction geared to sc. shaft driving 1 FP propeller Total Power: 1,471kW (2,000hp) 11.5kn Niigata 6M34AET 1 x 4 Stroke 6 Cy. 340 x 620 1471kW (2000bhp) Niigata Engineering Co Ltd-Japan AuxGen: 2 x 128kW 445V a.c Fuel: 255.0 (r.f.)
8737295 - -	**SATIA SAMUDERA 03** **PT Sinar Haluan Samudra** - *Samarinda* *Indonesia*	**207** 63 -	Class: KI	**2008-06 CV Sunjaya Abadi — Samarinda** Loa 29.00 Br ex - Dght 2.990 Lbp 26.50 Br md 8.00 Dpth 3.60 Welded, 1 dk	**(B32A2ST) Tug**	**2 oil engines** driving 2 Propellers Total Power: 1,618kW (2,200hp) Yanmar 6GL-ST 2 x 4 Stroke 6 Cy. 240 x 290 each-809kW (1100bhp) (made 1985, fitted 2008) Yanmar Diesel Engine Co Ltd-Japan
8749779 *YDA6345* -	**SATIA SAMUDERA 05** **PT Sinar Haluan Samudra** - *Samarinda* *Indonesia*	**212** 64 -	Class: KI	**2010-01 CV Sunjaya Abadi — Samarinda** Loa 29.00 Br ex - Dght 3.060 Lbp 27.16 Br md 8.00 Dpth 3.75 Welded, 1 dk	**(B32A2ST) Tug**	**2 oil engines** reduction geared to sc. shafts driving 2 Propellers Total Power: 1,764kW (2,398hp) Yanmar 6GL-ET 2 x 4 Stroke 6 Cy. 240 x 290 each-882kW (1199bhp) (made 1985, fitted 2010) Yanmar Diesel Engine Co Ltd-Japan AuxGen: 2 x 50kW 400/225V a.c
8651659 *YDA6509* -	**SATIA SAMUDERA 07** **PT Sinar Haluan Samudra** - *Samarinda* *Indonesia*	**212** 64 -	Class: KI	**2010-10 CV Sunjaya Abadi — Samarinda** Loa 28.50 Br ex - Dght 2.700 Lbp 26.30 Br md 8.00 Dpth 3.75 Welded, 1 dk	**(B32A2ST) Tug**	**2 oil engines** reduction geared to sc. shafts driving 2 Propellers Total Power: 1,766kW (2,402hp) Yanmar 2 x each-883kW (1201bhp) Yanmar Diesel Engine Co Ltd-Japan
8659247 *YDA6633* -	**SATIA SAMUDERA 09** **PT Sinar Haluan Samudra** - *Samarinda* *Indonesia*	**198** 60 -	Class: KI	**2011-06 CV Sunjaya Abadi — Samarinda** Loa 27.00 Br ex - Dght 2.710 Lbp 24.96 Br md 7.50 Dpth 3.50 Welded, 1 dk	**(B32A2ST) Tug**	**2 oil engines** reduction geared to sc. shafts driving 2 FP propellers AuxGen: 2 x 50kW 400/225V a.c
9522738 *9HVQ9* -	**SATIGNY** *launched as* Universe 6 *-2009* **Massatlantic (Malta) Ltd** Massoel Ltd SatCom: Inmarsat C 424960110 *Valletta* *Malta* MMSI: 249601000 Official number: 9522738	**5,087** 2,625 7,300	Class: BV	**2009-01 Universe Shipbuilding (Yangzhou) Co Ltd — Yizheng JS** Yd No: 06-006 Loa 112.80 Br ex - Dght 6.900 Lbp 106.00 Br md 17.20 Dpth 9.10 Welded, 1 dk	**(A21A2BC) Bulk Carrier** Grain: 9,394 Compartments: 3 Ho, ER 3 Ha: ER Cranes: 2x25t	**1 oil engine** reduction geared to sc. shafts driving 1 FP propeller Total Power: 2,500kW (3,399hp) 12.0kn Daihatsu 8DKM-28 1 x 4 Stroke 8 Cy. 280 x 390 2500kW (3399bhp) Shaanxi Diesel Heavy Industry Co Lt-China AuxGen: 3 x 250kW 50Hz a.c
9091301 *LXAA* -	**SATINE** **Comsea SA** Luxembourg Marine Services SA (LMS) SatCom: Inmarsat C 425304410 *Luxembourg* *Luxembourg* MMSI: 253044000	**247** 74 -	Class: GL (AB)	**2001-07 Azimut-Benetti SpA — Viareggio** Yd No: BC09 Loa 34.95 Br ex - Dght 1.920 Lbp 28.80 Br md 7.62 Dpth 3.80 Welded, 1 dk	**(X11A2YP) Yacht**	**2 oil engines** geared to sc. shafts driving 2 Propellers Total Power: 1,576kW (2,142hp) M.T.U. 12V2000M70 2 x Vee 4 Stroke 12 Cy. 130 x 150 each-788kW (1071bhp) MTU Friedrichshafen GmbH-Friedrichshafen
8109357 *VTDX* -	**SATNAM** **Uni General** Unimarine Pvt Ltd *Mumbai* *India* Official number: 1940	*115* 38 81	Class: IR (LR) ✠ Classed LR until 23/2/94	**1982-01 B.V. Scheepswerf "De Hoop" — Hardinxveld-Giessendam** Yd No: 762 Loa 23.68 Br ex 6.58 Dght 2.909 Lbp 21.24 Br md 6.51 Dpth 3.43 Welded, 1 dk	**(B11A2FT) Trawler** Ins: 70	**1 oil engine** with clutches, flexible couplings & sr reverse geared to sc. shaft driving 1 FP propeller Total Power: 405kW (551hp) Caterpillar 3408TA 1 x Vee 4 Stroke 8 Cy. 137 x 152 405kW (551bhp) Caterpillar Tractor Co-USA AuxGen: 2 x 12kW 380V 50Hz a.c
9518701 - -	**SATO** *ex* Dsct 501 *-2011* *ex* Wayne F *-2009* **Tanzania Ports Authority** - *Dar es Salaam* *Tanzania*	**140** 42 70	Class: (BV)	**2008-12 Damen Shipyards Cape Town — Cape Town (Hull)** **2008-12 B.V. Scheepswerf Damen — Gorinchem** Yd No: 509649 Loa 22.57 Br ex - Dght 3.160 Lbp 20.42 Br md 7.84 Dpth 3.74 Welded, 1 dk	**(B32A2ST) Tug**	**2 oil engines** reduction geared to sc. shafts driving 2 FP propellers Total Power: 2,200kW (2,992hp) 10.0kn Caterpillar 3512B-TA 2 x Vee 4 Stroke 12 Cy. 170 x 190 each-1100kW (1496bhp) Caterpillar Inc-USA AuxGen: 2 x 51kW 50Hz a.c

IMO / Call sign	Name / Owner	Tonnage	Class	Build / Dimensions	Type	Machinery
7314852 *EACY* -	**SATO BALEARES** *ex* Nash 5605 *-1992* *ex* V. H. en B. 5605 *-1980* **Sociedad Anonima Trabajos y Obras (SATO)** - *Las Palmas de Gran Canaria* *Spain* MMSI: 224290750	**558** 167 1,212	Class: (BV)	**1971 Plocka Stocznia Rzeczna — Plock** Loa 57.00 Br ex - Dght 3.048 Lbp 54.79 Br md 9.50 Dpth 3.76 Welded, 1 dk	**(B34A2SH) Hopper, Motor**	**2 oil engines** driving 2 Directional propellers Total Power: 442kW (600hp) Caterpillar D343TA 2 x 4 Stroke 6 Cy. 137 x 165 each-221kW (300bhp) Caterpillar Tractor Co-USA
8970598 *EAJY* -	**SATO CANTABRIA** *ex* Marineco Baloo *-2008* *ex* Mariska 2 *-2004* **Bancantabria Renting SL** Sociedad Anonima Trabajos y Obras (SATO) *Vigo* *Spain* Official number: 5-3/2008	**101** 28 -	Class: (BV)	**2002-03 AO Sudostroitelnyy i Sudorem. Zavod im. "Limenda"-Arkhangelsk** (Hull launched by) **2000* Neptune Shipyards BV — Aalst (Nl)** (Hull completed by) Yd No: 241 Loa 20.20 Br ex 8.04 Dght - Lbp 18.77 Br md 8.00 Dpth 2.40 Welded, 1 dk	**(B34T2QR) Work/Repair Vessel**	**2 oil engines** geared to sc. shafts driving 2 FP propellers Total Power: 882kW (1,200hp) Cummins KTA-19-M3 2 x 4 Stroke 6 Cy. 159 x 159 each-441kW (600bhp) Cummins Engine Co Inc-USA
9404297 *ECNH* -	**SATO GALICIA** - **Caja Laboral Popular Cooperativa de Credito** Sociedad Anonima Trabajos y Obras (SATO) *Vigo* *Spain* MMSI: 225363000 Official number: 5-3/2007	**993** 298 1,755		**2007-10 Francisco Cardama, SA — Vigo** Yd No: 225 Loa 66.00 Br ex - Dght 3.150 Lbp 62.00 Br md 12.50 Dpth 4.00 Welded, 1 dk	**(B33B2DT) Trailing Suction Hopper Dredger** Hopper: 1,000	**2 oil engines** driving 2 Directional propellers Total Power: 1,082kW (1,472hp) Thrusters: 1 Tunnel thruster (f)
7727279 *EHTD* -	**SATO GRAN CANARIA** - **Sociedad Anonima Trabajos y Obras (SATO)** - *Seville* *Spain* MMSI: 224013760 Official number: 5-5/1996	**659** 197 1,254	Class: (BV)	**1979 Astilleros Canarios S.A. (ASTICAN) — Las Palmas** Yd No: 2 Loa 53.24 Br ex - Dght 3.652 Lbp 51.62 Br md 10.96 Dpth 4.09 Welded	**(B34A2SH) Hopper, Motor** Hopper: 704	**2 oil engines** driving 2 FP propellers 6.8kn Deutz SBV8M540 2 x 4 Stroke 8 Cy. 370 x 400 Kloeckner Humboldt Deutz AG-West Germany
7727281 *EHTC* -	**SATO TENERIFE** - **Sociedad Anonima Trabajos y Obras (SATO)** - *Seville* *Spain* MMSI: 224013770 Official number: 5-6/1996	**659** 197 1,254	Class: (BV)	**1979 Astilleros Canarios S.A. (ASTICAN) — Las Palmas** Yd No: 3 Loa 53.24 Br ex - Dght 3.652 Lbp 51.62 Br md 10.96 Dpth 4.09 Welded	**(B34A2SH) Hopper, Motor** Hopper: 704	**2 oil engines** driving 2 FP propellers 6.8kn Deutz SBV8M540 2 x 4 Stroke 8 Cy. 370 x 400 Kloeckner Humboldt Deutz AG-West Germany
8631398 *PONH* -	**SATOMI** *ex* Satomi Maru No. 8 *-2013* **PT Indo Shipping Operator** - *Tanjung Priok* *Indonesia*	**987** 625 -	Class: KI	**1987-11 K.K. Kamishima Zosensho — Osakikamijima** Yd No: 216 Lengthened-2013 Loa 68.80 Br ex 11.02 Dght 3.950 Lbp 63.60 Br md 11.00 Dpth 5.10 Welded, 1 dk	**(A31A2GX) General Cargo Ship** Cranes: 1	**1 oil engine** driving 1 FP propeller Total Power: 662kW (900hp) Matsui MS25GSC 1 x 4 Stroke 6 Cy. 250 x 470 662kW (900bhp) Matsui Iron Works Co Ltd-Japan AuxGen: 1 x 70kW 225V a.c
9049932 - -	**SATRIA 01** - **CV Berkat Fortuna** - *Samarinda* *Indonesia*	**115** 69 -	Class: KI	**2003-12 C.V. Swadaya Utama — Samarinda** Loa 23.50 Br ex - Dght - Lbp 21.93 Br md 6.50 Dpth 3.00 Welded, 1 dk	**(B32A2ST) Tug**	**2 oil engines** geared to sc. shafts driving 2 Propellers Total Power: 810kW (1,102hp) 7.0kn Mitsubishi 10DC11-1A 2 x Vee 4 Stroke 10 Cy. 141 x 152 each-405kW (551bhp) Mitsubishi Heavy Industries Ltd-Japan AuxGen: 2 x 90kW 400V a.c
9029188 - -	**SATRIA 02** - **CV Berkat Fortuna** - *Samarinda* *Indonesia*	**148** 45 -	Class: KI	**2003-07 C.V. Swadaya Utama — Samarinda** Loa - Br ex - Dght 1.910 Lbp 30.80 Br md 6.50 Dpth 2.30 Welded, 1 dk	**(A35D2RL) Landing Craft** Bow ramp (centre)	**2 oil engines** geared to sc. shafts driving 2 Propellers Total Power: 470kW (640hp) Mitsubishi 8DC90A 2 x Vee 4 Stroke 8 Cy. 135 x 140 each-235kW (320bhp) Mitsubishi Heavy Industries Ltd-Japan AuxGen: 1 x 12kW 415V a.c, 1 x 13kW 415V a.c
8651960 - -	**SATRIA DHARMA** - **PT Pelayaran Laju Bersama** - *Pontianak* *Indonesia*	**104** 31 -	Class: KI	**2010-09 CV Sarana Kapuas — Pontianak** Loa - Br ex - Dght - Lbp 19.48 Br md 6.50 Dpth 3.00 Welded, 1 dk	**(B32A2ST) Tug**	**2 oil engines** reduction geared to sc. shafts driving 2 Propellers
8746090 - -	**SATRIA LAKSANA 78** *ex* Jhoni II *-2010* **PT Artha Gunung Mas** - *Samarinda* *Indonesia*	**204** 62 -	Class: KI	**2009-06 C.V. Karya Lestari Industri — Samarinda** Loa 28.00 Br ex - Dght 2.800 Lbp 25.82 Br md 8.00 Dpth 3.60 Welded, 1 dk	**(B32A2ST) Tug**	**2 oil engines** reduction geared to sc. shafts driving 2 Propellers AuxGen: 2 x 41kW 415V 50Hz a.c
8742824 - -	**SATRIA LAKSANA 88** *ex* Jhoni III *-2009* **PT Artha Gunung Mas** - *Samarinda* *Indonesia*	**199** 60 -	Class: KI	**2009-10 C.V. Karya Lestari Industri — Samarinda** Loa 28.00 Br ex - Dght 2.800 Lbp 25.82 Br md 8.00 Dpth 3.60 Welded, 1 dk	**(B32A2ST) Tug**	**2 oil engines** reduction geared to sc. shafts driving 2 Propellers Total Power: 1,552kW (2,110hp) 10.0kn Mitsubishi S12A2-MPTK 2 x Vee 4 Stroke 12 Cy. 150 x 160 each-776kW (1055bhp) Mitsubishi Heavy Industries Ltd-Japan AuxGen: 2 x 41kW 415V 50Hz a.c
8653839 - -	**SATRIA LAKSANA 98** - **PT Artha Gunung Mas** - *Samarinda* *Indonesia*	**207** 63 -	Class: KI	**2010-11 C.V. Karya Lestari Industri — Samarinda** Loa 28.00 Br ex - Dght 2.910 Lbp 26.16 Br md 8.00 Dpth 3.60 Welded, 1 dk	**(B32A2ST) Tug**	**2 oil engines** reduction geared to sc. shafts driving 2 Propellers Total Power: 1,716kW (2,334hp) Mitsubishi S12A2-MPTK 2 x Vee 4 Stroke 12 Cy. 150 x 160 each-858kW (1167bhp) Mitsubishi Heavy Industries Ltd-Japan AuxGen: 2 x 37kW 440V a.c
8735429 *YD6097* -	**SATRIA LAKSANA 128** *ex* Layar Sakti 28 *-2013* **PT Artha Gunung Mas** - *Samarinda* *Indonesia*	**189** 57 -	Class: KI	**2008-06 PT Muji Rahayu Shipyard — Tenggarong** Loa 27.50 Br ex - Dght 2.950 Lbp 26.30 Br md 7.50 Dpth 3.60 Welded, 1 dk	**(B32A2ST) Tug**	**2 oil engines** driving 2 Propellers Total Power: 1,220kW (1,658hp) Yanmar 6AYM-ETE 2 x 4 Stroke 6 Cy. 155 x 180 each-610kW (829bhp) Yanmar Diesel Engine Co Ltd-Japan
9512197 *YDA4337* -	**SATRIA LAKSANA 168** - **PT Artha Gunung Mas** - *Jakarta* *Indonesia*	**158** 48 146	Class: (NK)	**2008-04 Sapor Shipbuilding Industries Sdn Bhd — Sibu** Yd No: S19/2007 Loa 23.90 Br ex - Dght 2.912 Lbp 21.86 Br md 7.30 Dpth 3.50 Welded, 1 dk	**(B32A2ST) Tug**	**2 oil engines** reduction geared to sc. shafts driving 2 Propellers Total Power: 970kW (1,318hp) Yanmar 6AYM-STE 2 x 4 Stroke 6 Cy. 155 x 180 each-485kW (659bhp) Yanmar Diesel Engine Co Ltd-Japan AuxGen: 2 x 56kW a.c Fuel: 90.0
9607253 *YDA4765* -	**SATRIA LAKSANA 178** *launched as* Tsm 1 *-2011* **PT Artha Gunung Mas** - *Jakarta* *Indonesia*	**137** 42 127	Class: (NK)	**2011-02 Hung Seng Shipbuilding Sdn Bhd — Sibu** Yd No: 23 Loa 23.50 Br ex - Dght 2.712 Lbp 21.99 Br md 7.32 Dpth 3.20 Welded, 1 dk	**(B32A2ST) Tug**	**2 oil engines** reduction geared to sc. shafts driving 2 FP propellers Total Power: 894kW (1,216hp) Cummins KTA-19-M3 2 x 4 Stroke 6 Cy. 159 x 159 each-447kW (608bhp) Cummins Engine Co Inc-USA Fuel: 90.0
9607265 *YDA4764* -	**SATRIA LAKSANA 188** *ex* Tsm 3 *-2011* **PT Artha Gunung Mas** - *Jakarta* *Indonesia*	**137** 42 130	Class: NK	**2011-02 Hung Seng Shipbuilding Sdn Bhd — Sibu** Yd No: 24 Loa 23.50 Br ex - Dght 2.712 Lbp 21.99 Br md 7.32 Dpth 3.20 Welded, 1 dk	**(B32A2ST) Tug**	**2 oil engines** reduction geared to sc. shafts driving 2 FP propellers Total Power: 894kW (1,216hp) Cummins KTA-19-M3 2 x 4 Stroke 6 Cy. 159 x 159 each-447kW (608bhp) Cummins Engine Co Inc-USA Fuel: 93.0 (d.f.)
8658841 - -	**SATRIA LAKSANA 268** - **PT Artha Gunung Mas** - *Samarinda* *Indonesia*	**128** 39 -	Class: KI	**2011-05 C.V. Karya Lestari Industri — Samarinda** Loa 23.50 Br ex - Dght 2.080 Lbp 21.79 Br md 6.50 Dpth 2.75 Welded, 1 dk	**(B32A2ST) Tug**	**2 oil engines** reduction geared to sc. shafts driving 2 FP propellers Total Power: 970kW (1,318hp) Yanmar 6AYM-STE 2 x 4 Stroke 6 Cy. 155 x 180 each-485kW (659bhp) Yanmar Diesel Engine Co Ltd-Japan AuxGen: 2 x 40kW 415V a.c

IMO / Call sign	Name / Owner	Tonnage	Class	Builder / Dimensions	Type	Machinery
7853092 *YFHP* -	**SATRIA NUSANTARA** *ex* Iwojima *-1996* *ex* Ferry Choshu No. 1 *-1995* **PT Jembatan Nusantara** - *Jakarta* *Indonesia*	**656** 196 260	Class: KI	**1974**-10 **Kuwata Dock K.K. — Onomichi** Loa 54.51 Br ex - Dght 2.701 Lbp 43.52 Br md 12.01 Dpth 3.61 Welded, 1 dk	**(A36A2PR) Passenger/Ro-Ro Ship (Vehicles)** Passengers: 92	**2 oil engines** geared to sc. shafts driving 2 FP propellers Total Power: 1,472kW (2,002hp) 11.0kn Makita GNLH6275 2 x 4 Stroke 6 Cy. 275 x 450 each-736kW (1001bhp) (made 1974) Makita Diesel Co Ltd-Japan
8627206 *YDST* -	**SATRIA NUSANTARA 01** *ex* De Yun *-2009* *ex* Feng Shun 18 *-2003* *ex* Sakuyahime *-1998* *ex* Shinei Maru *-1988* **PT Citra Baru Adinusantara** - *Tanjung Priok* *Indonesia*	**1,372** 758 1,598	Class: KI	**1984**-08 **Kyoei Zosen KK — Mihara HS** Yd No: 138 Loa 70.20 Br ex - Dght 4.220 Lbp 68.54 Br md 11.80 Dpth 6.81 Welded, 1 dk	**(A31A2GX) General Cargo Ship** Grain: 2,952; Bale: 2,815	**1 oil engine** driving 1 FP propeller Total Power: 956kW (1,300hp) 11.8kn Hanshin 6LUN28ARG 1 x 4 Stroke 6 Cy. 280 x 480 956kW (1300bhp) The Hanshin Diesel Works Ltd-Japan
6502725 *YFLU* -	**SATRIA PRATAMA** *ex* Midorikawa Maru *-1996* **PT Prima Vista** - *Semarang* *Indonesia* MMSI: 525002091	**1,026** 308 189	Class: KI	**1964**-09 **Taguma Zosen KK — Onomichi HS** Yd No: 32 Converted From: Ferry (Passenger only)-1964 Loa 49.84 Br ex 13.26 Dght 2.515 Lbp 44.56 Br md 13.21 Dpth 3.81 Riveted\Welded, 1 dk	**(A36A2PR) Passenger/Ro-Ro Ship (Vehicles)** Passengers: unberthed: 475	**2 oil engines** driving 2 FP propellers Total Power: 1,176kW (1,598hp) 13.0kn Hanshin Z6VSH 2 x 4 Stroke 6 Cy. 280 x 450 each-588kW (799bhp) Hanshin Nainenki Kogyo-Japan AuxGen: 3 x 44kW 200V a.c Fuel: 29.5 5.5pd
9188489 *PMKK* -	**SATRIA SATU** - **PT Wintermar** - *Jakarta* *Indonesia* MMSI: 525019395	**1,499** 556 1,625 T/cm 8.2	Class: KI (AB)	**1998**-04 **Jingjiang Traffic Shipyard — Jingjiang JS** Yd No: POET1078 Loa 65.00 (BB) Br ex - Dght 3.792 Lbp 60.44 Br md 15.00 Dpth 5.20 Welded, 1 dk	**(A13B2TP) Products Tanker** Double Bottom Entire Compartment Length Compartments: 10 Wing Ta, ER 3 Cargo Pump (s): 2x150m³/hr, 1x50m³/hr	**2 oil engines** with clutches, flexible couplings & sr reverse geared to sc. shafts driving 2 FP propellers Total Power: 1,176kW (1,598hp) 10.0kn Yanmar 6N165-EN 2 x 4 Stroke 6 Cy. 165 x 232 each-588kW (799bhp) Yanmar Diesel Engine Co Ltd-Japan AuxGen: 3 x 240kW 440V 50Hz a.c Fuel: 170.0 (d.f.) 30.9 (r.f.) 10.4pd
7808504 - -	**SATRIA TIGA** - **Encik Sim Chek Siang** -	*157* 22 -	Class: (AB)	**1978**-07 **Asiaweld Shipbuilding Pte Ltd — Singapore** Yd No: 96 Loa - Br ex - Dght 2.150 Lbp 26.01 Br md 7.41 Dpth 3.03 Welded, 1 dk	**(B34L2QU) Utility Vessel**	**2 oil engines** driving 2 FP propellers Total Power: 1,074kW (1,460hp) 12.0kn Caterpillar 3406PCTA 2 x 4 Stroke 6 Cy. 137 x 165 each-537kW (730bhp) Caterpillar Tractor Co-USA AuxGen: 2 x 40kW
7925584 - -	**SATRO 21** - **-** -	*796* 465 750	Class: (AB)	**1980**-11 **Bel-Aire Shipyard Ltd — North Vancouver BC** Yd No: 278A Loa 58.20 Br ex 12.22 Dght 3.642 Lbp 54.86 Br md 12.20 Dpth 4.27 Welded, 1 dk	**(B21A2OS) Platform Supply Ship**	**2 oil engines** reverse reduction geared to sc. shafts driving 2 FP propellers Total Power: 1,654kW (2,248hp) 12.0kn Caterpillar D399SCAC 2 x Vee 4 Stroke 16 Cy. 159 x 203 each-827kW (1124bhp) Caterpillar Tractor Co-USA AuxGen: 2 x 100kW Thrusters: 1 Thwart. FP thruster (f)
7925596 *PP7186* -	**SATRO 23** - **Sociedade Auxiliar da Industria de Petroleo Ltda (SATRO)** - *Rio de Janeiro* *Brazil* Official number: 3810317772	*694* 208 750	Class: (AB)	**1980**-10 **Bel-Aire Shipyard Ltd — North Vancouver BC** Yd No: 278B Loa 58.20 Br ex 12.22 Dght 3.642 Lbp 54.86 Br md 12.20 Dpth 4.27 Welded, 1 dk	**(B21A2OS) Platform Supply Ship**	**2 oil engines** reverse reduction geared to sc. shafts driving 2 FP propellers Total Power: 1,654kW (2,248hp) 12.0kn Caterpillar D399SCAC 2 x Vee 4 Stroke 16 Cy. 159 x 203 each-827kW (1124bhp) Caterpillar Tractor Co-USA AuxGen: 2 x 100kW Thrusters: 1 Thwart. FP thruster (f)
7925601 *PP7187* -	**SATRO 25** - **Astromaritima Navegacao SA** - *Rio de Janeiro* *Brazil* MMSI: 710999991 Official number: 3810317837	**796** 465 900	Class: (AB)	**1980**-11 **Vancouver Shipyards Co Ltd — North Vancouver BC** Yd No: 90 Loa 58.20 Br ex 12.22 Dght 3.642 Lbp 54.86 Br md 12.20 Dpth 4.27 Welded, 1 dk	**(B21A2OS) Platform Supply Ship**	**2 oil engines** reverse reduction geared to sc. shafts driving 2 FP propellers Total Power: 1,654kW (2,248hp) 12.0kn Caterpillar D399SCAC 2 x Vee 4 Stroke 16 Cy. 159 x 203 each-827kW (1124bhp) Caterpillar Tractor Co-USA AuxGen: 2 x 100kW Thrusters: 1 Thwart. FP thruster (f)
7913000 - -	**SATSUKI** - **Pacific Maritime Holdings Ltd** -	*123* - 43		**1979**-06 **Kanbara Zosen K.K. — Onomichi** Yd No: 240 Loa 27.50 Br ex - Dght 2.000 Lbp 24.00 Br md 6.50 Dpth 2.90 Welded, 1 dk	**(B32A2ST) Tug**	**2 oil engines** driving 2 FP propellers Total Power: 632kW (860hp) Yanmar 6ML-HT 2 x 4 Stroke 6 Cy. 200 x 240 each-316kW (430bhp) Yanmar Diesel Engine Co Ltd-Japan
5070189 - -	**SATSUKI** *ex* Chihaya *-2002* *ex* Kiyu Maru No. 7 *-2001* *ex* Chihaya *-2000* - - *South Korea*	*177* - -		**1961 Hitachi Zosen Corp — Osaka OS** Yd No: 3909 Loa 33.00 Br ex 8.51 Dght - Lbp - Br md 8.49 Dpth 3.99 Riveted\Welded, 1 dk	**(B32A2ST) Tug**	**2 oil engines** driving 2 FP propellers Total Power: 1,456kW (1,980hp) 11.0kn B&W 6-26MTBF-40 2 x 4 Stroke 6 Cy. 260 x 400 each-728kW (990bhp) Hitachi Zosen Corp-Japan Fuel: 27.5
9153068 *9V2580* -	**SATSUKI** - **Satsuki Shipping Pte Ltd** Asiatic Lloyd Shipping Pte Ltd *Singapore* *Singapore* MMSI: 564324000 Official number: 399194	**14,089** 7,023 17,705	Class: NK	**1997**-08 **Imabari Shipbuilding Co Ltd — Imabari EH (Imabari Shipyard)** Yd No: 534 Loa 163.66 (BB) Br ex - Dght 8.916 Lbp 152.00 Br md 26.00 Dpth 13.40 Welded, 1 dk	**(A33A2CC) Container Ship (Fully Cellular)** TEU 1177 incl 200 ref C. 16 Ha: 2 (12.8 x 8.2)2 (12.8 x 10.8)12 (12.9 x 11.1)ER Cranes: 2x40t	**1 oil engine** driving 1 FP propeller Total Power: 9,628kW (13,090hp) 18.0kn Mitsubishi 7UEC50LSII 1 x 2 Stroke 7 Cy. 500 x 1950 9628kW (13090bhp) Akasaka Tekkosho KK (Akasaka DieselLtd)-Japan AuxGen: 3 x a.c Thrusters: 1 Tunnel thruster (f) Fuel: 1880.0
8742549 *JD2802* -	**SATSUKI MARU** - **KK Enomoto Kaisoten** - *Tokyo* *Japan* Official number: 140851	*497* - 1,600		**2008**-10 **Kotobuki Kogyo KK — Ichikikushikino KS** Yd No: 132 Loa 76.30 Br ex - Dght 4.030 Lbp 70.50 Br md 12.00 Dpth 6.95 Welded, 1 dk	**(A31A2GX) General Cargo Ship** 1 Ha: ER (40.1 x 9.5)	**1 oil engine** driving 1 Propeller Total Power: 1,471kW (2,000hp) Hanshin LH34LAG 1 x 4 Stroke 6 Cy. 340 x 640 1471kW (2000bhp) The Hanshin Diesel Works Ltd-Japan
8891730 - -	**SATSUMA** *ex* Satsuma No. 18 *-1995* *ex* Koei Maru No. 8 *-1995* **-**	*171* 101 351		**1977**-04 **YK Furumoto Tekko Zosensho — Osakikamijima** Loa 40.00 Br ex - Dght 3.800 Lbp 37.00 Br md 7.00 Dpth 4.80 Welded, 1 dk	**(A31A2GX) General Cargo Ship** Compartments: 1 Ho, ER 1 Ha: (20.4 x 5.1)ER	**1 oil engine** driving 1 FP propeller Total Power: 368kW (500hp) 8.0kn Yanmar 1 x 4 Stroke 368kW (500bhp) Yanmar Diesel Engine Co Ltd-Japan
9191503 *JNYL* -	**SATSUMA** - **Government of Japan (Ministry of Land, Infrastructure & Transport) (The Coastguard)** - *Tokyo* *Japan* MMSI: 431063000 Official number: 136748	*1,362* - -		**1999**-10 **Kawasaki Heavy Industries Ltd — Kobe HG** Yd No: 1493 Loa 91.40 Br ex 11.50 Dght 4.000 Lbp 87.00 Br md 11.00 Dpth 5.00 Welded, 1 dk	**(B34H2SQ) Patrol Vessel**	**2 oil engines** driving 2 FP propellers Total Power: 5,140kW (6,988hp) Niigata 8MG32CLX 2 x 4 Stroke 8 Cy. 320 x 420 each-2570kW (3494bhp) Niigata Engineering Co Ltd-Japan
9223526 *JG5383* -	**SATSUMA MARU** - **Tokyo Kisen KK** - *Yokohama, Kanagawa* *Japan* Official number: 136755	*166* - -		**1999**-12 **Kanagawa Zosen — Kobe** Yd No: 480 Loa 38.00 Br ex - Dght 2.760 Lbp 33.50 Br md 8.40 Dpth 3.40 Welded, 1 dk	**(B32A2ST) Tug**	**2 oil engines** Geared Integral to driving 2 Z propellers Total Power: 2,280kW (3,100hp) 15.3kn Niigata 6L25HX 2 x 4 Stroke 6 Cy. 250 x 350 each-1140kW (1550bhp) Niigata Engineering Co Ltd-Japan
8631518 - -	**SATSUMA No. 8** *ex* Toyofuku Maru No. 8 *-1995* **Yuzana Co Ltd** -	*146* - 402		**1988**-02 **YK Furumoto Tekko Zosensho — Osakikamijima** Loa 48.00 Br ex 8.02 Dght 3.400 Lbp 43.06 Br md 8.00 Dpth 4.90 Welded, 1 dk	**(A31A2GX) General Cargo Ship**	**1 oil engine** driving 1 FP propeller Total Power: 368kW (500hp) 10.0kn Yanmar MF24-HT 1 x 4 Stroke 6 Cy. 240 x 420 368kW (500bhp) Matsue Diesel KK-Japan

IMO / Call sign	Name / Owner / Manager / Port / Flag	GT / NT / DWT	Class	Built / Builder / Dimensions	Type / Cargo	Machinery
9258258 *JIQR* -	**SATSUMASEIUN MARU** **Government of Japan (Kagoshima Prefecture)** *Kagoshima, Kagoshima* *Japan* MMSI: 432321000 Official number: 136833	*645* - 400		**2002-03 Niigata Engineering Co Ltd — Niigata NI** Yd No: 2501 Loa 64.25 (BB) Br ex - Dght 3.900 Lbp 55.50 Br md 9.90 Dpth 4.15 Welded, 1 dk	**(B34K2QT) Training Ship**	**1 oil engine** driving 1 FP propeller Total Power: 1,618kW (2,200hp) Niigata 6L28HX 1 x 4 Stroke 6 Cy. 280 x 370 1618kW (2200bhp) Niigata Engineering Co Ltd-Japan Thrusters: 1 Thwart. FP thruster (f)
8021464 *V4YD2* -	**SATSUNAN** *ex* Amber *-2014* *ex* Seikai *-2011* *ex* Satsunan *-1998* **Topway Corp LP** - *St Kitts & Nevis* MMSI: 341198000 Official number: SKN 1002661	**346** 103 -	Class: GM	**1981-02 Niigata Engineering Co Ltd — Niigata NI** Yd No: 1707 Converted From: Fishing Vessel-2006 Loa 45.70 Br ex 9.20 Dght 3.152 Lbp 38.51 Br md 8.01 Dpth 3.46 Welded, 1 dk	**(B12B2FC) Fish Carrier** Ins: 34	**1 oil engine** reduction geared to sc. shaft driving 1 CP propeller Total Power: 1,030kW (1,400hp) 14.0kn Niigata 6MG25CX 1 x 4 Stroke 6 Cy. 250 x 320 1030kW (1400bhp) Niigata Engineering Co Ltd-Japan AuxGen: 1 x 300kW 225V a.c, 1 x 200kW 225V a.c
8019461 - -	**SATTAHIP 1** **Port Authority of Thailand (Marine Department)** - *Bangkok* *Thailand*	*292* 79 -	Class: (AB)	**1980-10 Sing Koon Seng Pte Ltd — Singapore** Yd No: SKS530 Loa - Br ex - Dght - Lbp 29.72 Br md 9.31 Dpth 4.63 Welded, 1 dk	**(B32A2ST) Tug**	**2 oil engines** geared to sc. shafts driving 2 FP propellers Total Power: 2,354kW (3,200hp) Yanmar 6Z-ST 2 x 4 Stroke 6 Cy. 280 x 340 each-1177kW (1600bhp) Yanmar Diesel Engine Co Ltd-Japan
9040479 - -	**SATTAR** *ex* Belstar *-2001* **Alicia Marine Co Ltd** IranoHind Shipping Co Ltd	**24,155** 14,291 43,419 T/cm 49.1	Class: BV (NV)	**1992-10 Oshima Shipbuilding Co Ltd — Saikai NS** Yd No: 10156 Loa 184.80 (BB) Br ex - Dght 11.241 Lbp 176.80 Br md 30.50 Dpth 15.80 Welded, 1 dk	**(A21A2BC) Bulk Carrier** Grain: 54,290; Bale: 53,240 Compartments: 5 Ho, ER 5 Ha: (14.4 x 15.3)4 (19.2 x 15.3)ER Cranes: 4x30t	**1 oil engine** driving 1 FP propeller Total Power: 7,025kW (9,551hp) 14.3kn Sulzer 6RTA52 1 x 2 Stroke 6 Cy. 520 x 1800 7025kW (9551bhp) Diesel United Ltd.-Aioi AuxGen: 3 x 410kW 440V 60Hz a.c
7828308 - -	**SATTHA** *ex* Mustika *-2005* *ex* Uniana *-2001* *ex* Ming Star *-1998* *ex* Kojin Maru No. 32 *-1992* *ex* Ohama Maru No. 32 *-1989* **Sta Inc** -	*245* 73 -		**1979-05 K.K. Yoshida Zosen Tekko — Kesennuma** Yd No: 268 Converted From: Fishing Vessel Loa 39.25 (BB) Br ex - Dght 2.401 Lbp 32.57 Br md 6.46 Dpth 2.75 Welded, 1 dk	**(A31A2GX) General Cargo Ship**	**1 oil engine** driving 1 FP propeller Total Power: 736kW (1,001hp) Hanshin 6LU28 1 x 4 Stroke 6 Cy. 280 x 440 736kW (1001bhp) Hanshin Nainenki Kogyo-Japan
9240330 *9VPQ2* -	**SATTHA BHUM** **Regional Container Lines Pte Ltd** RCL Shipmanagement Pte Ltd SatCom: Inmarsat C 456424610 *Singapore* *Singapore* MMSI: 564246000 Official number: 394309	**32,060** 12,580 38,948	Class: GL	**2009-06 Stocznia Gdynia SA — Gdynia** Yd No: 8184/22 Loa 210.97 (BB) Br ex - Dght 12.000 Lbp 196.00 Br md 32.26 Dpth 19.00 Welded, 1 dk	**(A33A2CC) Container Ship (Fully Cellular)** TEU 2732 C Ho 1222 TEU C Dk 1510 TEU incl 450 ref C. Compartments: ER, 8 Cell Ho 16 Ha: (12.8 x 17.9) (12.8 x 23.2)ER 14 (12.8 x 28.3)	**1 oil engine** driving 1 FP propeller Total Power: 21,770kW (29,598hp) 21.6kn MAN-B&W 7S70MC-C 1 x 2 Stroke 7 Cy. 700 x 2800 21770kW (29598bhp) H Cegielski Poznan SA-Poland AuxGen: 4 x 1200kW 450/220V 60Hz a.c Thrusters: 1 Thwart. CP thruster (f) Fuel: 258.9 (d.f.) 5704.0 (r.f.) 166.0pd
9287651 - -	**SATURN** **Lizingovaya Kompaniya Rybolovetskikh Kolkhozov OAO (Collective Fish Farm Leasing Co Ltd)** -	**189** 57 73	Class: RR (RS)	**2002-06 OAO Astrakhanskaya Sudoverf — Astrakhan** Yd No: 125 Loa 31.85 Br ex - Dght 2.100 Lbp 27.80 Br md 7.80 Dpth 3.15 Welded, 1 dk	**(B11B2FV) Fishing Vessel**	**1 oil engine** geared to sc. shaft driving 1 FP propeller Total Power: 232kW (315hp) 10.2kn Daldizel 6CHNSP18/22 1 x 4 Stroke 6 Cy. 180 x 220 232kW (315bhp) Daldizel-Khabarovsk AuxGen: 2 x 25kW Fuel: 14.0 (d.f.)
9400851 *V7PE6* -	**SATURN** **Seasafe Navigation Inc** National Shipping SA *Majuro* *Marshall Islands* MMSI: 538003215 Official number: 3215	**8,542** 4,117 13,051 T/cm 22.9	Class: AB	**2009-03 Sekwang Heavy Industries Co Ltd — Ulsan** Yd No: 1167 Loa 128.60 (BB) Br ex - Dght 8.714 Lbp 120.40 Br md 20.40 Dpth 11.50 Welded, 1 dk	**(A12B2TR) Chemical/Products Tanker** Double Hull (13F) Liq: 13,399; Liq (Oil): 13,399 Cargo Heating Coils Compartments: 12 Wing Ta, 2 Wing Slop Ta, ER 12 Cargo Pump (s): 12x300m³/hr Manifold: Bow/CM: 59.6m	**1 oil engine** driving 1 FP propeller Total Power: 4,200kW (5,710hp) 13.4kn MAN-B&W 6S35MC 1 x 2 Stroke 6 Cy. 350 x 1400 4200kW (5710bhp) AuxGen: 3 x a.c Thrusters: 1 Tunnel thruster (f)
9396634 *V2DM5* -	**SATURN** *ex* Montego *-2013* *launched as* Rickmers Vietnam *-2008* **ms 'Saturn' Schiffahrts GmbH & Co KG** Alpha Shipmanagement GmbH & Co KG *Saint John's* *Antigua & Barbuda* MMSI: 305270000 Official number: 4479	**16,162** 6,128 17,350	Class: GL (BV)	**2008-09 Jiangsu Yangzijiang Shipbuilding Co Ltd — Jiangyin JS** Yd No: 2006-729C Loa 161.30 (BB) Br ex - Dght 9.500 Lbp 149.60 Br md 25.00 Dpth 14.90 Welded, 1 dk	**(A33A2CC) Container Ship (Fully Cellular)** TEU 1345 Co Ho 556 TEU C Dk 789 TEU incl 449 ref C. Compartments: 4 Cell Ho, ER Cranes: 2x45t	**1 oil engine** driving 1 FP propeller Total Power: 12,640kW (17,185hp) 19.3kn MAN-B&W 8S50MC-C 1 x 2 Stroke 8 Cy. 500 x 2000 12640kW (17185bhp) AuxGen: 2 x 1520kW 450V a.c, 2 x 1140kW 450V a.c Thrusters: 1 Tunnel thruster (f)
9378175 *UBHH9* -	**SATURN** *ex* Havila Saturn *-2011* **Gaztechleasing Ltd** OOO Gazflot *Kaliningrad* *Russia* MMSI: 273356920	**2,806** 857 2,859	Class: RS (LR) ✠ Classed LR until 20/5/11	**2008-02 Cemre Muhendislik Gemi Insaat Sanayi ve Ticaret Ltd Sti-Pendik** (Hull) **2008-02 Havyard Leirvik AS — Leirvik i Sogn** Yd No: 092 Loa 74.50 (BB) Br ex 17.60 Dght 5.500 Lbp 64.80 Br md 17.20 Dpth 8.00 Welded, 1 dk	**(B21B20A) Anchor Handling Tug Supply** Passengers: cabins: 18 Cranes: 1x5t Ice Capable	**2 oil engines** with clutches, flexible couplings & sr reverse geared to sc. shafts driving 2 CP propellers Total Power: 12,000kW (16,316hp) 15.0kn MaK 12M32C 2 x Vee 4 Stroke 12 Cy. 320 x 420 each-6000kW (8158bhp) Caterpillar Motoren GmbH & Co. KG-Germany AuxGen: 2 x 550kW 440V 60Hz a.c, 2 x 3000kW 440V 60Hz a.c Boilers: HWH (o.f.) Thrusters: 1 Thwart. CP thruster (f); 1 Thwart. CP thruster (a); 1 Retract. directional thruster (f) Fuel: 935.0 (d.f.)
9315410 *ES2607* -	**SATURN** **PKL AS (PKL Ltd)** - *Tallinn* *Estonia* MMSI: 276588000 Official number: 1T04J05	**144** 44 46	Class: RS (NV)	**2004-09 Stocznia Polnocna SA (Northern Shipyard) — Gdansk** Yd No: B840/1 Loa 19.10 Br ex 9.85 Dght 2.850 Lbp 17.73 Br md 9.00 Dpth 3.80 Welded, 1 dk	**(B32A2ST) Tug** Ice Capable	**2 oil engines** geared to sc. shafts driving 2 Z propellers Total Power: 2,100kW (2,856hp) 10.0kn Caterpillar 3512B 2 x Vee 4 Stroke 12 Cy. 170 x 190 each-1050kW (1428bhp) Caterpillar Inc-USA
7832397 *UOPN* -	**SATURN** **Uralkasprybokhrana** - *Aqtau* *Kazakhstan* Official number: 790272	*163* 39 88	Class: (RS)	**1980 Astrakhanskaya Sudoverf im. "Kirova" — Astrakhan** Yd No: 127 Converted From: Fishing Vessel Loa 34.01 Br ex 7.09 Dght 2.899 Lbp 29.98 Br md - Dpth 3.69 Welded, 1 dk	**(B12D2FP) Fishery Patrol Vessel** Bale: 115 Compartments: 1 Ho, ER 1 Ha: (1.6 x 1.3) Derricks: 2x2t; Winches: 2 Ice Capable	**1 oil engine** driving 1 FP propeller Total Power: 224kW (305hp) 9.5kn S.K.L. 8NVD36-1U 1 x 4 Stroke 8 Cy. 240 x 360 224kW (305bhp) VEB Schwermaschinenbau "KarlLiebknecht" (SKL)-Magdeburg AuxGen: 2 x 75kW, 1 x 28kW Fuel: 16.0 (d.f.)
7938701 - -	**SATURN** *ex* Katy Lelia *-2011* **E Ebanks** - *Roatan* *Honduras* Official number: U-1921494	*112* 76 -		**1978 Steiner Shipyard, Inc. — Bayou La Batre, Al** L reg 20.46 Br ex 6.71 Dght - Lbp - Br md - Dpth 3.43 Welded, 1 dk	**(B11A2FT) Trawler**	**1 oil engine** geared to sc. shaft driving 1 FP propeller Total Power: 268kW (364hp) Cummins KTA-1150-M 1 x 4 Stroke 6 Cy. 159 x 159 268kW (364bhp) Cummins Engine Co Inc-USA
8035465 *UBBY* -	**SATURN** *ex* Hyocheon No. 7 *-2006* *ex* Kyoriki Maru *-2000* *ex* Seiyu Maru *-1993* **Marine Ecology Co Ltd (OOO 'Ekologiya Morya')** - *Petropavlovsk-Kamchatskiy* *Russia*	**323** 96 365	Class: RS	**1981-06 Kogushi Zosen K.K. — Okayama** Yd No: 229 Converted From: Chemical Tanker Loa 44.30 Br ex 7.72 Dght 2.890 Lbp 39.96 Br md 7.70 Dpth 3.35 Welded, 1 dk	**(A13B2TP) Products Tanker** Liq: 360; Liq (Oil): 360	**1 oil engine** driving 1 FP propeller Total Power: 552kW (750hp) 9.0kn Hanshin 6L26BGSH 1 x 4 Stroke 6 Cy. 260 x 400 552kW (750bhp) The Hanshin Diesel Works Ltd-Japan Fuel: 22.0 (d.f.)
8033340 - -	**SATURN** **Sevastopol Port Authority** - *Sevastopol* *Ukraine* Official number: 811229	*149* 101 20	Class: (RS)	**1981 Ilyichyovskiy Sudoremontnyy Zavod im. "50-letiya SSSR" — Ilyichyovsk** Yd No: 13 Loa 28.70 Br ex 6.35 Dght 1.480 Lbp 27.00 Br md - Dpth 2.50 Welded, 1 dk	**(A37B2PS) Passenger Ship** Passengers: unberthed: 250	**2 oil engines** driving 2 FP propellers Total Power: 220kW (300hp) 10.4kn Barnaultransmash 3D6C 2 x 4 Stroke 6 Cy. 150 x 180 each-110kW (150bhp) Barnaultransmash-Barnaul AuxGen: 2 x 1kW Fuel: 2.0 (d.f.)

IMO / Call sign	Name, owner, flag	Tonnage	Class	Build / dimensions	Type	Machinery
5314573 *WH5439* -	**SATURN** *ex* Muriel McAllister *ex* Saturn *-1980* *ex* Bern *-1956* **Jon B Johansen** - *Winterport, ME* *United States of America* Official number: 204605	*252* 171 -		**1907 Neafie & Levy Ship & Engine Building Co. — Philadelphia, Pa** Yd No: 1011 Loa 34.14 Br ex 7.50 Dght - Lbp - Br md - Dpth - Riveted, 1 dk	**(B32A2ST) Tug**	**1 oil engine** driving 1 FP propeller Total Power: 1,250kW (1,700hp) General Motors 16-278-A 1 x Vee 2 Stroke 16 Cy. 222 x 267 1250kW (1700bhp) (new engine 1980) General Motors Corp-USA
5416357 *LZPC* -	**SATURN** *ex* Lady Cecilia *-1964* **Port Fleet-99 SLtd (Portovi Flot-99)** - *Varna* *Bulgaria* Official number: 89	**157** 47 -	Class: (LR) (BR) ✠ Classed LR until 10/66	**1963-11 Charles D. Holmes & Co. Ltd. — Beverley** Yd No: 985 Loa 29.21 Br ex 7.52 Dght 3.241 Lbp 25.91 Br md 7.32 Dpth 3.81 Welded, 1 dk	**(B32A2ST) Tug**	**1 oil engine** sr reverse geared to sc. shaft driving 1 FP propeller Total Power: 677kW (920hp) Ruston 7VEBCM 1 x 4 Stroke 7 Cy. 260 x 368 677kW (920bhp) Ruston & Hornsby Ltd.-Lincoln AuxGen: 1 x 20kW 400V a.c, 1 x 10kW 400V a.c
6604690 *OUHO2* -	**SATURN** *ex* Dorca *-1989* *ex* Douro Star *-1979* *ex* Wilma Frank *-1972* **M/S Saturn Norresundby ApS** Norresundby Shipping A/S SatCom: Inmarsat C 422000061 *Norresundby* *Denmark (DIS)* MMSI: 219000245 Official number: D2051	**627** 297 772	Class: GL	**1966-07 N.V. Scheepswerf "Vooruitgang" Gebr. Suurmeijer — Foxhol** Yd No: 213 Loa 53.60 Br ex 9.40 Dght 3.447 Lbp 49.05 Br md 9.30 Dpth 5.41 Welded, 1 dk	**(A31A2GX) General Cargo Ship** Grain: 1,543; Bale: 1,435 Compartments: 1 Ho, ER 1 Ha: (26.6 x 6.1)ER Ice Capable	**1 oil engine** reverse reduction geared to sc. shaft driving 1 FP propeller Total Power: 221kW (300hp) 10.5kn MWM TRH435SU 1 x 4 Stroke 6 Cy. 250 x 350 221kW (300bhp) Motoren Werke Mannheim AG (MWM)-West Germany Fuel: 38.5 (d.f.) 2.5pd
7740635 - -	**SATURN** - **National JSC 'Chernomorneftegaz'** -	**1,167** 350 440	Class: (RS)	**1978 Yaroslavskiy Sudostroitelnyy Zavod — Yaroslavl** Yd No: 210 Loa 58.55 Br ex 12.68 Dght 4.692 Lbp 51.62 Br md - Dpth 5.90 Welded, 1 dk	**(B32A2ST) Tug** Ice Capable	**2 diesel electric oil engines** driving 2 gen. each 1000kW 900V Connecting to 1 elec. Motor of (1900kW) driving 1 FP propeller Total Power: 2,208kW (3,002hp) 13.2kn Kolomna 6CHN30/38 2 x 4 Stroke 6 Cy. 300 x 380 each-1104kW (1501bhp) Kolomenskiy Zavod-Kolomna AuxGen: 2 x 300kW 400V a.c, 2 x 160kW 400V a.c Fuel: 385.0 (d.f.)
7615490 *GXID* -	**SATURN** - **Caledonian Maritime Assets Ltd** CalMac Ferries Ltd *Glasgow* *United Kingdom* MMSI: 232003374 Official number: 377012	**899** 297 259		**1978-02 Ailsa Shipbuilding Co Ltd — Troon** Yd No: 552 Loa 69.53 Br ex 13.77 Dght 2.440 Lbp 66.53 Br md 13.42 Dpth 3.97 Welded, 1 dk	**(A36A2PR) Passenger/Ro-Ro Ship (Vehicles)** Passengers: unberthed: 694 Stern door/ramp Len: 4.76 Wid: 3.72 Swl: - Side door/ramp (p) Len: 4.80 Wid: 6.12 Swl: - Side door/ramp (s) Len: 4.80 Wid: 6.12 Swl: - Lane-Len: 184 Lane-Wid: 3.60 Lorries: 5, Cars: 20	**2 oil engines** geared to sc. shafts driving 2 Directional propellers Total Power: 1,794kW (2,440hp) 14.0kn Blackstone ESL8MK2 2 x 4 Stroke 8 Cy. 222 x 292 each-897kW (1220bhp) Mirrlees Blackstone (Stamford)Ltd.-Stamford AuxGen: 2 x 120kW a.c, 1 x 25kW a.c
9009516 - -	**SATURN** *ex* Saga *-2011* *ex* Sea Fox *-2009* *ex* Kaiyo Maru *-2008* *ex* Kaiyo Maru No. 38 *-2005* **Sea Gate Transportation Inc**	**435** 210 -	Class: IS	**1990-11 Fujishin Zosen K.K. — Kamo** Yd No: 565 Converted From: Fishing Vessel-1990 Loa 48.01 Br ex - Dght 3.470 Lbp 41.20 Br md 8.00 Dpth 3.48 Welded	**(B12B2FC) Fish Carrier**	**1 oil engine** with clutches & sr reverse geared to sc. shaft driving 1 CP propeller Total Power: 736kW (1,001hp) 13.8kn Niigata 6M28BFT 1 x 4 Stroke 6 Cy. 280 x 480 736kW (1001bhp) Niigata Engineering Co Ltd-Japan
8903064 *E5U2738* -	**SATURN** *ex* Union Saturn *-2013* *ex* Short Sea Trader *-2001* **Saturn Shipping Ltd** Vestra Ltd *Avatiu* *Cook Islands* MMSI: 518791000 Official number: 1827	**2,236** 1,244 3,263	Class: GL	**1991-06 Cochrane Shipbuilders Ltd. — Selby** Yd No: 168 Loa 99.73 Br ex - Dght 4.746 Lbp 96.00 Br md 12.60 Dpth 6.35 Welded, 1 dk	**(A31A2GX) General Cargo Ship** Grain: 4,575; Bale: 4,477 TEU 114 C.Ho 86/20' C.Dk 28/20' Compartments: 2 Ho, ER 1 Ha: (70.2 x 10.1)ER	**1 oil engine** with clutches, flexible couplings & sr geared to sc. shaft driving 1 CP propeller Total Power: 1,080kW (1,468hp) 10.5kn Alpha 8L23/30 1 x 4 Stroke 8 Cy. 225 x 300 1080kW (1468bhp) MAN B&W Diesel A/S-Denmark AuxGen: 1 x 324kW 220/380V a.c, 3 x 84kW 220/380V a.c Thrusters: 1 Thwart. FP thruster (f)
8841773 *WBN3026* -	**SATURN** - **Crowley Marine Services Inc** - *San Francisco, CA* *United States of America* MMSI: 366888770 Official number: 518570	**172** 51 -		**1969 Mangone Shipbuilding Co. — Houston, Tx** Yd No: 89 Loa - Br ex - Dght 3.556 Lbp 27.74 Br md 8.84 Dpth 4.04 Welded, 1 dk	**(B32A2ST) Tug**	**2 oil engines** geared to sc. shafts driving 2 FP propellers Total Power: 1,766kW (2,402hp) Caterpillar D399 2 x Vee 4 Stroke 16 Cy. 159 x 203 each-883kW (1201bhp) Caterpillar Tractor Co-USA
7639276 - -	**SATURN BUNKER I** *ex* Young Nam No. 1 *-2006* *ex* MSC Star *-1993* *ex* Fukuyoshi Maru No. 3 *-1991* **PT Krida Shipping International** - *Indonesia*	**701** 318 1,150	Class: (KR)	**1976-11 Omishima Dock K.K. — Imabari** Yd No: 1055 Loa 58.05 Br ex 10.04 Dght 4.150 Lbp 53.75 Br md 10.00 Dpth 4.35 Welded, 1 dk	**(B34E2SW) Waste Disposal Vessel** Liq: 1,026	**1 oil engine** geared to sc. shaft driving 1 FP propeller Total Power: 883kW (1,201hp) 10.8kn Akasaka AH28R 1 x 4 Stroke 6 Cy. 280 x 440 883kW (1201bhp) Akasaka Tekkosho KK (Akasaka DieselLtd)-Japan AuxGen: 2 x 56kW 225V a.c
6825701 *HQTP4* -	**SATURN II** *ex* Leone *-1999* *ex* Gemini I *-1999* *ex* Athina I *-1999* *ex* Phoenix *-1996* *ex* Phoenix I *-1991* *ex* Antares *-1991* *ex* Hawk *-1990* *ex* Audacity *-1990* **Seneca Maritime Corp** - *San Lorenzo* *Honduras* Official number: L-1327009	**699** 453 1,616	Class: (LR) (HR) ✠ Classed LR until 7/91	**1968-11 Goole SB. & Repairing Co. Ltd. — Goole** Yd No: 564 Loa 69.90 Br ex 11.10 Dght 4.390 Lbp 67.09 Br md 10.98 Dpth 4.80 Welded, 1 dk	**(A13B2TP) Products Tanker** Liq: 2,081; Liq (Oil): 2,081 Cargo Heating Coils Compartments: 10 Ta, ER	**1 oil engine** driving 1 FP propeller Total Power: 1,015kW (1,380hp) 11.0kn Deutz RBV6M358 1 x 4 Stroke 6 Cy. 400 x 580 1015kW (1380bhp) (new engine 1972) Kloeckner Humboldt Deutz AG-West Germany AuxGen: 2 x 50kW 220V d.c, 1 x 30kW 220V d.c
8626604 *YB4453* -	**SATURN III** *ex* Dong Yung 33 *-2003* *ex* Tomoe Maru *-2001* **PT Krida Shipping International** - *Jakarta* *Indonesia*	*315* 104 550	Class: (KI)	**1985-04 Kato Zosen Tekko — Japan** Loa 46.34 Br ex - Dght 3.190 Lbp 42.00 Br md 7.70 Dpth 3.45 Welded, 1 dk	**(A12A2TC) Chemical Tanker**	**1 oil engine** driving 1 FP propeller Total Power: 478kW (650hp) 10.0kn Yanmar MF24-DT 1 x 4 Stroke 6 Cy. 240 x 420 478kW (650bhp) Yanmar Diesel Engine Co Ltd-Japan
7908419 *CL2008* -	**SATURNO** *ex* Casablanca *-1997* *ex* Caribbean Export *-1995* *ex* State Swan *-1987* **SERMAR** - *Cuba*	*182* 124 1,000	Class: RC (AB)	**1980-03 Zigler Shipyards Inc — Jennings LA** Yd No: 270 Loa - Br ex - Dght 3.074 Lbp 45.73 Br md 10.67 Dpth 3.69 Welded, 1 dk	**(B21A2OS) Platform Supply Ship**	**2 oil engines** reverse reduction geared to sc. shafts driving 2 FP propellers Total Power: 1,030kW (1,400hp) 11.0kn G.M. (Detroit Diesel) 12V-149 2 x Vee 2 Stroke 12 Cy. 146 x 146 each-515kW (700bhp) General Motors Detroit DieselAllison Divn-USA AuxGen: 2 x 75kW a.c
9348845 *HC4748* -	**SATURNO** - **Superintendencia del Terminal Petrolero de Balao (SUINBA)** - *Balao* *Ecuador* Official number: R-02-0077	**317** 95 -	Class: (BV)	**2005-12 Francisco Cardama, SA — Vigo** Yd No: 217 Loa 30.00 Br ex - Dght 4.000 Lbp 27.50 Br md 9.00 Dpth 4.80 Welded, 1 dk	**(B32A2ST) Tug**	**2 oil engines** geared to sc. shafts driving 2 CP propellers Total Power: 3,282kW (4,462hp) Caterpillar 3516B-TA 2 x Vee 4 Stroke 16 Cy. 170 x 190 each-1641kW (2231bhp) Caterpillar Inc-USA AuxGen: 1 x 130kW 110/440V 60Hz a.c
9239599 *XCNY3* -	**SATURNO** *ex* Troms Falken *-2008* *ex* Normand Produce *-2005* *ex* Troms Falken *-2005* **Maritime Oil Services Ltd** Cotemar SA de CV *Isla del Carmen* *Mexico* MMSI: 345070262	**2,165** 1,086 3,350	Class: NV	**2001-09 Brevik Construction AS — Brevik** Yd No: 19 Loa 71.90 Br ex 16.03 Dght 5.900 Lbp 66.80 Br md 16.00 Dpth 7.00 Welded, 1 dk	**(B21A2OS) Platform Supply Ship** Ice Capable	**2 oil engines** reduction geared to sc. shafts driving 2 CP propellers Total Power: 4,016kW (5,460hp) Normo KRMB-9 2 x 4 Stroke 9 Cy. 250 x 300 each-2008kW (2730bhp) Rolls Royce Marine AS-Norway AuxGen: 2 x a.c, 2 x a.c Thrusters: 2 Thwart. CP thruster (f); 1 Thwart. CP thruster (a)
9209180 *CUFC7* A-3514-C	**SATURNO** - **Arrastoes Reunidos Lda** - *Aveiro* *Portugal*	**215** 65 -	Class: BV	**1999-11 Astilleros Armon SA — Navia** Yd No: 503 Loa 24.80 Br ex - Dght 3.890 Lbp 21.67 Br md 7.80 Dpth 5.70 Welded, 1 dk	**(B11B2FV) Fishing Vessel**	**1 oil engine** geared to sc. shaft driving 1 CP propeller Total Power: 441kW (600hp) 10.0kn Yanmar M220-EN 1 x 4 Stroke 6 Cy. 220 x 300 441kW (600bhp) Yanmar Diesel Engine Co Ltd-Japan

IMO / Call sign / Fishing no.	Name / Owner / Manager / Port / Flag	Tonnage	Class	Builder / Dimensions	Type	Machinery
9440540 *PS9237* -	**SATURNO** **Saveiros Camuyrano - Servicos Maritimos SA** - *Santos* *Brazil* MMSI: 710003470 Official number: 401-082204-0	**250** 75 116	Class: LR ✠**100A1** SS 10/2012 tug Brazailian coastal service **LMC** **UMS** Eq.Ltr: F; Cable: 275.0/17.5 U2 (a)	2007-10 **Wilson, Sons SA — Guaruja** (Hull) Yd No: 084 2007-10 **B.V. Scheepswerf Damen — Gorinchem** Yd No: 512219 Loa 24.47 Br ex 11.33 Dght 5.350 Lbp 20.80 Br md 10.70 Dpth 4.60 Welded, 1 dk	**(B32A2ST) Tug**	**2 oil engines** gearing integral to driving 2 Directional propellers Total Power: 4,200kW (5,710hp) Caterpillar 3516B-TA 2 x Vee 4 Stroke 16 Cy. 170 x 190 each-2100kW (2855bhp) Caterpillar Inc-USA AuxGen: 2 x 55kW 440V 60Hz a.c
9382724 *LAFW7* -	**SATURNUS** **S-Bulk KS** Seven Seas Carriers AS *Bergen* *Norway (NIS)* MMSI: 259790000	**30,273** 16,969 50,292 T/cm 52.2	Class: NV	2008-08 **P.T. PAL Indonesia — Surabaya** Yd No: 230 Loa 189.90 (BB) Br ex - Dght 12.820 Lbp 182.00 Br md 30.50 Dpth 17.50 Welded, 1 dk	**(A21A2BC) Bulk Carrier** Double Hull Grain: 60,557; Bale: 58,269 Compartments: 5 Ho, ER 5 Ha: 4 (20.0 x 25.5)ER (8.8 x 25.0) Cranes: 4x35t	**1 oil engine** driving 1 FP propeller Total Power: 9,480kW (12,889hp) 14.0kn MAN-B&W 6S50MC-C 1 x 2 Stroke 6 Cy. 500 x 2000 9480kW (12889bhp) STX Engine Co Ltd-South Korea AuxGen: 3 x 720kW a.c Fuel: 90.0 (d.f.) 1850.0 (r.f.) 37.0pd
7902441 *EI8999* WD 47	**SATURNUS** **Joseph G Whelan** - *Wexford* *Irish Republic* MMSI: 250000764 Official number: 402918	**187** 56 -		1980-08 **Scheepswerven Beliard Oostende N.V. — Oostende** Yd No: 234 Loa 27.89 Br ex 7.57 Dght 3.301 Lbp 23.88 Br md 7.51 Dpth 3.92 Welded, 1 dk	**(B11A2FT) Trawler**	**1 oil engine** reduction geared to sc. shaft driving 1 FP propeller Total Power: 596kW (810hp) A.B.C. 6MDXC 1 x 4 Stroke 6 Cy. 242 x 320 596kW (810bhp) Anglo Belgian Co NV (ABC)-Belgium
7719052 *PBTV* -	**SATURNUS** *ex Bugsier 8 -2009* **Amsterdam Tugs BV** Sleepdienst B Iskes & Zoon BV *IJmuiden* *Netherlands* MMSI: 246604000 Official number: 53210	*190* 57 -	Class: GL	1978-03 **Schiffswerft u. Maschinenfabrik Max Sieghold — Bremerhaven** Yd No: 180 Loa 26.29 Br ex 8.84 Dght 2.801 Lbp 23.80 Br md 8.81 Dpth 3.61 Welded, 1 dk	**(B32A2ST) Tug** Ice Capable	**2 oil engines** geared to sc. shafts driving 2 Directional propellers Total Power: 1,280kW (1,740hp) Deutz SBA6M528 2 x 4 Stroke 6 Cy. 220 x 280 each-640kW (870bhp) Kloeckner Humboldt Deutz AG-West Germany
8906951 *OXMP2* -	**SATURNUS** *ex Furevik -2005* **Partrederiet mt Saturnus** Sirius Chartering AB *Laeso* *Denmark (DIS)* MMSI: 219153000	**5,774** 2,556 8,490 T/cm 16.8	Class: GL RS (Class contemplated) (BV) (NV)	1990-12 **FEAB-Marstrandverken — Marstrand** (Hull) Yd No: 190 1990-12 **Soviknes Verft AS — Sovik** Yd No: 97 Loa 119.98 (BB) Br ex 17.83 Dght 7.870 Lbp 110.00 Br md 17.50 Dpth 9.90 Welded, 1 dk	**(A12B2TR) Chemical/Products Tanker** Double Hull Liq: 8,715; Liq (Oil): 8,715 Cargo Heating Coils Compartments: 12 Wing Ta, 2 Wing Slop Ta, ER 12 Cargo Pump (s): 12x340m³/hr Manifold: Bow/CM: 58.5m Ice Capable	**1 oil engine** reduction geared to sc. shaft driving 1 CP propeller Total Power: 2,939kW (3,996hp) 13.0kn MaK 8M453C 1 x 4 Stroke 8 Cy. 320 x 420 2939kW (3996bhp) Krupp MaK Maschinenbau GmbH-Kiel AuxGen: 1 x 515kW 440V 60Hz a.c, 4 x 321kW 440V 60Hz a.c Thrusters: 1 Thwart. FP thruster (f) Fuel: 100.0 (d.f.) 300.0 (r.f.)
9005998 - KY 43	**SATURNUS** *ex Harmtje Pieter -2009* **M C Fishing Co Ltd** - *Kirkcaldy* *United Kingdom* Official number: C19468	**156** 46 38	Class: (GL)	1990-04 **Scheepswerf Visser B.V. — Den Helder** Yd No: 129 Loa 24.00 Br ex 6.79 Dght 3.001 Lbp 21.30 Br md 6.70 Dpth 4.00 Welded, 1 dk	**(B11A2FT) Trawler** Ins: 100	**1 oil engine** with clutches, flexible couplings & sr geared to sc. shaft driving 1 FP propeller Total Power: 220kW (299hp) 9.0kn Stork DRO216K 1 x 4 Stroke 6 Cy. 210 x 300 220kW (299bhp) Stork Wartsila Diesel BV-Netherlands AuxGen: 2 x 52kW 220/380V 50Hz a.c Thrusters: 1 Thwart. FP thruster (f)
8839471 - -	**SATYA BERJAYA** *ex Katingan Express -2012* *ex Choai Maru No. 8 -2007* **PT Srijaya Segara Utama** - *Jakarta* *Indonesia*	*483* 156 1,046		1989-12 **K.K. Kamishima Zosensho — Osakikamijima** Yd No: 302 Loa 66.63 Br ex - Dght 3.700 Lbp 60.00 Br md 10.70 Dpth 6.20 Welded, 1 dk	**(A31A2GX) General Cargo Ship** 1 Ha: (37.5 x 8.5)ER	**1 oil engine** driving 1 FP propeller Total Power: 736kW (1,001hp) 10.0kn Hanshin 6LU28G 1 x 4 Stroke 6 Cy. 280 x 440 736kW (1001bhp) The Hanshin Diesel Works Ltd-Japan
7851721 *YEST* -	**SATYA DHARMA** *ex Dharma Cakra -2007* *ex Sakurajima Maru No. 3 -1992* **PT Dharma Lautan Utama** - *Surabaya* *Indonesia* MMSI: 525000012	**435** 145 150	Class: KI	1969-09 **Hitachi Zosen Corp — Onomichi HS (Mukaishima Shipyard)** Yd No: 4258 Loa 48.94 Br ex - Dght 2.300 Lbp 42.91 Br md 12.40 Dpth 3.41 Welded, 1 dk	**(A36A2PR) Passenger/Ro-Ro Ship (Vehicles)** Passengers: 486	**2 oil engines** driving 2 FP propellers Total Power: 662kW (900hp) 10.5kn Hanshin 6L26AGS 2 x 4 Stroke 6 Cy. 260 x 400 each-331kW (450bhp) The Hanshin Diesel Works Ltd-Japan
7912434 *PMBG* -	**SATYA KENCANA** *ex Nanakuni -2004* **PT Dharma Lautan Utama** - *Surabaya* *Indonesia*	*319* 96 355	Class: KI	1980-03 **Binan Senpaku Kogyo K.K. — Onomichi** Yd No: 5402 Loa 41.31 Br ex 10.22 Dght 1.980 Lbp 29.80 Br md 9.01 Dpth 2.80 Welded, 1 dk	**(A37B2PS) Passenger Ship**	**1 oil engine** geared to sc. shaft driving 1 FP propeller Total Power: 552kW (750hp) Daihatsu 6PSHTCM-26E 1 x 4 Stroke 6 Cy. 260 x 320 552kW (750bhp) Daihatsu Diesel Manufacturing Co Lt-Japan
7126437 *YFBY* -	**SATYA KENCANA I** *ex Pradipta Dharma -2005 ex Chita Line -1994* *ex Blue Line No. 2 -1988 ex Blue Line -1987* **PT Dharma Lautan Utama** - *Surabaya* *Indonesia* MMSI: 525015384	*806* 241 163	Class: KI	1970-11 **Sanuki Shipbuilding & Iron Works Co Ltd — Mitoyo KG** Yd No: 552 Loa 51.01 Br ex 10.42 Dght 2.502 Lbp 47.00 Br md 10.39 Dpth 3.51 Welded, 1 dk	**(A37B2PS) Passenger Ship** Passengers: unberthed: 400	**2 oil engines** driving 2 FP propellers Total Power: 1,472kW (2,002hp) 13.5kn Niigata 6M28KGHS 2 x 4 Stroke 6 Cy. 280 x 440 each-736kW (1001bhp) Niigata Engineering Co Ltd-Japan AuxGen: 1 x 60kW a.c, 1 x 40kW a.c
8904563 *POES* -	**SATYA KENCANA III** *ex Ferry Osumi No. 6 -2011* **PT Dharma Lautan Utama** - *Surabaya* *Indonesia* MMSI: 525015879	**2,825** 1,310 -	Class: KI	1989-11 **Hayashikane Dockyard Co Ltd — Nagasaki NS** Yd No: 975 Loa 76.88 Br ex - Dght 3.501 Lbp 71.13 Br md 13.31 Dpth 4.73 Welded	**(A36A2PR) Passenger/Ro-Ro Ship (Vehicles)** Passengers: unberthed: 737 Bow door/ramp Stern door/ramp Lane-Len: 140 Trailers: 14	**2 oil engines** driving 2 FP propellers Total Power: 3,382kW (4,598hp) 15.5kn Daihatsu 6DLM-32 2 x 4 Stroke 6 Cy. 320 x 400 each-1691kW (2299bhp) Daihatsu Diesel Manufacturing Co Lt-Japan AuxGen: 2 x 740kW 445V a.c Thrusters: 1 Thwart. FP thruster (f) Fuel: 91.5 (d.f.)
9584786 *YDA4714* -	**SATYA MANDIRI** **Pelayaran Josh Tirto PT** - *Pontianak* *Indonesia*	**146** 44 132	Class: KI (NK)	2010-06 **Tuong Aik Shipyard Sdn Bhd — Sibu** Yd No: 2922 Loa 23.90 Br ex - Dght 2.862 Lbp 22.29 Br md 7.32 Dpth 3.35 Welded, 1 dk	**(B32A2ST) Tug**	**2 oil engines** reduction geared to sc. shafts driving 2 Propellers Total Power: 970kW (1,318hp) Yanmar 6AYM-STE 2 x 4 Stroke 6 Cy. 155 x 180 each-485kW (659bhp) Yanmar Diesel Engine Co Ltd-Japan Fuel: 121.0
9471460 - -	**SATYAJAYA** **Transworld Shipping Agent** - *Honduras*	**296** 89 318		2007-06 **KPN Thai Teck Co Ltd — Bangkok** Yd No: 002 Loa 45.00 Br ex - Dght 3.600 Lbp 41.10 Br md 7.80 Dpth 3.60 Welded, 1 dk	**(B12B2FC) Fish Carrier**	**1 oil engine** geared to sc. shaft driving 1 Propeller Cummins 1 x 4 Stroke Cummins Engine Co Inc-USA
8901963 *VWVE* -	**SATYAM** *ex Atco Marwa -1999* **Shiv Vani Oil & Gas Exploration Services Ltd** Modest Maritime Services Pvt Ltd *Mumbai* *India* MMSI: 419072200 Official number: 2857	**122** 36 30	Class: IR (AB)	1988 **Halter Marine, Inc. — New Orleans, La** Yd No: 1146 Loa 30.99 Br ex 6.48 Dght 1.520 Lbp 29.07 Br md 6.40 Dpth 2.90 Welded	**(B21A2OC) Crew/Supply Vessel** Hull Material: Aluminium Alloy	**3 oil engines** reverse reduction geared to sc. shafts driving 3 FP propellers Total Power: 1,125kW (1,530hp) 15.0kn G.M. (Detroit Diesel) 12V-71-TI 3 x Vee 2 Stroke 12 Cy. 108 x 127 each-375kW (510bhp) General Motors Detroit DieselAllison Divn-USA AuxGen: 2 x 30kW 220V 60Hz a.c Fuel: 14.0 (d.f.)
8028008 - -	**SATYAM** **Shivam Engineers Pvt Ltd** - SatCom: Inmarsat C 441900171 *Panaji* *India* Official number: 122	*501* 309 600	Class: IR (BV)	1981-09 **Shivam Engineers Pvt. Ltd. — Goa** Yd No: 004 Loa 52.02 Br ex 9.33 Dght 2.201 Lbp 50.02 Br md 9.01 Dpth 2.82 Welded, 1 dk	**(A31A2GX) General Cargo Ship**	**3 oil engines** geared to sc. shafts driving 3 FP propellers Total Power: 330kW (450hp) 8.8kn Ruston 6YDM 3 x 4 Stroke 6 Cy. 111 x 127 each-110kW (150bhp) Ruston & Hornsby (India) Ltd-India
8664979 *XVJL* -	**SAU DUNG 09-ALCI** **Sau Dung Maritime Transport Co Ltd** - *Haiphong* *Vietnam* Official number: VN-2567-VT	**1,598** 1,062 3,146	Class: VR	2008-05 **Nam Ha Shipyard — Nam Ha** Yd No: TKB11-11 Loa 79.80 Br ex 12.82 Dght 5.100 Lbp 74.80 Br md 12.80 Dpth 6.08 Welded, 1 dk	**(A31A2GX) General Cargo Ship** Grain: 4,432; Bale: 4,029 Compartments: 2 Ho, ER 2 Ha: ER 2 (20.4 x 8.4)	**1 oil engine** driving 1 FP propeller Total Power: 970kW (1,319hp) 9.5kn S.K.L. 8NVD48A-2U 1 x 4 Stroke 8 Cy. 320 x 480 970kW (1319bhp) (made 1991, fitted 2008) SKL Motoren u. Systemtechnik AG-Magdeburg AuxGen: 2 x 36kW 400V a.c

Identity / Owner	Tonnage	Class	Build / Dimensions	Type	Machinery
8984044 **SAUDADES** *CQRF* *ex* Ariadne - **Ancura Yacht Transportes Maritimos Lda** Atlantic Madeira Yacht Management Lda *Madeira Portugal (MAR)* Official number: 1277	**106** 64 -		**1976 Baglietto S.p.A. — Varazze** Loa 27.00 Br ex - Dght 1.920 Lbp - Br md 5.80 Dpth 2.14 Welded, 1 dk	**(X11A2YP) Yacht** Hull Material: Aluminium Alloy Passengers: cabins: 4; berths: 8	**2 oil engines** driving 2 Propellers Total Power: 2,030kW (2,760hp) 22.0kn M.T.U. 2 x 4 Stroke each-1015kW (1380bhp) MTU Friedrichshafen GmbH-Friedrichshafen
5191919 **SAUHOLM** *LFDB* *ex* Sagholm *-1974* *ex* Koloyholm *-1967* - *ex* Trafik 3 *-1955* **Daafjord Laks AS** - *Stokmarknes Norway*	*121* 64 152	Class: (NV)	**1903 AS Akers Mekaniske Verksted — Oslo** Yd No: 226 Loa 28.99 Br ex 5.67 Dght 2.540 Lbp - Br md 5.64 Dpth 2.60 Riveted, 1 dk	**(A31A2GX) General Cargo Ship** Compartments: 1 Ho, ER 1 Ha: (9.2 x 2.6)ER Derricks: 1x2t; Winches: 1	**1 oil engine** driving 1 FP propeller Total Power: 162kW (220hp) 9.0kn Fuel: 3.0 (d.f.) 1.0pd
8732520 **SAUIPE** *PS6271* - **Sulnorte Servicos Maritimos Ltda** H Dantas Comercio Navegacao e Industrias Ltda *Rio de Janeiro Brazil* Official number: 3810511501	**193** - -		**2003-01 Detroit Brasil Ltda — Itajai** Loa 25.50 Br ex - Dght 3.000 Lbp - Br md 8.65 Dpth 4.26 Welded, 1 dk	**(B32A2ST) Tug**	**2 oil engines** reduction geared to sc. shafts driving 2 Directional propellers Total Power: 2,080kW (2,828hp) Volvo Penta D49 2 x Vee 4 Stroke 12 Cy. 170 x 180 each-1040kW (1414bhp) AB Volvo Penta-Sweden
6813710 **SAUJANA** *9MBS8* *ex* Perkasa *-1991* *ex* Kurogane *-1989* - *ex* V. S. P. Kurogane Maru *-1981* - - *Port Klang Malaysia* Official number: 327016	**336** 101 350	Class: (NK)	**1968 Osaka Shipbuilding Co Ltd — Osaka OS** Yd No: 279 Loa 36.30 Br ex - Dght 3.747 Lbp 35.00 Br md 9.80 Dpth 4.40 Riveted\Welded, 1 dk	**(B32A2ST) Tug**	**2 oil engines** reduction geared to sc. shafts driving 2 Directional propellers Total Power: 2,354kW (3,200hp) 13.9kn Niigata 6L31AX 2 x 4 Stroke 6 Cy. 310 x 380 each-1177kW (1600bhp) Niigata Engineering Co Ltd-Japan AuxGen: 2 x 64kW a.c
8898506 **SAULES KRASTAS** *V4PQ* *ex* Saulkrasti *-2004* - **UAB Green Line (JSC Green Line)** Ekohidrotehnika un Ko (Ekohidrotehnika & Co) *Basseterre St Kitts & Nevis* MMSI: 341405000	**949** 284 1,060	Class: RS	**1980-11 Santierul Naval Drobeta-Turnu Severin S.A. — Drobeta-Turnu S.** Yd No: 1 Loa 56.19 Br ex 11.21 Dght 3.700 Lbp 53.20 Br md 11.00 Dpth 4.44 Welded, 1 dk	**(B34A2SH) Hopper, Motor** Hopper: 600 Ice Capable	**2 oil engines** driving 2 FP propellers Total Power: 588kW (800hp) 8.9kn S.K.L. 6NVD26A-3 2 x 4 Stroke 6 Cy. 180 x 260 each-294kW (400bhp) VEB Schwermaschinenbau "KarlLiebknecht" (SKL)-Magdeburg AuxGen: 2 x 100kW a.c Fuel: 123.0 (d.f.)
8899122 **SAULUS** *9HPC8* *ex* SM-PRC-111 *-2006* - **Emarine Ltd** - *Valletta Malta* MMSI: 256269000 Official number: 8899122	**540** 171 1,104	Class: PR	**1976-04 Plocka Stocznia Rzeczna — Plock** Yd No: SM660/631 Converted From: General Cargo Ship-2005 Loa 58.96 Br ex 9.50 Dght 2.910 Lbp 57.77 Br md - Dpth 3.35 Welded, 1 dk	**(B34A2SH) Hopper, Motor**	**2 oil engines** reduction geared to sc. shafts driving 2 FP propellers Total Power: 382kW (520hp) 7.8kn Deutz BF12L714 2 x Vee 4 Stroke 12 Cy. 120 x 140 each-191kW (260bhp) Kloeckner Humboldt Deutz AG-West Germany AuxGen: 2 x 28kW 400V a.c
4902945 **SAURIA** *9LD2363* *ex* Oilstone *-2011* - **Allantone Supplies Ltd** - *Freetown Sierra Leone* MMSI: 667005063 Official number: SL105063	**362** 109 250	Class: IS (LR) ✠	**1968-06 Appledore Shipbuilders Ltd — Bideford** Yd No: A.S. 42 Loa 42.46 Br ex 7.62 Dght 2.490 Lbp 39.62 Br md 7.47 Dpth - Welded, 1 dk	**(A13B2TP) Products Tanker** Liq: 370; Liq (Oil): 370	**1 oil engine** reduction geared to sc. shaft driving 1 FP propeller Total Power: 298kW (405hp) 10.0kn Blackstone ES6 1 x 4 Stroke 6 Cy. 222 x 292 298kW (405bhp) Mirrlees Blackstone (Stamford)Ltd.-Stamford AuxGen: 3 x 75kW 220V d.c Fuel: 17.0
8957546 **SAUSALITO** *DUA2861* *ex* Diana Dos *-1999* - **Oilexpress Corp** Great Swiss Maritime Services Inc *Manila Philippines* Official number: 00-0000239	**680** 204 1,200	Class: (BV)	**1999 Padaco Marine Works & Shipbuilding Corp. — Manila** Yd No: 98-04 Loa 63.30 Br ex - Dght 2.770 Lbp 60.62 Br md 12.80 Dpth 3.50 Welded, 1 dk	**(A13B2TP) Products Tanker** Compartments: 10 Ta, ER	**2 oil engines** driving 2 FP propellers Total Power: 716kW (974hp) 8.0kn Caterpillar 3408TA 2 x Vee 4 Stroke 8 Cy. 137 x 152 each-358kW (487bhp) Caterpillar Inc-USA
9010747 **SAUVEUR DU MONDE** *FGEW* BL 735032 **Cyriaque Ramet** - SatCom: Inmarsat C 422710290 *Boulogne France* MMSI: 227102900 Official number: 735032	*101* - 34		**1990-06 Forges Caloin — Etaples** Yd No: 57 Loa 24.00 Br ex 6.80 Dght - Lbp 20.50 Br md 6.62 Dpth 3.60 Welded	**(B11A2FS) Stern Trawler**	**1 oil engine** with clutches, flexible couplings & sr geared to sc. shaft driving 1 CP propeller Total Power: 526kW (715hp) Caterpillar 3508TA 1 x Vee 4 Stroke 8 Cy. 170 x 190 526kW (715bhp) Caterpillar Inc-USA
9013177 **SAUZON** *FQHN* *ex* Amporelle *-2008* - **Naviland SA** - *Ile d'Yeu France* MMSI: 227004400 Official number: 425434	*345* 258 100	Class: BV	**1991-12 Soc. Francaise de Cons. Nav. — Villeneuve-la-Garenne** Yd No: 869 Loa 38.00 Br ex - Dght 1.350 Lbp 33.50 Br md 7.75 Dpth 3.40 Welded, 1 dk	**(A37B2PS) Passenger Ship** Passengers: unberthed: 370	**2 oil engines** with clutches, flexible couplings & sr geared to sc. shafts driving 2 Water jets Total Power: 3,398kW (4,620hp) 28.0kn MWM TBD604BV16 2 x Vee 4 Stroke 16 Cy. 170 x 195 each-1699kW (2310bhp) Motoren Werke Mannheim AG (MWM)-Mannheim AuxGen: 2 x 60kW 380V 50Hz a.c Fuel: 10.4 (d.f.)
8420103 **SAVA** *9LD2386* *ex* See Adler *-2011* *ex* Petersburg *-2010* - *ex* Peter S *-1993* **Mimosa Management Ltd** Wakes & Co Ltd SatCom: Inmarsat C 466700531 *Freetown Sierra Leone* MMSI: 667005086 Official number: SL105086	**1,838** 963 2,285 T/cm 9.2	Class: PX (GL)	**1985-09 JG Hitzler Schiffswerft und Masch GmbH & Co KG — Lauenburg** Yd No: 787 Loa 80.60 Br ex 12.70 Dght 4.171 Lbp 75.21 Br md 12.62 Dpth 4.65 Welded, 2 dks	**(A31A2GX) General Cargo Ship** Grain: 3,228; Bale: 3,146 TEU 96 C.Ho 62/20' (40') C.Dk 34/20' (40') Compartments: 1 Ho, ER 1 Ha: (51.3 x 10.1)ER Cranes: 2x6t Ice Capable	**1 oil engine** with flexible couplings & sr reverse geared to sc. shaft driving 1 FP propeller Total Power: 1,019kW (1,385hp) 11.0kn Deutz SBV6M628 1 x 4 Stroke 6 Cy. 240 x 280 1019kW (1385bhp) Kloeckner Humboldt Deutz AG-West Germany AuxGen: 2 x 86kW 380V 50Hz a.c, 1 x 72kW 380V 50Hz a.c, 1 x 60kW 380V 50Hz a.c Thrusters: 1 Thwart. FP thruster (f) Fuel: 7.5 (d.f.) 148.5 (r.f.)
8719073 **SAVA LAKE** *J8B4272* - **Sordic Shipping Co Ltd** Mestex Shipping & Trading Ltd *Kingstown St Vincent & The Grenadines* MMSI: 377691000 Official number: 10745	**2,030** 911 3,050	Class: RS (NV)	**1990-07 Brodogradiliste 'Sava' — Macvanska Mitrovica** Yd No: 297 Loa 74.65 (BB) Br ex 12.70 Dght 6.020 Lbp 69.70 Br md - Dpth 8.62 Welded, 1 dk	**(A31A2GX) General Cargo Ship** Grain: 3,792 TEU 98 C.Ho 20/20' C.Dk 78/20' Compartments: 1 Ho, ER, 1 Tw Dk 1 Ha: (47.0 x 10.2)ER Ice Capable	**1 oil engine** sr geared to sc. shaft driving 1 CP propeller Total Power: 1,470kW (1,999hp) 12.0kn Normo KRM-8 1 x 4 Stroke 8 Cy. 250 x 300 1470kW (1999bhp) Bergen Diesel AS-Norway AuxGen: 1 x 440kW 220V 50Hz a.c, 2 x 176kW 220V 50Hz a.c Thrusters: 1 Thwart. CP thruster (f)
8856390 **SAVAGE** *WAQ3499* - **Savage Inc** - *Ketchikan, AK United States of America* MMSI: 368213000 Official number: 648797	*115* 78 -		**1982 La Force Shipyard Inc — Coden AL** Loa - Br ex - Dght - Lbp 21.61 Br md 6.71 Dpth 3.29 Welded, 1 dk	**(B11B2FV) Fishing Vessel**	**1 oil engine** driving 1 FP propeller
9419187 **SAVAHEL** *9BRJ* *ex* Anugerah Perdana 07 *-2008* - **Sahlizadgan A** - *Bandar Abbas Iran* MMSI: 422764000 Official number: 11564	**460** 138 750	Class: AS (KI)	**2006-09 PT Anugerah Wijaya Bersaudara — Samarinda** Yd No: 700/02 Loa 56.45 Br ex 12.10 Dght 2.180 Lbp 53.00 Br md 11.94 Dpth 3.00 Welded, 1 dk	**(A35D2RL) Landing Craft** Bow ramp (centre)	**2 oil engines** reduction geared to sc. shafts driving 2 Propellers Total Power: 850kW (1,156hp) Caterpillar 3408TA 2 x Vee 4 Stroke 8 Cy. 137 x 152 each-425kW (578bhp) Caterpillar Inc-USA AuxGen: 2 x 80kW 400V a.c
9026057 **SAVANNA** - *ex* Hai Au *-2009* - **Kien Giang Tourism Co** - *Saigon Vietnam* Official number: VNSG-2001-TK	**270** 100 29	Class: VR	**2003-12 189 Company — Haiphong** Yd No: ST-180 Loa 33.30 Br ex 9.30 Dght 1.600 Lbp 30.00 Br md 8.54 Dpth 3.45 Welded, 1 dk	**(A37B2PS) Passenger Ship** Hull Material: Aluminium Alloy	**2 oil engines** geared to sc. shafts driving 2 Propellers Total Power: 3,478kW (4,728hp) 33.0kn M.T.U. 12V4000M70 2 x Vee 4 Stroke 12 Cy. 165 x 190 each-1739kW (2364bhp) MTU Friedrichshafen GmbH-Friedrichshafen

IMO / Call sign / Flag	Name / Owner	Tonnage	Class	Build / Dimensions	Type	Machinery
8205448 - -	**SAVANNA III** *ex* Vervenne Jr *-2011* *ex* Govert Kruijff *-2003* *ex* Regge *-1994* *ex* Sarah B *-1991* *ex* Sarah 7 *-1990* **Sabrutrans BV** - *Amsterdam* *Netherlands* Official number: 3968	**106** 32 -	Class: (BV)	**1983**-03 **Constructie en Scheepsbouw van Santen B.V. — Sliedrecht** (Hull) Yd No: 232 **1983**-03 **B.V. Scheepswerf Damen — Gorinchem** Yd No: 2717 Loa 22.62 Br ex - Dght 2.571 Lbp 20.42 Br md 6.61 Dpth 3.43 Welded, 1 dk	**(B32A2ST) Tug**	**2 oil engines** reduction geared to sc. shafts driving 2 FP propellers Total Power: 706kW (960hp) Caterpillar 2 x each-353kW (480bhp) (, fitted 1983)
8992651 *WDF9415* -	**SAVANNAH** **Regents of the University System of Georgia** - *Savannah, GA* *United States of America* MMSI: 303117000 Official number: 1110385	*265* 79 -		**2001**-01 **Washburn & Doughty Associates Inc — East Boothbay ME** Loa 27.91 Br ex - Dght 2.590 Lbp 24.99 Br md 8.23 Dpth 3.96 Welded, 1 dk	**(B31A2SR) Research Survey Vessel**	**2 oil engines** Reduction geared to sc. shafts driving 2 FP propellers Total Power: 820kW (1,114hp) 9.0kn Caterpillar 3406E-TA 2 x 4 Stroke 6 Cy. 137 x 165 each-410kW (557bhp) Caterpillar Inc-USA AuxGen: 2 x 90kW 208V 60Hz a.c Thrusters: 1 Tunnel thruster (f)
8968507 *WCZ7045* -	**SAVANNAH** - **Capt Elliott's Party Boats Inc** Texas Crewboats Inc *Freeport, TX* *United States of America* MMSI: 366778490 Official number: 1092236	**227** 68 -		**2000**-03 **Gulf Craft Inc — Patterson LA** Yd No: 433 Loa 39.62 Br ex - Dght - Lbp - Br md 7.92 Dpth 3.38 Welded, 1 dk	**(B21A20C) Crew/Supply Vessel** Hull Material: Aluminium Alloy	**4 oil engines** reduction geared to sc. shafts driving 2 FP propellers Total Power: 2,060kW (2,800hp) 23.0kn Cummins KTA-19-M4 4 x 4 Stroke 6 Cy. 159 x 159 each-515kW (700bhp) Cummins Engine Co Inc-USA AuxGen: 2 x 50kW a.c
9121194 *S6AK* -	**SAVANNAH** *ex* Eagle Sagitta *-2004* *ex* N O L Sagitta *-2000* **Jensal Shipping Inc** Eastern Pacific Shipping Pte Ltd SatCom: Inmarsat C 456394810 *Singapore* *Singapore* MMSI: 563948000 Official number: 386779	**28,433** 12,369 47,172 T/cm 50.3	Class: NK	**1996**-04 **Onomichi Dockyard Co Ltd — Onomichi HS** Yd No: 398 Loa 182.50 (BB) Br ex 32.23 Dght 12.667 Lbp 172.00 Br md 32.20 Dpth 19.10 Welded, 1 dk	**(A13A2TW) Crude/Oil Products Tanker** Double Hull (13F) Liq: 50,335; Liq (Oil): 50,335 Cargo Heating Coils Compartments: 2 Ta, 12 Wing Ta, 2 Wing Slop Ta, ER 4 Cargo Pump (s): 4x1000m³/hr Manifold: Bow/CM: 93m	**1 oil engine** driving 1 FP propeller Total Power: 8,562kW (11,641hp) 14.8kn B&W 6S50MC 1 x 2 Stroke 6 Cy. 500 x 1910 8562kW (11641bhp) Mitsui Engineering & Shipbuilding CLtd-Japan AuxGen: 3 x 420kW 450V 60Hz a.c Fuel: 130.0 (d.f.) 1483.0 (r.f.) 30.0pd
9269738 *WDD9810* -	**SAVANNAH** - **Crescent Towing & Salvage Co Inc** - *Savannah, GA* *United States of America* Official number: 1128392	**290** 87 -		**2002**-09 **Bollinger Machine Shop & Shipyard, Inc. — Lockport, La** Yd No: 410 Loa 29.26 Br ex - Dght - Lbp 27.92 Br md 10.40 Dpth 4.50 Welded, 1 dk	**(B32A2ST) Tug**	**2 oil engines** gearing integral to driving 2 Z propellers Total Power: 2,942kW (4,000hp) Caterpillar 3516B 2 x Vee 4 Stroke 16 Cy. 170 x 190 each-1471kW (2000bhp) Caterpillar Inc-USA AuxGen: 2 x 90kW a.c
9294989 *DNDD* -	**SAVANNAH EXPRESS** - **Beteiligungs KG ms 'Northern Julie' Schiffahrts GmbH & Co** Norddeutsche Reederei H Schuldt GmbH & Co KG *Hamburg* *Germany* MMSI: 211693000 Official number: 20146	**94,483** 55,670 108,180	Class: GL	**2005**-04 **Daewoo Shipbuilding & Marine Engineering Co Ltd — Geoje** Yd No: 4102 Loa 332.41 (BB) Br ex 43.32 Dght 14.500 Lbp 317.20 Br md 43.20 Dpth 24.50 Welded, 1 dk	**(A33A2CC) Container Ship (Fully Cellular)** Double Bottom Entire Compartment Length TEU 8411 C Ho 3967 TEU C Dk 4444 TEU incl 700 ref C. Compartments: 9 Ho, ER 19 Ha: (12.6 x 28.1) (12.6 x 33.2)16 (12.6 x 38.3)ER (12.6 x 18.1)	**1 oil engine** driving 1 FP propeller Total Power: 68,490kW (93,119hp) 25.0kn MAN-B&W 12K98ME-C 1 x 2 Stroke 12 Cy. 980 x 2400 68490kW (93119bhp) Doosan Engine Co Ltd-South Korea AuxGen: 4 x 3360kW 440/220V 60Hz a.c Thrusters: 1 Thwart. CP thruster (f) Fuel: 275.0 (d.f.) 10686.0 (r.f.)
8316699 *C6JD7* -	**SAVANNAH PEARL** *ex* Wren Arrow *-2013* *ex* Charles L D *-1990* **Savannah Pearl Shipping Co Ltd** SMT Shipping (Cyprus) Ltd SatCom: Inmarsat A 1103306 *Nassau* *Bahamas* MMSI: 308268000 Official number: 716252	**27,824** 12,607 43,003 T/cm 48.6	Class: NV (BV)	**1985**-07 **Hyundai Heavy Industries Co Ltd — Ulsan** Yd No: 337 Loa 187.51 (BB) Br ex 29.47 Dght 12.350 Lbp 177.00 Br md 29.01 Dpth 16.92 Welded, 1 dk	**(A31A2GO) Open Hatch Cargo Ship** Double Sides Entire Compartment Length Grain: 47,671; Bale: 46,280 TEU 1584 C Ho 1044 TEU C Dk 540 TEU Compartments: 7 Ho, ER 7 Ha: (12.4 x 17.0)3 (24.6 x 23.0)3 (12.4 x 23.0)ER Gantry cranes: 2x35t	**1 oil engine** driving 1 FP propeller Total Power: 6,055kW (8,232hp) 13.1kn B&W 6L60MCE 1 x 2 Stroke 6 Cy. 600 x 1944 6055kW (8232bhp) Hyundai Engine & Machinery Co Ltd-South Korea AuxGen: 3 x 750kW 450V 60Hz a.c Thrusters: 1 Thwart. CP thruster (f) Fuel: 101.0 (d.f.) 2009.5 (r.f.) 23.5pd
8124199 *WDF8237* -	**SAVANNAH RAY** *ex* Golden Sable *-2011* *ex* Pacific Invader *-1989* **Mystic Blue LLC** - SatCom: Inmarsat C 433842310 *Seward, AK* *United States of America* MMSI: 367492820 Official number: 625096	*199* 135 -		**1980**-08 **Bender Shipbuilding & Repair Co Inc — Mobile AL** Yd No: 135 L reg 24.88 Br ex 7.32 Dght - Lbp - Br md - Dpth 3.69 Welded, 1 dk	**(B11A2FS) Stern Trawler**	**1 oil engine** driving 1 FP propeller Total Power: 496kW (674hp) General Motors 1 x 2 Stroke 496kW (674bhp) General Motors Corp-USA
8225929 *WDF4805* -	**SAVANNAH RIVER** *ex* Snow River *-1996* *ex* Melena Theriot *-1991* **Ranger Remuda LLC** Ranger Offshore Inc *Morgan City, LA* *United States of America* MMSI: 368165000 Official number: 586452	**624** 187 700		**1977** **Universal Iron Works — Houma, La** Yd No: 147 Converted From: Offshore Supply Ship-2010 Loa - Br ex - Dght 3.450 Lbp 50.30 Br md 12.20 Dpth 3.97 Welded, 1 dk	**(B22A20V) Diving Support Vessel** Cranes: 1x50t	**2 oil engines** reduction geared to sc. shafts driving 2 FP propellers Total Power: 1,324kW (1,800hp) 9.0kn G.M. (Detroit Diesel) 16V-149 2 x Vee 2 Stroke 16 Cy. 146 x 146 each-662kW (900bhp) General Motors Detroit DieselAllison Divn-USA AuxGen: 2 x 75kW 60Hz a.c Thrusters: 1 Tunnel thruster (f)
5314810 *TCSA* -	**SAVARONA** *ex* Gunes Dil *-1951* *ex* Savarona *-1938* **Gemi Kurtarma Denizcilik ve Turizm AS** - SatCom: Inmarsat A 1740315 *Istanbul* *Turkey* MMSI: 271000250 Official number: 5739	**4,701** 1,410 1,540	Class: RI (LR) ✠	**1931**-07 **Blohm & Voss KG auf Aktien — Hamburg** Yd No: 490 Converted From: Training Vessel-1992 Converted From: Yacht-1951 Loa 124.30 Br ex 16.11 Dght 6.120 Lbp 104.65 Br md 16.08 Dpth 9.75 Riveted, 3 dks	**(X11A2YP) Yacht** Passengers: cabins: 18; berths: 36	**2 oil engines** reduction geared to sc. shafts driving 2 FP propellers Total Power: 2,706kW (3,680hp) Caterpillar 3608TA 2 x 4 Stroke 8 Cy. 280 x 300 each-1353kW (1840bhp) (new engine 1996) Caterpillar Inc-USA AuxGen: 3 x 280kW 220V a.c
9546942 *J8B4377* -	**SAVE RIVER** *ex* Dsct 503 *-2012* **Smit Amandla Marine Pty Ltd** - *Kingstown* *St Vincent & The Grenadines* MMSI: 377044000 Official number: 10850	**103** 103 70	Class: BV	**2010**-08 **Damen Shipyards Cape Town — Cape Town** (Hull) Yd No: (509651) **2010**-08 **B.V. Scheepswerf Damen — Gorinchem** Yd No: 509651 Loa 22.57 Br ex - Dght 3.160 Lbp 20.41 Br md 7.84 Dpth 3.74 Welded, 1 dk	**(B32A2ST) Tug**	**2 oil engines** reduction geared to sc. shafts driving 2 FP propellers Total Power: 1,940kW (2,638hp) Caterpillar 3512B 2 x Vee 4 Stroke 12 Cy. 170 x 190 each-970kW (1319bhp) Caterpillar Inc-USA AuxGen: 2 x 49kW 50Hz a.c
9256690 *PS4977* -	**SAVEIROS ALBATROZ** - **Wilson Sons Offshore SA** - *Rio de Janeiro* *Brazil* MMSI: 710000390 Official number: 4010812028	**2,150** 645 3,275	Class: LR ✠**100A1** SS 03/2013 offshore supply ship ✠**LMC** **UMS** Eq.Ltr: S; Cable: 467.5/38.0 U3 (a)	**2003**-03 **Wilson, Sons SA — Guaruja** Yd No: 097 Loa 71.90 Br ex 16.44 Dght 5.800 Lbp 66.80 Br md 16.00 Dpth 7.00 Welded, 1 dk	**(B21A20S) Platform Supply Ship**	**2 oil engines** with clutches & sr geared to sc. shafts driving 2 CP propellers Total Power: 4,010kW (5,452hp) 12.5kn Bergens KRMB-9 2 x 4 Stroke 9 Cy. 250 x 300 each-2005kW (2726bhp) Rolls Royce Marine AS-Norway AuxGen: 2 x 1440kW 440V 60Hz a.c, 2 x 260kW 440V 60Hz a.c Thrusters: 2 Thwart. CP thruster (f); 1 Thwart. CP thruster (a)
9424986 *PPOF* -	**SAVEIROS ATOBA** - **Wilson Sons Offshore SA** - *Rio de Janeiro* *Brazil* MMSI: 710000090 Official number: 3813868516	**2,429** 728 3,100	Class: LR ✠**100A1** SS 09/2013 offshore supply ship LI **LMC** **UMS** Eq.Ltr: T; Cable: 495.0/42.0 U3 (a)	**2008**-09 **Wilson, Sons SA — Guaruja** (Hull) Yd No: 101 **2008**-09 **B.V. Scheepswerf Damen — Gorinchem** Yd No: 552012 Loa 71.50 (BB) Br ex 16.04 Dght 6.200 Lbp 64.80 Br md 16.00 Dpth 7.50 Welded, 1 dk	**(B21A20S) Platform Supply Ship**	**4 diesel electric oil engines** driving 4 gen. each 1100kW 690V a.c Connecting to 2 elec. motors each (1500kW) driving 2 Directional propellers Total Power: 4,960kW (6,744hp) 11.8kn Caterpillar 3512B-TA 4 x Vee 4 Stroke 12 Cy. 170 x 190 each-1240kW (1686bhp) Caterpillar Inc-USA Thrusters: 2 Thwart. CP thruster (f)
9364332 *PPUD* -	**SAVEIROS FRAGATA** - **Wilson Sons Offshore SA** - SatCom: Inmarsat C 471011176 *Rio de Janeiro* *Brazil* MMSI: 710003090 Official number: 3810518239	**2,429** 728 3,249	Class: LR ✠**100A1** SS 03/2012 offshore supply ship LI **LMC** **UMS** Eq.Ltr: T; Cable: 495.0/42.0 U3 (a)	**2007**-03 **Wilson, Sons SA — Guaruja** (Hull) Yd No: 099 **2007**-03 **B.V. Scheepswerf Damen — Gorinchem** Yd No: 552004 Loa 71.85 (BB) Br ex 16.04 Dght 6.200 Lbp 64.88 Br md 16.00 Dpth 7.50 Welded, 1 dk	**(B21A20S) Platform Supply Ship**	**4 diesel electric oil engines** driving 4 gen. each 1100kW 440V a.c Connecting to 2 elec. motors each (1500kW) driving 2 Directional propellers Total Power: 4,960kW (6,744hp) 11.8kn Caterpillar 3512B-HD 4 x Vee 4 Stroke 12 Cy. 170 x 215 each-1240kW (1686bhp) Caterpillar Inc-USA Thrusters: 2 Thwart. CP thruster (f)

9258387 *PS5611* -	**SAVEIROS GAIVOTA** **Wilson Sons Offshore SA** - SatCom: Inmarsat C 471000071 *Rio de Janeiro* *Brazil* MMSI: 710001000 Official number: 4010812036	**1,851** 555 1,575	Class: LR ✠ **100A1** SS 05/2013 offshore supply ship ✠ **LMC** **UMS** Eq.Ltr: S; Cable: 467.5/38.0 U3 (a)	**2003-05 Wilson, Sons SA — Guaruja** Yd No: 098 Loa 62.40 Br ex 16.44 Dght 5.800 Lbp 57.45 Br md 16.00 Dpth 7.00 Welded, 1 dk	**(B21A2OS) Platform Supply Ship**	**2 oil engines** with clutches & sr geared to sc. shafts driving 2 CP propellers Total Power: 3,570kW (4,854hp) 12.0kn Bergens KRMB-8 2 x 4 Stroke 8 Cy. 250 x 300 each-1785kW (2427bhp) Rolls Royce Marine AS-Norway AuxGen: 2 x 1280kW 440V 60Hz a.c, 2 x 260kW 440V 60Hz a.c Thrusters: 2 Thwart. CP thruster (f); 1 Thwart. CP thruster (a)
9424962 *PPVP* -	**SAVEIROS PELICANO** **Wilson Sons Offshore SA** - *Rio de Janeiro* *Brazil* MMSI: 710003820 Official number: 3810521841	**2,429** 728 3,249	Class: LR ✠ **100A1** SS 05/2013 offshore supply ship LI **LMC** **UMS** Eq.Ltr: T; Cable: 495.0/42.0 U3 (a)	**2008-05 Wilson, Sons SA — Guaruja** (Hull) Yd No: 100 **2008-05 B.V. Scheepswerf Damen — Gorinchem** Yd No: 552011 Loa 71.85 (BB) Br ex 16.04 Dght 6.000 Lbp 64.80 Br md 16.00 Dpth 7.50 Welded, 1 dk	**(B21A2OS) Platform Supply Ship**	**4 diesel electric oil engines** driving 4 gen. each 1100kW 690V a.c Connecting to 2 elec. motors each (1500kW) driving 2 Directional propellers Total Power: 4,960kW (6,744hp) 11.8kn Caterpillar 3512B-TA 4 x Vee 4 Stroke 12 Cy. 170 x 190 each-1240kW (1686bhp) Caterpillar Inc-USA Thrusters: 2 Thwart. CP thruster (f)
8033223 *UGUZ* -	**SAVELOVO** **Alyye Parusa Co Ltd** - *Petropavlovsk-Kamchatskiy* *Russia* MMSI: 273847110 Official number: 811623	**782** 234 332	Class: RS	**1981 Zavod "Leninskaya Kuznitsa" — Kiyev** Yd No: 253 Loa 53.75 (BB) Br ex 10.72 Dght 4.333 Lbp 47.92 Br md 10.50 Dpth 6.02 Welded, 1 dk	**(B11A2FG) Factory Stern Trawler** Ins: 218 Compartments: 1 Ho, ER 1 Ha: (1.6 x 1.6) Derricks: 2x1.5t Ice Capable	**1 oil engine** driving 1 CP propeller Total Power: 971kW (1,320hp) 12.8kn S.K.L. 8NVD48A-2U 1 x 4 Stroke 8 Cy. 320 x 480 971kW (1320bhp) VEB Schwermaschinenbau "KarlLiebknecht" (SKL)-Magdeburg AuxGen: 1 x 300kW a.c, 3 x 160kW a.c Fuel: 164.0 (d.f.)
9427316 *V7WH4* -	**SAVINA** **Savina Transportation Corp** Neda Maritime Agency Co Ltd *Majuro* *Marshall Islands* MMSI: 538004301 Official number: 4301	**91,374** 57,770 176,382 T/cm 120.6	Class: BV	**2011-12 Shanghai Waigaoqiao Shipbuilding Co Ltd — Shanghai** (Hull) Yd No: 1135 Loa 292.00 (BB) Br ex 45.05 Dght 18.323 Lbp 282.00 Br md 45.00 Dpth 24.80 Welded, 1 dk	**(A21A2BC) Bulk Carrier** Grain: 194,179; Bale: 183,425 Compartments: 9 Ho, ER 9 Ha: ER	**1 oil engine** driving 1 FP propeller Total Power: 16,860kW (22,923hp) 14.0kn MAN-B&W 6S70MC 1 x 2 Stroke 6 Cy. 700 x 2674 16860kW (22923bhp) CSSC MES Diesel Co Ltd-China AuxGen: 3 x 900kW 60Hz a.c Fuel: 4700.0
7741354 - -	**SAVINSK** - - -	**774** 232 332	Class: (RS)	**1979-06 Zavod "Leninskaya Kuznitsa" — Kiyev** Yd No: 241 Loa 53.73 (BB) Br ex 10.72 Dght 4.290 Lbp 47.92 Br md - Dpth 6.00 Welded, 1 dk	**(B11A2FS) Stern Trawler** Ins: 220 Compartments: 1 Ho, ER 2 Ha: 2 (1.6 x 1.6) Derricks: 2x3.3t Ice Capable	**1 oil engine** driving 1 CP propeller Total Power: 971kW (1,320hp) 12.5kn S.K.L. 8NVD48A-2U 1 x 4 Stroke 8 Cy. 320 x 480 971kW (1320bhp) VEB Schwermaschinenbau "KarlLiebknecht" (SKL)-Magdeburg Thrusters: 1 Thwart. FP thruster (f); 1 Tunnel thruster (a)
8900440 *IVXN* -	**SAVIO** **Secomar SpA** - *Ravenna* *Italy* MMSI: 247180600 Official number: 10694	*374* 211 662	Class: RI	**1989-06 Cantiere Navale di Pesaro SpA (CNP) — Pesaro** Yd No: 63 Loa 39.52 Br ex 10.02 Dght 2.709 Lbp 38.14 Br md 10.00 Dpth 3.20 Welded, 1 dk	**(A13B2TU) Tanker (unspecified)** Liq: 749; Liq (Oil): 749 Compartments: 9 Ta, ER	**2 oil engines** driving 2 Directional propellers Total Power: 440kW (598hp) 8.4kn MWM TBD234V6 2 x Vee 4 Stroke 6 Cy. 128 x 140 each-220kW (299bhp) Motoren Werke Mannheim AG (MWM)-West Germany
9076325 *JZDJ* -	**SAVIOUR** *ex* Clipper Falcon *-2013* *ex* Bg Fighter *-2012* *ex* CEC Fighter *-2011* *ex* Arktis Fighter *-2002* *ex* CEC Fighter *-2001* *ex* Arktis Fighter *-2001* *ex* Ville de Rodae *-1996* *ex* Arktis Fighter *-1996* **PT Multi Synergy Line** - *Indonesia* MMSI: 525024119	**4,980** 2,230 7,121 T/cm 16.6	Class: (LR) (BV) Classed LR until 15/5/12	**1994-04 Aarhus Flydedok A/S — Aarhus** Yd No: 208 Loa 101.10 (BB) Br ex 19.20 Dght 7.320 Lbp 93.70 Br md 18.80 Dpth 9.30 Welded, 1 dk	**(A31A2GX) General Cargo Ship** Grain: 8,020 TEU 444 C.Ho 154/20' C.Dk 290/20' incl. 50 ref C. Compartments: 1 Ho, ER 1 Ha: (58.9 x 15.2)ER Cranes: 2x70t	**1 oil engine** with flexible couplings & reduction geared to sc. shaft driving 1 CP propeller Total Power: 4,502kW (6,121hp) 14.5kn MaK 6M552C 1 x 4 Stroke 6 Cy. 450 x 520 4502kW (6121bhp) Krupp MaK Maschinenbau GmbH-Kiel AuxGen: 1 x 600kW 220/440V 60Hz a.c, 3 x 344kW 220/440V 60Hz a.c Boilers: TOH New (o.f.) 7.1kgf/cm² (7.0bar), TOH (ex.g.) 10.2kgf/cm² (10.0bar) Thrusters: 1 Thwart. FP thruster (f)
7368308 - -	**SAVITRI** *ex* Nand Maina *-1986* *ex* Seeb *-1976* **Mercator Ltd** Mercator Shipping & Ship Management Ltd *Mumbai* *India* Official number: 1727	*499* 408 825	Class: IR (LR) ✠ Classed LR until 5/92	**1974-07 B.V. Scheepswerf Schouten Muiden — Muiden** (Aft & pt cargo sections) Yd No: 809 **1974-07 Scheepsbouw Hoja B.V. — Aalst (Nl)** (Fwd & pt cargo sections) Yd No: 1742 Loa 50.02 Br ex 9.61 Dght 2.877 Lbp 48.37 Br md 9.50 Dpth 3.51 Welded, 1 dk	**(A31A2GX) General Cargo Ship**	**2 oil engines** driving 2 Directional propellers Total Power: 772kW (1,050hp) G.M. (Detroit Diesel) 12V-71-TI 2 x Vee 2 Stroke 12 Cy. 108 x 127 each-386kW (525bhp) General Motors Corp-USA AuxGen: 1 x 40kW 220/380V 50Hz a.c
9090022 *AUKE* -	**SAVITRI BAI PHULE** **Government of The Republic of India (Coast Guard)** - *India* Official number: 235	**350** 105 54	Class: (AB) (IR)	**2006-10 Goa Shipyard Ltd. — Goa** Yd No: 1192 Loa 48.14 Br ex 7.51 Dght 2.100 Lbp 44.12 Br md 7.50 Dpth 4.35 Welded, 1 dk	**(B34H2SQ) Patrol Vessel** Hull Material: Aluminium Alloy	**3 oil engines** reduction geared to sc. shafts driving 3 Water jets Total Power: 8,160kW (11,094hp) M.T.U. 16V4000M90 3 x Vee 4 Stroke 16 Cy. 165 x 190 each-2720kW (3698bhp) MTU Friedrichshafen GmbH-Friedrichshafen AuxGen: 2 x 120kW 415V 50Hz a.c Fuel: 35.0 (d.f.)
9167253 *EPBL6* -	**SAVIZ** *ex* Azalea *-2012* *ex* Lantana *-2011* *ex* Ocean Candle *-2009* *ex* Iran Lorestan *-2008* **Oghiaanous Khoroushan Shipping Lines Co of Kish** Rahbaran Omid Darya Ship Management Co *Bandar Abbas* *Iran* MMSI: 422026600 Official number: 1043	**16,694** 8,416 23,176	Class: (GL) (NV)	**1999-02 Guangzhou Shipyard International Co Ltd — Guangzhou GD** Yd No: 6130005 Loa 174.00 (BB) Br ex - Dght 9.500 Lbp 162.00 Br md 26.00 Dpth 13.90 Welded, 2 dks	**(A31A2GX) General Cargo Ship** Grain: 30,014; Bale: 29,114 TEU 980 C Ho 486 TEU C Dk 494 TEU incl 42 ref C. Compartments: 5 Ho, ER, 5 Tw Dk 9 Ha: (12.7 x 12.7)8 (19.1 x 10.1)ER Cranes: 4x30t	**1 oil engine** driving 1 FP propeller Total Power: 9,484kW (12,894hp) 16.9kn B&W 6S50MC-C 1 x 2 Stroke 6 Cy. 500 x 2000 9484kW (12894bhp) Hudong Heavy Machinery Co Ltd-China AuxGen: 3 x 600kW 220/440V 60Hz a.c Fuel: 159.0 (d.f.) (Heating Coils) 1459.0 (r.f.) 37.3pd
8730326 - -	**SAVONA** **State Enterprise Mariupol Sea Commercial Port** - *Mariupol* *Ukraine* MMSI: 272001900 Official number: 892495	**205** 62 34	Class: (RS)	**1989-10 Ilyichyovskiy Sudoremontnyy Zavod im. "50-letiya SSSR" — Ilyichyovsk** Yd No: 20 Loa 37.60 Br ex 7.21 Dght 1.690 Lbp 34.03 Br md - Dpth 2.90 Welded	**(A37B2PS) Passenger Ship** Passengers: unberthed: 215	**3 oil engines** reduction geared to sc. shafts driving 3 FP propellers Total Power: 960kW (1,306hp) 16.5kn Barnaultransmash 3D6C 2 x 4 Stroke 6 Cy. 150 x 180 each-110kW (150bhp) Barnaultransmash-Barnaul Zvezda M401A-1 1 x Vee 4 Stroke 12 Cy. 180 x 200 740kW (1006bhp) "Zvezda"-Leningrad
9328699 *9MQK2* -	**SAVVY** **HL Adamas Sdn Bhd** Hong Lam Marine Pte Ltd *Port Klang* *Malaysia* MMSI: 533180011 Official number: 334568	**6,694** 3,785 10,327 T/cm 19.9	Class: NK	**2005-01 K.K. Miura Zosensho — Saiki** Yd No: 1287 Loa 120.00 (BB) Br ex 20.52 Dght 7.614 Lbp 114.60 Br md 20.50 Dpth 10.00 Welded, 1 dk	**(A13B2TP) Products Tanker** Double Hull (13F) Liq: 12,573; Liq (Oil): 12,830 Compartments: 10 Wing Ta, 1 Slop Ta, ER 2 Cargo Pump (s): 2x1000m³/hr Manifold: Bow/CM: 65.2m	**1 oil engine** driving 1 FP propeller Total Power: 2,942kW (4,000hp) 12.0kn Hanshin LH46L 1 x 4 Stroke 6 Cy. 460 x 880 2942kW (4000bhp) The Hanshin Diesel Works Ltd-Japan AuxGen: 2 x 250kW a.c Thrusters: 1 Tunnel thruster (f) Fuel: 65.0 (d.f.) 312.0 (r.f.)
9114749 *E3GA* -	**SAWA** **Assab Port Administration** - *Eritrea*	**198** 59 361	Class: (LR) ✠ Classed LR until 28/3/01	**1999-06 Stocznia Tczew Sp z oo — Tczew** (Hull) **1999-06 B.V. Scheepswerf Damen — Gorinchem** Yd No: 8802 Loa 25.86 Br ex 8.94 Dght 3.655 Lbp 20.97 Br md 8.90 Dpth 4.30 Welded, 1 dk	**(B32A2ST) Tug**	**2 oil engines** reduction geared to sc. shafts driving 2 Directional propellers Total Power: 1,940kW (2,638hp) 11.5kn Cummins KTA-38-M2 2 x Vee 4 Stroke 12 Cy. 159 x 159 each-970kW (1319bhp) Cummins Engine Co Inc-USA AuxGen: 2 x 51kW 400V 50Hz a.c
9171565 *TJPAK* -	**SAWA I** **Societe Camerounaise de Leasing Maritime** - *Douala* *Cameroon*	**202** 69 -		**1998-03 Factoria Naval de Marin S.A. — Marin** Yd No: 81 Loa 27.50 Br ex - Dght 3.000 Lbp 22.50 Br md 7.20 Dpth 3.35 Welded, 1 dk	**(B11A2FS) Stern Trawler** Compartments: 1 Ho 1 Ha:	**1 oil engine** reduction geared to sc. shaft driving 1 FP propeller Total Power: 519kW (706hp) 9.7kn Caterpillar 3508TA 1 x Vee 4 Stroke 8 Cy. 170 x 190 519kW (706bhp) Caterpillar Inc-USA

IMO / Call sign / Flag	Name / Owner / Port	Tonnage	Class	Builder / Dimensions	Type	Machinery
9171577 *TJPAL* -	**SAWA II** **Societe Camerounaise de Leasing Maritime** - *Douala* *Cameroon*	**202** 69 -		**1998-04 Factoria Naval de Marin S.A. — Marin** Yd No: 82 Loa 27.50 Br ex - Dght 3.000 Lbp 22.50 Br md 7.20 Dpth 3.35 Welded, 1 dk	**(B11A2FS) Stern Trawler** Compartments: 1 Ho 1 Ha:	**1 oil engine** reduction geared to sc. shaft driving 1 FP propeller Total Power: 519kW (706hp) 9.7kn Caterpillar 3508TA 1 x Vee 4 Stroke 8 Cy. 170 x 190 519kW (706bhp) Caterpillar Inc-USA
9171589 *TJPAT* -	**SAWA III** **Societe Camerounaise de Leasing Maritime** - *Douala* *Cameroon*	**202** 69 -		**1998-04 Factoria Naval de Marin S.A. — Marin** Yd No: 83 Loa 27.50 Br ex - Dght 3.000 Lbp 22.50 Br md 7.20 Dpth 3.35 Welded, 1 dk	**(B11A2FS) Stern Trawler** Compartments: 1 Ho 1 Ha:	**1 oil engine** reduction geared to sc. shaft driving 1 FP propeller Total Power: 519kW (706hp) 9.7kn Caterpillar 3508TA 1 x Vee 4 Stroke 8 Cy. 170 x 190 519kW (706bhp) Caterpillar Inc-USA
9171591 *TJPAU* -	**SAWA IV** **Societe Camerounaise de Leasing Maritime** - *Douala* *Cameroon*	**202** 69 -		**1998-04 Factoria Naval de Marin S.A. — Marin** Yd No: 84 Loa 27.50 Br ex - Dght 3.000 Lbp 22.50 Br md 7.20 Dpth 3.35 Welded, 1 dk	**(B11A2FS) Stern Trawler** Compartments: 1 Ho 1 Ha:	**1 oil engine** reduction geared to sc. shaft driving 1 FP propeller Total Power: 519kW (706hp) 9.7kn Caterpillar 3508TA 1 x Vee 4 Stroke 8 Cy. 170 x 190 519kW (706bhp) Caterpillar Inc-USA
7528726 *A9D2436* -	**SAWAD** *ex Arad -1979* **Arab Shipbuilding & Repair Yard Co (ASRY)** - *Bahrain* *Bahrain* Official number: A1428	*204* - 134	Class: LR ✠ **100A1** SS 04/2013 tug Arabian Gulf and Gulf of Oman service, west of a line from Muscat to Chah Bahar ✠ **LMC** Eq.Ltr: (F) D; Cable: U2	**1976-09 Estaleiros Sao Jacinto S.A. — Aveiro** Yd No: 117 Loa 33.38 Br ex 8.97 Dght 3.825 Lbp 30.00 Br md 8.50 Dpth 4.30 Welded, 1 dk	**(B32A2ST) Tug**	**1 oil engine** reverse reduction geared to sc. shaft driving 1 FP propeller Total Power: 1,765kW (2,400hp) MWM TBD500-8 1 x 4 Stroke 8 Cy. 360 x 450 1765kW (2400bhp) Motoren Werke Mannheim AG (MWM)-West Germany AuxGen: 1 x 48kW 380/220V 50Hz a.c, 1 x 32kW 380/220V 50Hz a.c
8224626 - -	**SAWAHIL-140** - **Government of The State of Kuwait (Ministry of Interior)** - *Kuwait*	*100* - -		**1984-02 Swiftships Maroil (S) Pte Ltd — Singapore** Yd No: 011 Loa - Br ex - Dght - Lbp - Br md - Dpth - Welded, 1 dk	**(B34M2QS) Search & Rescue Vessel**	**2 oil engines** geared to sc. shafts driving 2 FP propellers Total Power: 1,956kW (2,660hp) M.T.U. 12V396TC82 2 x Vee 4 Stroke 12 Cy. 165 x 185 each-978kW (1330bhp) MTU Friedrichshafen GmbH-Friedrichshafen
8224638 - -	**SAWAHIL-145** - **Government of The State of Kuwait (Ministry of Interior)** - *Kuwait*	*100* - -		**1984-02 Swiftships Maroil (S) Pte Ltd — Singapore** Yd No: SM012 Loa - Br ex - Dght - Lbp - Br md - Dpth - Welded, 1 dk	**(B34M2QS) Search & Rescue Vessel**	**2 oil engines** geared to sc. shafts driving 2 FP propellers Total Power: 1,956kW (2,660hp) M.T.U. 12V396TC82 2 x Vee 4 Stroke 12 Cy. 165 x 185 each-978kW (1330bhp) MTU Friedrichshafen GmbH-Friedrichshafen
8224640 - -	**SAWAHIL-150** - **Government of The State of Kuwait (Ministry of Interior)** - *Kuwait*	*100* - -		**1984-02 Swiftships Maroil (S) Pte Ltd — Singapore** Yd No: 013 Loa - Br ex - Dght - Lbp - Br md - Dpth - Welded, 1 dk	**(B34M2QS) Search & Rescue Vessel**	**2 oil engines** geared to sc. shafts driving 2 FP propellers Total Power: 1,956kW (2,660hp) M.T.U. 12V396TC82 2 x Vee 4 Stroke 12 Cy. 165 x 185 each-978kW (1330bhp) MTU Friedrichshafen GmbH-Friedrichshafen
9692234 *JZNM* -	**SAWAHLUNTO** **PT Indobaruna Bulk Transport** - *Jakarta* *Indonesia* MMSI: 525019655 Official number: 4920	**6,943** 2,179 9,649	Class: NK	**2014-01 Fukuoka Shipbuilding Co Ltd — Fukuoka FO** Yd No: 1298 Loa 109.90 (BB) Br ex - Dght 6.518 Lbp 106.00 Br md 23.80 Dpth 9.00 Welded, 1 dk	**(A24A2BT) Cement Carrier**	**1 oil engine** reduction geared to sc. shaft driving 1 Propeller Total Power: 4,020kW (5,466hp) Daihatsu 8DCM-32 1 x 4 Stroke 8 Cy. 320 x 400 4020kW (5466bhp) Daihatsu Diesel Manufacturing Co Lt-Japan
8112354 - -	**SAWAKIN** **Sea Ports Corp** - *Port Sudan* *Sudan*	*125* 37 52	Class: (LR) (BV) ✠ Classed LR until 14/2/88	**1986-07 Scheepswerf Aalst/'t Gilde B.V. — Aalst (Nl)** (Hull) **1986-07 B.V. Scheepswerf Damen — Gorinchem** Yd No: 2707 Loa 25.66 Br ex 6.94 Dght 2.909 Lbp 23.80 Br md 6.61 Dpth 3.43 Welded, 1 dk	**(B32A2ST) Tug**	**2 oil engines** with clutches, flexible couplings & sr reverse geared to sc. shafts driving 2 FP propellers Total Power: 1,176kW (1,598hp) MAN 6L20/27 2 x 4 Stroke 6 Cy. 200 x 270 each-588kW (799bhp) MAN B&W Diesel GmbH-Augsburg AuxGen: 2 x 38kW 220/380V 50Hz a.c
9036698 *JJ3781* -	**SAWANISHI MARU No. 3** **Sawanishi Kensetsu KK** - *Himeji, Hyogo* *Japan* Official number: 132280	*493* - 1,303		**1991-11 Hitachi Zosen Mukaishima Marine Co Ltd — Onomichi HS** Yd No: 52 Loa 65.60 Br ex 13.22 Dght 4.120 Lbp 60.00 Br md 13.20 Dpth 6.20 Welded, 1 dk	**(B33A2DU) Dredger (unspecified)** Grain: 944 Compartments: 1 Ho, ER 1 Ha: ER	**1 oil engine** with clutches & reverse geared to sc. shaft driving 1 FP propeller Total Power: 736kW (1,001hp) Hanshin 6LU35G 1 x 4 Stroke 6 Cy. 350 x 550 736kW (1001bhp) The Hanshin Diesel Works Ltd-Japan
9122526 *D7LJ* -	**SAWASDEE BANGKOK** *ex Helvetia -2012 ex CMA CGM Serengeti -2009* *ex Helvetia -2009 ex TS Shanghai -2008* *ex Helvetia -2004 ex Columbus Pacific -2003* *ex Sea Amazon -1998 ex Helvetia -1996* *ex Columbus Olinda -1996* *launched as Helvetia -1996* **Sinokor Merchant Marine Co Ltd** - *Jeju* *South Korea* MMSI: 441855000 Official number: JJR121029	**15,859** 8,023 20,084	Class: GL KR	**1996-04 Blohm + Voss AG — Hamburg** Yd No: 963 Loa 166.87 (BB) Br ex - Dght 9.600 Lbp 156.68 Br md 27.40 Dpth 13.20 Welded, 1 dk	**(A33A2CC) Container Ship (Fully Cellular)** TEU 1519 C Ho 588 TEU C Dk 931 TEU incl 150 ref C. Compartments: 5 Cell Ho, ER 8 Ha: (12.7 x 8.0) (12.8 x 18.1)6 (12.8 x 23.1)ER Cranes: 2x40t,1x36t	**1 oil engine** driving 1 CP propeller Total Power: 12,365kW (16,811hp) 19.0kn Mitsubishi 7UEC60LS 1 x 2 Stroke 7 Cy. 600 x 2200 12365kW (16811bhp) Mitsubishi Heavy Industries Ltd-Japan AuxGen: 1 x 1300kW 440/220V 60Hz a.c, 2 x 720kW 440/220V 60Hz a.c Thrusters: 1 Thwart. CP thruster (f) Fuel: 216.0 (d.f.) 1493.0 (r.f.) 56.0pd
9119660 *DSRK2* -	**SAWASDEE HONGKONG** *ex San Felipe -2013 ex Puerto Limon -2004* *ex San Felipe -2002 ex Columbus Mexico -2001* *ex Lykes Eagle -2000 ex Ivaran Eagle -1999* *ex San Felipe -1998* **Sinokor Merchant Marine Co Ltd** - *Jeju* *South Korea* MMSI: 441888000	**15,859** 8,023 20,058 T/cm 37.0	Class: KR (GL)	**1996-12 Thyssen Nordseewerke GmbH — Emden** Yd No: 513 Loa 166.87 (BB) Br ex 27.62 Dght 9.620 Lbp 156.68 Br md 27.40 Dpth 13.20 Welded, 1 dk	**(A33A2CC) Container Ship (Fully Cellular)** TEU 1512 C Ho 588 TEU C Dk 924 TEU incl 150 ref C. Compartments: 5 Cell Ho, ER 8 Ha: ER Cranes: 2x40t Ice Capable	**1 oil engine** driving 1 CP propeller Total Power: 12,355kW (16,798hp) 19.6kn Mitsubishi 7UEC60LS 1 x 2 Stroke 7 Cy. 600 x 2200 12355kW (16798bhp) Mitsubishi Heavy Industries Ltd-Japan AuxGen: 1 x 1300kW a.c, 2 x 720kW a.c Thrusters: 1 Thwart. CP thruster (f) Fuel: 217.0 (d.f.) 1561.0 (r.f.) 51.0pd
9081019 *DSRJ9* -	**SAWASDEE JAKARTA** *ex San Francisco -2013 ex Lykes Pilot -2006* *ex Maersk Apapa -2004 ex San Francisco -2001* *ex Lykes Raven -2000 ex Ivaran Raven -1999* *ex San Francisco -1998* *ex Contship Brasil -1997 ex Francisco -1996* **Sinokor Merchant Marine Co Ltd** - *Jeju* *South Korea* MMSI: 441887000 Official number: JJR-131010	**15,741** 8,023 20,072 T/cm 35.4	Class: GL KR	**1996-04 Thyssen Nordseewerke GmbH — Emden** Yd No: 511 Loa 166.62 (BB) Br ex 27.85 Dght 9.600 Lbp 156.00 Br md 27.40 Dpth 13.20 Welded, 1 dk	**(A33A2CC) Container Ship (Fully Cellular)** TEU 1512 C Ho 588 TEU C Dk 924 TEU incl 150 ref C. Compartments: ER, 5 Cell Ho 9 Ha: ER Cranes: 3x40t	**1 oil engine** driving 1 CP propeller Total Power: 12,355kW (16,798hp) 19.0kn Mitsubishi 7UEC60LS 1 x 2 Stroke 7 Cy. 600 x 2200 12355kW (16798bhp) Mitsubishi Heavy Industries Ltd-Japan AuxGen: 1 x 1300kW 440V 60Hz a.c, 2 x 720kW 440V 60Hz a.c Thrusters: 1 Thwart. CP thruster (f) Fuel: 217.0 (d.f.) 1493.0 (r.f.) 40.0pd
9046253 *DSRJ6* -	**SAWASDEE LAEMCHABANG** *ex San Clemente -2012* *ex Canmar Fortune -2005* *ex San Clemente -2004 ex Cielo del Cile -2003* *ex San Clemente -2001* *ex Columbus Bahia -2001* *ex San Clemente -1999* **Sinokor Merchant Marine Co Ltd** Fair Shipmanagement Co Ltd *Jeju* *South Korea* MMSI: 441884000 Official number: JJR-121064	**15,707** 7,787 20,528 T/cm 37.0	Class: KR (GL)	**1994-12 Thyssen Nordseewerke GmbH — Emden** Yd No: 505 Loa 166.81 (BB) Br ex 27.62 Dght 9.600 Lbp 156.68 Br md 27.40 Dpth 13.20 Welded, 1 dk	**(A33A2CC) Container Ship (Fully Cellular)** TEU 1512 C Ho 588 TEU C Dk 924 TEU incl 150 ref C. Compartments: 5 Cell Ho, ER 9 Ha: ER Cranes: 2x40t Ice Capable	**1 oil engine** driving 1 CP propeller Total Power: 12,355kW (16,798hp) 19.5kn Mitsubishi 7UEC60LS 1 x 2 Stroke 7 Cy. 600 x 2200 12355kW (16798bhp) Mitsubishi Heavy Industries Ltd-Japan AuxGen: 1 x 1300kW 220/440V a.c, 2 x 720kW 220/440V a.c Thrusters: 1 Thwart. CP thruster (f) Fuel: 217.3 (d.f.) 1464.3 (r.f.) 40.0pd

9081021 *DSRJ7* -	**SAWASDEE SINGAPORE** *ex* San Cristobal *-2012* *ex* Maersk Abidjan *-2004* *ex* San Cristobal *-2001* *ex* Lykes Hawk *-2000* *ex* San Cristobal *-1999* *ex* CGM Saint Exupery *-1998* *ex* Equinox *-1997* *ex* San Cristobal *-1995* **Chokang Shipping Co Ltd** Fair Shipmanagement Co Ltd *Jeju* *South Korea* MMSI: 441885000 Official number: JJR-121062	**15,707** 7,787 20,156 T/cm 36.5	Class: KR (GL)	**1995**-12 **Thyssen Nordseewerke GmbH — Emden** Yd No: 510 Loa 166.62 (BB) Br ex - Dght 9.600 Lbp 156.70 Br md 27.40 Dpth 13.20 Welded, 1 dk	**(A33A2CC) Container Ship (Fully Cellular)** TEU 1512 C Ho 588 TEU C Dk 924 TEU incl 150 ref C. Compartments: 5 Cell Ho, ER 8 Ha: (12.7 x 8.0) (12.8 x 18.1)6 (12.8 x 23.1)ER Cranes: 2x40t Ice Capable	**1 oil engine** driving 1 CP propeller Total Power: 12,355kW (16,798hp) 19.7kn Mitsubishi 7UEC60LS 1 x 2 Stroke 7 Cy. 600 x 2200 12355kW (16798bhp) Mitsubishi Heavy Industries Ltd-Japan AuxGen: 1 x 1300kW a.c, 2 x 720kW a.c Thrusters: 1 Thwart. CP thruster (f) Fuel: 218.0 (d.f.) 1493.0 (r.f.) 51.0pd
8911255 *POOF* -	**SAWITA** *ex* New Hoyo *-2012* **PT Bukit Merapin Nusantara Lines** - *Tanjung Priok* *Indonesia* MMSI: 525005055	*699* 210 371	Class: KI	**1990**-01 **Usuki Shipyard Co Ltd — Usuki OT** Yd No: 1601 Loa 71.50 (BB) Br ex 13.02 Dght 3.300 Lbp 64.32 Br md 12.60 Dpth 4.45 Welded, 2 dks	**(A36A2PR) Passenger/Ro-Ro Ship (Vehicles)** Passengers: unberthed: 424 Bow ramp Len: 4.90 Wid: 4.00 Swl: - Stern ramp Len: 4.90 Wid: 4.00 Swl: - Cars: 43	**2 oil engines** with flexible couplings & reverse reduction geared to sc. shafts driving 2 FP propellers Total Power: 2,942kW (4,000hp) 16.0kn Daihatsu 6DLM-28S 2 x 4 Stroke 6 Cy. 280 x 360 each-1471kW (2000bhp) Daihatsu Diesel Manufacturing Co Lt-Japan AuxGen: 2 x 266kW 225V a.c Thrusters: 1 Thwart. CP thruster (f)
7522356 - -	**SAWITTO** *ex* Enterprise *-2004* *ex* Consort Jupiter *-1992* *ex* Bintang Jaya II *-1990* *ex* Ryuwa Maru *-1987* **Fieldhead Corporation Sdn Bhd** -	**848** 543 1,370 T/cm 5.2	Class: (NK)	**1975**-12 **Sasaki Shipbuilding Co Ltd — Osakikamijima HS** Yd No: 300 Loa 57.96 Br ex 10.01 Dght 4.462 Lbp 57.00 Br md 9.99 Dpth 5.00 Welded, 1 dk	**(A13B2TP) Products Tanker** Liq: 1,685; Liq (Oil): 1,685 Compartments: 8 Ta, ER 2 Cargo Pump (s): 2x500m³/hr Manifold: Bow/CM: 34m	**1 oil engine** driving 1 FP propeller Total Power: 1,103kW (1,500hp) 11.0kn Makita GNLH630 1 x 4 Stroke 6 Cy. 300 x 480 1103kW (1500bhp) Makita Diesel Co Ltd-Japan AuxGen: 2 x 72kW Fuel: 4.5 (d.f.) 25.5 (r.f.) 2.0pd
9391244 *A4BA5* -	**SAWQRAH** **Government of The Sultanate of Oman (Ministry of Economy)** National Ferries Co SAOC *Port Sultan Qaboos* *Oman* MMSI: 461000093	**1,228** 368 68	Class: NV (RI)	**2010**-04 **Rodriquez Cantieri Navali SpA — Messina** Yd No: 354 Loa 52.00 Br ex - Dght 1.900 Lbp 45.50 Br md 15.50 Dpth 5.20 Welded, 1 dk	**(A36A2PR) Passenger/Ro-Ro Ship (Vehicles)** Hull Material: Aluminium Alloy Passengers: 100	**4 oil engines** reduction geared to sc. shafts driving 4 Water jets Total Power: 9,860kW (13,404hp) 40.5kn M.T.U. 16V4000M71 4 x Vee 4 Stroke 16 Cy. 165 x 190 each-2465kW (3351bhp) MTU Friedrichshafen GmbH-Friedrichshafen
9227132 *CNA2652* -	**SAWSANE** *ex* Big Fair 307 *-2000* **Offshore Maroc SA** - *Casablanca* *Morocco* MMSI: 242064000	**203** 61 399	Class: LR (NV) **✠100A1** SS 08/2010 tug **LMC**	**2000**-09 **Zhuhai Shipbuilding Industry Corp — Zhuhai GD** Yd No: 148 Loa 26.80 Br ex 8.40 Dght 3.000 Lbp 24.10 Br md 8.00 Dpth 3.80 Welded, 1 dk	**(B32A2ST) Tug**	**2 oil engines** geared to sc. shafts driving 2 FP propellers Total Power: 1,766kW (2,402hp) Cummins KTA-38-M2 2 x Vee 4 Stroke 12 Cy. 159 x 159 each-883kW (1201bhp) Chongqing Cummins Engine Co Ltd-China
9351373 *PNBK* -	**SAWU SEA** *ex* Team Partner *-2009* *ex* Sloman Supplier *-2009* *ex* S. Arctic *-2009* *ex* Team Partner *-2008* **PT Amas Iscindo Utama** Marco Shipping Co (Pte) Ltd *Jakarta* *Indonesia* MMSI: 525016541	**8,472** 4,223 11,172	Class: AB KI (LR) (GL) Classed LR until 3/12/11	**2008**-05 **YS Heavy Industries Co Ltd — Yeosu** Yd No: H506 Loa 129.41 (BB) Br ex - Dght 8.700 Lbp 120.60 Br md 19.00 Dpth 11.65 Welded, 1 dk	**(A31A2GX) General Cargo Ship** Double Hull Grain: 13,800 TEU 676 C Ho 272 TEU C Dk 404 TEU incl 60 ref C. Compartments: 2 Ho, ER 2 Ha: (58.1 x 15.6)ER (18.9 x 15.6) Cranes: 2x60t	**1 oil engine** reduction geared to sc. shaft driving 1 CP propeller Total Power: 6,000kW (8,158hp) 16.0kn MaK 6M43C 1 x 4 Stroke 6 Cy. 430 x 610 6000kW (8158bhp) Caterpillar Motoren GmbH & Co. KG-Germany AuxGen: 1 x 700kW 450V a.c, 3 x 360kW 450V a.c Thrusters: 1 Tunnel thruster (f) Fuel: 170.0 (d.f.) 801.0 (r.f.)
9201035 *SKHW* -	**SAXAREN** *ex* Waxholm *-1999* **Waxholms Angfartygs AB** - *Vaxholm* *Sweden* MMSI: 265512110	**274** 112 30		**1999**-04 **Batservice Holding AS — Mandal** Yd No: 20 Loa 37.35 Br ex - Dght - Lbp 35.00 Br md 7.50 Dpth 2.78 Welded	**(A37B2PS) Passenger Ship** Hull Material: Aluminium Alloy Passengers: unberthed: 340	**2 oil engines** with clutches, flexible couplings & sr geared to sc. shafts driving 2 CP propellers Total Power: 1,220kW (1,658hp) 18.0kn Deutz TBD616V12 2 x Vee 4 Stroke 12 Cy. 132 x 160 each-610kW (829bhp) Deutz AG-Koeln AuxGen: 2 x 60kW 400V 50Hz a.c Fuel: 6.0 (d.f.)
6811310 *TFPF* SH 050	**SAXHAMAR** *ex* Sjofn *-2006* *ex* Saeljon *-2006* *ex* Sigurdur Thorleifsson *-2006* *ex* Hrafn Sveinbjarnarson *-1990* **Utnes Ehf** - *Rif* *Iceland* MMSI: 251084110 Official number: 1028	**391** 115 -		**1967 VEB Elbewerft — Boizenburg** Loa 34.90 Br ex 7.22 Dght 2.699 Lbp 29.60 Br md 7.19 Dpth 3.61 Welded, 1 dk	**(B11B2FV) Fishing Vessel**	**1 oil engine** geared to sc. shaft driving 1 FP propeller Total Power: 485kW (659hp) Blackstone ERS8M 1 x 4 Stroke 8 Cy. 222 x 292 485kW (659bhp) Lister Blackstone Marine Ltd.-Dursley
8733263 *ZR4107* -	**SAXON** **Sceptre Fishing (Pty) Ltd & Saxon Offshore Fishing (Pty) Ltd** - *Cape Town* *South Africa* MMSI: 601500000 Official number: 10308	*269* 80 -		**2003**-01 **Tallie Marine Pty Ltd — St Helena Bay** Loa 26.73 Br ex - Dght - Lbp - Br md 8.50 Dpth 4.34 Bonded, 1 dk	**(B11B2FV) Fishing Vessel** Hull Material: Reinforced Plastic	**1 oil engine** driving 1 Propeller
5314987 *VJT5748* -	**SAXON ONWARD** **Norman Brinkman** - SatCom: Inmarsat C 450300258 *Port Adelaide, SA* *Australia* MMSI: 503316000 Official number: 301828	*209* 66 -	Class: (LR) ✠Classed LR until 19/1/83	**1960**-05 **J. S. Doig (Grimsby) Ltd. — Grimsby** Yd No: 67 L reg 32.16 Br ex 7.12 Dght - Lbp 31.70 Br md 7.01 Dpth 3.43 Riveted\Welded	**(B11A2FT) Trawler**	**1 oil engine** with flexible couplings & sr reverse geared to sc. shaft driving 1 FP propeller Total Power: 482kW (655hp) 12.5kn Ruston 5ATXM 1 x 4 Stroke 5 Cy. 318 x 368 482kW (655bhp) Ruston & Hornsby Ltd.-Lincoln Fuel: 40.5
5314999 *VM5869* -	**SAXON PROGRESS** **Fechner Engineering Pty Ltd** - SatCom: Inmarsat C 450300275 *Hobart, Tas* *Australia* Official number: 301848	*196* 65 -	Class: (LR) ✠Classed LR until 7/7/82	**1961**-02 **J. S. Doig (Grimsby) Ltd. — Grimsby** Yd No: 70 Converted From: Trawler L reg 32.16 Br ex 7.12 Dght - Lbp 31.70 Br md 7.01 Dpth 3.43 Riveted\Welded	**(B11A2FS) Stern Trawler**	**1 oil engine** with flexible couplings & sr reverse geared to sc. shaft driving 1 FP propeller Total Power: 482kW (655hp) Ruston 5ATXM 1 x 4 Stroke 5 Cy. 318 x 368 482kW (655bhp) Ruston & Hornsby Ltd.-Lincoln
9371024 *A8HT3* -	**SAXONA** *ex* Hai Hong Da 39 *-2005* **Saxona Navigaton Ltd** INTRESCO GmbH *Monrovia* *Liberia* MMSI: 636012771 Official number: 12771	**2,987** 1,672 5,069	Class: RS	**2005**-07 **Taizhou Haibin Shipbuilding & Repairing Co Ltd — Sanmen County ZJ** Yd No: 1 Loa 99.80 (BB) Br ex - Dght 5.650 Lbp 92.90 Br md 15.80 Dpth 7.10 Welded, 1 dk	**(A31A2GX) General Cargo Ship** Grain: 6,427 Compartments: 4 Ho, ER 2 Ha: (28.6 x 10.4)ER (28.0 x 10.4)	**1 oil engine** reduction geared to sc. shaft driving 1 FP propeller Total Power: 1,765kW (2,400hp) 11.0kn Chinese Std. Type G8300ZC 1 x 4 Stroke 8 Cy. 300 x 380 1765kW (2400bhp) Ningbo CSI Power & Machinery GroupCo Ltd-China AuxGen: 2 x 90kW a.c
9219393 *CQIG* -	**SAXONIA** *ex* X-Press Godavari *-2013* *ex* Saxonia *-2013* *ex* Emirates Ganges *-2013* *ex* TS Dubai *-2012* *launched as* Azalea *-2006* *ex* APL Shanghai *-2003* **ms 'Saxonia' Schiffahrtsgesellschaft mbH & Co KG** Hammonia Reederei GmbH & Co KG *Madeira* *Portugal (MAR)* MMSI: 255805556 Official number: 90825	**35,824** 14,444 41,850 T/cm 62.0	Class: LR (NV) (GL) **100A1** SS 07/2013 container ship *IWS LI **LMC** **UMS**	**2003**-07 **Stocznia Szczecinska Nowa Sp z oo — Szczecin** Yd No: B178/I/06 Loa 220.00 (BB) Br ex 32.30 Dght 12.000 Lbp 210.00 Br md 32.24 Dpth 18.70 Welded, 1 dk	**(A33A2CC) Container Ship (Fully Cellular)** Grain: 62,500; Bale: 50,000 TEU 3091 C Ho 1408 TEU C Dk 1683 TEU incl 500 ref C. Compartments: 6 Cell Ho, ER 11 Ha: (12.6 x 18.0)10 (12.6 x 28.3)ER	**1 oil engine** driving 1 FP propeller Total Power: 25,228kW (34,300hp) 22.5kn B&W 7K80MC-C 1 x 2 Stroke 7 Cy. 800 x 2300 25228kW (34300bhp) H Cegielski Poznan SA-Poland AuxGen: 2 x 1200kW a.c, 2 x 1000kW a.c Thrusters: 1 Thwart. CP thruster (f) Fuel: 3397.0 (r.f.)

IMO / Call sign / Flag	Ship name, former names, owners, port, flag	Tonnage	Classification	Builder / Dimensions	Ship type / Cargo	Machinery
9197818 *ZDEH8* -	**SAXUM** *launched as* Gerhard G *-2000* **Briese Schiffahrts GmbH & Co KG ms 'Saxum'** Briese Schiffahrts GmbH & Co KG *Gibraltar* *Gibraltar (British)* MMSI: 236125000	**2,301** 1,289 3,158 T/cm 9.0	Class: GL	**2000-10 Daewoo-Mangalia Heavy Industries S.A. — Mangalia** (Hull) Yd No: 1008 **2000-10 Scheepswerf Pattje B.V. — Waterhuizen** Yd No: 417 Loa 82.51 Br ex 12.60 Dght 5.250 Lbp 78.90 Br md 12.40 Dpth 6.80 Welded, 1 dk	**(A31A2GX) General Cargo Ship** Double Hull Grain: 4,740 TEU 132 C.Ho 96/20' (40') C.Dk 36/20' (40') Compartments: 1 Ho, ER 1 Ha: (56.3 x 10.2)ER Ice Capable	**1 oil engine** with flexible couplings & reductiongeared to sc. shaft driving 1 CP propeller Total Power: 1,800kW (2,447hp) 11.5kn MaK 6M25 1 x 4 Stroke 6 Cy. 255 x 400 1800kW (2447bhp) MaK Motoren GmbH & Co. KG-Kiel AuxGen: 1 x 240kW 230/400V 50Hz a.c, 2 x 90kW 230/400V 50Hz a.c Thrusters: 1 Thwart. FP thruster (f) Fuel: 16.0 (d.f.) 168.0 (r.f.) 6.5pd
9563768 *DUH2659* -	**SAYAH** *ex* Hsc International 002 *-2009* **Castaway Shipping & Project Logistics Inc** *Cebu* *Philippines* MMSI: 548814000 Official number: CEB1008135	*281* 191 -		**2009-06 HSC International Ship Corp — Consolacion** Yd No: 002 Loa 35.74 Br ex - Dght 1.710 Lbp - Br md 13.00 Dpth 3.00 Welded, 1 dk	**(B21A20C) Crew/Supply Vessel**	**2 oil engines** geared to sc. shafts driving 2 FP propellers Total Power: 3,200kW (4,350hp) Caterpillar 3516B-TA 2 x Vee 4 Stroke 16 Cy. 170 x 190 each-1600kW (2175bhp) Caterpillar Inc-USA
9073000 *DSRD2* -	**SAYAKA** *ex* Seiun Maru No. 38 *-2011* **Yu Jin Shipping Co Ltd** *Jeju* *South Korea* MMSI: 441781000 Official number: JJR-111026	**1,470** - 1,706	Class: KR	**1993-06 Yamanaka Zosen K.K. — Imabari** Yd No: 537 Loa 74.60 Br ex - Dght 4.250 Lbp 69.70 Br md 11.50 Dpth 7.20 Welded, 1 dk	**(A31A2GX) General Cargo Ship**	**1 oil engine** reverse geared to sc. shaft driving 1 FP propeller Total Power: 883kW (1,201hp) 13.4kn Hanshin LH30LG 1 x 4 Stroke 6 Cy. 300 x 600 883kW (1201bhp) The Hanshin Diesel Works Ltd-Japan AuxGen: 3 x 96kW 225V a.c
9124043 *JK5416* -	**SAYAMA 2** **Seitoku Kaiun Co Ltd** Auru KK *Kure, Hiroshima* *Japan* MMSI: 431400476 Official number: 134714	*2,926* - 2,682	Class: NK	**1995-09 Kegoya Dock K.K. — Kure** Yd No: 975 Loa 115.50 (BB) Br ex - Dght 5.114 Lbp 108.00 Br md 17.20 Dpth 11.95 Welded, 1 dk	**(A35B2RV) Vehicles Carrier** Quarter stern door/ramps (wing) Cars: 557	**1 oil engine** driving 1 FP propeller Total Power: 4,531kW (6,160hp) 16.0kn B&W 7L35MC 1 x 2 Stroke 7 Cy. 350 x 1050 4531kW (6160bhp) Makita Corp-Japan Thrusters: 1 Thwart. CP thruster (f) Fuel: 195.0 (r.f.)
9651852 *9HA3059* -	**SAYAN PRINCESS** **Sayan Princess Ltd** Hoyland Offshore AS *Valletta* *Malta* MMSI: 229086000	**2,925** 903 3,800	Class: NV	**2012-12 ATVT Sudnobudivnyi Zavod "Zaliv" — Kerch** (Hull) Yd No: 832 **2012-12 Bogazici Denizcilik Sanayi ve Ticaret AS — Altinova** Yd No: 1021 Loa 78.60 (BB) Br ex - Dght 6.600 Lbp 69.00 Br md 17.60 Dpth 7.70 Welded, 1 dk	**(B21A20S) Platform Supply Ship**	**4 diesel electric oil engines** driving 4 gen. each 1700kW a.c Connecting to 2 elec. motors driving 2 Azimuth electric drive units Total Power: 7,060kW (9,600hp) Caterpillar 3512C 4 x Vee 4 Stroke 12 Cy. 170 x 215 each-1765kW (2400bhp) Caterpillar Inc-USA Thrusters: 2 Tunnel thruster (f)
7733723 *UCXS* -	**SAYANOGORSK** **UTRF-Holding JSC (OAO 'UTRF-Holding')** *Petropavlovsk-Kamchatskiy* *Russia* MMSI: 273844210 Official number: 771498	**738** 221 350	Class: (RS)	**1978 Volgogradskiy Sudostroitelnyy Zavod — Volgograd** Yd No: 877 Loa 53.73 (BB) Br ex 10.72 Dght 4.290 Lbp 47.92 Br md - Dpth 6.02 Welded, 1 dk	**(B11A2FS) Stern Trawler** Ins: 218 Compartments: 1 Ho, ER 2 Ha: 2 (1.6 x 1.6) Derricks: 2x1.5t Ice Capable	**1 oil engine** driving 1 CP propeller Total Power: 971kW (1,320hp) 12.5kn S.K.L. 8NVD48A-2U 1 x 4 Stroke 8 Cy. 320 x 480 971kW (1320bhp) VEB Schwermaschinenbau "KarlLiebknecht" (SKL)-Magdeburg Thrusters: 1 Thwart. FP thruster (f); 1 Tunnel thruster (a)
8986298 *H02768* -	**SAYAR** *ex* Judy I *-2008* *ex* Admiral 2 *-2007* *ex* Khurais 1 *-2006* **Silver Ocean Marine Consultancy FZE** - *Panama* *Panama* Official number: 35593PEXT2	**125** 45 -		**1974-06 B.V. Scheepswerf Damen — Gorinchem** Yd No: 768 Loa 20.00 Br ex - Dght 1.850 Lbp - Br md 6.20 Dpth 2.80 Welded, 1 dk	**(B32A2ST) Tug**	**2 oil engines** geared to sc. shafts driving 2 Propellers Total Power: 552kW (750hp) Caterpillar D353 2 x 4 Stroke 6 Cy. 159 x 203 each-276kW (375bhp) Caterpillar Tractor Co-USA
7504196 *UGTI* -	**SAYDA** *ex* Saida *-1995* *ex* Nonhamar *-1992* **Grumant Joint Stock Co (A/O 'Grumant')** - *St Petersburg* *Russia* MMSI: 273521100	**1,205** 362 700	Class: RS (NV)	**1976-11 Fiskerstrand Verft AS — Fiskarstrand** Yd No: 29 Loa 57.03 Br ex 9.50 Dght 5.004 Lbp 50.63 Br md - Dpth 7.37 Welded, 2 dks	**(B11A2FS) Stern Trawler** Ins: 700 Ice Capable	**1 oil engine** driving 1 CP propeller Total Power: 1,800kW (2,447hp) 12.5kn Wichmann 9AXA 1 x 2 Stroke 9 Cy. 300 x 450 1800kW (2447bhp) Wichmann Motorfabrikk AS-Norway AuxGen: 4 x 170kW 380V 50Hz a.c
8033170 *UHTT* -	**SAYFULA KADI** *ex* Dauriya *-2001* **Sayfula Kadi Shipping Ltd** State Enterprise Makhachkala International Sea Commercial Port SatCom: Inmarsat C 427322222 *Taganrog* *Russia* MMSI: 273426570	**4,143** 1,432 6,234 T/cm 19.1	Class: (RS)	**1981-10 Volgogradskiy Sudostroitelnyy Zavod — Volgograd** Converted From: General Cargo Ship-2002 Loa 125.06 Br ex 16.63 Dght 4.830 Lbp 121.12 Br md - Dpth 6.90 Welded, 1 dk	**(A13B2TP) Products Tanker** Grain: 988; Liq: 5,903; Liq (Oil): 5,903 Compartments: 12 Wing Ta, ER Ice Capable	**2 oil engines** driving 2 FP propellers Total Power: 2,294kW (3,118hp) 11.3kn Dvigatel Revolyutsii 6CHRNP36/45 2 x 4 Stroke 6 Cy. 360 x 450 each-1147kW (1559bhp) Zavod "Dvigatel Revolyutsii"-Gorkiy AuxGen: 4 x 160kW Fuel: 487.0 (r.f.)
7819242 - -	**SAYID MOHAMED** **Government of The Democratic Republic of Somalia** - *Mogadiscio* *Somalia*	*121* 62 103		**1979-12 Brodogradiliste Greben — Vela Luka** Yd No: 808 Loa 23.19 Br ex 7.07 Dght 3.571 Lbp 21.21 Br md 6.85 Dpth 3.71 Bonded, 1 dk	**(B11A2FS) Stern Trawler** Hull Material: Reinforced Plastic	**1 oil engine** with clutches, flexible couplings & sr reverse geared to sc. shaft driving 1 FP propeller Total Power: 265kW (360hp) Caterpillar 3408PCTA 1 x Vee 4 Stroke 8 Cy. 137 x 152 265kW (360bhp) Caterpillar Tractor Co-USA AuxGen: 1 x 20kW 231/400V 50Hz a.c
7102900 - -	**SAYO MARU No. 26** **Katsuse Gyogyo KK** -	*164* 60 -		**1970 Tokushima Zosen K.K. — Fukuoka** Yd No: 1012 Loa 34.80 Br ex 6.86 Dght 2.998 Lbp 31.81 Br md 6.81 Dpth 3.31 Welded, 1 dk	**(B11B2FV) Fishing Vessel**	**1 oil engine** driving 1 FP propeller Total Power: 441kW (600hp) Daihatsu 6PSHTB-26D 1 x 4 Stroke 6 Cy. 260 x 320 441kW (600bhp) Daihatsu Diesel Manufacturing Co Lt-Japan
8713938 - -	**SAYURALA** *ex* Vigraha *-2009* **Government of The Democratic Socialist Republic of Sri Lanka (Navy Department)** - *Sri Lanka*	**1,247** 750 220	Class: (IR) (AB)	**1990-03 Mazagon Dock Ltd. — Mumbai** Yd No: 787 Loa 74.10 Br ex 11.42 Dght 3.500 Lbp 69.00 Br md 11.40 Dpth 7.90 Welded, 1 dk	**(B34H2SQ) Patrol Vessel**	**2 oil engines** with clutches, hydraulic couplings & epicyclic geared to sc. shafts driving 2 CP propellers Total Power: 9,416kW (12,802hp) 22.0kn Pielstick 16PA6V280 2 x Vee 4 Stroke 16 Cy. 280 x 290 each-4708kW (6401bhp) Kirloskar Oil Engines Ltd-India AuxGen: 4 x 212kW 415V 50Hz a.c, 1 x 159kW 415V 50Hz a.c Fuel: 111.0 (d.f.)
9144809 *4PKG* -	**SAYURI** **National Hydrographic Office** - *Colombo* *Sri Lanka*	**103** 31 20	Class: (GL)	**1996-11 Scheepswerf Visser B.V. — Den Helder** Yd No: 148 Loa 21.25 Br ex - Dght 1.606 Lbp 19.50 Br md 6.00 Dpth 3.00 Welded, 1 dk	**(B31A2SR) Research Survey Vessel**	**2 oil engines** reduction geared to sc. shafts driving 2 FP propellers Total Power: 298kW (406hp) 9.0kn MAN D2866LE 2 x 4 Stroke 6 Cy. 128 x 155 each-149kW (203bhp) MAN Nutzfahrzeuge AG-Nuernberg AuxGen: 1 x 40kW 380V 50Hz a.c
9587740 *JD3118* -	**SAYURI MARU** **Japan Railway Construction, Transport & Technology Agency & Nissan Kisen KK** Nissan Kisen KK *Imabari, Ehime* *Japan* MMSI: 431001931 Official number: 141329	*749* - 1,622	Class: NK	**2010-10 Yamanaka Zosen K.K. — Imabari** Yd No: 805 Loa 72.32 Br ex - Dght 4.620 Lbp 68.00 Br md 11.40 Dpth 5.30 Welded, 1 dk	**(A12B2TR) Chemical/Products Tanker** Double Hull (13F) Liq: 1,470; Liq (Oil): 1,470	**1 oil engine** driving 1 FP propeller Total Power: 1,618kW (2,200hp) Hanshin LA32G 1 x 4 Stroke 6 Cy. 320 x 680 1618kW (2200bhp) The Hanshin Diesel Works Ltd-Japan
9085302 *A6E2422* -	**SAYYAF** **Abu Dhabi Petroleum Ports Operating Co (IRSHAD)** - *Abu Dhabi* *United Arab Emirates* MMSI: 470679000 Official number: 3688	**680** 204 -	Class: LR ✠ **100A1** SS 12/2009 tug fire fighting ship 1 (2400 cubic metre/hr) with water spray Arabian Gulf service ✠ **LMC** Eq.Ltr: (K) ; Cable: 715.0/30.0 U2	**1994-12 McTay Marine — Bromborough** Yd No: 114 Loa 40.65 Br ex 12.10 Dght 4.442 Lbp 35.75 Br md 11.62 Dpth 5.20 Welded, 1 dk	**(B32A2ST) Tug**	**2 oil engines** with clutches, flexible couplings & sr reverse geared to sc. shafts driving 2 CP propellers Total Power: 3,200kW (4,350hp) 12.0kn Caterpillar 3606TA 2 x 4 Stroke 6 Cy. 280 x 300 each-1600kW (2175bhp) Caterpillar Inc-USA AuxGen: 3 x 200kW 380V 50Hz a.c Thrusters: 1 Thwart. FP thruster (f) Fuel: 104.5 (d.f.) 14.0pd

IMO / Call sign / Flag	Name / Owner / Port	Tonnage	Class	Build / Dimensions	Type	Machinery
7633856 *9MAS9* -	**SAZ SUPPLY** *ex* O. I. L. Supply 4 *-1987* **Ajang Shipping Sdn Bhd** - *Kuching* *Malaysia* MMSI: 533000411 Official number: 326012	*477* 146 516	Class: BV	**1977-07 Singapore Shipbuilding & Engineering Pte Ltd — Singapore** Yd No: 124 Loa 49.97 Br ex - Dght 2.590 Lbp 42.58 Br md 10.93 Dpth 3.41 Welded, 1 dk	**(B21A2OS) Platform Supply Ship** Liq: 180 Compartments: 6 Ta, ER	**2 oil engines** geared to sc. shafts driving 2 FP propellers Total Power: 1,544kW (2,100hp) 10.5kn Kromhout 6FDHD240 2 x 4 Stroke 6 Cy. 240 x 260 each-772kW (1050bhp) Stork Werkspoor Diesel BV-Netherlands
8966224 *TCCJ3* -	**SAZAN** **Ibrahim Avinal, Bahriye Avinal & Emine Avinal** Pirireis Denizcilik Gemi Acenteligi Gumrukleme Turizm Nakliyat ve Ticaret Ltd Sti (Pirireis Shipping Ltd Corp) *Istanbul* *Turkey* MMSI: 271002370 Official number: 373	**629** 317 1,210		**1951 in West Germany** Converted From: Fishing Vessel Lengthened-1998 Lengthened-1991 Lengthened-1987 Loa 54.34 Br ex - Dght 4.330 Lbp 49.40 Br md 9.81 Dpth 5.05 Welded, 1 dk	**(A31A2GX) General Cargo Ship**	**1 oil engine** driving 1 FP propeller Total Power: 224kW (305hp) S.K.L. 6NVD36-1U 1 x 4 Stroke 6 Cy. 240 x 360 224kW (305bhp) (new engine 1998) VEB Schwermaschinenbau "KarlLiebknecht" (SKL)-Magdeburg
7831123 *UFEE* -	**SAZHINSK** **Dalfin Co Ltd (OOO Kompaniya 'Dalfin')** - *Vladivostok* *Russia*	**739** 221 341	Class: (RS)	**1980-03 Zavod "Leninskaya Kuznitsa" — Kiyev** Yd No: 243 Loa 53.75 (BB) Br ex 10.72 Dght 4.290 Lbp 47.92 Br md - Dpth 6.00 Welded, 1 dk	**(B11A2FS) Stern Trawler** Ins: 218 Compartments: 1 Ho, ER 1 Ha: (1.6 x 1.6) Derricks: 1x3.3t Ice Capable	**1 oil engine** driving 1 FP propeller Total Power: 971kW (1,320hp) 12.8kn S.K.L. 8NVD48A-2U 1 x 4 Stroke 8 Cy. 320 x 480 971kW (1320bhp) VEB Schwermaschinenbau "KarlLiebknecht" (SKL)-Magdeburg
8972297 *UBWH4* -	**SB-1** *ex* Black Deep *-2009* *ex* Navodari 1 *-2002* **Shipping & Dredging Invest Ltd** Nargen OU *Kaliningrad* *Russia* MMSI: 273353440	**440** 132 700	Class: RS (BV)	**1985 Santierul Naval Drobeta-Turnu Severin S.A. — Drobeta-Turnu S.** Loa 49.38 Br ex 12.00 Dght 1.950 Lbp 47.38 Br md 11.70 Dpth 2.50 Welded, 1 dk	**(B34A2SH) Hopper, Motor**	**2 oil engines** gearing integral to driving 2 Z propellers Total Power: 318kW (432hp) Maybach MB836B 2 x 4 Stroke 6 Cy. 175 x 205 each-159kW (216bhp) Uzina 23 August Bucuresti-Bucuresti
7419482 - -	**SB 42** **Government of The Republic of Indonesia (Direktorat Jenderal Perhubungan Laut - Ministry of Sea Communications)** PT (Persero) Pengerukan Indonesia *Surabaya* *Indonesia*	*439* 132 640	Class: (KI)	**1975-04 Hikari Kogyo K.K. — Yokosuka** Yd No: 268 L reg 49.00 Br ex - Dght 2.670 Lbp 48.10 Br md 10.02 Dpth 3.07 Welded, 1 dk	**(B34E2SW) Waste Disposal Vessel**	**2 oil engines** geared to sc. shafts driving 2 Propellers Total Power: 412kW (560hp) Isuzu E120T-MF6A 2 x 4 Stroke 6 Cy. 135 x 140 each-206kW (280bhp) Isuzu Marine Engine Inc-Japan
7408201 - -	**SB 51** **PT Pelabuhan Indonesia II (Persero) Cabang Pelabuhan Tanjung Priok (Indonesia Port Corp II, Tanjung Priok)** PT (Persero) Pengerukan Indonesia *Jakarta* *Indonesia*	*822* 752 836	Class: (KI)	**1975-02 Yokohama Zosen — Chiba** Yd No: 1358 Converted From: General Cargo Ship-2009 Loa 56.00 Br ex 11.24 Dght 2.800 Lbp 55.00 Br md 11.00 Dpth 3.60 Welded, 1 dk	**(B34E2SW) Waste Disposal Vessel**	**2 oil engines** driving 2 FP propellers Total Power: 454kW (618hp) Isuzu E120T-MF6R 2 x 4 Stroke 6 Cy. 135 x 140 each-227kW (309bhp) (made 1974) Isuzu Marine Engine Inc-Japan
8826280 *YGKV* -	**SB 53** **Government of The Republic of Indonesia (Direktorat Jenderal Perhubungan Laut - Ministry of Sea Communications)** - *Jakarta* *Indonesia* Official number: 439/BA	*552* 166 -	Class: (KI)	**1981-01 P.T. Dok & Perkapalan Tanjung Priok — Jakarta** Loa 50.30 Br ex 9.50 Dght 3.330 Lbp - Br md - Dpth 3.75 Welded, 1 dk	**(B34E2SW) Waste Disposal Vessel**	**2 oil engines** driving 2 FP propellers Total Power: 1,088kW (1,480hp) Caterpillar 3408TA 2 x Vee 4 Stroke 8 Cy. 137 x 152 each-544kW (740bhp) Caterpillar Tractor Co-USA
8826319 - -	**SB 54** **Government of The Republic of Indonesia (Direktorat Jenderal Perhubungan Laut - Ministry of Sea Communications)** - *Jakarta* *Indonesia*	*523* 192 -	Class: KI	**1981 P.T. Dok & Perkapalan Tanjung Priok — Jakarta** Loa 50.30 Br ex 9.50 Dght 3.330 Lbp - Br md - Dpth 3.75 Welded, 1 dk	**(B34E2SW) Waste Disposal Vessel**	**2 oil engines** driving 2 FP propellers Total Power: 544kW (740hp) 8.0kn Caterpillar 3408T 2 x Vee 4 Stroke 8 Cy. 137 x 152 each-272kW (370bhp) Caterpillar Tractor Co-USA AuxGen: 1 x 40kW 400V a.c
8826321 - -	**SB 55** **Government of The Republic of Indonesia (Direktorat Jenderal Perhubungan Laut - Ministry of Sea Communications)** - *Jakarta* *Indonesia*	*512* 287 -	Class: (KI)	**1981 P.T. Pelita Bahari — Jakarta** Loa 54.58 Br ex 10.00 Dght 3.000 Lbp 52.96 Br md - Dpth 3.50 Welded, 1 dk	**(B34E2SW) Waste Disposal Vessel**	**2 oil engines** driving 2 FP propellers Total Power: 970kW (1,318hp) Deutz BF12L413F 2 x Vee 4 Stroke 12 Cy. 120 x 125 each-485kW (659bhp) Kloeckner Humboldt Deutz AG-West Germany AuxGen: 1 x 16kW 230V a.c
8826333 - -	**SB 56** **Government of The Republic of Indonesia (Direktorat Jenderal Perhubungan Laut - Ministry of Sea Communications)** - *Jakarta* *Indonesia*	*649* 628 -	Class: KI	**1981 P.T. Kodja (Unit I) — Jakarta** Yd No: 20 Loa 54.11 Br ex 10.00 Dght 3.000 Lbp 52.40 Br md - Dpth 3.50 Welded, 1 dk	**(B34E2SW) Waste Disposal Vessel**	**2 oil engines** reduction geared to sc. shafts driving 2 FP propellers Total Power: 442kW (600hp) Deutz BF12L413F 2 x Vee 4 Stroke 12 Cy. 120 x 125 each-221kW (300bhp) Kloeckner Humboldt Deutz AG-West Germany
8126563 *UFCG* -	**SB-408** *ex* Tsavliris Challenger *-1995* *ex* Hulk *-1993* *ex* SB-408 *-1993* **Sovfracht JSC (A/O 'Sovfrakht')** Tsavliris Russ (Worldwide Salvage & Towage) Ltd *Vladivostok* *Russia* MMSI: 273442150	**2,050** 615 810	Class: (RS) (BV)	**1984-06 Rauma-Repola Oy — Uusikaupunki** Yd No: 317 Loa 69.19 Br ex 15.40 Dght 5.100 Lbp 60.10 Br md 15.02 Dpth 7.01 Welded, 1 dk	**(B32A2ST) Tug** Ice Capable	**2 oil engines** with clutches & sr geared to sc. shafts driving 2 CP propellers Total Power: 5,738kW (7,802hp) 16.0kn Pielstick 6PC2-5L-400 2 x 4 Stroke 6 Cy. 400 x 460 each-2869kW (3901bhp) Mashinostroitelnyy Zavod"Russkiy-Dizel"-Leningrad Thrusters: 1 Thwart. CP thruster (f)
9134488 *DSFY5* -	**SB COUNT** *ex* Bum Woo *-2013* **ShippingBank Co Ltd** KSIM Co Ltd (Korea Ship Investment & Management) *Jeju* *South Korea* MMSI: 441250000 Official number: JJR-029344	**5,929** 3,389 11,042 T/cm 19.7	Class: KR	**1997-07 Daedong Shipbuilding Co Ltd — Busan** Yd No: 414 Loa 114.57 (BB) Br ex - Dght 8.370 Lbp 107.00 Br md 18.20 Dpth 10.70 Welded, 1 dk	**(A12B2TR) Chemical/Products Tanker** Double Hull (13F) Liq: 11,922; Liq (Oil): 11,922 Manifold: Bow/CM: 65.5m	**1 oil engine** driving 1 FP propeller Total Power: 4,193kW (5,701hp) 13.5kn B&W 6S35MC 1 x 2 Stroke 6 Cy. 350 x 1400 4193kW (5701bhp) Ssangyong Heavy Industries Co Ltd-South Korea
9193903 - -	**SB. MELATI** *ex* Melati *-2013* **Government of The Republic of Indonesia (Direktorat Jenderal Perhubungan Laut - Ministry of Sea Communications)** PT (Persero) Pengerukan Indonesia *Jakarta* *Indonesia*	**541** 163 300	Class: KI	**2007-11 P.T. Jasa Marina Indah — Semarang** Yd No: 042/JMI Loa 48.63 Br ex - Dght 3.339 Lbp 45.02 Br md 9.75 Dpth 3.66 Welded, 1 dk	**(B34A2SH) Hopper, Motor** Hopper: 500	**2 oil engines** geared to sc. shafts driving 2 FP propellers Total Power: 706kW (960hp) Caterpillar 3408 2 x Vee 4 Stroke 8 Cy. 137 x 152 each-353kW (480bhp) Caterpillar Inc-USA AuxGen: 2 x 66kW a.c
9134476 *DSOU5* -	**SB PRINCESS** *ex* Bum Mi *-2013* **ShippingBank Co Ltd** KSIM Co Ltd (Korea Ship Investment & Management) *Jeju* *South Korea* MMSI: 440350000 Official number: JJR-069510	**6,341** 3,202 11,049 T/cm 19.7	Class: KR	**1997-04 Daedong Shipbuilding Co Ltd — Busan** Yd No: 413 Lengthened-2006 Loa 122.50 (BB) Br ex - Dght 8.463 Lbp 114.57 Br md 18.20 Dpth 10.70 Welded, 1 dk	**(A12B2TR) Chemical/Products Tanker** Double Hull (13F) Liq: 11,040; Liq (Oil): 12,574 Cargo Heating Coils 18 Cargo Pump (s): 1x250m³/hr, 13x200m³/hr, 4x100m³/hr Manifold: Bow/CM: 62m	**1 oil engine** driving 1 FP propeller Total Power: 4,193kW (5,701hp) 13.5kn B&W 6S35MC 1 x 2 Stroke 6 Cy. 350 x 1400 4193kW (5701bhp) Ssangyong Heavy Industries Co Ltd-South Korea Thrusters: 1 Tunnel thruster (f) Fuel: 125.0 (d.f.) 575.0 (r.f.)
9193898 - -	**SB SERUNI** **Government of The Republic of Indonesia (Direktorat Jenderal Perhubungan Laut - Ministry of Sea Communications)** PT (Persero) Pengerukan Indonesia *Jakarta* *Indonesia* Official number: GT. 541 NO. 880/GA	**541** 163 -	Class: KI	**2007-11 P.T. Jasa Marina Indah — Semarang** Yd No: 041/JMI Loa 48.63 Br ex - Dght 3.339 Lbp 44.64 Br md 9.75 Dpth 3.66 Welded, 1 dk	**(B34A2SH) Hopper, Motor** Double Hull Hopper: 500	**2 oil engines** geared to sc. shafts driving 2 FP propellers Total Power: 706kW (960hp) Caterpillar 3408 2 x Vee 4 Stroke 8 Cy. 137 x 152 each-353kW (480bhp) Caterpillar Inc-USA AuxGen: 2 x 66kW a.c

9578268 *YDA6962* -	**SB101** **PT Bahtera Energi Samudra Tuah** - *Banjarmasin* *Indonesia*	**273** 82 -	Class: BV	**2010-07 Tuong Aik Shipyard Sdn Bhd — Sibu** Yd No: 2829 Loa 29.00 Br ex - Dght 3.600 Lbp 27.84 Br md 8.60 Dpth 4.20 Welded, 1 dk	**(B32A2ST) Tug**	**2 oil engines** reduction geared to sc. shafts driving 2 FP propellers Total Power: 2,080kW (2,828hp) 10.0kn Mitsubishi S12R-MPTK 2 x Vee 4 Stroke 12 Cy. 170 x 180 each-1040kW (1414bhp) Mitsubishi Heavy Industries Ltd-Japan AuxGen: 2 x 80kW 50Hz a.c Fuel: 185.0 (d.f.)
9575644 *9V9251* -	**SB102** *ex* Dragonet XIV *-2011* **Sun Paradise Shipping Pte Ltd** - *Singapore* *Singapore* Official number: 396837	**281** 85 303	Class: NK	**2011-03 Kaibuok Shipyard (M) Sdn Bhd — Sibu** Yd No: 0712 Loa 30.20 Br ex - Dght 3.812 Lbp 27.20 Br md 9.00 Dpth 4.60 Welded, 1 dk	**(B32A2ST) Tug**	**2 oil engines** reduction geared to sc. shafts driving 2 Propellers Total Power: 1,518kW (2,064hp) Mitsubishi S6R2-MPTK3 2 x 4 Stroke 6 Cy. 170 x 220 each-759kW (1032bhp) Mitsubishi Heavy Industries Ltd-Japan
8737271 *YDA3570* -	**SBD** **PT Sumber Bahari Makmur** - *Batam* *Indonesia* MMSI: 525016382	**148** 45 -	Class: KI	**2009-02 PT Sumber Samudra Makmur — Batam** Loa 25.00 Br ex - Dght 2.590 Lbp 22.02 Br md 7.00 Dpth 3.60 Welded, 1 dk	**(B32A2ST) Tug**	**2 oil engines** driving 2 Propellers Total Power: 1,176kW (1,598hp) Caterpillar D398 2 x Vee 4 Stroke 12 Cy. 159 x 203 each-588kW (799bhp) Caterpillar Inc-USA
9093581 *YD3389* -	**SBE** **PT Pelayaran Sumber Bahari** - *Batam* *Indonesia*	**201** 61 -	Class: KI	**2006-12 PT Sumber Samudra Makmur — Batam** Loa 27.00 Br ex - Dght - Lbp 24.48 Br md 8.20 Dpth 4.00 Welded, 1 dk	**(B32A2ST) Tug**	**2 oil engines** geared to sc. shafts driving 2 Propellers Total Power: 1,176kW (1,598hp) Caterpillar D398 2 x Vee 4 Stroke 12 Cy. 159 x 203 each-588kW (799bhp) Caterpillar Inc-USA
8625492 *UBNE7* -	**SBK-01** *ex* Junsho Maru No. 8 *-2007* **Sakhalin Bunkering Co (OOO 'Sakhalinskaya Bunkerovochnaya Kompaniya')** - *Korsakov* *Russia* MMSI: 273312480	**218** 85 280	Class: RS	**1986-02 Tokuoka Zosen K.K. — Naruto** Yd No: 138 Converted From: Oil Tanker-2007 Loa 37.75 Br ex - Dght 2.730 Lbp 34.02 Br md 7.00 Dpth 3.00 Welded, 1 dk	**(B35E2TF) Bunkering Tanker** Liq: 170; Liq (Oil): 319	**1 oil engine** reduction geared to sc. shaft driving 1 FP propeller Total Power: 272kW (370hp) 9.5kn Yanmar 6MAL-T 1 x 4 Stroke 6 Cy. 200 x 240 272kW (370bhp) Yanmar Diesel Engine Co Ltd-Japan
9095802 *YD3373* -	**SBL** **PT Wahana Mitra Bahari** - *Batam* *Indonesia* MMSI: 525015152	**230** 69 -	Class: KI	**2006-12 PT Sumber Samudra Makmur — Batam** Loa 29.30 Br ex - Dght - Lbp 26.78 Br md 8.20 Dpth 4.20 Welded, 1 dk	**(B32A2ST) Tug**	**2 oil engines** geared to sc. shafts driving 2 Propellers Total Power: 1,766kW (2,402hp) Caterpillar D399 2 x Vee 4 Stroke 16 Cy. 159 x 203 each-883kW (1201bhp) Caterpillar Inc-USA
7731036 *DSAI9* -	**SBM 5** *ex* Seorin No. 1 *-1998* *ex* Hyundai HT-113 *-1996* *ex* Tokuei Maru No. 27 *-1977* **KPS Co Ltd** - *Ulsan* *South Korea* MMSI: 440102400 Official number: USR-710080	**466** 159 -	Class: KR	**1971 Kochiken Zosen — Kochi** Yd No: 406 Loa 41.41 Br ex - Dght 4.159 Lbp 37.50 Br md 10.00 Dpth 4.50 Welded, 1 dk	**(B32A2ST) Tug**	**2 oil engines** driving 2 FP propellers Total Power: 2,648kW (3,600hp) 12.0kn Nippon Hatsudoki HS6NV238 2 x 4 Stroke 6 Cy. 380 x 580 each-1324kW (1800bhp) Nippon Hatsudoki-Japan AuxGen: 2 x 80kW 230V a.c
7314503 - -	**SBM 6** *ex* Hikita Maru *-1998* **Kum Woo Marine Co Ltd** - *Busan* *South Korea* Official number: BSR-961802	**203** - 95	Class: (KR)	**1973 Towa Zosen K.K. — Shimonoseki** Yd No: 445 Loa 33.20 Br ex 9.61 Dght 3.150 Lbp 28.00 Br md 9.58 Dpth 4.20 Welded, 1 dk	**(B32A2ST) Tug**	**2 oil engines** driving 2 FP propellers Total Power: 2,354kW (3,200hp) 13.8kn Hanshin 6MUH28 2 x 4 Stroke 6 Cy. 280 x 340 each-1177kW (1600bhp) Hanshin Nainenki Kogyo-Japan
7913787 - -	**SBM 7** *ex* Luna *-1997* *ex* Take Maru No. 78 *-1997* *ex* Kirishima Maru *-1989* **SK Shipping Co Ltd** KPS Co Ltd *Ulsan* *South Korea* MMSI: 440135780 Official number: USR-970594	**224** - 93	Class: KR	**1979-08 Sagami Zosen Tekko K.K. — Yokosuka** Yd No: 202 Loa 36.20 Br ex - Dght - Lbp 31.50 Br md 9.80 Dpth 4.30 Welded, 1 dk	**(B32A2ST) Tug**	**2 oil engines** driving 2 FP propellers Total Power: 2,354kW (3,200hp) 14.2kn Niigata 6MG28BX 2 x 4 Stroke 6 Cy. 280 x 320 each-1177kW (1600bhp) Niigata Engineering Co Ltd-Japan
9624988 *C6ZZ8* -	**SBM INSTALLER** **SBM Installer Sarl** SBM Offshore Contractors Inc *Nassau* *Bahamas* MMSI: 311073300 Official number: 8002045	**11,197** 3,360 5,200	Class: NV	**2013-09 Keppel Singmarine Pte Ltd — Singapore** Yd No: 366 Loa 111.20 (BB) Br ex 25.03 Dght 7.700 Lbp 102.05 Br md 25.00 Dpth 10.20 Welded, 1 dk	**(B22A20V) Diving Support Vessel** Cranes: 1x250t	**6 diesel electric oil engines** driving 4 gen. each 2810kW 2 gen. Connecting to 2 elec. motors each (3000kW) reduction geared to sc. shaft driving 2 CP propellers Total Power: 14,980kW (20,364hp) Wartsila 6L26 4 x 4 Stroke 6 Cy. 260 x 320 each-1870kW (2542bhp) Wartsila Italia SpA-Italy Wartsila 9L26 2 x 4 Stroke 9 Cy. 260 x 320 each-2810kW (3820bhp) Wartsila Italia SpA-Italy Thrusters: 2 Tunnel thruster (f); 1 Tunnel thruster (f); 2 Tunnel thruster (a)
9639361 - -	**SBM NO. 9** **KPS Co Ltd** - *Ulsan* *South Korea* MMSI: 440148970 Official number: USR-114808	**267** - 242	Class: KR	**2011-08 Yeunsoo Shipbuilding Co Ltd — Janghang** Yd No: 145 Loa 38.24 Br ex - Dght 3.587 Lbp 31.15 Br md - Dpth 4.50 Welded, 1 dk	**(B32A2ST) Tug**	**2 oil engines** reduction geared to sc. shafts driving 2 Propellers Total Power: 3,240kW (4,406hp) 13.5kn Yanmar 6EY26 2 x 4 Stroke 6 Cy. 260 x 385 each-1620kW (2203bhp) Yanmar Diesel Engine Co Ltd-Japan
8330530 - -	**SBORSHCHIK-1** -	**235** 120 455	Class: (RS)	**1984 Bakinskiy Sudostroitelnyy Zavod im Vano Sturua — Baku** Yd No: 371 Loa 35.17 Br ex 8.01 Dght 3.120 Lbp 33.25 Br md - Dpth 3.60 Welded, 1 dk	**(B34G2SE) Pollution Control Vessel** Liq: 468; Liq (Oil): 468 Compartments: 10 Ta Ice Capable	**1 oil engine** geared to sc. shaft driving 1 FP propeller Total Power: 166kW (226hp) 8.0kn Daldizel 6CHNSP18/22 1 x 4 Stroke 6 Cy. 180 x 220 166kW (226bhp) Daldizel-Khabarovsk AuxGen: 1 x 50kW a.c, 1 x 30kW a.c
8728660 - -	**SBORSHCHIK-4** **Ust-Dunaysk Port (Ust-Dunayskiy MTP)** - *Ust-Dunaysk* *Ukraine* Official number: 810067	*243* 108 442	Class: (RS)	**1981-12 Bakinskiy Sudostroitelnyy Zavod im Vano Sturua — Baku** Yd No: 350 Loa 35.17 Br ex 8.01 Dght 3.120 Lbp 33.25 Br md - Dpth 3.60 Welded, 1 dk	**(B34G2SE) Pollution Control Vessel** Liq: 468; Liq (Oil): 468 Compartments: 10 Ta Ice Capable	**1 oil engine** geared to sc. shaft driving 1 FP propeller Total Power: 166kW (226hp) 7.5kn Daldizel 6CHNSP18/22 1 x 4 Stroke 6 Cy. 180 x 220 166kW (226bhp) Daldizel-Khabarovsk AuxGen: 1 x 50kW a.c, 1 x 30kW a.c Fuel: 12.0 (d.f.)
8330542 - -	**SBORSHCHIK-7** **Ust-Dunaysk Port (Ust-Dunayskiy MTP)** -	**235** 120 455	Class: (RS)	**1984 Bakinskiy Sudostroitelnyy Zavod im Vano Sturua — Baku** Yd No: 373 Loa 35.17 Br ex 8.01 Dght 3.120 Lbp 33.25 Br md - Dpth 3.60 Welded, 1 dk	**(B34G2SE) Pollution Control Vessel** Liq: 468; Liq (Oil): 468 Compartments: 10 Ta Ice Capable	**1 oil engine** geared to sc. shaft driving 1 FP propeller Total Power: 166kW (226hp) 8.0kn Daldizel 6CHNSP18/22 1 x 4 Stroke 6 Cy. 180 x 220 166kW (226bhp) Daldizel-Khabarovsk AuxGen: 1 x 50kW a.c, 1 x 30kW a.c Fuel: 12.0 (d.f.)
8872954 - -	**SBORSHCHIK-306** **State Enterprise Mariupol Sea Commercial Port** - *Mariupol* *Ukraine* Official number: 750699	**193** 82 326	Class: (RS)	**1976 Bakinskiy Sudostroitelnyy Zavod im Vano Sturua — Baku** Yd No: 306 Loa 29.17 Br ex 8.01 Dght 3.120 Lbp 28.50 Br md - Dpth 3.60 Welded, 1 dk	**(B34G2SE) Pollution Control Vessel** Liq: 336; Liq (Oil): 336 Compartments: 8 Ta Ice Capable	**1 oil engine** geared to sc. shaft driving 1 FP propeller Total Power: 165kW (224hp) 7.5kn Daldizel 6CHNSP18/22 1 x 4 Stroke 6 Cy. 180 x 220 165kW (224bhp) Daldizel-Khabarovsk AuxGen: 1 x 50kW, 1 x 25kW Fuel: 15.0 (d.f.)
8929094 - -	**SBORSHCHIK-311** **State Enterprise Kerch Sea Trading Port** - *Kerch* *Ukraine* Official number: 760760	*205* 77 326	Class: (RS)	**1977 Bakinskiy Sudostroitelnyy Zavod im Vano Sturua — Baku** Yd No: 311 Loa 29.17 Br ex 8.01 Dght 3.120 Lbp 28.50 Br md - Dpth 3.60 Welded, 1 dk	**(B34G2SE) Pollution Control Vessel** Liq: 336; Liq (Oil): 336 Compartments: 8 Ta Ice Capable	**1 oil engine** geared to sc. shaft driving 1 FP propeller Total Power: 165kW (224hp) 7.5kn Daldizel 6CHNSP18/22 1 x 4 Stroke 6 Cy. 180 x 220 165kW (224bhp) Daldizel-Khabarovsk AuxGen: 1 x 50kW a.c, 1 x 30kW a.c Fuel: 16.0 (d.f.)

IMO / Call sign	Name / Owner / Registry	Tonnage	Class	Builder / Dimensions	Type / Cargo	Machinery
8929111 - -	**SBORSHCHIK-325** **Chernomorskiy Shipbuilding Yard JSC (Chernomorskiy Sudostroitelnyy Zavod)** *Nikolayev* *Ukraine* Official number: 780425	*205* 77 326	Class: (RS)	**1978 Bakinskiy Sudostroitelnyy Zavod im Vano Sturua — Baku** Yd No: 325 Loa 29.17 Br ex 8.01 Dght 3.120 Lbp 28.50 Br md - Dpth 3.60 Welded, 1 dk	**(B34G2SE) Pollution Control Vessel** Liq: 386; Liq (Oil): 386 Compartments: 8 Ta Ice Capable	**1 oil engine** geared to sc. shaft driving 1 FP propeller Total Power: 165kW (224hp) 7.5kn Daldizel 6CHNSP18/22 1 x 4 Stroke 6 Cy. 180 x 220 165kW (224bhp) Daldizel-Khabarovsk AuxGen: 1 x 50kW a.c, 1 x 30kW a.c Fuel: 15.0 (d.f.)
8872966 - -	**SBORSHCHIK-335** **State Enterprise Mariupol Sea Commercial Port** *Mariupol* *Ukraine* Official number: 800510	**194** 86 326	Class: (RS)	**1980-09 Bakinskiy Sudostroitelnyy Zavod im Vano Sturua — Baku** Yd No: 335 Loa 29.17 Br ex 8.01 Dght 3.120 Lbp 28.50 Br md - Dpth 3.60 Welded, 1 dk	**(B34G2SE) Pollution Control Vessel** Liq: 336; Liq (Oil): 336 Compartments: 8 Ta Ice Capable	**1 oil engine** geared to sc. shaft driving 1 FP propeller Total Power: 165kW (224hp) 7.5kn Daldizel 6CHNSP18/22 1 x 4 Stroke 6 Cy. 180 x 220 165kW (224bhp) Daldizel-Khabarovsk AuxGen: 1 x 50kW, 1 x 30kW Fuel: 15.0 (d.f.)
8728701 - -	**SBORSHCHIK-387** **State Enterprise Mariupol Sea Commercial Port** *Mariupol* *Ukraine* Official number: 860475	**235** 120 455	Class: (RS)	**1986-10 Bakinskiy Sudostroitelnyy Zavod im Vano Sturua — Baku** Yd No: 387 Loa 35.17 Br ex 8.01 Dght 3.120 Lbp 33.23 Br md - Dpth 3.60 Welded, 1 dk	**(B34G2SE) Pollution Control Vessel** Liq: 468; Liq (Oil): 468 Compartments: 10 Ta Ice Capable	**1 oil engine** geared to sc. shaft driving 1 FP propeller Total Power: 166kW (226hp) 8.1kn Daldizel 6CHNSP18/22 1 x 4 Stroke 6 Cy. 180 x 220 166kW (226bhp) Daldizel-Khabarovsk AuxGen: 1 x 50kW a.c, 1 x 30kW a.c Fuel: 15.0 (d.f.)
8728622 - -	**SBORSHCHIK-401** **State Enterprise Berdyansk Commercial Sea Port** *Berdyansk* *Ukraine* Official number: 884157	**235** 120 455	Class: (RS)	**1989-03 Bakinskiy Sudostroitelnyy Zavod im Vano Sturua — Baku** Yd No: 401 Loa 35.18 Br ex 8.01 Dght 3.122 Lbp 33.28 Br md - Dpth 3.61 Welded, 1 dk	**(B34G2SE) Pollution Control Vessel** Liq: 468; Liq (Oil): 468 Compartments: 10 Ta Ice Capable	**1 oil engine** geared to sc. shaft driving 1 FP propeller Total Power: 166kW (226hp) 8.1kn Daldizel 6CHNSP18/22 1 x 4 Stroke 6 Cy. 180 x 220 166kW (226bhp) Daldizel-Khabarovsk AuxGen: 1 x 50kW, 1 x 30kW Fuel: 11.0 (d.f.)
9572252 *YDA3605* -	**SBP** **PT Pelayaran Sumber Bahari** - *Batam* *Indonesia*	**238** 72 144	Class: KI	**2009-05 PT Sumber Samudra Makmur — Batam** Loa 29.30 Br ex - Dght 3.560 Lbp 27.07 Br md 8.20 Dpth 4.20 Welded, 1 dk	**(B32A2ST) Tug**	**2 oil engines** reduction geared to sc. shafts driving 2 Propellers Total Power: 1,722kW (2,342hp) Yanmar T260-ST 2 x 4 Stroke 6 Cy. 260 x 330 each-861kW (1171bhp) Yanmar Diesel Engine Co Ltd-Japan AuxGen: 2 x 41kW 400/230V a.c
8746404 *YD3670* -	**SBS** **PT Pelayaran Sumber Bahari** - *Batam* *Indonesia*	**142** 43 75	Class: KI	**2009-12 PT Sumber Samudra Makmur — Batam** Loa 23.00 Br ex - Dght 2.490 Lbp 21.12 Br md 7.00 Dpth 3.25 Welded, 1 dk	**(B32A2ST) Tug**	**2 oil engines** reduction geared to sc. shafts driving 2 Propellers Total Power: 806kW (1,096hp) Caterpillar 3412B 2 x Vee 4 Stroke 12 Cy. 137 x 152 each-403kW (548bhp) Caterpillar Inc-USA AuxGen: 2 x 70kW 380V a.c
8406999 *ZQZF9* -	**SBS CIRRUS** *ex Active Duke -2001* **Viking Supply Ships Ltd** *Lerwick* *United Kingdom* MMSI: 235001580 Official number: 904109	**2,562** 768 3,250	Class: NV	**1985-05 Liaaen Nordfjord AS — Nordfjordeid** Yd No: 141 Loa 80.78 Br ex - Dght 4.965 Lbp 76.21 Br md 18.01 Dpth 7.12 Welded, 1 dk	**(B21A20S) Platform Supply Ship** Passengers: cabins: 8; berths: 12	**2 oil engines** with clutches, flexible couplings & sr geared to sc. shafts driving 2 CP propellers Total Power: 4,414kW (6,002hp) 12.5kn Wartsila 6R32 2 x 4 Stroke 6 Cy. 320 x 350 each-2207kW (3001bhp) Oy Wartsila Ab-Finland AuxGen: 2 x 1560kW 440V 60Hz a.c, 2 x 312kW 440V 60Hz a.c Thrusters: 2 Thwart. CP thruster (f); 2 Tunnel thruster (a) Fuel: 1042.5 (d.f.)
9366835 *MLTG8* -	**SBS TEMPEST** **Viking Supply Ships Ltd** *Aberdeen* *United Kingdom* MMSI: 235010790 Official number: 911726	**2,596** 1,131 3,677	Class: NV	**2006-06 Societatea Comerciala Severnav S.A. — Drobeta-Turnu Severin** (Hull) Yd No: 0250003 **2006-06 Karmsund Maritime Service AS — Kopervik** Yd No: 25 Loa 73.40 (BB) Br ex 16.60 Dght 6.500 Lbp 64.00 Br md 16.60 Dpth 7.60 Welded, 1 dk	**(B21A20S) Platform Supply Ship**	**2 oil engines** reduction geared to sc. shafts driving 2 CP propellers Total Power: 4,900kW (6,662hp) 12.0kn MaK 8M25 2 x 4 Stroke 8 Cy. 255 x 400 each-2450kW (3331bhp) Caterpillar Motoren GmbH & Co. KG-Germany AuxGen: 2 x 1300kW 440/220V a.c, 2 x 370kW 440/220V a.c Thrusters: 2 Tunnel thruster (f); 2 Tunnel thruster (a)
9355965 *MPQN8* -	**SBS TYPHOON** **SBS Typhoon KS** Viking Supply Ships Ltd *Aberdeen* *United Kingdom* MMSI: 232964000 Official number: 912326	**2,574** 1,110 3,662	Class: NV	**2006-11 OAO Vyborgskiy Sudostroitelnyy Zavod — Vyborg** (Hull) Yd No: 044 **2006-11 Aker Yards AS Aukra — Aukra** Yd No: 122 Loa 73.40 (BB) Br ex - Dght 6.500 Lbp 64.00 Br md 16.60 Dpth 7.60 Welded, 1 dk	**(B21A20S) Platform Supply Ship**	**2 oil engines** reduction geared to sc. shafts driving 2 CP propellers Total Power: 4,060kW (5,520hp) 12.0kn Caterpillar 3606 2 x 4 Stroke 6 Cy. 280 x 300 each-2030kW (2760bhp) Caterpillar Inc-USA AuxGen: 2 x 240kW 440/220V a.c, 2 x 1300kW 400/220V a.c Thrusters: 2 Tunnel thruster (f); 2 Tunnel thruster (a) Fuel: 942.7 (r.f.)
8737269 *YD3554* -	**SBT** **PT Sumber Bahari Makmur** *Batam* *Indonesia* MMSI: 525016323	**148** 45 -	Class: KI	**2008-12 PT Sumber Samudra Makmur — Batam** Loa 25.00 Br ex - Dght 2.590 Lbp 22.02 Br md 7.00 Dpth 3.60 Welded, 1 dk	**(B32A2ST) Tug**	**2 oil engines** driving 2 Propellers Total Power: 1,204kW (1,636hp) Mitsubishi S6R2-MPTK 2 x 4 Stroke 6 Cy. 170 x 220 each-602kW (818bhp) Mitsubishi Heavy Industries Ltd-Japan
8930316 - -	**SC-667** - - *China*	**104** 36 -	Class: (VR)	**1996 in the People's Republic of China** Loa 28.50 Br ex - Dght 2.200 Lbp 23.90 Br md 5.50 Dpth 2.85 Welded, 1 dk	**(B11B2FV) Fishing Vessel**	**3 oil engines** reduction geared to sc. shafts driving 3 FP propellers Total Power: 336kW (456hp) 10.0kn Gardner 6LXB 3 x 4 Stroke 6 Cy. 121 x 152 each-112kW (152bhp) L. Gardner & Sons Ltd.-Manchester AuxGen: 1 x a.c
7800540 *C6SA2* -	**SC ABERDEEN** *ex Tungenes -2001 ex Astrea -1992* *launched as Erik Jarl -1979* **Sea-Cargo Skips AS** Seatrans AS *Nassau* *Bahamas* MMSI: 311264000 Official number: 8000354	**4,234** 1,271 3,041	Class: NV	**1979-07 Fosen Mek. Verksteder AS — Rissa** Yd No: 25 Loa 109.00 Br ex 16.51 Dght 4.820 Lbp 100.41 Br md 16.50 Dpth 10.06 Welded, 2 dks	**(A35A2RR) Ro-Ro Cargo Ship** Stern door/ramp (a) Len: 7.50 Wid: 4.60 Swl: 42 Side door (s) Lane-Len: 348 Grain: 10,126; Bale: 9,963 TEU 75 Compartments: 2 Ho, ER 1 Ha: (13.6 x 8.0)ER Cranes: 1x28t Ice Capable	**2 oil engines** driving 2 FP propellers Total Power: 4,400kW (5,982hp) 15.5kn MaK 6M453C 2 x 4 Stroke 6 Cy. 320 x 420 each-2200kW (2991bhp) (new engine 1993) Krupp MaK Maschinenbau GmbH-Kiel AuxGen: 2 x 420kW 400V 50Hz a.c Thrusters: 1 Thwart. FP thruster (f) Fuel: 1065.5 (d.f.) 14.0pd
8911736 *9HA3206* -	**SC AHTELA** *ex Ahtela -2012 ex Finnoak -2008* *ex Ahtela -1997* **Sea-Cargo Skips AS** Seatrans AS *Valletta* *Malta* MMSI: 229288000 Official number: 8911736	**8,610** 2,710 6,700 T/cm 18.1	Class: NV	**1991-12 Brodogradiliste 'Sava' — Macvanska Mitrovica** (Hull) Yd No: 305 **1991-12 Fosen Mek. Verksteder AS — Rissa** Yd No: 46 Lengthened-1998 Loa 139.50 (BB) Br ex - Dght 6.173 Lbp 129.50 Br md 19.00 Dpth 12.04 Welded, 2 dks	**(A35A2RR) Ro-Ro Cargo Ship** Stern door/ramp (a) Len: - Wid: - Swl: 70 Lane-Len: 1590 Lane-clr ht: 5.00 Bale: 12,000 TEU 359 incl 20 ref C. Ice Capable	**1 oil engine** with flexible couplings & sr geared to sc. shaft driving 1 CP propeller Total Power: 3,310kW (4,500hp) 16.5kn Wartsila 16V32D 1 x Vee 4 Stroke 16 Cy. 320 x 350 3310kW (4500bhp) Wartsila Diesel Oy-Finland AuxGen: 1 x 600kW 440V 60Hz a.c, 2 x 328kW 440V 60Hz a.c Thrusters: 1 Thwart. CP thruster (f) Fuel: 47.0 (d.f.) 600.0 (r.f.) 24.0pd
8917895 *C6ZL8* -	**SC ASTREA** *ex Astrea -2011* **Sea-Cargo Skips AS** Seatrans AS *Nassau* *Bahamas* MMSI: 311059100 Official number: 8001942	**9,528** 2,858 6,672	Class: NV	**1990-12 Tangen Verft AS — Kragero** (Hull) Yd No: 98 **1990-12 Langsten Slip & Baatbyggeri AS — Tomrefjord** Yd No: 150 Loa 129.10 (BB) Br ex 21.36 Dght 6.710 Lbp 120.00 Br md 21.00 Dpth 13.25 Welded, 2 dks	**(A35A2RR) Ro-Ro Cargo Ship** Stern door/ramp (a) Len: 13.00 Wid: 13.50 Swl: 120 Lane-Len: 824 Lane-clr ht: 6.70 TEU 451 C Ho 206 TEU C Dk 245 TEU incl 10 ref C. 1 Ha: (79.0 x 17.7)ER Ice Capable	**1 oil engine** sr geared to sc. shaft driving 1 CP propeller Total Power: 4,857kW (6,604hp) 13.5kn Wartsila 12V32E 1 x Vee 4 Stroke 12 Cy. 320 x 350 4857kW (6604bhp) Wartsila Diesel Oy-Finland AuxGen: 1 x 797kW 380V 50Hz a.c, 2 x 400kW 380V 50Hz a.c Thrusters: 1 Thwart. CP thruster (f) Fuel: 34.7 (d.f.) 518.0 (r.f.) 18.0pd

IMO / Call sign / Name / Owner / Manager	Tonnage	Class	Builder / Dimensions	Type / Cargo	Machinery
9175133 *VREW2* - **SC ATHENA** *ex* Zhi Hui Nv Shen *-2007* *ex* SC Athena *-2006* *ex* Dong Myung No. 2 *-2005* **Sea Dragon Shipping Co Ltd** Aoxing Ship Management (Shanghai) Ltd *Hong Kong* *Hong Kong* MMSI: 477189100 Official number: HK-2327	**1,997** 1,029 3,209 T/cm 9.7	Class: CC (KR)	**1997-09 Ilheung Shipbuilding & Engineering Co Ltd — Mokpo** Yd No: 96-71 Loa 85.40 (BB) Br ex 14.00 Dght 5.544 Lbp 78.01 Br md 14.00 Dpth 6.60 Welded, 1 dk	**(A12B2TR) Chemical/Products Tanker** Double Bottom Entire Compartment Length Liq: 3,708; Liq (Oil): 3,708 Cargo Heating Coils Compartments: 5 Ta, 10 Wing Ta, 2 Wing Slop Ta, ER 3 Cargo Pump (s): 3x400m³/hr Manifold: Bow/CM: 34.5m	**1 oil engine** driving 1 FP propeller Total Power: 1,618kW (2,200hp) 14.4kn Akasaka A34S 1 x 4 Stroke 6 Cy. 340 x 660 1618kW (2200bhp) Hyundai Heavy Industries Co Ltd-South Korea AuxGen: 2 x a.c Fuel: 49.1 (d.f.) 140.5 (r.f.)
9158331 *VREL7* - **SC AURORA** *ex* Li Ming Nv Shen *-2007* *ex* SC Aurora *-2006* *ex* Dong Myung No. 103 *-2005* *ex* Bu Yong *-2001* **Sea Phoenix Shipping Co Ltd** Aoxing Ship Management (Shanghai) Ltd *Hong Kong* *Hong Kong* MMSI: 477136500 Official number: HK-2245	**1,991** 1,105 3,372	Class: CC (KR)	**1996-11 Ilheung Shipbuilding & Engineering Co Ltd — Mokpo** Yd No: 95-63 Loa 85.40 (BB) Br ex - Dght 5.600 Lbp 78.00 Br md 14.00 Dpth 6.60 Welded, 1 dk	**(A12B2TR) Chemical/Products Tanker** Liq: 4,023; Liq (Oil): 4,023	**1 oil engine** driving 1 FP propeller Total Power: 1,618kW (2,200hp) 13.5kn Akasaka A34 1 x 4 Stroke 6 Cy. 340 x 660 1618kW (2200bhp) Hyundai Heavy Industries Co Ltd-South Korea AuxGen: 3 x 250kW 440V a.c Fuel: 188.0 (d.f.)
9471604 *VRFL2* - **SC BEIHAI** *completed as* Dong Xin 3 *-2009* **Hongkong Beihai Shipping Ltd** Donghai International Ship Management Ltd SatCom: Inmarsat C 447702133 *Hong Kong* *Hong Kong* MMSI: 477542500 Official number: HK-2446	**11,709** 5,615 17,777	Class: CC	**2009-06 No 4807 Shipyard of PLA — Fu'an FJ** Yd No: 223 Loa 151.79 Br ex 23.32 Dght 9.000 Lbp 142.60 Br md 23.30 Dpth 12.60 Welded, 1 dk	**(A12B2TR) Chemical/Products Tanker** Double Hull (13F) Liq: 19,841; Liq (Oil): 19,843 Compartments: 12 Wing Ta, 2 Wing Slop Ta, ER 12 Cargo Pump (s): 12x375m³/hr Manifold: Bow/CM: 77.5m Ice Capable	**1 oil engine** driving 1 FP propeller Total Power: 4,440kW (6,037hp) 13.0kn MAN-B&W 6S35MC 1 x 2 Stroke 6 Cy. 350 x 1400 4440kW (6037bhp) Yichang Marine Diesel Engine Co Ltd-China AuxGen: 3 x 436kW 400V a.c
9572185 *VRGU7* - **SC CHENGDU** **SC Chengdu Shipping Co Ltd** Sinochem Shipping Co Ltd (Hainan) *Hong Kong* *Hong Kong* MMSI: 477779200 Official number: HK-2734	**6,028** 2,740 9,182 T/cm 18.5	Class: CC	**2010-07 Chongqing Chuandong Shipbuilding Industry Co Ltd — Chongqing** Yd No: HT0104 Loa 115.74 (BB) Br ex - Dght 7.800 Lbp 108.00 Br md 18.60 Dpth 10.00 Welded, 1 dk	**(A12B2TR) Chemical/Products Tanker** Double Hull (13F) Liq: 8,568; Liq (Oil): 8,568 Cargo Heating Coils Compartments: 10 Wing Ta, 2 Wing Slop Ta, ER 10 Cargo Pump (s): 4x150m³/hr, 6x250m³/hr Manifold: Bow/CM: 56.2m	**1 oil engine** reduction geared to sc. shaft driving 1 FP propeller Total Power: 3,310kW (4,500hp) 13.1kn Yanmar 8N330-EN 1 x 4 Stroke 8 Cy. 330 x 440 3310kW (4500bhp) Qingdao Zichai Boyang Diesel EngineCo Ltd-China AuxGen: 3 x 500kW 400V a.c Thrusters: 1 Tunnel thruster (f) Fuel: 87.0 (d.f.) 510.0 (r.f.)
9425045 *VRIZ7* - **SC CHONGQING** *ex* Shui Shan *-2011* *ex* SC Chongqing *-2010* **SC Chongqing Shipping Co Ltd** Aoxing Ship Management (Shanghai) Ltd *Hong Kong* *Hong Kong* MMSI: 477950900 Official number: HK-3185	**6,028** 2,740 9,167 T/cm 18.5	Class: CC	**2010-01 Chongqing Chuandong Shipbuilding Industry Co Ltd — Chongqing** Yd No: HT0103 Loa 115.74 (BB) Br ex - Dght 7.800 Lbp 108.00 Br md 18.60 Dpth 10.00 Welded, 1 dk	**(A12B2TR) Chemical/Products Tanker** Double Hull (13F) Liq: 8,576; Liq (Oil): 9,509 Cargo Heating Coils Compartments: 10 Wing Ta, 2 Wing Slop Ta, ER 10 Cargo Pump (s): 6x250m³/hr, 4x150m³/hr Manifold: Bow/CM: 56.2m	**1 oil engine** reduction geared to sc. shaft driving 1 FP propeller Total Power: 3,310kW (4,500hp) 13.1kn Yanmar 8N330-EN 1 x 4 Stroke 8 Cy. 330 x 440 3310kW (4500bhp) Zibo Diesel Engine Factory-China AuxGen: 3 x 500kW 400V 60Hz a.c Thrusters: 1 Tunnel thruster (f) Fuel: 58.0 (d.f.) 518.0 (r.f.)
9430454 *VREQ7* - **SC DALIAN** **SC Dalian Ltd** Aoxing Ship Management (Shanghai) Ltd *Hong Kong* *Hong Kong* MMSI: 477177500 Official number: HK-2285	**8,539** 4,117 13,034 T/cm 23.2	Class: CC (AB)	**2009-02 21st Century Shipbuilding Co Ltd — Tongyeong** Yd No: 245 Loa 128.60 (BB) Br ex - Dght 8.714 Lbp 120.40 Br md 20.40 Dpth 11.50 Welded, 1 dk	**(A12B2TR) Chemical/Products Tanker** Double Hull (13F) Liq: 13,672; Liq (Oil): 14,094 Cargo Heating Coils Compartments: 12 Wing Ta, 2 Wing Slop Ta, ER 12 Cargo Pump (s): 12x300m³/hr Manifold: Bow/CM: 62.2m	**1 oil engine** driving 1 FP propeller Total Power: 4,400kW (5,982hp) 13.4kn MAN-B&W 6S35MC 1 x 2 Stroke 6 Cy. 350 x 1400 4400kW (5982bhp) STX Engine Co Ltd-South Korea AuxGen: 3 x 480kW a.c Thrusters: 1 Tunnel thruster (f) Fuel: 75.0 (d.f.) 661.0 (r.f.)
9492945 *A8YR5* - **SC DONGHAI** *completed as* Dong Xin 5 *-2009* **National Shipping SA** - *Monrovia* *Liberia* MMSI: 636015115 Official number: 15115	**11,709** 5,615 17,777	Class: LR (CC) **100A1** SS 05/2009 Double Hull oil & chemical tanker, Ship Type 2 ESP LI **LMC**	**2009-05 No 4807 Shipyard of PLA — Fu'an FJ** Yd No: 225 Loa 151.79 Br ex 23.32 Dght 9.000 Lbp 142.60 Br md 23.30 Dpth 12.60 Welded, 1 dk	**(A12B2TR) Chemical/Products Tanker** Double Hull (13F) Liq: 19,697; Liq (Oil): 19,697 Compartments: 12 Wing Ta, 2 Wing Slop Ta, ER 12 Cargo Pump (s): 12x375m³/hr Manifold: Bow/CM: 77.5m Ice Capable	**1 oil engine** driving 1 FP propeller Total Power: 4,440kW (6,037hp) 13.0kn MAN-B&W 6S35MC 1 x 2 Stroke 6 Cy. 350 x 1400 4440kW (6037bhp) Yichang Marine Diesel Engine Co Ltd-China AuxGen: 3 x 436kW 400V a.c
9429912 *HSB4577* - **SC EMERALD** *ex* Crest Emerald *-2011* **SC Offshore Services Co Ltd** SC Management Co Ltd *Bangkok* *Thailand* MMSI: 567431000	**1,470** 441 1,411	Class: AB (BV)	**2007-12 Guangzhou Hangtong Shipbuilding & Shipping Co Ltd — Jiangmen GD** Yd No: 062003 Loa 58.70 Br ex - Dght 4.750 Lbp 54.12 Br md 14.60 Dpth 5.50 Welded, 1 dk	**(B21B20A) Anchor Handling Tug Supply**	**2 oil engines** reduction geared to sc. shafts driving 2 CP propellers Total Power: 3,840kW (5,220hp) 13.5kn Caterpillar 3516B-HD 2 x Vee 4 Stroke 16 Cy. 170 x 215 each-1920kW (2610bhp) Caterpillar Inc-USA AuxGen: 3 x 315kW 50Hz a.c
9417854 *HSB3575* - **SC GLORY** **SC Offshore Co Ltd** SC Management Co Ltd *Bangkok* *Thailand* MMSI: 567051400 Official number: 490003246	**244** 83 80	Class: AB	**2006-11 Sam Aluminium Engineering Pte Ltd — Singapore** Yd No: H70 Loa 36.50 Br ex - Dght 1.300 Lbp 33.65 Br md 7.80 Dpth 3.40 Welded, 1 dk	**(B21A20C) Crew/Supply Vessel** Hull Material: Aluminium Alloy	**3 oil engines** reduction geared to sc. shafts driving 3 Propellers Total Power: 3,132kW (4,257hp) Caterpillar C32 3 x Vee 4 Stroke 12 Cy. 145 x 162 each-1044kW (1419bhp) Caterpillar Inc-USA AuxGen: 2 x 90kW a.c Fuel: 94.0
9606144 *HSB4572* - **SC GLORY 2** **SC Management Co Ltd** - *Bangkok* *Thailand* MMSI: 567427000 Official number: TG 54014	**236** 71 110	Class: AB	**2011-04 Penguin Shipyard International Pte Ltd — Singapore** Yd No: 168 Loa 36.00 Br ex - Dght 1.850 Lbp 33.20 Br md 7.60 Dpth 3.65 Welded, 1 dk	**(B21A20C) Crew/Supply Vessel** Hull Material: Aluminium Alloy	**3 oil engines** reduction geared to sc. shafts driving 3 FP propellers Total Power: 3,021kW (4,107hp) 20.0kn Cummins KTA-38-M2 3 x Vee 4 Stroke 12 Cy. 159 x 159 each-1007kW (1369bhp) Cummins Engine Co Inc-USA AuxGen: 2 x 100kW 415/220V 50Hz a.c
9606156 *HSB4581* - **SC GLORY 3** **SC Management Co Ltd** - *Bangkok* *Thailand* MMSI: 567432000	**236** 71 113	Class: AB	**2011-05 Penguin Shipyard International Pte Ltd — Singapore** Yd No: 169 Loa 36.00 Br ex - Dght 1.850 Lbp 33.20 Br md 7.60 Dpth 3.65 Welded, 1 dk	**(B21A20C) Crew/Supply Vessel** Hull Material: Aluminium Alloy	**3 oil engines** reduction geared to sc. shafts driving 3 FP propellers Total Power: 3,021kW (4,107hp) 20.0kn Cummins KTA-38-M2 3 x Vee 4 Stroke 12 Cy. 159 x 159 each-1007kW (1369bhp) Cummins Engine Co Ltd-United Kingdom AuxGen: 2 x 80kW 415/220V 50Hz a.c Thrusters: 1 Tunnel thruster (f)
9694672 *HSB4916* - **SC GLORY 4** **SC Management Co Ltd** - *Bangkok* *Thailand* MMSI: 567063500 Official number: TG 57003	**257** 77 133	Class: NK (BV)	**2013-10 PT Kim Seah Shipyard Indonesia — Batam (Hull)** Yd No: (212) **2013-10 Penguin Shipyard International Pte Ltd — Singapore** Yd No: 212 Loa 38.00 Br ex - Dght 1.890 Lbp 34.96 Br md 7.60 Dpth 3.65 Welded, 1 dk	**(B21A20C) Crew/Supply Vessel** Hull Material: Aluminium Alloy	**3 oil engines** reduction geared to sc. shafts driving 3 Propellers Total Power: 2,424kW (3,297hp) 25.9kn Baudouin 12M26.2P2 3 x Vee 4 Stroke 12 Cy. 150 x 150 each-808kW (1099bhp) Societe des Moteurs Baudouin SA-France Thrusters: 1 Tunnel thruster (f) Fuel: 65.0
9492957 *3FNT7* - **SC GUANGZHOU** *launched as* Dong Xin 6 *-2008* **SFL Chemical Tanker II Ltd** Aoxing Ship Management (Shanghai) Ltd *Panama* *Panama* MMSI: 370948000 Official number: 4018409	**11,709** 5,615 17,777 T/cm 30.6	Class: CC (LR) Classed LR until 17/4/09	**2008-10 No 4807 Shipyard of PLA — Fu'an FJ** Yd No: 217 Loa 151.79 (BB) Br ex 23.32 Dght 9.000 Lbp 142.60 Br md 23.30 Dpth 12.60 Welded, 1 dk	**(A12B2TR) Chemical/Products Tanker** Double Hull (13F) Liq: 19,843; Liq (Oil): 20,523 Cargo Heating Coils Compartments: 12 Wing Ta, 2 Wing Slop Ta, ER 12 Cargo Pump (s): 12x375m³/hr Manifold: Bow/CM: 77.5m Ice Capable	**1 oil engine** driving 1 FP propeller Total Power: 4,440kW (6,037hp) 13.0kn MAN-B&W 6S35MC 1 x 2 Stroke 6 Cy. 350 x 1400 4440kW (6037bhp) Yichang Marine Diesel Engine Co Ltd-China AuxGen: 3 x 436kW 400V 50Hz a.c Boilers: e (ex.g.) 8.0kgf/cm² (7.8bar), AuxB (o.f.) 8.0kgf/cm² (7.8bar) Thrusters: 1 Tunnel thruster (f) Fuel: 131.0 (d.f.) 768.0 (r.f.)

9350733 *VRCH2* -	**SC GUOJI** **Pole Star Shipping Corp Ltd** Aoxing Ship Management (Shanghai) Ltd SatCom: Inmarsat Mini-M 763675861 *Hong Kong* *Hong Kong* MMSI: 477581500 Official number: HK-1791	**8,562** 4,095 13,107 T/cm 23.3	Class: CC (KR)	**2006**-12 **21st Century Shipbuilding Co Ltd — Tongyeong** Yd No: 225 Loa 128.60 (BB) Br ex 20.40 Dght 8.714 Lbp 120.40 Br md 20.40 Dpth 11.50 Welded, 1 dk	**(A12B2TR) Chemical/Products Tanker** Double Hull (13F) Liq: 13,402; Liq (Oil): 13,402 Cargo Heating Coils Compartments: 12 Wing Ta, 2 Wing Slop Ta, ER 12 Cargo Pump (s): 12x300m³/hr Manifold: Bow/CM: 61.4m	**1 oil engine** driving 1 FP propeller Total Power: 4,440kW (6,037hp) 13.4kn MAN-B&W 6S35MC 1 x 2 Stroke 6 Cy. 350 x 1400 4440kW (6037bhp) STX Engine Co Ltd-South Korea AuxGen: 3 x 500kW 450V a.c Thrusters: 1 Tunnel thruster (f) Fuel: 75.0 (d.f.) 661.0 (r.f.)
9430430 *VRFC4* -	**SC HAIKOU** **SC Haikou Shipping Co Ltd** Sinochem Shipping Co Ltd (Hainan) SatCom: Inmarsat C 447701750 *Hong Kong* *Hong Kong* MMSI: 477218200 Official number: HK-2377	**8,562** 4,095 13,009 T/cm 22.9	Class: CC (KR)	**2009**-06 **21st Century Shipbuilding Co Ltd — Tongyeong** Yd No: 251 Loa 128.60 (BB) Br ex - Dght 8.714 Lbp 120.40 Br md 20.40 Dpth 11.50 Welded, 1 dk	**(A12B2TR) Chemical/Products Tanker** Double Hull (13F) Liq: 13,388; Liq (Oil): 13,359 Cargo Heating Coils Compartments: 12 Wing Ta, 2 Wing Slop Ta, ER 12 Cargo Pump (s): 12x300m³/hr Manifold: Bow/CM: 52.1m	**1 oil engine** driving 1 FP propeller Total Power: 4,440kW (6,037hp) 13.4kn MAN-B&W 6S35MC 1 x 2 Stroke 6 Cy. 350 x 1400 4440kW (6037bhp) STX Engine Co Ltd-South Korea AuxGen: 3 x 480kW 440V a.c Thrusters: 1 Tunnel thruster (f) Fuel: 40.0 (d.f.) 520.0 (r.f.)
9187904 *VRJP9* -	**SC HONGKONG** *ex* Maria Knutsen *-2011* *launched as* Chembulk Barcelona *-2007* **Hai Kuo Shipping 1371 Ltd** Aoxing Ship Management (Shanghai) Ltd SatCom: Inmarsat C 447784710 *Hong Kong* *Hong Kong* MMSI: 477847700 Official number: HK-3315	**13,753** 7,006 22,171 T/cm 32.9	Class: LR **✠100A1** SS 07/2011 oil & chemical tanker, Ship Type 2* CR (s.stl) SG 1.85 in all tanks ESP *IWS LI **✠LMC** **UMS IGS** Eq.Ltr: G†; Cable: 577.5/60.0 U3 (a)	**2001**-07 **Naval Gijon S.A. (NAGISA) — Gijon** Yd No: 556 Loa 159.62 (BB) Br ex 23.02 Dght 10.315 Lbp 149.79 Br md 23.00 Dpth 13.54 Welded, 1 dk	**(A12B2TR) Chemical/Products Tanker** Double Hull (13F) Liq: 23,453; Liq (Oil): 23,731 Cargo Heating Coils Compartments: 24 Wing Ta, ER 24 Cargo Pump (s): 24x200m³/hr Manifold: Bow/CM: 78.6m	**1 oil engine** driving 1 CP propeller Total Power: 7,134kW (9,699hp) 15.5kn B&W 5S50MC 1 x 2 Stroke 5 Cy. 500 x 1910 7134kW (9699bhp) Manises Diesel Engine Co. S.A.-Valencia AuxGen: 1 x 700kW 440V 60Hz a.c, 3 x 610kW 440V 60Hz a.c Boilers: 2 AuxB (o.f.) 10.4kgf/cm² (10.2bar), e (ex.g.) 11.2kgf/cm² (11.0bar) Thrusters: 1 Thwart. CP thruster (f) Fuel: 91.0 (d.f.) (Heating Coils) 1096.0 (r.f.)
9244879 *VRCD6* -	**SC IRIS** *ex* Feng Shou Nu Shen *-2006* *ex* SC Iris *-2005* *ex* Samho Global *-2004* **Lucky Harvest Shipping Co Ltd** Aoxing Ship Management (Shanghai) Ltd SatCom: Inmarsat Mini-M 763922165 *Hong Kong* *Hong Kong* MMSI: 477880400 Official number: HK-1763	**2,270** 1,220 3,713 T/cm 9.0	Class: CC (KR)	**2001**-04 **Haedong Shipbuilding Co Ltd — Tongyeong** Yd No: 1031 Loa 86.95 (BB) Br ex 14.23 Dght 5.948 Lbp 79.50 Br md 14.20 Dpth 7.00 Welded, 1 dk	**(A12B2TR) Chemical/Products Tanker** Double Hull (13F) Liq: 3,755; Liq (Oil): 3,755 Cargo Heating Coils Compartments: 8 Wing Ta, 1 Ta, 1 Slop Ta, ER 9 Cargo Pump (s): 9x200m³/hr Manifold: Bow/CM: 47.2m	**1 oil engine** reduction geared to sc. shaft driving 1 FP propeller Total Power: 1,960kW (2,665hp) 12.1kn MAN-B&W 8L28/32A 1 x 4 Stroke 8 Cy. 280 x 320 1960kW (2665bhp) Ssangyong Heavy Industries Co Ltd-South Korea AuxGen: 3 x 262kW 400V a.c Thrusters: 1 Tunnel thruster (f) Fuel: 52.0 (d.f.) 159.0 (r.f.)
9215048 *C6WF2* -	**SC LAURA** *ex* Maersk Pointer *-2007* **Majorna Mobiliengesellschaft mbH & Co KG** Sigma Tankers Inc SatCom: Inmarsat B 330806810 *Nassau* *Bahamas* MMSI: 308068000 Official number: 8001372	**61,764** 24,204 109,325 T/cm 89.9	Class: LR **✠100A1** SS 07/2010 Double Hull oil tanker ESP *IWS SPM LI **ShipRight** (SDA, FDA, CM) **✠LMC** **UMS IGS** Eq.Ltr: U†; Cable: 715.0/92.0 U3 (a)	**2001**-08 **Dalian New Shipbuilding Heavy Industries Co Ltd — Dalian LN** Yd No: PC1100-10 Loa 244.53 (BB) Br ex 42.03 Dght 15.450 Lbp 233.00 Br md 42.00 Dpth 22.20 Welded, 1 dk	**(A13B2TP) Products Tanker** Double Hull (13F) Liq: 117,921; Liq (Oil): 117,921 Cargo Heating Coils Compartments: 12 Wing Ta, 2 Wing Slop Ta, ER 3 Cargo Pump (s): 3x3000m³/hr Manifold: Bow/CM: 120.3m	**1 oil engine** driving 1 FP propeller Total Power: 15,540kW (21,128hp) 15.3kn Sulzer 7RTA62U 1 x 2 Stroke 7 Cy. 620 x 2150 15540kW (21128bhp) Dalian Marine Diesel Works-China AuxGen: 3 x 780kW 450V 60Hz a.c Boilers: 2 AuxB (o.f.) 18.4kgf/cm² (18.0bar), AuxB (ex.g.) 8.2kgf/cm² (8.0bar)
9428310 *VREU8* -	**SC LIAONING** **SC Liaoning Shipping Co Ltd** Aoxing Ship Management (Shanghai) Ltd *Hong Kong* *Hong Kong* MMSI: 477185400 Official number: HK-2317	**8,562** 4,095 13,029 T/cm 23.2	Class: CC (KR)	**2009**-01 **21st Century Shipbuilding Co Ltd — Tongyeong** Yd No: 246 Loa 128.60 (BB) Br ex - Dght 8.714 Lbp 120.40 Br md 20.40 Dpth 11.50 Welded, 1 dk	**(A12B2TR) Chemical/Products Tanker** Double Hull (13F) Liq: 13,388; Liq (Oil): 13,389 Cargo Heating Coils Compartments: 12 Wing Ta, 2 Wing Slop Ta, ER 12 Cargo Pump (s): 12x300m³/hr Manifold: Bow/CM: 61m	**1 oil engine** driving 1 FP propeller Total Power: 4,440kW (6,037hp) 13.4kn MAN-B&W 6S35MC 1 x 2 Stroke 6 Cy. 350 x 1400 4440kW (6037bhp) STX Engine Co Ltd-South Korea AuxGen: 3 x 600kW 445V a.c Thrusters: 1 Tunnel thruster (f) Fuel: 76.0 (d.f.) 644.0 (r.f.)
9425461 *A8Q08* -	**SC LOTTA** *launched as* Phoenix Grace *-2009* **Midir Mobiliengesellschaft mbH & Co KG** Kleimar NV SatCom: Inmarsat C 463704333 *Monrovia* *Liberia* MMSI: 636091625 Official number: 91625	**88,397** 57,037 169,057	Class: LR **✠100A1** SS 02/2014 bulk carrier CSR BC-A GRAB (20) Nos. 2, 4, 6 & 8 holds may be empty ESP **ShipRight** (CM) *IWS LI **✠LMC** **UMS** Eq.Ltr: A*; Cable: 742.5/102.0 U3 (a)	**2009**-02 **Sungdong Shipbuilding & Marine Engineering Co Ltd — Tongyeong** Yd No: 1035 Loa 287.50 (BB) Br ex 45.06 Dght 17.700 Lbp 279.00 Br md 45.00 Dpth 24.10 Welded, 1 dk	**(A21A2BC) Bulk Carrier** Grain: 191,654; Bale: 182,071 Compartments: 9 Ho, ER 9 Ha: 7 (15.5 x 20.6) (15.5 x 17.2)ER (14.6 x 17.2)	**1 oil engine** driving 1 FP propeller Total Power: 16,860kW (22,923hp) 14.6kn MAN-B&W 6S70MC 1 x 2 Stroke 6 Cy. 700 x 2674 16860kW (22923bhp) Hyundai Heavy Industries Co Ltd-South Korea AuxGen: 3 x 720kW 450V 60Hz a.c Boilers: AuxB (Comp) 8.0kgf/cm² (7.8bar) Fuel: 248.0 (d.f.) 3328.0 (r.f.)
9302578 *V7NF9* -	**SC MARA** *ex* MSC Mara *-2014* **Castle Lugano LLC** Bernhard Schulte Shipmanagement (China) Co Ltd *Majuro* *Marshall Islands* MMSI: 538002955 Official number: 2955	**54,214** 31,226 68,165 T/cm 83.2	Class: AB (GL)	**2006**-06 **Hanjin Heavy Industries & Construction Co Ltd — Busan** Yd No: 146 Loa 294.09 (BB) Br ex - Dght 13.500 Lbp 283.00 Br md 32.20 Dpth 21.60 Welded, 1 dk	**(A33A2CC) Container Ship (Fully Cellular)** TEU 5059 C Ho 2216 TEU C Dk 2843 TEU incl 454 ref C. Ice Capable	**1 oil engine** driving 1 FP propeller Total Power: 41,130kW (55,920hp) 23.0kn MAN-B&W 9K90MC-C 1 x 2 Stroke 9 Cy. 900 x 2300 41130kW (55920bhp) Doosan Engine Co Ltd-South Korea AuxGen: 4 x 1890kW 440/220V 60Hz a.c Thrusters: 1 Thwart. CP thruster (f) Fuel: 479.0 (d.f.) 6672.0 (r.f.)
9444168 *VRET4* -	**SC NINGBO** **SC Ningbo Ltd** Aoxing Ship Management (Shanghai) Ltd SatCom: Inmarsat C 447701589 *Hong Kong* *Hong Kong* MMSI: 477197700 Official number: HK-2306	**8,539** 4,117 13,083 T/cm 22.9	Class: CC (AB)	**2009**-03 **21st Century Shipbuilding Co Ltd — Tongyeong** Yd No: 250 Loa 128.60 (BB) Br ex - Dght 8.714 Lbp 120.40 Br md 20.40 Dpth 11.50 Welded, 1 dk	**(A12B2TR) Chemical/Products Tanker** Double Hull (13F) Liq: 13,388; Liq (Oil): 14,094 Cargo Heating Coils Compartments: 12 Wing Ta, 2 Wing Slop Ta, ER 12 Cargo Pump (s): 12x300m³/hr Manifold: Bow/CM: 49.7m	**1 oil engine** driving 1 FP propeller Total Power: 4,440kW (6,037hp) 13.4kn MAN-B&W 6S35MC 1 x 2 Stroke 6 Cy. 350 x 1400 4440kW (6037bhp) STX Engine Co Ltd-South Korea AuxGen: 3 x 480kW 445V a.c Thrusters: 1 Tunnel thruster (f) Fuel: 76.0 (d.f.) 653.0 (r.f.)
8516990 *OZ2140* -	**SC NORDIC** *ex* Trans Nordia *-2001* **Sp/f SC Nordic** Norresundby Shipping A/S *Torshavn* *Faeroe Islands (Danish)* MMSI: 231211000	**4,876** 1,823 4,020	Class: NV RI	**1986**-10 **Kleven Mek Verksted AS — Ulsteinvik** Yd No: 96 Loa 110.50 Br ex 17.61 Dght 5.713 Lbp 102.50 Br md 17.50 Dpth 11.03 Welded, 2 dks	**(A31B2GP) Palletised Cargo Ship** Side doors (s) Ice Capable	**1 oil engine** geared to sc. shaft driving 1 CP propeller Total Power: 2,998kW (4,076hp) 13.0kn Wartsila 8R32 1 x 4 Stroke 8 Cy. 320 x 350 2998kW (4076bhp) Oy Wartsila Ab-Finland AuxGen: 1 x 428kW 380V 50Hz a.c, 1 x 404kW 380V 50Hz a.c Thrusters: 1 Thwart. CP thruster (f)
9428308 *VREJ9* -	**SC QINGDAO** **SC Qingdao Shipping Co Ltd** Sinochem Shipping Co Ltd (Hainan) *Hong Kong* *Hong Kong* MMSI: 477115300 Official number: HK-2231	**8,562** 4,095 13,019 T/cm 23.2	Class: CC (KR)	**2008**-09 **21st Century Shipbuilding Co Ltd — Tongyeong** Yd No: 244 Loa 128.60 (BB) Br ex - Dght 8.700 Lbp 119.92 Br md 20.40 Dpth 11.50 Welded, 1 dk	**(A12B2TR) Chemical/Products Tanker** Double Hull (13F) Liq: 13,398; Liq (Oil): 14,094 Cargo Heating Coils Compartments: 12 Wing Ta, 2 Wing Slop Ta, ER 12 Cargo Pump (s): 12x300m³/hr Manifold: Bow/CM: 60.7m	**1 oil engine** driving 1 FP propeller Total Power: 4,400kW (5,982hp) 13.4kn MAN-B&W 6S35MC 1 x 2 Stroke 6 Cy. 350 x 1400 4400kW (5982bhp) STX Engine Co Ltd-South Korea AuxGen: 3 x 550kW a.c Thrusters: 1 Tunnel thruster (f) Fuel: 76.0 (d.f.) 644.0 (r.f.)
9224336 *V7KF5* -	**SC QINGDAO** *ex* CSCL Qingdao *-2013* **Kalapa Mobiliengesellschaft mbH & Co KG (KGAL)** China Shipping Container Lines Co Ltd *Majuro* *Marshall Islands* MMSI: 538090238 Official number: 90238	**39,941** 24,458 50,953 T/cm 70.4	Class: LR **✠100A1** SS 12/2011 container ship *IWS LI **ShipRight** (SDA, FDA, CM) **✠LMC** **UMS** Eq.Ltr: S†; Cable: 687.5/87.0 U3 (a)	**2001**-12 **Samsung Heavy Industries Co Ltd — Geoje** Yd No: 1345 Loa 259.80 (BB) Br ex 32.35 Dght 12.620 Lbp 244.80 Br md 32.25 Dpth 19.30 Welded, 1 dk	**(A33A2CC) Container Ship (Fully Cellular)** TEU 4253 C Ho 1584 TEU C Dk 2669 TEU incl 400 ref C. Compartments: ER, 7 Cell Ho 14 Ha: ER	**1 oil engine** driving 1 FP propeller Total Power: 36,515kW (49,646hp) 23.3kn B&W 8K90MC-C 1 x 2 Stroke 8 Cy. 900 x 2300 36515kW (49646bhp) Doosan Engine Co Ltd-South Korea AuxGen: 4 x 1700kW 450V 60Hz a.c Boilers: AuxB (Comp) 8.0kgf/cm² (7.8bar) Thrusters: 1 Thwart. FP thruster (f)

IMO / Call sign	Name / Owner / Manager	Tonnage	Class	Builder / Dimensions	Type / Cargo	Machinery
9224348 *V7KF4* -	**SC ROTTERDAM** *ex* CSCL Rotterdam *-2012* **Kintari Mobiliengesellschaft mbH & Co KG** Orient Overseas Container Line Ltd (OOCL) *Majuro* *Marshall Islands* MMSI: 538090237 Official number: 90237	**39,941** 24,458 50,953 T/cm 70.4	Class: LR ✠**100A1** SS 05/2012 container ship *IWS LI **ShipRight** (SDA, FDA, CM) ✠**LMC** **UMS** Eq.Ltr: S†; Cable: 687.5/87.0 U3 (a)	**2002-05 Samsung Heavy Industries Co Ltd — Geoje** Yd No: 1346 Loa 259.80 (BB) Br ex - Dght 12.600 Lbp 244.80 Br md 32.25 Dpth 19.30 Welded, 1 dk	**(A33A2CC) Container Ship (Fully Cellular)** TEU 4253 C Ho 1584 TEU C Dk 2669 TEU incl 400 ref C. Compartments: 7 Cell Ho, ER	**1 oil engine** driving 1 FP propeller Total Power: 36,540kW (49,680hp) 23.3kn B&W 8K90MC-C 1 x 2 Stroke 8 Cy. 900 x 2300 36540kW (49680bhp) Doosan Engine Co Ltd-South Korea AuxGen: 4 x 1700kW 450V 60Hz a.c Boilers: AuxB (Comp) 8.1kgf/cm² (7.9bar) Thrusters: 1 Thwart. CP thruster (f)
9230971 *A8LT7* -	**SC SARA** *ex* Nordatlantic *-2007* **Liwa Mobiliengesellschaft mbH & Co KG** Sigma Tankers Inc *Monrovia* *Liberia* MMSI: 636091297 Official number: 91297	**56,346** 32,059 105,344 T/cm 89.2	Class: AB (NV)	**2001-10 Sumitomo Heavy Industries Ltd. — Yokosuka Shipyard, Yokosuka** Yd No: 1282 Loa 239.00 (BB) Br ex 42.03 Dght 14.880 Lbp 229.00 Br md 42.00 Dpth 21.30 Welded, 1 dk	**(A13A2TV) Crude Oil Tanker** Double Hull (13F) Liq: 115,570; Liq (Oil): 115,570 Compartments: 12 Wing Ta, ER, 2 Wing Slop Ta 3 Cargo Pump (s): 3x3000m³/hr Manifold: Bow/CM: 115.6m	**1 oil engine** driving 1 FP propeller Total Power: 12,004kW (16,321hp) 15.0kn Sulzer 6RTA58T 1 x 2 Stroke 6 Cy. 580 x 2416 12004kW (16321bhp) Diesel United Ltd.-Aioi
9352054 *VRJF5* -	**SC SHANGHAI** *ex* Guohuai *-2011* *ex* Sc Shanghai *-2010* **Top Glory Enterprises Corp Ltd** Aoxing Ship Management (Shanghai) Ltd SatCom: Inmarsat C 447703758 *Hong Kong* *Hong Kong* MMSI: 477346700 Official number: HK3233	**8,562** 4,095 13,083 T/cm 23.3	Class: CC (KR)	**2007-02 21st Century Shipbuilding Co Ltd — Tongyeong** Yd No: 226 Loa 128.60 (BB) Br ex 20.43 Dght 8.714 Lbp 120.40 Br md 20.40 Dpth 11.50 Welded, 1 dk	**(A12B2TR) Chemical/Products Tanker** Double Hull (13F) Liq: 14,094; Liq (Oil): 14,094 Cargo Heating Coils Compartments: 12 Wing Ta, 2 Wing Slop Ta, ER 12 Cargo Pump (s): 12x300m³/hr Manifold: Bow/CM: 61.4m	**1 oil engine** driving 1 FP propeller Total Power: 4,440kW (6,037hp) 13.4kn MAN-B&W 6S35MC 1 x 2 Stroke 6 Cy. 350 x 1400 4440kW (6037bhp) (made 2006) STX Engine Co Ltd-South Korea AuxGen: 3 x 480kW 440V 60Hz a.c Thrusters: 1 Tunnel thruster (f) Fuel: 150.0 (d.f.) 1322.0 (r.f.)
9161871 *VRIL3* -	**SC SHANTOU** *ex* Chemstar King *-2011* **Sea Wealth Shipping Co Ltd** Aoxing Ship Management (Shanghai) Ltd *Hong Kong* *Hong Kong* MMSI: 477514800 Official number: HK-3075	**11,951** 5,765 19,508 T/cm 30.0	Class: NK	**1998-01 Shin Kurushima Dockyard Co. Ltd. — Akitsu** Yd No: 2960 Loa 147.83 (BB) Br ex 24.30 Dght 9.230 Lbp 141.00 Br md 24.20 Dpth 12.80 Welded, 1 dk	**(A12B2TR) Chemical/Products Tanker** Double Hull (13F) Liq: 21,439; Liq (Oil): 21,860 Cargo Heating Coils Compartments: 20 Wing Ta, ER 20 Cargo Pump (s): 20x200m³/hr Manifold: Bow/CM: 74m	**1 oil engine** driving 1 FP propeller Total Power: 6,179kW (8,401hp) 14.7kn Mitsubishi 7UEC45LA 1 x 2 Stroke 7 Cy. 450 x 1350 6179kW (8401bhp) Akasaka Tekkosho KK (Akasaka DieselLtd)-Japan AuxGen: 3 x 300kW 450V 60Hz a.c Fuel: 77.8 (d.f.) 723.1 (r.f.)
9185865 *VRGO4* -	**SC SHENZHEN** *ex* Chemstar Angel *-2009* *ex* Jipro Dream *-2007* **SC Shenzhen Shipping Co Ltd** Sinochem Shipping Co Ltd (Hainan) *Hong Kong* *Hong Kong* MMSI: 477742200 Official number: HK-2683	**11,962** 5,765 19,477 T/cm 30.0	Class: NK	**1999-10 Shin Kurushima Dockyard Co. Ltd. — Akitsu** Yd No: 5007 Loa 147.83 (BB) Br ex 24.22 Dght 9.230 Lbp 141.00 Br md 24.20 Dpth 12.80 Welded, 1 dk	**(A12B2TR) Chemical/Products Tanker** Double Hull (13F) Liq: 20,196; Liq (Oil): 21,414 Cargo Heating Coils Compartments: 20 Wing Ta (s.stl), 2 Wing Slop Ta (s.stl), ER 20 Cargo Pump (s): 20x200m³/hr Manifold: Bow/CM: 74m	**1 oil engine** driving 1 FP propeller Total Power: 6,178kW (8,400hp) 14.7kn Mitsubishi 7UEC45LA 1 x 2 Stroke 7 Cy. 450 x 1350 6178kW (8400bhp) Kobe Hatsudoki KK-Japan AuxGen: 3 x 320kW 450V 60Hz a.c Fuel: 91.0 (d.f.) (Heating Coils) 1050.0 (r.f.) 24.0pd
9340702 *C6WI7* -	**SC STEALTH** *ex* Beffen *-2010* **Armor Chems Inc** Sinochem Shipping Co Ltd (Hainan) SatCom: Inmarsat C 430814810 *Nassau* *Bahamas* MMSI: 308148000 Official number: 8001395	**11,729** 6,285 19,959 T/cm 29.8	Class: BV	**2007-08 Fukuoka Shipbuilding Co Ltd — Fukuoka FO** Yd No: 1266 Loa 144.09 (BB) Br ex 24.23 Dght 9.620 Lbp 136.46 Br md 24.19 Dpth 12.90 Welded, 1 dk	**(A12B2TR) Chemical/Products Tanker** Double Hull (13F) Liq: 21,280; Liq (Oil): 21,280 Cargo Heating Coils Compartments: 18 Ta, 2 Slop Ta, ER 18 Cargo Pump (s): 12x300m³/hr, 6x200m³/hr Manifold: Bow/CM: 72.9m	**1 oil engine** driving 1 FP propeller Total Power: 6,150kW (8,362hp) 14.5kn MAN-B&W 6S42MC 1 x 2 Stroke 6 Cy. 420 x 1764 6150kW (8362bhp) Makita Corp-Japan AuxGen: 3 x 560kW 440/110V a.c Thrusters: 1 Tunnel thruster (f) Fuel: 125.0 (d.f.) 920.0 (r.f.)
8601446 *3EXP6* -	**SC SUNNY** *ex* Seneca Maiden *-2013* *ex* Asian Manila *-1995* *ex* Lady Rose *-1994* *ex* ALS Prosperity *-1991* **Ever Sunny Shipping Ltd** Brother Marine Co Ltd *Panama* *Panama* MMSI: 355006000 Official number: 44262PEXT	**12,301** 7,385 19,764	Class: RI (LR) (NK) (PR) Classed LR until 18/1/13	**1986-10 K.K. Uwajima Zosensho — Uwajima** Yd No: 2481 Loa 155.03 (BB) Br ex 23.02 Dght 9.500 Lbp 145.01 Br md 23.00 Dpth 13.01 Welded, 1 dk	**(A31A2GX) General Cargo Ship** Grain: 26,697; Bale: 23,818 TEU 440 Compartments: 4 Ho, ER 4 Ha: (20.0 x 11.2)3 (20.0 x 14.4)ER Cranes: 2x41.6t,2x25.4t	**1 oil engine** driving 1 FP propeller Total Power: 5,074kW (6,899hp) 14.0kn Mitsubishi 6UEC52LA 1 x 2 Stroke 6 Cy. 520 x 1600 5074kW (6899bhp) Kobe Hatsudoki KK-Japan AuxGen: 1 x 513kW 450V 60Hz a.c, 2 x 425kW 450V 60Hz a.c Boilers: AuxB (o.f.) 7.0kgf/cm² (6.9bar) Fuel: 960.0 (r.f.)
9175535 *VRJM4* -	**SC TAIPEI** *ex* Isabel Knutsen *-2011* *ex* Chembulk Savannah *-2000* **SC Taipei Shipping Co Ltd** Aoxing Ship Management (Shanghai) Ltd *Hong Kong* *Hong Kong* MMSI: 477108300 Official number: HK-3288	**13,753** 7,006 22,377 T/cm 32.9	Class: LR ✠**100A1** SS 09/2010 oil & chemical tanker, Ship Type 2* CR (s.stl), SG 1.85 all tanks ESP LI *IWS ✠**LMC** **UMS IGS** Eq.Ltr: G†; Cable: 577.5/60.0 U3 (a)	**2000-06 Naval Gijon S.A. (NAGISA) — Gijon** Yd No: 553 Loa 159.62 (BB) Br ex 23.02 Dght 9.515 Lbp 149.79 Br md 23.00 Dpth 13.54 Welded, 1 dk	**(A12B2TR) Chemical/Products Tanker** Double Hull (13F) Liq: 23,738; Liq (Oil): 23,727 Cargo Heating Coils Compartments: 24 Wing Ta (s.stl), ER 24 Cargo Pump (s): 24x200m³/hr Manifold: Bow/CM: 78.2m	**1 oil engine** driving 1 CP propeller Total Power: 7,134kW (9,699hp) 15.5kn MAN-B&W 5S50MC 1 x 2 Stroke 5 Cy. 500 x 1910 7134kW (9699bhp) Manises Diesel Engine Co. S.A.-Valencia AuxGen: 1 x 700kW 440V 60Hz a.c, 3 x 610kW 440V 60Hz a.c Boilers: e (ex.g.) 11.7kgf/cm² (11.5bar), AuxB (o.f.) 10.5kgf/cm² (10.3bar), AuxB (o.f.) 11.1kgf/cm² (10.9bar) Thrusters: 1 Thwart. FP thruster (f) Fuel: 247.0 (d.f.) 1654.0 (r.f.)
9378333 *VRCT5* -	**SC TIANJIN** **SC Tianjin Shipping Co Ltd** Aoxing Ship Management (Shanghai) Ltd *Hong Kong* *Hong Kong* MMSI: 477797300 Official number: HK-1890	**8,458** 4,031 12,929 T/cm 22.9	Class: CC (KR)	**2007-04 Samho Shipbuilding Co Ltd — Tongyeong** Yd No: 1076 Loa 127.20 (BB) Br ex - Dght 8.714 Lbp 119.00 Br md 20.40 Dpth 11.50 Welded, 1 dk	**(A12B2TR) Chemical/Products Tanker** Double Hull (13F) Liq: 13,078; Liq (Oil): 13,410 Cargo Heating Coils Compartments: 12 Wing Ta, 2 Wing Slop Ta, ER 12 Cargo Pump (s): 12x300m³/hr Manifold: Bow/CM: 59.1m	**1 oil engine** driving 1 FP propeller Total Power: 4,457kW (6,060hp) 13.4kn MAN-B&W 6S35MC 1 x 2 Stroke 6 Cy. 350 x 1400 4457kW (6060bhp) STX Engine Co Ltd-South Korea AuxGen: 3 x 480kW 445V 60Hz a.c Thrusters: 1 Tunnel thruster (f) Fuel: 77.0 (d.f.) 663.0 (r.f.)
9224324 *V7KF6* -	**SC TIANJIN** *ex* CSAV Lanco *-2013* *ex* CSCL Tianjin *-2010* **Kalapa Mobiliengesellschaft mbH & Co KG (KGAL)** Yang Ming Marine Transport Corp *Majuro* *Marshall Islands* MMSI: 538090239 Official number: 90239	**39,941** 24,458 50,953 T/cm 70.4	Class: LR ✠**100A1** SS 11/2011 container ship *IWS LI **ShipRight** (SDA, FDA, CM) ✠**LMC** **UMS** Eq.Ltr: S†; Cable: 687.5/87.0 U3 (a)	**2001-11 Samsung Heavy Industries Co Ltd — Geoje** Yd No: 1344 Loa 259.80 (BB) Br ex 32.35 Dght 12.620 Lbp 244.80 Br md 32.25 Dpth 19.30 Welded, 1 dk	**(A33A2CC) Container Ship (Fully Cellular)** TEU 4253 C Ho 1584 TEU C Dk 2669 TEU incl 400 ref C. Compartments: ER, 7 Cell Ho 14 Ha: ER	**1 oil engine** driving 1 FP propeller Total Power: 36,515kW (49,646hp) 23.3kn B&W 8K90MC-C 1 x 2 Stroke 8 Cy. 900 x 2300 36515kW (49646bhp) Doosan Engine Co Ltd-South Korea AuxGen: 4 x 1700kW 450V 60Hz a.c Boilers: AuxB (Comp) 8.2kgf/cm² (8.0bar) Thrusters: 1 Thwart. FP thruster (f)
9252759 *VREL6* -	**SC VENUS** *ex* Earth Phoenix *-2005* **Sea Lucky Shipping Co Ltd** Aoxing Ship Management (Shanghai) Ltd *Hong Kong* *Hong Kong* MMSI: 477136400 Official number: HK-2244	**2,635** 1,087 3,557 T/cm 10.6	Class: NK (BV)	**2001-07 Sasaki Shipbuilding Co Ltd — Osakikamijima HS** Yd No: 636 Loa 89.80 (BB) Br ex 14.62 Dght 5.712 Lbp 83.00 Br md 14.60 Dpth 7.00 Welded, 1 dk	**(A12B2TR) Chemical/Products Tanker** Double Hull (13F) Liq: 3,795; Liq (Oil): 3,937 Cargo Heating Coils Compartments: 8 Wing Ta, 2 Wing Slop Ta, ER 8 Cargo Pump (s): 8x150m³/hr Manifold: Bow/CM: 44m	**1 oil engine** driving 1 FP propeller Total Power: 2,427kW (3,300hp) 13.0kn Akasaka A41 1 x 4 Stroke 6 Cy. 410 x 800 2427kW (3300bhp) Akasaka Tekkosho KK (Akasaka DieselLtd)-Japan AuxGen: 2 x 280kW 445V 60Hz a.c Thrusters: 1 Thwart. FP thruster (f) Fuel: 67.0 (d.f.) 204.0 (r.f.) 10.7pd
9452309 *HSB4800* -	**SC VICTOR** *ex* Swiwar Victor *-2013* **SC Offshore Services Co Ltd** SC Management Co Ltd *Bangkok* *Thailand* MMSI: 567482000 Official number: 560001388	**1,678** 503 1,385	Class: AB	**2007-11 Fujian Southeast Shipyard — Fuzhou FJ** Yd No: DN59M-17 Loa 59.25 Br ex - Dght 4.950 Lbp 52.20 Br md 14.95 Dpth 6.10 Welded, 1 dk	**(B21B20T) Offshore Tug/Supply Ship**	**2 oil engines** reduction geared to sc. shafts driving 2 Propellers Total Power: 3,840kW (5,220hp) 11.0kn Caterpillar 3516B-HD 2 x Vee 4 Stroke 16 Cy. 170 x 215 each-1920kW (2610bhp) Caterpillar Inc-USA AuxGen: 3 x 315kW a.c Fuel: 530.0 (d.f.)
9430442 *VRFF8* -	**SC XIAMEN** **SC Xiamen Shipping Co Ltd** Aoxing Ship Management (Shanghai) Ltd SatCom: Inmarsat C 447701756 *Hong Kong* *Hong Kong* MMSI: 477225700 Official number: HK-2404	**8,562** 4,095 13,040 T/cm 22.9	Class: CC (KR)	**2009-06 21st Century Shipbuilding Co Ltd — Tongyeong** Yd No: 252 Loa 128.60 (BB) Br ex - Dght 8.714 Lbp 120.40 Br md 20.40 Dpth 11.50 Welded, 1 dk	**(A12B2TR) Chemical/Products Tanker** Double Hull (13F) Liq: 14,382; Liq (Oil): 13,389 Cargo Heating Coils Compartments: 12 Wing Ta, 2 Wing Slop Ta, ER 12 Cargo Pump (s): 12x300m³/hr Manifold: Bow/CM: 52.1m	**1 oil engine** driving 1 FP propeller Total Power: 4,440kW (6,037hp) 13.4kn MAN-B&W 6S35MC 1 x 2 Stroke 6 Cy. 350 x 1400 4440kW (6037bhp) STX Engine Co Ltd-South Korea AuxGen: 3 x 600kW 445V a.c Thrusters: 1 Tunnel thruster (f) Fuel: 65.0 (d.f.) 570.0 (r.f.)

Ship	Tonnage	Class	Builder / Dimensions	Type / Cargo	Machinery
9185841 **SC ZHUHAI** *VRHQ7* *ex* Chemstar Venus *-2010* - **SC Wuhan Shipping Co Ltd** Sinochem Shipping Co Ltd (Hainan) *Hong Kong* *Hong Kong* MMSI: 477963900 Official number: HK-2911	11,951 5,765 19,455 T/cm 30.0	Class: NK	**1999-02 Shin Kurushima Dockyard Co. Ltd. — Akitsu** Yd No: 5005 Loa 147.83 (BB) Br ex 24.22 Dght 9.230 Lbp 141.00 Br md 24.20 Dpth 12.80 Welded, 1 dk	**(A12B2TR) Chemical/Products Tanker** Double Hull (13F) Liq: 20,198; Liq (Oil): 21,401 Cargo Heating Coils Compartments: 20 Wing Ta, ER, 2 Wing Slop Ta, 10 Ta 22 Cargo Pump (s): 22x200m^3/hr Manifold: Bow/CM: 74.4m	**1 oil engine** driving 1 FP propeller Total Power: 6,179kW (8,401hp) 14.7kn Mitsubishi 7UEC45LA 1 x 2 Stroke 7 Cy. 450 x 1350 6179kW (8401bhp) Kobe Hatsudoki KK-Japan AuxGen: 3 x 300kW 450V 60Hz a.c Fuel: 91.0 (d.f.) (Heating Coils) 1050.0 (r.f.)
9370628 **SCALA** *A8HS9* *ex* Qinfeng 107 *-2005* - **Scala Navigation Ltd** INTRESCO GmbH *Monrovia* *Liberia* MMSI: 636012769 Official number: 12769	4,446 2,752 6,826	Class: RS (CC)	**2005-08 Wenling Hexing Shipbuilding & Repair Yard — Wenling ZJ** Yd No: 1 Loa 115.10 Br ex - Dght 5.680 Lbp 107.20 Br md 17.20 Dpth 7.45 Welded, 1 dk	**(A31A2GX) General Cargo Ship** Grain: 9,838 Compartments: 4 Ho, ER 2 Ha: (32.2 x 11.8)ER (32.9 x 11.8)	**1 oil engine** reduction geared to sc. shaft driving 1 FP propeller Total Power: 2,001kW (2,721hp) 11.0kn Chinese Std. Type G8300ZC 1 x 4 Stroke 8 Cy. 300 x 380 2001kW (2721bhp) Ningbo CSI Power & Machinery GroupCo Ltd-China AuxGen: 3 x 120kW a.c
9566306 **SCALI DEL PONTINO** *9HA2924* - **G & H Shipping Srl** Lauritzen Kosan A/S SatCom: Inmarsat C 425675510 *Valletta* *Malta* MMSI: 256755000 Official number: 9566306	3,430 1,029 3,811 T/cm 11.0	Class: BV RI	**2011-11 Besiktas Gemi Insa AS — Altinova** Yd No: 10 Loa 88.40 (BB) Br ex 15.00 Dght 6.500 Lbp 82.50 Br md 14.80 Dpth 7.80 Welded, 1 dk	**(A11B2TG) LPG Tanker** Liq (Gas): 3,361 2 x Gas Tank (s); 2 independent (stl) cyl horizontal 2 Cargo Pump (s): 2x200m^3/hr Manifold: Bow/CM: 51m	**1 oil engine** reduction geared to sc. shaft driving 1 CP propeller Total Power: 1,950kW (2,651hp) 14.0kn Wartsila 6L26 1 x 4 Stroke 6 Cy. 260 x 320 1950kW (2651bhp) Wartsila Italia SpA-Italy AuxGen: 3 x 350kW 450V 60Hz a.c, 1 x 650kW 450V 60Hz a.c Thrusters: 1 Tunnel thruster (f) Fuel: 95.0 (d.f.) 381.0 (r.f.)
9566289 **SCALI DEL TEATRO** *9HA3541* - **G & H Shipping Srl** Lauritzen Kosan A/S *Valletta* *Malta* MMSI: 229713000 Official number: 9566289	3,430 1,029 3,824	Class: BV RI	**2014-02 Cide Gemi ve Yat Sanayi Ticaret AS — Cide** (Hull launched by) Yd No: 08 **2014-02 Besiktas Gemi Insa AS — Altinova** (Hull completed by) Loa 87.50 Br ex 15.00 Dght 6.500 Lbp 82.50 Br md 15.00 Dpth 7.80 Welded, 1 dk	**(A11B2TG) LPG Tanker** Liq (Gas): 3,700	**1 oil engine** driving 1 Propeller Total Power: 2,040kW (2,774hp) 14.6kn Wartsila 6L26 1 x 4 Stroke 6 Cy. 260 x 320 2040kW (2774bhp)
9566291 **SCALI REALI** *9HA2486* - **G & H Shipping Srl** Lauritzen Kosan A/S *Valletta* *Malta* MMSI: 248730000 Official number: 9566291	3,430 1,029 3,804 T/cm 11.0	Class: BV RI	**2010-08 Besiktas Gemi Insa AS — Altinova** (Hull completed by) Yd No: 09 **2010-08 Cide Gemi ve Yat Sanayi Ticaret AS — Cide** (Hull launched by) Loa 87.50 (BB) Br ex 15.00 Dght 6.500 Lbp 82.60 Br md 14.80 Dpth 7.80 Welded, 1 dk	**(A11B2TG) LPG Tanker** Double Hull Liq (Gas): 3,295 2 x Gas Tank (s); 2 (s.stl) 2 Cargo Pump (s): 2x200m^3/hr Manifold: Bow/CM: 51m	**1 oil engine** reduction geared to sc. shaft driving 1 CP propeller Total Power: 1,950kW (2,651hp) 13.5kn Wartsila 6L26 1 x 4 Stroke 6 Cy. 260 x 320 1950kW (2651bhp) Wartsila Italia SpA-Italy AuxGen: 3 x 350kW 440V 60Hz a.c, 1 x 650kW 440V 60Hz a.c Thrusters: 1 Tunnel thruster (f) Fuel: 70.0 (d.f.) 280.0 (r.f.)
9417361 **SCALI SANLORENZO** *9HA2400* - **G & H Shipping Srl** Lauritzen Kosan A/S *Valletta* *Malta* MMSI: 248532000 Official number: 9417361	3,430 1,029 3,801 T/cm 11.0	Class: BV RI	**2010-05 ZAO Sudostroitelnyy Zavod 'Naval' — Nikolayev** (Hull launched by) Yd No: 701 **2010-09 Besiktas Gemi Insa AS — Altinova** (Hull completed by) Yd No: 07 Loa 87.50 (BB) Br ex 15.00 Dght 6.500 Lbp 82.50 Br md 14.80 Dpth 7.80 Welded, 1 dk	**(A11B2TG) LPG Tanker** Double Hull Liq (Gas): 3,500 2 Cargo Pump (s): 2x200m^3/hr Manifold: Bow/CM: 51m	**1 oil engine** reduction geared to sc. shaft driving 1 CP propeller Total Power: 1,950kW (2,651hp) 14.0kn Wartsila 6L26 1 x 4 Stroke 6 Cy. 260 x 320 1950kW (2651bhp) AuxGen: 3 x 350kW 440V 60Hz a.c Thrusters: 1 Tunnel thruster (f)
8767513 **SCAMP** *HO2507* *ex* Alyce Danos *-2005* - **Hercules Liftboat Co LLC** - *Panama* *Panama* Official number: 3492509A	280 84 -		**1984 Blue Streak Industries, Inc. — Chalmette, La** Yd No: BLU JB 67 Loa 24.04 Br ex - Dght - Lbp - Br md 11.58 Dpth 2.44 Welded, 1 dk	**(B22A2ZM) Offshore Construction Vessel, jack up** Cranes: 1x40t	**2 oil engines** reduction geared to sc. shafts driving 2 Propellers Total Power: 500kW (680hp) 8.0kn G.M. (Detroit Diesel) 12V-71-N 2 x Vee 2 Stroke 12 Cy. 108 x 127 each-250kW (340bhp) Detroit Diesel Corporation-Detroit, Mi AuxGen: 2 x 75kW a.c
7700609 **SCAN FJELL** *OZ2141* *ex* Trans Fjell *-2002* - **Scan Carrier A/S** Norresundby Shipping A/S *Torshavn* *Faeroe Islands (Danish)* MMSI: 231212000	2,195 743 1,970	Class: RI (NV)	**1978-05 Loland Verft AS — Leirvik i Sogn** Yd No: 41 Loa 76.96 Br ex 14.03 Dght 5.440 Lbp 70.20 Br md 14.01 Dpth 9.00 Welded, 1 dk & S dk	**(A31A2GX) General Cargo Ship** Side door/ramp (s) Len: 6.70 Wid: 5.08 Swl: - Grain: 2,764; Bale: 2,764 TEU 36 C. 36/20' Compartments: 1 Ho, ER 1 Ha: (19.1 x 10.2)ER Derricks: 1x35t Ice Capable	**1 oil engine** driving 1 CP propeller Total Power: 1,442kW (1,961hp) 12.5kn Wichmann 7AXA 1 x 2 Stroke 7 Cy. 300 x 450 1442kW (1961bhp) Wichmann Motorfabrikk AS-Norway AuxGen: 2 x 102kW 220V 50Hz a.c Thrusters: 1 Thwart. FP thruster (f) Fuel: 107.5 (r.f.) 7.0pd
8015879 **SCAN FJORD** *8PWR* *ex* Carten Elina *-2011* *ex* Lysholmen *-2003* - **Rederiet Scan-Fjord AS** KTM Shipping AS SatCom: Inmarsat C 431431810 *Bridgetown* *Barbados* MMSI: 314318000	2,876 1,040 3,319 T/cm 10.4	Class: NV	**1981-10 Th Hellesoy Skipsbyggeri AS — Lofallstrand** Yd No: 104 Lengthened-1994 Loa 94.70 (BB) Br ex 13.83 Dght 5.125 Lbp 87.20 Br md 13.80 Dpth 9.22 Welded, 2 dks	**(A31A2GX) General Cargo Ship** Side door (s) TEU 52 C. 52/20' Compartments: 2 Ho, ER 2 Ha: 2 (15.4 x 9.0)ER Cranes: 1 Ice Capable	**1 oil engine** sr geared to sc. shaft driving 1 CP propeller Total Power: 2,460kW (3,345hp) 12.0kn Wartsila 6R32LN 1 x 4 Stroke 6 Cy. 320 x 350 2460kW (3345bhp) Wartsila Finland Oy-Finland AuxGen: 1 x 186kW 380V 50Hz a.c, 2 x 184kW 380V 50Hz a.c Thrusters: 1 Tunnel thruster (f) Fuel: 202.0 (d.f.) 8.2pd
7224277 **SCAN MASTER** *LFWS* *ex* Norsel *-2009* *ex* Rose-Marie S *-1994* - **Grontvedt Shipping AS** - *Trondheim* *Norway* MMSI: 257776000 Official number: 7224277	1,093 352 1,242	Class: (GL)	**1972 Gutehoffnungshuette Sterkrade AG Rheinwerft Walsum — Duisburg** Yd No: 1090 Converted From: Chemical Tanker-1995 Loa 71.28 (BB) Br ex 11.59 Dght 3.558 Lbp 67.52 Br md 11.51 Dpth 5.52 Welded, 2 dks	**(A13B2TP) Products Tanker** Double Hull Liq: 950; Liq (Oil): 950 Compartments: 4 Ta, ER 2 Cargo Pump (s): 2x120m^3/hr Ice Capable	**1 oil engine** driving 1 FP propeller Total Power: 736kW (1,001hp) 12.0kn Deutz RBV8M545 1 x 4 Stroke 8 Cy. 320 x 450 736kW (1001bhp) Kloeckner Humboldt Deutz AG-West Germany AuxGen: 3 x 72kW 380V 50Hz a.c Thrusters: 1 Thwart. FP thruster (f) Fuel: 43.5 (d.f.) 4.0pd
8883018 **SCAN PIPE II** *LGWY* *ex* Innherredsferja II *-2001* - **SR Seaservice AS** - *Levanger* *Norway*	241 69 -	Class: (NV)	**1962-07 Ulstein Mek. Verksted AS — Ulsteinvik** Yd No: 20 Loa - Br ex - Dght - Lbp - Br md - Dpth - Welded, 1 dk	**(A35A2RR) Ro-Ro Cargo Ship**	**3 oil engines** geared to sc. shaft driving 1 FP propeller Total Power: 279kW (378hp) Volvo Penta MD96B 3 x 4 Stroke 6 Cy. 121 x 140 each-93kW (126bhp) Volvo Pentaverken-Sweden
4906393 **SCAN SCARAB** *GZGX* *ex* Scarab *-1997* - **Echoscan Ltd** - *Fleetwood* *United Kingdom* MMSI: 232003722 Official number: 900317	284 85 -	Class: LR ✠ **100A1** SS 07/2002 U.K. coasting and between River Elbe and Brest ✠ **LMC** Eq.Ltr: D; Cable: 137.0/19.0	**1971-10 Charles D. Holmes & Co. Ltd. — Beverley** Yd No: 1022 Loa 35.24 Br ex 9.03 Dght 3.770 Lbp 30.38 Br md 8.56 Dpth 4.16 Welded, 1 dk	**(B34P2QV) Salvage Ship**	**1 oil engine** sr reverse geared to sc. shaft driving 1 FP propeller Total Power: 485kW (659hp) 12.0kn Blackstone ERS8M 1 x 4 Stroke 8 Cy. 222 x 292 485kW (659bhp) Lister Blackstone Marine Ltd.-Dursley AuxGen: 1 x 110kW 440V 50Hz a.c, 1 x 30kW 440V 60Hz a.c
7039426 **SCAN TRANS** *JXGT* *ex* Terningen *-2004* *ex* Sakkestad *-1994* - *ex* Lena *-1989* *ex* Semi *-1977* **Grontvedt Shipping AS** - *Trondheim* *Norway* MMSI: 257228000 Official number: 17252	499 175 750	Class: (NV)	**1970 Lindstols Skips- & Baatbyggeri AS — Risor** Yd No: 269 Lengthened-1984 Loa 51.64 Br ex 9.02 Dght 3.920 Lbp 46.70 Br md 9.00 Dpth 5.85 Welded, 2 dks	**(A31A2GX) General Cargo Ship** Grain: 1,331 Compartments: 1 Ho, ER 1 Ha: (30.5 x 6.2)ER Derricks: 1x5t,1x3t; Winches: 2 Ice Capable	**1 oil engine** geared to sc. shaft driving 1 FP propeller Total Power: 392kW (533hp) 9.5kn Caterpillar 3508TA 1 x Vee 4 Stroke 8 Cy. 170 x 190 392kW (533bhp) (new engine 1985) Caterpillar Tractor Co-USA AuxGen: 2 x 25kW 220V 50Hz a.c, 1 x 15kW 220V 50Hz a.c
7810143 **SCAN VIKING** *LHWJ* *ex* Seifjord *-2006* *ex* Vassoyfisk *-1994* - *ex* Utsira *-1994* **Grontvedt Shipping AS** - *Trondheim* *Norway* MMSI: 257060400	317 95 40	Class: (NV)	**1979-03 Karmsund Verft & Mek. Verksted — Avaldsnes** Yd No: 22 Loa 27.44 Br ex - Dght - Lbp 23.63 Br md 7.33 Dpth 3.81 Welded, 1 dk	**(A32A2GF) General Cargo/Passenger Ship** Compartments: 1 Ho, ER 1 Ha: (3.5 x 2.2)ER	**1 oil engine** geared to sc. shaft driving 1 FP propeller Total Power: 416kW (566hp) Caterpillar D379SCAC 1 x Vee 4 Stroke 8 Cy. 159 x 203 416kW (566bhp) Caterpillar Tractor Co-USA AuxGen: 1 x 45kW 220V 50Hz a.c, 1 x 31kW 220V 50Hz a.c Thrusters: 1 Thwart. FP thruster (f)

IMO / Call sign	Name / Owner	Tonnage	Class	Builder / Dimensions	Type / Capacity	Machinery
8129383 *SKFZ* -	**SCANDICA** **Government of The Kingdom of Sweden (Rederiet Sjofartsverket) Swedish Maritime Administration** - *Norrkoping* *Sweden* MMSI: 265724000	**980** 294 361	Class: (NV)	**1983-01 AB Asi-Verken — Amal** Yd No: 134 Loa 56.76 Br ex 12.04 Dght 3.820 Lbp 50.02 Br md 12.01 Dpth 5.01 Welded, 1 dk	**(B34Q2QB) Buoy Tender** Compartments: 1 Ho, ER 1 Ha: ER Cranes: 1x16t,1x12t Ice Capable	**2 oil engines** with clutches, flexible couplings & sr geared to sc. shaft driving 1 CP propeller Total Power: 2,588kW (3,518hp) 15.0kn Hedemora V16A/12 2 x Vee 4 Stroke 16 Cy. 185 x 210 each-1294kW (1759bhp) Hedemora Diesel AB-Sweden AuxGen: 4 x 232kW 380V 50Hz a.c Thrusters: 1 Thwart. FP thruster (f); 1 Tunnel thruster (a)
7933529 *WDC7308* -	**SCANDIES ROSE** *ex* Enterprise *-1989* **Scandies LP** SatCom: Inmarsat M 636760110 *Dutch Harbor, AK* *United States of America* MMSI: 367601000 Official number: 602351	*195* 132 -		**1978 Bender Welding & Machine Co Inc — Mobile AL** Yd No: 747 L reg 35.51 Br ex - Dght - Lbp - Br md 10.37 Dpth 3.43 Welded, 1 dk	**(B11B2FV) Fishing Vessel**	**2 oil engines** geared to sc. shafts driving 2 FP propellers Total Power: 1,176kW (1,598hp) G.M. (Detroit Diesel) 12V-149-TI 2 x Vee 2 Stroke 12 Cy. 146 x 146 each-588kW (799bhp) General Motors Detroit DieselAllison Divn-USA
7826788 *C6TA7* -	**SCANDINAVIA** *ex* Visborg *-2003* *ex* Visby *-2003* *ex* Stena Felicity *-1997* *ex* Felicity *-1990* *ex* Visby *-1990* **Adabar Co Ltd** Polish Baltic Shipping Co (POLFERRIES) (Polska Zegluga Baltycka SA) *Nassau* *Bahamas* MMSI: 311561000 Official number: 8000667	**23,842** 11,083 2,800	Class: NV	**1980-10 Oresundsvarvet AB — Landskrona** Yd No: 278 Loa 145.65 (BB) Br ex 25.50 Dght 5.710 Lbp 132.56 Br md 24.01 Dpth 16.57 Welded, 5 dks	**(A36A2PR) Passenger/Ro-Ro Ship (Vehicles)** Passengers: unberthed: 730; cabins: 287; berths: 1142 Bow door/ramp Len: 18.50 Wid: 8.00 Swl: 15 Stern door/ramp (p) Len: 14.20 Wid: 3.50 Swl: 2 Stern door/ramp (s) Len: 14.20 Wid: 3.50 Swl: 2 Stern door/ramp (centre) Len: 15.80 Wid: 10.51 Swl: 15 Lane-Len: 2205 Lane-Wid: 2.50 Lane-clr ht: 4.50 Cars: 515 Ice Capable	**4 oil engines** sr geared to sc. shafts driving 2 CP propellers Total Power: 21,480kW (29,204hp) 21.0kn B&W 8K45GFC 4 x 2 Stroke 8 Cy. 450 x 900 each-5370kW (7301bhp) AB Gotaverken-Sweden AuxGen: 2 x 1700kW 380V 50Hz a.c, 3 x 1660kW 380V 50Hz a.c Thrusters: 2 Thwart. CP thruster (f) Fuel: 88.9 (d.f.) 840.9 (r.f.) 77.0pd
9487873 *ZDJR4* -	**SCANDINAVIAN EXPRESS** *ex* Ocean Premium *-2010* **Panamax Bulk I BV** Vroon BV *Gibraltar* *Gibraltar (British)* MMSI: 236555000	**51,209** 30,733 93,038 T/cm 80.9	Class: LR ✠ **100A1** SS 02/2010 bulk carrier CSR BC-A GRAB (20) Nos. 2, 4 & 6 holds may be empty ESP **ShipRight** (CM) *IWS LI ✠ **LMC** **UMS** Cable: 687.5/87.0 U3	**2010-02 COSCO (Dalian) Shipyard Co Ltd — Dalian LN** Yd No: N239 Loa 229.17 (BB) Br ex 38.05 Dght 14.900 Lbp 221.98 Br md 38.00 Dpth 20.70 Welded, 1 dk	**(A21A2BC) Bulk Carrier** Grain: 110,300 Compartments: 7 Ho, ER 7 Ha: ER	**1 oil engine** driving 1 FP propeller Total Power: 12,240kW (16,642hp) 14.1kn MAN-B&W 6S60MC 1 x 2 Stroke 6 Cy. 600 x 2292 12240kW (16642bhp) Doosan Engine Co Ltd-South Korea AuxGen: 3 x 700kW 450V 60Hz a.c Boilers: AuxB (Comp) 9.2kgf/cm² (9.0bar) Fuel: 2800.0 42.0pd
8917560 *C6UL9* -	**SCANDINAVIAN REEFER** **Byron Shipping Co** NYKCool AB *Nassau* *Bahamas* MMSI: 311955000 Official number: 8000992	**7,944** 4,632 11,095 T/cm 22.5	Class: BV (LR) ✠ Classed LR until 2/12/04	**1992-11 Kvaerner Kleven Leirvik AS — Leirvik i Sogn** Yd No: 246 Loa 140.50 (BB) Br ex 19.73 Dght 9.600 Lbp 130.00 Br md 19.70 Dpth 13.01 Welded, 1 dk, 2nd & 3rd dks in Nos. 1 to 4 holds, 4th dk in Nos. 2 to 4 holds	**(A34A2GR) Refrigerated Cargo Ship** Ins: 12,015 TEU 204 C Ho 108 TEU C Dk 96 TEU incl 42 ref C Compartments: 4 Ho, ER, 11 Tw Dk 4 Ha: (12.6 x 5.4)3 (12.6 x 10.6)ER Cranes: 2x36t,2x8t	**1 oil engine** with flexible couplings & sr geared to sc. shaft driving 1 CP propeller Total Power: 11,925kW (16,213hp) 21.9kn MAN 9L58/64 1 x 4 Stroke 9 Cy. 580 x 640 11925kW (16213bhp) MAN B&W Diesel AG-Augsburg AuxGen: 1 x 1800kW 450V 60Hz a.c, 4 x 650kW 450V 60Hz a.c Boilers: TOH (o.f.) 10.2kgf/cm² (10.0bar), TOH (ex.g.) 10.2kgf/cm² (10.0bar) Thrusters: 1 Thwart. CP thruster (f) Fuel: 200.0 (d.f.) 1524.0 (r.f.) 58.8pd
9019054 *5BRU3* -	**SCANDOLA** *ex* Ionian Star *-1999* *ex* Via Ligure *-1994* **Compagnie Meridionale de Navigation** *Limassol* *Cyprus* MMSI: 210133000	**19,308** 5,792 5,985	Class: BV (LR) (RI) ✠ Classed LR until 11/3/98	**1992-06 van der Giessen-de Noord BV — Krimpen a/d IJssel** Yd No: 957 Converted From: Ferry (Passenger/Vehicle)-1994 Loa 150.43 (BB) Br ex 23.43 Dght 6.015 Lbp 137.33 Br md 23.40 Dpth 13.40 Welded, 2 dks	**(A36A2PR) Passenger/Ro-Ro Ship (Vehicles)** Passengers: unberthed: 750; cabins: 85; berths: 250 Stern door/ramp (a) Len: 6.80 Wid: 15.50 Swl: 100 Lane-Len: 1850 Lane-clr ht: 4.90 Trailers: 141	**2 oil engines** with flexible couplings & sr geared to sc. shafts driving 2 CP propellers Total Power: 18,000kW (24,472hp) 19.0kn Sulzer 8ZAL40S 2 x 4 Stroke 8 Cy. 400 x 560 each-9000kW (12236bhp) Zaklady Urzadzen Technicznych'Zgoda' SA-Poland AuxGen: 2 x 800kW 440V 60Hz a.c, 2 x 800kW 440V 60Hz a.c Thrusters: 1 Thwart. CP thruster (f) Fuel: 44.9 (d.f.) 644.0 (r.f.) 42.0pd
8505915 *J8B3399* -	**SCANLARK** *ex* RMS Scanlark *-2009* *ex* Oland *-2006* *ex* Drochtersen *-1998* **Scan Maritime Inc** AS Vista Shipping Agency *Kingstown* *St Vincent & The Grenadines* MMSI: 375354000 Official number: 9871	**1,371** 752 1,520	Class: GL	**1985-12 Gebr. Koetter Schiffswerft - Saegewerk — Haren/Ems** Yd No: 78 Loa 75.17 (BB) Br ex 10.80 Dght 4.320 Lbp 71.02 Br md 10.71 Dpth 5.57 Welded, 2 dks	**(A31A2GX) General Cargo Ship** Grain: 2,652; Bale: 2,639 Compartments: 1 Ho, ER 1 Ha: (48.1 x 8.5)ER Ice Capable	**1 oil engine** with flexible couplings & sr reverse geared to sc. shaft driving 1 FP propeller Total Power: 599kW (814hp) 11.0kn MaK 6M332AK 1 x 4 Stroke 6 Cy. 240 x 330 599kW (814bhp) Krupp MaK Maschinenbau GmbH-Kiel AuxGen: 2 x 76kW 380/220V a.c Thrusters: 1 Tunnel thruster (f)
6607989 *HO3879* -	**SCANNER** *ex* Geo Scanner *-2005* *ex* Ankenes *-1981* **Scanner Maritime SA** Corinthian Maritime SA *Panama* *Panama* MMSI: 355203000 Official number: 3097005	**1,001** 300 630	Class: (NV)	**1965-12 C. Luehring — Brake** Yd No: 6502 Converted From: Palletised Cargo Ship-1981 Loa 58.35 Br ex 10.52 Dght 3.620 Lbp 51.77 Br md 10.49 Dpth 4.09 Riveted\Welded, 1 dk & S dk	**(B31A2SR) Research Survey Vessel** Grain: 1,756; Bale: 1,437; Ins: 205 Compartments: 1 Ho, ER 1 Ha: (7.7 x 2.9)ER Derricks: 1x10t; Winches: 1 Ice Capable	**1 oil engine** driving 1 CP propeller Total Power: 883kW (1,201hp) 12.0kn MaK 8M451AK 1 x 4 Stroke 8 Cy. 320 x 450 883kW (1201bhp) Maschinenbau Kiel AG (MaK)-Kiel AuxGen: 2 x 200kW 380V 50Hz a.c Fuel: 40.5 (d.f.)
7340966 *LW4416* -	**SCANNER I** *ex* Orionman *-1994* **Naviera Scan SA** Sirius Tankers SA *Buenos Aires* *Argentina* MMSI: 701025000 Official number: 02381	*2,632* - 6,176	Class: (LR) (RI) ✠ Classed LR until 11/7/07	**1975-05 Hall, Russell & Co. Ltd. — Aberdeen** Yd No: 964 Converted From: Chemical Tanker-1987 Loa 103.64 Br ex 14.97 Dght 7.100 Lbp 97.54 Br md 14.94 Dpth 7.93 Welded, 1 dk	**(A13B2TP) Products Tanker** Double Bottom Entire Compartment Length Liq: 7,082; Liq (Oil): 7,082 Compartments: 15 Ta, ER 7 Cargo Pump (s): 4x250m³/hr, 3x70m³/hr	**1 oil engine** with clutches, flexible couplings & sr geared to sc. shaft driving 1 CP propeller Total Power: 2,589kW (3,520hp) 12.5kn Ruston 16RKCM 1 x Vee 4 Stroke 16 Cy. 254 x 305 2589kW (3520bhp) Ruston Paxman Diesels Ltd.-Colchester AuxGen: 3 x 144kW 415V 50Hz a.c Boilers: db 9.1kgf/cm² (8.9bar) Thrusters: 1 Thwart. FP thruster (f) Fuel: 309.5 (d.f.) 19.5pd
8634091 *SCBD* VY 76	**SCANO** *ex* Bokoland *-2009* **VK 190 Fiskeri AB** *Handelop* *Sweden* MMSI: 266045000	**149** 44 -		**1991 Sydvest Stalbatar AB — Jarfalla** Lengthened-1998 Loa 23.70 Br ex - Dght 3.200 Lbp - Br md 6.04 Dpth - Welded, 1 dk	**(B11B2FV) Fishing Vessel**	**1 oil engine** geared to sc. shaft driving 1 FP propeller Total Power: 404kW (549hp) Grenaa 1 x 4 Stroke 404kW (549bhp) A/S Grenaa Motorfabrik-Denmark
5079551 *JXQJ* R-717-K	**SCANTANK** *ex* Vesterled *-2006* *ex* Hordafisk *-2002* *ex* Lopus *-2000* *ex* Norli *-1995* *ex* Kryssgrunn *-1994* *ex* Corall *-1970* **Grontvedt Shipping AS** - *Trondheim* *Norway* MMSI: 259134000	**228** 73 -	Class: (NV)	**1961 Flekkefjord Slipp & Maskinfabrikk AS AS — Flekkefjord** Yd No: 55 Lengthened-1973 Loa 31.63 Br ex 6.71 Dght 4.341 Lbp 28.63 Br md 6.68 Dpth 5.90 Welded, 1 dk	**(B11B2FV) Fishing Vessel** Compartments: 1 Ho, 2 Ta, ER 3 Ha: (0.9 x 1.3)2 (1.4 x 1.4)ER Derricks: 1x1t; Winches: 1 Ice Capable	**1 oil engine** geared to sc. shaft driving 1 FP propeller Total Power: 625kW (850hp) 11.5kn Caterpillar D398SCAC 1 x Vee 4 Stroke 12 Cy. 159 x 203 625kW (850bhp) (new engine 1982) Caterpillar Tractor Co-USA AuxGen: 1 x 4kW 24V d.c, 1 x 2kW 24V d.c
7734727 *E5U2628* -	**SCANTUG 2** *ex* Mocarz *-2012* **Dolphin Maritime LLC** - *Avatiu* *Cook Islands* MMSI: 518681000 Official number: 1717	**105** 32 -	Class: PR	**1978-03 Stocznia Remontowa 'Nauta' SA — Gdynia** Yd No: H900/374 Loa 25.68 Br ex 6.81 Dght 2.601 Lbp 23.53 Br md - Dpth 3.56 Welded, 1 dk	**(B32A2ST) Tug**	**1 oil engine** driving 1 CP propeller Total Power: 688kW (935hp) 11.5kn Sulzer 6ASL25/30 1 x 4 Stroke 6 Cy. 250 x 300 688kW (935bhp) Zaklady Przemyslu Metalowego 'HCegielski' SA-Poznan AuxGen: 2 x 41kW 400V a.c

IMO / Call sign	Name / Owner / Manager / Registry	Tonnage	Class	Builder / Dimensions	Type / Capacity	Machinery
9237577 *H07694* -	**SCAPINO** *ex* Pacific 1 *-2006* *ex* Pac-Union *-2005* **Globeco SpA** Asaker Marine & Shipping Agency *Panama* *Panama* MMSI: 372937000 Official number: 45191PEXTF	**497** 149 297	Class: IR RI (AB)	**2005-10 ABG Shipyard Ltd — Surat** Yd No: 213 Loa 34.63 Br ex 11.22 Dght 4.700 Lbp 30.00 Br md 11.20 Dpth 5.50 Welded, 1 dk	**(B32A2ST) Tug**	**2 oil engines** reduction geared to sc. shafts driving 2 Directional propellers Total Power: 3,240kW (4,406hp) Wartsila 9L20 2 x 4 Stroke 9 Cy. 200 x 280 each-1620kW (2203bhp) Wartsila France SA-France AuxGen: 3 x 168kW a.c
8502298 *FHAD* LR 612366	**SCAPIRIA I** **Carfin SARL** Huos Garcia Yanez *La Rochelle* *France* MMSI: 227883000 Official number: 612366	*159* 60 152	Class: (BV)	**1984-09 Ateliers du Bastion SA — Les Sables-d'Olonne** Yd No: 617 Loa 30.31 Br ex 7.73 Dght 3.501 Lbp 26.01 Br md 7.60 Dpth 4.02 Welded, 1 dk	**(B11A2FS) Stern Trawler**	**1 oil engine** geared to sc. shaft driving 1 CP propeller Total Power: 552kW (750hp) 12.5kn Crepelle 4SN3 1 x 4 Stroke 4 Cy. 260 x 280 552kW (750bhp) Crepelle et Cie-France Fuel: 65.0 (d.f.)
7006431 - -	**SCARABEO** - -	*194* 91 -		**1969 Cant. Nav. M. Morini & C. — Ancona** Yd No: 118 Loa 32.42 Br ex 6.96 Dght 2.896 Lbp 25.10 Br md 6.81 Dpth 3.61 Welded, 2 dks	**(B11A2FT) Trawler**	**1 oil engine** driving 1 FP propeller Total Power: 386kW (525hp) MAN G6V30/45ATL 1 x 4 Stroke 6 Cy. 300 x 450 386kW (525bhp) Maschinenbau Augsburg Nuernberg (MAN)-Augsburg
8754970 *C6AD7* -	**SCARABEO 5** **SAIPEM SpA (Societa Azionaria Italiana Perforazioni e Montaggi SpA)** - *Nassau* *Bahamas* MMSI: 311076700 Official number: 8002069	**29,611** 8,883 -	Class: AB (RI)	**1990-04 Fincantieri-Cant. Nav. Italiani S.p.A. — Genova** Yd No: 5833 Loa 80.80 Br ex 68.80 Dght 7.300 Lbp - Br md - Dpth 7.30 Welded, 1 dk	**(Z11C3ZE) Drilling Rig, semi Submersible** Cranes: 2x60t Ice Capable	**8 diesel electric oil engines** driving 8 gen. each 3840kW 6000V a.c Connecting to 8 elec. motors each (2350kW) driving 8 Azimuth electric drive units 6.0kn Thrusters: 8 Thwart. FP thruster
8758861 *C6NZ9* -	**SCARABEO 7** *ex* Safe Supporter *-1997* *ex* Treasure Supporter *-1986* **SAIPEM (Portugal) Comercio Maritima Sociedade Unipessoal Lda** SAIPEM SpA (Societa Azionaria Italiana Perforazioni e Montaggi SpA) *Nassau* *Bahamas* MMSI: 309598000 Official number: 728082	**23,595** 5,713 -	Class: NV	**1980-03 Gotaverken Arendal AB — Goteborg** Yd No: 912 Converted From: Accommodation Vessel, Offshore-1999 Loa 106.10 Br ex 64.80 Dght 9.880 Lbp - Br md - Dpth 33.83 Welded, 1 dk	**(Z11C3ZE) Drilling Rig, semi Submersible** Passengers: berths: 107 Cranes: 1x80t,1x50t	**5 diesel electric oil engines** driving 5 gen. each 1880kW 440V a.c Connecting to 4 elec. motors each (2400kW) driving 4 Directional propellers Total Power: 9,415kW (12,800hp) Nohab F212V 5 x Vee 4 Stroke 12 Cy. 250 x 300 each-1883kW (2560bhp) Nohab Diesel AB-Sweden
9480423 *C6YV7* -	**SCARABEO 9** **SAIPEM (Portugal) Comercio Maritima Sociedade Unipessoal Lda** SAIPEM SpA (Societa Azionaria Italiana Perforazioni e Montaggi SpA) *Nassau* *Bahamas* MMSI: 311046800 Official number: 8001835	**36,863** 11,059 23,965	Class: NV	**2011-08 Yantai Raffles Shipyard Co Ltd — Yantai SD** (Hull launched by) Yd No: YRF2006-189 **2011-08 Keppel FELS Ltd — Singapore** (Hull completed by) Loa 115.00 Br ex 78.00 Dght 23.600 Lbp - Br md - Dpth 42.40 Welded, 1 dk	**(Z11C3ZE) Drilling Rig, semi Submersible** Passengers: berths: 200 Cranes: 2x100t	**8 diesel electric oil engines** driving 8 gen. each 5400kW 11000V a.c Connecting to 8 elec. motors each (4300kW) driving 8 Azimuth electric drive units Total Power: 45,440kW (61,784hp) Wartsila 12V32 8 x Vee 4 Stroke 12 Cy. 320 x 400 each-5680kW (7723bhp) Thrusters: 4 Retract. directional thruster 2 (p) 2 (s)
8500836 - -	**SCARBOROUGH** **State Transit - Sydney Ferries** - *Sydney, NSW* *Australia*	*186* 76 200 T/cm 1.0	Class: (LR) ✠ Classed LR until 19/3/87	**1986-03 Carrington Slipways Pty Ltd — Newcastle NSW** Yd No: 178 Loa 25.38 Br ex 10.01 Dght - Lbp 23.40 Br md 9.61 Dpth 2.04 Welded, 1 dk	**(A37B2PS) Passenger Ship** Hull Material: Aluminium Alloy Passengers: unberthed: 400	**2 oil engines** with clutches, flexible couplings & sr reverse geared to sc. shafts driving 2 FP propellers Total Power: 900kW (1,224hp) 12.5kn M.T.U. 6V396TC62 2 x Vee 4 Stroke 6 Cy. 165 x 185 each-450kW (612bhp) MTU Friedrichshafen GmbH-Friedrichshafen AuxGen: 2 x 64kW 24V d.c Fuel: 8.5 (d.f.) 2.5pd
9544059 *3FYE3* -	**SCARLET CARDINAL** **Kikyou Ship Holding SA** Taiyo Nippon Kisen Co Ltd *Panama* *Panama* MMSI: 351684000 Official number: 45439TJ	**43,010** 27,239 82,165 T/cm 70.2	Class: NK	**2014-02 Tsuneishi Shipbuilding Co Ltd — Fukuyama HS** Yd No: 1512 Loa 228.99 Br ex - Dght 14.429 Lbp 222.00 Br md 32.26 Dpth 20.05 Welded, 1 dk	**(A21A2BC) Bulk Carrier** Grain: 97,294 Compartments: 1 Ho, 6 Ho, ER 7 Ha: 6 (17.8 x 15.4)ER (16.2 x 13.8)	**1 oil engine** driving 1 FP propeller Total Power: 9,710kW (13,202hp) 14.5kn MAN-B&W 6S60MC-C 1 x 2 Stroke 6 Cy. 600 x 2400 9710kW (13202bhp) Mitsui Engineering & Shipbuilding CLtd-Japan AuxGen: 3 x 400kW a.c Fuel: 3180.0
8702745 - -	**SCARLET CHORD** *ex* Ingun *-1998* -	**176** 51 -		**1987-06 Gotaverken Arendal AB — Goteborg** (Hull) Yd No: 643-037 **1987-06 Ronnangs Svets AB — Ronnang** Yd No: 113 Loa 22.64 Br ex - Dght 3.501 Lbp - Br md 6.89 Dpth 4.68	**(B11A2FS) Stern Trawler**	**1 oil engine** driving 1 FP propeller Total Power: 346kW (470hp) Volvo Penta TAMD162 1 x 4 Stroke 6 Cy. 144 x 165 346kW (470bhp) AB Volvo Penta-Sweden
9273832 *HPWV* -	**SCARLET IBIS** **Luci Shipholding SA** Nippon Yusen Kabushiki Kaisha (NYK Line) *Panama* *Panama* MMSI: 356773000 Official number: 2962704C	**30,411** 11,876 46,719 T/cm 53.9	Class: NK	**2004-01 Iwagi Zosen Co Ltd — Kamijima EH** Yd No: 223 Loa 185.93 (BB) Br ex 32.23 Dght 11.866 Lbp 179.00 Br md 32.20 Dpth 19.05 Welded, 1 dk	**(A12B2TR) Chemical/Products Tanker** Double Hull (13F) Liq: 56,019; Liq (Oil): 54,898 Part Cargo Heating Coils Compartments: 20 Wing Ta, 2 Wing Slop Ta, ER 20 Cargo Pump (s): 20x350m³/hr Manifold: Bow/CM: 93m	**1 oil engine** driving 1 FP propeller Total Power: 11,060kW (15,037hp) 16.2kn MAN-B&W 7S50MC-C 1 x 2 Stroke 7 Cy. 500 x 2000 11060kW (15037bhp) Mitsui Engineering & Shipbuilding CLtd-Japan AuxGen: 3 x 800kW a.c Fuel: 265.0 (d.f.) 2787.0 (r.f.)
9290828 *V7TJ4* -	**SCARLET STAR** **Scarlet Star Shipping Ltd** International Andromeda Shipping SAM *Majuro* *Marshall Islands* MMSI: 538003816 Official number: 3816	**23,298** 10,195 37,252 T/cm 46.1	Class: LR ✠ **100A1** SS 01/2010 Double Hull oil tanker ESP *IWS LI EP (B) **ShipRight** (SDA, FDA, CM) Ice Class 1B at 11.466M draught Max/min draughts fwd 11.466/5.907m Max/min draughts aft 11.967/7.617m Power required 9267kw, installed 9480kw ✠ **LMC** **UMS IGS** Eq.Ltr: J†; Cable: 605.0/66.0 U3 (a)	**2005-01 Hyundai Mipo Dockyard Co Ltd — Ulsan** Yd No: 0327 Converted From: Chemical/Products Tanker-2007 Loa 182.55 Br ex 27.38 Dght 11.217 Lbp 175.00 Br md 27.34 Dpth 16.70 Welded, 1 dk	**(A13B2TP) Products Tanker** Double Hull (13F) Liq: 41,328; Liq (Oil): 42,171 Compartments: 12 Wing Ta, 2 Wing Slop Ta, ER 10 Cargo Pump (s): 10x500m³/hr Manifold: Bow/CM: 91.8m Ice Capable	**1 oil engine** driving 1 FP propeller Total Power: 9,460kW (12,862hp) 14.5kn B&W 6S50MC-C 1 x 2 Stroke 6 Cy. 500 x 2000 9460kW (12862bhp) Hyundai Heavy Industries Co Ltd-South Korea AuxGen: 3 x 740kW 450V 60Hz a.c Boilers: e (ex.g.) 11.8kgf/cm² (11.6bar), WTAuxB (o.f.) 9.1kgf/cm² (8.9bar) Thrusters: 1 Thwart. FP thruster (f) Fuel: 152.0 (d.f.) 1004.0 (r.f.)
9392078 *3FOQ3* -	**SCARLETT** **Golden Helm Shipping Co SA** Osaka Shipping Co Ltd (Osaka Senpaku KK) SatCom: Inmarsat C 435466811 *Panama* *Panama* MMSI: 354668000 Official number: 4091509	**21,192** 11,444 33,371	Class: NK	**2009-10 Shin Kochi Jyuko K.K. — Kochi** Yd No: 7225 Loa 179.99 (BB) Br ex - Dght 10.031 Lbp 172.00 Br md 28.20 Dpth 14.30 Welded, 1 dk	**(A21A2BC) Bulk Carrier** Double Hull Grain: 44,642; Bale: 43,765 Compartments: 5 Ho, ER 5 Ha: ER Cranes: 4x30t	**1 oil engine** driving 1 FP propeller Total Power: 6,250kW (8,498hp) 14.3kn Mitsubishi 6UEC52LA 1 x 2 Stroke 6 Cy. 520 x 1600 6250kW (8498bhp) Kobe Hatsudoki KK-Japan Fuel: 1490.0
9585077 *WDF2816* -	**SCARLETT ISABELLA** **Scarlett Isabella Inc** *Cape May, NJ* *United States of America* Official number: 1218735	**430** 129 -		**2009-12 Raymond & Associates LLC — Coden AL** Yd No: 417 Loa 39.62 Br ex - Dght - Lbp - Br md 10.35 Dpth 3.80 Welded, 1 dk	**(B21A20S) Platform Supply Ship**	**2 oil engines** reduction geared to sc. shafts driving 2 Propellers

Identity / Owner / Manager	Tonnage	Class	Builder / Dimensions	Type / Cargo	Machinery
7437680 **SCATTERBRAIN** *WDE7517* - **Last Island Fisheries Inc** - *Brownsville, TX* *United States of America* MMSI: 367157360 Official number: 547785	*103* 70 -		**1973 Marine Mart, Inc. — Port Isabel, Tx** Yd No: 113 L reg 19.69 Br ex 6.13 Dght - Lbp - Br md - Dpth 3.43 Welded, 1 dk	**(B11A2FT) Trawler**	**1 oil engine** driving 1 FP propeller Total Power: 268kW (364hp) Caterpillar D353SCAC 1 x 4 Stroke 6 Cy. 159 x 203 268kW (364bhp) Caterpillar Tractor Co-USA
9025297 **SCC STAR** - - **PT Indotrans Sejahtera** - *Samarinda* *Indonesia*	**152** 46 -	Class: (KI)	**2002-07 in Indonesia** L reg 32.60 Br ex - Dght - Lbp 28.00 Br md 7.20 Dpth 2.15 Welded, 1 dk	**(A35D2RL) Landing Craft** Bow ramp (centre)	**2 oil engines** geared to sc. shafts driving 2 Propellers Total Power: 544kW (740hp) Nissan RD8 2 x Vee 4 Stroke 8 Cy. 135 x 125 each-272kW (370bhp) Nissan Diesel Motor Co. Ltd.-Ageo
9285366 **SCELVERINGHE** *PGAA* - **Scelveringhe Scheepvaart BV** - *Yerseke* *Netherlands* MMSI: 244476000 Official number: 41701	**5,116** 1,534 7,745	Class: LR ✠ **100A1** SS 06/2009 hopper dredger ✠ **LMC** **UMS** Eq.Ltr: V†; Cable: 471.0/42.0 U3 (a)	**2004-06 SC Aker Braila SA — Braila** (Hull) Yd No: 1422 **2004-06 Scheepswerf K Damen BV — Hardinxveld** Yd No: 743 Loa 116.50 (BB) Br ex 18.60 Dght 6.400 Lbp 110.00 Br md 18.00 Dpth 8.30 Welded, 1 dk	**(B33B2DT) Trailing Suction Hopper Dredger** Hopper: 3,880 Compartments: 1 Ho, ER	**1 oil engine** with clutches, flexible couplings & dr geared to sc. shaft driving 1 CP propeller Total Power: 4,320kW (5,873hp) 13.0kn MaK 9M32C 1 x 4 Stroke 9 Cy. 320 x 480 4320kW (5873bhp) Caterpillar Motoren GmbH & Co. KG-Germany AuxGen: 1 x 1800kW 440V 60Hz a.c, 1 x 190kW 440V 60Hz a.c Thrusters: 1 Thwart. FP thruster (f) Fuel: 600.0 (d.f.) 16.0pd
9577056 **SCF ALPINE** *A8XQ2* - **Anubis Shipholding Ltd** SCF Unicom Singapore Pte Ltd SatCom: Inmarsat C 463708966 *Monrovia* *Liberia* MMSI: 636014957 Official number: 14957	**42,208** 22,056 74,602 T/cm 68.5	Class: LR ✠ **100A1** SS 11/2010 Double Hull oil tanker CSR ESP **ShipRight** (ACS (B), CM) *IWS LI SPM4 EP (bar above) ✠ **LMC** **UMS IGS** Cable: 632.5/81.0 U3 (a)	**2010-11 Hyundai Mipo Dockyard Co Ltd — Ulsan** Yd No: 2290 Loa 228.50 (BB) Br ex 32.23 Dght 14.500 Lbp 219.00 Br md 32.20 Dpth 20.90 Welded, 1 dk	**(A13A2TW) Crude/Oil Products Tanker** Double Hull (13F) Liq: 82,360; Liq (Oil): 82,360 Compartments: 12 Wing Ta, 2 Wing Slop Ta, ER 12 Cargo Pump (s): 12x900m³/hr Manifold: Bow/CM: 112.4m	**1 oil engine** driving 1 FP propeller Total Power: 13,560kW (18,436hp) 14.5kn MAN-B&W 6S60MC-C 1 x 2 Stroke 6 Cy. 600 x 2400 13560kW (18436bhp) Hyundai Heavy Industries Co Ltd-South Korea AuxGen: 3 x 800kW 450V 60Hz a.c Boilers: WTAuxB (o.f.) 9.0kgf/cm² (8.8bar), WTAuxB (Comp) 9.0kgf/cm² (8.8bar) Fuel: 230.0 (d.f.) 2160.0 (r.f.)
9224439 **SCF ALTAI** *ELZP3* - **Galea Corp** Unicom Management Services (Cyprus) Ltd SatCom: Inmarsat C 463694260 *Monrovia* *Liberia* MMSI: 636011490 Official number: 11490	**81,085** 52,045 159,417 T/cm 117.2	Class: NV (AB)	**2001-12 Hyundai Heavy Industries Co Ltd — Ulsan** Yd No: 1333 Loa 274.48 (BB) Br ex 48.04 Dght 17.072 Lbp 264.00 Br md 48.00 Dpth 23.10 Welded, 1 dk	**(A13A2TV) Crude Oil Tanker** Double Hull (13F) Liq: 167,829; Liq (Oil): 167,829 Cargo Heating Coils Compartments: 12 Wing Ta, 2 Wing Slop Ta, ER 3 Cargo Pump (s): 3x4000m³/hr Manifold: Bow/CM: 138m	**1 oil engine** driving 1 FP propeller Total Power: 18,624kW (25,321hp) 15.7kn MAN-B&W 6S70MC-C 1 x 2 Stroke 6 Cy. 700 x 2800 18624kW (25321bhp) Hyundai Heavy Industries Co Ltd-South Korea AuxGen: 3 x 908kW 60Hz a.c Fuel: 185.5 (d.f.) 3898.5 (r.f.)
9333436 **SCF AMUR** *A8JX5* - **Carrier Tanker Inc** Unicom Management Services (Cyprus) Ltd *Monrovia* *Liberia* MMSI: 636013003 Official number: 13003	**29,844** 12,025 47,095 T/cm 51.7	Class: NV	**2007-12 STX Shipbuilding Co Ltd — Changwon (Jinhae Shipyard)** Yd No: 2017 Loa 183.00 (BB) Br ex 32.24 Dght 12.430 Lbp 173.90 Br md 32.20 Dpth 19.10 Welded, 1 dk	**(A13B2TP) Products Tanker** Double Hull (13F) Liq: 51,662; Liq (Oil): 51,662 Compartments: 12 Wing Ta, 2 Wing Slop Ta, ER 14 Cargo Pump (s): 12x600m³/hr, 2x300m³/hr Manifold: Bow/CM: 92.7m Ice Capable	**1 oil engine** driving 1 CP propeller Total Power: 9,480kW (12,889hp) 14.5kn MAN-B&W 6S50MC-C 1 x 2 Stroke 6 Cy. 500 x 2000 9480kW (12889bhp) STX Engine Co Ltd-South Korea AuxGen: 3 x 900kW 450V 60Hz a.c Fuel: 115.0 (d.f.) 2887.0 (r.f.)
6910702 **SCF ARCTIC** *A8KT2* *ex* Methane Arctic *-2006* *ex* Arctic Tokyo *-1993* - **Violet Tankers SA** Unicom Management Services (Cyprus) Ltd *Monrovia* *Liberia* MMSI: 636013122 Official number: 13122	**48,454** 14,536 40,585	Class: AB	**1969-12 Kockums Mekaniska Verkstads AB — Malmo** Yd No: 517 Loa 243.34 Br ex 34.04 Dght 10.037 Lbp 230.00 Br md 33.99 Dpth 21.21 Welded, 1 dk	**(A11A2TN) LNG Tanker** Double Hull Liq (Gas): 71,500 6 x Gas Tank (s); 6 membrane Gas Transport (36% Ni.stl) pri horizontal Ice Capable	**1 Steam Turb** reduction geared to sc. shaft driving 1 FP propeller Total Power: 14,710kW (20,000hp) 18.3kn De Laval 1 x steam Turb 14710kW (20000shp) Kockums Mekaniska Verkstads AB-Sweden AuxGen: 2 x 1000kW 440V 60Hz a.c Fuel: 2491.5 (r.f.) (Heating Coils) 91.5pd
9422457 **SCF BAIKAL** *A8SW9* *ex* SCF Vankor *-2010* - **Camber Shipping Inc** SCF Unicom Singapore Pte Ltd SatCom: Inmarsat C 463707442 *Monrovia* *Liberia* MMSI: 636014311 Official number: 14311	**81,339** 52,257 158,097 T/cm 118.4	Class: AB	**2010-03 Hyundai Heavy Industries Co Ltd — Ulsan** Yd No: 2036 Loa 274.00 (BB) Br ex 48.05 Dght 17.171 Lbp 264.00 Br md 48.00 Dpth 23.14 Welded, 1 dk	**(A13A2TW) Crude/Oil Products Tanker** Double Hull (13F) Liq: 167,118; Liq (Oil): 158,000 Cargo Heating Coils Compartments: 12 Wing Ta, 2 Wing Slop Ta, ER 3 Cargo Pump (s): 3x4000m³/hr Manifold: Bow/CM: 137.4m	**1 oil engine** driving 1 FP propeller Total Power: 18,622kW (25,318hp) 15.7kn MAN-B&W 6S70ME-C 1 x 2 Stroke 6 Cy. 700 x 2800 18622kW (25318bhp) Hyundai Heavy Industries Co Ltd-South Korea AuxGen: 3 x 850kW a.c Fuel: 405.0 (d.f.) 3690.0 (r.f.)
9305568 **SCF BALTICA** *A8IA5* - **Ashbourne Navigation Ltd** Unicom Management Services (Cyprus) Ltd SatCom: Inmarsat Mini-M 764552266 *Monrovia* *Liberia* MMSI: 636012813 Official number: 12813	**65,293** 35,715 117,153 T/cm 98.3	Class: NV	**2005-12 Hyundai Heavy Industries Co Ltd — Ulsan** Yd No: 1622 Loa 249.80 (BB) Br ex 44.07 Dght 15.422 Lbp 239.00 Br md 44.00 Dpth 22.00 Welded, 1 dk	**(A13A2TV) Crude Oil Tanker** Double Hull (13F) Liq: 130,213; Liq (Oil): 130,213 Compartments: 12 Wing Ta, 2 Wing Slop Ta, ER 3 Cargo Pump (s): 3x3000m³/hr Manifold: Bow/CM: 125.1m Ice Capable	**1 oil engine** driving 1 FP propeller Total Power: 16,660kW (22,651hp) 14.5kn MAN-B&W 7S60ME-C 1 x 2 Stroke 7 Cy. 600 x 2400 16660kW (22651bhp) Hyundai Heavy Industries Co Ltd-South Korea AuxGen: 3 x 950kW 440/220V 60Hz a.c Fuel: 189.0 (d.f.) (Heating Coils) 2842.0 (r.f.) 60.0pd
9224441 **SCF CAUCASUS** *ELZP4* - **Gulfstar Corp** SCF Unicom Singapore Pte Ltd SatCom: Inmarsat C 463694336 *Monrovia* *Liberia* MMSI: 636011491 Official number: 11491	**81,085** 52,045 159,173 T/cm 117.2	Class: NV (AB)	**2002-03 Hyundai Heavy Industries Co Ltd — Ulsan** Yd No: 1334 Loa 274.48 (BB) Br ex 48.04 Dght 17.071 Lbp 264.00 Br md 48.00 Dpth 23.10 Welded, 1 dk	**(A13A2TV) Crude Oil Tanker** Double Hull (13F) Liq: 167,931; Liq (Oil): 167,931 Cargo Heating Coils Compartments: 12 Wing Ta, 2 Wing Slop Ta, ER 3 Cargo Pump (s): 3x4000m³/hr Manifold: Bow/CM: 138m	**1 oil engine** driving 1 FP propeller Total Power: 18,881kW (25,671hp) 15.7kn MAN-B&W 6S70MC-C 1 x 2 Stroke 6 Cy. 700 x 2800 18881kW (25671bhp) Hyundai Heavy Industries Co Ltd-South Korea AuxGen: 3 x 908kW 60Hz a.c Fuel: 185.5 (d.f.) 3898.5 (r.f.)
8992493 **SCF EXPLORER** *WDE2863* *ex* Delane Waxler *-2013* *ex* Sivi Shirah *-2009* - *ex* Gladys *-2004* *ex* Charles Burden *-2004* *ex* City of Evansville *-2004* **SCF Waxler Barge Line LLC** SCF Waxler Marine LLC *New Orleans, LA* *United States of America* MMSI: 367330620 Official number: 260630	*234* 149 -		**1950-01 Maxon Marine Industries Inc. — Tell City, In** L reg 35.36 Br ex - Dght - Lbp - Br md 8.23 Dpth 2.44 Welded, 1 dk	**(B32A2ST) Tug**	**1 oil engine** driving 1 Propeller
9224453 **SCF KHIBINY** *ELZP5* - **Wilshire Corp** SCF Novoship JSC (Novorossiysk Shipping Co) SatCom: Inmarsat C 463694420 *Monrovia* *Liberia* MMSI: 636011492 Official number: 11492	**81,085** 52,045 159,196 T/cm 117.2	Class: NV (AB)	**2002-05 Hyundai Heavy Industries Co Ltd — Ulsan** Yd No: 1335 Loa 274.48 (BB) Br ex 48.04 Dght 17.072 Lbp 264.00 Br md 48.00 Dpth 23.10 Welded, 1 dk	**(A13A2TV) Crude Oil Tanker** Double Hull (13F) Liq: 167,930; Liq (Oil): 167,930 Cargo Heating Coils Compartments: 12 Wing Ta, 2 Wing Slop Ta, ER 3 Cargo Pump (s): 3x4000m³/hr Manifold: Bow/CM: 137.9m	**1 oil engine** driving 1 FP propeller Total Power: 18,623kW (25,320hp) 15.7kn MAN-B&W 6S70MC-C 1 x 2 Stroke 6 Cy. 700 x 2800 18623kW (25320bhp) Hyundai Heavy Industries Co Ltd-South Korea AuxGen: 3 x 908kW 60Hz a.c Fuel: 185.5 (d.f.) 3898.5 (r.f.)
9333400 **SCF NEVA** *UBVI2* - **Krusso Shipping Co Ltd** Unicom Management Services (St Petersburg) Ltd *St Petersburg* *Russia* MMSI: 273350570	**29,902** 12,025 47,125 T/cm 52.0	Class: NV RS	**2006-10 STX Shipbuilding Co Ltd — Changwon (Jinhae Shipyard)** Yd No: 2014 Loa 183.00 (BB) Br ex 32.20 Dght 12.430 Lbp 173.90 Br md 32.20 Dpth 19.10 Welded, 1 dk	**(A13B2TP) Products Tanker** Double Hull (13F) Liq: 51,662; Liq (Oil): 51,662 Compartments: 12 Wing Ta, 2 Wing Slop Ta, ER 12 Cargo Pump (s): 12x600m³/hr Manifold: Bow/CM: 91.5m Ice Capable	**1 oil engine** driving 1 CP propeller Total Power: 9,480kW (12,889hp) 14.5kn MAN-B&W 6S50MC-C 1 x 2 Stroke 6 Cy. 500 x 2000 9480kW (12889bhp) STX Engine Co Ltd-South Korea AuxGen: 3 x 900kW a.c Fuel: 115.3 (d.f.) 1442.8 (r.f.)

IMO / Call sign	Name / Owner / Manager / Flag	Tonnage	Class	Builder / Dimensions	Type / Cargo	Machinery
9577068 *D5AE7* -	**SCF PACIFICA** *ex Megacore Pacifica -2011* **Norwick Shipping Ltd** SCF Unicom Singapore Pte Ltd *Monrovia* *Liberia* MMSI: 636015361 Official number: 15361	**42,208** 22,056 74,534 T/cm 68.5	Class: LR **✠100A1** SS 01/2011 Double Hull oil tanker CSR ESP **ShipRight** (ACS (B),CM) *IWS LI SPM4 EP (bar above) **✠LMC** **UMS IGS** Cable: 687.5/81.0 U3 (a)	**2011-01 Hyundai Mipo Dockyard Co Ltd — Ulsan** Yd No: 2291 Loa 228.48 (BB) Br ex 32.24 Dght 14.500 Lbp 219.00 Br md 32.20 Dpth 20.90 Welded, 1 dk	**(A13A2TW) Crude/Oil Products Tanker** Double Hull (13F) Liq: 82,360; Liq (Oil): 82,360 Compartments: 12 Wing Ta, 2 Wing Slop Ta, ER 12 Cargo Pump (s): 12x900m³/hr Manifold: Bow/CM: 112.4m	**1 oil engine** driving 1 FP propeller Total Power: 13,560kW (18,436hp) 14.5kn MAN-B&W 6S60MC-C 1 x 2 Stroke 6 Cy. 600 x 2400 13560kW (18436bhp) Hyundai Heavy Industries Co Ltd-South Korea AuxGen: 3 x 800kW 450V 60Hz a.c Boilers: WTAuxB (o.f.) 9.1kgf/cm² (8.9bar), WTAuxB (Comp) 9.1kgf/cm² (8.9bar) Fuel: 230.0 (d.f.) 2160.0 (r.f.)
9577109 *D5AE5* -	**SCF PEARL** **Twister Navigation Inc (Twister Navigation Liberia Inc)** SCF Unicom Singapore Pte Ltd SatCom: Inmarsat C 463711095 *Monrovia* *Liberia* MMSI: 636015359 Official number: 15359	**42,208** 22,056 74,552 T/cm 68.6	Class: LR **✠100A1** SS 10/2011 Double Hull oil tanker CSR ESP **ShipRight** (ACS (B),CM) *IWS LI SPM4 EP (bar above) **✠LMC** **UMS IGS** Cable: 687.5/81.0 U3 (a)	**2011-10 Hyundai Mipo Dockyard Co Ltd — Ulsan** Yd No: 2296 Loa 228.50 (BB) Br ex 32.24 Dght 14.520 Lbp 219.00 Br md 32.20 Dpth 20.90 Welded, 1 dk	**(A13A2TW) Crude/Oil Products Tanker** Double Hull (13F) Liq: 82,356; Liq (Oil): 82,360 Compartments: 12 Wing Ta, 2 Wing Slop Ta, 1 Slop Ta, ER 12 Cargo Pump (s): 12x900m³/hr Manifold: Bow/CM: 112.1m	**1 oil engine** driving 1 FP propeller Total Power: 13,560kW (18,436hp) 14.5kn MAN-B&W 6S60MC-C 1 x 2 Stroke 6 Cy. 600 x 2400 13560kW (18436bhp) Hyundai Heavy Industries Co Ltd-South Korea AuxGen: 3 x 800kW 450V 60Hz a.c Boilers: WTAuxB (o.f.) 9.0kgf/cm² (8.8bar), WTAuxB (Comp) 9.2kgf/cm² (9.0bar) Fuel: 287.0 (d.f.) 1708.0 (r.f.)
9333424 *A8JX4* -	**SCF PECHORA** **Duport Marine Services Inc** Unicom Management Services (Cyprus) Ltd *Monrovia* *Liberia* MMSI: 636013002 Official number: 13002	**29,844** 12,025 47,218 T/cm 51.5	Class: NV	**2007-11 STX Shipbuilding Co Ltd — Changwon (Jinhae Shipyard)** Yd No: 2016 Loa 183.00 (BB) Br ex 32.23 Dght 12.430 Lbp 173.90 Br md 32.20 Dpth 19.10 Welded, 1 dk	**(A13B2TP) Products Tanker** Double Hull (13F) Liq: 51,662; Liq (Oil): 51,662 Compartments: 12 Wing Ta, 2 Wing Slop Ta, ER 12 Cargo Pump (s): 12x600m³/hr Manifold: Bow/CM: 92m Ice Capable	**1 oil engine** driving 1 CP propeller Total Power: 13,560kW (18,436hp) 14.5kn MAN-B&W 6S60MC-C 1 x 2 Stroke 6 Cy. 600 x 2400 13560kW (18436bhp) STX Engine Co Ltd-South Korea AuxGen: 3 x 900kW 440/220V 60Hz a.c Fuel: 170.0 (d.f.) 1320.0 (r.f.)
9577070 *A8YG6* -	**SCF PIONEER** **Sorel Shipping Ltd** SCF Unicom Singapore Pte Ltd 773131284 *Monrovia* *Liberia* MMSI: 636015049 Official number: 15049	**42,208** 22,056 74,552 T/cm 67.2	Class: LR **✠100A1** SS 03/2011 Double Hull oil tanker CSR ESP **ShipRight** (ACS (B),CM) *IWS LI SPM4 EP (bar above) **✠LMC** **UMS IGS** Cable: 687.5/81.0 U3 (a)	**2011-03 Hyundai Mipo Dockyard Co Ltd — Ulsan** Yd No: 2292 Loa 228.48 (BB) Br ex 32.24 Dght 14.500 Lbp 219.00 Br md 32.20 Dpth 20.90 Welded, 1 dk	**(A13A2TW) Crude/Oil Products Tanker** Double Hull (13F) Liq: 82,354; Liq (Oil): 82,360 Compartments: 12 Wing Ta, 2 Wing Slop Ta, ER 12 Cargo Pump (s): 12x900m³/hr Manifold: Bow/CM: 112.1m	**1 oil engine** driving 1 FP propeller Total Power: 13,560kW (18,436hp) 14.5kn MAN-B&W 6S60MC-C 1 x 2 Stroke 6 Cy. 600 x 2400 13560kW (18436bhp) Hyundai Heavy Industries Co Ltd-South Korea AuxGen: 3 x 800kW 450V 60Hz a.c Boilers: WTAuxB (o.f.) 9.2kgf/cm² (9.0bar), WTAuxB (Comp) 9.2kgf/cm² (9.0bar) Fuel: 230.0 (d.f.) 2160.0 (r.f.)
9456927 *D5AE8* -	**SCF PLYMOUTH** *ex Megacore Philothea -2011* **Norwick Shipping Ltd** SCF Unicom Singapore Pte Ltd *Monrovia* *Liberia* MMSI: 636015362 Official number: 15362	**42,208** 22,056 74,606 T/cm 68.5	Class: LR (AB) **100A1** SS 01/2011 Double Hull oil tanker CSR ESP *IWS LI SPM4 EP (bar above) **LMC** **UMS IGS**	**2011-01 Hyundai Mipo Dockyard Co Ltd — Ulsan** Yd No: 2289 Loa 228.48 (BB) Br ex 32.25 Dght 14.500 Lbp 219.00 Br md 32.20 Dpth 20.90 Welded, 1 dk	**(A13A2TW) Crude/Oil Products Tanker** Double Hull (13F) Liq: 82,360; Liq (Oil): 82,000 Compartments: 12 Wing Ta, 2 Wing Slop Ta, ER 12 Cargo Pump (s): 12x900m³/hr Manifold: Bow/CM: 112.4m	**1 oil engine** driving 1 FP propeller Total Power: 13,560kW (18,436hp) 14.5kn MAN-B&W 6S60MC-C8 1 x 2 Stroke 6 Cy. 600 x 2400 13560kW (18436bhp) Hyundai Heavy Industries Co Ltd-South Korea AuxGen: 3 x 800kW a.c Fuel: 230.0 (d.f.) 2160.0 (r.f.)
9577082 *A8YG7* -	**SCF PRIME** **Rozel Shipping Ltd** SCF Unicom Singapore Pte Ltd SatCom: Inmarsat C 463709515 *Monrovia* *Liberia* MMSI: 636015050 Official number: 15050	**42,208** 22,056 74,581 T/cm 68.6	Class: LR **✠100A1** SS 04/2011 Double Hull oil tanker CSR ESP **ShipRight** (ACS (B),CM) *IWS LI SPM4 EP (bar above) **✠LMC** **UMS IGS** Eq.Ltr: U; Cable: 687.5/81.0 U3 (a)	**2011-04 Hyundai Mipo Dockyard Co Ltd — Ulsan** Yd No: 2293 Loa 228.48 (BB) Br ex 32.24 Dght 14.530 Lbp 219.00 Br md 32.20 Dpth 20.90 Welded, 1 dk	**(A13A2TW) Crude/Oil Products Tanker** Double Hull (13F) Liq: 82,354; Liq (Oil): 82,360 Cargo Heating Coils Compartments: 12 Wing Ta, 2 Wing Slop Ta, ER 12 Cargo Pump (s): 12x900m³/hr Manifold: Bow/CM: 112.1m	**1 oil engine** driving 1 FP propeller Total Power: 13,560kW (18,436hp) 14.5kn MAN-B&W 6S60MC-C 1 x 2 Stroke 6 Cy. 600 x 2400 13560kW (18436bhp) Hyundai Heavy Industries Co Ltd-South Korea AuxGen: 3 x 800kW 450V 60Hz a.c Boilers: WTAuxB (o.f.) 9.1kgf/cm² (8.9bar), WTAuxB (Comp) 9.3kgf/cm² (9.1bar) Fuel: 175.0 (d.f.) 1610.0 (r.f.)
9421960 *A8SW6* -	**SCF PRIMORYE** **Lumber Marine SA** SCF Unicom Singapore Pte Ltd SatCom: Inmarsat C 463705734 *Monrovia* *Liberia* MMSI: 636014308 Official number: 14308	**84,029** 49,212 158,070 T/cm 118.3	Class: NV	**2009-09 Daewoo Shipbuilding & Marine Engineering Co Ltd — Geoje** Yd No: 5310 Loa 274.00 (BB) Br ex Dght 17.000 Lbp 264.00 Br md 48.00 Dpth 23.70 Welded, 1 dk	**(A13A2TV) Crude Oil Tanker** Double Hull (13F) Liq: 168,553; Liq (Oil): 168,553 Cargo Heating Coils Compartments: 12 Wing Ta, 2 Wing Slop Ta, ER 3 Cargo Pump (s): 3x3500m³/hr Manifold: Bow/CM: 137.5m	**1 oil engine** driving 1 FP propeller Total Power: 16,860kW (22,923hp) 15.2kn MAN-B&W 6S70MC-C 1 x 2 Stroke 6 Cy. 700 x 2800 16860kW (22923bhp) Doosan Engine Co Ltd-South Korea AuxGen: 3 x 1000kW a.c Fuel: 251.0 (d.f.) 3006.0 (r.f.)
9577111 *A8YG9* -	**SCF PROGRESS** **Plemont Shipping Ltd** SCF Unicom Singapore Pte Ltd *Monrovia* *Liberia* MMSI: 636015052 Official number: 15052	**42,208** 22,056 74,588 T/cm 68.5	Class: LR **✠100A1** SS 01/2012 Double Hull oil tanker CSR ESP **ShipRight** (ACS (B),CM) *IWS LI SPM4 EP (bar above) **✠LMC** **UMS IGS** Cable: 687.5/81.0 U3 (a)	**2012-01 Hyundai Mipo Dockyard Co Ltd — Ulsan** Yd No: 2297 Loa 228.50 (BB) Br ex 32.25 Dght 14.520 Lbp 219.00 Br md 32.20 Dpth 20.90 Welded, 1 dk	**(A13A2TW) Crude/Oil Products Tanker** Double Hull (13F) Liq: 82,360; Liq (Oil): 82,360 Compartments: 12 Wing Ta, 2 Wing Slop Ta, ER 12 Cargo Pump (s): 12x900m³/hr Manifold: Bow/CM: 112.4m	**1 oil engine** driving 1 FP propeller Total Power: 13,560kW (18,436hp) 14.5kn MAN-B&W 6S60MC-C 1 x 2 Stroke 6 Cy. 600 x 2400 13560kW (18436bhp) Hyundai Heavy Industries Co Ltd-South Korea AuxGen: 3 x 800kW 450V 60Hz a.c Boilers: WTAuxB (o.f.) 9.1kgf/cm² (8.9bar), WTAuxB (Comp) 9.3kgf/cm² (9.1bar) Fuel: 230.0 (d.f.) 2160.0 (r.f.)
9577094 *A8YG8* -	**SCF PROVIDER** **Gorey Shipping Ltd** SCF Unicom Singapore Pte Ltd SatCom: Inmarsat C 463709521 *Monrovia* *Liberia* MMSI: 636015051 Official number: 15051	**42,208** 22,056 74,548 T/cm 68.5	Class: LR **✠100A1** SS 03/2011 Double Hull oil tanker CSR ESP **ShipRight** (ACS (B),CM) *IWS LI SPM4 EP (bar above) **✠LMC** **UMS IGS** Cable: 687.5/81.0 U3 (a)	**2011-03 Hyundai Mipo Dockyard Co Ltd — Ulsan** Yd No: 2294 Loa 228.50 (BB) Br ex 32.24 Dght 14.500 Lbp 219.00 Br md 32.20 Dpth 20.90 Welded, 1 dk	**(A13A2TW) Crude/Oil Products Tanker** Double Hull (13F) Liq: 82,360; Liq (Oil): 82,360 Compartments: 12 Wing Ta, 2 Wing Slop Ta, ER 12 Cargo Pump (s): 12x900m³/hr Manifold: Bow/CM: 112.4m	**1 oil engine** driving 1 FP propeller Total Power: 13,560kW (18,436hp) 14.5kn MAN-B&W 6S60MC-C 1 x 2 Stroke 6 Cy. 600 x 2400 13560kW (18436bhp) Hyundai Heavy Industries Co Ltd-South Korea AuxGen: 3 x 800kW 450V 60Hz a.c Boilers: AuxB (Comp) 9.2kgf/cm² (9.0bar), WTAuxB (o.f.) 9.0kgf/cm² (8.8bar) Fuel: 230.0 (d.f.) 2160.0 (r.f.)
9577123 *D5AE6* -	**SCF PRUDENCIA** **Typhoon Navigation Inc** SCF Unicom Singapore Pte Ltd *Monrovia* *Liberia* MMSI: 636015360 Official number: 15360	**42,208** 22,056 74,565 T/cm 68.5	Class: LR **✠100A1** SS 03/2012 Double Hull oil tanker CSR ESP **ShipRight** (ACS (B), CM) *IWS LI SPM4 EP (bar above) **✠LMC** **UMS IGS** Cable: 687.5/81.0 U3 (a)	**2012-03 Hyundai Mipo Dockyard Co Ltd — Ulsan** Yd No: 2298 Loa 228.00 (BB) Br ex 32.24 Dght 14.500 Lbp 219.00 Br md 32.20 Dpth 20.90 Welded, 1 dk	**(A13A2TW) Crude/Oil Products Tanker** Double Hull (13F) Liq: 82,360; Liq (Oil): 82,360 Compartments: 12 Wing Ta, 2 Wing Slop Ta, ER 12 Cargo Pump (s): 12x900m³/hr Manifold: Bow/CM: 112.4m	**1 oil engine** driving 1 FP propeller Total Power: 13,560kW (18,436hp) 14.5kn MAN-B&W 6S60MC-C 1 x 2 Stroke 6 Cy. 600 x 2400 13560kW (18436bhp) Hyundai Heavy Industries Co Ltd-South Korea AuxGen: 3 x 800kW 450V 60Hz a.c Boilers: WTAuxB (o.f.) 9.0kgf/cm² (8.8bar), WTAuxB (Comp) 9.2kgf/cm² (9.0bar) Fuel: 230.0 (d.f.) 2160.0 (r.f.)

9307724 **SCF SAKHALIN**
UHME *ex* FESCO Sakhalin *-2010*
- **SCF Sakhalin Vessels Ltd**
Sovcomflot Varandey Ltd (OOO Sovcomflot Varandey)
Vladivostok *Russia*
MMSI: 273318120
Official number: 9307724

6,882
2,065
4,298

Class: NV RS

2005-06 **Aker Finnyards Oy — Helsinki** Yd No: 504
Loa 99.90 Br ex 21.54 Dght 7.500
Lbp 93.50 Br md 20.95 Dpth 11.00
Welded, 1 dk

(B21B20T) Offshore Tug/Supply Ship
Passengers: 40
Cranes: 1x10t
Ice Capable

3 diesel electric oil engines driving 3 gen. Connecting to 2 elec. motors each (7500kW) driving 2 Azimuth electric drive units
Total Power: 17,400kW (23,658hp) 15.0kn
Wartsila 8L38B
3 x 4 Stroke 8 Cy. 380 x 475 each-5800kW (7886bhp)
Wartsila Finland Oy-Finland
AuxGen: 3 x 1080kW 3000/400V 50Hz a.c
Thrusters: 2 Thwart. CP thruster (f)
Fuel: 1548.0 (d.f.) 1594.0 (r.f.) 76.6pd

9421972 **SCF SAMOTLOR**
A8SW7 *launched as* SCF Sakhalin *-2010*
- **Chamber Marine SA**
SCF Unicom Singapore Pte Ltd
SatCom: Inmarsat C 463707262
Monrovia *Liberia*
MMSI: 636014309
Official number: 14309

84,029
49,212
158,070
T/cm
118.3

Class: NV

2010-02 **Daewoo Shipbuilding & Marine Engineering Co Ltd — Geoje** Yd No: 5311
Loa 274.00 (BB) Br ex 48.03 Dght 17.024
Lbp 264.00 Br md 48.00 Dpth 23.70
Welded, 1 dk

(A13A2TV) Crude Oil Tanker
Double Hull (13F)
Liq: 168,552; Liq (Oil): 168,552
Cargo Heating Coils
Compartments: 12 Wing Ta, 2 Wing Slop Ta, ER
3 Cargo Pump (s): 3x3500m³/hr
Manifold: Bow/CM: 137.5m

1 oil engine driving 1 FP propeller
Total Power: 18,660kW (25,370hp) 15.2kn
MAN-B&W 6S70MC-C
1 x 2 Stroke 6 Cy. 700 x 2800 18660kW (25370bhp)
Doosan Engine Co Ltd-South Korea
AuxGen: 3 x 1000kW a.c
Fuel: 200.0 (d.f.) 2900.0 (r.f.)

9224465 **SCF SAYAN**
ELZP6
- **Amber Tankers Inc**
Unicom Management Services (Cyprus) Ltd
SatCom: Inmarsat C 463694486
Monrovia *Liberia*
MMSI: 636011493
Official number: 11493

81,085
52,045
159,184
T/cm
117.2

Class: NV (AB)

2002-08 **Hyundai Heavy Industries Co Ltd — Ulsan** Yd No: 1336
Loa 274.48 (BB) Br ex 48.04 Dght 17.072
Lbp 264.00 Br md 48.00 Dpth 23.10
Welded, 1 dk

(A13A2TV) Crude Oil Tanker
Double Hull (13F)
Liq: 167,930; Liq (Oil): 167,930
Cargo Heating Coils
Compartments: 12 Wing Ta, 2 Wing Slop Ta, ER
3 Cargo Pump (s): 3x4000m³/hr
Manifold: Bow/CM: 138m

1 oil engine driving 1 FP propeller
Total Power: 18,623kW (25,320hp) 15.7kn
MAN-B&W 6S70MC-C
1 x 2 Stroke 6 Cy. 700 x 2800 18623kW (25320bhp)
Hyundai Heavy Industries Co Ltd-South Korea
AuxGen: 3 x 850kW a.c
Fuel: 185.5 (d.f.) (Heating Coils) 3898.5 (r.f.)

9625968 **SCF SHANGHAI**
D5EQ8
- **Langford Navigation SA**
SCF Novoship JSC (Novorossiysk Shipping Co)
Monrovia *Liberia*
MMSI: 636016138
Official number: 16138

167,578
110,076
320,701
T/cm
180.0

Class: NV RS

2014-02 **Bohai Shipbuilding Heavy Industry Co Ltd — Huludao LN** Yd No: BH518G1-8
Loa 332.00 (BB) Br ex 60.04 Dght 22.600
Lbp 320.00 Br md 60.00 Dpth 30.50
Welded, 1 dk

(A13A2TV) Crude Oil Tanker
Double Hull (13F)
Liq: 340,000; Liq (Oil): 340,000
Compartments: 5 Wing Ta, 5 Ta, 5 Wing Ta, 1 Wing Slop Ta, 1 Wing Slop Ta, ER
3 Cargo Pump (s): 3x5500m³/hr

1 oil engine driving 1 FP propeller
Total Power: 31,640kW (43,018hp) 15.5kn
Wartsila 7RT-flex82T
1 x 2 Stroke 7 Cy. 820 x 3375 31640kW (43018bhp)
Wartsila Switzerland Ltd-Switzerland
AuxGen: 2 x 1200kW a.c

9120322 **SCF SUEK**
A8TM7 *ex* Gianni D *-2009* *ex* St. Nicholas *-2002*
- *completed as* Kiev *-1998*
Abital Carrier Co
Sovcomflot (UK) Ltd
Monrovia *Liberia*
MMSI: 636014382
Official number: 14382

40,538
24,216
69,100

Class: NV

1998-04 **OAO Sudostroitelnyy Zavod 'Okean' — Nikolayev** Yd No: 501
Loa 224.90 (BB) Br ex - Dght 13.868
Lbp 217.30 Br md 32.20 Dpth 18.85
Welded, 1 dk

(A21A2BC) Bulk Carrier
Grain: 86,330
Compartments: 7 Ho, ER
7 Ha: 7 (16.7 x 15.2)ER
Ice Capable

1 oil engine driving 1 FP propeller
Total Power: 10,500kW (14,276hp) 14.3kn
B&W 6S60MC
1 x 2 Stroke 6 Cy. 600 x 2292 10500kW (14276bhp)
AO Bryanskiy MashinostroitelnyyZavod (BMZ)-Bryansk
AuxGen: 2 x 600kW 220/380V 50Hz a.c, 1 x 520kW 220/380V 50Hz a.c

---

9422445 **SCF SURGUT**
A8SW8
- **Gatson Shipping Ltd**
SCF Unicom Singapore Pte Ltd
SatCom: Inmarsat C 463706582
Monrovia *Liberia*
MMSI: 636014310
Official number: 14310

81,339
52,257
158,096
T/cm
118.4

Class: AB

2009-12 **Hyundai Heavy Industries Co Ltd — Ulsan** Yd No: 2035
Loa 274.00 (BB) Br ex 48.04 Dght 17.171
Lbp 264.00 Br md 48.00 Dpth 23.14
Welded, 1 dk

(A13A2TV) Crude Oil Tanker
Double Hull (13F)
Liq: 167,118; Liq (Oil): 158,000
Cargo Heating Coils
Compartments: 12 Wing Ta, 2 Wing Slop Ta, ER
3 Cargo Pump (s): 3x4000m³/hr
Manifold: Bow/CM: 137.4m

1 oil engine driving 1 FP propeller
Total Power: 18,660kW (25,370hp) 15.7kn
MAN-B&W 6S70ME-C
1 x 2 Stroke 6 Cy. 700 x 2800 18660kW (25370bhp)
Hyundai Heavy Industries Co Ltd-South Korea
AuxGen: 3 x 850kW a.c
Fuel: 2888.5 (d.f.) 395.3 (d.f.)

9324746 **SCF TOBOLSK**
A8IZ7
- **Corrad Shipping Corp**
SCF Unicom Singapore Pte Ltd
Monrovia *Liberia*
MMSI: 636012909
Official number: 12909

23,003
6,900
26,424
T/cm
41.4

Class: LR
✠ **100A** SS 12/2011
liquefied gas carrier, Ship Type 2G,
Propane, butane, butylene, propylene, anhydrous ammonia and Butadiene in independent tanks Type A, maximum SG 0.70, partial loading vinyl chloride monomer with SG 0.97, maximum vapour pressure 0.25 bar (0.45 in harbour), minimum cargo temperature minus 48 degree C,
ShipRight (SDA)
*IWS
LI
✠ **LMC UMS +Lloyd's RMC (LG)**
Eq.Ltr: K†;
Cable: 632.5/68.0 U3 (a)

2006-12 **Hyundai Heavy Industries Co Ltd — Ulsan** Yd No: 1758
Loa 174.20 (BB) Br ex 28.02 Dght 9.500
Lbp 165.00 Br md 28.00 Dpth 17.80
Welded, 1 dk

(A11B2TG) LPG Tanker
Double Hull
Liq (Gas): 34,487
3 x Gas Tank (s); 3 independent (C.mn.stl) pri horizontal
6 Cargo Pump (s): 6x400m³/hr
Manifold: Bow/CM: 102m

1 oil engine driving 1 FP propeller
Total Power: 9,480kW (12,889hp) 16.5kn
MAN-B&W 6S50MC-C
1 x 2 Stroke 6 Cy. 500 x 2000 9480kW (12889bhp)
Hyundai Heavy Industries Co Ltd-South Korea
AuxGen: 2 x 1215kW 450V 60Hz a.c, 1 x 740kW 450V 60Hz a.c
Boilers: AuxB (Comp) 8.2kgf/cm² (8.0bar)
Fuel: 186.7 (d.f.) 1772.0 (r.f.)

9326598 **SCF TOMSK**
A8IZ8
- **Nodrog Shipping Corp**
SCF Unicom Singapore Pte Ltd
Monrovia *Liberia*
MMSI: 636012910
Official number: 12910

23,003
6,900
26,424
T/cm
41.4

Class: LR
✠ **100A1** SS 01/2012
liquefied gas carrier, Ship Type 2G,
Propane, butane, butylene, propylene, anhydrous ammonia and Butadiene in independent tanks Type A, maximum SG 0.70, partial loading vinyl chloride monomer with maximum SG 0.97, maximum vaopur pressure 0.25 bar (0.45 bar in harbour), mimimum cargo temperature minus 48 degree C,
ShipRight (SDA)
*IWS
LI
✠ **LMC UMS +Lloyd's RMC (LG)**
Eq.Ltr: K†;
Cable: 632.5/68.0 U3 (a)

2007-01 **Hyundai Heavy Industries Co Ltd — Ulsan** Yd No: 1759
Loa 174.20 (BB) Br ex 28.02 Dght 9.500
Lbp 165.00 Br md 28.00 Dpth 17.80
Welded, 1 dk

(A11B2TG) LPG Tanker
Double Bottom Entire Compartment Length
Liq (Gas): 34,487
3 x Gas Tank (s); 3 independent (C.mn.stl) pri horizontal
6 Cargo Pump (s): 6x400m³/hr
Manifold: Bow/CM: 88.3m

1 oil engine driving 1 FP propeller
Total Power: 9,480kW (12,889hp) 16.5kn
MAN-B&W 6S50MC-C
1 x 2 Stroke 6 Cy. 500 x 2000 9480kW (12889bhp)
Hyundai Heavy Industries Co Ltd-South Korea
AuxGen: 2 x 1215kW 450V 60Hz a.c, 1 x 740kW 450V 60Hz a.c
Boilers: AuxB (Comp) 8.2kgf/cm² (8.0bar)
Fuel: 448.0 (d.f.) 3652.0 (r.f.)

9231509 **SCF URAL**
ELZP7
- **Beautiful Seaways Inc**
Unicom Management Services (Cyprus) Ltd
SatCom: Inmarsat C 463694545
Monrovia *Liberia*
MMSI: 636011494
Official number: 11494

81,085
52,045
159,314
T/cm
117.2

Class: NV (AB)

2002-11 **Hyundai Heavy Industries Co Ltd — Ulsan** Yd No: 1350
Loa 274.48 (BB) Br ex 48.04 Dght 17.072
Lbp 264.00 Br md 48.00 Dpth 23.10
Welded, 1 dk

(A13A2TV) Crude Oil Tanker
Double Hull (13F)
Liq: 167,930; Liq (Oil): 167,930
Cargo Heating Coils
Compartments: 12 Wing Ta, 2 Wing Slop Ta, ER
3 Cargo Pump (s): 3x4000m³/hr
Manifold: Bow/CM: 138m

1 oil engine driving 1 FP propeller
Total Power: 18,623kW (25,320hp) 15.7kn
MAN-B&W 6S70MC-C
1 x 2 Stroke 6 Cy. 700 x 2800 18623kW (25320bhp)
Hyundai Heavy Industries Co Ltd-South Korea
AuxGen: 3 x 850kW a.c
Fuel: 185.5 (d.f.) 3898.5 (r.f.)

9232864 **SCF VALDAI**
ELZP8
- **Eastbank Holdings Ltd**
Unicom Management Services (Cyprus) Ltd
SatCom: Inmarsat C 463694581
Monrovia *Liberia*
MMSI: 636011495
Official number: 11495

81,085
52,045
159,313
T/cm
117.2

Class: NV (AB)

2003-02 **Hyundai Heavy Industries Co Ltd — Ulsan** Yd No: 1351
Loa 274.48 (BB) Br ex 48.04 Dght 17.050
Lbp 264.00 Br md 48.00 Dpth 23.10
Welded, 1 dk

(A13A2TV) Crude Oil Tanker
Double Hull (13F)
Liq: 167,930; Liq (Oil): 167,930
Compartments: 12 Wing Ta, 2 Wing Slop Ta, ER
3 Cargo Pump (s): 3x4000m³/hr
Manifold: Bow/CM: 138m

1 oil engine driving 1 FP propeller
Total Power: 18,881kW (25,671hp) 15.7kn
MAN-B&W 6S70MC-C
1 x 2 Stroke 6 Cy. 700 x 2800 18881kW (25671bhp)
Hyundai Heavy Industries Co Ltd-South Korea
AuxGen: 3 x 850kW 440V 60Hz a.c
Fuel: 185.5 (d.f.) (Heating Coils) 3898.5 (r.f.) 67.0pd

9333412 **SCF YENISEI** **29,844** Class: NV
A8JA2 12,025
\- **Machanter Shipping Corp** 47,187
Unicom Management Services (Cyprus) Ltd T/cm
Monrovia *Liberia* 51.5
MMSI: 636012912
Official number: 12912

2007-11 STX Shipbuilding Co Ltd — Changwon (Jinhae Shipyard) Yd No: 2015
Loa 183.00 (BB) Br ex 32.23 Dght 12.430
Lbp 173.90 Br md 32.20 Dpth 19.10
Welded, 1 dk

(A13B2TP) Products Tanker
Double Hull (13F)
Liq: 51,662; Liq (Oil): 51,662
Compartments: 12 Wing Ta, 2 Wing Slop Ta, ER
12 Cargo Pump (s): 12x600m³/hr
Manifold: Bow/CM: 92.7m
Ice Capable

1 oil engine driving 1 CP propeller
Total Power: 9,480kW (12,889hp) 14.5kn
MAN-B&W 6S50MC-C
1 x 2 Stroke 6 Cy. 500 x 2000 9480kW (12889bhp)
STX Engine Co Ltd-South Korea
AuxGen: 3 x 900kW 450V 60Hz a.c
Fuel: 90.0 (d.f.) 1311.0 (r.f.)

9111010 **SCH 3** **107** Class: IR (GL)
VTBE *ex* Tri-Swift *-1996* 33
\- **Dolphin Offshore Shipping Ltd** -
\-
Mumbai *India*
MMSI: 419008900
Official number: 2725

1994-04 Kiong Nguong Shipbuilding Contractor Co — Sibu Yd No: 008
Loa 22.00 Br ex 6.12 Dght 1.800
Lbp 20.51 Br md 6.10 Dpth 3.05
Welded, 1 dk

(B32A2ST) Tug

2 oil engines reduction geared to sc. shafts driving 2 FP propellers
Total Power: 522kW (710hp) 10.0kn
Cummins KTA-19-M
2 x 4 Stroke 6 Cy. 159 x 159 each-261kW (355bhp)
Chongqing Automotive Engine Factory-China
AuxGen: 2 x 10kW 400V 50Hz a.c
Fuel: 46.0 (d.f.)

5010323 **SCHAARHOERN** *140* Class: GL
DJAB *ex* Alexandra *-2011* 54
\- - -
\-
Flensburg *Germany*
MMSI: 211263680

1908 Schiffswerft und Maschinenfabrik Janssen & Schmilinsky AG — Hamburg Yd No: 495
Converted From: Ferry (Passenger only)-1986
Loa 33.63 Br ex 7.17 Dght 2.601
Lbp - Br md - Dpth 2.80
Riveted, 1 dk

(X11A2YP) Yacht

1 Steam Recip driving 1 FP propeller
Total Power: 309kW (420hp) 12.0kn
1 x Steam Recip. 309kW (420ihp)
Schiffswerft und MaschinenfabrikJanssen & Schmilinsky AG-Germany

---

8111738 **SCHAARTOR** **994** Class: (GL) (BV)
\- *ex* Red Stork *-1988* 299
\- - 1,142
\-

1982-06 JG Hitzler Schiffswerft und Masch GmbH & Co KG — Lauenburg Yd No: 771
Loa 60.00 Br ex 13.34 Dght 4.245
Lbp 54.36 Br md 13.06 Dpth 4.90
Welded, 1 dk

(B21B20A) Anchor Handling Tug Supply
Passengers: berths: 22
Grain: 170; Bale: 145

2 oil engines sr geared to sc. shafts driving 2 CP propellers
Total Power: 3,236kW (4,400hp) 13.0kn
MaK 6M453AK
2 x 4 Stroke 6 Cy. 320 x 420 each-1618kW (2200bhp)
Krupp MaK Maschinenbau GmbH-Kiel
AuxGen: 2 x 350kW 230/380V 50Hz a.c, 2 x 200kW 230/380V 50Hz a.c, 1 x 100kW 220/380V 50Hz a.c
Thrusters: 1 Thwart. CP thruster (f)
Fuel: 563.5 (d.f.)

7725166 **SCHACKENBORG** **14,805** Class: RI (LR)
3FTU9 *ex* Dana Caribia *-1984* 4,441 ✠ Classed LR until 23/10/03
\- **Nordana Shipping (Singapore) Pte Ltd** 10,470
Jutha Maritime Public Co Ltd T/cm
Panama *Panama* 26.1
MMSI: 355934000
Official number: 4332912

1979-12 Nippon Kokan KK (NKK Corp) — Shizuoka SZ Yd No: 378
2002 Cindemir Makina Gemi Onarim ve Tersanecilik AS — Istanbul (Tuzla)
(Additional cargo section)
Lengthened-2002
Loa 161.40 (BB) Br ex 24.29 Dght 6.413
Lbp 150.40 Br md 24.01 Dpth 14.36
Welded, 2 dks, Upr intermediate hoistable dk fwd & Lwr hoistable dk aft light cargoes only

(A35A2RR) Ro-Ro Cargo Ship
Stern door & ramp
Len: 14.50 Wid: 8.50 Swl: 200
Side door (s)
Lane-Len: 1884
Lane-Wid: 6.00
Lane-clr ht: 6.30
Trailers: 149
Bale: 18,569
TEU 654 C Ho 280 TEU C Dk 374 TEU incl 12 ref C.
Compartments: 1 Ho, ER
2 Ha: (26.6 x 8.0) (21.3 x 9.0)ER
Cranes: 1x36t; Derricks: 1x120t

1 oil engine driving 1 FP propeller
Total Power: 5,913kW (8,039hp) 15.3kn
B&W 6L55GF
1 x 2 Stroke 6 Cy. 550 x 1380 5913kW (8039bhp)
Mitsui Engineering & Shipbuilding CLtd-Japan
AuxGen: 3 x 920kW 220/390V 50Hz a.c
Boilers: AuxB (o.f.) 8.0kgf/cm² (7.8bar), AuxB (ex.g.) 8.0kgf/cm² (7.8bar)
Thrusters: 1 Thwart. CP thruster (f)
Fuel: 72.0 (d.f.) (Heating Coils) 1735.0 (r.f.) 27.2pd

5317305 **SCHALL** **318** Class: GL
DNBQ *ex* Luke *-1971* *ex* Seefalke *-1968* 95
\- **Anja Tonjes** 29
Capt Kronisch GmbH
SatCom: Inmarsat M 621191010
Bremerhaven *Germany*
MMSI: 211236290
Official number: 1021

1962 Schiffswerft H. Rancke — Hamburg Yd No: 189
Converted From: General Cargo Ship-1971
Lengthened-1985
Loa 49.15 Br ex 7.32 Dght 1.590
Lbp 45.50 Br md 7.24 Dpth 2.75
Riveted\Welded, 1 dk

(B31A2SR) Research Survey Vessel

1 oil engine reduction geared to sc. shaft driving 1 CP propeller
Total Power: 439kW (597hp) 10.0kn
MAN D2842LE
1 x Vee 4 Stroke 12 Cy. 128 x 142 439kW (597bhp) (new engine 1997)
MAN Nutzfahrzeuge AG-Nuernberg

7349455 **SCHARHORN** **1,305** Class: GL
DGOQ *ex* Ostertor *-1982* 391
\- **Government of The Federal Republic of Germany (Bundesminister fuer Verkehr-WSV)** 908
Government of The Federal Republic of Germany (Wasser- und Schiffahrtsamt Luebeck)
SatCom: Inmarsat A 1123443
Kiel *Germany*
MMSI: 211219990
Official number: 11900

1974-04 Gutehoffnungshuette Sterkrade AG Rheinwerft Walsum — Duisburg Yd No: 1112
Converted From: Offshore Supply Ship-1983
Loa 56.14 Br ex 14.33 Dght 4.683
Lbp 51.24 Br md 14.00 Dpth 5.19
Welded, 1 dk

(B34G2SE) Pollution Control Vessel
Ice Capable

2 oil engines driving 2 FP propellers
Total Power: 2,574kW (3,500hp) 13.0kn
MWM TBD441V12
2 x Vee 4 Stroke 12 Cy. 230 x 270 each-1287kW (1750bhp)
Motoren Werke Mannheim AG (MWM)-West Germany
AuxGen: 3 x 112kW 220/380V 50Hz a.c
Thrusters: 1 Thwart. FP thruster (f)

7355911 **SCHASTLIVAYA ZVEZDA** **547** Class: (RS) (KR)
\- *ex* Hansung-31 *-2001* 265
\- *ex* Han Sung No. 31 *-1998* 486
Sakhalin Co Ltd (OOO 'Sakhalin')

1973 Korea Shipbuilding & Engineering Corp — Busan Yd No: 175
Loa 52.63 Br ex - Dght 3.350
Lbp 47.27 Br md 8.41 Dpth 3.81
Welded, 1 dk

(B11B2FV) Fishing Vessel
Ins: 542
4 Ha: 2 (1.0 x 0.9)2 (1.6 x 1.6)
Derricks: 1x1t

1 oil engine driving 1 FP propeller
Total Power: 736kW (1,001hp) 13.0kn
Hanshin 6LUD26G
1 x 4 Stroke 6 Cy. 260 x 440 736kW (1001bhp)
Hanshin Nainenki Kogyo-Japan
AuxGen: 2 x 200kW 230V a.c

7308504 **SCHATZE** *103*
WY2489 70
\- -
\-
Aransas Pass, TX *United States of America*
Official number: 509920

1967 Rockport Yacht & Supply Co. (RYSCO) — Rockport, Tx Yd No: 155
L reg 21.37 Br ex 6.56 Dght -
Lbp - Br md - Dpth 2.39
Welded

(B11B2FV) Fishing Vessel

1 oil engine driving 1 FP propeller
Total Power: 221kW (300hp)

8114857 **SCHEDAR** *196*
4DEC4 *ex* Daiko Maru *-2009* *ex* Utsumi *-1991* 92
Harbor Star Shipping Services Inc -
\-
Batangas *Philippines*
Official number: 04-0000335

1981-12 Sanyo Zosen K.K. — Onomichi Yd No: 825
L reg 27.01 Br ex - Dght 2.801
Lbp 26.01 Br md 8.62 Dpth 3.61
Welded, 1 dk

(B32A2ST) Tug

2 oil engines Geared Integral to driving 2 Z propellers
Total Power: 1,912kW (2,600hp) 13.5kn
Niigata 6L25BX
2 x 4 Stroke 6 Cy. 250 x 320 each-956kW (1300bhp)
Niigata Engineering Co Ltd-Japan

9065405 **SCHELDE HIGHWAY** **8,659** Class: LR
H9DC *ex* Feederchief *-2004* 2,597 ✠ **100A1** SS 10/2013
\- **Feederchief Shipping SA** 3,222 vehicle carrier
Stargate Shipmanagement GmbH
SatCom: Inmarsat A 1256731
Panama *Panama*
MMSI: 355444000
Official number: 2788101CH

moveable deck
Ice Class 1C
Max ice load waterline draught 5.719m
Ice light waterline draught forward 3.312m
Ice light waterline draught aft 4.612m
✠ **LMC**
Eq.Ltr: X; Cable: 495.0/52.0 U2

1993-10 Usuki Shipyard Co Ltd — Usuki OT Yd No: 1622
Loa 99.90 (BB) Br ex 20.53 Dght 5.612
Lbp 93.00 Br md 20.50 Dpth 6.60
Welded, 6 dks

(A35B2RV) Vehicles Carrier
Stern door/ramp (centre)
Len: 12.00 Wid: 5.00 Swl: 30
Side door/ramp (s)
Len: 15.50 Wid: 5.00 Swl: 7
Cars: 805
Cargo Heating Coils
Ice Capable

1 oil engine driving 1 CP propeller
Total Power: 3,177kW (4,319hp) 14.2kn
B&W 6L35MC
1 x 2 Stroke 6 Cy. 350 x 1050 3177kW (4319bhp)
The Hanshin Diesel Works Ltd-Japan
AuxGen: 3 x 360kW 450V 60Hz a.c
Boilers: AuxB (o.f.) 7.0kgf/cm² (6.9bar)
Thrusters: 1 Thwart. CP thruster (f)
Fuel: 27.6 (d.f.) (Heating Coils) 503.0 (r.f.) 12.4pd

9264752 **SCHELDE TRADER** **6,704** Class: GL
PBKZ *ex* Mekong Chaiyo *-2009* 3,557
\- *ex* Schelde Trader *-2005* 8,015
\- T/cm
\- 20.7
Winschoten *Netherlands*
MMSI: 245694000
Official number: 42295

2003-09 Zhejiang Yangfan Ship Group Co Ltd — Zhoushan ZJ Yd No: 2008
Loa 132.60 (BB) Br ex - Dght 7.220
Lbp 123.40 Br md 19.20 Dpth 9.20
Welded, 1 dk

(A33A2CC) Container Ship (Fully Cellular)
Double Bottom Entire Compartment Length
TEU 660 C Ho 188 TEU C Dk 472 TEU incl 116 ref C.
Cranes: 2x50t

1 oil engine geared to sc. shaft driving 1 CP propeller
Total Power: 6,300kW (8,565hp) 17.0kn
MaK 7M43
1 x 4 Stroke 7 Cy. 430 x 610 6300kW (8565bhp)
Caterpillar Motoren GmbH & Co. KG-Germany
AuxGen: 3 x 360kW 380V a.c, 1 x 1200kW 380V a.c
Thrusters: 1 Tunnel thruster (f)

9439474 **SCHELDEBANK** **2,999** Class: BV
PBJM 1,643
\- **Bankship IV BV** 4,500
Pot Scheepvaart BV
Delfzijl *Netherlands*
MMSI: 244870000
Official number: 51297

2007-09 Ferus Smit Leer GmbH — Leer Yd No: 382
Loa 89.78 (BB) Br ex - Dght 5.950
Lbp 84.97 Br md 14.00 Dpth 7.50
Welded, 1 dk

(A31A2GX) General Cargo Ship
Grain: 6,088
Ice Capable

1 oil engine reduction geared to sc. shaft driving 1 CP propeller
Total Power: 2,640kW (3,589hp) 13.0kn
MaK 8M25
1 x 4 Stroke 8 Cy. 255 x 400 2640kW (3589bhp)
Caterpillar Motoren GmbH & Co. KG-Germany
Thrusters: 1 Tunnel thruster (f)

IMO / Call sign / Fishing no.	Name / Owner / Manager / Port / Flag	GT / NT / DWT	Classification	Builder / Dimensions	Type / Cargo	Machinery
9194048 - -	**SCHELDEDIEP** *ex* Lunamar *-2011* *ex* Scheldediep *-2007* **Beheermaatschappij ms 'Scheldediep II' BV** Rederi AB Swedish Bulk *Limassol* *Cyprus* MMSI: 212385000	**3,170** 1,876 4,550	Class: GL	**2000-01 Rousse Shipyard JSC — Rousse** Yd No: 402 Loa 98.94 Br ex - Dght 5.740 Lbp 92.50 Br md 13.80 Dpth 7.40 Welded, 1 dk	**(A31A2GX) General Cargo Ship** Grain: 6,255 TEU 282 C. 282/20' (40') Compartments: 1 Ho, ER 1 Ha: (70.4 x 11.2)ER Ice Capable	**1 oil engine** reduction geared to sc. shaft driving 1 CP propeller Total Power: 2,880kW (3,916hp) 14.0kn MaK 6M32 1 x 4 Stroke 6 Cy. 320 x 480 2880kW (3916bhp) MaK Motoren GmbH & Co. KG-Kiel AuxGen: 1 x 328kW 220/380V a.c, 2 x 160kW 220/380V a.c Fuel: 254.0 (d.f.)
9514925 *PBMR* -	**SCHELDEDIJK** **Beheermaatschappij ms 'Scheldedijk' BV** Navigia Shipmanagement BV *Groningen* *Netherlands* MMSI: 245060000 Official number: 50329	**2,984** 1,551 4,891	Class: GL (BV)	**2010-02 Chowgule & Co Pvt Ltd — Goa** Yd No: 189 Loa 89.95 (BB) Br ex - Dght 6.220 Lbp 84.94 Br md 14.40 Dpth 7.85 Welded, 1 dk	**(A31A2GX) General Cargo Ship** Grain: 5,818 Compartments: 1 Ho, ER 1 Ha: ER (62.3 x 11.7)	**1 oil engine** reduction geared to sc. shaft driving 1 CP propeller Total Power: 1,980kW (2,692hp) 11.5kn MaK 6M25 1 x 4 Stroke 6 Cy. 255 x 400 1980kW (2692bhp) Caterpillar Motoren GmbH & Co. KG-Germany AuxGen: 1 x 312kW 415V 50Hz a.c, 1 x 160kW 415V 50Hz a.c Thrusters: 1 Tunnel thruster (f) Fuel: 35.0 (d.f.) 280.0 (r.f.)
9202510 *PFAQ* -	**SCHELDEGRACHT** **Rederij Scheldegracht** Spliethoff's Bevrachtingskantoor BV *Amsterdam* *Netherlands* MMSI: 244730000 Official number: 38770	**16,639** 6,730 21,250 T/cm 35.1	Class: LR ✠**100A1** SS 09/2010 strengthened for heavy cargoes, container cargoes in holds on upper deck and on upper deck covers timber deck cargoes tanktop suitable for regular discharge by grabs LI *IWS Ice Class 1A (Finnish-Swedish Ice Class Rules 1985) Max draught midship 10.959m Max/min draught aft 11.47/6.6m Max/min draught fwd 11.47/4.2m ✠**LMC** **UMS** Eq.Ltr: If; Cable: 620.4/64.0 U3 (a)	**2000-12 Stocznia Szczecinska Porta Holding SA — Szczecin** Yd No: B587/IV/2 Loa 172.00 (BB) Br ex 25.50 Dght 10.600 Lbp 160.29 Br md 25.30 Dpth 14.60 Welded, 1 dk	**(A31A2GX) General Cargo Ship** Grain: 22,200 TEU 1127 C Ho 478 TEU C Dk 649 TEU incl 120 ref C. Cargo Heating Coils Compartments: 3 Ho, ER 4 Ha: (6.4 x 7.5) (25.6 x 15.2)Tappered (38.4 x 17.8) (32.0 x 20.4)ER Cranes: 3x120t Ice Capable	**1 oil engine** with flexible couplings & sr gearedto sc. shaft driving 1 CP propeller Total Power: 12,060kW (16,397hp) 19.1kn Wartsila 6L64 1 x 4 Stroke 6 Cy. 640 x 900 12060kW (16397bhp) Wartsila Italia SpA-Italy AuxGen: 1 x 1000kW 445V 60Hz a.c, 3 x 450kW 445V 60Hz a.c Boilers: TOH (o.f.) 10.2kgf/cm² (10.0bar), TOH (ex.g.) 10.2kgf/cm² (10.0bar) Thrusters: 1 Thwart. FP thruster (f) Fuel: 275.0 (d.f.) (Heating Coils) 1750.0 (r.f.) 45.0pd
8985103 *PBJO* BRU 2	**SCHELDESTROOM** **De Koning Mosselkweek BV** - *Bruinisse* *Netherlands* MMSI: 245575000 Official number: 26141	**148** 44 -		**1937 N.V. Scheepswerven Gebr. van der Windt — Vlaardingen** Loa 35.00 Br ex 7.16 Dght - Lbp 33.15 Br md 6.89 Dpth 2.06 Welded, 1 dk	**(B11B2FV) Fishing Vessel**	**1 oil engine** geared to sc. shaft driving 1 Propeller Total Power: 448kW (609hp) Caterpillar 3412C 1 x Vee 4 Stroke 12 Cy. 137 x 152 448kW (609bhp) Caterpillar Tractor Co-USA
8925256 *PHHW* YE 83	**SCHELPDIER** **Gebr Vette BV** - *Yerseke* *Netherlands* MMSI: 244212000 Official number: 26895	**168** 50 -		**1983 Gebr. Kooiman B.V. Scheepswerf en Machinefabriek — Zwijndrecht** Yd No: 131 Loa 35.93 Br ex - Dght 1.850 Lbp 33.70 Br md 7.00 Dpth 2.47 Welded, 1 dk	**(B11B2FV) Fishing Vessel**	**1 oil engine** driving 1 FP propeller Total Power: 382kW (519hp) Mitsubishi S6N-MPTK 1 x 4 Stroke 6 Cy. 160 x 180 382kW (519bhp) Mitsubishi Heavy Industries Ltd-Japan
9277266 *PBHG*	**SCHEURRAK** **Government of The Kingdom of The Netherlands (Rijkswaterstaat Directie Noordzee)** - *Rijswijk, Zuid Holland* *Netherlands* MMSI: 246316000 Official number: 41223	**161** 48 10	Class: LR ✠**100A1** SS 12/2010 patrol catamaran SSC HSC G2 **LMC** Cable: 9.0/22.0 U3 (a)	**2005-12 Scheepsbouw en Machinefabriek De Greuns B.V. — Leeuwarden** (Hull) Yd No: 242 **2005-12 B.V. Scheepswerf Damen Hardinxveld — Hardinxveld-Giessendam** Yd No: 2242 Loa 26.55 Br ex 10.20 Dght 1.000 Lbp 23.95 Br md 10.00 Dpth 2.80 Welded	**(B31A2SR) Research Survey Vessel** Hull Material: Aluminium Alloy	**2 oil engines** driving 1 gen. of 57kW with clutches, flexible couplings & sr geared to sc. shafts driving 2 Water jets Total Power: 1,576kW (2,142hp) 22.0kn M.T.U. 12V2000M70 2 x Vee 4 Stroke 12 Cy. 130 x 150 each-788kW (1071bhp) MTU Friedrichshafen GmbH-Friedrichshafen AuxGen: 1 x 57kW 400V 50Hz a.c, 1 x 17kW 400V 50Hz a.c
9188233 *PCHC* -	**SCHIEBORG** **K/S UL 677** Wagenborg Shipping BV SatCom: Inmarsat C 424574911 *Delfzijl* *Netherlands* MMSI: 245749000 Official number: 36244	**21,005** 10,601 12,457 T/cm 38.6	Class: BV	**2000-04 Flender Werft AG — Luebeck** Yd No: 677 Loa 183.10 (BB) Br ex - Dght 7.500 Lbp 173.00 Br md 25.20 Dpth 15.30 Welded, 2 dks	**(A35A2RR) Ro-Ro Cargo Ship** Passengers: cabins: 6; driver berths: 12 Stern door/ramp (a) Len: 16.00 Wid: 22.70 Swl: 100 Lane-Len: 2475 Lane-clr ht: 5.30 Trailers: 136	**1 oil engine** driving 1 CP propeller Total Power: 10,920kW (14,847hp) 18.0kn Sulzer 7RTA52U 1 x 2 Stroke 7 Cy. 520 x 1800 10920kW (14847bhp) HSD Engine Co Ltd-South Korea AuxGen: 2 x 990kW a.c Thrusters: 2 Thwart. CP thruster (f); 1 Tunnel thruster (a)
7944736 - -	**SCHIEDAM** *ex* Mms Gagah *-2011* *ex* Kingpin *-2007* *ex* Roland *-2004* **Mammoet Trading BV** Mammoet Salvage BV *Basseterre* *St Kitts & Nevis* Official number: SKN1002162	**2,390** 717 5,000	Class: GL	**1971-07 Howaldtswerke-Deutsche Werft AG (HDW) — Kiel** Yd No: 530290 Loa 75.98 Br ex 24.01 Dght 3.301 Lbp - Br md - Dpth 4.68 Welded, 1 dk	**(Y11B4WL) Sheerlegs Pontoon** A-frames: 1x1000t	**2 oil engines** reduction geared to sc. shafts driving 2 Directional propellers Total Power: 882kW (1,200hp) Deutz SBF16M716 2 x Vee 4 Stroke 16 Cy. 135 x 160 each-441kW (600bhp) Kloeckner Humboldt Deutz AG-West Germany
8202616 - -	**SCHILDTURM** - -	**887** 266 952	Class: (GL)	**1983-04 Teraoka Shipyard Co Ltd — Minamiawaji HG** Yd No: 218 Loa 57.49 Br ex 12.07 Dght 4.222 Lbp 51.80 Br md 12.01 Dpth 4.78 Welded, 1 dk	**(B21B20A) Anchor Handling Tug Supply**	**2 oil engines** reverse reduction geared to sc. shafts driving 2 FP propellers Total Power: 2,942kW (4,000hp) 12.5kn Yanmar 6Z280L-ST 2 x 4 Stroke 6 Cy. 280 x 360 each-1471kW (2000bhp) Yanmar Diesel Engine Co Ltd-Japan Thrusters: 1 Thwart. FP thruster (f)
8605507 *DJOV* -	**SCHILKSEE** **Schlepp- und Fahrgesellschaft Kiel mbH-SFK** *Kiel* *Germany* MMSI: 211897000 Official number: 2489	**159** 71 35	Class: (GL)	**1986-10 Schiffswerft u. Masch. Paul Lindenau GmbH & Co. KG — Kiel** Yd No: 223 Loa 28.02 Br ex 7.37 Dght 1.851 Lbp 25.96 Br md 7.00 Dpth 2.85 Welded, 1 dk	**(A37B2PS) Passenger Ship** Passengers: unberthed: 245	**1 oil engine** with flexible couplings & reverse reduction geared to sc. shaft driving 1 FP propeller Total Power: 215kW (292hp) 11.5kn MWM TBD604BL6 1 x 4 Stroke 6 Cy. 170 x 195 215kW (292bhp) Motoren Werke Mannheim AG (MWM)-West Germany
8100612 *PHJJ* HA 36	**SCHILLHORN** **Meromar Shipping BV** - *Harlingen* *Netherlands* MMSI: 245647000 Official number: 26090	*257* 75 -	Class: (GL)	**1981-10 Schiffswerft Gebr Schloemer Oldersum — Moormerland** Yd No: 281 Lengthened-2011 Loa 39.30 Br ex 8.06 Dght 2.291 Lbp 33.10 Br md 8.02 Dpth 3.36 Welded, 1 dk	**(B11B2FV) Fishing Vessel**	**1 oil engine** driving 1 FP propeller Total Power: 270kW (367hp) Volvo Penta TAMD121C 1 x 4 Stroke 6 Cy. 130 x 150 270kW (367bhp) (new engine 1988) AB Volvo Penta-Sweden
9505405 *ZDKV2* -	**SCHILLIG** **Briese Schiffahrts GmbH & Co KG ms 'Schillig'** Briese Schiffahrts GmbH & Co KG *Gibraltar* *Gibraltar (British)* MMSI: 236111817	**2,415** 1,361 3,194	Class: GL	**2012-07 LISEMCO — Haiphong** Yd No: LS-015 / 008 Loa 86.02 (BB) Br ex - Dght 5.300 Lbp 82.42 Br md 12.40 Dpth 6.70 Welded, 1 dk	**(A31A2GX) General Cargo Ship** Grain: 4,971; Bale: 4,971 TEU 138 Compartments: 1 Ho, ER 1 Ha: ER (59.6 x 11.0) Ice Capable	**1 oil engine** reduction geared to sc. shaft driving 1 CP propeller Total Power: 1,980kW (2,692hp) 12.0kn MaK 6M25C 1 x 4 Stroke 6 Cy. 255 x 400 1980kW (2692bhp) Caterpillar Motoren GmbH & Co. KG-Germany AuxGen: 1 x 288kW 400V a.c, 2 x 112kW 400V a.c Thrusters: 1 Tunnel thruster (f)
9652454 *DBMZ* -	**SCHILLIG** **Government of The Federal Republic of Germany (Bundesminister fuer Verkehr-WSV)** Government of The Federal Republic of Germany (Wasser- und Schiffahrtsamt Tonning) *Wilhelmshaven* *Germany* MMSI: 211591710	**444** 133 430	Class: GL	**2013-03 Schiffs- und Stahlbau Berne GmbH & Co KG (SSB) — Berne** (Hull) Yd No: 1136644 **2013-02 Fr Fassmer GmbH & Co KG — Berne** Yd No: 09/1/5012 Loa 43.98 Br ex 9.54 Dght 1.600 Lbp 35.50 Br md 8.90 Dpth 3.20 Welded, 1 dk	**(B34Q2QB) Buoy Tender** Cranes: 1x8.5t	**2 oil engines** reduction geared to sc. shafts driving 2 Voith-Schneider propellers Total Power: 750kW (1,020hp) MAN D2842LE 2 x Vee 4 Stroke 12 Cy. 128 x 142 each-375kW (510bhp) MAN Nutzfahrzeuge AG-Nuernberg Thrusters: 1 Tunnel thruster (f)

IMO / Call sign	Name / Owner	Tonnage	Classification	Build / Dimensions	Type / Capacity	Machinery
9505285 *ZDJJ8* -	**SCHILLPLATE** **Briese Schiffahrts GmbH & Co KG ms 'Schillplate'** Briese Schiffahrts GmbH & Co KG *Gibraltar* *Gibraltar (British)* MMSI: 236111603	2,415 1,036 3,175	Class: GL	**2009-09 LISEMCO — Haiphong** Yd No: 002 Loa 85.97 Br ex - Dght 5.300 Lbp 82.42 Br md 12.40 Dpth 6.70 Welded, 1 dk	**(A31A2GX) General Cargo Ship** Grain: 4,971; Bale: 4,971 TEU 138 C Ho 102 TEU C Dk 36 TEU Compartments: 1 Ho, 1 Tw Dk, ER 1 Ha: (59.6 x 11.0)ER Ice Capable	**1 oil engine** reduction geared to sc. shaft driving 1 CP propeller Total Power: 1,800kW (2,447hp) 12.5kn MaK 6M25 1 x 4 Stroke 6 Cy. 255 x 400 1800kW (2447bhp) Caterpillar Motoren GmbH & Co. KG-Germany AuxGen: 1 x 280kW 400V a.c, 1 x 120kW 400V a.c Thrusters: 1 Tunnel thruster (f) Fuel: 46.0 (d.f.) 205.0 (r.f.)
9662409 *9HA3268* -	**SCHINOUSA** **Rudo Enterprises Ltd** Minerva Marine Inc *Valletta* *Malta* MMSI: 229361000 Official number: 9662409	91,374 57,770 176,000 T/cm 120.6	Class: BV	**2014-03 Shanghai Jiangnan Changxing Shipbuilding Co Ltd — Shanghai** Yd No: H1257 Loa 292.00 (BB) Br ex 48.00 Dght 18.300 Lbp 282.00 Br md 45.00 Dpth 24.80 Welded, 1 dk	**(A21A2BC) Bulk Carrier** Grain: 194,486; Bale: 183,425	**1 oil engine** driving 1 FP propeller Total Power: 19,620kW (26,675hp) 14.0kn MAN-B&W 6S70MC-C8 1 x 2 Stroke 6 Cy. 700 x 2800 19620kW (26675bhp) CSSC MES Diesel Co Ltd-China
9197363 *PCGR* -	**SCHIPPERSGRACHT** **Rederij Schippersgracht** Spliethoff's Bevrachtingskantoor BV *Amsterdam* *Netherlands* MMSI: 245578000 Official number: 36732	16,641 6,700 21,402 T/cm 35.1	Class: LR **✠100A1** SS 11/2013 strengthened for heavy cargoes, container cargoes in holds, on upper deck and on upper deck hatch covers, timber deck cargoes LA LI *IWS Ice Class 1A at a draught of 10.943m Max/min draughts fwd 11.47/4.2m Max/min draughts aft 11.47/6.6m Power required 8512kw, power installed 12060kw **✠LMC** **UMS**	**2000-01 Mitsubishi Heavy Industries Ltd. — Shimonoseki** Yd No: 1060 Loa 168.14 (BB) Br ex 25.40 Dght 10.710 Lbp 159.14 Br md 25.20 Dpth 14.60 Welded, 1 dk	**(A31A2GX) General Cargo Ship** Grain: 23,786; Bale: 23,786 TEU 1127 C Ho 478 TEU C Dk 649 TEU incl 120 ref C. Cargo Heating Coils Compartments: 3 Ho, ER 3 Ha: (26.6 x 15.2)Tappered (38.4 x 17.8) (31.9 x 20.4)ER Cranes: 3x120t Ice Capable	**1 oil engine** reverse reduction geared to sc. shaft driving 1 CP propeller Total Power: 12,060kW (16,397hp) 19.5kn Wartsila 6L64 1 x 4 Stroke 6 Cy. 640 x 900 12060kW (16397bhp) Wartsila Italia SpA-Italy AuxGen: 1 x 1000kW 445V 60Hz a.c, 3 x 450kW 445V 60Hz a.c Boilers: TOH (o.f.) 10.2kgf/cm² (10.0bar), TOH (ex.g.) 10.2kgf/cm² (10.0bar) Thrusters: 1 Thwart. CP thruster (f) Fuel: 275.0 (d.f.) (Heating Coils) 1750.0 (r.f.) 45.0pd
9604378 *DKBI* -	**SCHLESWIG-HOLSTEIN** **Neue Pellwormer Dampfschiffahrts GmbH** - *Wyk auf Foehr* *Germany* MMSI: 211551940 Official number: 73056	3,202 995 434	Class: GL	**2011-12 Neptun Werft GmbH — Rostock** (Hull) Yd No: S518 **2011-12 Meyer Werft GmbH — Papenburg** Yd No: S518 Loa 75.85 Br ex 16.40 Dght 1.850 Lbp 72.00 Br md 15.80 Dpth 3.40 Welded, 1 dk	**(A36A2PR) Passenger/Ro-Ro Ship (Vehicles)** Passengers: unberthed: 1200 Bow door (centre) Stern door (centre) Cars: 75	**4 oil engines** reduction geared to sc. shafts driving 4 Voith-Schneider propellers Total Power: 3,212kW (4,368hp) 12.0kn Caterpillar 3508C 4 x Vee 4 Stroke 8 Cy. 170 x 190 each-803kW (1092bhp) Caterpillar Inc-USA
6603828 *CB2582* -	**SCHLESWIG-HOLSTEIN** **Viento Sur (Sociedad Pesquera) Ltda** - *Valparaiso* *Chile* Official number: 2056	*139* 59 -	Class: (BV) (GL)	**1965 Evers-Werft — Niendorf/Ostsee** Yd No: 496 Loa 30.00 Br ex 6.81 Dght 2.801 Lbp - Br md - Dpth 3.41 Welded, 1 dk	**(B11A2FT) Trawler**	**1 oil engine** driving 1 FP propeller Total Power: 441kW (600hp) 11.5kn Frichs 8185CU 1 x 4 Stroke 8 Cy. 185 x 260 441kW (600bhp) (, fitted 1974) Frichs A/S-Denmark
9151539 *DMLM* -	**SCHLESWIG-HOLSTEIN** **Moldossa Vermietungsgesellschaft mbH & Co FS Schleswig-Holstein KG** Scandlines Deutschland GmbH SatCom: Inmarsat C 421119010 *Puttgarden* *Germany* MMSI: 211190000 Official number: 52566	15,187 4,556 2,904	Class: LR (GL) **100A1** SS 07/2012 passenger, vehicle and train ferry for service between Putgarden and Rodby *IWS Ice Class 1C **LMC** **UMS** Eq.Ltr: E†; Cable: 550.0/54.0 U3	**1997-07 van der Giessen-de Noord BV — Krimpen a/d IJssel** Yd No: 969 Loa 142.00 (BB) Br ex 25.40 Dght 5.800 Lbp 134.06 Br md 24.80 Dpth 14.05 Welded, 1 dk	**(A36A2PT) Passenger/Ro-Ro Ship (Vehicles/Rail)** Passengers: unberthed: 1040 Bow door Len: 4.90 Wid: 7.50 Swl: - Stern door Len: 4.90 Wid: 7.50 Swl: - Lane-Len: 1454 Lane-Wid: 2.50 Lane-clr ht: 5.55 Cars: 304 Ice Capable	**5 diesel electric oil engines** driving 2 gen. each 2240kW 6600V a.c 3 gen. each 2696kW 6600V a.c Connecting to 4 elec. motors each (3100kW) driving 4 Contra-rotating propellers 2 fwd and 2 aft Total Power: 17,600kW (23,930hp) 15.5kn MaK 8M32 5 x 4 Stroke 8 Cy. 320 x 480 each-3520kW (4786bhp) MaK Motoren GmbH & Co. KG-Kiel Boilers: HWH (ex.g.) (fitted: 1997) 6.2kgf/cm² (6.1bar) Fuel: 432.0 (d.f.) 42.5pd
9431599 *PBWZ* -	**SCHOKLAND** **H Buter** Amasus Shipping BV SatCom: Inmarsat C 424665510 *Urk* *Netherlands* MMSI: 246655000 Official number: 51259	2,702 810 3,300	Class: BV	**2010-07 Hong Ha Shipbuilding Co Ltd — Haiphong** Yd No: 07 Loa 89.98 (BB) Br ex - Dght 4.920 Lbp 84.98 Br md 13.75 Dpth 6.25 Welded, 1 dk	**(A31A2GX) General Cargo Ship** Grain: 4,870; Bale: 4,870 TEU 300 Compartments: 1 Ho, ER 1 Ha: ER (61.8 x 10.8) Ice Capable	**1 oil engine** reduction geared to sc. shaft driving 1 CP propeller Total Power: 1,980kW (2,692hp) 13.0kn MaK 6M25 1 x 4 Stroke 6 Cy. 255 x 400 1980kW (2692bhp) Caterpillar Motoren GmbH & Co. KG-Germany AuxGen: 1 x 468kW 400V 50Hz a.c, 2 x 232kW 400V 50Hz a.c Thrusters: 1 Tunnel thruster (f)
7812581 *WDB3505* -	**SCHOONER TIDE** *ex* Ensco Schooner *-2003* *ex* Clipper Cozumel *-1990* **Twenty Grand Offshore Inc** Tidewater Marine LLC *New Orleans, LA* *United States of America* MMSI: 366887830 Official number: 608347	656 196 700	Class: AB	**1979-07 Blount Marine Corp. — Warren, RI** Yd No: 220 Loa 53.97 Br ex 12.10 Dght 3.661 Lbp 50.62 Br md 11.89 Dpth 4.27 Welded, 1 dk	**(B21B20T) Offshore Tug/Supply Ship**	**2 oil engines** reverse reduction geared to sc. shafts driving 2 FP propellers Total Power: 1,368kW (1,860hp) 10.0kn G.M. (Detroit Diesel) 16V-149 2 x Vee 2 Stroke 16 Cy. 146 x 146 each-684kW (930bhp) General Motors Detroit DieselAllison Divn-USA AuxGen: 2 x 99kW Thrusters: 1 Thwart. FP thruster (f)
8215857 *PHJO* -	**SCHORPIOEN** *ex* Skylark *-1988* **Zinkcon Dekker BV** - *Papendrecht* *Netherlands* MMSI: 245735000 Official number: 306	290 87 422	Class: GL (BV)	**1982-11 Deltawerf BV — Sliedrecht** Yd No: 645 Loa 35.41 Br ex - Dght 1.990 Lbp 34.40 Br md 10.00 Dpth 3.25 Welded, 1 dk	**(A31C2GD) Deck Cargo Ship** Cranes: 1x4.5t	**2 oil engines** with clutches & sr reverse geared to sc. shafts driving 2 FP propellers Total Power: 536kW (728hp) 9.0kn Caterpillar 3408TA 2 x Vee 4 Stroke 8 Cy. 137 x 152 each-268kW (364bhp) Caterpillar Tractor Co-USA AuxGen: 1 x 70kW 220/380V a.c
7357646 - -	**SCHOTLAND** *ex* Wenduine *-1990* **Malta Towage Ltd** -	125 37 -	Class: (LR) ✠ Classed LR until 13/9/07	**1975-01 N.V. Scheepswerf van Rupelmonde — Rupelmonde** Yd No: 426 Loa 28.00 Br ex 7.47 Dght 2.661 Lbp 25.11 Br md 7.00 Dpth 3.30 Welded, 1 dk	**(B32A2ST) Tug**	**1 oil engine** driving 1 FP propeller Total Power: 1,103kW (1,500hp) 12.8kn Deutz RBV8M545 1 x 4 Stroke 8 Cy. 320 x 450 1103kW (1500bhp) Kloeckner Humboldt Deutz AG-West Germany AuxGen: 2 x 60kW 380V 50Hz a.c
8843836 *PBKT* -	**SCHOTSMAN** *ex* Cincobulk *-2003* *ex* Steinvang *-1999* *ex* Marpol Baltic *-1995* *ex* Eide Rescue I *-1994* *ex* Kuhlung *-1991* **Zeezand II BV** - *Terneuzen* *Netherlands* MMSI: 244795000 Official number: 41018	2,104 631 2,150	Class: NV (BV)	**1983-08 VEB Schiffswerft Neptun — Rostock** Yd No: 1422/134 Converted From: General Cargo Ship-2003 Converted From: Standby Safety Vessel-1995 Converted From: Replenishment Dry Cargo Vessel-1991 Lengthened-1999 Loa 89.97 (BB) Br ex - Dght 5.495 Lbp 87.74 Br md 12.37 Dpth 6.80 Welded, 1 dk	**(B33B2DT) Trailing Suction Hopper Dredger** Hopper: 1,523 Compartments: 1 Ho, ER 1 Ha: ER Ice Capable	**1 oil engine** reduction geared to sc. shaft driving 1 CP propeller Total Power: 1,079kW (1,467hp) 12.0kn Stork-Werkspoor 6SW280 1 x 4 Stroke 6 Cy. 280 x 300 1079kW (1467bhp) (made 1980, fitted 1999) Stork Wartsila Diesel BV-Netherlands AuxGen: 4 x 130kW Thrusters: 1 Tunnel thruster (f)
8227147 - -	**SCHS-1001** **Adzhar Fishing Fleet Administration (Adzharskoye Upravleniye Rybolovnogo Flota)** -	104 31 31	Class: (RS)	**1983 Azovskaya Sudoverf — Azov** Yd No: 1001 Loa 26.50 Br ex 6.58 Dght 2.361 Lbp 22.90 Br md - Dpth 3.05 Welded, 1 dk	**(B11B2FV) Fishing Vessel**	**1 oil engine** geared to sc. shaft driving 1 FP propeller Total Power: 166kW (226hp) 9.3kn Daldizel 6CHNSP18/22 1 x 4 Stroke 6 Cy. 180 x 220 166kW (226bhp) Daldizel-Khabarovsk AuxGen: 2 x 30kW a.c Fuel: 7.0 (d.f.)
8726739 - -	**SCHS-1006** **1 May Fishing Collective (Rybolovetskiy Kolkhoz imeni 1 Maya)** - *Kerch* *Ukraine*	109 32 58	Class: (RS)	**1986-01 Azovskaya Sudoverf — Azov** Yd No: 1006 Loa 26.50 Br ex 6.59 Dght 2.360 Lbp 22.90 Br md 6.50 Dpth 3.05 Welded, 1 dk	**(B11A2FS) Stern Trawler**	**1 oil engine** geared to sc. shaft driving 1 FP propeller Total Power: 165kW (224hp) 9.3kn Daldizel 6CHNSP18/22 1 x 4 Stroke 6 Cy. 180 x 220 165kW (224bhp) Daldizel-Khabarovsk AuxGen: 2 x 30kW a.c Fuel: 7.0 (d.f.)

8726741 - -	**SCHS-1007** **Lenin Fishing Collective (Rybolovetskiy Kolkhoz imeni Lenina)** -	**104** 31 58	Class: (RS)	**1986**-04 **Azovskaya Sudoverf — Azov** Yd No: 1007 Loa 26.50 Br ex 6.59 Dght 2.360 Lbp 22.90 Br md - Dpth 3.05 Welded, 1 dk	**(B11A2FS) Stern Trawler**	**1 oil engine** geared to sc. shaft driving 1 FP propeller Total Power: 165kW (224hp) 9.3kn Daldizel 6CHNSP18/22 1 x 4 Stroke 6 Cy. 180 x 220 165kW (224bhp) Daldizel-Khabarovsk AuxGen: 2 x 30kW a.c Fuel: 9.0 (d.f.)
8726777 - -	**SCHS-1014** **Chernomorets Fishing Collective (Rybolovetskiy Kolkhoz 'Chernomorets')** -	**104** 31 58	Class: (RS)	**1986**-11 **Azovskaya Sudoverf — Azov** Yd No: 1014 Loa 26.50 Br ex 6.59 Dght 2.360 Lbp 22.90 Br md - Dpth 3.05 Welded, 1 dk	**(B11A2FS) Stern Trawler**	**1 oil engine** geared to sc. shaft driving 1 FP propeller Total Power: 165kW (224hp) 9.3kn Daldizel 6CHNSP18/22 1 x 4 Stroke 6 Cy. 180 x 220 165kW (224bhp) Daldizel-Khabarovsk AuxGen: 2 x 30kW a.c Fuel: 8.0 (d.f.)
8726791 - -	**SCHS-1016** *ex* Milda *ex* Lyly *-1993* *ex* SCHS-1016 *-1992* **V I Lenina Fishing Collective (Rybolovetskiy Kolkhoz Imeni V I Lenina)** -	**104** 31 58	Class: (RS)	**1987**-03 **Azovskaya Sudoverf — Azov** Yd No: 1016 Loa 26.50 Br ex 6.59 Dght 2.360 Lbp 22.90 Br md - Dpth 3.05 Welded, 1 dk	**(B11A2FS) Stern Trawler**	**1 oil engine** geared to sc. shaft driving 1 FP propeller Total Power: 165kW (224hp) 9.3kn Daldizel 6CHNSP18/22 1 x 4 Stroke 6 Cy. 180 x 220 165kW (224bhp) Daldizel-Khabarovsk AuxGen: 2 x 30kW a.c Fuel: 9.0 (d.f.)
8726806 - -	**SCHS-1018** **Kotovskiy Fishing Collective (Rybolovetskiy Kolkhoz imeni Kotovskogo)** -	**104** 31 58	Class: (RS)	**1987**-05 **Azovskaya Sudoverf — Azov** Yd No: 1018 Loa 26.50 Br ex 6.59 Dght 2.360 Lbp 22.90 Br md - Dpth 3.05 Welded, 1 dk	**(B11A2FS) Stern Trawler**	**1 oil engine** geared to sc. shaft driving 1 FP propeller Total Power: 165kW (224hp) 9.3kn Daldizel 6CHNSP18/22 1 x 4 Stroke 6 Cy. 180 x 220 165kW (224bhp) Daldizel-Khabarovsk AuxGen: 2 x 30kW a.c Fuel: 9.0 (d.f.)
8726844 *ENZY* -	**SCHS-1028** **Ryboselskokhozyaystvennoye Kollektivnoye Predpriyatiye 'Vitchizna'** - *Illichevsk* *Ukraine* Official number: 873850	**104** 31 58	Class: (RS)	**1988**-08 **Azovskaya Sudoverf — Azov** Yd No: 1028 Loa 26.50 Br ex 6.59 Dght 2.360 Lbp 22.90 Br md - Dpth 3.05 Welded, 1 dk	**(B11A2FS) Stern Trawler**	**1 oil engine** geared to sc. shaft driving 1 FP propeller Total Power: 165kW (224hp) 9.3kn Daldizel 6CHNSP18/22 1 x 4 Stroke 6 Cy. 180 x 220 165kW (224bhp) Daldizel-Khabarovsk AuxGen: 2 x 30kW a.c Fuel: 9.0 (d.f.)
8726868 - -	**SCHS-1031** **Chernomorets Fishing Collective (Rybolovetskiy Kolkhoz 'Chernomorets')** -	**104** 31 58	Class: (RS)	**1988**-12 **Azovskaya Sudoverf — Azov** Yd No: 1031 Loa 26.50 Br ex 6.59 Dght 2.360 Lbp 22.90 Br md - Dpth 3.05 Welded, 1 dk	**(B11A2FS) Stern Trawler**	**1 oil engine** geared to sc. shaft driving 1 FP propeller Total Power: 165kW (224hp) 9.3kn Daldizel 6CHNSP18/22 1 x 4 Stroke 6 Cy. 180 x 220 165kW (224bhp) Daldizel-Khabarovsk AuxGen: 2 x 30kW a.c Fuel: 9.0 (d.f.)
8729781 - -	**SCHS-1032** **Ukraina Fishing Collective (Rybolovetskiy Kolkhoz 'Ukraina')** -	**104** 31 58	Class: (RS)	**1989**-03 **Azovskaya Sudoverf — Azov** Yd No: 1032 Loa 26.52 Br ex 6.59 Dght 2.361 Lbp 22.92 Br md - Dpth 3.08 Welded, 1 dk	**(B11A2FS) Stern Trawler**	**1 oil engine** geared to sc. shaft driving 1 FP propeller Total Power: 165kW (224hp) 9.3kn Daldizel 6CHNSP18/22 1 x 4 Stroke 6 Cy. 180 x 220 165kW (224bhp) Daldizel-Khabarovsk AuxGen: 2 x 30kW a.c Fuel: 9.0 (d.f.)
8730352 *EOFP* -	**SCHS-1035** **Lenin Fishing Collective (Rybolovetskiy Kolkhoz imeni Lenina)** - *Illichevsk* *Ukraine* Official number: 886193	**104** 31 58	Class: (RS)	**1989**-09 **Azovskaya Sudoverf — Azov** Yd No: 1035 Loa 26.52 Br ex 6.59 Dght 2.361 Lbp 22.92 Br md - Dpth 3.08 Welded, 1 dk	**(B11A2FS) Stern Trawler**	**1 oil engine** geared to sc. shaft driving 1 FP propeller Total Power: 165kW (224hp) 9.3kn Daldizel 6CHNSP18/22 1 x 4 Stroke 6 Cy. 180 x 220 165kW (224bhp) Daldizel-Khabarovsk AuxGen: 2 x 30kW a.c Fuel: 9.0 (d.f.)
8833946 - -	**SCHS-1038** - -	**104** 31 58	Class: (RS)	**1990**-02 **Azovskaya Sudoverf — Azov** Yd No: 1038 Loa 26.50 Br ex 6.60 Dght 2.361 Lbp 22.90 Br md - Dpth 3.08 Welded, 1dk	**(B11A2FS) Stern Trawler**	**1 oil engine** geared to sc. shaft driving 1 FP propeller Total Power: 165kW (224hp) 9.3kn Daldizel 6CHNSP18/22 1 x 4 Stroke 6 Cy. 180 x 220 165kW (224bhp) Daldizel-Khabarovsk AuxGen: 2 x 30kW a.c Fuel: 9.0 (d.f.)
8847088 *UWRG* -	**SCHS-1047** **Interfish-Biotech Ltd** - *Mariupol* *Ukraine* Official number: 903098	**104** 31 58	Class: (RS)	**1991**-08 **Azovskaya Sudoverf — Azov** Yd No: 1047 Loa 26.50 Br ex 6.59 Dght 2.360 Lbp 22.90 Br md - Dpth 3.05 Welded, 1 dk	**(B11A2FS) Stern Trawler** Ins: 48	**1 oil engine** geared to sc. shaft driving 1 FP propeller Total Power: 165kW (224hp) 9.3kn Daldizel 6CHNSP18/22 1 x 4 Stroke 6 Cy. 180 x 220 165kW (224bhp) Daldizel-Khabarovsk AuxGen: 2 x 30kW a.c Fuel: 9.0 (d.f.)
9076868 *UGXL* -	**SCHS-1060** **Chumbur Fishing Collective (Rybolovetskiy Kolkhoz 'Chumbur')** - *Makhachkala* *Russia* Official number: 920924	**104** 31 58	Class: (RS)	**1992**-12 **AO Azovskaya Sudoverf — Azov** Yd No: 1060 Loa 26.50 Br ex 6.59 Dght 2.360 Lbp 22.90 Br md 6.50 Dpth 3.05 Welded, 1 dk	**(B11A2FS) Stern Trawler**	**1 oil engine** geared to sc. shaft driving 1 FP propeller Total Power: 165kW (224hp) 9.3kn Daldizel 6CHNSP18/22 1 x 4 Stroke 6 Cy. 180 x 220 165kW (224bhp) Daldizel-Khabarovsk AuxGen: 2 x 30kW a.c Fuel: 9.0 (d.f.)
9101948 *UANI* -	**SCHS-1067** *ex* Alvand *-2002* **Fishko** - *Novorossiysk* *Russia* Official number: 921541	**104** 31 58	Class: RS	**1993**-06 **AO Azovskaya Sudoverf — Azov** Yd No: 1067 Loa 26.50 Br ex 6.59 Dght 2.360 Lbp 22.90 Br md - Dpth 3.05 Welded, 1 dk	**(B11A2FS) Stern Trawler** Ins: 48 Compartments: 1 Ho 1 Ha: (1.2 x 0.8) Derricks: 1x1t	**1 oil engine** geared to sc. shaft driving 1 FP propeller Total Power: 165kW (224hp) 9.3kn Daldizel 6CHNSP18/22 1 x 4 Stroke 6 Cy. 180 x 220 165kW (224bhp) Daldizel-Khabarovsk AuxGen: 2 x 30kW Fuel: 9.0 (d.f.)
9101950 *UAWO* -	**SCHS-1068** *ex* Damavand *-2002* **Fishko** - *Novorossiysk* *Russia* Official number: 921908	**104** 31 58	Class: RS	**1993**-06 **AO Azovskaya Sudoverf — Azov** Yd No: 1068 Loa 26.50 Br ex 6.59 Dght 2.360 Lbp 22.90 Br md 6.50 Dpth 3.05 Welded, 1 dk	**(B11A2FS) Stern Trawler** Ins: 48 Compartments: 1 Ho 1 Ha: (1.2 x 0.8) Derricks: 1x1t	**1 oil engine** geared to sc. shaft driving 1 FP propeller Total Power: 165kW (224hp) 9.3kn Daldizel 6CHNSP18/22 1 x 4 Stroke 6 Cy. 180 x 220 165kW (224bhp) Daldizel-Khabarovsk AuxGen: 2 x 30kW Fuel: 9.0 (d.f.)
8726894 - -	**SCHS-2009** - - *Nigeria*	**104** 31 61	Class: (RS)	**1986**-12 **Yeyskiy Sudostroitelnyy Zavod — Yeysk** Yd No: 2009 Loa 26.50 Br ex 6.59 Dght 2.340 Lbp 22.90 Br md - Dpth 3.05 Welded, 1 dk	**(B11A2FS) Stern Trawler**	**1 oil engine** geared to sc. shaft driving 1 FP propeller Total Power: 165kW (224hp) 9.3kn Daldizel 6CHNSP18/22 1 x 4 Stroke 6 Cy. 180 x 220 165kW (224bhp) Daldizel-Khabarovsk AuxGen: 2 x 30kW a.c Fuel: 10.0 (d.f.)
8726909 - -	**SCHS-2010** **Kherson Fishermen Rental Fishing Cooperative** - *Kherson* *Ukraine*	**104** 31 61	Class: (RS)	**1987**-07 **Yeyskiy Sudostroitelnyy Zavod — Yeysk** Yd No: 2010 Loa 26.50 Br ex 6.59 Dght 2.340 Lbp 22.90 Br md 6.00 Dpth 3.05 Welded, 1 dk	**(B11A2FS) Stern Trawler**	**1 oil engine** geared to sc. shaft driving 1 FP propeller Total Power: 165kW (224hp) 9.3kn Daldizel 6CHNSP18/22 1 x 4 Stroke 6 Cy. 180 x 220 165kW (224bhp) Daldizel-Khabarovsk AuxGen: 2 x 30kW a.c Fuel: 10.0 (d.f.)
8726911 - -	**SCHS-2011** *ex* Miranda II *-1994* *ex* SCHS-2011 *-1993* **Chernomorets Fishing Collective (Rybolovetskiy Kolkhoz 'Chernomorets')** -	**104** 31 61	Class: (RS)	**1987**-11 **Yeyskiy Sudostroitelnyy Zavod — Yeysk** Yd No: 2011 Loa 26.50 Br ex 6.59 Dght 2.340 Lbp 23.20 Br md - Dpth 3.05 Welded, 1 dk	**(B11A2FS) Stern Trawler**	**1 oil engine** geared to sc. shaft driving 1 FP propeller Total Power: 165kW (224hp) 9.3kn Daldizel 6CHNSP18/22 1 x 4 Stroke 6 Cy. 180 x 220 165kW (224bhp) Daldizel-Khabarovsk AuxGen: 2 x 30kW a.c Fuel: 10.0 (d.f.)

IMO / Call sign	Name / Owner	Tonnage	Class	Build / Dimensions	Type	Machinery
8730364 - -	**SCHS-2015** **Sukhumi Fishing Combine (Sukhumskiy Rybokombinat)** -	**104** 31 61	Class: (RS)	**1989-11 Yeyskiy Sudostroitelnyy Zavod — Yeysk** Yd No: 2015 Loa 26.52 Br ex 6.59 Dght 2.340 Lbp 22.90 Br md - Dpth 3.08 Welded, 1 dk	**(B11A2FS) Stern Trawler**	**1 oil engine** geared to sc. shaft driving 1 FP propeller Total Power: 165kW (224hp) 9.3kn Daldizel 6CHNSP18/22 1 x 4 Stroke 6 Cy. 180 x 220 165kW (224bhp) Daldizel-Khabarovsk AuxGen: 2 x 30kW a.c Fuel: 10.0 (d.f.)
8839421 - -	**SCHS-2017** **Kherson Fishermen Rental Fishing Cooperative** *Kherson* *Ukraine* Official number: 882075	**104** 31 61	Class: (RS)	**1990-09 Yeyskiy Sudostroitelnyy Zavod — Yeysk** Yd No: 2017 Loa 26.52 Br ex 6.60 Dght 2.340 Lbp 22.90 Br md - Dpth 3.08 Welded, 1 dk	**(B11A2FS) Stern Trawler**	**1 oil engine** geared to sc. shaft driving 1 FP propeller Total Power: 165kW (224hp) 9.3kn Daldizel 6CHSPN2A18-225 1 x 4 Stroke 6 Cy. 180 x 220 165kW (224bhp) Daldizel-Khabarovsk AuxGen: 2 x 30kW a.c Fuel: 10.0 (d.f.)
8847090 - -	**SCHS-2019** **Akva Ltd (Proizvodstvennoye Kommercheskoye 'Akva' Ltd)** -	**104** 31 61	Class: (RS)	**1991-06 Yeyskiy Sudostroitelnyy Zavod — Yeysk** Yd No: 2019 Loa 26.50 Br ex 6.59 Dght 2.340 Lbp 23.20 Br md - Dpth 3.05 Welded, 1 dk	**(B11A2FS) Stern Trawler**	**1 oil engine** geared to sc. shaft driving 1 FP propeller Total Power: 165kW (224hp) 9.3kn Daldizel 6CHSPN2A18-225 1 x 4 Stroke 6 Cy. 180 x 220 165kW (224bhp) Daldizel-Khabarovsk AuxGen: 2 x 30kW a.c Fuel: 10.0 (d.f.)
8862454 - -	**SCHS-2020** **Chernomorets Fishing Collective (Rybolovetskiy Kolkhoz 'Chernomorets')** -	**104** 31 61	Class: (RS)	**1991-11 Yeyskiy Sudostroitelnyy Zavod — Yeysk** Yd No: 2020 Loa 26.50 Br ex 6.59 Dght 2.340 Lbp 22.90 Br md - Dpth 3.05 Welded, 1 dk	**(B11B2FV) Fishing Vessel**	**1 oil engine** geared to sc. shaft driving 1 FP propeller Total Power: 165kW (224hp) 9.3kn Daldizel 6CHSPN2A18-225 1 x 4 Stroke 6 Cy. 180 x 220 165kW (224bhp) Daldizel-Khabarovsk AuxGen: 2 x 30kW a.c Fuel: 10.0 (d.f.)
8953485 - -	**SCHS-2024** **Magnetik Co Ltd** -	**104** 31 61	Class: (RS)	**1999 Yeyskiy Sudostroitelnyy Zavod — Yeysk** Yd No: 2024 Loa 26.50 Br ex 6.59 Dght 2.340 Lbp 23.90 Br md - Dpth 3.05 Welded, 1 dk	**(B11B2FV) Fishing Vessel** Grain: 66 Compartments: 1 Ho 1 Ha: (1.0 x 1.4)	**1 oil engine** geared to sc. shaft driving 1 FP propeller Total Power: 165kW (224hp) 9.3kn Daldizel 6CHSPN18/22 1 x 4 Stroke 6 Cy. 180 x 220 165kW (224bhp) Daldizel-Khabarovsk AuxGen: 2 x 30kW Fuel: 10.0 (d.f.)
8826838 - -	**SCHS-3208** **Chernomor Cooperative Business (Kooperativnoye Predpriyatiye 'Chernomor')** -	**104** 31 58	Class: (RS)	**1989-06 Rybinskaya Sudoverf — Rybinsk** Yd No: 8 Loa 26.50 Br ex 6.50 Dght 2.321 Lbp 23.61 Br md - Dpth 3.05 Welded	**(B11A2FS) Stern Trawler**	**1 oil engine** driving 1 FP propeller Total Power: 220kW (299hp) 9.5kn S.K.L. 6NVD26A-2 1 x 4 Stroke 6 Cy. 180 x 260 220kW (299bhp) VEB Schwermaschinenbau "KarlLiebknecht" (SKL)-Magdeburg AuxGen: 2 x 30kW a.c Fuel: 9.0 (d.f.)
8330554 - -	**SCHS-7007** **Priboy Fishing Collective Enterprise (Kollektivnoye Rybolovnoye Khozyaystvo 'Priboy')** -	**104** 31 61	Class: (RS)	**1979 Azovskaya Sudoverf — Azov** Yd No: 7007 Loa 26.50 Br ex 6.59 Dght 2.330 Lbp 22.90 Br md - Dpth 3.05 Welded, 1 dk	**(B11B2FV) Fishing Vessel**	**1 oil engine** geared to sc. shaft driving 1 FP propeller Total Power: 165kW (224hp) 9.3kn Daldizel 6CHNSP18/22 1 x 4 Stroke 6 Cy. 180 x 220 165kW (224bhp) Daldizel-Khabarovsk AuxGen: 2 x 30kW a.c Fuel: 10.0 (d.f.)
8330566 - -	**SCHS-7037** **Ukraina Fishing Collective (Rybolovetskiy Kolkhoz 'Ukraina')** -	**104** 31 61	Class: (RS)	**1983 Azovskaya Sudoverf — Azov** Yd No: 7037 Loa 26.50 Br ex 6.58 Dght 2.331 Lbp 22.90 Br md - Dpth 3.05 Welded, 1 dk	**(B11B2FV) Fishing Vessel**	**1 oil engine** geared to sc. shaft driving 1 FP propeller Total Power: 165kW (224hp) 9.3kn Daldizel 6CHNSP18/22 1 x 4 Stroke 6 Cy. 180 x 220 165kW (224bhp) Daldizel-Khabarovsk AuxGen: 2 x 30kW a.c Fuel: 10.0 (d.f.)
8330621 - -	**SCHS-7043** **OOO 'Epsilon Invest'** - *Kerch* *Ukraine* Official number: 831576	**104** 31 61	Class: (RS)	**1984 Azovskaya Sudoverf — Azov** Yd No: 7043 Loa 26.50 Br ex 6.58 Dght 2.340 Lbp 22.90 Br md - Dpth 3.05 Welded, 1 dk	**(B11B2FV) Fishing Vessel**	**1 oil engine** geared to sc. shaft driving 1 FP propeller Total Power: 165kW (224hp) 9.3kn Daldizel 6CHNSP18/22 1 x 4 Stroke 6 Cy. 180 x 220 165kW (224bhp) Daldizel-Khabarovsk AuxGen: 2 x 30kW a.c Fuel: 10.0 (d.f.)
8330669 - -	**SCHS-7048** - - *Nigeria*	**104** 31 61	Class: (RS)	**1984 Azovskaya Sudoverf — Azov** Yd No: 7048 Loa 26.50 Br ex 6.58 Dght 2.340 Lbp 22.90 Br md - Dpth 3.05 Welded, 1 dk	**(B11B2FV) Fishing Vessel**	**1 oil engine** geared to sc. shaft driving 1 FP propeller Total Power: 165kW (224hp) 9.3kn Daldizel 6CHNSP18/22 1 x 4 Stroke 6 Cy. 180 x 220 165kW (224bhp) Daldizel-Khabarovsk AuxGen: 2 x 30kW a.c Fuel: 10.0 (d.f.)
8330671 - -	**SCHS-7049** **Marine Ecological Systems Co Ltd (OOO 'Morskiye Ekologicheskiye Sistemy')** -	**104** 31 61	Class: (RS)	**1984-12 Azovskaya Sudoverf — Azov** Yd No: 7049 Converted From: Fishing Vessel Loa 26.50 Br ex 6.58 Dght 2.340 Lbp 22.90 Br md - Dpth 3.51 Welded, 1 dk	**(A31A2GX) General Cargo Ship**	**1 oil engine** geared to sc. shaft driving 1 FP propeller Total Power: 165kW (224hp) 9.3kn Daldizel 6CHNSP18/22 1 x 4 Stroke 6 Cy. 180 x 220 165kW (224bhp) Daldizel-Khabarovsk AuxGen: 2 x 30kW a.c Fuel: 10.0 (d.f.)
8726789 - -	**SCHS RUS** *ex* SCHS-1015 *-2001* *ex* Agoy *-1996* *ex* SCHS-1015 *-1994* **Azovskiy Rybak Fishing Collective (Rybolovetskaya Artel 'Azovskiy Rybak')** -	**104** 31 58	Class: (RS)	**1987-01 Azovskaya Sudoverf — Azov** Yd No: 1015 Loa 26.50 Br ex 6.59 Dght 2.360 Lbp 22.90 Br md - Dpth 3.05 Welded, 1 dk	**(B11A2FS) Stern Trawler**	**1 oil engine** geared to sc. shaft driving 1 FP propeller Total Power: 165kW (224hp) 9.3kn Daldizel 6CHNSP18/22 1 x 4 Stroke 6 Cy. 180 x 220 165kW (224bhp) Daldizel-Khabarovsk AuxGen: 2 x 30kW a.c Fuel: 9.0 (d.f.)
8837980 *UUJM* -	**SCHS VOYKOVETS** *ex* Voykovets *-1990* **Interfish Plus Ltd** - *Mariupol* *Ukraine* Official number: 894339	**104** 31 58	Class: (RS)	**1990-12 Azovskaya Sudoverf — Azov** Yd No: 1043 Loa 26.52 Br ex 6.60 Dght 2.361 Lbp 22.92 Br md - Dpth 3.08 Welded, 1 dk	**(B11A2FS) Stern Trawler** Ins: 48	**1 oil engine** geared to sc. shaft driving 1 FP propeller Total Power: 165kW (224hp) 9.3kn Daldizel 6CHNSP18/22 1 x 4 Stroke 6 Cy. 180 x 220 165kW (224bhp) Daldizel-Khabarovsk AuxGen: 2 x 30kW a.c Fuel: 9.0 (d.f.)
9194086 *PFAZ* -	**SCHUITENDIEP** *ex* Samba *-2012* *ex* Schuitendiep *-2011* **Hartmann Schiffahrts GmbH & Co KG (Hartmann Reederei)** Feederlines BV *Groningen* *Netherlands* MMSI: 244830000 Official number: 36287	**3,170** 1,876 4,555	Class: (GL)	**2000-10 Rousse Shipyard JSC — Rousse** Yd No: 406 Loa 98.94 Br ex - Dght 5.750 Lbp 92.50 Br md 13.80 Dpth 7.40 Welded, 1 dk	**(A31A2GX) General Cargo Ship** Grain: 6,255 TEU 282 C. 282/20' (40') 1 Ha: ER Ice Capable	**1 oil engine** geared to sc. shaft driving 1 CP propeller Total Power: 2,880kW (3,916hp) 14.0kn MaK 6M32 1 x 4 Stroke 6 Cy. 320 x 480 2880kW (3916bhp) MaK Motoren GmbH & Co. KG-Kiel AuxGen: 1 x 328kW 220/380V a.c, 2 x 160kW 220/380V a.c
8900804 *PBYE* -	**SCHUITENGAT** **Government of The Kingdom of The Netherlands (Rijkswaterstaat Directie Noordzee)** - *Rijswijk, Zuid Holland* *Netherlands* MMSI: 244652000 Official number: 18850	**288** 86 -	Class: BV	**1990-09 Scheepswerf Bijlholt B.V. — Foxhol** (Hull) Yd No: 671 **1990-09 B.V. Scheepswerf Damen — Gorinchem** Yd No: 8682 Loa 38.20 Br ex - Dght 1.700 Lbp 34.70 Br md 8.70 Dpth 2.75 Welded, 1 dk	**(B34Q2QB) Buoy Tender** Ice Capable	**2 oil engines** geared to sc. shafts driving 2 FP propellers Total Power: 486kW (660hp) Deutz SBA8M816 2 x 4 Stroke 8 Cy. 142 x 160 each-243kW (330bhp) Kloeckner Humboldt Deutz AG-West Germany Thrusters: 1 Tunnel thruster (f)

IMO / Call sign	Name / Owner	Tonnage	Class	Built / Dimensions	Type	Machinery
8802313 *PF8488* -	**SCHULPENGAT** **Texels Eigen Stoomboot Onderneming NV (TESO)** - *Texel* *Netherlands* MMSI: 244100526 Official number: 18990	**8,311** 2,493 1,215	Class: LR ✠ **100A1** SS 12/2010 ferry extended protected waters service from the port of Texel ✠ **LMC** Cable: 300.0/42.0 U3	**1990-12 Verolme Scheepswerf Heusden B.V. — Heusden** Yd No: 1012 Loa 110.40 Br ex 18.70 Dght 3.800 Lbp 108.00 Br md 18.20 Dpth 6.95 Welded, 1dk	**(A36A2PR) Passenger/Ro-Ro Ship (Vehicles)** Passengers: unberthed: 1750 Bow door (lwr) Bow door (upr) Stern door (lwr) Stern door (upr) Lorries: 25, Cars: 156	**6 diesel electric oil engines** driving 6 gen. each 1300kW 3000V a.c Connecting to 8 elec. motors each (625kW) driving 4 Voith-Schneider propellers Total Power: 8,310kW (11,298hp) 11.6kn Caterpillar 3606TA 1 x 4 Stroke 6 Cy. 280 x 300 1385kW (1883bhp) (new engine 2003) Caterpillar Inc-USA Caterpillar 3606TA 5 x 4 Stroke 6 Cy. 280 x 300 each-1385kW (1883bhp) Caterpillar Inc-USA Fuel: 460.0 (d.f.)
8519966 *HSB4794* -	**SCHUMI** *ex* Maple 1 *-2013* *ex* Chelsea Bridge *-2011* *ex* Berge Kobe *-2005* *ex* Co-Op Sunrise *-2005* **Siam Lucky Marine Co Ltd** - *Thailand* MMSI: 567481000	**47,249** 15,957 51,466 T/cm 71.5	Class: NV (NK)	**1987-03 Hitachi Zosen Corp — Onomichi HS (Innoshima Shipyard)** Yd No: 4826 Loa 219.74 (BB) Br ex 38.44 Dght 11.023 Lbp 210.71 Br md 38.41 Dpth 21.01 Welded, 1 dk	**(A11B2TG) LPG Tanker** Double Hull Liq (Gas): 76,194 4 x Gas Tank (s); 4 independent (9% Ni.stl) pri horizontal 9 Cargo Pump (s): 8x600m³/hr, 1x500m³/hr Manifold: Bow/CM: 94.8m	**1 oil engine** driving 1 FP propeller Total Power: 12,578kW (17,101hp) 16.1kn B&W 8S60MC 1 x 2 Stroke 8 Cy. 600 x 2292 12578kW (17101bhp) Hitachi Zosen Corp-Japan AuxGen: 3 x 740kW 450V 60Hz a.c, 1 x 600kW 450V 60Hz a.c Fuel: 496.0 (d.f.) 2920.9 (r.f.) 53.5pd
9638408 *VRMK4* -	**SCHUYLER TRADER** **Clara Shipping Co Pte Ltd** Raffles Shipmanagement Services Pte Ltd *Hong Kong* *Hong Kong* MMSI: 477752600	**23,405** 11,922 35,800	Class: BV	**2013-11 Qingshan Shipyard — Wuhan HB** Yd No: QS36000-1 Loa 179.90 (BB) Br ex - Dght 10.000 Lbp 175.00 Br md 30.00 Dpth 14.60 Welded, 1 dk	**(A21A2BC) Bulk Carrier** Grain: 48,635; Bale: 46,500 Compartments: 5 Ho, ER 5 Ha: 4 (20.0 x 20.0)ER (16.8 x 16.0) Cranes: 4x30t	**1 oil engine** driving 1 FP propeller Total Power: 6,400kW (8,701hp) 14.0kn MAN-B&W 5S50ME-B9 1 x 2 Stroke 5 Cy. 500 x 2214 6400kW (8701bhp) STX Engine Co Ltd-South Korea Fuel: 1690.0
8894732 *XUDZ5* -	**SCHWERFASSBAR** *ex* Koei Maru No. 31 *-2011* *ex* Shunyo Maru No. 88 *-2011* **Ever Transportation Ltd** *Phnom Penh* *Cambodia* MMSI: 515529000 Official number: 1186884	**174** 52 -		**1986-06 Kidoura Shipyard Co Ltd — Kesennuma MG** Yd No: 532 L reg 28.50 Br ex - Dght - Lbp - Br md 6.15 Dpth 2.55 Welded, 1 dk	**(B11B2FV) Fishing Vessel**	**1 oil engine** driving 1 FP propeller Total Power: 294kW (400hp) Matsui MS25GTSC-3 1 x 4 Stroke 6 Cy. 250 x 470 294kW (400bhp) Matsui Iron Works Co Ltd-Japan
8308460 *VWQL* -	**SCI-02** **The Shipping Corporation of India Ltd (SCI)** - SatCom: Inmarsat C 441959010 *Mumbai* *India* MMSI: 419256000 Official number: 2039	**1,310** 393 1,776	Class: IR (NV)	**1984-11 Robin Shipyard Pte Ltd — Singapore** Yd No: 335 Loa 58.60 Br ex 13.01 Dght 5.936 Lbp 51.62 Br md 12.98 Dpth 6.76 Welded, 2 dks	**(B21B20A) Anchor Handling Tug Supply**	**4 oil engines** with clutches, flexible couplings & sr geared to sc. shafts driving 2 CP propellers Total Power: 3,972kW (5,400hp) Daihatsu 6DSM-26A 4 x 4 Stroke 6 Cy. 260 x 300 each-993kW (1350bhp) Daihatsu Diesel Manufacturing Co Lt-Japan AuxGen: 2 x 680kW 380V 50Hz a.c, 2 x 245kW 380V 50Hz a.c Thrusters: 1 Thwart. CP thruster (f)
8308472 *VWQN* -	**SCI-03** **The Shipping Corporation of India Ltd (SCI)** - SatCom: Inmarsat C 441945210 *Mumbai* *India* MMSI: 419257000 Official number: 2040	**1,310** 393 1,772	Class: IR (NV)	**1984-11 Robin Shipyard Pte Ltd — Singapore** Yd No: 336 Loa 58.60 Br ex 13.01 Dght 5.936 Lbp 51.62 Br md 12.98 Dpth 6.76 Welded, 2 dks	**(B21B20A) Anchor Handling Tug Supply**	**4 oil engines** with clutches, flexible couplings & sr geared to sc. shafts driving 2 CP propellers Total Power: 3,972kW (5,400hp) Daihatsu 6DSM-26A 4 x 4 Stroke 6 Cy. 260 x 300 each-993kW (1350bhp) Daihatsu Diesel Manufacturing Co Lt-Japan AuxGen: 2 x 680kW 380V 50Hz a.c, 2 x 245kW 380V 50Hz a.c Thrusters: 1 Thwart. CP thruster (f)
9547257 *AVFU* -	**SCI AHIMSA** **The Shipping Corporation of India Ltd (SCI)** - *Mumbai* *India* MMSI: 419000125 Official number: 3703	**2,067** 704 1,970	Class: IR (AB)	**2012-08 Cochin Shipyard Ltd — Ernakulam** Yd No: BY-79 Loa 65.80 Br ex 16.40 Dght 5.700 Lbp 57.00 Br md 16.00 Dpth 6.80 Welded, 1 dk	**(B21B20A) Anchor Handling Tug Supply**	**2 oil engines** reduction geared to sc. shafts driving 2 CP propellers Total Power: 8,000kW (10,876hp) 13.0kn Wartsila 8L32 2 x 4 Stroke 8 Cy. 320 x 400 each-4000kW (5438bhp) Wartsila Finland Oy-Finland AuxGen: 2 x 1800kW a.c, 2 x 250kW a.c Fuel: 220.0 (d.f.)
9418298 *AUTR* -	**SCI CHENNAI** **The Shipping Corporation of India Ltd (SCI)** - SatCom: Inmarsat C 441901272 *Mumbai* *India* MMSI: 419739000 Official number: 3406	**43,679** 21,391 57,790	Class: BV IR	**2008-10 Hyundai Samho Heavy Industries Co Ltd — Samho** Yd No: S371 Loa 264.00 (BB) Br ex 32.28 Dght 13.200 Lbp 249.00 Br md 32.25 Dpth 19.30 Welded, 1 dk	**(A33A2CC) Container Ship (Fully Cellular)** TEU 4469 incl 350 ref C	**1 oil engine** driving 1 FP propeller Total Power: 36,160kW (49,163hp) 24.0kn Wartsila 8RTA82C 1 x 2 Stroke 8 Cy. 820 x 2646 36160kW (49163bhp) Hyundai Heavy Industries Co Ltd-South Korea Thrusters: 1 Tunnel thruster (f)
9547245 - -	**SCI KUNDAN** **The Shipping Corporation of India Ltd (SCI)** - *Mumbai* *India* MMSI: 419000298 Official number: 3837	**2,067** 704 1,970	Class: IR (AB)	**2012-04 Cochin Shipyard Ltd — Ernakulam** Yd No: BY-78 Loa 65.80 Br ex 16.40 Dght 5.700 Lbp 57.00 Br md 16.00 Dpth 6.80 Welded, 1 dk	**(B21B20A) Anchor Handling Tug Supply** Liq: 628	**2 oil engines** reduction geared to sc. shafts driving 2 CP propellers Total Power: 8,000kW (10,876hp) 13.0kn Wartsila 8L32 2 x 4 Stroke 8 Cy. 320 x 400 each-4000kW (5438bhp) Wartsila Finland Oy-Finland AuxGen: 2 x 1800kW a.c, 2 x a.c Fuel: 220.0 (d.f.)
9524918 *AUZY* -	**SCI MUKTA** **The Shipping Corporation of India Ltd (SCI)** - *Mumbai* *India* MMSI: 419779000 Official number: 3568	**2,039** 686 4,200	Class: IR	**2012-02 Bharati Shipyard Ltd — Ratnagiri** Yd No: 397 Loa 64.79 (BB) Br ex - Dght 6.290 Lbp 56.40 Br md 15.70 Dpth 7.00 Welded, 1 dk	**(B21B20A) Anchor Handling Tug Supply**	**2 oil engines** reduction geared to sc. shafts driving 2 CP propellers Total Power: 5,280kW (7,178hp) 14.0kn MaK 8M25C 2 x 4 Stroke 8 Cy. 255 x 400 each-2640kW (3589bhp) Caterpillar Motoren GmbH & Co. KG-Germany AuxGen: 2 x 300kW a.c, 2 x 1500kW a.c Thrusters: 2 Tunnel thruster (f); 1 Tunnel thruster (a)
9419539 *AUTQ* -	**SCI MUMBAI** **The Shipping Corporation of India Ltd (SCI)** - *Mumbai* *India* MMSI: 419738000 Official number: 3405	**43,679** 21,391 57,790	Class: BV IR	**2008-10 Hyundai Samho Heavy Industries Co Ltd — Samho** Yd No: S372 Loa 264.00 (BB) Br ex 32.28 Dght 13.200 Lbp 249.00 Br md 32.20 Dpth 19.50 Welded, 1 dk	**(A33A2CC) Container Ship (Fully Cellular)** TEU 4469 incl 350 ref C	**1 oil engine** driving 1 FP propeller Total Power: 49,177kW (66,861hp) 24.0kn Wartsila 8RTA82C 1 x 2 Stroke 8 Cy. 820 x 2646 49177kW (66861bhp) Hyundai Heavy Industries Co Ltd-South Korea Thrusters: 1 Tunnel thruster (f)
9575606 *AVFV* -	**SCI NALANDA** **The Shipping Corporation of India Ltd (SCI)** - *Mumbai* *India* MMSI: 419000126 Official number: 3704	**2,633** 997 3,093	Class: IR NV	**2012-08 Cochin Shipyard Ltd — Ernakulam** Yd No: BY-85 Loa 78.70 (BB) Br ex - Dght 5.830 Lbp 70.10 Br md 16.00 Dpth 7.00 Welded, 1 dk	**(B21A20S) Platform Supply Ship** Liq: 695	**4 diesel electric oil engines** driving 4 gen. Connecting to 2 elec. motors driving 2 Azimuth electric drive units Total Power: 3,640kW (4,948hp) 14.0kn Caterpillar C32 2 x Vee 4 Stroke 12 Cy. 145 x 162 each-910kW (1237bhp) Caterpillar Inc-USA Thrusters: 2 Tunnel thruster (f)
9290414 *A8RL5* -	**SCI NHAVA SHEVA** *ex* Santa Patricia *-2012* *ex* Cap Scott *-2012* *ex* Santa Patricia *-2010* *ex* Maersk Dolores *-2010* *ex* P&O Nedlloyd Delft *-2005* **KG ms 'Santa Patricia' Offen Reederei GmbH & Co** Reederei Claus-Peter Offen GmbH & Co KG *Monrovia* *Liberia* MMSI: 636091672 Official number: 91672	**54,809** 34,226 67,255	Class: GL	**2005-05 Hyundai Heavy Industries Co Ltd — Ulsan** Yd No: 1567 Loa 294.51 (BB) Br ex - Dght 13.650 Lbp 283.20 Br md 32.20 Dpth 22.10 Welded, 1 dk	**(A33A2CC) Container Ship (Fully Cellular)** TEU 5047 C Ho 2295 TEU C Dk 2752 TEU incl 550 ref C	**1 oil engine** driving 1 FP propeller Total Power: 45,778kW (62,240hp) 25.0kn Sulzer 8RTA96C 1 x 2 Stroke 8 Cy. 960 x 2500 45778kW (62240bhp) Hyundai Heavy Industries Co Ltd-South Korea AuxGen: 2 x 1800kW 450/230V 60Hz a.c, 2 x 2400kW 450/230V 60Hz a.c Thrusters: 1 Thwart. CP thruster (f)

9524889 *AVAB* -	**SCI PANNA** - **The Shipping Corporation of India Ltd (SCI)** - SatCom: Inmarsat C 441922995 *Mumbai* *India* MMSI: 419783000 Official number: 3571	**2,040** 686 2,001	Class: IR	**2011-08 Bharati Shipyard Ltd — Ratnagiri** Yd No: 394 Loa 64.79 (BB) Br ex - Dght 6.290 Lbp 56.40 Br md 15.70 Dpth 7.00 Welded, 1 dk	**(B21B20A) Anchor Handling Tug Supply**	**2 oil engines** reduction geared to sc. shafts driving 2 Propellers Total Power: 5,280kW (7,178hp) 14.0kn MaK 8M25C 2 x 4 Stroke 8 Cy. 255 x 400 each-2640kW (3589bhp) Caterpillar Motoren GmbH & Co. KG-Germany AuxGen: 2 x 300kW a.c, 2 x 1500kW a.c Thrusters: 2 Tunnel thruster (f); 1 Tunnel thruster (a)
9547233 *AVLI* -	**SCI PAWAN** - **The Shipping Corporation of India Ltd (SCI)** - SatCom: Inmarsat C 441923045 *Mumbai* *India* MMSI: 419000294 Official number: 3834	**2,048** 614 1,970	Class: IR (AB)	**2011-11 Cochin Shipyard Ltd — Ernakulam** Yd No: BY-77 Loa 65.80 Br ex 16.40 Dght 4.800 Lbp 57.00 Br md 16.00 Dpth 6.80 Welded, 1 dk	**(B21B20A) Anchor Handling Tug Supply**	**2 oil engines** reduction geared to sc. shafts driving 2 CP propellers Total Power: 8,000kW (10,876hp) 13.0kn Wartsila 8L32 2 x 4 Stroke 8 Cy. 320 x 400 each-4000kW (5438bhp) Wartsila Finland Oy-Finland AuxGen: 2 x 1800kW 50Hz a.c, 2 x 250kW 50Hz a.c Fuel: 220.0 (d.f.)
9524906 *AUZZ* -	**SCI RATNA** - **The Shipping Corporation of India Ltd (SCI)** - SatCom: Inmarsat C 441923121 *Mumbai* *India* MMSI: 419781000 Official number: 3569	**2,039** 686 3,762	Class: IR	**2011-10 Bharati Shipyard Ltd — Ratnagiri** Yd No: 396 Loa 64.79 (BB) Br ex - Dght 6.290 Lbp 56.40 Br md 15.70 Dpth 7.00 Welded, 1 dk	**(B21B20A) Anchor Handling Tug Supply**	**2 oil engines** reduction geared to sc. shafts driving 2 CP propellers Total Power: 5,280kW (7,178hp) 14.0kn MaK 8M25C 2 x 4 Stroke 8 Cy. 255 x 400 each-2640kW (3589bhp) Caterpillar Motoren GmbH & Co. KG-Germany AuxGen: 2 x 300kW a.c, 2 x 1500kW a.c Thrusters: 2 Tunnel thruster (f); 1 Tunnel thruster (a)
9547269 *AVFW* -	**SCI URJA** - **The Shipping Corporation of India Ltd (SCI)** - *Mumbai* *India* MMSI: 419000127 Official number: 3705	**2,048** 614 1,970	Class: AB IR	**2013-02 Cochin Shipyard Ltd — Ernakulam** Yd No: BY-80 Loa 65.80 Br ex - Dght 5.700 Lbp 57.00 Br md 16.00 Dpth 6.80 Welded, 1 dk	**(B21B20A) Anchor Handling Tug Supply**	**2 oil engines** reduction geared to sc. shafts driving 2 CP propellers Total Power: 8,000kW (10,876hp) 13.0kn Wartsila 8L32 2 x 4 Stroke 8 Cy. 320 x 400 each-4000kW (5438bhp) Cummins Engine Co Inc-USA AuxGen: 2 x 1800kW a.c, 2 x 250kW a.c Fuel: 220.0 (d.f.)
9575618 *AVFX* -	**SCI YAMUNA** - **The Shipping Corporation of India Ltd (SCI)** - *Mumbai* *India* MMSI: 419000128 Official number: 3706	**2,633** 997 3,095	Class: IR NV	**2012-11 Cochin Shipyard Ltd — Ernakulam** Yd No: BY-86 Loa 78.70 (BB) Br ex 16.03 Dght 5.830 Lbp 70.10 Br md 16.00 Dpth 7.00 Welded, 1 dk	**(B21A20S) Platform Supply Ship** Liq: 695	**4 diesel electric oil engines** driving 4 gen. each 1000kW a.c Connecting to 2 elec. motors driving 2 Azimuth electric drive units Total Power: 3,640kW (4,948hp) 14.0kn Caterpillar C32 4 x Vee 4 Stroke 12 Cy. 145 x 162 each-910kW (1237bhp) Caterpillar Inc-USA Thrusters: 2 Tunnel thruster (f)
5265813 *HQBH5* -	**SCIENTIFIC KING** *ex* Rey Mar *-1986* *ex* United Star *-1986* *ex* Halcyon Star *-1976* *ex* Ortoire *-1974* **Scientific Sun SA & Wind Laboratory Ltd** - *San Lorenzo* *Honduras* Official number: L-1321598	*992* 473 1,463	Class: (LR) ✠ Classed LR until 11/4/84	**1959-12 Clelands (Successors) Ltd. — Wallsend** Yd No: 238 Loa 66.55 Br ex 11.00 Dght 4.274 Lbp 62.18 Br md 10.67 Dpth 5.01 Welded, 1 dk	**(A12B2TR) Chemical/Products Tanker**	**1 oil engine** with flexible couplings & dr reverse geared to sc. shaft driving 1 FP propeller Total Power: 780kW (1,060hp) 10.0kn Crossley HRN8 1 x 2 Stroke 8 Cy. 267 x 343 780kW (1060bhp) Crossley Bros. Ltd.-Manchester
8219906 *IBBW* -	**SCILLA** - **Rete Ferroviaria Italiana (RFI)** - *Catania* *Italy* MMSI: 247052200 Official number: 246	*5,619* 2,577 2,395	Class: RI	**1985-03 Fincantieri-Cant. Nav. Italiani S.p.A. — Castellammare di Stabia** Yd No: 4402 Loa 145.01 Br ex 18.80 Dght 5.850 Lbp 138.61 Br md 18.41 Dpth 7.73 Welded	**(A36A2PT) Passenger/Ro-Ro Ship (Vehicles/Rail)** Passengers: unberthed: 1500 Bow door Stern door/ramp Len: 6.00 Wid: 4.50 Swl: - Lane-Len: 445 Lane-clr ht: 2.08 Cars: 170, Rail Wagons: 45	**4 oil engines** sr geared to sc. shafts driving 2 CP propellers Total Power: 12,356kW (16,800hp) 19.0kn GMT A420.6L 4 x 4 Stroke 6 Cy. 420 x 500 each-3089kW (4200bhp) Fincantieri Cantieri NavalItaliani SpA-Italy AuxGen: 4 x 900kW 440V 60Hz a.c Thrusters: 1 Thwart. CP thruster (f); 1 Tunnel thruster (a) Fuel: 567.0 (d.f.)
7527796 *GWOS* -	**SCILLONIAN III** - **Lyonesse Shipping Co Ltd** Isles of Scilly Shipping Co Ltd *Scilly* *United Kingdom* MMSI: 232001270 Official number: 377666	**1,346** 421 262	Class: LR ✠ **100A1** SS 03/2014 for service between Cornwall & the Scilly Isles & Plymouth ✠ **LMC** Eq.Ltr: M; Cable: U2	**1977-05 Appledore Shipbuilders Ltd — Bideford** Yd No: A.S.115 Loa 68.00 Br ex 11.87 Dght 2.941 Lbp 60.00 Br md 11.26 Dpth 6.91 Welded, 2 dks	**(A32A2GF) General Cargo/Passenger Ship** Passengers: unberthed: 600 Grain: 924; Liq: 38 TEU 14 C.Ho 14/20' Compartments: 2 Ho, ER, 1 Tw Dk 1 Ha: (10.0 x 3.0)ER Cranes: 1x5t	**2 oil engines** reverse reduction geared to sc. shafts driving 2 FP propellers Total Power: 1,794kW (2,440hp) 15.5kn Blackstone ESL8MK2 2 x 4 Stroke 8 Cy. 222 x 292 each-897kW (1220bhp) Mirrlees Blackstone (Stamford)Ltd.-Stamford AuxGen: 3 x 100kW 415V 50Hz a.c Thrusters: 2 Thwart. FP thruster
8917687 *ELVO5* -	**SCIO SUN** *ex* Duburg *-2010* *ex* Kota Perkasa *-2002* *ex* Japan Senator *-1998* **Piccadilly Finance Corp** Varship Shipping Co Ltd *Monrovia* *Liberia* MMSI: 636014892 Official number: 14892	**18,000** 10,484 26,288	Class: NK (GL)	**1990-10 Bremer Vulkan AG Schiffbau u. Maschinenfabrik — Bremen** Yd No: 51 Loa 176.57 (BB) Br ex - Dght 10.510 Lbp 166.96 Br md 27.50 Dpth 14.30 Welded, 1 dk	**(A33A2CC) Container Ship (Fully Cellular)** Grain: 36,170 TEU 1752 C Ho 708 TEU C Dk 1044 TEU incl 140 ref C. Compartments: 3 Cell Ho, ER 9 Ha: ER Ice Capable	**1 oil engine** driving 1 FP propeller Vane wheel Total Power: 12,180kW (16,560hp) 19.0kn B&W 7L60MC 1 x 2 Stroke 7 Cy. 600 x 1944 12180kW (16560bhp) Bremer Vulkan AG Schiffbau u.Maschinenfabrik-Bremen AuxGen: 1 x 800kW 220/440V a.c, 4 x 524kW 220/440V a.c Thrusters: 1 Thwart. FP thruster (f) Fuel: 2400.0
8703490 - -	**SCIROCCO** *ex* Choko Maru No. 68 *-2010* **Pesquera Comercial SA** - *Argentina* Official number: 02574	*893* - 950		**1987-09 Kitanihon Zosen K.K. — Hachinohe** Yd No: 217 Loa 67.87 (BB) Br ex - Dght 3.952 Lbp 60.00 Br md 10.22 Dpth 6.05 Welded	**(B11B2FV) Fishing Vessel** Ins: 1,254	**1 oil engine** driving 1 FP propeller Total Power: 1,177kW (1,600hp) Akasaka K28S 1 x 4 Stroke 6 Cy. 280 x 500 1177kW (1600bhp) Akasaka Tekkosho KK (Akasaka DieselLtd)-Japan
9407835 *A8QZ6* -	**SCIROCCO** - **Optim Ltd** Dynacom Tankers Management Ltd SatCom: Inmarsat C 463704952 *Monrovia* *Liberia* MMSI: 636014043 Official number: 14043	**42,010** 22,361 73,382 T/cm 67.1	Class: AB	**2009-07 New Times Shipbuilding Co Ltd — Jingjiang JS** Yd No: 0307360 Loa 228.60 (BB) Br ex - Dght 14.498 Lbp 219.70 Br md 32.26 Dpth 20.80 Welded, 1 dk	**(A13B2TP) Products Tanker** Double Hull (13F) Liq: 84,076; Liq (Oil): 81,500 Cargo Heating Coils Compartments: 12 Wing Ta, 2 Wing Slop Ta, ER 3 Cargo Pump (s): 3x2300m³/hr Manifold: Bow/CM: 116.4m	**1 oil engine** driving 1 FP propeller Total Power: 11,300kW (15,363hp) 14.5kn MAN-B&W 5S60MC-C 1 x 2 Stroke 5 Cy. 600 x 2400 11300kW (15363bhp) Hyundai Heavy Industries Co Ltd-South Korea AuxGen: 3 x 1125kW a.c
9359959 *HBEM* -	**SCL AKWABA** *ex* Safmarine Akwaba *-2013* **SCL Akwaba AG** Enzian Ship Management AG *Basel* *Switzerland* MMSI: 269868000 Official number: 190	**9,938** 4,265 12,576	Class: GL (LR) ✠ Classed LR until 23/5/09	**2008-04 Tianjin Xingang Shipbuilding Industry Co Ltd — Tianjin** Yd No: 343-3 Loa 139.96 (BB) Br ex 21.76 Dght 8.400 Lbp 133.50 Br md 21.51 Dpth 11.65 Welded, 1 dk	**(A31A2GX) General Cargo Ship** Grain: 16,194 TEU 702 C Ho 288 TEU C Dk 414 TEU incl. 138 ref C. Compartments: 3 Ho, ER 3 Ha: ER Cranes: 3x45t	**1 oil engine** driving 1 FP propeller Total Power: 7,860kW (10,686hp) 16.0kn MAN-B&W 6S46MC-C 1 x 2 Stroke 6 Cy. 460 x 1932 7860kW (10686bhp) Yichang Marine Diesel Engine Co Ltd-China AuxGen: 3 x 680kW 450V 60Hz a.c Boilers: AuxB (Comp) 8.2kgf/cm² (8.0bar) Thrusters: 1 Thwart. CP thruster (f)
9359961 *HBEN* -	**SCL ANDISA** *ex* Safmarine Andisa *-2013* *launched as* Safmarine Anita *-2008* **SCL Andisa AG** Enzian Ship Management AG *Basel* *Switzerland* MMSI: 269927000 Official number: 192	**9,938** 4,263 12,641	Class: GL (LR) ✠ Classed LR until 19/6/09	**2008-06 Tianjin Xingang Shipbuilding Industry Co Ltd — Tianjin** Yd No: 343-4 Loa 139.94 (BB) Br ex 21.78 Dght 8.400 Lbp 133.50 Br md 21.51 Dpth 11.65 Welded, 1 dk	**(A31A2GX) General Cargo Ship** Grain: 16,194 TEU 702 C Ho 288 C Dk 414 incl 138 ref C. Compartments: 3 Ho, ER Cranes: 3x45t	**1 oil engine** driving 1 FP propeller Total Power: 7,860kW (10,686hp) 16.0kn MAN-B&W 6S46MC-C 1 x 2 Stroke 6 Cy. 460 x 1932 7860kW (10686bhp) Yichang Marine Diesel Engine Co Ltd-China AuxGen: 3 x 680kW 450V 60Hz a.c Boilers: AuxB (Comp) 8.2kgf/cm² (8.0bar) Thrusters: 1 Thwart. CP thruster (f)
9359935 *HBEK* -	**SCL ANGELA** *ex* Safmarine Angela *-2012* *ex* Safmarine Akwaba *-2007* **mv Marie-Jeanne AG** Enzian Ship Management AG *Basel* *Switzerland* MMSI: 269668000 Official number: 188	**9,938** 4,265 12,605	Class: GL (LR) ✠ Classed LR until 20/2/10	**2007-12 Tianjin Xingang Shipyard — Tianjin** Yd No: 343-1 Loa 139.96 (BB) Br ex 21.78 Dght 8.400 Lbp 133.50 Br md 21.51 Dpth 11.65 Welded, 1 dk	**(A31A2GX) General Cargo Ship** Grain: 16,194 TEU 706 C Ho 292 TEU C Dk 414 TEU Compartments: 3 Ho, ER 3 Ha: (39.2 x 17.9) (25.9 x 17.9)ER (20.3 x 10.8) Cranes: 3x45t	**1 oil engine** driving 1 FP propeller Total Power: 7,860kW (10,686hp) 16.0kn MAN-B&W 6S46MC-C 1 x 2 Stroke 6 Cy. 460 x 1932 7860kW (10686bhp) Yichang Marine Diesel Engine Co Ltd-China AuxGen: 3 x 680kW 450V 60Hz a.c Boilers: WTAuxB New (Comp) 8.2kgf/cm² (8.0bar) Thrusters: 1 Thwart. CP thruster (f) Fuel: 121.0 (d.f.) 982.0 (r.f.)

IMO / Call sign	Name / Owner / Manager	Tonnage	Class	Builder / Dimensions	Type / Capacity	Machinery
9359947 *HBEL* -	**SCL ANITA** *ex* Safmarine Anita *-2013* *launched as* Safmarine Andisa *-2008* **SCL Anita AG** Enzian Ship Management AG *Basel* *Switzerland* MMSI: 269669000 Official number: 189	**9,938** 4,263 12,560	Class: LR ✠ **100A1** SS 01/2013 strengthened for heavy cargoes container cargoes in all holds and on upper deck and all hatch covers LI ✠ **LMC** **UMS** Eq.Ltr: D†; Cable: 550.0/54.0 U3	**2008**-01 **Tianjin Xingang Shipyard — Tianjin** Yd No: 343-2 Loa 139.99 (BB) Br ex 21.78 Dght 8.400 Lbp 133.50 Br md 21.50 Dpth 11.65 Welded, 1 dk	**(A31A2GX) General Cargo Ship** Grain: 16,194 TEU 702 C Ho 288 C Dk 414 incl. 138 ref C. Compartments: 3 Ho, ER Cranes: 3x45t	**1 oil engine** driving 1 FP propeller Total Power: 7,860kW (10,686hp) 16.0kn MAN-B&W 6S46MC-C 1 x 2 Stroke 6 Cy. 460 x 1932 7860kW (10686bhp) Yichang Marine Diesel Engine Co Ltd-China AuxGen: 3 x 680kW 450V 60Hz a.c Boilers: AuxB (Comp) 8.2kgf/cm² (8.0bar) Thrusters: 1 Thwart. CP thruster (f)
9539377 *HBLG* -	**SCL BASILISK** **SCL Basilisk AG** Enzian Ship Management AG *Basel* *Switzerland* MMSI: 269021000	**14,859** 6,310 17,809	Class: GL (LR) ✠ Classed LR until 5/8/13	**2013**-08 **Wuhu Xinlian Shipbuilding Co Ltd — Wuhu AH** Yd No: W0823 Loa 161.47 (BB) Br ex 25.22 Dght 8.600 Lbp 153.52 Br md 25.20 Dpth 12.41 Welded, 1 dk	**(A31A2GX) General Cargo Ship** Grain: 25,500; Bale: 25,500 TEU 1054 TEU C Ho 426 TEU C Dk 628 incl 145 ref C Compartments: 3 Ho, ER 3 Ha: ER Cranes: 3x80t	**1 oil engine** driving 1 FP propeller Total Power: 9,960kW (13,542hp) 17.0kn MAN-B&W 6S50MC-C 1 x 2 Stroke 6 Cy. 500 x 2000 9960kW (13542bhp) Doosan Engine Co Ltd-South Korea AuxGen: 3 x 960kW 450V 60Hz a.c Boilers: AuxB (Comp) 9.2kgf/cm² (9.0bar) Thrusters: 1 Thwart. CP thruster (f) Fuel: 180.0 (d.f.) 1700.0 (r.f.)
9304461 *HBEG* -	**SCL BERN** *ex* SITC Bern *-2006* *ex* SCL Bern *-2005* **SCL Bern AG** Enzian Ship Management AG *Basel* *Switzerland* MMSI: 269074000 Official number: 170	**9,990** 4,483 12,578	Class: GL (Class contemplated) (LR) ✠ Classed LR until 14/2/14	**2005**-02 **Kyokuyo Shipyard Corp — Shimonoseki YC** Yd No: 455 Loa 139.95 (BB) Br ex 21.53 Dght 8.420 Lbp 133.50 Br md 21.50 Dpth 11.65 Welded, 1 dk	**(A31A2GX) General Cargo Ship** Grain: 17,010; Bale: 17,010 TEU 766 C Ho 306 TEU C Dk 460 TEU incl 120 ref C. Compartments: 3 Ho, ER 3 Ha: (51.8 x 17.9) (13.3 x 17.9)ER (26.6 x 17.9) Cranes: 2x80t	**1 oil engine** driving 1 FP propeller Total Power: 8,208kW (11,160hp) 17.0kn MAN-B&W 8S42MC 1 x 2 Stroke 8 Cy. 420 x 1764 8208kW (11160bhp) Hitachi Zosen Corp-Japan AuxGen: 3 x 680kW 450V 60Hz a.c Boilers: AuxB (Comp) 7.0kgf/cm² (6.9bar) Thrusters: 1 Thwart. CP thruster (f) Fuel: 91.8 (d.f.) 1043.3 (r.f.)
9381421 *A8TS7*	**SCL ELISE** *launched as* Transitorius *-2009* **SCL Elise Shipping Ltd** Enzian Ship Management AG SatCom: Inmarsat C 463705867 *Monrovia* *Liberia* MMSI: 636014420 Official number: 14420	**5,599** 2,883 7,694 T/cm 17.8	Class: GL	**2009**-07 **Tianjin Xinhe Shipbuilding Heavy Industry Co Ltd — Tianjin** Yd No: SB510 Loa 108.12 (BB) Br ex - Dght 6.820 Lbp 103.90 Br md 18.20 Dpth 9.00 Welded, 1 dk	**(A31A2GX) General Cargo Ship** Grain: 10,194; Bale: 10,194 Compartments: 3 Ho, ER 3 Ha: ER Ice Capable	**1 oil engine** driving 1 CP propeller Total Power: 2,800kW (3,807hp) 12.0kn MAN-B&W 7S26MC 1 x 2 Stroke 7 Cy. 260 x 980 2800kW (3807bhp) STX Engine Co Ltd-South Korea AuxGen: 2 x 355kW 440V a.c Thrusters: 1 Tunnel thruster (f)
9381419 *A8MT8*	**SCL MARGRIT** **SCL Margrit GmbH & Co KG** Enzian Ship Management AG *Monrovia* *Liberia* MMSI: 636091368 Official number: 91368	**5,599** 2,883 7,775 T/cm 17.8	Class: GL (LR) ✠ 5/2/09	**2009**-02 **Tianjin Xinhe Shipbuilding Heavy Industry Co Ltd — Tianjin** Yd No: SB509 Loa 108.18 (BB) Br ex - Dght 6.820 Lbp 103.90 Br md 18.20 Dpth 9.00 Welded, 1 dk	**(A31A2GX) General Cargo Ship** Grain: 10,194; Bale: 10,194 Compartments: 3 Ho, ER 3 Ha: ER Ice Capable	**1 oil engine** driving 1 CP propeller Total Power: 2,800kW (3,807hp) 12.0kn MAN-B&W 7S26MC 1 x 2 Stroke 7 Cy. 260 x 980 2800kW (3807bhp) STX Engine Co Ltd-South Korea AuxGen: 2 x 365kW 440V a.c Thrusters: 1 Tunnel thruster (f)
9381433 *A8TX4*	**SCL NICOLE** *completed as* Merwedelta *-2009* **SCL Nicole Shipping Ltd** Enzian Ship Management AG *Monrovia* *Liberia* MMSI: 636014452 Official number: 14452	**5,599** 2,883 7,678 T/cm 17.8	Class: GL (LR) **100A1** 10/2009 Class contemplated	**2009**-10 **Tianjin Xinhe Shipbuilding Heavy Industry Co Ltd — Tianjin** Yd No: SB511 Loa 108.15 (BB) Br ex - Dght 6.820 Lbp 103.90 Br md 18.20 Dpth 9.00 Welded, 1 dk	**(A31A2GX) General Cargo Ship** Grain: 10,194; Bale: 10,194 Compartments: 3 Ho, ER 3 Ha: ER Ice Capable	**1 oil engine** driving 1 CP propeller Total Power: 2,800kW (3,807hp) 12.0kn MAN-B&W 7S26MC 1 x 2 Stroke 7 Cy. 260 x 980 2800kW (3807bhp) STX Engine Co Ltd-South Korea AuxGen: 2 x 365kW 440V a.c Thrusters: 1 Tunnel thruster (f)
9614701 *HBEH* -	**SCL TRUDY** **SCL Trudy AG** Enzian Ship Management AG *Basel* *Switzerland* MMSI: 269075000 Official number: 208	**14,941** 6,300 17,577	Class: GL	**2013**-08 **Taizhou Sanfu Ship Engineering Co Ltd — Taizhou JS** Yd No: SF100112 Loa 161.37 (BB) Br ex - Dght 8.600 Lbp 153.50 Br md 25.20 Dpth 12.40 Welded, 1 dk	**(A31A2GX) General Cargo Ship** Grain: 25,500 Compartments: 3 Ho, ER 3 Ha: ER Cranes: 3x80t	**1 oil engine** driving 1 FP propeller Total Power: 9,960kW (13,542hp) 17.2kn MAN-B&W 6S50MC-C8 1 x 2 Stroke 6 Cy. 500 x 2000 9960kW (13542bhp) Hyundai Heavy Industries Co Ltd-South Korea Thrusters: 1 Tunnel thruster (f)
9210309 *V2OI1* -	**SCM ELPIDA** *ex* BBC Pacific *-2005* *ex* Westkap *-2002* **Krey Schiffahrts GmbH & Co ms 'Westkap' KG** Krey Schiffahrts GmbH *Saint John's* *Antigua & Barbuda* MMSI: 304188000 Official number: 3787	**6,170** 2,958 7,725	Class: GL	**2000**-11 **Stocznia Gdanska - Grupa Stoczni Gdynia SA — Gdansk** Yd No: 8203/07 Loa 107.75 (BB) Br ex - Dght 7.806 Lbp 102.10 Br md 18.20 Dpth 10.10 Welded, 1 dk	**(A31A2GX) General Cargo Ship** Grain: 10,401; Bale: 10,401 TEU 371 C. 371/20' (40') Compartments: 2 Ho, ER 2 Ha: Cranes: 2x80t Ice Capable	**1 oil engine** reduction geared to sc. shaft driving 1 CP propeller Total Power: 3,456kW (4,699hp) 14.3kn MAN 8L32/40 1 x 4 Stroke 8 Cy. 320 x 400 3456kW (4699bhp) H Cegielski Poznan SA-Poland AuxGen: 1 x 424kW 220/380V a.c, 2 x 312kW 220/380V a.c Fuel: 421.0 (r.f.)
8414776 *3FSV* -	**SCM FEDRA** *ex* Jaco Spirit *-2009* *ex* Thor Svendborg *-2008* *ex* SCM Tepuy II *-2006* *ex* Kotor Bay *-2004* *ex* Nikolay Malakhov *-2004* *ex* Tauranga Chief *-2002* *ex* Nikolay Malakhov *-2001* *ex* Niugini Chief *-1999* *ex* Nikolay Malakhov *-1998* *ex* Capitaine Kermadec *-1997* *ex* Nicole Green *-1996* *ex* Nikolay Malakhov *-1995* *ex* Carpulp *-1987* **Temple Marine Ltd** Naviera Ulises Ltd *Panama* *Panama* MMSI: 370950000 Official number: 4072409	**6,031** 3,603 9,650 T/cm 18.5	Class: (LR) (NV) (RS) ✠ Classed LR until 10/87	**1987**-04 **Miho Zosensho K.K. — Shimizu** Yd No: 1256 Loa 113.01 (BB) Br ex 19.03 Dght 8.540 Lbp 106.03 Br md 18.92 Dpth 11.28 Welded, 2 dks	**(A31A2GX) General Cargo Ship** Grain: 12,582; Bale: 11,528 TEU 564 C Ho 234 TEU C Dk 330 TEU incl 50 ref C. Compartments: 1 Ho, ER, 1 Tw Dk 2 Ha: (33.6 x 15.7) (35.7 x 15.7)ER Cranes: 2x50t Ice Capable	**1 oil engine** driving 1 CP propeller Total Power: 4,413kW (6,000hp) 12.5kn Hanshin 6LF58 1 x 4 Stroke 6 Cy. 580 x 1050 4413kW (6000bhp) The Hanshin Diesel Works Ltd-Japan AuxGen: 1 x 600kW 445V 60Hz a.c, 3 x 200kW 445V 60Hz a.c Fuel: 106.0 (d.f.) 534.0 (r.f.)
8202812 *PCJQ* SCH 27	**SCOMBRUS** *ex* Hendrika Johanna *-1989* **Diepzee Visserij Maatschappij Cornelis Vrolijk V BV** - *Scheveningen* *Netherlands* MMSI: 245454000 Official number: 1748	**2,125** 637 1,872	Class: BV	**1982**-12 **"Welgelegen" Scheepswerf en Machinefabriek B.V. — Harlingen** Yd No: 105 Loa 78.24 (BB) Br ex 13.52 Dght 5.550 Lbp 71.61 Br md 13.28 Dpth 8.36 Welded, 2 dks	**(B11A2FS) Stern Trawler** Ins: 2,357 Compartments: 1 Ho, ER 2 Ha: ER	**1 oil engine** with flexible couplings & sr gearedto sc. shaft driving 1 CP propeller Total Power: 2,942kW (4,000hp) 15.0kn Werkspoor 6TM410 1 x 4 Stroke 6 Cy. 410 x 470 2942kW (4000bhp) Stork Werkspoor Diesel BV-Netherlands AuxGen: 1 x 900kW 220/380V 50Hz a.c, 2 x 620kW 220/380V 50Hz a.c
7505499 *LMCH* M-5-SA	**SCOMBRUS** *ex* Soroyfisk *-2011* *ex* Nystrom *-2011* *ex* Stella Viking *-2010* *ex* Stephens *-2006* **Tollevik AS** - *Aalesund* *Norway* MMSI: 257583600	*474* 267 -		**1976**-06 **Scheepswerf Vooruit B.V. — Zaandam** Yd No: 351 Loa 27.01 Br ex - Dght - Lbp 25.40 Br md 7.82 Dpth 4.12 Welded, 1 dk	**(B11B2FV) Fishing Vessel**	**1 oil engine** geared to sc. shaft driving 1 FP propeller Total Power: 736kW (1,001hp) 12.0kn Blackstone ESL8 1 x 4 Stroke 8 Cy. 222 x 292 736kW (1001bhp) Mirrlees Blackstone (Stamford)Ltd.-Stamford
8819275 *V4XU2* -	**SCOMBRUS** *ex* Indian Reefer *-2014* *ex* Erikson Reefer *-1992* **ESJA Investments Ltd** Norbulk Shipping UK Ltd *St Kitts & Nevis* MMSI: 341176000 Official number: SKN 1002652	**5,084** 3,163 6,120	Class: NV	**1991**-02 **Solisnor - Estaleiros Navais SA — Setubal** (Hull) Yd No: 142 **1991**-02 **Kvaerner Kleven Ulsteinvik AS — Ulsteinvik** Yd No: 111 Loa 109.02 (BB) Br ex - Dght 6.801 Lbp 100.01 Br md 18.01 Dpth 9.81 Welded, 3 dks	**(A34A2GR) Refrigerated Cargo Ship** Ins: 7,525 TEU 108 C Ho 48 TEU C Dk 60 icle 20 ref C Compartments: 4 Ho, ER 4 Ha: 4 (9.8 x 8.5)ER Cranes: 4x6t	**1 oil engine** geared to sc. shaft driving 1 FP propeller Total Power: 4,043kW (5,497hp) 16.0kn Wartsila 12V32D 1 x Vee 4 Stroke 12 Cy. 320 x 350 4043kW (5497bhp) Wartsila Diesel Oy-Finland AuxGen: 1 x 890kW 440V 60Hz a.c, 1 x 470kW 440V 60Hz a.c, 2 x 390kW 440V 60Hz a.c Thrusters: 1 Thwart. FP thruster (f) Fuel: 114.0 (d.f.) 565.0 (r.f.)
7327495 *LW6829*	**SCOMBRUS 1** *ex* Ryusho Maru No. 8 *-1987* **Harengus SA** - *Puerto Madryn* *Argentina* MMSI: 701000544 Official number: 0509	**240** 107 -	Class: (NK) (RI)	**1973** **Niigata Engineering Co Ltd — Niigata NI** Yd No: 1231 Loa 35.92 Br ex 7.42 Dght 2.261 Lbp 31.98 Br md 7.40 Dpth 4.65 Welded, 1 dk	**(B11A2FT) Trawler**	**1 oil engine** driving 1 FP propeller Total Power: 758kW (1,031hp) Niigata 6L25BXB 1 x 4 Stroke 6 Cy. 250 x 320 758kW (1031bhp) Niigata Engineering Co Ltd-Japan

IMO / Call sign	Name / Owner / Port / Flag	Tonnage	Class	Builder / Dimensions	Type / Cargo	Machinery
9345805 *9HNY8* -	**SCOPE** **CVI Scope LLC** Cargill Inc SatCom: Inmarsat C 425620110 *Valletta* *Malta* MMSI: 256201000 Official number: 9345805	**88,930** 58,083 174,008 T/cm 119.0	Class: AB	**2006-11 Shanghai Waigaoqiao Shipbuilding Co Ltd — Shanghai** Yd No: 1047 Loa 289.00 (BB) Br ex 45.05 Dght 18.120 Lbp 279.00 Br md 45.00 Dpth 24.65 Welded, 1 dk	**(A21A2BC) Bulk Carrier** Grain: 193,247; Bale: 183,425 Compartments: 9 Ho, ER 9 Ha: 7 (15.5 x 20.0)ER 2 (15.5 x 16.5)	**1 oil engine** driving 1 FP propeller Total Power: 16,860kW (22,923hp) 14.5kn MAN-B&W 6S70MC 1 x 2 Stroke 6 Cy. 700 x 2674 16860kW (22923bhp) Hudong Heavy Machinery Co Ltd-China AuxGen: 3 x 750kW a.c Fuel: 322.5 (d.f.) 4508.5 (r.f.)
8514576 *FHFT* -	**SCORFF** **CCIM Port De Commerce De Lorient** - *Lorient* *France* MMSI: 227019500 Official number: 686039	**204** 61 -	Class: BV	**1986-10 C.E.R.N.A.T. — Nantes** Yd No: 43278 Loa 28.10 Br ex - Dght 3.261 Lbp 25.51 Br md 8.21 Dpth 3.84 Welded, 1 dk	**(B32A2ST) Tug**	**2 oil engines** driving 2 Directional propellers Total Power: 1,860kW (2,528hp) MWM TBD604BV12 2 x Vee 4 Stroke 12 Cy. 170 x 195 each-930kW (1264bhp) Motoren Werke Mannheim AG (MWM)-West Germany
8627725 *YGZS* -	**SCORPIO** *ex* K. K. 32 *-2007* *ex* Yamataka Maru No. 3 *-2001* **PT Fajar Indah Tirta Abadi** - *Cirebon* *Indonesia*	**597** 180 900	Class: KI	**1986-03 Amakusa Zosen K.K. — Amakusa** Converted From: Grab Dredger-2001 Loa 51.01 Br ex - Dght 3.190 Lbp 45.00 Br md 10.00 Dpth 5.10 Welded, 1 dk	**(A31A2GX) General Cargo Ship**	**1 oil engine** reverse geared to sc. shaft driving 1 FP propeller Total Power: 625kW (850hp) 10.0kn Akasaka DM26K 1 x 4 Stroke 6 Cy. 260 x 440 625kW (850bhp) Akasaka Tekkosho KK (Akasaka DieselLtd)-Japan AuxGen: 1 x 75kW 225V a.c
9112595 *YDA6004* -	**SCORPIO** *ex* Kimtrans Scorpio *-2008* **Pelayaran Salim Samudra Pacific Line** - *Samarinda* *Indonesia*	**111** 34 120	Class: KI (NK)	**1994-07 Kian Juan Dockyard Sdn Bhd — Miri** Yd No: 82 Loa 23.17 Br ex - Dght 2.409 Lbp 21.80 Br md 6.70 Dpth 2.90 Welded, 1 dk	**(B32A2ST) Tug**	**2 oil engines** reduction geared to sc. shafts driving 2 FP propellers Total Power: 692kW (940hp) 9.0kn Caterpillar 3408TA 2 x Vee 4 Stroke 8 Cy. 137 x 152 each-346kW (470bhp) Caterpillar Inc-USA AuxGen: 2 x 16kW a.c Fuel: 75.0 (d.f.)
9389071 *SVA07* -	**SCORPIO** **Fantasea Navigation Ltd** TMS Tankers Ltd SatCom: Inmarsat C 424086410 *Piraeus* *Greece* MMSI: 240864000 Official number: 11855	**58,418** 32,391 107,157 T/cm 93.9	Class: AB	**2009-03 Shanghai Waigaoqiao Shipbuilding Co Ltd — Shanghai** Yd No: 1084 Loa 243.80 (BB) Br ex - Dght 15.100 Lbp 233.00 Br md 42.00 Dpth 21.40 Welded, 1 dk	**(A13A2TW) Crude/Oil Products Tanker** Double Hull (13F) Liq: 118,000; Liq (Oil): 118,000 Compartments: 12 Wing Ta, 2 Wing Slop Ta, ER 3 Cargo Pump (s): 3x2800m³/hr Manifold: Bow/CM: 121.7m	**1 oil engine** driving 1 FP propeller Total Power: 13,560kW (18,436hp) 15.0kn MAN-B&W 6S60MC-C 1 x 2 Stroke 6 Cy. 600 x 2400 13560kW (18436bhp) Hudong Heavy Machinery Co Ltd-China AuxGen: 3 x 800kW a.c Fuel: 245.0 (d.f.) 3000.0 (r.f.)
9253947 *9V6214* -	**SCORPIO** **PSA Marine Pte Ltd** - *Singapore* *Singapore* MMSI: 563003450 Official number: 389796	**246** 73 90	Class: LR (AB) **100A1** SS 05/2012 TOC contemplated	**2002-05 Keppel Singmarine Pte Ltd — Singapore** Yd No: 240 Loa 26.33 Br ex - Dght 3.750 Lbp 22.50 Br md 9.00 Dpth 4.70 Welded, 1 dk	**(B32A2ST) Tug**	**2 oil engines** driving 2 Directional propellers Total Power: 2,354kW (3,200hp) 12.0kn Yanmar 8N21A-EN 2 x 4 Stroke 8 Cy. 210 x 290 each-1177kW (1600bhp) Yanmar Diesel Engine Co Ltd-Japan AuxGen: 2 x 85kW
9550761 *WDF2159* -	**SCORPIO** **San Francisco Bay Area Water Emergency Transportation Authority (WETA)** - *San Francisco, CA* *United States of America* Official number: 1215086	**317** - 249		**2009-12 Nichols Bros. Boat Builders, Inc. — Freeland, Wa** (Hull) Yd No: S-157 **2009-12 Kvichak Marine Industries — Seattle, Wa** Yd No: 420 Loa 36.00 Br ex 8.80 Dght 1.900 Lbp 34.60 Br md 8.50 Dpth 3.80 Welded, 1 dk	**(A37B2PS) Passenger Ship** Hull Material: Aluminium Alloy Passengers: unberthed: 208	**2 oil engines** geared to sc. shafts driving 2 FP propellers Total Power: 2,100kW (2,856hp) 25.0kn M.T.U. 16V2000M70 2 x Vee 4 Stroke 16 Cy. 130 x 150 each-1050kW (1428bhp) MTU Friedrichshafen GmbH-Friedrichshafen AuxGen: 2 x 99kW a.c
7026974 *HO8773* -	**SCORPIO DEL GOLFO** *ex* Big Orange VI *-1981* *ex* Aquarius *-1974* *ex* Keeneland *-1974* **Intermarine de Panama SA** Intermarine (Sharjah) Ltd *Panama* *Panama* MMSI: 356511000 Official number: 1267082C	*408* 122 122	Class: AB	**1969 Burton Shipyard Co., Inc. — Port Arthur, Tx** Yd No: 460 Loa 47.20 Br ex 11.59 Dght 3.372 Lbp 47.20 Br md 11.57 Dpth 3.97 Welded, 1 dk	**(B21A2OS) Platform Supply Ship**	**2 oil engines** reverse reduction geared to sc. shafts driving 2 FP propellers Total Power: 1,654kW (2,248hp) 12.0kn Caterpillar D399 2 x Vee 4 Stroke 16 Cy. 159 x 203 each-827kW (1124bhp) Caterpillar Tractor Co-USA
8220644 *9V3804* -	**SCORPIO I** **South Sumatra Richfield Marine Pte Ltd** Pacific Richfield Marine Pte Ltd SatCom: Inmarsat C 456336010 *Singapore* *Singapore* MMSI: 563360000 Official number: 385535	*1,001* 300 1,500	Class: AB	**1983-07 Santan Engineering Pte Ltd — Singapore** Yd No: 8234 Loa - Br ex - Dght 4.514 Lbp 55.61 Br md 13.61 Dpth 5.21 Welded, 1 dk	**(B21A2OS) Platform Supply Ship**	**2 oil engines** reverse reduction geared to sc. shafts driving 2 FP propellers Total Power: 2,206kW (3,000hp) 12.0kn Yanmar 6T260L-ET 2 x 4 Stroke 6 Cy. 260 x 330 each-1103kW (1500bhp) Yanmar Diesel Engine Co Ltd-Japan AuxGen: 2 x 200kW Thrusters: 1 Thwart. FP thruster (f)
8128353 *9LB2325* -	**SCORPION** *ex* Taymyr *-2007* **Multi Group International FZE** - *Freetown* *Sierra Leone* MMSI: 667002165 Official number: SL102165	**1,490** 447 658	Class: IS (HR) (RR)	**1983-06 IHC Smit BV — Kinderdijk** Yd No: C01158 Loa 86.52 Br ex - Dght 2.390 Lbp 73.51 Br md 14.01 Dpth 3.51 Welded, 1 dk	**(B33A2DC) Cutter Suction Dredger**	**2 oil engines** with clutches & sr reverse geared to sc. shafts driving 2 FP propellers Total Power: 1,324kW (1,800hp) Bolnes 6DNL150/600 2 x 2 Stroke 6 Cy. 190 x 350 each-662kW (900bhp) 'Bolnes' Motorenfabriek BV-Netherlands
9633393 *2ETH2* -	**SCORPION** **Sea Breeze Charters Ltd** Ocean Management GmbH *Douglas* *Isle of Man (British)* MMSI: 235087977 Official number: 742863	**338** 101 45	Class: AB	**2011-08 Cant. Nav. San Lorenzo SpA — Viareggio** Yd No: 109/40 Loa 40.00 Br ex - Dght 1.660 Lbp 35.30 Br md 7.90 Dpth 3.90 Welded, 1 dk	**(X11A2YP) Yacht** Hull Material: Aluminium Alloy	**2 oil engines** reduction geared to sc. shafts driving 2 FP propellers Total Power: 4,680kW (6,362hp) 26.0kn M.T.U. 12V4000M93 2 x Vee 4 Stroke 12 Cy. 170 x 190 each-2340kW (3181bhp) MTU Friedrichshafen GmbH-Friedrichshafen AuxGen: 2 x 70kW a.c Fuel: 30.0 (d.f.)
7726990 *ERNZ* -	**SCORPION 1** *ex* Sherin *-2012* *ex* Mari *-2011* *ex* Anne *-1998* *ex* Pentland *-1995* *ex* Mara *-1993* *ex* Trabant *-1991* **Ask-Shipping92 Co** Tartousi Shipping Ltd *Moldova* MMSI: 214181426	**1,925** 854 2,265	Class: MB (GL)	**1978-08 J.J. Sietas KG Schiffswerft GmbH & Co. — Hamburg** Yd No: 865 Loa 79.79 Br ex 12.83 Dght 4.432 Lbp 74.50 Br md 12.80 Dpth 4.50 Welded, 2 dks	**(A31A2GX) General Cargo Ship** Grain: 3,594; Bale: 3,506 TEU 145 C. 145/20' Compartments: 1 Ho, ER 1 Ha: (50.3 x 10.2)ER Ice Capable	**1 oil engine** driving 1 FP propeller Total Power: 1,103kW (1,500hp) 12.0kn MaK 8M452AK 1 x 4 Stroke 8 Cy. 320 x 450 1103kW (1500bhp) MaK Maschinenbau GmbH-Kiel AuxGen: 3 x 63kW 380/220V a.c Thrusters: 1 Tunnel thruster (f)
7433725 *PS3302* -	**SCORPIUS** **Saveiros Camuyrano - Servicos Maritimos SA** Wilson Sons Agencia Maritima Ltda *Rio de Janeiro* *Brazil* Official number: 3810248398	*184* 76	Class: (LR) ✠ Classed LR until 16/8/07	**1976-11 Maclaren Estaleiros e Servicos Maritimos S.A. — Rio de Janeiro** Yd No: 219 Loa 24.36 Br ex 7.17 Dght 3.401 Lbp 21.52 Br md 7.01 Dpth 4.02 Welded, 1 dk	**(B32A2ST) Tug**	**2 oil engines** reverse reduction geared to sc. shaft driving 1 Directional propeller Total Power: 1,236kW (1,680hp) MAN G7V235/330ATL 2 x 4 Stroke 7 Cy. 235 x 330 each-618kW (840bhp) Mecanica Pesada SA-Brazil AuxGen: 2 x 48kW 450V 60Hz a.c Fuel: 41.0 (d.f.)
7210783 *WDD8770* -	**SCORPIUS** *ex* Kekoa *-2007* *ex* Barbara R. McAllister *-1990* *ex* Paris Theriot *-1979* **Taurus Marine Inc** Cross Link Inc (Westar Marine Services) *San Francisco, CA* *United States of America* MMSI: 367302540 Official number: 506606	**382** 114 -	Class: (AB)	**1967-01 Nolty J. Theriot Inc. — Golden Meadow, La** Yd No: 20 Loa - Br ex - Dght 4.214 Lbp 35.92 Br md 9.61 Dpth 4.86 Welded, 1 dk	**(B32A2ST) Tug**	**2 oil engines** reverse reduction geared to sc. shafts driving 2 FP propellers Total Power: 4,230kW (5,752hp) EMD (Electro-Motive) 16-645-E5 2 x Vee 2 Stroke 16 Cy. 230 x 254 each-2115kW (2876bhp) General Motors Corp-USA AuxGen: 2 x 100kW Fuel: 233.5 (d.f.)
9096882 *CUFD4* A-3570-C	**SCORPIUS** **Testa y Cunhas SA** - *Aveiro* *Portugal*	**277** 68 -	Class: BV	**2001-11 Astilleros Ria de Aviles SL — Nieva** Yd No: 79 Loa 27.90 Br ex - Dght 3.440 Lbp 22.96 Br md 7.50 Dpth 5.50 Welded, 2 dks	**(B11A2FS) Stern Trawler**	**1 oil engine** geared to sc. shaft driving 1 CP propeller Total Power: 588kW (799hp) 11.0kn GUASCOR F360-SP 1 x Vee 4 Stroke 12 Cy. 152 x 165 588kW (799bhp) Gutierrez Ascunce Corp (GUASCOR)-Spain

9012707 - -	**SCORPIUS** **M3nergy Offshore Ltd** M3nergy Bhd	**52,176** 27,904 94,225 T/cm 88.5	Class: AB (RI)	**1994-06 Fincantieri-Cant. Nav. Italiani S.p.A. — Ancona** Yd No: 5905 Loa 233.26 (BB) Br ex 42.65 Dght 14.018 Lbp 223.97 Br md 42.60 Dpth 19.84 Welded, 1 dk	**(A13A2TV) Crude Oil Tanker** Double Hull (13F) Liq: 98,365; Liq (Oil): 98,365 Cargo Heating Coils Compartments: 7 Ta, ER 3 Cargo Pump (s): 3x2500m^3/hr Manifold: Bow/CM: 116m	**1 oil engine** driving 1 FP propeller Total Power: 9,415kW (12,801hp) 13.9kn Sulzer 7RTA62 1 x 2 Stroke 7 Cy. 620 x 2150 9415kW (12801bhp) Fincantieri Cantieri Navaliltaliani SpA-Italy AuxGen: 2 x 1100kW 450V 60Hz a.c, 1 x 700kW 450V 60Hz a.c Fuel: 284.0 (d.f.) (Heating Coils) 1815.0 (r.f.) 34.0pd
9318228 *OXGJ2* -	**SCORPIUS** *launched as* Besiktas Ireland *-2006* **P/R mt 'Scorpius'** Sirius Shipping ApS *Laeso* *Denmark (DIS)* MMSI: 219178000 Official number: D4477	**7,636** 3,644 11,249 T/cm 22.0	Class: NV (BV)	**2006-03 Gisan Gemi Ins. San — Istanbul** Yd No: 36 Loa 129.75 (BB) Br ex - Dght 8.000 Lbp 123.20 Br md 19.60 Dpth 10.40 Welded, 1 dk	**(A12B2TR) Chemical/Products Tanker** Double Hull (13F) Liq: 12,394; Liq (Oil): 12,394 Compartments: 12 Wing Ta, 2 Wing Slop Ta, ER 12 Cargo Pump (s): 12x300m^3/hr Manifold: Bow/CM: 67m Ice Capable	**1 oil engine** reduction geared to sc. shaft driving 1 CP propeller Total Power: 4,320kW (5,873hp) 13.5kn MaK 9M32C 1 x 4 Stroke 9 Cy. 320 x 480 4320kW (5873bhp) Caterpillar Motoren GmbH & Co. KG-Germany AuxGen: 3 x 500kW 400/230V 50Hz a.c, 1 x 1500kW 400/230V 50Hz a.c Thrusters: 1 Thwart. FP thruster (f) Fuel: 100.0 (d.f.) 540.0 (r.f.)
9137208 *MGMT3* -	**SCOT CARRIER** *ex* Dependia *-2004* **Scot Carrier Shipping Ltd** Intrada Ships Management Ltd *Inverness* *United Kingdom* MMSI: 235008290 Official number: 909611	**1,882** 1,020 2,508	Class: GL (BV)	**1997-05 Societatea Comerciala Navol S.A. Oltenita — Oltenita** Yd No: 108 Loa 81.88 (BB) Br ex 12.50 Dght 4.250 Lbp 78.00 Br md 12.40 Dpth 5.40 Welded, 1 dk	**(A31A2GX) General Cargo Ship** Bale: 3,680 TEU 144 C. 144/20' Compartments: 1 Ho, ER 1 Ha: (55.8 x 10.2)ER Ice Capable	**1 oil engine** with flexible couplings & sr reverse geared to sc. shaft driving 1 FP propeller Total Power: 999kW (1,358hp) 11.0kn A.B.C. 6DZC 1 x 4 Stroke 6 Cy. 256 x 310 999kW (1358bhp) Anglo Belgian Corp NV (ABC)-Belgium Thrusters: 1 Thwart. FP thruster (f)
9137193 *VQUR2* -	**SCOT EXPLORER** *ex* Bornrif *-2004* **Scot Explorer Shipping Ltd** Intrada Ships Management Ltd SatCom: Inmarsat C 423500479 *Rochester* *United Kingdom* MMSI: 235007950 Official number: 909266	**1,882** 1,020 2,521	Class: GL	**1996-09 Societatea Comerciala Navol S.A. Oltenita — Oltenita** Yd No: 107 Loa 81.68 (BB) Br ex 12.50 Dght 4.250 Lbp 78.00 Br md 12.40 Dpth 5.40 Welded, 1 dk	**(A31A2GX) General Cargo Ship** Bale: 3,680 TEU 144 C. 144/20' Compartments: 1 Ho, ER 1 Ha: ER Ice Capable	**1 oil engine** with flexible couplings & sr reverse geared to sc. shaft driving 1 FP propeller Total Power: 1,103kW (1,500hp) 11.0kn A.B.C. 6MDZC 1 x 4 Stroke 6 Cy. 256 x 310 1103kW (1500bhp) Anglo Belgian Corp NV (ABC)-Belgium Thrusters: 1 Thwart. FP thruster (f)
9243930 *MPTH7* -	**SCOT ISLES** *ex* Somers Isles *-2006* **Hohebank Shipping Ltd** Intrada Ships Management Ltd *Rochester* *United Kingdom* MMSI: 232974000 Official number: 912366	**2,595** 1,402 3,154	Class: GL (LR) (BV) ✠ Classed LR until 14/12/01	**2001-12 Tille Scheepsbouw Kootstertille B.V. — Kootstertille** Yd No: 341 Loa 91.25 (BB) Br ex - Dght 4.920 Lbp 84.99 Br md 13.75 Dpth 6.25 Welded, 1 dk	**(A31A2GX) General Cargo Ship** Double Hull Grain: 5,196 TEU 197 C.Ho 99/20' C.Dk 98/20' Compartments: 1 Ho, ER 1 Ha: (58.8 x 10.8)ER Ice Capable	**1 oil engine** reduction geared to sc. shaft driving 1 CP propeller Total Power: 1,950kW (2,651hp) 13.0kn Wartsila 6L26 1 x 4 Stroke 6 Cy. 260 x 320 1950kW (2651bhp) Wartsila NSD Nederland BV-Netherlands AuxGen: 1 x 312kW a.c, 2 x 124kW 400V 50Hz a.c Thrusters: 1 Thwart. FP thruster (f) Fuel: 283.0 (d.f.)
9243916 *ZNQQ9* -	**SCOT MARINER** **Scot Mariner Shipping Ltd** Intrada Ships Management Ltd *Rochester* *United Kingdom* MMSI: 235002520 Official number: 905006	**2,594** 1,395 3,313	Class: GL (LR) ✠ Classed LR until 11/4/03	**2001-09 Tille Scheepsbouw Kootstertille B.V. — Kootstertille** Yd No: 339 Loa 89.98 (BB) Br ex - Dght 4.920 Lbp 84.98 Br md 13.75 Dpth 6.25 Welded, 1 dk	**(A31A2GX) General Cargo Ship** Grain: 4,870 TEU 158 Compartments: 1 Ho, ER 1 Ha: (61.9 x 10.8)ER Ice Capable	**1 oil engine** with flexible couplings & sr geared to sc. shaft driving 1 CP propeller Total Power: 1,950kW (2,651hp) 13.0kn Wartsila 6L26 1 x 4 Stroke 6 Cy. 260 x 320 1950kW (2651bhp) Wartsila NSD Nederland BV-Netherlands AuxGen: 1 x 424kW 400/220V 50Hz a.c, 2 x 147kW 400/220V 50Hz a.c Thrusters: 1 Thwart. CP thruster (f) Fuel: 238.0 (d.f.) 8.7pd
9331347 *2ALZ7* -	**SCOT PIONEER** *ex* Harns *-2008* **Scot Pioneer Shipping Ltd** Intrada Ships Management Ltd *Inverness* *United Kingdom* MMSI: 235060914 Official number: 914003	**2,528** 1,053 3,638	Class: GL (LR) ✠ Classed LR until 19/11/12	**2006-12 Leda doo — Korcula** (Hull) **2006-12 Scheepswerf Peters B.V. — Kampen** Yd No: 1206 Loa 89.99 (BB) Br ex 12.58 Dght 5.429 Lbp 84.95 Br md 12.50 Dpth 8.00 Welded, 1 dk	**(A31A2GX) General Cargo Ship** Grain: 4,927 TEU 157 C Ho 105 TEU C Dk 52 TEU Compartments: 1 Ho, ER 1 Ha: ER	**1 oil engine** with clutches, flexible couplings & sr geared to sc. shaft driving 1 CP propeller Total Power: 1,800kW (2,447hp) 13.0kn Wartsila 9L20 1 x 4 Stroke 9 Cy. 200 x 280 1800kW (2447bhp) Wartsila Nederland BV-Netherlands AuxGen: 1 x 168kW 400V 50Hz a.c, 1 x 250kW 400V 50Hz a.c Thrusters: 1 Thwart. FP thruster (f)
9138769 *MZKS5* -	**SCOT RANGER** **Scot Ranger Shipping Ltd** Intrada Ships Management Ltd *Inverness* *United Kingdom* MMSI: 232004332 Official number: 902400	**2,260** 1,128 3,419	Class: GL (LR) ✠ Classed LR until 24/1/00	**1997-03 Yorkshire D.D. Co. Ltd. — Hull** Yd No: 341 Loa 84.90 Br ex 12.70 Dght 5.112 Lbp 80.20 Br md 12.60 Dpth 6.70 Welded, 2 dks	**(A31A2GX) General Cargo Ship** Grain: 4,131 Compartments: 1 Ho, ER 1 Ha: (53.4 x 10.2)ER	**1 oil engine** with clutches, flexible couplings & sr geared to sc. shaft driving 1 CP propeller Total Power: 1,710kW (2,325hp) 11.5kn MaK 9M20 1 x 4 Stroke 9 Cy. 200 x 300 1710kW (2325bhp) MaK Motoren GmbH & Co. KG-Kiel AuxGen: 1 x 90kW 415V 50Hz a.c, 1 x 80kW 415V 50Hz a.c Thrusters: 1 Thwart. CP thruster (f) Fuel: 120.0 (d.f.)
9243928 *VSSO2* -	**SCOT VENTURE** **Scot Venture Shipping Ltd** Intrada Ships Management Ltd SatCom: Inmarsat C 423543710 *Inverness* *United Kingdom* MMSI: 235437000 Official number: 905518	**2,602** 1,395 3,262	Class: GL (LR) ✠ Classed LR until 7/4/03	**2002-04 Tille Scheepsbouw Kootstertille B.V. — Kootstertille** Yd No: 340 Loa 89.98 (BB) Br ex - Dght 4.920 Lbp 84.98 Br md 13.75 Dpth 6.25 Welded, 1 dk	**(A31A2GX) General Cargo Ship** Grain: 4,870 TEU 162 C.Ho 102/20' (40') C.Dk 60/ 20' (40') Compartments: 1 Ho, ER 1 Ha: (61.9 x 10.8)ER Ice Capable	**1 oil engine** reduction geared to sc. shaft driving 1 CP propeller Total Power: 1,950kW (2,651hp) 13.5kn Wartsila 6L26 1 x 4 Stroke 6 Cy. 260 x 320 1950kW (2651bhp) Wartsila NSD Nederland BV-Netherlands AuxGen: 1 x 424kW 400V 50Hz a.c, 2 x 147kW 400V 50Hz a.c Thrusters: 1 Thwart. CP thruster (f)
9615092 *5IXA86* -	**SCOTER** *ex* Sunrise *-2014* *launched as* Myth *-2013* **NITC** - *Zanzibar* *Tanzania (Zanzibar)* MMSI: 677008500	**8,750** - 11,000	Class: CC (Class contemplated) NV (Class contemplated)	**2013-01 Yangzhou Dayang Shipbuilding Co Ltd — Yangzhou JS** Yd No: DY904 Loa 138.00 Br ex 21.62 Dght 9.300 Lbp 130.00 Br md 21.60 Dpth 11.90 Welded, 1 dk	**(A11B2TG) LPG Tanker** Liq (Gas): 12,000	**1 oil engine** driving 1 FP propeller Total Power: 6,480kW (8,810hp) 15.0kn MAN-B&W 6S42MC 1 x 2 Stroke 6 Cy. 420 x 1764 6480kW (8810bhp)
9594420 *5BFS3* -	**SCOTER** **Andria Shipping Ltd** Navarone SA SatCom: Inmarsat C 420945610 *Limassol* *Cyprus* MMSI: 209456000 Official number: 9594420	**33,042** 18,700 56,837 T/cm 58.8	Class: GL	**2012-05 Yangfan Group Co Ltd — Zhoushan ZJ** Yd No: 2149 Loa 189.90 (BB) Br ex - Dght 12.800 Lbp 185.00 Br md 32.26 Dpth 18.00 Welded, 1 dk	**(A21A2BC) Bulk Carrier** Grain: 71,634; Bale: 68,200 Compartments: 5 Ho, ER 5 Ha: 4 (21.3 x 18.3)ER (18.9 x 18.3) Cranes: 4x30t	**1 oil engine** driving 1 FP propeller Total Power: 9,480kW (12,889hp) 14.2kn MAN-B&W 6S50MC-C8 1 x 2 Stroke 6 Cy. 500 x 2000 9480kW (12889bhp) STX Engine Co Ltd-South Korea
9144249 *MXHR6* -	**SCOTIA** **Government of Scotland (The Scottish Ministers)** Marine Scotland SatCom: Inmarsat B 323497310 *Leith* *United Kingdom* MMSI: 234973000 Official number: 900894	**2,619** 785 850	Class: LR ✠ **100A1** CS 03/2013 Ice Class 1D ✠ **LMC** **UMS** Eq.Ltr: R; Cable: 442.4/40.0 U2	**1998-03 Ferguson Shipbuilders Ltd — Port Glasgow** Yd No: 704 Loa 68.60 (BB) Br ex 15.02 Dght 5.671 Lbp 61.20 Br md 15.00 Dpth 8.60 Welded, 2 dks	**(B12D2FR) Fishery Research Vessel** Ice Capable	**3 diesel electric oil engines** driving 3 gen. each 1400kW 660V a.c Connecting to 2 elec. motors each (1500kW) driving 1 FP propeller Total Power: 4,455kW (6,057hp) 11.0kn Wartsila 9L20 3 x 4 Stroke 9 Cy. 200 x 280 each-1485kW (2019bhp) Wartsila NSD Finland Oy-Finland AuxGen: 1 x 258kW 415V 50Hz a.c Thrusters: 1 Thwart. FP thruster (f); 1 Thwart. FP thruster (a) Fuel: 275.0 (r.f.)
8953588 - -	**SCOTIA MARINER** **Good Venture Fishing Co Ltd** - *Lunenburg, NS* *Canada* MMSI: 316308000 Official number: 821382	*117* 88 -		**1999 Chantier Naval Matane Inc — Matane QC** L reg 18.50 Br ex - Dght - Lbp - Br md 7.26 Dpth 3.91 Welded, 1 dk	**(B11B2FV) Fishing Vessel**	**1 oil engine** driving 1 FP propeller Total Power: 469kW (638hp) 10.0kn

9487885 *ZDKL5* -	**SCOTIAN EXPRESS** **Panamax Bulk 2 BV** Vroon BV *Gibraltar* *Gibraltar (British)* MMSI: 236621000	**51,209** 31,195 93,019 T/cm 80.9	Class: LR ✠ **100A1** SS 08/2011 bulk carrier CSR BC-A GRAB (20) Nos. 2, 4 & 6 holds may be empty ESP **ShipRight** (CM) *IWS LI ✠ **LMC** **UMS** Eq.Ltr: S†; Cable: 687.5/87.0 U3 (a)	**2011-08 COSCO (Dalian) Shipyard Co Ltd — Dalian LN** Yd No: N240 Loa 229.17 (BB) Br ex 38.04 Dght 14.900 Lbp 221.98 Br md 38.00 Dpth 20.70 Welded, 1 dk	**(A21A2BC) Bulk Carrier** Grain: 110,300 Compartments: 7 Ho, ER 7 Ha: ER	**1 oil engine** driving 1 FP propeller Total Power: 12,240kW (16,642hp) 14.1kn MAN-B&W 6S60MC 1 x 2 Stroke 6 Cy. 600 x 2292 12240kW (16642bhp) Mitsui Engineering & Shipbuilding CLtd-Japan AuxGen: 3 x 730kW 450V 60Hz a.c Boilers: WTAuxB (Comp) 9.2kgf/cm² (9.0bar)
9163025 *XJBF* -	**SCOTIAN SEA** *ex* Havila Runde *-2013* *ex* Rescue Saga *-1998* **3260813 Nova Scotia Ltd** Secunda Canada LP *Halifax, NS* *Canada* MMSI: 316024142 Official number: 837282	**2,017** 775 2,700	Class: NV	**1997-07 Kvaerner Kleven Leirvik AS — Leirvik i Sogn** Yd No: 277 Loa 69.00 (BB) Br ex - Dght 6.008 Lbp 63.60 Br md 16.00 Dpth 7.00 Welded, 1 dk	**(B21A2OS) Platform Supply Ship**	**2 oil engines** reduction geared to sc. shafts driving 2 CP propellers Total Power: 5,084kW (6,912hp) 11.5kn Caterpillar 3608TA 2 x 4 Stroke 8 Cy. 280 x 300 each-2542kW (3456bhp) Caterpillar Inc-USA AuxGen: 2 x 1920kW 220/450V 60Hz a.c, 1 x 1070kW 220/450V 60Hz a.c Thrusters: 1 Thwart. FP thruster (f); 1 Retract. directional thruster (f); 2 Thwart. FP thruster (a)
7312311 - -	**SCOTIAN SHORE** *ex* Western Salvor *-1997* *ex* Fred J. Agnich *-1996* *ex* Western Crest *-1996* *ex* Fred J. Agnich *-1994* *ex* Scotian Shore *-1980* **Petra Services Ltd** Petramar Management SA	**939** 282 893	Class: (LR) (AB) ✠ Classed LR until 31/7/96	**1973-07 Ferguson Industries Ltd — Pictou NS** Yd No: 194 Converted From: Offshore Tug/Supply Ship-1980 Loa 56.52 Br ex 12.15 Dght 4.604 Lbp 50.91 Br md 11.89 Dpth 5.14 Welded, 1 dk	**(B31A2SR) Research Survey Vessel** Ice Capable	**2 oil engines** reverse reduction geared to sc. shafts driving 2 FP propellers Total Power: 2,942kW (4,000hp) 11.0kn Blackstone EWSL16 2 x Vee 4 Stroke 16 Cy. 222 x 292 each-1471kW (2000bhp) Mirrlees Blackstone (Stamford)Ltd.-Stamford AuxGen: 2 x 250kW 440V 60Hz a.c, 1 x 112kW 440V 60Hz a.c Thrusters: 1 Thwart. FP thruster (f) Fuel: 600.0 (d.f.)
9429883 *2EKA4* -	**SCOTSMAN** *ex* Corvin *-2011* *launched as* Ulupinar *-2007* **SMS Towage Ltd** - *Hull* *United Kingdom* MMSI: 235085775 Official number: 917869	**192** 57 -	Class: LR (GL) (RI) **100A1** SS 10/2012 tug **LMC**	**2007-10 Pirlant Shipyard — Tuzla** Yd No: 11 Loa 24.39 Br ex - Dght 4.420 Lbp 23.20 Br md 9.15 Dpth 4.04 Welded, 1 dk	**(B32A2ST) Tug**	**2 oil engines** reduction geared to sc. shafts driving 2 Z propellers Total Power: 2,460kW (3,344hp) Caterpillar 3512B 2 x Vee 4 Stroke 12 Cy. 170 x 190 each-1230kW (1672bhp) Caterpillar Inc-USA AuxGen: 2 x 59kW a.c Fuel: 74.0 (d.f.)
9127289 *GCUP* -	**SCOTT** **Government of The United Kingdom** Government of The United Kingdom (The Secretary of State for Defence) (Commodore Royal Fleet Auxiliary) *United Kingdom* MMSI: 233844000	**9,498** 2,849 8,600	Class: LR ✠ **100A1** SS 06/2008 *IWS LI Ice Class 1A ✠ **LMC** **UMS** Eq.Ltr: C†; Cable: 550.0/54.0 U3	**1997-06 Appledore Shipbuilders Ltd — Bideford** Yd No: A.S.166 Loa 131.13 (BB) Br ex 21.55 Dght 8.300 Lbp 120.35 Br md 21.50 Dpth 14.00 Welded, 1 dk	**(B31A2SR) Research Survey Vessel** Ice Capable	**2 oil engines** with clutches, flexible couplings & sr geared to sc. shaft driving 1 CP propeller Total Power: 8,640kW (11,746hp) 17.6kn MaK 9M32 2 x 4 Stroke 9 Cy. 320 x 480 each-4320kW (5873bhp) MaK Motoren GmbH & Co. KG-Kiel AuxGen: 4 x 600kW 450V 60Hz a.c Thrusters: 1 Retract. directional thruster (f)
9466142 *C6YA8* -	**SCOTT SPIRIT** **Scott Spirit LLC** Teekay Navion Offshore Loading Pte Ltd *Nassau* *Bahamas* MMSI: 311027400 Official number: 9000332	**66,563** 29,517 109,335 T/cm 98.3	Class: NV	**2011-07 Samsung Heavy Industries Co Ltd — Geoje** Yd No: 1828 Loa 248.58 (BB) Br ex 43.82 Dght 15.020 Lbp 235.00 Br md 43.80 Dpth 22.40 Welded, 1 dk	**(A13A2TS) Shuttle Tanker** Double Hull (13F) Liq: 116,448; Liq (Oil): 119,250 Compartments: 12 Wing Ta, 2 Wing Slop Ta, ER 4 Cargo Pump (s): 4x3000m³/hr Manifold: Bow/CM: 126.3m	**2 oil engines** driving 2 CP propellers Total Power: 18,960kW (25,778hp) 14.6kn MAN-B&W 6S50MC-C 2 x 2 Stroke 6 Cy. 500 x 2000 each-9480kW (12889bhp) Doosan Engine Co Ltd-South Korea AuxGen: 4 x 2640kW 450V a.c Thrusters: 1 Tunnel thruster (f); 2 Directional thruster (f); 1 Directional thruster (a) Fuel: 658.0 (d.f.) 2830.0 (r.f.)
8890322 *WDC3384* -	**SCOTT T. SLATTEN** **Bisso Towboat Co Inc** - *New Orleans, LA* *United States of America* MMSI: 367007070 Official number: 1029550	**276** 82 -	Class: (AB)	**1995 Main Iron Works, Inc. — Houma, La** Yd No: 394 Loa 32.00 Br ex - Dght 3.210 Lbp 30.69 Br md 10.33 Dpth 3.65 Welded, 1 dk	**(B32A2ST) Tug**	**3 oil engines** reverse reduction geared to sc. shafts driving 3 FP propellers Total Power: 2,925kW (3,978hp) 12.5kn G.M. (Detroit Diesel) 16V-149-TI 3 x Vee 2 Stroke 16 Cy. 146 x 146 each-975kW (1326bhp) Detroit Diesel Corporation-Detroit, Mi Fuel: 206.0 (d.f.)
9203356 *WCY7989* -	**SCOTT TURECAMO** **Moran Towing Corp** - SatCom: Inmarsat C 436677110 *New York, NY* *United States of America* Official number: 1067705	**585** 175 500	Class: AB	**1998-11 Moss Point Marine, Inc. — Escatawpa, Ms** Yd No: 147 Loa 36.90 Br ex - Dght 4.270 Lbp 36.90 Br md 10.97 Dpth 5.18 Welded, 1 dk	**(B32B2SA) Articulated Pusher Tug**	**2 oil engines** reverse reduction geared to sc. shafts driving 2 FP propellers Total Power: 4,120kW (5,602hp) 12.0kn EMD (Electro-Motive) 12-645-F7B 2 x Vee 2 Stroke 12 Cy. 230 x 254 each-2060kW (2801bhp) General Motors Corp.Electro-Motive Div.-La Grange
5315838 *MCIB* -	**SCOTTISH KING** *ex* Grampian King *-1995* *ex* Scottish King *-1978* **Mr S Ding** - *Whitby* *United Kingdom* Official number: 301576	*274* 86 -	Class: (LR) ✠ Classed LR until 16/4/82	**1959-10 J. Lewis & Sons Ltd. — Aberdeen** Yd No: 286 Converted From: Trawler-1980 L reg 36.87 Br ex 7.88 Dght 3.233 Lbp 36.12 Br md 7.78 Dpth 3.89 Riveted\Welded, 1 dk	**(B22G2OY) Standby Safety Vessel**	**1 oil engine** driving 1 FP propeller Total Power: 531kW (722hp) 11.0kn Mirrlees KSSDM-6 1 x 4 Stroke 6 Cy. 381 x 457 531kW (722bhp) Mirrlees, Bickerton & Day-Stockport AuxGen: 2 x 20kW 220V d.c Fuel: 46.5 (d.f.)
9435454 *IBDZ* -	**SCOTTISH VIKING** **Visemar di Navigazione Srl** *Bari* *Italy* MMSI: 247265800	**26,904** 8,912 7,800	Class: RI	**2009-04 Cantiere Navale Visentini Srl — Porto Viro** Yd No: 221 Loa 186.44 (BB) Br ex - Dght 6.790 Lbp 177.40 Br md 25.60 Dpth 15.00 Welded, 1 dk	**(A36A2PR) Passenger/Ro-Ro Ship (Vehicles)** Passengers: unberthed: 57; cabins: 107; berths: 432 Lane-Len: 2250 Lane-Wid: 3.00 Lane-clr ht: 5.10 Trailers: 120 Ice Capable	**2 oil engines** reduction geared to sc. shafts driving 2 CP propellers Total Power: 21,600kW (29,368hp) 23.5kn MAN-B&W 9L48/60B 2 x 4 Stroke 9 Cy. 480 x 600 each-10800kW (14684bhp) MAN B&W Diesel AG-Augsburg Thrusters: 2 Tunnel thruster (f)
7620689 *WDC3611* -	**SCOTTY SKY** *ex* Marine Fuel Oil *-1996* *ex* L. G. Laduca *-1991* **American Petroleum & Transport Inc** - *New York, NY* *United States of America* MMSI: 367011150 Official number: 281507	*296* 270	Class: (AB)	**1960 Blount Marine Corp. — Warren, RI** Yd No: 61 Loa 35.59 Br ex 9.61 Dght 3.074 Lbp 35.39 Br md 9.56 Dpth 3.66 Welded, 1 dk	**(A13B2TU) Tanker (unspecified)** Compartments: 8 Ta, ER	**2 oil engines** reverse reduction geared to sc. shafts driving 2 FP propellers Total Power: 324kW (440hp) 12.5kn General Motors 6-110 2 x 2 Stroke 6 Cy. 127 x 142 each-162kW (220bhp) General Motors Corp-USA AuxGen: 1 x 20kW d.c
1011238 *ZGDP4* -	**SCOUT** *ex* Karia *-2013* **Bark Ltd** Yacht Logistics Inc *George Town* *Cayman Islands (British)* MMSI: 319058900 Official number: 744433	**496** 148 56	Class: LR ✠ **100A1** SS 08/2012 SSC Yacht, mono, G6 ✠ **LMC** **UMS** Cable: 307.0/22.0 U2 (a)	**2012-08 R.M.K. Tersanesi — Tuzla** Yd No: 80 Loa 44.94 (BB) Br ex 9.21 Dght 3.000 Lbp 30.24 Br md 9.01 Dpth 4.45 Welded, 1 dk	**(X11A2YP) Yacht**	**2 oil engines** with clutches, flexible couplings & dr reverse geared to sc. shafts driving 2 FP propellers Total Power: 1,940kW (2,638hp) 14.5kn Caterpillar C32 2 x Vee 4 Stroke 12 Cy. 145 x 162 each-970kW (1319bhp) Caterpillar Inc-USA AuxGen: 2 x 125kW 400V 50Hz a.c Thrusters: 1 Tunnel thruster (f)
9188570 *WCZ2046* -	**SCOUT** **Vessel Management Services Inc** - *San Francisco, CA* *United States of America* Official number: 1063759	**366** 109 -		**1999-03 Nichols Bros. Boat Builders, Inc. — Freeland, Wa** Yd No: S-131 Loa 31.39 Br ex - Dght 4.318 Lbp 29.87 Br md 10.97 Dpth 4.57 Welded, 1 dk	**(B32A2ST) Tug**	**2 oil engines** gearing integral to driving 2 Voith-Schneider propellers Total Power: 3,530kW (4,800hp) 14.0kn Caterpillar 3516B 2 x Vee 4 Stroke 16 Cy. 170 x 190 each-1765kW (2400bhp) Caterpillar Inc-USA AuxGen: 2 x 105kW 60Hz a.c Fuel: 39.8 (d.f.) 14.5pd

IMO / Call sign	Name / Owner	Tonnage	Class	Builder / Dimensions	Type	Machinery
9184706 *V2OR6* -	**SCOUT** *ex* OXL Scout *-2009* *ex* AS Africa *-2008* *ex* Arnarnes *-2006* *ex* Radeplein *-2004* **Nordica Schiffahrtsgesellschaft mbH & Co KG ms 'Bochum'** Held Bereederungs GmbH & Co KG *Saint John's* *Antigua & Barbuda* MMSI: 304664000 Official number: 3873	**2,615** 1,226 3,479	Class: GL (BV)	**1999-05 Tille Scheepsbouw Kootstertille B.V. — Kootstertille** Yd No: 323 Loa 92.85 Br ex 15.95 Dght 4.880 Lbp 84.95 Br md 15.85 Dpth 6.18 Welded, 1 dk	**(A31A2GX) General Cargo Ship** TEU 294 C.Ho 72/20' C.Dk 222/20' Compartments: 1 Ho, ER Cranes: 2x40t	**1 oil engine** reduction geared to sc. shaft driving 1 CP propeller Total Power: 3,250kW (4,419hp) 13.0kn Wartsila 8R32E 1 x 4 Stroke 8 Cy. 320 x 350 3250kW (4419bhp) Wartsila NSD Finland Oy-Finland AuxGen: 1 x 504kW 220/400V 50Hz a.c
9283071 *9YFM* -	**SCOUT** **Miller Marine Group** Mid Atlantic Ltd *Port of Spain* *Trinidad & Tobago* MMSI: 362010000	**319** 95 -	Class: AB	**2002-12 Breaux Brothers Enterprises, Inc. — Loreauville, La** Yd No: 1274 Loa 47.24 Br ex - Dght - Lbp 41.76 Br md 9.14 Dpth 3.69 Welded, 1 dk	**(B21A2OC) Crew/Supply Vessel** Hull Material: Aluminium Alloy	**4 oil engines** geared to sc. shafts driving 4 FP propellers Total Power: 3,236kW (4,400hp) Yanmar 12LAK (M)-STE2 4 x Vee 4 Stroke 12 Cy. 150 x 165 each-809kW (1100bhp) Showa Precision Mchy. Co. Ltd.-Amagasaki AuxGen: 2 x 75kW a.c
9319492 *V3RY6* -	**SCOUT** *ex* Jaya Scout *-2013* **Markabi Ltd** Trelco Marine Services Co WLL *Belize City* *Belize* MMSI: 312424000 Official number: 701320037	**1,690** 507 1,349	Class: AB	**2004-11 Fujian Southeast Shipyard — Fuzhou FJ** Yd No: 840 Loa 59.25 Br ex - Dght 4.950 Lbp 52.20 Br md 14.95 Dpth 6.10 Welded, 1 dk	**(B21B20A) Anchor Handling Tug Supply**	**2 oil engines** reduction geared to sc. shafts driving 2 CP propellers Total Power: 3,542kW (4,816hp) 11.0kn Caterpillar 3516B-HD 2 x Vee 4 Stroke 16 Cy. 170 x 215 each-1771kW (2408bhp) Caterpillar Inc-USA AuxGen: 3 x 320kW 415V 50Hz a.c Thrusters: 1 Tunnel thruster (f) Fuel: 520.0
9723825 - -	**SCP 01** **PT Samudra Cahaya Prima** - *Batam* *Indonesia*	**256** 77 194	Class: NK	**2013-12 PT Palma Progress Shipyard — Batam** Yd No: 550 Loa 28.05 Br ex - Dght 3.312 Lbp 25.76 Br md 8.60 Dpth 4.30 Welded, 1 dk	**(B32A2ST) Tug**	**2 oil engines** reduction geared to sc. shafts driving 2 Propellers
9728899 - -	**SCP 02** **PT Samudra Cahaya Prima** - *Batam* *Indonesia*	**256** 77 196	Class: NK	**2014-02 PT Palma Progress Shipyard — Batam** Yd No: 551 Loa 28.05 Br ex - Dght 3.312 Lbp 26.77 Br md 8.60 Dpth 4.30 Welded, 1 dk	**(B32A2ST) Tug**	**2 oil engines** reduction geared to sc. shafts driving 2 Propellers Total Power: 1,116kW (1,518hp) 10.0kn
9530151 *VREK8* -	**SCSC FORTUNE** **SCSC Fortune Shipping Co Ltd** Shanghai Changjiang Shipping Corp SatCom: Inmarsat C 447701787 *Hong Kong* *Hong Kong* MMSI: 477264600 Official number: HK-2238	**6,550** 2,854 8,411	Class: CC	**2009-08 Wusong Shipyard — Shanghai** Yd No: S08-8000T-01 Loa 117.80 Br ex - Dght 7.000 Lbp 111.40 Br md 18.00 Dpth 10.40 Welded, 2 dks	**(A31A2GX) General Cargo Ship** Grain: 11,900; Bale: 11,900 Compartments: 2 Ho, 2 Tw Dk, ER 2 Ha: (44.8 x 15.0)ER (25.9 x 15.0)Tappered Cranes: 2x40t Ice Capable	**1 oil engine** reduction geared to sc. shaft driving 1 Propeller Total Power: 2,501kW (3,400hp) 11.6kn Daihatsu 8DKM-28 1 x 4 Stroke 8 Cy. 280 x 390 2501kW (3400bhp) Shaanxi Diesel Heavy Industry Co Lt-China AuxGen: 3 x 256kW 400V a.c
9530163 *VREK7* -	**SCSC LUCK** **SCSC Luck Shipping Co Ltd** Shanghai Changjiang Shipping Corp *Hong Kong* *Hong Kong* MMSI: 477682300 Official number: HK-2237	**6,550** 2,854 8,397	Class: CC	**2010-02 Wusong Shipyard — Shanghai** Yd No: S08-8000T-02 Loa 117.80 Br ex - Dght 7.000 Lbp 111.40 Br md 18.00 Dpth 10.40 Welded, 2 dks	**(A31A2GX) General Cargo Ship** Grain: 11,900; Bale: 11,900 Compartments: 2 Ho, 2 Tw Dk, ER 2 Ha: (44.8 x 15.0)ER (25.9 x 15.0) Cranes: 2x40t Ice Capable	**1 oil engine** reduction geared to sc. shaft driving 1 Propeller Total Power: 3,089kW (4,200hp) 11.6kn Chinese Std. Type GN8320ZC 1 x 4 Stroke 8 Cy. 320 x 380 3089kW (4200bhp) Ningbo CSI Power & Machinery GroupCo Ltd-China AuxGen: 3 x 256kW 400V a.c
9553361 *VRHF6* -	**SCSC WEALTH** **SCSC International Merchant & Shipping (Hong Kong) Co Ltd** Shanghai Changjiang Shipping Corp SatCom: Inmarsat C 447702952 *Hong Kong* *Hong Kong* MMSI: 477932100 Official number: HK-2821	**6,550** 2,854 8,394	Class: CC	**2010-12 Wusong Shipyard — Shanghai** Yd No: S08-8000T-04 Loa 117.80 Br ex - Dght 7.000 Lbp 111.40 Br md 18.00 Dpth 10.40 Welded, 2 dks	**(A31A2GX) General Cargo Ship** Grain: 11,900; Bale: 11,900 Compartments: 2 Ho, 2 Tw Dk, ER 2 Ha: (44.8 x 15.0)ER (25.9 x 15.0) Cranes: 2x30t Ice Capable	**1 oil engine** reduction geared to sc. shaft driving 1 FP propeller Total Power: 2,500kW (3,399hp) 11.6kn Daihatsu 8DKM-28 1 x 4 Stroke 8 Cy. 280 x 390 2500kW (3399bhp) Shaanxi Diesel Heavy Industry Co Lt-China AuxGen: 3 x 250kW 400V a.c
9302554 *V7NF8* -	**SCT CHILE** *ex* MSC Debra *-2011* **Castle Basel LLC** Bernhard Schulte Shipmanagement (China) Co Ltd *Majuro* *Marshall Islands* MMSI: 538002954 Official number: 2954	**54,214** 31,226 68,080 T/cm 83.2	Class: AB (GL)	**2006-04 Hanjin Heavy Industries & Construction Co Ltd — Busan** Yd No: 144 Loa 294.10 (BB) Br ex - Dght 13.500 Lbp 283.00 Br md 32.20 Dpth 21.60 Welded, 1 dk	**(A33A2CC) Container Ship (Fully Cellular)** TEU 5059 C Ho 2216 TEU C Dk 2843 TEU incl 454 ref C. Ice Capable	**1 oil engine** driving 1 FP propeller Total Power: 41,130kW (55,920hp) 23.0kn MAN-B&W 9K90MC-C 1 x 2 Stroke 9 Cy. 900 x 2300 41130kW (55920bhp) Doosan Engine Co Ltd-South Korea AuxGen: 4 x 1680kW 60Hz a.c Thrusters: 1 Thwart. CP thruster (f) Fuel: 430.0 (d.f.) 6670.0 (r.f.)
9158501 *V7LX3* -	**SCT PERU** *ex* Boxford *-2010* *ex* CSAV Peru *-2010* *ex* NYK Esperanza *-2003* *ex* Laura S *-2002* *ex* Lykes Innovator *-2001* *ex* TMM Manzanillo *-2000* *ex* Laura S *-1999* *launched as* Thea S *-1998* **SeaCT Containership Shipco 1 LLC** Seacastle Singapore Pte Ltd *Majuro* *Marshall Islands* MMSI: 538002821 Official number: 2821	**25,624** 12,733 33,914 T/cm 45.0	Class: LR (GL) **100A1** SS 07/2013 container ship *IWS LI **LMC** **UMS** Eq.Ltr: D; Cable: 676.0/76.0 U3 (a)	**1998-07 Volkswerft Stralsund GmbH — Stralsund** Yd No: 419 Loa 207.40 (BB) Br ex - Dght 11.400 Lbp 195.40 Br md 29.80 Dpth 16.40 Welded, 1 dk	**(A33A2CC) Container Ship (Fully Cellular)** TEU 2474 C Ho 992 TEU C Dk 1482 TEU incl 320 ref C. Compartments: 5 Cell Ho, ER 10 Ha: (12.6 x 15.4) (12.6 x 20.4)8 (12.6 x 25.4)ER Cranes: 3x45t Ice Capable	**1 oil engine** driving 1 FP propeller Total Power: 17,220kW (23,412hp) 21.0kn B&W 6L70MC 1 x 2 Stroke 6 Cy. 700 x 2268 17220kW (23412bhp) Dieselmotorenwerk Rostock GmbH-Rostock AuxGen: 3 x 1520kW 220/440V 60Hz a.c Boilers: AuxB (Comp) 9.2kgf/cm² (9.0bar) Thrusters: 1 Thwart. FP thruster (f)
9302566 *V7NF7* -	**SCT SANTIAGO** *ex* MSC Benedetta *-2011* **Castle Geneva LLC** Bernhard Schulte Shipmanagement (China) Co Ltd *Majuro* *Marshall Islands* MMSI: 538002953 Official number: 2953	**54,214** 31,226 68,126 T/cm 83.2	Class: AB (GL)	**2006-05 Hanjin Heavy Industries & Construction Co Ltd — Busan** Yd No: 145 Loa 294.09 (BB) Br ex - Dght 13.500 Lbp 283.00 Br md 32.20 Dpth 21.60 Welded, 1 dk	**(A33A2CC) Container Ship (Fully Cellular)** TEU 5059 C Ho 2216 TEU C Dk 2843 TEU incl 454 ref C. Ice Capable	**1 oil engine** driving 1 FP propeller Total Power: 41,130kW (55,920hp) 24.0kn MAN-B&W 9K90MC-C 1 x 2 Stroke 9 Cy. 900 x 2300 41130kW (55920bhp) Doosan Engine Co Ltd-South Korea AuxGen: 4 x 1680kW a.c Thrusters: 1 Tunnel thruster (f)
9302580 *V7NG2* -	**SCT ZURICH** *ex* MSC Olga *-2011* **Castle Zurich LLC** Bernhard Schulte Shipmanagement (China) Co Ltd *Majuro* *Marshall Islands* MMSI: 538002956 Official number: 2956	**54,214** 31,226 68,135 T/cm 83.2	Class: AB (GL)	**2006-09 Hanjin Heavy Industries & Construction Co Ltd — Busan** Yd No: 147 Loa 294.10 (BB) Br ex - Dght 13.500 Lbp 283.00 Br md 32.20 Dpth 21.60 Welded, 1 dk	**(A33A2CC) Container Ship (Fully Cellular)** Double Bottom Entire Compartment Length TEU 5059 C Ho 2216 TEU C Dk 2843 TEU incl 454 ref C. Ice Capable	**1 oil engine** driving 1 FP propeller Total Power: 41,107kW (55,889hp) 24.3kn MAN-B&W 9K90MC-C 1 x 2 Stroke 9 Cy. 900 x 2300 41107kW (55889bhp) Doosan Engine Co Ltd-South Korea AuxGen: 4 x 1890kW 440V 60Hz a.c Thrusters: 1 Thwart. CP thruster (f) Fuel: 479.0 (d.f.) 6672.0 (r.f.)
8663327 *FGIG* PL 686777	**SCUDERIA** *ex* Nathalie Patricia 3 *-1998* - - *Paimpol* *France* MMSI: 227593000	**113** - -		**1988-01 Chantier de Bretagne Sud — Belz** Loa 20.60 Br ex - Dght - Lbp 17.15 Br md 6.54 Dpth - Welded, 1 dk	**(B11A2FS) Stern Trawler**	**1 oil engine** reduction geared to sc. shaft driving 1 Propeller Total Power: 405kW (551hp)
9541746 *PP9309* -	**SCULPTOR** **Saveiros Camuyrano - Servicos Maritimos SA** - *Rio de Janeiro* *Brazil* MMSI: 710000003 Official number: 3813877604	**374** - 273	Class: LR ✠ **100A1** SS 10/2010 tug, (fire-fighting Ship 1 (2400m3/h) with water spray) *IWS **LMC** **UMS** Eq.Ltr: H; Cable: 302.5/22.0 U2 (a)	**2010-10 Wilson, Sons SA — Guaruja** (Hull) Yd No: 092 **2010-10 B.V. Scheepswerf Damen — Gorinchem** Yd No: 511218 Loa 32.22 Br ex 11.70 Dght 4.250 Lbp 29.01 Br md 10.60 Dpth 5.00 Welded, 1 dk	**(B32A2ST) Tug**	**2 oil engines** reduction geared to sc. shafts driving 2 Directional propellers Total Power: 4,180kW (5,684hp) Caterpillar 3516B 2 x Vee 4 Stroke 16 Cy. 170 x 190 each-2090kW (2842bhp) Caterpillar Inc-USA AuxGen: 2 x 99kW 440V 60Hz a.c

9365441 *3ELR3* -	**SCUTUM** **Asian Prosperity 3 Shipping Co SA** Shinsung Shipping Co Ltd *Panama* *Panama* MMSI: 351578000 Official number: 3313707A	**4,594** 2,193 6,588	Class: KR	**2007-08 Mokpo Shipbuilding & Engineering Co Ltd — Mokpo** Yd No: 05-172 Loa 109.50 (BB) Br ex - Dght 6.763 Lbp 102.00 Br md 16.60 Dpth 8.70 Welded, 1 dk	**(A31A2GX) General Cargo Ship** Grain: 7,459; Bale: 7,459 2 Ha: (29.4 x 11.1)ER (28.7 x 11.1)	**1 oil engine** driving 1 FP propeller Total Power: 2,942kW (4,000hp) 14.5kn Hanshin LH46L 1 x 4 Stroke 6 Cy. 460 x 880 2942kW (4000bhp) (made 2006) The Hanshin Diesel Works Ltd-Japan AuxGen: 2 x 280kW 445V a.c
9229623 *P3GN9* -	**SCYTHIA GRAECA** **Scythia Graeca Shipping Ltd** Angelakos (Hellas) SA *Limassol* *Cyprus* MMSI: 210718000 Official number: 9229623	**39,035** 25,246 74,133 T/cm 66.3	Class: LR ✠**100A1** SS 06/2012 bulk carrier strengthened for heavy cargoes, Nos. 2, 4 & 6 holds may b e empty ESP ESN *IWS LI **ShipRight** (SDA, FDA, CM) ✠**LMC** **UMS** Eq.Ltr: N†; Cable: 660.0/76.0 U3 (a)	**2002-06 Namura Shipbuilding Co Ltd — Imari SG** Yd No: 220 Loa 224.89 (BB) Br ex 32.24 Dght 13.962 Lbp 215.00 Br md 32.20 Dpth 19.30 Welded, 1 dk	**(A21A2BC) Bulk Carrier** Grain: 89,246 Compartments: 7 Ho, ER 7 Ha: 6 (16.8 x 14.8)ER (16.8 x 13.2)	**1 oil engine** driving 1 FP propeller Total Power: 11,044kW (15,015hp) 14.9kn B&W 7S50MC-C 1 x 2 Stroke 7 Cy. 500 x 2000 11044kW (15015bhp) Hitachi Zosen Corp-Japan AuxGen: 3 x 500kW 450V 60Hz a.c Boilers: WTAuxB (Comp) 7.0kgf/cm² (6.9bar)
7902324 *GZAW* -	**SD ADEPT** *ex Adept -2008* **SD Marine Services Ltd** Serco Ltd SatCom: Inmarsat M 623200021 *London* *United Kingdom* MMSI: 232002648 Official number: 913788	**384** 115 85	Class: LR ✠**100A1** SS 02/2012 tug ✠**LMC** Eq.Ltr: F; Cable: 275.0/19.0 U2 (a)	**1980-10 R. Dunston (Hessle) Ltd. — Hessle** Yd No: H922 Loa 38.83 Br ex 9.43 Dght 3.400 Lbp 37.00 Br md 9.10 Dpth 4.25 Welded, 1 dk	**(B32A2ST) Tug**	**2 oil engines** gearing integral to driving 2 Voith-Schneider propellers Total Power: 1,920kW (2,610hp) 12.0kn Ruston 6RKCM 2 x 4 Stroke 6 Cy. 254 x 305 each-960kW (1305bhp) Ruston Diesels Ltd.-Newton-le-Willows AuxGen: 3 x 98kW 440V 60Hz a.c
9533787 *2CHE8* -	**SD BOUNTIFUL** **SD Marine Services Ltd** Serco Ltd *London* *United Kingdom* MMSI: 235072757 Official number: 916327	**271** 81 -	Class: LR ✠**100A1** SS 03/2010 tug United Kingdom coastal service **LMC** **UMS** Eq.Ltr: E; Cable: 151.0/16.0 U2 (a)	**2010-03 'Crist' Sp z oo — Gdansk** (Hull launched by) **2010-03 B.V. Scheepswerf Maaskant — Stellendam** (Hull completed by) Yd No: 600 **2010-03 B.V. Scheepswerf Damen — Gorinchem** Yd No: 545302 Loa 29.14 Br ex 9.59 Dght 4.800 Lbp 26.40 Br md 9.45 Dpth 4.00 Welded, 1 dk	**(B32A2ST) Tug**	**2 oil engines** gearing integral to driving 2 Z propellers Total Power: 2,850kW (3,874hp) 12.0kn Caterpillar 3512B-HD 2 x Vee 4 Stroke 12 Cy. 170 x 190 each-1425kW (1937bhp) Caterpillar Inc-USA AuxGen: 2 x 98kW 440V 60Hz a.c
9150119 *GCUS* -	**SD BOVISAND** *ex Bovisand -2008* **SD Marine Services Ltd** Serco Ltd *London* *United Kingdom* MMSI: 232002184	*226* 180 20	Class: LR ✠**100A1** SS 09/2012 SSC passenger (A) pilot swath HSC G2 service area ✠**LMC** **UMS** Cable: 110.0/16.0 U2 (a)	**1997-09 FBM Marine Ltd. — Cowes** Yd No: 1438 Loa 23.95 Br ex - Dght 2.250 Lbp 20.16 Br md 11.10 Dpth 4.95 Welded, 1 dk	**(B21A20C) Crew/Supply Vessel** Hull Material: Aluminium Alloy	**2 oil engines** with clutches, flexible couplings & sr reverse geared to sc. shafts driving 2 Water jets Total Power: 896kW (1,218hp) 15.5kn Caterpillar 3408TA 2 x Vee 4 Stroke 8 Cy. 137 x 152 each-448kW (609bhp) Caterpillar Inc-USA AuxGen: 2 x 34kW 440V 60Hz a.c
7902336 - -	**SD BUSTLER** *ex Bustler -2008* **Marine Salvage Ltd** -	**384** 115 85	Class: (LR) ✠ Classed LR until 17/7/13	**1981-04 R. Dunston (Hessle) Ltd. — Hessle** Yd No: H923 Loa 38.83 Br ex 9.43 Dght 3.400 Lbp 37.00 Br md 9.10 Dpth 4.00 Welded, 1 dk	**(B32A2ST) Tug**	**2 oil engines** gearing integral to driving 2 Voith-Schneider propellers Total Power: 1,912kW (2,600hp) 12.0kn Ruston 6RKCM 2 x 4 Stroke 6 Cy. 254 x 305 each-956kW (1300bhp) Ruston Diesels Ltd.-Newton-le-Willows AuxGen: 3 x 98kW 440V 60Hz a.c
7902350 *GZAZ* -	**SD CAREFUL** *ex Careful -2008* **SD Marine Services Ltd** Serco Ltd *London* *United Kingdom* MMSI: 232002652 Official number: 913792	**384** 115 85	Class: LR ✠**100A1** SS 11/2012 tug U.K. coasting service ✠**LMC** Eq.Ltr: F; Cable: 277.0/19.0 U2 (a)	**1982-03 R. Dunston (Hessle) Ltd. — Hessle** Yd No: H925 Loa 38.82 Br ex 9.43 Dght 2.488 Lbp 37.01 Br md 9.10 Dpth 3.99 Welded, 1 dk	**(B32A2ST) Tug**	**2 oil engines** dr geared to sc. shafts driving 2 Voith-Schneider propellers Total Power: 1,920kW (2,610hp) Ruston 6RKCM 2 x 4 Stroke 6 Cy. 254 x 305 each-960kW (1305bhp) Ruston Diesels Ltd.-Newton-le-Willows AuxGen: 3 x 98kW 440V 60Hz a.c
9150107 *GCUT* -	**SD CAWSAND** *ex Cawsand -2008* **SD Marine Services Ltd** Serco Ltd *London* *United Kingdom* MMSI: 232002185	*226* 180 20	Class: LR ✠**100A1** SS 08/2012 SSC passenger (A) pilot swath HSC G2 service area ✠**LMC** **UMS** Cable: 110.0/16.0 U2 (a)	**1997-08 FBM Marine Ltd. — Cowes** Yd No: 1437 Loa 23.95 Br ex - Dght 2.250 Lbp 21.16 Br md 11.10 Dpth 4.95 Welded, 1 dk	**(B21A20C) Crew/Supply Vessel** Hull Material: Aluminium Alloy	**2 oil engines** with clutches, flexible couplings & sr reverse geared to sc. shafts driving 2 Water jets Total Power: 896kW (1,218hp) 15.5kn Caterpillar 3408TA 2 x Vee 4 Stroke 8 Cy. 137 x 152 each-448kW (609bhp) Caterpillar Inc-USA AuxGen: 2 x 34kW 440V 60Hz a.c
9533751 *2CPN3* -	**SD CHRISTINA** **SD Marine Services Ltd** Serco Ltd *London* *United Kingdom* MMSI: 235074703	**121** - -	Class: LR ✠**100A1** SS 07/2010 tug United Kingdom coastal service **LMC** **UMS** Eq.Ltr: A†; Cable: 110.0/12.5 U2 (a)	**2010-07 Damen Shipyards Gdynia SA — Gdynia** (Hull) Yd No: 512403 **2010-07 B.V. Scheepswerf Damen — Gorinchem** Yd No: 512403 Loa 21.19 Br ex 9.43 Dght 3.600 Lbp 19.00 Br md 8.90 Dpth 4.00 Welded, 1 dk	**(B32A2ST) Tug**	**2 oil engines** gearing integral to driving 2 Directional propellers Total Power: 1,492kW (2,028hp) 11.0kn Caterpillar 3508B-TA 2 x Vee 4 Stroke 8 Cy. 170 x 190 each-746kW (1014bhp) Caterpillar Inc-USA AuxGen: 2 x 76kW 440V 60Hz a.c Thrusters: 1 Tunnel thruster (f) Fuel: 19.0
9533763 *2CNO2* -	**SD DEBORAH** **SD Marine Services Ltd** Serco Ltd *London* *United Kingdom* MMSI: 235074296 Official number: 916833	**121** - 45	Class: LR ✠**100A1** SS 11/2010 tug, United Kingdom coastal service **LMC** **UMS** Eq.Ltr: A†; Cable: 110.0/12.5 U2 (a)	**2010-11 Damen Shipyards Gdynia SA — Gdynia** (Hull) Yd No: 512404 **2010-11 B.V. Scheepswerf Damen — Gorinchem** Yd No: 512404 Loa 21.19 Br ex 9.43 Dght 3.600 Lbp 19.00 Br md 8.90 Dpth 4.00 Welded, 1 dk	**(B32A2ST) Tug**	**2 oil engines** gearing integral to driving 2 Directional propellers Total Power: 1,492kW (2,028hp) 11.0kn Caterpillar 3508B-TA 2 x Vee 4 Stroke 8 Cy. 170 x 190 each-746kW (1014bhp) Caterpillar Inc-USA AuxGen: 2 x 76kW 440V 60Hz a.c Thrusters: 1 Tunnel thruster (f) Fuel: 19.0
9533804 *2CHL5* -	**SD DEPENDABLE** **SD Marine Services Ltd** Serco Ltd *London* *United Kingdom* Official number: 916401	**271** 81 -	Class: LR ✠**100A1** SS 07/2010 tug, United Kingdom coastal service **LMC** **UMS** Eq.Ltr: E; Cable: 137.5/16.0 U2 (a)	**2010-07 'Crist' Sp z oo — Gdansk** (Hull launched by) **2010-07 B.V. Scheepswerf Maaskant — Stellendam** (Hull completed by) Yd No: 602 **2010-07 B.V. Scheepswerf Damen — Gorinchem** Yd No: 545304 Loa 29.14 Br ex 9.59 Dght 4.800 Lbp 26.40 Br md 9.45 Dpth 4.00 Welded, 1 dk	**(B32A2ST) Tug**	**2 oil engines** gearing integral to driving 2 Z propellers Total Power: 2,850kW (3,874hp) 12.0kn Caterpillar 3512B-HD 2 x Vee 4 Stroke 12 Cy. 170 x 215 each-1425kW (1937bhp) Caterpillar Inc-USA AuxGen: 2 x 98kW 440V 60Hz a.c
9631034 *9HA3301* -	**SD DOLPHIN** **Elisabeth Ltd** - *Valletta* *Malta* MMSI: 229398000	**453** 135 200	Class: LR ✠**100A1** SS 04/2013 escort tug *IWS EP **LMC** **UMS** Eq.Ltr: H; Cable: 330.0/22.0 U2 (a)	**2013-04 Song Cam Shipyard — Haiphong** (Hull) Yd No: (512506) **2013-04 B.V. Scheepswerf Damen — Gorinchem** Yd No: 512506 Loa 32.70 Br ex 12.82 Dght 4.100 Lbp 28.84 Br md 12.20 Dpth 5.35 Welded, 1 dk	**(B32A2ST) Tug**	**2 oil engines** gearing integral to driving 2 Directional propellers Total Power: 5,050kW (6,866hp) Caterpillar 3516C-HD 2 x Vee 4 Stroke 16 Cy. 170 x 215 each-2525kW (3433bhp) Caterpillar Inc-USA AuxGen: 2 x 100kW 400V 50Hz a.c
9533737 *2CNO2* -	**SD EILEEN** **SD Marine Services Ltd** Serco Ltd *London* *United Kingdom* Official number: 916357	**121** - -	Class: LR ✠**100A1** SS 04/2010 tug, United Kingdom coastal service **LMC** **UMS** Eq.Ltr: A; Cable: 110.0/12.5 U2 (a)	**2010-03 Damen Shipyards Gdynia SA — Gdynia** (Hull) Yd No: 512401 **2010-04 B.V. Scheepswerf Damen — Gorinchem** Yd No: 512401 Loa 21.19 Br ex 9.43 Dght 3.600 Lbp 19.00 Br md 8.90 Dpth 4.00 Welded, 1 dk	**(B32A2ST) Tug**	**2 oil engines** gearing integral to driving 2 Directional propellers Total Power: 1,492kW (2,028hp) 11.0kn Caterpillar 3508B-TA 2 x Vee 4 Stroke 8 Cy. 170 x 190 each-746kW (1014bhp) Caterpillar Inc-USA AuxGen: 2 x 76kW 440V 60Hz a.c Thrusters: 1 Thwart. FP thruster (f) Fuel: 19.0

IMO / Call sign / Flag	Name / Owner	Tonnage	Classification	Builder / Dimensions	Type	Machinery
9447512 *9V7132* -	**SD EMERALD** *ex* Cathay 5 *-2009* **Sindo Damai Holdings Pte Ltd** - *Singapore* *Singapore* Official number: 392959	**153** 46 115	Class: NK	**2007**-06 **Tuong Aik Shipyard Sdn Bhd — Sibu** Yd No: 2620 Loa 23.50 Br ex - Dght 2.712 Lbp 21.96 Br md 7.32 Dpth 3.20 Welded, 1 dk	**(B32A2ST) Tug**	**2 oil engines** reduction geared to sc. shafts driving 2 FP propellers Total Power: 894kW (1,216hp) Cummins KTA-19-M3 2 x 4 Stroke 6 Cy. 159 x 159 each-447kW (608bhp) Cummins Engine Co Inc-USA Fuel: 100.0 (d.f.)
8973112 *ZNHS4* -	**SD ENGINEER** *ex* Forth Engineer *-2008* **SD Marine Services Ltd** Serco Ltd *London* *United Kingdom* MMSI: 235002008 Official number: 903906	**102** 40 -		**1996 B.V. Scheepswerf Damen — Gorinchem** Loa 17.49 Br ex 8.06 Dght 1.800 Lbp - Br md 8.00 Dpth 2.75 Welded, 1 dk	**(B34T2QR) Work/Repair Vessel** Cranes: 1	**2 oil engines** geared to sc. shafts driving 2 FP propellers Total Power: 442kW (600hp) 8.0kn Caterpillar 3406C 2 x 4 Stroke 6 Cy. 137 x 165 each-221kW (300bhp) Caterpillar Inc-USA AuxGen: 1 x 40kW 220/380V 50Hz a.c Fuel: 27.0 (d.f.)
9535670 *2BRX3* -	**SD EVA** **SD Marine Services Ltd** Serco Ltd *London* *United Kingdom* MMSI: 235068803 Official number: 915951	**168** 49 30	Class: LR (BV) **100A1** SS 08/2009 SSC passenger (A), mono HSC G2 intended for service in waters where the range to refuge is 20 nautical miles or less, vessel not to operate in sea conditions when the significant wave height exceeds that as shown in the operational envelope **LMC**	**2009**-08 **van Noorloos Lasbedrijf B.V. — Sliedrecht** (Hull) Yd No: (544813) **2009**-08 **B.V. Scheepswerf Damen — Gorinchem** Yd No: 544813 Loa 33.50 Br ex 7.40 Dght 1.540 Lbp 32.00 Br md 6.50 Dpth 3.30 Welded, 1 dk	**(B21A20C) Crew/Supply Vessel** Hull Material: Aluminium Alloy Passengers: unberthed: 80	**2 oil engines** reduction geared to sc. shafts driving 2 FP propellers Total Power: 1,640kW (2,230hp) 22.0kn Caterpillar C32 2 x Vee 4 Stroke 12 Cy. 145 x 162 each-820kW (1115bhp) Caterpillar Inc-USA AuxGen: 2 x 61kW a.c Thrusters: 1 Tunnel thruster (f)
8401494 *GAAH* -	**SD FAITHFUL** *ex* Faithful *-2008* **SD Marine Services Ltd** Serco Ltd *London* *United Kingdom* MMSI: 232002651 Official number: 913797	**384** 115 85	Class: LR ✠**100A1** SS 08/2012 tug ✠**LMC** Eq.Ltr: F; Cable: 277.0/19.0 U2 (a)	**1985**-12 **R. Dunston (Hessle) Ltd. — Hessle** Yd No: H947 Loa 38.84 Br ex 9.43 Dght 2.501 Lbp 35.54 Br md 9.11 Dpth 4.02 Welded, 1 dk	**(B32A2ST) Tug**	**2 oil engines** gearing integral to driving 2 Voith-Schneider propellers Total Power: 1,930kW (2,624hp) 12.0kn Ruston 6RKCM 2 x 4 Stroke 6 Cy. 254 x 305 each-965kW (1312bhp) Ruston Diesels Ltd.-Newton-le-Willows AuxGen: 3 x 131kW 440V 60Hz a.c Fuel: 22.0 (d.f.)
8401468 *GAAE* -	**SD FORCEFUL** *ex* Forceful *-2008* **SD Marine Services Ltd** Serco Ltd *London* *United Kingdom* MMSI: 232002650 Official number: 913799	**384** 115 85	Class: LR ✠**100A1** SS 05/2013 tug coasting service ✠**LMC** Eq.Ltr: F; Cable: 275.0/19.0 U2 (a)	**1985**-03 **R. Dunston (Hessle) Ltd. — Hessle** Yd No: H944 Loa 38.82 Br ex 9.43 Dght 3.401 Lbp 37.00 Br md 9.10 Dpth 4.00 Welded, 1 dk	**(B32A2ST) Tug**	**2 oil engines** gearing integral to driving 2 Voith-Schneider propellers Total Power: 1,930kW (2,624hp) 12.5kn Ruston 6RKCM 2 x 4 Stroke 6 Cy. 254 x 305 each-965kW (1312bhp) Ruston Diesels Ltd.-Newton-le-Willows AuxGen: 3 x 131kW 440V 60Hz a.c Fuel: 22.0 (d.f.)
9476317 *2BJH2* -	**SD HERCULES** **SD Marine Services Ltd** Serco Ltd *London* *United Kingdom* MMSI: 235066588 Official number: 915312	**134** - 382	Class: LR ✠**100A1** SS 01/2014 tug United Kingdom coastal service **LMC** **UMS** Eq.Ltr: B; Cable: 137.5/14.0 U2 (a)	**2009**-01 **Stocznia Tczew Sp z oo — Tczew** (Hull) **2009**-01 **B.V. Scheepswerf Damen — Gorinchem** Yd No: 509823 Loa 26.61 Br ex 8.44 Dght 3.390 Lbp 23.69 Br md 7.90 Dpth 4.05 Welded, 1 dk	**(B32A2ST) Tug**	**2 oil engines** with clutches, flexible couplings & sr geared to sc. shafts driving 2 FP propellers Total Power: 1,640kW (2,230hp) Caterpillar 3508B-TA 2 x Vee 4 Stroke 8 Cy. 170 x 190 each-820kW (1115bhp) Caterpillar Inc-USA AuxGen: 2 x 99kW 440V 60Hz a.c
9050802 *GCOX* -	**SD IMPETUS** *ex* Impetus *-2008* **SD Marine Services Ltd** Serco Ltd *London* *United Kingdom* MMSI: 232001490 Official number: 913804	**319** 95 92	Class: LR ✠**100A1** SS 06/2013 tug ✠**LMC** **UMS** Eq.Ltr: G; Cable: 302.5/20.5 U2	**1993**-06 **R. Dunston (Hessle) Ltd. — Hessle** Yd No: H1003 Loa 32.53 Br ex 10.42 Dght 4.000 Lbp 27.75 Br md 10.00 Dpth 5.20 Welded, 1 dk	**(B32A2ST) Tug**	**2 oil engines** with clutches, flexible couplings & sr geared to sc. shafts driving 2 Directional propellers Total Power: 2,536kW (3,448hp) 12.8kn Allen 8PBCS12-F 2 x 4 Stroke 8 Cy. 242 x 305 each-1268kW (1724bhp) NEI Allen Ltd.-Bedford AuxGen: 2 x 370kW 440V 60Hz a.c Thrusters: 1 Thwart. FP thruster (f)
9050797 *GCOW* -	**SD IMPULSE** *ex* Impulse *-2008* **SD Marine Services Ltd** Serco Ltd *London* *United Kingdom* MMSI: 232001480 Official number: 913805	**319** 95 92	Class: LR ✠**100A1** SS 03/2013 tug ✠**LMC** **UMS** Eq.Ltr: G; Cable: 302.5/20.5 U2	**1993**-03 **R. Dunston (Hessle) Ltd. — Hessle** Yd No: H1002 Loa 32.53 Br ex 10.42 Dght 3.890 Lbp 27.75 Br md 10.00 Dpth 5.20 Welded, 1 dk	**(B32A2ST) Tug**	**2 oil engines** with clutches, flexible couplings & sr geared to sc. shafts driving 2 Directional propellers Total Power: 2,538kW (3,450hp) 12.5kn Allen 8S12-D 2 x 4 Stroke 8 Cy. 241 x 305 each-1269kW (1725bhp) (made 1992) NEI Allen Ltd.-Bedford AuxGen: 2 x 370kW 440V 60Hz a.c Thrusters: 1 Thwart. FP thruster (f) Fuel: 65.0 (d.f.) 13.0pd
9539808 *2BZL9* -	**SD INDEPENDENT** **SD Marine Services Ltd** Serco Ltd *London* *United Kingdom* MMSI: 235070762 Official number: 916009	**186** - -	Class: LR ✠**100A1** SS 10/2009 tug United Kingdom coastal service **LMC** **UMS** Eq.Ltr: B; Cable: 137.5/16.0 U2 (a)	**2009**-10 **Stocznia Tczew Sp z oo — Tczew** (Hull) Yd No: (510821) **2009**-10 **B.V. Scheepswerf Damen — Gorinchem** Yd No: 510821 Loa 26.09 Br ex 9.44 Dght 3.890 Lbp 23.00 Br md 8.90 Dpth 4.30 Welded, 1 dk	**(B32A2ST) Tug**	**2 oil engines** gearing integral to driving 2 Directional propellers Total Power: 2,610kW (3,548hp) Caterpillar 3512B-HD 2 x Vee 4 Stroke 12 Cy. 170 x 215 each-1305kW (1774bhp) Caterpillar Inc-USA AuxGen: 2 x 99kW 440V 60Hz a.c Thrusters: 1 Thwart. FP thruster (f)
9540285 *2BZM2* -	**SD INDULGENT** **SD Marine Services Ltd** Serco Ltd *London* *United Kingdom* MMSI: 235070763 Official number: 916010	**186** - -	Class: LR ✠**100A1** SS 01/2010 tug United Kingdom coastal service **LMC** **UMS** Eq.Ltr: H; Cable: 137.5/16.0 U2 (a)	**2010**-01 **Stocznia Tczew Sp z oo — Tczew** (Hull) Yd No: (510822) **2010**-01 **B.V. Scheepswerf Damen — Gorinchem** Yd No: 510822 Loa 26.09 Br ex 9.44 Dght 3.890 Lbp 23.00 Br md 8.90 Dpth 4.30 Welded, 1 dk	**(B32A2ST) Tug**	**2 oil engines** gearing integral to driving 2 Directional propellers Total Power: 2,610kW (3,548hp) Caterpillar 3512B-HD 2 x Vee 4 Stroke 12 Cy. 170 x 215 each-1305kW (1774bhp) Caterpillar Inc-USA AuxGen: 2 x 98kW 440V 60Hz a.c Thrusters: 1 Thwart. FP thruster (f)
9174567 *PIAM* -	**SD JACOBA** *ex* Atlantic Fir *-1998* **K & K International BV** Sleepdienst Adriaan Kooren BV (Tugboat Company Adriaan Kooren) - KOTUG *Rotterdam* *Netherlands* MMSI: 244216000 Official number: 36667	**392** 117 145	Class: LR ✠**100A1** SS 05/2013 tug the European waters limited in the North and West by the straight lines drawn from Cape Kanin (North coast Russia) over the points of 72N and 25E, 60N and 11W, 36N and 11W to Cape Spartal (North coast Morocco), the Mediterranean Sea and the Black Sea, with the exemption of the Gulf of Sidra, South of the parallel of 33N ✠**LMC** **UMS** Eq.Ltr: G; Cable: 302.5/20.5 U2 (a)	**1998**-05 **East Isle Shipyard Ltd — Georgetown PE** Yd No: 66 Loa 30.80 Br ex - Dght 4.780 Lbp 28.97 Br md 11.14 Dpth 5.21 Welded, 1 dk	**(B32A2ST) Tug**	**2 oil engines** gearing integral to driving 2 Z propellers Total Power: 2,982kW (4,054hp) 12.5kn Caterpillar 3516TA 2 x Vee 4 Stroke 16 Cy. 170 x 190 each-1491kW (2027bhp) Caterpillar Inc-USA AuxGen: 2 x 165kW 440V 60Hz a.c Fuel: 181.5 (d.f.)
9476331 *2BME7* -	**SD JUPITER** **SD Marine Services Ltd** Serco Ltd *London* *United Kingdom* MMSI: 235067375 Official number: 915574	**134** - 382	Class: LR ✠**100A1** SS 06/2009 tug United Kingdom coastal service **LMC** **UMS** Eq.Ltr: B; Cable: 137.5/14.0 U2 (a)	**2009**-06 **Stocznia Tczew Sp z oo — Tczew** (Hull) Yd No: (509825) **2009**-06 **B.V. Scheepswerf Damen — Gorinchem** Yd No: 509825 Loa 26.16 Br ex 8.44 Dght 3.390 Lbp 23.69 Br md 7.94 Dpth 4.05 Welded, 1 dk	**(B32A2ST) Tug**	**2 oil engines** with clutches, flexible couplings & sr geared to sc. shafts driving 2 FP propellers Total Power: 1,640kW (2,230hp) Caterpillar 3508B-TA 2 x Vee 4 Stroke 8 Cy. 170 x 190 each-820kW (1115bhp) Caterpillar Inc-USA AuxGen: 2 x 99kW 440V 60Hz a.c

9176735 *MQX04* -	**SD KYLE OF LOCHALSH** *ex MCS Lenie -2008* **SD Marine Services Ltd** Serco Ltd *London* *United Kingdom* MMSI: 235003636 Official number: 900538	**120** - -	Class: LR (BV) **100A1** SS 08/2012 tug United Kingdom coastal service **LMC**	**1997-08 David Abels, Boatbuilders — Bristol** Yd No: 64 Loa 24.35 Br ex - Dght 2.900 Lbp 23.95 Br md 9.00 Dpth 3.45 Welded, 1 dk	**(B32A2ST) Tug**	**2 oil engines** with clutches, flexible couplings & sr geared to sc. shafts driving 2 FP propellers Total Power: 1,640kW (2,230hp) 12.0kn Caterpillar 3508TA 2 x Vee 4 Stroke 8 Cy. 170 x 190 each-820kW (1115bhp) Caterpillar Inc-USA AuxGen: 2 x 38kW 380V 50Hz a.c Thrusters: 1 Tunnel thruster (f) Fuel: 75.0 (d.f.) 3.5pd
9476329 *2BME6* -	**SD MARS** **SD Marine Services Ltd** Serco Ltd *London* *United Kingdom* MMSI: 235067374 Official number: 915533	**134** - 382	Class: LR **✠100A1** SS 04/2009 tug, United Kingdom coastal service **LMC** **UMS** Eq.Ltr: B; Cable: 137.5/14.0 U2 (a)	**2009-04 Stocznia Tczew Sp z oo — Tczew** (Hull) **2009-04 B.V. Scheepswerf Damen — Gorinchem** Yd No: 509824 Loa 26.28 Br ex 8.44 Dght 3.390 Lbp 23.69 Br md 7.90 Dpth 4.05 Welded, 1 dk	**(B32A2ST) Tug**	**2 oil engines** with clutches, flexible couplings & sr geared to sc. shafts driving 2 FP propellers Total Power: 1,640kW (2,230hp) Caterpillar 3508B-TA 2 x Vee 4 Stroke 8 Cy. 170 x 190 each-820kW (1115bhp) Caterpillar Inc-USA AuxGen: 2 x 99kW 440V 60Hz a.c Thrusters: 1 Tunnel thruster (f)
8003668 - -	**SD MENAI** *ex Menai -2008* **SD Marine Services Ltd** Serco Ltd *London* *United Kingdom* MMSI: 235004346	*117* 88 -	Class: LR **✠100A1** SS 09/2012 U.K. coastal service up to sixty miles from safe haven **✠LMC** Eq.Ltr: C; Cable: 247.5/17.5 U1	**1981-11 R. Dunston Ltd. — Thorne** Yd No: T1366 Loa 24.34 Br ex 6.71 Dght 2.140 Lbp 22.86 Br md 6.41 Dpth 3.51 Welded	**(B34R2QY) Supply Tender**	**1 oil engine** sr reverse geared to sc. shaft driving 1 FP propeller Total Power: 243kW (330hp) Blackstone ERS4M 1 x 4 Stroke 4 Cy. 222 x 292 243kW (330bhp) Mirrlees Blackstone (Stamford)Ltd.-Stamford AuxGen: 1 x 34kW 440V 60Hz a.c, 1 x 13kW 440V 60Hz a.c
8807959 *GACY* -	**SD MOORFOWL** *ex Moorfowl -2008* **SD Marine Services Ltd** Serco Ltd *London* *United Kingdom* MMSI: 235004366 Official number: 913889	**438** 131 140	Class: LR **✠100A1** SS 04/2011 diving support vessel UK coastal service **✠LMC** Eq.Ltr: I; Cable: 192.5/24.0 U2	**1989-06 McTay Marine — Bromborough** Yd No: 83 Converted From: Mooring Vessel-2010 Loa 37.75 Br ex 11.90 Dght 2.000 Lbp 30.10 Br md 11.50 Dpth 3.80 Welded, 1 dk	**(B22A2OV) Diving Support Vessel**	**2 oil engines** with flexible couplings & reductiongeared to sc. shafts driving 2 Directional propellers Total Power: 594kW (808hp) Cummins KTA-19-M 2 x 4 Stroke 6 Cy. 159 x 159 each-297kW (404bhp) Cummins Engine Co Inc-USA AuxGen: 2 x 225kW 440V 60Hz a.c Thrusters: 1 Thwart. FP thruster (f)
8807947 *GACX* -	**SD MOORHEN** *ex Moorhen -2008* **SD Marine Services Ltd** Serco Ltd *London* *United Kingdom* MMSI: 232002927 Official number: 913888	**438** 131 140	Class: LR **✠100A1** SS 02/2011 diving support vessel UK coastal service **✠LMC** Eq.Ltr: I; Cable: 192.5/27.0 U2	**1989-05 McTay Marine — Bromborough** Yd No: 82 Converted From: Mooring Vessel-2009 Loa 37.75 Br ex 11.90 Dght 2.000 Lbp 30.10 Br md 11.50 Dpth 3.80 Welded, 1 dk	**(B22A2OV) Diving Support Vessel**	**2 oil engines** with flexible couplings & reductiongeared to sc. shafts driving 2 Directional propellers Total Power: 594kW (808hp) Cummins KTA-19-M 2 x 4 Stroke 6 Cy. 159 x 159 each-297kW (404bhp) Cummins Engine Co Inc-USA AuxGen: 2 x 225kW 440V 60Hz a.c Thrusters: 1 Thwart. FP thruster (f)
9533414 *2CCG6* -	**SD NAVIGATOR** **SD Marine Services Ltd** Serco Ltd *London* *United Kingdom* MMSI: 235071537	**150** 65 -	Class: LR **✠100A1** SS 07/2009 not exceeding 60 nautical miles from United Kingdom coastal service **LMC** **UMS** Cable: 192.5/22.0 U2 (a)	**2009-07 ZPUH Magra — Gdynia** (Hull) Yd No: (519302) **2009-07 B.V. Scheepswerf Damen — Gorinchem** Yd No: 519302 Loa 25.54 Br ex 10.64 Dght 2.550 Lbp 23.90 Br md 10.00 Dpth 3.35 Welded, 1 dk	**(B34L2QU) Utility Vessel**	**2 oil engines** with clutches, flexible couplings & sr reverse geared to sc. shafts driving 2 FP propellers Total Power: 714kW (970hp) 8.0kn Caterpillar C18 2 x 4 Stroke 6 Cy. 145 x 183 each-357kW (485bhp) Caterpillar Inc-USA AuxGen: 2 x 55kW 440V 60Hz a.c Thrusters: 1 Thwart. FP thruster (f)
9179323 *2FDV4* -	**SD NORTHERN RIVER** *ex Northern River -2011* **SD Marine Services Ltd** Serco Ltd *London* *United Kingdom* MMSI: 235090402 Official number: 918025	**3,612** 1,468 4,550	Class: LR (NV) **100A1** SS 02/2012 offshore supply ship **LMC** **UMS**	**1998-03 Bourgas Shipyards Co Ltd — Bourgas** (Hull) Yd No: 061/001 **1998-03 Myklebust Mek. Verksted AS — Gursken** Yd No: 18 Loa 83.80 Br ex 18.80 Dght 6.336 Lbp 76.20 Br md 18.00 Dpth 7.80 Welded, 1 dk	**(B21A2OS) Platform Supply Ship** Cranes: 1x50t,1x20t	**2 oil engines** reduction geared to sc. shafts driving 2 CP propellers Total Power: 7,060kW (9,598hp) 12.0kn Normo BRM-8 2 x 4 Stroke 8 Cy. 320 x 360 each-3530kW (4799bhp) Ulstein Bergen AS-Norway AuxGen: 2 x 1920kW 220/440V 60Hz a.c, 2 x 350kW 220/440V 60Hz a.c Thrusters: 1 Thwart. FP thruster (f); 1 Retract. directional thruster (f); 2 Thwart. FP thruster (a) Fuel: 1117.0
9185542 *YDA4401*	**SD PEARL** *ex Cathay I -2008* **PT Pelayaran Sukses Sindo Damai** - *Tanjung Priok* *Indonesia*	*132* 40 118	Class: KI (NK)	**1998-06 Super-Light Shipbuilding Contractor — Sibu** Yd No: 36 Loa 23.17 Br ex - Dght 2.412 Lbp 21.68 Br md 7.00 Dpth 2.90 Welded, 1 dk	**(B32A2ST) Tug**	**2 oil engines** reduction geared to sc. shafts driving 2 FP propellers Total Power: 744kW (1,012hp) Cummins KTA-19-M 2 x 4 Stroke 6 Cy. 159 x 159 each-372kW (506bhp) Cummins Engine Co Inc-USA AuxGen: 2 x 20kW a.c
5274462 - -	**SD PERAKI** *ex Angelita Iv -2008 ex Peraki -2003* **F F Maritime Corp** - *Iloilo* *Philippines* Official number: ILO3006918	*1,896* 753 2,108	Class: (LR) ✠ Classed LR until 19/3/01	**1960-11 Simons-Lobnitz Ltd. — Renfrew** Yd No: 1157 Loa 81.69 Br ex 15.12 Dght 5.144 Lbp 76.21 Br md 14.66 Dpth 6.40 Welded, 1 dk	**(B33B2DS) Suction Hopper Dredger** Hopper: 1,472 7 Ha: (8.8 x 8.8)6 (7.0 x 7.0) Derricks: 1x8t	**2 Steam Recips** driving 2 FP propellers 10.5kn Simons Lobnitz Ltd.-Renfrew AuxGen: 2 x 100kW 220V d.c Fuel: 254.0 (r.f.)
8401482 *GAAG* -	**SD POWERFUL** *ex Powerful -2008* **SD Marine Services Ltd** Serco Ltd *London* *United Kingdom* MMSI: 232002939 Official number: 913819	**384** 115 89	Class: LR **✠100A1** SS 06/2012 tug **✠LMC** Eq.Ltr: F; Cable: 275.0/19.0 U2 (a)	**1985-10 R. Dunston (Hessle) Ltd. — Hessle** Yd No: H946 Loa 38.79 Br ex 9.43 Dght 4.250 Lbp 37.01 Br md 9.11 Dpth 4.02 Welded, 1 dk	**(B32A2ST) Tug**	**2 oil engines** gearing integral to driving 2 Voith-Schneider propellers Total Power: 1,930kW (2,624hp) 12.0kn Ruston 6RKCM 2 x 4 Stroke 6 Cy. 254 x 305 each-965kW (1312bhp) Ruston Diesels Ltd.-Newton-le-Willows AuxGen: 3 x 131kW 440V 60Hz a.c Fuel: 22.0 (d.f.)
9533426 *2CTC6* -	**SD RAASAY** **SD Marine Services Ltd** Serco Ltd *London* *United Kingdom* Official number: 916317	**146** - -	Class: LR **✠100A1** SS 12/2009 United Kingdom coastal service **LMC** **UMS** Eq.Ltr: B; Cable: 137.5/16.0 U2 (a)	**2009-12 ZPUH Magra — Gdynia** (Hull) **2009-12 B.V. Scheepswerf Damen — Gorinchem** Yd No: 519303 Loa 25.54 Br ex - Dght 2.550 Lbp - Br md 10.00 Dpth 3.35 Welded, 1 dk	**(B34R2QY) Supply Tender**	**2 oil engines** with clutches, flexible couplings & sr reverse geared to sc. shafts driving 2 FP propellers Total Power: 714kW (970hp) 8.0kn Caterpillar C18 2 x 4 Stroke 6 Cy. 145 x 183 each-357kW (485bhp) Caterpillar Inc-USA AuxGen: 2 x 55kW 440V 60Hz a.c Thrusters: 1 Thwart. FP thruster (f)
9600712 *UBEK4* -	**SD RANGER** **Kolendo Shipping Ltd** JSC Rosnefteflot *Murmansk* *Russia* MMSI: 273338060	**294** 88 627	Class: LR RS **✠100A1** SS 03/2012 tug **LMC** **UMS** Eq.Ltr: F; Cable: 275.0/19.0 U2 (a)	**2012-03 Santierul Naval Damen Galati S.A. — Galati** (Hull) Yd No: 1203 **2012-03 B.V. Scheepswerf Damen — Gorinchem** Yd No: 511574 Loa 28.67 Br ex 10.43 Dght 3.740 Lbp 25.78 Br md 9.80 Dpth 4.60 Welded, 1 dk	**(B32A2ST) Tug**	**2 oil engines** gearing integral to driving 2 Z propellers Total Power: 3,728kW (5,068hp) Caterpillar 3516C 2 x Vee 4 Stroke 16 Cy. 170 x 215 each-1864kW (2534bhp) Caterpillar Inc-USA AuxGen: 2 x 86kW 400V 50Hz a.c Fuel: 72.0 (d.f.)
9600774 *9HA3067* -	**SD REBEL** **SD Rebel Ltd** Sleepdienst Adriaan Kooren BV (Tugboat Company Adriaan Kooren) - KOTUG *Valletta* *Malta* MMSI: 229097000 Official number: 9600774	**294** 88 629	Class: LR **✠100A1** SS 03/2012 tug **LMC** **UMS** Eq.Ltr: F; Cable: 275.0/19.0 U2 (a)	**2012-03 Santierul Naval Damen Galati S.A. — Galati** (Hull) Yd No: (511581) **2012-03 B.V. Scheepswerf Damen — Gorinchem** Yd No: 511581 Loa 28.60 Br ex 10.13 Dght 3.750 Lbp 25.78 Br md 9.80 Dpth 4.60 Welded, 1 dk	**(B32A2ST) Tug**	**2 oil engines** gearing integral to driving 2 Z propellers Total Power: 3,728kW (5,068hp) Caterpillar 3516C 2 x Vee 4 Stroke 16 Cy. 170 x 215 each-1864kW (2534bhp) Caterpillar Inc-USA AuxGen: 2 x 86kW 400V 50Hz a.c
9533402 *2BZL7* -	**SD RELIABLE** **SD Marine Services Ltd** Serco Ltd *London* *United Kingdom* MMSI: 235070759 Official number: 915991	**271** 81 -	Class: LR **✠100A** SS 11/2009 tug U.K. coastal service **LMC** **UMS** Eq.Ltr: E; Cable: 137.5/16.0 U2 (a)	**2009-11 'Crist' Sp z oo — Gdansk** (Hull launched by) **2009-11 B.V. Scheepswerf Maaskant — Stellendam** (Hull completed by) Yd No: 599 **2009-11 B.V. Scheepswerf Damen — Gorinchem** Yd No: 545301 Loa 29.14 Br ex 9.59 Dght 4.800 Lbp 26.40 Br md 9.45 Dpth 4.00 Welded, 1 dk	**(B32A2ST) Tug**	**2 oil engines** gearing integral to driving 2 Z propellers Total Power: 3,000kW (4,078hp) 12.0kn Caterpillar 3512B-HD 2 x Vee 4 Stroke 12 Cy. 170 x 190 each-1500kW (2039bhp) Caterpillar Inc-USA AuxGen: 2 x 98kW 440V 60Hz a.c

IMO / Call sign	Name / Owner	Tonnage	Class	Builder / Dimensions	Type	Machinery
9533799 *2CHL4* -	**SD RESOURCEFUL** **SD Marine Services Ltd** Serco Ltd *London* *United Kingdom* Official number: 916328	**271** 81 -	Class: LR **✠100A1** SS 05/2010 tug United Kingdom coastal service **LMC** **UMS** Eq.Ltr: E; Cable: 151.0/16.0 U2 (a)	**2010-05 'Crist' Sp z oo — Gdansk** (Hull launched by) **2010-05 B.V. Scheepswerf Maaskant — Stellendam** (Hull completed by) Yd No: 601 **2010-05 B.V. Scheepswerf Damen — Gorinchem** Yd No: 545303 Loa 29.14 Br ex 9.59 Dght 4.800 Lbp 26.40 Br md 9.45 Dpth 4.00 Welded, 1 dk	**(B32A2ST) Tug**	**2 oil engines** gearing integral to driving 2 Z propellers Total Power: 3,000kW (4,078hp) 12.0kn Caterpillar 3512B-HD 2 x Vee 4 Stroke 12 Cy. 170 x 215 each-1500kW (2039bhp) Caterpillar Inc-USA AuxGen: 2 x 98kW 440V 60Hz a.c
9618745 *9HA3065* -	**SD ROVER** **SD Rover Ltd** Sleepdienst Adriaan Kooren BV (Tugboat Company Adriaan Kooren) - KOTUG *Valletta* *Malta* MMSI: 229095000 Official number: 9618745	**294** 88 626	Class: LR **✠100A1** SS 03/2012 tug **LMC** **UMS** Eq.Ltr: F; Cable: 275.0/19.0 U2 (a)	**2012-03 Santierul Naval Damen Galati S.A. — Galati** (Hull) Yd No: (511583) **2012-03 B.V. Scheepswerf Damen — Gorinchem** Yd No: 511583 Loa 28.67 Br ex 10.13 Dght 3.750 Lbp 25.78 Br md 9.80 Dpth 4.60 Welded, 1 dk	**(B32A2ST) Tug**	**2 oil engines** gearing integral to driving 2 Z propellers Total Power: 3,728kW (5,068hp) Caterpillar 3516C 2 x Vee 4 Stroke 16 Cy. 170 x 215 each-1864kW (2534bhp) Caterpillar Inc-USA AuxGen: 2 x 86kW 400V 50Hz a.c
9551911 *9HA2375* -	**SD SALVOR** *ex* BOA Njord *-2013* **Elisabeth Ltd** Kotug International BV *Valletta* *Malta* MMSI: 248465000 Official number: 9551911	**490** 147 -	Class: NV (BV)	**2010-03 Medyilmaz Gemi Sanayi ve Ticaret AS — Karadeniz Eregli** Yd No: 16 Loa 32.00 Br ex - Dght 4.560 Lbp 30.46 Br md 11.60 Dpth 5.36 Welded, 1 dk	**(B32A2ST) Tug**	**2 oil engines** reduction geared to sc. shafts driving 2 Directional propellers Total Power: 3,372kW (4,584hp) Caterpillar 3516B-HD 2 x Vee 4 Stroke 16 Cy. 170 x 215 each-1686kW (2292bhp) Caterpillar Inc-USA AuxGen: 2 x a.c Thrusters: 1 Tunnel thruster (f)
9448190 *9HIX9* -	**SD SEAHORSE** **SD Seahorse Ltd** Sleepdienst Adriaan Kooren BV (Tugboat Company Adriaan Kooren) - KOTUG SatCom: Inmarsat C 424903910 *Valletta* *Malta* MMSI: 249039000 Official number: 9448190	**483** 145 -	Class: BV	**2008-06 Medyilmaz Gemi Sanayi ve Ticaret AS — Karadeniz Eregli** Yd No: 07 Loa 32.00 Br ex - Dght 3.850 Lbp - Br md 11.60 Dpth 5.36 Welded, 1 dk	**(B32A2ST) Tug**	**2 oil engines** reduction geared to sc. shafts driving 2 Z propellers Total Power: 3,838kW (5,218hp) Caterpillar 3516B 2 x Vee 4 Stroke 16 Cy. 170 x 190 each-1919kW (2609bhp) Caterpillar Inc-USA AuxGen: 2 x 194kW 50Hz a.c
9448188 *9HIW9* -	**SD SEAL** **SD Seal Ltd** Sleepdienst Adriaan Kooren BV (Tugboat Company Adriaan Kooren) - KOTUG SatCom: Inmarsat C 424904012 *Valletta* *Malta* MMSI: 249040000 Official number: 9448188	**483** 145 -	Class: BV	**2008-05 Medyilmaz Gemi Sanayi ve Ticaret AS — Karadeniz Eregli** Yd No: 06 Loa 32.00 Br ex - Dght 3.600 Lbp 30.46 Br md 11.60 Dpth 5.36 Welded, 1 dk	**(B32A2ST) Tug**	**2 oil engines** reduction geared to sc. shafts driving 2 Z propellers Total Power: 3,840kW (5,220hp) Caterpillar 3516B 2 x Vee 4 Stroke 16 Cy. 170 x 190 each-1920kW (2610bhp) Caterpillar Inc-USA AuxGen: 2 x 159kW a.c
9410715 *9HBU9* -	**SD SHARK** **SD Shark Ltd** Kotug International BV SatCom: Inmarsat C 425675910 *Valletta* *Malta* MMSI: 256759000 Official number: 9410715	**483** 145 -	Class: BV	**2008-03 Medyilmaz Gemi Sanayi ve Ticaret AS — Karadeniz Eregli** Yd No: 04 Loa 32.00 Br ex - Dght 4.300 Lbp 30.46 Br md 11.60 Dpth 5.36 Welded, 1 dk	**(B32A2ST) Tug**	**2 oil engines** reduction geared to sc. shafts driving 2 Z propellers Total Power: 3,788kW (5,150hp) Caterpillar 3516B-HD 2 x Vee 4 Stroke 16 Cy. 170 x 215 each-1894kW (2575bhp) Caterpillar Inc-USA AuxGen: 2 x 194kW 50Hz a.c
9165047 *DSOY3* -	**SD SKY** *ex* Lilium Gas *-2006* **Shinhan Capital Co Ltd** CPL Shipping Co Ltd *Jeju* *South Korea* MMSI: 440621000 Official number: JJR-069824	**2,362** 709 2,000 T/cm 9.4	Class: KR (NK)	**1997-11 K.K. Miura Zosensho — Saiki** Yd No: 1178 Loa 89.50 (BB) Br ex - Dght 5.342 Lbp 83.00 Br md 13.80 Dpth 6.40 Welded, 1 dk	**(A11B2TG) LPG Tanker** Double Bottom Entire Compartment Length Liq (Gas): 2,461 2 x Gas Tank (s); 2 independent horizontal 2 Cargo Pump (s): 2x300m³/hr Manifold: Bow/CM: 40.9m	**1 oil engine** driving 1 FP propeller Total Power: 2,427kW (3,300hp) 13.0kn Akasaka A41 1 x 4 Stroke 6 Cy. 410 x 800 2427kW (3300bhp) Akasaka Tekkosho KK (Akasaka DieselLtd)-Japan AuxGen: 2 x 240kW a.c Fuel: 74.0 (d.f.) 339.0 (r.f.) 8.2pd
9577238 *9HA3326* -	**SD SPARTA** *ex* Titan *-2013* **SD Sparta Ltd** Kotug International BV *Valletta* *Malta* MMSI: 229435000 Official number: 9577238	**484** 145 225	Class: BV	**2013-02 Eregli Gemi Insa Sanayi ve Ticaret AS — Karadeniz Eregli** Yd No: 37 Loa 32.00 Br ex - Dght 4.180 Lbp 30.24 Br md 11.60 Dpth 5.36 Welded, 1 dk	**(B32A2ST) Tug**	**2 oil engines** reduction geared to sc. shafts driving 2 Directional propellers Total Power: 3,840kW (5,220hp) 12.0kn Caterpillar 3516B-HD 2 x Vee 4 Stroke 16 Cy. 170 x 215 each-1920kW (2610bhp) Caterpillar Inc-USA AuxGen: 2 x 175kW 60Hz a.c Fuel: 150.0 (d.f.)
9448176 *9HBT9* -	**SD STINGRAY** **SD Stingray Ltd** Kotug International BV SatCom: Inmarsat C 425675813 *Valletta* *Malta* MMSI: 256758000 Official number: 9448176	**483** 145 -	Class: BV	**2008-04 Medyilmaz Gemi Sanayi ve Ticaret AS — Karadeniz Eregli** Yd No: 05 Loa - Br ex - Dght 3.850 Lbp 32.00 Br md 11.60 Dpth 5.36 Welded, 1 dk	**(B32A2ST) Tug**	**2 oil engines** reduction geared to sc. shafts driving 2 Z propellers Total Power: 3,840kW (5,220hp) Caterpillar 3516B 2 x Vee 4 Stroke 16 Cy. 170 x 190 each-1920kW (2610bhp) Caterpillar Inc-USA AuxGen: 2 x 174kW a.c
9533749 *2COB9* -	**SD SUZANNE** **SD Marine Services Ltd** Serco Ltd *Portsmouth* *United Kingdom* MMSI: 235074416 Official number: 916411	**121** - -	Class: LR **✠100A1** SS 06/2010 tug United Kingdom coastal service **LMC** **UMS** Eq.Ltr: A†; Cable: 110.0/12.5 U2 (a)	**2010-06 Damen Shipyards Gdynia SA — Gdynia** (Hull) Yd No: 512402 **2010-06 B.V. Scheepswerf Damen — Gorinchem** Yd No: 512402 Loa 21.19 Br ex 9.43 Dght 3.600 Lbp 19.00 Br md 8.90 Dpth 4.00 Welded, 1 dk	**(B32A2ST) Tug**	**2 oil engines** gearing integral to driving 2 Directional propellers Total Power: 1,492kW (2,028hp) 11.0kn Caterpillar 3508B-TA 2 x Vee 4 Stroke 8 Cy. 170 x 190 each-746kW (1014bhp) Caterpillar Inc-USA AuxGen: 2 x 76kW 440V 60Hz a.c Thrusters: 1 Tunnel thruster (f) Fuel: 19.0
7510274 *GUZX* -	**SD TEESDALE** *ex* Teesdale H *-2008* *ex* Wilks *-1986* **SD Marine Services Ltd** Serco Ltd *London* *United Kingdom* MMSI: 232003495 Official number: 366101	**499** 301 1,050	Class: (LR) (BV) ✠ Classed LR until 2/9/88	**1976-03 Yorkshire D.D. Co. Ltd. — Hull** Yd No: 238 Converted From: General Cargo Ship-1986 Loa 43.90 Br ex 9.96 Dght 3.901 Lbp 40.77 Br md 9.50 Dpth 4.75 Welded, 1 dk	**(A13B2TU) Tanker (unspecified)** Double Hull (13F) Liq: 1,136; Liq (Oil): 1,136 Compartments: 5 Ta, ER	**2 oil engines** reduction geared to sc. shafts driving 2 Directional propellers Total Power: 344kW (468hp) 7.0kn Caterpillar D343 2 x 4 Stroke 6 Cy. 137 x 165 each-172kW (234bhp) Caterpillar Tractor Co-USA AuxGen: 1 x 2kW 24V d.c Fuel: 15.0 (d.f.)
9534107 *2BRX2* -	**SD VICTORIA** **SD Marine Services Ltd** Serco Ltd *London* *United Kingdom* MMSI: 235068802	**3,522** 1,056 1,088	Class: LR **✠100A1** SS 06/2010 **✠LMC** **UMS** Eq.Ltr: T; Cable: 467.5/38.0 U3 (a)	**2010-06 Santierul Naval Damen Galati S.A. — Galati** (Hull) Yd No: 551011 **2010-06 B.V. Scheepswerf Damen — Gorinchem** Yd No: 551011 Loa 83.00 (BB) Br ex 16.03 Dght 4.250 Lbp 74.86 Br md 16.00 Dpth 7.20 Welded, 1 dk	**(B22A20R) Offshore Support Vessel** Cranes: 2	**2 oil engines** with clutches, flexible couplings & sr geared to sc. shafts driving 2 CP propellers Total Power: 2,984kW (4,058hp) 15.4kn Caterpillar 3516B-TA 2 x Vee 4 Stroke 16 Cy. 170 x 190 each-1492kW (2029bhp) Caterpillar Inc-USA AuxGen: 2 x 524kW 440V 60Hz a.c, 1 x 640kW 440V 60Hz a.c Thrusters: 1 Tunnel thruster (f)
8807600 *GACZ* -	**SD WARDEN** *ex* Warden *-2008* **SD Marine Services Ltd** Serco Ltd *London* *United Kingdom* MMSI: 232002653 Official number: 913890	*691* 207 -	Class: LR **✠100A1** SS 07/2011 **✠LMC** Eq.Ltr: J; Cable: 358.0/26.0 U2 (a)	**1989-11 Richards (Shipbuilders) Ltd — Lowestoft** Yd No: 579 Loa 48.63 Br ex 10.95 Dght 3.475 Lbp 42.02 Br md 10.51 Dpth 5.01 Welded, 1 dk	**(B34S2QM) Mooring Vessel**	**2 oil engines** with clutches, flexible couplings & sr geared to sc. shafts driving 2 CP propellers Total Power: 2,840kW (3,862hp) 15.0kn Ruston 8RK3CM 2 x Vee 4 Stroke 8 Cy. 254 x 305 each-1420kW (1931bhp) Ruston Diesels Ltd.-Newton-le-Willows AuxGen: 2 x 750kW 440V 60Hz a.c, 2 x 160kW 440V 60Hz a.c Thrusters: 1 Thwart. CP thruster (f)

IMO / Call sign	Name / Owner	Tonnage	Class	Builder / Dimensions	Type	Machinery
7703053 *GXHF* -	**SD WATERMAN** *ex* Waterman *-2008* **Allantone Supplies Ltd** - *London* *United Kingdom* MMSI: 232003847 Official number: 913827	**290** 87 300	✠ **100A1** SS 06/2009 ✠ **LMC** Eq.Ltr: F; Cable: 275.0/25.0 U1 (b)	**1978**-06 **R. Dunston (Hessle) Ltd. — Hessle** Yd No: H914 Converted From: Water Tanker-1978 Loa 40.11 Br ex 7.85 Dght 2.540 Lbp 37.52 Br md 7.56 Dpth 3.51 Welded, 1 dk	**(A14A2LO) Water Tanker** Liq: 300 Compartments: 4 Ta, ER	**1 oil engine** reverse reduction geared to sc. shaft driving 1 FP propeller Total Power: 485kW (659hp) 10.2kn Blackstone ES8 1 x 4 Stroke 8 Cy. 222 x 292 485kW (659bhp) Mirrlees Blackstone (Stamford)Ltd.-Stamford AuxGen: 2 x 70kW 440V 60Hz a.c, 1 x 24kW 440V 50Hz a.c Fuel: 22.0
8602000 *OYES2* -	**SDK SPAIN** *ex* Sea Box *-2009* *ex* Gorch Fock *-2005* *ex* RMS Scotia *-2000* *ex* Gorch Fock *-1999* **Partrederiet SDK Spain** Venus Shipping ApS *Fredericia* *Denmark (DIS)* MMSI: 220394000 Official number: D4177	**1,525** 594 1,506	Class: GL	**1986**-06 **Hermann Suerken GmbH & Co. KG — Papenburg** Yd No: 346 Loa 74.33 Br ex 12.43 Dght 3.602 Lbp 69.53 Br md 12.41 Dpth 5.72 Welded, 2 dks	**(A31A2GX) General Cargo Ship** Grain: 2,703; Bale: 2,686 TEU 84 C.Ho 56/20' (40') C.Dk 28/20' (40') Compartments: 1 Ho, ER 1 Ha: (43.8 x 10.6)ER	**1 oil engine** with clutches, flexible couplings & sr geared to sc. shaft driving 1 FP propeller Total Power: 600kW (816hp) 10.0kn Deutz SBV6M628 1 x 4 Stroke 6 Cy. 240 x 280 600kW (816bhp) Kloeckner Humboldt Deutz AG-West Germany AuxGen: 1 x 94kW 220/380V 50Hz a.c, 1 x 34kW 220/380V 50Hz a.c Thrusters: 1 Thwart. FP thruster (f)
9357822 *3EDG9* -	**SDL KOBE** **KS Lines SA** Marukichi Commerce Co Ltd *Panama* *Panama* MMSI: 371613000 Official number: 3125906B	**2,986** 1,370 3,918	Class: NK	**2005**-12 **K.K. Matsuura Zosensho — Osakikamijima** Yd No: 556 Loa 87.00 (BB) Br ex - Dght 5.845 Lbp 81.00 Br md 14.80 Dpth 6.10 Welded, 1 dk	**(A31A2GX) General Cargo Ship** Grain: 6,179; Bale: 5,983 2 Ha: (25.2 x 12.0)ER (12.6 x 12.0) Derricks: 1x25t,2x15t	**1 oil engine** driving 1 FP propeller Total Power: 1,514kW (2,058hp) 11.0kn Hanshin LH36L 1 x 4 Stroke 6 Cy. 360 x 670 1514kW (2058bhp) The Hanshin Diesel Works Ltd-Japan Fuel: 270.0
9384784 *3EFX3* -	**SDL MAYA** **KS Maya Lines SA** Marukichi Commerce Co Ltd *Panama* *Panama* MMSI: 353645000 Official number: 3186406A	**2,986** 1,370 3,913	Class: NK	**2006**-05 **K.K. Matsuura Zosensho — Osakikamijima** Yd No: 557 Loa 87.00 (BB) Br ex 14.82 Dght 5.845 Lbp 81.00 Br md 14.80 Dpth 8.95 Welded, 1 dk	**(A31A2GX) General Cargo Ship** Grain: 6,179; Bale: 5,983 Derricks: 3x15t	**1 oil engine** driving 1 FP propeller Total Power: 2,059kW (2,799hp) 11.0kn Hanshin LH38L 1 x 4 Stroke 6 Cy. 380 x 760 2059kW (2799bhp) The Hanshin Diesel Works Ltd-Japan Fuel: 265.0
9380336 *3EET3* -	**SDL ROKKO** **KS Rokko Lines SA** Marukichi Commerce Co Ltd SatCom: Inmarsat C 437180710 *Panama* *Panama* MMSI: 371807000 Official number: 3175006A	**2,957** 1,671 4,837	Class: NK	**2006**-05 **Amakusa Zosen K.K. — Amakusa** Yd No: 167 Loa 80.40 (BB) Br ex 14.20 Dght 7.162 Lbp 76.10 Br md 14.20 Dpth 9.60 Welded, 2 dks	**(A31A2GX) General Cargo Ship** Grain: 6,005; Bale: 5,676	**1 oil engine** driving 1 FP propeller Total Power: 2,059kW (2,799hp) 11.0kn Hanshin LH38L 1 x 4 Stroke 6 Cy. 380 x 760 2059kW (2799bhp) The Hanshin Diesel Works Ltd-Japan Fuel: 245.0
8925464 *YD6737* -	**SDM I** *ex* Obor III *-2001* **Sea Devil Marine Pte Ltd** - *Banjarmasin* *Indonesia*	**226** 68 -	Class: KI (BV)	**1996 Guangzhou Fishing Vessel Shipyard — Guangzhou GD** Yd No: XY-2072 Loa 29.80 Br ex - Dght 3.350 Lbp 27.08 Br md 8.20 Dpth 4.10 Welded, 1 dk	**(B32A2ST) Tug**	**2 oil engines** driving 2 FP propellers Total Power: 1,382kW (1,878hp) 12.0kn Cummins KTA-38-M1 2 x Vee 4 Stroke 12 Cy. 159 x 159 each-691kW (939bhp) Cummins Engine Co Ltd-United Kingdom AuxGen: 2 x 65kW 416V 50Hz a.c Fuel: 157.0 (d.f.)
9025314 - -	**SDS 2** **PT Surachman** - *Jakarta* *Indonesia*	**227** 136 -	Class: KI	**1991**-04 **P.T. Tirta Jaya — Pontianak** L reg 25.00 Br ex - Dght 2.750 Lbp 22.00 Br md 7.00 Dpth 3.50 Welded, 1 dk	**(B32A2ST) Tug**	**2 oil engines** geared to sc. shafts driving 2 Propellers Total Power: 736kW (1,000hp) 8.0kn Cummins KTA-19-M 2 x 4 Stroke 6 Cy. 159 x 159 each-368kW (500bhp) (made 1988) Cummins Engine Co Ltd-United Kingdom
8834720 - -	**SDS-004** **OOO 'Istok-DV'** -	**353** 105 155	Class: (RS)	**1990**-01 **Sretenskiy Sudostroitelnyy Zavod — Sretensk** Yd No: 204 Loa 39.90 Br ex 8.90 Dght 3.201 Lbp 36.25 Br md - Dpth 4.63 Welded, 1 dk	**(B11A2FS) Stern Trawler** Ins: 95	**1 oil engine** geared to sc. shaft driving 1 CP propeller Total Power: 441kW (600hp) 9.5kn Daldizel 6CHNSP18/22-600 1 x 4 Stroke 6 Cy. 180 x 220 441kW (600bhp) Daldizel-Khabarovsk AuxGen: 3 x 75kW a.c Fuel: 60.0 (d.f.)
9025338 *YD4347* -	**SDS 8** **PT Trada Maritime** - *Jakarta* *Indonesia*	**133** 79 -	Class: KI	**1992**-04 **P.T. Indomarine — Jakarta** L reg 20.17 Br ex - Dght 2.000 Lbp 19.60 Br md 6.10 Dpth 2.75 Welded, 1 dk	**(B32A2ST) Tug**	**2 oil engines** geared to sc. shafts driving 2 Propellers Total Power: 514kW (698hp) Cummins NTA-855-M 2 x 4 Stroke 6 Cy. 140 x 152 each-257kW (349bhp) (made 1990) Cummins Engine Co Ltd-United Kingdom
8874689 - -	**SDS 10** **PT Pelayaran Bhineka Eka Karya** - *Jakarta* *Indonesia*	**143** 85 -	Class: KI	**1993**-12 **P.T. Indomarine — Jakarta** Loa 20.90 Br ex - Dght - Lbp 19.15 Br md 6.10 Dpth 2.75 Welded, 1 dk	**(B32A2ST) Tug**	**2 oil engines** geared to sc. shafts driving 2 FP propellers Total Power: 700kW (952hp) 9.0kn Cummins NTA-855-M 2 x 4 Stroke 6 Cy. 140 x 152 each-350kW (476bhp) Cummins Engine Co Inc-USA AuxGen: 2 x 22kW 380V a.c
9025326 *YD6083* -	**SDS 16** *ex* Cendana I *-2001* **PT Wintermar** - *Samarinda* *Indonesia*	**152** - -	Class: (KI)	**1992**-01 **P.T. Rejeki Abadi Sakti — Samarinda** L reg 26.20 Br ex - Dght - Lbp 23.65 Br md 7.00 Dpth 3.73 Welded, 1 dk	**(B32A2ST) Tug**	**2 oil engines** geared to sc. shaft driving 1 Propeller Total Power: 1,214kW (1,650hp) Caterpillar D398 2 x Vee 4 Stroke 12 Cy. 159 x 203 each-607kW (825bhp) Caterpillar Inc-USA
9025340 - -	**SDS 18** **PT Surachman** - *Jakarta* *Indonesia*	**126** 75 -	Class: KI	**1998**-03 **P.T. Mariana Bahagia — Palembang** L reg 23.00 Br ex - Dght 2.400 Lbp 21.63 Br md 7.00 Dpth 3.00 Welded, 1 dk	**(B32A2ST) Tug**	**2 oil engines** geared to sc. shafts driving 2 Propellers Total Power: 810kW (1,102hp) 10.0kn Yanmar 6LAAM-UTE 2 x 4 Stroke 6 Cy. 148 x 165 each-405kW (551bhp) (made 1997) Yanmar Diesel Engine Co Ltd-Japan
9025352 - -	**SDS 20** *ex* FC-1 *-2001* **PT Castbay Marine** - *Jakarta* *Indonesia*	**126** 75 -	Class: KI	**1998**-07 **P.T. Mariana Bahagia — Palembang** L reg 23.00 Br ex - Dght 2.390 Lbp 21.96 Br md 7.00 Dpth 3.00 Welded, 1 dk	**(B32A2ST) Tug**	**2 oil engines** geared to sc. shafts driving 2 Propellers Total Power: 794kW (1,080hp) 10.0kn Caterpillar 3412 2 x Vee 4 Stroke 12 Cy. 137 x 152 each-397kW (540bhp) (made 1992, fitted 1998) Caterpillar Inc-USA
9025364 - -	**SDS 24** **PT Wintermar** - *Palembang* *Indonesia*	**131** 78 -	Class: KI	**2001**-08 **P.T. Mariana Bahagia — Palembang** Yd No: 35 Loa 23.00 Br ex - Dght - Lbp 21.63 Br md 7.00 Dpth 3.00 Welded, 1 dk	**(B32A2ST) Tug**	**2 oil engines** geared to sc. shafts driving 2 Propellers Total Power: 882kW (1,200hp) 10.0kn Yanmar 6LAHM-STE3 2 x 4 Stroke 6 Cy. 150 x 165 each-441kW (600bhp) (made 2000) Yanmar Diesel Engine Co Ltd-Japan
9260110 *YDA4063* -	**SDS 28** **PT Sentosa Segara Mulia Shipping** PT Wintermar *Jakarta* *Indonesia*	**143** 43 112	Class: KI (NK)	**2001**-12 **Tuong Aik (Sarawak) Sdn Bhd — Sibu** Yd No: 2104 Loa 23.50 Br ex - Dght 2.712 Lbp 21.76 Br md 7.32 Dpth 3.20 Welded, 1 dk	**(B32A2ST) Tug**	**2 oil engines** geared to sc. shafts driving 2 FP propellers Total Power: 942kW (1,280hp) Yanmar 6LAHM-STE3 2 x 4 Stroke 6 Cy. 150 x 165 each-471kW (640bhp) Yanmar Diesel Engine Co Ltd-Japan AuxGen: 2 x 40kW 415V a.c Fuel: 95.0
9282120 *YD4984* -	**SDS 30** **PT Sumber Wahyu Samudera** - *Jakarta* *Indonesia* Official number: BA3578/L	**130** 78 116	Class: KI (NK)	**2002**-11 **Yii Brothers Shipbuilding Contractor Co — Sibu** Yd No: 99 Loa 23.50 Br ex - Dght 2.712 Lbp 21.76 Br md 7.32 Dpth 3.20 Welded, 1 dk	**(B32A2ST) Tug**	**2 oil engines** reduction geared to sc. shafts driving 2 FP propellers Total Power: 942kW (1,280hp) Yanmar 6LAHM-STE3 2 x 4 Stroke 6 Cy. 150 x 165 each-471kW (640bhp) Yanmar Diesel Engine Co Ltd-Japan AuxGen: 2 x 30kW 415V 50Hz a.c

Ship / Owner	Tonnage	Class	Builder / Dimensions	Type	Machinery
9342308 **SDS 36** *YDA4034* - **PT Pelabuhan Indonesia II (Persero) (Indonesia Port Corp II) (PELINDO II)** - *Tanjung Priok* *Indonesia*	**139** 42 119	Class: KI (NK)	**2004**-12 **Lingco Shipbuilding Pte Ltd — Singapore** Yd No: 4204 Loa 23.50 Br ex - Dght 2.712 Lbp 21.77 Br md 7.32 Dpth 3.20 Welded, 1 dk	**(B32A2ST) Tug**	**2 oil engines** geared to sc. shaft driving 2 FP propellers Total Power: 912kW (1,240hp) Yanmar 6LAHM-STE3 2 x 4 Stroke 6 Cy. 150 x 165 each-456kW (620bhp) Yanmar Diesel Engine Co Ltd-Japan
9376323 **SDS 42** *YDA4081* *ex* Jana Bosds 42 *-2005* - **PT Wintermar** - *Jakarta* *Indonesia*	**121** 37 -	Class: KI	**2005**-07 **Jana Seribu Shipbuilding (M) Sdn Bhd — Sibu** Loa 22.95 Br ex - Dght - Lbp 20.73 Br md 7.01 Dpth 2.89 Welded, 1 dk	**(B32A2ST) Tug**	**2 oil engines** reduction geared to sc. shafts driving 2 FP propellers Total Power: 736kW (1,000hp) 10.0kn Cummins KTA-19-M 2 x 4 Stroke 6 Cy. 159 x 159 each-368kW (500bhp) Cummins Engine Co Inc-USA AuxGen: 2 x 30kW 420V a.c
9375628 **SDS 44** *YDA4112* - **PT Wintermar** - *Jakarta* *Indonesia*	**197** 60 -	Class: KI (GL)	**2005**-09 **Forward Shipbuilding Enterprise Sdn Bhd — Sibu** Yd No: 103 Loa 26.00 Br ex - Dght 3.000 Lbp 23.86 Br md 8.00 Dpth 3.65 Welded, 1 dk	**(B32A2ST) Tug**	**2 oil engines** reduction geared to sc. shafts driving 2 Propellers Total Power: 1,516kW (2,062hp) Mitsubishi S6R2-MPTK2 2 x 4 Stroke 6 Cy. 170 x 220 each-758kW (1031bhp) Mitsubishi Heavy Industries Ltd-Japan AuxGen: 2 x 45kW 415V a.c
9380348 **SDS 46** *YDA4144* - **PT Alfa Trans Raya** - *Jakarta* *Indonesia*	**192** 58 146	Class: NK	**2006**-03 **Fulsail Sdn Bhd — Sibu** Yd No: 7500 Loa 27.00 Br ex - Dght 2.835 Lbp 25.01 Br md 8.20 Dpth 3.60 Welded, 1 dk	**(B32A2ST) Tug**	**2 oil engines** reduction geared to sc. shafts driving 2 Propellers Total Power: 1,518kW (2,064hp) Mitsubishi S6R2-MPTK 1 x 4 Stroke 6 Cy. 170 x 220 759kW (1032bhp) Mitsubishi Heavy Industries Ltd-Japan Mitsubishi S6R2-MPTK3L 1 x 4 Stroke 6 Cy. 170 x 220 759kW (1032bhp) Mitsubishi Heavy Industries Ltd-Japan Fuel: 125.0 (d.f.)
9405679 **SDS 48** *YDA4171* - **PT Wintermar** PT Wintermar Offshore Marine *Jakarta* *Indonesia*	**192** 58 152	Class: NK	**2006**-08 **Fulsail Sdn Bhd — Sibu** Yd No: 7501 Loa 27.00 Br ex - Dght 2.835 Lbp 25.01 Br md 8.20 Dpth 3.60 Welded, 1 dk	**(B32A2ST) Tug**	**2 oil engines** reduction geared to sc. shafts driving 2 Propellers Total Power: 1,518kW (2,064hp) Mitsubishi S6R2-MTKL 2 x 4 Stroke 6 Cy. 170 x 220 each-759kW (1032bhp) Mitsubishi Heavy Industries Ltd-Japan AuxGen: 2 x 194kW a.c Fuel: 125.0 (d.f.)
9452294 **SDS 50** *YDA4268* - **PT Wintermar** - *Palembang* *Indonesia* MMSI: 525019366	**183** 55 -	Class: KI	**2007**-05 **P.T. Mariana Bahagia — Palembang** Yd No: 046 Loa 25.00 Br ex - Dght 2.700 Lbp 22.00 Br md 7.60 Dpth 3.50 Welded, 1 dk	**(B32A2ST) Tug**	**2 oil engines** reduction geared to sc. shafts driving 2 Propellers Total Power: 1,220kW (1,658hp) Yanmar 6AYM-ETE 2 x 4 Stroke 6 Cy. 155 x 180 each-610kW (829bhp) Yanmar Diesel Engine Co Ltd-Japan AuxGen: 2 x 35kW 400V a.c
8834732 **SDS-501** - - **Formant Co Ltd** -	**358** 107 125	Class: (RS)	**1990**-12 **SSZ im. "Oktyabrskoy Revolyutsii" — Blagoveshchensk** Yd No: 501 Loa 41.89 Br ex 8.90 Dght 3.182 Lbp 37.17 Br md - Dpth 4.63 Welded, 1 dk	**(B11A2FS) Stern Trawler** Ins: 133	**1 oil engine** geared to sc. shaft driving 1 CP propeller Total Power: 441kW (600hp) 10.0kn Daldizel 6CHSPN3A18-600 1 x 4 Stroke 6 Cy. 180 x 220 441kW (600bhp) Daldizel-Khabarovsk AuxGen: 3 x 75kW a.c Fuel: 55.0 (d.f.)
8860676 **SDS-502** - - **Sea World Co Ltd (ZAO 'Mir Morya')** -	**374** 112 125	Class: (RS)	**1991**-12 **SSZ im. "Oktyabrskoy Revolyutsii" — Blagoveshchensk** Yd No: 502 Loa 41.87 Br ex - Dght 3.180 Lbp 37.15 Br md 8.90 Dpth 4.60 Welded, 1 dk	**(B11A2FS) Stern Trawler** Ice Capable	**1 oil engine** reduction geared to sc. shaft driving 1 CP propeller Total Power: 331kW (450hp) 10.0kn S.K.L. 6VD18/15AL-2 1 x 4 Stroke 6 Cy. 150 x 180 331kW (450bhp) (made 1990) VEB Schwermaschinenbau "KarlLiebknecht" (SKL)-Magdeburg
8884907 **SDS-504** - - - -	**415** 124 125	Class: (RS)	**1993**-12 **AO SSZ im. "Oktyabrskoy Revolyutsii" — Blagoveshchensk** Yd No: 504 Loa 41.87 Br ex 9.25 Dght 3.210 Lbp 37.12 Br md 8.90 Dpth 4.60 Welded, 1 dk	**(B11A2FS) Stern Trawler**	**1 oil engine** driving 1 CP propeller Total Power: 450kW (612hp) 10.0kn S.K.L. 6VD18/15AL-2 1 x 4 Stroke 6 Cy. 150 x 180 450kW (612bhp) SKL Motoren u. Systemtechnik AG-Magdeburg AuxGen: 2 x 75kW a.c Fuel: 60.0 (d.f.)
9210256 **SDS RAIN** *IBGR* *ex* Ostkap *-2005* - **SDS Navigation Srl** - *Naples* *Italy* MMSI: 247153300	**6,204** 2,958 8,278	Class: RI (GL)	**2000**-06 **Stocznia Gdanska - Grupa Stoczni Gdynia SA — Gdansk** Yd No: 8203/02 Loa 107.68 Br ex - Dght 7.800 Lbp 102.10 Br md 18.20 Dpth 10.10 Welded, 1 dk	**(A31A2GX) General Cargo Ship** Double Bottom Entire Compartment Length Grain: 10,401; Bale: 10,401 TEU 371 C. 371/20' Compartments: 2 Ho, ER, 2 Tw Dk 2 Ha: ER Cranes: 2x35t Ice Capable	**1 oil engine** reduction geared to sc. shaft driving 1 CP propeller Total Power: 3,840kW (5,221hp) 14.3kn MAN 8L32/40 1 x 4 Stroke 8 Cy. 320 x 400 3840kW (5221bhp) H Cegielski Poznan SA-Poland AuxGen: 1 x 424kW 380V a.c, 2 x 312kW 380V a.c Thrusters: 1 Thwart. FP thruster (f) Fuel: 421.0 (r.f.)
9338125 **SDS WIND** *ICZW* *ex* Atlas-C *-2006* - **SDS Navigation Srl** - *Naples* *Italy* MMSI: 247182200	**5,581** 2,835 7,600 T/cm 17.8	Class: RI (GL)	**2005**-10 **Jiangsu Yangzijiang Shipbuilding Co Ltd — Jiangyin JS** Yd No: 2004-687C Loa 108.20 (BB) Br ex - Dght 7.010 Lbp 103.90 Br md 18.20 Dpth 9.00 Welded, 1 dk	**(A31A2GX) General Cargo Ship** Grain: 10,255; Bale: 10,255 Compartments: 3 Ho, ER 3 Ha: ER	**1 oil engine** driving 1 CP propeller Total Power: 2,800kW (3,807hp) 12.4kn MAN-B&W 7S26MC 1 x 2 Stroke 7 Cy. 260 x 980 2800kW (3807bhp) STX Engine Co Ltd-South Korea AuxGen: 2 x 280kW 450/230V 60Hz a.c Thrusters: 1 Thwart. CP thruster (f)
9166596 **SE** *CSIG* - **Transtejo-Transportes Tejo EP** - *Lisbon* *Portugal* MMSI: 263700018 Official number: LX-3182-TL	**445** 176 63	Class: LR ✠ **100A1** SS 03/2013 HSC passenger catamaran ferry, group 2 estuary of the River Tejo ✠ **LMC** **CCS** Eq.Ltr: F; Cable: 13.5/19.0 U1	**1998**-03 **FBM Marine Ltd. — Cowes** Yd No: 1444 Loa 48.25 Br ex 12.20 Dght 1.390 Lbp 45.25 Br md 11.80 Dpth 2.90 Welded, 1 dk	**(A37B2PS) Passenger Ship** Hull Material: Aluminium Alloy Passengers: unberthed: 496	**2 oil engines** with clutches, flexible couplings & reduction geared to sc. shafts driving 2 Water jets Total Power: 2,480kW (3,372hp) 23.0kn M.T.U. 12V396TE74 2 x Vee 4 Stroke 12 Cy. 165 x 185 each-1240kW (1686bhp) MTU Friedrichshafen GmbH-Friedrichshafen AuxGen: 2 x 46kW 380V 50Hz a.c Fuel: 20.1 (d.f.) 6.3pd
9655169 **SE CERULEAN** *9V9934* - **Starleena Shipping Pte Ltd** SE Shipping Lines Pte Ltd *Singapore* *Singapore* MMSI: 566819000 Official number: 397762	**19,454** 8,055 25,000	Class: NV	**2013**-06 **Sainty Shipbuilding (Yangzhou) Corp Ltd — Yizheng JS** Yd No: SAM 10018M Loa 167.70 (BB) Br ex 26.28 Dght 10.500 Lbp 158.23 Br md 26.00 Dpth 14.30 Welded, 1 dk	**(A31A2GX) General Cargo Ship** TEU 1280 Compartments: 2 Ho, ER 2 Ha: ER Cranes: 2x450t	**2 oil engines** reduction geared to sc. shafts driving 2 CP propellers Total Power: 9,000kW (12,236hp) 16.5kn Bergens B32: 40L9P 2 x 4 Stroke 9 Cy. 320 x 400 each-4500kW (6118bhp) Rolls Royce Ind'l Power Group Crossley Engines-Manchester AuxGen: 2 x a.c, 1 x a.c Thrusters: 1 Tunnel thruster (f)
9066796 **SE EUN** - *ex* Sankyo Maru *-2012* - **Se Eun Marine Co Ltd** - *Busan* *South Korea* Official number: BSR-120068	*563* - 1,250	Class: KR	**1994**-03 **Ishikawajima Ship & Chemical Plant Co Ltd — Tokyo** Yd No: 598 Loa 61.39 Br ex 10.60 Dght 4.200 Lbp 60.90 Br md 10.00 Dpth 4.70 Welded, 1 dk	**(A12A2TC) Chemical Tanker** Compartments: 8 Ta, ER	**1 oil engine** reverse geared to sc. shaft driving 1 FP propeller Total Power: 1,103kW (1,500hp) Hanshin LH28LG 1 x 4 Stroke 6 Cy. 280 x 530 1103kW (1500bhp) The Hanshin Diesel Works Ltd-Japan

IMO / Call sign	Name / Owner	Tonnage	Class	Builder / Dimensions	Type / Capacity	Machinery	Speed / Model
7322627 *H03751* -	**SE HEUN** *ex* Ocean Blue *-2004* *ex* Yustina *-2004* *ex* Sea Pride *-1994* *ex* Amigo II *-1994* *ex* Tamayoshi Maru No. 16 *-1988* **Tristar Shipping Trading Ltd** - SatCom: Inmarsat C 435550010 *Panama* *Panama* MMSI: 355500000 Official number: 3069005	**1,313** 753 -		**1973**-06 **Tokushima Zosen Sangyo K.K. — Komatsushima** Yd No: 362 Converted From: Bulk Aggregates Carrier-1988 L reg 70.32 Br ex 13.02 Dght - Lbp 70.00 Br md 13.00 Dpth 6.30 Riveted\Welded, 1 dk	**(A31A2GX) General Cargo Ship**	**1 oil engine** driving 1 FP propeller Total Power: 1,471kW (2,000hp) Hanshin 1 x 4 Stroke 6 Cy. 380 x 580 1471kW (2000bhp) Hanshin Nainenki Kogyo-Japan	11.0kn 6LU38
5429524 *6MDB* -	**SE HO No. 2** *ex* Yong Jin No. 2 *-1978* *ex* Yoshicho Maru No. 23 *-1971* **Se Ho Trade Ltd** - *Busan* *South Korea* Official number: BS-A-360	*226* 115 -	Class: (KR)	**1963 Yamanishi Shipbuilding Co Ltd — Ishinomaki MG** Yd No: 433 Loa 42.75 Br ex 7.45 Dght - Lbp 37.98 Br md 7.40 Dpth 3.41 Welded, 1 dk	**(B11B2FV) Fishing Vessel** Ins: 322	**1 oil engine** driving 1 FP propeller Total Power: 515kW (700hp) Hanshin 1 x 4 Stroke 6 Cy. 320 x 450 515kW (700bhp) Hanshin Nainenki Kogyo-Japan AuxGen: 2 x 96kW 230V a.c	11.8kn V6
8031483 *6LQM* -	**SE IL No. 81** *ex* Dong Shin No. 1 *-1986* *ex* Kum Soo No. 303 *-1984* **Kim Chan-Se** - *Busan* *South Korea* Official number: BS0201-A1887	*129* 52 105	Class: (KR)	**1980 Jinhae Ship Construction Industrial Co Ltd — Changwon** Loa 34.45 Br ex - Dght - Lbp 29.21 Br md 6.00 Dpth 2.75 Welded, 1 dk	**(B11A2FS) Stern Trawler** Ins: 77 4 Ha: 4 (7.7 x 7.4)	**1 oil engine** driving 1 FP propeller Total Power: 552kW (750hp) Matsui 1 x 4 Stroke 6 Cy. 230 x 380 552kW (750bhp) Matsui Iron Works Co Ltd-Japan AuxGen: 2 x 40kW 225V a.c	10.0kn MU623DSC
8031495 *6LQG* -	**SE IL No. 82** *ex* Dong Shin No. 2 *-1986* *ex* Kum Soo No. 307 *-1984* **Kim Chan-Se** - *Busan* *South Korea* Official number: BS0201-A1888	*129* 53 105	Class: (KR)	**1980 Jinhae Ship Construction Industrial Co Ltd — Changwon** Loa 34.45 Br ex - Dght 2.534 Lbp 29.21 Br md 6.00 Dpth 2.75 Welded, 1 dk	**(B11A2FS) Stern Trawler** Ins: 77 4 Ha: 4 (7.7 x 7.3)	**1 oil engine** driving 1 FP propeller Total Power: 552kW (750hp) Matsui 1 x 4 Stroke 6 Cy. 230 x 380 552kW (750bhp) Matsui Iron Works Co Ltd-Japan AuxGen: 2 x 40kW 225V a.c	10.0kn MU623DSC
6517940 *6MES* -	**SE IN No. 101** *ex* Dong Jin No. 55 *-1991* *ex* Shinei Maru No. 6 *-1971* **Se In Fishery Co Ltd** - *Busan* *South Korea* Official number: BS02-A482	*226* 113 288	Class: (KR)	**1965 KK Kanasashi Zosen — Shizuoka SZ** Yd No: 707 Loa 41.41 Br ex 7.57 Dght 3.122 Lbp 37.98 Br md 7.50 Dpth 3.38 Welded, 1 dk	**(B11B2FV) Fishing Vessel** Ins: 341	**1 oil engine** driving 1 FP propeller Total Power: 515kW (700hp) Fuji 1 x 4 Stroke 6 Cy. 300 x 430 515kW (700bhp) Fuji Diesel Co Ltd-Japan AuxGen: 2 x 72kW 230V a.c	11.3kn 6SD30
9431460 *9V8831* -	**SE PACIFICA** *ex* Ellensborg *-2009* **Saphir Shipping Pte Ltd** SE Shipping Lines Pte Ltd *Singapore* *Singapore* MMSI: 565227000 Official number: 396291	**9,627** 4,260 12,649	Class: GL	**2009**-06 **Taizhou Sanfu Ship Engineering Co Ltd — Taizhou JS** Yd No: SF060106 Loa 138.51 (BB) Br ex 21.30 Dght 8.000 Lbp 130.00 Br md 21.00 Dpth 11.00 Welded, 1 dk	**(A31A2GX) General Cargo Ship** Double Hull Grain: 15,952; Bale: 15,952 TEU 665 C Ho 334 TEU C Dk 331 TEU incl 50 ref C. Compartments: 3 Ho, 3 Tw Dk, ER 3 Ha: (42.0 x 17.5) (25.5 x 17.5)ER (18.7 x 15.0)Tappered Cranes: 2x150t Ice Capable	**1 oil engine** reduction geared to sc. shaft driving 1 CP propeller Total Power: 5,400kW (7,342hp) MaK 1 x 4 Stroke 6 Cy. 430 x 610 5400kW (7342bhp) Caterpillar Motoren GmbH & Co. KG-Germany Thrusters: 1 Tunnel thruster (f)	15.0kn 6M43C
9431434 *9V8828* -	**SE PANTHEA** *ex* Elsborg *-2009* **Saphire Shipping Pte Ltd** SE Shipping Lines Pte Ltd *Singapore* *Singapore* MMSI: 564217000 Official number: 396288	**9,627** 4,260 12,747	Class: GL	**2009**-01 **Taizhou Sanfu Ship Engineering Co Ltd — Taizhou JS** Yd No: SF060105 Loa 138.54 (BB) Br ex 21.30 Dght 8.000 Lbp 130.00 Br md 21.00 Dpth 11.00 Welded, 1 dk	**(A31A2GX) General Cargo Ship** Grain: 15,953; Bale: 15,952 TEU 665 C Ho 334 TEU C Dk 331 TEU incl 50 ref C. Compartments: 3 Ho, 3 Tw Dk, ER 3 Ha: (42.0 x 17.5) (25.5 x 17.5)ER (18.7 x 15.0)Tappered Cranes: 2x150t Ice Capable	**1 oil engine** reduction geared to sc. shaft driving 1 CP propeller Total Power: 5,400kW (7,342hp) MaK 1 x 4 Stroke 6 Cy. 430 x 610 5400kW (7342bhp) Caterpillar Motoren GmbH & Co. KG-Germany Thrusters: 1 Tunnel thruster (f)	15.0kn 6M43C
9453781 *9V8834* -	**SE PELAGICA** *ex* Billesborg *-2010* **Shanica Shipping Pte Ltd** SE Shipping Lines Pte Ltd *Singapore* *Singapore* MMSI: 566222000	**9,627** 4,261 12,737	Class: GL	**2010**-03 **Taizhou Sanfu Ship Engineering Co Ltd — Taizhou JS** Yd No: SF070102 Loa 138.54 (BB) Br ex 21.19 Dght 8.000 Lbp 130.00 Br md 21.00 Dpth 11.00 Welded, 1 dk	**(A31A2GX) General Cargo Ship** Grain: 15,953; Bale: 15,952 TEU 665 C Ho 334 TEU C Dk 331 TEU incl. 50 ref C Compartments: 3 Ho, 3 Tw Dk, ER 3 Ha: (42.0 x 17.5) (25.5 x 17.5)ER (18.7 x 15.0)Tappered Cranes: 2x150t Ice Capable	**1 oil engine** reduction geared to sc. shafts driving 1 CP propeller Total Power: 5,400kW (7,342hp) MaK 1 x 4 Stroke 6 Cy. 430 x 610 5400kW (7342bhp) Caterpillar Motoren GmbH & Co. KG-Germany AuxGen: 1 x 700kW 400V a.c, 3 x 500kW 400V a.c Thrusters: 1 Tunnel thruster (f)	15.0kn 6M43C
9431472 *9V8833* -	**SE POTENTIA** *launched as* Brattingsborg *-2009* **Shaneaka Shipping Pte Ltd** SE Shipping Lines Pte Ltd *Singapore* *Singapore* MMSI: 566204000 Official number: 396293	**9,627** 4,261 12,767	Class: GL	**2009**-12 **Taizhou Sanfu Ship Engineering Co Ltd — Taizhou JS** Yd No: SF070101 Loa 138.53 (BB) Br ex 21.19 Dght 8.000 Lbp 130.00 Br md 21.00 Dpth 11.00 Welded, 1 dk	**(A31A2GX) General Cargo Ship** Grain: 15,952; Bale: 15,952 TEU 665 C Ho 334 TEU C Dk 331 TEU Compartments: 3 Ho, 3 Tw Dk, ER 3 Ha: (42.0 x 17.5) (25.5 x 17.5)ER (18.7 x 15.0)Tappered Cranes: 2x150t Ice Capable	**1 oil engine** reduction geared to sc. shaft driving 1 CP propeller Total Power: 5,400kW (7,342hp) MaK 1 x 4 Stroke 6 Cy. 430 x 610 5400kW (7342bhp) Caterpillar Motoren GmbH & Co. KG-Germany AuxGen: 1 x 700kW 400V a.c, 3 x 532kW 400V a.c Thrusters: 1 Tunnel thruster (f)	15.0kn 6M43C
7221201 *6LGM* -	**SE WON No. 106** *ex* Dong Wha No. 106 *-1991* *ex* Tong Wha No. 106 *-1984* **Park Sun-Ae & Besides One** - *Busan* *South Korea* Official number: BS02-A2894	*184* 109 235	Class: (KR)	**1968 Dae Sun Shipbuilding & Engineering Co Ltd — Busan** Loa 43.41 Br ex - Dght 2.835 Lbp 38.74 Br md 6.90 Dpth 3.20 Welded, 1 dk	**(B11B2FV) Fishing Vessel** Ins: 222 3 Ha: 3 (1.2 x 1.2)ER	**1 oil engine** driving 1 FP propeller Total Power: 478kW (650hp) Hanshin 1 x 4 Stroke 6 Cy. 270 x 400 478kW (650bhp) Hanshin Nainenki Kogyo-Japan AuxGen: 2 x 100kW 230V a.c	10.3kn Z76
9135353 *DSPN9* -	**SE YANG** *ex* Nisshin Maru *-2010* **C& Merchant Marine Co Ltd** - *Busan* *South Korea* MMSI: 441762000 Official number: BSR105245	*746* - 2,181	Class: KR	**1996**-01 **K.K. Miura Zosensho — Saiki** Yd No: 1152 Loa 69.99 Br ex - Dght - Lbp 66.00 Br md 12.50 Dpth 4.95 Welded, 1 dk	**(A13B2TP) Products Tanker** Liq: 2,181; Liq (Oil): 2,181	**1 oil engine** driving 1 FP propeller Total Power: 1,324kW (1,800hp) Hanshin 1 x 4 Stroke 6 Cy. 300 x 600 1324kW (1800bhp) The Hanshin Diesel Works Ltd-Japan	11.0kn LH30LG
9285964 *DSNO3* -	**SE YANG** - **Tong Yang Cement Corp** - *Busan* *South Korea* MMSI: 441411000 Official number: BSR-040491	**4,771** 1,764 6,500	Class: KR	**2004**-04 **INP Heavy Industries Co Ltd — Ulsan** Yd No: 1130 Loa 110.63 Br ex - Dght 6.100 Lbp 103.00 Br md 18.00 Dpth 8.90 Welded, 1 dk	**(A24A2BT) Cement Carrier** Grain: 6,866 Compartments: 6 Ho/Ta, ER 6 Ha: ER	**1 oil engine** driving 1 FP propeller Total Power: 3,354kW (4,560hp) B&W 1 x 2 Stroke 6 Cy. 350 x 1050 3354kW (4560bhp) STX Corp-South Korea	13.3kn 6L35MC
9044085 *DSNO7* -	**SE YANG ACE** *ex* Aro Forest *-2012* *ex* Sea Orientalroad *-2004* **C& Merchant Marine Co Ltd** - *Busan* *South Korea* MMSI: 440152280 Official number: BSR-049363	**3,240** 1,558 4,999 T/cm 12.8	Class: KR (NK)	**1992**-07 **Daedong Shipbuilding Co Ltd — Busan** Yd No: 379 Loa 99.80 (BB) Br ex 15.83 Dght 5.974 Lbp 93.06 Br md 15.80 Dpth 7.85 Welded, 1 dk	**(A12B2TR) Chemical/Products Tanker** Double Bottom Entire Compartment Length Liq: 5,305; Liq (Oil): 5,382 Cargo Heating Coils Compartments: 10 Wing Ta, ER, 2 Wing Slop Ta 3 Cargo Pump (s): 2x500m³/hr, 1x200m³/hr Manifold: Bow/CM: 46.2m	**1 oil engine** driving 1 FP propeller Total Power: 2,167kW (2,946hp) MAN-B&W 1 x 2 Stroke 6 Cy. 260 x 980 2167kW (2946bhp) Ssangyong Heavy Industries Co Ltd-South Korea AuxGen: 2 x 199kW 440V 60Hz a.c Fuel: 91.0 (d.f.) (Part Heating Coils) 278.0 (r.f.) 8.0pd	12.4kn 6S26MC
6715449 *6LUO* -	**SE YANG No. 31** *ex* Sam In No. 5 *-2004* *ex* Daien Maru No. 11 *-1969* **Se Yang Fisheries Co Ltd** - *Busan* *South Korea* Official number: BS-A-465	*400* 212 -	Class: (KR)	**1967 Miho Zosensho K.K. — Shimizu** Yd No: 597 Loa 54.34 Br ex 8.26 Dght 3.404 Lbp 48.54 Br md 8.23 Dpth 3.79 Welded, 1 dk	**(B11B2FV) Fishing Vessel** Ins: 487 2 Ha: (1.3 x 1.0) (2.1 x 2.1)ER	**1 oil engine** driving 1 FP propeller Total Power: 956kW (1,300hp) Niigata 1 x 4 Stroke 6 Cy. 370 x 540 956kW (1300bhp) Niigata Engineering Co Ltd-Japan AuxGen: 2 x 164kW 225V a.c	11.0kn 6M37HS

IMO / Call sign	Name / Owner / Manager / Port / Flag	Tonnage	Class	Builder / Dimensions	Type	Machinery
7831240 *6LDZ* -	**SE YANG No. 51** - **Se Yang Fisheries Co Ltd** - *Busan* *South Korea* Official number: BS02-A1530	**408** - 503	Class: (KR)	**1978 Daedong Shipbuilding Co Ltd — Busan** Loa 55.17 Br ex - Dght 3.956 Lbp 49.00 Br md 8.60 Dpth 4.02 Welded, 1 dk	**(B11B2FV) Fishing Vessel** Ins: 542 3 Ha: 2 (1.3 x 0.9) (1.7 x 1.7)	**1 oil engine** reverse geared to sc. shaft driving 1 FP propeller Total Power: 993kW (1,350hp) 12.8kn Akasaka AH28R 1 x 4 Stroke 6 Cy. 280 x 440 993kW (1350bhp) Akasaka Tekkosho KK (Akasaka DieselLtd)-Japan AuxGen: 2 x 200kW 225V a.c
7734703 *6KVK* -	**SE YANG No. 55** *ex* Lucky Star No. 107 *-1983* *ex* Shinmei Maru No. 27 *-1983* **Shin Heung Fisheries Co Ltd** - *Busan* *South Korea* Official number: BS-A-2034	*201* 91 156	Class: (KR)	**1964-03 Hakata Dock K.K. — Fukuoka** L reg 34.51 Br ex - Dght 2.950 Lbp 34.02 Br md 6.90 Dpth 3.10 Welded, 1 dk	**(B11B2FV) Fishing Vessel** Ins: 252 3 Ha: 3 (1.4 x 1.4)	**1 oil engine** driving 1 FP propeller Total Power: 427kW (581hp) 10.0kn Hanshin DB6 1 x 4 Stroke 6 Cy. 290 x 410 427kW (581bhp) Hanshin Nainenki Kogyo-Japan AuxGen: 2 x 64kW 225V a.c
8623781 *HLHC* -	**SE YANG No. 300** - **Park Yang-Boo** - *Busan* *South Korea* Official number: BS-A-2418	*129* - 486	Class: (KR)	**1986 Jinhae Ship Construction Industrial Co Ltd — Changwon** Loa 40.49 Br ex - Dght - Lbp 32.31 Br md 7.31 Dpth 3.00 Welded, 1 dk	**(B11B2FV) Fishing Vessel**	**1 oil engine** driving 1 FP propeller Total Power: 1,412kW (1,920hp) Fuji 1 x 4 Stroke 8 Cy. 320 x 380 1412kW (1920bhp) Fuji Diesel Co Ltd-Japan AuxGen: 1 x 128kW 225V a.c
6519871 *6KEW* -	**SE YANG No. 337** *ex* Nam Hae No. 219 *-1983* **Korea Marine Industry Development Corp** - *Incheon* *South Korea* Official number: IF1905	*159* 57 168	Class: (KR)	**1965 Ateliers et Chantiers du Havre — Le Havre** Yd No: B17 Loa 30.00 Br ex 6.53 Dght 2.515 Lbp 25.00 Br md 6.51 Dpth 3.10 Welded, 1 dk	**(B11B2FV) Fishing Vessel** Ins: 119 Compartments: 3 Ho, ER 3 Ha: 3 (0.8 x 0.8)ER	**1 oil engine** driving 1 FP propeller Total Power: 338kW (460hp) 10.0kn Fiat L230.8S 1 x 4 Stroke 8 Cy. 230 x 350 338kW (460bhp) SA Fiat SGM-Torino Fuel: 70.0 (d.f.)
6620400 *HLLU* -	**SE YOUNG No. 2** *ex* Keo Mun No. 502 *-1985* **Lee Soo-In** - *Busan* *South Korea* Official number: BF43165	*223* 80 -	Class: (KR)	**1966 Ateliers et Chantiers de La Manche — Dieppe** Yd No: 1191 Loa 32.29 Br ex 7.50 Dght 3.099 Lbp 26.98 Br md 7.47 Dpth 3.81 Welded, 1 dk	**(B11A2FS) Stern Trawler** Ins: 142 Compartments: 1 Ho, ER 2 Ha: 2 (0.9 x 0.9)ER Derricks: 4x0.5t; Winches: 2	**1 oil engine** driving 1 FP propeller Total Power: 471kW (640hp) 11.0kn Fiat L230.8S 1 x 4 Stroke 8 Cy. 230 x 350 471kW (640bhp) SA Fiat SGM-Torino
6906737 *IRMI* -	**SEA** *ex* Parat *-1980* **Ocean Srl** - *Trieste* *Italy* Official number: 739	*134* 24 100	Class: RI (GL)	**1969 Schulte & Bruns Schiffswerft — Emden** Yd No: 255 Loa 27.79 Br ex 7.90 Dght 2.852 Lbp 24.49 Br md 7.50 Dpth 3.48 Welded, 1 dk	**(B32A2ST) Tug**	**1 oil engine** reverse reduction geared to sc. shaft driving 1 FP propeller Total Power: 662kW (900hp) 11.5kn MaK 6M451AK 1 x 4 Stroke 6 Cy. 320 x 450 662kW (900bhp) Atlas MaK Maschinenbau GmbH-Kiel AuxGen: 2 x 37kW 24V d.c Fuel: 49.0 (d.f.)
9350537 *V3RK2* -	**SEA** - **Sea Bulk Inc** Jessy Shipping Co Ltd (Dzhessi Shipping Ko Ltd) *Belize City* *Belize* MMSI: 312260000 Official number: 071130135	**6,290** 3,711 10,131	Class: (RS) (CC)	**2005-10 Zhejiang Fanshun Shipbuilding Industry Co Ltd — Yueqing ZJ** Yd No: 3 Loa 128.00 (BB) Br ex 18.04 Dght 7.400 Lbp 117.00 Br md 18.00 Dpth 9.70 Welded, 1 dk	**(A31A2GX) General Cargo Ship** Grain: 12,684 Compartments: 2 Ho, ER 2 Ha: (24.7 x 10.4)ER (14.9 x 10.4) Cranes: 2x20t	**1 oil engine** geared to sc. shaft driving 1 FP propeller Total Power: 2,513kW (3,417hp) 10.5kn Daihatsu 8DKM-28 1 x 4 Stroke 8 Cy. 280 x 390 2513kW (3417bhp) Shaanxi Diesel Heavy Industry Co Lt-China AuxGen: 3 x 160kW a.c, 1 x 200kW a.c Fuel: 320.0 (r.f.)
8858609 - -	**SEA-1** *ex* Feniks *-2008* *ex* Palana *-2006* *ex* Astronavt *-1996* - -	**683** 233 529	Class: (RS)	**1992-02 Khabarovskiy Sudostroitelnyy Zavod im Kirova — Khabarovsk** Yd No: 886 Loa 54.99 Br ex 9.49 Dght 4.460 Lbp 50.04 Br md - Dpth 5.16 Welded, 1 dk	**(B12B2FC) Fish Carrier** Ice Capable	**1 oil engine** driving 1 FP propeller Total Power: 588kW (799hp) 11.3kn S.K.L. 6NVD48A-2U 1 x 4 Stroke 6 Cy. 320 x 480 588kW (799bhp) SKL Motoren u. Systemtechnik AG-Magdeburg
8716863 *5NQY5* -	**SEA ADVENTURER** *ex* Hilda Knutsen *-2011* **Sea Transport Services Nigeria Ltd** Oceanic Shipping Services Pvt Ltd *Lagos* *Nigeria* MMSI: 657826000 Official number: 377827	**11,425** 4,319 14,910 T/cm 29.5	Class: GL (NV)	**1989-11 SA Juliana Constructora Gijonesa — Gijon** Yd No: 321 Loa 141.50 Br ex 23.05 Dght 8.014 Lbp 133.83 Br md 23.00 Dpth 11.80 Welded, 1 dk	**(A12B2TR) Chemical/Products Tanker** Double Hull (13F) Liq: 17,159; Liq (Oil): 17,850 Compartments: 10 Wing Ta, ER 10 Cargo Pump (s): 10x240m³/hr Manifold: Bow/CM: 66m Ice Capable	**1 oil engine** driving 1 CP propeller Total Power: 5,237kW (7,120hp) 13.5kn B&W 4S50MC 1 x 2 Stroke 4 Cy. 500 x 1910 5237kW (7120bhp) Astilleros Espanoles SA (AESA)-Spain AuxGen: 2 x 900kW 440V 60Hz a.c, 1 x 750kW 440V 60Hz a.c Thrusters: 1 Thwart. FP thruster (f) Fuel: 84.0 (d.f.) 764.0 (r.f.)
7391422 *C6PG6* -	**SEA ADVENTURER** *ex* Clipper Adventurer *-2012* *ex* Alla Tarasova *-1997* **Adventurer Owner Ltd** FleetPro Ocean Inc SatCom: Inmarsat C 430999710 *Nassau* *Bahamas* MMSI: 309997000 Official number: 730585	**4,376** 1,347 1,465	Class: BV (LR) (RS) Classed LR until 4/11/13	**1975-12 Brodogradiliste 'Titovo' — Kraljevica** Yd No: 408 Converted From: Cruise Ship-1998 Loa 100.01 (BB) Br ex 16.24 Dght 4.650 Lbp 90.00 Br md 16.20 Dpth 6.99 Welded, 3 dks. 2 Superstructure dks.	**(A37A2PC) Passenger/Cruise** Passengers: cabins: 61; berths: 122 Ice Capable	**2 oil engines** driving 2 CP propellers Total Power: 3,884kW (5,280hp) 17.0kn B&W 8-35VF-62 2 x 2 Stroke 8 Cy. 350 x 620 each-1942kW (2640bhp) Tvornica Dizel Motora 'Uljanik'-Yugoslavia AuxGen: 4 x 320kW 400V 50Hz a.c Boilers: 2 AuxB (o.f.) Thrusters: 1 Thwart. FP thruster (f) Fuel: 395.0 (d.f.)
9039585 *3FMJ4* -	**SEA AEOLIS** *ex* Tosei Maru *-2013* **Sea Aeolis Maritime Ltd** Mediterranean Car-Carriers Line SA (MCCL) *Panama* *Panama* MMSI: 353430000 Official number: 44754PEXT2	*9,259* 6,485 2,550	Class: NK	**1992-02 Naikai Shipbuilding & Engineering Co Ltd — Onomichi HS (Setoda Shipyard)** Yd No: 572 Loa 108.22 (BB) Br ex 20.02 Dght 5.516 Lbp 99.98 Br md 20.00 Dpth 6.45 Welded, 2 dks	**(A35B2RV) Vehicles Carrier** Stern door/ramp Cars: 686	**1 oil engine** driving 1 FP propeller Total Power: 4,708kW (6,401hp) 16.5kn B&W 8L35MC 1 x 2 Stroke 8 Cy. 350 x 1050 4708kW (6401bhp) Hitachi Zosen Corp-Japan AuxGen: 2 x 560kW a.c Thrusters: 1 Thwart. CP thruster (f) Fuel: 320.0 (r.f.)
9466271 *PHSA* -	**SEA ALFA** - **Sea Alfa BV** Seacontractors BV *Vlissingen* *Netherlands* MMSI: 245168000 Official number: 51395	**309** 92 -	Class: BV	**2008-02 Damen Shipyards Kozle Sp z oo — Kedzierzyn-Kozle (Hull)** Yd No: 1116 **2008-02 B.V. Scheepswerf Damen Hardinxveld — Hardinxveld-Giessendam** Yd No: 1581 Loa 30.09 Br ex 9.10 Dght 3.200 Lbp 27.99 Br md - Dpth 4.40 Welded, 1 dk	**(B32A2ST) Tug** Passengers: berths: 7 Cranes: 1	**2 oil engines** reduction geared to sc. shafts driving 2 FP propellers Total Power: 2,460kW (3,344hp) 11.0kn Caterpillar 3512B 2 x Vee 4 Stroke 12 Cy. 170 x 190 each-1230kW (1672bhp) Caterpillar Inc-USA AuxGen: 2 x 96kW 400/230V 50Hz a.c Thrusters: 1 Tunnel thruster (f) Fuel: 148.8 (d.f.)
9104263 *9HA2388* -	**SEA AMAZON** *ex* Jasmine Ace *-2010* *ex* RoRo Hidaka *-2004* *ex* Yutoku Maru *-2004* **Sea Amazon Shipping Ltd** Mediterranean Car-Carriers Line SA (MCCL) *Valletta* *Malta* MMSI: 248497000 Official number: 9104263	**13,038** 4,921 4,910	Class: NK	**1995-02 Kyokuyo Shipyard Corp — Shimonoseki YC** Yd No: 391 Loa 134.66 (BB) Br ex 22.42 Dght 6.314 Lbp 125.00 Br md 22.40 Dpth 11.75 Welded, 4 dks	**(A35A2RR) Ro-Ro Cargo Ship** Quarter stern door/ramp (p) Len: - Wid: 5.50 Swl: 55 Lane-Len: 1116 Lorries: 15, Cars: 178, Trailers: 76	**1 oil engine** driving 1 CP propeller Total Power: 9,989kW (13,581hp) 20.0kn B&W 7S50MC 1 x 2 Stroke 7 Cy. 500 x 1910 9989kW (13581bhp) Hitachi Zosen Corp-Japan Thrusters: 1 Thwart. CP thruster (f) Fuel: 855.0 (r.f.)
9407043 *VRMK3* -	**SEA AMBITION** *ex* Bow Lima *-2013* **Top Sailing Enterprise Ltd** Aoxing Ship Management (Shanghai) Ltd *Hong Kong* *Hong Kong* MMSI: 477652800 Official number: HK-3898	**11,722** 6,324 19,971 T/cm 29.8	Class: NK	**2007-09 Fukuoka Shipbuilding Co Ltd — Nagasaki NS** Yd No: 2013 Loa 144.09 (BB) Br ex 24.23 Dght 9.625 Lbp 136.00 Br md 24.19 Dpth 12.90 Welded, 1 dk	**(A12B2TR) Chemical/Products Tanker** Double Hull (13F) Liq: 21,715; Liq (Oil): 32,538 Cargo Heating Coils Compartments: 20 Wing Ta (s.stl), ER 20 Cargo Pump (s): 10x200m³/hr, 10x300m³/hr Manifold: Bow/CM: 72m	**1 oil engine** driving 1 FP propeller Total Power: 6,150kW (8,362hp) 14.5kn MAN-B&W 6S42MC 1 x 2 Stroke 6 Cy. 420 x 1764 6150kW (8362bhp) Makita Corp-Japan AuxGen: 3 x 560kW 440/110V 60Hz a.c Thrusters: 1 Tunnel thruster (f) Fuel: 105.0 (d.f.) 1003.0 (r.f.)
9222558 *ELYL6* -	**SEA AMITY** - **Sea Amity Maritime Inc** Lihai International Shipping Ltd *Monrovia* *Liberia* MMSI: 636011334 Official number: 11334	**17,859** 9,828 28,290	Class: NK	**2001-01 Naikai Zosen Corp — Onomichi HS (Setoda Shipyard)** Yd No: 669 Loa 171.93 (BB) Br ex - Dght 9.573 Lbp 164.90 Br md 27.00 Dpth 13.60 Welded, 1 dk	**(A21A2BC) Bulk Carrier** Grain: 38,215; Bale: 36,680 Compartments: 5 Ho, ER 5 Ha: (12.7 x 16.0)4 (20.1 x 17.6)ER Cranes: 4x30t	**1 oil engine** driving 1 FP propeller Total Power: 7,135kW (9,701hp) 14.0kn B&W 5S50MC 1 x 2 Stroke 5 Cy. 500 x 1910 7135kW (9701bhp) Hitachi Zosen Corp-Japan Fuel: 1430.0 (r.f.)

IMO / Call sign	Ship / Former names / Owner / Registry	Tonnage	Class	Builder / Dimensions	Type	Machinery
8319524 *H9OC* -	**SEA AMORE** *ex* Lady Bushra *-2011* *ex* Mount Fuji *-2004* *ex* Hero *-2004* *ex* Mount Fuji *-1990* **MCD Shipping SA** - *Panama* *Panama* MMSI: 357019000 Official number: 32617PEXT2	**11,356** 6,551 19,505 T/cm 27.2	Class: NK RS (Class contemplated)	**1984**-03 **Sasebo Heavy Industries Co. Ltd. — Sasebo Yard, Sasebo** Yd No: 331 Loa 148.00 (BB) Br ex - Dght 9.319 Lbp 138.82 Br md 23.11 Dpth 12.70 Welded, 1 dk	**(A21A2BC) Bulk Carrier** Grain: 23,790; Bale: 23,103 Compartments: 4 Ho, ER 4 Ha: (17.6 x 9.6)3 (19.2 x 11.2)ER Derricks: 4x25t	**1 oil engine** driving 1 FP propeller Total Power: 4,266kW (5,800hp) 13.8kn Mitsubishi 6UEC52HA 1 x 2 Stroke 6 Cy. 520 x 1250 4266kW (5800bhp) Kobe Hatsudoki KK-Japan AuxGen: 2 x 300kW Fuel: 1055.0 (r.f.)
8017891 *3EQR2* -	**SEA ANEMOS** *ex* Lamia *-2008* *ex* Edsel *-2004* *ex* Millenium Jaguar *-2002* *ex* Fortuna II *-2001* *ex* Nissho Maru *-1998* **Sea Anemos Shipping Co SA** Mediterranean Car-Carriers Line SA (MCCL) *Panama* *Panama* MMSI: 357121000 Official number: 3418608A	**6,525** 2,488 2,709	Class: NK	**1980**-08 **Nishi Shipbuilding Co Ltd — Imabari EH** Yd No: 307 Loa 106.06 (BB) Br ex - Dght 5.814 Lbp 98.02 Br md 17.26 Dpth 7.85 Welded, 6 dks, incl. 5 hoistable dks	**(A35B2RV) Vehicles Carrier** Quarter stern ramp1 (p) 1 (s) Lorries: 11, Cars: 560	**1 oil engine** driving 1 FP propeller Total Power: 3,884kW (5,281hp) 13.0kn B&W 6K45GFC 1 x 2 Stroke 6 Cy. 450 x 900 3884kW (5281bhp) Mitsui Engineering & Shipbuilding CLtd-Japan AuxGen: 2 x 360kW 450V 60Hz a.c, 1 x 200kW 450V 60Hz a.c Fuel: 76.2 (d.f.) (Heating Coils) 424.2 (r.f.) 11.0pd
8656271 *HP5131* -	**SEA ANGEL** *ex* Queen *-2012* **Newtech International Services LLC** - *Panama* *Panama* MMSI: 353523000 Official number: 39980PEXT2	**489** 242 -		**2007 UR-Dock — Basrah** Loa 44.00 Br ex - Dght - Lbp - Br md 11.00 Dpth 6.25 Welded, 1 dk	**(A13B2TP) Products Tanker**	**2 oil engines** reduction geared to sc. shafts driving 2 Propellers Total Power: 1,176kW (1,598hp) Caterpillar 2 x each-588kW (799bhp) Caterpillar Inc-USA
5270533 - -	**SEA ANGEL** *ex* Grampian Avenger II *-2005* *ex* Pitufo *-1999* *ex* Putford Eagle *-1986* *ex* Paramount *-1984* **Arranbrae Ltd** -	**283** 84 -	Class: (LR) Eq.Ltr: i; ✠ Classed LR until 20/5/08	**1959**-10 **T. Mitchison Ltd. — Gateshead** Yd No: 94 Converted From: Standby Safety Vessel-1986 Converted From: Trawler-1976 Loa 38.65 Br ex 7.73 Dght 3.353 Lbp 34.50 Br md 7.62 Dpth 3.81 Welded	**(B11A2FT) Trawler**	**1 oil engine** driving 1 FP propeller Total Power: 559kW (760hp) Mirrlees KSSDM-6 1 x 4 Stroke 6 Cy. 381 x 457 559kW (760bhp) Mirrlees, Bickerton & Day-Stockport AuxGen: 1 x 126kW 220V a.c, 1 x 76kW 220V a.c Boilers: (db) (3.5kgf/cm² (3.4bar))
8860353 *WDB7176* -	**SEA ANGEL** *ex* Princess V *-2004* **Mario Lopez** - *Palacios, TX* *United States of America* Official number: 984167	*136* 108 -		**1992 Master Boat Builders, Inc. — Coden, Al** Yd No: 154 Loa - Br ex - Dght - Lbp 23.50 Br md 6.71 Dpth 3.66 Welded, 1 dk	**(B11B2FV) Fishing Vessel**	**1 oil engine** driving 1 FP propeller
8958461 *WDD3154* -	**SEA ANGEL** *ex* Sea Commander *-2006* **SAH Corp** - *Galveston, TX* *United States of America* MMSI: 367126440 Official number: 1084904	**148** 44 -		**1999 Master Boat Builders, Inc. — Coden, Al** L reg 24.87 Br ex - Dght - Lbp - Br md 7.31 Dpth 3.81 Welded, 1 dk	**(B11B2FV) Fishing Vessel**	**1 oil engine** driving 1 FP propeller
8958590 - -	**SEA ANGEL** *ex* Sea Angel II *-2005* **Sea Angel II Inc** - *New York, NY* *United States of America* Official number: 1088683	**106** 84 -		**1999 Kannin Pham — Chalmette, La** L reg 21.94 Br ex - Dght - Lbp - Br md 6.70 Dpth 3.04 Welded, 1 dk	**(B11B2FV) Fishing Vessel**	**1 oil engine** driving 1 FP propeller
9551222 *WDE5879* -	**SEA ANGEL** - **Capt Elliott's Party Boats Inc** Texas Crewboats Inc *Freeport, TX* *United States of America* MMSI: 367372810 Official number: 1214786	**367** 110 -		**2008**-09 **Neuville Boat Works, Inc. — New Iberia, La** Yd No: 154-6 Loa 48.76 Br ex - Dght - Lbp - Br md 9.08 Dpth 3.81 Welded, 1 dk	**(B21A2OC) Crew/Supply Vessel** Hull Material: Aluminium Alloy	**4 oil engines** geared to sc. shafts driving 4 Propellers Total Power: 3,580kW (4,868hp) 25.0kn Cummins KTA-38-M2 4 x Vee 4 Stroke 12 Cy. 159 x 159 each-895kW (1217bhp) Cummins Engine Co Inc-USA Thrusters: 1 Tunnel thruster (f)
8133293 - -	**SEA ANGEL I** *ex* Papa's Girls *-2005* *ex* Midnight Special *-1994* **Bonacca Shipping S de RL** - *Roatan* *Honduras* Official number: U-1828121	*182* 124 -		**1980**-01 **Marine Builders, Inc. — Mobile, Al** Yd No: 123 L reg 27.16 Br ex 7.93 Dght - Lbp - Br md - Dpth 2.27 Welded, 1 dk	**(B11B2FV) Fishing Vessel**	**2 oil engines** driving 2 FP propellers Total Power: 626kW (852hp) G.M. (Detroit Diesel) 16V-71 2 x Vee 2 Stroke 16 Cy. 108 x 127 each-313kW (426bhp) General Motors Detroit DieselAllison Divn-USA
8940622 - -	**SEA ANGELS** - **Nhi Nguyen** - *Biloxi, MS* *United States of America* Official number: 1048326	**134** 40 -		**1996 Rodriguez Boat Builders, Inc. — Coden, Al** Yd No: 159 L reg 24.63 Br ex - Dght - Lbp - Br md 7.32 Dpth 3.75 Welded, 1 dk	**(B11B2FV) Fishing Vessel**	**1 oil engine** driving 1 FP propeller
9097525 *WDE6973* -	**SEA ANGELS** *ex* Sea Angels Ii *-2011* **Atlantic Carolina Trawling Inc** - *Beaufort, NC* *United States of America* MMSI: 367387260 Official number: 1125310	*185* 55 -		**2002**-01 Yd No: 234 L reg 26.94 Br ex - Dght - Lbp - Br md 7.92 Dpth 3.81 Welded, 1 dk	**(B11B2FV) Fishing Vessel**	**1 oil engine** driving 1 Propeller
8956657 *YYV3487* -	**SEA ANGELUS** *ex* Lady Dana *-2004* *ex* Explorer *-2004* *ex* Colonel *-2004* *ex* Aegean Sea *-2004* **Servicios Efega CA** - *Maracaibo* *Venezuela* Official number: AJZL - 27.936	**232** 163 203		**1980 Swiftships Inc — Morgan City LA** Yd No: 259 L reg 35.00 Br ex 8.50 Dght 2.950 Lbp - Br md 8.00 Dpth 3.00 Welded, 1 dk	**(B21A2OS) Platform Supply Ship**	**2 oil engines** driving 2 FP propellers Total Power: 1,132kW (1,540hp) 12.0kn G.M. (Detroit Diesel) 12V-149 2 x Vee 2 Stroke 12 Cy. 146 x 146 each-566kW (770bhp) Detroit Diesel Corporation-Detroit, Mi
9350513 *C4TL2* -	**SEA ANGLER** - **DESS PSV Ltd** Deep Sea Supply Management (Singapore) Pte Ltd *Limassol* *Cyprus* MMSI: 212755000	**2,160** 1,036 3,250	Class: NV	**2007**-07 **Cochin Shipyard Ltd — Ernakulam** Yd No: BY-58 Loa 71.90 (BB) Br ex - Dght 5.830 Lbp 66.80 Br md 16.00 Dpth 7.00 Welded, 1 dk	**(B21A2OS) Platform Supply Ship**	**2 oil engines** redeuction geared to sc. shafts driving 2 CP propellers Total Power: 4,010kW (5,452hp) 11.0kn Bergens KRMB-9 2 x 4 Stroke 9 Cy. 250 x 300 each-2005kW (2726bhp) Rolls Royce Marine AS-Norway AuxGen: 2 x 250kW 440V 60Hz a.c, 2 x 1280kW 440V 60Hz a.c Thrusters: 2 Thwart. CP thruster (f); 2 Thwart. CP thruster (a)
9375381 *3EOB4* -	**SEA APACHE** - **Gulf Marine Far East Pte Ltd** GulfMark Offshore Inc *Panama* *Panama* MMSI: 354674000 Official number: 3385208	**2,943** 883 2,694	Class: AB	**2008**-01 **Keppel Singmarine Pte Ltd — Singapore** Yd No: 311 Loa 76.00 Br ex - Dght 6.200 Lbp 68.40 Br md 17.00 Dpth 7.60 Welded, 1 dk	**(B21B20A) Anchor Handling Tug Supply** Cranes: 1x5t	**4 oil engines** reduction geared to sc. shafts driving 2 CP propellers Total Power: 7,920kW (10,768hp) 14.0kn MaK 6M25 4 x 4 Stroke 6 Cy. 255 x 400 each-1980kW (2692bhp) Caterpillar Motoren GmbH & Co. KG-Germany AuxGen: 3 x 550kW a.c Thrusters: 2 Tunnel thruster (f); 1 Tunnel thruster (a) Fuel: 1091.4 (d.f.)
9047087 *DSPA9* -	**SEA ARIRANG** *ex* Tpc Arirang *-2013* *ex* Ionian Father *-2007* *ex* Cemtex General *-2006* *ex* Gaurav *-2005* *ex* Ispat Gaurav *-2002* *ex* Christitsa *-1996* **Hanaro Shipping Co Ltd** - *Jeju* *South Korea* MMSI: 440720000 Official number: JJR-079266	**38,136** 23,928 71,535 T/cm 65.8	Class: KR (AB)	**1994**-01 **Hitachi Zosen Corp — Maizuru KY** Yd No: 4868 Loa 223.70 (BB) Br ex - Dght 13.461 Lbp 215.57 Br md 32.20 Dpth 18.60 Welded, 1 dk	**(A21A2BC) Bulk Carrier** Grain: 85,108; Bale: 82,337 Compartments: 7 Ho, ER 7 Ha: (16.2 x 13.0)6 (17.9 x 14.6)ER	**1 oil engine** driving 1 FP propeller Total Power: 9,003kW (12,240hp) 14.5kn B&W 6S60MCE 1 x 2 Stroke 6 Cy. 600 x 2292 9003kW (12240bhp) Hitachi Zosen Corp-Japan AuxGen: 3 x 480kW 450V 60Hz a.c

LR/IMO No. / Call sign	Name, former names, owner, manager, port, flag	Tonnage	Class	Build, yard, dimensions	Type, cargo	Machinery
7803229 *9LB2361* -	**SEA ARROW** *ex* Andreas *-2008* *ex* Al Furkan *-2007* *ex* Andreas Boye *-2003* **Vi-Za Sun Ltd** - *Freetown* *Sierra Leone* MMSI: 667002237 Official number: SL102237	**1,167** 593 1,304	Class: UA (BV)	**1979-04 A/S Nordsovaerftet — Ringkobing** Yd No: 136 Loa 69.80 Br ex 10.44 Dght 3.552 Lbp 64.83 Br md 10.41 Dpth 6.02 Welded, 2 dks	**(A31A2GX) General Cargo Ship** Grain: 2,873; Bale: 2,604 TEU 48 C.Ho 32/20' C.Dk 16/20' ref C. Compartments: 2 Ho, ER 2 Ha: 2 (18.5 x 7.4)ER Derricks: 2x10t; Winches: 2 Ice Capable	**1 oil engine** driving 1 CP propeller Total Power: 647kW (880hp) 11.0kn Callesen 8-427-HTKO 1 x 4 Stroke 8 Cy. 270 x 400 647kW (880bhp) Aabenraa Motorfabrik, HeinrichCallesen A/S-Denmark AuxGen: 2 x 80kW 380V 50Hz a.c, 1 x 35kW 380V 50Hz a.c Fuel: 101.5 3.0pd
9535864 *V7BW6* -	**SEA ATHENA** *ex* Fortune Apricot *-2014* **Athena Shipowning Co** Seatankers Management Co Ltd *Majuro* *Marshall Islands* MMSI: 538005487 Official number: 5487	**33,036** 19,270 57,034 T/cm 58.8	Class: AB	**2010-06 Taizhou Sanfu Ship Engineering Co Ltd — Taizhou JS** Yd No: SF060103 Loa 189.99 (BB) Br ex - Dght 12.800 Lbp 185.00 Br md 32.26 Dpth 18.00 Welded, 1 dk	**(A21A2BC) Bulk Carrier** Grain: 71,634; Bale: 68,200 Compartments: 5 Ho, ER 5 Ha: 4 (21.3 x 18.3)ER (18.9 x 18.3) Cranes: 4x30t	**1 oil engine** driving 1 FP propeller Total Power: 9,480kW (12,889hp) 14.2kn MAN-B&W 6S50MC-C 1 x 2 Stroke 6 Cy. 500 x 2000 9480kW (12889bhp) STX Engine Co Ltd-South Korea AuxGen: 3 x 600kW a.c Fuel: 120.0 (d.f.) 2200.0 (r.f.)
9636644 *V7AB8* -	**SEA AUVA** **Sea Hull 2341 Corp** Highlander Tankers AS *Majuro* *Marshall Islands* MMSI: 538004959 Official number: 4959	**23,297** 9,919 37,538 T/cm 45.3	Class: BV	**2013-07 Hyundai Mipo Dockyard Co Ltd — Ulsan** Yd No: 2341 Loa 184.00 (BB) Br ex 27.43 Dght 11.515 Lbp 176.00 Br md 27.40 Dpth 17.20 Welded, 1 dk	**(A12B2TR) Chemical/Products Tanker** Double Hull (13F) Liq: 40,755; Liq (Oil): 40,760 Cargo Heating Coils Compartments: 7 Wing Ta, 5 Wing Ta, 1 Wing Slop Ta, 1 Wing Slop Ta, ER 12 Cargo Pump (s): 10x500m³/hr, 2x300m³/hr Manifold: Bow/CM: 92.6m	**1 oil engine** driving 1 FP propeller Total Power: 7,860kW (10,686hp) 15.0kn MAN-B&W 6S46MC-C8 1 x 2 Stroke 6 Cy. 460 x 1932 7860kW (10686bhp) Hyundai Heavy Industries Co Ltd-South Korea AuxGen: 3 x 740kW 60Hz a.c Thrusters: 1 Tunnel thruster (f) Fuel: 163.0 (d.f.) 1070.0 (r.f.)
9420019 *3FMT9* -	**SEA BADGER** **DESS Cyprus Ltd** Deep Sea Supply Plc *Panama* *Panama* MMSI: 370054000 Official number: 4490113	**1,943** 646 1,575	Class: NV	**2011-06 ABG Shipyard Ltd — Surat** Yd No: 273 Loa 63.40 Br ex - Dght 5.100 Lbp 56.53 Br md 15.80 Dpth 6.80 Welded, 1 dk	**(B21B20A) Anchor Handling Tug Supply**	**2 oil engines** reduction geared to sc. shafts driving 2 CP propellers Total Power: 5,002kW (6,800hp) 10.5kn Yanmar 8N280-EN 2 x 4 Stroke 8 Cy. 280 x 380 each-2501kW (3400bhp) Yanmar Diesel Engine Co Ltd-Japan AuxGen: 3 x 425kW 440V 60Hz a.c Thrusters: 1 Tunnel thruster (f)
9134036 *3FIH8* -	**SEA BAILO** **Xin Zhu Hai Shipping Co Ltd** Qingdao Ocean Shipping Co Ltd (COSCO QINGDAO) SatCom: Inmarsat B 335460210 *Panama* *Panama* MMSI: 354602000 Official number: 2569198CH	**17,172** 9,770 26,611 T/cm 39.4	Class: CC (LR) ✠ Classed LR until 24/12/00	**1998-04 Tianjin Xingang Shipyard — Tianjin** Yd No: 309 Loa 172.00 (BB) Br ex 26.05 Dght 9.520 Lbp 164.00 Br md 26.00 Dpth 13.40 Welded, 1 dk	**(A21A2BC) Bulk Carrier** Double Bottom Entire Compartment Length Grain: 36,782; Bale: 34,984 Compartments: 5 Ho, ER 5 Ha: (13.3 x 13.1)4 (19.5 x 17.1)ER Cranes: 4x30t	**1 oil engine** driving 1 FP propeller Total Power: 6,650kW (9,041hp) 14.0kn B&W 5L50MC 1 x 2 Stroke 5 Cy. 500 x 1620 6650kW (9041bhp) Hudong Shipyard-China AuxGen: 3 x 530kW 450V 60Hz a.c Fuel: 168.4 (d.f.) (Part Heating Coils) 1390.4 (r.f.) 25.5pd
9125815 *3FWU7* -	**SEA BAISEN** **Xin Zhen Hai Shipping Co Ltd** Qingdao Ocean Shipping Co Ltd (COSCO QINGDAO) SatCom: Inmarsat B 335175010 *Panama* *Panama* MMSI: 351750000 Official number: 2559598C	**17,172** 9,770 26,613 T/cm 39.4	Class: CC (LR) ✠ Classed LR until 8/1/10	**1998-01 Tianjin Xingang Shipyard — Tianjin** Yd No: 308 Loa 172.00 (BB) Br ex 26.05 Dght 9.520 Lbp 164.00 Br md 26.00 Dpth 13.40 Welded, 1 dk	**(A21A2BC) Bulk Carrier** Double Bottom Entire Compartment Length Grain: 36,782; Bale: 34,984 Compartments: 5 Ho, ER 5 Ha: (13.3 x 13.1)4 (19.5 x 17.1)ER Cranes: 4x30t	**1 oil engine** driving 1 FP propeller Total Power: 6,650kW (9,041hp) 14.3kn B&W 5L50MC 1 x 2 Stroke 5 Cy. 500 x 1620 6650kW (9041bhp) Hudong Shipyard-China AuxGen: 3 x 530kW 450V 60Hz a.c Boilers: AuxB (Comp) 8.1kgf/cm² (7.9bar) Fuel: 168.4 (d.f.) (Part Heating Coils) 1390.4 (r.f.) 25.5pd
9125803 *3FKS7* -	**SEA BAISI** **Sea Baisi Maritime Inc** Qingdao Ocean Shipping Co Ltd (COSCO QINGDAO) SatCom: Inmarsat B 335128810 *Panama* *Panama* MMSI: 351288000 Official number: 2558998C	**17,172** 9,770 26,637 T/cm 39.4	Class: CC (LR) ✠ Classed LR until 20/8/11	**1997-08 Tianjin Xingang Shipyard — Tianjin** Yd No: 307 Loa 172.00 (BB) Br ex 26.05 Dght 9.520 Lbp 164.00 Br md 26.00 Dpth 13.40 Welded, 1 dk	**(A21A2BC) Bulk Carrier** Grain: 36,782; Bale: 34,984 Compartments: 5 Ho, ER 5 Ha: (13.3 x 13.1)4 (19.5 x 17.1)ER Cranes: 4x30t	**1 oil engine** driving 1 FP propeller Total Power: 6,650kW (9,041hp) 14.2kn B&W 5L50MC 1 x 2 Stroke 5 Cy. 500 x 1620 6650kW (9041bhp) Hudong Shipyard-China AuxGen: 3 x 530kW 450V 60Hz a.c Boilers: AuxB (Comp) 8.0kgf/cm² (7.8bar)
8109981 - -	**SEA BARON** *ex* Sea Bridge *-1994* **PT Putra Tanjungpura** -	**10,313** 3,093 10,377	Class: (NK)	**1982-09 Kawasaki Heavy Industries Ltd — Kobe HG** Yd No: 1341 Loa 150.00 (BB) Br ex 32.24 Dght 5.025 Lbp 143.01 Br md 32.20 Dpth 8.01 Welded, 1 dk	**(A38C2GH) Heavy Load Carrier** Stern door/ramp Len: 7.00 Wid: 20.00 Swl: - Grain: 5,175; Bale: 4,760 Compartments: 1 Ho, ER 2 Ha: (12.3 x 4.4) (12.3 x 6.0)ER Cranes: 1x430t,2x12.5t	**2 oil engines** with flexible couplings & sr gearedto sc. shafts driving 2 CP propellers Total Power: 5,736kW (7,798hp) 13.9kn Pielstick 6PC2-5L-400 2 x 4 Stroke 6 Cy. 400 x 460 each-2868kW (3899bhp) Nippon Kokan KK (NKK Corp)-Japan AuxGen: 2 x 520kW Thrusters: 1 Thwart. CP thruster (f) Fuel: 303.5 (d.f.) (Heating Coils) 1427.0 (r.f.) 18.0pd
8206923 - -	**SEA BASS** *ex* TPS 226 *-2010* *ex* Halliburton 226 *-2002* **Fal Engineering Services Ltd** - *Port of Spain* *Trinidad & Tobago*	**298** 89 -	Class: (AB)	**1982-08 Rockport Yacht & Supply Co. (RYSCO) — Rockport, Tx** Yd No: 506 Loa 39.81 Br ex 10.09 Dght - Lbp 37.95 Br md 10.06 Dpth 2.16 Welded, 1 dk	**(B22A20R) Offshore Support Vessel**	**2 oil engines** reverse reduction geared to sc. shafts driving 2 FP propellers Total Power: 626kW (852hp) 10.0kn Caterpillar 3412TA 2 x Vee 4 Stroke 12 Cy. 137 x 152 each-313kW (426bhp) Caterpillar Tractor Co-USA AuxGen: 2 x 75kW
9387190 *5BAL2* -	**SEA BASS** **DESS PSV Ltd** Deep Sea Supply Navegacao Maritima Ltda SatCom: Inmarsat C 421200059 *Limassol* *Cyprus* MMSI: 212870000 Official number: 9387190	**2,160** 1,036 3,250	Class: NV	**2008-01 Cochin Shipyard Ltd — Ernakulam** Yd No: BY-60 Loa 71.90 Br ex 16.03 Dght 5.830 Lbp 66.80 Br md 16.00 Dpth 7.01 Welded, 1 dk	**(B21A20S) Platform Supply Ship**	**2 oil engines** reduction geared to sc. shafts driving 2 CP propellers Total Power: 4,010kW (5,452hp) 11.0kn Bergens KRMB-9 2 x 4 Stroke 9 Cy. 250 x 300 each-2005kW (2726bhp) Rolls Royce Marine AS-Norway AuxGen: 2 x 250kW 440V 60Hz a.c, 2 x 1280kW 440V 60Hz a.c Thrusters: 2 Thwart. CP thruster (f); 1 Thwart. CP thruster (a) Fuel: 850.0 (d.f.) 17.0pd
9670195 *9VLD3* -	**SEA BASS** **An Yi Shipping Pte Ltd** Ocean Tankers (Pte) Ltd *Singapore* *Singapore* MMSI: 563022820	**295** 89 89	Class: BV	**2012-11 Wuxi Hongqi Shipyard Co Ltd — Wuxi JS** Yd No: ATE-011-P216 Loa 30.00 Br ex - Dght 3.600 Lbp 23.50 Br md 9.50 Dpth 4.70 Welded, 1 dk	**(B32A2ST) Tug**	**2 oil engines** reduction geared to sc. shafts driving 2 Z propellers Total Power: 2,942kW (4,000hp) Niigata 6L26HLX 2 x 4 Stroke 6 Cy. 260 x 350 each-1471kW (2000bhp) Niigata Engineering Co Ltd-Japan AuxGen: 2 x 96kW 50Hz a.c Fuel: 140.0 (d.f.)
9122277 *YDA4875* -	**SEA BASSET** **PT Salam Bahagia** PT Wintermar *Jakarta* *Indonesia* MMSI: 525300219	**210** 63 110	Class: NK (BV)	**1995-09 Matsuura Tekko Zosen K.K. — Osakikamijima** Yd No: 389 Loa 24.00 Br ex 9.10 Dght 3.712 Lbp 22.57 Br md 8.50 Dpth 4.70 Welded, 1 dk	**(B32A2ST) Tug**	**2 oil engines** gearing integral to driving 2 Z propellers Total Power: 2,206kW (3,000hp) 12.6kn Niigata 6L25CXE 2 x 4 Stroke 6 Cy. 250 x 320 each-1103kW (1500bhp) Niigata Engineering Co Ltd-Japan AuxGen: 1 x 100kW 415V 50Hz a.c Fuel: 57.0 (d.f.) 4.5pd
9439539 *VRER9* -	**SEA BAY** **Golden Hope Inc** Teekay Shipping Ltd SatCom: Inmarsat C 447701542 *Hong Kong* *Hong Kong* MMSI: 477170700 Official number: HK-2295	**60,193** 33,762 108,760 T/cm 91.3	Class: AB	**2009-04 Zhoushan Jinhaiwan Shipyard Co Ltd — Daishan County ZJ** Yd No: J0001 Loa 243.00 (BB) Br ex 42.03 Dght 15.400 Lbp 233.00 Br md 42.00 Dpth 22.00 Welded, 1 dk	**(A13B2TP) Products Tanker** Double Hull (13F) Liq: 123,020; Liq (Oil): 123,020 Cargo Heating Coils Compartments: 12 Wing Ta, 2 Wing Slop Ta, ER 3 Cargo Pump (s): 3x2500m³/hr Manifold: Bow/CM: 122.2m	**1 oil engine** driving 1 FP propeller Total Power: 13,570kW (18,450hp) 15.0kn MAN-B&W 7S60MC 1 x 2 Stroke 7 Cy. 600 x 2292 13570kW (18450bhp) AuxGen: 3 x 680kW a.c Fuel: 145.0 (d.f.) 3000.0 (r.f.)
8802583 *VTPT* -	**SEA BAY II** **Sea Bay Venture Pvt Ltd** - *Kochi* *India* Official number: 2327	*116* 35 76	Class: (IR)	**1989-06 Goa Shipyard Ltd. — Goa** Yd No: 1146 Loa 23.43 Br ex 6.62 Dght 2.758 Lbp 21.00 Br md 6.51 Dpth 3.41 Welded, 1 dk	**(B11B2FV) Fishing Vessel** Ins: 80	**1 oil engine** with clutches & sr reverse geared to sc. shaft driving 1 FP propeller Total Power: 294kW (400hp) Cummins KT-1150-M 1 x 4 Stroke 6 Cy. 159 x 159 294kW (400bhp) Kirloskar Cummins Ltd-India AuxGen: 2 x 88kW 415V 50Hz a.c Fuel: 45.0 (d.f.)

7017521 *HP4997* -
SEA BEACH
ex Inagua Beach *-1987*
Cross Caribbean Services Ltd
-
SatCom: Inmarsat C 435602920
Panama *Panama*
MMSI: 356029000
Official number: 14235PEXT5
1,436 430 2,035 Class: (AB)
1970-09 Levingston SB. Co. — Orange, Tx Yd No: 688
Loa 81.51 Br ex 15.68 Dght 3.490
Lbp 77.63 Br md 15.55 Dpth 4.88
Welded, 1 dk
(A35D2RL) Landing Craft
Bow door/ramp
3 oil engines reverse reduction geared to sc. shafts driving 3 FP propellers
Total Power: 1,899kW (2,583hp) 12.0kn
Caterpillar D398TA
3 x Vee 4 Stroke 12 Cy. 159 x 203 each-633kW (861bhp)
Caterpillar Tractor Co-USA
AuxGen: 1 x 250kW 460V 60Hz a.c, 2 x 135kW 460V 60Hz a.c
Fuel: 713.5 (d.f.) 9.0pd

9185932 *C4RR2* -
SEA BEAR
ex Amadon Tide *-2006* *ex* Torm Osprey *-2001*
SFL Sea Bear Ltd
Deep Sea Supply Management (Singapore) Pte Ltd
Limassol *Cyprus*
MMSI: 209717000
Official number: 9185932
2,590 777 2,854 Class: AB (LR)
1999-01 Kvaerner Kleven AS — Ulsteinvik Yd No: 271
Loa 73.50 Br ex 16.80 Dght 6.900
Lbp 66.60 Br md 16.40 Dpth 8.00
Welded, 1 dk
(B21B20A) Anchor Handling Tug Supply
Passengers: cabins: 12
2 oil engines with clutches, flexible couplings & sr geared to sc. shafts driving 2 CP propellers
Total Power: 11,040kW (15,010hp) 15.0kn
Wartsila 12V32
2 x Vee 4 Stroke 12 Cy. 320 x 350 each-5520kW (7505bhp)
Wartsila NSD Finland Oy-Finland
AuxGen: 2 x 1800kW 450V 60Hz a.c, 2 x 300kW 450V 60Hz a.c
Thrusters: 1 Thwart. CP thruster (f); 1 Retract. directional thruster (f); 1 Thwart. CP thruster (a)
Fuel: 940.0 (d.f.) 22.0pd

7513379 *WCY2047* -
SEA BEE
Omega Protein Inc
-
Moss Point, MS *United States of America*
Official number: 549886
497 338 -
1973 Patterson Shipyard Inc. — Patterson, La
Loa 49.44 Br ex 9.76 Dght -
Lbp - Br md - Dpth 3.38
Welded, 1 dk
(B11A2FT) Trawler
1 oil engine driving 1 FP propeller
Total Power: 1,324kW (1,800hp)

8847272 - -
SEA BELL-3
ex Yug-03 *-1993*
Sea Bell JSC (A/O 'Morskoy Kolokol')
-
104 31 58 Class: (RS)
1991-08 Rybinskaya Sudoverf — Rybinsk Yd No: 18
Loa 26.50 Br ex 6.50 Dght 2.320
Lbp 23.61 Br md - Dpth 3.05
Welded, 1 dk
(B11A2FS) Stern Trawler
1 oil engine driving 1 FP propeller
Total Power: 220kW (299hp) 9.5kn
S.K.L. 6NVD26A-2
1 x 4 Stroke 6 Cy. 180 x 260 220kW (299bhp)
SKL Motoren u. Systemtechnik AG-Magdeburg
AuxGen: 2 x 25kW a.c
Fuel: 9.0 (d.f.)

8861943 - -
SEA BELL-6
ex Yug-04 *-1993*
Sea Bell JSC (A/O 'Morskoy Kolokol')
-
104 31 58 Class: (RS)
1991-10 Rybinskaya Sudoverf — Rybinsk Yd No: 19
Loa 26.50 Br ex 6.50 Dght 2.320
Lbp 23.61 Br md - Dpth 3.05
Welded
(B11A2FS) Stern Trawler
1 oil engine driving 1 FP propeller
Total Power: 220kW (299hp) 9.5kn
S.K.L. 6NVD26A-2
1 x 4 Stroke 6 Cy. 180 x 260 220kW (299bhp)
SKL Motoren u. Systemtechnik AG-Magdeburg
AuxGen: 2 x 25kW a.c
Fuel: 9.0 (d.f.)

8835956 - -
SEA BELL-12
ex Ariel *-1993*
Sea Bell JSC (A/O 'Morskoy Kolokol')
-
104 31 58 Class: (RS)
1990-10 Rybinskaya Sudoverf — Rybinsk Yd No: 15
Loa 26.50 Br ex 6.50 Dght 2.321
Lbp 23.61 Br md - Dpth 3.05
Welded
(B11A2FS) Stern Trawler
1 oil engine driving 1 FP propeller
Total Power: 220kW (299hp) 9.5kn
S.K.L. 6NVD26A-2
1 x 4 Stroke 6 Cy. 180 x 260 220kW (299bhp)
VEB Schwermaschinenbau "KarlLiebknecht" (SKL)-Magdeburg

8945206 - -
SEA BIRD
ex Jasmine *-2006*
Alvin A Que
-
Zamboanga *Philippines*
Official number: ZAM2D00159
188 117 -
1993 at Zamboanga
L reg 36.00 Br ex - Dght -
Lbp - Br md - Dpth -
Welded, 1 dk
(A31A2GX) General Cargo Ship
1 oil engine driving 1 FP propeller
Total Power: 331kW (450hp)
Niigata
1 x 4 Stroke 331kW (450bhp)
Niigata Engineering Co Ltd-Japan

6909026 *BYPO* -
SEA BIRD
ex Paulmy Star *-1975* *ex* Ocean Pioneer *-1975*
ex Chuyo Maru No. 16 *-1975*
Ming Tai Marine Products Co Ltd
-
Kaohsiung *Chinese Taipei*
Official number: 3497
591 312 436 Class: (CR)
1968 Hayashikane Shipbuilding & Engineering Co Ltd — Yokosuka KN Yd No: 675
Loa 50.20 Br ex 8.82 Dght 3.501
Lbp 44.66 Br md 8.81 Dpth 5.90
Welded, 2 dks
(B11B2FV) Fishing Vessel
Ins: 437
Compartments: 3 Ho, ER
3 Ha: ER
Derricks: 2x2t,2x1.5t; Winches: 4
1 oil engine driving 1 CP propeller
Total Power: 1,324kW (1,800hp) 12.0kn
Akasaka 6DH38SS
1 x 4 Stroke 6 Cy. 380 x 560 1324kW (1800bhp)
Akasaka Tekkosho KK (Akasaka DieselLtd)-Japan
AuxGen: 2 x 100kW 445V a.c

8202941 *5VCF9* -
SEA BIRD
ex Necdet-K *-2013* *ex* Ayder *-1993*
ex Kenan Kolotoglu *-1988*
Lovely Corp
GMZ Ship Management Co SA
Lome *Togo*
MMSI: 671389000
Official number: TG-00466L
4,337 2,851 7,650 Class: IV (TL) (AB) (BV)
1985-01 Kok Tersanecilik A.S. — Tuzla Yd No: 2
Loa 106.36 (BB) Br ex - Dght 7.300
Lbp 96.22 Br md 17.01 Dpth 9.22
Welded, 1 dk
(A31A2GX) General Cargo Ship
Grain: 9,996; Bale: 8,835
1 oil engine sr geared to sc. shaft driving 1 FP propeller
Total Power: 3,310kW (4,500hp) 13.0kn
MAN 6L40/45
1 x 4 Stroke 6 Cy. 400 x 450 3310kW (4500bhp)
MAN B&W Diesel AG-Augsburg
AuxGen: 2 x 180kW a.c, 1 x 80kW a.c

8644981 *WCW9687* -
SEA BIRD
ex Ghost *-1988* *ex* FS-289 *-1988*
Sea Bird Ventures LLC
-
Seattle, WA *United States of America*
MMSI: 368340000
Official number: 1047746
603 180 -
1944-11 Wheeler's Shipyard — New York, NY Yd No: 103
L reg 50.68 Br ex - Dght -
Lbp - Br md 9.75 Dpth 4.51
Welded, 1 dk
(B11B2FV) Fishing Vessel
1 oil engine driving 1 Propeller

8605480 *9LD2569* -
SEA BIRD
ex Eda *-2014* *ex* Meganisi *-2012* *ex* Ash *-2005*
ex Jackie Moon *-2005* *ex* Medwave *-2001*
ex Truso *-1996*
Ghinwa Shipping Inc
-
Freetown *Sierra Leone*
MMSI: 667069000
1,616 699 2,264 Class: IC (RS) (RI) (GL)
1986-06 Schiffs. Hugo Peters Wewelsfleth Peters & Co. GmbH — Wewelsfleth Yd No: 623
Loa 82.45 Br ex 11.36 Dght 4.190
Lbp 76.82 Br md 11.31 Dpth 5.41
Welded, 2 dks
(A31A2GX) General Cargo Ship
Grain: 2,953; Bale: 2,945
TEU 76 C. 76/20' (40')
Compartments: 1 Ho, ER
1 Ha: (49.8 x 9.0)ER
Ice Capable
1 oil engine with clutches, flexible couplings & sr reverse geared to sc. shaft driving 1 FP propeller
Total Power: 599kW (814hp) 10.5kn
MWM TBD440-6K
1 x 4 Stroke 6 Cy. 230 x 270 599kW (814bhp)
Motoren Werke Mannheim AG (MWM)-West Germany
AuxGen: 1 x 190kW 380V 50Hz a.c, 2 x 82kW 380V 50Hz a.c
Thrusters: 1 Thwart. FP thruster (f)
Fuel: 96.0 (d.f.) 3.0pd

7616016 *5IM350* -
SEA BIRD 3
ex Saaba Vii *-2013* *ex* Pacific Hawk *-2013*
ex Hawk Aki *-1980* *ex* Pacific Hawk 1 *-1978*
Sea Bird International Shipping Inc
-
Zanzibar *Tanzania (Zanzibar)*
MMSI: 677025000
Official number: 300105
248 74 184 Class: (AB) (NK)
1977-12 Imamura Zosen — Kure Yd No: 216
Loa 32.52 Br ex 8.54 Dght 3.309
Lbp 28.02 Br md 8.51 Dpth 3.61
Welded, 1 dk
(B32A2ST) Tug
2 oil engines reverse reduction geared to sc. shafts driving 2 FP propellers
Total Power: 1,104kW (1,500hp) 11.5kn
Yanmar 6MHL-UT
2 x 4 Stroke 6 Cy. 200 x 240 each-552kW (750bhp)
Yanmar Diesel Engine Co Ltd-Japan
AuxGen: 2 x 112kW 440V 60Hz a.c
Fuel: 107.0 (d.f.) 4.5pd

5183340 - -
SEA BIRD No. 82
ex Seisho Maru No. 7 *-1978*
ex Kasuga Maru No. 38 *-1978*
-
-
344 185 - Class: (KR)
1961-12 KK Kanasashi Zosen — Shizuoka SZ Yd No: 437
L reg 44.29 Br ex 7.83 Dght 3.175
Lbp 43.69 Br md 7.80 Dpth 3.81
Welded, 1 dk
(B11B2FV) Fishing Vessel
Ins: 555
4 Ha: 4 (1.6 x 1.4)ER
1 oil engine driving 1 FP propeller
Total Power: 736kW (1,001hp) 11.5kn
Akasaka SR6SS
1 x 4 Stroke 6 Cy. 350 x 500 736kW (1001bhp)
Akasaka Tekkosho KK (Akasaka DieselLtd)-Japan
AuxGen: 2 x 104kW 225V a.c
Fuel: 197.0

7048441 - -
SEA BIRD No. 83
ex Daisho Maru No. 8 *-1982*
ex Sanei Maru No. 28 *-1978*
-
-
164 78 -
1970 Uchida Zosen — Ise Yd No: 694
Loa - Br ex 6.84 Dght -
Lbp 33.74 Br md 6.81 Dpth 3.00
Riveted\Welded, 1 dk
(B11B2FV) Fishing Vessel
1 oil engine driving 1 FP propeller
Total Power: 515kW (700hp)
Hanshin 6L26AGSH
1 x 4 Stroke 6 Cy. 260 x 400 515kW (700bhp)
Hanshin Nainenki Kogyo-Japan

8331912 *3EHX2* -
SEA BIRD No. 87
ex Hamazen Maru No. 55 *-1982*
Yu Sung Co SA
Kaigai Gyogyo KK (Oversea Fisheries Corp)
Panama *Panama*
Official number: 10173YJ
289 155 -
1962 in Japan
Loa 46.16 Br ex 7.57 Dght -
Lbp 40.54 Br md 7.51 Dpth 3.61
Welded, 1 dk
(A31A2GX) General Cargo Ship
1 oil engine driving 1 FP propeller

7736270 *WSN8011* -	**SEA BLAZER** - **Vessel Conversions LLC** - *Seattle, WA* *United States of America* Official number: 588240	*127* 87 -		**1977 Desco Marine — Saint Augustine, Fl** Yd No: 231-F L reg 20.97 Br ex - Dght - Lbp - Br md 6.74 Dpth 3.81 Bonded, 1 dk	**(B11B2FV) Fishing Vessel** Hull Material: Reinforced Plastic	**1 oil engine** driving 1 FP propeller Total Power: 268kW (364hp)
8915108 *9V6441* -	**SEA BLESS** *ex* Zen *-2004* *ex* Falcon Jaya *-2003* *ex* Manpo Maru *-2003* **Nautical Bunkering (S) Pte Ltd** - *Singapore* *Singapore* MMSI: 563004890 Official number: 390464	**318** 95 525	Class: LR **100A1** SS 02/2014 Double Hull oil tanker carriage of oils with a FP exceeding 60 degree C for Singapore Port and 30 miles seawards service **LMC** Eq.Ltr: F; Cable: 275.0/28.0 U2	**1990-05 Murakami Hide Zosen K.K. — Imabari** Yd No: 311 Loa 47.42 (BB) Br ex 8.16 Dght 3.311 Lbp 44.00 Br md 8.00 Dpth 3.50 Welded, 1 dk	**(A13B2TU) Tanker (unspecified)** Double Hull	**1 oil engine** driving 1 FP propeller Total Power: 588kW (799hp) 10.3kn Yanmar MF26-HT 1 x 4 Stroke 6 Cy. 260 x 500 588kW (799bhp) Yanmar Diesel Engine Co Ltd-Japan AuxGen: 1 x 48kW 225V 60Hz a.c, 1 x 80kW 225V 60Hz a.c
8739047 *MNZL5* -	**SEA BLUEZ** - **CaddickLtd** - *Douglas* *Isle of Man (British)* MMSI: 232873000 Official number: 737847	**299** 89 -	Class: AB	**2006-08 Azimut-Benetti SpA — Viareggio** Yd No: BC103 Loa 35.80 Br ex - Dght 2.220 Lbp 30.80 Br md 7.86 Dpth 3.93 Bonded, 1 dk	**(X11A2YP) Yacht** Hull Material: Reinforced Plastic	**2 oil engines** reverse reduction geared to sc. shafts driving 2 Z propellers Total Power: 2,238kW (3,042hp) 20.0kn M.T.U. 12V2000M91 2 x Vee 4 Stroke 12 Cy. 130 x 150 each-1119kW (1521bhp) MTU Friedrichshafen GmbH-Friedrichshafen AuxGen: 2 x 80kW a.c Fuel: 38.0 (d.f.)
9539444 *3FDN7* -	**SEA BONANZA** *launched as* White Sanko *-2012* **White Panama SA** The Sanko Steamship Co Ltd (Sanko Kisen KK) SatCom: Inmarsat C 437346510 *Panama* *Panama* MMSI: 373465000 Official number: 4395012	**21,213** 11,615 33,628	Class: NK	**2012-06 Shin Kurushima Dockyard Co. Ltd. — Onishi** Yd No: 5618 Loa 179.99 Br ex - Dght 10.101 Lbp 172.00 Br md 28.20 Dpth 14.30 Welded, 1 dk	**(A21A2BC) Bulk Carrier** Double Hull Grain: 44,039; Bale: 43,164 Compartments: 5 Ho, ER 5 Ha: 3 (20.8 x 23.8) (19.2 x 23.8)ER (16.8 x 17.2) Cranes: 4x30t	**1 oil engine** driving 1 FP propeller Total Power: 6,250kW (8,498hp) 14.2kn Mitsubishi 6UEC45LSE 1 x 2 Stroke 6 Cy. 450 x 1840 6250kW (8498bhp) Kobe Hatsudoki KK-Japan Fuel: 1620.0
8723737 - -	**SEA BORN** *ex* Biruza *-1996* *ex* Birzai *-1996* *ex* Birzhay *-1992* **Mar Del Plata Shipping Ltd** -	**359** 107 129	Class: (RS)	**1986-12 Sudostroitelnyy Zavod "Avangard" — Petrozavodsk** Yd No: 606 Loa 35.72 Br ex 8.92 Dght 3.490 Lbp 31.00 Br md - Dpth 6.07 Welded, 2 dks	**(B11A2FS) Stern Trawler** Ice Capable	**1 oil engine** driving 1 FP propeller Total Power: 589kW (801hp) 10.9kn S.K.L. 6NVD48A-2U 1 x 4 Stroke 6 Cy. 320 x 480 589kW (801bhp) VEB Schwermaschinenbau "KarlLiebknecht" (SKL)-Magdeburg AuxGen: 2 x 200kW a.c
8996188 *WDE5895* -	**SEA BOUNTY** *ex* Yung Da Fa No. 168 *-2008* **Sea Bounty LLC** Sea Global Fisheries LLC *Pago Pago, AS* *United States of America* MMSI: 367084000 Official number: 1214841	**1,415** 515 1,490		**2003-09 Fong Kuo Shipbuilding Co Ltd — Kaohsiung** Yd No: 396 Loa 72.37 Br ex - Dght 5.440 Lbp 61.85 Br md 12.20 Dpth 7.20 Welded, 1 dk	**(B11B2FV) Fishing Vessel**	**1 oil engine** geared to sc. shaft driving 1 Propeller Total Power: 2,354kW (3,200hp) Daihatsu 8DLM-32 1 x 4 Stroke 8 Cy. 320 x 400 2354kW (3200bhp) Daihatsu Diesel Manufacturing Co Lt-Japan
1008255 *ZCIT2* -	**SEA BOWLD** - **Sea Bowld Marine Group** - *George Town* *Cayman Islands (British)* MMSI: 319934000 Official number: 736021	**498** 87 110	Class: GL	**2004-04 Oceanfast Pty Ltd — Fremantle WA** Yd No: 78 Loa 53.00 Br ex 8.87 Dght 2.650 Lbp 48.68 Br md 8.65 Dpth 4.90 Welded, 1 dk	**(X11A2YP) Yacht** Hull Material: Aluminium Alloy	**2 oil engines** geared to sc. shafts driving 2 FP propellers Total Power: 5,500kW (7,478hp) M.T.U. 16V4000M90 2 x Vee 4 Stroke 16 Cy. 165 x 190 each-2750kW (3739bhp) MTU Friedrichshafen GmbH-Friedrichshafen
9122265 - -	**SEA BOXER** - **PSA Marine Pte Ltd** Jurong Marine Services Pte Ltd *Saigon* *Vietnam*	**210** 63 109	Class: (BV)	**1995-08 Matsuura Tekko Zosen K.K. — Osakikamijima** Yd No: 388 Loa 24.00 Br ex 9.10 Dght 3.712 Lbp 19.50 Br md 8.50 Dpth 4.70 Welded, 1 dk	**(B32A2ST) Tug**	**2 oil engines** gearing integral to driving 2 Z propellers Total Power: 2,206kW (3,000hp) 12.7kn Niigata 6L25CXE 2 x 4 Stroke 6 Cy. 250 x 320 each-1103kW (1500bhp) Niigata Engineering Co Ltd-Japan AuxGen: 1 x 100kW 415V 50Hz a.c Fuel: 58.0 (d.f.) 4.5pd
9573440 *PYWQ* -	**SEA BRASIL** - **Deep Sea Supply Navegacao Maritima Ltda** Deep Sea Supply Plc *Rio de Janeiro* *Brazil* MMSI: 710011210	**3,938** 1,258 4,700	Class: NV	**2012-09 STX OSV Niteroi SA — Niteroi** Yd No: PRO-28 Loa 87.90 (BB) Br ex 19.02 Dght 6.600 Lbp 79.38 Br md 19.00 Dpth 8.00 Welded, 1 dk	**(B21A20S) Platform Supply Ship**	**4 diesel electric oil engines** driving 4 gen. Connecting to 2 elec. motors driving 2 Azimuth electric drive units Total Power: 7,060kW (9,600hp) 11.0kn Caterpillar 3512C 4 x Vee 4 Stroke 12 Cy. 170 x 215 each-1765kW (2400bhp) Caterpillar Inc-USA Thrusters: 2 Tunnel thruster (f)
9279551 *V7UC5* -	**SEA BRAVE** *ex* POS Brave *-2010* **Sea Brave Shipping & Trading SA** Genimar Shipping & Trading SA *Majuro* *Marshall Islands* MMSI: 538003930 Official number: 3930	**17,679** 10,133 28,657	Class: NK	**2004-03 Shin Kochi Jyuko K.K. — Kochi** Yd No: 7167 Loa 176.63 (BB) Br ex 26.00 Dght 9.633 Lbp 169.40 Br md 26.00 Dpth 13.60 Welded, 1 dk	**(A21A2BC) Bulk Carrier** Grain: 39,052; Bale: 37,976 Compartments: 5 Ho, ER 5 Ha: 4 (19.5 x 17.8)ER (17.9 x 12.8) Cranes: 4x30.8t	**1 oil engine** driving 1 FP propeller Total Power: 5,900kW (8,022hp) 14.1kn Mitsubishi 5UEC52LA 1 x 2 Stroke 5 Cy. 520 x 1600 5900kW (8022bhp) Kobe Hatsudoki KK-Japan AuxGen: 3 x 364kW a.c Fuel: 93.0 (d.f.) 1024.0 (r.f.)
9487029 *PHSB* -	**SEA BRAVO** - **Sea Bravo BV** Seacontractors BV *Vlissingen* *Netherlands* MMSI: 244468000 Official number: 52431	**327** 98 -	Class: BV	**2008-11 Damen Shipyards Kozle Sp z oo — Kedzierzyn-Kozle (Hull)** Yd No: 1123 **2008-11 B.V. Scheepswerf Damen Hardinxveld — Hardinxveld-Giessendam** Yd No: 1595 Loa 32.08 Br ex - Dght 3.400 Lbp 31.38 Br md 9.10 Dpth 4.40 Welded, 1 dk	**(B32A2ST) Tug** Passengers: cabins: 5; berths: 7 Cranes: 1x5.3t	**2 oil engines** reduction geared to sc. shafts driving 2 FP propellers Total Power: 2,460kW (3,344hp) Caterpillar 3512B-TA 2 x Vee 4 Stroke 12 Cy. 170 x 190 each-1230kW (1672bhp) Caterpillar Inc-USA AuxGen: 2 x 96kW 400/230V 50Hz a.c Thrusters: 1 Thwart. FP thruster (f) Fuel: 202.0
9436654 *2BMD9* -	**SEA BREEZE** - **Blenheim Shipping UK Ltd** - SatCom: Inmarsat C 423591634 *Douglas* *Isle of Man (British)* MMSI: 235067366 Official number: 740833	**51,130** 30,678 91,913	Class: LR ✠**100A1** SS 05/2009 bulk carrier CSR BC-A GRAB (20) Nos. 2, 4 & 6 holds may be empty ESP **ShipRight** (CM) *IWS LI ✠ **LMC** **UMS** Eq.Ltr: S†; Cable: 687.5/87.0 U3 (a)	**2009-05 Sungdong Shipbuilding & Marine Engineering Co Ltd — Tongyeong** Yd No: 1038 Loa 229.50 (BB) Br ex 37.12 Dght 14.700 Lbp 221.60 Br md 36.92 Dpth 20.50 Welded, 1 dk	**(A21A2BC) Bulk Carrier** Grain: 109,085; Bale: 103,631 Compartments: 7 Ho, ER 7 Ha: ER	**1 oil engine** driving 1 FP propeller Total Power: 11,060kW (15,037hp) 13.8kn MAN-B&W 7S50MC-C 1 x 2 Stroke 7 Cy. 500 x 2000 11060kW (15037bhp) Hyundai Heavy Industries Co Ltd-South Korea AuxGen: 3 x 600kW 450V 60Hz a.c Boilers: AuxB (Comp) 7.0kgf/cm² (6.9bar)
9672923 *OUWS2* -	**SEA BREEZE** *ex* Fob Swath 2 *-2012* **FOB Swath AS** A2SEA A/S *Fredericia* *Denmark (DIS)* MMSI: 219459000 Official number: A552	**244** 73 65	Class: NV	**2012-12 Danish Yachts A/S — Skagen** Yd No: 119 Loa 25.70 (BB) Br ex - Dght 2.490 Lbp 23.55 Br md 10.60 Dpth 5.37 Bonded, 1 dk	**(B21A20C) Crew/Supply Vessel** Hull Material: Carbon Fibre Sandwich Passengers: unberthed: 24	**2 oil engines** reduction geared to sc. shafts driving 2 CP propellers Total Power: 1,800kW (2,448hp) 22.0kn M.T.U. 10V2000M72 1 x Vee 4 Stroke 10 Cy. 135 x 156 900kW (1224bhp) MTU Friedrichshafen GmbH-Friedrichshafen Thrusters: 2 Tunnel thruster (f); 2 Tunnel thruster (a)
9668568 - -	**SEA BREEZE** - **Mohamed Ali Ali Amer** Sea Breeze for Marine & Petroleum Services *Alexandria* *Egypt* Official number: 9718	**367** 197 -	Class: HR (Class contemplated)	**2012-04 El Maadawy Workshop — Rashid** Yd No: 173 Loa 32.40 Br ex - Dght - Lbp 30.35 Br md 9.00 Dpth - Welded, 1 dk	**(B21A20C) Crew/Supply Vessel**	**2 oil engines** reduction geared to sc. shafts driving 2 Propellers Total Power: 2,060kW (2,800hp) General Motors 2 x each-1030kW (1400bhp) General Motors Corp-USA

IMO / Call sign	Name / Owner / Manager / Port	Tonnage	Class	Builder / Dimensions	Type / Cargo	Machinery
9086423 - -	**SEA BREEZE** - -	200 28 50		**1994-09 SBF Shipbuilders (1977) Pty Ltd — Fremantle WA** Yd No: 932 Loa 19.90 Br ex 7.00 Dght - Lbp - Br md - Dpth - Welded, 1 dk	**(A37B2PS) Passenger Ship** Hull Material: Aluminium Alloy Passengers: unberthed: 100	**2 oil engines** with flexible couplings & reverse reduction geared to sc. shafts driving 2 FP propellers Total Power: 1,100kW (1,496hp) 25.0kn M.T.U. 12V183TE62 2 x Vee 4 Stroke 12 Cy. 128 x 142 each-550kW (748bhp) MTU Friedrichshafen GmbH-Friedrichshafen
9057850 *JG5136* -	**SEA BREEZE** - - *Kagoshima, Kagoshima* *Japan* Official number: 133790	*197* - -		**1992-07 Kanagawa Zosen — Kobe** Yd No: 376 L reg 31.20 Br ex - Dght 3.000 Lbp 30.00 Br md 9.00 Dpth 4.00 Welded, 1 dk	**(B32A2ST) Tug**	**2 oil engines** Geared Integral to driving 2 Z propellers Total Power: 2,354kW (3,200hp) Niigata 6L25HX 2 x 4 Stroke 6 Cy. 250 x 350 each-1177kW (1600bhp) Niigata Engineering Co Ltd-Japan
8906250 *8PTW* -	**SEA BREEZE** *ex* Sea Hawk *-2013* *ex* Christa K *-2006* *ex* Mindful *-1999* *launched as* Christian R *-1989* **Camrose Shipping Ltd** Shipmar Co Ltd SatCom: Inmarsat C 431424110 *Bridgetown* *Barbados* MMSI: 314241000 Official number: 733496	1,959 963 3,015	Class: (GL) (NV) **100A1** SS 12/2009 strengthened for heavy cargoes **LMC** **UMS** Cable: 412.5/34.0 U2 (a)	**1989-12 Liesbosch Staal B.V. — Nieuwegein** (Hull) Yd No: 195 **1989-12 B.V. Scheepswerf Damen — Gorinchem** Yd No: 8243 Loa 87.70 (BB) Br ex - Dght 4.607 Lbp 84.39 Br md 12.50 Dpth 6.50 Welded, 1 dk	**(A31A2GX) General Cargo Ship** Grain: 3,998 TEU 158 C.Ho 78/20' C.Dk 80/20' Compartments: 1 Ho, ER 1 Ha: (62.7 x 10.1)ER Ice Capable	**1 oil engine** with flexible couplings & sr reverse geared to sc. shaft driving 1 FP propeller Total Power: 600kW (816hp) 11.0kn Deutz SBV6M628 1 x 4 Stroke 6 Cy. 240 x 280 600kW (816bhp) Kloeckner Humboldt Deutz AG-West Germany AuxGen: 2 x 80kW 380V 50Hz a.c Thrusters: 1 Thwart. FP thruster (f)
7501871 - -	**SEA BREEZE** *ex* Arados H *-2012* *ex* Samali S *-2005* *ex* Nordholm *-2001* **Openseas Maritime SA** Arados Shipping Co Srl	5,306 2,891 8,176	Class: (GL) (BV)	**1976-07 Watanabe Zosen KK — Imabari EH** Yd No: 183 Loa 117.61 (BB) Br ex 18.04 Dght 7.301 Lbp 110.01 Br md 18.00 Dpth 9.00 Welded, 1 dk	**(A21A2BC) Bulk Carrier** Grain: 10,134; Bale: 9,928 Compartments: 3 Ho, ER 3 Ha: (11.8 x 9.7)2 (20.2 x 9.7)ER Derricks: 2x20t,3x15t	**1 oil engine** driving 1 FP propeller Total Power: 4,560kW (6,200hp) 14.0kn Mitsubishi 6UEC52/105D 1 x 2 Stroke 6 Cy. 520 x 1050 4560kW (6200bhp) Kobe Hatsudoki KK-Japan AuxGen: 2 x 280kW 440V 60Hz a.c Fuel: 86.5 (d.f.) 548.5 (r.f.) 17.5pd
7404114 *WBN3019* -	**SEA BREEZE** *ex* Robin XII *-1984* **Crowley Foreign Towing Inc** - *San Francisco, CA* *United States of America* MMSI: 366888830 Official number: 569926	421 126 -	Class: AB	**1976-02 McDermott Shipyards Inc — Morgan City LA** Yd No: 209 Loa - Br ex 10.37 Dght 4.496 Lbp 36.61 Br md 10.32 Dpth 5.01 Welded, 1 dk	**(B32A2ST) Tug**	**2 oil engines** reverse reduction geared to sc. shafts driving 2 FP propellers Total Power: 3,574kW (4,860hp) 13.0kn Alco 12V251E 2 x Vee 4 Stroke 12 Cy. 229 x 267 each-1787kW (2430bhp) White Industrial Power Inc-USA AuxGen: 2 x 75kW Fuel: 254.0 (d.f.)
9179660 *3EYR3* -	**SEA BREEZE III** *ex* Amor *-2012* *ex* Scorpio *-2012* **Jambo Jet Maritime Co** Paoletta Services Inc *Panama* *Panama* Official number: 43714PEXT1	11,347 3,404 1,200	Class: (RI) (AB)	**1999-06 Fincantieri-Cant. Nav. Italiani S.p.A. — Riva Trigoso** Yd No: 6047 Loa 145.81 Br ex - Dght 3.941 Lbp 128.60 Br md 22.00 Dpth 12.60 Welded	**(A36A2PR) Passenger/Ro-Ro Ship (Vehicles)** Passengers: unberthed: 1800 Stern ramp Lane-Len: 800 Lorries: 30, Cars: 460	**4 oil engines & 2 Gas Turbs** reduction geared to sc. shafts driving 4 Water jets , boosters Total Power: 92,390kW (125,614hp) 40.0kn M.T.U. 20V1163TB73 4 x Vee 4 Stroke 20 Cy. 230 x 280 each-6701kW (9111bhp) MTU Friedrichshafen GmbH-Friedrichshafen GE Marine LM2500 2 x Gas Turb each-32793kW (44585shp) GE Marine Engines-Cincinnati, Oh Thrusters: 2 Thwart. FP thruster (f)
9151888 *V4YQ2* -	**SEA BREEZER** *ex* Sea Breeze *-2014* *ex* Vento Di Ponente *-2011* *ex* Sea Breeze *-2011* *ex* CMA CGM Fes *-2008* *ex* Sea Breeze *-2007* *ex* Action F. *-2006* *ex* Steamers Prestige *-2004* **OSS Lines Inc** Ocean Shell Shipping LLC *St Kitts & Nevis* MMSI: 341276000	7,171 3,580 8,965	Class: GL (LR) ✠ Classed LR until 15/5/04	**1999-02 Jinling Shipyard — Nanjing JS** Yd No: 96-7014 Loa 126.80 (BB) Br ex 20.04 Dght 7.900 Lbp 117.80 Br md 20.00 Dpth 10.60 Welded, 1 dk	**(A33A2CC) Container Ship (Fully Cellular)** TEU 779 C Ho 240 TEU C Dk 539 TEU incl 80 ref C. Compartments: 3 Cell Ho, ER 6 Ha: ER Cranes: 2x40t	**1 oil engine** with flexible couplings & sr gearedto sc. shaft driving 1 CP propeller Total Power: 6,300kW (8,565hp) 17.5kn Wartsila 6R46C 1 x 4 Stroke 6 Cy. 460 x 580 6300kW (8565bhp) Wartsila NSD Finland Oy-Finland AuxGen: 1 x 800kW 450V 60Hz a.c, 3 x 500kW 450V 60Hz a.c Boilers: AuxB (Comp) 9.2kgf/cm² (9.0bar) Thrusters: 1 Thwart. CP thruster (f) Fuel: 96.0 (d.f.) (Heating Coils) 777.0 (r.f.) 29.0pd
8033039 *BNCF* -	**SEA BRIDGE No. 1** - **Sea Bridge Inc** - *Kaohsiung* *Chinese Taipei*	*217* 139 218	Class: (CR)	**1978 San Yang Shipbuilding Co., Ltd. — Kaohsiung** Loa 31.50 Br ex 7.68 Dght 2.301 Lbp 29.01 Br md 7.41 Dpth 3.10 Welded, 1 dk	**(A12A2TC) Chemical Tanker**	**1 oil engine** driving 1 FP propeller Total Power: 250kW (340hp) 8.0kn G.M. (Detroit Diesel) 12V-71-N 1 x Vee 2 Stroke 12 Cy. 108 x 127 250kW (340bhp) General Motors Corp-USA AuxGen: 1 x 16kW 225V a.c
8033041 *BNCG* -	**SEA BRIDGE No. 2** - **Sea Bridge Inc** - *Kaohsiung* *Chinese Taipei*	*217* 140 218	Class: (CC) (CR)	**1978 San Yang Shipbuilding Co., Ltd. — Kaohsiung** Loa 31.50 Br ex 7.68 Dght 2.301 Lbp 29.01 Br md 7.41 Dpth 3.10 Welded, 1 dk	**(A12A2TC) Chemical Tanker**	**1 oil engine** driving 1 FP propeller Total Power: 250kW (340hp) 8.0kn G.M. (Detroit Diesel) 12V-71-N 1 x Vee 2 Stroke 12 Cy. 108 x 127 250kW (340bhp) General Motors Corp-USA AuxGen: 1 x 16kW 225V a.c
9103609 *HSB3434* -	**SEA BRIGHTON** *ex* Brighton *-2006* *ex* Eastern Hero *-2004* **Sang Thai Transport Co Ltd** Sinsimon Navigation Co Ltd *Bangkok* *Thailand* MMSI: 567050100 Official number: 490001163	5,601 2,301 6,903	Class: NK	**1994-03 Shin Kurushima Dockyard Co. Ltd. — Akitsu** Yd No: 2808 Loa 98.17 (BB) Br ex 18.82 Dght 7.429 Lbp 89.95 Br md 18.80 Dpth 12.90 Welded, 2 dks	**(A31A2GX) General Cargo Ship** Grain: 13,473; Bale: 12,472 Compartments: 2 Ho, ER 2 Ha: 2 (20.3 x 12.7)ER Cranes: 2x30t; Derricks: 2x25t	**1 oil engine** driving 1 FP propeller Total Power: 2,427kW (3,300hp) 12.4kn Hanshin 6EL40 1 x 4 Stroke 6 Cy. 400 x 800 2427kW (3300bhp) The Hanshin Diesel Works Ltd-Japan Fuel: 520.0 (r.f.)
7647182 *WDC3114* -	**SEA BROOKE** *ex* Cheramie Bo-Truc No. 27 *-1977* **Rockin 'D' Marine Services LLC** - *New Orleans, LA* *United States of America* MMSI: 367002760 Official number: 578598	*197* 134 500		**1977-01 Bollinger Machine Shop & Shipyard, Inc. — Lockport, La** Yd No: 102 Loa 50.32 Br ex - Dght 3.174 Lbp 48.21 Br md 10.98 Dpth 3.66 Welded, 1 dk	**(B21A2OS) Platform Supply Ship**	**2 oil engines** geared to sc. shafts driving 2 FP propellers Total Power: 1,704kW (2,316hp) G.M. (Detroit Diesel) 16V-149 2 x Vee 2 Stroke 16 Cy. 146 x 146 each-852kW (1158bhp) General Motors Detroit DieselAllison Divn-USA
8899586 *9YBQ* -	**SEA BULL** *ex* BCS Mariner *-1977* **Tucker Marine Services Ltd** - *Port of Spain* *Trinidad & Tobago*	133 40 -		**1966 Universal Iron Works — Houma, La** Yd No: 948 Loa 28.37 Br ex 7.32 Dght - Lbp - Br md - Dpth - Welded, 1 dk	**(B21A2OS) Platform Supply Ship**	**2 oil engines** driving 2 FP propellers Total Power: 882kW (1,200hp) G.M. (Detroit Diesel) 16V-71 2 x Vee 2 Stroke 16 Cy. 108 x 127 each-441kW (600bhp) Detroit Diesel Corporation-Detroit, Mi
7392696 - -	**SEA BULL SEC CINQUE** *ex* Almond *-1997* **Garnett Italiana Srl** Societa' Esercizio Cantieri (SEC) SpA SatCom: Inmarsat C 424735020 *Livorno* *Italy*	304 91 -	Class: (LR) (RI) ✠ Classed LR until 15/6/98	**1976-09 Richards (Shipbuilders) Ltd — Lowestoft** Yd No: 527 Loa 38.00 Br ex 9.63 Dght 3.826 Lbp 34.02 Br md 9.21 Dpth 4.50 Welded, 1 dk	**(B32A2ST) Tug**	**1 oil engine** sr geared to sc. shaft driving 1 CP propeller Total Power: 1,942kW (2,640hp) 14.0kn Ruston 12RKCM 1 x Vee 4 Stroke 12 Cy. 254 x 305 1942kW (2640bhp) Ruston Paxman Diesels Ltd.-Colchester AuxGen: 2 x 108kW 440V 50Hz a.c, 1 x 30kW 440V 50Hz a.c
7407922 *WBJ2333* -	**SEA BYRD** *ex* Sea Dragon *-2006* *ex* Warrior *-1991* *ex* Gulf Sun II *-1990* **Joann Alvarez** - *Tampa, FL* *United States of America* Official number: 555705	*583* 175 -		**1974-03 Desco Marine — Saint Augustine, Fl** Yd No: 168-F Loa 22.86 Br ex - Dght 2.744 Lbp 20.99 Br md 6.74 Dpth 3.81 Bonded, 1 dk	**(B11A2FT) Trawler** Hull Material: Reinforced Plastic	**1 oil engine** driving 1 FP propeller Total Power: 268kW (364hp) Caterpillar D343SCAC 1 x 4 Stroke 6 Cy. 137 x 165 268kW (364bhp) Caterpillar Tractor Co-USA
9358060 *9HA3034* -	**SEA-CARGO EXPRESS** - **Sea-Cargo Skips AS** Seatrans AS SatCom: Inmarsat C 422906110 *Valletta* *Malta* MMSI: 229061000 Official number: 9358060	6,693 3,855 5,000	Class: NV	**2012-04 Pinky Shipyard Pvt Ltd — Goa** Yd No: 324 Loa 117.38 (BB) Br ex - Dght 6.500 Lbp 110.70 Br md 18.00 Dpth 12.50 Welded, 1 dk	**(A35A2RR) Ro-Ro Cargo Ship** Double Hull Stern door/ramp (a) Side door (s) Lane-Len: 500 Trailers: 35 TEU 118 Cranes: 1x50t	**1 oil engine** reduction geared to sc. shaft driving 1 CP propeller Total Power: 4,500kW (6,118hp) 16.0kn Wartsila 9L32 1 x 4 Stroke 9 Cy. 320 x 400 4500kW (6118bhp) Wartsila Finland Oy-Finland AuxGen: 3 x a.c, 1 x a.c Thrusters: 1 Tunnel thruster (f)

Number / Call sign	Ship / Owner / Manager / Port	Tonnage	Class	Builder / Dimensions	Type	Machinery
9366122 *9V7734* -	**SEA CARRIER** *ex* Oslo Carrier 1 *-2013* *ex* Western Carrier *-2013* **Oslo Carriers Pte Ltd** Bulkship Management AS *Singapore* *Singapore* MMSI: 566837000 Official number: 398312	**6,668** 3,625 9,302	Class: GL	**2010-03 Zhejiang Zhenyu Shipbuilding Co Ltd — Xiangshan County ZJ** Yd No: MPC68-1 Loa 107.00 (BB) Br ex - Dght 8.000 Lbp 103.00 Br md 18.20 Dpth 10.50 Welded, 1 dk	**(A31A2GX) General Cargo Ship** Grain: 11,770; Bale: 11,770 TEU 132 Compartments: 3 Ho, 3 Tw Dk, ER 3 Ha: 2 (25.9 x 15.2)ER (16.1 x 15.2) Cranes: 2x35t Ice Capable	**1 oil engine** reverse reduction geared to sc. shafts driving 1 CP propeller Total Power: 3,840kW (5,221hp) 13.0kn MaK 8M32C 1 x 4 Stroke 8 Cy. 320 x 480 3840kW (5221bhp) Caterpillar Motoren GmbH & Co. KG-Germany AuxGen: 2 x 380kW a.c, 1 x 500kW a.c Thrusters: 1 Tunnel thruster (f)
9069853 *ZR4896* -	**SEA CARRIER** *ex* Leslie G *-1999* **Servest Pty Ltd** - *Cape Town* *South Africa* MMSI: 601175000 Official number: 19903	**159** 47 -		**1982-10 Offshore Trawlers, Inc. — Bayou La Batre, Al** L reg 25.45 Br ex - Dght - Lbp - Br md 7.31 Dpth 2.13 Welded, 1 dk	**(B21A2OS) Platform Supply Ship**	**1 oil engine** driving 1 Propeller Total Power: 500kW (680hp)
8220319 *YFGK* -	**SEA CARRIER I** *ex* Offshore III *-1983* **PT Rig Tenders Indonesia Tbk** - *Jakarta* *Indonesia* MMSI: 525019077	**527** 159 750	Class: AB KI	**1983-01 Tonoura Dock Co. Ltd. — Miyazaki** Yd No: 56 Loa 40.01 Br ex 10.04 Dght 3.849 Lbp 36.00 Br md 10.00 Dpth 4.22 Welded, 1 dk	**(B21A2OS) Platform Supply Ship**	**2 oil engines** dr reverse geared to sc. shafts driving 2 FP propellers Total Power: 2,060kW (2,800hp) 13.0kn Yanmar T260L-ST 2 x 4 Stroke 6 Cy. 260 x 330 each-1030kW (1400bhp) Yanmar Diesel Engine Co Ltd-Japan Thrusters: 1 Thwart. FP thruster (f)
8622385 *9MQG4* -	**SEA CASSANDRA** *ex* Kyuho Maru *-2012* **Sky Yield International Ltd** - *Port Klang* *Malaysia* MMSI: 533130965 Official number: 334531	*489* - 1,289		**1983 Imura Zosen K.K. — Komatsushima** Yd No: 213 Loa 60.81 Br ex - Dght 4.331 Lbp 56.01 Br md 9.81 Dpth 4.60 Welded, 1 dk	**(A13B2TP) Products Tanker**	**1 oil engine** driving 1 FP propeller Total Power: 736kW (1,001hp) 10.0kn Akasaka DM28AR 1 x 4 Stroke 6 Cy. 280 x 460 736kW (1001bhp) Akasaka Tekkosho KK (Akasaka DieselLtd)-Japan
9226231 *HSB4373* -	**SEA CASTLE** *ex* White Melati *-2009* **Sang Thai Transport Co Ltd** Sinsimon Navigation Co Ltd *Bangkok* *Thailand* MMSI: 567384000 Official number: 520083934	**4,967** 2,928 7,963	Class: NK	**2000-04 Seibu Zosen K.K. — Hiroshima** Yd No: 1022 Loa 101.30 Br ex - Dght 7.888 Lbp 92.75 Br md 18.00 Dpth 11.00 Welded, 1 dk	**(A31A2GX) General Cargo Ship** Grain: 11,649; Bale: 10,752 Compartments: 2 Ho, ER 2 Ha: (19.6 x 10.5) (32.9 x 10.5)ER Derricks: 2x30t,1x25t	**1 oil engine** driving 1 FP propeller Total Power: 2,942kW (4,000hp) 12.0kn Mitsubishi 6UEC37LA 1 x 2 Stroke 6 Cy. 370 x 880 2942kW (4000bhp) Akasaka Tekkosho KK (Akasaka DieselLtd)-Japan Fuel: 616.0 (r.f.)
7802500 *WDC6244* -	**SEA CECILE** *ex* Cheramie Bo-Truc No. 30 *-2005* **Rockin 'D' Marine Services LLC** - *New Orleans, LA* *United States of America* MMSI: 367053440 Official number: 585710	**510** 153 500		**1977-11 Bollinger Machine Shop & Shipyard, Inc. — Lockport, La** Yd No: 104 Loa 50.30 Br ex - Dght 3.098 Lbp 48.16 Br md 10.98 Dpth 3.66 Welded, 1 dk	**(B21A2OS) Platform Supply Ship**	**2 oil engines** geared to sc. shafts driving 2 FP propellers Total Power: 1,704kW (2,316hp) G.M. (Detroit Diesel) 16V-149 2 x Vee 2 Stroke 16 Cy. 146 x 146 each-852kW (1158bhp) General Motors Detroit DieselAllison Divn-USA
7116004 *HSCI* -	**SEA CELEBRITY** *ex* Sang Thai Ceramic *-2000* *ex* Ho Hai *-1982* *ex* Pacific Satu *-1981* *ex* Gurjan *-1979* *ex* Yuwa Maru *-1975* **Sinsimon Navigation Co Ltd** - *Bangkok* *Thailand* MMSI: 567008900 Official number: 251030165	**2,837** 1,708 4,836	Class: (NK)	**1971-08 Nishi Shipbuilding Co Ltd — Imabari EH** Yd No: 133 Loa 94.01 Br ex 15.04 Dght 6.250 Lbp 87.90 Br md 15.02 Dpth 7.52 Welded, 1 dk	**(A31A2GX) General Cargo Ship** Grain: 5,934; Bale: 5,588 Compartments: 2 Ho, ER 2 Ha: (18.2 x 7.5) (32.2 x 7.5)ER Derricks: 4x15t; Winches: 9	**1 oil engine** driving 1 FP propeller Total Power: 2,648kW (3,600hp) 12.0kn Akasaka 6DM51SS 1 x 4 Stroke 6 Cy. 510 x 840 2648kW (3600bhp) Akasaka Tekkosho KK (Akasaka DieselLtd)-Japan AuxGen: 2 x 132kW 445V 60Hz a.c Fuel: 377.0 13.0pd
8969850 *WDA5052* -	**SEA CHALLENGER** **Sea Challenger Corp** - *Galveston, TX* *United States of America* MMSI: 366815930 Official number: 1112875	**195** 58 -		**2001 Kennedy Ship & Repair, LP — Galveston, Tx** Yd No: H-102 Loa 32.00 Br ex - Dght - Lbp - Br md 8.22 Dpth 4.05 Welded, 1 dk	**(B11B2FV) Fishing Vessel**	**2 oil engines** reduction geared to sc. shaft driving 1 FP propeller Total Power: 794kW (1,080hp) Caterpillar 3412TA 2 x Vee 4 Stroke 12 Cy. 137 x 152 each-397kW (540bhp) Caterpillar Inc-USA
9322114 *V7KQ6* -	**SEA CHALLENGER** **Sea Challenger Shipholding SA** Perosea Shipping Co SA *Majuro* *Marshall Islands* MMSI: 538002661 Official number: 2661	**8,539** 4,117 13,089 T/cm 23.2	Class: BV (AB)	**2007-01 21st Century Shipbuilding Co Ltd — Tongyeong** Yd No: 215 Loa 128.60 (BB) Br ex - Dght 8.700 Lbp 120.40 Br md 20.40 Dpth 11.50 Welded, 1 dk	**(A12B2TR) Chemical/Products Tanker** Double Hull (13F) Liq: 13,408; Liq (Oil): 13,402 Cargo Heating Coils Compartments: 12 Wing Ta, 2 Wing Slop Ta, ER 12 Cargo Pump (s): 12x300m³/hr Manifold: Bow/CM: 61.4m	**1 oil engine** driving 1 FP propeller Total Power: 4,440kW (6,037hp) 13.4kn MAN-B&W 6S35MC 1 x 2 Stroke 6 Cy. 350 x 1400 4440kW (6037bhp) STX Engine Co Ltd-South Korea AuxGen: 3 x 550kW a.c Thrusters: 1 Tunnel thruster (f) Fuel: 69.2 (d.f.) 678.4 (r.f.)
9658290 *OWLQ2* -	**SEA CHALLENGER** **A2SEA A/S** - *Fredericia* *Denmark* MMSI: 219019002 Official number: D4623	**15,934** 4,781 15,771	Class: NV	**2014-03 COSCO (Nantong) Shipyard Co Ltd — Nantong JS** Yd No: N488 Loa 133.25 Br ex - Dght 5.800 Lbp 121.68 Br md 39.00 Dpth 9.00 Welded, 1 dk	**(B22A2ZM) Offshore Construction Vessel, jack up** Cranes: 1x900t	**6 diesel electric oil engines** driving 6 gen. each 3020kW 6600V a.c Connecting to 3 elec. motors each (800kW) driving 3 Voith-Schneider propellers Total Power: 17,820kW (24,228hp) MaK 9M25 6 x 4 Stroke 9 Cy. 255 x 400 each-2970kW (4038bhp) Caterpillar Motoren GmbH & Co. KG-Germany Thrusters: 2 Tunnel thruster (f); 1 Retract. directional thruster (f)
7626281 *HP9470* -	**SEA CHALLENGER I** *ex* Gulf Fleet No. 19 *-1998* **Green Ocean Supplier Ltd** Global Marine Ship Management & Operations LLC *Panama* *Panama* MMSI: 357113000 Official number: 27738PEXT2	**723** 217 700	Class: BV (AB)	**1977-06 Quality Equipment Inc — Houma LA** Yd No: 139 Loa 56.37 Br ex - Dght 3.712 Lbp 51.72 Br md 11.59 Dpth 4.58 Welded, 1 dk	**(B21A2OS) Platform Supply Ship**	**2 oil engines** reverse reduction geared to sc. shafts driving 2 FP propellers Total Power: 2,206kW (3,000hp) 12.0kn EMD (Electro-Motive) 12-645-E6 2 x Vee 2 Stroke 12 Cy. 230 x 254 each-1103kW (1500bhp) General Motors Corp.Electro-Motive Div.-La Grange AuxGen: 2 x 75kW 440V 60Hz a.c Thrusters: 1 Thwart. FP thruster (f)
8659211 *9LH2009* -	**SEA CHAMPION** **Ships & Boats Oil Services** - *Freetown* *Sierra Leone* Official number: SL109009	**177** 77 -		**2008-01 Port Said Marine Shipyard — Port Said** Yd No: 775 Loa 28.00 Br ex - Dght - Lbp - Br md 8.56 Dpth 3.60 Welded, 1 dk	**(B32A2ST) Tug**	**2 oil engines** reduction geared to sc. shafts driving 2 Propellers Total Power: 1,324kW (1,800hp) MWM TBD440-6 2 x 4 Stroke 6 Cy. 230 x 270 each-662kW (900bhp) (made 1980, fitted 2008) Kloeckner Humboldt Deutz AG-West Germany
9155676 *PECB* -	**SEA CHARENTE** *ex* Fisker *-1997* **Charente Shipping BV** Amasus Support BV *Lemmer* *Netherlands* MMSI: 246362000 Official number: 30725	**1,638** 837 2,100	Class: BV	**1996-09 Rechytskiy Sudostroitelnyy Zavod — Rechytsa** (Hull) **1996-09 B.V. Scheepswerf Damen Bergum — Bergum** Yd No: 9981 Loa 82.34 Br ex - Dght 3.700 Lbp 78.97 Br md 11.30 Dpth 4.80 Welded, 1 dk	**(A31A2GX) General Cargo Ship** Grain: 3,088 Compartments: 1 Ho, ER 1 Ha: (51.1 x 9.3)ER	**1 oil engine** with clutches, flexible couplings & sr geared to sc. shaft driving 1 FP propeller Total Power: 1,020kW (1,387hp) 11.2kn Kromhout 6FHD240G 1 x 4 Stroke 6 Cy. 240 x 260 1020kW (1387bhp) Stork Wartsila Diesel BV-Netherlands AuxGen: 2 x 64kW 220/380V 50Hz a.c Thrusters: 1 Thwart. FP thruster (f)
7739507 *WBF3639* -	**SEA CHARGER** **Westbank Corp** Daybrook Fisheries Inc *New Orleans, LA* *United States of America* MMSI: 367166270 Official number: 589550	*468* 318 -		**1978 Patterson Shipyard Inc. — Patterson, La** Yd No: 033 L reg 49.44 Br ex 9.45 Dght - Lbp - Br md - Dpth 3.43 Welded, 1 dk	**(B11B2FV) Fishing Vessel**	**1 oil engine** driving 1 FP propeller Total Power: 1,324kW (1,800hp)

IMO / Call sign	Name / Owner / Port / Flag	Tonnage	Class	Builder / Dimensions	Type	Machinery
9475923 *PHSC* -	**SEA CHARLIE** *ex* SMS Shoalbuster *-2009* **Sea Bravo BV** Seacontractors BV *Vlissingen* *Netherlands* MMSI: 244177000 Official number: 53279	**212** 63 200	Class: BV	**2008**-03 **Damen Shipyards Kozle Sp z oo — Kedzierzyn-Kozle** (Hull) Yd No: 1114 **2008**-03 **B.V. Scheepswerf Damen Hardinxveld — Hardinxveld-Giessendam** Yd No: 1575 Loa 26.02 Br ex - Dght 2.650 Lbp 23.36 Br md 9.10 Dpth 3.50 Welded, 1 dk	**(B32A2ST) Tug**	**2 oil engines** reduction geared to sc. shafts driving 2 FP propellers Total Power: 1,640kW (2,230hp) 10.0kn Caterpillar 3508B-TA 2 x Vee 4 Stroke 8 Cy. 170 x 190 each-820kW (1115bhp) Caterpillar Inc-USA AuxGen: 2 x 78kW 50Hz a.c Thrusters: 1 Tunnel thruster (f) Fuel: 130.0 (d.f.)
9252412 *V7DC4* -	**SEA CHARM** *ex* Sea Of Gracia *-2013* *ex* Efrossini *-2010* **Sea Charm Maritime Ltd** Hellenic Star Shipping Co SA *Majuro* *Marshall Islands* MMSI: 538005364 Official number: 5364	**40,002** 26,101 75,932 T/cm 67.7	Class: KR (LR) ✠ Classed LR until 9/3/11	**2003**-02 **Tsuneishi Shipbuilding Co Ltd — Fukuyama HS** Yd No: 1244 Loa 225.00 (BB) Br ex 32.30 Dght 14.040 Lbp 217.81 Br md 32.20 Dpth 19.15 Welded, 1 dk	**(A21A2BC) Bulk Carrier** Grain: 91,180 Compartments: 7 Ho, ER 7 Ha: (17.3 x 15.4)5 (17.3 x 15.4)ER (15.6 x 12.8)	**1 oil engine** driving 1 FP propeller Total Power: 8,550kW (11,625hp) 14.5kn B&W 6S60MC 1 x 2 Stroke 6 Cy. 600 x 2292 8550kW (11625bhp) Mitsui Engineering & Shipbuilding CLtd-Japan AuxGen: 3 x 600kW 450V 60Hz a.c Boilers: AuxB (Comp) 7.1kgf/cm² (7.0bar)
9407079 *VRMF3* -	**SEA CHARMING** *ex* Bow Cape *-2013* **Top Sailing Enterprise Ltd** Aoxing Ship Management (Shanghai) Ltd *Hong Kong* *Hong Kong* MMSI: 477220300 Official number: HK-3857	**11,722** 6,324 19,975 T/cm 29.8	Class: NK	**2008**-04 **Fukuoka Shipbuilding Co Ltd — Nagasaki NS** Yd No: 2017 Loa 144.09 (BB) Br ex 24.23 Dght 9.652 Lbp 136.00 Br md 24.19 Dpth 12.90 Welded, 1 dk	**(A12B2TR) Chemical/Products Tanker** Double Hull (13F) Liq: 20,375; Liq (Oil): 21,715 Cargo Heating Coils Compartments: 20 Wing Ta, ER 20 Cargo Pump (s): 10x200m³/hr, 10x300m³/hr Manifold: Bow/CM: 72m	**1 oil engine** driving 1 FP propeller Total Power: 6,150kW (8,362hp) 14.5kn MAN-B&W 6S42MC 1 x 2 Stroke 6 Cy. 420 x 1764 6150kW (8362bhp) Makita Corp-Japan AuxGen: 3 x 450kW a.c Thrusters: 1 Tunnel thruster (f) Fuel: 98.0 (d.f.) 1003.0 (r.f.)
8707044 - -	**SEA CHATEAU** - **Far Ping Maritime Transportation & Passenger Steamship Co Ltd** - *Chinese Taipei*	*166* - 22		**1987**-04 **Sanuki Shipbuilding & Iron Works Co Ltd — Mitoyo KG** Yd No: 103A Loa 35.30 Br ex - Dght 1.040 Lbp 29.20 Br md 9.30 Dpth 3.02 Welded, 1 dk	**(A37B2PS) Passenger Ship** Hull Material: Aluminium Alloy Passengers: unberthed: 150	**2 oil engines** driving 2 FP propellers Total Power: 2,522kW (3,428hp) 27.0kn MWM TBD604BV12 2 x Vee 4 Stroke 12 Cy. 170 x 195 each-1261kW (1714bhp) Mitsui Deutz Diesel Eng. Co.Ltd.-Tokyo AuxGen: 1 x 32kW 225V 60Hz a.c
8614340 *JL5541* -	**SEA CHATEAU No. 2** - **KK Marine Kanko Kaihatsu** - *Naha, Okinawa* *Japan* Official number: 129047	*145* - 13		**1986**-07 **Sanuki Shipbuilding & Iron Works Co Ltd — Mitoyo KG** Yd No: 102A Loa 33.00 Br ex - Dght 1.040 Lbp 26.70 Br md 9.11 Dpth 3.05 Welded, 1 dk	**(A37B2PS) Passenger Ship** Hull Material: Aluminium Alloy Passengers: unberthed: 96	**2 oil engines** with clutches & sr geared to sc. shafts driving 2 FP propellers Total Power: 1,472kW (2,002hp) Yanmar 12LAAK-UT1 2 x Vee 4 Stroke 12 Cy. 148 x 165 each-736kW (1001bhp) Yanmar Diesel Engine Co Ltd-Japan
8121159 *AUZF* -	**SEA CHEETAH** *ex* Maersk Terrier *-2009* *ex* Takapu *-1990* **Hind Offshore Pvt Ltd** - *Mumbai* *India* MMSI: 419084700 Official number: 3550	**1,621** 486 1,710	Class: IR LR ✠ **100A1** SS 01/2012 offshore tug/supply ship Ice Class 1* ✠ **LMC** **UMS** Eq.Ltr: Q; Cable: 770.0/36.0 U3	**1983**-08 **Hyundai Heavy Industries Co Ltd — Ulsan** Yd No: 0708 Loa 67.65 Br ex 14.86 Dght 5.884 Lbp 59.80 Br md 14.51 Dpth 6.91 Welded, 1 dk	**(B21B20A) Anchor Handling Tug Supply** Ice Capable	**4 oil engines** with clutches, flexible couplings & sr geared to sc. shafts driving 2 CP propellers Total Power: 8,828kW (12,004hp) 12.0kn Normo KVMB-12 4 x Vee 4 Stroke 12 Cy. 250 x 300 each-2207kW (3001bhp) AS Bergens Mek Verksteder-Norway AuxGen: 2 x 1570kW 450V 60Hz a.c, 2 x 248kW 450V 60Hz a.c, 1 x 75kW 450V 60Hz a.c Thrusters: 2 Tunnel thruster (f); 1 Tunnel thruster (a) Fuel: 930.0 (d.f.)
9188051 *9MGN8* -	**SEA CHEETAH** - **Sang Muara Sdn Bhd** PSA Marine Pte Ltd *Port Klang* *Malaysia* Official number: 330475	**285** 85 164	Class: BV	**1998**-04 **Imamura Zosen — Kure** Yd No: 401 Loa 29.00 Br ex - Dght 3.750 Lbp 23.50 Br md 9.50 Dpth 4.70 Welded, 1 dk	**(B32A2ST) Tug**	**2 oil engines** gearing integral to driving 2 Z propellers Total Power: 2,942kW (4,000hp) Yanmar 6N260-EN 2 x 4 Stroke 6 Cy. 260 x 360 each-1471kW (2000bhp) Yanmar Diesel Engine Co Ltd-Japan
9369629 *C4SE2* -	**SEA CHEETAH** - **SFL Sea Cheetah Ltd** Deep Sea Supply Navegacao Maritima Ltda *Limassol* *Cyprus* MMSI: 210465000 Official number: 9369629	**2,952** 885 2,301	Class: AB	**2007**-02 **Jaya Shipbuilding & Engineering Pte Ltd — Singapore** Yd No: 858 Loa 75.40 Br ex - Dght 6.100 Lbp 67.16 Br md 16.80 Dpth 7.50 Welded, 1 dk	**(B21B20A) Anchor Handling Tug Supply**	**2 oil engines** reduction geared to sc. shafts driving 2 CP propellers Total Power: 11,032kW (15,000hp) 12.0kn Wartsila 12V32 2 x Vee 4 Stroke 12 Cy. 320 x 400 each-5516kW (7500bhp) Wartsila Finland Oy-Finland AuxGen: 2 x 370kW 440V 60Hz a.c, 2 x 2300kW a.c Thrusters: 2 Thwart. CP thruster (f); 1 Thwart. CP thruster (a)
9421192 *3FR03* -	**SEA CHEROKEE** - **Gulf Marine Far East Pte Ltd** GulfMark Offshore Inc *Panama* *Panama* MMSI: 351875000 Official number: 4027909	**2,943** 883 2,728	Class: AB	**2009**-01 **Keppel Nantong Shipyard Co Ltd — Nantong JS** (Hull) Yd No: 007 **2009**-01 **Keppel Singmarine Pte Ltd — Singapore** Yd No: 313 Loa 76.00 Br ex - Dght 6.200 Lbp 68.40 Br md 17.00 Dpth 7.60 Welded, 1 dk	**(B21B20A) Anchor Handling Tug Supply**	**4 oil engines** reduction geared to sc. shafts driving 2 CP propellers Total Power: 7,920kW (10,768hp) 14.0kn MaK 6M25 4 x 4 Stroke 6 Cy. 255 x 400 each-1980kW (2692bhp) Caterpillar Motoren GmbH & Co. KG-Germany AuxGen: 3 x 550kW a.c Thrusters: 1 Retract. directional thruster (f); 1 Tunnel thruster (f); 1 Tunnel thruster (a) Fuel: 1250.0
9375379 *3ENG8* -	**SEA CHEYENNE** - **Gulf Marine Far East Pte Ltd** GulfMark Offshore Inc *Panama* *Panama* MMSI: 371174000 Official number: 3405908A	**2,943** 883 2,711	Class: AB	**2007**-10 **Keppel Singmarine Pte Ltd — Singapore** Yd No: 310 Loa 76.00 Br ex - Dght 6.200 Lbp 68.40 Br md 17.00 Dpth 7.60 Welded, 1 dk	**(B21B20A) Anchor Handling Tug Supply**	**4 oil engines** reduction geared to sc. shafts driving 2 CP propellers Total Power: 7,920kW (10,768hp) 14.0kn MaK 6M25 4 x 4 Stroke 6 Cy. 255 x 400 each-1980kW (2692bhp) Caterpillar Motoren GmbH & Co. KG-Germany AuxGen: 3 x 550kW a.c Thrusters: 1 Retract. directional thruster (f); 1 Tunnel thruster (a); 1 Tunnel thruster (f)
8991633 - -	**SEA CHIEF** *ex* LT-1944 *-1990* **Basic Towing Inc** - *Escanaba, MI* *United States of America* Official number: 1105613	**196** 133 -		**1952**-12 **Avondale Marine Ways Inc. — Westwego, La** Yd No: 403 L reg 30.60 Br ex - Dght - Lbp - Br md 8.08 Dpth 4.57 Welded, 1 dk	**(B32A2ST) Tug**	**1 oil engine** driving 1 Propeller
9375408 *3ERZ6* -	**SEA CHOCTAW** - **Gulf Marine Far East Pte Ltd** GulfMark Offshore Inc *Panama* *Panama* MMSI: 370224000 Official number: 3446808A	**2,943** 883 2,700	Class: AB	**2008**-07 **Keppel Singmarine Pte Ltd — Singapore** Yd No: 314 Loa 76.00 Br ex - Dght 6.200 Lbp 68.40 Br md 17.00 Dpth 7.60 Welded, 1 dk	**(B21B20A) Anchor Handling Tug Supply**	**4 oil engines** reduction geared to sc. shafts driving 2 CP propellers Total Power: 7,920kW (10,768hp) 14.0kn MaK 6M25 4 x 4 Stroke 6 Cy. 255 x 400 each-1980kW (2692bhp) Caterpillar Motoren GmbH & Co. KG-Germany AuxGen: 3 x 550kW a.c Thrusters: 1 Retract. directional thruster (f); 1 Tunnel thruster (f); 1 Tunnel thruster (a) Fuel: 1250.0 (d.f.)
8810671 *9MPT4* -	**SEA CHOLBURI** *ex* Trans Cholburi *-2012* *ex* Heisei Maru *-2006* **Skips Marine Services Sdn Bhd** - *Port Klang* *Malaysia* MMSI: 533001430 Official number: 334430	**718** 339 1,285	Class: (NK)	**1989**-04 **Teraoka Shipyard Co Ltd — Minamiawaji HG** Yd No: 277 Loa 64.95 (BB) Br ex - Dght 4.169 Lbp 62.00 Br md 10.00 Dpth 4.50 Welded, 1 dk	**(A12B2TR) Chemical/Products Tanker** Grain: 1,387; Liq: 1,507; Liq (Oil): 1,507	**1 oil engine** reverse geared to sc. shaft driving 1 FP propeller Total Power: 883kW (1,201hp) Akasaka K26SR 1 x 4 Stroke 6 Cy. 260 x 480 883kW (1201bhp) Akasaka Tekkosho KK (Akasaka DieselLtd)-Japan
5207158 *HO2050* -	**SEA CLASS VOYAGER** *ex* Behrmann Express *-2000* *ex* Tidy Bowl *-1993* *ex* Carib Haven *-1993* *ex* Lago Primero *-1985* *ex* Transamerican *-1980* *ex* Leuvehaven *-1972* **Sea Class Shipping Inc** - *Panama* *Panama* MMSI: 353696000 Official number: 28894PEXT	*381* 157 611	Class: (BV)	**1955**-04 **N.V. Scheepswerf "Waterhuizen" J. Pattje — Waterhuizen** Yd No: 222 Loa 57.54 Br ex 8.64 Dght 3.220 Lbp 51.97 Br md 8.62 Dpth 5.34 Riveted\Welded, 2 dks	**(A31A2GX) General Cargo Ship** Grain: 1,472 Compartments: 1 Ho, ER 1 Ha: (22.9 x 4.9)ER Derricks: 4x2t; Winches: 2	**1 oil engine** reduction geared to sc. shaft driving 1 FP propeller Total Power: 846kW (1,150hp) 11.0kn Caterpillar 1 x 4 Stroke 846kW (1150bhp) (new engine 1999) Caterpillar Inc-USA AuxGen: 1 x 10kW 110V d.c Fuel: 60.0 (d.f.)

IMO / Call sign	Name / Owner	Tonnage	Class	Builder / Dimensions	Type	Machinery
7520633 *WCZ2553* -	**SEA CLIPPER** **Sea Clipper LLC** - *Westport, WA United States of America* MMSI: 366765940 Official number: 553396	*181* 154 -		**1973 Bender Welding & Machine Co Inc — Mobile AL** L reg 25.06 Br ex 7.32 Dght - Lbp - Br md - Dpth 3.43 Welded, 1 dk	**(B11B2FV) Fishing Vessel**	**1 oil engine** driving 1 FP propeller Total Power: 588kW (799hp) G.M. (Detroit Diesel) 12V-149 1 x Vee 2 Stroke 12 Cy. 146 x 146 588kW (799bhp) General Motors Detroit DieselAllison Divn-USA
8843446 *9HOM2* -	**SEA CLOUD** *ex* Sea Cloud of Grand Cayman *-1987* *ex* Sea Cloud *-1980* *ex* Antarna *-1979* *ex* Patria *-1964* *ex* Angelita *-1961* *ex* Sea Cloud *-1952* *ex* Hussar *-1935* **Hansa Cloud Sailing Ltd** Hansa Shipping GmbH & Co KG SatCom: Inmarsat A 1256105 *Valletta Malta* MMSI: 256084000 Official number: 8843446	**2,532** 760 788	Class: GL (LR) ✠ Classed LR until 3/65	**1931-09 Fried. Krupp Germaniawerft AG — Kiel** Yd No: 519 Converted From: Yacht-1979 Converted From: Research Vessel-1947 Converted From: Yacht-1942 Loa 96.35 Br ex 15.24 Dght 4.880 Lbp 77.42 Br md 14.93 Dpth 8.53 Welded, 1 dk	**(A37A2PC) Passenger/Cruise** Passengers: cabins: 32; berths: 64	**4 oil engines** sr reverse geared to sc. shafts driving 2 FP propellers Total Power: 3,676kW (4,996hp) Enterprise DMG-38 4 x 4 Stroke 8 Cy. 305 x 381 each-919kW (1249bhp) (new engine 1957) Enterprise Engine & Foundry Co-USA AuxGen: 1 x 350kW 220/380V a.c, 1 x 276kW 220/380V a.c, 1 x 104kW 220/380V a.c
9171292 *9HUE6* -	**SEA CLOUD II** **Schiffahrts-Gesellschaft 'Sea Cloud II' mbH & Co KG** Hansa Shipping GmbH & Co KG *Valletta Malta* MMSI: 248953000 Official number: 7042	**3,849** 1,154 780	Class: GL	**2000-12 Astilleros Gondan SA — Castropol** Yd No: 405 Loa 117.00 Br ex - Dght 5.300 Lbp 81.50 Br md 16.00 Dpth 9.00 Welded	**(A37A2PC) Passenger/Cruise** Passengers: cabins: 48; berths: 94	**2 oil engines** reduction geared to sc. shafts driving 2 CP propellers Total Power: 2,500kW (3,400hp) 14.0kn MaK 8M20 2 x 4 Stroke 8 Cy. 200 x 300 each-1250kW (1700bhp) MaK Motoren GmbH & Co. KG-Kiel AuxGen: 2 x 520kW 380V 50Hz a.c, 1 x 250kW 380V 50Hz a.c Thrusters: 1 Thwart. CP thruster (f) Fuel: 360.0 (d.f.) 11.0pd
8507987 *D6DB7* -	**SEA COLINS** *ex* Ocean Sword *-2010* *ex* Fraih 30 *-2005* *ex* Sea Vixen *-2001* *ex* Asie VI *-1995* **Ocean Oil Field Services FZE** - *Moroni Union of Comoros* MMSI: 616410000 Official number: 1200479	**111** 33 -	Class: BV (AB)	**1985-06 Halter Marine, Inc. — Chalmette, La** Yd No: 1120 Loa 30.99 Br ex - Dght 1.677 Lbp - Br md 6.46 Dpth 2.90 Welded, 1 dk	**(B21A20C) Crew/Supply Vessel**	**2 oil engines** reverse reduction geared to sc. shafts driving 2 FP propellers Total Power: 1,126kW (1,530hp) G.M. (Detroit Diesel) 12V-71 2 x Vee 2 Stroke 12 Cy. 108 x 127 each-563kW (765bhp) General Motors Detroit DieselAllison Divn-USA AuxGen: 2 x 30kW a.c
9421207 *HP9712* -	**SEA COMANCHE** **Gulf Marine Far East Pte Ltd** GulfMark Offshore Inc SatCom: Inmarsat C 437283310 *Panama Panama* MMSI: 372833000 Official number: 4064409	**2,943** 883 2,718	Class: AB	**2009-06 Keppel Nantong Shipyard Co Ltd — Nantong JS** (Hull) Yd No: 008 **2009-06 Keppel Singmarine Pte Ltd — Singapore** Yd No: 315 Loa 76.00 Br ex - Dght 6.200 Lbp 69.00 Br md 17.00 Dpth 7.60 Welded, 1 dk	**(B21B20A) Anchor Handling Tug Supply**	**4 oil engines** reduction geared to sc. shafts driving 2 CP propellers Total Power: 7,920kW (10,768hp) 14.0kn MaK 6M25 4 x 4 Stroke 6 Cy. 255 x 400 each-1980kW (2692bhp) Caterpillar Motoren GmbH & Co. KG-Germany AuxGen: 3 x 550kW a.c Thrusters: 1 Retract. directional thruster (f); 1 Tunnel thruster (f); 1 Tunnel thruster (f) Fuel: 1250.0 (d.f.) 29.0pd
7128863 *HO3019* -	**SEA COMMAND** *ex* Seabulk Command *-2002* *ex* GMMOS Command *-1997* *ex* Saeed *-1992* *ex* Maersk Handler *-1980* **Seaport International Shipping Co LLC** - *Panama Panama* MMSI: 356858000 Official number: 3306207A	**591** 177 780	Class: (BV) (GL)	**1972-09 Rolandwerft Dockbetrieb GmbH Ganspe — Berne** (Hull launched by) Yd No: 983 **1972-09 Aarhus Flydedok A/S — Aarhus** (Hull completed by) Yd No: 153 Loa 53.35 Br ex 11.23 Dght 3.480 Lbp 50.02 Br md 11.00 Dpth 4.02 Welded, 1 dk	**(B21B20A) Anchor Handling Tug Supply** Liq: 612 Compartments: 8 Ta, 1 Ho, ER Derricks: 1x3t; Winches: 1 Ice Capable	**2 oil engines** driving 2 FP propellers Total Power: 2,794kW (3,798hp) 9.0kn MaK 8MU452AK 2 x 4 Stroke 8 Cy. 320 x 450 each-1397kW (1899bhp) MaK Maschinenbau GmbH-Kiel AuxGen: 3 x 128kW 220/380V a.c Thrusters: 1 Thwart. FP thruster (f) Fuel: 284.0 (d.f.) 11.0pd
6620644 *VGGC* -	**SEA COMMANDER** *ex* Seaspan Commander *-1990* *ex* Gulf Joan *-1979* **Sea-Link Marine Services Ltd** - *Vancouver, BC Canada* MMSI: 316001043 Official number: 325683	*661* 43 396		**1945 Marietta Manufacturing Co. — Point Pleasant, WV** L reg 43.50 Br ex 10.06 Dght - Lbp - Br md - Dpth 5.80 Welded, 1 dk	**(B32A2ST) Tug** Compartments: 1 Ho, ER 3 Ha: (1.3 x 0.9) (0.7 x 0.7) (1.0 x 1.0) Cranes: 1x5t	**4 oil engines** geared to sc. shaft driving 1 FP propeller Total Power: 2,252kW (3,060hp) 10.0kn Caterpillar D398TA 4 x Vee 4 Stroke 12 Cy. 159 x 203 each-563kW (765bhp) (new engine 1965) Caterpillar Tractor Co-USA AuxGen: 2 x 75kW 440V 60Hz a.c Fuel: 249.0 (d.f.)
9287209 *3EAP4* -	**SEA CONFIDENCE** **Greenfield Shipholding Co SA** Interocean Ship Management & Services Ltd *Panama Panama* MMSI: 351682000 Official number: 3080305A	**29,377** 17,592 52,300	Class: BV	**2005-06 Oshima Shipbuilding Co Ltd — Saikai NS** Yd No: 10392 Loa 189.90 (BB) Br ex - Dght 12.100 Lbp 179.00 Br md 32.26 Dpth 17.15 Welded, 1 dk	**(A21A2BC) Bulk Carrier** Double Hull Grain: 66,300; Bale: 65,295 Compartments: 5 Ho, ER 5 Ha: (19.0 x 18.6)2 (21.0 x 18.6) (22.0 x 18.6)ER (17.0 x 18.6) Cranes: 4x30t	**1 oil engine** driving 1 FP propeller Total Power: 8,900kW (12,100hp) 14.5kn MAN-B&W 6S50MC-C 1 x 2 Stroke 6 Cy. 500 x 2000 8900kW (12100bhp) Kawasaki Heavy Industries Ltd-Japan AuxGen: 3 x 520kW
9690963 *J8B4823* -	**SEA CONQUEST** **QMS 2 Offshore Services Ltd** Zakher Marine International Inc *Kingstown St Vincent & The Grenadines* MMSI: 375851000 Official number: 11296	**2,512** 753 1,679	Class: AB	**2013-09 POET (China) Shipbuilding & Engineering Co Ltd — Taixing JS** (Hull) Yd No: (1525) **2013-09 Pacific Ocean Engineering & Trading Pte Ltd (POET) — Singapore** Yd No: 1525 Loa 65.00 (BB) Br ex - Dght 4.500 Lbp 57.00 Br md 16.20 Dpth 6.00 Welded, 1 dk	**(B22A20R) Offshore Support Vessel** Cranes: 1x36t	**2 diesel electric oil engines** driving 4 gen. each 560kW a.c Connecting to 2 elec. motors driving 2 Propellers Total Power: 2,884kW (3,921hp) Niigata 2 x 4 Stroke each-1439kW (1956bhp) Niigata Engineering Co Ltd-Japan Fuel: 110.0 (d.f.)
7430541 *AUJB* -	**SEA CONQUEST** *ex* Indonesia Eagle *-1996* *ex* Osa Leopard *-1990* **Hind Offshore Pvt Ltd** Glory Shipmanagement Pvt Ltd *Mumbai India* MMSI: 419551000 Official number: 3144	**997** 299 1,135	Class: IR (LR) (AB) (GL) ✠ Classed LR until 19/8/82	**1977-07 Taiwan Shipbuilding Corp — Keelung** Yd No: N-077 Loa 56.70 Br ex 13.52 Dght 4.192 Lbp 51.49 Br md 13.11 Dpth 4.81 Welded, 1 dk	**(B21B20A) Anchor Handling Tug Supply** Compartments: 16 Ta, ER Derricks: 1x8t	**2 oil engines** reverse reduction geared to sc. shafts driving 2 FP propellers Total Power: 2,574kW (3,500hp) 10.0kn Deutz SBA12M528 2 x Vee 4 Stroke 12 Cy. 220 x 280 each-1287kW (1750bhp) Kloeckner Humboldt Deutz AG-West Germany AuxGen: 2 x 220kW 440V 60Hz a.c, 1 x 350kW 440V 60Hz a.c Thrusters: 1 Thwart. CP thruster (f) Fuel: 689.0 (d.f.)
7920675 *9HOH5* -	**SEA COQUETTE** *ex* Naniama *-1997* *ex* Nagasaki Maru *-1994* *ex* Asaka Maru No. 1 *-1993* **Sea Coquette Maritime Ltd** Mediterranean Car-Carriers Line SA (MCCL) *Valletta Malta* MMSI: 248009000 Official number: 05723	**2,823** 1,831 2,113	Class: NK (BV) (CC)	**1980-04 Honda Zosen — Saiki** Yd No: 676 Loa 84.51 Br ex - Dght 5.341 Lbp 78.01 Br md 13.50 Dpth 7.78 Welded, 2 dks	**(A35B2RV) Vehicles Carrier** Side door/ramp (p) Side door/ramp (s)	**1 oil engine** driving 1 FP propeller Total Power: 2,501kW (3,400hp) 15.0kn Hanshin 6LU46A 1 x 4 Stroke 6 Cy. 460 x 740 2501kW (3400bhp) The Hanshin Diesel Works Ltd-Japan AuxGen: 2 x 144kW 445V 60Hz a.c Fuel: 179.0 (d.f.) 12.5pd
9499955 *3FPV9* -	**SEA CORAL** *ex* Higaki 622 *-2008* **Dawn Shipping SA** Setouchi Enterprise Co Ltd *Panama Panama* MMSI: 370851000 Official number: 4003509	**9,932** 4,569 14,384 T/cm 22.0	Class: NK	**2008-11 Higaki Zosen K.K. — Imabari** Yd No: 622 Loa 127.66 (BB) Br ex - Dght 9.446 Lbp 119.50 Br md 19.60 Dpth 14.50 Welded, 1 dk	**(A31A2GX) General Cargo Ship** Grain: 20,085; Bale: 18,818 Compartments: 2 Ho, 2 Tw Dk, ER 2 Ha: ER Cranes: 3x30.7t; Derricks: 1x30t	**1 oil engine** driving 1 FP propeller Total Power: 4,200kW (5,710hp) 13.5kn MAN-B&W 6S35MC 1 x 2 Stroke 6 Cy. 350 x 1400 4200kW (5710bhp) Makita Corp-Japan Fuel: 750.0
9188049 *9MGN9* -	**SEA COUGAR** **Sang Muara Sdn Bhd** PSA Marine Pte Ltd *Port Klang Malaysia* Official number: 330476	**285** 85 164	Class: BV	**1998-03 Imamura Zosen — Kure** Yd No: 400 Loa 29.00 Br ex - Dght 3.750 Lbp 23.50 Br md 9.50 Dpth 4.70 Welded, 1 dk	**(B32B2SP) Pusher Tug**	**2 oil engines** gearing integral to driving 2 Z propellers Total Power: 2,942kW (4,000hp) Yanmar 6N260-EN 2 x 4 Stroke 6 Cy. 260 x 360 each-1471kW (2000bhp) Yanmar Diesel Engine Co Ltd-Japan
8661824 *HP9436* -	**SEA CRAWLER** *ex* Jose Ivan *-2011* **Marine Supply Services Co Corp** - *Panama Panama* Official number: 4221311	**235** 76 -		**2004-01 Astillero Jose Murillo — Buenaventura** Yd No: 001-2004 L reg 33.10 Br ex - Dght - Lbp - Br md 8.20 Dpth 3.30 Welded, 1 dk	**(B34R2QY) Supply Tender**	**1 oil engine** reduction geared to sc. shaft driving 1 Propeller Total Power: 530kW (721hp) G.M. (Detroit Diesel) 1 x 530kW (721bhp) General Motors Corp-USA

7910254 - - **SEA CREST** | Radil Bros Fishing Co Ltd | A C Radil & Associates | *Vancouver, BC* *Canada* | MMSI: 316005669 | Official number: 393357 | *147* 53 - | **1979-12 Vancouver Shipyards Co Ltd — North Vancouver BC** Yd No: 89 | Loa 24.08 Br ex - Dght - | Lbp 22.56 Br md 7.62 Dpth 3.43 | Welded, 1 dk | **(B11A2FS) Stern Trawler** | **1 oil engine** geared to sc. shaft driving 1 FP propeller | Total Power: 662kW (900hp) | General Motors | 1 x 2 Stroke 662kW (900bhp) | General Motors Detroit DieselAllison Divn-USA

8817100 *3EAT5* - **SEA CRUISER 1** | *ex* Toyofuji Maru *-2005* | **Feng Li Maritime Corp** | ASP Ship Management Ltd | SatCom: Inmarsat C 435408610 | *Panama* *Panama* | MMSI: 354086000 | Official number: 3073205A | **7,694** 2,406 3,184 | Class: NK | **1989-08 Kambara Marine Development & Shipbuilding Co Ltd — Fukuyama HS** Yd No: OE-160 | Loa 113.05 (BB) Br ex 18.02 Dght 5.516 | Lbp 105.00 Br md 18.00 Dpth 6.01 | Welded | **(A35B2RV) Vehicles Carrier** | Quarter bow door/ramp (p. a.) | Quarter bow door/ramp (s. a.) | Cars: 600 | Grain: 27,600 | **1 oil engine** driving 1 CP propeller | Total Power: 3,678kW (5,001hp) 16.0kn | B&W 7L35MC | 1 x 2 Stroke 7 Cy. 350 x 1050 3678kW (5001bhp) | Makita Diesel Co Ltd-Japan | AuxGen: 2 x 480kW a.c | Thrusters: 1 Thwart. CP thruster (f) | Fuel: 85.0 (d.f.) 305.0 (r.f.) 15.0pd

---

9512135 *3FBD4* - **SEA CRYSTAL** | *ex* Samho Family *-2011* *ex* Samho Gold *-2010* | **HR Crystal SA** | Hanaro Shipping Co Ltd | *Panama* *Panama* | MMSI: 371399000 | Official number: 40428PEXT2 | **11,290** 5,263 17,602 T/cm 28.7 | Class: KR | **2010-03 Samho Shipbuilding Co Ltd — Tongyeong** Yd No: 1108 | Loa 144.06 (BB) Br ex - Dght 9.214 | Lbp 136.00 Br md 22.60 Dpth 12.50 | Welded, 1 dk | **(A12B2TR) Chemical/Products Tanker** | Double Hull (13F) | Liq: 18,617; Liq (Oil): 19,020 | Compartments: 14 Wing Ta, 2 Wing Slop Ta, ER | 14 Cargo Pump (s): 14x300m³/hr | Manifold: Bow/CM: 72.3m | **1 oil engine** driving 1 FP propeller | Total Power: 5,920kW (8,049hp) 14.0kn | MAN-B&W 8S35MC | 1 x 2 Stroke 8 Cy. 350 x 1400 5920kW (8049bhp) | STX Engine Co Ltd-South Korea | AuxGen: 4 x 750kW 450V a.c | Thrusters: 1 Tunnel thruster (f) | Fuel: 100.0 (d.f.) 830.0 (r.f.)

7011149 *T8ZA* - **SEA CZAR** | *ex* Al Widadia *-2014* *ex* Nice *-1994* | *ex* Kalba Nice *-1994* *ex* Amina *-1992* | *ex* Hasnaa *-1987* *ex* Midorikai Maru No. 1 *-1980* | **Sanjeeb & Marine Service LLC** | - | *Malakal Harbour* *Palau* | MMSI: 511012010 | *1,452* 758 3,125 | Class: (HR) (NK) | **1969-06 Watanabe Zosen KK — Imabari EH** Yd No: 105 | Loa 83.27 Br ex 12.22 Dght 5.639 | Lbp 77.02 Br md 12.20 Dpth 6.20 | Welded, 1 dk | **(A13B2TP) Products Tanker** | Liq: 3,392; Liq (Oil): 3,392 | Compartments: 4 Ta, ER | 2 Cargo Pump (s) | **1 oil engine** driving 1 FP propeller | Total Power: 1,765kW (2,400hp) 12.5kn | Fuji 8S40BH | 1 x 4 Stroke 8 Cy. 400 x 580 1765kW (2400bhp) | Fuji Diesel Co Ltd-Japan | AuxGen: 2 x 104kW 445V 60Hz a.c, 1 x 40kW 445V 60Hz a.c | Fuel: 134.0 (d.f.) 8.5pd

---

8735716 *ZCIC9* - **SEA D** | *ex* Vinidrea II *-2007* | **Danforth Ventures Inc** | Ocean Management GmbH | *George Town* *Cayman Islands (British)* | MMSI: 319759000 | Official number: 735564 | **398** - - | Class: AB | **2002 Proteksan-Turquoise Yachts Inc — Tuzla** Yd No: 40 | Loa 39.50 Br ex - Dght 1.900 | Lbp 32.81 Br md 8.50 Dpth 4.10 | Welded, 1 dk | **(X11A2YP) Yacht** | Hull Material: Aluminium Alloy | **2 oil engines** geared to sc. shafts driving 2 Propellers | Total Power: 4,480kW (6,092hp) 21.0kn | M.T.U. 16V396TE94 | 2 x Vee 4 Stroke 16 Cy. 165 x 185 each-2240kW (3046bhp) | MTU Friedrichshafen GmbH-Friedrichshafen

---

9193721 *VRMS6* - **SEA DANUTA** | *ex* BW Danuta *-2013* *ex* Berge Danuta *-2011* | **Silvana Ltd** | Sinogas Management Pte Ltd | *Hong Kong* *Hong Kong* | MMSI: 477942300 | Official number: HK-3965 | **49,288** 14,787 56,824 T/cm 71.8 | Class: NV | **2000-09 Stocznia Gdynia SA — Gdynia** Yd No: 8185/1 | Loa 225.75 (BB) Br ex 36.40 Dght 12.522 | Lbp 218.58 Br md 36.36 Dpth 22.02 | Welded, 1 dk | **(A11B2TG) LPG Tanker** | Double Hull | Liq (Gas): 76,980 | 4 x Gas Tank (s); 4 independent (C.mn.stl) pri | 10 Cargo Pump (s): 10x600m³/hr | Manifold: Bow/CM: 111.8m | **1 oil engine** driving 1 FP propeller | Total Power: 17,640kW (23,983hp) 18.0kn | Sulzer 6RTA68T-B | 1 x 2 Stroke 6 Cy. 680 x 2720 17640kW (23983bhp) | H Cegielski Poznan SA-Poland | AuxGen: 1 x 1000kW 440V 60Hz a.c, 3 x 1000kW 440V 60Hz a.c | Fuel: 221.0 (d.f.) 4040.0 (r.f.) 68.0pd

---

9047843 *DSQE7* - **SEA DAON** | *ex* Sun Queen *-2008* | **Sea Bright Maritime Co Ltd** | Sung Kyung Maritime Co Ltd (SK Maritime) | *Jeju* *South Korea* | MMSI: 441550000 | Official number: JJR-084594 | **1,509** 678 1,580 | Class: KR (NK) | **1992-04 Honda Zosen — Saiki** Yd No: 835 | Loa 76.52 Br ex - Dght 4.120 | Lbp 70.00 Br md 12.00 Dpth 7.10 | Welded, 1 dk | **(A31A2GX) General Cargo Ship** | Compartments: 1 Ho, ER | 1 Ha: (40.2 x 9.3)ER | **1 oil engine** with clutches, flexible couplings & sr reverse geared to sc. shaft driving 1 FP propeller | Total Power: 883kW (1,201hp) 11.5kn | Niigata 6M31AFTE | 1 x 4 Stroke 6 Cy. 310 x 530 883kW (1201bhp) | Niigata Engineering Co Ltd-Japan | AuxGen: 2 x 120kW 220V 60Hz a.c

---

8996190 *WDD8934* - **SEA DEFENDER** | *ex* Yung Da Fa No. 668 *-2007* | **Sea Defender LLC** | Sea Global Fisheries LLC | *Pago Pago, AS* *United States of America* | MMSI: 368046000 | Official number: 1202621 | **1,415** 515 - | **2003-11 Fong Kuo Shipbuilding Co Ltd — Kaohsiung** Yd No: 397 | L reg 72.40 Br ex - Dght - | Lbp - Br md - Dpth - | Welded, 1 dk | **(B11B2FV) Fishing Vessel** | **1 oil engine** driving 1 Propeller

---

9695767 *PCWR* - **SEA DELTA** | **Global Ship Leasing 15 BV** | Seacontractors Brokerage BV | *Vlissingen* *Netherlands* | MMSI: 244810134 | Official number: 23262M | **221** 66 200 | Class: BV | **2013-07 Albwardy Marine Engineering LLC — Dubai (Hull)** Yd No: 571693 | **2013-07 B.V. Scheepswerf Damen Hardinxveld — Hardinxveld-Giessendam** Yd No: 571693 | Loa 27.02 Br ex 9.34 Dght 2.630 | Lbp 23.84 Br md 9.10 Dpth 3.60 | Welded, 1 dk | **(B32A2ST) Tug** | Cranes: 1 | **2 oil engines** reduction geared to sc. shafts driving 2 FP propellers | Total Power: 2,206kW (3,000hp) | Caterpillar 3512B | 2 x Vee 4 Stroke 12 Cy. 170 x 190 each-1103kW (1500bhp) | Caterpillar Inc-USA | AuxGen: 2 x 69kW 50Hz a.c | Thrusters: 1 Tunnel thruster (f) | Fuel: 125.0

9374181 *V7PI4* - **SEA DIAMOND** | *ex* S. Nicole *-2011* *ex* Nicole *-2008* | **HD Ltd** | Hanaro Shipping Co Ltd | *Majuro* *Marshall Islands* | MMSI: 538003234 | Official number: 3234 | **40,690** 25,762 77,096 | Class: KR (NK) | **2007-03 Namura Shipbuilding Co Ltd — Imari SG** Yd No: 293 | Loa 224.99 (BB) Br ex - Dght 14.078 | Lbp 217.00 Br md 32.26 Dpth 19.50 | Welded, 1 dk | **(A21A2BC) Bulk Carrier** | Grain: 92,128 | Compartments: 7 Ho, ER | 7 Ha: 6 (17.2 x 15.1)ER (17.2 x 13.4) | **1 oil engine** driving 1 FP propeller | Total Power: 9,930kW (13,501hp) 14.0kn | MAN-B&W 6S60MC | 1 x 2 Stroke 6 Cy. 600 x 2292 9930kW (13501bhp) | Hitachi Zosen Corp-Japan

---

9098725 *LXKL* - **SEA DIAMOND** | *ex* M. J. Taknm *-2008* *ex* Taknm *-2003* | *ex* Swing *-2003* | **Sea Diamond Yachting Ltd** | Navilux SA | *Luxembourg* *Luxembourg* | MMSI: 253342000 | Official number: 8-58 | **140** 48 - | Class: AB | **2002-06 Overmarine SpA — Viareggio** Yd No: 105/16 | Loa 31.04 Br ex - Dght 1.200 | Lbp 27.61 Br md 6.63 Dpth 3.20 | Bonded, 1 dk | **(X11A2YP) Yacht** | Hull Material: Reinforced Plastic | **2 oil engines** reverse reduction geared to sc. shafts driving 2 Propellers | Total Power: 3,840kW (5,220hp) | M.T.U. 12V396TB94 | 2 x Vee 4 Stroke 12 Cy. 165 x 185 each-1920kW (2610bhp) | MTU Friedrichshafen GmbH-Friedrichshafen

---

8719815 - - **SEA DIAMOND** | **Xuan T Nguyen** | *Freeport, TX* *United States of America* | Official number: 909622 | *120* 81 - | **1987-01 Rodriguez Boat Builders, Inc. — Coden, Al** Yd No: 53 | Loa 25.61 Br ex - Dght - | Lbp 21.97 Br md 6.76 Dpth 3.38 | Welded, 1 dk | **(B11A2FT) Trawler** | **1 oil engine** geared to sc. shaft driving 1 FP propeller | Total Power: 530kW (721hp) | Caterpillar 3412T | 1 x Vee 4 Stroke 12 Cy. 137 x 152 530kW (721bhp) | Caterpillar Inc-USA

7624647 *HO5201* - **SEA DIAMOND** | *ex* Karan 6 *-2005* | **GMV Marine Services Inc** | - | *Panama* *Panama* | Official number: 3494409A | *254* 77 175 | Class: (AB) | **1978-07 Dynamarine Corp. — Bauan** Yd No: 150 | Loa 37.80 Br ex 9.83 Dght 2.744 | Lbp 35.06 Br md 9.61 Dpth 3.59 | Welded, 1 dk | **(B21A2OS) Platform Supply Ship** | **2 oil engines** reverse reduction geared to sc. shafts driving 2 FP propellers | Total Power: 588kW (800hp) 11.0kn | Caterpillar 3406PCTA | 2 x 4 Stroke 6 Cy. 137 x 165 each-294kW (400bhp) | Caterpillar Tractor Co-USA | AuxGen: 2 x 90kW

7409592 *AUPP* - **SEA DIAMOND II** | *ex* Mawddy Tide *-2000* | **Kei-Rsos Maritime Ltd** | - | *Visakhapatnam* *India* | MMSI: 419649000 | Official number: 3300 | **646** 194 978 | Class: IR (AB) | **1975-01 Halter Marine, Inc. — Moss Point, Ms** Yd No: 462 | Loa 51.80 Br ex 11.60 Dght 3.690 | Lbp 50.37 Br md 11.56 Dpth 4.25 | Welded, 1 dk | **(B21B2OT) Offshore Tug/Supply Ship** | **2 oil engines** reverse reduction geared to sc. shafts driving 2 FP propellers | Total Power: 2,354kW (3,200hp) 12.0kn | EMD (Electro-Motive) 16-567-BC | 2 x Vee 2 Stroke 16 Cy. 216 x 254 each-1177kW (1600bhp) | (Re-engined ,made 1965, Reconditioned & fitted 1975) | General Motors Corp-USA | AuxGen: 2 x 99kW 450V 60Hz a.c | Thrusters: 1 Thwart. FP thruster (f) | Fuel: 239.0 (d.f.)

7349792 *H02971* -	**SEA DIAMOND V** *ex* Argo I *-2002* *ex* Bison I *-1997* *ex* Bison *-1979* **Kulamakkattu Valiyaveetil Varghese** Asaker Marine & Shipping Agency *Panama* *Panama* MMSI: 356645000 Official number: 3260507A	**600** 180 -	Class: (BV) (HR) (NV)	**1974-01 D.W. Kremer Sohn — Elmshorn** Yd No: 1159 Loa 42.33 Br ex 10.85 Dght 4.649 Lbp 36.30 Br md 10.83 Dpth 5.57 Welded, 1 dk	**(B32A2ST) Tug** Ice Capable	**2 oil engines** driving 2 CP propellers Total Power: 3,162kW (4,300hp) 13.5kn MaK 8M452AK 2 x 4 Stroke 8 Cy. 320 x 450 each-1581kW (2150bhp) MaK Maschinenbau GmbH-Kiel AuxGen: 2 x 150kW 220V 50Hz a.c Thrusters: 1 Thwart. FP thruster (f) Fuel: 30.5 (d.f.) 14.0pd
7523166 *HZNF* -	**SEA DIAMOND X** *ex* Gulf Battler *-2005* *ex* Battler *-1995* *ex* Maersk Battler *-1994* **Kulamakkattu Valiyaveetil Varghese** Asaker Marine & Shipping Agency *Saudi Arabia* MMSI: 403087000	**762** 228 560	Class: AB IR (LR) ✠ Classed LR until 2/3/99	**1976-12 Odense Staalskibsvaerft A/S — Munkebo (Lindo Shipyard)** Yd No: 505 Loa 45.70 Br ex 12.37 Dght 4.970 Lbp 39.50 Br md 12.00 Dpth 6.00 Welded, 1 dk, 2nd dk except in machinery space	**(B21B20A) Anchor Handling Tug Supply** Passengers: berths: 23 Ice Capable	**2 oil engines** sr geared to sc. shafts driving 2 CP propellers Total Power: 6,252kW (8,500hp) 10.0kn MaK 12M453AK 2 x Vee 4 Stroke 12 Cy. 320 x 420 each-3126kW (4250bhp) MaK Maschinenbau GmbH-Kiel AuxGen: 3 x 175kW 380V 50Hz a.c Thrusters: 1 Thwart. FP thruster (f) Fuel: 559.0 31.0pd
8006000 *3EYJ4* -	**SEA DIAMOND XI** *ex* Seabulk Alkatar *-2007* *ex* Ocean King 1 *-1997* *ex* Imsalv Tiger *-1995* *ex* Gallant I *-1986* *ex* Gallant *-1983* **Kulamakkattu Valiyaveetil Varghese** Asaker Marine & Shipping Agency SatCom: Inmarsat A 1332315 *Panama* *Panama* MMSI: 352780000 Official number: 1535486H	*723* 222 549	Class: BV (GL) (AB)	**1981-03 Yokohama Zosen — Chiba** Yd No: 1387 Loa 40.09 Br ex 11.61 Dght 4.880 Lbp 39.63 Br md 11.59 Dpth 5.80 Welded, 1 dk	**(B21B20A) Anchor Handling Tug Supply**	**2 oil engines** reverse reduction geared to sc. shafts driving 2 CP propellers Total Power: 4,230kW (5,752hp) 14.0kn EMD (Electro-Motive) 16-645-E7 2 x Vee 2 Stroke 16 Cy. 230 x 254 each-2115kW (2876bhp) General Motors Corp.Electro-Motive Div.-La Grange AuxGen: 1 x 360kW 380V 50Hz a.c, 2 x 202kW 380V 50Hz a.c Thrusters: 1 Thwart. CP thruster (f) Fuel: 643.0 (d.f.) 13.0pd
8216423 *HP9763* -	**SEA DIAMOND XIV** *ex* Seacor Force *-2008* *ex* Nicor Force *-1991* **K H Varghese Moonstar International** Asaker Marine & Shipping Agency *Panama* *Panama* MMSI: 370753000 Official number: 4025209	**999** 299 1,200	Class: AB IR	**1985-03 Halter Marine, Inc. — Lockport, La** Yd No: 1089 Loa 65.84 Br ex 12.83 Dght 4.266 Lbp 55.17 Br md 12.81 Dpth 4.88 Welded, 1 dk	**(B21B20A) Anchor Handling Tug Supply** Ice Capable	**2 oil engines** reverse reduction geared to sc. shafts driving 2 FP propellers Total Power: 4,516kW (6,140hp) 12.0kn EMD (Electro-Motive) 16-645-E7B 2 x Vee 2 Stroke 16 Cy. 230 x 254 each-2258kW (3070bhp) General Motors Corp.Electro-Motive Div.-La Grange AuxGen: 2 x 150kW 120/440V 60Hz a.c Thrusters: 1 Thwart. FP thruster (f) Fuel: 378.0 (d.f.) 12.0pd
9255543 *3FGI8* -	**SEA DIAMOND XVI** *ex* Hadi XI *-2010* **Kulamakkattu Valiyaveetil Varghese** Asaker Marine & Shipping Agency *Panama* *Panama* MMSI: 371195000 Official number: 4203910	**1,592** 477 1,787	Class: AB IR	**2002-03 Keppel Singmarine Dockyard Pte Ltd — Singapore** Yd No: 257 Loa 60.00 Br ex 16.03 Dght 4.850 Lbp 56.39 Br md 16.00 Dpth 5.50 Welded, 1 dk	**(B21B20A) Anchor Handling Tug Supply**	**2 oil engines** reduction geared to sc. shafts driving 2 CP propellers Total Power: 4,100kW (5,574hp) 11.0kn Deutz SBV9M628 2 x 4 Stroke 9 Cy. 240 x 280 each-2050kW (2787bhp) Deutz AG-Koeln AuxGen: 2 x 350kW 440V 60Hz a.c, 1 x 450kW 440V 60Hz a.c Thrusters: 1 Thwart. CP thruster (f) Fuel: 510.0
9336634 *HP7391* -	**SEA DIAMOND XVII** *ex* BOA Mighty *-2012* *ex* Miclyn Might *-2007* **Kulamakkattu Valiyaveetil Varghese** Asaker Marine & Shipping Agency *Panama* *Panama* MMSI: 373032000 Official number: 4420212	**1,047** 318 775	Class: BV IR (LR) ✠ Classed LR until 31/3/12	**2006-03 Nautica Nova Shipbuilding & Engineering Sdn Bhd — Butterworth** Yd No: A0266 Loa 48.00 Br ex 13.05 Dght 5.200 Lbp 40.56 Br md 13.00 Dpth 6.00 Welded, 1 dk	**(B21B20A) Anchor Handling Tug Supply**	**2 oil engines** with clutches, flexible couplings & sr reverse geared to sc. shafts driving 2 CP propellers Total Power: 5,080kW (6,906hp) 12.0kn MaK 8M25 2 x 4 Stroke 8 Cy. 255 x 400 each-2540kW (3453bhp) Caterpillar Motoren GmbH & Co. KG-Germany AuxGen: 3 x 430kW 415V 50Hz a.c Thrusters: 1 Thwart. CP thruster (f)
9535876 *V7EL7* -	**SEA DIAS** *ex* Fortune Plum *-2014* **Dias Shipowning Inc** Seatankers Management Co Ltd *Majuro* *Marshall Islands* MMSI: 538005491 Official number: 5491	**33,036** 19,270 57,053 T/cm 58.8	Class: AB	**2010-07 Taizhou Sanfu Ship Engineering Co Ltd — Taizhou JS** Yd No: SF060104 Loa 189.99 (BB) Br ex - Dght 12.800 Lbp 185.00 Br md 32.26 Dpth 18.00 Welded, 1 dk	**(A21A2BC) Bulk Carrier** Grain: 71,634; Bale: 68,200 Compartments: 5 Ho, ER 5 Ha: 4 (21.3 x 18.3)ER (18.9 x 18.3) Cranes: 4x30t	**1 oil engine** driving 1 FP propeller Total Power: 9,488kW (12,900hp) 14.2kn MAN-B&W 6S50MC-C 1 x 2 Stroke 6 Cy. 500 x 2000 9488kW (12900bhp) STX Engine Co Ltd-South Korea AuxGen: 3 x 600kW a.c Fuel: 120.0 (d.f.) 2200.0 (r.f.)
9213131 *C6YZ8* -	**SEA DISCOVERER** *ex* Clipper Discoverer *-2009* *ex* Coastal Queen 2 *-2009* *ex* Cape Cod Light *-2007* **Clipper Cruises Ltd** FleetPro Ocean Inc SatCom: Inmarsat C 430895112 *Nassau* *Bahamas* MMSI: 311050300 Official number: 9000374	**4,954** 1,486 695	Class: LR **100A1** SS 08/2011 passenger ship **LMC**	**2004-12 Atlantic Marine — Jacksonville, Fl** Yd No: 4243 Loa 91.44 Br ex - Dght 3.810 Lbp - Br md 15.24 Dpth 6.10 Welded	**(A37A2PC) Passenger/Cruise** Passengers: cabins: 114; berths: 226	**2 oil engines** geared to sc. shafts driving 2 Directional propellers Total Power: 2,942kW (4,000hp) 10.0kn Caterpillar 3516TA 2 x Vee 4 Stroke 16 Cy. 170 x 190 each-1471kW (2000bhp) Caterpillar Inc-USA AuxGen: 2 x 1815kW a.c Thrusters: 1 Thwart. FP thruster (f) Fuel: 249.0 (d.f.) 15.5pd
9516131 *5BGR3* -	**SEA DISCOVERY** **CA Sea Discovery Shipping Ltd** Interorient Marine Services Ltd SatCom: Inmarsat C 420918510 *Limassol* *Cyprus* MMSI: 209185000 Official number: 9516131	**6,872** 3,410 9,382	Class: GL	**2012-01 Penglai Bohai Shipyard Co Ltd — Penglai SD** Yd No: PBZ07-89 Loa 109.83 (BB) Br ex - Dght 8.000 Lbp 105.80 Br md 18.20 Dpth 10.50 Welded, 1 dk	**(A31A2GX) General Cargo Ship** Grain: 11,770; Bale: 11,770 TEU 276 Compartments: 3 Ho, ER 3 Ha: ER Cranes: 2x60t Ice Capable	**1 oil engine** reduction geared to sc. shaft driving 1 Propeller Total Power: 4,000kW (5,438hp) 13.0kn MAN-B&W 8L32/40 1 x 4 Stroke 8 Cy. 320 x 400 4000kW (5438bhp) Shaanxi Diesel Heavy Industry Co Lt-China Thrusters: 1 Tunnel thruster (f)
8852514 *WDB7914* -	**SEA DOG** *ex* Captain Thanh-Lap *-2004* *ex* Thanh Lap *-2001* *ex* Capt. Man *-1998* **Kenneth A Roma** - *Barnegat Light, NJ* *United States of America* MMSI: 366949730 Official number: 912043	*129* 88 -		**1987 National Fisherman's Cooperative — Biloxi, Ms** Loa - Br ex - Dght - Lbp 23.71 Br md 6.71 Dpth 3.51 Welded, 1 dk	**(B11B2FV) Fishing Vessel**	**1 oil engine** driving 1 FP propeller
9486427 *V7XL9* -	**SEA DOLPHIN C** **Milford Shipping Ltd** Cebi Denizcilik ve Ticaret AS *Majuro* *Marshall Islands* MMSI: 538004513 Official number: 4513	**23,236** 11,502 33,811	Class: AB (BV)	**2011-12 21st Century Shipbuilding Co Ltd — Tongyeong** Yd No: 1006 Loa 181.10 (BB) Br ex - Dght 9.900 Lbp 172.00 Br md 30.00 Dpth 14.80 Welded, 1 dk	**(A21A2BC) Bulk Carrier** Grain: 47,558; Bale: 45,180 Compartments: 5 Ho, ER 5 Ha: ER Cranes: 4x30.7t	**1 oil engine** driving 1 FP propeller Total Power: 6,480kW (8,810hp) 14.5kn MAN-B&W 6S42MC 1 x 2 Stroke 6 Cy. 420 x 1764 6480kW (8810bhp) Hyundai Heavy Industries Co Ltd-South Korea AuxGen: 3 x 570kW a.c Fuel: 130.0 (d.f.) 1600.0 (r.f.)
7035937 *A9D3259* -	**SEA DOLPHIN I** *ex* Koper *-2008* *ex* Emzari *-2005* *ex* Mini Mika *-2004* *ex* Sakura I *-2002* *ex* Sakura *-1998* *ex* Mini Sakura *-1996* *launched as* Mini Leg *-1970* **United Cement Co Bscc** - *Bahrain* *Bahrain* MMSI: 408573000	**1,639** 1,026 3,213	Class: BV (RS) (AB)	**1970-11 Hashimoto Zosensho — Kobe** (Hull) Yd No: 330 **1970-11 The Hakodate Dock Co Ltd — Japan** Yd No: 526 Loa 65.49 Br ex 15.32 Dght 4.947 Lbp 62.82 Br md 15.30 Dpth 6.61 Welded, 1 dk	**(A31A2GX) General Cargo Ship** Grain: 3,789; Bale: 3,672 Compartments: 2 Ho, ER 2 Ha: 2 (17.0 x 9.8)ER Cranes: 1x8t	**2 oil engines** reverse reduction geared to sc. shafts driving 2 FP propellers Total Power: 1,104kW (1,500hp) 10.3kn Daihatsu 6PSHTCM-26D 2 x 4 Stroke 6 Cy. 260 x 320 each-552kW (750bhp) Daihatsu Diesel Manufacturing Co Lt-Japan AuxGen: 2 x 104kW 445V 60Hz a.c Fuel: 106.5 (d.f.)
8941121 *WCX5465* -	**SEA DOPHIN** **Thuong Van Dang** - *Biloxi, MS* *United States of America* MMSI: 367187790 Official number: 1051108	**148** 44 -		**1997 Master Boat Builders, Inc. — Coden, Al** Yd No: 242 L reg 24.87 Br ex - Dght - Lbp - Br md 7.32 Dpth 3.81 Welded, 1 dk	**(B11B2FV) Fishing Vessel**	**1 oil engine** driving 1 FP propeller
7017363 - -	**SEA DOVE** *ex* Mina *-1997* *ex* Amina *-1995* *ex* Lion City *-1993* *ex* Lemujan *-1989* - -	**525** 157 347	Class: (BV)	**1970 Vosper Thornycroft Uniteers Pte Ltd — Singapore** Yd No: B.887 Loa 56.09 Br ex 11.76 Dght 2.032 Lbp 51.90 Br md 11.43 Dpth 3.36 Welded, 1 dk	**(B21A20S) Platform Supply Ship** Liq: 333; Liq (Oil): 333 Compartments: 6 Ta, ER	**2 oil engines** sr geared to sc. shafts driving 2 FP propellers Total Power: 832kW (1,132hp) 11.0kn Caterpillar D379SCAC 2 x Vee 4 Stroke 8 Cy. 159 x 203 each-416kW (566bhp) Caterpillar Tractor Co-USA AuxGen: 3 x 61kW 220/440V 50Hz a.c

8653413 - -	**SEA DOVE** *ex* Erick Jose *-2012* *ex* Lady Marguerite *-1991* *ex* Meridian Express *-1991* *ex* Mar 7 *-1991* **John Henry Francis** - *San Lorenzo* *Honduras* Official number: L1511582	**233** 70 -		**1980 Marine Fabricators, Inc. — Green Cove Springs, Fl** Loa 32.61 Br ex - Dght 1.520 Lbp - Br md 8.23 Dpth 3.65 Welded, 1 dk	**(B21A20S) Platform Supply Ship**	**2 oil engines** reduction geared to sc. shafts driving 2 Propellers Total Power: 898kW (1,220hp) 12.0kn Caterpillar 3412 2 x Vee 4 Stroke 12 Cy. 137 x 152 each-449kW (610bhp) Caterpillar Tractor Co-USA
8414221 *HSB2782* -	**SEA DRAGON** *ex* Damar Wulan *-1999* *ex* Asian Seaways *-1996* *ex* Sea Cosmos *-1990* *ex* Tropical Star *-1987* *ex* Sun Lotus *-1986* **S Ship Management 2000 Co Ltd** Sinsimon Navigation Co Ltd *Bangkok* *Thailand* MMSI: 567195000 Official number: 441000843	**5,463** 2,257 7,017	Class: (NK)	**1984-04 Imai Shipbuilding Co Ltd — Kochi KC** Yd No: 524 Loa 98.18 (BB) Br ex - Dght 7.548 Lbp 89.95 Br md 18.00 Dpth 13.00 Welded, 1 dk	**(A31A2GX) General Cargo Ship** Grain: 13,001; Bale: 12,103 Compartments: 2 Ho, ER 2 Ha: (22.3 x 9.8) (24.7 x 9.8)ER Derricks: 1x25t,3x15t	**1 oil engine** driving 1 FP propeller Total Power: 2,582kW (3,510hp) 12.0kn B&W 6L35MCE 1 x 2 Stroke 6 Cy. 350 x 1050 2582kW (3510bhp) Hitachi Zosen Corp-Japan AuxGen: 2 x 200kW a.c Fuel: 565.0 (r.f.)
8319330 *9LY2595* -	**SEA DRAGON** *ex* Nan You 12 *-2013* *ex* Zhong Hao 9 *-2007* *ex* Dong Zhao *-2007* *ex* Shin Iwaki Maru *-1998* **Grand Rich International Marine Co Ltd** Sino Chance Enterprise Inc *Freetown* *Sierra Leone* MMSI: 667003398 Official number: SL103398	**4,718** 2,642 5,674	Class: (CC) (NK)	**1984-11 Mitsubishi Heavy Industries Ltd. — Nagasaki** Yd No: 1955 Loa 103.94 (BB) Br ex 17.02 Dght 6.960 Lbp 97.00 Br md 17.00 Dpth 10.42 Welded, 1 dk	**(A13E2LD) Coal/Oil Mixture Tanker** Liq: 4,799; Liq (Oil): 4,799 Compartments: 8 Ta, ER 4 Cargo Pump (s): 4x350m³/hr	**1 oil engine** driving 1 FP propeller Total Power: 2,427kW (3,300hp) 12.8kn Hanshin 6EL40 1 x 4 Stroke 6 Cy. 400 x 800 2427kW (3300bhp) The Hanshin Diesel Works Ltd-Japan AuxGen: 2 x 350kW 440V 60Hz a.c Thrusters: 1 Thwart. CP thruster (f)
8021933 *XVBW* -	**SEA DRAGON** *ex* Duong Dong 02 *-2010* *ex* Bao Vinh 01 *-2006* *ex* Phuoc Thang 09 *-2006* *ex* Thanh Hoa 01 *-2006* *ex* Miyajima Maru *-1985* **Hai Long Co Ltd** - SatCom: Inmarsat C 457445610 *Haiphong* *Vietnam* MMSI: 574456000 Official number: VNSG-1658-TD	**1,229** 705 2,000	Class: VR (NK)	**1981-03 Matsuura Tekko Zosen K.K. — Osakikamijima** Yd No: 284 Converted From: General Cargo Ship-1998 Loa 71.05 Br ex 12.02 Dght 5.200 Lbp 67.01 Br md 12.01 Dpth 6.23 Welded, 1 dk	**(A13B2TP) Products Tanker** Liq: 2,331; Liq (Oil): 2,331	**1 oil engine** reduction geared to sc. shaft driving 1 FP propeller Total Power: 1,324kW (1,800hp) 12.8kn Fuji 6S37C 1 x 4 Stroke 6 Cy. 370 x 550 1324kW (1800bhp) Fuji Diesel Co Ltd-Japan AuxGen: 2 x 96kW a.c
8940309 - -	**SEA DRAGON** *ex* Thanh Nga *-2005* **Bonacca Shipping S de RL** - *Roatan* *Honduras* Official number: U-1828100	**127** 39 -		**1996 Ocean Marine, Inc. — Bayou La Batre, Al** Yd No: 314 L reg 24.69 Br ex - Dght - Lbp - Br md 7.01 Dpth 3.69 Welded, 1 dk	**(B11A2FT) Trawler**	**1 oil engine** reduction geared to sc. shaft driving 1 Propeller Total Power: 449kW (610hp) Caterpillar 3412 1 x Vee 4 Stroke 12 Cy. 137 x 152 449kW (610bhp) (made 1996) Caterpillar Inc-USA
8910354 *V4KC2* -	**SEA DRAGON** *ex* Mamzar *-2012* *ex* Kakushun Maru No. 8 *-2004* **Al Shahama Shipping & Trading Co Ltd** Meramar Shipping & Trading Co Inc *Charlestown* *St Kitts & Nevis* MMSI: 341913000 Official number: SKN 1002267	**2,995** 1,990 4,998	Class: IS (BV) (NK)	**1989-11 Hakata Zosen K.K. — Imabari** Yd No: 505 Loa 103.68 (BB) Br ex 15.52 Dght 6.900 Lbp 96.00 Br md 15.50 Dpth 8.15 Welded, 1 dk	**(A13B2TP) Products Tanker** Double Bottom Entire Compartment Length Liq: 5,438; Liq (Oil): 5,438 Compartments: 8 Ta, ER 3 Cargo Pump (s): 2x1800m³/hr, 1x750m³/hr Manifold: Bow/CM: 46m	**1 oil engine** driving 1 CP propeller Total Power: 3,236kW (4,400hp) 13.6kn Hanshin 6EL44 1 x 4 Stroke 6 Cy. 440 x 880 3236kW (4400bhp) The Hanshin Diesel Works Ltd-Japan AuxGen: 3 x 221kW 450V 60Hz a.c Thrusters: 1 Thwart. CP thruster (f) Fuel: 65.6 (d.f.) 371.1 (r.f.) 15.5pd
8852394 *WUV5035* -	**SEA DRAGON** - **Long Thanh Nguyen** - *Honolulu, HI* *United States of America* MMSI: 367140270 Official number: 916874	*103* 82 -		**1988 National Fisherman's Cooperative — Biloxi, Ms** Yd No: 8 Loa - Br ex - Dght - Lbp 21.95 Br md 6.86 Dpth 2.90 Welded, 1 dk	**(B11B2FV) Fishing Vessel**	**1 oil engine** driving 1 FP propeller
9031739 *3FR05* -	**SEA DRAGON** *ex* Speedy *-2012* *ex* Sichem Marbella *-2009* *ex* J. M. S. Emerald *-2004* *ex* Sun Emerald *-2003* *ex* Stolt Otome *-2000* **Choice Shipping Co Ltd** Artemiz Marine Services JLT SatCom: Inmarsat C 435230511 *Panama* *Panama* MMSI: 352305000 Official number: 39215PEXT4	**4,954** 2,557 7,715 T/cm 16.0	Class: BV (LR) (NK) Classed LR until 29/10/12	**1991-07 Higaki Zosen K.K. — Imabari** Yd No: 397 Loa 114.12 (BB) Br ex - Dght 6.774 Lbp 106.01 Br md 18.20 Dpth 8.10 Welded, 1 dk	**(A12B2TR) Chemical/Products Tanker** Double Bottom Entire Compartment Length Liq: 9,116; Liq (Oil): 9,116 Cargo Heating Coils Compartments: 12 Wing Ta, ER 12 Cargo Pump (s): 12x200m³/hr Manifold: Bow/CM: 58m	**1 oil engine** driving 1 FP propeller Total Power: 3,310kW (4,500hp) 12.5kn Hanshin 6LF50A 1 x 4 Stroke 6 Cy. 500 x 800 3310kW (4500bhp) The Hanshin Diesel Works Ltd-Japan AuxGen: 2 x 360kW 450V 60Hz a.c Boilers: e (ex.g.) 10.0kgf/cm² (9.8bar), AuxB (o.f.) 7.0kgf/cm² (6.9bar) Fuel: 104.0 (d.f.) 407.0 (r.f.)
9498858 *A9D3153* -	**SEA DRAGON** *ex* Bgp Supply I *-2012* **Al Jazeera Shipping Co** Al Jazeera Shipping Co WLL (AJS) *Bahrain* *Bahrain* MMSI: 408438000 Official number: BN 6052	**398** 120 460	Class: GL (CC)	**2007-12 Hung Seng Shipbuilding Sdn Bhd — Sibu** Yd No: 048 Loa 34.00 Br ex - Dght 4.210 Lbp 31.35 Br md 10.60 Dpth 4.95 Welded, 1 dk	**(B21A20S) Platform Supply Ship**	**2 oil engines** geared to sc. shafts driving 2 Propellers Total Power: 2,984kW (4,058hp) 12.0kn Cummins KTA-50-M2 2 x Vee 4 Stroke 16 Cy. 159 x 159 each-1492kW (2029bhp) Cummins Engine Co Ltd-United Kingdom AuxGen: 2 x 80kW 415V a.c
9216341 *3WBT* -	**SEA DRAGON** *ex* White Saga *-2009* *ex* Koyo Maru *-2000* **Seagull Shipping JSC (SESCO) (Cong Ty Co Phan Van Tai Bien Hai Au)** - SatCom: Inmarsat C 457492810 *Saigon* *Vietnam* MMSI: 574928000 Official number: VNSG-1962-TH	**4,963** 3,084 7,950	Class: NK VR	**1999-09 Seibu Zosen K.K. — Hiroshima** Yd No: 1021 Loa 101.30 Br ex - Dght 7.904 Lbp 92.75 Br md 18.00 Dpth 11.00 Welded, 1 dk	**(A31A2GX) General Cargo Ship** Grain: 11,641; Bale: 10,645 Compartments: 2 Ho, ER 2 Ha: (19.6 x 10.5) (32.9 x 10.5)ER Derricks: 2x30t,1x25t	**1 oil engine** driving 1 FP propeller Total Power: 2,942kW (4,000hp) 12.5kn Mitsubishi 6UEC37LA 1 x 2 Stroke 6 Cy. 370 x 880 2942kW (4000bhp) Akasaka Tekkosho KK (Akasaka DieselLtd)-Japan Fuel: 616.0 (r.f.)
9242429 *WCZ9564* -	**SEA DRAGON** - **Hien Nguyen** - *Sugar Land, TX* *United States of America* Official number: 1100337	**178** 53 -		**2000 Williams Fabrication, Inc. — Coden, Al** Yd No: WF103 Loa - Br ex - Dght - Lbp 26.09 Br md 7.57 Dpth 4.06 Welded, 1 dk	**(B11B2FV) Fishing Vessel**	**1 oil engine** driving 1 FP propeller
9658197 *YDA3165* -	**SEA DRAGON 01** - **PT Bima Maritimindo** - *Batam* *Indonesia*	**272** 82 287	Class: (NK)	**2012-05 Hung Seng Shipbuilding Sdn Bhd — Sibu** Yd No: 36 Loa 30.00 Br ex 8.60 Dght 3.512 Lbp 27.71 Br md 8.60 Dpth 4.12 Welded, 1 dk	**(B32A2ST) Tug**	**2 oil engines** reduction geared to sc. shafts driving 2 FP propellers Total Power: 1,518kW (2,064hp) Mitsubishi S6R2-MTK3L 2 x 4 Stroke 6 Cy. 170 x 220 each-759kW (1032bhp) Mitsubishi Heavy Industries Ltd-Japan Fuel: 220.0 (d.f.)
8954192 *XVSM* -	**SEA DRAGON 01** *ex* Nhat Thuan 02 *-2012* *ex* Sa Lan 20/7 *-2012* **Binh Thuan Transport & Commercial Co Ltd (Cong ty Tnhh Van Tai Va Thuong Mai Binh Thuan)** - *Saigon* *Vietnam* MMSI: 574012151 Official number: VNSG-1407-TD	**998** 553 1,800	Class: VR	**1969-01 Bach Dang Shipyard — Haiphong** Loa 73.50 Br ex 11.02 Dght 4.900 Lbp 66.50 Br md 11.00 Dpth 5.56 Welded, 1 dk	**(A13B2TP) Products Tanker** Liq: 2,076; Liq (Oil): 2,076	**1 oil engine** driving 1 FP propeller Total Power: 919kW (1,249hp) 12.0kn Akasaka AH28 1 x 4 Stroke 6 Cy. 280 x 440 919kW (1249bhp) Akasaka Tekkosho KK (Akasaka DieselLtd)-Japan AuxGen: 1 x 60kW a.c, 1 x 50kW a.c
9706114 *YDA3466* -	**SEA DRAGON 03** - **PT Bima Maritimindo** - *Batam* *Indonesia* MMSI: 525012285	**253** 76 295	Class: NK	**2013-09 Hung Seng Shipbuilding Sdn Bhd — Sibu** Yd No: 48 Loa 30.00 Br ex - Dght 3.512 Lbp 28.05 Br md 8.60 Dpth 4.12 Welded, 1 dk	**(B32A2ST) Tug**	**2 oil engines** reduction geared to sc. shafts driving 2 Directional propellers Total Power: 1,518kW (2,064hp) 11.0kn Mitsubishi 1 x 759kW (1032bhp) Mitsubishi Heavy Industries Ltd-Japan Mitsubishi S6R2-MTK3L 1 x 4 Stroke 6 Cy. 170 x 220 759kW (1032bhp) Mitsubishi Heavy Industries Ltd-Japan Fuel: 220.0

8958411 **SEA DRAGON II** *WCZ5821* - **Sea Dragon II Inc** - *Honolulu, HI* *United States of America* Official number: 1089137	**149** 44 -		**1999 Master Boat Builders, Inc. — Coden, Al** Yd No: 270 L reg 22.73 Br ex - Dght - Lbp - Br md 7.31 Dpth 3.81 Welded, 1 dk	**(B11B2FV) Fishing Vessel**	**1 oil engine** driving 1 FP propeller
8941236 **SEA DRAGON III** *WDD4105* *ex Topcat -2006* - **Long Thanh Nguyen** - *Honolulu, HI* *United States of America* MMSI: 367140260 Official number: 1051110	**119** 35 -		**1997 Ocean Marine, Inc. — Bayou La Batre, Al** Yd No: 331 L reg 22.68 Br ex - Dght - Lbp - Br md 7.01 Dpth 3.72 Welded, 1 dk	**(B11B2FV) Fishing Vessel**	**1 oil engine** driving 1 FP propeller
7927257 **SEA DRAGON NO. 88** - *ex Yoha 9 -2000 ex Yoha -1999* - *ex Isuzu Maru No. 23 -1985* - -	**574** 204 345		**1980-03 Miho Zosensho K.K. — Shimizu** Yd No: 1158 Loa 48.49 Br ex 8.44 Dght 3.231 Lbp 42.07 Br md 8.41 Dpth 3.56 Welded, 1 dk	**(B11B2FV) Fishing Vessel**	**1 oil engine** driving 1 FP propeller Total Power: 809kW (1,100hp) Akasaka DM28AR 1 x 4 Stroke 6 Cy. 280 x 460 809kW (1100bhp) Akasaka Tekkosho KK (Akasaka DieselLtd)-Japan
8666264 **SEA DREAM** - - **Yasa Turizm ve Tic AS** - *Bodrum* *Turkey* Official number: 45	**292** 88 -	Class: NK	**2005-07 Aegean Yacht Services — Bodrum** Yd No: 31 Loa 39.00 Br ex - Dght - Lbp 28.80 Br md 9.55 Dpth 4.80 Welded, 1 dk	**(X11A2YP) Yacht** Passengers: berths: 12	**2 oil engines** reduction geared to sc. shafts driving 2 Propellers Total Power: 994kW (1,352hp) MAN 2 x 4 Stroke Dbl.Act. 12 Cy. 128 x 142 each-497kW (676bhp) MAN Nutzfahrzeuge AG-Nuernberg Fuel: 10.0
9027336 **SEA DREAM** *MLRZ6* *ex Uniwest -2006 ex Bermie -2000* - *ex Aliosha VII of Rurik -1994* **Caribes Des Mers SA** Ocra Marine Services Ltd SatCom: Inmarsat M 600852749 *Douglas* *Isle of Man (British)* MMSI: 235010730 Official number: 738503	**498** 281 -	Class: BV (AB)	**1991-06 Cantieri SIAR SpA — Fano** Yd No: 89/01 Loa 43.00 Br ex - Dght 2.900 Lbp 37.57 Br md 9.20 Dpth 5.35 Bonded, 1 dk	**(X11A2YP) Yacht** Hull Material: Reinforced Plastic	**2 oil engines** geared to sc. shafts driving 2 FP propellers Total Power: 2,000kW (2,720hp) 16.0kn Caterpillar 3512B 2 x Vee 4 Stroke 12 Cy. 170 x 190 each-1000kW (1360bhp) Caterpillar Inc-USA AuxGen: 3 x 168kW 380/220V a.c Fuel: 116.5 (d.f.)
9302322 **SEA DREAM** *J7AD4* *ex Mutha Princess -2008* - *ex Asme Emerald -2006* **Blue Marine Logistics (S) Pte Ltd** Blue Marine Logistics Pvt Ltd *Portsmouth* *Dominica* Official number: 50276	**193** 58 163	Class: IR (NK)	**2003-09 Tang Tiew Hee & Sons Sdn Bhd — Sibu** Yd No: 11 Loa 26.00 Br ex - Dght 3.271 Lbp 24.35 Br md 8.00 Dpth 3.65 Welded, 1 dk	**(B32A2ST) Tug**	**2 oil engines** geared to sc. shafts driving 2 FP propellers Total Power: 1,220kW (1,658hp) 10.0kn Mitsubishi S6R2-MPTK 2 x 4 Stroke 6 Cy. 170 x 220 each-610kW (829bhp) Mitsubishi Heavy Industries Ltd-Japan AuxGen: 2 x 104kW 415V 50Hz a.c
9407653 **SEA DREAM** *3WON* - **Seagull Shipping JSC (SESCO) (Cong Ty Co Phan Van Tai Bien Hai Au)** - *Saigon* *Vietnam* MMSI: 574445000 Official number: VNSG-1798-TH	**8,216** 5,295 13,268	Class: NK VR	**2006-12 Ha Long Shipbuilding Co Ltd — Ha Long** Yd No: HLS-205 Loa 136.49 (BB) Br ex 20.23 Dght 8.365 Lbp 126.00 Br md 20.20 Dpth 11.30 Welded, 1 dk	**(A31A2GX) General Cargo Ship** Grain: 18,601; Bale: 17,744 Compartments: 4 Ho, ER 4 Ha: (18.7 x 11.4)2 (19.4 x 11.4)ER (18.3 x 10.8) Derricks: 4x25t	**1 oil engine** driving 1 FP propeller Total Power: 3,965kW (5,391hp) 13.2kn Mitsubishi 7UEC33LSII 1 x 2 Stroke 7 Cy. 330 x 1050 3965kW (5391bhp) Akasaka Tekkosho KK (Akasaka DieselLtd)-Japan Fuel: 710.0
9560259 **SEA DREAM** *IJBS2* - **Oromare SpA** - *Genoa* *Italy* MMSI: 247315800	**322** 96 -	Class: RI **100A1** 09/2011 Class contemplated	**2011-09 Santierul Naval Damen Galati S.A. — Galati** (Hull) Yd No: 1178 **2011-09 B.V. Scheepswerf Damen — Gorinchem** Yd No: 511628 Loa 35.30 Br ex - Dght 3.650 Lbp 34.65 Br md 8.84 Dpth 4.40 Welded, 1 dk	**(B32A2ST) Tug**	**2 oil engines** reduction geared to sc. shafts driving 2 FP propellers Total Power: 3,460kW (4,704hp) Caterpillar C280-6 2 x 4 Stroke 6 Cy. 280 x 300 each-1730kW (2352bhp) Caterpillar Inc-USA
9619696 **SEA DREAM** *9V9744* - **Transport Energy Marine Pte Ltd** HM Ship Management Pte Ltd *Singapore* *Singapore* MMSI: 566332000 Official number: 397535	**2,994** 1,400 4,993	Class: BV	**2012-01 Taizhou Yuanhang Shipyard Co Ltd — Wenling ZJ** Yd No: YH0707 Loa 79.90 Br ex - Dght 6.600 Lbp 76.50 Br md 16.40 Dpth 8.60 Welded, 1 dk	**(A13B2TP) Products Tanker** Double Hull (13F) Liq: 4,800; Liq (Oil): 4,886 Compartments: 5 Wing Ta, 5 Wing Ta, ER	**2 oil engines** reduction geared to sc. shafts driving 2 FP propellers Total Power: 1,920kW (2,610hp) 11.0kn MAN-B&W 6L23/30A 2 x 4 Stroke 6 Cy. 225 x 300 each-960kW (1305bhp) Zhenjiang Marine Diesel Works-China AuxGen: 2 x 140kW 50Hz a.c Fuel: 282.0
9406817 **SEA DUKE** *HP4851* *ex Fordeco 67 -2009* - **STFA Deniz Insaati Insaat Sanayi ve Ticaret AS** - *Panama* *Panama* MMSI: 354172000 Official number: 4231511A	**197** 60 -	Class: GL	**2006-09 Forward Shipbuilding Enterprise Sdn Bhd — Sibu** Yd No: 106 Loa 26.00 Br ex 8.02 Dght 3.000 Lbp 23.86 Br md 8.00 Dpth 3.65 Welded, 1 dk	**(B32A2ST) Tug**	**2 oil engines** reverse reduction geared to sc. shafts driving 2 FP propellers Total Power: 1,538kW (2,092hp) Mitsubishi S6R2-MPTK2 2 x 4 Stroke 6 Cy. 170 x 220 each-769kW (1046bhp) Mitsubishi Heavy Industries Ltd-Japan AuxGen: 2 x 50kW 50Hz a.c
9254006 **SEA DWELLER** *P3YX9* *ex Samho Friend -2004* - **Azolimnos Marine Co Ltd** Coral Shipping Corp *Limassol* *Cyprus* MMSI: 209249000 Official number: 9254006	**2,440** 1,084 3,420 T/cm 10.2	Class: GL (KR)	**2002-05 Samho Shipbuilding Co Ltd — Tongyeong** Yd No: 1035 Loa 87.31 (BB) Br ex 14.22 Dght 5.813 Lbp 79.80 Br md 14.00 Dpth 7.30 Welded, 1 dk	**(A12B2TR) Chemical/Products Tanker** Double Hull (13F) Liq: 3,722; Liq (Oil): 3,800 Cargo Heating Coils Compartments: 1 Ta, 8 Wing Ta, 2 Wing Slop Ta, ER 10 Cargo Pump (s): 10x200m³/hr Manifold: Bow/CM: 46m	**1 oil engine** driving 1 FP propeller Total Power: 1,912kW (2,600hp) 11.5kn Hanshin LH36LA 1 x 4 Stroke 6 Cy. 360 x 670 1912kW (2600bhp) The Hanshin Diesel Works Ltd-Japan AuxGen: 3 x 260kW 440V a.c Thrusters: 1 Thwart. FP thruster (f) Fuel: 49.0 (d.f.) 165.0 (r.f.)
8742264 **SEA DWELLER** *V7SI8* *ex No Escape -2010* - **Nachala Ltd** Ocean Management GmbH *Bikini* *Marshall Islands* MMSI: 538080071 Official number: 80071	**417** 125 -	Class: AB	**1999-04 Heesen Shipyards B.V. — Oss** Yd No: 10446 Loa 45.86 Br ex - Dght 1.650 Lbp 38.66 Br md 8.50 Dpth 3.77 Welded, 1 dk	**(X11A2YP) Yacht** Hull Material: Aluminium Alloy	**2 oil engines** reverse reduction geared to sc. shafts driving 2 Propellers Total Power: 4,480kW (6,092hp) M.T.U. 16V396TE94 2 x Vee 4 Stroke 16 Cy. 165 x 185 each-2240kW (3046bhp) MTU Friedrichshafen GmbH-Friedrichshafen
8719839 **SEA EAGLE** *UBYD* *ex Sea Eagle II -2005 ex Sea Eagle -2004* - **OOO 'Severo-Vostochnaya Kompaniya'** - *Petropavlovsk-Kamchatskiy* *Russia* Official number: 876844	**138** 41 110	Class: RS	**1987-11 Rodriguez Boat Builders, Inc. — Coden, Al** Yd No: 69 Loa 26.83 Br ex 7.36 Dght 2.880 Lbp 23.84 Br md 7.32 Dpth 3.54 Welded, 1 dk	**(B11A2FS) Stern Trawler**	**1 oil engine** reduction geared to sc. shaft driving 1 FP propeller Total Power: 497kW (676hp) 11.5kn Cummins VTA-28-M 1 x Vee 4 Stroke 12 Cy. 140 x 152 497kW (676bhp) Cummins Engine Co Inc-USA
8719504 **SEA EAGLE** *WDC4819* - **Sea Eagle Inc** - *Galveston, TX* *United States of America* Official number: 921492	*117* 79 -		**1987-10 Deep Sea Boat Builders, Inc. — Bayou La Batre, Al** Loa 25.91 Br ex - Dght - Lbp 22.21 Br md 6.82 Dpth 2.86 Welded, 1 dk	**(B11A2FT) Trawler**	**1 oil engine** geared to sc. shaft driving 1 FP propeller Total Power: 530kW (721hp) Caterpillar 3412T 1 x Vee 4 Stroke 12 Cy. 137 x 152 530kW (721bhp) Caterpillar Inc-USA
7831202 **SEA EAGLE** - *ex Blagovest -2009 ex Kapitan Rolzing -2001* - *ex Rosskor -2000 ex Dong Won No. 303 -1992* **West Khan SA** East Shine Shipping Co Ltd	**713** 335 498	Class: (RS) (KR)	**1978 Daedong Shipbuilding Co Ltd — Busan** Loa 55.16 Br ex 8.60 Dght 3.600 Lbp 49.00 Br md - Dpth 6.60 Welded, 1 dk	**(B11B2FV) Fishing Vessel** Ins: 542 3 Ha: 2 (1.2 x 0.9) (1.7 x 1.7)	**1 oil engine** reverse geared to sc. shaft driving 1 FP propeller Total Power: 993kW (1,350hp) 13.5kn Akasaka AH28R 1 x 4 Stroke 6 Cy. 280 x 440 993kW (1350bhp) Akasaka Tekkosho KK (Akasaka DieselLtd)-Japan AuxGen: 2 x 200kW 225V a.c Fuel: 246.0 (d.f.)
8331716 **SEA EAGLE** *WDG5235* *ex Miss Barbara -2001* - **Northcliffe Ocean Shipping & Trading Co Inc** - *United States of America* MMSI: 367544720 Official number: 636149	*108* 73 -		**1981 Rayco Shipbuilders & Repairs, Inc. — Bourg, La** Yd No: 83 Loa - Br ex - Dght - Lbp 18.35 Br md 7.32 Dpth 2.71 Welded, 1 dk	**(B32A2ST) Tug**	**1 oil engine** driving 1 FP propeller Total Power: 1,324kW (1,800hp)

IMO / Call sign	Name / Owner	Tonnage	Class	Builder / Dimensions	Type	Machinery
7200099 *WTX7605* -	**SEA EAGLE** *ex* E. D. Smith *-1980* *ex* Shamrock *-1980* *ex* YP 56 *-1980* *ex* Naugatuck *-1980* **Oscar Niemeth Towing Inc** - *Oakland, CA* *United States of America* MMSI: 367010910 Official number: 253073	*140* 29 -		**1926-01 Defoe Boat & Motor Works — Bay City, Mi** Loa - Br ex 7.19 Dght - Lbp 29.88 Br md - Dpth 3.20 Welded, 1 dk	**(B32A2ST) Tug**	**2 oil engines** driving 2 FP propellers Total Power: 1,324kW (1,800hp) Winton 2 x 6 Cy. each-662kW (900bhp) Winton Engineering Corp.-Cleveland, Oh
9219915 *WCY5079* -	**SEA EAGLE** **Kirby Offshore Marine Operating LLC** - *Charleston, SC* *United States of America* MMSI: 366756360 Official number: 1066709	**693** 207 -	Class: AB	**1998-09 Moss Point Marine, Inc. — Escatawpa, Ms** Yd No: 143 Loa 37.60 Br ex - Dght 6.125 Lbp 36.58 Br md 10.52 Dpth 6.71 Welded, 1 dk	**(B32B2SA) Articulated Pusher Tug**	**2 oil engines** reduction geared to sc. shafts driving 2 FP propellers Total Power: 4,288kW (5,830hp) Alco 16V251F 2 x Vee 4 Stroke 16 Cy. 229 x 267 each-2144kW (2915bhp) Coltec Industries, FairbanksMorse Eng. Div -Beloit
9600346 *J8B4546* -	**SEA EAGLE** *launched as* Bogazici 9 *-2011* **Sea Eagles Offshore Services Pte Ltd** Sea Eagles Shipping LLC *Kingstown* *St Vincent & The Grenadines* MMSI: 377576000 Official number: 11019	**463** 139 -	Class: BV	**2011-07 Dentas Gemi Insaat ve Onarim Sanayii A.S. — Istanbul** Yd No: 06-014 Loa 32.50 Br ex - Dght 4.300 Lbp 27.60 Br md 11.70 Dpth 5.60 Welded, 1 dk	**(B32A2ST) Tug**	**2 oil engines** reduction geared to sc. shafts driving 2 Z propellers Total Power: 4,200kW (5,710hp) Caterpillar 3516B-HD 2 x Vee 4 Stroke 16 Cy. 170 x 215 each-2100kW (2855bhp) Caterpillar Inc-USA AuxGen: 2 x 150kW 50Hz a.c Fuel: 200.0
9605932 *9V9031* -	**SEA EAGLE** **Tian San Shipping (Pte) Ltd** - *Singapore* *Singapore*	**196** 74 -	Class: BV	**2011-01 Hin Lee (Zhuhai) Shipyard Co Ltd — Zhuhai GD** (Hull) Yd No: 225 **2011-01 Cheoy Lee Shipyards Ltd — Hong Kong** Yd No: 5014 Loa 28.00 Br ex - Dght 2.000 Lbp 25.38 Br md 7.10 Dpth 4.60 Welded, 1 dk	**(A37B2PS) Passenger Ship** Hull Material: Aluminium Alloy	**3 oil engines** reduction geared to sc. shafts driving 3 FP propellers Total Power: 2,460kW (3,345hp) 24.5kn Caterpillar C32 1 x Vee 4 Stroke 12 Cy. 145 x 162 820kW (1115bhp) Caterpillar Motoren (Guangdong) CoLtd-China Caterpillar C32 2 x Vee 4 Stroke 12 Cy. 145 x 162 each-820kW (1115bhp) Caterpillar Motoren (Guangdong) CoLtd-China
9421037 *A9D2896* -	**SEA EAGLE** **Al Jazeera Shipping Co** Al Jazeera Shipping Co WLL (AJS) *Bahrain* *Bahrain* MMSI: 408815000 Official number: 4073	**366** 109 -	Class: BV	**2007-02 Yong Choo Kui Shipyard Sdn Bhd — Sibu** (Hull) Yd No: 25107 **2007-02 Greenbay Marine Pte Ltd — Singapore** Yd No: 152 Loa 32.00 Br ex - Dght 3.500 Lbp 29.30 Br md 9.76 Dpth 4.30 Welded, 1 dk	**(B32A2ST) Tug**	**2 oil engines** reduction geared to sc. shafts driving 2 FP propellers Total Power: 2,354kW (3,200hp) Cummins KTA-50-M2 2 x Vee 4 Stroke 16 Cy. 159 x 159 each-1177kW (1600bhp) Cummins Engine Co Inc-USA AuxGen: 2 x 78kW a.c
9494890 *9WNA9* -	**SEA EAGLE 1** **Deep Sea Supply Labuan Ltd** Deep Sea Supply Plc *Labuan* *Malaysia* MMSI: 533130059 Official number: 900024	**2,952** 885 2,182	Class: AB	**2009-04 Jaya Shipbuilding & Engineering Pte Ltd — Singapore** Yd No: 878 Loa 75.40 Br ex - Dght 6.100 Lbp 67.16 Br md 16.80 Dpth 7.50 Welded, 1 dk	**(B21B20A) Anchor Handling Tug Supply**	**2 oil engines** reduction geared to sc. shafts driving 2 CP propellers Total Power: 9,000kW (12,236hp) Wartsila 9L32 2 x 4 Stroke 9 Cy. 320 x 400 each-4500kW (6118bhp) Wartsila Finland Oy-Finland AuxGen: 2 x 2300kW a.c, 2 x 370kW a.c Fuel: 1260.0
7631860 *CZ9890* -	**SEA EAGLE II** *ex* Canmar Sea Eagle *-1990* *ex* Sea Eagle *-1981* **St Marys Cement Inc** Fettes Shipping Inc *Edmonton, AB* *Canada* MMSI: 316002063 Official number: 800891	*627* 188 245	Class: LR (AB) **100A1** Lake SS 03/2012 tug winters in the Great Lakes **LMC** Eq.Ltr: C; Cable: 548.0/28.5 U2	**1979-06 Modern Marine Power, Inc. — Houma, La** Yd No: 17 Loa 40.23 Br ex 10.67 Dght 3.500 Lbp 39.84 Br md - Dpth 5.74 Welded, 1 dk	**(B32B2SA) Articulated Pusher Tug**	**2 oil engines** reverse reduction geared to sc. shafts driving 2 FP propellers Total Power: 5,296kW (7,200hp) 12.0kn EMD (Electro-Motive) 20-645-E7 2 x Vee 2 Stroke 20 Cy. 230 x 254 each-2648kW (3600bhp) General Motors Corp.Electro-Motive Div.-La Grange AuxGen: 2 x 100kW 460V 60Hz a.c
9444663 *PHLP* -	**SEA ECHO** *ex* Odin *-2010* **Sea Alfa BV** Seacontractors BV *Vlissingen* *Netherlands* MMSI: 244905000 Official number: 50403	**123** 37 -	Class: BV	**2007-09 Damen Shipyards Kozle Sp z oo — Kedzierzyn-Kozle** (Hull) Yd No: 1115 **2007-09 B.V. Scheepswerf Damen Hardinxveld — Hardinxveld-Giessendam** Yd No: 1582 Loa 23.35 Br ex 8.64 Dght 2.050 Lbp 22.16 Br md 8.00 Dpth 2.99 Welded, 1 dk	**(B32A2ST) Tug**	**2 oil engines** reduction geared to sc. shafts driving 2 FP propellers Total Power: 1,302kW (1,770hp) Caterpillar 3412D 2 x Vee 4 Stroke 12 Cy. 145 x 162 each-651kW (885bhp) Caterpillar Inc-USA Thrusters: 1 Tunnel thruster (f)
7425601 *XUEN8* -	**SEA EFFORT** *ex* Century 7 *-2002* *ex* Ocean Ace *-2001* *ex* Shinnichifuji Maru *-2001* **Garten Holding Inc** Silver Star Ltd *Phnom Penh* *Cambodia* MMSI: 515178000 Official number: 0282131	**1,548** 973 3,373		**1975-03 Sasaki Shipbuilding Co Ltd — Osakikamijima HS** Yd No: 193 Loa 83.80 Br ex 13.01 Dght 5.792 Lbp 78.01 Br md 12.98 Dpth 7.65 Riveted\Welded, 1 dk	**(A31A2GX) General Cargo Ship** Grain: 4,696; Bale: 3,634 Compartments: 1 Ho, ER 1 Ha: (40.3 x 9.1)ER	**1 oil engine** driving 1 FP propeller Total Power: 1,839kW (2,500hp) 12.0kn Makita KSLH637 1 x 4 Stroke 6 Cy. 370 x 590 1839kW (2500bhp) Makita Tekkosho-Japan AuxGen: 2 x 144kW 450V 60Hz a.c Fuel: 36.0 (d.f.) 150.0 (r.f.) 9.0pd
9249269 *YJSL4* -	**SEA ELEGANCE** **Stevens Line Co Ltd** Sato Steamship Co Ltd (Sato Kisen KK) *Port Vila* *Vanuatu* MMSI: 576768000 Official number: 1406	**28,665** 17,978 51,097	Class: NK	**2002-06 Oshima Shipbuilding Co Ltd — Saikai NS** Yd No: 10327 Loa 189.99 (BB) Br ex - Dght 11.918 Lbp 182.00 Br md 32.26 Dpth 16.67 Welded, 1 dk	**(A21A2BC) Bulk Carrier** Grain: 65,252; Bale: 64,000 Compartments: 5 Ho, ER 5 Ha: (17.9 x 17.6)3 (20.4 x 17.6) (18.7 x 17.6)ER Cranes: 4x30t	**1 oil engine** driving 1 FP propeller Total Power: 9,488kW (12,900hp) 14.5kn MAN-B&W 6S50MC-C 1 x 2 Stroke 6 Cy. 500 x 2000 9488kW (12900bhp) Kawasaki Heavy Industries Ltd-Japan Fuel: 1610.0
9383601 *V7OC9* -	**SEA EMPEROR** **Sea Emperor Shipholding SA** Perosea Shipping Co SA *Majuro* *Marshall Islands* MMSI: 538003062 Official number: 3062	**8,503** 4,173 13,083 T/cm 23.2	Class: BV (AB)	**2008-06 21st Century Shipbuilding Co Ltd — Tongyeong** Yd No: 239 Loa 128.60 (BB) Br ex - Dght 8.700 Lbp 120.40 Br md 20.40 Dpth 11.50 Welded, 1 dk	**(A12B2TR) Chemical/Products Tanker** Double Hull (13F) Liq: 14,563; Liq (Oil): 14,563 Cargo Heating Coils Compartments: 14 Wing Ta, ER 14 Cargo Pump (s): 12x300m³/hr, 2x100m³/hr Manifold: Bow/CM: 61.4m	**1 oil engine** driving 1 FP propeller Total Power: 4,440kW (6,037hp) 13.4kn MAN-B&W 6S35MC 1 x 2 Stroke 6 Cy. 350 x 1400 4440kW (6037bhp) STX Engine Co Ltd-South Korea AuxGen: 3 x 500kW a.c Thrusters: 1 Tunnel thruster (f) Fuel: 66.0 (d.f.) 571.0 (r.f.)
9431537 *3FNP9* -	**SEA EMPIRE** *ex* Jin Empire *-2010* **Empire Shipping Line SA** Eastern Media International Corp (EMIC) *Panama* *Panama* MMSI: 371120000 Official number: 4165010	**43,537** 26,550 79,372 T/cm 71.9	Class: KR	**2010-04 Jiangsu Eastern Heavy Industry Co Ltd — Jingjiang JS** Yd No: 06C-069 Loa 229.00 (BB) Br ex - Dght 14.639 Lbp 222.00 Br md 32.26 Dpth 20.25 Welded, 1 dk	**(A21A2BC) Bulk Carrier** Double Hull Grain: 97,000; Bale: 90,784 Compartments: 7 Ho, ER 7 Ha: 5 (18.3 x 15.0) (15.7 x 15.0)ER (13.1 x 13.2)	**1 oil engine** driving 1 FP propeller Total Power: 11,060kW (15,037hp) 14.0kn MAN-B&W 7S50MC-C 1 x 2 Stroke 7 Cy. 500 x 2000 11060kW (15037bhp) STX Engine Co Ltd-South Korea AuxGen: 3 x 700kW 450V 60Hz a.c Fuel: 2670.0
9142526 *V2BR6* -	**SEA EMS** *ex* Holland *-2006* *ex* Ladon *-2005* **Fehn Schiffahrts GmbH & Co KG ms 'Sea Ems'** Fehn Ship Management GmbH & Co KG *Saint John's* *Antigua & Barbuda* MMSI: 304905000	**1,682** 957 2,503	Class: BV	**1996-02 Scheepswerf Bijlsma BV — Wartena** Yd No: 675 Loa 81.70 Br ex 11.10 Dght 4.450 Lbp 78.25 Br md 11.00 Dpth 5.67 Welded, 1 dk	**(A31A2GX) General Cargo Ship** Grain: 3,552; Bale: 3,240 Compartments: 1 Ho, ER 1 Ha: (57.8 x 9.2)ER Ice Capable	**1 oil engine** with clutches, flexible couplings & sr reverse geared to sc. shaft driving 1 FP propeller Total Power: 1,020kW (1,387hp) 10.5kn MaK 6M20 1 x 4 Stroke 6 Cy. 200 x 300 1020kW (1387bhp) Krupp MaK Maschinenbau GmbH-Kiel AuxGen: 1 x 95kW 380/220V 50Hz a.c, 1 x 57kW 380/220V 50Hz a.c Thrusters: 1 Thwart. FP thruster (f)
7823360 *WTF4069* -	**SEA ENCOUNTER** **Desilva Sea Encounter Corp** - SatCom: Inmarsat C 433853910 *Long Beach, CA* *United States of America* MMSI: 338539000 Official number: 604592	**2,077** 1,123 -		**1979-04 J M Martinac Shipbuilding Corp — Tacoma WA** Yd No: 216 Loa 71.02 Br ex 12.81 Dght - Lbp 59.34 Br md - Dpth 4.65 Welded, 2 dks	**(B11B2FV) Fishing Vessel**	**1 oil engine** geared to sc. shaft driving 1 FP propeller Total Power: 2,648kW (3,600hp) 16.0kn EMD (Electro-Motive) 20-645-E7 1 x Vee 2 Stroke 20 Cy. 230 x 254 2648kW (3600bhp) General Motors Corp.Electro-Motive Div.-La Grange AuxGen: 3 x 300kW Thrusters: 1 Thwart. FP thruster (f)

7915163 - -	**SEA ENDEAVOUR I** *ex* Sea Endeavour *-2006* **Saga Shipping & Trading Corp Ltd** -	**221** 66 119	Class: (LR) ✠ Classed LR until 11/7/07	**1980-08 Richards (Shipbuilders) Ltd — Great Yarmouth** Yd No: 549 Loa 30.48 Br ex 9.05 Dght 3.622 Lbp 26.60 Br md 8.50 Dpth 4.32 Welded, 1 dk	**(B32A2ST) Tug**	**1 oil engine** reverse reduction geared to sc. shaft driving 1 FP propeller Total Power: 2,207kW (3,001hp) 12.0kn Ruston 12RKCM 1 x Vee 4 Stroke 12 Cy. 254 x 305 2207kW (3001bhp) Ruston Diesels Ltd.-Newton-le-Willows AuxGen: 2 x 70kW 440V 50Hz a.c
9516179 *5BQB3* -	**SEA ENDURANCE** **CA Sea Endurance Shipping Ltd** Interorient Marine Services Ltd *Limassol* *Cyprus* MMSI: 210084000 Official number: 9516179	**6,872** 3,414 9,387	Class: GL	**2012-06 Penglai Bohai Shipyard Co Ltd — Penglai SD** Yd No: PBZ07-93 Loa 109.83 (BB) Br ex - Dght 8.000 Lbp 105.80 Br md 18.20 Dpth 10.50 Welded, 1 dk	**(A31A2GX) General Cargo Ship** Grain: 11,770; Bale: 11,770 TEU 276 Compartments: 3 Ho, ER 3 Ha: 2 (25.9 x 15.2)ER (16.1 x 15.2) Cranes: 2x60t Ice Capable	**1 oil engine** reduction geared to sc. shaft driving 1 Propeller Total Power: 4,000kW (5,438hp) 13.0kn MAN-B&W 8L32/40 1 x 4 Stroke 8 Cy. 320 x 400 4000kW (5438bhp) Shaanxi Diesel Heavy Industry Co Lt-China
8502092 *P3AT8* -	**SEA ENTERPRISER** *ex* Sea Enterprise *-2005* *ex* Volonga *-2002* *launched as* Mikhail Panfilov *-1998* **S E S Sea Enterprise Shipping Ltd** Interorient Marine Services Ltd *Limassol* *Cyprus* MMSI: 209196000 Official number: 8502092	**6,418** 2,840 7,049	Class: GL (RS)	**1998-06 Malta Shipbuilding Co. Ltd. — Marsa** (Assembled by) Yd No: 172 **1998-06 Malta Drydocks — Cospicua** (Parts for assembly by) Yd No: 172 Loa 131.60 Br ex 19.40 Dght 7.000 Lbp 122.00 Br md 19.30 Dpth 8.80 Welded, 1 dk	**(A31A2GX) General Cargo Ship** Grain: 9,871; Bale: 9,398 TEU 274 C. 274/20' Compartments: 4 Ho, ER 4 Ha: ER Cranes: 4x12.5t Ice Capable	**1 oil engine** driving 1 FP propeller Total Power: 4,690kW (6,377hp) 14.8kn B&W 7L45GBE 1 x 2 Stroke 7 Cy. 450 x 1200 4690kW (6377bhp) H Cegielski Poznan SA-Poland AuxGen: 3 x 400kW 220/380V a.c
7308542 *WDD6685* -	**SEA ERN** **Sea Ern LLC** - SatCom: Inmarsat C 436774310 *Seattle, WA* *United States of America* MMSI: 367176240 Official number: 504144	**215** 64 -		**1966 Pacific Fishermen, Inc. — Seattle, Wa** Yd No: 174 L reg 25.18 Br ex 7.93 Dght - Lbp - Br md - Dpth 2.87 Welded	**(B11B2FV) Fishing Vessel**	**1 oil engine** driving 1 FP propeller Total Power: 368kW (500hp)
7647780 *WDE6409* -	**SEA EXPLORER** *ex* Maria Angela *-2004* **Tyler Fishing LLC** - *New Bedford, MA* *United States of America* MMSI: 367379940 Official number: 579484	**124** 37 -		**1977 Bender Welding & Machine Co Inc — Mobile AL** Yd No: 356 L reg 22.96 Br ex 6.71 Dght - Lbp - Br md - Dpth 3.38 Welded, 1dk	**(B11B2FV) Fishing Vessel**	**1 oil engine** driving 1 FP propeller Total Power: 416kW (566hp)
7504249 *C6NG6* -	**SEA EXPLORER** *ex* Marjata II *-1995* *ex* Marjata *-1994* **Gardline Geosurvey Ltd** - SatCom: Inmarsat C 430932520 *Nassau* *Bahamas* MMSI: 309325000 Official number: 726167	**1,385** 415 659	Class: NV	**1976-02 AS Mjellem & Karlsen — Bergen** Yd No: 118 Lengthened-1983 Loa 58.86 Br ex 11.00 Dght 4.836 Lbp 55.35 Br md 10.98 Dpth 7.12 Welded, 2 dks	**(B31A2SR) Research Survey Vessel** Ice Capable	**2 oil engines** driving 2 CP propellers Total Power: 1,912kW (2,600hp) 12.5kn MaK 6M452AK 2 x 4 Stroke 6 Cy. 320 x 450 each-956kW (1300bhp) MaK Maschinenbau GmbH-Kiel AuxGen: 2 x 424kW 220V 50Hz a.c, 2 x 144kW 220V 50Hz a.c Thrusters: 1 Tunnel thruster (f); 1 Tunnel thruster (a)
8802882 *V7WD8* -	**SEA EXPLORER** *ex* Corinthian Ii *-2013* *ex* Island Sun *-2005* *ex* Sun *-2004* *ex* Renai I *-2003* *ex* Renaissance Seven *-2001* *ex* Regina Renaissance *-1998* *ex* Renaissance Seven *-1992* **Corinthian II Owner Ltd** FleetPro Ocean Inc *Majuro* *Marshall Islands* MMSI: 538004274 Official number: 4274	**4,200** 1,263 645	Class: LR (BV) (NV) (RI) ✠ **100A1** CS 08/2011 passenger ship Ice Class 1C at 3.95m draught Max/min draught fwd 3.95/3.52m Max/min draught aft 3.95/3.52m **LMC** Cable: 467.5/36.0 U3 (a)	**1991-12 Nuovi Cantieri Apuania SpA — Carrara** Yd No: 1146 Loa 90.36 (BB) Br ex 15.30 Dght 4.050 Lbp 78.95 Br md 15.27 Dpth 4.20 Welded, 3 dks	**(A37A2PC) Passenger/Cruise** Passengers: cabins: 59; berths: 120 Ice Capable	**2 oil engines** with flexible couplings & sr geared to sc. shafts driving 2 CP propellers Total Power: 3,520kW (4,786hp) 16.0kn Alpha 8L28/32 2 x 4 Stroke 8 Cy. 280 x 320 each-1760kW (2393bhp) MAN B&W Diesel A/S-Denmark AuxGen: 2 x 1100kW 440V 60Hz a.c, 2 x 1100kW 440V 50Hz a.c Boilers: WTAuxB (o.f.) 9.2kgf/cm² (9.0bar) Thrusters: 1 Thwart. FP thruster (f) Fuel: 47.0 (d.f.) 260.0 (r.f.)
8856297 - -	**SEA EXPLORER** **Versaggi Shrimp Corp** - *Tampa, FL* *United States of America* Official number: 664463	*117* 88 -		**1983 St Augustine Trawlers, Inc. — Saint Augustine, Fl** Loa 23.16 Br ex - Dght - Lbp 20.60 Br md 6.19 Dpth 3.38 Bonded, 1 dk	**(B11B2FV) Fishing Vessel** Hull Material: Reinforced Plastic	**1 oil engine** driving 1 FP propeller Total Power: 530kW (721hp) Caterpillar 3412TA 1 x Vee 4 Stroke 12 Cy. 137 x 152 530kW (721bhp) Caterpillar Tractor Co-USA
9516155 *5BQC3* -	**SEA EXPLORER** **CA Sea Explorer Shipping Ltd** Interorient Marine Services Ltd *Limassol* *Cyprus* MMSI: 210112000 Official number: 9516155	**6,872** 3,410 9,386	Class: GL	**2012-10 Penglai Bohai Shipyard Co Ltd — Penglai SD** Yd No: PBZ07-91 Loa 109.83 Br ex - Dght 8.000 Lbp 105.80 Br md 18.20 Dpth 10.50 Welded, 1 dk	**(A31A2GX) General Cargo Ship** Grain: 11,770; Bale: 11,770 TEU 276 Compartments: 3 Ho, ER 3 Ha: ER Cranes: 2x60t Ice Capable	**1 oil engine** driving 1 Propeller Total Power: 4,000kW (5,438hp) 13.0kn MAN-B&W 8L32/40 1 x 4 Stroke 8 Cy. 320 x 400 4000kW (5438bhp) Shaanxi Diesel Heavy Industry Co Lt-China
9553218 *V7YX4* -	**SEA EXPRESS** *ex* Peruvian Express *-2013* **Pontos Shipping Inc** Seatankers Management Co Ltd *Majuro* *Marshall Islands* MMSI: 538004757 Official number: 4757	**43,692** 27,808 79,252 T/cm 71.9	Class: LR ✠ **100A1** SS 07/2012 bulk carrier CSR BC-A Nos. 2, 4 & 6 holds may be empty GRAB (25) ESP **ShipRight** (ACS (B),CM) *IWS LI ✠ **LMC** **UMS** Eq.Ltr: Q†; Cable: 687.5/81.0 U3 (a)	**2012-07 COSCO (Dalian) Shipyard Co Ltd — Dalian LN** Yd No: N268 Loa 229.04 (BB) Br ex 32.29 Dght 14.580 Lbp 222.03 Br md 32.26 Dpth 20.25 Welded, 1 dk	**(A21A2BC) Bulk Carrier** Grain: 97,000; Bale: 90,784 Compartments: 7 Ho, ER 7 Ha: ER	**1 oil engine** driving 1 FP propeller Total Power: 11,060kW (15,037hp) 14.0kn MAN-B&W 7S50MC-C 1 x 2 Stroke 7 Cy. 500 x 2000 11060kW (15037bhp) Hyundai Heavy Industries Co Ltd-South Korea AuxGen: 3 x 730kW 450V 60Hz a.c Boilers: AuxB (Comp) 9.2kgf/cm² (9.0bar)
8952065 *ZR8338* -	**SEA EXPRESS** *ex* Marcia G *-1999* **Clipper Marine Services Pty Ltd** - *Cape Town* *South Africa* MMSI: 601126900 Official number: 11001	**159** 47 -	Class: (BV)	**1978 Graham Boats, Inc. — Pascagoula, Ms** Loa 29.26 Br ex - Dght 2.510 Lbp 26.55 Br md 7.31 Dpth 3.58 Welded, 1 dk	**(B21A2OS) Platform Supply Ship**	**2 oil engines** reduction geared to sc. shafts driving 2 FP propellers Total Power: 1,014kW (1,378hp) 9.5kn G.M. (Detroit Diesel) 12V-71 2 x Vee 2 Stroke 12 Cy. 108 x 127 each-507kW (689bhp) General Motors Detroit DieselAllison Divn-USA AuxGen: 2 x 30kW 220/110V 60Hz a.c
8739425 - -	**SEA EXPRESS** **Fawzy Moaaz** - *Egypt*	**221** 130 -		**2009-05 Port Said Marine Shipyard — Port Said** Yd No: 514 Loa 30.00 Br ex - Dght 1.800 Lbp 27.50 Br md 8.00 Dpth - Welded, 1 dk	**(B34J2SD) Crew Boat** Passengers: unberthed: 40	**3 oil engines** reduction geared to sc. shafts driving 3 FP propellers Total Power: 1,545kW (2,100hp) G.M. (Detroit Diesel) 12V-92-TA 3 x Vee 2 Stroke 12 Cy. 123 x 127 each-515kW (700bhp) Detroit Diesel Corporation-Detroit, Mi AuxGen: 2 x 60kW 220V a.c
7828281 *DUA6371* -	**SEA EXPRESS** *ex* Marusan Maru No. 88 *-1998* **Royale Fishing Corp** - *Manila* *Philippines* Official number: MNLD010178	*150* 86 -		**1979-05 K.K. Izutsu Zosensho — Nagasaki** Yd No: 800 Loa 38.26 Br ex - Dght 2.401 Lbp 31.50 Br md 6.30 Dpth 2.85 Welded, 1 dk	**(B11B2FV) Fishing Vessel**	**1 oil engine** driving 1 FP propeller Total Power: 647kW (880hp) Daihatsu 6DSM-26 1 x 4 Stroke 6 Cy. 260 x 320 647kW (880bhp) Daihatsu Diesel Manufacturing Co Lt-Japan
8737659 *5IM034* -	**SEA EXPRESS I** *ex* Freedom Of The Isles *-2009* **Fast Ferries Ltd** - *Zanzibar* *Tanzania* Official number: 100053	**149** 39 -		**2003-03 Eagle Farm Marine Fabrications — Brisbane QLD** Yd No: VLBA0023A303 Loa 23.90 Br ex - Dght 1.600 Lbp 23.40 Br md 7.80 Dpth 2.30 Welded, 1 dk	**(A37B2PS) Passenger Ship**	**2 oil engines** geared to sc. shafts driving 2 FP propellers Total Power: 1,206kW (1,640hp) M.T.U. 2 x 4 Stroke each-603kW (820bhp) MTU Friedrichshafen GmbH-Friedrichshafen

IMO / Call sign	Name / Owner	Tonnage	Class	Builder / Dimensions	Type	Machinery
7023518 - -	**SEA EXPRESS II** *ex* Arbi Traje *-2007* *ex* Leyla *-2005* *ex* Alex II *-2004* *ex* Nika *-2002* *ex* Sabur *-2000* *ex* Duso *-1998* *ex* Kolga *-1997* *ex* Fricis Gaylis *-1992* *ex* Jocon *-1971* *launched as* Nienhagen *-1970* **Isadora Navigation Ltd** -	**885** 301 1,032	Class: KC (RS)	**1970-03 VEB Elbewerften Boizenburg/Rosslau — Boizenburg** Yd No: 274 Loa 57.87 (BB) Br ex 10.14 Dght 3.960 Lbp 52.00 Br md 10.06 Dpth 5.80 Welded, 2 dks	**(A31A2GX) General Cargo Ship** Grain: 1,532; Bale: 1,400 Compartments: 1 Ho, ER 1 Ha: (27.2 x 7.7)ER Ice Capable	**1 oil engine** driving 1 CP propeller Total Power: 853kW (1,160hp) 12.0kn S.K.L. 8NVD48A-2U 1 x 4 Stroke 8 Cy. 320 x 480 853kW (1160bhp) VEB Schwermaschinenbau "KarlLiebknecht" (SKL)-Magdeburg AuxGen: 1 x 128kW 390V 50Hz a.c, 1 x 116kW 390V 50Hz a.c, 1 x 77kW 390V 50Hz a.c Fuel: 65.0 (d.f.)
9400966 *H04619* -	**SEA EXPRESS II** **Caribship LLC** G & G Marine Inc *Panama* *Panama* MMSI: 356449000 Official number: 3224506A	**487** 146 850		**2006-08 St Augustine Marine, Inc. — St Augustine, Fl** Yd No: 403123 Loa 59.74 Br ex 11.89 Dght 2.250 Lbp 53.44 Br md 11.58 Dpth 3.05 Welded, 1 dk	**(A35D2RL) Landing Craft** Bow ramp (centre)	**3 oil engines** reduction geared to sc. shafts driving 3 FP propellers Total Power: 1,656kW (2,250hp) 11.0kn Caterpillar 3412C 3 x Vee 4 Stroke 12 Cy. 137 x 152 each-552kW (750bhp) Caterpillar Inc-USA
8328173 *9HA2829*	**SEA EXPRESS III** *ex* Gac Tempest *-2011* *ex* Island Trader *-1994* *ex* Marenco Alpha *-1987* *ex* Rom 1 *-1987* *ex* Island Trader *-1987* **Polaris Marine Services Co Ltd** - *Valletta* *Malta* MMSI: 256324000 Official number: 8328173	**309** 92 271	Class: (BV) (NV)	**1983 Santierul Naval Galati S.A. — Galati** Yd No: 775 Loa 36.85 Br ex 10.22 Dght 2.750 Lbp 32.80 Br md 10.20 Dpth 4.45 Welded, 1 dk	**(B21A20S) Platform Supply Ship** Passengers: berths: 7	**2 oil engines** reduction geared to sc. shafts driving 2 CP propellers Total Power: 424kW (576hp) 8.0kn Volvo Penta TAMD120A 2 x 4 Stroke 6 Cy. 130 x 150 each-212kW (288bhp) AB Volvo Penta-Sweden AuxGen: 3 x 380/220V Fuel: 48.0 (d.f.)
9258674 *V7IZ3* -	**SEA FAITH** *ex* Ioannis P *-2011* *ex* Jag Prakash *-2005* **Benjamin Maritime SA** Sea World Management & Trading Inc *Majuro* *Marshall Islands* MMSI: 538002476 Official number: 2476	**27,627** 12,769 46,349 T/cm 51.1	Class: NV (IR)	**2003-02 Hanjin Heavy Industries & Construction Co Ltd — Busan** Yd No: 110 Loa 182.85 (BB) Br ex 32.23 Dght 12.215 Lbp 174.00 Br md 32.20 Dpth 18.10 Welded, 1 dk	**(A13A2TW) Crude/Oil Products Tanker** Double Hull (13F) Liq: 50,692; Liq (Oil): 50,692 Compartments: 16 Wing Ta, 2 Wing Slop Ta, ER 4 Cargo Pump (s) Manifold: Bow/CM: 94.3m	**1 oil engine** driving 1 FP propeller Total Power: 8,562kW (11,641hp) 14.5kn B&W 6S50MC 1 x 2 Stroke 6 Cy. 500 x 1910 8562kW (11641bhp) Hyundai Heavy Industries Co Ltd-South Korea Fuel: 126.0 (d.f.) 1068.0 (r.f.)
9251298 *9V6070* -	**SEA FALCON** **Tian San Shipping (Pte) Ltd** - *Singapore* *Singapore* Official number: 389378	**196** 74 50	Class: BV	**2001-09 Cheoy Lee Shipyards Ltd — Hong Kong** Yd No: 4769 Loa 28.00 Br ex - Dght - Lbp 26.06 Br md 7.14 Dpth 2.35 Welded	**(A37B2PS) Passenger Ship** Hull Material: Aluminium Alloy Passengers: unberthed: 200	**3 oil engines** reduction geared to sc. shafts driving 3 FP propellers Total Power: 2,364kW (3,213hp) 27.0kn M.T.U. 12V2000M70 3 x Vee 4 Stroke 12 Cy. 130 x 150 each-788kW (1071bhp) MTU Friedrichshafen GmbH-Friedrichshafen AuxGen: 2 x 40kW a.c Fuel: 4.3 (d.f.)
9572018 *J8B4544* -	**SEA FALCON** *launched as* Bogazici 8 *-2011* **Sea Eagles Offshore Services Pte Ltd** Sea Eagles Shipping LLC *Kingstown* *St Vincent & The Grenadines* MMSI: 377209000 Official number: 11017	**463** 139 -	Class: BV	**2011-05 Dentas Gemi Insaat ve Onarim Sanayii A.S. — Istanbul** Yd No: 06-013 Loa 32.50 Br ex - Dght 4.300 Lbp 27.60 Br md 11.70 Dpth 5.60 Welded, 1 dk	**(B32A2ST) Tug**	**2 oil engines** reduction geared to sc. shafts driving 2 Z propellers Total Power: 4,268kW (5,802hp) Caterpillar 3516B 2 x Vee 4 Stroke 16 Cy. 170 x 215 each-2134kW (2901bhp) Caterpillar Inc-USA AuxGen: 2 x 150kW 380V 50Hz a.c Fuel: 208.0 (d.f.)
9645683 *5BUM3* -	**SEA FALCON** **PSV Holding Inc** Deep Sea Supply Management (Singapore) Pte Ltd *Limassol* *Cyprus* MMSI: 210401000	**4,003** 1,533 4,543	Class: NV	**2013-02 Zhejiang Shipbuilding Co Ltd — Fenghua ZJ** Yd No: ZJ2013 Loa 88.80 Br ex 19.70 Dght 6.650 Lbp 82.00 Br md 19.00 Dpth 8.00 Welded, 1 dk	**(B21A20S) Platform Supply Ship** Ice Capable	**4 diesel electric oil engines** driving 4 gen. Connecting to 2 elec. motors driving 2 Azimuth electric drive units Total Power: 7,060kW (9,600hp) 13.0kn Caterpillar 3512C 4 x Vee 4 Stroke 12 Cy. 170 x 215 each-1765kW (2400bhp) Caterpillar Inc-USA Thrusters: 2 Tunnel thruster (f)
7534660 *WCY3585* -	**SEA FALCON** **Westbank Corp** Daybrook Fisheries Inc *New Orleans, LA* *United States of America* Official number: 563349	*497* 338 -		**1975-01 Patterson Shipyard Inc. — Patterson, La** L reg 49.44 Br ex 9.76 Dght - Lbp - Br md - Dpth 3.38 Welded, 1 dk	**(B11B2FV) Fishing Vessel**	**2 oil engines** driving 2 FP propellers Total Power: 1,704kW (2,316hp) G.M. (Detroit Diesel) 16V-149-TI 2 x Vee 2 Stroke 16 Cy. 146 x 146 each-852kW (1158bhp) General Motors Detroit DieselAllison Divn-USA
7408897 *D5EC5* -	**SEA FALCON** *ex* Iremis Falcon *-2013* *ex* Gulmar Falcon *-2012* *ex* Fisher Cavalier *-2003* *ex* Oceanic Cavalier *-2000* *ex* Lowland Cavalier *-1999* *ex* Seaway Falcon *-1987* **Traxstar Holdings Ltd** Ocean Marine International FZE *Monrovia* *Liberia* MMSI: 636016039 Official number: 16039	**2,645** 794 1,310	Class: NV	**1975-06 Martin Jansen GmbH & Co. KG Schiffsw. u. Masch. — Leer** Yd No: 135 Loa 80.93 Br ex 16.03 Dght 4.376 Lbp 73.97 Br md 16.00 Dpth 7.11 Welded, 2 dks	**(B22A20V) Diving Support Vessel** Cranes: 1x30t,1x2t Ice Capable	**4 diesel electric oil engines** driving 4 gen. each 1440kW 600V a.c Connecting to 4 elec. motors driving 2 CP propellers Total Power: 6,060kW (8,240hp) 13.5kn Hedemora V18A/12 4 x Vee 4 Stroke 18 Cy. 185 x 210 each-1515kW (2060bhp) (new engine 1980) Hedemora Diesel AB-Sweden AuxGen: 1 x 163kW 440V 60Hz a.c Thrusters: 2 Thwart. CP thruster (f); 2 Tunnel thruster (a) Fuel: 460.0 (d.f.) 14.0pd
8851754 *WDF4034* -	**SEA FALCON** **Frank D Crabtree** - *Lincoln City, OR* *United States of America* MMSI: 367447140 Official number: 649608	*129* 38 -		**1982 Steiner Shipyard, Inc. — Bayou La Batre, Al** Yd No: 124 Converted From: Ferry (Passenger only)-2001 Loa - Br ex - Dght - Lbp 25.69 Br md 6.71 Dpth 1.92 Welded, 1 dk	**(B11B2FV) Fishing Vessel**	**1 oil engine** driving 1 FP propeller Total Power: 338kW (460hp)
8991140 *ZGDK9* -	**SEA FALCON 2** *ex* Elle *-2013* *ex* Zaza *-2007* *ex* Fortunate Sun *-2005* *ex* Dream *-1999* *ex* Samantha Lin *-1995* **Aquarius Star Ltd** - *United Kingdom*	**480** 144 134	Class: AB	**1993-11 Puglia Engineering Inc. — Tacoma, Wa** Yd No: 490 Loa 45.35 Br ex - Dght 2.960 Lbp 38.74 Br md 9.14 Dpth 4.65 Welded, 1 dk	**(X11A2YP) Yacht** Passengers: cabins: 5; berths: 10	**2 oil engines** reverse reduction geared to sc. shafts driving 2 Propellers Total Power: 1,140kW (1,550hp) 15.0kn Caterpillar 3508TA 2 x Vee 4 Stroke 8 Cy. 170 x 190 each-570kW (775bhp) Caterpillar Inc-USA AuxGen: 2 x 99kW
9127734 *9WHV9* -	**SEA FARING** **WTK Realty Sdn Bhd** - *Kuching* *Malaysia* Official number: 327621	**117** 36 112	Class: (NK)	**1995-01 Yii Brothers Shipbuilding Contractor Co — Sibu** Yd No: 56 L reg 21.76 Br ex - Dght 2.388 Lbp 21.76 Br md 7.00 Dpth 2.90 Welded, 1 dk	**(B32A2ST) Tug**	**2 oil engines** geared to sc. shafts driving 2 FP propellers Total Power: 794kW (1,080hp) Caterpillar 2 x 4 Stroke each-397kW (540bhp) Caterpillar Inc-USA
8885597 *WDD2039* -	**SEA FARMER II** *ex* Atlantis *-2005* **Sandler Fisheries Inc** - *Boston, MA* *United States of America* MMSI: 367110160 Official number: 937222	**145** 44 -		**1988 Johnson Shipbuilding & Repair — Bayou La Batre, Al** Yd No: 15 L reg 23.07 Br ex - Dght - Lbp - Br md 6.95 Dpth 3.96 Welded, 1 dk	**(B11B2FV) Fishing Vessel**	**1 oil engine** driving 1 FP propeller
8664010 *E5U2690* -	**SEA FEVER** **Longford Investments Pty Ltd** - *Avatiu* *Cook Islands* MMSI: 518743000 Official number: 1779	**111** - -		**1983-09 Kailis Marine — Fremantle WA** Loa 22.50 Br ex - Dght - Lbp - Br md - Dpth - Welded, 1 dk	**(B34L2QU) Utility Vessel**	**1 oil engine** driving 1 Propeller

8101537 *3EQP4* -	**SEA FEYZ** *ex* Ayberk *-2010* *ex* Tore Secondo *-2008* *ex* Romeo Secondo *-2000* *ex* Uralar Quinto *-1992* **Camlica Corp** Feyz Denizcilik Lojistik Ic ve Dis Ticaret Sanayi Ltd Sti *Panama* *Panama* MMSI: 357155000 Official number: 3421208A	**2,765** 1,543 4,196	Class: TL (RI) (BV)	**1982**-07 **S.A. Balenciaga — Zumaya** Yd No: 303 Loa 91.29 Br ex - Dght 6.626 Lbp 83.01 Br md 14.41 Dpth 8.72 Welded, 2 dks	**(A31A2GX) General Cargo Ship** Grain: 5,404; Bale: 5,251 Compartments: 2 Ho, ER 2 Ha: (52.3 x 10.4)ER	**1 oil engine** sr geared to sc. shaft driving 1 FP propeller Total Power: 1,471kW (2,000hp) 12.0kn Deutz RBV6M358 1 x 4 Stroke 6 Cy. 400 x 580 1471kW (2000bhp) Hijos de J Barreras SA-Spain AuxGen: 2 x 112kW 220V 50Hz a.c, 1 x 50kW 220V 50Hz a.c Fuel: 192.0 (d.f.) 5.0pd
8990627 - -	**SEA FISH** *ex* Thien An *-2007* **Russell Portier** - *Chauvin, LA* *United States of America* Official number: 1032691	*114* 34 -		**1995 Allied Shipyard, Inc. — Larose, La** Yd No: 162 L reg 22.89 Br ex - Dght - Lbp - Br md 6.71 Dpth 3.66 Welded, 1 dk	**(B11B2FV) Fishing Vessel**	**1 oil engine** driving 1 Propeller
7048984 *WCD9851* -	**SEA FISHER** *ex* Aleutian Queen *-1989* *ex* Richwill *-1989* *ex* Colgan *-1989* *ex* HA 6 *-1989* **Marine Service International Inc** - *Seattle, WA* *United States of America* Official number: 296512	*490* 220 -	Class: (AB)	**1943 Sturgeon Bay Shipbuilding & Dry Dock Corp — Sturgeon Bay WI** Yd No: 137 Converted From: General Cargo Ship Loa 45.24 Br ex 9.91 Dght - Lbp - Br md - Dpth 4.37 Welded, 1 dk	**(B11B2FV) Fishing Vessel**	**1 oil engine** driving 1 FP propeller Total Power: 441kW (600hp)
8120167 - -	**SEA FISHER 11** - - - *United States of America*	*135* - -		**1980**-09 **Quality Marine, Inc. — Bayou La Batre, Al** Yd No: 145 Loa 25.33 Br ex - Dght - Lbp - Br md 7.01 Dpth 3.69 Welded, 1 dk	**(B11A2FS) Stern Trawler**	**1 oil engine** driving 1 FP propeller Total Power: 382kW (519hp) Caterpillar 3412TA 1 x Vee 4 Stroke 12 Cy. 137 x 152 382kW (519bhp) Caterpillar Tractor Co-USA
7053238 *CPB855* -	**SEA FLOWER** *ex* Sea Master *-2005* *ex* Baltic Meteor *-2001* *ex* Rivagijon *-1994* **Hartdale Enterprises Corp S de RL** - *La Paz* *Bolivia* Official number: 0001-07 10 2 2	**1,817** 1,368 1,223	Class: (BV)	**1971**-04 **Astilleros de Murueta S.A. — Gernika-Lumo** Yd No: 106 Loa 75.01 Br ex 13.16 Dght 4.242 Lbp 68.03 Br md 13.01 Dpth 7.22 Welded, 1 dk & S dk	**(A35A2RR) Ro-Ro Cargo Ship** Stern door/ramp Lane-Len: 320 Trailers: 25 Bale: 3,658	**1 oil engine** sr geared to sc. shaft driving 1 FP propeller Total Power: 1,765kW (2,400hp) 13.0kn MWM TBRHS345AU 1 x 4 Stroke 8 Cy. 360 x 450 1765kW (2400bhp) Naval Stork Werkspoor SA-Spain
9223356 *D9QH* -	**SEA FLOWER** *ex* Dolphin Ulsan *-2007* *ex* Triumphant *-2002* **Dae A Express Shipping Co Ltd** - *Pohang* *South Korea* MMSI: 440150000 Official number: PHR-076523	**584** - 269	Class: KR (NV)	**2002**-04 **North West Bay Ships Pty Ltd — Margate TAS** Yd No: 9901 Loa 54.50 Br ex 15.30 Dght 2.180 Lbp - Br md 15.00 Dpth 3.07 Welded, 1 dk	**(A37B2PS) Passenger Ship** Passengers: unberthed: 484	**3 oil engines** geared to sc. shafts driving 3 Water jets Total Power: 6,960kW (9,462hp) 40.0kn M.T.U. 16V4000M70 3 x Vee 4 Stroke 16 Cy. 165 x 190 each-2320kW (3154bhp) (made 2001) MTU Friedrichshafen GmbH-Friedrichshafen AuxGen: 2 x 160kW a.c Thrusters: 2 Thwart. FP thruster (f)
8814469 *D9QC* -	**SEA FLOWER II** *ex* Patria *-2004* **Dae A Express Shipping Co Ltd** - *Pohang* *South Korea* MMSI: 440145000 Official number: PHR-046585	**555** 191 110	Class: KR (NV)	**1990**-02 **FBM Marine Ltd. — Cowes** Yd No: 1244 Loa 36.40 (BB) Br ex 13.00 Dght 2.700 Lbp 31.70 Br md - Dpth 5.80 Welded	**(A37B2PS) Passenger Ship** Hull Material: Aluminium Alloy Passengers: unberthed: 400	**2 oil engines** geared to sc. shafts driving 2 FP propellers Total Power: 3,002kW (4,082hp) 30.0kn M.T.U. 16V396TB84 2 x Vee 4 Stroke 16 Cy. 165 x 185 each-1501kW (2041bhp) MTU Friedrichshafen GmbH-Friedrichshafen AuxGen: 2 x 84kW 220V 50Hz a.c
9645695 *5BWA3* -	**SEA FLYER** - **PSV Holding Inc** Deep Sea Supply Management (Singapore) Pte Ltd *Limassol* *Cyprus* MMSI: 209861000	**4,003** 1,533 4,700	Class: NV	**2013**-05 **Zhejiang Shipbuilding Co Ltd — Fenghua ZJ** Yd No: ZJ2014 Loa 88.80 Br ex 19.70 Dght 6.600 Lbp 81.98 Br md 18.99 Dpth 8.00 Welded, 1 dk	**(B21A20S) Platform Supply Ship** Ice Capable	**4 diesel electric oil engines** driving 4 gen. driving 2 Azimuth electric drive units Total Power: 7,060kW (9,600hp) 13.0kn Caterpillar 3512C 4 x Vee 4 Stroke 12 Cy. 170 x 215 each-1765kW (2400bhp) Caterpillar Inc-USA Thrusters: 2 Tunnel thruster (f)
9129768 - -	**SEA FLYTE II** - **Banwell Pty Ltd** - *Fremantle, WA* *Australia*	**136** - 33		**1995**-11 **WaveMaster International Pty Ltd — Fremantle WA** Yd No: 132 Loa 35.00 Br ex 7.00 Dght - Lbp - Br md - Dpth - Welded, 1 dk	**(A37B2PS) Passenger Ship** Hull Material: Aluminium Alloy Passengers: unberthed: 270	**2 oil engines** geared to sc. shafts driving 2 FP propellers Total Power: 1,472kW (2,002hp) 30.0kn Wartsila UD19L6M4D 2 x 4 Stroke 6 Cy. 127 x 145 each-736kW (1001bhp) Wartsila SACM Diesel SA-France
7033056 *A9D2884* -	**SEA FORCE** *ex* Hana *-2006* *ex* Sami *-2002* *ex* Salam *-2000* *ex* Eagle 1 *-1998* *ex* Porniroo *-1996* *ex* Black Eagle I *-1992* *ex* Klostertor *-1985* **Sea Eagles Shipping LLC** - *Bahrain* *Bahrain* MMSI: 408807000 Official number: BN 4065	**553** 166 669	Class: GL (AB)	**1970**-12 **JG Hitzler Schiffswerft und Masch GmbH & Co KG — Lauenburg** Yd No: 718 Loa 54.51 Br ex 11.33 Dght 3.440 Lbp 49.43 Br md 11.03 Dpth 3.97 Welded, 1 dk	**(B21B20T) Offshore Tug/Supply Ship** Cranes: 1x50t Ice Capable	**2 oil engines** reduction geared to sc. shafts driving 2 FP propellers Total Power: 2,206kW (3,000hp) 11.0kn MAN V6V22/30ATL 2 x Vee 4 Stroke 12 Cy. 220 x 300 each-1103kW (1500bhp) Maschinenbau Augsburg Nuernberg (MAN)-Augsburg AuxGen: 3 x 112kW 400V 50Hz a.c Thrusters: 1 Thwart. FP thruster (f) Fuel: 279.5 (d.f.)
9625322 *VHEO* -	**SEA FORCE** *ex* Sapor 5 *-2012* **Comcove Pty Ltd (Marine Diesel Traders)** - *Brisbane, Qld* *Australia* MMSI: 503659700 Official number: 860376	**277** 84 310	Class: NK	**2011**-06 **Sapor Shipbuilding Industries Sdn Bhd — Sibu** Yd No: SAPOR 54 Loa 30.20 Br ex - Dght 3.812 Lbp 28.42 Br md 9.00 Dpth 4.60 Welded, 1 dk	**(B32A2ST) Tug**	**2 oil engines** reduction geared to sc. shafts driving 2 Propellers Total Power: 1,518kW (2,064hp) Mitsubishi S6R2-MTK3L 2 x 4 Stroke 6 Cy. 170 x 220 each-759kW (1032bhp) Mitsubishi Heavy Industries Ltd-Japan Fuel: 240.0
9322102 *V7KG5* -	**SEA FORCE** - **Champion Navigation SA** Perosea Shipping Co SA SatCom: Inmarsat M 600843414 *Majuro* *Marshall Islands* MMSI: 538002617 Official number: 2617	**8,539** 4,117 13,078 T/cm 23.2	Class: BV (AB)	**2006**-09 **21st Century Shipbuilding Co Ltd — Tongyeong** Yd No: 213 Loa 128.60 (BB) Br ex - Dght 8.714 Lbp 120.40 Br md 20.40 Dpth 11.50 Welded, 1 dk	**(A12B2TR) Chemical/Products Tanker** Double Hull (13F) Liq: 13,402; Liq (Oil): 13,402 Cargo Heating Coils Compartments: 12 Wing Ta, 2 Wing Slop Ta, ER 12 Cargo Pump (s): 12x300m³/hr Manifold: Bow/CM: 60.7m	**1 oil engine** driving 1 FP propeller Total Power: 4,440kW (6,037hp) 13.4kn MAN-B&W 6S35MC 1 x 2 Stroke 6 Cy. 350 x 1400 4440kW (6037bhp) STX Engine Co Ltd-South Korea AuxGen: 3 x 550kW a.c Thrusters: 1 Tunnel thruster (f) Fuel: 80.0 (d.f.) 675.0 (r.f.)
9522037 *2BFN4* -	**SEA FORCE ONE** - **Locat SpA** - *London* *United Kingdom* MMSI: 235065689 Official number: 915183	**942** 282 171	Class: AB	**2008**-08 **T. Mariotti SpA — Genova** Yd No: MAR-Y001 Loa 53.80 (BB) Br ex - Dght 2.900 Lbp 45.80 Br md 10.50 Dpth 5.28 Welded, 1 dk	**(X11A2YP) Yacht**	**2 oil engines** reduction geared to sc. shafts driving 2 FP propellers Total Power: 3,372kW (4,584hp) 15.0kn Caterpillar 3516B-HD 2 x Vee 4 Stroke 16 Cy. 170 x 215 each-1686kW (2292bhp) Caterpillar Inc-USA AuxGen: 2 x a.c
9263057 *HSB4555* -	**SEA FOREST** *ex* White Amanda *-2011* **S Carrier 2000 Co Ltd** Sinsimon Navigation Co Ltd *Bangkok* *Thailand* MMSI: 567421000 Official number: TG 54006	**7,436** 3,415 10,302	Class: NK	**2002**-02 **Nishi Shipbuilding Co Ltd — Imabari EH** Yd No: 429 Loa 110.67 (BB) Br ex - Dght 8.564 Lbp 102.00 Br md 19.20 Dpth 13.50 Welded, 2 dks	**(A31A2GX) General Cargo Ship** Grain: 15,760; Bale: 14,681 Compartments: 2 Ho, ER 2 Ha: (20.3 x 14.0) (33.6 x 14.0)ER Cranes: 2x30.7t; Derricks: 1x30t	**1 oil engine** driving 1 FP propeller Total Power: 3,900kW (5,302hp) 13.3kn MAN-B&W 6L35MC 1 x 2 Stroke 6 Cy. 350 x 1050 3900kW (5302bhp) Makita Corp-Japan Fuel: 710.0
9656723 *5BWQ3* -	**SEA FORTH** - **PSV Holding Inc** Deep Sea Supply Management (Singapore) Pte Ltd *Limassol* *Cyprus* MMSI: 210738000	**4,003** 1,533 4,700	Class: NV	**2013**-08 **Zhejiang Shipbuilding Co Ltd — Fenghua ZJ** Yd No: ZJ2015 Loa 88.80 Br ex 19.70 Dght 6.600 Lbp 82.00 Br md 19.00 Dpth 8.00 Welded, 1 dk	**(B21A20S) Platform Supply Ship** Ice Capable	**4 diesel electric oil engines** driving 4 gen. Connecting to 2 elec. motors driving 2 Azimuth electric drive units Total Power: 7,060kW (9,600hp) 13.0kn Caterpillar 3512C 4 x Vee 4 Stroke 12 Cy. 170 x 215 each-1765kW (2400bhp) Caterpillar Inc-USA Thrusters: 2 Tunnel thruster (f)
8031770 - -	**SEA FORTUNE** *ex* Silver Energy *-2011* *ex* Dae Chang *-2006* **PT Pelayaran Niaga Indoshima Sakti** -	**1,300** 907 2,611	Class: (KR)	**1978**-07 **Korea Tacoma Marine Industries Ltd — Changwon** Yd No: 10030 Loa 77.20 Br ex - Dght 5.487 Lbp 70.52 Br md 11.21 Dpth 5.85 Welded, 1 dk	**(A13B2TP) Products Tanker** Liq: 2,739; Liq (Oil): 2,739	**1 oil engine** driving 1 FP propeller Total Power: 1,103kW (1,500hp) 11.5kn Hanshin 6LUN28 1 x 4 Stroke 6 Cy. 280 x 480 1103kW (1500bhp) Hanshin Nainenki Kogyo-Japan AuxGen: 2 x 44kW 445V a.c

IMO / Call sign	Name / Owner	Tonnage	Class	Builder / Dimensions	Type	Machinery
8319067 *S6DS* -	**SEA FORTUNE** *ex* Dolson *-2002* *ex* Kyokusei Maru *-1999* **Prosperbiz Petroleum (s) Pte Ltd** Shipmate Pte Ltd *Singapore* *Singapore* MMSI: 564367000 Official number: 388586	**1,999** 967 3,368 T/cm 9.0	Class: NK	**1984-11 Kitanihon Zosen K.K. — Hachinohe** Yd No: 186 Loa 86.02 Br ex - Dght 5.857 Lbp 80.02 Br md 14.01 Dpth 6.91 Welded, 1 dk	**(A13B2TP) Products Tanker** Liq: 3,395; Liq (Oil): 3,395	**1 oil engine** driving 1 FP propeller Total Power: 2,152kW (2,926hp) 12.0kn B&W 5L35MCE 1 x 2 Stroke 5 Cy. 350 x 1050 2152kW (2926bhp) Makita Diesel Co Ltd-Japan AuxGen: 3 x 240kW a.c Fuel: 230.0 (r.f.)
9141974 *D5FV9* -	**SEA FORTUNE** *ex* Seawind *-2010* *ex* Jasper *-2003* **Excelsior Navigation Co** Athenian Ship Management Inc *Monrovia* *Liberia* MMSI: 636016373 Official number: 16373	**38,775** 25,534 74,012 T/cm 65.5	Class: BV (NK)	**1996-04 Imabari Shipbuilding Co Ltd — Marugame KG (Marugame Shipyard)** Yd No: 1250 Loa 224.97 (BB) Br ex - Dght 14.009 Lbp 215.00 Br md 32.20 Dpth 19.30 Welded, 1 dk	**(A21A2BC) Bulk Carrier** Grain: 89,407 Compartments: 7 Ho, ER 7 Ha: (13.0 x 12.8)5 (17.9 x 15.6) (16.3 x 15.6)ER	**1 oil engine** driving 1 FP propeller Total Power: 12,269kW (16,681hp) 14.3kn B&W 6S60MC 1 x 2 Stroke 6 Cy. 600 x 2292 12269kW (16681bhp) Mitsui Engineering & Shipbuilding CLtd-Japan
9293741 *S6HA2*	**SEA FORTUNE 1** *ex* Sea Fortune *-2006* **DS-Rendite-Fonds Nr 100 VLCC 'Sea Fortune' GmbH & Co Tankschiff KG** Epic Ship Management Pte Ltd SatCom: Inmarsat C 456512010 *Singapore* *Singapore* MMSI: 565120000 Official number: 392051	**159,730** 96,326 299,097 T/cm 184.6	Class: CC NV	**2003-12 Nantong COSCO KHI Ship Engineering Co Ltd (NACKS) — Nantong JS** Yd No: 013 Loa 333.04 (BB) Br ex 60.04 Dght 18.680 Lbp 320.03 Br md 60.00 Dpth 29.30 Welded, 1 dk	**(A13A2TV) Crude Oil Tanker** Double Hull (13F) Liq: 331,333; Liq (Oil): 331,333 Compartments: 5 Ta, 10 Wing Ta, 2 Wing Slop Ta, ER 3 Cargo Pump (s) Manifold: Bow/CM: 164m	**1 oil engine** driving 1 FP propeller Total Power: 22,648kW (30,792hp) 15.7kn B&W 7S80MC 1 x 2 Stroke 7 Cy. 800 x 3056 22648kW (30792bhp) Hudong Heavy Machinery Co Ltd-China AuxGen: 3 x 880kW a.c
9419993 *5BCP3* -	**SEA FOX** **DESS Cyprus Ltd** Deep Sea Supply Navegacao Maritima Ltda SatCom: Inmarsat C 420901310 *Limassol* *Cyprus* MMSI: 209013000	**1,943** 646 1,905	Class: NV	**2011-01 ABG Shipyard Ltd — Surat** Yd No: 271 Loa 63.40 Br ex - Dght 5.100 Lbp 56.53 Br md 15.80 Dpth 6.80 Welded, 1 dk	**(B21B20A) Anchor Handling Tug Supply**	**2 oil engines** reduction geared to sc. shafts driving 2 CP propellers Total Power: 5,002kW (6,800hp) 10.5kn Yanmar 8N280-EN 2 x 4 Stroke 8 Cy. 280 x 380 each-2501kW (3400bhp) Yanmar Diesel Engine Co Ltd-Japan AuxGen: 3 x 425kW 440V 60Hz a.c Thrusters: 1 Thwart. CP thruster (f)
9097329 *WDE2381* -	**SEA FOX** **Sea Fox LLC** Sea Global Fisheries LLC *Pago Pago, AS* *United States of America* MMSI: 338394000 Official number: 1207469	**1,517** 605 -		**2008-02 Jong Shyn Shipbuilding Co., Ltd. — Kaohsiung** Yd No: 159 L reg 63.12 (BB) Br ex - Dght - Lbp - Br md 12.31 Dpth 7.25 Welded, 1 dk	**(B11B2FV) Fishing Vessel**	**1 oil engine** driving 1 Propeller Daihatsu 1 x 4 Stroke Daihatsu Diesel Manufacturing Co Lt-Japan
7032349 *ATTX* -	**SEA FOX** **New India Fisheries Ltd** - *Kolkata* *India* Official number: 1813	*134* 44 107		**1970 Kanmon Zosen K.K. — Shimonoseki** Yd No: 299 Loa 29.14 Br ex 6.84 Dght 2.591 Lbp 25.00 Br md 6.81 Dpth 3.00 Welded, 1 dk	**(B11A2FT) Trawler**	**1 oil engine** driving 1 FP propeller Total Power: 331kW (450hp) Daihatsu 6PSTCM-22 1 x 4 Stroke 6 Cy. 220 x 280 331kW (450bhp) Daihatsu Diesel Manufacturing Co Lt-Japan
7308566 - -	**SEA FOX** **Westbank Corp** - *New Orleans, LA* *United States of America* Official number: 281435	*274* 186 -		**1960 Patterson Shipyard Inc. — Patterson, La** L reg 43.41 Br ex 7.35 Dght - Lbp - Br md - Dpth 3.00 Welded, 1 dk	**(B11B2FV) Fishing Vessel**	**1 oil engine** driving 1 FP propeller Total Power: 736kW (1,001hp) General Motors 1 x 2 Stroke 736kW (1001bhp) (made 1956) General Motors Corp-USA
7322976 *HP5954* -	**SEA FOX** *ex* Taisei Maru No. 7 *-1990* *ex* Owari Maru No. 36 *-1984* *ex* Matsuo Maru No. 28 *-1980* *ex* Matsuo Maru No. 18 *-1980* **Inter Ocean Line** - *Panama* *Panama* Official number: D3761789PEXT	*154* - -		**1973 Usuki Iron Works Co Ltd — Usuki OT** Yd No: 885 Loa 35.84 Br ex 6.23 Dght 2.896 Lbp 31.91 Br md 6.20 Dpth 2.52 Welded, 1 dk	**(B11B2FV) Fishing Vessel**	**1 oil engine** driving 1 FP propeller Total Power: 552kW (750hp) Daihatsu 6DSM-26 1 x 4 Stroke 6 Cy. 260 x 320 552kW (750bhp) Daihatsu Diesel Manufacturing Co Lt-Japan
9605449 *PHSF*	**SEA FOXTROT** **Global Ship Leasing 12 BV** Seacontractors Brokerage BV *Vlissingen* *Netherlands* MMSI: 244184000 Official number: 54455	**327** 98 -	Class: BV	**2011-09 Damen Shipyards Kozle Sp z oo — Kedzierzyn-Kozle** (Hull) Yd No: 1161 **2011-09 B.V. Scheepswerf Damen Hardinxveld — Hardinxveld-Giessendam** Yd No: 571651 Loa 32.27 Br ex - Dght 3.300 Lbp 30.52 Br md 9.35 Dpth 4.40 Welded, 1 dk	**(B32A2ST) Tug** Cranes: 1x7.9t	**2 oil engines** reduction geared to sc. shafts driving 2 FP propellers Total Power: 2,498kW (3,396hp) Caterpillar 3512B-TA 2 x Vee 4 Stroke 12 Cy. 170 x 190 each-1249kW (1698bhp) Caterpillar Inc-USA AuxGen: 2 x 86kW 400/230V 50Hz a.c Thrusters: 1 Thwart. FP thruster (f) Fuel: 220.0 (d.f.)
5318608 *HO6348* -	**SEA FREEZE II** *ex* Straitfish II *-1982* *ex* Seisho Maru No. 18 *-1969* **Deerness Shipping Ltd** - *Panama* *Panama* Official number: 1249782	*212* 146 -	Class: (NK)	**1959-05 Yamanishi Shipbuilding Co Ltd — Ishinomaki MG** Yd No: 362 Converted From: Fishing Vessel Loa 40.70 Br ex 6.86 Dght 3.141 Lbp 35.21 Br md 6.81 Dpth 3.33 Riveted\Welded, 1 dk	**(A31A2GX) General Cargo Ship**	**1 oil engine** driving 1 FP propeller Total Power: 515kW (700hp) 9.0kn Fuji 6SD30 1 x 4 Stroke 6 Cy. 300 x 430 515kW (700bhp) (new engine 1963) Fuji Diesel Co Ltd-Japan AuxGen: 2 x 96kW a.c
9125982 *JK5233* -	**SEA FRIEND** **Setonaikai Kisen Co Ltd** - *Hiroshima, Hiroshima* *Japan* Official number: 134725	*312* 144		**1995-01 Naikai Zosen Corp — Onomichi HS (Setoda Shipyard)** Yd No: 600 Loa 49.90 Br ex 11.01 Dght 2.610 Lbp 38.90 Br md 10.00 Dpth 3.60 Welded, 1 dk	**(A36A2PR) Passenger/Ro-Ro Ship (Vehicles)** Passengers: unberthed: 350 Cars: 4	**1 oil engine** with clutches, flexible couplings & sr geared to sc. shaft driving 2 FP propellers 1 fwd and 1 aft Total Power: 1,030kW (1,400hp) 11.0kn Daihatsu 6DLM-26FSL 1 x 4 Stroke 6 Cy. 260 x 340 1030kW (1400bhp) Daihatsu Diesel Manufacturing Co Lt-Japan
8911126 *S6AJ2*	**SEA FRONTIER** *ex* Eishin Maru No. 8 *-2004* **Searights Maritime Services Pte Ltd** - *Singapore* *Singapore* MMSI: 563012120 Official number: 390817	**3,113** 1,517 4,999 T/cm 12.0	Class: LR (NK) **100A1** SS 12/2009 oil tanker, carriage of oils with FP exceeding 60 degree C voyages within the Singapore 30 mile limits in the course of which the vessel shall not be more than 20 miles from the nearest land ESP **LMC** Eq.Ltr: R; Cable: 495.0/40.0 U2 (a)	**1989-12 Shin Kurushima Dockyard Co. Ltd. — Hashihama, Imabari** Yd No: 2658 Loa 103.52 (BB) Br ex 15.02 Dght 6.980 Lbp 96.00 Br md 15.00 Dpth 7.90 Welded, 1 dk	**(A13B2TP) Products Tanker** Single Hull Liq: 5,522; Liq (Oil): 5,522 Compartments: 9 Ta, ER	**1 oil engine** driving 1 CP propeller Total Power: 2,940kW (3,997hp) 11.5kn Akasaka A45 1 x 4 Stroke 6 Cy. 450 x 880 2940kW (3997bhp) Akasaka Tekkosho KK (Akasaka DieselLtd)-Japan AuxGen: 2 x 300kW 450V 60Hz a.c Boilers: AuxB (Comp) 9.7kgf/cm² (9.5bar) Thrusters: 1 Thwart. FP thruster (f)
7200453 - -	**SEA FRONTIER** *ex* Great Tide *-2004* **Ahmed Jaffar Mohamed Ali & Mohamed Jaffar Mohamed Ali** Sea Frontier Marine	**198** - 712	Class: (NK)	**1965 Burton Shipyard Co., Inc. — Port Arthur, Tx** Yd No: 381 Loa 48.76 Br ex 11.60 Dght 2.998 Lbp 46.94 Br md 11.58 Dpth 3.66 Welded, 1 dk	**(B21A20S) Platform Supply Ship**	**2 oil engines** geared to sc. shafts driving 2 FP propellers Total Power: 1,126kW (1,530hp) Caterpillar D398TA 2 x Vee 4 Stroke 12 Cy. 159 x 203 each-563kW (765bhp) Caterpillar Tractor Co-USA
9656735 *5BXM3* -	**SEA FROST** **Deep Sea Supply Shipowning III BV** Deep Sea Supply Management (Singapore) Pte Ltd *Limassol* *Cyprus* MMSI: 210637000	**4,003** 1,533 4,700	Class: NV	**2013-11 Zhejiang Shipbuilding Co Ltd — Fenghua ZJ** Yd No: ZJ2016 Loa 88.80 Br ex 19.70 Dght 6.650 Lbp 82.00 Br md 19.00 Dpth 8.00 Welded, 1 dk	**(B21A20S) Platform Supply Ship** Ice Capable	**4 diesel electric oil engines** driving 4 gen. Connecting to 2 elec. motors driving 2 Azimuth electric drive units Total Power: 7,060kW (9,600hp) 13.0kn Caterpillar 3512C 4 x Vee 4 Stroke 12 Cy. 170 x 215 each-1765kW (2400bhp) Caterpillar Inc-USA Thrusters: 2 Tunnel thruster (f)

7907702 *A9D2871* -	**SEA FURY** *ex* Misfah 5 *-2006* *ex* J. O. R. C. 5 *-1983* **Al Jazeera Shipping Co** Al Jazeera Shipping Co WLL (AJS) *Bahrain* *Bahrain* MMSI: 408806000	*377* - -	Class: BV (LR) (NV) ✠ Classed LR until 28/3/01	**1980-06 Martin Jansen GmbH & Co. KG Schiffsw. u. Masch. — Leer** Yd No: 155 Loa 36.50 Br ex 11.00 Dght 4.312 Lbp 34.14 Br md 10.60 Dpth 5.19 Welded, 1 dk	**(B32A2ST) Tug**	**2 oil engines** reverse reduction geared to sc. shafts driving 2 FP propellers Total Power: 2,060kW (2,800hp) 13.5kn MWM TBD440-8K 2 x 4 Stroke 8 Cy. 230 x 270 each-1030kW (1400bhp) Motoren Werke Mannheim AG (MWM)-West Germany AuxGen: 3 x 50kW 400V 50Hz a.c
9672935 *OUWY2* -	**SEA GALE** *ex* Fob Swath 3 *-2013* **FOB Swath AS** A2SEA A/S *Fredericia* *Denmark (DIS)* MMSI: 219460000 Official number: A 553	**244** 73 65	Class: NV	**2013-05 Danish Yachts A/S — Skagen** Yd No: 120 Loa 24.65 (BB) Br ex 10.83 Dght 2.490 Lbp 23.55 Br md 10.60 Dpth 5.39 Bonded, 1 dk	**(B21A20C) Crew/Supply Vessel** Hull Material: Carbon Fibre Sandwich Passengers: unberthed: 24	**2 oil engines** reduction geared to sc. shafts driving 2 CP propellers Total Power: 1,800kW (2,448hp) 22.0kn M.T.U. 10V2000M72 1 x Vee 4 Stroke 10 Cy. 135 x 156 900kW (1224bhp) MTU Friedrichshafen GmbH-Friedrichshafen Thrusters: 2 Tunnel thruster (f); 2 Tunnel thruster (a)
8037413 *HP6110* -	**SEA GARNET** *ex* Ahmed III *-2009* *ex* Sarah *-1993* *ex* Offshore Orleans *-1978* **GMV Shipping Management & Operation LLC** - *Panama* *Panama* MMSI: 371779000 Official number: 43858PEXT	**369** 124 -	Class: (HR) (AB)	**1957 Ingalls SB. Corp. — Pascagoula, Ms** Yd No: 1043 Loa - Br ex - Dght 3.055 Lbp 41.15 Br md 10.37 Dpth 3.66 Welded, 1 dk	**(B21A20S) Platform Supply Ship**	**2 oil engines** sr geared to sc. shafts driving 2 FP propellers Total Power: 736kW (1,000hp) 10.0kn Caterpillar D399TA 2 x Vee 4 Stroke 16 Cy. 159 x 203 each-368kW (500bhp) Caterpillar Tractor Co-USA AuxGen: 1 x 90kW a.c, 1 x 75kW a.c
7528001 - -	**SEA GEM** - **Tuna Atlantic Ltda** - *Cartagena de Indias* *Colombia* MMSI: 730017000 Official number: MC-05-550	**1,468** 440 -		**1975-12 J M Martinac Shipbuilding Corp — Tacoma WA** Yd No: 205 Loa 68.08 Br ex - Dght - Lbp 59.26 Br md 12.81 Dpth 5.57 Welded, 1 dk	**(B11B2FV) Fishing Vessel**	**1 oil engine** driving 1 FP propeller Total Power: 2,648kW (3,600hp) EMD (Electro-Motive) 20-645-E7 1 x Vee 2 Stroke 20 Cy. 230 x 254 2648kW (3600bhp) General Motors Corp-USA
8828056 *VB5385* -	**SEA GEM** - **Gary Daley Ltd** - *St John's, NL* *Canada* MMSI: 316001956 Official number: 809104	*102* 50 -		**1988 Glovertown Shipyards Ltd — Glovertown NL** Loa 18.80 Br ex 6.70 Dght - Lbp - Br md - Dpth 2.30 Welded	**(B11A2FS) Stern Trawler**	**1 oil engine** driving 1 FP propeller Total Power: 331kW (450hp) 10.0kn
9236779 *A9D2873* -	**SEA GEM** *ex* Kim Heng 1188 *-2006* **Al Jazeera Shipping Co** Al Jazeera Shipping Co WLL (AJS) *Bahrain* *Bahrain* MMSI: 408009240 Official number: BN 9240	**142** 43 118	Class: AB (NK)	**2000-08 Tuong Aik (Sarawak) Sdn Bhd — Sibu** Yd No: 2002 Loa 23.50 Br ex - Dght 2.712 Lbp 21.07 Br md 7.32 Dpth 3.20 Welded, 1 dk	**(B32B2SP) Pusher Tug**	**2 oil engines** reduction geared to sc. shafts driving 2 FP propellers Total Power: 806kW (1,096hp) 12.0kn Caterpillar 3412TA 2 x Vee 4 Stroke 12 Cy. 137 x 152 each-403kW (548bhp) Caterpillar Inc-USA Fuel: 114.0 (d.f.)
9598218 *V7DX8* -	**SEA GEMINI** *launched as* Hb Phoenix *-2014* **Gemini Shipowning Inc** Seatankers Management Co Ltd *Majuro* *Marshall Islands* MMSI: 538005446 Official number: 5446	**44,276** 27,327 81,716 T/cm 72.3	Class: AB (Class contemplated) (CC)	**2014-01 Qingdao Wuchuan Heavy Industry Co Ltd — Qingdao SD** Yd No: A243M Loa 229.00 (BB) Br ex - Dght 14.450 Lbp 225.42 Br md 32.26 Dpth 20.10 Welded, 1 dk	**(A21A2BC) Bulk Carrier** Grain: 97,000 Compartments: 7 Ho, ER 7 Ha: 6 (15.6 x 15.0)ER (13.8 x 12.8)	**1 oil engine** driving 1 FP propeller Total Power: 11,300kW (15,363hp) 14.5kn MAN-B&W 5S60MC-C 1 x 2 Stroke 5 Cy. 600 x 2400 11300kW (15363bhp) Dalian Marine Diesel Co Ltd-China AuxGen: 3 x a.c
8623028 - -	**SEA GEMS 204** *ex* Don Leoncio K *-2014* *ex* Nichiei Maru No. 82 *-1982* **Zamboanga Universal Fishing Co** - *Zamboanga* *Philippines* Official number: ZAM2F00108	*213* 80 -		**1965 in Japan** Loa 38.99 Br ex 6.63 Dght 2.890 Lbp 34.98 Br md 6.61 Dpth 3.28 Welded, 1 dk	**(B11A2FT) Trawler**	**1 oil engine** driving 1 FP propeller Total Power: 515kW (700hp) Akasaka 1 x 4 Stroke 515kW (700bhp) Akasaka Tekkosho KK (Akasaka DieselLtd)-Japan
6900666 *5NML* -	**SEA GIANT** *ex* Seven Haleluyah *-2008* *ex* Putford Teal *-1996* *ex* Grampian Kestrel *-1991* *ex* Kinnaird *-1988* *ex* Pacific Service *-1985* *ex* Pacific Shore *-1980* **Moen Marine Shipping** - *Nigeria* Official number: 377328	**734** 220 920	Class: (LR) (NV) ✠ Classed LR until 6/93	**1969-03 Cochrane & Sons Ltd. — Selby** Yd No: 1523 Converted From: Offshore Tug/Supply Ship-1987 Loa 54.03 Br ex 11.69 Dght 4.172 Lbp 48.09 Br md 11.43 Dpth 4.73 Welded, 1 dk	**(B22G20Y) Standby Safety Vessel** Derricks: 1x2t	**2 oil engines** reverse reduction geared to sc. shafts driving 2 FP propellers Total Power: 1,766kW (2,402hp) 12.5kn Blackstone ESSL12 2 x Vee 4 Stroke 12 Cy. 222 x 292 each-883kW (1201bhp) Lister Blackstone Marine Ltd.-Dursley AuxGen: 2 x 125kW 220V d.c, 1 x 60kW 220V d.c Thrusters: 1 Water jet (f) Fuel: 61.0 (d.f.)
7509665 - -	**SEA GLOBAL 5** *ex* Endeavour *-2000* *ex* Sirichai Endeavour *-2000* *ex* Taiki Maru No. 38 *-1991* -	**285** 143 -		**1975-05 Goriki Zosensho — Ise** Yd No: 776 Loa - Br ex 8.21 Dght 3.201 Lbp 43.11 Br md 8.18 Dpth 3.56 Riveted\Welded, 1 dk	**(B11B2FV) Fishing Vessel** Ins: 335	**1 oil engine** driving 1 FP propeller Total Power: 736kW (1,001hp) 12.5kn Sumiyoshi S631SS 1 x 4 Stroke 6 Cy. 310 x 480 736kW (1001bhp) Sumiyoshi Tekkosho-Japan AuxGen: 2 x 250kW 225V a.c
6818643 *HP8586* -	**SEA GLOBAL I** *ex* Sea Lady I *-2003* *ex* Transdiesel *-2000* *ex* Ebella *-1996* *ex* Navichem Arcturus *-1992* *ex* Donald *-1989* *ex* Takis N. E. *-1989* *ex* Erik *-1988* **Sea Global Petroleum Suppliers Inc** - *Panama* *Panama* MMSI: 356617000 Official number: 25079PEXT4	**1,993** 1,170 3,209 T/cm 9.4	Class: (GL)	**1968-07 Elsflether Werft AG — Elsfleth** Yd No: 363 Lengthened-1976 Loa 91.28 Br ex 12.68 Dght 5.195 Lbp 84.56 Br md 12.60 Dpth 7.40 Welded, 1 dk.	**(A13B2TP) Products Tanker** Liq: 3,848; Liq (Oil): 3,848 Cargo Heating Coils Compartments: 12 Ta, ER 3 Cargo Pump (s): 1x405m³/hr, 2x245m³/hr Manifold: Bow/CM: 57m Ice Capable	**1 oil engine** driving 1 FP propeller Total Power: 1,324kW (1,800hp) 12.3kn Deutz RBV6M358 1 x 4 Stroke 6 Cy. 400 x 580 1324kW (1800bhp) Kloeckner Humboldt Deutz AG-West Germany AuxGen: 2 x 64kW 230/380V 50Hz a.c, 1 x 26kW 230/380V 50Hz a.c Fuel: 132.0 (d.f.) 6.0pd
7852359 *HP6191* -	**SEA GLORY** *ex* Sea Intellect *-1991* *ex* Daiei Maru No. 7 *-1991* **Seagull Petroleum Pte Ltd** - *Panama* *Panama* Official number: 20737PEXT	*444* 242 1,300		**1971 Y.K. Okajima Zosensho — Matsuyama** Yd No: 160 Loa 53.19 Br ex - Dght 4.501 Lbp 52.00 Br md 9.50 Dpth 6.05 Welded, 1 dk	**(A31A2GX) General Cargo Ship**	**1 oil engine** driving 1 FP propeller Total Power: 956kW (1,300hp) 11.5kn Makita ESLHC633 1 x 4 Stroke 6 Cy. 330 x 550 956kW (1300bhp) Makita Diesel Co Ltd-Japan
7910814 *5NMO* -	**SEA GLORY** *ex* Paul *-2005* **Upton Maritime Ltd** - *Lagos* *Nigeria* Official number: 377749	**3,003** 1,524 5,166 T/cm 11.0	Class: (RI) (GL)	**1980-03 Kroegerwerft Rendsburg GmbH — Schacht-Audorf** Yd No: 1501 Lengthened-1984 Loa 104.02 Br ex 15.04 Dght 5.660 Lbp 84.03 Br md 15.02 Dpth 5.80 Welded, 1 dk.	**(A12B2TR) Chemical/Products Tanker** Liq: 4,673; Liq (Oil): 4,673 Cargo Heating Coils Compartments: 10 Ta, ER 4 Cargo Pump (s): 4x275m³/hr Manifold: Bow/CM: 49m Ice Capable	**1 oil engine** sr geared to sc. shaft driving 1 FP propeller Total Power: 1,820kW (2,474hp) 12.3kn MWM TBD501-6 1 x 4 Stroke 6 Cy. 360 x 450 1820kW (2474bhp) Motoren Werke Mannheim AG (MWM)-West Germany Fuel: 65.5 (d.f.) 76.0 (r.f.) 8.0pd
9162459 *ELUD6* -	**SEA GLORY** *ex* Hai Chang *-1997* **Log Carriers Navigation Inc** Lihai International Shipping Ltd SatCom: Inmarsat B 363659110 *Monrovia* *Liberia* MMSI: 636010648 Official number: 10648	**18,093** 9,442 27,279 T/cm 38.9	Class: NK (AB)	**1997-05 Hudong Shipbuilding Group — Shanghai** Yd No: H1235A Loa 175.00 (BB) Br ex - Dght 9.816 Lbp 165.00 Br md 26.00 Dpth 13.90 Welded, 1 dk	**(A21A2BC) Bulk Carrier** Grain: 36,723; Bale: 35,621 Compartments: 5 Ho, ER 5 Ha: (14.2 x 12.9)4 (19.2 x 14.4)ER Cranes: 4x30t	**1 oil engine** driving 1 FP propeller Total Power: 5,845kW (7,947hp) 14.7kn B&W 5L50MC 1 x 2 Stroke 5 Cy. 500 x 1620 5845kW (7947bhp) Hudong Shipyard-China AuxGen: 3 x 440kW a.c Fuel: 1350.0
9009695 *T3DS2* -	**SEA GLORY** *ex* Lyra *-2012* *ex* Reefer Pioneer *-2002* **Shandong Zhonglu Fishery Shipping Co Ltd** - *Tarawa* *Kiribati* MMSI: 529523000 Official number: K-15911265	**4,444** 2,287 5,226	Class: NK (BV) (NV)	**1991-03 Kyokuyo Shipyard Corp — Shimonoseki YC** Yd No: 368 Loa 120.70 (BB) Br ex - Dght 6.914 Lbp 112.90 Br md 16.60 Dpth 10.00 Welded, 1 dk, 2nd & 3rd dk in holds only	**(A34A2GR) Refrigerated Cargo Ship** Bale: 5,954; Ins: 6,719 Compartments: 3 Ho, ER, 6 Tw Dk 3 Ha: (7.1 x 5.4)2 (7.1 x 6.4)ER Derricks: 6x5t	**1 oil engine** driving 1 FP propeller Total Power: 4,121kW (5,603hp) 15.8kn Mitsubishi 8UEC37LA 1 x 2 Stroke 8 Cy. 370 x 880 4121kW (5603bhp) Kobe Hatsudoki KK-Japan AuxGen: 4 x 366kW a.c Thrusters: 1 Thwart. CP thruster (f) Fuel: 90.0 (d.f.) 750.0 (r.f.)

IMO / Call sign	Name / Owner	Tonnage	Class	Builder / Dimensions	Type	Machinery
9436599 *A6E2891* -	**SEA GLORY** *ex* Surya Ratna 3 *-2008* **Target Engineering Construction Co (LLC)** - *Abu Dhabi* *United Arab Emirates* MMSI: 470694000 Official number: 5839	**265** 80 274	Class: NK	**2007-07 Hung Seng Shipbuilding Sdn Bhd — Sibu** Yd No: 042 Loa 30.00 Br ex - Dght 3.512 Lbp 28.08 Br md 8.60 Dpth 4.12 Welded, 1 dk	**(B32A2ST) Tug**	**2 oil engines** reduction geared to sc. shafts driving 2 FP propellers Total Power: 1,518kW (2,064hp) Mitsubishi S6R2-MTK3L 2 x 4 Stroke 6 Cy. 170 x 220 each-759kW (1032bhp) Mitsubishi Heavy Industries Ltd-Japan Fuel: 170.0 (d.f.)
9319519 *YDA4680* -	**SEA GLORY 6** **PT Mitra Bahtera Segara Sejati Tbk** - *Jakarta* *Indonesia*	**167** 51 -	Class: AB (GL)	**2004-07 P.T. Tunas Karya Bahari Indonesia — Indonesia** Yd No: 19 Loa 25.00 Br ex - Dght 2.700 Lbp 22.89 Br md 7.32 Dpth 3.35 Welded, 1 dk	**(B32A2ST) Tug**	**2 oil engines** reverse reduction geared to sc. shafts. driving 2 FP propellers Total Power: 942kW (1,280hp) Yanmar 6LAHM-STE3 2 x 4 Stroke 6 Cy. 150 x 165 each-471kW (640bhp) Yanmar Diesel Engine Co Ltd-Japan AuxGen: 2 x 20kW 415/20V a.c
9319521 *9V6514* -	**SEA GLORY 8** **Kian Hiap Holdings Pte Ltd** - *Singapore* *Singapore* Official number: 390649	**167** 51 -	Class: (BV) (GL)	**2004-07 P.T. Tunas Karya Bahari Indonesia — Indonesia** Yd No: 20 Loa 25.00 Br ex - Dght 2.700 Lbp 22.89 Br md 7.32 Dpth 3.35 Welded, 1 dk	**(B32A2ST) Tug**	**2 oil engines** reverse reduction geared to sc. shafts. driving 2 FP propellers Total Power: 942kW (1,280hp) Yanmar 6LAHM-STE3 2 x 4 Stroke 6 Cy. 150 x 165 each-471kW (640bhp) Yanmar Diesel Engine Co Ltd-Japan AuxGen: 2 x 20kW 415/220V a.c
8877203 *H04029* -	**SEA GLORY I** *ex* Poseidon *-2005* *ex* Sukok *-2003* *ex* S. K. Trader *-2003* *ex* Naniwa Maru No. 11 *-1992* *ex* Shinfukuju Maru *-1992* **Copa Fisheries Co Ltd** - *Panama* *Panama* MMSI: 371288000 Official number: 33469PEXT	**493** 299 585		**1977-02 Mategata Zosen K.K. — Namikata** Loa 50.40 Br ex - Dght 3.300 Lbp 45.90 Br md 8.80 Dpth 5.20 Welded, 1 dk	**(B12B2FC) Fish Carrier** Grain: 1,111; Bale: 1,056	**1 oil engine** driving 1 FP propeller Total Power: 552kW (750hp) 10.5kn Daihatsu 1 x 4 Stroke 552kW (750bhp) Daihatsu Diesel Manufacturing Co Lt-Japan
8855516 *WDE8357* -	**SEA GODDESS** *ex* Washington I *-1992* **Capt Washington I Inc** - *Honolulu, HI* *United States of America* Official number: 929439	*145* 99 -		**1988 Custom Vessel Fabricators — Houma, La** Yd No: 104 Loa - Br ex - Dght - Lbp 25.48 Br md 7.16 Dpth 3.38 Welded, 1 dk	**(B11B2FV) Fishing Vessel**	**1 oil engine** driving 1 FP propeller
8938863 - -	**SEA GODDESS** *ex* Sea Farer *-2005* **Sea Goddess LLC** - *Bayou La Batre, AL* *United States of America* Official number: 1037551	**156** 46 -		**1995 Allied Shipyard, Inc. — Larose, La** Yd No: 164 L reg 24.57 Br ex - Dght - Lbp - Br md 7.32 Dpth 3.81 Welded, 1 dk	**(B11B2FV) Fishing Vessel**	**1 oil engine** driving 1 FP propeller
8300353 *9LY2169* -	**SEA GODDESS** *ex* Angel No. 9 *-2012* *ex* Universe *-2009* *ex* Pioneer *-2003* *ex* Fuji Braves *-1996* *ex* Tomoe 325 *-1990* **Gold Advance Corp** - *Freetown* *Sierra Leone* MMSI: 667870000 Official number: SL100870	**6,378** 3,511 6,847 T/cm 19.2	Class: (KR) (NK)	**1983-11 Asakawa Zosen K.K. — Imabari** Yd No: 318 Loa 123.63 (BB) Br ex - Dght 6.057 Lbp 115.60 Br md 18.22 Dpth 9.81 Welded, 1 dk	**(A12B2TR) Chemical/Products Tanker** Double Bottom Entire Compartment Length Liq: 12,012; Liq (Oil): 12,012 Cargo Heating Coils Compartments: 12 Ta, ER 5 Cargo Pump (s): 5x600m³/hr Manifold: Bow/CM: 57m	**1 oil engine** driving 1 FP propeller Total Power: 4,413kW (6,000hp) 13.5kn Mitsubishi 6UEC45HA 1 x 2 Stroke 6 Cy. 450 x 1150 4413kW (6000bhp) Akasaka Tekkosho KK (Akasaka DieselLtd)-Japan AuxGen: 2 x 320kW 445V 60Hz a.c, 1 x 240kW 445V 60Hz a.c Fuel: 135.0 (d.f.) 826.0 (r.f.) 19.5pd
7316525 *H03518* -	**SEA GOLD** *ex* Khor Fakkan *-2004* *ex* Nazek *-2004* *ex* Winn *-1984* **Ruby Marine Services & Trading Inc** - *Panama* *Panama* MMSI: 355292000 Official number: 32003PEXT2	**255** 110 -		**1955 Burton Construction & Shipbuilding Corp. — Port Arthur, Tx** Yd No: 208 L reg 36.58 Br ex 9.15 Dght - Lbp 37.80 Br md 9.08 Dpth 2.60 Welded, 1 dk	**(B21A20S) Platform Supply Ship**	**2 oil engines** geared to sc. shafts driving 2 FP propellers Total Power: 882kW (1,200hp) 8.0kn Caterpillar D399TA 2 x Vee 4 Stroke 16 Cy. 159 x 203 each-441kW (600bhp) Caterpillar Tractor Co-USA
9405382 *PBSS* -	**SEA GOLF** *ex* Bever *-2010* **Sea Golf BV** Seacontractors BV *Vlissingen* *Netherlands* MMSI: 246590000 Official number: 49170	**221** 66 -	Class: BV	**2007-04 Damen Shipyards Kozle Sp z oo — Kedzierzyn-Kozle** (Hull) Yd No: 1110 **2007-04 B.V. Scheepswerf Damen Hardinxveld — Hardinxveld-Giessendam** Yd No: 1573 Loa 27.19 Br ex 9.30 Dght 2.630 Lbp 23.84 Br md 9.10 Dpth 3.60 Welded, 1 dk	**(B32A2ST) Tug** Cranes: 1x18t	**2 oil engines** reduction geared to sc. shafts driving 2 FP propellers Total Power: 2,206kW (3,000hp) Caterpillar 3512B 2 x Vee 4 Stroke 12 Cy. 170 x 190 each-1103kW (1500bhp) Caterpillar Inc-USA AuxGen: 2 x 76kW 400/220V 50Hz a.c Thrusters: 1 Tunnel thruster (f) Fuel: 136.0 (d.f.)
8913538 *ELPG7* -	**SEA GRACE** *ex* Alberto Topic *-2009* *ex* Eline *-1992* **Rubus Transport Inc** Mariteam Services Inc SatCom: Inmarsat C 463607110 *Monrovia* *Liberia* MMSI: 636009758 Official number: 9758	**25,778** 14,032 43,473 T/cm 50.4	Class: NK (LR) (NV) Classed LR until 17/6/11	**1991-06 Hashihama Shipbuilding Co Ltd — Tadotsu KG** (Hull) Yd No: 876 **1991-06 Tsuneishi Shipbuilding Co Ltd — Fukuyama HS** Yd No: 648 Loa 185.84 (BB) Br ex 30.44 Dght 11.323 Lbp 177.00 Br md 30.40 Dpth 16.20 Welded, 1 dk	**(A21A2BC) Bulk Carrier** Grain: 53,593; Bale: 52,269 TEU 1082 C Ho 516 TEU C Dk 566 TEU Compartments: 5 Ho, ER 5 Ha: (19.2 x 15.3)4 (20.8 x 15.3)ER Cranes: 4x30t Ice Capable	**1 oil engine** driving 1 FP propeller Total Power: 7,116kW (9,675hp) 14.0kn B&W 6L60MCE 1 x 2 Stroke 6 Cy. 600 x 1944 7116kW (9675bhp) Mitsui Engineering & Shipbuilding CLtd-Japan AuxGen: 3 x 440kW 440V 60Hz a.c Boilers: WTAuxB (Comp) 7.0kgf/cm² (6.9bar) Fuel: 276.0 (d.f.) 1574.0 (r.f.) 27.0pd
8844268 *C4UB2* -	**SEA GRACE** **NGK Shipping Ltd** - *Limassol* *Cyprus*	**305** 103 -		**1990-07 Nippon Hikoki (Airplane) K.K. — Yokohama** Loa 31.00 Br ex - Dght 1.500 Lbp 29.00 Br md 9.28 Dpth 3.22 Bonded, 1 dk	**(A37B2PS) Passenger Ship** Hull Material: Reinforced Plastic	**2 oil engines** driving 2 FP propellers Total Power: 2,428kW (3,302hp) Yanmar 16LAK-ST1 2 x Vee 4 Stroke 16 Cy. 150 x 165 each-1214kW (1651bhp) Yanmar Diesel Engine Co Ltd-Japan
8806682 *5NQY6* -	**SEA GRACE** *ex* Torill Knutsen *-2011* *ex* Vinga Knutsen *-1990* **Sea Transport Services Nigeria Ltd** Oceanic Shipping Services Pvt Ltd *Lagos* *Nigeria* MMSI: 657827000	**11,425** 4,319 14,910 T/cm 29.5	Class: GL (NV)	**1990-05 SA Juliana Constructora Gijonesa — Gijon** Yd No: 322 Loa 141.50 Br ex 23.05 Dght 7.985 Lbp 133.83 Br md 23.00 Dpth 11.82 Welded, 1 dk	**(A12B2TR) Chemical/Products Tanker** Double Hull (13F) Liq: 17,850; Liq (Oil): 17,850 Compartments: 10 Wing Ta, 2 Wing Slop Ta, ER 10 Cargo Pump (s): 10x240m³/hr Manifold: Bow/CM: 67m Ice Capable	**1 oil engine** driving 1 CP propeller Total Power: 5,237kW (7,120hp) 13.5kn B&W 4S50MC 1 x 2 Stroke 4 Cy. 500 x 1910 5237kW (7120bhp) Astilleros Espanoles SA (AESA)-Spain AuxGen: 2 x 770kW 440V 60Hz a.c, 1 x 750kW 440V 60Hz a.c Thrusters: 1 Thwart. FP thruster (f) Fuel: 63.0 (d.f.) 632.0 (r.f.)
9373096 *A9D2892* -	**SEA GRANDEUR** *ex* Profit Grandeur *-2006* **Al Jazeera Shipping Co WLL (AJS)** - *Bahrain* *Bahrain* MMSI: 408819000 Official number: BN 4083	**179** 54 -	Class: GL	**2006-01 Forward Marine Enterprise Sdn Bhd — Sibu** Yd No: FM-6 Loa 25.00 Br ex 8.12 Dght 3.000 Lbp 23.37 Br md 8.10 Dpth 3.60 Welded, 1 dk	**(B32A2ST) Tug**	**2 oil engines** reverse reduction geared to sc. shafts driving 2 Directional propellers Total Power: 1,248kW (1,696hp) Caterpillar 3412D 2 x Vee 4 Stroke 12 Cy. 145 x 162 each-624kW (848bhp) Caterpillar Inc-USA AuxGen: 2 x 50kW 415/230V a.c
9406295 *BR3464* -	**SEA GREEN 15** *ex* A. M. S. 23 *-2011* *ex* Swissco 188 *-2008* **Seagreen Enterprise Co Ltd** - *Kaohsiung* *Chinese Taipei* MMSI: 416004191 Official number: 015116	**321** 97 -	Class: (GL)	**2006-08 Singapore Marine Logistic Pte Ltd — Singapore** Yd No: 56 Loa 32.00 Br ex - Dght 2.575 Lbp - Br md 11.00 Dpth 3.25 Welded, 1 dk	**(B34T2QR) Work/Repair Vessel**	**2 oil engines** reverse reduction geared to sc. shafts driving 2 FP propellers Total Power: 1,074kW (1,460hp) Caterpillar 3412D 2 x Vee 4 Stroke 12 Cy. 145 x 162 each-537kW (730bhp) Caterpillar Inc-USA AuxGen: 2 x 96kW 415V a.c
5316064 - -	**SEA GRIFFON** **Coastal Marine Ltd** - *United Kingdom*	*117* 34 -	Class: (LR) ✠ Classed LR until 29/8/01	**1962-03 J. Lewis & Sons Ltd. — Aberdeen** Yd No: 321 Loa 26.85 Br ex 7.35 Dght 3.188 Lbp 24.41 Br md 7.01 Dpth 3.36 Riveted\Welded	**(B32A2ST) Tug**	**1 oil engine** sr reverse geared to sc. shaft driving 1 FP propeller Total Power: 588kW (799hp) National Gas FSM6 1 x 4 Stroke 6 Cy. 305 x 381 588kW (799bhp) National Gas & Oil Eng. Co.-Ashton-under-Lyne AuxGen: 2 x 15kW 220V d.c

IMO / Call sign	Ship / Owner	Tonnage	Class	Built / Dimensions	Type	Machinery
5316973 - -	**SEA GUARD I** *ex* Grampian Petrel *-1992* *ex* Seaward Petrel *-1982* **Alexander van't Hoff Delmay Holdings Ltd** -	*214* 75 -	Class: (LR) ✠ Classed LR until 4/5/83	**1959**-12 **J. Lewis & Sons Ltd. — Aberdeen** Yd No: 289 Converted From: Trawler-1984 L reg 32.28 Br ex 7.12 Dght - Lbp 31.81 Br md 7.01 Dpth 3.66 Riveted\Welded, 1 dk	**(B22G20Y) Standby Safety Vessel**	**1 oil engine** reverse reduction geared to sc. shaft driving 1 FP propeller Total Power: 522kW (710hp) 10.5kn Blackstone ETS8 1 x 4 Stroke 8 Cy. 222 x 292 522kW (710bhp) (made 1971, fitted 1972) Mirrlees Blackstone (Stamford)Ltd.-Stamford
9337573 *3EFU8* -	**SEA GUARDIAN** **Gulf Marine Far East Pte Ltd** - *Panama* *Panama* MMSI: 354518000 Official number: 3199406B	**1,470** 441 1,472	Class: AB (BV)	**2006**-03 **Guangzhou Southern Shipbuilding Co Ltd — Guangzhou GD** Yd No: 0402 Loa 58.70 Br ex - Dght 4.500 Lbp 53.20 Br md 14.60 Dpth 5.50 Welded, 1 dk	**(B21B20A) Anchor Handling Tug Supply**	**2 oil engines** reduction geared to sc. shafts driving 2 CP propellers Total Power: 3,840kW (5,220hp) 13.5kn Caterpillar 3516B-HD 1 x Vee 4 Stroke 16 Cy. 170 x 190 1920kW (2610bhp) Caterpillar Inc-USA Caterpillar 3516B-HD 1 x Vee 4 Stroke 16 Cy. 170 x 215 1920kW (2610bhp) Caterpillar Inc-USA AuxGen: 3 x 320kW a.c Thrusters: 1 Tunnel thruster (f) Fuel: 480.0 (d.f.)
6603165 *HOLV* -	**SEA GULF** *ex* Safeer I *-2004* *ex* Rania *-2000* *ex* Lisa *-1999* *ex* Al Falah *-1995* *ex* Arkadia *-1994* *ex* Sidon *-1988* *ex* Bellona *-1978* *ex* Lisa *-1975* **Ghorban Asgari Jafarabadi** - *Panama* *Panama* MMSI: 353359000 Official number: 32676PEXT	**2,102** 1,218 3,184 T/cm 9.0	Class: (HR) (BV) (NV)	**1966**-05 **Lodose Varv AB — Lodose** Yd No: 145 Loa 87.79 Br ex 12.53 Dght 5.804 Lbp 80.02 Br md 12.50 Dpth 6.10 Welded, 1 dk	**(A13B2TP) Products Tanker** Liq: 4,246; Liq (Oil): 4,246 Cargo Heating Coils Compartments: 2 Wing Ta, 5 Ta, ER 2 Cargo Pump (s): 2x500m³/hr Ice Capable	**1 oil engine** sr geared to sc. shaft driving 1 CP propeller Total Power: 1,618kW (2,200hp) 12.5kn MWM 1 x 4 Stroke 8 Cy. 360 x 450 1618kW (2200bhp) Motoren Werke Mannheim AG (MWM)-West Germany AuxGen: 3 x 84kW 380V 50Hz a.c Fuel: 274.5 (d.f.)
7707542 - -	**SEA GULL** *ex* Nord Star *-2009* *ex* Kava Sound *-1994* *ex* Ordinence *-1989* - - *Limbe* *Cameroon*	**460** 283 727	Class: (LR) ✠ Classed LR until 16/9/10	**1978**-10 **Cubow Ltd. — Woolwich, London** Yd No: 709 Loa 49.26 Br ex 8.95 Dght 3.206 Lbp 46.49 Br md 8.86 Dpth 3.81 Welded, 1 dk	**(A31A2GX) General Cargo Ship** Grain: 1,036; Bale: 997 Compartments: 1 Ho, ER 1 Ha: (26.5 x 6.4)ER	**1 oil engine** reverse reduction geared to sc. shaft driving 1 FP propeller Total Power: 344kW (468hp) 10.0kn Blackstone ES6 1 x 4 Stroke 6 Cy. 222 x 292 344kW (468bhp) Mirrlees Blackstone (Stamford)Ltd.-Stamford AuxGen: 3 x 2kW 24V d.c
7822964 - -	**SEA GULL** - **PSA Corp Ltd** -	*150* - 20		**1979 Singapore Shipbuilding & Engineering Pte Ltd — Singapore** Yd No: 149 Loa 31.77 Br ex - Dght - Lbp 30.80 Br md 6.71 Dpth 2.59 Welded, 1 dk	**(A37B2PS) Passenger Ship** Passengers: unberthed: 220	**2 oil engines** geared to sc. shafts driving 2 FP propellers Total Power: 394kW (536hp) 12.0kn Deutz SBA6M816 2 x 4 Stroke 6 Cy. 142 x 160 each-197kW (268bhp) Kloeckner Humboldt Deutz AG-West Germany
8739827 - -	**SEA GULL** *ex* Ptsc - Binh An 2007 *-2012* *ex* Binh An 2007 *-2010* **South East Asia Maritime Service JSC** - *Saigon* *Vietnam* Official number: VNSG-2125-TK	**116** 35 -	Class: VR	**2007**-08 **An Phu Works — Ho Chi Minh City** Loa 24.20 Br ex 7.62 Dght 3.050 Lbp 21.08 Br md 7.42 Dpth 4.19 Welded, 1 dk	**(B32A2ST) Tug**	**2 oil engines** reduction geared to sc. shafts driving 2 Propellers Total Power: 786kW (1,068hp) 12.0kn Caterpillar 3406 2 x 4 Stroke 6 Cy. 137 x 165 each-393kW (534bhp) Caterpillar Inc-USA
8952039 - -	**SEA GULL** *ex* Lyngvig *-1993* **Tonny Thomsen P/R**	**106** 31 -		**1970 AEroskobing Skibs- og Baadebyggeri — AEroskobing** L reg 21.78 Br ex - Dght - Lbp - Br md 6.14 Dpth 2.84 Welded, 1 dk	**(A31A2GX) General Cargo Ship**	**1 oil engine** driving 1 FP propeller Total Power: 298kW (405hp) Callesen 5-427-EO 1 x 4 Stroke 5 Cy. 270 x 400 298kW (405bhp) Aabenraa Motorfabrik, HeinrichCallesen A/S-Denmark
8955835 - -	**SEA GULL** *ex* Ryujin Maru No. 8 *-1995* *ex* Eiryu Maru No. 35 *-1995* **Naviera Columbus Co Ltd** -	**142** 42 -		**1982 Higashi Kyushu Shipbuilding Co Ltd — Usuki OT** Loa 30.79 Br ex - Dght - Lbp - Br md 5.50 Dpth 2.35 Bonded, 1 dk	**(B12B2FC) Fish Carrier** Hull Material: Reinforced Plastic	**1 oil engine** driving 1 FP propeller Total Power: 287kW (390hp) 11.0kn Yanmar 1 x 4 Stroke 287kW (390bhp) Yanmar Diesel Engine Co Ltd-Japan
6926309 *V4ES* -	**SEA GULL I** *ex* Sea Eagle II *-2005* *ex* Steinturm *-1984* **Mencast Subsea Pte Ltd** 38 Marine & Offshore Pte Ltd *Basseterre* *St Kitts & Nevis* MMSI: 341122000 Official number: SKN 1001122	*469* 165 689	Class: AB (GL)	**1969**-03 **JG Hitzler Schiffswerft und Masch GmbH & Co KG — Lauenburg** Yd No: 709 Loa 54.51 Br ex 11.28 Dght 3.371 Lbp 49.20 Br md 11.00 Dpth 3.97 Welded, 1 dk	**(B21A20S) Platform Supply Ship** Derricks: 1x5t Ice Capable	**2 oil engines** driving 2 FP propellers Total Power: 2,016kW (2,740hp) 12.5kn MWM TB16RS18/22 2 x Vee 4 Stroke 16 Cy. 180 x 220 each-1008kW (1370bhp) Motoren Werke Mannheim AG (MWM)-West Germany AuxGen: 3 x 112kW 380V 50Hz a.c Thrusters: 1 Thwart. FP thruster (f) Fuel: 279.5 (d.f.)
7009873 *3FHS9* -	**SEA GULL II** *ex* Koral I *-2005* *ex* Kora *-2003* *ex* Mada *-1999* *ex* Liliana d'Alesio *-1992* **Comercializadora Internacional de Servicios Maritimos** - SatCom: Inmarsat C 435739210 *Panama* *Panama* MMSI: 357392000 Official number: 2717500A	**1,777** 1,112 3,237	Class: (RI)	**1970**-06 **Cant. Nav. Giuliano — Trieste** Yd No: 85 Loa 90.81 Br ex 13.24 Dght 5.698 Lbp 82.00 Br md 13.21 Dpth 6.81 Welded, 1 dk	**(A13B2TP) Products Tanker** Liq: 4,040; Liq (Oil): 4,040 Cargo Heating Coils Compartments: 8 Ta, ER 2 Cargo Pump (s): 2x600m³/hr	**1 oil engine** driving 1 FP propeller Total Power: 1,317kW (1,791hp) 12.5kn Werkspoor TMABS398 1 x 4 Stroke 8 Cy. 390 x 680 1317kW (1791bhp) Stork Werkspoor Diesel BV-Netherlands
9222649 *9HA3471* -	**SEA HALCYONE** *ex* Unique Sunshine *-2013* **Halcyone Maritime Co Ltd** Sea World Management & Trading Inc *Valletta* *Malta* MMSI: 229636000 Official number: 9222649	**28,553** 12,369 47,087 T/cm 50.2	Class: AB (NK)	**2001**-01 **Onomichi Dockyard Co Ltd — Onomichi HS** Yd No: 457 Loa 182.50 (BB) Br ex - Dght 12.667 Lbp 172.00 Br md 32.20 Dpth 19.10 Welded, 1 dk	**(A13B2TP) Products Tanker** Double Hull (13F) Liq: 53,616; Liq (Oil): 53,616 Compartments: 2 Ta, 12 Wing Ta, ER 4 Cargo Pump (s): 4x1000m³/hr Manifold: Bow/CM: 93m	**1 oil engine** driving 1 FP propeller Total Power: 8,562kW (11,641hp) 15.3kn B&W 6S50MC 1 x 2 Stroke 6 Cy. 500 x 1910 8562kW (11641bhp) Mitsui Engineering & Shipbuilding CLtd-Japan AuxGen: 3 x 420kW 450V 60Hz a.c Fuel: 128.9 (d.f.) (Heating Coils) 1575.4 (r.f.) 36.5pd
9350501 *C4TJ2* -	**SEA HALIBUT** **SFL Sea Halibut Ltd** Deep Sea Supply Navegacao Maritima Ltda *Limassol* *Cyprus* MMSI: 212696000	**2,160** 1,036 3,250	Class: NV	**2007**-04 **Cochin Shipyard Ltd — Ernakulam** Yd No: BY-57 Loa 71.90 Br ex - Dght 5.830 Lbp 66.32 Br md 16.00 Dpth 7.00 Welded, 1 dk	**(B21A20S) Platform Supply Ship**	**2 oil engines** reduction geared to sc. shafts driving 2 CP propellers Total Power: 4,010kW (5,452hp) 11.0kn Bergens KRMB-9 2 x 4 Stroke 9 Cy. 250 x 300 each-2005kW (2726bhp) Rolls Royce Marine AS-Norway AuxGen: 2 x 250kW 440V 60Hz a.c, 2 x 1280kW 440V 60Hz a.c Thrusters: 2 Thwart. CP thruster (f); 1 Thwart. CP thruster (a) Fuel: 950.0 (d.f.)
9339791 *3EAM7* -	**SEA HARMONY** **Kingship Lines SA** Santoku Senpaku Co Ltd *Panama* *Panama* MMSI: 352501000 Official number: 3071505B	**16,960** 10,498 28,409 T/cm 39.7	Class: NK	**2005**-04 **Imabari Shipbuilding Co Ltd — Imabari EH (Imabari Shipyard)** Yd No: 622 Loa 169.26 (BB) Br ex - Dght 9.779 Lbp 160.40 Br md 27.20 Dpth 13.60 Welded, 1 dk	**(A21A2BC) Bulk Carrier** Grain: 37,523; Bale: 35,762 Compartments: 5 Ho, ER 5 Ha: 4 (19.2 x 17.6)ER (13.6 x 16.0) Cranes: 4x30.5t	**1 oil engine** driving 1 FP propeller Total Power: 5,850kW (7,954hp) 14.0kn MAN-B&W 6S42MC 1 x 2 Stroke 6 Cy. 420 x 1764 5850kW (7954bhp) Makita Corp-Japan Fuel: 1250.0
9394349 *9VCN2* -	**SEA HARMONY** *ex* En Voyager *-2012* *ex* Ariadne *-2007* **En Maritimes Pte Ltd** Equatorial Marine Fuel Management Services Pte Ltd SatCom: Inmarsat C 456569010 *Singapore* *Singapore* MMSI: 565690000 Official number: 393650	**5,052** 1,672 6,404 T/cm 16.1	Class: NK (AB)	**2007**-10 **Zhenjiang Sopo Shiprepair & Building Co Ltd — Zhenjiang JS** Yd No: SP07 Loa 99.60 (BB) Br ex 18.30 Dght 6.510 Lbp 94.00 Br md 18.00 Dpth 9.60 Welded, 1 dk	**(A13B2TP) Products Tanker** Double Hull (13F) Liq: 6,933; Liq (Oil): 7,253 Compartments: 6 Wing Ta, 6 Wing Ta (s.stl), 1 Wing Slop Ta, 1 Wing Slop Ta (s.stl), ER 2 Cargo Pump (s): 2x750m³/hr	**1 oil engine** reduction geared to sc. shaft driving 1 CP propeller Total Power: 2,970kW (4,038hp) 12.5kn MaK 9M25 1 x 4 Stroke 9 Cy. 255 x 400 2970kW (4038bhp) Caterpillar Motoren GmbH & Co. KG-Germany AuxGen: 3 x 285kW a.c Fuel: 99.1 (d.f.) 282.7 (r.f.)

8914166 8PMA -
SEA HARMONY
ex Graf Uko *-2013* *ex* Nordstrand *-2005*
ex MF Malta *-2001* *ex* Intermodal Malta *-1996*
ex Wannsee *-1994* *ex* Zelo *-1994*
ex Wannsee *-1994* *ex* Medeur Terzo *-1992*
ex Wannsee *-1992*
Saturn Shipping Ltd
Torbulk Ltd
Bridgetown *Barbados*
MMSI: 314025000
Official number: 725397
2,481 1,206 2,900 Class: GL (NV)
1991-05 Estaleiros Navais de Viana do Castelo S.A. — Viana do Castelo Yd No: 156
Loa 87.48 Br ex - Dght 5.027
Lbp 82.12 Br md 13.00 Dpth 7.10
Welded, 1 dk
(A31A2GX) General Cargo Ship
Grain: 4,650
TEU 202 C. 202/20' incl. 30 ref C.
Compartments: 1 Ho, ER
1 Ha: (57.4 x 10.2)ER
Ice Capable
1 oil engine with clutches & sr geared to sc. shaft driving 1 CP propeller
Total Power: 1,320kW (1,795hp) 12.0kn
Alpha 6L28/32A
1 x 4 Stroke 6 Cy. 280 x 320 1320kW (1795bhp)
MAN B&W Diesel A/S-Denmark
AuxGen: 1 x 250kW 220/380V a.c, 2 x 149kW 220/380V a.c
Thrusters: 1 Thwart. FP thruster (f)

9521382 - -
SEA HARRIER
ex Sabalo *-2009*
Morvarid Parsian Kish Co
-
168 50 40 Class: (BV)
2008-10 Damen Shipyards Singapore Pte Ltd — Singapore (Hull) Yd No: (544808)
2008-10 B.V. Scheepswerf Damen — Gorinchem Yd No: 544808
Loa 33.57 Br ex - Dght 1.650
Lbp 33.50 Br md 6.70 Dpth 3.30
Welded, 1 dk
(B21A2OC) Crew/Supply Vessel
Hull Material: Aluminium Alloy
Passengers: unberthed: 80
3 oil engines reduction geared to sc. shafts driving 3 FP propellers
Total Power: 2,460kW (3,345hp)
Caterpillar C32
3 x Vee 4 Stroke 12 Cy. 145 x 162 each-820kW (1115bhp)
Caterpillar Inc-USA

9358644 VRLY3 -
SEA HARVEST
ex Stolt Swazi *-2013*
Sea Harvest Shipping Co Ltd
Sinochem Shipping Co Ltd (Hainan)
Hong Kong *Hong Kong*
MMSI: 477243800
Official number: HK-3801
11,676 6,336 19,996 T/cm 29.8 Class: NK
2007-02 Fukuoka Shipbuilding Co Ltd — Fukuoka FO Yd No: 1263
Loa 144.09 (BB) Br ex 24.23 Dght 9.656
Lbp 136.00 Br md 24.19 Dpth 12.90
Welded, 1 dk
(A12B2TR) Chemical/Products Tanker
Double Hull (13F)
Liq: 21,715; Liq (Oil): 21,715
Cargo Heating Coils
Compartments: 20 Wing Ta, ER
22 Cargo Pump (s): 14x200m³/hr, 8x115m³/hr
Manifold: Bow/CM: 72.1m
1 oil engine driving 1 FP propeller
Total Power: 6,230kW (8,470hp) 14.5kn
Mitsubishi 7UEC45LA
1 x 2 Stroke 7 Cy. 450 x 1350 6230kW (8470bhp)
Akasaka Tekkosho KK (Akasaka DieselLtd)-Japan
AuxGen: 3 x 450kW a.c
Thrusters: 1 Tunnel thruster (f)
Fuel: 117.0 (d.f.) 458.0 (r.f.)

9222546 ELYL5
SEA HARVEST

Sea Harvest Maritime Inc
Lihai International Shipping Ltd
Monrovia *Liberia*
MMSI: 636011333
Official number: 11333
17,859 9,828 28,294 Class: NK
2000-11 Naikai Zosen Corp — Onomichi HS (Setoda Shipyard) Yd No: 668
Loa 171.93 (BB) Br ex - Dght 9.573
Lbp 164.90 Br md 27.00 Dpth 13.60
Welded, 1 dk
(A21A2BC) Bulk Carrier
Grain: 38,215; Bale: 36,680
Compartments: 5 Ho, ER
5 Ha: (12.7 x 16.0)4 (20.1 x 17.6)ER
Cranes: 4x30t
1 oil engine driving 1 FP propeller
Total Power: 5,392kW (7,331hp) 14.0kn
B&W 5S50MC
1 x 2 Stroke 5 Cy. 500 x 1910 5392kW (7331bhp)
Hitachi Zosen Corp-Japan
AuxGen: 3 x 440kW a.c
Fuel: 1462.0 (r.f.)

8501610 3FVI3 -
SEA HARVEST
ex Great Harvest *-2013* *ex* Agie Sb *-2004*
ex Sky Duke *-1997* *ex* Halla Fortune *-1996*
ex New Amity *-1996* *ex* Hokoku Maru *-1987*
H & C Shipping SA
Shipping Allied Corp
Panama *Panama*
MMSI: 372783000
Official number: 45368PEXT
37,057 22,421 68,192 T/cm 64.6 Class: (AB) (KR) (NK) (CR)
1986-03 Koyo Dockyard Co Ltd — Mihara HS Yd No: 1083
Loa 224.52 (BB) Br ex 32.24 Dght 13.224
Lbp 215.02 Br md 32.21 Dpth 18.32
Welded, 1 dk
(A21A2BC) Bulk Carrier
Grain: 79,948; Bale: 76,126
Compartments: 7 Ho, ER
7 Ha: 7 (17.4 x 14.4)ER
1 oil engine driving 1 FP propeller
Total Power: 8,017kW (10,900hp) 13.5kn
B&W 5L70MCE
1 x 2 Stroke 5 Cy. 700 x 2268 8017kW (10900bhp)
Mitsui Engineering & Shipbuilding CLtd-Japan
AuxGen: 4 x 335kW a.c

8333178 - -
SEA HAWK
ex YTM-774 *-1987*
Marex SA
-
194 131 -
1945 Commercial Iron Works — Portland, Or Yd No: 243
Loa - Br ex - Dght -
Lbp 28.73 Br md 7.62 Dpth 3.48
Welded, 1 dk
(B32A2ST) Tug
1 oil engine driving 1 FP propeller

8005977 V4CJ2 -
SEA HAWK
ex Sea Condor *-2001* *ex* Jinwei *-1998*
ex Shozui Maru *-1995*
GP 1 Pte Ltd
Shipmate Pte Ltd
SatCom: Inmarsat C 434187311
Basseterre *St Kitts & Nevis*
MMSI: 341873000
Official number: SKN 1002051
3,348 1,523 4,977 T/cm 13.4 Class: (GL) (NK)
1980-09 Usuki Iron Works Co Ltd — Usuki OT Yd No: 1516
Loa 105.36 Br ex - Dght 6.173
Lbp 98.02 Br md 15.51 Dpth 7.83
Welded, 1 dk
(A13A2TW) Crude/Oil Products Tanker
Double Bottom Entire Compartment Length
Liq: 5,541; Liq (Oil): 5,541
Cargo Heating Coils
Compartments: 10 Ta, ER
3 Cargo Pump (s): 2x1500m³/hr, 1x700m³/hr
Manifold: Bow/CM: 54m
1 oil engine driving 1 FP propeller
Total Power: 3,678kW (5,001hp) 14.3kn
Hanshin 6LU54A
1 x 4 Stroke 6 Cy. 540 x 850 3678kW (5001bhp)
The Hanshin Diesel Works Ltd-Japan
AuxGen: 2 x 280kW 445V 60Hz a.c
Fuel: 52.5 (d.f.) (Part Heating Coils) 237.5 (r.f.) 16.5pd

7729526 WDD9287 -
SEA HAWK

Kirby Offshore Marine Pacific LLC

Seattle, WA *United States of America*
MMSI: 367309440
Official number: 589839
404 121 - Class: (AB)
1978-06 Modern Marine Power, Inc. — Houma, La Yd No: 21
Loa - Br ex 9.78 Dght 4.363
Lbp 35.36 Br md 9.76 Dpth 5.06
Welded, 1 dk
(B32A2ST) Tug
2 oil engines reverse reduction geared to sc. shafts driving 2 FP propellers
Total Power: 2,868kW (3,900hp) 12.0kn
EMD (Electro-Motive) 16-645-E6
2 x Vee 2 Stroke 16 Cy. 230 x 254 each-1434kW (1950bhp)
General Motors Corp.Electro-Motive Div.-La Grange
AuxGen: 2 x 75kW

7229485 - -
SEA HAWK
ex South Fish *-1993*
Faget Nigeria Ltd

Lagos *Nigeria*
Official number: 376544
251 27 200 Class: (BV)
1972 Chantiers et Ateliers de La Perriere — Lorient Yd No: 372
Loa 41.18 Br ex 7.57 Dght 3.001
Lbp 38.51 Br md 7.51 Dpth 3.79
Welded, 1 dk
(B21B20A) Anchor Handling Tug Supply
Passengers: berths: 12
2 oil engines driving 2 CP propellers
Total Power: 1,618kW (2,200hp) 14.0kn
MGO 16V175ASHR
2 x Vee 4 Stroke 16 Cy. 175 x 180 each-809kW (1100bhp)
Societe Alsacienne de ConstructionsMecaniques (SACM)-France
AuxGen: 2 x 102kW 380V 50Hz a.c
Thrusters: 1 Thwart. FP thruster (f)
Fuel: 69.0 (d.f.)

8735053 9H2572 -
SEA HAWK
ex Geier *-1987*
Captain Morgan Leisure Ltd
-
Valletta *Malta*
Official number: 1656
105 32 -
1955-01 Burmester Yacht- u. Bootswerft — Bremen
Converted From: Patrol Vessel-1987
Loa 25.58 Br ex - Dght -
Lbp - Br md 5.36 Dpth 3.00
Welded, 1 dk
(A37B2PS) Passenger Ship
1 oil engine reduction geared to sc. shaft driving 1 Propeller
Total Power: 257kW (349hp)
Dorman 12QV
1 x Vee 4 Stroke 12 Cy. 257kW (349bhp)
Dorman Diesels Ltd.-Stafford

9256846 WDA7448 -
SEA HAWK

Kirby Offshore Marine Operating LLC

Charleston, SC *United States of America*
MMSI: 366843420
Official number: 1123632
863 258 - Class: AB
2002-05 Alabama Shipyard, Inc. — Mobile, Al Yd No: 93
Loa 37.90 Br ex - Dght 5.790
Lbp 37.60 Br md 12.20 Dpth 6.70
Welded, 1 dk
(B32B2SA) Articulated Pusher Tug
2 oil engines reverse reduction geared to sc. shafts driving 2 FP propellers
Total Power: 5,884kW (8,000hp)
EMD (Electro-Motive) 16-710-G7B
2 x Vee 2 Stroke 16 Cy. 230 x 279 each-2942kW (4000bhp)
General Motors Corp.Electro-Motive Div.-La Grange

9605944 9V9030 -
SEA HAWK

Tian San Shipping (Pte) Ltd
-
SatCom: Inmarsat C 456448310
Singapore *Singapore*
MMSI: 563016950
196 74 - Class: BV
2011-03 Hin Lee (Zhuhai) Shipyard Co Ltd — Zhuhai GD (Hull) Yd No: 226
2011-03 Cheoy Lee Shipyards Ltd — Hong Kong Yd No: 5015
Loa 28.00 Br ex - Dght 2.000
Lbp 25.78 Br md 7.10 Dpth 2.35
Welded, 1 dk
(A37B2PS) Passenger Ship
Hull Material: Aluminium Alloy
Passengers: unberthed: 200
3 oil engines reduction geared to sc. shafts driving 3 FP propellers
Total Power: 2,460kW (3,345hp) 24.5kn
Caterpillar C32
1 x Vee 4 Stroke 12 Cy. 145 x 162 820kW (1115bhp)
Caterpillar Motoren (Guangdong) CoLtd-China
Caterpillar C32
2 x Vee 4 Stroke 12 Cy. 145 x 162 each-820kW (1115bhp)
Caterpillar Motoren (Guangdong) CoLtd-China
AuxGen: 2 x 56kW 50Hz a.c

9662681 J8B4702 -
SEA HAWK
ex Zakher Hawk *-2013*
QMS 2 Offshore Services Ltd
Zakher Marine International Inc
Kingstown *St Vincent & The Grenadines*
MMSI: 376187000
Official number: 11175
1,657 497 1,487 Class: AB
2013-01 Nanjing East Star Shipbuilding Co Ltd — Nanjing JS Yd No: ESS100108
Loa 59.66 Br ex - Dght 5.000
Lbp 52.20 Br md 15.00 Dpth 6.10
Welded, 1 dk
(B22A2OR) Offshore Support Vessel
Cranes: 1x3t
2 oil engines reduction geared to sc. shafts driving 2 CP propellers
Total Power: 3,840kW (5,220hp) 12.0kn
Caterpillar 3516B-HD
2 x Vee 4 Stroke 16 Cy. 170 x 215 each-1920kW (2610bhp)
Caterpillar Inc-USA
AuxGen: 2 x 900kW 415V 50Hz a.c, 3 x 350kW 415V 50Hz a.c
Thrusters: 1 Tunnel thruster (f)
Fuel: 1000.0 (d.f.)

9494888 9WNB4 -
SEA HAWK 1

JSE Offshore (Labuan) Pte Ltd
Venus Marine Services Sdn Bhd
Labuan *Malaysia*
MMSI: 533130901
Official number: 900029
2,952 885 2,193 Class: AB
2010-01 Jaya Shipbuilding & Engineering Pte Ltd — Singapore Yd No: 875
Loa 75.40 Br ex - Dght 6.080
Lbp 67.16 Br md 16.80 Dpth 7.50
Welded, 1 dk
(B21B20A) Anchor Handling Tug Supply
2 oil engines reduction geared to sc. shafts driving 2 CP propellers
Total Power: 9,000kW (12,236hp) 12.0kn
Wartsila 9L32
2 x 4 Stroke 9 Cy. 320 x 400 each-4500kW (6118bhp)
Wartsila Finland Oy-Finland
AuxGen: 2 x 370kW 440V 60Hz a.c, 2 x 2300kW 440V 60Hz a.c
Thrusters: 2 Tunnel thruster (f); 1 Tunnel thruster (a)

IMO / Call sign	Name / Owner / Manager / Port / Flag	Tonnage	Class	Builder / Dimensions	Type / Capacity	Machinery
9014652 *ZMA3510* -	**SEA HAWKE II** - **Waikawa Fishing Co Ltd** - SatCom: Inmarsat C 451200591 *Napier* *New Zealand* MMSI: 512002725 Official number: 875269	*174* 131 -		**1990 Australian Shipbuilding Industries (WA) Pty Ltd — Fremantle WA** Loa 24.95 Br ex - Dght 3.000 Lbp 22.04 Br md 7.42 Dpth 3.84 Welded	**(B11A2FS) Stern Trawler**	**1 oil engine** geared to sc. shaft driving 1 FP propeller Total Power: 465kW (632hp) 10.0kn Caterpillar 3412TA 1 x Vee 4 Stroke 12 Cy. 137 x 152 465kW (632bhp) Caterpillar Inc-USA
9279719 *9HA3224* -	**SEA HELIOS** *ex* Avonden *-2013* *ex* Kudu *-2011* **Helios Shipping Co Ltd** Sea World Management & Trading Inc *Valletta* *Malta* MMSI: 229315000 Official number: 9279719	**28,069** 11,553 45,948 T/cm 50.6	Class: BV	**2004-03 Shin Kurushima Dockyard Co. Ltd. — Onishi** Yd No: 5195 Loa 179.88 (BB) Br ex 32.23 Dght 12.022 Lbp 172.00 Br md 32.20 Dpth 18.70 Welded, 1 Dk.	**(A13B2TP) Products Tanker** Double Hull (13F) Liq: 50,754; Liq (Oil): 50,753 Cargo Heating Coils Compartments: 14 Wing Ta, 1 Slop Ta, 2 Wing Slop Ta, ER 4 Cargo Pump (s): 4x1000m³/hr Manifold: Bow/CM: 91.3m	**1 oil engine** driving 1 FP propeller Total Power: 9,481kW (12,890hp) 15.1kn MAN-B&W 6S50MC-C 1 x 2 Stroke 6 Cy. 500 x 2000 9481kW (12890bhp) Mitsui Engineering & Shipbuilding CLtd-Japan AuxGen: 3 x 720kW 450/100V 60Hz a.c Fuel: 183.0 (d.f.) 1850.0 (r.f.)
9328728 *H9JT* -	**SEA HELLINIS** *ex* Celestial Wing *-2014* **Sea Hellinis Shipping SA** Mediterranean Car-Carriers Line SA (MCCL) *Panama* *Panama* MMSI: 356145000 Official number: 32974PEXT2	**45,232** 13,570 14,962	Class: NK	**2005-03 Mitsubishi Heavy Industries Ltd. — Shimonoseki** Yd No: 1109 Loa 180.00 (BB) Br ex 30.03 Dght 9.222 Lbp 171.70 Br md 30.00 Dpth 13.10 Welded, 10 dks. incl. 2 liftable dks.	**(A35B2RV) Vehicles Carrier** Side door/ramp (s) Len: - Wid: - Swl: 25 Quarter stern door/ramp (s. a.) Len: - Wid: - Swl: 100 Cars: 3,505	**1 oil engine** driving 1 FP propeller Total Power: 11,560kW (15,717hp) 19.9kn Mitsubishi 8UEC50LSII 1 x 2 Stroke 8 Cy. 500 x 1950 11560kW (15717bhp) Mitsubishi Heavy Industries Ltd-Japan AuxGen: 3 x 875kW 450V 60Hz a.c Thrusters: 1 Thwart. CP thruster (f) Fuel: 2090.0 (r.f.)
9279733 *9HA3226* -	**SEA HERMES** *ex* Oakden *-2012* *ex* High Trader *-2011* **Hermes Maritime Co Ltd** Sea World Management & Trading Inc *Valletta* *Malta* MMSI: 229317000 Official number: 9279733	**28,150** 11,553 45,879 T/cm 50.6	Class: BV	**2004-06 Shin Kurushima Dockyard Co. Ltd. — Onishi** Yd No: 5197 Loa 179.88 (BB) Br ex 32.23 Dght 12.022 Lbp 172.00 Br md 32.20 Dpth 18.70 Welded, 1 dk	**(A13B2TP) Products Tanker** Double Hull (13F) Liq: 50,753; Liq (Oil): 50,753 Cargo Heating Coils Compartments: 14 Wing Ta, 1 Slop Ta, ER 4 Cargo Pump (s): 4x1000m³/hr Manifold: Bow/CM: 91.3m	**1 oil engine** driving 1 FP propeller Total Power: 9,481kW (12,890hp) 15.1kn MAN-B&W 6S50MC-C 1 x 2 Stroke 6 Cy. 500 x 2000 9481kW (12890bhp) Mitsui Engineering & Shipbuilding CLtd-Japan AuxGen: 3 x 740kW 450/100V 60Hz a.c Fuel: 183.0 (d.f.) 1850.0 (r.f.)
9603154 *V7AI6* -	**SEA HERMES** *ex* Guanrong *-2013* **Hermes Shipping Inc** Golden Ocean Management AS *Majuro* *Marshall Islands* MMSI: 538005003 Official number: 5003	**44,047** 27,575 81,708 T/cm 71.9	Class: NV (GL)	**2013-01 Xiamen Shipbuilding Industry Co Ltd — Xiamen FJ** Yd No: XSI482A Loa 229.04 (BB) Br ex - Dght 14.470 Lbp 225.50 Br md 32.26 Dpth 20.05 Welded, 1 dk	**(A21A2BC) Bulk Carrier** Grain: 96,000; Bale: 90,784 Compartments: 7 Ho, ER 7 Ha: ER	**1 oil engine** driving 1 FP propeller Total Power: 11,900kW (16,179hp) 14.1kn MAN-B&W 5S60ME-C8 1 x 2 Stroke 5 Cy. 600 x 2400 11900kW (16179bhp) Wuxi Antai Power Machinery Co Ltd-China AuxGen: 3 x a.c
8827090 *V3NN* -	**SEA HERON** *ex* Pelican 33 *-2009* *ex* Penguin 33 *-2007* *ex* Tridaya Baruna IV *-1997* **Searching Offshore Pte Ltd** - *Belize City* *Belize* MMSI: 312018000 Official number: 130910822	**135** 41 -	Class: (AB) (KI)	**1978 Swiftships Inc — Morgan City LA** Yd No: 210 Loa 30.48 Br ex - Dght 1.257 Lbp - Br md 6.58 Dpth 2.89 Welded, 1 dk	**(B21A20C) Crew/Supply Vessel**	**3 oil engines** driving 3 FP propellers Total Power: 1,125kW (1,530hp) 17.0kn G.M. (Detroit Diesel) 12V-71-TI 3 x Vee 2 Stroke 12 Cy. 108 x 127 each-375kW (510bhp) General Motors Detroit DieselAllison Divn-USA AuxGen: 1 x 60kW 48V a.c
9142100 *3FZQ6* -	**SEA HONEST** *ex* Sea Honesty *-2009* **MSV Shipping & Transport Co** Vera Denizcilik Ithalat ve Ihracat Ticaret Ltd (Vera Shipping Import & Export Ltd) SatCom: Inmarsat B 335209710 *Panama* *Panama* MMSI: 352097000 Official number: 2376697CH	**17,429** 9,829 28,564 T/cm 39.3	Class: NK	**1997-02 Kanda Zosensho K.K. — Kawajiri** Yd No: 374 Loa 170.00 (BB) Br ex - Dght 9.750 Lbp 162.00 Br md 27.00 Dpth 13.80 Welded, 1 dk	**(A21A2BC) Bulk Carrier** Grain: 37,694; Bale: 36,665 Compartments: 5 Ho, ER 5 Ha: (14.1 x 15.0)4 (19.2 x 18.0)ER Cranes: 4x30t	**1 oil engine** driving 1 FP propeller Total Power: 5,884kW (8,000hp) 14.0kn Mitsubishi 5UEC52LA 1 x 2 Stroke 5 Cy. 520 x 1600 5884kW (8000bhp) Akasaka Tekkosho KK (Akasaka DieselLtd)-Japan AuxGen: 2 x 400kW 450V a.c Fuel: 1240.0 (r.f.) 21.0pd
9426116 *3FSI9* -	**SEA HONESTY** *ex* Aegean Sea *-2013* *ex* Susy *-2010* **Shunli Shipping SA** SW Shipping Co Ltd *Panama* *Panama* MMSI: 373223000 Official number: 44656PEXT	**51,255** 31,192 93,336 T/cm 80.9	Class: KR (AB) (RI)	**2010-08 Jiangsu Newyangzi Shipbuilding Co Ltd — Jingjiang JS** Yd No: YZJ2006-779 Loa 229.20 (BB) Br ex - Dght 14.900 Lbp 222.00 Br md 38.00 Dpth 20.70 Welded, 1 dk	**(A21A2BC) Bulk Carrier** Grain: 110,330 Compartments: 7 Ho, ER 7 Ha: 5 (17.9 x 17.0)ER 2 (15.3 x 14.6)	**1 oil engine** driving 1 FP propeller Total Power: 13,560kW (18,436hp) 14.1kn MAN-B&W 6S60MC-C 1 x 2 Stroke 6 Cy. 600 x 2400 13560kW (18436bhp) STX Engine Co Ltd-South Korea AuxGen: 3 x 730kW a.c Fuel: 200.0 (d.f.) 3500.0 (r.f.)
9517276 *WDE4114* -	**SEA HONOR** - **Sea Honor LLC** Sea Global Fisheries LLC *Pago Pago, AS* *United States of America* MMSI: 367344000 Official number: 1210858	**1,517** 605 -		**2008-06 Jong Shyn Shipbuilding Co., Ltd. — Kaohsiung** Yd No: 161 Loa 70.59 Br ex - Dght - Lbp - Br md 12.31 Dpth 7.25 Welded, 1 dk	**(B11B2FV) Fishing Vessel**	**1 oil engine** driving 1 Propeller Daihatsu 1 x 4 Stroke Daihatsu Diesel Manufacturing Co Lt-Japan
9140437 *HSB4391* -	**SEA HONOUR** *ex* Sentosa *-2009* *ex* Iligan *-2002* *ex* Cotabato *-2001* *ex* Jurong *-1998* **S Navigation Co Ltd** Sinsimon Navigation Co Ltd *Bangkok* *Thailand* MMSI: 567386000 Official number: 520085376	**6,264** 3,891 8,663	Class: NK	**1996-06 Shin Kurushima Dockyard Co. Ltd. — Akitsu** Yd No: 2901 Loa 100.59 (BB) Br ex 18.83 Dght 8.219 Lbp 93.50 Br md 18.80 Dpth 13.00 Welded, 1 dk	**(A31A2GX) General Cargo Ship** Grain: 13,941; Bale: 13,096 Compartments: 2 Ho, ER 2 Ha: 2 (24.0 x 12.6)ER Cranes: 2x30t; Derricks: 2x25t	**1 oil engine** driving 1 FP propeller Total Power: 3,236kW (4,400hp) 12.4kn B&W 5L35MC 1 x 2 Stroke 5 Cy. 350 x 1050 3236kW (4400bhp) Makita Corp-Japan Fuel: 650.0 (r.f.)
9439541 *VRES2* -	**SEA HOPE** - **Golden Delfina Inc** Teekay Shipping Ltd SatCom: Inmarsat C 447701540 *Hong Kong* *Hong Kong* MMSI: 477170800 Official number: HK-2296	**60,193** 33,762 108,701 T/cm 91.3	Class: AB	**2009-04 Zhoushan Jinhaiwan Shipyard Co Ltd — Daishan County ZJ** Yd No: J0002 Loa 243.00 (BB) Br ex 42.03 Dght 15.350 Lbp 233.00 Br md 42.00 Dpth 22.00 Welded, 1 dk	**(A13B2TP) Products Tanker** Double Hull (13F) Liq: 123,030; Liq (Oil): 123,030 Cargo Heating Coils Compartments: 12 Wing Ta, 2 Wing Slop Ta, ER 3 Cargo Pump (s): 3x2500m³/hr Manifold: Bow/CM: 122.2m	**1 oil engine** driving 1 FP propeller Total Power: 14,280kW (19,415hp) 15.0kn MAN-B&W 7S60MC 1 x 2 Stroke 7 Cy. 600 x 2292 14280kW (19415bhp) Hudong Heavy Machinery Co Ltd-China AuxGen: 3 x 680kW a.c Fuel: 121.0 (d.f.) 2518.0 (r.f.)
8828458 *A6E2685* -	**SEA HOPPER** *ex* GMMOS Hopper *-1997* *ex* Mattar *-1993* *ex* Matter *-1988* *ex* Misty Skye *-1985* *ex* Odom Sea Trac *-1984* **Seaport International Shipping Co LLC** - *Sharjah* *United Arab Emirates* Official number: 3486	*218* 67 -	Class: BV (AB)	**1979 Bollinger Machine Shop & Shipyard, Inc. — Lockport, La** Yd No: 119 Loa 35.05 Br ex - Dght 2.560 Lbp 32.00 Br md 7.92 Dpth 3.56 Welded, 1 dk	**(B34L2QU) Utility Vessel**	**2 oil engines** reverse reduction geared to sc. shafts driving 2 FP propellers Total Power: 698kW (950hp) 10.0kn G.M. (Detroit Diesel) 16V-71 2 x Vee 2 Stroke 16 Cy. 108 x 127 each-349kW (475bhp) General Motors Detroit DieselAllison Divn-USA AuxGen: 2 x 50kW a.c
7718967 *HSOU* -	**SEA HORIZON** *ex* Harmonic *-2000* *ex* Sang Thai Zenith *-2000* *ex* Ann *-1992* *ex* Otto *-1984* *ex* Mermaid I *-1984* **NGV A Transport Service Co Ltd** - *Bangkok* *Thailand* MMSI: 567139000 Official number: 351001133	**5,485** 2,979 8,298	Class: (LR) (NK) ✠ Classed LR until 7/10/90	**1979-04 Watanabe Zosen KK — Imabari EH** Yd No: 199 Loa 118.41 (BB) Br ex 18.09 Dght 7.211 Lbp 110.03 Br md 18.04 Dpth 7.99 Welded, 1 dk	**(A31A2GX) General Cargo Ship** Grain: 10,338; Bale: 10,144 Compartments: 4 Ho, ER 4 Ha: 4 (14.0 x 14.4)ER Derricks: 4x22t; Winches: 4	**1 oil engine** driving 1 FP propeller Total Power: 3,898kW (5,300hp) 11.5kn B&W 6K45GF 1 x 2 Stroke 6 Cy. 450 x 900 3898kW (5300bhp) Hitachi Zosen Corp-Japan AuxGen: 3 x 210kW 445V 60Hz a.c Fuel: 97.5 (d.f.) 565.5 (r.f.) 16.0pd
9258026 *9HA3225* -	**SEA HORIZON** *ex* Eskden *-2013* *ex* Eland *-2011* **Hesperos Maritime Co Ltd** Sea World Management & Trading Inc *Valletta* *Malta* MMSI: 229316000 Official number: 9258026	**28,529** 12,369 47,149 T/cm 50.6	Class: AB (BV)	**2003-09 Onomichi Dockyard Co Ltd — Onomichi HS** Yd No: 493 Loa 182.50 (BB) Br ex 32.23 Dght 12.666 Lbp 173.13 Br md 32.20 Dpth 19.10 Welded, 1 dk	**(A13B2TP) Products Tanker** Double Hull (13F) Liq: 50,332; Liq (Oil): 50,332 Cargo Heating Coils Compartments: 2 Ta, 12 Wing Ta, 2 Wing Slop Ta, ER 4 Cargo Pump (s): 4x1000m³/hr Manifold: Bow/CM: 91.7m	**1 oil engine** driving 1 FP propeller Total Power: 8,580kW (11,665hp) 14.5kn B&W 6S50MC 1 x 2 Stroke 6 Cy. 500 x 1910 8580kW (11665bhp) Mitsui Engineering & Shipbuilding CLtd-Japan AuxGen: 3 x 420kW 440/220V 60Hz a.c Fuel: 132.0 (d.f.) 1636.0 (r.f.) 36.0pd

IMO / Call sign	Name / Former names / Owner / Port	Tonnage	Class	Builder / Dimensions	Type / Capacity	Machinery
7315583 *5VAG5* -	**SEA HORSE** *ex* Sanie *-2009* *ex* Ibn Siraj *-2003* **Mas Maritimes SA** Sealink Sarl *Lome* *Togo* MMSI: 671049000	**4,932** 3,067 7,435	Class: (GL)	**1973-06 Schlichting-Werft GmbH — Luebeck** Yd No: 1378 Loa 116.69 (BB) Br ex 17.25 Dght 7.502 Lbp 107.96 Br md 17.20 Dpth 9.89 Welded, 2 dks	**(A31A2GX) General Cargo Ship** Grain: 10,675; Bale: 10,028 TEU 226 C. 226/20' Compartments: 3 Ho, ER 3 Ha: (13.0 x 7.7)2 (19.5 x 10.5)ER Derricks: 1x60t,10x10t,1x1t Ice Capable	**1 oil engine** sr geared to sc. shaft driving 1 FP propeller Total Power: 2,942kW (4,000hp) 15.5kn MaK 8M551AK 1 x 4 Stroke 8 Cy. 450 x 550 2942kW (4000bhp) MaK Maschinenbau GmbH-Kiel AuxGen: 2 x 256kW 220/380V 50Hz a.c, 1 x 136kW 220/380V 50Hz a.c Fuel: 69.0 (d.f.) 294.0 (r.f.)
7404085 *WBN4382* -	**SEA HORSE** *ex* Robin IX *-1984* **Crowley Foreign Towing Inc** - *San Francisco, CA* *United States of America* MMSI: 366887940 Official number: 567812	**421** 126 -	Class: AB	**1975 McDermott Shipyards Inc — Morgan City LA** Yd No: 206 Loa - Br ex 10.37 Dght 4.290 Lbp 36.63 Br md 10.32 Dpth 5.01 Welded, 1 dk	**(B32A2ST) Tug**	**2 oil engines** reverse reduction geared to sc. shafts driving 2 FP propellers Total Power: 3,574kW (4,860hp) 13.0kn Alco 12V251E 2 x Vee 4 Stroke 12 Cy. 229 x 267 each-1787kW (2430bhp) Alco Engine Co-USA AuxGen: 2 x 75kW Fuel: 254.0 (d.f.)
8212439 *A6E2710* -	**SEA HORSE** *ex* Amir Express *-2000* **Global Marine Services** - *Sharjah* *United Arab Emirates* Official number: SHJ/1074	**213** 63 500	Class: LR (AB) **100A1** SS 06/2012 supply ship, Gulf and Arabian coastal service **LMC**	**1982-06 Master Boat Builders, Inc. — Coden, Al** Yd No: 55 Loa 33.53 Br ex - Dght 2.917 Lbp 30.18 Br md 7.93 Dpth 3.20 Welded, 1 dk	**(B21A2OS) Platform Supply Ship** Passengers: berths: 22 Cranes: 1x10t	**2 oil engines** reverse reduction geared to sc. shafts driving 2 FP propellers Total Power: 1,030kW (1,400hp) 10.0kn G.M. (Detroit Diesel) 16V-71 2 x Vee 2 Stroke 16 Cy. 108 x 127 each-515kW (700bhp) General Motors Detroit DieselAllison Divn-USA AuxGen: 2 x 50kW Thrusters: 1 Tunnel thruster (f) Fuel: 100.0 (d.f.)
8305729 - -	**SEA HORSE** - **Versaggi Shrimp Corp** - *Tampa, FL* *United States of America* Official number: 651654	*119* 92 -		**1982-10 St Augustine Trawlers, Inc. — Saint Augustine, Fl** Yd No: F-43 Loa - Br ex 6.71 Dght - Lbp 23.17 Br md - Dpth 2.75 Bonded, 1 dk	**(B11B2FV) Fishing Vessel** Hull Material: Reinforced Plastic Ins: 81 Compartments: 1 Ho, ER 1 Ha:	**1 oil engine** geared to sc. shaft driving 1 FP propeller Total Power: 305kW (415hp) Caterpillar 3412T 1 x Vee 4 Stroke 12 Cy. 137 x 152 305kW (415bhp) Caterpillar Tractor Co-USA
8941157 *WDB8790* -	**SEA HORSE** *ex* Seahorse *-2009* *ex* Sea Gull II *-2005* **Tran Van ha** - *Garrison, TX* *United States of America* Official number: 1050022	**149** 44 -		**1997 Master Boat Builders, Inc. — Coden, Al** Yd No: 236 L reg 24.87 Br ex - Dght - Lbp - Br md 7.32 Dpth 3.81 Welded, 1 dk	**(B11B2FV) Fishing Vessel**	**2 oil engines** geared to sc. shafts driving 2 Propellers Caterpillar 3408T 2 x Vee 4 Stroke 8 Cy. 137 x 152 Caterpillar Inc-USA AuxGen: 2 x 60kW
8854902 *WDE6126* -	**SEA HORSE** *ex* Mistake *-2013* **Jerry Murphy's Repairs LLC** - *Pascagoula, MS* *United States of America* MMSI: 367376140 Official number: 912964	*115* 92 -		**1987 Utila, Inc. — Pascagoula, Ms** Loa - Br ex - Dght - Lbp 23.47 Br md 5.94 Dpth 3.51 Welded, 1 dk	**(B11B2FV) Fishing Vessel**	**1 oil engine** driving 1 FP propeller
8886101 *WDA6031* -	**SEA HORSE** *ex* St. Mary Magdalen *-2004* **Sea Horse** - *Abbeville, LA* *United States of America* MMSI: 366826970 Official number: 923929	*125* 85 -		**1987 Tuocem Ba Nguyen — Orange, Tx** L reg 23.64 Br ex - Dght - Lbp - Br md 7.01 Dpth 2.15 Welded, 1 dk	**(B11B2FV) Fishing Vessel**	**1 oil engine** driving 1 FP propeller
8940672 *WDD3311* -	**SEA HORSE II** *ex* Ocean Goddess *-2006* **Quang Van Tran** - *Port Arthur, TX* *United States of America* MMSI: 367128730 Official number: 1045802	**137** 41 -		**1996 T.M. Jemison Construction Co., Inc. — Bayou La Batre, Al** Yd No: 101 L reg 24.14 Br ex - Dght - Lbp - Br md 7.32 Dpth 3.63 Welded, 1 dk	**(B11B2FV) Fishing Vessel**	**1 oil engine** driving 1 FP propeller
9184110 - -	**SEA HORSE II** - **Southern Towing Ltd** - *Port of Spain* *Trinidad & Tobago* Official number: 9184110	**443** 132 540		**1997-12 Bollinger Machine Shop & Shipyard, Inc. — Lockport, La** Yd No: 319 Loa 44.70 Br ex - Dght 3.500 Lbp 44.34 Br md 10.97 Dpth 3.51 Welded, 1 dk	**(B21A2OS) Platform Supply Ship**	**2 oil engines** geared to sc. shafts driving 2 FP propellers Total Power: 1,104kW (1,500hp) 10.0kn Cummins KTA-38-M 2 x Vee 4 Stroke 12 Cy. 159 x 159 each-552kW (750bhp) Cummins Engine Co Inc-USA Thrusters: 1 Tunnel thruster (f)
6718350 *HO9565* -	**SEA HORSE II** *ex* Losange *-2006* *ex* Seaview *-1979* **Trawlers Leasing Inc** - *Panama* *Panama* Official number: 1009580B	*130* 104 -		**1967 East Gulf Shipyards — Panama City, Fl** Yd No: 6 Loa - Br ex - Dght - Lbp 24.39 Br md 7.01 Dpth 3.66 Welded, 1 dk	**(B11A2FT) Trawler**	**1 oil engine** driving 1 FP propeller Total Power: 279kW (379hp) Caterpillar 1 x 4 Stroke 6 Cy. 279kW (379bhp) Caterpillar Tractor Co-USA
7200702 *HO6364* -	**SEA HORSE III** *ex* Jupiter I *-1986* *ex* Jupiter *-1982* **Ivor Mansions Inc** - *Panama* *Panama* Official number: 9816PEXT1	*181* 123 -		**1965 Mangone Shipbuilding Co. — Houston, Tx** Yd No: 66 Loa - Br ex 10.98 Dght - Lbp 43.03 Br md - Dpth 3.81 Welded, 1 dk	**(B21A2OS) Platform Supply Ship**	**2 oil engines** geared to sc. shafts driving 2 FP propellers Total Power: 956kW (1,300hp) 13.0kn G.M. (Detroit Diesel) 12V-71 2 x Vee 2 Stroke 12 Cy. 108 x 127 each-478kW (650bhp) General Motors Corp-USA
6716182 *HP5637* -	**SEA HORSE IV** *ex* Daiyu Maru No. 15 *-1990* **Evermast Capital Corp** - *Panama* *Panama* Official number: D2651789PEXT	*199* - -		**1966 Nagasaki Zosen K.K. — Nagasaki** Yd No: 128 Loa 34.98 Br ex 6.58 Dght 2.820 Lbp 34.45 Br md 6.56 Dpth 3.20 Welded, 1 dk	**(B12B2FC) Fish Carrier**	**1 oil engine** driving 1 FP propeller Total Power: 478kW (650hp) Makita 1 x 4 Stroke 6 Cy. 290 x 430 478kW (650bhp) Makita Tekkosho-Japan
5429457 - -	**SEA HORSE ONE** *ex* Remolcanosa Cuatro *-1981* *ex* Vulcano *-1981* -	**164** - -	Class: (LR) ✠ Classed LR until 27/7/94	**1964-07 Enrique Lorenzo y Cia SA — Vigo** Yd No: 290 L reg 25.00 Br ex 7.01 Dght - Lbp 28.55 Br md 7.00 Dpth 3.76 Welded, 1 dk	**(B32A2ST) Tug**	**1 oil engine** driving 1 CP propeller Total Power: 772kW (1,050hp) 11.0kn MWM 1 x 4 Stroke 8 Cy. 320 x 480 772kW (1050bhp) Motoren Werke Mannheim AG (MWM)-West Germany AuxGen: 2 x 30kW 220V d.c
8964496 *WDF6981* -	**SEA HORSE VI** - **GIS Marine LLC** - *New Orleans, LA* *United States of America* MMSI: 367479880 Official number: 1103038	**454** 136 -		**2000-12 Bollinger Machine Shop & Shipyard, Inc. — Lockport, La** Yd No: 391 Loa 44.34 Br ex - Dght 3.046 Lbp 39.86 Br md 10.97 Dpth 3.50 Welded, 1 dk	**(B21A2OS) Platform Supply Ship**	**2 oil engines** geared to sc. shafts driving 2 FP propellers Total Power: 1,104kW (1,500hp) 10.0kn Cummins KTA-38-M0 2 x Vee 4 Stroke 12 Cy. 159 x 159 each-552kW (750bhp) Cummins Engine Co Ltd-United Kingdom Thrusters: 1 Tunnel thruster (f)
8951425 - -	**SEA HOSS** *ex* Scottie Lee *-1999* *ex* Willie G *-1995* **Kenol Luxama** - *San Lorenzo* *Honduras* Official number: L-0327459	**165** 52 -		**1976 Offshore Trawlers, Inc. — Bayou La Batre, Al** Yd No: 26 L reg 24.45 Br ex - Dght - Lbp - Br md 7.31 Dpth 2.13 Welded, 1 dk	**(A31A2GX) General Cargo Ship**	**1 oil engine** driving 1 FP propeller Total Power: 500kW (680hp) General Motors 1 x 500kW (680bhp) General Motors Corp-USA
9695779 *PCWS* -	**SEA HOTEL** - **Global Ship Leasing 16 BV** Seacontractors Brokerage BV *Vlissingen* *Netherlands* MMSI: 244810135	**221** 66 200	Class: BV	**2013-10 Albwardy Marine Engineering LLC — Dubai** (Hull) Yd No: 571694 **2013-10 B.V. Scheepswerf Damen Hardinxveld — Hardinxveld-Giessendam** Yd No: 571694 Loa 27.02 Br ex 9.35 Dght 3.000 Lbp 23.84 Br md 9.31 Dpth 3.60 Welded, 1 dk	**(B32A2ST) Tug**	**2 oil engines** reduction geared to sc. shafts driving 2 FP propellers Total Power: 2,206kW (3,000hp) Caterpillar 3512B 2 x Vee 4 Stroke 12 Cy. 170 x 190 each-1103kW (1500bhp) Caterpillar Inc-USA AuxGen: 2 x 70kW 50Hz a.c Thrusters: 1 Tunnel thruster (f) Fuel: 125.0

IMO / Call sign	Name / Owner	Tonnage	Class	Build / Dimensions	Type	Machinery
9151292 - -	**SEA HOUND** *ex* Sang Hound *-2004* *ex* Sea Hound *-1997* **PSA Marine Pte Ltd** -	**255** 76 -	Class: BV	**1997**-02 **Kanagawa Zosen — Kobe** Yd No: 436 Loa 27.50 Br ex - Dght 3.500 Lbp 25.90 Br md 8.50 Dpth 4.70 Welded, 1 dk	**(B32A2ST) Tug**	**2 oil engines** driving 2 FP propellers Total Power: 2,352kW (3,198hp) 12.5kn Niigata 6MG25HX 2 x 4 Stroke 6 Cy. 250 x 350 each-1176kW (1599bhp) Niigata Engineering Co Ltd-Japan
8940220 *WDC3196* -	**SEA HUNT** *ex* Master Ricky II *-2004* **Leland F Oldenburg** - *Honolulu, HI* *United States of America* MMSI: 367003760 Official number: 1046666	**134** 40 -		**1996 Master Boat Builders, Inc. — Coden, Al** Yd No: 235 L reg 23.68 Br ex - Dght - Lbp - Br md 7.32 Dpth 3.81 Welded, 1 dk	**(B11B2FV) Fishing Vessel**	**1 oil engine** driving 1 FP propeller
8914154 *8PUY* -	**SEA HUNTER** *ex* Sirius P *-2007* *ex* Highland *-1999* *ex* Sirrah *-1995* **Boddingtons Shipping Ltd** Torbulk Ltd *Bridgetown* *Barbados* MMSI: 314270000	**2,443** 1,182 3,148	Class: GL (NV)	**1990**-12 **Estaleiros Navais de Viana do Castelo S.A. — Viana do Castelo** Yd No: 155 Loa 87.47 (BB) Br ex 13.02 Dght 4.827 Lbp 82.10 Br md 13.00 Dpth 7.10 Welded, 1 dk	**(A31A2GX) General Cargo Ship** Grain: 4,650 TEU 153 C.Ho 104/20' C.Dk 49/20' Compartments: 1 Ho, ER 1 Ha: (57.4 x 10.2)ER Ice Capable	**1 oil engine** with clutches & sr geared to sc. shaft driving 1 CP propeller Total Power: 1,320kW (1,795hp) 12.0kn Alpha 6L28/32A 1 x 4 Stroke 6 Cy. 280 x 320 1320kW (1795bhp) MAN B&W Diesel A/S-Denmark AuxGen: 1 x 216kW 220/380V a.c, 2 x 135kW 220/380V a.c Thrusters: 1 Thwart. FP thruster (f) Fuel: 123.0 (d.f.) 7.3pd
8905737 *UBIF9* -	**SEA HUNTER** *ex* Sunna *-2008* *ex* Vaka *-1992* **Pacific Fishery Co Ltd (OOO Tikhookeanskaya Rybopromyshlennaya Kompaniya)** - *Magadan* *Russia* MMSI: 273336810	**1,042** 250 829	Class: RS (NV)	**1991**-03 **Astilleros Gondan SA — Castropol** Yd No: 296 Loa 53.17 (BB) Br ex 10.52 Dght 6.040 Lbp 46.37 Br md 10.50 Dpth 7.00 Welded, 2 dks	**(B11A2FS) Stern Trawler** Ins: 800 Ice Capable	**1 oil engine** with clutches, flexible couplings & sr geared to sc. shaft driving 1 CP propeller Total Power: 2,638kW (3,587hp) 14.0kn Alpha 12V28/32 1 x Vee 4 Stroke 12 Cy. 280 x 320 2638kW (3587bhp) MAN B&W Diesel A/S-Denmark AuxGen: 1 x 1520kW 380V a.c, 1 x 376kW 380V a.c Thrusters: 1 Thwart. CP thruster (f); 1 Thwart. CP thruster (a)
8811326 *LIVI* M-80-SJ	**SEA HUNTER** *ex* Trygvason *-2009* *ex* Solvar Jr. *-2004* *ex* Solvar Viking *-2004* *ex* Astrid *-1997* **Havoy Kystfiske AS** - *Aalesund* *Norway* MMSI: 259447000	**498** 154 171		**1988**-11 **Strandby Skibsvaerft I/S — Strandby** Yd No: 93 Loa 44.95 (BB) Br ex - Dght - Lbp - Br md 8.30 Dpth 5.28 Welded	**(B11B2FV) Fishing Vessel**	**1 oil engine** driving 1 CP propeller Total Power: 1,580kW (2,148hp) Nohab F38A 1 x Vee 4 Stroke 8 Cy. 250 x 300 1580kW (2148bhp) Wartsila Diesel Oy-Finland
8990421 - -	**SEA HUNTER** *ex* Queen Corinne *-2009* **Blue Maritime Inc** - *West Palm Beach, FL* *United States of America* Official number: 1153890	**126** 101		**2004 Capt. Russ, Jr., Inc. — Chauvin, La** Yd No: 153 L reg 23.77 Br ex - Dght - Lbp - Br md 8.22 Dpth 2.74 Welded, 1 dk	**(B11B2FV) Fishing Vessel**	**1 oil engine** driving 1 Propeller
8975732 - -	**SEA HUNTER** - -	**172** - -		**2001** Yd No: 219 L reg 26.94 Br ex - Dght - Lbp - Br md 7.62 Dpth 3.80 Welded, 1 dk	**(B11A2FT) Trawler**	**1 oil engine** geared to sc. shaft driving 1 Propeller Total Power: 395kW (537hp) Caterpillar 3412 1 x Vee 4 Stroke 12 Cy. 137 x 152 395kW (537bhp) Caterpillar Inc-USA
7819694 *WDB6726* -	**SEA HUNTER** *ex* Gallant Fox *-2008* *ex* H. O. S. Gallant Fox *-1996* *ex* Florence A *-1994* **Sea Hunters LP** - *Portland, ME* *United States of America* MMSI: 338123459 Official number: 598425	**830** 249 1,180	Class: AB	**1978**-10 **Halter Marine, Inc. — Lockport, La** Yd No: 758 Lengthened-1983 Loa 65.23 Br ex 12.20 Dght 3.555 Lbp 49.33 Br md 11.59 Dpth 4.27 Welded, 1 dk	**(B21A20S) Platform Supply Ship**	**2 oil engines** reverse reduction geared to sc. shafts driving 2 FP propellers Total Power: 2,648kW (3,600hp) 12.0kn EMD (Electro-Motive) 16-645-E2 2 x Vee 2 Stroke 16 Cy. 230 x 254 each-1324kW (1800bhp) (Re-engined ,made 1956, Reconditioned & fitted 1978) General Motors Corp.Electro-Motive Div.-La Grange AuxGen: 2 x 99kW
9349916 *UBAI8* -	**SEA HUNTER** *ex* Garfield *-2011* **Lion Sea Transport SA** East Shine Shipping Co Ltd *Korsakov* *Russia* MMSI: 273352740	**422** 126 -	Class: BV	**2005**-03 **Dearsan Gemi Insaat ve Sanayii Koll. Sti. — Tuzla** Yd No: 23 Loa 40.34 Br ex - Dght 3.420 Lbp 36.77 Br md 9.55 Dpth 4.57 Welded, 1 dk	**(X11A2YP) Yacht**	**2 oil engines** reduction geared to sc. shafts driving 2 Propellers Total Power: 1,268kW (1,724hp) 13.0kn Caterpillar 3508B 2 x Vee 4 Stroke 8 Cy. 170 x 190 each-634kW (862bhp) Caterpillar Inc-USA
9611307 *ZR8553* -	**SEA HUNTER** **Starlight Fishing CC** - *Cape Town* *South Africa* MMSI: 601137900 Official number: 11020	**170** - -		**2010**-09 **Tallie Marine Pty Ltd — St Helena Bay** Yd No: T78 (02) Loa 24.00 (BB) Br ex - Dght - Lbp - Br md 7.20 Dpth 3.42 Bonded, 1 dk	**(B11B2FV) Fishing Vessel** Hull Material: Reinforced Plastic	**1 oil engine** reduction geared to sc. shaft driving 1 Propeller Total Power: 533kW (725hp) 9.5kn Caterpillar C18 1 x 4 Stroke 6 Cy. 145 x 183 533kW (725bhp) Caterpillar Inc-USA
8940385 *WDE4422* -	**SEA HUNTERS PRIDE** *ex* Alexander *-2009* *ex* Maria Madalena *-2009* *ex* Lucky Cathy *-2004* **Sea Hunter's Pride Inc** - *Brownsville, TX* *United States of America* MMSI: 366942890 Official number: 1048325	**128** 39 -		**1996 Ocean Marine, Inc. — Bayou La Batre, Al** Yd No: 327 L reg 24.69 Br ex - Dght - Lbp - Br md 7.01 Dpth 3.69 Welded, 1 dk	**(B11B2FV) Fishing Vessel**	**1 oil engine** driving 1 FP propeller
7050561 *WDD2403* -	**SEA HUNTRESS** *ex* Neptune I *-2001* *ex* Iron Horse *-2001* **Ark Bait Co Inc** - *Fall River, MA* *United States of America* Official number: 516505	*131* 89 -		**1968 Marine Builders, Inc. — Mobile, Al** L reg 22.86 Br ex 6.84 Dght - Lbp - Br md - Dpth 3.41 Welded, 1 dk	**(B11B2FV) Fishing Vessel**	**1 oil engine** driving 1 FP propeller Total Power: 257kW (349hp)
9672959 *OUXA2* -	**SEA HURRICANE** *launched as* Fob Swath 5 *-2013* **FOB Swath AS** A2SEA A/S *Fredericia* *Denmark (DIS)* MMSI: 219464000 Official number: A 555	**244** 73 65	Class: NV	**2013**-12 **Danish Yachts A/S — Skagen** Yd No: 122 Loa 24.65 (BB) Br ex 10.83 Dght 2.490 Lbp 23.55 Br md 10.60 Dpth 5.37 Bonded, 1 dk	**(B21A20C) Crew/Supply Vessel** Hull Material: Carbon Fibre Sandwich	**2 oil engines** reduction geared to sc. shafts driving 2 CP propellers Total Power: 1,800kW (2,448hp) 22.0kn M.T.U. 10V2000M72 1 x Vee 4 Stroke 10 Cy. 135 x 156 900kW (1224bhp) MTU Friedrichshafen GmbH-Friedrichshafen AuxGen: 2 x 80kW 50Hz a.c Thrusters: 2 Tunnel thruster (f); 2 Tunnel thruster (a)
9151280 - -	**SEA HUSKY** *ex* Sang Husky *-2004* *ex* Sea Husky *-1997* **PSA Marine Pte Ltd** -	**255** 76 136	Class: BV	**1996**-12 **Kanagawa Zosen — Kobe** (Hull) Yd No: 435 **1996**-12 **Mitsubishi Heavy Industries Ltd. — Kobe** Yd No: 1218 Loa 27.50 Br ex - Dght 3.500 Lbp 25.90 Br md 8.50 Dpth 4.70 Welded, 1 dk	**(B32A2ST) Tug**	**2 oil engines** driving 2 FP propellers Total Power: 2,352kW (3,198hp) 12.5kn Niigata 6MG25HX 2 x 4 Stroke 6 Cy. 250 x 350 each-1176kW (1599bhp) Niigata Engineering Co Ltd-Japan Fuel: 64.0 (d.f.)
8946860 *V4MH2* -	**SEA HUSTLER** **WESK Ltd** - *Charlestown* *St Kitts & Nevis* MMSI: 341186000 Official number: SKN 1002324	*137* 58 -		**1976 Gulf Craft Inc — Patterson LA** Converted From: Offshore Supply Ship-1988 L reg 30.35 Br ex - Dght - Lbp - Br md 8.10 Dpth 1.98 Welded, 1 dk	**(A36A2PR) Passenger/Ro-Ro Ship (Vehicles)** Hull Material: Aluminium Alloy	**2 oil engines** driving 2 FP propellers Total Power: 670kW (910hp) 12.0kn G.M. (Detroit Diesel) 8V-71 2 x Vee 2 Stroke 8 Cy. 108 x 127 each-335kW (455bhp) Detroit Diesel Corporation-Detroit, Mi

8017750 - -	**SEA IDOL** *ex* Pobratim *-2009* *ex* Dunkan *-2005* *ex* Sunny *-2003* *ex* Pobratim *-2003* *ex* Dunkan *-2000* *ex* Lobana-1 *-2000* *ex* Arka No. 55 *-1996* *ex* Iwachi Maru No. 77 *-1996* *ex* Kaiho Maru No. 55 *-1989* - -	**549** 204 271	Class: (RS)	**1980**-12 **Miho Zosensho K.K. — Shimizu** Yd No: 1185 Loa 50.14 Br ex 8.51 Dght 3.240 Lbp 43.52 Br md 8.50 Dpth 3.59 Welded, 1 dk	**(B11B2FV) Fishing Vessel**	**1 oil engine** reduction geared to sc. shaft driving 1 FP propeller Total Power: 809kW (1,100hp) 11.5kn Niigata 6M28AFT 1 x 4 Stroke 6 Cy. 280 x 480 809kW (1100bhp) Niigata Engineering Co Ltd-Japan
9646481 *OYPY2* -	**SEA INSTALLER** - **A2SEA A/S** - *Esbjerg* *Denmark (DIS)* MMSI: 219456000 Official number: D4507	**15,966** 4,790 5,000	Class: NV	**2012**-10 **COSCO (Nantong) Shipyard Co Ltd — Nantong JS** Yd No: N370 Loa 132.34 Br ex - Dght 5.800 Lbp 121.68 Br md 39.00 Dpth 9.00 Welded, 1 dk	**(B22A2ZM) Offshore Construction Vessel, jack up** Cranes: 1x800t	**6 diesel electric oil engines** driving 6 gen. each 3050kW 6600V a.c Connecting to 3 elec. motors each (800kW) driving 3 Voith-Schneider propellers Total Power: 17,820kW (24,228hp) MaK 9M25 6 x 4 Stroke 9 Cy. 255 x 400 each-2970kW (4038bhp) Caterpillar Motoren GmbH & Co. KG-Germany Thrusters: 2 Tunnel thruster (f); 1 Retract. directional thruster (f) Fuel: 1000.0
9337561 *HO4201* -	**SEA INTREPID** - **Gulf Marine Far East Pte Ltd** - *Panama* *Panama* MMSI: 371615000 Official number: 3182206B	**1,470** 441 1,500	Class: AB (BV)	**2005**-09 **Guangzhou Southern Shipbuilding Co Ltd — Guangzhou GD** Yd No: 0401 Loa 58.70 Br ex - Dght 4.500 Lbp 53.20 Br md 14.60 Dpth 5.50 Welded, 1 dk	**(B21A2OS) Platform Supply Ship**	**2 oil engines** reduction geared to sc. shafts driving 2 CP propellers Total Power: 3,840kW (5,220hp) 13.5kn Caterpillar 3516B-TA 2 x Vee 4 Stroke 16 Cy. 170 x 190 each-1920kW (2610bhp) Caterpillar Inc-USA AuxGen: 3 x 320kW a.c Thrusters: 1 Tunnel thruster (f) Fuel: 464.0 (d.f.)
9425916 *3EXY4* -	**SEA IRIS** - **Lucretia Shipping SA** Santoku Senpaku Co Ltd *Panama* *Panama* MMSI: 351012000 Official number: 4189910	**32,287** 19,458 58,117 T/cm 57.4	Class: NK	**2010**-09 **Tsuneishi Heavy Industries (Cebu) Inc — Balamban** Yd No: SC-124 Loa 189.99 (BB) Br ex - Dght 12.826 Lbp 185.60 Br md 32.26 Dpth 18.00 Welded, 1 dk	**(A21A2BC) Bulk Carrier** Grain: 72,689; Bale: 70,122 Compartments: 5 Ho, ER 5 Ha: ER Cranes: 4x30t	**1 oil engine** driving 1 FP propeller Total Power: 8,400kW (11,421hp) 14.5kn MAN-B&W 6S50MC-C 1 x 2 Stroke 6 Cy. 500 x 2000 8400kW (11421bhp) Mitsui Engineering & Shipbuilding CLtd-Japan Fuel: 2388.0 (r.f.)
9420007 *5BET3* -	**SEA JACKAL** - **DESS Cyprus Ltd** Deep Sea Supply Plc SatCom: Inmarsat C 420926810 *Limassol* *Cyprus* MMSI: 209268000	**1,943** 645 1,898	Class: NV	**2011**-03 **ABG Shipyard Ltd — Surat** Yd No: 272 Loa 63.40 Br ex - Dght 4.600 Lbp 56.53 Br md 15.80 Dpth 6.80 Welded, 1 dk	**(B21B20A) Anchor Handling Tug Supply**	**2 oil engines** reduction geared to sc. shafts driving 2 CP propellers Total Power: 5,002kW (6,800hp) 10.5kn Yanmar 8N280-EN 2 x 4 Stroke 8 Cy. 280 x 380 each-2501kW (3400bhp) Yanmar Diesel Engine Co Ltd-Japan AuxGen: 3 x 425kW 440V 60Hz a.c Thrusters: 1 Thwart. CP thruster (f)
7805904 *5IM343* -	**SEA JADE** *ex* Samurai *-2011* *ex* Laffan 1 *-2011* *ex* Laffan *-2010* **Jade Marine Services & Trading Inc** - *Zanzibar* *Tanzania (Zanzibar)* MMSI: 677024300 Official number: 300099	**275** 82 286	Class: (LR) ✠ Classed LR until 2/3/10	**1978**-10 **Sing Koon Seng Pte Ltd — Singapore** Yd No: SKS479 Loa 33.79 Br ex 8.67 Dght 3.163 Lbp 30.99 Br md 8.51 Dpth 3.51 Welded, 1 dk	**(B21B20T) Offshore Tug/Supply Ship**	**2 oil engines** reverse reduction geared to sc. shafts driving 2 FP propellers Total Power: 736kW (1,000hp) Kelvin TBSC8 2 x 4 Stroke 8 Cy. 165 x 184 each-368kW (500bhp) GEC Diesels Ltd.Kelvin Marine Div.-Glasgow AuxGen: 2 x 40kW 415V 50Hz a.c
8626549 - -	**SEA JADE** *ex* Sea Chart 2 *-2007* *ex* Horyu Maru *-2000* *ex* Feng Long *-1999* *ex* Horyu Maru *-1999* - -	**786** 422 1,327		**1985 Sasaki Shipbuilding Co Ltd — Osakikamijima HS** Loa 67.75 Br ex - Dght 4.271 Lbp 62.01 Br md 10.00 Dpth 4.50 Welded, 1 dk	**(A13B2TP) Products Tanker** Liq: 1,599; Liq (Oil): 1,599	**1 oil engine** driving 1 FP propeller Total Power: 1,103kW (1,500hp) 11.5kn Makita LS33L 1 x 4 Stroke 6 Cy. 330 x 640 1103kW (1500bhp) Makita Diesel Co Ltd-Japan
7232482 *WYZ8479* -	**SEA JADE** *ex* Gemini I *-1978* **Arthur Thornton True Sr** - *Brunswick, GA* *United States of America* Official number: 543866	*125* 85 -		**1972 Desco Marine — Saint Augustine, Fl** Yd No: 112-F L reg 20.97 Br ex 6.74 Dght - Lbp - Br md - Dpth 3.81 Bonded	**(B11B2FV) Fishing Vessel** Hull Material: Reinforced Plastic Ins: 45	**1 oil engine** driving 1 FP propeller Total Power: 268kW (364hp) Caterpillar 3408PCTA 1 x Vee 4 Stroke 8 Cy. 137 x 152 268kW (364bhp) Caterpillar Tractor Co-USA
9140188 *9V5297* -	**SEA JAGUAR** - **PSA Marine Pte Ltd** - *Singapore* *Singapore* MMSI: 563003290 Official number: 387155	**244** 73 100	Class: BV	**1996**-06 **Matsuura Tekko Zosen K.K. — Osakikamijima** Yd No: 395 Loa 27.50 Br ex 9.10 Dght 3.500 Lbp 23.00 Br md 8.50 Dpth 4.70 Welded, 1 dk	**(B32A2ST) Tug**	**2 oil engines** gearing integral to driving 2 Z propellers Total Power: 2,352kW (3,198hp) 12.8kn Niigata 6L25CXE 2 x 4 Stroke 6 Cy. 250 x 320 each-1176kW (1599bhp) Niigata Engineering Co Ltd-Japan AuxGen: 2 x 92kW 415V 50Hz a.c Fuel: 52.0 (d.f.) 4.4pd
9095046 - -	**SEA JAGUAR** *ex* Camellia *-2007* *ex* Fujisan Maru No. 8 *-2000* - -	*149* 69 260		**1984**-05 **Kanbara Zosen K.K. — Onomichi** Yd No: 288 Loa 30.70 Br ex - Dght 2.650 Lbp 28.00 Br md 6.80 Dpth 2.90 Welded, 1 dk	**(A13B2TU) Tanker (unspecified)**	**1 oil engine** driving 1 Propeller Total Power: 221kW (300hp) Yanmar 1 x 4 Stroke 221kW (300bhp) Yanmar Diesel Engine Co Ltd-Japan
9369631 *C4UA2* -	**SEA JAGUAR** - **SFL Sea Jaguar Ltd** Deep Sea Supply Management (Singapore) Pte Ltd *Limassol* *Cyprus* MMSI: 212517000	**2,952** 885 2,273	Class: AB	**2007**-07 **Jaya Shipbuilding & Engineering Pte Ltd — Singapore** Yd No: 859 Loa 75.40 Br ex - Dght 6.080 Lbp 67.16 Br md 16.80 Dpth 7.50 Welded, 1 dk	**(B21B20A) Anchor Handling Tug Supply**	**2 oil engines** reduction geared to sc. shafts driving 2 CP propellers Total Power: 11,032kW (15,000hp) 14.0kn Wartsila 12V32 2 x Vee 4 Stroke 12 Cy. 320 x 400 each-5516kW (7500bhp) Wartsila Finland Oy-Finland AuxGen: 2 x 370kW 440V 60Hz a.c, 2 x 2300kW a.c Thrusters: 2 Thwart. CP thruster (f); 1 Thwart. CP thruster (a) Fuel: 1240.0
9209489 *HO3623* -	**SEA JAGUAR** *ex* Najade *-2004* **Seaport International Shipping Co Ltd** Seaport International Shipping Co LLC *Panama* *Panama* MMSI: 354762000 Official number: 3225507C	**172** 68 50	Class: (BV) (NV)	**1999**-07 **SBF Shipbuilders (1977) Pty Ltd — Fremantle WA** Yd No: 982 Loa 30.97 Br ex 6.82 Dght 1.680 Lbp 27.00 Br md 6.46 Dpth 1.70 Welded, 1 dk	**(A37B2PS) Passenger Ship** Passengers: unberthed: 184	**3 oil engines** reduction geared to sc. shafts driving 3 Water jets Total Power: 2,370kW (3,222hp) 30.0kn M.T.U. 12V2000M70 3 x Vee 4 Stroke 12 Cy. 130 x 150 each-790kW (1074bhp) MTU Friedrichshafen GmbH-Friedrichshafen AuxGen: 2 x 40kW 380V 50Hz a.c Fuel: 7.9 (d.f.)
7701079 *5NHU* -	**SEA JAGUAR I** *ex* Sea Jaguar *-1995* *ex* Sanyo *-1987* **Ship & Shore Services Ltd** - *Lagos* *Nigeria* Official number: 377391	**227** 69 108	Class: LR (BV) **100A1** SS 06/2012 tug Nigerian coastal service **LMC** Eq.Ltr: D; Cable: 250.0/22.0 U2	**1977**-03 **Kegoya Dock K.K. — Kure** Yd No: 752 Loa 31.72 Br ex 8.62 Dght 2.898 Lbp 29.72 Br md 8.60 Dpth 3.51 Welded, 1 dk	**(B32A2ST) Tug**	**2 oil engines** driving 2 Directional propellers Total Power: 1,912kW (2,600hp) 12.5kn Yanmar G250-ET 2 x 4 Stroke 6 Cy. 250 x 290 each-956kW (1300bhp) Yanmar Diesel Engine Co Ltd-Japan AuxGen: 2 x 66kW 100/445V 60Hz a.c Fuel: 35.0 (d.f.)
8654510 *9WGG9* -	**SEA JET 2** - **Joystar Capital Sdn Bhd** - *Kuching* *Malaysia* MMSI: 533036200 Official number: 330651	**135** 58 -	Class: MY	**2005**-05 **Far East Shipyard Co Sdn Bhd — Sibu** Yd No: FES/07/2005 Loa 41.00 Br ex - Dght - Lbp 37.55 Br md 4.22 Dpth 1.60 Welded, 1 dk	**(A37B2PS) Passenger Ship**	**2 oil engines** reduction geared to sc. shafts driving 2 Propellers Total Power: 1,598kW (2,172hp) Mitsubishi 2 x each-799kW (1086bhp) Mitsubishi Heavy Industries Ltd-Japan

9185085 SX6800 -
SEA JET 2
ex Mirage -1999
Sea Jet II Shipping Co
Seajets Catamaran Joint Venture
Piraeus — Greece
MMSI: 237006600
Official number: 10571
499 / 149 / 50
Class: LR (NV) **100A1** SS 03/2013 SSC passenger HSC G3 **LMC** **UMS**
1998-06 Batservice Holding AS — Mandal Yd No: 17
Loa 42.00 Br ex - Dght 1.863
Lbp 37.37 Br md 10.00 Dpth 4.07
Welded, 1 dk
(A37B2PS) Passenger Ship
Hull Material: Aluminium Alloy
Passengers: unberthed: 386
4 oil engines with clutches, flexible couplings & sr geared to sc. shafts driving 4 Water jets
Total Power: 7,000kW (9,516hp) 39.0kn
M.T.U. 12V396TE74
2 x Vee 4 Stroke 12 Cy. 165 x 185 each-1500kW (2039bhp)
MTU Friedrichshafen GmbH-Friedrichshafen
M.T.U. 16V396TE74L
2 x Vee 4 Stroke 16 Cy. 165 x 185 each-2000kW (2719bhp)
MTU Friedrichshafen GmbH-Friedrichshafen
AuxGen: 2 x 122kW 400V 50Hz a.c
Fuel: 15.2 (d.f.) 1.4pd

9607722 3EYU9 -
SEA JEWEL
Arab Maritime Petroleum Transport Co (AMPTC)
-
Panama — Panama
MMSI: 353221000
Official number: 44367PEXT
62,255 / 33,984 / 112,081
Class: AB
2013-03 Hyundai Heavy Industries Co Ltd — Ulsan Yd No: 2492
Loa 250.00 (BB) Br ex 44.03 Dght 14.700
Lbp 239.00 Br md 44.00 Dpth 21.00
Welded, 1 dk
(A13A2TW) Crude/Oil Products Tanker
Double Hull (13F)
Liq: 123,220; Liq (Oil): 123,220
Compartments: 6 Wing Ta, 6 Wing Ta, 1 Wing Slop Ta, 1 Slop Ta, 1 Wing Slop Ta, ER
3 Cargo Pump (s): 3x3000m³/hr
1 oil engine driving 1 FP propeller
Total Power: 14,280kW (19,415hp) 15.0kn
MAN-B&W 7S60MC-C8
1 x 2 Stroke 7 Cy. 600 x 2400 14280kW (19415bhp)
Hyundai Heavy Industries Co Ltd-South Korea
AuxGen: 3 x 850kW a.c
Fuel: 96.0 (d.f.) 3640.0 (r.f.)

8980256 - -
SEA JEWEL BRAVO
ex Time For Us -2013 ex Chevy Toy -2013
-
-
George Town — Cayman Islands (British)
251 / - / -
1999-01 Trinity Yachts LLC — New Orleans LA Yd No: 010
Loa 36.00 Br ex - Dght 1.800
Lbp - Br md 8.50 Dpth -
Welded, 1 dk
(X11A2YP) Yacht
Hull Material: Aluminium Alloy
2 oil engines geared to sc. shafts driving 2 Propellers
Total Power: 1,140kW (1,550hp) 14.5kn
Caterpillar 3412B
2 x Vee 4 Stroke 12 Cy. 137 x 152 each-570kW (775bhp)
Caterpillar Inc-USA
Thrusters: 1 Tunnel thruster (f)

9468499 3FF16 -
SEA JOY
ex Bandai III -2011
Perle Belle Marine SA
Kokuka Sangyo Co Ltd
SatCom: Inmarsat C 435561210
Panama — Panama
MMSI: 355612000
Official number: 4115110A
2,826 / 1,105 / 3,456 / T/cm 11.2
Class: BV
2009-12 Chongqing Chuandong Shipbuilding Industry Co Ltd — Chongqing Yd No: HT0115
Loa 91.22 (BB) Br ex - Dght 5.400
Lbp 87.00 Br md 15.00 Dpth 7.40
Welded, 1 dk
(A12A2TC) Chemical Tanker
Double Hull (13F)
Liq: 3,829
Cargo Heating Coils
Compartments: 10 Wing Ta, 2 Wing Slop Ta, ER
10 Cargo Pump (s): 10x150m³/hr
Manifold: Bow/CM: 50.8m
1 oil engine driving 1 FP propeller
Total Power: 2,426kW (3,298hp) 12.8kn
Hanshin LH41L
1 x 4 Stroke 6 Cy. 410 x 800 2426kW (3298bhp) (new engine 2009)
The Hanshin Diesel Works Ltd-Japan
AuxGen: 3 x 265kW 60Hz a.c
Fuel: 51.0 (d.f.) 194.0 (r.f.)

7725946 AVPY -
SEA JUMBO
ex Ios Jumbo -2012 ex Bourbon Trader -2004
ex Havila Trader -2003 ex Boa Trader -1998
ex Strathfarrar -1996 ex Stad Troll -1988
Hind Offshore Pvt Ltd
-
Mumbai — India
MMSI: 419000420
Official number: 3925
2,478 / 743 / 4,114
Class: IR NV
1979-05 Molde Verft AS — Hjelset (Hull) Yd No: (162)
1979-05 Ulstein Hatlo AS — Ulsteinvik Yd No: 162
Loa 80.77 Br ex 18.04 Dght 5.610
Lbp 76.21 Br md 18.01 Dpth 7.12
Welded, 2 dks
(B21A20S) Platform Supply Ship
Liq: 2,468
Compartments: 16 Ta, ER
2 oil engines geared to sc. shafts driving 2 CP propellers
Total Power: 3,384kW (4,600hp) 12.0kn
Nohab F212V
2 x Vee 4 Stroke 12 Cy. 250 x 300 each-1692kW (2300bhp)
AB Bofors NOHAB-Sweden
AuxGen: 2 x 808kW 450V 60Hz a.c, 1 x 250kW 450V 60Hz a.c, 1 x 125kW 450V 60Hz a.c
Thrusters: 2 Thwart. FP thruster (f); 1 Thwart. FP thruster (a)

7929657 9V5424 -
SEA KESTREL
ex Sea Rider -2001 ex Urakaze -1997
Tian San Shipping (Pte) Ltd
-
Singapore — Singapore
Official number: 387677
123 / 46 / 14
1979-12 K.K. Miho Zosensho — Osaka Yd No: 273
Loa 25.95 Br ex - Dght 0.960
Lbp 23.38 Br md 5.80 Dpth 2.60
Welded, 1 dk
(A37B2PS) Passenger Ship
Hull Material: Aluminium Alloy
Passengers: unberthed: 136
2 oil engines reduction geared to sc. shafts driving 2 FP propellers
Total Power: 810kW (1,102hp) 25.0kn
Maybach MB820BB
2 x Vee 4 Stroke 12 Cy. 175 x 205 each-405kW (551bhp)
Ikegai Tekkosho-Japan

9006459 ZCIW7 -
SEA KESTREL
ex Union Sapphire -2004 ex Hoo Kestrel -2003
Northern Coasters Ltd
Torbulk Ltd
SatCom: Inmarsat Mini-M 762102490
George Town — Cayman Islands (British)
MMSI: 319922000
Official number: 722234
1,382 / 794 / 2,225 / T/cm 8.0
Class: GL (LR) (BV)
Classed LR until 28/4/13
1993-04 Yorkshire D.D. Co. Ltd. — Hull Yd No: 328
Loa 77.80 (BB) Br ex 11.10 Dght 4.020
Lbp 72.30 Br md 11.00 Dpth 5.10
Welded, 1 dk
(A31A2GX) General Cargo Ship
Grain: 2,921; Bale: 2,810
Compartments: 2 Ho, ER
2 Ha: ER
2 oil engines with clutches, flexible couplings & dr geared to sc. shafts driving 2 Directional propellers
Total Power: 954kW (1,298hp) 10.0kn
Cummins KTA-19-M
2 x 4 Stroke 6 Cy. 159 x 159 each-477kW (649bhp)
Cummins Charleston Inc-USA
AuxGen: 3 x 52kW 415V 50Hz a.c
Fuel: 50.8 (d.f.) 4.1pd

8975744 WDB2250
SEA KING
Thoa Nguyen
-
New Orleans, LA — United States of America
MMSI: 366873920
Official number: 1128473
201 / - / -
2001 Master Boat Builders, Inc. — Coden, Al Yd No: 331
L reg 27.27 Br ex - Dght -
Lbp - Br md 8.20 Dpth 4.10
Welded, 1 dk
(B11B2FV) Fishing Vessel
1 oil engine driving 1 Propeller

7947439 WDC2201 -
SEA KING
ex Daddys Dream -2005
Ronald Yow
-
Mayport, FL — United States of America
MMSI: 366989420
Official number: 609677
172 / 116 / -
1979 Master Boat Builders, Inc. — Coden, Al Yd No: 3
L reg 26.89 Br ex 7.47 Dght -
Lbp - Br md - Dpth 3.51
Welded, 1 dk
(B11B2FV) Fishing Vessel
1 oil engine driving 1 FP propeller
Total Power: 515kW (700hp)

7936454 - -
SEA KING
ex Kosei Maru No. 18 -2003 ex East Star -2000
ex Sea Dragon No. 58 -2000
ex Tsuiki Maru No. 58 -1998
ex Taisei Maru No. 18 -1997
ex Kofuku Maru No. 58 -1989
ex Daiyu Maru No. 3 -1987
ex Mikasa Maru No. 3 -1983
Cargo Shipping Co Ltd
Marusan Hokuyo Suisan YK
298 / 89 / -
1980-04 Tonoura Dock Co. Ltd. — Miyazaki Yd No: 5
Loa 37.80 Br ex 7.12 Dght 2.450
Lbp 32.31 Br md 6.80 Dpth 2.75
Welded, 1 dk
(B11B2FV) Fishing Vessel
1 oil engine driving 1 FP propeller
Total Power: 346kW (470hp)
Otsuka SODHS6S26
1 x 4 Stroke 6 Cy. 260 x 410 346kW (470bhp)
KK Otsuka Diesel-Japan

8034423 - -
SEA KING
-
-
105 / 71 / -
1981 Steiner Shipyard, Inc. — Bayou La Batre, Al
Loa 22.81 Br ex - Dght 2.401
Lbp 20.12 Br md 6.71 Dpth 3.36
Welded, 1 dk
(B11A2FT) Trawler
1 oil engine reduction geared to sc. shaft driving 1 FP propeller
Total Power: 268kW (364hp)
Cummins KT-1150-M
1 x 4 Stroke 6 Cy. 159 x 159 268kW (364bhp)
Cummins Engine Co Inc-USA

8119211 9LB2288 -
SEA KING
ex Cambridge Service -2010
Ships & Boats Oil Services
Blue Marine Shipping Services Co
Freetown — Sierra Leone
MMSI: 667209900
Official number: SL102099
1,021 / 306 / 987
Class: BV (LR) (AB)
✠ Classed LR until 30/10/97
1983-01 Clelands Shipbuilders Ltd. — Wallsend Yd No: 359
Loa 60.03 Br ex 13.06 Dght 4.490
Lbp 53.57 Br md 12.81 Dpth 5.36
Welded, 1 dk
(B21B20A) Anchor Handling Tug Supply
2 oil engines with clutches, flexible couplings & sr geared to sc. shafts driving 2 CP propellers
Total Power: 3,108kW (4,226hp) 12.5kn
Mirrlees 6MB275
2 x 4 Stroke 6 Cy. 275 x 305 each-1554kW (2113bhp)
Mirrlees Blackstone (Stockport)Ltd.-Stockport
AuxGen: 2 x 500kW 440V 60Hz a.c, 1 x 250kW 440V 60Hz a.c
Thrusters: 1 Thwart. CP thruster (f)
Fuel: 198.0 (d.f.) 10.0pd

7734430 WYL9552 -
SEA KING
ex Sea Crest II -2010
TJM LLC
-
Boston, MA — United States of America
MMSI: 366835940
Official number: 586970
111 / 76 / -
1977 Steiner Shipyard, Inc. — Bayou La Batre, Al
L reg 20.46 Br ex - Dght -
Lbp - Br md 6.71 Dpth 3.43
Welded, 1 dk
(B11B2FV) Fishing Vessel
1 oil engine driving 1 FP propeller
Total Power: 268kW (364hp)
Caterpillar 3406TA
1 x 4 Stroke 6 Cy. 137 x 165 268kW (364bhp)
Caterpillar Tractor Co-USA

9326641 V7OC7 -
SEA KING
Sea King Shipholding SA
Perosea Shipping Co SA
Majuro — Marshall Islands
MMSI: 538003060
Official number: 3060
8,503 / 4,173 / 13,105 / T/cm 23.2
Class: BV (AB)
2008-02 21st Century Shipbuilding Co Ltd — Tongyeong Yd No: 222
Loa 128.60 (BB) Br ex - Dght 8.700
Lbp 120.40 Br md 20.40 Dpth 11.50
Welded, 1 dk
(A12B2TR) Chemical/Products Tanker
Double Hull (13F)
Liq: 13,402; Liq (Oil): 13,402
Cargo Heating Coils
Compartments: 12 Wing Ta, ER, 1 Wing Slop Ta
12 Cargo Pump (s): 12x300m³/hr
Manifold: Bow/CM: 61.4m
1 oil engine driving 1 FP propeller
Total Power: 4,440kW (6,037hp) 13.5kn
MAN-B&W 6S35MC
1 x 2 Stroke 6 Cy. 350 x 1400 4440kW (6037bhp)
STX Engine Co Ltd-South Korea
AuxGen: 3 x 550kW a.c
Thrusters: 1 Tunnel thruster (f)
Fuel: 74.0 (d.f.) 644.0 (r.f.)

Number / Call sign	Name / Owner / Port	Tonnage	Class	Built	Type	Machinery
8305602 - -	**SEA KING I** **Sea King I Inc** - *Brownsville, TX* *United States of America* Official number: 649985	*104* 94 -		**1982-07 Marine Mart, Inc. — Port Isabel, Tx** Yd No: 223 Loa - Br ex 6.10 Dght - Lbp 21.34 Br md - Dpth 3.66 Welded, 1 dk	**(B11A2FS) Stern Trawler** Compartments: 1 Ho, ER 1 Ha: ER	**1 oil engine** sr geared to sc. shaft driving 1 FP propeller Total Power: 268kW (364hp) Caterpillar 3408TA 1 x Vee 4 Stroke 8 Cy. 137 x 152 268kW (364bhp) Caterpillar Tractor Co-USA
7201524 *5IM612* -	**SEA KING VI** *ex* Sea King V *-2013* *ex* Family Rose Philomene *-2009* *ex* Gallant Man *-2009* **Yoruma Shipping Co SA** - *Zanzibar* *Tanzania (Zanzibar)* MMSI: 677051200 Official number: 300357	**374** 254 -		**1963 Patterson Shipyard Inc. — Patterson, La** Loa 47.50 Br ex 8.54 Dght - Lbp - Br md 8.50 Dpth 3.20 Welded, 1 dk	**(B11B2FV) Fishing Vessel**	**1 oil engine** driving 1 FP propeller Total Power: 809kW (1,100hp)
9375393 *3EPZ5* -	**SEA KIOWA** **GulfMark Offshore Inc** - *Panama* *Panama* MMSI: 352009000 Official number: 3414008	**2,943** 883 2,693	Class: AB	**2008-03 Keppel Singmarine Pte Ltd — Singapore** Yd No: 312 Loa 76.00 Br ex - Dght 6.200 Lbp 68.40 Br md 17.00 Dpth 7.60 Welded, 1 dk	**(B21B20A) Anchor Handling Tug Supply**	**4 oil engines** driving 1 gen. of 550kW a.c 1 gen. of 550kW a.c 1 gen. of 550kW a.c reduction geared to sc. shafts driving 2 CP propellers Total Power: 7,920kW (10,768hp) 14.0kn MaK 6M25 4 x 4 Stroke 6 Cy. 255 x 400 each-1980kW (2692bhp) Caterpillar Motoren GmbH & Co. KG-Germany AuxGen: 3 x a.c Thrusters: 1 Tunnel thruster (f); 1 Tunnel thruster (a); 1 Retract. directional thruster (f) Fuel: 1250.0 (d.f.)
8744494 *9V5598* -	**SEA KITE** **Tian San Shipping (Pte) Ltd** - *Singapore* *Singapore* Official number: 388171	**146** - -		**1985-04 K.K. Miho Zosensho — Osaka** Yd No: 300 Loa 28.12 Br ex - Dght - Lbp - Br md 5.90 Dpth - Welded, 1 dk	**(A37B2PS) Passenger Ship** Hull Material: Aluminium Alloy	**2 oil engines** reduction geared to sc. shafts driving 2 Propellers Total Power: 1,470kW (1,998hp)
7900754 *DUA6393* -	**SEA KNIGHT** *ex* Ming Hai *-1999* *ex* Shofuku Maru No. 35 *-1997* *ex* Kaiun Maru No. 35 *-1984* **Royale Fishing Corp** - *Manila* *Philippines* Official number: MNLD010319	*149* 79 200		**1979-05 Nagasaki Zosen K.K. — Nagasaki** Yd No: 683 Loa 36.00 Br ex 6.84 Dght 2.352 Lbp 33.02 Br md 6.80 Dpth 2.77 Welded, 1 dk	**(B12B2FC) Fish Carrier**	**1 oil engine** driving 1 FP propeller Total Power: 662kW (900hp) Hanshin 6LU28G 1 x 4 Stroke 6 Cy. 280 x 440 662kW (900bhp) The Hanshin Diesel Works Ltd-Japan
8855920 - -	**SEA KNIGHT '88** **BEV Processors Inc** - *Georgetown* *Guyana* Official number: 0000256	*112* 76 -		**1988 Steiner Shipyard, Inc. — Bayou La Batre, Al** Loa - Br ex - Dght - Lbp 19.75 Br md 6.71 Dpth 3.23 Welded, 1 dk	**(B11B2FV) Fishing Vessel**	**1 oil engine** driving 1 FP propeller
9189811 *9V5627* -	**SEA LABRADOR** **PSA Marine Pte Ltd** - *Singapore* *Singapore* MMSI: 564628000 Official number: 388250	**298** 89 200	Class: BV	**1998-07 Matsuura Tekko Zosen K.K. — Osakikamijima** Yd No: 508 Loa 31.00 Br ex - Dght 3.950 Lbp 25.50 Br md 9.50 Dpth 4.95 Welded, 1 dk	**(B32A2ST) Tug**	**2 oil engines** gearing integral to driving 2 Z propellers Total Power: 2,942kW (4,000hp) 13.0kn Yanmar 6N260-EN 2 x 4 Stroke 6 Cy. 260 x 360 each-1471kW (2000bhp) Yanmar Diesel Engine Co Ltd-Japan
8505692 *MNFC5* TN 20	**SEA LADY** *ex* Lady T Emiel *-2010* *ex* Andrea *-2000* *ex* Fokke Grietje *-1991* **TN Trawlers Ltd** - *Troon* *United Kingdom* MMSI: 235000340 Official number: B12151	**239** 72 101	Class: (GL)	**1986-01 Scheepswerf en Constructiebedrijf Marcon — Hoogezand** Yd No: 3/110 Loa 32.87 Br ex - Dght - Lbp - Br md 7.31 Dpth 3.81 Welded, 1 dk	**(B11B2FV) Fishing Vessel**	**1 oil engine** with clutches, flexible couplings & sr reverse geared to sc. shaft driving 1 FP propeller Total Power: 588kW (799hp) 10.8kn Mitsubishi S6U-MPTK 1 x 4 Stroke 6 Cy. 240 x 260 588kW (799bhp) Mitsubishi Heavy Industries Ltd-Japan AuxGen: 1 x 96kW 380V a.c, 2 x 76kW 380V a.c Fuel: 63.0 (d.f.)
7417214 *SSIS*	**SEA LADY** *ex* MISR GULF III *-2011* *ex* Abu El Hool 5 *-1999* *ex* Chap *-1995* *ex* Chap Tide *-1989* **Ships & Boats Oil Services** - *Alexandria* *Egypt*	**920** 180 -	Class: BV (AB)	**1976-06 Halter Marine, Inc. — Moss Point, Ms** Yd No: 484 Loa - Br ex - Dght 4.496 Lbp 54.77 Br md 12.20 Dpth 5.21 Welded, 1 dk	**(B21B20T) Offshore Tug/Supply Ship**	**2 oil engines** reverse reduction geared to sc. shafts driving 2 FP propellers Total Power: 3,162kW (4,300hp) 14.0kn EMD (Electro-Motive) 12-645-E5 2 x Vee 2 Stroke 12 Cy. 230 x 254 each-1581kW (2150bhp) General Motors Corp.Electro-Motive Div.-La Grange AuxGen: 2 x 150kW Thrusters: 1 Thwart. FP thruster (f)
9259599 *MBBU8* -	**SEA LADY** **Blenheim Shipping UK Ltd** - SatCom: Inmarsat B 323572810 *Douglas* *Isle of Man (British)* MMSI: 235728000 Official number: 736396	**56,204** 32,082 105,611 T/cm 89.2	Class: LR ✠ **100A1** SS 05/2013 Double Hull oil tanker ESP LI *IWS **ShipRight** (SDA, FDA, CM) ✠ **LMC** **UMS** Eq.Ltr: R†; Cable: 692.6/84.0 U3 (a)	**2003-08 Sumitomo Heavy Industries Marine & Engineering Co., Ltd. — Yokosuka** Yd No: 1295 Loa 239.00 (BB) Br ex 42.03 Dght 14.878 Lbp 229.00 Br md 42.00 Dpth 21.30 Welded, 1 dk	**(A13A2TV) Crude Oil Tanker** Double Hull (13F) Liq: 115,572; Liq (Oil): 115,572 Compartments: 12 Wing Ta, 2 Wing Slop Ta, ER 3 Cargo Pump (s): 3x2500m³/hr Manifold: Bow/CM: 117.9m	**1 oil engine** driving 1 FP propeller Total Power: 12,000kW (16,315hp) 14.9kn Wartsila 6RT-flex58T 1 x 2 Stroke 6 Cy. 580 x 2416 12000kW (16315bhp) Diesel United Ltd.-Aioi AuxGen: 3 x 720kW 450V 60Hz a.c Boilers: e (ex.g.) 22.0kgf/cm² (21.6bar), WTAuxB (o.f.) 18.0kgf/cm² (17.7bar) Fuel: 261.0 (d.f.) 2792.0 (r.f.)
9266188 *V7XH9* -	**SEA LADY** *ex* Free Lady *-2011* *ex* Snow Falcon *-2008* **Sea Lady Shipping & Trading SA** Genimar Shipping & Trading SA SatCom: Inmarsat C 453836888 *Majuro* *Marshall Islands* MMSI: 538004485 Official number: 4485	**27,986** 17,077 50,246 T/cm 53.3	Class: BV (NK)	**2003-04 Mitsui Eng. & SB. Co. Ltd. — Tamano** Yd No: 1572 Loa 189.80 (BB) Br ex - Dght 11.925 Lbp 181.00 Br md 32.26 Dpth 16.90 Welded, 1 dk	**(A21A2BC) Bulk Carrier** Double Bottom Entire Compartment Length Grain: 63,198; Bale: 60,713 Compartments: 5 Ho, ER 5 Ha: 4 (20.2 x 18.0)ER (17.6 x 18.0) Cranes: 4x30.5t	**1 oil engine** driving 1 FP propeller Total Power: 8,090kW (10,999hp) 14.5kn B&W 6S50MC-C 1 x 2 Stroke 6 Cy. 500 x 2000 8090kW (10999bhp) Mitsui Engineering & Shipbuilding CLtd-Japan AuxGen: 3 x 480kW 450V 60Hz a.c Fuel: 113.0 (d.f.) 1883.0 (r.f.)
8208749 *OXRB* -	**SEA LAND** *ex* Anguteq Ittuk *-2006* **Royal Arctic Bygdeservice AS** - *Nuuk* *Denmark* Official number: D2875	**375** 150 240	Class: NV	**1983-07 Marstal Staalskibsvaerft og Maskinfabrik A/S — Marstal** Yd No: 103 Loa 32.72 Br ex - Dght 3.310 Lbp 30.15 Br md 9.52 Dpth 4.20 Welded, 1 dk	**(A32A2GF) General Cargo/Passenger Ship** Compartments: 3 Ho, ER 3 Ha: (8.6 x 6.3)2 (3.1 x 2.5) Derricks: 1x7t; Winches: 1 Ice Capable	**1 oil engine** driving 1 CP propeller Total Power: 324kW (441hp) Alpha 404-26VO 1 x 2 Stroke 4 Cy. 260 x 400 324kW (441bhp) B&W Alpha Diesel A/S-Denmark
9106170 *VRMD7* -	**SEA-LAND CHAMPION** **Maersk Shipping Hong Kong Ltd** The Maersk Co Ltd *Hong Kong* *Hong Kong* MMSI: 477004400 Official number: HK-3845	**49,985** 28,968 59,840 T/cm 79.7	Class: AB	**1995-06 Ishikawajima-Harima Heavy Industries Co Ltd (IHI) — Chita AI** Yd No: 3055 Loa 292.15 (BB) Br ex - Dght 13.028 Lbp 273.00 Br md 32.20 Dpth 21.20 Welded, 1 dk	**(A33A2CC) Container Ship (Fully Cellular)** TEU 4082 C Ho 1961 TEU C Dk 2121 TEU incl 350 ref C. Compartments: ER, 8 Cell Ho 34 Ha: ER	**1 oil engine** driving 1 FP propeller Total Power: 36,476kW (49,593hp) 24.0kn Sulzer 9RTA84C 1 x 2 Stroke 9 Cy. 840 x 2400 36476kW (49593bhp) Diesel United Ltd.-Aioi AuxGen: 3 x 2200kW a.c Fuel: 6307.0 (r.f.)
9143001 *WDB9948* -	**SEA-LAND CHARGER** **Maersk Line Ltd** - *Norfolk, VA* *United States of America* MMSI: 303279000 Official number: 1163273	**49,985** 28,968 59,961 T/cm 79.7	Class: AB	**1997-03 Ishikawajima-Harima Heavy Industries Co Ltd (IHI) — Kure** Yd No: 3077 Loa 292.15 (BB) Br ex - Dght 13.028 Lbp 273.00 Br md 32.20 Dpth 21.20 Welded, 1 dk	**(A33A2CC) Container Ship (Fully Cellular)** TEU 4082 C Ho 1961 TEU C Dk 2121 TEU incl 350 ref C. Compartments: ER, 8 Cell Ho 17 Ha: ER	**1 oil engine** driving 1 FP propeller Total Power: 36,470kW (49,585hp) 24.0kn Sulzer 9RTA84C 1 x 2 Stroke 9 Cy. 840 x 2400 36470kW (49585bhp) Diesel United Ltd.-Aioi AuxGen: 3 x 2200kW 440V 50Hz a.c Fuel: 5729.0 (r.f.) (Heating Coils)

IMO / Call sign	Name / Owner / Manager	Tonnage	Class	Builder / Dimensions	Type / Cargo	Machinery
9106182 WDB9950 -	**SEA-LAND COMET** - **Maersk Line Ltd** *Norfolk, VA* *United States of America* MMSI: 338420000 Official number: 1163271	**49,985** 28,968 59,840 T/cm 79.7	Class: AB	**1995-10 Ishikawajima-Harima Heavy Industries Co Ltd (IHI) — Chita AI** Yd No: 3056 Loa 292.15 (BB) Br ex - Dght 13.028 Lbp 273.00 Br md 32.20 Dpth 21.20 Welded, 1 dk	**(A33A2CC) Container Ship (Fully Cellular)** TEU 4082 C Ho 1961 TEU C Dk 2121 TEU incl 350 ref C. Compartments: ER, 8 Cell Ho 34 Ha: ER	**1 oil engine** driving 1 FP propeller Total Power: 36,476kW (49,593hp) 24.0kn Sulzer 9RTA84C 1 x 2 Stroke 9 Cy. 840 x 2400 36476kW (49593bhp) Diesel United Ltd.-Aioi AuxGen: 3 x 2200kW a.c Fuel: 5828.0 (r.f.)
9143013 VRMD9 -	**SEA LAND EAGLE** - **Maersk Shipping Hong Kong Ltd** Maersk Line Ltd *Hong Kong* *Hong Kong* MMSI: 477195300 Official number: HK-3847	**49,985** 28,968 59,840 T/cm 79.8	Class: AB	**1997-06 Ishikawajima-Harima Heavy Industries Co Ltd (IHI) — Kure** Yd No: 3078 Loa 292.15 (BB) Br ex - Dght 13.000 Lbp 274.41 Br md 32.20 Dpth 21.20 Welded, 1 dk	**(A33A2CC) Container Ship (Fully Cellular)** TEU 4082 C Ho 1961 TEU C Dk 2121 TEU incl 350 ref C. Compartments: ER, 8 Cell Ho 17 Ha: ER	**1 oil engine** driving 1 FP propeller Total Power: 36,470kW (49,585hp) 24.0kn Sulzer 9RTA84C 1 x 2 Stroke 9 Cy. 840 x 2400 36470kW (49585bhp) Diesel United Ltd.-Aioi AuxGen: 3 x 2200kW 440V 60Hz a.c Fuel: 413.6 (d.f.) 5315.3 (r.f.) 150.0pd
5127657 - -	**SEA LAND EXPRESS** *ex* Caribbean Queens *-1995* *ex* General *-1993* **Caribbean Queens Inc** -	*499* 301 -	Class: (AB)	**1925-12 Bethlehem Steel Co. — San Francisco, Ca** Yd No: 5327 Converted From: Products Tank Barge, Non-propelled-1957 Loa 53.80 Br ex 9.81 Dght 3.709 Lbp 51.82 Br md 9.76 Dpth 4.27 Riveted, 1 dk	**(A31A2GX) General Cargo Ship**	**2 diesel electric oil engines** Connecting to 1 elec. Motor driving 1 FP propeller Total Power: 368kW (500hp) Imperial 2 x 4 Stroke 6 Cy. 292 x 381 each-184kW (250bhp) Atlas Imperial Diesel Engine Co-USA Fuel: 17.5
9143025 WDB9949 -	**SEA-LAND INTREPID** *ex* CSX Intrepid *-2000* *ex* Sea-Land Intrepid *-2000* **Maersk Line Ltd** - *Norfolk, VA* *United States of America* MMSI: 366882000 Official number: 1163268	**49,985** 28,968 59,840 T/cm 79.8	Class: AB	**1997-08 Ishikawajima-Harima Heavy Industries Co Ltd (IHI) — Kure** Yd No: 3079 Loa 292.15 (BB) Br ex - Dght 13.000 Lbp 273.00 Br md 32.20 Dpth 21.20 Welded, 1 dk	**(A33A2CC) Container Ship (Fully Cellular)** TEU 4082 C Ho 1961 TEU C Dk 2121 TEU incl 350 ref C. Compartments: ER, 8 Cell Ho 17 Ha: ER	**1 oil engine** driving 1 FP propeller Total Power: 36,470kW (49,585hp) 24.0kn Sulzer 9RTA84C 1 x 2 Stroke 9 Cy. 840 x 2400 36470kW (49585bhp) Diesel United Ltd.-Aioi AuxGen: 3 x 2200kW 440V 60Hz a.c Fuel: 413.6 (d.f.) 5315.3 (r.f.) 150.0pd
9143037 WDB9986 -	**SEA-LAND LIGHTNING** - **Maersk Line Ltd** *Norfolk, VA* *United States of America* MMSI: 303316000 Official number: 1163272	**49,985** 28,968 59,840 T/cm 79.8	Class: AB	**1997-09 Ishikawajima-Harima Heavy Industries Co Ltd (IHI) — Kure** Yd No: 3080 Loa 292.15 (BB) Br ex - Dght 13.000 Lbp 273.00 Br md 32.20 Dpth 21.20 Welded, 1 dk	**(A33A2CC) Container Ship (Fully Cellular)** TEU 4082 C Ho 1961 TEU C Dk 2121 TEU incl 350 ref C. Compartments: ER, 8 Cell Ho 17 Ha: ER	**1 oil engine** driving 1 FP propeller Total Power: 36,470kW (49,585hp) 24.0kn Sulzer 9RTA84C 1 x 2 Stroke 9 Cy. 840 x 2400 36470kW (49585bhp) Diesel United Ltd.-Aioi AuxGen: 3 x 2200kW 440V 60Hz a.c Fuel: 413.6 (d.f.) 5315.3 (r.f.) 150.0pd
9106194 VRMD8 -	**SEA LAND MERCURY** *ex* CSX Mercury *-2000* *ex* Sea-Land Mercury *-2000* **Maersk Shipping Hong Kong Ltd** Maersk Line Ltd *Hong Kong* *Hong Kong* MMSI: 477195400 Official number: HK-3846	**49,985** 28,968 59,961 T/cm 79.7	Class: AB	**1995-11 Ishikawajima-Harima Heavy Industries Co Ltd (IHI) — Kure** Yd No: 3057 Loa 292.15 (BB) Br ex - Dght 13.028 Lbp 273.00 Br md 32.20 Dpth 21.20 Welded, 1 dk	**(A33A2CC) Container Ship (Fully Cellular)** TEU 4082 C Ho 1961 TEU C Dk 2121 TEU incl 350 ref C. Compartments: ER, 8 Cell Ho 34 Ha: ER	**1 oil engine** driving 1 FP propeller Total Power: 36,470kW (49,585hp) 24.0kn Sulzer 9RTA84C 1 x 2 Stroke 9 Cy. 840 x 2400 36470kW (49585bhp) Diesel United Ltd.-Aioi AuxGen: 3 x 2200kW 450V a.c Fuel: 321.8 (d.f.) 5828.0 (r.f.) 148.0pd
9106209 VRMD6 -	**SEA-LAND METEOR** - **Maersk Shipping Hong Kong Ltd** A P Moller - Maersk A/S *Hong Kong* *Hong Kong* MMSI: 477004500 Official number: HK-3844	**49,985** 28,968 59,940 T/cm 79.7	Class: AB	**1996-01 Ishikawajima-Harima Heavy Industries Co Ltd (IHI) — Chita AI** Yd No: 3058 Loa 292.15 (BB) Br ex - Dght 13.028 Lbp 273.00 Br md 32.20 Dpth 21.20 Welded, 1 dk	**(A33A2CC) Container Ship (Fully Cellular)** TEU 4082 C Ho 1961 TEU C Dk 2121 TEU incl 350 ref C. Compartments: ER, 8 Cell Ho 34 Ha: ER	**1 oil engine** driving 1 FP propeller Total Power: 36,476kW (49,593hp) 24.0kn Sulzer 9RTA84C 1 x 2 Stroke 9 Cy. 840 x 2400 36476kW (49593bhp) Diesel United Ltd.-Aioi AuxGen: 3 x 2200kW a.c Fuel: 5729.0 (r.f.)
7820899 - -	**SEA-LAND PATRIOT** - **US Bank National Association** Maersk Line Ltd	**32,629** 13,998 36,277	Class: (AB)	**1980-01 Mitsubishi Heavy Industries Ltd. — Kobe** Yd No: 1106 **1985 Mitsubishi Heavy Industries Ltd. — Hiroshima** (Additional cargo section) Lengthened-1985 Loa 257.51 (BB) Br ex 30.69 Dght 11.000 Lbp 243.49 Br md 30.61 Dpth 16.51 Welded, 1 dk	**(A33A2CC) Container Ship (Fully Cellular)** TEU 2816 incl 261 ref C. Compartments: ER 14 Ha: (14.2 x 8.0)ER 13 (12.6 x 8.0) 24 Wing Ha: 2 (14.2 x 8.1)18 (12.6 x 8.1)4 (12.6 x 5.5)	**1 oil engine** driving 1 FP propeller Total Power: 22,175kW (30,149hp) 20.7kn Sulzer 9RND90M 1 x 2 Stroke 9 Cy. 900 x 1550 22175kW (30149bhp) Mitsubishi Heavy Industries Ltd-Japan AuxGen: 2 x 1300kW 450V 60Hz a.c, 1 x 900kW 450V 60Hz a.c, 1 x 650kW 450V 60Hz a.c, 1 x 240kW 450V 60Hz a.c Fuel: 615.0 (d.f.) 3477.5 (r.f.) 76.0pd
9116890 VRME2 -	**SEA-LAND RACER** *ex* MSC Everest *-2009* *ex* Sea-Land Racer *-2007* **Maersk Shipping Hong Kong Ltd** Maersk Line Ltd *Hong Kong* *Hong Kong* MMSI: 477195200 Official number: HK-3848	**49,985** 28,968 59,964 T/cm 79.7	Class: AB	**1996-02 Ishikawajima-Harima Heavy Industries Co Ltd (IHI) — Kure** Yd No: 3059 Loa 292.15 (BB) Br ex 32.26 Dght 13.027 Lbp 273.00 Br md 32.20 Dpth 21.20 Welded, 1 dk	**(A33A2CC) Container Ship (Fully Cellular)** TEU 4082 C Ho 1961 TEU C Dk 2121 TEU incl 350 ref C. Compartments: ER, 8 Cell Ho 17 Ha: ER	**1 oil engine** driving 1 FP propeller Total Power: 32,820kW (44,622hp) 24.4kn Sulzer 9RTA84C 1 x 2 Stroke 9 Cy. 840 x 2400 32820kW (44622bhp) Diesel United Ltd.-Aioi AuxGen: 3 x 2200kW 440V 60Hz a.c Fuel: 414.0 (d.f.) (Heating Coils) 5315.0 (r.f.) 145.0pd
8836285 - -	**SEA LANDER** *ex* Beachcomber I *-2011* *ex* F 33 *-1989* **Al Jazeera Shipping Co WLL (AJS)** - *Bahrain* *Bahrain* Official number: 6280	**147** 44 -	Class: AB	**1976 Kanrei Zosen K.K. — Tokushima** (Hull) **1976 Mitsui Ocean Development & Eng. Co. Ltd. — Japan** Yd No: S-073 Converted From: Landing Craft-1989 Loa 29.93 Br ex - Dght 1.794 Lbp 29.24 Br md 8.02 Dpth 2.50 Welded, 1 dk	**(B34P2QV) Salvage Ship**	**3 oil engines** reverse reduction geared to sc. shafts driving 3 FP propellers Total Power: 531kW (723hp) 10.0kn G.M. (Detroit Diesel) 8V-71 3 x Vee 2 Stroke 8 Cy. 108 x 127 each-177kW (241bhp) Detroit Diesel Corporation-Detroit, Mi AuxGen: 1 x 9kW a.c, 3 x 5kW a.c
9287156 VRAN4 -	**SEA LANTANA** - **NCN Corp** COSCO Bulk Carrier Co Ltd (COSCO BULK) *Hong Kong* *Hong Kong* MMSI: 477720100 Official number: HK-1424	**30,081** 17,927 52,471 T/cm 55.5	Class: AB	**2004-11 Tsuneishi Corp — Tadotsu KG** Yd No: 1274 Loa 190.00 (BB) Br ex - Dght 12.000 Lbp 182.00 Br md 32.26 Dpth 17.00 Welded, 1 dk	**(A21A2BC) Bulk Carrier** Grain: 67,756; Bale: 65,600 Compartments: 5 Ho, ER 5 Ha: ER Cranes: 4x30t	**1 oil engine** driving 1 FP propeller Total Power: 7,800kW (10,605hp) 14.5kn B&W 6S50MC 1 x 2 Stroke 6 Cy. 500 x 1910 7800kW (10605bhp) Mitsui Engineering & Shipbuilding CLtd-Japan AuxGen: 3 x 440kW a.c Fuel: 199.0 (d.f.) 2387.0 (r.f.)
8417974 9HX08 -	**SEA LARK** *ex* Sider Lark *-2010* *ex* Lark *-2005* *ex* Diana I *-2001* *ex* Sea Dian *-1997* *ex* Princess Dian *-1996* **Foxtrot Navigation Inc** Silo Management SA *Valletta* *Malta* MMSI: 256567000 Official number: 8417974	**12,368** 7,621 21,520	Class: PR (BV) (NK)	**1985-05 Watanabe Zosen KK — Imabari EH** Yd No: 232 Loa 151.95 (BB) Br ex - Dght 9.689 Lbp 142.32 Br md 24.01 Dpth 13.21 Welded, 1 dk	**(A21A2BC) Bulk Carrier** Grain: 28,300; Bale: 27,000 Compartments: 4 Ho, ER 4 Ha: (17.6 x 12.7)3 (20.0 x 12.7)ER Cranes: 3x50t; Derricks: 1x25t	**1 oil engine** driving 1 FP propeller Total Power: 4,670kW (6,349hp) 13.0kn B&W 5L50MC 1 x 2 Stroke 5 Cy. 500 x 1620 4670kW (6349bhp) Kawasaki Heavy Industries Ltd-Japan
8333180 WYP6844 -	**SEA LARK** *ex* Port Blakely *-1997* *ex* Pocahontas (YTB 266) *-1976* **Sea Lark Inc** - *San Francisco, CA* *United States of America* Official number: 548701	*196* 60 -	Class: (AB)	**1942 Birchfield Boiler, Inc. — Tacoma, Wa** Yd No: 2 Loa - Br ex - Dght - Lbp 28.73 Br md 7.62 Dpth 4.12 Welded, 1 dk	**(B32A2ST) Tug**	**1 oil engine** driving 1 FP propeller Total Power: 1,471kW (2,000hp) Enterprise 1 x 4 Stroke 8 Cy. 400 x 508 1471kW (2000bhp) Enterprise Engine & Foundry Co-USA
9133812 ELUH7 -	**SEA LAUNCH COMMANDER** - **Sea Launch ACS Ltd** Barber Moss Ship Management AS SatCom: Inmarsat B 363666910 *Monrovia* *Liberia* MMSI: 636010677 Official number: 10677	**50,023** 15,007 10,430	Class: NV	**1997-12 Kvaerner Govan Ltd — Glasgow** Yd No: 312 Loa 203.40 (BB) Br ex 32.29 Dght 8.250 Lbp 182.60 Br md 32.26 Dpth 26.00 Welded, 1 dk	**(B31A2SR) Research Survey Vessel** Stern door Len: 8.50 Wid: 11.00 Swl: - Stern ramp Len: 48.00 Wid: 8.00 Swl: 190 Side door/ramp (p) Len: 5.80 Wid: 3.00 Swl: 5 Ice Capable	**2 oil engines** with clutches, flexible couplings & sr geared to sc. shaft driving 1 CP propeller Total Power: 15,600kW (21,210hp) 19.6kn Wartsila 8L46B 2 x 4 Stroke 8 Cy. 460 x 580 each-7800kW (10605bhp) Wartsila Diesel Oy-Finland AuxGen: 2 x 5000kW 380/600V 50Hz a.c, 4 x 1220kW 380/600V 50Hz a.c Thrusters: 2 Thwart. FP thruster (f); 1 Retract. directional thruster (a) Fuel: 3931.0 (d.f.) 75.0pd

9254989 9HJH7 -
SEA LAVENDER
Prose Shipping Ltd
Eastern Mediterranean Maritime Ltd
Valletta *Malta*
MMSI: 215295000
Official number: 7908
27,989 17,077 50,341 T/cm 53.5
Class: BV (NK)
2002-09 Kawasaki Heavy Industries Ltd — Kobe HG Yd No: 1528
Loa 189.80 Br ex - Dght 11.925
Lbp 181.00 Br md 32.26 Dpth 16.90
Welded, 1 dk
(A21A2BC) Bulk Carrier
Grain: 63,198; Bale: 60,713
Compartments: 5 Ho, ER
5 Ha: 4 (20.2 x 18.0)ER (17.6 x 18.0)
Cranes: 4x30.5t
1 oil engine driving 1 FP propeller
Total Power: 8,090kW (10,999hp) 14.0kn
B&W 6S50MC-C
1 x 2 Stroke 6 Cy. 500 x 2000 8090kW (10999bhp)
Kawasaki Heavy Industries Ltd-Japan

9381744 3FOY9 -
SEA LEGEND
Arab Maritime Petroleum Transport Co (AMPTC)
SatCom: Inmarsat C 437085811
Panama *Panama*
MMSI: 370858000
Official number: 4012209
62,629 33,875 112,511 T/cm 98.5
Class: AB
2008-12 Hyundai Heavy Industries Co Ltd — Ulsan Yd No: 1902
Loa 249.97 (BB) Br ex - Dght 14.621
Lbp 239.00 Br md 44.00 Dpth 21.00
Welded, 1 dk
(A13A2TW) Crude/Oil Products Tanker
Double Hull (13F)
Liq: 124,705; Liq (Oil): 128,800
Cargo Heating Coils
Compartments: 12 Wing Ta, 2 Wing Slop Ta, ER
3 Cargo Pump (s): 3x3000m³/hr
Manifold: Bow/CM: 125.4m
1 oil engine driving 1 FP propeller
Total Power: 14,280kW (19,415hp) 15.4kn
MAN-B&W 7S60MC
1 x 2 Stroke 7 Cy. 600 x 2292 14280kW (19415bhp)
Hyundai Heavy Industries Co Ltd-South Korea
AuxGen: 3 x 838kW a.c
Fuel: 229.0 (d.f.) 3315.0 (r.f.) 55.0pd

7908407 J8AA5 -
SEA LEGEND
ex Bywater Ludlow *-2011* *ex* Sabine Seal *-2008*
ex State Flamingo *-1996*
Bywater Ludlow LLC
-
Kingstown *St Vincent & The Grenadines*
MMSI: 377901003
413 123 1,000
Class: (AB)
1980-04 Zigler Shipyards Inc — Jennings LA Yd No: 269
Loa - Br ex - Dght 3.074
Lbp 45.73 Br md 10.67 Dpth 3.69
Welded, 1 dk
(B21A20S) Platform Supply Ship
2 oil engines reverse reduction geared to sc. shafts driving 2 FP propellers
Total Power: 1,030kW (1,400hp) 11.0kn
G.M. (Detroit Diesel) 12V-149
2 x Vee 2 Stroke 12 Cy. 146 x 146 each-515kW (700bhp)
General Motors Detroit DieselAllison Divn-USA
AuxGen: 2 x 75kW

9189809 9V5552 -
SEA LEOPARD
PSA Marine Pte Ltd
-
Singapore *Singapore*
MMSI: 564627000
Official number: 388040
298 89 200
Class: BV
1998-06 Matsuura Tekko Zosen K.K. — Osakikamijima Yd No: 507
Loa 31.00 Br ex - Dght 3.950
Lbp 25.50 Br md 9.50 Dpth 4.95
Welded, 1 dk
(B32A2ST) Tug
2 oil engines gearing integral to driving 2 Z propellers
Total Power: 2,942kW (4,000hp) 13.0kn
Yanmar 6N260-EN
2 x 4 Stroke 6 Cy. 260 x 360 each-1471kW (2000bhp)
Yanmar Diesel Engine Co Ltd-Japan

9166364 5BBT2 -
SEA LEOPARD
ex William R Croyle *-2006*
ex Leopard Bay *-2003*
SFL Sea Leopard Ltd
Deep Sea Supply Navegacao Maritima Ltda
Limassol *Cyprus*
MMSI: 212570000
Official number: 9166364
2,556 810 2,900
Class: NV
1998-06 Kvaerner Leirvik AS — Leirvik i Sogn Yd No: 276
Loa 73.50 Br ex 16.40 Dght 6.900
Lbp 68.68 Br md 16.40 Dpth 8.00
Welded, 1 dk
(B21B20A) Anchor Handling Tug Supply
Passengers: cabins: 12
2 oil engines reduction geared to sc. shafts driving 2 CP propellers
Total Power: 11,240kW (15,282hp) 15.0kn
Wartsila 12V32
2 x Vee 4 Stroke 12 Cy. 320 x 400 each-5620kW (7641bhp)
Wartsila NSD Finland Oy-Finland
AuxGen: 2 x 1920kW 220/440V 60Hz a.c, 2 x 300kW 220/440V 60Hz a.c
Thrusters: 1 Thwart. FP thruster (f); 1 Retract. directional thruster (f); 1 Tunnel thruster (a)
Fuel: 782.0 (d.f.) 35.0pd

8965517 H02521 -
SEA LEVEL
ex Lauch Faircloth *-2003*
ex Southport Ft. Fisher *-2003*
ex Sea Level *-1972*
Ocean Pollution Control SA
-
Panama *Panama*
Official number: 29753PEXT1
229 156 -
1959 Wiley Mfg. Co. — Port Deposit, Md Yd No: 524
Converted From: Ferry (Passenger/Vehicle)-2008
Loa 37.00 Br ex - Dght 2.000
Lbp - Br md 13.40 Dpth 2.99
Welded, 1 dk
(B34G2SE) Pollution Control Vessel
2 oil engines driving 2 FP propellers
Total Power: 626kW (852hp) 12.0kn
Caterpillar
2 x 4 Stroke each-313kW (426bhp)
Caterpillar Tractor Co-USA

9677727 WDG2955 -
SEA LEVEL
State of North Carolina (Ferry Division)
-
Manns Harbor, NC *United States of America*
Official number: 1237503
1,081 - -
2012-04 Orange Shipbuilding, Inc. — Orange, Tx Yd No: 425
L reg 61.56 Br ex - Dght -
Lbp - Br md 15.24 Dpth 3.81
Welded, 1 dk
(A36A2PR) Passenger/Ro-Ro Ship (Vehicles)
Passengers: unberthed: 300
Bow door (centre)
Stern door (centre)
Vehicles: 50
2 oil engines reduction geared to sc. shafts driving 2 Propellers

---

6505026 HO3226 -
SEA LIFE
ex Assaf *-2007* *ex* Coruna *-1998*
Assaf Shipping Co SA
-
Panama *Panama*
MMSI: 372996000
Official number: 35886PEXT
1,204 406 1,211
Class: (LR)
✠ Classed LR until 21/3/01
1964-10 Ast. de Palma S.A. — Palma de Mallorca Yd No: 124
Loa 72.70 Br ex 11.03 Dght 4.484
Lbp 66.81 Br md 11.00 Dpth 6.35
Welded, 2 dks
(A34A2GR) Refrigerated Cargo Ship
Ins: 1,724
Ice Capable
1 oil engine driving 1 FP propeller
Total Power: 1,655kW (2,250hp) 15.0kn
MAN G9V40/60
1 x 4 Stroke 9 Cy. 400 x 600 1655kW (2250bhp)
Maschinenbau Augsburg Nuernberg (MAN)-Augsburg

7648966 8QPF -
SEA LIFT
ex Seifuku Maru *-1989*
Sealift Maldives (Pvt) Ltd
-
Male *Maldives*
Official number: 200/10-T
197 - 650
1970 Shinhama Dockyard Co. Ltd. — Anan Yd No: 627
Loa 48.11 Br ex - Dght 3.001
Lbp 42.85 Br md 8.50 Dpth 5.01
Welded, 2dks
(A31A2GX) General Cargo Ship
Bale: 955
1 Ha: (25.9 x 6.1)
1 oil engine driving 1 FP propeller
Total Power: 515kW (700hp) 9.5kn
Makita
1 x 4 Stroke 515kW (700bhp)
Makita Diesel Co Ltd-Japan

8130320 YBLQ -
SEA LIFT NO. 1
ex Hajoo 2000 *-2006* *ex* Mie Maru No. 38 *-2004*
PT Jaya Samudra Karunia
-
Jakarta *Indonesia*
1,594 479 1,830
Class: (KI)
1982-07 K.K. Miura Zosensho — Saiki Yd No: 656
Converted From: Work/Repair Vessel-2006
Loa 55.80 Br ex - Dght 3.250
Lbp 53.01 Br md 22.01 Dpth 3.81
Welded, 1 dk
(B34W2QJ) Trans Shipment Vessel
Cranes: 2x18t
2 oil engines geared to sc. shafts driving 2 FP propellers
Total Power: 1,472kW (2,002hp) 6.0kn
Daihatsu 6PSHTBM-26H
2 x 4 Stroke 6 Cy. 260 x 320 each-736kW (1001bhp)
Daihatsu Diesel Manufacturing Co Lt-Japan

5205423 - -
SEA LIGHT
ex Mwafak 1 *-2010* *ex* Leona *-2009*
ex Klik II *-2008* *ex* Leona *-2008*
ex Marigo *-2006* *ex* Sekavin IV *-2004*
ex Seifallah *-1992* *ex* Leendert Broere *-1975*
Ishraq Jasmim Mohiammed Al-Zubaidi
-
553 242 798
Class: (LR)
✠ Classed LR until 21/5/04
1960-09 D.W. Kremer Sohn — Elmshorn Yd No: 1085
Loa 59.31 Br ex 8.69 Dght 3.506
Lbp 54.89 Br md 8.60 Dpth 3.74
Riveted\Welded, 1 dk
(A13B2TU) Tanker (unspecified)
Single Hull
Liq: 915; Liq (Oil): 915
Compartments: 10 Ta, ER
1 oil engine driving 1 FP propeller
Total Power: 478kW (650hp) 11.0kn
Deutz RBV6M545
1 x 4 Stroke 6 Cy. 320 x 450 478kW (650bhp)
Kloeckner Humboldt Deutz AG-West Germany
AuxGen: 2 x 10kW 110V d.c
Boilers: db (o.f.) 10.4kgf/cm² (10.2bar)
Fuel: 24.0 (d.f.) 3.0pd

9287144 VRAJ9 -
SEA LILY
Sedon (Hong Kong) Ltd
COSCO Bulk Carrier Co Ltd (COSCO BULK)
Hong Kong *Hong Kong*
MMSI: 477600800
Official number: HK-1397
30,081 17,927 52,471 T/cm 55.5
Class: AB
2004-09 Tsuneishi Corp — Tadotsu KG Yd No: 1273
Loa 189.99 Br ex - Dght 12.000
Lbp 182.00 Br md 32.26 Dpth 17.00
Welded, 1 dk
(A21A2BC) Bulk Carrier
Grain: 67,756; Bale: 65,600
Compartments: 5 Ho, ER
5 Ha: ER
Cranes: 4x30t
1 oil engine driving 1 FP propeller
Total Power: 7,800kW (10,605hp) 14.5kn
B&W 6S50MC
1 x 2 Stroke 6 Cy. 500 x 1910 7800kW (10605bhp)
Mitsui Engineering & Shipbuilding CLtd-Japan
Fuel: 199.0 (d.f.) 2387.0 (r.f.)

7212444 - -
SEA LINK CARIBE
ex Marantha Express *-1975* *ex* Carol M *-1987*
ex Geomar II *-1986* *ex* Dearborn 47 *-1981*
ESSCO Ltd
-
981 686 610
Class: (AB)
1972 Burton Shipyard Co., Inc. — Port Arthur, Tx Yd No: 485
Loa 50.30 Br ex 11.69 Dght 3.372
Lbp 47.15 Br md 11.59 Dpth 3.97
Welded, 1 dk
(B21A20S) Platform Supply Ship
2 oil engines reverse reduction geared to sc. shafts driving 2 FP propellers
Total Power: 1,654kW (2,248hp) 10.0kn
Caterpillar D399TA
2 x Vee 4 Stroke 16 Cy. 159 x 203 each-827kW (1124bhp)
Caterpillar Tractor Co-USA
AuxGen: 2 x 100kW

8744688 - -
SEA-LINK PUSHER
ex Constant II *-2006*
ex Hyannis (YTB 817) *-1997*
Sea-Link Marine Services Ltd
-
Vancouver, BC *Canada*
Official number: 829405
221 66 -
1973-01 Marinette Marine Corp — Marinette WI Yd No: 817
Converted From: Tug-2006
L reg 30.36 Br ex - Dght -
Lbp - Br md 8.84 Dpth 5.14
Welded, 1 dk
(B32B2SP) Pusher Tug
1 oil engine reduction geared to sc. shaft driving 1 Propeller
Total Power: 2,290kW (3,113hp) 12.0kn
GE Marine 12V228
1 x Vee 4 Stroke 12 Cy. 229 x 267 2290kW (3113bhp) (new engine 2006)
General Electric Co.-Lynn, Ma

8659871 - -
SEA LION
ex KBS 308 *-2011*
CV KBS Marine
-
Samarinda *Indonesia*
230 103 -
Class: KI
2011-06 CV KBS Marine — Tenggarong
Loa 39.50 Br ex - Dght -
Lbp 37.70 Br md 8.00 Dpth 2.40
Welded, 1 dk
(A35D2RL) Landing Craft
Bow ramp (centre)
2 oil engines reduction geared to sc. shafts driving 2 Propellers
Total Power: 662kW (900hp)
Caterpillar
2 x each-331kW (450bhp)
Caterpillar Inc-USA
AuxGen: 2 x 46kW 400V a.c

IMO / Call sign	Name / Owner	Tonnage	Class	Builder / Dimensions	Type	Machinery
8913746 *9V5533* -	**SEA LION** **PSA Marine Pte Ltd** - *Singapore* *Singapore* MMSI: 563001370 Official number: 387966	**332** 101 -	Class: (AB)	**1990**-08 **Sembawang Bethlehem Pte Ltd — Singapore** Yd No: 202 Loa 29.50 Br ex - Dght - Lbp 28.40 Br md 9.80 Dpth 4.20 Welded, 1 dk	**(B32A2ST) Tug**	**2 oil engines** geared to sc. shafts driving 2 Directional propellers Total Power: 2,206kW (3,000hp) 12.0kn Kromhout 8FHD240 2 x 4 Stroke 8 Cy. 240 x 260 each-1103kW (1500bhp) Stork Wartsila Diesel BV-Netherlands AuxGen: 2 x 89kW 415V a.c Fuel: 124.0 (d.f.)
9050101 *V2GI2* -	**SEA LION** *ex* Industrial Venture *-2001* *ex* Sea Lion *-2000* *ex* Industrial Faith *-1997* *ex* Sea Lion *-1995* *ex* IAL Premier *-1995* *ex* Sea Lion *-1993* **Bischoff Schiffahrts GmbH & Co KG ms 'Scotland'** Bischoff Schiffahrts Beteiligung GmbH *Saint John's* *Antigua & Barbuda* MMSI: 305942000 Official number: 5028	**2,815** 1,532 4,037	Class: NK (BV)	**1993**-06 **Esbjerg Oilfield Services A/S — Esbjerg** Yd No: 64 Loa 88.40 Br ex - Dght 6.000 Lbp 80.30 Br md 15.00 Dpth 7.50 Welded, 1 dk	**(A31A2GX) General Cargo Ship** Grain: 2,757; Bale: 2,454 TEU 247 C Ho 93 TEU C Dk 154 TEU incl 20 ref C. Compartments: 1 Ho, ER, 1 Tw Dk 1 Ha: (50.0 x 11.8)ER Cranes: 2x25t Ice Capable	**1 oil engine** reduction geared to sc. shaft driving 1 CP propeller Total Power: 2,200kW (2,991hp) 14.0kn MaK 6M453C 1 x 4 Stroke 6 Cy. 320 x 420 2200kW (2991bhp) Krupp MaK Maschinenbau GmbH-Kiel AuxGen: 1 x 315kW 220/380V 50Hz a.c Thrusters: 1 Tunnel thruster (f) Fuel: 323.0
7115567 *H9FM* -	**SEA LION** *ex* Marmouset *-2006* *ex* Gulf King 57 *-2001* *ex* Marie Andree I *-1995* *ex* Marmouset *-1995* **Sea Lion Fishing Inc** Aquatic Marine Ltd *Panama* *Panama* MMSI: 352399000 Official number: 2883502E	**803** 240 406	Class: (BV)	**1971 Soc Industrielle et Commerciale de Consts Navales (SICCNa) — St-Malo** Yd No: 113 Loa 50.00 Br ex 10.32 Dght 4.801 Lbp 46.72 Br md 10.22 Dpth 6.00 Welded, 2 dks	**(B11A2FS) Stern Trawler** Ins: 390 Compartments: 1 Ho, ER 2 Ha: 2 (1.3 x 0.9)ER	**1 oil engine** reduction geared to sc. shaft driving 1 FP propeller Total Power: 1,361kW (1,850hp) 10.0kn Crepelle 12PSN 1 x Vee 4 Stroke 12 Cy. 260 x 280 1361kW (1850bhp) Crepelle et Cie-France AuxGen: 1 x 250kW, 2 x 120kW, 1 x 75kW Fuel: 178.5 (d.f.)
7114472 *DUH2264* -	**SEA LION** *ex* Kowan Maru No. 3 *-1995* *ex* Myojo Maru No. 101 *-1982* **Salvmarine Corp** - *Cebu* *Philippines* Official number: CEB1001159	*185* 123 -		**1970**-09 **Niigata Engineering Co Ltd — Niigata NI** Yd No: 1016 Converted From: Fishing Vessel-1982 Loa 34.63 Br ex 7.04 Dght 2.445 Lbp 31.60 Br md 7.01 Dpth 4.68 Welded, 1 dk	**(B32A2ST) Tug**	**1 oil engine** driving 1 FP propeller Total Power: 758kW (1,031hp) Niigata 6MG25AX 1 x 4 Stroke 6 Cy. 250 x 320 758kW (1031bhp) Niigata Engineering Co Ltd-Japan
7346336 *5NCJ* -	**SEA LION** **Nigerian Ports Authority (NPA)** - *Lagos* *Nigeria* MMSI: 657010000 Official number: 375562	*3,981* 1,940 5,550	Class: (BV)	**1975**-06 **Scheepswerven St. Pieter N.V. — Hemiksem** Yd No: 263 Loa 103.00 Br ex 16.62 Dght 6.401 Lbp 93.00 Br md 16.59 Dpth 7.98 Welded, 1 dk	**(B33B2DT) Trailing Suction Hopper Dredger** Hopper: 3,750	**2 oil engines** reduction geared to sc. shafts driving 2 FP propellers Total Power: 2,854kW (3,880hp) 12.0kn Blackstone ESL16MK2 2 x Vee 4 Stroke 16 Cy. 222 x 292 each-1427kW (1940bhp) Mirrlees Blackstone (Stamford)Ltd.-Stamford AuxGen: 4 x 170kW 220/440V 50Hz a.c
9277046 *9KCN* -	**SEA LION** **Arabian Gulf Mechanical Service & Contracting Co Ltd** - *Kuwait* *Kuwait* MMSI: 447094000 Official number: KT1676	**1,232** 367 1,255	Class: AB	**2002**-09 **Guangxi Guijiang Shipyard — Wuzhou GX** Yd No: 01-2001-02 Loa 58.30 Br ex - Dght 4.200 Lbp 52.00 Br md 13.80 Dpth 5.50 Welded, 1 dk	**(B21A20S) Platform Supply Ship**	**2 oil engines** geared to sc. shafts driving 2 FP propellers Total Power: 2,942kW (4,000hp) 12.5kn Yanmar 6N260-EN 2 x 4 Stroke 6 Cy. 260 x 360 each-1471kW (2000bhp) Yanmar Diesel Engine Co Ltd-Japan
9237620 *SVBR9*	**SEA LION** *ex* Samco America *-2013* **Chelsea Navigation Co** Pantheon Tankers Management Ltd *Piraeus* *Greece* MMSI: 241238000	**160,889** 110,470 318,509 T/cm 180.3	Class: NV (AB)	**2003**-04 **Hyundai Samho Heavy Industries Co Ltd — Samho** Yd No: S152 Loa 333.00 (BB) Br ex 60.04 Dght 22.500 Lbp 319.00 Br md 60.00 Dpth 30.40 Welded, 1 dk	**(A13A2TV) Crude Oil Tanker** Double Hull (13F) Liq: 339,052; Liq (Oil): 346,979 Compartments: 5 Ta, 10 Wing Ta, 2 Wing Slop Ta, ER 3 Cargo Pump (s): 3x5000m³/hr Manifold: Bow/CM: 165.2m	**1 oil engine** driving 1 FP propeller Total Power: 29,346kW (39,899hp) 15.5kn MAN-B&W 6S90MC-C 1 x 2 Stroke 6 Cy. 900 x 3188 29346kW (39899bhp) Hyundai Heavy Industries Co Ltd-South Korea AuxGen: 3 x 1150kW 440/220V 60Hz a.c Fuel: 400.0 (d.f.) (Heating Coils) 9290.0 (r.f.)
9622368 - -	**SEA LION** *ex* Selaco-02 *-2012* **Southern Waterborne Transport Service & Labour Export JSC** - *Saigon* *Vietnam* Official number: VNSG-2058-TK	**209** 63 177	Class: VR	**2010**-10 **Yard N.51 — Vietnam** Loa 28.09 Br ex 8.72 Dght 2.900 Lbp 24.81 Br md 8.50 Dpth 3.80 Welded, 1 dk	**(B32A2ST) Tug**	**2 oil engines** reduction geared to sc. shafts driving 2 FP propellers Total Power: 2,984kW (4,058hp) Cummins KTA-50-M2 2 x Vee 4 Stroke 16 Cy. 159 x 159 each-1492kW (2029bhp) Cummins Engine Co Inc-USA AuxGen: 2 x 40kW 380V a.c
9326639 *V7MO4* -	**SEA LION I** **Sea Lion Shipholding SA** Perosea Shipping Co SA SatCom: Inmarsat C 453832645 *Majuro* *Marshall Islands* MMSI: 538002879 Official number: 2879	**8,503** 4,173 13,116 T/cm 23.2	Class: BV (AB)	**2007**-07 **21st Century Shipbuilding Co Ltd — Tongyeong** Yd No: 219 Loa 128.60 (BB) Br ex 20.40 Dght 8.700 Lbp 120.40 Br md 20.40 Dpth 11.50 Welded, 1 dk	**(A12B2TR) Chemical/Products Tanker** Double Hull (13F) Liq: 13,402; Liq (Oil): 13,402 Cargo Heating Coils Compartments: 12 Wing Ta, 2 Wing Slop Ta, ER 12 Cargo Pump (s): 12x300m³/hr Manifold: Bow/CM: 61.4m	**1 oil engine** driving 1 FP propeller Total Power: 4,440kW (6,037hp) 13.4kn MAN-B&W 6S35MC 1 x 2 Stroke 6 Cy. 350 x 1400 4440kW (6037bhp) STX Engine Co Ltd-South Korea AuxGen: 3 x 550kW a.c Thrusters: 1 Tunnel thruster (f) Fuel: 69.2 (d.f.) 678.4 (r.f.)
8941468 *WCY4101* -	**SEA LION I** **Khang Van Dang** - *Biloxi, MS* *United States of America* Official number: 1045282	**157** 47 -		**1997 Toche Boat Builders, Inc. — Ocean Springs, Ms** Yd No: 224 L reg 25.54 Br ex - Dght - Lbp - Br md 7.32 Dpth 3.78 Welded, 1 dk	**(B11B2FV) Fishing Vessel**	**1 oil engine** driving 1 FP propeller
7018733 *HQIV4* -	**SEA LION II** *ex* Stella No. 1 *-1991* *ex* Hosho Maru No. 21 *-1991* *ex* Ryuo Maru No. 8 *-1980* **Neptune Trading S de RL** - *San Lorenzo* *Honduras* Official number: L-1924038	*229* 149 -		**1969 Miho Zosensho K.K. — Shimizu** Yd No: 713 Loa 50.40 Br ex 8.23 Dght 3.048 Lbp 44.20 Br md 8.21 Dpth 3.61 Welded, 1 dk	**(B11B2FV) Fishing Vessel**	**1 oil engine** driving 1 FP propeller Total Power: 699kW (950hp) Hanshin 6LU28 1 x 4 Stroke 6 Cy. 280 x 440 699kW (950bhp) Hanshin Nainenki Kogyo-Japan
9413975 - -	**SEA LION II** **Delta Sea Falcon Ltd** - *Jersey* *Jersey*	**176** 52 15		**2006**-07 **C.R.N. Cant. Nav. Ancona S.r.l. — Ancona** Yd No: 97/02 Loa 30.85 Br ex - Dght 1.500 Lbp 27.00 Br md 7.00 Dpth 3.07 Bonded, 1 dk	**(X11A2YP) Yacht** Hull Material: Reinforced Plastic	**2 oil engines** reduction geared to sc. shafts driving 2 FP propellers Total Power: 3,530kW (4,800hp) M.T.U. 16V2000M93 2 x Vee 4 Stroke 16 Cy. 135 x 156 each-1765kW (2400bhp) MTU Friedrichshafen GmbH-Friedrichshafen
5314729 - -	**SEA LION V** *ex* Cap Saumon *-1981* *ex* Sault-au-Mouton *-1964* - -	*450* 236 554	Class: (LR) ✠ Classed LR until 3/64	**1945**-07 **Geo T Davie & Sons Ltd — Levis QC** Yd No: 34 Loa 50.02 Br ex 9.81 Dght 2.902 Lbp 47.55 Br md 9.76 Dpth 3.59 Riveted\Welded, 1 dk	**(A31A2GX) General Cargo Ship** Compartments: 1 Ho, ER 4 Ha: 4 (4.2 x 5.4)ER	**2 oil engines** driving 2 FP propellers 8.0kn Fairbanks, Morse 2 x 2 Stroke 5 Cy. 255 x 320 Fairbanks Morse & Co.-New Orleans, La Fuel: 6.0
8969915 *WDA9792* -	**SEA LION V** **Khang Van Dang** - *Biloxi, MS* *United States of America* MMSI: 366869040 Official number: 1113356	**172** 51 -		**2001 La Force Shipyard Inc — Coden AL** Yd No: 111 L reg 26.18 Br ex - Dght - Lbp - Br md 7.62 Dpth 3.71 Welded, 1 dk	**(B11B2FV) Fishing Vessel**	**1 oil engine** driving 1 FP propeller
8979996 *WDD9669* -	**SEA LION VI** **Khang Van Dang** - *Biloxi, MS* *United States of America* MMSI: 367314660 Official number: 1125327	*173* 51 -		**2002**-01 **La Force Shipyard Inc — Coden AL** Yd No: 127 L reg 26.18 Br ex - Dght - Lbp - Br md 7.62 Dpth 3.65 Welded, 1 dk	**(B11B2FV) Fishing Vessel**	**1 oil engine** driving 1 Propeller

9105231 *9HA2487* -	**SEA LORD** *ex* Seaflower *-2010* *ex* Safflower *-2003* *ex* Rubin Safflower *-2000* **Melia Shipholding SA** Athenian Ship Management Inc *Valletta* *Malta* MMSI: 248731000 Official number: 9105231	**35,884** 23,407 69,128 T/cm 64.0	Class: NK	**1995**-01 **Koyo Dockyard Co Ltd — Mihara HS** (Hull) Yd No: 2057 **1995**-01 **Imabari Shipbuilding Co Ltd — Marugame KG (Marugame Shipyard)** Yd No: 1215 Loa 224.98 (BB) Br ex 32.24 Dght 13.298 Lbp 215.00 Br md 32.20 Dpth 18.30 Welded, 1 dk	**(A21A2BC) Bulk Carrier** Grain: 82,025 Compartments: 7 Ho, ER 7 Ha: (13.0 x 12.8) (16.3 x 14.4)4 (17.9 x 14.4) (14.7 x 14.4)ER	**1 oil engine** driving 1 FP propeller Total Power: 11,651kW (15,841hp) 14.5kn Sulzer 6RTA62 1 x 2 Stroke 6 Cy. 620 x 2150 11651kW (15841bhp) Mitsubishi Heavy Industries Ltd-Japan AuxGen: 3 x 440kW 450V 60Hz a.c Fuel: 157.0 (d.f.) 2569.0 (r.f.) 32.8pd
8314885 *V3TH* -	**SEA LORD** *ex* Tamoyo Maiden *-2012* *ex* Sea Pantheon *-2005* *ex* Express Progress *-2004* *ex* Clipper Mandarin *-2000* *ex* Sifnos Island *-1989* **Blooming Shipholding Co** GMZ Ship Management Co SA *Belize City* *Belize* MMSI: 312942000 Official number: 141230243	**10,511** 6,280 17,297	Class: NK (LR) (BV) (AB) Classed LR until 3/1/14	**1986**-02 **Ishikawajima-Harima Heavy Industries Co Ltd (IHI) — Aioi HG** Yd No: 2862 Loa 145.50 (BB) Br ex 21.04 Dght 9.451 Lbp 137.71 Br md 21.00 Dpth 13.10 Welded, 1 dk, 2nd dk portable	**(A31A2GX) General Cargo Ship** Grain: 21,266; Bale: 21,096 TEU 558 C Ho 334 TEU C Dk 224 TEU Compartments: 5 Ho, ER, 5 Tw Dk 5 Ha: (15.0 x 9.9) (12.7 x 15.6)3 (15.0 x 15.6)ER Cranes: 5x25t	**1 oil engine** with clutches, flexible couplings & sr geared to sc. shaft driving 1 CP propeller Total Power: 3,972kW (5,400hp) 14.5kn Pielstick 10PC2-6V-400 1 x Vee 4 Stroke 10 Cy. 400 x 460 3972kW (5400bhp) Ishikawajima Harima Heavy IndustrieCo Ltd (IHI)-Japan AuxGen: 1 x 550kW 450V 60Hz a.c, 1 x 190kW 450V 60Hz a.c Boilers: AuxB (o.f.) 5.1kgf/cm² (5.0bar) Fuel: 128.0 (d.f.) 732.5 (r.f.) 17.5pd
8601587 *D5FS3* -	**SEA LORD** *ex* Sea Toucan *-2014* *ex* Seabulk Toucan *-2009* *ex* Red Toucan *-2000* *ex* Cadimare *-1995* **Seawise Maritime Corp** Seaport International Shipping Co LLC *Monrovia* *Liberia* MMSI: 636016347 Official number: 16347	**1,352** 405 1,500	Class: BV (RI)	**1987**-07 **Cant. Navale "Ferrari" S.p.A. — La Spezia** Yd No: 50 Loa 62.01 Br ex 14.25 Dght 5.814 Lbp 54.01 Br md 14.10 Dpth 6.81 Welded, 1 dk	**(B21B20T) Offshore Tug/Supply Ship**	**4 oil engines** with clutches, flexible couplings & sr geared to sc. shafts driving 2 CP propellers Total Power: 6,200kW (8,430hp) Wartsila 12V22HF 2 x Vee 4 Stroke 12 Cy. 220 x 240 each-1860kW (2529bhp) Wartsila Diesel Oy-Finland Wartsila 8R22HF 2 x 4 Stroke 8 Cy. 220 x 240 each-1240kW (1686bhp) Wartsila Diesel Oy-Finland Thrusters: 2 Thwart. CP thruster (f)
9499462 *D5AE4* -	**SEA LOYALTY** **New Age Enterprises Ltd** Blue Sea Shipping SAM *Monrovia* *Liberia* MMSI: 636015358 Official number: 15358	**32,839** 19,559 58,018 T/cm 59.2	Class: NK (BV)	**2012**-01 **Yangzhou Dayang Shipbuilding Co Ltd — Yangzhou JS** Yd No: DY3071 Loa 189.99 (BB) Br ex - Dght 12.970 Lbp 185.00 Br md 32.26 Dpth 18.00 Welded, 1 dk	**(A21A2BC) Bulk Carrier** Grain: 71,549; Bale: 69,760 Compartments: 5 Ho, ER 5 Ha: ER Cranes: 4x36t	**1 oil engine** driving 1 FP propeller Total Power: 8,700kW (11,829hp) 14.3kn MAN-B&W 6S50MC-C 1 x 2 Stroke 6 Cy. 500 x 2000 8700kW (11829bhp) Doosan Engine Co Ltd-South Korea AuxGen: 3 x 650kW 60Hz a.c Fuel: 2260.0 32.0pd
9261619 *9HA2024* -	**SEA LUCK III** *ex* Livia *-2010* **Sphinx Shipping Ltd** Eastern Mediterranean Maritime Ltd SatCom: Inmarsat B 324982214 *Valletta* *Malta* MMSI: 249822000 Official number: 9261619	**57,314** 32,728 105,869 T/cm 91.9	Class: LR **100A1** SS 07/2013 Double Hull oil tanker ESP SPM *IWS LI **ShipRight** (SDA, FDA, CM) ✠ **LMC** **UMS IGS** Eq.Ltr: T†; Cable: 715.0/87.0 U3 (a)	**2003**-07 **Hyundai Samho Heavy Industries Co Ltd — Samho** Yd No: S184 Loa 244.00 (BB) Br ex 42.03 Dght 14.919 Lbp 234.00 Br md 42.00 Dpth 21.00 Welded, 1 dk	**(A13A2TV) Crude Oil Tanker** Double Hull (13F) Liq: 115,702; Liq (Oil): 120,300 Cargo Heating Coils Compartments: 12 Wing Ta, 2 Wing Slop Ta, ER 3 Cargo Pump (s): 3x3000m³/hr Manifold: Bow/CM: 122.8m	**1 oil engine** driving 1 FP propeller Total Power: 11,344kW (15,423hp) 14.5kn B&W 6L60MC 1 x 2 Stroke 6 Cy. 600 x 1944 11344kW (15423bhp) Hyundai Heavy Industries Co Ltd-South Korea AuxGen: 3 x 730kW 440/220V 60Hz a.c Boilers: AuxB (Comp) 8.1kgf/cm² (7.9bar), WTAuxB (o.f.) 18.4kgf/cm² (18.0bar) Fuel: 230.0 (d.f.) 2849.0 (r.f.)
8203701 *3EQD9* -	**SEA LUCKY I** *ex* Captain Kharlamov *-2008* *ex* Strelets *-2007* *ex* Ibn Seena *-2002* *ex* Union Rich *-2000* *ex* Union Lucky *-1996* *ex* Euro Courier *-1992* *ex* Caribe Courier *-1991* *ex* Euro Courier *-1989* *ex* E. M. T. C. Lusitania *-1989* *ex* Rewia *-1988* *ex* Rewi *-1987* *ex* RMS Riviera *-1986* *ex* Rewi *-1985* **Justice Marine Co Ltd** Sung Kyung Maritime Co Ltd (SK Maritime) *Panama* *Panama* MMSI: 354955000 Official number: 3409108A	**4,702** 2,333 6,076	Class: IB (CC) (GL)	**1983**-09 **Schiffswerft und Maschinenfabrik Cassens GmbH — Emden** Yd No: 163 Loa 101.61 (BB) Br ex 18.24 Dght 6.087 Lbp 95.20 Br md 18.22 Dpth 7.80 Welded, 2 dks	**(A31A2GA) General Cargo Ship (with Ro-Ro facility)** Stern door/ramp Len: 11.00 Wid: 6.50 Swl: 100 Lane-Wid: 7.00 Bale: 8,376 TEU 402 C.Ho 176/20' (40') C.Dk 226/20' (40') incl. 20 ref C. Compartments: 1 Ho, ER 1 Ha: (63.7 x 15.2)ER Cranes: 2x25t	**1 oil engine** with flexible couplings & sr gearedto sc. shaft driving 1 FP propeller Total Power: 2,398kW (3,260hp) 11.0kn MaK 8M453AK 1 x 4 Stroke 8 Cy. 320 x 420 2398kW (3260bhp) Krupp MaK Maschinenbau GmbH-Kiel Thrusters: 1 Thwart. FP thruster (f) Fuel: 129.5 (d.f.) 295.2 (r.f.)
9178410 *LNUA* -	**SEA LYNX** *ex* Howard Hogue *-2005* *ex* Torm Heron *-2004* *ex* Leo Bay *-1999* **Deep Sea Supply Shipowning AS** Deep Sea Supply Management (Singapore) Pte Ltd *Arendal* *Norway* MMSI: 258567000	**2,556** 810 2,900	Class: NV	**1999**-06 **Kvaerner Leirvik AS — Leirvik i Sogn** Yd No: 281 Loa 73.50 Br ex 16.43 Dght 6.880 Lbp 66.68 Br md 16.40 Dpth 8.00 Welded, 1 dk	**(B21B20A) Anchor Handling Tug Supply** Passengers: cabins: 12	**2 oil engines** reduction geared to sc. shafts driving 2 CP propellers Total Power: 11,240kW (15,282hp) 14.0kn Wartsila 12V32 2 x Vee 4 Stroke 12 Cy. 320 x 400 each-5620kW (7641bhp) Wartsila NSD Finland Oy-Finland AuxGen: 2 x 1800kW 220/440V 60Hz a.c, 2 x 300kW 220/440V 60Hz a.c Thrusters: 1 Retract. directional thruster (f); 1 Thwart. FP thruster (f); 1 Tunnel thruster (a)
9290775 *9HA3463* -	**SEA LYNX** *ex* Eagle Vienna *-2013* **Barkley Ltd** Pantheon Tankers Management Ltd *Valletta* *Malta* MMSI: 229628000 Official number: 9290775	**161,233** 110,526 318,000 T/cm 180.5	Class: LR ✠ **100A1** SS 11/2009 Double Hull oil tanker ESP *IWS LI SPM **ShipRight** (SDA, FDA Plus, CM) ✠ **LMC** **UMS IGS** Eq.Ltr: D*; Cable: 770.0/114.0 U3 (a)	**2004**-11 **Hyundai Samho Heavy Industries Co Ltd — Samho** Yd No: S222 Loa 333.00 (BB) Br ex 60.05 Dght 22.500 Lbp 319.00 Br md 60.00 Dpth 30.40 Welded, 1 dk	**(A13A2TV) Crude Oil Tanker** Double Hull (13F) Liq: 346,389; Liq (Oil): 346,389 Compartments: 5 Ta, 10 Wing Ta, ER, 2 Wing Slop Ta 3 Cargo Pump (s): 3x5000m³/hr Manifold: Bow/CM: 164m	**1 oil engine** driving 1 FP propeller Total Power: 29,340kW (39,891hp) 15.5kn MAN-B&W 6S90MC-C 1 x 2 Stroke 6 Cy. 900 x 3188 29340kW (39891bhp) Hyundai Heavy Industries Co Ltd-South Korea AuxGen: 3 x 1100kW 450V 60Hz a.c Boilers: e (ex.g.) 22.1kgf/cm² (21.7bar), WTAuxB New (o.f.) 18.0kgf/cm² (17.7bar) Fuel: 352.0 (d.f.) 9758.0 (r.f.)
7308645 *WDE7018* -	**SEA MAC** **Sea Mac Seafoods LLC** - *Kodiak, AK* *United States of America* MMSI: 338604000 Official number: 525516	**199** 59 -		**1970** **Allied Shipyard, Inc. — Larose, La** Yd No: 134 L reg 19.97 Br ex 6.43 Dght - Lbp - Br md - Dpth 2.75 Welded	**(B11B2FV) Fishing Vessel**	**1 oil engine** driving 1 FP propeller Total Power: 250kW (340hp)
8985921 *MXAK2* -	**SEA MAGIC** *ex* Leo Rising *-2013* *ex* Cheetah Moon *-2013* **Synseal Marine LLP** - *London* *United Kingdom* MMSI: 234692000 Official number: 900269	*114* - -		**1997** **Cantieri Navali Versil Srl — Viareggio** Loa 24.40 Br ex - Dght 2.080 Lbp - Br md 5.85 Dpth 3.28 Bonded, 1 dk	**(X11A2YP) Yacht** Hull Material: Reinforced Plastic Passengers: cabins: 4; berths: 8	**2 oil engines** driving 2 Propellers Total Power: 1,766kW (2,402hp) 22.0kn MAN 2 x 4 Stroke each-883kW (1201bhp) MAN B&W Diesel AG-Augsburg
7822976 - -	**SEA MAIDEN** - - -	*150* - 20		**1980**-02 **Singapore Shipbuilding & Engineering Pte Ltd — Singapore** Yd No: 150 Loa 31.77 Br ex - Dght - Lbp 30.80 Br md 6.71 Dpth 2.59 Welded, 1 dk	**(A37B2PS) Passenger Ship** Passengers: unberthed: 220	**2 oil engines** geared to sc. shafts driving 2 FP propellers Total Power: 394kW (536hp) 12.0kn Deutz SBA6M816 2 x 4 Stroke 6 Cy. 142 x 160 each-197kW (268bhp) Kloeckner Humboldt Deutz AG-West Germany
7505762 *A9D2987* -	**SEA MAINTAINER** *ex* Safaniya 2 *-2008* **Al Jazeera Shipping Co WLL (AJS)** - *Manama* *Bahrain* MMSI: 408331000 Official number: BN 5009	**777** 233 836	Class: AB	**1976**-05 **Vosper Thornycroft Pte Ltd — Singapore** Yd No: B.968 Loa 56.09 Br ex 11.61 Dght 2.828 Lbp 52.33 Br md 11.49 Dpth 3.43 Welded, 1 dk	**(B22D2OZ) Production Testing Vessel** Compartments: 6 Ta, 4 Wing Ta, ER Cranes: 1x25t	**2 oil engines** reverse reduction geared to sc. shafts driving 2 FP propellers Total Power: 1,214kW (1,650hp) 10.8kn Caterpillar D398TA 2 x Vee 4 Stroke 12 Cy. 159 x 203 each-607kW (825bhp) Caterpillar Tractor Co-USA AuxGen: 2 x 210kW a.c, 1 x 40kW a.c Thrusters: 1 Water jet (f)

9419046 *A9HS* -	**SEA MAJESTIC** *ex* Profit Majestic *-2007* **Al Jazeera Shipping Co WLL (AJS)** - *Bahrain* *Bahrain* MMSI: 408325000 Official number: BN 5006	**298** 90 234	Class: GL (NK)	**2007-01 Forward Marine Enterprise Sdn Bhd — Sibu** Yd No: FM-13 Loa 32.10 Br ex - Dght 3.512 Lbp 29.69 Br md 9.00 Dpth 4.20 Welded, 1 dk	**(B32A2ST) Tug**	**2 oil engines** reduction geared to sc. shafts driving 2 Propellers Total Power: 2,080kW (2,828hp) Mitsubishi S12R-MPTK 2 x Vee 4 Stroke 12 Cy. 170 x 180 each-1040kW (1414bhp) Mitsubishi Heavy Industries Ltd-Japan Fuel: 175.0
9363285 *3EQS8* -	**SEA MAJESTY** **Lucretia Shipping SA** Santoku Senpaku Co Ltd *Panama* *Panama* MMSI: 354768000 Official number: 3405308A	**20,236** 10,947 32,250 T/cm 43.8	Class: NK	**2008-05 Kanda Zosensho K.K. — Kawajiri** Yd No: 485 Loa 177.13 (BB) Br ex - Dght 10.020 Lbp 168.50 Br md 28.40 Dpth 14.25 Welded, 1 dk	**(A31A2GO) Open Hatch Cargo Ship** Double Hull Grain: 42,595; Bale: 41,124 Compartments: 5 Ho, ER 5 Ha: ER Cranes: 4x30.5t	**1 oil engine** driving 1 FP propeller Total Power: 6,620kW (9,001hp) 14.3kn Mitsubishi 6UEC52LA 1 x 2 Stroke 6 Cy. 520 x 1600 6620kW (9001bhp) Kobe Hatsudoki KK-Japan AuxGen: 2 x 450kW a.c Fuel: 1740.0
8808161 *DSOP5* -	**SEA MANSION** *ex* Sekino V *-1999* *ex* Sekino Maru *-1994* **Shipping Land Co Ltd** Daeyoung Shipping Co Ltd *Jeju* *South Korea* MMSI: 441032000 Official number: JJR-068905	**2,426** 850 2,267	Class: KR (NK)	**1988-09 KK Kanasashi Zosen — Toyohashi AI** Yd No: 3180 Loa 86.33 (BB) Br ex 14.53 Dght 4.972 Lbp 80.00 Br md 14.50 Dpth 5.00 Welded, 2 dks	**(A34A2GR) Refrigerated Cargo Ship** Ins: 3,520 Compartments: 4 Ho, ER, 4 Tw Dk 4 Ha: ER Derricks: 4x5t	**1 oil engine** driving 1 FP propeller Total Power: 1,471kW (2,000hp) 12.8kn B&W 6S26MC 1 x 2 Stroke 6 Cy. 260 x 980 1471kW (2000bhp) The Hanshin Diesel Works Ltd-Japan AuxGen: 2 x 360kW 450V 60Hz a.c Fuel: 367.0 (d.f.) 326.0 (r.f.) 5.5pd
9176670 *H3CS* -	**SEA MAPLE** **C & I Shipholding SA** COSCO (HK) Shipping Co Ltd *Panama* *Panama* MMSI: 352359000 Official number: 2698400CH	**26,136** 14,872 45,710 T/cm 49.8	Class: NK	**2000-03 Tsuneishi Shipbuilding Co Ltd — Fukuyama HS** Yd No: 1155 Loa 185.74 (BB) Br ex - Dght 11.620 Lbp 177.00 Br md 30.40 Dpth 16.50 Welded, 1 dk	**(A21A2BC) Bulk Carrier** Grain: 57,208; Bale: 55,564 Compartments: 5 Ho, ER 5 Ha: (15.3 x 12.8)4 (17.0 x 15.4)ER Cranes: 4x25t	**1 oil engine** driving 1 FP propeller Total Power: 7,172kW (9,751hp) 14.0kn B&W 6S50MC 1 x 2 Stroke 6 Cy. 500 x 1910 7172kW (9751bhp) Kawasaki Heavy Industries Ltd-Japan Fuel: 1610.0
7320837 *HQGS4* -	**SEA MARINA** *ex* Shoei Maru No. 8 *-1990* **Sea Marina Shipping Corp** - SatCom: Inmarsat A 1334316 *San Lorenzo* *Honduras* Official number: L-0323454	*704* 327 660		**1973-03 Hakata Zosen K.K. — Imabari** Yd No: 132 Loa - Br ex 11.03 Dght 3.048 Lbp 44.99 Br md 11.00 Dpth 5.49 Riveted\Welded, 1 dk	**(A24D2BA) Aggregates Carrier**	**1 oil engine** driving 1 FP propeller Total Power: 956kW (1,300hp) Daihatsu 6DSM-26FS 1 x 4 Stroke 6 Cy. 260 x 320 956kW (1300bhp) Daihatsu Diesel Manufacturing Co Lt-Japan
8317423 *3FUJ9* -	**SEA MARK** *ex* Cool Lady *-2001* *ex* San Diego *-1997* *ex* Reefer Dragon *-1996* **Habitat International Corp** Shandong Zhonglu Fishery Shipping Co Ltd *Panama* *Panama* MMSI: 355643000 Official number: 4307611	**5,321** 2,658 6,376	Class: NK	**1984-01 K.K. Taihei Kogyo — Akitsu** Yd No: 1638 Loa 125.67 (BB) Br ex 17.81 Dght 7.316 Lbp 117.02 Br md 17.80 Dpth 10.22 Welded, 3 dks	**(A34A2GR) Refrigerated Cargo Ship** Side doors (p) Cars: 212 Ins: 7,503 Compartments: 3 Ho, ER 4 Ha: 4 (6.1 x 6.1)ER Derricks: 8x5t; Winches: 8	**1 oil engine** driving 1 FP propeller Total Power: 5,148kW (6,999hp) 17.0kn Mitsubishi 7UEC45HA 1 x 2 Stroke 7 Cy. 450 x 1150 5148kW (6999bhp) Akasaka Tekkosho KK (Akasaka DieselLtd)-Japan AuxGen: 3 x 480kW 450V 60Hz a.c Fuel: 319.0 (d.f.) 787.0 (r.f.) 21.0pd
9419981 *5BYN2* -	**SEA MARTEN** **Nico Middle East Ltd (Topaz Marine)** - *Limassol* *Cyprus* MMSI: 212146000	**1,943** 583 1,575	Class: NV	**2010-05 ABG Shipyard Ltd — Surat** Yd No: 270 Loa 63.40 Br ex - Dght 4.800 Lbp 56.53 Br md 15.80 Dpth 6.80 Welded, 1 dk	**(B21B20A) Anchor Handling Tug Supply**	**2 oil engines** reduction geared to sc. shafts driving 2 CP propellers Total Power: 5,002kW (6,800hp) 10.5kn Yanmar 8N280-EN 2 x 4 Stroke 8 Cy. 280 x 380 each-2501kW (3400bhp) Yanmar Diesel Engine Co Ltd-Japan AuxGen: 4 x 425kW 440V 60Hz a.c Thrusters: 1 Tunnel thruster (f)
9228411 *SVBT5* -	**SEA MASTER** *ex* Star Sea Breeze *-2013* *ex* Sea Breeze Bulker *-2009* **Voyager Shiptrade SA** Mega Shipping Line Corp *Piraeus* *Greece* MMSI: 241263000	**28,019** 16,034 48,500 T/cm 54.4	Class: BV	**2001-04 Ishikawajima-Harima Heavy Industries Co Ltd (IHI) — Tokyo** Yd No: 3140 Loa 189.96 (BB) Br ex - Dght 10.700 Lbp 181.20 Br md 32.20 Dpth 16.50 Welded, 1 dk	**(A21A2BC) Bulk Carrier** Grain: 61,553; Bale: 59,844 Compartments: 5 Ho, ER 5 Ha: (17.8 x 17.0)4 (20.0 x 17.0)ER Cranes: 4x30t	**1 oil engine** driving 1 FP propeller Total Power: 7,700kW (10,469hp) 14.5kn Sulzer 6RTA48T 1 x 2 Stroke 6 Cy. 480 x 2000 7700kW (10469bhp) Diesel United Ltd.-Aioi AuxGen: 3 x 520kW 450V 60Hz a.c Fuel: 200.0 (d.f.) 1900.0 (r.f.)
9672856 - -	**SEA MASTER** **PT Lius Indah Abadi** - *Samarinda* *Indonesia* Official number: 4441/IIK	**218** 66 -	Class: KI	**2010-10 Galangan Kapal Pusaka Lestari — Samarinda** Yd No: GP.002 Loa 29.53 Br ex - Dght 2.840 Lbp 27.67 Br md 8.20 Dpth 3.80 Welded, 1 dk	**(B32A2ST) Tug**	**2 oil engines** reduction geared to sc. shafts driving 2 FP propellers Total Power: 1,472kW (2,002hp) Yanmar 6RY17P-GV 2 x 4 Stroke 6 Cy. 165 x 219 each-736kW (1001bhp) Yanmar Diesel Engine Co Ltd-Japan AuxGen: 2 x 44kW 400V a.c
7644398 *WYG6635* -	**SEA MASTER** **Harrington Trawlers Inc** - *Brownsville, TX* *United States of America* Official number: 575341	*114* 78 -		**1976 S & R Boat Builders, Inc. — Bayou La Batre, Al** Yd No: 26 L reg 21.98 Br ex 6.76 Dght - Lbp - Br md - Dpth 3.38 Welded, 1 dk	**(B11A2FT) Trawler**	**1 oil engine** driving 1 FP propeller Total Power: 268kW (364hp)
4603478 *OWOT2* -	**SEA MASTER** *ex* Sea Master 1 *-2013* *ex* Sea Master *-2013* *ex* Garsoy *-2010* **TP Offshore A/S** - *Grenaa* *Denmark (DIS)* Official number: D 4639	**192** 63 -	Class: RI	**1988-01 Brodrene Aa Baatbyggeri AS — Hyen** Yd No: 3/203 Converted From: Patrol Vessel-2009 Loa 34.00 Br ex - Dght 1.800 Lbp 30.20 Br md 7.00 Dpth 2.73 Bonded, 1 dk	**(B21A20C) Crew/Supply Vessel** Hull Material: Reinforced Plastic	**2 oil engines** reduction geared to sc. shafts driving 2 CP propellers 18.0kn MWM TBD6048V8 Motoren Werke Mannheim AG (MWM)-West Germany Thrusters: 1 Thwart. FP thruster (f)
9125827 *9V5196* -	**SEA MASTIFF** **Jurong Marine Services Pte Ltd** - *Singapore* *Singapore* Official number: 386791	**297** 89 160	Class: BV (LR) ✠ Classed LR until 12/2/97	**1995-11 Tianjin Xinhe Shipyard — Tianjin** Yd No: SB66881 Loa 30.50 Br ex 10.55 Dght 3.800 Lbp 28.44 Br md 9.60 Dpth 4.60 Welded, 1 dk	**(B32A2ST) Tug**	**2 oil engines** with clutches, flexible couplings & sr geared to sc. shafts driving 2 Directional propellers Total Power: 2,354kW (3,200hp) 13.0kn Kromhout 8FHD240 2 x 4 Stroke 8 Cy. 240 x 260 each-1177kW (1600bhp) Stork Wartsila Diesel BV-Netherlands AuxGen: 2 x 90kW 415V 50Hz a.c, 1 x 23kW 415V 50Hz a.c Fuel: 117.0 (d.f.) 11.7pd
9140401 *9V6725* -	**SEA MATRIX** *ex* Masayoshi Maru No. 18 *-2005* **Grandeur Trading & Services Pte Ltd** Equatorial Marine Fuel Management Services Pte Ltd *Singapore* *Singapore* MMSI: 563006520 Official number: 391402	**1,999** 890 2,602 T/cm 9.0	Class: NK	**1996-01 Sasaki Shipbuilding Co Ltd — Osakikamijima HS** Yd No: 601 Loa 89.93 Br ex - Dght 5.136 Lbp 85.00 Br md 13.20 Dpth 6.50 Welded, 1 dk	**(A13B2TP) Products Tanker** Liq: 3,249; Liq (Oil): 3,249 2 Cargo Pump (s): 2x1000m³/hr	**1 oil engine** driving 1 FP propeller Total Power: 2,427kW (3,300hp) 13.5kn Hanshin LH41L 1 x 4 Stroke 6 Cy. 410 x 800 2427kW (3300bhp) The Hanshin Diesel Works Ltd-Japan AuxGen: 2 x a.c Fuel: 180.0 (r.f.)
9710256 *AWFC* -	**SEA ME SMILE** **A K Shipping Pvt Ltd** New Horizons Shipmanagement Pvt Ltd *Mumbai* *India* MMSI: 419000854 Official number: 43791	**2,460** 864 3,004	Class: IR	**2014-01 Nantong Tongde Shipyard Co Ltd — Nantong JS** Yd No: 084 Loa 82.00 Br ex - Dght 3.767 Lbp 78.60 Br md 16.00 Dpth 5.50 Welded, 1 dk	**(A31A2GX) General Cargo Ship**	**2 oil engines** reduction geared to sc. shafts driving 2 Propellers Cummins Cummins Engine Co Inc-USA

IMO / Call sign	Name / Owner	Tonnage	Class	Builder / Dimensions	Type / Cargo	Machinery
8215089 *T3JG2* -	**SEA MEADOW 01** *ex* Sylvia Tide *-2013* *ex* Lamtide 301 *-1997* *ex* Tadrib *-1992* *ex* Tadrib Express *-1991* **Seascape Meadow Invest Inc** Hai Duong Co Ltd (HADUCO) *Tarawa* *Kiribati* MMSI: 529633000 Official number: K16841397	**1,003** 300 1,387	Class: AB VR (Class contemplated)	**1984**-07 **Offshore Shipbuilding Inc — Palatka FL** Yd No: 32 Loa 60.97 Br ex 12.20 Dght 3.987 Lbp 56.70 Br md 12.18 Dpth 4.58 Welded, 1 dk	**(B21A20S) Platform Supply Ship**	**2 oil engines** reverse reduction geared to sc. shafts driving 2 FP propellers Total Power: 2,868kW (3,900hp) 12.0kn EMD (Electro-Motive) 16-645-E6 1 x Vee 2 Stroke 16 Cy. 230 x 254 1434kW (1950bhp) (Re-engined ,made 1960, Reconditioned & fitted 1984) General Motors Corp.Electro-Motive Div.-La Grange EMD (Electro-Motive) 16-645-E6 1 x Vee 2 Stroke 16 Cy. 230 x 254 1434kW (1950bhp) (Re-engined ,made 1973, Reconditioned & fitted 1984) General Motors Corp.Electro-Motive Div.-La Grange AuxGen: 2 x 150kW Thrusters: 1 Thwart. FP thruster (f)
7724746 *AUNA* -	**SEA MELODY** *ex* Melody 3 *-2006* *ex* Salvenus *-2003* *ex* Ocean Discoverer *-1981* **Hind Offshore Pvt Ltd** - *Mumbai* *India* MMSI: 419611000 Official number: 3235	**969** 291 704	Class: IR (NK)	**1978**-04 **Kochi Jyuko K.K. — Kochi** Yd No: 1247 Loa 54.01 Br ex 11.02 Dght 4.573 Lbp 48.01 Br md 11.00 Dpth 5.01 Riveted\Welded, 1 dk	**(B32A2ST) Tug** 2 Ha: 2 (3.2 x 1.5) Derricks: 1x60t,1x10t	**2 oil engines** sr geared to sc. shafts driving 2 CP propellers Total Power: 3,090kW (4,202hp) 10.0kn Niigata 6L31EZ 2 x 4 Stroke 6 Cy. 310 x 380 each-1545kW (2101bhp) Niigata Engineering Co Ltd-Japan AuxGen: 2 x 200kW 440V 60Hz a.c Thrusters: 1 Tunnel thruster (f) Fuel: 569.0 (d.f.)
9006382 *8PAG7* -	**SEA MELODY** *ex* Marianne K. *-2012* *ex* Corona *-2000* **Saturn Shipping Ltd** Torbulk Ltd *Bridgetown* *Barbados* MMSI: 314392000 Official number: 733656	**2,450** 1,380 3,713	Class: GL	**1994**-12 **Peene-Werft GmbH — Wolgast** Yd No: 413 Loa 87.84 (BB) Br ex - Dght 5.460 Lbp 81.83 Br md 12.80 Dpth 7.10 Welded, 2 dks	**(A31A2GX) General Cargo Ship** Double Bottom Entire Compartment Length Grain: 4,666; Bale: 4,635 TEU 252 C Ho 180 TEU C Dk 72 TEU inc 6 ref C. Compartments: 1 Ho, ER 1 Ha: (56.6 x 10.2)ER Ice Capable	**1 oil engine** reduction geared to sc. shaft driving 1 FP propeller Total Power: 1,500kW (2,039hp) 10.0kn Deutz SBV8M628 1 x 4 Stroke 8 Cy. 240 x 280 1500kW (2039bhp) Motoren Werke Mannheim AG (MWM)-Mannheim AuxGen: 2 x 240kW 220/380V a.c Thrusters: 1 Thwart. FP thruster (f) Fuel: 122.0 (d.f.)
9425904 *3EWV8* -	**SEA MELODY** **Lucretia Shipping SA** Santoku Senpaku Co Ltd *Panama* *Panama* MMSI: 355465000 Official number: 4140210	**32,287** 19,458 58,117 T/cm 57.4	Class: NK	**2010**-04 **Tsuneishi Heavy Industries (Cebu) Inc — Balamban** Yd No: SC-123 Loa 189.99 (BB) Br ex - Dght 12.826 Lbp 185.60 Br md 32.26 Dpth 18.00 Welded, 1 dk	**(A21A2BC) Bulk Carrier** Grain: 72,689; Bale: 70,122 Compartments: 5 Ho, ER 5 Ha: ER Cranes: 4x30t	**1 oil engine** driving 1 FP propeller Total Power: 8,400kW (11,421hp) 14.5kn MAN-B&W 6S50MC-C 1 x 2 Stroke 6 Cy. 500 x 2000 8400kW (11421bhp) Mitsui Engineering & Shipbuilding CLtd-Japan Fuel: 2150.0 (r.f.)
9580118 *9HA2508* -	**SEA MELODY** **Sea Melody Co** DD Shipping Ltd SA SatCom: Inmarsat C 424877510 *Valletta* *Malta* MMSI: 248775000 Official number: 9580118	**23,453** 11,522 34,468	Class: KR NV (AB)	**2010**-11 **SPP Shipbuilding Co Ltd — Tongyeong** Yd No: H4061 Loa 180.00 (BB) Br ex 30.04 Dght 9.900 Lbp 172.95 Br md 30.00 Dpth 14.70 Welded, 1 dk	**(A21A2BC) Bulk Carrier** Grain: 48,766; Bale: 46,815 Compartments: 5 Ho, ER 5 Ha: ER Cranes: 4x35t	**1 oil engine** driving 1 FP propeller Total Power: 7,900kW (10,741hp) 14.0kn MAN-B&W 5S50MC-C 1 x 2 Stroke 5 Cy. 500 x 2000 7900kW (10741bhp) Doosan Engine Co Ltd-South Korea AuxGen: 3 x 600kW a.c Fuel: 185.0 (d.f.) 1560.0 (r.f.)
9207780 *V7CU8* -	**SEA MELODY I** *ex* Red Seto *-2013* *ex* Santa Margherita *-2006* **Sea Melody Maritime Ltd** Hellenic Star Shipping Co SA *Majuro* *Marshall Islands* MMSI: 538005338 Official number: 5338	**40,030** 25,920 75,957 T/cm 67.8	Class: BV (AB) (NK)	**2002**-11 **Tsuneishi Shipbuilding Co Ltd — Fukuyama HS** Yd No: 1169 Loa 225.00 Br ex - Dght 14.028 Lbp 217.00 Br md 32.26 Dpth 19.30 Welded, 1 dk	**(A21A2BC) Bulk Carrier** Grain: 91,311 Compartments: 7 Ho, ER 7 Ha: 6 (17.3 x 15.4)ER (15.6 x 12.8)	**1 oil engine** driving 1 FP propeller Total Power: 9,010kW (12,250hp) 14.0kn B&W 6S60MC 1 x 2 Stroke 6 Cy. 600 x 2292 9010kW (12250bhp) Mitsui Engineering & Shipbuilding CLtd-Japan Fuel: 3282.0 (r.f.)
8221131 *DUH2309* -	**SEA MERCHANT** *ex* Shintatsu Maru No. 5 *-1996* **Fortune Sea Carrier Inc** - *Cebu* *Philippines* Official number: CEB1001928	*248* 174 300		**1982** **Sokooshi Zosen K.K. — Osakikamijima** Yd No: 281 Loa 46.13 (BB) Br ex - Dght - Lbp 45.01 Br md 8.21 Dpth 5.01 Welded, 1 dk	**(A31A2GX) General Cargo Ship** Compartments: 1 Ho, ER 1 Ha: ER	**1 oil engine** driving 1 FP propeller Total Power: 515kW (700hp) Niigata 6M26KGHS 1 x 4 Stroke 6 Cy. 260 x 400 515kW (700bhp) Niigata Engineering Co Ltd-Japan
8010908 *5IM546* -	**SEA MERCHANT** *ex* Patriot R *-2011* *ex* Sea Patriot *-2004* *ex* Express Patriot *-2002* *ex* Promoter *-1998* *ex* Poros Island *-1987* *ex* Suntairona *-1985* *ex* Poros Island *-1982* **Yasmine Shipping Inc** Al Ryadh Trading FZCO *Zanzibar* *Tanzania (Zanzibar)* MMSI: 677044600 Official number: 300288	**10,322** 5,657 16,799	Class: IK (LR) (AB) Classed LR until 3/4/12	**1981**-07 **Ishikawajima-Harima Heavy Industries Co Ltd (IHI) — Tokyo** Yd No: 2763 Loa 145.52 (BB) Br ex 21.04 Dght 9.484 Lbp 137.01 Br md 21.01 Dpth 13.11 Welded, 1 dk, 2nd dk portable	**(A31A2GX) General Cargo Ship** Grain: 21,173; Bale: 21,073 TEU 367 C Ho 311 TEU C Dk 56 TEU Compartments: 5 Ho, ER, 5 Tw Dk 5 Ha: (15.0 x 9.8) (12.6 x 15.6)3 (14.9 x 15.6)ER Cranes: 5x25t	**1 oil engine** with clutches, flexible couplings & sr geared to sc. shaft driving 1 CP propeller Total Power: 4,476kW (6,086hp) 14.5kn Pielstick 12PC2-2V-400 1 x Vee 4 Stroke 12 Cy. 400 x 460 4476kW (6086bhp) Ishikawajima Harima Heavy IndustrieCo Ltd (IHI)-Japan AuxGen: 1 x 520kW 450V 60Hz a.c, 1 x 190kW 450V 60Hz a.c Boilers: AuxB (ex.g.) 7.0kgf/cm² (6.9bar), AuxB (o.f.) 7.0kgf/cm² (6.9bar) Fuel: 144.0 (d.f.) 1033.0 (r.f.) 22.5pd
9637662 *9V9601* -	**SEA MERLIN** *ex* Rua Cap. Lucio R. *-2012* **An Yi Shipping Pte Ltd** Ocean Tankers (Pte) Ltd *Singapore* *Singapore* MMSI: 563019440 Official number: 397340	**295** 89 89	Class: BV	**2012**-08 **Wuxi Hongqi Shipyard Co Ltd — Wuxi JS** Yd No: ATE-007-P212 Loa 30.00 Br ex - Dght 3.760 Lbp 23.50 Br md 9.50 Dpth 4.70 Welded, 1 dk	**(B32A2ST) Tug**	**2 oil engines** gearing integral to driving 2 Z propellers Total Power: 2,942kW (4,000hp) Niigata 6L26HLX 2 x 4 Stroke 6 Cy. 260 x 350 each-1471kW (2000bhp) Niigata Engineering Co Ltd-Japan AuxGen: 2 x 115kW 50Hz a.c Fuel: 140.0
8401212 *HSGA* -	**SEA MIRACLE** *ex* Bonlite *-2003* *ex* Vantage *-1995* *ex* Bornion Dua *-1993* **Sang Thai Shipping Co Ltd** Sinsimon Navigation Co Ltd SatCom: Inmarsat C 456746610 *Bangkok* *Thailand* MMSI: 567253000 Official number: 460004327	**2,820** 1,786 5,186	Class: (NK)	**1983**-12 **K.K. Imai Seisakusho — Kamijima** Loa 93.71 Br ex - Dght 6.152 Lbp 86.88 Br md 16.01 Dpth 7.60 Welded, 1 dk	**(A31A2GX) General Cargo Ship** Grain: 6,253; Bale: 5,573 Compartments: 2 Ho, ER 2 Ha: (17.4 x 8.5) (31.8 x 8.5)ER Derricks: 1x30t,2x15t	**1 oil engine** driving 1 FP propeller Total Power: 2,059kW (2,799hp) 11.5kn Hanshin 6EL38 1 x 4 Stroke 6 Cy. 380 x 760 2059kW (2799bhp) The Hanshin Diesel Works Ltd-Japan AuxGen: 2 x 160kW
9293375 *A8IX2* -	**SEA MIRAGE** **SIS Offshore Inc** Seaport International Shipping Co LLC *Monrovia* *Liberia* MMSI: 636012899 Official number: 12899	**250** 75 146	Class: BV (AB)	**2003**-12 **Penguin Shipyard International Pte Ltd — Singapore** Yd No: 132 Loa 39.58 Br ex - Dght 1.850 Lbp 36.40 Br md 7.50 Dpth 3.65 Welded, 1 dk	**(B21A20C) Crew/Supply Vessel** Hull Material: Aluminium Alloy	**3 oil engines** geared to sc. shafts driving 3 FP propellers Total Power: 2,880kW (3,915hp) Caterpillar 3512B 3 x Vee 4 Stroke 12 Cy. 170 x 190 each-960kW (1305bhp) Caterpillar Inc-USA
7000932 *HMZD7* -	**SEA MIST** *ex* Raneem Moon *-2006* *ex* Molly *-2004* *ex* Antares *-2002* *ex* Gardwill *-1991* *ex* Amazone *-1986* *ex* Bele *-1975* *ex* Tor Ireland *-1975* *ex* Bele *-1973* **Sylvester Arthur Ollivierre** Seatrade Shippers Traders & Charters *Wonsan* *North Korea* MMSI: 445924000 Official number: 1903012	**1,371** 516 1,370	Class: KC (BV) (GL)	**1969**-11 **Husumer Schiffswerft — Husum** Yd No: 1285 Loa 76.18 Br ex 11.94 Dght 3.937 Lbp 68.30 Br md 11.90 Dpth 6.40 Welded, 1 dk	**(A31A2GX) General Cargo Ship** Grain: 2,845; Bale: 2,690 TEU 72 C. 72/20' Compartments: 1 Ho, ER 1 Ha: (43.7 x 7.6)ER Ice Capable	**1 oil engine** driving 1 FP propeller Total Power: 1,103kW (1,500hp) 13.0kn Deutz RBV8M545 1 x 4 Stroke 8 Cy. 320 x 450 1103kW (1500bhp) Kloeckner Humboldt Deutz AG-West Germany AuxGen: 2 x 64kW 220/380V 50Hz a.c, 1 x 48kW 220/380V 50Hz a.c
9006435 *MPEK8* -	**SEA MITHRIL** *ex* Bowcliffe *-2005* *ex* Fast Ken *-1999* *ex* Bowcliffe *-1994* **White Horse (Malta) Ltd** Torbulk Ltd SatCom: Inmarsat C 423501127 *Hull* *United Kingdom* MMSI: 232002147 Official number: 720331	**1,382** 794 2,220 T/cm 8.0	Class: GL (LR) (BV) Classed LR until 22/10/12	**1992**-04 **Yorkshire D.D. Co. Ltd. — Hull** Yd No: 326 Loa 77.80 Br ex 11.10 Dght 4.026 Lbp 72.30 Br md 11.00 Dpth 5.10 Welded, 1 dk	**(A31A2GX) General Cargo Ship** Grain: 2,921; Bale: 2,810 Compartments: 2 Ho, ER 2 Ha: ER	**2 oil engines** with clutches, flexible couplings & dr geared to sc. shafts driving 2 Directional propellers Total Power: 954kW (1,298hp) 10.0kn Cummins KTA-19-M 2 x 4 Stroke 6 Cy. 159 x 159 each-477kW (649bhp) Cummins Charleston Inc-USA AuxGen: 3 x 52kW 415V 50Hz a.c Fuel: 50.8 (d.f.) 4.1pd

IMO / Call sign	Name / Owner / Port	Tonnage	Class	Builder / Dimensions	Type	Machinery
7127998 *WX6783* -	**SEA MONARCH** **Crowley Marine Services Inc** - *San Francisco, CA* *United States of America* Official number: 504597	*190* 88 -	Class: (AB)	**1966 Pacific Coast Eng. Co. — Alameda, Ca** Yd No: 213 Loa - Br ex - Dght 4.509 Lbp 35.13 Br md 9.45 Dpth 5.03 Welded, 1 dk	**(B32A2ST) Tug**	**2 oil engines** sr geared to sc. shafts driving 2 FP propellers Total Power: 2,114kW (2,874hp) 14.0kn EMD (Electro-Motive) 16-645-E5 2 x Vee 2 Stroke 16 Cy. 230 x 254 each-1057kW (1437bhp) General Motors Corp-USA AuxGen: 2 x 60kW 208V 60Hz a.c Fuel: 274.5 (d.f.)
9543847 *A9IT* -	**SEA MONARCH** **Al Jazeera Shipping Co** Al Jazeera Shipping Co WLL (AJS) *Bahrain* *Bahrain* MMSI: 408353000 Official number: BN6004	**450** 135 -	Class: BV	**2009-04 Celtug Service Shipyard Sdn Bhd — Sibu** Yd No: 0704 Loa 36.00 Br ex - Dght 3.800 Lbp 31.50 Br md 10.40 Dpth 5.00 Welded, 1 dk	**(B32A2ST) Tug**	**2 oil engines** reduction geared to sc. shafts driving 2 FP propellers Total Power: 3,238kW (4,402hp) 10.0kn Cummins QSK60-M 2 x Vee 4 Stroke 16 Cy. 159 x 190 each-1619kW (2201bhp) Cummins Engine Co Ltd-United Kingdom AuxGen: 2 x 275kW 50Hz a.c Thrusters: 1 Tunnel thruster (f) Fuel: 340.0 (d.f.)
7003867 *WF3716* -	**SEA MONSTER** *ex* Mars **Team Adventure Education Foundation Inc** - *Boston, MA* *United States of America* Official number: 266853	*192* 77 -	Class: (AB)	**1953 Gulfport Shipbuilding Corp. — Port Arthur, Tx** Yd No: 427 Converted From: Tug-1953 Loa 31.40 Br ex 7.90 Dght 3.547 Lbp 29.47 Br md 7.66 Dpth 3.94 Riveted\Welded, 1 dk	**(B34K2QT) Training Ship**	**1 diesel electric oil engine** driving 1 gen. of 814kW 560V d.c Connecting to 1 elec. Motor driving 1 FP propeller Total Power: 872kW (1,186hp) 11.0kn General Motors 12-278A 1 x Vee 2 Stroke 12 Cy. 222 x 267 872kW (1186bhp) General Motors Corp-USA Fuel: 60.0 (r.f.)
9429053 *V7YD3* -	**SEA MOON** **Sea Moon Co Ltd** Hellenic Star Shipping Co SA *Majuro* *Marshall Islands* MMSI: 538004631 Official number: 4631	**33,044** 19,231 57,012 T/cm 58.8	Class: BV	**2009-10 Qingshan Shipyard — Wuhan HB** Yd No: 20060359 Loa 189.99 (BB) Br ex - Dght 12.800 Lbp 185.00 Br md 32.26 Dpth 18.00 Welded, 1 dk	**(A21A2BC) Bulk Carrier** Grain: 71,634; Bale: 68,200 Compartments: 5 Ho, ER 5 Ha: ER Cranes: 4x30t	**1 oil engine** driving 1 FP propeller Total Power: 9,480kW (12,889hp) 14.2kn MAN-B&W 6S50MC-C 1 x 2 Stroke 6 Cy. 500 x 2000 9480kW (12889bhp) STX Engine Co Ltd-South Korea AuxGen: 3 x 660kW 60Hz a.c
8854445 *WDD3291* -	**SEA MOON I** *ex* Garden Sun *-2006* *ex* Jason Le *-1992* **Sea Moon I LLC** - *Honolulu, HI* *United States of America* Official number: 927176	*119* 81 -		**1987 Fred Falgout & Lee Guidry — Houma, La** Loa - Br ex - Dght - Lbp 23.44 Br md 6.71 Dpth 2.74 Welded, 1 dk	**(B11B2FV) Fishing Vessel**	**1 oil engine** driving 1 FP propeller
9125839 *9V5197* -	**SEA MUSANG** **Jurong Marine Services Pte Ltd** - *Singapore* *Singapore* MMSI: 564138000 Official number: 386792	**297** 89 160	Class: LR ✠ **100A1** SS 12/2010 tug Singapore, east & west Malaysiaand Indonesian waters which includethe west and southwest coasts of Sumatra, the south coast of Jara and the south coasts of the islandslying due east of Jara shall be excluded from these limits between mid April and mid October each year ✠ **LMC** Eq.Ltr: F; Cable: 275.0/19.0 U2 (a)	**1995-12 Tianjin Xinhe Shipyard — Tianjin** Yd No: SB66882 Loa 32.00 Br ex 10.55 Dght 3.800 Lbp 26.90 Br md 9.60 Dpth 4.36 Welded, 1 dk	**(B32A2ST) Tug**	**2 oil engines** gearing integral to driving 2 Z propellers Total Power: 2,354kW (3,200hp) 13.0kn Kromhout 8FHD240 2 x 4 Stroke 8 Cy. 240 x 260 each-1177kW (1600bhp) Stork Wartsila Diesel BV-Netherlands AuxGen: 2 x 90kW 415V 50Hz a.c, 1 x 23kW 415V 50Hz a.c Fuel: 117.0 (d.f.) 11.7pd
9212773 *ERSB* -	**SEA MUSIC** *ex* Achment *-2012* *ex* Civra *-2011* **Sea Music Maritime SA** Power Full Marine SA *Moldova* MMSI: 214181902	**5,392** 3,071 8,382	Class: GM (RI)	**2005-07 Selah Makina Sanayi ve Ticaret A.S. — Tuzla, Istanbul** (Hull) Yd No: (16) **2005-07 Ceksan Tersanesi — Turkey** Yd No: 16 Loa 116.00 Br ex - Dght 7.704 Lbp 107.60 Br md 17.20 Dpth 9.80 Welded, 1 dk	**(A31A2GX) General Cargo Ship** Compartments: 3 Ho, ER 3 Ha: (25.4 x 12.8) (18.9 x 12.8)ER (12.4 x 7.8)	**1 oil engine** reduction geared to sc. shaft driving 1 FP propeller Total Power: 4,250kW (5,778hp) 11.5kn Wartsila 8L46B 1 x 4 Stroke 8 Cy. 460 x 580 4250kW (5778bhp) Wartsila NSD Nederland BV-Netherlands Thrusters: 1 Tunnel thruster (f)
6922262 *HQEX4* -	**SEA NASS** *ex* Mini Luck *-1989* **United Cement Co Bscc** - *San Lorenzo* *Honduras* MMSI: 334597000 Official number: L-0332958	*1,355* 832 3,259	Class: BV (AB)	**1969-03 The Hakodate Dock Co Ltd — Hakodate HK** Yd No: 447 Loa 65.51 Br ex 15.32 Dght 4.947 Lbp 62.82 Br md 15.30 Dpth 6.45 Welded, 1 dk	**(A31A2GX) General Cargo Ship** Grain: 3,785; Bale: 3,669 Compartments: 2 Ho, ER 2 Ha: 2 (14.6 x 7.7)ER	**2 oil engines** reverse reduction geared to sc. shafts driving 2 FP propellers Total Power: 736kW (1,000hp) 10.3kn Daihatsu 6PSTCM-22 2 x 4 Stroke 6 Cy. 220 x 280 each-368kW (500bhp) Daihatsu Kogyo-Japan AuxGen: 1 x 104kW 445V 60Hz a.c, 1 x 48kW 445V 60Hz a.c Fuel: 83.5
9603142 *V7AM2* -	**SEA NEPTUNE** *ex* Guanhua *-2013* **Neptune Shipowning Inc** Golden Ocean Group Ltd (GOGL) *Majuro* *Marshall Islands* MMSI: 538005025 Official number: 5025	**44,047** 27,575 81,631 T/cm 71.9	Class: GL NV	**2013-03 Xiamen Shipbuilding Industry Co Ltd — Xiamen FJ** Yd No: XSI482B Loa 229.06 (BB) Br ex - Dght 14.450 Lbp 225.50 Br md 32.26 Dpth 20.05 Welded, 1 dk	**(A21A2BC) Bulk Carrier** Grain: 96,000; Bale: 90,784 Compartments: 7 Ho, ER 7 Ha: 5 (18.3 x 15.0) (15.7 x 15.1)ER (13.1 x 13.2)	**1 oil engine** driving 1 FP propeller Total Power: 11,900kW (16,179hp) 14.1kn MAN-B&W 5S60ME-C8 1 x 2 Stroke 5 Cy. 600 x 2400 11900kW (16179bhp) AuxGen: 3 x a.c
7637553 *HSB2989* -	**SEA NETWORK** *ex* Anusorn Reefer *-2012* *ex* Maya *-2004* **Sea Network Co Ltd** - *Bangkok* *Thailand* MMSI: 567227000 Official number: 460001298	**2,989** 1,555 2,510	Class: (BV)	**1978-10 Nieuwe Noord Nederlandse Scheepswerven B.V. — Groningen** Yd No: 394 Lengthened-1983 Loa 101.94 (BB) Br ex 14.46 Dght 5.320 Lbp 92.56 Br md 14.00 Dpth 8.01 Welded, 2 dks	**(A34A2GR) Refrigerated Cargo Ship** Ins: 5,136 Compartments: 4 Ho, ER 4 Ha: 4 (10.6 x 6.4)ER Derricks: 4x5t	**1 oil engine** reduction geared to sc. shaft driving 1 CP propeller Total Power: 2,207kW (3,001hp) 14.0kn Deutz SBV6M540 1 x 4 Stroke 6 Cy. 370 x 400 2207kW (3001bhp) Kloeckner Humboldt Deutz AG-West Germany AuxGen: 4 x 230kW 440V 60Hz a.c Thrusters: 1 Thwart. CP thruster (f) Fuel: 162.0 (d.f.) 390.0 (r.f.) 11.5pd
9103570 *DSRA3* -	**SEA NOA** *ex* Yae Maru No. 3 *-2009* **Sea Bright Maritime Co Ltd** Sung Kyung Maritime Co Ltd (SK Maritime) *Jeju* *South Korea* MMSI: 441776000 Official number: JJR-106981	**1,524** 700 2,790	Class: KR	**1994-03 Namikata Shipbuilding Co Ltd — Imabari EH** Yd No: 185 Loa 76.67 Br ex - Dght 5.813 Lbp 68.16 Br md 11.80 Dpth 7.32 Welded, 1 dk	**(A31A2GX) General Cargo Ship** Compartments: 1 Ho, ER 1 Ha: (38.4 x 9.1)ER	**1 oil engine** geared to sc. shaft driving 1 FP propeller Total Power: 736kW (1,001hp) 11.5kn Hanshin LH30L 1 x 4 Stroke 6 Cy. 300 x 600 736kW (1001bhp) The Hanshin Diesel Works Ltd-Japan
9114531 *3FEC5* -	**SEA NOBLE** *ex* Pansy *-2012* *ex* Daisy-T *-2008* **DY Pacific SA** LodeStar Marine Co Ltd SatCom: Inmarsat C 435513211 *Panama* *Panama* MMSI: 355132000 Official number: 2213095E	**8,015** 3,172 8,642	Class: KR (NK)	**1995-05 KK Kanasashi — Shizuoka SZ** Yd No: 3357 Loa 109.98 (BB) Br ex - Dght 7.815 Lbp 99.95 Br md 20.20 Dpth 13.20 Welded, 2 dks	**(A31A2GA) General Cargo Ship (with Ro-Ro facility)** Angled stern door/ramp (s. a.) Bale: 15,014 Compartments: 2 Ho, ER 2 Ha: 2 (30.0 x 16.2)ER Cranes: 2x30.5t	**1 oil engine** driving 1 FP propeller Total Power: 3,089kW (4,200hp) 13.0kn Mitsubishi 6UEC37LA 1 x 2 Stroke 6 Cy. 370 x 880 3089kW (4200bhp) Akasaka Tekkosho KK (Akasaka DieselLtd)-Japan Fuel: 610.0 (r.f.)
8331091 *ECDV* 1-CT-4-1-0	**SEA NOSTROMO CUARTO** *ex* Sea Nos Tromos II *-2004* *ex* Roompot *-2002* *ex* Midgard III *-1985* *ex* Ulrich Ellers *-1985* *ex* Midgard 15 *-1985* **Balearia Eurolineas Maritimas SA** - *Cartagena* *Spain* MMSI: 224088930 Official number: 1-1/2003	*124* 37 -	Class: (LR) Classed LR until 13/12/00	**1961-10 N.V. Scheepswerven v/h H.H. Bodewes — Millingen a/d Rijn** Yd No: 581 Loa 27.61 Br ex 6.96 Dght - Lbp 24.97 Br md 6.61 Dpth 3.64 Welded, 1 dk	**(B32A2ST) Tug**	**1 oil engine** with clutches, flexible couplings & sr reverse geared to sc. shaft driving 1 Propeller Total Power: 780kW (1,060hp) Deutz SBV8M545 1 x 4 Stroke 8 Cy. 320 x 450 780kW (1060bhp) Kloeckner Humboldt Deutz AG-West Germany AuxGen: 2 x 1kW 24V d.c

8877825 *DSOF5* -	**SEA NURI** *ex* Sea Bright *-2008* *ex* Jangho Sun *-2008* *ex* Daifuku Maru No. 11 *-2003* **Sea Bright Maritime Co Ltd** Sung Kyung Maritime Co Ltd (SK Maritime) *Jeju* *South Korea* MMSI: 440588000 Official number: JJR-031176	**1,775** 933 3,175	Class: KR	**1994-06 Koike Zosen Kaiun KK — Osakikamijima** Yd No: 181 Lengthened-2005 Loa 74.75 Br ex - Dght 5.763 Lbp 67.65 Br md 13.20 Dpth 7.20 Welded, 1 dk	**(A31A2GX) General Cargo Ship** Grain: 3,821; Bale: 3,317 Compartments: 1 Ho, ER 1 Ha: (36.3 x 9.6)ER	**1 oil engine** driving 1 FP propeller Total Power: 1,471kW (2,000hp) 11.0kn Hanshin LH34LG 1 x 4 Stroke 6 Cy. 340 x 640 1471kW (2000bhp) The Hanshin Diesel Works Ltd-Japan Fuel: 135.0
7006390 *J8PO* -	**SEA OCEAN** *ex* Oassys II *-2010* *ex* Julie *-1999* *ex* Seaction *-1993* *ex* Sannida *-1990* *ex* Scheldeborg *-1989* **Yiobalka International Trading SA** Seastar Management Services Inc *Kingstown* *St Vincent & The Grenadines* MMSI: 377986000 Official number: 400801	**2,021** 913 3,556	Class: (BV)	**1970-03 Fa C Amels & Zoon Scheepswerf & Machinefabriek 'Welgelegen' — Makkum** Yd No: 311 Loa 81.95 Br ex 12.45 Dght 5.131 Lbp 73.39 Br md 12.35 Dpth 6.53 Welded, 1 dk & S dk	**(A31A2GX) General Cargo Ship** Grain: 3,377 Compartments: 1 Ho, ER 3 Ha: (13.7 x 10.0) (15.0 x 10.0) (12.0 x 10.0)ER Cranes: 3x5t Ice Capable	**1 oil engine** driving 1 FP propeller Total Power: 1,765kW (2,400hp) 13.0kn MWM TBD500-8 1 x 4 Stroke 8 Cy. 360 x 450 1765kW (2400bhp) Motoren Werke Mannheim AG (MWM)-West Germany AuxGen: 1 x 117kW 380V 50Hz a.c, 1 x 56kW 380V 50Hz a.c Fuel: 167.5 (d.f.)
9387023 *9WNC5* -	**SEA OCELOT** **Deep Sea Supply Labuan II Ltd** Deep Sea Supply Management (Malaysia) Sdn Bhd *Labuan* *Malaysia* MMSI: 533130085 Official number: 900032	**2,708** 812 2,150	Class: AB	**2007-09 Jaya Shipbuilding & Engineering Pte Ltd — Singapore** Yd No: 855 Loa 70.00 Br ex - Dght 6.080 Lbp 61.80 Br md 16.80 Dpth 7.50 Welded, 1 dk	**(B21B20A) Anchor Handling Tug Supply** Passengers: cabins: 26	**2 oil engines** reduction geared to sc. shafts driving 2 CP propellers Total Power: 8,000kW (10,876hp) 14.0kn Wartsila 8L32 2 x 4 Stroke 8 Cy. 320 x 400 each-4000kW (5438bhp) Wartsila Finland Oy-Finland AuxGen: 2 x 2300kW a.c, 2 x 375kW a.c Thrusters: 2 Thwart. FP thruster (f); 1 Tunnel thruster (a) Fuel: 1250.0 (d.f.)
9303132 *3EGI6* -	**SEA ODYSSEY** **Cygnet Bulk Carriers SA** Kyokuto Shipping Co Ltd *Panama* *Panama* MMSI: 373944000 Official number: 3215506A	**45,011** 14,110 51,976	Class: NK	**2006-09 Sanoyas Hishino Meisho Corp — Kurashiki OY** Yd No: 1237 Loa 203.50 (BB) Br ex 37.20 Dght 10.518 Lbp 196.00 Br md 37.20 Dpth 21.60 Welded, 1 dk	**(A24B2BW) Wood Chips Carrier** Grain: 111,471 Compartments: 6 Ho, ER 6 Ha: ER Cranes: 3x15.5t	**1 oil engine** driving 1 FP propeller Total Power: 9,120kW (12,400hp) 14.5kn MAN-B&W 6S50MC-C 1 x 2 Stroke 6 Cy. 500 x 2000 9120kW (12400bhp) Mitsui Engineering & Shipbuilding CLtd-Japan AuxGen: 3 x a.c Fuel: 2790.0
9351232 - -	**SEA ODYSSEY** *ex* Aristocat V *-2013* *ex* Aristocat *-2012* **Cruise Whitsundays Pty Ltd** *Port Douglas, Qld* *Australia* Official number: 857967	**156** 52 21		**2010-01 North West Bay Ships Pty Ltd — Margate TAS** Yd No: 015 Loa 30.70 Br ex - Dght 2.100 Lbp 27.00 Br md 8.30 Dpth 2.70 Welded, 1 dk	**(A37B2PS) Passenger Ship** Passengers: unberthed: 117	**2 oil engines** reduction geared to sc. shafts driving 2 FP propellers Total Power: 2,030kW (2,760hp) 33.0kn M.T.U. 10V2000M92 2 x Vee 4 Stroke 10 Cy. 135 x 156 each-1015kW (1380bhp) MTU Friedrichshafen GmbH-Friedrichshafen AuxGen: 2 x a.c
9288459 *V7SQ4* -	**SEA OF FUTURE** *ex* Ikan Kerapu *-2009* **Sea of Future Holdings Co Ltd** STX Marine Service Co Ltd *Majuro* *Marshall Islands* MMSI: 538003701 Official number: 3701	**39,964** 25,889 76,454 T/cm 67.8	Class: KR (NK)	**2005-02 Tsuneishi Corp — Tadotsu KG** Yd No: 1283 Loa 225.00 Br ex - Dght 14.028 Lbp 217.00 Br md 32.26 Dpth 19.30 Welded, 1 dk	**(A21A2BC) Bulk Carrier** Grain: 91,357 Compartments: 7 Ho, ER 7 Ha: 6 (17.3 x 15.4)ER (15.6 x 12.8)	**1 oil engine** driving 1 FP propeller Total Power: 9,350kW (12,712hp) 14.0kn MAN-B&W 7S50MC-C 1 x 2 Stroke 7 Cy. 500 x 2000 9350kW (12712bhp) Mitsui Engineering & Shipbuilding CLtd-Japan Fuel: 3000.0 (r.f.)
9375915 *3FJH9* -	**SEA OF HARVEST** *launched as* Star of Kilakarai *-2009* **Sea of Harvest Holdings SA** STX Marine Service Co Ltd SatCom: Inmarsat C 435335710 *Panama* *Panama* MMSI: 353357000 Official number: 4091309	**42,751** 26,554 81,383 T/cm 69.7	Class: KR (NV)	**2009-06 Universal Shipbuilding Corp — Maizuru KY** Yd No: 102 Loa 224.90 (BB) Br ex - Dght 14.408 Lbp 222.00 Br md 32.26 Dpth 20.00 Welded, 1 dk	**(A21A2BC) Bulk Carrier** Grain: 96,030 Compartments: 7 Ho, ER 7 Ha: ER	**1 oil engine** driving 1 FP propeller Total Power: 11,060kW (15,037hp) 14.6kn MAN-B&W 7S50MC-C 1 x 2 Stroke 7 Cy. 500 x 2000 11060kW (15037bhp) Hitachi Zosen Corp-Japan AuxGen: 3 x a.c
9161869 *3FBC8* -	**SEA ORCHID** *ex* Siam Orchid *-2004* **Bayfield Shipping SA** Stavros Roussos Management & Chartering SA *Panama* *Panama* MMSI: 351895000 Official number: 2521298CH	**6,079** 3,290 9,994 T/cm 15.6	Class: NK	**1997-12 Shin Kurushima Dockyard Co. Ltd. — Akitsu** Yd No: 2953 Loa 113.33 (BB) Br ex - Dght 7.993 Lbp 107.00 Br md 19.40 Dpth 10.40 Welded, 1 dk	**(A21A2BC) Bulk Carrier** Double Bottom Entire Compartment Length Grain: 11,061; Bale: 10,701 Compartments: 3 Ho, ER 3 Ha: 2 (20.0 x 12.6) (14.6 x 10.6)ER Cranes: 2x30t; Derricks: 1x25t	**1 oil engine** driving 1 FP propeller Total Power: 3,884kW (5,281hp) 13.6kn B&W 6L35MC 1 x 2 Stroke 6 Cy. 350 x 1050 3884kW (5281bhp) Makita Corp-Japan AuxGen: 2 x 280kW 450V 60Hz a.c Fuel: 142.8 (d.f.) (Heating Coils) 521.2 (r.f.) 14.6pd
8910873 *DSPR9* -	**SEA ORION** *ex* Kaishin Maru No. 35 *-2007* **Seo Kwang Shipping Co Ltd** Sung Kyung Maritime Co Ltd (SK Maritime) *Jeju* *South Korea* MMSI: 441432000 Official number: JJR-072130	**1,513** - 1,376	Class: KR	**1989-11 K.K. Murakami Zosensho — Naruto** Yd No: 185 Loa 75.50 (BB) Br ex - Dght 4.073 Lbp 70.00 Br md 11.50 Dpth 7.00 Welded, 2 dks	**(A31A2GX) General Cargo Ship** Grain: 3,437; Bale: 3,321 Compartments: 1 Ho, ER 1 Ha: ER	**1 oil engine** with clutches, flexible couplings & reduction geared to sc. shaft driving 1 FP propeller Total Power: 1,214kW (1,651hp) 13.5kn Hanshin 6LU32RG 1 x 4 Stroke 6 Cy. 320 x 510 1214kW (1651bhp) The Hanshin Diesel Works Ltd-Japan
9376268 - -	**SEA ORYX** *ex* Petrolink 6 *-2013* *ex* Sealink Maju 7 *-2007* *ex* Sealink 130 *-2006* **Al Jazeera Shipping Co WLL (AJS)** - *Bahrain* *Bahrain*	**254** 76 267	Class: BV	**2006-05 Sealink Shipyard Sdn Bhd — Miri** Yd No: 130 Loa 30.00 Br ex - Dght 3.500 Lbp 27.60 Br md 8.60 Dpth 4.12 Welded, 1 dk	**(B32A2ST) Tug**	**2 oil engines** reduction geared to sc. shafts driving 2 FP propellers Total Power: 1,472kW (2,002hp) Caterpillar 3508B 2 x Vee 4 Stroke 8 Cy. 170 x 190 each-736kW (1001bhp) Caterpillar Inc-USA AuxGen: 2 x 56kW 415/220V 50Hz a.c
8968557 *9V6097* -	**SEA OSPREY** **Tian San Shipping (Pte) Ltd** *Singapore* *Singapore* Official number: 389420	**196** 74 50	Class: BV	**2001-08 Cheoy Lee Shipyards Ltd — Hong Kong** Yd No: 4770 Loa 28.00 Br ex - Dght 2.000 Lbp 26.06 Br md 7.14 Dpth 2.40 Welded, 1 dk	**(A37B2PS) Passenger Ship** Hull Material: Aluminium Alloy Passengers: unberthed: 200	**3 oil engines** reduction geared to sc. shafts driving 3 FP propellers Total Power: 2,364kW (3,213hp) 27.0kn M.T.U. 12V2000M70 3 x Vee 4 Stroke 12 Cy. 130 x 150 each-788kW (1071bhp) MTU Friedrichshafen GmbH-Friedrichshafen AuxGen: 2 x 40kW a.c Fuel: 4.3 (d.f.)
9369552 *C4VH2* -	**SEA OTTER** **Nico Middle East Ltd (Topaz Marine)** - *Limassol* *Cyprus* MMSI: 210514000	**1,943** 650 1,575	Class: NV	**2007-08 ABG Shipyard Ltd — Surat** Yd No: 237 Loa 63.40 Br ex 15.83 Dght 5.100 Lbp 54.00 Br md 15.80 Dpth 6.80 Welded, 1 dk	**(B21B20A) Anchor Handling Tug Supply** Cranes: 1x3t	**2 oil engines** reduction geared to sc. shafts driving 2 CP propellers Total Power: 4,790kW (6,512hp) 10.5kn Bergens C25: 33L8P 2 x 4 Stroke 8 Cy. 250 x 330 each-2390kW (3249bhp) Rolls Royce Marine AS-Norway AuxGen: 3 x 425kW 440V 60Hz a.c Thrusters: 1 Thwart. CP thruster (f)
9589334 *ZGAG3* -	**SEA OWL** **Sea Owl II Ltd** IMA Yachts LLC *George Town* *Cayman Islands (British)* Official number: 742387	**473** 141 79	Class: AB	**2010-08 Burger Boat Co — Manitowoc Wi** Yd No: 507C Loa 43.43 Br ex - Dght 2.170 Lbp 39.08 Br md 8.53 Dpth 3.99 Welded, 1 dk	**(X11A2YP) Yacht** Hull Material: Aluminium Alloy	**2 oil engines** reduction geared to sc. shafts driving 2 Propellers Total Power: 1,000kW (1,360hp) Caterpillar 3412E 2 x Vee 4 Stroke 12 Cy. 137 x 152 each-500kW (680bhp) Caterpillar Inc-USA AuxGen: 2 x 99kW a.c
1011604 *C6AO7* -	**SEA OWL** **Sea Owl III Inc** Edge Yachts Ltd *Nassau* *Bahamas* MMSI: 311000106 Official number: Y0010	**1,494** 448 236	Class: LR ✠ **100A1** SS 07/2013 SSC Yacht, mono, G6 ✠ **LMC** **UMS** Cable: 389.4/28.0 U2 (a)	**2013-07 NMC Alblasserdam BV — Alblasserdam** (Hull) Yd No: (807) **2013-07 Jacht- en Scheepswerf C. van Lent & Zonen B.V. — Kaag** Yd No: 807 Loa 62.00 Br ex 12.20 Dght 3.800 Lbp 52.30 Br md 11.80 Dpth 6.20 Welded, 1 dk	**(X11A2YP) Yacht**	**2 oil engines** with clutches, flexible couplings & sr reverse geared to sc. shafts driving 2 FP propellers Total Power: 3,040kW (4,134hp) M.T.U. 16V4000M53R 2 x Vee 4 Stroke 16 Cy. 170 x 210 each-1520kW (2067bhp) MTU Friedrichshafen GmbH-Friedrichshafen AuxGen: 2 x 308kW 400V 50Hz a.c Thrusters: 1 Thwart. FP thruster (f); 1 Directional thruster (a)

5379066 *HQAN* -	**SEA PAL** *ex* Neenai *-1988* *ex* Maria Beti *-1986* *ex* Mawar *-1985* *ex* Ministar *-1974* *ex* Vesta *-1974* **Neena Shipping Co SA** - *San Lorenzo* *Honduras* Official number: L-0300835	*1,336* 598 1,775	Class: (LR) (NV) ✠ Classed LR until 24/8/79	**1952**-09 **N.V. Werf Jan Smit Czn. — Alblasserdam** Yd No: 549 Loa 75.29 Br ex 11.33 Dght 4.865 Lbp 69.19 Br md 11.31 Dpth 5.52 Riveted\Welded, 1 dk	**(A31A2GX) General Cargo Ship** Grain: 2,504; Bale: 2,351 2 Ha: (9.9 x 5.9) (17.4 x 5.9)ER Derricks: 6x3t; Winches: 6 Ice Capable	**1 oil engine** driving 1 FP propeller Total Power: 809kW (1,100hp) 11.0kn Werkspoor TMAS398 1 x 4 Stroke 8 Cy. 390 x 680 809kW (1100bhp) NV Werkspoor-Netherlands AuxGen: 2 x 75kW 220V d.c, 1 x 25kW 220V d.c Fuel: 86.5 (d.f.)
9162760 *HSB4454* -	**SEA PALACE** *ex* Marine Amethyst *-2010* *ex* Shinken Ace *-2005* **Sang Thai Transport Co Ltd** Sinsimon Navigation Co Ltd *Bangkok* *Thailand* MMSI: 567061100 Official number: 530000970	**6,154** 3,097 8,527	Class: NK	**1997**-05 **Nishi Shipbuilding Co Ltd — Imabari EH** Yd No: 403 Loa 100.64 Br ex - Dght 8.192 Lbp 92.75 Br md 18.80 Dpth 13.00 Welded, 1 dk	**(A31A2GX) General Cargo Ship** Grain: 14,711; Bale: 13,536 Compartments: 2 Ho, ER 2 Ha: (21.7 x 12.8) (25.2 x 12.8)ER Cranes: 1x30.5t; Derricks: 2x25t	**1 oil engine** driving 1 FP propeller Total Power: 3,236kW (4,400hp) 12.5kn B&W 5L35MC 1 x 2 Stroke 5 Cy. 350 x 1050 3236kW (4400bhp) The Hanshin Diesel Works Ltd-Japan AuxGen: 2 x 240kW 450V 60Hz a.c Fuel: 130.3 (d.f.) 398.8 (r.f.)
8705369 - -	**SEA PALLAS** - **PSA Marine Pte Ltd** -	**174** 52 122 T/cm 1.7	Class: (LR) (AB) ✠ Classed LR until 24/9/97	**1988**-01 **Singapore Shipbuilding & Engineering Pte Ltd — Singapore** Yd No: 212 Loa 26.17 Br ex 8.62 Dght 2.801 Lbp 25.51 Br md 7.61 Dpth 3.61 Welded, 1 dk	**(B32A2ST) Tug**	**2 oil engines** with clutches, flexible couplings & dr geared to sc. shafts driving 2 Directional propellers Total Power: 1,194kW (1,624hp) 12.0kn Blackstone ESL5MK2 2 x 4 Stroke 5 Cy. 222 x 292 each-597kW (812bhp) Mirrlees Blackstone (Stamford)Ltd.-Stamford AuxGen: 2 x 32kW 415V 50Hz a.c Fuel: 53.5 (d.f.)
8705357 - -	**SEA PANTHER** - **PSA Marine Pte Ltd** -	**174** 52 122 T/cm 1.7	Class: (LR) (AB) ✠ Classed LR until 4/8/97	**1987**-12 **Singapore Shipbuilding & Engineering Pte Ltd — Singapore** Yd No: 211 Loa 27.13 Br ex 8.62 Dght 3.012 Lbp 23.04 Br md 7.61 Dpth 3.61 Welded, 1 dk	**(B32A2ST) Tug**	**2 oil engines** with clutches, flexible couplings & dr geared to sc. shafts driving 2 Directional propellers Total Power: 1,176kW (1,598hp) 12.0kn Blackstone ESL5MK2 2 x 4 Stroke 5 Cy. 222 x 292 each-588kW (799bhp) Mirrlees Blackstone (Stamford)Ltd.-Stamford AuxGen: 2 x 32kW 415V 50Hz a.c Fuel: 42.0 (d.f.)
9171747 *5BDR3* -	**SEA PANTHER** *ex* Billy Joe Ramey *-2006* *ex* Maersk Detector *-2004* **Deep Sea Supply Shipowning AS** Deep Sea Supply Plc *Limassol* *Cyprus* MMSI: 209121000	**2,556** 810 2,900	Class: NV	**1999**-02 **Kvaerner Leirvik AS — Leirvik i Sogn** Yd No: 279 Loa 73.50 Br ex - Dght 6.900 Lbp 66.68 Br md 16.40 Dpth 8.00 Welded, 1 dk	**(B21B20A) Anchor Handling Tug Supply** Passengers: cabins: 12 Cranes: 1x5t	**2 oil engines** reduction geared to sc. shafts driving 2 FP propellers Total Power: 11,040kW (15,010hp) 15.0kn Wartsila 12V32 2 x Vee 4 Stroke 12 Cy. 320 x 400 each-5520kW (7505bhp) Wartsila NSD Finland Oy-Finland AuxGen: 2 x 1800kW 220/440V 60Hz a.c, 2 x 300kW 220/440V 60Hz a.c Thrusters: 1 Thwart. FP thruster (f); 1 Retract. directional thruster (f); 1 Tunnel thruster (a) Fuel: 782.0 (d.f.) 35.0pd
8016299 *A6E2681* -	**SEA PANTHER** *ex* El Alat 9 *-1997* **Seaport International Shipping Co LLC** - *Sharjah* *United Arab Emirates* Official number: SHS/4249	*117* 32 -	Class: (AB)	**1980**-10 **Halter Marine, Inc. — Chalmette, La** Yd No: 947 Loa 26.67 Br ex 6.89 Dght 3.106 Lbp 23.78 Br md 6.86 Dpth 3.66 Welded, 1 dk	**(B34N2QP) Pilot Vessel**	**2 oil engines** reverse reduction geared to sc. shafts driving 2 FP propellers Total Power: 1,266kW (1,722hp) 14.0kn G.M. (Detroit Diesel) 16V-92-TA 2 x Vee 2 Stroke 16 Cy. 123 x 127 each-633kW (861bhp) General Motors Detroit DieselAllison Divn-USA AuxGen: 2 x 30kW
7528635 *3EUM3* -	**SEA PARTNER** *ex* Stena Partner *-2011* *ex* Freeway *-2002* *ex* European Freeway *-2002* *ex* Cerdic Ferry *-1991* *ex* Stena Transporter *-1986* *ex* Syria *-1983* *ex* Alpha Enterprise *-1979* **Partner SIA** SIA Sea Lines Ltd (Stena SeaLine) *Panama* *Panama* MMSI: 370176000 Official number: 4462513	**21,162** 6,348 8,408	Class: RI (LR) ✠ Classed LR until 21/11/12	**1978**-05 **Hyundai Heavy Industries Co Ltd — Ulsan** Yd No: 649 **1981 Hapag-Lloyd Werft GmbH — Bremerhaven** (Additional cargo section) Converted From: Ro-Ro Cargo Ship-1979 Lengthened-1981 Widened-1979 Loa 184.61 (BB) Br ex 25.28 Dght 6.370 Lbp 170.59 Br md 23.50 Dpth 14.65 Welded, 2 dks, 2nd dk for light cargoes only, 3rd dk movable in holds	**(A36A2PR) Passenger/Ro-Ro Ship (Vehicles)** Passengers: cabins: 45; berths: 166; driver berths: 166 Stern door/ramp (lwr) Len: 16.80 Wid: 12.30 Swl: 50 Stern door/ramp (upr) Len: 10.30 Wid: 6.30 Swl: - Lane-Len: 2382 Lane-Wid: 6.00 Lane-clr ht: 5.80 Trailers: 180 TEU 290 incl 52 ref C	**2 oil engines** with flexible couplings & sr gearedto sc. shafts driving 2 CP propellers Total Power: 11,638kW (15,824hp) 17.0kn Pielstick 12PC2-5V-400 2 x Vee 4 Stroke 12 Cy. 400 x 460 each-5819kW (7912bhp) Nippon Kokan KK (NKK Corp)-Japan AuxGen: 2 x 760kW 450V 60Hz a.c, 2 x 520kW 450V 60Hz a.c Boilers: 2 e 8.0kgf/cm² (7.8bar), AuxB (o.f.) 8.0kgf/cm² (7.8bar) Thrusters: 1 Thwart. CP thruster (f) Fuel: 200.0 (d.f.) 820.0 (r.f.) 38.0pd
8214097 *9HA2402* -	**SEA PATRON** *ex* Sancte Ioseph *-2014* *ex* Sancte Josefe *-2010* *ex* Smit Sumatera *-2010* **Patron Group Ltd** - *Valletta* *Malta* MMSI: 248537000 Official number: 8214097	**622** 186 493	Class: AB	**1983**-07 **Sing Koon Seng Pte Ltd — Singapore** Yd No: 607 Loa 42.02 Br ex 11.43 Dght 4.596 Lbp 36.00 Br md 11.41 Dpth 5.01 Welded, 1 dk	**(B21B20A) Anchor Handling Tug Supply** Cranes: 1	**2 oil engines** sr geared to sc. shafts driving 2 CP propellers Total Power: 2,148kW (2,920hp) 12.0kn Kromhout 8FHD240 2 x 4 Stroke 8 Cy. 240 x 260 each-1074kW (1460bhp) Stork Werkspoor Diesel BV-Netherlands AuxGen: 2 x 250kW 440V 60Hz a.c, 2 x 195kW 440V 60Hz a.c Thrusters: 1 Thwart. CP thruster (f) Fuel: 260.0 (d.f.) 9.5pd
9214848 *V7EL3* -	**SEA PEACE D** *ex* Sea Peace *-2014* *ex* Tarapaca *-2013* **Pax Navigation Inc** Baru Delta Maritime Inc *Majuro* *Marshall Islands* MMSI: 538005488 Official number: 5488	**26,084** 15,577 46,786 T/cm 50.2	Class: NK (Class contemplated) (CC)	**2000**-06 **Kanasashi Heavy Industries Co Ltd — Toyohashi AI** Yd No: 3521 Loa 183.04 (BB) Br ex - Dght 11.671 Lbp 174.30 Br md 31.00 Dpth 16.47 Welded, 1 dk	**(A21A2BC) Bulk Carrier** Grain: 59,077; Bale: 58,014 Compartments: 5 Ho, ER 5 Ha: (14.4 x 15.0)4 (20.0 x 15.6)ER Cranes: 4x30t	**1 oil engine** driving 1 FP propeller Total Power: 7,488kW (10,181hp) 14.3kn Mitsubishi 6UEC52LS 1 x 2 Stroke 6 Cy. 520 x 1850 7488kW (10181bhp) Kobe Hatsudoki KK-Japan Fuel: 1910.0
7917056 - -	**SEA PEARL** *ex* Dammam 30 *-2006* **Al Jazeera Shipping Co WLL (AJS)** - *Bahrain* *Bahrain* Official number: BN 4064	*578* 192 -	Class: (AB)	**1980**-06 **Buesumer Werft GmbH — Buesum** (Hull) **1980**-06 **Schlichting-Werft GmbH — Luebeck** Yd No: 1419 Converted From: Supply Tender-2006 Loa 43.69 Br ex 12.02 Dght 2.709 Lbp 43.59 Br md 12.01 Dpth 3.51 Welded, 1 dk	**(B34E2SV) Incinerator**	**2 oil engines** driving 2 Directional propellers Total Power: 882kW (1,200hp) 7.8kn M.T.U. 6V396TC62 2 x Vee 4 Stroke 6 Cy. 165 x 185 each-441kW (600bhp) MTU Friedrichshafen GmbH-Friedrichshafen AuxGen: 3 x 235kW
8302179 *V7MQ8* -	**SEA PEARL** *ex* Alanya *-2007* *ex* Rio Purus *-1993* **Sea Pearl Ltd** SMT Shipmanagement & Transport Gdynia Ltd Sp z oo *Majuro* *Marshall Islands* MMSI: 538002888 Official number: 2888	**27,013** 11,510 38,760	Class: LR (AB) **100A1** SS 07/2011 strengthened for carriage of heavy cargoes, Nos. 3 or 2 & 4 holds may be empty, container cargoes in hold Nos. 2 & 4 and on all hatch covers **LMC** **UMS** Eq.Ltr: M†; Cable: 632.5/73.0 U3 (a)	**1986**-07 **Stocznia im Komuny Paryskiej — Gdynia** Yd No: B541/01 Loa 183.25 (BB) Br ex 29.04 Dght 11.718 Lbp 175.30 Br md 29.00 Dpth 16.40 Welded, 1 dk	**(A31A2GO) Open Hatch Cargo Ship** Grain: 43,610; Bale: 42,000 TEU 588 C Ho 432 TEU C Dk 156 TEU Compartments: 5 Ho, ER 5 Ha: 3 (25.6 x 23.0)2 (20.8 x 20.4)ER Gantry cranes: 2x25t	**1 oil engine** driving 1 FP propeller Total Power: 9,600kW (13,052hp) 13.0kn B&W 6L67GFCA 1 x 2 Stroke 6 Cy. 670 x 1700 9600kW (13052bhp) Zaklady Przemyslu Metalowego 'HCegielski' SA-Poznan AuxGen: 1 x 1250kW 440V 60Hz a.c, 2 x 960kW 440V 60Hz a.c Boilers: e (ex.g.) 7.1kgf/cm² (7.0bar), AuxB (o.f.) 7.1kgf/cm² (7.0bar) Fuel: 161.0 (d.f.) 2810.5 (r.f.)
7315818 - -	**SEA PEARL** *ex* Lady Camilla *-2004* *ex* Lubchem *-1998* *ex* Mobil Lubchem *-1991* - -	**1,999** 1,004 3,310 T/cm 10.4	Class: (LR) ✠ Classed LR until 22/10/03	**1973**-06 **Ast. del Cantabrico y de Riera — Factoria de G. Riera, Gijon** Yd No: R.114 Loa 93.33 (BB) Br ex 14.03 Dght 5.360 Lbp 85.50 Br md 14.00 Dpth 6.30 Welded, 1 dk	**(A12A2TC) Chemical Tanker** Double Bottom Entire Compartment Length Liq: 3,691 Cargo Heating Coils Compartments: 10 Ta, ER 10 Cargo Pump (s) Ice Capable	**1 oil engine** driving 1 CP propeller Total Power: 1,765kW (2,400hp) 12.8kn Deutz RBV8M358 1 x 4 Stroke 8 Cy. 400 x 580 1765kW (2400bhp) Hijos de J Barreras SA-Spain AuxGen: 3 x 130kW 440V 60Hz a.c Boilers: db 5.0kgf/cm² (4.9bar), db (New boiler: 1973) 12.0kgf/cm² (11.8bar) Fuel: 205.0 (d.f.) 10.5pd
5423972 - -	**SEA PEARL** *ex* Regina Chatarina *-1999* *ex* Spica *-1993* *ex* Frisk *-1972* *ex* Fri *-1965* *ex* Carlso *-1961* *ex* Drochtersen *-1955* *ex* Dirk *-1955* - -	*130* 59 162		**1916 N.V. Scheepswerven Gebr. van der Windt — Vlaardingen** Converted From: Yacht Converted From: Fishing Vessel Converted From: General Cargo Ship-1953 Converted From: Fishing Vessel-1931 Loa 26.98 Br ex 6.61 Dght - Lbp - Br md 6.56 Dpth 3.00 Riveted, 1 dk	**(A37A2PC) Passenger/Cruise** Passengers: cabins: 8; berths: 18 2 Ha: (7.4 x 3.9) (2.2 x 1.9)ER Derricks: 1x1t; Winches: 1	**1 oil engine** driving 1 FP propeller Total Power: 74kW (101hp) Deutz SV2M245 1 x 4 Stroke 2 Cy. 280 x 450 74kW (101bhp) (new engine 1931) Humboldt Deutmotoren AG-Koeln

1007421 *ZCOO3* -	**SEA PEARL** *ex Pegasus Ii -2011 ex Pegasus -2008* *ex Aviva II -2007 ex Alfa Four -2005* *ex Ambrosiana -2004* **Hampshire Investments Holdings Ltd** Yachting Partners International (Monaco) SAM *George Town Cayman Islands (British)* MMSI: 319609000 Official number: 738482	**1,184** 355 191	Class: LR ✠ **100A1** SS 06/2009 SSC Yacht (P), mono, G6 **LMC UMS** Cable: 165.0/22.0 U3 (a)	**2004-06 Southern African Shipyards (Pty.) Ltd. — Durban** (Hull) Yd No: 563 **2004-06 Oceanco Shipyards (Alblasserdam) B.V. — Alblasserdam** Loa 60.00 Br ex 10.50 Dght 3.600 Lbp 47.71 Br md 10.00 Dpth 5.92 Welded, 1 dk	**(X11A2YP) Yacht**	**2 oil engines** with clutches, flexible couplings & sr reverse geared to sc. shafts driving 2 FP propellers Total Power: 2,462kW (3,348hp) 16.0kn Caterpillar 3512B 2 x Vee 4 Stroke 12 Cy. 170 x 190 each-1231kW (1674bhp) Caterpillar Inc-USA AuxGen: 2 x 155kW 400V 50Hz a.c Thrusters: 1 Thwart. FP thruster (f)
8950524 *WDG5675* -	**SEA PEARL** *ex Argent No. 1 -2012 ex Discovery Isle -2012* **Tomich Brothers Logistics LLC** - *San Pedro, CA United States of America* MMSI: 367549080 Official number: CF7336UH	*135* 43 -		**1977 Thompson Machine Works Ltd — Parksville BC** L reg 20.40 Br ex - Dght - Lbp - Br md - Dpth - Welded, 1 dk	**(B11B2FV) Fishing Vessel**	**1 oil engine** driving 1 FP propeller
8856778 *WDE5691* -	**SEA PEARL** *ex Paradise Queen -2012* **Vessel Management Associates Inc** - *Honolulu, HI United States of America* MMSI: 367192360 Official number: 982518	**201** 60 -		**1991 Johnson Shipbuilding & Repair — Bayou La Batre, Al** Yd No: 121 Loa - Br ex - Dght - Lbp 26.61 Br md 7.92 Dpth 3.87 Welded, 1 dk	**(B11B2FV) Fishing Vessel**	**1 oil engine** driving 1 FP propeller
8020305 - -	**SEA PEARL II** **Premium Seafoods Int Pty Ltd** SatCom: Inmarsat C 450301640 *Fremantle, WA Australia* Official number: 385835	*138* 84 -		**1980-07 Australian Shipbuilding Industries (WA) Pty Ltd — Fremantle WA** Yd No: 183 Loa 22.59 Br ex - Dght 2.941 Lbp 21.37 Br md 6.27 Dpth 3.79 Welded, 1 dk	**(B11A2FT) Trawler**	**1 oil engine** driving 1 FP propeller Total Power: 268kW (364hp) Caterpillar 3408TA 1 x Vee 4 Stroke 8 Cy. 137 x 152 268kW (364bhp) Caterpillar Tractor Co-USA
6810251 *3EMI3* -	**SEA PET I** *ex Libra Gas I -2007 ex Tine Kosan -1994* *ex Tine Tholstrup -1990* **Sea Bay Shipping Inc** - *Panama Panama* MMSI: 351691000 Official number: 36065PEXT	**1,324** 468 1,622 T/cm 6.7	Class: (LR) (BV) Classed LR until 24/9/07	**1968-01 Jos L Meyer — Papenburg** Yd No: 548 Loa 71.19 (BB) Br ex 12.04 Dght 4.630 Lbp 65.10 Br md 12.00 Dpth 5.50 Welded, 1 dk	**(A11B2TG) LPG Tanker** Liq (Gas): 1,622 2 x Gas Tank (s); 2 independent (stl) cyl horizontal 2 Cargo Pump (s): 2x125m³/hr Ice Capable	**1 oil engine** driving 1 FP propeller Total Power: 883kW (1,201hp) 10.0kn Deutz RBV8M545 1 x 4 Stroke 8 Cy. 320 x 450 883kW (1201bhp) Kloeckner Humboldt Deutz AG-West Germany AuxGen: 3 x 160kW 380V 50Hz a.c Fuel: 213.5 (d.f.) 6.0pd
8512499 - -	**SEA PHANTOM** *ex Satrya Express -2001* **Seaport International Shipping Co LLC** - *Sharjah United Arab Emirates* Official number: 4742	**127** 38 65	Class: BV (KI) (NV)	**1984-12 SBF Shipbuilders (1977) Pty Ltd — Fremantle WA** Yd No: 103 Loa 31.32 Br ex 6.56 Dght 2.000 Lbp 26.75 Br md 6.51 Dpth 3.51 Welded, 1 dk	**(A37B2PS) Passenger Ship** Hull Material: Aluminium Alloy Passengers: unberthed: 80	**2 oil engines** with clutches & sr geared to sc. shafts driving 2 FP propellers Total Power: 2,148kW (2,920hp) M.T.U. 12V396TB93 2 x Vee 4 Stroke 12 Cy. 165 x 185 each-1074kW (1460bhp) MTU Friedrichshafen GmbH-Friedrichshafen AuxGen: 2 x 26kW 415V 50Hz a.c
9326653 *V7OC8* -	**SEA PHANTOM** **Sea Phantom Shipholding SA** Perosea Shipping Co SA *Majuro Marshall Islands* MMSI: 538003061 Official number: 3061	**8,503** 4,173 13,115 T/cm 23.2	Class: AB	**2008-03 21st Century Shipbuilding Co Ltd — Tongyeong** Yd No: 223 Loa 128.60 (BB) Br ex 20.43 Dght 8.714 Lbp 120.86 Br md 20.40 Dpth 11.50 Welded, 1 dk	**(A12B2TR) Chemical/Products Tanker** Double Hull (13F) Liq: 13,400; Liq (Oil): 13,400 Cargo Heating Coils Compartments: 12 Wing Ta, 2 Wing Slop Ta, ER 12 Cargo Pump (s): 12x300m³/hr Manifold: Bow/CM: 60.9m	**1 oil engine** driving 1 FP propeller Total Power: 4,440kW (6,037hp) 13.4kn MAN-B&W 6S35MC 1 x 2 Stroke 6 Cy. 350 x 1400 4440kW (6037bhp) STX Engine Co Ltd-South Korea AuxGen: 3 x 550kW a.c Thrusters: 1 Thwart. FP thruster (f) Fuel: 79.6 (d.f.) 607.1 (r.f.)
9045156 *A8NM8* -	**SEA PHOENIX** *ex Amber Cherry -1996* **Sea Phoenix Inc** Roswell Navigation Corp *Monrovia Liberia* MMSI: 636013524 Official number: 13524	**7,303** 4,812 8,056	Class: NK (BV)	**1992-09 Shin Kochi Jyuko K.K. — Kochi** Yd No: 7021 Loa 134.02 (BB) Br ex - Dght 6.200 Lbp 125.00 Br md 20.80 Dpth 10.17 Welded, 1 dk, 2nd & 3rd dks in holds only	**(A34A2GR) Refrigerated Cargo Ship** Cars: 291 Ins: 11,165 TEU 12 incl 12 ref C Compartments: 4 Ho, ER, 1 Tw Dk in Fo'c's'l, 7 Tw Dk 4 Ha: 4 (7.4 x 7.3)ER Derricks: 8x5t	**1 oil engine** driving 1 FP propeller Total Power: 7,061kW (9,600hp) 19.3kn Mitsubishi 8UEC45LA 1 x 2 Stroke 8 Cy. 450 x 1350 7061kW (9600bhp) Kobe Hatsudoki KK-Japan AuxGen: 4 x 387kW a.c
9350525 *C4YJ2* -	**SEA PIKE** **SFL Sea Pike Ltd** Deep Sea Supply Navegacao Maritima Ltda SatCom: Inmarsat C 420917410 *Limassol Cyprus* MMSI: 209174000 Official number: 9350525	**2,160** 1,036 3,250	Class: NV	**2007-10 Cochin Shipyard Ltd — Ernakulam** Yd No: BY-59 Loa 71.90 (BB) Br ex - Dght 5.830 Lbp 66.31 Br md 16.00 Dpth 7.00 Welded, 1 dk	**(B21A20S) Platform Supply Ship**	**2 oil engines** reduction geared to sc. shafts driving 2 CP propellers Total Power: 4,010kW (5,452hp) 11.0kn Bergens KRMB-9 2 x 4 Stroke 9 Cy. 250 x 300 each-2005kW (2726bhp) Rolls Royce Marine AS-Norway AuxGen: 2 x 250kW 440V 60Hz a.c, 2 x 1280kW 440V 60Hz a.c Thrusters: 2 Thwart. CP thruster (f); 1 Thwart. CP thruster (a)
7404229 *LAYD* -	**SEA PILOT** *ex Siddis Pilot -2006* **Sea Supply AS** Chriship AS *Sortland Norway* MMSI: 258361000 Official number: 18685	**1,171** 352 726	Class: NV	**1976-01 Nieuwe Noord Nederlandse Scheepswerven B.V. — Groningen** Yd No: 386 Loa 58.27 Br ex 12.02 Dght 4.122 Lbp 51.34 Br md 12.00 Dpth 5.90 Welded, 1 dk	**(B21B20A) Anchor Handling Tug Supply**	**2 oil engines** reduction geared to sc. shafts driving 2 CP propellers Total Power: 4,530kW (6,158hp) 12.0kn Polar SF116VS-F 2 x Vee 4 Stroke 16 Cy. 250 x 300 each-2265kW (3079bhp) AB Bofors NOHAB-Sweden AuxGen: 2 x 170kW 440V 60Hz a.c, 1 x 56kW 440V 60Hz a.c Thrusters: 1 Thwart. FP thruster (f); 1 Retract. directional thruster (f)
9011466 *5NQY* -	**SEA PIONEER** *ex Rohas Ria -2008* **Sea Transport Services Nigeria Ltd** Oceanic Shipping Services Pvt Ltd *Lagos Nigeria* MMSI: 657438000 Official number: 377772	**3,727** 2,431 7,028 T/cm 14.7	Class: (AB)	**1991-11 Malaysia Shipyard & Engineering Sdn Bhd — Pasir Gudang** Yd No: 047 Loa 104.30 Br ex - Dght 6.730 Lbp 98.70 Br md 16.80 Dpth 8.30 Welded, 1 dk	**(A13B2TP) Products Tanker** Single Hull Liq: 8,322; Liq (Oil): 8,322 Compartments: 12 Wing Ta, ER, 2 Wing Slop Ta 2 Cargo Pump (s): 2x700m³/hr	**1 oil engine** reverse reduction geared to sc. shaft driving 1 FP propeller Total Power: 2,611kW (3,550hp) 11.5kn Blackstone ESL16MK2 1 x Vee 4 Stroke 16 Cy. 222 x 292 2611kW (3550bhp) Mirrlees Blackstone (Stamford)Ltd.-Stamford Fuel: 377.0
9339650 *V7PC8* -	**SEA PIONEER** *ex Karisma -2012 ex Trust Pioneer -2010* *ex Alam Comel -2008* **Bondi Ship Holding SA** Trinity Ships Inc *Majuro Marshall Islands* MMSI: 538003210 Official number: 3210	**22,184** 9,431 34,671 T/cm 41.5	Class: LR (RI) ✠ **100A1** SS 09/2012 Double Hull oil and chemical tanker, Ship Type 3 ESP **ShipRight** (SDA, FDA, CM) *IWS SPM LI ✠ **LMC UMS IGS** Eq.Ltr: Jt; Cable: 605.0/66.0 U3 (a)	**2007-09 Dalian Shipbuilding Industry Co Ltd — Dalian LN (No 1 Yard)** Yd No: PC350-14 Converted From: Products Tanker-2008 Converted From: Chemical/Products Tanker-2008 Loa 171.20 (BB) Br ex 27.44 Dght 11.815 Lbp 162.00 Br md 27.40 Dpth 17.30 Welded, 1 dk	**(A12B2TR) Chemical/Products Tanker** Double Hull (13F) Liq: 36,767; Liq (Oil): 36,767 Compartments: 12 Wing Ta, 2 Wing Slop Ta, ER 12 Cargo Pump (s): 10x500m³/hr, 2x300m³/hr Manifold: Bow/CM: 83.3m	**1 oil engine** driving 1 FP propeller Total Power: 7,150kW (9,721hp) 14.5kn MAN-B&W 5S50MC 1 x 2 Stroke 5 Cy. 500 x 1910 7150kW (9721bhp) Dalian Marine Diesel Works-China AuxGen: 3 x 910kW 450V 60Hz a.c Boilers: AuxB (ex.g.) 8.7kgf/cm² (8.5bar), WTAuxB (o.f.) 8.7kgf/cm² (8.5bar) Fuel: 110.0 (d.f.) 1156.0 (r.f.)
9319557 *9HA2144* -	**SEA PIONEER** *ex Olympian Racer -2009* *ex Sinotrans Tokyo -2008* *ex Olympian Racer -2005* **Sea Pioneer Maritime Ltd** Interorient Marine Services (Germany) GmbH & Co KG *Valletta Malta* MMSI: 248046000 Official number: 9319557	**9,910** 5,032 14,003 T/cm 28.0	Class: GL	**2005-05 SC Aker Tulcea SA — Tulcea** Yd No: 313 Loa 147.82 (BB) Br ex - Dght 8.506 Lbp 140.30 Br md 23.25 Dpth 11.50 Welded, 1 dk	**(A33A2CC) Container Ship (Fully Cellular)** Grain: 16,000; Bale: 16,000 TEU 1102 C Ho 334 TEU C Dk 768 incl 220 ref C	**1 oil engine** Reduction geared to sc. shaft driving 1 CP propeller Total Power: 9,600kW (13,052hp) 19.0kn MAN-B&W 8L48/60B 1 x 4 Stroke 8 Cy. 480 x 600 9600kW (13052bhp) MAN B&W Diesel AG-Augsburg AuxGen: 3 x 680kW 450/230V 60Hz a.c, 1 x 1275kW 450/230V 60Hz a.c Thrusters: 1 Tunnel thruster (f)

9084750 *XUGQ9* -	**SEA PLAIN STAR** *ex* Chun Wei *-2007* *ex* Shinyo Maru No. 1 *-2005* **Sunton Management Ltd** Sea Plain Shipping Co Ltd *Phnom Penh* *Cambodia* MMSI: 515765000 Official number: 0593012	**1,980** 1,021 1,471	Class: UM (UB)	**1993**-12 **Hitachi Zosen Mukaishima Marine Co Ltd — Onomichi HS** Yd No: 78 Loa 66.93 Br ex 13.10 Dght 4.560 Lbp 61.00 Br md 13.00 Dpth 7.53 Welded, 2 dks	**(A31A2GX) General Cargo Ship** Grain: 1,248 Compartments: 1 Ho, ER 1 Ha: ER	**1 oil engine** reverse geared to sc. shaft driving 1 FP propeller Total Power: 736kW (1,001hp) Hanshin LH34LG 1 x 4 Stroke 6 Cy. 340 x 640 736kW (1001bhp) The Hanshin Diesel Works Ltd-Japan
7410307 *9GGK* -	**SEA PLUS 87** *ex* Sea Plus 88 *-2008* *ex* Ghako 101 *-2008* *ex* Hae Chang No. 101 *-1983* **D-H Fisheries Co Ltd** - *Takoradi* *Ghana* Official number: 316691	*417* 202 497	Class: (KR) (NK)	**1975**-05 **Miho Zosensho K.K. — Shimizu** Yd No: 1025 Loa 55.45 Br ex 9.38 Dght 3.549 Lbp 47.00 Br md 8.49 Dpth 3.94 Welded, 1 dk	**(B11B2FV) Fishing Vessel** Ins: 418 13 Ha: (1.6 x 1.6)10 (1.3 x 1.3)2 (1.0 x 1.0) Derricks: 1x0.5t	**1 oil engine** driving 1 FP propeller Total Power: 1,177kW (1,600hp) 12.0kn Niigata 6M31X 1 x 4 Stroke 6 Cy. 310 x 460 1177kW (1600bhp) Niigata Engineering Co Ltd-Japan AuxGen: 2 x 200kW 225V a.c Fuel: 227.5 6.0pd
7410266 *9GEY* AFT 20	**SEA PLUS 89** *ex* Gbese 6 *-2004* *ex* Baek Du San No. 6 *-1982* **D-H Fisheries Co Ltd** - *Takoradi* *Ghana* MMSI: 627682000 Official number: 316682	*416* 209 489	Class: (KR) (NK)	**1975**-01 **Miho Zosensho K.K. — Shimizu** Yd No: 1021 Loa 55.45 Br ex 8.51 Dght 3.549 Lbp 47.00 Br md 8.49 Dpth 3.94 Welded, 1 dk	**(B11B2FV) Fishing Vessel** Bale: 418 12 Ha: (1.6 x 1.6)10 (1.3 x 1.3) (1.0 x 1.0)	**1 oil engine** driving 1 FP propeller Total Power: 1,177kW (1,600hp) 12.0kn Niigata 6M31X 1 x 4 Stroke 6 Cy. 310 x 460 1177kW (1600bhp) Niigata Engineering Co Ltd-Japan AuxGen: 2 x 200kW Fuel: 227.5 6.0pd
7408275 *9GDB* AFT 29	**SEA PLUS 97** *ex* Victory No. 1 *-2012* *ex* Afko 313 *-2007* *ex* Kaas 107 *-1987* *ex* Dong Won No. 807 *-1983* *ex* Baek Du San No. 5 *-1977* **D-H Fisheries Co Ltd** - *Takoradi* *Ghana* MMSI: 627695000 Official number: 316695	*454* 214 559	Class: (KR)	**1974**-07 **Miho Zosensho K.K. — Shimizu** Yd No: 991 Loa 57.43 Br ex 10.32 Dght 3.696 Lbp 48.98 Br md 9.00 Dpth 4.09 Welded, 1 dk	**(B11B2FV) Fishing Vessel** Ins: 417 7 Ha: 7 (1.6 x 1.6)	**1 oil engine** driving 1 FP propeller Total Power: 1,324kW (1,800hp) 12.0kn Akasaka AH33 1 x 4 Stroke 6 Cy. 330 x 500 1324kW (1800bhp) Akasaka Tekkosho KK (Akasaka DieselLtd)-Japan AuxGen: 2 x 264kW 445V a.c
9609146 *V7CP9* -	**SEA PLUTO** *ex* Very Mighty *-2013* **Pluto Shipowning Inc** Golden Ocean Management Asia Pte Ltd *Majuro* *Marshall Islands* MMSI: 538005303 Official number: 5303	**44,025** 27,679 81,007 T/cm 71.9	Class: LR ✠ **100A1** SS 11/2013 bulk carrier CSR BC-A GRAB (25) Nos. 2, 4 & 6 holds may be empty ESP **ShipRight** (CM, ACS (B)) *IWS LI EP (R) ✠ **LMC** **UMS** Eq.Ltr: Q†; Cable: 700.0/81.0 U3 (a)	**2013**-11 **New Times Shipbuilding Co Ltd — Jingjiang JS** Yd No: 0108207 Loa 229.00 Br ex 32.30 Dght 14.450 Lbp 225.50 Br md 32.26 Dpth 20.05 Welded, 1 dk	**(A21A2BC) Bulk Carrier** Grain: 97,000; Bale: 90,784 Compartments: 7 Ho, ER 7 Ha: 5 (18.3 x 15.0) (15.7 x 15.1)ER (13.1 x 13.2)	**1 oil engine** driving 1 FP propeller Total Power: 11,900kW (16,179hp) 14.1kn MAN-B&W 5S60MC-C8 1 x 2 Stroke 5 Cy. 600 x 2400 11900kW (16179bhp) STX Engine Co Ltd-South Korea AuxGen: 3 x 710kW 440V 60Hz a.c Boilers: AuxB (Comp) 9.2kgf/cm² (9.0bar)
9061021 *YDA4873* -	**SEA POINTER** *ex* Sang Pointer *-2008* *ex* Sea Pointer *-2003* *ex* Sang Pointer *-1999* *ex* Sea Pointer *-1995* **PT Salam Pacific Offshore** - *Jakarta* *Indonesia* MMSI: 525024016	**297** 89 216	Class: NK (LR) ✠ Classed LR until 1/9/13	**1994**-02 **Tianjin Xinhe Shipyard — Tianjin** Yd No: 22882 Loa 30.50 Br ex 10.60 Dght 3.500 Lbp 29.50 Br md 9.60 Dpth 4.36 Welded, 1 dk	**(B32A2ST) Tug** Passengers: unberthed: 10	**2 oil engines** gearing integral to driving 2 Z propellers Total Power: 2,520kW (3,426hp) 13.0kn Kromhout 8FGHD240 2 x 4 Stroke 8 Cy. 240 x 260 each-1260kW (1713bhp) Stork Wartsila Diesel BV-Netherlands AuxGen: 2 x 90kW 415V 50Hz a.c Fuel: 136.0
9392951 *5BDL2* -	**SEA POLLOCK** **DESS PSV Ltd** Deep Sea Supply Navegacao Maritima Ltda SatCom: Inmarsat C 420932010 *Limassol* *Cyprus* MMSI: 209320000 Official number: 9392951	**2,160** 1,036 3,250	Class: NV (IR)	**2008**-04 **Cochin Shipyard Ltd — Ernakulam** Yd No: BY-61 Loa 71.90 Br ex 16.03 Dght 5.830 Lbp 66.80 Br md 16.00 Dpth 7.00 Welded, 1 dk	**(B21A2OS) Platform Supply Ship**	**2 oil engines** reduction geared to sc. shafts driving 2 CP propellers Total Power: 4,009kW (5,451hp) 11.0kn Bergens KRMB-9 2 x 4 Stroke 9 Cy. 250 x 300 each-2004kW (2725bhp) Rolls Royce Marine AS-Norway AuxGen: 2 x 225kW 440V 60Hz a.c, 2 x 1280kW 440V 60Hz a.c Thrusters: 2 Thwart. CP thruster (f); 1 Thwart. CP thruster (a)
9322126 *V7LV4* -	**SEA POWER** **Sea Power Shipholding SA** Perosea Shipping Co SA SatCom: Inmarsat Mini-M 764614987 *Majuro* *Marshall Islands* MMSI: 538002814 Official number: 2814	**8,539** 4,117 13,096 T/cm 23.2	Class: BV (AB)	**2007**-04 **21st Century Shipbuilding Co Ltd — Tongyeong** Yd No: 217 Loa 128.60 (BB) Br ex 20.43 Dght 8.714 Lbp 120.40 Br md 20.40 Dpth 11.50 Welded, 1 dk	**(A12B2TR) Chemical/Products Tanker** Double Hull (13F) Liq: 13,402; Liq (Oil): 13,402 Cargo Heating Coils Compartments: 12 Wing Ta, 2 Wing Slop Ta, ER 12 Cargo Pump (s): 12x300m³/hr Manifold: Bow/CM: 61.4m	**1 oil engine** driving 1 FP propeller Total Power: 4,440kW (6,037hp) 13.4kn MAN-B&W 6S35MC 1 x 2 Stroke 6 Cy. 350 x 1400 4440kW (6037bhp) STX Engine Co Ltd-South Korea AuxGen: 3 x 550kW a.c Thrusters: 1 Tunnel thruster (f) Fuel: 76.0 (d.f.) 678.0 (r.f.)
9002049 *OUVL2* -	**SEA POWER** *ex* Ocean Hanne *-2005* *ex* Elisabeth *-1998* *ex* Ocean Hanne *-1997* *ex* Maersk Pacific *-1994* *ex* Ocean Hanne *-1993* **K/S Sea Power & Energy** A2SEA A/S SatCom: Inmarsat C 421907910 *Esbjerg* *Denmark (DIS)* MMSI: 219079000 Official number: D3361	**3,422** 999 3,095 T/cm 12.8	Class: GL (LR) (BV) ✠ Classed LR until 18/8/93	**1991**-05 **Orskov Christensens Staalskibsvaerft A/S — Frederikshavn** Yd No: 168 Converted From: General Cargo Ship (with Ro-Ro Facility)-2001 Loa 91.50 (BB) Br ex - Dght 4.250 Lbp 84.98 Br md 21.60 Dpth 6.90 Welded, 1 dk	**(B22A2ZM) Offshore Construction Vessel, jack up** Stern ramp (s) Len: 9.16 Wid: 4.70 Swl: - Cranes: 1x100t,1x27t Ice Capable	**2 oil engines** with clutches, flexible couplings & sr geared to sc. shafts driving 2 CP propellers Total Power: 2,400kW (3,264hp) 14.0kn MaK 6M332C 2 x 4 Stroke 6 Cy. 240 x 330 each-1200kW (1632bhp) Krupp MaK Maschinenbau GmbH-Kiel AuxGen: 2 x 750kW 380V 50Hz a.c, 1 x 139kW 380V 50Hz a.c Thrusters: 1 Thwart. CP thruster (f) Fuel: 349.4 (d.f.) 9.8pd
8890970 *A9D2856* -	**SEA POWER** *ex* Profit Power *-2006* **Al Jazeera Shipping Co WLL (AJS)** - *Bahrain* *Bahrain* Official number: BN 9184	**150** 45 135	Class: AB (NK)	**1995**-07 **Super-Light Shipbuilding Contractor — Sibu** Yd No: 17 Loa 23.25 Br ex - Dght 2.712 Lbp 21.77 Br md 7.32 Dpth 3.20 Welded, 1 dk	**(B32B2SP) Pusher Tug**	**2 oil engines** reduction geared to sc. shafts driving 2 FP propellers Total Power: 806kW (1,096hp) 10.0kn Caterpillar 3412 2 x Vee 4 Stroke 12 Cy. 137 x 152 each-403kW (548bhp) Caterpillar Inc-USA AuxGen: 2 x 20kW a.c
7730850 *H04692* -	**SEA POWER** *ex* Green Vile 2 *-2013* *ex* Greenville II *-2005* *ex* Mansal 38 *-1991* *ex* Reem *-1987* *ex* San-e Maru *-1987* **Zaki Radi Al Zair** Sea Eagles Shipping LLC *Panama* *Panama* MMSI: 356373000 Official number: 3251407A	**387** 116 -	Class: IS (RS) (AB) (NK)	**1972 Murakami Hide Zosen K.K. — Imabari** Yd No: 97 Loa - Br ex - Dght 3.960 Lbp 30.51 Br md 9.50 Dpth 4.22 Welded, 1 dk	**(B32A2ST) Tug**	**2 oil engines** reverse reduction geared to sc. shafts driving 2 FP propellers Total Power: 2,060kW (2,800hp) Makita FSHC633 2 x 4 Stroke 6 Cy. 330 x 500 each-1030kW (1400bhp) Makita Diesel Co Ltd-Japan AuxGen: 2 x 80kW Fuel: 200.0
7113179 *A6E2945* -	**SEA POWER** *ex* Rahhal *-2006* *ex* Spica I *-2001* *ex* BUE Orsay *-2000* *ex* Transporter *-1999* *ex* Hornbeck Transporter *-1996* *ex* Safe Transporter *-1995* *ex* Stevns Transporter *-1990* *ex* Maersk Server *-1987* **Middle East Fuel Distribution Co LLC** - *Sharjah* *United Arab Emirates* MMSI: 470641000 Official number: 4732	**718** 216 356	Class: GL (LR) (BV) ✠ Classed LR until 1/12/87	**1971**-07 **Aarhus Flydedok A/S — Aarhus** Yd No: 146 Converted From: Offshore Tug/Supply Ship-1990 Loa 53.35 Br ex 11.23 Dght 3.455 Lbp 50.02 Br md 11.00 Dpth 4.02 Welded, 1 dk	**(B21A2OS) Platform Supply Ship** Liq: 612 Compartments: 8 Ta, 1 Ho, ER Derricks: 1x3t; Winches: 1 Ice Capable	**2 oil engines** driving 2 FP propellers Total Power: 2,788kW (3,790hp) 13.0kn MaK 8MU452AK 2 x 4 Stroke 8 Cy. 320 x 450 each-1394kW (1895bhp) Atlas MaK Maschinenbau GmbH-Kiel AuxGen: 3 x 128kW 220/380V 50Hz a.c Thrusters: 1 Thwart. CP thruster (f) Fuel: 280.0 (d.f.)
9299252 - -	**SEA PRELUDE** - -	**499** 241 599 T/cm 4.2	Class: (NK)	**2003**-09 **Guangzhou Shipyard International Co Ltd — Guangzhou GD** Yd No: 02-2008 Loa 42.89 Br ex - Dght 2.956 Lbp 40.07 Br md 10.80 Dpth 4.00 Welded, 1 dk	**(A13B2TP) Products Tanker** Single Hull Liq: 811; Liq (Oil): 811 5 Cargo Pump (s): 4x58m³/hr, 1x72m³/hr Manifold: Bow/CM: 18m	**2 oil engines** geared to sc. shafts driving 2 FP propellers Total Power: 940kW (1,278hp) 9.0kn Yanmar 6LAH-STE3 2 x 4 Stroke 6 Cy. 150 x 165 each-470kW (639bhp) Yanmar Diesel Engine Co Ltd-Japan Fuel: 80.0

IMO / Call sign	Name, former names, owners, flag	Tonnage	Class	Builder, dimensions	Type	Machinery
9342956 *A9D2925* -	**SEA PRIDE** *ex* Uni Haul Mabel *-2007* **Al Jazeera Shipping Co** Al Jazeera Shipping Co WLL (AJS) *Bahrain* *Bahrain* MMSI: 408821000	**299** 89 350	Class: BV	**2005-05 Guangzhou Panyu Lingshan Shipyard Ltd — Guangzhou GD** (Hull) Yd No: 124 **2005-05 Cheoy Lee Shipyards Ltd — Hong Kong** Yd No: 4852 Loa 31.80 Br ex 10.10 Dght 3.200 Lbp 28.00 Br md 9.60 Dpth 4.15 Welded, 1 dk	**(B32A2ST) Tug**	**2 oil engines** reduction geared to sc. shafts driving 2 FP propellers Total Power: 2,238kW (3,042hp) 11.0kn Caterpillar 3512B 2 x Vee 4 Stroke 12 Cy. 170 x 190 each-1119kW (1521bhp) Caterpillar Inc-USA AuxGen: 2 x 85kW 400V 50Hz a.c Fuel: 190.0 (d.f.)
9582166 - -	**SEA PRINCE** *launched as* Fast Eagle *-2010* **Seatrade Offshore Services for Marine Companies** -	**202** 75 150	Class: (BV)	**2010-10 Port Said Engineering Works — Port Said** Yd No: 67890 Loa 31.00 Br ex - Dght - Lbp - Br md 7.50 Dpth - Welded, 1 dk	**(B34L2QU) Utility Vessel**	**2 oil engines** reduction geared to sc. shafts driving 2 Propellers Total Power: 1,640kW (2,230hp) Caterpillar C32 2 x Vee 4 Stroke 12 Cy. 145 x 162 each-820kW (1115bhp) Caterpillar Inc-USA
9553593 - -	**SEA PRINCE** **Ships & Boats Marine Management & Supplies** *Port Said* *Egypt* Official number: 6537	**454** 136 -		**2008-11 Port Said Engineering Works — Port Said** Yd No: 512 Loa 39.00 Br ex - Dght 2.400 Lbp 37.00 Br md 9.00 Dpth - Welded, 1 dk	**(B21A2OS) Platform Supply Ship**	**2 oil engines** reduction geared to sc. shafts driving 2 Propellers Total Power: 2,206kW (3,000hp) 11.5kn Caterpillar 3512 2 x Vee 4 Stroke 12 Cy. 170 x 190 each-1103kW (1500bhp) Caterpillar Inc-USA AuxGen: 2 x 150kW 480V 60Hz a.c Thrusters: 1 Tunnel thruster (f) Fuel: 150.0
9702259 *WDG7955* -	**SEA PRINCE** **Robert W Nelson** *Kasilof, AK* *United States of America* MMSI: 367572550 Official number: 1243484	*106* 85 -		**2012-10 Freddy's Marine LLC — Homer AK** L reg 17.67 Br ex - Dght - Lbp - Br md 6.10 Dpth 4.17 Bonded, 1 dk	**(B11B2FV) Fishing Vessel** Hull Material: Reinforced Plastic	**1 oil engine** reduction geared to sc. shaft driving 1 Propeller Thrusters: 1 Tunnel thruster (f)
6921373 - -	**SEA PRINCE** *ex* Rusalka *-2008* *ex* Sea Prince *-2007* *ex* Leonidas *-2007* *ex* Chahira *-2006* *ex* Leonidas *-2003* *ex* Lucky III *-2002* *ex* Star I *-2002* *ex* Nasnas *-2001* *ex* Theodora *-2001* *ex* Vassilis VII *-1998* *ex* Dwejra II *-1987* *ex* ASD Iris *-1976* *ex* Iris *-1973* **Ali N Abbas** -	**2,426** 1,519 3,750	Class: NA (LR) (GL) Classed LR until 1/3/00	**1969-07 N.V. Scheepswerf en Machinefabriek "De Biesbosch" — Dordrecht** Yd No: 520 Loa 84.26 (BB) Br ex 14.38 Dght 6.679 Lbp 75.01 Br md 14.20 Dpth 8.31 Welded, 2 dks	**(A31A2GX) General Cargo Ship** Grain: 5,317; Bale: 4,937 Compartments: 2 Ho, ER 2 Ha: (13.5 x 8.9) (31.4 x 11.0)ER Derricks: 3x12t	**1 oil engine** driving 1 FP propeller Total Power: 1,765kW (2,400hp) 14.5kn MWM RHS345AU 1 x 4 Stroke 8 Cy. 360 x 450 1765kW (2400bhp) Motoren Werke Mannheim AG (MWM)-West Germany AuxGen: 3 x 85kW 380V 50Hz a.c, 1 x 22kW 380V 50Hz a.c
6903711 - -	**SEA PRINCE** *ex* Kofuji Maru No. 22 *-1982* - -	*194* 122 27		**1968 Matsuura Tekko Zosen K.K. — Osakikamijima** Yd No: 193 Loa 35.77 Br ex 6.02 Dght 1.728 Lbp 31.98 Br md 6.00 Dpth 2.65 Welded, 1 dk	**(A37B2PS) Passenger Ship** Passengers: unberthed: 445	**1 oil engine** driving 1 FP propeller Total Power: 588kW (799hp) 12.5kn Hanshin 6LUS24 1 x 4 Stroke 6 Cy. 240 x 405 588kW (799bhp) Hanshin Nainenki Kogyo-Japan AuxGen: 1 x 12kW 225V a.c Fuel: 7.0 3.0pd
7614109 *A9D2526* -	**SEA PRINCE** *ex* Karan 2 *-1991* **Al Jazeera Shipping Co WLL (AJS)** *Bahrain* *Bahrain* Official number: 1077	*178* - -	Class: BV	**1976-02 Halter Marine, Inc. — New Orleans, La** Loa 30.48 Br ex - Dght 2.136 Lbp - Br md 7.32 Dpth 3.05 Welded	**(B21A2OS) Platform Supply Ship**	**1 oil engine** driving 1 FP propeller Total Power: 500kW (680hp) General Motors 1 x 2 Stroke 500kW (680bhp) General Motors Corp-USA
7367160 *WYT8569* -	**SEA PRINCE** *ex* Robin VII *-1983* **Crowley Marine Services Inc** *San Francisco, CA* *United States of America* MMSI: 366888750 Official number: 555271	**421** 126 -	Class: AB	**1974-02 McDermott Shipyards Inc — Morgan City LA** Yd No: 189 Loa 38.41 Br ex - Dght 4.255 Lbp 36.63 Br md 10.34 Dpth 5.01 Welded, 1 dk	**(B32A2ST) Tug**	**2 oil engines** reverse reduction geared to sc. shafts driving 2 FP propellers Total Power: 3,574kW (4,860hp) 13.0kn Alco 12V251E 2 x Vee 4 Stroke 12 Cy. 229 x 267 each-1787kW (2430bhp) Alco Engine Co-USA AuxGen: 2 x 75kW a.c Fuel: 457.0 (d.f.)
8883408 *YB3443* -	**SEA PRINCE** *ex* Nishi Nikko No. 3 *-1992* **PT Batam Fast** *Indonesia* MMSI: 525023092	**115** 73 -		**1976-10 Setouchi Zosen K.K. — Osakikamijima** Loa 23.00 Br ex - Dght - Lbp - Br md 5.40 Dpth 2.50 Welded, 1 dk	**(A37B2PS) Passenger Ship** Hull Material: Aluminium Alloy	**1 oil engine** driving 1 FP propeller
8853348 *WDF5374* -	**SEA PRINCESS** *ex* Sea Queen IV *-2013* *ex* Capt. Chau *-1994* - *Galliano, LA* *United States of America* MMSI: 367462440 Official number: 666946	*132* 106		**1984 Coastal Shipbuilding — Ocean Springs, Ms** Yd No: 79-10 Loa - Br ex - Dght - Lbp 22.86 Br md 6.71 Dpth 3.51 Welded, 1 dk	**(B11B2FV) Fishing Vessel**	**1 oil engine** driving 1 FP propeller
9150913 *ZCBU3* -	**SEA PRINCESS** *ex* Adonia *-2005* *ex* Sea Princess *-2003* **Princess Cruise Lines Ltd** *Hamilton* *Bermuda (British)* MMSI: 310465000 -	**77,499** 44,202 8,293	Class: LR (RI) ✠ **100A1** CS 11/2008 passenger ship *IWS ✠ **LMC** **CCS** Eq.Ltr: U†; Cable: 715.0/90.0 U3 (a)	**1998-11 Fincantieri-Cant. Nav. Italiani S.p.A. — Monfalcone** Yd No: 5998 Loa 261.31 (BB) Br ex 32.28 Dght 8.116 Lbp 221.40 Br md 32.25 Dpth 11.30 Welded, 5 dks plus 8 superstructure decks	**(A37A2PC) Passenger/Cruise** Passengers: cabins: 1011; berths: 2342	**4 diesel electric oil engines** driving 4 gen. each 11128kW 6600V a.c Connecting to 2 elec. motors each (14000kW) driving 2 FP propellers Total Power: 46,600kW (63,356hp) 19.5kn Sulzer 16ZAV40S 4 x Vee 4 Stroke 16 Cy. 400 x 560 each-11650kW (15839bhp) Grandi Motori Trieste-Italy AuxGen: 1 x 600kW 440V 60Hz a.c Boilers: e (ex.g.) 11.2kgf/cm² (11.0bar), AuxB (o.f.) 11.2kgf/cm² (11.0bar) Thrusters: 2 Thwart. CP thruster (f); 2 Thwart. CP thruster (a) Fuel: 266.0 (d.f.) (Heating Coils) 2963.0 (r.f.) 153.0pd
8516108 - -	**SEA PRINCESS** *ex* Reef Link II *-1992* -	*313* 129 43	Class: (NV)	**1987-05 North Queensland Engineers & Agents Pty Ltd — Cairns QLD** Yd No: 147 Loa 29.21 Br ex 11.46 Dght 2.171 Lbp 25.51 Br md 11.20 Dpth 3.30 Welded, 1 dk	**(A37B2PS) Passenger Ship** Hull Material: Aluminium Alloy Passengers: unberthed: 403	**2 oil engines** with clutches, flexible couplings & sr reverse geared to sc. shaft driving 2 FP propellers Total Power: 2,520kW (3,426hp) MWM TBD604BV12 2 x Vee 4 Stroke 12 Cy. 170 x 195 each-1260kW (1713bhp) Motoren Werke Mannheim AG (MWM)-West Germany AuxGen: 2 x 90kW 415V 50Hz a.c
8607634 *3FHU* -	**SEA PRINCESS** *ex* Flegra *-2013* *ex* Agia Theodora *-2010* *ex* Ocean Onyx *-2008* *ex* Tong Sheng *-2006* *ex* Mostfar *-2004* *ex* Witty *-1999* *ex* You Yi 24 *-1996* **Great Eastern Investments Inc** Prime Tankers LLC *Panama* *Panama* MMSI: 357559000 Official number: 4305111A	**4,492** 1,347 4,586	Class: BV (KR) (CC)	**1993-03 SC Santierul Naval SA Braila — Braila** Yd No: 1308 Converted From: General Cargo Ship-2006 Loa 101.50 Br ex - Dght 6.852 Lbp 94.13 Br md 16.60 Dpth 8.60 Welded, 1 dk	**(A13C2LA) Asphalt/Bitumen Tanker** Liq: 4,650; Liq (Oil): 4,650 2 Cargo Pump (s): 2x250m³/hr	**1 oil engine** geared to sc. shaft driving 1 FP propeller Total Power: 2,758kW (3,750hp) 12.0kn MAN 6L40/54A 1 x 4 Stroke 6 Cy. 400 x 540 2758kW (3750bhp) U.C.M. Resita S.A.-Resita AuxGen: 3 x 250kW 380V a.c Fuel: 107.0 (d.f.) 148.0 (r.f.) 6.0pd
9628025 *J8B4625* -	**SEA PRINCESS** *ex* Zakher Princess *-2013* **QMS 2 Offshore Services Ltd** Zakher Marine International Inc *Kingstown* *St Vincent & The Grenadines* MMSI: 376453000 Official number: 11098	**499** 149 360	Class: BV	**2011-12 Tuong Aik Shipyard Sdn Bhd — Sibu** Yd No: 2825 Loa 40.00 Br ex - Dght 4.400 Lbp 38.40 Br md 11.40 Dpth 4.95 Welded, 1 dk	**(B21B20A) Anchor Handling Tug Supply**	**2 oil engines** reduction geared to sc. shafts driving 2 FP propellers Total Power: 3,310kW (4,500hp) 12.0kn Mitsubishi S16R-MPTK2 2 x Vee 4 Stroke 16 Cy. 170 x 180 each-1655kW (2250bhp) Mitsubishi Heavy Industries Ltd-Japan AuxGen: 2 x 175kW 415V 50Hz a.c Thrusters: 1 Tunnel thruster (f) Fuel: 300.0

IMO / Call sign	Name / Owner	Tonnage	Class	Builder / Dimensions	Type / Cargo	Machinery
7718814 - -	**SEA PRINCESS II** *ex* Sedra *-2007* *ex* Sedra I *-1989* *ex* Neptank I *-1987* *ex* Tamaei Maru *-1985* - -	**1,902** 902 3,399	Class: (NK)	**1977-10 Teraoka Shipyard Co Ltd — Minamiawaji HG** Yd No: 171 Loa 81.51 (BB) Br ex 13.00 Dght 5.810 Lbp 74.95 Br md 13.00 Dpth 6.71 Riveted\Welded, 1 dk	**(A13B2TP) Products Tanker** Double Bottom Entire Compartment Length Liq: 3,367; Liq (Oil): 3,367	**1 oil engine** driving 1 FP propeller Total Power: 2,794kW (3,799hp) 11.8kn Hanshin 6LUS40 1 x 4 Stroke 6 Cy. 400 x 640 2794kW (3799bhp) Hanshin Nainenki Kogyo-Japan AuxGen: 2 x 144kW 445V 60Hz a.c Fuel: 48.5 (d.f.) 61.5 (r.f.) 10.5pd
8104072 - -	**SEA PRINCESS - S** - **Sarunic Bros Pty Ltd** - *Port Adelaide, SA* *Australia* Official number: 396607	**315** 99 220	Class: (NV)	**1982-03 Port Lincoln Ship Construction Pty Ltd — Port Lincoln SA** Yd No: 2 Loa 32.31 Br ex 8.41 Dght - Lbp 27.79 Br md - Dpth 4.02 Welded, 1 dk	**(B11B2FV) Fishing Vessel** Ins: 120; Liq: 139 Compartments: 8 Ho, ER 8 Ha:	**1 oil engine** sr geared to sc. shaft driving 1 CP propeller Total Power: 871kW (1,184hp) MWM TBD440-8 1 x 4 Stroke 8 Cy. 230 x 270 871kW (1184bhp) Motoren Werke Mannheim AG (MWM)-West Germany AuxGen: 1 x 104kW 415V 50Hz a.c, 1 x 66kW 415V 50Hz a.c
6510930 - -	**SEA PRODUCER** *ex* Nelco I *-1985* *ex* FS 211 (Col. Percival E. Gabel) *-1985* - -	**657** 197 528	Class: (RS) (AB)	**1944-01 Higgins Industries, Inc. — New Orleans, La** Yd No: 77 Converted From: General Cargo Ship-1944 Loa 54.86 Br ex 9.81 Dght 3.540 Lbp 50.68 Br md 9.76 Dpth 4.35 Welded, 1 dk	**(B11B2FV) Fishing Vessel** Compartments: 2 Ho, ER 2 Ha:	**2 oil engines** geared to sc. shafts driving 2 FP propellers Total Power: 930kW (1,264hp) 12.5kn Caterpillar 3412TA 2 x Vee 4 Stroke 12 Cy. 137 x 152 each-465kW (632bhp) (new engine 1990) Caterpillar Inc-USA AuxGen: 4 x 165kW a.c Fuel: 111.0 (d.f.)
9054614 *5NQY3* -	**SEA PROGRESS** *ex* Aegina *-2010* *ex* Dilesi *-2008* *ex* Aldebaran *-2003* **Sea Transport Services Nigeria Ltd** Oceanic Shipping Services Pvt Ltd *Lagos* *Nigeria* MMSI: 657530000 Official number: 377795	**4,999** 3,026 9,268 T/cm 17.1	Class: NK	**1992-07 Higaki Zosen K.K. — Imabari** Yd No: 410 Loa 115.28 (BB) Br ex 18.62 Dght 7.627 Lbp 108.00 Br md 18.60 Dpth 9.55 Welded, 1 dk	**(A12B2TR) Chemical/Products Tanker** Double Bottom Entire Compartment Length Liq: 10,488; Liq (Oil): 10,488 Cargo Heating Coils Compartments: 5 Ta, 10 Wing Ta, ER 15 Cargo Pump (s): 10x150m³/hr, 5x250m³/hr Manifold: Bow/CM: 62.9m	**1 oil engine** driving 1 FP propeller Total Power: 4,502kW (6,121hp) 14.0kn Mitsubishi 6UEC45LA 1 x 2 Stroke 6 Cy. 450 x 1350 4502kW (6121bhp) Akasaka Tekkosho KK (Akasaka DieselLtd)-Japan AuxGen: 4 x 263kW a.c Fuel: 620.0 (r.f.)
7827184 *HP9466* -	**SEA PROMISE** *ex* Al-Mojil 21 *-1998* *ex* Al-Mojil XXIV *-1993* *ex* Big Chip *-1992* *ex* Sherry Hebert *-1987* **Shell Pacific International Ltd** Seaport International Shipping Co LLC *Panama* *Panama* MMSI: 357114000 Official number: 2696600CH	**653** 196 1,200	Class: (AB)	**1979-06 Halter Marine, Inc. — Lockport, La** Yd No: 811 Loa 54.86 Br ex 11.61 Dght 3.677 Lbp 51.85 Br md 11.59 Dpth 4.27 Welded, 1 dk	**(B21A20S) Platform Supply Ship**	**2 oil engines** reverse reduction geared to sc. shafts driving 2 FP propellers Total Power: 2,206kW (3,000hp) 12.0kn EMD (Electro-Motive) 12-645-E6 2 x Vee 2 Stroke 12 Cy. 230 x 254 each-1103kW (1500bhp) General Motors Corp.Electro-Motive Div.-La Grange AuxGen: 2 x 75kW Thrusters: 1 Thwart. FP thruster (f)
9516143 *5BGQ3* -	**SEA PROSPECT** - **CA Sea Prospect Shipping Ltd** Interorient Marine Services Ltd *Limassol* *Cyprus* MMSI: 209179000 Official number: 9516143	**6,872** 3,410 9,385	Class: GL	**2012-06 Penglai Bohai Shipyard Co Ltd — Penglai SD** Yd No: PBZ07-90 Loa 109.83 Br ex - Dght 8.000 Lbp 105.80 Br md 18.20 Dpth 10.50 Welded, 1 dk	**(A31A2GX) General Cargo Ship** Grain: 11,770; Bale: 11,770 TEU 276 Compartments: 3 Ho, ER 3 Ha: ER Cranes: 2x60t Ice Capable	**1 oil engine** reduction geared to sc. shaft driving 1 Propeller Total Power: 4,000kW (5,438hp) 13.0kn MAN-B&W 8L32/40 1 x 4 Stroke 8 Cy. 320 x 400 4000kW (5438bhp) Shaanxi Diesel Heavy Industry Co Lt-China Thrusters: 1 Tunnel thruster (f)
9201061 *SVBW2* -	**SEA PROSPERITY** *ex* Star Sea Cosmos *-2013* **Sea Prosperity Shipping Inc** Mega Shipping Line Corp *Piraeus* *Greece* MMSI: 241288000	**28,015** 16,034 48,893 T/cm 54.4	Class: BV	**2000-03 Ishikawajima-Harima Heavy Industries Co Ltd (IHI) — Tokyo** Yd No: 3115 Loa 189.60 (BB) Br ex 32.23 Dght 11.620 Lbp 181.00 Br md 32.20 Dpth 16.50 Welded, 1 dk	**(A21A2BC) Bulk Carrier** Grain: 61,553; Bale: 59,844 Compartments: 5 Ho, ER 5 Ha: (17.6 x 17.0)4 (20.0 x 17.0)ER Cranes: 4x25t	**1 oil engine** driving 1 FP propeller Total Power: 7,700kW (10,469hp) 14.5kn Sulzer 6RTA48T 1 x 2 Stroke 6 Cy. 480 x 2000 7700kW (10469bhp) Diesel United Ltd.-Aioi
9593830 *V7AU3* -	**SEA PROTEUS** - **Proteus Shipping Inc** Golden Ocean Group Ltd (GOGL) *Majuro* *Marshall Islands* MMSI: 538005068 Official number: 5068	**43,951** 27,698 81,762 T/cm 71.6	Class: LR ✠ **100A1** SS 07/2013 bulk carrier CSR BC-A GRAB (20) Nos. 2, 4 & 6 holds may be empty ESP **ShipRight** (CM,ACS (B)) *IWS LI ✠ **LMC** **UMS** Eq.Ltr: N†; Cable: 687.5/81.0 U3 (a)	**2013-07 Wuhu Xinlian Shipbuilding Co Ltd — Wuhu AH** Yd No: W1021 Loa 229.00 (BB) Br ex 32.30 Dght 14.500 Lbp 225.50 Br md 32.26 Dpth 20.05 Welded, 1 dk	**(A21A2BC) Bulk Carrier** Grain: 95,700 Compartments: 7 Ho, ER 7 Ha: ER	**1 oil engine** driving 1 FP propeller Total Power: 11,900kW (16,179hp) 14.1kn MAN-B&W 5S60ME-C 1 x 2 Stroke 5 Cy. 600 x 2400 11900kW (16179bhp) Jiangsu Antai Power Machinery Co Lt-China AuxGen: 3 x 600kW 450V 60Hz a.c Boilers: AuxB (Comp) 9.2kgf/cm² (9.0bar)
9061033 *YDA4874* -	**SEA PULI** - **PT Salam Pacific Offshore** - *Jakarta* *Indonesia* MMSI: 525024017	**297** 89 160	Class: NK (Class contemplated) (LR) ✠ Classed LR until 4/2/14	**1994-02 Tianjin Xinhe Shipyard — Tianjin** Yd No: 22883 Loa 31.90 Br ex 10.60 Dght 3.500 Lbp 27.00 Br md 9.60 Dpth 4.50 Welded, 1 dk	**(B32A2ST) Tug**	**2 oil engines** gearing integral to driving 2 Z propellers Total Power: 2,500kW (3,400hp) 13.0kn Kromhout 8FGHD240 2 x 4 Stroke 8 Cy. 240 x 260 each-1250kW (1700bhp) Stork Wartsila Diesel BV-Netherlands AuxGen: 2 x 90kW 415V 50Hz a.c
9324112 *3EIA6* -	**SEA PULL** - **Golden Sunlight SA** Hisamoto Kisen Co Ltd (Hisamoto Kisen KK) SatCom: Inmarsat C 437205410 *Panama* *Panama* MMSI: 372054000 Official number: 3230307A	**88,523** 58,950 177,533 T/cm 119.0	Class: NK	**2006-10 Mitsui Eng. & SB. Co. Ltd., Chiba Works — Ichihara** Yd No: 1623 Loa 289.00 (BB) Br ex - Dght 17.975 Lbp 279.00 Br md 45.00 Dpth 24.40 Welded, 1 dk	**(A21A2BC) Bulk Carrier** Grain: 197,049 Compartments: 9 Ho, ER 9 Ha: 8 (15.5 x 20.6)ER (15.5 x 15.0)	**1 oil engine** driving 1 FP propeller Total Power: 16,860kW (22,923hp) 15.0kn MAN-B&W 6S70MC 1 x 2 Stroke 6 Cy. 700 x 2674 16860kW (22923bhp) Mitsui Engineering & Shipbuilding CLtd-Japan Fuel: 3970.0
7416973 - -	**SEA PUMA** *ex* Gulf Salvor *-2000* *ex* Seahorse *-1996* *ex* Alaskan Seahorse *-1994* *launched as* Dearborn 205 *-1976* **Global Offshore International Ltd** Global Pipeline Plus Nigeria Ltd	**856** 256 922	Class: (AB)	**1976-02 Bellinger Shipyards, Inc. — Jacksonville, Fl** Yd No: 112 Loa 60.51 Br ex 12.20 Dght 4.395 Lbp 55.40 Br md 12.15 Dpth 5.03 Welded, 1 dk	**(B21B20T) Offshore Tug/Supply Ship** Ice Capable	**2 oil engines** reverse reduction geared to sc. shafts driving 2 FP propellers Total Power: 3,678kW (5,000hp) 12.0kn Alco 12V251F 2 x Vee 4 Stroke 12 Cy. 229 x 267 each-1839kW (2500bhp) White Industrial Power Inc-USA AuxGen: 2 x 200kW Thrusters: 1 Thwart. FP thruster (f) Fuel: 408.5 (d.f.)
8037023 - -	**SEA QUEEN** - **Halfrank William Hydes** - *Roatan* *Honduras* Official number: U-1812095	*105* 71 -		**1980 Steiner Shipyard, Inc. — Bayou La Batre, Al** L reg 20.33 Br ex 6.71 Dght - Lbp - Br md - Dpth 3.28 Welded, 1 dk	**(B11B2FV) Fishing Vessel**	**1 oil engine** driving 1 FP propeller Total Power: 268kW (364hp)
8419946 - -	**SEA QUEEN** - **Primlaks Frozen Ltd** - *Port Harcourt* *Nigeria*	*140* 46 92	Class: (BV)	**1984-12 Astilleros Armon SA — Navia** Yd No: 106 Loa 24.01 Br ex - Dght 3.201 Lbp 20.91 Br md 6.96 Dpth 3.46 Welded, 1 dk	**(B11A2FT) Trawler** Ins: 105	**1 oil engine** with clutches, flexible couplings & reverse reduction geared to sc. shaft driving 1 FP propeller Total Power: 331kW (450hp) 10.0kn Caterpillar 3412T 1 x Vee 4 Stroke 12 Cy. 137 x 152 331kW (450bhp) Caterpillar Tractor Co-USA
8942137 *WDD6500* -	**SEA QUEEN** - **Francis VI Inc** - *Dulac, LA* *United States of America* MMSI: 367173670 Official number: 923317	**101** 81 -		**1988 Hung V. Le — Cut Off, La** L reg 21.95 Br ex - Dght - Lbp - Br md 6.40 Dpth 3.05 Welded, 1 dk	**(B11B2FV) Fishing Vessel**	**1 oil engine** driving 1 FP propeller

8748311 *JD3030* -	**SEA QUEEN** - **Kyushu Shosen Co Ltd** - *Nagasaki, Nagasaki* *Japan* Official number: 141195	*115* - 17		**2010-02 Setouchi Craft Co Ltd — Onomichi** Yd No: 288 Loa 30.50 Br ex - Dght 1.100 Lbp 26.00 Br md 6.30 Dpth 2.61 Welded, 1 dk	**(A37B2PS) Passenger Ship** Hull Material: Aluminium Alloy Passengers: unberthed: 140	**2 oil engines** reduction geared to sc. shafts driving 2 Propellers Total Power: 2,880kW (3,916hp) 30.0kn M.T.U. 16V2000M72 2 x Vee 4 Stroke 16 Cy. 135 x 156 each-1440kW (1958bhp) MTU Friedrichshafen GmbH-Friedrichshafen
9529176 - -	**SEA QUEEN** - **Ships & Boats Marine Management & Supplies** - *Alexandria* *Egypt* Official number: 8814	**152** 62 -	Class: BV	**2008-05 Port Said Engineering Works — Port Said** Yd No: 508 Loa 23.50 Br ex - Dght 1.000 Lbp 22.00 Br md 8.00 Dpth 2.00 Welded, 1 dk	**(B21B20T) Offshore Tug/Supply Ship**	**2 oil engines** reduction geared to sc. shafts driving 2 FP propellers Total Power: 588kW (800hp) 8.0kn Caterpillar 3406 2 x 4 Stroke 6 Cy. 137 x 165 each-294kW (400bhp) Caterpillar Inc-USA AuxGen: 2 x 80kW 380V 50Hz a.c Fuel: 80.0
8826955 - -	**SEA QUEEN 87** *ex* Asahi Maru No. 5 *-2005* **Hai Huang Fishery Co Ltd** -	*119* - -		**1986-03 Higashi Kyushu Shipbuilding Co Ltd — Usuki OT** L reg 28.10 Br ex - Dght 2.000 Lbp - Br md 6.10 Dpth 2.40 Bonded, 1 dk	**(B11B2FV) Fishing Vessel** Hull Material: Reinforced Plastic	**1 oil engine** driving 1 FP propeller
9018438 - -	**SEA QUEEN 88** *ex* Yuryo Maru No. 1 *-2005* - - *China*	*119* - -		**1990-02 Katsuura Dockyard Co. Ltd. — Nachi-Katsuura** Yd No: 305 L reg 30.00 Br ex - Dght 2.200 Lbp - Br md 6.60 Dpth 2.70 Welded	**(B11B2FV) Fishing Vessel**	**1 oil engine** driving 1 FP propeller
8885494 *WDE5203* -	**SEA QUEEN II** - **Thoai Van Nguyen** - *Cut Off, LA* *United States of America* Official number: 939008	*130* 104 -		**1989 Hung V. Le — Cut Off, La** L reg 23.98 Br ex - Dght - Lbp - Br md 7.02 Dpth 3.21 Welded, 1 dk	**(B11B2FV) Fishing Vessel**	**1 oil engine** driving 1 FP propeller
7731282 - -	**SEA QUEEN II** *ex* Sea Queen *-2005* *ex* Pandion I *-2005* **Dardanel Su Urunleri AS**	*121* 85 -		**1974 Bender Welding & Machine Co Inc — Mobile AL** L reg 20.85 Br ex - Dght - Lbp - Br md 6.71 Dpth 3.38 Welded, 1 dk	**(B11B2FV) Fishing Vessel**	**1 oil engine** driving 1 FP propeller Total Power: 530kW (721hp) Caterpillar 1 x 4 Stroke 530kW (721bhp) Caterpillar Tractor Co-USA
9429065 *9HA2111* -	**SEA QUEEN II** - **Sea Queen Navigation Ltd** Hellenic Star Shipping Co SA *Valletta* *Malta* MMSI: 249976000 Official number: 9429065	**33,044** 19,231 57,000 T/cm 58.8	Class: BV (GL)	**2010-10 Qingshan Shipyard — Wuhan HB** Yd No: 20060360 Loa 189.99 (BB) Br ex - Dght 12.800 Lbp 185.00 Br md 32.26 Dpth 18.00 Welded, 1 dk	**(A21A2BC) Bulk Carrier** Grain: 71,634; Bale: 68,200 Compartments: 5 Ho, ER 5 Ha: ER Cranes: 4x30t	**1 oil engine** driving 1 FP propeller Total Power: 9,480kW (12,889hp) 14.2kn MAN-B&W 6S50MC-C 1 x 2 Stroke 6 Cy. 500 x 2000 9480kW (12889bhp) STX Engine Co Ltd-South Korea AuxGen: 3 x 600kW 60Hz a.c
8970304 *WDA5004* -	**SEA QUEEN IIA** *ex* Miss Valarie II *-2013* - - *San Francisco, CA* *United States of America* Official number: 1110939	**164** 49 -		**2001 Ocean Marine, Inc. — Bayou La Batre, Al** Yd No: 392 L reg 25.35 Br ex - Dght - Lbp - Br md 7.62 Dpth 4.05 Welded, 1 dk	**(B11B2FV) Fishing Vessel**	**1 oil engine** driving 1 FP propeller
8885389 *WDC8244* -	**SEA QUEEN III** - **Sea Queen III Corp** - *Cut Off, LA* *United States of America* MMSI: 367083920 Official number: 995485	*100* 80 -		**1993 Thua V. Le — Larose, La** L reg 23.00 Br ex - Dght - Lbp - Br md 6.11 Dpth 3.05 Welded, 1 dk	**(B11B2FV) Fishing Vessel**	**1 oil engine** driving 1 FP propeller
8939910 *WDA3481* -	**SEA QUEST** - **Sea Quest Inc** - *Cape May, NJ* *United States of America* MMSI: 366798950 Official number: 1044127	**144** 98 -		**1996 in the United States of America** Yd No: 136 L reg 22.80 Br ex - Dght - Lbp - Br md 7.01 Dpth 3.93 Welded, 1 dk	**(B11B2FV) Fishing Vessel**	**1 oil engine** driving 1 FP propeller
9097355 *WDD9174* -	**SEA QUEST** - **Sea Quest LLC** Sea Global Fisheries LLC *Pago Pago, AS* *United States of America* MMSI: 366903000 Official number: 1203206	**1,416** 515 -		**2007-09 Ching Fu Shipbuilding Co Ltd — Kaohsiung** Yd No: 068 L reg 63.76 Br ex - Dght - Lbp - Br md 12.19 Dpth 7.25 Welded, 1 dk	**(B11B2FV) Fishing Vessel**	**1 oil engine** geared to sc. shaft driving 1 Propeller Total Power: 2,354kW (3,200hp) Daihatsu 8DLM-32 1 x 4 Stroke 8 Cy. 320 x 400 2354kW (3200bhp) Daihatsu Diesel Manufacturing Co Lt-Japan
9098373 - -	**SEA QUEST** *ex* Dylan's Quest *-2008* **Southern Towing Ltd** - *Port of Spain* *Trinidad & Tobago* MMSI: 362060000	**307** 92 -		**1999-06 La Force Shipyard Inc — Coden AL** Yd No: 91 Loa 37.49 Br ex - Dght 3.050 Lbp - Br md 9.14 Dpth 3.66 Welded, 1 dk	**(B21A20S) Platform Supply Ship**	**2 oil engines** reduction geared to sc. shafts driving 2 Propellers Total Power: 1,140kW (1,550hp) Caterpillar 3412 2 x Vee 4 Stroke 12 Cy. 137 x 152 each-570kW (775bhp) Caterpillar Inc-USA
9351402 *VJQ4737* -	**SEA QUEST II** *ex* Sea Quest *-2012* **Ecrolight Pty Ltd** - *Cairns, Qld* *Australia* Official number: 857942	**120** - -		**2004-12 New Wave Catamarans Pty Ltd — Brisbane QLD** Loa 23.50 Br ex - Dght 1.750 Lbp 21.65 Br md 7.50 Dpth 2.54 Welded, 1 dk	**(A37B2PS) Passenger Ship** Hull Material: Aluminium Alloy Passengers: unberthed: 130	**2 oil engines** geared to sc. shafts driving 2 FP propellers Total Power: 1,470kW (1,998hp) 27.0kn M.T.U. 12V183TE72 2 x Vee 4 Stroke 12 Cy. 128 x 142 each-735kW (999bhp) MTU Friedrichshafen GmbH-Friedrichshafen
9214252 *3FXL3* -	**SEA RACER** *ex* Sea Grace *-2008* *ex* Changi Hope *-2008* **Olive Sea Shipping Inc** Technomar Shipping Inc *Panama* *Panama* MMSI: 370890000 Official number: 4042909	**11,194** 6,784 18,320 T/cm 28.1	Class: NK	**2000-04 Shikoku Dockyard Co. Ltd. — Takamatsu** Yd No: 895 Loa 148.17 Br ex - Dght 9.120 Lbp 135.95 Br md 22.80 Dpth 12.20 Welded, 1 dk	**(A21A2BC) Bulk Carrier** Double Bottom Entire Compartment Length Grain: 23,212; Bale: 22,337 Compartments: 4 Ho, ER 4 Ha: (16.3 x 12.0)3 (19.0 x 12.0)ER Cranes: 3x30t	**1 oil engine** driving 1 FP propeller Total Power: 4,983kW (6,775hp) 13.5kn B&W 5L42MC 1 x 2 Stroke 5 Cy. 420 x 1360 4983kW (6775bhp) Mitsui Engineering & Shipbuilding CLtd-Japan AuxGen: 3 x 360kW 450V 60Hz a.c Fuel: 148.6 (d.f.) (Part Heating Coils) 974.2 (r.f.) 21.6pd
9095929 *ZCTZ7* -	**SEA RACER** *ex* Detroit Eagle *-2007* **Eagle Holdings International Ltd** Quorum Management Co *George Town* *Cayman Islands (British)* MMSI: 319284000 Official number: 740611	**516** 154 -	Class: AB	**2001-04 de Vries Scheepsbouw B.V. — Aalsmeer** Yd No: 661 Loa 46.60 Br ex 9.20 Dght 2.000 Lbp 39.05 Br md 8.80 Dpth 2.68 Welded, 1 dk	**(X11A2YP) Yacht** Hull Material: Aluminium Alloy	**2 oil engines & 1 Gas Turb** geared to sc. shafts driving 2 FP propellers , 1 Water jet Total Power: 9,124kW (12,405hp) M.T.U. 16V4000M70 1 x Vee 4 Stroke 16 Cy. 165 x 190 2320kW (3154bhp) Detroit Diesel Corporation-Detroit, Mi M.T.U. 16V4000M90 1 x Vee 4 Stroke 16 Cy. 165 x 190 2685kW (3651bhp) Detroit Diesel Corporation-Detroit, Mi Avco TF50 1 x Gas Turb 4119kW (5600shp) Detroit Diesel Corporation-Detroit, Mi AuxGen: 2 x 100kW a.c Fuel: 41.5 (d.f.)
7611810 *DZOO* -	**SEA RAIDER** - **Superior Shipping Corp** - *Manila* *Philippines* Official number: MNLD004498	*881* 523 1,200		**1985-06 Superior (SG) Engineering Co. — Tanza** Yd No: 0276 Loa 59.52 Br ex 10.67 Dght 3.963 Lbp 53.40 Br md 10.66 Dpth 5.49 Welded, 3 dks	**(A31A2GX) General Cargo Ship**	**2 oil engines** geared to sc. shafts driving 2 FP propellers Total Power: 1,104kW (1,500hp) Mitsubishi 6SAC 2 x 4 Stroke 6 Cy. 200 x 240 each-552kW (750bhp) Mitsubishi Heavy Industries Ltd-Japan

6709012 *WYZ7659* -	**SEA RAIDER II** **Vernon Nelson** - *New Orleans, LA* *United States of America* Official number: 505116	*365* 248 -		**1966**-01 **Patterson Shipyard Inc. — Patterson, La** Yd No: 20 L reg 42.65 Br ex - Dght - Lbp - Br md 9.20 Dpth - Welded, 1 dk	**(B11A2FT) Trawler**	**2 oil engines** driving 2 FP propellers Total Power: 1,074kW (1,460hp) General Motors 2 x each-537kW (730bhp) General Motors Corp-USA
8623858 *YB3240* -	**SEA RAIDER II** *ex* Sea Raider *-1997* **PT Pelayaran Bintan Baruna Sakti** PT Batam Fast *Indonesia* MMSI: 525023055	**142** 43 -		**1985 WaveMaster International Pty Ltd — Fremantle WA** L reg 30.39 Br ex - Dght 2.206 Lbp - Br md 6.51 Dpth 2.95 Welded, 1 dk	**(A37B2PS) Passenger Ship** Passengers: unberthed: 252	**1 oil engine** driving 1 FP propeller
8851560 *WUS7382* -	**SEA RAMBLER** **Sea Watch Fishing Co Inc** - *Freeport, NY* *United States of America* Official number: 937929	*123* 83 -		**1988 Rodriguez Boat Builders, Inc. — Coden, Al** Yd No: 78 Loa - Br ex - Dght - Lbp 22.01 Br md 6.74 Dpth 3.38 Welded, 1 dk	**(B11B2FV) Fishing Vessel**	**1 oil engine** driving 1 FP propeller
7817402 *WDE2684* -	**SEA RANGER** *ex* Eagle *-1997* **Bronco Fisheries Inc** - *Fairhaven, MA* *United States of America* MMSI: 367328270 Official number: 602018	*179* 122 -		**1979**-02 **Atlantic Marine — Jacksonville, Fl** Yd No: 180 Loa 28.99 Br ex 7.68 Dght 3.201 Lbp 26.14 Br md 7.62 Dpth 4.12 Welded, 1 dk	**(B11B2FV) Fishing Vessel** Grain: 178	**1 oil engine** geared to sc. shaft driving 1 FP propeller Total Power: 382kW (519hp) Caterpillar D398TA 1 x Vee 4 Stroke 12 Cy. 159 x 203 382kW (519bhp) (Reconditioned , Reconditioned & fitted 1978) Caterpillar Tractor Co-USA
1004900 *ZCYU9* -	**SEA RANGER** *ex* Lone Ranger *-2013* *ex* Simson S *-1997* *ex* Simson *-1994* **GSP Bigfoot 5 Corp** SC Grup Servicii Petroliere SA (GSP) *George Town* *Cayman Islands (British)* MMSI: 319023300	**1,890** 567 -	Class: BV (LR) (GL) Classed LR until 30/6/09	**1973**-05 **Schichau-Unterweser AG — Bremerhaven** Yd No: 1757 Converted From: Tug-1994 Loa 77.73 Br ex 13.60 Dght 5.770 Lbp 69.55 Br md 13.20 Dpth 6.60 Welded, 1 dk	**(X11A2YP) Yacht**	**2 oil engines** with flexible couplings & dr geared to sc. shafts driving 2 CP propellers Total Power: 6,472kW (8,800hp) 16.0kn Deutz RBV12M350 2 x Vee 4 Stroke 12 Cy. 400 x 500 each-3236kW (4400bhp) Kloeckner Humboldt Deutz AG-West Germany Thrusters: 1 Thwart. FP thruster (f)
7806506 *WCY8374* -	**SEA RAVEN** *ex* Dixie Commander *-1999* *ex* Star Providence *-1993* *ex* Sea Skimmer *-1990* *ex* Gemini *-1980* **Kirby Offshore Marine Operating LLC** - *Charleston, SC* *United States of America* MMSI: 366760320 Official number: 629923	**695** 208 -	Class: AB	**1941 Weaver Shipyards — Orange, Tx** (Aft section) Yd No: 575+578 **1980 Todd Shipyards Corp. — Galveston, Tx** (Fwd section) Yd No: 55 Converted From: Tug-1955 Lengthened-1980 Loa - Br ex - Dght - Lbp 36.68 Br md 10.67 Dpth 6.79 Welded, 1 dk	**(B32B2SA) Articulated Pusher Tug**	**2 oil engines** reverse reduction geared to sc. shafts driving 2 FP propellers Total Power: 3,728kW (5,068hp) 12.3kn EMD (Electro-Motive) 20-645-E7 2 x Vee 2 Stroke 20 Cy. 230 x 254 each-1864kW (2534bhp) (made 1975, fitted 1980) General Motors Corp.Electro-Motive Div.-La Grange AuxGen: 2 x 99kW
7813884 *5NLP* -	**SEA RAY** *ex* Wabecotanker *-2011* *ex* Lough Fisher *-2005* *ex* Cableman *-1998* **Haske Enterprises Ltd** Ship & Shore Services Ltd *Lagos* *Nigeria* MMSI: 657261000 Official number: 377637	**4,777** 2,446 8,399 T/cm 16.8	Class: LR ✠ **100A1** SS 10/2012 oil tanker (cc) ESP ✠ **LMC** **UMS** Eq.Ltr: W; Cable: 498.0/44.0 U3 (a)	**1980**-10 **Appledore Shipbuilders Ltd — Bideford** Yd No: A.S.129 Loa 117.20 (BB) Br ex 17.53 Dght 7.203 Lbp 109.63 Br md 17.51 Dpth 9.02 Welded, 1 dk	**(A13B2TP) Products Tanker** Single Hull Liq: 10,344; Liq (Oil): 10,344 Cargo Heating Coils Compartments: 5 Ta, 10 Wing Ta, 1 Slop Ta, ER 4 Cargo Pump (s): 2x450m³/hr, 2x550m³/hr Manifold: Bow/CM: 59.2m	**1 oil engine** with flexible couplings & sr geared to sc. shaft driving 1 CP propeller Total Power: 2,983kW (4,056hp) 10.5kn Ruston 16RKCM 1 x Vee 4 Stroke 16 Cy. 254 x 305 2983kW (4056bhp) Ruston Diesels Ltd.-Newton-le-Willows AuxGen: 4 x 200kW 415V 50Hz a.c Boilers: AuxB (o.f.) 8.3kgf/cm² (8.1bar), AuxB (ex.g.) 6.1kgf/cm² (6.0bar) Thrusters: 1 Thwart. FP thruster (f) Fuel: 86.0 (d.f.) 247.0 (d.f.) 7.0pd
9502075 *A9II* -	**SEA REGAL** **Al Jazeera Shipping Co WLL (AJS)** - *Bahrain* *Bahrain* MMSI: 408340000 Official number: BN 5080	**299** 90 320	Class: GL	**2008**-08 **Forward Marine Enterprise Sdn Bhd — Sibu** Yd No: FM-46 Loa 31.10 Br ex - Dght 3.570 Lbp 28.72 Br md 9.50 Dpth 4.20 Welded, 1 dk	**(B32A2ST) Tug**	**2 oil engines** reverse reduction geared to sc. shafts driving 2 FP propellers Total Power: 2,386kW (3,244hp) Cummins KTA-50-M2 2 x Vee 4 Stroke 16 Cy. 159 x 159 each-1193kW (1622bhp) Cummins Engine Co Ltd-United Kingdom AuxGen: 2 x 80kW 400V a.c
9275878 *WEOB* -	**SEA RELIANCE** **Vessel Management Services Inc** Intrepid Ship Management Inc *San Francisco, CA* *United States of America* MMSI: 369567000 Official number: 1122832	**950** 285 449	Class: AB	**2002**-05 **Moss Point Marine, Inc. — Escatawpa, Ms** Yd No: 1924 Loa - Br ex - Dght 5.940 Lbp 40.00 Br md 12.80 Dpth 6.70 Welded, 1 dk	**(B32B2SA) Articulated Pusher Tug**	**2 oil engines** reduction geared to sc. sha fts driving 2 FP propellers Total Power: 6,826kW (9,280hp) Caterpillar 3612TA 2 x Vee 4 Stroke 12 Cy. 280 x 300 each-3413kW (4640bhp) Caterpillar Inc-USA AuxGen: 2 x 190kW a.c Fuel: 640.0
7527605 *HQJM3* -	**SEA RESPECT** *ex* Horse *-1998* *ex* 0101 Mobydick *-1998* *ex* Dragon Dream *-1998* *ex* Prince King Queen *-1998* *ex* Mahrt *-1998* *ex* Fareast Empire *-1998* *ex* Yasaka *-1998* **Ark Shipping S de RL** - *San Lorenzo* *Honduras* Official number: L-0324154	**1,125** 584 1,600		**1975**-12 **Namikata Shipbuilding Co Ltd — Imabari EH** Yd No: 87 Loa - Br ex 11.03 Dght - Lbp 61.98 Br md 11.00 Dpth 6.30 Welded, 1 dk	**(A31A2GX) General Cargo Ship**	**1 oil engine** driving 1 FP propeller Total Power: 1,030kW (1,400hp) Hanshin 6LU32 1 x 4 Stroke 6 Cy. 320 x 510 1030kW (1400bhp) Hanshin Nainenki Kogyo-Japan
1010648 *ZGCA3* -	**SEA RHAPSODY** **Solston Shipping Ltd** Ocean Management GmbH *George Town* *Cayman Islands (British)* MMSI: 319020900	**1,503** 450 -	Class: LR ✠ **100A1** SS 03/2012 SSC Yacht (P), mono, G6 ✠ **LMC** **UMS** Cable: 385.0/26.0 U3 (a)	**2012**-03 **Schelde Scheepsnieuwbouw B.V. — Vlissingen** (Hull) Yd No: 900012 **2012**-03 **Amels BV — Vlissingen** Yd No: 6502 Loa 65.50 Br ex 12.18 Dght 3.800 Lbp 59.30 Br md 11.88 Dpth 6.45 Welded, 1 dk	**(X11A2YP) Yacht**	**2 oil engines** with clutches, flexible couplings & sr reverse geared to sc. shafts driving 2 FP propellers Total Power: 4,000kW (5,438hp) 17.0kn Caterpillar 3516C 2 x Vee 4 Stroke 16 Cy. 170 x 215 each-2000kW (2719bhp) Caterpillar Inc-USA AuxGen: 3 x 160kW 400V 50Hz a.c Thrusters: 1 Thwart. FP thruster (f)
9005833 *3FYN9* -	**SEA RHYME** *ex* Fgm Beauty *-2013* *ex* Cape Byron *-2010* *ex* Tiger Byron *-2003* *ex* Cape Byron *-2002* *ex* Tiger Cape *-1999* *ex* Cape Byron *-1999* *ex* Eagle Reliance *-1998* *ex* Maersk Asia Primo *-1995* *ex* Maersk Asia Prima *-1994* *ex* Range *-1994* *ex* Cape Byron *-1993* **Waves Shipping Ltd** Cassiopeia Seaway Inc *Panama* *Panama* MMSI: 372487000 Official number: 40142PEXT2	**8,944** 5,174 12,841 T/cm 23.2	Class: PR (GL)	**1993**-03 **Dorbyl Marine Pty. Ltd. — Durban** Yd No: 107 Converted From: Container Ship (Fully Cellular)-2010 Loa 139.90 (BB) Br ex 23.00 Dght 8.664 Lbp 126.40 Br md 22.70 Dpth 10.80 Welded, 1 dk	**(A31A2GX) General Cargo Ship** Grain: 16,935; Bale: 16,167 Compartments: 3 Ho, ER 3 Ha: (32.2 x 17.8)2 (25.2 x 17.8)ER Cranes: 2x40t Ice Capable	**1 oil engine** with flexible couplings & sr geared to sc. shaft driving 1 CP propeller Total Power: 6,599kW (8,972hp) 17.0kn MaK 6M601C 1 x 4 Stroke 6 Cy. 580 x 600 6599kW (8972bhp) Krupp MaK Maschinenbau GmbH-Kiel AuxGen: 1 x 1500kW 220/440V 60Hz a.c, 3 x 430kW 220/440V 60Hz a.c Thrusters: 1 Thwart. FP thruster (f) Fuel: 130.0 (d.f.) 670.0 (r.f.) 29.0pd
9237280 *ELYL7* -	**SEA RICHES** **Sea Riches Maritime Inc** Lihai International Shipping Ltd *Monrovia* *Liberia* MMSI: 636011335 Official number: 11335	**17,859** 9,828 28,287	Class: NK	**2001**-09 **Naikai Zosen Corp — Onomichi HS (Setoda Shipyard)** Yd No: 670 Loa 171.93 (BB) Br ex - Dght 9.573 Lbp 164.90 Br md 27.00 Dpth 13.60 Welded, 1 dk	**(A21A2BC) Bulk Carrier** Grain: 38,232; Bale: 36,736 Compartments: 5 Ho, ER 5 Ha: (12.7 x 16.0)4 (20.1 x 17.6)ER Cranes: 4x30t	**1 oil engine** driving 1 FP propeller Total Power: 5,390kW (7,328hp) 14.0kn B&W 5S50MC 1 x 2 Stroke 5 Cy. 500 x 1910 5390kW (7328bhp) Hitachi Zosen Corp-Japan AuxGen: 3 x 440kW a.c Fuel: 1305.0
9212412 *V7MB6* -	**SEA RIDER** *ex* King Edwin *-2012* *ex* Nordeuropa *-2007* **Flourish Shipping Co** Sea World Management & Trading Inc *Majuro* *Marshall Islands* MMSI: 538090294 Official number: 4611	**23,740** 8,832 35,775 T/cm 44.6	Class: NV	**2000**-10 **Daedong Shipbuilding Co Ltd — Changwon (Jinhae Shipyard)** Yd No: 1044 Loa 183.00 (BB) Br ex 27.43 Dght 11.017 Lbp 174.50 Br md 27.40 Dpth 17.60 Welded, 1 dk	**(A12B2TR) Chemical/Products Tanker** Double Hull (13F) Liq: 41,327; Liq (Oil): 41,327 Cargo Heating Coils Compartments: 12 Wing Ta, 2 Wing Slop Ta, ER 12 Cargo Pump (s): 10x500m³/hr, 2x300m³/hr Manifold: Bow/CM: 88.6m	**1 oil engine** driving 1 FP propeller Total Power: 7,878kW (10,711hp) 14.0kn B&W 6S46MC-C 1 x 2 Stroke 6 Cy. 460 x 1932 7878kW (10711bhp) Hyundai Heavy Industries Co Ltd-South Korea AuxGen: 3 x 500kW 60Hz a.c Thrusters: 1 Thwart. FP thruster (f) Fuel: 111.4 (d.f.) (Heating Coils) 1232.2 (r.f.) 32.0pd

IMO / Call sign / Flag	Name / Former names / Owner / Port	Tonnage	Class	Builder / Dimensions	Type	Machinery
8856302 - -	**SEA RIDER** - **Versaggi Shrimp Corp** - *Tampa, FL* *United States of America* Official number: 660557	*118* 88 -		**1983 St Augustine Trawlers, Inc. — Saint Augustine, Fl** Yd No: F-47 Loa 23.16 Br ex - Dght - Lbp 20.60 Br md 6.19 Dpth 3.38 Bonded, 1 dk	**(B11B2FV) Fishing Vessel** Hull Material: Reinforced Plastic	**1 oil engine** driving 1 FP propeller Total Power: 530kW (721hp) Caterpillar 3412TA 1 x Vee 4 Stroke 12 Cy. 137 x 152 530kW (721bhp) Caterpillar Tractor Co-USA
8855944 - -	**SEA RIDER II** - -	*101* 69 -		**1983 at Bayou La Batre, Al** Loa - Br ex - Dght - Lbp 20.33 Br md 6.71 Dpth 3.32 Welded, 1 dk	**(B11B2FV) Fishing Vessel**	**1 oil engine** driving 1 FP propeller
5235363 *HQBE7* -	**SEA RIM** *ex* Khattar *ex* Mumarim I *-1986* *ex* Petrolina IV *-1983* *ex* Milvia *-1977* *ex* Adria *-1953* **Fawaz El Kheir** - *San Lorenzo* *Honduras* Official number: L-0324037	*496* 268 750	Class: (HR) (RI)	**1953 "Navalmeccanica" Cant. Nav. — Senigallia** Yd No: 9 Loa 55.00 Br ex 9.68 Dght 3.455 Lbp 51.01 Br md 9.66 Dpth 3.79 Welded, 1 dk	**(A31A2GX) General Cargo Ship** Compartments: 1 Ho, ER	**1 oil engine** driving 1 FP propeller Total Power: 441kW (600hp) 10.0kn Ansaldo 1 x 4 Stroke 6 Cy. 370 x 560 441kW (600bhp) Ansaldo SpA-Italy
9030216 *PHQV* -	**SEA RISS** *ex* Solon *-1997* **CV Scheepvaartonderneming Aludra** *Buinen* *Netherlands* MMSI: 245862000 Official number: 20475	**1,595** 907 2,200	Class: BV	**1992-04 Scheepswerf Bijlsma BV — Wartena** Yd No: 657 Loa 79.90 Br ex - Dght 4.160 Lbp 75.00 Br md 11.00 Dpth 5.20 Welded, 1 dk	**(A31A2GX) General Cargo Ship** Grain: 3,355 TEU 164 C. 164/20' Compartments: 1 Ho, ER 1 Ha: (57.8 x 8.9)ER Ice Capable	**1 oil engine** reduction geared to sc.shaft driving 1 FP propeller Total Power: 955kW (1,298hp) Caterpillar 3512TA 1 x Vee 4 Stroke 12 Cy. 170 x 190 955kW (1298bhp) Caterpillar Inc-USA Thrusters: 1 Tunnel thruster (f)
8745228 - -	**SEA ROAMER** *ex* Free Enterprise Ii *-1997* **Sea Roamer Marine Services Ltd** - *Victoria, BC* *Canada* Official number: 195802	**104** 65 -		**1954 S Madill Ltd — Nanaimo BC** L reg 23.99 Br ex - Dght - Lbp - Br md 9.14 Dpth 1.28 Welded, 1 dk	**(A31A2GA) General Cargo Ship (with Ro-Ro facility)**	**3 oil engines** reduction geared to sc. shafts driving 3 Propellers Total Power: 429kW (582hp) 9.0kn
8766064 *WDC6580* -	**SEA ROBIN** *ex* Superior Outlook *-2005* *ex* Raya *-2004* **All Coast LLC** - *New Orleans, LA* *United States of America* MMSI: 367058120 Official number: 678621	**209** 62 -		**1984 Crown Point Industries — Marrero, La** Yd No: 10686 L reg 22.25 Br ex - Dght - Lbp - Br md 9.75 Dpth 2.13 Welded, 1 dk	**(B22A2ZM) Offshore Construction Vessel, jack up**	**2 oil engines** driving 2 Propellers
8974142 *J8B3699* -	**SEA ROBIN** *ex* Miss Anna *-2005* **Stanford Marine LLC** - *Kingstown* *St Vincent & The Grenadines* MMSI: 376351000 Official number: 10172	**211** 63 -	Class: AB	**1989-04 Breaux Brothers Enterprises, Inc. — Loreauville, La** Yd No: 146 Loa 39.62 Br ex 7.93 Dght 1.821 Lbp 35.72 Br md - Dpth 3.56 Welded, 1 dk	**(B21A20C) Crew/Supply Vessel** Hull Material: Aluminium Alloy Passengers: unberthed: 64	**4 oil engines** driving 2 gen. each 40kW a.c reverse reduction geared to sc. shafts driving 4 FP propellers Total Power: 1,484kW (2,016hp) 18.0kn G.M. (Detroit Diesel) 12V-71-TI 4 x Vee 2 Stroke 12 Cy. 108 x 127 each-371kW (504bhp) Detroit Diesel Corporation-Detroit, Mi AuxGen: 2 x 30kW a.c
7210496 *WYP8820* -	**SEA ROBIN** *ex* Pat Powers *-1981* *ex* R. Paul Guidry *-1976* **Allied Transportation LLC** - *Norfolk, VA* *United States of America* MMSI: 366836950 Official number: 535624	**294** 88 -	Class: AB	**1971 Main Iron Works, Inc. — Houma, La** Yd No: 241 Loa - Br ex - Dght 3.836 Lbp 32.44 Br md 9.15 Dpth 4.42 Welded, 1 dk	**(B32A2ST) Tug**	**2 oil engines** driving 2 FP propellers Total Power: 4,414kW (6,002hp) Alco 12V251E 2 x Vee 4 Stroke 12 Cy. 229 x 267 each-2207kW (3001bhp) (new engine 1988) White Industrial Power Inc-USA
8134027 - -	**SEA ROCK** *ex* Gulf Siren *-1987* *ex* Aljoumeira *-1981* *ex* Lionel Tim *-1970* -	*193* 131 -		**1964 Bollinger Machine Shop & Shipyard, Inc. — Lockport, La** Yd No: 47 Loa - Br ex - Dght 3.155 Lbp 26.29 Br md 7.93 Dpth 3.51 Welded, 1 dk	**(B32A2ST) Tug**	**2 oil engines** geared to sc. shafts driving 2 FP propellers Total Power: 1,472kW (2,002hp) Caterpillar D398TA 2 x Vee 4 Stroke 12 Cy. 159 x 203 each-736kW (1001bhp) Caterpillar Tractor Co-USA
7930498 *5IM289* -	**SEA ROSE** *ex* Golden Harvest *-2013* *ex* Sky Light *-2012* *ex* Zamzam *-2011* *ex* Vassilios VI *-2009* *ex* Silva *-1999* *ex* Asian Explorer *-1999* *ex* Samurai I *-1998* *ex* Hokuryu Maru *-1991* **Qimat Al Mazaya Fuel Supply Services** - *Zanzibar* *Tanzania (Zanzibar)* MMSI: 677018900 Official number: 300046	**1,516** 644 2,231 T/cm 8.0	Class: (BV) (NK)	**1980-01 Yamanishi Shipbuilding Co Ltd — Ishinomaki MG** Yd No: 863 Converted From: Chemical/Products Tanker-2010 Loa 86.06 Br ex - Dght 5.014 Lbp 78.42 Br md 12.00 Dpth 5.85 Welded, 1 dk	**(A12A2TC) Chemical Tanker** Liq: 2,300; Liq (Oil): 2,300 Compartments: 11 Ta 2 Cargo Pump (s)	**1 oil engine** driving 1 FP propeller Total Power: 1,692kW (2,300hp) 12.5kn Hanshin 6LU38 1 x 4 Stroke 6 Cy. 380 x 580 1692kW (2300bhp) The Hanshin Diesel Works Ltd-Japan AuxGen: 1 x 160kW 445V 60Hz a.c, 1 x 128kW 445V 60Hz a.c, 1 x 64kW 445V 60Hz a.c Fuel: 40.5 (d.f.) 173.0 (r.f.) 5.5pd
7381611 - -	**SEA ROSE** *ex* Sea Rose 1 *-2007* *ex* Seabulk Voyager *-2007* *ex* Selat Faith *-1997* *ex* Mansal 40 *-1995* *ex* Ahmed *-1987* *ex* Ibis Three *-1979* **Sea Rose Shipping & Trading Ltd** -	**908** 272 813	Class: (BV) (NV)	**1974-05 B.V. Scheepswerf "Waterhuizen" J. Pattje — Waterhuizen** Yd No: 304 Loa 53.78 Br ex 11.69 Dght 3.823 Lbp - Br md 11.50 Dpth 5.50 Welded, 2 dks	**(B21A2OS) Platform Supply Ship**	**2 oil engines** geared to sc. shafts driving 2 FP propellers Total Power: 1,472kW (2,002hp) 12.0kn De Industrie 6D7HD 2 x 4 Stroke 6 Cy. 305 x 460 each-736kW (1001bhp) B.V. Motorenfabriek "De Industrie"-Alphen a/d Rijn AuxGen: 2 x 172kW 220/440V 60Hz a.c, 1 x 56kW 220/440V 60Hz a.c Thrusters: 1 Thwart. FP thruster (f) Fuel: 385.0 (d.f.) 7.0pd
9115004 *9HA2027* -	**SEA ROSE** *ex* Amulet *-2009* *ex* Ever Gloria *-2004* **Gerald Shipholding Co** Athenian Ship Management Inc *Valletta* *Malta* MMSI: 249827000 Official number: 9115004	**25,997** 14,834 45,700 T/cm 49.8	Class: BV (NK)	**1995-06 Hashihama Shipbuilding Co Ltd — Tadotsu KG** Yd No: 1074 Loa 185.74 (BB) Br ex - Dght 11.600 Lbp 177.00 Br md 30.40 Dpth 16.50 Welded, 1 dk	**(A21A2BC) Bulk Carrier** Grain: 57,208; Bale: 55,565 Compartments: 5 Ho, ER 5 Ha: (20.0 x 15.3)4 (20.8 x 15.3)ER Cranes: 4x30t	**1 oil engine** driving 1 FP propeller Total Power: 7,172kW (9,751hp) 14.0kn B&W 6S50MC 1 x 2 Stroke 6 Cy. 500 x 1910 7172kW (9751bhp) Mitsui Engineering & Shipbuilding CLtd-Japan AuxGen: 3 x 400kW 450V a.c Fuel: 60.4 (d.f.) 1424.0 (r.f.) 25.5pd
8849385 - -	**SEA ROSE** *ex* Gulf Orchid *-2010* *ex* MPL I *-2005* **Target Engineering Construction Co (LLC)** - *Abu Dhabi* *United Arab Emirates*	*440* 132 -	Class: (AB)	**1991-04 Uni-France Offshore Engineering Pte Ltd — Singapore** Loa - Br ex - Dght - Lbp 38.40 Br md 12.00 Dpth 3.00 Welded, 1 dk	**(A35D2RL) Landing Craft** Bow door/ramp	**2 oil engines** sr geared to sc. shafts driving 2 FP propellers Total Power: 346kW (470hp) Caterpillar 3306TA 2 x 4 Stroke 6 Cy. 121 x 152 each-173kW (235bhp) Caterpillar Inc-USA AuxGen: 2 x 48kW a.c
9419979 - -	**SEA ROSE** *ex* Yong Cheng 16 *-2006* **Zhoushan Yongcheng Marine Co Ltd** - *Zhoushan, Zhejiang* *China*	**1,574** 881 2,500		**2006-02 Zhoushan Zhengpei Shipbuilding & Repair Co Ltd — Zhoushan ZJ** Loa 84.65 Br ex - Dght - Lbp - Br md 12.00 Dpth 5.60 Welded, 1 dk	**(A12A2TC) Chemical Tanker** Single Hull	**1 oil engine** reduction geared to sc. shaft driving 1 FP propeller Total Power: 735kW (999hp) 8.0kn Chinese Std. Type G6300ZCA 1 x 4 Stroke 6 Cy. 300 x 380 735kW (999bhp) Ningbo CSI Power & Machinery GroupCo Ltd-China
7398303 - -	**SEA ROVER** - **Sea Rover LLC** Pesquera Costa Roca SA de CV *Mexico*	*199* 139 -		**1973 Marine Construction & Design Co. (MARCO) — Seattle, Wa** Yd No: 238 L reg 27.99 Br ex - Dght - Lbp 27.97 Br md 8.31 Dpth 2.82 Welded, 1 dk	**(B11B2FV) Fishing Vessel**	**1 oil engine** driving 1 FP propeller Total Power: 625kW (850hp) Caterpillar D398SCAC 1 x Vee 4 Stroke 12 Cy. 159 x 203 625kW (850bhp) Caterpillar Tractor Co-USA
7335947 - -	**SEA ROYALE** *ex* Rantsevo *-2006* - -	**617** 185 304	Class: (RS)	**1973 Khabarovskiy Sudostroitelnyy Zavod im Kirova — Khabarovsk** Yd No: 237 Loa 54.84 Br ex 9.38 Dght 3.810 Lbp 49.99 Br md - Dpth 4.73 Welded, 1 dk	**(B11A2FT) Trawler** Ins: 284 Compartments: 2 Ho, ER 2 Ha: 2 (1.5 x 1.6) Derricks: 1x3t; Winches: 1 Ice Capable	**1 oil engine** driving 1 CP propeller Total Power: 588kW (799hp) 11.8kn S.K.L. 8NVD48-2U 1 x 4 Stroke 8 Cy. 320 x 480 588kW (799bhp) VEB Schwermaschinenbau "KarlLiebknecht" (SKL)-Magdeburg AuxGen: 3 x 88kW

IMO / Call sign	Name / Owner	Tonnage	Class	Builder / Dimensions	Type	Machinery
9006447 *ZCIX8* -	**SEA RUBY** *ex* Union Ruby *-2004* *ex* Hoo Larch *-2003* **Boddingtons Shipping Ltd & The Firth Shipping Co Ltd** Torbulk Ltd SatCom: Inmarsat C 431993210 *George Town* *Cayman Islands (British)* MMSI: 319932000 Official number: 722169	**1,382** 794 2,222 T/cm 8.0	Class: GL (LR) (BV) Classed LR until 4/9/12	**1992-11 Yorkshire D.D. Co. Ltd. — Hull** Yd No: 327 Loa 77.80 (BB) Br ex 11.10 Dght 4.020 Lbp 72.30 Br md 11.00 Dpth 5.10 Welded, 1 dk	**(A31A2GX) General Cargo Ship** Grain: 2,921; Bale: 2,810 Compartments: 2 Ho, ER 2 Ha: ER	**2 oil engines** with clutches, flexible couplings & sr geared to sc. shafts driving 2 Directional propellers Total Power: 954kW (1,298hp) 10.0kn Cummins KTA-19-M 2 x 4 Stroke 6 Cy. 159 x 159 each-477kW (649bhp) Cummins Charleston Inc-USA AuxGen: 3 x 52kW 415V 50Hz a.c Fuel: 53.0 (d.f.) 4.2pd
9541277 *3ETW6* -	**SEA RUBY** *ex* Samho Freedom *-2011* *ex* Samho Silver *-2010* **HR Ruby SA** KSIM Co Ltd (Korea Ship Investment & Management) SatCom: Inmarsat C 435199910 *Panama* *Panama* MMSI: 351999000 Official number: 40348PEXT3	**11,290** 5,263 17,541 T/cm 28.7	Class: KR	**2010-03 Samho Shipbuilding Co Ltd — Tongyeong** Yd No: 1110 Loa 144.06 (BB) Br ex - Dght 9.210 Lbp 136.00 Br md 22.60 Dpth 12.50 Welded, 1 dk	**(A12B2TR) Chemical/Products Tanker** Double Hull (13F) Liq: 18,623; Liq (Oil): 18,623 Compartments: 14 Wing Ta, 2 Wing Slop Ta, Wing ER 14 Cargo Pump (s): 14x300m³/hr Manifold: Bow/CM: 72.3m	**1 oil engine** driving 1 FP propeller Total Power: 5,349kW (7,273hp) 14.3kn MAN-B&W 8S35MC 1 x 2 Stroke 8 Cy. 350 x 1400 5349kW (7273bhp) STX Engine Co Ltd-South Korea AuxGen: 3 x 750kW 450V 60Hz a.c Thrusters: 1 Tunnel thruster (f) Fuel: 112.0 (d.f.) 914.0 (r.f.)
8932467 *IZMR* -	**SEA RUNNER** *ex* George Pickett *-1997* **Bambini Srl** - *Ravenna* *Italy* MMSI: 247093200 Official number: 65	**163** 49 165	Class: RI (AB)	**1982-01 Swiftships Inc — Morgan City LA** Yd No: 254 Loa 35.71 Br ex 7.60 Dght 1.100 Lbp 33.10 Br md 7.50 Dpth 3.04 Welded, 1 dk	**(B21A20C) Crew/Supply Vessel** Hull Material: Aluminium Alloy Passengers: unberthed: 47	**4 oil engines** geared to sc. shafts driving 2 FP propellers Total Power: 2,060kW (2,800hp) G.M. (Detroit Diesel) 12V-92 4 x Vee 2 Stroke 12 Cy. 123 x 127 each-515kW (700bhp) General Motors Detroit DieselAllison Divn-USA
7000293 *HQEU7* -	**SEA SABAH** *ex* Mini Lance *-1989* **United Cement Co Bscc** - *San Lorenzo* *Honduras* MMSI: 334599000 Official number: L-0332926	*1,355* 832 3,217	Class: BV (AB)	**1969-11 The Hakodate Dock Co Ltd — Muroran HK** Yd No: 450 Loa 65.51 Br ex 15.32 Dght 4.947 Lbp 62.82 Br md 15.30 Dpth 6.45 Welded, 1 dk	**(A31A2GX) General Cargo Ship** Grain: 3,785; Bale: 3,669 Compartments: 2 Ho, ER 2 Ha: 2 (14.6 x 7.7)ER Cranes: 1x8t	**2 oil engines** reverse reduction geared to sc. shafts driving 2 FP propellers Total Power: 736kW (1,000hp) 10.3kn Daihatsu 6PSTCM-22 2 x 4 Stroke 6 Cy. 220 x 280 each-368kW (500bhp) (new engine 1981) Daihatsu Kogyo-Japan AuxGen: 1 x 104kW 445V 60Hz a.c, 1 x 48kW 445V 60Hz a.c Fuel: 106.5 (d.f.)
8220656 *HO2151* -	**SEA SAFE** *ex* Sapphire *-2013* *ex* Seabulk Sapphire *-2011* *ex* Gray Vanguard *-1997* **Hede Ferrominas Pvt Ltd** - *Panama* *Panama* MMSI: 355689000 Official number: 10370PEXT5	**793** 238 1,500	Class: AB	**1983-06 Santan Engineering Pte Ltd — Singapore** Yd No: 8235 Loa 55.59 Br ex - Dght 4.536 Lbp 55.59 Br md 13.61 Dpth 5.21 Welded, 1 dk	**(B21B20A) Anchor Handling Tug Supply**	**2 oil engines** reverse reduction geared to sc. shaft driving 2 FP propellers Total Power: 2,118kW (2,880hp) 13.0kn Blackstone ESL8MK2 2 x 4 Stroke 8 Cy. 222 x 292 each-1059kW (1440bhp) Mirrlees Blackstone (Stamford)Ltd.-Stamford AuxGen: 2 x 175kW Thrusters: 1 Thwart. FP thruster (f) Fuel: 439.2
7129130 *LNDH* -	**SEA SAFETY** *ex* Strilbas *-2007* *ex* Ocean Safe *-1988* *ex* West Avocet *-1985* **Sea Supply AS** Chriship AS *Sortland* *Norway* MMSI: 258165000	**947** 284 711	Class: NV	**1972-02 B.V. Scheepswerf "Waterhuizen" J. Pattje — Waterhuizen** Yd No: 295 Loa 53.15 Br ex 11.52 Dght 3.772 Lbp 49.34 Br md 11.46 Dpth 5.52 Welded, 2 dks	**(B21B20T) Offshore Tug/Supply Ship** Liq: 104 Compartments: 3 Ta, ER A-frames: 1x13t; Winches: 1	**2 oil engines** driving 2 CP propellers Total Power: 3,236kW (4,400hp) 12.0kn De Industrie 8D8HD 2 x 4 Stroke 8 Cy. 400 x 600 each-1618kW (2200bhp) NV Motorenfabriek 'De Industrie'-Netherlands AuxGen: 2 x 170kW 440V 60Hz a.c, 1 x 56kW 440V 60Hz a.c Thrusters: 1 Thwart. FP thruster (f); 1 Retract. directional thruster (f); 2 Tunnel thruster (a) Fuel: 357.5 (d.f.) 15.0pd
7421837 *LAJP3* -	**SEA SAILOR** *ex* Siddis Sailor *-2006* **Sea Supply AS** Chriship AS *Sortland* *Norway (NIS)*	**1,324** 397 893	Class: NV	**1975-08 Scheepswerf Hoogezand B.V. — Hoogezand** Yd No: 179 Lengthened-1995 Loa 68.80 Br ex 12.02 Dght 4.118 Lbp 60.37 Br md 11.99 Dpth 6.00 Welded, 2 dks	**(B21B20A) Anchor Handling Tug Supply**	**2 oil engines** reduction geared to sc. shafts driving 2 FP propellers Total Power: 2,132kW (2,898hp) 10.0kn Alpha 10V23L-VO 2 x Vee 4 Stroke 10 Cy. 225 x 300 each-1066kW (1449bhp) Alpha Diesel A/S-Denmark AuxGen: 2 x 170kW 440V 60Hz a.c, 1 x 56kW 440V 60Hz a.c Thrusters: 2 Thwart. FP thruster (f)
9640803 *9V9660* -	**SEA SALMON** - **An Yi Shipping Pte Ltd** Ocean Tankers (Pte) Ltd *Singapore* *Singapore* MMSI: 566521000 Official number: 397440	**495** 148 200	Class: AB	**2012-06 Tongfang Jiangxin Shipbuilding Co Ltd — Hukou County JX** Yd No: JX637 Loa 32.00 Br ex 12.20 Dght 3.850 Lbp 30.02 Br md 11.60 Dpth 5.38 Welded, 1 dk	**(B32A2ST) Tug**	**2 oil engines** reduction geared to sc. shafts driving 2 Z propellers Total Power: 3,676kW (4,998hp) Niigata 6L28HX 2 x 4 Stroke 6 Cy. 280 x 370 each-1838kW (2499bhp) Niigata Engineering Co Ltd-Japan AuxGen: 2 x 215kW a.c Fuel: 170.0 (d.f.)
9203100 *9HZZ5* -	**SEA SALVOR** - **Government of The Republic of Malta (Department for Civil Defence)** Tug Malta Ltd *Valletta* *Malta* MMSI: 248324000 Official number: 6212	**323** 96 100	Class: LR RI **100A1** SS 11/2008 tug fire fighting ship 1 (3600 cubic m/h) with water spray **LMC** Eq.Ltr: F; Cable: 275.0/0.0	**1998-11 Cant. Navale "Ferrari" S.p.A. — La Spezia** Yd No: 230 Loa 29.95 Br ex - Dght 3.220 Lbp 29.30 Br md 10.20 Dpth 3.90 Welded, 1 dk	**(B32A2ST) Tug**	**2 oil engines** geared to sc. shafts driving 2 Directional propellers Total Power: 3,360kW (4,568hp) Deutz SBV8M628 2 x 4 Stroke 8 Cy. 240 x 280 each-1680kW (2284bhp) Motoren Werke Mannheim AG (MWM)-Mannheim AuxGen: 2 x 40kW 380V 50Hz a.c
9557226 *3EYH2* -	**SEA SAPPHIRE** *ex* Jin Hyang *-2013* **HR Sapphire SA** Hanaro Shipping Co Ltd *Panama* *Panama* MMSI: 351250000 Official number: 4533913	**20,141** 11,367 32,550	Class: KR (BV)	**2010-03 Zhejiang Hongxin Shipbuilding Co Ltd — Taizhou ZJ** Yd No: 2007-08 Loa 177.40 (BB) Br ex - Dght 10.217 Lbp 168.00 Br md 28.20 Dpth 14.20 Welded, 1 dk	**(A21A2BC) Bulk Carrier** Double Hull Grain: 40,161; Bale: 38,849 Compartments: 5 Ho, ER 5 Ha: 4 (19.2 x 21.0)ER (14.4 x 15.2) Cranes: 4x30t	**1 oil engine** driving 1 FP propeller Total Power: 6,480kW (8,810hp) 14.2kn MAN-B&W 6S42MC 1 x 2 Stroke 6 Cy. 420 x 1764 6480kW (8810bhp) STX Engine Co Ltd-South Korea AuxGen: 3 x 500kW 450V a.c Fuel: 1400.0
9640815 *9V9661* -	**SEA SARDINE** - **An Yi Shipping Pte Ltd** Ocean Tankers (Pte) Ltd *Singapore* *Singapore* MMSI: 566536000 Official number: 397441	**495** 148 204	Class: AB	**2012-06 Tongfang Jiangxin Shipbuilding Co Ltd — Hukou County JX** Yd No: JX638 Loa 32.00 Br ex 12.20 Dght 3.850 Lbp 30.02 Br md 11.60 Dpth 5.38 Welded, 1 dk	**(B32A2ST) Tug**	**2 oil engines** reduction geared to sc. shafts driving 2 Z propellers Total Power: 3,676kW (4,998hp) Niigata 6L28HX 2 x 4 Stroke 6 Cy. 280 x 370 each-1838kW (2499bhp) Niigata Engineering Co Ltd-Japan AuxGen: 2 x 215kW a.c Fuel: 170.0 (d.f.)
9124744 *HSB4521* -	**SEA SAWASDEE** *ex* Global Hime *-2010* *ex* Global Express *-2005* **Seamanship Co Ltd** - *Bangkok* *Thailand* MMSI: 567408000 Official number: 530003449	**3,516** 1,055 4,187 T/cm 12.6	Class: NK	**1995-09 Honda Zosen — Saiki** Yd No: 880 Loa 99.80 (BB) Br ex 16.80 Dght 5.564 Lbp 92.00 Br md 16.40 Dpth 7.10 Welded, 1 dk	**(A11B2TG) LPG Tanker** Double Bottom Entire Compartment Length Liq (Gas): 3,510 2 x Gas Tank (s); 2 (stl) cyl horizontal 3 Cargo Pump (s): 3x360m³/hr Manifold: Bow/CM: 45.5m	**1 oil engine** driving 1 FP propeller Total Power: 3,089kW (4,200hp) 12.5kn Mitsubishi 6UEC37LA 1 x 2 Stroke 6 Cy. 370 x 880 3089kW (4200bhp) Akasaka Tekkosho KK (Akasaka DieselLtd)-Japan AuxGen: 2 x 280kW 450V 60Hz a.c Fuel: 112.0 (d.f.) 545.0 (r.f.)
8417352 *HO9346* -	**SEA SCAN 1** *ex* Algosaibi 26 *-2013* **Seaterra Geophysik & Kampfmittel Dienstleistungen GmbH** - *Panama* *Panama* MMSI: 355012000 Official number: 45035PEXT1	*496* 149 276	Class: AB	**1985-05 ShinA Shipbuilding Co Ltd — Tongyeong** Yd No: 279 Loa 45.76 Br ex - Dght 3.201 Lbp 41.51 Br md 10.41 Dpth 4.37 Welded, 1 dk	**(B21A20S) Platform Supply Ship**	**2 oil engines** with clutches, flexible couplings & sr geared to sc. shafts driving 2 Directional propellers Total Power: 1,800kW (2,448hp) 11.0kn MAN 9L20/27 2 x 4 Stroke 9 Cy. 200 x 270 each-900kW (1224bhp) MAN B&W Diesel GmbH-Augsburg Thrusters: 1 Directional thruster (f)
8973198 *D6DS4* -	**SEA SCOUT** *ex* Al-Mojil IX *-2013* *ex* Flo Cheramie *-1982* **Seaport International Shipping Co LLC** - *Moroni* *Union of Comoros* Official number: 1200612	**254** 76 -	Class: (AB)	**1981-08 Continental Shipbuilders — Larose, La** Yd No: 007 Loa 33.53 Br ex - Dght 3.090 Lbp 33.53 Br md 9.75 Dpth 3.35 Welded, 1 dk	**(B21A20S) Platform Supply Ship**	**2 oil engines** geared to sc. shafts driving 2 FP propellers Total Power: 716kW (974hp) 12.0kn G.M. (Detroit Diesel) 16V-71 2 x Vee 2 Stroke 16 Cy. 108 x 127 each-358kW (487bhp) General Motors Detroit DieselAllison Divn-USA AuxGen: 2 x 50kW

9601120 *WDG2181* -	**SEA SCOUT** **C & C Technologies Inc** - *New Iberia, LA* *United States of America* MMSI: 368079000 Official number: 1237094	**419** 125 95	Class: (AB)	**2012-02 All American Marine Inc — Bellingham WA** Yd No: TD40-34AA Loa 40.84 Br ex - Dght 2.000 Lbp - Br md 10.80 Dpth 3.93 Welded, 1 dk	**(B31A2SR) Research Survey Vessel** Hull Material: Aluminium Alloy A-frames: 1	**4 oil engines** reduction geared to sc. shafts driving 2 Propellers Total Power: 2,534kW (3,446hp) 20.0kn Caterpillar C18 ACERT 2 x 4 Stroke 6 Cy. 145 x 183 each-447kW (608bhp) Caterpillar Inc-USA Caterpillar C32 ACERT 2 x Vee 4 Stroke 12 Cy. 145 x 162 each-820kW (1115bhp) Caterpillar Inc-USA AuxGen: 2 x 99kW 60Hz a.c
7437070 *HP4813* -	**SEA SEARCH** *ex* Obi VI *ex* Lamco *-1981* **Elite Freight Services** - *Panama* *Panama* Official number: 43770PEXT	**343** 103 309		**1965 Zigler Shipyards Inc — Jennings LA** Yd No: 166 Loa 42.67 Br ex 10.36 Dght 2.865 Lbp 40.53 Br md 10.06 Dpth 3.05 Welded, 1 dk	**(B21A2OS) Platform Supply Ship**	**2 oil engines** geared to sc. shafts driving 2 FP propellers Total Power: 758kW (1,030hp) 8.5kn Caterpillar 2 x Vee 4 Stroke 8 Cy. each-379kW (515bhp) Caterpillar Tractor Co-USA
7435319 - -	**SEA SEARCHER** *ex* Golden Eagle *-1996* *ex* Osa Puma *-1989* **Gulf Marine Far East Pte Ltd**	**992** 297 1,055	Class: (AB) (GL)	**1976-10 Vosper Thornycroft Pte Ltd — Singapore** Yd No: B.966 Loa 56.95 Br ex 13.14 Dght 4.211 Lbp 51.52 Br md 13.12 Dpth 4.78 Welded, 1 dk	**(B21B20A) Anchor Handling Tug Supply**	**2 oil engines** sr geared to sc. shafts driving 2 CP propellers Total Power: 2,831kW (3,849hp) 11.0kn Deutz SBA12M528 2 x Vee 4 Stroke 12 Cy. 220 x 280 each-1415kW (1924bhp) Kloeckner Humboldt Deutz AG-West Germany AuxGen: 3 x 350kW a.c
9573036 *A9JY* -	**SEA SERPENT** *ex* TS Express *-2012* **Al Jazeera Shipping Co WLL (AJS)** - *Bahrain* *Bahrain* MMSI: 408840000 Official number: BN6062	**249** 74 127	Class: AB	**2011-03 Bengbu Shenzhou Machinery Co Ltd — Bengbu AH** (Hull) Yd No: (1422) **2011-03 Pacific Ocean Engineering & Trading Pte Ltd (POET) — Singapore** Yd No: 1422 Loa 29.50 Br ex 9.02 Dght 3.900 Lbp 27.00 Br md 9.00 Dpth 4.16 Welded, 1 dk	**(B32A2ST) Tug**	**2 oil engines** reduction geared to sc. shafts driving 2 Propellers Total Power: 2,648kW (3,600hp) Yanmar 8N21A-EN 2 x 4 Stroke 8 Cy. 210 x 290 each-1324kW (1800bhp) Yanmar Diesel Engine Co Ltd-Japan AuxGen: 2 x 130kW a.c
7366427 *A9D2834* -	**SEA SERV 501** *ex* Aquamarine 501 *-1986* **Sea Eagle Marine Services** Sea Eagles Shipping LLC *Bahrain* *Bahrain*	**704** 211 798	Class: GL (BV) (AB)	**1974-02 Burton Shipyard Co., Inc. — Port Arthur, Tx** Yd No: 504 Loa 54.84 Br ex 12.20 Dght 3.887 Lbp 50.07 Br md 12.17 Dpth 4.58 Welded, 1 dk	**(B21B20T) Offshore Tug/Supply Ship**	**3 oil engines** reverse reduction geared to sc. shafts driving 3 FP propellers Total Power: 3,618kW (4,920hp) 9.0kn EMD (Electro-Motive) 16-645-E2 3 x Vee 2 Stroke 16 Cy. 230 x 254 each-1206kW (1640bhp) (Re-engined ,made 1952, Reconditioned & fitted 1974) General Motors Corp.Electro-Motive Div.-La Grange AuxGen: 2 x 150kW 220/110V 60Hz a.c Thrusters: 1 Thwart. FP thruster (f)
7423421 *P3PE3* -	**SEA SERV 503** *ex* Aquamarine 503 *-1986* **Sea Care Shipping Co Ltd** Sea Services Ltd *Limassol* *Cyprus* Official number: 709004	**745** 223 850	Class: AB	**1976-12 South Texas Shipyard, Inc. — Corpus Christi, Tx** Yd No: 103 Loa 56.39 Br ex - Dght 3.588 Lbp 49.99 Br md 12.20 Dpth 4.55 Welded, 1 dk	**(B21B20T) Offshore Tug/Supply Ship**	**3 oil engines** reverse reduction geared to sc. shafts driving 3 FP propellers Total Power: 3,618kW (4,920hp) 14.0kn EMD (Electro-Motive) 16-567-BC 3 x Vee 2 Stroke 16 Cy. 216 x 254 each-1206kW (1640bhp) (Re-engined , Reconditioned & fitted 1977) General Motors Corp.Electro-Motive Div.-La Grange AuxGen: 2 x 150kW Thrusters: 1 Thwart. FP thruster (f) Fuel: 363.5 (d.f.)
7643708 *WDA4909* -	**SEA SERVICE** *ex* Sea Star *-2001* *ex* Capt. Paul *-1989* **Hornbeck Offshore Transportation LLC** - *New Orleans, LA* *United States of America* MMSI: 366814440 Official number: 570691	**338** 101 -		**1976-04 Halter Marine, Inc. — Pierre Part, La** Yd No: 469 Loa 33.53 Br ex - Dght 4.220 Lbp 33.23 Br md 9.45 Dpth 4.88 Welded, 1 dk	**(B32A2ST) Tug**	**2 oil engines** driving 2 FP propellers Total Power: 1,654kW (2,248hp) Caterpillar D399TA 2 x Vee 4 Stroke 16 Cy. 159 x 203 each-827kW (1124bhp) Caterpillar Tractor Co-USA
8658114 *WDF9972* -	**SEA SERVICE 1** **Sea Ventures II LLC** Gulf Offshore Logistics LLC (GOL) *New Orleans, LA* *United States of America* MMSI: 367510770 Official number: 1236101	**791** - 949		**2011-12 Thoma-Sea Marine Constructors LLC — Houma LA** Yd No: 146 Loa 54.86 Br ex - Dght 3.410 Lbp - Br md 12.20 Dpth 4.26 Welded, 1 dk	**(B21A2OS) Platform Supply Ship**	**2 oil engines** reduction geared to sc. shafts driving 2 Propellers Total Power: 1,492kW (2,028hp) 10.0kn Caterpillar 3508B 2 x Vee 4 Stroke 8 Cy. 170 x 190 each-746kW (1014bhp) Caterpillar Inc-USA AuxGen: 2 x 250kW 60Hz a.c Thrusters: 1 Thwart. FP thruster (f)
9160047 *PCEF* -	**SEA SHANNON** *launched as* Joriston *-1998* **Shannon Shipping BV** Amasus Shipping BV *Lemmer* *Netherlands* MMSI: 245334000 Official number: 32152	**1,670** 834 2,268 T/cm 8.7	Class: LR (BV) **100A1** SS 05/2013 **LMC**	**1998-05 Rechytskiy Sudostroitelnyy Zavod — Rechytsa** (Hull) **1998-05 B.V. Scheepswerf Damen Bergum — Bergum** Yd No: 9983 Loa 82.45 Br ex - Dght 4.050 Lbp 78.66 Br md 11.30 Dpth 5.13 Welded, 1 dk	**(A31A2GX) General Cargo Ship** Grain: 3,088 Compartments: 1 Ho, ER 1 Ha: (51.1 x 9.3)ER	**1 oil engine** with clutches, flexible couplings & sr geared to sc. shaft driving 1 FP propeller Total Power: 1,020kW (1,387hp) 10.0kn Kromhout 6FHD240G 1 x 4 Stroke 6 Cy. 240 x 260 1020kW (1387bhp) Wartsila NSD Nederland BV-Netherlands AuxGen: 2 x 80kW 220/380V 50Hz a.c Thrusters: 1 Thwart. FP thruster (f) Fuel: 79.6 (d.f.) 3.5pd
8316338 *E5U2539* -	**SEA SHARK** *ex* Explorius *-2012* *ex* Clipper Mustang *-2001* *ex* Millenium Trader *-2001* *ex* East Trader *-1999* *ex* Diligence Trader *-1993* *ex* Sanko Diligence *-1987* **IMT Shipping Co Ltd** ISM Group Sarl *Avatiu* *Cook Islands* MMSI: 518592000 Official number: 1628	**15,786** 9,209 26,536 T/cm 37.6	Class: NK	**1985-03 KK Kanasashi Zosen — Toyohashi AI** Yd No: 3061 Loa 167.20 (BB) Br ex - Dght 9.541 Lbp 160.00 Br md 26.00 Dpth 13.30 Welded, 1 dk	**(A21A2BC) Bulk Carrier** Grain: 33,867; Bale: 32,650 Compartments: 5 Ho, ER 5 Ha: (13.9 x 13.1)4 (19.3 x 13.1)ER Cranes: 4x25.4t	**1 oil engine** driving 1 FP propeller Total Power: 5,075kW (6,900hp) 14.0kn B&W 6L50MCE 1 x 2 Stroke 6 Cy. 500 x 1620 5075kW (6900bhp) Mitsui Engineering & Shipbuilding CLtd-Japan AuxGen: 3 x 360kW 450V 60Hz a.c Fuel: 127.0 (d.f.) (Heating Coils) 1254.5 (r.f.) 20.0pd
7009196 *A9D3244* -	**SEA SHEIKH** *ex* Mini Lane *-1989* **United Cement Co Bscc** - *Bahrain* *Bahrain* MMSI: 408567000	*1,355* 832 3,213	Class: BV (AB)	**1970-02 The Hakodate Dock Co Ltd — Muroran HK** Yd No: 452 Loa 65.49 Br ex 15.32 Dght 4.947 Lbp 62.82 Br md 15.30 Dpth 6.45 Welded, 1 dk	**(A31A2GX) General Cargo Ship** Grain: 3,785; Bale: 3,669 Compartments: 2 Ho, ER 2 Ha: 2 (14.6 x 7.7)ER Cranes: 1x8t	**2 oil engines** reverse reduction geared to sc. shafts driving 2 FP propellers Total Power: 736kW (1,000hp) 10.3kn Daihatsu 6PSTCM-22 2 x 4 Stroke 6 Cy. 220 x 280 each-368kW (500bhp) Daihatsu Kogyo-Japan AuxGen: 1 x 104kW 445V 60Hz a.c, 1 x 48kW 445V 60Hz a.c Fuel: 83.5
8662244 *E5U2278* -	**SEA SHELL** **Sea Shell Navigation LLC** MS Yachts *Rarotonga* *Cook Islands* MMSI: 518328000 Official number: 1362	**260** 120 160	Class: (AB)	**2010-10 Fittipaldi Yachts — Angra dos Reis** Yd No: F110.02 Loa 33.70 (BB) Br ex - Dght 2.000 Lbp 28.70 Br md 8.00 Dpth 3.00 Welded, 1 dk	**(X11A2YP) Yacht** Hull Material: Aluminium Alloy	**2 oil engines** reduction geared to sc. shafts driving 2 Propellers Total Power: 1,066kW (1,450hp) Caterpillar C18 2 x 4 Stroke 6 Cy. 145 x 183 each-533kW (725bhp) Caterpillar Inc-USA
5212440 *WB5610* -	**SEA SHEPHERD** *ex* Los Angeles *-1989* *ex* WSA 19 *-1989* *ex* DPC 72 *-1989* **Ted A Dunn Marine Consultants** - *Los Angeles, CA* *United States of America* Official number: 244510	*146* 99 -	Class: (AB)	**1943-11 Decatur Iron & Steel Co. — Decatur, Al** Yd No: 72 Loa - Br ex 7.37 Dght 2.439 Lbp 25.00 Br md 7.32 Dpth 3.20 Welded, 1 dk	**(B32A2ST) Tug**	**1 oil engine** sr geared to sc. shaft driving 1 FP propeller Total Power: 515kW (700hp) EMD (Electro-Motive) 8-567 1 x Vee 2 Stroke 8 Cy. 216 x 254 515kW (700bhp) General Motors Corp-USA Fuel: 78.0
8879653 - -	**SEA SHUTTLE 1** **Excursion Services Ltd** Empresas Maritimas Asociadas SA (EMASA)	**111** 43 -		**1994 Sterling Yacht & Shipbuilding Co. (Pty.) Ltd. — Cape Town** Yd No: 225/1 Loa 22.50 Br ex 7.28 Dght 0.900 Lbp 20.87 Br md 7.20 Dpth 2.06 Bonded, 1 dk	**(A37B2PS) Passenger Ship** Hull Material: Reinforced Plastic Passengers: unberthed: 117	**2 oil engines** driving 2 Water jets Total Power: 2,300kW (3,128hp) 33.0kn Deutz TBD616V16 2 x Vee 4 Stroke 16 Cy. 132 x 160 each-1150kW (1564bhp) Gasmotoren Fabrik Deutz AG-Koeln

IMO / Call sign	Name / Owner	Tonnage	Class	Builder / Dimensions	Type	Machinery
7939315 *WYW9770* -	**SEA SIREN** **Sea Siren Fisheries Inc** Kevin Dawsons Boat Settlement *New Bedford, MA* *United States of America* Official number: 600188	*140* 95 -		**1978 St Augustine Trawlers, Inc. — Saint Augustine, Fl** L reg 21.43 Br ex 6.74 Dght - Lbp - Br md - Dpth 3.51 Welded, 1 dk	**(B11B2FV) Fishing Vessel**	**1 oil engine** driving 1 FP propeller Total Power: 371kW (504hp) Caterpillar 3412TA 1 x Vee 4 Stroke 12 Cy. 137 x 152 371kW (504bhp) Caterpillar Tractor Co-USA
9663867 - -	**SEA SKY - 1** **Nurjahan Group** - *Bangladesh*	**1,000** - 1,300	Class: GL (Class contemplated)	**2013-04 Western Marine Shipyard Ltd — Chittagong** Yd No: 086 Loa 65.00 Br ex - Dght 4.000 Lbp - Br md 11.00 Dpth 5.50 Welded, 1 dk	**(A12E2LE) Edible Oil Tanker** Double Hull (13F)	**1 oil engine** driving 1 Propeller
8922644 - -	**SEA SKY N 1** **Taipesar SA** - *Argentina* Official number: 0399	**426** 188 -		**1986 Lien Ho Shipbuilding Co, Ltd — Kaohsiung** Loa - Br ex - Dght - Lbp 59.10 Br md 9.40 Dpth 4.05 Welded, 1 dk	**(B11B2FV) Fishing Vessel**	**1 oil engine** driving 1 FP propeller 11.0kn Akasaka 1 x 4 Stroke 6 Cy. Akasaka Tekkosho KK (Akasaka DieselLtd)-Japan
9113252 *WDD5033* -	**SEA SLICE** *ex Slice -2001* **Mudminers LLC** - *Baltimore, MD* *United States of America* Official number: 1048894	**249** 74 50		**1997 Pacific Marine & Supply Co. — Honolulu, Hi** Yd No: HSI002 Loa - Br ex - Dght - Lbp - Br md - Dpth - Welded, 1 dk	**(A37B2PS) Passenger Ship** Hull Material: Aluminium Alloy	**2 oil engines** reduction geared to sc. shafts driving 2 CP propellers Total Power: 5,038kW (6,850hp) 30.0kn M.T.U. 16V396TB94 2 x Vee 4 Stroke 16 Cy. 165 x 185 each-2519kW (3425bhp) MTU Friedrichshafen GmbH-Friedrichshafen AuxGen: 2 x 180kW a.c
9615107 *D5BT2*	**SEA SMILE** **Lucretia Shipping SA** Santoku Senpaku Co Ltd *Monrovia* *Liberia* MMSI: 636015598 Official number: 15598	**23,273** 12,139 38,109 T/cm 48.6	Class: NK (KR)	**2012-04 Shimanami Shipyard Co Ltd — Imabari EH** Yd No: 563 Loa 179.97 (BB) Br ex - Dght 10.540 Lbp 173.00 Br md 29.80 Dpth 15.00 Welded, 1 dk	**(A21A2BC) Bulk Carrier** Grain: 47,125; Bale: 45,369 Compartments: 5 Ho, ER 5 Ha: ER Cranes: 4x30.5t	**1 oil engine** driving 1 FP propeller Total Power: 7,860kW (10,686hp) 14.7kn MAN-B&W 6S46MC-C 1 x 2 Stroke 6 Cy. 460 x 1932 7860kW (10686bhp) Makita Corp-Japan Fuel: 1940.0
9296511 *VRS4325* -	**SEA SMOOTH** *ex Park Island 6 -2011* **Hong Kong & Kowloon Ferry Ltd** - *Hong Kong* *Hong Kong* MMSI: 477995071	**274** 80 34		**2003-02 Hin Lee (Zhuhai) Shipyard Co Ltd — Zhuhai GD** (Hull) **2003-03 Cheoy Lee Shipyards Ltd — Hong Kong** Loa 28.00 Br ex - Dght 2.500 Lbp 25.40 Br md 8.10 Dpth 3.09 Bonded, 1 dk	**(A37B2PS) Passenger Ship** Hull Material: Reinforced Plastic Passengers: unberthed: 400	**2 oil engines** geared to sc. shafts driving 2 FP propellers Total Power: 1,912kW (2,600hp) 25.0kn Cummins KTA-38-M2 2 x Vee 4 Stroke 12 Cy. 159 x 159 each-956kW (1300bhp) Cummins Engine Co Inc-USA
8939350 - -	**SEA SNAKE** *ex Lucky Jimmy -2009* **LBJ LLC** - *Leeville, LA* *United States of America* MMSI: 366722250 Official number: 1033234	**123** 37 -		**1995 Ocean Marine, Inc. — Bayou La Batre, Al** Yd No: 309 L reg 24.69 Br ex - Dght - Lbp - Br md 7.01 Dpth 3.69 Welded, 1 dk	**(B11A2FT) Trawler**	**1 oil engine** geared to sc. shaft driving 1 Propeller Total Power: 397kW (540hp) Caterpillar 3412 1 x Vee 4 Stroke 12 Cy. 137 x 152 397kW (540bhp) Caterpillar Inc-USA
8824282 *V3NC5*	**SEA SONG** *ex Tsugaru Maru -2010 ex Kazuryu -1999* **Sea Song International Shipping Ltd** Sea Bridge International Shipping Ltd *Belize City* *Belize* MMSI: 312124000 Official number: 611020006	**1,495** 875 1,476	Class: IT	**1989-06 K.K. Kamishima Zosensho — Osakikamijima** Yd No: 235 Loa 76.22 Br ex - Dght 4.050 Lbp 70.00 Br md 12.00 Dpth 7.00 Welded, 1 dk	**(A31A2GX) General Cargo Ship**	**1 oil engine** reverse geared to sc. shaft driving 1 FP propeller Total Power: 736kW (1,001hp) 12.0kn Akasaka A31R 1 x 4 Stroke 6 Cy. 310 x 600 736kW (1001bhp) Akasaka Tekkosho KK (Akasaka DieselLtd)-Japan
8502377 *5IM292* -	**SEA SOUL 1** *ex Terry Dos -2013 ex Holsatia -2004* *ex P&O Nedlloyd Calais -2000* *ex Point Lisas -1998 ex Lys Carrier -1991* *ex Holsatia -1989* **Sea Soul Marine & Trading Co SA** Lale International Srl *Zanzibar* *Tanzania (Zanzibar)* MMSI: 677019200	**2,472** 953 3,050	Class: (GL)	**1985-10 Seebeckwerft AG — Bremerhaven** Yd No: 1054 Loa 90.02 (BB) Br ex 13.70 Dght 4.431 Lbp 86.52 Br md 13.62 Dpth 6.76 Welded, 2 dks	**(A31A2GX) General Cargo Ship** Grain: 4,445; Bale: 4,419 TEU 134 C.Ho 72/20' (40') C.Dk 62/20' (40') Compartments: 1 Ho, ER 1 Ha: (55.9 x 11.0)ER Cranes: 2x25t Ice Capable	**1 oil engine** with flexible couplings & sr gearedto sc. shaft driving 1 CP propeller Total Power: 1,348kW (1,833hp) 11.5kn Deutz SBV9M628 1 x 4 Stroke 9 Cy. 240 x 280 1348kW (1833bhp) Kloeckner Humboldt Deutz AG-West Germany AuxGen: 1 x 248kW 450V, 1 x 240kW 220/440V 60Hz a.c, 1 x 73kW 220/440V 60Hz a.c Thrusters: 1 Thwart. FP thruster (f) Fuel: 56.0 (d.f.) 172.5 (r.f.) 6.5pd
9376139 *3EHA4*	**SEA SOVEREIGN** **Gulf Marine Far East Pte Ltd** - *Panama* *Panama* MMSI: 371189000 Official number: 3231307B	**1,951** 585 1,875	Class: AB	**2006-09 P.T. Jaya Asiatic Shipyard — Batam** Yd No: 857 Loa 70.05 Br ex 15.00 Dght 4.950 Lbp 63.00 Br md 14.95 Dpth 6.10 Welded, 1 dk	**(B21B20A) Anchor Handling Tug Supply**	**2 oil engines** reduction geared to sc. shafts driving 2 CP propellers Total Power: 4,050kW (5,506hp) 11.0kn Wartsila 6L26 2 x 4 Stroke 6 Cy. 260 x 320 each-2025kW (2753bhp) Wartsila Finland Oy-Finland AuxGen: 2 x 370kW a.c Thrusters: 2 Tunnel thruster (f); 1 Tunnel thruster (a) Fuel: 810.0
9656620 *5BXK3* -	**SEA SPARK** **Deep Sea Supply Shipowning III BV** Deep Sea Supply Management (Singapore) Pte Ltd *Limassol* *Cyprus* MMSI: 209877000	**4,007** 1,533 4,700	Class: NV	**2013-10 Zhejiang Shipbuilding Co Ltd — Fenghua ZJ** Yd No: ZJ2019 Loa 88.80 Br ex 19.01 Dght 6.650 Lbp 82.00 Br md 19.00 Dpth 8.00 Welded, 1 dk	**(B21A20S) Platform Supply Ship** Ice Capable	**4 diesel electric oil engines** driving 4 gen. Connecting to 2 elec. motors driving 2 Azimuth electric drive units Total Power: 7,060kW (9,600hp) 13.0kn Caterpillar 3512C 4 x Vee 4 Stroke 12 Cy. 170 x 215 each-1765kW (2400bhp) Caterpillar Inc-USA Thrusters: 2 Tunnel thruster (f)
9389552 *A6E2843* -	**SEA SPARROW** *ex Marina Adventure 2 -2011* **Target Engineering Construction Co (LLC)** - *Abu Dhabi* *United Arab Emirates* Official number: 0081279843	**267** 81 274	Class: NK	**2006-06 Tang Tiew Hee & Sons Sdn Bhd — Sibu** Yd No: 26 Loa 30.00 Br ex - Dght 3.512 Lbp 28.08 Br md 8.60 Dpth 4.12 Welded, 1 dk	**(B32A2ST) Tug**	**2 oil engines** reduction geared to sc. shafts driving 2 Propellers Total Power: 1,518kW (2,064hp) 11.0kn Mitsubishi S6R2-MTK3L 2 x 4 Stroke 6 Cy. 170 x 220 each-759kW (1032bhp) Mitsubishi Heavy Industries Ltd-Japan Fuel: 235.0 (d.f.)
9656632 *5BYB3* -	**SEA SPEAR** **Deep Sea Supply Shipowning III BV** Deep Sea Supply Management (Singapore) Pte Ltd *Limassol* *Cyprus* MMSI: 210811000 Official number: 9656632	**4,007** 1,533 4,700	Class: NV	**2014-01 Zhejiang Shipbuilding Co Ltd — Fenghua ZJ** Yd No: ZJ2020 Loa 88.34 Br ex - Dght 6.650 Lbp 81.96 Br md 18.99 Dpth 8.00 Welded, 1 dk	**(B21A20S) Platform Supply Ship**	**4 diesel electric oil engines** driving 4 gen. Connecting to 2 elec. motors driving 2 Azimuth electric drive units Total Power: 7,060kW (9,600hp) 13.0kn Caterpillar 3512C 4 x Vee 4 Stroke 12 Cy. 170 x 215 each-1765kW (2400bhp) Caterpillar Inc-USA Thrusters: 2 Tunnel thruster (f)
9656644 *5BYZ3* -	**SEA SPIDER** **Deep Sea Supply Shipowning III BV** Deep Sea Supply Management (Singapore) Pte Ltd *Limassol* *Cyprus* MMSI: 210829000	**4,007** 1,533 4,700	Class: NV	**2014-01 Zhejiang Shipbuilding Co Ltd — Fenghua ZJ** Yd No: ZJ2021 Loa 88.80 Br ex - Dght 6.650 Lbp 81.95 Br md 19.00 Dpth 8.00 Welded, 1 dk	**(B21A20S) Platform Supply Ship**	**4 diesel electric oil engines** driving 4 gen. Connecting to 2 elec. motors driving 2 Azimuth electric drive units Total Power: 7,060kW (9,600hp) 13.0kn Caterpillar 3512C 4 x Vee 4 Stroke 12 Cy. 170 x 215 each-1765kW (2400bhp) Caterpillar Inc-USA Thrusters: 2 Tunnel thruster (f)
8308604 *WCZ9938* -	**SEA SPIDER** *ex Bayou Star -2013 ex Captain Eric II -2009* *ex Makandra No. 17 -2001* **Sea Spider LLC** - *Bayou La Batre, AL* *United States of America* Official number: 992032	*134* 91 -		**1983 Master Marine, Inc. — Bayou La Batre, Al** Yd No: 259 Loa 25.30 Br ex - Dght 3.000 Lbp 21.67 Br md 6.72 Dpth 3.81 Welded, 1 dk	**(B11A2FT) Trawler** Ins: 91	**1 oil engine** reduction geared to sc. shaft driving 1 FP propeller Total Power: 331kW (450hp) Caterpillar 3412T 1 x Vee 4 Stroke 12 Cy. 137 x 152 331kW (450bhp) Caterpillar Tractor Co-USA

8802868 *C6PJ8* -	**SEA SPIRIT** *ex* Spirit of Oceanus *-2010* *ex* Megastar Sagittarius *-2001* *ex* Sun Viva *-2000* *ex* Renaissance Five *-1997* *ex* Hanseatic Renaissance *-1992* *launched as* Renaissance Five *-1991* **TN Cruise K/S** FleetPro Ocean Inc SatCom: Inmarsat B 330922410 *Nassau* *Bahamas* MMSI: 309224000 Official number: 730911	**4,200** 1,263 645	Class: BV (AB) (RI) (NV)	**1991**-03 **Nuovi Cantieri Apuania SpA — Carrara** Yd No: 1144 Loa 90.36 (BB) Br ex 15.31 Dght 4.200 Lbp 78.82 Br md 15.27 Dpth 8.55 Welded	**(A37A2PC) Passenger/Cruise** Passengers: cabins: 60; berths: 120 Ice Capable	**2 oil engines** with clutches, flexible couplings & sr geared to sc. shafts driving 2 CP propellers Total Power: 3,518kW (4,784hp) 16.0kn Alpha 8L28/32 2 x 4 Stroke 8 Cy. 280 x 320 each-1759kW (2392bhp) MAN B&W Diesel A/S-Denmark AuxGen: 2 x 1000kW 440/220V 60Hz a.c, 2 x 800kW 440/220V 60Hz a.c Thrusters: 1 Thwart. FP thruster (f) Fuel: 78.0 (d.f.) 156.0 (r.f.)
9221322 *3EMW5* -	**SEA SPIRIT II** *ex* United Spirit *-2008* *ex* Russel Portier *-2007* **Ro-Ro Co Ltd** - *Panama* *Panama* MMSI: 354833000 Official number: 3483309	**498** 149 750		**1999 Russell Portier, Inc. — Chauvin, La** Loa 50.54 Br ex - Dght - Lbp - Br md 11.58 Dpth 3.05 Welded, 1 dk	**(A31A2GX) General Cargo Ship**	**2 oil engines** reduction geared to sc. shafts driving 2 FP propellers Total Power: 1,060kW (1,442hp) 12.0kn Caterpillar 3412TA 2 x Vee 4 Stroke 12 Cy. 137 x 152 each-530kW (721bhp) Caterpillar Inc-USA
8900244 *VRS4276* -	**SEA SPLENDID** *ex* Flying Swift *-2007* *ex* Discovery Bay 18 *-2007* **Hong Kong & Kowloon Ferry Ltd** - *Hong Kong* *Hong Kong* MMSI: 477995082	*125* - 30		**1989**-01 **Cheoy Lee Shipyards Ltd — Hong Kong** Yd No: 4281 Loa 22.86 Br ex 5.76 Dght - Lbp - Br md 5.45 Dpth 2.92 Welded	**(A37B2PS) Passenger Ship**	**2 oil engines** with flexible couplings & sr reverse geared to sc. shafts driving 2 FP propellers Total Power: 1,324kW (1,800hp) 25.0kn G.M. (Detroit Diesel) 16V-92-TA 2 x Vee 2 Stroke 16 Cy. 123 x 127 each-662kW (900bhp) General Motors Corp-USA
9575101 *VRJO7* -	**SEA SPLENDOR** - **Sea Splendor Co Ltd** Big Horizon Shipping Agencies Ltd *Hong Kong* *Hong Kong* MMSI: 477083500 Official number: HK-3307	**157,039** 99,110 297,123 T/cm 177.9	Class: NV	**2012**-03 **Dalian Shipbuilding Industry Co Ltd — Dalian LN (No 2 Yard)** Yd No: T3000-45 Loa 330.00 (BB) Br ex 60.03 Dght 21.500 Lbp 317.40 Br md 59.99 Dpth 29.70 Welded, 1 dk	**(A13A2TV) Crude Oil Tanker** Double Hull (13F) Liq: 324,600; Liq (Oil): 324,600 Compartments: 5 Ta, 10 Wing Ta, 2 Wing Slop Ta, ER 3 Cargo Pump (s): 3x5500m³/hr	**1 oil engine** driving 1 FP propeller Total Power: 25,480kW (34,643hp) 15.5kn MAN-B&W 7S80MC 1 x 2 Stroke 7 Cy. 800 x 3056 25480kW (34643bhp) Doosan Engine Co Ltd-South Korea AuxGen: 3 x a.c
9057630 *EIMG* S 89	**SEA SPRAY** *ex* Vea *-2004* **Cloughlin Fisheries Ltd** Margaret Downey *Skibbereen* *Irish Republic* MMSI: 250036000 Official number: 403765	**622** 209 -	Class: NV	**1993**-12 **Stocznia Remontowa 'Nauta' SA — Gdynia** (Hull) Yd No: TN43.2 **1993**-12 **Ludvig Hystad Slip & Mek. Verksted AS — Kopervik** Loa 43.20 Br ex - Dght - Lbp 37.20 Br md 10.00 Dpth 6.90 Welded, 2 dks	**(B11B2FV) Fishing Vessel**	**1 oil engine** geared to sc. shaft driving 1 FP propeller Total Power: 1,600kW (2,175hp) MaK 8M332C 1 x 4 Stroke 8 Cy. 240 x 330 1600kW (2175bhp) Krupp MaK Maschinenbau GmbH-Kiel
7365904 - -	**SEA SPRAY** *ex* Freda W *-1998* *ex* Edward Brough *-1982* - - *Guyana*	*428* 249 645	Class: (LR) (BV) ✠ Classed LR until 7/87	**1974**-05 **Scheepswerf Gebr. Coops B.V. — Hoogezand** Yd No: 264 Loa 47.76 Br ex 8.82 Dght 3.125 Lbp 44.00 Br md 8.70 Dpth 3.46 Welded, 1 dk	**(A31A2GX) General Cargo Ship** Grain: 915; Bale: 863 Compartments: 1 Ho, ER 1 Ha: (24.1 x 5.6)ER	**1 oil engine** reverse reduction geared to sc. shaft driving 1 FP propeller Total Power: 298kW (405hp) 9.0kn Blackstone ESL6MK2 1 x 4 Stroke 6 Cy. 222 x 292 298kW (405bhp) Mirrlees Blackstone (Stamford)Ltd.-Stamford AuxGen: 1 x 16kW 380/220V 50Hz a.c, 1 x 12kW 380/220V 50Hz a.c, 1 x 6kW 380/220V 50Hz a.c Fuel: 24.5 (d.f.) 2.0pd
9656656 *5BZS3* -	**SEA SPRINGER** - **Deep Sea SA** Deep Sea Supply Management AS *Limassol* *Cyprus* MMSI: 210841000	**4,007** 1,533 4,700	Class: NV	**2014**-04 **Zhejiang Shipbuilding Co Ltd — Fenghua ZJ** Yd No: ZJ2022 Loa 88.40 Br ex 19.04 Dght 6.650 Lbp 81.96 Br md 18.99 Dpth 8.00 Welded, 1 dk	**(B21A20S) Platform Supply Ship**	**4 diesel electric oil engines** driving 4 gen. Connecting to 2 elec. motors driving 2 Azimuth electric drive units Total Power: 7,060kW (9,600hp) 13.0kn Caterpillar 3512C 2 x Vee 4 Stroke 12 Cy. 170 x 215 each-1765kW (2400bhp) Caterpillar Inc-USA Thrusters: 2 Tunnel thruster (f)
9563433 *A6E2791* -	**SEA STALLION** *ex* Ss Stallion *-2011* **Target Engineering Construction Co (LLC)** - *Abu Dhabi* *United Arab Emirates* Official number: 1475513527	**280** 84 299	Class: NK	**2009**-09 **Yong Choo Kui Shipyard Sdn Bhd — Sibu** Yd No: 27133 Loa 29.00 Br ex - Dght 3.612 Lbp 26.78 Br md 9.00 Dpth 4.20 Welded, 1 dk	**(B32A2ST) Tug**	**2 oil engines** reduction geared to sc. shafts driving 2 Propellers Total Power: 2,238kW (3,042hp) Cummins KTA-38-M2 2 x Vee 4 Stroke 12 Cy. 159 x 159 each-1119kW (1521bhp) Cummins Engine Co Inc-USA
9498779 *A9D2967* -	**SEA STALLION** *ex* Allgo Hingis *-2008* **Al Jazeera Shipping Co WLL (AJS)** - *Bahrain* *Bahrain* MMSI: 408335000 Official number: BN 5043	**154** 47 113	Class: GL (NK)	**2008**-03 **SC Yii Brothers Shipyard Sdn Bhd — Sibu** Yd No: 121 Loa 24.00 Br ex - Dght 2.512 Lbp 22.33 Br md 8.00 Dpth 3.10 Welded, 1 dk	**(B32A2ST) Tug**	**2 oil engines** reduction geared to sc. shafts driving 2 FP propellers Total Power: 894kW (1,216hp) Cummins KTA-19-M3 2 x 4 Stroke 6 Cy. 159 x 159 each-447kW (608bhp) Cummins Engine Co Inc-USA AuxGen: 2 x 40kW a.c Fuel: 99.0 (d.f.)
9490557 *A8SY4* -	**SEA STAR** - **New Sea Star Steam Ships (Hong Kong) Co Ltd** Sea Star Ships Management Co Ltd *Monrovia* *Liberia* MMSI: 636014316 Official number: 14316	**50,697** 30,722 92,500 T/cm 80.9	Class: BV	**2010**-02 **Yangfan Group Co Ltd — Zhoushan ZJ** Yd No: 2089 Loa 230.00 (BB) Br ex - Dght 14.900 Lbp 222.00 Br md 38.00 Dpth 20.70 Welded, 1 dk	**(A21A2BC) Bulk Carrier** Grain: 110,300 Compartments: 7 Ho, ER 7 Ha: 5 (17.9 x 17.0)ER 2 (15.3 x 14.6)	**1 oil engine** driving 1 FP propeller Total Power: 12,240kW (16,642hp) 14.1kn MAN-B&W 6S60MC 1 x 2 Stroke 6 Cy. 600 x 2292 12240kW (16642bhp) Hyundai Heavy Industries Co Ltd-South Korea AuxGen: 3 x 700kW 60Hz a.c
9552680 *3WBN* -	**SEA STAR** - **Agribank Leasing Co II** Bac Hai Maritime Shipping Co Ltd *Haiphong* *Vietnam* MMSI: 574979000 Official number: VN-3096-VT	**2,803** 1,698 4,880	Class: VR	**2010**-03 **Hoang Phong Shipbuilding JSC — Xuan Truong** Yd No: V07-003.02 Loa 92.05 Br ex 15.02 Dght 6.000 Lbp 84.97 Br md 15.00 Dpth 7.50 Welded, 1 dk	**(A21A2BC) Bulk Carrier** Grain: 6,014; Bale: 5,418 Compartments: 2 Ho, ER 2 Ha: (20.0 x 10.0)ER (21.0 x 10.0)	**1 oil engine** reduction geared to sc. shaft driving 1 FP propeller Total Power: 1,765kW (2,400hp) 11.0kn Chinese Std. Type G8300ZC 1 x 4 Stroke 8 Cy. 300 x 380 1765kW (2400bhp) Ningbo CSI Power & Machinery GroupCo Ltd-China AuxGen: 2 x 144kW 400V a.c Fuel: 220.0
9536181 *D6ER7* -	**SEA STAR** - **Merchant Marine Shipping Ltd** MGK-Transforward SatCom: Inmarsat C 461671410 *Moroni* *Union of Comoros* MMSI: 616714000 Official number: 1200836	**2,981** 1,863 5,168	Class: UA (RS)	**2009**-05 **Anhui Ma'anshan Meihua Shipbuilding Co Ltd — Dangtu County AH** Yd No: 800002 Loa 96.90 Br ex 15.82 Dght 5.750 Lbp 90.00 Br md 15.80 Dpth 7.40 Welded, 1 dk	**(A31A2GX) General Cargo Ship** Grain: 6,736; Bale: 6,736 Compartments: 2 Ho, ER 2 Ha: (26.9 x 9.4)ER (25.6 x 9.4) Ice Capable	**1 oil engine** reduction geared to sc. shaft driving 1 FP propeller Total Power: 1,765kW (2,400hp) 12.0kn Chinese Std. Type 8300ZC 1 x 4 Stroke 8 Cy. 300 x 380 1765kW (2400bhp) Wuxi Antai Power Machinery Co Ltd-China AuxGen: 2 x 120kW a.c Fuel: 197.0 (d.f.)
9607710 *3FKJ6* -	**SEA STAR** - **Arab Maritime Petroleum Transport Co (AMPTC)** - *Panama* *Panama* MMSI: 373594000 Official number: 43489PEXT	**62,255** 33,984 112,147	Class: AB	**2012**-07 **Hyundai Heavy Industries Co Ltd — Ulsan** Yd No: 2491 Loa 249.97 (BB) Br ex 44.03 Dght 14.700 Lbp 239.00 Br md 44.00 Dpth 21.00 Welded, 1 dk	**(A13A2TW) Crude/Oil Products Tanker** Double Hull (13F) Liq: 123,220; Liq (Oil): 125,727 Compartments: 6 Wing Ta, 6 Wing Ta, 1 Wing Slop Ta, 1 Slop Ta, 1 Wing Slop Ta, ER 3 Cargo Pump (s): 3x3000m³/hr	**1 oil engine** driving 1 FP propeller Total Power: 14,280kW (19,415hp) 15.0kn MAN-B&W 7S60MC-C8 1 x 2 Stroke 7 Cy. 600 x 2400 14280kW (19415bhp) Hyundai Heavy Industries Co Ltd-South Korea AuxGen: 3 x 850kW a.c Fuel: 96.4 (d.f.) 3639.6 (r.f.)
9604835 - -	**SEA STAR** - **Myung Sung Machine Industry Ltd Partnership** Seaspovill Co Ltd *Gangneung* *South Korea* MMSI: 440600390 Official number: DHR-115304	**590** 206 70	Class: KR (BV)	**2010**-12 **Damen Shipyards Singapore Pte Ltd — Singapore** Yd No: (538728) **2010**-12 **B.V. Scheepswerf Damen — Gorinchem** Yd No: 538728 **2010* Afai Southern Shipyard (Panyu Guangzhou) Ltd — Guangzhou GD** (Hull) Yd No: (538728) Loa 42.16 (BB) Br ex 11.60 Dght 1.570 Lbp 40.18 Br md 11.30 Dpth 3.80 Welded, 1 dk	**(A37B2PS) Passenger Ship** Hull Material: Aluminium Alloy Passengers: unberthed: 450	**4 oil engines** reduction geared to sc. shafts driving 4 Water jets Total Power: 5,760kW (7,832hp) 38.5kn M.T.U. 16V2000M72 4 x Vee 4 Stroke 16 Cy. 135 x 156 each-1440kW (1958bhp) MTU Friedrichshafen GmbH-Friedrichshafen AuxGen: 2 x 86kW 440/230V 50Hz a.c Fuel: 13.0 (d.f.)

IMO / Call sign	Name / Owners / Flag	Tonnage	Class	Builder / Dimensions	Type / Capacity	Machinery
9624500 *V7DE4* -	**SEA STAR** *launched as* Centrans Star *-2014* **Star Shipowning Inc** SeaTeam Management Pte Ltd *Majuro* *Marshall Islands* MMSI: 538005376 Official number: 5376	**33,042** 19,132 56,591 T/cm 58.8	Class: GL NV	**2014-01 Jiangdong Shipyard — Wuhu AH** Yd No: JD57000-7 Loa 189.94 (BB) Br ex - Dght 12.800 Lbp 185.00 Br md 32.26 Dpth 18.00 Welded, 1 dk	**(A21A2BC) Bulk Carrier** Grain: 71,634; Bale: 68,200 Compartments: 1 Ho, 4 Ho, ER Cranes: 4x30t	**1 oil engine** driving 1 FP propeller Total Power: 9,480kW (12,889hp) 14.2kn MAN-B&W 6S50MC-C8 1 x 2 Stroke 6 Cy. 500 x 2000 9480kW (12889bhp) Hefei Rong'an Power Machinery Co Lt-China AuxGen: 3 x a.c
9346897 *A6E3008* -	**SEA STAR** *ex* Kim Heng 1700 *-2005* **Target Engineering Construction Co (LLC)** - *Abu Dhabi* *United Arab Emirates* MMSI: 470845000 Official number: 5081	**188** 57 162	Class: NK	**2005-04 Yong Choo Kui Shipyard Sdn Bhd — Sibu** Yd No: 5801 Loa 25.00 Br ex - Dght 2.862 Lbp 23.23 Br md 8.10 Dpth 3.60 Welded, 1 dk	**(B32A2ST) Tug**	**2 oil engines** reduction geared to sc. shafts driving 2 FP propellers Total Power: 1,266kW (1,722hp) Caterpillar 3412B 2 x Vee 4 Stroke 12 Cy. 137 x 152 each-633kW (861bhp) Caterpillar Inc-USA AuxGen: 2 x 78kW 97/97V 50Hz a.c Fuel: 120.0 (d.f.)
7703247 *9LD2428* -	**SEA STAR** *ex* Tri Star *-2012* *ex* Rosy River *-1999* *ex* Atlantis *-1993* *ex* Alybello *-1987* *ex* Atlantis *-1986* *ex* Maria Catharina *-1986* *ex* Baltic Link *-1983* *ex* Maria Catharina *-1980* **Ayan Navigation Ltd** GMZ Ship Management Co SA *Freetown* *Sierra Leone* MMSI: 667005128 Official number: SL105128	**4,168** 2,124 4,122	Class: DR IV (BV) (CC) (GL)	**1978-06 Schiffswerft Hugo Peters — Wewelsfleth** Yd No: 565 Loa 104.22 (BB) Br ex 16.03 Dght 6.730 Lbp 94.21 Br md 16.01 Dpth 8.51 Welded, 2 dks	**(A31A2GX) General Cargo Ship** Grain: 8,643; Bale: 8,273 TEU 330 C.Ho 138/20' C.Dk 192/20' incl. 55 ref C. Compartments: 1 Ho, ER 2 Ha: (63.5 x 12.7) Gantry cranes: 1 Ice Capable	**1 oil engine** reduction geared to sc. shaft driving 1 FP propeller Total Power: 2,942kW (4,000hp) 15.0kn MaK 6M551AK 1 x 4 Stroke 6 Cy. 450 x 550 2942kW (4000bhp) MaK Maschinenbau GmbH-Kiel AuxGen: 4 x 168kW 220/380V 50Hz a.c Thrusters: 1 Thwart. FP thruster (f)
5090282 *SX9874* -	**SEA STAR** *ex* Magdalini *-2002* *ex* Unity III *-2001* *ex* Island *-1990* *ex* Olaf *-1984* *ex* Brise II *-1983* *ex* Dora Reith *-1968* *ex* Dinklage *-1964* **Sea Star Shipping Co** Papoutsoglou Brothers & Ioannis Papoutsoglou *Piraeus* *Greece* MMSI: 237504800 Official number: 10973	*978* - 2,148	Class: (HR) (BV)	**1957-07 Alfred Hagelstein Masch. u. Schiffswerft — Luebeck** Yd No: 588 Lengthened & Deepened-1968 Loa 80.22 Br ex 10.85 Dght 5.004 Lbp 73.89 Br md 10.80 Dpth 6.25 Riveted\Welded, 1 dk	**(A31A2GX) General Cargo Ship** Grain: 2,977; Bale: 2,755 Compartments: 1 Ho, ER 2 Ha: (15.0 x 6.0) (23.5 x 6.0)ER Ice Capable	**1 oil engine** driving 1 FP propeller Total Power: 736kW (1,001hp) 11.0kn Deutz RBV8M545 1 x 4 Stroke 8 Cy. 320 x 450 736kW (1001bhp) Kloeckner Humboldt Deutz AG-West Germany AuxGen: 2 x 60kW 380V 50Hz a.c, 1 x 30kW 380V 50Hz a.c
5385326 - -	**SEA STAR** *ex* Walana *-1982* **Al Marjan Shipping & Trading Co**	*217* - -	Class: (LR) ✠ Classed LR until 30/11/85	**1960-12 Adelaide Ship Construction Pty Ltd — Port Adelaide SA** Yd No: 5 Loa 32.36 Br ex 8.54 Dght 3.658 Lbp 28.96 Br md 8.08 Dpth 4.09 Welded, 1 dk	**(B32A2ST) Tug**	**1 oil engine** driving 1 FP propeller Total Power: 765kW (1,040hp) 11.5kn National Gas F4AUDM8 1 x 4 Stroke 8 Cy. 305 x 380 765kW (1040bhp) National Gas & Oil Eng. Co.-Ashton-under-Lyne
7010274 *5NWD* -	**SEA STAR** *ex* Aristides S *-1996* *ex* Mar Manso *-1993* *ex* Kakuryo Maru No. 11 *-1979* **Amyntas NG Co Ltd** - *Lagos* *Nigeria*	*997* 585 2,470	Class: (NK)	**1969 Imabari Shipbuilding Co Ltd — Imabari EH (Imabari Shipyard)** Yd No: 245 Loa 71.40 Br ex 11.43 Dght 5.490 Lbp 67.01 Br md 10.94 Dpth 5.77 Riveted\Welded, 1 dk	**(A13B2TP) Products Tanker** Liq: 2,638; Liq (Oil): 2,638 Compartments: 4 Ta, ER	**1 oil engine** driving 1 FP propeller Total Power: 1,324kW (1,800hp) 11.0kn Makita FSHC638 1 x 4 Stroke 6 Cy. 380 x 540 1324kW (1800bhp) Makita Tekkosho-Japan AuxGen: 2 x 40kW
7048271 *WDD7346* -	**SEA STAR** - **Ljay Fisheries LLC** - SatCom: Inmarsat C 430348110 *Seattle, WA* *United States of America* MMSI: 367185190 Official number: 521201	*191* 129 -		**1969 Marine Construction & Design Co. (MARCO) — Seattle, Wa** Loa 28.66 Br ex 7.62 Dght - Lbp - Br md - Dpth 3.64 Welded	**(B11B2FV) Fishing Vessel**	**1 oil engine** driving 1 FP propeller Total Power: 533kW (725hp) Caterpillar D348SCAC 1 x Vee 4 Stroke 12 Cy. 137 x 165 533kW (725bhp) Caterpillar Tractor Co-USA
9034286 *9AA7257* -	**SEA STAR** - **Jadranska Krstarenja doo** - *Dubrovnik* *Croatia* MMSI: 238958340 Official number: 7T485	**887** 275 100	Class: CS	**1991-05 Scheepswerf v/h P. & A. Ruijtenberg B.V. — Raamsdonksveer** (Hull) **1991-05 Scheepswerf van Zelzate — Zelzate** Loa 45.02 Br ex - Dght 2.480 Lbp 32.25 Br md 10.55 Dpth 3.30 Welded	**(A37B2PS) Passenger Ship** Passengers: unberthed: 400	**2 oil engines** geared to sc. shafts driving 2 FP propellers Total Power: 1,268kW (1,724hp) 14.0kn Cummins KTA-38-M0 2 x Vee 4 Stroke 12 Cy. 159 x 159 each-634kW (862bhp) Cummins Engine Co Inc-USA
9102370 - -	**SEA STAR** *ex* Korea Sand Carry *-2005* *ex* Namyoung 99 *-1995* - -	**3,343** - 5,110	Class: (KR)	**1993-04 Ilheung Shipbuilding & Engineering Co Ltd — Mokpo** Yd No: 91-39 Loa 81.90 Br ex - Dght 4.714 Lbp 81.20 Br md 19.50 Dpth 6.00 Welded, 1 dk	**(A13B2TP) Products Tanker** Liq: 5,338; Liq (Oil): 5,338 Cargo Heating Coils	**2 oil engines** driving 2 FP propellers Total Power: 2,060kW (2,800hp) 10.1kn Niigata 6M28AFTE 2 x 4 Stroke 6 Cy. 280 x 480 each-1030kW (1400bhp) Ssangyong Heavy Industries Co Ltd-South Korea AuxGen: 3 x 130kW 445V a.c
8914221 *T3YU* -	**SEA STAR** *ex* Polestar *-2011* **Habitat International Corp** Shandong Zhonglu Fishery Shipping Co Ltd *Tarawa* *Kiribati* MMSI: 529382000 Official number: K13901194	**4,574** 2,474 5,470	Class: NK	**1990-02 Fukuoka Shipbuilding Co Ltd — Fukuoka FO** Yd No: 1154 Loa 120.20 (BB) Br ex - Dght 7.164 Lbp 109.80 Br md 16.40 Dpth 9.95 Welded, 1 dk	**(A34A2GR) Refrigerated Cargo Ship** Ins: 6,610 Compartments: 9 Ho, ER 9 Ha: ER Derricks: 6x3t	**1 oil engine** driving 1 FP propeller Total Power: 4,119kW (5,600hp) 16.0kn Mitsubishi 8UEC37LA 1 x 2 Stroke 8 Cy. 370 x 880 4119kW (5600bhp) Akasaka Tekkosho KK (Akasaka DieselLtd)-Japan Fuel: 620.0 (r.f.)
7811109 *HQXI3* -	**SEA STAR 1** *ex* Atik *-2011* *ex* Roysenes *-2004* *ex* Ryving *-1994* *ex* Sylvester *-1992* *ex* Boston Sea Harrier *-1985* **Nedria Investments (UK) Ltd** - *San Lorenzo* *Honduras* MMSI: 334911000 Official number: L-1528405	**405** 121 281	Class: (LR) (NV) ✠ Classed LR until 13/10/93	**1979-08 Richards (Shipbuilders) Ltd — Great Yarmouth** Yd No: 545 Loa 33.23 Br ex 9.22 Dght 4.041 Lbp 29.01 Br md 9.16 Dpth 4.78 Welded, 1 dk	**(B11A2FS) Stern Trawler**	**1 oil engine** sr geared to sc. shaft driving 1 CP propeller Total Power: 883kW (1,201hp) 11.5kn Blackstone ESL12 1 x Vee 4 Stroke 12 Cy. 222 x 292 883kW (1201bhp) Mirrlees Blackstone (Stamford)Ltd.-Stamford AuxGen: 1 x 180kW 220/440V 50Hz a.c, 2 x 64kW 220/440V 50Hz a.c Fuel: 107.0 (d.f.)
9405708 *YD3351* -	**SEA STAR 01** - **PT Cipta Pesona Armada** PT Tanito Harum *Batam* *Indonesia*	**251** 76 197	Class: NK	**2006-09 PT Palma Progress Shipyard — Batam** Yd No: 246 Loa 28.05 Br ex 8.60 Dght 3.312 Lbp 25.77 Br md 8.60 Dpth 4.30 Welded, 1 dk	**(B32A2ST) Tug**	**2 oil engines** reduction geared to sc. shafts driving 2 FP propellers Total Power: 1,518kW (2,064hp) Mitsubishi S6R2-MPTK3 2 x 4 Stroke 6 Cy. 170 x 220 each-759kW (1032bhp) Mitsubishi Heavy Industries Ltd-Japan AuxGen: 2 x 150kW a.c Fuel: 195.0 (d.f.)
9408504 *YD3369* -	**SEA STAR 02** - **PT Cipta Pesona Armada** - *Batam* *Indonesia* Official number: 1356/PPM	**251** 76 192	Class: NK	**2006-10 PT Palma Progress Shipyard — Batam** Yd No: 247 Loa 28.05 Br ex - Dght 3.312 Lbp 25.77 Br md 8.60 Dpth 4.30 Welded, 1 dk	**(B32A2ST) Tug**	**2 oil engines** reduction geared to sc. shafts driving 2 FP propellers Total Power: 1,518kW (2,064hp) Mitsubishi S6R2-MPTK 2 x 4 Stroke 6 Cy. 170 x 220 each-759kW (1032bhp) Mitsubishi Heavy Industries Ltd-Japan Fuel: 200.0 (d.f.)
9396921 *YD3353* -	**SEA STAR 03** - **PT Cipta Pesona Armada** PT Tanito Harum *Batam* *Indonesia*	**251** 76 195	Class: NK	**2006-08 PT Palma Progress Shipyard — Batam** Yd No: 248 Loa 28.05 Br ex 8.60 Dght 3.512 Lbp 25.77 Br md 8.60 Dpth 4.30 Welded, 1 dk	**(B32A2ST) Tug**	**2 oil engines** reduction geared to sc. shafts driving 2 FP propellers Total Power: 1,518kW (2,064hp) Mitsubishi S6R2-MPTK3 2 x 4 Stroke 6 Cy. 170 x 220 each-759kW (1032bhp) Mitsubishi Heavy Industries Ltd-Japan AuxGen: 2 x 150kW a.c Fuel: 200.0 (d.f.)
7626932 - -	**SEA STAR 3** *ex* Sanyo Maru *-1991* - -	*499* 302 1,150		**1976-12 Suzuki Shipyard Co. Ltd. — Yokkaichi** Yd No: 273 Loa - Br ex - Dght 4.101 Lbp 51.01 Br md 9.81 Dpth 4.70 Welded, 1 dk	**(A12A2TC) Chemical Tanker**	**1 oil engine** driving 1 FP propeller Total Power: 1,177kW (1,600hp) Akasaka DM33 1 x 4 Stroke 6 Cy. 330 x 500 1177kW (1600bhp) Akasaka Tekkosho KK (Akasaka DieselLtd)-Japan

8864464 *3ESN6* -	**SEA STAR 5** *ex* Katsu Maru No. 18 *-2008* **Hong Kong Seastar Shipping Ltd** *Panama* *Panama* MMSI: 370366000 Official number: 3472409	**2,642** 1,610 1,095	Class: IB	**1992-05 Azumi Zosen Kensetsu K.K. — Himeji** Yd No: 110 Loa 60.40 Br ex - Dght 4.470 Lbp 55.00 Br md 12.50 Dpth 6.70 Welded, 1 dk	**(A24D2BA) Aggregates Carrier**	**1 oil engine** reverse geared to sc. shaft driving 1 FP propeller Total Power: 736kW (1,001hp) 11.5kn Hanshin 6LU32G 1 x 4 Stroke 6 Cy. 320 x 510 736kW (1001bhp) The Hanshin Diesel Works Ltd-Japan
9408516 *YD3370* -	**SEA STAR 05** **PT Cipta Pesona Armada** PT Tanito Harum *Batam* *Indonesia* Official number: 1363/PPM	**251** 76 196	Class: NK	**2006-10 PT Palma Progress Shipyard — Batam** Yd No: 249 Loa 28.05 Br ex - Dght 3.312 Lbp 25.77 Br md 8.60 Dpth 4.30 Welded, 1 dk	**(B32A2ST) Tug**	**2 oil engines** reduction geared to sc. shafts driving 2 FP propellers Total Power: 1,518kW (2,064hp) Mitsubishi S6R2-MPTK 2 x 4 Stroke 6 Cy. 170 x 220 each-759kW (1032bhp) Mitsubishi Heavy Industries Ltd-Japan AuxGen: 2 x 150kW a.c Fuel: 200.0 (d.f.)
8310396 *3EPM6* -	**SEA STAR 7** *ex* Ai Rui Xin *-2013* *ex* Winner *-2009* *ex* Seizanmaru *-2003* *ex* Tenyo *-2001* *ex* Ryokoh 5 *-1996* *ex* Tenyo *-1990* *ex* Tenyo Maru *-1988* *ex* Koyo Maru *-1986* **Surplus Star (Hong Kong) Ltd** Hong Kong Seastar Shipping Ltd *Panama* *Panama* MMSI: 352819000 Official number: 1791088I	**4,136** 2,371 6,478	Class: (NK)	**1984-01 Murakami Hide Zosen K.K. — Imabari** Yd No: 218 Loa 105.00 Br ex - Dght 6.866 Lbp 98.00 Br md 16.80 Dpth 8.40 Welded, 1 dk	**(A31A2GX) General Cargo Ship** Grain: 8,290; Bale: 7,828 Compartments: 2 Ho, ER 2 Ha: (25.2 x 9.0) (28.0 x 9.0)ER Cranes: 2x25.5t; Derricks: 2x15t	**1 oil engine** driving 1 FP propeller Total Power: 2,380kW (3,236hp) 12.0kn B&W 6L35MCE 1 x 2 Stroke 6 Cy. 350 x 1050 2380kW (3236bhp) Mitsui Engineering & Shipbuilding CLtd-Japan AuxGen: 2 x 280kW 445V 60Hz a.c Fuel: 81.5 (d.f.) 505.0 (r.f.) 7.5pd
9001291 - -	**SEA STAR CRUISE** *ex* Star Cruise *-2011* *ex* New Nagato *-2010* **Sea World Express Ferry Co Ltd** *Mokpo* *South Korea* MMSI: 440320740 Official number: MPR-105146	*15,089* - 5,155	Class: KR	**1991-01 Kanda Zosensho K.K. — Kawajiri** Yd No: 332 Loa 185.50 (BB) Br ex - Dght 6.651 Lbp 170.23 Br md 26.80 Dpth 9.40 Welded	**(A36A2PR) Passenger/Ro-Ro Ship (Vehicles)** Passengers: unberthed: 698; cabins: 109; berths: 368 Bow door & ramp Stern door/ramp Lane-Len: 1530 Lane-clr ht: 4.20 Cars: 110, Trailers: 180	**2 oil engines** sr geared to sc. shafts driving 2 CP propellers Total Power: 23,832kW (32,402hp) 22.9kn Pielstick 9PC40L570 2 x 4 Stroke 9 Cy. 570 x 750 each-11916kW (16201bhp) Diesel United Ltd.-Aioi AuxGen: 2 x 1996kW, 1 x 996kW Thrusters: 2 Thwart. CP thruster (f) Fuel: 410.8 (d.f.) 86.4pd
9177351 - -	**SEA STAR I** *ex* Lake Star I *-1998* *ex* Lada Enam *-1998* **Sea Star Services SA** - *Zanzibar* *Tanzania* MMSI: 677012800 Official number: 100041	**191** 76 26		**1998-09 WaveMaster International Pty Ltd — Fremantle WA** Yd No: 155 Loa 30.50 Br ex 6.75 Dght 1.200 Lbp 25.30 Br md 6.50 Dpth 3.80 Welded, 1 dk	**(A37B2PS) Passenger Ship** Hull Material: Aluminium Alloy Passengers: unberthed: 179	**3 oil engines** geared to sc. shafts driving 3 Water jets Total Power: 1,980kW (2,691hp) 30.0kn M.T.U. 12V183TE92 3 x Vee 4 Stroke 12 Cy. 128 x 142 each-660kW (897bhp) MTU Friedrichshafen GmbH-Friedrichshafen
9177375 - -	**SEA STAR II** *ex* Lake Star II *-1998* *ex* Lada Tuluh *-1998* **Sea Star Services SA** - *Zanzibar* *Tanzania* MMSI: 677012700 Official number: 100042	**191** 76 26		**1998-10 WaveMaster International Pty Ltd — Fremantle WA** Yd No: 157 Loa 30.50 Br ex 6.75 Dght 1.200 Lbp 25.20 Br md 6.50 Dpth 3.80 Welded	**(A37B2PS) Passenger Ship** Hull Material: Aluminium Alloy Passengers: unberthed: 179	**3 oil engines** geared to sc. shafts driving 3 Water jets Total Power: 1,980kW (2,691hp) 28.8kn M.T.U. 12V183TE92 3 x Vee 4 Stroke 12 Cy. 128 x 142 each-660kW (897bhp) MTU Friedrichshafen GmbH-Friedrichshafen
5063588 *HP9103* -	**SEA STAR II** *ex* Emmanuel II *-1997* *ex* East Pacific *-1997* *ex* Satu *-1990* *ex* Vagabund *-1988* *ex* Carina *-1975* **Emmanuel II Inc** - *Panama* *Panama* Official number: 26595PEXT	*425* 247 889	Class: (HR) (GL)	**1960 J.J. Sietas Schiffswerft — Hamburg** Yd No: 475 Loa 56.22 Br ex 9.45 Dght 3.820 Lbp 50.02 Br md 9.40 Dpth 5.90 Riveted\Welded, 1 dk	**(A31A2GX) General Cargo Ship** Grain: 1,486; Bale: 1,342 Compartments: 1 Ho, ER 2 Ha: (8.7 x 5.4) (17.0 x 5.4)ER Derricks: 3x2t; Winches: 3 Ice Capable	**1 oil engine** driving 1 CP propeller Total Power: 368kW (500hp) 9.5kn Deutz RV6M545 1 x 4 Stroke 6 Cy. 320 x 450 368kW (500bhp) Kloeckner Humboldt Deutz AG-West Germany Fuel: 30.5
6525686 - -	**SEA STAR No. 1** *ex* Gloria No. 3 *-1995* *ex* Dong Won No. 501 *-1992* *ex* Ensanada No. 1 *-1986* *ex* Atlanta No. 1 *-1986* *ex* Dong Won No. 501 *-1983* *ex* Shoun Maru No. 1 *-1970* **Puk Wang Fisheries Co** - *Busan* *South Korea* Official number: 9501021-6210008	*309* 157 298	Class: (KR)	**1965 Niigata Engineering Co Ltd — Niigata NI** Yd No: 617 Loa 42.83 Br ex 8.03 Dght 3.258 Lbp 37.19 Br md 8.01 Dpth 3.61 Welded, 2 dks	**(B11A2FS) Stern Trawler** Ins: 290 3 Ha: (2.1 x 1.6)2 (1.6 x 2.1)	**1 oil engine** driving 1 FP propeller Total Power: 552kW (750hp) 10.0kn Niigata 6M28KEHS 1 x 4 Stroke 6 Cy. 280 x 440 552kW (750bhp) Niigata Engineering Co Ltd-Japan AuxGen: 2 x 36kW 220V a.c
7397361 *V4IE2* -	**SEA STAR V** *ex* Sea Star *-2008* *ex* Mansoor - 1 *-2008* *ex* Sarwaguna Empat *-1998* **Sea Eagles Shipping LLC** - *Basseterre* *St Kitts & Nevis* MMSI: 341019000 Official number: SKN 1002210	*485* 146 252	Class: IS (KI)	**1975-12 Singapore Shipbuilding & Engineering Pte Ltd — Singapore** Yd No: 98 Loa 48.04 Br ex 12.20 Dght 2.131 Lbp 44.84 Br md 12.17 Dpth 2.98 Welded, 1 dk	**(A35D2RL) Landing Craft** Bow ramp (centre)	**2 oil engines** driving 2 FP propellers Total Power: 898kW (1,220hp) 8.0kn Caterpillar 3412 2 x Vee 4 Stroke 12 Cy. 137 x 152 each-449kW (610bhp) (new engine 2000) Caterpillar Inc-USA AuxGen: 2 x 35kW 415V a.c
9366158 *9V7746* -	**SEA STEAMER** *ex* Western Steamer *-2013* **Oslo Carriers Pte Ltd** Bulkship Management AS *Singapore* *Singapore* MMSI: 566840000 Official number: 398315	**6,668** 3,500 9,384	Class: GL	**2011-10 Zhejiang Zhenyu Shipbuilding Co Ltd — Xiangshan County ZJ** Yd No: MPC68-4 Loa 107.00 (BB) Br ex - Dght 8.000 Lbp 103.00 Br md 18.20 Dpth 10.50 Welded, 1 dk	**(A31A2GX) General Cargo Ship** Grain: 11,770; Bale: 11,770 TEU 132 Compartments: 3 Ho, 3 Tw Dk, ER 3 Ha: 2 (25.9 x 15.2)ER (16.1 x 15.2) Cranes: 2x60t Ice Capable	**1 oil engine** reduction geared to sc. shaft driving 1 CP propeller Total Power: 3,840kW (5,221hp) 13.0kn MaK 8M32C 1 x 4 Stroke 8 Cy. 320 x 480 3840kW (5221bhp) Caterpillar Motoren GmbH & Co. KG-Germany AuxGen: 2 x 399kW a.c, 1 x 500kW a.c Thrusters: 1 Tunnel thruster (f)
9607318 *5NXF* -	**SEA STERLING** *ex* Sea Stallion *-2013* *ex* Ya Hang 18 *-2013* **Sea Petroleum & Gas Co Ltd** - *Lagos* *Nigeria* MMSI: 657993000	**4,126** 1,717 6,000	Class: BV	**2012-05 Taizhou Hongda Shipbuilding Co Ltd — Linhai ZJ** Yd No: HD8105 Loa 112.10 Br ex 16.44 Dght 6.000 Lbp 105.50 Br md 16.20 Dpth 8.00 Welded, 1 dk	**(A13B2TP) Products Tanker** Double Hull (13F) Liq: 5,763; Liq (Oil): 5,763 Compartments: 5 Wing Ta, 5 Wing Ta, ER Ice Capable	**1 oil engine** reduction geared to sc. shafts driving 1 FP propeller Total Power: 2,574kW (3,500hp) 12.5kn Yanmar 6N330-EN 1 x 4 Stroke 6 Cy. 330 x 440 2574kW (3500bhp) Qingdao Zichai Boyang Diesel EngineCo Ltd-China AuxGen: 3 x 200kW 50Hz a.c Fuel: 486.0
9420033 *5BMH3* -	**SEA STOAT** **DESS Cyprus Ltd** Deep Sea Supply Plc *Limassol* *Cyprus* MMSI: 209409000	**1,943** 646 1,923	Class: IR NV	**2011-12 ABG Shipyard Ltd — Surat** Yd No: 275 Loa 63.40 Br ex - Dght 5.100 Lbp 56.50 Br md 15.80 Dpth 6.80 Welded, 1 dk	**(B21B20A) Anchor Handling Tug Supply**	**2 oil engines** reduction geared to sc. shafts driving 2 CP propellers Total Power: 5,002kW (6,800hp) 10.5kn Yanmar 8N280-EN 2 x 4 Stroke 8 Cy. 280 x 380 each-2501kW (3400bhp) Yanmar Diesel Engine Co Ltd-Japan AuxGen: 3 x 425kW 440V 60Hz a.c Thrusters: 1 Thwart. CP thruster (f)
9672947 *OUWZ2* -	**SEA STORM** *ex* Fob Swath 4 *-2013* **FOB Swath AS** - *Fredericia* *Denmark* MMSI: 219463000 Official number: A554	**275** 73 65	Class: NV	**2013-09 Danish Yachts A/S — Skagen** Yd No: 121 Loa 24.65 (BB) Br ex 10.83 Dght 2.490 Lbp 23.55 Br md 10.60 Dpth 5.37 Bonded, 1 dk	**(B21A20C) Crew/Supply Vessel** Hull Material: Carbon Fibre Sandwich Passengers: unberthed: 24	**2 oil engines** reduction geared to sc. shafts driving 2 CP propellers Total Power: 1,800kW (2,448hp) 22.0kn M.T.U. 10V2000M72 1 x Vee 4 Stroke 10 Cy. 135 x 156 900kW (1224bhp) MTU Friedrichshafen GmbH-Friedrichshafen AuxGen: 2 x a.c Thrusters: 2 Tunnel thruster (f); 2 Tunnel thruster (a)
8103042 *WDC7865* -	**SEA STORM** *ex* Dona Genoveva *-1992* **Sea Storm Ltd Partnership** Arctic Storm Inc SatCom: Inmarsat C 436740310 *Seattle, WA* *United States of America* Official number: 628959	*199* 148 94		**1980-11 Marine Construction & Design Co. (MARCO) — Seattle, Wa** Yd No: 386 Loa 37.57 Br ex - Dght - Lbp - Br md 9.72 Dpth 4.37 Welded, 1 dk	**(B11A2FS) Stern Trawler** Cranes: 1	**1 oil engine** geared to sc. shaft driving 1 FP propeller Total Power: 1,379kW (1,875hp) 12.0kn Caterpillar 3516TA 1 x Vee 4 Stroke 16 Cy. 170 x 190 1379kW (1875bhp) (new engine 1992) Caterpillar Inc-USA AuxGen: 1 x 155kW

Ship	Tonnage	Class	Build / Dimensions	Type	Machinery
8978241 **SEA STOUT** - *ex* Keith G *-2004* - **Saleem Contractors Ltd** - *Port of Spain* *Trinidad & Tobago*	**193** 59 202		**1977**-02 **Offshore Trawlers, Inc. — Bayou La Batre, Al** Yd No: 21 Loa 33.52 Br ex - Dght 2.740 Lbp 29.56 Br md 7.92 Dpth 3.75 Welded, 1 dk	**(B34L2QU) Utility Vessel**	**2 oil engines** geared to sc. shafts driving 2 Propellers Total Power: 882kW (1,200hp) G.M. (Detroit Diesel) 16V-92 2 x Vee 2 Stroke 16 Cy. 123 x 127 each-441kW (600bhp) General Motors Corp-USA
8971839 **SEA STOUT** *A6E2711* *ex* Sharief Express *-1993* *ex* Masco IV *-1993* - **Global Marine Services** - *Sharjah* *United Arab Emirates* MMSI: 470876000 Official number: UAE/SHJ/3071	*212* 63 -	Class: LR (AB) **100A1** SS 06/2012 supply ship Gulf service, Arabian Sea service **LMC**	**1985**-01 **Master Boat Builders, Inc. — Coden, Al** Yd No: 66 Loa 33.52 Br ex - Dght 2.440 Lbp 30.18 Br md 7.92 Dpth 3.20 Welded, 1 dk	**(B21A20S) Platform Supply Ship** Passengers: cabins: 3; berths: 15	**2 oil engines** reverse reduction geared to sc. shafts driving 2 Propellers Total Power: 882kW (1,200hp) 11.0kn G.M. (Detroit Diesel) 16V-92 2 x Vee 2 Stroke 16 Cy. 123 x 127 each-441kW (600bhp) Detroit Diesel Corporation-Detroit, Mi AuxGen: 2 x 60kW 220V 50Hz a.c Fuel: 100.0 (d.f.)
9652105 **SEA STRENGTH** *HP5882* - **A R Singh Contractors Ltd** - *Panama* *Panama* MMSI: 371673000 Official number: 43132PEXT	**494** 148 -		**2012**-04 **St Johns Ship Building Inc — Palatka FL** Yd No: 020 Loa 47.80 Br ex 11.69 Dght 2.920 Lbp - Br md 11.50 Dpth 3.50 Welded, 1 dk	**(B22A20R) Offshore Support Vessel**	**2 oil engines** reverse reduction geared to sc. shaft (s) driving 2 Propellers Total Power: 1,250kW (1,700hp) 12.0kn Caterpillar C32 1 x Vee 4 Stroke 12 Cy. 145 x 162 625kW (850bhp) Caterpillar Inc-USA AuxGen: 2 x 99kW a.c Thrusters: 1 Tunnel thruster (f)
7647821 **SEA STRIKER** *WYQ4240* - **G B L Inc** - *New Orleans, LA* *United States of America* Official number: 579660	*468* 318 -		**1977** **Patterson Shipyard Inc. — Patterson, La** Yd No: 32 L reg 49.44 Br ex 9.45 Dght - Lbp - Br md - Dpth 3.46 Welded, 1dk	**(B11B2FV) Fishing Vessel**	**1 oil engine** driving 1 FP propeller Total Power: 1,324kW (1,800hp)
9174816 **SEA SUCCESS** *ELUL8* - **Sea Success Maritime Inc** Lihai International Shipping Ltd SatCom: Inmarsat B 363669710 *Monrovia* *Liberia* MMSI: 636010709 Official number: 10709	**18,093** 9,442 27,287 T/cm 38.9	Class: NK (AB)	**1998**-01 **Hudong Shipbuilding Group — Shanghai** Yd No: H1238A Loa 175.00 (BB) Br ex - Dght 9.816 Lbp 165.00 Br md 26.00 Dpth 13.90 Welded, 1 dk	**(A21A2BC) Bulk Carrier** Grain: 36,723; Bale: 35,621 Compartments: 5 Ho, ER 5 Ha: (14.2 x 12.8)4 (19.2 x 14.4)ER Cranes: 4x30t	**1 oil engine** driving 1 FP propeller Total Power: 5,763kW (7,835hp) 14.7kn B&W 5L50MC 1 x 2 Stroke 5 Cy. 500 x 1620 5763kW (7835bhp) Hudong Shipyard-China AuxGen: 3 x 460kW a.c Fuel: 1350.0
8402462 **SEA SUNNY** *HSAA* *ex* Worldline 2 *-2004* *ex* Ocean Forest *-2000* - *ex* Laguna 2 *-1996* *ex* Baja California *-1992* **Sang Thai Shipping Co Ltd** - SatCom: Inmarsat C 456748510 *Bangkok* *Thailand* MMSI: 567267000 Official number: 470000927	**4,010** 2,428 6,265	Class: (NK)	**1984**-06 **K.K. Taihei Kogyo — Akitsu** Yd No: 1674 Loa 106.48 Br ex - Dght 6.705 Lbp 97.95 Br md 16.41 Dpth 8.21 Welded, 1 dk	**(A31A2GX) General Cargo Ship** Grain: 8,346; Bale: 7,653 Compartments: 2 Ho, ER 2 Ha: (28.5 x 8.4) (28.6 x 8.4)ER Derricks: 4x15t	**1 oil engine** driving 1 FP propeller Total Power: 2,869kW (3,901hp) 12.8kn Mitsubishi 6UEC37H 1 x 2 Stroke 6 Cy. 370 x 880 2869kW (3901bhp) Akasaka Tekkosho KK (Akasaka DieselLtd)-Japan AuxGen: 2 x 160kW a.c
7041156 **SEA SUPPLIER I** *A6E2659* *ex* Hana Glory *-2013* *ex* Arab Gold *-2011* - *ex* Union Gold *-1990* *ex* Gulf Gold *-1980* **Standard Oil Marine Inc** Al Taawon Shipping Co LLC *United Arab Emirates* MMSI: 470105000	**635** 191 750	Class: (LR) (NK) ✠ Classed LR until 4/7/80	**1971**-07 **Vosper Thornycroft Uniteers Pte Ltd — Singapore** Yd No: B.903 Loa 48.77 Br ex 11.76 Dght 4.298 Lbp 44.93 Br md 11.59 Dpth 4.91 Welded, 1 dk	**(B21B20T) Offshore Tug/Supply Ship** Liq: 789 Compartments: 16 Ta, ER	**2 oil engines** driving 2 FP propellers Total Power: 1,838kW (2,498hp) 11.0kn Fuji 6L27.5G 2 x 4 Stroke 6 Cy. 275 x 320 each-919kW (1249bhp) (new engine 1984) Fuji Diesel Co Ltd-Japan AuxGen: 2 x 200kW 415/240V 50Hz a.c Thrusters: 1 Thwart. FP thruster (f) Fuel: 252.0 (d.f.)
9390745 **SEA SUPPORTER** *3EMS4* - **Gulf Marine Far East Pte Ltd** GulfMark Offshore Inc *Panama* *Panama* MMSI: 371183000 Official number: 3397608A	**2,344** 703 2,605	Class: AB	**2007**-10 **P.T. Jaya Asiatic Shipyard — Batam** Yd No: 861 Loa 70.05 Br ex - Dght 5.900 Lbp 63.00 Br md 15.60 Dpth 7.20 Welded, 1 dk	**(B21B20A) Anchor Handling Tug Supply**	**2 oil engines** reduction geared to sc. shafts driving 2 CP propellers Total Power: 5,850kW (7,954hp) 12.0kn Wartsila 9L26 2 x 4 Stroke 9 Cy. 260 x 320 each-2925kW (3977bhp) Wartsila Finland Oy-Finland AuxGen: 2 x 370kW a.c, 2 x 1800kW a.c Thrusters: 2 Tunnel thruster (f); 1 Tunnel thruster (a) Fuel: 1150.0 (d.f.)
9217010 **SEA SUPREME** *VRS4297* - **Hong Kong & Kowloon Ferry Ltd** - *Hong Kong* *Hong Kong* MMSI: 477995074	*277* 177 20		**1999**-07 **Cheoy Lee Shipyards Ltd — Hong Kong** Yd No: 4734 Loa 28.04 Br ex - Dght 1.310 Lbp 25.96 Br md 8.08 Dpth 3.10 Bonded, 1 dk	**(A37B2PS) Passenger Ship** Hull Material: Reinforced Plastic Passengers: unberthed: 380	**2 oil engines** reverse reduction geared to sc. shafts driving 2 FP propellers Total Power: 1,472kW (2,002hp) 23.0kn Cummins KTA-38-M1 2 x Vee 4 Stroke 12 Cy. 159 x 159 each-736kW (1001bhp) Cummins Engine Co Inc-USA AuxGen: 2 x 40kW a.c
7809223 **SEA SURVEY** *A9D3052* *ex* Chiyoda Maru No. 5 *-2010* *ex* Fraih 12 *-2010* - **Sea Eagles Shipping LLC** - *Bahrain* *Bahrain* Official number: 4350	**149** 44 -	Class: AB	**1978**-07 **Yokohama Zosen — Chiba** Yd No: 1375 Loa 27.01 Br ex 6.81 Dght 2.259 Lbp 24.01 Br md 6.61 Dpth 3.00 Welded, 1 dk	**(B34L2QU) Utility Vessel**	**2 oil engines** reverse reduction geared to sc. shafts driving 2 FP propellers Total Power: 588kW (800hp) 12.0kn G.M. (Detroit Diesel) 12V-71-N 2 x Vee 2 Stroke 12 Cy. 108 x 127 each-294kW (400bhp) General Motors Detroit DieselAllison Divn-USA AuxGen: 2 x 80kW
7813901 **SEA SURVEYOR** *C6QL6* *ex* Magnet *-1998* - **Gardline Shipping Ltd** Gardline Geosurvey Ltd SatCom: Inmarsat C 430801410 *Nassau* *Bahamas* MMSI: 308014000 Official number: 732193	**1,275** 382 545	Class: GL (LR) ✠ Classed LR until 7/12/10	**1979**-11 **Clelands Shipbuilding Co. Ltd — Wallsend** Yd No: 344 Converted From: Degaussing Vessel-1998 Lengthened-1998 Loa 64.10 Br ex 11.78 Dght 3.510 Lbp 58.01 Br md 11.40 Dpth 6.67 Welded, 2 dks	**(B31A2SR) Research Survey Vessel**	**2 oil engines** geared to sc. shafts driving 2 FP propellers Total Power: 1,214kW (1,650hp) 10.0kn Blackstone ESL6 2 x 4 Stroke 6 Cy. 222 x 292 each-607kW (825bhp) Mirrlees Blackstone (Stamford)Ltd.-Stamford AuxGen: 3 x 390kW 440V 60Hz a.c, 3 x 98kW 440V 60Hz a.c Thrusters: 1 Thwart. FP thruster (f); 1 Tunnel thruster (a)
8500331 **SEA SWALLOW** *P2V4851* *ex* Seawell No. 8 *-1998* - *ex* Putra Belait No. 2 *-1991* **Bismark Maritime Ltd** - *Port Moresby* *Papua New Guinea* MMSI: 553111144	**384** 115 420	Class: PA (BV) (GL)	**1984** **Greenbay Marine Pte Ltd — Singapore** Yd No: 48 Loa 45.20 Br ex 10.44 Dght 2.530 Lbp 43.20 Br md 10.40 Dpth 2.82 Welded, 1 dk	**(A35D2RL) Landing Craft** Bow door/ramp Cranes: 1x40t	**2 oil engines** reverse reduction geared to sc. shafts driving 2 FP propellers Total Power: 736kW (1,000hp) 10.0kn Caterpillar 3412T 2 x Vee 4 Stroke 12 Cy. 137 x 152 each-368kW (500bhp) Caterpillar Tractor Co-USA
7807641 **SEA SWIFT** *A6E2775* *ex* Harris M. Callais *-1991* - **Ahmad Hassan Shipping & Fuel Bunkering Establishment** - *Sharjah* *United Arab Emirates* MMSI: 470586000 Official number: 4634	**576** 177 1,000	Class: AB	**1978**-12 **Halter Marine, Inc. — Patterson, La** Yd No: 760 Loa 49.33 Br ex 11.61 Dght 3.393 Lbp 48.77 Br md 11.59 Dpth 3.97 Welded, 1 dk	**(B21A20S) Platform Supply Ship**	**2 oil engines** reverse reduction geared to sc. shafts driving 2 FP propellers Total Power: 1,704kW (2,316hp) 12.0kn G.M. (Detroit Diesel) 16V-149-TI 2 x Vee 2 Stroke 16 Cy. 146 x 146 each-852kW (1158bhp) General Motors Detroit DieselAllison Divn-USA AuxGen: 2 x 75kW Thrusters: 1 Thwart. FP thruster (f)
9306859 **SEA SWIFT** *9VAS3* - **Hong Lam Marine Pte Ltd** - *Singapore* *Singapore* MMSI: 564261000 Official number: 390209	**2,673** 1,510 4,998	Class: BV (CC)	**2003**-11 **Guangzhou Hangtong Shipbuilding & Shipping Co Ltd — Jiangmen GD** Yd No: 022009 Loa 91.72 Br ex - Dght 5.000 Lbp 87.72 Br md 15.30 Dpth 7.00 Welded, 1 dk	**(A13B2TP) Products Tanker** Double Bottom Entire Compartment Length Liq: 5,133; Liq (Oil): 5,133 Compartments: 12 Wing Ta, ER 4 Cargo Pump (s): 2x800m³/hr, 2x100m³/hr	**2 oil engines** reduction geared to sc. shafts driving 2 FP propellers Total Power: 1,912kW (2,600hp) 10.0kn Yanmar 6N21A-EN 2 x 4 Stroke 6 Cy. 210 x 290 each-956kW (1300bhp) Yanmar Diesel Engine Co Ltd-Japan AuxGen: 2 x 160kW 380V a.c

7219014 *D6BK3* -	**SEA SYMPHONY** *ex* Sea Song *-1998* *ex* A. H. 1 *-1996* *ex* Gray Sound *-1994* *ex* Hakim *-1979* **Technical London Ltd** SDS Shipping (Pvt) Ltd *Moroni* *Union of Comoros* MMSI: 616084000 Official number: 1200116	**126** 38 81	Class: (LR) (GL) ✠ Classed LR until 4/88	**1972-07 James & Stone (Brightlingsea) Ltd. — Brightlingsea** Yd No: 468 Loa 30.33 Br ex 6.96 Dght 2.057 Lbp 27.44 Br md 6.71 Dpth 2.90 Welded, 1 dk	**(B32A2ST) Tug**	**2 oil engines** reverse reduction geared to sc. shafts driving 2 FP propellers Total Power: 470kW (640hp) 8.0kn Kelvin TS8 2 x 4 Stroke 8 Cy. 165 x 184 each-235kW (320bhp) English Electric Diesels Ltd.-Glasgow AuxGen: 2 x 75kW 415V 50Hz a.c
6504735 - -	**SEA SYSTEMS** *ex* Montco *-1970* *ex* Bob Charles *-1966* **P G L Smith** - *Bahrain*	*189* 128 -		**1964 American Marine Corp. — New Orleans, La** Yd No: 887 Loa 39.48 Br ex 10.06 Dght 3.112 Lbp 36.89 Br md 9.76 Dpth 3.66 Welded, 1 dk	**(B21A2OS) Platform Supply Ship**	**2 oil engines** driving 2 FP propellers Total Power: 1,030kW (1,400hp) G.M. (Detroit Diesel) 16V-71 2 x Vee 2 Stroke 16 Cy. 108 x 127 each-515kW (700bhp) General Motors Corp-USA
9677480 *9V2259* -	**SEA TANKER** - **Sea Hub Tankers Pte Ltd** - *Singapore* *Singapore* MMSI: 563283000 Official number: 398811	**894** 303 1,303	Class: BV	**2013-08 Zhuhai Shipbuilding Industry Corp — Zhuhai GD** Yd No: 1-466 Loa 51.39 (BB) Br ex - Dght 4.400 Lbp 48.88 Br md 11.80 Dpth 5.50 Welded, 1 dk	**(A13B2TP) Products Tanker** Double Hull (13F) Liq: 1,159; Liq (Oil): 1,159 Compartments: 4 Wing Ta, 4 Wing Ta, ER	**2 oil engines** reduction geared to sc. shafts driving 2 FP propellers Total Power: 882kW (1,200hp) 10.0kn Cummins KTA-19-M3 2 x 4 Stroke 6 Cy. 159 x 159 each-441kW (600bhp) Cummins Diesel International Ltd-USA AuxGen: 2 x 100kW 50Hz a.c Fuel: 90.0
9662837 *S6LP3* -	**SEA TANKER I** - **ES Shipping Pte Ltd** Sea Hub Tankers Pte Ltd *Singapore* *Singapore* MMSI: 566666000 Official number: 397913	**2,714** 978 3,590	Class: NK	**2012-11 ES Offshore & Marine Eng (Thailand) Co Ltd — Prachuap Khiri Khan** Yd No: P904 Loa 90.46 (BB) Br ex 15.02 Dght 5.212 Lbp 85.00 Br md 15.00 Dpth 6.80 Welded, 1 dk	**(A13B2TP) Products Tanker** Double Hull (13F) Liq: 3,522; Liq (Oil): 3,522	**2 oil engines** reduction geared to sc. shaft (s) driving 2 Propellers Total Power: 1,912kW (2,600hp) 11.2kn Yanmar 6N21A-EV 2 x 4 Stroke 6 Cy. 210 x 290 each-956kW (1300bhp) Yanmar Diesel Engine Co Ltd-Japan AuxGen: 2 x 563kW a.c Fuel: 190.0
9664483 *9VAX8* -	**SEA TANKER II** - **Sea Hub Tankers Pte Ltd** - *Singapore* *Singapore* MMSI: 566736000 Official number: 398132	**2,714** 978 3,592	Class: NK	**2013-02 ES Offshore & Marine Eng (Thailand) Co Ltd — Prachuap Khiri Khan** Yd No: P905 Loa 90.45 Br ex - Dght 5.212 Lbp 85.00 Br md 15.00 Dpth 6.80 Welded, 1 dk	**(A13B2TP) Products Tanker** Double Hull (13F) Liq: 3,490; Liq (Oil): 3,550	**2 oil engines** reduction geared to sc. shafts driving 2 Propellers Total Power: 1,912kW (2,600hp) 10.0kn Yanmar 6N21A-EV 2 x 4 Stroke 6 Cy. 210 x 290 each-956kW (1300bhp) Yanmar Diesel Engine Co Ltd-Japan Fuel: 190.0
9575620 *5BUS3* -	**SEA TANTALUS** - **PSV Holding Inc** Deep Sea Supply Management (Singapore) Pte Ltd *Limassol* *Cyprus* MMSI: 209833000 Official number: 9575620	**3,455** 1,036 4,000	Class: NV	**2013-03 Cochin Shipyard Ltd — Ernakulam** Yd No: BY-89 Loa 82.20 (BB) Br ex 17.03 Dght 6.300 Lbp 74.10 Br md 17.00 Dpth 7.60 Welded, 1 dk	**(B21A2OS) Platform Supply Ship**	**4 diesel electric oil engines** driving 4 gen. each 1200kW Connecting to 2 elec. motors each (1600kW) driving 2 Azimuth electric drive units Total Power: 5,968kW (8,116hp) 11.0kn Cummins KTA-50-M1 4 x Vee 4 Stroke 16 Cy. 159 x 159 each-1492kW (2029bhp) Cummins Engine Co Inc-USA Thrusters: 2 Tunnel thruster (f)
8519497 - -	**SEA TARO** *ex* Kosho Maru *-2009* **Armco Marine Services Pte Ltd**	*199* - 441		**1986-04 Uchida Zosen — Ise** Yd No: 841 Loa 46.81 Br ex - Dght 3.400 Lbp 43.00 Br md 7.61 Dpth 3.46 Welded, 1 dk	**(A12A2TC) Chemical Tanker** Liq: 290 Compartments: 6 Ta, ER	**1 oil engine** driving 1 FP propeller Total Power: 441kW (600hp) Yanmar MF24-HT 1 x 4 Stroke 6 Cy. 240 x 420 441kW (600bhp) Yanmar Diesel Engine Co Ltd-Japan
9263485 *A9D2872* -	**SEA TEMPEST** *ex* Profit United *-2002* **Al Jazeera Shipping Co WLL (AJS)** - *Bahrain* *Bahrain* Official number: BN 9215	**144** 44 112	Class: AB (NK)	**2002-01 Forward Shipbuilding Enterprise Sdn Bhd — Sibu** Yd No: 79 Loa 23.50 Br ex - Dght 2.712 Lbp 21.79 Br md 7.32 Dpth 3.20 Welded, 1 dk	**(B32B2SP) Pusher Tug**	**2 oil engines** geared to sc. shafts driving 2 FP propellers Total Power: 940kW (1,278hp) Yanmar 6LAHM-STE3 2 x 4 Stroke 6 Cy. 150 x 165 each-470kW (639bhp) Yanmar Diesel Engine Co Ltd-Japan AuxGen: 2 x 20kW a.c Fuel: 114.0 (d.f.)
8968014 *9V6007* -	**SEA TERRIER** - **PSA Marine Pte Ltd** - *Singapore* *Singapore* MMSI: 563002930	**282** 85 -	Class: BV	**2001-12 Greenbay Marine Pte Ltd — Singapore** Yd No: 138 Loa 29.00 Br ex - Dght 3.500 Lbp 23.50 Br md 9.50 Dpth 4.70 Welded, 1 dk	**(B32B2SP) Pusher Tug**	**2 oil engines** gearing integral to driving 2 Z propellers Total Power: 2,942kW (4,000hp) Yanmar 6N260-EN 2 x 4 Stroke 6 Cy. 260 x 360 each-1471kW (2000bhp) Yanmar Diesel Engine Co Ltd-Japan
8020343 - -	**SEA THIEF** *ex* Jar Sea Thief *-2008* **Austral Fisheries Pty Ltd** - *Fremantle, WA* *Australia* Official number: 385900	*223* 140 -		**1980-12 Australian Shipbuilding Industries (WA) Pty Ltd — Fremantle WA** Yd No: 187 Loa 22.03 Br ex 7.68 Dght 3.001 Lbp 20.38 Br md 7.48 Dpth 4.07 Welded, 1 dk	**(B11A2FT) Trawler**	**1 oil engine** reverse reduction geared to sc. shaft driving 1 FP propeller Total Power: 342kW (465hp) 9.5kn Caterpillar 3412T 1 x Vee 4 Stroke 12 Cy. 137 x 152 342kW (465bhp) Caterpillar Tractor Co-USA
7522083 *9LH2029* -	**SEA THUNDER** *ex* Gulf Balder *-2013* *ex* Laga *-1996* **Gold Fleet Ltd** Tidewater Marine International Inc *Sierra Leone* MMSI: 667009029	**823** 246 765	Class: AB (LR) ✠ Classed LR until 30/6/98	**1976-09 D.W. Kremer Sohn — Elmshorn** Yd No: 1172 Loa 44.61 Br ex 12.37 Dght 5.501 Lbp 41.38 Br md 12.01 Dpth 6.28 Welded, 1 dk	**(B21B20A) Anchor Handling Tug Supply** Ice Capable	**2 oil engines** sr geared to sc. shafts driving 2 CP propellers Total Power: 5,458kW (7,420hp) 13.5kn Alpha 14U28L-VO 2 x Vee 4 Stroke 14 Cy. 280 x 320 each-2729kW (3710bhp) Alpha Diesel A/S-Denmark AuxGen: 3 x 220kW 450V 60Hz a.c, 1 x 80kW 450V 60Hz a.c Thrusters: 1 Thwart. CP thruster (f)
9166376 *5BDQ3* -	**SEA TIGER** *ex* Ray J Hope *-2006* *ex* Maersk Dispatcher *-2003* **Deep Sea Supply Shipowning AS** Deep Sea Supply Management (Singapore) Pte Ltd *Limassol* *Cyprus* MMSI: 210727000	**2,556** 810 2,802	Class: NV (AB)	**1998-11 Kvaerner Leirvik AS — Leirvik i Sogn** Yd No: 278 Loa 73.60 Br ex - Dght 6.900 Lbp 66.60 Br md 16.40 Dpth 8.00 Welded, 1 dk	**(B21B20A) Anchor Handling Tug Supply** Passengers: cabins: 12	**2 oil engines** reduction geared to sc. shafts driving 2 CP propellers Total Power: 11,034kW (15,002hp) 14.0kn Wartsila 12V32 2 x Vee 4 Stroke 12 Cy. 320 x 400 each-5517kW (7501bhp) Wartsila NSD Finland Oy-Finland AuxGen: 2 x 1800kW 220/440V 60Hz a.c, 2 x 300kW 220/440V 60Hz a.c Thrusters: 1 Thwart. FP thruster (f); 1 Retract. directional thruster (f); 1 Tunnel thruster (a) Fuel: 782.0 (d.f.) 35.0pd
9168295 - -	**SEA TIGER** - **SP-PSAM Tugboat Co Ltd** - *Saigon* *Vietnam*	**269** 80 140	Class: (BV)	**1997-06 Matsuura Tekko Zosen K.K. — Osakikamijima** Yd No: 502 Loa 29.00 Br ex - Dght 3.760 Lbp 23.50 Br md 9.00 Dpth 4.70 Welded, 1 dk	**(B32A2ST) Tug**	**2 oil engines** gearing integral to driving 2 Z propellers Total Power: 2,648kW (3,600hp) 13.4kn Niigata 6L25HX 2 x 4 Stroke 6 Cy. 250 x 350 each-1324kW (1800bhp) Niigata Engineering Co Ltd-Japan Fuel: 90.0 (d.f.)
8805470 *5VBU6*	**SEA TIGER** *ex* Thelema T *-2011* *ex* Balta *-2008* *ex* Perseverance *-2003* *completed as* Mosor Sky *-1990* **Sea Tiger Tankers SA** Sopetro Marine Ltd *Lome* *Togo* MMSI: 671312000	**22,607** 11,801 40,392 T/cm 49.3	Class: BV (LR) (RI) ✠ Classed LR until 18/7/09	**1990-11 Brodogradiliste 'Jozo Lozovina-Mosor' (Brodomosor) — Trogir** Yd No: 199 Converted From: Chemical/Products Tanker-2008 Loa 175.79 (BB) Br ex 32.02 Dght 11.180 Lbp 168.77 Br md 31.99 Dpth 15.08 Welded, 1 dk	**(A13A2TW) Crude/Oil Products Tanker** Double Bottom Entire Compartment Length Liq: 38,377; Liq (Oil): 38,377 Cargo Heating Coils Compartments: 6 Ta, 10 Wing Ta, 2 Wing Slop Ta, ER 4 Cargo Pump (s): 4x1200m³/hr Manifold: Bow/CM: 88m	**1 oil engine** driving 1 FP propeller Total Power: 7,651kW (10,402hp) 15.0kn B&W 5L60MC 1 x 2 Stroke 5 Cy. 600 x 1944 7651kW (10402bhp) Tvornica Dizel Motora 'Uljanik'-Yugoslavia AuxGen: 3 x 584kW 450V 60Hz a.c Boilers: 2 AuxB (o.f.) 16.8kgf/cm² (16.5bar), e (ex.g.) 18.4kgf/cm² (18.0bar) Fuel: 280.5 (d.f.) 1492.3 (r.f.)
9220378 *A6E2960* -	**SEA TIGER** *ex* Surya Wira 9 *-2004* **Target Engineering Construction Co (LLC)** - *Abu Dhabi* *United Arab Emirates* MMSI: 470769000 Official number: 4955	**120** 36 112	Class: NK	**2000-01 Yii Brothers Shipbuilding Contractor Co — Sibu** Yd No: 83 Loa 23.17 Br ex - Dght 2.388 Lbp 21.76 Br md 7.00 Dpth 2.90 Welded, 1 dk	**(B32A2ST) Tug**	**2 oil engines** reduction geared to sc. shafts driving 2 FP propellers Total Power: 806kW (1,096hp) 12.0kn Caterpillar 3412TA 2 x Vee 4 Stroke 12 Cy. 137 x 152 each-403kW (548bhp) Caterpillar Inc-USA Fuel: 75.0 (d.f.)

IMO / Call sign	Name / Owner	Tonnage	Class	Builder / Dimensions	Type / Cargo	Machinery
9276949 *HSB4766* -	**SEA TIMBER** *ex* Infinite Wisdom *-2013* **S Ship Management 2000 Co Ltd** Sinsimon Navigation Co Ltd *Bangkok* *Thailand* MMSI: 567478000 Official number: TG56001	**7,295** 4,822 12,540	Class: NK	**2003-05 Higaki Zosen K.K. — Imabari** Yd No: 553 Loa 127.82 Br ex - Dght 8.184 Lbp 119.83 Br md 19.60 Dpth 11.00 Welded, 1 dk	**(A31A2GX) General Cargo Ship** Grain: 17,150; Bale: 16,236 3 Ha: (35.7 x 9.8)ER 2 (18.9 x 9.8) Cranes: 2x30.5t; Derricks: 1x30t	**1 oil engine** driving 1 FP propeller Total Power: 3,883kW (5,279hp) 13.3kn B&W 6L35MC 1 x 2 Stroke 6 Cy. 350 x 1050 3883kW (5279bhp) The Hanshin Diesel Works Ltd-Japan AuxGen: 2 x 315kW a.c Fuel: 780.0
9575632 *5BVT3* -	**SEA TITUS** **PSV Holding Inc** Deep Sea Supply Management (Singapore) Pte Ltd *Limassol* *Cyprus* MMSI: 210620000	**3,455** 1,406 4,000	Class: NV	**2014-01 Cochin Shipyard Ltd — Ernakulam** Yd No: BY-90 Loa 82.20 (BB) Br ex - Dght 6.300 Lbp 74.10 Br md 17.00 Dpth 7.60 Welded, 1 dk	**(B21A20S) Platform Supply Ship**	**4 diesel electric oil engines** driving 4 gen. each 1200kW a.c Connecting to 2 elec. motors each (1600kW) driving 2 Azimuth electric drive units Total Power: 5,968kW (8,116hp) 11.0kn Cummins KTA-50-M2 4 x Vee 4 Stroke 16 Cy. 159 x 159 each-1492kW (2029bhp) STX Engine Co Ltd-South Korea Thrusters: 2 Tunnel thruster (f)
9557240 *3EYX2* -	**SEA TOPAZ** *ex* Chang Pyung *-2013* **HR Topaz SA** Hanaro Shipping Co Ltd *Panama* *Panama* MMSI: 357017000 Official number: 4534013	**20,198** 11,367 32,484	Class: KR (BV)	**2010-09 Zhejiang Hongxin Shipbuilding Co Ltd — Taizhou ZJ** Yd No: 2007-10 Loa 177.40 (BB) Br ex - Dght 10.217 Lbp 168.00 Br md 28.20 Dpth 14.20 Welded, 1 dk	**(A21A2BC) Bulk Carrier** Double Hull Grain: 40,161; Bale: 38,849 Compartments: 5 Ho, ER 5 Ha: 4 (19.2 x 21.0)ER (14.4 x 15.2) Cranes: 4x30t	**1 oil engine** driving 1 FP propeller Total Power: 6,480kW (8,810hp) 14.2kn MAN-B&W 6S42MC 1 x 2 Stroke 6 Cy. 420 x 1764 6480kW (8810bhp) STX Engine Co Ltd-South Korea
9624744 *5BXN3* -	**SEA TORTUGA** **PSV Holding Inc** Deep Sea Supply Management (Singapore) Pte Ltd *Limassol* *Cyprus* MMSI: 210646000 Official number: 9624744	**3,455** 1,406 4,000	Class: NV	**2014-02 Cochin Shipyard Ltd — Ernakulam** Yd No: BY-91 Loa 82.20 (BB) Br ex 17.03 Dght 6.300 Lbp 74.10 Br md 17.00 Dpth 7.60 Welded, 1 dk	**(B21A20S) Platform Supply Ship**	**4 diesel electric oil engines** driving 4 gen. Connecting to 2 elec. motors each (1600kW) driving 2 Azimuth electric drive units Total Power: 4,800kW (6,528hp) 11.0kn Cummins KTA-50-M1 4 x Vee 4 Stroke 16 Cy. 159 x 159 each-1200kW (1632bhp) STX Engine Co Ltd-South Korea Thrusters: 2 Tunnel thruster (f)
8919893 *T3TC* -	**SEA TRADER** *ex* Nova Flandria *-2009* *ex* Sohya Star *-2005* *ex* Sohya *-1997* **Habitat International Corp** Shandong Zhonglu Fishery Shipping Co Ltd *Tarawa* *Kiribati* MMSI: 529244000 Official number: K-12900919	**4,574** 2,474 5,517	Class: BV (NK)	**1990-12 Fukuoka Shipbuilding Co Ltd — Fukuoka FO** Yd No: 1159 Loa 120.20 (BB) Br ex - Dght 7.164 Lbp 109.80 Br md 16.40 Dpth 9.95 Welded	**(A34A2GR) Refrigerated Cargo Ship** Ins: 6,371 Compartments: 9 Ho, ER 9 Ha: ER	**1 oil engine** driving 1 FP propeller Total Power: 4,119kW (5,600hp) 16.0kn Mitsubishi 8UEC37LA 1 x 2 Stroke 8 Cy. 370 x 880 4119kW (5600bhp) Akasaka Tekkosho KK (Akasaka DieselLtd)-Japan AuxGen: 2 x 500kW 450V 60Hz a.c Fuel: 154.5 (d.f.) 16.4pd
9097379 *WDE2379* -	**SEA TRADER** **Sea Trader LLC** Sea Global Fisheries LLC *Pago Pago, AS* *United States of America* MMSI: 338074000 Official number: 1207470	**1,416** 515 -		**2008-01 Ching Fu Shipbuilding Co Ltd — Kaohsiung** Yd No: 070 L reg 63.76 Br ex - Dght - Lbp - Br md 12.19 Dpth 7.25 Welded, 1 dk	**(B11B2FV) Fishing Vessel**	**1 oil engine** geared to sc. shaft driving 1 Propeller Total Power: 2,354kW (3,200hp) Daihatsu 8DLM-32 1 x 4 Stroke 8 Cy. 320 x 400 2354kW (3200bhp) Daihatsu Diesel Manufacturing Co Lt-Japan
9003093 *DSPU9* -	**SEA TRADER** *ex* Genco Trader *-2008* *ex* Top Trader *-2005* *ex* Nova Spirit *-1995* **KT Capital Corp** Shipping Allied Corp *Jeju* *South Korea* MMSI: 441458000 Official number: JJR-089331	**35,890** 23,407 69,338 T/cm 64.4	Class: KR (LR) (AB) (NK) (NV) Classed LR until 7/9/05	**1990-07 Imabari Shipbuilding Co Ltd — Marugame KG (Marugame Shipyard)** Yd No: 1181 Loa 224.98 (BB) Br ex 32.24 Dght 13.295 Lbp 215.02 Br md 32.20 Dpth 18.30 Welded, 1 dk	**(A21A2BC) Bulk Carrier** Grain: 81,215 Compartments: 7 Ho, ER 7 Ha: (12.8 x 12.8) (16.3 x 14.4)4 (17.9 x 14.4) (14.7 x 14.4)ER	**1 oil engine** driving 1 FP propeller Total Power: 8,091kW (11,001hp) 13.5kn Sulzer 6RTA62 1 x 2 Stroke 6 Cy. 620 x 2150 8091kW (11001bhp) Mitsubishi Heavy Industries Ltd-Japan AuxGen: 2 x 480kW 440V 60Hz a.c, 1 x 750kW 440V 60Hz a.c Boilers: WTAuxB (Comp) 8.0kgf/cm² (7.8bar) Fuel: 250.1 (d.f.) 2556.7 (r.f.) 28.5pd
7517698 *WDE7566* -	**SEA TRADER** *ex* Ocean Marlin *-1989* **Trident Seafoods Corp** - SatCom: Inmarsat C 436770210 *Seattle, WA* *United States of America* MMSI: 367647000 Official number: 573519	**3,185** 1,048 1,496	Class: AB	**1976-06 American Marine Corp. — New Orleans, La** Yd No: 1137 **2002-09 Dakota Creek Industries Inc — Anacortes WA** (Additional cargo section) Converted From: Offshore Tug/Supply Ship-1993 Lengthened-2002 Widened-1993 Loa - Br ex - Dght 4.670 Lbp 84.73 Br md 18.90 Dpth 5.51 Welded, 1 dk	**(A31A2GX) General Cargo Ship** TEU 150 C.Dk 75/40'	**2 oil engines** reverse reduction geared to sc. shafts driving 2 FP propellers Total Power: 4,766kW (6,480hp) 16.0kn Alco 16V251F 2 x Vee 4 Stroke 16 Cy. 229 x 267 each-2383kW (3240bhp) White Industrial Power Inc-USA AuxGen: 2 x 150kW Thrusters: 1 Thwart. FP thruster (f)
6618861 *V3YF4* -	**SEA TRADER** *ex* Pegasus *-1999* *ex* Aqueduct *-1999* *ex* Shell 70 *-1999* **Marine Tankers Services AS** Maritime Management LLC *Belize City* *Belize* MMSI: 312547000 Official number: 010211590	**481** 234 734	Class: BV NV (GL)	**1965 Schiffswerft Scheel & Joehnk GmbH — Hamburg** Yd No: 447 Loa 59.47 Br ex 9.35 Dght 2.599 Lbp 56.01 Br md 9.00 Dpth 3.35 Welded, 1 dk	**(A13B2TP) Products Tanker** Liq: 1,000; Liq (Oil): 1,000 2 Cargo Pump (s)	**1 oil engine** driving 1 FP propeller Total Power: 427kW (581hp) 8.5kn MWM RH348SU 1 x 4 Stroke 6 Cy. 320 x 480 427kW (581bhp) Motoren Werke Mannheim AG (MWM)-West Germany
8105947 *DUH2318* -	**SEA TRADER** *ex* Ekishu Maru *-1996* **Fortune Sea Carrier Inc** - *Cebu* *Philippines* Official number: CEB1002009	*495* 337 1,100		**1981-08 K.K. Matsuo Tekko Zosensho — Matsue** Yd No: 2010 L reg 60.51 Br ex - Dght 4.001 Lbp 59.01 Br md 10.61 Dpth 5.80 Welded, 1 dk	**(A31A2GX) General Cargo Ship**	**1 oil engine** reduction geared to sc. shaft driving 1 FP propeller Total Power: 883kW (1,201hp) Hanshin 6LU28RG 1 x 4 Stroke 6 Cy. 280 x 440 883kW (1201bhp) The Hanshin Diesel Works Ltd-Japan
7109960 *HQXC4* -	**SEA TRADER 1** *ex* Noha 1 *-2008* *ex* Cape *-2007* *ex* Capetanios *-2007* *ex* Mini Liner *-1997* **United Cement Co Bscc** - SatCom: Inmarsat C 433400025 *San Lorenzo* *Honduras* MMSI: 334687000 Official number: L-0338289	**1,639** 1,026 2,914	Class: BV RS (AB)	**1971-07 K.K. Taihei Kogyo — Akitsu** (Hull) Yd No: 256 **1971-07 The Hakodate Dock Co Ltd — Japan** Yd No: 490 Loa 65.49 Br ex 15.32 Dght 4.947 Lbp 62.82 Br md 15.30 Dpth 6.61 Welded, 1 dk	**(A31A2GX) General Cargo Ship** Grain: 1,783 TEU 78 Compartments: 2 Ho, ER 4 Ha: 4 (19.5 x 5.1)ER Cranes: 2x15t	**2 oil engines** reverse reduction geared to sc. shafts driving 2 FP propellers Total Power: 1,104kW (1,500hp) 10.3kn Daihatsu 6PSHTCM-26D 2 x 4 Stroke 6 Cy. 260 x 320 each-552kW (750bhp) Daihatsu Diesel Manufacturing Co Lt-Japan AuxGen: 2 x 240kW 445V 60Hz a.c Fuel: 112.0 (d.f.)
8327777 *V4WY* -	**SEA TRADER 8** *ex* Western Targa III *-1993* *ex* Golden Dragon III *-1992* *ex* Koyo Maru No. 2 *-1984* **Faber Marine Pte Ltd** - *Basseterre* *St Kitts & Nevis* MMSI: 341595000 Official number: SKN 1001595	**319** 170 583 T/cm 7.5	Class: IS (NK)	**1973-04 YK Furumoto Tekko Zosensho — Osakikamijima** Yd No: 338 Loa 46.95 Br ex - Dght 3.183 Lbp 44.01 Br md 7.80 Dpth 3.26 Welded, 1 dk	**(A13B2TU) Tanker (unspecified)** Liq: 650; Liq (Oil): 650 Compartments: 6 Wing Ta, ER 2 Cargo Pump (s): 2x200m³/hr Manifold: Bow/CM: 30m	**1 oil engine** driving 1 FP propeller Total Power: 552kW (750hp) 10.0kn Hanshin 6L26BGSH 1 x 4 Stroke 6 Cy. 260 x 400 552kW (750bhp) The Hanshin Diesel Works Ltd-Japan AuxGen: 2 x 16kW a.c
7393169 *HO2883* -	**SEA TRIDENT** *ex* Western Trident *-1991* *ex* Anvil Scout *-1984* *ex* Kirsten Bravo *-1984* **Gardline Shipping Ltd** Gardline Geosurvey Ltd SatCom: Inmarsat A 1335140 *Panama* *Panama* MMSI: 357229000 Official number: 1413384G	**964** 289 1,010	Class: NV	**1974-10 Martin Jansen GmbH & Co. KG Schiffsw. u. Masch. — Leer** Yd No: 130 Loa 57.91 Br ex 10.21 Dght 3.745 Lbp 53.67 Br md 10.19 Dpth 6.35 Welded, 2 dks	**(B31A2SR) Research Survey Vessel** Grain: 1,770; Bale: 1,657 Compartments: 1 Ho, ER, 1 Tw Dk 2 Ha: (19.2 x 8.0) (6.0 x 5.0)ER Derricks: 1x3t; Winches: 1 Ice Capable	**1 oil engine** driving 1 CP propeller Total Power: 1,140kW (1,550hp) 12.0kn Alpha 10V23L-VO 1 x Vee 4 Stroke 10 Cy. 225 x 300 1140kW (1550bhp) Alpha Diesel A/S-Denmark AuxGen: 2 x 400kW 440V 60Hz a.c, 1 x 96kW 440V 60Hz a.c Thrusters: 1 Water jet (f) Fuel: 119.0 (d.f.) 5.0pd
9581760 *3EZA9* -	**SEA TRIUMPH** **Shoei Kisen Kaisha Ltd & Paraiso Shipping SA** Shoei Kisen Kaisha Ltd *Panama* *Panama* MMSI: 373802000 Official number: 4353012A	**92,752** 60,504 181,415 T/cm 125.0	Class: NK (AB)	**2012-02 Koyo Dockyard Co Ltd — Mihara HS** Yd No: 2362 Loa 291.98 (BB) Br ex - Dght 18.237 Lbp 283.80 Br md 45.00 Dpth 24.70 Welded, 1 dk	**(A21A2BC) Bulk Carrier** Grain: 201,243 Compartments: 9 Ho, ER 9 Ha: ER	**1 oil engine** driving 1 FP propeller Total Power: 18,660kW (25,370hp) 14.0kn MAN-B&W 6S70MC-C 1 x 2 Stroke 6 Cy. 700 x 2800 18660kW (25370bhp) Hitachi Zosen Corp-Japan Fuel: 5800.0

IMO / Call sign / Flag	Name / Owner / Port	Tonnage	Class	Build / Dimensions	Type	Machinery
5316466 *E5U2611* -	**SEA TROJAN** **Dolphin Maritime LLC** - *Avatiu* *Cook Islands* MMSI: 518664000 Official number: 1700	*117* 34 -	Class: LR ✠ **100A1** SS 01/2010 tug ✠ **LMC** Eq.Ltr: (a) ;	**1962-02 J. Lewis & Sons Ltd. — Aberdeen** Yd No: 320 Loa 26.85 Br ex 7.35 Dght 3.188 Lbp 24.41 Br md 7.01 Dpth 3.36 Riveted\Welded, 1 dk	**(B32A2ST) Tug**	**1 oil engine** driving 1 FP propeller Total Power: 588kW (799hp) 10.0kn National Gas FSM6 1 x 4 Stroke 6 Cy. 305 x 381 588kW (799bhp) National Gas & Oil Eng. Co.-Ashton-under-Lyne AuxGen: 2 x 15kW 220V d.c
8306058 - -	**SEA TROUT** - **Guyana Fisheries Ltd** - *Georgetown* *Guyana* Official number: 385135	*108* 48 98		**1983-06 Bender Shipbuilding & Repair Co Inc — Mobile AL** Yd No: 178 Loa - Br ex - Dght 2.590 Lbp 21.95 Br md 6.10 Dpth 3.28 Welded, 1 dk	**(B11A2FT) Trawler**	**1 oil engine** sr geared to sc. shaft driving 1 FP propeller Total Power: 268kW (364hp) 9.3kn Caterpillar 3408TA 1 x Vee 4 Stroke 8 Cy. 137 x 152 268kW (364bhp) Caterpillar Tractor Co-USA AuxGen: 2 x 3kW 32V d.c Fuel: 43.5 (d.f.) 1.0pd
9579377 *HKB13*	**SEA TROUT** *ex* GB Sea Trout *-2010* **Towage Services Developments Inc** International Tugs SA (INTERTUG) *Cartagena de Indias* *Colombia* MMSI: 730079000 Official number: MC-05-627	**475** 142 143	Class: LR (BV) **100A1** SS 06/2010 tug **LMC** Cable: 357.5/26.0 U2 (a)	**2010-06 Zhuhai Chenlong Shipyard Co Ltd — Zhuhai GD** Yd No: SI-015-P181 Loa 36.00 Br ex - Dght 4.000 Lbp 31.71 Br md 10.80 Dpth 5.00 Welded, 1 dk	**(B21B20A) Anchor Handling Tug Supply**	**2 oil engines** with flexible couplings & reverse geared to sc. shafts driving 2 Directional propellers Total Power: 3,282kW (4,462hp) Cummins QSK60-M 2 x Vee 4 Stroke 16 Cy. 159 x 190 each-1641kW (2231bhp) Cummins Engine Co Ltd-United Kingdom AuxGen: 2 x 240kW 415V 50Hz a.c Thrusters: 1 Thwart. FP thruster (f) Fuel: 335.0 (d.f.)
9420186 *LAUA*	**SEA TROUT** *launched as* Stril Mariner *-2008* **Deep Sea Supply Shipowning AS** Deep Sea Supply Management (Singapore) Pte Ltd SatCom: Inmarsat C 425841110 *Arendal* *Norway* MMSI: 258411000	**2,589** 901 3,678	Class: NV	**2008-06 OAO Vyborgskiy Sudostroitelnyy Zavod — Vyborg** (Hull) Yd No: 046 **2008-06 Karmsund Maritime Service AS — Kopervik** Yd No: 32 Loa 73.40 Br ex - Dght 6.500 Lbp 64.00 Br md 16.60 Dpth 7.60 Welded, 1 dk	**(B21A20S) Platform Supply Ship**	**2 oil engines** reduction geared to sc. shafts driving 2 CP propellers Total Power: 3,956kW (5,378hp) Caterpillar 3606 2 x 4 Stroke 6 Cy. 280 x 300 each-1978kW (2689bhp) Caterpillar Inc-USA AuxGen: 2 x a.c, 2 x a.c Thrusters: 2 Tunnel thruster (f); 2 Tunnel thruster (a)
7611509 *A6E2529* -	**SEA TRUCK** *ex* Jeddah N. M. I *-2007* *ex* Brando *-1979* *ex* Minigirl *-1977* **Mubarak Marine LLC** - *Dubai* *United Arab Emirates* MMSI: 470384000 Official number: 7141	*688* 321 1,246	Class: IR (LR) (NV) ✠ Classed LR until 23/9/83	**1977-05 Oy Pontoon Ab — Kristiinankaupunki** Yd No: 5 Loa 55.45 Br ex 12.43 Dght 3.010 Lbp 51.57 Br md 12.40 Dpth 4.02 Welded, 1 dk	**(A31C2GD) Deck Cargo Ship** Bow door/ramp	**1 oil engine** sr geared to sc. shafts driving 1 Directional propeller Total Power: 736kW (1,001hp) 7.5kn Yanmar 6RY17P-GV 1 x 4 Stroke 6 Cy. 165 x 219 736kW (1001bhp) (new engine 2005) Yanmar Diesel Engine Co Ltd-Japan AuxGen: 2 x 80kW 380V 50Hz a.c Fuel: 43.0 (d.f.)
7049926 - -	**SEA TRUKER** *ex* Miss Lurleen *-2013* - - *La Ceiba* *Honduras* Official number: S-3328333	*133* 90 -		**1968 Childress Co. — Bon Secour, Al** Yd No: 1 L reg 21.13 Br ex 7.14 Dght - Lbp - Br md - Dpth 3.33 Welded, 1 dk	**(B11B2FV) Fishing Vessel**	**1 oil engine** driving 1 FP propeller Total Power: 257kW (349hp)
9392963 *5BJY2* -	**SEA TURBOT** - **DESS PSV Ltd** Deep Sea Supply Navegacao Maritima Ltda SatCom: Inmarsat C 421203010 *Limassol* *Cyprus* MMSI: 212034000 Official number: 9392963	**2,160** 1,036 3,250	Class: NV	**2008-08 Cochin Shipyard Ltd — Ernakulam** Yd No: BY-62 Loa 71.90 Br ex 16.03 Dght 5.840 Lbp 66.80 Br md 16.00 Dpth 7.00 Welded, 1 dk	**(B21A20S) Platform Supply Ship**	**2 oil engines** reduction geared to sc. shafts driving 2 CP propellers Total Power: 4,009kW (5,451hp) 11.0kn Bergens KRMB-9 2 x 4 Stroke 9 Cy. 250 x 300 each-2004kW (2725bhp) Rolls Royce Marine AS-Norway AuxGen: 2 x 225kW 440V 60Hz a.c, 2 x 1280kW 440V 60Hz a.c Thrusters: 2 Thwart. CP thruster (f); 1 Thwart. CP thruster (a)
9244233 *C4GS2* -	**SEA URCHIN** *ex* Guinomar Bastion *-2006* **Keel Marine Co Ltd** Alert Shipmanagement Ltd *Limassol* *Cyprus* MMSI: 209927000 Official number: 9244233	**38,938** 24,972 74,193 T/cm 66.3	Class: NK	**2001-07 Namura Shipbuilding Co Ltd — Imari SG** Yd No: 215 Loa 224.89 (BB) Br ex - Dght 13.952 Lbp 215.00 Br md 32.20 Dpth 19.30 Welded, 1 dk	**(A21A2BC) Bulk Carrier** Grain: 89,246 Compartments: 7 Ho, ER 7 Ha: (16.8 x 13.2)6 (16.8 x 14.9)ER	**1 oil engine** driving 1 FP propeller Total Power: 8,680kW (11,801hp) 14.5kn B&W 7S50MC 1 x 2 Stroke 7 Cy. 500 x 1910 8680kW (11801bhp) Hitachi Zosen Corp-Japan AuxGen: 3 x 455kW a.c Fuel: 1960.0
7429920 - -	**SEA UTILITY** *ex* Sang Thai Uranus *-2000* *ex* Hanrasan No. 1 *-1993* *ex* Hanrasan *-1987* *ex* Sorabol *-1985* *ex* Taegu *-1984* *ex* Taga Maru *-1984* **NGV A Transport Service Co Ltd**	**5,986** 3,618 10,016	Class: (NK)	**1975-11 Kurushima Dockyard Co. Ltd. — Imabari** Yd No: 863 Loa 120.95 Br ex 19.21 Dght 7.895 Lbp 111.49 Br md 19.18 Dpth 10.24 Welded, 1 dk	**(A31A2GX) General Cargo Ship** Grain: 12,344; Bale: 12,054 Compartments: 2 Ho, ER 2 Ha: (34.5 x 9.8) (33.0 x 9.8)ER Derricks: 4x20t	**1 oil engine** driving 1 FP propeller Total Power: 4,560kW (6,200hp) 13.5kn Mitsubishi 6UEC52/105D 1 x 2 Stroke 6 Cy. 520 x 1050 4560kW (6200bhp) Akasaka Tekkosho KK (Akasaka DieselLtd)-Japan AuxGen: 2 x 216kW 445V a.c
9477012 *3EZM* -	**SEA VALIANT** - **Gulf Marine Far East Pte Ltd** - *Panama* *Panama* MMSI: 372775000 Official number: 4206710	**2,301** 690 2,058	Class: AB	**2010-06 Stocznia Polnocna SA (Northern Shipyard) — Gdansk** (Hull) Yd No: B844/20 **2010-06 Gdanska Stocznia 'Remontowa' SA — Gdansk** Yd No: 1674/20 Loa 70.00 Br ex - Dght 5.100 Lbp 63.60 Br md 15.50 Dpth 6.60 Welded, 1 dk	**(B21B20A) Anchor Handling Tug Supply**	**2 oil engines** reduction geared to sc. shafts driving 2 CP propellers Total Power: 10,062kW (13,680hp) 14.0kn Caterpillar C280-12 2 x Vee 4 Stroke 12 Cy. 280 x 300 each-5031kW (6840bhp) Caterpillar Inc-USA AuxGen: 2 x 1724kW 60Hz a.c, 2 x 250kW 60Hz a.c Thrusters: 2 Tunnel thruster (f); 1 Tunnel thruster (a) Fuel: 805.0 (d.f.)
7929839 *DUA6388* -	**SEA VALOR D.R.** *ex* Sea Valor *-1984* *ex* Kaisei Maru No. 23 *-1984* *ex* Taikei Maru No. 53 *-1988* **Philmariner Aqua Ventures Corp** - *Manila* *Philippines* Official number: MNLD010308	*145* 79 171		**1979-10 K.K. Murakami Zosensho — Ishinomaki** Yd No: 1037 Loa 41.18 (BB) Br ex 6.81 Dght 2.661 Lbp 29.52 Br md 6.51 Dpth 2.65 Welded, 1 dk	**(B11B2FV) Fishing Vessel**	**1 oil engine** driving 1 FP propeller Total Power: 478kW (650hp) Yanmar MF24-ST 1 x 4 Stroke 6 Cy. 240 x 420 478kW (650bhp) Yanmar Diesel Engine Co Ltd-Japan
7227994 *AUQZ* -	**SEA VENTURE** *ex* Total Venture *-2007* *ex* Aladin *-2001* *ex* Mermaid Marauder *-1991* *ex* Southern Tide *-1987* **Hind Offshore Pvt Ltd** - *Mumbai* *India* MMSI: 419070400 Official number: 3336	**817** 245 730	Class: IR (AB)	**1972-09 Adelaide Ship Construction Pty Ltd — Port Adelaide SA** Yd No: 74 Loa 51.82 Br ex 12.50 Dght 4.261 Lbp 48.87 Br md 12.20 Dpth 5.03 Welded, 1 dk	**(B21B20A) Anchor Handling Tug Supply**	**2 oil engines** reverse reduction geared to sc. shafts driving 2 FP propellers Total Power: 2,942kW (4,000hp) 10.0kn EMD (Electro-Motive) 16-645-E6 2 x Vee 2 Stroke 16 Cy. 230 x 254 each-1471kW (2000bhp) General Motors Corp.Electro-Motive Div.-La Grange AuxGen: 2 x 100kW 415V 50Hz a.c, 1 x 60kW 415V 50Hz a.c Thrusters: 1 Thwart. FP thruster (f) Fuel: 237.0 (d.f.)
7308683 *WX6176* -	**SEA VENTURE** - **War Eagle Inc** - *Houma, LA* *United States of America* Official number: 502839	*120* 86 -		**1966 Atlantic Marine — Jacksonville, Fl** L reg 20.30 Br ex 6.15 Dght - Lbp - Br md - Dpth 3.69 Welded	**(B11B2FV) Fishing Vessel**	**1 oil engine** driving 1 FP propeller Total Power: 221kW (300hp)
7019232 *WDD7333* -	**SEA VENTURE** *ex* Flood Tide *-1980* **Gunn Sea Venture LLC** - *Seattle, WA* *United States of America* MMSI: 367185050 Official number: 525572	**231** 69 -		**1970 Marine Construction & Design Co. (MARCO) — Seattle, Wa** Yd No: 208 Loa 31.70 Br ex - Dght - Lbp 28.71 Br md 7.90 Dpth 3.66 Welded, 1 dk	**(B11B2FV) Fishing Vessel**	**1 oil engine** driving 1 FP propeller Total Power: 588kW (799hp) 12.0kn G.M. (Detroit Diesel) 12V-149 1 x Vee 2 Stroke 12 Cy. 146 x 146 588kW (799bhp) General Motors Corp-USA AuxGen: 2 x 100kW 220V 60Hz a.c Fuel: 35.5

IMO / Call sign	Ship / Owner	Tonnage	Class	Builder / Dimensions	Type	Machinery
9347413 *WDC5952* -	**SEA VENTURE** *ex* W. H. Dietrich *-2005* **Mega Marine LLC** Chouest Offshore Services LLC *Galliano, LA* *United States of America* MMSI: 303422000 Official number: 1169958	**9,926** 2,977 5,644	Class: AB	**2005-09 North American Shipbuilding LLC — Larose LA** Yd No: 224 Loa 106.07 (BB) Br ex - Dght 6.940 Lbp 98.17 Br md 21.34 Dpth 8.54 Welded, 1 dk	**(B31A2SR) Research Survey Vessel**	**2 oil engines** reduction geared to sc. shafts driving 2 CP propellers Total Power: 8,640kW (11,746hp) 14.0kn MaK 9M32C 2 x 4 Stroke 9 Cy. 320 x 480 each-4320kW (5873bhp) Caterpillar Motoren GmbH & Co. KG-Germany AuxGen: 3 x 1360kW a.c, 2 x 2201kW a.c Fuel: 2220.0
5049453 - -	**SEA VENTURER** *ex* Boston Whirlwind *-1996* **Agustin Pousada Barreiro** -	**219** 65 -	Class: (LR) ✠ Classed LR until 29/11/00	**1962-04 Richards Iron Works Ltd — Lowestoft** Yd No: 466 Converted From: Standby Safety Vessel-1987 Converted From: Trawler-1979 L reg 28.50 Br ex 6.81 Dght 2.598 Lbp 27.74 Br md 6.71 Dpth 3.28 Riveted\Welded	**(B11A2FT) Trawler**	**1 oil engine** with flexible couplings & sr reverse geared to sc. shaft driving 1 FP propeller Total Power: 349kW (475hp) National Gas F4AUDM5 1 x 4 Stroke 5 Cy. 305 x 381 349kW (475bhp) National Gas & Oil Eng. Co.-Ashton-under-Lyne AuxGen: 2 x 15kW 220V d.c
8916152 *DSPT5* -	**SEA VENUS** *ex* Maratha Explorer *-2008* *ex* Oceanic Explorer *-2006* **Shipping Allied Corp** - *Jeju* *South Korea* MMSI: 441444000 Official number: JJR-089224	**36,741** 22,917 68,849 T/cm 65.2	Class: KR (NK) (AB)	**1990-07 Namura Shipbuilding Co Ltd — Imari SG** Yd No: 905 Loa 224.95 (BB) Br ex - Dght 13.222 Lbp 217.00 Br md 32.20 Dpth 18.20 Welded, 1 dk	**(A21A2BC) Bulk Carrier** Grain: 80,811 Compartments: 7 Ho, ER 7 Ha: (16.6 x 13.2) (16.6 x 14.9)5 (16.6 x 14.9)ER	**1 oil engine** driving 1 FP propeller Total Power: 7,503kW (10,201hp) 13.9kn Sulzer 6RTA62 1 x 2 Stroke 6 Cy. 620 x 2150 7503kW (10201bhp) Mitsubishi Heavy Industries Ltd-Japan AuxGen: 3 x 460kW 450V 60Hz a.c Fuel: 123.7 (d.f.) 2020.3 (r.f.) 29.8pd
9609134 *V7CP8* -	**SEA VENUS** *launched as* Verykoko *-2013* **Venus Shipowning Inc** Golden Ocean Management Asia Pte Ltd *Majuro* *Marshall Islands* MMSI: 538005302 Official number: 5302	**44,025** 27,682 80,888 T/cm 71.9	Class: LR ✠ **100A1** SS 10/2013 bulk carrier CSR BC-A GRAB (20) Nos. 2, 4 & 6 holds may be empty ESP **ShipRight** (CM, ACS (B)) *IWS LI EP (R) ✠ **LMC** **UMS** Eq.Ltr: Q†; Cable: 700.0/81.0 U3 (a)	**2013-10 New Century Shipbuilding Co Ltd — Jingjiang JS** Yd No: 0108206 Loa 229.00 Br ex 32.30 Dght 14.450 Lbp 225.50 Br md 32.26 Dpth 20.05 Welded, 1 dk	**(A21A2BC) Bulk Carrier** Grain: 97,000; Bale: 90,784 Compartments: 7 Ho, ER 7 Ha: 5 (18.3 x 15.0) (15.7 x 15.1)ER (13.1 x 13.2)	**1 oil engine** driving 1 FP propeller Total Power: 11,900kW (16,179hp) 14.1kn MAN-B&W 5S60MC-C8 1 x 2 Stroke 5 Cy. 600 x 2400 11900kW (16179bhp) STX Engine Co Ltd-South Korea AuxGen: 3 x 710kW 440V 60Hz a.c Boilers: AuxB (Comp) 9.2kgf/cm² (9.0bar)
9477024 *3EVV8* -	**SEA VICTOR** **Gulf Marine Far East Pte Ltd** - *Panama* *Panama* MMSI: 355949000 Official number: 4206610	**2,301** 690 2,058	Class: AB	**2010-07 Stocznia Polnocna SA (Northern Shipyard) — Gdansk** (Hull) Yd No: B844/21 **2010-07 Gdanska Stocznia 'Remontowa' SA — Gdansk** Yd No: 1674/21 Loa 70.00 Br ex - Dght 5.100 Lbp 63.60 Br md 15.50 Dpth 6.60 Welded, 1 dk	**(B21B20A) Anchor Handling Tug Supply** Cranes: 1	**2 oil engines** reduction geared to sc. shafts driving 2 CP propellers Total Power: 10,062kW (13,680hp) 14.0kn Caterpillar C280-12 2 x Vee 4 Stroke 12 Cy. 280 x 300 each-5031kW (6840bhp) Caterpillar Inc-USA AuxGen: 2 x 1724kW a.c, 2 x 250kW a.c Thrusters: 2 Tunnel thruster (f); 1 Tunnel thruster (a) Fuel: 820.0 (d.f.)
9309837 - -	**SEA VICTOR** **U Kyaw Thien** - *Indonesia*	**251** 170 -		**2003-11 Mahachai Dockyard Co., Ltd. — Samut Sakhon** Yd No: 5215 Loa 36.50 Br ex 7.50 Dght 2.950 Lbp 31.50 Br md 6.50 Dpth 3.50 Welded, 1 dk	**(B11B2FV) Fishing Vessel**	**1 oil engine** geared to sc. shaft driving 1 FP propeller Total Power: 728kW (990hp) Cummins 1 x 4 Stroke 728kW (990bhp) Cummins Engine Co Inc-USA
7390753 *WCY6777* -	**SEA VICTORY** *ex* Independent Victory *-1992* *ex* Martha *-1988* *ex* Martha Theriot *-1984* **Crowley Marine Services Inc** - *San Francisco, CA* *United States of America* MMSI: 367671000 Official number: 561652	**930** 279 -	Class: AB	**1974-07 Equitable Equipment Co. — New Orleans, La** Yd No: 1650 Loa 45.73 Br ex 12.20 Dght 6.147 Lbp 43.24 Br md 12.17 Dpth 6.71 Welded, 1 dk	**(B32A2ST) Tug** Ice Capable	**2 oil engines** sr reverse geared to sc. shafts driving 2 FP propellers Total Power: 1,766kW (2,402hp) 11.0kn G.M. (Detroit Diesel) 16V-149-TI 2 x Vee 2 Stroke 16 Cy. 146 x 146 each-883kW (1201bhp) (new engine 1976) General Motors Detroit DieselAllison Divn-USA AuxGen: 2 x 99kW a.c Fuel: 803.5 (d.f.)
8427371 *DUG2180* -	**SEA VID** *ex* Good Hope *-2010* *ex* Midway *-2010* **Rovi Navigation Lines Inc** - *Bacolod* *Philippines* Official number: 06-0000871	*452* 339 600		**1973 at Legaspi** Loa - Br ex 8.56 Dght 2.601 Lbp 47.71 Br md 8.54 Dpth 2.75 Welded, 1 dk	**(A31A2GX) General Cargo Ship**	**1 oil engine** driving 1 FP propeller Total Power: 147kW (200hp)
6500404 *EI3619* -	**SEA VIGILANT** *ex* Ventnor *-1993* - - *Cork* *Irish Republic* Official number: 402811	*173* - -	Class: (LR) ✠ Classed LR until 12/88	**1965-01 R. Dunston (Hessle) Ltd. — Hessle** Yd No: S818 Loa 31.40 Br ex 8.23 Dght - Lbp 28.35 Br md 7.78 Dpth 3.81 Welded, 1 dk	**(B32A2ST) Tug**	**1 oil engine** with flexible couplings & sr reverse geared to sc. shaft driving 1 FP propeller Total Power: 883kW (1,201hp) 12.0kn Crossley HGN8 1 x 2 Stroke 8 Cy. 267 x 343 883kW (1201bhp) Crossley Bros. Ltd.-Manchester AuxGen: 3 x 15kW 220V d.c
9020481 *HSB4488* -	**SEA VISIONS** *ex* Syracuse *-2010* *ex* Victoria Lucy *-2005* *ex* Magnapragos I *-1994* *ex* Victoria Lucy *-1992* **Seamanship Co Ltd** - *Bangkok* *Thailand* MMSI: 567403000 Official number: 530002037	**3,247** 975 3,785 T/cm 14.0	Class: NK	**1992-07 Murakami Hide Zosen K.K. — Imabari** Yd No: 331 Loa 99.50 (BB) Br ex 15.83 Dght 5.500 Lbp 92.50 Br md 15.80 Dpth 7.10 Welded, 1 dk	**(A11B2TG) LPG Tanker** Double Bottom Entire Compartment Length Liq (Gas): 3,311 2 x Gas Tank (s); 2 (s.stl) cyl horizontal 2 Cargo Pump (s): 2x300m³/hr Manifold: Bow/CM: 44.3m	**1 oil engine** driving 1 FP propeller Total Power: 2,236kW (3,040hp) 12.3kn B&W 4L35MC 1 x 2 Stroke 4 Cy. 350 x 1050 2236kW (3040bhp) Makita Corp-Japan AuxGen: 2 x 250kW a.c Fuel: 77.0 (d.f.) 562.0 (r.f.)
9420021 *5BKK3* -	**SEA VIXEN** **DESS Cyprus Ltd** Deep Sea Supply Plc *Limassol* *Cyprus* MMSI: 209981000 Official number: 9420021	**1,943** 646 1,350	Class: NV	**2011-09 ABG Shipyard Ltd — Surat** Yd No: 274 Loa 63.37 Br ex - Dght 5.100 Lbp 56.48 Br md 15.80 Dpth 6.80 Welded, 1 dk	**(B21B20A) Anchor Handling Tug Supply**	**2 oil engines** reduction geared to sc. shafts driving 2 CP propellers Total Power: 5,002kW (6,800hp) 10.5kn Yanmar 8N280-EN 2 x 4 Stroke 8 Cy. 280 x 380 each-2501kW (3400bhp) Yanmar Diesel Engine Co Ltd-Japan AuxGen: 3 x 425kW 440V 60Hz a.c Thrusters: 1 Tunnel thruster (f)
9408310 *V7QU2* -	**SEA VOYAGER** **Arlene Navigation Inc** ST Shipping & Transport Pte Ltd SatCom: Inmarsat C 453833649 *Majuro* *Marshall Islands* MMSI: 538003439 Official number: 3439	**60,205** 32,143 107,506 T/cm 95.2	Class: AB	**2009-01 Tsuneishi Holdings Corp Tsuneishi Shipbuilding Co — Tadotsu KG** Yd No: 1417 Loa 243.80 (BB) Br ex 42.03 Dght 14.578 Lbp 237.00 Br md 42.00 Dpth 21.30 Welded, 1 dk	**(A13A2TV) Crude Oil Tanker** Double Hull (13F) Liq: 121,065; Liq (Oil): 120,650 Cargo Heating Coils Compartments: 12 Wing Ta, 2 Wing Slop Ta, ER 3 Cargo Pump (s): 3x3000m³/hr Manifold: Bow/CM: 118.2m	**1 oil engine** driving 1 FP propeller Total Power: 10,599kW (14,410hp) 15.5kn MAN-B&W 6S60MC 1 x 2 Stroke 6 Cy. 600 x 2292 10599kW (14410bhp) Mitsui Engineering & Shipbuilding CLtd-Japan AuxGen: 3 x 640kW a.c Fuel: 270.0 (d.f.) 3800.0 (r.f.)
9213129 *C6YZ9* -	**SEA VOYAGER** *ex* Cape May Light *-2009* **Voyager Owner LLC** FleetPro Ocean Inc *Nassau* *Bahamas* MMSI: 311050400 Official number: 9000376	**4,954** 1,486 200	Class: LR (AB) **100A1** SS 02/2010 passenger ship **LMC** Cable: U2 (a)	**2001-04 Atlantic Marine — Jacksonville, Fl** Yd No: 4242 Loa 91.44 Br ex - Dght 3.810 Lbp 90.22 Br md 15.24 Dpth 6.10 Welded, 6 dks	**(A37A2PC) Passenger/Cruise** Passengers: cabins: 114; berths: 224	**2 oil engines** reduction geared to sc. shafts driving 2 Directional propellers Total Power: 2,982kW (4,054hp) 10.0kn Caterpillar 3516B 2 x Vee 4 Stroke 16 Cy. 170 x 190 each-1491kW (2027bhp) Caterpillar Inc-USA AuxGen: 2 x 1815kW 440/120V 60Hz a.c Thrusters: 1 Thwart. FP thruster (f) Fuel: 249.0 (d.f.) 15.5pd

9044073 *5NQY4* -	**SEA VOYAGER** *ex* Al Wahda *-2010* **Sea Voyager Ltd** Oceanic Shipping Services Pvt Ltd *Lagos* *Nigeria* Official number: 377804	**4,176** 2,255 6,666	Class: LR ✠ **100A1** SS 11/2012 oil tanker ESP ✠ **LMC** Eq.Ltr: V; Cable: 495.0/48.0 U2	**1992**-11 **Daedong Shipbuilding Co Ltd — Busan** Yd No: 378 Loa 109.20 (BB) Br ex 16.52 Dght 6.749 Lbp 101.20 Br md 16.50 Dpth 8.40 Welded, 1 dk	**(A13B2TP) Products Tanker** Double Bottom Entire Compartment Length Liq: 7,695; Liq (Oil): 7,695 Compartments: 10 Ta, ER 12 Cargo Pump (s)	**1 oil engine** driving 1 CP propeller Total Power: 2,942kW (4,000hp) 13.0kn B&W 6L35MC 1 x 2 Stroke 6 Cy. 350 x 1050 2942kW (4000bhp) Ssangyong Heavy Industries Co Ltd-South Korea AuxGen: 3 x 400kW 380V 50Hz a.c Boilers: AuxB (Comp) 9.2kgf/cm^2 (9.0bar) Thrusters: 1 Thwart. CP thruster (f)
7417317 *WCX9106* -	**SEA VOYAGER** *ex* Independent Voyager *-1992* *ex* Joshua *-1988* *ex* Marine Voyager *-1985* *ex* Joshua T. *-1983* **Crowley Marine Services Inc** - *San Francisco, CA* *United States of America* MMSI: 366888840 Official number: 573747	**930** 279 -	Class: AB	**1976**-06 **Equitable Equipment Co. — Madisonville, La** Yd No: 1662 Loa - Br ex 12.20 Dght 6.147 Lbp 43.24 Br md 12.15 Dpth 6.71 Welded, 1 dk	**(B32A2ST) Tug**	**2 oil engines** reverse reduction geared to sc. shafts driving 2 FP propellers Total Power: 5,296kW (7,200hp) 13.0kn EMD (Electro-Motive) 20-645-E5 2 x Vee 2 Stroke 20 Cy. 230 x 254 each-2648kW (3600bhp) General Motors Corp.Electro-Motive Div.-La Grange AuxGen: 2 x 99kW a.c Fuel: 804.5 (d.f.)
9030022 - -	**SEA VOYAGER II** - **Montrose Genge** - *St John's, NL* *Canada* MMSI: 316002174 Official number: 811394	*136* 66 -		**1989 Modern Marine Industries Ltd — Freshwater, NL** Loa 19.81 Br ex - Dght - Lbp 18.32 Br md 7.62 Dpth 3.66 Bonded	**(B11A2FS) Stern Trawler** Hull Material: Reinforced Plastic	**1 oil engine** with clutches & sr reverse geared to sc. shaft driving 1 FP propeller Total Power: 638kW (867hp) 10.0kn Caterpillar 3508TA 1 x Vee 4 Stroke 8 Cy. 170 x 190 638kW (867bhp) Caterpillar Inc-USA
6703123 - -	**SEA WARRIOR** *ex* Island Warrior II *-2001* *ex* Seaspan Warrior *-1991* *ex* Island Warrior *-1971* **Island Tug & Barge Ltd** - *Victoria, BC* *Canada* Official number: 311798	*215* 16 -		**1959 Marine Industries Ltee (MIL) — Sorel QC** Yd No: 258 Converted From: General Cargo Barge, Non-propelled-1966 Loa 29.32 Br ex 7.96 Dght - Lbp - Br md 7.95 Dpth 4.05 Welded, 1 dk	**(B32A2ST) Tug**	**2 oil engines** geared to sc. shaft driving 1 FP propeller Total Power: 1,126kW (1,530hp) 12.0kn Caterpillar D398TA 2 x Vee 4 Stroke 12 Cy. 159 x 203 each-563kW (765bhp) (new engine 1966, added 1966) Caterpillar Tractor Co-USA AuxGen: 2 x 60kW 460V a.c Fuel: 107.0 (d.f.)
8851651 *WBF3637* -	**SEA WASP** - **Westbank Corp** Daybrook Fisheries Inc *New Orleans, LA* *United States of America* MMSI: 367166280 Official number: 632370	*468* 318 -		**1981 Patterson Shipyard Inc. — Patterson, La** Yd No: 36 Loa - Br ex - Dght - Lbp 49.44 Br md 9.45 Dpth 3.44 Welded, 1 dk	**(B11B2FV) Fishing Vessel**	**1 oil engine** driving 1 FP propeller
8988973 *WDC3594* -	**SEA WATCHER I** - **f/v Misty Dawn Inc** - *Atlantic City, NJ* *United States of America* MMSI: 367010820 Official number: 1160720	**453** 135 -		**2004 Patti Shipyard, Inc. — Pensacola, Fl** Yd No: 163 Loa 40.85 Br ex - Dght - Lbp - Br md 10.36 Dpth 4.57 Welded, 1 dk	**(B11A2FS) Stern Trawler**	**1 oil engine** driving 1 Propeller
8885535 - -	**SEA WAVE** - **Sea Wave Corp** - *Monterey, CA* *United States of America* Official number: 951443	*206* 165 -		**1989 at Moss Landing, Ca** L reg 23.77 Br ex - Dght - Lbp - Br md 6.77 Dpth 5.49 Bonded, 1 dk	**(B11B2FV) Fishing Vessel** Hull Material: Reinforced Plastic	**1 oil engine** driving 1 FP propeller
7435565 *A9D2860* -	**SEA WAVE** *ex* Libra 7 *-2006* *ex* Permina Supply No. 27 *-2004* **Sea Eagle Marine Services** Sea Eagles Shipping LLC *Bahrain* *Bahrain* MMSI: 408805000 Official number: BN 4048	**1,243** 372 1,244	Class: AB (KI)	**1976**-05 **Nipponkai Heavy Ind. Co. Ltd. — Toyama** Yd No: 185 Loa 61.91 Br ex - Dght 4.901 Lbp 55.23 Br md 12.51 Dpth 6.41 Welded, 1 dk	**(B21B20A) Anchor Handling Tug Supply**	**2 oil engines** reverse reduction geared to sc. shafts driving 2 FP propellers Total Power: 4,414kW (6,002hp) 13.5kn Niigata 12MGV28BX 2 x Vee 4 Stroke 12 Cy. 280 x 320 each-2207kW (3001bhp) Niigata Engineering Co Ltd-Japan AuxGen: 3 x 160kW Thrusters: 1 Thwart. FP thruster (f) Fuel: 599.5 (d.f.)
8009557 *5IM382* -	**SEA WAVE** *ex* Gulluk *-2011* *ex* Al Safi *-2001* *ex* Trans Friendship *-1995* *ex* Gazania *-1987* **Sea Falcon Marine Inc** Al Ryadh Trading FZCO *Zanzibar* *Tanzania (Zanzibar)* MMSI: 677028200 Official number: 300136	**10,922** 6,410 17,605	Class: (LR) (TL) (NK) Classed LR until 23/11/01	**1980**-11 **Shikoku Dockyard Co. Ltd. — Takamatsu** Yd No: 811 Loa 148.10 Br ex 21.74 Dght 9.351 Lbp 136.68 Br md 21.70 Dpth 12.20 Welded, 1 dk	**(A21A2BC) Bulk Carrier** Grain: 21,818; Bale: 21,329 Compartments: 4 Ho, ER 4 Ha: (14.0 x 8.9)3 (20.2 x 10.5) Derricks: 4x25t	**1 oil engine** driving 1 FP propeller Total Power: 5,804kW (7,891hp) 14.5kn B&W 8L45GFCA 1 x 2 Stroke 8 Cy. 450 x 1200 5804kW (7891bhp) Mitsui Engineering & Shipbuilding CLtd-Japan AuxGen: 2 x 360kW 440V 60Hz a.c
8219621 *9LH2027* -	**SEA WAVE** *ex* Field Express *-2013* *ex* Normand Sky *-1988* **Ships & Boats Oil Services** - *Freetown* *Sierra Leone* MMSI: 667009027 Official number: SL109027	**1,299** 471 1,861	Class: BV (Class contemplated) RI (LR) (NV) ✠ Classed LR until 27/3/08	**1984**-08 **Jiangnan Shipyard — Shanghai** Yd No: 2152 Loa 58.16 Br ex 13.20 Dght 5.930 Lbp 51.62 Br md 13.01 Dpth 6.75 Welded, 1 dk	**(B21B20A) Anchor Handling Tug Supply**	**2 oil engines** with clutches, flexible couplings & sr geared to sc. shafts driving 2 CP propellers Total Power: 4,502kW (6,120hp) Normo KVMB-12 2 x Vee 4 Stroke 12 Cy. 250 x 300 each-2251kW (3060bhp) AS Bergens Mek Verksteder-Norway AuxGen: 2 x 725kW 440/220V 60Hz a.c, 2 x 172kW 440/220V 60Hz a.c Thrusters: 1 Thwart. CP thruster (f) Fuel: 614.0 (d.f.)
8010635 *3EKZ4* -	**SEA WAY** *ex* Mert N *-2007* *ex* Esterel *-2005* *ex* Este *-2003* *ex* Balcaria Este *-1995* *ex* Playa de Sardineiro *-1992* *ex* Illa de Ons *-1988* **Yagmur Deniz Tasimaciligi Ticaret Ltd Sti SA** Alpmar Shipping SatCom: Inmarsat C 437288211 *Panama* *Panama* MMSI: 372882000 Official number: 3323407C	**1,763** 893 2,149	Class: TL (RP) (BV)	**1981**-08 **Ast. y Talleres Celaya S.A. — Bilbao** Yd No: 180 Loa 69.91 Br ex 13.62 Dght 3.601 Lbp 65.61 Br md 13.61 Dpth 5.41 Welded, 1 dk	**(A31A2GX) General Cargo Ship** Grain: 2,735 Compartments: 1 Ho, ER 1 Ha: ER Ice Capable	**1 oil engine** geared to sc. shaft driving 1 FP propeller Total Power: 1,306kW (1,776hp) 11.0kn Waukesha L5792DSIM 1 x Vee 4 Stroke 12 Cy. 216 x 216 1306kW (1776bhp) Waukesha Engine Div. DresserIndustries Inc.-Waukesha, Wi AuxGen: 3 x 96kW 220/380V 50Hz a.c
7622182 *3FGT* -	**SEA WAY STAR** *ex* Mary D *-2009* *ex* Kells *-2008* *ex* Gotaland *-1988* **Enridan Management SA** - *Panama* *Panama* MMSI: 352490000 Official number: 40058PEXT	**1,986** 1,061 2,655	Class: (GL)	**1977**-04 **Rinkai Kogyo K.K. — Onomichi** Yd No: 34 Loa 79.20 (BB) Br ex 12.43 Dght 4.771 Lbp 73.50 Br md 12.40 Dpth 7.22 Welded, 2 dks	**(A31A2GX) General Cargo Ship** Grain: 4,023; Bale: 3,928 TEU 104 C. 104/20' Compartments: 1 Ho, ER 1 Ha: (43.8 x 9.9)ER Cranes: 1 Ice Capable	**1 oil engine** geared to sc. shaft driving 1 FP propeller Total Power: 1,177kW (1,600hp) 10.5kn Yanmar 6Z-ST 1 x 4 Stroke 6 Cy. 280 x 340 1177kW (1600bhp) Yanmar Diesel Engine Co Ltd-Japan Thrusters: 1 Tunnel thruster (f)
9369605 *9MLQ8* -	**SEA WEASEL** - **Sea Weasel Ltd** Deep Sea Supply Management (Singapore) Pte Ltd *Port Klang* *Malaysia* MMSI: 533002050 Official number: 334322	**1,943** 583 1,575	Class: NV	**2009**-10 **ABG Shipyard Ltd — Surat** Yd No: 258 Loa 63.40 Br ex - Dght 4.600 Lbp 54.00 Br md 15.80 Dpth 6.80 Welded, 1 dk	**(B21B20A) Anchor Handling Tug Supply**	**2 oil engines** reduction geared to sc. shafts driving 2 CP propellers Total Power: 4,780kW (6,498hp) 10.5kn Bergens C25: 33L8P 2 x 4 Stroke 8 Cy. 250 x 330 each-2390kW (3249bhp) Rolls Royce Marine AS-Norway AuxGen: 3 x 425kW 440V 60Hz a.c Thrusters: 1 Thwart. CP thruster (f); 1 Tunnel thruster (a) Fuel: 693.0 (d.f.)

IMO / Call sign	Name / Owner	Tonnage	Class	Builder / Dimensions	Type	Machinery
8921822 *3EQQ2* -	**SEA WELLINGTON** *ex* TPC Wellington *-2012* *ex* Triumph *-2005* *ex* Multi-Purpose 5 *-2003* *ex* Golden Lady *-1996* *ex* Skautopp *-1993* *ex* Western Skautopp *-1991* **HR Wellington SA** Hanaro Shipping Co Ltd *Panama* *Panama* MMSI: 357507000 Official number: 37113PEXT2	**23,257** 13,690 42,004 T/cm 47.6	Class: KR (LR) (NV) Classed LR until 3/6/05	**1990**-11 **Oshima Shipbuilding Co Ltd — Saikai NS** Yd No: 10133 Loa 179.99 (BB) Br ex 30.53 Dght 11.228 Lbp 172.00 Br md 30.50 Dpth 15.80 Welded, 1 dk	**(A21A2BC) Bulk Carrier** Grain: 52,125; Bale: 51,118 Compartments: 5 Ho, ER 5 Ha: (14.4 x 15.3)4 (19.2 x 15.3)ER Cranes: 4x25t	**1 oil engine** driving 1 FP propeller Total Power: 6,230kW (8,470hp) 14.0kn Sulzer 6RTA52 1 x 2 Stroke 6 Cy. 520 x 1800 6230kW (8470bhp) Diesel United Ltd.-Aioi AuxGen: 3 x 410kW 440V 60Hz a.c Boilers: AuxB (Comp) 7.0kgf/cm² (6.9bar) Fuel: 107.8 (d.f.) 1346.2 (r.f.) 23.0pd
8944587 *HP8328* -	**SEA WESTERN** *ex* Independent I *-1995* **Seamist Navigation SA** - *Panama* *Panama* MMSI: 351269000 Official number: 2311896A	**140** 42 -		**1958 Scheepsw. en Ghbw. v/h Jonker & Stans N.V. — Hendrik-Ido-Ambacht** Yd No: 281 Loa 29.20 Br ex - Dght - Lbp - Br md 6.92 Dpth 2.61 Welded, 1 dk	**(B32A2ST) Tug**	**2 oil engines** driving 2 FP propellers Total Power: 530kW (720hp) 8.0kn Bolnes 2 x 2 Stroke each-265kW (360bhp) NV Machinefabriek 'Bolnes' v/h JHvan Cappellen-Netherlands
9027661 *HQXK3* -	**SEA WIN I** *ex* Tanjung Bahari 8 *-2003* *ex* Lotus 8 *-2002* **Logos Shipping Pte Ltd** - *San Lorenzo* *Honduras* Official number: L-3828403	**109** 33 -	Class: (KI)	**1995**-07 **Sanmarine Engineering Sdn Bhd — Sandakan** Yd No: SE017 Loa 21.70 Br ex - Dght 2.320 Lbp 20.00 Br md 6.80 Dpth 3.43 Welded, 1 dk	**(B32A2ST) Tug**	**2 oil engines** geared to sc. shafts driving 2 Propellers Total Power: 514kW (698hp) 13.0kn Cummins NTA-855-M 2 x 4 Stroke 6 Cy. 140 x 152 each-257kW (349bhp) (made 1991) Cummins Engine Co Ltd-United Kingdom
7304405 *A9D2842* -	**SEA WIND** *ex* Azraq *-2005* *ex* Hunter Creek *-1994* *ex* Hunter *-1984* *ex* Lady Vilma *-1984* **Sea Eagles Shipping LLC** - *Bahrain* *Bahrain* MMSI: 408790000 Official number: BN 4026	**924** 277 1,056	Class: LR ✠ **100A1** SS 08/2010 ✠ **LMC** Cable: U1 (a)	**1973**-02 **Carrington Slipways Pty Ltd — Newcastle NSW** Yd No: 84 Loa 57.92 Br ex 13.26 Dght 4.390 Lbp 51.74 Br md 12.80 Dpth 4.90 Welded, 1 dk	**(B21B20A) Anchor Handling Tug Supply**	**4 oil engines** with clutches, flexible couplings & dr geared to sc. shafts driving 2 FP propellers Total Power: 2,944kW (4,004hp) 12.0kn Daihatsu 8PSHTCM-26D 4 x 4 Stroke 8 Cy. 260 x 320 each-736kW (1001bhp) Daihatsu Diesel Manufacturing Co Lt-Japan AuxGen: 2 x 200kW 415V 50Hz a.c Thrusters: 1 Thwart. CP thruster (f) Fuel: 350.0 (d.f.) 13.0pd
7128332 *SDNE* -	**SEA WIND** *ex* Saga Wind *-1989* *ex* Svealand *-1984* **Tallinn Swedish Line Ltd** HT Laevateenindus OU (HT Shipmanagement Ltd) *Stockholm* *Sweden* MMSI: 265126000 Official number: 11254	**15,879** 4,843 4,000	Class: NV	**1972**-03 **Helsingor Skibsvaerft og Maskinbyggeri A/S — Helsingor** Yd No: 397 Converted From: Ferry (Passenger/Vehicle)-1989 Lengthened & Widened-1984 Loa 154.41 (BB) Br ex 21.04 Dght 5.020 Lbp 142.07 Br md 21.01 Dpth 13.47 Welded, 2 dks	**(A36A2PT) Passenger/Ro-Ro Ship (Vehicles/Rail)** Passengers: cabins: 100; berths: 300 Bow door/ramp Stern door/ramp Len: 10.51 Wid: 8.00 Swl: - Side door (s) Lane-Len: 1270 Trailers: 100 Ice Capable	**4 oil engines** with flexible couplings & sr gearedto sc. shafts driving 2 CP propellers Total Power: 7,356kW (10,000hp) 18.0kn MaK 8M453AK 4 x 4 Stroke 8 Cy. 320 x 420 each-1839kW (2500bhp) (new engine 1984) Krupp MaK Maschinenbau GmbH-Kiel AuxGen: 5 x 140kW 380V 50Hz a.c, 2 x a.c Thrusters: 2 Thwart. CP thruster (f) Fuel: 626.0 (r.f.) 40.0pd
8602361 *A8UK3* -	**SEA WIND** *ex* Boe Sea *-2009* *ex* Zultan *-2004* *ex* Multimax Cadiz *-2003* *ex* Zilina *-2002* *ex* Vltava *-1995* **Wind Shipping Co SA** Venus Enterprises SA *Monrovia* *Liberia* MMSI: 636014510 Official number: 14510	**6,425** 3,320 7,938 T/cm 17.6	Class: BV (LR) ✠ Classed LR until 26/11/04	**1988**-04 **Tianjin Xingang Shipyard — Tianjin** Yd No: 260 Loa 119.00 Br ex - Dght 7.713 Lbp 109.99 Br md 18.61 Dpth 10.42 Welded, 2 dks	**(A31A2GX) General Cargo Ship** Grain: 11,651; Bale: 10,751 TEU 126 C. 126/20' Cranes: 4x15t Ice Capable	**1 oil engine** driving 1 FP propeller Total Power: 3,399kW (4,621hp) 13.4kn Sulzer 5RTA38 1 x 2 Stroke 5 Cy. 380 x 1100 3399kW (4621bhp) Shanghai Diesel Engine Co Ltd-China AuxGen: 3 x 320kW 400V 50Hz a.c Boilers: AuxB (Comp) 7.9kgf/cm² (7.7bar) Fuel: 104.2 (d.f.) 625.1 (r.f.) 15.5pd
8423739 - -	**SEA WINNER** *ex* Edelweiss-13 *-2012* *ex* Elusive *-2011* *ex* Alpha *-2010* *ex* Spartak *-2010* *ex* Will *-2010* *ex* Swift *-2010* *ex* Polaris *-2010* *ex* Ortol *-2010* *ex* Apsari No. 21 *-2004* *ex* Soho Maru No. 68 *-2000* **Government of The Russian Federation (Territorial Department of Federal Agency on Management of Federal Property at Leningrad Oblast)** -	**252** 77 -		**1985 Kakusei Zosen K.K. — Hachinohe** Yd No: 168 L reg 29.91 Br ex - Dght 2.650 Lbp - Br md 6.90 Dpth 2.90 Welded	**(B11A2FS) Stern Trawler**	**1 oil engine** driving 1 FP propeller
9687033 *3WHA9* -	**SEA WINNER** **Hai Van Shipping Service Co Ltd** - *Saigon* *Vietnam* Official number: VNSG-2126-TK	**346** 104 313	Class: VR	**2012**-12 **Binh Trieu Shbldg & Rpr Yard — Ho Chi Minh City** Loa 37.03 Br ex 9.80 Dght 3.500 Lbp 33.06 Br md 9.50 Dpth 4.40 Welded, 1 dk	**(B32A2ST) Tug**	**2 oil engines** reduction geared to sc. shafts driving 2 FP propellers Total Power: 3,520kW (4,786hp) Chinese Std. Type CW16V200ZC 2 x Vee 4 Stroke 16 Cy. 200 x 270 each-1760kW (2393bhp) Weichai Power Co Ltd-China
9392975 *5BLT2* -	**SEA WITCH** **DESS PSV Ltd** Deep Sea Supply Management (Singapore) Pte Ltd SatCom: Inmarsat C 421257910 *Limassol* *Cyprus* MMSI: 212579000 Official number: 9392975	**2,160** 1,036 3,250	Class: NV	**2008**-12 **Cochin Shipyard Ltd — Ernakulam** Yd No: BY-63 Loa 71.90 Br ex 16.03 Dght 5.830 Lbp 66.31 Br md 16.00 Dpth 7.00 Welded, 1 dk	**(B21A20S) Platform Supply Ship** Cranes: 1x3t	**2 oil engines** reduction geared to sc. shafts driving 2 CP propellers Total Power: 4,010kW (5,452hp) 11.0kn Bergens KRMB-9 2 x 4 Stroke 9 Cy. 250 x 300 each-2005kW (2726bhp) Rolls Royce Marine AS-Norway AuxGen: 2 x 225kW 440/220V 60Hz a.c, 2 x 1280kW 440/220V 60Hz a.c Thrusters: 2 Thwart. CP thruster (f); 1 Thwart. CP thruster (a)
8501270 - -	**SEA WITCH** - - *Nigeria*	*139* 89 -		**1984**-12 **Quality Shipyards Inc — Houma LA** Yd No: 171 Loa 27.16 Br ex - Dght - Lbp - Br md - Dpth - Welded, 1 dk	**(B11A2FT) Trawler**	**1 oil engine** driving 1 FP propeller Total Power: 460kW (625hp) Caterpillar 3412PCTA 1 x Vee 4 Stroke 12 Cy. 137 x 152 460kW (625bhp) Caterpillar Tractor Co-USA
8623793 - -	**SEA WOLF** **Trans Nautica International (Gibraltar) Ltd**	*305* 91 -		**1985 Thor Marine — Stockton-on-Tees** Loa 39.54 Br ex 8.25 Dght - Lbp - Br md 4.08 Dpth 3.06 Welded, 1 dk	**(A37B2PS) Passenger Ship**	**2 oil engines** driving 2 FP propellers Cummins 2 x 4 Stroke Cummins Engine Co Inc-USA
8036263 *WBF3641* -	**SEA WOLF** **Westbank Corp** Daybrook Fisheries Inc *New Orleans, LA* *United States of America* MMSI: 367166260 Official number: 617276	*468* 318		**1980**-01 **Patterson Shipyard Inc. — Patterson, La** Yd No: 35 L reg 49.44 Br ex 9.45 Dght - Lbp - Br md - Dpth 3.43 Welded, 1 dk	**(B11B2FV) Fishing Vessel**	**1 oil engine** driving 1 FP propeller Total Power: 1,324kW (1,800hp)
7926590 *WCW9770* -	**SEA WOLF** **Sea Wolf Alaska LLC** Alaska Boat Co LLC *Unalaska, AK* *United States of America* MMSI: 367088480 Official number: 609823	*199* 135 -		**1979 Marine Construction & Design Co. (MARCO) — Seattle, Wa** Yd No: 378 Lengthened-1989 Loa 43.60 (BB) Br ex - Dght 4.271 Lbp - Br md 9.56 Dpth 4.45 Welded, 1 dk	**(B11B2FV) Fishing Vessel** Ins: 350 Compartments: 3 Ho, ER 3 Ha: Cranes: 1x8t	**1 oil engine** reverse reduction geared to sc. shaft driving 1 FP propeller Total Power: 1,250kW (1,700hp) 12.0kn Caterpillar D399SCAC 1 x Vee 4 Stroke 16 Cy. 159 x 203 1250kW (1700bhp) Caterpillar Tractor Co-USA AuxGen: 2 x 155kW, 1 x 90kW
5144289 - -	**SEA WOLF** *ex* Sea Wolf Quest *-2000* *ex* Jakobsen Quest *-2000* *ex* Silvia G *-2000* *ex* Palais Maritime *-2000* *ex* Marine Prospector *-2000* *ex* Striloy *-1986* *ex* Havnoy *-1984* **Naviera Sacremento S de RL** - *San Lorenzo* *Honduras* Official number: L-0201665	*136* 38 -	Class: (NV)	**1958**-06 **Hatlo Verksted AS — Ulsteinvik** Yd No: 6 Loa 28.96 Br ex 6.51 Dght - Lbp 26.07 Br md 6.41 Dpth 3.05 Welded, 1 dk	**(B32A2ST) Tug** Compartments: 1 Ho, ER 1 Ha: (5.4 x 2.2) Derricks: 1x4t	**1 oil engine** driving 1 CP propeller Total Power: 294kW (400hp) 9.5kn Wichmann 4ACA 1 x 2 Stroke 4 Cy. 280 x 420 294kW (400bhp) Wichmann Motorfabrikk AS-Norway AuxGen: 1 x 12kW 220V 50Hz a.c, 1 x 8kW 220V 50Hz a.c Fuel: 10.0 (d.f.)

8975615 *A6E2961* -	**SEA WOLF** *ex* Putra Jaya *-2004* *ex* Poet Vanda *-2003* **Target Engineering Construction Co (LLC)** *Abu Dhabi* *United Arab Emirates* MMSI: 470770000	**122** 37 80	Class: BV (NV)	**2002-12 Pacific Ocean Engineering & Trading Pte Ltd (POET) — Singapore** Yd No: 1121 Loa 21.00 Br ex - Dght 2.420 Lbp 19.25 Br md 6.99 Dpth 3.30 Welded, 1 dk	**(B32A2ST) Tug**	**2 oil engines** geared to sc. shafts driving 2 FP propellers Total Power: 736kW (1,000hp) Cummins KTA-19-M1 2 x 4 Stroke 6 Cy. 159 x 159 each-368kW (500bhp) Cummins Engine Co Inc-USA AuxGen: 2 x 40kW a.c
9147930 *P3KT7* -	**SEA WOLF** *ex* Caribbean Sea Wolf *-1997* **Dobletto Shipping Co Ltd** Empresa de Navegacion Caribe *Limassol* *Cyprus* Official number: 710901	**131** 39 48	Class: LR (GL) **100A1** SS 03/2012 tug, Cuban coastal service **LMC**	**1996-12 Damex Shipbuilding & Engineering AVV — Santiago de Cuba** Yd No: 6527 Loa 22.50 Br ex 7.25 Dght 3.500 Lbp 20.00 Br md 7.20 Dpth 3.70 Welded, 1 dk	**(B32A2ST) Tug**	**2 oil engines** reduction geared to sc. shafts driving 2 FP propellers Total Power: 1,412kW (1,920hp) 11.4kn Caterpillar 3508TA 2 x Vee 4 Stroke 8 Cy. 170 x 190 each-706kW (960bhp) Caterpillar Inc-USA
7210070 - -	**SEA WOLF 1** *ex* Kiku Maru No. 63 *-1986* *ex* Kiku Maru No. 23 *-1981* **Delsan Transport Lines Inc** - *Manila* *Philippines*	*114* 42 -		**1972 Nagasaki Zosen K.K. — Nagasaki** Yd No: 310 Loa 33.79 Br ex 6.33 Dght 2.350 Lbp 29.29 Br md 6.30 Dpth 2.80 Welded, 1 dk	**(B11B2FV) Fishing Vessel**	**1 oil engine** driving 1 FP propeller Total Power: 515kW (700hp) Niigata 6L25BX 1 x 4 Stroke 6 Cy. 250 x 320 515kW (700bhp) Niigata Engineering Co Ltd-Japan
7210082 - -	**SEA WOLF 2** *ex* Kiku Maru No. 65 *-1986* *ex* Kiku Maru No. 25 *-1981* **Delsan Transport Lines Inc** - *Manila* *Philippines* Official number: S0456	*114* 42 -		**1972 Nagasaki Zosen K.K. — Nagasaki** Yd No: 311 Loa 33.79 Br ex 6.33 Dght 2.350 Lbp 29.29 Br md 6.30 Dpth 2.80 Welded, 1 dk	**(B11B2FV) Fishing Vessel**	**1 oil engine** driving 1 FP propeller Total Power: 515kW (700hp) Niigata 6L25BX 1 x 4 Stroke 6 Cy. 250 x 320 515kW (700bhp) Niigata Engineering Co Ltd-Japan
7225128 *9H6602* -	**SEA WOLF II** *ex* Tatsu Maru No. 6 *-1985* **Cassar Enterprises Ltd** - *Valletta* *Malta* Official number: 1208	*122* 41 -		**1972 Ando Shipbuilding Co. Ltd. — Tokyo** Yd No: 220 Converted From: Tug-1987 Loa 21.49 Br ex 9.02 Dght 1.982 Lbp 19.51 Br md 9.00 Dpth 2.70 Welded, 1 dk	**(B34T2QR) Work/Repair Vessel** A-frames: 1x45t	**2 oil engines** driving 2 FP propellers Total Power: 956kW (1,300hp) 9.0kn Daihatsu 6RSNTM-26E 2 x 4 Stroke 6 Cy. 260 x 320 each-478kW (650bhp) Daihatsu Diesel Manufacturing Co Lt-Japan
8306371 - -	**SEA WOLF II** **Agropesquera Industrial Bahia Cupica Ltda CI** - *Buenaventura* *Colombia* Official number: MC-01-466	*107* 89 161		**1982 Steiner Shipyard, Inc. — Bayou La Batre, Al** Yd No: 127 Loa 22.81 Br ex - Dght 2.401 Lbp 20.12 Br md 6.71 Dpth 3.36 Welded, 1 dk	**(B11A2FT) Trawler**	**1 oil engine** geared to sc. shaft driving 1 FP propeller Total Power: 268kW (364hp) Cummins KT-1150-M 1 x 4 Stroke 6 Cy. 159 x 159 268kW (364bhp) Cummins Engine Co Inc-USA
7006211 *XUBX7* -	**SEA WORKER** *ex* Leja *-2000* *ex* Krasnoborsk *-1995* **SMI Shipping Ltd** Selet Marine Vanino Co Ltd *Phnom Penh* *Cambodia* MMSI: 514015000 Official number: 0370040	**2,736** 1,402 3,950	Class: IC (RS)	**1970-07 Hollming Oy — Rauma** Yd No: 180 Loa 102.27 Br ex 14.05 Dght 6.211 Lbp 93.20 Br md 14.03 Dpth 6.89 Welded, 1 dk	**(A31A2GX) General Cargo Ship** Grain: 5,171; Bale: 4,785 Compartments: ER, 4 Ho 4 Ha: (9.9 x 7.0)ER 3 (9.9 x 8.3) Derricks: 8x5t; Winches: 8 Ice Capable	**1 oil engine** driving 1 FP propeller Total Power: 2,133kW (2,900hp) 13.5kn B&W 5-50VTBF-110 1 x 2 Stroke 5 Cy. 500 x 1100 2133kW (2900bhp) Valmet Oy-Finland Fuel: 30.5 (d.f.) 254.0 (r.f.)
8977912 - -	**SEA WORKER** *ex* Bk 26014 *-2010* **Al Jazeera Shipping Co** Al Jazeera Shipping Co WLL (AJS) *Bahrain* *Bahrain*	**170** 51 -	Class: BV	**1978 Scheepswerf Lanser B.V. — Sliedrecht** Yd No: 671 Loa 23.00 Br ex - Dght 1.780 Lbp 22.08 Br md 11.00 Dpth 2.80 Welded, 1 dk	**(B34B2SC) Crane Vessel** Cranes: 1x110t,2x13.5t	**2 oil engines** geared to sc. shafts driving 2 FP propellers Total Power: 412kW (560hp) 8.0kn Caterpillar 3406 2 x 4 Stroke 6 Cy. 137 x 165 each-206kW (280bhp) Caterpillar Tractor Co-USA AuxGen: 2 x 56kW 380/220V a.c
9049528 - -	**SEA WORLD I** **PT Sea World** - *Samarinda* *Indonesia*	**154** 47 -	Class: KI	**2005-07 P.T. Kaltim Shipyard — Samarinda** Loa 23.00 Br ex - Dght 2.500 Lbp 21.00 Br md 7.60 Dpth 3.50 Welded, 1 dk	**(B32A2ST) Tug**	**2 oil engines** geared to sc. shafts driving 2 Propellers Total Power: 780kW (1,060hp) G.M. (Detroit Diesel) 12V-92-TA 1 x Vee 2 Stroke 12 Cy. 123 x 127 390kW (530bhp) Detroit Diesel Co.-Detroit, Mi G.M. (Detroit Diesel) 12V-92-TA 1 x Vee 2 Stroke 12 Cy. 123 x 127 390kW (530bhp) Detroit Diesel Eng. Co.-Detroit, Mi AuxGen: 2 x 40kW 380V a.c
9049530 - -	**SEA WORLD II** **PT Sea World** - *Samarinda* *Indonesia*	**154** 47 -	Class: KI	**2005-08 P.T. Kaltim Shipyard — Samarinda** Loa 23.00 Br ex Dght 2.500 Lbp 21.00 Br md 7.60 Dpth 3.50 Welded, 1 dk	**(B32A2ST) Tug**	**2 oil engines** geared to sc. shafts driving 2 Propellers Total Power: 794kW (1,080hp) Caterpillar 3412B 2 x Vee 4 Stroke 12 Cy. 137 x 152 each-397kW (540bhp) Caterpillar Inc-USA AuxGen: 2 x 40kW 380V a.c
8975756 *WDA9104* -	**SEA WORLD II** **Hoang Nguyen** - *New Orleans, LA* *United States of America* MMSI: 366861460 Official number: 1128476	**164** 49 -		**2001 Master Boat Builders, Inc. — Coden, Al** Yd No: 332 L reg 28.95 Br ex - Dght - Lbp - Br md 7.62 Dpth 3.75 Welded, 1 dk	**(B11B2FV) Fishing Vessel**	**1 oil engine** driving 1 Propeller
9049475 - -	**SEA WORLD III** **PT Sea World** - *Samarinda* *Indonesia*	**132** 40 -	Class: KI	**2005-08 P.T. Kaltim Shipyard — Samarinda** Loa 22.00 Br ex - Dght - Lbp 19.75 Br md 7.00 Dpth 3.00 Welded, 1 dk	**(B32A2ST) Tug**	**2 oil engines** geared to sc. shafts driving 2 Propellers Total Power: 758kW (1,030hp) Caterpillar 3408 2 x Vee 4 Stroke 8 Cy. 137 x 152 each-379kW (515bhp) Caterpillar Inc-USA AuxGen: 2 x 40kW 380V a.c
7516266 *6NGJ* -	**SEA WORLD NO. 101** *ex* Bang Joo No. 7 *-2005* *ex* Hyang Rim No. 7 *-2005* *ex* Acacia No. 7 *-1994* **Sea World Corp** - *Busan* *South Korea* Official number: 9511020-6477703	**660** 249 460	Class: (KR)	**1975-01 Busan Shipbuilding Co Ltd — Busan** Yd No: 131 Loa 54.89 Br ex 9.15 Dght 3.742 Lbp 49.05 Br md 9.00 Dpth 3.95 Welded, 1 dk	**(B11B2FV) Fishing Vessel** Ins: 671 5 Ha: (1.8 x 1.8)3 (1.3 x 0.9) (1.3 x 1.0) Derricks: 2x1t,2x0.5t	**1 oil engine** driving 1 FP propeller Total Power: 956kW (1,300hp) 13.1kn Niigata 6L28X 1 x 4 Stroke 6 Cy. 280 x 440 956kW (1300bhp) Niigata Engineering Co Ltd-Japan AuxGen: 2 x 200kW 230V a.c
8519459 *HSB3376* -	**SEA ZENITH** *ex* Orchid Star *-2005* *ex* Gati 2 *-2004* *ex* Tamdhu *-2001* *ex* Gafu *-1993* **S Ship Management 2000 Co Ltd** - *Bangkok* *Thailand* MMSI: 567316000 Official number: 490000426	**5,548** 3,407 9,379	Class: KR (NK) (IR)	**1987-03 Taihei Kogyo K.K. — Hashihama, Imabari** Yd No: 1871 Loa 98.17 (BB) Br ex - Dght 9.021 Lbp 89.95 Br md 18.81 Dpth 12.91 Welded, 1 dk	**(A31A2GX) General Cargo Ship** Grain: 13,560; Bale: 12,554 TEU 175 C. 175/20' (40') Compartments: 2 Ho, ER 2 Ha: 2 (20.3 x 12.7)ER Derricks: 2x30t,2x25t	**1 oil engine** driving 1 FP propeller Total Power: 2,501kW (3,400hp) 12.9kn B&W 5L35MCE 1 x 2 Stroke 5 Cy. 350 x 1050 2501kW (3400bhp) Hitachi Zosen Corp-Japan AuxGen: 3 x a.c Fuel: 593.0
8765888 *WDC4896* -	**SEABASS** *ex* Les Waters *-1993* **All Coast LLC** - *New Orleans, LA* *United States of America* MMSI: 367032470 Official number: 659365	*186* 127 -		**1982-01 Sun Contractors, Inc. — Harvey, La** Yd No: LB-85 Loa - Br ex - Dght - Lbp 30.48 Br md 14.02 Dpth 2.43 Welded, 1 dk	**(B22A2ZM) Offshore Construction Vessel, jack up**	**2 oil engines** geared to sc. shafts driving 2 Propellers G.M. (Detroit Diesel) 12V-71 2 x Vee 2 Stroke 12 Cy. 108 x 127 Detroit Diesel Corporation-Detroit, Mi AuxGen: 2 x 100kW a.c
9251640 *DLDY* -	**SEABASS** **tms 'Seabass' Sea Tanker GmbH & Co KG** German Tanker Shipping GmbH & Co KG *Bremen* *Germany* MMSI: 218551000 Official number: SSR4845	**21,353** 8,390 32,445 T/cm 42.0	Class: GL	**2001-12 Lindenau GmbH Schiffswerft u. Maschinenfabrik — Kiel** Yd No: 243 Loa 177.75 (BB) Br ex 28.16 Dght 11.000 Lbp 169.00 Br md 28.00 Dpth 16.80 Welded, 1 dk	**(A13B2TP) Products Tanker** Double Hull (13F) Liq: 36,690; Liq (Oil): 36,690 Compartments: 6 Wing Ta, 6 Wing Ta, ER 10 Cargo Pump (s): 10x500m^3/hr Manifold: Bow/CM: 85m Ice Capable	**1 oil engine** geared to sc. shaft driving 1 CP propeller Total Power: 8,340kW (11,339hp) 14.0kn MAN 6L58/64 1 x 4 Stroke 6 Cy. 580 x 640 8340kW (11339bhp) MAN B&W Diesel AG-Augsburg Thrusters: 1 Thwart. FP thruster (f)

IMO / Call sign	Name / Owner	Tonnage	Class	Builder / Dimensions	Type	Machinery
9489651 *LARF7* -	**SEABED PRINCE** *ex* GSP Prince *-2012* *launched as* Acergy Merlin *-2009* **Volstad Shipping AS** Swire Seabed Shipping AS *Bergen* *Norway (NIS)* MMSI: 258647000	**4,398** 1,320 2,325	Class: NV	**2009-09 Yildirim Gemi Insaat Sanayii A.S. — Tuzla** (Hull) Yd No: 114 **2009-09 Baatbygg AS — Raudeberg** Yd No: 7 Loa 85.30 (BB) Br ex 18.62 Dght 6.800 Lbp 75.00 Br md 18.00 Dpth 9.10 Welded, 1 dk	**(B31A2SR) Research Survey Vessel** Passengers: berths: 62 Cranes: 1x70t Ice Capable	**4 diesel electric oil engines** driving 4 gen. each 1800kW 690V a.c Connecting to 2 elec. motors each (2200kW) driving 2 Azimuth electric drive units Total Power: 7,604kW (10,340hp) 12.5kn Caterpillar 3516B 4 x Vee 4 Stroke 16 Cy. 170 x 215 each-1901kW (2585bhp) Caterpillar Inc-USA Thrusters: 2 Thwart. CP thruster (f); 1 Retract. directional thruster (f) Fuel: 1050.0
9671632 *9V2431* -	**SEABED SUPPORTER** **Swire Pacific Offshore Operations Pte Ltd** - *Singapore* *Singapore* MMSI: 563784000 Official number: 399010	**4,224** 1,267 2,000	Class: RI (Class contemplated)	**2013-07 Fjellstrand AS — Omastrand** Yd No: 1688 Loa 89.80 (BB) Br ex 17.00 Dght 5.100 Lbp 82.69 Br md 16.52 Dpth - Welded, 1 dk	**(B22A2OR) Offshore Support Vessel** Cranes: 1x80t	**4 oil engines** driving 4 gen. each 1750kW Connecting to 2 elec. motors each (2000kW) reduction geared to sc. shafts driving 2 Azimuth electric drive units Total Power: 7,000kW (9,516hp) 12.0kn M.T.U. 4 x each-1750kW (2379bhp) MTU Friedrichshafen GmbH-Friedrichshafen Thrusters: 2 Tunnel thruster (f); 1 Directional thruster (f)
9533244 *LAGI7* -	**SEABED WORKER** **Seabed AS** Swire Seabed Shipping AS *Bergen* *Norway (NIS)* MMSI: 259889000	**3,923** 1,177 2,350	Class: NV	**2009-02 OAO Zavod "Krasnyye Barrikady" — Krasnyye Barrikady** (Hull) Yd No: 11/07 **2009-02 Fjellstrand AS — Omastrand** Yd No: 1679 Loa 88.80 (BB) Br ex 16.12 Dght 7.150 Lbp 78.20 Br md 16.00 Dpth 9.13 Welded, 1 dk	**(B22A2OR) Offshore Support Vessel** Cranes: 1x100t	**4 diesel electric oil engines** driving 4 gen. each 1800kW Connecting to 2 elec. motors each (2500kW) driving 2 Voith-Schneider propellers Total Power: 7,200kW (9,788hp) 14.5kn Cummins QSK60-M 4 x Vee 4 Stroke 16 Cy. 159 x 190 each-1800kW (2447bhp) Cummins Engine Co Inc-USA Thrusters: 2 Tunnel thruster (f); 1 Retract. directional thruster (f)
8909185 *V4PR* -	**SEABEE** *ex* Alara *-2010* *ex* Vedette *-2010* **Otto Shipping Co Ltd** Talya Denizcilik Ltd *Basseterre* *St Kitts & Nevis* MMSI: 341985000 Official number: SKN 1001986	**2,033** 1,168 3,502	Class: BV (LR) (GL) ✠ Classed LR until 26/2/09	**1990-12 Bodewes' Scheepswerven B.V. — Hoogezand** Yd No: 560 Loa 86.00 Br ex 14.23 Dght 5.285 Lbp 79.79 Br md 14.00 Dpth 6.64 Welded, 1dk	**(A31A2GX) General Cargo Ship** Grain: 4,262; Bale: 4,259 TEU 152 C.Ho 60/20' C.Dk 92/20' Compartments: 2 Ho, ER 2 Ha: 2 (24.9 x 11.0)ER	**1 oil engine** with flexible couplings & sr geared to sc. shaft driving 1 FP propeller Total Power: 1,320kW (1,795hp) 9.8kn MaK 6M452AK 1 x 4 Stroke 6 Cy. 320 x 450 1320kW (1795bhp) Krupp MaK Maschinenbau GmbH-Kiel AuxGen: 3 x 74kW 380V 50Hz a.c Fuel: 140.0 (d.f.)
8504789 - -	**SEABIRD** *ex* Oryong No. 702 *-2008* *ex* Haeng Bok No. 103 *-2003* **Unicorp Trading Inc** -	*629* 285 415	Class: (KR)	**1985-11 Dae Sun Shipbuilding & Engineering Co Ltd — Busan** Yd No: 290 Loa 53.29 (BB) Br ex - Dght 3.626 Lbp 46.89 Br md 8.73 Dpth 3.75 Welded, 1 dk	**(B11B2FV) Fishing Vessel**	**1 oil engine** with clutches, flexible couplings & sr geared to sc. shaft driving 1 FP propeller Total Power: 736kW (1,001hp) Niigata 6M28AFTE 1 x 4 Stroke 6 Cy. 280 x 480 736kW (1001bhp) Ssangyong Heavy Industries Co Ltd-South Korea AuxGen: 2 x 280kW 225V a.c
8657342 *T3DN2* -	**SEABLUE 1288** *ex* Gan Shangrao Cai 1288 *-2012* **Seablue Dredge & Land Reclamation Pte Ltd** - *Tarawa* *Kiribati* Official number: K-15051259	**1,227** 368 -		**2005-03 in the People's Republic of China** Loa 63.00 Br ex 12.00 Dght - Lbp - Br md 11.80 Dpth 3.80 Welded, 1 dk	**(B33A2DS) Suction Dredger**	**2 oil engines** reduction geared to sc. shafts driving 2 Propellers Total Power: 382kW (520hp) Chinese Std. Type 2 x each-191kW (260bhp) Zibo Diesel Engine Factory-China
9393589 *5BAW3* -	**SEABOARD AMERICA** **Kerasato Shipping Co Ltd** Athena Marine Co Ltd *Limassol* *Cyprus* MMSI: 210815000	**19,128** 9,736 25,747	Class: GL	**2010-09 Huanghai Shipbuilding Co Ltd — Rongcheng SD** Yd No: HCY-61 Loa 159.80 (BB) Br ex - Dght 9.800 Lbp 152.00 Br md 27.40 Dpth 13.50 Welded, 1 dk	**(A31A2GX) General Cargo Ship** Double Hull Grain: 34,000; Bale: 34,000 TEU 1571 C Ho 649 TEU C Dk 922 incl 150 ref C Compartments: 4 Ho, ER 4 Ha: 2 (33.6 x 23.0) (19.0 x 23.0)ER (19.0 x 18.0) Cranes: 2x120t,1x60t Ice Capable	**1 oil engine** driving 1 FP propeller Total Power: 6,810kW (9,259hp) 15.5kn MAN-B&W 6S40ME-B9 1 x 2 Stroke 6 Cy. 400 x 1770 6810kW (9259bhp) STX Engine Co Ltd-South Korea AuxGen: 3 x 600kW 450V 60Hz a.c Thrusters: 1 Tunnel thruster (f) Fuel: 150.0 (d.f.) 1400.0 (r.f.) 31.0pd
9395563 *D5DC5* -	**SEABOARD ATLANTIC** *ex* Mare *-2012* **Seaboard Atlantic Ltd** Seaboard Marine Ltd Inc *Monrovia* *Liberia* MMSI: 636015840 Official number: 15840	**8,273** 4,002 11,007	Class: GL	**2009-04 Detlef Hegemann Rolandwerft GmbH & Co. KG — Berne** Yd No: 247 Loa 139.60 (BB) Br ex - Dght 7.364 Lbp 133.25 Br md 22.20 Dpth 9.50 Welded, 1 dk	**(A33A2CC) Container Ship (Fully Cellular)** TEU 974 C Ho 218 TEU C Dk 756 TEU incl 170 ref C. Compartments: 3 Cell Ho, ER Ice Capable	**1 oil engine** reduction geared to sc. shaft driving 1 CP propeller Total Power: 8,402kW (11,423hp) 18.1kn MaK 9M43C 1 x 4 Stroke 9 Cy. 430 x 610 8402kW (11423bhp) Caterpillar Motoren GmbH & Co. KG-Germany AuxGen: 1 x 1196kW 450V a.c, 2 x 430kW 450V a.c Thrusters: 1 Tunnel thruster (f)
9393565 *5BXJ2* -	**SEABOARD CHILE** *launched as* Pacific Action *-2010* **Melato Shipping Co Ltd** Mastermind Shipmanagement Ltd *Limassol* *Cyprus* MMSI: 212314000	**19,128** 9,736 25,732	Class: GL	**2010-04 Huanghai Shipbuilding Co Ltd — Rongcheng SD** Yd No: HCY-59 Loa 159.89 (BB) Br ex - Dght 9.800 Lbp 152.00 Br md 27.40 Dpth 13.50 Welded, 1 dk	**(A31A2GX) General Cargo Ship** Double Hull Grain: 34,000; Bale: 34,000 TEU 1571 C Ho 649 TEU C Dk 922 incl 150 ref C Compartments: 4 Ho, ER 4 Ha: 2 (33.6 x 23.0) (19.0 x 23.0)ER (19.0 x 18.0) Cranes: 2x120t,1x60t Ice Capable	**1 oil engine** driving 1 FP propeller Total Power: 6,810kW (9,259hp) 15.5kn MAN-B&W 6S40ME-B9 1 x 2 Stroke 6 Cy. 400 x 1770 6810kW (9259bhp) STX Engine Co Ltd-South Korea AuxGen: 3 x 600kW 450V 60Hz a.c Thrusters: 1 Tunnel thruster (f) Fuel: 150.0 (d.f.) 1400.0 (r.f.) 31.0pd
9383285 *A8SB7* -	**SEABOARD OCEAN** *ex* Frisia Spree *-2011* **Container-Schiffahrt GmbH & Co ms 'Frisia Spree' KG** Hartmann Schiffahrts GmbH & Co KG (Hartmann Reederei) *Monrovia* *Liberia* MMSI: 636091623 Official number: 91731	**9,948** 5,020 13,670 T/cm 28.0	Class: GL	**2008-10 Yangzhou Dayang Shipbuilding Co Ltd — Yangzhou JS** Yd No: DY209 Loa 147.80 (BB) Br ex - Dght 8.500 Lbp 140.30 Br md 23.25 Dpth 11.50 Welded, 1 dk	**(A33A2CC) Container Ship (Fully Cellular)** Grain: 16,000; Bale: 16,000 TEU 1114 C Ho 334 TEU C Dk 780 TEU incl 220 ref C	**1 oil engine** reduction geared to sc. shaft driving 1 FP propeller Total Power: 9,730kW (13,229hp) 19.6kn MAN-B&W 7L58/64 1 x 4 Stroke 7 Cy. 580 x 640 9730kW (13229bhp) MAN B&W Diesel AG-Augsburg AuxGen: 3 x 570kW a.c, 1 x 1400kW 450V a.c Thrusters: 1 Tunnel thruster (f) Fuel: 230.0 (d.f.) 1400.0 (r.f.)
9393553 *5BVW2* -	**SEABOARD PACIFIC** *launched as* Pacific Alliance *-2010* **Katrizio Shipping Co Ltd** Athena Marine Co Ltd *Limassol* *Cyprus* MMSI: 210843000	**19,128** 9,736 25,733	Class: GL	**2010-01 Huanghai Shipbuilding Co Ltd — Rongcheng SD** Yd No: HCY-58 Loa 159.89 (BB) Br ex - Dght 9.800 Lbp 152.00 Br md 27.40 Dpth 13.50 Welded, 1 dk	**(A31A2GX) General Cargo Ship** Double Hull Grain: 34,000; Bale: 34,000 TEU 1571 C Ho 649 TEU C Dk 922 incl 150 ref C Compartments: 5 Ho 4 Ha: 2 (33.6 x 23.0) (19.0 x 23.0)ER (19.0 x 18.0) Cranes: 2x120t,1x45t Ice Capable	**1 oil engine** driving 1 FP propeller Total Power: 6,810kW (9,259hp) 15.5kn MAN-B&W 6S40ME-B9 1 x 2 Stroke 6 Cy. 400 x 1770 6810kW (9259bhp) STX Engine Co Ltd-South Korea AuxGen: 3 x 600kW 450V 60Hz a.c Thrusters: 1 Tunnel thruster (f) Fuel: 150.0 (d.f.) 1400.0 (r.f.) 31.0pd
9393577 *5BZE2* -	**SEABOARD PERU** **Fitorio Shipping Co Ltd** Athena Marine Co Ltd *Limassol* *Cyprus* MMSI: 212287000	**19,128** 9,736 25,774	Class: GL	**2010-06 Huanghai Shipbuilding Co Ltd — Rongcheng SD** Yd No: HCY-60 Loa 159.89 (BB) Br ex - Dght 9.800 Lbp 152.00 Br md 27.40 Dpth 13.50 Welded, 1 dk	**(A31A2GX) General Cargo Ship** Double Hull Grain: 34,000; Bale: 34,000 TEU 1571 C Ho 649 TEU C Dk 922 incl 150 ref C Compartments: 4 Ho, ER 4 Ha: 2 (33.6 x 23.0) (19.0 x 23.0)ER (19.0 x 18.0) Cranes: 2x120t,1x60t Ice Capable	**1 oil engine** driving 1 FP propeller Total Power: 6,810kW (9,259hp) 15.5kn MAN-B&W 6S40ME-B9 1 x 2 Stroke 6 Cy. 400 x 1770 6810kW (9259bhp) STX Engine Co Ltd-South Korea AuxGen: 3 x 600kW 450V 60Hz a.c Thrusters: 1 Tunnel thruster (f) Fuel: 150.0 (d.f.) 1400.0 (r.f.) 31.0pd

IMO / Call sign	Name / Owner / Manager / Registry	Tonnage	Class	Builder / Dimensions	Ship type / Capacity	Machinery
9178111 *V2HA5* -	**SEABOARD PRIDE** *ex* APL Quetzal *-2007* *ex* Stor Trader *-2003* *ex* Seaboard Pride *-2003* *ex* Stor Trader *-2001* *ex* Seaboard Pride *-2000* *launched as* Stor Trader *-1998* **Einundvierzigste Grosse Bleichen Schiffahrtsgesellschaft mbH & Co KG** Hermann Buss GmbH & Cie KG *Saint John's* *Antigua & Barbuda* MMSI: 304243000	**6,674** 3,560 8,329	Class: GL	**1998**-05 **Peterswerft Wewelsfleth GmbH & Co. — Wewelsfleth** Yd No: 658 Loa 132.48 (BB) Br ex 19.50 Dght 7.219 Lbp 123.40 Br md 19.20 Dpth 9.20 Welded, 1 dk	**(A33A2CC) Container Ship (Fully Cellular)** Grain: 22,950 TEU 660 C Ho 228 TEU C Dk 432 TEU incl 80 ref C. Compartments: 3 Cell Ho, ER 3 Ha: ER Cranes: 2x50t	**1 oil engine** with flexible couplings & sr gearedto sc. shaft driving 1 CP propeller Total Power: 5,940kW (8,076hp) 17.0kn Wartsila 9L38 1 x 4 Stroke 9 Cy. 380 x 475 5940kW (8076bhp) Wartsila NSD Nederland BV-Netherlands Thrusters: 1 Thwart. FP thruster (f)
9383297 *A8RF7* -	**SEABOARD RANGER** *ex* Mell Saraca *-2011* *ex* Frisia Rhein *-2009* **Container Schiffahrt GmbH & Co ms 'Frisia Rhein' KG** Hartmann Schiffahrts GmbH & Co KG (Hartmann Reederei) *Monrovia* *Liberia* MMSI: 636091654 Official number: 91654	**9,948** 5,020 13,684 T/cm 28.0	Class: GL	**2009**-07 **Yangzhou Dayang Shipbuilding Co Ltd — Yangzhou JS** Yd No: DY210 Loa 147.80 (BB) Br ex - Dght 8.500 Lbp 140.30 Br md 23.25 Dpth 11.50 Welded, 1 dk	**(A33A2CC) Container Ship (Fully Cellular)** Grain: 16,000; Bale: 16,000 TEU 1114 C Ho 334 TEU C Dk 780 incl 220 ref C Cranes: 2x45t	**1 oil engine** reduction geared to sc. shaft driving 1 CP propeller Total Power: 9,730kW (13,229hp) 19.6kn MAN-B&W 7L58/64 1 x 4 Stroke 7 Cy. 580 x 640 9730kW (13229bhp) MAN B&W Diesel AG-Augsburg AuxGen: 1 x 1400kW 450V a.c, 3 x 570kW a.c Thrusters: 1 Tunnel thruster (f) Fuel: 230.0 (d.f.) 1400.0 (r.f.)
9014030 *A8MR2* -	**SEABOARD SUN** *ex* Romea *-2007* **Seaboard Sun Ltd** Wilhelmsen Ship Management Ltd *Monrovia* *Liberia* MMSI: 636013398 Official number: 13398	**7,567** 2,270 7,748	Class: RI	**1991**-09 **Cantiere Navale Visentini di Visentini F e C SAS — Porto Viro** Yd No: 161 Loa 138.09 (BB) Br ex 21.59 Dght 6.113 Lbp 124.41 Br md 21.58 Dpth 10.50 Welded, 1 dk	**(A35A2RR) Ro-Ro Cargo Ship** Passengers: cabins: 5; berths: 12 Stern door/ramp (centre) Lane-Len: 900 Lane-clr ht: 6.10 Trailers: 78 TEU 470 C Ho 170 TEU C Dk 200 TEU	**1 oil engine** with flexible couplings & sr reverse geared to sc. shaft driving 1 CP propeller Total Power: 4,920kW (6,689hp) 17.0kn Wartsila 12V32E 1 x Vee 4 Stroke 12 Cy. 320 x 350 4920kW (6689bhp) Wartsila Diesel Oy-Finland AuxGen: 3 x 560kW 220/380V 50Hz a.c, 1 x 520kW 220/380V 50Hz a.c Thrusters: 1 Thwart. FP thruster (f) Fuel: 126.8 (d.f.) 477.6 (r.f.) 20.0pd
9288746 *9HZR7* -	**SEABORN** **Coral Waters Marine Ltd** Thenamaris (Ships Management) Inc SatCom: Inmarsat B 321578110 *Valletta* *Malta* MMSI: 215781000 Official number: 9088	**57,296** 32,526 105,042 T/cm 92.0	Class: LR ✠ **100A1** SS 01/2010 Double Hull oil tanker ESP *IWS LI SPM Ice Class 1C FS at draught of 15.253m Max/min draught fwd 15.253/6.24m Max/min draught aft 15.253/8.36m **ShipRight** (SDA, FDA Plus, CM) ✠ **LMC** **UMS IGS** Eq.Ltr: T†; Cable: 715.0/87.0 U3 (a)	**2005**-01 **Hyundai Samho Heavy Industries Co Ltd — Samho** Yd No: S213 Loa 243.96 (BB) Br ex 42.04 Dght 14.900 Lbp 234.02 Br md 42.00 Dpth 21.00 Welded, 1 dk	**(A13A2TW) Crude/Oil Products Tanker** Double Hull (13F) Liq: 115,604; Liq (Oil): 115,604 Cargo Heating Coils Compartments: 12 Wing Ta, 2 Wing Slop Ta, ER 3 Cargo Pump (s): 3x3000m³/hr Manifold: Bow/CM: 122.8m Ice Capable	**1 oil engine** driving 1 FP propeller Total Power: 11,324kW (15,396hp) 14.5kn B&W 6S60MC 1 x 2 Stroke 6 Cy. 600 x 2292 11324kW (15396bhp) Hyundai Heavy Industries Co Ltd-South Korea AuxGen: 3 x 780kW 440/220V 60Hz a.c Boilers: AuxB (Comp) 8.2kgf/cm² (8.0bar), WTAuxB (o.f.) 18.3kgf/cm² (17.9bar) Fuel: 191.9 (d.f.) 2660.9 (r.f.)
9247833 *VRYG4* -	**SEABORNE** *ex* Seaconstellation *-2003* **Good Ventures Maritime Inc** Valles Steamship (Canada) Inc *Hong Kong* *Hong Kong* MMSI: 477336000 Official number: HK-0954	**57,529** 32,194 106,638 T/cm 91.7	Class: NV	**2003**-02 **Tsuneishi Shipbuilding Co Ltd — Fukuyama HS** Yd No: 1238 Loa 240.50 (BB) Br ex 42.03 Dght 14.868 Lbp 230.00 Br md 42.00 Dpth 21.20 Welded, 1 dk	**(A13A2TV) Crude Oil Tanker** Double Hull (13F) Liq: 121,000; Liq (Oil): 121,000 Compartments: 12 Wing Ta, ER 3 Cargo Pump (s) Manifold: Bow/CM: 123m	**1 oil engine** driving 1 FP propeller Total Power: 11,840kW (16,098hp) 15.0kn B&W 6S60MC 1 x 2 Stroke 6 Cy. 600 x 2292 11840kW (16098bhp) Mitsui Engineering & Shipbuilding CLtd-Japan AuxGen: 3 x a.c Fuel: 215.8 (d.f.) (Heating Coils) 3128.0 (r.f.) 43.6pd
9288332 *9HXV7* -	**SEABOSS** **Aboma Holding Ltd** Thenamaris (Ships Management) Inc *Valletta* *Malta* MMSI: 215714000 Official number: 8984	**30,936** 18,158 55,426 T/cm 56.3	Class: NV	**2004**-09 **Nantong COSCO KHI Ship Engineering Co Ltd (NACKS) — Nantong JS** Yd No: 024 Loa 189.98 (BB) Br ex 32.30 Dght 12.520 Lbp 185.02 Br md 32.26 Dpth 17.80 Welded, 1 dk	**(A21A2BC) Bulk Carrier** Grain: 69,452; Bale: 66,110 Compartments: 5 Ho, ER 5 Ha: 4 (20.5 x 18.6)ER (17.8 x 18.6) Cranes: 4x30t	**1 oil engine** driving 1 FP propeller Total Power: 8,200kW (11,149hp) 14.6kn B&W 6S50MC-C 1 x 2 Stroke 6 Cy. 500 x 2000 8200kW (11149bhp) Dalian Marine Diesel Works-China AuxGen: 3 x 460kW
9008598 *C6FR6* -	**SEABOURN LEGEND** *ex* Queen Odyssey *-1996* *ex* Royal Viking Queen *-1995* **Star Legend Ltd** - SatCom: Inmarsat A 1316175 *Nassau* *Bahamas* MMSI: 311085000 Official number: 8000346	**9,961** 3,019 790	Class: NV	**1992**-02 **Schichau Seebeckwerft AG — Bremerhaven** Yd No: 1071 Loa 135.00 (BB) Br ex 20.50 Dght 5.420 Lbp 112.40 Br md 19.00 Dpth 12.40 Welded, 5 dks plus 4 superstructure dks	**(A37A2PC) Passenger/Cruise** Passengers: cabins: 106; berths: 214 Ice Capable	**4 oil engines** with clutches & dr geared to sc. shafts driving 2 CP propellers Total Power: 7,280kW (9,898hp) 16.0kn Normo KRMB-8 2 x 4 Stroke 8 Cy. 250 x 300 each-1460kW (1985bhp) Bergen Diesel AS-Norway Normo KVMB-12 2 x Vee 4 Stroke 12 Cy. 250 x 300 each-2180kW (2964bhp) Bergen Diesel AS-Norway AuxGen: 2 x 1200kW 440V 60Hz a.c, 1 x 880kW 440V 60Hz a.c Thrusters: 1 Thwart. CP thruster (f) Fuel: 35.0 (d.f.) 392.0 (r.f.) 33.0pd
9417086 *C6XC6* -	**SEABOURN ODYSSEY** **Seabourn Cruise Line Ltd** - SatCom: Inmarsat C 430941610 *Nassau* *Bahamas* MMSI: 309416000 Official number: 9000277	**32,346** 10,532 5,000	Class: RI	**2009**-06 **T. Mariotti SpA — Genova** Yd No: 62 Loa 198.19 (BB) Br ex 25.60 Dght 6.400 Lbp 169.20 Br md 25.60 Dpth 15.25 Welded	**(A37A2PC) Passenger/Cruise** Passengers: cabins: 225; berths: 450	**4 diesel electric oil engines** driving 4 gen. each 5536kW 6600V a.c Connecting to 2 elec. motors driving 2 FP propellers Total Power: 24,000kW (32,632hp) 19.0kn Wartsila 12V32 2 x Vee 4 Stroke 12 Cy. 320 x 400 each-6000kW (8158bhp) Wartsila Finland Oy-Finland Thrusters: 2 Tunnel thruster (f) Fuel: 1000.0 (r.f.)
8707343 *C6FR5* -	**SEABOURN PRIDE** **Windstar Pride Ltd** - SatCom: Inmarsat B 331108410 *Nassau* *Bahamas* MMSI: 311084000 Official number: 8000345	**9,975** 3,023 800	Class: NV	**1988**-11 **Schichau Seebeckwerft AG — Bremerhaven** Yd No: 1065 Loa 133.40 (BB) Br ex 20.50 Dght 5.001 Lbp 112.40 Br md 19.00 Dpth 12.40 Welded, 5 dks plus 4 superstructure dks	**(A37A2PC) Passenger/Cruise** Passengers: cabins: 106; berths: 208 Ice Capable	**4 oil engines** with clutches & dr geared to sc. shafts driving 2 CP propellers Total Power: 7,280kW (9,898hp) 16.0kn Normo KVMB-12 2 x Vee 4 Stroke 12 Cy. 250 x 300 each-2180kW (2964bhp) AS Bergens Mek Verksteder-Norway Normo KVMB-8 2 x Vee 4 Stroke 8 Cy. 250 x 300 each-1460kW (1985bhp) AS Bergens Mek Verksteder-Norway AuxGen: 2 x 1200kW 220/440V 60Hz a.c, 1 x 880kW 220/440V 60Hz a.c Thrusters: 1 Thwart. CP thruster (f) Fuel: 35.0 (d.f.) 392.0 (r.f.) 33.0pd
9483126 *C6YZ5* -	**SEABOURN QUEST** **Seabourn Cruise Line Ltd** - *Nassau* *Bahamas* MMSI: 311038900 Official number: 9000368	**32,346** 10,532 5,000	Class: RI	**2011**-05 **T. Mariotti SpA — Genova** Yd No: 64 **2011**-05 **Shipyard 'Viktor Lenac' dd — Rijeka** (Hull) Loa 198.19 (BB) Br ex - Dght 6.400 Lbp 169.19 Br md 26.00 Dpth 11.85 Welded, 1 dk	**(A37A2PC) Passenger/Cruise** Passengers: berths: 450	**4 diesel electric oil engines** driving 4 gen. each 5536kW 6600V a.c Connecting to 2 elec. motors driving 2 FP propellers Total Power: 24,000kW (32,632hp) 19.0kn Wartsila 12V32 1 x Vee 4 Stroke 12 Cy. 320 x 400 6000kW (8158bhp) Wartsila Finland Oy-Finland Wartsila 12V32 2 x Vee 4 Stroke 12 Cy. 320 x 400 each-6000kW (8158bhp) Wartsila Finland Oy-Finland Thrusters: 1 Tunnel thruster (f)
9417098 *C6YA5* -	**SEABOURN SOJOURN** **Seabourn Cruise Line Ltd** - SatCom: Inmarsat C 431100744 *Nassau* *Bahamas* MMSI: 311027100 Official number: 9000325	**32,346** 10,532 5,000	Class: RI	**2010**-04 **T. Mariotti SpA — Genova** Yd No: 63 Loa 198.19 (BB) Br ex - Dght 6.700 Lbp 169.19 Br md 26.00 Dpth 11.85 Welded	**(A37A2PC) Passenger/Cruise** Passengers: cabins: 225; berths: 462	**4 diesel electric oil engines** driving 4 gen. each 5536kW 6600V a.c Connecting to 2 elec. motors driving 2 CP propellers Total Power: 24,000kW (32,632hp) 19.0kn Wartsila 12V32 2 x Vee 4 Stroke 12 Cy. 320 x 400 each-6000kW (8158bhp) Wartsila Finland Oy-Finland Thrusters: 2 Tunnel thruster (f)

8807997 *C6FR4* -	**SEABOURN SPIRIT** - **Star Voyager Ltd** - SatCom: Inmarsat B 331108310 *Nassau* *Bahamas* MMSI: 311083000 Official number: 8000343	**9,975** 3,023 800	Class: NV	**1989-11 Schichau Seebeckwerft AG — Bremerhaven** Yd No: 1070 Loa 133.80 (BB) Br ex 20.50 Dght 5.170 Lbp 112.40 Br md 19.00 Dpth 12.40 Welded, 5 dks plus 4 superstructure dks	**(A37A2PC) Passenger/Cruise** Passengers: cabins: 106; berths: 208 Ice Capable	**4 oil engines** with clutches & dr geared to sc. shafts driving 2 CP propellers Total Power: 7,280kW (9,898hp) 16.0kn Normo KVMB-12 2 x Vee 4 Stroke 12 Cy. 250 x 300 each-2180kW (2964bhp) Bergen Diesel AS-Norway Normo KVMB-8 2 x Vee 4 Stroke 8 Cy. 250 x 300 each-1460kW (1985bhp) Bergen Diesel AS-Norway AuxGen: 2 x 1200kW 220/440V 60Hz a.c, 1 x 880kW 220/440V 60Hz a.c Thrusters: 1 Thwart. CP thruster (f) Fuel: 35.0 (d.f.) 392.0 (r.f.) 33.0pd
9436070 *9HA2412* -	**SEABOXER III** *ex Viking Kestrel -2010* **Melody Investment & Financing Inc** Thenamaris (Ships Management) Inc *Valletta* *Malta* MMSI: 248560000 Official number: 9436070	**18,485** 10,282 23,695 T/cm 38.0	Class: GL	**2010-06 Guangzhou Wenchong Shipyard Co Ltd — Guangzhou GD** Yd No: 361 Loa 176.84 (BB) Br ex - Dght 10.900 Lbp 166.40 Br md 27.40 Dpth 14.30 Welded, 1 dk	**(A33A2CC) Container Ship (Fully Cellular)** TEU 1740 C Ho 700 TEU C Dk 1040 TEU incl 300 ref C. Compartments: 5 Cell Ho, ER Cranes: 2x45t	**1 oil engine** driving 1 FP propeller Total Power: 16,660kW (22,651hp) 20.6kn MAN-B&W 7S60MC-C 1 x 2 Stroke 7 Cy. 600 x 2400 16660kW (22651bhp) Hudong Heavy Machinery Co Ltd-China AuxGen: 3 x 1520kW 450V 60Hz a.c Thrusters: 1 Tunnel thruster (f) Fuel: 170.0 (d.f.) 1700.0 (r.f.)
9288734 *9HZS7* -	**SEABRAVERY** - **Sea Gain Marine Co Ltd** Thenamaris (Ships Management) Inc *Valletta* *Malta* MMSI: 215782000 Official number: 9089	**57,296** 32,526 105,042 T/cm 82.0	Class: LR ✠**100A1** SS 01/2010 Double Hull oil tanker ESP *IWS LI SPM Ice Class 1C FS at draught of 15.253m Max/min draught fwd 15.253/6.24m Max/min draught aft 15.253/8.36m **ShipRight** (SDA, FDA Plus, CM) ✠**LMC** **UMS IGS** Eq.Ltr: T†; Cable: 715.0/87.0 U3 (a)	**2005-01 Hyundai Samho Heavy Industries Co Ltd — Samho** Yd No: S212 Loa 244.00 (BB) Br ex 42.04 Dght 14.900 Lbp 234.02 Br md 42.00 Dpth 21.00 Welded, 1 dk	**(A13A2TW) Crude/Oil Products Tanker** Double Hull (13F) Liq: 118,084; Liq (Oil): 118,084 Compartments: 12 Wing Ta, 2 Wing Slop Ta, ER 3 Cargo Pump (s): 3x3000m^3/hr Manifold: Bow/CM: 114.4m Ice Capable	**1 oil engine** driving 1 FP propeller Total Power: 11,324kW (15,396hp) 14.5kn B&W 6S60MC 1 x 2 Stroke 6 Cy. 600 x 2292 11324kW (15396bhp) Hyundai Heavy Industries Co Ltd-South Korea AuxGen: 3 x 780kW 440/220V 60Hz a.c Boilers: AuxB (Comp) 8.0kgf/cm^2 (7.8bar), WTAuxB (o.f.) 18.3kgf/cm^2 (17.9bar) Fuel: 2880.0 (r.f.)
7701495 *HSB2138* -	**SEABREEZ EXPRESS** *ex Seatran Express -2012 ex Sea Hawk 3 -1990* *ex Sea Hawk -1990* **PP Marine Travel Co Ltd** - *Bangkok* *Thailand* Official number: 331001163	**388** 248 29		**1977-04 Mitsubishi Heavy Industries Ltd. — Shimonoseki** Yd No: 784 Loa 45.01 Br ex 7.83 Dght 1.250 Lbp 41.00 Br md 7.79 Dpth 3.92 Welded, 1 dk	**(A37B2PS) Passenger Ship** Hull Material: Aluminium Alloy Passengers: 290	**2 oil engines** geared to sc. shafts driving 2 FP propellers Total Power: 3,236kW (4,400hp) 26.5kn M.T.U. 16V652TB81 2 x Vee 4 Stroke 16 Cy. 190 x 230 each-1618kW (2200bhp) Ikegai Tekkosho-Japan
9143312 *V3QG9* -	**SEABREEZE** *ex Tien Hau -2011 ex Brother Ace -2003* **Trans Holdings Overseas SA** Trans-Service Maritime Agency Ltd *Belize City* *Belize* MMSI: 312256000 Official number: 361130106	**11,478** 6,091 18,469 T/cm 28.8	Class: BV (NK)	**1996-02 Cheunggu Marine Industry Co Ltd — Ulsan** Yd No: 1089 Loa 145.00 (BB) Br ex - Dght 9.065 Lbp 133.50 Br md 24.00 Dpth 12.80 Welded, 1 dk	**(A31A2GX) General Cargo Ship** Grain: 22,695; Bale: 21,106 Compartments: 4 Ho, ER 4 Ha: (11.7 x 12.6) (18.2 x 14.0) (20.3 x 14.0) (16.8 x 14.0)ER Cranes: 3x25t	**1 oil engine** driving 1 FP propeller Total Power: 4,891kW (6,650hp) 14.7kn B&W 7S35MC 1 x 2 Stroke 7 Cy. 350 x 1400 4891kW (6650bhp) Ssangyong Heavy Industries Co Ltd-South Korea AuxGen: 2 x 400kW 60Hz a.c Fuel: 125.0 (d.f.) 862.0 (r.f.)
9343986 *9HA3104* -	**SEABREEZE** *ex Freja Fionia -2012* **Silene Shipping Ltd** Thenamaris (Ships Management) Inc *Valletta* *Malta* MMSI: 229045000 Official number: 9343986	**31,433** 14,001 53,714 T/cm 54.3	Class: NK	**2007-07 Shin Kurushima Dockyard Co. Ltd. — Onishi** Yd No: 5392 Loa 185.93 (BB) Br ex 32.23 Dght 13.025 Lbp 179.95 Br md 32.20 Dpth 19.67 Welded, 1 dk	**(A13B2TP) Products Tanker** Double Hull (13F) Liq: 56,767; Liq (Oil): 60,000 Cargo Heating Coils Compartments: 12 Wing Ta, 2 Wing Slop Ta, ER 4 Cargo Pump (s): 4x1000m^3/hr Manifold: Bow/CM: 91.7m	**1 oil engine** driving 1 FP propeller Total Power: 10,620kW (14,439hp) 15.8kn Mitsubishi 6UEC60LS 1 x 2 Stroke 6 Cy. 600 x 2200 10620kW (14439bhp) Kobe Hatsudoki KK-Japan AuxGen: 3 x 700kW a.c Fuel: 180.0 (d.f.) 1887.0 (r.f.)
8972273 *V3RT5* -	**SEABREEZE I** *ex Seabreeze -2011 ex Sibriz -2008* *ex Seabreeze -2004 ex Volzhskiy-25 -2003* **Saluta Shipping Ltd** Kent Shipping & Chartering Ltd *Belize City* *Belize* MMSI: 312411000 Official number: 141120199	**4,992** 2,364 5,354	Class: RS (RR)	**1988-10 Navashinskiy Sudostroitelnyy Zavod 'Oka' — Navashino** Yd No: 1027 Loa 138.30 Br ex 16.70 Dght 3.810 Lbp 135.00 Br md 16.50 Dpth 5.50 Welded, 1 dk	**(A31A2GX) General Cargo Ship** Grain: 9,358; Bale: 9,358 Compartments: 2 Ho, ER 2 Ha: 2 (28.8 x 13.3)ER Ice Capable	**2 oil engines** driving 2 FP propellers Total Power: 1,766kW (2,402hp) 10.6kn Dvigatel Revolyutsii 6CHRN36/45 2 x 4 Stroke 6 Cy. 360 x 450 each-883kW (1201bhp) Zavod "Dvigatel Revolyutsii"-Gorkiy
8657615 *V4OH* -	**SEABRIDGE** *ex LCU 1618 -2007* **Sea Bridge (St Kitts & Nevis) Inc** - *Charlestown* *St Kitts & Nevis* MMSI: 341370000 Official number: SKN 1001370	**224** 67 -		**1959-06 Gunderson Brothers Engineering Corp — Portland OR** Loa - Br ex - Dght - Lbp - Br md - Dpth - Welded, 1 dk	**(A35D2RL) Landing Craft** Bow ramp (centre)	**1 oil engine** driving 1 Propeller
8657627 *V4AK* -	**SEABRIDGE 2** *ex LCU 1649 -2008* **Sea Bridge (St Kitts & Nevis) Inc** - *Charlestown* *St Kitts & Nevis* MMSI: 341689000 Official number: SKN1001689	**182** 55 -		**1971-02 Defoe Shipbuilding Co. — Bay City, Mi** Loa - Br ex - Dght - Lbp - Br md - Dpth - Welded, 1 dk	**(A35D2RL) Landing Craft** Bow ramp (centre)	**1 oil engine** driving 1 Propeller
7908237 *WDC4069* -	**SEABROOKE** - **Angel Pacific Fisheries Inc** - *Kodiak, AK* *United States of America* MMSI: 367018620 Official number: 614410	*198* 134 -		**1980-05 Mitchel Duane Phares — Los Angeles, La** Yd No: 34 Loa 33.38 Br ex 9.15 Dght 3.536 Lbp 30.48 Br md - Dpth 4.14 Welded, 1 dk	**(B11B2FV) Fishing Vessel** Compartments: 4 Ho, ER Cranes: 1	**2 oil engines** driving 2 FP propellers Total Power: 764kW (1,038hp) Caterpillar 3412TA 2 x Vee 4 Stroke 12 Cy. 137 x 152 each-382kW (519bhp) Caterpillar Tractor Co-USA
9319507 *V7GU6* -	**SEABULK ADVANTAGE** - **SEACOR Offshore (Marshall Islands) Ltd** Seabulk Offshore Dubai Inc *Majuro* *Marshall Islands* MMSI: 538002175 Official number: 2175	**1,677** 503 1,511	Class: BV (AB)	**2004-09 Fujian Southeast Shipyard — Fuzhou FJ** (Hull) **2004-09 Jaya Shipbuilding & Engineering Pte Ltd — Singapore** Yd No: 841 Loa 59.25 Br ex - Dght 4.960 Lbp 52.20 Br md 14.95 Dpth 6.10 Welded, 1 dk	**(B21B20A) Anchor Handling Tug Supply** Passengers: berths: 24	**2 oil engines** reduction geared to sc. shafts driving 2 CP propellers Total Power: 3,542kW (4,816hp) 11.0kn Caterpillar 3516B-TA 2 x Vee 4 Stroke 16 Cy. 170 x 190 each-1771kW (2408bhp) Caterpillar Inc-USA AuxGen: 3 x 315kW 415/220V 50Hz a.c Thrusters: 1 Thwart. CP thruster (f) Fuel: 450.0 (d.f.)
9267039 *A8BR7* -	**SEABULK AFRICA** - **Seabulk Offshore LLC** SEACOR Offshore Dubai LLC *Monrovia* *Liberia* MMSI: 636011843 Official number: 11843	**2,150** 997 3,350	Class: BV (NV)	**2003-01 SIMEK AS — Flekkefjord** Yd No: 103 Loa 71.90 Br ex 16.03 Dght 5.810 Lbp 66.00 Br md 16.00 Dpth 7.00 Welded, 1 dk	**(B21A20S) Platform Supply Ship** Double Hull	**2 oil engines** reduction geared to sc. shafts driving 2 CP propellers Total Power: 4,010kW (5,452hp) 12.0kn Bergens KRMB-9 2 x 4 Stroke 9 Cy. 250 x 300 each-2005kW (2726bhp) Rolls Royce Marine AS-Norway AuxGen: 2 x 1280kW 440V 60Hz a.c, 2 x 260kW 440V 60Hz a.c Thrusters: 2 Thwart. CP thruster (a); 2 Thwart. CP thruster (f)
9321146 *V7HL2* -	**SEABULK ANGOLA** - **Seabulk Offshore Vessel Holdings Inc** Seabulk Offshore Dubai Inc *Majuro* *Marshall Islands* MMSI: 538002248 Official number: 2248	**1,323** 397 752	Class: BV	**2005-05 PT Nanindah Mutiara Shipyard — Batam** Yd No: T130 Loa 49.50 Br ex - Dght 5.750 Lbp - Br md 15.00 Dpth 6.75 Welded, 1 dk	**(B32A2ST) Tug**	**2 oil engines** geared to sc. shafts driving 2 Z propellers Total Power: 5,940kW (8,076hp) 14.0kn MaK 9M25 2 x 4 Stroke 9 Cy. 255 x 400 each-2970kW (4038bhp) Caterpillar Motoren GmbH & Co. KG-Germany AuxGen: 3 x 500kW 415/230V 50Hz a.c Thrusters: 1 Tunnel thruster (f)

9303508 **SEABULK ANGRA**
PPQF
\- **SEACOR Offshore do Brasil Ltda**
Seabulk International Inc
SatCom: Inmarsat C 4710000121
Rio de Janeiro *Brazil*
MMSI: 710000720
Official number: 3810513211

2,160 Class: AB
1,002
3,250

2005-01 Aker Promar SA — Niteroi Yd No: PRO-11
Loa 71.90 Br ex 16.44 Dght 5.900
Lbp 66.80 Br md 16.00 Dpth 7.00
Welded, 1 dk

(B21A2OS) Platform Supply Ship
Cranes: 1x30t

2 oil engines reduction geared to sc. shafts driving 2 CP propellers
Total Power: 4,010kW (5,452hp) 12.0kn
Bergens KRMB-9
2 x 4 Stroke 9 Cy. 250 x 300 each-2005kW (2726bhp)
Rolls Royce Marine AS-Norway
AuxGen: 2 x 260kW a.c, 2 x 1280kW a.c
Thrusters: 2 Tunnel thruster (f); 1 Tunnel thruster (a)

9131371 **SEABULK ARCTIC**
WCY7054 *ex* HMI Cape Lookout Shoals *-2001*
\- *ex* Makronissos *-1998*
Lightship Tankers IV LLC
Seabulk Tankers Inc
SatCom: Inmarsat B 336682610
Port Everglades, FL *United States of America*
MMSI: 366826000
Official number: 1072069

30,415 Class: AB
11,125
46,103
T/cm
52.5

1998-09 Newport News Shipbuilding — Newport News, Va Yd No: 649C
Loa 183.00 (BB) Br ex - Dght 12.216
Lbp 174.30 Br md 32.20 Dpth 19.15
Welded, 1 dk

(A13B2TP) Products Tanker
Double Hull (13F)
Liq: 52,787; Liq (Oil): 52,787
Cargo Heating Coils
Compartments: 14 Wing Ta, ER, 2 Wing Slop Ta
7 Cargo Pump (s): 3x1400m³/hr, 4x494m³/hr
Manifold: Bow/CM: 93.1m

1 oil engine driving 1 FP propeller
Total Power: 8,056kW (10,953hp) 14.0kn
B&W 6L60MC
1 x 2 Stroke 6 Cy. 600 x 1944 8056kW (10953bhp)
Kawasaki Heavy Industries Ltd-Japan
Fuel: 241.9 (d.f.) (Heating Coils) 1449.2 (r.f.) 31.0pd

9191096 **SEABULK ARIZONA**
WDE4781
\- **Wilmington Trust Co, as Trustee**
Seabulk Offshore LLC
Miami, FL *United States of America*
MMSI: 366750490
Official number: 1066216

1,099 Class: AB
329
2,108

1998-07 Halter Marine, Inc. — Lockport, La Yd No: 1790
Loa 62.48 Br ex 14.02 Dght 4.420
Lbp 62.00 Br md 13.80 Dpth 5.18
Welded, 1 dk

(B21A2OS) Platform Supply Ship

2 oil engines reverse reduction geared to sc. shafts driving 2 FP propellers
Total Power: 3,090kW (4,202hp) 11.0kn
Caterpillar 3516B-TA
2 x Vee 4 Stroke 16 Cy. 170 x 190 each-1545kW (2101bhp)
Caterpillar Inc-USA
AuxGen: 2 x 105kW 440/220V 60Hz a.c
Thrusters: 1 Retract. directional thruster (f)

9267376 **SEABULK ASIA**
V7QK2 *completed as* Active Princess *-2003*
\- **Cypress Ckor LLC**
Seabulk Offshore Dubai Inc
Majuro *Marshall Islands*
MMSI: 538003381
Official number: 3381

2,148 Class: BV (NV)
1,005
3,310

2003-09 SC Aker Tulcea SA — Tulcea (Hull) Yd No: 297
2003-09 Brattvaag Skipsverft AS — Brattvaag Yd No: 84
Loa 72.00 Br ex 16.03 Dght 5.910
Lbp 66.80 Br md 16.00 Dpth 7.00
Welded, 1 dk

(B21A2OS) Platform Supply Ship

2 oil engines reduction geared to sc. shafts driving 2 CP propellers
Total Power: 4,010kW (5,452hp) 12.0kn
Bergens KRMB-9
2 x 4 Stroke 9 Cy. 250 x 300 each-2005kW (2726bhp)
Rolls Royce Marine AS-Norway
AuxGen: 2 x 230kW 440V 60Hz a.c, 2 x 1280kW 440V 60Hz a.c
Thrusters: 2 Tunnel thruster (f); 1 Tunnel thruster (a)

9287405 **SEABULK BADAMYAR**
V7MA8
\- **Seabulk Overseas Transport Inc**
Seabulk Offshore Dubai Inc
Majuro *Marshall Islands*
MMSI: 538002830
Official number: 2830

1,041 Class: BV
312
674

2003-03 PT Nanindah Mutiara Shipyard — Batam Yd No: T102
Loa 49.00 Br ex - Dght 3.700
Lbp 45.68 Br md 13.20 Dpth 5.80
Welded, 1 dk

(B21B20A) Anchor Handling Tug Supply

2 oil engines reduction geared to sc. shafts driving 2 Directional propellers
Total Power: 2,880kW (3,916hp) 11.0kn
Wartsila 8L20
2 x 4 Stroke 8 Cy. 200 x 280 each-1440kW (1958bhp)
Wartsila Finland Oy-Finland
AuxGen: 3 x 190kW 440/230V 60Hz a.c
Thrusters: 1 Tunnel thruster (f)

9292072 **SEABULK BRASIL**
PPQG
\- **SEACOR Offshore do Brasil Ltda**
Seabulk International Inc
SatCom: Inmarsat C 471000099
Rio de Janeiro *Brazil*
MMSI: 710000490
Official number: 3810512362

2,160 Class: AB
973
3,250

2004-10 Aker Promar SA — Niteroi Yd No: PRO-10
Loa 71.90 Br ex 16.44 Dght 5.900
Lbp 66.80 Br md 16.00 Dpth 7.00
Welded, 1 dk

(B21A2OS) Platform Supply Ship
Cranes: 1x30t

2 oil engines reduction geared to sc. shafts driving 2 CP propellers
Total Power: 4,016kW (5,460hp) 12.0kn
Bergens KRMB-9
2 x 4 Stroke 9 Cy. 250 x 300 each-2008kW (2730bhp)
Rolls Royce Marine AS-Norway
AuxGen: 2 x 1280kW 60Hz a.c, 2 x 260kW 60Hz a.c
Thrusters: 2 Tunnel thruster (f); 1 Tunnel thruster (a)

8964408 **SEABULK CARMEN**
WDC3918 *ex* C/Centurion *-2005*
\- **Seabulk Offshore LLC**
SEACOR Marine LLC
Miami, FL *United States of America*
MMSI: 366756040
Official number: 1065310

824
247
1,219

1998-09 Houma Fabricators Inc — Houma LA Yd No: 114
Loa 57.90 Br ex - Dght 3.870
Lbp 53.00 Br md 12.80 Dpth 4.57
Welded, 1 dk

(B21A2OS) Platform Supply Ship

2 oil engines reduction geared to sc. shafts driving 2 FP propellers
Total Power: 1,940kW (2,638hp) 10.0kn
Caterpillar 3512
2 x Vee 4 Stroke 12 Cy. 170 x 190 each-970kW (1319bhp)
Caterpillar Inc-USA
AuxGen: 2 x 105kW a.c
Thrusters: 1 Tunnel thruster (f)

7816551 **SEABULK CHALLENGE**
KNJL *ex* HMI Petrochem *-2001* *ex* OMI Hudson *-1996*
\- *ex* Ogden Hudson *-1986*
Seabulk Petroleum Transport Inc
Seabulk Tankers Inc
SatCom: Inmarsat C 430310410
Port Everglades, FL *United States of America*
MMSI: 303104000
Official number: 642151

29,763 Class: AB
16,905
49,636
T/cm
56.6

1981-12 Avondale Shipyards Inc. — Avondale, La Yd No: 2319
Conv to DH-2008
Loa 191.81 (BB) Br ex - Dght 13.190
Lbp 185.93 Br md 32.26 Dpth 18.29
Welded, 1 dk

(A12B2TR) Chemical/Products Tanker
Double Hull (13F)
Liq: 46,752; Liq (Oil): 57,370
Cargo Heating Coils
Compartments: 20 Ta, ER, 2 Wing Slop Ta
18 Cargo Pump (s): 2x335m³/hr, 2x305m³/hr, 4x270m³/hr, 1x255m³/hr, 1x205m³/hr, 2x170m³/hr, 6x140m³/hr
Manifold: Bow/CM: 89m

2 oil engines reverse reduction geared to sc. shaft driving 1 FP propeller
Total Power: 10,520kW (14,302hp) 16.3kn
B&W 8K45GF
2 x 2 Stroke 8 Cy. 450 x 900 each-5260kW (7151bhp)
Hitachi Zosen Corp-Japan
AuxGen: 4 x 800kW
Fuel: 3437.0 (r.f.) 42.0pd

9183001 **SEABULK GALAXIE**
\- *ex* Galaxie *-2012*
\- **Seabulk Offshore Operators Nigeria Ltd**
\-
Lagos *Nigeria*
MMSI: 657915000
Official number: SR1932

1,183 Class: AB
355
1,637

1997-11 Houma Fabricators Inc — Houma LA Yd No: 113
Loa 66.29 Br ex - Dght 4.108
Lbp 63.14 Br md 13.41 Dpth 4.87
Welded, 1 dk

(B21A2OS) Platform Supply Ship

2 oil engines reverse reduction geared to sc. shafts driving 2 FP propellers
Total Power: 2,868kW (3,900hp) 10.0kn
EMD (Electro-Motive) 16-645-E6
2 x Vee 2 Stroke 16 Cy. 230 x 254 each-1434kW (1950bhp)
General Motors Corp.Electro-Motive Div.-La Grange
AuxGen: 2 x 150kW 440/220V 60Hz a.c
Thrusters: 1 Tunnel thruster (f); 1 Tunnel thruster (a)
Fuel: 280.0 (d.f.)

9274680 **SEABULK IPANEMA**
PR5543 *ex* Norskan Ipanema *-2004*
\- **SEACOR Offshore do Brasil Ltda**
Agencia Maritima Offshore Continental Ltda
SatCom: Inmarsat C 471000457
Rio de Janeiro *Brazil*

319 Class: NV
95
294

2002-03 Transnave Estaleiros Reparos eConstrucao Naval S/A Yd No: 12
Loa 36.60 Br ex - Dght 3.150
Lbp 32.48 Br md 8.70 Dpth 3.90
Welded, 1 dk

(B21B20T) Offshore Tug/Supply Ship

2 oil engines reduction geared to sc. shafts driving 2 FP propellers
Total Power: 1,864kW (2,534hp)
Caterpillar 3512TA
2 x Vee 4 Stroke 12 Cy. 170 x 190 each-932kW (1267bhp)
Caterpillar Inc-USA
AuxGen: 2 x a.c

9198496 **SEABULK KANSAS**
WDE4694
\- **General Electric Capital Corp**
Seabulk Offshore LLC
Miami, FL *United States of America*
MMSI: 366928000
Official number: 1071486

1,099 Class: AB
329
2,108

1998-12 Halter Marine, Inc. — Lockport, La Yd No: 1792
Loa 62.48 Br ex 14.02 Dght 4.420
Lbp 62.00 Br md 14.00 Dpth 5.18
Welded, 1 dk

(B21A2OS) Platform Supply Ship

2 oil engines reduction geared to sc. shafts driving 2 FP propellers
Total Power: 3,090kW (4,202hp) 11.0kn
Caterpillar 3516B-TA
2 x Vee 4 Stroke 16 Cy. 170 x 190 each-1545kW (2101bhp)
Caterpillar Inc-USA
AuxGen: 2 x 99kW 60Hz a.c
Thrusters: 1 Retract. directional thruster (f)

7423847 **SEABULK KNIGHT**
\- *ex* GMMOS Knight *-1997* *ex* Majid *-1993*
\- *ex* SML Seladang *-1979*
\-
\-

240 Class: (AB)
72
\-

1975-06 Singapore Slipway & Engineering Co. Pte Ltd — Singapore Yd No: 69
Loa 28.81 Br ex 8.89 Dght 3.639
Lbp 28.05 Br md 8.82 Dpth 4.25
Welded, 1 dk

(B32A2ST) Tug

2 oil engines reverse reduction geared to sc. shafts driving 2 FP propellers
Total Power: 1,552kW (2,110hp) 12.0kn
Caterpillar 3512TA
2 x Vee 4 Stroke 12 Cy. 170 x 190 each-776kW (1055bhp) (new engine 1982)
Caterpillar Tractor Co-USA
AuxGen: 2 x 70kW
Fuel: 127.4 (d.f.)

9324227 **SEABULK LUANDA**
V7IU8
\- **Seabulk Offshore Vessel Holdings Inc**
Seabulk Offshore Dubai Inc
Majuro *Marshall Islands*
MMSI: 538002456
Official number: 2456

2,063 Class: BV
619
1,886

2005-08 PT Nanindah Mutiara Shipyard — Batam Yd No: T133
Loa 65.20 Br ex - Dght 5.800
Lbp 63.99 Br md 15.00 Dpth 6.80
Welded, 1 dk

(B21B20A) Anchor Handling Tug Supply

2 oil engines reduction geared to sc. shafts driving 2 CP propellers
Total Power: 5,884kW (8,000hp) 12.0kn
MaK 9M25
2 x 4 Stroke 9 Cy. 255 x 400 each-2942kW (4000bhp)
Caterpillar Motoren GmbH & Co. KG-Germany
AuxGen: 2 x 1200kW 440/230V 60Hz a.c, 2 x 580kW 440/230V 60Hz a.c
Thrusters: 2 Tunnel thruster (f); 1 Tunnel thruster (a)

IMO / Call sign	Name / Owner	Tonnage	Class	Builder / Dimensions	Type	Machinery
8973629 *J7ABI* -	**SEABULK MONROE** **Seabulk Offshore LLC** Seabulk Offshore Dubai Inc *Portsmouth* *Dominica* MMSI: 325500010	**250** 75 242	Class: BV	**1993-01 Breaux Brothers Enterprises, Inc. — Loreauville, La** Yd No: 1207 Loa 39.92 Br ex - Dght 2.400 Lbp - Br md 8.40 Dpth 3.52 Welded, 1 dk	**(B21A20C) Crew/Supply Vessel** Hull Material: Aluminium Alloy Passengers: unberthed: 47	**4 oil engines** geared to sc. shafts driving 4 FP propellers Total Power: 2,248kW (3,056hp) 19.0kn Caterpillar 3412TA 4 x Vee 4 Stroke 12 Cy. 137 x 152 each-562kW (764bhp) Caterpillar Inc-USA AuxGen: 2 x 50kW 208/120V 60Hz a.c
9203071 *WDF9501* -	**SEABULK NEBRASKA** **Banc of America Leasing & Capital LLC** - *Miami, FL* *United States of America* MMSI: 338446000 Official number: 1073983	**1,099** 329 2,108	Class: AB	**1999-01 Halter Marine, Inc. — Lockport, La** Yd No: 1799 Loa 62.50 Br ex - Dght 4.420 Lbp 62.00 Br md 14.00 Dpth 5.20 Welded, 1 dk	**(B21A20S) Platform Supply Ship**	**2 oil engines** reduction geared to sc. shafts driving 2 CP propellers Total Power: 3,090kW (4,202hp) 11.0kn Caterpillar 3516B 2 x Vee 4 Stroke 16 Cy. 170 x 190 each-1545kW (2101bhp) Caterpillar Inc-USA AuxGen: 2 x 105kW 60Hz a.c Thrusters: 1 Retract. directional thruster (f) Fuel: 408.4 (d.f.)
8964666 *5NSX2* -	**SEABULK NIGER** *ex* Blair Mccall *-2009* **Seabulk Offshore Operators Nigeria Ltd** - *Lagos* *Nigeria* MMSI: 657547000 Official number: SR1468	**376** 112 -		**1987-11 Gulf Craft Inc — Patterson LA** Yd No: 300 Loa 47.24 Br ex - Dght 2.410 Lbp 42.36 Br md 9.14 Dpth 3.24 Welded, 1 dk	**(B21A20C) Crew/Supply Vessel** Hull Material: Aluminium Alloy	**5 oil engines** reverse reduction geared to sc. shafts driving 5 FP propellers Total Power: 2,355kW (3,200hp) 23.0kn Cummins KTA-19-M 5 x 4 Stroke 6 Cy. 159 x 159 each-471kW (640bhp) Cummins Engine Co Inc-USA AuxGen: 4 x 40kW a.c
9287390 *V7MA9* -	**SEABULK NILAR** **Seabulk Overseas Transport Inc** Seabulk Offshore Dubai Inc *Majuro* *Marshall Islands* MMSI: 538002831 Official number: 2831	**1,034** 310 749	Class: BV	**2003-02 PT Nanindah Mutiara Shipyard — Batam** Yd No: T101 Loa 49.00 Br ex - Dght 3.700 Lbp 45.68 Br md 13.20 Dpth 5.80 Welded, 1 dk	**(B21A20S) Platform Supply Ship**	**2 oil engines** reduction geared to sc. shafts driving 2 Directional propellers Total Power: 2,880kW (3,916hp) 12.0kn Wartsila 8L20 2 x 4 Stroke 8 Cy. 200 x 280 each-1440kW (1958bhp) Wartsila Finland Oy-Finland AuxGen: 3 x 190kW 440/230V 60Hz a.c Thrusters: 1 Tunnel thruster (f)
7807691 *5NSX* -	**SEABULK PENNINGTON** *ex* Seabulk Hawaii *-2008* *ex* Aleutian Command *-2008* **Seabulk Offshore Operators Nigeria Ltd** *Lagos* *Nigeria* Official number: SR1467	*663* 198 1,000	Class: AB	**1978-09 Quality Equipment Inc — Houma LA** Yd No: 148 Loa 54.87 Br ex - Dght 3.658 Lbp 51.85 Br md 11.60 Dpth 4.27 Welded, 1 dk	**(B34R2QY) Supply Tender**	**2 oil engines** driving 2 CP propellers Total Power: 2,206kW (3,000hp) 9.0kn Wichmann 5AXA 2 x 2 Stroke 5 Cy. 300 x 450 each-1103kW (1500bhp) Wichmann Motorfabrikk AS-Norway AuxGen: 2 x 99kW 450/225V 60Hz a.c Thrusters: 1 Thwart. FP thruster (f) Fuel: 277.0
8978411 *5NSX3* -	**SEABULK RAMOS** *ex* Jered Mccall *-2009* **Seabulk Offshore Operators Nigeria Ltd** - *Lagos* *Nigeria* Official number: SR1469	**390** 117 282		**1990-01 Gulf Craft Inc — Patterson LA** Yd No: 348 Loa 49.00 Br ex - Dght 2.000 Lbp 44.34 Br md 9.14 Dpth 3.24 Welded, 1 dk	**(B21A20C) Crew/Supply Vessel** Hull Material: Aluminium Alloy Passengers: unberthed: 56; cabins: 4	**6 oil engines** with clutches, flexible couplings & sr reverse geared to sc. shafts driving 6 FP propellers Total Power: 3,000kW (4,080hp) 21.0kn Cummins KTA-19-M 6 x 4 Stroke 6 Cy. 159 x 159 each-500kW (680bhp) Cummins Engine Co Inc-USA Fuel: 44.0 (d.f.) 12.6pd
7911088 *3FPG3* -	**SEABULK RAVEN** *ex* Red Raven *-1998* *ex* Far Sailor *-1993* *ex* Stad Sailor *-1986* **Translord Enterprises Inc** Hai Duong Co Ltd (HADUCO) *Panama* *Panama* MMSI: 355328000 Official number: 4309611	**1,608** 483 2,015	Class: NV	**1980-05 Ulstein Hatlo AS — Ulsteinvik** Yd No: 166 Loa 68.03 Br ex 14.71 Dght 5.946 Lbp 60.79 Br md 14.51 Dpth 6.91 Welded, 2 dks	**(B21B20A) Anchor Handling Tug Supply** Ice Capable	**4 oil engines** with clutches, flexible couplings & sr geared to sc. shafts driving 2 CP propellers Total Power: 7,768kW (10,560hp) 16.0kn Normo KVM-12 4 x Vee 4 Stroke 12 Cy. 250 x 300 each-1942kW (2640bhp) AS Bergens Mek Verksteder-Norway AuxGen: 2 x 1256kW 440V 60Hz a.c, 2 x 244kW 440V 60Hz a.c Thrusters: 2 Thwart. CP thruster (f); 1 Tunnel thruster (a) Fuel: 1000.0 (d.f.) 38.0pd
9269506 *V7QD9* -	**SEABULK SOUTH ATLANTIC** *ex* Troms Supporter *-2003* **Seabulk South Atlantic LLC** Seabulk Offshore Dubai Inc *Majuro* *Marshall Islands* MMSI: 538003339 Official number: 3339	*2,085* 766 2,100	Class: BV (NV)	**2003-05 SC Aker Braila SA — Braila** (Hull) **2003-05 Brevik Construction AS — Brevik** Yd No: 27 Loa 68.95 Br ex - Dght 6.000 Lbp 60.45 Br md 15.50 Dpth 7.00 Welded	**(B21B20A) Anchor Handling Tug Supply**	**2 oil engines** reduction geared to sc. shafts driving 2 CP propellers Total Power: 7,950kW (10,808hp) 13.0kn Bergens BRM-9 2 x 4 Stroke 9 Cy. 320 x 360 each-3975kW (5404bhp) Rolls Royce Marine AS-Norway AuxGen: 2 x 320kW 450V 60Hz a.c, 2 x 1600kW 450V 60Hz a.c Thrusters: 2 Tunnel thruster (f); 1 Tunnel thruster (a) Fuel: 839.0 (d.f.) 34.5pd
9117002 - -	**SEABULK ST. CHARLES** *ex* Royal Runner *-2003* **St Charles VZ LLC** Seabulk Offshore LLC *Las Piedras* *Venezuela* Official number: AMMT-2845	**309** 92 -		**1993-01 Breaux Bay Craft, Inc. — Loreauville, La** Yd No: 1656 Loa 46.32 Br ex - Dght 2.030 Lbp 42.36 Br md 9.14 Dpth 4.00 Welded, 1 dk	**(B21A20C) Crew/Supply Vessel** Hull Material: Aluminium Alloy Passengers: 72	**5 oil engines** geared to sc. shafts driving 5 FP propellers Total Power: 2,650kW (3,605hp) 22.0kn Caterpillar 3412TA 5 x Vee 4 Stroke 12 Cy. 137 x 152 each-530kW (721bhp) Caterpillar Inc-USA
9171228 *YYT4721* -	**SEABULK ST. FRANCES** *ex* Seabulk St. Francis *-1999* **North B Towing Inc** Inversiones Navol CA *Las Piedras* *Venezuela* MMSI: 775326000 Official number: AMMT-2664	**309** 92 -	Class: (AB)	**1996-11 Breaux Bay Craft, Inc. — Loreauville, La** Yd No: 1690 Loa 45.71 Br ex - Dght 2.190 Lbp 42.36 Br md 9.14 Dpth 3.80 Welded, 1 dk	**(B21A20C) Crew/Supply Vessel** Hull Material: Aluminium Alloy	**4 oil engines** reduction geared to sc. shafts driving 4 FP propellers Total Power: 3,280kW (4,460hp) 22.0kn Cummins KTA-38-M1 4 x Vee 4 Stroke 12 Cy. 159 x 159 each-820kW (1115bhp) (Re-engined 2006, refitted 2006) Cummins Engine Co Inc-USA AuxGen: 2 x 50kW a.c Fuel: 34.0
8973186 *YYT4720* -	**SEABULK ST. LANDRY** *ex* Marathon Runner *-2000* **North B Towing Inc** Inversiones Navol CA *Las Piedras* *Venezuela* MMSI: 775327000 Official number: AMMT-2663	**309** 92 -	Class: AB	**1996 Breaux Bay Craft, Inc. — Loreauville, La** Yd No: 1669 Loa 46.33 Br ex - Dght 2.200 Lbp 42.30 Br md 9.14 Dpth 3.81 Welded, 1 dk	**(B21A20C) Crew/Supply Vessel** Hull Material: Aluminium Alloy	**4 oil engines** reduction geared to sc. shafts driving 4 FP propellers Total Power: 809kW (1,100hp) 22.0kn G.M. (Detroit Diesel) 16V-92-TA 4 x Vee 2 Stroke 16 Cy. 123 x 127 General Motors Detroit DieselAllison Divn-USA AuxGen: 2 x 50kW
9117014 *YYT4722* -	**SEABULK ST. MARTIN** *ex* Massive Runner *-2000* **North B Towing Inc** Inversiones Navol CA *Las Piedras* *Venezuela* MMSI: 775328000 Official number: AMMT-2665	**309** 92 -	Class: (AB)	**1993-01 Breaux Bay Craft, Inc. — Loreauville, La** Yd No: 1667 Loa 46.32 Br ex - Dght 2.210 Lbp 42.37 Br md 9.14 Dpth 3.91 Welded, 1 dk	**(B21A20C) Crew/Supply Vessel** Hull Material: Aluminium Alloy	**4 oil engines** reverse reduction geared to sc. shafts driving 4 FP propellers Total Power: 3,280kW (4,460hp) 28.0kn Cummins KTA-38-M1 4 x Vee 4 Stroke 12 Cy. 159 x 159 each-820kW (1115bhp) (new engine 2007) Cummins Engine Co Inc-USA AuxGen: 2 x 50kW a.c Fuel: 50.0
8201143 *A6E2770* -	**SEABULK STAR** *ex* Shell Star *-2004* *ex* Seabulk Shell Star *-1999* *ex* Shell Star *-1997* *ex* GMMOS Horizon *-1995* *ex* C/Centurion *-1992* **Orient Oil Co Ltd** Orient Oil Co LLC *Sharjah* *United Arab Emirates* MMSI: 470577000 Official number: 6154	**579** 173 950	Class: AB	**1982-06 Houma Fabricators Inc — Houma LA** Yd No: 74 Loa 51.21 Br ex - Dght 3.682 Lbp 51.21 Br md 11.60 Dpth 4.35 Welded, 1 dk	**(B21A20S) Platform Supply Ship**	**2 oil engines** reverse reduction geared to sc. shafts driving 2 FP propellers Total Power: 1,368kW (1,860hp) 10.0kn G.M. (Detroit Diesel) 16V-149-NA 2 x Vee 2 Stroke 16 Cy. 146 x 146 each-684kW (930bhp) General Motors Detroit DieselAllison Divn-USA AuxGen: 2 x 75kW 225/440V Thrusters: 1 Thwart. FP thruster (f) Fuel: 272.6 (d.f.) 7.4pd
8136386 - -	**SEABULK TAURUS** *ex* Taurus *-1997* **Seabulk Taurus Inc** Seabulk Offshore International Inc	*146* 43 -	Class: (AB)	**1982-01 Gulf Marine Maintenance & Offshore Service Co (GMMOS) — Dubai** Yd No: 107 Loa 24.38 Br ex - Dght 2.688 Lbp 22.26 Br md 7.32 Dpth 2.90 Welded, 1 dk	**(B32A2ST) Tug**	**2 oil engines** reverse reduction geared to sc. shafts driving 2 FP propellers Total Power: 994kW (1,352hp) 9.0kn G.M. (Detroit Diesel) 12V-149 2 x Vee 2 Stroke 12 Cy. 146 x 146 each-497kW (676bhp) General Motors Detroit DieselAllison Divn-USA AuxGen: 2 x 40kW 208V 60Hz a.c Fuel: 138.0 (d.f.) 7.6pd

7912812 *H09648* -	**SEABULK TIMS I** *ex Tims-I -1999 launched as Petrobel I -1979* **Seabulk Tims Inc & Timsah Shipbuilding Co** Seabulk Offshore International Inc *Panama* Panama MMSI: 353023000 Official number: 1007280F	**1,424** 427 1,499	Class: AB	**1979**-12 **Imamura Zosen — Kure** Yd No: 258 Loa 70.10 Br ex - Dght 3.661 Lbp 66.43 Br md 16.16 Dpth 4.58 Welded, 1 dk	**(B21B20T) Offshore Tug/Supply Ship**	**2 oil engines** reverse reduction geared to sc. shafts driving 2 CP propellers Total Power: 3,310kW (4,500hp) 13.5kn MaK 6M453AK 2 x 4 Stroke 6 Cy. 320 x 420 each-1655kW (2250bhp) Ube Industries Ltd-Japan AuxGen: 2 x 215kW Thrusters: 1 Thwart. FP thruster (f) Fuel: 480.7
7816549 *KNJK* -	**SEABULK TRADER** *ex HMI Dynachem -2001* *ex OMI Dynachem -1996* *ex Ogden Dynachem -1985* **Seabulk Energy Transport Inc** Seabulk Tankers Inc SatCom: Inmarsat A 1542465 *Port Everglades, FL* United States of America MMSI: 303105000 Official number: 638899	**29,763** 16,257 49,990 T/cm 53.5	Class: AB	**1981**-09 **Avondale Shipyards Inc. — Avondale, La** Yd No: 2318 Conv to DH-2007 Loa 191.81 Br ex 32.29 Dght 13.180 Lbp 185.93 Br md 32.26 Dpth 18.29 Welded, 1 dk	**(A12B2TR) Chemical/Products Tanker** Double Hull (13F) Liq: 57,370; Liq (Oil): 57,370 Cargo Heating Coils Compartments: 20 Ta, ER 12 Cargo Pump (s): 2x355m³/hr, 2x305m³/hr, 2x270m³/hr, 1x255m³/hr, 1x205m³/hr, 1x170m³/hr, 3x140m³/hr Manifold: Bow/CM: 88.4m	**2 oil engines** sr geared to sc. shaft driving 1 FP propeller Total Power: 10,370kW (14,100hp) 16.3kn B&W 8K45GF 2 x 2 Stroke 8 Cy. 450 x 900 each-5185kW (7050bhp) Hitachi Zosen Corp-Japan AuxGen: 4 x 800kW Fuel: 3231.0 (r.f.)
9195523 *WCY6329* -	**SEABULK WISCONSIN** - **Banc of America Leasing & Capital LLC** Seabulk Offshore LLC *New Orleans, LA* United States of America MMSI: 366624000 Official number: 1069832	**1,099** 329 2,108	Class: AB	**1998**-10 **Halter Marine, Inc. — Lockport, La** Yd No: 1791 Loa 62.48 Br ex - Dght 4.420 Lbp 58.22 Br md 14.02 Dpth 5.18 Welded, 1 dk	**(B21A20S) Platform Supply Ship**	**2 oil engines** reverse reduction geared to sc. shafts driving 2 FP propellers Total Power: 3,090kW (4,202hp) 11.0kn Caterpillar 3516B 2 x Vee 4 Stroke 16 Cy. 170 x 190 each-1545kW (2101bhp) Caterpillar Inc-USA AuxGen: 2 x 105kW 60Hz a.c Thrusters: 1 Retract. directional thruster (f)
6803961 *5NTV3* -	**SEABULL 22** *ex Notre Dame -2011 ex Mare -2003* *ex Mare Serenitatis -2003* - - Nigeria	*631* 299 587	Class: (RI)	**1968** **Cant. Nav. Giuliano — Trieste** Yd No: 80 Loa 58.98 Br ex 9.00 Dght 4.014 Lbp 52.84 Br md 8.97 Dpth 4.75 Welded, 1 dk	**(B11A2FT) Trawler** Ins: 445 Compartments: 1 Ho (comb), ER 2 Ha: 2 (1.3 x 1.0)ER Cranes: 1x12t	**1 oil engine** geared to sc. shaft driving 1 FP propeller Total Power: 1,065kW (1,448hp) Deutz SBV6M628 1 x 4 Stroke 6 Cy. 240 x 280 1065kW (1448bhp) (new engine 1986) Kloeckner Humboldt Deutz AG-West Germany
9040340 - -	**SEACAPTURE** **f/v Seacapture Inc** - *Montauk, NY* United States of America Official number: 974233	*130* - -		**1991**-04 **Washburn & Doughty Associates Inc — East Boothbay ME** Yd No: 40 Loa 25.00 Br ex 6.70 Dght - Lbp - Br md - Dpth 2.89 Welded, 1 dk	**(B11B2FV) Fishing Vessel** Ins: 57	**1 oil engine** with clutches & sr geared to sc. shaft driving 1 FP propeller Total Power: 405kW (551hp) Caterpillar 3408TA 1 x Vee 4 Stroke 8 Cy. 137 x 152 405kW (551bhp) Caterpillar Inc-USA
7705130 *DQHS* -	**SEACAT** *ex Haffskattan -2008 ex Sundskattan -1993* *ex Skagen Express -1992* *ex Bornholm Express -1991 ex Steigtind -1986* **Michael Kopp** Peene-Werft GmbH *Rostock* Germany	**191** 66 30	Class: (GL) (NV)	**1977**-06 **Westermoen Hydrofoil AS — Alta** Yd No: 65 Converted From: Ferry (Passenger only)-2011 Loa 26.65 Br ex 9.02 Dght - Lbp 26.12 Br md - Dpth 2.73 Welded, 1 dk	**(X11A2YP) Yacht** Hull Material: Aluminium Alloy Passengers: unberthed: 166	**2 oil engines** geared to sc. shafts driving 2 FP propellers Total Power: 1,618kW (2,200hp) 26.0kn M.T.U. 12V493TY70 2 x Vee 4 Stroke 12 Cy. 175 x 205 each-809kW (1100bhp) MTU Friedrichshafen GmbH-Friedrichshafen
8717362 *DUH2331* -	**SEACAT 32** *ex Ocean Raider I -1998* *ex Bahtera Princess -1997 ex Intan Sari -1990* **ACG Joy Express Liner** - *Cebu* Philippines Official number: CEB1002187	**378** 114 48	Class: (KI) (NV)	**1988**-12 **Precision Marine Holding Pty Ltd — Fremantle WA** Yd No: 832 Loa 31.00 Br ex 13.10 Dght 1.700 Lbp 27.26 Br md 12.90 Dpth 3.78 Welded, 1 dk	**(A37B2PS) Passenger Ship** Hull Material: Aluminium Alloy Passengers: unberthed: 370	**2 oil engines** with clutches, flexible couplings & sr reverse geared to sc. shafts driving 2 FP propellers Total Power: 2,354kW (3,200hp) 27.0kn G.M. (Detroit Diesel) 16V-149-TI 2 x Vee 2 Stroke 16 Cy. 146 x 146 each-1177kW (1600bhp) General Motors Detroit DieselAllison Divn-USA AuxGen: 2 x 58kW 380V 50Hz a.c
9001538 - -	**SEACAT MOOREA** *ex Mandarin -2009 ex Ocean Flower -2004* *ex Avant -2002 ex Stena Lynx -1999* *ex Stena Sea Lynx -1996* - -	**3,231** 969 700	Class: (KR) (NV)	**1993**-06 **International Catamarans Pty Ltd — Hobart TAS** Yd No: 031 Loa 74.15 Br ex 26.00 Dght 2.610 Lbp 60.48 Br md 24.46 Dpth 7.23 Welded, 1 dk	**(A36A2PR) Passenger/Ro-Ro Ship (Vehicles)** Hull Material: Aluminium Alloy Passengers: unberthed: 582 Bow door/ramp Cars: 90	**4 oil engines** driving 4 Water jets Total Power: 16,188kW (22,008hp) 35.0kn Ruston 16RK270 4 x Vee 4 Stroke 16 Cy. 270 x 305 each-4047kW (5502bhp) Ruston Diesels Ltd.-Newton-le-Willows AuxGen: 4 x 124kW 240/415V 50Hz a.c Fuel: 28.3 (d.f.) 70.9pd
8322117 *UBYF6* -	**SEACHAMPION** *ex S d'Urville -2005 ex Sofrana d'Urville -2004* *ex Ajax -2003 ex Sofrana Bligh -2001* *ex Capitaine Bligh -2001 ex Ajax -2000* *ex Explorer -1999 ex Frisian Explorer -1987* *ex Samsun Express -1985* **Tranco-DV LLC** Transport-Forwarding Company JSC Kamchatka Lines *Vladivostok* Russia MMSI: 273330730	**3,949** 2,419 6,025	Class: RS (LR) ✠ Classed LR until 8/3/05	**1984**-11 **Scheepswerf en Machinefabriek de Groot & van Vliet B.V. — Bolnes** Yd No: 409 Loa 106.63 (BB) Br ex 18.09 Dght 6.590 Lbp 99.60 Br md 17.90 Dpth 8.51 Riveted\Welded, 2 dks	**(A31A2GX) General Cargo Ship** Grain: 8,149; Bale: 7,800 TEU 419 C Ho 142 TEU C Dk 277 TEU Compartments: 3 Ho, ER, 1 Tw Dk 3 Ha: (25.4 x 12.7)2 (18.7 x 12.7)ER Cranes: 2x63t Ice Capable	**1 oil engine** with flexible couplings & sr gearedto sc. shaft driving 1 CP propeller Total Power: 2,942kW (4,000hp) 14.5kn Werkspoor 6TM410 1 x 4 Stroke 6 Cy. 410 x 470 2942kW (4000bhp) Stork Werkspoor Diesel BV-Netherlands AuxGen: 1 x 499kW 380V 50Hz a.c, 3 x 224kW 380V 50Hz a.c Boilers: TOH (o.f.) 10.2kgf/cm² (10.0bar), TOH (ex.g.) 10.2kgf/cm² (10.0bar) Thrusters: 1 Thwart. FP thruster (f) Fuel: 466.0 (r.f.) 13.5pd
9314088 *9HA3125* -	**SEACHANCE** *ex Ruby River -2012 ex Ruby Queen -2004* **Atherstone Shipping Inc** Thenamaris (Ships Management) Inc *Valletta* Malta MMSI: 229172000 Official number: 9314088	**58,136** 31,909 107,081 T/cm 91.0	Class: AB	**2004**-10 **Koyo Dockyard Co Ltd — Mihara HS** Yd No: 2201 Loa 246.80 (BB) Br ex - Dght 14.790 Lbp 235.00 Br md 42.00 Dpth 21.30 Welded, 1 dk	**(A13A2TV) Crude Oil Tanker** Double Hull (13F) Liq: 116,632; Liq (Oil): 116,632 Cargo Heating Coils Compartments: 12 Wing Ta, 2 Wing Slop Ta, ER 3 Cargo Pump (s) Manifold: Bow/CM: 124m	**1 oil engine** driving 3 gen. each 925kW driving 1 FP propeller Total Power: 13,530kW (18,395hp) 14.5kn B&W 6S60MC-C 1 x 2 Stroke 6 Cy. 600 x 2400 13530kW (18395bhp) Mitsui Engineering & Shipbuilding CLtd-Japan AuxGen: 3 x 925kW a.c Fuel: 312.0 (d.f.) 3916.0 (r.f.)
9553139 *3EXM6* -	**SEACLIFF** **Luster Maritime SA** Shoei Kisen Kaisha Ltd SatCom: Inmarsat C 437047111 *Panama* Panama MMSI: 370471000 Official number: 4114910	**17,018** 10,109 28,343 T/cm 39.7	Class: NK	**2009**-12 **Imabari Shipbuilding Co Ltd — Marugame KG (Marugame Shipyard)** Yd No: 1546 Loa 169.37 (BB) Br ex - Dght 9.800 Lbp 160.40 Br md 27.20 Dpth 13.60 Welded, 1 dk	**(A21A2BC) Bulk Carrier** Grain: 37,320; Bale: 35,742 Compartments: 5 Ho, ER 5 Ha: ER Cranes: 4x30.5t	**1 oil engine** driving 1 FP propeller Total Power: 5,850kW (7,954hp) 14.0kn MAN-B&W 6S42MC 1 x 2 Stroke 6 Cy. 420 x 1764 5850kW (7954bhp) Makita Corp-Japan AuxGen: 3 x a.c Fuel: 1240.0
9570101 *VRME9* -	**SEACLIPPER** **Crawford Enterprises Inc** Valles Steamship (Canada) Inc *Hong Kong* Hong Kong MMSI: 477519100 Official number: HK-3855	**30,302** 14,058 48,554 T/cm 54.0	Class: NV	**2013**-10 **Guangzhou Shipyard International Co Ltd — Guangzhou GD** Yd No: 08130009 Loa 183.20 (BB) Br ex 32.50 Dght 12.320 Lbp 176.00 Br md 32.20 Dpth 18.20 Welded, 1 dk	**(A12B2TR) Chemical/Products Tanker** Double Hull (13F) Liq: 51,470; Liq (Oil): 51,470	**1 oil engine** driving 1 FP propeller Total Power: 9,960kW (13,542hp) 15.0kn MAN-B&W 6S50MC-C 1 x 2 Stroke 6 Cy. 500 x 2000 9960kW (13542bhp) Dalian Marine Diesel Co Ltd-China AuxGen: 3 x a.c
5425413 - -	**SEACLOSE** **Joseph Yambode & Co Ltd** - *Lagos* Nigeria Official number: 185406	*110* 63 193		**1954**-01 **R. Dunston Ltd. — Thorne** Yd No: T898 Loa 27.44 Br ex 6.10 Dght 1.982 Lbp - Br md 6.05 Dpth - Welded, 1 dk	**(A31A2GX) General Cargo Ship** Compartments: 1 Ho, ER 1 Ha: (12.8 x 4.1)ER Derricks: 1x2t	**2 oil engines** driving 2 FP propellers Total Power: 98kW (134hp) Kelvin K3 2 x 4 Stroke 3 Cy. 152 x 229 each-49kW (67bhp) Bergius Co. Ltd.-Glasgow
9352315 *DDPW* -	**SEACOD** **tms 'Seacod' GmbH & Co KG** German Tanker Shipping GmbH & Co KG *Bremen* Germany MMSI: 218019000 Official number: 4953	**26,548** 10,288 40,558 T/cm 53.0	Class: GL	**2006**-11 **Lindenau GmbH Schiffswerft u. Maschinenfabrik — Kiel** Yd No: 273 Loa 188.33 (BB) Br ex - Dght 11.000 Lbp 179.50 Br md 32.20 Dpth 17.05 Welded, 1 dk	**(A13B2TP) Products Tanker** Double Hull (13F) Liq: 47,376; Liq (Oil): 47,376 Compartments: 10 Wing Ta, 2 Wing Slop Ta, ER 10 Cargo Pump (s): 10x600m³/hr Manifold: Bow/CM: 97.2m Ice Capable	**1 oil engine** reduction geared to sc. shaft driving 1 CP propeller Total Power: 11,200kW (15,228hp) 15.5kn MAN-B&W 8L58/64 1 x 4 Stroke 8 Cy. 580 x 640 11200kW (15228bhp) MAN B&W Diesel AG-Augsburg AuxGen: 3 x 1140kW 400/230V 50Hz a.c, 1 x 1360kW 400/230V 50Hz a.c Thrusters: 1 Thwart. FP thruster (f)

IMO / Call sign	Name / Owner	Tonnage	Class	Builder / Dimensions	Type	Machinery
9432256 *HORX* -	**SEACON 6** *completed as* Herman *-2012* **Seacon 6 Ltd** Seacon Ships Management Co Ltd SatCom: Inmarsat C 437351810 *Panama* *Panama* MMSI: 373518000 Official number: 43423PEXT1	**33,044** 19,231 57,000 T/cm 58.8	Class: BV	**2012-06 Ningbo Beilun Lantian Shipbuilding Co Ltd — Ningbo ZJ** (Hull launched by) Yd No: HB2007 **2012-06 Zhejiang Zengzhou Shipyard Co Ltd — Zhoushan ZJ** (Hull completed by) Yd No: (HB2007) Loa 189.99 (BB) Br ex - Dght 12.800 Lbp 185.00 Br md 32.26 Dpth 18.00 Welded, 1 dk	**(A21A2BC) Bulk Carrier** Grain: 71,634; Bale: 70,557 Compartments: 5 Ho, ER 5 Ha: 4 (21.3 x 18.3)ER (18.9 x 18.3) Cranes: 4x30t	**1 oil engine** driving 1 FP propeller Total Power: 9,480kW (12,889hp) 14.2kn MAN-B&W 6S50MC-C 1 x 2 Stroke 6 Cy. 500 x 2000 9480kW (12889bhp) Hyundai Heavy Industries Co Ltd-South Korea AuxGen: 3 x 600kW 60Hz a.c Fuel: 120.0 (d.f.) 2200.0 (r.f.)
9487665 *HOHN* -	**SEACON 7** **Seacon 7 Ltd** Seacon Ships Management Co Ltd SatCom: Inmarsat C 437351610 *Panama* *Panama* MMSI: 373516000 Official number: 4439112A	**33,044** 19,231 57,000 T/cm 58.8	Class: BV	**2012-06 Ningbo Beilun Lantian Shipbuilding Co Ltd — Ningbo ZJ** (Hull launched by) Yd No: HB2004 **2012-06 Zhejiang Zengzhou Shipyard Co Ltd — Zhoushan ZJ** (Hull completed by) Yd No: (HB2004) Loa 189.99 Br ex - Dght 12.800 Lbp 185.00 Br md 32.26 Dpth 18.00 Welded, 1 dk	**(A21A2BC) Bulk Carrier** Grain: 71,634; Bale: 68,200 Compartments: 5 Ho, ER 5 Ha: Cranes: 4x35t	**1 oil engine** driving 1 FP propeller Total Power: 9,480kW (12,889hp) 14.2kn MAN-B&W 6S50MC-C 1 x 2 Stroke 6 Cy. 500 x 2000 9480kW (12889bhp) STX Engine Co Ltd-South Korea
9433107 *3FBQ3* -	**SEACON 8** **Fast Champ Shipping Ltd** Seacon Ships Management Co Ltd SatCom: Inmarsat C 437352010 *Panama* *Panama* MMSI: 373520000 Official number: 4440112A	**33,044** 19,232 57,000 T/cm 58.8	Class: BV	**2012-06 Ningbo Beilun Lantian Shipbuilding Co Ltd — Ningbo ZJ** (Hull launched by) Yd No: HB2008 **2012-06 Zhejiang Zengzhou Shipyard Co Ltd — Zhoushan ZJ** (Hull completed by) Yd No: (HB2008) Loa 189.99 Br ex - Dght 12.800 Lbp 185.00 Br md 32.26 Dpth 18.00 Welded, 1 dk	**(A21A2BC) Bulk Carrier** Grain: 71,634; Bale: 70,557 Compartments: 5 Ho, ER 5 Ha: ER Cranes: 4x30t	**1 oil engine** driving 1 FP propeller Total Power: 9,480kW (12,889hp) 14.2kn MAN-B&W 6S50MC-C 1 x 2 Stroke 6 Cy. 500 x 2000 9480kW (12889bhp) Hyundai Heavy Industries Co Ltd-South Korea AuxGen: 3 x 600kW 60Hz a.c Fuel: 2370.0
9440394 *3EZM4* -	**SEACON 9** **East Joy Shipping Ltd** Seacon Ships Management Co Ltd SatCom: Inmarsat C 437351910 *Panama* *Panama* MMSI: 373519000 Official number: 4449513	**42,263** 25,537 74,844	Class: LR ✠ **100A1** SS 06/2012 bulk carrier CSR BC-A Nos. 2, 4 & 6 holds may be empty GRAB (20) ESP LI *IWS ✠ **LMC** **UMS** Cable: 660.0/78.0 U3 (a)	**2012-06 Ningbo Beilun Lantian Shipbuilding Co Ltd — Ningbo ZJ** Yd No: HF2001 **2012-06 Zhejiang Zengzhou Shipyard Co Ltd — Zhoushan ZJ** Yd No: 006 Loa 225.00 (BB) Br ex 32.30 Dght 14.200 Lbp 217.00 Br md 32.26 Dpth 19.60 Welded, 1 dk	**(A21A2BC) Bulk Carrier** Grain: 90,000 Compartments: 7 Ho, ER 7 Ha: ER	**1 oil engine** driving 1 FP propeller Total Power: 11,300kW (15,363hp) 14.5kn MAN-B&W 5S60MC-C 1 x 2 Stroke 5 Cy. 600 x 2400 11300kW (15363bhp) Dalian Marine Diesel Co Ltd-China AuxGen: 3 x 560kW 450V 60Hz a.c Boilers: AuxB (Comp) 8.5kgf/cm² (8.3bar)
9352298 *DEJY* -	**SEACONGER** **tms 'Seaconger' GmbH & Co KG** German Tanker Shipping GmbH & Co KG *Bremen* *Germany* MMSI: 211822000 Official number: 4926	**21,329** 8,429 32,200 T/cm 42.0	Class: GL	**2005-12 Lindenau GmbH Schiffswerft u. Maschinenfabrik — Kiel** Yd No: 271 Loa 177.75 (BB) Br ex - Dght 11.000 Lbp 168.00 Br md 28.00 Dpth 16.80 Welded, 1 dk	**(A13B2TP) Products Tanker** Double Hull (13F) Liq: 35,890; Liq (Oil): 37,116 Compartments: 10 Wing Ta, 2 Wing Slop Ta, 1 Slop Ta, ER 10 Cargo Pump (s): 10x500m³/hr Manifold: Bow/CM: 85m Ice Capable	**1 oil engine** reduction geared to sc. shaft driving 1 CP propeller Total Power: 8,340kW (11,339hp) 15.0kn MAN-B&W 6L58/64 1 x 4 Stroke 6 Cy. 580 x 640 8340kW (11339bhp) MAN B&W Diesel AG-Augsburg AuxGen: 1 x 1120kW 400V 50Hz a.c, 3 x 960kW 400V 50Hz a.c Thrusters: 1 Tunnel thruster (f) Fuel: 300.0 (d.f.) 690.0 (r.f.)
9498676 *WDE2921* -	**SEACOR CABRAL** **SEACOR Offshore LLC** SEACOR Marine LLC *New Orleans, LA* *United States of America* MMSI: 366321000 Official number: 1207381	**1,111** 333 1,674	Class: AB	**2008-01 Master Boat Builders, Inc. — Coden, Al** Yd No: 402 Loa 58.20 Br ex 14.72 Dght 4.120 Lbp 55.47 Br md 14.63 Dpth 4.80 Welded, 1 dk	**(B21A20S) Platform Supply Ship**	**2 oil engines** reduction geared to sc. shafts driving 2 FP propellers Total Power: 1,940kW (2,638hp) 12.0kn Caterpillar 3512B 2 x Vee 4 Stroke 12 Cy. 170 x 190 each-970kW (1319bhp) Caterpillar Inc-USA AuxGen: 3 x 550kW a.c Thrusters: 2 Tunnel thruster (f); 1 Tunnel thruster (a) Fuel: 561.0 (d.f.) 14.3pd
8765034 *WDG3598* -	**SEACOR CHAMPION** *ex* Superior Champion *-2012* **SEACOR LB Offshore LLC** SEACOR Liftboats LLC *New Orleans, LA* *United States of America* MMSI: 367527690 Official number: 1115859	**1,312** 393 -		**2001 Orange Shipbuilding, Inc. — Orange, Tx** Yd No: 332 Loa 40.10 Br ex 23.77 Dght 3.416 Lbp - Br md 20.72 Dpth 4.26 Welded, 1 dk	**(B22A2ZM) Offshore Construction Vessel, jack up** Cranes: 1x200t,1x30t	**2 oil engines** reduction geared to sc. shafts driving 2 Propellers Total Power: 772kW (1,050hp) 4.0kn Caterpillar 3408 2 x Vee 4 Stroke 8 Cy. 137 x 152 each-386kW (525bhp) Caterpillar Inc-USA AuxGen: 2 x 60Hz a.c
9429493 *WDD9039* -	**SEACOR CHEETAH** **Sea-Cat Crewzer LLC** SEACOR Marine LLC *New Orleans, LA* *United States of America* MMSI: 367164000 Official number: 1197517	**498** 149 185	Class: AB	**2008-02 Gulf Craft LLC — Patterson LA** Yd No: 465 Loa 50.30 Br ex - Dght 2.130 Lbp 44.51 Br md 11.58 Dpth 4.47 Welded, 1 dk	**(B21A20C) Crew/Supply Vessel** Hull Material: Aluminium Alloy Passengers: unberthed: 150	**4 oil engines** reduction geared to sc. shafts driving 4 Water jets Total Power: 9,860kW (13,404hp) 36.0kn M.T.U. 16V4000M71 4 x Vee 4 Stroke 16 Cy. 165 x 190 each-2465kW (3351bhp) MTU Friedrichshafen GmbH-Friedrichshafen AuxGen: 2 x 270kW a.c Thrusters: 2 Retract. directional thruster (f) Fuel: 100.0 (d.f.)
9458793 *WDE2494* -	**SEACOR COLUMBUS** **SEACOR Offshore LLC** SEACOR Marine LLC *New Orleans, LA* *United States of America* MMSI: 368160000 Official number: 1199424	**1,111** 333 1,651	Class: AB	**2007-12 Master Boat Builders, Inc. — Coden, Al** Yd No: 401 Loa 58.20 Br ex 14.72 Dght 4.000 Lbp 55.47 Br md 14.63 Dpth 4.80 Welded, 1 dk	**(B21A20S) Platform Supply Ship**	**2 oil engines** reduction geared to sc. shafts driving 2 FP propellers Total Power: 2,852kW (3,878hp) 12.0kn Caterpillar 3512B 2 x Vee 4 Stroke 12 Cy. 170 x 190 each-1426kW (1939bhp) Caterpillar Inc-USA AuxGen: 3 x 550kW 60Hz a.c Thrusters: 2 Tunnel thruster (f); 1 Tunnel thruster (a) Fuel: 650.0 (d.f.)
8767410 *WDG3586* -	**SEACOR CONQUEROR** *ex* Superior Conqueror *-2012* *ex* J. A. Holleman *-2012* *ex* Southern Cross Two *-2012* **SEACOR LB Offshore LLC** SEACOR Liftboats LLC *New Orleans, LA* *United States of America* MMSI: 367527560 Official number: 642928	*185* 125 -		**1981 Blue Streak Industries, Inc. — Chalmette, La** Yd No: BLU JB 53 Loa 24.69 Br ex 11.58 Dght - Lbp - Br md - Dpth 2.43 Welded, 1 dk	**(B22A2ZM) Offshore Construction Vessel, jack up** Cranes: 1x70t,1x24t	**2 oil engines** reduction geared to sc. shafts driving 2 Propellers Total Power: 588kW (800hp) 7.8kn G.M. (Detroit Diesel) 12V-71 2 x Vee 2 Stroke 12 Cy. 108 x 127 each-294kW (400bhp) Detroit Diesel Corporation-Detroit, Mi AuxGen: 2 x 30kW 60Hz a.c
9207900 *WDA9650* -	**SEACOR CONQUEST** **OFS Marine One Inc** SEACOR Marine LLC SatCom: Inmarsat C 433854310 *New Orleans, LA* *United States of America* MMSI: 338144000 Official number: 1082888	**1,099** 329 1,689	Class: AB	**1999-06 Halter Marine, Inc. — Lockport, La** Yd No: 1800 Loa 62.49 Br ex - Dght 4.419 Lbp 58.29 Br md 14.02 Dpth 5.18 Welded, 1 dk	**(B21A20S) Platform Supply Ship**	**2 oil engines** with clutches, flexible couplings & sr reverse geared to sc. shafts driving 2 FP propellers Total Power: 3,090kW (4,202hp) 11.0kn Caterpillar 3516B 2 x Vee 4 Stroke 16 Cy. 170 x 190 each-1545kW (2101bhp) Caterpillar Inc-USA AuxGen: 2 x 105kW 480V 60Hz a.c Thrusters: 1 Retract. directional thruster (f) Fuel: 440.0 (d.f.) 14.4pd
9551296 *4JNW* -	**SEACOR COUGAR** **Sea-Cat Crewzer LLC** SEACOR Marine LLC *Baku* *Azerbaijan* MMSI: 423333100 Official number: BR-024	**498** 149 185	Class: AB	**2009-03 Gulf Craft LLC — Patterson LA** Yd No: 468 Loa 50.30 Br ex - Dght 2.130 Lbp 44.51 Br md 11.58 Dpth 4.50 Welded, 1 dk	**(B21A20C) Crew/Supply Vessel** Hull Material: Aluminium Alloy Passengers: unberthed: 136	**4 oil engines** reduction geared to sc. shafts driving 4 Water jets Total Power: 9,860kW (13,404hp) 36.0kn M.T.U. 16V4000M71 4 x Vee 4 Stroke 16 Cy. 165 x 190 each-2465kW (3351bhp) MTU Friedrichshafen GmbH-Friedrichshafen AuxGen: 2 x 290kW a.c Thrusters: 2 Retract. directional thruster (f)

IMO / Call sign	Name / Owner / Manager	Tonnage	Class	Builder / Dimensions	Type	Machinery
9464302 *WDE6053* -	**SEACOR DAVIS** **Graham Offshore LLC** SEACOR Marine LLC *New Orleans, LA* *United States of America* MMSI: 338128000 Official number: 1205368	2,188 829 2,473	Class: AB	**2009-01 Bender Shipbuilding & Repair Co Inc — Mobile AL** Yd No: 7878 Loa 80.77 (BB) Br ex - Dght 4.720 Lbp 73.76 Br md 15.85 Dpth 5.79 Welded, 1 dk	**(B21B20A) Anchor Handling Tug Supply** A-frames: 1x150t	**4 diesel electric oil engines** driving 1 gen. of 2100kW 690V a.c 3 gen. each 1825kW 690V a.c reduction geared to sc. shafts driving 2 FP propellers Total Power: 7,448kW (10,126hp) 12.0kn Caterpillar 3516B-TA 3 x Vee 4 Stroke 16 Cy. 170 x 190 each-1641kW (2231bhp) Caterpillar Inc-USA Caterpillar 3516C 1 x Vee 4 Stroke 16 Cy. 170 x 215 2525kW (3433bhp) Caterpillar Inc-USA AuxGen: 1 x 425kW 690/480V 60Hz a.c Thrusters: 2 Tunnel thruster (f); 1 Tunnel thruster (a) Fuel: 530.0
9225495 *WDF5354* -	**SEACOR DIAMOND** *ex* DMT Diamond *-2012* *ex* Nicki Candies *-2005* **SEACOR Marine LLC** - *New Orleans, LA* *United States of America* MMSI: 368151000 Official number: 1091373	2,227 668 2,620	Class: AB	**2000-01 Bender Shipbuilding & Repair Co Inc — Mobile AL** Yd No: 6910 Loa 72.50 Br ex - Dght 4.940 Lbp 68.20 Br md 16.50 Dpth 6.10 Welded, 1 dk	**(B21A20S) Platform Supply Ship** Cranes: 1x80t	**2 oil engines** gearing integral to driving 2 Z propellers Total Power: 2,868kW (3,900hp) 11.0kn EMD (Electro-Motive) 16-645-E6 2 x Vee 2 Stroke 16 Cy. 230 x 254 each-1434kW (1950bhp) General Motors Corp.Electro-Motive Div.-La Grange AuxGen: 3 x 250kW a.c Thrusters: 2 Thwart. CP thruster (f)
8768995 *WDG9999* -	**SEACOR EAGLE** *ex* Eagle *-2013* **SEACOR Eagle LLC** SEACOR Liftboats LLC *Galliano, LA* *United States of America* MMSI: 367593360 Official number: 1196599	1,313 393 -	Class: AB	**2007-06 Bollinger Machine Shop & Shipyard, Inc. — Lockport, La** Yd No: 515 L reg 45.00 Br ex 28.04 Dght - Lbp 41.91 Br md - Dpth 3.96 Welded, 1 dk	**(B22A2ZM) Offshore Construction Vessel, jack up** Cranes: 1x175t,1x50t,1x25t	**2 oil engines** driving 1 FP propeller Total Power: 2,350kW (3,196hp) Caterpillar 3512B-TA 2 x Vee 4 Stroke 12 Cy. 170 x 190 each-1175kW (1598bhp) Caterpillar Inc-USA AuxGen: 2 x a.c Thrusters: 1 Retract. directional thruster (f) Fuel: 107.2 (r.f.)
8763048 *WDG3593* -	**SEACOR EDGE** *ex* Superior Edge *-2012* *ex* Power VIII *-2004* *ex* Blue Streak Rabbit *-1994* **SEACOR LB Offshore II LLC** SEACOR Liftboats LLC *New Orleans, LA* *United States of America* Official number: 692549	*194* 180 -		**1985 Blue Streak Industries, Inc. — Chalmette, La** Yd No: BLU JB 70 Loa 26.52 Br ex 12.80 Dght 1.820 Lbp - Br md - Dpth 2.74 Welded, 1 dk	**(B22A2ZM) Offshore Construction Vessel, jack up** Cranes: 1x60t	**2 oil engines** geared to sc. shafts driving 2 Propellers Total Power: 882kW (1,200hp) G.M. (Detroit Diesel) 16V-92 2 x Vee 2 Stroke 16 Cy. 123 x 127 each-441kW (600bhp) Detroit Diesel Corporation-Detroit, Mi
8766038 *WDG3588* -	**SEACOR ENDEAVOR** *ex* Superior Endeavor *-2012* *ex* W. Lopez *-1998* **SEACOR LB Offshore LLC** SEACOR Liftboats LLC *New Orleans, LA* *United States of America* MMSI: 367527580 Official number: 1060683	717 215 -		**1998-01 Bollinger Machine Shop & Shipyard, Inc. — Lockport, La** Yd No: 320 Loa 35.52 Br ex 14.90 Dght 1.906 Lbp - Br md - Dpth 3.04 Welded, 1 dk	**(B22A2ZM) Offshore Construction Vessel, jack up** Cranes: 1x100t,1x25t	**2 oil engines** reduction geared to sc. shafts driving 2 Propellers Total Power: 1,492kW (2,028hp) 4.0kn Caterpillar 3508B 2 x Vee 4 Stroke 8 Cy. 170 x 190 each-746kW (1014bhp) Caterpillar Inc-USA AuxGen: 2 x 95kW 60Hz a.c
8763050 *WDG3589* -	**SEACOR ENDURANCE** *ex* Superior Endurance *-2012* *ex* Gulf Island I *-2012* **SEACOR LB Offshore II LLC** SEACOR Liftboats LLC *New Orleans, LA* *United States of America* MMSI: 366817820 Official number: 653622	*289* 196 -		**1983-02 Crown Point Industries — Marrero, La** Yd No: 106 Loa 32.01 Br ex 13.72 Dght 1.680 Lbp - Br md - Dpth 2.74 Welded, 1 dk	**(B22A2ZM) Offshore Construction Vessel, jack up** Cranes: 1x70t	**2 oil engines** geared to sc. shafts driving 2 Propellers Total Power: 736kW (1,000hp) G.M. (Detroit Diesel) 16V-71 2 x Vee 2 Stroke 16 Cy. 108 x 127 each-368kW (500bhp) Detroit Diesel Corporation-Detroit, Mi
8899275 - -	**SEACOR EXPRESS** *ex* Acadian Express *-2012* *ex* Evan Christopher *-2012* - -	118 35 -		**1979 Camcraft, Inc. — Crown Point, La** Yd No: 198 L reg 30.48 Br ex - Dght 1.260 Lbp - Br md 6.40 Dpth 2.59 Welded, 1 dk	**(B21A20C) Crew/Supply Vessel** Hull Material: Aluminium Alloy	**3 oil engines** reverse reduction geared to sc. shafts driving 3 FP propellers Total Power: 1,164kW (1,584hp) 23.0kn G.M. (Detroit Diesel) 12V-71-TI 3 x Vee 2 Stroke 12 Cy. 108 x 127 each-388kW (528bhp) General Motors Detroit DieselAllison Divn-USA AuxGen: 2 x 40kW a.c Fuel: 8.0 (d.f.)
9336232 *V7KS2* -	**SEACOR EXPRESS** **Seacor Supplyships 1 KS** Seabulk Offshore Dubai Inc *Majuro* *Marshall Islands* MMSI: 538002669 Official number: 2669	1,759 527 1,494	Class: AB	**2006-07 PT Nanindah Mutiara Shipyard — Batam** Yd No: T148 Loa 63.00 Br ex - Dght 5.170 Lbp 55.80 Br md 15.00 Dpth 6.10 Welded, 1 dk	**(B21B20A) Anchor Handling Tug Supply** Cranes: 1x11t	**2 oil engines** reduction geared to sc. shafts driving 2 CP propellers Total Power: 5,280kW (7,178hp) 11.0kn MaK 8M25 2 x 4 Stroke 8 Cy. 255 x 400 each-2640kW (3589bhp) Caterpillar Motoren GmbH & Co. KG-Germany AuxGen: 2 x 370kW 440/220V 60Hz a.c, 2 x 1200kW 440/220V 60Hz a.c Thrusters: 2 Thwart. CP thruster (f); 1 Thwart. CP thruster (a)
8770376 *WDG3602* -	**SEACOR FUTURE** *ex* Superior Future *-2012* **SEACOR LB Offshore II LLC** SEACOR Liftboats LLC *New Orleans, LA* *United States of America* MMSI: 367527740 Official number: 1212034	440 123 288		**2008-06 Halimar Shipyard LLC — Morgan City, La** (Hull launched by) Yd No: 148 **2008-06 Marine Industrial Fabrication, Inc. — New Iberia, La** (Hull completed by) Yd No: (148) Loa 33.60 Br ex 21.22 Dght 2.060 Lbp 29.20 Br md - Dpth 2.74 Welded, 1 dk	**(B22A2ZM) Offshore Construction Vessel, jack up** Cranes: 1x100t,1x26t	**2 oil engines** reduction geared to sc. shafts driving 2 Propellers Total Power: 810kW (1,102hp) 6.0kn Caterpillar 3412 2 x Vee 4 Stroke 12 Cy. 137 x 152 each-405kW (551bhp) Caterpillar Inc-USA AuxGen: 2 x 99kW a.c
8765541 *WDG3600* -	**SEACOR GALE** *ex* Superior Gale *-2012* **SEACOR LB Offshore LLC** SEACOR Liftboats LLC SatCom: Inmarsat C 436971110 *New Orleans, LA* *United States of America* MMSI: 367527720 Official number: 1124970	1,303 390 -	Class: LR (AB) **OU100A** SS 10/2012 self elevating unit **LMC**	**2002-12 Bollinger Marine Fabricators LLC — Amelia LA** Yd No: 399 Loa 40.20 Br ex 28.04 Dght - Lbp - Br md - Dpth 3.96 Welded, 1 dk	**(B22A2ZM) Offshore Construction Vessel, jack up** Cranes: 1x250t,1x30t	**2 oil engines** reduction geared to sc. shafts driving 2 Propellers Total Power: 2,236kW (3,040hp) 4.0kn Caterpillar 3512TA 2 x Vee 4 Stroke 12 Cy. 170 x 190 each-1118kW (1520bhp) Caterpillar Inc-USA AuxGen: 2 x 95kW a.c
9214915 *WDB7425* -	**SEACOR GLORY** **General Electric Capital Corp** SEACOR Marine LLC *New Orleans, LA* *United States of America* MMSI: 338501000 Official number: 1076923	2,252 871 3,465	Class: AB	**1999-07 Moss Point Marine, Inc. — Escatawpa, Ms** Yd No: 154 Loa 76.50 Br ex - Dght 5.746 Lbp 71.63 Br md 16.50 Dpth 7.10 Welded, 1 dk	**(B21A20S) Platform Supply Ship**	**3 diesel electric oil engines** driving 3 gen. each 1825kW 600V a.c Connecting to 2 elec. motors each (1839kW) driving 2 Azimuth electric drive units Total Power: 5,445kW (7,404hp) 11.4kn Caterpillar 3516B 3 x Vee 4 Stroke 16 Cy. 170 x 190 each-1815kW (2468bhp) Caterpillar Inc-USA Thrusters: 1 Retract. directional thruster (f); 1 Thwart. CP thruster (f) Fuel: 1002.9 (d.f.) 13.6pd
9407794 *V7UQ9* -	**SEACOR GRANT** **SEACOR Grant AS** SEACOR Offshore Dubai LLC *Majuro* *Marshall Islands* MMSI: 538004008 Official number: 4008	2,188 799 2,603	Class: AB	**2008-06 Bender Shipbuilding & Repair Co Inc — Mobile AL** Yd No: 7875 Loa 80.80 (BB) Br ex - Dght 4.700 Lbp 78.30 Br md 15.80 Dpth 5.80 Welded, 1 dk	**(B21B20A) Anchor Handling Tug Supply**	**4 diesel electric oil engines** driving 3 gen. each 1825kW 690V a.c 1 gen. of 2100kW 690V a.c Connecting to 2 elec. motors reduction geared to sc. shafts driving 2 FP propellers Total Power: 8,525kW (11,590hp) 12.0kn Caterpillar 3516B 3 x Vee 4 Stroke 16 Cy. 170 x 190 each-2000kW (2719bhp) Caterpillar Inc-USA Caterpillar 3516C 1 x Vee 4 Stroke 16 Cy. 170 x 215 2525kW (3433bhp) Caterpillar Inc-USA Thrusters: 2 Tunnel thruster (f); 1 Tunnel thruster (a) Fuel: 540.0
8769004 *WDD8788* -	**SEACOR HAWK** *ex* Hawk *-2014* **SEACOR Hawk LLC** SEACOR Liftboats LLC *Galliano, LA* *United States of America* MMSI: 367450000 Official number: 1200276	1,313 393 -	Class: AB	**2007-11 Bollinger Machine Shop & Shipyard, Inc. — Lockport, La** Yd No: 516 Loa 41.91 Br ex - Dght - Lbp - Br md 28.04 Dpth 3.96 Welded, 1 dk	**(B22A2ZM) Offshore Construction Vessel, jack up** Cranes: 1x175t,1x50t,1x25t	**2 oil engines** reduction geared to sc. shafts driving 2 FP propellers Total Power: 2,350kW (3,196hp) Caterpillar 3512 2 x Vee 4 Stroke 12 Cy. 170 x 190 each-1175kW (1598bhp) Caterpillar Inc-USA Thrusters: 1 Retract. directional thruster (f) Fuel: 107.2 (r.f.)

IMO / Call sign	Name / Owner	Tonnage	Class	Build / Dimensions	Type	Machinery
8770895 *WDG3604* -	**SEACOR INFLUENCE** *ex* Superior Influence *-2012* **Banc of America Leasing & Capital LLC** SEACOR Liftboats LLC *New Orleans, LA* *United States of America* MMSI: 367527760 Official number: 1218130	**1,799** 539 -	Class: AB	**2008**-02 **Boconco, Inc. — Bayou La Batre, Al** Yd No: 128 Loa 44.20 Br ex 33.50 Dght 2.710 Lbp 42.50 Br md - Dpth 3.84 Welded, 1 dk	**(B22A2ZM) Offshore Construction Vessel, jack up** Cranes: 1x200t,1x70t	**2 oil engines** reduction geared to sc. shafts driving 2 Propellers Total Power: 1,492kW (2,028hp) 5.6kn Caterpillar C32 2 x Vee 4 Stroke 12 Cy. 145 x 162 each-746kW (1014bhp) Caterpillar Inc-USA AuxGen: 2 x 300kW 60Hz a.c Fuel: 80.0 (d.f.)
8763062 *WDG3596* -	**SEACOR INTEGRITY** *ex* Superior Integrity *-2012* *ex* Gulf Island II *-2004* **SEACOR LB Offshore II LLC** SEACOR Liftboats LLC *New Orleans, LA* *United States of America* MMSI: 367527670 Official number: 663833	**333** 100 -		**1983 Crown Point Industries — Marrero, La** Yd No: 108 Loa 27.43 Br ex 12.19 Dght 1.670 Lbp - Br md 12.19 Dpth 2.43 Welded, 1 dk	**(B22A2ZM) Offshore Construction Vessel, jack up** Cranes: 1x70t	**2 oil engines** geared to sc. shafts driving 2 Propellers Total Power: 662kW (900hp) G.M. (Detroit Diesel) 12V-71 2 x Vee 2 Stroke 12 Cy. 108 x 127 each-331kW (450bhp) Detroit Diesel Corporation-Detroit, Mi
8766040 *WDG3583* -	**SEACOR INTERVENTION** *ex* Superior Intervention *-2012* *ex* Superior Challenge *-2006* *ex* J. Hankins *-2006* *ex* D. L. Hanson *-1997* **SEACOR LB Offshore II LLC** SEACOR Liftboats LLC *New Orleans, LA* *United States of America* MMSI: 367527530 Official number: 1052908	**660** 198 249	Class: LR **OU100A** SS 10/2011 self elevating unit Gulf of Mexico **LMC**	**1997**-06 **Bollinger Machine Shop & Shipyard, Inc. — Lockport, La** Yd No: 317 Loa 35.67 Br ex 14.94 Dght 1.920 Lbp - Br md - Dpth 3.04 Welded, 1 dk	**(B22A2ZM) Offshore Construction Vessel, jack up** Cranes: 1x100t,1x25t	**2 oil engines** reduction geared to sc. shafts driving 2 Propellers Total Power: 1,290kW (1,754hp) 5.2kn Cummins KTA-38-M0 2 x Vee 4 Stroke 12 Cy. 159 x 159 each-645kW (877bhp) Cummins Engine Co Inc-USA AuxGen: 2 x 125kW 60Hz a.c
9298985 *WDB5002* -	**SEACOR JEFFERSON** **SEACOR Worldwide Inc** SEACOR Marine LLC *New Orleans, LA* *United States of America* MMSI: 369312000 Official number: 1145691	**1,598** 479 2,315	Class: AB	**2004**-01 **Bollinger Machine Shop & Shipyard, Inc. — Lockport, La** Yd No: 439 Loa 63.09 Br ex - Dght 5.080 Lbp 59.43 Br md 16.15 Dpth 5.79 Welded, 1 dk	**(B21A2OS) Platform Supply Ship** Passengers: 25	**2 oil engines** gearing integral to driving 2 Z propellers Total Power: 3,542kW (4,816hp) 11.0kn Caterpillar 3516B-HD 2 x Vee 4 Stroke 16 Cy. 170 x 215 each-1771kW (2408bhp) Caterpillar Inc-USA AuxGen: 2 x 370kW a.c Thrusters: 2 Thwart. CP thruster (f) Fuel: 620.0 (d.f.) 8.0pd
9464297 *WDE4932* -	**SEACOR LEE** **Banc of America Leasing & Capital LLC** SEACOR Marine LLC *New Orleans, LA* *United States of America* MMSI: 367362000 Official number: 1205367	**2,188** 829 4,500	Class: AB	**2008**-10 **Bender Shipbuilding & Repair Co Inc — Mobile AL** Yd No: 7877 Loa 80.77 (BB) Br ex - Dght 4.720 Lbp 73.76 Br md 15.80 Dpth 5.79 Welded, 1 dk	**(B21B20A) Anchor Handling Tug Supply**	**4 diesel electric oil engines** driving 1 gen. of 2100kW 690V a.c 3 gen. each 1825kW 690V a.c Connecting to 2 elec. motors each (3580kW) driving 2 FP propellers Total Power: 7,448kW (10,126hp) 12.0kn Caterpillar 3516B 3 x Vee 4 Stroke 16 Cy. 170 x 190 each-1641kW (2231bhp) Caterpillar Inc-USA Caterpillar 3516C 1 x Vee 4 Stroke 16 Cy. 170 x 215 2525kW (3433bhp) Caterpillar Inc-USA AuxGen: 1 x 425kW 690V 60Hz a.c Thrusters: 2 Tunnel thruster (f); 1 Tunnel thruster (a) Fuel: 600.0
8765046 *WDG3590* -	**SEACOR LEGACY** *ex* Dixie Legacy *-2012* **SEACOR LB Offshore LLC** SEACOR Liftboats LLC *New Orleans, LA* *United States of America* MMSI: 367527610 Official number: 1095071	*2,259* 677 -	Class: AB	**2001**-05 **Semco LLC — Lafitte, La** Yd No: 1004 Loa 47.70 Br ex 31.39 Dght 2.670 Lbp - Br md - Dpth 3.96 Welded, 1 dk	**(B22A2ZM) Offshore Construction Vessel, jack up** Cranes: 2x175t	**4 oil engines** reduction geared to sc. shafts driving 4 Propellers Total Power: 2,548kW (3,464hp) Caterpillar 3508TA 4 x Vee 4 Stroke 8 Cy. 170 x 190 each-637kW (866bhp) Caterpillar Inc-USA AuxGen: 2 x 425kW
9665384 *V7BB8* -	**SEACOR LEOPARD** **Sea-Cat Crewzer II LLC** SEACOR Marine LLC *Majuro* *Marshall Islands* MMSI: 538005110 Official number: 5110	**497** 149 196	Class: AB	**2013**-09 **Gulf Craft LLC — Franklin LA** Yd No: 476 Loa 57.30 Br ex - Dght 1.730 Lbp 53.64 Br md 12.49 Dpth 4.27 Welded, 1 dk	**(B21A20C) Crew/Supply Vessel** Hull Material: Aluminium Alloy Passengers: unberthed: 150	**4 oil engines** reduction geared to sc. shaft (s) driving 4 Water jets Total Power: 11,520kW (15,664hp) 40.0kn M.T.U. 16V4000M73L 1 x Vee 4 Stroke 16 Cy. 170 x 190 2880kW (3916bhp) MTU Friedrichshafen GmbH-Friedrichshafen M.T.U. 16V4000M73L 3 x Vee 4 Stroke 16 Cy. 170 x 190 each-2880kW (3916bhp) MTU Friedrichshafen GmbH-Friedrichshafen AuxGen: 2 x 290kW a.c Thrusters: 2 Tunnel thruster 1 (p) 1 (s) Fuel: 109.0 (d.f.)
8770259 *WDG3601* -	**SEACOR LIBERTY** *ex* Superior Liberty *-2012* **SEACOR LB Offshore II LLC** SEACOR Liftboats LLC *New Orleans, LA* *United States of America* Official number: 1208449	**440** 132 288	Class: LR **OU100A** SS 03/2013 self elevating unit Gulf of Mexico restricted service, within 12 hours of a harbour of safe refuge or a location where the vessel can elevate to survive 100 knot wind **LMC** Cable: 100.0/12.5 U2	**2008**-02 **Halimar Shipyard LLC — Morgan City, La** (Hull) Yd No: 147 **2008**-02 **Marine Industrial Fabrication, Inc. — New Iberia, La** Yd No: (147) Loa 33.60 Br ex 21.20 Dght 2.300 Lbp 29.20 Br md 21.18 Dpth 2.75 Welded, 1 dk	**(B22A2ZM) Offshore Construction Vessel, jack up** Cranes: 1x100t,1x26t	**2 oil engines** with clutches & dr reverse geared to sc. shafts driving 2 FP propellers Total Power: 1,302kW (1,770hp) 6.0kn Caterpillar 3412 2 x Vee 4 Stroke 12 Cy. 137 x 152 each-651kW (885bhp) Caterpillar Inc-USA AuxGen: 2 x 99kW 220V 60Hz a.c
9665372 *V7ZK9* -	**SEACOR LYNX** **SEACOR Marine LLC** SEACOR Offshore Dubai LLC *Majuro* *Marshall Islands* MMSI: 538004850 Official number: 4850	**497** 149 195	Class: AB	**2013**-03 **Gulf Craft LLC — Franklin LA** Yd No: 475 Loa 58.60 Br ex - Dght 2.040 Lbp 53.95 Br md 12.50 Dpth 4.27 Welded, 1 dk	**(B21A20C) Crew/Supply Vessel** Hull Material: Aluminium Alloy Passengers: unberthed: 150	**4 oil engines** reduction geared to sc. shaft (s) driving 4 Water jets Total Power: 11,520kW (15,664hp) 40.0kn M.T.U. 16V4000M73L 1 x Vee 4 Stroke 16 Cy. 170 x 190 2880kW (3916bhp) MTU Friedrichshafen GmbH-Friedrichshafen M.T.U. 16V4000M73L 3 x Vee 4 Stroke 16 Cy. 170 x 190 each-2880kW (3916bhp) MTU Friedrichshafen GmbH-Friedrichshafen AuxGen: 2 x 290kW a.c Thrusters: 2 Retract. directional thruster 1 (p) 1 (s) Fuel: 100.0
9292319 *WDD5977* -	**SEACOR MADISON** **Siemens Financial Inc** SEACOR Marine LLC *New Orleans, LA* *United States of America* MMSI: 369257000 Official number: 1136167	**1,598** 479 2,319	Class: AB	**2003**-06 **Bollinger Machine Shop & Shipyard, Inc. — Lockport, La** Yd No: 435 Loa 63.09 Br ex - Dght 5.080 Lbp 59.41 Br md 16.16 Dpth 5.79 Welded, 1 dk	**(B21A20S) Platform Supply Ship**	**2 oil engines** gearing integral to driving 2 Z propellers Total Power: 3,544kW (4,818hp) 11.0kn Caterpillar 3516B-TA 2 x Vee 4 Stroke 16 Cy. 170 x 190 each-1772kW (2409bhp) Caterpillar Inc-USA AuxGen: 2 x 370kW a.c Thrusters: 2 Thwart. CP thruster (f)
9267261 *V7QW9* -	**SEACOR MARINER** *launched as* C-Mariner *-2002* **SEACOR Offshore (Marshall Islands) Ltd** Seabulk Offshore Dubai Inc *Majuro* *Marshall Islands* MMSI: 538003454 Official number: 3454	**495** 148 530	Class: BV (AB)	**2002**-09 **Bollinger Machine Shop & Shipyard, Inc. — Lockport, La** Yd No: 430 Loa 44.50 Br ex - Dght 3.040 Lbp 39.86 Br md 10.97 Dpth 3.65 Welded, 1 dk	**(B21A20S) Platform Supply Ship** Cranes: 1x8t	**2 oil engines** reduction geared to sc. shafts driving 2 FP propellers Total Power: 1,258kW (1,710hp) 10.0kn Caterpillar 3508B 2 x Vee 4 Stroke 8 Cy. 170 x 190 each-629kW (855bhp) Caterpillar Inc-USA AuxGen: 2 x 99kW a.c Thrusters: 1 Tunnel thruster (f); 1 Tunnel thruster (a)
9267259 *V7TX2* -	**SEACOR MASTER** *ex* C-Master *-2003* **Yarnell Offshore (MI) Ltd** SEACOR Offshore Dubai LLC *Majuro* *Marshall Islands* MMSI: 538003901 Official number: 3901	**497** 149 530	Class: BV (AB)	**2002**-06 **Bollinger Machine Shop & Shipyard, Inc. — Lockport, La** Yd No: 429 Loa 44.35 Br ex - Dght 3.500 Lbp 39.86 Br md 10.97 Dpth 3.65 Welded, 1 dk	**(B21A20S) Platform Supply Ship** Cranes: 1x10t	**2 oil engines** reduction geared to sc. shafts driving 2 FP propellers Total Power: 1,258kW (1,710hp) 10.0kn Cummins KTA-38-M 2 x Vee 4 Stroke 12 Cy. 159 x 159 each-629kW (855bhp) Cummins Engine Co Inc-USA AuxGen: 2 x 99kW a.c Thrusters: 1 Tunnel thruster (f); 1 Tunnel thruster (a)

9267273 *V7RX8* - 	**SEACOR MERCHANT** *launched as* C-Merchant *-2002* **Yarnell Offshore (MI) Ltd** SEACOR Offshore Dubai LLC *Majuro* *Marshall Islands* MMSI: 538003598 Official number: 3598	**498** 149 530 Class: BV (AB)	**2002-12 Bollinger Machine Shop & Shipyard, Inc. — Lockport, La** Yd No: 437 Loa 46.00 Br ex - Dght 3.048 Lbp 39.86 Br md 10.97 Dpth 3.65 Welded, 1 dk	**(B21A20S) Platform Supply Ship** Cranes: 1x9t	**2 oil engines** reduction geared to sc. shafts driving 2 FP propellers Total Power: 1,250kW (1,700hp) 10.0kn Caterpillar 3508B 2 x Vee 4 Stroke 8 Cy. 170 x 190 each-625kW (850bhp) Caterpillar Inc-USA AuxGen: 2 x 99kW 60Hz a.c Thrusters: 1 Tunnel thruster (f); 1 Tunnel thruster (a)
8765682 *WDG3592* -	**SEACOR POWER** *ex* Dixie Endeavor *-2012* **SEACOR LB Offshore LLC** SEACOR Liftboats LLC *New Orleans, LA* *United States of America* MMSI: 367527630 Official number: 1115290	**2,276** 682 695 Class: AB	**2002-04 Semco LLC — Lafitte, La** Yd No: 1009 Loa 50.74 Br ex 31.39 Dght 4.090 Lbp - Br md - Dpth 3.96 Welded, 1 dk	**(B22A2ZM) Offshore Construction Vessel, jack up** Cranes: 2x175t	**4 oil engines** reduction geared to sc. shafts driving 4 Propellers Total Power: 2,864kW (3,892hp) 4.3kn Caterpillar 3508TA 4 x Vee 4 Stroke 8 Cy. 170 x 190 each-716kW (973bhp) Caterpillar Inc-USA Thrusters: 1 Tunnel thruster (f)
9283564 *XCSG8* -	**SEACOR PRIDE** **Mantenimiento Express Maritimo S de RL de CV (Mexmar)** - *Dos Bocas* *Mexico* MMSI: 345050201 Official number: 2701348832-3	**1,243** 413 1,889 Class: AB	**2004-01 Halter Marine, Inc. — Moss Point, Ms** Yd No: 1950 Loa 66.19 Br ex 14.14 Dght 4.247 Lbp 64.33 Br md 14.02 Dpth 5.18 Welded, 1 dk	**(B21A20S) Platform Supply Ship**	**2 oil engines** gearing integral to driving 2 Z propellers Total Power: 2,982kW (4,054hp) 11.0kn Caterpillar 3516B 2 x Vee 4 Stroke 16 Cy. 170 x 190 each-1491kW (2027bhp) Caterpillar Inc-USA AuxGen: 2 x 170kW 480/220V 60Hz a.c Thrusters: 1 Tunnel thruster (f) Fuel: 577.0 (d.f.) 12.0pd
9226281 *WCZ6034* -	**SEACOR RELENTLESS** *ex* Stella Rowan *-2005* **SEACOR Worldwide Inc** - *Galliano, LA* *United States of America* MMSI: 338667000 Official number: 1090362	**2,137** 714 2,918 Class: AB	**2000-03 North American Shipbuilding LLC — Larose LA** Yd No: 202 Converted From: Offshore Supply Ship-2013 Loa 74.40 Br ex - Dght 5.500 Lbp 70.10 Br md 17.10 Dpth 6.40 Welded, 1 dk	**(B21B20A) Anchor Handling Tug Supply**	**2 oil engines** gearing integral to driving 2 Z propellers Total Power: 5,346kW (7,268hp) 12.0kn Caterpillar 3608TA 2 x 4 Stroke 8 Cy. 280 x 300 each-2673kW (3634bhp) Caterpillar Inc-USA AuxGen: 2 x 500kW a.c Thrusters: 1 Thwart. FP thruster (f); 1 Retract. directional thruster (f) Fuel: 665.0 (d.f.)
9213026 *WCZ2533* -	**SEACOR RELIANT** *ex* Merle Rowan *-2005* **SEACOR Worldwide Inc** - *Galliano, LA* *United States of America* MMSI: 338471000 Official number: 1082755	**2,137** 714 2,918 Class: AB	**1999-07 North American Shipbuilding LLC — Larose LA** Yd No: 201 Converted From: Offshore Supply Ship-2013 Loa 74.37 Br ex - Dght 5.500 Lbp 68.88 Br md 17.06 Dpth 6.40 Welded, 1 dk	**(B21B20A) Anchor Handling Tug Supply**	**2 oil engines** gearing integral to driving 2 Z propellers Total Power: 5,346kW (7,268hp) 12.0kn Caterpillar 3608TA 2 x 4 Stroke 8 Cy. 280 x 300 each-2673kW (3634bhp) Caterpillar Inc-USA AuxGen: 2 x 500kW a.c Thrusters: 1 Thwart. FP thruster (f); 1 Retract. directional thruster (f)
9706176 *WDG9332* -	**SEACOR RESOLUTE** **Seacor Resolute LLC** SEACOR Marine LLC *New Orleans, LA* *United States of America* MMSI: 338126000 Official number: 1248706	**1,445** 433 2,049 Class: AB	**2013-12 Master Boat Builders, Inc. — Coden, Al** Yd No: 431 Loa 61.30 Br ex 14.72 Dght 4.660 Lbp 58.50 Br md 14.63 Dpth 5.48 Welded, 1 dk	**(B22A20R) Offshore Support Vessel**	**2 oil engines** reduction geared to sc. shafts driving 2 Propellers Total Power: 2,850kW (3,874hp) 10.5kn Caterpillar 3512C-HD 2 x Vee 4 Stroke 12 Cy. 170 x 215 each-1425kW (1937bhp) Caterpillar Inc-USA AuxGen: 2 x 910kW 480V 60Hz a.c Thrusters: 2 Tunnel thruster (f); 2 Tunnel thruster (a) Fuel: 530.0 (d.f.)
9232735 *WCZ7513* -	**SEACOR RESOLVE** *ex* Heddie Rowe *-2005* **SEACOR Offshore LLC** SEACOR Worldwide Inc *Galliano, LA* *United States of America* MMSI: 338721000 Official number: 1093264	**2,137** 714 2,949 Class: AB	**2000-05 North American Shipbuilding LLC — Larose LA** Yd No: 205 Converted From: Offshore Supply Ship-2013 Loa 74.40 Br ex - Dght 5.500 Lbp 70.10 Br md 17.10 Dpth 6.40 Welded, 1 dk	**(B21B20A) Anchor Handling Tug Supply**	**2 oil engines** reduction geared to sc. shafts driving 2 Z propellers Total Power: 5,422kW (7,372hp) 12.0kn Caterpillar 3608 2 x 4 Stroke 8 Cy. 280 x 300 each-2711kW (3686bhp) Caterpillar Inc-USA AuxGen: 2 x 500kW 60Hz a.c Thrusters: 1 Retract. directional thruster (f); 1 Tunnel thruster (f)
8770900 *WDG3606* -	**SEACOR RESPECT** *ex* Superior Respect *-2012* **SEACOR LB Offshore II LLC** SEACOR Liftboats LLC *New Orleans, LA* *United States of America* MMSI: 367527780 Official number: 1218277	**1,799** 539 - Class: AB	**2008-02 Boconco, Inc. — Bayou La Batre, Al** Yd No: 129 Loa 44.20 Br ex 33.50 Dght 2.710 Lbp 42.50 Br md - Dpth 3.84 Welded, 1 dk	**(B22A2ZM) Offshore Construction Vessel, jack up** Cranes: 1x200t,1x70t	**2 oil engines** reduction geared to sc. shafts driving 2 Propellers Total Power: 1,492kW (2,028hp) 5.0kn Caterpillar C32 2 x Vee 4 Stroke 12 Cy. 145 x 162 each-746kW (1014bhp) Caterpillar Inc-USA AuxGen: 2 x 300kW 60Hz a.c Fuel: 80.0 (d.f.)
9236937 *WCZ9586* -	**SEACOR RIGOROUS** *ex* Louise Provine *-2005* **SEACOR Offshore LLC** SEACOR Worldwide Inc *Galliano, LA* *United States of America* MMSI: 338280100 Official number: 1096765	**2,137** 714 2,925 Class: AB	**2000-09 North American Shipbuilding LLC — Larose LA** Yd No: 206 Converted From: Offshore Supply Ship-2013 Loa 74.37 Br ex - Dght 5.376 Lbp 68.88 Br md 17.07 Dpth 6.40 Welded, 1 dk	**(B21B20A) Anchor Handling Tug Supply**	**2 oil engines** reduction geared to sc. shafts driving 2 Directional propellers Total Power: 5,344kW (7,266hp) 12.0kn Caterpillar 3608TA 2 x 4 Stroke 8 Cy. 280 x 300 each-2672kW (3633bhp) Caterpillar Inc-USA AuxGen: 2 x 500kW a.c Thrusters: 1 Tunnel thruster (f); 1 Retract. directional thruster (f)
9190664 *XCVL3* -	**SEACOR SPIRIT** **Compania Empresarial del Mar y Navegacion SA de CV** SEACOR Marine LLC *Dos Bocas* *Mexico* MMSI: 345070400	**1,106** 331 1,758 Class: AB	**1998-04 Moss Point Marine, Inc. — Escatawpa, Ms** Yd No: 142 Loa 59.99 Br ex - Dght 4.340 Lbp 58.22 Br md 14.02 Dpth 5.18 Welded, 1 dk	**(B21A20S) Platform Supply Ship** Grain: 239	**2 oil engines** reduction geared to sc. shafts driving 2 Z propellers Total Power: 2,868kW (3,900hp) 11.0kn EMD (Electro-Motive) 16-645-E6 2 x Vee 2 Stroke 16 Cy. 230 x 254 each-1434kW (1950bhp) General Motors Corp.Electro-Motive Div.-La Grange AuxGen: 2 x 99kW a.c Thrusters: 1 Thwart. FP thruster (f) Fuel: 398.2 (d.f.) 7.5pd
8765400 *WDG3599* -	**SEACOR STORM** *ex* Superior Storm *-2012* **SEACOR LB Offshore LLC** SEACOR Liftboats LLC *New Orleans, LA* *United States of America* MMSI: 367527710 Official number: 1120898	**1,142** 342 - Class: AB	**2002-05 Bollinger Marine Fabricators LLC — Amelia LA** Yd No: 398 Loa 40.55 Br ex 28.04 Dght - Lbp - Br md - Dpth 3.96 Welded, 1 dk	**(B22A2ZM) Offshore Construction Vessel, jack up** Cranes: 1x250t,1x30t	**2 oil engines** reduction geared to sc. shafts driving 2 Propellers Total Power: 2,236kW (3,040hp) Caterpillar 3512TA 2 x Vee 4 Stroke 12 Cy. 170 x 190 each-1118kW (1520bhp) Caterpillar Inc-USA AuxGen: 2 x 95kW 480V 60Hz a.c
8763012 *WDG3594* -	**SEACOR STRENGTH** *ex* Superior Spirit *-2012* *ex* Power IV *-2004* *ex* Dickson IV *-2000* *ex* Power IV *-1992* **SEACOR LB Offshore II LLC** SEACOR Liftboats LLC *New Orleans, LA* *United States of America* MMSI: 367527650 Official number: 680240	**194** 140 -	**1985 Crown Point Industries — Marrero, La** Yd No: 10688 Loa 30.48 Br ex 12.19 Dght 1.830 Lbp - Br md - Dpth 2.43 Welded, 1 dk	**(B22A2ZM) Offshore Construction Vessel, jack up** Cranes: 1x50t	**2 oil engines** geared to sc. shafts driving 2 Propellers Total Power: 662kW (900hp) G.M. (Detroit Diesel) 12V-71 2 x Vee 2 Stroke 12 Cy. 108 x 127 each-331kW (450bhp) Detroit Diesel Corporation-Detroit, Mi
9690004 *WDG7424* -	**SEACOR STRONG** **SEACOR Strong LLC** SEACOR Marine LLC *New Orleans, LA* *United States of America* MMSI: 303523000 Official number: 1245523	**1,445** 433 2,068 Class: AB	**2013-08 Master Boat Builders, Inc. — Coden, Al** Yd No: 430 Loa 62.00 Br ex 14.72 Dght 4.660 Lbp 58.52 Br md 14.63 Dpth 4.88 Welded, 1 dk	**(B22A20R) Offshore Support Vessel**	**2 oil engines** reduction geared to sc. shafts driving 2 FP propellers Total Power: 2,850kW (3,874hp) 10.5kn Caterpillar 3512C-HD 2 x Vee 4 Stroke 12 Cy. 170 x 215 each-1425kW (1937bhp) Caterpillar Inc-USA AuxGen: 2 x 910kW 480V 60Hz a.c Thrusters: 2 Tunnel thruster (f); 2 Tunnel thruster (a)
8766052 *WDG3587* -	**SEACOR SUPPORTER** *ex* Superior Vision *-2012* *ex* P. G. Jones *-1998* **SEACOR LB Offshore LLC** SEACOR Liftboats LLC *New Orleans, LA* *United States of America* MMSI: 366817990 Official number: 1062039	**717** 215 -	**1998-02 Bollinger Machine Shop & Shipyard, Inc. — Lockport, La** Yd No: 321 Loa 35.52 Br ex 14.93 Dght 1.906 Lbp - Br md - Dpth 3.04 Welded, 1 dk	**(B22A2ZM) Offshore Construction Vessel, jack up** Cranes: 1x100t,1x25t	**2 oil engines** reduction geared to sc. shafts driving 2 Propellers Total Power: 1,492kW (2,028hp) 4.0kn Caterpillar 3508B 2 x Vee 4 Stroke 8 Cy. 170 x 190 each-746kW (1014bhp) Caterpillar Inc-USA AuxGen: 2 x 95kW 60Hz a.c

IMO / Call sign	Name / Owner / Manager / Flag	Tonnage	Class	Built / Builder / Dimensions	Type	Machinery
8109797 - - -	**SEACOR SURF** *ex* Western Surf *-1991* - -	**547** 164 -	Class: (AB)	**1982-03 Quality Shipbuilders Inc. — Moss Point, Ms** Yd No: 115 Loa 42.68 Br ex 10.11 Dght 3.920 Lbp 39.35 Br md 10.08 Dpth 4.14 Welded, 1 dk	**(B31A2SR) Research Survey Vessel**	**2 oil engines** sr reverse geared to sc. shafts driving 2 FP propellers Total Power: 1,250kW (1,700hp) 12.0kn Caterpillar D398SCAC 2 x Vee 4 Stroke 12 Cy. 159 x 203 each-625kW (850bhp) Caterpillar Tractor Co-USA AuxGen: 2 x 175kW 460V 60Hz a.c Thrusters: 1 Thwart. FP thruster (f)
9214939 *V7DF4* -	**SEACOR VALOR** **SEACOR Offshore LLC** SEACOR Marine LLC *Majuro* *Marshall Islands* MMSI: 538005380 Official number: 5380	**1,508** 452 1,990	Class: AB	**1999-07 Halter Marine Panama City, Inc. — Panama City, Fl** Yd No: 152 Loa 67.06 Br ex - Dght 5.000 Lbp 64.31 Br md 14.20 Dpth 6.10 Welded, 1 dk	**(B21B20A) Anchor Handling Tug Supply**	**2 oil engines** dr geared to sc. shafts driving 2 CP propellers Total Power: 5,968kW (8,114hp) 11.0kn EMD (Electro-Motive) 16-710-G7B 2 x Vee 2 Stroke 16 Cy. 230 x 279 each-2984kW (4057bhp) General Motors Corp.Electro-Motive Div.-La Grange AuxGen: 2 x 180kW 60Hz a.c Thrusters: 1 Thwart. FP thruster (f) Fuel: 565.2 (d.f.) 16.0pd
9163336 *WDC3760* -	**SEACOR VANGUARD** **SEACOR Offshore LLC** SEACOR Marine LLC *New Orleans, LA* *United States of America* MMSI: 368900000 Official number: 1059683	**2,983** 894 3,314	Class: AB	**1998-06 Halter Marine Pascagoula, Inc. — Pascagoula, Ms** Yd No: 257 Loa 77.72 (BB) Br ex - Dght 6.710 Lbp 74.68 Br md 18.29 Dpth 7.92 Welded, 1 dk	**(B21B20A) Anchor Handling Tug Supply** Passengers: berths: 24 Cranes: 1x20t	**4 oil engines** with flexible couplings & sr gearedto sc. shafts driving 2 CP propellers Total Power: 10,296kW (14,000hp) 12.3kn EMD (Electro-Motive) 16-645-F7B 4 x Vee 2 Stroke 16 Cy. 230 x 254 each-2574kW (3500bhp) General Motors Detroit DieselAllison Divn-USA AuxGen: 2 x 2000kW 480V 60Hz a.c, 1 x 400kW 480V 60Hz a.c Thrusters: 2 Thwart. FP thruster (f); 2 Tunnel thruster (a) Fuel: 986.6 (d.f.) 54.0pd
9196694 *WCY5598* -	**SEACOR VANTAGE** **SEACOR Offshore LLC** SEACOR Marine LLC *New Orleans, LA* *United States of America* MMSI: 366259000 Official number: 1065404	**2,283** 684 2,439	Class: AB	**1998-07 Moss Point Marine, Inc. — Escatawpa, Ms** Yd No: 141 Loa 73.46 Br ex - Dght 5.762 Lbp 70.41 Br md 15.85 Dpth 6.71 Welded	**(B21B20A) Anchor Handling Tug Supply** Grain: 224 Cranes: 1x5t	**4 oil engines** dr geared to sc. shafts driving 2 CP propellers Total Power: 9,032kW (12,280hp) 11.0kn EMD (Electro-Motive) 16-645-E7B 4 x Vee 2 Stroke 16 Cy. 230 x 254 each-2258kW (3070bhp) General Motors Corp-USA AuxGen: 2 x 1600kW a.c, 1 x 350kW a.c Thrusters: 2 Thwart. FP thruster (f); 1 Thwart. FP thruster (a) Fuel: 765.4 (d.f.) 18.0pd
9226865 *WDA5518* -	**SEACOR VENTURE** **Graham Offshore Inc** SEACOR Marine LLC *New Orleans, LA* *United States of America* MMSI: 338449000 Official number: 1065402	**1,576** 472 2,088	Class: AB	**2000-03 Moss Point Marine, Inc. — Escatawpa, Ms** Yd No: 153 Loa 67.06 Br ex - Dght 5.130 Lbp 64.31 Br md 14.63 Dpth 6.10 Welded, 1 dk	**(B21B20A) Anchor Handling Tug Supply**	**2 oil engines** with flexible couplings & dr gearedto sc. shafts driving 2 CP propellers Total Power: 5,884kW (8,000hp) 11.0kn EMD (Electro-Motive) 16-710-G7 2 x Vee 2 Stroke 16 Cy. 230 x 279 each-2942kW (4000bhp) General Motors Corp.Electro-Motive Div.-La Grange AuxGen: 2 x 185kW 480V 60Hz a.c Thrusters: 1 Tunnel thruster (f) Fuel: 716.8 (d.f.) 24.0pd
8764810 *WDG3597* -	**SEACOR VICTORY** *ex* Superior Victory *-2012* **SEACOR LB Offshore LLC** SEACOR Liftboats LLC *New Orleans, LA* *United States of America* MMSI: 367527680 Official number: 1098667	**674** 202 -		**2000 Conrad Industries, Inc. — Morgan City, La** Yd No: 679 Loa 35.05 Br ex 20.30 Dght 2.900 Lbp 33.90 Br md - Dpth 3.05 Welded, 1 dk	**(B22A2ZM) Offshore Construction Vessel, jack up** Cranes: 1x125t,1x25t	**2 oil engines** driving 2 FP propellers Total Power: 898kW (1,220hp) 5.0kn Caterpillar 3412 2 x Vee 4 Stroke 12 Cy. 137 x 152 each-449kW (610bhp) Caterpillar Inc-USA AuxGen: 2 x 95kW a.c
9533696 *XCTE8* -	**SEACOR VIKING** **Mantenimiento Express Maritimo S de RL de CV (Mexmar)** - *Ensenada* *Mexico* MMSI: 345070708	**3,601** 1,429 5,131	Class: AB	**2012-03 Fujian Mawei Shipbuilding Ltd — Fuzhou FJ** Yd No: 619-15 Loa 87.08 (BB) Br ex - Dght 6.050 Lbp 82.96 Br md 18.80 Dpth 7.40 Welded, 1 dk	**(B21A20S) Platform Supply Ship** Cranes: 1x2t	**4 diesel electric oil engines** driving 4 gen. each 1700kW Connecting to 2 elec. motors each (2000kW) driving 2 Azimuth electric drive units Total Power: 6,864kW (9,332hp) 12.0kn Cummins QSK60-M 4 x Vee 4 Stroke 16 Cy. 159 x 190 each-1716kW (2333bhp) Cummins Engine Co Inc-USA Thrusters: 1 Thwart. CP thruster (f); 1 Retract. directional thruster (f) Fuel: 970.0 (d.f.)
9206839 *V7YP6* -	**SEACOR VOYAGER** **SEACOR Offshore (Marshall Islands) Ltd** SEACOR Offshore Dubai LLC *Majuro* *Marshall Islands* MMSI: 538004705 Official number: 4705	**1,508** 452 2,194	Class: AB BV (Class contemplated)	**1998-12 Moss Point Marine, Inc. — Escatawpa, Ms** Yd No: 149 Loa 67.06 Br ex - Dght 5.169 Lbp 64.31 Br md 14.15 Dpth 6.10 Welded, 1 dk	**(B21B20A) Anchor Handling Tug Supply** Grain: 237	**2 oil engines** dr geared to sc. shafts driving 2 CP propellers Total Power: 5,884kW (8,000hp) 11.0kn EMD (Electro-Motive) 16-710-G7 2 x Vee 2 Stroke 16 Cy. 230 x 279 each-2942kW (4000bhp) General Motors Corp.Electro-Motive Div.-La Grange AuxGen: 2 x 185kW 480V 60Hz a.c Thrusters: 1 Thwart. FP thruster (f) Fuel: 594.6 (d.f.) 16.0pd
9533701 *XCVE4* -	**SEACOR WARRIOR** **Mantenimiento Express Maritimo S de RL de CV (Mexmar)** SEACOR Offshore Dubai LLC *Dos Bocas* *Mexico* MMSI: 345050041 Official number: 2701351032-6	**3,601** 1,429 5,145	Class: AB	**2012-07 Fujian Mawei Shipbuilding Ltd — Fuzhou FJ** Yd No: 619-16 Loa 87.08 (BB) Br ex - Dght 5.900 Lbp 82.96 Br md 18.80 Dpth 7.40 Welded, 1 dk	**(B21A20S) Platform Supply Ship**	**4 diesel electric oil engines** driving 4 gen. each 1825kW Connecting to 2 elec. motors each (2000kW) driving 2 Z propellers Total Power: 6,864kW (9,332hp) 12.0kn Cummins QSK60-M 4 x Vee 4 Stroke 16 Cy. 159 x 190 each-1716kW (2333bhp) Cummins Engine Co Inc-USA Thrusters: 1 Tunnel thruster (f); 1 Retract. directional thruster (f)
9296353 *WDD5978* -	**SEACOR WASHINGTON** **Siemens Financial Inc** SEACOR Marine LLC *New Orleans, LA* *United States of America* MMSI: 369297000 Official number: 1141431	**1,598** 479 2,315	Class: AB	**2003-09 Bollinger Machine Shop & Shipyard, Inc. — Lockport, La** Yd No: 436 Loa 63.09 Br ex - Dght 5.080 Lbp 59.43 Br md 16.15 Dpth 5.79 Welded, 1 dk	**(B21A20S) Platform Supply Ship** Passengers: 25	**2 oil engines** gearing integral to driving 2 Z propellers Total Power: 3,542kW (4,816hp) 11.0kn Caterpillar 3516B-HD 2 x Vee 4 Stroke 16 Cy. 170 x 215 each-1771kW (2408bhp) Caterpillar Inc-USA AuxGen: 2 x 370kW a.c Thrusters: 2 Thwart. CP thruster (f) Fuel: 720.0 (d.f.) 18.0pd
9112519 - - -	**SEACORAL DANIO** *ex* Kadya Banjar 11 *-2000* *ex* Regal I *-1995* - -	**177** 53 -	Class: (AB)	**1994 Hangzhou Dongfeng Shipyard — Hangzhou ZJ** Yd No: TS25-1 Loa 25.20 Br ex - Dght 2.394 Lbp 23.36 Br md 7.94 Dpth 2.97 Welded, 1 dk	**(B32A2ST) Tug**	**2 oil engines** reverse reduction geared to sc. shafts driving 2 FP propellers Total Power: 1,176kW (1,598hp) 12.0kn MWM TBD234V16 2 x Vee 4 Stroke 16 Cy. 128 x 140 each-588kW (799bhp) Motoren Werke Mannheim AG (MWM)-Mannheim AuxGen: 2 x 45kW a.c
9619335 *PNYV* -	**SEACOVE KNIGHT** **PT Wintermar** - *Jakarta* *Indonesia* MMSI: 525019586 Official number: 3272/PPM	**936** 280 865	Class: AB	**2011-01 P.T. Mariana Bahagia — Palembang** Yd No: 52 Loa 49.80 Br ex 12.90 Dght 4.500 Lbp 46.36 Br md 12.60 Dpth 5.30 Welded, 1 dk	**(B21B20A) Anchor Handling Tug Supply**	**2 oil engines** reduction geared to sc. shafts driving 2 Propellers Total Power: 3,680kW (5,004hp) Yanmar 6EY26 2 x 4 Stroke 6 Cy. 260 x 385 each-1840kW (2502bhp) Yanmar Diesel Engine Co Ltd-Japan AuxGen: 3 x 225kW a.c Thrusters: 1 Tunnel thruster (f) Fuel: 370.0
9695391 *JZIH* -	**SEACOVE NOBLE** **PT Sentosa Segara Mulia Shipping** PT Wintermar *Jakarta* *Indonesia*	**495** 166 -	Class: KI (Class contemplated) RI	**2013-04 P.T. Mariana Bahagia — Palembang** Yd No: 58 Loa 45.00 Br ex - Dght - Lbp - Br md 11.00 Dpth 4.00 Welded, 1 dk	**(B21B20A) Anchor Handling Tug Supply**	**2 oil engines** reduction geared to sc. shafts driving 2 Propellers Total Power: 2,460kW (3,344hp) Caterpillar 3512B 2 x Vee 4 Stroke 12 Cy. 170 x 190 each-1230kW (1672bhp) Caterpillar Inc-USA AuxGen: 3 x 257kW 380V a.c

9723796 *T2P04* -	**SEACOVE PEARL** **Seacove Overseas Ltd** - *Funafuti* *Tuvalu* MMSI: 572680210 Official number: 30111313	**387** - 400	Class: RI	**2014-01 P.T. Mariana Bahagia — Palembang** Yd No: 059 L reg 38.60 Br ex - Dght 3.200 Lbp 35.20 Br md 10.00 Dpth 4.00 Welded, 1 dk	**(B21B20T) Offshore Tug/Supply Ship**	**2 oil engines** reduction geared to sc. shafts driving 2 FP propellers Total Power: 1,220kW (1,658hp) AuxGen: 2 x 130kW a.c
7023087 - -	**SEACREST** *ex* Vermland *-2012* *ex* Gerd Gaustadnes *-1974* **Seatrans-UK Ltd** -	**608** 303 386	Class: (NV)	**1970 Lindstols Skips- & Baatbyggeri AS — Risor** Yd No: 268 Lengthened-1979 Loa 49.97 Br ex 9.02 Dght 3.240 Lbp 44.66 Br md 9.00 Dpth 5.87 Welded, 2 dks	**(A31A2GX) General Cargo Ship** Grain: 1,220; Bale: 1,110 Compartments: 1 Ho, ER 1 Ha: (28.5 x 6.2)ER Derricks: 1x5t,1x3t; Winches: 2 Ice Capable	**1 oil engine** geared to sc. shaft driving 1 FP propeller Total Power: 662kW (900hp) 11.5kn Grenaa 6FR24TK 1 x 4 Stroke 6 Cy. 240 x 300 662kW (900bhp) (made 1982, fitted 1995) A/S Grenaa Motorfabrik-Denmark AuxGen: 1 x 36kW 220V 50Hz a.c, 1 x 28kW 220V 50Hz a.c, 1 x 24kW 220V 50Hz a.c Fuel: 20.5 (d.f.) 2.0pd
9588421 *9WKI3* -	**SEACREST WARRIOR** **Vegasa Shipping Sdn Bhd** - *Kuching* *Malaysia* MMSI: 533036400 Official number: 333214	**379** 113 -	Class: BV	**2010-08 Sapor Shipbuilding Industries Sdn Bhd — Sibu** Yd No: SAPOR 31 Loa 33.20 Br ex - Dght 3.500 Lbp 29.30 Br md 9.70 Dpth 4.30 Welded, 1 dk	**(B32A2ST) Tug**	**2 oil engines** reduction geared to sc. shafts driving 2 FP propellers Total Power: 2,984kW (4,058hp) Cummins KTA-50-M2 2 x Vee 4 Stroke 16 Cy. 159 x 159 each-1492kW (2029bhp) Cummins Engine Co Ltd-United Kingdom AuxGen: 2 x 80kW 50Hz a.c
9297890 *C6UY2* -	**SEACROSS** **Narcissus Enterprises SA** Thenamaris (Ships Management) Inc SatCom: Inmarsat Mini-M 764556344 *Nassau* *Bahamas* MMSI: 309401000 Official number: 8001090	**84,601** 53,710 163,288 T/cm 123.1	Class: AB	**2006-01 Hyundai Samho Heavy Industries Co Ltd — Samho** Yd No: S247 Loa 274.19 (BB) Br ex 50.00 Dght 17.000 Lbp 264.00 Br md 49.97 Dpth 23.10 Welded, 1 dk	**(A13A2TV) Crude Oil Tanker** Double Hull (13F) Liq: 173,947; Liq (Oil): 173,947 Cargo Heating Coils Compartments: 12 Wing Ta, 2 Wing Slop Ta, ER 3 Cargo Pump (s): 3x4000m³/hr Manifold: Bow/CM: 135.9m Ice Capable	**1 oil engine** driving 1 FP propeller Total Power: 18,630kW (25,329hp) 15.5kn MAN-B&W 6S70MC-C 1 x 2 Stroke 6 Cy. 700 x 2800 18630kW (25329bhp) Hyundai Heavy Industries Co Ltd-South Korea AuxGen: 3 x 950kW 440/220V 60Hz a.c Fuel: 154.9 (d.f.) 4330.3 (r.f.)
9248801 *9HA2846* -	**SEACROWN I** *ex* Seacrown *-2011* **Felicia Seaways Co** Thenamaris (Ships Management) Inc *Valletta* *Malta* MMSI: 256337000 Official number: 9248801	**25,287** 10,185 40,039 T/cm 49.9	Class: NV	**2003-01 Hyundai Mipo Dockyard Co Ltd — Ulsan** Yd No: 0102 Loa 176.00 (BB) Br ex - Dght 11.100 Lbp 168.00 Br md 31.00 Dpth 17.00 Welded, 1 dk	**(A12B2TR) Chemical/Products Tanker** Double Hull (13F) Liq: 42,564; Liq (Oil): 42,564 Cargo Heating Coils Compartments: 12 Wing Ta, 2 Wing Slop Ta, ER 12 Cargo Pump (s): 12x450m³/hr Manifold: Bow/CM: 89.4m	**1 oil engine** driving 1 FP propeller Total Power: 8,580kW (11,665hp) 14.5kn B&W 6S50MC 1 x 2 Stroke 6 Cy. 500 x 1910 8580kW (11665bhp) Hyundai Heavy Industries Co Ltd-South Korea AuxGen: 3 x 740kW 450V 60Hz a.c Thrusters: 1 Thwart. FP thruster (f) Fuel: 201.0 (d.f.) 1414.0 (r.f.)
9183300 *9HJO9* -	**SEADANCE** *ex* Valiant *-2008* **Chalet Shipping Ltd** Eastern Mediterranean Maritime Ltd SatCom: Inmarsat B 324906510 *Valletta* *Malta* MMSI: 249065000 Official number: 9183300	**57,066** 32,719 105,477 T/cm 92.0	Class: AB	**1999-12 Hyundai Heavy Industries Co Ltd — Ulsan** Yd No: 1178 Loa 243.86 (BB) Br ex 42.00 Dght 14.920 Lbp 234.09 Br md 42.00 Dpth 21.00 Welded, 1 dk	**(A13A2TV) Crude Oil Tanker** Double Hull (13F) Liq: 115,536; Liq (Oil): 115,536 Cargo Heating Coils Compartments: 12 Wing Ta, 2 Wing Slop Ta, ER 3 Cargo Pump (s): 3x2500m³/hr Manifold: Bow/CM: 120.2m	**1 oil engine** driving 1 FP propeller Total Power: 12,269kW (16,681hp) 14.6kn MAN-B&W 6S60MC 1 x 2 Stroke 6 Cy. 600 x 2292 12269kW (16681bhp) Hyundai Heavy Industries Co Ltd-South Korea AuxGen: 3 x 762kW a.c Fuel: 165.0 (d.f.) 3277.0 (r.f.)
9297888 *C6UX9* -	**SEADANCER** **Kingsbury Navigation Ltd** Thenamaris (Ships Management) Inc SatCom: Inmarsat Mini-M 764556340 *Nassau* *Bahamas* MMSI: 309287000 Official number: 8001089	**84,601** 53,710 163,288 T/cm 123.1	Class: AB	**2006-01 Hyundai Samho Heavy Industries Co Ltd — Samho** Yd No: S246 Loa 274.19 (BB) Br ex 50.00 Dght 17.000 Lbp 264.01 Br md 49.97 Dpth 23.10 Welded, 1 dk	**(A13A2TV) Crude Oil Tanker** Double Hull (13F) Liq: 173,947; Liq (Oil): 173,947 Cargo Heating Coils Compartments: 12 Wing Ta, ER, 2 Wing Slop Ta 3 Cargo Pump (s): 3x4000m³/hr Manifold: Bow/CM: 135.9m Ice Capable	**1 oil engine** driving 1 FP propeller Total Power: 18,630kW (25,329hp) 15.5kn MAN-B&W 6S70MC-C 1 x 2 Stroke 6 Cy. 700 x 2800 18630kW (25329bhp) Hyundai Heavy Industries Co Ltd-South Korea AuxGen: 3 x 950kW 440/220V 60Hz a.c Fuel: 154.9 (d.f.) (Heating Coils) 4330.0 (r.f.)
7437692 *WBB5945* -	**SEADAWN** *ex* Virgo *-1989* *ex* Scorpio *-1978* **FY Fisheries Inc** *Newport, OR* *United States of America* MMSI: 367372000 Official number: 548685	**348** 104 -		**1973 John A. Martinolich Shipbuilding Corp. — Tacoma, Wa** L reg 28.53 Br ex 8.84 Dght - Lbp - Br md - Dpth 2.72 Welded, 1 dk	**(B11B2FV) Fishing Vessel**	**1 oil engine** driving 1 FP propeller Total Power: 625kW (850hp) Caterpillar D398SCAC 1 x Vee 4 Stroke 12 Cy. 159 x 203 625kW (850bhp) Caterpillar Tractor Co-USA
9386536 *9HA3530* -	**SEADELTA** *ex* Stealth Haralambos *-2014* *launched as* Cape Alba *-2009* **Tank Pasha Inc** Thenamaris (Ships Management) Inc *Valletta* *Malta* MMSI: 229700000 Official number: 9386536	**62,775** 34,934 113,021 T/cm 99.7	Class: AB	**2009-01 New Times Shipbuilding Co Ltd — Jingjiang JS** Yd No: 0311512 Loa 249.96 (BB) Br ex 44.04 Dght 14.800 Lbp 240.00 Br md 44.00 Dpth 21.00 Welded, 1 dk	**(A13A2TW) Crude/Oil Products Tanker** Double Hull (13F) Liq: 124,679; Liq (Oil): 127,453 Cargo Heating Coils Compartments: 12 Wing Ta, 2 Wing Slop Ta, ER 3 Cargo Pump (s): 3x3000m³/hr Manifold: Bow/CM: 122.5m	**1 oil engine** driving 1 FP propeller Total Power: 15,820kW (21,509hp) 15.0kn MAN-B&W 7S60MC-C 1 x 2 Stroke 7 Cy. 600 x 2400 15820kW (21509bhp) Doosan Engine Co Ltd-South Korea AuxGen: 3 x 1125kW a.c Fuel: 225.0 (d.f.) 3000.0 (r.f.)
7129506 *HO5031* -	**SEADIVER** *ex* Seaquest I *-2009* *ex* Trinity Seal *-2008* *ex* Gulf Responder *-1996* *ex* Jade *-1991* *ex* Baltic Seahorse *-1991* **Seamar Marine Services LLC** - *Panama* *Panama* MMSI: 351719000 Official number: 3465909B	**604** 181 975	Class: (AB)	**1972 Burton Shipyard Co., Inc. — Port Arthur, Tx** Yd No: 482 Loa 53.65 Br ex 11.64 Dght 3.371 Lbp 50.88 Br md 11.59 Dpth 3.97 Welded, 1 dk	**(B21B20T) Offshore Tug/Supply Ship**	**2 oil engines** driving 2 FP propellers Total Power: 1,654kW (2,248hp) 12.0kn Caterpillar D399TA 2 x Vee 4 Stroke 16 Cy. 159 x 203 each-827kW (1124bhp) Caterpillar Tractor Co-USA AuxGen: 2 x 75kW 440V 60Hz a.c Thrusters: 1 Thwart. FP thruster (f) Fuel: 253.0 (d.f.)
9632832 *9HA3399* -	**SEADREAM** **Rainbow Shipholding SA** Thenamaris (Ships Management) Inc *Valletta* *Malta* MMSI: 229550000 Official number: 9632832	**52,467** 29,753 62,603	Class: LR ✠ **100A1** SS 01/2014 container ship **ShipRight** (SDA, FDA plus, CM, ACS (B)) CCSA *IWS LI EP (Bt,Ede,I) ✠ **LMC** **UMS** Eq.Ltr: V†; Cable: 715.0/92.0 U3 (a)	**2014-01 Hyundai Samho Heavy Industries Co Ltd — Samho** Yd No: S617 Loa 255.40 (BB) Br ex 37.43 Dght 13.500 Lbp 242.00 Br md 37.40 Dpth 22.10 Welded, 1 dk	**(A33A2CC) Container Ship (Fully Cellular)** TEU 5071 C Ho 1982 TEU C Dk 3089 TEU incl 770 ref C Compartments: 7 Cell Ho, ER 7 Ha: ER	**1 oil engine** driving 1 FP propeller Total Power: 26,700kW (36,301hp) 21.5kn MAN-B&W 6G80ME-C9 1 x 2 Stroke 6 Cy. 800 x 3720 26700kW (36301bhp) Hyundai Heavy Industries Co Ltd-South Korea AuxGen: 4 x 2300kW 450V 60Hz a.c Boilers: e (ex.g.) 12.2kgf/cm² (12.0bar), AuxB (o.f.) 9.2kgf/cm² (9.0bar) Thrusters: 1 Thwart. CP thruster (f)
8203438 *C6PW8*	**SEADREAM I** *ex* Seabourn Goddess I *-2001* *ex* Sea Goddess I *-2000* **SeaDream Yacht Club AS** SeaDream Yacht Club Management AS SatCom: Inmarsat A 1320363 *Nassau* *Bahamas* MMSI: 308908000 Official number: 731014	**4,333** 1,299 450	Class: LR (NV) **100A1** CS 03/2009 passenger ship **LMC** Eq.Ltr: S; Cable: 467.5/36.0 U3 (a)	**1984-03 Oy Wartsila Ab — Helsinki** Yd No: 466 Loa 104.83 (BB) Br ex - Dght 4.001 Lbp 90.56 Br md 14.51 Dpth 6.00 Welded, 3 dks	**(A37A2PC) Passenger/Cruise** Passengers: cabins: 58; berths: 113	**2 oil engines** with clutches, flexible couplings & sr geared to sc. shafts driving 2 CP propellers Total Power: 3,540kW (4,812hp) 17.5kn Wartsila 12V22HF 2 x Vee 4 Stroke 12 Cy. 220 x 240 each-1770kW (2406bhp) Oy Wartsila Ab-Finland AuxGen: 3 x 496kW 450V 60Hz a.c Boilers: e (ex.g.) 8.2kgf/cm² (8.0bar), AuxB (o.f.) 8.2kgf/cm² (8.0bar) Thrusters: 1 Thwart. CP thruster (f) Fuel: 19.0 (d.f.) 297.5 (r.f.) 16.5pd

IMO / Call sign	Name / Owner / Manager / Flag	Tonnage	Class	Builder / Dimensions	Type	Machinery
8203440 *C6PW9* -	**SEADREAM II** *ex* Seabourn Goddess II *-2001* *ex* Sea Goddess II *-2000* **SeaDream Yacht Club AS** SeaDream Yacht Club Management AS *Nassau* *Bahamas* MMSI: 308311000 Official number: 731015	**4,333** 1,300 450	Class: LR (NV) **100A1** CS 11/2009 passenger ship **LMC** Eq.Ltr: S; Cable: 467.5/36.0 U3 (a)	**1985**-04 **Hollming Oy — Rauma** (Hull) **1985**-04 **Oy Wartsila Ab — Helsinki** Yd No: 467 Loa 104.81 (BB) Br ex - Dght 4.001 Lbp 90.56 Br md 14.61 Dpth 6.00 Welded, 3 dks	**(A37A2PC) Passenger/Cruise** Passengers: cabins: 58; berths: 113	**2 oil engines** with clutches, flexible couplings & sr geared to sc. shafts driving 2 CP propellers Total Power: 3,540kW (4,812hp) 17.5kn Wartsila 12V22HF 2 x Vee 4 Stroke 12 Cy. 220 x 240 each-1770kW (2406bhp) Oy Wartsila Ab-Finland AuxGen: 3 x 496kW 450V 60Hz a.c Boilers: e (ex.g.) 7.0kgf/cm² (6.9bar), WTAuxB (o.f.) 7.0kgf/cm² (6.9bar) Thrusters: 1 Thwart. CP thruster (f) Fuel: 19.0 (d.f.) 297.5 (r.f.) 16.5pd
9153056 *9HA3271* -	**SEAEAGLE** *ex* Cemtex Renaissance *-2013* **Rosemary Shipping Ltd** Eastern Mediterranean Maritime Ltd *Valletta* *Malta* MMSI: 229364000 Official number: 9153056	**37,709** 23,950 71,663 T/cm 65.8	Class: BV (AB) (CR)	**1998**-01 **Hitachi Zosen Corp — Maizuru KY** Yd No: 4917 Loa 223.70 (BB) Br ex - Dght 13.430 Lbp 215.00 Br md 32.20 Dpth 18.60 Welded, 1 dk	**(A21A2BC) Bulk Carrier** Grain: 85,136; Bale: 82,337 Compartments: 7 Ho, ER 7 Ha: (16.2 x 13.0)6 (17.0 x 14.5)ER	**1 oil engine** driving 1 FP propeller Total Power: 8,702kW (11,831hp) 14.5kn B&W 6S60MC 1 x 2 Stroke 6 Cy. 600 x 2292 8702kW (11831bhp) Hitachi Zosen Corp-Japan
9667851 *J8B4821* -	**SEAEAGLES COMMANDER** **Sea Eagles Shipping LLC** - *Kingstown* *St Vincent & The Grenadines* MMSI: 375847000 Official number: 11294	**294** 88 160	Class: BV (Class contemplated) LR ✠ **100A1** SS 03/2013 escort tug fire-fighting Ship 1 (2400m3/h) *IWS **LMC** **UMS** Eq.Ltr: F; Cable: 275.0/19.0 U2 (a)	**2013**-03 **Santierul Naval Damen Galati S.A. — Galati** (Hull) Yd No: 1235 **2013**-03 **B.V. Scheepswerf Damen — Gorinchem** Yd No: 512318 Loa 28.67 Br ex 10.43 Dght 4.800 Lbp 27.90 Br md 9.80 Dpth 4.60 Welded, 1 dk	**(B32A2ST) Tug**	**2 oil engines** gearing integral to driving 2 Directional propellers Total Power: 3,728kW (5,068hp) Caterpillar 3516C-HD 2 x Vee 4 Stroke 16 Cy. 170 x 215 each-1864kW (2534bhp) Caterpillar Inc-USA AuxGen: 2 x 86kW 400V 50Hz a.c
9667849 *J8B4803* -	**SEAEAGLES LEADER** **Sea Eagles Shipping LLC** - *Kingstown* *St Vincent & The Grenadines* MMSI: 375815000 Official number: 11276	**294** 88 160	Class: BV (Class contemplated) LR ✠ **100A1** SS 02/2013 escort tug, fire-fighting Ship 1 (2400m3/h) *IWS **LMC** **UMS** Eq.Ltr: F; Cable: 275.0/19.0 U2 (a)	**2013**-02 **Santierul Naval Damen Galati S.A. — Galati** (Hull) Yd No: 1234 **2013**-02 **B.V. Scheepswerf Damen — Gorinchem** Yd No: 512317 Loa 28.67 Br ex 10.43 Dght 4.800 Lbp 27.90 Br md 9.80 Dpth 4.60 Welded, 1 dk	**(B32A2ST) Tug**	**2 oil engines** reduction geared to sc. shafts driving 2 Directional propellers Total Power: 3,728kW (5,068hp) Caterpillar 3516B-HD 2 x Vee 4 Stroke 16 Cy. 170 x 215 each-1864kW (2534bhp) Caterpillar Inc-USA AuxGen: 2 x 86kW 400V 50Hz a.c
9236755 *9HFA7* -	**SEAEMPRESS** **Eternal Navigation Ltd** Thenamaris (Ships Management) Inc *Valletta* *Malta* MMSI: 215171000 Official number: 7605	**23,241** 10,113 39,443 T/cm 46.1	Class: NV	**2002**-02 **Hyundai Mipo Dockyard Co Ltd — Ulsan** Yd No: 0019 Converted From: Chemical/Products Tanker-2005 Loa 182.55 Br ex 27.34 Dght 11.722 Lbp 175.00 Br md 27.30 Dpth 16.70 Welded, 1 dk	**(A13B2TP) Products Tanker** Double Hull (13F) Liq: 41,343; Liq (Oil): 43,119 Cargo Heating Coils Compartments: 12 Wing Ta, 2 Wing Slop Ta, ER 12 Cargo Pump (s): 2x300m³/hr, 10x500m³/hr Manifold: Bow/CM: 91.5m	**1 oil engine** driving 1 FP propeller Total Power: 9,467kW (12,871hp) 14.5kn B&W 6S50MC-C 1 x 2 Stroke 6 Cy. 500 x 2000 9467kW (12871bhp) Hyundai Heavy Industries Co Ltd-South Korea AuxGen: 3 x a.c Fuel: 95.0 (d.f.) 1000.0 (r.f.)
9248796 *9HJI7* -	**SEAEXPLORER** **Beloved Enterprises Ltd** Thenamaris (Ships Management) Inc *Valletta* *Malta* MMSI: 215311000 Official number: 7909	**25,287** 10,185 39,975 T/cm 49.9	Class: NV	**2003**-01 **Hyundai Mipo Dockyard Co Ltd — Ulsan** Yd No: 0101 Loa 175.93 (BB) Br ex 31.03 Dght 11.116 Lbp 168.00 Br md 31.00 Dpth 17.00 Welded, 1 dk	**(A12B2TR) Chemical/Products Tanker** Double Hull (13F) Liq: 42,685; Liq (Oil): 42,685 Cargo Heating Coils Compartments: 12 Wing Ta, 2 Wing Slop Ta, ER 12 Cargo Pump (s): 12x450m³/hr Manifold: Bow/CM: 88m	**1 oil engine** driving 1 FP propeller Total Power: 8,580kW (11,665hp) 14.5kn B&W 6S50MC 1 x 2 Stroke 6 Cy. 500 x 1910 8580kW (11665bhp) Hyundai Heavy Industries Co Ltd-South Korea AuxGen: 3 x 740kW 450V 60Hz a.c Thrusters: 1 Tunnel thruster (f) Fuel: 220.0 (d.f.) 1425.0 (r.f.)
9344019 *9HA3260* -	**SEAEXPRESS** **Savoy Trading Co** Thenamaris (Ships Management) Inc *Valletta* *Malta* MMSI: 229353000 Official number: 9344019	**28,069** 11,597 45,976 T/cm 50.6	Class: NK (BV)	**2007**-10 **Shin Kurushima Dockyard Co. Ltd. — Onishi** Yd No: 5426 Loa 179.88 (BB) Br ex 32.23 Dght 12.022 Lbp 172.00 Br md 32.20 Dpth 18.70 Welded, 1 dk	**(A13B2TP) Products Tanker** Double Hull (13F) Liq: 51,988; Liq (Oil): 51,789 Cargo Heating Coils Compartments: 14 Wing Ta, 2 Wing Slop Ta, ER 4 Cargo Pump (s): 4x1000m³/hr Manifold: Bow/CM: 91.3m	**1 oil engine** driving 1 FP propeller Total Power: 9,480kW (12,889hp) 15.1kn MAN-B&W 6S50MC-C 1 x 2 Stroke 6 Cy. 500 x 2000 9480kW (12889bhp) Mitsui Engineering & Shipbuilding CLtd-Japan AuxGen: 3 x 720kW 450/220V 60Hz a.c Fuel: 170.0 (d.f.) 1700.0 (r.f.)
8650722 *4LHN2* -	**SEAF-TSITSINATELA** *ex* Ihsan Usta *-2011* **Madai Ltd** - *Poti* *Georgia* MMSI: 213831000 Official number: C-01401	**133** 48 122	Class: MG	**2001**-12 **Surmene Tersanesi — Trabzon** Loa 22.40 Br ex 8.60 Dght - Lbp - Br md - Dpth 2.35 Welded, 1 dk	**(B11B2FV) Fishing Vessel**	**2 oil engines** reduction geared to sc. shafts driving 2 Propellers Iveco Aifo AB Volvo Penta-Sweden
9185279 *9HVU6* -	**SEAFAITH II** *ex* Stavanger Solveig *-2000* **Cordelia Shipping Co** Thenamaris (Ships Management) Inc *Valletta* *Malta* MMSI: 248915000 Official number: 7133	**57,951** 32,370 109,280 T/cm 90.8	Class: AB (NV)	**2000**-08 **Dalian New Shipbuilding Heavy Industries Co Ltd — Dalian LN** Yd No: PC1100-6 Loa 244.60 (BB) Br ex - Dght 15.517 Lbp 233.00 Br md 42.00 Dpth 22.20 Welded, 1 dk	**(A13A2TW) Crude/Oil Products Tanker** Double Hull (13F) Liq: 117,919; Liq (Oil): 117,919 Cargo Heating Coils Compartments: 12 Wing Ta, 2 Wing Slop Ta, ER 3 Cargo Pump (s): 3x300m³/hr	**1 oil engine** driving 1 FP propeller Total Power: 15,550kW (21,142hp) 15.3kn Sulzer 7RTA62U 1 x 2 Stroke 7 Cy. 620 x 2150 15550kW (21142bhp) Dalian Marine Diesel Works-China AuxGen: 3 x 820kW 450V 60Hz a.c Fuel: 195.0 (d.f.) 3055.0 (r.f.)
7805485 *4RCU* -	**SEAFALCON** *ex* Sea Falcon III *-1996* *ex* Kyoyu Maru *-1995* **GSM Puteri Maritime SA** Golden Star Marine Pte Ltd *Colombo* *Sri Lanka* MMSI: 417222376 Official number: 1334	**1,187** 688 2,024	Class: NK	**1978**-08 **Sasaki Shipbuilding Co Ltd — Osakikamijima HS** Yd No: 325 Loa 74.95 Br ex - Dght 4.717 Lbp 70.00 Br md 11.50 Dpth 5.20 Welded, 1 dk	**(A13B2TP) Products Tanker**	**2 oil engines** driving 2 FP propellers Total Power: 1,176kW (1,598hp) 10.0kn Matsui 6M26KR 2 x 4 Stroke 6 Cy. 260 x 400 each-588kW (799bhp) Matsui Iron Works Co Ltd-Japan Fuel: 68.0 (d.f.)
9231212 *9HA2814* -	**SEAFALCON** *ex* Dubai Legend *-2011* *ex* Oinoussian Spirit *-2006* *launched as* Golden Sea *-2002* **Dolphin Bay Marine SA** Thenamaris (Ships Management) Inc *Valletta* *Malta* MMSI: 256078000 Official number: 9231212	**62,247** 33,887 112,661 T/cm 98.4	Class: LR ✠ **100A1** SS 02/2012 Double Hull oil tanker ESP *IWS SPM LI **ShipRight** (SDA, FDA, CM) ✠ **LMC** **UMS IGS** Eq.Ltr: U†; Cable: 715.0/90.0 U3 (a)	**2002**-02 **Samho Heavy Industries Co Ltd — Samho** Yd No: 129 Loa 249.97 (BB) Br ex 44.00 Dght 14.618 Lbp 239.00 Br md 44.00 Dpth 21.00 Welded, 1 dk	**(A13A2TV) Crude Oil Tanker** Double Hull (13F) Liq: 123,785; Liq (Oil): 123,785 Compartments: 12 Wing Ta, ER, 2 Wing Slop Ta 3 Cargo Pump (s): 3x3000m³/hr Manifold: Bow/CM: 124.2m	**1 oil engine** driving 1 FP propeller Total Power: 14,280kW (19,415hp) 15.0kn B&W 7S60MC 1 x 2 Stroke 7 Cy. 600 x 2292 14280kW (19415bhp) Hyundai Heavy Industries Co Ltd-South Korea AuxGen: 3 x 750kW 220/440V 60Hz a.c Boilers: e (ex.g.) 20.4kgf/cm² (20.0bar), WTAuxB (o.f.) 18.4kgf/cm² (18.0bar) Fuel: 232.4 (d.f.) (Heating Coils) 3056.0 (r.f.) 52.0pd
8506414 *3FBD2* -	**SEAFARER** *ex* Irbe Venta *-2010* *ex* Sophie O *-2006* *ex* Bremer Anna *-2003* *ex* Aros News *-2002* *ex* Nioba *-1997* *ex* Bremer Import *-1991* *ex* Nioba *-1989* *ex* Rudolf Karstens *-1987* **Afloat Leasing Ltd** Sea Link Shipping LLC *Panama* *Panama* MMSI: 353678000 Official number: 40954PEXT2	**2,816** 1,526 3,674	Class: GL	**1985**-12 **Muetzelfeldtwerft GmbH — Cuxhaven** Yd No: 205 Loa 91.17 (BB) Br ex 13.85 Dght 5.240 Lbp 84.46 Br md 13.81 Dpth 6.76 Welded, 2 dks	**(A31A2GX) General Cargo Ship** Grain: 5,219; Bale: 5,172 TEU 187 C.Ho 105/20' (40') C.Dk 82/20' (40') incl. 8 ref C. Compartments: 1 Ho, ER 1 Ha: (57.1 x 11.0)ER Cranes: 2x25t Ice Capable	**1 oil engine** with flexible couplings & sr gearedto sc. shaft driving 1 CP propeller Total Power: 1,739kW (2,364hp) 12.5kn Wartsila 6R32 1 x 4 Stroke 6 Cy. 320 x 350 1739kW (2364bhp) Oy Wartsila Ab-Finland AuxGen: 2 x 220kW 380V 50Hz a.c, 2 x 192kW 380V 50Hz a.c, 2 x 50kW 380V 50Hz a.c Thrusters: 1 Thwart. FP thruster (f) Fuel: 54.5 (d.f.) 203.0 (r.f.) 7.5pd
8701753 *VVMW* -	**SEAFARER** **Sri Murugan Fisheries Co Pvt Ltd** - *Mormugao* *India* Official number: 2218	*127* 38 75	Class: (IR)	**1987**-12 **Chowgule & Co Pvt Ltd — Goa** Yd No: 94 Loa 24.01 Br ex 7.40 Dght 2.636 Lbp 20.02 Br md 7.21 Dpth 3.41 Welded, 1 dk	**(B11A2FS) Stern Trawler** Ins: 45	**1 oil engine** with clutches & sr geared to sc. shaft driving 1 FP propeller Total Power: 331kW (450hp) Caterpillar 3412T 1 x Vee 4 Stroke 12 Cy. 137 x 152 331kW (450bhp) Caterpillar Inc-USA AuxGen: 2 x 16kW 415V 50Hz a.c Fuel: 5.3 (d.f.)

IMO / Call sign	Name / Owner	Tonnage	Class	Build / Dimensions	Type	Machinery
8855932 *WDD6933* -	**SEAFARER** **Jessie Jean Enterprises Inc** *Point Judith, RI* *United States of America* MMSI: 367179650 Official number: 675048	*158* 107 -		**1984 La Force Shipyard Inc — Coden AL** Yd No: 18 Loa - Br ex - Dght - Lbp 23.38 Br md 7.32 Dpth 3.60 Welded, 1 dk	**(B11B2FV) Fishing Vessel**	**1 oil engine** driving 1 FP propeller
9057991 *HSHE*	**SEAFDEC** **The South East Asian Fisheries Development Center** - SatCom: Inmarsat C 456700910 *Bangkok* *Thailand* MMSI: 567072000 Official number: 350900855	**1,178** 354 745	Class: NK	**1993-02 Miho Zosensho K.K. — Shimizu** Yd No: 1419 Loa 65.03 (BB) Br ex - Dght 5.008 Lbp 58.46 Br md 12.00 Dpth 7.10 Welded, 1 dk	**(B12D2FR) Fishery Research Vessel** Ins: 148	**1 oil engine** with clutches, flexible couplings & sr geared to sc. shaft driving 1 CP propeller Total Power: 2,060kW (2,801hp) 14.3kn Yanmar 6N330-UN 1 x 4 Stroke 6 Cy. 330 x 440 2060kW (2801bhp) Yanmar Diesel Engine Co Ltd-Japan AuxGen: 3 x 330kW a.c Thrusters: 1 Thwart. CP thruster (f) Fuel: 390.0 (r.f.)
9296937 *HSHU*	**SEAFDEC 2** **The South East Asian Fisheries Development Center** - *Bangkok* *Thailand* Official number: 460002765	**211** 64 107	Class: NK	**2004-02 Niigata Shipbuilding & Repair Inc — Niigata NI** Yd No: 0001 Loa 33.24 (BB) Br ex - Dght 3.023 Lbp 27.00 Br md 7.20 Dpth 3.00 Welded, 1 dk	**(B12D2FR) Fishery Research Vessel** Grain: 28; Bale: 20	**1 oil engine** geared to sc. shaft driving 1 CP propeller Total Power: 736kW (1,001hp) 12.0kn Yanmar 6N18A-EV 1 x 4 Stroke 6 Cy. 180 x 280 736kW (1001bhp) Yanmar Diesel Engine Co Ltd-Japan AuxGen: 1 x 160kW a.c Thrusters: 1 Tunnel thruster (f) Fuel: 50.0 (d.f.)
7433907 *WDD6122* -	**SEAFISHER** *ex Savage -1991* **M/V Savage Inc** Kemp Pacific Fisheries Inc SatCom: Inmarsat A 1502756 *Seattle, WA* *United States of America* MMSI: 367658000 Official number: 575587	**1,453** 586 1,000	Class: (AB)	**1976-08 Halter Marine, Inc. — Moss Point, Ms** Yd No: 520 Converted From: Offshore Supply Ship-1991 Loa 54.87 Br ex 12.20 Dght 3.683 Lbp 49.92 Br md 12.15 Dpth 4.27 Welded, 1 dk	**(B11B2FV) Fishing Vessel**	**2 oil engines** reverse reduction geared to sc. shafts driving 2 FP propellers Total Power: 2,206kW (3,000hp) 12.0kn EMD (Electro-Motive) 12-645-E2 2 x Vee 2 Stroke 12 Cy. 230 x 254 each-1103kW (1500bhp) General Motors Corp.Electro-Motive Div.-La Grange AuxGen: 2 x 150kW a.c Fuel: 222.5 (d.f.)
8924393 *UBIE6* -	**SEAFLIGHT-I** *ex Katran-4 -1998* **Black Sea Express Lines Co Ltd (OOO 'Chernomorskiye Skorostnyye Linii LC')** - *Novorossiysk* *Russia* MMSI: 273310870	**135** 52 15	Class: (RS) (RI)	**1996-11 OAO Volgogradskiy Sudostroitelnyy Zavod — Volgograd** Yd No: S-604 Loa 34.50 Br ex 10.30 Dght 1.140 Lbp 30.93 Br md 5.80 Dpth 1.80 Welded, 1 dk	**(A37B2PS) Passenger Ship** Passengers: 124	**2 oil engines** geared to sc. shafts driving 2 FP propellers Total Power: 2,520kW (3,426hp) M.T.U. 12V396TE74 2 x Vee 4 Stroke 12 Cy. 165 x 185 each-1260kW (1713bhp) MTU Friedrichshafen GmbH-Friedrichshafen AuxGen: 2 x 8kW a.c
8894615 *UGWD* -	**SEAFLIGHT II** *ex Katran-1 -1998* **Black Sea Express Lines Co Ltd (OOO 'Chernomorskiye Skorostnyye Linii LC')** - *Novorossiysk* *Russia*	*135* 53 15	Class: RS (RI)	**1994-12 OAO Volgogradskiy Sudostroitelnyy Zavod — Volgograd** Yd No: S-601 Loa 34.50 Br ex 10.30 Dght 1.140 Lbp 30.00 Br md 5.80 Dpth 1.80 Welded, 1 dk	**(A37B2PS) Passenger Ship** Hull Material: Aluminium Alloy Passengers: 121	**2 oil engines** geared to sc. shafts driving 2 FP propellers Total Power: 2,104kW (2,860hp) 34.0kn M.T.U. 12V396TC82 2 x Vee 4 Stroke 12 Cy. 165 x 185 each-1052kW (1430bhp) MTU Friedrichshafen GmbH-Friedrichshafen AuxGen: 2 x 8kW a.c Fuel: 2.0 (d.f.)
1007067 *ZCG06* -	**SEAFLOWER** **Seaflower Holdings Ltd** Master Yachts Consultancy SL *George Town* *Cayman Islands (British)* MMSI: 319689000 Official number: 735449	**405** 121 78	Class: LR ✠ **100A1** SS 04/2012 SSC Yacht, mono, G6 **LMC** **UMS** Cable: 278.0/17.5 U2 (a)	**2002-04 Jacht- en Scheepswerf C. van Lent & Zonen B.V. — Kaag** Yd No: 787 Loa 40.00 Br ex 9.00 Dght 3.490 Lbp 35.04 Br md 8.70 Dpth 4.65 Welded, 1 dk	**(X11A2YP) Yacht**	**2 oil engines** with clutches, flexible couplings & sr reverse geared to sc. shafts driving 2 FP propellers Total Power: 1,060kW (1,442hp) 13.0kn Caterpillar 3412TA 2 x Vee 4 Stroke 12 Cy. 137 x 152 each-530kW (721bhp) Caterpillar Inc-USA AuxGen: 2 x 85kW 400V 50Hz a.c Thrusters: 1 Thwart. FP thruster (f)
8623248 *YB3431*	**SEAFLYTE** *ex Seaflyte H34 -1985* **PT Batam Fast** - *Indonesia* MMSI: 525023095	**127** 59 -		**1981 SBF Shipbuilders (1977) Pty Ltd — Fremantle WA** Loa 29.55 Br ex 6.46 Dght - Lbp - Br md 6.42 Dpth 3.20 Welded, 1 dk	**(A37B2PS) Passenger Ship** Passengers: 240	**2 oil engines** driving 2 FP propellers M.T.U. 2 x Vee 4 Stroke 8 Cy. MTU Friedrichshafen GmbH-Friedrichshafen
9082582 *ZM2673* -	**SEAFLYTE** **Fullers Group Ltd** - *Auckland* *New Zealand* Official number: 876063	**143** 107 19	Class: (BV)	**1994-09 WaveMaster International Pty Ltd — Fremantle WA** Yd No: 051 Loa 21.50 Br ex 8.05 Dght - Lbp 19.30 Br md 7.70 Dpth 2.50 Welded	**(A37B2PS) Passenger Ship** Hull Material: Aluminium Alloy Passengers: unberthed: 159	**2 oil engines** with clutches, flexible couplings & sr reverse geared to sc. shafts driving 2 FP propellers Total Power: 810kW (1,102hp) 22.0kn M.T.U. 8V183TE72 2 x Vee 4 Stroke 8 Cy. 128 x 142 each-405kW (551bhp) MTU Friedrichshafen GmbH-Friedrichshafen
6912499 *HP3778*	**SEAFORCE** *ex Framfjord -2010 ex Sotra -2008* *ex Sture-Goran -2005 ex Sirafjord -1985* **Northsea Offshore Services BV** GloMar Shipmanagement BV *Panama* *Panama* MMSI: 370522000 Official number: 4301411	**193** 57 39	Class: RI	**1969 Georg Eides Sonner AS — Hoylandsbygd** Yd No: 85 Converted From: Salvage Vessel-1986 Converted From: Ferry (Passenger only)-1979 Lengthened-1978 Loa 30.15 Br ex 6.74 Dght 2.560 Lbp 23.50 Br md 6.70 Dpth 3.41 Welded, 1 dk	**(B22G2OY) Standby Safety Vessel** Bale: 130	**1 oil engine** reduction geared to sc. shaft driving 1 CP propeller Total Power: 653kW (888hp) 10.0kn Caterpillar 3508 1 x Vee 4 Stroke 8 Cy. 170 x 190 653kW (888bhp) (new engine 2000) Caterpillar Inc-USA AuxGen: 2 x 160kW 50Hz a.c Thrusters: 1 Thwart. FP thruster (f) Fuel: 30.0 (d.f.)
8628119 *DUH2498*	**SEAFORD 5** *ex Shinriki Maru No. 2 -2002* **Seaford Shipping Lines Inc** *Cebu* *Philippines* Official number: CEB1006111	*249* 166 683		**1986 K.K. Kamishima Zosensho — Osakikamijima** Yd No: 183 Loa 56.32 Br ex - Dght 3.290 Lbp 51.01 Br md 9.50 Dpth 5.52 Welded, 1 dk	**(A31A2GX) General Cargo Ship**	**1 oil engine** geared to sc. shaft driving 1 FP propeller Total Power: 625kW (850hp) 8.5kn Hanshin 6LU26G 1 x 4 Stroke 6 Cy. 260 x 440 625kW (850bhp) The Hanshin Diesel Works Ltd-Japan
8408167 *DUH2379* -	**SEAFORD 7** *ex Lucila -2002 ex Shinko Maru No. 21 -1998* **Seaford Shipping Lines Inc** - *Cebu* *Philippines* Official number: CD07004924	*299* 203 942		**1984-06 Namikata Shipbuilding Co Ltd — Imabari EH** Yd No: 117 Loa 64.42 Br ex - Dght 3.452 Lbp 59.52 Br md 10.51 Dpth 6.02 Welded, 1 dk	**(A31A2GX) General Cargo Ship** Grain: 1,379 Compartments: 1 Ho, ER 1 Ha: ER	**1 oil engine** driving 1 FP propeller Total Power: 736kW (1,001hp) Makita LS31 1 x 4 Stroke 6 Cy. 310 x 600 736kW (1001bhp) Makita Diesel Co Ltd-Japan
8110344 *DUK2382* -	**SEAFORD 8** *ex Pierce -2006 ex Eileen -2000* *ex Seiyu -1998 ex Seiyu Maru -1997* **Seaford Shipping Lines Inc** *Cagayan de Oro* *Philippines* Official number: CD07004925	*159* - 1,519		**1981-04 Sasaki Shipbuilding Co Ltd — Osakikamijima HS** Yd No: 275 Loa 69.35 Br ex 11.54 Dght 4.123 Lbp 65.03 Br md 11.51 Dpth 6.02 Welded, 1 dk	**(A31A2GX) General Cargo Ship** Grain: 2,792; Bale: 2,504 Compartments: 1 Ho, ER 1 Ha: ER	**1 oil engine** driving 1 FP propeller Total Power: 1,177kW (1,600hp) Hanshin 6LU32 1 x 4 Stroke 6 Cy. 320 x 510 1177kW (1600bhp) The Hanshin Diesel Works Ltd-Japan
8975495 *ZM2456* -	**SEAFORT** *ex Kinsei Maru -2001* **Richard John Prentice** *Timaru* *New Zealand* Official number: 876099	**122** 36 -		**1980-03 Narasaki Zosen KK — Muroran HK** L reg 26.80 (BB) Br ex - Dght - Lbp - Br md 6.55 Dpth 2.10 Welded, 1 dk	**(B11B2FV) Fishing Vessel**	**1 oil engine** geared to sc. shaft driving 1 Propeller Total Power: 510kW (693hp) 11.0kn Yanmar 1 x 4 Stroke 510kW (693bhp) Yanmar Diesel Engine Co Ltd-Japan
9598737 *2FEP5* -	**SEAFOX 5** **Seafox 5 Ltd** Workfox BV *Douglas* *Isle of Man (British)* MMSI: 235090598 Official number: 742807	**19,697** 5,909 11,013	Class: AB	**2012-09 Keppel FELS Ltd — Singapore** Yd No: B317 Loa 151.00 Br ex - Dght 5.790 Lbp 115.00 Br md 49.98 Dpth 9.75 Welded, 1 dk	**(B22A2ZM) Offshore Construction Vessel, jack up** Cranes: 1x1200t,1x50t	**4 diesel electric oil engines** driving 4 gen. Connecting to 4 elec. motors each (3000kW) driving 4 Directional propellers Total Power: 11,768kW (16,000hp) 8.0kn EMD (Electro-Motive) 16-710-G7C 4 x Vee 2 Stroke 16 Cy. 230 x 279 each-2942kW (4000bhp) Electro Motive Diesel Inc-USA Fuel: 1440.0

IMO / Call sign	Name / Owner	Tonnage	Class	Builder / Dimensions	Type / Capacity	Machinery
6931043 *WDE7203* -	**SEAFREEZE ALASKA** *ex* Arctic Trawler *-1999* *ex* Polyarniy *-1997* *ex* Arctic Trawler *-1995* *ex* Seafreeze Atlantic *-1980* **Seafreeze Alaska I LLC** United States Seafoods LLC *Dutch Harbor, AK* *United States of America* MMSI: 367390380 Official number: 517242	**2,729** 1,085 1,719	Class: NV (AB)	**1968**-07 **Maryland Shipbuilding & Drydock Co. — Baltimore, Md** Yd No: 142 Loa 89.92 Br ex 13.52 Dght 5.790 Lbp 80.02 Br md 13.49 Dpth 6.00 Welded, 2 dks	**(B11A2FG) Factory Stern Trawler** Ins: 1,189 Derricks: 2x2t Ice Capable	**3 diesel electric oil engines** driving 2 gen. each 1000kW d.c 1 gen. of 670kW d.c Connecting to 2 elec. motors driving 1 FP propeller Total Power: 3,309kW (4,500hp) EMD (Electro-Motive) 12-645-E2 3 x Vee 2 Stroke 12 Cy. 230 x 254 each-1103kW (1500bhp) General Motors Corp.Electro-Motive Div.-La Grange AuxGen: 2 x 400kW Thrusters: 1 Tunnel thruster (f) Fuel: 825.0
8990964 *WDA7384* -	**SEAFREEZE AMERICA** *ex* Cape Flattery *-2012* *ex* Cape Flattery (YTT-9) *-2000* *ex* YTT-9 *-1992* **Seafreeze America LLC** United States Seafoods LLC *Dutch Harbor, AK* *United States of America* MMSI: 369001000 Official number: 1111595	**1,011** 303 1,168	Class: (AB)	**1990**-09 **McDermott Shipyards Inc — Amelia LA** Yd No: 283 Converted From: Torpedo Trials Vessel-2000 Loa 56.69 Br ex - Dght 3.353 Lbp 54.10 Br md 12.19 Dpth 4.88 Welded, 1 dk	**(B31A2SR) Research Survey Vessel** Cranes: 1x11t	**1 oil engine** geared to sc. shafts driving 1 FP propeller Total Power: 932kW (1,267hp) 11.0kn Cummins KTA-50-M 1 x Vee 4 Stroke 16 Cy. 159 x 159 932kW (1267bhp) Cummins Engine Co Inc-USA AuxGen: 3 x 395kW a.c Thrusters: 1 Thwart. FP thruster (f); 2 Directional thruster (a)
9629574 *9HA3308* -	**SEAFRIEND** **Rosebay Marine SA** Thenamaris (Ships Management) Inc *Valletta* *Malta* MMSI: 229407000 Official number: 9629574	**29,925** 13,626 50,908 T/cm 52.0	Class: AB	**2013**-05 **STX Offshore & Shipbuilding Co Ltd — Changwon (Jinhae Shipyard)** Yd No: 1534 Loa 183.00 (BB) Br ex 32.23 Dght 13.100 Lbp 173.90 Br md 32.20 Dpth 19.10 Welded, 1 dk	**(A12B2TR) Chemical/Products Tanker** Double Hull (13F) Liq: 52,170; Liq (Oil): 52,170 Compartments: 6 Wing Ta, 6 Wing Ta, 1 Wing Slop Ta, 1 Slop Ta, 1 Wing Slop Ta, ER 12 Cargo Pump (s): 12x600m³/hr Manifold: Bow/CM: 93.1m	**1 oil engine** driving 1 FP propeller Total Power: 9,019kW (12,262hp) 14.5kn MAN-B&W 6S50ME-C8 1 x 2 Stroke 6 Cy. 500 x 2000 9019kW (12262bhp) STX Engine Co Ltd-South Korea AuxGen: 3 x 740kW a.c Fuel: 160.0 (d.f.) 1570.0 (r.f.)
9457268 *VRHA3* -	**SEAFRONTIER** **Dorchester Associates Inc** Valles Steamship (Canada) Inc *Hong Kong* *Hong Kong* MMSI: 477881600 Official number: HK-2778	**30,241** 14,702 50,500 T/cm 55.4	Class: NV	**2011**-05 **Guangzhou Shipyard International Co Ltd — Guangzhou GD** Yd No: 06130089 Converted From: Chemical/Products Tanker-2011 Loa 183.20 (BB) Br ex 32.20 Dght 12.600 Lbp 176.00 Br md 32.20 Dpth 18.20 Welded, 1 dk	**(A13B2TP) Products Tanker** Double Hull (13F) Liq: 56,354; Liq (Oil): 51,470 Compartments: 6 Wing Ta, 6 Wing Ta, 1 Wing Slop Ta, 1 Wing Slop Ta, ER 12 Cargo Pump (s): 12x550m³/hr Manifold: Bow/CM: 90.4m	**1 oil engine** driving 1 FP propeller Total Power: 9,480kW (12,889hp) 15.0kn MAN-B&W 6S50MC-C 1 x 2 Stroke 6 Cy. 500 x 2000 9480kW (12889bhp) Dalian Marine Diesel Co Ltd-China AuxGen: 3 x 910kW a.c Fuel: 201.7 (d.f.) 1947.2 (r.f.)
8517061 *A8KP6* -	**SEAFROST** *ex* Kapitan Korotaev *-2006* *ex* Kapitan Korotayev *-1994* **Cain Marine Co** Alison Management Corp *Monrovia* *Liberia* MMSI: 636013103 Official number: 13103	**11,013** 5,050 17,400 T/cm 27.8	Class: GL (NV) (RS)	**1988**-10 **Brodogradiliste 'Uljanik' — Pula** Yd No: 374 Converted From: Chemical/Products Tanker-2000 Conv to DH-2007 Loa 151.34 (BB) Br ex 22.45 Dght 9.440 Lbp 142.94 Br md 22.40 Dpth 12.15 Welded, 1 dk	**(A13A2TW) Crude/Oil Products Tanker** Double Hull Liq: 17,049; Liq (Oil): 20,065 Compartments: 6 Ta, 10 Wing Ta, 2 Wing Slop Ta, ER 16 Cargo Pump (s): 16x250m³/hr Manifold: Bow/CM: 72.9m Ice Capable	**1 oil engine** driving 1 CP propeller Total Power: 5,696kW (7,744hp) 15.1kn B&W 5L50MC 1 x 2 Stroke 5 Cy. 500 x 1620 5696kW (7744bhp) Tvornica Dizel Motora 'Uljanik'-Yugoslavia AuxGen: 1 x 760kW 220/380V 50Hz a.c, 2 x 540kW 220/380V 50Hz a.c Thrusters: 1 Thwart. CP thruster (f) Fuel: 141.0 (d.f.) 937.2 (r.f.)
8207824 - -	**SEAFURY** **M G Kailis Pty Ltd** - *Fremantle, WA* *Australia* Official number: 396416	*112* 92 42		**1982**-02 **K Shipyard Construction Co — Fremantle WA** Loa 22.51 Br ex 6.10 Dght 2.501 Lbp 20.91 Br md 6.01 Dpth 3.13 Welded, 1 dk	**(B11A2FT) Trawler**	**1 oil engine** with clutches & sr reverse geared to sc. shaft driving 1 FP propeller Total Power: 247kW (336hp) Mercedes Benz 0M404 1 x Vee 4 Stroke 12 Cy. 125 x 142 247kW (336bhp) Daimler Benz AG-West Germany AuxGen: 1 x 104kW 450V 50Hz a.c Fuel: 32.0 (d.f.)
9198977 *OJIW* -	**SEAGARD** **Bore Ltd (Bore Oy Ab)** - *Mariehamn* *Finland* MMSI: 230927000 Official number: 55167	**10,488** 3,146 7,226 T/cm 25.0	Class: LR (GL) **100A1** SS 06/2009 roll on - roll off cargo ship containers on weather deck, in association with a summer moulded draught of 7.00m Ice Class 1AS Max draught midship 7.128m Max/min draught aft 7.136/5.670m Max/min draught forward 7.138/4.222m **LMC** **UMS** Cable: 550.0/52.0 U3	**1999**-06 **J.J. Sietas KG Schiffswerft GmbH & Co. — Hamburg** Yd No: 1187 Loa 153.45 (BB) Br ex 20.85 Dght 7.000 Lbp 142.80 Br md 20.60 Dpth 8.42 Welded, 2 dks	**(A35A2RR) Ro-Ro Cargo Ship** Passengers: berths: 12; driver berths: 12 Stern ramp (p) Len: 14.01 Wid: 12.00 Swl: 200 Stern ramp (s) Len: 14.00 Wid: 4.50 Swl: 200 Lane-Len: 1605 Lane-Wid: 2.90 Lane-clr ht: 5.00 Trailers: 120 Bale: 14,264 TEU 303 incl 50 ref C Ice Capable	**1 oil engine** with flexible couplings & sr gearedto sc. shaft driving 1 CP propeller Total Power: 15,598kW (21,207hp) 21.0kn Wartsila 16V46B 1 x Vee 4 Stroke 16 Cy. 460 x 580 15598kW (21207bhp) Wartsila NSD Finland Oy-Finland AuxGen: 1 x 1500kW 400V 50Hz a.c, 2 x 534kW 400V 50Hz a.c Boilers: 2 TOH (ex.g.), TOH (o.f.) Thrusters: 1 Thwart. CP thruster (f); 1 Thwart. CP thruster (a) Fuel: 132.0 (d.f.) (Heating Coils) 945.0 (r.f.) 50.0pd
5220057 *HQLJ5* -	**SEAGARTH** *ex* Maplegarth *-1990* - - *San Lorenzo* *Honduras* Official number: L-1724698	*212* - -	Class: (LR) ✠ Classed LR until 14/3/89	**1962**-03 **P K Harris & Sons Ltd — Bideford** Yd No: 137 Loa 30.48 Br ex 8.64 Dght 3.506 Lbp 27.89 Br md 8.08 Dpth 4.20 Welded	**(B32A2ST) Tug**	**2 oil engines** with fluid couplings & sr reverse geared to sc. shaft driving 1 FP propeller Total Power: 956kW (1,300hp) 12.0kn Ruston 6ARM 2 x 4 Stroke 6 Cy. 260 x 368 each-478kW (650bhp) Ruston & Hornsby Ltd.-Lincoln Fuel: 40.5
7382691 *SDMO* -	**SEAGAS** *ex* Fjalir *-2012* **AGA Gas AB** - *Stockholm* *Sweden* MMSI: 265704520	**626** 187 203	Class: NV	**1974**-09 **Loland Verft AS — Leirvik i Sogn** Yd No: 37 Converted From: Ferry (Passenger/Vehicle)-2013 Loa 49.65 Br ex 11.55 Dght 3.130 Lbp 46.75 Br md 11.25 Dpth 4.22 Welded, 1 dk	**(A11A2TN) LNG Tanker** Liq (Gas): 170 1 x Gas Tank (s); 1 cyl horizontal Ice Capable	**1 oil engine** driving 2 Propellers aft, 1 fwd Total Power: 735kW (999hp) Wichmann 5ACA 1 x 2 Stroke 5 Cy. 280 x 420 735kW (999bhp) Wichmann Motorfabrikk AS-Norway
8129814 *C4HM2* -	**SEAGAS GENERAL** *ex* Sigas General *-2005* *ex* Kilgas General *-2001* *ex* Balder Phenix *-1998* **KJP Seagas General Ltd** - *Limassol* *Cyprus* MMSI: 212009000 Official number: 8129814	**4,605** 1,382 4,597 T/cm 15.1	Class: LR (NK) **100A1** SS 05/2011 liquefied gas carrier, Ship Type 2PG Anhydrous ammonia, butadiene, n-butane, iso butane, n-iso-butane mixture, isoprene, propane, butane/propane mixture, propylene, vinyl chloride, butylene in four independent spherical tanks (Type C) max. vapour pressure 6.9 bar min. temp. minus 45 degree C design ambient temp. minus 18 degree C **LMC**	**1982**-12 **Fukuoka Shipbuilding Co Ltd — Fukuoka FO** Yd No: 1098 Loa 105.62 (BB) Br ex 17.66 Dght 5.910 Lbp 96.81 Br md 17.61 Dpth 7.70 Welded, 1 dk	**(A11B2TG) LPG Tanker** Double Bottom Entire Compartment Length Liq (Gas): 3,539 4 x Gas Tank (s); 4 independent (C.mn.stl) sph horizontal 4 Cargo Pump (s): 4x150m³/hr Manifold: Bow/CM: 44.1m	**1 oil engine** driving 1 FP propeller Total Power: 2,868kW (3,899hp) 13.0kn Mitsubishi 6UEC37/88H 1 x 2 Stroke 6 Cy. 370 x 880 2868kW (3899bhp) Akasaka Tekkosho KK (Akasaka DieselLtd)-Japan AuxGen: 2 x 360kW Fuel: 155.0 (d.f.) 670.0 (r.f.)
8219932 *C4KW2* -	**SEAGAS GOVERNOR** *ex* Sigas Governor *-2006* *ex* Kilgas Governor *-2001* *ex* Gaz Polaris *-1997* *ex* Polaris Gas *-1995* *ex* Gas Crest *-1991* **KJP Seagas Governor Ltd** - *Limassol* *Cyprus* MMSI: 210712000 Official number: 8219932	**4,658** 1,397 4,563 T/cm 15.1	Class: LR (NK) **100A1** SS 10/2012 liquefied gas carrier, Ship Type 2PG Anhydrous ammonia, butadiene, n-butane, iso butane, n-iso-butane mixture, isoprene, propane, butane/propane mixture, propylene, vinyl chloride, butylene, in four independent spherical tanks (Type C), max vapour pressure 6.9 bar, min temp minus 45 degree C, design ambient temp minus 18 degree C **LMC** Eq.Ltr: V; Cable: 495.0/48.0 U2 (a)	**1983**-09 **Fukuoka Shipbuilding Co Ltd — Fukuoka FO** Yd No: 1097 Loa 105.62 (BB) Br ex 17.66 Dght 5.914 Lbp 96.80 Br md 17.60 Dpth 7.70 Welded, 1 dk	**(A11B2TG) LPG Tanker** Double Bottom Entire Compartment Length Liq (Gas): 3,463 4 x Gas Tank (s); 4 independent (stl) sph 4 Cargo Pump (s): 4x150m³/hr Manifold: Bow/CM: 44.1m	**1 oil engine** driving 1 FP propeller Total Power: 2,868kW (3,899hp) 13.0kn Mitsubishi 6UEC37/88H 1 x 2 Stroke 6 Cy. 370 x 880 2868kW (3899bhp) Akasaka Tekkosho KK (Akasaka DieselLtd)-Japan AuxGen: 3 x 360kW 440V 60Hz a.c Boilers: AuxB (o.f.) 8.2kgf/cm² (8.0bar) Fuel: 159.0 (d.f.) 709.0 (r.f.)

9498925 *V7P04* -	**SEAGLASS II** - **Nikka Finance Inc** Primebulk Shipmanagement Ltd *Majuro* *Marshall Islands* MMSI: 538003264 Official number: 3264	**18,499** 10,335 29,124	Class: NK	**2008-11 Nantong Nikka Shipbuilding Co Ltd — Nantong JS** Yd No: 002 Loa 169.99 (BB) Br ex - Dght 10.058 Lbp 163.60 Br md 27.00 Dpth 14.20 Welded, 1 dk	**(A21A2BC) Bulk Carrier** Grain: 39,988; Bale: 39,296 Compartments: 5 Ho, ER 5 Ha: 4 (20.1 x 17.7)ER (12.1 x 16.0) Cranes: 4x30t	**1 oil engine** driving 1 FP propeller Total Power: 5,730kW (7,791hp) 14.2kn MAN-B&W 5S50MC 1 x 2 Stroke 5 Cy. 500 x 1910 5730kW (7791bhp) Hitachi Zosen Corp-Japan Fuel: 1383.0 (r.f.)
9253478 *9HA3325* -	**SEAGLORY** *ex* St. Pauli *-2013* **Seaglory Maritime Ltd** Eastern Mediterranean Maritime Ltd *Valletta* *Malta* MMSI: 229434000 Official number: 9253478	**28,552** 12,369 47,149 T/cm 50.6	Class: NK	**2003-05 Onomichi Dockyard Co Ltd — Onomichi HS** Yd No: 485 Loa 182.50 (BB) Br ex 32.20 Dght 12.650 Lbp 172.00 Br md 32.20 Dpth 19.10 Welded, 1 dk	**(A13B2TP) Products Tanker** Double Hull (13F) Liq: 50,332; Liq (Oil): 50,332 Cargo Heating Coils Compartments: 2 Ta, 12 Wing Ta, 2 Wing Slop Ta, ER 4 Cargo Pump (s): 4x1000m^3/hr Manifold: Bow/CM: 91.7m	**1 oil engine** driving 1 FP propeller Total Power: 8,580kW (11,665hp) 15.3kn MAN-B&W 6S50MC 1 x 2 Stroke 6 Cy. 500 x 1910 8580kW (11665bhp) Mitsui Engineering & Shipbuilding CLtd-Japan AuxGen: 3 x 420kW a.c Fuel: 112.5 (d.f.) 1554.0 (r.f.)
9313905 *OZDB2* -	**SEAGO ANTWERP** *ex* Maersk Boston *-2012* *ex* Boston *-2012* *ex* Maersk Boston *-2010* **A P Moller - Maersk A/S** A P Moller *Copenhagen* *Denmark (DIS)* MMSI: 219216000 Official number: D4072	**48,788** 16,832 53,701	Class: AB (LR) ✠ Classed LR until 15/5/09	**2006-05 Volkswerft Stralsund GmbH — Stralsund** Yd No: 459 Loa 293.83 (BB) Br ex 32.28 Dght 12.200 Lbp 278.20 Br md 32.18 Dpth 21.40 Welded, 1 dk	**(A33A2CC) Container Ship (Fully Cellular)** TEU 4504 incl 1400 ref C Compartments: 8 Cell Ho, ER 8 Ha: ER	**1 oil engine** driving 1 FP propeller Total Power: 68,640kW (93,323hp) 21.0kn Sulzer 12RT-flex96C 1 x 2 Stroke 12 Cy. 960 x 2500 68640kW (93323bhp) Doosan Engine Co Ltd-South Korea AuxGen: 4 x 2765kW 450/230V 60Hz a.c Boilers: AuxB (ex.g.) 9.3kgf/cm^2 (9.1bar), WTAuxB (o.f.) 9.3kgf/cm^2 (9.1bar) Thrusters: 1 Thwart. CP thruster (f); 1 Thwart. CP thruster (a)
9313967 *OXVA2* -	**SEAGO BREMERHAVEN** *ex* Maersk Beaumont *-2012* *ex* Beaumont *-2012* *ex* Maersk Beaumont *-2010* **Nordea Finans Sverige AB** The Maersk Co Ltd *Copenhagen* *Denmark (DIS)* MMSI: 219118000 Official number: D4078	**48,788** 16,832 53,890	Class: AB (LR) ✠ Classed LR until 25/11/08	**2007-12 Volkswerft Stralsund GmbH — Stralsund** Yd No: 465 Loa 293.83 (BB) Br ex 32.28 Dght 12.200 Lbp 278.20 Br md 32.18 Dpth 21.40 Welded, 1 dk	**(A33A2CC) Container Ship (Fully Cellular)** TEU 4504 incl 1400 ref C Compartments: 8 Cell Ho, ER	**1 oil engine** driving 1 FP propeller Total Power: 68,640kW (93,323hp) 21.0kn Wartsila 12RT-flex96C 1 x 2 Stroke 12 Cy. 960 x 2500 68640kW (93323bhp) Doosan Engine Co Ltd-South Korea AuxGen: 4 x 2765kW 450V 60Hz a.c Boilers: e (ex.g.) 9.5kgf/cm^2 (9.3bar), WTAuxB (o.f.) 9.5kgf/cm^2 (9.3bar) Thrusters: 1 Thwart. CP thruster (f); 1 Thwart. CP thruster (a)
9313917 *OZCX2* -	**SEAGO FELIXSTOWE** *ex* Baltimore *-2012* *ex* Maersk Baltimore *-2010* **A P Moller - Maersk A/S** A P Moller *Copenhagen* *Denmark (DIS)* MMSI: 219196000 Official number: D4073	**48,788** 16,832 53,700	Class: LR ✠ **100A1** SS 08/2011 container ship *IWS LI **ShipRight** (SDA, FDA, CM) ✠ **LMC** **UMS** Eq.Ltr: A†; Cable: 732.0/90.0 U3 (a)	**2006-08 Volkswerft Stralsund GmbH — Stralsund** Yd No: 460 Loa 294.10 (BB) Br ex 32.28 Dght 12.200 Lbp 278.20 Br md 32.18 Dpth 21.40 Welded, 1 dk	**(A33A2CC) Container Ship (Fully Cellular)** TEU 4504 incl 1400 ref C Compartments: 8 Cell Ho, ER 8 Ha: ER	**1 oil engine** driving 1 FP propeller Total Power: 68,640kW (93,323hp) 21.0kn Sulzer 12RT-flex96C 1 x 2 Stroke 12 Cy. 960 x 2500 68640kW (93323bhp) Doosan Engine Co Ltd-South Korea AuxGen: 4 x 2765kW 450V 60Hz a.c Boilers: e (ex.g.) 9.3kgf/cm^2 (9.1bar), WTAuxB (o.f.) 9.3kgf/cm^2 (9.1bar) Thrusters: 1 Thwart. CP thruster (f); 1 Thwart. CP thruster (a)
9313943 *OXVE2* -	**SEAGO ISTANBUL** *ex* Maersk Buffalo *-2012* *ex* Buffalo *-2012* *ex* Maersk Buffalo *-2011* *launched as* Maersk *-2007* **Nordea Finans Sverige AB** The Maersk Co Ltd *Copenhagen* *Denmark (DIS)* MMSI: 219116000 Official number: D4076	**48,788** 16,832 53,701	Class: LR ✠ **100A1** SS 06/2012 container ship *IWS LI **ShipRight** (SDA, FDA, CM) ✠ **LMC** **UMS** Eq.Ltr: T†; Cable: 715.0/87.0 U3 (a)	**2007-06 Volkswerft Stralsund GmbH — Stralsund** Yd No: 463 Loa 294.10 (BB) Br ex 32.28 Dght 12.200 Lbp 278.20 Br md 32.18 Dpth 21.40 Welded, 1 dk	**(A33A2CC) Container Ship (Fully Cellular)** TEU 4504 incl 1400 ref C Compartments: 8 Cell Ho, ER	**1 oil engine** driving 1 FP propeller Total Power: 68,640kW (93,323hp) 21.0kn Wartsila 12RT-flex96C 1 x 2 Stroke 12 Cy. 960 x 2500 68640kW (93323bhp) Doosan Engine Co Ltd-South Korea AuxGen: 4 x 2765kW 450V 60Hz a.c Boilers: e (ex.g.) 9.3kgf/cm^2 (9.1bar), WTAuxB (o.f.) 9.3kgf/cm^2 (9.1bar) Thrusters: 1 Thwart. CP thruster (f); 1 Thwart. CP thruster (a)
9313955 *OXVD2* -	**SEAGO PIRAEUS** *ex* Maersk Brownsville *-2013* *ex* Brownsville *-2012* *ex* Maersk Brownsville *-2011* **Nordea Finans Sverige AB** The Maersk Co Ltd *Copenhagen* *Denmark (DIS)* MMSI: 219117000 Official number: D4077	**48,788** 16,832 53,807	Class: AB (LR) ✠ Classed LR until 25/6/09	**2007-09 Volkswerft Stralsund GmbH — Stralsund** Yd No: 464 Loa 294.10 (BB) Br ex 32.28 Dght 12.200 Lbp 278.20 Br md 32.18 Dpth 21.40 Welded, 1 dk	**(A33A2CC) Container Ship (Fully Cellular)** TEU 4504 incl 1400 ref C Compartments: 8 Cell Ho, ER	**1 oil engine** driving 1 FP propeller Total Power: 68,640kW (93,323hp) 21.0kn Wartsila 12RT-flex96C 1 x 2 Stroke 12 Cy. 960 x 2500 68640kW (93323bhp) Doosan Engine Co Ltd-South Korea AuxGen: 4 x 2756kW 450V 60Hz a.c Boilers: e (ex.g.) 9.5kgf/cm^2 (9.3bar), WTAuxB (o.f.) 9.5kgf/cm^2 (9.3bar) Thrusters: 1 Thwart. CP thruster (f); 1 Thwart. CP thruster (a)
9343015 *9V6626*	**SEAGOOD CASSANDRA 2** - **Sea-Good Pte Ltd** - *Singapore* *Singapore* MMSI: 563257000 Official number: 391030	**496** 148 593	Class: AB	**2005-02 Sealink Shipyard Sdn Bhd — Miri** Yd No: 120 Loa 48.00 Br ex 11.50 Dght 2.500 Lbp 46.20 Br md 11.00 Dpth 3.50 Welded, 1 dk	**(B21A20S) Platform Supply Ship**	**2 oil engines** reverse reduction geared to sc. shafts driving 2 FP propellers Total Power: 1,074kW (1,460hp) Caterpillar 3412TA 2 x Vee 4 Stroke 12 Cy. 137 x 152 each-537kW (730bhp) Caterpillar Inc-USA AuxGen: 2 x 150kW a.c Thrusters: 1 Tunnel thruster (f)
9420409 *9WHA2*	**SEAGOOD VICTORIA 6** - **Seabright Sdn Bhd** Sealink Sdn Bhd *Kuching* *Malaysia* MMSI: 533000547 Official number: 330861	**488** 146 650	Class: LR **100A1** SS 08/2012 ✠ **LMC** Cable: 440.0/26.0 U2 (a)	**2007-08 Kian Juan Dockyard Sdn Bhd — Miri** Yd No: 109 Loa 43.72 Br ex - Dght 2.400 Lbp 42.10 Br md 10.90 Dpth 3.20 Welded, 1 dk	**(A35D2RL) Landing Craft** Bow ramp (centre)	**2 oil engines** with clutches & sr reverse geared to sc. shafts driving 2 FP propellers Total Power: 1,074kW (1,460hp) 11.0kn Caterpillar 3412TA 2 x Vee 4 Stroke 12 Cy. 137 x 152 each-537kW (730bhp) Caterpillar Inc-USA AuxGen: 2 x 80kW 415V 50Hz a.c
9290309 *9HA3307*	**SEAGRACE** *ex* Pacific Alliance *-2013* **Cooper Navigation Ltd** Thenamaris (Ships Management) Inc *Valletta* *Malta* MMSI: 229406000 Official number: 9290309	**57,226** 32,671 105,941 T/cm 92.0	Class: NK	**2004-07 Hyundai Heavy Industries Co Ltd — Ulsan** Yd No: 1538 Loa 243.96 Br ex - Dght 14.918 Lbp 234.00 Br md 42.00 Dpth 21.00 Welded, 1 dk	**(A13A2TW) Crude/Oil Products Tanker** Double Hull (13F) Liq: 120,739; Liq (Oil): 120,739 Cargo Heating Coils Compartments: 12 Wing Ta, 2 Wing Slop Ta, ER 3 Cargo Pump (s) Manifold: Bow/CM: 122m	**1 oil engine** driving 1 FP propeller Total Power: 13,548kW (18,420hp) 15.1kn B&W 6S60MC-C 1 x 2 Stroke 6 Cy. 600 x 2400 13548kW (18420bhp) Hyundai Heavy Industries Co Ltd-South Korea AuxGen: 3 x 660kW Fuel: 3370.0
8708050 - -	**SEAGRAN 1** *ex* Fukutoku Maru No. 78 *-2004* - -	*409* - -		**1987-09 KK Kanasashi Zosen — Toyohashi AI** Yd No: 3138 Loa 56.09 (BB) Br ex 8.03 Dght 3.452 Lbp 49.61 Br md 8.01 Dpth 3.87 Welded	**(B11B2FV) Fishing Vessel** Ins: 667	**1 oil engine** driving 1 FP propeller Total Power: 736kW (1,001hp) Niigata 6M28BFT 1 x 4 Stroke 6 Cy. 280 x 480 736kW (1001bhp) Niigata Engineering Co Ltd-Japan
8520202 *UBP15*	**SEAGRAND** *ex* Corn Hill *-2011* *ex* Poolgracht *-2006* **Vostokmorservice Co Ltd** - *Vladivostok* *Russia* MMSI: 273351860	**5,998** 3,600 9,672 T/cm 19.1	Class: RS (LR) ✠ Classed LR until 27/4/12	**1986-10 Miho Zosensho K.K. — Shimizu** Yd No: 1284 Loa 113.14 (BB) Br ex 18.98 Dght 8.532 Lbp 106.03 Br md 18.92 Dpth 11.31 Welded, 2 dks	**(A31A2GX) General Cargo Ship** Grain: 12,738; Bale: 12,006 TEU 487 C.Ho 234/20' (40') C.Dk 253/20' (40') Compartments: 1 Ho, ER, 1 Tw Dk 2 Ha: (33.6 x 15.7) (35.7 x 15.7)ER Cranes: 2x50t	**1 oil engine** driving 1 CP propeller Total Power: 4,413kW (6,000hp) 14.0kn Hanshin 6LF58 1 x 4 Stroke 6 Cy. 580 x 1050 4413kW (6000bhp) The Hanshin Diesel Works Ltd-Japan AuxGen: 1 x 400kW 445V 60Hz a.c, 3 x 200kW 445V 60Hz a.c Boilers: TOH (o.f.) 10.2kgf/cm^2 (10.0bar), TOH (ex.g.) 10.2kgf/cm^2 (10.0bar) Fuel: 125.0 (d.f.) 629.0 (r.f.)
7721029 - -	**SEAGRAND** *ex* Moon Bird *-2003* *ex* Protea Trader *-1990* *ex* Black Bird *-1990* *ex* Alamar *-1987* *ex* Alamak *-1985* **Mar Runners Shipping Co Ltd** Grand Marine Co Ltd	**3,457** 2,248 3,787	Class: IS (GL)	**1978-09 B.V. Scheepswerf Jonker & Stans — Hendrik-Ido-Ambacht** Yd No: 344 Loa 82.12 (BB) Br ex 17.02 Dght 6.412 Lbp 74.81 Br md 17.01 Dpth 10.01 Welded, 2 dks	**(A31A2GX) General Cargo Ship** Grain: 7,305; Bale: 7,079 TEU 30 C.Dk 30/20' Compartments: 2 Ho, ER 2 Ha: 2 (19.0 x 13.5)ER Derricks: 1x100t,4x10t	**1 oil engine** reduction geared to sc. shaft driving 1 CP propeller Total Power: 2,207kW (3,001hp) 12.5kn MWM TBD501-8 1 x 4 Stroke 8 Cy. 360 x 450 2207kW (3001bhp) Motoren Werke Mannheim AG (MWM)-West Germany AuxGen: 1 x 244kW 440V 60Hz a.c, 2 x 200kW 440V 60Hz a.c Fuel: 140.0 (d.f.) 415.5 (r.f.)
5076195 - -	**SEAGUARD** *ex* Dawn Saviour *-1993* *ex* Saltrou *-1987* *ex* Clova *-1982* **Marine Industries & Investments Ltd** - *Israel* Official number: MS.339	*281* 94 -	Class: (LR) ✠ Classed LR until 8/7/93	**1960-04 J. Lewis & Sons Ltd. — Aberdeen** Yd No: 293 Converted From: Trawler-1975 L reg 36.89 Br ex 7.88 Dght 3.125 Lbp 36.23 Br md 7.78 Dpth 3.89 Riveted\Welded	**(B22G20Y) Standby Safety Vessel**	**1 oil engine** sr geared to sc shaft driving 1 FP propeller Total Power: 485kW (659hp) Blackstone ERS8M 1 x 4 Stroke 8 Cy. 222 x 292 485kW (659bhp) (made 1972, fitted 1987) Lister Blackstone Marine Ltd.-Dursley AuxGen: 1 x 35kW 220V d.c, 1 x 30kW 220V d.c, 1 x 25kW 220V d.c

9174268 *9HHP7* -	**SEAGUARDIAN** *ex* Golden Disa *-2002* **Jiacaranda Shipping Ltd** Eastern Mediterranean Maritime Ltd *Valletta* *Malta* MMSI: 215247000 Official number: 7782	**39,714** 25,189 75,462 T/cm 67.3	Class: AB	**1999-03 Hitachi Zosen Corp — Maizuru KY** Yd No: 5889 Loa 224.95 (BB) Br ex - Dght 13.841 Lbp 217.00 Br md 32.20 Dpth 19.15 Welded, 1 dk	**(A21A2BC) Bulk Carrier** Grain: 89,423; Bale: 86,925 Compartments: 7 Ho, ER 7 Ha: (16.3 x 13.0)6 (17.2 x 14.6)ER	**1 oil engine** driving 1 FP propeller Total Power: 9,261kW (12,591hp) 14.5kn B&W 6S60MC 1 x 2 Stroke 6 Cy. 600 x 2292 9261kW (12591bhp) Hitachi Zosen Corp-Japan
9112545 *MVB02* BF 74	**SEAGULL** **MV Seagull** - *Banff* *United Kingdom* MMSI: 233714000 Official number: B14307	**349** 160 -		**1995-04 Yorkshire D.D. Co. Ltd. — Hull** (Hull) Yd No: 337 **1995-04 Macduff Shipyards Ltd — Macduff** Yd No: 579 Loa 27.41 (BB) Br ex 8.52 Dght 4.900 Lbp - Br md - Dpth - Welded, 1 dk	**(B11A2FS) Stern Trawler**	**1 oil engine** driving 1 FP propeller Total Power: 1,380kW (1,876hp) 11.5kn Deutz TBD620BV12 1 x Vee 4 Stroke 12 Cy. 170 x 195 1380kW (1876bhp) Motoren Werke Mannheim AG (MWM)-West Germany
8902149 - -	**SEAGULL** *ex* Seagull No. 2 *-1998* **Juma Said Abdul Rahman** -	*567* - 100		**1989-12 Mitsui Eng. & SB. Co. Ltd. — Tamano** Yd No: TH-1702 Loa 39.30 Br ex - Dght 3.252 Lbp 33.70 Br md 15.60 Dpth 6.80 Welded	**(A37B2PS) Passenger Ship** Hull Material: Aluminium Alloy Passengers: unberthed: 410	**4 oil engines** with clutches & reverse geared to sc. shafts driving 2 FP propellers Total Power: 7,884kW (10,720hp) 30.6kn M.T.U. 16V396TB84 4 x Vee 4 Stroke 16 Cy. 165 x 185 each-1971kW (2680bhp) MTU Friedrichshafen GmbH-Friedrichshafen AuxGen: 2 x 220kW 450V 60Hz a.c Thrusters: 2 Thwart. CP thruster (f)
8929599 *5NKS* -	**SEAGULL** *ex* Seagull (5001) *-1970* **Aqua Seals Ltd** - *Nigeria* Official number: SR648	*248* 74 -		**1970-01 Fairmile Construction Co. Ltd. — Berwick-on-Tweed** Yd No: 655 Loa 36.66 Br ex - Dght 2.100 Lbp 33.52 Br md 7.16 Dpth 4.42 Welded, 1 dk	**(B34P2QV) Salvage Ship**	**2 oil engines** reduction geared to sc. shafts driving 2 FP propellers Total Power: 2,942kW (4,000hp) 21.0kn Paxman 16YJCM 2 x Vee 4 Stroke 16 Cy. 197 x 216 each-1471kW (2000bhp) Davey, Paxman & Co. Ltd.-Colchester Fuel: 31.0 (d.f.)
7050884 *EMGE* -	**SEAGULL** *ex* Dmitriy Manuilskiy *-1991* **LLC 'Capital Shipping Co'** - *Kherson* *Ukraine* MMSI: 272067000 Official number: 700370	**2,466** 988 2,925	Class: UA (RS)	**1970-06 Sudostroitelnyy Zavod "Krasnoye Sormovo" — Gorkiy** Yd No: 21 Loa 114.20 Br ex 13.21 Dght 3.420 Lbp 108.01 Br md 13.00 Dpth 5.54 Welded, 1 dk	**(A31A2GX) General Cargo Ship** Bale: 4,297 Compartments: 4 Ho, ER 4 Ha: (17.6 x 9.3)3 (18.0 x 9.3) Ice Capable	**2 oil engines** driving 2 FP propellers Total Power: 970kW (1,318hp) 10.8kn S.K.L. 6NVD48A-U 2 x 4 Stroke 6 Cy. 320 x 480 each-485kW (659bhp) VEB Schwermaschinenbau "KarlLiebknecht" (SKL)-Magdeburg AuxGen: 3 x 50kW a.c Fuel: 111.0 (d.f.)
7301960 - -	**SEAGULL** *ex* Shun Da *-2003* *ex* Ming Yuan 8 *-2003* *ex* Hua Fu 6 *-2003* *ex* Kyokuho Maru No. 10 *-1996* - -	*739* 413 958 T/cm 0.1		**1973 Watanabe Zosen KK — Imabari EH** Yd No: 151 Loa 52.74 Br ex 10.04 Dght 3.860 Lbp 48.11 Br md 10.01 Dpth 4.10 Riveted\Welded, 1 dk	**(A12A2TC) Chemical Tanker** Liq: 896 Compartments: 8 Ta, ER 2 Cargo Pump (s): 2x150m³/hr	**1 oil engine** geared to sc. shaft driving 1 FP propeller Total Power: 736kW (1,001hp) 10.0kn Daihatsu 6DSM-22 1 x 4 Stroke 6 Cy. 220 x 280 736kW (1001bhp) Daihatsu Diesel Manufacturing Co Lt-Japan Fuel: 36.5 (d.f.) 2.0pd
9244427 *JM6693* -	**SEAGULL** **Kyodo Ferry KK** - *Kamiamakusa, Kumamoto* *Japan* Official number: 136441	*132* - 80		**2001-06 Shitanoe Shipbuilding Co Ltd — Usuki OT** Yd No: 1217 Loa 37.47 Br ex - Dght - Lbp 29.28 Br md 8.30 Dpth 3.20 Welded	**(A36A2PR) Passenger/Ro-Ro Ship (Vehicles)**	**1 oil engine** driving 1 FP propeller Total Power: 611kW (831hp) 10.4kn Niigata 6NSDL-M 1 x 4 Stroke 6 Cy. 160 x 235 611kW (831bhp) Niigata Engineering Co Ltd-Japan
9452505 *9HA2364* -	**SEAGULL** *ex* Thalassini Niki *-2012* **Catalina Shipping Co** Trade Fortune Inc *Valletta* *Malta* MMSI: 248435000 Official number: 9452505	**34,374** 19,565 58,609 T/cm 59.1	Class: NK (AB)	**2010-05 SPP Plant & Shipbuilding Co Ltd — Sacheon** Yd No: H1031 Loa 196.00 (BB) Br ex - Dght 13.020 Lbp 189.00 Br md 32.26 Dpth 18.60 Welded, 1 dk	**(A21A2BC) Bulk Carrier** Grain: 75,531; Bale: 70,734 Compartments: 5 Ho, ER 5 Ha: ER Cranes: 4x36t	**1 oil engine** driving 1 FP propeller Total Power: 9,960kW (13,542hp) 14.5kn MAN-B&W 6S50MC-C8 1 x 2 Stroke 6 Cy. 500 x 2000 9960kW (13542bhp) Doosan Engine Co Ltd-South Korea AuxGen: 3 x 600kW a.c Fuel: 137.0 (d.f.) 2177.0 (r.f.)
9666223 *V5GU* -	**SEAGULL** **Namport (Namibian Port Authority)** - *Walvis Bay* *Namibia*	**100** 30 16	Class: RI	**2012-10 Astilleros Armon Burela SA — Burela** (Hull) Yd No: (AN-123) **2012-10 Auxiliar Naval del Principado SA — Puerto de Vega** Yd No: AN-123 Loa 27.00 Br ex - Dght 2.200 Lbp 23.87 Br md 6.00 Dpth 3.50 Welded, 1 dk	**(B34N2QP) Pilot Vessel**	**2 oil engines** reduction geared to sc. shafts driving 2 FP propellers Total Power: 1,492kW (2,028hp) 15.1kn Caterpillar C32 2 x Vee 4 Stroke 12 Cy. 145 x 162 each-746kW (1014bhp) Caterpillar Inc-USA
9698678 *OWNZ2* -	**SEAGULL** **Global Ship Leasing 11 BV** World Marine Offshore A/S *Marstal* *Denmark* MMSI: 219489000	**167** 50 -	Class: BV	**2013-06 Damen Shipyards Singapore Pte Ltd — Singapore** (Hull) Yd No: (532516) **2013-06 B.V. Scheepswerf Damen — Gorinchem** Yd No: 532516 Loa 25.75 Br ex - Dght 1.800 Lbp 23.73 Br md 10.06 Dpth 3.50 Welded, 1 dk	**(B21A20C) Crew/Supply Vessel** Hull Material: Aluminium Alloy	**2 oil engines** reduction geared to sc. shafts driving 2 FP propellers Total Power: 1,790kW (2,434hp) 22.0kn Caterpillar C32 ACERT 2 x Vee 4 Stroke 12 Cy. 145 x 162 each-895kW (1217bhp) Caterpillar Inc-USA AuxGen: 2 x 23kW 50Hz a.c Thrusters: 2 Tunnel thruster (f)
6808947 - -	**SEAGULL 1** *ex* Metwally *-2005* *ex* Eagle Star *-2004* *ex* Paola *-1991* *ex* Takis *-1988* *ex* Takis E *-1987* *ex* Captain Lucas *-1987* *ex* Hokushun Maru *-1980* *ex* Shinko Maru *-1980* **Ashraf Khalil Ibrahim Al Sharif & Luay S Sabri Al Qaisy** -	**566** 330 1,040	Class: KC (HR)	**1968 Hashihama Shipbuilding Co Ltd — Imabari EH** Yd No: 231 Loa 54.51 Br ex 8.82 Dght 4.192 Lbp 49.51 Br md 8.79 Dpth 4.40 Riveted\Welded, 1 dk	**(A13B2TU) Tanker (unspecified)** Compartments: 4 Ta, ER	**1 oil engine** driving 1 FP propeller Total Power: 625kW (850hp) 10.5kn Nippon Hatsudoki HS6NV325 1 x 4 Stroke 6 Cy. 325 x 460 625kW (850bhp) Nippon Hatsudoki-Japan AuxGen: 2 x 28kW 225V a.c Fuel: 45.5 3.0pd
7913610 - -	**SEAGULL 2** *ex* Ferry Matsushima *-2011* *ex* Kinoe Maru *-1999* *ex* Ehime No. 16 *-1988* **Baobab Beach Bungalows Ltd** -	*199* - 200		**1979-12 Nakatani Shipyard Co. Ltd. — Etajima** Yd No: 456 Loa 35.16 Br ex 10.01 Dght 2.201 Lbp 34.50 Br md 8.60 Dpth 3.00 Welded, 1 dk	**(A37B2PS) Passenger Ship**	**1 oil engine** driving 1 FP propeller Total Power: 883kW (1,201hp) Yanmar 6GAL-ET 1 x 4 Stroke 6 Cy. 240 x 290 883kW (1201bhp) Yanmar Diesel Engine Co Ltd-Japan
9320219 - -	**SEAGULL 3** *ex* Da Nang 18 *-2006* **Seagull Marine Services - India** -	**499** 361 935	Class: (VR)	**2004-05 Trung Hai Private Enterprise — Haiphong** Loa 56.45 Br ex 9.17 Dght 3.310 Lbp 52.70 Br md 9.15 Dpth 4.05 Welded, 1 dk	**(A31A2GX) General Cargo Ship** Compartments: 2 Ho, ER 2 Ha: ER 2 (13.2 x 5.2)	**1 oil engine** reduction geared to sc. shaft driving 1 FP propeller Total Power: 300kW (408hp) S.K.L. 8NVD36-1U 1 x 4 Stroke 8 Cy. 240 x 360 300kW (408bhp) SKL Motoren u. Systemtechnik AG-Magdeburg
8014382 *3EIY3* -	**SEAGULL D** *ex* Pangor *-2009* *ex* Bolkar *-2007* *ex* Star Gemini *-2001* *ex* Aditya Usha *-1997* *ex* Targa *-1988* *ex* Anna K *-1987* *ex* San Vicente Ferrer *-1987* *ex* Saint Vincent *-1985* **Seagull Shipping Co** Al Fadel Shipping Co Sarl *Panama* *Panama* MMSI: 372434000 Official number: 3262807A	**11,412** 6,540 18,427 T/cm 28.5	Class: RS (KR) (AB) (IR) (BV)	**1981-03 Minaminippon Shipbuilding Co Ltd — Usuki OT** Yd No: 539 Loa 154.50 (BB) Br ex 22.89 Dght 9.150 Lbp 143.20 Br md 22.86 Dpth 12.50 Welded, 1 dk	**(A21A2BC) Bulk Carrier** Grain: 23,898; Bale: 23,095 Compartments: 4 Ho, ER 4 Ha: (15.2 x 9.8)3 (16.8 x 11.2)ER Derricks: 4x25t	**1 oil engine** driving 1 FP propeller Total Power: 5,913kW (8,039hp) 14.5kn B&W 6L55GFC 1 x 2 Stroke 6 Cy. 550 x 1380 5913kW (8039bhp) Mitsui Engineering & Shipbuilding CLtd-Japan AuxGen: 3 x 360kW 445V 60Hz a.c Fuel: 1379.0 (r.f.) 24.0pd
8962101 *9MCW8* -	**SEAGULL EXPRESS 3** - - *Port Klang* *Malaysia* Official number: 328259	**121** 75 32		**1997 P.T. Asia Marine Fibrindo — Tangerang** Loa - Br ex - Dght 1.782 Lbp 29.20 Br md 4.87 Dpth 2.80 Bonded, 1 dk	**(A37B2PS) Passenger Ship** Hull Material: Reinforced Plastic	**2 oil engines** geared to sc. shafts driving 2 FP propellers Total Power: 1,472kW (2,002hp) M.T.U. 12V183TE72 2 x Vee 4 Stroke 12 Cy. 128 x 142 each-736kW (1001bhp) MTU Friedrichshafen GmbH-Friedrichshafen
8960074 - -	**SEAGULL I** **Hoang Van Nguyen** - *Ocean Springs, MS* *United States of America* Official number: 1103636	**172** 51 -		**2000 La Force Shipyard Inc — Coden AL** Yd No: 102 Loa 26.18 Br ex - Dght - Lbp - Br md 7.62 Dpth 3.72 Welded, 1 dk	**(B11B2FV) Fishing Vessel**	**1 oil engine** driving 1 FP propeller

IMO / Call sign	Name / Owner	Tonnage	Class	Builder / Dimensions	Type	Machinery
5382996 *9HQH8* -	**SEAGULL II** *ex* Seagull I *-2006* *ex* Biser Jadrana *-2002* *ex* Porec *-2002* *ex* Vladimir Nazor *-1986* - - *Valletta* *Malta* MMSI: 256282000 Official number: 10216	*430* 189 -	Class: (CS) (JR)	**1952**-12 **Brodogradiliste 'Uljanik' — Pula** Yd No: 138 Converted From: Ferry (Passenger only)-2006 Loa 54.21 Br ex 8.56 Dght 2.915 Lbp 50.65 Br md 8.51 Dpth 3.51 Welded, 1 dk	**(X11A2YP) Yacht**	**2 oil engines** driving 2 FP propellers Total Power: 772kW (1,050hp) 14.0kn Sulzer 5TD29 2 x 2 Stroke 5 Cy. 290 x 500 each-386kW (525bhp) Sulzer Bros Ltd-Switzerland AuxGen: 3 x 27kW 220V a.c
8969939 - -	**SEAGULL III** **Hoang Van Nguyen** - *Youngsville, LA* *United States of America* Official number: 1117493	**172** 51 -		**2001 La Force Shipyard Inc — Coden AL** Yd No: 114 L reg 26.18 Br ex - Dght - Lbp - Br md 7.62 Dpth 3.71 Welded, 1 dk	**(B11B2FV) Fishing Vessel**	**1 oil engine** driving 1 FP propeller
8323159 *5IM297* -	**SEAGULL-K** *ex* Harbour Gemini *-2012* *ex* Zhong Qiang *-2006* *ex* Worldline 3 *-2003* *ex* Siti Azlina *-2000* **Sea Pride Maritime Co SA** Island Navigators Management Co SatCom: Inmarsat C 467400226 *Zanzibar* *Tanzania (Zanzibar)* MMSI: 677019700 Official number: 300054	**4,908** 3,102 7,988	Class: BR (CC) (BV) (NK)	**1984**-05 **Imai Shipbuilding Co Ltd — Kochi KC** Yd No: 525 Loa 110.34 Br ex - Dght 7.253 Lbp 102.01 Br md 18.30 Dpth 9.35 Welded, 1 dk	**(A31A2GX) General Cargo Ship** Grain: 10,439; Bale: 9,831 Compartments: 2 Ho, ER 2 Ha: (29.4 x 10.2) (32.2 x 10.2)ER Derricks: 1x130t,4x25t	**1 oil engine** driving 1 FP propeller Total Power: 4,330kW (5,887hp) 13.0kn B&W 7L35MC 1 x 2 Stroke 7 Cy. 350 x 1050 4330kW (5887bhp) Hitachi Zosen Corp-Japan AuxGen: 2 x 200kW
9652507 *3FJD5* -	**SEAGULL WIND** **Sangria Pioneer Four SA** MC Shipping Ltd *Panama* *Panama* MMSI: 351528000 Official number: 4486013	**43,656** 27,221 82,908 T/cm 71.0	Class: NK	**2013**-04 **Sanoyas Shipbuilding Corp — Kurashiki OY** Yd No: 1330 Loa 229.00 (BB) Br ex - Dght 14.648 Lbp 225.00 Br md 32.24 Dpth 20.20 Welded, 1 dk	**(A21A2BC) Bulk Carrier** Grain: 95,891 Compartments: 7 Ho, ER 7 Ha: ER	**1 oil engine** driving 1 FP propeller Total Power: 9,750kW (13,256hp) 14.0kn MAN-B&W 6S60MC-C8 1 x 2 Stroke 6 Cy. 600 x 2400 9750kW (13256bhp) Mitsui Engineering & Shipbuilding CLtd-Japan AuxGen: 3 x 580kW a.c Fuel: 2680.0
9255488 *DEEI* -	**SEAHAKE** **tms 'Seahake' GmbH & Co KG** German Tanker Shipping GmbH & Co KG *Bremen* *Germany* MMSI: 211409100 Official number: 4883	**21,329** 8,387 32,464 T/cm 42.0	Class: GL	**2003**-11 **Lindenau GmbH Schiffswerft u. Maschinenfabrik — Kiel** Yd No: 251 Loa 177.72 (BB) Br ex 28.09 Dght 11.000 Lbp 168.00 Br md 28.00 Dpth 16.80 Welded, 1 dk	**(A13B2TP) Products Tanker** Double Hull (13F) Liq: 36,671; Liq (Oil): 36,671 Compartments: 10 Wing Ta, 2 Wing Slop Ta, ER 12 Cargo Pump (s): 10x500m³/hr, 2x200m³/hr Ice Capable	**1 oil engine** geared to sc. shaft driving 1 CP propeller Total Power: 8,340kW (11,339hp) 15.1kn MAN 6L58/64 1 x 4 Stroke 6 Cy. 580 x 640 8340kW (11339bhp) MAN B&W Diesel AG-Augsburg Thrusters: 1 Tunnel thruster (f)
9669366 *2GHA7* -	**SEAHAWK** *launched as* Sea Hawk Of Malta *-2013* **Ox Pasture Chartering Ltd** - *Peel* *Isle of Man (British)* MMSI: 235097329	**491** 147 60	Class: AB	**2013**-11 **Perini Navi SpA (Divisione Picchiotti) — Viareggio** Yd No: 2193 Loa 58.60 Br ex 11.39 Dght 12.300 Lbp 50.43 Br md 11.14 Dpth - Welded, 1 dk	**(X11A2YS) Yacht (Sailing)** Hull Material: Aluminium Alloy	**2 oil engines** reduction geared to sc. shafts driving 2 Propellers Total Power: 1,440kW (1,958hp) M.T.U. 8V2000M72 2 x Vee 4 Stroke 8 Cy. 135 x 156 each-720kW (979bhp) MTU Friedrichshafen GmbH-Friedrichshafen AuxGen: 3 x 90kW a.c Fuel: 47.0 (d.f.)
7929695 - -	**SEAHAWK 2** - **United International Ltd** -	*519* - 39		**1980**-05 **Mitsubishi Heavy Industries Ltd. — Shimonoseki** Yd No: 818 Loa 48.30 Br ex 8.22 Dght 1.450 Lbp 44.00 Br md 8.20 Dpth 3.90 Welded, 1 dk	**(A37B2PS) Passenger Ship** Hull Material: Aluminium Alloy Passengers: 401	**2 oil engines** reverse reduction geared to sc. shafts driving 2 FP propellers Total Power: 3,560kW (4,840hp) 26.5kn M.T.U. 16V652TB91 2 x Vee 4 Stroke 16 Cy. 190 x 230 each-1780kW (2420bhp) Ikegai Tekkosho-Japan
9299599 *VRBE3* -	**SEAHERITAGE** **Omega Maritime Inc** Valles Steamship (Canada) Inc SatCom: Inmarsat C 447700190 *Hong Kong* *Hong Kong* MMSI: 477998200 Official number: HK-1559	**60,208** 33,762 109,229 T/cm 91.3	Class: AB	**2005**-08 **Hudong-Zhonghua Shipbuilding (Group) Co Ltd — Shanghai** Yd No: H1361A Loa 243.00 (BB) Br ex 42.03 Dght 15.350 Lbp 233.00 Br md 42.00 Dpth 22.00 Welded, 1 dk	**(A13A2TV) Crude Oil Tanker** Double Hull (13F) Liq: 123,030; Liq (Oil): 125,440 Cargo Heating Coils Compartments: 12 Wing Ta, ER, 2 Wing Slop Ta 3 Cargo Pump (s): 3x2500m³/hr Manifold: Bow/CM: 119.5m	**1 oil engine** driving 1 FP propeller Total Power: 9,981kW (13,570hp) 14.5kn MAN-B&W 7S60MC 1 x 2 Stroke 7 Cy. 600 x 2292 9981kW (13570bhp) Hudong Heavy Machinery Co Ltd-China AuxGen: 3 x 680kW a.c Fuel: 150.0 (d.f.) 2984.0 (r.f.)
9554690 - -	**SEAHOME SAPPHIRE** *ex* Haiphong Fishery Ht-109.01 *-2009* **Agribank Leasing Co II** Gia Hai Shipping Corp SatCom: Inmarsat C 457483010 *Saigon* *Vietnam* MMSI: 574830000	**2,989** 1,927 5,083	Class: VR	**2009**-02 **Haiphong Fishery Shipbuilding JSC — Haiphong** Yd No: HT-109.01 Loa 92.25 Br ex 15.33 Dght 6.480 Lbp 84.96 Br md 15.30 Dpth 7.85 Welded, 1 dk	**(A31A2GX) General Cargo Ship** Grain: 6,959 Compartments: 2 Ho, ER 2 Ha: (23.8 x 9.4)ER (15.8 x 9.4) Derricks: 2x10t	**1 oil engine** reduction geared to sc. shaft driving 1 FP propeller Total Power: 1,765kW (2,400hp) 10.0kn Chinese Std. Type G8300ZC 1 x 4 Stroke 8 Cy. 300 x 380 1765kW (2400bhp) (made 2008) Ningbo CSI Power & Machinery GroupCo Ltd-China
9425485 *3WPO* -	**SEAHOME SKY** *launched as* Dai Hung 45 *-2007* **Agribank Leasing Co II** Long Thinh Shipping Trading Co Ltd SatCom: Inmarsat C 457444910 *Haiphong* *Vietnam* MMSI: 574449000	**1,598** 1,022 2,050	Class: VR	**2007**-12 **Nam Ha Shipyard — Nam Ha** Loa 79.90 Br ex - Dght 5.000 Lbp 74.80 Br md 12.80 Dpth 6.08 Welded, 1 dk	**(A31A2GX) General Cargo Ship** Grain: 3,867	**1 oil engine** geared to sc. shaft driving 1 FP propeller Total Power: 1,103kW (1,500hp) Chinese Std. Type 8300 1 x 4 Stroke 8 Cy. 300 x 380 1103kW (1500bhp) Zibo Diesel Engine Factory-China
9486013 *9HA2233* -	**SEAHOPE II** **Online Shipping Inc** Thenamaris (Ships Management) Inc *Valletta* *Malta* MMSI: 248185000 Official number: 9486013	**33,036** 19,270 56,894 T/cm 58.8	Class: AB	**2010**-02 **Taizhou Sanfu Ship Engineering Co Ltd — Taizhou JS** Yd No: SF060101 Loa 189.99 (BB) Br ex - Dght 12.800 Lbp 185.00 Br md 32.26 Dpth 18.00 Welded, 1 dk	**(A21A2BC) Bulk Carrier** Grain: 71,634; Bale: 68,200 Compartments: 5 Ho, ER 5 Ha: ER Cranes: 4x36t	**1 oil engine** driving 1 FP propeller Total Power: 9,480kW (12,889hp) 14.2kn MAN-B&W 6S50MC-C 1 x 2 Stroke 6 Cy. 500 x 2000 9480kW (12889bhp) STX Engine Co Ltd-South Korea AuxGen: 3 x 660kW a.c Fuel: 124.0 (d.f.) 2246.0 (r.f.)
8213744 *PCAP* -	**SEAHORSE** *ex* Seahorse I *-1998* *ex* Snimos Ace *-1994* **Deeprock CV** Tideway BV SatCom: Inmarsat A 1716531 *Vlissingen* *Netherlands* MMSI: 244137000 Official number: 36290	**19,516** 5,854 20,958	Class: LR (NK) **100A1** SS 05/2009 **LMC** **UMS** Eq.Ltr: I†; Cable: 605.0/73.0 U2	**1983**-06 **Mitsubishi Heavy Industries Ltd. — Nagasaki** Yd No: 1917 Converted From: Heavy Load Carrier-1999 Loa 162.01 (BB) Br ex 38.05 Dght 6.371 Lbp 152.63 Br md 38.00 Dpth 9.02 Welded, 1 dk	**(B22K2OB) Pipe Burying Vessel**	**2 oil engines** with flexible couplings & sr gearedto sc. shafts driving 2 Directional propellers Total Power: 6,524kW (8,870hp) 13.1kn MAN 7L40/54A 2 x 4 Stroke 7 Cy. 400 x 540 each-3262kW (4435bhp) Mitsubishi Heavy Industries Ltd-Japan AuxGen: 3 x 480kW 450V 60Hz a.c Boilers: 2 e (ex.g.) 6.0kgf/cm² (5.9bar), AuxB (o.f.) 6.0kgf/cm² (5.9bar) Thrusters: 1 Thwart. CP thruster (f); 2 Directional thruster (f); 2 Directional thruster (a) Fuel: 280.0 (d.f.) 2760.0 (r.f.) 27.5pd
8427967 *DUA2686* -	**SEAHORSE** **Seven Seas Tugs & Barges Corp** - *Manila* *Philippines* Official number: MNLD000196	*245* 152 -		**1980 at Manila** Loa - Br ex 7.35 Dght - Lbp 40.85 Br md 7.32 Dpth 3.00 Welded, 1 dk	**(A13B2TU) Tanker (unspecified)**	**1 oil engine** driving 1 FP propeller Total Power: 151kW (205hp)
6517574 *WDD6925* -	**SEAHORSE** *ex* Skilak *-2005* **Arctic Wolf Marine Inc** - *Naknek, AK* *United States of America* MMSI: 367179520 Official number: 292012	*171* 116 230 T/cm 1.1	Class: (BV)	**1963 Pacific Coast Eng. Co. — Alameda, Ca** Yd No: 200 Loa 35.29 Br ex 11.03 Dght - Lbp - Br md 10.98 Dpth 2.16 Welded, 1 dk	**(A35D2RL) Landing Craft** Bow door/ramp Liq: 494; Liq (Oil): 494 Compartments: 5 Ta, ER	**2 oil engines** driving 2 FP propellers Total Power: 618kW (840hp) 8.5kn Caterpillar D343TA 2 x 4 Stroke 6 Cy. 137 x 165 each-309kW (420bhp) Caterpillar Tractor Co-USA

IMO / Call sign / Flag	Name / Owner	Tonnage	Class	Builder / Dimensions	Type	Machinery
7101889 *H04018* -	**SEAHORSE** *ex* Titan *-2005* *ex* Laura Rosa *-2000* **Oil Trading Corp** Bunker Vessel Management SA *Panama* *Panama* MMSI: 371256000 Official number: 3137606B	*166* 50 -	Class: (AB)	**1970**-01 **Halter Marine Services, Inc. — New Orleans, La** Yd No: 261 Loa 26.22 Br ex 7.93 Dght 3.556 Lbp 25.10 Br md 7.90 Dpth 3.89 Welded, 1 dk	**(B32A2ST) Tug**	**2 oil engines** reverse reduction geared to sc. shafts driving 2 FP propellers Total Power: 1,126kW (1,530hp) 10.0kn Caterpillar D398TA 2 x Vee 4 Stroke 12 Cy. 159 x 203 each-563kW (765bhp) Caterpillar Tractor Co-USA AuxGen: 2 x 40kW Fuel: 132.0
8992819 *WAG4795* -	**SEAHORSE** - **Northern Marine Salvage Inc** - *Seattle, WA* *United States of America* Official number: 285363	*160* 108 -		**1942**-01 **United States Navy Yard, Puget Sound — Bremerton, Wa** L reg 30.08 Br ex - Dght - Lbp - Br md 9.14 Dpth 2.13 Welded, 1 dk	**(B34L2QU) Utility Vessel** Cranes: 1	**2 oil engines** driving 2 FP propellers Total Power: 610kW (830hp) Caterpillar D343 2 x 4 Stroke 6 Cy. 137 x 165 each-305kW (415bhp) Caterpillar Inc-USA
7228431 *MZHO9* -	**SEAHORSE 2** *ex* Sesso *-2005* *ex* Sessoy *-1987* **Argyll Workboats** - *United Kingdom* MMSI: 232004949	**144** 43 -		**1972 Sigbjorn Iversen — Flekkefjord** Yd No: 21 Converted From: Ferry (Passenger/Vehicle)-2004 Loa 25.40 Br ex 7.47 Dght - Lbp 23.75 Br md 7.12 Dpth 2.52 Welded, 1 dk	**(B22A20V) Diving Support Vessel**	**1 oil engine** geared to sc. shaft driving 1 CP propeller Total Power: 279kW (379hp) 11.0kn Volvo Penta TAMD122A 1 x 4 Stroke 6 Cy. 130 x 150 279kW (379bhp) (new engine 2004) AB Volvo Penta-Sweden AuxGen: 2 x 24kW 220V 50Hz a.c Thrusters: 1 Thwart. CP thruster (f)
8979300 - -	**SEAHORSE CHUDITCH** - **DMS Maritime Pty Ltd** - *Fremantle, WA* *Australia* Official number: 857227	**139** - -		**2003 Super-Light Shipbuilding Contractor — Sibu** Loa 23.50 Br ex - Dght 2.850 Lbp - Br md 7.32 Dpth 2.85 Welded, 1 dk	**(B32A2ST) Tug**	**2 oil engines** geared to sc. shafts driving 2 Propellers Total Power: 530kW (720hp) Caterpillar 3412C 2 x Vee 4 Stroke 12 Cy. 137 x 152 each-265kW (360bhp) Caterpillar Inc-USA
6413259 *HP5300* -	**SEAHORSE II** *ex* Ryan Atlantic *-2010* *ex* Cape Norman *-1985* **Island Charters SA** - *Panama* *Panama* Official number: 4251711	*359* 122 -	Class: (LR) ✠ Classed LR until 3/65	**1964**-07 **Halifax Shipyards Ltd — Halifax NS** Yd No: 33 Converted From: Trawler-2011 Loa 43.01 Br ex 8.11 Dght - Lbp 37.24 Br md 8.01 Dpth 4.07 Welded	**(X11A2YP) Yacht**	**1 oil engine** driving 1 FP propeller Total Power: 221kW (300hp) Deutz RBV6M545 1 x 4 Stroke 6 Cy. 320 x 450 221kW (300bhp) Kloeckner Humboldt Deutz AG-West Germany
9188594 *VHN8774* -	**SEAHORSE MERCATOR** - **KV Equipment Rentals Pty Ltd** DMS Maritime Pty Ltd *Sydney, NSW* *Australia* Official number: 856305	**212** 64 60	Class: (LR) ✠ Classed LR until 25/11/03	**1998**-11 **Tenix Shipbuilding WA — Fremantle WA** Yd No: 347 Loa 32.50 Br ex 8.21 Dght 2.400 Lbp 27.60 Br md 8.10 Dpth 4.10 Welded, 1 dk	**(B34K2QT) Training Ship**	**2 oil engines** with clutches, flexible couplings & sr geared to sc. shafts driving 2 FP propellers Total Power: 1,566kW (2,130hp) 15.0kn Caterpillar 3412C-TA 2 x Vee 4 Stroke 12 Cy. 137 x 152 each-783kW (1065bhp) Caterpillar Inc-USA AuxGen: 2 x 50kW 415V 50Hz a.c
1006532 *VJN3995* -	**SEAHORSE P** *ex* Seahorse *-2012* *ex* Tigre D'or *-2010* **Royvis Pty Ltd** - *Sydney, NSW* *Australia* MMSI: 503741000 Official number: 860262	**609** 182 -	Class: LR ✠ **100A1** SS 11/2009 SSC Yacht (P) mono G6 service area ✠ **LMC** **UMS** Cable: 391.0/22.0	**1999**-11 **Damen Shipyards Gdynia SA — Gdynia** (Hull) **1999**-11 **Amels Holland BV — Makkum** Yd No: 434 Loa 51.69 Br ex 9.42 Dght 3.200 Lbp 44.94 Br md 9.00 Dpth 4.90 Welded, 1 dk	**(X11A2YP) Yacht**	**2 oil engines** with clutches, flexible couplings & sr reverse geared to sc. shafts driving 2 FP propellers Total Power: 1,790kW (2,434hp) 15.0kn Cummins KTA-38-M2 2 x Vee 4 Stroke 12 Cy. 159 x 159 each-895kW (1217bhp) Cummins Engine Co Ltd-United Kingdom AuxGen: 2 x 136kW 380V 50Hz a.c Thrusters: 1 Thwart. FP thruster (f)
8979312 - -	**SEAHORSE QUENDA** - **DMS Maritime Pty Ltd** - *Sydney, NSW* *Australia* Official number: 857228	**139** - -		**2003 Super-Light Shipbuilding Contractor — Sibu** Loa 23.50 Br ex - Dght 2.850 Lbp - Br md 7.32 Dpth - Welded, 1 dk	**(B32A2ST) Tug**	**2 oil engines** geared to sc. shafts driving 2 Propellers Total Power: 530kW (720hp) Caterpillar 3412C 2 x Vee 4 Stroke 12 Cy. 137 x 152 each-265kW (360bhp) Caterpillar Inc-USA
7623904 *VNFG* -	**SEAHORSE SPIRIT** *ex* British Viking *-1998* *ex* Balder Hudson *-1986* **DMS Maritime Pty Ltd** - *Melbourne, Vic* *Australia* MMSI: 503040000 Official number: 855907	**2,090** 627 2,170	Class: BV (NV)	**1980**-06 **Marystown Shipyard Ltd — Marystown NL** Yd No: 26 Converted From: Trials Support Vessel-2010 Converted From: Offshore Supply Ship-1998 Loa 72.07 Br ex 16.01 Dght 5.265 Lbp 66.60 Br md - Dpth 6.51 Welded, 2 dks	**(B21A20S) Platform Supply Ship** Cranes: 1x5t Ice Capable	**2 oil engines** sr reverse geared to sc. shafts driving 2 CP propellers Total Power: 4,030kW (5,480hp) 8.0kn Alco 12V251F 2 x Vee 4 Stroke 12 Cy. 229 x 267 each-2015kW (2740bhp) Bombardier Inc-Canada AuxGen: 2 x 960kW 220/440V 60Hz a.c, 3 x 388kW 220/440V 60Hz a.c Thrusters: 2 Thwart. CP thruster (f); 1 Tunnel thruster (a); 1 Tunnel thruster (a) Fuel: 850.0 (d.f.) 20.0pd
7623930 *VNFW* -	**SEAHORSE STANDARD** *ex* British Magnus *-1998* *ex* Balder Cabot *-1985* **DMS Maritime Pty Ltd** - *Fremantle, WA* *Australia* MMSI: 503044000 Official number: 856117	**2,090** 627 1,982	Class: BV (NV)	**1981**-03 **Marystown Shipyard Ltd — Marystown NL** Yd No: 29 Converted From: Trials Support Vessel-2010 Converted From: Offshore Supply Ship-1998 Loa 72.07 Br ex 16.41 Dght 5.253 Lbp 66.60 Br md 16.01 Dpth 6.51 Welded, 2 dks	**(B21A20S) Platform Supply Ship** Cranes: 1x5t Ice Capable	**2 oil engines** sr reverse geared to sc. shafts driving 2 CP propellers Total Power: 4,030kW (5,480hp) 8.0kn Alco 12V251F 2 x Vee 4 Stroke 12 Cy. 229 x 267 each-2015kW (2740bhp) Bombardier Inc-Canada AuxGen: 2 x 960kW 220/440V 60Hz a.c, 3 x 388kW 220/440V 60Hz a.c Thrusters: 2 Thwart. CP thruster (f); 1 Tunnel thruster (a); 1 Tunnel thruster (a) Fuel: 850.0 (d.f.) 20.0pd
8716722 *9LD2573* -	**SEAIR QUEEN** *ex* Cesaria *-2014* *ex* Overseas Primar *-2009* *ex* Primar *-2005* *ex* BP Advocate *-1993* *launched as* Onomichi Spirit *-1988* **Maritime Ventures Fund Ltd** Doehle Danautic India Pvt Ltd *Freetown* *Sierra Leone* MMSI: 667073000 Official number: SL105273	**25,368** 10,927 39,538 T/cm 47.5	Class: PX (RS) (AB)	**1988**-08 **Onomichi Dockyard Co Ltd — Onomichi HS** Yd No: 327 Loa 182.30 (BB) Br ex 31.42 Dght 10.970 Lbp 172.02 Br md 31.40 Dpth 17.20 Welded, 1 dk	**(A13B2TP) Products Tanker** Double Sides Entire Compartment Length Liq: 47,889; Liq (Oil): 47,889 Cargo Heating Coils Compartments: 7 Ta, 2 Wing Slop Ta, ER, 1 Slop Ta 3 Cargo Pump (s): 3x1300m³/hr Manifold: Bow/CM: 91.2m	**1 oil engine** driving 1 FP propeller Total Power: 7,967kW (10,832hp) 14.5kn B&W 6S50MC 1 x 2 Stroke 6 Cy. 500 x 1910 7967kW (10832bhp) Mitsui Engineering & Shipbuilding CLtd-Japan AuxGen: 3 x 420kW a.c Fuel: 115.8 (d.f.) 1497.9 (r.f.)
6228238 - -	**SEAJACK** *ex* Luna Sea *-2010* *ex* Alliance *-2004* *ex* Massachusetts *-2003* **Tropic Tuna Ltd** -	*199* 85 187	Class: (AB)	**1962 Sturgeon Bay Shipbuilding & Dry Dock Corp — Sturgeon Bay WI** Yd No: 257 L reg 34.90 Br ex 7.12 Dght - Lbp 34.29 Br md 7.09 Dpth 3.89 Welded, 1 dk	**(B11A2FT) Trawler** Compartments: 1 Ho, ER 2 Ha:	**1 oil engine** reverse reduction geared to sc. shaft driving 1 FP propeller Total Power: 607kW (825hp) General Motors 8-278 1 x Vee 2 Stroke 8 Cy. 216 x 267 607kW (825bhp) General Motors Corp-USA AuxGen: 1 x 21kW, 2 x 20kW Fuel: 43.5
9522207 *3ESD6* -	**SEAJACKS KRAKEN** - **Seajacks 1 Ltd** Seajacks UK Ltd *Panama* *Panama* MMSI: 370267000 Official number: 3477109A	**5,186** 1,555 1,683	Class: AB	**2009**-03 **Lamprell Energy Ltd — Dubai** Yd No: 07-001 Loa 76.00 Br ex - Dght 3.650 Lbp 61.00 Br md 36.00 Dpth 6.00 Welded, 1 dk	**(B22A2ZM) Offshore Construction Vessel, jack up** Cranes: 1x300t,1x50t	**4 diesel electric oil engines** driving 4 gen. each 1600kW 690V a.c Connecting to 4 elec. motors each (1500kW) driving 4 Azimuth electric drive units Total Power: 6,000kW (8,156hp) 8.0kn Caterpillar 3516 4 x Vee 4 Stroke 16 Cy. 170 x 190 each-1500kW (2039bhp) Caterpillar Inc-USA Fuel: 454.0 (r.f.)
9522219 *3ESC6* -	**SEAJACKS LEVIATHAN** - **Seajacks 2 Ltd** Seajacks UK Ltd SatCom: Inmarsat C 437026210 *Panama* *Panama* MMSI: 370262000 Official number: 3494509B	**5,186** 1,555 1,683	Class: AB	**2009**-06 **Lamprell Energy Ltd — Dubai** Yd No: 07-002 Loa 76.00 Br ex - Dght 3.650 Lbp 61.00 Br md 36.00 Dpth 6.00 Welded, 1 dk	**(B22A2ZM) Offshore Construction Vessel, jack up** Cranes: 1x400t	**4 diesel electric oil engines** driving 4 gen. each 1600kW 690V a.c Connecting to 4 elec. motors each (1500kW) reduction geared to sc. shafts driving 4 Azimuth electric drive units Total Power: 6,000kW (8,156hp) 8.0kn Caterpillar 3516 4 x Vee 4 Stroke 16 Cy. 170 x 190 each-1500kW (2039bhp) Caterpillar Inc-USA AuxGen: 4 x 1600kW a.c Fuel: 454.0 (r.f.)

IMO / Call sign	Name / Owner / Flag	Tonnage	Class	Builder / Dimensions	Type / Capacity	Machinery
9596571 *3FJW7* -	**SEAJACKS ZARATAN** **Seajacks 3 Ltd** Seajacks UK Ltd *Panama* *Panama* MMSI: 373322000 Official number: 4386012	**9,704** 2,911 3,597	Class: AB	**2012-05 Lamprell Energy Ltd — Sharjah** Yd No: 104 Loa 81.00 Br ex - Dght 5.300 Lbp - Br md 41.00 Dpth 7.00 Welded, 1 dk	**(B22A2ZM) Offshore Construction Vessel, jack up** Passengers: berths: 90 Cranes: 1x800t,2x12.5t	**6 diesel electric oil engines** driving 4 gen. each 1600kW 690V a.c 2 gen. each 1200kW 690V a.c Connecting to 6 elec. motors each (1500kW) driving 3 Azimuth electric drive units Total Power: 8,800kW (11,964hp) 9.1kn Thrusters: 1 Tunnel thruster (wing) Fuel: 680.0
9213820 *9HGN7* -	**SEAJOY** *ex Big Ocean -2002* **Sage Shipping Ltd** Eastern Mediterranean Maritime Ltd *Valletta* *Malta* MMSI: 215208000 Official number: 7698	**38,367** 24,622 73,454 T/cm 65.4	Class: RI (NK)	**2000-10 Sumitomo Heavy Industries Ltd. — Yokosuka Shipyard, Yokosuka** Yd No: 1264 Loa 225.00 (BB) Br ex - Dght 13.871 Lbp 217.00 Br md 32.26 Dpth 19.20 Welded, 1 dk	**(A21A2BC) Bulk Carrier** Grain: 87,298 Compartments: 7 Ho, ER 7 Ha: (16.3 x 13.4)6 (16.3 x 15.0)ER	**1 oil engine** driving 1 FP propeller Total Power: 8,877kW (12,069hp) 14.5kn Sulzer 7RTA48T 1 x 2 Stroke 7 Cy. 480 x 2000 8877kW (12069bhp) Diesel United Ltd.-Aioi
8333221 - -	**SEAKA** *ex Ohau -1997 ex Komine Maru No. 31 -1985* - -	*146* 47 -		**1973-01 Kesennuma Tekko — Kesennuma** Loa - Br ex 7.07 Dght - Lbp 30.18 Br md 7.05 Dpth 2.43 Welded, 1 dk	**(B11B2FV) Fishing Vessel**	**1 oil engine** driving 1 FP propeller Total Power: 246kW (334hp) Niigata 6M26CR 1 x 4 Stroke 6 Cy. 260 x 400 246kW (334bhp) Niigata Engineering Co Ltd-Japan
9292187 *C6UC7* -	**SEAKING** **Scope Navigation Inc** Thenamaris (Ships Management) Inc SatCom: Inmarsat C 431187310 *Nassau* *Bahamas* MMSI: 311873000 Official number: 8000917	**161,382** 110,526 318,669 T/cm 181.0	Class: LR ✠ **100A1** SS 02/2010 Double Hull oil tanker ESP *IWS LI SPM **ShipRight** (SDA, FDA plus, CM) ✠ **LMC** **UMS IGS** Eq.Ltr: D*; Cable: 770.0/117.0 U3 (a)	**2005-02 Hyundai Heavy Industries Co Ltd — Ulsan** Yd No: 1609 Loa 333.00 (BB) Br ex 60.04 Dght 22.500 Lbp 319.00 Br md 60.00 Dpth 30.40 Welded, 1 dk	**(A13A2TV) Crude Oil Tanker** Double Hull (13F) Liq: 339,180; Liq (Oil): 352,000 3 Cargo Pump (s) Manifold: Bow/CM: 167m	**1 oil engine** driving 1 FP propeller Total Power: 29,326kW (39,872hp) 15.7kn B&W 6S90MC-C 1 x 2 Stroke 6 Cy. 900 x 3188 29326kW (39872bhp) Hyundai Heavy Industries Co Ltd-South Korea AuxGen: 3 x 1180kW 450V 60Hz a.c Boilers: e (ex.g.) 25.5kgf/cm² (25.0bar), AuxB (o.f.) 22.4kgf/cm² (22.0bar)
8962814 *H02821* -	**SEAL** *ex Nymfen II -2002 ex Nymfen -2002* **Sea Star S de RL** Pacific Maritime Co Ltd *Panama* *Panama* Official number: 30403PEXT	*192* 60 -		**1963 Orlogsvaerftet (Naval Dockyard) — Copenhagen** Converted From: Patrol Vessel, Naval Loa 37.00 Br ex - Dght - Lbp 36.13 Br md 6.76 Dpth 3.49 Welded, 1 dk	**(X11A2YP) Yacht**	**3 oil engines** driving 2 FP propellers Total Power: 1,986kW (2,701hp) 20.0kn Foden 1 x 74kW (101bhp) Fodens Ltd.-Sandbach Maybach 2 x 4 Stroke each-956kW (1300bhp) Maybach Motorenbau GmbH-Friedrichshafen
8929604 *5NLB* -	**SEAL** *ex Seal (5000) -1967* **Aqua Seals Ltd** *Nigeria*	*251* 74 64		**1967-08 Brooke Marine Ltd. — Lowestoft** Yd No: 356 Loa 36.66 Br ex - Dght 2.100 Lbp 33.52 Br md 7.16 Dpth 4.42 Welded, 1 dk	**(B34P2QV) Salvage Ship**	**2 oil engines** reduction geared to sc. shafts driving 2 FP propellers Total Power: 2,942kW (4,000hp) 21.0kn Paxman 16YJCM 2 x Vee 4 Stroke 16 Cy. 197 x 216 each-1471kW (2000bhp) Davey, Paxman & Co. Ltd.-Colchester Fuel: 31.0 (d.f.)
8208828 *GDDT* -	**SEAL CARR** **City Leasing Ltd** Forth Estuary Towage Ltd *Leith* *United Kingdom* MMSI: 235040683 Official number: 398733	**251** 75 107	Class: BV (LR) ✠ Classed LR until 15/3/85	**1983-05 McTay Marine Ltd. — Bromborough** Yd No: 47 Loa 29.42 Br ex 8.92 Dght 3.061 Lbp 27.51 Br md 8.60 Dpth 3.61 Welded, 1 dk	**(B32A2ST) Tug**	**2 oil engines** with flexible couplings & sr gearedto sc. shafts driving 2 Directional propellers Total Power: 1,342kW (1,824hp) 11.5kn Allen 6PS12-F 2 x 4 Stroke 6 Cy. 241 x 305 each-671kW (912bhp) NEI A.P.E. Ltd. W. H. Allen-Bedford AuxGen: 2 x 80kW 415V 50Hz a.c Fuel: 20.0 (d.f.) 7.0pd
8510867 *VVWX* -	**SEAL I** *ex Nestor -1988* **Seal Fisheries Ltd** - *Visakhapatnam* *India*	*160* 47 80	Class: (IR) (NV)	**1986 Australian Shipbuilding Industries (WA) Pty Ltd — Fremantle WA** Yd No: 233 Loa 24.95 Br ex 7.50 Dght - Lbp 22.05 Br md 7.45 Dpth 4.09 Welded, 1 dk	**(B11A2FT) Trawler** Ins: 110	**1 oil engine** with clutches, flexible couplings & sr geared to sc. shaft driving 1 FP propeller Total Power: 370kW (503hp) Caterpillar 3412T 1 x Vee 4 Stroke 12 Cy. 137 x 152 370kW (503bhp) Caterpillar Tractor Co-USA AuxGen: 2 x 50kW 415V 50Hz a.c
8802557 *VVWY* -	**SEAL II** **Seal Fisheries Ltd** - *Visakhapatnam* *India*	*155* 47 80	Class: (IR) (NV)	**1988-03 Australian Shipbuilding Industries (WA) Pty Ltd — Fremantle WA** Yd No: 260 Loa - (BB) Br ex 7.45 Dght 3.001 Lbp 24.90 Br md 7.42 Dpth 3.85 Welded, 1 dk	**(B11A2FT) Trawler** Ins: 110	**1 oil engine** with flexible couplings & sr gearedto sc. shaft driving 1 CP propeller Total Power: 372kW (506hp) Caterpillar 3412T 1 x Vee 4 Stroke 12 Cy. 137 x 152 372kW (506bhp) Caterpillar Inc-USA AuxGen: 2 x 50kW 415V 50Hz a.c
7315727 *GSAZ* -	**SEAL SANDS** **PD Teesport Ltd** - *Middlesbrough* *United Kingdom* MMSI: 232004108 Official number: 341858	**731** 219 887	Class: (LR) ✠ Classed LR until 15/11/10	**1973-08 R. Dunston (Hessle) Ltd. — Hessle** Yd No: S890 Loa 48.21 Br ex 12.35 Dght 4.077 Lbp 44.66 Br md 12.01 Dpth 4.65 Welded, 1 dk	**(B33B2DU) Hopper/Dredger (unspecified)** Hopper: 500	**2 oil engines** reverse reduction geared to sc. shafts driving 2 FP propellers Total Power: 1,014kW (1,378hp) 10.0kn Polar SF15RS-C 2 x 4 Stroke 5 Cy. 250 x 300 each-507kW (689bhp) British Polar Engines Ltd.-Glasgow AuxGen: 3 x 49kW 415V 50Hz a.c
9104421 *9HJM7* -	**SEALADY** *ex Grand Success -2002* **Sunshine Maritime Ltd** Eastern Mediterranean Maritime Ltd *Valletta* *Malta* MMSI: 215297000 Official number: 7916	**23,263** 13,807 42,183 T/cm 47.6	Class: RI (NK)	**1995-03 Oshima Shipbuilding Co Ltd — Saikai NS** Yd No: 10179 Loa 180.00 (BB) Br ex 30.53 Dght 11.228 Lbp 172.88 Br md 30.50 Dpth 15.80 Welded, 1 dk	**(A21A2BC) Bulk Carrier** Grain: 52,125; Bale: 51,118 Compartments: 5 Ho, ER 5 Ha: (14.4 x 15.3)4 (19.2 x 15.3)ER Cranes: 4x25t	**1 oil engine** driving 1 FP propeller Total Power: 6,230kW (8,470hp) 14.0kn Sulzer 6RTA52 1 x 2 Stroke 6 Cy. 520 x 1800 6230kW (8470bhp) Diesel United Ltd.-Aioi
9060039 - -	**SEALANCE TWO** **Lloyd James Hart** - *St John's, NL* *Canada* Official number: 813716	*134* 57 -		**1992-05 Glovertown Shipyards Ltd — Glovertown NL** Yd No: 53 Loa 19.80 Br ex - Dght - Lbp 18.53 Br md 7.32 Dpth 3.63 Welded, 1 dk	**(B11B2FV) Fishing Vessel**	**1 oil engine** with clutches & sr reverse geared to sc. shaft driving 1 FP propeller Total Power: 497kW (676hp) Cummins VTA-28-M2 1 x Vee 4 Stroke 12 Cy. 140 x 152 497kW (676bhp) Cummins Engine Co Inc-USA
9197545 *9HA3372* -	**SEALAND ILLINOIS** **Miko Shipping Co** Costamare Shipping Co SA *Valletta* *Malta* MMSI: 229487000 Official number: 9197545	**74,583** 41,490 81,577 T/cm 105.0	Class: GL	**2000-12 Hyundai Heavy Industries Co Ltd — Ulsan** Yd No: 1212 Loa 304.16 (BB) Br ex 40.10 Dght 14.000 Lbp 292.16 Br md 40.00 Dpth 24.20 Welded, 1 dk	**(A33A2CC) Container Ship (Fully Cellular)** TEU 6420 C Ho 3130 TEU C Dk 3290 TEU incl 500 ref C. Compartments: ER, 8 Cell Ho 17 Ha: (12.6 x 15.5) (12.6 x 25.6)Tappered (12.6 x 31.1)Tappered ER 14 (12.6 x 35.8)	**1 oil engine** driving 1 FP propeller Total Power: 57,059kW (77,577hp) 26.0kn B&W 10K98MC-C 1 x 2 Stroke 10 Cy. 980 x 2400 57059kW (77577bhp) Hyundai Heavy Industries Co Ltd-South Korea AuxGen: 4 x 2280kW 220/440V a.c Thrusters: 1 Tunnel thruster (f)
9196864 *9HA3390* -	**SEALAND MICHIGAN** **Dino Shipping Co** Costamare Shipping Co SA *Valletta* *Malta* MMSI: 229538000 Official number: 9196864	**74,583** 41,490 81,574 T/cm 105.0	Class: BV (GL)	**2000-10 Hyundai Heavy Industries Co Ltd — Ulsan** Yd No: 1211 Loa 304.16 (BB) Br ex 40.10 Dght 14.000 Lbp 292.00 Br md 40.00 Dpth 24.20 Welded, 1 dk	**(A33A2CC) Container Ship (Fully Cellular)** TEU 6420 C Ho 3130 TEU C Dk 3290 TEU incl 500 ref C. Compartments: ER, 8 Cell Ho 17 Ha: (12.6 x 15.5) (12.6 x 25.6)Tappered (12.6 x 31.1)Tappered ER 14 (12.6 x 35.8)	**1 oil engine** driving 1 FP propeller Total Power: 57,059kW (77,577hp) 26.0kn B&W 10K98MC-C 1 x 2 Stroke 10 Cy. 980 x 2400 57059kW (77577bhp) Hyundai Heavy Industries Co Ltd-South Korea AuxGen: 4 x 2280kW 220/440V Thrusters: 1 Thwart. CP thruster (f)
9196838 *9HA3394* -	**SEALAND NEW YORK** **Costis Maritime Corp** Costamare Shipping Co SA *Valletta* *Malta* MMSI: 229544000 Official number: 9196838	**74,661** 41,490 81,462 T/cm 105.0	Class: BV (GL)	**2000-05 Hyundai Heavy Industries Co Ltd — Ulsan** Yd No: 1208 Loa 304.16 (BB) Br ex 40.10 Dght 14.000 Lbp 292.00 Br md 40.00 Dpth 24.20 Welded, 1 dk	**(A33A2CC) Container Ship (Fully Cellular)** TEU 6420 C Ho 3130 TEU C Dk 3290 TEU incl 500 ref C. Compartments: ER, 8 Cell Ho 17 Ha: (12.6 x 15.5) (12.6 x 25.6)Tappered (12.6 x 31.1)Tappered ER 14 (12.6 x 35.8)	**1 oil engine** driving 1 FP propeller Total Power: 57,059kW (77,577hp) 26.0kn B&W 10K98MC-C 1 x 2 Stroke 10 Cy. 980 x 2400 57059kW (77577bhp) Hyundai Heavy Industries Co Ltd-South Korea AuxGen: 4 x 2280kW 220/440V Thrusters: 1 Thwart. FP thruster (f)

IMO / Call sign	Name / Owner / Manager	Tonnage	Class	Builder / Dimensions	Type	Machinery
9196852 *9HA3421* -	**SEALAND WASHINGTON** **Christos Maritime Corp** Costamare Shipping Co SA *Valletta* *Malta* MMSI: 229577000 Official number: 9196852	**74,586** 41,490 81,556 T/cm 105.0	Class: LR (GL) **100A1** SS 09/2010 container ship *IWS LI **LMC** **UMS**	**2000-08 Hyundai Heavy Industries Co Ltd — Ulsan** Yd No: 1210 Loa 304.16 (BB) Br ex 40.10 Dght 14.000 Lbp 292.00 Br md 40.00 Dpth 24.20 Welded, 1 dk	**(A33A2CC) Container Ship (Fully Cellular)** TEU 6420 C Ho 3130 TEU C Dk 3290 TEU incl 500 ref C. Compartments: ER, 8 Cell Ho 17 Ha: (12.6 x 15.5) (12.6 x 25.6)Tappered (12.6 x 31.1)Tappered ER 14 (12.6 x 35.8)	**1 oil engine** driving 1 FP propeller Total Power: 57,059kW (77,577hp) 26.0kn B&W 10K98MC-C 1 x 2 Stroke 10 Cy. 980 x 2400 57059kW (77577bhp) Hyundai Heavy Industries Co Ltd-South Korea AuxGen: 4 x 2280kW 220/440V Thrusters: 1 Thwart. CP thruster (f)
8647103 *DUA2065* -	**SEALANE** *ex* Mari-Ed *-2005* **Seatrans Corp** Translift Ship Management Inc *Batangas* *Philippines* Official number: BAT5001084	*248* 158 -		**1991-01 at Manila** Loa 47.09 Br ex - Dght - Lbp - Br md 7.01 Dpth 2.09 Welded, 1 dk	**(A13B2TU) Tanker (unspecified)**	**1 oil engine** driving 1 Propeller Cummins 1 x 4 Stroke Cummins Engine Co Inc-USA
7017765 - -	**SEALIFE II** - **E J LeBlanc & Sons Seiners Ltd** - *Pictou, NS* *Canada* MMSI: 316004202 Official number: 323540	*287* 142 -		**1970 Ferguson Industries Ltd — Pictou NS** Yd No: 185 Loa 30.79 Br ex 8.67 Dght - Lbp - Br md 8.62 Dpth 4.30 Welded, 1 dk	**(B11A2FT) Trawler** Derricks: 2x5t	**1 oil engine** driving 1 CP propeller Total Power: 736kW (1,001hp) 12.0kn Ruston 6AP3 1 x 4 Stroke 6 Cy. 203 x 273 736kW (1001bhp) English Electric Diesels Ltd.-Glasgow AuxGen: 2 x 40kW 220V 60Hz a.c Fuel: 40.5 (d.f.)
6724672 - - -	**SEALIFT 22** *ex* Johann Petersen *-1983* - -	*192* - -	Class: (GL)	**1967 Johann Oelkers KG — Hamburg** Yd No: 555 Loa 30.66 Br ex 7.98 Dght 3.709 Lbp 27.61 Br md 7.93 Dpth 4.12 Welded, 1 dk	**(B32A2ST) Tug** Ice Capable	**2 diesel electric oil engines** driving 2 gen. each 550kW 500V d.c Connecting to 2 elec. motors driving 1 FP propeller Total Power: 1,176kW (1,598hp) 13.0kn MAN G8V235/33MA 2 x 4 Stroke 8 Cy. 235 x 330 each-588kW (799bhp) Maschinenbau Augsburg Nuernberg (MAN)-Augsburg AuxGen: 3 x 75kW 220V d.c, 1 x 14kW 220V d.c
8873245 - -	**SEALINE 1** *ex* Atco Rasha *-2013* **Sea Line Shipping Services LLC** - *Dubai* *United Arab Emirates* Official number: 7146	**124** 37 -	Class: RI (AB)	**1992-02 Neuville Boat Works, Inc. — New Iberia, La** Yd No: 100-13 Loa 30.48 Br ex 6.71 Dght 1.520 Lbp 30.48 Br md 6.71 Dpth 2.90 Welded, 1 dk	**(B21A20C) Crew/Supply Vessel** Hull Material: Aluminium Alloy	**2 oil engines** reverse reduction geared to sc. shafts driving 2 FP propellers Total Power: 750kW (1,020hp) 18.0kn G.M. (Detroit Diesel) 12V-71-TI 2 x Vee 2 Stroke 12 Cy. 108 x 127 each-375kW (510bhp) General Motors Detroit DieselAllison Divn-USA AuxGen: 2 x 30kW a.c
9251652 *DECO* -	**SEALING** **tms 'Sealing' GmbH & Co KG** German Tanker Shipping GmbH & Co KG *Bremen* *Germany* MMSI: 211397660 Official number: 4871	**21,356** 8,390 32,428 T/cm 42.0	Class: GL	**2003-05 Lindenau GmbH Schiffswerft u. Maschinenfabrik — Kiel** Yd No: 257 Loa 177.74 (BB) Br ex 28.09 Dght 11.000 Lbp 168.00 Br md 28.00 Dpth 16.80 Welded, 1 dk	**(A13B2TP) Products Tanker** Double Hull (13F) Liq: 36,760; Liq (Oil): 36,760 Compartments: 10 Wing Ta, ER 10 Cargo Pump (s): 10x500m³/hr Manifold: Bow/CM: 84.9m Ice Capable	**1 oil engine** reduction geared to sc. shaft driving 1 CP propeller Total Power: 8,340kW (11,339hp) 15.1kn MAN 6L58/64 1 x 4 Stroke 6 Cy. 580 x 640 8340kW (11339bhp) MAN B&W Diesel AG-Augsburg AuxGen: 1 x 1120kW 400V 50Hz a.c, 3 x 960kW 400V 50Hz a.c Thrusters: 1 Thwart. CP thruster (f) Fuel: 373.0 (d.f.) 856.0 (r.f.)
9480813 *9WKQ3* -	**SEALINK 161** **Sealink Offshore (L) Ltd** Sealink Sdn Bhd *Kuching* *Malaysia* MMSI: 533000966 Official number: 333081	**1,896** 568 1,788	Class: AB	**2010-09 Sealink Engineering & Slipway Sdn Bhd — Miri** Yd No: 161 Loa 61.25 Br ex - Dght 5.100 Lbp 58.70 Br md 16.00 Dpth 6.00 Welded, 1 dk	**(B21B20A) Anchor Handling Tug Supply**	**2 oil engines** reduction geared to sc. shafts driving 2 CP propellers Total Power: 3,840kW (5,220hp) 11.0kn Yanmar 6EY26 2 x 4 Stroke 6 Cy. 260 x 385 each-1920kW (2610bhp) Yanmar Diesel Engine Co Ltd-Japan AuxGen: 3 x 380kW a.c, 1 x 800kW a.c Thrusters: 1 Tunnel thruster (f)
9645217 *9V9385* -	**SEALINK 178** **Seabright Singapore Pte Ltd** Sealink Sdn Bhd *Singapore* *Singapore* MMSI: 566793000 Official number: 397003	**5,174** 1,552 4,642	Class: AB	**2013-04 Jiangsu Zhenjiang Shipyard Co Ltd — Zhenjiang JS** Yd No: SSS178A Loa 84.80 (BB) Br ex - Dght 6.800 Lbp 75.00 Br md 22.00 Dpth 8.30 Welded, 1 dk	**(B21B20A) Anchor Handling Tug Supply**	**2 oil engines** reduction geared to sc. shafts driving 2 Propellers Total Power: 6,120kW (8,320hp) Wartsila 9L26 2 x 4 Stroke 9 Cy. 260 x 320 each-3060kW (4160bhp) Wartsila Italia SpA-Italy AuxGen: 2 x 1500kW a.c, 2 x 1664kW a.c
9645229 *9WOK5* -	**SEALINK 179** **Sealink Antarabangsa Ltd** - *Kuching* *Malaysia* MMSI: 533170084 Official number: 334737	**5,174** 1,552 4,598	Class: AB	**2013-08 Jiangsu Zhenjiang Shipyard Co Ltd — Zhenjiang JS** Yd No: SSS179A Loa 84.80 (BB) Br ex - Dght 6.000 Lbp 75.00 Br md 22.00 Dpth 8.30 Welded, 1 dk	**(B21B20A) Anchor Handling Tug Supply**	**2 diesel electric oil engines** reduction geared to sc. shafts driving 2 Propellers Total Power: 6,120kW (8,320hp) 12.0kn Wartsila 9L26 2 x 4 Stroke 9 Cy. 260 x 320 each-3060kW (4160bhp) Wartsila Finland Oy-Finland AuxGen: 2 x 1664kW a.c Thrusters: 2 Tunnel thruster (f); 2 Tunnel thruster (a) Fuel: 1330.0 (d.f.)
9278961 *9WED4* -	**SEALINK CASSANDRA** **Seabright Sdn Bhd** Sealink Sdn Bhd *Kuching* *Malaysia* MMSI: 533422000 Official number: 329772	**490** 147 575	Class: AB	**2002-08 Sealink Shipyard Sdn Bhd — Miri** Yd No: 108 Loa 48.00 Br ex 11.00 Dght 2.800 Lbp 46.20 Br md 11.00 Dpth 3.50 Welded, 1 Dk.	**(B21A20S) Platform Supply Ship**	**2 oil engines** reverse reduction geared to sc. shafts driving 2 FP propellers Total Power: 1,074kW (1,460hp) 10.0kn Caterpillar 3412TA 2 x Vee 4 Stroke 12 Cy. 137 x 152 each-537kW (730bhp) Caterpillar Inc-USA AuxGen: 2 x 96kW a.c Thrusters: 1 Thwart. FP thruster (f) Fuel: 600.0 (d.f.)
8881606 *VNDN* -	**SEALINK DARWIN** *ex* Sealink Indah *-2010* **Conlon Murphy Pty Ltd (QAL Specialised Transport NT)** - *Darwin, NT* *Australia* MMSI: 503620000 Official number: 859239	**479** 172 -	Class: AB	**1994-08 Nam Cheong Dockyard Sdn Bhd — Miri** Yd No: 389 Loa 46.20 Br ex - Dght 2.500 Lbp 42.86 Br md 10.90 Dpth 3.20 Welded, 1 dk	**(A35D2RL) Landing Craft** Bow ramp (centre)	**2 oil engines** driving 2 FP propellers Total Power: 692kW (940hp) Caterpillar 3408TA 2 x Vee 4 Stroke 8 Cy. 137 x 152 each-346kW (470bhp) Caterpillar Inc-USA AuxGen: 1 x 85kW a.c
9258844 *9WCZ5* -	**SEALINK MAJU 2** **Sealink Pacific Sdn Bhd** Sealink Sdn Bhd *Kuching* *Malaysia* MMSI: 533000335 Official number: 328174	**257** 77 177	Class: AB	**2001-10 Sealink Shipyard Sdn Bhd — Miri** Yd No: 109 Loa 29.00 Br ex - Dght 3.950 Lbp 27.01 Br md 9.00 Dpth 4.25 Welded, 1 dk	**(B32A2ST) Tug**	**2 oil engines** with clutches, flexible couplings & sr geared to sc. shafts driving 2 FP propellers Total Power: 1,806kW (2,456hp) 8.9kn Caterpillar 3512TA 2 x Vee 4 Stroke 12 Cy. 170 x 190 each-903kW (1228bhp) Caterpillar Inc-USA AuxGen: 2 x 135kW 415V 50Hz a.c Thrusters: 1 Thwart. FP thruster (f) Fuel: 185.0 (d.f.)
9371000 *9WHS4* -	**SEALINK MAJU 4** **Era Surplus Sdn Bhd** Sealink Sdn Bhd *Kuching* *Malaysia* Official number: 332964	**248** 74 -	Class: AB	**2005-12 Nantong Huigang Ship-Propeller Co Ltd — Qidong JS** Yd No: 2003-09 Loa 29.00 Br ex - Dght 3.500 Lbp 26.50 Br md 9.00 Dpth 4.25 Welded, 1 dk	**(B32A2ST) Tug**	**2 oil engines** reduction geared to sc. shafts driving 2 Propellers Total Power: 2,402kW (3,266hp) Cummins KTA-50-M2 2 x Vee 4 Stroke 16 Cy. 159 x 159 each-1201kW (1633bhp) Cummins Engine Co Inc-USA
9373101 *9WHS5* -	**SEALINK MAJU 5** **Era Surplus Sdn Bhd** Sealink Sdn Bhd *Kuching* *Malaysia* Official number: 332965	**248** 74 -	Class: AB	**2005-12 Nantong Huigang Ship-Propeller Co Ltd — Qidong JS** Yd No: 2003-10 Loa 29.00 Br ex - Dght 3.900 Lbp 26.50 Br md 9.00 Dpth 4.25 Welded, 1 dk	**(B32A2ST) Tug**	**2 oil engines** reduction geared to sc. shafts driving 2 FP propellers Total Power: 2,354kW (3,200hp) Cummins KTA-50-M2 2 x Vee 4 Stroke 16 Cy. 159 x 159 each-1177kW (1600bhp) Cummins Engine Co Inc-USA AuxGen: 2 x 90kW a.c

9376256 *9WEX4* -	**SEALINK MAJU 6** **Sealink Pacific Sdn Bhd** Sealink Sdn Bhd *Kuching* *Malaysia* MMSI: 533786000 Official number: 330038	**254** 76 -	Class: BV	**2006**-01 **Sealink Shipyard Sdn Bhd — Miri** Yd No: 129 Loa 30.00 Br ex - Dght 3.500 Lbp 27.73 Br md 8.60 Dpth 4.12 Welded, 1 dk	**(B32A2ST) Tug**	**2 oil engines** reduction geared to sc. shafts driving 2 FP propellers Total Power: 1,472kW (2,002hp) Caterpillar 3508B 2 x Vee 4 Stroke 8 Cy. 170 x 190 each-736kW (1001bhp) Caterpillar Inc-USA AuxGen: 2 x 56kW 415/220V 50Hz a.c
9480851 *9WHK8* -	**SEALINK MAJU 8** **Sealink Sdn Bhd** - *Kuching* *Malaysia* MMSI: 533000743 Official number: 330995	**499** 149 349	Class: AB	**2008**-08 **Sealink Shipyard Sdn Bhd — Miri** Yd No: 166 Loa 38.00 Br ex - Dght 3.800 Lbp 33.40 Br md 11.80 Dpth 4.80 Welded, 1 dk	**(B21B20A) Anchor Handling Tug Supply**	**2 oil engines** reverse reduction geared to sc. shafts driving 2 Propellers Total Power: 2,352kW (3,198hp) Cummins KTA-50-M2 2 x Vee 4 Stroke 16 Cy. 159 x 159 each-1176kW (1599bhp) Cummins Engine Co Inc-USA AuxGen: 2 x 150kW a.c Thrusters: 1 Tunnel thruster (f) Fuel: 330.0
9373589 *9WGK2* -	**SEALINK MAJU 21** **Seabright Sdn Bhd** Sealink Sdn Bhd *Kuching* *Malaysia* MMSI: 533793000 Official number: 330669	**499** 149 423	Class: AB	**2006**-07 **Sealink Shipyard Sdn Bhd — Miri** Yd No: 121 Loa 38.00 Br ex - Dght 3.800 Lbp 33.40 Br md 11.80 Dpth 4.80 Welded, 1 dk	**(B21B20A) Anchor Handling Tug Supply**	**2 oil engines** reduction geared to sc. shafts driving 2 FP propellers Total Power: 2,388kW (3,246hp) Cummins KTA-50-M2 2 x Vee 4 Stroke 16 Cy. 159 x 159 each-1194kW (1623bhp) Cummins Engine Co Inc-USA AuxGen: 2 x 151kW a.c Fuel: 330.0
9558608 *9WCK7* -	**SEALINK MAJU 27** **Godrimaju Sdn Bhd** Sealink Sdn Bhd *Kuching* *Malaysia* MMSI: 533000828 Official number: 333122	**499** 149 314	Class: AB	**2009**-10 **Sealink Shipyard Sdn Bhd — Miri** Yd No: 176 Loa 38.00 Br ex - Dght 3.800 Lbp 33.40 Br md 11.80 Dpth 4.80 Welded, 1 dk	**(B21B20A) Anchor Handling Tug Supply**	**2 oil engines** reverse reduction geared to sc. shaft (s) driving 2 FP propellers Total Power: 3,282kW (4,462hp) Cummins QSK60-M 2 x Vee 4 Stroke 16 Cy. 159 x 190 each-1641kW (2231bhp) Cummins Engine Co Inc-USA AuxGen: 3 x 245kW a.c Thrusters: 1 Tunnel thruster (f) Fuel: 320.0
9558610 *9WCK8* -	**SEALINK MAJU 28** **Sealink Shipyard Sdn Bhd** Sealink Sdn Bhd *Kuching* *Malaysia* MMSI: 533979000 Official number: 333123	**499** 149 327	Class: AB	**2010**-07 **Sealink Shipyard Sdn Bhd — Miri** Yd No: 186 Loa 38.00 Br ex - Dght 3.800 Lbp 35.01 Br md 11.80 Dpth 4.80 Welded, 1 dk	**(B21B20A) Anchor Handling Tug Supply**	**2 oil engines** reverse reduction geared to sc. shaft driving 2 FP propellers Total Power: 3,282kW (4,462hp) Cummins QSK60-M 2 x Vee 4 Stroke 16 Cy. 159 x 190 each-1641kW (2231bhp) Cummins Engine Co Inc-USA AuxGen: 3 x 245kW a.c Fuel: 320.0
9367566 *9WGJ7* -	**SEALINK VANESSA 4** **Sealink Sdn Bhd** - *Kuching* *Malaysia* MMSI: 533781000 Official number: 329664	**496** 149 541	Class: AB	**2005**-11 **Sealink Shipyard Sdn Bhd — Miri** Yd No: 127 Loa 48.00 Br ex - Dght 2.800 Lbp 46.20 Br md 11.00 Dpth 3.50 Welded, 1 dk	**(B21A20S) Platform Supply Ship**	**2 oil engines** reverse reduction geared to sc. shafts driving 2 FP propellers Total Power: 2,538kW (3,450hp) Cummins KTA-50-M2 2 x Vee 4 Stroke 16 Cy. 159 x 159 each-1269kW (1725bhp) Cummins Engine Co Inc-USA AuxGen: 2 x 150kW a.c Thrusters: 1 Tunnel thruster (f)
9420552 *9WGX2* -	**SEALINK VANESSA 6** **Sealink Sdn Bhd** - *Kuching* *Malaysia* MMSI: 533000519 Official number: 330822	**494** 148 512	Class: LR **100A1** SS 04/2012 offshore tug/supply ship ✠ **LMC** Cable: 495.0/34.0 U2 (a)	**2007**-04 **Sealink Shipyard Sdn Bhd — Miri** Yd No: 134 Loa 48.00 Br ex - Dght 2.500 Lbp 46.20 Br md 11.00 Dpth 3.50 Welded, 1 dk	**(B21B20T) Offshore Tug/Supply Ship**	**2 oil engines** with clutches & sr reverse geared to sc. shafts driving 2 FP propellers Total Power: 1,790kW (2,434hp) 12.0kn Cummins KTA-38-M2 2 x Vee 4 Stroke 12 Cy. 159 x 159 each-895kW (1217bhp) Cummins Engine Co Inc-USA AuxGen: 2 x 150kW 415V 50Hz a.c Thrusters: 1 Thwart. FP thruster (f)
9421570 *9WGW9* -	**SEALINK VANESSA 7** **Sealink Sdn Bhd** - *Kuching* *Malaysia* MMSI: 533000689 Official number: 330821	**494** 148 512	Class: LR **100A1** SS 09/2012 offshore tug/supply ship ✠ **LMC** Cable: 495.0/26.0 U2 (a)	**2007**-09 **Sealink Shipyard Sdn Bhd — Miri** Yd No: 154 Loa 48.00 Br ex - Dght 2.500 Lbp 46.20 Br md 11.00 Dpth 3.50 Welded, 1 dk	**(B21B20T) Offshore Tug/Supply Ship**	**2 oil engines** with clutches & sr reverse geared to sc. shafts driving 2 FP propellers Total Power: 1,790kW (2,434hp) Cummins KTA-38-M2 2 x Vee 4 Stroke 12 Cy. 159 x 159 each-895kW (1217bhp) Cummins Engine Co Inc-USA AuxGen: 2 x 150kW 415V 50Hz a.c Thrusters: 1 Thwart. FP thruster (f)
9361055 *9WET5* -	**SEALINK VICTORIA 4** **Cergas Maju Sama Sdn Bhd** Sealink Sdn Bhd *Kuching* *Malaysia* MMSI: 533778000 Official number: 329988	**492** 147 650	Class: AB	**2005**-09 **Kian Juan Dockyard Sdn Bhd — Miri** Yd No: 98 Loa 45.50 Br ex - Dght 2.200 Lbp 42.10 Br md 10.90 Dpth 3.20 Welded, 1 dk	**(A35D2RL) Landing Craft** Bow ramp (centre)	**2 oil engines** reduction geared to sc. shafts driving 2 FP propellers Total Power: 1,060kW (1,442hp) 11.0kn Caterpillar 3412TA 2 x Vee 4 Stroke 12 Cy. 137 x 152 each-530kW (721bhp) Caterpillar Inc-USA AuxGen: 2 x 85kW a.c
9357418 - -	**SEALINK VICTORIA 5** - -	**226** 68 350	Class: (BV)	**2005**-07 **Sealink Shipyard Sdn Bhd — Miri** Yd No: 123 Loa 35.50 Br ex - Dght 2.000 Lbp 32.86 Br md 9.00 Dpth 2.55 Welded, 1 dk	**(B21A20S) Platform Supply Ship**	**2 oil engines** reduction geared to sc. shafts driving 2 FP propellers Total Power: 514kW (698hp) 9.0kn Cummins NTA-855-M 2 x 4 Stroke 6 Cy. 140 x 152 each-257kW (349bhp) Cummins Engine Co Inc-USA AuxGen: 2 x 50kW 415/230V 50Hz a.c
9377810 *A8SW2* -	**SEALION** *launched as Mikator -2009* **Blue Light Marine Ltd** Alison Management Corp *Monrovia* *Liberia* MMSI: 636014306 Official number: 14306	**3,978** 1,793 5,698 T/cm 14.5	Class: BV (AB)	**2009**-04 **Qingdao Hyundai Shipbuilding Co Ltd — Jiaonan SD** Yd No: 211 Loa 105.50 (BB) Br ex 16.60 Dght 6.600 Lbp 98.00 Br md 16.60 Dpth 8.60 Welded, 1 dk	**(A12B2TR) Chemical/Products Tanker** Double Hull (13F) Liq: 6,115; Liq (Oil): 6,446 Cargo Heating Coils Compartments: 10 Wing Ta, 2 Wing Slop Ta, ER 12 Cargo Pump (s): 12x200m³/hr Manifold: Bow/CM: 56.3m	**1 oil engine** reduction geared to sc. shaft driving 1 CP propeller Total Power: 3,000kW (4,079hp) 14.0kn Wartsila 6L32 1 x 4 Stroke 6 Cy. 320 x 400 3000kW (4079bhp) Wartsila Finland Oy-Finland AuxGen: 3 x 480kW a.c, 1 x 1500kW a.c Thrusters: 1 Tunnel thruster (f) Fuel: 60.0 (d.f.) 248.0 (r.f.)
1003748 *9H9735* -	**SEALION** **Sealion Yachting Ltd** - *Valletta* *Malta* Official number: 1003748	**208** 62 -	Class: LR ✠ **100A1** SS 05/2012 Yacht **LMC**	**1992**-03 **Scheepsbouw en Machinefabriek Hakvoort B.V. — Monnickendam** Loa 31.55 Br ex 7.50 Dght 2.400 Lbp 26.85 Br md - Dpth 3.95 Welded, 1 dk	**(X11A2YP) Yacht**	**2 oil engines** geared to sc. shafts driving 2 FP propellers Total Power: 280kW (380hp) Gardner 6LYTI 2 x 4 Stroke 6 Cy. 140 x 168 each-140kW (190bhp) L. Gardner & Sons Ltd.-Manchester
9202819 *VM2214* -	**SEALION 2000** **Australia Inbound Pty Ltd** Kangaroo Island Sealink Pty Ltd (SeaLink Travel Group) *Port Adelaide, SA* *Australia* MMSI: 503608000 Official number: 856002	**800** 250 400		**1998**-08 **Tenix Shipbuilding WA — Fremantle WA** Yd No: 343 Loa 49.00 Br ex - Dght 2.500 Lbp 48.80 Br md 16.00 Dpth 5.00 Welded, 1 dk	**(A36A2PR) Passenger/Ro-Ro Ship (Vehicles)** Passengers: unberthed: 353 Cars: 63	**2 oil engines** geared to sc. shafts driving 2 FP propellers Total Power: 2,156kW (2,932hp) Caterpillar 3512TA 2 x Vee 4 Stroke 12 Cy. 170 x 190 each-1078kW (1466bhp) Caterpillar Inc-USA
9620906 *AWEY* -	**SEALION ACE** **Sea Sparkle Harbour Services Pvt Ltd** - *Kochi* *India* MMSI: 419000850 Official number: 4129	**471** 141 187	Class: AB IR	**2013**-08 **Guangzhou Southern Shipbuilding Co Ltd — Guangzhou GD (Hull)** Yd No: (HY2180) **2013**-08 **Bonny Fair Development Ltd — Hong Kong** Yd No: HY2180 Loa 32.00 Br ex 11.30 Dght 4.300 Lbp 30.07 Br md 11.00 Dpth 5.60 Welded, 1 dk	**(B32A2ST) Tug**	**2 oil engines** reduction geared to sc. shafts driving 2 Propellers Total Power: 3,676kW (4,998hp) Niigata 6L28HX 2 x 4 Stroke 6 Cy. 280 x 370 each-1838kW (2499bhp) Niigata Engineering Co Ltd-Japan AuxGen: 2 x 156kW a.c Fuel: 210.0 (d.f.)

IMO / Call sign	Name / Owner	Tonnage	Class	Builder / Dimensions	Type	Machinery
9517733 *AVKW* -	**SEALION ADMIRAL** **Sealion Sparkle Port & Terminal Services (Dahej) Ltd** - *Mumbai* *India* MMSI: 419000282 Official number: 3822	**472** 141 307	Class: IR (LR) ✠ Classed LR until 3/4/12	**2011-01 Yuexin Shipbuilding Co Ltd — Guangzhou GD** Yd No: 3106 Loa 31.98 Br ex 12.23 Dght 4.560 Lbp 25.87 Br md 11.60 Dpth 5.36 Welded, 1 dk	**(B32A2ST) Tug**	**2 oil engines** gearing integral to driving 2 Z propellers Total Power: 3,676kW (4,998hp) Niigata 6L28HX 2 x 4 Stroke 6 Cy. 280 x 370 each-1838kW (2499bhp) Niigata Engineering Co Ltd-Japan AuxGen: 2 x 136kW 415V 50Hz a.c
9279305 *AUDL* -	**SEALION AGILE** *ex* Nectar *-2003* **Ocean Sparkle Ltd** - *Mumbai* *India* MMSI: 419042100 Official number: 3048	*298* 89 137	Class: IR (LR) ✠ Classed LR until 9/8/08	**2003-10 ASL Shipyard Pte Ltd — Singapore** Yd No: 288 Loa 30.00 Br ex 10.34 Dght 5.400 Lbp 26.63 Br md 10.30 Dpth 3.80 Welded, 1 dk	**(B32A2ST) Tug**	**2 oil engines** geared to sc. shaft driving 2 Directional propellers Total Power: 3,308kW (4,498hp) 10.0kn Niigata 6L28HX 2 x 4 Stroke 6 Cy. 280 x 370 each-1654kW (2249bhp) Niigata Engineering Co Ltd-Japan AuxGen: 2 x 83kW 415V 50Hz a.c Fuel: 118.0 (r.f.)
9274862 *PPQZ* -	**SEALION AMAZONIA** **Sealion do Brasil Navegacao Ltda** - SatCom: Inmarsat C 471000157 *Rio de Janeiro* *Brazil* MMSI: 710001550 Official number: 3810514951	**2,865** 917 2,750	Class: NV	**2005-12 Estaleiro Itajai S.A. (EISA) — Itajai** Yd No: 140 Loa 73.80 (BB) Br ex 16.05 Dght 6.300 Lbp 65.00 Br md 16.00 Dpth 7.40 Welded, 1 dk	**(B21A20S) Platform Supply Ship** A-frames: 1x50t; Cranes: 1x10t	**4 diesel electric oil engines** driving 4 gen. each 1292kW 690V a.c Connecting to 2 elec. motors each (1500kW) geared to sc. shafts driving 2 Azimuth electric drive units Total Power: 5,440kW (7,396hp) 12.0kn MaK 8M20 4 x 4 Stroke 8 Cy. 200 x 300 each-1360kW (1849bhp) Caterpillar Motoren GmbH & Co. KG-Germany Thrusters: 2 Tunnel thruster (f) Fuel: 819.0
9279290 *AUDI* -	**SEALION APEX** *ex* Navigator *-2003* **Ocean Sparkle Ltd** - *Mumbai* *India* MMSI: 419041700 Official number: 3045	*298* 89 120	Class: IR (LR) ✠ Classed LR until 9/8/08	**2003-10 ASL Shipyard Pte Ltd — Singapore** Yd No: 287 Loa 30.00 Br ex 10.34 Dght 5.400 Lbp 28.40 Br md 10.30 Dpth 3.88 Welded, 1 dk	**(B32A2ST) Tug**	**2 oil engines** geared to sc. shaft driving 2 Directional propellers Total Power: 3,308kW (4,498hp) 10.0kn Niigata 6L28HX 2 x 4 Stroke 6 Cy. 280 x 370 each-1654kW (2249bhp) Niigata Engineering Co Ltd-Japan AuxGen: 2 x 83kW 415V 50Hz a.c Fuel: 108.0 (d.f.)
9246229 *AUDK* -	**SEALION SENTINEL** *ex* Sentinel *-2003* **Sealion Sparkle Port & Terminal Services (Dahej) Ltd** - *Mumbai* *India* MMSI: 419041900 Official number: 3047	**286** 85 200	Class: IR (LR) ✠ Classed LR until 9/8/08	**2001-11 ASL Shipyard Pte Ltd — Singapore** Yd No: 218 Loa 29.95 Br ex 9.82 Dght 3.800 Lbp 26.27 Br md 9.80 Dpth 4.80 Welded, 1 dk	**(B32A2ST) Tug**	**2 oil engines** reduction geared to sc. shafts driving 2 Directional propellers Total Power: 3,326kW (4,522hp) 12.0kn Deutz SBV8M628 2 x 4 Stroke 8 Cy. 240 x 280 each-1663kW (2261bhp) Deutz AG-Koeln AuxGen: 2 x 83kW 415V 50Hz a.c Fuel: 133.0 (d.f.)
9246217 *AUDJ* -	**SEALION STERLING** *ex* Sterling *-2003* **Sealion Sparkle Port & Terminal Services (Dahej) Ltd** - *Mumbai* *India* MMSI: 419041800 Official number: 3046	**286** 85 200	Class: IR (LR) ✠ Classed LR until 9/8/08	**2001-10 ASL Shipyard Pte Ltd — Singapore** Yd No: 217 Loa 29.95 Br ex 9.82 Dght 3.800 Lbp 26.27 Br md 9.80 Dpth 4.80 Welded, 1 dk	**(B32A2ST) Tug**	**2 oil engines** with flexible couplings & reduction geared to sc. shafts driving 2 Directional propellers Total Power: 3,326kW (4,522hp) 12.0kn Deutz SBV8M628 2 x 4 Stroke 8 Cy. 240 x 280 each-1663kW (2261bhp) Deutz AG-Koeln AuxGen: 2 x 83kW 415V 50Hz a.c Fuel: 133.0 (d.f.)
9387621 *3FZT5* -	**SEALORD** *ex* Lord *-2010* **Lord Shipping Co Ltd** Shipping Co Marinebulk Ltd *Panama* *Panama* MMSI: 352240000 Official number: 4233911	**7,345** 4,208 10,860	Class: RS	**2006-11 Zhejiang Donghong Shipbuilding Co Ltd — Xiangshan County ZJ** Yd No: 03 Loa 126.60 (BB) Br ex 18.64 Dght 7.800 Lbp 117.50 Br md 18.60 Dpth 10.10 Welded, 1 dk	**(A31A2GX) General Cargo Ship** Grain: 15,857 Compartments: 3 Ho, ER 3 Ha: ER 3 (25.2 x 12.6) Cranes: 2x20t Ice Capable	**1 oil engine** reduction geared to sc. shaft driving 1 FP propeller Total Power: 3,310kW (4,500hp) 12.0kn Yanmar 8N330-EN 1 x 4 Stroke 8 Cy. 330 x 440 3310kW (4500bhp) Qingdao Zichai Boyang Diesel EngineCo Ltd-China AuxGen: 3 x 250kW a.c, 1 x 120kW a.c Fuel: 770.0
9302970 *9HA3567* -	**SEALOYALTY** *ex* Garden City River *-2014* **Fortune Shipping & Maritime Inc** Thenamaris (Ships Management) Inc *Valletta* *Malta* MMSI: 229740000 Official number: 9302970	**56,146** 32,671 106,468 T/cm 91.0	Class: NK	**2005-05 Universal Shipbuilding Corp — Nagasu KM (Ariake Shipyard)** Yd No: 018 Loa 243.07 (BB) Br ex - Dght 14.753 Lbp 233.00 Br md 42.00 Dpth 20.70 Welded, 1 dk	**(A13A2TV) Crude Oil Tanker** Double Hull (13F) Liq: 113,458; Liq (Oil): 113,458 Cargo Heating Coils Compartments: 12 Wing Ta, 2 Wing Slop Ta, ER 3 Cargo Pump (s): 3x2500m³/hr Manifold: Bow/CM: 123.5m	**1 oil engine** driving 1 FP propeller Total Power: 14,000kW (19,034hp) 15.2kn Sulzer 7RTA58T 1 x 2 Stroke 7 Cy. 580 x 2416 14000kW (19034bhp) Diesel United Ltd.-Aioi AuxGen: 3 x 680kW 450V 60Hz a.c Fuel: 239.0 (d.f.) 3041.9 (r.f.)
7808152 *WAK7089* -	**SEALTH** **State of Washington (Department of Transportation)** Washington State Department of Transportation (Washington State Ferries) *Seattle, WA* *United States of America* MMSI: 366710820 Official number: 662478	*2,477* 1,772 1,910	Class: (AB)	**1982-04 Marine Power & Equipment Co. Ltd. — Seattle, Wa** Yd No: 348 Loa 100.13 Br ex 23.98 Dght 5.182 Lbp 96.78 Br md 23.93 Dpth 7.22 Welded, 2 dks	**(A36A2PR) Passenger/Ro-Ro Ship (Vehicles)** Passengers: unberthed: 1200 Vehicles: 100	**2 oil engines** sr geared to sc. shafts driving 2 CP propellers aft, 1 fwd Total Power: 3,678kW (5,000hp) 15.8kn General Electric 7FDM12 2 x Vee 4 Stroke 12 Cy. 229 x 267 each-1839kW (2500bhp) General Electric Co.-Lynn, Ma AuxGen: 2 x 300kW
9288344 *9HXU7* -	**SEALUCK II** **Wilderness Shipping Ltd** Thenamaris (Ships Management) Inc *Valletta* *Malta* MMSI: 215713000 Official number: 8983	**30,936** 18,154 55,452 T/cm 56.3	Class: NV	**2004-10 Nantong COSCO KHI Ship Engineering Co Ltd (NACKS) — Nantong JS** Yd No: 025 Loa 189.98 (BB) Br ex 32.30 Dght 12.520 Lbp 185.01 Br md 32.26 Dpth 17.80 Welded, 1 dk	**(A21A2BC) Bulk Carrier** Grain: 69,452; Bale: 66,110 Compartments: 5 Ho, ER 5 Ha: 4 (20.5 x 18.6)ER (17.8 x 18.6) Cranes: 4x30t	**1 oil engine** driving 1 FP propeller Total Power: 8,200kW (11,149hp) 14.6kn B&W 6S50MC-C 1 x 2 Stroke 6 Cy. 500 x 2000 8200kW (11149bhp) Dalian Marine Diesel Works-China AuxGen: 3 x 740kW a.c
4902593 *ZDDN7* -	**SEALYHAM** **Pooltide Ltd** - *Gibraltar* *Gibraltar (British)* MMSI: 236000450 Official number: 730153	**142** - 106	Class: LR ✠ **100A1** SS 08/2012 tug extended protected waters service from Port of Gibraltar ✠ **LMC** Cable: 138.0/25.0	**1967-05 Appledore Shipbuilders Ltd — Bideford** Yd No: A.S. 25 Loa 28.67 Br ex 7.72 Dght - Lbp 25.90 Br md 7.39 Dpth 3.66 Welded, 1 dk	**(B32A2ST) Tug**	**2 oil engines** sr reverse geared to sc. shafts driving 2 FP propellers Total Power: 970kW (1,318hp) 12.0kn Blackstone ERS8 2 x 4 Stroke 8 Cy. 222 x 292 each-485kW (659bhp) Blackstone & Co. Ltd.-Stamford AuxGen: 2 x 40kW 220V d.c
9450260 - -	**SEALYON** *ex* Lady Illusion *-2010* *ex* Illusion *-2010* **Sealyon Marine Ltd** - *George Town* *Cayman Islands (British)*	**235** 70 -	Class: RI	**2007-07 ISA Produzione Srl — Ancona** Yd No: 120.05 Loa 36.44 Br ex - Dght 1.500 Lbp 30.00 Br md 7.40 Dpth 3.61 Welded, 1 dk	**(X11A2YP) Yacht**	**3 oil engines** reduction geared to sc. shafts driving 3 FP propellers Total Power: 4,413kW (6,000hp) M.T.U. 16V2000M91 3 x Vee 4 Stroke 16 Cy. 130 x 150 each-1471kW (2000bhp) MTU Friedrichshafen GmbH-Friedrichshafen
9447603 *2CGJ2* -	**SEALYON** *ex* Candyscape Ii *-2013* **Farncombe Holdings Ltd** YCO SAM *Douglas* *Isle of Man (British)* MMSI: 235072538 Official number: 740890	**990** 700 -	Class: RI	**2009-07 Viareggio SuperYachts Srl — Viareggio** Yd No: 1 Loa 61.80 Br ex 10.80 Dght 3.100 Lbp 51.60 Br md 10.65 Dpth 5.33 Welded, 1 dk	**(X11A2YP) Yacht**	**2 oil engines** driving 2 Propellers Total Power: 4,000kW (5,438hp) 15.0kn Caterpillar 3516B-HD 2 x Vee 4 Stroke 16 Cy. 170 x 215 each-2000kW (2719bhp) Caterpillar Inc-USA
9317949 *9HOE9* -	**SEAMAGIC** *ex* Polar Merchant *-2008* **Poseidon Shipping & Maritime Corp** Thenamaris (Ships Management) Inc SatCom: Inmarsat C 424926610 *Valletta* *Malta* MMSI: 249266000 Official number: 9317949	**67,032** 35,024 116,995 T/cm 98.0	Class: NV	**2007-03 Hyundai Heavy Industries Co Ltd — Ulsan** Yd No: 1702 Loa 249.85 (BB) Br ex 44.03 Dght 15.420 Lbp 238.99 Br md 44.00 Dpth 22.70 Welded, 1 dk	**(A13B2TP) Products Tanker** Double Hull (13F) Liq: 134,589; Liq (Oil): 134,589 Cargo Heating Coils Compartments: 12 Wing Ta, 2 Wing Slop Ta, ER 3 Cargo Pump (s): 3x3000m³/hr Manifold: Bow/CM: 124.9m Ice Capable	**1 oil engine** driving 1 FP propeller Total Power: 15,806kW (21,490hp) 15.1kn MAN-B&W 7S60MC-C 1 x 2 Stroke 7 Cy. 600 x 2400 15806kW (21490bhp) Hyundai Heavy Industries Co Ltd-South Korea AuxGen: 3 x 1050kW 440/220V 60Hz a.c Fuel: 232.5 (d.f.) 3083.9 (r.f.)

Ship no. / Call sign	Name / Owner	Tonnage	Class	Build / Dimensions	Type	Machinery
7437707 - -	**SEAMAN BROTHERS** - -	*116* 79 -		**1973 Superior Fabricators, Inc. — Bayou La Batre, Al** L reg 20.58 Br ex 6.71 Dght - Lbp - Br md - Dpth 3.56 Welded, 1 dk	**(B11A2FT) Trawler**	**1 oil engine** driving 1 FP propeller Total Power: 268kW (364hp) Caterpillar D353SCAC 1 x 4 Stroke 6 Cy. 159 x 203 268kW (364bhp) Caterpillar Tractor Co-USA
8410691 *9LA2125* -	**SEAMAN GUARD OHIO** *ex* Timor Navigator *-2012* *ex* Kaio Maru *-2011* **Seaman Guard Inc** AdvanFort Co *Freetown* *Sierra Leone* MMSI: 667004026 Official number: SL10426	**394** 118 197		**1984-10 Narasaki Zosen KK — Muroran HK** Yd No: 1064 Converted From: Fishery Patrol Vessel-2012 Loa 45.93 Br ex 7.32 Dght 3.271 Lbp 43.31 Br md 7.31 Dpth 3.71 Welded, 1 dk	**(B34H2SQ) Patrol Vessel**	**2 oil engines** with clutches, flexible couplings & sr geared to sc. shafts driving 2 FP propellers Total Power: 2,060kW (2,800hp) Pielstick 6PA5 2 x 4 Stroke 6 Cy. 255 x 270 each-1030kW (1400bhp) Niigata Engineering Co Ltd-Japan
8654314 *9LA2126* -	**SEAMAN GUARD VIRGINIA** *ex* Badtz Maru *-2012* *ex* Redpole *-2000* *ex* Sea Otter (5002) *-1985* **Seaman Guard Inc** AdvanFort Co *Freetown* *Sierra Leone* MMSI: 667004027 Official number: SL104027	**240** 72 -	Class: OM (Class contemplated)	**1970-12 Fairmile Construction Co. Ltd. — Berwick-on-Tweed** Yd No: 656 Converted From: Yacht-2000 Converted From: Patrol Vessel, Naval-2000 Loa 36.60 Br ex - Dght 2.000 Lbp 33.88 Br md 7.16 Dpth 4.42 Welded, 1 dk	**(B34H2SQ) Patrol Vessel**	**2 oil engines** reduction geared to sc. shafts driving 2 Propellers Total Power: 2,942kW (4,000hp) Paxman 16YJCM 2 x Vee 4 Stroke 16 Cy. 197 x 216 each-1471kW (2000bhp) Davey, Paxman & Co. Ltd.-Colchester
9096595 *HC4904* -	**SEAMAN II** - **Cruising Galapagos SA** - *Puerto Baquerizo Moreno* *Ecuador* Official number: TN-00-00532	**249** 74 -		**2007-02 Botto Astilleros y Marina — Guayaquil** Loa 27.60 Br ex 11.00 Dght 1.450 Lbp - Br md - Dpth 3.52 Bonded, 1 dk	**(A37A2PC) Passenger/Cruise** Hull Material: Reinforced Plastic Passengers: cabins: 9; berths: 16	**2 oil engines** geared to sc. shafts driving 2 Propellers Total Power: 522kW (710hp) 12.0kn Cummins QSM11-M 2 x 4 Stroke 6 Cy. 125 x 147 each-261kW (355bhp) Cummins Engine Co Inc-USA Fuel: 11.0 (d.f.)
8516184 *HP7550* -	**SEAMAR III** *ex* Seamar *-1994* **Marsea Ship Co Ltd** Seamar - Servicios de Apoio Maritimo Ltda *Panama* *Panama* MMSI: 353944000 Official number: 2188395C	**1,597** 481 1,171	Class: (NV)	**1988-06 Industrias Reunidas Caneco SA — Rio de Janeiro** Yd No: 298 Loa 63.02 Br ex - Dght 4.211 Lbp 56.90 Br md 15.41 Dpth 5.01 Welded, 1 dk	**(B22D2OZ) Production Testing Vessel**	**2 oil engines** geared to sc. shafts driving 2 FP propellers Total Power: 2,398kW (3,260hp) MAN 12V20/27 2 x Vee 4 Stroke 12 Cy. 200 x 270 each-1199kW (1630bhp) Mecanica Pesada SA-Brazil AuxGen: 4 x 280kW 440V 60Hz a.c Thrusters: 1 Thwart. FP thruster (f)
8503515 *ZDJF2* -	**SEAMAR SPLENDID** *ex* Highland Sprite *-2009* *ex* Wimpey Seasprite *-1988* **SeaMar Shipping BV** SeaMar Services BV *Gibraltar* *Gibraltar (British)* MMSI: 236519000	**1,199** 385 1,442 T/cm 6.5	Class: BV NV (LR) ✠ Classed LR until 30/4/01	**1986-07 Cochrane Shipbuilders Ltd. — Selby** Yd No: 133 Converted From: Offshore Supply Ship-2009 Converted From: Offshore Supply Ship-1999 Loa 59.21 Br ex 14.13 Dght 4.401 Lbp 54.01 Br md 12.80 Dpth 5.21 Welded, 1 dk	**(B31A2SR) Research Survey Vessel**	**2 oil engines** with clutches, flexible couplings & sr geared to sc. shafts driving 2 CP propellers Total Power: 2,640kW (3,590hp) 13.3kn Alpha 6L28/32A 2 x 4 Stroke 6 Cy. 280 x 320 each-1320kW (1795bhp) MAN B&W Diesel A/S-Denmark AuxGen: 3 x 250kW 440V 60Hz a.c Thrusters: 1 Thwart. CP thruster (f); 1 Tunnel thruster (a) Fuel: 306.0 (d.f.) 7.0pd
9199921 *5NIUZ* -	**SEAMARK** - **Rangk Ltd** - *Lagos* *Nigeria* MMSI: 657153000 Official number: SR196	**242** 72 -	Class: AB	**1998-07 Swiftships Inc — Morgan City LA** Yd No: 492 Loa 44.19 Br ex 8.15 Dght 1.790 Lbp 42.79 Br md 8.07 Dpth 3.60 Welded, 1 dk	**(B21A2OC) Crew/Supply Vessel** Hull Material: Aluminium Alloy	**3 oil engines** reverse reduction geared to sc. shafts driving 3 Water jets Total Power: 1,821kW (2,475hp) 21.0kn Caterpillar 3412TA 3 x Vee 4 Stroke 12 Cy. 137 x 152 each-607kW (825bhp) Caterpillar Inc-USA AuxGen: 2 x 50kW
9380489 *DDSL* -	**SEAMARLIN** - **German Tanker Shipping GmbH & Co KG** - *Bremen* *Germany* MMSI: 218085000 Official number: 4966	**26,548** 10,304 40,549 T/cm 53.0	Class: GL	**2007-07 Lindenau GmbH Schiffswerft u. Maschinenfabrik — Kiel** Yd No: 275 Loa 188.33 (BB) Br ex - Dght 11.000 Lbp 179.50 Br md 32.20 Dpth 17.05 Welded, 1 dk	**(A13B2TP) Products Tanker** Double Hull (13F) Liq: 42,894; Liq (Oil): 42,894 Compartments: 10 Wing Ta, 2 Wing Slop Ta, ER 10 Cargo Pump (s): 10x600m³/hr Manifold: Bow/CM: 97.2m Ice Capable	**1 oil engine** reduction geared to sc. shaft driving 1 CP propeller Total Power: 11,200kW (15,228hp) 15.5kn MAN-B&W 8L58/64 1 x 4 Stroke 8 Cy. 580 x 640 11200kW (15228bhp) MAN B&W Diesel AG-Augsburg AuxGen: 3 x 1140kW 400/230V 50Hz a.c, 1 x 1350kW 400/230V 50Hz a.c Thrusters: 1 Thwart. FP thruster (f) Fuel: 470.0 (d.f.) 1510.0 (r.f.)
9452749 *V7NC2* -	**SEAMASTER** - **Rosso Shipholding Corp** Coral Shipping Corp SatCom: Inmarsat C 453832830 *Majuro* *Marshall Islands* MMSI: 538002940 Official number: 2940	**2,526** 1,288 4,114 T/cm 10.3	Class: GL (BV)	**2007-11 Rui'an Jiangnan Shiprepair & Building Yard — Rui'an ZJ** Yd No: 0516 Loa 90.38 (BB) Br ex - Dght 6.180 Lbp 83.16 Br md 13.80 Dpth 7.28 Welded, 1 dk	**(A13B2TP) Products Tanker** Double Hull (13F) Liq: 4,605; Liq (Oil): 4,605 Cargo Heating Coils Compartments: 5 Wing Ta, 5 Wing Ta, 1 Wing Slop Ta, 1 Wing Slop Ta, ER Cranes: 1x3t 2 Cargo Pump (s): 2x500m³/hr Manifold: Bow/CM: 47.4m	**1 oil engine** reduction geared to sc. shafts driving 1 FP propeller Total Power: 2,207kW (3,001hp) 12.3kn Yanmar 6N330-UN 1 x 4 Stroke 6 Cy. 330 x 440 2207kW (3001bhp) Zibo Diesel Engine Factory-China AuxGen: 3 x 160kW a.c Thrusters: 1 Tunnel thruster (f) Fuel: 32.3 (d.f.) 120.6 (r.f.)
9625920 *9HA3425* -	**SEAMASTER** - **Pansy Shipping Ltd** Eastern Mediterranean Maritime Ltd *Valletta* *Malta* MMSI: 229584000 Official number: 9625920	**20,239** 7,688 24,129	Class: BV GL	**2013-10 SPP Shipbuilding Co Ltd — Sacheon** Yd No: H4078 Loa 170.10 (BB) Br ex - Dght 8.500 Lbp 160.00 Br md 29.80 Dpth 14.50 Welded, 1 dk	**(A33A2CC) Container Ship (Fully Cellular)** TEU 1756 incl 350 ref C Cranes: 3x40t	**1 oil engine** driving 1 FP propeller Total Power: 14,280kW (19,415hp) 18.5kn MAN-B&W 6S60ME-B8 1 x 2 Stroke 6 Cy. 600 x 2400 14280kW (19415bhp) AuxGen: 3 x 1670kW a.c Thrusters: 1 Tunnel thruster (f) Fuel: 2150.0
7647077 - -	**SEAMASTER** *ex* Ocean *-1977* **Libexim Bulk Handling SA** Seabulk Shipping SA	**390** 117 -	Class: (AB)	**1974 K.K. Imai Seisakusho — Kamijima** Yd No: 136 Loa - Br ex - Dght - Lbp 34.14 Br md 9.20 Dpth 4.25 Welded, 1 dk	**(B32A2ST) Tug**	**2 oil engines** reverse reduction geared to sc. shafts driving 2 FP propellers Total Power: 2,354kW (3,200hp) 12.5kn Niigata 16V25X 2 x Vee 4 Stroke 16 Cy. 250 x 320 each-1177kW (1600bhp) Niigata Engineering Co Ltd-Japan AuxGen: 2 x 80kW
9304825 *9HA3547* -	**SEAMASTER IV** *ex* Seamaster *-2014* **Prime Marine Co SA** Thenamaris (Ships Management) Inc *Valletta* *Malta* MMSI: 229719000 Official number: 9304825	**60,208** 33,762 109,266 T/cm 91.3	Class: AB	**2006-05 Hudong-Zhonghua Shipbuilding (Group) Co Ltd — Shanghai** Yd No: H1368A Loa 243.00 (BB) Br ex 42.03 Dght 15.335 Lbp 233.00 Br md 42.00 Dpth 22.00 Welded, 1 dk	**(A13A2TV) Crude Oil Tanker** Double Hull (13F) Liq: 123,030; Liq (Oil): 123,030 Cargo Heating Coils Compartments: 12 Wing Ta, ER, 2 Wing Slop Ta 3 Cargo Pump (s): 3x2500m³/hr Manifold: Bow/CM: 119.5m	**1 oil engine** driving 1 FP propeller Total Power: 13,570kW (18,450hp) 14.5kn MAN-B&W 7S60MC 1 x 2 Stroke 7 Cy. 600 x 2292 13570kW (18450bhp) Hudong Heavy Machinery Co Ltd-China AuxGen: 3 x 680kW a.c Fuel: 145.5 (d.f.) 2966.4 (r.f.)
9182459 *JL6375* -	**SEAMAX** - **Ishizaki Kisen KK** - *Matsuyama, Ehime* *Japan* MMSI: 431500847 Official number: 135491	*284* - 2,823		**1998-02 Hitachi Zosen Corp — Kawasaki KN** Yd No: 117324 Loa 39.00 Br ex - Dght 1.880 Lbp 37.50 Br md 11.40 Dpth 3.70 Welded, 1 dk	**(A37B2PS) Passenger Ship** Passengers: unberthed: 200	**4 oil engines** with clutches, flexible couplings & reverse reduction geared to sc. shafts driving 2 Water jets Total Power: 8,092kW (11,000hp) 45.0kn Niigata 16V16FX 4 x Vee 4 Stroke 16 Cy. 165 x 185 each-2023kW (2750bhp) Niigata Engineering Co Ltd-Japan
8626903 *HP7013* -	**SEAMAX SARIYA** *ex* Atco Sariya *-2012* *ex* Peggy *-1988* **Sea Max Ship Management LLC** - *Panama* *Panama* MMSI: 370038000 Official number: 4527213	**273** 82 -	Class: AB (BV)	**1981 Universal Iron Works — Houma, La** Yd No: 177 Loa 37.01 Br ex - Dght 2.501 Lbp 34.29 Br md 8.54 Dpth 3.15 Welded, 1 dk	**(B21A2OS) Platform Supply Ship**	**2 oil engines** driving 2 FP propellers Total Power: 1,066kW (1,450hp) 12.5kn G.M. (Detroit Diesel) 16V-92-TA 2 x Vee 2 Stroke 16 Cy. 123 x 127 each-533kW (725bhp) General Motors Detroit DieselAllison Divn-USA AuxGen: 2 x 40kW 225V a.c Thrusters: 1 Thwart. FP thruster (f)
8873233 *HO9242* -	**SEAMAX STAR** *ex* Atco Badya *-2013* **Sea Max Ship Management LLC & Suparna C** Sea Max Ship Management LLC *Panama* *Panama* MMSI: 356887000 Official number: 4541713	**124** 37 46	Class: RI (AB)	**1989-08 Neuville Boat Works, Inc. — New Iberia, La** Yd No: 100-11 Loa 32.00 Br ex 6.71 Dght 1.680 Lbp 30.48 Br md - Dpth 2.75 Welded, 1 dk	**(B21A2OC) Crew/Supply Vessel** Hull Material: Aluminium Alloy	**3 oil engines** reverse reduction geared to sc. shafts driving 3 FP propellers Total Power: 1,140kW (1,551hp) 18.0kn G.M. (Detroit Diesel) 12V-71-TI 3 x Vee 2 Stroke 12 Cy. 108 x 127 each-380kW (517bhp) General Motors Detroit DieselAllison Divn-USA AuxGen: 2 x 30kW a.c

8121862 *HP9384* -	**SEAMAX SUPREME** *ex* Atco Farah *-2013* **Sea Max Ship Management LLC** - *Panama* *Panama* MMSI: 357718000 Official number: 4527013	**186** 55 250	Class: AB	**1991-12 Swiftships Inc — Morgan City LA** Yd No: 290 Loa 35.05 Br ex - Dght 2.950 Lbp 29.92 Br md 7.93 Dpth 3.35 Welded, 1 dk	**(B21A20S) Platform Supply Ship**	**2 oil engines** driving 2 FP propellers Total Power: 992kW (1,348hp) 11.0kn G.M. (Detroit Diesel) 16V-92 2 x Vee 2 Stroke 16 Cy. 123 x 127 each-496kW (674bhp) General Motors Detroit DieselAllison Divn-USA
8873221 *HP2815* -	**SEAMAX SWIFT** *ex* Atco Faten *-2013* **Sea Max Ship Management LLC** - *Panama* *Panama* MMSI: 354553000 Official number: 4541313	**124** 37 46	Class: RI (AB)	**1991-10 Neuville Boat Works, Inc. — New Iberia, La** Yd No: 100-12 Loa 32.00 Br ex 6.71 Dght - Lbp 30.48 Br md 6.71 Dpth 2.74 Welded, 1 dk	**(B21A20C) Crew/Supply Vessel** Hull Material: Aluminium Alloy	**3 oil engines** reverse reduction geared to sc. shafts driving 3 FP propellers Total Power: 1,125kW (1,530hp) 18.0kn G.M. (Detroit Diesel) 12V-71-TI 3 x Vee 2 Stroke 12 Cy. 108 x 127 each-375kW (510bhp) General Motors Detroit DieselAllison Divn-USA AuxGen: 2 x 30kW a.c
8216019 *VTTP* -	**SEAMEC I** *ex* Peerless Stena 1 *-2000* *ex* Drive Ocean *-1994* *ex* British Providence *-1988* *ex* Tender Tartan *-1986* **SEAMEC Ltd** - SatCom: Inmarsat Mini-M 762483777 *Mumbai* *India* MMSI: 419224000 Official number: 2408	**2,557** 767 1,751	Class: IR NV	**1983-05 Tangen Verft AS — Kragero** (Hull launched by) Yd No: 78 **1983-05 Langsten AS — Tomrefjord** (Hull completed by) Yd No: 100 Loa 76.38 (BB) Br ex - Dght 5.510 Lbp 68.43 Br md 16.24 Dpth 7.37 Welded, 1 dk	**(B21A20S) Platform Supply Ship** Passengers: berths: 60 Ice Capable	**2 oil engines** reduction geared to sc. shafts driving 2 CP propellers Total Power: 4,560kW (6,200hp) 12.0kn Wichmann 10AXAG 2 x 2 Stroke 10 Cy. 300 x 450 each-2280kW (3100bhp) Wichmann Motorfabrikk AS-Norway AuxGen: 4 x 312kW 600V 60Hz a.c, 2 x 1440kW 600V 60Hz a.c Thrusters: 2 Thwart. CP thruster (f); 2 Tunnel thruster (a) Fuel: 386.0 (r.f.)
8109292 *VTPN* -	**SEAMEC II** *ex* Peerless Stena II *-2001* *ex* Nand Shamik *-1995* *ex* Shearwater Sapphire *-1988* **SEAMEC Ltd** - *Mumbai* *India* MMSI: 419227000 Official number: 2322	**4,503** 1,351 2,067	Class: IR LR ✠ **100A1** SS 06/2012 diving support ship/fire fighting ship 2 (7200 cub.m/hour) with waterspray helicopter deck Ice Class 3 ✠ **LMC** **UMS**	**1982-08 B.V. Scheepswerf "De Hoop" — Lobith** Yd No: 297 Loa 95.56 Br ex 23.20 Dght 5.215 Lbp 76.20 Br md 18.00 Dpth 7.60 Welded, 2 dks	**(B22A20V) Diving Support Vessel** Passengers: berths: 90 Cranes: 1x50t,1x10t Ice Capable	**4 diesel electric oil engines** driving 4 gen. each 1630kW 6000V a.c Connecting to 2 elec. motors each (1880kW) driving 2 Directional propellers Total Power: 6,800kW (9,244hp) 12.0kn MAN 9L25/30 4 x 4 Stroke 9 Cy. 250 x 300 each-1700kW (2311bhp) Brons Industrie NV-Netherlands Boilers: 2 AuxB (o.f.) 10.1kgf/cm² (9.9bar) Thrusters: 2 Thwart. CP thruster (f) Fuel: 889.0 (d.f.) 636.5 (r.f.) 18.5pd
8128339 *VWZX* -	**SEAMEC III** *ex* Peerless Stena III *-2001* *ex* Nand Rewant *-2001* *ex* Shearwater Topaz *-1985* **SEAMEC Ltd** - *Mumbai* *India* MMSI: 419228000 Official number: 2074	*4,327* 1,298 2,067	Class: IR LR ✠ **100A1** SS 05/2013 diving support ship/fire fighting ship 2 (7200 cub.m/hour) with waterspray helicopter deck Ice Class 3 ✠ **LMC** **UMS**	**1983-04 B.V. Scheepswerf "De Hoop" — Lobith** Yd No: 298 Loa 92.82 Br ex 18.45 Dght 5.201 Lbp 76.23 Br md 18.01 Dpth 7.62 Welded, 2 dks	**(B22A20V) Diving Support Vessel** Passengers: berths: 90 Cranes: 1x50t,1x10t Ice Capable	**4 diesel electric oil engines** driving 4 gen. each 1630kW 6000V a.c Connecting to 2 elec. motors each (1880kW) driving 2 Directional propellers Total Power: 6,620kW (9,000hp) 12.0kn MAN 9L25/30 4 x 4 Stroke 9 Cy. 250 x 300 each-1655kW (2250bhp) Brons Industrie NV-Netherlands AuxGen: 2 x 200kW 440V 60Hz a.c Boilers: 2 AuxB (o.f.) 10.1kgf/cm² (9.9bar) Thrusters: 2 Thwart. CP thruster (f) Fuel: 889.5 (d.f.) 636.5 (r.f.) 18.5pd
8302959 *AUNJ* -	**SEAMEC PRINCESS** *ex* Oceanic Princess *-2006* *ex* Finnpine *-2000* *ex* Solano *-1994* **SEAMEC Ltd** - *Mumbai* *India* MMSI: 419603000 Official number: 3243	**8,709** 3,337 6,700	Class: IR NV	**1984-09 Rauma-Repola Oy — Rauma** Yd No: 286 Converted From: Cable-layer-2008 Converted From: Ro-Ro Cargo Ship-2001 Loa 120.20 Br ex 21.04 Dght 6.715 Lbp 111.20 Br md 21.01 Dpth 14.51 Welded, 2 dks	**(B22A20V) Diving Support Vessel** Lane-Len: 1184 Ice Capable	**4 diesel electric oil engines** driving 4 gen. Connecting to 2 elec. motors driving 2 Azimuth electric drive units Total Power: 10,940kW (14,874hp) 12.0kn Wartsila 6R32 2 x 4 Stroke 6 Cy. 320 x 350 each-2340kW (3181bhp) (new engine 2000) Wartsila NSD Finland Oy-Finland Wartsila 8R32 2 x 4 Stroke 8 Cy. 320 x 350 each-3130kW (4256bhp) (new engine 2000) Wartsila NSD Finland Oy-Finland Thrusters: 3 Thwart. FP thruster (f)
9559793 *XVAP* -	**SEAMEN** - **Agribank Leasing Co II** Viet Long Transport & Chartering Co Ltd SatCom: Inmarsat C 457493610 *Haiphong* *Vietnam* MMSI: 574936000	**2,551** 1,497 4,374	Class: VR	**2009-08 Dai Duong Shipbuilding Co Ltd — Haiphong** Yd No: HP703-14 Loa 90.72 Br ex 13.00 Dght 6.160 Lbp 84.96 Br md 12.98 Dpth 7.60 Welded, 1 dk	**(A31A2GX) General Cargo Ship** Grain: 4,850 Compartments: 2 Ho, ER 2 Ha: ER 2 (21.0 x 8.0) Cranes: 2x10t	**1 oil engine** driving 1 FP propeller Total Power: 1,500kW (2,039hp) 11.0kn Chinese Std. Type G8300ZC 1 x 4 Stroke 8 Cy. 300 x 380 1500kW (2039bhp) Wuxi Antai Power Machinery Co Ltd-China AuxGen: 2 x 170kW 400V a.c Fuel: 228.0 (r.f.)
9260005 *9HA3292* -	**SEAMERCURY** *ex* Baltic Adonia I *-2013* *ex* Arctic Point *-2009* *launched as* Baltic Adonia *-2003* **Champlain Navigation Corp** Thenamaris (Ships Management) Inc *Valletta* *Malta* MMSI: 229388000 Official number: 9260005	**23,235** 10,129 37,198 T/cm 46.1	Class: GL NK (NV)	**2003-06 Hyundai Mipo Dockyard Co Ltd — Ulsan** Yd No: 0122 Loa 182.55 Br ex 27.38 Dght 11.217 Lbp 175.00 Br md 27.34 Dpth 16.70 Welded, 1 dk	**(A12B2TR) Chemical/Products Tanker** Double Hull (13F) Liq: 41,343; Liq (Oil): 41,343 Cargo Heating Coils Compartments: 12 Wing Ta, 2 Wing Slop Ta, ER 12 Cargo Pump (s): 10x500m³/hr, 2x320m³/hr Manifold: Bow/CM: 91.8m Ice Capable	**1 oil engine** driving 1 FP propeller Total Power: 9,480kW (12,889hp) 14.5kn B&W 6S50MC-C 1 x 2 Stroke 6 Cy. 500 x 2000 9480kW (12889bhp) Hyundai Heavy Industries Co Ltd-South Korea AuxGen: 3 x 740kW 450V 60Hz a.c Thrusters: 1 Thwart. FP thruster (f) Fuel: 149.9 (d.f.) (Heating Coils) 1155.0 (r.f.)
9462897 *VRIK8* -	**SEAMERIDIAN** - **City Express Shipping Ltd** Valles Steamship (Canada) Inc *Hong Kong* *Hong Kong* MMSI: 477229100 Official number: HK-3072	**30,241** 14,702 50,309 T/cm 55.4	Class: NV	**2011-09 Guangzhou Shipyard International Co Ltd — Guangzhou GD** Yd No: 06130091 Loa 183.20 (BB) Br ex 32.23 Dght 12.600 Lbp 176.00 Br md 32.20 Dpth 18.20 Welded, 1 dk	**(A13B2TP) Products Tanker** Double Hull (13F) Liq: 56,354; Liq (Oil): 51,470	**1 oil engine** driving 1 FP propeller Total Power: 9,480kW (12,889hp) 15.0kn MAN-B&W 6S50MC-C 1 x 2 Stroke 6 Cy. 500 x 2000 9480kW (12889bhp) Dalian Marine Diesel Co Ltd-China AuxGen: 3 x 910kW a.c
9247481 *9HHS7* -	**SEAMERIT** - **Ocean Star Navigation Ltd** Thenamaris (Ships Management) Inc *Valletta* *Malta* MMSI: 215263000 Official number: 7794	**23,236** 10,113 39,441 T/cm 46.1	Class: NV	**2002-09 Hyundai Mipo Dockyard Co Ltd — Ulsan** Yd No: 0029 Converted From: Chemical/Products Tanker-2005 Loa 182.55 (BB) Br ex - Dght 11.720 Lbp 175.00 Br md 27.34 Dpth 16.70 Welded, 1 dk	**(A13B2TP) Products Tanker** Double Hull (13F) Liq: 43,119; Liq (Oil): 43,119 14 Cargo Pump (s)	**1 oil engine** driving 1 FP propeller Total Power: 9,466kW (12,870hp) 14.5kn MAN-B&W 6S50MC-C 1 x 2 Stroke 6 Cy. 500 x 2000 9466kW (12870bhp) Hyundai Heavy Industries Co Ltd-South Korea
9115858 *DUH2600* -	**SEAMINE 2** *ex* Es Star *-2003* **Seamine Ventures Inc** - *Cebu* *Philippines* Official number: CEB1006858	**118** 33 112	Class: (NK)	**1994-08 Super-Light Shipbuilding Contractor — Sibu** Yd No: 11 Loa 23.17 Br ex - Dght 2.388 Lbp 21.76 Br md 7.00 Dpth 2.90 Welded, 1 dk	**(B32A2ST) Tug**	**2 oil engines** reduction geared to sc. shafts driving 2 FP propellers Total Power: 692kW (940hp) 9.0kn Caterpillar 3408TA 2 x Vee 4 Stroke 8 Cy. 137 x 152 each-346kW (470bhp) Caterpillar Inc-USA AuxGen: 2 x 16kW a.c
7820057 *ZMAT* -	**SEAMOUNT ENTERPRISE** - **Anton's Trawling Co Ltd** - *Auckland* *New Zealand* Official number: 876085	**221** 66 -		**1982-02 Fami Fabrications Pty Ltd — Port Kembla NSW** Yd No: 78/1 Loa 29.82 Br ex 8.03 Dght 3.401 Lbp 26.32 Br md 7.61 Dpth 4.02 Welded, 1 dk	**(B11A2FS) Stern Trawler**	**1 oil engine** with clutches, flexible couplings & sr geared to sc. shaft driving 1 CP propeller Total Power: 897kW (1,220hp) 12.0kn Blackstone ESL8MK2 1 x 4 Stroke 8 Cy. 222 x 292 897kW (1220bhp) Mirrlees Blackstone (Stamford)Ltd.-Stamford AuxGen: 2 x 72kW 415V 50Hz a.c, 1 x 20kW 415V 50Hz a.c
8614211 *ZMOI* -	**SEAMOUNT EXPLORER** *ex* Europa *-1997* **Anton's Trawling Co Ltd** - SatCom: Inmarsat C 421120796 *Auckland* *New Zealand* MMSI: 512000030 Official number: 876211	**671** 201 345	Class: GL	**1987-06 Sieghold Werft Bremerhaven GmbH & Co. — Bremerhaven** Yd No: 201 Loa 44.02 Br ex 10.67 Dght 4.501 Lbp 33.02 Br md 10.61 Dpth 7.01 Welded, 2 dks	**(B11A2FG) Factory Stern Trawler** Ins: 302 Ice Capable	**1 oil engine** with clutches, flexible couplings & sr geared to sc. shaft driving 1 CP propeller Total Power: 1,620kW (2,203hp) 13.6kn Alpha 8L28/32 1 x 4 Stroke 8 Cy. 280 x 320 1620kW (2203bhp) MAN B&W Diesel A/S-Denmark AuxGen: 1 x 880kW 220/380V a.c, 1 x 384kW 220/380V a.c Thrusters: 1 Thwart. CP thruster (f)

IMO / Call sign	Name / Owner	Tonnage	Class	Builder / Dimensions	Type	Machinery
9204776 *DEBQ* -	**SEAMULLET** **tms 'Seamullet' GmbH & Co KG** German Tanker Shipping GmbH & Co KG *Bremen* *Germany* MMSI: 211379750 Official number: 4858	**21,353** 8,389 32,238 T/cm 42.0	Class: GL	**2001-04 Lindenau GmbH Schiffswerft u. Maschinenfabrik — Kiel** Yd No: 242 Loa 177.78 (BB) Br ex - Dght 11.000 Lbp 168.00 Br md 28.00 Dpth 16.80 Welded, 1 dk	**(A13B2TP) Products Tanker** Double Hull (13F) Liq: 36,716; Liq (Oil): 36,716 Compartments: 10 Wing Ta, ER 10 Cargo Pump (s): 10x600m^3/hr Manifold: Bow/CM: 85m Ice Capable	**1 oil engine** reduction geared to sc. shaft driving 1 CP propeller Total Power: 8,340kW (11,339hp) 15.1kn MAN 6L58/64 1 x 4 Stroke 6 Cy. 580 x 640 8340kW (11339bhp) MAN B&W Diesel AG-Augsburg AuxGen: 1 x 1120kW 240/400V a.c, 3 x 960kW 240/400V 50Hz a.c Thrusters: 1 Thwart. FP thruster (f) Fuel: 321.0 (d.f.) 811.0 (r.f.)
9382700 *9HA3561* -	**SEAMUSE** *ex Belaia -2014* **Planet Marine SA** Thenamaris (Ships Management) Inc *Valletta* *Malta* MMSI: 229734000 Official number: 9382700	**28,799** 13,234 48,673 T/cm 51.8	Class: NK	**2007-03 Iwagi Zosen Co Ltd — Kamijima EH** Yd No: 254 Loa 179.99 (BB) Br ex 32.23 Dght 12.616 Lbp 172.00 Br md 32.20 Dpth 19.05 Welded, 1 dk	**(A13A2TW) Crude/Oil Products Tanker** Double Hull (13F) Liq: 54,753; Liq (Oil): 54,753 Cargo Heating Coils Compartments: 16 Wing Ta, ER, 2 Wing Slop Ta 4 Cargo Pump (s): 4x1250m^3/hr Manifold: Bow/CM: 83.4m	**1 oil engine** driving 1 FP propeller Total Power: 9,480kW (12,889hp) 15.1kn MAN-B&W 6S50MC-C 1 x 2 Stroke 6 Cy. 500 x 2000 9480kW (12889bhp) Mitsui Engineering & Shipbuilding CLtd-Japan Fuel: 313.0 (d.f.) 1910.0 (r.f.)
9407445 *9HZL9* -	**SEAMUSIC** *ex King Charles -2009* **Blue Light Development Corp** Thenamaris (Ships Management) Inc SatCom: Inmarsat C 424974610 *Valletta* *Malta* MMSI: 249746000 Official number: 9407445	**62,775** 34,934 112,931 T/cm 99.7	Class: AB	**2009-06 New Times Shipbuilding Co Ltd — Jingjiang JS** Yd No: 0311508 Loa 250.00 (BB) Br ex 44.04 Dght 14.800 Lbp 240.00 Br md 44.00 Dpth 21.00 Welded, 1 dk	**(A13A2TW) Crude/Oil Products Tanker** Double Hull (13F) Liq: 127,223; Liq (Oil): 129,500 Cargo Heating Coils Compartments: 12 Wing Ta, 2 Wing Slop Ta, ER 3 Cargo Pump (s): 3x3000m^3/hr Manifold: Bow/CM: 122.5m	**1 oil engine** driving 1 FP propeller Total Power: 15,820kW (21,509hp) 15.0kn MAN-B&W 7S60MC-C 1 x 2 Stroke 7 Cy. 600 x 2400 15820kW (21509bhp) Hyundai Heavy Industries Co Ltd-South Korea AuxGen: 3 x 1125kW a.c
7427568 *IRDK* -	**SEAN CHRISTOPHER** *ex Lombardia -1998* **Oromare SpA** - SatCom: Inmarsat C 424748720 *Genoa* *Italy* MMSI: 247007900 Official number: 47	*197* 26 287	Class: RI	**1976-10 Cantieri Navali Campanella SpA — Savona** Yd No: 81 Loa 31.11 Br ex 8.84 Dght 3.946 Lbp 26.52 Br md 8.41 Dpth 4.42 Welded, 1 dk	**(B32A2ST) Tug**	**1 oil engine** reduction geared to sc. shaft driving 1 CP propeller Total Power: 1,839kW (2,500hp) 13.6kn Nohab F212V 1 x Vee 4 Stroke 12 Cy. 250 x 300 1839kW (2500bhp) AB Bofors NOHAB-Sweden
7528829 *POEQ* -	**SEAN MARINE I** *ex Heritage Service -2011* **PT Sufie Bahari Lines** - *Batam* *Indonesia*	**1,058** 317 960	Class: AB KI	**1978-06 Campbell Industries — San Diego, Ca** Yd No: 119 Converted From: Offshore Tug/Supply Ship-1990 Loa 63.20 Br ex 12.25 Dght 4.541 Lbp 55.35 Br md 12.19 Dpth 5.18 Welded, 1 dk	**(B34G2SE) Pollution Control Vessel** Ice Capable	**2 oil engines** sr geared to sc. shafts driving 2 CP propellers Total Power: 4,230kW (5,752hp) 12.0kn EMD (Electro-Motive) 16-645-E5 2 x Vee 2 Stroke 16 Cy. 230 x 254 each-2115kW (2876bhp) General Motors Corp.Electro-Motive Div.-La Grange AuxGen: 2 x 150kW a.c, 2 x 100kW a.c Thrusters: 1 Thwart. FP thruster (f)
9216004 *EI5775* S 22	**SEAN OISIN** *ex Ardent -2007* **Paul Flannery** - *Skibbereen* *Irish Republic* MMSI: 250184000 Official number: 403465	**233** 70 -	Class: (BV)	**2001-02 Chantiers Piriou — Concarneau** Yd No: 214 Loa 24.90 Br ex - Dght 3.500 Lbp 21.79 Br md 8.00 Dpth 3.90 Welded, 1 dk	**(B11A2FT) Trawler**	**1 oil engine** reduction geared to sc. shaft driving 1 FP propeller Total Power: 600kW (816hp) 10.0kn Caterpillar 3512 1 x Vee 4 Stroke 12 Cy. 170 x 190 600kW (816bhp) Caterpillar Inc-USA
1011501 *2ETL3* -	**SEANNA** **Skycat Ltd** Nigel Burgess Ltd (BURGESS) SatCom: Inmarsat C 423592829 *Douglas* *Isle of Man (British)* MMSI: 235088016 Official number: 742864	**1,426** 427 -	Class: LR ✠ **100A1** SS 07/2011 SSC Yacht, mono, G6 **LMC** **UMS** Cable: 192.0/24.0 U3 (a)	**2011-07 Azimut-Benetti SpA — Livorno** Yd No: FB254 Loa 64.50 (BB) Br ex - Dght 3.370 Lbp 54.47 Br md 12.10 Dpth 6.25 Welded, 1 dk	**(X11A2YP) Yacht**	**2 oil engines** with clutches, flexible couplings & sr reverse geared to sc. shafts driving 2 FP propellers Total Power: 3,370kW (4,582hp) Caterpillar 3516B-HD 2 x Vee 4 Stroke 16 Cy. 170 x 215 each-1685kW (2291bhp) Caterpillar Inc-USA AuxGen: 3 x 200kW 400V 50Hz a.c Thrusters: 1 Thwart. FP thruster (f)
9259185 *VRAO6* -	**SEANOSTRUM** **Seanostrum Tanker Ltd** Valles Steamship (Canada) Inc *Hong Kong* *Hong Kong* MMSI: 477760900 Official number: HK-1434	**57,979** 31,829 107,144 T/cm 91.0	Class: NK	**2002-11 Imabari Shipbuilding Co Ltd — Saijo EH (Saijo Shipyard)** Yd No: 8010 Loa 246.80 (BB) Br ex 42.03 Dght 14.900 Lbp 235.00 Br md 42.00 Dpth 21.30 Welded, 1 dk	**(A13A2TV) Crude Oil Tanker** Double Hull (13F) Liq: 116,592; Liq (Oil): 122,858 Compartments: 14 Wing Ta, ER, 2 Wing Slop Ta 3 Cargo Pump (s): 3x2500m^3/hr Manifold: Bow/CM: 123.8m	**1 oil engine** driving 1 FP propeller Total Power: 13,548kW (18,420hp) 14.7kn B&W 6S60MC 1 x 2 Stroke 6 Cy. 600 x 2292 13548kW (18420bhp) Mitsui Engineering & Shipbuilding CLtd-Japan Fuel: 299.0 (d.f.) 4073.0 (r.f.)
9290361 *9HBO8* -	**SEAOATH** **Seacargo Shipping Ltd** Thenamaris (Ships Management) Inc *Valletta* *Malta* MMSI: 215810000 Official number: 9293	**57,162** 32,768 105,472 T/cm 92.0	Class: AB	**2005-02 Hyundai Heavy Industries Co Ltd — Ulsan** Yd No: 1555 Loa 243.98 (BB) Br ex 42.00 Dght 14.920 Lbp 234.00 Br md 42.00 Dpth 21.00 Welded,.1 dk	**(A13A2TW) Crude/Oil Products Tanker** Double Hull (13F) Liq: 118,281; Liq (Oil): 120,695 Cargo Heating Coils Compartments: 12 Wing Ta, 2 Wing Slop Ta, ER 3 Cargo Pump (s) Manifold: Bow/CM: 121.9m Ice Capable	**1 oil engine** driving 1 FP propeller Total Power: 11,327kW (15,400hp) 14.6kn B&W 6S60MC 1 x 2 Stroke 6 Cy. 600 x 2292 11327kW (15400bhp) Hyundai Heavy Industries Co Ltd-South Korea AuxGen: 3 x 660kW 440/220V 60Hz a.c Fuel: 175.7 (d.f.) (Heating Coils) 2772.8 (r.f.)
8888276 *ZHEJ3* -	**SEAOIL GRACE** *ex PBR/228 -2007* **Sea Oil Marine Services Inc** Marflex Navegacao Ltda *George Town* *Cayman Islands (British)* MMSI: 319622000 Official number: 710598	**270** 81 -	Class: AB	**1980 Service Machine & Shipbuilding Co — Amelia LA** Yd No: 133 Loa - Br ex - Dght 3.160 Lbp 35.96 Br md 8.53 Dpth 3.50 Welded, 1 dk	**(B21B20T) Offshore Tug/Supply Ship**	**2 oil engines** reverse reduction geared to sc. shafts driving 2 FP propellers Total Power: 1,560kW (2,120hp) 12.0kn G.M. (Detroit Diesel) 16V-92 2 x Vee 2 Stroke 16 Cy. 123 x 127 each-780kW (1060bhp) General Motors Corp-USA AuxGen: 2 x 50kW a.c
8888288 *PQ5043* -	**SEAOIL MARY** *ex PBR/229 -2007* **Sea Oil Marine Services Inc** Marflex Navegacao Ltda *Rio de Janeiro* *Brazil*	**270** 81 -	Class: AB	**1980 Service Machine & Shipbuilding Co — Amelia LA** Yd No: 135 Loa - Br ex - Dght 3.160 Lbp 35.96 Br md 8.53 Dpth 3.50 Welded, 1 dk	**(B21B20T) Offshore Tug/Supply Ship**	**2 oil engines** reverse reduction geared to sc. shafts driving 2 FP propellers Total Power: 1,560kW (2,120hp) 12.0kn G.M. (Detroit Diesel) 16V-92 2 x Vee 2 Stroke 16 Cy. 123 x 127 each-780kW (1060bhp) General Motors Corp-USA AuxGen: 2 x 50kW a.c
9693721 - -	**SEAOP 3** - CNPC South-East Asia Pipeline Co Ltd *Yangon* *Myanmar* Official number: 6868 (A)	**440** 132 146	Class: CC	**2014-04 Guangdong Yuexin Ocean Engineering Co Ltd — Guangzhou GD** Yd No: 3182 Loa 38.40 Br ex - Dght 3.600 Lbp 32.60 Br md 10.60 Dpth 4.80 Welded, 1 dk	**(B32A2ST) Tug**	**2 oil engines** reduction geared to sc. shafts driving 2 Directional propellers Total Power: 3,678kW (5,000hp) Yanmar 2 x 4 Stroke each-1839kW (2500bhp)
9693733 - -	**SEAOP 4** - CNPC South-East Asia Pipeline Co Ltd *Yangon* *Myanmar* Official number: 6869 (A)	**440** 132 148	Class: CC	**2014-04 Guangdong Yuexin Ocean Engineering Co Ltd — Guangzhou GD** Yd No: 3183 Loa 38.40 Br ex - Dght 3.600 Lbp 32.60 Br md 10.60 Dpth 4.80 Welded, 1 dk	**(B32A2ST) Tug**	**2 oil engines** reduction geared to sc. shafts driving 2 Directional propellers Total Power: 3,678kW (5,000hp) Yamaha 2 x 4 Stroke each-1839kW (2500bhp)
9661182 - -	**SEAOP 5** *launched as Yong Li 2 -2014* **Government of The Union of Myanmar (Ministry of Energy - Myanmar Oil & Gas Enterprise)** CNPC South-East Asia Pipeline Co Ltd *Yangon* *Myanmar* Official number: 6870A	**492** 147 148	Class: CC	**2014-04 Guangdong Yuexin Ocean Engineering Co Ltd — Guangzhou GD** Yd No: 3185 Loa 39.40 Br ex - Dght 3.600 Lbp 33.60 Br md 10.60 Dpth 4.80 Welded, 1 dk	**(B32A2ST) Tug**	**2 oil engines** reduction geared to sc. shafts driving 2 Directional propellers Total Power: 3,678kW (5,000hp) Yanmar 2 x 4 Stroke each-1839kW (2500bhp) AuxGen: 2 x a.c
9486025 *9HA2223* -	**SEAPACE** **Courtecy Shipping Inc** Thenamaris (Ships Management) Inc *Valletta* *Malta* MMSI: 248184000 Official number: 9486025	**33,036** 19,270 56,894 T/cm 58.8	Class: AB	**2010-03 Taizhou Sanfu Ship Engineering Co Ltd — Taizhou JS** Yd No: SF060102 Loa 189.99 (BB) Br ex - Dght 12.800 Lbp 185.00 Br md 32.26 Dpth 18.00 Welded, 1 dk	**(A21A2BC) Bulk Carrier** Grain: 71,634; Bale: 68,200 Compartments: 5 Ho, ER 5 Ha: ER Cranes: 4x36t	**1 oil engine** driving 1 FP propeller Total Power: 9,480kW (12,889hp) 14.2kn MAN-B&W 6S50MC-C 1 x 2 Stroke 6 Cy. 500 x 2000 9480kW (12889bhp) STX Engine Co Ltd-South Korea AuxGen: 3 x 600kW a.c Fuel: 124.0 (d.f.) 2250.0 (r.f.)

9304356 **SEAPACIS**
VRBE2
-
Seaway Navigation Ltd
Valles Steamship (Canada) Inc
SatCom: Inmarsat Mini-M 764471984
Hong Kong *Hong Kong*
MMSI: 477999500
Official number: HK-1558

56,489 Class: AB
32,667
105,747
T/cm
90.5

2005-09 Namura Shipbuilding Co Ltd — Imari SG
Yd No: 261
Loa 241.03 (BB) Br ex - Dght 14.953
Lbp 232.00 Br md 42.00 Dpth 21.20
Welded, 1 dk

(A13A2TV) Crude Oil Tanker
Double Hull (13F)
Liq: 113,307; Liq (Oil): 122,268
Cargo Heating Coils
Compartments: 12 Wing Ta, 2 Wing Slop Ta, ER
3 Cargo Pump (s): 3x2500m³/hr
Manifold: Bow/CM: 119m

1 oil engine driving 1 FP propeller
Total Power: 12,240kW (16,642hp) 15.0kn
MAN-B&W 6S60MC
1 x 2 Stroke 6 Cy. 600 x 2292 12240kW (16642bhp)
Hitachi Zosen Corp-Japan
AuxGen: 3 x 600kW a.c
Fuel: 239.0 (d.f.) 2725.5 (r.f.)

9089633 **SEAPATROLLER**
ZMSP *ex Hinau (P 3556) -2007*
- **S & K Day Ltd**
Seaworks Ltd
Wellington *New Zealand*
Official number: 876424

119
35
-

1985-10 Whangarei Eng. & Construction Co. Ltd. — Whangarei Yd No: 165
Converted From: Patrol Vessel-2007
Loa 26.82 Br ex - Dght -
Lbp - Br md 6.10 Dpth 2.25
Welded, 1 dk

(B34H2SQ) Patrol Vessel

2 oil engines geared to sc. shafts driving 2 Propellers
Total Power: 522kW (710hp) 12.0kn
Cummins KT-1150-M
2 x 4 Stroke 6 Cy. 159 x 159 each-261kW (355bhp)
Cummins Engine Co Inc-USA

6423462 **SEAPEARL**
A9D2381 *ex Seagull -1980 ex No. 5 -1974*
- **Bahrain Bulk Trade WLL**
Abdulla Ahmed Nass Co
Bahrain

122 Class: (LR) (BV)
- ✠ Classed LR until 4/5/84
-

1965-04 R. Dunston (Hessle) Ltd. — Hessle
Yd No: S816
Loa 26.57 Br ex 7.50 Dght 2.096
Lbp 24.31 Br md 7.17 Dpth 2.65
Welded, 1 dk

(B32A2ST) Tug

1 oil engine driving 1 FP propeller
Total Power: 485kW (659hp)
Brons 8GV-E
1 x Vee 2 Stroke 8 Cy. 220 x 380 485kW (659bhp)
Drypool Eng. & D.D. Co. Ltd.-Hull

9423449 **SEAPIKE**
D5CO4
-
tms 'Seapike' GmbH & Co KG
German Tanker Shipping GmbH & Co KG
Monrovia *Liberia*
MMSI: 636092435
Official number: 92435

28,449 Class: GL
11,293
43,550

2009-06 Lindenau GmbH Schiffswerft u. Maschinenfabrik — Kiel Yd No: 280
Loa 199.53 (BB) Br ex 32.25 Dght 11.000
Lbp 190.70 Br md 32.20 Dpth 17.05
Welded, 1 dk

(A13B2TP) Products Tanker
Double Hull (13F)
Liq: 50,182; Liq (Oil): 47,370
Compartments: 12 Wing Ta, 1 Slop Ta, 1 Wing Slop Ta, ER
12 Cargo Pump (s): 10x600m³/hr, 2x250m³/hr
Manifold: Bow/CM: 102.8m
Ice Capable

1 oil engine reduction geared to sc. shaft driving 1 CP propeller
Total Power: 11,200kW (15,228hp) 15.5kn
MAN-B&W 8L58/64
1 x 4 Stroke 8 Cy. 580 x 640 11200kW (15228bhp)
MAN B&W Diesel AG-Augsburg
AuxGen: 3 x 1360kW 400V a.c, 1 x 1140kW 400V a.c
Thrusters: 1 Tunnel thruster (f)
Fuel: 380.0 (d.f.) 1200.0 (r.f.)

8912572 **SEAPOL ONE**
JVSW3 *ex Aichi -2007 ex Aichi Maru -2007*
- **Ocean Connection Pte Ltd**
Seaport Shipping Pvt Ltd
Ulaanbaatar *Mongolia*
MMSI: 457013000
Official number: 23460890

675 Class: RS
202
445

1990-03 Niigata Engineering Co Ltd — Niigata NI
Yd No: 2165
Loa 55.12 (BB) Br ex - Dght 3.732
Lbp 47.50 Br md 9.00 Dpth 3.90
Welded, 1 dk

(B11B2FV) Fishing Vessel
Ins: 112

1 oil engine with clutches, flexible couplings & sr reverse geared to sc. shaft driving 1 FP propeller
Total Power: 1,030kW (1,400hp)
Niigata 6M28BFT
1 x 4 Stroke 6 Cy. 280 x 480 1030kW (1400bhp)
Niigata Engineering Co Ltd-Japan

7376161 **SEAPOWER**
HP3705 *ex Weatherly -2007*
- **Assef Navegacion SA**
-
Panama *Panama*
Official number: 41016PEXT2

1,154 Class: (AB)
346
2,200

1975-12 Teraoka Shipyard Co Ltd — Minamiawaji HG Yd No: 141
Loa 65.84 Br ex - Dght 4.719
Lbp 60.41 Br md 12.81 Dpth 5.80
Welded, 1 dk

(B21A20S) Platform Supply Ship
Ice Capable

2 oil engines sr geared to sc. shafts driving 2 CP propellers
Total Power: 5,178kW (7,040hp) 15.0kn
Nohab F216V
2 x Vee 4 Stroke 16 Cy. 250 x 300 each-2589kW (3520bhp)
AB NOHAB-Sweden
AuxGen: 2 x 150kW a.c, 1 x 75kW a.c
Thrusters: 1 Thwart. FP thruster (f)

9629562 **SEAPRIDE**
9HA3272
-
Calmseas Shipping SA
Thenamaris (Ships Management) Inc
SatCom: Inmarsat C 422936510
Valletta *Malta*
MMSI: 229365000
Official number: 9629562

29,925 Class: AB
13,626
50,908
T/cm
52.0

2013-02 STX Offshore & Shipbuilding Co Ltd — Changwon (Jinhae Shipyard) Yd No: 1533
Loa 183.00 (BB) Br ex 32.23 Dght 13.150
Lbp 173.90 Br md 32.20 Dpth 19.10
Welded, 1 dk

(A12B2TR) Chemical/Products Tanker
Double Hull (13F)
Liq: 52,209; Liq (Oil): 52,170
Cargo Heating Coils
Compartments: 6 Wing Ta, 6 Wing Ta, 1 Wing Slop Ta, 1 Wing Slop Ta, ER
12 Cargo Pump (s): 12x600m³/hr
Manifold: Bow/CM: 91.9m

1 oil engine driving 1 FP propeller
Total Power: 9,109kW (12,385hp) 14.5kn
MAN-B&W 6S50ME-C8
1 x 2 Stroke 6 Cy. 500 x 2000 9109kW (12385bhp)
STX Engine Co Ltd-South Korea
AuxGen: 3 x 740kW a.c
Fuel: 160.0 (d.f.) 1540.0 (r.f.)

8868460 **SEAPRIMFICO 02**
-
-
Vietnam Soviet Fishery Joint Venture Co (SEAPRIMFICO) (Xi Nghiep Lien Doanh Thuy San Viet Xo)
-
Saigon *Vietnam*

380 Class: (VR)
114
625

1990 Ho Chi Minh City Shipyard — Ho Chi Minh City
Loa 43.80 Br ex - Dght 3.400
Lbp - Br md 8.15 Dpth 4.00
Welded, 1 dk

(A34A2GR) Refrigerated Cargo Ship
Ins: 312
Compartments: 1 Ho, ER

1 oil engine reduction geared to sc. shaft driving 1 FP propeller
Total Power: 552kW (750hp) 9.0kn
Sulzer 6AL20/24
1 x 4 Stroke 6 Cy. 200 x 240 552kW (750bhp) (Re-engined ,made 1964, Reconditioned & fitted 1990)
Zaklady Przemyslu Metalowego 'HCegielski' SA-Poznan
AuxGen: 1 x 150kW a.c, 2 x 100kW a.c

9241607 **SEAPRINCE**
SVQD
-
Crystalsea Maritime Inc
Thenamaris (Ships Management) Inc
SatCom: Inmarsat C 424065410
Piraeus *Greece*
MMSI: 240654000
Official number: 11705

84,598 Class: AB
46,548
149,878
T/cm
121.8

2002-05 Samho Heavy Industries Co Ltd — Samho Yd No: 128
Loa 274.19 (BB) Br ex 50.04 Dght 15.848
Lbp 264.00 Br md 50.00 Dpth 23.10
Welded, 1 dk

(A13A2TW) Crude/Oil Products Tanker
Liq: 173,947; Liq (Oil): 178,373
Cargo Heating Coils
Compartments: 12 Wing Ta, 2 Wing Slop Ta, ER
3 Cargo Pump (s): 3x4000m³/hr
Manifold: Bow/CM: 136.9m

1 oil engine driving 1 FP propeller
Total Power: 18,624kW (25,321hp) 15.5kn
MAN-B&W 6S70MC-C
1 x 2 Stroke 6 Cy. 700 x 2800 18624kW (25321bhp)
Hyundai Heavy Industries Co Ltd-South Korea
AuxGen: 3 x 950kW a.c
Fuel: 165.0 (d.f.) 3780.0 (r.f.)

9373668 **SEAPRINCESS**
9HJZ9 *ex Neverland Sky -2008*
- **Dolphin Maritime Services Ltd**
Thenamaris (Ships Management) Inc
SatCom: Inmarsat C 424907810
Valletta *Malta*
MMSI: 249078000
Official number: 9373668

61,248 Class: AB
35,402
115,949
T/cm
99.1

2008-09 Samsung Heavy Industries Co Ltd — Geoje Yd No: 1659
Loa 248.96 (BB) Br ex 43.83 Dght 14.919
Lbp 239.00 Br md 43.80 Dpth 21.00
Welded, 1 dk

(A13A2TV) Crude Oil Tanker
Double Hull (13F)
Liq: 123,642; Liq (Oil): 117,712
Cargo Heating Coils
Compartments: 12 Wing Ta, 2 Wing Slop Ta, ER
3 Cargo Pump (s): 3x2800m³/hr
Manifold: Bow/CM: 124.9m

1 oil engine driving 1 FP propeller
Total Power: 13,560kW (18,436hp) 15.3kn
MAN-B&W 6S60MC-C
1 x 2 Stroke 6 Cy. 600 x 2400 13560kW (18436bhp)
Doosan Engine Co Ltd-South Korea
AuxGen: 3 x 850kW a.c
Fuel: 150.0 (d.f.) 3450.0 (r.f.)

8839029 **SEAPRODEX 04**
-
-
Seaprodex Import-Export & Shipping Co (SEAPROSHIMEX) (Cong Ty Van Tai Bien Va Xnk Thuoc Seaprodex)
-
Saigon *Vietnam*

340 Class: (VR)
-
150

1988 Ha Long Shipbuilding Engineering JSC — Haiphong
L reg 35.80 Br ex - Dght 3.100
Lbp - Br md 7.60 Dpth 3.65
Welded, 1 dk

(A34A2GR) Refrigerated Cargo Ship

1 oil engine driving 1 FP propeller
Total Power: 736kW (1,001hp)
Niigata 6M28KGHS
1 x 4 Stroke 6 Cy. 280 x 440 736kW (1001bhp)
Niigata Engineering Co Ltd-Japan
AuxGen: 2 x 100kW a.c

7210329 **SEAPRODEX 06**
- *ex Khanh Hoi -1989 ex Taiyo Maru No. 2 -1989*
- *ex Kasuga Maru No. 18 -1979*
Seaprodex Import-Export & Shipping Co (SEAPROSHIMEX) (Cong Ty Van Tai Bien Va Xnk Thuoc Seaprodex)
-
Saigon *Vietnam*

299 Class: (VR)
155
520

1972 KK Kanasashi Zosen — Shizuoka SZ
Yd No: 1063
Loa 49.52 Br ex 8.23 Dght 3.296
Lbp 44.00 Br md 8.21 Dpth 3.66
Welded, 1 dk

(B11B2FV) Fishing Vessel

1 oil engine driving 1 FP propeller
Total Power: 919kW (1,249hp) 13.0kn
Akasaka AH28
1 x 4 Stroke 6 Cy. 280 x 440 919kW (1249bhp)
Akasaka Tekkosho KK (Akasaka DieselLtd)-Japan
AuxGen: 2 x 385kW a.c

9247479 **SEAPROMISE**
9HGK7
-
Oceanic Navigation Ltd
Thenamaris (Ships Management) Inc
Valletta *Malta*
MMSI: 215220000
Official number: 7682

23,236 Class: NV
10,113
39,480
T/cm
46.4

2002-05 Hyundai Mipo Dockyard Co Ltd — Ulsan
Yd No: 0028
Converted From: Chemical/Products Tanker-2005
Loa 182.55 Br ex - Dght 11.720
Lbp 175.00 Br md 27.34 Dpth 16.70
Welded, 1 dk

(A13B2TP) Products Tanker
Double Hull (13F)
Liq: 41,343; Liq (Oil): 43,119
Cargo Heating Coils
Compartments: 10 Wing Ta, 2 Wing Slop Ta, ER
12 Cargo Pump (s): 2x300m³/hr, 10x500m³/hr
Manifold: Bow/CM: 92.2m

1 oil engine driving 1 FP propeller
Total Power: 9,466kW (12,870hp) 14.5kn
MAN-B&W 6S50MC-C
1 x 2 Stroke 6 Cy. 500 x 2000 9466kW (12870bhp)
Hyundai Heavy Industries Co Ltd-South Korea
AuxGen: 3 x 740kW 450V 60Hz a.c
Thrusters: 1 Tunnel thruster (f)
Fuel: 189.0 (d.f.) 1088.0 (r.f.)

8889050 **SEAQUAL**
- *ex Chokyu Maru No. 32 -1999*
- *ex Kifuku Maru No. 51 -1999*
- *ex Yoshi Maru Go No. 31 -1999*
-
-

177
53
-

1980-12 Minami-Kyushu Zosen KK — Ichikikushikino KS
L reg 27.50 Br ex - Dght -
Lbp - Br md 6.00 Dpth 2.40
Welded, 1 dk

(B11B2FV) Fishing Vessel

1 oil engine driving 1 FP propeller

9288863 **SEAQUEEN**
9HHY9 *ex Neverland Soul -2008 ex HS Norma -2006*
- **Sealion Enterprises Ltd**
Thenamaris (Ships Management) Inc
SatCom: Inmarsat C 424901210
Valletta *Malta*
MMSI: 249012000
Official number: 9288863

62,796 Class: NV (RI)
34,548
115,639
T/cm
99.9

2004-11 Samsung Heavy Industries Co Ltd — Geoje Yd No: 1468
Loa 249.87 (BB) Br ex - Dght 14.925
Lbp 239.00 Br md 43.87 Dpth 21.30
Welded, 1 dk

(A13A2TV) Crude Oil Tanker
Double Hull (13F)
Liq: 124,258; Liq (Oil): 124,092
Cargo Heating Coils
Compartments: 12 Wing Ta, 2 Wing Slop Ta, ER
3 Cargo Pump (s): 3x2800m³/hr
Manifold: Bow/CM: 125.6m

1 oil engine driving 1 FP propeller
Total Power: 13,548kW (18,420hp) 15.3kn
B&W 6S60MC-C
1 x 2 Stroke 6 Cy. 600 x 2400 13548kW (18420bhp) (made 2004)
AuxGen: 3 x 924kW 440/220V 60Hz a.c
Fuel: 140.0 (d.f.) 3178.0 (r.f.)

Ship / Owner	Tonnage	Class	Build / Dimensions	Type	Machinery
9502659 **SEAQUEST** *ZCXD4* - **RDV International Marine Ltd** - *George Town* *Cayman Islands (British)* MMSI: 319302000 Official number: 740641	**492** 149 98	Class: AB	**2008-05 Westport Shipyard, Inc. — Westport, Wa** Yd No: 5004 Loa 49.94 Br ex - Dght 2.360 Lbp 44.80 Br md 9.31 Dpth 4.19 Bonded, 1 dk	**(X11A2YP) Yacht** Hull Material: Reinforced Plastic	**2 oil engines** reduction geared to sc. shafts driving 2 FP propellers Total Power: 5,370kW (7,302hp) M.T.U. 16V4000M90 2 x Vee 4 Stroke 16 Cy. 165 x 190 each-2685kW (3651bhp) Detroit Diesel Corporation-Detroit, Mi
9227443 **SEARACER** *9HDX7* - **Seafeatures Navigation SA** Thenamaris (Ships Management) Inc SatCom: Inmarsat C 421514211 *Valletta* *Malta* MMSI: 215142000 Official number: 7543	**84,598** 46,548 149,830 T/cm 121.8	Class: AB	**2002-01 Samho Heavy Industries Co Ltd — Samho** Yd No: 125 Loa 274.00 Br ex - Dght 15.826 Lbp 264.00 Br md 50.00 Dpth 23.10 Welded, 1 dk	**(A13A2TW) Crude/Oil Products Tanker** Double Hull (13F) Liq: 178,372; Liq (Oil): 178,372 Cargo Heating Coils Compartments: 12 Wing Ta, ER 3 Cargo Pump (s): 3x4000m³/hr Manifold: Bow/CM: 137m	**1 oil engine** driving 1 FP propeller Total Power: 18,624kW (25,321hp) 15.0kn B&W 6S70MC-C 1 x 2 Stroke 6 Cy. 700 x 2800 18624kW (25321bhp) Hyundai Heavy Industries Co Ltd-South Korea AuxGen: 3 x 950kW 220/450V 60Hz a.c Fuel: 138.1 (d.f.) (Heating Coils) 4048.0 (r.f.) 70.0pd
9236743 **SEARAMBLER** *9HCN7* - **Celebrity Shipping Ltd** Thenamaris (Ships Management) Inc *Valletta* *Malta* MMSI: 215107000 Official number: 7483	**23,236** 10,113 39,551 T/cm 46.1	Class: NV	**2001-10 Hyundai Mipo Dockyard Co Ltd — Ulsan** Yd No: 0018 Converted From: Chemical/Products Tanker-2003 Loa 182.55 (BB) Br ex 27.40 Dght 11.700 Lbp 175.00 Br md 27.34 Dpth 16.70 Welded, 1 dk	**(A13B2TP) Products Tanker** Double Hull (13F) Liq: 43,119; Liq (Oil): 43,119 14 Cargo Pump (s) Ice Capable	**1 oil engine** driving 1 FP propeller Total Power: 9,467kW (12,871hp) 14.5kn B&W 6S50MC-C 1 x 2 Stroke 6 Cy. 500 x 2000 9467kW (12871bhp) Hyundai Heavy Industries Co Ltd-South Korea
9442158 **SEARANGER** *VREG3* - **Ocean Navigation Ltd** Valles Steamship (Canada) Inc SatCom: Inmarsat C 447700674 *Hong Kong* *Hong Kong* MMSI: 477192100 Official number: HK-2201	**60,193** 33,762 109,165 T/cm 91.3	Class: AB	**2009-04 Hudong-Zhonghua Shipbuilding (Group) Co Ltd — Shanghai** Yd No: H1509A Loa 243.00 (BB) Br ex 42.03 Dght 15.370 Lbp 233.00 Br md 42.00 Dpth 22.00 Welded, 1 dk	**(A13A2TV) Crude Oil Tanker** Double Hull (13F) Liq: 123,030; Liq (Oil): 103,056 Cargo Heating Coils Compartments: 12 Wing Ta, 2 Wing Slop Ta, ER 3 Cargo Pump (s): 3x2500m³/hr Manifold: Bow/CM: 119.5m	**1 oil engine** driving 1 FP propeller Total Power: 13,570kW (18,450hp) 14.5kn MAN-B&W 7S60MC 1 x 2 Stroke 7 Cy. 600 x 2292 13570kW (18450bhp) Hudong Heavy Machinery Co Ltd-China AuxGen: 3 x 680kW a.c Fuel: 120.0 (d.f.) 2585.0 (r.f.)
9255490 **SEARAY** *DEEV* - **German Tanker Shipping GmbH & Co KG** - *Bremen* *Germany* MMSI: 211422510 Official number: 4890	**21,329** 8,381 32,310 T/cm 42.0	Class: GL	**2004-05 Lindenau GmbH Schiffswerft u. Maschinenfabrik — Kiel** Yd No: 254 Loa 177.69 (BB) Br ex 28.03 Dght 11.000 Lbp 168.00 Br md 28.00 Dpth 16.80 Welded, 1 dk	**(A13B2TP) Products Tanker** Double Hull (13F) Liq: 36,692; Liq (Oil): 37,413 Compartments: 10 Wing Ta, ER, 2 Wing Slop Ta 10 Cargo Pump (s): 10x500m³/hr Manifold: Bow/CM: 84.9m Ice Capable	**1 oil engine** geared to sc. shaft driving 1 CP propeller Total Power: 8,340kW (11,339hp) 15.1kn MAN-B&W 6L58/64 1 x 4 Stroke 6 Cy. 580 x 640 8340kW (11339bhp) AuxGen: 3 x 960kW 400/230V 50Hz a.c, 1 x 1120kW a.c Thrusters: 1 Thwart. CP thruster (f)
8014411 **SEARCH** *LARE4* - *ex* Polar Search *-2007* *ex* Mobil Search *-1993* **Exploration Vessel Resources AS** GC Rieber Shipping AS SatCom: Inmarsat C 425871010 *Bergen* *Norway (NIS)* MMSI: 258710000 Official number: N01261	**4,084** 1,226 1,442	Class: NV (AB)	**1982-06 Mitsubishi Heavy Industries Ltd. — Shimonoseki** Yd No: 837 Loa 98.51 (BB) Br ex - Dght 5.360 Lbp 89.01 Br md 15.41 Dpth 7.95 Welded, 2 dks	**(B31A2SR) Research Survey Vessel** Bale: 316 Ice Capable	**4 oil engines** with clutches, flexible couplings & dr geared to sc. shafts driving 2 CP propellers Total Power: 7,062kW (9,602hp) 17.3kn Daihatsu 6DSM-28 2 x 4 Stroke 6 Cy. 280 x 340 each-1324kW (1800bhp) Daihatsu Diesel Manufacturing Co Lt-Japan Daihatsu 8DSM-32 2 x 4 Stroke 8 Cy. 320 x 380 each-2207kW (3001bhp) Daihatsu Diesel Manufacturing Co Lt-Japan AuxGen: 2 x 2200kW 460V 60Hz a.c, 2 x 1200kW 460V 60Hz a.c Thrusters: 1 Thwart. CP thruster (f) Fuel: 1030.0 (d.f.) 32.0pd
7807433 **SEARCHER** - - **Aquashield Oil & Marine Services Ltd** - *Nigeria*	**171** 34 -		**1979-08 Brooke Marine Ltd. — Lowestoft** Yd No: 423 Loa 32.87 Br ex 6.33 Dght 1.524 Lbp 30.48 Br md 6.10 Dpth 3.61 Welded, 1 dk	**(B34H2SQ) Patrol Vessel**	**2 oil engines** reverse reduction geared to sc. shafts driving 2 FP propellers Total Power: 2,978kW (4,048hp) Paxman 12YJCM 2 x Vee 4 Stroke 12 Cy. 197 x 216 each-1489kW (2024bhp) Paxman Diesels Ltd.-Colchester
8717491 **SEARCHER** *MKJF6* BF 205 *ex* Philip Borum *-1999* **Tarlair Fishing Co Ltd** - SatCom: Inmarsat C 423200050 *Banff* *United Kingdom* MMSI: 235003110 Official number: B10135	**227** 78		**1988-12 James N. Miller & Sons Ltd. — St. Monans** Yd No: 1036 Loa 23.71 Br ex 7.42 Dght - Lbp 21.21 Br md 7.36 Dpth 2.98 Welded, 2 dks	**(B11A2FS) Stern Trawler** Ins: 170	**1 oil engine** with clutches, flexible couplings & sr geared to sc. shaft driving 1 CP propeller Total Power: 459kW (624hp) Caterpillar 3412TA 1 x Vee 4 Stroke 12 Cy. 137 x 152 459kW (624bhp) Caterpillar Inc-USA
8981884 **SEARCHER** *WDA6100* - *ex* Isle of June *-2002* **Medical Foundation for the Study of the Environment & the Human Body** - *Honolulu, HI* *United States of America* MMSI: 366828690 Official number: 1103056	**197** 59 -	Class: (AB)	**2000-12 Rodriguez Boat Builders, Inc. — Coden, Al** Yd No: 192 Loa - Br ex - Dght - Lbp 24.68 Br md 7.92 Dpth 3.65 Welded, 1 dk	**(X11A2YP) Yacht**	**2 oil engines** reverse reduction geared to sc. shafts driving 2 Propellers Total Power: 358kW (486hp) 11.0kn Caterpillar 3406TA 2 x 4 Stroke 6 Cy. 137 x 165 each-179kW (243bhp) Caterpillar Inc-USA AuxGen: 2 x 60kW
9234800 **SEARCHER** *ZQNK9* - **Government of The United Kingdom (Home Office Border Force, Maritime & Aviation Operations)** - *United Kingdom* MMSI: 235081000	**238** 71 -	Class: (LR) ✠ 10/01	**2001-10 Scheepswerf Made B.V. — Made** (Hull) Yd No: 00029 **2001-10 B.V. Scheepswerf Damen — Gorinchem** Yd No: 549853 Loa 42.80 Br ex - Dght 2.100 Lbp 38.30 Br md 6.80 Dpth 3.77 Welded, 1 dk	**(B34H2SQ) Patrol Vessel**	**2 oil engines** reduction geared to sc. shafts driving 2 CP propellers Total Power: 4,176kW (5,678hp) 24.0kn Caterpillar 3516B-TA 2 x Vee 4 Stroke 16 Cy. 170 x 190 each-2088kW (2839bhp) Caterpillar Inc-USA
8914831 **SEAROAD MERSEY** *VJBA* - **Commonwealth Bank of Australia** SeaRoad Shipping Pty Ltd *Devonport, Tas* *Australia* MMSI: 503000035 Official number: 853962	**7,928** 2,378 4,824 T/cm 19.2	Class: NV	**1991-04 Singmarine Dockyard & Engineering Pte Ltd — Singapore** Yd No: 178 Lengthened-1996 Loa 119.39 (BB) Br ex 18.52 Dght 5.512 Lbp 109.35 Br md 18.50 Dpth 13.60 Welded, 2 dk	**(A35A2RR) Ro-Ro Cargo Ship** Stern door/ramp Len: 8.00 Wid: 9.00 Swl: 100 Stern door/ramp Len: 6.00 Wid: 4.00 Swl: 50 Lane-Len: 350 Lane-Wid: 3.00 Lane-clr ht: 7.00 Cars: 28, Trailers: 30 TEU 186	**2 oil engines** sr geared to sc. shafts driving 2 CP propellers Total Power: 6,556kW (8,914hp) 15.5kn Wartsila 8R32E 2 x 4 Stroke 8 Cy. 320 x 350 each-3278kW (4457bhp) Wartsila Diesel Oy-Finland AuxGen: 2 x 680kW 440V 60Hz a.c, 1 x 550kW 440V 60Hz a.c Thrusters: 1 Thwart. CP thruster (f) Fuel: 47.0 (d.f.) 461.0 (r.f.) 24.0pd
8917429 **SEAROAD TAMAR** *VNGO* - **Commonwealth Bank of Australia** SeaRoad Shipping Pty Ltd *Launceston, Tas* *Australia* MMSI: 503000039 Official number: 854168	**13,965** 4,189 9,958	Class: NV	**1991-06 Carrington Slipways Pty Ltd — Newcastle NSW** Yd No: 212 Loa 147.00 (BB) Br ex 23.03 Dght 6.614 Lbp 135.00 Br md 23.00 Dpth 14.70 Welded, 2 dks	**(A35A2RR) Ro-Ro Cargo Ship** Stern door/ramp (p) Len: 5.20 Wid: 7.50 Swl: - Stern door/ramp (s) Len: 8.00 Wid: 7.50 Swl: - Lane-Len: 925 Lane-clr ht: 7.00 Trailers: 59 TEU 340 incl 40 ref C.	**2 oil engines** with clutches, flexible couplings & sr geared to sc. shafts driving 2 CP propellers Total Power: 9,920kW (13,488hp) 16.5kn MaK 8M552C 2 x 4 Stroke 8 Cy. 450 x 520 each-4960kW (6744bhp) Krupp MaK Maschinenbau GmbH-Kiel Thrusters: 1 Thwart. CP thruster (f)
9274501 **SEAROSE FPSO** *VOXS* - *ex* Sea Rose Fpso *-2004* **Husky Oil Operations Ltd** - *St John's, NL* *Canada* MMSI: 316317000 Official number: 824325	**95,887** 40,132 139,950	Class: NV	**2004-02 Samsung Heavy Industries Co Ltd — Geoje** Yd No: 1424 Loa 272.00 Br ex - Dght 18.600 Lbp 258.78 Br md 46.00 Dpth 26.60 Welded, 1 dk	**(B22E2OF) FPSO, Oil** Double Hull (13F) Liq: 148,226; Liq (Oil): 148,226 Compartments: 12 Wing Ta, 2 Wing Slop Ta, ER 3 Cargo Pump (s): 3x4000m³/hr Ice Capable	**2 oil engines** geared to sc. shafts driving 2 CP propellers Total Power: 15,600kW (21,210hp) 12.5kn Wartsila 8L46B 2 x 4 Stroke 8 Cy. 460 x 580 each-7800kW (10605bhp) Wartsila Finland Oy-Finland AuxGen: 2 x 2430kW 60Hz a.c Fuel: 3700.0 (d.f.) 58.3pd
9506540 **SEARUBY** *5BGD3* - *ex* Mell Shepherd *-2013* *launched as* Searuby *-2012* **Chiamo Island Shipping Co Ltd** Marlow Navigation Co Ltd *Limassol* *Cyprus* MMSI: 209660000	**15,636** 6,717 16,866	Class: GL	**2012-03 AVIC Weihai Shipyard Co Ltd — Weihai SD** Yd No: SN325 Loa 160.86 (BB) Br ex - Dght 9.900 Lbp 151.00 Br md 25.00 Dpth 13.90 Welded, 1 dk	**(A33A2CC) Container Ship (Fully Cellular)** TEU 1304 C Ho 492 TEU C Dk 812 TEU incl 258 ref C. Cranes: 2x45t Ice Capable	**1 oil engine** driving 1 FP propeller Total Power: 13,560kW (18,436hp) 19.0kn MAN-B&W 6S60MC-C 1 x 2 Stroke 6 Cy. 600 x 2400 13560kW (18436bhp) Hyundai Heavy Industries Co Ltd-South Korea AuxGen: 3 x 960kW 450V a.c Thrusters: 1 Tunnel thruster (f)

9500871 *T2KR3* -	**SEASAFE SALVO** **Workboats 1 Ltd** Go Offshore Pty Ltd *Funafuti* *Tuvalu* Official number: 30340914	**2,042** 612 1,624	Class: AB	**2010-03 Taishan Winde Shipbuilding Co Ltd — Taishan GD** Yd No: 0704 Loa 61.20 Br ex - Dght 4.500 Lbp 58.40 Br md 16.00 Dpth 6.00 Welded, 1 dk	**(B34L2QU) Utility Vessel**	**2 oil engines** reduction geared to sc. shafts driving 2 Propellers Total Power: 2,942kW (4,000hp) Niigata 6L26HLX 2 x 4 Stroke 6 Cy. 260 x 350 each-1471kW (2000bhp) Niigata Engineering Co Ltd-Japan AuxGen: 2 x 410kW a.c Thrusters: 1 Tunnel thruster (f)
9500869 *V3MF9* -	**SEASAFE SUPPORTER** **Koi Marine Ltd** Go Offshore (Asia) Pte Ltd SatCom: Inmarsat C 431204610 *Belize City* *Belize* MMSI: 312046000 Official number: 130920811	**2,150** 645 1,624	Class: AB	**2009-03 Taishan Winde Shipbuilding Co Ltd — Taishan GD** Yd No: 0703 Loa 61.20 Br ex - Dght 4.500 Lbp 58.40 Br md 16.00 Dpth 6.00 Welded, 1 dk	**(B22A2OR) Offshore Support Vessel** Cranes: 1x45t	**2 oil engines** geared to sc. shafts driving 2 FP propellers Total Power: 2,942kW (4,000hp) 12.5kn Niigata 6L26HLX 2 x 4 Stroke 6 Cy. 260 x 350 each-1471kW (2000bhp) Niigata Engineering Co Ltd-Japan AuxGen: 2 x 410kW a.c Thrusters: 1 Tunnel thruster (f) Fuel: 490.0
7340617 *9WEU2* -	**SEASAFE SYNERGY** *ex* Seabulk Takzim *-2010* *ex* Seabulk Freedom *-2005* *ex* GMMOS Freedom *-1997* *ex* Valle Bianca *-1993* *ex* Wimpey Sealion *-1985* **Amsbach Marine (M) Sdn Bhd** Nautika Sdn Bhd *Port Klang* *Malaysia* MMSI: 533001400 Official number: 329993	**1,532** 459 1,494	Class: BV (LR) (RI) ✠ Classed LR until 4/86	**1973-11 Appledore Shipbuilders Ltd — Bideford** Yd No: A.S. 96 Loa 59.01 Br ex 12.76 Dght 5.269 Lbp 53.93 Br md 12.50 Dpth 6.05 Welded, 1 dk	**(B21B20A) Anchor Handling Tug Supply** Passengers: berths: 12 Derricks: 1x5t Ice Capable	**2 oil engines** with clutches, flexible couplings & sr geared to sc. shafts driving 2 CP propellers Total Power: 3,310kW (4,500hp) 14.0kn Alpha 18V23HU 2 x Vee 4 Stroke 18 Cy. 225 x 300 each-1655kW (2250bhp) Alpha Diesel A/S-Denmark AuxGen: 3 x 200kW 440V 60Hz a.c Thrusters: 1 Thwart. FP thruster (f) Fuel: 548.5 (d.f.)
9629550 *9HA3228* -	**SEASALVIA** **Blue Waves Marine SA** Thenamaris (Ships Management) Inc SatCom: Inmarsat C 422931911 *Valletta* *Malta* MMSI: 229319000 Official number: 9629550	**29,925** 13,626 50,908 T/cm 52.0	Class: AB	**2013-01 STX Offshore & Shipbuilding Co Ltd — Changwon (Jinhae Shipyard)** Yd No: 1532 Loa 183.00 (BB) Br ex 32.23 Dght 13.100 Lbp 173.90 Br md 32.20 Dpth 19.10 Welded, 1 dk	**(A12B2TR) Chemical/Products Tanker** Double Hull (13F) Liq: 52,209; Liq (Oil): 52,170 Cargo Heating Coils Compartments: 6 Wing Ta, 6 Wing Ta, 1 Wing Slop Ta, 1 Wing Slop Ta, ER 12 Cargo Pump (s): 12x600m³/hr Manifold: Bow/CM: 91.9m	**1 oil engine** driving 1 FP propeller Total Power: 9,019kW (12,262hp) 14.5kn MAN-B&W 6S50ME-C8 1 x 2 Stroke 6 Cy. 500 x 2000 9019kW (12262bhp) STX Engine Co Ltd-South Korea AuxGen: 3 x 740kW a.c Fuel: 443.0 (d.f.) 1291.0 (r.f.)
9255660 *9HSM7* -	**SEASCOUT** **Valiant Sailor Marine Inc** Thenamaris (Ships Management) Inc *Valletta* *Malta* MMSI: 215535000 Official number: 8503	**57,301** 32,526 105,330 T/cm 92.0	Class: LR ✠ **100A1** SS 01/2014 Double Hull oil tanker ESP *IWS SPM LI **ShipRight** (SDA, FDA Plus, CM) ✠ **LMC** **UMS IGS** Eq.Ltr: T†; Cable: 715.0/87.0 U3 (a)	**2004-01 Hyundai Samho Heavy Industries Co Ltd — Samho** Yd No: S172 Loa 244.00 (BB) Br ex 42.03 Dght 14.900 Lbp 234.00 Br md 42.00 Dpth 21.00 Welded, 1 dk	**(A13A2TW) Crude/Oil Products Tanker** Double Hull (13F) Liq: 115,604; Liq (Oil): 118,080 Cargo Heating Coils Compartments: 12 Wing Ta, 2 Wing Slop Ta, ER 3 Cargo Pump (s): 3x3000m³/hr Manifold: Bow/CM: 122.8m	**1 oil engine** driving 1 FP propeller Total Power: 11,344kW (15,423hp) 14.5kn B&W 6S60MC 1 x 2 Stroke 6 Cy. 600 x 2292 11344kW (15423bhp) Hyundai Heavy Industries Co Ltd-South Korea AuxGen: 3 x 730kW 440/220V 60Hz a.c Boilers: e (ex.g.) 8.2kgf/cm² (8.0bar), WTAuxB (o.f.) 18.2kgf/cm² (17.8bar) Fuel: 195.0 (d.f.) (Heating Coils) 2417.0 (r.f.)
9304368 *VRCA7* -	**SEASENATOR** **Reliance Finance Co Ltd** Valles Steamship (Canada) Inc *Hong Kong* *Hong Kong* MMSI: 477607200 Official number: HK-1740	**56,489** 32,667 105,715 T/cm 90.0	Class: AB	**2007-01 Namura Shipbuilding Co Ltd — Imari SG** Yd No: 262 Loa 241.03 (BB) Br ex - Dght 14.930 Lbp 233.29 Br md 42.00 Dpth 21.20 Welded, 1 dk	**(A13A2TV) Crude Oil Tanker** Double Hull (13F) Liq: 113,300; Liq (Oil): 122,268 Compartments: 12 Wing Ta, 2 Wing Slop Ta, ER 3 Cargo Pump (s): 3x2500m³/hr Manifold: Bow/CM: 119m	**1 oil engine** driving 1 FP propeller Total Power: 12,240kW (16,642hp) 15.3kn MAN-B&W 6S60MC 1 x 2 Stroke 6 Cy. 600 x 2292 12240kW (16642bhp) Hitachi Zosen Corp-Japan AuxGen: 3 x 600kW a.c Fuel: 239.0 (d.f.) 2725.5 (r.f.)
9298193 *DEIG* -	**SEASHARK** **tms 'Seashark' GmbH & Co KG** German Tanker Shipping GmbH & Co KG *Bremen* *Germany* MMSI: 211135000 Official number: 4906	**21,329** 8,370 32,302 T/cm 42.0	Class: GL	**2004-10 Lindenau GmbH Schiffswerft u. Maschinenfabrik — Kiel** Yd No: 270 Loa 177.78 (BB) Br ex 28.03 Dght 11.000 Lbp 168.00 Br md 28.00 Dpth 16.80 Welded, 1 dk	**(A13B2TP) Products Tanker** Double Hull (13F) Liq: 36,664; Liq (Oil): 36,664 Compartments: 10 Wing Ta, 2 Wing Slop Ta, ER 10 Cargo Pump (s): 10x500m³/hr Manifold: Bow/CM: 85m Ice Capable	**1 oil engine** geared to sc. shaft driving 1 CP propeller Total Power: 8,340kW (11,339hp) 15.1kn MAN-B&W 6L58/64 1 x 4 Stroke 6 Cy. 580 x 640 8340kW (11339bhp) MAN B&W Diesel AG-Augsburg AuxGen: 1 x 1120kW 400/230V a.c, 3 x 960kW 400/230V a.c Thrusters: 1 Tunnel thruster (f)
8230314 *XUBP4* -	**SEASHELL** *ex* Volgo-Balt 201 *-2010* **Seashell Shipping Ltd** MD Shipping Co *Phnom Penh* *Cambodia* MMSI: 515325000 Official number: 1077612	**2,457** 1,191 2,893	Class: UA (RS) (RR)	**1977 Zavody Tazkeho Strojarstva (ZTS) — Komarno** Yd No: 1930 Loa 113.87 Br ex 13.20 Dght 3.640 Lbp 110.00 Br md 13.01 Dpth 5.50 Welded, 1 dk	**(A31A2GX) General Cargo Ship** Grain: 4,720 Compartments: 4 Ho, ER 4 Ha: (18.6 x 11.2)2 (18.8 x 11.2) (20.3 x 11.2)ER	**2 oil engines** driving 2 FP propellers Total Power: 1,030kW (1,400hp) 10.0kn Skoda 6L275A2 2 x 4 Stroke 6 Cy. 275 x 350 each-515kW (700bhp) Skoda-Praha Fuel: 110.0 (d.f.)
5219541 *DUTL2* -	**SEASIA 1** *ex* Philippine Sea *-2006* *ex* China Sea *-1978* *ex* Maria Aurora II *-1976* **Mamsar Construction & Industrial Corp** - *Cagayan de Oro* *Philippines* Official number: 0000033	*293* 110 -	Class: (LR) Eq.Ltr: (f) ; ✠ Classed LR until 5/4/07	**1938-08 Scott & Sons — Bowling** Yd No: 348 Loa 39.17 Br ex 9.89 Dght 3.861 Lbp 36.66 Br md 9.45 Dpth 4.27 Riveted	**(B32A2ST) Tug** Winches: 1	**1 oil engine** sr reverse geared to sc. shaft driving 1 FP propeller Total Power: 919kW (1,249hp) 10.0kn Mirrlees KSSDM-6 1 x 4 Stroke 6 Cy. 381 x 457 919kW (1249bhp) (new engine 1962) Mirrlees, Bickerton & Day-Stockport AuxGen: 2 x 20kW 220V d.c, 1 x 13kW 220V d.c
9070943 *DUTN6* -	**SEASIA 4** *ex* Kowa 9210 *-2006* **Mamsar Construction & Industrial Corp** - *Cagayan de Oro* *Philippines* Official number: 10-0000036	**126** 38 -	Class: (AB)	**1992-11 P.T. Kacaba Marga Marina — Batam** Yd No: 36 Loa - Br ex - Dght 2.257 Lbp 21.38 Br md 7.49 Dpth 3.20 Welded, 1 dk	**(B32A2ST) Tug**	**2 oil engines** reverse reduction geared to sc. shafts driving 2 FP propellers Total Power: 740kW (1,006hp) 10.0kn Caterpillar 3412TA 2 x Vee 4 Stroke 12 Cy. 137 x 152 each-370kW (503bhp) Caterpillar Inc-USA AuxGen: 2 x 36kW a.c
8843551 *DUTR2* -	**SEASIA 201** *ex* Scorpio *-2007* **Mamsar Construction & Industrial Corp** - *Cagayan de Oro* *Philippines* Official number: 10-0000032	**941** 282 1,680	Class: (LR) Classed LR until 17/10/01	**1978-05 Dynamarine Corp. — Bauan** Converted From: General Cargo Barge, Non-propelled-2006 Loa 59.10 Br ex 15.55 Dght 2.740 Lbp - Br md 15.54 Dpth 3.35 Welded, 1 dk	**(A35D2RL) Landing Craft** Compartments: 4 Ho	**2 oil engines** driving 2 FP propellers Total Power: 662kW (900hp) 8.0kn Cummins 2 x 4 Stroke each-331kW (450bhp) (new engine 2006) Cummins Engine Co Inc-USA
9632820 *9HA3361* -	**SEASMILE** **Quick Star Marine SA** Thenamaris (Ships Management) Inc *Valletta* *Malta* MMSI: 229474000 Official number: 9632820	**52,467** 29,753 51,020	Class: LR ✠ **100A1** SS 08/2013 container ship **ShipRight** (SDA,FDA Plus,CM,ACS (B)) CCSA *IWS LI EP (Bt,Ede,I) ✠ **LMC** **UMS** Eq.Ltr: V†; Cable: 715.0/92.0 U3 (a)	**2013-08 Hyundai Samho Heavy Industries Co Ltd — Samho** Yd No: S616 Loa 255.40 (BB) Br ex 37.43 Dght 13.500 Lbp 242.00 Br md 37.00 Dpth 22.10 Welded, 1 dk	**(A33A2CC) Container Ship (Fully Cellular)** TEU 5071 C Ho 1982 TEU C Dk 3089 TEU incl 770 ref C Compartments: 7 Cell Ho, ER	**1 oil engine** driving 1 FP propeller Total Power: 24,800kW (33,718hp) 21.5kn MAN-B&W 6G80ME-C9 1 x 2 Stroke 6 Cy. 800 x 3720 24800kW (33718bhp) Hyundai Heavy Industries Co Ltd-South Korea AuxGen: 4 x 2300kW 450V 60Hz a.c Boilers: e (ex.g.) 12.2kgf/cm² (12.0bar), AuxB (o.f.) 9.2kgf/cm² (9.0bar) Thrusters: 1 Thwart. CP thruster (f)
8941341 *WCY5538* -	**SEASNAIL** **Jonathan Claypool** - *Eureka, CA* *United States of America* MMSI: 338769000 Official number: 1057008	*123* 98 -		**1997 Seasnail — Fields Landing, Ca** L reg 22.77 Br ex - Dght - Lbp - Br md 6.95 Dpth 3.29 Welded, 1 dk	**(B11B2FV) Fishing Vessel**	**1 oil engine** driving 1 FP propeller

IMO / Call sign / Flag	Name / Owner / Manager	Tonnage	Class	Builder / Dimensions	Type	Machinery
9290438 *9HBP8* -	**SEASONG** **Rose Navigation Ltd** Thenamaris (Ships Management) Inc *Valletta* Malta MMSI: 215811000 Official number: 9294	**57,162** 32,768 105,472 T/cm 92.0	Class: AB	**2005-03 Hyundai Heavy Industries Co Ltd — Ulsan** Yd No: 1569 Loa 244.00 (BB) Br ex 42.03 Dght 14.900 Lbp 234.00 Br md 42.00 Dpth 21.00 Welded, 1 dk	**(A13A2TW) Crude/Oil Products Tanker** Double Hull (13F) Liq: 118,281; Liq (Oil): 120,695 Cargo Heating Coils Compartments: 12 Wing Ta, 2 Wing Slop Ta, ER 3 Cargo Pump (s): 3x300m³/hr Manifold: Bow/CM: 121.9m Ice Capable	**1 oil engine** driving 1 FP propeller Total Power: 11,323kW (15,395hp) 14.6kn B&W 6S60MC 1 x 2 Stroke 6 Cy. 600 x 2292 11323kW (15395bhp) Hyundai Heavy Industries Co Ltd-South Korea AuxGen: 3 x 660kW a.c Fuel: 176.0 (d.f.) 2773.0 (r.f.)
7434808 *CZ5656* -	**SEASPAN CAVALIER** **Seaspan ULC** - *Vancouver, BC* Canada MMSI: 316003659 Official number: 369522	*149* 15 -		**1975-03 Vancouver Shipyards Co Ltd — North Vancouver BC** Yd No: 53 Loa 25.23 Br ex - Dght - Lbp 23.63 Br md 7.55 Dpth 3.89 Welded, 1 dk	**(B32A2ST) Tug**	**2 oil engines** geared to sc. shafts driving 2 FP propellers Total Power: 1,176kW (1,598hp) 12.0kn G.M. (Detroit Diesel) 12V-149-TI 2 x Vee 2 Stroke 12 Cy. 146 x 146 each-588kW (799bhp) Detroit Diesel-Detroit, Mi
7017789 *VDLT* -	**SEASPAN CHALLENGER** *ex* Hecate Crown *-1985* **Seaspan ULC** - *Vancouver, BC* Canada MMSI: 316003900 Official number: 344602	**486** 145 295	Class: LR ✠ **100A1** SS 03/2011 tug ✠ **LMC** Eq.Ltr: (g) ; Cable: U2	**1970-07 Star Shipyards (Mercer's) Ltd — New Westminster BC** Yd No: 399 Loa 40.59 Br ex 10.22 Dght 4.903 Lbp 36.05 Br md 9.77 Dpth 5.39 Welded, 1 dk	**(B32A2ST) Tug**	**1 oil engine** sr reverse geared to sc. shaft driving 1 FP propeller Total Power: 2,648kW (3,600hp) 15.0kn EMD (Electro-Motive) 20-645-E5 1 x Vee 2 Stroke 20 Cy. 230 x 254 2648kW (3600bhp) General Motors Corp-USA AuxGen: 2 x 75kW 460V 60Hz a.c Fuel: 294.5 (d.f.)
7041235 *VDPS* -	**SEASPAN CHAMPION** *ex* Island Champion *-1971* **Seaspan ULC** - *Vancouver, BC* Canada MMSI: 316003661 Official number: 344714	*150* 6 -		**1970 Benson Bros Shipbuilding Co (1960) Ltd — Vancouver BC** Yd No: 30 Loa 27.13 Br ex 7.32 Dght - Lbp 24.67 Br md 6.71 Dpth 4.27 Welded, 1 dk	**(B32A2ST) Tug** 1 Ha: (1.2 x 0.9)	**1 oil engine** driving 1 CP propeller Total Power: 1,066kW (1,449hp) 12.0kn EMD (Electro-Motive) 8-645-E6 1 x Vee 2 Stroke 8 Cy. 230 x 254 1066kW (1449bhp) General Motors Corp.Electro-Motive Div.-La Grange AuxGen: 2 x 50kW 120/208V 60Hz a.c Fuel: 101.5 (d.f.)
6704866 *CY8261* -	**SEASPAN CHIEF** *ex* Island Chief *-1972* **Seaspan ULC** - *Victoria, BC* Canada MMSI: 316003662 Official number: 327101	*149* 12 -		**1966 McKay-Cormack Ltd — Victoria BC** Yd No: 68 Loa 26.52 Br ex 7.42 Dght 4.115 Lbp 25.91 Br md 7.01 Dpth 4.17 Welded, 1 dk	**(B32A2ST) Tug**	**1 oil engine** driving 1 FP propeller Total Power: 883kW (1,201hp) 12.0kn EMD (Electro-Motive) 12-567-BC 1 x Vee 2 Stroke 12 Cy. 216 x 254 883kW (1201bhp) General Motors Corp-USA AuxGen: 2 x 30kW 110/208V 60Hz a.c Fuel: 75.0 (d.f.)
9224312 *VRBH3* -	**SEASPAN CHIWAN** *ex* CSCL Chiwan *-2013* **Seaspan Corp** Seaspan Ship Management Ltd *Hong Kong* Hong Kong MMSI: 477014500 Official number: HK-1583	**39,941** 24,458 50,488 T/cm 70.0	Class: NV (LR) ✠ Classed LR until 20/9/01	**2001-09 Samsung Heavy Industries Co Ltd — Geoje** Yd No: 1343 Loa 259.80 (BB) Br ex 32.35 Dght 12.600 Lbp 244.80 Br md 32.25 Dpth 19.30 Welded, 1 dk	**(A33A2CC) Container Ship (Fully Cellular)** TEU 4253 C Ho 1584 TEU C Dk 2669 TEU incl 400 ref C. Compartments: ER, 7 Cell Ho 14 Ha: ER	**1 oil engine** driving 1 FP propeller Total Power: 36,515kW (49,646hp) 23.3kn B&W 8K90MC-C 1 x 2 Stroke 8 Cy. 900 x 2300 36515kW (49646bhp) Doosan Engine Co Ltd-South Korea AuxGen: 4 x 1680kW 450V 60Hz a.c Boilers: AuxB (Comp) 8.0kgf/cm² (7.8bar) Thrusters: 1 Thwart. FP thruster (f)
7043336 *VCZQ* -	**SEASPAN COMMANDER** *ex* Evco Buccaneer *-2013* *ex* Seaspan Commander *-1976* *ex* Le Beau *-1971* **Seaspan ULC** - *Vancouver, BC* Canada Official number: 345111	*148* 9 -		**1970 Star Shipyards (Mercer's) Ltd — New Westminster BC** Yd No: 400 Loa 25.84 Br ex 7.78 Dght 3.404 Lbp 24.08 Br md 7.47 Dpth 4.20 Welded, 1 dk	**(B32A2ST) Tug**	**2 oil engines** geared to sc. shafts driving 2 CP propellers Total Power: 1,500kW (2,040hp) 14.0kn Caterpillar D398TA 2 x Vee 4 Stroke 12 Cy. 159 x 203 each-750kW (1020bhp) Caterpillar Tractor Co-USA AuxGen: 2 x 50kW 120/208V 60Hz a.c Fuel: 69.0 (d.f.)
7343683 *CZ5530* -	**SEASPAN COMMODORE** **Seaspan ULC** - *Vancouver, BC* Canada MMSI: 316004100 Official number: 369068	**667** 200 467	Class: LR ✠ **100A1** SS 12/2011 tug ✠ **LMC** Eq.Ltr: J; Cable: U2	**1974-11 Vancouver Shipyards Co Ltd — North Vancouver BC** Yd No: 48 Loa 43.92 (BB) Br ex 11.41 Dght 5.800 Lbp 39.22 Br md 10.93 Dpth 6.20 Welded, 1 dk	**(B32A2ST) Tug**	**2 oil engines** reverse reduction geared to sc. shafts driving 2 FP propellers Total Power: 4,230kW (5,752hp) 14.5kn EMD (Electro-Motive) 16-645-E6 2 x Vee 2 Stroke 16 Cy. 230 x 254 each-2115kW (2876bhp) General Motors Corp-USA AuxGen: 2 x 125kW 480V 60Hz a.c
7434779 *CZ6447* -	**SEASPAN CORSAIR** **Seaspan ULC** - *Vancouver, BC* Canada MMSI: 316003663 Official number: 370217	*149* 14 -		**1975-09 Vancouver Shipyards Co Ltd — North Vancouver BC** Yd No: 63 Loa 25.23 Br ex 7.57 Dght 3.887 Lbp 23.63 Br md 7.55 Dpth 4.25 Welded, 1 dk	**(B32A2ST) Tug**	**2 oil engines** reverse reduction geared to sc. shafts driving 2 FP propellers Total Power: 1,176kW (1,598hp) 12.0kn G.M. (Detroit Diesel) 12V-149-TI 2 x Vee 2 Stroke 12 Cy. 146 x 146 each-588kW (799bhp) Detroit Diesel-Detroit, Mi
7343671 *CZ3943* -	**SEASPAN CRUSADER** **Seaspan ULC** - *Vancouver, BC* Canada MMSI: 316003665 Official number: 348499	*148* 15 -		**1974-02 Vancouver Shipyards Co Ltd — North Vancouver BC** Yd No: 47 Loa 25.46 Br ex 7.83 Dght 3.633 Lbp 23.63 Br md 7.42 Dpth 3.89 Welded, 2 dks	**(B32A2ST) Tug**	**2 oil engines** geared to sc. shafts driving 2 FP propellers Total Power: 1,176kW (1,598hp) G.M. (Detroit Diesel) 12V-149-TI 2 x Vee 2 Stroke 12 Cy. 146 x 146 each-588kW (799bhp) Detroit Diesel-Detroit, Mi
7434781 *CFN6638* -	**SEASPAN CUTLASS** **Seaspan ULC** - *Vancouver, BC* Canada MMSI: 316003666 Official number: 370250	*149* 14 -		**1975-11 Vancouver Shipyards Co Ltd — North Vancouver BC** Yd No: 64 Loa 25.23 Br ex 7.57 Dght 3.861 Lbp 23.60 Br md 7.55 Dpth 4.25 Welded, 1 dk	**(B32A2ST) Tug**	**2 oil engines** reduction geared to sc. shaft (s) driving 2 FP propellers Total Power: 1,268kW (1,724hp) 12.0kn Cummins KTA-38-M0 2 x Vee 4 Stroke 12 Cy. 159 x 159 each-634kW (862bhp) (new engine 2013) Cummins Engine Co Inc-USA
9227027 *VRBH4* -	**SEASPAN DALIAN** *ex* CSCL Dalian *-2012* **Seaspan Corp** Seaspan Ship Management Ltd *Hong Kong* Hong Kong MMSI: 477014600 Official number: HK-1584	**39,941** 24,458 50,789 T/cm 70.4	Class: NV (LR) ✠ Classed LR until 4/9/02	**2002-09 Samsung Heavy Industries Co Ltd — Geoje** Yd No: 1348 Loa 259.80 (BB) Br ex 32.35 Dght 12.600 Lbp 244.80 Br md 32.25 Dpth 19.30 Welded, 1 dk	**(A33A2CC) Container Ship (Fully Cellular)** TEU 4253 C Ho 1584 TEU C Dk 2669 TEU incl 400 ref C. Compartments: 7 Cell Ho, ER 7 Ha: ER	**1 oil engine** driving 1 FP propeller Total Power: 36,540kW (49,680hp) 23.3kn B&W 8K90MC-C 1 x 2 Stroke 8 Cy. 900 x 2300 36540kW (49680bhp) Doosan Engine Co Ltd-South Korea AuxGen: 4 x 1680kW 450/230V 60Hz a.c Thrusters: 1 Thwart. CP thruster (f)
8315827 *CY5559* -	**SEASPAN DISCOVERY** **Seaspan ULC** - *Vancouver, BC* Canada MMSI: 316003523 Official number: 804174	*435* 249 -		**1984-05 Vancouver Shipyards Co Ltd — North Vancouver BC** Yd No: 107 Loa 32.62 Br ex - Dght 3.441 Lbp 29.72 Br md 10.67 Dpth 3.97 Welded, 1 dk	**(B32A2ST) Tug**	**2 oil engines** gearing integral to driving 2 Z propellers Total Power: 2,648kW (3,600hp) Niigata 6L28BXE 2 x 4 Stroke 6 Cy. 280 x 320 each-1324kW (1800bhp) Niigata Engineering Co Ltd-Japan AuxGen: 2 x 75kW 460V 60Hz a.c Fuel: 160.5 (d.f.)
6801925 *VGTD* -	**SEASPAN DORIS** *ex* Doris Yorke *-1974* **Seaspan ULC** - *Victoria, BC* Canada MMSI: 316003655 Official number: 328327	*2,612* 1,287 2,000	Class: (AB)	**1968-04 Victoria Machinery Depot Co Ltd — Victoria BC** Yd No: 145 Loa 99.07 Br ex 17.28 Dght 3.353 Lbp 91.75 Br md 17.23 Dpth 5.72 Welded, 1 dk	**(A36A2PT) Passenger/Ro-Ro Ship (Vehicles/Rail)** Lorries: 42, Rail Wagons: 18	**4 oil engines** reverse reduction geared to sc. shafts driving 2 FP propellers Total Power: 1,472kW (2,000hp) 12.0kn Caterpillar D379TA 4 x Vee 4 Stroke 8 Cy. 159 x 203 each-368kW (500bhp) Caterpillar Tractor Co-USA AuxGen: 2 x 50kW Fuel: 180.0 (d.f.) 9.0pd
9432971 *CFN6642* -	**SEASPAN EAGLE** *ex* Seaspan Terminal IV *-2011* *ex* Ramparts 2800-4 *-2011* **Seaspan ULC** - *Vancouver, BC* Canada MMSI: 316020871 Official number: 835966	**441** 132 176	Class: AB	**2011-07 Pirlant Shipyard — Tuzla** Yd No: 16 Loa 28.20 Br ex - Dght 2.830 Lbp 26.17 Br md 12.60 Dpth 5.30 Welded, 1 dk	**(B32A2ST) Tug**	**2 oil engines** reduction geared to sc. shafts driving 2 Z propellers Total Power: 3,678kW (5,000hp) Caterpillar 3516B-HD 2 x Vee 4 Stroke 16 Cy. 170 x 215 each-1839kW (2500bhp) Caterpillar Inc-USA AuxGen: 2 x 96kW a.c

9072393 **SEASPAN FALCON** *189*
VG6987 42
\- **Seaspan ULC** 58
\-
Vancouver, BC *Canada*
MMSI: 316003667
Official number: 816602

1993-09 **Vancouver Shipyards Co Ltd — North Vancouver BC** Yd No: 133
Loa 25.45 Br ex 9.75 Dght 2.520
Lbp 18.90 Br md 9.14 Dpth 4.07
Welded, 1 dk

(B32A2ST) Tug

2 oil engines gearing integral to driving 2 Z propellers
Total Power: 2,354kW (3,200hp) 11.0kn
G.M. (Detroit Diesel) 16V-149-TI
2 x Vee 2 Stroke 16 Cy. 146 x 146 each-1177kW (1600bhp)
General Motors Detroit DieselAllison Divn-USA
AuxGen: 2 x 125kW 460V 60Hz a.c
Fuel: 50.0 (d.f.)

9227039 **SEASPAN FELIXSTOWE** **39,941** Class: NV (LR)
VRBH8 *ex* CSCL Felixstowe *-2012* 24,458 ✠ Classed LR until 16/10/02
\- **Seaspan Corp** 50,790
Seaspan Ship Management Ltd T/cm
Hong Kong *Hong Kong* 70.4
MMSI: 477020100
Official number: HK-1588

2002-10 **Samsung Heavy Industries Co Ltd — Geoje** Yd No: 1349
Loa 259.80 (BB) Br ex 32.35 Dght 12.600
Lbp 244.80 Br md 32.25 Dpth 19.30
Welded, 1 dk

(A33A2CC) Container Ship (Fully Cellular)
TEU 4253 C Ho 1584 TEU C Dk 2669 TEU incl 400 ref C.
Compartments: 7 Cell Ho, ER

1 oil engine driving 1 FP propeller
Total Power: 36,515kW (49,646hp) 23.3kn
B&W 8K90MC-C
1 x 2 Stroke 8 Cy. 900 x 2300 36515kW (49646bhp)
Doosan Engine Co Ltd-South Korea
AuxGen: 4 x 1680kW 450V 60Hz a.c
Boilers: AuxB (Comp) 8.0kgf/cm² (7.8bar)
Thrusters: 1 Thwart. CP thruster (f)

6420484 **SEASPAN GREG** *2,493* Class: (AB)
VGNK *ex* Greg Yorke *-1974* 1,232
\- **Seaspan ULC** -
\-
Vancouver, BC *Canada*
MMSI: 316003668
Official number: 323224

1964-03 **Allied Shipbuilders Ltd — North Vancouver BC** Yd No: 142
Loa 99.07 Br ex 17.28 Dght 3.858
Lbp 97.54 Br md 17.23 Dpth 5.72
Welded, 1 dk

(A36A2PT) Passenger/Ro-Ro Ship (Vehicles/Rail)
Trailers: 24

2 oil engines driving 2 FP propellers
Total Power: 1,454kW (1,976hp) 12.0kn
Caterpillar D399TA
2 x Vee 4 Stroke 16 Cy. 159 x 203 each-727kW (988bhp)
(new engine 1970)
Caterpillar Tractor Co-USA
Fuel: 180.0 (d.f.) 9.0pd

7414107 **SEASPAN GUARDIAN** *149*
CFN6634 *ex* Gulf Irene *-1978* 22
\- **Seaspan ULC** -
\-
Vancouver, BC *Canada*
MMSI: 316003669
Official number: 369175

1974-12 **Vito Steel Boat & Barge Construction Ltd — Delta BC** Yd No: 143
Loa 23.32 Br ex 7.32 Dght -
Lbp 22.26 Br md - Dpth 4.12
Welded, 1 dk

(B32A2ST) Tug

2 oil engines driving 2 FP propellers
Total Power: 1,066kW (1,450hp) 11.0kn
G.M. (Detroit Diesel) 12V-149
2 x Vee 2 Stroke 12 Cy. 146 x 146 each-533kW (725bhp)
General Motors Detroit DieselAllison Divn-USA

9224300 **SEASPAN HAMBURG** **39,941** Class: NV (LR)
VRBH6 *ex* CSAV Licanten *-2013* 24,458 ✠
\- *ex* CSCL Hamburg *-2010* 50,790
Seaspan Corp T/cm
Seaspan Ship Management Ltd 70.0
Hong Kong *Hong Kong*
MMSI: 477014800
Official number: HK-1586

2001-07 **Samsung Heavy Industries Co Ltd — Geoje** Yd No: 1342
Loa 259.80 (BB) Br ex 32.35 Dght 12.600
Lbp 244.80 Br md 32.25 Dpth 19.30
Welded, 1 dk

(A33A2CC) Container Ship (Fully Cellular)
TEU 4253 C Ho 1584 TEU C Dk 2669 TEU incl 400 ref C.
Compartments: ER, 7 Cell Ho
14 Ha: ER

1 oil engine driving 1 FP propeller
Total Power: 36,515kW (49,646hp) 23.3kn
B&W 8K90MC-C
1 x 2 Stroke 8 Cy. 900 x 2300 36515kW (49646bhp)
Doosan Engine Co Ltd-South Korea
AuxGen: 4 x 1680kW 450V 60Hz a.c
Thrusters: 1 Thwart. FP thruster (f)
Fuel: 235.0 (d.f.) 6106.0 (r.f.) 146.0pd

9072408 **SEASPAN HAWK** *189*
VG6972 42
\- **Seaspan ULC** 58
\-
Vancouver, BC *Canada*
MMSI: 316005715
Official number: 816601

1993-09 **Vancouver Shipyards Co Ltd — North Vancouver BC** Yd No: 132
Loa 25.45 Br ex 9.75 Dght 2.520
Lbp 18.90 Br md 9.14 Dpth 4.07
Welded, 1 dk

(B32A2ST) Tug

2 oil engines gearing integral to driving 2 Z propellers
Total Power: 2,354kW (3,200hp) 11.0kn
G.M. (Detroit Diesel) 16V-149-TI
2 x Vee 2 Stroke 16 Cy. 146 x 146 each-1177kW (1600bhp)
General Motors Detroit DieselAllison Divn-USA
AuxGen: 2 x 125kW 460V 60Hz a.c
Fuel: 50.0 (d.f.)

8881541 **SEASPAN III** **643** Class: (IR) (HR)
ATVU *ex* Irini *-1997* 193
\- **Seaspan Shipping Ltd** 595
Mumbai *India*
Official number: 2675

1990
Loa 50.26 Br ex 9.42 Dght 2.460
Lbp 45.70 Br md 9.40 Dpth 3.65
Welded, 1 dk

(A37B2PS) Passenger Ship

2 oil engines driving 2 FP propellers
Total Power: 1,472kW (2,002hp) 12.0kn
S.K.L. 6NVD48A-2U
2 x 4 Stroke 6 Cy. 320 x 480 each-736kW (1001bhp)
VEB Schwermaschinenbau "KarlLiebknecht" (SKL)-Magdeburg
AuxGen: 3 x 100kW 400V 50Hz a.c
Fuel: 48.0 (d.f.)

9623130 **SEASPAN KESTREL** **441** Class: AB
CFN6303 *ex* Sanmar Terminal VI *-2012* 132
\- **Seaspan ULC** 140
\-
Vancouver, BC *Canada*
MMSI: 316020869
Official number: 836505

2011-12 **Gemsan Gemi Insa ve Gemi Isletmeciligi San. Ltd. — Tuzla** Yd No: 54
Loa 25.00 Br ex - Dght 5.300
Lbp 20.00 Br md 12.60 Dpth 6.00
Welded, 1 dk

(B32A2ST) Tug

2 oil engines reduction geared to sc. shafts driving 2 Z propellers
Total Power: 4,700kW (6,390hp)
Caterpillar 3516C-HD
2 x Vee 4 Stroke 16 Cy. 170 x 215 each-2350kW (3195bhp)
Caterpillar Inc-USA
AuxGen: 2 x 96kW a.c
Fuel: 120.0 (d.f.)

6823052 **SEASPAN KING** *498* Class: LR
VGXJ *ex* Island King *-1971* 131 ✠ **100A1** SS 03/2009
\- **Seaspan ULC** - tug
\- **LMC**
Vancouver, BC *Canada* Eq.Ltr: g; Cable: U2
MMSI: 316003800
Official number: 330317

1968-10 **Star Shipyards (Mercer's) Ltd — New Westminster BC** Yd No: 392
Loa 40.59 Br ex 10.22 Dght 4.573
Lbp 36.05 Br md 9.77 Dpth 5.39
Welded, 1 dk

(B32A2ST) Tug

1 oil engine sr reverse geared to sc. shaft driving 1 FP propeller
Total Power: 2,648kW (3,600hp) 14.0kn
EMD (Electro-Motive) 20-645-E5
1 x Vee 2 Stroke 20 Cy. 230 x 254 2648kW (3600bhp)
General Motors Corp-USA
AuxGen: 2 x 75kW 460V 60Hz a.c
Fuel: 386.0 (d.f.)

5212385 **SEASPAN LORNE** *149*
\- *ex* Lorne Yorke *-1974* 43
\- **Seaspan ULC** -
\-
Vancouver, BC *Canada*
MMSI: 316003673
Official number: 313751

1961-04 **Star Shipyards (Mercer's) Ltd — New Westminster BC** Yd No: 352
Loa 28.20 Br ex 7.62 Dght 2.744
Lbp - Br md - Dpth -
Welded, 1 dk

(B32A2ST) Tug

2 oil engines driving 2 FP propellers
Total Power: 744kW (1,012hp)
Caterpillar D379TA
2 x Vee 4 Stroke 8 Cy. 159 x 203 each-372kW (506bhp)
Caterpillar Tractor Co-USA

7636028 **SEASPAN MONARCH** **376** Class: LR
CFK9611 *ex* Jervis Crown *-1994* 112 ✠ **100A1** SS 06/2012
\- **Seaspan ULC** - tug
\- ✠ **LMC**
Vancouver, BC *Canada* Eq.Ltr: H; Cable: 330.0/28.0 U2
MMSI: 316004500
Official number: 383384

1977-11 **John Manly Shipyard Ltd — Vancouver BC** Yd No: 527
Loa 35.06 Br ex 9.53 Dght 4.104
Lbp 31.58 Br md 9.15 Dpth 4.83
Welded, 1 dk

(B32A2ST) Tug

2 oil engines sr geared to sc. shafts driving 2 FP propellers
Total Power: 1,942kW (2,640hp)
Nohab F26R
2 x 4 Stroke 6 Cy. 250 x 300 each-971kW (1320bhp)
AB Bofors NOHAB-Sweden
AuxGen: 2 x 95kW 460V 60Hz a.c

7043324 **SEASPAN NAVIGATOR** *148*
VDPW *ex* La Garde *-1971* 9
\- **Seaspan ULC** -
\-
Vancouver, BC *Canada*
MMSI: 316003658
Official number: 345112

1970 **Vancouver Shipyards Co Ltd — North Vancouver BC** Yd No: 9
Loa 25.84 Br ex 7.78 Dght 3.404
Lbp 24.08 Br md 7.47 Dpth 4.20
Welded, 1 dk

(B32A2ST) Tug

2 oil engines geared to sc. shafts driving 2 FP propellers
Total Power: 626kW (852hp)
Caterpillar D398TA
2 x Vee 4 Stroke 12 Cy. 159 x 203 each-313kW (426bhp)
Caterpillar Tractor Co-USA

9227015 **SEASPAN NINGBO** **39,941** Class: NV (LR)
VRBH5 *ex* CSCL Ningbo *-2012* 24,458 ✠
\- **Seaspan Corp** 50,790
Seaspan Ship Management Ltd T/cm
Hong Kong *Hong Kong* 70.4
MMSI: 477014700
Official number: HK-1585

2002-06 **Samsung Heavy Industries Co Ltd — Geoje** Yd No: 1347
Loa 259.80 (BB) Br ex 32.35 Dght 12.600
Lbp 244.80 Br md 32.25 Dpth 19.30
Welded, 1 dk

(A33A2CC) Container Ship (Fully Cellular)
TEU 4253 C Ho 1584 TEU C Dk 2669 TEU incl 400 ref C.
Compartments: ER, 7 Cell Ho

1 oil engine driving 1 FP propeller
Total Power: 36,515kW (49,646hp) 23.3kn
B&W 8K90MC-C
1 x 2 Stroke 8 Cy. 900 x 2300 36515kW (49646bhp)
Doosan Engine Co Ltd-South Korea
AuxGen: 4 x 1680kW 440/220V 60Hz a.c
Boilers: AuxB New (Comp) 8.0kgf/cm² (7.8bar)
Thrusters: 1 Thwart. CP thruster (f)
Fuel: 250.0 (d.f.) 6100.0 (r.f.) 146.0pd

9623128 **SEASPAN OSPREY** **441** Class: AB
CFN6644 *ex* Sanmar Terminal V *-2011* 132
\- **Seaspan ULC** 132
\-
Vancouver, BC *Canada*
MMSI: 316020868
Official number: 836296

2011-10 **Gemsan Gemi Insa ve Gemi Isletmeciligi San. Ltd. — Tuzla** Yd No: 53
Loa 28.20 Br ex - Dght 5.300
Lbp 26.17 Br md 12.60 Dpth 5.30
Welded, 1 dk

(B32A2ST) Tug

2 oil engines reduction geared to sc. shafts driving 2 Z propellers
Total Power: 4,700kW (6,390hp)
Caterpillar 3516C-HD
2 x Vee 4 Stroke 16 Cy. 170 x 215 each-2350kW (3195bhp)
Caterpillar Inc-USA
AuxGen: 2 x 90kW a.c

6722325 **SEASPAN PACER** *203*
VXSS *ex* Le Mars *-1971* 25
\- **Seaspan ULC** -
\-
Vancouver, BC *Canada*
MMSI: 316003676
Official number: 328843

1967 **Star Shipyards (Mercer's) Ltd — New Westminster BC** Yd No: 378
Loa 29.04 Br ex 7.90 Dght -
Lbp 28.20 Br md 7.62 Dpth 4.25
Welded, 1 dk

(B32A2ST) Tug
2 Ha: (0.9 x 1.5) (0.6 x 0.6)

2 oil engines driving 2 FP propellers
Total Power: 1,654kW (2,248hp) 11.3kn
Caterpillar 3512B
2 x Vee 4 Stroke 12 Cy. 170 x 190 each-827kW (1124bhp)
(new engine 2000)
Caterpillar Inc-USA
AuxGen: 2 x 75kW 120/208V 60Hz a.c
Fuel: 124.0 (d.f.)

IMO / Call sign	Name / Owner	Tonnage	Class	Builder / Dimensions	Type	Machinery
7406693 *CZ5427* -	**SEASPAN PROTECTOR** *ex* Gulf Sally *-1978* **Seaspan ULC** - *Vancouver, BC* *Canada* MMSI: 316003677 Official number: 368710	*149* 22 -		**1974-08 Vito Steel Boat & Barge Construction Ltd — Delta BC** Loa 23.32 Br ex 7.32 Dght 4.115 Lbp 22.26 Br md 7.27 Dpth - Welded, 1 dk	**(B32A2ST) Tug**	**2 oil engines** geared to sc. shafts driving 2 FP propellers Total Power: 1,176kW (1,598hp) 11.0kn G.M. (Detroit Diesel) 12V-149-TI 2 x Vee 2 Stroke 12 Cy. 146 x 146 each-588kW (799bhp) General Motors Corp-USA
6503731 *CY7444* -	**SEASPAN QUEEN** *ex* La Reine *-1971* **Seaspan ULC** - *Vancouver, BC* *Canada* MMSI: 316003678 Official number: 323220	*207* 42 -		**1964 Star Shipyards (Mercer's) Ltd — New Westminster BC** Loa 29.04 Br ex 7.93 Dght - Lbp 28.20 Br md 7.62 Dpth 3.66 Welded, 1 dk	**(B32A2ST) Tug**	**2 oil engines** driving 2 FP propellers Total Power: 1,258kW (1,710hp) Caterpillar 3512 2 x Vee 4 Stroke 12 Cy. 170 x 190 each-629kW (855bhp) (new engine 2000) Caterpillar Inc-USA Fuel: 118.0
9432957 *CFN6643* -	**SEASPAN RAVEN** *ex* Seaspan Terminal III *-2011* *ex* Sanmar Terminal III *-2010* *launched as* Ramparts 2800-3 *-2010* **Seaspan ULC** - *Vancouver, BC* *Canada* MMSI: 316018851 Official number: 835230	**441** 132 149	Class: AB	**2010-10 Pirlant Shipyard — Tuzla** Yd No: 15 Loa 28.20 Br ex - Dght 5.100 Lbp 26.17 Br md 12.60 Dpth 5.30 Welded, 1 dk	**(B32A2ST) Tug**	**2 oil engines** Reduction geared to sc. shafts driving 2 Z propellers Total Power: 3,678kW (5,000hp) Caterpillar 3516B 2 x Vee 4 Stroke 16 Cy. 170 x 190 each-1839kW (2500bhp) Caterpillar Inc-USA AuxGen: 2 x 96kW a.c Fuel: 119.0
7503805 *VG2885* -	**SEASPAN REGENT** **Seaspan ULC** - *Vancouver, BC* *Canada* MMSI: 316004400 Official number: 356755	**621** 186 480	Class: LR ✠ **100A-** SS 05/2004 tug ✠ **LMC** Eq.Ltr: (J) ;	**1976-06 Bel-Aire Shipyard Ltd — North Vancouver BC** Yd No: 246 Loa 43.36 Br ex 12.37 Dght 5.335 Lbp 39.25 Br md 10.93 Dpth 5.82 Welded, 1 dk	**(B32A2ST) Tug**	**2 oil engines** reverse reduction geared to sc. shafts driving 2 FP propellers Total Power: 4,230kW (5,752hp) 14.0kn EMD (Electro-Motive) 16-645-E7 2 x Vee 2 Stroke 16 Cy. 230 x 254 each-2115kW (2876bhp) General Motors Corp.Electro-Motive Div.-La Grange AuxGen: 2 x 125kW 480V 60Hz a.c
9537147 *CFK9083* -	**SEASPAN RESOLUTION** **Seaspan ULC** - *Vancouver, BC* *Canada* MMSI: 316014995 Official number: 833674	**469** 140 174	Class: LR **100A1** SS 06/2009 tug, British Columbia coast waters, east of Race Rocks and south of Cambell River, coastal service within 25 nautical miles from shore and within 25 nautical miles from place of refuge ✠ **LMC** Eq.Ltr: F; Cable: 130.0/25.0 U2 (a)	**2009-06 J M Martinac Shipbuilding Corp — Tacoma WA** Yd No: 252 Loa 29.87 Br ex 13.08 Dght 4.960 Lbp 24.43 Br md 12.19 Dpth 5.31 Welded, 1 dk	**(B32A2ST) Tug**	**2 oil engines** gearing integral to driving 2 Z propellers Total Power: 4,476kW (6,086hp) 12.0kn EMD (Electro-Motive) 12-710-G7C 2 x Vee 2 Stroke 12 Cy. 230 x 279 each-2238kW (3043bhp) General Motors Corp.Electro-Motive Div.-La Grange AuxGen: 1 x 99kW 480V 60Hz a.c, 1 x 259kW 480V 60Hz a.c
8020018 *VY7102* -	**SEASPAN ROYAL** *ex* Captain Bob *-2011* *ex* Smit Capt. Bob *-2010* *ex* Rivtow Capt. Bob *-2008* **Seaspan ULC** - *Vancouver, BC* *Canada* MMSI: 316003600 Official number: 801519	**975** 322 -	Class: AB	**1982-04 John Manly Shipyard Ltd — Vancouver BC** Yd No: 580 Loa 43.90 Br ex - Dght 5.871 Lbp 39.50 Br md 11.89 Dpth 6.35 Welded, 1 dk	**(B32A2ST) Tug**	**2 oil engines** reverse reduction geared to sc. shafts driving 2 FP propellers Total Power: 4,538kW (6,170hp) 14.0kn EMD (Electro-Motive) 16-645-E7 2 x Vee 2 Stroke 16 Cy. 230 x 254 each-2269kW (3085bhp) General Motors Corp.Electro-Motive Div.-La Grange AuxGen: 2 x 125kW 440V 60Hz a.c Fuel: 559.0 (d.f.) 21.5pd
5164916 *VDZP* -	**SEASPAN SOVEREIGN** *ex* Island Sovereign *-1972* *ex* LT-62 *-1954* **Seaspan ULC** - *Victoria, BC* *Canada* MMSI: 316272000 Official number: 192879	*432* 95 -		**1944 Calumet Shipyard & Dry Dock Co. — Chicago, Il** Yd No: 158 Loa 37.50 Br ex 9.15 Dght 5.501 Lbp - Br md - Dpth - Welded, 1 dk	**(B32A2ST) Tug**	**1 oil engine** driving 1 FP propeller Total Power: 1,581kW (2,150hp) EMD (Electro-Motive) 16-567-C 1 x Vee 2 Stroke 16 Cy. 216 x 254 1581kW (2150bhp) (new engine 1965) General Motors Corp-USA
7005889 *CY9526* -	**SEASPAN VALIANT** *ex* Island Valiant *-1971* **Seaspan ULC** - *Vancouver, BC* *Canada* MMSI: 316003679 Official number: 331847	*110* 7 -		**1970 Bel-Aire Shipyard Ltd — North Vancouver BC** Loa 22.56 Br ex 7.32 Dght 3.810 Lbp - Br md 6.90 Dpth - Welded, 1 dk	**(B32A2ST) Tug** 1 Ha: (0.7 x 0.6)	**1 oil engine** geared to sc. shaft driving 1 CP propeller Total Power: 750kW (1,020hp) 11.0kn Caterpillar D398TA 1 x Vee 4 Stroke 12 Cy. 159 x 203 750kW (1020bhp) Caterpillar Tractor Co-USA AuxGen: 2 x 23kW 110/208V 60Hz a.c Fuel: 40.5 (d.f.)
7041247 *VDPB* -	**SEASPAN VICTOR** *ex* Island Victor *-1971* **Seaspan ULC** - *Vancouver, BC* *Canada* MMSI: 316003681 Official number: 331229	*110* 7 -		**1970 Bel-Aire Shipyard Ltd — North Vancouver BC** Yd No: 191 Loa 22.56 Br ex 6.91 Dght - Lbp 20.50 Br md 6.89 Dpth 3.81 Welded, 1 dk	**(B32A2ST) Tug**	**1 oil engine** geared to sc. shaft driving 1 CP propeller Total Power: 750kW (1,020hp) Caterpillar D398TA 1 x Vee 4 Stroke 12 Cy. 159 x 203 750kW (1020bhp) Caterpillar Tractor Co-USA
6826872 - -	**SEASPAN VOYAGER** *ex* Gulf Jean *-1980* - -	*147* 9 -		**1968 BC Marine Shipbuilders Ltd — Vancouver BC** Yd No: 15 Loa 23.78 Br ex 7.78 Dght 3.963 Lbp 22.00 Br md 7.35 Dpth 3.46 Welded, 1 dk	**(B32A2ST) Tug**	**1 oil engine** geared to sc. shaft driving 1 CP propeller Total Power: 827kW (1,124hp) 12.0kn Caterpillar D398TA 1 x Vee 4 Stroke 12 Cy. 159 x 203 827kW (1124bhp) Caterpillar Tractor Co-USA
8873441 *A6E2801* -	**SEASPEED EXPRESS** *ex* Stanford Hawk *-2009* *ex* Atco Amira *-2001* *ex* Matss Hind *-2001* **Seaspeed Marine Management LLC** - *Sharjah* *United Arab Emirates* MMSI: 470606000 Official number: 4678	**156** 48 -	Class: AB	**1982 Camcraft, Inc. — Marrero, La** Yd No: 280 Loa 33.53 Br ex 7.80 Dght 2.230 Lbp 29.51 Br md 7.72 Dpth 3.43 Welded, 1 dk	**(B21A20S) Platform Supply Ship** Hull Material: Aluminium Alloy	**3 oil engines** reduction geared to sc. shafts driving 3 FP propellers Total Power: 1,125kW (1,530hp) 21.9kn G.M. (Detroit Diesel) 12V-71-TI 3 x Vee 2 Stroke 12 Cy. 108 x 127 each-375kW (510bhp) Detroit Diesel Corporation-Detroit, Mi AuxGen: 2 x 40kW a.c
9380477 *DDSJ* -	**SEASPRAT** - **tms 'Seasprat' GmbH & Co KG** German Tanker Shipping GmbH & Co KG *Bremen* *Germany* MMSI: 218057000 Official number: 4965	**26,548** 10,304 40,597 T/cm 53.0	Class: GL	**2007-03 Lindenau GmbH Schiffswerft u. Maschinenfabrik — Kiel** Yd No: 274 Loa 188.33 (BB) Br ex - Dght 11.000 Lbp 179.50 Br md 32.20 Dpth 17.05 Welded, 1 dk	**(A13B2TP) Products Tanker** Double Hull (13F) Liq: 47,370; Liq (Oil): 47,370 Compartments: 10 Wing Ta, 2 Wing Slop Ta, ER 10 Cargo Pump (s): 10x600m³/hr Manifold: Bow/CM: 97.2m Ice Capable	**1 oil engine** reduction geared to sc. shaft driving 1 CP propeller Total Power: 11,200kW (15,228hp) 16.3kn MAN-B&W 8L58/64 1 x 4 Stroke 8 Cy. 580 x 640 11200kW (15228bhp) MAN B&W Diesel AG-Augsburg AuxGen: 1 x 1360kW 400/230V 60Hz a.c, 3 x 1140kW 400/230V 60Hz a.c Thrusters: 1 Tunnel thruster (f)
5267201 *GJBH* -	**SEASPRING** *ex* Otterspool *-1976* **Seaspring Ltd** - *London* *United Kingdom* MMSI: 232003431 Official number: 187163	*775* 278 1,205	Class: (LR) ✠ Classed LR until 3/64	**1957-06 Henry Scarr Ltd. — Hessle** Yd No: 735 Converted From: Research Vessel-1991 Converted From: Hopper-1976 Loa 60.05 Br ex 11.82 Dght - Lbp 56.70 Br md 11.43 Dpth 4.20 Riveted, 1 dk	**(B34G2SE) Pollution Control Vessel** Compartments: 1 Ho, ER	**1 oil engine** sr geared to sc. shaft driving 1 FP propeller Total Power: 777kW (1,056hp) 9.5kn Paxman 12YLCM 1 x Vee 4 Stroke 12 Cy. 248 x 267 777kW (1056bhp) Davey, Paxman & Co. Ltd.-Colchester AuxGen: 2 x 50kW 220V d.c
9373656 *9HAV9* -	**SEASTAR** *ex* Neverland Gold *-2008* **Seavalue Shipping SA** Thenamaris (Ships Management) Inc SatCom: Inmarsat C 425670210 *Valletta* *Malta* MMSI: 256702000 Official number: 9373656	**61,248** 35,402 115,639 T/cm 99.0	Class: AB	**2008-03 Samsung Heavy Industries Co Ltd — Geoje** Yd No: 1658 Loa 248.96 (BB) Br ex 43.87 Dght 14.925 Lbp 239.00 Br md 43.80 Dpth 21.30 Welded, 1 dk	**(A13A2TV) Crude Oil Tanker** Double Hull (13F) Liq: 124,092; Liq (Oil): 124,092 Cargo Heating Coils Compartments: 12 Wing Ta, ER, 2 Wing Slop Ta 3 Cargo Pump (s): 3x2800m³/hr Manifold: Bow/CM: 125.6m	**1 oil engine** driving 1 FP propeller Total Power: 12,240kW (16,642hp) 15.3kn MAN-B&W 6S60MC 1 x 2 Stroke 6 Cy. 600 x 2292 12240kW (16642bhp) Doosan Engine Co Ltd-South Korea AuxGen: 3 x 850kW a.c

9185683 - -	**SEASTAR 3** *ex* Flyingcat 2 *-2012* *ex* Flying Dolphin 2000 *-2000* **Jeong Sang General Construction Co Ltd** Seaspovill Co Ltd *Gangneung* South Korea MMSI: 440153350 Official number: DHR-125314	**950** 271 65	Class: KR (GL)	**1998-06 Austal Ships Pty Ltd — Fremantle WA** Yd No: 64 Loa 47.60 (BB) Br ex - Dght 1.630 Lbp 43.13 Br md 13.00 Dpth 4.00 Welded	**(A37B2PS) Passenger Ship** Hull Material: Aluminium Alloy Passengers: unberthed: 516	**4 oil engines** with clutches, flexible couplings & sr geared to sc. shafts driving 4 Water jets steerable Total Power: 9,280kW (12,616hp) 42.0kn M.T.U. 16V4000M70 4 x Vee 4 Stroke 16 Cy. 165 x 190 each-2320kW (3154bhp) MTU Friedrichshafen GmbH-Friedrichshafen AuxGen: 2 x 205kW 380V 50Hz a.c Fuel: 22.0 (d.f.) 42.0pd
9602693 *3FQE2* -	**SEASTAR EMPRESS** **Pinta Shipping Five Ltd** Norbulk Shipping UK Ltd *Panama* Panama MMSI: 371246000 Official number: 4313111	**22,409** 12,013 35,000	Class: BV	**2011-06 Nantong Jinghua Shipbuilding Co Ltd — Nantong JS** Yd No: BC350-8 Loa 179.90 (BB) Br ex - Dght 10.800 Lbp 171.50 Br md 28.40 Dpth 15.00 Welded, 1 dk	**(A21A2BC) Bulk Carrier** Grain: 44,272 Compartments: 5 Ho, ER 5 Ha: ER Cranes: 4x30t	**1 oil engine** driving 1 FP propeller Total Power: 7,600kW (10,333hp) 14.0kn MAN-B&W 6S50MC-C 1 x 2 Stroke 6 Cy. 500 x 2000 7600kW (10333bhp) STX Engine Co Ltd-South Korea AuxGen: 3 x 600kW 60Hz a.c
9588873 *3FNU6* -	**SEASTAR ENDURANCE** **Pinta Shipping One Ltd** Navig8 Bulk Asia Pte Ltd *Panama* Panama MMSI: 351120000 Official number: 4326411	**22,137** 11,328 33,500 T/cm 44.4	Class: BV	**2011-09 Zhejiang Jingang Shipbuilding Co Ltd — Wenling ZJ** Yd No: 029 Loa 179.50 (BB) Br ex - Dght 10.650 Lbp 172.00 Br md 28.00 Dpth 15.20 Welded, 1 dk	**(A21A2BC) Bulk Carrier** Grain: 44,075 Compartments: 5 Ho, ER 5 Ha: ER Cranes: 4x30t	**1 oil engine** driving 1 FP propeller Total Power: 6,480kW (8,810hp) 14.0kn MAN-B&W 6S42MC 1 x 2 Stroke 6 Cy. 420 x 1764 6480kW (8810bhp) Hyundai Heavy Industries Co Ltd-South Korea AuxGen: 3 x 520kW 60Hz a.c Fuel: 1470.0
8409056 *3FL09* -	**SEASTEADER I** *ex* Opus Casino *-2012* *ex* Liquid Vegas *-2010* *ex* Royal Star *-2008* *ex* Liberty II *-2000* *ex* Liberty I *-1998* *ex* Royal Empress *-1997* *ex* Punta Pedrera *-1995* **The Seasteading Institute** - *Panama* Panama Official number: 43791PEXT	**2,040** 630 182	Class: (RI) (BV)	**1985-09 Union Naval de Levante SA (UNL) — Valencia** Yd No: 152 Loa 67.62 Br ex - Dght 3.012 Lbp 58.40 Br md 12.77 Dpth 4.10 Welded	**(A36A2PR) Passenger/Ro-Ro Ship (Vehicles)** Passengers: unberthed: 250 Stern door/ramp (centre) Len: 3.60 Wid: 6.14 Swl: - Lane-clr ht: 2.70 Cars: 43	**2 oil engines** with clutches, flexible couplings & sr reverse geared to sc. shafts driving 2 FP propellers Total Power: 2,736kW (3,720hp) 17.5kn Alpha 12V23LU 2 x Vee 4 Stroke 12 Cy. 225 x 300 each-1368kW (1860bhp) Construcciones Echevarria SA-Spain AuxGen: 2 x 216kW a.c
9270270 *WDE4031* -	**SEASTREAK HIGHLANDS** **Citicapital Commercial Leasing Corp** SeaStreak America Inc *Atlantic Highlands, NJ* United States of America MMSI: 367347670 Official number: 1151440	**417** 156 100		**2004-02 Gladding-Hearn SB. Duclos Corp. — Somerset, Ma** Yd No: P-343 Loa 42.90 Br ex 10.43 Dght 2.000 Lbp - Br md - Dpth 4.00 Welded, 1 dk	**(A37B2PS) Passenger Ship** Hull Material: Aluminium Alloy Passengers: unberthed: 505	**4 oil engines** geared to sc. shafts driving 4 Water jets Total Power: 5,516kW (7,500hp) 35.0kn Cummins KTA-50-M2 4 x Vee 4 Stroke 16 Cy. 159 x 159 each-1379kW (1875bhp) Cummins Engine Co Inc-USA
8968272 *WDE4029* -	**SEASTREAK NEW JERSEY** **SeaStreak LLC** SeaStreak America Inc *Atlantic Highlands, NJ* United States of America MMSI: 367347640 Official number: 1118507	**417** 156 100		**2001-08 Gladding-Hearn SB. Duclos Corp. — Somerset, Ma** Yd No: P-328 Loa 42.90 Br ex - Dght 1.960 Lbp - Br md 10.45 Dpth 3.38 Welded, 1 dk	**(A37B2PS) Passenger Ship** Hull Material: Aluminium Alloy Passengers: unberthed: 505	**4 oil engines** driving 2 gen. each 95kW a.c reduction geared to sc shafts driving 4 Water jets Total Power: 5,516kW (7,500hp) 38.3kn Cummins KTA-50-M2 4 x Vee 4 Stroke 16 Cy. 159 x 159 each-1379kW (1875bhp) Cummins Engine Co Inc-USA Fuel: 9.0 (d.f.)
8967620 *WDE3997* -	**SEASTREAK NEW YORK** **SeaStreak LLC** SeaStreak America Inc *Atlantic Highlands, NJ* United States of America MMSI: 367347130 Official number: 1105798	**431** 159 100		**2001-05 Gladding-Hearn SB. Duclos Corp. — Somerset, Ma** Yd No: P-327 Loa 42.90 Br ex - Dght 1.960 Lbp - Br md 10.45 Dpth 3.35 Welded, 1 dk	**(A37B2PS) Passenger Ship** Hull Material: Aluminium Alloy Passengers: unberthed: 505	**4 oil engines** driving 2 gen. each 95kW a.c reduction geared to sc shafts driving 4 Water jets Total Power: 5,516kW (7,500hp) 38.3kn Cummins KTA-50-M2 4 x Vee 4 Stroke 16 Cy. 159 x 159 each-1379kW (1875bhp) Cummins Engine Co Inc-USA Fuel: 9.0 (d.f.)
8982010 *WDE4030* -	**SEASTREAK WALL STREET** **Citicapital Commercial Leasing Corp** SeaStreak America Inc *Somerset, MA* United States of America MMSI: 367347650 Official number: 1145690	**417** 156 100		**2003-09 Gladding-Hearn SB. Duclos Corp. — Somerset, Ma** Yd No: P-342 Loa 42.90 Br ex 10.43 Dght 2.000 Lbp - Br md - Dpth 4.00 Welded, 1 dk	**(A37B2PS) Passenger Ship** Hull Material: Aluminium Alloy Passengers: unberthed: 505	**2 oil engines** reduction geared to sc. shafts driving 2 CP propellers Total Power: 2,758kW (3,750hp) 32.0kn M.T.U. 16V4000M53 2 x Vee 4 Stroke 16 Cy. 170 x 210 each-1379kW (1875bhp) (new engine 2012) MTU Friedrichshafen GmbH-Friedrichshafen
8824543 - -	**SEASURVEYOR** *ex* New Tobishima *-2011* **S & K Day Ltd** Seaworks Ltd *Wellington* New Zealand Official number: 876264	**356** 106 250		**1989-05 Mitsui Eng. & SB. Co. Ltd. — Tamano** Yd No: 1611 Converted From: Ferry (Passenger only)-2010 Loa 38.95 Br ex - Dght 2.900 Lbp 36.00 Br md 10.00 Dpth 3.60 Welded, 1 dk	**(B31A2SR) Research Survey Vessel**	**2 oil engines** geared to sc. shafts driving 2 FP propellers Total Power: 2,796kW (3,802hp) 10.0kn Pielstick 12PA4V185VG 2 x Vee 4 Stroke 12 Cy. 185 x 210 each-1398kW (1901bhp) Fuji Diesel Co Ltd-Japan
7727190 - -	**SEASURVEYOR** *ex* Geomarine 1 *-1995* **S & K Day Ltd** Seaworks Ltd	**180** 54 -	Class: (BV)	**1978-05 Selco Shipyard Pte Ltd — Singapore** Yd No: H279 Loa 28.00 Br ex - Dght 2.300 Lbp 27.00 Br md 7.70 Dpth 3.00 Welded, 1 dk	**(B31A2SR) Research Survey Vessel**	**2 oil engines** reduction geared to sc. shafts driving 2 FP propellers Total Power: 536kW (728hp) 11.5kn Caterpillar D343SCAC 2 x 4 Stroke 6 Cy. 137 x 165 each-268kW (364bhp) Caterpillar Tractor Co-USA AuxGen: 2 x 110kW 220/440V 50Hz a.c Fuel: 40.0 (d.f.)
8617524 *V4EP2* -	**SEATANK** *ex* Andhika Andalantama *-2000* **Seatank Pte Ltd** Sentek Marine & Trading Pte Ltd *Basseterre* St Kitts & Nevis MMSI: 341390000	**2,734** 1,349 3,912 T/cm 12.8	Class: IS (NK)	**1987-03 Higaki Zosen K.K. — Imabari** Yd No: 346 Loa 89.95 (BB) Br ex - Dght 4.799 Lbp 85.02 Br md 18.01 Dpth 6.02 Welded, 1 dk	**(A13B2TP) Products Tanker** Liq: 4,707; Liq (Oil): 4,707 Compartments: 10 Ta, ER 3 Cargo Pump (s)	**1 oil engine** driving 1 FP propeller Total Power: 1,765kW (2,400hp) 11.0kn Hanshin 6EL35 1 x 4 Stroke 6 Cy. 350 x 700 1765kW (2400bhp) The Hanshin Diesel Works Ltd-Japan Fuel: 380.0 (r.f.)
7901045 *VJT34307* 0669	**SEATAS 3** *ex* Khalf 3 *-2003* **Lukin Fisheries Pty Ltd (Lukin & Sons)** SatCom: Inmarsat C 450300325 *Melbourne, Vic* Australia Official number: 852900	*271* 81 321	Class: (LR) ✠ Classed LR until 28/1/87	**1979-11 Maebata Zosen Tekko K.K. — Sasebo** Yd No: 133 Loa 30.23 Br ex 8.21 Dght 3.701 Lbp 26.50 Br md 8.01 Dpth 4.37 Welded, 1 dk	**(B11B2FV) Fishing Vessel**	**1 oil engine** sr geared to sc. shaft driving 1 CP propeller Total Power: 588kW (799hp) Yanmar T220-UT 1 x 4 Stroke 6 Cy. 220 x 280 588kW (799bhp) Yanmar Diesel Engine Co Ltd-Japan AuxGen: 2 x 52kW 380V 50Hz a.c
8325779 *PJFS* -	**SEATEAM OMEGA** *ex* Oceanix Omega *-2013* *ex* Miclyn Surveyor *-2007* *ex* Merdeka 1 *-1997* **Oceanix Omega NV** Seateam Offshore Ltd *Willemstad* Curacao MMSI: 306847000 Official number: 2008-C-1938	**1,245** 373 829	Class: BV	**1983-12 Mickon Marine Industries Pte Ltd — Singapore** Yd No: 233 Loa 56.19 Br ex - Dght 2.700 Lbp 51.80 Br md 13.72 Dpth 3.69 Welded, 1 dk	**(B22A20R) Offshore Support Vessel** Cranes: 1x5t	**2 oil engines** driving 2 FP propellers Total Power: 920kW (1,250hp) 10.0kn G.M. (Detroit Diesel) 16V-92-N 2 x Vee 2 Stroke 16 Cy. 123 x 127 each-460kW (625bhp) General Motors Detroit DieselAllison Divn-USA AuxGen: 3 x 150kW 415V 50Hz a.c Thrusters: 1 Thwart. FP thruster (f)
8014356 *XUCB7* -	**SEATIGER** *ex* Kestrel *-2004* *ex* Bakengracht *-1999* **Delouna Shipping Co Ltd** Grand Marine Co Ltd *Phnom Penh* Cambodia MMSI: 515515000 Official number: 0381172	**3,433** 2,186 6,156	Class: (LR) (RS) ✠ Classed LR until 12/7/04	**1981-03 Miho Zosensho K.K. — Shimizu** Yd No: 1183 Loa 80.22 (BB) Br ex 16.11 Dght 8.470 Lbp 74.86 Br md 16.01 Dpth 10.52 Welded, 2 dks	**(A31A2GX) General Cargo Ship** Grain: 7,181; Bale: 7,045 TEU 189 C.Ho 124/20' (40') C.Dk 65/20' (40') Compartments: 1 Ho, ER, 1 Tw Dk 1 Ha: (44.4 x 12.8)ER Cranes: 2x15t Ice Capable	**1 oil engine** driving 1 CP propeller Total Power: 2,207kW (3,001hp) 12.8kn Hanshin 6LUS40 1 x 4 Stroke 6 Cy. 400 x 640 2207kW (3001bhp) Hanshin Nainenki Kogyo-Japan AuxGen: 3 x 200kW 445V 60Hz a.c, 1 x 132kW 445V 60Hz a.c Fuel: 57.8 (d.f.) 314.2 (r.f.) 10.0pd
9253997 *V7JL5* -	**SEATIZEN** *ex* Samho Triton *-2006* **Fortland Maritime Corp** Coral Shipping Corp *Majuro* Marshall Islands MMSI: 538002542 Official number: 2542	**2,440** 1,084 3,447 T/cm 10.1	Class: GL (KR)	**2002-04 Samho Shipbuilding Co Ltd — Tongyeong** Yd No: 1034 Loa 87.30 (BB) Br ex - Dght 5.800 Lbp 79.80 Br md 14.00 Dpth 7.30 Welded, 1 dk	**(A12B2TR) Chemical/Products Tanker** Double Hull (13F) Liq: 3,724; Liq (Oil): 3,930 Cargo Heating Coils Compartments: 1 Ta, 8 Wing Ta, 2 Wing Slop Ta, ER 10 Cargo Pump (s): 10x200m³/hr Manifold: Bow/CM: 46.1m	**1 oil engine** reduction geared to sc. shaft driving 1 FP propeller Total Power: 1,960kW (2,665hp) 12.3kn MAN-B&W 8L28/32A 1 x 4 Stroke 8 Cy. 280 x 320 1960kW (2665bhp) STX Corp-South Korea AuxGen: 3 x 260kW 440V a.c Thrusters: 1 Thwart. FP thruster (f) Fuel: 51.0 (d.f.) 166.0 (r.f.)

Ship	Tonnage / Class	Build	Type / Capacity	Machinery
9517331 **SEATON** *V7XK7* *ex* Global Hemera *-2011* *ex* Sider Cat *-2008* - **Seaton Shipping Co Ltd** Briese Schiffahrts GmbH & Co KG *Majuro* *Marshall Islands* MMSI: 538004503 Official number: 4503	**5,164** Class: BV 2,913 7,394 T/cm 17.5	**2008-08 Ningbo Xinle Shipbuilding Co Ltd — Ningbo ZJ** Yd No: XL-116 Loa 119.95 (BB) Br ex 16.84 Dght 6.265 Lbp 112.99 Br md 16.80 Dpth 8.20 Welded, 1 dk	**(A21A2BC) Bulk Carrier** Grain: 10,106; Bale: 9,903 Compartments: 2 Ho, ER 2 Ha: ER 2 (29.9 x 12.6)	**1 oil engine** reduction geared to sc. shaft driving 1 FP propeller Total Power: 2,500kW (3,399hp) 11.5kn Daihatsu 8DKM-28 1 x 4 Stroke 8 Cy. 280 x 390 2500kW (3399bhp) Daihatsu Diesel Manufacturing Co Lt-Japan AuxGen: 2 x a.c
8803898 **SEATRAN DISCOVERY 4** - *ex* White Marine *-2007* - **Seatran Ferry Co Ltd** - *Bangkok* *Thailand* Official number: 500055157	*135* 49 50	**1988-07 Iisaku Zosen K.K. — Nishi-Izu** Yd No: 88138 Loa 32.40 Br ex - Dght 1.750 Lbp 27.00 Br md 6.00 Dpth 2.52 Welded, 1 dk	**(A37B2PS) Passenger Ship** Hull Material: Aluminium Alloy	**2 oil engines** with clutches & sr reverse geared to sc. shafts driving 2 FP propellers Total Power: 1,472kW (2,002hp) Yanmar 12LAAK-UT1 2 x Vee 4 Stroke 12 Cy. 148 x 165 each-736kW (1001bhp) Yanmar Diesel Engine Co Ltd-Japan
8916619 **SEATRAN DISCOVERY 5** *T2QQ4* *ex* Sea Hawk *-2014* - **Seatran Ferry Co Ltd** - *Funafuti* *Tuvalu* Official number: 30479014	*304* Class: IZ - 40	**1990-02 Mitsubishi Heavy Industries Ltd. — Shimonoseki** Yd No: 940 Loa 48.50 Br ex - Dght 1.450 Lbp 44.00 Br md 8.20 Dpth 3.90 Welded, 1 dk	**(A37B2PS) Passenger Ship** Hull Material: Aluminium Alloy	**2 oil engines** with clutches, flexible couplings & sr reverse geared to sc. shafts driving 2 FP propellers Total Power: 4,046kW (5,500hp) Ikegai 16V190ATC 2 x Vee 4 Stroke 16 Cy. 190 x 230 each-2023kW (2750bhp) Ikegai Tekkosho-Japan
8712233 **SEATRAN FERRY 1** - *ex* Blue Line 2 *-2002* *ex* Blue Line *-2000* - **Seatran Ferry Co Ltd** - *Thailand* Official number: 451000324	*1,109* 906 249	**1987-10 Fujiwara Zosensho — Imabari** Yd No: 106 Loa - Br ex - Dght 2.852 Lbp 59.52 Br md 13.80 Dpth 3.76 Welded, 1 dk	**(A36A2PR) Passenger/Ro-Ro Ship (Vehicles)** Passengers: unberthed: 488 Cars: 60, Trailers: 25	**2 oil engines** driving 2 FP propellers Total Power: 2,354kW (3,200hp) 14.0kn Niigata 6M31AFTE 2 x 4 Stroke 6 Cy. 310 x 530 each-1177kW (1600bhp) Niigata Engineering Co Ltd-Japan
8216813 **SEATRAN FERRY 4** - *ex* Ferry Osumi No. 5 *-2002* - **Seatran Ferry Co Ltd** - *Thailand* Official number: 451001613	*961* 708 464	**1984-03 Hayashikane Shipbuilding & Engineering Co Ltd — Nagasaki NS** Yd No: 912 Loa 71.25 Br ex 13.87 Dght 3.501 Lbp 65.00 Br md 13.30 Dpth 4.70 Welded, 1 dk	**(A36A2PR) Passenger/Ro-Ro Ship (Vehicles)** Passengers: unberthed: 488 Bow door/ramp Stern door/ramp Lane-Len: 90 Cars: 61	**2 oil engines** with clutches & sr reverse geared to sc. shafts driving 2 FP propellers Total Power: 3,090kW (4,202hp) 15.5kn Daihatsu 6DSM-32 2 x 4 Stroke 6 Cy. 320 x 380 each-1545kW (2101bhp) Daihatsu Diesel Manufacturing Co Lt-Japan AuxGen: 2 x 500kW 445V 60Hz a.c Thrusters: 1 Thwart. CP thruster (f)
8319407 **SEATRAN FERRY 5** *HSB3127* *ex* Ise Maru *-2004* - **Seatran Ferry Co Ltd** - *Bangkok* *Thailand* Official number: 460004911	**1,099** 698 455	**1984-03 Naikai Shipbuilding & Engineering Co Ltd — Onomichi HS (Taguma Shipyard)** Yd No: 488 Loa 64.32 (BB) Br ex - Dght 3.301 Lbp 60.03 Br md 13.01 Dpth 4.53 Welded, 1 dk	**(A36A2PR) Passenger/Ro-Ro Ship (Vehicles)** Passengers: unberthed: 583 Stern door/ramp Lane-clr ht: 4.00 Cars: 42	**2 oil engines** with clutches, flexible couplings & sr reverse geared to sc. shafts driving 2 FP propellers Total Power: 2,648kW (3,600hp) 14.0kn Niigata 6MG28BX 2 x 4 Stroke 6 Cy. 280 x 320 each-1324kW (1800bhp) Niigata Engineering Co Ltd-Japan AuxGen: 2 x 200kW 445V 60Hz a.c Thrusters: 1 Thwart. CP thruster (f) Fuel: 10.5 (d.f.) 39.0 (r.f.) 11.0pd
8613504 **SEATRAN FERRY 6** - *ex* Shima Maru *-2005* - **Seatran Ferry Co Ltd** - *Bangkok* *Thailand* Official number: 480000686	**1,076** 571 394	**1986-11 Kanda Zosensho K.K. — Kawajiri** Yd No: 300 Loa 64.29 (BB) Br ex - Dght 3.152 Lbp 60.00 Br md 13.50 Dpth 4.53 Welded, 1 dk	**(A36A2PR) Passenger/Ro-Ro Ship (Vehicles)** Passengers: unberthed: 584 Bow door/ramp Len: 3.30 Wid: 5.35 Swl: - Stern door/ramp Len: 3.35 Wid: 5.60 Swl: - Vehicles: 42	**2 oil engines** with clutches, flexible couplings & sr reverse geared to sc. shafts driving 2 FP propellers Total Power: 2,648kW (3,600hp) 15.2kn Daihatsu 6DLM-28 2 x 4 Stroke 6 Cy. 280 x 360 each-1324kW (1800bhp) Daihatsu Diesel Manufacturing Co Lt-Japan Thrusters: 1 Thwart. CP thruster (f)
8920713 **SEATRAN FERRY 7** *HSB3660* *ex* Kokusai Maru No. 31 *-2007* - **Seatran Ferry Co Ltd** - *Bangkok* *Thailand* Official number: 500053862	*815* 270 257	**1990-04 Fujiwara Zosensho — Imabari** Yd No: 116 Loa 63.70 (BB) Br ex 14.70 Dght 3.020 Lbp 59.00 Br md 12.80 Dpth 4.00 Welded	**(A36A2PR) Passenger/Ro-Ro Ship (Vehicles)** Passengers: unberthed: 490	**2 oil engines** sr reverse geared to sc. shafts driving 2 FP propellers Total Power: 4,120kW (5,602hp) Hanshin 6MU37 2 x 4 Stroke 6 Cy. 370 x 430 each-2060kW (2801bhp) The Hanshin Diesel Works Ltd-Japan Thrusters: 1 Thwart. CP thruster (f); 1 Thwart. CP thruster (a)
8613671 **SEATRAN FERRY 8** - *ex* Daihatsu Maru No. 8 *-2009* - - - -	*1,163* - 1,078	**1986-12 K.K. Taihei Kogyo — Akitsu** Yd No: 1941 Loa 76.03 (BB) Br ex - Dght 4.112 Lbp 70.01 Br md 13.01 Dpth 7.57 Welded	**(A35B2RV) Vehicles Carrier**	**1 oil engine** reverse reduction geared to sc. shaft driving 1 FP propeller Total Power: 1,471kW (2,000hp) Daihatsu 6DLM-32 1 x 4 Stroke 6 Cy. 320 x 400 1471kW (2000bhp) Daihatsu Diesel Manufacturing Co Lt-Japan
8621850 **SEATRAN PORT 3** - *ex* Nikko Maru No. 68 *-2005* - **Seatran Port Co Ltd** - *Bangkok* *Thailand* Official number: 4800-03919	**1,007** 303 1,250	**1984 Kyoei Zosen KK — Mihara HS** Yd No: 136 Loa 55.50 Br ex - Dght 3.501 Lbp 51.80 Br md 15.00 Dpth 3.51 Welded, 1 dk	**(B33A2DU) Dredger (unspecified)**	**1 oil engine** driving 1 FP propeller Total Power: 221kW (300hp) 7.3kn Yanmar 1 x 4 Stroke 221kW (300bhp) Yanmar Diesel Engine Co Ltd-Japan
8742795 **SEATRANS** *YD8029* **PT Pacific Seatrans Lines** - *Bitung* *Indonesia*	**106** Class: (KI) 32 -	**2009-06 PT Maritim Jaya Shipyard — Batam** Yd No: 123 Loa 21.07 Br ex - Dght 2.720 Lbp 20.00 Br md 6.70 Dpth 3.20 Welded, 1 dk	**(B32A2ST) Tug**	**2 oil engines** reduction geared to sc. shafts driving 2 Propellers Total Power: 760kW (1,034hp) Cummins KT-19-M 2 x 4 Stroke 6 Cy. 159 x 159 each-380kW (517bhp) Cummins Engine Co Inc-USA
9247821 **SEATRANSPORT** *VRYB7* - **Prosperous Maritime Corp** Valles Steamship (Canada) Inc *Hong Kong* *Hong Kong* MMSI: 477238000 Official number: HK-0916	**57,529** Class: NV 32,194 106,638 T/cm 91.7	**2002-10 Tsuneishi Shipbuilding Co Ltd — Fukuyama HS** Yd No: 1233 Loa 240.50 (BB) Br ex 42.03 Dght 14.868 Lbp 230.00 Br md 42.00 Dpth 21.20 Welded, 1 dk	**(A13A2TV) Crude Oil Tanker** Double Hull (13F) Liq: 121,000; Liq (Oil): 121,000 Compartments: 12 Wing Ta, ER 3 Cargo Pump (s) Manifold: Bow/CM: 123m	**1 oil engine** driving 1 FP propeller Total Power: 12,240kW (16,642hp) 15.0kn B&W 6S60MC 1 x 2 Stroke 6 Cy. 600 x 2292 12240kW (16642bhp) Mitsui Engineering & Shipbuilding CLtd-Japan AuxGen: 3 x a.c Fuel: 215.8 (d.f.) (Heating Coils) 3128.0 (r.f.) 43.6pd
9629548 **SEATREASURE** *9HA3207* **Blue Skies Shipping SA** Thenamaris (Ships Management) Inc SatCom: Inmarsat C 422928910 *Valletta* *Malta* MMSI: 229289000 Official number: 9629548	**29,925** Class: AB 13,626 50,908 T/cm 52.0	**2013-01 STX Offshore & Shipbuilding Co Ltd — Changwon (Jinhae Shipyard)** Yd No: 1531 Loa 183.00 (BB) Br ex 32.23 Dght 13.150 Lbp 173.90 Br md 32.20 Dpth 19.10 Welded, 1 dk	**(A12B2TR) Chemical/Products Tanker** Double Hull (13F) Liq: 52,207; Liq (Oil): 51,800 Cargo Heating Coils Compartments: 6 Wing Ta, 6 Wing Ta, 1 Wing Slop Ta, 1 Wing Slop Ta, ER 12 Cargo Pump (s): 12x600m³/hr Manifold: Bow/CM: 91.9m	**1 oil engine** driving 1 FP propeller Total Power: 9,019kW (12,262hp) 14.5kn MAN-B&W 6S50ME-C8 1 x 2 Stroke 6 Cy. 500 x 2000 9019kW (12262bhp) STX Engine Co Ltd-South Korea AuxGen: 3 x 740kW a.c Fuel: 443.0 (d.f.) 1291.0 (r.f.)
9227455 **SEATRIUMPH** *9HDY7* - **Maritime Connection Inc** Thenamaris (Ships Management) Inc SatCom: Inmarsat C 421515511 *Valletta* *Malta* MMSI: 215155000 Official number: 7544	**84,598** Class: AB 53,710 149,953 T/cm 121.9	**2002-01 Samho Heavy Industries Co Ltd — Samho** Yd No: 126 Loa 274.00 Br ex - Dght 15.850 Lbp 264.00 Br md 50.00 Dpth 23.10 Welded, 1 dk	**(A13A2TW) Crude/Oil Products Tanker** Double Hull (13F) Liq: 178,372; Liq (Oil): 178,372 Cargo Heating Coils Compartments: 12 Wing Ta, ER 3 Cargo Pump (s): 3x4000m³/hr Manifold: Bow/CM: 137m	**1 oil engine** driving 1 FP propeller Total Power: 18,624kW (25,321hp) 15.5kn B&W 6S70MC-C 1 x 2 Stroke 6 Cy. 700 x 2800 18624kW (25321bhp) Hyundai Heavy Industries Co Ltd-South Korea AuxGen: 3 x 950kW 220/440V 60Hz a.c Fuel: 163.0 (d.f.) (Heating Coils) 4336.0 (r.f.) 75.0pd
9352303 **SEATROUT** *DDPN* - **tms 'Seatrout' GmbH & Co KG** German Tanker Shipping GmbH & Co KG *Bremen* *Germany* MMSI: 211881000 Official number: 4942	**26,548** Class: GL 10,288 40,600 T/cm 53.0	**2006-05 Lindenau GmbH Schiffswerft u. Maschinenfabrik — Kiel** Yd No: 272 Loa 188.33 (BB) Br ex - Dght 11.000 Lbp 179.50 Br md 32.20 Dpth 17.05 Welded, 1 dk	**(A13B2TP) Products Tanker** Double Hull (13F) Liq: 42,894; Liq (Oil): 42,894 Compartments: 10 Wing Ta, 2 Wing Slop Ta, ER 10 Cargo Pump (s): 10x600m³/hr Manifold: Bow/CM: 97.2m Ice Capable	**1 oil engine** reduction geared to sc. shaft driving 1 CP propeller Total Power: 11,200kW (15,228hp) 15.5kn MAN-B&W 8L58/64 1 x 4 Stroke 8 Cy. 580 x 640 11200kW (15228bhp) MAN B&W Diesel AG-Augsburg AuxGen: 3 x 1140kW 400/230V 50Hz a.c, 1 x 1360kW 400/230V 50Hz a.c Thrusters: 1 Thwart. FP thruster (f) Fuel: 470.0 (d.f.) 1510.0 (r.f.)

9350678 *5BKW2* -	**SEATRUCK PACE** *ex* Clipper Pace *-2012* **Pace & Point Shipping Ltd** Seatruck Ferries Shipholding Ltd *Limassol* *Cyprus* MMSI: 212400000	**14,759** 4,428 5,125	Class: NV	**2009-02 Ast. de Huelva S.A. — Huelva** Yd No: 821 Loa 142.00 (BB) Br ex - Dght 5.700 Lbp 133.18 Br md 23.00 Dpth 16.30 Welded	**(A35A2RR) Ro-Ro Cargo Ship** Stern door/ramp (p. a.) Len: 9.50 Wid: 6.50 Swl: - Stern door/ramp (s. a.) Len: 9.50 Wid: 12.30 Swl: - Lane-Len: 1830 Lane-clr ht: 6.80 Trailers: 120	**2 oil engines** geared to sc. shafts driving 2 CP propellers Total Power: 18,480kW (25,126hp) 22.0kn Wartsila 8L46 2 x 4 Stroke 8 Cy. 460 x 580 each-9240kW (12563bhp) Wartsila Finland Oy-Finland AuxGen: 3 x 645kW a.c, 2 x 1200kW a.c Thrusters: 2 Thwart. CP thruster (f) Fuel: 150.0 (d.f.) 891.0 (r.f.)
9372676 *5BKX2* -	**SEATRUCK PANORAMA** *ex* Clipper Panorama *-2011* *launched as* Clipper Pennant *-2008* **Seatruck Panorama Ltd** Seatruck Ferries Ltd SatCom: Inmarsat C 421239210 *Limassol* *Cyprus* MMSI: 212392000	**14,759** 4,428 5,125	Class: NV	**2008-11 Astilleros de Sevilla SA — Seville** (Hull) **2008-11 Ast. de Huelva S.A. — Huelva** Yd No: 822 Loa 142.00 (BB) Br ex - Dght 5.700 Lbp 133.18 Br md 23.00 Dpth 16.30 Welded	**(A35A2RR) Ro-Ro Cargo Ship** Stern door/ramp (p. a.) Len: 9.50 Wid: 6.50 Swl: - Stern door/ramp (s. a.) Len: 9.50 Wid: 12.30 Swl: - Lane-Len: 1830 Lane-clr ht: 6.80 Trailers: 120	**2 oil engines** reduction geared to sc. shafts driving 2 CP propellers Total Power: 18,480kW (25,126hp) 22.0kn Wartsila 8L46 2 x 4 Stroke 8 Cy. 460 x 580 each-9240kW (12563bhp) Wartsila Finland Oy-Finland AuxGen: 2 x 1200kW a.c, 3 x 645kW a.c Thrusters: 2 Thwart. CP thruster (f) Fuel: 150.0 (d.f.) 891.0 (r.f.)
9506215 *2FCX7* -	**SEATRUCK POWER** **Seatruck Ferries Two Ltd** Seatruck Ferries Ltd *Douglas* *Isle of Man (British)* MMSI: 235090183	**19,722** 5,917 5,300	Class: NV	**2012-02 Flensburger Schiffbau-Ges. mbH & Co. KG — Flensburg** Yd No: 747 Loa 142.00 (BB) Br ex - Dght 5.700 Lbp 133.46 Br md 25.00 Dpth 21.35 Welded, 4 dks	**(A35A2RR) Ro-Ro Cargo Ship** Passengers: driver berths: 12 Stern door/ramp (centre) Len: 19.00 Wid: 17.60 Swl: - Lane-Len: 2166 Trailers: 151	**2 oil engines** reduction geared to sc. shafts driving 2 CP propellers Total Power: 16,000kW (21,754hp) 21.0kn MAN-B&W 7L48/60CR 2 x 4 Stroke 7 Cy. 480 x 600 each-8000kW (10877bhp) MAN B&W Diesel AG-Augsburg AuxGen: 2 x 1200kW a.c, 2 x 800kW a.c Thrusters: 2 Tunnel thruster (f)
9506203 *2EUK3* -	**SEATRUCK PROGRESS** **Seatruck Ferries One Ltd** Seatruck Ferries Ltd *Douglas* *Isle of Man (British)* MMSI: 235088244 Official number: 742867	**19,722** 5,917 5,300	Class: NV	**2011-11 Flensburger Schiffbau-Ges. mbH & Co. KG — Flensburg** Yd No: 746 Loa 142.00 (BB) Br ex - Dght 5.700 Lbp 133.46 Br md 25.00 Dpth 21.35 Welded, 4 dks	**(A35A2RR) Ro-Ro Cargo Ship** Passengers: driver berths: 12 Stern door/ramp (centre) Len: 19.00 Wid: 17.60 Swl: - Lane-Len: 2166 Trailers: 151	**2 oil engines** reduction geared to sc. shafts driving 2 CP propellers Total Power: 16,000kW (21,754hp) 21.0kn MAN-B&W 7L48/60CR 2 x 4 Stroke 7 Cy. 480 x 600 each-8000kW (10877bhp) MAN B&W Diesel AG-Augsburg AuxGen: 2 x 1200kW a.c, 2 x 800kW a.c Thrusters: 2 Tunnel thruster (f) Fuel: 100.0 (d.f.) 830.0 (r.f.)
9220988 *P3UX8* -	**SEATTLE** *ex* UBC Seattle *-2004* *ex* Stornes *-2001* **Mundi Shipping Co Ltd** Athena Marine Co Ltd *Limassol* *Cyprus* MMSI: 209316000 Official number: 9220988	**19,743** 10,718 31,923 T/cm 41.0	Class: GL	**2000-12 Saiki Heavy Industries Co Ltd — Saiki OT** Yd No: 1108 Loa 171.60 (BB) Br ex - Dght 10.400 Lbp 163.60 Br md 27.00 Dpth 14.80 Welded, 1 dk	**(A21A2BC) Bulk Carrier** Grain: 41,755; Bale: 41,137 Compartments: 5 Ho, ER 5 Ha: (13.4 x 15.0)3 (20.5 x 22.8) (19.7 x 18.0)ER Cranes: 4x30t Ice Capable	**1 oil engine** driving 1 FP propeller Total Power: 7,061kW (9,600hp) 14.5kn Mitsubishi 6UEC52LA 1 x 2 Stroke 6 Cy. 520 x 1600 7061kW (9600bhp) Akasaka Tekkosho KK (Akasaka DieselLtd)-Japan AuxGen: 2 x 480kW 450V 60Hz a.c Fuel: 319.0 (d.f.) (Heating Coils) 1327.0 (r.f.) 27.1pd
8965880 - -	**SEATTLE** - -	*194*		**1970 Astilleros Marco Chilena Ltda. — Iquique** L reg 30.05 Br ex - Dght - Lbp - Br md 7.65 Dpth 3.68 Welded, 1 dk	**(B11B2FV) Fishing Vessel**	**1 oil engine** driving 1 FP propeller
9560352 *3FFH5* -	**SEATTLE BRIDGE** **Yuti Shipping SA** 'K' Line Ship Management Co Ltd (KLSM) SatCom: Inmarsat C 435390311 *Panama* *Panama* MMSI: 353903000 Official number: 4173310	**71,787** 26,914 72,890 T/cm 95.3	Class: NK	**2010-05 Koyo Dockyard Co Ltd — Mihara HS** Yd No: 2285 Loa 293.18 (BB) Br ex - Dght 14.021 Lbp 276.00 Br md 40.00 Dpth 24.30 Welded, 1 dk	**(A33A2CC) Container Ship (Fully Cellular)** TEU 6350 C Ho 2912 TEU C Dk 3438 TEU incl 500 ref C. Compartments: ER, 9 Cell Ho 9 Ha: ER	**1 oil engine** driving 1 FP propeller Total Power: 62,920kW (85,546hp) 25.0kn MAN-B&W 11K98MC 1 x 2 Stroke 11 Cy. 980 x 2660 62920kW (85546bhp) Mitsui Engineering & Shipbuilding CLtd-Japan AuxGen: 5 x 2000kW a.c Thrusters: 1 Tunnel thruster (f) Fuel: 8900.0 (r.f.)
7318949 *WDB4541* -	**SEATTLE ENTERPRISE** *ex* Grant Neptune *-1987* *ex* Polar 902 *-1982* **Trident Seafoods Corp** - SatCom: Inmarsat A 1511660 *Seattle, WA* *United States of America* MMSI: 369604000 Official number: 904767	**2,292** 687 -	Class: (AB)	**1973-07 Burton Shipyard Co., Inc. — Port Arthur, Tx** Yd No: 503 Converted From: Research Vessel-1988 Converted From: Offshore Tug/Supply Ship-1982 Lengthened-1988 Loa 82.33 Br ex 13.42 Dght 4.747 Lbp 61.01 Br md - Dpth 5.49 Welded, 1 dk	**(B11A2FG) Factory Stern Trawler**	**2 oil engines** driving 2 CP propellers Total Power: 2,868kW (3,900hp) EMD (Electro-Motive) 16-645-E6 2 x Vee 2 Stroke 16 Cy. 230 x 254 each-1434kW (1950bhp) (new engine 1988) General Motors Corp.Electro-Motive Div.-U.S.A. AuxGen: 2 x 780kW a.c, 2 x 250kW a.c Thrusters: 1 Thwart. FP thruster (f)
9450375 *9HA3473* -	**SEATTLE EXPRESS** **KG ms 'CPO Hamburg' Offen Reederei GmbH & Co** Reederei Claus-Peter Offen GmbH & Co KG *Valletta* *Malta* MMSI: 229638000 Official number: 9450375	**91,203** 55,360 103,845	Class: GL	**2009-12 Hyundai Heavy Industries Co Ltd — Ulsan** Yd No: 2074 Loa 334.11 (BB) Br ex - Dght 14.610 Lbp 319.00 Br md 42.80 Dpth 24.80 Welded, 1 dk	**(A33A2CC) Container Ship (Fully Cellular)** TEU 8580 C Ho 3832 TEU C Dk 4748 incl 700 ref C.	**1 oil engine** driving 1 FP propeller Total Power: 72,240kW (98,218hp) 25.6kn MAN-B&W 12K98MC-C 1 x 2 Stroke 12 Cy. 980 x 2400 72240kW (98218bhp) Hyundai Heavy Industries Co Ltd-South Korea AuxGen: 4 x 2699kW 6600/450V 60Hz a.c Thrusters: 1 Tunnel thruster (f)
7807500 *WCW5082* -	**SEATTLE SLEW** *ex* H. O. S. Seattle Slew *-1997* *ex* Oryx *-1993* **T Benetee LLC** Tidewater Marine LLC *New Orleans, LA* *United States of America* Official number: 603700	**717** 215 1,000	Class: AB	**1979-03 Halter Marine, Inc. — New Orleans, La** Yd No: 711 Loa 56.39 Br ex 12.22 Dght 3.658 Lbp 54.87 Br md 12.20 Dpth 4.27 Welded, 1 dk	**(B21A20S) Platform Supply Ship**	**2 oil engines** reverse reduction geared to sc. shafts driving 2 FP propellers Total Power: 1,654kW (2,248hp) 12.0kn Caterpillar D399SCAC 2 x Vee 4 Stroke 16 Cy. 159 x 203 each-827kW (1124bhp) Caterpillar Tractor Co-USA AuxGen: 2 x 125kW
7736139 - -	**SEATUCK** *ex* Lady Dawn *-2005* *ex* Rachel R *-1992* *ex* Dee Jay *-1992* **Off Shore Diving Corp** - *New York, NY* *United States of America* Official number: 588061	*115* 79 -		**1977 Steiner Shipyard, Inc. — Bayou La Batre, Al** L reg 20.12 Br ex - Dght - Lbp - Br md 6.71 Dpth 3.23 Welded, 1 dk	**(B11B2FV) Fishing Vessel**	**1 oil engine** driving 1 FP propeller Total Power: 268kW (364hp) Caterpillar 3406TA 1 x 4 Stroke 6 Cy. 137 x 165 268kW (364bhp) Caterpillar Tractor Co-USA
9204764 *DDTS* -	**SEATURBOT** **tms 'Seaturbot' GmbH & Co KG** German Tanker Shipping GmbH & Co KG *Bremen* *Germany* MMSI: 211330520 Official number: 4820	**21,353** 8,389 32,230 T/cm 42.0	Class: GL	**2000-06 Lindenau GmbH Schiffswerft u. Maschinenfabrik — Kiel** Yd No: 241 Loa 177.75 (BB) Br ex 28.16 Dght 11.000 Lbp 168.00 Br md 28.00 Dpth 16.80 Welded, 1 dk	**(A13A2TW) Crude/Oil Products Tanker** Double Hull (13F) Liq: 36,690; Liq (Oil): 36,690 Compartments: 10 Wing Ta, ER, 2 Wing Slop Ta 10 Cargo Pump (s): 10x600m³/hr Manifold: Bow/CM: 85m Ice Capable	**1 oil engine** reduction geared to sc. shaft driving 1 CP propeller Total Power: 8,340kW (11,339hp) 14.7kn MAN 6L58/64 1 x 4 Stroke 6 Cy. 580 x 640 8340kW (11339bhp) MAN B&W Diesel AG-Augsburg AuxGen: 1 x 1120kW 240/400V 50Hz a.c, 3 x 960kW 240/400V 50Hz a.c Thrusters: 1 Thwart. CP thruster (f) Fuel: 321.6 (d.f.) 811.4 (r.f.) 30.0pd
9315771 *9HA2304* -	**SEAVALOUR** *ex* Gan-Valour *-2010* **Universal Maritime Ventures SA** Thenamaris (Ships Management) Inc *Valletta* *Malta* MMSI: 248298000 Official number: 9315771	**29,348** 12,036 46,702 T/cm 52.2	Class: NV	**2007-03 Hyundai Mipo Dockyard Co Ltd — Ulsan** Yd No: 0324 Loa 183.20 (BB) Br ex - Dght 12.217 Lbp 174.00 Br md 32.20 Dpth 18.80 Welded, 1 dk	**(A12B2TR) Chemical/Products Tanker** Double Hull (13F) Liq: 51,909; Liq (Oil): 51,909 Compartments: 12 Wing Ta, 2 Wing Slop Ta, ER 12 Cargo Pump (s): 12x600m³/hr Manifold: Bow/CM: 91.7m	**1 oil engine** driving 1 FP propeller Total Power: 9,488kW (12,900hp) 14.5kn MAN-B&W 6S50MC-C 1 x 2 Stroke 6 Cy. 500 x 2000 9488kW (12900bhp) Hyundai Heavy Industries Co Ltd-South Korea AuxGen: 3 x 740kW a.c Fuel: 187.0 (d.f.) 1315.0 (r.f.)
9205940 *9HG07* -	**SEAVENUS** *ex* Nord Cecilie *-2002* **Squid Line Shipping Ltd** Eastern Mediterranean Maritime Ltd *Valletta* *Malta* MMSI: 215209000 Official number: 7699	**28,632** 17,569 50,913 T/cm 54.2	Class: BV (NV)	**2000-08 Oshima Shipbuilding Co Ltd — Saikai NS** Yd No: 10280 Loa 189.99 (BB) Br ex 32.29 Dght 11.918 Lbp 182.00 Br md 32.26 Dpth 16.67 Welded, 1 dk	**(A21A2BC) Bulk Carrier** Grain: 65,252; Bale: 64,000 Compartments: 5 Ho, ER 5 Ha: (17.9 x 17.6) (18.7 x 17.6)3 (20.4 x 17.6)ER Cranes: 4x30t	**1 oil engine** driving 1 FP propeller Total Power: 9,467kW (12,871hp) 14.5kn B&W 6S50MC-C 1 x 2 Stroke 6 Cy. 500 x 2000 9467kW (12871bhp) Kawasaki Heavy Industries Ltd-Japan AuxGen: 3 x 450kW 450V 60Hz a.c Fuel: 111.0 (d.f.) (Heating Coils) 1625.0 (r.f.)

IMO / Call sign	Name / Owner	Tonnage	Class	Builder / Dimensions	Type / Cargo	Machinery
6908993 *HSB4649* -	**SEAVIC AREMAR** *ex* Aremar *-1999* **Seavic Reefer Line Co Ltd** Seavic Food Industries Co Ltd *Bangkok* *Thailand* MMSI: 567451000 Official number: 550000225	**2,649** 1,009 2,435	Class: LR ✠ **100A1** SS 08/2009 ✠ **LMC** **+Lloyd's RMC** Eq.Ltr: R; Cable: U2	**1969-11 Astilleros Argentinos Rio de La Plata S.A. (ASTARSA) — Tigre** Yd No: 127 Loa 99.57 (BB) Br ex 13.62 Dght 5.411 Lbp 89.41 Br md 13.61 Dpth 8.82 Welded, 2 dks, 3rd dk (sparred) in Nos. 2 & 3 holds	**(A34A2GR) Refrigerated Cargo Ship** Ins: 3,951; Liq: 90 Compartments: 1 Dp Ta in Hold, 2 Ho, ER, 3 Tw Dk 4 Ha: 2 (5.7 x 4.3)2 (6.4 x 4.3)ER Cranes: 2; Derricks: 2x3t	**1 oil engine** sr geared to sc. shaft driving 1 CP propeller Total Power: 3,530kW (4,799hp) 13.5kn Fiat A420.12SS 1 x Vee 4 Stroke 12 Cy. 420 x 500 3530kW (4799bhp) Grandes Motores Diesel SAIC (FIAT Concord)-Argentina AuxGen: 3 x 218kW 400V 50Hz a.c Boilers: (AuxB) (10.0kgf/cm^2 (9.8bar)) Fuel: 130.0 (d.f.) 430.0 (r.f.) 11.0pd
7819034 *HSB2579* -	**SEAVIC PRINSES** *ex* Apirachai Reefer 2 *-2012* *ex* Saronic Pride *-1999* *ex* Pacific Princess *-1996* **Seavic Reefer Line Co Ltd** Seavic Food Industries Co Ltd *Bangkok* *Thailand* MMSI: 567004800 Official number: 417400061	**2,988** 1,448 3,878	Class: (LR) ✠ Classed LR until 22/3/06	**1979-05 Scheepswerf en Mfbk. Ysselwerf B.V. — Capelle a/d IJssel** Yd No: 192 **1983-10 van der Giessen-de Noord BV — Krimpen a/d IJssel** (Additional cargo section) Lengthened-1983 Loa 96.98 (BB) Br ex 15.09 Dght 5.423 Lbp 88.91 Br md 15.02 Dpth 8.01 Welded, 2 dks	**(A34A2GR) Refrigerated Cargo Ship** Ins: 5,132 Compartments: 4 Ho, ER, 4 Tw Dk 4 Ha: 4 (8.7 x 8.8)ER Cranes: 2x3t; Derricks: 4x5t Ice Capable	**1 oil engine** sr geared to sc. shaft driving 1 CP propeller Total Power: 2,060kW (2,801hp) 14.5kn MaK 8M453AK 1 x 4 Stroke 8 Cy. 320 x 420 2060kW (2801bhp) Krupp MaK Maschinenbau GmbH-Kiel AuxGen: 1 x 360kW 380V 50Hz a.c, 2 x 224kW 380V 50Hz a.c Boilers: 2 e (ex.g.) (fitted: 1979) 9.2kgf/cm^2 (9.0bar), 2 AuxB (o.f.) (fitted: 1979) 8.7kgf/cm^2 (8.5bar) Fuel: 342.0
7724186 *HSB4761* -	**SEAVIC REEFER** *ex* Rade *-1993* *ex* Azur Trader *-1993* *ex* Fresh Carrier *-1989* *ex* Chion Med *-1987* *ex* Shereen *-1982* *ex* Nor Freeze I *-1981* **Seavic Reefer Line Co Ltd** - *Bangkok* *Thailand* MMSI: 567476000	**2,305** 733 2,480	Class: NV	**1979-05 Kaarbos Mek. Verksted AS — Harstad** Yd No: 89 Loa 80.65 Br ex 15.30 Dght 5.023 Lbp 72.13 Br md - Dpth 7.73 Welded, 1 dk & S dk	**(A34A2GR) Refrigerated Cargo Ship** Ins: 3,795 Compartments: 2 Ho, ER 3 Ha: (9.6 x 5.7)2 (7.7 x 5.7) Cranes: 2x5t Ice Capable	**1 oil engine** driving 1 FP propeller Total Power: 2,721kW (3,699hp) 14.0kn Normo KVMB-18 1 x Vee 4 Stroke 18 Cy. 250 x 300 2721kW (3699bhp) AS Bergens Mek Verksteder-Norway AuxGen: 3 x 312kW 380V 50Hz a.c Thrusters: 1 Thwart. FP thruster (f)
9315783 *9HA2305* -	**SEAVICTORY** *ex* Gan-Victory *-2010* **Highlander Seaways Inc** Thenamaris (Ships Management) Inc *Valletta* *Malta* MMSI: 248299000 Official number: 9315783	**29,348** 12,036 46,702 T/cm 52.2	Class: NV	**2007-06 Hyundai Mipo Dockyard Co Ltd — Ulsan** Yd No: 0325 Loa 183.20 (BB) Br ex 32.23 Dght 12.217 Lbp 174.00 Br md 32.20 Dpth 18.80 Welded, 1 dk	**(A12B2TR) Chemical/Products Tanker** Double Hull (13F) Liq: 51,909; Liq (Oil): 51,909 Compartments: 12 Wing Ta, 2 Wing Slop Ta, ER 12 Cargo Pump (s): 12x600m^3/hr Manifold: Bow/CM: 91.7m	**1 oil engine** driving 1 FP propeller Total Power: 9,488kW (12,900hp) 14.5kn MAN-B&W 6S50MC-C 1 x 2 Stroke 6 Cy. 500 x 2000 9488kW (12900bhp) Hyundai Heavy Industries Co Ltd-South Korea AuxGen: 3 x 740kW a.c Fuel: 200.6 (d.f.) 1335.4 (r.f.)
9318096 *9HUM8* -	**SEAVOYAGER** - **Lanel Navigation Corp** Thenamaris (Ships Management) Inc SatCom: Inmarsat C 425643910 *Valletta* *Malta* MMSI: 256439000 Official number: 9318096	**81,339** 52,080 159,233 T/cm 118.0	Class: NV	**2007-07 Hyundai Samho Heavy Industries Co Ltd — Samho** Yd No: S276 Loa 274.26 (BB) Br ex 48.04 Dght 17.071 Lbp 264.00 Br md 48.00 Dpth 23.10 Welded, 1 dk	**(A13A2TV) Crude Oil Tanker** Double Hull (13F) Liq: 167,531; Liq (Oil): 167,531 Cargo Heating Coils Compartments: 12 Wing Ta, 2 Wing Slop Ta, ER 3 Cargo Pump (s): 3x4000m^3/hr Manifold: Bow/CM: 138.4m	**1 oil engine** driving 1 FP propeller Total Power: 18,623kW (25,320hp) 15.7kn MAN-B&W 6S70MC-C 1 x 2 Stroke 6 Cy. 700 x 2800 18623kW (25320bhp) Hyundai Heavy Industries Co Ltd-South Korea AuxGen: 3 x a.c
9408762 *VRDT2* -	**SEAVOYAGER** - **Premium Shipping Co Ltd** Valles Steamship (Canada) Inc SatCom: Inmarsat C 447700640 *Hong Kong* *Hong Kong* MMSI: 477144300 Official number: HK-2096	**60,193** 33,762 109,085 T/cm 91.3	Class: AB	**2009-01 Hudong-Zhonghua Shipbuilding (Group) Co Ltd — Shanghai** Yd No: H1508A Loa 243.00 (BB) Br ex 42.03 Dght 15.350 Lbp 233.00 Br md 42.00 Dpth 22.00 Welded, 1 dk	**(A13A2TV) Crude Oil Tanker** Double Hull (13F) Liq: 123,030; Liq (Oil): 128,000 Cargo Heating Coils Compartments: 12 Wing Ta, 2 Wing Slop Ta, ER 3 Cargo Pump (s): 3x2500m^3/hr Manifold: Bow/CM: 119.5m	**1 oil engine** driving 1 FP propeller Total Power: 13,570kW (18,450hp) 14.5kn MAN-B&W 7S60MC 1 x 2 Stroke 7 Cy. 600 x 2292 13570kW (18450bhp) Hudong Heavy Machinery Co Ltd-China AuxGen: 3 x 680kW a.c Fuel: 150.0 (d.f.) 2800.0 (r.f.)
8822765 *ZMBU* -	**SEAWATCH** *ex* Little Mermaid *-1995* **S & K Day Ltd** Seaworks Ltd *Wellington* *New Zealand* Official number: 875089	*125* 94 -		**1976 Nautilus Marine — Nelson** Loa 23.00 Br ex 9.67 Dght 1.900 Lbp - Br md 9.65 Dpth 3.24 Welded, 1 dk	**(B34P2QV) Salvage Ship**	**2 oil engines** with clutches & reverse reduction geared to sc. shafts driving 2 FP propellers Total Power: 206kW (280hp) Lister JAS6 2 x 4 Stroke 6 Cy. 127 x 140 each-103kW (140bhp) Lister Marine, R. A. Lister &Co. Ltd., Marine Div.-Dursley
8410184 *5BFG2* -	**SEAWAY** *ex* Vaydagubskiy *-2000* **Baggermaatschappij Boskalis BV** - *Limassol* *Cyprus* MMSI: 212472000	**12,962** 3,888 22,664	Class: BV (RS)	**1986-09 Oy Wartsila Ab — Turku** Yd No: 1285 Converted From: Hopper/Suction Dredger-2001 Lengthened-2001 Loa 171.90 Br ex 22.35 Dght 8.820 Lbp 154.31 Br md 22.00 Dpth 12.50 Welded, 1 dk	**(B33B2DT) Trailing Suction Hopper Dredger** Hopper: 13,255 Ice Capable	**2 oil engines** reduction geared to sc. shafts driving 2 CP propellers Total Power: 8,804kW (11,970hp) 14.0kn Pielstick 8PC2-6L-400 2 x 4 Stroke 8 Cy. 400 x 460 each-4402kW (5985bhp) Oy Wartsila Ab-Finland AuxGen: 2 x 1600kW 400V 50Hz a.c, 2 x 3600kW 660V a.c Thrusters: 2 Tunnel thruster (f) Fuel: 2050.0
6610039 *5NLQ2* -	**SEAWAY AGBAMU** *ex* Seaway Rover *-2008* *ex* Ceanic Rover *-1999* *ex* Hornbeck Illustrious *-1998* *ex* Seaboard Illustrious *-1995* *ex* Ross Illustrious *-1982* **Peacegate Oil & Gas Ltd** Peacegate Group *Nigeria* MMSI: 657272000 Official number: SR783	**1,433** 429 2,300	Class: IS (LR) (BV) ✠ Classed LR until 20/10/82	**1966-09 Cochrane & Sons Ltd. — Selby** Yd No: 1504 Converted From: Stern Trawler-1983 Loa 65.72 Br ex 12.17 Dght 4.990 Lbp 60.97 Br md 12.04 Dpth 7.93 Welded, 2 dks	**(B22G2OY) Standby Safety Vessel**	**1 oil engine** driving 1 CP propeller Total Power: 1,581kW (2,150hp) 11.0kn Ruston 9ATCM 1 x 4 Stroke 9 Cy. 318 x 368 1581kW (2150bhp) Ruston & Hornsby Ltd.-Lincoln AuxGen: 2 x 300kW 220V d.c, 2 x 170kW 220V d.c
9049322 *YD6496* -	**SEAWAY CAMAR LAUT** *ex* Total Commitment *-2004* **PT Acergy Indonesia** - *Samarinda* *Indonesia*	**144** 44 -	Class: KI	**1968-01 Trawler Construction Group Pty Ltd — Fremantle WA** Loa 28.33 Br ex - Dght 2.000 Lbp 25.98 Br md 7.32 Dpth 2.67 Welded, 1 dk	**(B34L2QU) Utility Vessel**	**2 oil engines** geared to sc. shafts driving 2 Propellers Total Power: 354kW (482hp) Caterpillar D334 2 x 4 Stroke 6 Cy. 121 x 152 each-177kW (241bhp) Caterpillar Tractor Co-USA
7016644 *5VCJ3* -	**SEAWAY INVINCIBLE** *ex* Tidewater Invincible *-1998* *ex* Hornbeck Invincible *-1998* *ex* Seaboard Invincible *-1995* *ex* Invincible *-1982* **Seaway Invincible Ltd** Hallstrom Holdings Pte Ltd *Lome* *Togo* MMSI: 671408000	**1,461** 438 1,727	Class: PV (LR) (BV) (IS) ✠ Classed LR until 17/11/82	**1970-09 Cochrane & Sons Ltd. — Selby** Yd No: 1522 Converted From: Pollution Control Vessel-1988 Converted From: Stern Trawler-1983 Loa 65.54 Br ex 12.12 Dght 4.990 Lbp 61.50 Br md 12.04 Dpth 7.93 Welded, 2 dks	**(B22G2OY) Standby Safety Vessel** Compartments: 2 Ho, ER 6 Ha: 2 (2.4 x 2.7) (1.3 x 3.6)3 (0.9 x 0.9)	**1 oil engine** dr geared to sc. shaft driving 1 CP propeller Total Power: 1,589kW (2,160hp) 11.0kn Ruston 9ATCM 1 x 4 Stroke 9 Cy. 318 x 368 1589kW (2160bhp) English Electric Diesels Ltd.-Glasgow AuxGen: 2 x 300kW 220V d.c, 2 x 255kW 220V d.c Fuel: 406.5 (d.f.)
6908400 *HP4559* -	**SEAWAY SAPPHIRE** *ex* Kim Princess *-1989* *ex* Sea Treasure *-1987* *ex* Tomoe 8 *-1981* *ex* Taisei Maru No. 31 *-1978* **Seaway Marine Services Pte Ltd** - *Panama* *Panama* Official number: 17776PEXT4	**1,074** 545 1,910	Class: (GL) (BV)	**1968-11 Tokushima Zosen Sangyo K.K. — Komatsushima** Yd No: 278 Loa 70.36 Br ex 10.52 Dght 4.960 Lbp 65.00 Br md 10.49 Dpth 5.49 Riveted\Welded, 1 dk	**(A13B2TP) Products Tanker** Liq: 2,489; Liq (Oil): 2,489 Compartments: 4 Ta, ER	**1 oil engine** driving 1 FP propeller Total Power: 1,103kW (1,500hp) 11.5kn Niigata 6M37CHS 1 x 4 Stroke 6 Cy. 370 x 540 1103kW (1500bhp) Niigata Engineering Co Ltd-Japan AuxGen: 1 x 60kW 225V a.c
9215531 *J8B3149* -	**SEAWAYS 9** *ex* Britoil 37 *-2004* **Towage & Salvage Contractors Ltd** Seaways International LLC *Kingstown* *St Vincent & The Grenadines* MMSI: 375042000 Official number: 9621	**458** 137 362	Class: AB	**1999-08 Fujian Southeast Shipyard — Fuzhou FJ** Yd No: H8023 Loa 37.00 Br ex - Dght 4.279 Lbp 34.84 Br md 11.40 Dpth 4.95 Welded, 1 dk	**(B32A2ST) Tug**	**2 oil engines** with clutches, flexible couplings & reverse reduction geared to sc. shafts driving 2 FP propellers Total Power: 3,678kW (5,000hp) 11.5kn Yanmar 6N280-EN 2 x 4 Stroke 6 Cy. 280 x 380 each-1839kW (2500bhp) Yanmar Diesel Engine Co Ltd-Japan AuxGen: 2 x 80kW 220/440V 50Hz a.c Fuel: 200.0 (d.f.) 8.0pd
9322932 *J8B3261* -	**SEAWAYS 10** - **Sofia Marine Corp** Seaways International LLC *Kingstown* *St Vincent & The Grenadines* MMSI: 375157000 Official number: 9733	**919** 275 560	Class: AB (LR) ✠ Classed LR until 17/7/06	**2005-10 Dubai Drydocks — Dubai** Yd No: NB29 Loa 45.00 Br ex 13.10 Dght 5.432 Lbp 39.60 Br md 12.60 Dpth 6.00 Welded, 1 dk	**(B32A2ST) Tug** Passengers: berths: 22	**2 oil engines** with clutches, flexible couplings & sr reverse geared to sc. shafts driving 2 CP propellers Total Power: 5,440kW (7,396hp) 13.0kn MAN-B&W 8L27/38 2 x 4 Stroke 8 Cy. 270 x 380 each-2720kW (3698bhp) MAN B&W Diesel A/S-Denmark AuxGen: 2 x 500kW 380V 50Hz a.c, 1 x 245kW 380V 50Hz a.c Thrusters: 1 Thwart. CP thruster (f)

IMO / Call sign / Flag	Name / Owner / Port / MMSI	Tonnage	Class	Builder / Dimensions	Type	Machinery
9380207 *9V7232* -	**SEAWAYS 12** **Seaways International Pte Ltd** - *Singapore* *Singapore* MMSI: 565651000 Official number: 393382	**1,419** 425 1,146	Class: AB	**2007-11 Keppel Singmarine Pte Ltd — Singapore** Yd No: 324 Loa 51.00 Br ex - Dght 6.600 Lbp 44.40 Br md 15.00 Dpth 6.50 Welded, 1 dk	**(B21B20A) Anchor Handling Tug Supply**	**2 oil engines** reduction geared to sc. shafts driving 2 CP propellers Total Power: 5,940kW (8,076hp) 13.0kn MaK 9M25 2 x 4 Stroke 9 Cy. 255 x 400 each-2970kW (4038bhp) Caterpillar Motoren GmbH & Co. KG-Germany AuxGen: 2 x 500kW 380V 50Hz a.c Thrusters: 1 Tunnel thruster (f) Fuel: 792.2 (r.f.)
9361160 *9V6661* -	**SEAWAYS 15** *ex Uni Haul Doreen -2006* **Seaways International Pte Ltd** - *Singapore* *Singapore* MMSI: 565308000 Official number: 391169	**297** 89 -	Class: BV	**2006-01 Guangzhou Panyu Lingshan Shipyard Ltd — Guangzhou GD** (Hull) Yd No: 128 **2006-01 Cheoy Lee Shipyards Ltd — Hong Kong** Yd No: 4868 Loa 31.80 Br ex - Dght 3.200 Lbp 29.26 Br md 9.60 Dpth 4.15 Welded, 1 dk	**(B32A2ST) Tug**	**2 oil engines** reduction geared to sc. shafts driving 2 CP propellers Total Power: 2,236kW (3,040hp) Caterpillar 3512B 2 x Vee 4 Stroke 12 Cy. 170 x 190 each-1118kW (1520bhp) Caterpillar Inc-USA
9442287 *9V7233* -	**SEAWAYS 16** **Seaways International Pte Ltd** - *Singapore* *Singapore* MMSI: 565669000 Official number: 393383	**1,566** 469 929	Class: AB	**2010-07 Keppel Singmarine Pte Ltd — Singapore** Yd No: 335 Loa 51.00 Br ex 15.12 Dght 6.600 Lbp 44.40 Br md 15.00 Dpth 6.50 Welded, 1 dk	**(B21B20A) Anchor Handling Tug Supply** Cranes: 1x10t	**2 oil engines** driving 2 gen. reduction geared to sc. shafts driving 2 CP propellers Total Power: 5,940kW (8,076hp) 13.0kn MaK 9M25C 2 x 4 Stroke 9 Cy. 255 x 400 each-2970kW (4038bhp) Caterpillar Motoren GmbH & Co. KG-Germany AuxGen: 2 x 500kW 380V 50Hz a.c, 2 x 1200kW 380V 50Hz a.c Thrusters: 2 Thwart. CP thruster (f); 1 Thwart. CP thruster (a) Fuel: 680.0
9166819 *J8B3887* -	**SEAWAYS 18** *ex Koranui -2008 ex Sea-Tow 25 -2005* **All Weather Towage Contractors Ltd** Seaways International LLC *Kingstown* *St Vincent & The Grenadines* MMSI: 376874000 Official number: 10360	**491** 147 -	Class: BV	**1997-06 Ship Constructors Ltd — Whangarei** Yd No: 150 Loa 34.50 Br ex - Dght 4.850 Lbp 32.49 Br md 10.80 Dpth 6.09 Welded, 1 dk	**(B32A2ST) Tug**	**2 oil engines** reduction geared to sc. shafts driving 2 FP propellers Total Power: 2,194kW (2,982hp) 14.0kn EMD (Electro-Motive) 12-645-F7B 2 x Vee 2 Stroke 12 Cy. 230 x 254 each-1097kW (1491bhp) General Motors Corp.Electro-Motive Div.-La Grange AuxGen: 2 x 96kW 415/240V 50Hz a.c
9556636 *9V7689* -	**SEAWAYS 20** **Seaways International Pte Ltd** - SatCom: Inmarsat C 456624610 *Singapore* *Singapore* MMSI: 566246000 Official number: 394635	**1,691** 507 1,077	Class: AB	**2011-10 Keppel Singmarine Pte Ltd — Singapore** Yd No: 349 Loa 55.00 Br ex - Dght 5.800 Lbp 52.70 Br md 15.00 Dpth 6.75 Welded, 1 dk	**(B21B20A) Anchor Handling Tug Supply** Cranes: 1	**2 oil engines** reduction geared to sc. shafts driving 2 Z propellers Total Power: 5,940kW (8,076hp) 13.5kn MaK 9M25C 2 x 4 Stroke 9 Cy. 255 x 400 each-2970kW (4038bhp) Caterpillar Motoren GmbH & Co. KG-Germany AuxGen: 3 x 275kW a.c, 2 x 1200kW a.c Thrusters: 2 Tunnel thruster (f) Fuel: 600.0
9647954 *9V9961* -	**SEAWAYS 22** **Seaways International Pte Ltd** - *Singapore* *Singapore* MMSI: 566912000 Official number: 397794	**1,212** 363 590	Class: AB	**2013-09 Keppel Singmarine Pte Ltd — Singapore** Yd No: 369 Loa 44.55 Br ex 13.53 Dght 5.200 Lbp 42.80 Br md 13.50 Dpth 6.50 Welded, 1 dk	**(B21B20A) Anchor Handling Tug Supply**	**2 oil engines** reduction geared to sc. shafts driving 2 Propellers Total Power: 4,000kW (5,438hp) MaK 6M25C 2 x 4 Stroke 6 Cy. 255 x 400 each-2000kW (2719bhp) Caterpillar Motoren (Guangdong) CoLtd-China AuxGen: 2 x 350kW a.c Fuel: 480.0
7047540 - -	**SEAWELD VENTURE** *ex Parker Tide -1985 ex Algosaibi XII -1983* *ex Parker Tide -1983 ex Eastern Patriot -1974* *ex Wapiti -1972* **Michael J Fagg** -	*181* 106 -	Class: (AB)	**1969 Corpus Christi Marine Service — Corpus Christi, Tx** Yd No: 107 L reg 34.14 Br ex - Dght 3.074 Lbp 33.46 Br md 7.93 Dpth 3.74 Welded, 1 dk	**(B21A20S) Platform Supply Ship**	**2 oil engines** reverse reduction geared to sc. shafts driving 2 FP propellers Total Power: 992kW (1,348hp) G.M. (Detroit Diesel) 12V-149 2 x Vee 2 Stroke 12 Cy. 146 x 146 each-496kW (674bhp) General Motors Detroit DieselAllison Divn-USA
8324567 *GGXE* -	**SEAWELL** *ex CSO Seawell -2002 ex Stena Seawell -1995* **Helix Well Ops (UK) Ltd** - SatCom: Inmarsat B 323215910 *Aberdeen* *United Kingdom* MMSI: 232159000 Official number: 701184	**9,158** 2,747 4,615	Class: NV	**1987-03 North East Shipbuilders Ltd. — Pallion, Sunderland** Yd No: 24 Loa 111.41 Br ex - Dght 7.260 Lbp 100.01 Br md 22.51 Dpth 7.80 Welded	**(B22A20V) Diving Support Vessel** Passengers: berths: 147 Cranes: 2 Ice Capable	**6 diesel electric oil engines** driving 3 Directional propellers Contr. pitch Total Power: 12,666kW (17,220hp) 15.0kn Hedemora V18B/12 6 x Vee 4 Stroke 18 Cy. 210 x 210 each-2111kW (2870bhp) Hedemora Diesel AB-Sweden AuxGen: 2 x 2240kW Thrusters: 3 Thwart. CP thruster (f)
8623860 - -	**SEAWELL III** *ex Monarch I -1989 ex Hai Hin 42 -1987* **Amanan & Sons Marine Pte Ltd**	**157** 46 100	Class: (BV)	**1986 Indonesia Onshore/Offshore Pte Ltd — Singapore** Loa 25.89 Br ex 7.65 Dght 3.041 Lbp 23.17 Br md 7.62 Dpth 3.74 Welded, 1 dk	**(B32A2ST) Tug**	**2 oil engines** driving 2 FP propellers Total Power: 592kW (804hp) 9.0kn Caterpillar 3408TA 2 x Vee 4 Stroke 8 Cy. 137 x 152 each-296kW (402bhp) Caterpillar Tractor Co-USA AuxGen: 2 x 36kW 415V a.c
9305427 *ZR8025* CTA777	**SEAWIN DIAMOND** **ADR Fishing (Pty) Ltd** - *Cape Town* *South Africa* MMSI: 601061600 Official number: 10718	**151** 45 75	Class: (BV)	**2003-09 Fujian Southeast Shipyard — Fuzhou FJ** Yd No: 2002-15 Loa 24.46 Br ex 7.20 Dght 2.500 Lbp 21.50 Br md 7.00 Dpth 3.25 Welded, 1 dk	**(B11B2FV) Fishing Vessel**	**1 oil engine** geared to sc. shaft driving 1 FP propeller Total Power: 485kW (659hp) Cummins QSK19-M 1 x 4 Stroke 6 Cy. 159 x 159 485kW (659bhp) Cummins Engine Co Inc-USA
9305441 *ZR7997* -	**SEAWIN EMERALD** **ADR Fishing (Pty) Ltd** - *Cape Town* *South Africa* MMSI: 601073100 Official number: 10733	**151** 45 75	Class: (BV)	**2003-09 Fujian Southeast Shipyard — Fuzhou FJ** Yd No: 2002-17 Loa 24.46 Br ex 7.20 Dght 2.500 Lbp 21.50 Br md 7.00 Dpth 3.25 Welded, 1 dk	**(B11B2FV) Fishing Vessel**	**1 oil engine** geared to sc. shaft driving 1 FP propeller Total Power: 485kW (659hp) Cummins QSK19-M 1 x 4 Stroke 6 Cy. 159 x 159 485kW (659bhp) Cummins Engine Co Inc-USA
9305415 *ZR8313* -	**SEAWIN SAPPHIRE** **Winn Winn Fishing CC** - *Cape Town* *South Africa* MMSI: 601126200 Official number: 10719	**151** 45 75	Class: (BV)	**2003-09 Fujian Southeast Shipyard — Fuzhou FJ** Yd No: 2002-14 Loa 24.46 Br ex 7.20 Dght 2.500 Lbp 21.50 Br md 7.00 Dpth 3.25 Welded, 1 dk	**(B11B2FV) Fishing Vessel**	**1 oil engine** geared to sc. shaft driving 1 FP propeller Total Power: 597kW (812hp) Cummins QSK19-M 1 x 4 Stroke 6 Cy. 159 x 159 597kW (812bhp) Cummins Engine Co Inc-USA
9303144 *9HA3440* -	**SEAWIND** *ex Danann Island -2013* **Valley Trading Co** Thenamaris (Ships Management) Inc *Valletta* *Malta* MMSI: 229604000 Official number: 9303144	**38,891** 25,195 75,637 T/cm 66.5	Class: NK	**2006-05 Sanoyas Hishino Meisho Corp — Kurashiki OY** Yd No: 1238 Loa 225.00 (BB) Br ex 32.26 Dght 13.995 Lbp 217.00 Br md 32.26 Dpth 19.30 Welded, 1 dk	**(A21A2BC) Bulk Carrier** Grain: 89,201 Compartments: 7 Ho, ER 7 Ha: 6 (17.1 x 15.0)ER (16.3 x 13.4)	**1 oil engine** driving 4 gen. driving 1 FP propeller Total Power: 8,973kW (12,200hp) 14.0kn MAN-B&W 7S50MC-C 1 x 2 Stroke 7 Cy. 500 x 2000 8973kW (12200bhp) Mitsui Engineering & Shipbuilding CLtd-Japan AuxGen: 3 x 445kW 440/230V 60Hz a.c Fuel: 175.0 (d.f.) 2625.0 (r.f.)
9288186 *C6S2090* -	**SEAWIND** **Bahamas Ferries Ltd** - *Nassau* *Bahamas* MMSI: 311635000 Official number: 7000013	**485** 174 105		**2003-02 South Pacific Marine Pty Ltd — Burpengary QLD** Yd No: 694 Loa 45.96 Br ex 15.15 Dght 2.085 Lbp 42.43 Br md 15.00 Dpth 3.50 Welded	**(A36A2PR) Passenger/Ro-Ro Ship (Vehicles)** Hull Material: Aluminium Alloy Passengers: unberthed: 350 Cars: 36	**4 oil engines** geared to sc. shafts driving 2 FP propellers Total Power: 2,316kW (3,148hp) 17.0kn Daewoo V222TIM 4 x Vee 4 Stroke 12 Cy. 128 x 142 each-579kW (787bhp) Daewoo Heavy Industries & MachineryCo Ltd-South Korea
9359428 *VNW5765* -	**SEAWIND 1** *ex Seawind -2010 ex Mermaid Venture -2007* *ex Shin Yang 204 -2005* **Fodico Pty Ltd** - *Gladstone, Qld* *Australia* MMSI: 503495000 Official number: 857880	**492** 148 453	Class: BV	**2005-08 Shin Yang Shipyard Sdn Bhd — Miri** Yd No: 204 Loa 46.00 Br ex - Dght 2.500 Lbp 43.50 Br md 10.90 Dpth 3.20 Welded, 1 dk	**(A35D2RL) Landing Craft** Bow ramp (centre)	**2 oil engines** reduction geared to sc. shafts driving 2 FP propellers Total Power: 882kW (1,200hp) 10.0kn Cummins KTA-19-M3 2 x 4 Stroke 6 Cy. 159 x 159 each-441kW (600bhp) Cummins Engine Co Inc-USA AuxGen: 2 x 80kW 415/220V 50Hz a.c Thrusters: 1 Tunnel thruster (f)

8721143 UIQK -
SEAWIND 1
ex Kapitan Lomayev *-2001*
JSC Sakhalin Leasing Fleet (ZAO 'Sakhalin Leasing Flot')
-
Kholmsk *Russia*
MMSI: 273426670
Official number: 851866

4,407 1,322 1,810
Class: RS (LR)
Classed LR until 5/4/02

1987-06 GP Chernomorskiy Sudostroitelnyy Zavod — Nikolayev Yd No: 560
Loa 104.50 Br ex 16.03 Dght 5.900
Lbp 96.40 Br md 16.00 Dpth 10.20
Welded, 2 dks

(B11A2FG) Factory Stern Trawler
Ice Capable

2 oil engines geared to sc. shaft driving 1 CP propeller
Total Power: 5,148kW (7,000hp) 16.1kn
Russkiy 6CHN40/46
2 x 4 Stroke 6 Cy. 400 x 460 each-2574kW (3500bhp)
Mashinostroitelnyy Zavod"Russkiy-Dizel"-Leningrad
AuxGen: 2 x 1600kW 220/380V 50Hz a.c, 3 x 344kW 220/380V 50Hz a.c
Fuel: 1226.0 (d.f.)

9057434 3EPV9 -
SEAWING-4
-
Hydrofoils Holding Corp
-
Panama *Panama*
Official number: 21634PEXT

130 39 16
Class: (BV) (RS)

1992-04 Zavod im. "Ordzhonikidze" — Poti
Loa 34.50 Br ex 10.30 Dght 1.110
Lbp 32.25 Br md - Dpth 1.80
Welded

(A37B2PS) Passenger Ship
Hull Material: Aluminium Alloy
Passengers: unberthed: 155

2 oil engines geared to sc. shafts driving 2 FP propellers
Total Power: 1,912kW (2,600hp)
M.T.U. 12V396
2 x Vee 4 Stroke 12 Cy. 165 x 185 each-956kW (1300bhp)
MTU Friedrichshafen GmbH-Friedrichshafen

8853489 WDE7235 -
SEAWOLF
ex Genesee *-2001* *ex* Bagatell *-2001*
Research Federation of the State of New York
-
Port Jefferson, NY *United States of America*
MMSI: 367390740
Official number: 657422

122 97 -

1982 Washburn & Doughty Associates Inc — Woolwich ME Yd No: 13
Loa - Br ex - Dght -
Lbp 24.38 Br md 6.40 Dpth 2.83
Welded, 1 dk

(B11B2FV) Fishing Vessel

1 oil engine geared to sc. shaft driving 1 FP propeller
Total Power: 588kW (799hp)
Cummins KT-2300-M
1 x Vee 4 Stroke 12 Cy. 159 x 159 588kW (799bhp)
Cummins Engine Co Inc-USA

7802524 WDD9036 -
SEAWOLF
ex Ben Cheramie *-2007* *ex* Sea Wolf *-2006*
ex G/P IV Point *-1996* *ex* Southern Mar *-1991*
ex PBR/311 *-1987*
launched as Creole Atlantic *-1978*
Seamar Marine Services LLC
-
New Orleans, LA *United States of America*
MMSI: 367150770
Official number: 597499

258 176 700
Class: (AB)

1978-10 Bourg Dry Dock & Service Co., Inc. — Bourg, La Yd No: 45
Loa 54.89 Br ex 12.22 Dght 3.683
Lbp 50.30 Br md 12.20 Dpth 4.27
Welded, 1 dk

(B21A2OS) Platform Supply Ship

2 oil engines reverse reduction geared to sc. shafts driving 2 FP propellers
Total Power: 1,766kW (2,402hp) 12.5kn
EMD (Electro-Motive) 12-567-BC
2 x Vee 2 Stroke 12 Cy. 216 x 254 each-883kW (1201bhp)
(Re-engined ,made 1953, Reconditioned & fitted 1978)
General Motors Corp-USA
AuxGen: 2 x 75kW
Thrusters: 1 Thwart. FP thruster (f)
Fuel: 75.0 (d.f.)

5076298 V7JN3 -
SEAWOLF
ex Dolce Far Niente *-2008* *ex* Seawolfe C *-2006*
ex Seawolfe *-2004* *ex* Matsas Salvor *-2002*
ex Smit Salvor *-1978* *ex* Clyde *-1973*
6875904 Canada Inc
Fraser Yachts Florida Inc
Jaluit *Marshall Islands*
MMSI: 538070194
Official number: 70194

851 255
Class: AB (LR)
✠ Classed LR until 26/10/90

1957-01 J & K Smit's Scheepswerven NV — Kinderdijk Yd No: 858
2002-09 Ast. de Palma S.A. — Palma de Mallorca
Converted From: Tug-2002
Rebuilt
Loa 58.12 Br ex 11.23 Dght 4.966
Lbp 52.02 Br md 10.80 Dpth 5.44
Riveted\Welded, 1 dk

(X11A2YP) Yacht
Ice Capable

2 oil engines with hydroflex coupling & sr gear to sc. shaft driving 1 FP propeller
Total Power: 2,074kW (2,820hp) 12.4kn
MAN RB666
2 x 4 Stroke 6 Cy. 450 x 660 each-1037kW (1410bhp)
J & K Smit's Machinehandel NV-Netherlands
AuxGen: 2 x 220kW a.c
Thrusters: 1 Tunnel thruster (f)
Fuel: 220.0 (d.f.)

8764822 J8B3952 -
SEAWORK 1
ex Blake 101 *-2008* *ex* Mr. Jeremiah *-2004*
Pershing Inc
Workships Contractors BV
SatCom: Inmarsat C 437567610
Kingstown *St Vincent & The Grenadines*
MMSI: 375676000
Official number: 10425

1,072 321 -
Class: BV (LR)
✠ Classed LR until 30/1/09

2002-02 Oil Barges, Inc. — New Iberia, La Yd No: C-4294
Loa 38.92 Br ex - Dght 1.850
Lbp - Br md 21.12 Dpth 3.04
Welded, 1 dk

(B22A2ZM) Offshore Construction Vessel, jack up

2 oil engines geared to sc. shafts driving 2 FP propellers
Total Power: 884kW (1,202hp)
Caterpillar 3412C
2 x Vee 4 Stroke 12 Cy. 137 x 152 each-442kW (601bhp)
Caterpillar Inc-USA

9323273 ECHJ -
SEAWORLD
-
Excursiones Maritimas Benidorm SL
-
Alicante *Spain*
MMSI: 224133620
Official number: 2-1/2004

444 143 37

2004-11 Metalships & Docks, S.A. — Vigo Yd No: 272
Loa 33.37 Br ex - Dght -
Lbp - Br md 10.00 Dpth 4.00
Welded, 1 dk

(A37B2PS) Passenger Ship
Passengers: unberthed: 250

2 oil engines geared to sc. shafts driving 2 Propellers
Total Power: 3,480kW (4,732hp)
M.T.U. 12V4000M70
2 x Vee 4 Stroke 12 Cy. 165 x 190 each-1740kW (2366bhp)
MTU Friedrichshafen GmbH-Friedrichshafen

9654830 PBDG -
SEAZIP 1
-
SeaZip 1 Shipping BV
Seazip Offshore Service BV
Harlingen *Netherlands*
MMSI: 244770995

147 45 -
Class: GL (BV)

2012-10 Damen Shipyards Singapore Pte Ltd — Singapore (Hull) Yd No: (532506)
2012-10 B.V. Scheepswerf Damen — Gorinchem Yd No: 532506
Loa 25.75 Br ex - Dght 1.800
Lbp 23.98 Br md 10.40 Dpth 2.90
Welded, 1 dk

(B21A2OC) Crew/Supply Vessel
Hull Material: Aluminium Alloy

2 oil engines reduction geared to sc. shafts driving 2 FP propellers
Total Power: 1,492kW (2,028hp) 22.0kn
Caterpillar C32 ACERT
2 x Vee 4 Stroke 12 Cy. 145 x 162 each-746kW (1014bhp)
AuxGen: 2 x 22kW a.c
Thrusters: 2 Tunnel thruster (f)
Fuel: 14.2

9654842 PBQR -
SEAZIP 2
-
SeaZip 2 Shipping BV
Seazip Offshore Service BV
Harlingen *Netherlands*
MMSI: 244770997

147 126 -
Class: GL (BV)

2012-10 Damen Shipyards Singapore Pte Ltd — Singapore (Hull) Yd No: (532507)
2012-10 B.V. Scheepswerf Damen — Gorinchem Yd No: 532507
Loa 25.75 Br ex - Dght 1.800
Lbp 23.98 Br md 10.40 Dpth 2.90
Welded, 1 dk

(B21A2OC) Crew/Supply Vessel
Hull Material: Aluminium Alloy

2 oil engines reduction geared to sc. shafts driving 2 FP propellers
Total Power: 1,492kW (2,028hp) 22.0kn
Caterpillar C32 ACERT
2 x Vee 4 Stroke 12 Cy. 145 x 162 each-746kW (1014bhp)
AuxGen: 2 x 22kW a.c
Thrusters: 2 Tunnel thruster (f)

7511199 ODSK -
SEBA M
ex Hans Leonhardt *-1997*
Kinda Wazzi Moukahal & Maria Alida Yehia Kabbani
Rabunion Maritime Agency Sarl
Beirut *Lebanon*
MMSI: 450462000
Official number: B-4274

7,244 3,765 11,680
Class: TL (GL) (NK)

1976-03 Ujina Zosensho — Hiroshima Yd No: 547
Loa 129.27 (BB) Br ex 19.64 Dght 8.240
Lbp 120.02 Br md 19.60 Dpth 10.52
Welded, 1 dk

(A21A2BC) Bulk Carrier
Grain: 14,560; Bale: 14,005
TEU 260 C. 260/20'
Compartments: 3 Ho, ER
3 Ha: (13.3 x 9.7) (28.6 x 9.7) (14.0 x 9.7)ER
Derricks: 3x22t,1x17t
Ice Capable

1 oil engine driving 1 FP propeller
Total Power: 4,406kW (5,990hp) 14.0kn
B&W 7K45GF
1 x 2 Stroke 7 Cy. 450 x 900 4406kW (5990bhp)
Hitachi Zosen Corp-Japan
AuxGen: 3 x 240kW

8732946 - -
SEBAHATTIN REIS
-
-
-
Bandirma *Turkey*
Official number: 1080

194 59 -

1984-01 in Turkey
Loa 29.85 Br ex - Dght 2.300
Lbp - Br md 9.50 Dpth -
Welded, 1 dk

(B11B2FV) Fishing Vessel

1 oil engine driving 1 Propeller
Total Power: 331kW (450hp)
Volvo Penta
1 x 4 Stroke 331kW (450bhp)
AB Volvo Penta-Sweden

9039705 - -
SEBAK
-
Government of The People's Republic of Bangladesh (Navy Department)
-
Bangladesh

172 - -

1993-12 Dockyard & Engineering Works Ltd — Narayanganj (Assembled by) Yd No: 445
1993-12 B.V. Scheepswerf Damen — Gorinchem (Parts for assembly by) Yd No: 3173
Loa 25.68 Br ex 8.03 Dght -
Lbp 24.25 Br md 7.80 Dpth 4.05
Welded, 1 dk

(B32A2ST) Tug

2 oil engines geared to sc. shafts driving 2 FP propellers
Total Power: 1,342kW (1,824hp)
Caterpillar 3512TA
2 x Vee 4 Stroke 12 Cy. 170 x 190 each-671kW (912bhp)
Caterpillar Inc-USA

9141479 DSEH2 -
SEBANG T-3
ex Global T-3 *-2008*
Sebang Co Ltd
-
SatCom: Inmarsat C 444075012
Busan *South Korea*
MMSI: 440074000
Official number: BSR-958733

230 - 162
Class: KR

1996-01 Kangnam Corp — Busan Yd No: 695043
Loa 37.85 Br ex - Dght 3.590
Lbp 33.00 Br md 8.80 Dpth 3.80
Welded, 1 dk

(B32A2ST) Tug

2 oil engines geared to sc. shafts driving 2 FP propellers
Total Power: 2,560kW (3,480hp) 13.3kn
Alpha 8L23/30
2 x 4 Stroke 8 Cy. 225 x 300 each-1280kW (1740bhp)
Hyundai Heavy Industries Co Ltd-South Korea

7102962 DSOZ4 -
SEBANG T-7
ex Gerard *-2006* *ex* Sea Horse IV *-2002*
ex Kah Weng *-1990* *ex* Salvista *-1989*
ex Iris *-1981*
Korea Union Salvage Co Ltd
-
Busan *South Korea*
MMSI: 440667000
Official number: BSR-061252

1,054 316 1,146
Class: KR (LR) (NK)
Classed LR until 8/89

1970-12 Daiko Dockyard Co. Ltd. — Osaka Yd No: 67
Loa 63.89 Br ex 11.66 Dght 4.979
Lbp 57.99 Br md 11.41 Dpth 5.29
Riveted\Welded, 1 dk

(B32A2ST) Tug

2 oil engines driving 2 CP propellers
Total Power: 3,678kW (5,000hp)
Hanshin 6L46
2 x 4 Stroke 6 Cy. 460 x 680 each-1839kW (2500bhp)
The Hanshin Diesel Works Ltd-Japan
AuxGen: 2 x 176kW 445V 60Hz a.c
Fuel: 879.0 13.0pd

6924222 *SHGC* GG 564	**SEBASTIAN** *ex* Lipton *-2010* *ex* Roxen *-1998* *ex* Susi Ann *-1978* *ex* Desiree *-1970* **Andres Rojas med firma Moran Truck & Transport** - *Gothenburg* *Sweden* MMSI: 265717000	**309** 92 -	Class: (BV)	**1967**-12 **VEB Rosslauer Schiffswerft — Rosslau** Yd No: S.910/2 Loa 35.62 Br ex 7.32 Dght 3.099 Lbp 31.63 Br md 7.29 Dpth 3.66 Welded, 1 dk	**(B11A2FT) Trawler** Grain: 540 Compartments: 2 Ho, ER 4 Ha: 4 (1.2 x 1.2)ER	**1 oil engine** driving 1 CP propeller Total Power: 883kW (1,201hp) 13.0kn Polar SF18VS 1 x Vee 4 Stroke 8 Cy. 250 x 300 883kW (1201bhp) AB NOHAB-Sweden Fuel: 34.5 (d.f.)
8510960 *OVUW* S 105	**SEBASTIAN** *ex* Britta Brock *-2009* *ex* Jeanette *-2005* *ex* Kemila *-2004* **Jens Vinther Pedersen** - SatCom: Inmarsat C 421913910 *Skagen* *Denmark* MMSI: 219139000 Official number: H1563	**656** 270 495	Class: (BV)	**1986**-06 **A/S Nakskov Skibsvaerft — Nakskov** (Hull launched by) **1986**-06 **Marstal Team Staal ApS — Marstal** (Hull completed by) Yd No: 103 **1986**-06 **Poul Ree A/S — Stokkemarke** Yd No: 5252 Loa 45.11 (BB) Br ex - Dght - Lbp 38.99 Br md 9.01 Dpth 7.29 Welded, 1 dk	**(B11A2FT) Trawler**	**1 oil engine** geared to sc. shaft driving 1 FP propeller Total Power: 1,199kW (1,630hp) MaK 6M332AK 1 x 4 Stroke 6 Cy. 240 x 330 1199kW (1630bhp) Krupp MaK Maschinenbau GmbH-Kiel
8856481 *HQLK6* -	**SEBASTIAN** *ex* Vigilante *-1996* *ex* YW 123 *-1992* **Rossline Business International SA** - *San Lorenzo* *Honduras* MMSI: 334607000 Official number: L-1324696	**581** 285 -		**1945 Leathem D Smith Shipbuilding Co — Sturgeon Bay WI** Loa 53.04 Br ex 10.06 Dght - Lbp 50.65 Br md 9.76 Dpth 3.96 Welded, 1 dk	**(A14A2LO) Water Tanker**	**1 oil engine** geared to sc. shaft driving 1 FP propeller Total Power: 588kW (799hp) 10.0kn Caterpillar D398TA 1 x Vee 4 Stroke 12 Cy. 159 x 203 588kW (799bhp) Caterpillar Tractor Co-USA
9329021 *ECIF* -	**SEBASTIAN DE OCAMPO** - **Government of Spain (Xunta de Galicia - Conselleria Pesca y Asuntos Maritimos)** - *Santa Cruz de Tenerife* *Spain (CSR)* MMSI: 224111000 Official number: 8-38/2004	**771** 231 416	Class: BV	**2005**-06 **Francisco Cardama, SA — Vigo** Yd No: 215 Loa 41.00 Br ex - Dght 5.000 Lbp 36.20 Br md 13.00 Dpth 6.05 Welded, 1 dk	**(B34M2QS) Search & Rescue Vessel**	**2 oil engines** geared to sc. shafts driving 2 CP propellers Total Power: 3,282kW (4,462hp) 12.0kn Caterpillar 3516B-TA 2 x Vee 4 Stroke 16 Cy. 170 x 190 each-1641kW (2231bhp) Caterpillar Inc-USA
7914303 - -	**SEBASTIAN M** - **Antonio D'Antonia Pesquera SA**	**110** 83 130	Class: (AB)	**1983**-01 **SANYM S.A. — Buenos Aires** Yd No: 29 Loa 25.51 Br ex - Dght 3.001 Lbp 22.31 Br md 6.51 Dpth 3.31 Welded, 1 dk	**(B11A2FS) Stern Trawler** Ins: 140	**1 oil engine** with clutches, flexible couplings & sr reverse geared to sc. shaft driving 1 FP propeller Total Power: 313kW (426hp) 10.0kn Caterpillar D353SCAC 1 x 4 Stroke 6 Cy. 159 x 203 313kW (426bhp) Caterpillar Tractor Co-USA AuxGen: 2 x 24kW
9176723 *YD6924* -	**SEBASTIAN MITRA** *ex* QS Mitra *-2004* *ex* Fordeco 28 *-2003* *ex* Sane 1 *-2002* **Pelayaran Salim Samudra Pacific Line** - *Samarinda* *Indonesia*	**240** 72 -	Class: KI (BV)	**1997**-01 **Shanghai Fishing Vessel Shipyard — Shanghai** Yd No: XY-2074 Loa 29.80 Br ex - Dght - Lbp 27.08 Br md 8.20 Dpth 4.10 Welded, 1 dk	**(B32A2ST) Tug**	**2 oil engines** geared to sc. shafts driving 2 FP propellers Total Power: 1,492kW (2,028hp) 12.0kn Caterpillar 3508B-HD 2 x Vee 4 Stroke 8 Cy. 170 x 215 each-746kW (1014bhp) Caterpillar Inc-USA AuxGen: 2 x 95kW a.c
9278454 *IKYH* -	**SEBASTIANO** - **Augustea Imprese Marittime e di Salvataggi SpA** - *Catania* *Italy* MMSI: 247100900	**326** 90 326	Class: RI	**2004**-02 **Cant. Nav. Rosetti — Ravenna** Yd No: 64 Loa 31.30 Br ex - Dght 4.100 Lbp 29.80 Br md 10.00 Dpth 5.00 Welded	**(B32A2ST) Tug**	**2 oil engines** geared to sc. shafts driving 2 Directional propellers Total Power: 3,300kW (4,486hp) Wartsila 6L26 2 x 4 Stroke 6 Cy. 260 x 320 each-1650kW (2243bhp) Wartsila Finland Oy-Finland AuxGen: 2 x 95kW 380/220V 50Hz a.c Fuel: 100.0 (d.f.) 10.0pd
9505364 *LXIO* -	**SEBASTIANO CABOTO** - **Codralux SA** Dredging & Maritime Management SA SatCom: Inmarsat C 425333610 *Luxembourg* *Luxembourg* MMSI: 253336000	**3,824** 1,147 4,800	Class: BV CC (Class contemplated)	**2011**-09 **Tianjin Xinhe Shipbuilding Heavy Industry Co Ltd — Tianjin** Yd No: SB714 Loa 93.25 (BB) Br ex - Dght 5.000 Lbp 81.00 Br md 19.80 Dpth 7.00 Welded, 1 dk	**(B33B2DT) Trailing Suction Hopper Dredger**	**3 diesel electric oil engines** driving 3 gen. each 1360kW a.c Connecting to 2 elec. motors each (1000kW) driving 2 Azimuth electric drive units Total Power: 2,910kW (3,957hp) 11.5kn Caterpillar 3512B 3 x Vee 4 Stroke 12 Cy. 170 x 190 each-970kW (1319bhp) Caterpillar Inc-USA Thrusters: 1 Tunnel thruster (f) Fuel: 480.0
9602875 *PPOK* -	**SEBASTIAO CABOTO** - **Alianca Navegacao e Logistica Ltda** - *Manaus* *Brazil* MMSI: 710000596	**42,564** 17,234 52,065	Class: GL	**2013**-01 **Shanghai Shipyard Co Ltd — Shanghai** Yd No: 1205 Loa 228.00 (BB) Br ex - Dght 12.500 Lbp 217.50 Br md 37.30 Dpth 19.60 Welded, 1 dk	**(A33A2CC) Container Ship (Fully Cellular)** TEU 3868 incl 500 ref C	**1 oil engine** driving 1 FP propeller Total Power: 22,890kW (31,121hp) 20.0kn MAN-B&W 7S70ME-C8 1 x 2 Stroke 7 Cy. 700 x 2800 22890kW (31121bhp) Hyundai Heavy Industries Co Ltd-South Korea Thrusters: 1 Tunnel thruster (f)
9696204 *FAB9929* -	**SEBASTIEN VAUBAN** - **Conseil General de la Gironde - Direction des Transports Maritimes** - *Bordeaux* *France* MMSI: 227259890 Official number: BX 931 837	**810** - -	Class: BV (Class contemplated)	**2014**-03 **SOCARENAM — Boulogne** Yd No: 250 Loa 60.00 Br ex 12.96 Dght 1.700 Lbp - Br md 12.50 Dpth 3.30 Welded, 1 dk	**(A36A2PR) Passenger/Ro-Ro Ship (Vehicles)** Passengers: unberthed: 300 Vehicles: 40	**3 oil engines** reduction geared to sc. shafts driving 3 Propellers Total Power: 2,460kW (3,345hp) Caterpillar C32 3 x Vee 4 Stroke 12 Cy. 145 x 162 each-820kW (1115bhp) Caterpillar Inc-USA
8033792 *UHKY* -	**SEBEKS** *ex* Kastor *-1999* *ex* MTK-0104 *-1992* **Mart Ltd (OOO 'Mart')** - *Murmansk* *Russia* MMSI: 273423760	**156** 46 40	Class: RS	**1982**-01 **Sosnovskiy Sudostroitelnyy Zavod — Sosnovka** Yd No: 104 Loa 27.96 Br ex 6.76 Dght 2.910 Lbp 24.09 Br md - Dpth 3.71 Welded, 1 dk	**(B11B2FV) Fishing Vessel**	**1 oil engine** driving 1 FP propeller Total Power: 294kW (400hp) 10.0kn S.K.L. 8NVD26A-2 1 x 4 Stroke 8 Cy. 180 x 260 294kW (400bhp) VEB Schwermaschinenbau "KarlLiebknecht" (SKL)-Magdeburg AuxGen: 2 x 75kW Fuel: 26.0 (d.f.)
9194749 *A4DD7* -	**SEBET** - **Bahwan Lamnalco LLC** Smit Lamnalco Ltd *Port Sultan Qaboos* *Oman* MMSI: 461000007 Official number: 849	**191** 57 -	Class: BV	**1999**-07 **Stocznia Tczew Sp z oo — Tczew** (Hull) **1999**-07 **B.V. Scheepswerf Damen — Gorinchem** Yd No: 7007 Loa 26.15 Br ex 7.96 Dght 3.400 Lbp 25.22 Br md 7.80 Dpth 4.05 Welded, 1 dk	**(B32A2ST) Tug**	**2 oil engines** reduction geared to sc. shafts driving 2 FP propellers Total Power: 4,002kW (5,442hp) 12.8kn Caterpillar 3512B-HD 2 x Vee 4 Stroke 12 Cy. 170 x 215 each-2001kW (2721bhp) Caterpillar Inc-USA AuxGen: 2 x 48kW 230/400V 50Hz a.c Fuel: 62.3 (d.f.)
8901298 *5ARM* -	**SEBHA** - **National Fishing & Marketing Co (NAFIMCO)** - *Tripoli* *Libya*	*173* 54 -	Class: (LR) ✠ Classed LR until 11/9/96	**1991**-11 **Chungmu Shipbuilding Co Inc — Tongyeong** Yd No: 223 Loa 31.15 (BB) Br ex 7.72 Dght - Lbp 25.25 Br md 7.70 Dpth 3.50 Welded, 1 dk	**(B11A2FS) Stern Trawler** Ins: 100	**1 oil engine** with clutches, flexible couplings & sr geared to sc. shaft driving 1 CP propeller Total Power: 704kW (957hp) Blackstone ESL6MK2 1 x 4 Stroke 6 Cy. 222 x 292 704kW (957bhp) Mirrlees Blackstone (Stamford)Ltd.-Stamford AuxGen: 2 x 72kW 380V 50Hz a.c
9434321 *DUBV* -	**SEBRING EXPRESS** - **PCTC Express II BV** Vroon BV SatCom: Inmarsat C 454881710 *Manila* *Philippines* MMSI: 548817000 Official number: MNLA000733	**43,810** 13,143 15,154	Class: NK	**2009**-08 **Mitsubishi Heavy Industries Ltd. — Shimonoseki** Yd No: 1133 Loa 180.00 (BB) Br ex 30.03 Dght 9.222 Lbp 171.70 Br md 30.00 Dpth 33.52 Welded, 10 dks. incl. 2 liftable dks.	**(A35B2RV) Vehicles Carrier** Side door/ramp (s) Len: - Wid: - Swl: 25 Quarter stern door/ramp (s. a.) Len: - Wid: - Swl: 100 Cars: 3,205	**1 oil engine** driving 1 FP propeller Total Power: 11,900kW (16,179hp) 19.9kn Mitsubishi 8UEC50LSII 1 x 2 Stroke 8 Cy. 500 x 1950 11900kW (16179bhp) Mitsubishi Heavy Industries Ltd-Japan AuxGen: 3 x 875kW 450V 60Hz a.c Thrusters: 1 Thwart. CP thruster (f) Fuel: 2200.0 (r.f.)

IMO / Call sign	Name / Owner	Tonnage	Class	Build / Dimensions	Type	Machinery
8957950 *YD6377* -	**SEBUDI** *ex* Karya Budi Terang IV *-1999* **PT Etam Kalimantan Raya** - *Samarinda* *Indonesia*	**234** 140 -	Class: KI	**1997-12 Kuran Jaya Sakti — Samarinda** Loa 25.50 Br ex - Dght - Lbp - Br md - Dpth 3.80 Welded, 1 dk	**(B32A2ST) Tug**	**2 oil engines** reduction geared to sc. shafts driving 2 FP propellers Total Power: 882kW (1,200hp) Caterpillar D379TA 2 x Vee 4 Stroke 8 Cy. 159 x 203 each-441kW (600bhp) (Re-engined ,made 1975) Caterpillar Tractor Co-USA
9045883 - -	**SECHANG VICTORY** *ex* Ferry Ryukyu *-2006* *ex* Kairyu No. 11 *-2004* **Se Chang Co Ltd** - *Jeju* *South Korea* MMSI: 440155030 Official number: JJR-069541	**4,572** 1,979 2,966	Class: KR (NK)	**1992-09 Hayashikane Dockyard Co Ltd — Nagasaki NS** Yd No: 997 Loa 124.71 (BB) Br ex - Dght 6.064 Lbp 116.00 Br md 17.50 Dpth 9.00 Welded, 3 dks	**(A35A2RR) Ro-Ro Cargo Ship** Quarter bow door/ramp (s) Len: 20.00 Wid: 7.30 Swl: - Quarter stern door/ramp (s) Len: 19.00 Wid: 7.30 Swl: - Lane-Len: 300 Cars: 53, Trailers: 15 TEU 147 C Dk. 147 TEU	**1 oil engine** driving 1 FP propeller Total Power: 7,061kW (9,600hp) 19.7kn Mitsubishi 8UEC45LA 1 x 2 Stroke 8 Cy. 450 x 1350 7061kW (9600bhp) Akasaka Tekkosho KK (Akasaka DieselLtd)-Japan AuxGen: 3 x 394kW a.c Thrusters: 1 Thwart. FP thruster (f) Fuel: 283.0 (r.f.) 28.0pd
8879718 - -	**SECHIN** - **Sindicato Pesquero del Peru SA (SIPESA)** - *Chimbote* *Peru* Official number: CE-006143-PM	**277** 128 -	Class: (BV)	**1990 Astilleros Naves Industriales S.A. (NAVINSA) — Callao** Yd No: 78 Loa 32.50 Br ex - Dght 3.620 Lbp 29.00 Br md 7.70 Dpth 4.10 Welded, 1 dk	**(B11B2FV) Fishing Vessel**	**1 oil engine** reduction geared to sc. shaft driving 1 FP propeller Total Power: 421kW (572hp) 10.8kn Caterpillar D379TA 1 x Vee 4 Stroke 8 Cy. 159 x 203 421kW (572bhp) Caterpillar Inc-USA AuxGen: 1 x 3kW a.c Fuel: 22.0 (d.f.)
9570307 *OA2664* -	**SECHIN** - **Petrolera Transoceanica SA** - *Callao* *Peru* MMSI: 760122000 Official number: CO-35714-EM	**236** 70 -	Class: AB	**2010-09 SIMA Serv. Ind. de la Marina Callao (SIMAC) — Callao** Yd No: 1122 Loa 24.55 Br ex - Dght 3.780 Lbp 23.25 Br md 9.70 Dpth 4.45 Welded, 1 dk	**(B32A2ST) Tug**	**2 oil engines** reduction geared to sc. shafts driving 2 Directional propellers Total Power: 3,282kW (4,462hp) Caterpillar 3516B-TA 2 x Vee 4 Stroke 16 Cy. 170 x 190 each-1641kW (2231bhp) Caterpillar Inc-USA AuxGen: 2 x 99kW a.c Fuel: 120.0
8818489 - -	**SECHIN II** - **Sindicato Pesquero del Peru SA (SIPESA)** - *Pisco* *Peru* Official number: PS-010061-PM	**364** 153 -	Class: (BV)	**1991-05 Inversiones Navales S.A. (INSA) — Callao** Yd No: 078 Loa - Br ex - Dght 3.900 Lbp 38.60 Br md 8.60 Dpth 4.27 Welded	**(B11B2FV) Fishing Vessel**	**1 oil engine** geared to sc. shaft driving 1 FP propeller Caterpillar 1 x 4 Stroke Caterpillar Inc-USA
9060467 *OA4599* -	**SECHURA** *ex* Enco *-2009* **Petrolera Transoceanica SA** - *Callao* *Peru*	*239* 72 160	Class: LR ✠ **100A1** SS 05/2008 tug ✠ **LMC** Eq.Ltr: G; Cable: 412.5/20.5 U2	**1993-05 Astilleros y Servicios Navales S.A. (ASENAV) — Valdivia** Yd No: 103 Loa 30.85 Br ex 9.30 Dght 3.605 Lbp 26.96 Br md 9.00 Dpth 4.04 Welded, 1 dk	**(B32A2ST) Tug**	**2 oil engines** with clutches, flexible couplings & sr geared to sc. shafts driving 2 CP propellers Total Power: 2,074kW (2,820hp) 12.0kn Caterpillar 3516TA 2 x Vee 4 Stroke 16 Cy. 170 x 190 each-1037kW (1410bhp) Caterpillar Inc-USA AuxGen: 2 x 48kW 400V 50Hz a.c
9120451 - -	**SECHURA** - **Conservera Garrido SA** - *Lima* *Peru* Official number: PT-13533-PM	**310** - -	Class: (BV)	**1995-12 Astilleros Naves Industriales S.A. (NAVINSA) — Callao** Yd No: 10 Loa - Br ex - Dght - Lbp - Br md - Dpth - Welded, 1 dk	**(B11B2FV) Fishing Vessel**	**1 oil engine** geared to sc. shaft driving 1 FP propeller Total Power: 1,119kW (1,521hp) Caterpillar 3508TA 1 x Vee 4 Stroke 8 Cy. 170 x 190 1119kW (1521bhp) Caterpillar Inc-USA
7112371 *HP8061* -	**SECHURA EXPRESS** *ex* Essa 1 *-2006* *ex* El Daman *-2002* *ex* Essa 1 *-2001* *ex* Corona *-1994* *ex* Sea Pearl *-1976* **IMI Del Peru SAC** - *Panama* *Panama* Official number: 23814PEXT5	*500* 178 813	Class: (RI) (AB)	**1971-06 Mangone Shipbuilding Co. — Houston, Tx** Yd No: 99 Loa 56.32 Br ex 11.51 Dght 3.988 Lbp 51.24 Br md 11.47 Dpth 4.88 Welded, 1 dk	**(B21B20T) Offshore Tug/Supply Ship**	**2 oil engines** reverse reduction geared to sc. shafts driving 2 FP propellers Total Power: 2,868kW (3,900hp) 12.0kn EMD (Electro-Motive) 16-645-E6 2 x Vee 2 Stroke 16 Cy. 230 x 254 each-1434kW (1950bhp) General Motors Corp.Electro-Motive Div.-La Grange AuxGen: 2 x 150kW Fuel: 169.5 (d.f.) 14.0pd
6727519 *D3UC* -	**SECIL BENGO** - **Secil Maritima UEE** - *Luanda* *Angola* Official number: C-510	**975** 322 980	Class: (LR) (BV) ✠ Classed LR until 9/3/88	**1967-09 Sorefame — Lobito** Yd No: 36 Loa 62.00 Br ex 10.65 Dght 3.556 Lbp 57.60 Br md 10.50 Dpth 5.85 Welded, 1 dk & S dk	**(A31A2GX) General Cargo Ship** Grain: 1,759; Bale: 1,702; Ins: 49 Compartments: 2 Ho, ER 2 Ha: (10.5 x 5.7) (12.8 x 5.7)ER Cranes: 1x5t,1x3t	**1 oil engine** driving 1 FP propeller Total Power: 728kW (990hp) 12.0kn Alpha 498R 1 x 2 Stroke 8 Cy. 310 x 490 728kW (990bhp) Alpha Diesel A/S-Denmark AuxGen: 2 x 72kW 380V 50Hz a.c, 1 x 15kW 380V 50Hz a.c Fuel: 87.5 (d.f.)
5043461 *D3UD* -	**SECIL MAR** *ex* Bettina Bork *-1963* **Secil Maritima UEE** - *Luanda* *Angola* Official number: C-688	*499* 269 769	Class: (BV)	**1961 N.V. Scheepswerf Gebr. van der Werf — Deest** Yd No: 289 Loa 55.10 Br ex 9.33 Dght 3.480 Lbp 50.02 Br md 9.25 Dpth 3.89 Welded, 1 dk	**(A31A2GX) General Cargo Ship** Grain: 998; Bale: 935 Compartments: 1 Ho, ER 1 Ha: (22.0 x 5.4)ER Cranes: 2x2t	**1 oil engine** geared to sc. shaft driving 1 FP propeller Total Power: 412kW (560hp) 10.0kn MAN G8V30/45ATL 1 x 4 Stroke 8 Cy. 300 x 450 412kW (560bhp) Maschinenbau Augsburg Nuernberg (MAN)-Augsburg AuxGen: 1 x 20kW 220V d.c Fuel: 57.0 (d.f.)
8502975 *IMEQ* -	**SECOMAR QUATTRO** *ex* D'Bianca *-1996* **Secomar SpA** - SatCom: Inmarsat C 424702875 *Ravenna* *Italy* MMSI: 247072300 Official number: 3885	**377** 113 365	Class: RI (NK)	**1987-08 Metalurgia e Construcao Naval S.A. (CORENA) — Itajai** Yd No: 151 Loa 43.00 Br ex - Dght 3.020 Lbp 39.48 Br md 9.30 Dpth 3.50 Welded	**(B21A20S) Platform Supply Ship**	**2 oil engines** driving 2 FP propellers Total Power: 1,104kW (1,500hp) Daihatsu 6DSM-19A 2 x 4 Stroke 6 Cy. 190 x 230 each-552kW (750bhp) Daihatsu Diesel Manufacturing Co Lt-Japan AuxGen: 2 x 108kW 440V 60Hz a.c
7948548 - -	**SECOND GENERATION** *ex* Sandy *-1991* *ex* Miss Sandy *-1991* **Marinaldo Fisheries Inc** - *New Bedford, MA* *United States of America* Official number: 615482	*119* 81 -		**1979 St Augustine Trawlers, Inc. — Saint Augustine, Fl** Yd No: S-43 L reg 19.76 Br ex 6.71 Dght - Lbp - Br md - Dpth 3.13 Welded, 1 dk	**(B11B2FV) Fishing Vessel**	**1 oil engine** driving 1 FP propeller Total Power: 382kW (519hp) Caterpillar 3412TA 1 x Vee 4 Stroke 12 Cy. 137 x 152 382kW (519bhp) Caterpillar Tractor Co-USA
7948536 - -	**SECOND WIND** *ex* Mary Louise *-1992* *ex* Miss Roberta *-1992* **Diaz Fisheries Inc** - *United States of America* Official number: 615481	*119* 81 -		**1979 St Augustine Trawlers, Inc. — Saint Augustine, Fl** Yd No: S-44 L reg 19.76 Br ex 6.71 Dght - Lbp - Br md - Dpth 3.13 Welded, 1 dk	**(B11B2FV) Fishing Vessel**	**1 oil engine** driving 1 FP propeller Total Power: 382kW (519hp) Caterpillar 3412TA 1 x Vee 4 Stroke 12 Cy. 137 x 152 382kW (519bhp) Caterpillar Tractor Co-USA
7819709 *D6FC4* -	**SECRET** *ex* Sly Fox *-2009* *ex* H. O. S. Sly Fox *-1996* *ex* Rosalie G *-1994* **Mega Star Shipping Ltd** National Shipping & Investment Co *Moroni* *Union of Comoros* MMSI: 616795000 Official number: 1200928	**830** 249 900	Class: (AB)	**1978 Halter Marine, Inc. — Lockport, La** Yd No: 759 Lengthened-1984 Loa - Br ex - Dght 3.556 Lbp 65.23 Br md 12.20 Dpth 4.27 Welded, 1 dk	**(B34R2QY) Supply Tender**	**2 oil engines** reverse reduction geared to sc. shafts driving 2 FP propellers Total Power: 2,648kW (3,600hp) 12.0kn EMD (Electro-Motive) 16-645-E2 1 x Vee 2 Stroke 16 Cy. 230 x 254 1324kW (1800bhp) (Re-engined ,made 1968, Reconditioned & fitted 1978) General Motors Detroit DieselAllison Divn-USA EMD (Electro-Motive) 16-645-E2 1 x Vee 2 Stroke 16 Cy. 230 x 254 1324kW (1800bhp) (Re-engined ,made 1970, Reconditioned & fitted 1978) General Motors Detroit DieselAllison Divn-USA AuxGen: 2 x 99kW Thrusters: 1 Thwart. FP thruster (f)
1011795 *DMCC* -	**SECRET** - **Secret II Ltd** Nigel Burgess Ltd (BURGESS) *Germany* MMSI: 211594650 Official number: 743781	**2,240** 672 220	Class: LR ✠ **100A1** SS 05/2013 SSC Yacht, mono, G6 ✠ **LMC** **UMS** Cable: 387.7/30.0 U2 (a)	**2013-05 Stahlbau Nord GmbH — Bremen** (Hull) Yd No: (6493) **2013-05 Schiffs- u. Yachtwerft Abeking & Rasmussen GmbH & Co. — Lemwerder** Yd No: 6493 Loa 82.48 Br ex 12.75 Dght 3.450 Lbp 65.71 Br md 12.40 Dpth 6.45 Welded, 1 dk	**(X11A2YP) Yacht**	**2 oil engines** with clutches, flexible couplings & sr reverse geared to sc. shafts driving 2 FP propellers Total Power: 2,982kW (4,054hp) Caterpillar 3516B-TA 2 x Vee 4 Stroke 16 Cy. 170 x 190 each-1491kW (2027bhp) Caterpillar Inc-USA AuxGen: 3 x 412kW 400V 50Hz a.c Thrusters: 1 Thwart. FP thruster (f); 1 Water jet (a)

IMO / Call sign	Name / Owner / Port	Tonnage	Class	Builder / Dimensions	Type	Machinery
7513408 *WYT9655* -	**SECRET** **Pete Shrimp Co Inc** - *Brownsville, TX* *United States of America* Official number: 550725	*110* 75 -		**1973 Bender Welding & Machine Co Inc — Mobile AL** L reg 20.85 Br ex 6.71 Dght - Lbp - Br md - Dpth 3.38 Welded, 1 dk	**(B11A2FT) Trawler**	**1 oil engine** driving 1 FP propeller Total Power: 268kW (364hp) Caterpillar D353SCAC 1 x 4 Stroke 6 Cy. 159 x 203 268kW (364bhp) Caterpillar Tractor Co-USA
9513907 *V7YZ4* -	**SECRET** **Miraero SG No 3 SA** Genel Denizcilik Nakliyati AS (GEDEN LINES) *Majuro* *Marshall Islands* MMSI: 538004770 Official number: 4770	**32,795** 18,550 55,395 T/cm 57.1	Class: NV	**2013-01 Hyundai-Vinashin Shipyard Co Ltd — Ninh Hoa** Yd No: S049 Loa 187.88 (BB) Br ex 32.26 Dght 12.868 Lbp 182.50 Br md 32.24 Dpth 18.30 Welded, 1 dk	**(A21A2BC) Bulk Carrier** Grain: 70,814; Bale: 68,144 Compartments: 5 Ho, ER 5 Ha: ER Cranes: 4x35t	**1 oil engine** driving 1 FP propeller Total Power: 8,820kW (11,992hp) 14.5kn MAN-B&W 6S50MC-C8 1 x 2 Stroke 6 Cy. 500 x 2000 8820kW (11992bhp) Hyundai Heavy Industries Co Ltd-South Korea AuxGen: 3 x a.c Fuel: 110.0 (d.f.) 1807.0 (r.f.)
8852368 *WDE8463* -	**SECRET ISLAND** **Secret Island Fisheries LLC** - *Seattle, WA* *United States of America* Official number: 969494	**308** 92 -		**1990 Tri-Star Marine, Inc. — Seattle, Wa** Yd No: C-1101 Loa - Br ex - Dght - Lbp 30.21 Br md 8.53 Dpth 3.35 Welded, 1 dk	**(B11B2FV) Fishing Vessel**	**1 oil engine** driving 1 FP propeller
8985866 *VQBS6* -	**SECRET LIFE** *ex* Al Mahboba *-2002* *ex* Taiba III *-1990* *ex* The Big R *-1981* *ex* Jardell *-1981* **Pencil Reef Ltd** YDL Yachting Corp *London* *United Kingdom* MMSI: 235007542 Official number: 716048	**381** 114 -	Class: (AB)	**1973-10 de Vries Scheepsbouw B.V. — Aalsmeer** Yd No: 604 Loa 45.00 Br ex 8.90 Dght 2.900 Lbp - Br md 8.41 Dpth 4.74 Welded, 1 dk	**(X11A2YP) Yacht** Passengers: cabins: 6; berths: 12	**2 oil engines** geared to sc. shafts driving 1 FP propeller , 1 Propeller Total Power: 1,544kW (2,100hp) 13.0kn G.M. (Detroit Diesel) 16V-149 2 x Vee 2 Stroke 16 Cy. 146 x 146 each-772kW (1050bhp) General Motors Detroit DieselAllison Divn-USA AuxGen: 2 x 125kW 110/220V 50Hz a.c
1003762 *V7XB7* -	**SECRET LOVE** *ex* Amour Secret *-2001* *ex* Secret Love *-2000* **Talanda Trading Inc** - *Bikini* *Marshall Islands* MMSI: 538080088 Official number: 80088	*298* 89 -	Class: LR ✠ **100A1** SS 11/2009 Yacht **LMC**	**1990-03 Amels Holland BV — Makkum** Yd No: 422 Loa 36.50 Br ex 7.70 Dght 2.850 Lbp 31.00 Br md - Dpth 4.47 Welded, 1 dk	**(X11A2YP) Yacht**	**2 oil engines** driving 2 FP propellers Total Power: 1,000kW (1,360hp) Caterpillar 3512TA 2 x Vee 4 Stroke 12 Cy. 170 x 190 each-500kW (680bhp) Caterpillar Inc-USA
7923275 *WDF8787* -	**SECRETARIAT** *ex* H. O. S. Secretariat *-1996* *ex* Point T *-1991* **RP/PHL Marine Leasing LLC** - *Morgan City, LA* *United States of America* MMSI: 366808960 Official number: 626141	**544** 163 700	Class: (AB)	**1980 Halter Marine, Inc. — Mobile, Al** Yd No: 875 Loa - Br ex 11.21 Dght 3.884 Lbp 43.29 Br md 10.98 Dpth 4.27 Welded, 1 dk	**(B21A20S) Platform Supply Ship**	**2 oil engines** reverse reduction geared to sc. shafts driving 2 FP propellers Total Power: 1,472kW (2,002hp) 12.0kn G.M. (Detroit Diesel) 16V-149-NA 2 x Vee 2 Stroke 16 Cy. 146 x 146 each-736kW (1001bhp) General Motors Detroit DieselAllison Divn-USA AuxGen: 2 x 75kW Thrusters: 1 Thwart. FP thruster (f)
8892394 *5NWN5* -	**SECWAV 1** *ex* Bremen 3 *-2013* **West African Ventures Ltd** - *Lagos* *Nigeria* MMSI: 657972000 Official number: SR 2089	**163** 48 20	Class: GL	**1987 Fr Fassmer GmbH & Co KG — Berne** Yd No: 85/1001 Loa 30.47 Br ex - Dght 1.600 Lbp 28.00 Br md 6.60 Dpth 3.97 Welded, 1 dk	**(B34H2SQ) Patrol Vessel**	**3 oil engines** reduction geared to sc. shafts driving 2 CP propellers , 1 FP propeller Total Power: 2,520kW (3,426hp) 26.0kn MWM TBD234V12 2 x Vee 4 Stroke 12 Cy. 128 x 140 each-660kW (897bhp) MTU Friedrichshafen GmbH-Friedrichshafen MWM TBD604BV12 1 x Vee 4 Stroke 12 Cy. 170 x 195 1200kW (1632bhp) MTU Friedrichshafen GmbH-Friedrichshafen AuxGen: 2 x 58kW 220/380V a.c
9015931 *5NWN6* -	**SECWAV 2** *ex* Gluckstadt *-2013* **West African Ventures Ltd** - *Lagos* *Nigeria* Official number: SR2088	**138** 41 -	Class: GL	**1991-04 Fr Fassmer GmbH & Co KG — Berne** Yd No: 189/1201 Loa 28.50 Br ex 6.37 Dght 1.650 Lbp 26.00 Br md 6.20 Dpth 3.70 Welded, 1 dk	**(B34H2SQ) Patrol Vessel** Hull Material: Aluminium Alloy	**3 oil engines** with flexible couplings & sr geared to sc. shafts driving 1 CP propeller , 2 FP propellers Total Power: 2,475kW (3,366hp) 23.0kn MWM TBD604BV8 3 x Vee 4 Stroke 8 Cy. 170 x 195 each-825kW (1122bhp) Motoren Werke Mannheim AG (MWM)-Mannheim Thrusters: 1 Thwart. FP thruster (f)
8847105 *UGKG* -	**SEDANKA** **Novyy Mir Fishing Collective (Rybolovetskiy Kolkhoz 'Novyy Mir')** - *Nakhodka* *Russia* MMSI: 273824300 Official number: 901158	**763** 221 329	Class: RS	**1991-09 Yaroslavskiy Sudostroitelnyy Zavod — Yaroslavl** Yd No: 379 Loa 53.70 (BB) Br ex 10.71 Dght 4.360 Lbp 47.92 Br md 10.50 Dpth 6.00 Welded, 1 dk	**(B11A2FS) Stern Trawler** Ins: 248 Ice Capable	**1 oil engine** driving 1 CP propeller Total Power: 969kW (1,317hp) 12.6kn S.K.L. 8NVD48A-2U 1 x 4 Stroke 8 Cy. 320 x 480 969kW (1317bhp) SKL Motoren u. Systemtechnik AG-Magdeburg AuxGen: 1 x 300kW a.c, 3 x 150kW a.c
8832966 *UHTP* -	**SEDANKA** **Preobrazheniye Trawler Fleet Base (Preobrazhenskaya Baza Tralovogo Flota)** - *Nakhodka* *Russia* MMSI: 273826810	**741** 222 332	Class: RS	**1990-08 Volgogradskiy Sudostroitelnyy Zavod — Volgograd** Yd No: 261 Loa 53.75 (BB) Br ex 10.70 Dght 4.400 Lbp 47.93 Br md 10.50 Dpth 6.00 Welded, 1dk	**(B11A2FS) Stern Trawler** Ins: 218 Ice Capable	**1 oil engine** driving 1 CP propeller Total Power: 969kW (1,317hp) 12.7kn S.K.L. 8NVD48A-2U 1 x 4 Stroke 8 Cy. 320 x 480 969kW (1317bhp) VEB Schwermaschinenbau "KarlLiebknecht" (SKL)-Magdeburg AuxGen: 1 x 300kW a.c, 3 x 160kW a.c
8656178 *EPBT9* -	**SEDAR 1** *ex* Anugerah P8 *-2014* - - *Iran* MMSI: 422034100	**478** 159 1,000	Class: (KI)	**2011-12 P.T. Gunung Sebatung Shipyard — Samarinda** Yd No: 4/2011 Loa 62.00 Br ex - Dght 2.200 Lbp 60.20 Br md 12.00 Dpth 3.00 Welded, 1 dk	**(A35D2RL) Landing Craft**	**2 oil engines** reduction geared to sc. shafts driving 2 Propellers Total Power: 1,220kW (1,658hp) Mitsubishi S6R2-MPTK 2 x 4 Stroke 6 Cy. 170 x 220 each-610kW (829bhp) Mitsubishi Heavy Industries Ltd-Japan
8874811 - -	**SEDARI** **PT Etam Kalimantan Raya** - *Balikpapan* *Indonesia*	**134** 80 -	Class: (KI)	**1994-01 P.T. Galangan Tanjung Batu — Balikpapan** Loa 21.00 Br ex - Dght - Lbp 19.30 Br md 6.00 Dpth 2.70 Welded, 1 dk	**(B32A2ST) Tug**	**2 oil engines** reduction geared to sc. shafts driving 2 FP propellers Total Power: 692kW (940hp) 8.0kn Caterpillar 3408B 2 x Vee 4 Stroke 8 Cy. 137 x 152 each-346kW (470bhp) Caterpillar Inc-USA AuxGen: 1 x 40kW 220V a.c
9451458 *4JNL* -	**SEDATION A** *launched as* Sedation *-2007* **SOCAR-ASM LLC** - *Baku* *Azerbaijan* MMSI: 423275100 Official number: DGR0502	**458** 137 225	Class: AB RS	**2007-07 Heesen Shipyards B.V. — Oss** Yd No: 13644 Loa 44.17 Br ex 9.00 Dght 1.900 Lbp 36.30 Br md 8.50 Dpth 3.50 Welded, 1 dk	**(X11A2YP) Yacht** Hull Material: Aluminium Alloy	**2 oil engines** reduction geared to sc. shafts driving 2 FP propellers Total Power: 5,440kW (7,396hp) 25.0kn M.T.U. 16V4000M90 2 x Vee 4 Stroke 16 Cy. 165 x 190 each-2720kW (3698bhp) MTU Friedrichshafen GmbH-Friedrichshafen Fuel: 58.0 (d.f.)
8659077 *YDA4412* -	**SEDAYU-01** *ex* Sujin *-2008* **PT Ocean Buana Lines** - *Cirebon* *Indonesia*	**225** 68 -	Class: KI	**2000-05 Dongsung Shipbuilding Co Ltd — Pohang** Yd No: 225 Loa 27.00 Br ex - Dght 3.200 Lbp - Br md 8.00 Dpth 3.50 Welded, 1 dk	**(B32A2ST) Tug**	**2 oil engines** reduction geared to sc. shafts driving 2 Propellers Total Power: 1,912kW (2,600hp) 10.0kn Niigata 2 x each-956kW (1300bhp) Niigata Engineering Co Ltd-Japan

IMO / Call sign	Name / Owner	Tonnage	Class	Build / Dimensions	Type / Capacities	Machinery
8755118 *ELN05* -	**SEDCO 702** **Transocean Offshore Gulf of Guinea II Ltd** Transocean Offshore Deepwater Drilling Inc *Monrovia* *Liberia* MMSI: 636009404 Official number: 9404	**16,881** 5,064 12,729	Class: AB	**1973-03 Avondale Industries, Inc., Shipyards Div. — New Orleans, La** Yd No: 2051 Loa 89.92 Br ex 74.67 Dght 6.400 Lbp - Br md - Dpth 39.62 Welded, 1 dk	**(Z11C3ZE) Drilling Rig, semi Submersible** Passengers: berths: 108 Cranes: 2x85t,2x15t	**6 diesel electric oil engines** driving 6 gen. each 3640kW 11000V a.c Connecting to 8 elec. motors each (2250kW) driving 8 Azimuth electric drive units Total Power: 20,640kW (28,062hp) 5.0kn Caterpillar 3612 1 x Vee 4 Stroke 12 Cy. 280 x 300 3440kW (4677bhp) (new engine 2007) Caterpillar Inc-USA Caterpillar 3612 5 x Vee 4 Stroke 12 Cy. 280 x 300 each-3440kW (4677bhp) (new engine 2007) Caterpillar Inc-USA AuxGen: 3 x 2100kW a.c Thrusters: 4 Thwart. FP thruster
8755144 *ELLW6* -	**SEDCO 706** **Transocean Drilling Offshore Sarl** Transocean Offshore Deepwater Drilling Inc *Monrovia* *Liberia* MMSI: 636009053 Official number: 9053	**17,164** 5,149 -	Class: AB	**1976-08 Kaiser Steel Corp. — Oakland, Ca** Yd No: 631 Loa 89.92 Br ex 74.70 Dght 27.430 Lbp - Br md - Dpth 39.62 Welded, 1 dk	**(Z11C3ZE) Drilling Rig, semi Submersible** Passengers: berths: 133 Cranes: 2x50t	**6 diesel electric oil engines** driving 6 gen. each 3640kW a.c Connecting to 8 elec. motors each (2250kW) driving 8 Azimuth electric drive units Total Power: 20,640kW (28,062hp) Caterpillar 3612 1 x Vee 4 Stroke 12 Cy. 280 x 300 3440kW (4677bhp) (new engine 2007) Caterpillar Inc-USA Caterpillar 3612 4 x Vee 4 Stroke 12 Cy. 280 x 300 each-3440kW (4677bhp) (new engine 2007) Caterpillar Inc-USA Thrusters: 4 Thwart. FP thruster
8755156 *5MOU* -	**SEDCO 707** **Transocean Drilling Offshore Sarl** Transocean Inc *Monrovia* *Liberia* MMSI: 636005710 Official number: 5710	**14,233** 4,269 10,669	Class: AB	**1976-07 Avondale Industries, Inc., Shipyards Div. — New Orleans, La** Yd No: 2282 Loa 108.20 Br ex 74.67 Dght 24.410 Lbp - Br md - Dpth 34.29 Welded, 1 dk	**(Z11C3ZE) Drilling Rig, semi Submersible** Passengers: berths: 112 Cranes: 2x50t	**6 diesel electric oil engines** driving 6 gen. each 2500kW a.c Connecting to 8 elec. motors driving 8 Azimuth electric drive units Total Power: 20,640kW (28,062hp) Caterpillar 3612 6 x Vee 4 Stroke 12 Cy. 280 x 300 each-3440kW (4677bhp) (new engine 0000) Caterpillar Tractor Co-USA
8755170 *ELPE9* -	**SEDCO 709** **Triton Holdings Ltd** Transocean Inc *Monrovia* *Liberia* MMSI: 636009744 Official number: 9744	**12,763** 3,828 9,312	Class: AB	**1977-05 Hawker Siddeley Canada Ltd — Halifax NS** Yd No: 67 Loa 89.92 Br ex 74.70 Dght 24.410 Lbp - Br md - Dpth 34.29 Welded, 1 dk	**(Z11C3ZE) Drilling Rig, semi Submersible** Passengers: berths: 124 Cranes: 2x50t Ice Capable	**8 diesel electric oil engines** driving 8 gen. Connecting to 8 elec. motors driving 8 Azimuth electric drive units Thrusters: 8 Thwart. FP thruster
8755182 *ELNN4* -	**SEDCO 710** **Transocean Drilling Offshore Sarl** Transocean Offshore Deepwater Drilling Inc *Monrovia* *Liberia* MMSI: 636009395 Official number: 9395	**16,386** 4,915 9,891	Class: AB	**1983-03 Mitsui Eng. & SB. Co. Ltd. — Tamano** Yd No: F-588 Loa 90.00 Br ex 75.90 Dght 24.380 Lbp 89.92 Br md - Dpth 34.30 Welded, 1 dk	**(Z11C3ZE) Drilling Rig, semi Submersible** Passengers: berths: 118 Cranes: 2x65t Ice Capable	**6 diesel electric oil engines** driving 6 gen. each 2500kW a.c Connecting to 8 elec. motors driving 8 Azimuth electric drive units Total Power: 17,904kW (24,342hp) 8.0kn EMD (Electro-Motive) 20-645-E9B 1 x Vee 2 Stroke 20 Cy. 230 x 254 2984kW (4057bhp) (new engine 0000) General Motors Corp.Electro-Motive Div.-La Grange EMD (Electro-Motive) 20-645-E9B 5 x Vee 2 Stroke 20 Cy. 230 x 254 each-2984kW (4057bhp) (new engine 0000) General Motors Corp.Electro-Motive Div.-La Grange
8755211 *YJRD8* -	**SEDCO 711** *ex Sedco/BP 711 -1993* **Triton Holdings Ltd** Transocean Offshore (North Sea) Ltd *Port Vila* *Vanuatu* MMSI: 577050000 Official number: 2116	**14,073** 4,221 -	Class: AB	**1982-08 Hyundai Heavy Industries Co Ltd — Ulsan** Yd No: 711 Loa 89.96 Br ex 77.60 Dght 24.380 Lbp - Br md - Dpth 39.60 Welded, 1 dk	**(Z11C3ZE) Drilling Rig, semi Submersible** Passengers: berths: 100 Cranes: 2x51t,2x8t	**3 diesel electric oil engines** driving 3 gen. each 2200kW a.c Connecting to 4 elec. motors driving 4 Azimuth electric drive units Total Power: 7,326kW (9,960hp) 6.0kn EMD (Electro-Motive) 16-645-E9 3 x Vee 2 Stroke 16 Cy. 230 x 254 each-2442kW (3320bhp) (new engine 1982) General Motors Corp.Electro-Motive Div.-La Grange AuxGen: 3 x 2200kW a.c
8755209 *YJSA6* -	**SEDCO 714** **Triton Holdings Ltd** Transocean Offshore (North Sea) Ltd *Port Vila* *Vanuatu* MMSI: 577085000 Official number: 2150	**13,898** 4,169 -	Class: AB	**1983-12 Hyundai Heavy Industries Co Ltd — Ulsan** Yd No: 714 Loa 90.00 Br ex 76.00 Dght 25.908 Lbp 89.96 Br md - Dpth 39.62 Welded, 1 dk	**(Z11C3ZE) Drilling Rig, semi Submersible** Passengers: berths: 98 Cranes: 2x57t,2x10t	**3 diesel electric oil engines** driving 3 gen. Connecting to 4 elec. motors each (1000kW) driving 2 Azimuth electric drive units Total Power: 4,476kW (6,087hp) EMD (Electro-Motive) 16-645-E9 3 x Vee 2 Stroke 16 Cy. 230 x 254 each-1492kW (2029bhp) (new engine 1997) General Motors Corp.Electro-Motive Div.-La Grange AuxGen: 3 x 2200kW a.c
8764913 *ELXM2* -	**SEDCO ENERGY** **SEDCO FOREX International Inc** Transocean Offshore (UK) Inc *Monrovia* *Liberia* MMSI: 636011195 Official number: 11195	**23,404** 7,021 -	Class: AB	**2000-07 DCN INTERNATIONAL - Direction desConstructions Navales International** Yd No: 2-98 Loa 106.00 Br ex 69.00 Dght 20.000 Lbp - Br md - Dpth 34.00 Welded, 1 dk	**(Z11C3ZE) Drilling Rig, semi Submersible** Passengers: berths: 130 Cranes: 2x65t	**6 diesel electric oil engines** driving 6 gen. each 4400kW 11000V a.c Connecting to 4 elec. motors each (7000kW) driving 4 Azimuth electric drive units Total Power: 27,480kW (37,362hp) 8.0kn Caterpillar 3616 1 x Vee 4 Stroke 16 Cy. 280 x 300 4580kW (6227bhp) Caterpillar Inc-USA Caterpillar 3616 5 x Vee 4 Stroke 16 Cy. 280 x 300 each-4580kW (6227bhp) Caterpillar Inc-USA
8764901 *ELXM3* -	**SEDCO EXPRESS** **Triton Asset Leasing GmbH** Transocean Offshore Deepwater Drilling Inc *Monrovia* *Liberia* MMSI: 636011196 Official number: 11196	**24,175** 7,252 -	Class: AB	**2000-06 DCN INTERNATIONAL - Direction desConstructions Navales International** Yd No: 1-98 Loa 106.00 Br ex 69.00 Dght 20.000 Lbp - Br md - Dpth 34.00 Welded, 1 dk	**(Z11C3ZE) Drilling Rig, semi Submersible** Passengers: berths: 130 Cranes: 2x65t	**6 diesel electric oil engines** driving 6 gen. each 4400kW 11000V a.c Connecting to 4 elec. motors each (7000kW) driving 4 Azimuth electric drive units Total Power: 27,480kW (37,362hp) 8.0kn Caterpillar 3616 6 x Vee 4 Stroke 16 Cy. 280 x 300 each-4580kW (6227bhp) Caterpillar Inc-USA
9615901 *TCZX8* -	**SEDDULBAHIR** **Kolsan Insaat Otomativ Sanayi ve Ticaret AS** *Istanbul* *Turkey* MMSI: 271042594	**1,490** 1,055 800	Class: TL	**2011-06 Sefine Shipyard Co Inc — Altinova** Yd No: 06 Loa 86.72 Br ex 18.20 Dght 4.000 Lbp 81.10 Br md 17.80 Dpth 5.80 Welded, 1 dk	**(A36A2PR) Passenger/Ro-Ro Ship (Vehicles)** Passengers: unberthed: 200 Bow ramp (centre) Stern ramp (centre) Cars: 86	**2 oil engines** reduction geared to sc. shafts driving 2 Directional propellers Total Power: 2,420kW (3,290hp) 14.0kn Mitsubishi S12R-MPTK 2 x Vee 4 Stroke 12 Cy. 170 x 180 each-1210kW (1645bhp) Mitsubishi Heavy Industries Ltd-Japan AuxGen: 2 x 260kW a.c
8992699 *TC9243* -	**SEDEF-M** **Mercan Petrol Ve Den Tas Hc Ve Ltd Sti** - *Istanbul* *Turkey* Official number: 7434	**147** 76 258		**1998-11 Aykin Denizcilik San ve Tic Ltd Sti — Tuzla** Yd No: 02 Loa 36.95 Br ex - Dght 2.410 Lbp 32.76 Br md 6.00 Dpth 2.85 Welded, 1 dk	**(B35E2TF) Bunkering Tanker**	**1 oil engine** driving 1 Propeller Total Power: 441kW (600hp) 13.0kn MAN 1 x 4 Stroke 441kW (600bhp) MAN B&W Diesel AG-Augsburg
9041605 *9V6523* -	**SEDNA** *ex Seiwa Maru -2004* **Grandeur Trading & Services Pte Ltd** Equatorial Marine Fuel Management Services Pte Ltd *Singapore* *Singapore* MMSI: 563005260 Official number: 390673	**1,642** 711 2,641 T/cm 7.8	Class: NK	**1992-02 Kegoya Dock K.K. — Kure** Yd No: 928 Loa 74.95 (BB) Br ex 14.02 Dght 5.177 Lbp 70.50 Br md 14.00 Dpth 5.90 Welded, 1 dk	**(A13B2TP) Products Tanker** Ins: 3,729; Liq: 2,650; Liq (Oil): 2,650 Compartments: 8 Ta, ER 2 Cargo Pump (s): 2x900m³/hr	**1 oil engine** driving 1 CP propeller Total Power: 2,060kW (2,801hp) 13.1kn Hanshin 6EL38 1 x 4 Stroke 6 Cy. 380 x 760 2060kW (2801bhp) The Hanshin Diesel Works Ltd-Japan AuxGen: 3 x 186kW a.c Thrusters: 1 Thwart. CP thruster (f) Fuel: 145.0 (r.f.)

Ship	Tonnage	Class	Builder / Dimensions	Type	Machinery
8224298 **SEDNA** *9HGU9* *ex* Kale *-2007* *ex* Alert *-2004* - **Sedna Maritime Ltd** Megatrans Uluslararasi Deniz Nakliyat Sanayi ve Ticaret AS *Valletta* *Malta* MMSI: 256967000 Official number: 8224298	**2,970** 1,895 4,830	Class: BV	**1984-09 Bodewes' Scheepswerven B.V. — Hoogezand** Yd No: 548 Loa 88.73 Br ex 15.42 Dght 6.651 Lbp 81.01 Br md 15.21 Dpth 8.21 Welded, 1 dk	**(A31A2GX) General Cargo Ship** Grain: 6,060; Bale: 5,880 Compartments: 2 Ho, ER 2 Ha: ER	**1 oil engine** with clutches, flexible couplings & sr geared to sc. shaft driving 1 FP propeller Total Power: 1,320kW (1,795hp) 12.5kn MaK 6MU452AK 1 x 4 Stroke 6 Cy. 320 x 450 1320kW (1795bhp) Krupp MaK Maschinenbau GmbH-Kiel
9402093 **SEDNA DESGAGNES** *8PVW* *completed as* Beluga Festivity *-2009* - **Transport Desgagnes Inc** - *Bridgetown* *Barbados* MMSI: 314296000	**9,611** 4,260 12,612	Class: GL	**2009-02 Qingshan Shipyard — Wuhan HB** Yd No: 20060304 Loa 139.00 (BB) Br ex - Dght 8.000 Lbp 130.00 Br md 21.00 Dpth 11.00 Welded, 2 dks	**(A31A2GX) General Cargo Ship** Double Bottom Entire Compartment Length Grain: 15,952 TEU 665 C Ho 334 TEU C Dk 331 TEU incl. 25 ref C. Compartments: 3 Ho, 3 Tw Dk, ER 3 Ha: (42.3 x 18.0) (26.0 x 18.0)ER (19.3 x 15.4) Cranes: 2x180t Ice Capable	**1 oil engine** reduction geared to sc. shaft driving 1 CP propeller Total Power: 5,400kW (7,342hp) 14.0kn MaK 6M43C 1 x 4 Stroke 6 Cy. 430 x 610 5400kW (7342bhp) Caterpillar Motoren GmbH & Co. KG-Germany AuxGen: 3 x 395kW 400/230V 50Hz a.c, 1 x 700kW 400/230V 50Hz a.c Thrusters: 1 Thwart. FP thruster (f) Fuel: 130.0 (d.f.) 818.0 (r.f.)
5044312 **SEDNA IV** *CFN3024* *ex* Saint Kilda *-2002* *ex* Starfish *-1981* - *ex* Bielefeld *-1971* **Navigation Sedna Inc** - *Cap-aux-Meules, QC* *Canada* MMSI: 316327000 Official number: 820221	**394** 118 -	Class: (GL)	**1957 Yacht- u. Bootswerft Abeking & Rasmussen — Lemwerder** Yd No: 5169 Converted From: Fishing Vessel-1992 Loa 51.34 Br ex 7.95 Dght 4.200 Lbp 40.01 Br md 7.90 Dpth 5.34 Welded, 1 dk	**(X11A2YS) Yacht (Sailing)** Ice Capable	**1 oil engine** reduction geared to sc. shaft driving 1 CP propeller Total Power: 368kW (500hp) MWM TBD604BL6 1 x 4 Stroke 6 Cy. 170 x 195 368kW (500bhp) (new engine 1992, fitted 1992) Motoren Werke Mannheim AG (MWM)-Mannheim AuxGen: 3 x a.c Thrusters: 1 Thwart. FP thruster (f)
9542685 **SEDNA OCEAN** *3FA09* - **Sea Wealth Navigation SA** Daiichi Chuo Marine Co Ltd (DC Marine) *Panama* *Panama* MMSI: 352663000 Official number: 4320311	**19,815** 10,385 31,997 T/cm 45.1	Class: NK	**2011-11 The Hakodate Dock Co Ltd — Hakodate HK** Yd No: 844 Loa 175.50 Br ex - Dght 9.640 Lbp 167.00 Br md 29.40 Dpth 13.70 Welded, 1 dk	**(A21A2BC) Bulk Carrier** Double Hull Grain: 40,499; Bale: 39,279 Compartments: 5 Ho, ER 5 Ha: ER Cranes: 4x30t	**1 oil engine** driving 1 FP propeller Total Power: 6,840kW (9,300hp) 14.5kn Mitsubishi 6UEC45LSE 1 x 2 Stroke 6 Cy. 450 x 1840 6840kW (9300bhp) Kobe Hatsudoki KK-Japan Fuel: 1370.0
7946356 **SEDOV** *UELO* *ex* Kommodore Johnsen *-1945* - *ex* Magdalene Vinnen *-1936* **Murmansk State Technical University** - SatCom: Inmarsat A 1406720 *Murmansk* *Russia* MMSI: 273510000 Official number: 210019	**3,432** 1,029 1,171	Class: RS	**1921-09 Fried. Krupp Germaniawerft AG — Kiel** Yd No: 372 Loa 117.50 Br ex 14.62 Dght 6.310 Lbp 98.20 Br md 14.60 Dpth 8.72 Welded, 2 dks	**(X11B2QN) Sail Training Ship** Passengers: cabins: 24 Ice Capable	**1 oil engine** reduction geared to sc. shaft driving 1 FP propeller Total Power: 1,600kW (2,175hp) 10.4kn Wartsila 8L20 1 x 4 Stroke 8 Cy. 200 x 280 1600kW (2175bhp) (Re-engined 2008, refitted 2008) Wartsila Finland Oy-Finland AuxGen: 3 x 164kW a.c Fuel: 221.0 (d.f.)
9342372 **SEDRA II** *9KCH* - **Kuwait Oil Tanker Co SAK** - SatCom: Inmarsat C 444715411 *Kuwait* *Kuwait* MMSI: 447154000 Official number: KT1722	**3,962** 1,244 5,048 T/cm 15.0	Class: LR ✠**100A1** SS 04/2013 Double Hull oil tanker ESP *IWS LI ✠**LMC** **UMS** Eq.Ltr: W; Cable: 495.0/44.0 U3 (a)	**2008-05 Jurong SML Pte Ltd — Singapore** Yd No: 0885 Loa 90.00 (BB) Br ex 19.02 Dght 6.000 Lbp 83.50 Br md 19.00 Dpth 8.20 Welded, 1 dk	**(A13B2TP) Products Tanker** Double Hull (13F) Liq: 4,424; Liq (Oil): 4,424 Cargo Heating Coils Compartments: 8 Wing Ta, 2 Wing Slop Ta, ER 3 Cargo Pump (s): 2x600m³/hr, 1x300m³/hr Manifold: Bow/CM: 44.2m	**1 oil engine** with clutches, flexible couplings & reverse reduction geared to sc. shaft driving 1 FP propeller Total Power: 2,942kW (4,000hp) 12.0kn Daihatsu 6DKM-36 1 x 4 Stroke 6 Cy. 360 x 480 2942kW (4000bhp) Daihatsu Diesel Manufacturing Co Lt-Japan AuxGen: 2 x 500kW 450V 60Hz a.c, 1 x 740kW 450V 60Hz a.c Boilers: WTAuxB (o.f.) 9.2kgf/cm² (9.0bar) Thrusters: 1 Thwart. CP thruster (f) Fuel: 617.0 (d.f.) 92.0 (r.f.)
9099664 **SEE GOD I** - *ex* Fu Yuan Yu 300 *-2008* - **Bossgie Ltd** - *Takoradi* *Ghana* Official number: GSR 0056	**138** 48 -		**2002-01 Huanghai Shipbuilding Co Ltd — Rongcheng SD** Loa 32.54 Br ex - Dght - Lbp - Br md 6.20 Dpth 2.85 Welded, 1 dk	**(B11B2FV) Fishing Vessel**	**1 oil engine** reduction geared to sc. shaft driving 1 Propeller Total Power: 300kW (408hp) 11.0kn Chinese Std. Type 6300ZC 1 x 4 Stroke 6 Cy. 300 x 380 300kW (408bhp) Dalian Fishing Vessel Co-China
9099676 **SEE GOD II** - *ex* Fu Yuan Yu 301 *-2008* - **Bossgie Ltd** - *Takoradi* *Ghana* Official number: GSR 0057	**138** 48 -		**2002-01 Huanghai Shipbuilding Co Ltd — Rongcheng SD** Loa 32.54 Br ex - Dght - Lbp - Br md 6.20 Dpth 2.85 Welded, 1 dk	**(B11B2FV) Fishing Vessel**	**1 oil engine** reduction geared to sc. shaft driving 1 Propeller Total Power: 300kW (408hp) 11.0kn Chinese Std. Type 6300ZC 1 x 4 Stroke 6 Cy. 300 x 380 300kW (408bhp) Dalian Fishing Vessel Co-China
9704312 **SEE STAR** *9LH2021* *launched as* Sea Star *-2013* - **Ships & Boats Oil Services** - *Freetown* *Sierra Leone* Official number: SL109021	**145** 50 -	Class: BV (Class contemplated) IS	**2013-01 Gemak Sanayi ve Ticaret Koll. Sti. — Tuzla** Loa 32.07 Br ex - Dght 1.800 Lbp 30.00 Br md 6.70 Dpth 3.00 Welded, 1 dk	**(B21A20C) Crew/Supply Vessel** Hull Material: Aluminium Alloy	**2 oil engines** reduction geared to sc. shafts driving 2 Propellers Total Power: 1,250kW (1,700hp) Iveco Aifo 8291 SRM85 2 x Vee 4 Stroke 12 Cy. 145 x 130 each-625kW (850bhp) IVECO AIFO S.p.A.-Pregnana Milanese
9195561 **SEE-STERN** *V2BF2* - **Seetransit Bereederungs GmbH & Co KG ms 'See-Stern'** - *Saint John's* *Antigua & Barbuda* MMSI: 304809000 Official number: 3987	**1,552** 848 1,863	Class: GL (LR) ✠ Classed LR until 15/6/09	**2005-06 DAHK Chernomorskyi Sudnobudivnyi Zavod — Mykolayiv** (Hull) Yd No: 0203 **2005-06 B.V. Scheepswerf Damen Bergum — Bergum** Yd No: 9326 Loa 82.23 Br ex 11.40 Dght 3.404 Lbp 78.05 Br md 11.30 Dpth 4.45 Welded, 1 dk	**(A31A2GX) General Cargo Ship** TEU 48 Compartments: 1 Ho, ER 1 Ha: ER	**1 oil engine** with clutches, flexible couplings & sr reverse geared to sc. shaft driving 1 FP propeller Total Power: 954kW (1,297hp) 11.0kn Caterpillar 3512B-TA 1 x Vee 4 Stroke 12 Cy. 170 x 190 954kW (1297bhp) Caterpillar Inc-USA AuxGen: 2 x 67kW 400V 50Hz a.c Thrusters: 1 Water jet (f)
7390650 **SEE VIEW** *T8XT* *ex* Al Dawaliah 2 *-2014* *ex* Nico Jumeirah *-1997* - *ex* Viking Larak *-1988* *ex* Gus Tide *-1987* **Deep Ocean Shipping Ltd** - *Malakal Harbour* *Palau* MMSI: 511011054	**399** 119 853	Class: BV (NV) (AB)	**1974-07 American Marine Corp. — New Orleans, La** Yd No: 1118 Loa 52.30 Br ex 11.59 Dght 3.683 Lbp 50.62 Br md 11.56 Dpth 4.27 Welded, 1 dk	**(B21B20A) Anchor Handling Tug Supply** Cranes: 1x25t	**2 oil engines** reduction geared to sc. shafts driving 2 FP propellers Total Power: 2,206kW (3,000hp) 11.0kn EMD (Electro-Motive) 12-645-E2 2 x Vee 2 Stroke 12 Cy. 230 x 254 each-1103kW (1500bhp) General Motors Corp.Electro-Motive Div.-La Grange AuxGen: 2 x 75kW 220/110V 60Hz a.c Thrusters: 1 Tunnel thruster (f) Fuel: 287.5 (d.f.)
7827110 **SEE WIND** *9LE2094* *ex* Miriam Tide *-2013* *ex* Lacoste Tide *-1987* - *ex* Blue Cat *-1985* **Star Offshore Services Ltd** Ships & Boats Oil Services *Freetown* *Sierra Leone* MMSI: 667595000	**672** 201 906	Class: AB BV (Class contemplated) (RI)	**1979-08 Halter Marine, Inc. — Moss Point, Ms** Yd No: 803 Loa 56.39 Br ex - Dght 3.640 Lbp 51.82 Br md 12.19 Dpth 4.27 Welded, 1 dk	**(B21A20S) Platform Supply Ship**	**2 oil engines** reverse reduction geared to sc. shafts driving 2 FP propellers Total Power: 2,206kW (3,000hp) 12.0kn EMD (Electro-Motive) 12-645-E6 2 x Vee 2 Stroke 12 Cy. 230 x 254 each-1103kW (1500bhp) General Motors Corp.Electro-Motive Div.-U.S.A. AuxGen: 2 x 125kW Thrusters: 1 Thwart. FP thruster (f) Fuel: 160.0
9191541 **SEEADLER** *DBFC* - **Government of The Federal Republic of Germany (Bundesanstalt fuer Landwirtschaft und Ernahrung BLE) (Federal Office for Agriculture & Food)** - *Rostock* *Germany* MMSI: 211316340	**1,774** 532 465	Class: GL	**2000-06 Peene-Werft GmbH — Wolgast** Yd No: 489 Loa 72.40 (BB) Br ex 12.74 Dght 5.100 Lbp 67.20 Br md 12.50 Dpth 6.20 Welded, 1 dk	**(B12D2FP) Fishery Patrol Vessel** Ice Capable	**2 oil engines** with clutches, flexible couplings & sr geared to sc. shafts driving 2 CP propellers Total Power: 7,600kW (10,332hp) 19.0kn M.T.U. 16V595TE70 2 x Vee 4 Stroke 16 Cy. 190 x 210 each-3800kW (5166bhp) MTU Friedrichshafen GmbH-Friedrichshafen AuxGen: 2 x 1025kW 690V 50Hz a.c, 1 x 290kW 400V 50Hz a.c Thrusters: 1 Thwart. FP thruster (f) Fuel: 339.0 (d.f.)

IMO / Call sign	Name / Owner	Tonnage	Class	Built / Dimensions	Type	Machinery
9500716 *9HA2317* -	**SEEB** **Seeb Maritime Transportation Co Ltd** Oman Ship Management Co SAOC SatCom: Inmarsat C 424832310 *Valletta* *Malta* MMSI: 248323000 Official number: 9500716	**164,359** 108,547 319,439 T/cm 178.7	Class: LR (NV) **100A1** SS 11/2011 Double Hull oil tanker CSR ESP *IWS LI SPM4 EP (bar above) **LMC** **UMS IGS** Eq.Ltr: E*; Cable: 770.0/117.0 U3 (a)	**2011**-11 **Daewoo Shipbuilding & Marine Engineering Co Ltd — Geoje** Yd No: 5332 Loa 333.00 (BB) Br ex 60.04 Dght 22.500 Lbp 320.00 Br md 60.00 Dpth 30.50 Welded, 1 dk	**(A13A2TV) Crude Oil Tanker** Double Hull (13F) Liq: 340,600; Liq (Oil): 340,600 Compartments: 5 Ta, 10 Wing Ta, ER, 2 Wing Slop Ta 4 Cargo Pump (s): 1x3500m^3/hr, 3x5500m^3/hr Manifold: Bow/CM: 156.6m	**1 oil engine** driving 1 FP propeller Total Power: 29,400kW (39,972hp) 15.3kn MAN-B&W 6S90MC-C 1 x 2 Stroke 6 Cy. 900 x 3188 29400kW (39972bhp) Doosan Engine Co Ltd-South Korea AuxGen: 3 x 1190kW 450V 60Hz a.c Boilers: e (ex.g.) 22.9kgf/cm^2 (22.5bar), WTAuxB (Comp) 16.8kgf/cm^2 (16.5bar), WTAuxB (o.f.) 16.8kgf/cm^2 (16.5bar) Fuel: 350.0 (d.f.) 8255.0 (r.f.)
5317252 - -	**SEEBAER** - - -	*133* 47 -	Class: (DS)	**1958 VEB Elbewerft — Boizenburg** Loa 26.45 Br ex 6.71 Dght 3.550 Lbp 23.40 Br md - Dpth 3.66 Welded, 1 dk	**(B11B2FV) Fishing Vessel** Compartments: 1 Ho, ER 1 Ha: ER Ice Capable	**1 oil engine** driving 1 FP propeller Total Power: 221kW (300hp) 9.0kn S.K.L. 6NVD36 1 x 4 Stroke 6 Cy. 240 x 360 221kW (300bhp) VEB Maschinenbau Halberstadt-Halberstadt AuxGen: 2 x 29kW 110V d.c
9421233 *DBFI* -	**SEEFALKE** **Government of The Federal Republic of Germany (Bundesanstalt fuer Landwirtschaft und Ernahrung BLE) (Federal Office for Agriculture & Food)** - *Cuxhaven* *Germany* MMSI: 218692000	**1,981** 594 470	Class: GL	**2008**-11 **Peene-Werft GmbH — Wolgast** Yd No: 559 Loa 72.79 (BB) Br ex - Dght 5.140 Lbp 67.21 Br md 12.50 Dpth 6.80 Welded, 1 dk	**(B12D2FP) Fishery Patrol Vessel** Ice Capable	**2 diesel electric oil engines** Connecting to 2 elec. motors each (1050kW) reduction geared to sc. shafts driving 2 CP propellers Total Power: 7,200kW (9,790hp) M.T.U. 20V4000M72 2 x Vee 4 Stroke 20 Cy. 165 x 190 each-3600kW (4895bhp) MTU Friedrichshafen GmbH-Friedrichshafen AuxGen: 2 x 1370kW 690/400V a.c Thrusters: 1 Tunnel thruster (f)
5148716 *Y4EK* -	**SEEFUCHS** *ex* Heringshai **Seefuchs GbR** - *Sassnitz* *Germany* MMSI: 211362930	*133* 47 -	Class: (DS) (GL)	**1958 VEB Elbewerft — Boizenburg** Loa 26.45 Br ex 6.71 Dght 3.550 Lbp 23.40 Br md - Dpth 3.66 Welded, 1 dk	**(B11B2FV) Fishing Vessel** Compartments: 1 Ho, ER 1 Ha: ER Ice Capable	**1 oil engine** driving 1 FP propeller Total Power: 184kW (250hp) 9.0kn S.K.L. 6NVD36 1 x 4 Stroke 6 Cy. 240 x 360 184kW (250bhp) VEB Maschinenbau Halberstadt-Halberstadt AuxGen: 1 x 12kW 110V d.c, 1 x 11kW 110V d.c
7017014 - -	**SEEHUND** - -	*302* 105 -	Class: (DS) (GL)	**1957 VEB Elbewerft — Boizenburg** Yd No: 1812 Loa 47.96 Br ex 8.34 Dght 2.699 Lbp 46.72 Br md - Dpth 3.00 Welded, 1 dk	**(B34A2SH) Hopper, Motor**	**1 oil engine** driving 1 FP propeller Total Power: 160kW (218hp) 6.0kn S.K.L. 6NVD36-1U 1 x 4 Stroke 6 Cy. 240 x 360 160kW (218bhp) VEB Schwermaschinenbau "KarlLiebknecht" (SKL)-Magdeburg AuxGen: 1 x 16kW 220/380V 50Hz a.c, 1 x 7kW 220/380V 50Hz a.c
7437276 - -	**SEEKER** **Arabon Seafoods Pty Ltd** - *Mooloolaba, Qld* *Australia* Official number: 355452	*101* 69 -		**1974 R G & P G Morton — Launceston TAS** L reg 20.06 Br ex 6.48 Dght - Lbp - Br md - Dpth - Welded, 1 dk	**(B11B2FV) Fishing Vessel**	**1 oil engine** driving 1 FP propeller Total Power: 221kW (300hp) 12.0kn G.M. (Detroit Diesel) 12V-71-N 1 x Vee 2 Stroke 12 Cy. 108 x 127 221kW (300bhp) General Motors Corp-USA
7813896 - -	**SEEKER** **Aquashield Oil & Marine Services Ltd** - *Nigeria*	**171** 34 -		**1980**-03 **Brooke Marine Ltd. — Lowestoft** Yd No: 424 Loa 32.87 Br ex 6.33 Dght 1.524 Lbp 30.48 Br md 6.10 Dpth 3.61 Welded, 1 dk	**(B34H2SQ) Patrol Vessel**	**2 oil engines** reverse reduction geared to sc. shafts driving 2 FP propellers Total Power: 2,978kW (4,048hp) Paxman 12YJCM 2 x Vee 4 Stroke 12 Cy. 197 x 216 each-1489kW (2024bhp) Paxman Diesels Ltd.-Colchester
8506048 - -	**SEEKER** *ex* Hornbeck Seeker *-1996* *ex* Sunset Seeker *-1995* *ex* Far Seeker *-1993* *launched as* Rumi *-1991* **Tidewater Hulls Ltd** Mare Alta do Brasil Navegacao Ltda	**928** 278 850	Class: AB (BV)	**1991**-01 **Astilleros Luzuriaga SA — Pasaia** (Hull launched by) Yd No: 233 **1991**-01 **in Spain** (Hull completed by) Loa 53.01 Br ex - Dght 4.501 Lbp 46.00 Br md 12.01 Dpth 5.21 Welded, 1 dk	**(B21B20T) Offshore Tug/Supply Ship**	**2 oil engines** reduction geared to sc. shafts driving 2 CP propellers Total Power: 2,802kW (3,810hp) 13.8kn MAN 14V20/27 2 x Vee 4 Stroke 14 Cy. 200 x 270 each-1401kW (1905bhp) EN Bazan de Construcciones NavalesMilitares SA-Spain AuxGen: 2 x 440kW 220/380V 50Hz a.c, 2 x 158kW 220/380V 50Hz a.c
8942096 *WTE5329* -	**SEEKER** **f/v Seeker Inc** - *Newport, OR* *United States of America* Official number: 924585	*213* 63 -		**1987 Johnson Shipbuilding & Repair — Bayou La Batre, Al** Yd No: 9 L reg 26.55 Br ex - Dght - Lbp - Br md 7.92 Dpth 3.96 Welded, 1 dk	**(B11B2FV) Fishing Vessel**	**1 oil engine** driving 1 FP propeller
9227156 *9V8237* -	**SEEKER** **PSA Marine Pte Ltd** - *Singapore* *Singapore* MMSI: 563013410 Official number: 395493	**292** 87 216	Class: LR ✠ **100A1** SS 12/2010 tug ✠ **LMC** Eq.Ltr: F†; Cable: 275.0/19.0 U2	**2000**-12 **ASL Shipyard Pte Ltd — Singapore** Yd No: 187 Loa 29.95 Br ex 10.20 Dght 3.800 Lbp 26.27 Br md 9.80 Dpth 4.80 Welded, 1 dk	**(B32A2ST) Tug**	**2 oil engines** reduction geared to sc. shafts driving 2 Directional propellers Total Power: 2,648kW (3,600hp) 12.0kn Yanmar 8N21AL-EN 2 x 4 Stroke 8 Cy. 210 x 290 each-1324kW (1800bhp) Yanmar Diesel Engine Co Ltd-Japan AuxGen: 2 x 83kW 415V 50Hz a.c
9234795 *ZQNL2* -	**SEEKER** **Government of The United Kingdom (Home Office Border Force, Maritime & Aviation Operations)** - *United Kingdom* MMSI: 235082000	**238** 71 -	Class: (LR) ✠ 7/01	**2001**-07 **Scheepswerf Made B.V. — Made** (Hull) Yd No: 00026 **2001**-07 **B.V. Scheepswerf Damen — Gorinchem** Yd No: 549852 Loa 42.80 Br ex - Dght 2.100 Lbp 38.30 Br md 6.80 Dpth 3.77 Welded, 1 dk	**(B34H2SQ) Patrol Vessel**	**2 oil engines** reduction geared to sc. shafts driving 2 CP propellers Total Power: 4,176kW (5,678hp) 24.0kn Caterpillar 3516B-TA 2 x Vee 4 Stroke 16 Cy. 170 x 190 each-2088kW (2839bhp) Caterpillar Inc-USA
6611540 - -	**SEEKHPAR** **Karachi Port Trust** - *Karachi* *Pakistan*	*113* 61 37		**1965 Karachi Shipyard & Engineering Works Ltd. — Karachi** Yd No: 79 Loa 26.27 Br ex 7.22 Dght 1.829 Lbp 24.01 Br md 7.01 Dpth 2.90 Welded, 1 dk	**(A37B2PS) Passenger Ship**	**2 oil engines** driving 2 FP propellers MAN 2 x 4 Stroke 5 Cy. 175 x 220 Maschinenbau Augsburg Nuernberg (MAN)-Augsburg
9059066 *DBQP* -	**SEEKRABBE** **Niedersachsen Ports GmbH & Co KG** - *Norddeich* *Germany* MMSI: 211232950 Official number: 5516	**656** 196 531	Class: GL	**1993**-05 **Julius Diedrich Schiffswerft GmbH & Co KG — Moormerland** Yd No: 165 Loa 52.00 Br ex - Dght 2.080 Lbp 49.00 Br md 12.00 Dpth 3.00 Welded, 1 dk	**(B33B2DS) Suction Hopper Dredger** Hopper: 500 Compartments: 1 Ho, ER 1 Ha: (31.0 x 9.2)ER Ice Capable	**2 oil engines** with clutches, flexible couplings & sr geared to sc. shafts driving 2 Directional propellers Total Power: 574kW (780hp) 8.0kn Caterpillar 3406TA 2 x 4 Stroke 6 Cy. 137 x 165 each-287kW (390bhp) Caterpillar Inc-USA AuxGen: 1 x 86kW 220/380V a.c, 1 x 20kW 220/380V a.c Thrusters: 1 Tunnel thruster (f)
9301603 *MNUN2* -	**SEELAND** **ms 'Seeland' GmbH & Co KG** Schiffahrtskontor tom Worden GmbH & Co KG *Douglas* *Isle of Man (British)* MMSI: 235011600 Official number: DR146	**5,257** 2,697 7,064	Class: GL	**2006**-08 **Qingdao Hyundai Shipbuilding Co Ltd — Jiaonan SD** Yd No: 103 Loa 117.34 (BB) Br ex 16.80 Dght 6.000 Lbp 113.03 Br md 16.50 Dpth 7.95 Welded, 1 dk	**(A31A2GX) General Cargo Ship** Double Bottom Entire Compartment Length Grain: 9,317; Bale: 9,000 TEU 324 C Ho 180 TEU C Dk 144 TEU Compartments: 2 Ho, ER 2 Ha: (51.0 x 13.5)ER Ice Capable	**1 oil engine** reduction geared to sc. shaft driving 1 CP propeller Total Power: 3,840kW (5,221hp) 12.5kn MaK 8M32C 1 x 4 Stroke 8 Cy. 320 x 480 3840kW (5221bhp) Caterpillar Motoren GmbH & Co. KG-Germany AuxGen: 2 x 280kW 400/230V a.c, 1 x 480kW 400/230V a.c Thrusters: 1 Tunnel thruster (f)
9246528 *DBQM* -	**SEELOWE** **Niedersachsen Ports GmbH & Co KG** - *Norddeich* *Germany* MMSI: 211374390 Official number: 5439	**270** 81 171	Class: GL	**2003**-07 **Elbewerk GmbH (Boizenburg) — Boizenburg** Yd No: 102 Loa 32.57 Br ex - Dght 1.626 Lbp 27.00 Br md 9.00 Dpth 3.00 Welded, 1 dk	**(B34L2QU) Utility Vessel** Ice Capable	**2 oil engines** geared to sc. shafts driving 2 FP propellers Total Power: 600kW (816hp) 8.0kn MAN D2866LXE 2 x 4 Stroke 6 Cy. 128 x 155 each-300kW (408bhp) MAN Nutzfahrzeuge AG-Nuernberg Thrusters: 1 Tunnel thruster (f)

5171684 - -	**SEEMA** *ex Jentayu -1967* **K M Shafi** - *Chittagong* *Bangladesh*	*138* 66 122	Class: (LR) ✠ Classed LR until 12/53	**1951**-08 **Clelands (Successors) Ltd. — Wallsend** Yd No: 167 Loa 29.42 Br ex 6.13 Dght 1.905 Lbp - Br md 6.08 Dpth - Riveted\Welded, 1 dk	**(A31A2GX) General Cargo Ship** Bale: 175 Compartments: 1 Ho, ER 1 Ha: (7.6 x 3.6)ER Winches: 1	**2 oil engines** driving 2 FP propellers 8.5kn Thornycroft 2 x 4 Stroke 6 Cy. 120 x 165 John I Thornycroft & Co Ltd-United Kingdom Fuel: 7.0
8218196 *3FIK3* -	**SEER** *ex Al Jaber Iv -2010* **Seer Marine Services Corp** - *Panama* *Panama* MMSI: 353427000 Official number: 4253911	**1,154** 346 1,463	Class: (GL) (BV) (AB)	**1982**-12 **Santan Engineering Pte Ltd — Singapore** Yd No: 8238 Loa 68.51 Br ex - Dght 3.090 Lbp 61.02 Br md 14.01 Dpth 4.22 Welded, 1 dk	**(A35D2RL) Landing Craft** Bow door/ramp (centre)	**2 oil engines** reverse reduction geared to sc. shafts driving 2 FP propellers Total Power: 802kW (1,090hp) 10.0kn Caterpillar D379TA 2 x Vee 4 Stroke 8 Cy. 159 x 203 each-401kW (545bhp) Caterpillar Tractor Co-USA AuxGen: 2 x 170kW
8509052 *DFAC* NC 309	**SEEWOLF** - **'Seewolf' Fischereigesellschaft mbH** - *Cuxhaven* *Germany* MMSI: 211267780 Official number: 971	**261** 100 150	Class: (GL)	**1985**-11 **Sieghold Werft Bremerhaven GmbH & Co. — Bremerhaven** Yd No: 198 Loa 30.36 Br ex 8.01 Dght 3.252 Lbp 26.01 Br md 7.82 Dpth 3.97 Welded, 1 dk	**(B11A2FS) Stern Trawler**	**1 oil engine** with clutches, flexible couplings & sr geared to sc. shaft driving 1 CP propeller Total Power: 599kW (814hp) Deutz SBV6M628 1 x 4 Stroke 6 Cy. 240 x 280 599kW (814bhp) Kloeckner Humboldt Deutz AG-West Germany Thrusters: 1 Thwart. FP thruster (f)
5317410 - -	**SEEWOLF** - -	*133* 47 -	Class: (DS)	**1958 VEB Elbewerft — Boizenburg** Loa 26.45 Br ex 6.71 Dght 3.550 Lbp 23.40 Br md - Dpth 3.66 Welded, 1 dk	**(B11B2FV) Fishing Vessel** Compartments: 1 Ho, ER 1 Ha: ER Ice Capable	**1 oil engine** driving 1 FP propeller Total Power: 184kW (250hp) 9.0kn S.K.L. 8NVD36 1 x 4 Stroke 8 Cy. 240 x 360 184kW (250bhp) VEB Maschinenbau Halberstadt-Halberstadt AuxGen: 2 x 21kW 110V d.c
6610388 *TC5726* -	**SEFER GARIP** - **Turkiye Taskomuru Kuruma Genel Mudurlugu** - *Zonguldak* *Turkey* Official number: 519	*230* 119 436	Class: (LR) ✠ Classed LR until 7/68	**1966**-06 **Celiktrans Deniz Insaat Kizaklari Ltd. Sti — Tuzla,Ist** Yd No: 24 Loa 32.52 Br ex 9.02 Dght 1.800 Lbp 30.79 Br md 9.01 Dpth 2.80 Welded, 1 dk	**(B34A2SH) Hopper, Motor** Compartments: 1 Ho, ER	**1 oil engine** reverse geared to sc. shaft driving 1 FP propeller Total Power: 250kW (340hp) 9.0kn Alpha 404-24VO 1 x 2 Stroke 4 Cy. 240 x 400 250kW (340bhp) Alpha Diesel A/S-Denmark AuxGen: 1 x 15kW 220V d.c Fuel: 8.0 (d.f.)
9605126 *TCSE4* -	**SEFER KAPTAN 1** *ex Sefer Kaptan -2011* **Omer Hizarci-Sefer Hizarci Ort** - *Istanbul* *Turkey* Official number: G-1573	**299** 202 -	Class: TL	**2011**-10 **Turkoglu Gemi Insaa Sanayi Ticaret Ltd Sti — Altinova** Yd No: 009 Loa 41.98 Br ex - Dght 1.490 Lbp 39.36 Br md 10.00 Dpth 3.20 Welded, 1 dk	**(A37B2PS) Passenger Ship**	**2 oil engines** reduction geared to sc. shafts driving 2 Propellers Total Power: 1,176kW (1,598hp) 12.2kn Iveco Aifo 8291 SRM85 2 x Vee 4 Stroke 12 Cy. 145 x 130 each-588kW (799bhp) IVECO AIFO S.p.A.-Pregnana Milanese AuxGen: 2 x 90kW a.c
9437634 *9HXX8* -	**SEFERIS** *ex Giannis M -2013 ex Sider Tiger -2007* **Trinity Maritime Inc** Pacific & Atlantic (Shipmanagers) Inc *Valletta* *Malta* MMSI: 256584000 Official number: 9437634	**5,222** 2,913 7,448 T/cm 17.5	Class: BV	**2007**-05 **Ningbo Xinle Shipbuilding Co Ltd — Ningbo ZJ** Yd No: 2005-6 Loa 119.95 Br ex 16.84 Dght 6.280 Lbp 112.99 Br md 16.80 Dpth 8.20 Welded, 1 dk	**(A21A2BC) Bulk Carrier** Grain: 10,106; Bale: 9,904	**1 oil engine** reduction geared to sc. shaft driving 1 FP propeller Total Power: 2,500kW (3,399hp) 11.5kn Daihatsu 8DKM-28 1 x 4 Stroke 8 Cy. 280 x 390 2500kW (3399bhp) Shaanxi Diesel Heavy Industry Co Lt-China
8407321 *EQJS* -	**SEFFAIN** - **Bahregan Marine Services Co Ltd** - *Bushehr* *Iran* MMSI: 422106000 Official number: 441	**456** 137 350	Class: AS (NV)	**1984**-11 **Nagasaki Zosen K.K. — Nagasaki** Yd No: 875 Loa 38.00 Br ex - Dght 3.644 Lbp 35.01 Br md 10.01 Dpth 3.97 Welded, 1 dk	**(B34L2QU) Utility Vessel**	**2 oil engines** geared to sc. shafts driving 2 FP propellers Total Power: 2,060kW (2,800hp) 13.0kn Yanmar T260-ST 2 x 4 Stroke 6 Cy. 260 x 330 each-1030kW (1400bhp) Yanmar Diesel Engine Co Ltd-Japan AuxGen: 2 x 240kW 380V 50Hz a.c, 1 x 100kW 380V 50Hz a.c Thrusters: 1 Thwart. FP thruster (f)
9066045 *UICC* -	**SEG** - **CJSC 'Armator'** Neva Shipping Co (OOO Nevskaya Sudokhodnaya Kompaniya) *St Petersburg* *Russia* MMSI: 273413060	**1,596** 831 2,300	Class: RS	**1993**-05 **Arminius Werke GmbH — Bodenwerder** Yd No: 10524 Loa 81.44 Br ex 11.46 Dght 4.233 Lbp 77.40 Br md 11.30 Dpth 5.40 Welded, 1 dk	**(A31A2GX) General Cargo Ship** Grain: 2,926 TEU 72 C. 72/20' Compartments: 1 Ho, ER 1 Ha: (51.6 x 9.0)ER Ice Capable	**1 oil engine** with flexible couplings & sr reverse geared to sc. shaft driving 1 FP propeller Total Power: 1,000kW (1,360hp) 9.5kn MaK 6M332C 1 x 4 Stroke 6 Cy. 240 x 330 1000kW (1360bhp) Krupp MaK Maschinenbau GmbH-Kiel Thrusters: 1 Thwart. FP thruster (f)
7830492 *WDF8616* -	**SEGA** *ex Eva Bisso -2011 ex Captain Gary -2006* *ex Miss Marcia -2005* **Noah Towing LLC** - *Charleston, SC* *United States of America* MMSI: 367142070 Official number: 594031	*103* 70 -		**1978 Main Iron Works, Inc. — Houma, La** L reg 19.66 Br ex - Dght - Lbp - Br md 7.45 Dpth 2.82 Welded, 1 dk	**(B32A2ST) Tug**	**2 oil engines** reduction geared to sc. shaft driving 1 FP propeller Total Power: 1,132kW (1,540hp) G.M. (Detroit Diesel) 16V-92 2 x Vee 2 Stroke 16 Cy. 123 x 127 each-566kW (770bhp) General Motors Corp-USA AuxGen: 2 x 30kW a.c
7101683 *YCVZ* -	**SEGAR PACIFIC** *ex Rimba Raya -2005 ex Tatanusa 3 -2005* *ex Bima Raya -1989 ex Toko Maru No. 2 -1981* **PT Sejahtera Agung** - *Jakarta* *Indonesia* Official number: 94+PST	*1,185* 594 2,013	Class: (KI)	**1970**-08 **Honda Zosen — Saiki** Yd No: 580 Loa 71.91 Br ex 11.03 Dght 4.979 Lbp 66.81 Br md 11.00 Dpth 5.59 Welded, 1 dk	**(A31A2GX) General Cargo Ship** Grain: 2,201; Bale: 1,995 Compartments: 1 Ho, ER 1 Ha: (31.8 x 6.5)ER Derricks: 2x12t; Winches: 6	**1 oil engine** driving 1 FP propeller Total Power: 1,839kW (2,500hp) 14.5kn Hanshin 6L46SH 1 x 4 Stroke 6 Cy. 460 x 680 1839kW (2500bhp) Hanshin Nainenki Kogyo-Japan AuxGen: 2 x 104kW 450V a.c Fuel: 131.0 8.5pd
8664395 *JZWA* -	**SEGARA ANAK 1** *ex Qian Zhou 28 -2014 ex Xin Jin Gui -2003* **PT Majukarsa Perdana Jaya Line** - *Indonesia*	**2,547** 1,426 4,200	Class: IZ (Class contemplated)	**2003**-12 **Yueqing Donggang Shipbuilding Co Ltd — Yueqing ZJ** Loa 93.50 Br ex - Dght 5.750 Lbp 86.60 Br md 13.50 Dpth 7.00 Welded, 1 dk	**(A31A2GX) General Cargo Ship**	**1 oil engine** reduction geared to sc. shafts driving 1 Propeller Total Power: 1,323kW (1,799hp) Chinese Std. Type 1 x 1323kW (1799bhp) Wuxi Antai Power Machinery Co Ltd-China
8664187 *JZVZ* -	**SEGARA IBU** *ex Xin Zhong Shun -2014 ex Tong Jie 07 -2012* **PT Majukarsa Perdana Jaya Line** - *Indonesia*	**1,951** 1,092 3,305	Class: IZ	**2004**-04 **Zhejiang Hongguan Ship Industry Co Ltd — Linhai ZJ** Loa 82.80 Br ex - Dght 5.400 Lbp 76.50 Br md 12.80 Dpth 6.60 Welded, 1 dk	**(A31A2GX) General Cargo Ship**	**1 oil engine** reduction geared to sc. shaft driving 1 FP propeller Total Power: 1,103kW (1,500hp) Chinese Std. Type 1 x 1103kW (1500bhp) Ningbo CSI Power & Machinery GroupCo Ltd-China
7853298 *YFRW* -	**SEGARA JAYA** *ex Lungshan No. 28 -1997* *ex Shuho Maru No. 11 -1993* **PT Patria Nusasegara** - *Jakarta* *Indonesia*	**430** 177 670	Class: KI (NK)	**1977**-02 **Shinwa Sangyo K.K. — Osakikamijima** Loa 50.50 Br ex - Dght 3.701 Lbp 44.86 Br md 8.01 Dpth 4.09 Welded, 1 dk	**(A13B2TU) Tanker (unspecified)** Liq: 697; Liq (Oil): 697	**1 oil engine** driving 1 FP propeller Total Power: 588kW (799hp) 10.0kn Niigata 1 x 4 Stroke 588kW (799bhp) Niigata Engineering Co Ltd-Japan
8655708 - -	**SEGARA SEJATI 1** - **PT Mitra Bahtera Segara Sejati Tbk** - *Samarinda* *Indonesia*	**182** 55 -	Class: KI	**2011**-02 **PT Mangkupalas Mitra Makmur — Samarinda** Loa 26.00 Br ex - Dght 2.940 Lbp 24.50 Br md 8.00 Dpth 3.50 Welded, 1 dk	**(B32A2ST) Tug**	**2 oil engines** reduction geared to sc. shafts driving 2 FP propellers AuxGen: 2 x 44kW 380/220V a.c
8654091 - -	**SEGARA SEJATI 2** - **PT Mitra Bahtera Segara Sejati Tbk** - *Samarinda* *Indonesia*	**182** 55 -	Class: KI	**2011**-02 **PT Mangkupalas Mitra Makmur — Samarinda** Loa 26.00 Br ex - Dght 2.940 Lbp 24.50 Br md 8.00 Dpth 3.50 Welded, 1 dk	**(B32A2ST) Tug**	**2 oil engines** reduction geared to sc. shafts driving 2 FP propellers AuxGen: 2 x 44kW 380/220V a.c
8659120 *YDA6650* -	**SEGARA SEJATI 3** - **PT Mitra Bahtera Segara Sejati Tbk** - *Samarinda* *Indonesia*	**223** 67 -	Class: KI	**2011**-06 **PT Mangkupalas Mitra Makmur — Samarinda** Loa 29.00 Br ex - Dght 3.000 Lbp 27.02 Br md 8.00 Dpth 3.70 Welded, 1 dk	**(B32A2ST) Tug**	**2 oil engines** reduction geared to sc. shafts driving 2 FP propellers Total Power: 1,220kW (1,658hp) Yanmar 6AYM-ETE 2 x 4 Stroke 6 Cy. 155 x 180 each-610kW (829bhp) Yanmar Diesel Engine Co Ltd-Japan AuxGen: 2 x 43kW 415V a.c

8520692 *PNQU* -	**SEGARA SEJATI 8** *ex* Koei Maru No. 8 *-2010* **PT Mitra Bahtera Segara Sejati Tbk** - *Jakarta* *Indonesia* MMSI: 525015765	*642* - 1,421	Class: (NK)	**1986-05 Ube Dockyard Co. Ltd. — Ube** Yd No: 196 Loa 65.12 Br ex - Dght 4.258 Lbp 60.03 Br md 10.51 Dpth 4.73 Welded, 1 dk	**(A24A2BT) Cement Carrier** Grain: 1,183	**1 oil engine** geared to sc. shaft driving 1 FP propeller Total Power: 956kW (1,300hp) 10.6kn Yanmar T260-ST 1 x 4 Stroke 6 Cy. 260 x 330 956kW (1300bhp) Yanmar Diesel Engine Co Ltd-Japan Fuel: 40.0 (d.f.)
8914958 *PONY* -	**SEGARATAMA I** *ex* Takara *-2013* **PT Patra Segara Tama** - *Batam* *Indonesia*	**301** 91 480	Class: KI	**1990-06 Imura Zosen K.K. — Komatsushima** Yd No: 237 Loa 49.30 Br ex - Dght 3.201 Lbp 45.00 Br md 8.00 Dpth 3.40 Welded, 1 dk	**(A12A2TC) Chemical Tanker**	**1 oil engine** driving 1 FP propeller Total Power: 588kW (799hp) Sumiyoshi S25G 1 x 4 Stroke 6 Cy. 250 x 450 588kW (799bhp) Sumiyoshi Tekkosho-Japan AuxGen: 1 x 80kW 225/130V a.c
6605785 *9GUV* -	**SEGE** - **Ocean Fisheries Ltd** - *Takoradi* *Ghana* Official number: 316543	*1,077* 514 1,437	Class: (LR) Classed LR until 31/5/89	**1966-04 Shikoku Dockyard Co. Ltd. — Takamatsu** Yd No: 686 Loa 65.79 Br ex 11.03 Dght 4.515 Lbp 60.00 Br md 11.00 Dpth 5.31 Welded, 1 dk	**(B12B2FC) Fish Carrier** Ins: 1,170 Compartments: 2 Ho, ER 2 Ha: 2 (2.9 x 2.2)ER Derricks: 4x1.5t	**1 oil engine** driving 1 FP propeller Total Power: 1,133kW (1,540hp) 11.3kn B&W 5-35VBF-62 1 x 2 Stroke 5 Cy. 350 x 620 1133kW (1540bhp) Mitsui Shipbuilding & Engineering CLtd-Japan AuxGen: 2 x 150kW 445V 50Hz a.c Fuel: 318.0
9656876 *9V9968* -	**SEGER** - **NM Tankers Pte Ltd** New Maritime Pte Ltd *Singapore* *Singapore* MMSI: 566532000 Official number: 397802	**2,239** 926 3,606	Class: CC	**2012-06 Qinhuangdao China Harbour Shbldg Industry Co Ltd — Qinhuangdao HE** Yd No: 2010/38-02 Loa 78.00 Br ex - Dght 5.000 Lbp 74.00 Br md 15.30 Dpth 6.90 Welded, 1 dk	**(A13B2TP) Products Tanker** Double Hull (13F) Liq: 3,218; Liq (Oil): 3,218 Compartments: 4 Wing Ta, 4 Wing Ta, 1 Wing Slop Ta, 1 Wing Slop Ta, ER	**2 oil engines** driving 2 Propellers Total Power: 1,268kW (1,724hp) 10.5kn Cummins KTA-38-M0 2 x Vee 4 Stroke 12 Cy. 159 x 159 each-634kW (862bhp) Chongqing Cummins Engine Co Ltd-China AuxGen: 2 x 250kW 400V a.c
9165188 *DSPZ4* -	**SEGERO** - **KT Submarine Co Ltd** - *Jeju* *South Korea* MMSI: 441500000 Official number: JJR-089578	**8,323** 2,496 6,409	Class: KR (LR) ✠ Classed LR until 15/12/02	**1998-04 Hanjin Heavy Industries Co Ltd — Busan** Yd No: 058 Loa 115.38 (BB) Br ex 20.02 Dght 7.805 Lbp 95.60 Br md 20.00 Dpth 15.00 Welded, 2 dks	**(B34D2SL) Cable Layer** A-frames: 1x50t Ice Capable	**4 diesel electric oil engines** driving 2 gen. each 2300kW 3300V a.c 2 gen. each 3400kW 3300V a.c Connecting to 2 elec. motors each (2700kW) driving 2 Directional propellers Total Power: 10,662kW (14,497hp) 15.0kn Alpha 6L23/30 1 x 4 Stroke 6 Cy. 225 x 300 960kW (1305bhp) Ssangyong Heavy Industries Co Ltd-South Korea MAN 6L32/40 1 x 4 Stroke 6 Cy. 320 x 400 2646kW (3598bhp) Ssangyong Heavy Industries Co Ltd-South Korea MAN 8L32/40 2 x 4 Stroke 8 Cy. 320 x 400 each-3528kW (4797bhp) Ssangyong Heavy Industries Co Ltd-South Korea Thrusters: 2 Thwart. FP thruster (f); 1 Directional thruster (a)
9152038 *IFRT* -	**SEGESTA JET** - **Rete Ferroviaria Italiana (RFI)** - *Reggio Calabria* *Italy* MMSI: 247042300 Official number: 285	**392** 325 56	Class: (RI)	**1999-03 Rodriquez Cantieri Navali SpA — Messina** Yd No: 271 Loa 50.46 Br ex 9.20 Dght 1.477 Lbp 43.00 Br md 8.80 Dpth 4.20 Welded, 1 dk	**(A37B2PS) Passenger Ship** Hull Material: Aluminium Alloy Passengers: unberthed: 500	**2 oil engines** with clutches, flexible couplings & sr geared to sc. shafts driving 2 Water jets Total Power: 4,000kW (5,438hp) 28.5kn M.T.U. 16V396TE74L 2 x Vee 4 Stroke 16 Cy. 165 x 185 each-2000kW (2719bhp) MTU Friedrichshafen GmbH-Friedrichshafen Thrusters: 1 Thwart. FP thruster (f)
9288978 *LLZL* -	**SEGLA** - **Segla AS** - *Tromso* *Norway* MMSI: 258470000	**436** 130 -		**2002 Porsgrunn Verksted AS — Porsgrunn** Yd No: 131 Loa 36.40 (BB) Br ex 8.50 Dght 6.650 Lbp - Br md - Dpth 6.40 Welded, 1 dk	**(B11B2FV) Fishing Vessel**	**1 oil engine** reduction geared to sc. shaft driving 1 CP propeller Total Power: 880kW (1,196hp) 10.2kn Volvo Penta 1 x 4 Stroke 880kW (1196bhp) AB Volvo Penta-Sweden Thrusters: 1 Tunnel thruster (f)
8739762 *EA3299* 3-GI-81-00	**SEGMON** - **Pesquerias Luarquesa SL** - *Luarca* *Spain* Official number: 3-1/2000	**120** - -		**2000-03 Astilleros Armon SA — Navia** Loa 22.00 Br ex - Dght - Lbp 18.00 Br md 6.50 Dpth 2.70 Welded, 1 dk	**(B11B2FV) Fishing Vessel**	**1 oil engine** driving 1 Propeller Total Power: 420kW (571hp) 7.8kn
9069956 *PKGX* -	**SEGORO MAS** *ex* Xing Ning 19 *-2007* **PT Pelayaran Tempuran Emas Tbk (TEMAS Line)** - *Jakarta* *Indonesia* MMSI: 525019363	**2,999** 1,976 5,250	Class: KI	**2005-01 Zhejiang Hongguan Ship Industry Co Ltd — Linhai ZJ** Loa 96.50 (BB) Br ex - Dght 5.930 Lbp 90.80 Br md 15.80 Dpth 7.40 Welded, 1 dk	**(A33A2CC) Container Ship (Fully Cellular)** TEU 266	**1 oil engine** geared to sc. shaft driving 1 Propeller Total Power: 1,765kW (2,400hp) 11.0kn Chinese Std. Type G8300ZC 1 x 4 Stroke 8 Cy. 300 x 380 1765kW (2400bhp) Wuxi Antai Power Machinery Co Ltd-China
9549102 *YJQL4* -	**SEGOVIA TIDE** *ex* Pioneer 5151 *-2010* **Aqua Fleet Ltd** Tidewater Inc *Port Vila* *Vanuatu* MMSI: 576652000 Official number: 1959	**1,520** 456 1,385	Class: AB	**2010-04 Guangdong Hongsheng Shipbuilding Industry Co Ltd — Guangzhou GD** Yd No: HS0703 Loa 58.70 Br ex - Dght 4.500 Lbp 54.12 Br md 14.60 Dpth 5.50 Welded, 1 dk	**(B21B20A) Anchor Handling Tug Supply**	**2 oil engines** reduction geared to sc. shafts driving 2 CP propellers Total Power: 3,840kW (5,220hp) 13.5kn Caterpillar 3516B-HD 2 x Vee 4 Stroke 16 Cy. 170 x 215 each-1920kW (2610bhp) Caterpillar Inc-USA AuxGen: 3 x 400kW a.c Fuel: 480.0
8991671 *WDA3468* -	**SEGUIN** *ex* Campti (YTB 816) *-2000* **Hartley Marine Services** - *Boothbay Harbor, ME* *United States of America* MMSI: 366798810 Official number: 1105173	**235** 134		**1972 Marinette Marine Corp — Marinette WI** Yd No: 816 L reg 31.24 Br ex - Dght - Lbp - Br md 8.84 Dpth 5.12 Welded, 1 dk	**(B32A2ST) Tug**	**1 oil engine** reduction geared to sc. shaft driving 1 Propeller Total Power: 1,471kW (2,000hp) Fairbanks, Morse 1 x 1471kW (2000bhp) in the United States of America
9095216 *EABU* 3-CO-62-06	**SEGUNDA DEL MAR** - **Recesmar SL** - *Muros* *Spain* Official number: 3-2/2006	**217** 65 -		**2006-05 Astilleros Armon Burela SA — Burela** Yd No: 269 Loa 28.00 Br ex - Dght 3.500 Lbp 23.00 Br md 7.50 Dpth - Welded, 1 dk	**(B11A2FS) Stern Trawler**	**1 oil engine** driving 1 Propeller Total Power: 235kW (320hp)
8716394 *EDQD* -	**SEGUNDO RIBEL** - **Pesquera Lolo SL** - *La Guardia* *Spain* MMSI: 224099450 Official number: 3-3549/	**203** - 119		**1988-01 Astilleros Armon SA — Navia** Yd No: 155 Loa 28.02 (BB) Br ex - Dght 3.131 Lbp 23.86 Br md 6.51 Dpth 3.51 Welded, 1 dk	**(B11B2FV) Fishing Vessel** Ins: 145	**1 oil engine** with clutches, flexible couplings & reverse reduction geared to sc. shaft driving 1 FP propeller Total Power: 441kW (600hp) Caterpillar 3412TA 1 x Vee 4 Stroke 12 Cy. 137 x 152 441kW (600bhp) Caterpillar Inc-USA
8818099 *6WJA* DAK 1176	**SEGUNDO SAN RAFAEL** - **Armadora Paradela SL** - *Dakar* *Senegal*	*312* 94 -	Class: (BV)	**1989-07 Astilleros y Talleres Ferrolanos S.A. (ASTAFERSA) — Ferrol** Yd No: 297 Loa 34.85 Br ex - Dght 3.350 Lbp 27.51 Br md 8.11 Dpth 5.52 Welded	**(B11A2FS) Stern Trawler** Ins: 254	**1 oil engine** with clutches, flexible couplings & sr geared to sc. shaft driving 1 CP propeller Total Power: 522kW (710hp) 11.0kn Blackstone ESL5MK2 1 x 4 Stroke 5 Cy. 222 x 292 522kW (710bhp) Mirrlees Blackstone (Stamford)Ltd.-Stamford AuxGen: 1 x 149kW 380V a.c, 2 x 108kW 380V a.c
9105217 - -	**SEGUS 88** *ex* Hosei Maru No. 88 *-2012* - - *Indonesia*	*499* - 1,348	Class: (NK)	**1994-05 Honda Zosen — Saiki** Yd No: 858 Loa 71.30 Br ex - Dght 4.450 Lbp 65.00 Br md 12.50 Dpth 7.27 Welded, 1 dk	**(A31A2GX) General Cargo Ship** Grain: 1,535; Bale: 1,826 2 Ha: (15.0 x 9.2) (15.6 x 9.5)ER Cranes: 1x12t	**1 oil engine** driving 1 FP propeller Total Power: 736kW (1,001hp) Akasaka A34 1 x 4 Stroke 6 Cy. 340 x 660 736kW (1001bhp) Akasaka Tekkosho KK (Akasaka DieselLtd)-Japan

9187978 *TCCF3* -	**SEHER II** **Yagci Denizcilik ve Ticaret Ltd Sti (Yagci Shipping & Trading Co Ltd)** - *Istanbul* *Turkey* MMSI: 271002353 Official number: 7362	**1,220** 782 2,418 T/cm 7.1	Class: TL	**1998**-07 **Yakup Kacaranlioglu Tersanesi — Tuzla** Yd No: 1 Loa 73.80 (BB) Br ex 10.90 Dght 5.850 Lbp 67.00 Br md 9.40 Dpth 5.85 Welded, 2 dks	**(A31A2GX) General Cargo Ship** Grain: 2,961; Bale: 2,724 Compartments: 2 Ho, ER 2 Ha: (16.3 x 6.6) (18.7 x 6.6)ER Derricks: 2x5t	**1 oil engine** with clutches, flexible couplings & reverse reduction geared to sc. shaft driving 1 FP propeller Total Power: 864kW (1,175hp) 10.0kn S.K.L. 8NVD48A-2U 1 x 4 Stroke 8 Cy. 320 x 480 864kW (1175bhp) SKL Motoren u. Systemtechnik AG-Magdeburg AuxGen: 2 x 150kW 380V 50Hz a.c Fuel: 116.0 (d.f.) 116.0pd
8311522 *J8B2902* -	**SEHER YILDIZI** *ex* Phoros *-2003* *ex* Icaro *-2002* *ex* Naica *-2000* *ex* Ayca *-1991* **Yonkers Shipping Inc** Fener Denizcilik Sanayi ve Ticaret Ltd Sti SatCom: Inmarsat C 437758310 *Kingstown* *St Vincent & The Grenadines* MMSI: 377583000 Official number: 9374	**1,981** 996 3,250	Class: HR TL (GL) (RI)	**1984**-06 **Desan Deniz Insaat Sanayii — Istanbul** Yd No: 1 Loa 82.17 Br ex - Dght 5.830 Lbp 75.01 Br md 14.00 Dpth 7.00 Welded, 1 dk	**(A31A2GX) General Cargo Ship** Grain: 3,555 Compartments: 2 Ho, ER 2 Ha: (19.2 x 7.8) (19.2 x 10.2)ER Derricks: 4x5t	**1 oil engine** driving 1 FP propeller Total Power: 1,228kW (1,670hp) Skoda 9TSR35/50-2 1 x 4 Stroke 9 Cy. 350 x 500 1228kW (1670bhp) CKD Praha-Praha AuxGen: 2 x 1280kW 220/380V a.c
7389900 *TC5430* -	**SEHIT ADEM YAVUZ** **Istanbul Buyuksehir Belediye Baskanligi** Istanbul Sehir Hatlari Turizm Sanayi ve Ticaret AS *Istanbul* *Turkey* MMSI: 271002509 Official number: 4418	*456* 208 180	Class: (TL)	**1976**-09 **Denizcilik Bankasi T.A.O. — Halic, Istanbul** Yd No: 188 Loa 67.00 Br ex 11.03 Dght 2.600 Lbp 55.93 Br md 10.60 Dpth 3.90 Welded, 2 dks	**(A37B2PS) Passenger Ship**	**2 oil engines** reverse reduction geared to sc. shafts driving 2 FP propellers Total Power: 1,104kW (1,500hp) 14.0kn Stork DRO218K 2 x 4 Stroke 8 Cy. 210 x 300 each-552kW (750bhp) Stork Werkspoor Diesel BV-Netherlands AuxGen: 2 x 90kW a.c
7389948 *TC5441* -	**SEHIT CANER GONYELI** **Istanbul Buyuksehir Belediye Baskanligi** Istanbul Sehir Hatlari Turizm Sanayi ve Ticaret AS *Istanbul* *Turkey* MMSI: 271002512 Official number: 4537	*456* 208 180	Class: TL	**1977**-12 **Denizcilik Bankasi T.A.O. — Halic, Istanbul** Yd No: 192 Loa 58.20 Br ex 11.00 Dght 2.401 Lbp 55.93 Br md 10.60 Dpth 3.60 Welded, 2 dks	**(A37B2PS) Passenger Ship**	**2 oil engines** reverse reduction geared to sc. shafts driving 2 FP propellers Total Power: 1,104kW (1,500hp) 14.0kn Stork DRO218K 2 x 4 Stroke 8 Cy. 210 x 300 each-552kW (750bhp) Stork Werkspoor Diesel BV-Netherlands
7389950 *TCAP7* -	**SEHIT ILKER KARTER** **Istanbul Buyuksehir Belediye Baskanligi** Istanbul Sehir Hatlari Turizm Sanayi ve Ticaret AS *Istanbul* *Turkey* MMSI: 271002518 Official number: 4787	*456* 208 180	Class: TL	**1980**-06 **Denizcilik Bankasi T.A.O. — Halic, Istanbul** Yd No: 194 Loa 58.20 Br ex 11.00 Dght 2.600 Lbp 55.93 Br md 10.60 Dpth 3.60 Welded, 2 dks	**(A37B2PS) Passenger Ship**	**2 oil engines** reduction geared to sc. shafts driving 2 FP propellers Total Power: 1,104kW (1,500hp) Stork 8DRO210K 2 x 4 Stroke 8 Cy. 210 x 300 each-552kW (750bhp) Stork Werkspoor Diesel BV-Netherlands
7389912 *TC5419* -	**SEHIT KARAOGLANOGLU** **Istanbul Buyuksehir Belediye Baskanligi** Istanbul Sehir Hatlari Turizm Sanayi ve Ticaret AS *Istanbul* *Turkey* MMSI: 271002521 Official number: 4444	*456* 208 180	Class: TL	**1977**-04 **Denizcilik Bankasi T.A.O. — Halic, Istanbul** Yd No: 189 Loa 58.20 Br ex 11.03 Dght 2.401 Lbp 55.93 Br md 10.60 Dpth 3.60 Welded, 2 dks	**(A37B2PS) Passenger Ship**	**2 oil engines** reverse reduction geared to sc. shafts driving 2 FP propellers Total Power: 1,104kW (1,500hp) Stork DRO218K 2 x 4 Stroke 8 Cy. 210 x 300 each-552kW (750bhp) Stork Werkspoor Diesel BV-Netherlands
8113229 *TC5417* -	**SEHIT METIN SULUS** *ex* Metin Sulus *-1993* **Istanbul Buyuksehir Belediye Baskanligi** Istanbul Sehir Hatlari Turizm Sanayi ve Ticaret AS *Istanbul* *Turkey* MMSI: 271002523 Official number: 5466	*456* 208 150	Class: TL	**1986**-03 **Turkiye Gemi Sanayii A.S. — Halic, Istanbul** Yd No: 216 Loa 58.20 Br ex - Dght 2.920 Lbp 55.93 Br md 10.60 Dpth 3.60 Welded, 1 dk	**(A37B2PS) Passenger Ship**	**2 oil engines** driving 2 FP propellers Total Power: 1,104kW (1,500hp) Sulzer 6AL20/24 2 x 4 Stroke 6 Cy. 200 x 240 each-552kW (750bhp)
7638088 *TC5431* -	**SEHIT MUSTAFA AYDOGDU** **Istanbul Buyuksehir Belediye Baskanligi** Istanbul Sehir Hatlari Turizm Sanayi ve Ticaret AS *Istanbul* *Turkey* MMSI: 271002522 Official number: 4888	*456* 208 180	Class: TL	**1981**-04 **Denizcilik Bankasi T.A.O. — Istinye, Istanbul** Yd No: 41 Loa 58.20 Br ex 10.62 Dght 2.920 Lbp 52.81 Br md 10.60 Dpth 3.60 Welded, 2 dks	**(A37B2PS) Passenger Ship**	**2 oil engines** geared to sc. shafts driving 2 FP propellers Total Power: 552kW (750hp) A.B.C. 6MDXC 2 x 4 Stroke 6 Cy. 242 x 320 each-276kW (375bhp) Anglo Belgian Corp NV (ABC)-Belgium
8973966 *TCA2753* -	**SEHIT NADIR GUNES** **Adalar Belediye Baskanligi** - *Istanbul* *Turkey* Official number: 6879	**139** - -		**1987** **Gemak Sanayi ve Ticaret Koll. Sti. — Tuzla** Loa 23.95 Br ex - Dght 3.000 Lbp - Br md 7.70 Dpth - Welded, 1 dk	**(A37B2PS) Passenger Ship**	**2 oil engines** geared to sc. shafts driving 2 FP propellers Total Power: 492kW (668hp) Caterpillar 2 x 4 Stroke each-246kW (334bhp) Caterpillar Inc-USA AuxGen: 1 x
7389936 *TC5446* -	**SEHIT NECATI GURKAYA** *ex* Necati Gurkaya *-1994* **Istanbul Buyuksehir Belediye Baskanligi** Istanbul Sehir Hatlari Turizm Sanayi ve Ticaret AS *Istanbul* *Turkey* MMSI: 271002525 Official number: 4473	*456* 208 180	Class: (TL)	**1977**-04 **Denizcilik Bankasi T.A.O. — Halic, Istanbul** Yd No: 191 Loa 58.20 Br ex 11.03 Dght 2.920 Lbp 52.81 Br md 10.60 Dpth 3.60 Welded, 2 dks	**(A37B2PS) Passenger Ship**	**2 oil engines** reverse reduction geared to sc. shafts driving 2 FP propellers Total Power: 1,104kW (1,500hp) 14.0kn Stork DRO218K 2 x 4 Stroke 8 Cy. 210 x 300 each-552kW (750bhp) Stork Werkspoor Diesel BV-Netherlands
8113243 *TC5437* -	**SEHIT SAMI AKBULUT** *ex* Saraybumu *-2008* *launched as* Kadikoy *-1985* **Istanbul Buyuksehir Belediye Baskanligi** Istanbul Sehir Hatlari Turizm Sanayi ve Ticaret AS *Istanbul* *Turkey* MMSI: 271002527 Official number: 5428	*456* 208 150	Class: TL	**1985**-11 **Turkiye Gemi Sanayii A.S. — Halic, Istanbul** Yd No: 218 Loa 58.20 Br ex - Dght 2.401 Lbp 55.93 Br md 10.60 Dpth 3.60 Welded, 1 dk	**(A37B2PS) Passenger Ship**	**2 oil engines** driving 2 FP propellers Total Power: 1,104kW (1,500hp) Sulzer 6AL20/24 2 x 4 Stroke 6 Cy. 200 x 240 each-552kW (750bhp)
7638064 *TC5422* -	**SEHIT TEMEL SIMSIR** **TC Persembe Belediye Baskanligi** Istanbul Sehir Hatlari Turizm Sanayi ve Ticaret AS *Istanbul* *Turkey* MMSI: 271002528 Official number: 4736	*456* 208 180	Class: TL	**1979**-09 **Denizcilik Bankasi T.A.O. — Istinye, Istanbul** Yd No: 38 Loa 58.20 Br ex 10.62 Dght 2.920 Lbp 55.93 Br md 10.60 Dpth 3.60 Welded, 1 dk	**(A37B2PS) Passenger Ship**	**2 oil engines** geared to sc. shafts driving 2 FP propellers Total Power: 552kW (750hp) Stork 8DRO210K 2 x 4 Stroke 8 Cy. 210 x 300 each-276kW (375bhp) Stork Werkspoor Diesel BV-Netherlands
9614830 *TCVQ8* -	**SEHNAZ KA** **Genka Denizcilik ve Yatirim AS** *Istanbul* *Turkey* MMSI: 271043396	**7,087** 3,733 10,609	Class: BV	**2012**-11 **Kocatepe Gemi Cekek ve Insaat Sanayi Ltd Sti — Altinova** Yd No: 17 Loa 124.50 (BB) Br ex - Dght 7.800 Lbp 118.37 Br md 19.00 Dpth 10.20 Welded, 1 dk	**(A31A2GX) General Cargo Ship** Double Hull Grain: 13,218 Compartments: 3 Ho, ER 3 Ha: ER Ice Capable	**1 oil engine** reduction geared to sc. shaft driving 1 CP propeller Total Power: 2,610kW (3,549hp) 13.5kn Hyundai Himsen 9H25/33P 1 x 4 Stroke 9 Cy. 250 x 330 2610kW (3549bhp) Hyundai Heavy Industries Co Ltd-South Korea AuxGen: 2 x 320kW 50Hz a.c, 1 x 584kW 50Hz a.c Fuel: 360.0
5104253 *DMKD* -	**SEHO** *ex* Enez Sun II *-1973* **Reederei Mirko Stengel** - *Heiligenhafen* *Germany* MMSI: 211226940 Official number: 2516	**170** 55 19	Class: GL (BV)	**1962** **Chantiers et Ateliers de La Perriere — Lorient** Yd No: 25554 Converted From: Yacht-2010 Converted From: Ferry (Passenger only)-1995 Loa 27.92 Br ex 7.52 Dght 1.873 Lbp 25.02 Br md 7.50 Dpth 3.28 Riveted\Welded, 1 dk	**(A37B2PS) Passenger Ship** 2 Ha: 2 (2.7 x 3.9)ER Derricks: 1x2t; Winches: 1	**2 oil engines** reduction geared to sc. shafts driving 2 FP propellers Total Power: 442kW (600hp) 11.0kn Volvo Penta TAMD120AK 2 x 4 Stroke 6 Cy. 130 x 150 each-221kW (300bhp) (, fitted 1976) AB Volvo Penta-Sweden
9619505 *YEQG* -	**SEI DELI** **PT Pelabuhan Indonesia I (Persero) Cabang Belawan (Indonesia Port Corp I, Belawan Branch)** PT Pelabuhan Indonesia I (Persero) (Indonesia Port Corp I) (PELINDO I) *Surabaya* *Indonesia*	**347** 105 -	Class: KI	**2011**-06 **PT Dok dan Perkapalan Surabaya (Persero) — Surabaya** Yd No: 10603 Loa 32.00 Br ex 9.82 Dght 3.300 Lbp 30.24 Br md 9.80 Dpth 4.60 Welded, 1 dk	**(B32A2ST) Tug**	**2 oil engines** reduction geared to sc. shafts driving 2 Propellers Total Power: 2,942kW (4,000hp) Niigata 6L26HLX 2 x 4 Stroke 6 Cy. 260 x 350 each-1471kW (2000bhp) Niigata Engineering Co Ltd-Japan AuxGen: 2 x 160kW 380V a.c

IMO / Call sign	Name / Owner / Port	Tonnage	Class	Build	Type	Machinery
9670236 - -	**SEI DELI II** - **PT Pelabuhan Indonesia I (Persero) Cabang Belawan (Indonesia Port Corp I, Belawan Branch)** - *Batam* *Indonesia* Official number: 2012PPJNo.1738/L	379 114 -	Class: KI	**2012-08 PT Trikarya Alam Shipyard — Batam** Yd No: NBT-061 Loa 32.50 Br ex - Dght - Lbp - Br md 9.80 Dpth 5.00 Welded, 1 dk	**(B32A2ST) Tug**	**2 oil engines** reduction geared to sc. shafts driving 2 Propellers Total Power: 3,282kW (4,462hp) Caterpillar 3516B 2 x Vee 4 Stroke 16 Cy. 170 x 190 each-1641kW (2231bhp) Caterpillar Inc-USA
9672014 - -	**SEI DELI III** - **PT Pelabuhan Indonesia I (Persero) Cabang Belawan (Indonesia Port Corp I, Belawan Branch)** - *Belawan* *Indonesia* Official number: 2012 PPA No.4520/L	379 114 -	Class: KI	**2012-09 PT Trikarya Alam Shipyard — Batam** Yd No: NBT-062 Loa 32.50 Br ex - Dght - Lbp - Br md 9.80 Dpth 5.00 Welded, 1 dk	**(B32A2ST) Tug**	**2 oil engines** reduction geared to sc. shafts driving 2 Propellers Total Power: 3,282kW (4,462hp) Caterpillar 3516B 2 x Vee 4 Stroke 16 Cy. 170 x 190 each-1641kW (2231bhp) Caterpillar Inc-USA
9672026 - -	**SEI DELI IV** - **PT Pelabuhan Indonesia I (Persero) Cabang Belawan (Indonesia Port Corp I, Belawan Branch)** - *Dumai* *Indonesia* Official number: 2012 PPJ NO.1743/L	379 114 -	Class: KI	**2012-09 PT Trikarya Alam Shipyard — Batam** Yd No: NBT-063 Loa 32.50 Br ex - Dght - Lbp - Br md 9.80 Dpth 5.00 Welded, 1 dk	**(B32A2ST) Tug**	**2 oil engines** reduction geared to sc. shafts driving 2 FP propellers Total Power: 3,282kW (4,462hp) Caterpillar 3516B 2 x Vee 4 Stroke 16 Cy. 170 x 190 each-1641kW (2231bhp) Caterpillar Inc-USA
9509891 *PODV* -	**SEI PAKNING** - **PT PERTAMINA (PERSERO)** - *Jakarta* *Indonesia* MMSI: 525008069	24,167 7,251 29,756	Class: KI NV	**2011-08 Zhejiang Chenye Shipbuilding Co Ltd — Daishan County ZJ** Yd No: 0802 Loa 180.03 (BB) Br ex 30.52 Dght 9.000 Lbp 173.00 Br md 30.49 Dpth 15.91 Welded, 1 dk	**(A13B2TP) Products Tanker** Double Hull (13F) Liq: 33,000; Liq (Oil): 33,000	**1 oil engine** driving 1 FP propeller Total Power: 6,480kW (8,810hp) 14.0kn MAN-B&W 6S42MC 1 x 2 Stroke 6 Cy. 420 x 1764 6480kW (8810bhp) Hyundai Heavy Industries Co Ltd-South Korea
7703950 *UBTG3* -	**SEI WHALE** *ex* Seyval *-2010* *ex* Sei Whale *-2010* *ex* Yefim Krivosheyev *-2008* **Alians Marin Ltd** - *St Petersburg* *Russia* MMSI: 273353090	3,835 1,150 2,396	Class: RS	**1980-05 Stocznia Gdanska im Lenina — Gdansk** Yd No: B408/09 Loa 93.91 Br ex 15.92 Dght 6.200 Lbp 85.02 Br md 15.91 Dpth 10.01 Welded, 2 dks	**(B11A2FG) Factory Stern Trawler** Ins: 1,947 Compartments: 3 Ho, ER 4 Ha: (0.6 x 0.6)3 (2.4 x 2.1) Derricks: 6x3t Ice Capable	**1 oil engine** geared to sc. shaft driving 1 FP propeller Total Power: 3,825kW (5,200hp) 15.8kn Sulzer 8ZL40/48 1 x 4 Stroke 8 Cy. 400 x 480 3825kW (5200bhp) Zaklady Urzadzen Technicznych'Zgoda' SA-Poland AuxGen: 1 x 1200kW 400V 50Hz a.c, 1 x 760kW 400V 50Hz a.c, 2 x 350kW 320V 50Hz a.c Fuel: 1195.0 (r.f.)
8630265 *JK4712* -	**SEICHO MARU** - **Seino Kaiun YK** - *Karatsu, Saga* *Japan* MMSI: 431401624 Official number: 128034	*129* - 363		**1986-11 Y.K. Kaneko Zosensho — Hojo** Loa 42.50 Br ex 7.82 Dght 3.200 Lbp 38.00 Br md 7.80 Dpth 4.95 Welded, 1 dk	**(A31A2GX) General Cargo Ship**	**1 oil engine** driving 1 FP propeller Total Power: 331kW (450hp) 10.0kn Yanmar MF24-UT 1 x 4 Stroke 6 Cy. 240 x 420 331kW (450bhp) Matsue Nainenki Kogyo-Japan
8923818 *JL6459* -	**SEIEI** *ex* Shoei Maru *-2013* *ex* Shinei Maru *-2007* - - *Osakikamijima, Hiroshima* *Japan* MMSI: 431500501 Official number: 135170	*691* - 2,052		**1996-06 K.K. Uno Zosensho — Imabari** Yd No: 506 Loa 79.20 Br ex - Dght 4.730 Lbp 71.70 Br md 13.50 Dpth 7.60 Welded, 1 dk	**(A31A2GX) General Cargo Ship** Grain: 2,348; Bale: 2,273 Compartments: 1 Ho, ER 1 Ha: (28.7 x 10.5)ER Cranes: 1x20t	**1 oil engine** driving 1 FP propeller Total Power: 1,618kW (2,200hp) 12.5kn Hanshin LH34LA 1 x 4 Stroke 6 Cy. 340 x 640 1618kW (2200bhp) The Hanshin Diesel Works Ltd-Japan
8889957 *JM6458* -	**SEIEI** - **Eguchi Kaiun YK** - *Kamiamakusa, Kumamoto* *Japan* MMSI: 431600417 Official number: 134550	*199* - -		**1995-08 YK Furumoto Tekko Zosensho — Osakikamijima** Yd No: 617 Loa 57.50 Br ex - Dght - Lbp 51.00 Br md 9.50 Dpth 5.55 Welded, 1 dk	**(A31A2GX) General Cargo Ship**	**1 oil engine** driving 1 FP propeller Total Power: 883kW (1,201hp) 12.2kn Matsui ML627GSC 1 x 4 Stroke 6 Cy. 270 x 480 883kW (1201bhp) Matsui Iron Works Co Ltd-Japan
8895188 - -	**SEIEI MARU** *ex* Koei Maru No. 2 *-2007* - -	*195* - 499		**1977-09 K.K. Kawamoto Zosensho — Osakikamijima** Loa 46.00 Br ex - Dght 3.300 Lbp - Br md 7.50 Dpth 5.00 Welded, 1 dk	**(A31A2GX) General Cargo Ship** Compartments: 1 Ho, ER 1 Ha: (22.0 x 5.5)ER	**1 oil engine** driving 1 FP propeller Total Power: 441kW (600hp) 10.0kn Matsui 1 x 4 Stroke 441kW (600bhp) Matsui Iron Works Co Ltd-Japan
9012202 *JNYI* -	**SEIEI MARU** - **Nuclear Fuel Transport Co Ltd** Gennen Senpaku KK (Nuclear Fuel Shipping Co Ltd) *Rokkasho, Aomori* *Japan* MMSI: 431060000 Official number: 132820	4,053 - 3,206	Class: NK	**1991-09 Mitsubishi Heavy Industries Ltd. — Kobe** Yd No: 1186 Loa 99.89 (BB) Br ex - Dght 5.412 Lbp 95.00 Br md 16.00 Dpth 8.00 Welded, 1 dk	**(A38D2GN) Nuclear Fuel Carrier** Compartments: 7 Ho, ER 13 Ha: ER	**1 oil engine** driving 1 CP propeller Total Power: 2,869kW (3,901hp) 13.0kn Mitsubishi 6UEC37LA 1 x 2 Stroke 6 Cy. 370 x 880 2869kW (3901bhp) Mitsubishi Heavy Industries Ltd-Japan AuxGen: 5 x 220kW a.c Thrusters: 1 Thwart. CP thruster (f) Fuel: 320.0 (r.f.)
9033012 *JM6132* -	**SEIEI MARU** - **Ube Shipping & Logistics Ltd (Ube Kosan KK)** - *Ube, Yamaguchi* *Japan* MMSI: 431401143 Official number: 133459	*4,941* - 8,079	Class: NK	**1992-08 Fukuoka Shipbuilding Co Ltd — Fukuoka FO** Yd No: 1171 Loa 111.58 (BB) Br ex - Dght 7.514 Lbp 105.00 Br md 18.00 Dpth 9.30 Welded, 1 dk	**(A24A2BT) Cement Carrier** Grain: 5,785 Compartments: 9 Ho, ER	**1 oil engine** with clutches, flexible couplings & sr geared to sc. shaft driving 1 CP propeller Total Power: 3,089kW (4,200hp) 13.0kn Daihatsu 6DLM-40 1 x 4 Stroke 6 Cy. 400 x 480 3089kW (4200bhp) Daihatsu Diesel Manufacturing Co Lt-Japan AuxGen: 4 x 620kW a.c Thrusters: 1 Thwart. CP thruster (f); 1 Tunnel thruster (a) Fuel: 225.0 (r.f.)
9154658 *JL6516* -	**SEIEI MARU** - **Sanwa Kaiun KK & Seiyo Kisen KK** Seiyo Kisen KK *Imabari, Ehime* *Japan* Official number: 135543	*499* - 1,597		**1996-10 Yamanaka Zosen K.K. — Imabari** Yd No: 603 Loa - Br ex - Dght 4.080 Lbp 70.00 Br md 12.00 Dpth 7.01 Welded, 2 dks	**(A31A2GX) General Cargo Ship** Grain: 2,853	**1 oil engine** driving 1 FP propeller Total Power: 736kW (1,001hp) Hanshin LH30L 1 x 4 Stroke 6 Cy. 300 x 600 736kW (1001bhp) The Hanshin Diesel Works Ltd-Japan
9142344 *JK5435* -	**SEIEI MARU** - **Eimoto Kaiun YK** - *Kure, Hiroshima* *Japan* Official number: 134738	*197* - 600		**1996-04 Yamakawa Zosen Tekko K.K. — Kagoshima** Yd No: 735 Loa 57.50 Br ex - Dght 3.160 Lbp 51.50 Br md 9.00 Dpth 5.44 Welded, 1 dk	**(A31A2GX) General Cargo Ship**	**1 oil engine** driving 1 FP propeller Total Power: 736kW (1,001hp) 10.5kn Niigata 6M26AGTE 1 x 4 Stroke 6 Cy. 260 x 460 736kW (1001bhp) Niigata Engineering Co Ltd-Japan
9085027 *JG5233* -	**SEIEI MARU No. 7** - **KK Eiho Shipping** - *Yokohama, Kanagawa* *Japan* Official number: 134939	*104* - 318		**1994-12 K.K. Tago Zosensho — Nishi-Izu** Yd No: 257 Loa 37.00 Br ex - Dght 2.300 Lbp 35.00 Br md 7.00 Dpth 2.50 Welded, 1 dk	**(A13B2TP) Products Tanker** Liq: 360; Liq (Oil): 360	**1 oil engine** with clutches, flexible couplings & reverse geared to sc. shaft driving 1 FP propeller Total Power: 330kW (449hp) Yanmar MF24-ST 1 x 4 Stroke 6 Cy. 240 x 420 330kW (449bhp) Yanmar Diesel Engine Co Ltd-Japan
8815475 - -	**SEIEI MARU No. 8** - **PT Karya Cemerlang** - *Indonesia*	*460* - 630		**1988-11 K.K. Saidaiji Zosensho — Okayama** Yd No: 157 Loa 50.50 Br ex - Dght 3.220 Lbp 46.00 Br md 10.50 Dpth 5.40 Welded, 1 dk	**(B33A2DG) Grab Dredger**	**1 oil engine** driving 1 FP propeller Total Power: 552kW (750hp) Niigata 6M28BGT 1 x 4 Stroke 6 Cy. 280 x 480 552kW (750bhp) Niigata Engineering Co Ltd-Japan
8816376 *JK4756* -	**SEIEI MARU No. 18** - **Kaiyo Kisen YK** - *Himeji, Hyogo* *Japan* Official number: 130994	*499* - 1,548		**1988-10 Matsuura Tekko Zosen K.K. — Osakikamijima** Yd No: 346 Loa 67.50 (BB) Br ex 13.50 Dght 4.473 Lbp 61.10 Br md 13.20 Dpth 7.20 Welded, 2 dks	**(B33A2DG) Grab Dredger** Grain: 925 Compartments: 1 Ho, ER 1 Ha: ER	**1 oil engine** driving 1 FP propeller Total Power: 1,324kW (1,800hp) Fuji 6S32G 1 x 4 Stroke 6 Cy. 320 x 610 1324kW (1800bhp) Fuji Diesel Co Ltd-Japan Thrusters: 1 Thwart. CP thruster (f)

8704377 *JJ3541* -	**SEIEI MARU No. 21** - **Yamaichi Kogyo KK** - *Ieshima, Hyogo* *Japan* Official number: 129284	*496* - 1,155		**1987-05 Matsuura Tekko Zosen K.K. — Osakikamijima** Yd No: 330 Loa 63.02 (BB) Br ex 13.59 Dght 4.172 Lbp 58.02 Br md 13.50 Dpth 6.20 Welded, 2 dks	**(B33A2DG) Grab Dredger** Grain: 673 Compartments: 1 Ho, ER 1 Ha: ER	**1 oil engine** with clutches, flexible couplings & reverse geared to sc. shaft driving 1 FP propeller Total Power: 736kW (1,001hp) 9.0kn Fuji 6S32G2 1 x 4 Stroke 6 Cy. 320 x 610 736kW (1001bhp) Fuji Diesel Co Ltd-Japan Fuel: 50.0
8949276 - -	**SEIEI MARU No. 33** *ex* Yuei Maru No. 28 - -	*131* - -		**1972 K.K. Mukai Zosensho — Nagasaki** Loa 35.05 Br ex - Dght 2.565 Lbp 31.20 Br md 5.80 Dpth 2.85 Welded, 1 dk	**(B12B2FC) Fish Carrier**	**1 oil engine** driving 1 FP propeller Total Power: 463kW (629hp) Niigata 6MG25BX 1 x 4 Stroke 6 Cy. 250 x 320 463kW (629bhp) Niigata Engineering Co Ltd-Japan
8925115 *JJ3836* -	**SEIEI MARU No. 48** - **Seiko Kaiun YK** - *Himeji, Hyogo* *Japan* Official number: 134181	*498* - 1,349		**1996-09 K.K. Saidaiji Zosensho — Okayama** Yd No: 221 Loa 65.00 Br ex - Dght 4.470 Lbp 60.00 Br md 13.20 Dpth 7.30 Welded, 1 dk	**(A31A2GX) General Cargo Ship**	**1 oil engine** driving 1 FP propeller Total Power: 736kW (1,001hp) 12.0kn Niigata 6M34BGT 1 x 4 Stroke 6 Cy. 340 x 620 736kW (1001bhp) Niigata Engineering Co Ltd-Japan
7934781 *JL4654* -	**SEIEI MARU No. 68** *ex* Koryu Maru No. 25 *-1998* **Keiji Sato** - *Uwajima, Ehime* *Japan* Official number: 123065	*148* - 43		**1979-12 K.K. Mukai Zosensho — Nagasaki** Yd No: 377 Loa 38.51 Br ex - Dght 2.701 Lbp 33.00 Br md 6.41 Dpth 3.00 Welded, 1 dk	**(B12B2FC) Fish Carrier**	**1 oil engine** reverse geared to sc. shaft driving 1 FP propeller Total Power: 441kW (600hp) Matsui MU623CGHS 1 x 4 Stroke 6 Cy. 230 x 380 441kW (600bhp) Matsui Iron Works Co Ltd-Japan
9052575 *CB8777* -	**SEIFJORD** *ex* La Nina I *-2005* **CPT Empresas Maritimas SA** - *Valparaiso* *Chile* MMSI: 725014700 Official number: 3129	*831* 250 763 T/cm 3.9		**1993-08 Astilleros Marco Chilena Ltda. — Iquique** Yd No: 203 Converted From: Fishing Vessel-2005 Loa 48.40 (BB) Br ex 10.40 Dght 5.415 Lbp 43.30 Br md 10.20 Dpth 7.30 Welded, 2 dks	**(B12C2FL) Live Fish Carrier (Well Boat)** Ins: 850	**1 oil engine** with clutches & sr geared to sc. shaft driving 1 CP propeller Total Power: 1,824kW (2,480hp) 13.0kn Caterpillar 3606TA 1 x 4 Stroke 6 Cy. 280 x 300 1824kW (2480bhp) Caterpillar Inc-USA Thrusters: 1 Thwart. FP thruster (f); 1 Tunnel thruster (a)
9156723 *JK5342* SN1-200	**SEIFU** - **Shimane Prefecture** - *Matsue, Shimane* *Japan* MMSI: 431400636 Official number: 133677	*120* - -		**1997-02 Mitsubishi Heavy Industries Ltd. — Shimonoseki** Yd No: 1039 L reg 35.10 Br ex - Dght - Lbp - Br md 6.50 Dpth 3.14 Welded, 1 dk	**(B12D2FP) Fishery Patrol Vessel** Hull Material: Aluminium Alloy	**2 oil engines** geared to sc. shafts driving 2 FP propellers G.M. (Detroit Diesel) 16V-149-TI 2 x Vee 2 Stroke 16 Cy. 146 x 146 General Motors Detroit DieselAllison Divn-USA
9047726 *JM6118* -	**SEIFUKU MARU** - **Kiyotsugu Hashimoto** - *Kamiamakusa, Kumamoto* *Japan* Official number: 132687	*198* - 500		**1992-04 KK Ura Kyodo Zosensho — Awaji HG** Yd No: 287 L reg 44.00 Br ex - Dght - Lbp - Br md 8.00 Dpth 3.40 Welded, 1 dk	**(A13B2TP) Products Tanker**	**1 oil engine** driving 1 FP propeller Total Power: 625kW (850hp) Niigata 6M26BGT 1 x 4 Stroke 6 Cy. 260 x 460 625kW (850bhp) Niigata Engineering Co Ltd-Japan
8720618 *JK4871* -	**SEIFUKU MARU** - **Kiyoshi Sekioka** - *Hiroshima, Hiroshima* *Japan* Official number: 130944	*408* - 982		**1988-03 K.K. Miura Zosensho — Saiki** Yd No: 808 Loa 54.75 Br ex 11.82 Dght 4.040 Lbp 51.11 Br md 11.80 Dpth 5.90 Welded, 1 dk	**(A24D2BA) Aggregates Carrier**	**1 oil engine** driving 1 FP propeller Total Power: 736kW (1,001hp) 12.0kn Yanmar MF33-DT 1 x 4 Stroke 6 Cy. 330 x 620 736kW (1001bhp) Matsue Diesel KK-Japan
9243588 *JL6661* -	**SEIFUKU MARU No. 2** - **Yamaichi Unyu YK** - *Anan, Tokushima* *Japan* Official number: 136552	*499* - -		**2000-08 K.K. Murakami Zosensho — Naruto** Yd No: 232 Loa 74.99 Br ex - Dght - Lbp 70.00 Br md 12.30 Dpth 7.00 Welded, 1 dk	**(A31A2GX) General Cargo Ship** Compartments: 1 Ho, ER 1 Ha: (39.6 x 10.0)ER	**1 oil engine** driving 1 FP propeller Total Power: 1,305kW (1,774hp) 10.5kn Niigata 6M31BLGT 1 x 4 Stroke 6 Cy. 310 x 600 1305kW (1774bhp) Niigata Engineering Co Ltd-Japan Fuel: 62.0 (d.f.)
8743347 *JD2916* -	**SEIFUKU MARU NO. 6** - **Yamaichi Unyu YK** - *Anan, Tokushima* *Japan* Official number: 141021	*499* - 1,830		**2009-05 YK Nakanoshima Zosensho — Kochi KC** Yd No: 261 Loa 74.71 Br ex - Dght 4.330 Lbp 69.00 Br md 12.00 Dpth 7.35 Welded, 1 dk	**(A31A2GX) General Cargo Ship** Bale: 2,469 Compartments: 1 Ho, ER 1 Ha: ER (40.0 x 9.5)	**1 oil engine** driving 1 Propeller Total Power: 1,618kW (2,200hp) 12.5kn Niigata 6M34BGT 1 x 4 Stroke 6 Cy. 340 x 620 1618kW (2200bhp) Niigata Engineering Co Ltd-Japan
9606584 *JD3178* -	**SEIFUKU MARU NO. 7** - **Hashimoto Kaiun YK** - *Kamiamakusa, Kumamoto* *Japan* Official number: 141416	*297* - 610		**2011-06 KK Ura Kyodo Zosensho — Awaji HG** Yd No: 343 Loa 52.65 Br ex - Dght 3.500 Lbp 48.00 Br md 9.00 Dpth 3.70 Welded, 1 dk	**(A13B2TP) Products Tanker** Double Hull (13F)	**1 oil engine** reduction geared to sc. shaft driving 1 FP propeller Total Power: 800kW (1,088hp) Yanmar 6N21A-UV 1 x 4 Stroke 6 Cy. 210 x 290 800kW (1088bhp) Yanmar Diesel Engine Co Ltd-Japan
8961054 *JH2476* -	**SEIFUKU MARU No. 8** - - - *Kira, Aichi* *Japan* Official number: 111199	*172* - 431		**1971-03 Itoh Zosen K.K. — Nagoya** Loa 41.76 Br ex - Dght 2.940 Lbp 38.50 Br md 6.70 Dpth 3.13 Welded, 1 dk	**(A31A2GX) General Cargo Ship**	**1 oil engine** driving 1 FP propeller Total Power: 588kW (799hp) 10.0kn Yanmar 1 x 4 Stroke 588kW (799bhp) Yanmar Diesel Engine Co Ltd-Japan
8974594 *JH3481* -	**SEIFUKU MARU NO. 18** - **Sei Mizutani** - *Kihoku, Mie* *Japan* MMSI: 431258000 Official number: 135666	*119* - -		**2002-01 Higashi Kyushu Shipbuilding Co Ltd — Usuki OT** Yd No: 860 L reg 31.00 Br ex - Dght - Lbp - Br md 5.83 Dpth 2.60 Bonded, 1 dk	**(B11B2FV) Fishing Vessel** Hull Material: Reinforced Plastic	**1 oil engine** geared to sc. shaft driving 1 Propeller Total Power: 456kW (620hp) Yanmar 6N280-EN2 1 x 4 Stroke 6 Cy. 280 x 380 456kW (620bhp) Yanmar Diesel Engine Co Ltd-Japan
9036765 *JRQF* IT1-296	**SEIFUKU MARU No. 68** - **YK Hamada Gyogyobu** - *Miyako, Iwate* *Japan* MMSI: 432260000 Official number: 132184	*379* - -		**1991-09 Niigata Engineering Co Ltd — Niigata NI** Yd No: 2221 Loa 56.43 (BB) Br ex - Dght 3.440 Lbp 49.10 Br md 8.80 Dpth 3.80 Welded	**(B11B2FV) Fishing Vessel** Ins: 472	**1 oil engine** with clutches, flexible couplings & sr geared to sc. shaft driving 1 CP propeller Total Power: 699kW (950hp) Niigata 6M28BFT 1 x 4 Stroke 6 Cy. 280 x 480 699kW (950bhp) Niigata Engineering Co Ltd-Japan
9262792 *JPZG* IT1-703	**SEIFUKU MARU No. 78** - **YK Hamada Gyogyobu** - *Miyako, Iwate* *Japan* MMSI: 432353000 Official number: 133331	*379* - -		**2002-08 Niigata Engineering Co Ltd — Niigata NI** Yd No: 2503 Loa 65.00 Br ex - Dght - Lbp 56.43 Br md 8.80 Dpth 3.80 Welded, 1 dk	**(B11B2FV) Fishing Vessel**	**1 oil engine** reverse geared to sc. shaft driving 1 FP propeller Total Power: 736kW (1,001hp) Niigata 6M28BFT 1 x 4 Stroke 6 Cy. 280 x 480 736kW (1001bhp) Niigata Engineering Co Ltd-Japan
9634751 *7JKM* -	**SEIFUKU MARU NO. 88** - **YK Hamada Gyogyobu** - *Miyako, Iwate* *Japan* Official number: 141552	*387* - -		**2012-03 Niigata Shipbuilding & Repair Inc — Niigata NI** Yd No: 0057 Loa 56.51 Br ex - Dght 3.440 Lbp - Br md 8.80 Dpth 3.80 Welded, 1 dk	**(B11B2FV) Fishing Vessel**	**1 oil engine** reverse reduction geared to sc. shaft driving 1 Propeller Total Power: 1,029kW (1,399hp) Niigata 6M28BFT 1 x 4 Stroke 6 Cy. 280 x 480 1029kW (1399bhp) Niigata Engineering Co Ltd-Japan
9620853 *CA3621* -	**SEIFYR** - **CPT Empresas Maritimas SA** - *Valparaiso* *Chile* MMSI: 725000879 Official number: 3293	**1,299** 396 1,380	Class: AB	**2011-10 Guangzhou Southern Shipbuilding Co Ltd — Guangzhou GD** (Hull) **2011-10 Bonny Fair Development Ltd — Hong Kong** Yd No: HY2168 Loa 64.81 (BB) Br ex 12.60 Dght 4.800 Lbp 58.74 Br md 12.00 Dpth 5.74 Welded, 1 dk	**(B12C2FL) Live Fish Carrier (Well Boat)**	**1 oil engine** reduction geared to sc. shaft driving 1 CP propeller Total Power: 1,710kW (2,325hp) MaK 9M20C 1 x 4 Stroke 9 Cy. 200 x 300 1710kW (2325bhp) Caterpillar Inc-USA AuxGen: 2 x 450kW a.c, 2 x 150kW a.c

IMO / Call sign	Name / Owner / Port	Tonnage	Builder / Dimensions	Type / Capacity	Machinery
9264269 *LLUW* -	**SEIGRUNN** **Seigrunn AS** Seistar Holding AS *Bergen* *Norway* MMSI: 259673000	**993** Class: NV 301 1,200	**2002-09 Karmsund Maritime Service AS — Kopervik** Yd No: 23 Loa 49.80 Br ex - Dght 5.915 Lbp 45.40 Br md 11.60 Dpth 6.60 Welded, 1 dk	**(B12C2FL) Live Fish Carrier (Well Boat)** Liq: 1,200	**1 oil engine** geared to sc. shaft driving 1 FP propeller Total Power: 1,839kW (2,500hp) Caterpillar 3606TA 1 x 4 Stroke 6 Cy. 280 x 300 1839kW (2500bhp) Caterpillar Inc-USA
8903765 *CA3623* -	**SEIGRUNN** *ex* Allipen I *-2012* **Blumar Seafoods** *Valparaiso* *Chile* MMSI: 725000882 Official number: 3283	*906* 239 -	**1990-08 Astilleros Marco Chilena Ltda. — Iquique** Yd No: 194 Loa 47.00 (BB) Br ex 10.40 Dght - Lbp - Br md 10.32 Dpth 5.00 Welded	**(B11B2FV) Fishing Vessel** Ins: 750	**1 oil engine** with flexible couplings & sr geared to sc. shaft driving 1 CP propeller Total Power: 1,601kW (2,177hp) 14.5kn Deutz SBV6M628 1 x 4 Stroke 6 Cy. 240 x 280 1601kW (2177bhp) Kloeckner Humboldt Deutz AG-West Germany Thrusters: 1 Thwart. FP thruster (f); 1 Thwart. FP thruster (a)
7722956 - -	**SEIHO** *ex* Seiho Maru No. 3 *-1999* *ex* Sanko Maru *-1994* - -	*199* - 520	**1978-03 Takebe Zosen — Takamatsu** Yd No: 71 Loa - Br ex - Dght - Lbp 44.00 Br md 8.01 Dpth 3.31 Welded, 1 dk	**(A31A2GX) General Cargo Ship**	**1 oil engine** driving 1 FP propeller Total Power: 515kW (700hp) Matsui 6M26KS 1 x 4 Stroke 6 Cy. 260 x 400 515kW (700bhp) Matsui Iron Works Co Ltd-Japan
6921517 - -	**SEIHO MARU** *ex* Kiire Maru No. 6 *-1990* *ex* Choko Maru *-1990* - -	*288* 99 -	**1969 Towa Zosen K.K. — Shimonoseki** Yd No: 375 Loa 35.21 Br ex 10.04 Dght 3.150 Lbp 33.99 Br md 10.01 Dpth 4.42 Welded, 1 dk	**(B32A2ST) Tug**	**2 oil engines** geared to sc. shafts driving 2 FP propellers Total Power: 2,206kW (3,000hp) 13.0kn Fuji 6MD32H 2 x 4 Stroke 6 Cy. 320 x 380 each-1103kW (1500bhp) Fuji Diesel Co Ltd-Japan AuxGen: 2 x 40kW 225V 60Hz a.c Fuel: 50.0 11.0pd
8877667 *JL6149* -	**SEIHO MARU** **Hamaguchi Kaiun YK** *Shodoshima, Kagawa* *Japan* Official number: 133878	*498* - 1,599	**1994-04 Mategata Zosen K.K. — Namikata** Yd No: 1052 Loa 74.00 Br ex - Dght 4.130 Lbp 69.00 Br md 12.00 Dpth 6.90 Welded, 1 dk	**(A31A2GX) General Cargo Ship** Grain: 2,608; Bale: 2,201 Compartments: 1 Ho, ER 1 Ha: (39.0 x 8.5)ER	**1 oil engine** driving 1 FP propeller Total Power: 736kW (1,001hp) 11.0kn Hanshin LH30LG 1 x 4 Stroke 6 Cy. 300 x 600 736kW (1001bhp) The Hanshin Diesel Works Ltd-Japan
8949123 - -	**SEIHO MARU** - -	*108* - -	**1973-07 Manazuru Ozawa Zosen — Manazuru** Loa 23.00 Br ex - Dght 2.400 Lbp 20.99 Br md 8.50 Dpth 3.40 Welded, 1 dk	**(B32B2SP) Pusher Tug**	**1 oil engine** driving 1 FP propeller Total Power: 1,177kW (1,600hp) 11.5kn
9124110 *JM6438* -	**SEIHO MARU** *ex* Waka Maru *-2006* *ex* Kotobuki Maru *-2004* **Nikyo Kaiun YK** *Anan, Tokushima* *Japan* Official number: 134530	*498* - 1,340	**1995-06 K.K. Miura Zosensho — Saiki** Yd No: 1123 Loa 69.40 Br ex - Dght 3.900 Lbp 62.00 Br md 10.30 Dpth 4.60 Welded, 1 dk	**(A13B2TP) Products Tanker**	**1 oil engine** driving 1 FP propeller Total Power: 736kW (1,001hp) 11.8kn Niigata 6M30BGT 1 x 4 Stroke 6 Cy. 300 x 530 736kW (1001bhp) Niigata Engineering Co Ltd-Japan
9134361 *JM6496* -	**SEIHO MARU** *ex* Genkai Maru *-2003* **Shinomiya Tanker KK (Shinomiya Tanker Co Ltd)** - *Anan, Tokushima* *Japan* MMSI: 431400523 Official number: 134640	*999* Class: NK - 1,271	**1996-02 Shin Kochi Jyuko K.K. — Kochi** Yd No: 7077 Loa 71.01 (BB) Br ex - Dght 4.312 Lbp 66.00 Br md 12.20 Dpth 5.35 Welded, 1 dk	**(A11B2TG) LPG Tanker** Liq (Gas): 1,723 2 x Gas Tank (s);	**1 oil engine** driving 1 FP propeller Total Power: 1,912kW (2,600hp) Akasaka A37 1 x 4 Stroke 6 Cy. 370 x 720 1912kW (2600bhp) Akasaka Tekkosho KK (Akasaka DieselLtd)-Japan Fuel: 215.0 (d.f.)
9207479 *JL6559* -	**SEIHO MARU** **Sanwa Kaiun YK** *Imabari, Ehime* *Japan* Official number: 136461	*499* - 1,593	**1998-09 Yamanaka Zosen K.K. — Imabari** Yd No: 627 Loa 72.12 Br ex - Dght 4.060 Lbp 70.00 Br md 12.00 Dpth 7.01 Welded, 1 dk	**(A31A2GX) General Cargo Ship** Grain: 2,824; Bale: 2,761	**1 oil engine** driving 1 FP propeller Total Power: 1,324kW (1,800hp) Hanshin 1 x 4 Stroke 1324kW (1800bhp) The Hanshin Diesel Works Ltd-Japan
8858972 *JH3198* -	**SEIHO MARU No. 8** **Yoshitaka Suzuki** *Hazu, Aichi* *Japan* Official number: 131609	*220* - 299	**1991-07 K.K. Tago Zosensho — Nishi-Izu** Yd No: 233 Loa 42.01 Br ex - Dght 2.520 Lbp 38.00 Br md 7.80 Dpth 2.70 Welded, 1 dk	**(A31A2GX) General Cargo Ship** Grain: 634; Bale: 626	**1 oil engine** driving 1 FP propeller 7.8kn Sumiyoshi S23G 1 x 4 Stroke 6 Cy. 230 x 400 Sumiyoshi Tekkosho-Japan
8889799 *JK5380* -	**SEIHO MARU No. 28** **YK Jyusei Kaiun** *Kasaoka, Okayama* *Japan* Official number: 134762	*199* - 699	**1995-06 Yano Zosen K.K. — Imabari** Yd No: 157 Loa 57.50 Br ex - Dght 3.130 Lbp 53.00 Br md 9.50 Dpth 5.34 Welded, 1 dk	**(A31A2GX) General Cargo Ship** Bale: 1,111 Compartments: 1 Ho, ER 1 Ha: (30.3 x 7.5)ER	**1 oil engine** driving 1 FP propeller Total Power: 736kW (1,001hp) 10.8kn Matsui MA28GSC-33 1 x 4 Stroke 6 Cy. 280 x 540 736kW (1001bhp) Matsui Iron Works Co Ltd-Japan
7353585 - -	**SEIHO MARU No. 38** **Government of The Oriental Republic of Uruguay (Servicio Oceanografico y Pesca)** - *Uruguay*	*284* 141 -	**1973 Uchida Zosen — Ise** Yd No: 740 Loa - Br ex 8.23 Dght - Lbp 43.21 Br md 8.21 Dpth 3.56 Riveted\Welded, 1 dk	**(B11B2FV) Fishing Vessel**	**1 oil engine** driving 1 FP propeller Total Power: 736kW (1,001hp) Hanshin 6LU28G 1 x 4 Stroke 6 Cy. 280 x 440 736kW (1001bhp) Hanshin Nainenki Kogyo-Japan
8944238 *JK2867* -	**SEIJIN MARU** *ex* Kasuga Maru *-2003* **Sumikaju Takasu** *Hazu, Aichi* *Japan* Official number: 103113	*181* - 301	**1968-09 Kogushi Zosen K.K. — Okayama** Loa 33.00 Br ex - Dght 2.800 Lbp 31.20 Br md 6.85 Dpth 3.00 Welded, 1 dk	**(A31A2GX) General Cargo Ship** Compartments: 1 Ho, ER 1 Ha: (19.0 x 4.9)ER	**1 oil engine** driving 1 FP propeller Total Power: 169kW (230hp) 8.0kn Kubota 1 x 4 Stroke 169kW (230bhp) Kubota Corp-Japan
8962577 *JL3313* -	**SEIJU MARU** **Katsumi Ise** *Izumi-Sano, Osaka* *Japan* Official number: 107010	*171* - -	**1969-07 K.K. Miura Zosensho — Oseto** L reg 26.25 Br ex - Dght - Lbp - Br md 6.50 Dpth 2.60 Welded, 1 dk	**(A31A2GX) General Cargo Ship**	**1 oil engine** driving 1 FP propeller
8350968 - -	**SEIJU MARU** *ex* Yahata Maru No. 8 *-1985* - -	*423* - 463	**1983 Y.K. Takasago Zosensho — Naruto** Yd No: 117 Loa 38.99 Br ex 8.79 Dght 3.060 Lbp - Br md - Dpth - Welded, 1 dk	**(A31A2GX) General Cargo Ship**	**1 oil engine** driving 1 FP propeller Total Power: 441kW (600hp) Matsui 6M26KGHS 1 x 4 Stroke 6 Cy. 260 x 400 441kW (600bhp) Matsui Iron Works Co Ltd-Japan
9523354 *JD2871* -	**SEIJU MARU** **Seiyo Kisen KK** *Imabari, Ehime* *Japan* MMSI: 431000848 Official number: 140935	*748* - 2,385	**2009-01 Yamanaka Zosen K.K. — Imabari** Yd No: 771 Loa 83.12 Br ex - Dght 4.670 Lbp 77.50 Br md 13.00 Dpth 8.10 Welded, 1 dk	**(A31A2GX) General Cargo Ship** Grain: 3,804	**1 oil engine** driving 1 FP propeller Total Power: 1,471kW (2,000hp) 12.4kn Hanshin LH34LA 1 x 4 Stroke 6 Cy. 340 x 640 1471kW (2000bhp) The Hanshin Diesel Works Ltd-Japan
6804109 - -	**SEIJU MARU No. 2** - -	*298* 162 -	**1967 KK Kanasashi Zosen — Shizuoka SZ** Yd No: 801 Loa 43.69 Br ex 8.11 Dght 2.921 Lbp 38.38 Br md 8.08 Dpth 3.23 Welded, 2 dks	**(B11B2FV) Fishing Vessel**	**1 oil engine** driving 1 FP propeller Total Power: 699kW (950hp) Niigata 6M31HS 1 x 4 Stroke 6 Cy. 310 x 460 699kW (950bhp) Niigata Engineering Co Ltd-Japan
7851898 -	**SEIJU MARU No. 5** **Pohnpei Economic Progress Inc** *Kolonia, Pohnpei* *Micronesia*	*199* - 370	**1969 Yonomoto Zosen — Japan** Yd No: 135 Lengthened-1984 Loa 47.20 Br ex - Dght 3.101 Lbp - Br md 8.01 Dpth 4.50 Welded, 1 dk	**(A24D2BA) Aggregates Carrier**	**1 oil engine** driving 1 FP propeller Total Power: 478kW (650hp) 10.5kn Fuji 6S27.5GH 1 x 4 Stroke 6 Cy. 275 x 410 478kW (650bhp) Fuji Diesel Co Ltd-Japan

IMO / Call sign / Flag	Name / Owner	Tonnage	Class	Construction	Type	Machinery
8840793 - -	**SEIJU MARU No. 31** *ex* Koei Maru No. 11 - -	*134* - -		**1972 Yamanishi Shipbuilding Co Ltd — Ishinomaki MG** L reg 28.20 Br ex - Dght 2.100 Lbp - Br md 6.30 Dpth 2.60 Welded, 1 dk	**(B11B2FV) Fishing Vessel**	**1 oil engine** driving 1 FP propeller Total Power: 316kW (430hp) Niigata 1 x 4 Stroke 316kW (430bhp) Niigata Engineering Co Ltd-Japan
7856549 - -	**SEIKA** *ex* Seikai *-1996* - -	*167* 45 -		**1976 Ishikawajima-Harima Heavy Industries Co Ltd (IHI) — Aioi HG** Loa 25.00 Br ex - Dght 2.501 Lbp 23.30 Br md 10.80 Dpth 3.10 Welded, 1 dk	**(B34G2SE) Pollution Control Vessel**	**2 oil engines** driving 2 FP propellers Total Power: 706kW (960hp) 11.0kn
9668441 *JD3414* -	**SEIKAI** **Kagoshima Prefecture, Toshima-Mura** - *Kagoshima, Kagoshima* *Japan* Official number: 141766	*129* - -		**2013-03 Japan Marine United Corp (JMU) — Yokohama KN (Tsurumi Shipyard)** Yd No: 0080 Loa 38.00 Br ex - Dght 3.150 Lbp - Br md 6.80 Dpth - Welded, 1 dk	**(B12D2FP) Fishery Patrol Vessel** Hull Material: Aluminium Alloy	**1 oil engine** driving 1 Propeller
9250361 *JM6692*	**SEIKAI MARU** **YK Kiyomaru Kaiun** - *Kamiamakusa, Kumamoto* *Japan* Official number: 136440	*498* - 1,500		**2001-05 K.K. Yoshida Zosen Kogyo — Arida** Yd No: 525 Loa 75.01 Br ex - Dght - Lbp 70.00 Br md 12.20 Dpth 7.00 Welded, 1 dk	**(A31A2GX) General Cargo Ship** Compartments: 1 Ho, ER 1 Ha: (40.0 x 10.0)ER	**1 oil engine** driving 1 FP propeller Total Power: 1,618kW (2,200hp) 12.0kn Akasaka A34C 1 x 4 Stroke 6 Cy. 340 x 620 1618kW (2200bhp) Akasaka Tekkosho KK (Akasaka DieselLtd)-Japan Fuel: 73.0 (d.f.) 5.0pd
8743361 *JD2923* -	**SEIKAI MARU** **Inoshita Kaiun KK** - *Niihama, Ehime* *Japan* Official number: 141030	*499* - 1,700		**2009-05 Koike Zosen Kaiun KK — Osakikamijima** Yd No: 521 Loa 74.70 (BB) Br ex - Dght 4.150 Lbp 69.50 Br md 12.20 Dpth 7.10 Welded, 1 dk	**(A31A2GX) General Cargo Ship** Grain: 2,507; Bale: 2,487 Compartments: 1 Ho, ER 1 Ha: ER (40.1 x 9.7)	**1 oil engine** reduction geared to sc. shaft driving 1 FP propeller Total Power: 1,618kW (2,200hp) 12.0kn Daihatsu 6DKM-26 1 x 4 Stroke 6 Cy. 260 x 380 1618kW (2200bhp) Daihatsu Diesel Manufacturing Co Lt-Japan Thrusters: 1 Tunnel thruster (f)
9128893 *JM6430*	**SEIKAI MARU** **Nakatani Kaiun KK** - *Hyuga, Miyazaki* *Japan* Official number: 134525	*498* - 1,600		**1995-10 Shitanoe Shipbuilding Co Ltd — Usuki OT** Yd No: 1168 Loa - Br ex - Dght 4.120 Lbp 72.00 Br md 11.70 Dpth 7.05 Welded, 1 dk	**(A31A2GX) General Cargo Ship**	**1 oil engine** driving 1 FP propeller Total Power: 736kW (1,001hp) Hanshin LH30LG 1 x 4 Stroke 6 Cy. 300 x 600 736kW (1001bhp) The Hanshin Diesel Works Ltd-Japan
8997302 *JD2033* -	**SEIKAI MARU** **Seiyo Kisen KK** - *Imabari, Ehime* *Japan* Official number: 140069	*499* - 1,760		**2004-08 Yamanaka Zosen K.K. — Imabari** L reg 69.92 Br ex - Dght 4.340 Lbp 68.00 Br md 12.10 Dpth 7.34 Welded, 1 dk	**(A31A2GX) General Cargo Ship**	**1 oil engine** driving 1 Propeller Total Power: 1,324kW (1,800hp) Hanshin LH30L 1 x 4 Stroke 6 Cy. 300 x 600 1324kW (1800bhp) The Hanshin Diesel Works Ltd-Japan
7921071 - -	**SEIKAI No. 2** - - *South Korea*	*203* - -		**1980-03 Misaki Senpaku Kogyo K.K. — Miura** Yd No: 56 Loa 27.00 Br ex - Dght 2.000 Lbp 25.00 Br md 11.00 Dpth 3.60 Welded, 1 dk	**(B34G2SE) Pollution Control Vessel**	**2 oil engines** reduction geared to sc. shafts driving 2 FP propellers Total Power: 408kW (554hp) Mitsubishi S8A-T 2 x 4 Stroke 8 Cy. 145 x 160 each-204kW (277bhp) Mitsubishi Heavy Industries Ltd-Japan
9524322 *CB9839* -	**SEIKAPP** **CPT Empresas Maritimas SA** - *Valparaiso* *Chile* MMSI: 725004230 Official number: 3234	**1,159** 315 1,483	Class: AB	**2009-01 Bonny Fair Development Ltd — Hong Kong** Yd No: HY2157 Loa 60.84 (BB) Br ex - Dght 4.790 Lbp 56.84 Br md 12.00 Dpth 5.74 Welded, 1 dk	**(B12C2FL) Live Fish Carrier (Well Boat)**	**1 oil engine** reduction geared to sc. shaft driving 1 CP propeller Total Power: 1,710kW (2,325hp) 12.0kn MaK 9M20C 1 x 4 Stroke 9 Cy. 200 x 300 1710kW (2325bhp) Caterpillar Motoren GmbH & Co. KG-Germany AuxGen: 2 x 450kW a.c Thrusters: 1 Tunnel thruster (f); 1 Tunnel thruster (a)
9442653 *JD2501* -	**SEIKEI MARU** *ex* Yamanaka 752 *-2007* **Seiyo Kisen KK** - *Imabari, Ehime* *Japan* Official number: 140636	*499* - 1,860		**2007-10 Yamanaka Zosen K.K. — Imabari** Yd No: 752 Loa 74.20 Br ex - Dght 4.350 Lbp 68.00 Br md 12.10 Dpth 7.34 Welded, 1 dk	**(A31A2GX) General Cargo Ship** Compartments: 1 Ho, ER 1 Ha: ER (40.0 x 9.5)	**1 oil engine** driving 1 FP propeller Total Power: 1,324kW (1,800hp) Hanshin LH30L 1 x 4 Stroke 6 Cy. 300 x 600 1324kW (1800bhp) The Hanshin Diesel Works Ltd-Japan
9105384 *JL6098*	**SEIKEI MARU** **Kimura Kisen YK** - *Uchinomi, Kagawa* *Japan* Official number: 132988	*179* - 350		**1994-04 Masui Zosensho K.K. — Nandan** Yd No: 230 Loa - (BB) Br ex - Dght 3.200 Lbp - Br md - Dpth - Welded, 1 dk	**(A13B2TP) Products Tanker** Compartments: 8 Ta, ER	**1 oil engine** driving 1 FP propeller Total Power: 441kW (600hp) Matsui ML624GS 1 x 4 Stroke 6 Cy. 240 x 400 441kW (600bhp) Matsui Iron Works Co Ltd-Japan
9148013 *JJ3923*	**SEIKI 21** **Sonoda Kisen KK** - *Kobe, Hyogo* *Japan* Official number: 134237	*498* - 1,598		**1996-01 Kanawa Dockyard Co. Ltd. — Hiroshima** Yd No: 1014 Loa 75.25 Br ex - Dght 4.130 Lbp 70.50 Br md 12.00 Dpth 7.10 Welded, 1 dk	**(A31A2GX) General Cargo Ship** Grain: 2,891; Bale: 2,725	**1 oil engine** driving 1 FP propeller Total Power: 736kW (1,001hp) 9.5kn Hanshin LH34LAG 1 x 4 Stroke 6 Cy. 340 x 640 736kW (1001bhp) The Hanshin Diesel Works Ltd-Japan
9381031 *JD2308*	**SEIKI MARU** **Inoshita Kaiun KK** - *Niihama, Ehime* *Japan* Official number: 140389	*498* - 1,600		**2006-09 K.K. Watanabe Zosensho — Nagasaki** Yd No: 137 Loa 76.12 Br ex - Dght 4.300 Lbp 70.20 Br md 12.30 Dpth 7.00 Welded, 1 dk	**(A31A2GX) General Cargo Ship** 1 Ha: ER (40.0 x 10.0)	**1 oil engine** driving 1 FP propeller Total Power: 1,471kW (2,000hp) Hanshin LH34LAG 1 x 4 Stroke 6 Cy. 340 x 640 1471kW (2000bhp) The Hanshin Diesel Works Ltd-Japan
7903639 - -	**SEIKO** *ex* Navi *-2008* *ex* Lucky Star No. 1 *-2007* *ex* Chance No. 505 *-2007* *ex* Prince No. 505 *-1988* *ex* Daikichi Maru No. 88 *-1987*	**498** 230 409	Class: (KR)	**1979-08 Miho Zosensho K.K. — Shimizu** Yd No: 1142 Loa 52.41 Br ex - Dght 3.536 Lbp 46.00 Br md 8.81 Dpth 3.76 Welded, 1 dk	**(B11B2FV) Fishing Vessel**	**1 oil engine** driving 1 FP propeller Total Power: 1,214kW (1,651hp) 13.0kn Akasaka DM30 1 x 4 Stroke 6 Cy. 300 x 480 1214kW (1651bhp) Akasaka Tekkosho KK (Akasaka DieselLtd)-Japan AuxGen: 2 x 240kW 225V a.c
8132392 *YFOQ* -	**SEIKO** *ex* Seiko Maru *-1996* - - *Surabaya* *Indonesia*	*633* 404 690	Class: (KI)	**1981-09 Shitanoe Shipbuilding Co Ltd — Usuki OT** Yd No: 1020 Loa 55.85 Br ex - Dght 3.200 Lbp 53.01 Br md 9.30 Dpth 5.11 Welded, 1 dk	**(A31A2GX) General Cargo Ship**	**1 oil engine** driving 1 FP propeller Total Power: 625kW (850hp) Niigata 6M26ZE 1 x 4 Stroke 6 Cy. 260 x 400 625kW (850bhp) Niigata Engineering Co Ltd-Japan
6519182 *CB4104*	**SEIKO** *ex* Sjobris *-1977* **Alimentos Marinos SA (ALIMAR)** - *Valparaiso* *Chile* MMSI: 725008400 Official number: 2602	**468** 135 -	Class: (NV)	**1965-07 Smedvik Mek. Verksted AS — Tjorvaag** Yd No: 5 Lengthened & Deepened-1968 Loa 42.02 Br ex 8.26 Dght 4.350 Lbp 37.32 Br md 8.23 Dpth 6.46 Welded, 2 dks	**(B11B2FV) Fishing Vessel** Compartments: 1 Ho, 3 Ta, ER 4 Ha: (2.6 x 3.2)3 (2.4 x 1.7)ER Derricks: 1x3t; Winches: 1 Ice Capable	**1 oil engine** driving 1 FP propeller Total Power: 809kW (1,100hp) MaK 6MU451AK 1 x 4 Stroke 6 Cy. 320 x 450 809kW (1100bhp) Maschinenbau Kiel AG (MaK)-Kiel AuxGen: 1 x 156kW 220V 50Hz a.c, 1 x 152kW 220V 50Hz a.c Thrusters: 1 Thwart. FP thruster (f); 1 Tunnel thruster (a)
8866412 - -	**SEIKO 1** *ex* Tag 800 *-1977* *ex* Ag 80 *-1977* *ex* Impala I *-1994* *ex* Hayabusa Maru No. 5 *-1993*	*149* 47 -		**1969 Hayashikane Shipbuilding & Engineering Co Ltd — Nagasaki NS** Loa 32.80 Br ex - Dght 1.800 Lbp 28.20 Br md 6.90 Dpth 2.83 Welded, 1 dk	**(B32A2ST) Tug**	**1 oil engine** driving 1 FP propeller Total Power: 588kW (799hp) 10.0kn Niigata 1 x 4 Stroke 588kW (799bhp) Niigata Engineering Co Ltd-Japan
8961640 *JH2521* -	**SEIKO MARU** **Kenji Kamisaka** - *Handa, Aichi* *Japan* Official number: 112246	*175* - 300		**1971-11 Katahara Zosen K.K. — Gamagori** Loa 33.00 Br ex - Dght 2.800 Lbp 30.00 Br md 6.80 Dpth 3.00 Welded, 1 dk	**(A31A2GX) General Cargo Ship** Compartments: 1 Ho, ER 1 Ha: ER (22.0 x 5.0)	**1 oil engine** driving 1 FP propeller Total Power: 434kW (590hp) 10.0kn Mitsubishi 1 x 434kW (590bhp) Mitsubishi Heavy Industries Ltd-Japan

Number / Name / Owner	Tonnage	Class	Builder / Dimensions	Type / Cargo	Machinery
9103556 *JM6187* - **SEIKO MARU** *ex* Shoei Maru No. 18 *-2003* **Gunji Watanabe** - *Karatsu, Saga* *Japan* Official number: 133580	*198* - 600		**1993**-12 **Koike Zosen Kaiun KK — Osakikamijima** Yd No: 177 Loa 57.49 Br ex - Dght - Lbp 52.00 Br md 9.20 Dpth 5.50 Welded, 1 dk	**(A31A2GX) General Cargo Ship** Grain: 1,225; Bale: 1,199 Compartments: 1 Ho 1 Ha: (29.2 x 7.1)	**1 oil engine** driving 1 FP propeller Total Power: 736kW (1,001hp) 10.0kn Hanshin LH26G 1 x 4 Stroke 6 Cy. 260 x 440 736kW (1001bhp) The Hanshin Diesel Works Ltd-Japan
9078919 *JK5284* - **SEIKO MARU** - **Nakaei Marine Co Ltd** - *Okayama, Okayama* *Japan* MMSI: 431400201 Official number: 134040	*699* - 1,851	Class: NK	**1993**-08 **Shin Kurushima Dockyard Co. Ltd. — Hashihama, Imabari** Yd No: 2790 Loa 75.02 (BB) Br ex - Dght 4.662 Lbp 70.00 Br md 11.20 Dpth 5.10 Welded, 1 dk	**(A13B2TP) Products Tanker** Liq: 2,180; Liq (Oil): 2,180 Compartments: 10 Ta, ER	**1 oil engine** reverse geared to sc. shaft driving 1 FP propeller Total Power: 1,324kW (1,800hp) 11.8kn Hanshin LH30LG 1 x 4 Stroke 6 Cy. 300 x 600 1324kW (1800bhp) The Hanshin Diesel Works Ltd-Japan Fuel: 75.0 (d.f.)
8032229 *JL4905* - **SEIKO MARU** - **YK Imai Sangyo** - *Kami, Kochi* *Japan* Official number: 124150	*128* - -		**1979**-12 **Imai Shipbuilding Co Ltd — Kochi KC** Loa - Br ex - Dght - Lbp 21.49 Br md 8.01 Dpth 2.49 Welded, 1 dk	**(B33A2DB) Bucket Ladder Dredger**	**1 oil engine** driving 1 FP propeller
8312552 - - **SEIKO MARU** - **Kinsin Maritime Co Ltd** - *Chinese Taipei*	*699* 315 1,878		**1983**-08 **Kurinoura Dockyard Co Ltd — Yawatahama EH** Yd No: 185 Loa 76.50 Br ex - Dght 4.552 Lbp 72.01 Br md 11.21 Dpth 5.01 Welded, 1 dk	**(A13B2TP) Products Tanker** Liq: 2,150; Liq (Oil): 2,150 Compartments: 10 Ta, ER	**1 oil engine** with clutches, flexible couplings & sr geared to sc. shaft driving 1 CP propeller Total Power: 1,324kW (1,800hp) Hanshin 6EL30 1 x 4 Stroke 6 Cy. 300 x 600 1324kW (1800bhp) The Hanshin Diesel Works Ltd-Japan
8625583 *YHMM* - **SEIKO MARU** *ex* Konpira Maru No. 18 *-2005* **PT Armada Mandiri** - *Surabaya* *Indonesia*	*645* 261 700	Class: KI	**1986**-03 **K.K. Kamishima Zosensho — Osakikamijima** Yd No: 178 Loa 54.60 Br ex - Dght 3.420 Lbp 49.50 Br md 9.00 Dpth 5.50 Welded, 1 dk	**(A31A2GX) General Cargo Ship**	**1 oil engine** driving 1 FP propeller Total Power: 405kW (551hp) 9.8kn Hanshin 6LU26G 1 x 4 Stroke 6 Cy. 260 x 440 405kW (551bhp) The Hanshin Diesel Works Ltd-Japan
8627232 - - **SEIKO MARU** *ex* Kannon Maru *-1990* - - *Chinese Taipei*	*169* - 500		**1984 YK Furumoto Tekko Zosensho — Osakikamijima** Yd No: 531 Loa 49.99 Br ex - Dght 3.601 Lbp 45.01 Br md 8.31 Dpth 4.91 Welded, 1 dk	**(A31A2GX) General Cargo Ship** Grain: 1,059; Bale: 1,015	**1 oil engine** driving 1 FP propeller Total Power: 441kW (600hp) 10.5kn Matsui 6M26KGHS 1 x 4 Stroke 6 Cy. 260 x 400 441kW (600bhp) Matsui Iron Works Co Ltd-Japan
9413781 *JD2337* - **SEIKO MARU** - **Japan Railway Construction, Transport & Technology Agency & Shimobayashi Kisen Co Ltd** Shimobayashi Kisen YK *Bizen, Okayama* *Japan* Official number: 140430	*749* - 1,957		**2006**-12 **Imura Zosen K.K. — Komatsushima** Yd No: 318 Loa 72.20 Br ex - Dght 4.720 Lbp 67.20 Br md 12.00 Dpth 5.20 Welded, 1 dk	**(A13B2TP) Products Tanker** Double Hull (13F) Grain: 2,200	**1 oil engine** driving 1 FP propeller Total Power: 1,471kW (2,000hp) 12.5kn Hanshin LH34LA 1 x 4 Stroke 6 Cy. 340 x 640 1471kW (2000bhp) The Hanshin Diesel Works Ltd-Japan
8965115 *JM6688* - **SEIKO MARU No. 2** - **YK Daido Kaiun** - *Kamiamakusa, Kumamoto* *Japan* Official number: 136436	*499* - -		**2000**-10 **Amakusa Zosen K.K. — Amakusa** Yd No: 138 Loa 68.34 Br ex - Dght - Lbp 62.00 Br md 13.30 Dpth 7.20 Welded, 1 dk	**(A24D2BA) Aggregates Carrier**	**1 oil engine** driving 1 FP propeller Total Power: 1,471kW (2,000hp) Hanshin LH34LA 1 x 4 Stroke 6 Cy. 340 x 640 1471kW (2000bhp) The Hanshin Diesel Works Ltd-Japan
8839768 - - **SEIKO MARU No. 3** - - - *Indonesia*	*472* - 549		**1989**-10 **Katsuura Dockyard Co. Ltd. — Nachi-Katsuura** Loa 51.00 Br ex - Dght 3.270 Lbp 46.00 Br md 10.50 Dpth 5.40 Welded, 1 dk	**(A24D2BA) Aggregates Carrier**	**1 oil engine** geared to sc. shaft driving 1 FP propeller Total Power: 736kW (1,001hp) Hanshin LH28G 1 x 4 Stroke 6 Cy. 280 x 460 736kW (1001bhp) The Hanshin Diesel Works Ltd-Japan
9138434 *JL6522* - **SEIKO MARU No. 8** - - - *Saka, Hiroshima* *Japan* MMSI: 431000782 Official number: 135550	*691* - 2,000		**1996**-10 **Fujiwara Zosensho — Imabari** Yd No: 131 Loa - Br ex - Dght - Lbp 58.00 Br md 13.50 Dpth 4.70 Welded, 1 dk	**(A24D2BA) Aggregates Carrier**	**1 oil engine** driving 1 FP propeller Total Power: 1,471kW (2,000hp) Niigata 6M34AGT 1 x 4 Stroke 6 Cy. 340 x 620 1471kW (2000bhp) Niigata Engineering Co Ltd-Japan
9234977 *JG5598* - **SEIKO MARU No. 18** - **YK Seiko Maru** - *Kozushima, Tokyo* *Japan* Official number: 136775	*199* - -		**2000**-01 **ISB Co Ltd — Futtsu CH** Yd No: 501 Loa 57.30 Br ex - Dght - Lbp 52.00 Br md 9.20 Dpth 5.00 Welded, 1 dk	**(A31A2GX) General Cargo Ship** Grain: 1,112; Bale: 1,088	**1 oil engine** driving 1 FP propeller Total Power: 1,030kW (1,400hp) 12.0kn Yanmar DY28-UN 1 x 4 Stroke 6 Cy. 280 x 530 1030kW (1400bhp) Yanmar Diesel Engine Co Ltd-Japan Fuel: 20.0 (d.f.)
8408765 *JG2206* - **SEIKO MARU No. 21** - **YK Eiwa Kaiun** - *Kawasaki, Kanagawa* *Japan* Official number: 117783	*195* - 478		**1984**-08 **Suzuki Shipyard Co. Ltd. — Yokkaichi** Yd No: 505 Loa - Br ex - Dght 2.801 Lbp 43.01 Br md 8.31 Dpth 3.31 Welded, 1 dk	**(A13A2TV) Crude Oil Tanker** Liq: 550; Liq (Oil): 550 Compartments: 6 Ta, ER	**1 oil engine** driving 1 FP propeller Total Power: 588kW (799hp) Niigata 6M26AGT 1 x 4 Stroke 6 Cy. 260 x 460 588kW (799bhp) Niigata Engineering Co Ltd-Japan
8921901 *JM5895* - **SEIKO MARU No. 38** - **Taiyo A&F Co Ltd (Taiyo A&F KK)** - *Yaizu, Shizuoka* *Japan* Official number: 131292	*330* - -		**1990**-06 **K.K. Watanabe Zosensho — Nagasaki** Yd No: 1171 Loa 59.54 (BB) Br ex - Dght 4.001 Lbp 49.70 Br md 8.80 Dpth 4.45 Welded	**(B11B2FV) Fishing Vessel**	**1 oil engine** driving 1 FP propeller Total Power: 1,155kW (1,570hp) Niigata 8MG28HX 1 x 4 Stroke 8 Cy. 280 x 370 1155kW (1570bhp) Niigata Engineering Co Ltd-Japan
9152210 *JRZJ* KN1-725 **SEIKO MARU No. 52** - **Nanyo Suisan KK** - SatCom: Inmarsat B 343187310 *Miura, Kanagawa* *Japan* MMSI: 431873000 Official number: 134956	*499* - -		**1996**-07 **Miho Zosensho K.K. — Shimizu** Yd No: 1476 Loa 58.00 (BB) Br ex - Dght - Lbp 51.00 Br md 9.00 Dpth 3.00 Welded, 1 dk	**(B11B2FV) Fishing Vessel** Ins: 854	**1 oil engine** with flexible couplings & sr gearedto sc. shaft driving 1 FP propeller Total Power: 736kW (1,001hp) 12.7kn Niigata 6M28HFT 1 x 4 Stroke 6 Cy. 280 x 480 736kW (1001bhp) Niigata Engineering Co Ltd-Japan AuxGen: 2 x 320kW 445V a.c Fuel: 325.0 (d.f.) 3.0pd
7817048 *OIRO* - **SEILI** - **Meritaito Oy** - *Helsinki* *Finland* MMSI: 230110670 Official number: 12309	871 262 192		**1979**-12 **Rauma-Repola Oy — Savonlinna** Yd No: 430 Lengthened-2004 Loa 50.50 Br ex 12.60 Dght 3.801 Lbp - Br md 12.21 Dpth 5.01 Welded, 2 dks	**(B34Q2QB) Buoy Tender** Ice Capable	**3 diesel electric oil engines** Connecting to 2 elec. motors each (1100kW) geared to sc. shafts driving 2 Directional propellers Total Power: 2,400kW (3,264hp) 12.5kn Thrusters: 1 Tunnel thruster (f)
9733789 *JD3658* - **SEIMEI** - **Yamada Kisen YK** - *Japan*	*749* - 2,300	Class: FA	**2014**-02 **Koike Zosen Kaiun KK — Osakikamijima** Yd No: 560 Loa - Br ex - Dght - Lbp - Br md - Dpth - Welded, 1 dk	**(A31A2GX) General Cargo Ship**	**1 oil engine** driving 1 Propeller
5318309 *LLFL* - **SEIMSDAL** *ex* Petrolea *-1990* *ex* Skomvaer *-1990* **Sverre Mardal** - *Bergen* *Norway*	*108* 48 132		**1892 Nylands Verksted — Oslo** L reg 26.34 Br ex 5.24 Dght 3.169 Lbp - Br md 5.21 Dpth - Riveted	**(A31A2GX) General Cargo Ship** Compartments: 1 Ho, ER 1 Ha: (6.9 x 3.0)ER	**1 oil engine** driving 1 FP propeller Total Power: 88kW (120hp) 8.3kn Wichmann 1 x 2 Stroke 2 Cy. 320 x 320 88kW (120bhp) (made 1953, fitted 1969) Wichmann Motorfabrikk AS-Norway

8312461 *DSMN2* -	**SEIN OCEAN** *ex* Blue Ocean *-2009* *ex* Western Star *-2007* *ex* Nova Cotta *-2005* *ex* Isla Bonita *-1996* *ex* East Breeze *-1990* **Sein Shipping Co Ltd** - *Jeju* *South Korea* MMSI: 441725000 Official number: JJR-094064	**4,071** 2,449 5,563	Class: KT (KR) (BV) (NK)	**1983-09 Kitanihon Zosen K.K. — Hachinohe** Yd No: 178 Loa 110.00 (BB) Br ex 16.44 Dght 7.464 Lbp 100.44 Br md 16.40 Dpth 9.45 Welded, 3 dks	**(A34A2GR) Refrigerated Cargo Ship** Ins: 6,070 TEU 8 Compartments: 3 Ho, ER 3 Ha: 2 (7.6 x 6.1) (7.0 x 6.1)ER Cranes: 3x4t	**1 oil engine** driving 1 FP propeller Total Power: 4,781kW (6,500hp) 16.0kn Mitsubishi 6UEC45HA 1 x 2 Stroke 6 Cy. 450 x 1150 4781kW (6500bhp) Akasaka Tekkosho KK (Akasaka DieselLtd)-Japan AuxGen: 2 x 640kW 440V a.c Fuel: 114.5 (d.f.) 836.0 (r.f.) 22.0pd
8813623 *DSRO7* -	**SEIN SKY** *ex* Damaco Francia *-2013* *ex* Nova Francia *-2008* *ex* East Sea *-2006* *ex* Ice Sea *-2001* *ex* Amber Atlantic *-1996* **Sein Shipping Co Ltd** - *Jeju* *South Korea* MMSI: 440097000 Official number: JJR-131043	**5,476** 3,559 6,756	Class: KR (BV) (NV) (NK)	**1989-02 Shin Kurushima Dockyard Co. Ltd. — Akitsu** Yd No: 2596 Loa 124.70 (BB) Br ex - Dght 7.516 Lbp 117.00 Br md 17.80 Dpth 9.85 Welded, 1 dk	**(A34A2GR) Refrigerated Cargo Ship** Ins: 8,447 Compartments: 4 Ho, ER, 8 Tw Dk 4 Ha: 4 (6.2 x 7.3)ER Derricks: 8x5t	**1 oil engine** driving 1 FP propeller Total Power: 5,149kW (7,001hp) 16.9kn Mitsubishi 6UEC45LA 1 x 2 Stroke 6 Cy. 450 x 1350 5149kW (7001bhp) Kobe Hatsudoki KK-Japan AuxGen: 4 x 348kW a.c
8319029 *DSRN5* -	**SEIN STAR** *ex* Adriatic *-2009* *ex* White Reefer *-1990* **Sein Shipping Co Ltd** - *Jeju* *South Korea* MMSI: 441923000 Official number: JJR-131023	**3,498** 1,530 4,173	Class: KR (BV) (NK)	**1984-01 Kitanihon Zosen K.K. — Hachinohe** Yd No: 181 Loa 99.02 (BB) Br ex - Dght 6.713 Lbp 89.90 Br md 16.00 Dpth 7.10 Welded, 2 dks	**(A34A2GR) Refrigerated Cargo Ship** Ins: 5,178 Compartments: 3 Ho, ER 3 Ha: 2 (6.5 x 5.1) (6.4 x 5.0)ER Derricks: 6x5t	**1 oil engine** driving 1 FP propeller Total Power: 3,972kW (5,400hp) 15.5kn Mitsubishi 6UEC45HA 1 x 2 Stroke 6 Cy. 450 x 1150 3972kW (5400bhp) Akasaka Tekkosho KK (Akasaka DieselLtd)-Japan AuxGen: 2 x 560kW a.c
8415859 *DSQY9* -	**SEIN SUN** *ex* Nova Australia *-2009* *ex* Green Eskimo *-2000* *ex* Garnet Reefer *-1996* *ex* Winter Reefer *-1995* *ex* Atlas Rex *-1995* **KDB Capital Corp** Sein Shipping Co Ltd SatCom: Inmarsat C 444075910 *Jeju* *South Korea* MMSI: 441759000 Official number: JJR-106309	**4,427** 2,678 5,438	Class: KR (LR) (BV) (NV) (NK) Classed LR until 20/12/00	**1984-12 Kitanihon Zosen K.K. — Hachinohe** Yd No: 187 Loa 109.00 (BB) Br ex 16.42 Dght 7.665 Lbp 100.00 Br md 16.41 Dpth 10.01 Welded, 3 dks	**(A34A2GR) Refrigerated Cargo Ship** Ins: 6,644 Compartments: 3 Ho, ER 3 Ha: 3 (7.0 x 6.1)ER Derricks: 6x5t	**1 oil engine** driving 1 FP propeller Total Power: 4,781kW (6,500hp) 16.0kn Mitsubishi 6UEC45HA 1 x 2 Stroke 6 Cy. 450 x 1150 4781kW (6500bhp) Kobe Hatsudoki KK-Japan AuxGen: 3 x 400kW 440V 60Hz a.c
9585211 - -	**SEINA II** *ex* Surya Ratna 17 *-2010* **Seina Marine Ltd** - *Nigeria*	**298** 90 241	Class: (BV) (NK)	**2010-04 Hung Seng Shipbuilding Sdn Bhd — Sibu** Yd No: 12 Loa 32.10 Br ex - Dght 3.612 Lbp 29.38 Br md 9.00 Dpth 4.20 Welded, 1 dk	**(B32A2ST) Tug**	**2 oil engines** reduction geared to sc. shaft driving 2 Propellers Total Power: 2,386kW (3,244hp) Cummins KTA-50-M2 2 x Vee 4 Stroke 16 Cy. 159 x 159 each-1193kW (1622bhp) Cummins Engine Co Inc-USA Fuel: 200.0 (d.f.)
7726847 *PBAI* -	**SEINE** *ex* Paul Barrillon *-2002* **SHM Seine BV** Baggerbedrijf de Boer BV *Sliedrecht* *Netherlands* MMSI: 244300000 Official number: 41348	**5,291** 1,587 9,200	Class: BV	**1978-03 Dubigeon-Normandie S.A. — Grand Quevilly** Yd No: 2542 Loa 100.89 Br ex 18.45 Dght 6.880 Lbp 94.01 Br md 18.00 Dpth 8.21 Welded, 1 dk	**(B33B2DT) Trailing Suction Hopper Dredger** Hopper: 4,317	**2 oil engines** reverse reduction geared to sc. shafts driving 2 FP propellers Total Power: 2,060kW (2,800hp) 13.0kn AGO 240V16DSHR 2 x Vee 4 Stroke 16 Cy. 240 x 220 each-1030kW (1400bhp) Societe Alsacienne de ConstructionsMecaniques (SACM)-France Thrusters: 1 Tunnel thruster (f) Fuel: 1189.0 (d.f.)
9316311 *C6VJ7* -	**SEINE HIGHWAY** - **Seine Maritime Ltd** Ray Car Carriers Ltd *Nassau* *Bahamas* MMSI: 308654000 Official number: 8001181	**23,498** 7,050 8,100	Class: NV	**2007-02 Stocznia Gdynia SA — Gdynia** Yd No: 8245/4 Loa 147.93 (BB) Br ex 25.03 Dght 7.900 Lbp 134.00 Br md 25.00 Dpth 25.20 Welded	**(A35B2RV) Vehicles Carrier** Stern door/ramp (p. a.) Len: 18.80 Wid: 6.00 Swl: 70 Quarter stern door/ramp (s. a.) Len: 27.50 Wid: 6.00 Swl: 70 Cars: 2,130 Ice Capable	**1 oil engine** driving 1 FP propeller Total Power: 9,170kW (12,468hp) 18.9kn MAN-B&W 7S46MC-C 1 x 2 Stroke 7 Cy. 460 x 1932 9170kW (12468bhp) H Cegielski Poznan SA-Poland AuxGen: 3 x 1120kW a.c Thrusters: 1 Thwart. CP thruster (f); 1 Thwart. CP thruster (a)
9044970 *CB4828* -	**SEINES** *ex* Tolten I *-2013* - - *Valparaiso* *Chile* MMSI: 725001450 Official number: 2767	**918** 245 957		**1992-10 Astilleros Marco Chilena Ltda. — Iquique** Yd No: 200 Loa 48.40 (BB) Br ex 10.40 Dght - Lbp 43.30 Br md 10.20 Dpth 5.00 Welded, 2 dks	**(B11B2FV) Fishing Vessel** Ins: 770	**1 oil engine** with clutches & sr geared to sc. shaft driving 1 CP propeller Total Power: 1,651kW (2,245hp) 14.0kn Deutz SBV8M628 1 x 4 Stroke 8 Cy. 240 x 280 1651kW (2245bhp) Kloeckner Humboldt Deutz AG-Germany Thrusters: 1 Thwart. FP thruster (f); 1 Tunnel thruster (a)
8997065 *JF2103* -	**SEIO MARU** - **Taisei Kisen YK** - *Karatsu, Saga* *Japan* Official number: 140009	*199* - 650		**2004-09 Y.K. Okajima Zosensho — Matsuyama** Yd No: 259 Loa 60.29 Br ex - Dght 3.110 Lbp 52.80 Br md 9.60 Dpth 5.30 Welded, 1 dk	**(A31A2GX) General Cargo Ship**	**1 oil engine** driving 1 Propeller Total Power: 736kW (1,001hp) Hanshin LH28LG 1 x 4 Stroke 6 Cy. 280 x 530 736kW (1001bhp) The Hanshin Diesel Works Ltd-Japan
9016545 *V6P1164* -	**SEIPAL** *ex* Eikyu Maru No. 2 *-1990* - - *Micronesia*	*349* - -		**1990-12 Niigata Engineering Co Ltd — Niigata NI** Yd No: 2203 Loa 63.24 (BB) Br ex - Dght 4.460 Lbp 55.00 Br md 12.00 Dpth 7.27 Welded	**(B11B2FV) Fishing Vessel** Ins: 1,128	**1 oil engine** with clutches, flexible couplings & dr geared to sc. shaft driving 1 CP propeller Total Power: 1,986kW (2,700hp) Niigata 6M40CFX 1 x 4 Stroke 6 Cy. 400 x 600 1986kW (2700bhp) Niigata Engineering Co Ltd-Japan Thrusters: 1 Thwart. FP thruster (f)
9223124 *LLFV* M-123-SA	**SEIR** *ex* Saetring *-2007* **Seir AS** Oddvar Urkedal *Aalesund* *Norway* MMSI: 257225000	**850** 255 400	Class: NV	**2000-10 Stocznia Cenal Sp z oo — Gdansk** (Hull) Yd No: 124 **2000-10 Larsnes Mek. Verksted AS — Larsnes** Yd No: 37 Loa 39.90 Br ex - Dght 4.460 Lbp 35.80 Br md 10.60 Dpth 7.30 Welded, 1 dk	**(B11B2FV) Fishing Vessel** Ins: 405 Ice Capable	**1 oil engine** geared to sc. shaft driving 1 CP propeller Total Power: 956kW (1,300hp) Yanmar 6N21A-EN 1 x 4 Stroke 6 Cy. 210 x 290 956kW (1300bhp) Yanmar Diesel Engine Co Ltd-Japan AuxGen: 1 x 322kW a.c, 1 x 462kW a.c Thrusters: 1 Thwart. FP thruster (f)
8889725 *JK5422* -	**SEIREI MARU** *ex* Shorei Maru *-2009* **Omaezaki Kaiun KK** - *Osakikamijima, Hiroshima* *Japan* MMSI: 431400416 Official number: 134667	*446* - 949		**1995-04 Koike Zosen Kaiun KK — Osakikamijima** Loa 67.00 Br ex - Dght 3.920 Lbp 62.00 Br md 11.80 Dpth 6.25 Welded, 1 dk	**(A24D2BA) Aggregates Carrier** Compartments: 1 Ho, ER 1 Ha: (27.6 x 9.3)ER Cranes: 1x3t	**1 oil engine** driving 1 FP propeller Total Power: 736kW (1,001hp) 11.6kn Hanshin LH31G 1 x 4 Stroke 6 Cy. 310 x 530 736kW (1001bhp) The Hanshin Diesel Works Ltd-Japan
9004748 *JI3442* -	**SEIREN MARU No. 3** - **KK Tatsumi Shokai & Genkai Kisen KK** Genkai Kisen KK *Osaka, Osaka* *Japan* Official number: 131690	*201* - 546		**1990-09 Taiyo Shipbuilding Co Ltd — Sanyoonoda YC** Yd No: 221 Loa 48.17 Br ex - Dght 3.050 Lbp 44.00 Br md 8.00 Dpth 3.45 Welded, 1 dk	**(A12A2TC) Chemical Tanker** Liq: 342 Compartments: 6 Ta, ER 2 Cargo Pump (s): 2x150m³/hr	**1 oil engine** with clutches & geared to sc. shaft driving 1 FP propeller Total Power: 588kW (799hp) Yanmar MF24-UT 1 x 4 Stroke 6 Cy. 240 x 420 588kW (799bhp) Matsue Diesel KK-Japan
8961066 *JH2507* -	**SEIRIKI MARU** *ex* Jinsei Maru *-2002* **Masayasu Ozaki** - *Gamagori, Aichi* *Japan* Official number: 111258	*196* - 366		**1971-07 Itoh Zosen K.K. — Nagoya** Loa 36.20 Br ex - Dght 3.000 Lbp 32.00 Br md 6.80 Dpth 3.20 Welded, 1 dk	**(A31A2GX) General Cargo Ship**	**1 oil engine** driving 1 FP propeller Total Power: 169kW (230hp) 8.5kn
8617586 *JNNI* -	**SEIRYO MARU No. 1** - **Tokio Yonegawa** - SatCom: Inmarsat B 343175110 *Yaizu, Shizuoka* *Japan* MMSI: 431751000 Official number: 128608	*221* - -		**1987-03 Katsuura Dockyard Co. Ltd. — Nachi-Katsuura** Yd No: 286 Loa 44.50 (BB) Br ex - Dght 3.150 Lbp 37.01 Br md 7.51 Dpth 3.18 Welded, 1 dk	**(B11B2FV) Fishing Vessel** Ins: 260	**1 oil engine** driving 1 CP propeller Total Power: 625kW (850hp) 11.0kn Hanshin 6LU24 1 x 4 Stroke 6 Cy. 240 x 410 625kW (850bhp) The Hanshin Diesel Works Ltd-Japan AuxGen: 2 x 240kW a.c

Identity / Name / Owner	Tonnage	Class	Build / Dimensions	Type	Machinery
9037616 **SEIRYO MARU No. 2** *JE3050* - **YK Iwai Shoten** - *Kesennuma, Miyagi* *Japan* Official number: 132227	*119* - -		**1991**-11 **Kesennuma Tekko — Kesennuma** Yd No: 282 L reg 31.60 Br ex - Dght - Lbp 31.50 Br md 6.40 Dpth 2.80 Welded, 1 dk	**(B11B2FV) Fishing Vessel**	**1 oil engine** with clutches, flexible couplings & sr geared to sc. shaft driving 1 CP propeller Total Power: 592kW (805hp) Niigata 6M26AFTE 1 x 4 Stroke 6 Cy. 260 x 460 592kW (805bhp) Niigata Engineering Co Ltd-Japan
8509894 **SEIRYO MARU No. 8** *JHBC* MG1-1421 **Nihon Maguro Shigen Kenkyujo KK** - SatCom: Inmarsat A 1200274 *Kesennuma, Miyagi* *Japan* MMSI: 431702950 Official number: 128193	*409* - 387		**1985**-10 **Goriki Zosensho — Ise** Yd No: 873 Loa 53.88 Br ex - Dght 3.352 Lbp 46.69 Br md 8.01 Dpth 3.71 Welded, 1 dk	**(B11B2FV) Fishing Vessel** Ins: 476	**1 oil engine** sr geared to sc. shaft driving 1 CP propeller Total Power: 736kW (1,001hp) Niigata 6M28AFTE 1 x 4 Stroke 6 Cy. 280 x 480 736kW (1001bhp) Niigata Engineering Co Ltd-Japan
9041710 **SEIRYO MARU No. 12** *JQGF* MG1-1853 **Nihon Maguro Shigen Kenkyujo KK** - SatCom: Inmarsat A 1204674 *Kesennuma, Miyagi* *Japan* MMSI: 431702020 Official number: 132225	*379* - -		**1991**-10 **Niigata Engineering Co Ltd — Niigata NI** Yd No: 2225 Loa 56.43 (BB) Br ex - Dght 3.440 Lbp 49.10 Br md 8.80 Dpth 3.80 Welded, 1 dk	**(B11B2FV) Fishing Vessel** Ins: 478	**1 oil engine** with clutches, flexible couplings & sr geared to sc. shaft driving 1 CP propeller Total Power: 699kW (950hp) Niigata 6M28HFT 1 x 4 Stroke 6 Cy. 280 x 480 699kW (950bhp) Niigata Engineering Co Ltd-Japan
8876833 **SEIRYO MARU No. 35** *JD2479* - **YK Ohara Gyogyobu** - *Shiriuchi, Hokkaido* *Japan* Official number: 118696	*125* - -		**1980**-06 **Kyowa Zosen — Kesennuma** L reg 28.00 Br ex - Dght - Lbp 26.50 Br md 5.70 Dpth 2.80 Welded, 1 dk	**(B11B2FV) Fishing Vessel**	**1 oil engine** driving 1 FP propeller Niigata 1 x 4 Stroke Niigata Engineering Co Ltd-Japan
7700764 **SEIRYO MARU No. 38** - - **Fisheries Project Implementation Department Stats Trading Organization** - *Male* *Maldives*	*299* 154 -		**1977**-09 **Goriki Zosensho — Ise** Yd No: 788 Loa - Br ex - Dght 3.252 Lbp 43.77 Br md 8.31 Dpth 3.66 Welded, 1 dk	**(B11B2FV) Fishing Vessel**	**1 oil engine** driving 1 FP propeller Total Power: 736kW (1,001hp) Niigata 6L25BX 1 x 4 Stroke 6 Cy. 250 x 320 736kW (1001bhp) Niigata Engineering Co Ltd-Japan
9083689 **SEIRYO MARU No. 55** *JD2675* - **YK Ohara Gyogyobu** - *Shiriuchi, Hokkaido* *Japan* Official number: 128588	*119* - 153		**1993**-09 **Y.K. Yoshida Zosensho — Japan** Yd No: 383 Loa 38.25 (BB) Br ex - Dght 2.500 Lbp 31.25 Br md 6.40 Dpth 2.80 Welded	**(B11B2FV) Fishing Vessel** Bale: 137	**1 oil engine** with clutches, flexible couplings & sr geared to sc. shaft driving 1 CP propeller Total Power: 588kW (799hp) Niigata 6M26AFTE 1 x 4 Stroke 6 Cy. 260 x 460 588kW (799bhp) Niigata Engineering Co Ltd-Japan
9234874 **SEIRYO MARU No. 65** *JD2755* - **YK Ohara Gyogyobu** - *Shiriuchi, Hokkaido* *Japan* Official number: 135351	*183* - -		**2000**-03 **K.K. Yoshida Zosen Tekko — Kesennuma** Yd No: 517 L reg 34.30 Br ex - Dght - Lbp - Br md 7.00 Dpth 3.00 Welded, 1 dk	**(B11B2FV) Fishing Vessel**	**1 oil engine** driving 1 FP propeller Niigata 1 x 4 Stroke Niigata Engineering Co Ltd-Japan
9162344 **SEIRYU** *JL6546* *ex* Shinei Maru No. 11 *-2006* - **Seitoku Kaiun Kensetsu KK** - *Toba, Mie* *Japan* MMSI: 431500624 Official number: 135576	*716* - 2,100		**1997**-05 **Hitachi Zosen Mukaishima Marine Co Ltd — Onomichi HS** Yd No: 113 L reg 69.99 Br ex - Dght 4.830 Lbp 68.00 Br md 14.60 Dpth 8.06 Welded, 1 dk	**(A31A2GX) General Cargo Ship**	**1 oil engine** driving 1 FP propeller Total Power: 1,471kW (2,000hp) Hanshin LH38L 1 x 4 Stroke 6 Cy. 380 x 760 1471kW (2000bhp) The Hanshin Diesel Works Ltd-Japan
9135121 **SEIRYU MARU** *JK5471* - **Oshima Butsuryu Co Ltd** - *Shikokuchuo, Ehime* *Japan* Official number: 134784	*498* - 1,505		**1995**-11 **Kanmon Zosen K.K. — Shimonoseki** Yd No: 568 Loa 74.10 (BB) Br ex 12.52 Dght - Lbp 70.00 Br md 12.50 Dpth 3.79 Welded, 2 dks	**(A31A2GX) General Cargo Ship** Bale: 2,535 Compartments: 1 Ho, ER 1 Ha: ER	**1 oil engine** with clutches & reverse geared to sc. shaft driving 1 FP propeller Total Power: 736kW (1,001hp) Akasaka A31R 1 x 4 Stroke 6 Cy. 310 x 600 736kW (1001bhp) Akasaka Tekkosho KK (Akasaka DieselLtd)-Japan
8914984 **SEIRYU MARU** *JM5893* - **Nichiyo Kaiun KK** Nichiyo Kaiun YK *Shimonoseki, Yamaguchi* *Japan* MMSI: 431401059 Official number: 131290	*697* - 1,488	Class: NK	**1990**-03 **Kambara Marine Development & Shipbuilding Co Ltd — Fukuyama HS** Yd No: OE-166 Loa 68.98 (BB) Br ex 11.52 Dght 4.290 Lbp 65.00 Br md 11.50 Dpth 5.10 Welded, 1 dk	**(A24A2BT) Cement Carrier** Grain: 1,466 Compartments: 4 Ho, ER	**1 oil engine** with clutches, flexible couplings & sr geared to sc. shaft driving 1 CP propeller Total Power: 1,177kW (1,600hp) 11.3kn Yanmar 6Z280-EN 1 x 4 Stroke 6 Cy. 280 x 360 1177kW (1600bhp) Yanmar Diesel Engine Co Ltd-Japan AuxGen: 1 x 280kW 445V 60Hz a.c, 1 x 200kW 445V 60Hz a.c Fuel: 60.0 (d.f.)
8731708 **SEIRYU MARU** *JD2414* - **Koike Kisen KK** - *Onagawa, Miyagi* *Japan* Official number: 140539	*498* - 1,700		**2007**-03 **Namikata Shipbuilding Co Ltd — Imabari EH** Yd No: 222 Loa 74.50 Br ex - Dght 4.320 Lbp 68.00 Br md 12.00 Dpth 7.35 Welded, 1 dk	**(A31A2GX) General Cargo Ship** Compartments: 1 Ho, ER 1 Ha: ER (40.0 x 9.5)	**1 oil engine** driving 1 Propeller Total Power: 1,618kW (2,200hp) 11.5kn Hanshin LH34LA 1 x 4 Stroke 6 Cy. 340 x 640 1618kW (2200bhp) The Hanshin Diesel Works Ltd-Japan
8707991 **SEIRYU MARU** - *ex* Nikko Maru *-1991* - - *China*	*184* - -		**1987**-10 **Kanagawa Zosen — Kobe** Yd No: 299 Loa 33.20 Br ex - Dght 2.901 Lbp 29.88 Br md 8.81 Dpth 3.71 Welded, 1 dk	**(B32A2ST) Tug**	**2 oil engines** driving 2 FP propellers Total Power: 2,206kW (3,000hp) 14.0kn Niigata 6L25CXE 2 x 4 Stroke 6 Cy. 250 x 320 each-1103kW (1500bhp) Niigata Engineering Co Ltd-Japan AuxGen: 2 x 64kW 225V 60Hz a.c, 1 x 32kW 225V 60Hz a.c
8514708 **SEIRYU MARU** - - **Daiei Shipping Co Ltd** -	*694* - 1,517		**1985**-12 **Kochi Jyuko (Kaisei Zosen) K.K. — Kochi** Yd No: 1863 Loa 70.31 (BB) Br ex - Dght 4.152 Lbp 64.01 Br md 11.21 Dpth 4.81 Welded, 1 dk	**(B34E2SV) Incinerator**	**1 oil engine** driving 1 FP propeller Total Power: 1,324kW (1,800hp) Akasaka A31 1 x 4 Stroke 6 Cy. 310 x 600 1324kW (1800bhp) Akasaka Tekkosho KK (Akasaka DieselLtd)-Japan
9323285 **SEIRYU MARU** *7JAC* - **Government of Japan (Ministry of Land, Infrastructure & Transport - Bureau of Ports & Harbours - Chubu Regional Bureau)** - *Nagoya, Aichi* *Japan* MMSI: 432501000 Official number: 140055	**4,792** - 3,320		**2005**-03 **Mitsubishi Heavy Industries Ltd. — Kobe** Yd No: 1258 Loa 104.00 Br ex 17.66 Dght 5.600 Lbp 96.00 Br md 17.40 Dpth 7.50 Welded, 1 dk	**(B33B2DT) Trailing Suction Hopper Dredger** Hopper: 1,700	**2 oil engines** reduction geared to sc. shafts driving 2 Propellers Total Power: 5,720kW (7,776hp) Niigata 8L28HLX 2 x 4 Stroke 8 Cy. 280 x 400 each-2860kW (3888bhp) Niigata Engineering Co Ltd-Japan Thrusters: 1 Tunnel thruster (f)
9599975 **SEIRYU MARU** *JD3018* - **Inoshita Kaiun KK** - *Niihama, Ehime* *Japan* Official number: 141180	*498* - 1,600		**2010**-01 **K.K. Watanabe Zosensho — Nagasaki** Yd No: 166 Loa 76.12 Br ex - Dght 4.030 Lbp 70.20 Br md 12.30 Dpth 7.00 Welded, 1 dk	**(A31A2GX) General Cargo Ship** Bale: 2,506 1 Ha: ER (40.0 x 10.0)	**1 oil engine** reduction geared to sc. shaft driving 1 Propeller Total Power: 1,471kW (2,000hp) Hanshin LH34LG 1 x 4 Stroke 6 Cy. 340 x 640 1471kW (2000bhp) The Hanshin Diesel Works Ltd-Japan
9667667 **SEIRYU MARU** *JD3476* - **Nissei Unyu YK** - *Imabari, Ehime* *Japan* MMSI: 431004176 Official number: 141856	*270* - 820		**2013**-01 **Yamanaka Zosen K.K. — Imabari** Yd No: 832 Loa 60.80 Br ex - Dght 3.520 Lbp - Br md 9.80 Dpth - Welded, 1 dk	**(A31A2GX) General Cargo Ship**	**1 oil engine** driving 1 Propeller Total Power: 1,176kW (1,599hp) Hanshin LH28L 1 x 4 Stroke 6 Cy. 280 x 530 1176kW (1599bhp) The Hanshin Diesel Works Ltd-Japan

IMO / Call sign / Flag	Name / Owner	Tonnage	Class	Build / Dimensions	Type	Machinery
8989616 *JM6734* -	**SEIRYU MARU NO. 5** **YK Asano Suisan** - SatCom: Inmarsat C 443242510 *Nango, Miyazaki* *Japan* MMSI: 432425000 Official number: 136454	*119* - -		**2003-09 Higashi Kyushu Shipbuilding Co Ltd — Usuki OT** Loa 39.00 Br ex - Dght 2.040 Lbp - Br md 5.83 Dpth 2.60 Bonded, 1 dk	**(B11B2FV) Fishing Vessel** Hull Material: Reinforced Plastic	**1 oil engine** reduction geared to sc. shaft driving 1 Propeller Total Power: 721kW (980hp) Niigata 6MG28HX 1 x 4 Stroke 6 Cy. 280 x 370 721kW (980bhp) Niigata Engineering Co Ltd-Japan
9046643 *JK5175* -	**SEIRYU MARU No. 7** **Takashi Miyazaki** - *Hiroshima, Hiroshima* *Japan* Official number: 133054	*499* - 1,471		**1992-05 Hitachi Zosen Mukaishima Marine Co Ltd — Onomichi HS** Yd No: 60 Loa 66.93 (BB) Br ex 13.10 Dght 4.560 Lbp 61.00 Br md 13.00 Dpth 7.53 Welded, 2 dks	**(A31A2GX) General Cargo Ship** Grain: 1,248 Compartments: 1 Ho, ER 1 Ha: ER	**1 oil engine** with clutches & reverse geared to sc. shaft driving 1 FP propeller Total Power: 736kW (1,001hp) Niigata 6M34AGT 1 x 4 Stroke 6 Cy. 340 x 620 736kW (1001bhp) Niigata Engineering Co Ltd-Japan Thrusters: 1 Thwart. FP thruster (f)
8844854 *JL5821* -	**SEIRYU MARU NO. 8** *ex* Seifuku Maru No. 8 *-2005* **Hironaka Kaiun YK** - *Hirao, Yamaguchi* *Japan* Official number: 131479	*174* - 345		**1990-10 Hongawara Zosen K.K. — Fukuyama** Loa 41.70 Br ex - Dght 2.900 Lbp 37.00 Br md 7.20 Dpth 3.30 Welded, 1 dk	**(A12A2TC) Chemical Tanker** 1 Cargo Pump (s): 1x150m³/hr	**1 oil engine** driving 1 FP propeller Total Power: 441kW (600hp) 9.5kn Yanmar MF24-HT 1 x 4 Stroke 6 Cy. 240 x 420 441kW (600bhp) Yanmar Diesel Engine Co Ltd-Japan
8975902 *JM6732* -	**SEIRYU MARU NO. 18** **Seiryu Suisan YK** - SatCom: Inmarsat C 443236610 *Nango, Miyazaki* *Japan* MMSI: 432366000 Official number: 136452	*119* - -		**2002-10 Higashi Kyushu Shipbuilding Co Ltd — Usuki OT** Yd No: 873 L reg 31.00 Br ex - Dght - Lbp - Br md 5.83 Dpth 2.60 Bonded, 1 dk	**(B11B2FV) Fishing Vessel** Hull Material: Reinforced Plastic	**1 oil engine** driving 1 Propeller Niigata 6MG28HX 1 x 4 Stroke 6 Cy. 280 x 370 Niigata Engineering Co Ltd-Japan
7634379 *WBB8821* -	**SEIS SURVEYOR** *ex* Obi III *-1985* *ex* Lamco Carrier *-1981* **Fugro Properties Inc** - SatCom: Inmarsat A 1517242 *Patterson, LA* *United States of America* MMSI: 367074850 Official number: 575398	**573** 171 1,050		**1976-07 Zigler Shipyards Inc — Jennings LA** Yd No: 250 Converted From: Offshore Supply Ship-1976 Loa 45.73 Br ex 11.03 Dght 3.301 Lbp 41.46 Br md 10.98 Dpth 3.81 Welded	**(B31A2SR) Research Survey Vessel**	**1 oil engine** driving 1 FP propeller Total Power: 1,250kW (1,700hp) Caterpillar 1 x 4 Stroke 1250kW (1700bhp) Caterpillar Tractor Co-USA
9185580 *JM6633* -	**SEISEN MARU** **Kotoku Kisen KK** - *Sasebo, Nagasaki* *Japan* MMSI: 431601615 Official number: 136382	*999* - 1,310	Class: NK	**1998-10 K.K. Miura Zosensho — Saiki** Yd No: 1215 Loa 71.50 (BB) Br ex - Dght 4.513 Lbp 65.50 Br md 12.50 Dpth 5.50 Welded, 1 dk	**(A11B2TG) LPG Tanker** Liq (Gas): 1,829 2 x Gas Tank (s); 2 independent cyl horizontal 2 Cargo Pump (s): 2x500m³/hr	**1 oil engine** driving 1 FP propeller Total Power: 1,765kW (2,400hp) 12.8kn Akasaka A37 1 x 4 Stroke 6 Cy. 370 x 720 1765kW (2400bhp) Akasaka Tekkosho KK (Akasaka DieselLtd)-Japan Fuel: 210.0 (d.f.)
9156682 *JL6275* -	**SEISHIN MARU** **Inoshita Kaiun KK** - *Niihama, Ehime* *Japan* Official number: 134860	*499* - 1,600		**1996-10 K.K. Matsuura Zosensho — Osakikamijima** Yd No: 520 Loa - Br ex - Dght 4.200 Lbp 70.00 Br md 12.00 Dpth 7.20 Welded, 1 dk	**(A31A2GX) General Cargo Ship**	**1 oil engine** driving 1 FP propeller Total Power: 736kW (1,001hp) Hanshin LH30LG 1 x 4 Stroke 6 Cy. 300 x 600 736kW (1001bhp) The Hanshin Diesel Works Ltd-Japan
9523342 *JD2840* -	**SEISHIN MARU NO. 1** **Maruju Kaiun Co Ltd** - *Niihama, Ehime* *Japan* Official number: 140894	*499* - 1,835		**2008-11 Yamanaka Zosen K.K. — Imabari** Yd No: 770 Loa 74.24 Br ex - Dght 4.360 Lbp 68.00 Br md 12.00 Dpth 7.37 Welded, 1 dk	**(A31A2GX) General Cargo Ship** Grain: 2,921; Bale: 2,838 1 Ha: ER (40.0 x 9.5)	**1 oil engine** driving 1 FP propeller Total Power: 1,323kW (1,799hp) Hanshin LH30LG 1 x 4 Stroke 6 Cy. 300 x 600 1323kW (1799bhp) The Hanshin Diesel Works Ltd-Japan
8922618 *JM6359* -	**SEISHIN MARU No. 2** **Nishida Shoji KK** - *Sasebo, Nagasaki* *Japan* Official number: 134597	*362* - 709		**1996-03 KK Yanase Dock — Onomichi HS** Loa 58.00 Br ex - Dght 3.320 Lbp 52.00 Br md 12.00 Dpth 6.20 Welded, 1 dk	**(A24D2BA) Aggregates Carrier**	**1 oil engine** driving 1 FP propeller Total Power: 736kW (1,001hp) 11.0kn Yanmar DY28-EN 1 x 4 Stroke 6 Cy. 280 x 530 736kW (1001bhp) Yanmar Diesel Engine Co Ltd-Japan Thrusters: 1 Tunnel thruster (f)
9037680 *JM6122* -	**SEISHO MARU** **KK Nagai** - *Imari, Saga* *Japan* Official number: 132611	*183* - -		**1991-10 K.K. Odo Zosen Tekko — Shimonoseki** Yd No: 501 Loa 32.00 Br ex 9.24 Dght 3.000 Lbp 27.00 Br md 9.00 Dpth 3.80 Welded, 1 dk	**(B32A2ST) Tug**	**2 oil engines** Geared Integral to driving 2 Z propellers Total Power: 2,280kW (3,100hp) Niigata 6L25HX 2 x 4 Stroke 6 Cy. 250 x 350 each-1140kW (1550bhp) Niigata Engineering Co Ltd-Japan
9068079 *JK5358* -	**SEISHO MARU** *ex* Kaiyo Maru *-2008* **YK Miura Kaiun** - *Hazu, Aichi* *Japan* Official number: 134109	*492* - 1,000		**1993-12 Amakusa Zosen K.K. — Amakusa** Loa 50.54 Br ex - Dght - Lbp 43.50 Br md 12.00 Dpth 5.30 Welded, 1 dk	**(A24D2BA) Aggregates Carrier**	**1 oil engine** driving 1 FP propeller Total Power: 736kW (1,001hp) 10.0kn Niigata 6M28BGT 1 x 4 Stroke 6 Cy. 280 x 480 736kW (1001bhp) Niigata Engineering Co Ltd-Japan
9608037 *JD3182* -	**SEISHO MARU** **Inoshita Kaiun KK** - *Niihama, Ehime* *Japan* Official number: 141420	*499* - 1,700		**2011-04 Fujiwara Zosensho — Imabari** Yd No: 165 Loa 74.71 Br ex - Dght 4.150 Lbp 69.50 Br md 12.20 Dpth 7.10 Welded, 1 dk	**(A31A2GX) General Cargo Ship** Grain: 2,507; Bale: 2,507 1 Ha: ER (40.1 x 9.7)	**1 oil engine** driving 1 FP propeller Total Power: 1,618kW (2,200hp) Hanshin LA32G 1 x 4 Stroke 6 Cy. 320 x 680 1618kW (2200bhp) The Hanshin Diesel Works Ltd-Japan
9194828 *JI3655* -	**SEISHO MARU** **Matsuda Kisen KK** - *Osaka, Osaka* *Japan* Official number: 135957	*322* - 665		**1998-07 Hongawara Zosen K.K. — Fukuyama** Yd No: 493 Loa 52.70 Br ex - Dght 3.350 Lbp 47.95 Br md 9.00 Dpth 3.70 Welded, 1 dk	**(A12A2TC) Chemical Tanker** Liq: 597 Compartments: 3 Ta, ER 2 Cargo Pump (s): 2x220m³/hr	**1 oil engine** driving 1 FP propeller Total Power: 736kW (1,001hp) 11.0kn Hanshin LH26G 1 x 4 Stroke 6 Cy. 260 x 440 736kW (1001bhp) The Hanshin Diesel Works Ltd-Japan
9192131 *JG5533* -	**SEISHO MARU** **EPDC Coal Tech & Marine Co Ltd & Shinwa Naiko Kaiun KK** Shinwa Naiko Kaiun Kaisha Ltd *Tokyo* *Japan* MMSI: 431100544 Official number: 136590	*1,767* - 2,300 T/cm 9.6	Class: NK	**1998-06 Kanmon Zosen K.K. — Shimonoseki** Yd No: 600 Loa 86.52 (BB) Br ex - Dght 5.127 Lbp 80.00 Br md 14.00 Dpth 6.00 Welded, 1 dk	**(A24H2BZ) Powder Carrier** Grain: 2,700 Compartments: 6 Ho, ER 6 Ha: ER	**1 oil engine** driving 1 CP propeller Total Power: 2,207kW (3,001hp) 14.0kn Hanshin LH38L 1 x 4 Stroke 6 Cy. 380 x 760 2207kW (3001bhp) The Hanshin Diesel Works Ltd-Japan AuxGen: 2 x 435kW a.c Thrusters: 1 Thwart. CP thruster (f) Fuel: 135.0 (d.f.)
8910005 *JH3165* -	**SEISHO MARU NO. 1** *ex* Seiyo Maru No. 1 *-2002* **Seiyo Suisan YK** - *Minami-ise, Mie* *Japan* MMSI: 432280000 Official number: 130079	*135* - -		**1989-04 K.K. Watanabe Zosensho — Nagasaki** Yd No: 1156 Loa 46.46 (BB) Br ex - Dght 2.901 Lbp 37.00 Br md 7.90 Dpth 3.22 Welded, 1 dk	**(B11B2FV) Fishing Vessel**	**1 oil engine** with clutches, flexible couplings & dr geared to sc. shaft driving 1 CP propeller Total Power: 861kW (1,171hp) Niigata 6MG28HX 1 x 4 Stroke 6 Cy. 280 x 370 861kW (1171bhp) Niigata Engineering Co Ltd-Japan Thrusters: 1 Thwart. FP thruster (f)
9068093 *JH3328* -	**SEISHO MARU NO. 2** **Kazuhisa Miura** - *Hazu, Aichi* *Japan* Official number: 133240	*279* - 700		**1993-12 Y.K. Okajima Zosensho — Matsuyama** Yd No: 242 Loa 44.93 Br ex - Dght - Lbp 39.80 Br md 8.30 Dpth 4.00 Welded, 1 dk	**(A31A2GX) General Cargo Ship**	**1 oil engine** reduction geared to sc. shaft driving 1 FP propeller Total Power: 588kW (799hp) 9.5kn Yanmar 6N165-EN 1 x 4 Stroke 6 Cy. 165 x 232 588kW (799bhp) Yanmar Diesel Engine Co Ltd-Japan
7950395 - -	**SEISHO MARU No. 3** - -	*254* - -		**1974-01 Kochi Jyuko K.K. — Kochi** Yd No: 1197 L reg 42.10 Br ex - Dght - Lbp - Br md 7.80 Dpth 3.41 Welded, 1 dk	**(B11B2FV) Fishing Vessel**	**1 oil engine** driving 1 FP propeller Total Power: 662kW (900hp) Akasaka 1 x 4 Stroke 662kW (900bhp) Akasaka Tekkosho KK (Akasaka DieselLtd)-Japan

Number / Call sign / Flag	Name / Owner	Tonnage	Class	Built / Dimensions	Type	Machinery
8854017 *JH3197* -	**SEISHO MARU No. 8** **Nobuo Miura** - *Nishio, Aichi* Japan Official number: 131608	*242* - 299		**1991-04 Y.K. Okajima Zosensho — Matsuyama** Yd No: 234 Loa 42.00 Br ex - Dght 2.400 Lbp 38.50 Br md 7.80 Dpth 3.80 Welded, 1 dk	**(A31A2GX) General Cargo Ship**	**1 oil engine** driving 1 FP propeller Total Power: 287kW (390hp) 8.0kn Sumiyoshi S23G 1 x 4 Stroke 6 Cy. 230 x 400 287kW (390bhp) Sumiyoshi Marine Diesel Co Ltd-Japan
8811895 *JH3147* -	**SEISHO MARU NO. 18** *ex* Seiyo Maru No. 18 *-2002* **Seiyo Suisan YK** - *Minami-ise, Mie* Japan MMSI: 432281000 Official number: 128500	*199* - 300		**1988-03 Watanabe Zosen KK — Imabari EH** Yd No: 1131 Loa 48.30 (BB) Br ex 7.71 Dght - Lbp 40.50 Br md 7.70 Dpth 3.86 Welded	**(B12B2FC) Fish Carrier**	**1 oil engine** sr geared to sc. shaft driving 1 FP propeller Total Power: 861kW (1,171hp) Yanmar 6Z280-ET 1 x 4 Stroke 6 Cy. 280 x 360 861kW (1171bhp) Yanmar Diesel Engine Co Ltd-Japan Thrusters: 1 Thwart. FP thruster (f)
8849098 - -	**SEISHO MARU No. 28** *ex* Eiho Maru No. 81 *-1996* *ex* Miyajima Maru No. 32 *-1990* -	*138* - -		**1976-01 Ishimura Zosen — Kimaishi** L reg 30.20 Br ex - Dght - Lbp - Br md 6.20 Dpth 2.80 Welded, 1 dk	**(B11B2FV) Fishing Vessel**	**1 oil engine** driving 1 FP propeller Total Power: 346kW (470hp) Hanshin 1 x 4 Stroke 346kW (470bhp) The Hanshin Diesel Works Ltd-Japan
9032343 *JH3210* -	**SEISHO MARU NO. 35** *ex* Seiyo Maru No. 35 *-2002* **Seiyo Suisan YK** - *Minami-ise, Mie* Japan MMSI: 432283000 Official number: 131586	*283* - -		**1991-05 K.K. Watanabe Zosensho — Nagasaki** Yd No: 1183 Loa 51.73 (BB) Br ex 8.02 Dght 3.801 Lbp 43.01 Br md 8.00 Dpth 4.12 Welded	**(B12B2FC) Fish Carrier** Ins: 349	**1 oil engine** with clutches, flexible couplings & sr reverse geared to sc. shaft driving 1 CP propeller Total Power: 853kW (1,160hp) Yanmar 6Z280-EN 1 x 4 Stroke 6 Cy. 280 x 360 853kW (1160bhp) Yanmar Diesel Engine Co Ltd-Japan Thrusters: 1 Thwart. FP thruster (f)
9032355 *JH3209* -	**SEISHO MARU NO. 38** *ex* Seiyo Maru No. 38 *-2002* **Seiyo Suisan YK** - *Minami-ise, Mie* Japan MMSI: 432284000 Official number: 130110	*286* - -		**1991-03 K.K. Watanabe Zosensho — Nagasaki** Yd No: 1185 Loa 51.73 (BB) Br ex 8.02 Dght 3.801 Lbp 43.00 Br md 8.00 Dpth 4.10 Welded	**(B12B2FC) Fish Carrier** Ins: 349	**1 oil engine** with clutches, flexible couplings & sr reverse geared to sc. shaft driving 1 CP propeller Total Power: 853kW (1,160hp) Yanmar 6Z280-EN 1 x 4 Stroke 6 Cy. 280 x 360 853kW (1160bhp) Yanmar Diesel Engine Co Ltd-Japan Thrusters: 1 Thwart. FP thruster (f)
8814603 - -	**SEISHO MARU NO. 38** *ex* Koei Maru No. 6 *-2007* **Yamada Suisan KK** -	*173* - -		**1988-03 Kesennuma Tekko — Kesennuma** Yd No: 267 Loa - (BB) Br ex 6.62 Dght - Lbp 31.91 Br md 6.61 Dpth 2.80 Welded, 1 dk	**(B11B2FV) Fishing Vessel**	**1 oil engine** with clutches, flexible couplings & sr geared to sc. shaft driving 1 FP propeller Total Power: 705kW (959hp) Akasaka K28FD 1 x 4 Stroke 6 Cy. 280 x 480 705kW (959bhp) Akasaka Tekkosho KK (Akasaka DieselLtd)-Japan Thrusters: 1 Thwart. FP thruster (f); 1 Thwart. FP thruster (a)
8504715 *7KSJ* -	**SEISHO MARU NO. 78** *ex* Koei Maru No. 21 *-1994* **Oyama Gyogyo YK** - *Matsue, Shimane* Japan Official number: 126643	*127* - 156		**1985-07 Yamanishi Shipbuilding Co Ltd — Ishinomaki MG** Yd No: 908 Loa 37.60 (BB) Br ex 6.63 Dght - Lbp 30.51 Br md 6.61 Dpth 3.13 Welded, 1 dk	**(B11A2FS) Stern Trawler**	**1 oil engine** with clutches, flexible couplings & sr geared to sc. shaft driving 1 CP propeller Total Power: 883kW (1,201hp) Akasaka DM26K 1 x 4 Stroke 6 Cy. 260 x 440 883kW (1201bhp) Akasaka Tekkosho KK (Akasaka DieselLtd)-Japan
8743268 *7JEV* ME1-958	**SEISHO MARU NO. 88** **Seiyo Suisan YK** - *Minami-ise, Mie* Japan Official number: 140972	*195* - -		**2009-03 K.K. Watanabe Zosensho — Nagasaki** Yd No: 165 Loa 49.16 (BB) Br ex - Dght 3.670 Lbp - Br md 7.40 Dpth 3.80 Welded, 1 dk	**(B11B2FV) Fishing Vessel** Ins: 182	**1 oil engine** reduction geared to sc. shaft driving 1 Propeller Total Power: 1,840kW (2,502hp) Yanmar 6EY26 1 x 4 Stroke 6 Cy. 260 x 385 1840kW (2502bhp) Yanmar Diesel Engine Co Ltd-Japan
9651527 *7JNC* -	**SEISHO MARU NO. 88** **Nemuro Gyogyo Kyodo Kumiai** - *Nemuro, Hokkaido* Japan Official number: 141768	*199* - 230		**2012-12 K.K. Yoshida Zosen Tekko — Kesennuma** Yd No: 557 Loa 46.20 Br ex - Dght 2.900 Lbp - Br md 7.50 Dpth - Welded, 1 dk	**(B11B2FV) Fishing Vessel**	**1 oil engine** reduction geared to sc. shaft driving 1 Propeller Total Power: 1,838kW (2,499hp) Niigata 6MG28HX 1 x 4 Stroke 6 Cy. 280 x 370 1838kW (2499bhp) Niigata Engineering Co Ltd-Japan
8221076 - -	**SEISHO No. 8** *ex* Seisho Maru No. 8 *-1999* - -	*197* - 492		**1982 K.K. Mochizuki Zosensho — Osakikamijima** Yd No: 118 Loa 47.35 (BB) Br ex 8.23 Dght 3.220 Lbp 43.52 Br md 8.21 Dpth 4.81 Welded, 2 dks	**(A31A2GX) General Cargo Ship** Grain: 866; Bale: 793 Compartments: 1 Ho, ER 1 Ha: ER	**1 oil engine** reverse reduction geared to sc. shaft driving 1 FP propeller Total Power: 368kW (500hp) Akasaka MH22R 1 x 4 Stroke 6 Cy. 220 x 390 368kW (500bhp) Akasaka Tekkosho KK (Akasaka DieselLtd)-Japan
9072666 *JG5208* -	**SEISHU MARU** **Kyodo Syosen KK (Kyodo Syosen Co Ltd)** - *Tokyo* Japan MMSI: 431400149 Official number: 133860	*699* - 2,040		**1993-04 K.K. Matsuura Zosensho — Osakikamijima** Yd No: 500 Loa 81.22 (BB) Br ex 12.63 Dght 4.650 Lbp 75.00 Br md 12.60 Dpth 7.50 Welded, 2 dks	**(A31A2GX) General Cargo Ship** Compartments: 1 Ho, ER	**1 oil engine** reverse geared to sc. shaft driving 1 FP propeller Total Power: 1,618kW (2,200hp) Niigata 6M34AGT 1 x 4 Stroke 6 Cy. 340 x 620 1618kW (2200bhp) Niigata Engineering Co Ltd-Japan Thrusters: 1 Thwart. FP thruster (f)
9066306 *JIKD* ME1-877	**SEISHU MARU NO. 7** *ex* Otoshiro Maru No. 31 *-2006* **Otoshiro Gyogyo KK** - SatCom: Inmarsat B 343115910 *Minami-ise, Mie* Japan MMSI: 431159000 Official number: 133203	*349* - 771		**1993-01 Miho Zosensho K.K. — Shimizu** Yd No: 1423 Loa 63.00 (BB) Br ex - Dght 4.453 Lbp 55.00 Br md 12.00 Dpth 7.26 Welded, 1 dk	**(B11B2FV) Fishing Vessel**	**1 oil engine** with clutches, flexible couplings & sr reverse geared to sc. shaft driving 1 CP propeller Total Power: 1,912kW (2,600hp) Hanshin 6LUS40 1 x 4 Stroke 6 Cy. 400 x 640 1912kW (2600bhp) The Hanshin Diesel Works Ltd-Japan Thrusters: 1 Thwart. FP thruster (f)
8415249 *JGJK* -	**SEISHU MARU NO. 8** *ex* Kyoyo Maru *-1995* *ex* Kyoyo Maru No. 2 *-1995* **Otoshiro Gyogyo KK** - SatCom: Inmarsat A 1206257 *Minami-ise, Mie* Japan MMSI: 431559000 Official number: 127078	*499* - -		**1984-11 Goriki Zosensho — Ise** Yd No: 868 Loa 64.67 (BB) Br ex - Dght - Lbp 56.01 Br md 9.40 Dpth 4.40 Welded, 1 dk	**(B11B2FV) Fishing Vessel** Ins: 672	**1 oil engine** sr geared to sc. shaft driving 1 FP propeller Total Power: 1,471kW (2,000hp) Hanshin 6LU35 1 x 4 Stroke 6 Cy. 350 x 550 1471kW (2000bhp) The Hanshin Diesel Works Ltd-Japan
7322299 - -	**SEISHU MARU No. 38** *ex* Baek Du San No. 2 *-1976* **Jin Yang Fisheries Co Ltd** - South Korea	*431* 215 508		**1973 Miho Zosensho K.K. — Shimizu** Yd No: 903 Loa 57.46 Br ex 9.02 Dght 3.699 Lbp 49.00 Br md 9.01 Dpth 4.09 Welded, 1 dk	**(B11B2FV) Fishing Vessel**	**1 oil engine** driving 1 FP propeller Total Power: 1,324kW (1,800hp) Akasaka AH33 1 x 4 Stroke 6 Cy. 330 x 500 1324kW (1800bhp) Akasaka Tekkosho KK (Akasaka DieselLtd)-Japan
9084970 - -	**SEISHUN** *ex* Seishun Maru *-2013* - -	*190* - 438	Class: IZ	**1993-02 K.K. Tago Zosensho — Nishi-Izu** Yd No: 251 Loa 41.35 Br ex 8.20 Dght 2.900 Lbp 37.00 Br md 8.00 Dpth 3.00 Welded, 1 dk	**(A13B2TP) Products Tanker** Liq: 416; Liq (Oil): 416	**1 oil engine** reverse geared to sc. shaft driving 1 FP propeller Total Power: 736kW (1,001hp) Akasaka T26SR 1 x 4 Stroke 6 Cy. 260 x 440 736kW (1001bhp) Akasaka Tekkosho KK (Akasaka DieselLtd)-Japan
9369045 *POAS* -	**SEISMIC SUPPORTER** *ex* PWM Supply *-2011* *ex* Crest Supply 1 *-2010* **Miclyn Express Offshore Pte Ltd** - *Batam* Indonesia MMSI: 525024006	**621** 188 706	Class: BV KI (AB)	**2006-04 Yuexin Shipbuilding Co Ltd — Guangzhou GD** Yd No: 3058 Loa 45.00 Br ex 11.82 Dght 3.800 Lbp 39.40 Br md 11.80 Dpth 4.60 Welded, 1 dk	**(B21B2OT) Offshore Tug/Supply Ship**	**2 oil engines** reduction geared to sc. shafts driving 2 FP propellers Total Power: 2,610kW (3,548hp) 11.0kn Caterpillar 3512B 2 x Vee 4 Stroke 12 Cy. 170 x 190 each-1305kW (1774bhp) Caterpillar Inc-USA AuxGen: 3 x 225kW 415V 50Hz a.c Thrusters: 1 Tunnel thruster (f) Fuel: 550.0 (d.f.)

9064657 *LGKM3* -	**SEISRANGER** **Seisranger AS** Forland Shipping AS *Bergen* *Norway (NIS)* MMSI: 258335000	**5,475** 1,637 2,495	Class: NV	1993-04 **Nordfjord Skipsindustri AS — Nordfjordeid** (Hull) Yd No: 39 1993-04 **Th Hellesoy Skipsbyggeri AS — Lofallstrand** Yd No: 124 Loa 86.60 (BB) Br ex - Dght 6.563 Lbp 74.60 Br md 20.00 Dpth 7.40 Welded, 3 dks	**(B31A2SR) Research Survey Vessel** Passengers: berths: 58 A-frames: 1x40t	**4 diesel electric oil engines** driving 2 gen. each 2312kW 2 gen. each 1540kW Connecting to 2 elec. motors each (1901kW) driving 2 CP propellers Total Power: 8,102kW (11,016hp) 14.0kn Bergens KVGB-12 2 x Vee 4 Stroke 12 Cy. 250 x 300 each-2431kW (3305bhp) Bergen Diesel AS-Norway Normo KRM-8 2 x 4 Stroke 8 Cy. 250 x 300 each-1620kW (2203bhp) Bergen Diesel AS-Norway AuxGen: 2 x 1200kW 660V a.c Thrusters: 1 Thwart. FP thruster (f); 2 Tunnel thruster (f); 2 Tunnel thruster (a) Fuel: 1317.0 (d.f.)
9052587 *CB5092* -	**SEISTROM** *ex* Don Roberto I *-2013* - - *Valparaiso* *Chile* MMSI: 725003110 Official number: 2785	*998* 257 939 T/cm 4.0		1993-05 **Astilleros Marco Chilena Ltda. — Iquique** Yd No: 204 Loa 48.40 (BB) Br ex 10.40 Dght 5.868 Lbp 43.30 Br md 10.20 Dpth 7.30 Welded, 1 dk	**(B11B2FV) Fishing Vessel**	**1 oil engine** with clutches & sr geared to sc. shaft driving 1 CP propeller Total Power: 1,824kW (2,480hp) 13.0kn Caterpillar 3606TA 1 x 4 Stroke 6 Cy. 280 x 300 1824kW (2480bhp) Caterpillar Inc-USA Thrusters: 1 Thwart. FP thruster (f); 1 Tunnel thruster (a)
9494072 *7JEJ* -	**SEISUI MARU** **Government of Japan (Ministry of Education, Culture, Sports, Science & Technology)** Mie University (Mie Daigakusei Monoshigen) *Tsu, Mie* *Japan* MMSI: 432683000 Official number: 140890	*318* - 180		2009-01 **Mitsubishi Heavy Industries Ltd. — Shimonoseki** Yd No: 1142 Loa 50.90 (BB) Br ex - Dght 3.300 Lbp 42.50 Br md 8.60 Dpth 3.75 Welded, 1 dk	**(B31A2SR) Research Survey Vessel**	**1 diesel electric oil engine** Connecting to 1 elec. Motor of (1000kW) driving 1 CP propeller
9058775 *JJ3800* -	**SEISUI MARU No. 8** **Nikko Kaiun YK** - *Himeji, Hyogo* *Japan* Official number: 132302	*493* - 995		1993-01 **Mukaishima Zoki Co. Ltd. — Onomichi** Yd No: 281 Loa 61.47 Br ex 9.82 Dght 4.150 Lbp 56.75 Br md 9.80 Dpth 4.40 Welded, 1 dk	**(A12A2TC) Chemical Tanker** Liq: 825 Compartments: 6 Wing Ta, ER 2 Cargo Pump (s): 2x200m³/hr	**1 oil engine** reverse geared to sc. shaft driving 1 FP propeller Total Power: 883kW (1,201hp) Niigata 6M28BGT 1 x 4 Stroke 6 Cy. 280 x 480 883kW (1201bhp) Niigata Engineering Co Ltd-Japan
8630423 *UFTK* -	**SEISYO MARU-38** *ex* Pacific Wave *-2013* *ex* Seisho Maru No. 38 *-2007* **Akvaresurs-DV Co Ltd (OOO 'Akvaresurs-DV')** - *Vladivostok* *Russia* MMSI: 273315570	**222** 69 135	Class: RS	1984-01 **K.K. Yoshida Zosen Tekko — Kesennuma** Loa 37.30 Br ex 7.40 Dght 2.580 Lbp 31.88 Br md 6.20 Dpth 2.90 Welded, 1 dk	**(B11B2FV) Fishing Vessel**	**1 oil engine** reduction geared to sc. shaft driving 1 FP propeller Total Power: 617kW (839hp) 10.0kn Yanmar T240-ET2 1 x 4 Stroke 6 Cy. 240 x 310 617kW (839bhp) Yanmar Diesel Engine Co Ltd-Japan
8889787 *JK5379* -	**SEITOKU** *ex* Shuei Maru *-2003* **YK Taiko Kisen** - *Kure, Hiroshima* *Japan* Official number: 134761	*199* - 536		1995-05 **Hongawara Zosen K.K. — Fukuyama** Loa 47.20 Br ex - Dght 3.210 Lbp 43.00 Br md 8.00 Dpth 3.45 Welded, 1 dk	**(A13B2TU) Tanker (unspecified)** Liq: 572; Liq (Oil): 572 1 Cargo Pump (s): 1x500m³/hr	**1 oil engine** driving 1 FP propeller Total Power: 588kW (799hp) 11.0kn Yanmar MF24-UT 1 x 4 Stroke 6 Cy. 240 x 420 588kW (799bhp) Yanmar Diesel Engine Co Ltd-Japan
8869610 - -	**SEITOKU MARU No. 28** *ex* Tenyu Maru No. 81 *-1997* - -	**168** - -		1976-07 **Narasaki Senpaku Kogyo K.K. — Muroran** L reg 28.10 Br ex - Dght - Lbp - Br md 5.80 Dpth 2.30 Welded, 1 dk	**(B11B2FV) Fishing Vessel**	**1 oil engine** driving 1 FP propeller
9442677 *JD2469* -	**SEITOKU NO. 1** **YK Taiko Kisen** - *Kure, Hiroshima* *Japan* Official number: 140600	*498* - 1,279		2007-09 **Imura Zosen K.K. — Komatsushima** Yd No: 321 Loa 65.23 Br ex - Dght 4.060 Lbp 59.98 Br md 10.40 Dpth 4.50 Welded, 1 dk	**(A13B2TP) Products Tanker** Double Hull (13F) Liq: 1,200; Liq (Oil): 1,200 2 Cargo Pump (s): 2x600m³/hr	**1 oil engine** reduction geared to sc. shaft driving 1 Propeller Total Power: 541kW (736hp) 11.0kn Niigata 6M28NT 1 x 4 Stroke 6 Cy. 280 x 480 541kW (736bhp) Niigata Engineering Co Ltd-Japan
9177600 *JLLY* -	**SEIUN MARU** **Government of Japan (Ministry of Land, Infrastructure & Transport)** - SatCom: Inmarsat B 343110310 *Tokyo* *Japan* MMSI: 431103000 Official number: 135874	**5,890** 1,767 2,673		1997-09 **Sumitomo Heavy Industries Ltd. — Yokosuka Shipyard, Yokosuka** Yd No: 1220 Loa 116.00 Br ex - Dght 6.300 Lbp 105.00 Br md 17.90 Dpth 10.80 Welded, 3 dks	**(B34K2QT) Training Ship**	**1 oil engine** driving 1 CP propeller Total Power: 7,723kW (10,500hp) 19.5kn B&W 6L50MC 1 x 2 Stroke 6 Cy. 500 x 1620 7723kW (10500bhp) Mitsui Engineering & Shipbuilding CLtd-Japan AuxGen: 3 x 800kW a.c Thrusters: 1 Thwart. CP thruster (f) Fuel: 208.0 (d.f.) 1288.0 (r.f.) 25.2pd
9414539 *JD2384* -	**SEIUN MARU NO. 10** **Okamoto Kaiun YK** - *Shodoshima, Kagawa* *Japan* Official number: 140494	*499* - 1,820		2007-03 **Yamanaka Zosen K.K. — Imabari** Yd No: 735 Loa 74.20 Br ex - Dght 4.360 Lbp 68.00 Br md 12.00 Dpth 7.37 Welded, 1 dk	**(A31A2GX) General Cargo Ship** Grain: 2,662; Bale: 2,643 1 Ha: ER (40.0 x 9.5)	**1 oil engine** driving 1 FP propeller Total Power: 1,323kW (1,799hp) Hanshin LH30LG 1 x 4 Stroke 6 Cy. 300 x 600 1323kW (1799bhp) The Hanshin Diesel Works Ltd-Japan
8960828 *JH2469* -	**SEIUN MARU No. 11** **Aoki Kensetsu KK** - *Atami, Shizuoka* *Japan* Official number: 115043	*196* - -		1972-11 **Oshima Kogyo K.K. — Yokosuka** Loa 26.70 Br ex - Dght 1.400 Lbp 24.70 Br md 13.00 Dpth 2.60 Welded, 1 dk	**(B33A2DG) Grab Dredger**	**2 oil engines** driving 2 FP propellers Total Power: 220kW (300hp) 7.0kn Kubota 2 x 4 Stroke each-110kW (150bhp) Kubota Corp-Japan
8952467 *JL6621* -	**SEIUN MARU No. 18** **Okamoto Kaiun YK** - *Uchinomi, Kagawa* *Japan* Official number: 136481	*499* - -		1999-09 **Yamanaka Zosen K.K. — Imabari** Yd No: 638 Loa 76.23 Br ex - Dght - Lbp 70.00 Br md 12.00 Dpth 7.01 Welded, 1 dk	**(A31A2GX) General Cargo Ship** Grain: 2,732; Bale: 2,672	**1 oil engine** driving 1 FP propeller Total Power: 1,324kW (1,800hp) 12.7kn Hanshin LH30LG 1 x 4 Stroke 6 Cy. 300 x 600 1324kW (1800bhp) The Hanshin Diesel Works Ltd-Japan Fuel: 100.0 (d.f.)
9556272 *JD2920* -	**SEIUN MARU NO. 28** **Okamoto Kaiun YK** - *Shodoshima, Kagawa* *Japan* Official number: 141025	*499* - 1,840		2009-05 **Yamanaka Zosen K.K. — Imabari** Yd No: 776 Loa 74.20 Br ex - Dght 4.360 Lbp 68.00 Br md 12.00 Dpth 7.37 Welded, 1 dk	**(A31A2GX) General Cargo Ship** Grain: 2,921; Bale: 2,838 1 Ha: ER (40.0 x 9.5)	**1 oil engine** reduction geared to sc. shaft driving 1 FP propeller Total Power: 1,323kW (1,799hp) Hanshin LH30L 1 x 4 Stroke 6 Cy. 300 x 600 1323kW (1799bhp) The Hanshin Diesel Works Ltd-Japan
9614270 *JD3216* -	**SEIUN MARU NO. 38** **Japan Railway Construction, Transport & Technology Agency & Okamoto Kaiun YK** Okamoto Kaiun YK *Shodoshima, Kagawa* *Japan* Official number: 141470	*499* - 1,840		2011-05 **Yamanaka Zosen K.K. — Imabari** Yd No: 812 Loa 74.24 Br ex - Dght 4.360 Lbp 68.00 Br md 12.00 Dpth 7.37 Welded, 1 dk	**(A31A2GX) General Cargo Ship** Grain: 2,921; Bale: 2,838 1 Ha: ER (40.0 x 9.5)	**1 oil engine** reduction geared to sc. shafts driving 1 FP propeller Total Power: 1,324kW (1,800hp) Hanshin LH30L 1 x 4 Stroke 6 Cy. 300 x 600 1324kW (1800bhp) The Hanshin Diesel Works Ltd-Japan
8035647 - -	**SEIUN NO. 13** *ex* Seiun Maru No. 13 *-2009* **Palpal Underwater Co Ltd** - *South Korea*	*199* - -		1981-08 **Ishii Zosen K.K. — Futtsu** Yd No: 130 L reg 28.11 Br ex - Dght - Lbp - Br md 14.51 Dpth 2.60 Welded, 1 dk	**(B33A2DG) Grab Dredger**	**2 oil engines** driving 2 FP propellers Total Power: 294kW (400hp) 7.0kn Yanmar 2 x 4 Stroke each-147kW (200bhp) Yanmar Diesel Engine Co Ltd-Japan
7712913 *LHDO* H-19-AV	**SEIVAAG** *ex* Lafjord *-2008* **Seivaag Shipping AS** Seistar Holding AS SatCom: Inmarsat C 425816120 *Bergen* *Norway* Official number: 19190	**996** 299 900	Class: NV	1978-07 **Brodrene Lothe AS, Flytedokken — Haugesund** Yd No: 38 Loa 55.40 Br ex 9.86 Dght 6.500 Lbp 48.11 Br md 9.83 Dpth 7.29 Welded, 2 dks	**(B11A2FS) Stern Trawler** Compartments: 1 Ho, 6 Ta, ER 7 Ha: ER Ice Capable	**1 oil engine** driving 1 CP propeller Total Power: 1,545kW (2,101hp) 14.5kn Wichmann 7AXA 1 x 2 Stroke 7 Cy. 300 x 450 1545kW (2101bhp) Wichmann Motorfabrikk AS-Norway AuxGen: 2 x 160kW 380V 50Hz a.c, 1 x 99kW 380V 50Hz a.c Thrusters: 1 Thwart. FP thruster (f); 1 Tunnel thruster (a) Fuel: 36.0 (d.f.) 189.5 (r.f.) 10.0pd

Ship / Owner	Tonnage	Class	Builder / Dimensions	Type / Cargo	Machinery
7607120 **SEIVAG** *CB8197* *ex* Prosjekt Kopervik *-2000* *ex* Batsfjord *-1994* - **CPT Empresas Maritimas SA** - *Valparaiso* *Chile* MMSI: 725012400 Official number: 3103	**650** 208 -	Class: (NV)	**1976**-10 **Kleivset Baatbyggeri — Foldfjorden** (Hull) **1976**-10 **AS Storviks Mek. Verksted — Kristiansund** Yd No: 74 Converted From: Stern Trawler-2000 Loa 46.54 Br ex 9.40 Dght 4.533 Lbp 39.98 Br md 9.00 Dpth 6.51 Welded, 1 dk	**(A34A2GR) Refrigerated Cargo Ship** Ice Capable	**1 oil engine** driving 1 FP propeller Total Power: 1,214kW (1,651hp) 12.0kn MaK 8M451AK 1 x 4 Stroke 8 Cy. 320 x 450 1214kW (1651bhp) MaK Maschinenbau GmbH-Kiel AuxGen: 2 x 132kW 220V 50Hz a.c Fuel: 122.0 5.0pd
9021277 **SEIWA** *T3VQ* *ex* Seiwa Maru *-2007* - **Green World Panama SA** Green World Co Ltd *Tarawa* *Kiribati* MMSI: 529304000 Official number: K-12911095	**2,692** 1,064 2,830	Class: NK	**1991**-09 **Miyoshi Shipbuilding Co Ltd — Uwajima EH** Yd No: 293 Loa 94.00 Br ex - Dght 5.183 Lbp 84.80 Br md 14.00 Dpth 5.25 Welded, 1 dk	**(A34A2GR) Refrigerated Cargo Ship** Ins: 3,729 3 Ha: 3 (4.8 x 4.8)ER Derricks: 6x5t	**1 oil engine** driving 1 FP propeller Total Power: 2,427kW (3,300hp) 13.0kn Akasaka A41 1 x 4 Stroke 6 Cy. 410 x 800 2427kW (3300bhp) Akasaka Tekkosho KK (Akasaka DieselLtd)-Japan AuxGen: 2 x 360kW a.c Fuel: 730.0 (r.f.)
9033749 **SEIWA MARU** *JG5074* - - **Chiyoda Kaihatsu KK** - *Tokyo* *Japan* Official number: 133103	*446* - 906		**1991**-10 **Hitachi Zosen Mukaishima Marine Co Ltd — Onomichi HS** Yd No: 53 Loa 59.22 Br ex 9.62 Dght 3.800 Lbp 54.50 Br md 9.60 Dpth 4.30 Welded, 1 dk	**(A12A2TC) Chemical Tanker** Liq: 769 Compartments: 6 Ta, ER 2 Cargo Pump (s): 2x200m³/hr	**1 oil engine** with clutches & reverse geared to sc. shaft driving 1 FP propeller Total Power: 736kW (1,001hp) Hanshin LH28G 1 x 4 Stroke 6 Cy. 280 x 460 736kW (1001bhp) The Hanshin Diesel Works Ltd-Japan
9109574 **SEIWA MARU** *JL6203* *ex* Takasago 2 *-2008* - **Matsuda Kaiun KK** - *Komatsushima, Tokushima* *Japan* MMSI: 431500282 Official number: 133980	*999* - 1,248	Class: NK	**1994**-11 **Shin Kochi Jyuko K.K. — Kochi** Yd No: 7056 Loa 71.00 Br ex - Dght 4.240 Lbp 66.00 Br md 12.20 Dpth 5.35 Welded, 1 dk	**(A11B2TG) LPG Tanker** Liq (Gas): 1,725 2 x Gas Tank (s);	**1 oil engine** driving 1 FP propeller Total Power: 1,471kW (2,000hp) 12.6kn Akasaka A37 1 x 4 Stroke 6 Cy. 370 x 720 1471kW (2000bhp) Akasaka Tekkosho KK (Akasaka DieselLtd)-Japan AuxGen: 3 x a.c Fuel: 225.0 (d.f.)
9094250 **SEIWA MARU** *JD2151* - - **Inoshita Kaiun KK** - *Niihama, Ehime* *Japan* Official number: 140214	*499* - 1,600		**2005**-08 **K.K. Watanabe Zosensho — Nagasaki** Yd No: 127 Loa 76.15 Br ex - Dght 4.030 Lbp 70.20 Br md 12.30 Dpth 7.00 Welded, 1 dk	**(A31A2GX) General Cargo Ship** 1 Ha: ER (40.0 x 10.0)	**1 oil engine** driving 1 Propeller Total Power: 1,324kW (1,800hp) 11.5kn Hanshin LH30L 1 x 4 Stroke 6 Cy. 300 x 600 1324kW (1800bhp) The Hanshin Diesel Works Ltd-Japan
8954594 **SEIWA MARU** *JI3663* - - **Seiwa Kaiun KK** - *Osaka, Osaka* *Japan* Official number: 136787	*363* - -		**1999**-10 **Hongawara Zosen K.K. — Fukuyama** Yd No: 505 Loa 53.33 Br ex - Dght - Lbp - Br md 9.20 Dpth 4.10 Welded, 1 dk	**(A12A2TC) Chemical Tanker** Liq: 610 Compartments: 3 Ta, ER 1 Cargo Pump (s): 1x250m³/hr	**1 oil engine** driving 1 FP propeller Total Power: 736kW (1,001hp) Yanmar DY26-SN 1 x 4 Stroke 6 Cy. 260 x 440 736kW (1001bhp) Yanmar Diesel Engine Co Ltd-Japan Fuel: 40.7 (d.f.)
8889945 **SEIWA MARU** *JM6392* *ex* Yoshino Maru No. 3 *-2009* - **Kyowa Sekiyu KK** - *Yokohama, Kanagawa* *Japan* Official number: 134490	*149* - -		**1995**-09 **Mikami Zosen K.K. — Japan** Yd No: 350 L reg 36.20 Br ex - Dght - Lbp - Br md 7.30 Dpth 3.10 Welded, 1 dk	**(A13B2TU) Tanker (unspecified)**	**1 oil engine** driving 1 FP propeller Total Power: 515kW (700hp) 10.0kn Yanmar MF24-DT 1 x 4 Stroke 6 Cy. 240 x 420 515kW (700bhp) Yanmar Diesel Engine Co Ltd-Japan
9644407 **SEIWA MARU** *JD3227* - - **Kaiyo Kogyo KK** - *Yokohama, Kanagawa* *Japan* MMSI: 432816000 Official number: 141493	*309* - -		**2011**-07 **Hatayama Zosen KK — Yura WK** Yd No: 266 Loa 38.00 Br ex - Dght 3.700 Lbp 32.50 Br md 10.40 Dpth 4.70 Welded, 1 dk	**(B32A2ST) Tug**	**2 oil engines** reduction geared to sc. shafts driving 2 Propellers Total Power: 3,680kW (5,004hp) Yanmar 6EY26 2 x 4 Stroke 6 Cy. 260 x 385 each-1840kW (2502bhp) Yanmar Diesel Engine Co Ltd-Japan
9370927 **SEIWA MARU** *JD2205* - - **Seiyo Kisen KK** - *Imabari, Ehime* *Japan* Official number: 140276	*499* - 1,800		**2006**-01 **Yamanaka Zosen K.K. — Imabari** Yd No: 718 Loa 70.73 Br ex - Dght 4.350 Lbp 68.00 Br md 12.10 Dpth 7.34 Welded, 2 dks	**(A31A2GX) General Cargo Ship** Grain: 2,859; Bale: 2,815 1 Ha: ER (40.0 x 9.5)	**1 oil engine** driving 1 FP propeller Total Power: 1,324kW (1,800hp) 11.6kn Hanshin LH30L 1 x 4 Stroke 6 Cy. 300 x 600 1324kW (1800bhp) The Hanshin Diesel Works Ltd-Japan
9336933 **SEIWA MARU** *JD2213* - - **Fujitrans Corp** Kagoshima Senpaku Kaisha Ltd *Nagoya, Aichi* *Japan* MMSI: 431200693 Official number: 140284	*15,781* - 6,818	Class: NK	**2006**-02 **Mitsubishi Heavy Industries Ltd. — Shimonoseki** Yd No: 1116 Loa 167.00 (BB) Br ex - Dght 7.600 Lbp 158.00 Br md 30.20 Dpth 28.75 Welded,	**(A35B2RV) Vehicles Carrier** Quarter stern door/ramp (p. a.) Len: 25.00 Wid: 7.00 Swl: 65 Quarter stern door/ramp (s. a.) Len: 25.00 Wid: 7.00 Swl: 65 Cars: 846	**1 oil engine** driving 1 FP propeller Total Power: 20,460kW (27,817hp) 23.4kn Mitsubishi 12UEC52LSE 1 x 2 Stroke 12 Cy. 520 x 2000 20460kW (27817bhp) Mitsubishi Heavy Industries Ltd-Japan AuxGen: 2 x 1600kW a.c, 1 x 1600kW a.c Thrusters: 1 Tunnel thruster (f); 2 Tunnel thruster (f) Fuel: 2700.0 (r.f.)
8838427 **SEIWA MARU No. 1** - - - - -	*109* - -		**1977** **Nishii Dock Co. Ltd. — Ise** L reg 28.70 Br ex - Dght 2.100 Lbp - Br md 5.90 Dpth 2.60 Bonded, 1 dk	**(B11B2FV) Fishing Vessel** Hull Material: Reinforced Plastic	**1 oil engine** driving 1 FP propeller Total Power: 294kW (400hp) Yanmar 1 x 4 Stroke 294kW (400bhp) Yanmar Diesel Engine Co Ltd-Japan
9281102 **SEIWA MARU NO. 18** *JHQS* - ME1-836 **Koei Gyogyo KK** - *Owase, Mie* *Japan* MMSI: 432367000 Official number: 135669	*439* - -		**2002**-12 **Miho Zosensho K.K. — Shimizu** Yd No: 1503 Loa 57.41 Br ex 9.03 Dght 3.490 Lbp 50.50 Br md 9.00 Dpth 3.90 Welded, 1 Dk.	**(B11B2FV) Fishing Vessel**	**1 oil engine** geared to sc. shaft driving 1 FP propeller Total Power: 736kW (1,001hp) Hanshin LH28LG 1 x 4 Stroke 6 Cy. 280 x 530 736kW (1001bhp) The Hanshin Diesel Works Ltd-Japan
9019949 **SEIWA MARU NO. 81** *JM5997* *ex* Kyuei Maru No. 35 *-2006* - **YK Ishitani Gyogyo** - *Otaru, Hokkaido* *Japan* Official number: 131388	*107* - -		**1991**-03 **Fujishin Zosen K.K. — Kamo** Yd No: 566 Loa 37.00 Br ex - Dght 2.430 Lbp 31.00 Br md 6.50 Dpth 2.75 Welded	**(B11B2FV) Fishing Vessel**	**1 oil engine** with clutches & sr geared to sc. shaft driving 1 CP propeller Total Power: 617kW (839hp) Yanmar 6T240-ET 1 x 4 Stroke 6 Cy. 240 x 310 617kW (839bhp) Yanmar Diesel Engine Co Ltd-Japan
5318907 **SEIWAL** - - - - -	*133* 47 -	Class: (DS)	**1958** **VEB Elbewerft — Boizenburg** Loa 26.45 Br ex 6.71 Dght 3.550 Lbp 23.40 Br md - Dpth 3.66 Welded, 1 dk	**(B11B2FV) Fishing Vessel** Compartments: 1 Ho, ER 1 Ha: ER Ice Capable	**1 oil engine** driving 1 FP propeller Total Power: 221kW (300hp) 9.0kn S.K.L. 6NVD36 1 x 4 Stroke 6 Cy. 240 x 360 221kW (300bhp) VEB Maschinenbau Halberstadt-Halberstadt AuxGen: 2 x 21kW 110V d.c
8988076 **SEIYO** - *ex* Sheng Yang *-2005* *ex* Admiral *-2005* - **Vast Line Ltd** Dalian East Ocean Maritime Consulting Services Co Ltd	**1,245** 731 -		**1985** **Ningbo Jiangbei Shipyard — Ningbo ZJ** Loa - Br ex - Dght 4.550 Lbp 65.67 Br md 11.50 Dpth 6.20 Welded, 1 dk	**(A31A2GX) General Cargo Ship**	**1 oil engine** driving 1 Propeller Total Power: 1,103kW (1,500hp)
9104524 **SEIYO 18** *3EJK6* *ex* Apollo Tiga *-2003* - **Sea Prosperous Maritime SA** Dalian Sea Carrier Co Ltd *Panama* *Panama* MMSI: 372798000 Official number: 45711PEXT	**6,641** 2,801 8,629	Class: NK	**1994**-08 **Shin Kurushima Dockyard Co. Ltd. — Hashihama, Imabari** Yd No: 2831 Loa 100.61 (BB) Br ex - Dght 8.220 Lbp 93.50 Br md 18.80 Dpth 13.60 Welded, 1 dk	**(A31A2GX) General Cargo Ship** Grain: 15,212; Bale: 13,574 Compartments: 2 Ho, ER 2 Ha: (27.0 x 12.6) (21.0 x 12.6)ER Cranes: 1x30t,2x20t	**1 oil engine** driving 1 FP propeller Total Power: 3,089kW (4,200hp) 13.0kn B&W 5L35MC 1 x 2 Stroke 5 Cy. 350 x 1050 3089kW (4200bhp) Makita Corp-Japan Fuel: 625.0 (r.f.)
9135523 **SEIYO EXPLORER** *3FTI5* *ex* Global Explorer *-2012* - **Seiyo Explorer Co Ltd** Dalian Sea Carrier Co Ltd SatCom: Inmarsat C 437016610 *Panama* *Panama* MMSI: 370166000 Official number: 24765PEXT2	**20,398** 9,257 24,800	Class: NK	**1996**-01 **Shin Kurushima Dockyard Co. Ltd. — Onishi** Yd No: 2881 Loa 153.78 (BB) Br ex - Dght 10.050 Lbp 143.80 Br md 26.00 Dpth 16.00 Welded, 1 dk	**(A21A2BC) Bulk Carrier** Grain: 44,888; Bale: 43,766 Compartments: 4 Ho, ER 4 Ha: (16.0 x 17.4)2 (20.0 x 22.0) (20.0 x 20.0)ER Cranes: 4x30.5t	**1 oil engine** driving 1 FP propeller Total Power: 6,179kW (8,401hp) 14.3kn Mitsubishi 7UEC45LA 1 x 2 Stroke 7 Cy. 450 x 1350 6179kW (8401bhp) Kobe Hatsudoki KK-Japan Fuel: 1020.0 (r.f.)

IMO / Call sign	Name / Owner / Manager	Tonnage / Class	Builder / Dimensions	Type / Capacity	Machinery
9417048 *VRDA7* -	**SEIYO FORTUNE** **Seiyo Fortune Maritime SA** Dalian Sea Carrier Co Ltd *Hong Kong* *Hong Kong* MMSI: 477897400 Official number: HK-1949	**7,508** Class: NK 3,117 10,514	**2007-08 Liaoning Marine & Offshore Industrial Park Co Ltd — Yingkou LN** Yd No: 85-1 Loa 105.00 Br ex - Dght 8.810 Lbp 95.00 Br md 20.50 Dpth 13.60 Welded, 1 dk	**(A31A2GX) General Cargo Ship** Grain: 15,305; Bale: 14,003 Cranes: 1x30t; Derricks: 2x25t	**1 oil engine** driving 1 Propeller Total Power: 3,700kW (5,031hp) 13.5kn MAN-B&W 5S35MC 1 x 2 Stroke 5 Cy. 350 x 1400 3700kW (5031bhp) Yichang Marine Diesel Engine Co Ltd-China Fuel: 655.0
9413353 *3EGT6* -	**SEIYO GLORY** *ex Most Rich -2007* **Seiyo Glory Co Ltd** Dalian Sea Carrier Co Ltd *Panama* *Panama* MMSI: 372106000 Official number: 3250407A	**1,972** Class: CC 1,395 3,350	**2006-12 Zhejiang Hongxin Shipbuilding Co Ltd — Taizhou ZJ** Yd No: 0516 Loa 81.00 Br ex - Dght 5.500 Lbp 76.00 Br md 13.60 Dpth 6.80 Welded, 1 dk	**(A31A2GX) General Cargo Ship** Grain: 4,541 Compartments: 2 Ho, ER 2 Ha: ER 2 (18.6 x 9.0) Ice Capable	**1 oil engine** reduction geared to sc. shaft driving 1 FP propeller Total Power: 1,324kW (1,800hp) 12.0kn Chinese Std. Type G6300ZC 1 x 4 Stroke 6 Cy. 300 x 380 1324kW (1800bhp) Wuxi Antai Power Machinery Co Ltd-China AuxGen: 2 x 150kW 400V a.c
9581045 *VRHK6* -	**SEIYO GODDESS** **Sea Dove Maritime SA** Dalian Sea Carrier Co Ltd *Hong Kong* *Hong Kong* MMSI: 477932300 Official number: HK-2862	**9,130** Class: CC 4,017 12,217	**2010-09 Wuchang Shipbuilding Industry Co Ltd — Wuhan HB** Yd No: A196M Loa 120.00 Br ex - Dght 8.600 Lbp 112.00 Br md 20.80 Dpth 13.00 Welded, 1 dk	**(A31A2GX) General Cargo Ship** Grain: 16,805; Bale: 14,461 Compartments: 2 Ho, ER 2 Ha: (39.9 x 18.2)ER (38.5 x 18.2) Cranes: 2x30t Ice Capable	**1 oil engine** driving 1 FP propeller Total Power: 3,310kW (4,500hp) 11.8kn Hanshin LH46LA 1 x 4 Stroke 6 Cy. 460 x 880 3310kW (4500bhp) The Hanshin Diesel Works Ltd-Japan AuxGen: 3 x 250kW 400V a.c
9423619 *H02447* -	**SEIYO GROWTH** *ex Howa 1 -2008* **Seiyo Growth Maritime SA** Dalian Sea Carrier Co Ltd *Panama* *Panama* MMSI: 372518000 Official number: 3305407B	**2,919** Class: CC 1,377 3,976	**2007-04 Yangzhou Longchuan Shipbuilding Co Ltd — Jiangdu JS** Yd No: 505 Loa 87.00 Br ex - Dght 6.300 Lbp 79.98 Br md 14.20 Dpth 9.40 Welded, 1 dk	**(A31A2GX) General Cargo Ship** Grain: 6,028 Compartments: 2 Ho, ER 2 Ha: (28.0 x 9.0)ER (14.0 x 9.0)	**1 oil engine** reverse reduction geared to sc. shaft driving 1 FP propeller Total Power: 1,618kW (2,200hp) 11.0kn Niigata 6M34BFT 1 x 4 Stroke 6 Cy. 340 x 620 1618kW (2200bhp) Niigata Engineering Co Ltd-Japan AuxGen: 2 x 180kW 400V a.c
9447380 *JD2500* -	**SEIYO MARU** **Japan Railway Construction, Transport & Technology Agency & Nanyo Shipping Co Ltd** Nanyo Shipping Co Ltd (Nanyo Kaiun KK) *Tokyo* *Japan* MMSI: 431000334 Official number: 140634	*749* Class: NK - 1,883	**2007-10 K.K. Miura Zosensho — Saiki** Yd No: 1328 Loa 69.98 Br ex 12.00 Dght 4.742 Lbp 66.00 Br md 12.00 Dpth 5.20 Welded, 1 dk	**(A13B2TP) Products Tanker** Double Hull (13F) Liq: 2,200; Liq (Oil): 2,200	**1 oil engine** reduction geared to sc. shaft driving 1 FP propeller Total Power: 1,471kW (2,000hp) Hanshin LH34LG 1 x 4 Stroke 6 Cy. 340 x 640 1471kW (2000bhp) The Hanshin Diesel Works Ltd-Japan AuxGen: 2 x a.c Fuel: 75.0 (d.f.)
9572599 *JD2987* -	**SEIYO MARU** **Japan Railway Construction, Transport & Technology Agency & Nichiyo Kaiun KK** Azuma Kisen KK *Shimonoseki, Yamaguchi* *Japan* MMSI: 431001072 Official number: 141130	*232* - 370	**2009-10 Hongawara Zosen K.K. — Fukuyama** Yd No: 631 Loa 44.84 Br ex - Dght 2.900 Lbp 41.15 Br md 8.50 Dpth 3.15 Welded, 1 dk	**(A24A2BT) Cement Carrier**	**1 oil engine** reduction geared to sc. shaft driving 1 FP propeller Total Power: 736kW (1,001hp) Yanmar 6N18A-EV 1 x 4 Stroke 6 Cy. 180 x 280 736kW (1001bhp) Yanmar Diesel Engine Co Ltd-Japan
9310458 *JI3719* -	**SEIYO MARU** **Shoyo Kisen Kaisha Ltd** - *Osaka, Osaka* *Japan* Official number: 137245	*475* - -	**2004-01 Kanagawa Zosen — Kobe** Yd No: 522 Loa 44.20 Br ex - Dght 4.200 Lbp 39.00 Br md 10.80 Dpth 5.60 Welded, 1 dk	**(B32A2ST) Tug**	**2 oil engines** geared to sc. shafts driving 2 Z propellers Total Power: 4,412kW (5,998hp) Daihatsu 6DKM-32 2 x 4 Stroke 6 Cy. 320 x 360 each-2206kW (2999bhp) Daihatsu Diesel Manufacturing Co Lt-Japan AuxGen: 2 x 160kW 225V a.c
9169445 *JM6549* -	**SEIYO MARU** **Corporation for Advanced Transport & Technology & GK Nakatsuru Gumi** GK Nakatsuru Gumi *Tsukumi, Oita* *Japan* MMSI: 431400704 Official number: 135413	*4,396* Class: NK - 6,710	**1997-05 Tsuneishi Shipbuilding Co Ltd — Fukuyama HS** Yd No: OE-215 Loa 114.50 (BB) Br ex - Dght 6.618 Lbp 107.00 Br md 17.60 Dpth 8.30 Welded, 1 dk	**(A24A2BT) Cement Carrier** Grain: 5,294	**1 oil engine** driving 1 CP propeller Total Power: 2,648kW (3,600hp) 12.2kn Akasaka A45 1 x 4 Stroke 6 Cy. 450 x 880 2648kW (3600bhp) Akasaka Tekkosho KK (Akasaka DieselLtd)-Japan AuxGen: 1 x 450kW 450V a.c, 1 x 200kW 450V a.c Thrusters: 1 Thwart. FP thruster (f) Fuel: 44.0 (d.f.) 133.0 (r.f.) 10.8pd
9154646 *JL6511* -	**SEIYO MARU** **Taisei Kosan KK & Sanwa Kaiun KK** Taisei Kosan KK *Imabari, Ehime* *Japan* Official number: 135538	*499* - 1,598	**1996-08 Yamanaka Zosen K.K. — Imabari** Yd No: 602 Loa - Br ex - Dght 4.060 Lbp 70.00 Br md 12.00 Dpth 7.01 Welded, 2 dks	**(A31A2GX) General Cargo Ship** Grain: 2,853	**1 oil engine** driving 1 FP propeller Total Power: 736kW (1,001hp) Hanshin LH30L 1 x 4 Stroke 6 Cy. 300 x 600 736kW (1001bhp) The Hanshin Diesel Works Ltd-Japan
8701363 *JMFG* -	**SEIYO MARU** **Government of Japan (Ministry of Education, Culture, Sports, Science & Technology)** Tokyo University of Marine Science & Technology (Tokyo Kaiyo-Daigaku) *Tokyo* *Japan* MMSI: 431431000 Official number: 130180	*170* - 154	**1987-10 Miho Zosensho K.K. — Shimizu** Yd No: 1306 Loa 35.51 Br ex - Dght 2.801 Lbp 31.02 Br md 7.01 Dpth 3.41 Welded	**(B11A2FS) Stern Trawler** Ins: 505	**1 oil engine** with clutches, flexible couplings & dr geared to sc. shaft driving 1 CP propeller Total Power: 772kW (1,050hp) Pielstick 5PA5 1 x 4 Stroke 5 Cy. 225 x 270 772kW (1050bhp) Niigata Engineering Co Ltd-Japan Thrusters: 1 Thwart. CP thruster (f); 1 Tunnel thruster (a)
7335557 *H05430* -	**SEIYO MARU No. 2** *ex Kasuga Maru No. 2 -1981* **K Takahashi Co SA** - *Panama* *Panama* Official number: 9435PEXT1	*489* Class: (NK) 267 1,233	**1969 Watanabe Zosen KK — Imabari EH** Yd No: 111 Loa 54.21 Br ex 9.43 Dght 4.522 Lbp 49.51 Br md 9.40 Dpth 4.58 Welded, 1 dk	**(A31A2GX) General Cargo Ship** Grain: 1,708; Bale: 1,547 Compartments: 1 Ho, ER 1 Ha: (26.3 x 5.4)ER	**1 oil engine** driving 1 FP propeller Total Power: 736kW (1,001hp) 11.5kn Daihatsu 8PSHTCM-26D 1 x 4 Stroke 8 Cy. 260 x 320 736kW (1001bhp) Daihatsu Diesel Manufacturing Co Lt-Japan AuxGen: 2 x 20kW 225V a.c
6620515 - -	**SEIYO MARU No. 15** *ex Yuyo Maru -1981* **-** -	*168* 75 152	**1966 Nagasaki Zosen K.K. — Nagasaki** Yd No: 130 Loa 34.80 Br ex 6.63 Dght 2.769 Lbp 29.09 Br md 6.61 Dpth 3.18 Welded, 1 dk	**(B11B2FV) Fishing Vessel**	**1 oil engine** driving 1 FP propeller Total Power: 478kW (650hp) Niigata 6MG25AHS 1 x 4 Stroke 6 Cy. 250 x 320 478kW (650bhp) Niigata Engineering Co Ltd-Japan
7740300 - -	**SEIYO MARU No. 35** *ex Eisho Maru No. 12 -1990* **Victory Venture Fishing Corp** - *Philippines*	*178* - -	**1978-03 K.K. Murakami Zosensho — Ishinomaki** Yd No: 1004 L reg 35.39 Br ex - Dght - Lbp - Br md 7.00 Dpth 3.41 Welded, 1 dk	**(B12B2FC) Fish Carrier**	**1 oil engine** driving 1 FP propeller Daihatsu 1 x 4 Stroke Daihatsu Diesel Manufacturing Co Lt-Japan
9136668 *JK5427* -	**SEIYO NO. 3** *ex Koa Maru -2004* **KK SY Promotion** - *Tokyo* *Japan* Official number: 134802	*446* - 911	**1995-10 Matsuura Tekko Zosen K.K. — Osakikamijima** Yd No: 390 Loa 57.99 Br ex - Dght 3.830 Lbp 54.50 Br md 9.60 Dpth 4.30 Welded, 1 dk	**(A12A2TC) Chemical Tanker** Liq: 696 6 Cargo Pump (s): 6x100m³/hr	**1 oil engine** with clutches & reverse geared to sc. shaft driving 1 FP propeller Total Power: 736kW (1,001hp) Akasaka K28BR 1 x 4 Stroke 6 Cy. 280 x 480 736kW (1001bhp) Akasaka Tekkosho KK (Akasaka DieselLtd)-Japan
9315264 *JL6716* -	**SEIYO NO. 5** **Kotobuki Kaiun KK** - *Ozu, Ehime* *Japan* Official number: 136568	*498* - 1,198	**2004-04 Imura Zosen K.K. — Komatsushima** Yd No: 311 Loa 64.81 Br ex - Dght 4.200 Lbp 61.00 Br md 10.20 Dpth 4.50 Welded, 1 dk	**(A13B2TP) Products Tanker** Double Hull (13F) Liq: 1,240; Liq (Oil): 1,240	**1 oil engine** driving 1 Propeller Total Power: 736kW (1,001hp) Hanshin LH28G 1 x 4 Stroke 6 Cy. 280 x 460 736kW (1001bhp) The Hanshin Diesel Works Ltd-Japan
8706868 *JK4650* -	**SEIYO NO. 7** *ex Kotoku Maru No. 2 -2007* **KK SY Promotion** - *Kobe, Hyogo* *Japan* Official number: 129521	*120* - 295	**1987-08 Kochi Jyuko K.K. — Kochi** Yd No: 1966 Loa 34.61 Br ex - Dght 2.800 Lbp 31.00 Br md 7.00 Dpth 3.00 Welded, 1 dk	**(A13B2TP) Products Tanker** Liq: 340; Liq (Oil): 340 Compartments: 6 Ta, ER	**1 oil engine** geared to sc. shaft driving 1 FP propeller Total Power: 221kW (300hp) Yanmar 6M-T 1 x 4 Stroke 6 Cy. 200 x 240 221kW (300bhp) Yanmar Diesel Engine Co Ltd-Japan

IMO / Call sign	Name / Owner / Manager / Port	Tonnage	Class	Built / Dimensions	Type / Capacity	Machinery
8989678 *JJ4055* -	**SEIYO NO. 8** - **Meiwa Kaiun KK** - *Kobe, Hyogo* Japan Official number: 136009	*298* - -		**2004-03 KK Ura Kyodo Zosensho — Awaji HG** Yd No: 321 Loa 53.00 Br ex - Dght 3.200 Lbp 48.00 Br md 9.00 Dpth 3.70 Welded, 1 dk	**(A31A2GX) General Cargo Ship** Grain: 619	**1 oil engine** driving 1 Propeller Total Power: 736kW (1,001hp) 10.8kn Yanmar DY26-SN 1 x 4 Stroke 6 Cy. 260 x 440 736kW (1001bhp) Yanmar Diesel Engine Co Ltd-Japan
9145798 *3FBK7* -	**SEIYO PIONEER** *ex Global Pioneer -2012* **Sea Eagle Marine Co Ltd** Dalian Sea Carrier Co Ltd *Panama* Panama MMSI: 355098000 Official number: 2368397CH	**20,395** 9,257 24,814 T/cm 33.9	Class: NK	**1997-02 KK Kanasashi — Toyohashi AI** Yd No: 3423 Loa 153.80 (BB) Br ex - Dght 10.050 Lbp 143.80 Br md 26.00 Dpth 16.00 Welded, 1 dk	**(A21A2BC) Bulk Carrier** Grain: 44,888; Bale: 43,766 Compartments: 4 Ho, ER 4 Ha: (16.0 x 17.4)2 (20.0 x 22.0) (20.0 x 20.0)ER Cranes: 4x30.5t	**1 oil engine** driving 1 FP propeller Total Power: 6,179kW (8,401hp) 14.3kn Mitsubishi 7UEC45LA 1 x 2 Stroke 7 Cy. 450 x 1350 6179kW (8401bhp) Kobe Hatsudoki KK-Japan Fuel: 1100.0 (r.f.)
9159024 *3FAD7* -	**SEIYO SAPPHIRE** *ex Luna Azul -2011* **Seiyo Sapphire Co Ltd** Dalian Sea Carrier Co Ltd SatCom: Inmarsat M 654805410 *Panama* Panama MMSI: 353999000 Official number: 2369597E	**8,359** 2,931 8,421	Class: NK	**1997-03 Higaki Zosen K.K. — Imabari** Yd No: 480 Loa 118.00 (BB) Br ex - Dght 7.450 Lbp 108.00 Br md 19.60 Dpth 13.70 Welded, 1 dk	**(A31A2GA) General Cargo Ship (with Ro-Ro facility)** Quarter stern door/ramp (s. a.) Len: - Wid: - Swl: 40 Cars: 199 Grain: 19,036; Bale: 17,662 2 Ha: 2 (27.3 x 14.0) Cranes: 2x40t; Derricks: 2x25t	**1 oil engine** driving 1 FP propeller Total Power: 4,193kW (5,701hp) 13.7kn B&W 6S35MC 1 x 2 Stroke 6 Cy. 350 x 1400 4193kW (5701bhp) The Hanshin Diesel Works Ltd-Japan AuxGen: 2 x 400kW 450V a.c Fuel: 636.0 (r.f.) 16.7pd
9124213 *3FIM9* -	**SEIYO SPIRIT** *ex Golden Glint -2004* **Seiyo Spirit Maritime SA** Dalian Sea Carrier Co Ltd *Panama* Panama MMSI: 373538000 Official number: 4483513	**6,113** 3,108 8,514	Class: NK	**1995-06 Nishi Shipbuilding Co Ltd — Imabari EH** Yd No: 391 Loa 100.64 (BB) Br ex - Dght 8.250 Lbp 94.59 Br md 18.80 Dpth 13.00 Welded, 2 dks	**(A31A2GX) General Cargo Ship** Grain: 14,570; Bale: 13,321 Compartments: 2 Ho, ER 2 Ha: (17.5 x 12.8) (28.0 x 12.8)ER Cranes: 1x30t; Derricks: 2x25t	**1 oil engine** driving 1 FP propeller Total Power: 3,236kW (4,400hp) 12.5kn B&W 5L35MC 1 x 2 Stroke 5 Cy. 350 x 1050 3236kW (4400bhp) Makita Corp-Japan Fuel: 415.0 (r.f.)
9284398 *3FWQ9* -	**SEIYO SPRING** *ex Future Ace -2013* **Seiyo Marine Co Ltd** Dalian Sea Carrier Co Ltd *Panama* Panama MMSI: 355191000 Official number: 4531113	**7,443** 3,343 9,999	Class: NK	**2003-09 Nishi Shipbuilding Co Ltd — Imabari EH** Yd No: 436 Loa 110.67 Br ex - Dght 8.470 Lbp 102.00 Br md 19.20 Dpth 13.50 Welded, 1 dk	**(A31A2GX) General Cargo Ship** Grain: 15,504; Bale: 14,333 Cranes: 2x35t; Derricks: 1x30t	**1 oil engine** driving 1 Propeller Total Power: 3,900kW (5,302hp) 13.2kn B&W 6L35MC 1 x 2 Stroke 6 Cy. 350 x 1050 3900kW (5302bhp) The Hanshin Diesel Works Ltd-Japan Fuel: 710.0
9335214 *XUFX3* -	**SEIYO STAR** - **Seiyo Star Co Ltd** Dalian Sea Carrier Co Ltd SatCom: Inmarsat C 451571410 *Phnom Penh* Cambodia MMSI: 515714000 Official number: 0404229	**2,363** 1,607 3,800	Class: UM	**2004-10 Zhejiang Dongfang Shipbuilding Co Ltd — Yueqing ZJ** Yd No: DFG3506 Loa 84.40 Br ex - Dght 5.800 Lbp 76.50 Br md 14.20 Dpth 7.60 Welded, 1 dk	**(A31A2GX) General Cargo Ship**	**1 oil engine** reduction geared to sc. shaft driving 1 FP propeller Total Power: 1,545kW (2,101hp) Chinese Std. Type 6320ZC 1 x 4 Stroke 6 Cy. 320 x 440 1545kW (2101bhp) Guangzhou Diesel Engine Factory CoLtd-China
9414656 *DSRM4* -	**SEIYO SUNNY** *ex Outsailing 7 -2009* **KT Capital Corp** Shin Chang Shipping Co Ltd *Jeju* South Korea MMSI: 441914000 Official number: JJR-131017	**1,972** 1,271 3,323	Class: KR (CC)	**2007-01 Zhejiang Hongxin Shipbuilding Co Ltd — Taizhou ZJ** Loa 81.00 Br ex - Dght 5.500 Lbp 76.00 Br md 13.60 Dpth 6.80 Welded, 1 dk	**(A31A2GX) General Cargo Ship** Grain: 4,541 Compartments: 2 Ho, ER 2 Ha: ER 2 (18.6 x 9.0) Ice Capable	**1 oil engine** driving 1 FP propeller Total Power: 1,324kW (1,800hp) 10.8kn Hanshin LH31G 1 x 4 Stroke 6 Cy. 310 x 530 1324kW (1800bhp) The Hanshin Diesel Works Ltd-Japan AuxGen: 2 x 150kW 400V a.c
9624471 *JD3331* -	**SEIYOH 101** - **KK SY Promotion** - *Tokyo* Japan Official number: 141639	*499* - 1,254		**2012-03 KK Ura Kyodo Zosensho — Awaji HG** Yd No: 346 Loa 64.46 Br ex - Dght 4.212 Lbp 60.00 Br md 10.00 Dpth 4.50 Welded, 1 dk	**(A12A2TC) Chemical Tanker** Double Hull (13F) 2 Cargo Pump (s): 2x300m³/hr	**1 oil engine** geared to sc. shaft driving 1 Propeller Total Power: 1,030kW (1,400hp) 11.5kn Hanshin LH28G 1 x 4 Stroke 6 Cy. 280 x 460 1030kW (1400bhp) The Hanshin Diesel Works Ltd-Japan
9611151 *JD3189* -	**SEIYU MARU** - **Yoshu Kisen KK** - *Imabari, Ehime* Japan MMSI: 431500251 Official number: 141435	*498* - 1,650		**2011-03 Namikata Shipbuilding Co Ltd — Imabari EH** Yd No: 233 Loa 74.72 Br ex - Dght 4.123 Lbp 69.80 Br md 12.00 Dpth 7.07 Welded, 1 dk	**(A31A2GX) General Cargo Ship** Grain: 2,507; Bale: 2,487 1 Ha: ER (39.6 x 9.5)	**1 oil engine** driving 1 Propeller Total Power: 1,620kW (2,203hp) 11.5kn Akasaka A34C 1 x 4 Stroke 6 Cy. 340 x 620 1620kW (2203bhp) Akasaka Tekkosho KK (Akasaka DieselLtd)-Japan
9677222 *JD3554* -	**SEIYU MARU** - **Seiei Kaiun KK** - *Imabari, Ehime* Japan MMSI: 431004596 Official number: 141976	*267* - 800	Class: FA	**2013-07 Yano Zosen K.K. — Imabari** Yd No: 266 Loa 61.00 Br ex - Dght 3.440 Lbp - Br md 9.80 Dpth 6.00 Welded, 1 dk	**(A31A2GX) General Cargo Ship** Double Hull Grain: 1,371; Bale: 1,328 Compartments: 1 Ho, ER 1 Ha: ER (31.0 x 7.5)	**1 oil engine** reduction geared to sc. shaft driving 1 Propeller Total Power: 1,029kW (1,399hp) Niigata 6M28BGT 1 x 4 Stroke 6 Cy. 280 x 480 1029kW (1399bhp) Niigata Engineering Co Ltd-Japan
9682174 *JD3531* -	**SEIYU MARU** - **Sanwa Kaiun YK** - *Imabari, Ehime* Japan MMSI: 431004475 Official number: 141941	*270* - 820		**2013-05 Yamanaka Zosen K.K. — Imabari** Yd No: 838 Loa 60.83 Br ex - Dght 3.520 Lbp - Br md 9.80 Dpth - Welded, 1 dk	**(A31A2GX) General Cargo Ship** Compartments: 1 Ho, ER 1 Ha: ER	**1 oil engine** reduction geared to sc. shaft driving 1 Propeller Total Power: 1,176kW (1,599hp) Hanshin LH28L 1 x 4 Stroke 6 Cy. 280 x 530 1176kW (1599bhp) The Hanshin Diesel Works Ltd-Japan
9062386 *JL6141* -	**SEIYU MARU** - **Yuki Kisen KK** - *Shikokuchuo, Ehime* Japan Official number: 133896	*199* - 480 T/cm 3.1		**1993-06 Koa Sangyo KK — Takamatsu KG** Yd No: 572 Loa 49.59 Br ex - Dght 3.100 Lbp 45.00 Br md 7.80 Dpth 3.30 Welded, 1 dk	**(A12A2TC) Chemical Tanker** Liq: 390 Compartments: 2 Ta, ER 2 Cargo Pump (s): 2x150m³/hr	**1 oil engine** reverse geared to sc. shaft driving 1 FP propeller Total Power: 736kW (1,001hp) Hanshin LH26G 1 x 4 Stroke 6 Cy. 260 x 440 736kW (1001bhp) The Hanshin Diesel Works Ltd-Japan
8350891 - -	**SEIYU MARU** - - - China	*498* - 1,599		**1983 Yamanaka Zosen K.K. — Imabari** Yd No: 258 Loa 67.42 Br ex 11.51 Dght 4.370 Lbp - Br md - Dpth - Welded, 1 dk	**(A31A2GX) General Cargo Ship**	**1 oil engine** driving 1 FP propeller Total Power: 956kW (1,300hp) Niigata 6M31AFT 1 x 4 Stroke 6 Cy. 310 x 530 956kW (1300bhp) Niigata Engineering Co Ltd-Japan
8849086 *JH3183* IK1-323	**SEIYU MARU No. 5** - **Haruo Fuchu** - *Noto, Ishikawa* Japan Official number: 119893	*138* - -		**1977-03 KK Toyo Zosen Tekkosho — Kamaishi IW** L reg 30.20 Br ex - Dght - Lbp - Br md 6.20 Dpth 2.60 Welded, 1 dk	**(B11B2FV) Fishing Vessel**	**1 oil engine** driving 1 FP propeller Total Power: 280kW (381hp) Niigata 6MG22X 1 x 4 Stroke 6 Cy. 220 x 250 280kW (381bhp) Niigata Engineering Co Ltd-Japan
8951748 - -	**SEIYU MARU No. 21** - **Jaeson Tank Cleaning Co Ltd** - South Korea	*146* - 310		**1975-07 Sokooshi Zosen K.K. — Osakikamijima** Yd No: 239 Loa 31.11 Br ex - Dght 2.500 Lbp - Br md 6.20 Dpth 3.00 Welded, 1 dk	**(A13B2TU) Tanker (unspecified)**	**1 oil engine** geared to sc. shaft driving 1 FP propeller Total Power: 441kW (600hp) 8.5kn Yanmar 6U-UT 1 x 4 Stroke 6 Cy. 200 x 240 441kW (600bhp) Yanmar Diesel Engine Co Ltd-Japan
8889804 *JL6153* -	**SEIZAN MARU** - **Inoshita Kaiun KK** - *Niihama, Ehime* Japan Official number: 134853	*498* - 1,600		**1995-03 Yamanaka Zosen K.K. — Imabari** Yd No: 572 Loa 74.90 Br ex - Dght 4.100 Lbp 70.00 Br md 12.00 Dpth 7.01 Welded, 1 dk	**(A31A2GX) General Cargo Ship** Compartments: 1 Ho, ER 1 Ha: (38.0 x 9.7)ER	**1 oil engine** driving 1 FP propeller Total Power: 736kW (1,001hp) 11.0kn Hanshin LH30LG 1 x 4 Stroke 6 Cy. 300 x 600 736kW (1001bhp) The Hanshin Diesel Works Ltd-Japan

9176199 *JM6511* -	**SEIZAN MARU** - **Corporation for Advanced Transport & Technology & Yamaki Unyu KK** Ube Shipping & Logistics Ltd (Ube Kosan KK) *Ube, Yamaguchi* *Japan* MMSI: 431401335 Official number: 135450	*4,651* - 5,714	Class: NK	**1998**-08 **K.K. Miura Zosensho — Saiki** Yd No: 1211 Loa 115.35 Br ex - Dght 5.714 Lbp 108.00 Br md 18.00 Dpth 8.15 Welded, 1 dk	**(A24A2BT) Cement Carrier** Grain: 5,077	**1 oil engine** geared to sc. shaft driving 1 FP propeller Total Power: 3,310kW (4,500hp) Daihatsu 6DLM-40 1 x 4 Stroke 6 Cy. 400 x 480 3310kW (4500bhp) Daihatsu Diesel Manufacturing Co Lt-Japan Fuel: 240.0
9566033 *JD3025* -	**SEIZAN MARU** - **Seiyo Kisen KK** - *Imabari, Ehime* *Japan* Official number: 141190	*499* - 1,830		**2010**-01 **Yamanaka Zosen K.K. — Imabari** Yd No: 785 Loa 74.24 Br ex - Dght 4.360 Lbp 68.00 Br md 12.00 Dpth 7.37 Welded, 1 dk	**(A31A2GX) General Cargo Ship** Grain: 2,914; Bale: 2,831 1 Ha: ER (40.0 x 9.5)	**1 oil engine** driving 1 FP propeller Total Power: 1,323kW (1,799hp) 12.1kn Hanshin LH30L 1 x 4 Stroke 6 Cy. 300 x 600 1323kW (1799bhp) The Hanshin Diesel Works Ltd-Japan
8997819 *JD2062* -	**SEIZAN MARU 21** - **Watanabe Kowan Kaiun YK** - *Imabari, Ehime* *Japan* Official number: 140109	*498* - 1,550		**2004**-12 **Yamanaka Zosen K.K. — Imabari** Loa 72.04 Br ex - Dght 3.900 Lbp 70.00 Br md 12.50 Dpth 6.75 Welded, 1 dk	**(A31A2GX) General Cargo Ship**	**1 oil engine** reduction geared to sc. shaft driving 1 Propeller Total Power: 1,471kW (2,000hp) 13.0kn Daihatsu 6DKM-26 1 x 4 Stroke 6 Cy. 260 x 380 1471kW (2000bhp) Daihatsu Diesel Manufacturing Co Lt-Japan
8980490 *JL6706* -	**SEIZAN MARU NO. 8** - **Muraike Kaiun YK** - *Imabari, Ehime* *Japan* Official number: 137043	*498* - 1,550		**2002**-12 **Yamanaka Zosen K.K. — Imabari** L reg 72.04 Br ex - Dght - Lbp - Br md 12.50 Dpth 6.75 Welded, 1 dk	**(A31A2GX) General Cargo Ship**	**1 oil engine** driving 1 Propeller
9338008 *9WFW9* -	**SEJAHTERA 3** - **Jetacorp Sdn Bhd** - *Kuching* *Malaysia* MMSI: 533000536 Official number: 329860	**161** 73 -		**2004**-01 **Jana Seribu Shipbuilding (M) Sdn Bhd — Sibu** Yd No: 0305 Loa 42.06 Br ex 4.72 Dght 1.335 Lbp 37.70 Br md 4.62 Dpth 1.50 Welded, 1 dk	**(A37B2PS) Passenger Ship**	**2 oil engines** reduction geared to sc. shafts driving 2 Propellers Total Power: 1,692kW (2,300hp) Mitsubishi S12R-MTK 2 x Vee 4 Stroke 12 Cy. 170 x 180 each-846kW (1150bhp) Mitsubishi Heavy Industries Ltd-Japan
8824529 *YBWB* -	**SEJAHTERA 18** *ex* Tokai Maru No. 18 *-2006* **PT Pelayaran Nasional 'Sinar Pagoda'** - *Batam* *Indonesia*	*807* 410 610	Class: KI	**1989**-05 **K.K. Yoshida Zosen Kogyo — Arida** Converted From: Bulk Aggregates Carrier-2006 Lengthened-2006 Loa 55.99 Br ex - Dght 3.650 Lbp 52.35 Br md 11.00 Dpth 5.60 Welded, 1 dk	**(A31A2GX) General Cargo Ship** Compartments: 1 Ho, ER 1 Ha: (12.1 x 8.0)ER	**1 oil engine** driving 1 FP propeller Total Power: 588kW (799hp) Niigata 6M26AGTE 1 x 4 Stroke 6 Cy. 260 x 460 588kW (799bhp) Niigata Engineering Co Ltd-Japan AuxGen: 2 x 37kW 89V a.c
8823305 *PMBS* -	**SEJAHTERA 19** *ex* Shin Konpira Maru *-2009* **PT Pelayaran Nasional 'Sinar Pagoda'** - *Batam* *Indonesia*	**375** 145 259	Class: KI	**1989**-03 **Katsuura Dockyard Co. Ltd. — Nachi-Katsuura** Converted From: Grab Dredger-2009 Loa 41.00 Br ex - Dght 2.510 Lbp 37.15 Br md 8.80 Dpth 3.95 Welded, 1 dk	**(A31A2GX) General Cargo Ship** Compartments: 1 Ho, ER 1 Ha: (14.0 x 7.0)ER	**1 oil engine** driving 1 FP propeller Total Power: 272kW (370hp) Matsui 6M26KGHS 1 x 4 Stroke 6 Cy. 260 x 400 272kW (370bhp) Matsui Iron Works Co Ltd-Japan AuxGen: 1 x 85kW 225/130V a.c
8746571 *PMNT* -	**SEJAHTERA 20** - **PT Pelayaran Nasional 'Sinar Pagoda'** - *Batam* *Indonesia* MMSI: 525023101 Official number: 866/L	**715** 408 960	Class: KI RI	**2008**-09 **P.T. Bandar Victory Shipyard — Batam** Loa 55.77 Br ex - Dght 4.390 Lbp 50.32 Br md 9.60 Dpth 5.35 Welded, 1 dk	**(A31A2GX) General Cargo Ship**	**1 oil engine** reduction geared to sc. shaft driving 1 FP propeller Total Power: 610kW (829hp) 9.0kn Yanmar 6AYM-ETE 1 x 4 Stroke 6 Cy. 155 x 180 610kW (829bhp) Yanmar Diesel Engine Co Ltd-Japan AuxGen: 2 x 63kW 220/360V 50Hz a.c
8850889 *PMRH* -	**SEJAHTERA 21** *ex* Shinyo Maru No. 3 *-2008* **PT Pelayaran Nasional 'Sinar Pagoda'** - *Batam* *Indonesia* Official number: 1159/L	**681** 205 1,200	Class: KI	**1991**-03 **K.K. Tago Zosensho — Nishi-Izu** Yd No: 232 Converted From: Bulk Aggregates Carrier-1991 Lengthened-2009 Loa 60.30 Br ex - Dght 5.200 Lbp 57.85 Br md 10.50 Dpth 5.20 Welded, 1 dk	**(A31A2GX) General Cargo Ship**	**1 oil engine** reduction geared to sc. shaft driving 1 FP propeller Total Power: 478kW (650hp) 9.0kn Sumiyoshi S26G 1 x 4 Stroke 6 Cy. 260 x 470 478kW (650bhp) Sumiyoshi Marine Diesel Co Ltd-Japan
9047635 *PNHT* -	**SEJAHTERA 27** *ex* Koju Maru *-2009* *ex* Daitoku Maru *-2002* **PT Pelayaran Nasional 'Sinar Pagoda'** - *Jakarta* *Indonesia*	**641** 264 700	Class: KI	**1993**-01 **Katsuura Dockyard Co. Ltd. — Nachi-Katsuura** Yd No: 316 Loa 46.46 Br ex - Dght - Lbp 41.28 Br md 10.50 Dpth 4.80 Welded, 1 dk	**(A31A2GX) General Cargo Ship**	**1 oil engine** driving 1 FP propeller Total Power: 257kW (349hp) Matsui ML626GSC-2 1 x 4 Stroke 6 Cy. 260 x 480 257kW (349bhp) Matsui Iron Works Co Ltd-Japan
8844220 *PODF* -	**SEJAHTERA 28** *ex* Shoho Maru *-2011* **PT Pelayaran Nasional 'Sinar Pagoda'** - *Batam* *Indonesia*	**670** 371 700	Class: KI RI	**1990**-08 **Kyoei Zosen KK — Mihara HS** Loa 57.00 Br ex - Dght 3.200 Lbp 52.10 Br md 9.50 Dpth 5.40 Welded, 1 dk	**(A31A2GX) General Cargo Ship**	**1 oil engine** driving 1 FP propeller Total Power: 662kW (900hp) 10.5kn Niigata 6M26AGTE 1 x 4 Stroke 6 Cy. 260 x 460 662kW (900bhp) Niigata Engineering Co Ltd-Japan AuxGen: 1 x 88kW 225/130V a.c
8840987 - -	**SEJAHTERA 29** *ex* Yushin Maru No. 18 *-2011* *ex* National No. 2 *-1995* **PT Pelayaran Nasional 'Sinar Pagoda'** -	*489* - 441		**1990**-03 **Tokuoka Zosen K.K. — Naruto** Loa 46.61 Br ex - Dght 3.020 Lbp 40.00 Br md 11.50 Dpth 3.05 Welded, 1 dk	**(A24D2BA) Aggregates Carrier** Compartments: 1 Ho, ER 1 Ha: (15.4 x 9.3)ER	**1 oil engine** driving 1 FP propeller Sumiyoshi S26G 1 x 4 Stroke 6 Cy. 260 x 470 Sumiyoshi Marine Diesel Co Ltd-Japan
8840286 - -	**SEJAHTERA 31** *ex* Kawachi Maru *-2011* - - *Indonesia*	*177* - 449		**1990**-03 **KK Ouchi Zosensho — Matsuyama EH** Loa 49.00 Br ex - Dght 3.210 Lbp 45.00 Br md 8.30 Dpth 5.00 Welded, 1 dk	**(A31A2GX) General Cargo Ship**	**1 oil engine** driving 1 FP propeller Total Power: 427kW (581hp) 10.0kn Yanmar MF24-DT 1 x 4 Stroke 6 Cy. 240 x 420 427kW (581bhp) Yanmar Diesel Engine Co Ltd-Japan
9665322 - -	**SEJAHTERA 33** *ex* Zhe Ling Ji 138 *-2012* **PT Pelayaran Nasional 'Sinar Pagoda'** - *Indonesia*	**753** 421 -		**2012**-05 **Wenling Donghai Shipyard — Wenling ZJ** Yd No: 120 Loa 55.60 Br ex 9.33 Dght - Lbp 52.00 Br md 9.00 Dpth 5.30 Welded, 1 dk	**(A31A2GX) General Cargo Ship**	**1 oil engine** reduction geared to sc. shaft driving 1 Propeller Total Power: 900kW (1,224hp) 11.0kn Chinese Std. Type 8170ZLC 1 x 4 Stroke 8 Cy. 170 x 200 900kW (1224bhp) Zibo Diesel Engine Factory-China
7510028 *YFKA* -	**SEJAHTERA ABADI** *ex* Planet *-2003* *ex* Ebisu Maru No. 8 *-1994* *ex* Yamato *-1989* **PT Sinar Bahtera Pacific Lines** - *Jakarta* *Indonesia*	**612** 241 674	Class: KI	**1975**-07 **Namikata Shipbuilding Co Ltd — Imabari EH** Yd No: 86 Loa - Br ex 9.33 Dght 3.099 Lbp 49.00 Br md 9.30 Dpth 5.19 Riveted\Welded, 1 dk	**(A31A2GX) General Cargo Ship**	**1 oil engine** driving 1 FP propeller Total Power: 552kW (750hp) Makita GNLH623 1 x 4 Stroke 6 Cy. 230 x 410 552kW (750bhp) Makita Diesel Co Ltd-Japan
7374929 *YCHN* -	**SEJAHTERA LESTARI** *ex* Soopanava Inter 3 *-2006* *ex* Isla Leyte *-1999* *ex* Itogon *-1993* *ex* Antamok *-1986* *ex* Tamaraw Hope *-1984* *ex* Paraiso *-1979* *ex* Riman *-1979* **PT Pelayaran Sejahtera Bahtera Agung** - *Surabaya* *Indonesia*	**3,951** 2,602 6,700	Class: KI (AB) (NK)	**1976**-05 **Nishi Shipbuilding Co Ltd — Imabari EH** Yd No: 162 Loa 109.50 Br ex 16.54 Dght 6.930 Lbp 99.01 Br md 16.51 Dpth 8.51 Riveted\Welded, 1 dk	**(A31A2GX) General Cargo Ship** Grain: 9,028; Bale: 8,491 Compartments: 2 Ho, ER 2 Ha: (26.9 x 8.3) (28.7 x 8.3)ER Derricks: 1x50t,4x15t	**1 oil engine** driving 1 FP propeller Total Power: 3,016kW (4,101hp) 13.0kn Makita KSLH647 1 x 4 Stroke 6 Cy. 470 x 760 3016kW (4101bhp) Makita Diesel Co Ltd-Japan AuxGen: 2 x 184kW
9160762 *YD4693* -	**SEJAHTERA MAKMUR** *ex* Blue Ocean Star *-2000* **PT Pelayaran Suri Adidaya Kapuas** - *Pontianak* *Indonesia*	**132** 39 79	Class: (KI) (CC)	**1996**-12 **Jiangdu Shipyard — Jiangdu JS** Yd No: 95120 Loa - Br ex - Dght 2.030 Lbp 21.00 Br md 7.50 Dpth 3.20 Welded, 1 dk	**(B32A2ST) Tug**	**2 oil engines** geared to sc. shafts driving 1 FP propeller Total Power: 530kW (720hp) Chinese Std. Type 6160ZC 2 x 4 Stroke 6 Cy. 160 x 225 each-265kW (360bhp) Ningbo Zhonghua Dongli PowerMachinery Co Ltd -China
7334565 *PMCU* -	**SEJAHTERA SENTOSA** *ex* Five Star *-2008* *ex* Zhe Hai 716 *-2007* *ex* Kapor *-2004* **PT Samudera Sejahtera Lestari** - *Surabaya* *Indonesia*	**4,833** 1,982 7,898	Class: (KI) (BV)	**1973**-10 **Watanabe Zosen KK — Imabari EH** Yd No: 159 Loa 115.65 Br ex 17.45 Dght 7.011 Lbp 107.07 Br md 17.40 Dpth 8.69 Welded, 1 dk	**(A31A2GX) General Cargo Ship** Grain: 10,695; Bale: 10,221 Derricks: 4x15t	**1 oil engine** driving 1 FP propeller Total Power: 3,310kW (4,500hp) 12.8kn Mitsubishi 6UET45/80D 1 x 2 Stroke 6 Cy. 450 x 800 3310kW (4500bhp) Kobe Hatsudoki Seizosho-Japan

6711429 *YEKW* -	**SEJATI PRATAMA** *ex* Thanus *-1993* *ex* Thanassakis *-1989* *ex* Olimbos *-1987* *ex* Irafoss *-1985* *ex* Securitas *-1972* **PT Sejati Bina Segara Lines** - *Jakarta* *Indonesia* Official number: 4847	**1,457** 905 2,677	Class: (KI) (GL)	**1967**-05 **Scheepswerf 'Friesland' NV — Lemmer** Yd No: 44 Loa 80.30 Br ex 11.87 Dght 5.550 Lbp 69.02 Br md 11.70 Dpth 6.61 Welded, 2 dks	**(A31A2GX) General Cargo Ship** Grain: 3,418; Bale: 3,029 Compartments: 1 Ho, ER, 1 Tw Dk 2 Ha: (17.0 x 5.5) (16.4 x 5.5)ER Cranes: 2x3t; Derricks: 1x20t,1x3t; Winches: 2 Ice Capable	**1 oil engine** driving 1 FP propeller Total Power: 736kW (1,001hp) 12.0kn Deutz RBV6M358 1 x 4 Stroke 6 Cy. 400 x 580 736kW (1001bhp) Kloeckner Humboldt Deutz AG-West Germany AuxGen: 2 x 145kW 220/380V 50Hz a.c, 1 x 60kW 220/380V 50Hz a.c Fuel: 215.5 (d.f.)
9178185 *OZOH* -	**SEJEROFAERGEN** - **Kalundborg Kommune** Sejerofaergen *Sejero* *Denmark* MMSI: 219000584 Official number: A483	**1,433** 430 266 T/cm 4.7	Class: BV	**1998**-12 **Esbjerg Oilfield Services A/S — Esbjerg** Yd No: 68 Loa 48.50 Br ex - Dght 2.650 Lbp 42.90 Br md 11.70 Dpth 3.90 Welded, 1 dk plus Pt & Stbd hanging dks	**(A36A2PR) Passenger/Ro-Ro Ship (Vehicles)** Passengers: unberthed: 246 Bow door & ramp Len: 4.50 Wid: 4.00 Swl: - Stern ramp Len: 4.50 Wid: 4.00 Swl: - Lane-Len: 180 Lane-Wid: 4.00 Cars: 36 Ice Capable	**2 oil engines** geared to sc. shafts driving 2 Directional propellers Total Power: 1,276kW (1,734hp) 12.0kn Caterpillar 3508B 2 x Vee 4 Stroke 8 Cy. 170 x 190 each-638kW (867bhp) Caterpillar Inc-USA AuxGen: 2 x 310kW 400V 50Hz a.c Thrusters: 2 Thwart. FP thruster (f) Fuel: 65.6 (d.f.) 9.1pd
9223021 - -	**SEJONG NO. 1** *ex* Poong Yang Saechonyon No. 1 *-2004* **Il Shin Shipping Co Ltd** - *Sacheon* *South Korea* Official number: SPR-992939	*173* - 121	Class: (KR)	**1999**-12 **Mokpo Shipbuilding & Engineering Co Ltd — Mokpo** Yd No: 99-159 Lengthened Loa 48.85 Br ex - Dght 1.435 Lbp - Br md 8.50 Dpth 2.10 Welded, 1 dk	**(A37B2PS) Passenger Ship**	**2 oil engines** geared to sc. shafts driving 2 FP propellers Total Power: 1,060kW (1,442hp) 14.4kn M.T.U. 12V183 2 x Vee 4 Stroke 12 Cy. 128 x 142 each-530kW (721bhp) Daewoo Heavy Industries Ltd-South Korea
7430450 - -	**SEJONG T1** *ex* Nichiei Maru *-2004* *ex* Octagon *-1990* *ex* Hachiko Maru *-1985* **Sejong S & D Shipping Co Ltd** Sehan Industries Co Ltd *South Korea* MMSI: 440114230	**496** 148 -	Class: (NK)	**1975**-06 **Yokohama Yacht Co Ltd — Yokohama KN** Yd No: 711 Loa 33.00 Br ex 9.71 Dght 3.899 Lbp 30.76 Br md 9.68 Dpth 4.35 Welded, 1 dk	**(B32B2SA) Articulated Pusher Tug**	**2 oil engines** driving 2 FP propellers Total Power: 3,384kW (4,600hp) 13.8kn Hanshin 6LUS38 2 x 4 Stroke 6 Cy. 380 x 580 each-1692kW (2300bhp) The Hanshin Diesel Works Ltd-Japan AuxGen: 2 x 120kW a.c Fuel: 172.5 12.5pd
8701648 - - -	**SEJU FRONTIER** *ex* Sechang Frontier *-2011* *ex* Makwan Ferry *-2003* *ex* Ferry *-2001* *ex* Shinju Maru *-2001* **Seju Co Ltd** - *Busan* *South Korea* MMSI: 441092000 Official number: BSR-017035	**9,815** 2,944 5,411	Class: KR (NK)	**1988**-02 **Imabari Shipbuilding Co Ltd — Imabari EH (Imabari Shipyard)** Yd No: 467 Lengthened-1994 Loa 141.70 (BB) Br ex - Dght 6.063 Lbp 132.00 Br md 20.01 Dpth 14.71 Welded, 1 dk	**(A35A2RR) Ro-Ro Cargo Ship** Angled side door/ramp (p. f.) Len: 16.50 Wid: 7.00 Swl: 50 Quarter stern door/ramp (p) Len: 23.00 Wid: 7.00 Swl: 50 Lane-Len: 910 Lane-clr ht: 6.40	**1 oil engine** geared to sc. shaft driving 1 FP propeller Total Power: 6,620kW (9,001hp) 17.5kn Pielstick 6PC40L570 1 x 4 Stroke 6 Cy. 570 x 750 6620kW (9001bhp) Nippon Kokan KK (NKK Corp)-Japan AuxGen: 3 x 470kW a.c
8817069 - -	**SEJU PIONEER** *ex* Sechang Pioneer *-2011* *ex* Shinei Maru *-2003* **Seju Co Ltd** - *Busan* *South Korea* MMSI: 440103850 Official number: BSR-018817	*4,405* - 5,381	Class: KR (NK)	**1988**-12 **Imabari Shipbuilding Co Ltd — Imabari EH (Imabari Shipyard)** Yd No: 475 Loa 129.75 Br ex - Dght 6.062 Lbp 120.00 Br md 20.00 Dpth 6.40 Welded	**(A35A2RR) Ro-Ro Cargo Ship** Angled side door/ramp (p. f.) Len: 16.50 Wid: 7.00 Swl: 50 Quarter stern door/ramp (p) Len: 23.00 Wid: 7.00 Swl: 50 Lane-Len: 720 Lane-clr ht: 6.40 Trailers: 60	**1 oil engine** geared to sc. shaft driving 1 FP propeller Total Power: 6,620kW (9,001hp) 17.5kn Pielstick 6PC40L570 1 x 4 Stroke 6 Cy. 570 x 750 6620kW (9001bhp) Nippon Kokan KK (NKK Corp)-Japan AuxGen: 3 x 469kW a.c
9103764 *TCA2730* -	**SEKA** *ex* Baronen *-2007* **Altinnal Turizm Isletmecilik ve Yatirim AS** - *Istanbul* *Turkey* MMSI: 271010099 Official number: 9367	**172** 68 17	Class: NV	**1994**-05 **Holen Mek. Verksted AS — Langevaag** Yd No: 133 Loa 24.15 Br ex - Dght 1.215 Lbp 23.48 Br md 8.25 Dpth 3.40 Welded, 1 dk	**(A37B2PS) Passenger Ship** Hull Material: Aluminium Alloy Passengers: unberthed: 125	**2 oil engines** with clutches, flexible couplings & sr geared to sc. shafts driving 2 CP propellers Total Power: 1,470kW (1,998hp) 30.0kn M.T.U. 12V183TE92 2 x Vee 4 Stroke 12 Cy. 128 x 142 each-735kW (999bhp) MTU Friedrichshafen GmbH-Friedrichshafen AuxGen: 1 x 40kW a.c Fuel: 4.8 (d.f.)
8109656 *TC6578* -	**SEKA AKDENIZ I** - **Sumer Holding AS Tasucu Kagit Sanayii Isletmesi Mudurlugu (Tasucu Paper Industry Operations Directorate)** Seka Akdeniz Isletme Mudurlugu *Mersin* *Turkey* Official number: 16983	*299* 91 -	Class: TL (AB)	**1983**-12 **Sedef Gemi Endustrisi A.S. — Gebze** Yd No: 37 Loa 29.90 Br ex 9.45 Dght 3.850 Lbp 28.33 Br md 9.42 Dpth 4.73 Welded, 1 dk	**(B32A2ST) Tug**	**2 oil engines** with clutches, flexible couplings & sr reverse geared to sc. shafts driving 2 FP propellers Total Power: 1,250kW (1,700hp) 13.3kn Caterpillar D398SCAC 2 x Vee 4 Stroke 12 Cy. 159 x 203 each-625kW (850bhp) Caterpillar Tractor Co-USA AuxGen: 2 x 85kW
7709019 *TC6577* -	**SEKA AKDENIZ-II** *ex* Seka Akdeniz Ii *-2012* *launched as* Pendik I *-1984* **Sumer Holding AS Tasucu Kagit Sanayii Isletmesi Mudurlugu (Tasucu Paper Industry Operations Directorate)** - *Mersin* *Turkey* Official number: 17071	*108* 29 -	Class: TL	**1984**-05 **Denizcilik Bankasi T.A.O. — Halic, Istanbul** Yd No: 199 Loa 25.00 Br ex 6.74 Dght 2.620 Lbp 24.01 Br md 6.71 Dpth 4.78 Welded, 1 dk	**(B32A2ST) Tug**	**1 oil engine** driving 1 FP propeller Total Power: 919kW (1,249hp) Niigata 6L25BX 1 x 4 Stroke 6 Cy. 250 x 320 919kW (1249bhp) Niigata Engineering Co Ltd-Japan
8627696 *YHDW* -	**SEKAR PERMATA** *ex* Taisho Maru No. 68 *-2001* **PT Alexindo Yakin Prima** - *Batam* *Indonesia*	**1,253** 512 1,379	Class: KI	**1986**-06 **Nagashima Zosen KK — Kihoku ME** Converted From: Bulk Aggregates Carrier-2003 Loa 62.79 Br ex - Dght 4.241 Lbp 57.10 Br md 13.40 Dpth 6.23 Welded, 1 dk	**(A31A2GX) General Cargo Ship**	**1 oil engine** reduction geared to sc. shaft driving 1 FP propeller Total Power: 1,177kW (1,600hp) 11.0kn Hanshin 6LU32G 1 x 4 Stroke 6 Cy. 320 x 510 1177kW (1600bhp) The Hanshin Diesel Works Ltd-Japan AuxGen: 2 x 92kW 380V a.c
8982498 *YFSN* -	**SEKAR PURNAMA** - **PT Bintanindo Sentosa Daya** - *Tanjungpinang* *Indonesia* MMSI: 525023084 Official number: 1997GGA No. 3050/L	**673** 369 1,200	Class: KI	**1997**-08 **P.T. Bandar Victory Shipyard — Batam** Yd No: 059 Loa 55.60 Br ex - Dght 3.420 Lbp 51.25 Br md 9.90 Dpth 4.50 Welded, 1 dk	**(A31A2GX) General Cargo Ship** Compartments: 2 Ho, ER	**2 oil engines** geared to sc. shafts driving 2 FP propellers Total Power: 692kW (940hp) 9.0kn Caterpillar 3408 2 x Vee 4 Stroke 8 Cy. 137 x 152 each-346kW (470bhp) Caterpillar Inc-USA AuxGen: 2 x 47kW 220/380V 50Hz a.c Fuel: 50.0 (r.f.)
8626056 *YHXR* -	**SEKAR PUSPITA 2** *ex* Kikushima *-2004* *ex* Kosho Maru No. 5 *-1995* *ex* Shinei Maru *-1988* **PT Bintanindo Sentosa Daya** - *Tanjungpinang* *Indonesia*	**648** 278 550	Class: KI	**1984**-11 **Y.K. Kaneko Zosensho — Hojo** Loa 45.24 Br ex - Dght 3.500 Lbp 40.86 Br md 8.21 Dpth 4.96 Welded, 1 dk	**(A31A2GX) General Cargo Ship**	**1 oil engine** driving 1 FP propeller Total Power: 441kW (600hp) 9.0kn Matsui 6M26KGHS 1 x 4 Stroke 6 Cy. 260 x 400 441kW (600bhp) Matsui Iron Works Co Ltd-Japan
8622464 *YDJY* -	**SEKAR PUSPITA 3** *ex* Sekar Petrona *-2007* *ex* Fuyo Maru No. 18 *-2005* *ex* Saiwai Maru No. 12 *-1993* **PT Pelayaran Nasional 'Sinar Pagoda'** - *Tanjungpinang* *Indonesia*	*616* 185 1,000	Class: KI	**1983**-11 **Y.K. Takasago Zosensho — Naruto** Yd No: 126 Loa - Br ex - Dght 4.010 Lbp 46.21 Br md 10.00 Dpth 5.01 Welded, 1 dk	**(A31A2GX) General Cargo Ship**	**1 oil engine** driving 1 FP propeller Total Power: 736kW (1,001hp) 10.0kn Matsui MS25GSC 1 x 4 Stroke 6 Cy. 250 x 470 736kW (1001bhp) Matsui Iron Works Co Ltd-Japan
8625806 *YHOT* -	**SEKAR PUSPITA I** *ex* Akatsuki Maru No. 6 *-2004* *ex* Fukuei Maru *-1997* *ex* Akatsuki Maru No. 6 *-1992* *ex* Fukuei Maru *-1989* **PT Pelayaran Nasional 'Sinar Pagoda'** - *Batam* *Indonesia* Official number: PPM 300/L	*553* 322 596	Class: KI	**1985**-11 **K.K. Kamishima Zosensho — Osakikamijima** Yd No: 173 Loa 49.51 Br ex - Dght 3.310 Lbp 45.01 Br md 9.01 Dpth 5.01 Welded, 1 dk	**(A31A2GX) General Cargo Ship**	**1 oil engine** driving 1 FP propeller Total Power: 552kW (750hp) 10.0kn Matsui 6M26KGHS 1 x 4 Stroke 6 Cy. 260 x 400 552kW (750bhp) Matsui Iron Works Co Ltd-Japan

7128227 *SW5656* -	**SEKAVIN** *ex* Sara Hashim *-1989* *ex* Kikaku Maru No. 2 *-1983* **Zephiros Shipping Co** Sekavin SA *Piraeus* *Greece* MMSI: 237327000 Official number: 9583	*992* 686 2,147	Class: (HR) (AB) (NK)	**1971**-10 **Kishimoto Zosen — Osakikamijima** Yd No: 417 Loa 77.60 (BB) Br ex 12.07 Dght 4.790 Lbp 72.52 Br md 12.02 Dpth 5.49 Welded, 1 dk	**(B35E2TF) Bunkering Tanker** Liq: 2,820; Liq (Oil): 2,820 Compartments: 5 Ta, ER	**1 oil engine** driving 1 FP propeller Total Power: 1,692kW (2,300hp) 12.0kn Fuji 6S40B 1 x 4 Stroke 6 Cy. 400 x 580 1692kW (2300bhp) Fuji Diesel Co Ltd-Japan AuxGen: 2 x 40kW 225V a.c Fuel: 108.5
5398660 *SV4994* -	**SEKAVIN 1** *ex* Zetland *-1979* **Sekavin SA** - *Piraeus* *Greece* MMSI: 237026500 Official number: 2629	*138* 28 -	Class: (LR) (HR) ✠ Classed LR until 2/2/05	**1961**-06 **Grangemouth Dockyard Co. Ltd. — Grangemouth** Yd No: 528 Loa 25.91 Br ex 7.50 Dght 3.861 Lbp 22.86 Br md 7.17 Dpth 3.74 Riveted\Welded, 1 dk	**(B32A2ST) Tug**	**1 oil engine** with hydraulic coupling driving 1 CP propeller Total Power: 618kW (840hp) Alpha 497R 1 x 2 Stroke 7 Cy. 290 x 490 618kW (840bhp) Alpha Diesel A/S-Denmark
5419488 *SV4997* -	**SEKAVIN 2** *ex* Dalgrain *-1979* **Sekavin SA** - *Piraeus* *Greece* MMSI: 237025600 Official number: 2651	*139* 24 -	Class: (LR) (HR) ✠ Classed LR until 2/2/05	**1963**-10 **Grangemouth Dockyard Co. Ltd. — Grangemouth** Yd No: 532 Loa 26.42 Br ex 7.50 Dght - Lbp 22.86 Br md 7.17 Dpth 3.74 Riveted\Welded, 1 dk	**(B32A2ST) Tug**	**1 oil engine** with hydraulic coupling driving 1 CP propeller Total Power: 618kW (840hp) Alpha 498R 1 x 2 Stroke 8 Cy. 310 x 490 618kW (840bhp) Alpha Diesel A/S-Denmark
8737219 - -	**SEKAWAN ABADI I** **PT Sekawan Kontrindo** - *Samarinda* *Indonesia*	**168** 51 -	Class: KI	**2008**-09 **C.V. Dok & Galangan Kapal Perlun — Samarinda** Loa 38.60 Br ex - Dght - Lbp 32.20 Br md 7.20 Dpth 2.10 Welded, 1 dk	**(A35D2RL) Landing Craft**	**2 oil engines** driving 2 Propellers Total Power: 316kW (430hp) Mitsubishi 6D22 2 x 4 Stroke 6 Cy. 130 x 140 each-158kW (215bhp) Mitsubishi Heavy Industries Ltd-Japan
8618633 *9LY2657* -	**SEKI MARU** *ex* Ofuku Maru *-1997* *ex* Daifuku Maru *-1996* **PT Lintas Armada Indonesia** - *Freetown* *Sierra Leone* MMSI: 667059000 Official number: SL103460	*194* - 601		**1987**-05 **K.K. Miura Zosensho — Saiki** Yd No: 773 Loa 50.60 Br ex - Dght 3.160 Lbp 46.02 Br md 10.51 Dpth 5.20 Welded, 1 dk	**(B33A2DB) Bucket Ladder Dredger**	**1 oil engine** geared to sc. shaft driving 1 FP propeller Total Power: 552kW (750hp) Hanshin 6LU26G 1 x 4 Stroke 6 Cy. 260 x 440 552kW (750bhp) The Hanshin Diesel Works Ltd-Japan
9601376 *JD2960* -	**SEKIEI MARU** **Sekiei Kaiun YK** *Kure, Hiroshima* *Japan* Official number: 141084	*499* - 1,800		**2009**-08 **YK Nakanoshima Zosensho — Kochi KC** Yd No: 262 Loa 74.71 (BB) Br ex - Dght 4.330 Lbp 69.00 Br md 12.00 Dpth 7.35 Welded, 1 dk	**(A31A2GX) General Cargo Ship** Grain: 2,468 1 Ha: ER (40.0 x 9.5)	**1 oil engine** driving 1 Propeller Total Power: 1,618kW (2,200hp) Niigata 6M34BGT 1 x 4 Stroke 6 Cy. 340 x 620 1618kW (2200bhp) Niigata Engineering Co Ltd-Japan Thrusters: 1 Thwart. FP thruster (f)
8619170 *JM5671* -	**SEKIHO MARU** *ex* Nippo Maru *-2006* **Nishi Nippon Kaiun KK** *Kitakyushu, Fukuoka* *Japan* Official number: 129489	*198* - -		**1987**-04 **K.K. Odo Zosen Tekko — Shimonoseki** Yd No: 331 Loa 34.02 Br ex 9.45 Dght 2.731 Lbp 29.01 Br md 9.20 Dpth 4.20 Welded, 1 dk	**(B32A2ST) Tug**	**2 oil engines** with flexible couplings & dr gearedto sc. shafts driving 2 FP propellers Total Power: 2,500kW (3,400hp) Fuji 6L27.5G 2 x 4 Stroke 6 Cy. 275 x 320 each-1250kW (1700bhp) Fuji Diesel Co Ltd-Japan
8890877 *JL6425* -	**SEKIHO MARU** **Kanei Kisen YK** *Imabari, Ehime* *Japan* MMSI: 431500413 Official number: 135155	*157* - -		**1995**-12 **Kanbara Zosen K.K. — Onomichi** Yd No: 480 Loa 48.35 Br ex - Dght - Lbp 44.00 Br md 8.30 Dpth 5.20 Welded, 1 dk	**(A31A2GX) General Cargo Ship**	**1 oil engine** driving 1 FP propeller Total Power: 588kW (799hp) 10.0kn Hanshin 6LU24G 1 x 4 Stroke 6 Cy. 240 x 410 588kW (799bhp) The Hanshin Diesel Works Ltd-Japan
8210405 - -	**SEKIRYU MARU No. 3** *ex* Sekishin *-1998* *ex* Takatori Maru No. 58 *-1997* **Sunny Shipping Corp** -	*729* - 930		**1982**-05 **K.K. Matsuo Tekko Zosensho — Matsue** Yd No: 2013 Loa - Br ex - Dght 3.850 Lbp 50.02 Br md 12.01 Dpth 4.02 Welded, 1 dk	**(B33A2DG) Grab Dredger** Grain: 600 Compartments: 1 Ho, ER 1 Ha: ER	**1 oil engine** driving 1 FP propeller Total Power: 1,103kW (1,500hp) Hanshin 6LU32G 1 x 4 Stroke 6 Cy. 320 x 510 1103kW (1500bhp) The Hanshin Diesel Works Ltd-Japan
9068055 - -	**SEKISHU INDAH** *ex* Sekishu Maru *-2012* - - *Indonesia*	*184* - 350		**1993**-12 **KK Ouchi Zosensho — Matsuyama EH** Loa 51.75 Br ex - Dght - Lbp 47.00 Br md 8.50 Dpth 5.50 Welded, 1 dk	**(A31A2GX) General Cargo Ship**	**1 oil engine** driving 1 FP propeller Total Power: 736kW (1,001hp) 10.5kn Yanmar MF26-HT 1 x 4 Stroke 6 Cy. 260 x 500 736kW (1001bhp) Yanmar Diesel Engine Co Ltd-Japan
9668465 *JD3407* -	**SEKISHU MARU** **Sekishu Kisen YK** *Kure, Hiroshima* *Japan* Official number: 141757	*199* - 730		**2012**-09 **Yano Zosen K.K. — Imabari** Yd No: 261 Loa 58.30 (BB) Br ex - Dght 3.202 Lbp - Br md 9.80 Dpth 5.42 Welded, 1 dk	**(A31A2GX) General Cargo Ship** Double Hull Grain: 1,168; Bale: 1,168 Compartments: 1 Ho, ER 1 Ha: ER	**1 oil engine** reduction geared to sc. shaft driving 1 Propeller Total Power: 1,029kW (1,399hp) 12.3kn Niigata 6M28BGT 1 x 4 Stroke 6 Cy. 280 x 480 1029kW (1399bhp) Niigata Engineering Co Ltd-Japan Thrusters: 1 Thwart. FP thruster (f)
9172686 *7JIU* -	**SEKIYO** **Nippon Yusen Kabushiki Kaisha (NYK Line)** Hachiuma Steamship Co Ltd (Hachiuma Kisen KK) *Hamada, Shimane* *Japan* MMSI: 432799000 Official number: 141376	**52,665** 25,619 91,439 T/cm 90.0	Class: NK	**1998**-06 **Hitachi Zosen Corp — Nagasu KM** Yd No: 4932 Loa 234.93 (BB) Br ex - Dght 12.700 Lbp 225.00 Br md 43.00 Dpth 19.00 Welded, 1 dk	**(A21A2BC) Bulk Carrier** Double Hull Grain: 106,606 Cargo Heating Coils Compartments: 5 Ho, ER 5 Ha: (25.9 x 15.5) (18.1 x 18.9)3 (28.4 x 18.9)ER	**1 oil engine** driving 1 FP propeller Total Power: 12,460kW (16,941hp) 14.3kn B&W 7S60MC 1 x 2 Stroke 7 Cy. 600 x 2292 12460kW (16941bhp) Hitachi Zosen Corp-Japan AuxGen: 3 x 480kW 440V 60Hz a.c Fuel: 210.5 (d.f.) (Heating Coils) 3348.7 (r.f.) 43.8pd
8979776 *JL6709* -	**SEKIZEN NO. 2** - - *Imabari, Ehime* *Japan* Official number: 137051	*179* - -		**2003**-06 **Ishida Zosen Kensetsu KK — Onomichi HS** Yd No: 678 L reg 29.96 Br ex - Dght - Lbp - Br md 10.50 Dpth 2.94 Welded, 1 dk	**(A36A2PR) Passenger/Ro-Ro Ship (Vehicles)**	**1 oil engine** driving 1 Propeller Total Power: 603kW (820hp) Mitsubishi S6R2F-MTK 1 x 4 Stroke 6 Cy. 170 x 220 603kW (820bhp) Mitsubishi Heavy Industries Ltd-Japan
9266700 *VWSG* -	**SEKKIZHAR** **Chennai Port Trust** - *Chennai* *India* Official number: 2937	**397** 119 152	Class: (IR)	**2003**-03 **Goodwill Engineering Works — Pondicherry** Yd No: 46 Loa 32.60 Br ex 10.72 Dght 4.650 Lbp 31.00 Br md 10.70 Dpth 4.00 Welded, 1 dk	**(B32A2ST) Tug**	**2 oil engines** reduction geared to sc. shafts driving 2 FP propellers Total Power: 2,648kW (3,600hp) 12.0kn Yanmar 8N21A-EN 2 x 4 Stroke 8 Cy. 210 x 290 each-1324kW (1800bhp) Yanmar Diesel Engine Co Ltd-Japan AuxGen: 2 x 80kW 415V 50Hz a.c Fuel: 41.7 (d.f.)
5424328 *TUN2198* AN 924	**SEKOU BARADJI** *ex* Jean Charles *-1977* **Ivoirgel** - *Abidjan* *Cote d'Ivoire*	*175* 60 111	Class: (BV)	**1963 Haarlemsche Scheepsbouw Mij. N.V. — Haarlem** Yd No: 578 Loa 28.00 Br ex 6.79 Dght 3.341 Lbp 25.25 Br md 6.71 Dpth 3.61 Welded, 1 dk	**(B11A2FT) Trawler** 2 Ha: 2 (1.0 x 1.3) Derricks: 1x2t; Winches: 1	**1 oil engine** driving 1 FP propeller Total Power: 456kW (620hp) Deutz SBA8M528 1 x 4 Stroke 8 Cy. 220 x 280 456kW (620bhp) Kloeckner Humboldt Deutz AG-West Germany Fuel: 26.0 (d.f.)
8330487 - -	**SEKSTAN** *ex* Reydovyy-16 *-1985* **Ecoservis-DV Co Ltd** - *Vostochnyy* *Russia* MMSI: 273442810 Official number: 833336	**106** 32 14	Class: RS	**1984**-06 **Zavod "Krasnyy Moryak" — Rostov-na-Donu** Yd No: 16 Loa 23.15 Br ex 6.24 Dght 1.850 Lbp 20.00 Br md 6.01 Dpth 2.80 Welded, 1 dk	**(A37B2PS) Passenger Ship** Passengers: unberthed: 70 Ice Capable	**1 oil engine** geared to sc. shaft driving 1 FP propeller Total Power: 163kW (222hp) 9.6kn Daldizel 6CHNSP18/22-300 1 x 4 Stroke 6 Cy. 180 x 220 163kW (222bhp) Daldizel-Khabarovsk AuxGen: 1 x 16kW Fuel: 7.0 (d.f.)
8410158 *ES2800* -	**SEKTORI** **Meritaito Oy** Government of The Republic of Estonia (Estonian Maritime Administration) (Eesti Veeteede Amet) *Tallinn* *Estonia* MMSI: 276781000 Official number: 5T08L01	**215** 64 174		**1985**-05 **Rauma-Repola Oy — Savonlinna** Yd No: 467 Loa 33.02 Br ex - Dght 2.820 Lbp - Br md 7.90 Dpth 3.40 Welded, 1 dk	**(B34Q2QB) Buoy Tender**	**2 oil engines** with flexible couplings & sr gearedto sc. shaft driving 1 Directional propeller Total Power: 558kW (758hp) Scania DSI14 2 x Vee 4 Stroke 8 Cy. 127 x 140 each-279kW (379bhp) Saab Scania AB-Sweden Thrusters: 1 Thwart. FP thruster (f)

8038041 - -	**SEKUSHCHIY** - -	**770** Class: (RS) 231 332	**1982-08 Zavod "Leninskaya Kuznitsa" — Kiyev** Yd No: 256 Loa 53.75 (BB) Br ex 10.72 Dght 4.290 Lbp 47.92 Br md - Dpth 6.02 Welded, 1 dk	**(B11A2FS) Stern Trawler** Ins: 218 Compartments: 1 Ho, ER 1 Ha: (1.6 x 1.6) Derricks: 2x1.5t Ice Capable	**1 oil engine** driving 1 FP propeller Total Power: 971kW (1,320hp) 12.8kn S.K.L. 8NVD48-2U 1 x 4 Stroke 8 Cy. 320 x 480 971kW (1320bhp) VEB Schwermaschinenbau "KarlLiebknecht" (SKL)-Magdeburg
7913880 - -	**SEKYEONG NO. 1** *ex* Kaisei Maru *-2002* **Sekyeong Shipping Co Ltd** *Incheon* *South Korea* Official number: ICR-023038	**194** - -	**1979-11 Sanyo Zosen K.K. — Onomichi** Yd No: 786 Loa 32.28 Br ex 9.40 Dght 3.100 Lbp 30.00 Br md 9.21 Dpth 4.00 Welded, 1 dk	**(B32A2ST) Tug**	**2 oil engines** driving 2 FP propellers Total Power: 2,500kW (3,400hp) Daihatsu 6DSM-26 2 x 4 Stroke 6 Cy. 260 x 320 each-1250kW (1700bhp) (new engine 2002, added 2002) Daihatsu Diesel Manufacturing Co Lt-Japan
7903067 *DSFZ8* -	**SEKYEONG NO. 7** *ex* Shoho Maru *-2002* **KDB Capital Corp** Sekyeong Shipping Co Ltd *Busan* *South Korea* MMSI: 441265000 Official number: BSR-020310	**152** - -	**1979-05 Kanagawa Zosen — Kobe** Yd No: 198 Loa 30.30 Br ex - Dght 2.701 Lbp 25.50 Br md 8.62 Dpth 3.80 Welded, 1 dk	**(B32A2ST) Tug**	**2 oil engines** driving 2 FP propellers Total Power: 1,766kW (2,402hp) Daihatsu 6PSHTB-26D 2 x 4 Stroke 6 Cy. 260 x 320 each-883kW (1201bhp) Daihatsu Diesel Manufacturing Co Lt-Japan
5319341 - -	**SELADANG** - **Government of Malaysia (Office of The Federal Secretary for Sarawak)** - *Kuching* *Malaysia*	*230* 112 254	**1957 Cheoy Lee Shipyards Ltd — Hong Kong** Yd No: 690 Loa 35.03 Br ex 6.96 Dght 2.744 Lbp 32.97 Br md 6.71 Dpth 3.20 Riveted\Welded, 1 dk	**(A31A2GX) General Cargo Ship** Grain: 258 Compartments: 1 Ho, ER Derricks: 2x2t; Winches: 2	**1 oil engine** driving 1 FP propeller 9.0kn Blackstone E6 1 x 4 Stroke 6 Cy. 222 x 292 Blackstone & Co. Ltd.-Stamford Fuel: 14.0
9420162 *TCSS2* -	**SELAHATTIN ASLAN 2** - **ARINTAS Arslan Insaat Nakliyat Sanayi ve Ticaret AS** Selmar Denizcilik Sanayi ve Ticaret AS *Istanbul* *Turkey* MMSI: 271000965	**2,875** Class: BV 1,397 4,300	**2007-06 Selahattin Aslan Tersanesi — Tuzla** Yd No: 9 Loa 88.80 Br ex - Dght 6.630 Lbp 80.95 Br md 13.50 Dpth 7.80 Welded, 1 dk	**(A31A2GX) General Cargo Ship** Grain: 5,095	**1 oil engine** reduction geared to sc. shaft driving 1 FP propeller Total Power: 1,449kW (1,970hp) 13.0kn MAN-B&W 6L28/32A 1 x 4 Stroke 6 Cy. 280 x 320 1449kW (1970bhp) MAN Diesel A/S-Denmark
8972170 - -	**SELAMAT 17** - **Neptune Shipbuilding & Engineering Pte Ltd** -	**103** Class: (GL) 35 -	**1992-10 Maju Layar Sdn Bhd — Sibu** Yd No: 370-P Loa 18.98 Br ex 6.87 Dght 2.690 Lbp 18.22 Br md 6.60 Dpth 2.80 Welded, 1 dk	**(B32A2ST) Tug**	**2 oil engines** geared to sc. shafts driving 2 FP propellers Total Power: 520kW (706hp) Caterpillar 2 x 4 Stroke each-260kW (353bhp) Caterpillar Inc-USA
8826345 - -	**SELAMAT II** - **PT Bahar Budi Raya** - *Samarinda* *Indonesia*	*142* Class: (KI) 78 -	**1985 P.T. Tirta Kencana Overseas — Samarinda** Loa 31.90 Br ex 7.16 Dght 1.700 Lbp 29.15 Br md - Dpth 2.13 Welded, 1 dk	**(A35D2RL) Landing Craft** Bow door/ramp	**2 oil engines** geared to sc. shafts driving 2 FP propellers Total Power: 242kW (330hp) Yanmar 6KDGGE 2 x 4 Stroke 6 Cy. 145 x 170 each-121kW (165bhp) Yanmar Diesel Engine Co Ltd-Japan AuxGen: 1 x 16kW 220V a.c
8329335 *PLPG* -	**SELAMAT SENTOSA** *ex* Asahimas I *-2002* **PT Pelnus Sri Indrapura** - *Jakarta* *Indonesia*	*245* Class: (KI) 118 430	**1970 in Japan** Loa - Br ex - Dght - Lbp 35.01 Br md 8.01 Dpth 3.41 Welded, 1 dk	**(A31A2GX) General Cargo Ship**	**1 oil engine** driving 1 FP propeller Total Power: 353kW (480hp) Sumiyoshi 1 x 4 Stroke 6 Cy. 353kW (480bhp) Sumiyoshi Tekkosho-Japan
7218254 *YDA4113* -	**SELAMAT VI** *ex* Kame Maru *-2005* **PT Multi Agung Sarana Ananda** - *Tanjung Priok* *Indonesia*	*264* Class: KI 80 -	**1972-04 Hibikinada Dock Co. Ltd. — Kitakyushu** (Hull) Yd No: 119 **1972-04 Tokushima Zosen Sangyo K.K. — Komatsushima** Yd No: 330 Loa 29.01 Br ex 8.54 Dght 2.801 Lbp 26.52 Br md 8.51 Dpth 3.92 Welded, 1 dk	**(B32A2ST) Tug**	**2 oil engines** driving 2 FP propellers Total Power: 1,912kW (2,600hp) 11.0kn Daihatsu 6DSM-26 2 x 4 Stroke 6 Cy. 260 x 320 each-956kW (1300bhp) Daihatsu Diesel Manufacturing Co Lt-Japan Fuel: 81.5 11.0pd
9497335 *V2FK3* -	**SELANDIA** - **ms 'Selandia' Schiffahrtsgesellschaft mbH & Co KG** DT-Bereederungs GmbH & Co KG SatCom: Inmarsat C 430500437 *Saint John's* *Antigua & Barbuda* MMSI: 305701000 Official number: 4850	**43,717** Class: GL (LR) 26,502 ✠ Classed LR until 22/3/11 79,508 T/cm 71.9	**2011-03 Jiangsu Eastern Heavy Industry Co Ltd — Jingjiang JS** Yd No: 06C-014 Loa 229.00 (BB) Br ex 32.30 Dght 14.620 Lbp 222.00 Br md 32.26 Dpth 20.25 Welded, 1 dk	**(A21A2BC) Bulk Carrier** Grain: 97,000; Bale: 90,784 Compartments: 7 Ho, ER 7 Ha: ER Ice Capable	**1 oil engine** driving 1 FP propeller Total Power: 11,620kW (15,799hp) 14.0kn Wartsila 7RT-flex50 1 x 2 Stroke 7 Cy. 500 x 2050 11620kW (15799bhp) Diesel United Ltd.-Aioi AuxGen: 3 x 700kW 450V 60Hz a.c Boilers: AuxB (Comp) 8.4kgf/cm² (8.2bar)
9157284 *OWLH2* -	**SELANDIA SEAWAYS** *ex* Tor Selandia *-2010* **DFDS Seaways AB** - *Copenhagen* *Denmark (DIS)* MMSI: 219458000	**24,803** Class: NV 7,258 11,089 T/cm 41.0	**1998-12 Fincantieri-Cant. Nav. Italiani S.p.A. — Ancona** Yd No: 6020 Loa 197.02 (BB) Br ex 25.90 Dght 7.500 Lbp 180.00 Br md 25.20 Dpth 9.50 Welded, 3 dks including 1 hoistable	**(A35A2RR) Ro-Ro Cargo Ship** Passengers: 12 Stern door/ramp (a) Len: 14.00 Wid: 20.80 Swl: 180 Lane-Len: 2772 Lane-Wid: 2.95 Lane-clr ht: 6.00 Trailers: 198	**2 oil engines** with flexible couplings & sr gearedto sc. shafts driving 2 CP propellers Total Power: 21,600kW (29,368hp) 21.0kn Sulzer 9ZA50S 2 x 4 Stroke 9 Cy. 500 x 660 each-10800kW (14684bhp) Grandi Motori Trieste-Italy AuxGen: 2 x 1400kW 380V 50Hz a.c, 3 x 900kW 380V 50Hz a.c Thrusters: 2 Thwart. CP thruster (f) Fuel: 50.0 (d.f.) (Heating Coils) 708.0 (r.f.) 70.0pd
9371787 *OYIN2* -	**SELANDIA SWAN** *launched as* Besiktas Nordland *-2008* **Uni-Tankers mt 'Selandia Swan' ApS** Uni-Tankers A/S (UNI-TANKERS) SatCom: Inmarsat Mini-M 763479955 *Middelfart* *Denmark (DIS)* MMSI: 220545000 Official number: D4329	**11,711** Class: GL (BV) 6,020 17,998 T/cm 28.1	**2008-03 Gisan Gemi Ins. San — Istanbul** Yd No: 40 Loa 147.50 (BB) Br ex 22.43 Dght 9.490 Lbp 138.00 Br md 22.40 Dpth 12.60 Welded, 1 dk	**(A12B2TR) Chemical/Products Tanker** Double Hull (13F) Liq: 20,185; Liq (Oil): 21,300 Compartments: 14 Wing Ta, 2 Wing Slop Ta, ER 14 Cargo Pump (s): 14x380m³/hr Manifold: Bow/CM: 71.4m Ice Capable	**1 oil engine** reduction geared to sc. shaft driving 1 CP propeller Total Power: 6,300kW (8,565hp) 14.0kn MaK 7M43 1 x 4 Stroke 7 Cy. 430 x 610 6300kW (8565bhp) Caterpillar Motoren GmbH & Co. KG-Germany AuxGen: 3 x 800kW 440V 60Hz a.c, 1 x 1200kW 440V a.c Thrusters: 1 Tunnel thruster (f) Fuel: 173.0 (d.f.) 830.0 (r.f.) 23.0pd
7517789 *YCGK* -	**SELAT BALI** - **PT Pelabuhan Indonesia III (Persero) (Indonesia Port Corp III) (PELINDO III)** - *Jakarta* *Indonesia*	*212* Class: (KI) (AB) 144 169	**1977-03 Equitable Shipyards, Inc. — New Orleans, La** Yd No: 1683 Loa 29.11 Br ex 8.84 Dght 3.353 Lbp 26.52 Br md 8.63 Dpth 4.02 Welded, 1 dk	**(B32A2ST) Tug**	**2 oil engines** reverse reduction geared to sc. shafts driving 2 FP propellers Total Power: 1,250kW (1,700hp) 11.0kn Caterpillar D398SCAC 2 x Vee 4 Stroke 12 Cy. 159 x 203 each-625kW (850bhp) Caterpillar Tractor Co-USA AuxGen: 2 x 75kW
7517791 - -	**SELAT BANGKA** - **Government of The Republic of Indonesia (Direktorat Jenderal Perhubungan Laut - Ministry of Sea Communications)** PT Pelabuhan Indonesia II (Persero) (Indonesia Port Corp II) (PELINDO II) *Jakarta* *Indonesia*	*212* Class: KI (AB) 144 169	**1977-04 Equitable Shipyards, Inc. — New Orleans, La** Yd No: 1684 Loa 29.11 Br ex 8.84 Dght 3.353 Lbp 26.52 Br md 8.63 Dpth 4.02 Welded, 1 dk	**(B32A2ST) Tug**	**2 oil engines** reverse reduction geared to sc. shafts driving 2 FP propellers Total Power: 1,250kW (1,700hp) 11.0kn Caterpillar D398SCAC 2 x Vee 4 Stroke 12 Cy. 159 x 203 each-625kW (850bhp) Caterpillar Tractor Co-USA AuxGen: 2 x 85kW
8340444 - -	**SELAT BANGKA** - **PT Pelabuhan Indonesia II (Persero) Cabang Pelabuhan Tanjung Priok (Indonesia Port Corp II, Tanjung Priok)** PT Pelabuhan Indonesia II (Persero) (Indonesia Port Corp II) (PELINDO II) *Jakarta* *Indonesia*	**186** Class: (KI) 56 -	**1975 Promet Pte Ltd — Singapore** Loa - Br ex - Dght - Lbp 28.71 Br md 7.60 Dpth 3.87 Welded, 1 dk	**(B32A2ST) Tug**	**2 oil engines** geared to sc. shafts driving 2 FP propellers Total Power: 1,280kW (1,740hp) Deutz SBA6M528 2 x 4 Stroke 6 Cy. 220 x 280 each-640kW (870bhp) Kloeckner Humboldt Deutz AG-West Germany
7617060 *YCGT* -	**SELAT BUNGA LAUT** - **PT Pelabuhan Indonesia II (Persero) (Indonesia Port Corp II) (PELINDO II)** - *Jakarta* *Indonesia*	*159* Class: (KI) (NV) 1 -	**1977-11 Kleivset Baatbyggeri — Foldfjorden** (Hull) **1977-11 AS Storviks Mek. Verksted — Kristiansund** Yd No: 84 Loa 26.32 Br ex - Dght 3.001 Lbp 24.01 Br md 8.01 Dpth 3.81 Welded, 1 dk	**(B32A2ST) Tug**	**1 oil engine** geared to sc. shaft driving 1 FP propeller Total Power: 853kW (1,160hp) Deutz SBA8M528 1 x 4 Stroke 8 Cy. 220 x 280 853kW (1160bhp) Kloeckner Humboldt Deutz AG-West Germany

5319468 - -	**SELAT DURIAN** *ex* Penolong *-1961* *ex* Rose *-1961* **PT Pelabuhan Indonesia II (Persero) Cabang Pelabuhan Tanjung Priok (Indonesia Port Corp II, Tanjung Priok)** - *Jakarta* *Indonesia*	*102* - -	Class: (LR) ✠	**1929-01 The Taikoo Dockyard & Engineering Co — Hong Kong** Rebuilt-1961 Loa 28.96 Br ex 6.61 Dght 2.915 Lbp 28.66 Br md 6.48 Dpth 2.93 Riveted\Welded, 1 dk	**(B32A2ST) Tug**	**2 oil engines** driving 2 FP propellers Deutz RV6M345 2 x 4 Stroke 6 Cy. 280 x 450 Humboldt Deutmotoren AG-Koeln
8872071 *HP7371* -	**SELAT EAGLE** *ex* Seabulk Eagle *-2004* *ex* Imsalv Star *-1997* *ex* Lucy D. *-1994* **Blue Sky Marine Shipping Inc** - *Panama* *Panama* MMSI: 352782000 Official number: 22603PEXT5	*169* 50 3	Class: (BV) (GL)	**1979-06 Queen Craft, Inc. — Panama City, Fl** Loa 36.58 Br ex - Dght 3.050 Lbp 32.68 Br md 8.33 Dpth 3.35 Welded, 1 dk	**(B21A2OS) Platform Supply Ship**	**2 oil engines** reverse reduction geared to sc. shafts driving 2 FP propellers Total Power: 882kW (1,200hp) 13.0kn Caterpillar D379TA 2 x Vee 4 Stroke 8 Cy. 159 x 203 each-441kW (600bhp) Caterpillar Tractor Co-USA AuxGen: 2 x 50kW 220/440V a.c
8333283 *A6E3045* -	**SELAT FAITH** *ex* Singaora *-2003* **Selat Marine Services Co Ltd** - *Sharjah* *United Arab Emirates* MMSI: 470821464 Official number: 5200	**488** 146 -	Class: AB	**1984 Yamakawa Zosen Tekko K.K. — Kagoshima** Yd No: 673 Loa - Br ex - Dght 3.771 Lbp 38.99 Br md 10.00 Dpth 4.50 Welded, 1 dk	**(B22A2OV) Diving Support Vessel**	**2 oil engines** geared to sc. shafts driving 2 FP propellers Total Power: 1,618kW (2,200hp) 12.5kn Fuji 6M23C 2 x 4 Stroke 6 Cy. 230 x 260 each-809kW (1100bhp) Fuji Diesel Co Ltd-Japan AuxGen: 2 x 200kW a.c
9554963 *9V9655* -	**SELAT FALCON** - **Selat Offshore Pte Ltd** Selat Marine Services Co Ltd *Singapore* *Singapore* MMSI: 566297000 Official number: 397435	**453** 135 500	Class: BV	**2011-11 Guangzhou Panyu Yuefeng Shiprepair & Building Yard — Guangzhou GD** Yd No: GMG0784 Loa 36.50 Br ex - Dght 4.200 Lbp 31.02 Br md 10.40 Dpth 5.00 Welded, 1 dk	**(B32A2ST) Tug**	**3 oil engines** reduction geared to sc. shafts driving 2 FP propellers Total Power: 2,384kW (3,242hp) Cummins KTA-50-M2 2 x Vee 4 Stroke 16 Cy. 159 x 159 each-1192kW (1621bhp) Cummins Diesel International Ltd-USA Fuel: 350.0
8810279 *YHNF* -	**SELAT IGGAR** *ex* Putri Vania *-2011* *ex* Izumi Maru *-2003* **PT Selatiggar Lines** - *Surabaya* *Indonesia*	*619* 312 452	Class: KI	**1988-10 Honda Zosen — Saiki** Yd No: 785 Loa 49.75 Br ex - Dght 3.101 Lbp 45.45 Br md 10.22 Dpth 5.21 Welded	**(A31A2GX) General Cargo Ship**	**1 oil engine** driving 1 FP propeller Total Power: 405kW (551hp) Niigata 6M26AGTE 1 x 4 Stroke 6 Cy. 260 x 460 405kW (551bhp) Niigata Engineering Co Ltd-Japan AuxGen: 1 x 74kW 225/130V a.c, 1 x 37kW 225/130V a.c
7617046 *YCGQ* -	**SELAT KARIMATA** - **Government of The Republic of Indonesia (Direktorat Jenderal Perhubungan Laut - Ministry of Sea Communications)** PT Pelabuhan Indonesia II (Persero) (Indonesia Port Corp II) (PELINDO II) *Jakarta* *Indonesia*	*157* 48 75	Class: (KI) (NV)	**1977-09 Hjorungavaag Verksted AS — Hjorungavaag** Yd No: 29 Loa 26.32 Br ex - Dght 3.001 Lbp 24.01 Br md 8.01 Dpth 3.81 Welded, 1 dk	**(B32A2ST) Tug**	**1 oil engine** geared to sc. shaft driving 1 FP propeller Total Power: 853kW (1,160hp) 11.0kn Deutz SBA8M528 1 x 4 Stroke 8 Cy. 220 x 280 853kW (1160bhp) Kloeckner Humboldt Deutz AG-West Germany
7517765 - -	**SELAT LAUT** - **Government of The Republic of Indonesia (Direktorat Jenderal Perhubungan Laut - Ministry of Sea Communications)** PT Pelabuhan Indonesia I (Persero) Cabang Belawan (Indonesia Port Corp I, Belawan Branch) *Jakarta* *Indonesia*	*194* 59 169	Class: KI (AB)	**1977-02 Equitable Shipyards, Inc. — New Orleans, La** Yd No: 1681 Loa 29.11 Br ex 8.84 Dght 3.353 Lbp 26.52 Br md 8.63 Dpth 4.02 Welded, 1 dk	**(B32A2ST) Tug**	**2 oil engines** reverse reduction geared to sc. shafts driving 2 FP propellers Total Power: 1,250kW (1,700hp) 14.0kn Caterpillar D398SCAC 2 x Vee 4 Stroke 12 Cy. 159 x 203 each-625kW (850bhp) Caterpillar Tractor Co-USA
9099949 *YDA4311* -	**SELAT LEGUNDI-I 212** - **PT Pelabuhan Indonesia II (Persero) (Indonesia Port Corp II) (PELINDO II)** - *Jakarta* *Indonesia*	**291** 88 -	Class: KI	**2007-03 P.T. Daya Radar Utama — Jakarta** L reg 29.00 Br ex - Dght 3.490 Lbp 25.50 Br md 9.50 Dpth 4.58 Welded, 1 dk	**(B32A2ST) Tug**	**2 oil engines** geared to sc. shafts driving 2 Propellers Total Power: 1,766kW (2,402hp) Yanmar 6N21A-SV 2 x 4 Stroke 6 Cy. 210 x 290 each-883kW (1201bhp) Yanmar Diesel Engine Co Ltd-Japan
8654118 - -	**SELAT LEGUNDI-II.206** - **PT Pelabuhan Indonesia II (Persero) (Indonesia Port Corp II) (PELINDO II)** - *Samarinda* *Indonesia*	**129** 39 -	Class: KI	**2011-01 PT Succes Ocean Shipping — Samarinda** Loa 23.50 Br ex - Dght - Lbp 21.93 Br md 7.00 Dpth 3.10 Welded, 1 dk	**(B32A2ST) Tug**	**2 oil engines** reduction geared to sc. shafts driving 2 FP propellers AuxGen: 2 x 95kW a.c
7617058 *YCGN* -	**SELAT LEMBEH** - **Government of The Republic of Indonesia (Direktorat Jenderal Perhubungan Laut - Ministry of Sea Communications)** PT Pelabuhan Indonesia IV (Persero) Cabang Bitung (Indonesia Port Corp IV, Bitung) *Makassar* *Indonesia*	*160* 48 75	Class: KI (NV)	**1977-06 Kleivset Baatbyggeri — Foldfjorden** (Hull) **1977-06 AS Storviks Mek. Verksted — Kristiansund** Yd No: 83 Loa 26.29 Br ex - Dght 3.001 Lbp 24.01 Br md 8.01 Dpth 3.81 Welded, 1 dk	**(B32A2ST) Tug**	**1 oil engine** geared to sc. shaft driving 1 FP propeller Total Power: 853kW (1,160hp) Deutz SBA8M528 1 x 4 Stroke 8 Cy. 220 x 280 853kW (1160bhp) Kloeckner Humboldt Deutz AG-West Germany
8340456 - -	**SELAT LOMBOK** - **PT Pelabuhan Indonesia II (Persero) (Indonesia Port Corp II) (PELINDO II)** - *Jakarta* *Indonesia*	*198* 21 -	Class: (KI)	**1975 Promet Pte Ltd — Singapore** Loa - Br ex - Dght - Lbp 28.71 Br md 7.60 Dpth 3.87 Welded, 1 dk	**(B32A2ST) Tug**	**2 oil engines** geared to sc. shafts driving 2 FP propellers Total Power: 1,280kW (1,740hp) Deutz SBA6M528 2 x 4 Stroke 6 Cy. 220 x 280 each-640kW (870bhp) Kloeckner Humboldt Deutz AG-West Germany
8013302 *YB5176* -	**SELAT MADURA I** - **PT Jembatan Nusantara** - *Jakarta* *Indonesia*	*209* 79 50	Class: KI	**1981-02 P.T. Kodja (Unit I) — Jakarta** Yd No: 666 Loa 37.60 Br ex - Dght 1.901 Lbp 32.03 Br md 10.02 Dpth 2.57 Welded	**(A37B2PS) Passenger Ship**	**2 oil engines** geared to sc. shaft driving 1 FP propeller Total Power: 268kW (364hp) Deutz F8L413F 2 x Vee 4 Stroke 8 Cy. 120 x 125 each-134kW (182bhp) Kloeckner Humboldt Deutz AG-West Germany AuxGen: 1 x 22kW 400V a.c
8328484 *YB5177* -	**SELAT MADURA II** - **PT Jembatan Nusantara** - *Jakarta* *Indonesia*	*209* 79 50	Class: KI	**1981 P.T. Kodja (Unit I) — Jakarta** Loa 37.60 Br ex - Dght 1.901 Lbp 32.03 Br md 10.02 Dpth 2.57 Welded, 1 dk	**(A37B2PS) Passenger Ship**	**2 oil engines** geared to sc. shafts driving 2 FP propellers Total Power: 268kW (364hp) Deutz F8L413F 2 x Vee 4 Stroke 8 Cy. 120 x 125 each-134kW (182bhp) Kloeckner Humboldt Deutz AG-West Germany
9104146 *POQU* -	**SELAT MAS** *ex* Acx Cosmos *-2012* **PT Pelayaran Tempuran Emas Tbk (TEMAS Line)** - *Jakarta* *Indonesia* MMSI: 525005115	**13,941** 7,039 18,106	Class: NK	**1995-01 Imabari Shipbuilding Co Ltd — Imabari EH (Imabari Shipyard)** Yd No: 510 Loa 163.66 (BB) Br ex - Dght 8.915 Lbp 152.00 Br md 26.00 Dpth 13.40 Welded, 1 dk	**(A33A2CC) Container Ship (Fully Cellular)** TEU 1241 incl 197 ref C. Compartments: 4 Cell Ho 8 Ha: ER	**1 oil engine** driving 1 FP propeller Total Power: 9,628kW (13,090hp) 18.0kn Mitsubishi 7UEC50LSII 1 x 2 Stroke 7 Cy. 500 x 1950 9628kW (13090bhp) Kobe Hatsudoki KK-Japan AuxGen: 3 x 825kW 440V 60Hz a.c Thrusters: 1 Thwart. CP thruster (f) Fuel: 128.0 (d.f.) 1414.0 (r.f.) 36.0pd
8301216 *A6E2663* -	**SELAT PISCES** *ex* Bertram *-1998* *ex* TSS Bertram *-1992* *ex* Teratai *-1984* *ex* Osam Dragon 8 *-1984* **Selat Marine Services Co Ltd** - *Sharjah* *United Arab Emirates* MMSI: 470519000 Official number: SHJ4400	**386** 115 750	Class: AB	**1983-06 Goriki Zosensho — Ise** Yd No: 861 Loa 38.99 Br ex 9.53 Dght 3.215 Lbp 35.01 Br md 9.50 Dpth 3.61 Welded, 1 dk	**(B21A2OS) Platform Supply Ship**	**2 oil engines** sr reverse geared to sc. shafts driving 2 FP propellers Total Power: 1,176kW (1,598hp) 11.5kn Otsuka SODHS6X26 2 x 4 Stroke 6 Cy. 260 x 410 each-588kW (799bhp) KK Otsuka Diesel-Japan AuxGen: 1 x 128kW a.c, 1 x 100kW a.c Thrusters: 1 Thwart. FP thruster (f)
7617034 *YCGM* -	**SELAT RIAU** - **Government of The Republic of Indonesia (Direktorat Jenderal Perhubungan Laut - Ministry of Sea Communications)** - *Dumai* *Indonesia*	*158* 1 75	Class: (KI) (NV)	**1977-05 Hjorungavaag Verksted AS — Hjorungavaag** Yd No: 28 Loa 26.32 Br ex - Dght 3.001 Lbp 24.01 Br md 8.01 Dpth 3.81 Welded, 1 dk	**(B32A2ST) Tug**	**1 oil engine** geared to sc. shaft driving 1 CP propeller Total Power: 853kW (1,160hp) 11.0kn Deutz SBA8M528 1 x 4 Stroke 8 Cy. 220 x 280 853kW (1160bhp) Kloeckner Humboldt Deutz AG-West Germany

IMO / Call sign	Name / Owner / Flag	Tonnage	Class	Builder / Dimensions	Type / Capacity	Machinery
7517753 - -	**SELAT SIBERUT** **PT Pelabuhan Indonesia II (Persero) Cabang Teluk Bayur (Indonesia Port Corp II, Teluk Bayur)** - *Dumai* *Indonesia*	*212* 64 170	Class: (KI) (AB)	**1976-10 Equitable Shipyards, Inc. — New Orleans, La** Yd No: 1680 Loa 29.11 Br ex 8.84 Dght 3.353 Lbp 26.52 Br md 8.74 Dpth 4.53 Welded, 1 dk	**(B32A2ST) Tug**	**2 oil engines** reverse reduction geared to sc. shafts driving 2 FP propellers Total Power: 1,250kW (1,700hp) 14.0kn Caterpillar D398SCAC 2 x Vee 4 Stroke 12 Cy. 159 x 203 each-625kW (850bhp) Caterpillar Tractor Co-USA AuxGen: 2 x 75kW
9646170 *9V9748* -	**SELAT STAR** **Selat Offshore Pte Ltd** - *Singapore* *Singapore* MMSI: 566370000 Official number: 397539	**453** 135 500	Class: BV	**2012-01 Guangzhou Panyu Yuefeng Shiprepair & Building Yard — Guangzhou GD** Yd No: GMG0891 Loa 36.50 Br ex - Dght 4.200 Lbp 31.50 Br md 10.40 Dpth 5.00 Welded, 1 dk	**(B32A2ST) Tug**	**2 oil engines** reduction geared to sc. shafts driving 2 FP propellers Total Power: 3,244kW (4,410hp) Cummins 2 x Vee 4 Stroke 16 Cy. 159 x 159 each-1622kW (2205bhp) Cummins Diesel International Ltd-USA
9646015 *9V9749* -	**SELAT SUCCESS** **Selat Marine Services Co Ltd** - *Singapore* *Singapore* MMSI: 566343000 Official number: 397540	**375** 112 308	Class: BV	**2011-12 Guangzhou Panyu Lingshan Shipyard Ltd — Guangzhou GD** Yd No: 201 Loa 36.30 Br ex 10.12 Dght 3.500 Lbp 32.54 Br md 9.80 Dpth 4.30 Welded, 1 dk	**(B32A2ST) Tug**	**2 oil engines** reduction geared to sc. shafts driving 2 FP propellers Total Power: 1,492kW (2,028hp) Caterpillar 3508B 2 x Vee 4 Stroke 8 Cy. 170 x 190 each-746kW (1014bhp) Caterpillar Inc-USA AuxGen: 2 x 215kW 50Hz a.c Thrusters: 1 Tunnel thruster (f) Fuel: 260.0
7641322 - -	**SELAT SUNDA** **PT Pelabuhan Indonesia II (Persero) Cabang Pelabuhan Tanjung Priok (Indonesia Port Corp II, Tanjung Priok)** PT Pelabuhan Indonesia II (Persero) (Indonesia Port Corp II) (PELINDO II) *Jakarta* *Indonesia*	*188* 25 -	Class: (KI)	**1975 Promet Pte Ltd — Singapore** Loa - Br ex 7.62 Dght - Lbp 28.71 Br md 7.60 Dpth 3.84 Welded, 1 dk	**(B32A2ST) Tug**	**2 oil engines** geared to sc. shafts driving 2 FP propellers Total Power: 1,280kW (1,740hp) Deutz SBA6M528 2 x 4 Stroke 6 Cy. 220 x 280 each-640kW (870bhp) Kloeckner Humboldt Deutz AG-West Germany
7702607 *YCGO* -	**SELAT TANAKEKE** **Government of The Republic of Indonesia (Direktorat Jenderal Perhubungan Laut - Ministry of Sea Communications)** PT Pelabuhan Indonesia IV (Persero) (Indonesia Port Corp IV) (PELINDO IV) *Makassar* *Indonesia*	*158* 1 -	Class: (KI) (NV)	**1977-09 Sterkoder Mek. Verksted AS — Kristiansund** Yd No: 75 Loa 26.04 Br ex - Dght 3.001 Lbp 24.01 Br md 8.01 Dpth 3.08 Welded, 1 dk	**(B32A2ST) Tug**	**1 oil engine** geared to sc. shaft driving 1 FP propeller Total Power: 853kW (1,160hp) 12.0kn Deutz SBA8M528 1 x 4 Stroke 8 Cy. 220 x 280 853kW (1160bhp) Kloeckner Humboldt Deutz AG-West Germany
9182679 *YHSM* -	**SELATAN DATANG** *ex* Kota Datang *-2004* *ex* Selamat Datang *-2002* *ex* Nutra Idaman *-2002* *ex* Ngee Tai No. 5 *-2000* **PT Pelayaran Samudera Selatan** Pacific International Lines (Pte) Ltd *Jakarta* *Indonesia* MMSI: 525019219 Official number: 389736	**2,509** 753 3,956	Class: BV (NK)	**1997-11 Moxen Shipyard Sdn Bhd — Sibu** Yd No: 3495 Loa 77.00 Br ex - Dght 4.335 Lbp 71.79 Br md 21.34 Dpth 5.48 Welded, 1 dk	**(A31A2GX) General Cargo Ship** Grain: 4,860; Bale: 4,410 Compartments: 2 Ho, ER 2 Ha: ER	**2 oil engines** reduction geared to sc. shafts driving 2 FP propellers Total Power: 1,790kW (2,434hp) 11.0kn Yanmar M220-EN 2 x 4 Stroke 6 Cy. 220 x 300 each-895kW (1217bhp) Yanmar Diesel Engine Co Ltd-Japan AuxGen: 2 x 80kW 450/220V 50Hz a.c
7525877 *YGMY* -	**SELATAN MEGAH** *ex* Kota Megah *-2003* *ex* CGM Bretagne *-1992* *ex* Impala *-1985* **PT Salam Pacific Indonesia Lines** - *Jakarta* *Indonesia* MMSI: 525019047	**7,028** 3,933 8,512	Class: (KI) (BV) (GL)	**1977-03 Yamanishi Shipbuilding Co Ltd — Ishinomaki MG** Yd No: 810 Loa 129.32 (BB) Br ex 19.23 Dght 7.821 Lbp 119.31 Br md 19.21 Dpth 10.24 Welded, 2 dks	**(A31A2GX) General Cargo Ship** Grain: 12,875; Bale: 11,627 TEU 312 C Ho 180 TEU C Dk 132 TEU incl 30 ref C. Compartments: 3 Ho, ER, 3 Tw Dk 3 Ha: (12.3 x 10.3)2 (25.3 x 12.9)ER Derricks: 2x50t,3x30t Ice Capable	**1 oil engine** driving 1 FP propeller Total Power: 4,410kW (5,996hp) 16.5kn B&W 7K45GF 1 x 2 Stroke 7 Cy. 450 x 900 4410kW (5996bhp) Hitachi Zosen Corp-Japan AuxGen: 2 x 520kW 450V 60Hz a.c, 1 x 350kW 450V 60Hz a.c Fuel: 146.0 (d.f.) (Heating Coils) 904.0 (r.f.)
8870865 *TCBG6* -	**SELAY** **Selay Denizcilik Sanayi ve Ticaret Ltd Sti** - *Istanbul* *Turkey* MMSI: 271002100 Official number: 6411	**1,584** 944 2,878 T/cm 8.0	Class: BV	**1993-04 Hidrodinamik Gemi Sanayi ve Ticaret A.S. — Tuzla, Istanbul** Loa 80.00 Br ex - Dght 5.510 Lbp 71.05 Br md 12.20 Dpth 6.20 Welded, 1 dk	**(A13B2TP) Products Tanker** Liq: 2,922; Liq (Oil): 2,922 Cargo Heating Coils Compartments: 10 Ta, ER 2 Cargo Pump (s): 2x500m³/hr	**1 oil engine** reduction geared to sc. shaft driving 1 FP propeller Total Power: 970kW (1,319hp) 11.0kn S.K.L. 8NVD48A-2U 1 x 4 Stroke 8 Cy. 320 x 480 970kW (1319bhp) SKL Motoren u. Systemtechnik AG-Magdeburg
9405320 *TCPM9* -	**SELAY-S** **Sener Petrol Denizcilik Ticaret AS** - *Istanbul* *Turkey* MMSI: 271000894	**7,776** 3,865 11,796 T/cm 22.1	Class: BV	**2008-03 Yildirim Gemi Insaat Sanayii A.S. — Tuzla** Yd No: 110 Loa 130.12 (BB) Br ex - Dght 8.350 Lbp 123.67 Br md 19.60 Dpth 10.90 Welded, 1 dk	**(A12B2TR) Chemical/Products Tanker** Double Hull (13F) Liq: 13,010; Liq (Oil): 13,010 Cargo Heating Coils Compartments: 14 Wing Ta, 2 Wing Slop Ta, ER 14 Cargo Pump (s): 14x300m³/hr Manifold: Bow/CM: 67m Ice Capable	**1 oil engine** reduction geared to sc. shaft driving 1 FP propeller Total Power: 4,500kW (6,118hp) 15.0kn MAN-B&W 9L32/40 1 x 4 Stroke 9 Cy. 320 x 400 4500kW (6118bhp) MAN B&W Diesel AG-Augsburg AuxGen: 1 x 648kW 50Hz a.c, 2 x 550kW 50Hz a.c Thrusters: 1 Tunnel thruster (f) Fuel: 85.0 (d.f.) 548.0 (r.f.)
9553335 *LIXG* -	**SELBJORNSFJORD** **FosenNamsos Sjo AS** - *Bergen* *Norway* MMSI: 259094000	**2,989** 896 900	Class: NV	**2010-12 UAB Vakaru Laivu Remontas (JSC Western Shiprepair) — Klaipeda** (Hull) Yd No: (70) **2010-12 Fiskerstrand Verft AS — Fiskarstrand** Yd No: 70 Loa 113.96 Br ex 17.20 Dght 3.100 Lbp 105.00 Br md 16.80 Dpth 5.50 Welded, 1 dk	**(A36A2PR) Passenger/Ro-Ro Ship (Vehicles)** Passengers: unberthed: 249 Cars: 120	**3 diesel electric oil engines** driving 3 gen. Connecting to 2 elec. motors reduction geared to sc. shaft driving 2 Azimuth electric drive units 1 propeller fwd, 1 aft Total Power: 3,620kW (4,922hp) 13.0kn Mitsubishi GS12R-MPTA 1 x Vee 4 Stroke 12 Cy. 170 x 180 1200kW (1632bhp) Mitsubishi Heavy Industries Ltd-Japan Mitsubishi S12R-MPTK 2 x Vee 4 Stroke 12 Cy. 170 x 180 each-1210kW (1645bhp) Mitsubishi Heavy Industries Ltd-Japan
9540601 *TCMD9* -	**SELDENIZ** *launched as* Enver Aslan 2 *-2011* **Seldeniz Sel Denizcilik AS** Selmar Denizcilik Sanayi ve Ticaret AS *Istanbul* *Turkey* MMSI: 271042622	**2,861** 1,397 4,300	Class: BV	**2011-04 Seltas Denizcilik Sanayi ve Ticaret AS — Altinova** Yd No: 1 Loa 88.80 (BB) Br ex - Dght 6.500 Lbp 80.80 Br md 13.50 Dpth 7.80 Welded, 1 dk	**(A31A2GX) General Cargo Ship** Grain: 5,095 Compartments: 2 Ho, ER 2 Ha: ER	**1 oil engine** reduction geared to sc. shaft driving 1 CP propeller Total Power: 1,470kW (1,999hp) 14.5kn MAN-B&W 6L28/32A 1 x 4 Stroke 6 Cy. 280 x 320 1470kW (1999bhp) STX Engine Co Ltd-South Korea AuxGen: 2 x 150kW 50Hz a.c Thrusters: 1 Tunnel thruster (f)
8117158 *YDXR* -	**SELE/PERTAMINA 3006** **PT PERTAMINA (PERSERO)** - *Jakarta* *Indonesia* MMSI: 525008023	**21,338** 7,234 29,900 T/cm 47.0	Class: KI (LR) ✠ Classed LR until 8/12/01	**1982-09 Sasebo Heavy Industries Co. Ltd. — Sasebo Yard, Sasebo** Yd No: 307 Loa 180.02 (BB) Br ex 30.03 Dght 8.875 Lbp 171.00 Br md 30.00 Dpth 15.02 Welded, 1 dk	**(A13B2TP) Products Tanker** Single Hull Liq: 39,653; Liq (Oil): 39,653 Compartments: 10 Ta, ER 3 Cargo Pump (s) Manifold: Bow/CM: 90m	**1 oil engine** driving 1 FP propeller Total Power: 9,731kW (13,230hp) 15.0kn Sulzer 6RLB66 1 x 2 Stroke 6 Cy. 660 x 1400 9731kW (13230bhp) Ishikawajima Harima Heavy IndustrieCo Ltd (IHI)-Japan AuxGen: 3 x 680kW 450V 60Hz a.c Fuel: 195.5 (d.f.) (Heating Coils) 606.5 (r.f.)
9388297 *A8OD9* -	**SELECAO** **Bayswater Trading Co Ltd** Tsakos Columbia Shipmanagement (TCM) SA *Monrovia* *Liberia* MMSI: 636013614 Official number: 13614	**41,676** 21,792 74,296 T/cm 67.2	Class: AB	**2008-02 Sungdong Shipbuilding & Marine Engineering Co Ltd — Tongyeong** Yd No: 3003 Loa 228.00 (BB) Br ex 32.56 Dght 14.317 Lbp 219.00 Br md 32.24 Dpth 20.60 Welded, 1 dk	**(A13A2TW) Crude/Oil Products Tanker** Double Hull (13F) Liq: 78,928; Liq (Oil): 83,104 Cargo Heating Coils Compartments: 12 Wing Ta, 2 Wing Slop Ta, ER 3 Cargo Pump (s): 3x2000m³/hr Manifold: Bow/CM: 113.1m	**1 oil engine** driving 1 FP propeller Total Power: 12,240kW (16,642hp) 15.3kn MAN-B&W 6S60MC 1 x 2 Stroke 6 Cy. 600 x 2292 12240kW (16642bhp) STX Engine Co Ltd-South Korea AuxGen: 3 x 680kW a.c Fuel: 122.0 (d.f.) 2138.0 (r.f.)
9391610 *A8PS2* -	**SELECTA** *ex* Thai Binh Sea *-2011* **Selecta Steamship Ltd** INTRESCO GmbH *Monrovia* *Liberia* MMSI: 636013821 Official number: 13821	**31,670** 18,755 56,548 T/cm 56.9	Class: NK (VR)	**2010-07 Nam Trieu Shipbuilding Industry Co. Ltd. — Haiphong** Yd No: F56-NT01 Loa 190.00 (BB) Br ex - Dght 12.740 Lbp 185.00 Br md 32.26 Dpth 18.10 Welded, 1 dk	**(A21A2BC) Bulk Carrier** Grain: 72,111; Bale: 67,110 Compartments: 5 Ho, ER 5 Ha: ER Cranes: 4x30t	**1 oil engine** driving 1 FP propeller Total Power: 8,890kW (12,087hp) 14.5kn Wartsila 6RT-flex50 1 x 2 Stroke 6 Cy. 500 x 2050 8890kW (12087bhp) Diesel United Ltd.-Aioi Fuel: 2601.0 (r.f.)

IMO / Call sign	Name / Owner	Tonnage	Class	Builder / Dimensions	Type / Capacity	Machinery
9543316 *9HXK9* -	**SELEINA** *ex* Onego Seleina *-2011* *ex* Universe 7 *-2009* **Massmariner (Malta) Ltd** Massoel Ltd SatCom: Inmarsat C 424967610 *Valletta* *Malta* MMSI: 249676000 Official number: 9543316	**5,087** 2,625 7,300	Class: BV	**2009-04 Universe Shipbuilding (Yangzhou) Co Ltd — Yizheng JS** Yd No: 06-007 Loa 112.80 (BB) Br ex - Dght 6.900 Lbp 106.17 Br md 17.20 Dpth 9.10 Welded, 1 dk	**(A21A2BC) Bulk Carrier** Grain: 9,394 Compartments: 3 Ho, ER 3 Ha: ER Cranes: 2x25t	**1 oil engine** driving 1 FP propeller Total Power: 2,500kW (3,399hp) 12.0kn Daihatsu 8DKM-28 1 x 4 Stroke 8 Cy. 280 x 390 2500kW (3399bhp) Shaanxi Diesel Heavy Industry Co Lt-China AuxGen: 3 x 250kW 50Hz a.c
8887325 *UELZ* -	**SELEMDZHA** **JSC Baltic Technical Fleet (A/O 'Baltiyskiy Tekhnicheskiy Flot') (Balttekhflot)** - *St Petersburg* *Russia* MMSI: 273437350 Official number: 763237	**687** 206 973	Class: (RS)	**1978-11 Baltiyskiy Sudomekhanicheskiy Zavod — Leningrad** Yd No: 11 Loa 56.15 Br ex 10.27 Dght 3.710 Lbp 52.60 Br md - Dpth 4.30 Welded, 1 dk	**(B34A2SH) Hopper, Motor** Hopper: 450 Compartments: 1 Ho, ER 1 Ha: (21.1 x 6.1)ER Ice Capable	**2 oil engines** driving 2 FP propellers Total Power: 442kW (600hp) 8.0kn Pervomaysk 6CH25/34-2 2 x 4 Stroke 6 Cy. 250 x 340 each-221kW (300bhp) Pervomaydizelmash (PDM)-Pervomaysk AuxGen: 2 x 50kW a.c Fuel: 48.0 (d.f.)
9606209 - -	**SELENE** *ex* Pandora 3 *-2010* **Jumprope Ltd** - *Road Harbour* *British Virgin Islands*	**110** 100 -		**2010-10 SM Europe Ltd — Gdansk** Yd No: 117/1 Loa 35.45 Br ex - Dght 3.100 Lbp - Br md 6.50 Dpth 3.10 Welded, 1 dk	**(X11A2YS) Yacht (Sailing)**	**2 oil engines** reduction geared to sc. shafts driving 2 Propellers Iveco Aifo 2 x 4 Stroke IVECO AIFO S.p.A.-Pregnana Milanese
9498597 *3FTE6* -	**SELENE LEADER** **Granville Shipholding SA** Hachiuma Steamship Co Ltd (Hachiuma Kisen KK) *Panama* *Panama* MMSI: 356560000 Official number: 4173510	**59,637** 17,892 18,082	Class: NK	**2010-05 Shin Kurushima Toyohashi Shipbuilding Co Ltd — Toyohashi AI** Yd No: 3630 Loa 199.99 (BB) Br ex - Dght 9.625 Lbp 192.00 Br md 32.26 Dpth 35.80 Welded	**(A35B2RV) Vehicles Carrier** Side door/ramp (s) Quarter stern door/ramp (s. a.) Cars: 6,400	**1 oil engine** driving 1 FP propeller Total Power: 14,280kW (19,415hp) 19.8kn MAN-B&W 7S60MC 1 x 2 Stroke 7 Cy. 600 x 2292 14280kW (19415bhp) Mitsui Engineering & Shipbuilding CLtd-Japan Thrusters: 1 Tunnel thruster (f) Fuel: 2940.0 (r.f.)
9100059 *DCNG* -	**SELENE PRAHM** **Hammann & Prahm Reederei GmbH & Co ms KG 'Selene Prahm'** Hammann & Prahm Reederei GmbH *Leer* *Germany* MMSI: 211219630 Official number: 4470	**1,584** 878 2,422	Class: GL	**1994-06 Koetter-Werft GmbH — Haren/Ems** Yd No: 88 Loa 75.10 (BB) Br ex - Dght 4.380 Lbp 70.20 Br md 11.65 Dpth 6.70 Welded, 1 dk	**(A31A2GX) General Cargo Ship** Double Bottom Entire Compartment Length Grain: 3,115 Compartments: 1 Ho, ER 1 Ha: (49.2 x 9.3)ER Ice Capable	**1 oil engine** geared to sc. shaft driving 1 CP propeller Total Power: 830kW (1,128hp) 10.7kn Alpha 6L23/30A 1 x 4 Stroke 6 Cy. 225 x 300 830kW (1128bhp) MAN B&W Diesel A/S-Denmark Thrusters: 1 Thwart. FP thruster (f)
9262766 *HPOE* -	**SELENE TRADER** **Regulus Lines SA** Nova Tankers A/S SatCom: Inmarsat C 435107310 *Panama* *Panama* MMSI: 351073000 Official number: 2943403CH	**159,912** 97,520 300,727 T/cm 179.3	Class: NK	**2003-09 Mitsui Eng. & SB. Co. Ltd., Chiba Works — Ichihara** Yd No: 1558 Loa 333.00 (BB) Br ex - Dght 20.960 Lbp 320.00 Br md 60.00 Dpth 29.65 Welded, 1 dk	**(A13A2TV) Crude Oil Tanker** Double Hull (13F) Liq: 337,323; Liq (Oil): 337,323 3 Cargo Pump (s): 3x5000m³/hr	**1 oil engine** driving 1 FP propeller Total Power: 27,160kW (36,927hp) 15.9kn MAN-B&W 7S80MC-C 1 x 2 Stroke 7 Cy. 800 x 3200 27160kW (36927bhp) Mitsui Engineering & Shipbuilding CLtd-Japan Fuel: 7500.0
8820145 *UBMI4* -	**SELENGA** *ex* Phuhai 2 *-2012* *ex* Koei Maru No. 7 *-2006* **Paroos Co Ltd (Paroos OOO)** - *Nevelsk* *Russia* MMSI: 273358560	**683** 334 428	Class: RS	**1989-01 Goriki Zosensho — Ise** Yd No: 1007 Loa 57.02 Br ex - Dght 3.600 Lbp 49.80 Br md 9.10 Dpth 3.85 Welded, 1 dk	**(B11B2FV) Fishing Vessel** Ins: 540	**1 oil engine** driving 1 FP propeller Total Power: 736kW (1,001hp) 11.0kn Niigata 6M28BFT 1 x 4 Stroke 6 Cy. 280 x 480 736kW (1001bhp) Niigata Engineering Co Ltd-Japan
8714657 *UBSH8* -	**SELENGA** *ex* Lerici Star *-2011* *ex* Kapitan Grishin *-2007* *ex* Sofrana Kermadec *-2003* *ex* Capitaine Tasman *-2002* *ex* Kapitan Grishin *-2001* *ex* CMBT Tana *-2000* *ex* Kapitan Grishin *-1995* *launched as* Timca *-1988* **Sakhalin Shipping Co (SASCO)** - *Kholmsk* *Russia* MMSI: 273352140	**6,030** 3,602 9,589 T/cm 18.5	Class: RS (LR) (RI) (NV) ✠ Classed LR until 3/2/89	**1988-05 Miho Zosensho K.K. — Shimizu** Yd No: 1324 Loa 113.14 (BB) Br ex 19.23 Dght 8.532 Lbp 106.00 Br md 18.90 Dpth 11.28 Welded, 2 dks	**(A31A2GX) General Cargo Ship** Grain: 12,582; Bale: 11,528 TEU 564 C Ho 234 TEU C Dk 330 TEU incl 50 ref C. Compartments: 1 Ho, ER 2 Ha: (33.6 x 15.7) (35.7 x 15.7)ER Cranes: 2x50t Ice Capable	**1 oil engine** driving 1 CP propeller Total Power: 4,413kW (6,000hp) 12.5kn Hanshin 6LF58 1 x 4 Stroke 6 Cy. 580 x 1050 4413kW (6000bhp) The Hanshin Diesel Works Ltd-Japan AuxGen: 1 x 600kW 445V 60Hz a.c, 3 x 200kW 445V 60Hz a.c
9447067 *9HVO9* -	**SELENKA** **Selenka Shipping Ltd** Tune Chemical Tankers BV *Valletta* *Malta* MMSI: 249598000 Official number: 9447067	**7,260** 3,652 10,745 T/cm 22.0	Class: BV	**2009-02 Tersan Tersanecilik ve Tasimacilik AS — Istanbul (Tuzla)** Yd No: 024 Loa 131.84 (BB) Br ex - Dght 7.970 Lbp 124.21 Br md 18.90 Dpth 10.20 Welded, 1 dk	**(A12B2TR) Chemical/Products Tanker** Double Hull (13F) Liq: 12,272; Liq (Oil): 12,684 Cargo Heating Coils Compartments: 12 Wing Ta, 2 Wing Slop Ta, ER 12 Cargo Pump (s): 12x300m³/hr Manifold: Bow/CM: 67.2m Ice Capable	**1 oil engine** reduction geared to sc. shafts driving 1 CP propeller Total Power: 4,320kW (5,873hp) 14.6kn MAN-B&W 9L32/40 1 x 4 Stroke 9 Cy. 320 x 400 4320kW (5873bhp) MAN B&W Diesel AG-Augsburg AuxGen: 1 x 1440kW 440V a.c, 2 x 880kW 440V 60Hz a.c Thrusters: 1 Tunnel thruster (f) Fuel: 100.0 (d.f.) 596.0 (r.f.)
9709439 - -	**SELERA 3** **PT Anugrah Selera Insani** Daniel Timotius *Samarinda* *Indonesia* Official number: 6635	**205** 62 -	Class: KI (Class contemplated)	**2013-04 PT Anugrah Selera Insani — Samarinda** Yd No: 02712 Loa 28.93 Br ex - Dght - Lbp - Br md 8.00 Dpth 3.80 Welded, 1 dk	**(B32A2ST) Tug**	**2 oil engines** reduction geared to sc. shafts driving 2 Propellers Total Power: 1,220kW (1,658hp) Mitsubishi S6R2-MPTK2 2 x 4 Stroke 6 Cy. 170 x 220 each-610kW (829bhp) Mitsubishi Heavy Industries Ltd-Japan
9012472 *9MAG5* -	**SELESA EKSPRES** **Langkawi Saga Travel & Tours Sdn Bhd** - *Penang* *Malaysia* MMSI: 533000121 Official number: 325441	**349** 132 -	Class: NV	**1990-11 FBM Marinteknik (S) Pte Ltd — Singapore** Yd No: 117 Loa 36.00 Br ex - Dght 1.290 Lbp 36.00 Br md 9.40 Dpth 3.48 Welded	**(A37B2PS) Passenger Ship** Hull Material: Aluminium Alloy Passengers: unberthed: 350	**2 oil engines** geared to sc. shafts driving 2 Water jets Total Power: 2,798kW (3,804hp) M.T.U. 12V396TE84 2 x Vee 4 Stroke 12 Cy. 165 x 185 each-1399kW (1902bhp) MTU Friedrichshafen GmbH-Friedrichshafen AuxGen: 2 x 39kW 380V 50Hz a.c
8650289 *JXII* T-31-BG	**SELFJORDBUEN** **Juda Ben Hur AS** - *Harstad* *Norway*	**115** 46 -		**1987 Blokken Skipsverft & Mek Verksted AS — Sortland** Loa 23.05 Br ex - Dght - Lbp - Br md 6.00 Dpth 5.23 Welded, 1 dk	**(B11B2FV) Fishing Vessel**	**1 oil engine** reduction geared to sc. shaft driving 1 FP propeller
8914556 *V2RU* -	**SELFOSS** *ex* Hanne Sif *-1999* *ex* Vento di Ponente *-1996* *ex* Elisabeth Delmas *-1996* *ex* Hanne Sif *-1995* *ex* Maersk Euro Tertio *-1994* *launched as* Hanne Sif *-1991* **Sel Line Ltd** The Iceland Steamship Co Ltd (Eimskip Island Ehf) (Eimskip Ehf) *Saint John's* *Antigua & Barbuda* MMSI: 304263000 Official number: 2572	**7,676** 4,076 8,627 T/cm 20.6	Class: NV	**1991-11 Orskov Christensens Staalskibsvaerft A/S — Frederikshavn** Yd No: 183 Loa 126.63 (BB) Br ex 20.70 Dght 7.480 Lbp 113.30 Br md 20.50 Dpth 10.70 Welded, 1 dk	**(A33A2CC) Container Ship (Fully Cellular)** TEU 724 C Ho 254 TEU C Dk 470 TEU incl 144 ref C. Compartments: 4 Cell Ho, ER 6 Ha: (12.6 x 12.8) (14.0 x 15.5)4 (12.6 x 15.5)ER Cranes: 2x40t Ice Capable	**1 oil engine** with flexible couplings & sr reverse geared to sc. shaft driving 1 CP propeller Total Power: 5,397kW (7,338hp) 16.5kn MaK 8M552C 1 x 4 Stroke 8 Cy. 450 x 520 5397kW (7338bhp) Krupp MaK Maschinenbau GmbH-Kiel AuxGen: 1 x 1230kW 440V 60Hz a.c, 3 x 570kW 440V 60Hz a.c Thrusters: 1 Thwart. FP thruster (f); 1 Tunnel thruster (a)
8228725 - -	**SELIKHINO** **Kurilskiy Rassvet JSC (A/O 'Kurilskiy Rassvet')** -	**821** 246 270	Class: (RS)	**1984-11 Volgogradskiy Sudostroitelnyy Zavod — Volgograd** Yd No: 221 Loa 53.74 Br ex 10.71 Dght 4.330 Lbp 47.92 Br md 10.50 Dpth 6.00 Welded, 1 dk	**(B11A2FG) Factory Stern Trawler** Ins: 218 Compartments: 1 Ho, ER 1 Ha: (1.6 x 1.6) Ice Capable	**1 oil engine** driving 1 CP propeller Total Power: 971kW (1,320hp) 12.7kn S.K.L. 8NVD48A-2U 1 x 4 Stroke 8 Cy. 320 x 480 971kW (1320bhp) VEB Schwermaschinenbau "KarlLiebknecht" (SKL)-Magdeburg AuxGen: 1 x 300kW a.c, 3 x 160kW a.c Fuel: 182.0 (d.f.)

IMO / Call sign	Name / Owner	Tonnage	Class	Builder / Dimensions	Type / Cargo	Machinery
8728036 *ENJP* -	**SELIM** *ex* Ivan Akulov *-2011* **Private Enterprise Sea Star** SatCom: Inmarsat C 427207710 *Kherson* *Ukraine* MMSI: 272077000	*2,553* 1,408 2,893	Class: RR UA	**1979-06 Zavody Tazkeho Strojarstva (ZTS) — Komarno** Yd No: 1949 Loa 114.00 Br ex 13.23 Dght 3.600 Lbp 110.52 Br md - Dpth 5.50 Welded, 1 dk	**(A31A2GX) General Cargo Ship**	**2 oil engines** driving 2 FP propellers Total Power: 1,030kW (1,400hp) 10.0kn Skoda 6L275A2 2 x 4 Stroke 6 Cy. 275 x 350 each-515kW (700bhp) CKD Praha-Praha AuxGen: 2 x 80kW a.c
8727587 *UYAX* -	**SELIM-1** *ex* Andrey Bubnov *-2011* **Private Enterprise Sea Star** *Kherson* *Ukraine* MMSI: 272087000	**2,592** 1,196 2,850	Class: UA (RR)	**1976-07 Zavody Tazkeho Strojarstva (ZTS) — Komarno** Yd No: 1925 Loa 113.87 Br ex 13.19 Dght 3.600 Lbp 110.52 Br md - Dpth 5.50 Welded, 1 dk	**(A31A2GX) General Cargo Ship**	**2 oil engines** driving 2 FP propellers Total Power: 1,028kW (1,398hp) 10.0kn Skoda 6L275IIPN 2 x 4 Stroke 6 Cy. 275 x 350 each-514kW (699bhp) CKD Praha-Praha AuxGen: 2 x 80kW a.c
8805133 - -	**SELIN** *ex* Maruoka Maru No. 1 *-2010* -	*199* - 480		**1988-11 Mukaishima Zoki Co. Ltd. — Onomichi** Yd No: 252 Loa 47.78 Br ex 8.20 Dght 3.010 Lbp 43.20 Br md 8.00 Dpth 3.35 Welded, 1 dk	**(A12A2TC) Chemical Tanker** Liq: 325 Compartments: 6 Ta, ER	**1 oil engine** driving 1 FP propeller Total Power: 589kW (801hp) Yanmar MF24-UT 1 x 4 Stroke 6 Cy. 240 x 420 589kW (801bhp) Matsue Diesel KK-Japan
9178551 *9HA2573* -	**SELIN M** *ex* Royal Forest *-2010* **Black Funnel Shipping Ltd** Med Brokerage & Management Corp *Valletta* *Malta* MMSI: 248909000 Official number: 9178551	**19,731** 11,389 31,770 T/cm 45.4	Class: NK (BV)	**1998-11 The Hakodate Dock Co Ltd — Hakodate HK** Yd No: 772 Loa 176.75 (BB) Br ex - Dght 9.562 Lbp 168.00 Br md 29.40 Dpth 13.50 Welded, 1 dk	**(A21A2BC) Bulk Carrier** Grain: 42,178; Bale: 40,657 TEU 128 Compartments: 5 Ho, ER 5 Ha: (13.6 x 15.0)4 (20.0 x 19.6)ER Cranes: 4x30.5t	**1 oil engine** driving 1 FP propeller Total Power: 6,620kW (9,001hp) 14.0kn Mitsubishi 6UEC52LA 1 x 2 Stroke 6 Cy. 520 x 1600 6620kW (9001bhp) Akasaka Tekkosho KK (Akasaka DieselLtd)-Japan Fuel: 1365.0
9352169 *TCON9* -	**SELIN-S** **Sener Petrol Denizcilik Ticaret AS** SatCom: Inmarsat C 427122559 *Istanbul* *Turkey* MMSI: 271000863	**2,244** 1,035 3,336 T/cm 10.3	Class: BV	**2006-05 Yildirim Gemi Insaat Sanayii A.S. — Tuzla** Yd No: 106 Loa 92.80 (BB) Br ex - Dght 5.774 Lbp 85.60 Br md 13.20 Dpth 6.60 Welded, 1 dk	**(A12B2TR) Chemical/Products Tanker** Double Hull (13F) Liq: 3,682; Liq (Oil): 3,736 Compartments: 10 Wing Ta, 1 Slop Ta, ER 3 Cargo Pump (s): 3x300m³/hr Manifold: Bow/CM: 38.7m	**1 oil engine** reduction geared to sc. shaft driving 1 CP propeller Total Power: 1,470kW (1,999hp) 12.0kn MAN-B&W 6L28/32A 1 x 4 Stroke 6 Cy. 280 x 320 1470kW (1999bhp) MAN B&W Diesel A/S-Denmark AuxGen: 2 x 628kW 400V a.c Fuel: 54.0 (d.f.) 183.3 (r.f.)
7912068 - -	**SELINA** **Gulf Transport Co Ltd** *Bangkok* *Thailand* Official number: 221023780	*187* 124 300		**1979-08 Bangkok Shipbuilding Co. — Bangkok** Yd No: 033 Loa 31.42 Br ex - Dght 2.501 Lbp 29.82 Br md 7.01 Dpth 3.18 Welded, 1 dk	**(A14A2LO) Water Tanker** 2 Cargo Pump (s): 2x30m³/hr	**1 oil engine** driving 1 FP propeller Total Power: 386kW (525hp) G.M. (Detroit Diesel) 12V-71-N 1 x Vee 2 Stroke 12 Cy. 108 x 127 386kW (525bhp) General Motors Detroit DieselAllison Divn-USA Fuel: 20.0 (d.f.) 1.0pd
9163609 *9LD2546* -	**SELINAY S** *ex* Tunc *-2013* *ex* Mag Excellence *-2013* *ex* Sisu Cursa *-2013* *ex* Georg Mitchell *-2008* *ex* Scheldedijk *-2004* *ex* Batavier IX *-2000* *ex* Scheldedijk *-1999* *ex* Batavier VII *-1999* *launched as* Scheldedijk *-1998* **Themis Maritime Ltd** *Freetown* *Sierra Leone* Official number: SL105246	**2,599** 1,226 3,459	Class: (BV)	**1998-05 Tille Scheepsbouw Kootstertille B.V. — Kootstertille** (Hull) Yd No: 317 **1998-05 Niestern Sander B.V. — Delfzijl** Loa 92.75 (BB) Br ex - Dght 4.920 Lbp 84.95 Br md 15.85 Dpth 6.15 Welded, 1 dk	**(A33A2CC) Container Ship (Fully Cellular)** Grain: 4,162 TEU 301 C Ho 122 TEU C Dk 179 TEU incl 50 ref C Compartments: 1 Ho, ER 2 Ha: (25.2 x 10.6)Tappered (25.2 x 13.2)ER	**1 oil engine** reduction geared to sc. shaft driving 1 CP propeller Total Power: 3,280kW (4,459hp) 15.0kn Wartsila 8R32 1 x 4 Stroke 8 Cy. 320 x 350 3280kW (4459bhp) Wartsila NSD Finland Oy-Finland AuxGen: 2 x 264kW 230/400V 50Hz a.c Thrusters: 1 Thwart. FP thruster (f)
9607459 *CQLU* -	**SELINDA** **ms 'Selinda' Schiffahrtsgesellschaft mbH & Co KG** John T Essberger GmbH & Co KG *Madeira* *Portugal (MAR)* MMSI: 255805360	**24,341** 11,521 34,236 T/cm 49.6	Class: GL	**2013-04 Yangfan Group Co Ltd — Zhoushan ZJ** Yd No: 2182 Loa 179.96 Br ex - Dght 10.100 Lbp 176.75 Br md 30.00 Dpth 14.70 Welded, 1 dk	**(A21A2BC) Bulk Carrier** Double Hull Grain: 46,700; Bale: 45,684 Compartments: 5 Ho, ER 5 Ha: 4 (19.2 x 20.3)ER (16.0 x 18.7) Cranes: 4x35t Ice Capable	**1 oil engine** driving 1 FP propeller Total Power: 6,900kW (9,381hp) 14.2kn Wartsila 5RT-flex50 1 x 2 Stroke 5 Cy. 500 x 2050 6900kW (9381bhp) AuxGen: 3 x 570kW 450V a.c Fuel: 160.0 (d.f.) 1700.0 (r.f.)
9382956 *A8RL6* -	**SELINI** **Payton Shipping Corp** Tsakos Columbia Shipmanagement (TCM) SA *Monrovia* *Liberia* MMSI: 636014121 Official number: 14121	**41,676** 19,936 74,296 T/cm 67.2	Class: AB	**2009-01 Sungdong Shipbuilding & Marine Engineering Co Ltd — Tongyeong** Yd No: 3015 Loa 228.13 (BB) Br ex 32.56 Dght 14.317 Lbp 219.00 Br md 32.24 Dpth 20.60 Welded, 1 dk	**(A13A2TW) Crude/Oil Products Tanker** Double Hull (13F) Liq: 78,928; Liq (Oil): 83,104 Cargo Heating Coils Compartments: 12 Wing Ta, 2 Wing Slop Ta, ER 3 Cargo Pump (s): 3x2000m³/hr Manifold: Bow/CM: 113.1m	**1 oil engine** driving 1 FP propeller Total Power: 12,240kW (16,642hp) 15.3kn MAN-B&W 6S60MC 1 x 2 Stroke 6 Cy. 600 x 2292 12240kW (16642bhp) STX Engine Co Ltd-South Korea AuxGen: 3 x 680kW a.c Fuel: 122.0 (d.f.) 2138.0 (r.f.)
6407468 - -	**SELINUNTE** *ex* Terekie *-1978* **Antonino Giacalone** - *Mazara del Vallo* *Italy* Official number: 186	*197* - 110	Class: (BV)	**1964 Haarlemsche Scheepsbouw Mij. N.V. — Haarlem** Yd No: 585 Loa 35.72 Br ex 7.09 Dght 3.404 Lbp 30.00 Br md 7.01 Dpth 4.02 Welded, 1 dk	**(B11A2FT) Trawler** 2 Ha: 2 (1.2 x 0.9) Derricks: 1x1.5t	**1 oil engine** driving 1 FP propeller Total Power: 548kW (745hp) 11.5kn MAN G6V30/45ATL 1 x 4 Stroke 6 Cy. 300 x 450 548kW (745bhp) Maschinenbau Augsburg Nuernberg (MAN)-Augsburg Fuel: 49.5 (d.f.)
9152052 *IYZP* -	**SELINUNTE JET** **Bluferries Srl** Rete Ferroviaria Italiana (RFI) *Catania* *Italy* MMSI: 247042400	**493** 325 56	Class: RI	**1999-05 Rodriquez Cantieri Navali SpA — Messina** Yd No: 272 Loa 50.46 Br ex - Dght 1.477 Lbp 43.00 Br md 8.78 Dpth 4.20 Welded, 1 dk	**(A37B2PS) Passenger Ship** Hull Material: Aluminium Alloy Passengers: unberthed: 500	**2 oil engines** with clutches, flexible couplings & sr geared to sc. shafts driving 2 Water jets Total Power: 4,000kW (5,438hp) M.T.U. 16V396TE74L 2 x Vee 4 Stroke 16 Cy. 165 x 185 each-2000kW (2719bhp) MTU Friedrichshafen GmbH-Friedrichshafen
8919051 *LAJC7* -	**SELJE** *ex* Jo Selje *-2010* **Skibsaksjeselskapet Hassel** Jo Tankers A/S *Bergen* *Norway (NIS)* MMSI: 257471000	**22,415** 11,481 36,778 T/cm 48.0	Class: NV (LR) **IGS ✠** Classed LR until 26/10/04	**1993-11 Kvaerner Govan Ltd — Glasgow** Yd No: 305 Loa 182.30 (BB) Br ex 32.05 Dght 10.731 Lbp 176.10 Br md 32.00 Dpth 14.00 Welded, 1 dk	**(A12B2TR) Chemical/Products Tanker** Double Hull (13F) Liq: 38,475; Liq (Oil): 38,475 Cargo Heating Coils Compartments: 12 Ta (s.stl), 17 Wing Ta (s.stl), 3 Wing Ta, 5 Ta, ER 37 Cargo Pump (s): 2x600m³/hr, 4x500m³/hr, 15x300m³/hr, 10x200m³/hr, 6x125m³/hr Manifold: Bow/CM: 98.4m	**1 oil engine** driving 1 FP propeller Total Power: 10,422kW (14,170hp) 15.5kn B&W 6L60MC 1 x 2 Stroke 6 Cy. 600 x 1944 10422kW (14170bhp) Kawasaki Heavy Industries Ltd-Japan AuxGen: 3 x 952kW 450V 60Hz a.c Boilers: 2 AuxB (o.f.) 8.2kgf/cm² (8.0bar), sg 7.1kgf/cm² (7.0bar), e (ex.g.) 8.2kgf/cm² (8.0bar) Thrusters: 1 Thwart. CP thruster (f) Fuel: 286.0 (d.f.) 2144.0 (r.f.)
8610136 *JXNC* -	**SELJE** **Fjord1 AS** - *Maaloy* *Norway* MMSI: 257387700	**1,280** 383 662 T/cm 7.6	Class: (NV)	**1987-06 Tronderverftet AS — Hommelvik** Yd No: 60 Loa 83.50 Br ex 13.97 Dght 3.401 Lbp 73.79 Br md 13.71 Dpth 4.50 Welded, 1 dk	**(A36A2PR) Passenger/Ro-Ro Ship (Vehicles)** Passengers: unberthed: 399 Bow door & ramp Stern door & ramp Lane-Len: 480 Lane-Wid: 5.00 Lane-clr ht: 4.80 Cars: 106, Trailers: 12	**1 oil engine** with clutches, flexible couplings & sr geared to sc. shafts driving 2 CP propellers Total Power: 1,469kW (1,997hp) Normo KRMB-8 1 x 4 Stroke 8 Cy. 250 x 300 1469kW (1997bhp) AS Bergens Mek Verksteder-Norway AuxGen: 2 x 125kW 220V 50Hz a.c Fuel: 90.0 (d.f.)
9188960 *LKYA* SF-35-S	**SELJEVAER** *ex* Antarctic I *-2009* *ex* Argos Helena *-2000* *ex* Seljevaer *-2000* **Stadt Havfiske AS** Ervik Havfiske AS *Maaloy* *Norway* MMSI: 257155000	**1,155** 346 450	Class: BV (NV)	**1998-09 SC Santierul Naval SA Braila — Braila** (Hull) Yd No: 1389 **1998-09 Blaalid Slip & Mek Verksted AS — Raudeberg** Yd No: 31 Lengthened-2012 Loa 54.58 (BB) Br ex - Dght 4.600 Lbp 49.50 Br md 10.00 Dpth 6.90 Welded, 1 dk	**(B11A2FS) Stern Trawler** Ice Capable	**1 oil engine** reduction geared to sc. shaft driving 1 CP propeller Total Power: 1,118kW (1,520hp) 12.5kn Caterpillar 3512TA 1 x Vee 4 Stroke 12 Cy. 170 x 190 1118kW (1520bhp) Caterpillar Inc-USA AuxGen: 2 x 324kW 440/220V 60Hz a.c Thrusters: 1 Thwart. FP thruster (f)
9036167 *EAGO* -	**SELLA** **Remolques Gijoneses SA** - *Gijon* *Spain* MMSI: 224174240 Official number: 1-3/1992	**256** 77 -	Class: BV	**1992-05 S.L. Ardeag — Bilbao** Yd No: 175 Loa 28.85 Br ex - Dght 4.120 Lbp 25.60 Br md 8.70 Dpth 4.80 Welded, 1 dk	**(B32A2ST) Tug**	**2 oil engines** sr geared to sc. shafts driving 2 CP propellers Total Power: 2,006kW (2,728hp) 12.5kn Normo KRMB-9 2 x 4 Stroke 9 Cy. 250 x 300 each-1003kW (1364bhp) Bergen Diesel AS-Norway Thrusters: 1 Thwart. CP thruster (a) Fuel: 130.0 (d.f.)

9189043 *DUSA9* -	**SELNES** *ex* Tarifa No. 5 *-1999* *ex* Boada 7 *-1999* *launched as* Diana 701 *-1998* **Sun Warm Tuna Corp** - *Manila* *Philippines* MMSI: 548053100 Official number: MNLD010669	**930** 355 680	Class: (NV) (NK)	**1998**-05 **KK Kanasashi — Shizuoka SZ** Yd No: 3496 Loa 63.31 Br ex - Dght 4.100 Lbp 56.00 Br md 9.70 Dpth 4.20 Welded	**(A34A2GR) Refrigerated Cargo Ship** Ins: 972 Compartments: 3 Ho, ER 3 Ha: 2 (1.2 x 1.0) (1.9 x 1.9)ER	**1 oil engine** with clutches, flexible couplings & sr reverse geared to sc. shaft driving 1 FP propeller Total Power: 1,324kW (1,800hp) Hanshin 6LC28LG 1 x 4 Stroke 6 Cy. 280 x 530 1324kW (1800bhp) The Hanshin Diesel Works Ltd-Japan AuxGen: 2 x 400kW 220V 50Hz a.c
8658085 *TFHS* -	**SELUR I** **Hagtak hf** - *Hafnarfjordur* *Iceland* MMSI: 251169440 Official number: 5935	**131** 39 -		**1977**-12 **at Seydisfjordur** Loa 32.17 Br ex - Dght - Lbp 30.53 Br md 6.50 Dpth 2.40 Welded, 1 dk	**(A31A2GX) General Cargo Ship**	**1 oil engine** driving 1 Propeller
9052678 *J8B3801* -	**SELVAAGSUND** *ex* Aurora *-2008* *ex* Michel *-2006* *ex* Sea Rhine *-2005* *ex* Michel *-2002* **Berge Rederi AS** - SatCom: Inmarsat C 437713410 *Kingstown* *St Vincent & The Grenadines* MMSI: 377134000 Official number: 10274	**1,598** 819 2,246	Class: NV (BV)	**1993**-02 **Scheepswerf Bijlsma BV — Wartena** Yd No: 662 Loa 81.70 Br ex 11.10 Dght 4.500 Lbp 76.95 Br md 11.00 Dpth 6.20 Welded, 1 dk	**(A31A2GX) General Cargo Ship** Grain: 3,226 TEU 128 Compartments: 1 Ho, ER 1 Ha: (57.8 x 8.9)ER Gantry cranes: 1 Ice Capable	**1 oil engine** reduction geared to sc. shaft driving 1 FP propeller Total Power: 1,000kW (1,360hp) 10.5kn A.B.C. 6MDZC 1 x 4 Stroke 6 Cy. 256 x 310 1000kW (1360bhp) Anglo Belgian Corp NV (ABC)-Belgium AuxGen: 2 x 85kW 220/380V 50Hz a.c Thrusters: 1 Tunnel thruster (f) Fuel: 132.0 (d.f.) 4.2pd
9195793 *LJXW* -	**SELVAG SENIOR** **Selvag Senior AS** - SatCom: Inmarsat C 425962310 *Bodo* *Norway* MMSI: 259623000	**1,960** 588 2,350	Class: NV	**1999**-09 **SC Santierul Naval Tulcea SA — Tulcea** (Hull) **1999**-09 **Slipen Mek. Verksted AS — Sandnessjoen** Yd No: 64 Loa 67.40 (BB) Br ex - Dght 7.600 Lbp 60.60 Br md 13.00 Dpth 8.30 Welded, 1 dk	**(B11A2FS) Stern Trawler** Ins: 1,200 Ice Capable	**1 oil engine** reduction geared to sc. shaft driving 1 FP propeller Total Power: 5,520kW (7,505hp) 15.0kn Wartsila 12V32 1 x Vee 4 Stroke 12 Cy. 320 x 350 5520kW (7505bhp) Wartsila NSD Finland Oy-Finland AuxGen: 1 x 1100kW 440V 60Hz a.c Thrusters: 1 Thwart. CP thruster (f); 1 Tunnel thruster (a) Fuel: 20.0 (d.f.) 450.0 (r.f.) 15.0pd
8132445 *YGZA* -	**SELVI PRATAMA** *ex* K. K. 28 *-2004* *ex* Taiei Maru No. 1 *-2001* *ex* Kosei Maru No. 8 *-1991* *ex* Shinpuku Maru No. 12 *-1989* **PT Citra Baru Adinusantara** - *Cirebon* *Indonesia*	**658** 198 530	Class: (KI)	**1981**-11 **Y.K. Tokai Zosensho — Tsukumi** Yd No: 606 Loa 50.00 Br ex - Dght 3.100 Lbp 45.26 Br md 11.00 Dpth 5.01 Welded, 1 dk	**(A31A2GX) General Cargo Ship**	**1 oil engine** driving 1 FP propeller Total Power: 662kW (900hp) 10.0kn Niigata 1 x 4 Stroke 662kW (900bhp) Niigata Engineering Co Ltd-Japan
8627490 *YHWE* -	**SELVI UTAMI** *ex* Myoriki Maru No. 203 *-2004* **PT Citra Baru Adinusantara** - *Surabaya* *Indonesia*	*1,349* 652 -	Class: KI	**1986**-06 **Muneta Zosen K.K. — Akashi** Converted From: Bulk Aggregates Carrier-2006 Loa - Br ex - Dght 4.590 Lbp 57.46 Br md 13.50 Dpth 6.00 Welded, 1 dk	**(A31A2GX) General Cargo Ship**	**1 oil engine** driving 1 FP propeller Total Power: 956kW (1,300hp) Yanmar MF28-ST 1 x 4 Stroke 6 Cy. 280 x 450 956kW (1300bhp) Yanmar Diesel Engine Co Ltd-Japan AuxGen: 2 x 107kW 225V a.c
8738550 - -	**SELWYN 1** **PT Pacific Lestari Jaya** - *Samarinda* *Indonesia*	**250** 75 -	Class: KI	**2009**-04 **CV Sunjaya Abadi — Samarinda** Loa 30.30 Br ex - Dght - Lbp 27.90 Br md 8.60 Dpth 4.35 Welded, 1 dk	**(B32A2ST) Tug**	**2 oil engines** driving 2 Propellers Total Power: 1,618kW (2,200hp) Mitsubishi S12A2-MTK 2 x Vee 4 Stroke 12 Cy. 150 x 160 each-809kW (1100bhp) Mitsubishi Heavy Industries Ltd-Japan
9613991 - -	**SELWYN 2** **PT Pacific Lestari Jaya** - *Samarinda* *Indonesia*	**262** 79 -	Class: KI	**2010**-08 **CV Sunjaya Abadi — Samarinda** Loa 30.30 Br ex - Dght 3.250 Lbp 28.75 Br md 8.60 Dpth 4.35 Welded, 1 dk	**(B32A2ST) Tug**	**2 oil engines** reduction geared to sc. shafts driving 2 Propellers AuxGen: 2 x 47kW 400V a.c
9616993 *YDA6634* -	**SELWYN 3** **PT Mitra Bahtera Segara Sejati Tbk** - *Samarinda* *Indonesia* MMSI: 525010019 Official number: 100212750	**261** 79 -	Class: KI	**2010**-08 **CV Sunjaya Abadi — Samarinda** Yd No: 4443 Loa 30.30 Br ex - Dght 3.240 Lbp 28.70 Br md 8.60 Dpth 4.35 Welded, 1 dk	**(B32A2ST) Tug**	**2 oil engines** reduction geared to sc. shafts driving 2 Propellers Total Power: 1,618kW (2,200hp) Yanmar 12LAK (M)-STE2 2 x Vee 4 Stroke 12 Cy. 150 x 165 each-809kW (1100bhp) Yanmar Diesel Engine Co Ltd-Japan AuxGen: 2 x 47kW 400V a.c
6911677 - -	**SEMA** **Fehmi Akgul** - *Istanbul* *Turkey*	*149* - 305		**1968 Deniz Insaat Kizaklari — Fener** Yd No: 113 Loa 36.00 Br ex 7.27 Dght 2.604 Lbp 31.50 Br md 7.24 Dpth 2.90 Welded, 1 dk	**(A31A2GX) General Cargo Ship**	**1 oil engine** geared to sc. shaft driving 1 FP propeller Total Power: 243kW (330hp) Blackstone ER6M 1 x 4 Stroke 6 Cy. 222 x 292 243kW (330bhp) Lister Blackstone Marine Ltd.-Dursley
7320277 - -	**SEMA 1** *ex* Osema I *-2004* *ex* Abeille Medoc *-2002* *ex* Neromer *-1991* **Servicios Maritimos Portuarios (SEMAPORT)** - *Malabo* *Equatorial Guinea*	*282* 84 -	Class: (BV)	**1973**-10 **Chantiers et Ateliers de La Perriere — Lorient** Yd No: 375 Loa 34.50 Br ex - Dght 4.547 Lbp 29.93 Br md 8.79 Dpth 4.75 Welded, 1 dk	**(B32A2ST) Tug**	**1 oil engine** geared to sc. shaft driving 1 FP propeller Total Power: 1,471kW (2,000hp) 12.7kn Crepelle 12PSN 1 x Vee 4 Stroke 12 Cy. 260 x 280 1471kW (2000bhp) Crepelle et Cie-France AuxGen: 2 x 160kW 380V a.c Fuel: 112.0 (d.f.)
9021863 - -	**SEMA 2** *ex* Efstratios Z *-2007* **Servicios Maritimos Portuarios (SEMAPORT)** - *Equatorial Guinea*	**197** 29 -	Class: (HR)	**2005**-06 **Fotas Stamatis — Thessaloniki** Yd No: 001 Loa 26.45 Br ex - Dght - Lbp 22.38 Br md 8.50 Dpth 4.00 Welded, 1 dk	**(B32A2ST) Tug**	**2 oil engines** geared to sc. shafts driving 2 FP propellers Total Power: 1,939kW (2,636hp) 10.0kn Caterpillar 3512B 2 x Vee 4 Stroke 12 Cy. 170 x 190 each-969kW (1317bhp) Caterpillar Inc-USA
8633126 - -	**SEMA 11** *ex* Kasco No. 77 *-2007* *ex* Hai Soon No. 9 *-1987* **Semapesko SA** -	*198* 79 -	Class: (RI)	**1977 Sungpo Shipyard Co — Geoje** Yd No: 98 Loa 36.00 Br ex 7.17 Dght 2.700 Lbp 31.00 Br md 7.15 Dpth 3.35 Welded, 1 dk	**(B11B2FV) Fishing Vessel**	**1 oil engine** driving 1 FP propeller Total Power: 956kW (1,300hp) Niigata 6M31KGHS 1 x 4 Stroke 6 Cy. 310 x 460 956kW (1300bhp) Niigata Engineering Co Ltd-Japan
9378553 - -	**SEMA IV** *ex* Evyap M *-2009* **Servicios Maritimos Portuarios (SEMAPORT)** - *Malabo* *Equatorial Guinea*	**193** 114 -	Class: (BV)	**2006**-09 **Eregli Gemi Insa Sanayi ve Ticaret AS — Karadeniz Eregli** Yd No: 01 Loa 22.50 Br ex - Dght 3.110 Lbp 21.68 Br md 8.80 Dpth 3.66 Welded, 1 dk	**(B32A2ST) Tug**	**2 oil engines** reduction geared to sc. shafts driving 2 FP propellers Total Power: 2,316kW (3,148hp) Caterpillar 3512B 2 x Vee 4 Stroke 12 Cy. 170 x 190 each-1158kW (1574bhp) Caterpillar Inc-USA AuxGen: 2 x 54kW 380/220V a.c
8652005 - -	**SEMAH** **Government of The Republic of Indonesia (Direktorat Jenderal Perhubungan Darat - Ministry of Land Communications)** PT ASDP Indonesia Ferry (Persero) - Angkutan Sungai Danau & Penyeberangan *Pontianak* *Indonesia*	**226** 68 -	Class: KI	**2010**-08 **P.T. Indomarine — Jakarta** Loa 31.60 Br ex - Dght 1.800 Lbp 24.96 Br md 9.00 Dpth 2.70 Welded, 1 dk	**(A36A2PR) Passenger/Ro-Ro Ship (Vehicles)**	**2 oil engines** reduction geared to sc. shafts driving 2 Propellers Total Power: 514kW (698hp) Yanmar 6HA2M-HTE 2 x 4 Stroke 6 Cy. 130 x 165 each-257kW (349bhp) Yanmar Diesel Engine Co Ltd-Japan AuxGen: 2 x 90kW 380V a.c
8002482 - -	**SEMANEH** - -	*130* 36 84	Class: (LR) ✠ Classed LR until 20/1/84	**1981**-03 **Carl B Hoffmanns Maskinfabrik A/S — Esbjerg** (Hull) Yd No: 33 **1981**-03 **Soren Larsen & Sonners Skibsvaerft A/S — Nykobing Mors** Yd No: 147 Loa 24.64 Br ex 6.76 Dght 2.801 Lbp 21.42 Br md 6.71 Dpth 3.31 Welded	**(B11A2FS) Stern Trawler** Ins: 57	**1 oil engine** driving 1 CP propeller Total Power: 405kW (551hp) Alpha 405-26VO 1 x 2 Stroke 5 Cy. 270 x 400 405kW (551bhp) B&W Alpha Diesel A/S-Denmark AuxGen: 2 x 32kW 380V 50Hz a.c Fuel: 47.0 (d.f.)

IMO / Call sign	Name / Owner / Port	GT / NT / DWT	Class	Builder / Dimensions	Type	Machinery
9563653 *POUU* -	**SEMAR 81** **PT Baraka Alam Sari** - *Jakarta* *Indonesia* MMSI: 525005165	**372** 112 214	Class: LR ✠**100A1** SS 10/2012 tug *IWS ✠**LMC** Eq.Ltr: G; Cable: 302.5/20.5 U2 (a)	**2012**-10 **Keppel Singmarine Pte Ltd — Singapore** Yd No: 355 Loa 30.00 Br ex 10.80 Dght 4.200 Lbp 25.30 Br md 10.50 Dpth 4.90 Welded, 1 dk	**(B32A2ST) Tug**	**2 oil engines** gearing integral to driving 2 Z propellers Total Power: 3,308kW (4,498hp) Niigata 6L28HX 2 x 4 Stroke 6 Cy. 280 x 370 each-1654kW (2249bhp) Niigata Engineering Co Ltd-Japan AuxGen: 3 x 86kW 380V 50Hz a.c
9644287 *POZG* -	**SEMAR 82** **PT Baraka Alam Sari** - *Jakarta* *Indonesia*	**447** 75 112	Class: LR ✠**100A1** SS 02/2013 tug *IWS ✠**LMC** Eq.Ltr: H; Cable: 330.0/22.0 U2 (a)	**2013**-02 **Keppel Singmarine Pte Ltd — Singapore** Yd No: 376 Loa 30.50 Br ex 11.22 Dght 3.000 Lbp 28.52 Br md 11.20 Dpth 4.50 Welded, 1 dk	**(B32A2ST) Tug**	**2 oil engines** gearing integral to driving 2 Voith-Schneider propellers Total Power: 3,650kW (4,962hp) Caterpillar 3516C-HD 2 x Vee 4 Stroke 16 Cy. 170 x 215 each-1825kW (2481bhp) Caterpillar Inc-USA AuxGen: 2 x 100kW 380V 50Hz a.c
9644299 *JZBE* -	**SEMAR 83** **PT Baraka Alam Sari** - *Jakarta* *Indonesia*	**447** 75 107	Class: LR ✠**100A1** SS 02/2013 tug *IWS ✠**LMC** Eq.Ltr: H; Cable: 330.0/22.0 U2 (a)	**2013**-02 **Keppel Singmarine Pte Ltd — Singapore** Yd No: 377 Loa 30.50 Br ex 11.22 Dght 3.000 Lbp 28.50 Br md 11.20 Dpth 4.50 Welded, 1 dk	**(B32A2ST) Tug**	**2 oil engines** gearing integral to driving 2 Voith-Schneider propellers Total Power: 3,650kW (4,962hp) Caterpillar 3516C-HD 2 x Vee 4 Stroke 16 Cy. 170 x 215 each-1825kW (2481bhp) Caterpillar Inc-USA AuxGen: 2 x 100kW 380V 50Hz a.c
9028885 - -	**SEMAR DELAPAN** **PT Humpuss Transportasi Curah** PT Humpuss Intermoda Transportasi Tbk *Samarinda* *Indonesia*	**231** 70 -	Class: KI	**2005**-12 **CV Muji Rahayu — Tenggarong** Loa 30.50 Br ex - Dght - Lbp 27.98 Br md 8.50 Dpth 3.60 Welded, 1 dk	**(B32A2ST) Tug**	**2 oil engines** geared to sc. shafts driving 2 Propellers Total Power: 1,220kW (1,658hp) Yanmar 6AYM-ETE 2 x 4 Stroke 6 Cy. 155 x 180 each-610kW (829bhp) Yanmar Diesel Engine Co Ltd-Japan AuxGen: 2 x 82kW 380/220V a.c
8654106 *YD3789* -	**SEMAR DELAPAN BELAS** **PT Humpuss Transportasi Curah** - *Batam* *Indonesia*	**212** 64 -	Class: KI	**2010**-11 **PT Trikarya Alam Shipyard — Batam** Loa 27.00 Br ex - Dght 3.250 Lbp 24.96 Br md 8.20 Dpth 4.00 Welded, 1 dk	**(B32A2ST) Tug**	**2 oil engines** reduction geared to sc. shafts driving 2 FP propellers Total Power: 1,552kW (2,110hp) Mitsubishi S12A2-MPTK 2 x Vee 4 Stroke 12 Cy. 150 x 160 each-776kW (1055bhp) Mitsubishi Heavy Industries Ltd-Japan AuxGen: 2 x 63kW 415V a.c
9028847 - -	**SEMAR DUA** *ex Equator 01 -2005* **PT Wikasita Lawana** - *Samarinda* *Indonesia*	**227** 69 -	Class: KI	**2004**-07 **CV Muji Rahayu — Tenggarong** Loa 30.50 Br ex - Dght - Lbp 27.50 Br md 8.50 Dpth 3.60 Welded, 1 dk	**(B32A2ST) Tug**	**2 oil engines** driving 1 Propeller Total Power: 1,716kW (2,334hp) Mitsubishi S12A2-MPTK 2 x Vee 4 Stroke 12 Cy. 150 x 160 each-858kW (1167bhp) (made 2004) Mitsubishi Heavy Industries Ltd-Japan AuxGen: 2 x 90kW 380/220V a.c
9669689 - -	**SEMAR DUA PULUH DUA** **PT Humpuss Transportasi Curah** - *Batam* *Indonesia* Official number: GT.185NO.4310/PPm	**166** 56 -	Class: KI (BV)	**2012**-08 **PT Bandar Abadi — Batam** Yd No: 163 Loa 26.00 Br ex - Dght 3.000 Lbp 24.36 Br md 8.00 Dpth 3.65 Welded, 1 dk	**(B32A2ST) Tug**	**2 oil engines** reduction geared to sc. shafts driving 2 FP propellers Total Power: 1,220kW (1,658hp) Yanmar 6AYM-WST 2 x 4 Stroke 6 Cy. 155 x 180 each-610kW (829bhp) Yanmar Diesel Engine Co Ltd-Japan
9666144 *YDA3183* -	**SEMAR DUA PULUH SATU** **PT Humpuss Transportasi Curah** - *Batam* *Indonesia* Official number: GT.185NO.4219/PPM	**185** 56 -	Class: KI (BV)	**2012**-07 **PT Bandar Abadi — Batam** Yd No: 162 Loa 26.00 Br ex - Dght 3.000 Lbp 24.36 Br md 8.00 Dpth 3.65 Welded, 1 dk	**(B32A2ST) Tug**	**2 oil engines** reduction geared to sc. shafts driving 2 FP propellers Total Power: 1,220kW (1,658hp) Yanmar 6AYM-WST 2 x 4 Stroke 6 Cy. 155 x 180 each-610kW (829bhp) Yanmar Diesel Engine Co Ltd-Japan AuxGen: 2 x 59kW 50Hz a.c Fuel: 110.0 (d.f.)
9028914 - -	**SEMAR DUABELAS** **PT Humpuss Transportasi Curah** PT Humpuss Intermoda Transportasi Tbk *Samarinda* *Indonesia*	**231** 70 -	Class: KI	**2006**-03 **PT Muji Rahayu Shipyard — Tenggarong** Loa - Br ex - Dght - Lbp 28.12 Br md 8.50 Dpth 3.60 Welded, 1 dk	**(B32A2ST) Tug**	**2 oil engines** geared to sc. shafts driving 2 Propellers Total Power: 1,220kW (1,658hp) Yanmar 6AYM-ETE 2 x 4 Stroke 6 Cy. 155 x 180 each-610kW (829bhp) Yanmar Diesel Engine Co Ltd-Japan AuxGen: 2 x 82kW 380/220V a.c
9709453 - -	**SEMAR DUAPULUH TIGA** **PT Humpuss Transportasi Curah** - *Batam* *Indonesia* Official number: 2013 PPm No. 3157/L	**243** 73 -	Class: GL	**2013**-09 **PT Citra Shipyard — Batam** Yd No: TB 058 Loa 27.00 Br ex - Dght 3.400 Lbp 25.44 Br md 8.20 Dpth 4.00 Welded, 1 dk	**(B32A2ST) Tug**	**2 oil engines** reduction geared to sc. shafts driving 2 Propellers Total Power: 1,716kW (2,334hp) Mitsubishi S12A2-MPTK 2 x Vee 4 Stroke 12 Cy. 150 x 160 each-858kW (1167bhp) Mitsubishi Heavy Industries Ltd-Japan
9028861 - -	**SEMAR EMPAT** **PT Humpuss Transportasi Curah** - *Samarinda* *Indonesia*	**167** 51 -	Class: KI	**2004**-07 **CV Muji Rahayu — Tenggarong** Loa 27.00 Br ex - Dght 2.000 Lbp 24.34 Br md 7.50 Dpth 3.75 Welded, 1 dk	**(B32A2ST) Tug**	**2 oil engines** geared to sc. shafts driving 2 Propellers Total Power: 1,686kW (2,292hp) Yanmar 12LAA-UTE1 2 x Vee 4 Stroke 12 Cy. 148 x 165 each-843kW (1146bhp) (made 1997, fitted 2004) Yanmar Diesel Engine Co Ltd-Japan AuxGen: 2 x 90kW 380/220V a.c
9028873 - -	**SEMAR ENAM** **PT Humpuss Transportasi Curah** PT Humpuss Intermoda Transportasi Tbk *Samarinda* *Indonesia*	**231** 70 -	Class: KI	**2005**-07 **CV Muji Rahayu — Tenggarong** Loa 30.50 Br ex - Dght - Lbp 28.22 Br md 8.50 Dpth 3.60 Welded, 1 dk	**(B32A2ST) Tug**	**2 oil engines** geared to sc. shafts driving 2 Propellers Total Power: 1,220kW (1,658hp) Yanmar 6AYM-ETE 2 x 4 Stroke 6 Cy. 155 x 180 each-610kW (829bhp) Yanmar Diesel Engine Co Ltd-Japan AuxGen: 2 x 82kW 380/220V a.c
9029891 *YD6841* -	**SEMAR ENAMBELAS** *ex Modalwan 16106 -2006* **PT Humpuss Transportasi Curah** - *Samarinda* *Indonesia*	**164** 50 -	Class: KI (GL)	**2004**-12 **Bonafile Shipbuilders & Repairs Sdn Bhd — Sandakan** Yd No: 08/04 Loa 26.10 Br ex - Dght 2.848 Lbp 24.29 Br md 7.32 Dpth 3.35 Welded, 1 dk	**(B32A2ST) Tug**	**2 oil engines** reverse reduction geared to sc. shafts driving 2 FP propellers Total Power: 1,204kW (1,636hp) Mitsubishi S6R2-MPTK 2 x 4 Stroke 6 Cy. 170 x 220 each-602kW (818bhp) Mitsubishi Heavy Industries Ltd-Japan AuxGen: 2 x 40kW 380/220V a.c
9281401 *YD6767* -	**SEMAR LIMA** *ex Modalwan 1025 -2005* **PT Humpuss Transportasi Curah** PT Humpuss Intermoda Transportasi Tbk *Samarinda* *Indonesia*	**119** 38 92	Class: KI (NK)	**2002**-10 **Bonafile Shipbuilders & Repairs Sdn Bhd — Sandakan** Yd No: 2315T Loa 23.00 Br ex - Dght 2.879 Lbp 21.00 Br md 6.80 Dpth 3.43 Welded, 1 dk	**(B32A2ST) Tug**	**2 oil engines** geared to sc. shafts driving 2 FP propellers Total Power: 810kW (1,102hp) 10.0kn Yanmar 6LAAM-UTE 2 x 4 Stroke 6 Cy. 148 x 165 each-405kW (551bhp) Yanmar Diesel Engine Co Ltd-Japan AuxGen: 2 x 29kW a.c
9069607 *YDA4137* -	**SEMAR LIMABELAS** **PT Humpuss Transportasi Curah** - *Tanjung Priok* *Indonesia*	**219** 66 -	Class: KI	**2006**-03 **PT Karya Teknik Utama — Batam** Loa 27.00 Br ex - Dght - Lbp 24.85 Br md 7.00 Dpth 3.50 Welded, 1 dk	**(B32A2ST) Tug**	**2 oil engines** driving 2 Propellers Total Power: 1,516kW (2,062hp) Mitsubishi S6R2-MPTK 2 x 4 Stroke 6 Cy. 170 x 220 each-758kW (1031bhp) (made 2004) Mitsubishi Heavy Industries Ltd-Japan
9028823 *YDA4022* -	**SEMAR SATU** **PT Humpuss Transportasi Curah** - *Jakarta* *Indonesia*	**229** 68 -	Class: KI	**2004**-07 **PT Karya Teknik Utama — Batam** Loa 27.00 Br ex - Dght 3.000 Lbp 25.70 Br md 8.20 Dpth 4.00 Welded, 1 dk	**(B32A2ST) Tug**	**2 oil engines** geared to sc. shafts driving 2 Propellers Total Power: 1,516kW (2,062hp) 11.0kn Mitsubishi S6R-MPTK2 2 x 4 Stroke 6 Cy. 170 x 220 each-758kW (1031bhp) Mitsubishi Heavy Industries Ltd-Japan AuxGen: 2 x 90kW 380V a.c
9028902 - -	**SEMAR SEBELAS** **PT Humpuss Transportasi Curah** PT Humpuss Intermoda Transportasi Tbk *Samarinda* *Indonesia*	**231** 70 -	Class: KI	**2006**-03 **PT Muji Rahayu Shipyard — Tenggarong** Loa - Br ex - Dght - Lbp 28.12 Br md 8.50 Dpth 3.60 Welded, 1 dk	**(B32A2ST) Tug**	**2 oil engines** geared to sc. shafts driving 2 Propellers Total Power: 1,220kW (1,658hp) Yanmar 6AYM-ETE 2 x 4 Stroke 6 Cy. 155 x 180 each-610kW (829bhp) Yanmar Diesel Engine Co Ltd-Japan AuxGen: 2 x 82kW 380/220V a.c

IMO / Call sign	Name / Owner / Port	Tonnage	Class	Build / Dimensions	Type	Machinery
9028732 - -	**SEMAR SEMBILAN** **PT Humpuss Transportasi Curah** PT Humpuss Intermoda Transportasi Tbk *Samarinda* *Indonesia*	**231** 70 -	Class: KI	**2006-03 PT Muji Rahayu Shipyard — Tenggarong** Loa - Br ex - Dght - Lbp 27.98 Br md 8.50 Dpth 3.60 Welded, 1 dk	**(B32A2ST) Tug**	**2 oil engines** geared to sc. shafts driving 2 Propellers Total Power: 1,220kW (1,658hp) Yanmar 6AYM-ETE 2 x 4 Stroke 6 Cy. 155 x 180 each-610kW (829bhp) (made 2005) Yanmar Diesel Engine Co Ltd-Japan AuxGen: 2 x 82kW 380/220V a.c
9028897 - -	**SEMAR SEPULUH** **PT Humpuss Transportasi Curah** PT Humpuss Intermoda Transportasi Tbk *Samarinda* *Indonesia*	**231** 70 -	Class: KI	**2005-12 CV Muji Rahayu — Tenggarong** Loa - Br ex - Dght - Lbp 27.98 Br md 8.50 Dpth 3.60 Welded, 1 dk	**(B32A2ST) Tug**	**2 oil engines** geared to sc. shafts driving 2 Propellers Total Power: 1,220kW (1,658hp) Yanmar 6AYM-ETE 2 x 4 Stroke 6 Cy. 155 x 180 each-610kW (829bhp) Yanmar Diesel Engine Co Ltd-Japan AuxGen: 2 x 82kW 380/220V a.c
9028859 *YD6614* -	**SEMAR TIGA** *ex* Equator 02 *-2004* **PT Humpuss Transportasi Curah** - *Samarinda* *Indonesia*	**167** 51 -	Class: KI	**2004-08 CV Muji Rahayu — Tenggarong** Loa 27.00 Br ex - Dght 2.000 Lbp 24.30 Br md 7.50 Dpth 2.75 Welded, 1 dk	**(B32A2ST) Tug**	**2 oil engines** driving 2 Propellers Total Power: 1,060kW (1,442hp) Mitsubishi S6N-MTK 2 x 4 Stroke 6 Cy. 160 x 180 each-530kW (721bhp) (made 1998, fitted 2004) Mitsubishi Heavy Industries Ltd-Japan AuxGen: 2 x 92kW 380/220V a.c
9028835 - -	**SEMAR TUJUH** **PT Humpuss Transportasi Curah** PT Humpuss Intermoda Transportasi Tbk *Tanjung Priok* *Indonesia*	**230** 69 -	Class: KI	**2005-03 PT Karya Teknik Utama — Batam** Loa 27.00 Br ex - Dght 3.000 Lbp 25.70 Br md 8.20 Dpth 4.00 Welded, 1 dk	**(B32A2ST) Tug**	**2 oil engines** geared to sc. shafts driving 2 Propellers Total Power: 1,516kW (2,062hp) 11.0kn Mitsubishi S6R-MPTK2 2 x 4 Stroke 6 Cy. 170 x 220 each-758kW (1031bhp) (made 2004) Mitsubishi Heavy Industries Ltd-Japan AuxGen: 2 x 90kW 380V a.c
8934001 *YFNZ* -	**SEMARANG CARAKA JAYA NIAGA III-35** **PT Pann (Persero)** - *Jakarta* *Indonesia* MMSI: 525003010 Official number: 1379+BA	**3,401** 1,895 4,180	Class: KI	**1997-10 P.T. Dok & Perkapalan Kodja Bahari (Unit II) — Jakarta** Yd No: 1230 Loa 98.00 Br ex - Dght 5.500 Lbp 92.00 Br md 16.50 Dpth 7.80 Welded, 1 dk	**(A31A2GX) General Cargo Ship** TEU 208 C. 208/20'	**1 oil engine** geared to sc. shaft driving 1 FP propeller Total Power: 1,498kW (2,037hp) 11.9kn Pielstick 8PA5L 1 x 4 Stroke 8 Cy. 255 x 270 1498kW (2037bhp) Niigata Engineering Co Ltd-Japan AuxGen: 3 x 215kW a.c
9096428 - -	**SEMAYA** *ex* Athina-Mina *-2008* *ex* Athena I *-1998* *ex* Arcturus *-1974* **Semaya 2006 SL** - *Panama* *Panama*	*133* - 20	Class: (AB)	**1968-08 D. C. Anastassiades & A. Ch. Tsortanides — Perama** Yd No: 24 Loa 27.33 Br ex - Dght 2.520 Lbp 24.69 Br md 6.02 Dpth 3.20 Welded, 1 dk	**(X11A2YP) Yacht**	**2 oil engines** reduction geared to sc. shafts driving 2 FP propellers Total Power: 508kW (690hp) Caterpillar C12 2 x 4 Stroke 6 Cy. 130 x 150 each-254kW (345bhp) (new engine 2001) Caterpillar Inc-USA
8662567 *POGK*	**SEMBILANG** **Government of The Republic of Indonesia (Direktorat Jenderal Perhubungan Darat - Ministry of Land Communications)** - *Jakarta* *Indonesia* Official number: GT.560/3084/BA	**560** 168 -	Class: KI	**2011-09 PT Bayu Bahari Sentosa — Jakarta** Loa 45.50 Br ex - Dght 2.140 Lbp 40.57 Br md 12.00 Dpth 3.20 Welded, 1 dk	**(A36A2PR) Passenger/Ro-Ro Ship (Vehicles)**	**2 oil engines** reduction geared to sc. shafts driving 2 Propellers Total Power: 1,220kW (1,658hp) Yanmar 2 x each-610kW (829bhp) Yanmar Diesel Engine Co Ltd-Japan
9147875 *V2QG7* -	**SEMBRIA** *ex* Alina *-2011* **Medea Shipping Ltd** Mestex Shipping & Trading Ltd *Saint John's* *Antigua & Barbuda* MMSI: 304010760 Official number: 3089	**5,381** 2,626 6,790 T/cm 17.2	Class: GL	**1998-05 Turkiye Gemi Sanayii A.S. — Halic, Istanbul** Yd No: 241 Loa 107.57 (BB) Br ex - Dght 6.630 Lbp 103.00 Br md 18.20 Dpth 9.00 Welded, 1 dk	**(A31A2GX) General Cargo Ship** Double Hull Grain: 9,729 Compartments: 3 Ho, ER 3 Ha: (24.5 x 15.2) (28.4 x 15.2) (20.3 x 15.2)ER Ice Capable	**1 oil engine** driving 1 CP propeller Total Power: 2,400kW (3,263hp) 12.0kn B&W 6S26MC 1 x 2 Stroke 6 Cy. 260 x 980 2400kW (3263bhp) MAN B&W Diesel A/S-Denmark AuxGen: 2 x 250kW 440V a.c Thrusters: 1 Thwart. FP thruster (f)
8728763 *4JDY* -	**SEMED VURGUN** **Azerbaijan State Caspian Shipping Co (ASCSS)** Meridian Shipping & Management LLC *Baku* *Azerbaijan* MMSI: 423063100 Official number: DGR-0070	**4,134** 1,240 5,353 T/cm 19.1	Class: RS	**1987-11 Volgogradskiy Sudostroitelnyy Zavod — Volgograd** Yd No: 34 Loa 125.06 (BB) Br ex 16.63 Dght 4.150 Lbp 121.12 Br md 16.60 Dpth 6.90 Welded, 1 dk	**(A13B2TP) Products Tanker** Single Hull Liq: 5,904; Liq (Oil): 5,904 Compartments: 6 Ta, ER Ice Capable	**2 oil engines** driving 2 FP propellers Total Power: 2,296kW (3,122hp) 11.3kn Dvigatel Revolyutsii 6CHRNP36/45 2 x 4 Stroke 6 Cy. 360 x 450 each-1148kW (1561bhp) Zavod "Dvigatel Revolyutsii"-Gorkiy AuxGen: 4 x 160kW a.c Fuel: 79.0 (d.f.) 190.0 (r.f.)
9137727 *UBGK6* -	**SEMEN DEZHNEV** *ex* Thor Gitta *-2013* *ex* BBC Singapore *-2008* *ex* Bremer Timber *-2004* *ex* Ranzel *-1997* **Aspect Co Ltd (OOO 'Aspect')** - *Korsakov* *Russia* MMSI: 273333760	**4,078** 2,009 4,900	Class: RS (GL)	**1996-12 Stocznia Polnocna SA (Northern Shipyard) — Gdansk** Yd No: B196/2/1 Loa 101.30 (BB) Br ex 16.78 Dght 6.398 Lbp 93.80 Br md 16.60 Dpth 8.10 Welded, 2 dks	**(A31A2GX) General Cargo Ship** Grain: 6,800 TEU 390 C Ho 127 C Dk 263 TEU incl 50 ref C. Compartments: 1 Ho, ER 1 Ha: (57.8 x 13.4)ER Cranes: 2x60t Ice Capable	**1 oil engine** with flexible couplings & sr gearedto sc. shaft driving 1 CP propeller Total Power: 3,960kW (5,384hp) 15.0kn MAN 9L32/40 1 x 4 Stroke 9 Cy. 320 x 400 3960kW (5384bhp) MAN B&W Diesel AG-Augsburg AuxGen: 1 x 640kW 400V 50Hz a.c, 2 x 378kW 400V 50Hz a.c Thrusters: 1 Thwart. FP thruster (f) Fuel: 103.0 (d.f.) 442.0 (r.f.) 15.5pd
8956384 - -	**SEMEN SHAPURKO** *ex* Portovyy *-2000* **Novorossiysk Port Fleet JSC (ZAO 'Flot Novorossiyskogo Torgovogo Porta')** - *Novorossiysk* *Russia* MMSI: 273451950 Official number: 754420	**111** - 24	Class: RS	**1975 "Petrozavod" — Leningrad** Yd No: 577 Loa 24.20 Br ex 6.95 Dght 2.260 Lbp 22.55 Br md 6.90 Dpth 2.96 Welded, 1 dk	**(B32A2ST) Tug** Ice Capable	**2 oil engines** driving 2 Voith-Schneider propellers Total Power: 900kW (1,224hp) 9.8kn Pervomaysk 6CH25/34 2 x 4 Stroke 6 Cy. 250 x 340 each-450kW (612bhp) Pervomaydizelmash (PDM)-Pervomaysk
9543328 *9HA2044* -	**SEMENTINA** *ex* Onego Sementina *-2011* *completed as* Universe 8 *-2009* **Massmariner (Malta) Ltd** Massoel Ltd *Valletta* *Malta* MMSI: 249861000 Official number: 9543328	**5,087** 2,625 7,300	Class: BV	**2009-06 Universe Shipbuilding (Yangzhou) Co Ltd — Yizheng JS** Yd No: 06-008 Loa 112.80 (BB) Br ex - Dght 6.900 Lbp 106.00 Br md 17.20 Dpth 9.10 Welded, 1 dk	**(A21A2BC) Bulk Carrier** Grain: 9,394 Compartments: 3 Ho, ER 3 Ha: ER Cranes: 2x25t	**1 oil engine** reduction geared to sc. shaft driving 1 FP propeller Total Power: 2,500kW (3,399hp) 11.0kn Daihatsu 8DKM-28 1 x 4 Stroke 8 Cy. 280 x 390 2500kW (3399bhp) Shaanxi Diesel Heavy Industry Co Lt-China AuxGen: 3 x 250kW 50Hz a.c Fuel: 360.0
9617428 *ETSM* -	**SEMERA** **Ethiopian Shipping & Logistics Services Enterprise** - *Addis Ababa* *Ethiopia* MMSI: 624023000 Official number: 23/04	**21,024** 10,298 28,112	Class: AB	**2013-11 Huanghai Shipbuilding Co Ltd — Rongcheng SD** Yd No: HCY-143 Loa 166.49 Br ex 27.70 Dght 10.100 Lbp 158.32 Br md 27.40 Dpth 14.20 Welded, 1 dk	**(A31A2GX) General Cargo Ship** Grain: 39,100; Bale: 39,100 TEU 1696 Compartments: 4 Ho, ER 4 Ha: ER Ice Capable	**1 oil engine** driving 1 FP propeller Total Power: 6,810kW (9,259hp) 15.2kn MAN-B&W 6S40ME-B9 1 x 2 Stroke 6 Cy. 400 x 1770 6810kW (9259bhp) STX (Dalian) Engine Co Ltd-China AuxGen: 3 x 720kW a.c Fuel: 130.0 (d.f.) 1480.0 (r.f.)
7345150 *YBMU* -	**SEMERU** **PT PERTAMINA (PERSERO)** - *Jakarta* *Indonesia* Official number: 189+DA	*395* 47 -	Class: (KI) (AB)	**1974-05 Robin Shipyard Pte Ltd — Singapore** Yd No: 112 Loa - Br ex - Dght 3.937 Lbp 36.02 Br md 9.00 Dpth 4.50 Welded, 1 dk	**(B32A2ST) Tug**	**2 oil engines** driving 2 FP propellers Total Power: 2,354kW (3,200hp) 12.5kn Niigata 8MG25BX 2 x 4 Stroke 8 Cy. 250 x 320 each-1177kW (1600bhp) Niigata Engineering Co Ltd-Japan AuxGen: 2 x 80kW Fuel: 284.5 (d.f.)
9655573 *A7MG* -	**SEMESMA** **Qatar Navigation QSC (Milaha)** - *Doha* *Qatar* MMSI: 466084000	**495** - -	Class: LR (Class contemplated)	**2014-02 Nakilat Damen Shipyards Qatar Ltd — Ras Laffan** (Hull) Yd No: (513023) **2014-02 B.V. Scheepswerf Damen — Gorinchem** Yd No: 513023 Loa 32.14 Br ex - Dght - Lbp - Br md 12.50 Dpth 5.40 Welded, 1 dk	**(B32A2ST) Tug**	**2 oil engines** reduction geared to sc. shaft (s) driving 2 Directional propellers

7122003 *YFYF* -	**SEMI I** *ex* Teh Sun No. 707 *-2002* *ex* Kamo Maru No. 28 *-1986* **Husin Widjaya** - *Surabaya* *Indonesia*	*422* 200 -	Class: (KI)	**1970-02 KK Kanasashi Zosen — Shizuoka SZ** Yd No: 969 Loa 48.67 Br ex 8.13 Dght 3.252 Lbp 42.60 Br md 8.11 Dpth 3.61 Welded, 1 dk	**(B11B2FV) Fishing Vessel**	**1 oil engine** geared to sc. shaft driving 1 FP propeller Total Power: 699kW (950hp) 11.0kn Hanshin 6LU28 1 x 4 Stroke 6 Cy. 280 x 440 699kW (950bhp) Hanshin Nainenki Kogyo-Japan
9194531 - -	**SEMILANG VI** - **Government of Malaysia (Department of Fisheries)** -	**110** - -		**2001-12 Kay Marine Sdn Bhd — Kuala Terengganu** (Hull) **2001-12 B.V. Scheepswerf Damen — Gorinchem** Yd No: 5642 Loa 17.00 Br ex - Dght - Lbp - Br md 5.10 Dpth 2.60 Welded, 1 dk	**(B12D2FP) Fishery Patrol Vessel**	**2 oil engines** geared to sc. shafts driving 2 FP propellers MAN-B&W 2 x 4 Stroke MAN B&W Diesel AG-Augsburg
9603348 - -	**SEMINOLE** - **Government of The United States of America (Department of The Navy)** - *United States of America*	**352** 105 118	Class: (AB)	**2011-02 J M Martinac Shipbuilding Corp — Tacoma WA** Yd No: 251 Loa 27.43 Br ex - Dght - Lbp 25.07 Br md 11.65 Dpth 5.03 Welded, 1 dk	**(B32A2ST) Tug**	**2 oil engines** reduction geared to sc. shafts driving 2 Z propellers Total Power: 2,700kW (3,670hp) Caterpillar 3512C 2 x Vee 4 Stroke 12 Cy. 170 x 215 each-1350kW (1835bhp) Caterpillar Inc-USA AuxGen: 2 x 135kW a.c Fuel: 98.0 (d.f.)
7645550 *IBRV* -	**SEMINOLE** *ex* Global Seminole *-2011* *ex* Gal D. L. B. 900 *-1997* *ex* Mahavir *-1995* *ex* D. L. B. 701 *-1981* *ex* E. T. P. M. 701 *-1979* **Micoperi Srl** - *Ravenna* *Italy* MMSI: 247274900	**13,232** 3,969 10,969	Class: RI (BV) (IR)	**1975-07 Dubigeon-Normandie S.A. — Grand Quevilly** Loa 135.81 (BB) Br ex - Dght 4.501 Lbp 122.00 Br md 30.50 Dpth 9.00 Welded, 1 dk	**(B22C2OQ) Pipe Layer Crane Vessel** Passengers: berths: 193 Cranes: 1x295t	**4 diesel electric oil engines** driving 4 gen. each 1850kW 5500V a.c Connecting to 4 elec. motors driving 2 CP propellers Total Power: 6,184kW (8,408hp) 7.1kn Pielstick 16PA4V185VG 4 x Vee 4 Stroke 16 Cy. 185 x 210 each-1546kW (2102bhp) Chantiers de l'Atlantique-France AuxGen: 1 x 480kW 440V 60Hz a.c Fuel: 2088.0 (r.f.)
8890396 *9HVD4* -	**SEMINOLE** *ex* Fortuna I *-2003* **Prestige Shipmanagement Ltd** Misha Shipping Agency & Trade Ltd SatCom: Inmarsat C 424955910 *Valletta* *Malta* MMSI: 249559000 Official number: 4700	**4,976** 2,310 3,832	Class: RS	**1995-06 OAO Navashinskiy Sudostroitelnyy Zavod 'Oka' — Navashino** Yd No: 1060 Loa 107.40 Br ex 16.70 Dght 3.800 Lbp 101.20 Br md 16.50 Dpth 5.50 Welded, 1 dk	**(A31A2GX) General Cargo Ship** Grain: 4,706 Compartments: 3 Ho, ER 3 Ha: 3 (18.6 x 12.6)ER Ice Capable	**2 oil engines** driving 2 FP propellers Total Power: 1,766kW (2,402hp) 11.4kn Dvigatel Revolyutsii 6CHRN36/45 2 x 4 Stroke 6 Cy. 360 x 450 each-883kW (1201bhp) Zavod "Dvigatel Revolyutsii"-Nizhniy Novgorod AuxGen: 2 x 160kW a.c Thrusters: 1 Thwart. FP thruster (f) Fuel: 159.0 (d.f.)
9164160 *DYPA* -	**SEMINOLE PRINCESS** *ex* Clipper Flamingo *-2006* *ex* VOC Flamingo *-2004* *ex* Cielo di Calgary *-2001* *ex* Clipper Flamingo *-2000* *ex* Chuqui *-2000* *ex* Clipper Flamingo *-1997* **Adirondack Shipping LLC** Roymar Ship Management Inc *Manila* *Philippines* MMSI: 548749000 Official number: MNLA000678	**19,357** 9,135 29,516 T/cm 41.0	Class: LR (AB) **100A1** SS 01/2012 LI **LMC** **UMS** Eq.Ltr: H†; Cable: 605.0/62.0 U3 (a)	**1997-01 Dalian Shipyard Co Ltd — Dalian LN** Yd No: MC280-5 Loa 181.00 (BB) Br ex 26.06 Dght 10.040 Lbp 170.72 Br md 26.00 Dpth 14.40 Welded, 1 dk	**(A31A2GX) General Cargo Ship** Grain: 36,311; Bale: 35,452 TEU 1130 C Ho 680 TEU C Dk 450 TEU incl 12 ref C. Compartments: 5 Ho, ER, 5 Tw Dk 5 Ha: (19.2 x 15.2)Tappered 2 (25.2 x 22.5) (19.3 x 22.5) (19.2 x 12.8)Tappered ER Cranes: 5x30t	**1 oil engine** driving 1 FP propeller Total Power: 6,400kW (8,701hp) 14.5kn B&W 5S50MC 1 x 2 Stroke 5 Cy. 500 x 1910 6400kW (8701bhp) Dalian Marine Diesel Works-China AuxGen: 1 x 550kW 440V 60Hz a.c, 2 x 500kW 440V 60Hz a.c Boilers: AuxB (Comp) Fuel: 146.0 (d.f.) 1238.0 (r.f.) 26.0pd
8662892 - -	**SEMIRALICE** - **Oceanprime Ltd** - *London* *United Kingdom* Official number: 919391	**163** 49 -	Class: RI	**2006-03 Cantieri Navali Rizzardi Srl — Sabaudia** Yd No: 95/09 Loa 30.20 Br ex - Dght 1.800 Lbp 24.60 Br md 6.76 Dpth 3.08 Bonded, 1 dk	**(X11A2YP) Yacht** Hull Material: Reinforced Plastic	**2 oil engines** reduction geared to sc. shafts driving 2 Propellers Total Power: 3,580kW (4,868hp) M.T.U. 16V2000M93 2 x Vee 4 Stroke 16 Cy. 135 x 156 each-1790kW (2434bhp) MTU Friedrichshafen GmbH-Friedrichshafen
9658056 *D5CH2* -	**SEMIRAMIS** - **Red Rose Navigation Corp** Efnav Co Ltd *Monrovia* *Liberia* MMSI: 636015698 Official number: 15698	**44,827** 26,527 82,620 T/cm 71.9	Class: NV	**2013-08 STX Offshore & Shipbuilding Co Ltd — Changwon (Jinhae Shipyard)** Yd No: 1553 Loa 228.90 (BB) Br ex - Dght 14.500 Lbp 225.50 Br md 32.24 Dpth 20.20 Welded, 1 dk	**(A21A2BC) Bulk Carrier** Grain: 95,172 Compartments: 7 Ho, ER 7 Ha: ER	**1 oil engine** driving 1 FP propeller Total Power: 14,280kW (19,415hp) 14.5kn MAN-B&W 6S60ME-C 1 x 2 Stroke 6 Cy. 600 x 2400 14280kW (19415bhp) MAN Diesel A/S-Denmark AuxGen: 3 x a.c
9406893 *V7MN4* -	**SEMIRIO** *ex* Yue May *-2007* **Kili Shipping Co Inc** Diana Shipping Services SA SatCom: Inmarsat C 453832526 *Majuro* *Marshall Islands* MMSI: 538002875 Official number: 2875	**88,955** 58,078 174,261 T/cm 119.0	Class: BV (AB)	**2007-06 Shanghai Waigaoqiao Shipbuilding Co Ltd — Shanghai** Yd No: 1035 Loa 288.92 (BB) Br ex 45.05 Dght 18.120 Lbp 278.20 Br md 45.00 Dpth 24.50 Welded, 1 dk	**(A21A2BC) Bulk Carrier** Grain: 189,382; Bale: 183,425 Compartments: 9 Ho, ER 9 Ha: 7 (15.5 x 20.0)ER 2 (15.5 x 16.5)	**1 oil engine** driving 1 FP propeller Total Power: 16,860kW (22,923hp) 14.5kn MAN-B&W 6S70MC 1 x 2 Stroke 6 Cy. 700 x 2674 16860kW (22923bhp) Hudong Heavy Machinery Co Ltd-China AuxGen: 3 x 750kW a.c Fuel: 342.9 (d.f.) 4466.1 (r.f.)
7102235 *J8EE6* -	**SEMLOW** - **Dommel Maritime Corp** Motaku Shipping Agencies Ltd *Kingstown* *St Vincent & The Grenadines* MMSI: 376314000 Official number: 3155	**992** 372 718	Class: (BV) (DS) (GL)	**1971 VEB Elbewerften Boizenburg/Rosslau — Boizenburg** Yd No: 288 Loa 57.74 (BB) Br ex 10.32 Dght 3.680 Lbp 51.85 Br md 10.09 Dpth 5.80 Welded, 2 dks	**(A31A2GX) General Cargo Ship** Grain: 1,532; Bale: 1,400 Compartments: 2 Ho, ER 2 Ha: (8.9 x 7.7) (12.5 x 7.7)ER Cranes: 2x3t Ice Capable	**1 oil engine** driving 1 CP propeller Total Power: 853kW (1,160hp) 12.5kn S.K.L. 8NVD48A-2U 1 x 4 Stroke 8 Cy. 320 x 480 853kW (1160bhp) VEB Schwermaschinenbau "KarlLiebknecht" (SKL)-Magdeburg AuxGen: 1 x 128kW 390V 50Hz a.c, 1 x 116kW 390V 50Hz a.c, 1 x 77kW 390V 50Hz a.c Fuel: 65.0 (d.f.)
9443310 *YDA4275* -	**SEMPANA** - **PT Mitra Armada Laut** - *Pontianak* *Indonesia*	**192** 58 172	Class: KI (NK)	**2007-04 Tuong Aik Shipyard Sdn Bhd — Sibu** Yd No: 2615 Loa 26.00 Br ex - Dght 3.012 Lbp 24.29 Br md 8.00 Dpth 3.65 Welded, 1 dk	**(B32A2ST) Tug**	**2 oil engines** reduction geared to sc shafts driving 2 Propellers Total Power: 1,220kW (1,658hp) Yanmar 6AYM-ETE 2 x 4 Stroke 6 Cy. 155 x 180 each-610kW (829bhp) Yanmar Diesel Engine Co Ltd-Japan AuxGen: 2 x 35kW a.c
8654455 - -	**SEMPATI** *ex* Diamond I *-2012* **PT Pelayaran Intan** - *Pontianak* *Indonesia*	**132** 40 -	Class: KI	**2011-01 in Indonesia** Loa 26.00 Br ex - Dght - Lbp 22.08 Br md 7.30 Dpth 3.30 Welded, 1 dk	**(B32A2ST) Tug**	**2 oil engines** reduction geared to sc. shafts driving 2 FP propellers Total Power: 1,716kW (2,334hp) Mitsubishi S12A2-MPTK 2 x Vee 4 Stroke 12 Cy. 150 x 160 each-858kW (1167bhp) Mitsubishi Heavy Industries Ltd-Japan AuxGen: 2 x 48kW 400V a.c
9187021 *PIAL* YE 20	**SEMPER CONFIDENS** **Mosselkwekerij A M Verschuure BV** - *Yerseke* *Netherlands* MMSI: 244053000 Official number: 35720	**295** 88 -		**1998-09 Gebr. Kooiman B.V. Scheepswerf en Machinefabriek — Zwijndrecht** Yd No: 158 Loa 40.11 Br ex - Dght - Lbp - Br md - Dpth - Welded, 1 dk	**(B11B2FV) Fishing Vessel**	**2 oil engines** geared to sc. shafts driving 2 FP propellers Total Power: 800kW (1,088hp) M.T.U. 8V2000M60 2 x Vee 4 Stroke 8 Cy. 130 x 150 each-400kW (544bhp) MTU Friedrichshafen GmbH-Friedrichshafen
8838219 *XULZ8* -	**SEMPER PARATUS** *ex* Leonidas *-2014* *ex* Pontus 9 *-2011* *ex* Rybak *-2011* *ex* Gladys *-2008* *ex* Gloriya *-2008* *ex* Rybak *-2006* *ex* Alta *-2005* *ex* Gamma *-2004* *ex* Gloria V *-2003* *ex* Rybak *-2001* *ex* Ryosei Maru No. 25 *-1997* **Sunmoon Marine Co Ltd** TL Shipping Co Ltd *Phnom Penh* *Cambodia* MMSI: 514328000 Official number: 0681330	**241** 64 78	Class: RS	**1981-01 Ishimura Zosen — Kimaishi** Yd No: 521 Converted From: Fishing Vessel Lengthened & Widened-2005 Loa 36.63 Br ex 7.36 Dght 2.450 Lbp 29.66 Br md 6.16 Dpth 2.80 Welded, 1 dk	**(B11B2FV) Fishing Vessel** Ins: 124	**1 oil engine** driving 1 FP propeller Niigata 1 x 4 Stroke Niigata Engineering Co Ltd-Japan

IMO / Call sign / Owner	Tonnage	Class	Built	Type	Machinery
7945106 **SEMPRE AVANTI T II** *ISAH* - **Giuseppe Tudisco** - *Italy*	*121* 51 -	Class: (RI)	**1975**-09 **Cantieri Meridionali CINET Srl — Molfetta** Loa 26.73 Br ex 5.82 Dght 2.291 Lbp 21.59 Br md 5.81 Dpth 3.05 Welded, 1 dk	**(A37B2PS) Passenger Ship**	**1 oil engine** driving 1 FP propeller Total Power: 331kW (450hp) Baudouin 12P15.2 1 x Vee 4 Stroke 12 Cy. 150 x 150 331kW (450bhp) (new engine 1991) Societe des Moteurs Baudouin SA-France
9335288 **SEMPRE GALAICO** *ECCO* 3-VILL-52- **Hermanos Costa Rial SA** - *Cambados* *Spain* Official number: 3-2/2003	**124** 37 -		**2004**-12 **Astilleros Pineiro, S.L. — Moana** Yd No: 099 Loa 25.75 Br ex - Dght - Lbp 20.90 Br md - Dpth - Welded, 1 dk	**(B11B2FV) Fishing Vessel**	**1 oil engine** geared to sc. shaft driving 1 FP propeller Total Power: 530kW (721hp) Volvo Penta D30A MT 1 x 4 Stroke 6 Cy. 170 x 220 530kW (721bhp) Gutierrez Ascunce Corp (GUASCOR)-Spain
9396880 **SEMUA BAHAGIA** *9MFL5* - **Semua Shipping Sdn Bhd** - *Port Klang* *Malaysia* MMSI: 533000711 Official number: 332461	**5,182** 2,593 8,008 T/cm 16.5	Class: BV	**2008**-03 **Yangzhou Kejin Shipyard Co Ltd — Jiangdu JS** Yd No: 06015 Loa 106.40 (BB) Br ex - Dght 7.800 Lbp 99.60 Br md 18.60 Dpth 10.00 Welded, 1 dk	**(A13B2TP) Products Tanker** Double Hull (13F)	**1 oil engine** geared to sc. shaft driving 1 FP propeller Total Power: 3,310kW (4,500hp) 12.5kn Yanmar 8N330-EN 1 x 4 Stroke 8 Cy. 330 x 440 3310kW (4500bhp) Yanmar Diesel Engine Co Ltd-Japan AuxGen: 3 x 335kW a.c Fuel: 90.0 (d.f.) 330.0 (r.f.)
9396878 **SEMUA BERJAYA** *9MFJ8* - **Semua Shipping Sdn Bhd** - *Port Klang* *Malaysia* MMSI: 533629000 Official number: 332442	**5,182** 2,593 8,008 T/cm 16.5	Class: BV	**2008**-01 **Yangzhou Kejin Shipyard Co Ltd — Jiangdu JS** Yd No: 06013 Loa 105.83 (BB) Br ex - Dght 7.800 Lbp 99.60 Br md 18.60 Dpth 10.00 Welded, 1 dk	**(A13B2TP) Products Tanker** Double Hull (13F)	**1 oil engine** reduction geared to sc. shaft driving 1 FP propeller Total Power: 3,310kW (4,500hp) 12.5kn Yanmar 8N330-EN 1 x 4 Stroke 8 Cy. 330 x 440 3310kW (4500bhp) Yanmar Diesel Engine Co Ltd-Japan AuxGen: 3 x 335kW a.c Fuel: 90.0 (d.f.) 330.0 (r.f.)
9494917 **SEMUA GEMBIRA** *9MIE4* *ex Changmanhuanle -2009* - *ex Semua Gembira -2009* *ex Yangzhou Kejin 06030 -2009* **Semua Shipping Sdn Bhd** - *Port Klang* *Malaysia* MMSI: 533000793 Official number: 333974	**5,182** 2,593 8,008 T/cm 16.5	Class: BV	**2009**-02 **Yangzhou Kejin Shipyard Co Ltd — Jiangdu JS** Yd No: 07030 Loa 105.83 Br ex - Dght 7.800 Lbp 99.60 Br md 18.60 Dpth 10.25 Welded, 1 dk	**(A13B2TP) Products Tanker** Double Hull (13F) Liq: 8,923; Liq (Oil): 8,923 Compartments: 10 Wing Ta, ER	**1 oil engine** reduction geared to sc. shaft driving 1 FP propeller Total Power: 3,310kW (4,500hp) 12.5kn Yanmar 8N330-EN 1 x 4 Stroke 8 Cy. 330 x 440 3310kW (4500bhp) Qingdao Zichai Boyang Diesel EngineCo Ltd-China AuxGen: 3 x 335kW a.c
9494929 **SEMUA GEMILANG** *9MII2* - **Semua Shipping Sdn Bhd** - 773151191 *Port Klang* *Malaysia* MMSI: 533682000 Official number: 334010	**5,182** 2,593 8,034 T/cm 16.5	Class: BV	**2009**-03 **Yangzhou Kejin Shipyard Co Ltd — Jiangdu JS** Yd No: 07031 Loa 105.83 (BB) Br ex - Dght 7.800 Lbp 99.60 Br md 18.60 Dpth 10.25 Welded, 1 dk	**(A13B2TP) Products Tanker** Double Hull (13F) Liq: 8,740; Liq (Oil): 8,923 Compartments: 10 Wing Ta, 2 Wing Slop Ta, ER 3 Cargo Pump (s): 3x500m³/hr Manifold: Bow/CM: 53.5m	**1 oil engine** reduction geared to sc. shaft driving 1 FP propeller Total Power: 3,310kW (4,500hp) 12.5kn Yanmar 8N330-EN 1 x 4 Stroke 8 Cy. 330 x 440 3310kW (4500bhp) Qingdao Zichai Boyang Diesel EngineCo Ltd-China AuxGen: 3 x 335kW 60Hz a.c Thrusters: 1 Tunnel thruster (f) Fuel: 90.0 (d.f.) 330.0 (r.f.)
9548158 **SEMUA MUHIBBAH** *9MIN7* - **Semado Maritime Sdn Bhd** Semua Shipping Sdn Bhd *Port Klang* *Malaysia* MMSI: 533000861 Official number: 334070	**7,267** 3,441 11,134 T/cm 22.0	Class: BV	**2010**-05 **Yangzhou Kejin Shipyard Co Ltd — Jiangdu JS** Yd No: 07067 Loa 130.20 (BB) Br ex - Dght 8.000 Lbp 122.10 Br md 18.60 Dpth 10.80 Welded, 1 dk	**(A13B2TP) Products Tanker** Double Hull (13F) Liq: 11,729; Liq (Oil): 11,728 Compartments: 10 Wing Ta, 2 Wing Slop Ta, ER 10 Cargo Pump (s): 10x350m³/hr Manifold: Bow/CM: 61m	**1 oil engine** reduction geared to sc. shaft driving 1 FP propeller Total Power: 3,840kW (5,221hp) 13.0kn MAN-B&W 8L32/40 1 x 4 Stroke 8 Cy. 320 x 400 3840kW (5221bhp) Shaanxi Diesel Heavy Industry Co Lt-China AuxGen: 3 x 560kW 60Hz a.c Thrusters: 1 Tunnel thruster (f) Fuel: 50.0 (d.f.) 510.0 (r.f.)
9548160 **SEMUA MUTIARA** *9MIN6* - **Semado Maritime Sdn Bhd** Semua Shipping Sdn Bhd *Port Klang* *Malaysia* MMSI: 533036600 Official number: 334069	**7,267** 3,441 11,134 T/cm 22.0	Class: BV	**2010**-08 **Yangzhou Kejin Shipyard Co Ltd — Jiangdu JS** Yd No: 07068 Loa 130.20 (BB) Br ex - Dght 8.000 Lbp 122.10 Br md 18.60 Dpth 10.80 Welded, 1 dk	**(A13B2TP) Products Tanker** Double Hull (13F) Liq: 11,729; Liq (Oil): 11,729 Compartments: 10 Wing Ta, 2 Wing Slop Ta, ER 10 Cargo Pump (s): 10x350m³/hr Manifold: Bow/CM: 61m	**1 oil engine** reduction geared to sc. shaft driving 1 FP propeller Total Power: 3,840kW (5,221hp) 13.0kn MAN-B&W 8L32/40 1 x 4 Stroke 8 Cy. 320 x 400 3840kW (5221bhp) Shaanxi Diesel Heavy Industry Co Lt-China AuxGen: 3 x 560kW 60Hz a.c Thrusters: 1 Tunnel thruster (f) Fuel: 50.0 (d.f.) 510.0 (r.f.)
9439357 **SEMUA PERDANA** *V7SE2* - **NFC Labuan Shipleasing I Ltd** Semua Chemical Shipping Sdn Bhd SatCom: Inmarsat C 453834563 *Majuro* *Marshall Islands* MMSI: 538003630 Official number: 3630	**8,539** 4,117 13,062 T/cm 23.2	Class: AB	**2009**-09 **21st Century Shipbuilding Co Ltd — Tongyeong** Yd No: 259 Loa 128.60 (BB) Br ex 20.43 Dght 8.714 Lbp 120.40 Br md 20.40 Dpth 11.50 Welded, 1 dk	**(A12B2TR) Chemical/Products Tanker** Double Hull (13F) Liq: 13,395; Liq (Oil): 14,084 Compartments: 12 Wing Ta, 2 Wing Slop Ta, ER 12 Cargo Pump (s): 12x300m³/hr Manifold: Bow/CM: 61m	**1 oil engine** driving 1 FP propeller Total Power: 4,440kW (6,037hp) 13.4kn MAN-B&W 6S35MC 1 x 2 Stroke 6 Cy. 350 x 1400 4440kW (6037bhp) STX Engine Co Ltd-South Korea AuxGen: 3 x 500kW a.c Thrusters: 1 Tunnel thruster (f) Fuel: 45.0 (d.f.) 601.0 (r.f.)
9439369 **SEMUA PERKASA** *V7SE3* - **NFC Labuan Shipleasing I Ltd** Semua Chemical Shipping Sdn Bhd SatCom: Inmarsat C 453834598 *Majuro* *Marshall Islands* MMSI: 538003631 Official number: 3631	**8,539** 4,117 13,053 T/cm 23.2	Class: AB	**2009**-10 **21st Century Shipbuilding Co Ltd — Tongyeong** Yd No: 260 Loa 128.60 (BB) Br ex 20.43 Dght 8.714 Lbp 120.40 Br md 20.40 Dpth 11.50 Welded, 1 dk	**(A12B2TR) Chemical/Products Tanker** Double Hull (13F) Liq: 12,715; Liq (Oil): 12,715 Part Cargo Heating Coils Compartments: 12 Wing Ta, 2 Wing Slop Ta, ER 12 Cargo Pump (s): 12x300m³/hr Manifold: Bow/CM: 61m	**1 oil engine** driving 1 FP propeller Total Power: 4,440kW (6,037hp) 13.4kn MAN-B&W 6S35MC 1 x 2 Stroke 6 Cy. 350 x 1400 4440kW (6037bhp) STX Engine Co Ltd-South Korea AuxGen: 3 x 550kW a.c Thrusters: 1 Tunnel thruster (f) Fuel: 45.0 (d.f.) 600.0 (r.f.)
9417115 **SEMUA SEJATI** *9MHQ8* - **Semua Shipping Sdn Bhd** - *Port Klang* *Malaysia* MMSI: 533003390 Official number: 332481	**5,182** 2,593 8,008 T/cm 16.5	Class: BV	**2008**-06 **Yangzhou Kejin Shipyard Co Ltd — Jiangdu JS** Yd No: 06027 Loa 106.40 (BB) Br ex - Dght 7.800 Lbp 99.60 Br md 18.60 Dpth 10.00 Welded, 1 dk	**(A13B2TP) Products Tanker** Double Hull (13F) Liq: 9,000; Liq (Oil): 9,000 Compartments: 10 Wing Ta, 2 Wing Slop Ta, ER	**1 oil engine** reduction geared to sc. shaft driving 1 FP propeller Total Power: 3,310kW (4,500hp) 12.5kn Yanmar 8N330-EN 1 x 4 Stroke 8 Cy. 330 x 440 3310kW (4500bhp) Yanmar Diesel Engine Co Ltd-Japan AuxGen: 3 x 335kW a.c Fuel: 90.0 (d.f.) 330.0 (r.f.)
9417127 **SEMUA SELAMAT** *9MHW8* - **Semua Shipping Sdn Bhd** - *Port Klang* *Malaysia* MMSI: 533693000 Official number: 333859	**5,182** 2,593 8,008 T/cm 16.5	Class: BV	**2008**-11 **Yangzhou Kejin Shipyard Co Ltd — Jiangdu JS** Yd No: 06028 Loa 105.83 (BB) Br ex - Dght 7.800 Lbp 99.60 Br md 18.60 Dpth 10.25 Welded, 1 dk	**(A13B2TP) Products Tanker** Double Hull (13F) Liq: 8,740; Liq (Oil): 9,000 Compartments: 10 Wing Ta, 2 Wing Slop Ta, ER 3 Cargo Pump (s): 3x500m³/hr Manifold: Bow/CM: 53.5m	**1 oil engine** reduction geared to sc. shaft driving 1 FP propeller Total Power: 3,310kW (4,500hp) 12.5kn Yanmar 8N330-EN 1 x 4 Stroke 8 Cy. 330 x 440 3310kW (4500bhp) Yanmar Diesel Engine Co Ltd-Japan AuxGen: 3 x 335kW a.c Thrusters: 1 Tunnel thruster (f) Fuel: 90.0 (d.f.) 330.0 (r.f.)
9068952 **SEMUMU** *YFNA* - **Government of The Republic of Indonesia (Direktorat Jenderal Perhubungan Darat - Ministry of Land Communications)** PT ASDP Indonesia Ferry (Persero) - Angkutan Sungai Danau & Penyeberangan *Jakarta* *Indonesia*	**409** 122 -	Class: KI	**1996**-10 **P.T. Industri Kapal Indonesia (IKI) — Makassar** L reg 39.00 Br ex - Dght 1.800 Lbp 32.50 Br md 10.50 Dpth 2.90 Welded, 1 dk	**(A37B2PS) Passenger Ship**	**2 oil engines** geared to sc. shafts driving 2 Propellers Total Power: 896kW (1,218hp) 10.5kn Yanmar 6LAA-UTE 2 x 4 Stroke 6 Cy. 148 x 165 each-448kW (609bhp) Yanmar Diesel Engine Co Ltd-Japan
8720175 **SEMUTIK No. 1** - - **Semutik Sdn Bhd** -	*152* 88 -		**1974** **Sen Koh Shipbuilding Corp — Kaohsiung** Loa - Br ex - Dght - Lbp 30.64 Br md 6.01 Dpth 2.62 Welded, 1 dk	**(B11B2FV) Fishing Vessel**	**1 oil engine** driving 1 FP propeller Total Power: 206kW (280hp) 8.0kn Hanshin 6L24GSH 1 x 4 Stroke 6 Cy. 240 x 400 206kW (280bhp) The Hanshin Diesel Works Ltd-Japan

IMO / Call sign	Name / Owner	Tonnage	Class	Built / Dimensions	Type / Capacity	Machinery
8330279 *P3VP9* -	**SEMYACHIK** *ex* Langust *-2006* *ex* Bolsheretskiy *-2004* **Seamermaid Shipping Ltd** *Limassol* *Cyprus* MMSI: 209057000 Official number: 8330279	**697** 229 495	Class: (RS)	**1984 Khabarovskiy Sudostroitelnyy Zavod im Kirova — Khabarovsk** Yd No: 849 Loa 55.02 Br ex 9.53 Dght 4.341 Lbp 50.04 Br md - Dpth 5.19 Welded, 1 dk	**(B12B2FC) Fish Carrier** Ins: 632 Ice Capable	**1 oil engine** driving 1 FP propeller Total Power: 588kW (799hp) 11.3kn S.K.L. 6NVD48A-2U 1 x 4 Stroke 6 Cy. 320 x 480 588kW (799bhp) VEB Schwermaschinenbau "KarlLiebknecht" (SKL)-Magdeburg AuxGen: 3 x 150kW Fuel: 114.0 (d.f.)
7119446 *UIPF* -	**SEMYON DEZHNEV** **Federal State Unitary Enterprise Rosmorport** SatCom: Inmarsat C 427300146 *St Petersburg* *Russia* MMSI: 273123000 Official number: 712714	**2,315** 694 1,141	Class: RS	**1971-12 Admiralteyskiy Sudostroitelnyy Zavod — Leningrad** Yd No: 782 Loa 68.48 Br ex 18.09 Dght 6.050 Lbp 62.01 Br md 17.51 Dpth 8.31 Welded, 2 dks	**(B34C2SI) Icebreaker** Derricks: 2x1.5t Ice Capable	**3 diesel electric oil engines** driving 3 gen. each 1250kW Connecting to 1 elec. Motor of (1180kW) 2 elec. motors each (1760kW) driving 3 CP propellers 1 fwd and 2 aft Total Power: 3,750kW (5,100hp) 14.0kn Fairbanks, Morse 10-38D8-1/8 3 x 2 Stroke 10 Cy. 207 x 254 each-1250kW (1700bhp) in the U.S.S.R. AuxGen: 3 x 200kW a.c, 1 x 100kW a.c Fuel: 617.0 (d.f.)
7529639 *XUAH9* -	**SEMYON MOROZOV** **Amadea Shipping Ltd** Sea Way Investors Shipping Ltd *Phnom Penh* *Cambodia* MMSI: 514011000 Official number: 0875943	**2,466** 1,094 3,134	Class: UA (RS)	**1975-03 Sudostroitelnyy Zavod im Volodarskogo — Rybinsk** Yd No: 69 Loa 114.03 Br ex 13.21 Dght 3.650 Lbp 108.01 Br md 12.98 Dpth 5.52 Welded, 1 dk	**(A31A2GX) General Cargo Ship** Grain: 4,297 Compartments: 4 Ho, ER 4 Ha: (17.6 x 9.3)3 (18.0 x 9.3)ER Ice Capable	**2 oil engines** driving 2 FP propellers Total Power: 970kW (1,318hp) 10.8kn S.K.L. 6NVD48-2U 2 x 4 Stroke 6 Cy. 320 x 480 each-485kW (659bhp) VEB Schwermaschinenbau "KarlLiebknecht" (SKL)-Magdeburg
8133592 - -	**SEMYON OSIPENKO** *ex* Zador *-2004* **Trawling Fleet Corp 'Yugrybpoisk'** -	**171** 51 88	Class: (RS)	**1982 Astrakhanskaya Sudoverf im. "Kirova" — Astrakhan** Yd No: 157 Loa 34.01 Br ex 7.09 Dght 2.901 Lbp 29.98 Br md - Dpth 3.66 Welded, 1 dk	**(B11B2FV) Fishing Vessel** Ice Capable	**1 oil engine** driving 1 CP propeller Total Power: 224kW (305hp) 9.5kn S.K.L. 8VD36/24-1 1 x 4 Stroke 8 Cy. 240 x 360 224kW (305bhp) VEB Schwermaschinenbau "KarlLiebknecht" (SKL)-Magdeburg
8033912 *USEH* -	**SEMYON RUDNEV** **'Ukrrichflot' Joint Stock Shipping Co** *Kherson* *Ukraine* MMSI: 272075000 Official number: 810601	**2,466** 988 3,134	Class: UA (RS)	**1982-07 Sudostroitelnyy Zavod "Krasnoye Sormovo" — Gorkiy** Yd No: 71 Loa 114.03 Br ex 13.21 Dght 3.671 Lbp 108.03 Br md 13.00 Dpth 5.52 Welded, 1 dk	**(A31A2GX) General Cargo Ship** Bale: 4,297 Compartments: 4 Ho, ER 4 Ha: (17.6 x 9.3)3 (17.9 x 9.3)ER Ice Capable	**2 oil engines** driving 2 FP propellers Total Power: 970kW (1,318hp) 10.8kn S.K.L. 6NVD48-2U 2 x 4 Stroke 6 Cy. 320 x 480 each-485kW (659bhp) VEB Schwermaschinenbau "KarlLiebknecht" (SKL)-Magdeburg
8326539 - -	**SEN HAI** *ex* Sheng Li 9 *-1998* **Shenzhen Oceanwood Co Ltd** *Haikou, Hainan* *China*	**2,464** 1,195 3,576	Class: (CC)	**1979-07 Hudong Shipyard — Shanghai** Loa 102.10 Br ex - Dght 5.680 Lbp 92.00 Br md 13.80 Dpth 6.50 Welded, 1 dk	**(A13B2TP) Products Tanker** Liq: 4,239; Liq (Oil): 4,239 Compartments: 5 Ho, ER 2 Cargo Pump (s): 2x100m³/hr	**1 oil engine** driving 1 FP propeller Total Power: 2,207kW (3,001hp) 14.5kn Hudong 6ESDZ43/82C 1 x 2 Stroke 6 Cy. 430 x 820 2207kW (3001bhp) Hudong Shipyard-China AuxGen: 2 x 250kW 400V 50Hz a.c
9364411 *WDB8296* -	**SEN. JOHN J. MARCHI** *ex* Marinette *-2005* **New York City (Department of Transportation)** - *New York, NY* *United States of America* MMSI: 366952870 Official number: 1163079	**5,901** 1,770 1,000	Class: AB	**2005-03 Marinette Marine Corp — Marinette WI** Yd No: 512 Loa 94.50 Br ex - Dght 4.170 Lbp 91.60 Br md 21.30 Dpth 6.32 Welded, 1 dk	**(A36A2PR) Passenger/Ro-Ro Ship (Vehicles)** Passengers: unberthed: 4400 Cars: 30	**3 diesel electric oil engines** driving 3 gen. Connecting to 2 elec. motors driving 2 Propellers Total Power: 8,595kW (11,685hp) EMD (Electro-Motive) 16-710-G7B 3 x Vee 2 Stroke 16 Cy. 230 x 279 each-2865kW (3895bhp) General Motors Corp.Electro-Motive Div.-La Grange
9355159 *3EDP5* -	**SEN-OKU** **Primavera Montana SA** Shunzan Kaiun KK (Shunzan Kaiun Co Ltd) SatCom: Inmarsat C 435307312 *Panama* *Panama* MMSI: 353073000 Official number: 3204806A	**104,728** 66,443 206,306 T/cm 140.2	Class: NK	**2006-08 Imabari Shipbuilding Co Ltd — Saijo EH (Saijo Shipyard)** Yd No: 8028 Loa 299.94 (BB) Br ex - Dght 18.105 Lbp 291.40 Br md 50.00 Dpth 24.50 Welded, 1 dk	**(A21A2BC) Bulk Carrier** Grain: 220,022 Compartments: 9 Ho, ER 9 Ha: ER	**1 oil engine** driving 1 FP propeller Total Power: 18,629kW (25,328hp) 14.5kn MAN-B&W 6S70MC-C 1 x 2 Stroke 6 Cy. 700 x 2800 18629kW (25328bhp) Mitsui Engineering & Shipbuilding CLtd-Japan AuxGen: 4 x 2400kW a.c
9606596 *JD3265* -	**SEN OUU MARU** **Senko Co Ltd** *Osaka, Osaka* *Japan* MMSI: 431000670 Official number: 141551	*498* - 1,259		**2011-11 KK Ura Kyodo Zosensho — Awaji HG** Yd No: 345 Loa 64.46 Br ex - Dght 4.200 Lbp 60.00 Br md 10.00 Dpth 4.60 Welded, 1 dk	**(A12A2TC) Chemical Tanker** Double Hull (13F) Compartments: 8 Wing Ta, ER 2 Cargo Pump (s): 2x300m³/hr	**1 oil engine** reverse geared to sc. shaft driving 1 CP propeller Total Power: 1,030kW (1,400hp) 11.5kn Hanshin LH28G 1 x 4 Stroke 6 Cy. 280 x 460 1030kW (1400bhp) The Hanshin Diesel Works Ltd-Japan
9634907 *3FGM6* -	**SEN TREASURE** **SLSS Shipping SA** Nakanishi Marine Co Ltd *Panama* *Panama* MMSI: 373738000 Official number: 4455013	**18,462** 10,335 29,029	Class: NK	**2013-01 Nantong Nikka Shipbuilding Co Ltd — Nantong JS (Hull)** Yd No: NK-015 **2013-01 Nantong Yahua Shipbuilding Co Ltd — Nantong JS** Yd No: NK-015 Loa 169.99 (BB) Br ex 27.38 Dght 10.060 Lbp 163.60 Br md 27.00 Dpth 14.20 Welded, 1 dk	**(A21A2BC) Bulk Carrier** Grain: 39,995; Bale: 39,070 Compartments: 5 Ho, ER 5 Ha: 4 (20.1 x 17.7)ER (12.1 x 16.0) Cranes: 4x30t	**1 oil engine** driving 1 FP propeller Total Power: 5,810kW (7,899hp) 14.2kn MAN-B&W 6S46MC-C8 1 x 2 Stroke 6 Cy. 460 x 1932 5810kW (7899bhp) Hitachi Zosen Corp-Japan Fuel: 1710.0
8226947 *BRWE* -	**SEN YANG** *ex* Tie Shan *-2003* *ex* Hong Qi 088 *-1991* **Anhui Wanjiang Shipping Co** - *Nanjing, Jiangsu* *China*	*871* 393 1,181	Class: (CC)	**1970 Guangzhou Shipyard — Guangzhou GD** Loa 64.58 Br ex - Dght 4.201 Lbp 59.00 Br md 10.80 Dpth 5.10 Welded, 1 dk	**(A31A2GX) General Cargo Ship** Grain: 1,543; Bale: 1,414 Compartments: 2 Ho, ER 2 Ha: 2 (9.6 x 4.5)ER Derricks: 4x3t; Winches: 4	**1 oil engine** driving 1 FP propeller Total Power: 699kW (950hp) 12.0kn Fiat A300.6S 1 x 4 Stroke 6 Cy. 300 x 450 699kW (950bhp) SA Fiat SGM-Torino AuxGen: 3 x 48kW 230V d.c
8907761 *HP5519* -	**SENA** *launched as* Fiona *-1990* **High Fortune Development Ltd** *Panama* *Panama* Official number: 1886490A	**274** 118 381	Class: (LR) ✠ Classed LR until 21/2/96	**1989-12 Xiamen Shipyard — Xiamen FJ** Yd No: 806-3 Loa 38.50 Br ex - Dght 3.600 Lbp 34.00 Br md 8.20 Dpth 4.20 Welded, 1 dk	**(B11B2FV) Fishing Vessel**	**1 oil engine** with clutches, flexible couplings & sr reverse geared to sc. shaft driving 1 FP propeller Total Power: 660kW (897hp) MAN 6L20/27 1 x 4 Stroke 6 Cy. 200 x 270 660kW (897bhp) Sichuan Diesel Engine Factory-China AuxGen: 2 x 40kW 400V 50Hz a.c
9003160 *C9KA* -	**SENA** **Atlantic Investment International Co** *Maputo* *Mozambique*	**678** 211 791	Class: (NK)	**1990-07 Niigata Engineering Co Ltd — Niigata NI** Yd No: 2178 Loa 55.05 Br ex - Dght 4.016 Lbp 50.00 Br md 9.80 Dpth 4.50 Welded	**(B12B2FC) Fish Carrier** Grain: 352; Bale: 308; Ins: 307 TEU 2 C. 2/20' 2 Ha: (6.3 x 4.6) (2.5 x 2.5)ER Derricks: 4x5t	**1 oil engine** with clutches, flexible couplings & sr geared to sc. shaft driving 1 FP propeller Total Power: 736kW (1,001hp) Daihatsu 6DLM-22S 1 x 4 Stroke 6 Cy. 220 x 300 736kW (1001bhp) Daihatsu Diesel Manufacturing Co Lt-Japan AuxGen: 4 x 184kW a.c Thrusters: 1 Thwart. FP thruster (f)
6422602 *VC5234* -	**SENA II** *ex* Rio San Lorenzo *-1984* *ex* Gulf Guard *-1977* **Canadian Black Cod Fishing Corp** - *Victoria, BC* *Canada* MMSI: 316001125 Official number: 322139	*183* 59 78	Class: (LR) ✠ Classed LR until 6/69	**1965-07 Bathurst Marine Ltd — Bathurst NB** Yd No: 11 Loa 28.66 Br ex 6.74 Dght - Lbp 24.39 Br md 6.71 Dpth 3.66 Welded	**(B11A2FS) Stern Trawler** Compartments: 1 Ho, ER 2 Ha: (2.4 x 1.2) (0.6 x 0.4) Derricks: 1x3t	**1 oil engine** driving 1 CP propeller Total Power: 364kW (495hp) Normo RTG-7 1 x 4 Stroke 7 Cy. 250 x 360 364kW (495bhp) AS Bergens Mek Verksteder-Norway AuxGen: 1 x 30kW 110/208V 60Hz a.c, 1 x 20kW 110/208V 60Hz a.c
9318254 *V7JH2* -	**SENA KALKAVAN** **LESE Kalkavan Schiffseigentums GmbH & Co KG** Kalkavan Shipmanagement GmbH & Co KG *Majuro* *Marshall Islands* MMSI: 538090199 Official number: 90199	**10,308** 5,070 12,545	Class: AB	**2005-09 Sedef Gemi Endustrisi A.S. — Tuzla** Yd No: 134 Loa 149.60 (BB) Br ex - Dght 7.800 Lbp 137.80 Br md 22.70 Dpth 11.30 Welded, 1 dk	**(A33A2CC) Container Ship (Fully Cellular)** TEU 1147 incl 232 ref C. Ice Capable	**1 oil engine** driving 1 FP propeller Total Power: 10,500kW (14,276hp) 19.0kn B&W 7S50MC-C 1 x 2 Stroke 7 Cy. 500 x 2000 10500kW (14276bhp) AuxGen: 1 x 1800kW a.c, 3 x 570kW a.c Thrusters: 1 Tunnel thruster (f); 1 Thwart. CP thruster (a) Fuel: 91.0 (d.f.) 1259.0 (r.f.)

IMO / Call sign	Name / Owner	Tonnage	Class	Builder / Dimensions	Type	Machinery
8425608 *DUFM* -	**SENADO** *ex* Batasan **Majestic Shipping Corp** - *Manila* *Philippines* Official number: 00-0001354	*239* 150 -		**1981 R. Visitacion & Sons — Manila** Loa - Br ex 9.81 Dght - Lbp 55.66 Br md 9.77 Dpth 2.65 Welded, 1 dk	**(A35D2RL) Landing Craft**	**1 oil engine** driving 1 FP propeller Total Power: 368kW (500hp)
7805746 *YDLR* -	**SENANG** *ex* Koei Maru No. 5 *-2007* **PT Indobaruna Bulk Transport** - *Jakarta* *Indonesia* MMSI: 525019348	**5,003** 1,993 6,821	Class: KI (NK)	**1978-12 Ube Dockyard Co. Ltd. — Ube** Yd No: 156 Loa 118.07 Br ex 16.03 Dght 6.868 Lbp 110.01 Br md 16.01 Dpth 9.15 Welded, 1 dk	**(A24A2BT) Cement Carrier**	**1 oil engine** reduction geared to sc. shaft driving 1 FP propeller Total Power: 3,310kW (4,500hp) 14.0kn MaK 6M552AK 1 x 4 Stroke 6 Cy. 450 x 520 3310kW (4500bhp) Ube Industries Ltd-Japan AuxGen: 2 x 200kW 450V 60Hz a.c Fuel: 45.5 (d.f.) 229.5 (r.f.) 14.5pd
7603124 *YFRQ* -	**SENANG** *ex* Kocho Maru *-1995* *ex* Koryu Maru *-1987* **PT Sarana Bahari Prima** - *Jakarta* *Indonesia*	**1,314** 820 1,535	Class: KI	**1976-08 K.K. Miura Zosensho — Saiki** Yd No: 518 Loa 70.00 Br ex 11.22 Dght 4.306 Lbp 66.65 Br md 11.20 Dpth 6.28 Welded	**(A31A2GX) General Cargo Ship**	**1 oil engine** driving 1 FP propeller Total Power: 1,324kW (1,800hp) Makita GSLH633 1 x 4 Stroke 6 Cy. 330 x 530 1324kW (1800bhp) Makita Diesel Co Ltd-Japan
8905763 *9MAG4* -	**SENANG EKSPRES** - **Fast Ferry Ventures Sdn Bhd** - *Penang* *Malaysia* MMSI: 533000400 Official number: 325433	**111** 49 15		**1989-03 WaveMaster International Pty Ltd — Fremantle WA** Yd No: 018 Loa 26.01 Br ex 6.70 Dght 0.830 Lbp 23.40 Br md 6.01 Dpth 1.50 Welded, 1 dk	**(A37B2PS) Passenger Ship** Hull Material: Aluminium Alloy Passengers: unberthed: 140	**2 oil engines** reverse geared to sc. shafts driving 2 FP propellers Total Power: 2,942kW (4,000hp) MWM TBD604V8 2 x Vee 4 Stroke 8 Cy. 160 x 185 each-1471kW (2000bhp) Motoren Werke Mannheim AG (MWM)-West Germany
7393872 *YGNX* -	**SENANG JAYA** *ex* Dinamarca *-1990* **PT Sultra Lestari Lines** - *Jakarta* *Indonesia* MMSI: 525019058	*2,367* 1,358 2,105	Class: KI (LR) ✠ Classed LR until 17/5/95	**1976-04 Ast. de Mallorca S.A. — Palma de Mallorca** Yd No: 215 Loa 81.64 Br ex 14.13 Dght 4.573 Lbp 74.83 Br md 14.01 Dpth 7.70 Welded, 1 dk & S dk	**(A31A2GX) General Cargo Ship** Grain: 4,681; Bale: 4,353 Compartments: 1 Ho, ER 1 Ha: (40.8 x 10.2)ER Derricks: 2x5t; Winches: 2 Ice Capable	**1 oil engine** driving 1 FP propeller Total Power: 1,765kW (2,400hp) 12.0kn Deutz RBV8M358 1 x 4 Stroke 8 Cy. 400 x 580 1765kW (2400bhp) Hijos de J Barreras SA-Spain AuxGen: 2 x 160kW 380V 50Hz a.c Fuel: 222.5 (d.f.)
8746478 *PMXJ* -	**SENANGIN** - **Government of The Republic of Indonesia (Direktorat Jenderal Perhubungan Darat - Ministry of Land Communications)** - *Tanjung Priok* *Indonesia* Official number: GT.560/2600-BA	**560** 168 -	Class: KI	**2009-05 PT Bayu Bahari Sentosa — Jakarta** Loa 45.50 Br ex - Dght 2.150 Lbp 40.15 Br md 12.00 Dpth 3.20 Welded, 1 dk	**(A36A2PR) Passenger/Ro-Ro Ship (Vehicles)**	**2 oil engines** reduction geared to sc. shafts driving 2 Propellers Total Power: 1,220kW (1,658hp) Yanmar 6AYM-ETE 2 x 4 Stroke 6 Cy. 155 x 180 each-610kW (829bhp) Yanmar Diesel Engine Co Ltd-Japan AuxGen: 2 x 105kW 380V a.c
9491367 *TCMI3* -	**SENANUR CEBI** *completed as* Romito *-2011* **Cebi Gemi Isletmeciligi ve Ticaret AS** Cebi Denizcilik ve Ticaret AS *Istanbul* *Turkey* MMSI: 271042675	**31,763** 18,415 55,660 T/cm 57.0	Class: NK (RI)	**2011-05 Hyundai Mipo Dockyard Co Ltd — Ulsan** Yd No: 6076 Loa 187.88 (BB) Br ex - Dght 12.868 Lbp 182.50 Br md 32.26 Dpth 18.30 Welded, 1 dk	**(A21A2BC) Bulk Carrier** Grain: 70,733; Bale: 69,550 Compartments: 5 Ho, ER 5 Ha: ER Cranes: 4x30t	**1 oil engine** driving 1 FP propeller Total Power: 8,820kW (11,992hp) 14.5kn MAN-B&W 6S50MC-C 1 x 2 Stroke 6 Cy. 500 x 2000 8820kW (11992bhp) Hyundai Heavy Industries Co Ltd-South Korea Fuel: 2000.0
8131013 *9WAW7* -	**SENARI JAYA** *ex* Thai Hua *-2000* *ex* Senei Maru I *-1995* *ex* Senei Maru *-1994* - - *Kuching* *Malaysia* MMSI: 533654000 Official number: 327752	**1,227** 626 1,516	Class: (NK)	**1982-03 K.K. Uno Zosensho — Imabari** Yd No: 158 Loa 72.61 Br ex 11.02 Dght 4.450 Lbp 68.00 Br md 11.00 Dpth 6.15 Welded, 1 dk	**(A31A2GX) General Cargo Ship** Compartments: 1 Ho, ER 1 Ha: (39.0 x 8.0)ER	**1 oil engine** driving 1 FP propeller Total Power: 1,177kW (1,600hp) Makita GSLH633 1 x 4 Stroke 6 Cy. 330 x 530 1177kW (1600bhp) Makita Diesel Co Ltd-Japan
9451575 *A8PS4* -	**SENATA** *ex* Aspen *-2013* **Senata Navigation Ltd** INTRESCO GmbH *Monrovia* *Liberia* MMSI: 636013823 Official number: 13823	**8,289** 5,253 12,898	Class: GL (RI)	**2008-03 Linhai Hangchang Shipbuilding Co Ltd — Linhai ZJ** Yd No: 05-027 Loa 140.55 (BB) Br ex - Dght 7.500 Lbp 131.80 Br md 20.00 Dpth 10.30 Welded, 1 dk	**(A21A2BC) Bulk Carrier** Grain: 18,000 Cranes: 2x20t	**1 oil engine** reduction geared to sc. shafts driving 1 FP propeller Total Power: 3,310kW (4,500hp) 14.0kn Yanmar 8N330-EN 1 x 4 Stroke 8 Cy. 330 x 440 3310kW (4500bhp) Yanmar Diesel Engine Co Ltd-Japan AuxGen: 2 x 250kW 440V a.c
7938696 - -	**SENATOR** *ex* Red Snapper *-1993* *ex* El Paisa *-1993* *ex* Katy Adla *-1988*	*125* 100 -		**1978 Steiner Shipyard, Inc. — Bayou La Batre, Al** L reg 20.46 Br ex 6.71 Dght - Lbp - Br md - Dpth 3.43 Welded, 1 dk	**(B11A2FT) Trawler**	**1 oil engine** geared to sc. shaft driving 1 FP propeller Total Power: 268kW (364hp) Cummins KTA-1150-M 1 x 4 Stroke 6 Cy. 159 x 159 268kW (364bhp) Cummins Engine Co Inc-USA
6706125 *J8PD6* -	**SENATOR** *ex* Myraas *-1996* *ex* Kviksholm *-1985* *ex* Lady *-1984* *ex* Pollen *-1983* *ex* Pulpa *-1981* *ex* Clover Bres *-1974* *ex* Sligo *-1974* *ex* Clover Bres *-1972* **West Indies Transport Ltd** - *Kingstown* *St Vincent & The Grenadines* Official number: 400508	**687** 297 832	Class: (BV) (NV)	**1967-01 Batservice Verft AS — Mandal** Yd No: 529 Loa 55.28 Br ex 9.33 Dght 3.506 Lbp 50.02 Br md 9.30 Dpth 5.52 Welded, 2 dks	**(A31A2GX) General Cargo Ship** Grain: 1,523; Bale: 1,365 Compartments: 1 Ho, ER 2 Ha: 2 (13.3 x 6.0)ER Cranes: 1 Ice Capable	**1 oil engine** driving 1 CP propeller Total Power: 515kW (700hp) 10.0kn Alpha 406-26VO 1 x 2 Stroke 6 Cy. 260 x 400 515kW (700bhp) (new engine 1984) B&W Alpha Diesel A/S-Denmark AuxGen: 2 x 20kW 220V d.c, 1 x 15kW 220V d.c Fuel: 41.5 (d.f.) 2.0pd
8721296 *UFWE* -	**SENATOR** *ex* Amur-2503 *-2007* *ex* Volgo-Balt 251 *-1986* **Senator Shipping Ltd** TESK Sev In Transs Ltd (OOO 'TESK Sev In Transs') *Makhachkala* *Russia* MMSI: 273378200	**3,086** 999 3,340	Class: RS (RR)	**1984-09 Zavody Tazkeho Strojarstva (ZTS) — Komarno** Yd No: 2303 Loa 115.89 Br ex 13.42 Dght 4.130 Lbp 112.40 Br md 13.00 Dpth 6.00 Welded, 1 dk	**(A31A2GX) General Cargo Ship** Grain: 4,064 TEU 102 C.Ho 62/20' (40') C.Dk 40/20' (40') Compartments: 3 Ho, ER 3 Ha: (11.6 x 10.1) (23.0 x 10.1) (24.0 x 10.1)ER Ice Capable	**2 oil engines** reverse reduction geared to sc. shafts driving 2 FP propellers Total Power: 1,030kW (1,400hp) 10.0kn Skoda 6L275A2 2 x 4 Stroke 6 Cy. 275 x 350 each-515kW (700bhp) CKD Praha-Praha AuxGen: 3 x 120kW 220/380V a.c Thrusters: 1 Thwart. FP thruster (f) Fuel: 157.0 (d.f.)
8942668 *UBLG* -	**SENATOR-1** *ex* Bogsan-2 *-2008* *ex* Vyacheslav Aleksandrov *-2002* **Senator Shipping Ltd** TESK Sev In Transs Ltd (OOO 'TESK Sev In Transs') *Makhachkala* *Russia* MMSI: 273422660	**1,777** 576 1,844	Class: (RS) (RR)	**1986-06 RO Brodogradiliste Novi Sad — Novi Sad** Yd No: 260 Loa 88.70 Br ex 12.50 Dght 3.200 Lbp 82.00 Br md 12.20 Dpth 3.50 Welded, 1 dk	**(A31A2GX) General Cargo Ship**	**2 oil engines** driving 2 FP propellers Total Power: 920kW (1,250hp) 10.0kn Alpha 6T23LU 2 x 4 Stroke 6 Cy. 225 x 300 each-460kW (625bhp) in Yugoslavia
7436741 *HQWX2* -	**SENATORS** *ex* Apache *-2006* **Bluedeep Investments Corp** Saje Shipping (Nig) Ltd *San Lorenzo* *Honduras* MMSI: 334515000 Official number: L-1728191	**434** 130 -	Class: RS (AB)	**1968 Halter Marine Services, Inc. — New Orleans, La** Yd No: 176 Loa 37.04 Br ex - Dght 4.563 Lbp 34.55 Br md 10.37 Dpth 5.03 Welded, 1 dk	**(B32A2ST) Tug**	**2 oil engines** driving 2 FP propellers Total Power: 2,206kW (3,000hp) 13.5kn EMD (Electro-Motive) 12-645-E2 2 x Vee 2 Stroke 12 Cy. 230 x 254 each-1103kW (1500bhp) General Motors Corp-USA AuxGen: 2 x 115kW 220/440V 60Hz a.c Fuel: 313.0 (d.f.)
8508682 *3EAK5* -	**SENAWANG** *ex* Shin Kyowa Maru *-2002* **Senawang Tankers Pte Ltd** Petrojaya Marine Sdn Bhd *Panama* *Panama* MMSI: 352114000 Official number: 3092405A	**3,120** 1,469 4,999	Class: NK	**1985-06 Naikai Shipbuilding & Engineering Co Ltd — Onomichi HS (Setoda Shipyard)** Yd No: 504 Loa 102.04 Br ex 15.24 Dght 6.371 Lbp 95.03 Br md 15.21 Dpth 7.52 Welded, 1 dk	**(A13B2TP) Products Tanker** Liq: 5,348; Liq (Oil): 5,348 Compartments: 8 Ta, ER 2 Cargo Pump (s): 2x1200m³/hr Manifold: Bow/CM: 51m	**1 oil engine** geared to sc. shaft driving 1 CP propeller Total Power: 2,206kW (2,999hp) 12.5kn Akasaka A41 1 x 4 Stroke 6 Cy. 410 x 800 2206kW (2999bhp) Akasaka Tekkosho KK (Akasaka DieselLtd)-Japan AuxGen: 1 x 420kW 440V 60Hz a.c, 1 x 280kW 440V 60Hz a.c, 1 x 96kW 440V 60Hz a.c Thrusters: 1 Thwart. CP thruster (f) Fuel: 55.5 (d.f.) 224.0 (r.f.) 8.0pd

IMO / Call sign	Name / Owner	Tonnage	Class	Builder / Dimensions	Type	Machinery
8729303 *YLJJ* LR-1121	**SENCIS** *ex* MRTK-1121 *-1989* **Grants & Co Ltd (SIA 'Grants & Ko')** - *Riga* Latvia MMSI: 275151000 Official number: 0662	**117** 35 30	Class: (RS)	**1989-05 Sosnovskiy Sudostroitelnyy Zavod — Sosnovka** Yd No: 753 Loa 25.51 Br ex - Dght 2.391 Lbp 22.00 Br md 7.01 Dpth 3.31 Welded, 1 dk	**(B11A2FS) Stern Trawler** Ins: 64	**1 oil engine** driving 1 FP propeller Total Power: 221kW (300hp) 9.5kn S.K.L. 6NVD26A-2 1 x 4 Stroke 6 Cy. 180 x 260 221kW (300bhp) VEB Schwermaschinenbau "KarlLiebknecht" (SKL)-Magdeburg
8137213 *DDAW* -	**SENCKENBERG** **Senckenbergische Naturforschende Gesellschaft** KUK Nordseeforschungschiff- Bereederung GmbH *Wilhelmshaven* Germany MMSI: 211217760 Official number: 204	**185** 55 48	Class: GL	**1976 Julius Diedrich Schiffswerft GmbH & Co KG — Moormerland** Yd No: 132 Loa 29.72 Br ex 7.42 Dght - Lbp 26.00 Br md 7.40 Dpth 3.60 Welded, 1 dk	**(B12D2FR) Fishery Research Vessel** Ice Capable	**1 oil engine** reduction geared to sc. shaft driving 1 FP propeller Total Power: 346kW (470hp) 10.0kn Deutz SBF12M716 1 x Vee 4 Stroke 12 Cy. 135 x 160 346kW (470bhp) Kloeckner Humboldt Deutz AG-West Germany AuxGen: 1 x 56kW 220/380V a.c
8713433 *JNOK* -	**SENDAI** - **Government of Japan (Ministry of Land, Infrastructure & Transport) (The Coastguard)** - *Tokyo* Japan MMSI: 431600649 Official number: 130203	*330* - -		**1988-06 Shikoku Dockyard Co. Ltd. — Takamatsu** Yd No: 846 Loa 67.80 Br ex 7.92 Dght 2.810 Lbp 63.00 Br md 7.90 Dpth 4.40 Welded, 1 dk	**(B34H2SQ) Patrol Vessel**	**2 oil engines** driving 2 CP propellers Total Power: 2,206kW (3,000hp) 17.5kn Niigata 6M31EX 2 x 4 Stroke 6 Cy. 310 x 460 each-1103kW (1500bhp) Niigata Engineering Co Ltd-Japan AuxGen: 2 x 96kW 225V 60Hz a.c
9472555 *JD2669* -	**SENDAI MARU** - **Miyagi Marine Service KK** - *Shiogama, Miyagi* Japan Official number: 140768	*232* - -		**2008-05 Kanagawa Zosen — Kobe** Yd No: 579 Loa 37.20 Br ex - Dght 3.100 Lbp 32.70 Br md 9.80 Dpth 4.17 Welded, 1 dk	**(B32A2ST) Tug**	**2 oil engines** reduction geared to sc. shafts driving 2 Propellers Total Power: 2,942kW (4,000hp) 14.6kn Niigata 6L28HX 2 x 4 Stroke 6 Cy. 280 x 370 each-1471kW (2000bhp) Niigata Engineering Co Ltd-Japan
9370824 *3FYY9* -	**SENDAI SPIRIT** - **Kingship Lines SA** Santoku Senpaku Co Ltd *Panama* Panama MMSI: 370768000 Official number: 4001308A	**39,895** 21,193 49,520	Class: NK	**2008-11 Tsuneishi Holdings Corp Tsuneishi Shipbuilding Co — Fukuyama HS** Yd No: 1385 Loa 199.90 (BB) Br ex - Dght 11.547 Lbp 191.50 Br md 32.20 Dpth 22.75 Welded, 1 dk	**(A24B2BW) Wood Chips Carrier** Grain: 102,130 Compartments: 6 Ho, ER 6 Ha: ER Cranes: 3x14.7t	**1 oil engine** driving 1 FP propeller Total Power: 8,360kW (11,366hp) 14.0kn MAN-B&W 6S50MC 1 x 2 Stroke 6 Cy. 500 x 1910 8360kW (11366bhp) Kawasaki Heavy Industries Ltd-Japan Fuel: 2820.0
9069657 *YBRD* -	**SENDANG MAS** *ex* Xing Ning 18 *-2007* **PT Pelayaran Tempuran Emas Tbk (TEMAS Line)** - *Jakarta* Indonesia MMSI: 525019359	**4,225** 2,217 6,200	Class: KI	**2004-05 Zhejiang Hongguan Ship Industry Co Ltd — Linhai ZJ** Loa 112.23 (BB) Br ex - Dght 6.300 Lbp 104.62 Br md 16.20 Dpth 8.00 Welded, 1 dk	**(A33A2CC) Container Ship (Fully Cellular)** TEU 466	**1 oil engine** reduction geared to sc. shaft driving 1 Propeller Total Power: 2,059kW (2,799hp) 11.0kn Guangzhou 8320ZC 1 x 4 Stroke 8 Cy. 320 x 440 2059kW (2799bhp) Guangzhou Diesel Engine Factory CoLtd-China AuxGen: 3 x 118kW 400V a.c
5320003 - -	**SENDANGAN** - **PT Pelayaran Udjana Saka Ombak** - *Jakarta* Indonesia	*138* 66 90		**1957 P.T. Carya — Jakarta** L reg 27.68 Br ex 5.54 Dght - Lbp - Br md - Dpth - Welded, 1 dk	**(A31A2GX) General Cargo Ship** 1 Ha: (4.7 x 2.6)	**1 oil engine** driving 1 FP propeller Total Power: 118kW (160hp) 8.0kn
7360057 *ZCDP4* -	**SENDJE BERGE** *ex* Berge Charlotte *-2000* *ex* Alsace *-1997* *ex* Esso Normandie *-1995* **Sendje Berge Ltd** BW Offshore Norway AS *Hamilton* Bermuda (British) MMSI: 310484000 Official number: 733780	**133,871** 103,586 274,333 T/cm 161.6	Class: NV (BV) (AB)	**1974-12 Ch. de l'Atlantique — St. Nazaire** Yd No: R25 Converted From: Crude Oil Tanker-2000 Loa 348.75 (BB) Br ex 51.87 Dght 21.378 Lbp 330.78 Br md 51.82 Dpth 27.34 Welded, 1 dk	**(B22E2OF) FPSO, Oil** Liq: 326,930; Liq (Oil): 326,930 Compartments: 12 Ta, ER 4 Cargo Pump (s): 4x3000m³/hr Manifold: Bow/CM: 176m	**1 Steam Turb** tr & dr geared to sc. shaft driving 1 FP propeller Total Power: 23,864kW (32,445hp) 16.0kn Stal-Laval 1 x steam Turb 23864kW (32445shp) Chantiers de l'Atlantique-France AuxGen: 1 x 1900kW 440V 60Hz a.c, 2 x 750kW 440V 60Hz a.c Fuel: 11002.0 (r.f.) (Heating Coils) 232.0 (d.f.) 160.5pd
8870310 - -	**SENDRILLA** *ex* Baraka *-1994* **South Sinai Shipping Co** - *Alexandria* Egypt	*180* - -	Class: (GL)	**1990 Alexandria Shipyard — Alexandria** L reg 24.80 Br ex - Dght 1.500 Lbp - Br md 7.10 Dpth 3.69 Welded, 1 dk	**(A37B2PS) Passenger Ship**	**2 oil engines** reverse reduction geared to sc. shafts driving 2 FP propellers Total Power: 176kW (240hp) 9.0kn Perkins V8.510M 2 x Vee 4 Stroke 8 Cy. 108 x 114 each-88kW (120bhp) Perkins Engines Ltd.-Peterborough AuxGen: 2 x 80kW 220/380V a.c
5364889 *SV5863* -	**SENE II** *ex* Mina *-1994* *ex* Scene II *-1984* *ex* Midmar I *-1977* *ex* Topmast 16 *-1975* *ex* Segundo *-1955* *ex* LCT-474 *-1947* **Dorenco SACIM** State Lines *Piraeus* Greece Official number: 7616	*434* 215 -	Class: (LR) ✠ Classed LR until 9/5/84	**1943-01 Sir Wm. Arrol & Co. Ltd. — Meadowside** Converted From: General Cargo Ship-1955 Converted From: Tank Landing Craft-1947 Loa 58.53 Br ex 9.20 Dght 2.045 Lbp 53.09 Br md 9.17 Dpth 2.67 Welded, 1 dk	**(B34P2QV) Salvage Ship** Compartments: 1 Ho, ER 1 Ha: (8.5 x 5.7)	**2 oil engines** sr geared to sc. shafts driving 2 FP propellers Total Power: 352kW (478hp) 5.0kn Paxman 2 x Vee 4 Stroke 12 Cy. 178 x 197 each-176kW (239bhp) (made 1945, fitted 1966) Davey, Paxman & Co. Ltd.-Colchester Thrusters: 1 Water jet (f) Fuel: 25.0 (d.f.)
7224021 *WDC8537* -	**SENECA** *ex* Sara T *-1990* *ex* Adventuress *-1990* *ex* Olympic Miler *-1990* *ex* The Squire *-1990* **Pocahontas Inc** - *Boston, MA* United States of America Official number: 532569	*131* 108 -		**1971 Lantana Boatyard, Inc. — Lake Worth, Fl** Loa 23.78 Br ex 6.71 Dght 2.744 Lbp - Br md - Dpth 3.79 Welded	**(B11B2FV) Fishing Vessel** Hull Material: Aluminium Alloy	**1 oil engine** geared to sc. shaft driving 1 FP propeller Total Power: 268kW (364hp) 10.0kn Caterpillar 3408TA 1 x Vee 4 Stroke 8 Cy. 137 x 152 268kW (364bhp) Caterpillar Tractor Co-USA
9192727 *JG5357* -	**SENEI MARU** - **Corporation for Advanced Transport & Technology Fujiei Kaiun KK** Fujiei Sangyo KK *Kawasaki, Kanagawa* Japan MMSI: 431100477 Official number: 135245	*1,880* - 3,339	Class: NK	**1998-08 Hitachi Zosen Corp — Kawasaki KN** Yd No: 4953 Loa 77.30 Br ex - Dght 5.912 Lbp 72.00 Br md 15.00 Dpth 7.20 Welded, 1 dk	**(A31A2GX) General Cargo Ship** Grain: 1,860; Liq: 1,306 Compartments: 1 Ho, ER 1 Ha: (26.0 x 9.8)ER Cranes: 1x20t	**1 oil engine** driving 1 FP propeller Total Power: 2,207kW (3,001hp) Hanshin LH38L 1 x 4 Stroke 6 Cy. 380 x 760 2207kW (3001bhp) The Hanshin Diesel Works Ltd-Japan Thrusters: 1 Thwart. FP thruster (f) Fuel: 160.0
9646261 *JD3094* -	**SENEI MARU** - **Izumi Kisen KK (Izumi Shipping Co Ltd)** - *Tokyo* Japan MMSI: 431001782 Official number: 141292	*499* - 1,600		**2010-08 K.K. Murakami Zosensho — Naruto** Loa 75.00 Br ex - Dght 4.340 Lbp 69.60 Br md 12.00 Dpth 7.37 Welded, 1 dk	**(A31A2GX) General Cargo Ship**	**1 oil engine** geared to sc. shaft driving 1 Propeller Total Power: 1,176kW (1,599hp) Akasaka K31FD 1 x 4 Stroke 6 Cy. 310 x 530 1176kW (1599bhp) Akasaka Tekkosho KK (Akasaka DieselLtd)-Japan
8889830 *JL6356* -	**SENEI MARU NO. 5** *ex* Senei Maru *-2012* **Kinjo Kaiun YK** - *Imabari, Ehime* Japan Official number: 134928	*499* - 1,600		**1995-04 Namikata Shipbuilding Co Ltd — Imabari EH** Yd No: 188 Loa 75.92 Br ex - Dght 4.050 Lbp 71.00 Br md 12.00 Dpth 7.00 Welded, 1 dk	**(A31A2GX) General Cargo Ship** Grain: 2,543; Bale: 2,534 Compartments: 1 Ho, ER 1 Ha: (39.0 x 9.5)ER	**1 oil engine** driving 1 Z propeller Total Power: 736kW (1,001hp) 11.5kn Akasaka A31 1 x 4 Stroke 6 Cy. 310 x 600 736kW (1001bhp) Akasaka Tekkosho KK (Akasaka DieselLtd)-Japan
9152129 *JG5003* -	**SENEI MARU No. 5** - **Corporation for Advanced Transport & Technology Fujiei Kaiun KK** Fujiei Sangyo KK *Kawasaki, Kanagawa* Japan MMSI: 431100284 Official number: 134933	*1,598* - 2,901	Class: NK	**1996-11 KK Kanasashi — Shizuoka SZ** Yd No: 3426 Loa 74.41 Br ex - Dght 5.914 Lbp 68.00 Br md 14.20 Dpth 7.10 Welded, 1 dk	**(B34E2SW) Waste Disposal Vessel** Grain: 1,683; Liq: 1,225 2 Ha: 2 (13.0 x 8.6)ER Cranes: 1x20t	**1 oil engine** driving 1 FP propeller Total Power: 2,648kW (3,600hp) 12.8kn Hanshin 6LF46 1 x 4 Stroke 6 Cy. 460 x 740 2648kW (3600bhp) The Hanshin Diesel Works Ltd-Japan Thrusters: 1 Thwart. FP thruster (f) Fuel: 135.0 (d.f.)

IMO / Call sign	Name / Owner	Tonnage	Class	Builder / Dimensions	Type	Machinery
7051967 - DAK 631	**SENEPESCA STAR** *ex* Taiyo Maru No. 2 *-1981* **Societe Senegalaise pour l'Expansion de la Peche, Surgelation et Conditionnement des Aliments (SENEPESCA)** - *Dakar* *Senegal*	*625* 288 749	Class: (BV)	**1970 Hayashikane Shipbuilding & Engineering Co Ltd — Yokosuka KN** Yd No: 693 Loa 56.55 Br ex 9.89 Dght 2.710 Lbp 52.89 Br md 9.81 Dpth 6.84 Welded, 2 dks	**(B11A2FT) Trawler**	**1 oil engine** driving 1 CP propeller Total Power: 1,545kW (2,101hp) 13.5kn Niigata 6MG31X 1 x 4 Stroke 6 Cy. 310 x 380 1545kW (2101bhp) Niigata Engineering Co Ltd-Japan AuxGen: 2 x 176kW 445V a.c Fuel: 358.5
8517293 *3EOR2* -	**SENER 1** *ex* Marianne K *-2007* *ex* Wistaria *-2006* *ex* Marine Peace *-2003* *ex* Oh Poong *-2000* *ex* Fuji *-1997* **Aspana Shipping & Trading Corp** Sener Kardesler Denizcilik Sanayi ve Ticaret AS (Sener Brothers Shipping Industry & Trading) SatCom: Inmarsat C 437173310 *Panama* *Panama* MMSI: 371733000 Official number: 3368108B	**4,498** 2,154 8,150	Class: NK TL (KR)	**1985-12 Imai Shipbuilding Co Ltd — Kochi KC** Yd No: 540 Loa 97.64 Br ex - Dght 7.740 Lbp 89.97 Br md 18.51 Dpth 10.00 Welded, 2 dks	**(A31A2GX) General Cargo Ship** Grain: 10,582; Bale: 10,089 Compartments: 2 Ho, ER 2 Ha: (33.8 x 11.2) (17.6 x 11.2)ER Derricks: 3x25t	**1 oil engine** driving 1 FP propeller Total Power: 1,228kW (1,670hp) 10.0kn Hanshin 6EL38 1 x 4 Stroke 6 Cy. 380 x 760 1228kW (1670bhp) The Hanshin Diesel Works Ltd-Japan
8821412 *JKAJ* MG1-1682	**SENFUKU MARU NO. 1** *ex* Taiko Maru No. 28 *-2007* *ex* Sachi Maru No. 1 *-1996* **YK Senfuku Suisan** - SatCom: Inmarsat A 1200214 *Shizuoka, Shizuoka* *Japan* MMSI: 431703820 Official number: 130750	*390* - -		**1989-04 Niigata Engineering Co Ltd — Niigata NI** Yd No: 2128 Loa 54.07 (BB) Br ex - Dght 3.440 Lbp 47.90 Br md 8.70 Dpth 3.80 Welded	**(B11B2FV) Fishing Vessel** Ins: 497	**1 oil engine** with clutches, flexible couplings & sr geared to sc. shaft driving 1 CP propeller Total Power: 699kW (950hp) Niigata 6M28BFT 1 x 4 Stroke 6 Cy. 280 x 480 699kW (950bhp) Niigata Engineering Co Ltd-Japan
8614900 *JGQJ* -	**SENFUKU MARU NO. 11** *ex* Taiko Maru No. 78 *-2005* *ex* Ryusei Maru No. 78 *-1994* *ex* Taiko Maru No. 78 *-1990* **YK Senfuku Suisan** - SatCom: Inmarsat A 1204611 *Shizuoka, Shizuoka* *Japan* MMSI: 431704310 Official number: 129678	*409* - 470		**1986-11 Miho Zosensho K.K. — Shimizu** Yd No: 1291 Loa 54.60 (BB) Br ex 8.74 Dght 3.407 Lbp 48.00 Br md 8.70 Dpth 3.75 Welded, 1 dk	**(B11B2FV) Fishing Vessel** Ins: 650	**1 oil engine** with clutches, flexible couplings & dr geared to sc. shaft driving 1 FP propeller Total Power: 736kW (1,001hp) Niigata 6M28BFT 1 x 4 Stroke 6 Cy. 280 x 480 736kW (1001bhp) Niigata Engineering Co Ltd-Japan
9033464 *JPVA* -	**SENFUKU MARU NO. 22** *ex* Fukuyoshi Maru No. 85 *-2005* **YK Senfuku Suisan** - SatCom: Inmarsat A 1204531 *Shizuoka, Shizuoka* *Japan* MMSI: 431702360 Official number: 132209	*379* - -		**1991-06 Niigata Engineering Co Ltd — Niigata NI** Yd No: 2218 Loa 56.40 (BB) Br ex - Dght 3.440 Lbp 49.10 Br md 8.80 Dpth 3.80 Welded	**(B11B2FV) Fishing Vessel** Ins: 478	**1 oil engine** with clutches, flexible couplings & sr geared to sc. shaft driving 1 CP propeller Total Power: 699kW (950hp) Niigata 6M28BFT 1 x 4 Stroke 6 Cy. 280 x 480 699kW (950bhp) Niigata Engineering Co Ltd-Japan
8610112 *JGIT* -	**SENFUKU MARU NO. 61** *ex* Chiyo Maru No. 17 *-2004* **YK Senfuku Suisan** - SatCom: Inmarsat B 343184710 *Shizuoka, Shizuoka* *Japan* MMSI: 431847000 Official number: 129663	*409* - 479		**1986-09 Niigata Engineering Co Ltd — Niigata NI** Yd No: 2023 Loa 55.81 (BB) Br ex - Dght 3.000 Lbp 49.18 Br md 8.91 Dpth 3.81 Welded, 1 dk	**(B11B2FV) Fishing Vessel** Ins: 543	**1 oil engine** with clutches, flexible couplings & sr geared to sc. shaft driving 1 CP propeller Total Power: 699kW (950hp) Niigata 6M28AFTE 1 x 4 Stroke 6 Cy. 280 x 480 699kW (950bhp) Niigata Engineering Co Ltd-Japan
9053464 *JQGL* -	**SENFUKU MARU NO. 62** *ex* Jyutoku Maru No. 28 *-2004* *ex* Kinei Maru No. 8 *-1999* **YK Senfuku Suisan** - SatCom: Inmarsat A 1205224 *Shizuoka, Shizuoka* *Japan* MMSI: 431700010 Official number: 132264	*409* - -		**1992-12 KK Kanasashi — Shizuoka SZ** Yd No: 3272 Loa 56.70 (BB) Br ex 8.83 Dght 3.450 Lbp 49.60 Br md 8.80 Dpth 3.84 Welded, 1 dk	**(B11B2FV) Fishing Vessel** Ins: 523	**1 oil engine** with flexible couplings & sr reverse geared to sc. shaft driving 1 FP propeller Total Power: 736kW (1,001hp) Akasaka K28FD 1 x 4 Stroke 6 Cy. 280 x 480 736kW (1001bhp) Akasaka Tekkosho KK (Akasaka DieselLtd)-Japan
8712312 *JJLC* -	**SENFUKU MARU NO. 66** *ex* Shinsei Maru No. 65 *-2005* *ex* Kinei Maru No. 126 *-1999* **YK Senfuku Suisan** - SatCom: Inmarsat A 1202321 *Shizuoka, Shizuoka* *Japan* MMSI: 431633000 Official number: 129684	*379* - -		**1987-09 KK Kanasashi Zosen — Shizuoka SZ** Yd No: 3145 Loa 53.52 (BB) Br ex 8.74 Dght 3.401 Lbp 46.89 Br md 8.70 Dpth 3.76 Welded	**(B11B2FV) Fishing Vessel**	**1 oil engine** with clutches, flexible couplings & sr reverse geared to sc. shaft driving 1 FP propeller Total Power: 736kW (1,001hp) Niigata 6M28BFT 1 x 4 Stroke 6 Cy. 280 x 480 736kW (1001bhp) Niigata Engineering Co Ltd-Japan
8103420 *YDXX* -	**SENGETI/PERTAMINA 3007** - **PT PERTAMINA (PERSERO)** - *Jakarta* *Indonesia* MMSI: 525008024	**21,747** 7,541 29,952 T/cm 46.7	Class: KI (LR) ✠ Classed LR until 4/3/08	**1982-10 Onomichi Dockyard Co Ltd — Onomichi HS** Yd No: 303 Loa 180.02 (BB) Br ex 30.03 Dght 8.856 Lbp 171.00 Br md 30.00 Dpth 15.02 Welded, 1 dk	**(A13B2TP) Products Tanker** Single Hull Liq: 39,302; Liq (Oil): 39,302 Cargo Heating Coils Compartments: 10 Ta, ER 4 Cargo Pump (s): 4x1000m³/hr Manifold: Bow/CM: 90m	**1 oil engine** driving 1 FP propeller Total Power: 9,731kW (13,230hp) 15.0kn Sulzer 6RLB66 1 x 2 Stroke 6 Cy. 660 x 1400 9731kW (13230bhp) Ishikawajima Harima Heavy IndustrieCo Ltd (IHI)-Japan AuxGen: 3 x 680kW 450V 60Hz a.c Boilers: e (o.f.) 22.1kgf/cm² (21.7bar), AuxB (o.f.) 17.9kgf/cm² (17.6bar) Fuel: 213.0 (d.f.) (Heating Coils) 930.0 (r.f.) 39.0pd
9731810 - -	**SENGGORA ESCORT** - **PT Pelayaran Senggora** - *Batam* *Indonesia* Official number: 2014 PPm No.3393/L	**199** 60	Class: KI (Class contemplated)	**2014-01 PT Citra Shipyard — Batam** Yd No: TB 049 Loa 24.80 Br ex - Dght - Lbp - Br md 8.00 Dpth 3.65 Welded, 1 dk	**(B32A2ST) Tug**	**2 oil engines** reduction geared to sc. shafts driving 2 Propellers Total Power: 1,220kW (1,658hp) Yanmar 6AYM-WET 2 x 4 Stroke 6 Cy. 155 x 180 each-610kW (829bhp) Yanmar Diesel Engine Co Ltd-Japan
9696723 *YDA3384* -	**SENGGORA MARINER** - **PT Pelayaran Senggora** - *Batam* *Indonesia* Official number: 2013 PPM NO. 2945/L	**200** 61 -	Class: KI RI	**2013-01 PT Citra Shipyard — Batam** Yd No: TB 020 Loa 26.00 Br ex - Dght 2.990 Lbp - Br md 8.00 Dpth 3.65 Welded, 1 dk	**(B32A2ST) Tug**	**2 oil engines** reduction geared to sc.shafts driving 2 Propellers Total Power: 1,220kW (1,658hp) 11.0kn Yanmar 6AYM-WET 2 x 4 Stroke 6 Cy. 155 x 180 each-610kW (829bhp) Yanmar Diesel Engine Co Ltd-Japan
7946863 *TCAG4* -	**SENGUL K** *ex* Ak-Gul II *-2009* **Zafer Nakliyat - Ergun Zafer Tuzcu** - *Istanbul* *Turkey* MMSI: 271002632 Official number: 4467	*498* 295 1,000		**1977 Gemi-is Kolleketif Sirketi — Fener, Istanbul** Loa 48.32 Br ex - Dght 2.950 Lbp 44.00 Br md 8.01 Dpth 3.36 Welded, 1 dk	**(A31A2GX) General Cargo Ship** Derricks: 4	**1 oil engine** driving 1 FP propeller Total Power: 368kW (500hp) S.K.L. 6VD36/24A-1 1 x 4 Stroke 6 Cy. 240 x 360 368kW (500bhp) VEB Schwermaschinenbau "KarlLiebknecht" (SKL)-Magdeburg
6717136 - -	**SENHO MARU** *ex* Kuko No. 2 *-2001* *ex* Senho Maru *-1999* - - *South Korea*	*177* - -		**1967-03 Osaka Shipbuilding Co Ltd — Osaka OS** Yd No: 266 Loa 29.06 Br ex 8.26 Dght 2.794 Lbp 28.05 Br md 8.21 Dpth 3.89 Riveted\Welded, 1 dk	**(B32A2ST) Tug**	**2 oil engines** driving 2 FP propellers Total Power: 1,472kW (2,002hp) 13.0kn Fuji 6M32CH4C 2 x 4 Stroke 6 Cy. 320 x 380 each-736kW (1001bhp) Fuji Diesel Co Ltd-Japan AuxGen: 1 x 24kW 225V a.c Fuel: 30.5 6.0pd
9257890 *JK5609* -	**SENHO MARU** - **Nitto Tugboat KK** - *Kurashiki, Okayama* *Japan* Official number: 136161	*199* - -		**2001-11 Kanagawa Zosen — Kobe** Yd No: 502 Loa 37.10 Br ex - Dght - Lbp - Br md 9.00 Dpth 4.10 Welded, 1 dk	**(B32A2ST) Tug**	**2 oil engines** driving 2 FP propellers Total Power: 2,648kW (3,600hp) Yanmar 8N21A-EV 2 x 4 Stroke 8 Cy. 210 x 290 each-1324kW (1800bhp) Yanmar Diesel Engine Co Ltd-Japan

Ship	Tonnage / Class	Builder / Dimensions	Type	Machinery
7911727 **SENHOR DO BONFIM** - - - -	**766** Class: (AB) 230 1,021	**1982-08 Maclaren IC Estaleiros e Servicos S.A. — Niteroi** Yd No: 254 Loa 54.87 Br ex 11.64 Dght 3.990 Lbp 52.00 Br md 11.60 Dpth 4.63 Welded, 1 dk	**(B21A20S) Platform Supply Ship**	**2 oil engines** reverse reduction geared to sc. shafts driving 2 FP propellers Total Power: 1,824kW (2,480hp) 12.0kn Alpha 8V23LU 2 x Vee 4 Stroke 8 Cy. 225 x 300 each-912kW (1240bhp) Equipamentos Villares SA-Brazil AuxGen: 2 x 128kW Thrusters: 1 Thwart. FP thruster (f)
7937422 **SENHORA DA BOA VIAGEM** *WYC7688* *ex* Morning Star - **Boa Viagem Fishing Corp** - *New Bedford, MA* *United States of America* Official number: 598066	*140* 95 -	**1978 St Augustine Trawlers, Inc. — Saint Augustine, Fl** L reg 21.43 Br ex 6.74 Dght - Lbp - Br md - Dpth 3.51 Welded, 1 dk	**(B11B2FV) Fishing Vessel**	**1 oil engine** driving 1 FP propeller Total Power: 382kW (519hp) Caterpillar 3412TA 1 x Vee 4 Stroke 12 Cy. 137 x 152 382kW (519bhp) Caterpillar Tractor Co-USA
7931428 **SENHORA DA HORA** - - - -	*199* 58 117	**1981-09 Est. Navais da Figueira da Foz Lda. (FOZNAVE) — Figueira da Foz** Yd No: 043 Loa 33.91 Br ex 8.01 Dght 3.550 Lbp 28.61 Br md 7.82 Dpth 3.61 Welded, 1 dk	**(B11A2FS) Stern Trawler**	**1 oil engine** sr geared to sc. shaft driving 1 CP propeller Total Power: 1,066kW (1,449hp) Alpha 10V23L-VO 1 x Vee 4 Stroke 10 Cy. 225 x 300 1066kW (1449bhp) B&W Alpha Diesel A/S-Denmark
7106839 **SENHORA DE FATIMA** *VM5368* - **WA Seafood Exporters Pty Ltd** - *Fremantle, WA* *Australia* Official number: 332073	*198* 132 -	**1970 Dillingham Shipyards (WA) Pty Ltd — Fremantle WA** Yd No: 203 Loa 24.08 Br ex 6.89 Dght 3.201 Lbp 20.81 Br md 6.74 Dpth 4.04 Welded, 1 dk	**(B11A2FT) Trawler** Ins: 96	**1 oil engine** driving 1 FP propeller Total Power: 313kW (426hp) 10.0kn Caterpillar D343SCAC 1 x 4 Stroke 6 Cy. 137 x 165 313kW (426bhp) Caterpillar Tractor Co-USA AuxGen: 1 x 30kW 250/440V 50Hz a.c
7021209 **SENHORA MALAK** *CNNO* *ex* Senhora da Fe *-1983* - **Societe D'Armements et Peches Nord Africains** - *Casablanca* *Morocco*	*179* Class: (LR) 55 ✠ Classed LR until 5/74 71	**1970-10 Estaleiros Sao Jacinto S.A. — Aveiro** Yd No: 79 Loa 32.01 Br ex 7.45 Dght 2.763 Lbp 27.08 Br md 7.21 Dpth 3.41 Riveted\Welded	**(B11A2FS) Stern Trawler**	**1 oil engine** driving 1 CP propeller Total Power: 485kW (659hp) MaK 6M351AK 1 x 4 Stroke 6 Cy. 240 x 350 485kW (659bhp) Atlas MaK Maschinenbau GmbH-Kiel AuxGen: 2 x 28kW 380V 50Hz a.c
8701519 **SENIHA-S** *3FOG6* *ex* Eastwind Rhine *-2009* *ex* EW Hastings *-2008* - *ex* Hastings *-2004* *ex* Danube *-2000* *ex* Torm Estrid *-1995* *ex* Anatoli *-1995* **Bulk Blacksea Inc** Erler Denizcilik ve Ticaret Ltd Sti *Panama* *Panama* MMSI: 355347009 Official number: 39817PEXT	**17,895** Class: BV (LR) 9,137 ✠ Classed LR until 16/1/06 29,995 T/cm 37.9	**1990-01 Stocznia Szczecinska im A Warskiego — Szczecin** Yd No: B560/02 Converted From: Products Tanker-2008 Loa 170.01 (BB) Br ex 25.34 Dght 10.880 Lbp 161.88 Br md 25.32 Dpth 14.50 Welded, 1 dk	**(A21A2BC) Bulk Carrier** Single Hull Grain: 40,306 Compartments: 6 Ho, ER 6 Ha: ER Cranes: 3	**1 oil engine** driving 1 FP propeller Total Power: 6,500kW (8,837hp) 14.0kn B&W 6L50MC 1 x 2 Stroke 6 Cy. 500 x 1620 6500kW (8837bhp) Zaklady Przemyslu Metalowego 'HCegielski' SA-Poznan AuxGen: 3 x 640kW 380V 50Hz a.c Boilers: 2 AuxB (o.f.) 17.3kgf/cm² (17.0bar), AuxB (ex.g.) 7.1kgf/cm² (7.0bar) Fuel: 273.5 (d.f.) 1415.2 (r.f.)
8959099 **SENIO** *ISHB* - **Secomar SpA** - *Ravenna* *Italy* Official number: 10725	*145* Class: RI 97 250	**1990 Costruzioni Navali SpA — Travaco' Siccomario** Yd No: 51 L reg 32.00 Br ex - Dght 2.000 Lbp 31.30 Br md 7.00 Dpth 2.40 Welded, 1 dk	**(A13B2TU) Tanker (unspecified)** 2 Cargo Pump (s)	**1 oil engine** driving 1 FP propeller Total Power: 155kW (211hp) Fiat 821M 1 x 4 Stroke 6 Cy. 137 x 156 155kW (211bhp) (made 1976) AIFO, Appl. Ind. FIAT OM S.p.A-Pregnana Milanese
7712731 **SENIOR** *LGYT* *ex* Tromsoybuen *-2008* *ex* Grimsholm *-1998* N-200-B **Nyholmen AS** Hansen Dahl Fiskeri AS *Bodo* *Norway* MMSI: 257285000 Official number: 19157	**1,278** Class: NV 442 1,493	**1978-05 Batservice Verft AS — Mandal** (Hull) Yd No: 647 **1978-05 Ulstein Hatlo AS — Ulsteinvik** Yd No: 156 Loa 62.72 Br ex 11.64 Dght 6.430 Lbp 54.62 Br md 11.61 Dpth 8.01 Welded, 2 dks	**(B11B2FV) Fishing Vessel** Compartments: 6 Ta, 2 Ho, ER 8 Ha: 2 (2.5 x 2.5)6 (3.5 x 2.5)ER Ice Capable	**1 oil engine** geared to sc. shaft driving 1 CP propeller Total Power: 2,501kW (3,400hp) 15.0kn MaK 9M453AK 1 x 4 Stroke 9 Cy. 320 x 420 2501kW (3400bhp) MaK Maschinenbau GmbH-Kiel AuxGen: 2 x 198kW 380V 50Hz a.c, 1 x 128kW 380V 50Hz a.c Thrusters: 1 Thwart. FP thruster (f); 1 Tunnel thruster (a)
9285196 **SENIORITY** *2GJZ6* *launched as* Superiority *-2006* - **FSL-15 Inc** James Fisher (Shipping Services) Ltd *London* *United Kingdom* MMSI: 235098058	**3,859** Class: LR 1,276 ✠ **100A1** SS 09/2011 4,430 Double Hull oil and chemical tanker, Ship Type 2 T/cm ESP 13.6 LI ✠ **LMC** **UMS CCS** Eq.Ltr: U; Cable: 467.5/40.0 U3 (a)	**2006-09 Qingshan Shipyard — Wuhan HB** Yd No: 20020402 Loa 95.14 (BB) Br ex 17.12 Dght 5.892 Lbp 87.11 Br md 17.00 Dpth 7.70 Welded, 1 dk	**(A12B2TR) Chemical/Products Tanker** Double Hull (13F) Liq: 4,602; Liq (Oil): 4,602 Compartments: 6 Ta, 1 Slop Ta, ER 6 Cargo Pump (s): 6x375m³/hr Manifold: Bow/CM: 46.6m	**6 diesel electric oil engines** driving 6 gen. each 486kW 450V a.c Connecting to 2 elec. motors each (900kW) driving 2 FP propellers Total Power: 3,090kW (4,200hp) 11.0kn MAN D2840LE 6 x Vee 4 Stroke 10 Cy. 128 x 142 each-515kW (700bhp) MAN Nutzfahrzeuge AG-Nuernberg Boilers: HWH (o.f.) 3.9kgf/cm² (3.8bar) Thrusters: 1 Thwart. FP thruster (f) Fuel: 105.0 (d.f.)
9509918 **SENIPAH** *H3DE* - **PT PERTAMINA (PERSERO)** - *Panama* *Panama* MMSI: 352384000 Official number: 019922817PE	**24,167** Class: NV 7,253 29,756	**2014-03 Zhejiang Chenye Shipbuilding Co Ltd — Daishan County ZJ** Yd No: 0804 Loa 180.03 (BB) Br ex 30.53 Dght 9.000 Lbp 173.00 Br md 30.51 Dpth 15.90 Welded, 1 dk	**(A13B2TP) Products Tanker** Double Hull (13F) Liq: 33,000; Liq (Oil): 33,000	**1 oil engine** driving 1 FP propeller Total Power: 6,480kW (8,810hp) 14.0kn MAN-B&W 6S42MC 1 x 2 Stroke 6 Cy. 420 x 1764 6480kW (8810bhp) Hyundai Heavy Industries Co Ltd-South Korea AuxGen: 3 x a.c
8829177 **SENITE** *UETR* *ex* Fosforitovyy *-1992* - **Dalkrevetka Co Ltd** - *Nevelsk* *Russia* MMSI: 273828200	**683** Class: RS 233 529	**1990-05 Khabarovskiy Sudostroitelnyy Zavod im Kirova — Khabarovsk** Yd No: 876 Loa 54.99 Br ex 9.49 Dght 4.661 Lbp 50.04 Br md 9.30 Dpth 5.16 Welded, 1 dk	**(B12B2FC) Fish Carrier** Ins: 632 Ice Capable	**1 oil engine** driving 1 FP propeller Total Power: 588kW (799hp) 11.3kn S.K.L. 6NVD48A-2U 1 x 4 Stroke 6 Cy. 320 x 480 588kW (799bhp) VEB Schwermaschinenbau "KarlLiebknecht" (SKL)-Magdeburg AuxGen: 3 x 150kW a.c
8625222 **SENJA PAPUA** *PMSH* *ex* Cemara *-2011* - *ex* Kyotoku Maru No. 37 *-2008* **PT Persada Nusantara Timur** - *Surabaya* *Indonesia*	**683** Class: KI 253 599	**1987-05 K.K. Kamishima Zosensho — Osakikamijima** Yd No: 207 Loa 56.22 Br ex - Dght 3.071 Lbp 52.00 Br md 9.50 Dpth 5.30 Welded, 1 dk	**(A31A2GX) General Cargo Ship**	**1 oil engine** geared to sc. shaft driving 1 FP propeller Total Power: 552kW (750hp) 9.0kn Hanshin 6LU26G 1 x 4 Stroke 6 Cy. 260 x 440 552kW (750bhp) The Hanshin Diesel Works Ltd-Japan
8908349 **SENJALAND** *LLNQ* *ex* Stokke Senior *-2009* *ex* Bogo *-2001* T-9-TK **Oddbjorn Frantzen** - *Aalesund* *Norway* MMSI: 257570600	**172** 68 -	**1989-11 Bruces Verkstad AB — Landskrona** (Hull launched by) **1989-11 Kattegat Vaerft A/S — Grenaa** (Hull completed by) Loa 23.83 Br ex - Dght - Lbp 7.29 Br md 7.21 Dpth - Welded	**(B11A2FS) Stern Trawler**	**1 oil engine** geared to sc. shaft driving 1 FP propeller Total Power: 675kW (918hp) Caterpillar 3508TA 1 x Vee 4 Stroke 8 Cy. 170 x 190 675kW (918bhp) Caterpillar Inc-USA
8520111 **SENKO MARU** - - - -	*199* - 696	**1986-02 Kishigami Zosen K.K. — Akitsu** Yd No: 1875 Loa 53.47 (BB) Br ex - Dght 3.420 Lbp 49.50 Br md 9.00 Dpth 5.50 Welded, 2 dks	**(A31A2GX) General Cargo Ship** Compartments: 1 Ho, ER 1 Ha: ER	**1 oil engine** with clutches & reverse reduction geared to sc. shaft driving 1 FP propeller Total Power: 405kW (551hp) Akasaka A24R 1 x 4 Stroke 6 Cy. 240 x 450 405kW (551bhp) Akasaka Tekkosho KK (Akasaka DieselLtd)-Japan
9021265 **SENKOKU MARU** *JK5072* - **Senko Co Ltd** - *Osaka, Osaka* *Japan* Official number: 132497	*498* - 1,200	**1991-04 Miyoshi Shipbuilding Co Ltd — Uwajima EH** Yd No: 287 Loa - Br ex - Dght 4.252 Lbp 60.03 Br md 10.01 Dpth 4.53 Welded, 1 dk	**(A12A2TC) Chemical Tanker** Compartments: 8 Wing Ta, ER 2 Cargo Pump (s): 2x300m³/hr	**1 oil engine** geared to sc. shaft driving 1 FP propeller Total Power: 1,030kW (1,400hp) Hanshin LH28G 1 x 4 Stroke 6 Cy. 280 x 460 1030kW (1400bhp) The Hanshin Diesel Works Ltd-Japan
9457696 **SENKOMA MARU** *JD2515* - **Senko KK & Sinpo Kisen KK** - *Imabari, Ehime* *Japan* MMSI: 431000376 Official number: 140648	*498* - 1,550	**2007-12 K.K. Watanabe Zosensho — Nagasaki** Yd No: 146 Loa 76.12 Br ex - Dght 4.030 Lbp 70.20 Br md 12.30 Dpth 7.00 Welded, 1 dk	**(A31A2GX) General Cargo Ship** Bale: 2,494 Compartments: 1 Ho, ER 1 Ha: ER (40.0 x 10.1)	**1 oil engine** driving 1 FP propeller Total Power: 1,618kW (2,200hp) Hanshin LH34LA 1 x 4 Stroke 6 Cy. 340 x 640 1618kW (2200bhp) The Hanshin Diesel Works Ltd-Japan

9140449 *HSB4262* -	**SENNA** *ex* New Breeze *-2009* **Siam Lucky Marine Co Ltd** - *Bangkok* Thailand MMSI: 567359000 Official number: 520081178	**4,002** 1,201 3,700 T/cm 13.7	Class: NK	**1996-09 Shin Kurushima Dockyard Co. Ltd. — Akitsu** Yd No: 2903 Loa 105.92 (BB) Br ex 16.23 Dght 5.123 Lbp 99.90 Br md 16.20 Dpth 8.00 Welded, 1 dk	**(A11B2TG) LPG Tanker** Double Bottom Entire Compartment Length Liq (Gas): 3,534 3 x Gas Tank (s); 3 membrane (C.mn.stl) cyl horizontal 6 Cargo Pump (s): 6x350m^3/hr Manifold: Bow/CM: 60.8m	**1 oil engine** driving 1 FP propeller Total Power: 2,900kW (3,943hp) 14.0kn Mitsubishi 6UEC37LA 1 x 2 Stroke 6 Cy. 370 x 880 2900kW (3943bhp) Kobe Hatsudoki KK-Japan AuxGen: 2 x 200kW 450V 60Hz a.c Fuel: 105.0 (d.f.) 446.0 (r.f.)
9005182 *HSB4407* -	**SENNA 2** *ex* Nautica Segamat *-2009* *ex* Kelso *-2004* *ex* Golden Crux No. 11 *-1999* **Siam Lucky Marine Co Ltd** - *Bangkok* Thailand MMSI: 567388000 Official number: 520084760	**3,493** 1,048 4,421 T/cm 12.9	Class: BV (NK)	**1991-02 Usuki Shipyard Co Ltd — Usuki OT** Yd No: 1608 Loa 99.98 (BB) Br ex 16.43 Dght 5.913 Lbp 94.00 Br md 16.40 Dpth 7.50 Welded, 1 dk	**(A11B2TG) LPG Tanker** Double Sides Entire Compartment Length Liq (Gas): 3,523 3 x Gas Tank (s); 3 independent cyl horizontal 3 Cargo Pump (s): 3x300m^3/hr Manifold: Bow/CM: 57.2m	**1 oil engine** driving 1 CP propeller Total Power: 2,942kW (4,000hp) 13.5kn Mitsubishi 6UEC37LA 1 x 2 Stroke 6 Cy. 370 x 880 2942kW (4000bhp) Akasaka Tekkosho KK (Akasaka DieselLtd)-Japan AuxGen: 2 x 240kW 450V 60Hz a.c, 1 x 320kW 450V 60Hz a.c Fuel: 57.0 (d.f.) 596.0 (r.f.)
9179270 *HSB4486* -	**SENNA 3** *ex* Gas Jaya *-2010* **Siam Lucky Marine Co Ltd** - *Bangkok* Thailand MMSI: 567402000 Official number: 530003368	**3,499** 1,050 3,003 T/cm 12.7	Class: NK	**1998-12 Shin Kochi Jyuko K.K. — Kochi** Yd No: 7111 Loa 96.02 (BB) Br ex - Dght 4.517 Lbp 89.50 Br md 16.40 Dpth 7.20 Welded, 1 dk	**(A11B2TG) LPG Tanker** Double Sides Entire Compartment Length Liq (Gas): 3,531 Cargo Heating Coils 2 x Gas Tank (s); 2 independent (C.mn.stl) cyl horizontal 2 Cargo Pump (s): 2x300m^3/hr Manifold: Bow/CM: 44.1m	**1 oil engine** driving 1 FP propeller Total Power: 2,405kW (3,270hp) 13.5kn B&W 6S26MC 1 x 2 Stroke 6 Cy. 260 x 980 2405kW (3270bhp) Makita Corp-Japan AuxGen: 2 x 280kW 450V 60Hz a.c Fuel: 140.0 (d.f.) (Part Heating Coils) 539.0 (r.f.) 8.5pd
8717934 *HSB4532* -	**SENNA 4** *ex* Kinna *-2010* *ex* Kinna Kosan *-2001* *ex* Seoul Gas *-1999* **Siam Lucky Marine Co Ltd** - *Bangkok* Thailand MMSI: 567413000 Official number: 540001148	**3,901** 1,170 3,230 T/cm 13.8	Class: BV (GL) (KR)	**1989-07 Korea Shipbuilding & Engineering Corp — Busan** Yd No: 1046 Loa 105.90 (BB) Br ex 16.20 Dght 5.020 Lbp 99.90 Br md 16.10 Dpth 8.00 Welded, 1 dk	**(A11B2TG) LPG Tanker** Double Bottom Entire Compartment Length Liq (Gas): 3,932 3 x Gas Tank (s); 3 independent (stl) cyl horizontal 3 Cargo Pump (s): 3x350m^3/hr Manifold: Bow/CM: 60.5m	**1 oil engine** driving 1 FP propeller Total Power: 2,346kW (3,190hp) 13.5kn Mitsubishi 6UEC37LA 1 x 2 Stroke 6 Cy. 370 x 880 2346kW (3190bhp) Hyundai Engine & Machinery Co Ltd-South Korea AuxGen: 2 x 240kW 450/220V 60Hz a.c Fuel: 67.0 (d.f.) 227.0 (r.f.)
9006679 *HSB4553* -	**SENNA JUMBO** *ex* Noto Gloria *-2011* **Siam Lucky Marine Co Ltd** - *Bangkok* Thailand MMSI: 567419000 Official number: TG 54002	**42,286** 15,519 49,412 T/cm 67.1	Class: NK	**1992-02 Kawasaki Heavy Industries Ltd — Kobe HG** Yd No: 1429 Loa 224.05 (BB) Br ex - Dght 11.020 Lbp 212.00 Br md 36.00 Dpth 17.70 Welded, 1 dk	**(A11B2TG) LPG Tanker** Double Bottom Entire Compartment Length Liq (Gas): 75,203 4 x Gas Tank (s); 4 independent (C.mn.stl) pri horizontal 8 Cargo Pump (s): 8x600m^3/hr	**1 oil engine** driving 1 FP propeller Total Power: 9,121kW (12,401hp) 15.5kn B&W 5S70MCE 1 x 2 Stroke 5 Cy. 700 x 2674 9121kW (12401bhp) Kawasaki Heavy Industries Ltd-Japan AuxGen: 3 x 1040kW 450V 60Hz a.c Fuel: 563.7 (d.f.) (Heating Coils) 2100.0 (r.f.) 31.1pd
8917845 *HSB4712* -	**SENNA PRINCESS** *ex* Jag Viraj *-2012* *ex* Gaz Diamond *-2004* *ex* Spic Diamond *-2000* **Siam Lucky Marine Co Ltd** - *Bangkok* Thailand MMSI: 567464000 Official number: 550002748	**17,778** 5,333 17,577 T/cm 35.4	Class: NK (LR) (IR) (KR) ✠ Classed LR until 3/10/12	**1991-08 Hyundai Heavy Industries Co Ltd — Ulsan** Yd No: 700 Loa 159.96 (BB) Br ex 25.92 Dght 8.314 Lbp 153.50 Br md 25.90 Dpth 15.40 Welded, 1 dk	**(A11B2TG) LPG Tanker** Double Hull Liq (Gas): 22,472 3 x Gas Tank (s); 3 independent (s.stl) pri horizontal 6 Cargo Pump (s): 6x350m^3/hr Manifold: Bow/CM: 77.8m	**1 oil engine** driving 1 FP propeller Total Power: 6,986kW (9,498hp) 15.0kn B&W 6S50MC 1 x 2 Stroke 6 Cy. 500 x 1910 6986kW (9498bhp) Hyundai Heavy Industries Co Ltd-South Korea AuxGen: 3 x 860kW 390V 50Hz a.c Boilers: e (ex.g.) 11.7kgf/cm^2 (11.5bar), AuxB (o.f.) 8.0kgf/cm^2 (7.8bar) Fuel: 170.1 (d.f.) 1236.3 (r.f.)
8998667 - -	**SENO 27** *ex* Muara Kaltim Permai *-2010* **PT Seno Hidayat Lines** - *Samarinda* Indonesia	**183** 109 -	Class: KI	**1996-12 P.T. Muara Mahakam Indah — Samarinda** L reg 22.00 Br ex - Dght - Lbp 21.68 Br md 7.00 Dpth 2.30 Welded, 1 dk	**(B32A2ST) Tug**	**2 oil engines** reduction geared to sc. shafts driving 2 Propellers Total Power: 806kW (1,096hp) 12.0kn Caterpillar 3412 2 x Vee 4 Stroke 12 Cy. 137 x 152 each-403kW (548bhp) Caterpillar Inc-USA
6720602 *DUH2135* -	**SENOR SAN JOSE** *ex* Tanshu Maru *-1994* **San Juan Shipping Lines Corp** - *Cebu* Philippines Official number: CEB1000142	*498* 183 77		**1967 Hashihama Shipbuilding Co Ltd — Imabari EH** Yd No: 228 Loa 54.01 Br ex 8.03 Dght 2.388 Lbp 49.99 Br md 8.01 Dpth 3.61 Riveted\Welded, 1 dk	**(A37B2PS) Passenger Ship** Passengers: 558	**1 oil engine** driving 1 FP propeller Total Power: 1,103kW (1,500hp) 15.0kn Mitsubishi 6UET33/55 1 x 2 Stroke 6 Cy. 330 x 550 1103kW (1500bhp) Akasaka Tekkosho KK (Akasaka DieselLtd)-Japan AuxGen: 2 x 120kW 445V a.c Fuel: 28.5 6.0pd
7215408 *WY8422* -	**SENORA LINDA** *ex* Michael Lynwood *-2005* *ex* Madera Cruz *-2005* **Madlin Shrimp Co Inc** - *Port Isabel, TX* United States of America Official number: 524443	*103* 70 -		**1970 Marine Mart, Inc. — Port Isabel, Tx** Yd No: 59 L reg 19.69 Br ex 6.13 Dght - Lbp - Br md - Dpth 3.46 Welded	**(B11B2FV) Fishing Vessel**	**1 oil engine** driving 1 FP propeller Total Power: 268kW (364hp)
7603954 - -	**SENORA ROSA** *ex* Marlene F *-1990* *ex* Mr. Chip *-1978* **Nelson Richard Gough-Holness** - *Roatan* Honduras Official number: U-1812611	*114* 77 -		**1973 Heritage Marine — Freeport, Tx** L reg 20.06 Br ex - Dght - Lbp - Br md 6.43 Dpth 3.48 Welded, 1 dk	**(B11B2FV) Fishing Vessel**	**1 oil engine** driving 1 FP propeller Total Power: 268kW (364hp)
9384540 *LAEG7* -	**SENORITA** - **Ugland Shipping AS** Ugland Marine Services AS *Grimstad* Norway (NIS) MMSI: 259732000	**32,379** 19,353 58,300 T/cm 57.4	Class: LR (NK) **100A1** SS 03/2013 bulk carrier BC-A strengthened for heavy cargoes, Nos. 2 & 4 holds may be empty ESP ESN LI **LMC** Eq.Ltr: L†; Cable: 632.5/70.0 U3 (a)	**2008-03 Tsuneishi Heavy Industries (Cebu) Inc — Balamban** Yd No: SC-099 Loa 190.00 (BB) Br ex - Dght 12.800 Lbp 185.60 Br md 32.26 Dpth 18.00 Welded, 1 dk	**(A21A2BC) Bulk Carrier** Grain: 72,360; Bale: 70,557 Compartments: 5 Ho, ER 5 Ha: ER Cranes: 4x30t	**1 oil engine** driving 1 FP propeller Total Power: 7,140kW (9,708hp) 14.5kn MAN-B&W 6S50MC-C 1 x 2 Stroke 6 Cy. 500 x 2000 7140kW (9708bhp) Mitsui Engineering & Shipbuilding CLtd-Japan AuxGen: 3 x 496kW 450V 60Hz a.c Boilers: AuxB (Comp) 7.1kgf/cm^2 (7.0bar)
9070113 *JM6409* -	**SENPO MARU** - **Geneq Corp (KK Geneq)** Kitakyushu Unyu KK (Kitakyushu Transportation Co Ltd) *Kitakyushu, Fukuoka* Japan MMSI: 431600258 Official number: 134496	*4,910* - 7,496	Class: NK	**1994-09 Nippon Kokan KK (NKK Corp) — Yokohama KN (Tsurumi Shipyard)** Yd No: 1060 Loa 114.80 Br ex - Dght 7.085 Lbp 108.00 Br md 17.50 Dpth 9.30 Welded, 1 dk	**(A24A2BT) Cement Carrier** Grain: 6,021 Compartments: 8 Ho, ER	**1 oil engine** driving 1 FP propeller Total Power: 3,354kW (4,560hp) 12.8kn B&W 6L35MC 1 x 2 Stroke 6 Cy. 350 x 1050 3354kW (4560bhp) Hitachi Zosen Corp-Japan AuxGen: 2 x 500kW a.c, 1 x 340kW a.c Thrusters: 1 Thwart. CP thruster (f) Fuel: 191.0 (r.f.) 12.6pd
9046710 *JK5184* -	**SENREI MARU** *ex* Shinko Maru 36 *-2007* *ex* Kongo Maru No. 8 *-2006* **Senko Co Ltd** - *Osaka, Osaka* Japan MMSI: 431400024 Official number: 133041	*499* - 1,150		**1992-07 Kegoya Dock K.K. — Kure** Yd No: 933 Loa 65.00 Br ex 10.02 Dght 4.212 Lbp - Br md 10.00 Dpth 4.60 Welded, 1 dk	**(A13B2TP) Products Tanker** Compartments: 8 Ta, ER 2 Cargo Pump (s): 2x500m^3/hr	**1 oil engine** reverse geared to sc. shaft driving 1 Directional propeller Total Power: 736kW (1,001hp) 11.7kn Hanshin LH28G 1 x 4 Stroke 6 Cy. 280 x 460 736kW (1001bhp) The Hanshin Diesel Works Ltd-Japan AuxGen: 2 x 120kW 225V a.c
8351053 *YGJM* -	**SENRI JAYA** *ex* Senri Maru *-1999* **PT Patria Nusasegara** - *Jakarta* Indonesia	**497** 312 1,200	Class: KI	**1983-01 Shitanoe Shipbuilding Co Ltd — Usuki OT** Yd No: 1028 Loa 55.09 Br ex - Dght 4.220 Lbp 49.90 Br md 9.80 Dpth 4.50 Welded, 1 dk	**(A13B2TP) Products Tanker**	**1 oil engine** driving 1 FP propeller Total Power: 662kW (900hp) 9.5kn Akasaka 1 x 4 Stroke 6 Cy. 662kW (900bhp) Akasaka Tekkosho KK (Akasaka DieselLtd)-Japan

IMO / Call sign	Name / Owner / Manager / Port	Tonnage	Class	Builder / Dimensions	Type	Machinery
8877112 *YGJN* -	**SENRI JAYA I** *ex* Kencana Jaya I *-2000* *ex* Kasuga Maru No. 2 *-1999* **PT Patria Nusasegara** - *Jakarta* *Indonesia*	**325** 115 550	Class: KI	**1977-09 Ishida Zosen Kogyo YK — Onomichi HS** Loa 45.46 Br ex - Dght 3.300 Lbp 41.00 Br md 7.80 Dpth 3.40 Welded, 1 dk	**(A13B2TP) Products Tanker** Liq: 577; Liq (Oil): 577 Compartments: 4 Ta, ER	**1 oil engine** driving 1 FP propeller Total Power: 552kW (750hp) Hanshin 1 x 4 Stroke 552kW (750bhp) The Hanshin Diesel Works Ltd-Japan
9523330 *JD2862* -	**SENRIN MARU** - **Senko Co Ltd & Yoshiga Kaiun KK** Senko Co Ltd *Osaka, Osaka* *Japan* MMSI: 431000823 Official number: 140925	*747* - 892	Class: NK	**2009-01 Yamanaka Zosen K.K. — Imabari** Yd No: 768 Loa 66.96 Br ex - Dght 4.172 Lbp 63.00 Br md 11.50 Dpth 4.90 Welded, 1 dk	**(A11B2TG) LPG Tanker** Liq (Gas): 1,391	**1 oil engine** reverse reduction geared to sc. shaft driving 1 FP propeller Total Power: 1,471kW (2,000hp) Akasaka A34C 1 x 4 Stroke 6 Cy. 340 x 620 1471kW (2000bhp) Akasaka Tekkosho KK (Akasaka DieselLtd)-Japan Fuel: 100.0 (d.f.)
9309564 *JD2014* -	**SENRYU MARU** - **Senko Co Ltd & Yoshiga Kaiun KK** Senko Co Ltd *Osaka, Osaka* *Japan* MMSI: 431401993 Official number: 140043	*698* - 870	Class: NK	**2004-09 Nichizo Iron Works & Marine Corp — Onomichi HS** Yd No: 175 Loa 62.45 Br ex - Dght 4.130 Lbp 57.50 Br md 11.00 Dpth 5.10 Welded, 1 dk	**(A11B2TG) LPG Tanker** Liq (Gas): 1,193	**1 oil engine** reverse geared to sc. shaft driving 1 FP propeller Total Power: 1,176kW (1,599hp) 12.5kn Hanshin LH28LG 1 x 4 Stroke 6 Cy. 280 x 530 1176kW (1599bhp) The Hanshin Diesel Works Ltd-Japan AuxGen: 2 x 250kW a.c Fuel: 105.0
9094585 *JD2253* -	**SENRYU MARU** - **Izumi Kisen KK (Izumi Shipping Co Ltd)** - *Tokyo* *Japan* Official number: 140326	*498* - 1,800		**2006-05 Yamanaka Zosen K.K. — Imabari** Yd No: 718 Loa 72.70 Br ex - Dght 3.610 Lbp 68.00 Br md 12.30 Dpth 7.33 Welded, 1 dk	**(A31A2GX) General Cargo Ship** Bale: 2,600 1 Ha: ER (40.0 x 10.0)	**1 oil engine** driving 1 Propeller Total Power: 1,618kW (2,200hp) 10.0kn Niigata 6M34BGT 1 x 4 Stroke 6 Cy. 340 x 620 1618kW (2200bhp) Niigata Engineering Co Ltd-Japan
8522860 - -	**SENSATION** *ex* Lady Eleanor *-1999* **Pleny Gibson Hyde Rivera** - *Roatan* *Honduras* Official number: RH-U25432	*100* 75 -		**1984 Steiner Shipyard, Inc. — Bayou La Batre, Al** Loa 22.86 Br ex - Dght - Lbp - Br md 6.71 Dpth 3.51 Welded, 1 dk	**(B11A2FT) Trawler**	**1 oil engine** driving 1 FP propeller Total Power: 268kW (364hp) Caterpillar 3408PCTA 1 x Vee 4 Stroke 8 Cy. 137 x 152 268kW (364bhp) Caterpillar Tractor Co-USA
9433925 *ZCPY9* -	**SENSATION** - **Sensation Wealth Management Ltd** Fraser Worldwide SAM *George Town* *Cayman Islands (British)* MMSI: 319281000 Official number: 739786	**499** 149 -	Class: AB	**2007-03 Sensation New Zealand Ltd — Auckland** Yd No: 24 Loa 49.54 Br ex - Dght - Lbp 41.30 Br md 8.50 Dpth 4.10 Welded, 1 dk	**(X11A2YP) Yacht** Hull Material: Aluminium Alloy	**2 oil engines** geared to sc. shafts driving 2 FP propellers Total Power: 4,560kW (6,200hp) Caterpillar 3516B-TA 2 x Vee 4 Stroke 16 Cy. 170 x 190 each-2280kW (3100bhp) Caterpillar Inc-USA AuxGen: 2 x 99kW a.c
8744171 *LXSN* -	**SENSATION R** - **Sailing Properties SA** Non Plus Ultra SA *Luxembourg* *Luxembourg* Official number: 9-43	**114** 34 49		**1988 Sensation New Zealand Ltd — Auckland** Yd No: 001 Loa 35.17 Br ex 8.10 Dght - Lbp 28.44 Br md 6.64 Dpth 3.28 Welded, 1 dk	**(X11A2YP) Yacht**	**1 oil engine** driving 1 Propeller Total Power: 441kW (600hp) Lugger 1 x 4 Stroke 441kW (600bhp)
9084229 *3FRB7* -	**SENSEI** *ex* Kita Dake *-2013* *ex* Princess *-2004* *ex* Ocean Serene *-2002* **Diolkos Maritime SA** Karlog Shipping Co Ltd *Panama* *Panama* MMSI: 356843000 Official number: 45522PEXT	**13,865** 7,738 21,955	Class: NK	**1994-09 Saiki Heavy Industries Co Ltd — Saiki OT** (Hull) Yd No: 1035 **1994-09 Onomichi Dockyard Co Ltd — Onomichi HS** Yd No: 381 Loa 157.79 (BB) Br ex - Dght 9.115 Lbp 148.00 Br md 25.00 Dpth 12.70 Welded, 1 dk	**(A21A2BC) Bulk Carrier** Grain: 29,254; Bale: 28,299 Compartments: 4 Ho, ER 4 Ha: (20.0 x 17.5)3 (20.8 x 17.5)ER Cranes: 4x30t	**1 oil engine** driving 1 FP propeller Total Power: 5,295kW (7,199hp) 14.0kn Mitsubishi 6UEC45LA 1 x 2 Stroke 6 Cy. 450 x 1350 5295kW (7199bhp) Kobe Hatsudoki KK-Japan AuxGen: 2 x 400kW a.c Fuel: 80.0 (d.f.) 1130.0 (r.f.) 22.2pd
1006673 *ZGBE7* -	**SENSES** - **MY Senses LLC** YCO SAM *George Town* *Cayman Islands (British)* MMSI: 319833000 Official number: 731270	**993** 297 240	Class: LR ✠ **100A1** SS 10/2009 SSC Yacht (P) mono G6 service area ✠ **LMC** **CCS** Cable: 330.0/24.0 U3	**1999-10 Stahlbau Nord GmbH — Bremen** (Hull) **1999-10 Fr Schweers Schiffs- und Bootswerft GmbH & Co KG — Berne** Yd No: 6500 Loa 57.00 Br ex 12.90 Dght 3.200 Lbp 50.05 Br md 12.70 Dpth 6.20 Welded, 2 dks	**(X11A2YP) Yacht**	**2 oil engines** with clutches, flexible couplings & sr reverse geared to sc. shafts driving 2 FP propellers Total Power: 2,320kW (3,154hp) 15.0kn Deutz TBD620BV12 2 x Vee 4 Stroke 12 Cy. 170 x 195 each-1160kW (1577bhp) Deutz AG-Koeln AuxGen: 2 x 165kW 400V 50Hz a.c Thrusters: 1 Thwart. FP thruster (f)
8997833 *JD2065* -	**SENSHIN MARU** - **Izumi Kisen KK (Izumi Shipping Co Ltd)** - *Tokyo* *Japan* Official number: 140114	*499* - 1,600		**2005-01 K.K. Watanabe Zosensho — Nagasaki** Yd No: 123 Loa 76.15 Br ex - Dght 4.030 Lbp 70.20 Br md 12.30 Dpth 7.00 Welded, 1 dk	**(A31A2GX) General Cargo Ship**	**1 oil engine** driving 1 Propeller Total Power: 736kW (1,001hp) Niigata 1 x 4 Stroke 736kW (1001bhp) Niigata Engineering Co Ltd-Japan
8965311 *JL6603* -	**SENSHIN MARU** - **Senko Co Ltd** - *Imabari, Ehime* *Japan* Official number: 136527	*499* - -		**2000-10 Yamanaka Zosen K.K. — Imabari** Yd No: 658 Loa 76.38 Br ex - Dght - Lbp 70.18 Br md 12.30 Dpth 6.85 Welded, 1 dk	**(A31A2GX) General Cargo Ship** Compartments: 1 Ho, ER 1 Ha: (40.1 x 10.0)ER	**1 oil engine** driving 1 FP propeller Total Power: 1,471kW (2,000hp) 12.6kn Hanshin LH32LG 1 x 4 Stroke 6 Cy. 320 x 640 1471kW (2000bhp) The Hanshin Diesel Works Ltd-Japan Fuel: 110.0 (d.f.)
9152399 *JM6562* -	**SENSHIN MARU** - **Kyodo Ferry Unyu YK** - *Nishinoomote, Kagoshima* *Japan* MMSI: 431600668 Official number: 135423	*749* - 1,559		**1997-01 K.K. Miura Zosensho — Saiki** Yd No: 1177 Loa 69.70 Br ex - Dght 4.313 Lbp 65.00 Br md 11.50 Dpth 5.07 Welded, 1 dk	**(A24A2BT) Cement Carrier**	**1 oil engine** driving 1 FP propeller Total Power: 1,177kW (1,600hp) Niigata 6M28HFT 1 x 4 Stroke 6 Cy. 280 x 480 1177kW (1600bhp) Niigata Engineering Co Ltd-Japan
9284336 *JK5618* -	**SENSHO** - **Kissho Kaiun YK** - *Hofu, Yamaguchi* *Japan* Official number: 136183	**498** - 1,200		**2002-07 Nakatani Shipyard Co. Ltd. — Etajima** Yd No: 595 L reg 57.43 Br ex - Dght 4.200 Lbp - Br md 10.00 Dpth 4.50 Welded, 1 dk	**(A12A2TC) Chemical Tanker** Double Hull (13F) 6 Cargo Pump (s): 6x100m³/hr	**1 oil engine** geared to sc. shaft driving 1 Propeller Total Power: 441kW (600hp) Yanmar 6N165-EN 1 x 4 Stroke 6 Cy. 165 x 232 441kW (600bhp) Yanmar Diesel Engine Co Ltd-Japan
9240653 *JG5609* -	**SENSHO** - **Izumi Kisen KK (Izumi Shipping Co Ltd)** - *Tokyo* *Japan* MMSI: 431100886 Official number: 136961	*744* - 1,700		**2000-06 Yamanaka Zosen K.K. — Imabari** Yd No: 653 Loa 80.73 (BB) Br ex - Dght 4.402 Lbp 74.98 Br md 13.50 Dpth 7.59 Welded, 2 dks	**(A35A2RR) Ro-Ro Cargo Ship** Quarter stern ramp (p)	**1 oil engine** reduction geared to sc. shaft driving 1 FP propeller Total Power: 2,206kW (2,999hp) 13.8kn Daihatsu 8DKM-28 1 x 4 Stroke 8 Cy. 280 x 390 2206kW (2999bhp) Daihatsu Diesel Manufacturing Co Lt-Japan AuxGen: 2 x 240kW 445V a.c Thrusters: 1 Thwart. FP thruster (f) Fuel: 113.0 (d.f.)
9240627 *JL6659* -	**SENSHO MARU** - **Imura Kisen KK** - *Anan, Tokushima* *Japan* Official number: 136550	*497* - -		**2000-06 Shitanoe Shipbuilding Co Ltd — Usuki OT** Yd No: 1210 Loa 69.81 Br ex - Dght - Lbp 65.00 Br md 12.40 Dpth 7.30 Welded, 1 dk	**(A31A2GX) General Cargo Ship** Compartments: 1 Ho, ER 1 Ha: (20.4 x 10.0)ER Cranes: 1x3.5t	**1 oil engine** reverse geared to sc. shaft driving 1 FP propeller Total Power: 1,324kW (1,800hp) 11.5kn Akasaka A31R 1 x 4 Stroke 6 Cy. 310 x 600 1324kW (1800bhp) Akasaka Tekkosho KK (Akasaka DieselLtd)-Japan Fuel: 81.0 (d.f.)
9623075 *JD3228* -	**SENSHO MARU** *ex* Katsumaru *-2011* **Katsumaru Kaiun KK** - *Imabari, Ehime* *Japan* MMSI: 431002691 Official number: 141494	*499* - 1,710		**2011-06 Yamanaka Zosen K.K. — Imabari** Yd No: 813 Loa 75.23 Br ex - Dght 4.172 Lbp 69.00 Br md 12.00 Dpth 7.12 Welded, 1 dk	**(A31A2GX) General Cargo Ship** Grain: 2,937; Bale: 2,853 1 Ha: ER (40.0 x 9.5)	**1 oil engine** reduction geared to sc. shaft driving 1 FP propeller Total Power: 1,323kW (1,799hp) Hanshin LA28G 1 x 4 Stroke 6 Cy. 280 x 590 1323kW (1799bhp) The Hanshin Diesel Works Ltd-Japan

IMO / Call sign	Name / Owner	Tonnage	Class	Builder / Dimensions	Type	Machinery
9099470 *JD2221* -	**SENSHO MARU** - **Senko Co Ltd** - *Imabari, Ehime* Japan Official number: 140291	*283* - 800		**2006**-08 **Nantong Gangzha Shipyard — Nantong JS** (Hull) **2006**-08 **Daio Zoki K.K. — Japan** Yd No: 706 Loa 61.05 Br ex - Dght 3.420 Lbp 56.00 Br md 10.00 Dpth 5.50 Welded, 1 dk	**(A31A2GX) General Cargo Ship**	**1 oil engine** driving 1 Propeller Total Power: 1,030kW (1,400hp) 11.5kn Hanshin LH28G 1 x 4 Stroke 6 Cy. 280 x 460 1030kW (1400bhp) The Hanshin Diesel Works Ltd-Japan
8608365 *7KLR* -	**SENSHO MARU** - **Nippon Yusen Kabushiki Kaisha & Geneq Corp** Nippon Yusen Kabushiki Kaisha (NYK Line) *Kitakyushu, Fukuoka* Japan MMSI: 431601371 Official number: 129490	*4,905* - 7,606	Class: NK	**1987**-07 **Tohoku Shipbuilding Co Ltd — Shiogama MG** Yd No: 218 Loa 114.80 Br ex 17.53 Dght 7.086 Lbp 108.01 Br md 17.51 Dpth 9.30 Welded, 1 dk	**(A24A2BT) Cement Carrier** Grain: 6,021	**1 oil engine** with clutches, flexible couplings & reduction geared to sc. shaft driving 1 CP propeller Total Power: 2,714kW (3,690hp) 12.0kn Ito M506EUS 1 x 4 Stroke 6 Cy. 500 x 880 2714kW (3690bhp) Ito Tekkosho-Japan AuxGen: 5 x 294kW a.c Thrusters: 1 Thwart. CP thruster (f); 1 Thwart. CP thruster (a) Fuel: 200.0 (r.f.)
9176905 *JH3414* -	**SENSHO MARU No. 1** - **Norihiro Takemura** - *Kihoku, Mie* Japan Official number: 134456	*120* - -		**1997**-03 **Higashi Kyushu Shipbuilding Co Ltd — Usuki OT** L reg 29.70 Br ex - Dght - Lbp - Br md 5.47 Dpth 2.48 Bonded, 1 dk	**(B11B2FV) Fishing Vessel** Hull Material: Reinforced Plastic	**1 oil engine** driving 1 FP propeller Daihatsu 1 x 4 Stroke Daihatsu Diesel Manufacturing Co Lt-Japan
9167825 - -	**SENSHU MARU** - **Pegasus Inc** -	*187* - -		**1997**-07 **Niigata Engineering Co Ltd — Niigata NI** Yd No: 2328 Loa 42.00 (BB) Br ex - Dght - Lbp 35.06 Br md 7.40 Dpth 3.20 Welded, 1 dk	**(B11A2FS) Stern Trawler** Compartments: 1 Ho, ER 1 Ha: ER	**1 oil engine** with clutches, flexible couplings & sr geared to sc. shaft driving 1 CP propeller Total Power: 1,103kW (1,500hp) Niigata 6MG25HX 1 x 4 Stroke 6 Cy. 250 x 350 1103kW (1500bhp) Niigata Engineering Co Ltd-Japan AuxGen: 2 x 160kW 225V a.c Thrusters: 1 Thwart. CP thruster (f)
9058842 *JI3507* -	**SENSHU MARU** - **Tonan Kaiun KK** - *Osaka, Osaka* Japan Official number: 133421	*199* - 425		**1992**-08 **K.K. Odo Zosen Tekko — Shimonoseki** Yd No: 506 L reg 37.30 Br ex - Dght 3.200 Lbp - Br md 8.20 Dpth 3.40 Welded, 1 dk	**(A24A2BT) Cement Carrier** Grain: 337 Compartments: 2 Ho, ER	**1 oil engine** with clutches, flexible couplings & sr reverse geared to sc. shaft driving 1 FP propeller Total Power: 588kW (799hp) Yanmar M200-SN 1 x 4 Stroke 6 Cy. 200 x 260 588kW (799bhp) Yanmar Diesel Engine Co Ltd-Japan
8014473 *JCIR* -	**SENSHU MARU** - **Nippon Yusen Kaisha, Mitsui OSK Lines Ltd & Kawasaki Kisen Kaisha Ltd** Mitsui OSK Lines Ltd (MOL) SatCom: Inmarsat B 343102310 *Osaka, Osaka* Japan MMSI: 431023000 Official number: 126466	**102,330** 30,699 69,594	Class: NK	**1984**-02 **Mitsui Eng. & SB. Co. Ltd., Chiba Works — Ichihara** Yd No: 1230 Loa 283.00 (BB) Br ex - Dght 11.500 Lbp 270.01 Br md 44.81 Dpth 25.02 Welded, 1 dk	**(A11A2TN) LNG Tanker** Double Bottom Entire Compartment Length Liq (Gas): 125,835 5 x Gas Tank (s); 5 independent Kvaerner-Moss (alu) sph 10 Cargo Pump (s): 10x1000m³/hr	**1 Steam Turb** dr geared to sc. shaft driving 1 FP propeller Total Power: 29,420kW (39,999hp) 19.3kn Stal-Laval 1 x steam Turb 29420kW (39999shp) Mitsui Engineering & Shipbuilding CLtd-Japan AuxGen: 2 x 2500kW 450V 60Hz a.c, 1 x 1200kW 450V 60Hz a.c Thrusters: 1 Thwart. CP thruster (f) Fuel: 8844.5 (r.f.) 225.0 (d.f.) 186.0pd
9100425 *JIKV* ME1-802	**SENSHU MARU No. 1** *ex Senshu Maru -2002* **Yuki Yamamoto** - SatCom: Inmarsat B 343164410 *Minami-ise, Mie* Japan MMSI: 431644000 Official number: 133210	*495* - 579		**1994**-07 **Miho Zosensho K.K. — Shimizu** Yd No: 1434 Loa 59.00 (BB) Br ex - Dght 3.683 Lbp 52.00 Br md 9.00 Dpth 4.00 Welded, 1 dk	**(B11B2FV) Fishing Vessel** Ins: 725	**1 oil engine** with clutches, flexible couplings & sr geared to sc. shaft driving 1 FP propeller Total Power: 736kW (1,001hp) Akasaka E28 1 x 4 Stroke 6 Cy. 280 x 480 736kW (1001bhp) Akasaka Tekkosho KK (Akasaka DieselLtd)-Japan
7300112 *JI2019* -	**SENSHU MARU No. 2** - **Yoshio Ogawa** - *Osaka, Osaka* Japan Official number: 93278	*199* - 365		**1963**-09 **Nishi Shipbuilding Co Ltd — Imabari EH** Yd No: 111 Loa 32.82 Br ex 7.04 Dght 2.515 Lbp 29.93 Br md 7.01 Dpth 2.80 Welded, 1 dk	**(A31A2GX) General Cargo Ship** Compartments: 1 Ho, ER 1 Ha: (21.4 x 5.0)	**1 oil engine** driving 1 FP propeller Total Power: 88kW (120hp) 6.5kn Yanmar 4MS 1 x 4 Stroke 4 Cy. 200 x 280 88kW (120bhp) Yanmar Diesel Engine Co Ltd-Japan
9047908 *JRWC* ME1-883	**SENSHU MARU No. 3** *ex Junko Maru No. 8 -1999* **Yuki Yamamoto** - SatCom: Inmarsat A 1205116 *Minami-ise, Mie* Japan MMSI: 432611000 Official number: 133095	*466* - -		**1992**-03 **KK Kanasashi — Shizuoka SZ** Yd No: 3288 Loa 58.02 (BB) Br ex 9.02 Dght 3.600 Lbp 51.00 Br md 9.00 Dpth 3.95 Welded, 1 dk	**(B11B2FV) Fishing Vessel** Ins: 649	**1 oil engine** with clutches, flexible couplings & sr reverse geared to sc. shaft driving 1 FP propeller Total Power: 736kW (1,001hp) Akasaka A28FD 1 x 4 Stroke 6 Cy. 280 x 550 736kW (1001bhp) Akasaka Tekkosho KK (Akasaka DieselLtd)-Japan
7238761 - -	**SENSHU MARU No. 15** *ex Miyaura Maru No. 15 -1979* - -	*133* 55 -		**1972 Sanuki Shipbuilding & Iron Works Co Ltd — Mitoyo KG** Yd No: 665 Loa - Br ex 7.01 Dght - Lbp 30.92 Br md 6.99 Dpth 2.80 Riveted\Welded, 1 dk	**(B11B2FV) Fishing Vessel**	**1 oil engine** driving 1 FP propeller Total Power: 478kW (650hp) Hanshin 6L26AGSH 1 x 4 Stroke 6 Cy. 260 x 400 478kW (650bhp) Hanshin Nainenki Kogyo-Japan
8932285 - -	**SENSUI** *ex Sensui Maru -1997* **Sto Domingo Shipping Lines** - Philippines	*145* 92 300		**1969**-09 **Hokusatsu Zosen — Japan** Loa 29.20 Br ex 6.50 Dght 2.800 Lbp 22.60 Br md - Dpth 3.20 Welded, 1 dk	**(A31A2GX) General Cargo Ship**	**1 oil engine** driving 1 FP propeller 9.0kn
6812027 *PLOR* -	**SENTA 2** *ex Garsa Satu -1997 ex Shinsei Maru -1973* **PT Sentarum Lines** - *Jakarta* Indonesia Official number: 549	**3,895** 2,112 5,970	Class: (KI) (NK)	**1968**-03 **Hayashikane Shipbuilding & Engineering Co Ltd — Shimonoseki YC** Yd No: 1110 Loa 108.69 Br ex 16.44 Dght 6.590 Lbp 100.41 Br md 16.41 Dpth 8.21 Welded, 1 dk	**(A31A2GX) General Cargo Ship** Grain: 8,058; Bale: 7,740 Compartments: 3 Ho, ER 3 Ha: (12.5 x 8.0) (22.4 x 8.0) (11.9 x 8.0)ER Derricks: 1x15t,3x10t	**1 oil engine** driving 1 FP propeller Total Power: 2,795kW (3,800hp) 12.5kn Mitsubishi 6UET45/75C 1 x 2 Stroke 6 Cy. 450 x 750 2795kW (3800bhp) Kobe Hatsudoki Seizosho-Japan AuxGen: 2 x 180kW 445V 60Hz a.c Fuel: 70.0 (d.f.) 700.0 (r.f.) 12.0pd
9490404 *JD2823* -	**SENTAI MARU** *ex Ura 333 -2008* **Senko Co Ltd** Shibako Marine YK *Osaka, Osaka* Japan MMSI: 431000781 Official number: 140827	*498* - 1,199		**2008**-10 **KK Ura Kyodo Zosensho — Awaji HG** Yd No: 333 Loa 64.46 Br ex - Dght 4.210 Lbp 60.00 Br md 10.00 Dpth 4.50 Welded, 1 dk	**(A12A2TC) Chemical Tanker** Double Hull (13F) Liq: 1,230 Compartments: 8 Wing Ta, ER 2 Cargo Pump (s): 2x300m³/hr	**1 oil engine** driving 1 FP propeller Total Power: 1,030kW (1,400hp) 11.5kn Hanshin LH28G 1 x 4 Stroke 6 Cy. 280 x 460 1030kW (1400bhp) The Hanshin Diesel Works Ltd-Japan
9612492 - -	**SENTARUM** - **PT Sentarum Lines** - *Tanjung Priok* Indonesia	**224** 68 164	Class: KI	**2010**-03 **PT Karya Teknik Utama — Batam** Loa 27.00 Br ex - Dght 3.000 Lbp 24.67 Br md 8.20 Dpth 4.00 Welded, 1 dk	**(B32A2ST) Tug**	**2 oil engines** reduction geared to sc. shafts driving 2 Propellers Total Power: 1,618kW (2,200hp) Yanmar 12LAK (M)-STE2 2 x Vee 4 Stroke 12 Cy. 150 x 165 each-809kW (1100bhp) Yanmar Diesel Engine Co Ltd-Japan AuxGen: 2 x 60kW 400V a.c
9315616 *9VIN3* -	**SENTEK 8** - **Sentek Marine & Trading Pte Ltd** - *Singapore* Singapore MMSI: 564034000 Official number: 390367	**3,587** 1,464 4,943	Class: GL (CC)	**2004**-05 **Zhejiang Jiantiao Shipyard Co Ltd — Sanmen County ZJ** Yd No: JD0202 Loa 96.63 (BB) Br ex - Dght 5.760 Lbp 88.00 Br md 17.00 Dpth 7.50 Welded, 1 dk	**(A13B2TP) Products Tanker** Double Hull (13F) Cargo Heating Coils Compartments: 12 Wing Ta, ER 2 Cargo Pump (s)	**2 oil engines** reduction geared to sc. shafts driving 2 FP propellers Total Power: 1,622kW (2,206hp) 11.0kn Chinese Std. Type G6300ZC 2 x 4 Stroke 6 Cy. 300 x 380 each-811kW (1103bhp) Ningbo CSI Power & Machinery GroupCo Ltd-China AuxGen: 2 x 200kW 400V a.c, 1 x 95kW 400V a.c Thrusters: 1 Tunnel thruster (f)
9537161 *9V8555* -	**SENTEK 20** - **Sentek Resources Pte Ltd** Sentek Marine & Trading Pte Ltd SatCom: Inmarsat C 456376612 *Singapore* Singapore MMSI: 563766000 Official number: 395953	**1,602** 554 1,974	Class: RI (BV)	**2010**-07 **Lianyungang Shenghua Shipbuilding & Repair Co Ltd — Guannan County JS** Yd No: 540 Loa 68.40 Br ex 12.82 Dght 4.790 Lbp 62.98 Br md 12.80 Dpth 6.50 Welded, 1 dk	**(A13B2TP) Products Tanker** Double Hull (13F)	**2 oil engines** reduction geared to sc. shafts driving 2 FP propellers Total Power: 882kW (1,200hp) 10.0kn Chinese Std. Type 6300ZC 2 x 4 Stroke 6 Cy. 300 x 380 each-441kW (600bhp) Ningbo CSI Power & Machinery GroupCo Ltd-China Thrusters: 1 Tunnel thruster (f)

9537173 *9V8556* -	**SENTEK 21** **Sentek Resources Pte Ltd** Sentek Marine & Trading Pte Ltd SatCom: Inmarsat C 456497411 *Singapore* *Singapore* MMSI: 564974000 Official number: 395954	**1,602** 554 1,991	Class: RI (BV)	**2010-11 Lianyungang Shenghua Shipbuilding & Repair Co Ltd — Guannan County JS** Yd No: 541 Loa 68.40 Br ex 12.82 Dght 4.790 Lbp 62.98 Br md 12.80 Dpth 6.50 Welded, 1 dk	**(A13B2TP) Products Tanker** Double Hull (13F)	**2 oil engines** reduction geared to sc. shafts driving 2 FP propellers Total Power: 882kW (1,200hp) 10.0kn Chinese Std. Type 6300ZC 2 x 4 Stroke 6 Cy. 300 x 380 each-441kW (600bhp) Ningbo CSI Power & Machinery GroupCo Ltd-China Thrusters: 1 Tunnel thruster (f)
9601211 *9V8557* -	**SENTEK 22** **Sentek Shipping & Trading Pte Ltd** Sentek Marine & Trading Pte Ltd *Singapore* *Singapore* MMSI: 566065000	**1,602** 554 1,988	Class: RI	**2011-07 Lianyungang Shenghua Shipbuilding & Repair Co Ltd — Guannan County JS** Yd No: SH545 Loa 68.40 Br ex - Dght 4.800 Lbp 62.98 Br md 12.80 Dpth 6.50 Welded, 1 dk	**(B35E2TF) Bunkering Tanker** Double Hull (13F)	**2 oil engines** reduction geared to sc. shafts driving 2 FP propellers Total Power: 882kW (1,200hp) 10.0kn Weifang 8170ZC 2 x 4 Stroke 8 Cy. 170 x 200 each-441kW (600bhp) Ningbo CSI Power & Machinery GroupCo Ltd-China AuxGen: 2 x 150kW 400/240V 50Hz a.c
9601003 *9V8558* -	**SENTEK 23** **Sentek Marine & Trading Pte Ltd** - *Singapore* *Singapore* MMSI: 566066000	**1,602** 554 1,993	Class: RI	**2011-12 Lianyungang Shenghua Shipbuilding & Repair Co Ltd — Guannan County JS** Yd No: SH546 Loa 68.40 Br ex - Dght 4.800 Lbp 62.98 Br md 12.80 Dpth 6.50 Welded, 1 dk	**(B35E2TF) Bunkering Tanker** Double Hull (13F)	**2 oil engines** reduction geared to sc. shafts driving 2 FP propellers Total Power: 850kW (1,156hp) 10.5kn Weifang 8170ZC 2 x 4 Stroke 8 Cy. 170 x 200 each-425kW (578bhp) Ningbo CSI Power & Machinery GroupCo Ltd-China AuxGen: 2 x 150kW a.c
9537202 *9V9855* -	**SENTEK 25** **Sentek Tanker Pte Ltd** Sentek Marine & Trading Pte Ltd *Singapore* *Singapore* MMSI: 566724000 Official number: 397662	**1,589** 560 2,140	Class: RI	**2012-11 Lianyungang Shenghua Shipbuilding & Repair Co Ltd — Guannan County JS** Yd No: 547 Loa 68.40 Br ex - Dght 4.800 Lbp 62.98 Br md 12.80 Dpth 6.50 Welded, 1 dk	**(A13B2TP) Products Tanker** Double Hull (13F)	**2 oil engines** reduction geared to sc. shafts driving 2 FP propellers Total Power: 1,080kW (1,468hp) 9.0kn Chinese Std. Type 6200ZC 1 x 4 Stroke 6 Cy. 200 x 270 540kW (734bhp) Jinan Diesel Engine Co Ltd-China Chinese Std. Type 6300ZC 1 x 4 Stroke 6 Cy. 300 x 380 540kW (734bhp) Jinan Diesel Engine Co Ltd-China AuxGen: 2 x 150kW a.c
9537214 *9V9856* -	**SENTEK 26** **Sentek Tanker Pte Ltd** Sentek Marine & Trading Pte Ltd *Singapore* *Singapore* MMSI: 566824000 Official number: 397663	**1,589** 560 2,141	Class: RI	**2013-01 Lianyungang Shenghua Shipbuilding & Repair Co Ltd — Guannan County JS** Yd No: 548 Loa 68.40 Br ex - Dght 4.790 Lbp 62.98 Br md 12.80 Dpth 6.50 Welded, 1 dk	**(A13B2TP) Products Tanker** Double Hull (13F)	**2 oil engines** reduction geared to sc. shaft driving 2 FP propellers Total Power: 882kW (1,200hp) 10.0kn Chinese Std. Type 6300ZC 2 x 4 Stroke 6 Cy. 300 x 380 each-441kW (600bhp) Ningbo CSI Power & Machinery GroupCo Ltd-China AuxGen: 2 x 150kW 380/220V 50Hz a.c
9537226 *9V2147* -	**SENTEK 27** **Sentek Petroleum Trading Pte Ltd** Sentek Marine & Trading Pte Ltd *Singapore* *Singapore* MMSI: 563562000 Official number: 398674	**1,589** 560 2,151	Class: RI	**2013-10 Lianyungang Shenghua Shipbuilding & Repair Co Ltd — Guannan County JS** Yd No: 549 Loa 68.40 Br ex - Dght 4.790 Lbp 62.98 Br md 12.80 Dpth 6.50 Welded, 1 dk	**(A13B2TP) Products Tanker** Double Hull (13F)	**2 oil engines** reduction geared to sc. shaft driving 2 FP propellers Total Power: 1,080kW (1,468hp) 10.0kn Chinese Std. Type 6200ZC 2 x 4 Stroke 6 Cy. 200 x 270 each-540kW (734bhp) Jinan Diesel Engine Co Ltd-China AuxGen: 2 x 150kW 380/220V 50Hz a.c
9537238 *9V2148* -	**SENTEK 28** **Sentek Petroleum Trading Pte Ltd** Sentek Marine & Trading Pte Ltd *Singapore* *Singapore* MMSI: 563848000 Official number: 398675	**1,589** 560 2,151	Class: RI	**2013-12 Lianyungang Shenghua Shipbuilding & Repair Co Ltd — Guannan County JS** Yd No: 550 Loa 68.40 Br ex - Dght 4.790 Lbp 62.45 Br md 12.80 Dpth 6.50 Welded, 1 dk	**(A13B2TP) Products Tanker** Double Hull (13F)	**2 oil engines** reduction geared to sc. shaft driving 2 FP propellers Total Power: 882kW (1,200hp) 10.0kn Chinese Std. Type 6200ZC 2 x 4 Stroke 6 Cy. 200 x 270 each-441kW (600bhp) Jinan Diesel Engine Co Ltd-China
9567893 *9YHN* -	**SENTINEL** *launched as* Freedom *-2010* **Mid Atlantic Ltd** - *Port of Spain* *Trinidad & Tobago* MMSI: 362067000	**353** 105 348	Class: AB	**2010-09 Midship Marine, Inc. — New Orleans, La** Yd No: 332 Loa 47.34 Br ex - Dght 2.350 Lbp 43.07 Br md 9.15 Dpth 3.96 Welded, 1 dk	**(B21A2OC) Crew/Supply Vessel** Hull Material: Aluminium Alloy	**4 oil engines** reduction geared to sc. shafts driving 4 FP propellers Total Power: 3,236kW (4,400hp) Yanmar 12LAK (M)-STE2 4 x Vee 4 Stroke 12 Cy. 150 x 165 each-809kW (1100bhp) Yanmar Diesel Engine Co Ltd-Japan AuxGen: 2 x 93kW a.c
9665554 *D5FA7* -	**SENTINEL** **Auva Navigation Corp** Primerose Shipping Co Ltd *Monrovia* *Liberia* MMSI: 636016214 Official number: 16214	**35,812** 21,224 63,500 T/cm 62.1	Class: BV	**2013-09 Yangzhou Dayang Shipbuilding Co Ltd — Yangzhou JS** Yd No: DY4023 Loa 199.99 (BB) Br ex - Dght 13.300 Lbp 193.74 Br md 32.26 Dpth 18.50 Welded, 1 dk	**(A21A2BC) Bulk Carrier** Grain: 77,493; Bale: 75,555 Compartments: 5 Ho, ER 5 Ha: 4 (22.1 x 18.6)ER (14.8 x 17.0) Cranes: 4x35t	**1 oil engine** driving 1 FP propeller Total Power: 8,300kW (11,285hp) 14.5kn MAN-B&W 5S60ME-C8 1 x 2 Stroke 5 Cy. 600 x 2400 8300kW (11285bhp) Doosan Engine Co Ltd-South Korea AuxGen: 3 x 600kW 60Hz a.c Fuel: 2296.0
7106877 *IBXS* -	**SENTINEL** *ex* Scotia *-1998* **Diamar SpA** ARGO Ship Management & Services Srl SatCom: Inmarsat C 424728211 *Naples* *Italy* MMSI: 247282000	**1,702** 509 599	Class: RI	**1971-12 Ferguson Bros (Port Glasgow) Ltd — Port Glasgow** Yd No: 461 Converted From: Stern Trawler-2010 Loa 68.20 Br ex 13.52 Dght 4.573 Lbp 60.97 Br md 13.42 Dpth 7.17 Welded, 2 dks	**(B31A2SR) Research Survey Vessel** Cranes: 1	**3 diesel electric oil engines** driving 3 gen. each 700kW 500V d.c Connecting to 1 elec. Motor driving 1 Directional propeller Total Power: 2,649kW (3,603hp) 10.5kn Polar SF18VS-D 3 x Vee 4 Stroke 8 Cy. 250 x 300 each-883kW (1201bhp) British Polar Engines Ltd.-Glasgow AuxGen: 3 x 350kW 420V 50Hz a.c Thrusters: 1 Thwart. FP thruster (f); 2 Tunnel thruster (a) Fuel: 352.5 (d.f.)
7405077 *D6B02* -	**SENTINEL** *ex* Fivi *-2002* *ex* Mirfak *-1989* *ex* Bened *-1988* *ex* Lindewal *-1987* *ex* Cairnleader *-1982* *Moroni* *Union of Comoros* MMSI: 616115000 Official number: 1200148	**1,861** 1,065 3,117	Class: (LR) ✠ Classed LR until 31/3/03	**1975-09 Martin Jansen GmbH & Co. KG Schiffsw. u. Masch. — Leer** Yd No: 132 Loa 79.51 (BB) Br ex 13.62 Dght 5.538 Lbp 72.01 Br md 13.50 Dpth 6.66 Welded, 1 dk	**(A31A2GX) General Cargo Ship** Grain: 3,767; Bale: 3,342 TEU 72 C. 72/20' Compartments: 1 Ho, ER 2 Ha: 2 (18.5 x 10.2)ER Ice Capable	**1 oil engine** sr geared to sc. shaft driving 1 FP propeller Total Power: 1,765kW (2,400hp) 12.0kn MaK 8M452AK 1 x 4 Stroke 8 Cy. 320 x 450 1765kW (2400bhp) MaK Maschinenbau GmbH-Kiel AuxGen: 3 x 72kW 400/231V 50Hz a.c Fuel: 234.5 (d.f.) 8.0pd
7507370 *WBN6510* -	**SENTINEL** **Crowley Puerto Rico Services Inc** *San Francisco, CA* *United States of America* MMSI: 366766980 Official number: 573426	**538** 161 -	Class: AB	**1976-05 McDermott Shipyards Inc — Morgan City LA** Yd No: 218 Loa 41.46 Br ex 11.13 Dght 5.182 Lbp 39.22 Br md 11.08 Dpth 5.80 Welded, 1 dk	**(B32A2ST) Tug**	**2 oil engines** reverse reduction geared to sc. shafts driving 2 FP propellers Total Power: 5,148kW (7,000hp) 14.0kn EMD (Electro-Motive) 20-645-E7 2 x Vee 2 Stroke 20 Cy. 230 x 254 each-2574kW (3500bhp) General Motors Corp.Electro-Motive Div.-La Grange AuxGen: 2 x 90kW Fuel: 782.5 (d.f.)
7726249 *HP6707* -	**SENTINEL** *ex* Trinity River *-2011* *ex* Lena Candies *-1997* **Lanex Corp Inc** Blanco Offshore Logistics SA de CV *Panama* *Panama* MMSI: 354091000 Official number: 4336312	**952** 285 750	Class: (AB)	**1978-08 Burton Shipyard Co., Inc. — Port Arthur, Tx** Yd No: 524 Loa 53.35 Br ex - Dght 3.963 Lbp 51.36 Br md 13.42 Dpth 4.58 Welded, 1 dk	**(B21A2OS) Platform Supply Ship**	**2 oil engines** reverse reduction geared to sc. shafts driving 2 FP propellers Total Power: 1,810kW (2,460hp) 10.0kn EMD (Electro-Motive) 12-567-BC 2 x Vee 2 Stroke 12 Cy. 216 x 254 each-905kW (1230bhp) (Re-engined ,made 1960, Reconditioned & fitted 1978) General Motors Corp.Electro-Motive Div.-La Grange AuxGen: 3 x 150kW Thrusters: 1 Thwart. FP thruster (f)
7644817 *WDA7137* -	**SENTINEL** *ex* Jesse James *-2010* *ex* Sun-Dance *-2005* **Aqua King Fishery LLC** *United States of America* MMSI: 366840040 Official number: 575736	*119* 95 -		**1976-01 S & R Boat Builders, Inc. — Bayou La Batre, Al** L reg 21.98 Br ex 6.76 Dght - Lbp - Br md - Dpth 3.38 Welded, 1 dk	**(B11B2FV) Fishing Vessel**	**1 oil engine** driving 1 FP propeller Total Power: 313kW (426hp)

IMO / Call sign	Name / Owner / Manager	Tonnage	Class	Builder / Dimensions	Type / Capacity	Machinery
8020159 *VTFG* -	**SENTINEL** **Government of The Republic of India (Andaman & Nicobar Administration)** The Shipping Corporation of India Ltd (SCI) *Mumbai* *India* MMSI: 419318000 Official number: 1946	*2,408* 722 1,472	Class: IR (AB)	**1982-07 Mazagon Dock Ltd. — Mumbai** Yd No: 580 Loa 81.34 Br ex - Dght 4.111 Lbp 74.00 Br md 14.41 Dpth 7.29 Welded, 2 dks	**(A32A2GF) General Cargo/Passenger Ship** Grain: 803; Bale: 764 Compartments: 2 Ho, ER 2 Ha: ER Derricks: 4	**2 oil engines** sr reverse geared to sc. shafts driving 2 FP propellers Total Power: 1,560kW (2,120hp) 12.0kn MAN G5V30/45ATL 2 x 4 Stroke 5 Cy. 300 x 450 each-780kW (1060bhp) Garden Reach Shipbuilders &Engineers Ltd-India AuxGen: 3 x 212kW Fuel: 141.0 (d.f.)
8915354 *9LY2534* -	**SENTINEL** *ex* Seikai *-2012* **Amber Dragon Holdings Inc** Alpha Logistics Services (EPZ) Ltd *Freetown* *Sierra Leone* MMSI: 667003337 Official number: SL103337	*189* 57 -		**1989-09 Yamakawa Zosen Tekko K.K. — Kagoshima** Yd No: 686 Loa 43.70 Br ex - Dght 3.101 Lbp 38.00 Br md 6.80 Dpth 3.50 Welded, 1 dk	**(B12D2FP) Fishery Patrol Vessel**	**2 oil engines** with flexible couplings & sr geared to sc. shafts driving 2 FP propellers Total Power: 2,206kW (3,000hp) Daihatsu 6DLM-26S 2 x 4 Stroke 6 Cy. 260 x 340 each-1103kW (1500bhp) Daihatsu Diesel Manufacturing Co Lt-Japan
8980426 *MRXY4* -	**SENTINEL** **Government of The United Kingdom (Home Office Border Force, Maritime & Aviation Operations)** - *United Kingdom* MMSI: 234469000	**178** - -		**1993 Vosper Thornycroft (UK) Ltd — Southampton** Loa 36.00 Br ex - Dght - Lbp - Br md - Dpth - Welded, 1 dk	**(B34H2SQ) Patrol Vessel**	**3 oil engines** driving 2 Propellers , 1 Water jet Total Power: 3,200kW (4,350hp) Caterpillar 3516B-TA 1 x Vee 4 Stroke 16 Cy. 170 x 190 1600kW (2175bhp) Caterpillar Inc-USA Caterpillar 3516B-TA 1 x Vee 4 Stroke 16 Cy. 170 x 190 1600kW (2175bhp) (new engine 0000) Caterpillar Inc-USA Rolls Royce CV8M600 1 x Vee 4 Stroke 8 Cy. 135 x 152 Perkins Engines Ltd.-Peterborough
8309567 *A8MZ5* -	**SENTINEL I** *ex* Ocean Pearl *-2014* *ex* Synergy *-2008* *ex* Uqba Ibn Nafi *-2007* **Synergy Navigation SA** - SatCom: Inmarsat Mini-M 764805277 *Monrovia* *Liberia* MMSI: 636013442 Official number: 13442	**28,195** 15,331 51,546 T/cm 51.1	Class: BV (RS) (NV)	**1985-07 Daewoo Shipbuilding & Heavy Machinery Ltd — Geoje** Yd No: 2005 Converted From: Chemical Tanker-2013 Loa 180.03 (BB) Br ex 32.23 Dght 13.325 Lbp 170.00 Br md 32.21 Dpth 18.04 Welded, 1 dk	**(A12B2TR) Chemical/Products Tanker** Double Bottom Entire Compartment Length Liq: 51,001; Liq (Oil): 51,001 Compartments: 6 Ta, 8 Wing Ta, 2 Wing Slop Ta, ER 16 Cargo Pump (s): 4x200m^3/hr, 4x180m^3/hr, 6x170m^3/hr, 1x290m^3/hr, 1x320m^3/hr Manifold: Bow/CM: 87.3m	**1 oil engine** driving 1 FP propeller Total Power: 8,238kW (11,200hp) 14.0kn Sulzer 5RTA68 1 x 2 Stroke 5 Cy. 680 x 2000 8238kW (11200bhp) Hyundai Engine & Machinery Co Ltd-South Korea AuxGen: 3 x 850kW 440V 60Hz a.c, 1 x 650kW 440V 60Hz a.c Fuel: 200.0 (d.f.) 2200.0 (r.f.) 30.0pd
8018039 *ELBY4* -	**SENTINEL II** **Lib-Ore Steamship Co Inc** Wilhelmsen Ship Management Ltd SatCom: Inmarsat C 463609610 *Monrovia* *Liberia* MMSI: 636007200 Official number: 7200	**34,353** 13,078 47,353	Class: LR ✠ **100A1** SS 10/2010 caustic soda/heavy bulk carriers with 2 longitudinal bulkheads, strengthened for heavy cargoes, Nos. 2 & 4 holds or Nos. 1, 3 & 5 holds may be empty, & also carriage of caustic soda in Nos. 1, 3 & 5 wing tanks & slop tanks ESP ✠ **LMC** **UMS** Eq.Ltr: N†; Cable: 660.0/84.0 U2 (a)	**1982-03 Hitachi Zosen Corp — Onomichi HS (Innoshima Shipyard)** Yd No: 4687 Loa 209.00 Br ex 32.24 Dght 11.027 Lbp 200.01 Br md 32.21 Dpth 18.11 Welded, 1 dk	**(A21B2BO) Ore Carrier** Double Bottom Entire Compartment Length Grain: 45,875; Liq: 20,108 Cargo Heating Coils Compartments: 5 Ho, 8 Wing Ta, ER 5 Ha: 2 (19.2 x 14.4)2 (23.0 x 14.4) (19.2 x 12.6)ER	**1 oil engine** driving 1 FP propeller Total Power: 10,591kW (14,400hp) 14.8kn B&W 7L67GFCA 1 x 2 Stroke 7 Cy. 670 x 1700 10591kW (14400bhp) Hitachi Zosen Corp-Japan AuxGen: 3 x 960kW 450V 60Hz a.c, 1 x 120kW 450V 60Hz a.c Boilers: AuxB (o.f.) 17.0kgf/cm^2 (16.7bar), AuxB (ex.g.) htr 21.0kgf/cm^2 (20.6bar)rcv 17kgf/cm` (16,7bar) Thrusters: 1 Thwart. FP thruster (f) Fuel: 51.0 (d.f.) 2245.0 (r.f.)
8119596 *OZ2069* -	**SENTINEL RANGER** *ex* Ranger *-2014* *ex* Normand Ranger *-2007* **Team Beredskap Sp/f** Simon Mokster Shipping AS SatCom: Inmarsat C 423102610 *Torshavn* *Faeroe Islands (Danish)* MMSI: 231026000	**1,502** 401 1,400	Class: NV	**1982-10 Haugesund Mekaniske Verksted AS — Haugesund** Yd No: 67 Loa 64.42 Br ex - Dght 4.720 Lbp 56.42 Br md 13.81 Dpth 6.91 Welded, 2 dks	**(B21B20A) Anchor Handling Tug Supply**	**2 oil engines** reduction geared to sc. shafts driving 2 FP propellers Total Power: 5,296kW (7,200hp) 16.0kn Wichmann 9AXAG 2 x 2 Stroke 9 Cy. 300 x 450 each-2648kW (3600bhp) Wichmann Motorfabrikk AS-Norway AuxGen: 2 x 640kW 440V 60Hz a.c, 2 x 254kW 440V 60Hz a.c Thrusters: 1 Thwart. FP thruster (f); 1 Retract. directional thruster amid
9191345 *V7BP8* -	**SENTINEL SPIRIT** *ex* Sentinel *-2008* **1999 Sentinel Trust** Teekay Marine (Singapore) Pte Ltd *Majuro* *Marshall Islands* MMSI: 538001331 Official number: 1331	**58,288** 30,842 104,601 T/cm 92.1	Class: AB	**1999-11 Samsung Heavy Industries Co Ltd — Geoje** Yd No: 1278 Loa 243.56 (BB) Br ex 42.04 Dght 14.721 Lbp 233.00 Br md 41.75 Dpth 21.30 Welded, 1 dk	**(A13A2TV) Crude Oil Tanker** Double Hull (13F) Liq: 113,334; Liq (Oil): 117,881 Cargo Heating Coils Compartments: 12 Wing Ta, ER, 2 Wing Slop Ta 3 Cargo Pump (s): 3x2800m^3/hr Manifold: Bow/CM: 123.5m	**1 oil engine** driving 1 FP propeller Total Power: 12,004kW (16,321hp) 15.0kn Sulzer 6RTA58T 1 x 2 Stroke 6 Cy. 580 x 2416 12004kW (16321bhp) Samsung Heavy Industries Co Ltd-South Korea AuxGen: 3 x 700kW 450V 60Hz a.c Fuel: 159.3 (d.f.) (Heating Coils) 2269.2 (r.f.) 45.2pd
7406825 *LAWW3* -	**SENTINEL STAR** *ex* Ramco Star *-2014* *ex* Ocean Star *-2010* *ex* Norindo Sun *-1985* **Sentinel Marine Ltd** SatCom: Inmarsat A 131112642 *Bergen* *Norway (NIS)* MMSI: 258129000	**1,513** 453 890	Class: RI (NV)	**1975-12 Scheepswerf Hoogezand B.V. — Hoogezand** Yd No: 177 Lengthened-1986 Loa 69.85 Br ex 12.03 Dght 4.610 Lbp 63.07 Br md 11.99 Dpth 5.90 Welded, 2 dks	**(B21A20S) Platform Supply Ship** Passengers: berths: 12	**2 oil engines** driving 2 CP propellers Total Power: 2,280kW (3,100hp) 11.0kn Alpha 10V23L-VO 2 x Vee 4 Stroke 10 Cy. 225 x 300 each-1140kW (1550bhp) Alpha Diesel A/S-Denmark AuxGen: 2 x 170kW 440V 60Hz a.c, 1 x 56kW 440V 60Hz a.c Thrusters: 1 Thwart. FP thruster (f); 1 Retract. directional thruster (f) Fuel: 500.0 (r.f.) 13.0pd
7016694 *YDLA* -	**SENTOSA** *ex* Riama *-1985* *ex* Phoenix *-1983* *ex* Lim Glory *-1982* *ex* Shorei Maru *-1979* **PT Pelayaran Sumber Sakti Shipping Line Ltd** - *Jakarta* *Indonesia* MMSI: 525019493	**2,186** 1,214 3,764	Class: (NK) (KI)	**1969-09 Nishi Shipbuilding Co Ltd — Imabari EH** Yd No: 116 Loa 91.90 Br ex 14.03 Dght 5.160 Lbp 85.68 Br md 14.00 Dpth 6.81 Welded, 1 dk	**(A31A2GX) General Cargo Ship** Grain: 4,418; Bale: 4,061 Compartments: 2 Ho, ER 2 Ha: (17.6 x 7.0) (29.4 x 7.0)ER Derricks: 1x15t,2x10t; Winches: 3	**1 oil engine** driving 1 FP propeller Total Power: 1,765kW (2,400hp) 12.5kn Hanshin Z6L46SH 1 x 4 Stroke 6 Cy. 460 x 680 1765kW (2400bhp) Hanshin Nainenki Kogyo-Japan AuxGen: 2 x 100kW 440V a.c Fuel: 338.5 8.0pd
8202070 *HOGM* -	**SENTOSA** *ex* Smart *-2010* *ex* Radiant Polaris *-2003* *ex* Balaji Premium *-2001* *ex* Verona *-1995* *ex* Iris 1 *-1993* **Golden Fortune Ltd SA** Glory Ship Management Pte Ltd *Panama* *Panama* MMSI: 357865000 Official number: 2920103B	**22,308** 13,036 36,205	Class: BV (NV) (AB) (IR) (NK)	**1982-09 Imabari Shipbuilding Co Ltd — Marugame KG (Marugame Shipyard)** Yd No: 1106 Loa 189.74 (BB) Br ex 27.67 Dght 10.862 Lbp 178.01 Br md 27.60 Dpth 15.19 Welded, 1 dk	**(A21A2BC) Bulk Carrier** Grain: 48,797; Bale: 46,631 Compartments: 5 Ho, ER 5 Ha: (18.4 x 13.6)4 (20.0 x 15.3)ER Cranes: 4x25t	**1 oil engine** driving 1 FP propeller Total Power: 9,598kW (13,049hp) 14.5kn Sulzer 6RLB66 1 x 2 Stroke 6 Cy. 660 x 1400 9598kW (13049bhp) Mitsubishi Heavy Industries Ltd-Japan AuxGen: 2 x 500kW
7808970 *YHXF* -	**SENTOSA 6** *ex* Shun An Du 6 *-2007* *ex* Liao Lu Du 6 *-2000* *ex* Tomozuru Maru *-1993* **PT Sentosa Lestari Abadi** - *Jakarta* *Indonesia* MMSI: 525016218	*2,625* 788 629	Class: KI	**1978-11 Towa Zosen K.K. — Shimonoseki** Yd No: 522 Loa 71.57 Br ex 13.62 Dght 3.601 Lbp 65.03 Br md 13.61 Dpth 4.81 Welded, 2 dks	**(A36A2PR) Passenger/Ro-Ro Ship (Vehicles)** Passengers: unberthed: 600 Cars: 37, Trailers: 21	**2 oil engines** geared to sc. shafts driving 2 FP propellers Total Power: 2,354kW (3,200hp) 15.0kn Daihatsu 8DSM-26 2 x 4 Stroke 8 Cy. 260 x 320 each-1177kW (1600bhp) Daihatsu Diesel Manufacturing Co Lt-Japan AuxGen: 2 x 240kW 450V 60Hz a.c Fuel: 24.0 (d.f.) 89.5 (r.f.) 6.0pd
8313051 *YDZO* -	**SENTOSA 201** *ex* Huiwan 201 *-2007* *ex* Ryoun Maru *-1998* **PT Sentosa Lestari Abadi** - *Tanjung Priok* *Indonesia*	*610* 381 660	Class: KI	**1983-11 Nippon Zosen Tekko K.K. — Kitakyushu** Yd No: 286 Loa 53.70 Br ex 9.53 Dght 3.218 Lbp 49.51 Br md 9.50 Dpth 5.31 Welded, 2 dks	**(A31A2GX) General Cargo Ship** Grain: 1,385; Bale: 1,302 Compartments: 1 Ho, ER 1 Ha: ER	**1 oil engine** driving 1 FP propeller Total Power: 625kW (850hp) Niigata 6M26AGT 1 x 4 Stroke 6 Cy. 260 x 460 625kW (850bhp) Niigata Engineering Co Ltd-Japan
9097903 *YEAA* -	**SENTOSA 203** *ex* Shen Hang 563 *-2007* **PT Bangka Jaya Lines** - *Tanjung Priok* *Indonesia*	**617** 322 759	Class: KI	**1986-01 Guangdong New China Shipyard Co Ltd — Dongguan GD** Loa - Br ex - Dght - Lbp 52.00 Br md 9.00 Dpth 5.00 Welded, 1 dk	**(A31A2GX) General Cargo Ship**	**1 oil engine** driving 1 Propeller Total Power: 882kW (1,199hp) Niigata 6M26AGTE 1 x 4 Stroke 6 Cy. 260 x 460 882kW (1199bhp) Niigata Engineering Co Ltd-Japan

IMO / Call sign / Flag	Name / Owner / Port	Tonnage	Class	Builder / Dimensions	Type / Capacity	Machinery
9136993 *PNWT* -	**SENTOSA 205** *ex* Chisho Maru No. 3 *-2012* **PT Bangka Jaya Lines** - *Jakarta* *Indonesia*	**1,486** 846 1,600	Class: KI	**1995-07 Yamanaka Zosen K.K. — Imabari** Yd No: 576 Loa 74.95 (BB) Br ex - Dght 4.242 Lbp 70.00 Br md 11.50 Dpth 7.24 Welded, 1 dk	**(A31A2GX) General Cargo Ship** Grain: 2,229 Compartments: 1 Ho, ER 1 Ha: ER	**1 oil engine** reverse geared to sc. shaft driving 1 FP propeller Total Power: 1,324kW (1,800hp) Akasaka A31R 1 x 4 Stroke 6 Cy. 310 x 600 1324kW (1800bhp) Akasaka Tekkosho KK (Akasaka DieselLtd)-Japan Thrusters: 1 Thwart. FP thruster (f)
9054860 *PNZF* -	**SENTOSA 207** *ex* Yusho Cosmos *-2011* *ex* Daito Maru *-2001* **PT Bangka Jaya Lines** - *Jakarta* *Indonesia* MMSI: 525012085	**1,444** 487 1,516	Class: KI (BV)	**1992-10 Sanyo Zosen K.K. — Onomichi** Yd No: 1038 Loa 75.88 (BB) Br ex 12.02 Dght 4.164 Lbp 70.00 Br md 12.00 Dpth 7.00 Welded, 2 dks	**(A31A2GX) General Cargo Ship** Grain: 2,850; Bale: 2,800 Compartments: 1 Ho, ER 1 Ha: ER	**1 oil engine** with clutches & reverse geared to sc. shaft driving 1 FP propeller Total Power: 735kW (999hp) 13.0kn Akasaka A34 1 x 4 Stroke 6 Cy. 340 x 660 735kW (999bhp) Akasaka Tekkosho KK (Akasaka DieselLtd)-Japan AuxGen: 2 x 133kW 225V a.c, 1 x 46kW 225V a.c Thrusters: 1 Tunnel thruster (f)
7312763 *YD4863* -	**SENTOSA 3201** *ex* Karya 20 *-2007* *ex* Koyo Maru No. 8 *-2002* **PT Kebon Asri Nusa** - *Tanjung Priok* *Indonesia*	*274* 83 -	Class: (KI)	**1973-03 Daiko Dockyard Co. Ltd. — Osaka** Yd No: 76 Loa 30.15 Br ex 9.53 Dght 2.998 Lbp 26.52 Br md 9.50 Dpth 4.02 Riveted\Welded, 1 dk	**(B32A2ST) Tug**	**2 oil engines** driving 2 FP propellers Total Power: 2,354kW (3,200hp) Daihatsu 8DSM-26 2 x 4 Stroke 8 Cy. 260 x 320 each-1177kW (1600bhp) Daihatsu Diesel Manufacturing Co Lt-Japan
9069982 *YB6301* -	**SENTOSA ANUGERAH PERDANA** **PT Anugerah Wijaya Bersaudara** - *Samarinda* *Indonesia*	**213** 64 -	Class: (KI)	**2006-08 C.V. Dok & Galangan Kapal Perlun — Samarinda** L reg 39.20 Br ex - Dght - Lbp 35.10 Br md 8.00 Dpth 2.50 Welded, 1 dk	**(A35D2RL) Landing Craft** Bow ramp (centre)	**2 oil engines** geared to sc. shafts driving 2 Propellers Total Power: 514kW (698hp) Mitsubishi 8DC9 2 x Vee 4 Stroke 8 Cy. 135 x 140 each-257kW (349bhp) Mitsubishi Heavy Industries Ltd-Japan
9527996 *9V7779* -	**SENTOSA BULKER** **J Lauritzen Singapore Pte Ltd** - SatCom: Inmarsat C 456589512 *Singapore* *Singapore* MMSI: 565895000 Official number: 394831	**20,809** 11,689 32,755 T/cm 46.0	Class: NV (BV)	**2010-04 Jiangmen Nanyang Ship Engineering Co Ltd — Jiangmen GD** Yd No: 602 Loa 179.90 (BB) Br ex 28.44 Dght 10.150 Lbp 171.50 Br md 28.40 Dpth 14.10 Welded, 1 dk	**(A21A2BC) Bulk Carrier** Grain: 42,500; Bale: 40,280 Compartments: 5 Ho, ER 5 Ha: 3 (20.0 x 19.2) (18.4 x 19.2)ER (14.4 x 17.6) Cranes: 4x30.5t	**1 oil engine** driving 1 FP propeller Total Power: 6,480kW (8,810hp) 13.7kn MAN-B&W 6S42MC 1 x 2 Stroke 6 Cy. 420 x 1764 6480kW (8810bhp) Yichang Marine Diesel Engine Co Ltd-China AuxGen: 3 x a.c
7231567 *YDA4106* -	**SENTOSA DUA** *ex* K K Jaya 5 *-2009* *ex* Azuma Maru *-2005* **PT Kebon Asri Nusa** - *Tanjung Priok* *Indonesia*	**241** 73 -	Class: KI	**1972-09 Kanagawa Zosen — Kobe** Yd No: 120 Loa 33.33 Br ex 8.23 Dght 2.299 Lbp 29.49 Br md 8.21 Dpth 3.41 Riveted\Welded, 1 dk	**(B32A2ST) Tug**	**2 oil engines** Geared Integral to driving 2 Z propellers Total Power: 1,766kW (2,402hp) 13.0kn Niigata 6L25BX 2 x 4 Stroke 6 Cy. 250 x 320 each-883kW (1201bhp) Niigata Engineering Co Ltd-Japan
8740307 - -	**SENTOSA INDAH SEJATI** **PT Kembang Sentosa Bersama** - *Banjarmasin* *Indonesia*	**733** 220 -	Class: KI	**2009-07 Indah Sentosa Bahari — Banjarmasin** Loa 64.00 Br ex - Dght - Lbp 62.40 Br md 12.50 Dpth 3.66 Welded, 1 dk	**(A35D2RL) Landing Craft**	**2 oil engines** driving 2 Propellers Total Power: 1,472kW (2,002hp) M.T.U. 12V183TE92 2 x Vee 4 Stroke 12 Cy. 128 x 142 each-736kW (1001bhp) MTU Friedrichshafen GmbH-Friedrichshafen
9502427 *9V8224* -	**SENTOSA LEADER** **Ocean Sentosa (PCTC) Pte Ltd** United Ocean Ship Management Pte Ltd *Singapore* *Singapore* MMSI: 565349000 Official number: 395472	**51,917** 15,576 17,143	Class: NK	**2010-05 Tsuneishi Heavy Industries (Cebu) Inc — Balamban** Yd No: SC-140 Loa 179.90 (BB) Br ex - Dght 9.622 Lbp 170.00 Br md 32.20 Dpth 34.80 Welded, 12 dks. incl. 3 hoistable dks.	**(A35B2RV) Vehicles Carrier** Side door/ramp (s) Len: 20.00 Wid: 4.20 Swl: 15 Quarter stern door/ramp (s. a.) Len: 35.00 Wid: 13.50 Swl: 100 Cars: 5,195	**1 oil engine** driving 1 FP propeller Total Power: 14,120kW (19,198hp) 19.3kn MAN-B&W 7S60MC-C 1 x 2 Stroke 7 Cy. 600 x 2400 14120kW (19198bhp) Mitsui Engineering & Shipbuilding CLtd-Japan AuxGen: 3 x 950kW a.c Thrusters: 1 Tunnel thruster (f) Fuel: 3110.0 (r.f.)
9392822 *9VLV7* -	**SENTOSA RIVER** **'K' Line Pte Ltd (KLPL)** - *Singapore* *Singapore* MMSI: 563525000 Official number: 394119	**59,258** 36,052 115,146 T/cm 92.4	Class: AB	**2008-10 Sasebo Heavy Industries Co. Ltd. — Sasebo Yard, Sasebo** Yd No: 761 Loa 243.80 (BB) Br ex - Dght 15.600 Lbp 234.00 Br md 42.00 Dpth 21.50 Welded, 1 dk	**(A13A2TV) Crude Oil Tanker** Double Hull (13F) Liq: 119,528; Liq (Oil): 126,606 Cargo Heating Coils Compartments: 12 Wing Ta, 2 Wing Slop Ta, ER 3 Cargo Pump (s): 3x2500m³/hr Manifold: Bow/CM: 119.6m	**1 oil engine** driving 1 FP propeller Total Power: 13,560kW (18,436hp) 15.0kn MAN-B&W 6S60MC-C 1 x 2 Stroke 6 Cy. 600 x 2400 13560kW (18436bhp) Mitsui Engineering & Shipbuilding CLtd-Japan AuxGen: 3 x 700kW a.c Fuel: 70.0 (d.f.) 3000.0 (r.f.)
9507946 *J8B4122* -	**SENTRY** *ex* Fordeco 101 *-2009* **Borinken Towing & Salvage LLC** Borinken Towage & Salvage Corp *Kingstown* *St Vincent & The Grenadines* MMSI: 377193000 Official number: 10595	**290** 87 234	Class: GL	**2009-03 Tai Tung Hing Shipyard Sdn Bhd — Sibu** Yd No: 5 Loa 32.10 Br ex 9.02 Dght 3.570 Lbp 29.38 Br md 9.00 Dpth 4.20 Welded, 1 dk	**(B32A2ST) Tug**	**2 oil engines** reverse reduction geared to sc. shafts driving 2 FP propellers Total Power: 2,388kW (3,246hp) Cummins KTA-50-M2 2 x Vee 4 Stroke 16 Cy. 159 x 159 each-1194kW (1623bhp) Cummins Engine Co Inc-USA AuxGen: 2 x 80kW 415V a.c Fuel: 200.0
9576870 *9YHX* -	**SENTRY** **Mid Atlantic Ltd** - SatCom: Inmarsat C 436206910 *Port of Spain* *Trinidad & Tobago* MMSI: 362069000	**353** 105 345	Class: AB	**2010-12 Midship Marine, Inc. — New Orleans, La** Yd No: 333 Loa 48.78 Br ex - Dght 2.230 Lbp 47.26 Br md 9.15 Dpth 3.96 Welded, 1 dk	**(B21A20C) Crew/Supply Vessel** Hull Material: Aluminium Alloy	**4 oil engines** reduction geared to sc. shafts driving 4 FP propellers Total Power: 3,236kW (4,400hp) Yanmar 12LAK (M)-STE2 4 x Vee 4 Stroke 12 Cy. 150 x 165 each-809kW (1100bhp) Yanmar Diesel Engine Co Ltd-Japan AuxGen: 2 x 93kW a.c Fuel: 95.0 (d.f.)
7726500 *WBN3013* -	**SENTRY** **Crowley Puerto Rico Services Inc** - *San Francisco, CA* *United States of America* MMSI: 366766990 Official number: 579188	**538** 161 -	Class: AB	**1977-01 McDermott Shipyards Inc — Morgan City LA** Yd No: 225 Loa 41.46 Br ex - Dght 5.161 Lbp 39.22 Br md 11.14 Dpth 5.80 Welded, 1 dk	**(B32A2ST) Tug**	**2 oil engines** reverse reduction geared to sc. shafts driving 2 FP propellers Total Power: 5,296kW (7,200hp) 14.3kn EMD (Electro-Motive) 20-645-E7B 2 x Vee 2 Stroke 20 Cy. 230 x 254 each-2648kW (3600bhp) General Motors Corp.Electro-Motive Div.-La Grange AuxGen: 2 x 90kW
8860688 *UIMJ* -	**SENTYABR** **V M Gorbunov** - *Murmansk* *Russia* MMSI: 273557500 Official number: 903543	**104** 31 58	Class: (RS)	**1991-07 Azovskaya Sudoverf — Azov** Yd No: 1048 Loa 26.50 Br ex 6.59 Dght 2.360 Lbp 22.90 Br md 6.50 Dpth 3.05 Welded, 1 dk	**(B11A2FS) Stern Trawler** Ins: 48	**1 oil engine** geared to sc. shaft driving 1 FP propeller Total Power: 165kW (224hp) 9.3kn Daldizel 6CHNSP18/22 1 x 4 Stroke 6 Cy. 180 x 220 165kW (224bhp) Daldizel-Khabarovsk AuxGen: 2 x 30kW Fuel: 9.0 (d.f.)
8706882 - -	**SENWA MARU** - - *South Korea*	*198* - 557		**1987-06 Kurinoura Dockyard Co Ltd — Yawatahama EH** Yd No: 239 Loa 48.01 Br ex 8.03 Dght 3.300 Lbp 44.00 Br md 8.01 Dpth 3.41 Welded, 1 dk	**(A13A2TV) Crude Oil Tanker** Liq: 617; Liq (Oil): 617 Compartments: 6 Ta, ER	**1 oil engine** with clutches & reverse reduction geared to sc. shaft driving 1 FP propeller Total Power: 478kW (650hp) Niigata 6M26BGT 1 x 4 Stroke 6 Cy. 260 x 460 478kW (650bhp) Niigata Engineering Co Ltd-Japan
9703124 *9LY2632* -	**SENWAY 1** **Yisen Investment Ltd** Shanghai Vasteast International Shipping Management Co Ltd *Freetown* *Sierra Leone* MMSI: 667003435	**1,063** 605 1,418	Class: ZC (Class contemplated)	**2013-07 Lianyungang Wuzhou Shipbuilding Co Co Ltd — Guanyun County JS** Yd No: WZ-37 Loa 65.80 Br ex - Dght 2.300 Lbp 63.80 Br md 15.80 Dpth 3.50 Welded, 1 dk	**(A31A2GX) General Cargo Ship**	**2 oil engines** reduction geared to sc. shafts driving 2 FP propellers Total Power: 436kW (592hp) Chinese Std. Type Z6170ZLC 2 x 4 Stroke 6 Cy. 170 x 200 each-218kW (296bhp) Zibo Diesel Engine Factory-China
9070101 *JM6375* -	**SENYO MARU** **Geneq Corp (KK Geneq)** Kitakyushu Unyu KK (Kitakyushu Transportation Co Ltd) *Kitakyushu, Fukuoka* *Japan* MMSI: 431600175 Official number: 134465	*4,911* - 7,482	Class: NK	**1993-12 Nippon Kokan KK (NKK Corp) — Yokohama KN (Tsurumi Shipyard)** Yd No: 1059 Loa 114.80 Br ex 17.52 Dght 7.090 Lbp 108.00 Br md 17.50 Dpth 9.30 Welded, 1 dk	**(A24A2BT) Cement Carrier** Bale: 6,115	**1 oil engine** driving 1 FP propeller Total Power: 3,354kW (4,560hp) 12.8kn B&W 6L35MC 1 x 2 Stroke 6 Cy. 350 x 1050 3354kW (4560bhp) Hitachi Zosen Corp-Japan AuxGen: 2 x 500kW a.c, 1 x 340kW a.c Thrusters: 1 Thwart. CP thruster (f) Fuel: 230.0 (r.f.)

8998423 JD2096 -
SENYO MARU 499 - 1,750
Izumi Kisen KK (Izumi Shipping Co Ltd)
-
Tokyo *Japan*
Official number: 140154
2005-04 **K.K. Watanabe Zosensho — Nagasaki**
Loa 74.70 Br ex - Dght 4.350
Lbp 69.00 Br md 12.00 Dpth 7.38
Welded, 1 dk
(A31A2GX) General Cargo Ship
1 oil engine driving 1 Propeller
Total Power: 736kW (1,001hp) 11.5kn
Niigata 6M34BGT
1 x 4 Stroke 6 Cy. 340 x 620 736kW (1001bhp)
Niigata Engineering Co Ltd-Japan

9000405 9LY2548 -
SENYO MARU 3,576 - 6,097 Class: SL (NK)
Amiba Marine Co Ltd
Aoyang Marine Co Ltd
Freetown *Sierra Leone*
MMSI: 667003351
1990-06 **Nishi Shipbuilding Co Ltd — Imabari EH**
Yd No: 360
Loa 105.27 Br ex - Dght 6.931
Lbp 98.00 Br md 15.50 Dpth 8.80
Welded
(A31A2GX) General Cargo Ship
Grain: 7,657; Bale: 7,382
Compartments: 2 Ho, ER
2 Ha: (30.2 x 8.4) (29.3 x 8.4)ER
1 oil engine driving 1 FP propeller
Total Power: 2,427kW (3,300hp) 12.5kn
B&W 6L35MCE
1 x 2 Stroke 6 Cy. 350 x 1050 2427kW (3300bhp)
The Hanshin Diesel Works Ltd-Japan
Thrusters: 1 Thwart. FP thruster (f)
Fuel: 180.0 (r.f.)

9088627 JI3557 -
SENYO MARU 999 - 1,135 T/cm 6.4 Class: NK
Senko Co Ltd & Yoshiga Kaiun KK
Senko Co Ltd
Osaka, Osaka *Japan*
MMSI: 431300188
Official number: 134156
1994-06 **Shin Kurushima Dockyard Co. Ltd. — Hashihama, Imabari** Yd No: 2806
Loa 69.52 (BB) Br ex - Dght 4.042
Lbp 64.00 Br md 12.20 Dpth 5.20
Welded, 1 dk
(A11B2TG) LPG Tanker
Liq (Gas): 1,430
2 x Gas Tank (s); 2 independent (C.mn.stl) cyl horizontal
1 oil engine driving 1 CP propeller
Total Power: 1,618kW (2,200hp) 13.6kn
Akasaka A34
1 x 4 Stroke 6 Cy. 340 x 660 1618kW (2200bhp)
Akasaka Tekkosho KK (Akasaka DieselLtd)-Japan
AuxGen: 2 x 200kW 450V 60Hz a.c
Thrusters: 1 Thwart. CP thruster (f)
Fuel: 170.0 (d.f.) 6.3pd

7326477 - -
SENYO MARU 193 - -
Dae Sun Shipbuilding & Engineering Co Ltd
-
South Korea
1973-06 **Shin Yamamoto Shipbuilding & Engineering Co Ltd — Kochi KC**
Yd No: 169
Loa 30.45 Br ex - Dght 2.604
Lbp 27.00 Br md 8.60 Dpth 3.80
Riveted\Welded, 1 dk
(B32A2ST) Tug
2 oil engines Geared Integral to driving 2 Z propellers
Total Power: 1,766kW (2,402hp) 13.5kn
Niigata 6L25BX
2 x 4 Stroke 6 Cy. 250 x 320 each-883kW (1201bhp)
Niigata Engineering Co Ltd-Japan

8876924 JK5228 -
SENZAN MARU No. 5 476 - 1,098
Kawaoka Kisen YK
-
Bizen, Okayama *Japan*
Official number: 133079
1994-03 **Koike Zosen Kaiun KK — Osakikamijima**
Loa 75.00 Br ex - Dght 3.720
Lbp 68.50 Br md 11.50 Dpth 6.70
Welded, 1 dk
(A31A2GX) General Cargo Ship
Compartments: 1 Ho, ER
1 Ha: (39.6 x 8.5)ER
1 oil engine driving 1 FP propeller
Total Power: 736kW (1,001hp) 11.0kn
Niigata 6M28BGT
1 x 4 Stroke 6 Cy. 280 x 480 736kW (1001bhp)
Niigata Engineering Co Ltd-Japan

6808909 - -
SEO DONG 3 349 138 352 Class: (KR)
ex Kores 3 *-1998* *ex* Kyung Dong No. 3 *-1996*
ex Sun Light No. 26 *-1986*
ex Ryuho Maru No. 32 *-1975*
-
-
1968 Uchida Zosen — Ise Yd No: 653
Loa 47.20 Br ex 8.64 Dght 3.404
Lbp 42.80 Br md 8.62 Dpth 3.79
Riveted\Welded, 1 dk
(B11A2FS) Stern Trawler
Ins: 351
3 Ha: (1.6 x 1.3)2 (1.7 x 1.5)
1 oil engine driving 1 FP propeller
Total Power: 1,177kW (1,600hp) 11.5kn
Akasaka 6DH38SS
1 x 4 Stroke 6 Cy. 380 x 560 1177kW (1600bhp)
Akasaka Tekkosho KK (Akasaka DieselLtd)-Japan
AuxGen: 2 x 80kW 230V a.c

9183520 - -
SEO HAE NO. 8 **1,101** - 743 Class: (KR)
ex New Airport No. 1 *-2005*
Mirejet Co Ltd
-
Incheon *South Korea*
MMSI: 440003450
Official number: ICR-979251
1997-12 **Zhejiang Shipyard — Ningbo ZJ**
Yd No: 97-80
Loa 92.20 Br ex - Dght 2.462
Lbp 65.00 Br md 18.00 Dpth 3.50
Welded, 1 dk
(A37B2PS) Passenger Ship
Bow ramp (centre)
Stern ramp (centre)
2 oil engines reduction geared to sc. shafts driving 2 FP propellers
Total Power: 626kW (852hp) 10.1kn
Cummins KTA-19-M
2 x 4 Stroke 6 Cy. 159 x 159 each-313kW (426bhp)
Cummins Engine Co Ltd-United Kingdom
AuxGen: 1 x 180kW 440V a.c

9184500 - -
SEO HAE NO. 9 **1,101** 442 728 Class: (KR)
ex New Airport No. 2 *-2005*
Mirejet Co Ltd
-
Incheon *South Korea*
MMSI: 440003460
Official number: ICR-979290
1997-12 **Ilheung Shipbuilding & Engineering Co Ltd — Mokpo** Yd No: 97-78
Loa 92.20 Br ex - Dght 2.462
Lbp 65.00 Br md 18.00 Dpth 3.50
Welded, 1 dk
(A37B2PS) Passenger Ship
Bow ramp (centre)
Stern ramp (centre)
2 oil engines reduction geared to sc. shafts driving 2 FP propellers
Total Power: 626kW (852hp) 10.1kn
Cummins KTA-19-M
2 x 4 Stroke 6 Cy. 159 x 159 each-313kW (426bhp)
Cummins Engine Co Ltd-United Kingdom
AuxGen: 1 x 180kW 440V a.c

9117882 DSAN -
SEO JIN No. 9 **429** - 1,057 Class: (KR)
ex Hae Sung No. 33 *-1996*
Seo Jin Transportation Co Ltd
-
Incheon *South Korea*
Official number: ICR-934551
1994-01 **Koje Shipbuilding Co Ltd — Geoje**
Yd No: 357
Loa 53.00 Br ex - Dght 4.212
Lbp 47.01 Br md 9.50 Dpth 4.60
Welded, 1 dk
(A13B2TP) Products Tanker
Liq: 1,220; Liq (Oil): 1,220
1 oil engine geared to sc. shaft driving 1 FP propeller
Total Power: 716kW (973hp) 11.4kn
Caterpillar 3508TA
1 x Vee 4 Stroke 8 Cy. 170 x 190 716kW (973bhp)
Caterpillar Inc-USA
AuxGen: 1 x 104kW 225V a.c

7417903 6NEL -
SEO JIN No. 11 449 246 524 Class: (KR)
ex Jin Young No. 155 *-1999*
ex O Yang No. 88 *-1992*
Sang Ji Fisheries Co Ltd
-
Busan *South Korea*
MMSI: 440785000
Official number: 9512151-6260008
1974-11 **Dae Sun Shipbuilding & Engineering Co Ltd — Busan** Yd No: 181
Loa 55.50 Br ex 9.02 Dght 3.586
Lbp 49.05 Br md 9.01 Dpth 3.97
Riveted\Welded, 1 dk
(B11B2FV) Fishing Vessel
Ins: 770
3 Ha: 2 (1.3 x 0.9) (1.8 x 1.8)
1 oil engine driving 1 FP propeller
Total Power: 1,030kW (1,400hp) 13.7kn
Hanshin 6LUN28
1 x 4 Stroke 6 Cy. 280 x 480 1030kW (1400bhp)
Hanshin Nainenki Kogyo-Japan
AuxGen: 2 x 200kW 225V a.c

6507725 6MXS -
SEO KWANG 465 239 - Class: (KR)
ex Sam He No. 11 *-1979*
ex Kaki Maru No. 11 *-1979*
Seo Kwang Fisheries Co Ltd
-
Busan *South Korea*
Official number: BS-A-853
1964 Miho Zosensho K.K. — Shimizu Yd No: 518
Loa 54.51 Br ex 9.53 Dght -
Lbp 48.19 Br md 9.50 Dpth 4.04
Welded, 1 dk
(B11B2FV) Fishing Vessel
Ins: 644
3 Ha: (1.0 x 1.0)2 (1.9 x 1.9)
1 oil engine driving 1 FP propeller
Total Power: 956kW (1,300hp) 11.5kn
Akasaka YS6SS
1 x 4 Stroke 6 Cy. 400 x 570 956kW (1300bhp)
Akasaka Tekkosho KK (Akasaka DieselLtd)-Japan
AuxGen: 2 x 128kW 225V a.c

9032006 - -
SEO KYUNG ISLAND **11,607** 3,482 2,706 Class: KR (BV)
ex Santa Cruz De Tenerife *-2013*
Seo Kyung Co Ltd
International Maritime Services Pty Ltd
SatCom: Inmarsat C 444090830
Busan *South Korea*
MMSI: 441913000
Official number: BSR-130013
1994-01 **Union Naval de Levante SA (UNL) — Valencia** Yd No: 217
Loa 116.79 (BB) Br ex 20.72 Dght 5.400
Lbp 101.83 Br md 20.70 Dpth 7.50
Welded, 3 dks
(A36A2PR) Passenger/Ro-Ro Ship (Vehicles)
Passengers: unberthed: 378
Bow door/ramp
Len: 12.50 Wid: 5.00 Swl: -
Stern door/ramp
Len: 11.50 Wid: 8.40 Swl: -
Lane-Len: 993
Lane-Wid: 3.00
Lane-clr ht: 5.30
Cars: 280
2 oil engines with flexible couplings & sr geared to sc. shafts driving 2 CP propellers
Total Power: 5,808kW (7,896hp) 16.0kn
Alpha 12V28/32
2 x Vee 4 Stroke 12 Cy. 280 x 320 each-2904kW (3948bhp)
EN Bazan de Construcciones NavalesMilitares SA-Spain
AuxGen: 4 x 700kW 400V 50Hz a.c
Thrusters: 1 Thwart. CP thruster (f)
Fuel: 60.0 (d.f.) 300.0 (r.f.) 20.0pd

8741430 - -
SEO LIM **393** 117 - Class: (KR)
COSCO (Zhoushan) Shipyard Co Ltd
-
2008-07 **Geumgang Shipbuilding Co Ltd — Janghang** Yd No: GGS-02
Loa 37.40 Br ex - Dght -
Lbp 32.00 Br md 9.80 Dpth 4.40
Welded, 1 dk
(B32A2ST) Tug
2 oil engines reduction geared to sc. shafts driving 2 Propellers
Total Power: 2,434kW (3,310hp) 13.6kn
Niigata 6L28HX
2 x 4 Stroke 6 Cy. 280 x 370 each-1217kW (1655bhp)
Niigata Engineering Co Ltd-Japan

7417757 6MPQ -
SEO LIM No. 302 433 216 - Class: KR
ex O Dae Yang No. 302 *-1999*
Seo Lim Fisheries Co Ltd
-
Busan *South Korea*
MMSI: 440964000
Official number: 9502048-6210005
1974-08 **Daedong Shipbuilding Co Ltd — Busan**
Yd No: 128
Loa 55.94 Br ex - Dght 3.650
Lbp 49.51 Br md 8.60 Dpth 4.09
Welded, 1 dk
(B11B2FV) Fishing Vessel
Ins: 675
3 Ha: 2 (1.9 x 1.9) (1.3 x 0.9)ER
1 oil engine driving 1 FP propeller
Total Power: 993kW (1,350hp) 12.0kn
Akasaka AH28
1 x 4 Stroke 6 Cy. 280 x 440 993kW (1350bhp)
Akasaka Tekkosho KK (Akasaka DieselLtd)-Japan
AuxGen: 2 x 200kW 225V a.c

9031014 DSHH -
SEO NAM No. 1 107 - 57 Class: KR
Seonam Shipping Co Ltd
-
Yeosu *South Korea*
Official number: YSR-905149
1990-03 **Namyang Shipbuilding Co Ltd — Yeosu**
Yd No: 1015
Loa 27.51 Br ex 7.83 Dght 2.800
Lbp 24.49 Br md 7.61 Dpth 3.31
Welded, 1 dk
(B32A2ST) Tug
2 oil engines with clutches, flexible couplings & sr geared to sc. shafts driving 2 Directional propellers
Total Power: 956kW (1,300hp) 11.5kn
Niigata 6NSD-M
2 x 4 Stroke 6 Cy. 160 x 210 each-478kW (650bhp)
Ssangyong Heavy Industries Co Ltd-South Korea

8816508 6NIL -
SEO YANG No. 16 183 - 225 Class: (KR)
ex Jin Hae No. 158 *-1993*
Seoyang Moolsan Co Ltd
-
Busan *South Korea*
Official number: BS02-A2603
1988-03 **Jinhae Ship Construction Industrial Co Ltd — Changwon**
Loa 44.00 Br ex - Dght 3.010
Lbp 37.75 Br md 7.01 Dpth 3.41
Welded, 1 dk
(B12B2FC) Fish Carrier
Bale: 304
7 Ha: (2.9 x 2.6)2 (2.9 x 3.2) (2.9 x 2.3) (2.9 x 2.9) (2.9 x 2.1) (2.9 x 1.6)
1 oil engine driving 1 FP propeller
Total Power: 824kW (1,120hp) 12.5kn
Daihatsu
1 x 4 Stroke 6 Cy. 260 x 320 824kW (1120bhp)
Daihatsu Diesel Manufacturing Co Lt-Japan
AuxGen: 2 x 88kW 225V a.c

IMO / Call sign / Flag	Name / Owner / Port	Tonnage	Class	Builder / Dimensions	Type	Machinery
6921567 *6MEO* -	**SEO YANG No. 89** *ex* Dong Bang No. 111 *-1994* *ex* Kwang Il No. 51 *-1982* *ex* Fujiura Maru No. 3 *-1978* *ex* Daien Maru No. 11 *-1978* **Seoyang Moolsan Co Ltd** - *Busan* South Korea Official number: 9511039-6260007	*499* 264 553	Class: (KR)	**1969 Miho Zosensho K.K. — Shimizu** Yd No: 700 Loa 57.00 Br ex 9.91 Dght 3.880 Lbp 50.79 Br md 9.80 Dpth 4.15 Welded, 1 dk	**(B11B2FV) Fishing Vessel** Ins: 851 3 Ha: (1.3 x 0.9) (1.6 x 1.9) (1.9 x 1.9)	**1 oil engine** driving 1 FP propeller Total Power: 1,103kW (1,500hp) 11.8kn Niigata 6M37AHS 1 x 4 Stroke 6 Cy. 370 x 540 1103kW (1500bhp) Niigata Engineering Co Ltd-Japan AuxGen: 2 x 200kW 225V a.c
6720420 - -	**SEO YEUN** *ex* Ozuchi Maru *-1980* **Yong Nam Co Ltd** - *Incheon* South Korea Official number: ICR-675588	*287* 79 86	Class: (KR)	**1967 Shin Yamamoto Shipbuilding & Engineering Co Ltd — Kochi KC** Yd No: 88 Loa 31.81 Br ex 9.66 Dght 3.150 Lbp 29.01 Br md 9.58 Dpth 4.40 Riveted\Welded, 1 dk	**(B32A2ST) Tug**	**2 oil engines** driving 2 FP propellers Total Power: 1,066kW (1,450hp) 12.5kn MAN V6V22/30ATL 2 x Vee 4 Stroke 12 Cy. 220 x 300 each-533kW (725bhp) Kawasaki Dockyard Co Ltd-Japan AuxGen: 2 x 28kW 220V a.c
9208241 - -	**SEODONG CAR FERRY** *ex* Geogum Car Ferry No. 13 *-2012* **Seo Dong Maritime Co Ltd** - *Goheung* South Korea Official number: YSR-995625	**261** - 175	Class: (KR)	**1999-03 Moonchang Shipbuilding Dockyard Co Ltd — Mokpo** Yd No: 98-01 Loa 53.00 Br ex - Dght 1.861 Lbp 45.00 Br md 9.40 Dpth 2.70 Welded	**(A36A2PR) Passenger/Ro-Ro Ship (Vehicles)**	**1 oil engine** driving 1 FP propeller Total Power: 537kW (730hp) 13.4kn Caterpillar 3412TA 1 x Vee 4 Stroke 12 Cy. 137 x 152 537kW (730bhp) Caterpillar Inc-USA AuxGen: 1 x 104kW 225V a.c
9639139 - -	**SEODONG NO. 1** - **Mirae Shipping Co Ltd** - *Incheon* South Korea MMSI: 440013140 Official number: ICR-111824	*411* - 288	Class: KR	**2011-05 Moonchang Shipbuilding Dockyard Co Ltd — Mokpo** Yd No: 10-80 Loa 60.63 Br ex 12.00 Dght 2.040 Lbp 49.00 Br md 10.60 Dpth 2.85 Welded, 1 dk	**(A36A2PR) Passenger/Ro-Ro Ship (Vehicles)** Bow door/ramp (centre) Len: 9.00 Wid: 6.40 Swl: - Cars: 50	**2 oil engines** reverse reduction geared to sc. shaft (s) driving 2 FP propellers Total Power: 1,382kW (1,878hp) 14.0kn Mitsubishi S6R2-MTK2L 2 x 4 Stroke 6 Cy. 170 x 220 each-691kW (939bhp) Mitsubishi Heavy Industries Ltd-Japan
9637480 - -	**SEODONG NO. 2** - **Mirae Shipping Co Ltd** - *Incheon* South Korea Official number: ICR-111844	*399* - 288	Class: (KR)	**2011-06 Moonchang Shipbuilding Dockyard Co Ltd — Mokpo** Yd No: 10-81 Loa 60.63 Br ex 12.00 Dght 2.040 Lbp 49.00 Br md 10.60 Dpth 2.85 Welded, 1 dk	**(A36A2PR) Passenger/Ro-Ro Ship (Vehicles)** Passengers: unberthed: 250 Bow door/ramp (centre) Len: 9.00 Wid: 6.40 Swl: - Cars: 50	**2 oil engines** reverse reduction geared to sc. shaft (s) driving 2 FP propellers Total Power: 1,382kW (1,878hp) 14.0kn Mitsubishi S6R2-MTK2L 2 x 4 Stroke 6 Cy. 170 x 220 each-691kW (939bhp) Mitsubishi Heavy Industries Ltd-Japan AuxGen: 2 x 125kW 225V 60Hz a.c Fuel: 18.0 (d.f.)
9320192 - -	**SEODONG NO. 3** *ex* Cheong Ryong Car Ferry No. 501 *-2012* **Lee Sang Yun** - *Incheon* South Korea Official number: DSR-049066	*244* - 206	Class: KT (KR)	**2004-05 Moonchang Shipbuilding Dockyard Co Ltd — Mokpo** Yd No: 03-18 Loa 49.80 Br ex 12.00 Dght 1.812 Lbp 40.00 Br md 10.00 Dpth 2.40 Welded, 1 dk	**(A36A2PR) Passenger/Ro-Ro Ship (Vehicles)**	**2 oil engines** geared to sc. shafts driving 2 Propellers Total Power: 790kW (1,074hp) Cummins KTA-19-M 2 x 4 Stroke 6 Cy. 159 x 159 each-395kW (537bhp) Cummins India Ltd-India
9179878 *H3RM* -	**SEODONG SKY** *ex* Himawari No. 3 *-2013* *ex* Hakata Maru *-2004* **Seo Dong Maritime Co Ltd** - *Panama* Panama Official number: 019922752PE	*7,754* 2,326 4,120	Class: (NK)	**1997-11 Fukuoka Shipbuilding Co Ltd — Fukuoka FO** Yd No: 1200 Loa 132.82 (BB) Br ex - Dght 6.215 Lbp 123.00 Br md 21.40 Dpth 8.90 Welded, 1 dk	**(A36A2PR) Passenger/Ro-Ro Ship (Vehicles)** Passengers: 50 Angled stern door/ramp (p. a.) Trailers: 20 TEU 300 4 Ha: (11.9 x 10.6)3 (11.9 x 15.9)	**1 oil engine** driving 1 CP propeller Total Power: 12,379kW (16,830hp) 21.5kn Mitsubishi 9UEC50LSII 1 x 2 Stroke 9 Cy. 500 x 1950 12379kW (16830bhp) Kobe Hatsudoki KK-Japan Thrusters: 1 Thwart. CP thruster (f); 1 Tunnel thruster (a) Fuel: 600.0
9129691 *DSRB9* -	**SEOHAE GAS** *ex* Chiba Gas *-2011* *ex* Golden Crux No. 18 *-2010* **KDB Capital Corp** E Marine Co Ltd *Busan* South Korea MMSI: 440066000 Official number: BSR-101016	**2,991** 898 2,999 T/cm 11.6	Class: KR (NK)	**1995-12 Shin Kurushima Dockyard Co. Ltd. — Hashihama, Imabari** Yd No: 2892 Loa 95.92 (BB) Br ex 15.03 Dght 5.116 Lbp 89.95 Br md 15.00 Dpth 7.20 Welded, 1 dk	**(A11B2TG) LPG Tanker** Double Bottom Entire Compartment Length Liq (Gas): 3,273 2 x Gas Tank (s); 2 cyl horizontal 2 Cargo Pump (s): 2x300m³/hr Manifold: Bow/CM: 43.4m	**1 oil engine** driving 1 FP propeller Total Power: 2,869kW (3,901hp) 14.5kn Mitsubishi 6UEC37LA 1 x 2 Stroke 6 Cy. 370 x 880 2869kW (3901bhp) Akasaka Tekkosho KK (Akasaka DieselLtd)-Japan Fuel: 141.0 (d.f.) 453.0 (r.f.)
9213789 - -	**SEOHO NO. 7** *ex* Tatsumi *-2006* **Seoho Shipping Co Ltd** - *Yeosu* South Korea Official number: YSR-065639	**148** - 89	Class: KR	**2000-05 Niigata Engineering Co Ltd — Niigata NI** Yd No: 2370 Loa 31.02 Br ex - Dght 2.956 Lbp 27.00 Br md 8.80 Dpth 3.50 Welded, 1 dk	**(B32A2ST) Tug**	**2 oil engines** Geared Integral to driving 2 Z propellers Total Power: 2,354kW (3,200hp) Niigata 6L25HX 2 x 4 Stroke 6 Cy. 250 x 350 each-1177kW (1600bhp) Niigata Engineering Co Ltd-Japan AuxGen: 2 x 80kW 225V a.c
7362976 *DTBP2* -	**SEOHYUN 101** *ex* Guetndar *-2010* *ex* Sirius *-2001* *ex* Pole Star *-1999* *ex* Ain Chegag *-1994* *ex* Nam Yang *-1982* **Seokyung Corp** - *Busan* South Korea Official number: 0501001-6261402	**889** 435 -	Class: (PR) (AB)	**1974-12 Astilleros del Atlantico S.A. — Santander** Yd No: 158 Loa 64.70 Br ex - Dght 4.319 Lbp 57.00 Br md 10.60 Dpth 6.68 Welded, 1 dk	**(B11A2FS) Stern Trawler**	**1 oil engine** driving 1 FP propeller Total Power: 1,361kW (1,850hp) 11.0kn Deutz RBV6M358 1 x 4 Stroke 6 Cy. 400 x 580 1361kW (1850bhp) Hijos de J Barreras SA-Spain
8705319 *D7LY* -	**SEOKYUNG PARADISE** *ex* New Dong Chun *-2013* *ex* Huadong Pearl *-2006* *ex* Ferry Cosmo *-2002* *ex* Ferry Muroto *-2002* **Seokyung Car Ferry Co Ltd** - *Busan* South Korea MMSI: 441908000 Official number: BSR-130012	**12,961** 3,888 2,404	Class: KR	**1987-07 Kurushima Dockyard Co. Ltd. — Onishi** Yd No: 2516 Loa 127.41 (BB) Br ex 23.02 Dght 5.450 Lbp 123.02 Br md 23.00 Dpth 12.50 Welded	**(A36A2PR) Passenger/Ro-Ro Ship (Vehicles)** Passengers: unberthed: 855; cabins: 6; berths: 12 Bow door & ramp Stern door/ramp Lane-Len: 660 Lane-clr ht: 5.20 Lorries: 63, Cars: 48	**2 oil engines** with clutches, flexible couplings & sr geared to sc. shafts driving 2 CP propellers Total Power: 16,402kW (22,300hp) 21.0kn Pielstick 7PC40L570 2 x 4 Stroke 7 Cy. 570 x 620 each-8201kW (11150bhp) Ishikawajima Harima Heavy IndustrieCo Ltd (IHI)-Japan Thrusters: 1 Thwart. CP thruster (f); 1 Tunnel thruster (a)
9241748 - -	**SEOMSARANG NO. 1** - **Government of The Republic of South Korea (Ministry of Land, Transport & Maritime Affairs)** Hae Kwang Transport Ltd *Mokpo* South Korea Official number: MPR-004861	**101** - 57	Class: (KR)	**2000-11 Packcheon Shipbuilding & Engineering Co Ltd — Mokpo** Yd No: 00-163 Loa 36.70 Br ex - Dght 1.409 Lbp 29.90 Br md 7.00 Dpth 1.90 Welded	**(A36A2PR) Passenger/Ro-Ro Ship (Vehicles)**	**2 oil engines** geared to sc. shafts driving 2 FP propellers Total Power: 716kW (974hp) 11.5kn Caterpillar 3408C 2 x Vee 4 Stroke 8 Cy. 137 x 152 each-358kW (487bhp) Caterpillar Inc-USA Fuel: 11.0 (r.f.)
9260512 - -	**SEOMSARANG NO. 3** - **Government of The Republic of South Korea (Ministry of Oceans & Fisheries)** Hae Nam Transportation Co Ltd *Mokpo* South Korea Official number: MPR-014951	**124** - 226	Class: KR	**2001-11 Korea Shipyard Co Ltd — Mokpo** Yd No: 100 Loa 37.90 Br ex - Dght 1.400 Lbp 29.90 Br md 7.00 Dpth 1.90 Welded	**(A36A2PR) Passenger/Ro-Ro Ship (Vehicles)** Cars: 17	**2 oil engines** reduction geared to sc. shafts driving 2 FP propellers Total Power: 716kW (974hp) 12.5kn Caterpillar 3408C 2 x Vee 4 Stroke 8 Cy. 137 x 152 each-358kW (487bhp) Caterpillar Inc-USA
9281243 - -	**SEOMSARANG NO. 5** - **Government of The Republic of South Korea (Ministry of Land, Transport & Maritime Affairs)** - *Mokpo* South Korea MMSI: 440302010 Official number: MPR-024901	*150* - 89	Class: (KR)	**2002-10 Packcheon Shipbuilding & Engineering Co Ltd — Mokpo** Yd No: 02-165 Loa 44.50 Br ex 9.00 Dght 1.610 Lbp 35.50 Br md 8.00 Dpth 2.10 Welded, 1 Dk.	**(A36A2PR) Passenger/Ro-Ro Ship (Vehicles)** Cars: 18	**2 oil engines** geared to sc. shafts driving 2 Propellers Total Power: 794kW (1,080hp) 14.0kn Caterpillar 3412TA 2 x Vee 4 Stroke 12 Cy. 137 x 152 each-397kW (540bhp) Caterpillar Inc-USA
9305520 -	**SEOMSARANG NO. 6** - **Government of The Republic of South Korea (Ministry of Land, Transport & Maritime Affairs)** Mokpo Dae Heung Co *Mokpo* South Korea Official number: MPR-034931	**177** - -	Class: KR	**2003-10 Packcheon Shipbuilding & Engineering Co Ltd — Mokpo** Yd No: 03-166 Loa 49.80 Br ex - Dght 1.600 Lbp 40.99 Br md 8.00 Dpth 2.20 Welded, 1 dk	**(A37B2PS) Passenger Ship**	**2 oil engines** geared to sc. shafts driving 2 CP propellers Total Power: 904kW (1,230hp) 14.5kn Caterpillar 3412E 2 x Vee 4 Stroke 12 Cy. 137 x 152 each-452kW (615bhp) Caterpillar Inc-USA

9380702 - -	**SEOMSARANG NO. 7** **The Mokpo Regional Martime Affairs & Fisheries Office** Cheongsan Agricultural Cooperative Association *Mokpo* *South Korea* Official number: MPR-064841	**151** - 83	Class: KR	**2006-05 Packcheon Shipbuilding & Engineering Co Ltd — Mokpo** Yd No: 05-180 Loa 44.50 Br ex 9.00 Dght 1.610 Lbp 35.50 Br md - Dpth 2.10 Welded, 1 dk	**(A36A2PR) Passenger/Ro-Ro Ship (Vehicles)** Cars: 19	**2 oil engines** reduction geared to sc. shafts driving 2 FP propellers Total Power: 794kW (1,080hp) 13.0kn Caterpillar 3412E-TA 2 x Vee 4 Stroke 12 Cy. 137 x 152 each-397kW (540bhp) Caterpillar Inc-USA
9241700 *DSFS8* -	**SEONG HEE** **Pukwan Ferry Co Ltd** - *Jeju* *South Korea* MMSI: 441163000 Official number: JJR-028846	**16,875** 5,849 3,750	Class: KR	**2002-03 Hyundai Mipo Dockyard Co Ltd — Ulsan** Yd No: 0027 Loa 162.00 Br ex - Dght 5.600 Lbp 150.00 Br md 23.60 Dpth 14.55 Welded	**(A36A2PR) Passenger/Ro-Ro Ship (Vehicles)** Passengers: 560 Cars: 9, Trailers: 44 TEU 4 C. 4/20'	**2 oil engines** reduction geared to sc. shafts driving 2 CP propellers Total Power: 8,826kW (12,000hp) 18.7kn Daihatsu 8DLM-40A 2 x 4 Stroke 8 Cy. 400 x 480 each-4413kW (6000bhp) Daihatsu Diesel Manufacturing Co Lt-Japan
9458315 *DSQJ6* -	**SEONGHO ACE** **Seong Ho Shipping Co Ltd** - SatCom: Inmarsat C 444060110 *Jeju* *South Korea* MMSI: 441601000 Official number: JJR-092173	**8,577** 4,095 13,127 T/cm 23.2	Class: KR	**2009-06 Ilheung Shipbuilding & Engineering Co Ltd — Mokpo** Yd No: 07-140 Loa 128.60 (BB) Br ex - Dght 8.714 Lbp 119.92 Br md 20.40 Dpth 11.53 Welded, 1 dk	**(A12B2TR) Chemical/Products Tanker** Double Hull (13F) Liq: 13,400; Liq (Oil): 13,400 Cargo Heating Coils Compartments: 12 Wing Ta, 2 Wing Slop Ta, ER 12 Cargo Pump (s): 12x300m³/hr Manifold: Bow/CM: 61.3m	**1 oil engine** driving 1 FP propeller Total Power: 4,200kW (5,710hp) 13.4kn MAN-B&W 6S35MC 1 x 2 Stroke 6 Cy. 350 x 1400 4200kW (5710bhp) STX Engine Co Ltd-South Korea Thrusters: 1 Tunnel thruster (f) Fuel: 45.0 (d.f.) 540.0 (r.f.)
9427237 *DSPF9* -	**SEONGHO BONANZA** **Seong Ho Shipping Co Ltd** - *Jeju* *South Korea* MMSI: 440918000 Official number: JJR-079471	**3,690** 1,777 5,555 T/cm 13.8	Class: KR	**2007-06 Ilheung Shipbuilding & Engineering Co Ltd — Mokpo** Yd No: 06-135 Loa 101.00 (BB) Br ex - Dght 6.613 Lbp 94.12 Br md 16.00 Dpth 8.50 Welded, 1 dk	**(A12B2TR) Chemical/Products Tanker** Double Hull (13F) Liq: 6,049; Liq (Oil): 6,370 Cargo Heating Coils Compartments: 10 Wing Ta, 2 Wing Slop Ta, ER 12 Cargo Pump (s): 12x200m³/hr Manifold: Bow/CM: 55.5m	**1 oil engine** driving 1 FP propeller Total Power: 2,648kW (3,600hp) 14.5kn Hanshin LH41LA 1 x 4 Stroke 6 Cy. 410 x 800 2648kW (3600bhp) The Hanshin Diesel Works Ltd-Japan AuxGen: 3 x 260kW 440V a.c Fuel: 44.4 (d.f.) 239.0 (r.f.)
9427251 *D8QR* -	**SEONGHO GALAXY** **Seong Ho Shipping Co Ltd** - *Jeju* *South Korea* MMSI: 440133000 Official number: JJR-079977	**3,690** 1,777 5,526 T/cm 13.8	Class: KR	**2007-10 Ilheung Shipbuilding & Engineering Co Ltd — Mokpo** Yd No: 06-136 Loa 101.00 (BB) Br ex - Dght 6.610 Lbp 94.12 Br md 16.00 Dpth 8.50 Welded, 1 dk	**(A12B2TR) Chemical/Products Tanker** Double Hull (13F) Liq: 6,370; Liq (Oil): 6,370 Cargo Heating Coils Compartments: 10 Wing Ta, 2 Wing Slop Ta, ER 2 Cargo Pump (s): 2x200m³/hr Manifold: Bow/CM: 55.5m	**1 oil engine** driving 1 Propeller Total Power: 2,648kW (3,600hp) 14.5kn Hanshin LH41LA 1 x 4 Stroke 6 Cy. 410 x 800 2648kW (3600bhp) The Hanshin Diesel Works Ltd-Japan AuxGen: 4 x 260kW 440V a.c Fuel: 50.0 (d.f.) 251.0 (r.f.)
9321421 *DSOU9* -	**SEONGHO MERCURY** *ex* Minitank Four *-2006* **Seong Ho Shipping Co Ltd** - *Jeju* *South Korea* MMSI: 440367000 Official number: JJR-069559	**5,570** 2,524 8,033 T/cm 17.7	Class: KR (AB)	**2006-08 Nokbong Shipbuilding Co Ltd — Geoje** Yd No: 400 Loa 113.09 (BB) Br ex 18.20 Dght 7.463 Lbp 105.00 Br md 18.20 Dpth 9.60 Welded, 1 dk	**(A12B2TR) Chemical/Products Tanker** Double Hull (13F) Liq: 8,549; Liq (Oil): 8,549 Cargo Heating Coils Compartments: 10 Wing Ta, 2 Wing Slop Ta, ER 12 Cargo Pump (s): 12x200m³/hr Manifold: Bow/CM: 57.9m	**1 oil engine** driving 1 CP propeller Total Power: 3,375kW (4,589hp) 13.7kn Wartsila 9R32LN 1 x 4 Stroke 9 Cy. 320 x 350 3375kW (4589bhp) Wartsila Finland Oy-Finland AuxGen: 3 x 600kW 450V 60Hz a.c, 1 x 1200kW 450V 60Hz a.c Thrusters: 1 Tunnel thruster (f) Fuel: 73.0 (d.f.) 475.0 (r.f.)
9496094 *DSQF5* -	**SEONGHO PIOCE** **Seong Ho Shipping Co Ltd** - *Jeju* *South Korea* MMSI: 441556000 Official number: JJR-084647	**3,698** 1,777 5,538 T/cm 13.8	Class: KR	**2008-10 Ilheung Shipbuilding & Engineering Co Ltd — Mokpo** Yd No: 06-138 Loa 101.00 (BB) Br ex - Dght 6.613 Lbp 94.12 Br md 16.00 Dpth 8.50 Welded, 1 dk	**(A12B2TR) Chemical/Products Tanker** Double Hull (13F) Liq: 6,051; Liq (Oil): 6,051 Cargo Heating Coils Compartments: 10 Wing Ta, ER, 2 Wing Slop Ta 2 Cargo Pump (s): 2x200m³/hr Manifold: Bow/CM: 55.5m	**1 oil engine** driving 1 Propeller Total Power: 2,648kW (3,600hp) 14.5kn Hanshin LH41LA 1 x 4 Stroke 6 Cy. 410 x 800 2648kW (3600bhp) The Hanshin Diesel Works Ltd-Japan Fuel: 45.0 (d.f.) 230.0 (r.f.)
9193305 *DHBN* -	**SEOUL EXPRESS** *ex* Bremen Express *-2007* **Hapag-Lloyd AG** - *Hamburg* *Germany* MMSI: 211331640 Official number: 18795	**54,465** 23,876 66,971 T/cm 83.0	Class: GL	**2000-06 Hyundai Heavy Industries Co Ltd — Ulsan** Yd No: 1192 Loa 294.05 (BB) Br ex - Dght 13.550 Lbp 283.21 Br md 32.20 Dpth 21.80 Welded, 1 dk	**(A33A2CC) Container Ship (Fully Cellular)** TEU 4890 C Ho 2326 TEU C Dk 2564 TEU incl 370 ref C Compartments: 6 Cell Ho 17 Ha:	**1 oil engine** driving 1 FP propeller Total Power: 40,040kW (54,438hp) 24.0kn MAN-B&W 7K98MC 1 x 2 Stroke 7 Cy. 980 x 2660 40040kW (54438bhp) Hyundai Heavy Industries Co Ltd-South Korea AuxGen: 1 x 3000kW a.c, 2 x 2300kW a.c, 1 x 1750kW a.c Thrusters: 1 Thwart. FP thruster (f) Fuel: 335.0 (d.f.) (Heating Coils) 6612.0 (r.f.) 140.7pd
8619405 *DSOI4* -	**SEOUL GAS** *ex* OSM Brave *-2010* *ex* Sea Friend *-2009* *ex* Lingfield *-2005* *ex* Ulsan Gas *-1997* **Shinhan Capital Co Ltd** E Marine Co Ltd *Jeju* *South Korea* MMSI: 440717000 Official number: JJR-059346	**3,894** 1,168 3,240 T/cm 13.8	Class: KR (GL)	**1988-03 Korea Shipbuilding & Engineering Corp — Busan** Yd No: 1042 Loa 105.60 (BB) Br ex - Dght 5.028 Lbp 99.90 Br md 16.11 Dpth 8.01 Welded, 1 dk	**(A11B2TG) LPG Tanker** Double Hull (13F) Liq (Gas): 4,009 3 x Gas Tank (s); 3 membrane (stl) cyl horizontal 3 Cargo Pump (s): 3x350m³/hr Manifold: Bow/CM: 60.1m	**1 oil engine** driving 1 FP propeller Total Power: 2,346kW (3,190hp) 13.5kn Mitsubishi 6UEC37LA 1 x 2 Stroke 6 Cy. 370 x 880 2346kW (3190bhp) Hyundai Engine & Machinery Co Ltd-South Korea AuxGen: 2 x 240kW 450/220V 60Hz a.c Fuel: 74.5 (d.f.) 254.5 (r.f.)
9367839 *2BOC4* -	**SEOUL TOWER** **Kelpin Shipping Ltd** Zodiac Maritime Agencies Ltd *London* *United Kingdom* MMSI: 235067873 Official number: 915351	**26,638** 11,896 34,325 T/cm 47.0	Class: LR ✠ **100A1** SS 01/2014 container ship **ShipRight** (SDA, CM) *IWS LI ✠ **LMC** **UMS** Eq.Ltr: 0†; Cable: 660.0/78.0 U3 (a)	**2009-01 Xiamen Shipbuilding Industry Co Ltd — Xiamen FJ** Yd No: XSI405D Loa 211.85 (BB) Br ex 29.80 Dght 11.400 Lbp 199.95 Br md 29.80 Dpth 16.70 Welded, 1 dk	**(A33A2CC) Container Ship (Fully Cellular)** TEU 2578 C Ho 958 TEU C Dk 1620 TEU incl 354 ref C. Compartments: 5 Cell Ho, ER 10 Ha: ER Cranes: 3x45t	**1 oil engine** driving 1 FP propeller Total Power: 21,560kW (29,313hp) 22.0kn Wartsila 7RTA72U 1 x 2 Stroke 7 Cy. 720 x 2500 21560kW (29313bhp) Dalian Marine Diesel Co Ltd-China AuxGen: 3 x 2400kW 450V 60Hz a.c Boilers: WTAuxB (Comp) 9.2kgf/cm² (9.0bar) Thrusters: 1 Thwart. CP thruster (f)
9230268 *D7LH* -	**SEOYOUNG** *ex* Eagle Asia 06 *-2013* *ex* Global Eos *-2013* **Myungsan Shipping Co Ltd** - *Jeju* *South Korea* MMSI: 440036000 Official number: JJR-131049	**6,757** 3,763 11,679 T/cm 20.1	Class: KR (AB)	**2000-09 Higaki Zosen K.K. — Imabari** Yd No: 518 Loa 121.29 (BB) Br ex - Dght 8.500 Lbp 113.50 Br md 19.60 Dpth 11.40 Welded, 1 dk	**(A12A2TC) Chemical Tanker** Double Hull (13F) Cargo Heating Coils Compartments: 14 Wing Ta, ER 14 Cargo Pump (s): 6x200m³/hr, 8x300m³/hr Manifold: Bow/CM: 61m	**1 oil engine** driving 1 FP propeller Total Power: 4,565kW (6,207hp) 13.6kn Mitsubishi 6UEC45LA 1 x 2 Stroke 6 Cy. 450 x 1350 4565kW (6207bhp) Kobe Hatsudoki KK-Japan Fuel: 110.0 (d.f.) 513.0 (r.f.)
9620152 *A6E2227* -	**SEP-450** **National Petroleum Construction Co (NPCC)** - *Abu Dhabi* *United Arab Emirates* MMSI: 470340000 Official number: 0006872	**5,685** 1,705 -	Class: AB	**2012-04 National Petroleum Construction Co — Abu Dhabi** Yd No: 0098 Loa 77.30 Br ex - Dght 3.650 Lbp 61.00 Br md 36.00 Dpth 6.00 Welded, 1 dk	**(B22A2ZM) Offshore Construction Vessel, jack up**	**4 diesel electric oil engines** driving 4 gen. Connecting to 3 elec. motors each (1200kW) driving 3 Azimuth electric drive units Wartsila 4 x 4 Stroke Wartsila Diesel S.A.-Bermeo
9066162 - -	**SEP ASO** **Daiichi Kensetsu Kiko Co Ltd** - *Nishinomiya, Hyogo* *Japan*	**579** 173 -	Class: NK	**1992-10 Iguchi Zosen Y.K. — Onomichi** Yd No: 507 L reg 32.64 Br ex - Dght 1.710 Lbp 34.00 Br md 20.00 Dpth 3.00 Welded	**(Z11C4ZM) Support Platform, jack up**	**1 oil engine** driving 1 FP propeller
8503618 *9BSR* -	**SEPAHAN** *ex* Seasafe *-2009* *ex* Shinei Maru *-2006* - - *Iran* MMSI: 422800000	*403* - 850		**1985-09 Koa Sangyo KK — Takamatsu KG** Yd No: 522 Loa 55.00 Br ex - Dght 3.631 Lbp 50.02 Br md 9.01 Dpth 4.12 Welded, 1 dk	**(A12A2TC) Chemical Tanker** Liq: 626 Compartments: 6 Ta, ER	**1 oil engine** driving 1 FP propeller Total Power: 736kW (1,001hp) Yanmar MF28-ST 1 x 4 Stroke 6 Cy. 280 x 450 736kW (1001bhp) Yanmar Diesel Engine Co Ltd-Japan
9448061 *DUBZ* -	**SEPANG EXPRESS** **PCTC Express VII BV** Vroon BV SatCom: Inmarsat C 454882110 *Manila* *Philippines* MMSI: 548821000 Official number: MNLA000738	**43,810** 13,143 15,154	Class: NK	**2009-12 Mitsubishi Heavy Industries Ltd. — Shimonoseki** Yd No: 1134 Loa 180.00 (BB) Br ex 30.03 Dght 9.222 Lbp 171.70 Br md 30.00 Dpth 33.52 Welded, 10 dks. incl. 2 liftable dks.	**(A35B2RV) Vehicles Carrier** Side door/ramp (s) Len: - Wid: - Swl: 25 Quarter stern door/ramp (s. a.) Len: - Wid: - Swl: 100 Cars: 3,205	**1 oil engine** driving 1 FP propeller Total Power: 11,900kW (16,179hp) 19.9kn Mitsubishi 8UEC50LSII 1 x 2 Stroke 8 Cy. 500 x 1950 11900kW (16179bhp) Mitsubishi Heavy Industries Ltd-Japan AuxGen: 3 x 875kW 450V 60Hz a.c Thrusters: 1 Thwart. CP thruster (f) Fuel: 2320.0 (r.f.)

IMO / Call sign	Ship / Owner	Tonnage	Class	Builder / Dimensions	Type / Capacity	Machinery
9237292 *9BRE* -	**SEPANO** *ex* Trava *-2007* *ex* Kanin *-2007* **Parsian Golden Sea Shipping Co** - SatCom: Inmarsat C 442200016 *Bandar Anzali* *Iran* MMSI: 422756000 Official number: 893	**4,953** 1,645 6,239 T/cm 20.0	Class: AS (RS) (GL)	**2000-10 Sudostroitelnyy Zavod "Krasnoye Sormovo" — Nizhniy Novgorod** Yd No: 19610/43 Loa 139.93 Br ex 16.65 Dght 4.670 Lbp 135.97 Br md 16.40 Dpth 6.70 Welded, 1 dk	**(A31A2GX) General Cargo Ship** Grain: 6,843; Bale: 6,785 Ice Capable	**2 oil engines** geared to sc. shafts driving 2 FP propellers Total Power: 2,200kW (2,992hp) 10.0kn S.K.L. 6VDS29/24AL-2 2 x 4 Stroke 6 Cy. 240 x 290 each-1100kW (1496bhp) SKL Motoren u. Systemtechnik AG-Magdeburg Fuel: 380.0
8879500 *HMT4* -	**SEPAS** *ex* Shoryu *-2013* **Nejoum Al Bahar Shipping & Cargo LLC** *Wonsan* *North Korea* Official number: 195763	*199* 100 -		**1994-12 K.K. Kamishima Zosensho — Osakikamijima** Yd No: 572 Loa 53.77 Br ex - Dght - Lbp 47.00 Br md 9.00 Dpth 5.20 Welded, 1 dk	**(A31A2GX) General Cargo Ship** Bale: 1,059 Compartments: 1 Ho, ER 1 Ha: (27.5 x 7.0)ER	**1 oil engine** driving 1 FP propeller Total Power: 736kW (1,001hp) 10.5kn Hanshin LH26G 1 x 4 Stroke 6 Cy. 260 x 440 736kW (1001bhp) The Hanshin Diesel Works Ltd-Japan
8874495 *9BSO* -	**SEPAS** *ex* Arnold Ikkonen *-2008* **Parsian Golden Sea Shipping Co** - *Bandar Anzali* *Iran* MMSI: 422797000 Official number: 900	**4,110** 1,327 5,025	Class: AS (RS) (GL)	**1994-10 Sudostroitelnyy Zavod "Krasnoye Sormovo" — Nizhniy Novgorod** Yd No: 19611/31 Loa 117.39 Br ex 16.64 Dght 4.800 Lbp 111.40 Br md 16.60 Dpth 6.72 Welded, 1 dk	**(A31A2GX) General Cargo Ship** Grain: 5,087; Bale: 4,985 TEU 104 C. 104/20' Compartments: 3 Ho, ER 3 Ha: (22.0 x 11.8)2 (21.4 x 11.8)ER Ice Capable	**2 oil engines** driving 2 FP propellers Total Power: 1,940kW (2,638hp) 11.0kn S.K.L. 8NVDS48A-3U 2 x 4 Stroke 8 Cy. 320 x 480 each-970kW (1319bhp) SKL Motoren u. Systemtechnik AG-Magdeburg AuxGen: 3 x 150kW Thrusters: 1 Thwart. FP thruster (f) Fuel: 417.0 (r.f.) 11.4pd
8976683 - -	**SEPATI** **PT Etam Kalimantan Raya** *Balikpapan* *Indonesia*	**202** 61 -	Class: KI	**1998-06 P.T. Galangan Tanjung Batu — Balikpapan** Loa 28.90 Br ex - Dght - Lbp 24.90 Br md 8.00 Dpth 3.60 Welded, 1 dk	**(B32A2ST) Tug**	**2 oil engines** geared to sc. shafts driving 2 Propellers Total Power: 1,266kW (1,722hp) 10.0kn Caterpillar D398 2 x Vee 4 Stroke 12 Cy. 159 x 203 each-633kW (861bhp) Caterpillar Inc-USA AuxGen: 2 x 55kW 380V a.c
8721454 *EPCL7* -	**SEPEHR ARTIN** *ex* Georgiy Zhukov *-2013* *ex* Amur-2519 *-2007* **Sepehr Parsiyan Co** - *Iran* MMSI: 422049900	**3,086** 999 3,329	Class: RR (RS)	**1987-06 Zavody Tazkeho Strojarstva (ZTS) — Komarno** Yd No: 2319 Loa 115.70 Br ex 13.43 Dght 4.130 Lbp 111.20 Br md 13.00 Dpth 6.00 Welded, 1 dk	**(A31A2GX) General Cargo Ship** Grain: 4,064 TEU 102 C.Ho 62/20' (40') C.Dk 40/20' (40') Compartments: 3 Ho, ER 3 Ha: (11.6 x 10.1) (23.0 x 10.1) (24.0 x 10.1)ER	**2 oil engines** reverse reduction geared to sc. shafts driving 2 FP propellers Total Power: 1,030kW (1,400hp) 10.0kn Skoda 6L275A2 2 x 4 Stroke 6 Cy. 275 x 350 each-515kW (700bhp) CKD Praha-Praha AuxGen: 3 x 138kW 220/380V a.c, 1 x 25kW 220/380V a.c Thrusters: 1 Thwart. FP thruster (f) Fuel: 157.0 (d.f.)
9311385 *9AA6416* -	**SEPEN** *ex* LS Anne *-2009* *ex* Brovig Mistral *-2009* *ex* Vedrey Heimer *-2008* *ex* LS Anne *-2007* *ex* Veysel Bey *-2006* **Adriatic Chemical KS** Dinamarin doo *Rijeka* *Croatia* MMSI: 238256000	**2,701** 1,205 3,500 T/cm 10.8	Class: CS NV (GL) (BV)	**2004-10 Yildirim Gemi Insaat Sanayii A.S. — Tuzla** Yd No: 101 Loa 92.86 (BB) Br ex - Dght 5.700 Lbp 86.65 Br md 14.10 Dpth 7.20 Welded, 1 dk	**(A12B2TR) Chemical/Products Tanker** Double Hull (13F) Liq: 4,223; Liq (Oil): 4,223 Compartments: 10 Ta, 1 Slop Ta, ER 10 Cargo Pump (s): 10x300m^3/hr Manifold: Bow/CM: 41m Ice Capable	**1 oil engine** reduction geared to sc. shaft driving 1 CP propeller Total Power: 2,040kW (2,774hp) 12.0kn MAN-B&W 6L27/38 1 x 4 Stroke 6 Cy. 270 x 380 2040kW (2774bhp) MAN B&W Diesel AG-Augsburg AuxGen: 2 x 504kW 380/220V 50Hz a.c, 1 x 500kW 380/220V 50Hz a.c Thrusters: 1 Thwart. FP thruster (f) Fuel: 47.6 (d.f.) (Heating Coils) 208.5 (r.f.) 10.0pd
9496343 *D5FA2* -	**SEPETIBA BAY** *ex* Orient Approach *-2013* **P&B Shipping Co LLP** Companhia de Navegacao Norsul *Monrovia* *Liberia* MMSI: 636016208 Official number: 16208	**23,426** 11,082 33,755 T/cm 48.8	Class: NV	**2012-06 Samjin Shipbuilding Industries Co Ltd — Weihai SD** Yd No: 1020 Loa 180.00 (BB) Br ex - Dght 9.800 Lbp 172.00 Br md 30.00 Dpth 14.70 Welded, 1 dk	**(A21A2BC) Bulk Carrier** Grain: 46,284; Bale: 45,570 Compartments: 5 Ho, ER 5 Ha: ER Cranes: 4x35t	**1 oil engine** driving 1 FP propeller Total Power: 8,580kW (11,665hp) 14.0kn MAN-B&W 6S50MC 1 x 2 Stroke 6 Cy. 500 x 1910 8580kW (11665bhp) AuxGen: 3 x a.c
9369992 *D5DS4* -	**SEPHORA** *ex* Kt Venture *-2013* **Prospero Marine Ltd** Nordic Shipping AS *Monrovia* *Liberia* MMSI: 636015958 Official number: 15958	**30,766** 18,071 55,866 T/cm 56.1	Class: BV	**2007-06 Kawasaki Shipbuilding Corp — Kobe HG** Yd No: 1577 Loa 189.90 (BB) Br ex 32.26 Dght 12.520 Lbp 185.00 Br md 32.26 Dpth 17.80 Welded, 1 dk	**(A21A2BC) Bulk Carrier** Grain: 69,450; Bale: 66,368 Compartments: 5 Ho, ER 5 Ha: 4 (20.5 x 18.6)ER (17.8 x 18.6) Cranes: 4x30.5t	**1 oil engine** driving 1 FP propeller Total Power: 8,200kW (11,149hp) 14.6kn MAN-B&W 6S50MC-C 1 x 2 Stroke 6 Cy. 500 x 2000 8200kW (11149bhp) Kawasaki Heavy Industries Ltd-Japan AuxGen: 3 x a.c
9043201 - -	**SEPIA 1** *ex* Chefalu 13 *-1998* - -	**142** - 198	Class: (RN)	**1995-04 Santierul Naval Tulcea — Tulcea** Yd No: 7710 Loa 25.65 Br ex 7.20 Dght 2.407 Lbp 22.00 Br md - Dpth 3.40 Welded	**(B11B2FV) Fishing Vessel**	**1 oil engine** sr geared to sc. shaft driving 1 FP propeller Total Power: 220kW (299hp) 10.0kn S.K.L. 6VD18/15AL-1 1 x 4 Stroke 6 Cy. 150 x 180 220kW (299bhp) VEB Elbe Werk-Rosslau AuxGen: 2 x 28kW 380V 50Hz a.c Fuel: 12.0 (d.f.)
7128605 *9BMD* -	**SEPIDAN** *ex* Lillian XXII *-1991* *ex* Nanna Buur *-1974* **Mr H Momeni** - *Bushehr* *Iran* Official number: 16561	**232** 92 354	Class: AS (AB) (BV)	**1971-12 Blaalid Slip & Mek Verksted AS — Raudeberg** Yd No: 25 Converted From: General Cargo Ship Loa 33.05 Br ex 7.01 Dght 3.201 Lbp 30.99 Br md 7.00 Dpth 3.36 Welded, 1 dk	**(B22A2OV) Diving Support Vessel** Compartments: 1 Ho, ER 1 Ha: (16.9 x 5.0)ER Cranes: 1x4t; Derricks: 1x4t	**2 oil engines** driving 2 Directional propellers Total Power: 338kW (460hp) 10.0kn Scania DSI11 2 x 4 Stroke 6 Cy. 127 x 145 each-169kW (230bhp) Saab Scania do Brasil SA-Brazil AuxGen: 1 x 35kW 220V 50Hz a.c Fuel: 30.5 (d.f.)
8518091 *P2NC* -	**SEPIK COAST** *ex* Niugini Coast *-2005* **Anton Lee Transport Pty Ltd** Consort Express Lines Pty Ltd SatCom: Inmarsat C 455300046 *Port Moresby* *Papua New Guinea* MMSI: 553111131 Official number: 000386	**1,951** 1,223 2,323	Class: AB	**1986-08 Donghai Shipyard — Shanghai** Yd No: 102 Lengthened-1989 Loa 77.53 Br ex 13.85 Dght 4.905 Lbp 72.50 Br md 13.81 Dpth 6.10 Welded, 1 dk	**(A31A2GX) General Cargo Ship** Grain: 3,172; Bale: 2,888 Compartments: 1 Ho, ER 2 Ha: ER Cranes: 1x25t,1x15t	**1 oil engine** reverse reduction geared to sc. shaft driving 1 FP propeller Total Power: 883kW (1,201hp) 10.5kn Wartsila 6R22D 1 x 4 Stroke 6 Cy. 220 x 240 883kW (1201bhp) Wartsila Power Singapore Pte Ltd-Singapore AuxGen: 3 x 105kW 240/415V 50Hz a.c
5130692 - -	**SEPIK DESTINY** *ex* Gurubi *-1976* *ex* Gimada *-1976* **South Sea Lines Ltd** - *Port Moresby* *Papua New Guinea* Official number: 000050	*210* 70 -		**1955 Clelands (Successors) Ltd. — Wallsend** Yd No: 206 L reg 32.01 Br ex 7.93 Dght - Lbp - Br md - Dpth - Welded, 1 dk	**(A31A2GX) General Cargo Ship**	**2 oil engines** geared to sc. shafts driving 2 FP propellers Gardner 8L3B 2 x 4 Stroke 8 Cy. 140 x 197 L. Gardner & Sons Ltd.-Manchester
9116785 *P2V5546* -	**SEPIK EXPRESS** *ex* Dollart *-2013* **Bismark Maritime Ltd** - *Port Moresby* *Papua New Guinea* Official number: 001375	**2,532** 1,351 3,560	Class: GL	**1995-12 Slovenske Lodenice a.s. — Komarno** Yd No: 1408 Loa 87.92 (BB) Br ex - Dght 5.518 Lbp 81.85 Br md 12.80 Dpth 7.10 Welded, 2 dks	**(A31A2GX) General Cargo Ship** Grain: 4,600; Bale: 4,588 TEU 174 C.Ho 108/20' (40') C.Dk 66/20' (40') incl. 18 ref C. Compartments: 1 Ho, ER, 1 Tw Dk 1 Ha: (56.6 x 10.2)ER Cranes: 2x35t Ice Capable	**1 oil engine** with clutches, flexible couplings & sr geared to sc. shaft driving 1 CP propeller Total Power: 1,470kW (1,999hp) 11.5kn MaK 8M332C 1 x 4 Stroke 8 Cy. 240 x 330 1470kW (1999bhp) Krupp MaK Maschinenbau GmbH-Kiel AuxGen: 1 x 376kW 380V 50Hz a.c, 2 x 230kW 380V 50Hz a.c Thrusters: 1 Thwart. FP thruster (f) Fuel: 195.0 (d.f.)
8103432 *YDXT* -	**SEPINGGAN/PERTAMINA 3008** **PT PERTAMINA (PERSERO)** - *Jakarta* *Indonesia* MMSI: 525008025	**21,747** 7,541 29,941 T/cm 46.0	Class: KI (LR) ✠ Classed LR until 12/3/08	**1982-12 Onomichi Dockyard Co Ltd — Onomichi HS** Yd No: 304 Loa 180.02 (BB) Br ex 30.03 Dght 8.856 Lbp 171.00 Br md 30.00 Dpth 15.02 Welded, 1 dk	**(A13B2TP) Products Tanker** Single Hull Liq: 39,302; Liq (Oil): 39,302 Part Cargo Heating Coils Compartments: 10 Ta, ER 3 Cargo Pump (s): 3x1000m^3/hr Manifold: Bow/CM: 90m	**1 oil engine** driving 1 FP propeller Total Power: 9,731kW (13,230hp) 15.0kn Sulzer 6RLB66 1 x 2 Stroke 6 Cy. 660 x 1400 9731kW (13230bhp) Ishikawajima Harima Heavy IndustrieCo Ltd (IHI)-Japan AuxGen: 3 x 680kW 450V 60Hz a.c Boilers: e 22.5kgf/cm^2 (22.1bar), AuxB (o.f.) 18.0kgf/cm^2 (17.7bar) Fuel: 213.0 (d.f.) (Part Heating Coils) 930.0 (r.f.) 39.0pd

9099638 *FMDS* MA 917369	**SEPTIMANIE II** **Barba & Rico** - *Marseille* *France* MMSI: 228210900 Official number: 917369R	**149** - -		**2005-01 in France** Loa 24.90 (BB) Br ex - Dght - Lbp 22.40 Br md - Dpth - Welded, 1 dk	**(B11A2FS) Stern Trawler**	**1 oil engine** driving 1 Propeller Total Power: 316kW (430hp) Thrusters: 1 Thwart. FP thruster (f)
8733823 *EA3135* 3-GI-47-97	**SEPTIMO** **Nicolasin SL** - - *Santander* *Spain* Official number: 3-7/1997	**110** 33 -		**1997-01 Astilleros Ria de Aviles SL — Nieva** Loa 22.50 Br ex - Dght - Lbp 17.50 Br md 5.80 Dpth 2.75 Welded, 1 dk	**(B11B2FV) Fishing Vessel**	**1 oil engine** driving 1 Propeller Total Power: 198kW (269hp)
9627679 *ZGBE8* -	**SEPTIMUS** *ex* Satori *-2014* **IL Dono Ltd** Dohle Private Clients Ltd *George Town* *Cayman Islands (British)* MMSI: 319824000 Official number: 742982	**499** 149 -	Class: AB	**2011-05 Heesen Shipyards B.V. — Oss** Yd No: 15250 Loa 49.80 Br ex 8.95 Dght 1.980 Lbp 42.97 Br md 8.95 Dpth 4.03 Welded, 1 dk	**(X11A2YP) Yacht** Hull Material: Aluminium Alloy	**2 oil engines** reduction geared to sc. shafts driving 2 FP propellers Total Power: 3,520kW (4,786hp) M.T.U. 16V4000M60 2 x Vee 4 Stroke 16 Cy. 165 x 190 each-1760kW (2393bhp) MTU Friedrichshafen GmbH-Friedrichshafen
8129101 *P24374* -	**SEPURA** **Government of Papua New Guinea (Department of Transport & Civil Aviation)** - *Port Moresby* *Papua New Guinea* Official number: 000344	*636* 168 455	Class: (LR) ✠ Classed LR until 9/1/87	**1982-12 Sing Koon Seng Pte Ltd — Singapore** Yd No: 594 Loa 50.81 Br ex 9.73 Dght 2.952 Lbp 47.10 Br md 9.52 Dpth 3.81 Welded, 1 dk	**(B34Q2QL) Buoy & Lighthouse Tender** Grain: 410 Compartments: 1 Ho, ER 1 Ha: (6.0 x 4.0)ER Derricks: 1x10t	**2 oil engines** with clutches, flexible couplings & dr geared to sc. shaft driving 1 CP propeller Total Power: 812kW (1,104hp) 12.0kn Deutz SBA8M816 2 x 4 Stroke 8 Cy. 142 x 160 each-406kW (552bhp) Kloeckner Humboldt Deutz AG-West Germany AuxGen: 1 x 250kW 415V 50Hz a.c, 2 x 80kW 415V 50Hz a.c Thrusters: 1 Thwart. FP thruster (f) Fuel: 87.0 (d.f.) 5.0pd
8899536 - -	**SEPURI** **PT Etam Kalimantan Raya** - *Balikpapan* *Indonesia*	**140** 84 -	Class: KI	**1995-12 P.T. Galangan Tanjung Batu — Balikpapan** Loa 21.00 Br ex - Dght 2.390 Lbp 19.30 Br md 6.10 Dpth 3.00 Welded, 1 dk	**(B32A2ST) Tug**	**2 oil engines** reduction geared to sc. shafts driving 2 FP propellers Total Power: 592kW (804hp) Caterpillar 3408TA 2 x Vee 4 Stroke 8 Cy. 137 x 152 each-296kW (402bhp) Caterpillar Inc-USA
9619220 *9MLV8* -	**SEPUTEH** **Crossborder Scapes (M) Sdn Bhd** Baycorp Ship Management Sdn Bhd *Port Klang* *Malaysia* MMSI: 533062900 Official number: 334368	**226** 67 -	Class: BV	**2011-09 NGV Tech Sdn Bhd — Telok Panglima Garang** Yd No: 1175 Loa 34.00 Br ex - Dght 1.500 Lbp 31.67 Br md 7.85 Dpth 3.30 Welded, 1 dk	**(B34J2SD) Crew Boat** Hull Material: Aluminium Alloy	**3 oil engines** reduction geared to sc. shafts driving 3 FP propellers Total Power: 3,243kW (4,410hp) 25.0kn Caterpillar C32 ACERT 3 x Vee 4 Stroke 12 Cy. 145 x 162 each-1081kW (1470bhp) Caterpillar Inc-USA AuxGen: 2 x 112kW 50Hz a.c Fuel: 40.0 (d.f.)
9677856 *WDG4437* -	**SEQUEL** **Big Dog Fish Co Inc** - *Valdez, AK* *United States of America* MMSI: 367536560 Official number: 1240646	*101* 80 -		**2012-10 Delta Marine Industries, Inc. — Seattle, Wa** L reg 17.61 Br ex - Dght - Lbp - Br md 6.91 Dpth 3.50 Bonded, 1 dk	**(B11B2FV) Fishing Vessel** Hull Material: Reinforced Plastic	**1 oil engine** reduction geared to sc. shaft driving 1 Propeller
9544633 *ZCXA7* -	**SEQUEL P** **Va Bene Ltd** Dynamic Yacht Management LLC SatCom: Inmarsat C 431900155 *George Town* *Cayman Islands (British)* MMSI: 319008400 Official number: 740621	**710** 213 110	Class: AB	**2009-05 Proteksan-Turquoise Yachts Inc — Istanbul (Pendik)** Yd No: 50 Loa 54.70 Br ex - Dght 2.900 Lbp 47.61 Br md 9.30 Dpth 4.79 Welded, 1 dk	**(X11A2YP) Yacht** Passengers: 12; cabins: 6	**2 oil engines** reduction geared to sc. shaft driving 2 Propellers Total Power: 2,206kW (3,000hp) 14.0kn Caterpillar 3512B 2 x Vee 4 Stroke 12 Cy. 170 x 190 each-1103kW (1500bhp) Caterpillar Inc-USA AuxGen: 2 x 189kW a.c
9259989 - -	**SEQUOIA** **Government of The United States of America (US Coast Guard)** - *Guam, GU* *United States of America*	**1,930** 579 578	Class: (AB)	**2004-04 Marinette Marine Corp — Marinette WI** Yd No: 214 Loa 68.58 Br ex - Dght 3.960 Lbp 62.79 Br md 14.02 Dpth 5.98 Welded, 1 dk	**(B34Q2QB) Buoy Tender**	**2 oil engines** geared to sc. shaft driving 1 CP propeller Total Power: 4,626kW (6,290hp) Caterpillar 3608TA 2 x 4 Stroke 8 Cy. 280 x 300 each-2313kW (3145bhp) Caterpillar Inc-USA AuxGen: 2 x 450kW a.c Thrusters: 1 Tunnel thruster (f)
9574626 *3EYR8* -	**SEQUOIA DRAGON** **Three Friends International Shipping SA** Ningbo FTZ Cosnavi International Shipping Management Co Ltd *Panama* *Panama* MMSI: 353510000 Official number: 4139310	**5,286** 3,006 7,000	Class: BV	**2010-01 Zhejiang Tenglong Shipyard — Wenling ZJ** Yd No: KH-009 Loa 119.60 Br ex - Dght 6.300 Lbp 112.99 Br md 16.80 Dpth 8.20 Welded, 1 dk	**(A21A2BC) Bulk Carrier** Grain: 10,195 Compartments: 2 Ho, ER 2 Ha: ER	**1 oil engine** reduction geared to sc. shaft driving 1 FP propeller Total Power: 2,500kW (3,399hp) 12.5kn Daihatsu 8DKM-28 1 x 4 Stroke 8 Cy. 280 x 390 2500kW (3399bhp) Shaanxi Diesel Heavy Industry Co Lt-China AuxGen: 3 x 250kW 50Hz a.c
8038728 *HP7603* -	**SERA** *ex* Viking Lady *-2012* *ex* Lady Kay *-1993* **Colby Nigeria Ltd** - *Panama* *Panama*	**104** 78 -	Class: IS	**1980-09 Port Brownsville Shipyard — Brownsville, Tx** Yd No: 8058 L reg 29.78 Br ex - Dght - Lbp - Br md 7.92 Dpth 2.47 Welded, 1 dk	**(B21A2OC) Crew/Supply Vessel**	**2 oil engines** geared to sc. shafts driving 2 FP propellers Total Power: 882kW (1,200hp) G.M. (Detroit Diesel) 16V-92 2 x Vee 2 Stroke 16 Cy. 123 x 127 each-441kW (600bhp) General Motors Detroit DieselAllison Divn-USA AuxGen: 2 x
8817368 - -	**SERAFINA** *ex* Remsborg *-2012* *ex* Eemsborg *-2009* **Dennis Maritime Oy Ltd** - *Brando* *Finland*	**1,999** 1,203 3,015	Class: BV	**1990-09 Scheepswerf Ferus Smit BV — Westerbroek** Yd No: 256 Loa 82.04 Br ex 12.60 Dght 4.941 Lbp 78.59 Br md 12.50 Dpth 6.60 Welded, 2 dks	**(A31A2GX) General Cargo Ship** Grain: 4,519 TEU 128 C. 128/20' (40') Compartments: 1 Ho, ER 2 Ha: (26.8 x 10.3) (25.5 x 10.3)ER Ice Capable	**1 oil engine** geared to sc. shaft driving 1 CP propeller Total Power: 1,698kW (2,309hp) 12.0kn Caterpillar 3606TA 1 x 4 Stroke 6 Cy. 280 x 300 1698kW (2309bhp) Caterpillar Inc-USA
7104104 *YBNT* -	**SERAJU** **PT PERTAMINA (PERSERO)** - *Jakarta* *Indonesia*	*128* 109 94	Class: (AB)	**1971-03 Robin Shipyard Pte Ltd — Singapore** Yd No: 43 Loa 29.11 Br ex 7.62 Dght 2.848 Lbp 26.83 Br md 7.42 Dpth 3.36 Welded, 1 dk	**(B32A2ST) Tug**	**2 oil engines** driving 2 FP propellers Total Power: 860kW (1,170hp) 11.0kn Daihatsu 6PSHTCM-26D 2 x 4 Stroke 6 Cy. 260 x 320 each-430kW (585bhp) Daihatsu Diesel Manufacturing Co Lt-Japan AuxGen: 1 x 24kW, 1 x 10kW Fuel: 55.0 (d.f.)
8003515 *YCXL* -	**SERAM** **Government of The Republic of Indonesia (Direktorat Jenderal Perhubungan Laut - Ministry of Sea Communications)** PT (Persero) Pengerukan Indonesia *Jakarta* *Indonesia* MMSI: 525019033 Official number: 1989	*3,942* 1,183 4,165	Class: KI (IR) (BV)	**1981-07 IHC van Rees de Klop BV — Sliedrecht** Yd No: C01138 Loa 92.03 Br ex - Dght 6.603 Lbp 85.83 Br md 16.02 Dpth 8.03 Welded, 1 dk	**(B33B2DT) Trailing Suction Hopper Dredger** Hopper: 2,900	**2 oil engines** sr reverse geared to sc. shafts driving 2 FP propellers Total Power: 2,794kW (3,798hp) 12.5kn Bolnes 14VDNL150/600 2 x Vee 2 Stroke 14 Cy. 190 x 350 each-1397kW (1899bhp) 'Bolnes' Motorenfabriek BV-Netherlands AuxGen: 1 x 540kW 380V 50Hz a.c, 2 x 270kW 380V 50Hz a.c Thrusters: 1 Thwart. FP thruster (f) Fuel: 541.0 (d.f.)
8121173 *YDXS* -	**SERANG JAYA/PERTAMINA 3011** **PT PERTAMINA (PERSERO)** - *Jakarta* *Indonesia* MMSI: 525008028	**22,227** 11,363 29,990 T/cm 45.9	Class: KI (LR) ✠ Classed LR until 4/1/08	**1983-06 Korea Shipbuilding & Engineering Corp — Busan** Yd No: 2010 Loa 179.97 (BB) Br ex 30.03 Dght 9.119 Lbp 171.10 Br md 30.01 Dpth 15.02 Welded, 1 dk	**(A13B2TP) Products Tanker** Single Hull Liq: 38,786; Liq (Oil): 38,786 Compartments: 11 Ta, ER 3 Cargo Pump (s): 3x1000m^3/hr Manifold: Bow/CM: 92m	**1 oil engine** driving 1 FP propeller Total Power: 9,731kW (13,230hp) 15.5kn Sulzer 6RLB66 1 x 2 Stroke 6 Cy. 660 x 1400 9731kW (13230bhp) Mitsubishi Heavy Industries Ltd-Japan AuxGen: 3 x 500kW 450V 60Hz a.c Boilers: e 22.0kgf/cm^2 (21.6bar), AuxB (o.f.) 16.0kgf/cm^2 (15.7bar) Fuel: 173.0 (d.f.) (Part Heating Coils) 1333.0 (r.f.) 35.0pd

IMO / Call sign	Name / Owner / Port	Tonnage	Class	Build	Type	Machinery
9667069 *YDB4226* -	**SERASI 14** **PT Serasi Shipping Indonesia (SSI)** - *Jakarta* *Indonesia*	**145** 44 109	Class: KI	**2012-12 Capricorn Central Shipbuilding Sdn Bhd — Sibu** Yd No: 025 Loa 23.50 Br ex - Dght - Lbp - Br md 7.32 Dpth 3.20 Welded, 1 dk	**(B32A2ST) Tug**	**2 oil engines** reduction geared to sc. shafts driving 2 Propellers Yanmar 2 x 4 Stroke Yanmar Diesel Engine Co Ltd-Japan
9667071 *YDB4224* -	**SERASI 16** **PT Serasi Shipping Indonesia (SSI)** - *Jakarta* *Indonesia*	**145** 44 109	Class: KI	**2013-02 Capricorn Central Shipbuilding Sdn Bhd — Sibu** Yd No: 026 Loa 23.50 Br ex - Dght - Lbp - Br md 7.32 Dpth 3.20 Welded, 1 dk	**(B32A2ST) Tug**	**2 oil engines** reduction geared to sc. shafts driving 2 Propellers Yanmar 2 x 4 Stroke Yanmar Diesel Engine Co Ltd-Japan
8909123 *YDOJ* -	**SERASI I** *ex* Yufutsu Maru *-2006* **PT Toyofuji Serasi Indonesia (TFSI)** - *Jakarta* *Indonesia* MMSI: 525015105 Official number: 2006PSTNO.4031/L	**7,677** 2,304 2,457	Class: KI NK	**1990-01 Naikai Shipbuilding & Engineering Co Ltd — Onomichi HS (Setoda Shipyard)** Yd No: 551 Loa 107.14 (BB) Br ex - Dght 5.313 Lbp 99.98 Br md 18.30 Dpth 6.40 Welded, 5 dks	**(A35B2RV) Vehicles Carrier** Quarter stern door/ramp (p) Len: 18.00 Wid: 5.50 Swl: - Quarter stern door/ramp (s) Len: 18.00 Wid: 5.50 Swl: - Cars: 501	**1 oil engine** driving 1 FP propeller Total Power: 2,648kW (3,600hp) 15.0kn B&W 6L35MC 1 x 2 Stroke 6 Cy. 350 x 1050 2648kW (3600bhp) Hitachi Zosen Corp-Japan Thrusters: 1 Thwart. CP thruster (f); 1 Thwart. CP thruster (a) Fuel: 190.0 (r.f.)
8701325 *YDVK* -	**SERASI II** *ex* Shinpo Maru *-2006* *ex* Hoshin Maru *-2003* **PT Toyofuji Serasi Indonesia (TFSI)** - *Tanjung Priok* *Indonesia* MMSI: 525015144 Official number: 2006 BA NO 788/L	*7,733* 2,320 2,538	Class: KI NK	**1987-09 Kambara Marine Development & Shipbuilding Co Ltd — Fukuyama HS** Yd No: OE-150 Loa 108.01 (BB) Br ex - Dght 5.013 Lbp 100.01 Br md 18.41 Dpth 6.02 Welded	**(A35B2RV) Vehicles Carrier** Lorries: 305, Cars: 533	**1 oil engine** driving 1 CP propeller Total Power: 2,942kW (4,000hp) 16.0kn Mitsubishi 6UEC37LA 1 x 2 Stroke 6 Cy. 370 x 880 2942kW (4000bhp) Akasaka Tekkosho KK (Akasaka DieselLtd)-Japan AuxGen: 2 x 440kW 450V 60Hz a.c Fuel: 285.0 (r.f.)
8716162 *PMXN* -	**SERASI III** *ex* Trans Pacific 1 *-2009* *ex* Seiwa Maru *-2008* **PT Toyofuji Serasi Indonesia (TFSI)** - *Jakarta* *Indonesia* MMSI: 525015455 Official number: 2009 PST NO. 5831/L	**9,500** 2,751 2,618	Class: KI NK	**1988-08 Mitsubishi Heavy Industries Ltd. — Nagasaki** Yd No: 2018 Loa 115.00 (BB) Br ex 20.04 Dght 5.420 Lbp 105.00 Br md 20.00 Dpth 6.58 Welded, 4 dks	**(A35B2RV) Vehicles Carrier** Quarter stern door/ramp (p. a.) Quarter stern door/ramp (s. a.) Cars: 400	**1 oil engine** sr geared to sc. shaft driving 1 FP propeller Total Power: 3,089kW (4,200hp) 15.0kn Mitsubishi 6UEC37LA 1 x 2 Stroke 6 Cy. 370 x 880 3089kW (4200bhp) Mitsubishi Heavy Industries Ltd-Japan AuxGen: 3 x 570kW 450V a.c Thrusters: 1 Thwart. CP thruster (f); 1 Tunnel thruster (a) Fuel: 220.0 (r.f.)
9574781 *PNBR* -	**SERASI IX** *ex* Surya Samudra *-2009* **PT Serasi Shipping Indonesia (SSI)** - *Samarinda* *Indonesia* MMSI: 525009061	**790** 237 -	Class: KI	**2009-06 Galangan Kapal Tunas Harapan — Samarinda** Yd No: 25 Loa 68.80 Br ex - Dght 3.320 Lbp 61.20 Br md 12.70 Dpth 3.32 Welded, 1 dk	**(A35D2RL) Landing Craft** Bow door/ramp (centre)	**2 oil engines** geared to sc. shafts driving 2 Propellers Total Power: 980kW (1,332hp) Mitsubishi S6A3-MPTK 2 x 4 Stroke 6 Cy. 150 x 175 each-490kW (666bhp) Mitsubishi Heavy Industries Ltd-Japan
9039573 *PNTN* -	**SERASI V** *ex* Trans Dream 1 *-2010* *ex* Toyofuji Maru No. 16 *-2008* **PT Toyofuji Serasi Indonesia (TFSI)** - *Jakarta* *Indonesia* MMSI: 525015778 Official number: 2011 PST NO.6637/L	**10,245** 3,368 3,624	Class: KI NK	**1991-10 Naikai Shipbuilding & Engineering Co Ltd — Onomichi HS (Setoda Shipyard)** Yd No: 571 Loa 128.92 (BB) Br ex 20.02 Dght 6.016 Lbp 117.00 Br md 20.00 Dpth 6.38 Welded, 5 dks	**(A35B2RV) Vehicles Carrier** Quarter stern door/ramp (p) Len: 20.00 Wid: 5.25 Swl: - Quarter stern door/ramp (s) Len: 20.00 Wid: 5.25 Swl: - Cars: 803	**1 oil engine** driving 1 FP propeller Total Power: 5,973kW (8,121hp) 18.0kn B&W 7L42MC 1 x 2 Stroke 7 Cy. 420 x 1360 5973kW (8121bhp) Hitachi Zosen Corp-Japan AuxGen: 3 x 680kW a.c Thrusters: 1 Thwart. CP thruster (f); 1 Thwart. CP thruster (a) Fuel: 310.0 (r.f.)
9606649 *YDA4763* -	**SERASI VI** **PT Serasi Shipping Indonesia (SSI)** - *Jakarta* *Indonesia* Official number: 03071008	**194** 59 166	Class: KI (NK)	**2011-03 Capricorn Central Shipbuilding Sdn Bhd — Sibu** Yd No: 029 Loa 26.00 Br ex - Dght 3.012 Lbp 24.34 Br md 8.00 Dpth 3.65 Welded, 1 dk	**(B32A2ST) Tug**	**2 oil engines** reduction geared to sc. shafts driving 2 FP propellers Total Power: 1,220kW (1,658hp) Yanmar 6AYM-ETE 2 x 4 Stroke 6 Cy. 155 x 180 each-610kW (829bhp) Yanmar Diesel Engine Co Ltd-Japan Fuel: 130.0 (d.f.)
8921793 *POAM* -	**SERASI VIII** *ex* Aichi Maru *-2011* **PT Toyofuji Serasi Indonesia (TFSI)** - *Jakarta* *Indonesia* MMSI: 525015900	*5,411* - 4,979	Class: KI NK	**1991-01 Naikai Shipbuilding & Engineering Co Ltd — Onomichi HS (Setoda Shipyard)** Yd No: 558 Loa 148.22 (BB) Br ex 20.42 Dght 6.649 Lbp 137.00 Br md 20.40 Dpth 6.86 Welded, 1 dk	**(A35B2RV) Vehicles Carrier** Quarter stern door/ramp (p) Quarter stern door/ramp (s) Lane-clr ht: 4.20 Cars: 730	**1 oil engine** driving 1 FP propeller Total Power: 9,709kW (13,200hp) 20.0kn B&W 8L50MC 1 x 2 Stroke 8 Cy. 500 x 1620 9709kW (13200bhp) Hitachi Zosen Corp-Japan AuxGen: 3 x 640kW 450V 60Hz a.c Thrusters: 1 Thwart. CP thruster (f); 1 Thwart. CP thruster (a) Fuel: 491.9 (d.f.) 35.9pd
9144457 *POOG* -	**SERASI X** *ex* Paimpol *-2012* *ex* La Paimpolaise *-2007* *ex* Palamos *-2004* *ex* Fret Marne *-2003* *ex* Palamos *-2002* *ex* Scan Pacific *-2001* **PT Serasi Shipping Indonesia (SSI)** - *Jakarta* *Indonesia* MMSI: 525003152	**5,752** 2,579 5,100 T/cm 16.6	Class: BV (GL)	**1996-12 Peene-Werft GmbH — Wolgast** Yd No: 476 Loa 101.29 (BB) Br ex 18.90 Dght 6.627 Lbp 95.34 Br md 18.60 Dpth 9.70 Welded, 2 dks	**(A35A2RR) Ro-Ro Cargo Ship** Double Bottom Entire Compartment Length Stern door/ramp Len: - Wid: 10.00 Swl: 350 Lane-Len: 570 Trailers: 30 Bale: 9,800 TEU 501 C Ho 210 TEU C Dk 291 TEU incl 40 ref C. Compartments: 1 Ho, ER, 1 Tw Dk 1 Ha: (70.2 x 15.6)ER Cranes: 2x100t Ice Capable	**1 oil engine** with flexible couplings & sr gearedto sc. shaft driving 1 CP propeller Total Power: 5,280kW (7,179hp) 16.0kn MAN 12V32/40 1 x Vee 4 Stroke 12 Cy. 320 x 400 5280kW (7179bhp) MAN B&W Diesel AG-Augsburg AuxGen: 1 x 700kW a.c, 2 x 360kW a.c Thrusters: 1 Thwart. FP thruster (f)
7234492 - -	**SERAYA JAYA** *ex* Eastern Pioneer *-1991* *ex* Tarros Ilex *-1988* *ex* Zim Manila *-1981* *ex* Tarros Ilex *-1979* *ex* Marisud Prima *-1978* *ex* Tarros Ilex *-1977* *ex* Cheshire Venture *-1977* - - *Jakarta* *Indonesia* MMSI: 525019062 Official number: 5716	**1,907** 722 1,905	Class: (LR) (KI) ✠ Classed LR until 21/6/95	**1972-11 A. Vuijk & Zonen's Scheepswerven N.V. — Capelle a/d IJssel** Yd No: 859 Loa 85.32 Br ex 13.75 Dght 4.704 Lbp 79.15 Br md 13.70 Dpth 6.05 Welded, 1 dk	**(A33A2CR) Container Ship (Fully Cellular with Ro-Ro Facility)** Stern door/ramp Len: 7.25 Wid: 5.80 Swl: - Trailers: 30 TEU 113 C.Ho 44/20' (40') C.Dk 69/20' (40') incl. 33 ref C. Compartments: 2 Dp Ta in Hold, 1 Cell Ho, ER 1 Ha: (39.6 x 10.9)ER Ice Capable	**1 oil engine** reverse reduction geared to sc. shaft driving 1 CP propeller Total Power: 2,354kW (3,200hp) 15.0kn Mirrlees KMR-6 1 x 4 Stroke 6 Cy. 381 x 457 2354kW (3200bhp) (new engine 1977) Mirrlees Blackstone (Stockport)Ltd.-Stockport AuxGen: 3 x 144kW 380V 50Hz a.c Thrusters: 1 Thwart. FP thruster (f) Fuel: 243.0 (r.f.)
8329294 - -	**SERAYU** **PT PERTAMINA (PERSERO)** - *Jakarta* *Indonesia*	*153* 46 -	Class: KI	**1971 Robin Shipyard Pte Ltd — Singapore** Loa 29.49 Br ex - Dght 2.340 Lbp 27.26 Br md 7.54 Dpth 3.59 Welded, 1 dk	**(B32A2ST) Tug**	**2 oil engines** geared to sc. shafts driving 2 FP propellers Total Power: 882kW (1,200hp) Daihatsu 6PSHTM-26D 2 x 4 Stroke 6 Cy. 260 x 320 each-441kW (600bhp) Daihatsu Diesel Manufacturing Co Lt-Japan
9166003 *YFZH* -	**SERAYU** **Government of The Republic of Indonesia (Direktorat Jenderal Perhubungan Darat - Ministry of Land Communications)** PT ASDP Indonesia Ferry (Persero) - Angkutan Sungai Danau & Penyeberangan *Jakarta* *Indonesia*	**1,515** 452 150	Class: (KI) (GL)	**1998-11 Fr. Luerssen Werft GmbH & Co. — Bremen** Yd No: 13587 Loa 69.80 Br ex - Dght 2.000 Lbp 62.00 Br md 10.40 Dpth 7.30 Welded, 1 dk	**(A37B2PS) Passenger Ship** Hull Material: Aluminium Alloy Passengers: unberthed: 925	**4 oil engines** with flexible couplings & sr gearedto sc. shafts driving 4 Water jets Total Power: 15,220kW (20,692hp) 38.0kn M.T.U. 16V595TE70 4 x Vee 4 Stroke 16 Cy. 190 x 210 each-3805kW (5173bhp) MTU Friedrichshafen GmbH-Friedrichshafen AuxGen: 2 x 420kW a.c Thrusters: 1 Thwart. FP thruster (f)
9258765 *YD4891* -	**SERDADU JAYA** **PT Pelayaran Jasa Samudera Shipping** - *Cirebon* *Indonesia*	**125** 75 160	Class: KI	**2001-12 Nga Chai Shipyard Sdn Bhd — Sibu** Loa 23.50 Br ex - Dght 2.500 Lbp 21.36 Br md 7.30 Dpth 2.90 Welded, 1 dk	**(B32A2ST) Tug**	**2 oil engines** reduction geared to sc. shafts driving 2 FP propellers Total Power: 780kW (1,060hp) Yanmar 6LAA-UTE 2 x 4 Stroke 6 Cy. 148 x 165 each-390kW (530bhp) Yanmar Diesel Engine Co Ltd-Japan AuxGen: 1 x 22kW a.c

IMO / Call sign	Name / Owner	Tonnage	Class	Build / Dimensions	Type	Machinery
7630452 *UIHG* -	**SERDEZH** **Deepsea Global Co Ltd (OOO Dipsi Global)** - *Vladivostok* *Russia*	**739** 221 347	Class: (RS)	**1976-07 Volgogradskiy Sudostroitelnyy Zavod — Volgograd** Yd No: 867 Loa 53.73 (BB) Br ex 10.70 Dght 4.290 Lbp 47.92 Br md - Dpth 6.02 Welded, 1 dk	**(B11A2FS) Stern Trawler** Ins: 218 Compartments: 1 Ho, ER 2 Ha: 2 (1.6 x 1.6) Derricks: 2x1.5t; Winches: 2 Ice Capable	**1 oil engine** driving 1 CP propeller Total Power: 971kW (1,320hp) 12.5kn S.K.L. 8NVD48A-2U 1 x 4 Stroke 8 Cy. 320 x 480 971kW (1320bhp) VEB Schwermaschinenbau "KarlLiebknecht" (SKL)-Magdeburg AuxGen: 3 x 500kW a.c Thrusters: 1 Thwart. FP thruster (f); 1 Tunnel thruster (a) Fuel: 1833.0 (r.f.)
8330592 - -	**SERDOLIK** *ex* SCHS-7040 *-2003* **Southern Trading House Ltd (OOO 'Yuzhnyy Torgovyy Dom')** -	**109** 39 61	Class: (RS)	**1984 Azovskaya Sudoverf — Azov** Yd No: 7040 Loa 26.50 Br ex 6.58 Dght 2.340 Lbp 22.90 Br md - Dpth 3.05 Welded, 1 dk	**(B11B2FV) Fishing Vessel**	**1 oil engine** geared to sc. shaft driving 1 FP propeller Total Power: 165kW (224hp) 9.3kn Daldizel 6CHNSP18/22 1 x 4 Stroke 6 Cy. 180 x 220 165kW (224bhp) Daldizel-Khabarovsk AuxGen: 2 x 30kW a.c Fuel: 10.0 (d.f.)
9555333 *UCLN* -	**SERDOLIK** **GTLK Malta Ltd** JS North-Western Shipping Co (OAO 'Severo-Zapadnoye Parokhodstvo') *Moscow* *Russia* MMSI: 273334240	**3,505** 1,832 5,027	Class: BV (RS)	**2012-08 Qingdao Hyundai Shipbuilding Co Ltd — Jiaonan SD** Yd No: 308 Loa 89.96 (BB) Br ex 14.58 Dght 6.400 Lbp 84.72 Br md 14.50 Dpth 7.20 Welded, 1 dk	**(A31A2GX) General Cargo Ship** Double Hull Grain: 6,230 TEU 178 Compartments: 1 Ho, ER 1 Ha: ER (56.4 x 11.5) Ice Capable	**1 oil engine** reduction geared to sc. shaft driving 1 CP propeller Total Power: 2,640kW (3,589hp) 12.0kn MaK 8M25C 1 x 4 Stroke 8 Cy. 255 x 400 2640kW (3589bhp) Caterpillar Motoren GmbH & Co. KG-Germany AuxGen: 1 x 292kW 50Hz a.c, 2 x 180kW 50Hz a.c Thrusters: 1 Tunnel thruster (f) Fuel: 370.0
8929513 *UCJK* -	**SEREBRYANKA** **Government of The Russian Federation** Federal State Unitary Enterprise 'Atomflot' *Murmansk* *Russia* MMSI: 273133300	**2,925** 877 1,625	Class: RS	**1974-12 Navashinskiy Sudostroitelnyy Zavod 'Oka' — Navashino** Loa 102.00 Br ex 15.03 Dght 4.200 Lbp 88.90 Br md - Dpth 6.71 Welded, 1 dk	**(A38D2GN) Nuclear Fuel Carrier** Ice Capable	**2 oil engines** driving 2 FP propellers Total Power: 1,470kW (1,998hp) 11.5kn Russkiy 8DR30/50-4-3 2 x 2 Stroke 8 Cy. 300 x 500 each-735kW (999bhp) Mashinostroitelnyy Zavod"Russkiy-Dizel"-Leningrad AuxGen: 3 x 100kW a.c Fuel: 286.0 (d.f.)
8606111 *9HTC9* -	**SEREF KURU** *ex* Shahat *-2009* *ex* Jaref *-2008* **Dryson Shipping Ltd** Kuruoglu Denizcilik Insaat Sanayi ve Ticaret Ltd Sti *Valletta* *Malta* MMSI: 249478000 Official number: 8606111	**8,195** 4,456 9,561	Class: AB (NK)	**1987-12 Kyokuyo Shipyard Corp — Shimonoseki YC** Yd No: 2492 Loa 125.00 (BB) Br ex - Dght 7.519 Lbp 118.01 Br md 20.01 Dpth 11.82 Welded, 2 dks	**(A31A2GX) General Cargo Ship** Grain: 15,719; Bale: 14,748; Ins: 320 TEU 320 incl 20 ref C. Compartments: 4 Ho, ER 4 Ha: (12.8 x 10.2)2 (19.5 x 10.2) (13.5 x 10.2)ER Cranes: 2x26t,1x20.5t,1x15.3t	**1 oil engine** driving 1 FP propeller Total Power: 4,413kW (6,000hp) 14.5kn Mitsubishi 6UEC45LA 1 x 2 Stroke 6 Cy. 450 x 1350 4413kW (6000bhp) Kobe Hatsudoki KK-Japan AuxGen: 4 x 214kW
8405189 - -	**SEREIA** *ex* Hai Xiang *-2009* *ex* Rong Ping *-2006* *ex* Double Eagle *-2000* *ex* Tokin Maru *-1998* *ex* Tokin Maru No. 2 *-1997* *ex* Taijin Maru *-1989* **Aiman Comercio Geral**	**1,236** 692 1,599	Class: (CC)	**1984-06 Kochi Jyuko (Kaisei Zosen) K.K. — Kochi** Yd No: 1715 Loa 71.29 Br ex - Dght 4.950 Lbp 66.02 Br md 11.51 Dpth 6.51 Welded, 1 dk	**(A31A2GX) General Cargo Ship** Grain: 2,573; Bale: 2,289 Compartments: 1 Ho, ER 1 Ha: ER	**1 oil engine** sr geared to sc. shaft driving 1 CP propeller Total Power: 883kW (1,201hp) 11.5kn Hanshin 6LUN28A 1 x 4 Stroke 6 Cy. 280 x 480 883kW (1201bhp) The Hanshin Diesel Works Ltd-Japan
9706009 *J8B4993* -	**SEREIA** *ex* P&O Tug II *-2014* **P&O Maritime FZE** Redwise Maritime Services BV *Kingstown* *St Vincent & The Grenadines* MMSI: 375106000 Official number: 11466	**286** 86 400	Class: AB	**2014-01 Sanmar Denizcilik Makina ve Ticaret — Istanbul** Yd No: 18 Loa 25.20 Br ex - Dght 2.600 Lbp 22.71 Br md 12.00 Dpth 4.31 Welded, 1 dk	**(B32A2ST) Tug**	**2 oil engines** reduction geared to sc. shafts driving 2 Directional propellers Total Power: 2,536kW (3,448hp) Caterpillar 3512C-HD 2 x Vee 4 Stroke 12 Cy. 170 x 215 each-1268kW (1724bhp) Caterpillar Inc-USA
8844581 *YHUL* -	**SEREIA DOMAR** *ex* Elses 1 *-2004* *ex* Shuttle No. 2 *-2004* **PT Surya Timur Lines** - *Surabaya* *Indonesia*	*409* 123 -	Class: KI	**1990-06 Kanbara Zosen K.K. — Onomichi** Yd No: 401 Loa 49.00 Br ex - Dght 2.700 Lbp 40.22 Br md 9.50 Dpth 3.60 Welded, 1 dk	**(A36A2PR) Passenger/Ro-Ro Ship (Vehicles)**	**1 oil engine** geared to sc. shaft driving 1 FP propeller Total Power: 1,177kW (1,600hp) Daihatsu 6DLM-26FSL 1 x 4 Stroke 6 Cy. 260 x 340 1177kW (1600bhp) Daihatsu Diesel Manufacturing Co Lt-Japan AuxGen: 2 x 92kW 225V a.c
9458391 *VRLT6* -	**SEREN** *ex* Adelina *-2013* **Mega Trophy Ltd** Istanbul Denizcilik ve Deniz Tasimaciligi AS *Hong Kong* *Hong Kong* MMSI: 477243300 Official number: HK-3764	**20,965** 10,262 28,085	Class: GL	**2011-12 Huanghai Shipbuilding Co Ltd — Rongcheng SD** Yd No: HCY-85 Loa 166.42 (BB) Br ex - Dght 10.100 Lbp 158.32 Br md 27.40 Dpth 14.20 Welded, 1 dk	**(A31A2GX) General Cargo Ship** Grain: 39,100; Bale: 39,100 TEU 1735 Compartments: 4 Ho, ER 4 Ha: ER Cranes: 2x200t,1x45t Ice Capable	**1 oil engine** driving 1 FP propeller Total Power: 6,810kW (9,259hp) 15.2kn MAN-B&W 6S40ME-B9 1 x 2 Stroke 6 Cy. 400 x 1770 6810kW (9259bhp) STX Engine Co Ltd-South Korea AuxGen: 3 x 600kW 450V a.c
7505774 *TCHO* -	**SEREN AYANOGLU** *ex* Leyla Deval *-2008* *ex* Yesim F *-1989* **Aytrans Uluslararasi Denizcilik Nakliyat ve Ticaret Ltd Sti** - SatCom: Inmarsat C 427120350 *Istanbul* *Turkey* MMSI: 271000194 Official number: 5542	**3,523** 2,279 5,703	Class: RS TL (AB)	**1987-05 Celiktekne Sanayii ve Ticaret A.S. — Tuzla, Istanbul** Yd No: 8 Loa 110.00 Br ex - Dght 6.700 Lbp 100.01 Br md 15.41 Dpth 8.21 Welded, 1 dk	**(A31A2GX) General Cargo Ship** Grain: 8,326; Bale: 7,504 Compartments: 3 Ho, ER 3 Ha: ER	**1 oil engine** sr geared to sc. shaft driving 1 CP propeller Total Power: 3,199kW (4,349hp) 12.0kn Sulzer 6ZL40/48 1 x 4 Stroke 6 Cy. 400 x 480 3199kW (4349bhp) Zaklady Urzadzen Technicznych'Zgoda' SA-Poland AuxGen: 2 x 180kW a.c, 1 x 80kW a.c
8842959 *YBLO* -	**SERENA** *ex* Victoria 07 *-2007* *ex* Fortune No. 7 *-2006* *ex* Han Chang No. 3 *-2000* **PT Pelayaran Sherin Kapuas Raya** - *Pontianak* *Indonesia* MMSI: 525016143	*1,131* 646 2,116	Class: KI (KR)	**1990-06 Shinyoung Shipbuilding Industry Co Ltd — Yeosu** Loa 67.04 Br ex - Dght 5.160 Lbp 62.00 Br md 11.00 Dpth 5.60 Welded, 1 dk	**(A12B2TR) Chemical/Products Tanker** Liq: 2,378; Liq (Oil): 2,378	**1 oil engine** driving 1 FP propeller Total Power: 1,030kW (1,400hp) 13.5kn Hanshin 6LU32 1 x 4 Stroke 6 Cy. 320 x 510 1030kW (1400bhp) Hanshin Nainenki Kogyo-Japan AuxGen: 1 x 160kW 445V a.c
9294977 *DCGX2* -	**SERENA** **ms 'Serena' Schiffahrtsgesellschaft mbH & Co Reederei KG** Intersee Schiffahrtsgesellschaft mbH & Co KG *Haren/Ems* *Germany* Official number: 5309	**7,767** 3,856 10,649 T/cm 23.2	Class: GL (LR) ✠ Classed LR until 30/7/10	**2004-07 B.V. Scheepswerf Damen Hoogezand — Foxhol** Yd No: 839 **2004-07 Damen Shipyards Yichang Co Ltd — Yichang HB** (Hull) Loa 145.63 (BB) Br ex 18.36 Dght 7.350 Lbp 139.38 Br md 18.25 Dpth 10.30 Welded, 1 dk	**(A31A2GX) General Cargo Ship** Grain: 14,695; Bale: 13,975 TEU 679 C Ho 302 TEU C Dk 377 TEU incl 60 ref C. Compartments: 2 Ho, ER Cranes: 2x60t Ice Capable	**1 oil engine** with flexible couplings & sr geared to sc. shaft driving 1 CP propeller Total Power: 4,320kW (5,873hp) 14.8kn MaK 9M32C 1 x 4 Stroke 9 Cy. 320 x 480 4320kW (5873bhp) Caterpillar Motoren GmbH & Co. KG-Germany AuxGen: 1 x 440kW 400V 50Hz a.c, 3 x 350kW 400V 50Hz a.c Boilers: TOH (ex.g.) 10.2kgf/cm² (10.0bar), TOH (o.f.) 10.2kgf/cm² (10.0bar) Thrusters: 1 Thwart. CP thruster (f)
9468281 *PNWM* -	**SERENA III** *ex* Yong Xiang 12 *-2010* **PT Pelayaran Sherin Kapuas Raya** - *Pontianak* *Indonesia* MMSI: 525010062	**2,286** 1,049 3,050	Class: KI	**2005-12 Zhoushan Putuo Luomen Shiprepair & Building Co Ltd — Zhoushan ZJ** Loa 91.03 Br ex - Dght 5.400 Lbp 84.25 Br md 13.50 Dpth 6.35 Welded, 1 dk	**(A12B2TR) Chemical/Products Tanker** Double Hull (13F)	**1 oil engine** geared to sc. shaft driving 1 Propeller Total Power: 1,765kW (2,400hp) Chinese Std. Type 8300ZC 1 x 4 Stroke 8 Cy. 300 x 380 1765kW (2400bhp) Guangzhou Diesel Engine Factory CoLtd-China
9095149 - -	**SERENA JOYE** *ex* Ocean Island *-1988* **James Walkus Fishing Ltd** - *Nanaimo, BC* *Canada* MMSI: 316002916 Official number: 383909	*125* 37 -		**1979-01 Gooldrup Boat Building — Campbell River BC** L reg 22.19 Br ex - Dght - Lbp - Br md 7.32 Dpth 2.56 Bonded, 1 dk	**(B11B2FV) Fishing Vessel** Hull Material: Reinforced Plastic	**1 oil engine** driving 1 Propeller Total Power: 496kW (674hp) 12.0kn

Ship	Tonnage	Class	Builder / Dimensions	Type / Cargo	Machinery
9201865 **SERENADA** *9HA3341* *ex* Friesedijk *-2005* *ex* Admiral Moon *-2001* - *ex* Friesedijk *-2000* **Arlas Shipping Co International SA** Lumar SA *Valletta* *Malta* MMSI: 229453000 Official number: 9201865	**2,926** 1,444 3,820	Class: BV	**1999-10 Tille Scheepsbouw Kootstertille B.V. — Kootstertille** Yd No: 328 Loa 100.80 (BB) Br ex - Dght 4.880 Lbp 92.90 Br md 15.85 Dpth 6.18 Welded, 1 dk	**(A31A2GX) General Cargo Ship** Grain: 4,803; Bale: 4,803 TEU 344 C Ho 86 TEU C Dk 258 TEU incl 70 ref C. Compartments: 1 Ho, ER 3 Ha: (6.3 x 10.6)2 (25.2 x 13.2)ER Ice Capable	**1 oil engine** reduction geared to sc. shaft driving 1 CP propeller Total Power: 3,245kW (4,412hp) 14.5kn Wartsila 8R32 1 x 4 Stroke 8 Cy. 320 x 350 3245kW (4412bhp) Wartsila NSD Finland Oy-Finland AuxGen: 2 x 422kW 220/440V 50Hz a.c, 1 x 504kW 220/440V 50Hz a.c Thrusters: 1 Thwart. FP thruster (f) Fuel: 50.0 (d.f.) 260.0 (r.f.)
7116860 **SERENADE** *IBCZ* *ex* Serenity *-1993* *ex* Danae *-1988* - *ex* Negah *-1980* *ex* Otto Porr *-1978* **Blaik Corp** Nuova Naviservice Srl SatCom: Inmarsat C 424700116 *Naples* *Italy* MMSI: 247089800 Official number: 188	**4,257** 2,235 6,341	Class: RI (GL)	**1972-06 Arnhemsche Scheepsbouw Mij NV — Arnhem** Yd No: 461 **1992-05 Estaleiros Navais de Viana do Castelo S.A. — Viana do Castelo** (Additional cargo section) Yd No: 166 Lengthened & Rebuilt-1992 Loa 101.38 Br ex 16.03 Dght 7.217 Lbp 95.00 Br md 15.96 Dpth 9.22 Welded, 1 dk	**(A21A2BC) Bulk Carrier** Grain: 8,426; Bale: 8,040 Compartments: 3 Ho, ER 3 Ha: (12.9 x 10.9) (25.3 x 10.9) (19.3 x 10.9)ER Ice Capable	**1 oil engine** sr geared to sc. shaft driving 1 FP propeller Total Power: 2,207kW (3,001hp) 13.0kn MaK 6M551AK 1 x 4 Stroke 6 Cy. 450 x 550 2207kW (3001bhp) MaK Maschinenbau GmbH-Kiel AuxGen: 2 x 280kW 220/380V 50Hz a.c
9228344 **SERENADE OF THE SEAS** *C6FV8* - **Serenade of the Seas Inc** Royal Caribbean Cruises Ltd (RCCL) *Nassau* *Bahamas* MMSI: 311492000 Official number: 9000068	**90,090** 53,812 11,960	Class: NV	**2003-07 Jos L Meyer GmbH — Papenburg** Yd No: 657 Loa 293.20 (BB) Br ex - Dght 8.500 Lbp 263.20 Br md 32.20 Dpth 10.70 Welded, 15 dks	**(A37A2PC) Passenger/Cruise** Passengers: cabins: 1050; berths: 2500	**2 turbo electric Gas Turbs & 1 turbo electric Steam Turb** driving 1 gen. of 7500kW 11000V a.c 2 gen. each 25000kW 11000V a.c Connecting to 2 elec. motors each (20000kW) driving 2 Azimuth electric drive units Total Power: 61,408kW (83,490hp) 24.0kn GE Marine LM2500 2 x Gas Turb each-25000kW (33990shp) GE Marine Engines-Cincinnati, Oh GE Marine 1 x steam Turb 7500kW (10197shp) GE Marine Engines-Cincinnati, Oh AuxGen: 1 x 3120kW a.c Thrusters: 3 Thwart. CP thruster (f)
9362190 **SERENATA** *3EEE2* - **Belocean Shipping SA** Taiyo Nippon Kisen Co Ltd *Panama* *Panama* MMSI: 353408000 Official number: 3200706A	**39,736** 25,724 76,561 T/cm 66.6	Class: NK	**2006-07 Imabari Shipbuilding Co Ltd — Marugame KG (Marugame Shipyard)** Yd No: 1417 Loa 224.94 (BB) Br ex - Dght 14.139 Lbp 217.00 Br md 32.26 Dpth 19.50 Welded, 1 dk	**(A21A2BC) Bulk Carrier** Grain: 90,644 Compartments: 7 Ho, ER 7 Ha: 6 (17.1 x 15.6)ER (17.1 x 12.8)	**1 oil engine** driving 1 FP propeller Total Power: 12,240kW (16,642hp) 14.0kn MAN-B&W 6S60MC 1 x 2 Stroke 6 Cy. 600 x 2292 12240kW (16642bhp) Kawasaki Heavy Industries Ltd-Japan Fuel: 2740.0
9158082 **SERENAY 1** *3FUL4* *ex* Boterdiep *-2013* - **Su-Ay 1 Shipping Ltd** Kadir Colak Denizcilik Turizm ve Ticaret AS *Panama* *Panama* MMSI: 352080000 Official number: 04544PEXT	**5,638** 3,110 8,300	Class: LR ✠ **100A1** SS 06/2009 strenghtened for heavy cargoes, container cargoes in holds and on hatch covers ✠ **LMC** **UMS** Eq.Ltr: X; Cable: 502.4/46.0 U3	**1999-06 B.V. Scheepswerf Damen Hoogezand — Foxhol** Yd No: 802 **1999-06 Santierul Naval Damen Galati S.A. — Galati** (Hull) Yd No: 925 Loa 121.31 (BB) Br ex 15.89 Dght 7.400 Lbp 115.15 Br md 15.85 Dpth 9.75 Welded, 1 dk	**(A31A2GX) General Cargo Ship** Grain: 11,420 TEU 401 C. 401/20' Compartments: 2 Ho, ER 2 Ha: (38.2 x 13.2) (44.8 x 13.2)ER	**1 oil engine** with flexible couplings & sr gearedto sc. shaft driving 1 CP propeller Total Power: 3,840kW (5,221hp) 14.5kn MaK 8M32 1 x 4 Stroke 8 Cy. 320 x 480 3840kW (5221bhp) MaK Motoren GmbH & Co. KG-Kiel AuxGen: 1 x 452kW 400V 50Hz a.c, 2 x 264kW 400V 50Hz a.c Boilers: TOH (o.f.) 10.2kgf/cm² (10.0bar), TOH (ex.g.) 10.2kgf/cm² (10.0bar) Thrusters: 1 Thwart. FP thruster (f)
9438030 **SERENDIPITY** *V7EN6* *ex* Davakis G *-2014* - **Cien Maritime Co** - *Majuro* *Marshall Islands* MMSI: 538005500 Official number: 5500	**31,137** 17,993 54,051	Class: BV	**2008-05 Taizhou Kouan Shipbuilding Co Ltd — Taizhou JS** Yd No: KA215 Loa 189.99 (BB) Br ex - Dght 12.600 Lbp 183.36 Br md 32.26 Dpth 17.50 Welded, 1 dk	**(A21A2BC) Bulk Carrier** Double Hull Grain: 66,207 Compartments: 5 Ho, ER 5 Ha: ER Cranes: 4x36t	**1 oil engine** driving 1 FP propeller Total Power: 9,480kW (12,889hp) 14.5kn MAN-B&W 6S50MC-C 1 x 2 Stroke 6 Cy. 500 x 2000 9480kW (12889bhp) Hyundai Heavy Industries Co Ltd-South Korea AuxGen: 3 x 600kW a.c
9429728 **SERENE** *2CES9* LK 297 **Serene Fishing Co Ltd** LHD Ltd *Lerwick* *United Kingdom* MMSI: 235072137 Official number: C19520	**2,943** 826 2,800	Class: NV	**2009-08 CHT Denizcilik Gemi Insaa Sanayi Ticaret Ltd Sti — Istanbul (Tuzla)** (Hull) Yd No: 04 **2009-08 West Contractors AS — Olensvaag** Yd No: 31 Loa 71.66 (BB) Br ex - Dght 7.800 Lbp 62.40 Br md 15.60 Dpth 8.45 Welded, 1 dk	**(B11A2FS) Stern Trawler** Ins: 2,045 Ice Capable	**1 oil engine** reduction geared to sc. shaft driving 1 CP propeller Total Power: 6,000kW (8,158hp) 15.0kn MaK 12M32C 1 x Vee 4 Stroke 12 Cy. 320 x 420 6000kW (8158bhp) Caterpillar Motoren GmbH & Co. KG-Germany AuxGen: 1 x 1360kW 440V 60Hz a.c, 1 x 1060kW 440V 60Hz a.c, 1 x 2800kW 440V 60Hz a.c Thrusters: 1 Tunnel thruster (f); 1 Tunnel thruster (a) Fuel: 500.0
9234252 **SERENE** *9V7028* - **PSA Marine Pte Ltd** - *Singapore* *Singapore* MMSI: 563011370 Official number: 392565	**292** 87 110	Class: LR ✠ **100A1** SS 05/2011 tug ✠ **LMC** Eq.Ltr: F†; Cable: 275.0/19.0 U2 (a)	**2001-05 ASL Shipyard Pte Ltd — Singapore** Yd No: 207 Loa 29.95 Br ex - Dght 4.700 Lbp 26.10 Br md 9.80 Dpth 4.80 Welded, 1 dk	**(B32A2ST) Tug**	**2 oil engines** reduction geared to sc. shafts driving 2 Directional propellers Total Power: 3,326kW (4,522hp) 12.0kn Deutz SBV8M628 2 x 4 Stroke 8 Cy. 240 x 280 each-1663kW (2261bhp) Deutz AG-Koeln AuxGen: 2 x 83kW 415V 50Hz a.c
1010090 **SERENE** *ZGBA9* - **Serena Equity Ltd** YCO SAM *George Town* *Cayman Islands (British)* MMSI: 319021900 Official number: 742951	**8,231** 2,469 1,050	Class: LR ✠ **100A1** SS 07/2011 passenger ship *IWS EP Ice Class 1D at draught of 5.65m Max/min draughts fwd 6.05/4.086m Required power 1600kw, installed power 10400kw ✠ **LMC** **UMS** Eq.Ltr: X; Cable: 495.0/46.0 U3 (a)	**2011-07 Fincantieri-Cant. Nav. Italiani S.p.A. — La Spezia** Yd No: 6154 Loa 133.90 (BB) Br ex 19.00 Dght 5.600 Lbp 119.15 Br md 18.60 Dpth 9.95 Welded, 3 dks	**(X11A2YP) Yacht**	**8 diesel electric oil engines** driving 8 gen. each 2000kW 6600V a.c Connecting to 2 elec. motors each (5200kW) driving 2 CP propellers Total Power: 16,640kW (22,624hp) M.T.U. 16V4000M40 8 x Vee 4 Stroke 16 Cy. 165 x 190 each-2080kW (2828bhp) MTU Friedrichshafen GmbH-Friedrichshafen Thrusters: 2 Thwart. CP thruster (f); 2 Thwart. FP thruster (a)
7712834 **SERENE** - *ex* Antares *-1986* - - - -	**371** 130 305	Class: (LR) ✠ Classed LR until 7/4/92	**1978-11 Bentsen & Sonner Slip & Mek. Verksted — Sogne** (Hull) Yd No: (52) **1978-11 Sigbjorn Iversen — Flekkefjord** Yd No: 52 Lengthened-1981 Loa 38.82 (BB) Br ex 7.73 Dght 3.322 Lbp 34.24 Br md 7.62 Dpth 3.92 Welded, 2 dks	**(B11A2FT) Trawler**	**1 oil engine** sr geared to sc. shaft driving 1 CP propeller Total Power: 809kW (1,100hp) Blackstone ESL8MK2 1 x 4 Stroke 8 Cy. 222 x 292 809kW (1100bhp) Mirrlees Blackstone (Stamford)Ltd.-Stamford AuxGen: 2 x 72kW 220V 50Hz a.c Thrusters: 1 Thwart. FP thruster (f); 1 Tunnel thruster (a)
7508336 **SERENE REEFER** *HSB2752* *ex* Diamond Reefer *-2008* *ex* Green Rose *-2000* - *ex* Pacific Rose *-1994* *ex* Gomba Endeavour *-1981* **Dech Reefer Co Ltd** - SatCom: Inmarsat C 456700097 *Bangkok* *Thailand* MMSI: 567188000 Official number: 440900074	**3,624** 1,931 4,348	Class: (LR) ✠ Classed LR until 16/3/01	**1979-05 Mazagon Dock Ltd. — Mumbai** Yd No: 449 **1984-02 Nederlandse Scheepsbouw Mij. B.V. — Amsterdam** (Additional cargo section) Converted From: General Cargo Ship-1984 Lengthened-1984 Loa 107.68 (BB) Br ex 14.74 Dght 5.460 Lbp 99.98 Br md 14.71 Dpth 7.80 Welded, 2 dks	**(A34A2GR) Refrigerated Cargo Ship** Ins: 5,693 Compartments: 3 Ho, ER, 3 Tw Dk 3 Ha: 2 (13.2 x 10.5) (16.7 x 10.5)ER Cranes: 2x12.5t,1x10t	**1 oil engine** sr geared to sc. shaft driving 1 CP propeller Total Power: 2,339kW (3,180hp) 14.5kn Alpha 12U28L-VO 1 x Vee 4 Stroke 12 Cy. 280 x 320 2339kW (3180bhp) Alpha Diesel A/S-Denmark AuxGen: 3 x 170kW 380V 50Hz a.c Fuel: 50.0 (d.f.) 332.0 (r.f.)
9514353 **SERENE SKY** *3FUZ9* - **Sea Wealth Navigation SA** Daiichi Chuo Marine Co Ltd (DC Marine) SatCom: Inmarsat C 435122412 *Panama* *Panama* MMSI: 351224000 Official number: 4256211	**31,760** 18,653 56,119 T/cm 55.8	Class: NK	**2011-03 Mitsui Eng. & SB. Co. Ltd., Chiba Works — Ichihara** Yd No: 1775 Loa 189.99 (BB) Br ex - Dght 12.715 Lbp 182.00 Br md 32.25 Dpth 18.10 Welded, 1 dk	**(A21A2BC) Bulk Carrier** Grain: 71,345; Bale: 68,733 Compartments: 5 Ho, ER 5 Ha: ER Cranes: 4x30t	**1 oil engine** driving 1 FP propeller Total Power: 9,480kW (12,889hp) 14.5kn MAN-B&W 6S50MC-C 1 x 2 Stroke 6 Cy. 500 x 2000 9480kW (12889bhp) Mitsui Engineering & Shipbuilding CLtd-Japan Fuel: 2300.0 (r.f.)

9405423 *SVAC6* -	**SERENEA** **Serenea Special Maritime Enterprise (ENE)** Chandris (Hellas) Inc SatCom: Inmarsat C 424079710 *Chios* *Greece* MMSI: 240797000 Official number: 444	**81,502** 51,283 158,583 T/cm 119.7	Class: LR **✠100A1** SS 06/2009 Double Hull oil tanker CSR ESP **ShipRight** (CM) *IWS LI EP **✠LMC** **UMS IGS** Eq.Ltr: Y†; Cable: 742.5/97.0 U3 (a)	**2009-06 Samsung Heavy Industries Co Ltd — Geoje** Yd No: 1723 Loa 274.42 (BB) Br ex 48.04 Dght 17.025 Lbp 264.00 Br md 48.00 Dpth 23.20 Welded, 1 dk	**(A13A2TV) Crude Oil Tanker** Double Hull (13F) Liq: 167,441; Liq (Oil): 167,441 Cargo Heating Coils Compartments: 12 Wing Ta, 2 Wing Slop Ta, ER 3 Cargo Pump (s): 3x3800m^3/hr Manifold: Bow/CM: 136.4m	**1 oil engine** driving 1 FP propeller Total Power: 18,660kW (25,370hp) 15.5kn MAN-B&W 6S70ME-C 1 x 2 Stroke 6 Cy. 700 x 2800 18660kW (25370bhp) Doosan Engine Co Ltd-South Korea AuxGen: 3 x 538kW 450V 60Hz a.c Boilers: e (ex.g.) 22.4kgf/cm^2 (22.0bar), AuxB (o.f.) 18.2kgf/cm^2 (17.8bar) Fuel: 140.0 (d.f.) 3250.0 (r.f.)
9403554 *A8MI9* -	**SERENGETI** **Tidebay Ltd** Dynacom Tankers Management Ltd *Monrovia* *Liberia* MMSI: 636013348 Official number: 13348	**42,331** 21,943 74,998 T/cm 67.2	Class: AB	**2009-04 Sungdong Shipbuilding & Marine Engineering Co Ltd — Tongyeong** Yd No: 3034 Loa 228.00 (BB) Br ex 32.27 Dght 14.426 Lbp 219.00 Br md 32.24 Dpth 20.90 Welded, 1 dk	**(A13B2TP) Products Tanker** Double Hull (13F) Liq: 80,609; Liq (Oil): 83,104 Compartments: 12 Wing Ta, 2 Wing Slop Ta, ER 3 Cargo Pump (s): 3x2300m^3/hr Manifold: Bow/CM: 113.2m	**1 oil engine** driving 1 FP propeller Total Power: 12,240kW (16,642hp) 15.3kn MAN-B&W 6S60MC 1 x 2 Stroke 6 Cy. 600 x 2292 12240kW (16642bhp) Doosan Engine Co Ltd-South Korea AuxGen: 3 x 680kW a.c Fuel: 130.0 (d.f.) 2050.0 (r.f.)
5142657 *J8B4685* -	**SERENISSIMA** *ex* Andrea *-2012* *ex* Harald Jarl *-2002* **Premier Cruises Ltd** West Wind Ltd SatCom: Inmarsat C 437643910 *Kingstown* *St Vincent & The Grenadines* MMSI: 376439000 Official number: 11158	**2,598** 829 590	Class: CS (BV) (NV)	**1960-06 AS Trondhjems Mekaniske Verksted — Trondheim** Yd No: 244 Converted From: General Cargo/Passenger Ship-1960 Loa 87.41 Br ex 13.29 Dght 4.920 Lbp 79.25 Br md 13.26 Dpth 7.35 Riveted\Welded, 2 dks, pt 3rd dk	**(A37A2PC) Passenger/Cruise** Passengers: cabins: 57; berths: 117 Compartments: 2 Ho, ER 2 Ha: (3.0 x 3.0) (5.4 x 3.0)ER Derricks: 1x3t,2x1.5t Ice Capable	**1 oil engine** driving 1 CP propeller Total Power: 2,537kW (3,449hp) 16.0kn B&W 5-50VTBF-110/40 1 x 2 Stroke 5 Cy. 500 x 1100 2537kW (3449bhp) AS Akers Mek Verksted-Norway AuxGen: 3 x 720kW 60Hz a.c Thrusters: 1 Tunnel thruster (f) Fuel: 188.0 (r.f.) 10.0pd
1011317 *ZCGA* -	**SERENITY** **Serenity Marine Ltd** - *The Creek* *Cayman Islands (British)* MMSI: 319012800 Official number: 743646	**858** 257 -	Class: LR **✠100A1** SS 12/2011 SSC Yacht, mono, G6 **LMC** **UMS** Cable: 400.0/24.0 U2 (a)	**2011-12 Heesen Shipyards B.V. — Oss** Yd No: 15555 Loa 55.10 Br ex 10.02 Dght 3.000 Lbp 47.91 Br md 9.53 Dpth 5.20 Welded, 1 dk	**(X11A2YP) Yacht**	**2 oil engines** with clutches, flexible couplings & sr reverse geared to sc. shafts driving 2 FP propellers Total Power: 2,640kW (3,590hp) 15.0kn M.T.U. 12V4000M60 2 x Vee 4 Stroke 12 Cy. 165 x 190 each-1320kW (1795bhp) MTU Friedrichshafen GmbH-Friedrichshafen AuxGen: 2 x 175kW 400V 50Hz a.c Thrusters: 1 Thwart. FP thruster (f)
9240017 - -	**SERENITY** **Government of Bermuda (Department of Marine & Ports Services)** - *Hamilton* *Bermuda (British)*	**163** 72 26	Class: LR **✠100A1** SS 03/2012 SSC passenger catamaran, G2 Bermuda service **LMC** Cable: 110.0/9.0 U2 (a)	**2002-03 Gladding-Hearn SB. Duclos Corp. — Somerset, Ma** Yd No: P-331 Loa 25.72 Br ex 9.45 Dght 1.600 Lbp 23.11 Br md 9.20 Dpth 3.34 Welded, 1 dk	**(A37B2PS) Passenger Ship** Hull Material: Aluminium Alloy Passengers: 250	**2 oil engines** with clutches, flexible couplings & sr reverse geared to sc. shafts driving 2 FP propellers Total Power: 1,440kW (1,958hp) 25.0kn M.T.U. 12V2000M 2 x Vee 4 Stroke 12 Cy. 130 x 150 each-720kW (979bhp) Detroit Diesel Corporation-Detroit, Mi AuxGen: 2 x 40kW 120/240V 60Hz a.c
9391579 *C6WY5* -	**SERENITY ACE** **Serenity Maritime Ltd** Ray Car Carriers Ltd SatCom: Inmarsat C 431100126 *Nassau* *Bahamas* MMSI: 311002800 Official number: 8001487	**57,692** 21,037 21,004	Class: NV	**2008-12 Stocznia Gdynia SA — Gdynia** Yd No: 8168/23 Loa 199.98 (BB) Br ex - Dght 10.000 Lbp 188.28 Br md 32.25 Dpth 14.00 Welded, 11 dks. incl. Nos.1, 3, 5 & 7 dks hoistable	**(A35B2RV) Vehicles Carrier** Side door/ramp (s) Len: 25.00 Wid: 7.00 Swl: 22 Quarter stern door/ramp (s. a.) Len: 38.00 Wid: 7.00 Swl: 150 Cars: 6,658 Ice Capable	**1 oil engine** driving 1 FP propeller Total Power: 15,820kW (21,509hp) 20.0kn MAN-B&W 7S60ME-C 1 x 2 Stroke 7 Cy. 600 x 2400 15820kW (21509bhp) H Cegielski Poznan SA-Poland AuxGen: 3 x a.c Thrusters: 1 Tunnel thruster (centre)
9287998 *V7KT9* -	**SERENITY I** *ex* Delvina *-2006* *ex* Stiogeo *-2006* **Serenity Maritime Inc** Starbulk SA *Majuro* *Marshall Islands* MMSI: 538002678 Official number: 2678	**31,198** 18,361 53,688 T/cm 57.3	Class: LR **✠100A1** SS 04/2011 bulk carrier BC-A strengthened for heavy cargoes, Nos. 2 & 4 holds may be empty ESP LI **ShipRight** (SDA, FDA, CM) **✠LMC** **UMS** Eq.Ltr: M†; Cable: 632.5/73.0 U3 (a)	**2006-04 New Century Shipbuilding Co Ltd — Jingjiang JS** Yd No: 0105314 Loa 190.00 (BB) Br ex 32.29 Dght 12.490 Lbp 182.00 Br md 32.26 Dpth 17.20 Welded, 1 dk	**(A21A2BC) Bulk Carrier** Double Hull Grain: 65,500; Bale: 63,628 Compartments: 5 Ho, ER 5 Ha: 4 (21.6 x 22.4)ER (19.2 x 20.8) Cranes: 4x36t	**1 oil engine** driving 1 FP propeller Total Power: 9,480kW (12,889hp) 14.2kn MAN-B&W 6S50MC-C 1 x 2 Stroke 6 Cy. 500 x 2000 9480kW (12889bhp) Hudong Heavy Machinery Co Ltd-China AuxGen: 3 x 600kW 450V 60Hz a.c Boilers: AuxB (Comp) 8.2kgf/cm^2 (8.0bar) Fuel: 215.0 (d.f.) 2000.0 (r.f.) 33.4pd
9600841 *9HA2389* -	**SERENITY II** **Itatzel Marketing Inc** - *Valletta* *Malta* MMSI: 248499000 Official number: 9600841	**388** 116 -	Class: RI	**2010-08 Mengi Yay Yatcilik — Istanbul (Tuzla)** Yd No: 071 Loa 40.05 Br ex 8.00 Dght 2.470 Lbp 36.13 Br md 7.91 Dpth 4.08 Welded, 1 dk	**(X11A2YP) Yacht**	**2 oil engines** reduction geared to sc. shafts driving 2 Propellers Total Power: 1,640kW (2,230hp) Caterpillar C32 2 x Vee 4 Stroke 12 Cy. 145 x 162 each-820kW (1115bhp) Caterpillar Inc-USA
8984874 *ZGBT4* -	**SERENITY J** *ex* Serenity *-2011* *ex* Summer Time *-2004* *ex* Lady Halima *-2004* **Puma Light Ltd** - *George Town* *Cayman Islands (British)* MMSI: 319037700 Official number: 734906	**390** 117 290	Class: AB	**2001-09 Heesen Shipyards B.V. — Oss** Yd No: 11239 Loa 39.60 Br ex - Dght 2.800 Lbp 34.60 Br md 8.30 Dpth 4.22 Welded, 1 dk	**(X11A2YP) Yacht**	**2 oil engines** reverse reduction geared to sc. shafts driving 2 Propellers Total Power: 1,214kW (1,650hp) Caterpillar 3412C 2 x Vee 4 Stroke 12 Cy. 137 x 152 each-607kW (825bhp) Caterpillar Inc-USA AuxGen: 2 x 65kW
8917728 *PHMA* -	**SERENO** *ex* Passaden *-2007* *ex* ECL Captain *-1992* *completed as* Passaden *-1991* **Merweplein BV** Rederij Chr Kornet & Zonen BV *Werkendam* *Netherlands* MMSI: 244996000 Official number: 48214	**3,828** 2,016 4,452 T/cm 15.0	Class: BV (LR) (GL) Classed LR until 13/11/07	**1991-09 J.J. Sietas KG Schiffswerft GmbH & Co. — Hamburg** Yd No: 1059 Loa 103.50 (BB) Br ex 16.24 Dght 6.070 Lbp 96.90 Br md 16.00 Dpth 8.00 Welded, 1 dk	**(A31A2GX) General Cargo Ship** Grain: 6,820; Bale: 6,603 TEU 372 C Ho 134 TEU C Dk 238 TEU incl 50 ref C Compartments: 2 Ho, ER 3 Ha: (12.4 x 10.3)2 (25.1 x 12.8)ER Ice Capable	**1 oil engine** with flexible couplings & sr geared to sc. shaft driving 1 CP propeller Total Power: 3,330kW (4,527hp) 15.3kn Wartsila 9R32D 1 x 4 Stroke 9 Cy. 320 x 350 3330kW (4527bhp) Wartsila Diesel Oy-Finland AuxGen: 1 x 500kW 220/380V a.c, 2 x 228kW 220/380V a.c Thrusters: 1 Thwart. FP thruster (f)
7611274 - -	**SERGACH** **Ostrov Co Ltd** -	**739** 221 350	Class: (RS)	**1975 Yaroslavskiy Sudostroitelnyy Zavod — Yaroslavl** Yd No: 323 Loa 53.73 (BB) Br ex 10.70 Dght 4.287 Lbp 47.92 Br md - Dpth 6.02 Welded, 1 dk	**(B11A2FS) Stern Trawler** Ins: 218 Compartments: 1 Ho, ER 2 Ha: 2 (1.6 x 1.6) Derricks: 2x1.5t; Winches: 2 Ice Capable	**1 oil engine** driving 1 CP propeller Total Power: 971kW (1,320hp) 12.5kn S.K.L. 8NVD48A-2U 1 x 4 Stroke 8 Cy. 320 x 480 971kW (1320bhp) VEB Schwermaschinenbau "KarlLiebknecht" (SKL)-Magdeburg Thrusters: 1 Thwart. FP thruster (f); 1 Tunnel thruster (a)
6704177 *VC5728* -	**SERGE-LUC** *ex* Erin Colleen *-1979* *ex* Techno-Canada *-1979* **Les Pecheries Serge-Luc Inc** - *Gaspe, QC* *Canada* Official number: 320755	*128* 38 -	Class: (LR) ✠ Classed LR until 6/71	**1966-12 Les Chantiers Maritimes de Paspebiac Inc — Paspebiac QC** Yd No: 20 Loa 27.18 Br ex 6.63 Dght 2.896 Lbp 23.98 Br md - Dpth 3.36 Welded	**(B11A2FT) Trawler**	**1 oil engine** reverse reduction geared to sc. shaft driving 1 FP propeller Total Power: 496kW (674hp) 10.0kn Caterpillar D379SCAC 1 x Vee 4 Stroke 8 Cy. 159 x 203 496kW (674bhp) Caterpillar Tractor Co-USA AuxGen: 2 x 20kW 240V 60Hz a.c
8804309 *UBAG4* -	**SERGEY BOCHKAREV** *ex* Koshin Maru No. 1 *-2009* **Tral-Master Co Ltd** - *Sovetskaya Gavan* *Russia* MMSI: 273339930	*1,521* 460 796	Class: RS	**1988-10 Yamanishi Shipbuilding Co Ltd — Ishinomaki MG** Yd No: 965 Loa 73.00 (BB) Br ex 12.22 Dght 5.632 Lbp 64.00 Br md 12.20 Dpth 7.25 Welded	**(B11A2FS) Stern Trawler** Ins: 967	**1 oil engine** with clutches & sr geared to sc. shaft driving 1 CP propeller Total Power: 2,207kW (3,001hp) Hanshin 8LUS40 1 x 4 Stroke 8 Cy. 400 x 640 2207kW (3001bhp) The Hanshin Diesel Works Ltd-Japan
7332426 *UTDU* -	**SERGEY GRITSEVETS** **Ukrainian Danube Shipping Co** - SatCom: Inmarsat C 427213510 *Izmail* *Ukraine* MMSI: 272135000 Official number: 731330	**3,712** 1,404 4,625	Class: UA (RS)	**1973-07 Navashinskiy Sudostroitelnyy Zavod 'Oka' — Navashino** Yd No: 1062 Loa 123.53 Br ex 15.02 Dght 4.850 Lbp 117.00 Br md 14.99 Dpth 6.51 Welded, 1 dk	**(A31A2GX) General Cargo Ship** Bale: 4,940 Compartments: 4 Ho, ER 4 Ha: 2 (12.0 x 8.3)2 (13.7 x 8.3)ER Cranes: 2x8t Ice Capable	**2 oil engines** driving 2 FP propellers Total Power: 1,472kW (2,002hp) 11.8kn Russkiy 8DR30/50-4 2 x 2 Stroke 8 Cy. 300 x 500 each-736kW (1001bhp) Mashinostroitelnyy Zavod"Russkiy-Dizel"-Leningrad

7347378 *UCYL* -	**SERGEY KRAVKOV** **Government of The Russian Federation** Government of The Russian Federation (Federal State Unitary Hydrographic Department of Ministry of Transport of Russian Federation) SatCom: Inmarsat C 427300977 *Arkhangelsk* *Russia* MMSI: 273918000 Official number: 733412	**1,212** 363 643	Class: RS	**1974-05 Oy Laivateollisuus Ab — Turku** Yd No: 295 Loa 68.23 Br ex 11.89 Dght 4.150 Lbp 60.00 Br md 11.87 Dpth 6.00 Welded, 2 dks	**(B31A2SR) Research Survey Vessel** Bale: 445 Compartments: 2 Ho, ER 2 Ha: (5.8 x 3.2) (1.9 x 1.7) Cranes: 1x5t,1x2t Ice Capable	**1 oil engine** driving 1 CP propeller Total Power: 1,618kW (2,200hp) 13.5kn Deutz SBV6M358 1 x 4 Stroke 6 Cy. 400 x 580 1618kW (2200bhp) Kloeckner Humboldt Deutz AG-West Germany Thrusters: 1 Thwart. FP thruster (f) Fuel: 270.0 (d.f.)
8606276 *UAXN* -	**SERGEY KUZNETSOV** *ex* Mekong Fortune *-2002* *ex* Saigon Fortune *-1993* *ex* Fortune Bay *-1992* *ex* Markham Bay *-1991* *ex* Magdalena R *-1988* **LLC 'Obogatitelnaya Fabrika'** - *Arkhangelsk* *Russia* MMSI: 273449000 Official number: 866325	**2,610** 1,186 2,871	Class: RS (GL)	**1987-08 Detlef Hegemann Rolandwerft GmbH & Co. KG — Berne** Yd No: 139 Loa 83.29 (BB) Br ex - Dght 4.601 Lbp 82.75 Br md 13.01 Dpth 6.66 Welded, 2 dks	**(A31A2GX) General Cargo Ship** Grain: 4,755 TEU 153 C.Ho 105/20' C.Dk 48/20' Compartments: 1 Ho, ER 1 Ha: (55.9 x 10.2)ER Cranes: 2x25t Ice Capable	**1 oil engine** reduction geared to sc. shaft driving 1 CP propeller Total Power: 1,680kW (2,284hp) 11.8kn Alpha 8L28/32 1 x 4 Stroke 8 Cy. 280 x 320 1680kW (2284bhp) MAN B&W Diesel A/S-Denmark Thrusters: 1 Thwart. FP thruster (f)
8721222 *UGVG* -	**SERGEY NOVOSYOLOV** *ex* Atlantic Princess *-2007* *ex* Vladimir Simonok *-1995* **Collective Farm Fishery V Lenin (Rybolovetskiy Kolkhoz Imeni V I Lenina)** - *Petropavlovsk-Kamchatskiy* *Russia* MMSI: 273830200	**4,407** 1,322 1,810	Class: RS	**1987-03 GP Chernomorskiy Sudostroitelnyy Zavod — Nikolayev** Yd No: 558 Loa 104.50 Br ex 16.03 Dght 5.900 Lbp 96.40 Br md 16.00 Dpth 10.20 Welded, 2 dks	**(B11A2FG) Factory Stern Trawler** Ice Capable	**2 oil engines** geared to sc. shaft driving 1 CP propeller Total Power: 5,148kW (7,000hp) 16.1kn Russkiy 6CHN40/46 2 x 4 Stroke 6 Cy. 400 x 460 each-2574kW (3500bhp) Mashinostroitelnyy Zavod"Russkiy-Dizel"-Leningrad AuxGen: 2 x 1600kW 220/380V 50Hz a.c, 3 x 200kW 220/380V 50Hz a.c Fuel: 1226.0 (d.f.)
7831006 *V4UR2* -	**SERGEY POKHLEBAYEV** **Cherutsova Svetlana Alexeevna** - *Basseterre* *St Kitts & Nevis* MMSI: 341509000 Official number: SKN 1002564	*245* 103 51	Class: (RS)	**1979-12 Nakhodkinskiy Sudoremontnyy Zavod — Nakhodka** Yd No: 12 Loa 38.41 Br ex 6.71 Dght 2.201 Lbp 34.50 Br md - Dpth 2.90 Welded, 1 dk	**(A37B2PS) Passenger Ship** Passengers: unberthed: 180 Ice Capable	**2 oil engines** geared to sc. shafts driving 2 FP propellers Total Power: 464kW (630hp) 12.5kn Daldizel 8CHNSP18/22 2 x 4 Stroke 8 Cy. 180 x 220 each-232kW (315bhp) Daldizel-Khabarovsk AuxGen: 1 x 14kW, 2 x 13kW Fuel: 20.0 (d.f.)
8929496 - -	**SERGEY SLESAREVICH** **JSC P/O 'Sevmash' (Production Association North Machine Building Enterprise JSC)** - *Arkhangelsk* *Russia* Official number: 812306	*187* - 46	Class: RS	**1981-07 Gorokhovetskiy Sudostroitelnyy Zavod — Gorokhovets** Yd No: 401 Loa 29.30 Br ex 8.49 Dght 3.090 Lbp 27.00 Br md 8.30 Dpth 4.30 Welded, 1 dk	**(B32A2ST) Tug** Ice Capable	**2 oil engines** driving 2 CP propellers Total Power: 882kW (1,200hp) 11.4kn Russkiy 6D30/50-4-3 2 x 2 Stroke 6 Cy. 300 x 500 each-441kW (600bhp) Mashinostroitelnyy Zavod"Russkiy-Dizel"-Leningrad AuxGen: 2 x 25kW a.c Fuel: 36.0 (d.f.)
9489900 *PPWB* -	**SERGIO BUARQUE DE HOLANDA** **Petrobras Transporte SA (TRANSPETRO) - Fronape** - SatCom: Inmarsat C 471011492 *Rio de Janeiro* *Brazil* MMSI: 710010540	**29,077** 13,897 48,300	Class: LR ✠**100A1** SS 06/2012 Double Hull oil tanker CSR ESP **ShipRight** (CM) CG *IWS LI SPM ✠**LMC** **UMS IGS** Eq.Ltr: M†; Cable: 632.5/73.0 U3 (a)	**2012-06 Estaleiro Maua SA — Niteroi RJ** Yd No: M-200 Loa 182.88 (BB) Br ex 32.44 Dght 12.800 Lbp 174.00 Br md 32.20 Dpth 18.60 Welded, 1 dk	**(A13B2TP) Products Tanker** Double Hull (13F) Liq: 54,880; Liq (Oil): 54,880 Compartments: 12 Wing Ta, 2 Wing Slop Ta, ER	**1 oil engine** driving 1 FP propeller Total Power: 9,462kW (12,865hp) 14.5kn MAN-B&W 6S50ME-C 1 x 2 Stroke 6 Cy. 500 x 2000 9462kW (12865bhp) STX Engine Co Ltd-South Korea AuxGen: 3 x 875kW 450V 60Hz a.c Boilers: TOH (o.f.) 10.2kgf/cm² (10.0bar)
8741179 - -	**SERGIO GRACIA AGUILAR** *ex* Seorim 3 *-2009* **Maritima Isla Mujeres SA de CV** - *Mexico*	**364** 115 165		**2006-12 Moonchang Shipbuilding Dockyard Co Ltd — Mokpo** Lengthened & Widened-2010 Loa 54.14 Br ex - Dght 1.327 Lbp 38.50 Br md 10.00 Dpth 2.40 Welded, 1 dk	**(A36A2PR) Passenger/Ro-Ro Ship (Vehicles)** Passengers: unberthed: 190 Vehicles: 34	**2 oil engines** reduction geared to sc. shafts driving 2 Propellers Total Power: 898kW (1,220hp) 13.0kn Caterpillar 3412 2 x Vee 4 Stroke 12 Cy. 137 x 152 each-449kW (610bhp) Caterpillar Inc-USA
8878726 *UBTD* -	**SERGIY RADONEZHSKIY** **Kamchatskaya Ryba Co Ltd** - *Petropavlovsk-Kamchatskiy* *Russia* MMSI: 273416300 Official number: 920036	**772** 231 352	Class: (RS)	**1993-10 Khabarovskiy Sudostroitelnyy Zavod im Kirova — Khabarovsk** Yd No: 308 Loa 56.39 Br ex 9.52 Dght 4.140 Lbp 49.90 Br md 9.30 Dpth 5.00 Welded, 1 dk	**(B12B2FC) Fish Carrier** Ins: 200 Ice Capable	**1 oil engine** driving 1 CP propeller Total Power: 736kW (1,001hp) 11.8kn S.K.L. 6NVD48A-2U 1 x 4 Stroke 6 Cy. 320 x 480 736kW (1001bhp) SKL Motoren u. Systemtechnik AG-Magdeburg Fuel: 92.0 (d.f.)
8210792 *UBCI3* -	**SERGIY RADONEZHSKIY** *ex* Myojo Maru No. 101 *-2012* **Aquatehnologii LLC** - *Vladivostok* *Russia*	*264* - -	Class: RS	**1982-08 Niigata Engineering Co Ltd — Niigata NI** Yd No: 1761 Loa - Br ex - Dght 2.452 Lbp 30.82 Br md 7.41 Dpth 4.68 Welded, 1 dk	**(B11A2FS) Stern Trawler** Ins: 90 Compartments: 1 Ho, ER 1 Ha:	**1 oil engine** with clutches, flexible couplings & sr geared to sc. shaft driving 1 CP propeller Total Power: 883kW (1,201hp) Niigata 6MG28BX 1 x 4 Stroke 6 Cy. 280 x 320 883kW (1201bhp) Niigata Engineering Co Ltd-Japan
6713245 *UFBV* -	**SERGIY RADONEZHSKIY** *ex* Morskoy-6 *-2003* *ex* Pavel Khokhryakov *-2000* *ex* Morskoy-6 *-1979* **A G Misharin** Barents-Trans Shipping Co Ltd *Arkhangelsk* *Russia* MMSI: 273443130	**1,596** 717 2,210	Class: RS	**1967-06 Reposaaren Konepaja Oy — Pori** Yd No: 119 Loa 90.30 Br ex 12.35 Dght 3.650 Lbp 83.98 Br md 12.20 Dpth 5.14 Welded, 1 dk	**(A31A2GX) General Cargo Ship** Bale: 2,911 Compartments: 3 Ho, ER 3 Ha: 3 (13.1 x 8.5)ER Cranes: 2x2.5t Ice Capable	**2 oil engines** driving 2 FP propellers Total Power: 1,030kW (1,400hp) 11.0kn Russkiy 6DR30/50 2 x 2 Stroke 6 Cy. 300 x 500 each-515kW (700bhp) Mashinostroitelnyy Zavod"Russkiy-Dizel"-Leningrad AuxGen: 3 x 65kW a.c Fuel: 109.0 (d.f.)
9293832 *9MGL7* -	**SERI ALAM** *launched as* Puteri Intan Dua *-2005* **MISC Bhd** - SatCom: Inmarsat C 453392510 *Port Klang* *Malaysia* MMSI: 533925000 Official number: 330453	**95,729** 28,718 83,482 T/cm 100.0	Class: BV	**2005-09 Samsung Heavy Industries Co Ltd — Geoje** Yd No: 1502 Loa 283.06 (BB) Br ex - Dght 12.400 Lbp 270.00 Br md 43.40 Dpth 26.00 Welded, 1 dk	**(A11A2TN) LNG Tanker** Double Bottom Entire Compartment Length Liq (Gas): 145,572 5 x Gas Tank (s); 4 membrane (s.stl) pri horizontal, ER 8 Cargo Pump (s): 8x1700m³/hr Manifold: Bow/CM: 155.6m	**1 Steam Turb** reduction geared to sc. shaft driving 1 FP propeller Total Power: 24,877kW (33,823hp) 19.0kn Kawasaki UA-400 1 x steam Turb 24877kW (33823shp) Kawasaki Heavy Industries Ltd-Japan AuxGen: 2 x 3450kW 6600/220V 60Hz a.c, 1 x 3450kW 6600/220V 60Hz a.c Fuel: 505.7 (d.f.) 7075.0 (r.f.)
9293844 *9MGO9* -	**SERI AMANAH** **MISC Bhd** - SatCom: Inmarsat C 453393710 *Port Klang* *Malaysia* MMSI: 533937000 Official number: 330509	**95,729** 28,718 83,400 T/cm 102.2	Class: BV	**2006-03 Samsung Heavy Industries Co Ltd — Geoje** Yd No: 1503 Loa 283.07 (BB) Br ex - Dght 12.425 Lbp 270.00 Br md 43.40 Dpth 26.00 Welded, 1 dk	**(A11A2TN) LNG Tanker** Double Bottom Entire Compartment Length Liq (Gas): 142,795 5 x Gas Tank (s); 4 membrane (s.stl) pri horizontal, ER 8 Cargo Pump (s): 8x1700m³/hr Manifold: Bow/CM: 142.7m	**1 Steam Turb** reduction geared to sc. shaft driving 1 FP propeller Total Power: 24,877kW (33,823hp) 19.0kn Kawasaki UA-400 1 x steam Turb 24877kW (33823shp) Kawasaki Heavy Industries Ltd-Japan AuxGen: 2 x 3450kW 6600/220V 60Hz a.c, 1 x 3450kW 6600/220V 60Hz a.c Fuel: 505.0 (d.f.) 7075.0 (r.f.)
9321653 *9MGV4* -	**SERI ANGGUN** **MISC Bhd** - SatCom: Inmarsat C 453300562 *Port Klang* *Malaysia* MMSI: 533953000 Official number: 330567	**95,729** 28,718 83,395 T/cm 101.4	Class: BV	**2006-11 Samsung Heavy Industries Co Ltd — Geoje** Yd No: 1589 Loa 283.00 (BB) Br ex - Dght 12.400 Lbp 266.00 Br md 43.40 Dpth 26.00 Welded, 1 dk	**(A11A2TN) LNG Tanker** Double Bottom Entire Compartment Length Liq (Gas): 145,100 5 x Gas Tank (s); 4 membrane (s.stl) pri horizontal, ER 8 Cargo Pump (s): 8x1700m³/hr Manifold: Bow/CM: 142.7m	**1 Steam Turb** reduction geared to sc. shaft driving 1 FP propeller Total Power: 24,860kW (33,800hp) 19.0kn Kawasaki UA-400 1 x steam Turb 24860kW (33800shp) Kawasaki Heavy Industries Ltd-Japan AuxGen: 2 x 3450kW 6600/220V 60Hz a.c, 1 x 3450kW 6600/220V 60Hz a.c Thrusters: 1 Tunnel thruster (f) Fuel: 423.0 (d.f.) 6846.0 (r.f.)

9321665 *9MGW4* -	**SERI ANGKASA** **MISC Bhd** - SatCom: Inmarsat C 453395710 *Port Klang* *Malaysia* MMSI: 533957000 Official number: 330581	**95,729** 28,718 83,407 T/cm 102.3	Class: BV	**2006-12 Samsung Heavy Industries Co Ltd — Geoje** Yd No: 1590 Loa 283.07 (BB) Br ex - Dght 12.425 Lbp 266.00 Br md 43.40 Dpth 26.00 Welded, 1 dk	**(A11A2TN) LNG Tanker** Double Bottom Entire Compartment Length Liq (Gas): 142,786 5 x Gas Tank (s); 4 membrane (s.stl) pri , ER 8 Cargo Pump (s): 8x1700m^3/hr Manifold: Bow/CM: 143.1m	**1 Steam Turb** dr. geared to sc. shaft driving 1 FP propeller Total Power: 24,877kW (33,823hp) 19.0kn Kawasaki UA-400 1 x steam Turb 24877kW (33823shp) Kawasaki Heavy Industries Ltd-Japan AuxGen: 2 x 3450kW 6600/220V 60Hz a.c, 1 x 3450kW 6600/220V 60Hz a.c Fuel: 260.0 (d.f.) 6000.0 (r.f.)
8971401 *V8V2105* -	**SERI ANNA** **Interhill Industries Sdn Bhd** - *Muara* *Brunei* Official number: 0022A	*229* 68 35	Class: BV	**1999-09 Aluminium Fast Ferries Australia Pty Ltd — Brisbane QLD** Yd No: 002 Loa 32.31 Br ex - Dght 1.340 Lbp 29.97 Br md 8.18 Dpth 2.75 Welded, 2 dks	**(A37B2PS) Passenger Ship** Hull Material: Aluminium Alloy Passengers: unberthed: 264	**4 oil engines** reduction geared to sc. shafts driving 2 FP propellers , 2 Water jets Total Power: 2,596kW (3,528hp) 25.0kn M.T.U. 8V396TE74 4 x Vee 4 Stroke 8 Cy. 165 x 185 each-649kW (882bhp) (made 1978) MTU Friedrichshafen GmbH-Friedrichshafen AuxGen: 2 x 136kW 240V 50Hz a.c
9329679 *9MFE7* -	**SERI AYU** **MISC Bhd** - SatCom: Inmarsat C 453300221 *Port Klang* *Malaysia* MMSI: 533942000 Official number: 332383	**95,729** 28,718 83,365 T/cm 100.2	Class: BV	**2007-10 Samsung Heavy Industries Co Ltd — Geoje** Yd No: 1591 Loa 283.07 (BB) Br ex - Dght 12.400 Lbp 270.04 Br md 43.40 Dpth 26.00 Welded, 1 dk	**(A11A2TN) LNG Tanker** Double Bottom Entire Compartment Length Liq (Gas): 143,474 5 x Gas Tank (s); 4 membrane (s.stl) pri horizontal, ER 8 Cargo Pump (s): 8x1700m^3/hr Manifold: Bow/CM: 143.1m	**1 Steam Turb** reduction geared to sc. shaft driving 1 FP propeller Total Power: 24,877kW (33,823hp) 19.0kn Kawasaki UA-400 1 x steam Turb 24877kW (33823shp) Kawasaki Heavy Industries Ltd-Japan AuxGen: 2 x 3450kW 6600/220V 60Hz a.c, 1 x 3450kW 6600/220V 60Hz a.c Fuel: 505.0 (d.f.) 7075.0 (r.f.)
9331634 *9MGZ6* -	**SERI BAKTI** **MISC Bhd** - SatCom: Inmarsat Mini-M 761121780 *Port Klang* *Malaysia* MMSI: 533380000 Official number: 332319	**105,335** 31,600 90,065 T/cm 111.4	Class: LR ✠ **100A1** SS 06/2012 liquefied gas tanker, Ship Type 2G, methane in membrane tanks, maximum vapour pressure 0.25 bar minimum temperature minus 163 degree C **ShipRight** (SDA) *IWS LI ✠ **LMC** **UMS** Eq.Ltr: A*; Cable: 742.5/107.0 U3 (a)	**2007-06 Mitsubishi Heavy Industries Ltd. — Nagasaki** Yd No: 2220 Loa 289.80 (BB) Br ex 46.53 Dght 12.425 Lbp 276.80 Br md 46.50 Dpth 25.80 Welded, 1 dk	**(A11A2TN) LNG Tanker** Double Hull Liq (Gas): 149,886 5 x Gas Tank (s); 4 membrane (36% Ni.stl) pri horizontal, ER 8 Cargo Pump (s): 8x1650m^3/hr Manifold: Bow/CM: 144.9m	**1 Steam Turb** with flexible couplings & dr reverse geared to sc. shafts driving 1 CP propeller Total Power: 24,500kW (33,310hp) 19.0kn Mitsubishi MS36-2A 1 x steam Turb 24500kW (33310shp) Mitsubishi Heavy Industries Ltd-Japan AuxGen: 3 x 2900kW 450V 60Hz a.c Boilers: wtdb (o.f.) 78.5kgf/cm^2 (77.0bar) 67.3kgf/cm^2 (66.0bar) Fuel: 650.0 (d.f.) 8800.0 (r.f.)
9331660 *9MIB9* -	**SERI BALHAF** **MISC Bhd** - SatCom: Inmarsat Mini-M 764846898 *Port Klang* *Malaysia* MMSI: 533868000 Official number: 333905	**107,633** 32,289 91,201 T/cm 113.7	Class: BV	**2009-01 Mitsubishi Heavy Industries Ltd. — Nagasaki** Yd No: 2223 Loa 294.60 (BB) Br ex - Dght 12.400 Lbp 281.60 Br md 46.50 Dpth 25.80 Welded, 1 dk	**(A11A2TN) LNG Tanker** Double Hull Liq (Gas): 154,567 5 x Gas Tank (s); 4 membrane (36% Ni.stl) pri horizontal, ER 8 Cargo Pump (s): 8x1850m^3/hr Manifold: Bow/CM: 147.3m	**4 diesel electric oil engines** driving 3 gen. each 11000kW a.c 1 gen. of 5500kW a.c Connecting to 2 elec. motors each (13500kW) driving 1 CP propeller Total Power: 39,900kW (54,247hp) 19.5kn Wartsila 12V50DF 3 x Vee 4 Stroke 12 Cy. 500 x 580 each-11400kW (15499bhp) Wartsila France SA-France Wartsila 6L50DF 1 x 4 Stroke 6 Cy. 500 x 580 5700kW (7750bhp) Wartsila France SA-France Thrusters: 1 Tunnel thruster (f) Fuel: 5750.0 (d.f.)
9331672 *9MII5* -	**SERI BALQIS** **MISC Bhd** - SatCom: Inmarsat Mini-M 764890442 *Port Klang* *Malaysia* MMSI: 533894000 Official number: 334017	**107,633** 32,289 91,198 T/cm 113.7	Class: BV	**2009-03 Mitsubishi Heavy Industries Ltd. — Nagasaki** Yd No: 2224 Loa 294.60 (BB) Br ex - Dght 12.400 Lbp 281.60 Br md 46.50 Dpth 25.80 Welded, 1 dk	**(A11A2TN) LNG Tanker** Double Hull Liq (Gas): 154,747 4 x Gas Tank (s); 4 membrane (36% Ni.stl) pri horizontal 8 Cargo Pump (s): 8x1850m^3/hr Manifold: Bow/CM: 147.3m	**4 diesel electric oil engines** driving 3 gen. each 11000kW a.c 1 gen. of 5500kW a.c Connecting to 2 elec. motors each (13500kW) driving 1 CP propeller Total Power: 39,900kW (54,247hp) 19.5kn Wartsila 12V50DF 3 x Vee 4 Stroke 12 Cy. 500 x 580 each-11400kW (15499bhp) Wartsila France SA-France Wartsila 6L50DF 1 x 4 Stroke 6 Cy. 500 x 580 5700kW (7750bhp) Wartsila France SA-France Thrusters: 1 Tunnel thruster (f) Fuel: 5749.0 (d.f.)
9331646 *9MFJ6* -	**SERI BEGAWAN** **MISC Bhd** - SatCom: Inmarsat Mini-M 761155294 *Port Klang* *Malaysia* MMSI: 533016000 Official number: 332436	**105,335** 31,600 89,902 T/cm 111.4	Class: LR ✠ **100A1** SS 12/2012 liquefied gas carrier, Ship Type 2G methane (LNG) in membrane tanks maximum vapour pressure 0.25 bar minimum temperature minus 163 degree C **ShipRight** (SDA) *IWS LI ✠ **LMC** **UMS** Eq.Ltr: A*; Cable: 742.5/107.0 U3 (a)	**2007-12 Mitsubishi Heavy Industries Ltd. — Nagasaki** Yd No: 2221 Loa 289.80 (BB) Br ex 46.54 Dght 12.425 Lbp 276.80 Br md 46.50 Dpth 25.80 Welded, 1 dk.	**(A11A2TN) LNG Tanker** Double Hull Liq (Gas): 149,964 4 x Gas Tank (s); 4 membrane (36% Ni.stl) pri horizontal 8 Cargo Pump (s): 8x1650m^3/hr Manifold: Bow/CM: 144.9m	**1 Steam Turb** with flexible couplings & dr reverse geared to sc. shaft driving 1 CP propeller Total Power: 24,500kW (33,310hp) 19.0kn Mitsubishi MS36-2A 1 x steam Turb 24500kW (33310shp) Mitsubishi Heavy Industries Ltd-Japan AuxGen: 3 x 2900kW 450V 60Hz a.c Boilers: wtdb (o.f.) 78.0kgf/cm^2 (76.5bar) Superheater 515°C 65.3kgf/cm^2 (64.0bar) Fuel: 650.0 (d.f.) 8800.0 (r.f.)
9331658 *9MHQ7* -	**SERI BIJAKSANA** **MISC Bhd** - SatCom: Inmarsat Mini-M 761155294 *Port Klang* *Malaysia* MMSI: 533051000 Official number: 332480	**104,881** 31,464 89,953 T/cm 111.4	Class: AB	**2008-04 Mitsubishi Heavy Industries Ltd. — Nagasaki** Yd No: 2222 Loa 289.80 (BB) Br ex 46.54 Dght 12.400 Lbp 276.80 Br md 46.50 Dpth 25.80 Welded, 1 dk	**(A11A2TN) LNG Tanker** Double Hull Liq (Gas): 149,822 8 Cargo Pump (s): 8x1650m^3/hr Manifold: Bow/CM: 144.9m	**1 Steam Turb** reduction geared to sc. shaft driving 1 CP propeller Total Power: 22,050kW (29,979hp) 19.0kn Mitsubishi MS36-2A 1 x steam Turb 22050kW (29979shp) Mitsubishi Heavy Industries Ltd-Japan AuxGen: 3 x 2900kW a.c Fuel: 588.6 (d.f.) 6299.0 (r.f.)
8864294 - -	**SERI PESISIR** *ex* Rampai Pesisir *-2012* *ex* Kotoku Maru *-2007* *ex* Kaisei Maru No. 3 *-2005* **Gama Bistari Sdn Bhd** -	**1,082** 599 2,200	Class: IZ	**1992-01 Y.K. Takasago Zosensho — Naruto** Yd No: 182 Loa 73.70 (BB) Br ex - Dght 3.650 Lbp 67.00 Br md 11.20 Dpth 6.50 Welded, 1 dk	**(A31A2GX) General Cargo Ship**	**1 oil engine** reverse geared to sc. shaft driving 1 FP propeller Total Power: 736kW (1,001hp) 11.0kn Hanshin LH28G 1 x 4 Stroke 6 Cy. 280 x 460 736kW (1001bhp) The Hanshin Diesel Works Ltd-Japan
9081825 *SYNC*	**SERIFOPOULO** **Serifopoulo Special Maritime Enterprise (ENE)** **Eletson Corp** SatCom: Inmarsat A 1132304 *Piraeus* *Greece* MMSI: 239380000 Official number: 10273	**28,507** 12,161 46,699 T/cm 50.5	Class: LR (AB) **100A1** SS 02/2010 Double Hull oil tanker ESP LI **LMC** **UMS IGS** Eq.Ltr: M†; Cable: 632.5/73.0 U3	**1995-02 Hyundai Heavy Industries Co Ltd — Ulsan** Yd No: 879 Loa 182.76 (BB) Br ex 32.40 Dght 12.215 Lbp 172.50 Br md 32.20 Dpth 18.60 Welded, 1 dk	**(A13A2TW) Crude/Oil Products Tanker** Double Hull Liq: 50,782; Liq (Oil): 50,782 Cargo Heating Coils Compartments: 7 Ta, 2 Wing Slop Ta, ER 3 Cargo Pump (s): 3x1500m^3/hr Manifold: Bow/CM: 90m	**1 oil engine** driving 1 FP propeller Total Power: 6,618kW (8,998hp) 14.8kn B&W 6S50MC 1 x 2 Stroke 6 Cy. 500 x 1910 6618kW (8998bhp) Hyundai Heavy Industries Co Ltd-South Korea AuxGen: 1 x 700kW 450V 60Hz a.c, 2 x 550kW 450V 60Hz a.c Boilers: 2 AuxB (o.f.) 18.4kgf/cm^2 (18.0bar) Fuel: 152.4 (d.f.) (Heating Coils) 1394.3 (r.f.) 26.0pd
9081837 *SXDR*	**SERIFOS** **Serifos Special Maritime Enterprise (ENE)** **Eletson Corp** SatCom: Inmarsat C 423942110 *Piraeus* *Greece* MMSI: 239421000 Official number: 10312	**28,507** 12,161 46,700 T/cm 51.5	Class: LR (AB) **100A1** SS 05/2010 Double Hull oil tanker ESP **LMC** **UMS IGS** Eq.Ltr: M†; Cable: 632.5/73.0 U3	**1995-05 Hyundai Heavy Industries Co Ltd — Ulsan** Yd No: 880 Loa 182.76 (BB) Br ex 32.40 Dght 12.216 Lbp 172.50 Br md 32.20 Dpth 18.60 Welded, 1 dk	**(A13A2TW) Crude/Oil Products Tanker** Double Hull Liq: 50,782; Liq (Oil): 50,782 Cargo Heating Coils Compartments: 7 Ta, 2 Wing Slop Ta, ER 3 Cargo Pump (s): 3x1500m^3/hr Manifold: Bow/CM: 90m	**1 oil engine** driving 1 FP propeller Total Power: 6,618kW (8,998hp) 14.8kn B&W 6S50MC 1 x 2 Stroke 6 Cy. 500 x 1910 6618kW (8998bhp) Hyundai Heavy Industries Co Ltd-South Korea AuxGen: 1 x 700kW 450V 60Hz a.c, 2 x 550kW 450V 60Hz a.c Boilers: 2 AuxB (o.f.) 18.4kgf/cm^2 (18.0bar) Fuel: 151.4 (d.f.) (Heating Coils) 1394.3 (r.f.) 26.7pd

IMO / Call sign	Name / Owner	Tonnage	Class	Builder / Dimensions	Type	Machinery
9371256 *9VFJ9* -	**SERIFOS** **Serifos Shipping (Pte) Ltd** Aegean Bunkering (Singapore) Pte Ltd *Singapore* *Singapore* MMSI: 565576000 Official number: 393434	**3,220** 1,327 4,664	Class: AB	**2007-11 Fujian Southeast Shipyard — Fuzhou FJ** Yd No: 3500-2 Loa 90.22 (BB) Br ex - Dght 6.010 Lbp 85.00 Br md 15.60 Dpth 7.80 Welded, 1 dk	**(A13B2TP) Products Tanker** Double Hull (13F) Liq: 4,470; Liq (Oil): 4,470 Cargo Heating Coils Compartments: 10 Wing Ta, ER 3 Cargo Pump (s): 2x500m^3/hr, 1x300m^3/hr	**1 oil engine** reduction geared to sc. shaft driving 1 FP propeller Total Power: 2,480kW (3,372hp) Wartsila 8L26 1 x 4 Stroke 8 Cy. 260 x 320 2480kW (3372bhp) Wartsila Finland Oy-Finland AuxGen: 3 x 250kW a.c Fuel: 62.6 (d.f.) 289.7 (r.f.)
9036117 - -	**SERIN** *ex* Sol *-1994* - -	*171* 51 330	Class: (BV)	**1990 Stocznia 'Wisla' — Gdansk** Yd No: 1103 Loa 25.71 Br ex - Dght 3.682 Lbp 22.46 Br md 7.41 Dpth 4.02 Welded	**(B11A2FS) Stern Trawler**	**1 oil engine** reduction geared to sc. shaft driving 1 CP propeller Total Power: 419kW (570hp) 9.0kn MAN D2542MLE 1 x Vee 4 Stroke 12 Cy. 125 x 142 419kW (570bhp) MAN Nutzfahrzeuge AG-Nuernberg
9621534 *PBPB*	**SERKEBORG** **Noordereems BV** Wagenborg Kazakhstan BV *Delfzijl* *Netherlands* MMSI: 245141000	**1,520** 456 867	Class: BV	**2012-10 Niestern Sander B.V. — Delfzijl** Yd No: 845 Loa 68.20 Br ex 14.30 Dght 3.150 Lbp 64.89 Br md 14.00 Dpth - Welded, 1 dk	**(B21B20T) Offshore Tug/Supply Ship** Ice Capable	**2 diesel electric oil engines** driving 2 gen. each 1750kW 690V a.c Connecting to 2 elec. motors each (1750kW) driving 2 Azimuth electric drive units Total Power: 3,500kW (4,758hp) 12.0kn Thrusters: 1 Tunnel thruster (f) Fuel: 810.0
8618267 *OYCQ* GR 5 66	**SERMILIK** *ex* Freyja *-2006* **Royal Greenland AS** *Paamiut* *Denmark* MMSI: 331206000	**241** 72 -	Class: NV	**1987-12 Moen Slip og Mekanisk Verksted AS — Kolvereid** Yd No: 29 Loa 25.91 Br ex - Dght 4.050 Lbp 23.02 Br md 8.01 Dpth 6.25 Welded, 1 dk	**(B11A2FS) Stern Trawler** Ice Capable	**1 oil engine** geared to sc. shaft driving 1 FP propeller Total Power: 735kW (999hp) Alpha 6L23/30 1 x 4 Stroke 6 Cy. 225 x 300 735kW (999bhp) MAN B&W Diesel A/S-Denmark AuxGen: 1 x 210kW 380V 50Hz a.c, 1 x 92kW 380V 50Hz a.c
8600052 *LW9767* -	**SERMILIK** *ex* Helen Basse *-1992* **Sermilik SA** Harengus SA *Buenos Aires* *Argentina* MMSI: 701000925 Official number: 0505	**236** 85 250	Class: (BV)	**1985 Strandby Skibsvaerft I/S — Strandby** Yd No: 83 Loa 35.41 (BB) Br ex - Dght - Lbp 30.99 Br md 7.71 Dpth 6.46 Welded, 3 dks	**(B11A2FS) Stern Trawler** Ins: 275	**1 oil engine** with clutches, flexible couplings & sr geared to sc. shaft driving 1 CP propeller Total Power: 810kW (1,101hp) 12.5kn Alpha 5T23L-KVO 1 x 4 Stroke 5 Cy. 225 x 300 810kW (1101bhp) MAN B&W Diesel A/S-Denmark AuxGen: 2 x 260kW 220/380V a.c Thrusters: 1 Directional thruster (f) Fuel: 76.0 (d.f.)
7302378 *OW2202* -	**SERMILIK II** *ex* Manu *-2008* *ex* Umanak *-2004* *ex* Solbakur *-1998* *ex* Adalvik *-1990* *ex* Drangey *-1989* **P/F Thor** *Hosvik* *Faeroe Islands (Danish)* MMSI: 231835000 Official number: VN 668	**776** 232 359	Class: LR NV ✠**100A1** SS 12/2010 stern trawler Ice Class 3 ✠**LMC** Eq.Ltr: (l) J; Cable: U2	**1973-03 Narasaki Zosen KK — Muroran HK** Yd No: 808 Lengthened-1986 Loa 53.70 Br ex 9.53 Dght 4.300 Lbp 47.83 Br md 9.50 Dpth 6.51 Welded, 2 dks	**(B11A2FS) Stern Trawler** Ice Capable	**1 oil engine** sr geared to sc. shaft driving 1 FP propeller Total Power: 1,618kW (2,200hp) Crepelle 8SN3 1 x 4 Stroke 8 Cy. 260 x 280 1618kW (2200bhp) (new engine 1986) Moteurs Duvant Crepelle-France AuxGen: 1 x 292kW 380V 50Hz a.c, 1 x 292kW 400V 50Hz a.c
5320754 *CSNS*	**SERNACHE** **Eurodoca - Empresa de Pescas e Commercializacao de Pescado SA** *Lisbon* *Portugal* MMSI: 263532000 Official number: LX-30-N	*900* 470 773	Class: (LR) (RP) ✠ Classed LR until 1/8/90	**1948-07 Scheepswerf "De Gideon" v/h J. Koster Hzn. — Groningen** Yd No: 216 Loa 65.61 Br ex 9.76 Dght 4.820 Lbp 58.98 Br md 9.71 Dpth 5.21 Riveted\Welded, 1 dk	**(B11B2FV) Fishing Vessel** Ice Capable	**1 oil engine** driving 1 CP propeller Total Power: 1,103kW (1,500hp) Wichmann 5AXA 1 x 2 Stroke 5 Cy. 300 x 450 1103kW (1500bhp) (new engine 1978) Wichmann Motorfabrikk AS-Norway AuxGen: 3 x 210kW 380V 50Hz a.c Thrusters: 1 Thwart. FP thruster (f)
9076454 *UCLT*	**SEROGLAZKA** **Collective Farm Fishery V Lenin (Rybolovetskiy Kolkhoz Imeni V I Lenina)** - SatCom: Inmarsat A 1404616 *Petropavlovsk-Kamchatskiy* *Russia* MMSI: 273843200 Official number: 910744	**4,407** 1,322 1,810	Class: RS	**1992-11 DAHK Chernomorskyi Sudnobudivnyi Zavod — Mykolayiv** Yd No: 600 Loa 104.50 Br ex 16.03 Dght 5.900 Lbp 96.40 Br md 16.00 Dpth 10.20 Welded, 1 dk	**(B11A2FG) Factory Stern Trawler** Ice Capable	**2 oil engines** reduction geared to sc. shaft driving 1 CP propeller Total Power: 5,148kW (7,000hp) 16.1kn Russkiy 6CHN40/46 2 x 4 Stroke 6 Cy. 400 x 460 each-2574kW (3500bhp) Mashinostroitelnyy Zavod"Russkiy-Dizel"-Sankt-Peterburg AuxGen: 2 x 1600kW 220/380V 50Hz a.c, 3 x 200kW 220/380V 50Hz a.c Fuel: 1127.0 (d.f.) 23.0pd
8737398 *PMMG*	**SEROJA** **Government of The Republic of Indonesia (Direktorat Jenderal Perhubungan Laut - Ministry of Sea Communications)** *Jakarta* *Indonesia* MMSI: 525019540	**518** 156 909	Class: KI	**1998-09 in Indonesia** Loa 47.63 Br ex - Dght 3.200 Lbp 44.64 Br md 9.75 Dpth 3.66 Welded, 1 dk	**(B33A2DU) Dredger (unspecified)**	**2 oil engines** reduction geared to sc. shafts driving 2 Propellers Total Power: 706kW (960hp) 10.0kn Caterpillar 3408C 2 x Vee 4 Stroke 8 Cy. 137 x 152 each-353kW (480bhp) Caterpillar Inc-USA AuxGen: 2 x 40kW 400/230V a.c
9567673 *3FFV6* -	**SEROJA ENAM** *ex* APL Poland *-2014* *ex* Seroja Enam *-2013* **Sun Lanes Shipping SA** Nissen Kaiun Co Ltd (Nissen Kaiun KK) *Panama* *Panama* MMSI: 351109000 Official number: 42220PEXT3	**86,679** 47,960 90,480	Class: NK	**2011-08 Mitsubishi Heavy Industries Ltd. — Nagasaki** Yd No: 2269 Loa 316.00 (BB) Br ex - Dght 14.540 Lbp 302.00 Br md 45.60 Dpth 25.00 Welded, 1 dk	**(A33A2CC) Container Ship (Fully Cellular)** TEU 8540 C.Ho 3474 TEU C.Dk 5066 TEU incl 630 ref C.	**1 oil engine** driving 1 FP propeller Total Power: 62,810kW (85,396hp) 25.3kn MAN-B&W 11K98MC-C 1 x 2 Stroke 11 Cy. 980 x 2400 62810kW (85396bhp) Mitsui Engineering & Shipbuilding CLtd-Japan AuxGen: 4 x a.c Thrusters: 1 Tunnel thruster (f) Fuel: 8700.0
9596935 *PNSQ* -	**SEROJA I** **PT Usda Seroja Jaya** *Batam* *Indonesia* MMSI: 525015779	**1,869** 798 3,100	Class: KI	**2010-12 PT Usda Seroja Jaya — Rengat** Loa 87.26 Br ex - Dght 3.700 Lbp 83.16 Br md 15.60 Dpth 4.14 Welded, 1 dk	**(A13B2TP) Products Tanker** Double Hull (13F)	**2 oil engines** reduction geared to sc. shafts driving 2 Propellers Total Power: 376kW (512hp) 14.0kn Weifang X6170ZC 2 x 4 Stroke 6 Cy. 170 x 200 each-188kW (256bhp) Weifang Diesel Engine Factory-China
9662813 *POTB* -	**SEROJA II** **PT Usda Seroja Jaya** - *Batam* *Indonesia* MMSI: 525020122 Official number: USJ008	**2,280** 1,408 3,500	Class: KI	**2012-05 PT Usda Seroja Jaya — Rengat** Yd No: 08 Loa 87.26 Br ex - Dght 3.910 Lbp 83.36 Br md 15.60 Dpth 4.40 Welded, 1 dk	**(A13B2TP) Products Tanker** Double Hull (13F)	**2 oil engines** reduction geared to sc. shafts driving 2 FP propellers Total Power: 764kW (1,038hp) 10.3kn Weifang X6170ZC 2 x 4 Stroke 6 Cy. 170 x 200 each-382kW (519bhp) Weichai Power Co Ltd-China AuxGen: 2 x 60kW 400V a.c, 1 x 90kW 400V a.c
9662825 *POTC* -	**SEROJA III** **PT Usda Seroja Jaya** - *Batam* *Indonesia* MMSI: 525020127 Official number: USJ009	**2,280** 1,212 3,500	Class: KI	**2012-05 PT Usda Seroja Jaya — Rengat** Yd No: 09 Loa 87.26 Br ex - Dght 3.910 Lbp 83.36 Br md 15.60 Dpth 4.40 Welded, 1 dk	**(A13B2TP) Products Tanker** Double Hull (13F)	**2 oil engines** reduction geared to sc. shafts driving 2 FP propellers Total Power: 764kW (1,038hp) 10.3kn Weifang X6170ZC 2 x 4 Stroke 6 Cy. 170 x 200 each-382kW (519bhp) Weichai Power Co Ltd-China AuxGen: 2 x 60kW 400V a.c, 1 x 90kW 400V a.c
9658812 *POOQ* -	**SEROJA IV** **PT Usda Seroja Jaya** - *Batam* *Indonesia* MMSI: 525020082	**2,280** 1,151 3,500	Class: KI	**2012-04 PT Usda Seroja Jaya — Rengat** Yd No: 07 Loa 87.26 Br ex - Dght - Lbp 83.36 Br md 15.60 Dpth 5.20 Welded, 1 dk	**(A13B2TP) Products Tanker** Double Hull (13F)	**2 oil engines** reduction geared to sc. shafts driving 2 FP propellers Total Power: 764kW (1,038hp) 10.3kn Weifang X6170ZC 2 x 4 Stroke 6 Cy. 170 x 200 each-382kW (519bhp) Weichai Power Co Ltd-China AuxGen: 2 x 60kW 400V a.c, 1 x 90kW 400V a.c
9567661 *3FTU* -	**SEROJA LIMA** *ex* APL France *-2013* *ex* Seroja Lima *-2013* **Leo Ocean SA & Tokei Kaiun Ltd** Tokei Kaiun KK SatCom: Inmarsat C 435798810 *Panama* *Panama* MMSI: 357988000 Official number: 41739PEXT3	**86,682** 47,960 90,388	Class: NK	**2011-03 Mitsubishi Heavy Industries Ltd. — Nagasaki** Yd No: 2268 Loa 316.00 (BB) Br ex - Dght 14.535 Lbp 302.00 Br md 45.60 Dpth 25.00 Welded, 1 dk	**(A33A2CC) Container Ship (Fully Cellular)** TEU 8540 C.Ho 3474 TEU C.Dk 5066 TEU incl 630 ref C.	**1 oil engine** driving 1 FP propeller Total Power: 62,810kW (85,396hp) 25.3kn MAN-B&W 11K98MC-C 1 x 2 Stroke 11 Cy. 980 x 2400 62810kW (85396bhp) Mitsui Engineering & Shipbuilding CLtd-Japan AuxGen: 4 x a.c Thrusters: 1 Tunnel thruster (f) Fuel: 8792.0 (r.f.)

IMO / Call sign	Name / Owner / Registry	Tonnage	Class	Builder / Dimensions	Type	Machinery
9495038 *3FRZ3* -	**SEROJA TIGA** *ex* APL Zeebrugge *-2014* *ex* Seroja Tiga *-2010* **Southern Route Maritime SA & Nissen Kaiun Co Ltd** Nissen Kaiun Co Ltd (Nissen Kaiun KK) SatCom: Inmarsat C 435544310 *Panama* *Panama* MMSI: 355443000 Official number: 40558PEXT4	**86,679** 47,960 90,414	Class: NK	**2010-05 Mitsubishi Heavy Industries Ltd. — Nagasaki** Yd No: 2258 Loa 316.00 (BB) Br ex - Dght 14.530 Lbp 302.00 Br md 45.60 Dpth 25.00 Welded, 1 dk	**(A33A2CC) Container Ship (Fully Cellular)** TEU 8540 C Ho 3474 TEU C Dk 5066 TEU incl 630 ref C.	**1 oil engine** driving 1 FP propeller Total Power: 62,810kW (85,396hp) 25.3kn MAN-B&W 11K98MC-C 1 x 2 Stroke 11 Cy. 980 x 2400 62810kW (85396bhp) Mitsui Engineering & Shipbuilding CLtd-Japan AuxGen: 4 x a.c Thrusters: 1 Tunnel thruster (f) Fuel: 7920.0 (r.f.)
9658769 *POOR* -	**SEROJA V** - **PT Usda Seroja Jaya** - *Batam* *Indonesia* MMSI: 525015000	**2,280** 1,212 3,500	Class: KI	**2012-03 PT Usda Seroja Jaya — Rengat** Yd No: 06 Loa 87.26 Br ex - Dght 3.920 Lbp 83.36 Br md 15.60 Dpth 5.20 Welded, 1 dk	**(A13B2TP) Products Tanker**	**2 oil engines** reduction geared to sc. shafts driving 2 FP propellers Total Power: 764kW (1,038hp) 10.3kn Weifang X6170ZC 2 x 4 Stroke 6 Cy. 170 x 200 each-382kW (519bhp) Weichai Power Co Ltd-China AuxGen: 1 x 90kW 400V a.c, 2 x 60kW 400V a.c
9691462 *JZGO* -	**SEROJA VII** - **PT Usda Seroja Jaya** - *Batam* *Indonesia* MMSI: 525023164	**2,384** 1,335 3,500	Class: KI (Class contemplated)	**2013-04 PT Usda Seroja Jaya — Rengat** Yd No: 016 Loa 88.35 (BB) Br ex - Dght 4.500 Lbp 84.29 Br md 15.00 Dpth 4.80 Welded, 1 dk	**(A13B2TP) Products Tanker** Double Hull (13F)	**2 oil engines** reduction geared to sc. shafts driving 2 Propellers Total Power: 970kW (1,318hp) Yanmar 6AYM-WST 2 x 4 Stroke 6 Cy. 155 x 180 each-485kW (659bhp) Yanmar Diesel Engine Co Ltd-Japan
9691474 *JZGP* -	**SEROJA VIII** - **PT Usda Seroja Jaya** - *Batam* *Indonesia* MMSI: 525023160	**2,384** 1,335 3,500	Class: KI (Class contemplated)	**2013-05 PT Usda Seroja Jaya — Rengat** Yd No: 017 Loa 88.35 (BB) Br ex - Dght 4.500 Lbp 84.29 Br md 15.00 Dpth 4.80 Welded, 1 dk	**(A13B2TP) Products Tanker** Double Hull (13F)	**2 oil engines** reduction geared to sc. shafts driving 2 Propellers Total Power: 970kW (1,318hp) Yanmar 6AYM-WST 2 x 4 Stroke 6 Cy. 155 x 180 each-485kW (659bhp) Yanmar Diesel Engine Co Ltd-Japan
9735725 - -	**SEROJA X** *ex* New Britain I *-2014* **PT Usda Seroja Jaya** - *Indonesia* MMSI: 525020223	**2,253** 1,530 4,175	Class: RI (Class contemplated)	**2014-01 PT Usda Seroja Jaya — Rengat** Yd No: 020 Loa 89.34 Br ex - Dght 4.530 Lbp 84.66 Br md 15.00 Dpth 5.34 Welded, 1 dk	**(A12D2LV) Vegetable Oil Tanker** Double Hull (13F)	**2 oil engines** reduction geared to sc. shafts driving 2 Propellers Total Power: 970kW (1,318hp) Yanmar 6AYM-WST 2 x 4 Stroke 6 Cy. 155 x 180 each-485kW (659bhp) Yanmar Diesel Engine Co Ltd-Japan
8033235 *UINI* -	**SEROVO** - **Preobrazheniye Trawler Fleet Base (Preobrazhenskaya Baza Tralovogo Flota)** - *Nakhodka* *Russia* MMSI: 273825610 Official number: 802179	**840** 252 322	Class: RS	**1981-12 Yaroslavskiy Sudostroitelnyy Zavod — Yaroslavl** Yd No: 347 Loa 53.74 (BB) Br ex 10.71 Dght 4.290 Lbp 47.92 Br md - Dpth 6.00 Welded, 1 dk	**(B11A2FS) Stern Trawler** Ins: 218 Compartments: 1 Ho, ER 1 Ha: (1.6 x 1.6) Derricks: 2x1.5t Ice Capable	**1 oil engine** driving 1 FP propeller Total Power: 971kW (1,320hp) 12.8kn S.K.L. 8NVD48A-2U 1 x 4 Stroke 8 Cy. 320 x 480 971kW (1320bhp) VEB Schwermaschinenbau "KarlLiebknecht" (SKL)-Magdeburg Fuel: 195.0 (d.f.)
8216461 *EZCZ* -	**SERPAY** *ex* Valerie Anne *-2013* *ex* Willow River *-2009* *ex* Caribbean Sentry *-2009* *ex* Juanita Candies *-1988* **The Turkmen Marine Merchant Fleet Authority** - *Turkmenbashy* *Turkmenistan* MMSI: 434114100 Official number: 4206310	**899** 269 -	Class: BV (AB)	**1987-11 Halter Marine, Inc. — Lockport, La** Yd No: 1099 Converted From: Offshore Supply Ship-1988 Loa 57.92 Br ex - Dght 3.964 Lbp 56.39 Br md 13.42 Dpth 4.58 Welded, 1 dk	**(B22A2OR) Offshore Support Vessel**	**2 oil engines** reduction geared to sc. shafts driving 2 FP propellers Total Power: 2,834kW (3,854hp) 10.0kn EMD (Electro-Motive) 16-645-E6 2 x Vee 2 Stroke 16 Cy. 230 x 254 each-1417kW (1927bhp) General Motors Corp.Electro-Motive Div.-La Grange AuxGen: 3 x 150kW a.c Thrusters: 1 Tunnel thruster (f)
9335020 *LAED7* -	**SERPENTINE** - **S-Bulk KS** Seven Seas Carriers AS *Bergen* *Norway (NIS)* MMSI: 259717000	**30,273** 16,969 50,292 T/cm 52.2	Class: NV	**2008-02 P.T. PAL Indonesia — Surabaya** Yd No: 229 Loa 189.90 (BB) Br ex 30.56 Dght 12.820 Lbp 182.00 Br md 30.50 Dpth 17.50 Welded, 1 dk	**(A21A2BC) Bulk Carrier** Double Hull Grain: 60,557; Bale: 58,269 Compartments: 5 Ho, ER 5 Ha: 4 (20.0 x 25.5)ER (8.8 x 25.0) Cranes: 4x35t	**1 oil engine** driving 1 FP propeller Total Power: 9,480kW (12,889hp) 14.0kn MAN-B&W 6S50MC-C 1 x 2 Stroke 6 Cy. 500 x 2000 9480kW (12889bhp) AuxGen: 3 x 720kW a.c Fuel: 90.0 (d.f.) 1850.0 (r.f.) 37.2pd
8924185 *YD4960* -	**SERPONG** *ex* Ocean Echo *-2003* **PT Rig Tenders Indonesia Tbk** - *Jakarta* *Indonesia*	**135** 81 -	Class: KI (GL)	**1997-01 PT Nanindah Mutiara Shipyard — Batam** Yd No: T35 Loa 23.50 Br ex - Dght 2.500 Lbp 21.44 Br md 7.50 Dpth 3.10 Welded, 1 dk	**(B32A2ST) Tug**	**2 oil engines** reduction geared to sc. shafts driving 2 FP propellers Total Power: 940kW (1,278hp) 10.0kn Yanmar 6LAHM-STE 2 x 4 Stroke 6 Cy. 150 x 165 each-470kW (639bhp) Yanmar Diesel Engine Co Ltd-Japan AuxGen: 2 x 40kW 415V a.c
8725905 *UARU* M-0318	**SERPUKHOV** - **Andeg Fishing Collective (Rybolovetskiy Kolkhoz 'Andeg')** - *Murmansk* *Russia* MMSI: 273298100 Official number: 863914	**745** 223 414	Class: RS	**1986-10 Zavod "Leninskaya Kuznitsa" — Kiyev** Yd No: 1574 Loa 54.82 Br ex 9.95 Dght 4.140 Lbp 50.30 Br md 9.80 Dpth 5.00 Welded, 1 dk	**(B11A2FS) Stern Trawler** Ice Capable	**1 oil engine** driving 1 CP propeller Total Power: 853kW (1,160hp) 12.0kn S.K.L. 8NVD48A-2U 1 x 4 Stroke 8 Cy. 320 x 480 853kW (1160bhp) VEB Schwermaschinenbau "KarlLiebknecht" (SKL)-Magdeburg AuxGen: 4 x 160kW a.c
9579468 *TCZS8* -	**SERRA ATASOY** - **Atasoy Gemicilik Lojistik** Atasoy Group of Shipping Companies (Atasoy Grup Denizcilik Ticaret Ltd Sti) SatCom: Inmarsat C 427101256 *Istanbul* *Turkey* MMSI: 271042556 Official number: 1374	**2,870** 1,535 4,284	Class: BV	**2011-10 Kocatepe Gemi Cekek ve Insaat Sanayi Ltd Sti — Altinova** Yd No: 4 Loa 89.90 (BB) Br ex - Dght 5.350 Lbp 84.95 Br md 13.60 Dpth 6.90 Welded, 1 dk	**(A31A2GX) General Cargo Ship** Compartments: 1 Ho, ER 1 Ha: ER (61.6 x 11.4)	**1 oil engine** reduction geared to sc. shaft driving 1 CP propeller Total Power: 1,520kW (2,067hp) 11.5kn MaK 8M20C 1 x 4 Stroke 8 Cy. 200 x 300 1520kW (2067bhp) Caterpillar Motoren GmbH & Co. KG-Germany AuxGen: 1 x 282kW 400V a.c, 2 x 200kW 400V a.c Thrusters: 1 Tunnel thruster (f)
9466946 *9HA2537* -	**SERRA-MERT** - **Bossa Ticaret ve Sanayi Isletmeleri TAS** Marinpet Petrol Denizcilik Ticaret Ltd Sti *Valletta* *Malta* MMSI: 248833000 Official number: 9466946	**3,576** 1,640 5,384 T/cm 13.7	Class: BV	**2010-08 Celiktrans Deniz Insaat Kizaklari Ltd. Sti — Tuzla,Ist** Yd No: CS39 Loa 105.76 (BB) Br ex - Dght 6.250 Lbp 99.84 Br md 15.00 Dpth 7.75 Welded, 1 dk	**(A12B2TR) Chemical/Products Tanker** Double Hull (13F) Liq: 5,717; Liq (Oil): 5,739 Cargo Heating Coils Compartments: 12 Wing Ta, 2 Wing Slop Ta, ER 12 Cargo Pump (s): 12x150m³/hr Manifold: Bow/CM: 53m Ice Capable	**1 oil engine** reduction geared to sc. shaft driving 1 CP propeller Total Power: 2,640kW (3,589hp) 14.0kn MaK 8M25 1 x 4 Stroke 8 Cy. 255 x 400 2640kW (3589bhp) Caterpillar Motoren GmbH & Co. KG-Germany AuxGen: 3 x 365kW 60Hz a.c Thrusters: 1 Tunnel thruster (f) Fuel: 54.0 (d.f.) 299.0 (r.f.)
9229568 *PS4434* -	**SERRA NEVADA** - **Bravante Group** - SatCom: Inmarsat C 471000063 *Rio de Janeiro* *Brazil* MMSI: 710000031 Official number: 3810499676	**1,780** 874 3,338	Class: RI (BV)	**2003-05 Empresa Tecnica Nacional (ETN) — Belem** Yd No: 413 Loa 74.17 Br ex 14.52 Dght 4.500 Lbp 72.13 Br md 14.50 Dpth 6.20 Welded, 1 dk	**(A13B2TP) Products Tanker** Double Hull	**2 oil engines** geared to sc. shafts driving 2 FP propellers Total Power: 1,274kW (1,732hp) 10.0kn Caterpillar 3508TA 2 x Vee 4 Stroke 8 Cy. 170 x 190 each-637kW (866bhp) Caterpillar Inc-USA
9229570 *PS5933* -	**SERRA POLAR** - **Bravante Group** - *Rio de Janeiro* *Brazil* MMSI: 710000022 Official number: 3810499668	**1,785** 874 3,338	Class: RI (BV)	**2004-11 Empresa Tecnica Nacional (ETN) — Belem** Yd No: 414 Loa 74.17 Br ex 14.52 Dght 4.500 Lbp 72.13 Br md 14.50 Dpth 6.20 Welded, 1 dk	**(A13B2TP) Products Tanker** Double Hull (13F) Liq: 4,253; Liq (Oil): 4,253 Compartments: 4 Ta, ER 4 Cargo Pump (s): 4x700m³/hr	**2 oil engines** geared to sc. shafts driving 2 FP propellers Total Power: 1,274kW (1,732hp) 10.0kn Caterpillar 3508TA 2 x Vee 4 Stroke 8 Cy. 170 x 190 each-637kW (866bhp) Caterpillar Inc-USA AuxGen: 2 x 290kW 220V 60Hz a.c

IMO / Call sign	Name / Owner	Tonnage	Class	Build / Dimensions	Type	Machinery
9254965 *9V7323* -	**SERRA THERESA** **Herning Shipping Asia Pte Ltd** Risler SA SatCom: Inmarsat C 456574210 *Singapore* *Singapore* MMSI: 565742000 Official number: 393738	**1,074** 450 1,520 T/cm 6.5	Class: BV	**2003-06 R.M.K. Tersanesi — Tuzla** Yd No: 54 Loa 70.14 (BB) Br ex 10.50 Dght 4.190 Lbp 65.10 Br md 10.45 Dpth 5.10 Welded, 1 dk	**(A12A2TC) Chemical Tanker** Double Hull (13F) Liq: 1,614 Cargo Heating Coils Compartments: 1 Ta, 8 Wing Ta, ER 9 Cargo Pump (s): 9x100m³/hr Manifold: Bow/CM: 36.4m Ice Capable	**1 oil engine** geared to sc. shaft driving 1 CP propeller Total Power: 1,140kW (1,550hp) 10.5kn MaK 6M20 1 x 4 Stroke 6 Cy. 200 x 300 1140kW (1550bhp) Caterpillar Motoren GmbH & Co. KG-Germany AuxGen: 1 x 252kW 440/230V 60Hz a.c, 2 x 174kW 440/230V 60Hz a.c, 1 x 100kW 440/230V 60Hz a.c Thrusters: 1 Tunnel thruster (f) Fuel: 82.0 (d.f.) 5.0pd
6826042 - -	**SERRANO HEVIA** **Sun Fisheries Ltd** L & J Management Ltd	**252** 75 141	Class: (BV)	**1968 Ast. Neptuno — Valencia** Yd No: 26 Loa 30.17 Br ex 7.01 Dght 2.490 Lbp 27.01 Br md 6.79 Dpth 3.79 Welded, 1 dk	**(B11A2FT) Trawler** 2 Ha: 2 (1.0 x 1.0)ER	**1 oil engine** driving 1 FP propeller Total Power: 485kW (659hp) 12.7kn Stork RHO218K 1 x 4 Stroke 8 Cy. 210 x 300 485kW (659bhp) Naval Stork Werkspoor SA-Spain Fuel: 71.0 (d.f.)
9474979 *ICLH* -	**SERSER** *launched as* Aspat C *-2008* **Rimorchiatori Laziali Impresa di Salvataggio e Rimorchi SpA** Cafiservice SpA *Naples* *Italy* MMSI: 247245800	**3,040** 1,397 3,900	Class: BV (RI)	**2008-05 Arkadas Denizcilik Insaat Sanayi Ticaret Ltd Sti — Istanbul (Tuzla)** Yd No: 03 Loa 80.10 Br ex 15.02 Dght 5.830 Lbp 78.50 Br md 15.00 Dpth 7.20 Welded, 1 dk	**(A31A2GX) General Cargo Ship** Compartments: 1 Ho, ER 1 Ha: ER Cranes: 2x60t	**1 oil engine** reduction geared to sc. shaft driving 1 FP propeller Total Power: 1,980kW (2,692hp) 13.0kn MaK 6M25 1 x 4 Stroke 6 Cy. 255 x 400 1980kW (2692bhp) Caterpillar Motoren GmbH & Co. KG-Germany AuxGen: 2 x 500kW 50Hz a.c, 1 x 124kW 50Hz a.c Fuel: 247.0
9637715 *C6AN5* -	**SERTANEJO SPIRIT** **Sertanejo Spirit LLC** Teekay Shipping Ltd *Nassau* *Bahamas* MMSI: 311000096 Official number: 7000536	**83,882** 48,528 154,233	Class: AB	**2013-11 Samsung Heavy Industries Co Ltd — Geoje** Yd No: 2040 Loa 282.00 (BB) Br ex - Dght 16.200 Lbp 267.00 Br md 49.00 Dpth 23.60 Welded, 1 dk	**(A13A2TS) Shuttle Tanker** Double Hull (13F) Liq: 158,350; Liq (Oil): 158,350 Compartments: 6 Wing Ta, 6 Wing Ta, 1 Wing Slop Ta, 1 Wing Slop Ta, ER 3 Cargo Pump (s): 3x3500m³/hr	**1 oil engine** driving 1 CP propeller Total Power: 14,270kW (19,401hp) 15.0kn MAN-B&W 6S70ME-C8 1 x 2 Stroke 6 Cy. 700 x 2800 14270kW (19401bhp) Doosan Engine Co Ltd-South Korea AuxGen: 2 x 4300kW a.c, 2 x 2800kW a.c Fuel: 550.0 (d.f.) 3200.0 (r.f.)
9541203 *V7WX8* -	**SERTAO** **Dleif Drilling LLC** Schahin Petroleo e Gas SA *Majuro* *Marshall Islands* MMSI: 538004418 Official number: 4418	**60,316** 18,094 61,537	Class: BV (AB)	**2012-02 Samsung Heavy Industries Co Ltd — Geoje** Yd No: 1870 Loa 227.81 Br ex - Dght 13.000 Lbp 219.40 Br md 42.00 Dpth 19.00 Welded, 1 dk	**(B22B20D) Drilling Ship**	**6 diesel electric oil engines** driving 2 Azimuth electric drive units Total Power: 42,000kW (57,102hp) 12.0kn MAN-B&W 14V32/40 6 x Vee 4 Stroke 14 Cy. 320 x 400 each-7000kW (9517bhp)
9089384 *TCB2047* -	**SERTER AHMET-1** **Zafer Serter & Birol Serter** *Istanbul* *Turkey* MMSI: 271056075 Official number: 8822	**228** 68 -		**2005-03 Basaran Gemi Sanayi — Trabzon** Yd No: 73 Loa 30.60 (BB) Br ex - Dght - Lbp 26.64 Br md 10.50 Dpth 3.20 Welded, 1 dk	**(B12B2FC) Fish Carrier**	**3 oil engines** reduction geared to sc. shafts driving 3 Propellers Total Power: 1,030kW (1,400hp) Iveco Aifo 2 x 4 Stroke each-331kW (450bhp) Iveco Pegaso-Madrid S.K.L. 1 x 4 Stroke 368kW (500bhp) SKL Motoren u. Systemtechnik AG-Magdeburg
7212339 *EAPP* -	**SERTOSA CATORCE** **Sertosa Norte SL** - *Cadiz* *Spain* MMSI: 224227470 Official number: 1-4/1992	*261* 7 138	Class: (LR) ✠ Classed LR until 17/4/02	**1972-07 Sociedad Metalurgica Duro Felguera — Gijon** Yd No: 72 Loa 32.21 Br ex 8.84 Dght 3.753 Lbp 28.17 Br md 8.40 Dpth 4.32 Welded, 1 dk	**(B32A2ST) Tug**	**1 oil engine** sr geared to sc. shaft driving 1 FP propeller Total Power: 1,214kW (1,651hp) 12.5kn MWM TBD500-6 1 x 4 Stroke 6 Cy. 360 x 450 1214kW (1651bhp) Sociedad Espanola de ConstruccionNaval-Spain AuxGen: 2 x 80kW 380V 50Hz a.c, 1 x 60kW 380V 50Hz a.c
6504503 *EBXH* -	**SERTOSA CINCO** **Servicios Auxiliares de Puertos SA (SERTOSA)** - *Ceuta* *Spain* MMSI: 224042730 Official number: 1-2/1992	**192** 57 -	Class: LR ✠ **100A1** SS 05/2013 tug Spain & Portugal coasting service, also between Tangier and Melilla ✠ **LMC** **UMS** Eq.Ltr: b; Cable: U1 (b)	**1965-02 Hijos de J. Barreras S.A. — Vigo** Yd No: 1332 Loa 29.57 Br ex 8.16 Dght 3.601 Lbp 26.83 Br md 7.78 Dpth 3.89 Welded, 1 dk	**(B32A2ST) Tug**	**1 oil engine** with flexible couplings & sr geared to sc. shaft driving 1 CP propeller Total Power: 1,658kW (2,254hp) 12.5kn Deutz SBV9M628 1 x 4 Stroke 9 Cy. 240 x 280 1658kW (2254bhp) (new engine 1990) Hijos de J Barreras SA-Spain AuxGen: 1 x 60kW 380V 50Hz a.c, 2 x 32kW 220V 50Hz d.c Fuel: 56.0 (d.f.)
7901710 *EHWK* -	**SERTOSA DIECINUEVE** **Sertosa Norte SL** - *Cadiz* *Spain* Official number: 1-9/1992	*162* 11 92	Class: AB	**1980-01 S.A. Balenciaga — Zumaya** Yd No: 296 Loa 26.83 Br ex 7.93 Dght 3.350 Lbp 24.01 Br md 7.90 Dpth 3.97 Welded, 1 dk	**(B32A2ST) Tug**	**1 oil engine** reverse reduction geared to sc. shaft driving 1 CP propeller Total Power: 1,596kW (2,170hp) 12.0kn Alpha 14V23L-VO 1 x Vee 4 Stroke 14 Cy. 225 x 300 1596kW (2170bhp) Construcciones Echevarria SA-Spain AuxGen: 2 x 40kW a.c
7510561 *EHLP* -	**SERTOSA DIECIOCHO** **ING Lease (Espana) SA EFC** Servicios Auxiliares de Puertos SA (SERTOSA) *Santa Cruz de Tenerife* *Spain (CSR)* MMSI: 224020910 Official number: 13/2008	*290* 80 179	Class: LR ✠ **100A1** SS 06/2008 tug ✠ **LMC** **UMS** Eq.Ltr: G; Cable: 302.5/20.5 U2	**1977-12 Enrique Lorenzo y Cia SA — Vigo** Yd No: 385 Loa 33.51 Br ex 9.38 Dght 4.506 Lbp 29.93 Br md 8.86 Dpth 5.31 Welded, 1 dk	**(B32A2ST) Tug**	**2 oil engines** geared to sc. shaft driving 1 CP propeller Total Power: 2,864kW (3,894hp) 12.5kn Caterpillar 3516TA 2 x Vee 4 Stroke 16 Cy. 170 x 190 each-1432kW (1947bhp) (new engine 1998) Caterpillar Inc-USA AuxGen: 2 x 72kW 380V 50Hz a.c
7510559 *EHLO* -	**SERTOSA DIECISIETE** **ING Lease (Espana) SA EFC** Servicios Auxiliares de Puertos SA (SERTOSA) *Cadiz* *Spain* MMSI: 224020920	*262* 80 179	Class: LR ✠ **100A1** SS 04/2012 tug ✠ **LMC** **UMS** Eq.Ltr: G; Cable: 302.5/20.5 U2	**1977-11 Enrique Lorenzo y Cia SA — Vigo** Yd No: 384 Loa 33.51 Br ex 9.38 Dght 4.506 Lbp 29.93 Br md 8.86 Dpth 5.31 Welded, 1 dk	**(B32A2ST) Tug**	**2 oil engines** sr geared to sc. shaft driving 1 CP propeller Total Power: 2,368kW (3,220hp) 12.5kn Caterpillar 3516TA 2 x Vee 4 Stroke 16 Cy. 170 x 190 each-1184kW (1610bhp) (new engine 1996) Caterpillar Inc-USA AuxGen: 2 x 72kW 380V 50Hz a.c
6617881 *EFAA* -	**SERTOSA DIEZ** **Credit Agricole Leasing Sucursal en Espana** Servicios Auxiliares de Puertos SA (SERTOSA) *Cadiz* *Spain* MMSI: 224075770 Official number: 1-2/1992	**192** 57 -	Class: LR ✠ **100A1** SS 12/2011 tug Spain & Portugal coastal service, also between Tangier & Melilla ✠ **LMC** **UMS** Eq.Ltr: (b) ;	**1966-09 Hijos de J. Barreras S.A. — Vigo** Yd No: 1356 Loa 29.57 Br ex 8.16 Dght 3.601 Lbp 26.85 Br md 7.78 Dpth 3.89 Riveted\Welded, 1 dk	**(B32A2ST) Tug**	**1 oil engine** with flexible couplings & sr geared to sc. shaft driving 1 CP propeller Total Power: 1,658kW (2,254hp) 12.5kn Deutz SBV9M628 1 x 4 Stroke 9 Cy. 240 x 280 1658kW (2254bhp) (new engine 1991) Hijos de J Barreras SA-Spain AuxGen: 1 x 120kW 380V 50Hz a.c, 1 x 32kW 220V d.c Fuel: 56.0 (d.f.)
6523717 *EETL* -	**SERTOSA NUEVE** **Servicios Auxiliares de Puertos SA (SERTOSA)** - *Cadiz* *Spain* Official number: 1-1/1992	**192** 57 -	Class: LR ✠ **100A1** SS 11/2011 tug Spain & Portugal coastal service, also between Tangier and Melilla ✠ **LMC** **UMS** Eq.Ltr: (b) ;	**1966-04 Hijos de J. Barreras S.A. — Vigo** Yd No: 1358 Loa 29.57 Br ex 8.16 Dght 3.601 Lbp 26.85 Br md 7.78 Dpth 3.89 Riveted\Welded, 1 dk	**(B32A2ST) Tug**	**1 oil engine** with flexible couplings & sr geared to sc. shaft driving 1 CP propeller Total Power: 1,658kW (2,254hp) 12.5kn Deutz SBV9M628 1 x 4 Stroke 9 Cy. 240 x 280 1658kW (2254bhp) (new engine 1991) Hijos de J Barreras SA-Spain AuxGen: 1 x 60kW 380V 50Hz a.c, 2 x 32kW 380V 50Hz a.c Fuel: 56.0 (d.f.)
6520105 *EENY* -	**SERTOSA OCHO** **Servicios Auxiliares de Puertos SA (SERTOSA)** - *Ceuta* *Spain* MMSI: 224072840 Official number: 1-1/1992	**192** 57 -	Class: LR ✠ **100A1** SS 02/2011 tug Spain and Portugal coasting service, also between Tangier and Melilla ✠ **LMC** **UMS** Eq.Ltr: (b) ;	**1965-07 Hijos de J. Barreras S.A. — Vigo** Yd No: 1344 Loa 29.57 Br ex 8.16 Dght 3.601 Lbp 26.83 Br md 7.78 Dpth 3.89 Riveted\Welded, 1 dk	**(B32A2ST) Tug**	**1 oil engine** with flexible couplings & sr geared to sc. shaft driving 1 CP propeller Total Power: 1,658kW (2,254hp) 12.5kn Deutz SBV9M628 1 x 4 Stroke 9 Cy. 240 x 280 1658kW (2254bhp) (new engine 1991) Hijos de J Barreras SA-Spain AuxGen: 1 x 60kW 380V 50Hz a.c, 2 x 32kW 380V 50Hz a.c Fuel: 56.0 (d.f.)

7363530 *EDLS* -	**SERTOSA QUINCE** **Servicios Auxiliares de Puertos SA (SERTOSA)** - *Cadiz* *Spain* MMSI: 224042670 Official number: 1-5/1992	**240** 72 -	Class: LR ✠ **100A1** SS 11/2012 tug ✠ **LMC** **UMS** Eq.Ltr: (d) ; Cable: U2	**1974**-06 **Sociedad Metalurgica Duro Felguera — Gijon** Yd No: 95 Loa 30.32 Br ex 8.64 Dght - Lbp 28.55 Br md 8.08 Dpth 4.47 Welded	**(B32A2ST) Tug**	**1 oil engine** with clutches, flexible couplings & dr geared to sc. shaft driving 1 CP propeller Total Power: 1,353kW (1,840hp) 12.5kn MWM TBD645L6 1 x 4 Stroke 6 Cy. 330 x 450 1353kW (1840bhp) (new engine 1998) Motoren Werke Mannheim AG (MWM)-Mannheim AuxGen: 2 x 60kW 380V 50Hz a.c, 1 x 16kW 380V 50Hz a.c
9238014 *EBTP* -	**SERTOSA TREINTA** **Sertosa Norte SL** - *La Coruna* *Spain* MMSI: 224032190 Official number: 1-1/2001	**350** 105 415	Class: BV	**2001**-06 **S.A. Balenciaga — Zumaya** Yd No: 384 Loa 30.00 Br ex - Dght 4.400 Lbp 26.70 Br md 10.00 Dpth 5.10 Welded, 1 dk	**(B32A2ST) Tug**	**2 oil engines** reduction geared to sc. shafts driving 2 Directional propellers Total Power: 2,942kW (4,000hp) 12.0kn Deutz SBV6M628 2 x 4 Stroke 6 Cy. 240 x 280 each-1471kW (2000bhp) Deutz AG-Koeln AuxGen: 2 x 100kW 400V 50Hz a.c
9397432 *ECMS* -	**SERTOSA TREINTAYCUATRO** **Sertosa Norte SL** Compania de Remolcadores Ibaizabal SA SatCom: Inmarsat C 422500180 *Santa Cruz de Tenerife* *Spain (CSR)* MMSI: 224350690 Official number: 2/2009	**784** 235 705	Class: BV (LR) ✠ Classed LR until 13/8/09	**2008**-05 **Astilleros Armon SA — Navia** Yd No: 655 Loa 35.25 Br ex 14.00 Dght 6.700 Lbp 32.00 Br md 14.00 Dpth 6.70 Welded, 1 dk	**(B32A2ST) Tug**	**2 oil engines** with flexible couplings & reduction geared to sc. shafts driving 2 Directional propellers Total Power: 6,000kW (8,158hp) 12.0kn Bergens B32: 40L6P 2 x 4 Stroke 6 Cy. 320 x 400 each-3000kW (4079bhp) Rolls Royce Marine AS-Norway AuxGen: 3 x 184kW 400V 50Hz a.c Boilers: TOH (o.f.) 8.7kgf/cm² (8.5bar) Fuel: 296.0 (d.f.)
9260342 *EBZW* -	**SERTOSA TREINTAYDOS** **Flotanor SL** Sertosa Norte SL *La Coruna* *Spain* MMSI: 224057430 Official number: 1-2/2002	**380** 114 450	Class: BV	**2002**-07 **S.A. Balenciaga — Zumaya** Yd No: 387 Loa 31.20 Br ex - Dght 4.280 Lbp 27.10 Br md 10.00 Dpth 5.10 Welded, 1 dk	**(B32A2ST) Tug**	**2 oil engines** geared to sc. shafts driving 2 Directional propellers Total Power: 2,800kW (3,806hp) 12.0kn Deutz SBV6M628 2 x 4 Stroke 6 Cy. 240 x 280 each-1400kW (1903bhp) Deutz AG-Koeln Thrusters: 1 Tunnel thruster (f)
7905455 *EHVV* -	**SERTOSA VEINTE** **Sertosa Norte SL** - *Cadiz* *Spain* MMSI: 224084960 Official number: 1-10/1992	*162* 11 92	Class: (AB)	**1980**-05 **S.A. Balenciaga — Zumaya** Yd No: 297 Loa 26.83 Br ex 7.93 Dght 3.350 Lbp 24.01 Br md 7.90 Dpth 3.97 Welded, 1 dk	**(B32A2ST) Tug**	**1 oil engine** reverse reduction geared to sc. shaft driving 1 CP propeller Total Power: 1,596kW (2,170hp) 12.0kn Alpha 14V23L-VO 1 x Vee 4 Stroke 14 Cy. 225 x 300 1596kW (2170bhp) Construcciones Echevarria SA-Spain AuxGen: 2 x 40kW a.c
8506933 *EAXO* -	**SERTOSA VEINTICINCO** **Flotanor SL** Sertosa Norte SL *Cadiz* *Spain* MMSI: 224012970 Official number: 1-12/1992	**186** 56 159	Class: BV	**1986**-02 **S.A. Balenciaga — Zumaya** Yd No: 312 Loa 27.51 Br ex - Dght 3.301 Lbp 24.01 Br md 8.21 Dpth 4.42 Welded, 1 dk	**(B32A2ST) Tug**	**1 oil engine** geared to sc. shaft driving 1 CP propeller Total Power: 1,596kW (2,170hp) 13.3kn Alpha 14V23L-VO 1 x Vee 4 Stroke 14 Cy. 225 x 300 1596kW (2170bhp) Construcciones Echevarria SA-Spain
8506921 *EAXP* -	**SERTOSA VEINTICUATRO** **Servicios Auxiliares de Puertos SA (SERTOSA)** - *Cadiz* *Spain* MMSI: 224042680 Official number: 1-11/1992	**186** 56 159	Class: BV	**1985**-12 **S.A. Balenciaga — Zumaya** Yd No: 311 Loa 27.51 Br ex - Dght 3.301 Lbp 24.01 Br md 8.21 Dpth 4.42 Welded, 1 dk	**(B32A2ST) Tug**	**1 oil engine** geared to sc. shaft driving 1 CP propeller Total Power: 1,596kW (2,170hp) 13.3kn Alpha 14V23L-VO 1 x Vee 4 Stroke 14 Cy. 225 x 300 1596kW (2170bhp) Construcciones Echevarria SA-Spain
9133953 *EAIU* -	**SERTOSA VEINTIOCHO** **Flotanor SL** Sertosa Norte SL *Ceuta* *Spain* MMSI: 224830000 Official number: 1-1/1996	**331** 99 592	Class: BV	**1996**-02 **Construcciones Navales Santodomingo SA — Vigo** Yd No: 609 Loa 29.50 Br ex - Dght 4.500 Lbp 28.00 Br md 11.00 Dpth 4.00 Welded, 1 dk	**(B32A2ST) Tug**	**2 oil engines** gearing integral to driving 2 Voith-Schneider propellers Total Power: 2,800kW (3,806hp) 12.0kn Deutz SBV6M628 2 x 4 Stroke 6 Cy. 240 x 280 each-1400kW (1903bhp) Motoren Werke Mannheim AG (MWM)-Mannheim AuxGen: 2 x 95kW 380V 50Hz a.c Fuel: 150.0 (d.f.) 9.3pd
9057692 *EAJK* -	**SERTOSA VEINTISEIS** **Flotanor SL** Sertosa Norte SL *Algeciras* *Spain* MMSI: 224828000 Official number: 1-1/1993	**325** 98 576	Class: BV	**1993**-06 **Astilleros Zamakona SA — Santurtzi** Yd No: 263 Loa 29.95 Br ex - Dght 2.500 Lbp 28.00 Br md 11.00 Dpth 4.00 Welded, 1 dk	**(B32A2ST) Tug**	**2 oil engines** gearing integral to driving 2 Voith-Schneider propellers Total Power: 2,800kW (3,806hp) 12.0kn Deutz SBV6M628 2 x 4 Stroke 6 Cy. 240 x 280 each-1400kW (1903bhp) Motoren Werke Mannheim AG (MWM)-Mannheim AuxGen: 2 x 80kW 220/380V 50Hz a.c
9060974 *EAJZ* -	**SERTOSA VEINTISIETE** **Servicios Auxiliares de Puertos SA (SERTOSA)** - *La Coruna* *Spain* MMSI: 224337000 Official number: 1-1/1993	**325** 98 576	Class: BV	**1993**-09 **Astilleros Zamakona SA — Santurtzi** Yd No: 267 Loa 29.50 Br ex - Dght 2.500 Lbp 28.00 Br md 11.00 Dpth 4.00 Welded, 1 dk	**(B32A2ST) Tug**	**2 oil engines** gearing integral to driving 2 Voith-Schneider propellers Total Power: 2,800kW (3,806hp) 12.0kn Deutz SBV6M628 2 x 4 Stroke 6 Cy. 240 x 280 each-1400kW (1903bhp) Motoren Werke Mannheim AG (MWM)-Mannheim AuxGen: 2 x 80kW 220/380V 50Hz a.c
8101549 *EAXU* -	**SERTOSA VEINTITRES** *launched as* Betelgeuse *-1982* **Sertosa Norte SL** - *Algeciras* *Spain* Official number: 1-2/1992	*174* 24 92	Class: (AB)	**1982**-03 **S.A. Balenciaga — Zumaya** Yd No: 304 Loa 26.80 Br ex - Dght 3.350 Lbp 24.01 Br md 7.92 Dpth 3.97 Welded, 1 dk	**(B32A2ST) Tug**	**1 oil engine** sr geared to sc. shaft driving 1 CP propeller Total Power: 1,596kW (2,170hp) 13.0kn Alpha 14V23L-VO 1 x Vee 4 Stroke 14 Cy. 225 x 300 1596kW (2170bhp) Construcciones Echevarria SA-Spain AuxGen: 2 x 60kW 220V 50Hz a.c Fuel: 86.5 (d.f.) 6.5pd
7703704 *EHMN* -	**SERTOSA VEINTIUNO** *ex* Polaris *-1982* **Boat Service SA** Servicios Auxiliares de Puertos SA (SERTOSA) *Algeciras* *Spain* MMSI: 224024810 Official number: 1-1/1992	**164** 49 192	Class: BV (AB)	**1977**-07 **S.A. Balenciaga — Zumaya** Yd No: 288 Loa 26.83 Br ex - Dght 3.950 Lbp 24.01 Br md 7.90 Dpth 3.97 Welded, 1 dk	**(B32A2ST) Tug**	**1 oil engine** reverse reduction geared to sc. shaft driving 1 FP propeller Total Power: 1,493kW (2,030hp) 12.0kn Alpha 14V23LH 1 x Vee 4 Stroke 14 Cy. 225 x 300 1493kW (2030bhp) Construcciones Echevarria SA-Spain AuxGen: 2 x 32kW
9600176 *9WIZ4* -	**SERUDONG 7** **Serudong Shipping Sdn Bhd** - *Kota Kinabalu* *Malaysia* Official number: 332639	**146** 44 113	Class: NK	**2010**-12 **Tuong Aik Shipyard Sdn Bhd — Sibu** Yd No: 2927 Loa 23.50 Br ex - Dght 2.712 Lbp 21.56 Br md 7.32 Dpth 3.20 Welded, 1 dk	**(B32A2ST) Tug**	**2 oil engines** reduction geared to sc. shafts driving 2 FP propellers Total Power: 970kW (1,318hp) Yanmar 6AYM-STE 2 x 4 Stroke 6 Cy. 155 x 180 each-485kW (659bhp) Yanmar Diesel Engine Co Ltd-Japan AuxGen: 2 x 28kW a.c Fuel: 110.0 (d.f.)
9674995 *9WKN3* -	**SERUDONG 9** **Serudong Shipping Sdn Bhd** - *Kota Kinabalu* *Malaysia* Official number: 332690	**142** 43 120	Class: NK	**2013**-01 **Forward Marine Enterprise Sdn Bhd — Sibu** Yd No: FM-123 Loa 23.50 Br ex 7.33 Dght 2.712 Lbp 22.00 Br md 7.32 Dpth 3.20 Welded, 1 dk	**(B32A2ST) Tug**	**2 oil engines** reduction geared to sc. shafts driving 2 FP propellers Total Power: 970kW (1,318hp) Yanmar 6AYM-WST 2 x 4 Stroke 6 Cy. 155 x 180 each-485kW (659bhp) Yanmar Diesel Engine Co Ltd-Japan Fuel: 90.0 (d.f.)
7311082 *YDEK* -	**SERUI INDAH** *ex* Tanto Mulia *-1995* *ex* Dragon Maru *-1992* *ex* Tatsumi Maru No. 31 *-1982* **PT Sarana Bahari Prima** - *Jakarta* *Indonesia*	*1,459* 893 2,299	Class: KI	**1971**-04 **Fukushima Zosen Ltd. — Matsue** Yd No: 248 Loa 72.60 Br ex 12.02 Dght 4.827 Lbp 66.81 Br md 11.99 Dpth 5.60 Welded, 1 dk	**(A31A2GX) General Cargo Ship** Compartments: 2 Ho, ER 2 Ha: 2 (15.9 x 8.4)ER	**1 oil engine** driving 1 FP propeller Total Power: 1,471kW (2,000hp) Nippon Hatsudoki 6N38T 1 x 4 Stroke 6 Cy. 380 x 580 1471kW (2000bhp) Nippon Hatsudoki-Japan AuxGen: 2 x 64kW 445V a.c

7736555 *YFJH* -	**SERUNI** *ex* Fukuyoshi Maru *-1994* *ex* Shoun Maru No. 2 *-1985* **PT Suntraco Intim Transport Inc** - *Surabaya* *Indonesia*	*611* 268 900	Class: KI	**1978-04 K.K. Murakami Zosensho — Naruto** Yd No: 110 Loa 54.57 Br ex - Dght 3.900 Lbp 49.00 Br md 9.20 Dpth 5.15 Welded, 1 dk	**(A31A2GX) General Cargo Ship**	**1 oil engine** driving 1 FP propeller Total Power: 736kW (1,001hp) Hanshin 6LUD26 1 x 4 Stroke 6 Cy. 260 x 440 736kW (1001bhp) The Hanshin Diesel Works Ltd-Japan
6918390 *YCNK* -	**SERUNTING II** *ex* Kahuripan *-2004* *ex* Niaga XXV *-1985* *ex* Dacapo *-1979* *ex* Dorthe Ty *-1979* *ex* Balco *-1975* *ex* Lotte Nielsen *-1973* **PT Sumatra Jawa Line** - *Jakarta* *Indonesia* MMSI: 525015533	**1,239** 484 2,220	Class: KI (LR) ✠ Classed LR until 19/12/80	**1969-11 Aarhus Flydedok og Maskinkompagni A/S — Aarhus** Yd No: 141 Loa 70.44 Br ex 11.54 Dght 5.538 Lbp 65.26 Br md 11.51 Dpth 6.30 Welded, 1 dk & S dk	**(A31A2GX) General Cargo Ship** Grain: 2,832; Bale: 2,492 Compartments: 1 Ho, ER 2 Ha: (16.6 x 7.0) (17.5 x 7.0)ER Derricks: 1x10t,3x5t Ice Capable	**1 oil engine** driving 1 FP propeller Total Power: 1,178kW (1,602hp) 12.5kn MaK 8MU451AK 1 x 4 Stroke 8 Cy. 320 x 450 1178kW (1602bhp) Atlas MaK Maschinenbau GmbH-Kiel AuxGen: 1 x 80kW 380V 50Hz a.c Fuel: 205.0 (d.f.)
8898013 - -	**SERUYAN** **PT Pelayaran Nasional Bintan Golden** - *Samarinda* *Indonesia*	**116** 69 -	Class: KI	**1993 P.T. Karta Putra — Jakarta** Loa 20.00 Br ex - Dght 2.250 Lbp 18.00 Br md 6.00 Dpth 2.80 Welded, 1 dk	**(B32A2ST) Tug**	**2 oil engines** reduction geared to sc. shafts driving 2 FP propellers Total Power: 478kW (650hp) Caterpillar 3406B 2 x 4 Stroke 6 Cy. 137 x 165 each-239kW (325bhp) Caterpillar Inc-USA
7636365 *J8B4154* -	**SERVAL** *ex* Sun London *-2009* **Catharina Shipping Ltd** Westcoasting Towage Services Sp z oo *Kingstown* *St Vincent & The Grenadines* MMSI: 377103000 Official number: 10627	**275** 82 203	Class: PR (LR) ✠ Classed LR until 30/4/08	**1977-11 R. Dunston (Hessle) Ltd. — Hessle** Yd No: H912 Loa 32.92 Br ex 9.61 Dght 4.172 Lbp 29.01 Br md 9.15 Dpth 4.90 Welded, 1 dk	**(B32A2ST) Tug**	**1 oil engine** dr geared to sc. shaft driving 1 CP propeller Total Power: 1,942kW (2,640hp) 12.0kn Ruston 12RKCM 1 x Vee 4 Stroke 12 Cy. 254 x 305 1942kW (2640bhp) Ruston Paxman Diesels Ltd.-Colchester AuxGen: 3 x 60kW 440V 50Hz a.c Fuel: 92.0 (d.f.)
7308736 - -	**SERVAL** **Penrod Drilling Corp** - *Morgan City, LA* *United States of America* Official number: 528755	*137* 93 -		**1970 Breaux Bay Craft, Inc. — Loreauville, La** Loa - Br ex - Dght - Lbp 31.96 Br md 6.28 Dpth 3.03 Welded, 1 dk	**(B21A2OS) Platform Supply Ship** Hull Material: Aluminium Alloy	**2 oil engines** geared to sc. shafts driving 2 FP propellers Total Power: 1,324kW (1,800hp) Caterpillar D398TA 2 x Vee 4 Stroke 12 Cy. 159 x 203 each-662kW (900bhp) Caterpillar Tractor Co-USA
9443774 *TCMF7* -	**SERVET ANA** **Devmarin Denizcilik AS** Deval Transport AS *Istanbul* *Turkey* MMSI: 271042643 Official number: TUGS 2021	**19,999** 10,351 30,124 T/cm 43.5	Class: AB (NK)	**2011-04 Tsuji Heavy Industries (Jiangsu) Co Ltd — Zhangjiagang JS** Yd No: S1007 Loa 178.70 (BB) Br ex - Dght 9.790 Lbp 170.00 Br md 28.00 Dpth 14.00 Welded, 1 dk	**(A21A2BC) Bulk Carrier** Double Hull Grain: 40,633; Bale: 38,602 Compartments: 5 Ho, ER 5 Ha: 4 (20.8 x 21.0)ER (16.6 x 15.0) Cranes: 4x30t	**1 oil engine** driving 1 FP propeller Total Power: 6,232kW (8,473hp) 14.0kn MAN-B&W 6S42MC 1 x 2 Stroke 6 Cy. 420 x 1764 6232kW (8473bhp) Makita Corp-Japan AuxGen: 3 x 688kW a.c Fuel: 120.0 (d.f.) 1320.0 (r.f.)
7819450 *TCIV* -	**SERVET-KA** *ex* Ravanda *-2008* *ex* Tekmar I *-2001* *ex* Kaptan Ismail Cillioglu *-1992* **Garanti Finansal Kiralama AS (Garanti Leasing)** Adnil Denizcilik Ticaret Ltd Sti SatCom: Inmarsat C 427122543 *Istanbul* *Turkey* MMSI: 271002058 Official number: 128	**1,814** 128 2,893	Class: TL (AB)	**1981-03 Meltem Beykoz Tersanesi — Beykoz** Yd No: 32 Loa 81.21 Br ex 13.03 Dght 5.638 Lbp 71.20 Br md 13.01 Dpth 6.61 Welded, 1 dk	**(A31A2GX) General Cargo Ship** Grain: 3,737; Bale: 3,511 Compartments: 2 Ho, ER 2 Ha: (- x 8.0) (18.8 x 8.0)ER Derricks: 4x3.5t	**1 oil engine** driving 1 FP propeller Total Power: 1,214kW (1,651hp) 12.0kn Skoda 9L350IIPS 1 x 4 Stroke 9 Cy. 350 x 500 1214kW (1651bhp) CKD Praha-Praha AuxGen: 2 x 77kW a.c, 1 x 44kW a.c
9556399 *YDA4454* -	**SERVEWELL EAGER** **PT Logindo Samudramakmur** - *Jakarta* *Indonesia* MMSI: 525016010	**135** 41 -	Class: KI	**2009-02 PT Steadfast Marine — Pontianak** Yd No: 150108-016 Loa 24.00 Br ex - Dght 2.490 Lbp 22.64 Br md 7.60 Dpth 3.10 Welded, 1 dk	**(B32A2ST) Tug**	**2 oil engines** reduction geared to sc. shafts driving 2 Propellers Total Power: 794kW (1,080hp) Caterpillar 3412C 2 x Vee 4 Stroke 12 Cy. 137 x 152 each-397kW (540bhp) Caterpillar Inc-USA AuxGen: 2 x 37kW 380/220V a.c
9325594 *PNAJ* -	**SERVEWELL SINCERE** *ex* Jaya Fortune 6 *-2009* **PT Logindo Samudramakmur** - *Pontianak* *Indonesia* MMSI: 525016528	**1,337** 402 1,473	Class: BV	**2004-09 Yuexin Shipbuilding Co Ltd — Guangzhou GD** Yd No: YX-3301 Loa 57.50 Br ex - Dght 4.800 Lbp 52.00 Br md 13.80 Dpth 5.50 Welded, 1 dk	**(B21A2OS) Platform Supply Ship**	**2 oil engines** geared to sc. shafts driving 2 CP propellers Total Power: 3,494kW (4,750hp) 12.0kn Caterpillar 3512 2 x Vee 4 Stroke 12 Cy. 170 x 190 each-1747kW (2375bhp) Caterpillar Inc-USA
8950653 *PNJP* -	**SERVEWELL STABLE** *ex* Jaya Samson *-2010* **PT Logindo Samudramakmur** - *Jakarta* *Indonesia*	**314** 95 -	Class: BV KI	**1998-10 Guangzhou Fishing Vessel Shipyard — Guangzhou GD** Yd No: XY-2096 Loa 31.80 Br ex - Dght 3.200 Lbp 29.34 Br md 9.60 Dpth 4.15 Welded, 1 dk	**(B32A2ST) Tug**	**2 oil engines** reduction geared to sc. shafts driving 2 FP propellers Total Power: 1,884kW (2,562hp) 11.0kn Caterpillar 3512TA 2 x Vee 4 Stroke 12 Cy. 170 x 190 each-942kW (1281bhp) Caterpillar Inc-USA AuxGen: 2 x 70kW 380V 50Hz a.c
9131618 *YDA4591* -	**SERVEWELL STEADY** *ex* Jaya Coral *-2009* **PT Logindo Samudramakmur** - *Jakarta* *Indonesia* Official number: 386617	**285** 85 154	Class: AB KI	**1996-02 Jaya Shipbuilding & Engineering Pte Ltd — Singapore** Yd No: 809 Loa 26.02 Br ex - Dght 3.340 Lbp 24.38 Br md 8.89 Dpth 4.16 Welded, 1 dk	**(B32A2ST) Tug**	**2 oil engines** gearing integral to driving 2 Z propellers Total Power: 1,884kW (2,562hp) 9.0kn G.M. (Detroit Diesel) 16V-149-T 2 x Vee 2 Stroke 16 Cy. 146 x 146 each-942kW (1281bhp) Detroit Diesel Corporation-Detroit, Mi AuxGen: 2 x 90kW 415V 50Hz a.c Fuel: 80.0 (d.f.) 5.1pd
9571662 *YDA4519* -	**SERVEWELL STEWARD** **PT Logindo Samudramakmur** - *Pontianak* *Indonesia* MMSI: 525016524	**268** 81 77	Class: BV KI	**2009-08 Lung Teh Shipbuilding Co, Ltd — Suao** Yd No: NB385 Loa 36.00 Br ex - Dght 1.880 Lbp 33.00 Br md 7.60 Dpth 3.65 Welded, 1 dk	**(B34J2SD) Crew Boat** Hull Material: Aluminium Alloy Passengers: 110	**3 oil engines** reduction geared to sc shafts. driving 3 FP propellers Total Power: 2,910kW (3,957hp) 24.0kn Caterpillar C32 3 x Vee 4 Stroke 12 Cy. 145 x 162 each-970kW (1319bhp) Caterpillar Inc-USA AuxGen: 2 x 86kW 50Hz a.c Thrusters: 1 Tunnel thruster (f) Fuel: 35.0 (d.f.)
9314430 *POTG* -	**SERVEWELL VIGOR** *ex* Jaya Puffin 2 *-2012* **PT Servewell Offshore** - *Pontianak* *Indonesia* MMSI: 525016718	**499** 149 494	Class: BV KI	**2004-03 Tuong Aik Shipyard Sdn Bhd — Sibu** Yd No: 2210 Loa 45.00 Br ex - Dght 3.200 Lbp 41.08 Br md 11.00 Dpth 4.00 Welded, 1 dk	**(B21B20T) Offshore Tug/Supply Ship**	**2 oil engines** geared to sc. shafts driving 2 FP propellers Total Power: 2,574kW (3,500hp) 12.0kn Caterpillar 3512B-HD 2 x Vee 4 Stroke 12 Cy. 170 x 215 each-1287kW (1750bhp) Caterpillar Inc-USA AuxGen: 3 x 215kW 415V a.c Thrusters: 1 Thwart. FP thruster (f)
9656539 *YDB4284* -	**SERVEWELL VIRTUE** **PT Servewell Offshore** - *Jakarta* *Indonesia* MMSI: 525005200	**168** 51 -	Class: BV	**2012-06 PT Steadfast Marine — Pontianak** (Hull) Yd No: (544826) **2013-04 B.V. Scheepswerf Damen — Gorinchem** Yd No: 544826 Loa 34.30 Br ex 7.32 Dght 1.930 Lbp 32.00 Br md 6.50 Dpth 3.30 Welded, 1 dk	**(B21A2OC) Crew/Supply Vessel** Hull Material: Aluminium Alloy	**3 oil engines** reduction geared to sc. shafts driving 3 FP propellers Total Power: 2,238kW (3,042hp) 24.4kn Caterpillar C32 ACERT 3 x Vee 4 Stroke 12 Cy. 145 x 162 each-746kW (1014bhp) Caterpillar Inc-USA AuxGen: 2 x 69kW 60Hz a.c
5320871 *TC5625* -	**SERVIBURNU** **TDI Liman Isletmesi** - *Istanbul* *Turkey* Official number: 3284	*108* 30 -	Class: (GL)	**1961 D.W. Kremer Sohn — Elmshorn** Yd No: 1077 Loa 26.17 Br ex 6.71 Dght 2.579 Lbp - Br md - Dpth 3.46 Welded, 1 dk	**(B32A2ST) Tug**	**1 oil engine** driving 1 FP propeller Total Power: 588kW (799hp) Deutz SBV8M536 1 x 4 Stroke 8 Cy. 270 x 360 588kW (799bhp) Kloeckner Humboldt Deutz AG-West Germany AuxGen: 1 x 60kW 220V d.c
8925610 - -	**SERVICE 02** **Vung Tau Shipping & Service Co (Cong Ty Dich Vu Van Tai Bien Vung Tau)** - *Vung Tau* *Vietnam*	**120** - -	Class: (VR)	**1984 at Ho Chi Minh City** Loa - Br ex - Dght - Lbp 42.25 Br md 6.80 Dpth 3.40 Welded, 1 dk	**(A13B2TP) Products Tanker**	**1 oil engine** driving 1 FP propeller Total Power: 294kW (400hp) S.K.L. 8NVD26A-2 1 x 4 Stroke 8 Cy. 180 x 260 294kW (400bhp) VEB Schwermaschinenbau "KarlLiebknecht" (SKL)-Magdeburg AuxGen: 2 x 37kW a.c

ID	Name / Owners	Tonnage	Class	Builder / Dimensions	Type	Machinery
6814776 - -	**SERVICE VII** *ex* Bunair *-1990* *ex* Zubayya *-1985* *ex* Sharif 4 *-1982* *ex* Al Jabbar *-1981* **FAL Energy Co Ltd** FAL Bunkering Co Ltd	*126* - 85	Class: (LR) ✠ Classed LR until 29/7/92	**1968**-06 **R. Dunston (Hessle) Ltd. — Hessle** Yd No: S857 Loa 28.07 Br ex 7.75 Dght 2.744 Lbp 25.02 Br md 7.32 Dpth 3.41 Welded, 1 dk	**(B32A2ST) Tug**	**1 oil engine** reverse reduction geared to sc. shaft driving 1 FP propeller Total Power: 736kW (1,001hp) 10.8kn Blackstone EWSL8 1 x 4 Stroke 8 Cy. 222 x 292 736kW (1001bhp) Lister Blackstone Marine Ltd.-Dursley AuxGen: 2 x 30kW 440V 50Hz a.c Fuel: 38.0 (d.f.)
6416495 - -	**SERVICE XIX** *ex* Ghalla *-1990* *ex* Al Gattarah *-1990* *ex* Ilaria Montanari *-1977* *ex* Carlopia I *-1970* **FAL Energy Co Ltd** FAL Bunkering Co Ltd	*786* 531 1,166 T/cm 4.0	Class: (AB) (RI)	**1964 Cant. Nav. Soc. Nettuno — Reggio nell Emilia** Yd No: 14/B Loa 68.92 Br ex 9.53 Dght 2.871 Lbp 64.75 Br md 9.50 Dpth 3.41 Riveted\Welded, 1 dk	**(A13B2TP) Products Tanker** Liq: 1,598; Liq (Oil): 1,598 Compartments: 10 Ta, ER 1 Cargo Pump (s): 1x150m³/hr Manifold: Bow/CM: 36m	**2 oil engines** driving 2 FP propellers Total Power: 626kW (852hp) 7.0kn Alpha 405-24VO 2 x 2 Stroke 5 Cy. 240 x 400 each-313kW (426bhp) A/S Burmeister & Wain's Maskin ogSkibsbyggeri-Denmark AuxGen: 2 x 40kW a.c, 2 x 20kW a.c
8410421 *MCWS8* -	**SERVICEMAN** *ex* Shinano Maru *-2003* **SMS Towage Ltd** Specialist Marine Services Ltd *Hull* *United Kingdom* Official number: 908156	**295** 88 114	Class: LR **100A1** SS 11/2013 tug extended protected waters service Humber Estuary **LMC** Eq.Ltr: E; Cable: 275.0/16.0 U2 (a)	**1984**-10 **Hikari Kogyo K.K. — Yokosuka** Yd No: 336 Loa 31.35 Br ex 9.53 Dght 3.101 Lbp 26.50 Br md 9.50 Dpth 4.30 Welded, 1 dk	**(B32A2ST) Tug**	**2 oil engines** driving 2 Directional propellers Total Power: 2,574kW (3,500hp) Yanmar 6Z280L-ST 2 x 4 Stroke 6 Cy. 280 x 360 each-1287kW (1750bhp) Yanmar Diesel Engine Co Ltd-Japan AuxGen: 2 x 100kW 445V 60Hz a.c
8720838 *HKJV* -	**SERVIPORT I** *ex* Tracy P *-1989* *ex* Dragon Lady *-1989* **Sociedad Colombiana de Servicios Portuarios SA (SERVIPORT)** - *Cartagena de Indias* *Colombia* Official number: MC-05-439	*119* 65 -	Class: LR **100A1** SS 10/2009 tug Ecuadorian, Panamanian, Colombian and Venezuela coastla service **LMC** Eq.Ltr: F; Cable: 275.0/19.0 U2	**1982 Turnship Ltd. — Coden, Al** Loa 25.90 Br ex 8.64 Dght - Lbp 25.10 Br md 8.53 Dpth 3.66 Welded, 1 dk	**(B32A2ST) Tug**	**2 oil engines** sr geared to sc. shafts driving 2 FP propellers Total Power: 1,342kW (1,824hp) G.M. (Detroit Diesel) 16V-149 2 x Vee 2 Stroke 16 Cy. 146 x 146 each-671kW (912bhp) General Motors Corp-USA AuxGen: 2 x 50kW 440V 60Hz a.c
7340825 *HKQV* -	**SERVIPORT II** *ex* Moena *-1990* *ex* Seaforth Saga *-1990* *ex* Protector *-1990* *ex* Seaforth Saga *-1983* **Sociedad Colombiana de Servicios Portuarios SA (SERVIPORT)** - *Cartagena de Indias* *Colombia* MMSI: 730001200 Official number: MC-05-472	*871* 334 1,040	Class: LR ✠**100A1** SS 08/2010 tug ✠**LMC** Eq.Ltr: L; Cable: U2	**1975**-06 **Drypool Group Ltd. — England** Yd No: 1558 Converted From: Patrol Vessel-1988 Converted From: Offshore Tug/Supply Ship-1983 Loa 58.48 Br ex 12.04 Dght 4.522 Lbp 51.77 Br md 11.80 Dpth 5.21 Welded, 1 dk	**(B21B20T) Offshore Tug/Supply Ship**	**2 oil engines** reverse reduction geared to sc. shafts driving 2 FP propellers Total Power: 4,532kW (6,162hp) 13.5kn Polar SF116VS-F 2 x Vee 4 Stroke 16 Cy. 250 x 300 each-2266kW (3081bhp) British Polar Engines Ltd.-Glasgow AuxGen: 2 x 246kW 440V 60Hz a.c Thrusters: 1 Water jet (f) Fuel: 589.5 (d.f.)
7232731 *HKRH*	**SERVIPORT III** *ex* Bahia Utria *-2001* *ex* Panama Chief *-1991* *ex* Regent *-1986* *ex* Achilles *-1980* *ex* Edda Salvator *-1977* **Sociedad Colombiana de Servicios Portuarios SA (SERVIPORT)** - *Cartagena de Indias* *Colombia* Official number: MC-05-523	**937** 369 1,369	Class: (LR) (GL) (AB) (NV) ✠ Classed LR until 22/1/11	**1973**-01 **Scheepswerf Hoogezand N.V. — Hoogezand** Yd No: 165 Loa 59.91 Br ex 12.22 Dght 4.810 Lbp 54.00 Br md 11.90 Dpth 5.50 Welded, 1 dk	**(B21B20A) Anchor Handling Tug Supply** Cranes: 1x25t; Derricks: 1x20t,1x10t	**2 oil engines** with clutches, flexible couplings & sr reverse geared to sc. shafts driving 2 CP propellers Total Power: 4,530kW (6,158hp) 11.0kn Polar SF116VS-F 2 x Vee 4 Stroke 16 Cy. 250 x 300 each-2265kW (3079bhp) AB NOHAB-Sweden AuxGen: 1 x 247kW 440V 60Hz a.c, 1 x 245kW 440V 60Hz a.c Thrusters: 1 Thwart. CP thruster (f) Fuel: 600.0 (d.f.) 23.5pd
8209169 - -	**SERVIPORT IV** *ex* Manzanillo *-1998* *ex* Saba *-1994* - -	**184** 57 130	Class: (BV)	**1982**-06 **Dricon Scheepsconstructie B.V. — Drimmelen** Yd No: 640 Loa 26.52 Br ex 7.98 Dght 3.000 Lbp 24.46 Br md 7.66 Dpth 4.12 Welded, 1 dk	**(B32A2ST) Tug**	**2 oil engines** sr reverse geared to sc. shafts driving 2 FP propellers Total Power: 2,132kW (2,898hp) 12.9kn MWM TBD603V16 2 x Vee 4 Stroke 16 Cy. 160 x 185 each-1066kW (1449bhp) Motoren Werke Mannheim AG (MWM)-West Germany
7368621 - -	**SERVIS** *ex* Nesco Reefer *-2012* *ex* Green Flake *-2005* *ex* Mare Freezer *-1996* *ex* Atle Jarl *-1995* - -	**2,688** 1,060 1,284	Class: (LR) (NV) Classed LR until 14/11/07	**1976**-06 **Georg Eides Sonner AS — Hoylandsbygd** Yd No: 98 Loa 84.51 (BB) Br ex 16.62 Dght 4.949 Lbp 77.96 Br md 16.59 Dpth 7.19 Welded, 1 dk	**(A34A2GR) Refrigerated Cargo Ship** Side door (p) Ins: 3,545 TEU 24 C.Ho 12/20' C.Dk 12/20' Compartments: 2 Ho, ER, 2 Tw Dk 2 Ha: (14.1 x 9.2) (5.5 x 4.0)ER Cranes: 1x40t,1x7t; Derricks: 1x40t; Winches: 4 Ice Capable	**1 oil engine** with flexible couplings & reductiongeared to sc. shaft driving 1 CP propeller Total Power: 2,648kW (3,600hp) 15.0kn Mirrlees KMR-6 1 x 4 Stroke 6 Cy. 381 x 457 2648kW (3600bhp) Mirrlees Blackstone (Stockport)Ltd.-Stockport AuxGen: 3 x 180kW 380V 50Hz a.c Boilers: db (o.f.) 7.1kgf/cm² (7.0bar) Thrusters: 1 Thwart. FP thruster (f) Fuel: 376.0 (r.f.) 12.0pd
7020994 *SPS2065* -	**SERWAL** **Project Zegluga Sp z oo (Project Zegluga Ltd)** - *Szczecin* *Poland*	*115* 29 28	Class: PR	**1968**-12 **Gdynska Stocznia Remontowa — Gdynia** Yd No: H800/326 Loa 25.43 Br ex - Dght 2.501 Lbp 23.47 Br md 6.81 Dpth 3.41 Welded, 1 dk	**(B32A2ST) Tug** Ice Capable	**1 oil engine** driving 1 FP propeller Total Power: 588kW (799hp) S.K.L. 6NVD48A-2U 1 x 4 Stroke 6 Cy. 320 x 480 588kW (799bhp) VEB Schwermaschinenbau "KarlLiebknecht" (SKL)-Magdeburg AuxGen: 2 x 12kW 220V a.c
8738914 *SPS2475* -	**SERWAL 3** *ex* Multratug 14 *-2003* *ex* Petronella J. Goedkoop *-2003* **Multratug BV** Project Zegluga Sp z oo (Project Zegluga Ltd) *Szczecin* *Poland* MMSI: 261014570	**112** 33 -	Class: PR	**1962 Arnhemsche Scheepsbouw Mij NV — Arnhem** Yd No: 406 Loa 28.87 Br ex - Dght 2.600 Lbp 26.55 Br md 6.60 Dpth 3.20 Welded, 1 dk	**(B32A2ST) Tug**	**2 oil engines** driving 2 Propellers Total Power: 1,324kW (1,800hp) Bolnes 6DNL120/500 2 x 2 Stroke 6 Cy. 190 x 350 each-662kW (900bhp) NV Machinefabriek 'Bolnes' v/h JHvan Cappellen-Netherlands
6518308 *EROT* -	**SESILI** *ex* Alex *-2010* *ex* Star Trader *-1993* *ex* Star-Trader *-1982* *ex* Alexander *-1979* **Le Broni Ltd** - *Giurgiulesti* *Moldova* MMSI: 214181520	**492** 229 568	Class: MG (RS) (GL)	**1965**-07 **Ruhrorter Schiffswerft u. Maschinenfabrik GmbH — Duisburg** Yd No: 358 Loa 55.30 Br ex 9.07 Dght 3.020 Lbp 49.00 Br md - Dpth 3.51 Welded, 1 dk	**(A31A2GX) General Cargo Ship** Grain: 850; Bale: 818 Compartments: 1 Ho, ER 1 Ha: (25.4 x 5.9)ER Derricks: 2x3t; Winches: 2 Ice Capable	**1 oil engine** geared to sc. shaft driving 1 FP propeller Total Power: 368kW (500hp) 10.5kn MWM RH348SU 1 x 4 Stroke 6 Cy. 320 x 480 368kW (500bhp) Motoren Werke Mannheim AG (MWM)-West Germany
8866254 *UEUG* -	**SESKAR** *ex* Vasilios D *-2001* *ex* Mytos *-1998* *ex* Chernomorets *-1998* **OOO 'Kontur-SPB'** - *St Petersburg* *Russia* MMSI: 273421260	**895** 501 1,645	Class: (RS)	**1972 Shipbuilding & Shiprepairing Yard 'Ivan Dimitrov' — Rousse** Yd No: 91 Loa 59.69 Br ex 10.80 Dght 4.780 Lbp - Br md - Dpth 5.52 Welded, 1 dk	**(A13B2TP) Products Tanker** Ice Capable	**2 oil engines** driving 2 FP propellers Total Power: 588kW (800hp) 8.7kn S.K.L. 8NVD36-1U 2 x 4 Stroke 8 Cy. 240 x 360 each-294kW (400bhp) VEB Schwermaschinenbau "KarlLiebknecht" (SKL)-Magdeburg
9502491 *WDE7899* -	**SESOK** **US Bancorp Equipment Finance Inc** - *Naknek, Ak* *United States of America* MMSI: 367399110 Official number: 1217646	**166** 115 -		**2009**-06 **Diversified Marine, Inc. — Portland, Or** Yd No: 21 Loa 23.16 Br ex 10.20 Dght 1.060 Lbp 21.30 Br md 9.75 Dpth 1.98 Welded, 1 dk	**(B32A2ST) Tug**	**3 oil engines** reduction geared to sc. shafts driving 3 FP propellers Total Power: 1,002kW (1,362hp) 9.0kn Caterpillar C18 3 x 4 Stroke 6 Cy. 145 x 183 each-334kW (454bhp) Caterpillar Inc-USA AuxGen: 2 x 60kW a.c
9338797 *ECBK* -	**SESTAO KNUTSEN** **Norspan LNG IV AS** Knutsen OAS Shipping AS SatCom: Inmarsat C 422537210 *Santa Cruz de Tenerife* *Spain (CSR)* MMSI: 225372000 Official number: 8/2007	**90,478** 27,143 77,204 T/cm 86.6	Class: LR ✠**100A1** SS 11/2012 liquified gas tanker, Ship Type 2G*, methane in membrane tanks, max. pressure 0.25 bar min. temperature minus 163 degree C **ShipRight** (SDA) *IWS LI ✠**LMC** **UMS CCS** Eq.Ltr: Y†; Cable: 742.5/102.0 U3 (a)	**2007**-11 **Construcciones Navales del Norte SL — Sestao** Yd No: 331 Loa 284.38 (BB) Br ex 42.53 Dght 12.300 Lbp 271.00 Br md 42.50 Dpth 25.40 Welded, 1 dk.	**(A11A2TN) LNG Tanker** Double Bottom Entire Compartment Length Liq (Gas): 135,357 Cargo Heating Coils 4 x Gas Tank (s); 4 membrane (36% Ni.stl) pri horizontal 8 Cargo Pump (s): 8x1700m³/hr Manifold: Bow/CM: 137.3m	**1 Steam Turb** with flexible couplings & dr geared to sc. shaft driving 1 FP propeller Total Power: 28,000kW (38,069hp) 19.5kn Kawasaki UA-400 1 x steam Turb 28000kW (38069shp) Kawasaki Heavy Industries Ltd-Japan AuxGen: 1 x 3100kW 3300V 60Hz a.c, 2 x 3150kW 3300V 60Hz a.c Boilers: WTAuxB (o.f.) 79.5kgf/cm² (78.0bar) Superheater 515°C 64.2kgf/cm² (63.0bar) Thrusters: 1 Thwart. CP thruster (f) Fuel: 221.0 (d.f.) 4137.3 (r.f.)

9406659 *D5BH9* -	**SESTREA** **Amphinome Shipping Inc** Chandris (Hellas) Inc *Monrovia* *Liberia* MMSI: 636015522 Official number: 15522	**81,502** 51,283 158,519 T/cm 119.7	Class: LR ✠**100A1** SS 01/2012 Double Hull oil tanker CSR ESP **ShipRight** (CM) *IWS LI EP ✠**LMC** **UMS IGS** Eq.Ltr: Y†; Cable: 742.5/97.0 U3 (a)	**2009-09 Samsung Heavy Industries Co Ltd — Geoje** Yd No: 1724 Loa 274.42 (BB) Br ex - Dght 17.380 Lbp 264.00 Br md 48.04 Dpth 23.20 Welded, 1 dk	**(A13A2TV) Crude Oil Tanker** Double Hull (13F) Liq: 167,440; Liq (Oil): 167,440 Cargo Heating Coils Compartments: 12 Wing Ta, 2 Wing Slop Ta, ER 3 Cargo Pump (s): 3x3800m^3/hr Manifold: Bow/CM: 136.4m	**1 oil engine** driving 1 FP propeller Total Power: 18,660kW (25,370hp) 15.5kn MAN-B&W 6S70ME-C 1 x 2 Stroke 6 Cy. 700 x 2800 18660kW (25370bhp) Doosan Engine Co Ltd-South Korea AuxGen: 3 x 538kW 450V 60Hz a.c Boilers: e (ex.g.) 22.4kgf/cm^2 (22.0bar), AuxB (o.f.) 18.2kgf/cm^2 (17.8bar) Fuel: 330.0 (d.f.) 2700.0 (r.f.)
8215780 *9HHV9* -	**SESTRI STAR** *ex* Adria Celeste *-2007* *ex* Sofala *-2006* *ex* CMBT Limpopo *-2001* *ex* Oribi *-1998* *ex* FMG Cartagena *-1995* *ex* Maersk Kingston *-1995* *ex* Ursus Delmas *-1994* *ex* Zim Kingston III *-1993* *ex* Ursus *-1990* *ex* Cape York *-1988* *ex* Aqaba Crown *-1986* *launched as* Ursus *-1983* **Vittorio Bogazzi & Figli SpA** BNavi Ship Management Srl *Valletta* *Malta* MMSI: 249006000 Official number: 8215780	**8,386** 4,796 11,750 T/cm 23.1	Class: RI (GL)	**1983-04 J.J. Sietas KG Schiffswerft GmbH & Co. — Hamburg** Yd No: 912 Loa 133.48 (BB) Br ex 20.22 Dght 8.650 Lbp 122.97 Br md 20.21 Dpth 11.41 Welded, 2 dks	**(A31A2GX) General Cargo Ship** Grain: 15,625; Bale: 14,911 TEU 665 C Ho 286 C Dk 379 TEU incl 80 ref C. Compartments: 3 Ho, ER, 3 Tw Dk 3 Ha: (6.3 x 13.0)2 (37.8 x 15.3)ER Cranes: 2x35t Ice Capable	**1 oil engine** sr geared to sc. shaft driving 1 CP propeller Total Power: 4,413kW (6,000hp) 15.5kn MaK 6M601AK 1 x 4 Stroke 6 Cy. 580 x 600 4413kW (6000bhp) Krupp MaK Maschinenbau GmbH-Kiel AuxGen: 1 x 736kW 440V 60Hz a.c, 3 x 360kW 440V 60Hz a.c Thrusters: 1 Thwart. FP thruster (f)
7801867 *UBWJ* -	**SESTRORETSK** *ex* Sibirskiy-2104 *-1999* **Shipping Company 'Quadro Shipping Ltd'** Marship (Marine Recruitment & Shipping Co Ltd) *St Petersburg* *Russia* MMSI: 273343110 Official number: 794108	**3,415** 1,024 3,484	Class: RS	**1980-07 Valmet Oy — Turku** Yd No: 373 Loa 128.30 Br ex - Dght 3.170 Lbp 123.55 Br md 15.60 Dpth 5.44 Welded, 1 dk	**(A31A2GX) General Cargo Ship** Bale: 4,700 Ice Capable	**2 oil engines** driving 2 FP propellers Total Power: 1,324kW (1,800hp) 10.5kn Dvigatel Revolyutsii 6CHRN36/45 2 x 4 Stroke 6 Cy. 360 x 450 each-662kW (900bhp) Zavod "Dvigatel Revolyutsii"-Gorkiy AuxGen: 3 x 120kW a.c Thrusters: 1 Thwart. FP thruster (f) Fuel: 145.0 (d.f.)
6914655 *UEPK* -	**SESTRORETSK** *ex* MB-7015 *-1999* **OAO 'Tolyattiazot'** - *Novorossiysk* *Russia* Official number: 683189	**232** 70 91	Class: (RS)	**1969-04 VEB Schiffswerft "Edgar Andre" — Magdeburg** Yd No: 7015 Loa 34.78 Br ex 8.51 Dght 2.750 Lbp 30.41 Br md 8.21 Dpth 3.87 Welded, 1 dk	**(B32A2ST) Tug** Ice Capable	**1 oil engine** driving 1 CP propeller Total Power: 552kW (750hp) 11.3kn S.K.L. 6NVD48A-2U 1 x 4 Stroke 6 Cy. 320 x 480 552kW (750bhp) VEB Schwermaschinenbau "KarlLiebknecht" (SKL)-Magdeburg AuxGen: 2 x 42kW Fuel: 74.0 (d.f.)
9375563 - -	**SESTRORETSK** - **JSC 'Port Fleet Ltd' (ZAO 'Portovyy Flot')** - *St Petersburg* *Russia*	**188** 56 124	Class: RS	**2005-11 OAO Leningradskiy Sudostroitelnyy Zavod 'Pella' — Otradnoye** Yd No: 908 Loa 25.40 Br ex 9.30 Dght 3.300 Lbp 23.40 Br md 8.80 Dpth 4.30 Welded, 1 dk	**(B32A2ST) Tug** Ice Capable	**2 oil engines** gearing integral to driving 2 Directional propellers Total Power: 2,460kW (3,344hp) 12.0kn Caterpillar 3512B-TA 2 x Vee 4 Stroke 12 Cy. 170 x 190 each-1230kW (1672bhp) Caterpillar Inc-USA Fuel: 83.0 (d.f.)
9151711 *DTBH6* -	**SETA 56** - **Inter-Burgo Co Ltd** - *Busan* *South Korea* MMSI: 441134000 Official number: 0109006-6260008	**305** 91 245	Class: KR	**1996-07 Yongsung Shipbuilding Co Ltd — Geoje** Yd No: 151 Loa 45.05 Br ex - Dght - Lbp 37.50 Br md 7.20 Dpth 2.80 Welded, 1 dk	**(B11B2FV) Fishing Vessel**	**1 oil engine** reduction geared to sc. shaft driving 1 FP propeller Total Power: 736kW (1,001hp) 10.9kn Yanmar M220-UN 1 x 4 Stroke 6 Cy. 220 x 300 736kW (1001bhp) Yanmar Diesel Engine Co Ltd-Japan
9151723 *DTBH7* -	**SETA 57** - **Inter-Burgo Co Ltd** - *Busan* *South Korea* MMSI: 441135000 Official number: 0109007-6260007	**192** 91 242	Class: KR	**1996-07 Yongsung Shipbuilding Co Ltd — Geoje** Yd No: 152 Loa 45.05 Br ex - Dght 3.321 Lbp 37.50 Br md 7.20 Dpth 3.80 Welded, 1 dk	**(B11B2FV) Fishing Vessel**	**1 oil engine** reduction geared to sc. shaft driving 1 FP propeller Total Power: 736kW (1,001hp) 11.0kn Yanmar M220-UN 1 x 4 Stroke 6 Cy. 220 x 300 736kW (1001bhp) Yanmar Diesel Engine Co Ltd-Japan
8647531 - -	**SETA 59** - **Inter-Burgo SA** - *Luanda* *Angola* Official number: C-697-AC	**136** 41 -	Class: (KR)	**2000-03 Yongsung Shipbuilding Co Ltd — Geoje** Yd No: 165 Loa 28.19 Br ex - Dght 2.500 Lbp 24.00 Br md 6.60 Dpth 3.20 Welded, 1 dk	**(B11B2FV) Fishing Vessel** Ins: 102	**1 oil engine** reduction geared to sc. shaft driving 1 Propeller Total Power: 478kW (650hp) Yanmar 1 x 4 Stroke 6 Cy. 160 x 200 478kW (650bhp) Yanmar Diesel Engine Co Ltd-Japan
8647543 - -	**SETA 60** - **Inter-Burgo Co Ltd** - *Busan* *South Korea* Official number: 10060001-6261107	**136** 41 -	Class: (KR)	**2000-03 Yongsung Shipbuilding Co Ltd — Geoje** Yd No: 165 Loa 28.19 Br ex - Dght 2.500 Lbp 24.00 Br md 6.60 Dpth 3.20 Welded, 1 dk	**(B11B2FV) Fishing Vessel** Ins: 102	**1 oil engine** reduction geared to sc. shaft driving 1 Propeller Total Power: 478kW (650hp) Yanmar 1 x 4 Stroke 6 Cy. 160 x 200 478kW (650bhp) Yanmar Diesel Engine Co Ltd-Japan
8647555 - -	**SETA 61** - **Inter-Burgo SA** - *Luanda* *Angola* Official number: C-699-AC	**136** 41 -	Class: (KR)	**2000-03 Yongsung Shipbuilding Co Ltd — Geoje** Yd No: 165 Loa 28.19 Br ex - Dght 2.500 Lbp 24.00 Br md 6.60 Dpth 3.20 Welded, 1 dk	**(B11B2FV) Fishing Vessel** Ins: 102	**1 oil engine** reduction geared to sc. shaft driving 1 Propeller Total Power: 478kW (650hp) Yanmar 1 x 4 Stroke 6 Cy. 160 x 200 478kW (650bhp) Yanmar Diesel Engine Co Ltd-Japan
8647567 - -	**SETA 62** - **Inter-Burgo Co Ltd** - *Busan* *South Korea* Official number: 10060002-6261106	**136** 41 -	Class: (KR)	**2000-03 Yongsung Shipbuilding Co Ltd — Geoje** Yd No: 165 Loa 28.19 Br ex - Dght 2.500 Lbp 24.00 Br md 6.60 Dpth 3.20 Welded, 1 dk	**(B11B2FV) Fishing Vessel** Ins: 102	**1 oil engine** reduction geared to sc. shaft driving 1 Propeller Total Power: 478kW (650hp) Yanmar 1 x 4 Stroke 6 Cy. 160 x 200 478kW (650bhp) Yanmar Diesel Engine Co Ltd-Japan
9249001 *DTBE9* -	**SETA 70** - **Inter-Burgo Co Ltd** - *Busan* *South Korea* MMSI: 441080000 Official number: 0106003-6260007	**220** 119 334	Class: KR	**2001-04 Yongsung Shipbuilding Co Ltd — Geoje** Yd No: 173 Loa 46.04 Br ex - Dght - Lbp 37.50 Br md 7.20 Dpth 4.20 Welded, 1 dk	**(B11B2FV) Fishing Vessel** Ins: 360	**1 oil engine** geared to sc. shaft driving 1 FP propeller Total Power: 883kW (1,201hp) 13.0kn Yanmar M220-EN 1 x 4 Stroke 6 Cy. 220 x 300 883kW (1201bhp) Yanmar Diesel Engine Co Ltd-Japan
7913012 *JJ3205* -	**SETA MARU** - **Oita Eisen KK & KK Naikai Parking** - *Saiki, Oita* *Japan* Official number: 121121	*195* - -		**1979-11 Kanbara Zosen K.K. — Onomichi** Yd No: 241 Loa 31.50 Br ex - Dght 2.701 Lbp 27.01 Br md 8.81 Dpth 3.61 Welded, 1 dk	**(B32A2ST) Tug**	**2 oil engines** Geared Integral to driving 2 Z propellers Total Power: 1,912kW (2,600hp) Mitsubishi S16N-TK 2 x Vee 4 Stroke 16 Cy. 160 x 180 each-956kW (1300bhp) Mitsubishi Heavy Industries Ltd-Japan
6802058 *HQKD5* -	**SETA No. 2** *ex* Tala No. 1 *-1993* *ex* Dong Won No. 515 *-1982* *ex* Meisho Maru No. 15 *-1971* **Aroma Internacional SA** Inter-Burgo SA SatCom: Inmarsat C 424226110 *San Lorenzo* *Honduras* Official number: L-1924272	*339* 134 352	Class: (KR)	**1967 Uchida Zosen — Ise** Yd No: 699 Loa 47.20 Br ex 8.62 Dght 3.379 Lbp 42.80 Br md 8.59 Dpth 3.79 Riveted\Welded, 2 dks	**(B11A2FS) Stern Trawler**	**1 oil engine** driving 1 FP propeller Total Power: 1,177kW (1,600hp) 11.1kn Akasaka AH38 1 x 4 Stroke 6 Cy. 380 x 560 1177kW (1600bhp) Akasaka Tekkosho KK (Akasaka DieselLtd)-Japan AuxGen: 3 x 82kW 230V a.c

8715986 *HQCL2* -	**SETA No. 3** *ex* Tala-3 *-1995* *ex* Dae Sung No. 13 *-1989* **Aroma Internacional SA** Inter-Burgo SA *San Lorenzo* *Honduras* Official number: L-0201976	**137** - 307	Class: (KR)	**1987-04 Chungmu Shipbuilding Co Inc — Tongyeong** Yd No: 170 Loa 43.52 Br ex - Dght 3.494 Lbp 36.81 Br md 8.51 Dpth 5.62 Welded, 2 dks	**(B11A2FS) Stern Trawler** Ins: 310 Cranes: 4x2t	**1 oil engine** driving 1 FP propeller Total Power: 736kW (1,001hp) 10.4kn Yanmar T220L-UT 1 x 4 Stroke 6 Cy. 220 x 280 736kW (1001bhp) Yanmar Diesel Engine Co Ltd-Japan AuxGen: 2 x 136kW 385V a.c
7950230 *HQXA8* -	**SETA No. 23** *ex* Kyung Dong No. 51 *-1989* *ex* Acapulco Tercero *-1989* *ex* Shosei Maru *-1981* *ex* Asahi Maru No. 5 *-1979* **Inter-Burgo SA** - *San Lorenzo* *Honduras* Official number: L-1922658	*299* 154 460	Class: (KR)	**1971 Kochi Jyuko K.K. — Kochi** Yd No: 1160 Loa 49.73 Br ex - Dght - Lbp 43.20 Br md 8.31 Dpth 3.61 Welded, 1 dk	**(B11B2FV) Fishing Vessel**	**1 oil engine** driving 1 FP propeller Total Power: 736kW (1,001hp) Akasaka 1 x 4 Stroke 736kW (1001bhp) Akasaka Tekkosho KK (Akasaka DieselLtd)-Japan
9391763 *3FVC7* -	**SETAGAWA** - **IHI3247 Shipping SA** Kawasaki Kisen Kaisha Ltd (Kawasaki Kisen KK) ('K' Line) *Panama* *Panama* MMSI: 373604000 Official number: 4348112	**159,936** 97,268 299,998 T/cm 170.1	Class: NK	**2009-12 IHI Marine United Inc — Kure HS** Yd No: 3247 Loa 333.00 (BB) Br ex 60.04 Dght 20.549 Lbp 324.00 Br md 60.00 Dpth 29.00 Welded, 1 dk	**(A13A2TV) Crude Oil Tanker** Double Hull (13F) Liq: 330,158; Liq (Oil): 342,750 Compartments: 5 Ta, 10 Wing Ta, 2 Wing Slop Ta, ER 3 Cargo Pump (s): 3x5500m³/hr Manifold: Bow/CM: 163.6m	**1 oil engine** driving 1 FP propeller Total Power: 27,160kW (36,927hp) 15.3kn Wartsila 7RTA84T 1 x 2 Stroke 7 Cy. 840 x 3150 27160kW (36927bhp) Diesel United Ltd.-Aioi AuxGen: 3 x 1100kW a.c Fuel: 728.0 (d.f.) 6829.0 (r.f.)
8746088 *YB6295* -	**SETAGEN** - **PT Benua Raya Katulistiwa** - *Balikpapan* *Indonesia*	**299** 90 -	Class: KI	**2005 in Indonesia** Loa 42.00 Br ex - Dght - Lbp 40.32 Br md 10.00 Dpth 2.50 Welded, 1 dk	**(A37B2PS) Passenger Ship**	**2 oil engines** reduction geared to sc. shafts driving 2 Propellers Total Power: 470kW (640hp) Mitsubishi 8DC9 2 x Vee 4 Stroke 8 Cy. 135 x 140 each-235kW (320bhp) Mitsubishi Heavy Industries Ltd-Japan AuxGen: 2 x 235kW 380/220V a.c
7707504 *YGQF* -	**SETANGGI 2** *ex* Brastagi III *-2008* *ex* Everest *-2001* *ex* Capitaine Cook *-1995* *ex* New Orleans *-1993* *ex* Tiger Bay *-1991* *ex* New Orleans *-1990* *ex* Celinda *-1988* *ex* Frellsen Gunvor *-1986* *ex* Gunvor Frellsen *-1980* **PT Pelayaran Berkah Setanggi Timur** - *Jakarta* *Indonesia*	**3,849** 2,635 4,300	Class: KI (BV) (NV)	**1979-04 Sonderborg Skibsvaerft A/S — Sonderborg** Yd No: 82 Loa 100.01 Br ex 17.91 Dght 5.250 Lbp 91.32 Br md 17.01 Dpth 9.02 Welded, 2 dks	**(A31A2GX) General Cargo Ship** Grain: 9,218; Bale: 8,426 TEU 258 C. 258/20' incl. 20 ref C. Compartments: 2 Ho, ER 2 Ha: 2 (26.0 x 12.8)ER Derricks: 2x45t,2x22.5t Ice Capable	**1 oil engine** driving 1 CP propeller Total Power: 2,501kW (3,400hp) 12.0kn MaK 9M453AK 1 x 4 Stroke 9 Cy. 320 x 420 2501kW (3400bhp) MaK Maschinenbau GmbH-Kiel AuxGen: 2 x 262kW 380V 50Hz a.c, 1 x 141kW 380V 50Hz a.c Fuel: 67.0 (d.f.) 358.0 (r.f.) 11.0pd
9089504 *9BRX* -	**SETAREH BANDAR** *ex* Khaiyn Star *-2008* *ex* GBS-2 *-2007* *ex* Sin Matu 16 *-2006* **Jaber Moshtagedour** Alima Shipping & Cargo Co LLC *Khorramshahr* *Iran* MMSI: 422778000	**499** 398 1,250		**1994-01 Seri Modalwan Sdn Bhd — Sandakan** L reg 53.50 Br ex - Dght 2.800 Lbp 50.50 Br md 13.70 Dpth 3.04 Welded, 1 dk	**(A35D2RL) Landing Craft**	**2 oil engines** driving 2 Propellers Total Power: 458kW (622hp) 9.0kn Cummins 2 x 4 Stroke each-229kW (311bhp) Cummins Engine Co Inc-USA
5357707 *EPGG* -	**SETAREH DARYA** *ex* Thalassa *-1974* **Gulf Shipping Co SA** Gulf Agency Co (Iran) Ltd *Khorramshahr* *Iran*	*499* 272 681	Class: (BV)	**1956-04 N.V. Scheepswerf "Appingedam" v/h A. Apol C.V. — Appingedam** Yd No: 176 Loa 52.71 Br ex 8.51 Dght 3.353 Lbp 47.86 Br md 8.39 Dpth 3.59 Welded, 1 dk	**(A31A2GX) General Cargo Ship** Grain: 934; Bale: 892 Compartments: 1 Ho, ER 2 Ha: 2 (12.1 x 4.9)ER Derricks: 2x3t; Winches: 2	**1 oil engine** sr geared to sc. shaft driving 1 FP propeller Total Power: 405kW (551hp) 10.0kn Deutz RBA8M528 1 x 4 Stroke 8 Cy. 220 x 280 405kW (551bhp) (new engine 0000) Kloeckner Humboldt Deutz AG-West Germany AuxGen: 1 x 46kW Fuel: 50.0
8802167 *EPQH* -	**SETAREH JONOUB** - **Ferdos Seyd Co** - *Bandar Abbas* *Iran* MMSI: 422524000 Official number: 11265	**673** 201 350	Class: AS (GL)	**1991 Iran Marine Ind. Co. (IMICO) — Bushehr** Loa 45.50 Br ex 10.27 Dght 3.802 Lbp 40.26 Br md 10.00 Dpth 6.60 Welded, 1 dk	**(B11A2FT) Trawler** Ins: 320	**1 oil engine** with clutches, flexible couplings & sr reverse geared to sc. shaft driving 1 CP propeller Total Power: 1,176kW (1,599hp) 12.0kn Deutz SBV8M628 1 x 4 Stroke 8 Cy. 240 x 280 1176kW (1599bhp) Kloeckner Humboldt Deutz AG-Germany AuxGen: 1 x 320kW 220/380V a.c, 2 x 224kW 220/380V a.c Fuel: 231.0 (d.f.)
8037384 *9BRG* -	**SETAREH KHALIJ** *ex* Eagle Bluff *-2008* **Kamal Beik H** - *Bushehr* *Iran* Official number: 16942	*149* 93 -	Class: AS	**1977 Ocean Shipyards (WA) Pty Ltd — Fremantle WA** Loa 23.40 Br ex - Dght - Lbp - Br md 6.76 Dpth 2.47 Welded, 1 dk	**(B11A2FT) Trawler**	**1 oil engine** sr geared to sc. shaft driving 1 FP propeller Total Power: 530kW (721hp) 9.0kn Caterpillar 3412 1 x Vee 4 Stroke 12 Cy. 137 x 152 530kW (721bhp) (new engine 1977, fitted 1977) Caterpillar Inc-USA AuxGen: 1 x 72kW 440V 50Hz a.c Fuel: 51.0 (d.f.)
8657938 *9BHT* -	**SETAREH KHORRAMSHAHR** - **Omid Sharafi** - *Bandar Imam Khomeini* *Iran* Official number: 20210	**210** 140 -	Class: AS	**1980 in Iran** Loa 31.44 Br ex - Dght 2.430 Lbp 27.47 Br md 7.50 Dpth 3.20 Welded, 1 dk	**(A31A2GX) General Cargo Ship**	**2 oil engines** reduction geared to sc. shafts driving 2 Propellers Total Power: 2,000kW (2,720hp) Volvo Penta 2 x each-1000kW (1360bhp) AB Volvo Penta-Sweden
8991877 *9BJB* -	**SETAREH SHOMAL** *ex* North Star *-2006* **Mohammad Fardid** - *Bandar Abbas* *Iran* MMSI: 422545000 Official number: 846	**796** 239 -	Class: AS	**1997-03 in the Philippines** L reg 57.60 Br ex - Dght - Lbp - Br md 13.10 Dpth 3.89 Welded, 1 dk	**(A35D2RL) Landing Craft** Bow ramp (f)	**2 oil engines** reduction geared to sc. shafts driving 2 Propellers Total Power: 736kW (1,000hp) Caterpillar 3412 2 x Vee 4 Stroke 12 Cy. 137 x 152 each-368kW (500bhp) Caterpillar Inc-USA
9025584 - -	**SETCO PRIBUMI** - **PT Mega Lestari Samudra** - *Jakarta* *Indonesia*	**108** 64 -	Class: (KI)	**1977 Pan-Asia Shipyard & Engineering Co Pte Ltd — Singapore** L reg 23.70 Br ex 7.02 Dght 2.800 Lbp 21.22 Br md 7.00 Dpth 3.55 Welded, 1 dk	**(B32A2ST) Tug**	**2 oil engines** geared to sc. shafts driving 1 Propeller Total Power: 536kW (728hp) Caterpillar D343 2 x 4 Stroke 6 Cy. 137 x 165 each-268kW (364bhp) (made 1972) Caterpillar Tractor Co-USA
7533290 *HP8464* -	**SETE 3** *ex* Petrola Pente *-1995* *ex* Jorc V *-1981* *ex* Dekatessera *-1979* **SETE Energy Saudia for Industrial Projects Ltd** - *Panama* *Panama* Official number: 2333496C	*114* 26 139	Class: LR ✠ **100A1** SS 03/2009 tug for service within 15 miles or the ports of Jeddah, Thuwal & Rabigh and coastal voyages not exceeding 15 miles between ports **LMC** Eq.Ltr: (c) ; Cable: U2	**1976-03 Staalin B.V. — 's-Gravenhage** Yd No: 784 Loa 22.76 Br ex 6.89 Dght 2.661 Lbp 19.28 Br md 6.61 Dpth 3.43 Welded, 1 dk	**(B32A2ST) Tug**	**2 oil engines** reverse reduction geared to sc. shafts driving 2 FP propellers Total Power: 992kW (1,348hp) G.M. (Detroit Diesel) 12V-149 2 x Vee 2 Stroke 12 Cy. 146 x 146 each-496kW (674bhp) General Motors Detroit DieselAllison Divn-USA AuxGen: 2 x 25kW 380/220V 50Hz a.c
7533317 - -	**SETE 4** *ex* Petrola Exi *-1995* *ex* Jorc VI *-1981* *ex* Dekapende *-1979* **Huta-Sete Marine Works Ltd** Huta Marine Works Ltd *Saudi Arabia*	*114* 26 139	Class: (LR) ✠ Classed LR until 17/7/06	**1976-03 Rilaco B.V. — Krimpen a/d IJssel** (Hull) **1976-03 B.V. Scheepswerf Damen — Gorinchem** Yd No: 794 Loa 22.76 Br ex 6.89 Dght 2.661 Lbp 19.28 Br md 6.61 Dpth 3.43 Welded, 1 dk	**(B32A2ST) Tug**	**2 oil engines** reverse reduction geared to sc. shafts driving 2 FP propellers Total Power: 992kW (1,348hp) G.M. (Detroit Diesel) 12V-149 2 x Vee 2 Stroke 12 Cy. 146 x 146 each-496kW (674bhp) General Motors Detroit DieselAllison Divn-USA AuxGen: 2 x 25kW 380/220V 50Hz a.c
5353828 - -	**SETE 9** *ex* Pente *-1998* *ex* Taucher O. Wulf III *-1972* **Huta-Sete Marine Works Ltd** Huta Marine Works Ltd *Saudi Arabia*	*136* 70 -	Class: (GL)	**1941 J.J. Sietas — Hamburg** Yd No: 338 Converted From: Salvage Vessel-1972 L reg 27.97 Br ex 7.29 Dght - Lbp 26.01 Br md 7.26 Dpth 3.10 Welded, 1 dk	**(B32A2ST) Tug**	**1 oil engine** driving 1 FP propeller Total Power: 971kW (1,320hp) 10.0kn MWM TRH348AU 1 x 4 Stroke 8 Cy. 320 x 480 971kW (1320bhp) (new engine 1955) Motoren Werke Mannheim AG (MWM)-West Germany

5118761 *HZ2343* -	**SETE 10** *ex* Ikosidio *-1998* *ex* A. Moir *-1976* *ex* Foundation Vanguard *-1973* **Huta-Sete Marine Works Ltd** Huta Marine Works Ltd *Jeddah* *Saudi Arabia*	*207* 54 96	Class: (AB)	**1962 Davie Shipbuilding Ltd — Levis QC** Yd No: 636 Loa 30.00 Br ex 8.49 Dght 3.736 Lbp 27.03 Br md 8.18 Dpth 4.09 Welded, 1 dk	**(B32A2ST) Tug**	**1 oil engine** reverse reduction geared to sc. shaft driving 1 FP propeller Total Power: 736kW (1,001hp) 11.0kn Fairbanks, Morse 6-38D8-1/8 1 x 2 Stroke 6 Cy. 207 x 254 736kW (1001bhp) Canadian Locomotive Co Ltd-Canada AuxGen: 2 x 30kW 550V 60Hz a.c
9150432 *CSAJ* -	**SETE CIDADES** **TRANSINSULAR -Transportes Maritimos Insulares Sarl** S&C Shipmanagement & Crewing Lda (S&C Gestao de Navios e Tripulacoes Lda) *Lisbon* *Portugal* MMSI: 263755000 Official number: J-424	**3,979** 1,941 4,969 T/cm 14.0	Class: BV	**1999-12 Estaleiros Navais de Viana do Castelo S.A. — Viana do Castelo** Yd No: 205 Loa 100.60 (BB) Br ex - Dght 6.314 Lbp 93.00 Br md 16.50 Dpth 8.00 Welded, 1 dk	**(A33A2CC) Container Ship (Fully Cellular)** TEU 378 C Ho 127 TEU C Dk 251 TEU incl 50 ref C Compartments: 2 Cell Ho, ER 2 Ha: (25.6 x 13.2) (32.6 x 13.2)ER Cranes: 2x40t Ice Capable	**1 oil engine** with flexible couplings & sr gearedto sc. shaft driving 1 CP propeller Total Power: 3,472kW (4,721hp) 15.7kn MaK 8M32 1 x 4 Stroke 8 Cy. 320 x 480 3472kW (4721bhp) MaK Motoren GmbH & Co. KG-Kiel AuxGen: 1 x 700kW 380V 50Hz a.c, 2 x 240kW 380V 50Hz a.c Thrusters: 1 Thwart. FP thruster (f) Fuel: 76.8 (d.f.) (Heating Coils) 291.6 (r.f.) 15.5pd
9302310 *WDB7469* -	**SETH MCCALL** **SEACOR Offshore LLC** SEACOR Marine LLC *New Orleans, LA* *United States of America* MMSI: 369316000 Official number: 1146469	**436** 130 305	Class: AB	**2003-10 Gulf Craft LLC — Patterson LA** Yd No: 451 Loa 53.80 Br ex 9.14 Dght 2.440 Lbp 48.01 Br md - Dpth 4.11 Welded, 1 dk	**(B21A2OC) Crew/Supply Vessel** Hull Material: Aluminium Alloy Passengers: unberthed: 76	**4 oil engines** geared to sc. shafts driving 4 Water jets Total Power: 5,296kW (7,200hp) 28.0kn Cummins KTA-50-M2 4 x Vee 4 Stroke 16 Cy. 159 x 159 each-1324kW (1800bhp) Cummins Engine Co Inc-USA AuxGen: 2 x 99kW 60Hz a.c Thrusters: 1 Retract. directional thruster (f); 1 Tunnel thruster (f) Fuel: 112.0 (d.f.) 35.0pd
8898025 - -	**SETIA** **PT Sabda Bagan** - *Pontianak* *Indonesia*	**148** 45 -	Class: KI	**1996-04 P.T. Wahana Kapuas — Pontianak** Loa 22.00 Br ex - Dght - Lbp 20.24 Br md 7.00 Dpth 3.92 Welded, 1 dk	**(B32A2ST) Tug**	**2 oil engines** reduction geared to sc. shafts driving 2 FP propellers Total Power: 810kW (1,102hp) 10.0kn Yanmar 2 x 4 Stroke 6 Cy. each-405kW (551bhp) (made 1976) Yanmar Diesel Engine Co Ltd-Japan
8005874 *5IM607* -	**SETIA 3** *ex* Setia Abadi *-2013* *ex* Burong Layang *-1991* **Bunga Jaya Marin Sdn Bhd** - *Zanzibar* *Tanzania (Zanzibar)* MMSI: 677050700 Official number: 300352	**254** 76 -	Class: (BV) (NV) (AB)	**1980-06 Teraoka Shipyard Co Ltd — Minamiawaji HG** Yd No: 196 Loa 31.50 Br ex - Dght 2.312 Lbp 28.66 Br md 7.80 Dpth 3.00 Welded, 1 dk	**(B31A2SR) Research Survey Vessel**	**2 oil engines** reverse reduction geared to sc. shafts driving 2 FP propellers Total Power: 764kW (1,038hp) 8.0kn Caterpillar 3412TA 2 x Vee 4 Stroke 12 Cy. 137 x 152 each-382kW (519bhp) Caterpillar Tractor Co-USA AuxGen: 2 x 125kW 415V 50Hz a.c Fuel: 75.0 (d.f.) 3.5pd
8402149 *V3RZ7* -	**SETIA 5** *ex* Setia Damai *-2013* *ex* Permata *-2004* - - *Belize City* *Belize* MMSI: 312397000 Official number: 991310002	*278* 83 111	Class: AB (LR) ✠ Classed LR until 12/12/01	**1985-08 Limbongan Timor Sdn Bhd — Kuala Terengganu** Yd No: 10783 Loa 35.06 Br ex 10.37 Dght 2.171 Lbp 33.69 Br md 10.08 Dpth 2.77 Welded, 1 dk	**(B34Q2QB) Buoy Tender**	**2 oil engines** with clutches & sr geared to sc. shafts driving 2 FP propellers Total Power: 592kW (804hp) 7.0kn Caterpillar 3408C 2 x Vee 4 Stroke 8 Cy. 137 x 152 each-296kW (402bhp) Caterpillar Tractor Co-USA AuxGen: 2 x 80kW 416V 50Hz a.c Fuel: 500.0 (d.f.)
9025596 *YD6341* -	**SETIA ABADI** **PT Aneka Samudera Lintas** - *Samarinda* *Indonesia*	**127** 76 -	Class: KI	**1998-02 P.T. Galangan Teluk Bajau Kaltim — Samarinda** L reg 20.75 Br ex - Dght 2.250 Lbp 18.25 Br md 6.50 Dpth 2.80 Welded, 1 dk	**(B32A2ST) Tug**	**2 oil engines** reduction geared to sc. shafts driving 1 Propeller Total Power: 692kW (940hp) Caterpillar 3408C 2 x Vee 4 Stroke 8 Cy. 137 x 152 each-346kW (470bhp) Caterpillar Inc-USA Fuel: 75.0 (d.f.)
9529231 *9MII9* -	**SETIA AMAN** **Alam-Pe III (L) Inc** Alam Maritim (M) Sdn Bhd SatCom: Inmarsat C 453300790 *Port Klang* *Malaysia* MMSI: 533058300 Official number: 334021	**3,404** 1,125 2,131	Class: BV (AB)	**2010-05 Nantong MLC Tongbao Shipbuilding Co Ltd — Rugao JS** Yd No: MLC7802 Loa 78.00 Br ex - Dght 4.800 Lbp 70.55 Br md 20.00 Dpth 6.50 Welded, 1 dk	**(B22A2OR) Offshore Support Vessel** Passengers: berths: 188 Cranes: 1x30t	**2 oil engines** reduction geared to sc. shafts driving 2 FP propellers Total Power: 3,840kW (5,220hp) 13.0kn Yanmar 6EY26 2 x 4 Stroke 6 Cy. 260 x 385 each-1920kW (2610bhp) Yanmar Diesel Engine Co Ltd-Japan AuxGen: 3 x 750kW a.c Thrusters: 1 Tunnel thruster (f)
9448126 *9MFH5* -	**SETIA AZAM** **Alam Maritim (M) Sdn Bhd** - *Port Klang* *Malaysia* MMSI: 533377000 Official number: 332418	**641** 192 576	Class: NK (AB)	**2007-08 Yuexin Shipbuilding Co Ltd — Guangzhou GD** Yd No: 3078 Loa 45.00 Br ex - Dght 3.800 Lbp 39.40 Br md 11.80 Dpth 4.60 Welded, 1 dk	**(B21B20A) Anchor Handling Tug Supply** Passengers: cabins: 7; berths: 20	**2 oil engines** reduction geared to sc. shafts driving 2 FP propellers Total Power: 2,850kW (3,874hp) 9.0kn Caterpillar 3512B 2 x Vee 4 Stroke 12 Cy. 170 x 190 each-1425kW (1937bhp) Caterpillar Inc-USA AuxGen: 3 x 125kW a.c Thrusters: 1 Tunnel thruster (f) Fuel: 550.0 (d.f.)
9498030 *9MHT6* -	**SETIA BUDI** **Alam Maritim (M) Sdn Bhd** - SatCom: Inmarsat C 453300371 *Port Klang* *Malaysia* MMSI: 533017600 Official number: 333824	**481** 145 358	Class: NK	**2008-08 Pleasant Engineering Sdn Bhd — Sandakan** Yd No: 12/06 Loa 40.00 Br ex - Dght 3.812 Lbp 36.41 Br md 11.80 Dpth 4.60 Welded, 1 dk	**(B34L2QU) Utility Vessel**	**2 oil engines** geared to sc. shafts driving 2 FP propellers Total Power: 1,790kW (2,434hp) Cummins KTA-38-M2 2 x Vee 4 Stroke 12 Cy. 159 x 159 each-895kW (1217bhp) Cummins Engine Co Inc-USA AuxGen: 2 x 280kW 415V 50Hz a.c Thrusters: 1 Tunnel thruster (f) Fuel: 262.0 (r.f.)
7391989 *9MEU7* -	**SETIA CEKAL** *ex* Orient Explorer *-2003* *ex* Lady Gay *-1994* **Alam Maritim (M) Sdn Bhd** - *Port Klang* *Malaysia* MMSI: 533000015 Official number: 328537	**994** 299 1,063	Class: (LR) ✠ Classed LR until 1/2/04	**1974-12 Carrington Slipways Pty Ltd — Newcastle NSW** Yd No: 97 Converted From: Offshore Tug/Supply Ship-1997 Lengthened-1997 Loa 62.00 Br ex 13.26 Dght 4.400 Lbp 59.00 Br md 12.81 Dpth 4.88 Welded, 1 dk	**(B22A2OV) Diving Support Vessel** Passengers: berths: 48 Cranes: 1x10t	**4 oil engines** with clutches, flexible couplings & dr reverse geared to sc. shafts driving 1 CP propeller , 2 FP propellers Total Power: 3,088kW (4,200hp) 10.0kn Daihatsu 8PSHTCM-26E 4 x 4 Stroke 8 Cy. 260 x 320 each-772kW (1050bhp) Daihatsu Diesel Manufacturing Co Lt-Japan AuxGen: 2 x 250kW 415V 50Hz a.c Thrusters: 1 Thwart. CP thruster (f) Fuel: 604.0 (d.f.) 13.0pd
9358606 *9MFF7* -	**SETIA CEKAP** *ex* Jaya Puffin 3 *-2007* **Alam Maritim (M) Sdn Bhd** - *Port Klang* *Malaysia* MMSI: 533375000 Official number: 332398	**499** 149 516	Class: BV (AB)	**2005-10 Yuexin Shipbuilding Co Ltd — Guangzhou GD** Yd No: 3049 Loa 41.11 Br ex - Dght 3.400 Lbp 40.00 Br md 11.00 Dpth 4.00 Welded, 1 dk	**(B21B2OT) Offshore Tug/Supply Ship**	**2 oil engines** reduction geared to sc. shafts driving 2 FP propellers Total Power: 2,610kW (3,548hp) 10.0kn Caterpillar 3512B-HD 2 x Vee 4 Stroke 12 Cy. 170 x 215 each-1305kW (1774bhp) Caterpillar Inc-USA AuxGen: 3 x 245kW a.c Thrusters: 1 Tunnel thruster (f) Fuel: 280.0 (d.f.)
9510383 *9MIM5* -	**SETIA DERAS** **Alam Fast Boats (L) Inc** Trinity Offshore Pte Ltd SatCom: Inmarsat C 453300831 *Port Klang* *Malaysia* MMSI: 533043600 Official number: 334060	**270** 81 88	Class: BV (AB)	**2009-06 Sam Aluminium Engineering Pte Ltd — Singapore** Yd No: H80 Loa 40.25 Br ex - Dght 1.300 Lbp 40.00 Br md 7.80 Dpth 3.40 Welded, 1 dk	**(B34L2QU) Utility Vessel** Hull Material: Aluminium Alloy Passengers: unberthed: 80	**3 oil engines** reduction geared to sc. shafts driving 3 FP propellers Total Power: 3,090kW (4,200hp) 18.0kn Caterpillar C32 3 x Vee 4 Stroke 12 Cy. 145 x 162 each-1030kW (1400bhp) Caterpillar Inc-USA AuxGen: 2 x 90kW 415V 50Hz a.c Thrusters: 1 Tunnel thruster (f) Fuel: 100.0 (d.f.)
9303637 *9MGG7* -	**SETIA EMAS** **Alam Maritim (M) Sdn Bhd** - *Port Klang* *Malaysia* MMSI: 533000280 Official number: 330409	**964** 289 860	Class: BV	**2004-05 Fujian Southeast Shipyard — Fuzhou FJ** Yd No: 835 Loa 48.00 Br ex 13.20 Dght 4.200 Lbp 42.40 Br md 13.20 Dpth 5.20 Welded, 1 dk	**(B21B20A) Anchor Handling Tug Supply** Passengers: berths: 24	**2 oil engines** geared to sc. shafts driving 2 CP propellers Total Power: 3,494kW (4,750hp) 13.5kn Caterpillar 3516B 2 x Vee 4 Stroke 16 Cy. 170 x 190 each-1747kW (2375bhp) Caterpillar Inc-USA AuxGen: 3 x 315kW 415/220V 50Hz a.c Thrusters: 1 Tunnel thruster (f) Fuel: 520.0 (d.f.)

IMO / Call sign / Flag	Name / Owner	Tonnage	Class	Build / Dimensions	Type	Machinery
9543225 *9MLD4* -	**SETIA ERAT** **Alam-JV DP1 (L) Inc** Alam Maritim (M) Sdn Bhd *Port Klang* *Malaysia* MMSI: 533048900 Official number: 334137	**1,537** 461 1,475	Class: BV	**2010-02 Guangzhou Hangtong Shipbuilding & Shipping Co Ltd — Jiangmen GD** Yd No: 072012 Loa 58.70 Br ex - Dght 4.750 Lbp 53.20 Br md 14.60 Dpth 5.50 Welded, 1 dk	**(B21B20A) Anchor Handling Tug Supply**	**2 oil engines** reduction geared to sc.shafts driving 2 CP propellers Total Power: 3,282kW (4,462hp) 13.5kn Caterpillar 3516B-TA 2 x Vee 4 Stroke 16 Cy. 170 x 190 each-1641kW (2231bhp) Caterpillar Inc-USA AuxGen: 3 x 350kW 50Hz a.c Thrusters: 1 Tunnel thruster (f) Fuel: 460.0 (d.f.)
9324265 *9MGO9* -	**SETIA FAJAR** *ex Jaya Supplier 3 -2005* **Alam Maritim (L) Inc** Alam Maritim (M) Sdn Bhd *Port Klang* *Malaysia* MMSI: 533936000 Official number: 330488	**1,470** 441 1,475	Class: BV	**2005-09 Guangzhou Hangtong Shipbuilding & Shipping Co Ltd — Jiangmen GD** Yd No: 042001 Loa 58.70 Br ex - Dght 4.750 Lbp 53.20 Br md 14.60 Dpth 5.50 Welded, 1 dk	**(B21B20A) Anchor Handling Tug Supply**	**2 oil engines** geared to sc. shafts driving 2 CP propellers Total Power: 3,840kW (5,220hp) 13.5kn Caterpillar 3516B-HD 2 x Vee 4 Stroke 16 Cy. 170 x 215 each-1920kW (2610bhp) Caterpillar Inc-USA AuxGen: 3 x 340kW 415/220V 50Hz a.c Thrusters: 1 Tunnel thruster (f) Fuel: 470.0 (d.f.)
9297266 *9MGC9* -	**SETIA GAGAH** **Alam Maritim (M) Sdn Bhd** - *Port Klang* *Malaysia* MMSI: 533000086 Official number: 330360	**1,188** 356 859	Class: NK (AB)	**2003-09 P.T. Jaya Asiatic Shipyard — Batam** Yd No: 833 Loa 60.00 Br ex - Dght 4.510 Lbp 54.05 Br md 13.30 Dpth 6.00 Welded, 1 dk	**(B21B20A) Anchor Handling Tug Supply**	**2 oil engines** reduction geared to sc. shafts driving 2 CP propellers Total Power: 3,322kW (4,516hp) 10.0kn Caterpillar 3616-HD 2 x Vee 4 Stroke 16 Cy. 170 x 215 each-1661kW (2258bhp) Caterpillar Inc-USA AuxGen: 2 x 145kW a.c Thrusters: 1 Tunnel thruster (f) Fuel: 245.0 (d.f.)
9529217 *9MII7* -	**SETIA GIGIH** **Alam-Pe II (L) Inc** Alam Maritim (M) Sdn Bhd *Port Klang* *Malaysia* MMSI: 533042900 Official number: 334019	**1,454** 436 1,018	Class: BV (AB)	**2009-04 Nantong MLC Tongbao Shipbuilding Co Ltd — Rugao JS** Yd No: MLC6002 Loa 60.00 Br ex - Dght 4.500 Lbp 53.70 Br md 13.30 Dpth 6.00 Welded, 1 dk	**(B21B20T) Offshore Tug/Supply Ship**	**2 oil engines** reduction geared to sc. shafts driving 2 FP propellers Total Power: 3,840kW (5,220hp) Yanmar 6EY26 2 x 4 Stroke 6 Cy. 260 x 385 each-1920kW (2610bhp) Yanmar Diesel Engine Co Ltd-Japan AuxGen: 3 x 415kW a.c Thrusters: 1 Tunnel thruster (f) Fuel: 300.0 (d.f.)
9288631 *9MGC8* -	**SETIA HANDAL** **Alam Maritim (M) Sdn Bhd** - *Port Klang* *Malaysia* MMSI: 533000085 Official number: 330359	**688** 204 390	Class: BV (AB)	**2003-04 Yuexin Shipbuilding Co Ltd — Guangzhou GD** (Hull) Yd No: (4805) **2003-04 Cheoy Lee Shipyards Ltd — Hong Kong** Yd No: 4805 Loa 49.00 Br ex 11.83 Dght 3.050 Lbp 44.60 Br md 11.58 Dpth 4.20 Welded, 1 dk	**(B21B20A) Anchor Handling Tug Supply**	**2 oil engines** geared to sc. shafts driving 2 Propellers Total Power: 2,316kW (3,148hp) 10.0kn Caterpillar 3516TA 2 x Vee 4 Stroke 16 Cy. 170 x 190 each-1158kW (1574bhp) Caterpillar Inc-USA AuxGen: 2 x 145kW 440V 50Hz a.c Thrusters: 1 Tunnel thruster (f) Fuel: 165.0 (d.f.)
9529281 *9MIE2* -	**SETIA HEBAT** **Alam-Pe V (L) Inc** Alam Maritim (M) Sdn Bhd *Port Klang* *Malaysia* MMSI: 533880000 Official number: 333972	**1,530** 459 1,475	Class: BV	**2008-11 Grandview Shipbuilding & Engineering Co Ltd — Guangzhou GD** Yd No: GMG0627 Loa 58.70 Br ex - Dght 4.750 Lbp 53.20 Br md 14.60 Dpth 5.50 Welded, 1 dk	**(B21B20A) Anchor Handling Tug Supply**	**2 oil engines** reduction geared to sc. shafts driving 2 CP propellers Total Power: 3,676kW (4,998hp) 13.5kn Niigata 6MG28HX 2 x 4 Stroke 6 Cy. 280 x 370 each-1838kW (2499bhp) Niigata Engineering Co Ltd-Japan AuxGen: 3 x 315kW a.c Thrusters: 1 Tunnel thruster (f) Fuel: 475.0 (d.f.)
9664756 *9MQB8* -	**SETIA HIJRAH** **Alam Maritim (L) Inc** Alam Maritim (M) Sdn Bhd *Port Klang* *Malaysia* MMSI: 533130937 Official number: 334992	**3,709** 1,112 3,076	Class: AB	**2013-01 Guangxin Shipbuilding & Heavy Industry Co Ltd — Zhongshan GD** Yd No: GMG10122 Loa 76.00 Br ex 18.22 Dght 5.200 Lbp 67.50 Br md 18.00 Dpth 8.00 Welded, 1 dk	**(B21B20A) Anchor Handling Tug Supply**	**2 oil engines** reduction geared to sc. shafts driving 2 CP propellers Total Power: 9,000kW (12,236hp) MAN-B&W 9L32/40CD 2 x 4 Stroke 9 Cy. 320 x 400 each-4500kW (6118bhp) AuxGen: 2 x 1920kW a.c, 2 x 450kW a.c Fuel: 990.0
9587271 *9MLM8* -	**SETIA IMAN** **Alam-JV DP1 (L) Inc** Alam Maritim (M) Sdn Bhd *Port Klang* *Malaysia* MMSI: 533000833 Official number: 334278	**1,678** 503 1,353	Class: BV (AB)	**2010-07 Fujian Southeast Shipyard — Fuzhou FJ** Yd No: DN59M-80 Loa 59.25 Br ex - Dght 4.950 Lbp 52.20 Br md 14.95 Dpth 6.10 Welded, 1 dk	**(B21B20A) Anchor Handling Tug Supply**	**2 oil engines** reduction geared to sc. shafts driving 2 CP propellers Total Power: 3,840kW (5,220hp) 11.0kn Caterpillar 3516B-HD 2 x Vee 4 Stroke 16 Cy. 170 x 215 each-1920kW (2610bhp) Caterpillar Inc-USA AuxGen: 2 x 800kW a.c, 2 x 350kW a.c
9337559 *9MGP5* -	**SETIA INDAH** **Alam Maritim (L) Inc** Alam Maritim (M) Sdn Bhd *Port Klang* *Malaysia* MMSI: 533000122 Official number: 330495	**1,365** 409 1,500	Class: BV	**2005-09 Yuexin Shipbuilding Co Ltd — Guangzhou GD** Yd No: 3047 Loa 58.70 Br ex - Dght 4.500 Lbp 52.00 Br md 13.80 Dpth 5.50 Welded, 1 dk	**(B21B20A) Anchor Handling Tug Supply** Passengers: cabins: 17	**2 oil engines** reduction geared to sc. shafts driving 2 CP propellers Total Power: 3,542kW (4,816hp) 10.0kn Caterpillar 3516B-HD 2 x Vee 4 Stroke 16 Cy. 170 x 215 each-1771kW (2408bhp) Caterpillar Inc-USA AuxGen: 3 x 315kW 415V 50Hz a.c Thrusters: 1 Tunnel thruster (f) Fuel: 370.0 (d.f.) 7.0pd
9214707 *9MEX3* -	**SETIA JAGUH** *ex Jaya Commander -2003* **Alam Maritim (M) Sdn Bhd** - *Port Klang* *Malaysia* MMSI: 533000038 Official number: 330325	**2,032** 609 1,880	Class: BV	**1999-11 Yantai Raffles Shipyard Co Ltd — Yantai SD** Yd No: YRF97-94 Loa 64.00 Br ex - Dght 5.600 Lbp 57.00 Br md 15.00 Dpth 6.80 Welded, 1 dk	**(B21B20A) Anchor Handling Tug Supply** Passengers: berths: 32	**2 oil engines** geared to sc. shafts driving 2 CP propellers Total Power: 6,546kW (8,900hp) 14.2kn Wartsila 8R32 2 x 4 Stroke 8 Cy. 320 x 350 each-3273kW (4450bhp) Wartsila NSD Finland Oy-Finland AuxGen: 3 x 300kW 414/220V 60Hz a.c Thrusters: 1 Tunnel thruster (f) Fuel: 594.0 (d.f.)
9664768 *9MQE3* -	**SETIA JIHAD** **Alam Maritim (L) Inc** Alam Maritim (M) Sdn Bhd *Port Klang* *Malaysia* MMSI: 533130957 Official number: 334515	**3,709** 1,112 3,131	Class: AB	**2013-03 Guangxin Shipbuilding & Heavy Industry Co Ltd — Zhongshan GD** Yd No: GMG10123 Loa 76.00 Br ex 18.22 Dght 5.200 Lbp 67.50 Br md 18.00 Dpth 8.00 Welded, 1 dk	**(B21B20A) Anchor Handling Tug Supply**	**2 oil engines** reduction geared to sc. shafts driving 2 CP propellers Total Power: 9,000kW (12,236hp) MAN-B&W 9L32/40CD 2 x 4 Stroke 9 Cy. 320 x 400 each-4500kW (6118bhp) AuxGen: 2 x 1920kW a.c, 2 x 450kW a.c
8150772 *YFMA* -	**SETIA KARYA** *ex Sapporo -1997 ex Eagle No. 7 -1993* *ex Shinei Maru -1992* **CV Baringin Rattan Industri** - *Semarang* *Indonesia*	**505** 276 900	Class: (KI)	**1974-10 K.K. Saidaiji Zosensho — Okayama** Loa 53.00 Br ex - Dght 4.100 Lbp 48.26 Br md 8.01 Dpth 5.21 Welded, 1 dk	**(A31A2GX) General Cargo Ship**	**1 oil engine** driving 1 FP propeller Total Power: 588kW (799hp) 10.0kn Matsui 6M26KGHS 1 x 4 Stroke 6 Cy. 260 x 400 588kW (799bhp) Matsui Iron Works Co Ltd-Japan
9320570 *9MGQ8* -	**SETIA KASTURI** **Alam Maritim (L) Inc** Alam Maritim (M) Sdn Bhd *Port Klang* *Malaysia* MMSI: 533013400 Official number: 330508	**1,439** 431 1,258	Class: NK (AB)	**2005-10 Guangdong Hope Yue Shipbuilding Industry Ltd — Guangzhou GD** Yd No: 2127 Loa 60.00 Br ex - Dght 4.500 Lbp 53.70 Br md 13.30 Dpth 6.00 Welded, 1 dk	**(B21B20A) Anchor Handling Tug Supply**	**2 oil engines** reduction geared to sc. shafts driving 2 CP propellers Total Power: 3,544kW (4,818hp) 10.0kn Caterpillar 3516B-HD 2 x Vee 4 Stroke 16 Cy. 170 x 215 each-1772kW (2409bhp) Caterpillar Inc-USA AuxGen: 3 x 320kW 415V 50Hz a.c Thrusters: 1 Tunnel thruster (f) Fuel: 465.0 (d.f.)
9529205 *9MII6* -	**SETIA KENTAL** **Alam-Pe II (L) Inc** Alam Maritim (M) Sdn Bhd SatCom: Inmarsat C 453300768 *Port Klang* *Malaysia* MMSI: 533042700 Official number: 334018	**1,454** 436 1,005	Class: BV (AB)	**2009-06 Nantong MLC Tongbao Shipbuilding Co Ltd — Rugao JS** Yd No: MLC6001 Loa 60.00 Br ex - Dght 4.500 Lbp 53.70 Br md 13.30 Dpth 6.00 Welded, 1 dk	**(B21B20A) Anchor Handling Tug Supply**	**2 oil engines** reduction geared to sc. shafts driving 2 FP propellers Total Power: 3,840kW (5,220hp) Yanmar 6EY26 2 x 4 Stroke 6 Cy. 260 x 385 each-1920kW (2610bhp) Yanmar Diesel Engine Co Ltd-Japan AuxGen: 3 x 360kW a.c Thrusters: 1 Tunnel thruster (f) Fuel: 500.0 (d.f.)

IMO / Call sign / Flag	Name / Owner	Tonnage	Class	Build / Dimensions	Type	Machinery
9510395 *9MIS5* -	**SETIA KILAS** **Alam Fast Boats (L) Inc** Alam Maritim (M) Sdn Bhd *Port Klang* *Malaysia* MMSI: 533048300 Official number: 334113	**270** 81 88	Class: BV (AB)	**2009-10 Sam Aluminium Engineering Pte Ltd — Singapore** Yd No: H81 Loa 40.38 Br ex - Dght 1.300 Lbp 38.07 Br md 7.80 Dpth 3.40 Welded, 1 dk	**(B34L2QU) Utility Vessel** Hull Material: Aluminium Alloy Passengers: unberthed: 80	**3 oil engines** reduction geared to sc. shafts driving 3 FP propellers Total Power: 3,090kW (4,200hp) 18.0kn Caterpillar C32 3 x Vee 4 Stroke 12 Cy. 145 x 162 each-1030kW (1400bhp) Caterpillar Inc-USA AuxGen: 2 x 90kW a.c Thrusters: 1 Tunnel thruster (f) Fuel: 100.0 (d.f.)
9324253 *9MGN5* -	**SETIA LESTARI** *ex Jaya Supplier 2 -2005* **Alam Maritim (L) Inc** Alam Maritim (M) Sdn Bhd *Port Klang* *Malaysia* MMSI: 533932000 Official number: 330472	**1,470** 441 1,475	Class: BV	**2005-02 Guangzhou Hangtong Shipbuilding & Shipping Co Ltd — Jiangmen GD** Yd No: 032008 Loa 58.70 Br ex - Dght 4.750 Lbp 53.20 Br md 14.60 Dpth 5.50 Welded, 1 dk	**(B21B20A) Anchor Handling Tug Supply**	**2 oil engines** geared to sc. shafts driving 2 CP propellers Total Power: 3,494kW (4,750hp) 13.5kn Caterpillar 3516B-HD 2 x Vee 4 Stroke 16 Cy. 170 x 215 each-1747kW (2375bhp) Caterpillar Inc-USA AuxGen: 3 x 315kW 415/220V 50Hz a.c Thrusters: 1 Tunnel thruster (f) Fuel: 470.0 (d.f.)
9587283 *9ML02* -	**SETIA LUHUR** **Alam-JV DP1 (L) Inc** Alam Maritim (M) Sdn Bhd *Port Klang* *Malaysia* MMSI: 533058400 Official number: 334293	**1,678** 503 1,463	Class: BV (AB)	**2010-09 Fujian Southeast Shipyard — Fuzhou FJ** Yd No: DN59M-81 Loa 59.25 Br ex - Dght 4.950 Lbp 52.20 Br md 14.95 Dpth 6.10 Welded, 1 dk	**(B21B20A) Anchor Handling Tug Supply**	**2 oil engines** reduction geared to sc. shafts driving 2 CP propellers Total Power: 3,840kW (5,220hp) 11.0kn Caterpillar 3516B-HD 2 x Vee 4 Stroke 16 Cy. 170 x 215 each-1920kW (2610bhp) Caterpillar Inc-USA AuxGen: 2 x 800kW 415V 50Hz a.c, 2 x 350kW 415V 50Hz a.c Fuel: 520.0
9025601 - -	**SETIA MAKMUR** **PT Trimanunggal Nugraha** - *Samarinda* *Indonesia*	**206** 62 -	Class: (KI)	**1999-03 P.T. Galangan Teluk Bajau Kaltim — Samarinda** L reg 36.25 Br ex - Dght 1.690 Lbp 36.25 Br md 8.00 Dpth 2.30 Welded, 1 dk	**(A35D2RL) Landing Craft** Bow ramp (centre)	**2 oil engines** geared to sc. shafts driving 2 Propellers Total Power: 442kW (600hp) Mitsubishi 6D22 2 x 4 Stroke 6 Cy. 130 x 140 each-221kW (300bhp) Mitsubishi Heavy Industries Ltd-Japan
9049956 - -	**SETIA MAKMUR II** **H Suta Wijaya** - *Samarinda* *Indonesia*	**135** 81 -	Class: KI	**2004-08 PT Trimanunggal Nugraha — Samarinda** Loa - Br ex - Dght 2.040 Lbp 23.00 Br md 7.00 Dpth 3.25 Welded, 1 dk	**(B32A2ST) Tug**	**2 oil engines** geared to sc. shafts driving 2 Propellers Total Power: 810kW (1,102hp) Yanmar 6LAA-UTE 2 x 4 Stroke 6 Cy. 148 x 165 each-405kW (551bhp) Yanmar Diesel Engine Co Ltd-Japan AuxGen: 1 x 42kW 415/380V a.c, 1 x 65kW 415/380V a.c
9029334 *YD6780* -	**SETIA MAKMUR III** **H Suta Wijaya** - *Samarinda* *Indonesia*	**139** 42 -	Class: KI	**2005-07 in Indonesia** Loa 23.80 Br ex - Dght 2.550 Lbp 22.22 Br md 7.00 Dpth 3.25 Welded, 1 dk	**(B32A2ST) Tug**	**2 oil engines** geared to sc. shafts driving 2 Propellers Total Power: 882kW (1,200hp) Cummins KTA-19-M 2 x 4 Stroke 6 Cy. 159 x 159 each-441kW (600bhp) Cummins Engine Co Inc-USA AuxGen: 2 x 82kW 380/220V a.c
8651831 *YDA6480* -	**SETIA MAKMUR V** **PT Agus Suta Lines** - *Samarinda* *Indonesia* Official number: 4057//lik	**145** 44 -	Class: KI	**2009-11 PT Trimanunggal Nugraha — Samarinda** Yd No: 008 Loa 23.85 Br ex - Dght - Lbp 22.32 Br md 7.30 Dpth 3.05 Welded, 1 dk	**(B32A2ST) Tug**	**2 oil engines** reduction geared to sc. shafts driving 2 Propellers Total Power: 1,220kW (1,658hp) Yanmar 6LAAM-ETE 2 x 4 Stroke 6 Cy. 148 x 165 each-610kW (829bhp) Yanmar Diesel Engine Co Ltd-Japan
9358589 *9MGO7* -	**SETIA NURANI** **Alam Maritim (M) Sdn Bhd** - *Port Klang* *Malaysia* MMSI: 533934000 Official number: 330486	**1,523** 457 1,461	Class: BV (AB)	**2005-09 Guangzhou Panyu Lingshan Shipyard Ltd — Guangzhou GD** Yd No: 112 Loa 59.00 Br ex 14.78 Dght 4.750 Lbp 53.20 Br md 14.60 Dpth 5.50 Welded, 1 dk	**(B21B20A) Anchor Handling Tug Supply**	**2 oil engines** reduction geared to sc. shafts driving 2 CP propellers Total Power: 3,788kW (5,150hp) 13.5kn Caterpillar 3516B 2 x Vee 4 Stroke 16 Cy. 170 x 190 each-1894kW (2575bhp) Caterpillar Inc-USA AuxGen: 2 x 315kW 440V 60Hz a.c Thrusters: 1 Tunnel thruster (f) Fuel: 475.0 (d.f.)
9373022 *9MGR7* -	**SETIA PADU** **Alam Maritim (L) Inc** Alam Maritim (M) Sdn Bhd *Port Klang* *Malaysia* MMSI: 533943000 Official number: 330522	**1,470** 441 1,475	Class: BV	**2006-02 Guangzhou Hangtong Shipbuilding & Shipping Co Ltd — Jiangmen GD** Yd No: 042005 Loa 58.70 Br ex 14.62 Dght 4.750 Lbp 53.20 Br md 14.60 Dpth 5.50 Welded, 1 dk	**(B21B20A) Anchor Handling Tug Supply**	**2 oil engines** reduction geared to sc. shafts driving 2 CP propellers Total Power: 3,788kW (5,150hp) 13.5kn Caterpillar 3516B 2 x Vee 4 Stroke 16 Cy. 170 x 215 each-1894kW (2575bhp) Caterpillar Inc-USA AuxGen: 3 x 315kW 415/220V 50Hz a.c Fuel: 470.0 (d.f.)
9543213 *9MLD3* -	**SETIA QASEH** **Alam-JV DP1 (L) Inc** Alam Maritim (M) Sdn Bhd *Port Klang* *Malaysia* MMSI: 533049100 Official number: 334136	**1,537** 461 1,475	Class: BV	**2010-01 Guangzhou Hangtong Shipbuilding & Shipping Co Ltd — Jiangmen GD** Yd No: 072004 Loa 58.70 Br ex - Dght 4.750 Lbp 53.20 Br md 14.60 Dpth 5.50 Welded, 1 dk	**(B21B20A) Anchor Handling Tug Supply**	**2 oil engines** reduction geared to sc.shafts driving 2 CP propellers Total Power: 3,282kW (4,462hp) 13.5kn Caterpillar 3516B-TA 2 x Vee 4 Stroke 16 Cy. 170 x 190 each-1641kW (2231bhp) Caterpillar Inc-USA
9381304 *9MGV8* -	**SETIA RENTAS** **Alam Maritim (L) Inc** Alam Maritim (M) Sdn Bhd *Port Klang* *Malaysia* MMSI: 533956000 Official number: 330575	**1,536** 460 1,475	Class: BV	**2006-08 Yuexin Shipbuilding Co Ltd — Guangzhou GD** Yd No: 3055 Loa 58.70 Br ex 14.62 Dght 4.750 Lbp 54.12 Br md 14.60 Dpth 5.50 Welded, 1 dk	**(B21B20A) Anchor Handling Tug Supply**	**2 oil engines** reduction geared to sc. shafts driving 2 CP propellers Total Power: 3,788kW (5,150hp) 13.5kn Caterpillar 3516B 2 x Vee 4 Stroke 16 Cy. 170 x 190 each-1894kW (2575bhp) Caterpillar Inc-USA AuxGen: 3 x 340kW 440V 50Hz a.c Thrusters: 1 Thwart. CP thruster (f) Fuel: 470.0 (d.f.) 13.0pd
9408944 *9MHY4* -	**SETIA SAKTI** **Alam Synergy III (L) Inc** Alam Maritim (M) Sdn Bhd *Port Klang* *Malaysia* MMSI: 533861000 Official number: 333873	**2,996** 899 2,250	Class: BV (AB)	**2008-06 Yuexin Shipbuilding Co Ltd — Guangzhou GD** Yd No: 3079 Loa 76.00 Br ex - Dght 4.500 Lbp 68.15 Br md 20.00 Dpth 6.10 Welded, 1 dk	**(B22A20V) Diving Support Vessel**	**2 oil engines** reduction geared to sc. shafts driving 2 CP propellers Total Power: 3,840kW (5,220hp) 10.0kn Caterpillar 3516B 2 x Vee 4 Stroke 16 Cy. 170 x 190 each-1920kW (2610bhp) Caterpillar Inc-USA AuxGen: 2 x 500kW a.c, 2 x 1600kW a.c Thrusters: 2 Thwart. CP thruster (s) Fuel: 1032.0 (d.f.)
9408920 *9MFD8* -	**SETIA TANGKAS** **Alam Synergy I (L) Inc** Alam Maritim (M) Sdn Bhd *Port Klang* *Malaysia* MMSI: 533996000 Official number: 332371	**1,470** 441 1,475	Class: BV	**2007-06 Guangzhou Hangtong Shipbuilding & Shipping Co Ltd — Jiangmen GD** Yd No: 052007 Loa 58.70 Br ex - Dght 4.750 Lbp 53.20 Br md 14.60 Dpth 5.50 Welded, 1 dk	**(B21B20A) Anchor Handling Tug Supply** Passengers: cabins: 15	**2 oil engines** reduction geared to sc. shafts driving 2 CP propellers Total Power: 3,788kW (5,150hp) 13.5kn Caterpillar 3516B 2 x Vee 4 Stroke 16 Cy. 170 x 190 each-1894kW (2575bhp) Caterpillar Inc-USA AuxGen: 3 x 315kW 440V 60Hz a.c Fuel: 475.0 (d.f.)
9494711 *9MID5* -	**SETIA TEGAP** **Alam Maritim (M) Sdn Bhd** - *Port Klang* *Malaysia* MMSI: 533876000 Official number: 333965	**1,537** 461 1,475	Class: BV	**2008-09 Guangzhou Hangtong Shipbuilding & Shipping Co Ltd — Jiangmen GD** Yd No: 062011 Loa 58.70 Br ex - Dght 4.750 Lbp 53.20 Br md 14.60 Dpth 5.50 Welded, 1 dk	**(B21B20A) Anchor Handling Tug Supply**	**2 oil engines** reduction geared to sc. shafts driving 2 CP propellers Total Power: 3,676kW (4,998hp) 13.5kn Niigata 6L28HX 2 x 4 Stroke 6 Cy. 280 x 370 each-1838kW (2499bhp) Niigata Engineering Co Ltd-Japan

9488683 *9MHS2* - **SETIA TEGUH** **Alam Maritim (M) Sdn Bhd** - *Port Klang* *Malaysia* MMSI: 533062000 Official number: 332483 | **1,678** 503 1,342 | Class: BV (AB) | **2008**-01 **Fujian Southeast Shipyard — Fuzhou FJ** Yd No: DN59M-20 Loa 59.25 Br ex - Dght 4.950 Lbp 52.20 Br md 14.95 Dpth 6.10 Welded, 1 dk | **(B21B20A) Anchor Handling Tug Supply** | **2 oil engines** reduction geared to sc. shafts driving 2 CP propellers Total Power: 3,372kW (4,584hp) 11.0kn Caterpillar 3516B-HD 2 x Vee 4 Stroke 16 Cy. 170 x 215 each-1686kW (2292bhp) Caterpillar Inc-USA AuxGen: 3 x 315kW a.c Thrusters: 1 Tunnel thruster (f) Fuel: 456.0 (d.f.)

9529229 *9MII8* - **SETIA ULUNG** **Alam-Pe III (L) Inc** Alam Maritim (M) Sdn Bhd *Port Klang* *Malaysia* MMSI: 533042800 Official number: 334020 | **3,404** 1,125 2,182 | Class: BV (AB) | **2009**-10 **Nantong MLC Tongbao Shipbuilding Co Ltd — Rugao JS** Yd No: MLC7801 Loa 78.00 Br ex - Dght 4.820 Lbp 70.55 Br md 20.00 Dpth 6.50 Welded, 1 dk | **(B22A20R) Offshore Support Vessel** Passengers: berths: 188 Cranes: 1x24t | **2 oil engines** reduction geared to sc. vessel driving 2 FP propellers Total Power: 3,788kW (5,150hp) Yanmar 6EY26 2 x 4 Stroke 6 Cy. 260 x 385 each-1894kW (2575bhp) Yanmar Diesel Engine Co Ltd-Japan AuxGen: 3 x 750kW a.c Thrusters: 1 Tunnel thruster (f)

9429900 *9MHR2* - **SETIA UNGGUL** **Alam Synergy II (L) Inc** Alam Maritim (M) Sdn Bhd *Port Klang* *Malaysia* MMSI: 533045000 Official number: 332466 | **1,470** 441 1,475 | Class: BV | **2007**-12 **Guangzhou Hangtong Shipbuilding & Shipping Co Ltd — Jiangmen GD** Yd No: 062002 Loa 58.70 Br ex - Dght 4.750 Lbp 53.20 Br md 14.60 Dpth 5.50 Welded, 1 dk | **(B21B20A) Anchor Handling Tug Supply** | **2 oil engines** reduction geared to sc. shafts driving 2 CP propellers Total Power: 1,940kW (2,638hp) 13.5kn Caterpillar 3512B 2 x Vee 4 Stroke 12 Cy. 170 x 190 each-970kW (1319bhp) Caterpillar Inc-USA

9425588 *9MFE2* - **SETIA WANGSA** **Alam Maritim (M) Sdn Bhd** - *Port Klang* *Malaysia* MMSI: 533997000 Official number: 332372 | **1,678** 503 1,375 | Class: BV (AB) | **2007**-06 **Fujian Southeast Shipyard — Fuzhou FJ** Yd No: DN59M-16 Loa 59.25 Br ex - Dght 4.950 Lbp 52.20 Br md 14.95 Dpth 6.10 Welded, 1 dk | **(B21B20A) Anchor Handling Tug Supply** Passengers: cabins: 16 | **2 oil engines** reduction geared to sc. shafts driving 2 CP propellers Total Power: 3,788kW (5,150hp) 10.0kn Caterpillar 3516B-TA 2 x Vee 4 Stroke 16 Cy. 170 x 190 each-1894kW (2575bhp) Caterpillar Inc-USA AuxGen: 3 x 315kW 440V 50Hz a.c Fuel: 530.0 (d.f.)

9431329 *9MFE9* - **SETIA WIRA** **Alam Maritim (M) Sdn Bhd** - *Port Klang* *Malaysia* MMSI: 533374000 Official number: 332385 | **675** 202 970 | Class: BV | **2007**-09 **Guangzhou Panyu Lingshan Shipyard Ltd — Guangzhou GD** Yd No: 146 Loa 48.00 Br ex - Dght 3.800 Lbp 42.40 Br md 11.80 Dpth 4.60 Welded, 1 dk | **(B21B20A) Anchor Handling Tug Supply** | **2 oil engines** reduction geared to sc. shafts driving 2 FP propellers Total Power: 2,574kW (3,500hp) 10.0kn Caterpillar 3512B 2 x Vee 4 Stroke 12 Cy. 170 x 190 each-1287kW (1750bhp) Caterpillar Inc-USA AuxGen: 3 x 245kW a.c Thrusters: 1 Thwart. FP thruster (f) Fuel: 540.0 (d.f.)

9498042 *9MHW4* - **SETIA YAKIN** **Alam Maritim (M) Sdn Bhd** - *Port Klang* *Malaysia* MMSI: 533863000 Official number: 333866 | **496** 149 406 | Class: NK | **2008**-08 **Pleasant Engineering Sdn Bhd — Sandakan** Yd No: 13/06 Loa 45.00 Br ex - Dght 3.212 Lbp 40.99 Br md 11.00 Dpth 4.00 Welded, 1 dk | **(B34L2QU) Utility Vessel** | **2 oil engines** geared to sc. shafts driving 2 FP propellers Total Power: 2,386kW (3,244hp) Cummins KTA-50-M2 2 x Vee 4 Stroke 16 Cy. 159 x 159 each-1193kW (1622bhp) Cummins Engine Co Inc-USA AuxGen: 3 x 199kW a.c Fuel: 240.0

9481790 *9MFK4* - **SETIA ZAMAN** **Alam Maritim (M) Sdn Bhd** - *Port Klang* *Malaysia* MMSI: 533050000 Official number: 332450 | **481** 145 341 | Class: NK | **2008**-03 **Pleasant Engineering Sdn Bhd — Sandakan** Yd No: 11/06 Loa 40.00 Br ex - Dght 3.812 Lbp 36.41 Br md 11.80 Dpth 4.60 Welded, 1 dk | **(B34L2QU) Utility Vessel** | **2 oil engines** geared to sc. shafts driving 2 Propellers Total Power: 1,790kW (2,434hp) 11.0kn Cummins KTA-38-M2 2 x Vee 4 Stroke 12 Cy. 159 x 159 each-895kW (1217bhp) Cummins Engine Co Inc-USA Thrusters: 1 Tunnel thruster (f) Fuel: 305.0 (d.f.)

8661446 *YDA6034* - **SETIAWATI** **PT Aesel Samuderah** - *Samarinda* *Indonesia* Official number: 3497/IIK | **136** 41 - | Class: KI | **2007**-10 **PT Trimanunggal Nugraha — Samarinda** Yd No: 010 Loa 23.50 Br ex - Dght - Lbp 22.36 Br md 7.09 Dpth 3.25 Welded, 1 dk | **(B32A2ST) Tug** | **2 oil engines** reduction geared to sc. shafts driving 2 Propellers Total Power: 980kW (1,332hp) Mitsubishi S6A3-MPTK 2 x 4 Stroke 6 Cy. 150 x 175 each-490kW (666bhp) Mitsubishi Heavy Industries Ltd-Japan AuxGen: 2 x 81kW 400V a.c

8667787 *YDB6325* - **SETIAWATI I** **PT Aesel Samuderah** - *Samarinda* *Indonesia* Official number: 5577/IIK | **162** 49 - | Class: KI (Class contemplated) | **2013**-08 **PT Bunga Nusa Mahakam — Samarinda** Loa 24.91 Br ex - Dght 2.400 Lbp 23.28 Br md 7.30 Dpth 3.20 Welded, 1 dk | **(B32A2ST) Tug** | **2 oil engines** reduction geared to sc. shafts driving 2 Propellers Total Power: 980kW (1,332hp) Mitsubishi S6A3-MPTK 2 x 4 Stroke 6 Cy. 150 x 175 each-490kW (666bhp) Mitsubishi Heavy Industries Ltd-Japan

8986470 *JL6631* - **SETO** **Shikoku Kisen KK** - *Naoshima, Kagawa* *Japan* MMSI: 431501766 Official number: 137048 | *635* - - | | **2003**-10 **Fujiwara Zosensho — Imabari** Yd No: 152 L reg 60.66 Br ex - Dght - Lbp - Br md 14.70 Dpth 3.90 Welded, 1 dk | **(A36A2PR) Passenger/Ro-Ro Ship (Vehicles)** | **2 oil engines** reduction geared to sc. shafts driving 2 Propellers Total Power: 1,912kW (2,600hp) Yanmar 6N21A-EV 2 x 4 Stroke 6 Cy. 210 x 290 each-956kW (1300bhp) Yanmar Diesel Engine Co Ltd-Japan

9105451 *3FZB4* - **SETO** **Frontier Maritime Shipping IV SA** Nippon Yusen Kabushiki Kaisha (NYK Line) SatCom: Inmarsat A 1347561 *Panama* *Panama* MMSI: 354951000 Official number: 2207395CH | **77,307** 48,787 151,166 T/cm 106.0 | Class: NK | **1995**-03 **Nippon Kokan KK (NKK Corp) — Tsu ME** Yd No: 147 Loa 273.00 (BB) Br ex - Dght 17.419 Lbp 260.00 Br md 43.00 Dpth 23.90 Welded, 1 dk | **(A21A2BC) Bulk Carrier** Grain: 167,715 Compartments: 9 Ho, ER 9 Ha: (14.2 x 18.4)7 (14.2 x 19.8) (14.2 x 14.0)ER | **1 oil engine** driving 1 FP propeller Total Power: 15,403kW (20,942hp) 14.9kn B&W 6S70MC 1 x 2 Stroke 6 Cy. 700 x 2674 15403kW (20942bhp) Mitsui Engineering & Shipbuilding CLtd-Japan AuxGen: 2 x 560kW 450V 60Hz a.c, 1 x 480kW 450V 60Hz a.c Fuel: 197.0 (d.f.) (Heating Coils) 3895.0 (r.f.) 52.5pd

8315085 *JL5063* - **SETO** **Ehime Zosen Service KK** - *Imabari, Ehime* *Japan* Official number: 126254 | *145* - - | Class: (NK) | **1983**-03 **Kishigami Zosen K.K. — Akitsu** Yd No: 1588 Loa 29.32 Br ex - Dght 2.963 Lbp 27.34 Br md 8.01 Dpth 3.81 Welded, 1 dk | **(B32A2ST) Tug** | **2 oil engines** driving 2 FP propellers Total Power: 2,942kW (4,000hp) 11.3kn Daihatsu 6PSHTDM-26H 2 x 4 Stroke 6 Cy. 260 x 320 each-1471kW (2000bhp) Daihatsu Diesel Manufacturing Co Lt-Japan AuxGen: 2 x 44kW

9382712 *3EIS8* - **SETO EXPRESS** **La Darien Navegacion SA** Thome Ship Management Pte Ltd *Panama* *Panama* MMSI: 372383000 Official number: 3262507A | **28,799** 12,962 47,999 T/cm 51.8 | Class: NK | **2007**-01 **Iwagi Zosen Co Ltd — Kamijima EH** Yd No: 264 Loa 179.99 (BB) Br ex 32.23 Dght 12.486 Lbp 172.00 Br md 32.20 Dpth 19.05 Welded, 1 dk | **(A13A2TW) Crude/Oil Products Tanker** Double Hull (13F) Liq: 54,754; Liq (Oil): 54,754 Cargo Heating Coils Compartments: 16 Wing Ta, 2 Wing Slop Ta, ER 4 Cargo Pump (s): 4x1250m³/hr Manifold: Bow/CM: 92.4m | **1 oil engine** driving 1 FP propeller Total Power: 9,480kW (12,889hp) 15.1kn MAN-B&W 6S50MC-C 1 x 2 Stroke 6 Cy. 500 x 2000 9480kW (12889bhp) Mitsui Engineering & Shipbuilding CLtd-Japan AuxGen: 3 x 400kW a.c Fuel: 264.0 (d.f.) 2094.0 (r.f.)

8221105 - - **SETO I** *ex Seto -1995* **Tsuneishi Port Service Panama SA** Mitsui Warehouse Co Ltd (Mitsui-Soko Co Ltd) | **1,292** 387 - | | **1982** **Mitsui Eng. & SB. Co. Ltd. — Tamano** Yd No: F516251 Loa 42.52 Br ex - Dght 3.720 Lbp 38.28 Br md 25.01 Dpth 4.02 Welded, 1 dk | **(B34B2SC) Crane Vessel** | **1 diesel electric oil engine** driving 2 gen. each 270kW 450V a.c Connecting to 2 elec. motors driving 2 Directional propellers aft, 1 fwd Total Power: 310kW (421hp) Deutz SBA6M816 1 x 4 Stroke 6 Cy. 142 x 160 310kW (421bhp) Kloeckner Humboldt Deutz AG-West Germany

7432393 *JG3503* - **SETO MARU** *ex Ashigara Maru -1999* **Toko Kaiun KK** - *Hiroshima, Hiroshima* *Japan* Official number: 117714 | *197* - - | | **1975**-04 **Kanagawa Zosen — Kobe** Yd No: 150 Loa 33.30 Br ex 8.21 Dght 2.286 Lbp 29.49 Br md 8.18 Dpth 3.38 Riveted\Welded, 1 dk | **(B32A2ST) Tug** | **2 oil engines** Geared Integral to driving 2 Z propellers Total Power: 1,912kW (2,600hp) Niigata 2 x 4 Stroke each-956kW (1300bhp) Niigata Engineering Co Ltd-Japan

7424877 - -	SETO MARU - - -	*134* 59 -		1974 **N**agasaki Zosen K.K. — Nagasaki Yd No: 507 Loa 37.29 Br ex 7.22 Dght 2.413 Lbp 30.79 Br md 7.19 Dpth 4.60 Welded, 1 dk	**(B11B2FV) Fishing Vessel**	**1 oil engine** geared to sc. shaft driving 1 FP propeller Total Power: 736kW (1,001hp) Daihatsu 6PSHTCM-26E 1 x 4 Stroke 6 Cy. 260 x 320 736kW (1001bhp) Daihatsu Diesel Manufacturing Co Lt-Japan
8952493 *JI3662* -	**SETO MARU** - **K**yokuo Kaiun KK - *Osaka, Osaka* *Japan* MMSI: 431401808 Official number: 136786	*749* - 1,670		**1999-09 N**akatani Shipyard Co. Ltd. — Etajima Yd No: 587 Loa 69.92 (BB) Br ex - Dght 4.739 Lbp 65.00 Br md 11.20 Dpth 5.50 Welded, 1 dk	**(A12A2TC) Chemical Tanker** Liq: 872 Compartments: 8 Wing Ta, ER 2 Cargo Pump (s): 2x250m³/hr	**1 oil engine** driving 1 CP propeller Total Power: 1,471kW (2,000hp) 12.8kn Hanshin LH36L 1 x 4 Stroke 6 Cy. 360 x 670 1471kW (2000bhp) The Hanshin Diesel Works Ltd-Japan AuxGen: 3 x 104kW a.c Thrusters: 1 Thwart. FP thruster (f) Fuel: 95.0 (d.f.)
7514048 *JG3578* -	**SETO MARU NO. 2** *ex* Miyagi Maru 2 *-2009* *ex* Hirose Maru *-1989* **A**ki Marine KK - *Hiroshima, Hiroshima* *Japan* Official number: 117792	*197* - -		**1975-09 S**agami Zosen Tekko K.K. — Yokosuka Yd No: 180 Loa 30.50 Br ex 8.82 Dght 2.600 Lbp 27.00 Br md 8.80 Dpth 3.47 Welded, 1 dk	**(B32A2ST) Tug**	**2 oil engines** driving 2 FP propellers Total Power: 1,912kW (2,600hp) Niigata 6L25BX 2 x 4 Stroke 6 Cy. 250 x 320 each-956kW (1300bhp) Niigata Engineering Co Ltd-Japan
9083665 *JG5285* -	**SETOGIRI** *ex* Shikinami *-2000* **G**overnment of **J**apan (Ministry of Land, Infrastructure & Transport) (The Coastguard) - *Tokyo* *Japan* MMSI: 431300141 Official number: 134317	*113* - -		**1994-03 S**umidagawa Zosen K.K. — Tokyo Yd No: N5-12 Loa 35.00 Br ex - Dght 1.230 Lbp - Br md 6.30 Dpth 3.43 Welded	**(B34H2SQ) Patrol Vessel**	**2 oil engines** with clutches, flexible couplings & reverse reduction geared to sc. shafts driving 2 FP propellers Total Power: 2,942kW (4,000hp) 25.0kn M.T.U. 12V396TB94 2 x Vee 4 Stroke 12 Cy. 165 x 185 each-1471kW (2000bhp) MTU Friedrichshafen GmbH-Friedrichshafen
8914908 *JJ3744* -	**SETOUCHI MARU No. 2** - **T**aisei Kaiun YK - *Ieshima, Hyogo* *Japan* Official number: 131861	*410* - 1,106		**1990-02 H**amamoto Zosensho K.K. — Tokushima Yd No: 731 Loa 59.27 (BB) Br ex - Dght 4.222 Lbp 52.00 Br md 12.00 Dpth 5.90 Welded, 1 dk	**(A24D2BA) Aggregates Carrier** Compartments: 1 Ho, ER 1 Ha: ER	**1 oil engine** driving 1 FP propeller Total Power: 736kW (1,001hp) Niigata 6M30GT 1 x 4 Stroke 6 Cy. 300 x 530 736kW (1001bhp) Niigata Engineering Co Ltd-Japan
7917185 - -	**SETRA III** - **G**overnment of **M**exico (Secretaria de Communicaciones y Transportes Servicio de Transbordadores, Direccion General) - *Mexico*	*1,078* 323 618		**1986-11** Astilleros de **M**arina — Coatzacoalcos Yd No: 22 Loa 60.03 Br ex 15.63 Dght 1.801 Lbp 51.85 Br md 15.00 Dpth 3.03 Welded, 1 dk	**(A36A2PR) Passenger/Ro-Ro Ship (Vehicles)**	**2 oil engines** driving 2 Propellers aft, 1 fwd Total Power: 536kW (728hp) Dorman 2 x 4 Stroke 8 Cy. 159 x 165 each-268kW (364bhp) Dorman Diesels Ltd.-Stafford
7917197 - -	**SETRA VI** - **G**overnment of **M**exico (Secretaria de Communicaciones y Transportes Servicio de Transbordadores, Direccion General) - *Mexico*	*1,078* 323 618		**1982** Astilleros de **M**arina — Coatzacoalcos Yd No: 23 Loa 60.03 Br ex - Dght 1.800 Lbp 51.84 Br md 15.63 Dpth 3.00 Welded	**(A36A2PR) Passenger/Ro-Ro Ship (Vehicles)**	**2 oil engines** driving 2 FP propellers Total Power: 268kW (364hp) Dorman 8QTM 2 x 4 Stroke 8 Cy. 159 x 165 each-134kW (182bhp) (Re-engined ,made 1976, Reconditioned & fitted 1982) Dorman Diesels Ltd.-Stafford
9072721 *JM6197* -	**SETSU MARU** - **E**iwa Unyu KK - *Shimonoseki, Yamaguchi* *Japan* MMSI: 431400141 Official number: 133536	*1,582* - 3,037	Class: (NK)	**1993-04 M**urakami Hide Zosen K.K. — Imabari Yd No: 347 Loa 86.50 Br ex - Dght 5.200 Lbp 82.00 Br md 13.50 Dpth 6.40 Welded, 1 dk	**(A13B2TP) Products Tanker** Liq: 3,300; Liq (Oil): 3,300	**1 oil engine** reverse geared to sc. shaft driving 1 FP propeller Total Power: 2,060kW (2,801hp) Hanshin 6EL38G 1 x 4 Stroke 6 Cy. 380 x 760 2060kW (2801bhp) The Hanshin Diesel Works Ltd-Japan
9104316 *JM4153* -	**SETSU MARU** - **C**orporation for **A**dvanced Transport & Technology & Nansei Kaiun Co Ltd Nansei Kaiun KK SatCom: Inmarsat M 643165610 *Naha, Okinawa* *Japan* MMSI: 431656000 Official number: 133745	**1,484** 486 1,500	Class: NK	**1994-07 K.K. M**iura Zosensho — Saiki Yd No: 1107 Loa 81.55 Br ex - Dght 3.822 Lbp 74.50 Br md 12.50 Dpth 6.75 Welded, 1 dk	**(A31A2GX) General Cargo Ship** Grain: 2,596; Bale: 2,596 TEU 64 C. 64/20' Compartments: 1 Ho, ER 1 Ha: (42.6 x 10.2)ER	**1 oil engine** driving 1 CP propeller Total Power: 1,471kW (2,000hp) 13.3kn Hanshin 6EL40 1 x 4 Stroke 6 Cy. 400 x 800 1471kW (2000bhp) The Hanshin Diesel Works Ltd-Japan AuxGen: 2 x 144kW a.c Fuel: 92.0 (d.f.) 9.0pd
9028392 *TRSC* -	**SETTE CAMA** *ex* Panagia Tripiti *-2009* **C**ompagnie Nationale de Navigation Interieure - *Gabon* MMSI: 626901100	*705* 433 550	Class: (BV)	**1977-01 A**lsa Shipyard — Piraeus Loa 66.00 Br ex - Dght 2.300 Lbp 58.98 Br md 11.60 Dpth 2.75 Welded, 1 dk	**(A36A2PR) Passenger/Ro-Ro Ship (Vehicles)** Passengers: unberthed: 266 Bow ramp (f) Trailers: 15	**2 oil engines** driving 2 FP propellers Total Power: 610kW (830hp) 10.0kn Kelvin TASC8 2 x 4 Stroke 8 Cy. 165 x 184 each-305kW (415bhp) Kelvin Diesels Ltd.-Glasgow AuxGen: 2 x 80kW 380/220V 50Hz a.c
7023477 *ZR7015* -	**SETTE MARI** *ex* Quiet Waters Riv *-1997* *ex* Unity *-1995* *ex* Eshcol *-1993* *ex* Lunar Bow *-1978* **P**aternoster Vissery Beperk - *Saldanha* *South Africa* MMSI: 601523000 Official number: 10321	*267* 107 254	Class: (LR) Classed LR until 5/16/5/80	**1970-08 B**entsen & Sonner Slip & Mek. Verksted — Sogne (Hull) **1970-08 S**igbjorn **I**versen — Flekkefjord Yd No: 13 Lengthened-1974 Loa 32.49 Br ex 7.14 Dght - Lbp 29.04 Br md 7.05 Dpth 3.76 Welded	**(B11A2FT) Trawler** Compartments: 1 Ho, ER 2 Ha: (0.9 x 0.9) (1.4 x 0.9)ER Derricks: 1x2t	**1 oil engine** reverse reduction geared to sc. shaft driving 1 CP propeller Total Power: 416kW (566hp) 10.0kn Caterpillar D379TA 1 x Vee 4 Stroke 8 Cy. 159 x 203 416kW (566bhp) Caterpillar Tractor Co-USA AuxGen: 1 x 10kW 110V d.c Thrusters: 1 Thwart. FP thruster (f); 1 Tunnel thruster (a)
7103538 *SECT* GG59	**SETTE MARI** *ex* Sparkling Star *-2004* *ex* Ocean Star *-2000* *ex* Challenge *-2000* **R**ederi AB **E**ngesberg - *Gavle* *Sweden* MMSI: 266101000	**352** 112 -	Class: (NV)	**1971-02 S**igbjorn **I**versen — Flekkefjord Yd No: 15 Lengthened-1974 Loa 39.89 Br ex 7.09 Dght - Lbp 30.21 Br md 7.07 Dpth 3.76 Welded, 1 dk	**(B11B2FV) Fishing Vessel**	**1 oil engine** geared to sc. shaft driving 1 FP propeller Total Power: 313kW (426hp) 10.5kn Caterpillar D379SCAC 1 x Vee 4 Stroke 8 Cy. 159 x 203 313kW (426bhp) Caterpillar Tractor Co-USA
8137902 *IUIR* -	**SETTEBELLO** *ex* Enosis *-2000* **D**elcomar Srl - *Naples* *Italy* Official number: 1079	*338* 66 215	Class: (RI)	**1966 B**ekris & Eleftheropoulos — Piareus Loa 57.82 Br ex 9.02 Dght 1.691 Lbp 51.69 Br md 9.01 Dpth 1.81 Welded, 1 dk	**(A31A2GX) General Cargo Ship**	**2 oil engines** driving 2 FP propellers Total Power: 1,212kW (1,648hp) MWM 2 x Vee 4 Stroke 16 Cy. 140 x 180 each-606kW (824bhp) Motoren Werke Mannheim AG (MWM)-West Germany
4903365 - -	**SETTER** - **J**TI Organisation Nigeria Ltd - *Nigeria*	*152* - -	Class: (LR) ✠ Classed LR until 6/7/05	**1969-10 A**ppledore Shipbuilders Ltd — Bideford Yd No: A.S. 62 Loa 28.68 Br ex 7.74 Dght - Lbp 25.90 Br md 7.39 Dpth 3.66 Welded, 1 dk	**(B32A2ST) Tug**	**2 oil engines** sr reverse geared to sc. shafts driving 2 FP propellers Total Power: 970kW (1,318hp) 12.0kn Blackstone ERS8 2 x 4 Stroke 8 Cy. 222 x 292 each-485kW (659bhp) Blackstone & Co. Ltd.-Stamford AuxGen: 2 x 40kW 220V d.c
8036598 *WDE3914* -	**SETTLER** - **F**rontier Fishing Corp - *Mattapoisett, MA* *United States of America* MMSI: 367345930 Official number: 620472	*185* 130 -		**1980** Edward T **G**amage Inc — East Boothbay ME L reg 25.39 Br ex 7.14 Dght - Lbp - Br md - Dpth 3.76 Welded, 1 dk	**(B11B2FV) Fishing Vessel**	**1 oil engine** driving 1 FP propeller Total Power: 618kW (840hp) Caterpillar D398SCAC 1 x Vee 4 Stroke 12 Cy. 159 x 203 618kW (840bhp) Caterpillar Tractor Co-USA
8320949 *JQWO* -	**SETTSU** - **G**overnment of **J**apan (Ministry of Land, Infrastructure & Transport) (The Coastguard) - SatCom: Inmarsat B 343128210 *Tokyo* *Japan* MMSI: 431282000 Official number: 128066	*3,111* - 1,883		**1984-09 S**umitomo Heavy Industries Ltd. — Oppama Shipyard, Yokosuka Yd No: 1114 Loa 105.40 Br ex 14.64 Dght 5.170 Lbp 96.85 Br md 14.60 Dpth 8.00 Welded, 1 dk	**(B34H2SQ) Patrol Vessel**	**2 oil engines** sr geared to sc. shafts driving 2 CP propellers Total Power: 11,474kW (15,600hp) Pielstick 12PC2-5V-400 2 x Vee 4 Stroke 12 Cy. 400 x 460 each-5737kW (7800bhp) Ishikawajima Harima Heavy IndustrieCo Ltd (IHI)-Japan Thrusters: 1 Thwart. CP thruster (f)

IMO / Call sign	Name / Owner	Tonnage	Class	Construction	Type	Machinery
9151412 *3FTD7*	**SETTSU** **Supreme Shipholding Co SA** Interocean Shipping Co Ltd SatCom: Inmarsat C 435162110 *Panama* *Panama* MMSI: 351621000 Official number: 2514898CH	**13,448** 5,857 17,221 T/cm 31.5	Class: BV (NK)	**1997**-10 **Shin Kochi Jyuko K.K. — Kochi** Yd No: 7093 Loa 159.53 (BB) Br ex - Dght 8.718 Lbp 150.00 Br md 25.00 Dpth 12.80 Welded, 1 dk	**(A33A2CC) Container Ship (Fully Cellular)** TEU 1157 C Ho 464 TEU C Dk 673 TEU incl 120 ref C. 15 Ha: (9.8 x 8.5)2 (12.6 x 8.0)6 (12.8 x 10.6)6 (12.6 x 10.6)ER Cranes: 2x40t	**1 oil engine** driving 1 FP propeller Total Power: 9,628kW (13,090hp) 18.0kn Mitsubishi 7UEC50LSII 1 x 2 Stroke 7 Cy. 500 x 1950 9628kW (13090bhp) Kobe Hatsudoki KK-Japan AuxGen: 4 x 438kW 440/100V 60Hz a.c Thrusters: 1 Thwart. CP thruster (f) Fuel: 2067.0
8622347 - -	**SETTSU MARU No. 5** - - *China*	*393* - 1,131		**1983 Yoshiura Zosen — Kure** Yd No: 287 Loa 66.30 Br ex - Dght 3.920 Lbp 62.01 Br md 10.30 Dpth 6.00 Welded, 1 dk	**(A31A2GX) General Cargo Ship**	**1 oil engine** reduction geared to sc. shaft driving 1 FP propeller Total Power: 772kW (1,050hp) 10.5kn Hanshin 6LU26RG 1 x 4 Stroke 6 Cy. 260 x 440 772kW (1050bhp) The Hanshin Diesel Works Ltd-Japan
7432549 - -	**SETTSU No. 8** *ex* Settsu Maru No. 8 *-1993* -	*492* 316 1,200		**1975**-09 **Oura Dock — Imabari** Yd No: 103 L reg 60.66 Br ex 11.03 Dght - Lbp 58.98 Br md 11.00 Dpth 6.33 Riveted\Welded, 1 dk	**(A31A2GX) General Cargo Ship**	**1 oil engine** driving 1 FP propeller Total Power: 1,177kW (1,600hp) Hanshin 6LUD32 1 x 4 Stroke 6 Cy. 320 x 510 1177kW (1600bhp) Hanshin Nainenki Kogyo-Japan
8303800 *3EJA2* -	**SETUBAL I** *ex* Galp Setubal *-2007* *ex* Wind Sovereign *-1990* *ex* Aniara *-1989* *ex* Minerva *-1989* **Southgate Navigation Ltd SA** Maritime Management Synergy SA *Panama* *Panama* MMSI: 372452000 Official number: 3271907	**17,913** 8,316 29,997 T/cm 41.0	Class: RP (BV) (NV) (NK)	**1984**-07 **Kasado Dockyard Co Ltd — Kudamatsu YC** Yd No: 345 Loa 176.05 (BB) Br ex 26.60 Dght 9.966 Lbp 165.85 Br md - Dpth 14.50 Welded, 1 dk	**(A13B2TP) Products Tanker** Single Hull Liq: 44,119; Liq (Oil): 44,119 Compartments: 15 Ta, ER 3 Cargo Pump (s) Manifold: Bow/CM: 87m	**1 oil engine** driving 1 FP propeller Total Power: 4,926kW (6,697hp) 14.0kn B&W 6L60MCE 1 x 2 Stroke 6 Cy. 600 x 1944 4926kW (6697bhp) Mitsui Engineering & Shipbuilding CLtd-Japan AuxGen: 2 x 520kW 440V 60Hz a.c
9419931 *A8UZ4* -	**SETY** **Tenacious Shipping & Trading SA** Byzantine Maritime Corp *Monrovia* *Liberia* MMSI: 636014577 Official number: 14577	**31,532** 18,765 55,753 T/cm 56.9	Class: NK	**2010**-03 **IHI Marine United Inc — Yokohama KN** Yd No: 3262 Loa 189.96 (BB) Br ex - Dght 12.735 Lbp 185.00 Br md 32.26 Dpth 18.10 Welded, 1 dk	**(A21A2BC) Bulk Carrier** Grain: 72,062; Bale: 67,062 Compartments: 5 Ho, ER 5 Ha: 4 (20.9 x 18.6)ER (14.6 x 18.6) Cranes: 4x35t	**1 oil engine** driving 1 FP propeller Total Power: 8,890kW (12,087hp) 14.5kn Wartsila 6RT-flex50 1 x 2 Stroke 6 Cy. 500 x 2050 8890kW (12087bhp) Diesel United Ltd.-Aioi AuxGen: 3 x 430kW a.c Fuel: 2170.0 (r.f.)
7000085 - -	**SEUNG RI** *ex* Kano Maru *-1981* - -	*476* 147 211	Class: KC	**1969 Narasaki Zosen KK — Muroran HK** Yd No: 699 Loa 47.15 Br ex 8.64 Dght 3.455 Lbp 42.02 Br md 8.62 Dpth 3.48 Welded, 1 dk	**(B11B2FV) Fishing Vessel**	**1 oil engine** driving 1 FP propeller Total Power: 736kW (1,001hp) Niigata 6L25BX 1 x 4 Stroke 6 Cy. 250 x 320 736kW (1001bhp) Niigata Engineering Co Ltd-Japan
5321124 *DFNY* -	**SEUTE DEERN** **Reederei Cassen Eils GmbH & Co KG** - *Cuxhaven* *Germany* MMSI: 211208410 Official number: 632	**825** 309 -	Class: (GL)	**1961 Rheinstahl Nordseewerke GmbH — Emden** Yd No: 335 Lengthened-1979 Loa 64.17 Br ex 10.06 Dght 2.400 Lbp 57.38 Br md 10.04 Dpth 3.38 Welded, 1 dk	**(A32A2GF) General Cargo/Passenger Ship** Passengers: unberthed: 770 Grain: 145; Bale: 131 Compartments: 2 Ho, ER 2 Ha: (1.5 x 0.9) (2.9 x 1.9)ER Derricks: 1x1.5t Ice Capable	**2 oil engines** geared to sc. shafts driving 2 FP propellers Total Power: 2,000kW (2,720hp) 15.5kn Deutz SBV6M628 2 x 4 Stroke 6 Cy. 240 x 280 each-1000kW (1360bhp) (new engine 1992) Motoren Werke Mannheim AG (MWM)-Mannheim AuxGen: 2 x 65kW 220/380V 50Hz a.c
5321136 *VWSW* -	**SEVA** **Kolkata Port Trust** - *Kolkata* *India* Official number: 1075	*1,351* 364 667	Class: (LR) (IR) ✠ Classed LR until 8/9/78	**1963**-10 **Simons-Lobnitz Ltd. — Renfrew** Yd No: 1168 Loa 73.92 Br ex 12.35 Dght 3.890 Lbp 67.06 Br md 12.20 Dpth 5.19 Riveted\Welded, 1 dk, 2nd dk clear of mchy. space	**(B35X2XX) Vessel (function unknown)**	**2 Steam Recips** driving 2 FP propellers Simons Lobnitz Ltd.-Renfrew AuxGen: 2 x 120kW 220V d.c Fuel: 254.0 (r.f.)
8740125 *9V8945* -	**SEVAN BRASIL** *ex* Sevan Driller II *-2012* **Sevan Drilling Rig II Pte Ltd** Sevan Drilling Invest AS *Singapore* *Singapore* MMSI: 564594000 Official number: 396424	**52,254** 15,677 40,000	Class: NV	**2012**-02 **COSCO (Nantong) Shipyard Co Ltd — Nantong JS** Yd No: N280 Loa 99.00 Br ex 99.00 Dght 15.000 Lbp 75.00 Br md 75.00 Dpth 24.50 Welded, 1 dk	**(Z11C3ZE) Drilling Rig, semi Submersible** Cranes: 2x100t	**8 diesel electric oil engines** driving 8 gen. Connecting to 8 elec. motors each (3800kW) driving 8 Azimuth electric drive units Total Power: 48,000kW (65,264hp) 6.5kn Bergens B32: 40V12P 8 x Vee 4 Stroke 12 Cy. 320 x 400 each-6000kW (8158bhp) Rolls Royce Marine AS-Norway
8769846 *3EAN3* -	**SEVAN DRILLER** **Sevan Driller Ltd** Sevan Drilling ASA *Panama* *Panama* Official number: 45658PEXT	**50,663** 15,199 40,000	Class: NV	**2009**-11 **COSCO (Nantong) Shipyard Co Ltd — Nantong JS** Yd No: N111 Loa 84.00 Br ex 84.00 Dght 15.020 Lbp 72.00 Br md 75.00 Dpth 24.50 Welded, 1 dk	**(Z11C3ZE) Drilling Rig, semi Submersible**	**8 diesel electric oil engines** driving 8 gen. Connecting to 8 elec. motors each (3800kW) driving 8 Azimuth electric drive units Total Power: 48,000kW (65,264hp) Bergens B32: 40V12P 1 x Vee 4 Stroke 12 Cy. 320 x 400 6000kW (8158bhp) (new engine 2009) Rolls Royce Marine AS-Norway Bergens B32: 40V12P 7 x Vee 4 Stroke 12 Cy. 320 x 400 each-6000kW (8158bhp) (new engine 2009) Rolls Royce Marine AS-Norway
9679440 *3FMN7* -	**SEVAN LOUISIANA** *ex* Sevan Norway *-2013* **Sevan Drilling Rig V Pte Ltd** Sevan Drilling ASA *Panama* *Panama* MMSI: 355245000 Official number: 45140PEXT	**51,775** 15,533 40,000	Class: NV	**2013**-10 **COSCO (Qidong) Offshore Co Ltd — Qidong JS** Yd No: N418 Loa 99.00 Br ex 99.00 Dght 15.000 Lbp 75.00 Br md 84.00 Dpth 24.50 Welded, 1 dk	**(Z11C3ZE) Drilling Rig, semi Submersible**	**8 diesel electric oil engines** driving 8 gen. driving 8 Azimuth electric drive units Total Power: 48,000kW (65,264hp) 7.0kn Wartsila 12V32 8 x Vee 4 Stroke 12 Cy. 320 x 400 each-6000kW (8158bhp) Wartsila Finland Oy-Finland
8929458 - -	**SEVASTOPOL** **Sea Commercial Port of Odessa (Odesskiy Morskiy Port)** - *Odessa* *Ukraine* Official number: 753521	**126** 43 16	Class: (RS)	**1977**-08 **Ilyichyovskiy Sudoremontnyy Zavod im. "50-letiya SSSR" — Ilyichyovsk** Yd No: 47 Loa 33.48 Br ex 5.70 Dght 1.580 Lbp 30.00 Br md - Dpth 2.55 Welded, 1 dk	**(A37B2PS) Passenger Ship** Passengers: unberthed: 92	**2 oil engines** geared to sc. shafts driving 2 FP propellers Total Power: 442kW (600hp) 14.5kn Barnaultransmash 3D12A 2 x Vee 4 Stroke 12 Cy. 150 x 180 each-221kW (300bhp) Barnaultransmash-Barnaul AuxGen: 2 x 12kW a.c Fuel: 6.0 (d.f.)
8926298 - -	**SEVASTOPOL** **Nikolayev Clay Works (Nikolayevskiy Glinozemnyy Zavod)** - *Nikolayev* *Ukraine* Official number: 821150	*230* - 76	Class: (RS)	**1982 Brodogradiliste 'Tito' — Belgrade** Yd No: 1087 Loa 35.83 Br ex 9.30 Dght 3.040 Lbp 32.07 Br md - Dpth 4.50 Welded, 1 dk	**(B32A2ST) Tug** Ice Capable	**2 oil engines** geared to sc. shaft driving 1 CP propeller Total Power: 1,854kW (2,520hp) 13.2kn Sulzer 6ASL25/30 2 x 4 Stroke 6 Cy. 250 x 300 each-927kW (1260bhp) in Yugoslavia AuxGen: 2 x 100kW a.c Fuel: 60.0 (d.f.)
6904155 *EOLD* -	**SEVASTOPOL-1** *ex* Musson *-1999* **Ukraine Marine Ecology Research Centre** - SatCom: Inmarsat A 1401736 *Sevastopol* *Ukraine* MMSI: 272924000 Official number: 673261	**2,996** 911 1,101	Class: (RS)	**1967**-10 **Stocznia Szczecinska im A Warskiego — Szczecin** Yd No: B88/02 Converted From: Research Vessel-2000 Loa 97.11 Br ex 13.82 Dght 5.201 Lbp 88.42 Br md 13.80 Dpth 8.77 Welded, 2 dks	**(A37B2PS) Passenger Ship** Passengers: berths: 100 Bale: 150 Compartments: 1 Ho, ER 1 Ha: (4.1 x 4.1) Cranes: 1x3t; Winches: 2 Ice Capable	**2 oil engines** driving 2 FP propellers Total Power: 3,530kW (4,800hp) 16.0kn Sulzer 8TD48 2 x 2 Stroke 8 Cy. 480 x 700 each-1765kW (2400bhp) Zaklady Urzadzen Technicznych'Zgoda' SA-Poland
8929460 - -	**SEVASTOPOLETS** **State Enterprise 'Sevastopol Sea Fishing Port' (Derzhavne Pidpryyemstvo Sevastopolska Morskyy Rybnyy Port)** - *Sevastopol* *Ukraine* Official number: 710193	*187* - 46	Class: (RS)	**1971 "Petrozavod" — Leningrad** Yd No: 785 Loa 29.30 Br ex 8.49 Dght 3.090 Lbp 27.00 Br md - Dpth 4.35 Welded, 1 dk	**(B32A2ST) Tug** Ice Capable	**2 oil engines** driving 2 CP propellers Total Power: 882kW (1,200hp) 11.4kn Russkiy 6D30/50-4-2 2 x 2 Stroke 6 Cy. 300 x 500 each-441kW (600bhp) Mashinostroitelnyy Zavod"Russkiy-Dizel"-Leningrad AuxGen: 2 x 25kW a.c Fuel: 43.0 (d.f.)

Number	Name / Owner	Tonnage	Class	Builder / Dimensions	Type	Machinery
8728579 *UDLF* -	**SEVASTOPOLETS-1** **Government of The Russian Federation** Federal State Unitary Enterprise Rosmorport *Novorossiysk* *Russia* MMSI: 273155500 Official number: 851688	**1,208** 362 501	Class: RS	**1986-02 Sevastopolskiy Morskoy Zavod — Sevastopol** Yd No: 1 Loa 46.80 Br ex 21.40 Dght 2.600 Lbp 45.16 Br md 21.00 Dpth 4.00 Welded	**(B34B2SC) Crane Vessel** Cranes: 1x140t Ice Capable	**3 diesel electric oil engines** driving 1 gen. of 100kW Connecting to 4 elec. motors each (315kW) driving 2 Voith-Schneider propellers Total Power: 1,413kW (1,921hp) 7.2kn Pervomaysk 6CHNSP25/34 1 x 4 Stroke 6 Cy. 250 x 340 345kW (469bhp) Pervomaydizelmash (PDM)-Pervomaysk Pervomaysk 8CHNSP25/34 2 x 4 Stroke 8 Cy. 250 x 340 each-534kW (726bhp) Pervomaydizelmash (PDM)-Pervomaysk
8728593 - -	**SEVASTOPOLETS-3** **OAO 'Tolyattiazot'** -	**1,208** 362 501	Class: (RS)	**1987-11 Sevastopolskiy Morskoy Zavod — Sevastopol** Yd No: 3 Loa 46.80 Br ex 21.40 Dght 2.600 Lbp 45.60 Br md - Dpth 4.00 Welded, 1 dk	**(B34B2SC) Crane Vessel** Cranes: 1x140t Ice Capable	**3 diesel electric oil engines** driving 1 gen. of 100kW Connecting to 4 elec. motors each (315kW) driving 2 Voith-Schneider propellers Total Power: 1,413kW (1,921hp) 7.2kn Pervomaysk 6CHNSP25/34 1 x 4 Stroke 6 Cy. 250 x 340 345kW (469bhp) Pervomaydizelmash (PDM)-Pervomaysk Pervomaysk 8CHNSP25/34 2 x 4 Stroke 8 Cy. 250 x 340 each-534kW (726bhp) Pervomaydizelmash (PDM)-Pervomaysk
7418567 *UEJR* -	**SEVASTOPOLSKIY** **OOO 'ZBK'** *Kaliningrad* *Russia* Official number: 732296	**196** 58 70	Class: (RS)	**1974-05 Sudostroitelnyy Zavod "Avangard" — Petrozavodsk** Yd No: 274 Loa 31.60 Br ex 7.32 Dght 2.744 Lbp 29.15 Br md 7.20 Dpth 3.54 Welded, 1 dk	**(B11B2FV) Fishing Vessel** Ice Capable	**1 oil engine** driving 1 FP propeller Total Power: 224kW (305hp) 9.5kn S.K.L. 8NVD36-1U 1 x 4 Stroke 8 Cy. 240 x 360 224kW (305bhp) VEB Schwermaschinenbau "KarlLiebknecht" (SKL)-Magdeburg AuxGen: 2 x 64kW a.c Fuel: 36.0 (d.f.)
8615019 *V3TM* -	**SEVEN** *ex Bos -2009 ex Sea Rose -2009* *ex Eros -2007 ex Progress -2007* *ex Twins -2005 ex Aront -2005* *ex Morning Glory -2003 ex Sirius No. 2 -2003* *ex Shonan Maru -1999* **Coral Shipping Co Ltd** - *Belize City* *Belize* MMSI: 312939000 Official number: 161420802	**713** 213 505	Class: (RS)	**1987-02 Niigata Engineering Co Ltd — Niigata NI** Yd No: 2027 Loa 56.01 (BB) Br ex - Dght 3.836 Lbp 49.00 Br md 9.21 Dpth 4.02 Welded, 1 dk	**(B11B2FV) Fishing Vessel** Ins: 106	**1 oil engine** with clutches, flexible couplings & sr geared to sc. shaft driving 1 CP propeller Total Power: 1,030kW (1,400hp) 11.0kn Niigata 6M28AFTE 1 x 4 Stroke 6 Cy. 280 x 480 1030kW (1400bhp) Niigata Engineering Co Ltd-Japan
9419125 *2CBP2* -	**SEVEN ATLANTIC** **Subsea 7 Ltd** Subsea 7 International Contracting Ltd *Douglas* *Isle of Man (British)* MMSI: 235071342	**17,496** 5,248 11,885	Class: LR ✠ **100A1** SS 01/2010 diving support ship helicopter landing area LI EP work deck strengthened for load of 10t/m2 (from fr. 20 to fr. 66) ✠ **LMC** **UMS** Eq.Ltr: J†; Cable: 605.0/66.0 U3 (a)	**2010-01 Merwede Shipyard BV — Hardinxveld** Yd No: 713 Loa 144.79 Br ex - Dght 8.000 Lbp 128.96 Br md 26.00 Dpth 12.00 Welded, 1 dk	**(B22A2OV) Diving Support Vessel** Passengers: 150 Cranes: 1x120t,2x10t	**6 diesel electric oil engines** driving 6 gen. each 3240kW 6600V a.c Connecting to 3 elec. motors each (2950kW) driving 3 Directional propellers Total Power: 20,160kW (27,408hp) 13.6kn Wartsila 7L32 6 x 4 Stroke 7 Cy. 320 x 400 each-3360kW (4568bhp) Wartsila Finland Oy-Finland Thrusters: 2 Retract. directional thruster (f); 1 Thwart. FP thruster (f)
9452787 *C6YG8* -	**SEVEN BOREALIS** *ex Acergy Borealis -2012 ex Sembawang -2011* **Class 3 (UK) Ltd** Subsea 7 International Contracting Ltd SatCom: Inmarsat C 431101293 *Nassau* *Bahamas* MMSI: 311031900 Official number: 8001730	**49,735** 14,921 47,000	Class: NV	**2012-02 Nantong Yahua Shipbuilding Co Ltd — Nantong JS** (Hull) Yd No: (H07-02) **2012-02 Sembawang Shipyard Pte Ltd — Singapore** Yd No: H07-02 Loa 180.90 (BB) Br ex - Dght 11.000 Lbp 168.60 Br md 46.20 Dpth 16.10 Welded, 1 dk	**(B22C2OQ) Pipe Layer Crane Vessel** Passengers: cabins: 122 Cranes: 1x5000t,2x40t,1x36t	**6 diesel electric oil engines** driving 6 gen. Connecting to 2 elec. motors each (5500kW) driving 2 Azimuth electric drive units Total Power: 34,560kW (46,986hp) 14.0kn Bergens B32: 40V12P 6 x Vee 4 Stroke 12 Cy. 320 x 400 each-5760kW (7831bhp) Rolls Royce Marine AS-Norway Thrusters: 3 Retract. directional thruster (f); 1 Retract. directional thruster (a); 1 Tunnel thruster (f) Fuel: 2800.0 (r.f.)
8111879 *ELXL9* -	**SEVEN CONDOR** *ex Acergy Condor -2013* *ex Seaway Condor -2006* **Subsea 7 Offshore Resources (UK) Ltd** Subsea 7 MS Ltd SatCom: Inmarsat A 1447425 *Monrovia* *Liberia* MMSI: 636011194 Official number: 11194	**8,506** 2,552 4,550	Class: NV	**1982-05 Werft Nobiskrug GmbH — Rendsburg** Yd No: 710 Converted From: Diving Support Vessel-1994 Lengthened-2000 Loa 144.60 Br ex - Dght 6.010 Lbp 128.20 Br md 22.60 Dpth 10.72 Welded, 3 dks	**(B22C2OX) Pipe Layer** Passengers: berths: 100 A-frames: 1x250t; Cranes: 2x60t	**6 diesel electric oil engines** driving 6 gen. each 1200kW 660V a.c Connecting to 2 elec. motors driving 2 Directional propellers Total Power: 7,632kW (10,374hp) 11.0kn MaK 8M332AK 6 x 4 Stroke 8 Cy. 240 x 330 each-1272kW (1729bhp) Krupp MaK Maschinenbau GmbH-Kiel AuxGen: 1 x 472kW 440V 60Hz a.c Thrusters: 2 Tunnel thruster (f); 1 Tunnel thruster (f); 1 Retract. directional thruster (f); 1 Retract. directional thruster (a) Fuel: 1000.0 (d.f.) 1397.0 (r.f.) 22.0pd
8813910 *2EBF9* -	**SEVEN DISCOVERY** *ex Acergy Discovery -2013 ex Discovery -2006* **Subsea 7 Offshore Resources (UK) Ltd** Subsea 7 International Contracting Ltd *Douglas* *Isle of Man (British)* MMSI: 235083664 Official number: 737842	**8,248** 2,474 4,645	Class: NV (LR) ✠ Classed LR until 30/11/09	**1990-11 N.V. Boelwerf S.A. — Temse** Yd No: 1531 Loa 120.47 Br ex 19.73 Dght 6.514 Lbp 96.00 Br md 19.50 Dpth 11.00 Welded, 2 dks	**(B34D2SL) Cable Layer** Cranes: 1x140t,1x50t,1x8t Ice Capable	**4 diesel electric oil engines** driving 4 gen. each 2576kW 6000V a.c Connecting to 3 elec. motors each (2000kW) driving 3 Directional propellers Total Power: 9,720kW (13,216hp) 12.0kn Wartsila 6R32E 4 x 4 Stroke 6 Cy. 320 x 350 each-2430kW (3304bhp) Wartsila Diesel Oy-Finland Thrusters: 3 Tunnel thruster (f) Fuel: 1288.4 (d.f.) 23.4pd
9015905 *ELUB4* -	**SEVEN EAGLE** *ex Acergy Eagle -2012 ex Seaway Eagle -2006* *launched as Navigator -1997* **Subsea 7 Shipping Ltd** Subsea 7 International Contracting Ltd SatCom: Inmarsat B 363659610 *Monrovia* *Liberia* MMSI: 636010639 Official number: 10639	**9,556** 2,866 6,000	Class: NV (LR) ✠ Classed LR until 21/9/97	**1997-04 Boelwerf Vlaanderen N.V. — Temse** (Hull launched by) Yd No: 1540 **1997-04 Schelde Scheepsnieuwbouw B.V. — Vlissingen** (Hull completed by) Loa 142.39 Br ex 19.75 Dght 6.853 Lbp 116.44 Br md 19.50 Dpth 11.00 Welded, 2 dks	**(B21A2OP) Pipe Carrier** Passengers: berths: 101 Cranes: 1x250t,1x155t Ice Capable	**4 diesel electric oil engines** driving 4 gen. each 2576kW 6000V a.c Connecting to 3 elec. motors each (2000kW) driving 3 Directional propellers Total Power: 9,077kW (12,342hp) 13.0kn Wartsila 6R32E 4 x 4 Stroke 6 Cy. 320 x 350 each-1787kW (2430bhp) Wartsila Diesel Oy-Finland Thrusters: 3 Thwart. CP thruster (f)
9354519 *3ENS3* -	**SEVEN EXPRESS** **Cassiopeia Marine SA** Mitsui OSK Lines Ltd (MOL) SatCom: Inmarsat Mini-M 7648115832 *Panama* *Panama* MMSI: 352144000 Official number: 3346708A	**28,063** 11,804 45,998 T/cm 50.6	Class: NK	**2007-12 Shin Kurushima Dockyard Co. Ltd. — Onishi** Yd No: 5450 Loa 179.88 (BB) Br ex 32.23 Dght 12.102 Lbp 172.00 Br md 32.20 Dpth 18.70 Welded, 1 dk	**(A13B2TP) Products Tanker** Double Hull (13F) Liq: 50,781; Liq (Oil): 50,781 Cargo Heating Coils Compartments: 14 Wing Ta, 2 Wing Slop Ta, ER 3 Cargo Pump (s): 3x1000m³/hr Manifold: Bow/CM: 91.3m	**1 oil engine** driving 1 FP propeller Total Power: 9,267kW (12,599hp) 14.6kn Mitsubishi 6UEC60LA 1 x 2 Stroke 6 Cy. 600 x 1900 9267kW (12599bhp) Mitsubishi Heavy Industries Ltd-Japan AuxGen: 3 x 700kW a.c Fuel: 183.0 (d.f.) 1820.0 (r.f.)
9455167 *2EEN9* -	**SEVEN FALCON** *ex Seven Havila -2013* *launched as Acergy Havila -2011* **Subsea 7 (Cyprus) Ltd** Subsea 7 Vessel Management Group SatCom: Inmarsat C 423592668 *Ramsey* *Isle of Man (British)* MMSI: 235084424 Official number: 741805	**11,071** 3,321 7,250	Class: NV	**2011-02 Cemre Muhendislik Gemi Insaat Sanayi ve Ticaret Ltd Sti — Altinova** (Hull) Yd No: (088) **2011-02 Havyard Leirvik AS — Leirvik i Sogn** Yd No: 088 Loa 120.00 (BB) Br ex - Dght 8.250 Lbp 106.60 Br md 23.00 Dpth 10.04 Welded, 1 dk	**(B22A2OV) Diving Support Vessel** Double Hull Cranes: 1x250t,1x50t Ice Capable	**8 diesel electric oil engines** driving 8 gen. Connecting to 2 elec. motors each (3500kW) driving 2 Azimuth electric drive units Total Power: 12,648kW (17,200hp) 16.0kn Caterpillar 3516TA 8 x Vee 4 Stroke 16 Cy. 170 x 190 each-1581kW (2150bhp) Caterpillar Inc-USA Thrusters: 2 Tunnel thruster (f); 2 Retract. directional thruster (f); 1 Directional thruster (a) Fuel: 1335.0
9618094 *3FIZ5* -	**SEVEN INAGHA** **Subsea 7 Offshore Resources (UK) Ltd** Subsea 7 International Contracting Ltd *Panama* *Panama* MMSI: 373181000 Official number: 43111PEXT	**3,783** 1,134 1,104	Class: AB	**2012-04 Semco LLC — Lafitte, La** Yd No: 1015 Loa 59.45 Br ex - Dght 3.260 Lbp - Br md 39.30 Dpth 4.27 Welded, 1 dk	**(B22A2ZM) Offshore Construction Vessel, jack up**	**4 diesel electric oil engines** driving 4 gen. Connecting to 4 elec. motors reduction geared to sc. shafts driving 2 FP propellers Total Power: 7,000kW (9,516hp) 6.0kn Caterpillar 3512B 4 x Vee 4 Stroke 12 Cy. 170 x 190 each-1750kW (2379bhp) Caterpillar Inc-USA

8019576 *JJ3506* -	**SEVEN ISLAND AI** *ex* Jet No. 7 *-2002* *ex* Spirit of Friendship *-1987* *ex* Aries *-1985* *ex* Montevedeo Jet *-1982* **Tokai Kisen Co Ltd** - *Tokyo* *Japan* Official number: 129168	*279* - -	Class: (AB)	**1980-10 Boeing Marine Systems — Seattle, Wa** Yd No: 0017 Loa 27.43 Br ex - Dght 1.300 Lbp 24.16 Br md 8.53 Dpth 2.59 Welded, 1 dk	**(A37B2PS) Passenger Ship** Hull Material: Aluminium Alloy Passengers: unberthed: 250	**2 Gas Turbs** dr geared to sc. shafts driving 2 Water jets Total Power: 5,444kW (7,402hp) 43.0kn Allison 501-K20B 2 x Gas Turb each-2722kW (3701shp) General Motors Detroit DieselAllison Divn-USA AuxGen: 2 x 50kW 440V 60Hz a.c Thrusters: 1 Thwart. FP thruster (f)
7932068 *JG5664* -	**SEVEN ISLAND NIJI** *ex* Seajet Kara *-2002* *ex* Alderney Blizzard *-1999* *ex* Adler Blizzard *-1999* *ex* Princesse Clementine *-1998* **Tokai Kisen Co Ltd** - *Tokyo* *Japan* Official number: 137120	*281* 96 50	Class: (AB)	**1981-04 Boeing Marine Systems — Seattle, Wa** Yd No: 0019 Loa 27.44 Br ex 9.15 Dght - Lbp 23.93 Br md 8.54 Dpth 2.65 Welded, 1 dk	**(A37B2PS) Passenger Ship** Hull Material: Aluminium Alloy Passengers: unberthed: 340	**2 Gas Turbs** dr geared to sc. shafts driving 2 Water jets Total Power: 5,442kW (7,398hp) 43.0kn Allison 501-K20B 2 x Gas Turb each-2721kW (3699shp) General Motors Detroit DieselAllison Divn-USA AuxGen: 2 x 50kW 440V 60Hz a.c Thrusters: 1 Thwart. FP thruster (f)
8819160 *JM5778* -	**SEVEN ISLAND TOMO** *ex* Toppy 1 *-2013* *ex* Toppy *-2003* **Tokai Kisen Co Ltd** *Kagoshima, Kagoshima* *Japan* Official number: 131269	*164* - 20		**1989-06 Kawasaki Heavy Industries Ltd — Kobe HG** Yd No: F003 Loa 27.36 Br ex - Dght 1.560 Lbp 23.99 Br md 8.53 Dpth 2.59 Welded	**(A37B2PS) Passenger Ship** Hull Material: Aluminium Alloy Passengers: unberthed: 252	**2 Gas Turbs** geared to sc. shafts driving 2 Water jets Total Power: 5,590kW (7,600hp) 43.0kn Allison 501-KF 2 x Gas Turb each-2795kW (3800shp) General Motors Detroit DieselAllison Divn-USA AuxGen: 2 x 50kW 450V 60Hz a.c
7932070 *JG5665* -	**SEVEN ISLAND YUME** *ex* Seajet Kristen *-2002* *ex* Adler Wizard *-1999* *ex* Prinses Stephanie *-1998* **Tokai Kisen Co Ltd** - *Tokyo* *Japan* Official number: 137151	*280* 242 115	Class: (AB)	**1981-06 Boeing Marine Systems — Seattle, Wa** Yd No: 0020 Loa 27.44 Br ex - Dght 5.301 Lbp 23.93 Br md 8.53 Dpth 2.65 Welded, 1 dk	**(A37B2PS) Passenger Ship** Hull Material: Aluminium Alloy Passengers: unberthed: 340	**2 Gas Turbs** dr geared to sc. shafts driving 2 Water jets Total Power: 5,442kW (7,398hp) 43.0kn Allison 501-K20B 2 x Gas Turb each-2721kW (3699shp) General Motors Detroit DieselAllison Divn-USA AuxGen: 2 x 50kW 440V 60Hz a.c Thrusters: 1 Thwart. FP thruster (f)
9470624 *V7ZJ6* -	**SEVEN J'S** *ex* Slojo *-2012* **Seven J's MI Ltd** Fraser Yachts Florida Inc *Bikini* *Marshall Islands* MMSI: 538070886 Official number: 70886	**496** 149 -	Class: LR ✠ **100A1** SS 09/2013 SSC Yacht, mono, G6 Cable: 19.0/0.0 U2 (a)	**2008-09 Delta Marine Industries, Inc. — Seattle, Wa** Yd No: 156036 Loa 47.60 Br ex 8.99 Dght 2.130 Lbp 41.70 Br md 8.69 Dpth 3.81 Bonded, 1 dk	**(X11A2YP) Yacht** Hull Material: Reinforced Plastic	**2 oil engines** with clutches, flexible couplings & sr reverse geared to sc. shafts driving 2 FP propellers Total Power: 1,938kW (2,634hp) Caterpillar 3508B-TA 2 x Vee 4 Stroke 8 Cy. 170 x 190 each-969kW (1317bhp) Caterpillar Inc-USA AuxGen: 2 x 99kW 208V 60Hz a.c Thrusters: 1 Thwart. FP thruster (f)
9366823 *V2ZT4* -	**SEVEN MAKO** **Coastal Shipping Ltd** - *Saint John's* *Antigua & Barbuda* MMSI: 304184000 Official number: 1687	**290** 87 309	Class: (AB)	**2006-05 Zhuhai Shipbuilding Industry Corp — Zhuhai GD** Yd No: GMG0502 Loa 30.10 Br ex 9.40 Dght 3.400 Lbp 27.91 Br md 9.00 Dpth 4.10 Welded, 1 dk	**(B32A2ST) Tug**	**2 oil engines** reduction geared to sc. shafts driving 2 FP propellers Total Power: 1,766kW (2,402hp) 10.0kn Cummins KTA-38-M2 2 x Vee 4 Stroke 12 Cy. 159 x 159 each-883kW (1201bhp) Cummins Engine Co Ltd-United Kingdom
9230414 *2EBC3* -	**SEVEN MAR** *ex* Polar Queen *-2011* *ex* Knight *-2005* **Subsea 7 Offshore Resources (UK) Ltd** Subsea 7 International Contracting Ltd *Ramsey* *Isle of Man (British)* MMSI: 235083629 Official number: 741804	**14,502** 4,351 13,129	Class: NV	**2001-09 Hyundai Mipo Dockyard Co Ltd — Ulsan** Yd No: 0003 Converted From: Cable-layer-2006 Loa 144.60 (BB) Br ex 37.05 Dght 8.000 Lbp 128.60 Br md 27.00 Dpth 13.20 Welded	**(B22C20X) Pipe Layer** Passengers: berths: 121 A-frames: 1x60t; Cranes: 1x300t,1x20t	**4 diesel electric oil engines** driving 4 gen. each 3845kW a.c Connecting to 2 elec. motors each (4500kW) driving 2 Directional propellers Total Power: 15,360kW (20,884hp) 12.0kn MAN 8L32/40 2 x 4 Stroke 8 Cy. 320 x 400 each-3840kW (5221bhp) Hyundai Heavy Industries Co Ltd-South Korea AuxGen: 1 x 1135kW a.c Thrusters: 1 Tunnel thruster (f); 2 Retract. directional thruster (f)
9366249 *V2ZS4* -	**SEVEN MARLIN** **Bluefan Enterprises Ltd** Dutch Caribbean Towing & Shipping NV (DCTShipping) *Saint John's* *Antigua & Barbuda* MMSI: 304180000 Official number: 1686	**290** 87 303	Class: AB	**2006-05 Zhuhai Shipbuilding Industry Corp — Zhuhai GD** Yd No: GMG0501 Loa 30.10 Br ex 9.40 Dght 3.400 Lbp 27.91 Br md 9.00 Dpth 4.10 Welded, 1 dk	**(B32A2ST) Tug**	**2 oil engines** reduction geared to sc. shafts driving 2 FP propellers Total Power: 1,766kW (2,402hp) 10.0kn Cummins KTA-38-M2 2 x Vee 4 Stroke 12 Cy. 159 x 159 each-883kW (1201bhp) Cummins Engine Co Ltd-United Kingdom
9177856 *MZHR7* -	**SEVEN NAVICA** *ex* Skandi Navica *-2008* **Subsea 7 Navica AS** Subsea 7 International Contracting Ltd *Douglas* *Isle of Man (British)* MMSI: 232419000 Official number: 732669	**6,083** 1,825 9,560	Class: NV	**1999-12 SC Santierul Naval Tulcea SA — Tulcea** (Hull) Yd No: 297 **1999-12 Brattvaag Skipsverft AS — Brattvaag** Yd No: 90 Lengthened Loa 108.53 (BB) Br ex - Dght 7.165 Lbp 100.55 Br md 22.00 Dpth 9.00 Welded, 1 dk	**(B22C20X) Pipe Layer** Passengers: cabins: 50	**4 diesel electric oil engines** driving 2 gen. each 3200kW a.c 2 gen. each 2400kW a.c Connecting to 2 elec. motors each (3000kW) driving 2 Directional propellers contra rotating propellers Total Power: 12,600kW (17,132hp) 12.0kn Wartsila 6L32 2 x 4 Stroke 6 Cy. 320 x 400 each-2700kW (3671bhp) Wartsila NSD Norway AS-Norway Wartsila 8L32 2 x 4 Stroke 8 Cy. 320 x 400 each-3600kW (4895bhp) Wartsila NSD Norway AS-Norway Thrusters: 2 Thwart. FP thruster (f); 1 Retract. directional thruster (f) Fuel: 2316.0
9358826 *MQND3* -	**SEVEN OCEANS** **Subsea 7 Ltd** Subsea 7 International Contracting Ltd *Douglas* *Isle of Man (British)* MMSI: 235053116 Official number: 739302	**18,201** 5,460 12,430	Class: LR ✠ **100A1** SS 07/2012 upper deck strengthened for load 10t/m2 helicopter landing area LI EP *IWS ✠ **LMC** **UMS** Eq.Ltr: K†; Cable: 632.5/68.0 U3 (a)	**2007-07 Merwede Shipyard BV — Hardinxveld** Yd No: 709 Loa 157.31 Br ex - Dght 7.500 Lbp 138.32 Br md 28.40 Dpth 12.50 Welded, 3 dks	**(B22C20Q) Pipe Layer Crane Vessel** Passengers: cabins: 69 Cranes: 1x400t,1x40t,1x12t	**6 diesel electric oil engines** driving 6 gen. each 3240kW 6600V a.c Connecting to 3 elec. motors each (2950kW) driving 3 Azimuth electric drive units Total Power: 20,160kW (27,408hp) 13.0kn Wartsila 7L32 6 x 4 Stroke 7 Cy. 320 x 400 each-3360kW (4568bhp) Wartsila Nederland BV-Netherlands Boilers: TOH (o.f.) 13.3kgf/cm² (13.0bar) Thrusters: 2 Retract. directional thruster (f); 1 Tunnel thruster (f) Fuel: 2243.0 (d.f.) 1095.0 (r.f.)
8213392 *ELVE9* -	**SEVEN OSPREY** *ex* Acergy Osprey *-2013* *ex* Seaway Osprey *-2006* *ex* Norskald *-1990* *ex* Seacom *-1985* **Subsea 7 Offshore Resources (UK) Ltd** Subsea 7 International Contracting Ltd SatCom: Inmarsat B 363672610 *Monrovia* *Liberia* MMSI: 636010844 Official number: 10844	**6,254** 1,877 3,104	Class: NV (BV)	**1984-03 Chantiers du Nord et de La Mediterranee (NORMED) — La Seyne** Yd No: 1442 Loa 101.71 Br ex 21.60 Dght 5.750 Lbp 90.02 Br md 19.61 Dpth 10.70 Welded, 1 dk	**(B22A20V) Diving Support Vessel** Passengers: berths: 102 Cranes: 1x150t,1x40t	**6 diesel electric oil engines** driving 6 gen. each 1200kW 660V a.c Connecting to 2 elec. motors each (1103kW) 2 elec. motors each (1618kW) driving 2 Directional propellers Total Power: 7,722kW (10,500hp) Crepelle 8PSN3L 6 x 4 Stroke 8 Cy. 260 x 320 each-1287kW (1750bhp) Crepelle et Cie-France Thrusters: 2 Directional thruster (f); 1 Tunnel thruster (f) Fuel: 1021.0

Ship	Tonnage	Class	Builder / Dimensions	Type	Machinery
9518311 **SEVEN PACIFIC** *2DLM3* - **Subsea 7 Ltd** Subsea 7 International Contracting Ltd SatCom: Inmarsat C 423592517 *Douglas* *Isle of Man (British)* MMSI: 235080015 Official number: 742798	**12,084** 3,625 8,000	Class: LR ✠ **100A1** SS 11/2010 WDL (10t/m2 from frame 10 till frame 100) helicopter landing area LI EP (N) Ice Class 1C FS at a draught of 6.765m Max/min draughts fwd 6.90/4.90m max/min draughts aft 7.30/4.90m Power required 3228kw, power installed 6600kw ✠ **LMC** **UMS** Eq.Ltr: J†; Cable: 605.0/66.0 U3 (a)	**2010-11 IHC Offshore & Marine BV — Krimpen a/d IJssel** Yd No: 7719 Loa 133.15 Br ex 24.03 Dght 6.750 Lbp 121.15 Br md 24.00 Dpth 10.00 Welded, 1 dk	**(B22C2OQ) Pipe Layer Crane Vessel** Cranes: 1x250t,1x30t Ice Capable	**4 diesel electric oil engines** driving 2 gen. each 3280kW 6600V a.c 2 gen. each 2880kW 6600V a.c Connecting to 3 elec. motors each (2500kW) driving 3 Directional propellers Total Power: 14,400kW (19,578hp) 13.0kn Wartsila 7L32 2 x 4 Stroke 7 Cy. 320 x 400 each-3360kW (4568bhp) Wartsila Finland Oy-Finland Wartsila 8L32 2 x 4 Stroke 8 Cy. 320 x 400 each-3840kW (5221bhp) Wartsila Finland Oy-Finland Thrusters: 1 Directional thruster (f); 2 Thwart. FP thruster (f)
8420244 **SEVEN PELICAN** *C6RE7* *ex DSND Pelican -2008* - *ex Seaway Pelican -2000* **Subsea 7 (Cayman Vessel Co) Ltd** Subsea 7 International Contracting Ltd SatCom: Inmarsat A 1310420 *Nassau* *Bahamas* MMSI: 311007000 Official number: 8000125	**4,892** 1,468 2,333	Class: NV	**1985-12 AS Framnaes Mek. Vaerksted — Sandefjord** Yd No: 200 Loa 92.31 Br ex 18.32 Dght 6.550 Lbp 79.51 Br md 18.01 Dpth 9.50 Welded, 1 dk	**(B22A2OR) Offshore Support Vessel** Passengers: cabins: 62; berths: 105 Compartments: 3 Ta, ER Cranes: 1x120t,1x60t,1x10t	**4 diesel electric oil engines** driving 4 gen. each 2950kW Connecting to 2 elec. motors each (2757kW) driving 2 Azimuth electric drive units Total Power: 12,004kW (16,320hp) 10.0kn Wichmann WX28V10 4 x Vee 4 Stroke 10 Cy. 280 x 360 each-3001kW (4080bhp) Wichmann Motorfabrikk AS-Norway AuxGen: 1 x 160kW 220V 60Hz a.c Thrusters: 3 Tunnel thruster (f); 1 Tunnel thruster (a) Fuel: 1255.0 24.0pd
9268629 **SEVEN PETREL** *2HDR6* *ex Acergy Petrel -2013 ex Seaway Petrel -2007* - **Subsea 7 Petrel AS** Subsea 7 International Contracting Ltd *Douglas* *Isle of Man (British)* MMSI: 235102789	**3,371** 1,012 1,506	Class: NV	**2003-04 SC Aker Braila SA — Braila** (Hull) Yd No: 1417 **2003-04 Brattvaag Skipsverft AS — Brattvaag** Yd No: 101 Loa 76.45 (BB) Br ex 15.03 Dght 7.000 Lbp 64.20 Br md 15.00 Dpth 8.80 Welded, 1 dk	**(B31A2SR) Research Survey Vessel** Passengers: berths: 48 Cranes: 1x21t Ice Capable	**4 diesel electric oil engines** driving 4 gen. each 1960kW a.c Connecting to 2 elec. motors each (2000kW) driving 2 Directional propellers Total Power: 6,620kW (9,000hp) 13.0kn Mitsubishi S16R-MPTK 4 x Vee 4 Stroke 16 Cy. 170 x 180 each-1655kW (2250bhp) Mitsubishi Heavy Industries Ltd-Japan Thrusters: 2 Tunnel thruster (f); 1 Retract. directional thruster (f) Fuel: 710.0 (r.f.)
9250529 **SEVEN PHOENIX** *2EEZ6* *ex Pertinacia -2012* - **Subsea 7 Offshore Resources (UK) Ltd** Subsea 7 International Contracting Ltd *Douglas* *Isle of Man (British)* MMSI: 235084529 Official number: 742828	**13,116** 3,777 12,593	Class: NV (RI) (AB)	**2003-03 Cant. Nav. Fratelli Orlando Srl — Livorno** Yd No: 281 Converted From: Cable-layer-2006 Loa 129.90 (BB) Br ex 27.80 Dght 8.410 Lbp 112.93 Br md 23.40 Dpth 12.00 Welded, 1 dk	**(B22C2OX) Pipe Layer** A-frames: 1x60t; Cranes: 1x30t	**4 diesel electric oil engines** driving 4 gen. each 3240kW 6600V a.c Connecting to 2 elec. motors each (3300kW) driving 2 Directional propellers Total Power: 12,960kW (17,620hp) 12.0kn Wartsila 8R32 4 x 4 Stroke 8 Cy. 320 x 350 each-3240kW (4405bhp) Wartsila Finland Oy-Finland Thrusters: 1 Retract. directional thruster (f); 2 Thwart. FP thruster (f); 2 Directional thruster (a)
9362798 **SEVEN PHOENIX** *3EDI7* - **Pine Tanker SA** Kaisei Tsusho KK (Kaisei Tsusho Co Ltd) *Panama* *Panama* MMSI: 371580000 Official number: 3135706A	**1,930** 724 2,499 T/cm 8.6	Class: NK	**2005-11 KK Onishigumi Zosensho — Mihara HS** Yd No: 350 Loa 79.84 (BB) Br ex 13.12 Dght 5.409 Lbp 74.00 Br md 13.00 Dpth 6.50 Welded, 1 dk	**(A12B2TR) Chemical/Products Tanker** Double Hull (13F) Liq: 2,623; Liq (Oil): 2,709 Cargo Heating Coils Compartments: 1 Slop Ta, 8 Wing Ta, ER 9 Cargo Pump (s): 9x300m³/hr Manifold: Bow/CM: 38.6m	**1 oil engine** driving 1 FP propeller Total Power: 1,912kW (2,600hp) 12.9kn Hanshin LH36LA 1 x 4 Stroke 6 Cy. 360 x 670 1912kW (2600bhp) The Hanshin Diesel Works Ltd-Japan AuxGen: 2 x 264kW 445/110V 60Hz a.c Fuel: 60.0 (d.f.) 206.0 (r.f.) 7.2pd
8756772 **SEVEN POLARIS** *HO2654* *ex Acergy Polaris -2012* - *ex Seaway Polaris -2006* *ex D. L. B. Polaris -2000 ex Polaris -1986* **Class 3 Shipping Ltd** Subsea 7 Contracting (UK) Ltd *Panama* *Panama* MMSI: 357492000 Official number: 17576PEXT10	**16,455** 4,936 -	Class: BV	**1979-07 Mitsui Kaiyo — Japan** Yd No: S-133 Loa 137.60 Br ex 39.01 Dght 6.490 Lbp 137.16 Br md - Dpth 9.14 Welded, 1 dk	**(B22C2OQ) Pipe Layer Crane Vessel** Passengers: berths: 263 Cranes: 1x1440t	**4 oil engines** reduction geared to sc. shafts driving 4 Directional propellers Total Power: 14,120kW (19,196hp) 11.0kn Bergens BRM-8 4 x 4 Stroke 8 Cy. 320 x 360 each-3530kW (4799bhp) AS Bergens Mek Verksteder-Norway AuxGen: 3 x 1000kW 460V a.c, 2 x 1440kW 480V a.c Thrusters: 1 Tunnel thruster (f); 1 Tunnel thruster (a) Fuel: 2900.0
8210936 **SEVEN SEAS** *HSB2703* *ex Cambridge Reefer -1999* - **Seven Seas Transport Co Ltd** - *Bangkok* *Thailand* MMSI: 567176000 Official number: 430900284	**1,876** 600 2,178	Class: LR (NK) **100A1** SS 06/2009 refrigerated cargo ship **LMC** **Lloyd's RMC** Eq.Ltr: 0; Cable: 412.5/34.0 U2 (a)	**1982-10 Tokushima Zosen Sangyo K.K. — Komatsushima** Yd No: 1552 Loa 83.90 (BB) Br ex - Dght 5.022 Lbp 78.10 Br md 13.61 Dpth 5.06 Welded, 2 dks	**(A34A2GR) Refrigerated Cargo Ship** Ins: 2,950 Compartments: 3 Ho, ER, 3 Tw Dk 3 Ha: 3 (4.8 x 4.9)ER Derricks: 6x5t	**1 oil engine** driving 1 FP propeller Total Power: 1,471kW (2,000hp) 13.5kn Akasaka A37 1 x 4 Stroke 6 Cy. 370 x 720 1471kW (2000bhp) Akasaka Tekkosho KK (Akasaka DieselLtd)-Japan AuxGen: 2 x 360kW 440V 60Hz a.c Boilers: e (ex.g.) 10.0kgf/cm² (9.8bar), AuxB (o.f.) 8.0kgf/cm² (7.8bar)
1010777 **SEVEN SEAS** *ZGAZ5* - **Little Buoy Ltd** Vessel Safety Management LLC SatCom: Inmarsat C 431972910 *George Town* *Cayman Islands (British)* MMSI: 319729000 Official number: 742942	**2,658** 797 -	Class: LR ✠ **100A1** SS 11/2010 SSC Yacht (P), mono G6 **LMC** **UMS** Cable: 550.0/34.0 U3 (a)	**2010-11 Zwijnenburg BV — Krimpen a/d IJssel** (Hull) Yd No: 706 **2010-11 Aluship Technology Sp z oo — Gdansk** (Upper part) Yd No: 706 **2010-11 Oceanco Shipyards (Alblasserdam) B.V. — Alblasserdam** Yd No: 706 Loa 84.47 (BB) Br ex 13.80 Dght 3.900 Lbp 66.57 Br md 13.80 Dpth 7.10 Welded, 1 dk	**(X11A2YP) Yacht**	**2 oil engines** with clutches, flexible couplings & sr reverse geared to sc. shafts driving 2 FP propellers Total Power: 7,200kW (9,790hp) M.T.U. 16V595TE70 2 x Vee 4 Stroke 16 Cy. 190 x 210 each-3600kW (4895bhp) MTU Friedrichshafen GmbH-Friedrichshafen AuxGen: 2 x 308kW 400V 50Hz a.c, 1 x 612kW 400V 50Hz a.c Thrusters: 1 Thwart. FP thruster (f); 1 Thwart. FP thruster (a)
9384760 **SEVEN SEAS** *2AJJ2* - **Subsea 7 Ltd** Subsea 7 International Contracting Ltd SatCom: Inmarsat C 423590834 *Douglas* *Isle of Man (British)* MMSI: 235060176 Official number: 9384760	**18,367** 5,510 11,366	Class: LR ✠ **100A1** SS 06/2013 upper deck strengthened for load of 10T/m2 helicopter landing area EP LI *IWS ✠ **LMC** **UMS** Eq.Ltr: K†; Cable: 632.5/68.0 U3 (a)	**2008-06 Merwede Shipyard BV — Hardinxveld** Yd No: 710 Loa 157.31 Br ex 28.45 Dght 8.000 Lbp 138.32 Br md 28.40 Dpth 12.50 Welded, 3 dks	**(B22C2OQ) Pipe Layer Crane Vessel** Passengers: cabins: 69 Cranes: 1x400t,1x154t,1x40t	**6 diesel electric oil engines** driving 6 gen. each 3240kW 6600V a.c Connecting to 3 elec. motors each (2950kW) driving 3 Azimuth electric drive units Total Power: 20,160kW (27,408hp) 13.0kn Wartsila 7L32 6 x 4 Stroke 7 Cy. 320 x 400 each-3360kW (4568bhp) Wartsila Nederland BV-Netherlands Boilers: TOH (o.f.) 13.3kgf/cm² (13.0bar) Thrusters: 2 Retract. directional thruster (f); 1 Thwart. FP thruster (f) Fuel: 1283.0 (d.f.) 1216.0 (r.f.)
9238521 **SEVEN SEAS HIGHWAY** *9V9950* - **Global Gate Shipping (Pte) Ltd** Taiyo Nippon Kisen Co Ltd *Singapore* *Singapore* MMSI: 566454000 Official number: 397782	**55,493** 16,648 17,232 T/cm 51.2	Class: NK	**2001-11 Imabari Shipbuilding Co Ltd — Marugame KG (Marugame Shipyard)** Yd No: 1367 Loa 199.94 (BB) Br ex - Dght 9.616 Lbp 190.00 Br md 32.20 Dpth 33.74 Welded, 12 dks	**(A35B2RV) Vehicles Carrier** Side door/ramp1 (p) 1 (s) Len: 17.00 Wid: 4.50 Swl: 20 Quarter stern door/ramp (s. a.) Len: 32.55 Wid: 7.00 Swl: 100 Cars: 6,043	**1 oil engine** driving 1 FP propeller Total Power: 13,940kW (18,953hp) 20.0kn Mitsubishi 8UEC60LSII 1 x 2 Stroke 8 Cy. 600 x 2300 13940kW (18953bhp) Kobe Hatsudoki KK-Japan AuxGen: 3 x 1200kW 450V 60Hz a.c Thrusters: 1 Thwart. FP thruster (f) Fuel: 130.3 (d.f.) (Heating Coils) 3100.4 (r.f.) 52.8pd
8301137 **SEVEN SEAS I** *HP4761* *ex Subsea 7 -2013 ex Gulf Fleet No. 67 -2006* - **Subsea Petroleum Services** - *Panama* *Panama* MMSI: 354113000 Official number: 45412PEXT	*863* 258 1,128	Class: BV (AB)	**1984-07 St Louis Ship Division of Pott Industries Inc — St Louis, Mo** Yd No: 5048 Loa 57.94 Br ex - Dght 4.180 Lbp 50.91 Br md 12.20 Dpth 4.88 Welded, 1 dk	**(B21B2OT) Offshore Tug/Supply Ship** Passengers: berths: 24 Ice Capable	**2 oil engines** reverse reduction geared to sc. shafts driving 2 FP propellers Total Power: 3,390kW (4,610hp) 9.0kn EMD (Electro-Motive) 12-645-E7B 2 x Vee 2 Stroke 12 Cy. 230 x 254 each-1695kW (2305bhp) General Motors Corp.Electro-Motive Div.-La Grange AuxGen: 2 x 99kW 60Hz a.c Thrusters: 1 Thwart. FP thruster (f)

9210139 *C6VV8* -	**SEVEN SEAS MARINER** **Mariner LLC** Prestige Cruise Services LLC *Nassau* *Bahamas* MMSI: 311622000 Official number: 8001280	**48,075** 17,600 4,700 T/cm 46.6	Class: LR (NV) (BV) **100A1** SS 03/2011 TOC contemplated	**2001-03 Chantiers de l'Atlantique — St-Nazaire** Yd No: K31 Loa 216.00 (BB) Br ex - Dght 7.000 Lbp 187.00 Br md 28.80 Dpth 16.15 Welded, 12 dks	**(A37A2PC) Passenger/Cruise** Passengers: cabins: 366; berths: 730	**4 diesel electric oil engines** driving 4 gen. each 7650kW 6600V a.c Connecting to 2 elec. motors each (8500kW) driving 2 Azimuth electric drive units Total Power: 33,600kW (45,684hp) 19.5kn Wartsila 12V38 4 x Vee 4 Stroke 12 Cy. 380 x 475 each-8400kW (11421bhp) Wartsila Nederland BV-Netherlands Thrusters: 1 Tunnel thruster (f); 1 Tunnel thruster (a) Fuel: 136.4 (d.f.) (Heating Coils) 1629.3 (r.f.) 100.0pd
9064126 *C6ZI9* -	**SEVEN SEAS NAVIGATOR** *launched as* Akademik Nikolay Pilyugin *-1999* **Navigator Vessel Co LLC** Prestige Cruise Services LLC *Nassau* *Bahamas* MMSI: 311050600 Official number: 9000380	**28,803** 9,739 3,342	Class: LR (NV) (BV) (RI) **100A1** SS 08/2009 TOC contemplated	**1999-08 Admiralteyskiy Sudostroitelnyy Zavod — Sankt-Peterburg** (Hull launched by) Yd No: 02510 **1999-08 T. Mariotti SpA — Genova** (Hull completed by) Yd No: 6125 Loa 172.00 (BB) Br ex 24.83 Dght 7.302 Lbp 150.18 Br md 24.80 Dpth 12.30 Welded	**(A37A2PC) Passenger/Cruise** Passengers: cabins: 252; berths: 530 Ice Capable	**4 oil engines** reduction geared to sc. shafts driving 2 CP propellers Total Power: 15,536kW (21,124hp) 17.5kn Wartsila 8L38 4 x 4 Stroke 8 Cy. 380 x 475 each-3884kW (5281bhp) Wartsila NSD Nederland BV-Netherlands AuxGen: 3 x 2200kW a.c Thrusters: 1 Thwart. CP thruster (f)
9247144 *C6SW3* -	**SEVEN SEAS VOYAGER** **Voyager Vessel Co LLC** Prestige Cruise Services LLC *Nassau* *Bahamas* MMSI: 311513000 Official number: 8000610	**42,363** 15,525 5,400	Class: LR (NV) (RI) **100A1** SS 01/2013 TOC contemplated	**2003-02 Cantiere Navale Visentini Srl — Porto Viro** (Hull) Yd No: MAR001 **2003-02 T. Mariotti SpA — Genova** Loa 206.50 (BB) Br ex - Dght 7.100 Lbp 177.10 Br md 28.80 Dpth 15.70 Welded	**(A37A2PC) Passenger/Cruise** Passengers: cabins: 353; berths: 730	**4 diesel electric oil engines** driving 4 gen. Connecting to 2 elec. motors each (7000kW) driving 2 Azimuth electric drive units Total Power: 23,760kW (32,304hp) 20.0kn Wartsila 6R38 4 x 4 Stroke 6 Cy. 380 x 475 each-5940kW (8076bhp) Wartsila Finland Oy-Finland Thrusters: 2 Tunnel thruster (f) Fuel: 1500.0 (r.f.) 85.0pd
9350874 *ZCOD6* -	**SEVEN SINS** **Global Corporate Charter Co Ltd** - *George Town* *Cayman Islands (British)* MMSI: 319425000 Official number: 737678	**430** 129 270	Class: AB	**2005-04 Heesen Shipyards B.V. — Oss** Yd No: 12441 Loa 41.30 Br ex 8.30 Dght 2.400 Lbp 34.27 Br md 8.00 Dpth 4.22 Welded, 1 dk	**(X11A2YP) Yacht**	**2 oil engines** reduction geared to sc. shafts driving 2 Propellers Total Power: 1,472kW (2,002hp) Caterpillar 3412TA 2 x Vee 4 Stroke 12 Cy. 137 x 152 each-736kW (1001bhp) Caterpillar Inc-USA
9320130 *FMJR* -	**SEVEN SISTERS** **DFDS A/S** - *Dieppe* *France* MMSI: 228244700 Official number: 912387	**18,425** 5,527 3,608	Class: BV	**2006-10 Hijos de J. Barreras S.A. — Vigo** Yd No: 1646 Loa 142.45 (BB) Br ex - Dght 5.900 Lbp 125.00 Br md 24.20 Dpth 8.35 Welded	**(A36A2PR) Passenger/Ro-Ro Ship (Vehicles)** Passengers: 600; cabins: 196 Bow ramp (centre) Len: 12.40 Wid: 4.20 Swl: - Stern door/ramp (p. a.) Len: 16.00 Wid: 7.00 Swl: - Stern door/ramp (s. a.) Len: 16.00 Wid: 7.00 Swl: - Trailers: 62	**2 oil engines** geared to sc. shafts driving 2 CP propellers Total Power: 18,906kW (25,704hp) 22.0kn Wartsila 9L46C 2 x 4 Stroke 9 Cy. 460 x 580 each-9453kW (12852bhp) Wartsila Diesel S.A.-Bermeo AuxGen: 3 x 1125kW 400V 50Hz a.c Thrusters: 2 Thwart. CP thruster (f) Fuel: 78.2 (d.f.) 662.2 (r.f.)
9128611 - -	**SEVEN STAR** *ex* Asaka Maru *-2003* **Sun Hwa Co Ltd** - *Incheon* *South Korea* Official number: ICR-032750	*153* - -	Class: KR	**1995-06 Kanagawa Zosen — Kobe** Yd No: 420 Loa 31.80 Br ex - Dght - Lbp 29.36 Br md 8.80 Dpth 3.83 Welded, 1 dk	**(B32A2ST) Tug**	**2 oil engines** driving 2 FP propellers Total Power: 2,280kW (3,100hp) Niigata 6L25HX 2 x 4 Stroke 6 Cy. 250 x 350 each-1140kW (1550bhp) Niigata Engineering Co Ltd-Japan
8211198 *J8B3083* -	**SEVEN STAR** *ex* Aras III *-2007* *ex* Laura *-2004* *ex* Ilka *-1998* **High Seas Group Ltd** Haifa Marine Shipping Ltd *Kingstown* *St Vincent & The Grenadines* MMSI: 376001700 Official number: 9555	**1,939** 971 3,089	Class: RS (GL)	**1982-12 J.J. Sietas KG Schiffswerft GmbH & Co. — Hamburg** Yd No: 907 Loa 87.97 (BB) Br ex 11.33 Dght 4.880 Lbp 85.37 Br md 11.31 Dpth 6.70 Welded, 2 dks	**(A31A2GX) General Cargo Ship** Grain: 3,806; Bale: 3,763 TEU 90 C.Ho 54/20' C.Dk 36/20' Compartments: 1 Ho, ER 1 Ha: (55.9 x 9.3)ER	**1 oil engine** reverse reduction geared to sc. shaft driving 1 FP propeller Total Power: 734kW (998hp) 9.0kn Deutz SBV8M628 1 x 4 Stroke 8 Cy. 240 x 280 734kW (998bhp) Kloeckner Humboldt Deutz AG-West Germany AuxGen: 2 x 152kW 380V 50Hz a.c, 1 x 73kW 380V 50Hz a.c Thrusters: 1 Thwart. FP thruster (f) Fuel: 145.0 (r.f.) 45.0 (d.f.)
8304282 - -	**SEVEN STAR 1** *ex* Tokuhiro Maru No. 51 *-1993* **Primero Naviera Industria SA** - *San Lorenzo* *Honduras* Official number: L-1925307	**116** 53 -		**1983-05 Tokushima Zosen K.K. — Fukuoka** Yd No: 1500 Loa 40.52 Br ex - Dght 3.120 Lbp 33.51 Br md 6.71 Dpth 3.13 Welded, 1 dk	**(B11A2FS) Stern Trawler** Ins: 79	**1 oil engine** with clutches, flexible couplings & sr reverse geared to sc. shaft driving 1 CP propeller Total Power: 699kW (950hp) Niigata 6M28AFTE 1 x 4 Stroke 6 Cy. 280 x 480 699kW (950bhp) Niigata Engineering Co Ltd-Japan
8304294 - -	**SEVEN STAR 2** *ex* Tokuhiro Maru No. 52 *-1993* **Primero Naviera Industria SA** - *San Lorenzo* *Honduras* Official number: L-1925308	**116** 53 -		**1983-05 Tokushima Zosen K.K. — Fukuoka** Yd No: 1501 Loa 40.52 Br ex - Dght 3.120 Lbp 33.51 Br md 6.71 Dpth 3.13 Welded, 1 dk	**(B11A2FS) Stern Trawler** Ins: 79	**1 oil engine** with clutches, flexible couplings & sr reverse geared to sc. shaft driving 1 CP propeller Total Power: 699kW (950hp) Niigata 6M28AFTE 1 x 4 Stroke 6 Cy. 280 x 480 699kW (950bhp) Niigata Engineering Co Ltd-Japan
9619373 *LCPX* -	**SEVEN VIKING** **Eidesvik Seven AS** Eidesvik AS *Haugesund* *Norway* MMSI: 257973000	**11,266** 3,379 5,125	Class: NV	**2013-01 ATVT Sudnobudivnyi Zavod "Zaliv" — Kerch** (Hull) Yd No: (295) **2013-01 Ulstein Verft AS — Ulsteinvik** Yd No: 295 Loa 106.50 Br ex - Dght 8.000 Lbp 100.00 Br md 24.50 Dpth 11.50 Welded, 1 dk	**(B22A2OR) Offshore Support Vessel** Cranes: 1x135t Ice Capable	**4 diesel electric oil engines** driving 2 gen. each 4320kW a.c 2 gen. each 1824kW a.c Connecting to 3 elec. motors each (3000kW) driving 3 Azimuth electric drive units Contra-rotating Total Power: 12,960kW (17,620hp) 16.0kn MaK 6M25 2 x 4 Stroke 6 Cy. 255 x 400 each-1980kW (2692bhp) Caterpillar Motoren GmbH & Co. KG-Germany MaK 9M32C 2 x 4 Stroke 9 Cy. 320 x 480 each-4500kW (6118bhp) Caterpillar Motoren GmbH & Co. KG-Germany Thrusters: 2 Retract. directional thruster (f); 1 Tunnel thruster (f) Fuel: 2100.0 (d.f.)
9649029 *2GZA5* -	**SEVEN WAVES** **Subsea 7 Gestao Brazil SA** Subsea 7 International Contracting Ltd *Douglas* *Isle of Man (British)* MMSI: 235101697 Official number: 743895	**17,283** 5,185 11,312	Class: LR (Class contemplated) **100A1** 03/2014	**2014-03 IHC Offshore & Marine BV — Krimpen a/d IJssel** Yd No: 727 Loa 145.95 Br ex - Dght 8.300 Lbp 134.72 Br md 29.94 Dpth 13.00 Welded, 1 dk	**(B22C2OX) Pipe Layer** Passengers: unberthed: 120 Cranes: 1x400t,1x25t	**6 diesel electric oil engines** driving 6 gen. each 3840kW Connecting to 3 elec. motors each (2950kW) driving 3 Azimuth electric drive units Total Power: 23,040kW (31,326hp) 13.0kn Wartsila 8L32 6 x 4 Stroke 8 Cy. 320 x 400 each-3840kW (5221bhp) Wartsila Finland Oy-Finland Thrusters: 2 Tunnel thruster (f); 2 Retract. directional thruster (f) Fuel: 2197.0 (d.f.)
7800112 *3FZN* -	**SEVENHILL** *ex* Kibris Gunesi *-2012* *ex* Moondance *-2009* *ex* Merchant Victor *-1997* *ex* Emadala *-1990* **Sevenhill Maritime Inc** - *Panama* *Panama* MMSI: 351349000 Official number: 4372312	**5,881** 1,764 3,046	Class: GS (NV) (TL) (GL)	**1978-11 Rickmers Rhederei GmbH Rickmers Werft — Bremerhaven** Yd No: 395 Loa 116.30 (BB) Br ex 18.22 Dght 5.360 Lbp 103.00 Br md 17.42 Dpth 12.22 Welded, 2 dks	**(A35A2RR) Ro-Ro Cargo Ship** Stern door/ramp (centre) Len: 9.00 Wid: 8.00 Swl: 50 Lane-Len: 852 Cars: 37, Trailers: 71 Grain: 14,038; Bale: 12,995 TEU 210 incl 40 ref C. Ice Capable	**2 oil engines** reduction geared to sc. shafts driving 2 CP propellers Total Power: 4,414kW (6,002hp) 15.5kn MaK 8M453AK 2 x 4 Stroke 8 Cy. 320 x 420 each-2207kW (3001bhp) MaK Maschinenbau GmbH-Kiel AuxGen: 2 x 560kW a.c Thrusters: 1 Thwart. FP thruster (f) Fuel: 77.4 (d.f.) (Heating Coils) 423.7 (r.f.) 21.0pd
8728749 *UBME6* -	**SEVER** **Ecosoyuz Co Ltd** - *Murmansk* *Russia*	**204** 83 264	Class: RS	**1985-12 Sudoremontnyy Zavod "Yakor" — Sovetskaya Gavan** Yd No: 780 Loa 36.01 Br ex 7.65 Dght 2.500 Lbp 35.50 Br md 7.42 Dpth 3.10 Welded, 1 dk	**(B35E2TF) Bunkering Tanker** Liq: 253; Liq (Oil): 253 Compartments: 1 Ho, 6 Ta Ice Capable	**1 oil engine** geared to sc. shaft driving 1 FP propeller Total Power: 165kW (224hp) 7.0kn Daldizel 6CHNSP18/22 1 x 4 Stroke 6 Cy. 180 x 220 165kW (224bhp) Daldizel-Khabarovsk AuxGen: 1 x 30kW Fuel: 7.0 (d.f.)

8860690 **SEVER**
UIMK
\- **Nord Stream Ltd**
\-
Murmansk *Russia*
MMSI: 273558500
Official number: 910373
104 31 58
Class: (RS)
1991 Azovskaya Sudoverf — Azov Yd No: 1050
Loa 26.50 Br ex 6.59 Dght 2.360
Lbp 22.90 Br md 6.50 Dpth 3.05
Welded, 1 dk
(B11A2FS) Stern Trawler
Ins: 48
Ice Capable
1 oil engine geared to sc. shaft driving 1 FP propeller
Total Power: 165kW (224hp) 9.3kn
Daldizel 6CHNSP18/22
1 x 4 Stroke 6 Cy. 180 x 220 165kW (224bhp)
Daldizel-Khabarovsk
AuxGen: 2 x 30kW
Fuel: 9.0 (d.f.)

9353917 **SEVERINA**
UBWF6
\- **'Urengoygidromekhanizatsiya' JSC**
Taganrog *Russia*
MMSI: 273337330
659 157 92
Class: RS
2011-09 OAO Sudostroitelnyy Zavod 'Liman' — Nikolayev Yd No: 20-072
Loa 47.26 Br ex - Dght 1.980
Lbp 42.67 Br md 9.60 Dpth 3.97
Welded, 1 dk
(B34J2SD) Crew Boat
Ice Capable
2 oil engines reduction geared to sc. shafts driving 2 FP propellers
Total Power: 1,552kW (2,110hp) 14.0kn
AuxGen: 2 x 86kW a.c
Fuel: 80.0

9539078 **SEVERINE**
PCMU
\- **Shiplux VIII SA**
EuroShip Services Ltd
Hoek van Holland *Netherlands*
MMSI: 246171000
16,342 4,902 6,600
Class: BV
2012-01 Kyokuyo Shipyard Corp — Shimonoseki YC Yd No: 501
Loa 152.00 (BB) Br ex - Dght 5.400
Lbp 142.00 Br md 22.00 Dpth 16.20
Welded, 3 dks
(A35A2RR) Ro-Ro Cargo Ship
Stern door/ramp (centre)
Len: 14.50 Wid: 18.00 Swl: 150
Lane-Len: 1760
Lane-clr ht: 7.00
1 oil engine reduction geared to sc. shaft driving 1 CP propeller
Total Power: 7,000kW (9,517hp) 16.0kn
Wartsila 16V32
1 x Vee 4 Stroke 16 Cy. 320 x 400 7000kW (9517bhp)
Wartsila Finland Oy-Finland
AuxGen: 3 x 500kW 60Hz a.c
Thrusters: 1 Tunnel thruster (f); 1 Tunnel thruster (a)
Fuel: 760.0

9544231 **SEVERN**
WDE5806
\- **Vane Line Bunkering Inc**
Baltimore, MD *United States of America*
MMSI: 367371840
Official number: 1212431
327 98 200
2010-04 Thoma-Sea Marine Constructors LLC — Houma LA Yd No: 139
Loa 30.49 Br ex - Dght -
Lbp 30.26 Br md 10.37 Dpth 4.57
Welded, 1 dk
(B32B2SP) Pusher Tug
2 oil engines reverse reduction geared to sc. shafts driving 2 FP propellers
Total Power: 3,282kW (4,462hp)
Caterpillar 3516
2 x Vee 4 Stroke 16 Cy. 170 x 190 each-1641kW (2231bhp)
Caterpillar Inc-USA

8652043 **SEVERN SEA**
2DCG5
\- *ex Vista 5 -2010 ex Kalvsund -2010*
ex Mul 11 -1985
Severn Subsea Ltd
Keynvor Morlift Ltd
Bideford *United Kingdom*
MMSI: 235077754
Official number: 911453
147 44 -
1947 AB Gavle Varv — Gavle
Converted From: Minelayer-2011
Loa 30.14 Br ex - Dght 2.500
Lbp - Br md 7.21 Dpth 3.60
Welded, 1 dk
(B31A2SR) Research Survey Vessel
Passengers: 12
Cranes: 1
2 oil engines reduction geared to sc. shafts driving 2 FP propellers
Total Power: 558kW (758hp) 10.0kn
Volvo Penta TAMD122A
2 x 4 Stroke 6 Cy. 130 x 150 each-279kW (379bhp) (new engine 0000)
AB Volvo Penta-Sweden
AuxGen: 1 x 120kW a.c
Thrusters: 1 Tunnel thruster

7391628 **SEVERNAYA**
UDWX
\- **NSF Ltd**
Novorossiysk *Russia*
MMSI: 273435350
1,191 357 700
Class: RS
1977-03 Brodogradiliste 'Tito' — Belgrade Yd No: 904
Loa 68.20 Br ex 12.30 Dght 3.452
Lbp 63.40 Br md 11.99 Dpth 4.50
Welded, 1 dk
(B33A2DB) Bucket Ladder Dredger
Ice Capable
2 diesel electric oil engines Connecting to 2 elec. motors each (380kW) driving 2 FP propellers
Total Power: 1,700kW (2,312hp)
B&W 7-26MTBF-40
2 x 4 Stroke 7 Cy. 260 x 400 each-850kW (1156bhp)
Titovi Zavodi 'Litostroj'-Yugoslavia
AuxGen: 2 x 288kW, 1 x 100kW
Fuel: 219.0 (d.f.)

8206545 **SEVERNAYA ZEMLYA**
UBSE8
\- *ex Arneles -2007*
Zakharov-Vaqueiro Co Ltd
Pesquera Vaqueiro SA
Murmansk *Russia*
MMSI: 273340810
1,345 449 796
Class: BV
1984-08 Astilleros Gondan SA — Castropol Yd No: 234
Loa 73.80 Br ex - Dght 4.810
Lbp 66.70 Br md 10.51 Dpth 7.00
Welded, 1 dk
(B11B2FV) Fishing Vessel
Ins: 940
1 oil engine geared to sc. shaft driving 1 FP propeller
Total Power: 1,361kW (1,850hp) 12.3kn
Deutz RBV6M358
1 x 4 Stroke 6 Cy. 400 x 580 1361kW (1850bhp)
Hijos de J Barreras SA-Spain
AuxGen: 3 x 260kW 380V 50Hz a.c
Fuel: 750.0 (d.f.)

9551923 **SEVERNAYA ZEMLYA**
UBVF4
\- *completed as Victory -2009*
Murmansk Shipping Co (MSC)
\-
Murmansk *Russia*
MMSI: 273337230
15,868 7,206 23,645
Class: RS
2009-04 Chengxi Shipyard Co Ltd — Jiangyin JS Yd No: CX4267
Loa 180.50 Br ex 22.90 Dght 9.910
Lbp 173.28 Br md 22.86 Dpth 13.50
Welded, 1 dk
(A21A2BC) Bulk Carrier
Grain: 25,445
TEU 520
Compartments: 7 Ho, ER
7 Ha: 6 (12.8 x 13.5)ER (12.8 x 10.8)
Ice Capable
1 oil engine driving 1 FP propeller
Total Power: 9,480kW (12,889hp) 13.0kn
MAN-B&W 6S50MC-C
1 x 2 Stroke 6 Cy. 500 x 2000 9480kW (12889bhp)
AO Bryanskiy MashinostroitelnyyZavod (BMZ)-Bryansk
AuxGen: 3 x 680kW 60Hz a.c
Fuel: 1220.0 (r.f.)

8929434 **SEVERNAYA ZVEZDA**
UICK
\- **North Star Fishing Collective (Rybolovetskiy Kolhoz 'Severnaya Zvezda')**
\-
Murmansk *Russia*
MMSI: 273215000
Official number: 920642
743 217 414
Class: (RS)
1994-05 ATVT Zavod "Leninska Kuznya" — Kyyiv Yd No: 1660
Loa 54.82 Br ex 10.15 Dght 4.140
Lbp 50.30 Br md 9.80 Dpth 5.00
Welded, 1 dk
(B11A2FS) Stern Trawler
Ins: 400
Ice Capable
1 oil engine driving 1 CP propeller
Total Power: 852kW (1,158hp) 12.0kn
S.K.L. 8NVD48A-2U
1 x 4 Stroke 8 Cy. 320 x 480 852kW (1158bhp)
SKL Motoren u. Systemtechnik AG-Magdeburg
AuxGen: 4 x 160kW a.c
Fuel: 155.0 (d.f.)

8957285 **SEVERNOYE PRIMORYE**
\- *ex Liao Da Gan Yu 8714 -2000*
\- **Fasco Rybflot JSC**
115 39 85
Class: (RS)
1999-05 Rongcheng Shipbuilding Industry Co Ltd — Rongcheng SD Yd No: Y040199523
Loa 34.00 Br ex - Dght 2.100
Lbp 29.62 Br md 6.00 Dpth 2.70
Welded, 1 dk
(B11B2FV) Fishing Vessel
1 oil engine geared to sc. shaft driving 1 CP propeller
Total Power: 220kW (299hp) 11.5kn
Chinese Std. Type Z6170ZL
1 x 4 Stroke 6 Cy. 170 x 200 220kW (299bhp)
Zibo Diesel Engine Factory-China
AuxGen: 2 x 12kW
Fuel: 42.0 (d.f.)

8770998 **SEVERNOYE SIYANIYE**
UBUG3
\- **JSC Gazprom**
OOO Gazflot
Murmansk *Russia*
MMSI: 273354210
54,450 16,335 9,282
Class: RS
2011-06 Samsung Heavy Industries Co Ltd — Geoje (Hull) Yd No: 7075
2011-06 OAO Vyborgskiy Sudostroitelnyy Zavod — Vyborg Yd No: 107
Loa 122.54 Br ex 91.97 Dght 23.500
Lbp 118.56 Br md 72.72 Dpth 36.15
Welded, 1 dk
(Z11C3ZE) Drilling Rig, semi Submersible
6 diesel electric oil engines driving 6 gen. each 5200kW a.c Connecting to 4 elec. motors driving 4 Propellers
Total Power: 31,200kW (42,420hp)
Caterpillar 3616
6 x Vee 4 Stroke 16 Cy. 280 x 300 each-5200kW (7070bhp)
Caterpillar Inc-USA
Thrusters: 4 Thwart. FP thruster

8892306 **SEVERODONETSK**
UFVM
\- **JSC 'Lesosibirsk Port' (OAO Lesosibirskiy Port)**
JSC Yenisey River Shipping Co (A/O Yeniseyskoye Parokhodstvo)
Taganrog *Russia*
MMSI: 273314400
1,652 622 2,072
Class: RR
1964-08 Zavody Tazkeho Strojarstva (ZTS) — Komarno Yd No: 2050
Loa 103.60 Br ex 12.40 Dght 2.780
Lbp 100.05 Br md 12.20 Dpth 4.90
Welded, 1 dk
(A31A2GX) General Cargo Ship
2 oil engines driving 2 FP propellers
Total Power: 772kW (1,050hp)
Skoda 6L275PN
2 x 4 Stroke 6 Cy. 275 x 360 each-386kW (525bhp)
CKD Praha-Praha

8883965 **SEVERODVINETS**
\-
\- **Zvezda-DISSK Co Ltd (Far-Eastern Engineering Shipbuilding Co)**
Vladivostok *Russia*
Official number: 772838
187 - 46
Class: RS
1978 Gorokhovetskiy Sudostroitelnyy Zavod — Gorokhovets Yd No: 362
Loa 29.30 Br ex 8.49 Dght 3.090
Lbp 27.00 Br md 8.30 Dpth 4.30
Welded, 1 dk
(B32A2ST) Tug
Ice Capable
2 oil engines driving 2 CP propellers
Total Power: 882kW (1,200hp) 11.4kn
Russkiy 6D30/50-4-3
2 x 2 Stroke 6 Cy. 300 x 500 each-441kW (600bhp)
Mashinostroitelnyy Zavod"Russkiy-Dizel"-Leningrad
AuxGen: 2 x 30kW a.c
Fuel: 36.0 (d.f.)

6521915 **SEVERODVINSKIY**
\-
\- **Quor Construction Ltd**
JSC Chernomortekhflot
Ukraine
MMSI: 272725000
1,944 583 1,702
Class: (LR) (RS)
✠ Classed LR until 6/68
1966-09 Alexander Stephen & Sons Ltd — Glasgow Yd No: 686
Loa 82.05 Br ex 14.28 Dght 4.128
Lbp 76.82 Br md 13.72 Dpth 5.19
Welded, 1 dk
(B33B2DT) Trailing Suction Hopper Dredger
Hopper: 1,183
1 Ha: ER
Derricks: 2x6t
Ice Capable
2 diesel electric oil engines driving 2 gen. each 1000kW 835V Connecting to 2 elec. motors driving 2 FP propellers
Total Power: 2,206kW (3,000hp) 11.5kn
Mirrlees KSSDM-6
2 x 4 Stroke 6 Cy. 381 x 457 each-1103kW (1500bhp)
Mirrlees National Ltd.-Stockport
AuxGen: 1 x 350kW 220/380V 50Hz a.c, 2 x 150kW 220/380V 50Hz a.c
Thrusters: 1 Thwart. FP thruster (f)
Fuel: 230.0 (d.f.)

8860705 **SEVERYANIN**
UCSL
\- **Bagaj Co Ltd**
\-
Murmansk *Russia*
MMSI: 273550300
104 31 58
Class: (RS)
1992-06 AO Azovskaya Sudoverf — Azov Yd No: 1057
Loa 26.50 Br ex 6.95 Dght 2.360
Lbp 22.90 Br md 6.50 Dpth 3.05
Welded, 1 dk
(B11A2FS) Stern Trawler
Ins: 48
Ice Capable
1 oil engine geared to sc. shaft driving 1 FP propeller
Total Power: 165kW (224hp) 9.3kn
Daldizel 6CHNSP18/22
1 x 4 Stroke 6 Cy. 180 x 220 165kW (224bhp)
Daldizel-Khabarovsk
AuxGen: 2 x 30kW
Fuel: 9.0 (d.f.)

7311824 *UBIX* -	**SEVERYANIN II** *ex* Lofottral II *-2003* **Murmanrybflot-2 JSC (ZAO 'Murmanrybflot-2')** - SatCom: Inmarsat C 427322722 *Murmansk* *Russia* MMSI: 273448120 Official number: MI-0830	**546** 163 328	Class: NV RS	**1973-03 AS Storviks Mek. Verksted — Kristiansund** Yd No: 52 Loa 46.54 Br ex 9.02 Dght 4.534 Lbp 42.65 Br md 9.00 Dpth 6.51 Welded, 2 dks	**(B11A2FS) Stern Trawler** Compartments: 1 Ho, ER 1 Ha: (2.5 x 1.9)ER Ice Capable	**1 oil engine** driving 1 CP propeller Total Power: 1,103kW (1,500hp) 12.5kn Deutz RBV8M545 1 x 4 Stroke 8 Cy. 320 x 450 1103kW (1500bhp) Kloeckner Humboldt Deutz AG-West Germany AuxGen: 2 x 132kW 220V 50Hz a.c Fuel: 142.0 (d.f.) 5.0pd
8929472 - -	**SEVERYANKA** - **Murmansk Marine Fishing Port ('Murmanskiy Morskoy Rybnyy Port')** - *Murmansk* *Russia* MMSI: 273449020 Official number: 780904	*950* 495 1,621	Class: (RS)	**1978-09 Shipbuilding & Shiprepairing Yard 'Ivan Dimitrov' — Rousse** Yd No: 129 Loa 60.55 Br ex 11.00 Dght 4.780 Lbp 56.67 Br md - Dpth 5.50 Welded, 1 dk	**(B35E2TF) Bunkering Tanker** Liq: 1,701; Liq (Oil): 1,701 Compartments: 12 Ta, ER Ice Capable	**2 oil engines** driving 2 FP propellers Total Power: 448kW (610hp) 9.0kn S.K.L. 8NVD36-1U 2 x 4 Stroke 8 Cy. 240 x 360 each-224kW (305bhp) VEB Schwermaschinenbau "KarlLiebknecht" (SKL)-Magdeburg AuxGen: 1 x 34kW a.c, 2 x 25kW a.c Fuel: 129.0 (d.f.)
9458406 *VRLT7* -	**SEVGI** *ex* Consuela *-2013* **Sergio Ltd** Istanbul Denizcilik ve Deniz Tasimaciligi AS *Hong Kong* *Hong Kong* MMSI: 477486700	**20,965** 10,262 28,164	Class: GL	**2012-02 Huanghai Shipbuilding Co Ltd — Rongcheng SD** Yd No: HCY-86 Loa 166.40 (BB) Br ex - Dght 10.100 Lbp 158.32 Br md 27.40 Dpth 14.20 Welded, 1 dk	**(A31A2GX) General Cargo Ship** Grain: 38,319; Bale: 38,319 TEU 1746 Compartments: 4 Ho, ER 4 Ha: (24.9 x 23.0)2 (33.6 x 23.0)ER (19.0 x 18.0) Cranes: 2x200t,1x45t Ice Capable	**1 oil engine** driving 1 FP propeller Total Power: 6,810kW (9,259hp) 15.2kn MAN-B&W 6S40ME-B9 1 x 2 Stroke 6 Cy. 400 x 1770 6810kW (9259bhp) STX Engine Co Ltd-South Korea
7534505 *TCBT9* -	**SEVGIN** *ex* Fouad I *-1997* *ex* Skoni *-1995* *ex* Rea Spirit *-1993* *ex* Pronos *-1981* *ex* Sea Thand X *-1976* *ex* Rakusui Maru *-1976* **Azim Denizcilik Ticaret ve Sanayi Ltd Sti** - *Istanbul* *Turkey* Official number: 7054	*926* 544 1,588	Class: (HR)	**1965 Kurushima Dock Co. Ltd. — Japan** Yd No: 325 Loa 64.85 Br ex 10.04 Dght 4.217 Lbp 60.00 Br md 10.01 Dpth 5.31 Welded, 1 dk	**(A31A2GX) General Cargo Ship** Grain: 2,192; Bale: 2,097 Compartments: 1 Ho, ER 1 Ha: (34.0 x 6.4)	**1 oil engine** driving 1 FP propeller Total Power: 736kW (1,001hp) 10.0kn AuxGen: 2 x 25kW 225V a.c
9078488 *A8VF2* -	**SEVILLA CARRIER** - **Sevilla Shipping Corp** Norbulk Shipping UK Ltd *Monrovia* *Liberia* MMSI: 636014597 Official number: 14597	**5,994** 3,362 7,252	Class: NK	**1994-04 Kyokuyo Shipyard Corp — Shimonoseki YC** Yd No: 387 Loa 134.01 (BB) Br ex 20.23 Dght 7.116 Lbp 127.00 Br md 20.20 Dpth 9.93 Welded, 1 dk	**(A34A2GR) Refrigerated Cargo Ship** Bale: 8,729; Ins: 8,729 TEU 98 incl 98 ref C Compartments: 4 Ho, ER 4 Ha: 4 (7.3 x 7.0)ER Derricks: 8x5t	**1 oil engine** driving 1 FP propeller Total Power: 8,253kW (11,221hp) 18.5kn Mitsubishi 6UEC50LSII 1 x 2 Stroke 6 Cy. 500 x 1950 8253kW (11221bhp) Kobe Hatsudoki KK-Japan Fuel: 1150.0 (r.f.)
9414632 *EANB* -	**SEVILLA KNUTSEN** - **Norspan LNG VI AS** Knutsen OAS Shipping AS *Santa Cruz de Tenerife* *Spain (CSR)* MMSI: 224072000	**110,920** 34,573 97,730	Class: NV	**2010-05 Daewoo Shipbuilding & Marine Engineering Co Ltd — Geoje** Yd No: 2269 Loa 290.00 (BB) Br ex - Dght 12.900 Lbp 279.00 Br md 45.80 Dpth 26.50 Welded, 1 dk	**(A11A2TN) LNG Tanker** Liq (Gas): 173,400 4 x Gas Tank (s); 4 membrane (36% Ni.stl) pri horizontal 8 Cargo Pump (s)	**4 diesel electric oil engines** driving 3 gen. each 9778kW 6600V a.c 1 gen. of 8889kW 6600V a.c Connecting to 2 elec. motors each (13600kW) driving 2 FP propellers Total Power: 43,650kW (59,345hp) 19.5kn Wartsila 12V50DF 3 x Vee 4 Stroke 12 Cy. 500 x 580 each-11400kW (15499bhp) Wartsila Italia SpA-Italy Wartsila 9L50DF 1 x 4 Stroke 9 Cy. 500 x 580 9450kW (12848bhp) Wartsila Italia SpA-Italy Fuel: 6100.0 (r.f.)
9064592 - -	**SEVILLA UNO** - - *Morocco*	**151** - -		**1992-12 Montajes Cies S.L. — Vigo** Yd No: 6 Loa 27.50 Br ex - Dght 3.150 Lbp 22.00 Br md 6.50 Dpth 3.20 Welded	**(B11B2FV) Fishing Vessel**	**1 oil engine** driving 1 FP propeller Total Power: 320kW (435hp) Mitsubishi 1 x 320kW (435bhp) Mitsubishi Heavy Industries Ltd-Japan
8112976 - -	**SEVILLA WAVE** - -	**15,933** 10,335 26,858 T/cm 35.2	Class: (LR) ✠ Classed LR until 31/8/04	**1986-11 Astilleros Espanoles SA (AESA) — Seville** Yd No: 258 Loa 183.09 (BB) Br ex 22.46 Dght 10.511 Lbp 171.69 Br md 22.41 Dpth 14.23 Welded, 1 dk	**(A21A2BC) Bulk Carrier** Grain: 35,553; Bale: 30,263 Compartments: 7 Ho, ER 7 Ha: (10.1 x 11.4) (12.0 x 11.4) (8.0 x 11.4)2 (13.6 x 11.4) (14.4 x 11.4) (8.8 x 11.4)ER Cranes: 4x16t	**1 oil engine** driving 1 FP propeller Total Power: 7,000kW (9,517hp) 17.8kn Sulzer 5RND68M 1 x 2 Stroke 5 Cy. 680 x 1250 7000kW (9517bhp) Astilleros Espanoles SA (AESA)-Spain AuxGen: 3 x 460kW 440V 60Hz a.c Boilers: AuxB (Comp) 6.4kgf/cm² (6.3bar) Fuel: 150.0 (d.f.) 1259.5 (r.f.)
9362712 *A8OO9* -	**SEVILLIA** *launched as* Manchester Strait *-2008* **ms 'Sevillia' GmbH & Co KG** Ahrenkiel Shipmanagement GmbH & Co KG *Monrovia* *Liberia* MMSI: 636091493 Official number: 91493	**21,018** 9,156 25,884	Class: GL	**2008-01 Taizhou Kouan Shipbuilding Co Ltd — Taizhou JS** Yd No: KA506 Loa 179.74 (BB) Br ex 27.65 Dght 10.700 Lbp 167.20 Br md 27.60 Dpth 15.90 Welded, 1 dk	**(A33A2CC) Container Ship (Fully Cellular)** TEU 1794 C Ho 740 TEU C Dk 1054 TEU incl 319 ref C Cranes: 2x40t	**1 oil engine** driving 1 FP propeller Total Power: 16,664kW (22,656hp) 20.5kn MAN-B&W 7S60MC-C 1 x 2 Stroke 7 Cy. 600 x 2400 16664kW (22656bhp) Hudong Heavy Machinery Co Ltd-China AuxGen: 2 x 1709kW 450V a.c, 1 x 1330kW 450V a.c Thrusters: 1 Tunnel thruster (f)
6719756 *TCZX5* -	**SEVIM TURAN** *ex* Mehmet Sefa *-2011* *ex* Alkor-1 *-2010* *ex* Argo *-2001* *ex* Baltiyskiy-47 *-1997* *ex* Swift *-1993* *ex* Baltiyskiy-47 *-1991* **HNT Denizcilik ve Ticaret Ltd Sti** - SatCom: Inmarsat C 427101173 *Istanbul* *Turkey* MMSI: 271042591	**1,998** 1,012 3,007	Class: IS TL (RS)	**1966-03 Gorokhovetskiy Sudostroitelnyy Zavod — Gorokhovets** Yd No: 415 Loa 96.02 Br ex 13.21 Dght 4.170 Lbp 92.00 Br md 13.01 Dpth 5.52 Welded, 1 dk	**(A31A2GX) General Cargo Ship** Bale: 3,467 Compartments: 3 Ho, ER 3 Ha: 3 (16.5 x 9.3)ER Ice Capable	**2 oil engines** driving 2 FP propellers Total Power: 970kW (1,318hp) 10.0kn S.K.L. 6NVD48A-U 2 x 4 Stroke 6 Cy. 320 x 480 each-485kW (659bhp) VEB Schwermaschinenbau "KarlLiebknecht" (SKL)-Magdeburg AuxGen: 3 x 50kW a.c Fuel: 116.0 (d.f.)
9334313 *TCPK8* -	**SEVKETTIN SONAY** - **Haciogullari Hazir Beton Sac ve Yapi Malzemeleri Sanayi ve Ticaret AS** Sonay Denizcilik Ltd Sti (Sonay Shipping Co Ltd) *Istanbul* *Turkey* MMSI: 271000875	**9,490** 4,537 13,250	Class: BV	**2006-09 Celiktekne Sanayii ve Ticaret A.S. — Tuzla, Istanbul** Yd No: 59 Loa 143.41 (BB) Br ex - Dght 8.300 Lbp 143.00 Br md 21.70 Dpth 11.10 Welded, 1 dk	**(A31A2GX) General Cargo Ship** Grain: 16,306 Compartments: 4 Ho, ER 4 Ha: ER Cranes: 3x30t	**1 oil engine** driving 1 CP propeller Total Power: 4,440kW (6,037hp) 14.0kn MAN-B&W 6S35MC 1 x 2 Stroke 6 Cy. 350 x 1400 4440kW (6037bhp) MAN B&W Diesel A/S-Denmark AuxGen: 1 x 600kW a.c Thrusters: 1 Tunnel thruster (f)
8729810 *UHBY* -	**SEVMORPUT** - **Government of The Russian Federation** Federal State Unitary Enterprise 'Atomflot' SatCom: Inmarsat C 427321975 *Murmansk* *Russia* MMSI: 273137100 Official number: 840293	**38,226** 11,468 33,980	Class: (RS)	**1988-12 Sudostroitelnyy Zavod "Zaliv" — Kerch** Yd No: 401 Converted From: Barge Carrier-2006 Loa 260.31 Br ex - Dght 11.800 Lbp 236.61 Br md 32.21 Dpth 18.32 Welded, 1 dk	**(A31A2GX) General Cargo Ship** Barges/Lighters: 74 Gantry cranes: 1x500t Ice Capable	**1 Steam Turb** geared to sc. shaft driving 1 CP propeller Total Power: 21,625kW (29,401hp) 20.5kn Russkiy 1 x steam Turb 21625kW (29401shp) in the U.S.S.R. Boilers: NR New
8801187 *UCFU* MI-0001	**SEVRYBA-1** *launched as* Bjergun Senior *-1995* **Virma Co Ltd (OOO 'Virma')** - *Murmansk* *Russia* MMSI: 273523100	**1,448** 555 868	Class: RS (NV)	**1995-06 Construcciones Navales Santodomingo SA — Vigo** (Hull) Yd No: 566 **1995-06 Baatbygg AS — Raudeberg** Loa 56.40 (BB) Br ex - Dght 5.715 Lbp 50.41 Br md 11.90 Dpth 7.13 Welded, 2 dks	**(B11A2FS) Stern Trawler** Ins: 425 Ice Capable	**1 oil engine** sr geared to sc. shaft driving 1 CP propeller Total Power: 2,199kW (2,990hp) 13.0kn Wartsila 6R32D 1 x 4 Stroke 6 Cy. 320 x 350 2199kW (2990bhp) Construcciones Echevarria SA-Spain AuxGen: 1 x 1000kW 230/450V 60Hz a.c, 2 x 680kW 230/450V 60Hz a.c Thrusters: 1 Thwart. FP thruster (f)
9549982 *UBKF3* -	**SEVRYUGA** - **JSC 'Transportno-Logisticheskiy Kompleks'** - *St Petersburg* *Russia* MMSI: 273335020	**188** 56 119	Class: RS	**2008-12 OAO Leningradskiy Sudostroitelnyy Zavod 'Pella' — Otradnoye** Yd No: 916 Loa 25.40 Br ex 9.30 Dght 3.280 Lbp 23.40 Br md 8.80 Dpth 4.30 Welded, 1 dk	**(B32A2ST) Tug**	**2 oil engines** geared to sc. shafts driving 2 CP propellers Total Power: 2,984kW (4,058hp) 12.0kn Cummins KTA-50-M2 2 x Vee 4 Stroke 16 Cy. 159 x 159 each-1492kW (2029bhp) Cummins Engine Co Ltd-United Kingdom AuxGen: 2 x 84kW Fuel: 83.0 (d.f.)

IMO / Call sign	Name / Owner	Tonnage	Class	Builder / Dimensions	Type	Machinery
7222956 - -	**SEWA** - -	*392* 109 186	Class: (LR) ✠ Classed LR until 23/8/85	**1972**-10 **Scheepswerf en Machinefabriek "De Liesbosch" B.V. — Nieuwegein** Yd No: 132 Loa 36.58 Br ex 9.99 Dght 3.849 Lbp 33.28 Br md 9.45 Dpth 4.50 Welded, 1 dk	**(B32A2ST) Tug**	**2 oil engines** reverse reduction geared to sc. shafts driving 2 FP propellers Total Power: 1,618kW (2,200hp) 12.0kn Deutz SBA8M528 2 x 4 Stroke 8 Cy. 220 x 280 each-809kW (1100bhp) Kloeckner Humboldt Deutz AG-West Germany AuxGen: 2 x 128kW 415V 50Hz a.c, 1 x 50kW 415V 50Hz a.c
9025613 - -	**SEWALI** **PT Etam Kalimantan Raya** - *Balikpapan* *Indonesia*	**156** 47 -	Class: KI	**2001**-06 **P.T. Galangan Tanjung Batu — Balikpapan** L reg 26.90 Br ex - Dght - Lbp 24.10 Br md 7.00 Dpth 3.10 Welded, 1 dk	**(B32A2ST) Tug**	**2 oil engines** geared to sc. shafts driving 2 Propellers Total Power: 882kW (1,200hp) Caterpillar D379 2 x Vee 4 Stroke 8 Cy. 159 x 203 each-441kW (600bhp) Caterpillar Inc-USA
9096715 *PMNO* -	**SEWANGI I** *ex* Yong Tong A *-2009* *ex* Chang Sheng Tuo 9 *-2007* **PT Yiwan Shipping** - *Jakarta* *Indonesia* MMSI: 525015386	**624** 189 -	Class: (KI)	**2007**-05 **Qiyang Baishui Shipbuilding Co Ltd — Qiyang County HN** Yd No: 06003 Loa 47.00 Br ex 10.02 Dght 3.600 Lbp 42.20 Br md 10.00 Dpth 5.00 Welded, 1 dk	**(B32A2ST) Tug**	**2 oil engines** geared to sc. shafts driving 2 Propellers Total Power: 1,176kW (1,598hp) Chinese Std. Type 8300 2 x 4 Stroke 8 Cy. 300 x 380 each-588kW (799bhp) Wuxi Antai Power Machinery Co Ltd-China
7607833 - -	**SEWARD** *ex* Apolo *-2003* *ex* Dalmar Energy *-1993* *ex* Zamtug III *-1989* *ex* Sealift 23 *-1988* *ex* Sypesteyn *-1984* *ex* F 31 *-1981* **Portside Towing Ltd** - *Montego Bay* *Jamaica* Official number: JMR03008	*337* 49 -	Class: (AB)	**1976**-06 **K.K. Imai Seisakusho — Kamijima** (Hull) Yd No: 156 **1976**-06 **Mitsui Ocean Development & Eng. Co. Ltd. — Japan** Yd No: S-070 Loa - Br ex 9.22 Dght 3.988 Lbp 34.00 Br md 9.21 Dpth 4.25 Welded, 1 dk	**(B32A2ST) Tug**	**2 oil engines** reverse reduction geared to sc. shafts driving 2 FP propellers Total Power: 1,838kW (2,498hp) 11.5kn Niigata 6MG25BX 2 x 4 Stroke 6 Cy. 250 x 320 each-919kW (1249bhp) Niigata Engineering Co Ltd-Japan AuxGen: 2 x 144kW a.c, 1 x 24kW a.c
8408002 *HP5896* -	**SEWARD JOHNSON** **Deep Ocean Technology LLC** CEPEMAR Servicos de Consultoria em Meio Ambiente Ltda SatCom: Inmarsat C 437300129 *Panama* *Panama* MMSI: 351859000 Official number: 4303011	**879** 263 -	Class: (AB)	**1984**-07 **Atlantic Marine — Jacksonville, Fl** Yd No: 197 Loa 53.65 Br ex - Dght 4.023 Lbp 48.77 Br md 10.98 Dpth 4.88 Welded, 1 dk	**(B22A2OR) Offshore Support Vessel**	**2 oil engines** sr geared to sc. shafts driving 2 FP propellers Total Power: 1,250kW (1,700hp) 13.0kn Caterpillar 3512TA 2 x Vee 4 Stroke 12 Cy. 170 x 190 each-625kW (850bhp) Caterpillar Tractor Co-USA AuxGen: 3 x 270kW 470V 60Hz a.c Thrusters: 1 Directional thruster (f); 1 Directional thruster (a) Fuel: 198.0 (d.f.) 3.5pd
7517856 *WYJ6341* -	**SEWELLS POINT** **Moran Towing Corp** - *Wilmington, DE* *United States of America* MMSI: 367306860 Official number: 581156	*237* 161 -	Class: AB	**1977**-05 **Jakobson Shipyard, Inc. — Oyster Bay, NY** Yd No: 457 Loa - Br ex - Dght 3.950 Lbp 30.03 Br md 8.84 Dpth 5.03 Welded, 1 dk	**(B32A2ST) Tug**	**1 oil engine** reverse reduction geared to sc. shaft driving 1 FP propeller Total Power: 1,581kW (2,150hp) 12.5kn EMD (Electro-Motive) 12-645-E7B 1 x Vee 2 Stroke 12 Cy. 230 x 254 1581kW (2150bhp) General Motors Corp.Electro-Motive Div.-La Grange AuxGen: 2 x 60kW
9105205 - -	**SEWOL** *ex* Ferry Naminoue *-2012* **Chonghaejin Marine Co Ltd** - *South Korea*	**6,586** - 3,981		**1994**-06 **Hayashikane Dockyard Co Ltd — Nagasaki NS** Yd No: 1006 Loa 145.61 (BB) Br ex - Dght 6.260 Lbp 132.00 Br md 22.00 Dpth 14.00 Welded, 3 dks	**(A36A2PR) Passenger/Ro-Ro Ship (Vehicles)** Passengers: 804; cabins: 52 Angled side door/ramp (s. f.) Quarter stern door/ramp (p) Len: 18.00 Wid: 7.60 Swl: - Quarter stern door/ramp (s) Len: 18.00 Wid: 7.60 Swl: - Lorries: 60, Cars: 90 Compartments: 1 Ho 1 Ha: Derricks: 1	**2 oil engines** driving 2 FP propellers Total Power: 13,240kW (18,002hp) 21.5kn Pielstick 12PC2-6V-400 2 x Vee 4 Stroke 12 Cy. 400 x 460 each-6620kW (9001bhp) Diesel United Ltd.-Aioi AuxGen: 3 x 960kW a.c Fuel: 574.0 (d.f.) 56.0pd
9155652 - -	**SEWOLTARA** - **Korea Development Leasing Corp** Onbada Co Ltd *Yeosu* *South Korea* Official number: YSR-965150	**131** - 21	Class: (KR)	**1996**-11 **Semo Co Ltd — Donghae** Yd No: 213 Loa 28.40 Br ex 7.40 Dght 1.264 Lbp 25.50 Br md 7.20 Dpth 2.53 Welded, 1 dk	**(A37B2PS) Passenger Ship** Passengers: unberthed: 194	**2 oil engines** with clutches, flexible couplings & sr geared to sc. shafts driving 2 Water jets Total Power: 2,942kW (4,000hp) 32.0kn Niigata 12V16FX 2 x Vee 4 Stroke 12 Cy. 165 x 185 each-1471kW (2000bhp) Niigata Engineering Co Ltd-Japan
9165695 *9HA3405* -	**SEXTA** *ex* Ocean Star *-2013* **Sexta Marine SA** Medlink Management SA *Valletta* *Malta* MMSI: 229558000 Official number: 9165695	**11,376** 6,331 18,367 T/cm 28.9	Class: NK (VR) (AB)	**2000**-07 **INP Heavy Industries Co Ltd — Ulsan** Yd No: 1111 Loa 144.75 (BB) Br ex - Dght 9.050 Lbp 133.50 Br md 24.00 Dpth 12.80 Welded, 1 dk	**(A21A2BC) Bulk Carrier** Double Bottom Entire Compartment Length Grain: 24,017; Bale: 22,748 Compartments: 4 Ho, ER 4 Ha: (16.9 x 12.6)3 (17.5 x 14.0)ER Cranes: 3x30t,1x24t	**1 oil engine** driving 1 FP propeller Total Power: 5,590kW (7,600hp) 13.5kn B&W 8S35MC 1 x 2 Stroke 8 Cy. 350 x 1400 5590kW (7600bhp) Hyundai Heavy Industries Co Ltd-South Korea AuxGen: 2 x 350kW 450V 60Hz a.c Fuel: 115.7 (d.f.) (Heating Coils) 880.6 (r.f.)
9358321 *VRCS6* -	**SEXTANS** *ex* Overseas Sextans *-2010* **Pretty Urban Shipping SA** Parakou Shipmanagement Pte Ltd *Hong Kong* *Hong Kong* MMSI: 477768200 Official number: HK-1883	**30,068** 13,602 51,218 T/cm 52.0	Class: BV	**2007**-05 **STX Shipbuilding Co Ltd — Changwon (Jinhae Shipyard)** Yd No: 2024 Loa 183.06 (BB) Br ex 32.21 Dght 13.147 Lbp 173.90 Br md 32.20 Dpth 19.10 Welded, 1 dk	**(A12B2TR) Chemical/Products Tanker** Double Hull (13F) Liq: 52,047; Liq (Oil): 52,047 Cargo Heating Coils Compartments: 12 Wing Ta, 2 Wing Slop Ta, ER 12 Cargo Pump (s): 12x600m³/hr Manifold: Bow/CM: 92.1m	**1 oil engine** driving 1 FP propeller Total Power: 9,488kW (12,900hp) 14.2kn MAN-B&W 6S50MC-C 1 x 2 Stroke 6 Cy. 500 x 2000 9488kW (12900bhp) STX Engine Co Ltd-South Korea
7206782 *7TAQ* -	**SEYBOUSE 1** **Entreprise Portuaire de Skikda (EPS)** - *Skikda* *Algeria*	*261* 69 239	Class: BV	**1972 D.W. Kremer Sohn — Elmshorn** Yd No: 1151 Loa 33.48 Br ex - Dght 3.442 Lbp 29.70 Br md 8.92 Dpth 4.32 Welded	**(B32A2ST) Tug**	**1 oil engine** driving 1 FP propeller Total Power: 1,692kW (2,300hp) 13.0kn MaK 9M452AK 1 x 4 Stroke 9 Cy. 320 x 450 1692kW (2300bhp) MaK Maschinenbau GmbH-Kiel Fuel: 120.0 (d.f.)
7211414 *7TAR* -	**SEYBOUSE 2** **Entreprise Portuaire d'Arzew (EPA)** - *Alger* *Algeria*	*261* 69 -	Class: (BV)	**1973**-05 **D.W. Kremer Sohn — Elmshorn** Yd No: 1152 Loa 33.48 Br ex - Dght 3.455 Lbp 29.72 Br md 8.92 Dpth 4.32 Welded, 1 dk	**(B32A2ST) Tug**	**1 oil engine** driving 1 CP propeller Total Power: 1,692kW (2,300hp) 13.0kn MaK 9M452AK 1 x 4 Stroke 9 Cy. 320 x 450 1692kW (2300bhp) MaK Maschinenbau GmbH-Kiel AuxGen: 1 x 88kW 400V 50Hz a.c Fuel: 120.0 (d.f.)
7219052 *7TAT* -	**SEYBOUSE 3** **Entreprise Portuaire de Bejaia (EPB)** - *Alger* *Algeria*	*261* 69 -	Class: BV	**1972 D.W. Kremer Sohn — Elmshorn** Yd No: 1153 Loa 33.48 Br ex - Dght 3.455 Lbp 29.72 Br md 8.92 Dpth 4.32 Welded	**(B32A2ST) Tug**	**1 oil engine** driving 1 CP propeller Total Power: 1,692kW (2,300hp) 13.0kn MaK 9M452AK 1 x 4 Stroke 9 Cy. 320 x 450 1692kW (2300bhp) MaK Maschinenbau GmbH-Kiel AuxGen: 1 x 88kW 400V 50Hz a.c Fuel: 120.0 (d.f.)
7225908 *7TAU* -	**SEYBOUSE 4** **Entreprise Portuaire d'Arzew (EPA)** - *Alger* *Algeria*	*261* 69 -	Class: (BV)	**1972 D.W. Kremer Sohn — Elmshorn** Yd No: 1154 Loa 33.51 Br ex 9.38 Dght 3.690 Lbp 29.60 Br md 8.92 Dpth 4.30 Welded	**(B32A2ST) Tug**	**1 oil engine** driving 1 CP propeller Total Power: 1,692kW (2,300hp) 13.0kn MaK 9M452AK 1 x 4 Stroke 9 Cy. 320 x 450 1692kW (2300bhp) MaK Maschinenbau GmbH-Kiel AuxGen: 1 x 88kW 400V 50Hz a.c Fuel: 120.0 (d.f.)
7326439 - -	**SEYBOUSE 5** **Societe Nationale de Transport Maritime & Compagnie Nationale Algerienne de Navigation Maritime (SNTM/CNAN)** - *Alger* *Algeria*	*261* 69 -	Class: (BV)	**1973 D.W. Kremer Sohn — Elmshorn** Yd No: 1158 Loa 33.48 Br ex 9.38 Dght 3.455 Lbp 29.70 Br md 8.92 Dpth 4.32 Welded	**(B32A2ST) Tug**	**1 oil engine** driving 1 CP propeller Total Power: 1,692kW (2,300hp) 13.0kn MaK 9M452AK 1 x 4 Stroke 9 Cy. 320 x 450 1692kW (2300bhp) MaK Maschinenbau GmbH-Kiel AuxGen: 1 x 88kW 400V 50Hz a.c Fuel: 120.0 (d.f.)

IMO / Call sign	Name / Owner / Manager / Port / IDs	GT / NT / DWT	Class	Built / Builder / Dimensions	Type / Capacities	Machinery
9538232 *S7WR* -	**SEYCHELLES PARADISE** **Seychelles Petroleum Co Ltd** German Tanker Shipping GmbH & Co KG *Victoria* *Seychelles* MMSI: 664527000	**1,545** 485 1,786	Class: GL	**2009-10 Lindenau GmbH Schiffswerft u. Maschinenfabrik — Kiel** Yd No: 284 Loa 67.80 Br ex - Dght 4.200 Lbp 63.70 Br md 13.20 Dpth 5.20 Welded, 1 dk	**(A13B2TP) Products Tanker** Double Hull (13F) Liq: 1,650; Liq (Gas): 118; Liq (Oil): 1,650 Compartments: 6 Ta, ER	**2 oil engines** reduction geared to sc. shafts driving 2 CP propellers Total Power: 956kW (1,300hp) 10.2kn Volvo Penta D16MH 2 x 4 Stroke 6 Cy. 144 x 165 each-478kW (650bhp) AB Volvo Penta-Sweden AuxGen: 3 x 320kW 400V a.c Thrusters: 1 Tunnel thruster (f)
9365635 *S7VR* -	**SEYCHELLES PATRIOT** **Seychelles Patriot Ltd** German Tanker Shipping GmbH & Co KG *Victoria* *Seychelles* MMSI: 664445000	**27,007** 13,057 45,680 T/cm 54.0	Class: GL	**2008-02 Lindenau GmbH Schiffswerft u. Maschinenfabrik — Kiel** Yd No: 277 Loa 189.02 (BB) Br ex - Dght 11.810 Lbp 181.90 Br md 32.20 Dpth 17.05 Welded, 1 dk	**(A12B2TR) Chemical/Products Tanker** Double Hull (13F) Liq: 51,776; Liq (Oil): 51,500 Compartments: 12 Wing Ta, 2 Wing Slop Ta, ER 12 Cargo Pump (s): 12x500m³/hr Manifold: Bow/CM: 97m Ice Capable	**1 oil engine** reduction geared to sc. shaft driving 1 CP propeller Total Power: 11,200kW (15,228hp) 15.8kn MAN-B&W 8L58/64 1 x 4 Stroke 8 Cy. 580 x 640 11200kW (15228bhp) MAN B&W Diesel AG-Augsburg AuxGen: 3 x 1140kW 400V 60Hz a.c, 1 x 1360kW 400V 60Hz a.c Thrusters: 1 Tunnel thruster (f) Fuel: 200.0 (d.f.) 1600.0 (r.f.)
9255517 *S7SQ* -	**SEYCHELLES PIONEER** **Seychelles Pioneer Ltd Number Fifty** Seychelles Petroleum Co Ltd *Victoria* *Seychelles* MMSI: 664288000	**22,346** 10,920 37,500 T/cm 45.0	Class: GL	**2005-04 Lindenau GmbH Schiffswerft u. Maschinenfabrik — Kiel** Yd No: 258 Loa 185.00 (BB) Br ex 28.04 Dght 11.700 Lbp 175.20 Br md 28.00 Dpth 16.80 Welded, 1 dk	**(A12B2TR) Chemical/Products Tanker** Double Hull (13F) Liq: 42,327; Liq (Oil): 42,327 Compartments: 10 Wing Ta, 2 Wing Slop Ta, ER 10 Cargo Pump (s): 10x500m³/hr Manifold: Bow/CM: 92m Ice Capable	**1 oil engine** geared to sc. shaft driving 1 CP propeller Total Power: 8,340kW (11,339hp) 15.1kn MAN-B&W 6L58/64 1 x 4 Stroke 6 Cy. 580 x 640 8340kW (11339bhp) MAN B&W Diesel AG-Augsburg AuxGen: 3 x 960kW 400/230V 50Hz a.c, 1 x 1120kW 400/230V 50Hz a.c Thrusters: 1 Thwart. CP thruster (f) Fuel: 135.0 (d.f.) 1030.0 (r.f.) 33.5pd
9365623 *S7VK* -	**SEYCHELLES PRELUDE** **Seychelles Prelude Ltd** VicNav Ltd *Victoria* *Seychelles* MMSI: 664444000 Official number: 50180	**27,007** 13,057 45,680 T/cm 54.1	Class: GL	**2007-12 Lindenau GmbH Schiffswerft u. Maschinenfabrik — Kiel** Yd No: 276 Loa 189.00 (BB) Br ex - Dght 11.810 Lbp 181.90 Br md 32.20 Dpth 17.05 Welded, 1 dk	**(A12B2TR) Chemical/Products Tanker** Double Hull (13F) Liq: 50,741; Liq (Oil): 51,500 Compartments: 12 Wing Ta, 2 Wing Slop Ta, ER 12 Cargo Pump (s): 12x500m³/hr Manifold: Bow/CM: 91.5m Ice Capable	**1 oil engine** reduction geared to sc. shaft driving 1 CP propeller Total Power: 11,200kW (15,228hp) 16.0kn MAN-B&W 8L58/64 1 x 4 Stroke 8 Cy. 580 x 640 11200kW (15228bhp) MAN B&W Diesel AG-Augsburg AuxGen: 3 x 1140kW 400/230V 50Hz a.c, 1 x 1360kW 400/230V 50Hz a.c Thrusters: 1 Tunnel thruster (f) Fuel: 215.0 (d.f.) 1525.0 (r.f.)
9251664 *S7SP* -	**SEYCHELLES PRIDE** **Seychelles Petroleum Co Ltd** German Tanker Shipping GmbH & Co KG *Victoria* *Seychelles* MMSI: 664209000 Official number: 50039	**21,353** 8,390 32,580 T/cm 42.0	Class: GL	**2002-06 Lindenau GmbH Schiffswerft u. Maschinenfabrik — Kiel** Yd No: 244 Loa 177.77 (BB) Br ex 28.03 Dght 11.000 Lbp 169.00 Br md 28.00 Dpth 16.80 Welded, 1 dk	**(A13B2TP) Products Tanker** Double Hull (13F) Liq: 36,690; Liq (Oil): 37,440 Compartments: 10 Wing Ta, 2 Wing Slop Ta, ER 12 Cargo Pump (s): 10x500m³/hr, 2x200m³/hr Manifold: Bow/CM: 84.9m	**1 oil engine** geared to sc. shaft driving 1 CP propeller Total Power: 8,340kW (11,339hp) 15.1kn MAN 6L58/64 1 x 4 Stroke 6 Cy. 580 x 640 8340kW (11339bhp) AuxGen: 3 x 960kW 380V a.c, 1 x 1120kW 380V a.c Thrusters: 1 Thwart. FP thruster (f) Fuel: 863.0
9298181 *S7TQ* -	**SEYCHELLES PROGRESS** **Seychelles Progress Ltd** Seychelles Petroleum Co Ltd *Victoria* *Seychelles* MMSI: 664296000	**22,346** 10,928 37,557 T/cm 45.0	Class: GL	**2005-08 Lindenau GmbH Schiffswerft u. Maschinenfabrik — Kiel** Yd No: 259 Loa 185.00 (BB) Br ex 28.04 Dght 11.700 Lbp 175.20 Br md 28.00 Dpth 16.80 Welded, 1 dk	**(A12B2TR) Chemical/Products Tanker** Double Hull (13F) Liq: 43,300; Liq (Oil): 43,300 Compartments: 10 Wing Ta, ER, 2 Wing Slop Ta 10 Cargo Pump (s): 10x500m³/hr Manifold: Bow/CM: 92.2m Ice Capable	**1 oil engine** geared to sc. shaft driving 1 CP propeller Total Power: 8,340kW (11,339hp) 15.1kn MAN-B&W 6L58/64 1 x 4 Stroke 6 Cy. 580 x 640 8340kW (11339bhp) MAN B&W Diesel AG-Augsburg AuxGen: 3 x 960kW 400/240V 50Hz a.c, 1 x 1120kW 50Hz a.c Thrusters: 1 Thwart. CP thruster (f) Fuel: 134.0 (d.f.) 1058.0 (r.f.) 34.0pd
9153161 *TCCD2* -	**SEYDI ALI REIS-I** **Istanbul Deniz Otobusleri Sanayi ve Ticaret AS (IDO)** - *Istanbul* *Turkey* MMSI: 271002316 Official number: 4490	**395** 119 39	Class: TL (NV)	**1997-03 Kvaerner Fjellstrand AS — Omastrand** Yd No: 1636 Loa 35.00 Br ex - Dght 1.520 Lbp 32.22 Br md 10.10 Dpth 3.91 Welded, 2 dks	**(A37B2PS) Passenger Ship** Passengers: unberthed: 341	**4 oil engines** geared to sc. shafts driving 2 Water jets Total Power: 2,440kW (3,316hp) 32.0kn M.T.U. 12V183TE72 4 x Vee 4 Stroke 12 Cy. 128 x 142 each-610kW (829bhp) MTU Friedrichshafen GmbH-Friedrichshafen AuxGen: 2 x 71kW 230/400V 50Hz a.c
7431442 *6VKG* -	**SEYDOU NOROU TAAL II** *ex* Yene **Societe des Pecheries Senegalaises de l'Atlantique (SOPESEA)** - *Dakar* *Senegal* Official number: 0318	*282* 90 -	Class: (BV)	**1972 Zavod "Leninskaya Kuznitsa" — Kiyev** Loa 36.00 Br ex 8.11 Dght - Lbp 30.00 Br md - Dpth 4.14 Welded, 1 dk	**(B11B2FV) Fishing Vessel**	**1 oil engine** driving 1 FP propeller Total Power: 596kW (810hp) MGO 12V175ASH 1 x Vee 4 Stroke 12 Cy. 175 x 180 596kW (810bhp) (made 1969, fitted 1972) Societe Alsacienne de ConstructionsMecaniques (SACM)-France AuxGen: 3 x 83kW 380V 50Hz a.c Fuel: 80.5 (d.f.)
6512639 *9BGD* -	**SEYEDI 1** *ex* Mona 10 *-1997* *ex* Rk 17 *-1997* *ex* Resedco 1 *-1997* **Abbas Nezarat & Partners** - *Bandar Imam Khomeini* *Iran* MMSI: 422527000 Official number: 20323	*140* 42 -	Class: AS (GL)	**1965-03 Ruhrorter Schiffswerft u. Maschinenfabrik GmbH — Duisburg** Yd No: 333 Converted From: General Cargo Ship-2005 Converted From: Trawler-1997 Loa 29.49 Br ex 7.27 Dght 2.794 Lbp 22.00 Br md 7.22 Dpth 3.81 Welded, 1 dk	**(B32A2ST) Tug**	**1 oil engine** geared to sc. shaft driving 1 FP propeller Total Power: 621kW (844hp) Caterpillar D398 1 x Vee 4 Stroke 12 Cy. 159 x 203 621kW (844bhp) (new engine 2000, fitted 2000) Caterpillar Inc-USA
9069786 *TC9934* -	**SEYHAN-4** **Cemal Barbaros** - *Istanbul* *Turkey* MMSI: 271002604 Official number: TUGS 1108	**815** 246 -		**1992-05 in Turkey** Loa 40.00 Br ex - Dght 2.800 Lbp - Br md 11.00 Dpth - Welded, 1 dk	**(A37B2PS) Passenger Ship**	**2 oil engines** driving 2 Propellers Total Power: 442kW (600hp) Volvo Penta TAMD122A 2 x 4 Stroke 6 Cy. 130 x 150 each-221kW (300bhp) AB Volvo Penta-Sweden
9520388 *TCTN9* -	**SEYIT ALI** **Denizsan Gemi Isletmeciligi ve Ticaret AS** - *Istanbul* *Turkey* MMSI: 271002686	**2,976** 1,843 4,342 T/cm 11.5	Class: BV	**2009-02** Yd No: 030 Loa 93.62 (BB) Br ex - Dght 6.070 Lbp 84.73 Br md 14.55 Dpth 7.60 Welded, 1 dk	**(A31A2GX) General Cargo Ship** Grain: 3,894 Compartments: 2 Ho, ER 2 Ha: (28.0 x 11.8)ER (30.1 x 11.8)	**1 diesel electric oil engine** reduction geared to sc. shaft driving 1 FP propeller Total Power: 1,471kW (2,000hp) MAN-B&W 6L28/32A 1 x 4 Stroke 6 Cy. 280 x 320 1471kW (2000bhp) MAN Diesel A/S-Denmark
9544451 *TCZW6* -	**SEYIT ONBASI** **Government of The Republic of Turkey (Kiyi Emniyeti ve Gemicilik Kurtarma Isletmesi Genel Mudurlugu Gemicilik Kur Dairesi Bsk)** - *Istanbul* *Turkey* MMSI: 271042584	**939** 281 939	Class: BV	**2011-06 Gisan Gemi Ins. San — Istanbul** Yd No: 50 Loa 52.95 Br ex - Dght 4.000 Lbp 47.55 Br md 12.00 Dpth - Welded, 1 dk	**(B34G2SE) Pollution Control Vessel** Liq: 429; Liq (Oil): 429	**2 oil engines** reduction geared to sc. shafts driving 2 CP propellers Total Power: 3,306kW (4,494hp) 13.0kn Mitsubishi S16R-MPTA 2 x Vee 4 Stroke 16 Cy. 170 x 180 each-1653kW (2247bhp) Mitsubishi Heavy Industries Ltd-Japan AuxGen: 3 x 420kW 50Hz a.c Fuel: 69.0 (d.f.)
9596777 *9HA3396* -	**SEYMA** **Seyma Denizcilik Demir Celik Sanayi ve Ticaret AS** Atlantik Denizcilik Ticaret ve Sanayi AS *Valletta* *Malta* MMSI: 229546000 Official number: 9596777	**4,364** 2,500 6,342	Class: BV	**2013-12 Den-Ta Denizcilik Ticaret ve Sanayi Ltd Sti — Altinova** Yd No: 02 Loa 121.55 Br ex - Dght 6.320 Lbp 112.17 Br md 15.98 Dpth - Welded, 1 dk	**(A12B2TR) Chemical/Products Tanker** Double Hull (13F) Liq: 7,380; Liq (Oil): 7,380 Compartments: 7 Wing Ta, 7 Wing Ta, ER	**1 oil engine** reduction geared to sc. shaft driving 1 CP propeller Total Power: 2,321kW (3,156hp) 14.0kn Hyundai Himsen 8H25/33P 1 x 4 Stroke 8 Cy. 250 x 330 2321kW (3156bhp) Hyundai Heavy Industries Co Ltd-South Korea AuxGen: 3 x 482kW 60Hz a.c Fuel: 340.0

8138645 - -	**SEYSMORAZVEDCHIK** **Kaspmorneftegeofizrazvedka Trust (Caspian Oil Geophysical Research Trust)** -	*174* 52 37	Class: (RS)	**1983 Sretenskiy Sudostroitelnyy Zavod — Sretensk** Yd No: 18 Loa 33.97 Br ex 7.09 Dght 2.591 Lbp 30.00 Br md - Dpth 3.65 Welded, 1 dk	**(B31A2SR) Research Survey Vessel** Ice Capable	**1 oil engine** driving 1 FP propeller Total Power: 224kW (305hp) 9.1kn S.K.L. 8NVD36-1U 1 x 4 Stroke 8 Cy. 240 x 360 224kW (305bhp) VEB Schwermaschinenbau "KarlLiebknecht" (SKL)-Magdeburg AuxGen: 2 x 86kW, 1 x 28kW Fuel: 20.0 (d.f.)
9110339 *D5EY5* -	**SEZAI SELAH** *ex* Hanjin Houston *-2011* **ES International Ltd** Zigana Gemi Isletmeleri AS *Monrovia* *Liberia* MMSI: 636016195 Official number: 16195	**16,252** 9,669 27,209 T/cm 37.3	Class: BV (KR)	**1995-09 Hanjin Heavy Industries Co Ltd — Ulsan** Yd No: 624 Loa 167.00 (BB) Br ex 26.24 Dght 9.916 Lbp 158.00 Br md 26.20 Dpth 13.80 Welded, 1 dk	**(A21A2BC) Bulk Carrier** Grain: 35,155; Bale: 34,100 Compartments: 5 Ho, ER 5 Ha: (13.6 x 13.4)4 (17.6 x 13.4)ER Cranes: 4x25t	**1 oil engine** driving 1 FP propeller Total Power: 6,657kW (9,051hp) 14.0kn MAN-B&W 5L50MC 1 x 2 Stroke 5 Cy. 500 x 1620 6657kW (9051bhp) Hyundai Heavy Industries Co Ltd-South Korea
6411299 - -	**SEZOES** *ex* Roxanne *-2004* *ex* Gym *-1998* *ex* Mounts Bay *-1996* *ex* Beechgarth *-1996* **Lutamar-Prestacao de Servicos a Navegacao Lda** - *Setubal* *Portugal* Official number: S-40-RC	**207** - -	Class: (LR) ✠ Classed LR until 91	**1964-05 W. J. Yarwood & Sons Ltd. — Northwich** Yd No: 943 Loa 31.12 Br ex 8.62 Dght 3.528 Lbp 28.05 Br md 8.08 Dpth 4.12 Welded, 1 dk	**(B32A2ST) Tug**	**2 oil engines** with hydraulic couplings & sr reverse geared to sc. shaft driving 1 FP propeller Total Power: 956kW (1,300hp) Ruston 6VEBXM 2 x 4 Stroke 6 Cy. 260 x 368 each-478kW (650bhp) Ruston & Hornsby Ltd.-Lincoln
9441142 *EBXT* -	**SF ALHUCEMAS** **Balearia Eurolineas Maritimas SA** *Santa Cruz de Tenerife* *Spain (CSR)* MMSI: 224553000	**20,238** 6,125 3,520	Class: BV	**2009-12 Hijos de J. Barreras S.A. — Vigo** Yd No: 1662 Loa 154.51 (BB) Br ex - Dght 5.500 Lbp 137.00 Br md 24.20 Dpth 13.80 Welded, 1 dk	**(A36A2PR) Passenger/Ro-Ro Ship (Vehicles)** Passengers: cabins: 56; berths: 222 Bow door (f) Len: 15.78 Wid: 4.00 Swl: - Stern door/ramp (p. a.) Len: 16.00 Wid: 8.00 Swl: - Stern door/ramp (s. a.) Len: 16.00 Wid: 8.00 Swl: - Lane-Len: 1136 Lane-clr ht: 4.50 Cars: 125	**2 oil engines** reduction geared to sc. shafts driving 2 CP propellers Total Power: 18,006kW (24,480hp) 21.4kn MaK 9M43C 2 x 4 Stroke 9 Cy. 430 x 610 each-9003kW (12240bhp) Caterpillar Motoren GmbH & Co. KG-Germany AuxGen: 3 x 1100kW 400V 50Hz a.c, 2 x 1300kW 400V 50Hz a.c Thrusters: 2 Tunnel thruster (f) Fuel: 80.0 (d.f.) 560.0 (r.f.) 84.0pd
9003926 *DUE2256* -	**SF MARINER** *ex* Hoshin Maru *-2009* *ex* Toyotsu Maru *-2007* **Seaford Shipping Lines Inc** - *Cebu* *Philippines* Official number: CEB1008190	*497* 348 1,500		**1990-09 K.K. Miura Zosensho — Saiki** Yd No: 1003 L reg 68.03 Br ex - Dght 4.111 Lbp 67.00 Br md 12.01 Dpth 7.01 Welded	**(A31A2GX) General Cargo Ship**	**1 oil engine** driving 1 FP propeller Total Power: 1,177kW (1,600hp) Niigata 6M30FT 1 x 4 Stroke 6 Cy. 300 x 530 1177kW (1600bhp) Niigata Engineering Co Ltd-Japan
8921523 *DUH3061* -	**SF PROVIDER** *ex* Shinko Maru No. 38 *-2010* **Seaford Shipping Lines Inc** - *Cebu* *Philippines* Official number: CEB1008319	*498* 349 1,447		**1990-04 Shirahama Zosen K.K. — Honai** Yd No: 146 Loa 72.10 (BB) Br ex - Dght 4.201 Lbp 66.00 Br md 12.20 Dpth 7.00 Welded	**(A31A2GX) General Cargo Ship** Grain: 1,949	**1 oil engine** with clutches & reverse geared to sc. shaft driving 1 CP propeller Total Power: 1,324kW (1,800hp) Akasaka A31R 1 x 4 Stroke 6 Cy. 310 x 600 1324kW (1800bhp) Akasaka Tekkosho KK (Akasaka DieselLtd)-Japan Thrusters: 1 Thwart. CP thruster (f); 1 Thwart. CP thruster (a)
8823836 *DUH2834* -	**SF VOYAGER** *ex* Sumiho Maru No. 26 *-2010* *ex* Kyoyu Maru *-1993* **Seaford Shipping Lines Inc** - *Cebu* *Philippines* Official number: CEB1008246	*498* 349 1,532		**1988-10 K.K. Yoshida Zosen Kogyo — Arida** Loa 74.50 Br ex - Dght 4.170 Lbp 69.00 Br md 12.00 Dpth 7.15 Welded, 1 dk	**(A31A2GX) General Cargo Ship**	**1 oil engine** geared to sc. shaft driving 1 FP propeller Total Power: 1,324kW (1,800hp) Hanshin LH31G 1 x 4 Stroke 6 Cy. 310 x 530 1324kW (1800bhp) The Hanshin Diesel Works Ltd-Japan
9018787 *SVA4700* -	**SFAKIA** *ex* New Hiyama *-2010* **Anonymos Naftiliaki Eteria Notioditikis Kritis (ANENDYK)** - *Chania* *Greece* MMSI: 239637800 Official number: 33	*1,199* 510 649		**1991-05 Naikai Shipbuilding & Engineering Co Ltd — Onomichi HS (Setoda Shipyard)** Yd No: 566 Loa 76.61 (BB) Br ex 14.52 Dght 3.861 Lbp 70.00 Br md 14.50 Dpth 9.28 Welded, 1 dk	**(A36A2PR) Passenger/Ro-Ro Ship (Vehicles)** Passengers: unberthed: 540 Cars: 45	**2 oil engines** with clutches, flexible couplings & sr reverse geared to sc. shafts driving 2 FP propellers Total Power: 2,942kW (4,000hp) 17.0kn Daihatsu 6DLM-28 2 x 4 Stroke 6 Cy. 280 x 360 each-1471kW (2000bhp) Daihatsu Diesel Manufacturing Co Lt-Japan Thrusters: 1 Thwart. CP thruster (f)
8213342 *SV9176*	**SFAKIA** *ex* Serafim *-1985* **Naftiliakes Touristikes Epichirisis Notioditikis Kritis Sfakia SA** - *Piraeus* *Greece* MMSI: 237030800 Official number: 8152	*250* 150 -		**1985-05 Vassiliadis Yard — Ambelaki, Salamis** Yd No: 42 Loa 29.34 Br ex 6.84 Dght 1.891 Lbp 27.61 Br md 6.51 Dpth 2.80 Welded, 1 dk	**(A37B2PS) Passenger Ship**	**2 oil engines** driving 2 FP propellers Total Power: 648kW (882hp) Baudouin 12F11SRM 2 x Vee 4 Stroke 12 Cy. 115 x 105 each-324kW (441bhp) Societe des Moteurs Baudouin SA-France
9453391 *5BKQ3*	**SFAKIA WAVE** **Marina T Navigation Ltd** Teo Shipping Corp *Limassol* *Cyprus* MMSI: 209919000 Official number: 9453391	**47,984** 27,675 87,340	Class: LR ✠ **100A1** SS 11/2011 bulk carrier CSR BC-A GRAB (20) Nos. 2, 4 & 6 holds may be empty ESP **ShipRight** CM *IWS LI ✠ **LMC** **UMS** Eq.Ltr: R†; Cable: 687.5/84.0 U3 (a)	**2011-11 Hudong-Zhonghua Shipbuilding (Group) Co Ltd — Shanghai** Yd No: H1560A Loa 229.00 (BB) Br ex 36.84 Dght 14.200 Lbp 221.00 Br md 36.80 Dpth 19.90 Welded, 1 dk	**(A21A2BC) Bulk Carrier** Double Hull Grain: 100,097 Compartments: 7 Ho, ER 7 Ha: ER	**1 oil engine** driving 1 FP propeller Total Power: 10,500kW (14,276hp) 14.5kn MAN-B&W 6S60MC-C 1 x 2 Stroke 6 Cy. 600 x 2400 10500kW (14276bhp) Hudong Heavy Machinery Co Ltd-China AuxGen: 3 x 600kW 440V 60Hz a.c Boilers: e (ex.g.) 12.2kgf/cm² (12.0bar), AuxB (o.f.) 9.2kgf/cm² (9.0bar)
8657421 *9A8308* -	**SFERA** *ex* Sea World *-2002* **Goran, Ilija & Nenad Bacic** - *Rijeka* *Croatia* Official number: 2T-729	**146** 61 -	Class: CS	**1999 Rifler Basaran — Surmene** Loa 26.22 Br ex - Dght 1.644 Lbp 19.50 Br md 7.24 Dpth 2.75 Welded, 1 dk	**(A37B2PS) Passenger Ship**	**2 oil engines** reduction geared to sc. shafts driving 2 FP propellers Total Power: 302kW (410hp) 10.0kn MAN D2866E 2 x 4 Stroke 6 Cy. 128 x 155 each-151kW (205bhp) MAN Nutzfahrzeuge AG-Nuernberg
8656300 *UBNH8* G-0920	**SFERA NO. 2** *ex* Hsien Hua No. 2 *-1984* **LLC Go-Raizing Sakhalin** - *Nevelsk* *Russia* MMSI: 273358530 Official number: 847358	**801** 332 564	Class: RS	**1984-12 Fong Kuo Shipbuilding Co Ltd — Kaohsiung** Loa 59.30 Br ex - Dght 3.700 Lbp 52.40 Br md 9.50 Dpth 4.20 Welded, 1 dk	**(B11B2FV) Fishing Vessel**	**1 oil engine** reduction geared to sc. shaft driving 1 FP propeller Total Power: 1,044kW (1,419hp) 12.0kn Hanshin 1 x 1044kW (1419bhp) The Hanshin Diesel Works Ltd-Japan AuxGen: 1 x 360kW a.c, 1 x 240kW a.c Fuel: 255.0
8656283 *UBNH9* G-0921	**SFERA NO. 3** *ex* Hsien Hua No. 3 *-1989* **LLC Go-Raizing Sakhalin** - *Nevelsk* *Russia* MMSI: 273359530 Official number: 897268	**798** 335 744	Class: RS	**1989-05 Kaohsiung Shipbuilding Co. Ltd. — Kaohsiung** Loa 61.00 Br ex - Dght 3.900 Lbp 52.68 Br md 9.50 Dpth 4.35 Welded, 1 dk	**(B11B2FV) Fishing Vessel**	**1 oil engine** reduction geared to sc. shaft driving 1 FP propeller Total Power: 1,119kW (1,521hp) 12.0kn Hanshin LH28G 1 x 4 Stroke 6 Cy. 280 x 460 1119kW (1521bhp) The Hanshin Diesel Works Ltd-Japan AuxGen: 2 x 445kW a.c, 1 x 265kW a.c Fuel: 220.0 (d.f.)

IMO / Call sign	Name / Owner / Manager / Port	Tonnage	Class	Builder / Dimensions	Type	Machinery
9047788 *LW7122* -	**SFIDA** **Esfida SA** - *Mar del Plata* *Argentina* MMSI: 701006035 Official number: 01567	**137** 80 100	Class: (RI)	**1992**-08 **Ast. Naval Federico Contessi y Cia. S.A. — Mar del Plata** Yd No: 70 Loa 27.00 Br ex - Dght - Lbp 24.70 Br md 7.00 Dpth 3.65 Welded, 1 dk	**(B11B2FV) Fishing Vessel**	**1 oil engine** reduction geared to sc. shaft driving 1 FP propeller Total Power: 456kW (620hp) 10.0kn Caterpillar 3412TA 1 x Vee 4 Stroke 12 Cy. 137 x 152 456kW (620bhp) Caterpillar Inc-USA AuxGen: 2 x 32kW 220/380V 50Hz a.c
8728878 *USOZ* -	**SFINKS** **Black Sea Shipping Co (Chernomorskoye Morskoye Parokhodstvo) (BLASCO)** - *Odessa* *Ukraine* Official number: 875911	**165** 49 27	Class: (RS)	**1989**-01 **Brodogradiliste 'Boris Kidric' — Apatin** Yd No: 1093 Loa 23.53 Br ex 9.00 Dght 3.250 Lbp 21.04 Br md - Dpth 3.51 Welded, 1 dk	**(B32B2SP) Pusher Tug** Ice Capable	**2 oil engines** geared to sc. shafts driving 2 Directional propellers Total Power: 600kW (816hp) 10.0kn MAN D2840LE 2 x Vee 4 Stroke 10 Cy. 128 x 142 each-300kW (408bhp) MAN Nutzfahrzeuge AG-Nuernberg AuxGen: 2 x 50kW a.c
9638513 *YL2758* -	**SFINKSA** **Freeport of Riga Fleet (Rigas Brivostas Flote)** Freeport of Riga Authority (Rigas Brivostas Parvalde) *Riga* *Latvia* MMSI: 275415000 Official number: 3082	**277** 83 116	Class: (RS)	**2011**-11 **OAO Leningradskiy Sudostroitelnyy Zavod 'Pella' — Otradnoye** Yd No: 620 Loa 29.44 Br ex 10.10 Dght 3.500 Lbp 26.50 Br md 9.50 Dpth 4.82 Welded, 1 dk	**(B32A2ST) Tug**	**2 oil engines** reduction geared to sc. shafts driving 2 Directional propellers Total Power: 3,000kW (4,078hp) Caterpillar 3512B-HD 2 x Vee 4 Stroke 12 Cy. 170 x 215 each-1500kW (2039bhp) Caterpillar Inc-USA AuxGen: 2 x 86kW a.c Fuel: 66.0 (d.f.)
9455909 *V7UX8* -	**SFL AVON** **SFL Avon Inc** Frontline Ltd *Majuro* *Marshall Islands* MMSI: 538004074 Official number: 4074	**18,321** 10,202 23,232 T/cm 38.0	Class: NV (GL)	**2010**-10 **Guangzhou Wenchong Shipyard Co Ltd — Guangzhou GD** Yd No: 373 Loa 175.44 (BB) Br ex - Dght 10.850 Lbp 165.00 Br md 27.40 Dpth 14.30 Welded, 1 dk	**(A33A2CC) Container Ship (Fully Cellular)** TEU 1740 C Ho 700 TEU C Dk 1040 TEU incl 300 ref C. Compartments: 5 Cell Ho, ER Cranes: 2x45t Ice Capable	**1 oil engine** driving 1 FP propeller Total Power: 15,820kW (21,509hp) 19.5kn MAN-B&W 7S60MC-C 1 x 2 Stroke 7 Cy. 600 x 2400 15820kW (21509bhp) Hudong Heavy Machinery Co Ltd-China AuxGen: 3 x 1180kW 450V 60Hz a.c Thrusters: 1 Tunnel thruster (f) Fuel: 170.0 (d.f.) 1700.0 (r.f.)
9232632 *V7NM7* -	**SFL EUROPA** *ex* Montemar Europa *-2009* **SFL Europa Inc** Bernhard Schulte Shipmanagement (Singapore) Pte Ltd *Majuro* *Marshall Islands* MMSI: 538002981 Official number: 2981	**16,803** 8,673 22,900 T/cm 37.1	Class: NV (GL)	**2003**-10 **Stocznia Szczecinska Nowa Sp z oo — Szczecin** Yd No: B170/III/14 Loa 184.70 (BB) Br ex - Dght 9.850 Lbp 171.94 Br md 25.30 Dpth 13.50 Welded, 1 dk	**(A33A2CC) Container Ship (Fully Cellular)** Grain: 29,000; Bale: 29,000 TEU 1728 C Ho 634 TEU C Dk 1094 TEU incl 250 ref C. Cranes: 3x40t	**1 oil engine** driving 1 FP propeller Total Power: 13,327kW (18,119hp) 19.6kn Sulzer 6RTA62U 1 x 2 Stroke 6 Cy. 620 x 2150 13327kW (18119bhp) H Cegielski Poznan SA-Poland AuxGen: 3 x 1096kW 440/220V 60Hz a.c Thrusters: 1 Tunnel thruster (f)
9315927 *V7YA3* -	**SFL FALCON** *ex* Horizon Falcon *-2007* **Phoenix Falcon Inc** MCC Transport Singapore Pte Ltd *Majuro* *Marshall Islands* MMSI: 538004613 Official number: 4613	**28,927** 15,033 39,420 T/cm 56.7	Class: NV	**2007**-04 **Hyundai Mipo Dockyard Co Ltd — Ulsan** Yd No: 0409 Loa 222.17 (BB) Br ex 30.03 Dght 12.000 Lbp 210.00 Br md 30.00 Dpth 16.80 Welded, 1 dk	**(A33A2CC) Container Ship (Fully Cellular)** TEU 2824 C Ho 1026 TEU C Dk 1798 TEU incl 586 ref C.	**1 oil engine** driving 1 FP propeller Total Power: 25,270kW (34,357hp) 22.5kn MAN-B&W 7K80MC-C 1 x 2 Stroke 7 Cy. 800 x 2300 25270kW (34357bhp) Hyundai Heavy Industries Co Ltd-South Korea AuxGen: 4 x a.c Thrusters: 1 Tunnel thruster (f) Fuel: 215.0 (d.f.) 3241.0 (r.f.)
9303819 *V7YA4* -	**SFL HAWK** *ex* Horizon Hawk *-2012* *completed as* Irenes Resolve *-2007* **Phoenix Hawk Inc** MCC Transport Singapore Pte Ltd *Majuro* *Marshall Islands* MMSI: 538004614 Official number: 4614	**28,592** 14,769 39,418 T/cm 56.7	Class: AB (GL)	**2007**-03 **Hyundai Mipo Dockyard Co Ltd — Ulsan** Yd No: 0389 Loa 222.20 (BB) Br ex - Dght 12.000 Lbp 210.00 Br md 30.00 Dpth 16.80 Welded, 1 dk	**(A33A2CC) Container Ship (Fully Cellular)** TEU 2824 C Ho 1026 TEU C Dk 1798 TEU incl 586 ref C.	**1 oil engine** driving 1 FP propeller Total Power: 25,228kW (34,300hp) 22.5kn MAN-B&W 7K80MC-C 1 x 2 Stroke 7 Cy. 800 x 2300 25228kW (34300bhp) Hyundai Heavy Industries Co Ltd-South Korea AuxGen: 4 x 1600kW 440V 60Hz a.c Thrusters: 1 Tunnel thruster (f) Fuel: 458.0 (d.f.) 3308.0 (r.f.) 97.0pd
9525821 *V7VD7* -	**SFL HUDSON** *ex* Bao Wealth *-2010* **SFL Hudson Inc** Bernhard Schulte Shipmanagement (Singapore) Pte Ltd *Majuro* *Marshall Islands* MMSI: 538004096 Official number: 4096	**32,945** 19,231 56,836 T/cm 58.8	Class: BV (LR) ✠ Classed LR until 16/8/09	**2009**-08 **Jiangsu Hantong Ship Heavy Industry Co Ltd — Tongzhou JS** Yd No: 028 Loa 189.94 (BB) Br ex 32.30 Dght 12.800 Lbp 184.86 Br md 32.26 Dpth 18.00 Welded, 1 dk	**(A21A2BC) Bulk Carrier** Grain: 71,634; Bale: 68,200 Compartments: 5 Ho, ER 5 Ha: 4 (21.3 x 18.3)ER (18.9 x 18.3) Cranes: 4x35t	**1 oil engine** driving 1 FP propeller Total Power: 9,480kW (12,889hp) 14.2kn MAN-B&W 6S50MC-C 1 x 2 Stroke 6 Cy. 500 x 2000 9480kW (12889bhp) Doosan Engine Co Ltd-South Korea AuxGen: 3 x 600kW 440V 60Hz a.c Boilers: AuxB (Comp) 9.0kgf/cm² (8.8bar)
9615561 *VRIX5* -	**SFL HUMBER** **SFL Humber Inc** SFL Bulk Holding Ltd *Hong Kong* *Hong Kong* MMSI: 477095300 Official number: HK-3176	**33,055** 19,224 56,970 T/cm 58.8	Class: NV	**2012**-01 **Zhejiang Zhenghe Shipbuilding Co Ltd — Zhoushan ZJ** Yd No: 1038 Loa 189.99 (BB) Br ex 32.31 Dght 12.800 Lbp 185.00 Br md 32.26 Dpth 18.00 Welded, 1 dk	**(A21A2BC) Bulk Carrier** Grain: 71,634; Bale: 68,200 Compartments: 5 Ho, ER 5 Ha: ER Cranes: 4x30t	**1 oil engine** driving 1 FP propeller Total Power: 9,480kW (12,889hp) 14.2kn MAN-B&W 6S50MC-C 1 x 2 Stroke 6 Cy. 500 x 2000 9480kW (12889bhp) STX Engine Co Ltd-South Korea AuxGen: 3 x a.c
9303807 *V7YA5* -	**SFL HUNTER** *ex* Horizon Hunter *-2012* *launched as* Irenes Relief *-2006* **Phoenix Hunter Inc** Bernhard Schulte Shipmanagement (Singapore) Pte Ltd *Majuro* *Marshall Islands* MMSI: 538004615 Official number: 4615	**28,592** 14,769 39,266 T/cm 56.7	Class: AB (GL)	**2006**-11 **Hyundai Mipo Dockyard Co Ltd — Ulsan** Yd No: 0388 Loa 222.20 (BB) Br ex - Dght 12.000 Lbp 210.00 Br md 30.00 Dpth 16.80 Welded, 1 dk	**(A33A2CC) Container Ship (Fully Cellular)** TEU 2824 C Ho 1026 TEU C Dk 1798 TEU incl 586 ref C.	**1 oil engine** driving 1 FP propeller Total Power: 25,228kW (34,300hp) 22.5kn MAN-B&W 7K80MC-C 1 x 2 Stroke 7 Cy. 800 x 2300 25228kW (34300bhp) Hyundai Heavy Industries Co Ltd-South Korea AuxGen: 4 x 1680kW 440V 60Hz a.c Thrusters: 1 Thwart. CP thruster (f) Fuel: 220.0 (d.f.) 3308.0 (r.f.) 97.0pd
9615676 *VRIX3* -	**SFL KATE** **SFL Kate Inc** SFL Bulk Holding Ltd *Hong Kong* *Hong Kong* MMSI: 477434500 Official number: HK-3174	**32,964** 19,233 56,798 T/cm 58.8	Class: NV (CC)	**2011**-08 **Zhejiang Zhenghe Shipbuilding Co Ltd — Zhoushan ZJ** Yd No: 1037 Loa 189.99 (BB) Br ex - Dght 12.800 Lbp 185.64 Br md 32.26 Dpth 18.00 Welded, 1 dk	**(A21A2BC) Bulk Carrier** Grain: 71,634; Bale: 68,200 Compartments: 5 Ho, ER 5 Ha: ER Cranes: 4x30t	**1 oil engine** driving 1 FP propeller Total Power: 9,480kW (12,889hp) 14.2kn MAN-B&W 6S50MC-C 1 x 2 Stroke 6 Cy. 500 x 2000 9480kW (12889bhp) AuxGen: 3 x a.c
9508847 *VRKA8* -	**SFL KENT** **SFL Kent Inc** Golden Ocean Management AS *Hong Kong* *Hong Kong* MMSI: 477792200 Official number: HK-3402	**22,656** 11,369 34,061 T/cm 48.5	Class: NV	**2012**-03 **Jiangsu Yangzijiang Shipbuilding Co Ltd — Jiangyin JS** Yd No: YZJ2006-923 Loa 181.00 (BB) Br ex - Dght 9.800 Lbp 172.00 Br md 30.00 Dpth 14.60 Welded, 1 dk	**(A21A2BC) Bulk Carrier** Grain: 47,000 Compartments: 5 Ho, ER 5 Ha: ER Cranes: 4x30t	**1 oil engine** driving 1 FP propeller Total Power: 6,480kW (8,810hp) 13.9kn MAN-B&W 6S42MC 1 x 2 Stroke 6 Cy. 420 x 1764 6480kW (8810bhp) Zhenjiang Marine Diesel Works-China AuxGen: 3 x a.c
9587221 *VRJG3* -	**SFL MEDWAY** **SFL Medway Inc** Hong Xiang Shipping Holding (Hong Kong) Co Ltd *Hong Kong* *Hong Kong* MMSI: 477346800 Official number: HK-3239	**22,656** 11,380 34,060 T/cm 48.5	Class: NV	**2011**-10 **Jiangsu Yangzijiang Shipbuilding Co Ltd — Jiangyin JS** Yd No: YZJ2006-921 Loa 181.03 (BB) Br ex - Dght 9.816 Lbp 172.00 Br md 30.00 Dpth 14.60 Welded, 1 dk	**(A21A2BC) Bulk Carrier** Grain: 47,000 Compartments: 5 Ho, ER 5 Ha: ER Cranes: 4	**1 oil engine** driving 1 FP propeller Total Power: 6,480kW (8,810hp) 13.9kn MAN-B&W 6S42MC 1 x 2 Stroke 6 Cy. 420 x 1764 6480kW (8810bhp) Hudong Heavy Machinery Co Ltd-China AuxGen: 3 x 620kW a.c
9539834 *VRHZ6* -	**SFL SARA** **SFL Sara Inc** Golden Ocean Group Ltd (GOGL) SatCom: Inmarsat C 447703193 *Hong Kong* *Hong Kong* MMSI: 477866600	**33,044** 19,231 56,856 T/cm 58.8	Class: BV	**2011**-02 **Xiamen Shipbuilding Industry Co Ltd — Xiamen FJ** Yd No: XSI409B Loa 189.99 (BB) Br ex - Dght 12.800 Lbp 185.00 Br md 32.26 Dpth 18.00 Welded, 1 dk	**(A21A2BC) Bulk Carrier** Grain: 71,634; Bale: 68,200 Compartments: 5 Ho, ER 5 Ha: ER Cranes: 4x30t	**1 oil engine** driving 1 FP propeller Total Power: 9,480kW (12,889hp) 14.2kn MAN-B&W 6S50MC-C 1 x 2 Stroke 6 Cy. 500 x 2000 9480kW (12889bhp) Hyundai Heavy Industries Co Ltd-South Korea AuxGen: 3 x 600kW 60Hz a.c Fuel: 2400.0
9587219 *VRIX4* -	**SFL SPEY** **SFL Spey Inc** Hong Xiang Shipping Holding (Hong Kong) Co Ltd *Hong Kong* *Hong Kong* MMSI: 477353900 Official number: HK-3175	**22,656** 11,369 33,985 T/cm 48.5	Class: NV	**2011**-08 **Jiangsu Yangzijiang Shipbuilding Co Ltd — Jiangyin JS** Yd No: YZJ2006-920 Loa 181.00 (BB) Br ex - Dght 9.800 Lbp 172.00 Br md 30.00 Dpth 14.60 Welded, 1 dk	**(A21A2BC) Bulk Carrier** Grain: 47,000 Compartments: 5 Ho, ER 5 Ha: ER Cranes: 4x30t	**1 oil engine** driving 1 FP propeller Total Power: 6,480kW (8,810hp) 13.9kn MAN-B&W 6S42MC 1 x 2 Stroke 6 Cy. 420 x 1764 6480kW (8810bhp) Hudong Heavy Machinery Co Ltd-China AuxGen: 3 x a.c

IMO / Call sign	Name / Owner / Manager	Tonnage	Class	Built / Dimensions	Type / Cargo	Machinery
9303792 *V7YA6* -	**SFL TIGER** *ex* Horizon Tiger *-2012* *ex* Irenes Respect *-2007* **Phoenix Tiger Inc** MCC Transport Singapore Pte Ltd SatCom: Inmarsat C 453837467 *Majuro* *Marshall Islands* MMSI: 538004616 Official number: 4616	**28,592** 14,769 39,266 T/cm 56.7	Class: AB (GL)	**2006-07 Hyundai Mipo Dockyard Co Ltd — Ulsan** Yd No: 0387 Loa 222.15 (BB) Br ex - Dght 12.000 Lbp 210.00 Br md 30.00 Dpth 16.80 Welded, 1 dk	**(A33A2CC) Container Ship (Fully Cellular)** TEU 2824 C Ho 1026 TEU C Dk 1798 TEU incl 586 ref C. Compartments: 6 Cell Ho, ER	**1 oil engine** driving 1 FP propeller Total Power: 25,270kW (34,357hp) 22.5kn MAN-B&W 7K80MC-C 1 x 2 Stroke 7 Cy. 800 x 2300 25270kW (34357bhp) Hyundai Heavy Industries Co Ltd-South Korea AuxGen: 4 x 1500kW 440V 60Hz a.c Thrusters: 1 Tunnel thruster (f) Fuel: 215.0 (d.f.) 3241.0 (r.f.) 95.0pd
9587233 *VRJS6* -	**SFL TRENT** **SFL Trent Inc** Hong Xiang Shipping Holding (Hong Kong) Co Ltd *Hong Kong* *Hong Kong* MMSI: 477274500 Official number: HK-3336	**22,656** 11,380 34,025 T/cm 48.5	Class: NV	**2012-01 Jiangsu Yangzijiang Shipbuilding Co Ltd — Jiangyin JS** Yd No: YZJ2006-922 Loa 181.00 (BB) Br ex - Dght 9.820 Lbp 172.00 Br md 30.00 Dpth 14.60 Welded, 1 dk	**(A21A2BC) Bulk Carrier** Grain: 47,000 Compartments: 5 Ho, ER 5 Ha: ER Cranes: 4	**1 oil engine** driving 1 FP propeller Total Power: 6,480kW (8,810hp) 13.9kn MAN-B&W 6S42MC 1 x 2 Stroke 6 Cy. 420 x 1764 6480kW (8810bhp) Hudong Heavy Machinery Co Ltd-China AuxGen: 3 x 620kW a.c
9600839 *VRHQ3* -	**SFL YUKON** **SFL Yukon Inc** Golden Ocean Group Ltd (GOGL) SatCom: Inmarsat C 447703192 *Hong Kong* *Hong Kong* MMSI: 477746900 Official number: HK-2907	**33,044** 19,231 56,836 T/cm 58.8	Class: BV	**2010-12 Xiamen Shipbuilding Industry Co Ltd — Xiamen FJ** Yd No: XSI409A Loa 189.99 (BB) Br ex - Dght 12.800 Lbp 185.00 Br md 32.26 Dpth 18.00 Welded, 1 dk	**(A21A2BC) Bulk Carrier** Grain: 71,634; Bale: 68,200 Compartments: 5 Ho, ER 5 Ha: ER Cranes: 4x30t	**1 oil engine** driving 1 FP propeller Total Power: 9,480kW (12,889hp) 14.2kn MAN-B&W 6S50MC-C 1 x 2 Stroke 6 Cy. 500 x 2000 9480kW (12889bhp) Hyundai Heavy Industries Co Ltd-South Korea AuxGen: 3 x 600kW 60Hz a.c
8703866 *D7RK* -	**SG-2** *ex* Jinse 102 *-2010* *ex* Seolim No. 1 *-2008* *ex* Haeryong No. 3 *-2007* *ex* Korea No. 3 *-2004* **Jeung Heung-Jun** - *Masan* *South Korea* MMSI: 440101465 Official number: CMR-876597	**160** - 126	Class: (KR)	**1987-09 Dae Sun Shipbuilding & Engineering Co Ltd — Busan** Yd No: 319 Loa 32.19 Br ex - Dght 2.901 Lbp 28.55 Br md 8.81 Dpth 3.61 Welded, 1 dk	**(B32A2ST) Tug**	**2 oil engines** sr geared to sc. shafts driving 2 FP propellers Total Power: 2,354kW (3,200hp) 13.0kn Pielstick 6PA5L255 2 x 4 Stroke 6 Cy. 255 x 270 each-1177kW (1600bhp) Ssangyong Heavy Industries Co Ltd-South Korea AuxGen: 2 x 104kW 225V a.c
8106460 *D9YO* -	**SG-3** *ex* Chung Min *-2009* *ex* Chitashio *-1993* **Hwang Kyu-Kweon** - *Masan* *South Korea* MMSI: 440006820 Official number: MSR-932033	**212** - 124	Class: (KR)	**1981-07 Shimoda Dockyard Co. Ltd. — Shimoda** Yd No: 321 Loa 33.53 Br ex 9.89 Dght 3.564 Lbp 28.02 Br md 9.61 Dpth 4.12 Welded, 1 dk	**(B32A2ST) Tug**	**2 oil engines** reduction geared to sc. shafts driving 2 FP propellers Total Power: 2,500kW (3,400hp) 12.3kn Niigata 6L28BX 2 x 4 Stroke 6 Cy. 280 x 320 each-1250kW (1700bhp) Niigata Engineering Co Ltd-Japan AuxGen: 2 x 80kW 225V a.c
8818051 *SQSA* -	**SG-311** *ex* Kaper-1 *-2008* **Skarb Panstwa** - *Gdansk* *Poland* MMSI: 261003410	*376* 112 70	Class: PR	**1990-12 Stocznia 'Wisla' — Gdansk** Yd No: SKS40/01 Loa 42.50 Br ex - Dght 2.800 Lbp 39.36 Br md 8.19 Dpth 4.10 Welded, 1 dk	**(B12D2FP) Fishery Patrol Vessel**	**2 oil engines** reduction geared to sc. shafts driving 2 FP propellers Total Power: 3,520kW (4,786hp) 17.6kn Sulzer 8ATL25D 2 x 4 Stroke 8 Cy. 250 x 300 each-1760kW (2393bhp) Zaklady Przemyslu Metalowego 'HCegielski' SA-Poznan AuxGen: 2 x 145kW 400V a.c
8818063 *SQSP* -	**SG-312** *ex* Kaper-2 *-2008* **Baltic Division - Border Guard (Baltycki Dywizjon Strazy Granicznej)** - *Kolobrzeg* *Poland* MMSI: 261003420	*378* 113 66	Class: PR	**1992-03 Stocznia 'Wisla' — Gdansk** Yd No: SKS40/02 Loa 42.50 Br ex - Dght 2.500 Lbp 40.20 Br md 8.20 Dpth 4.60 Welded	**(B12D2FP) Fishery Patrol Vessel** Ice Capable	**2 oil engines** reduction geared to sc. shafts driving 2 FP propellers Total Power: 3,520kW (4,786hp) 17.6kn Sulzer 8ATL25D 2 x 4 Stroke 8 Cy. 250 x 300 each-1760kW (2393bhp) H Cegielski Poznan SA-Poland AuxGen: 2 x 145kW 400V a.c
9336995 *9VIJ5* -	**SG CAPITAL** **Pear Orion Pte Ltd** Nippon Yusen Kabushiki Kaisha (NYK Line) SatCom: Inmarsat C 456391110 *Singapore* *Singapore* MMSI: 563911000 Official number: 394032	**106,367** 64,038 207,912	Class: NK	**2008-12 Universal Shipbuilding Corp — Tsu ME** Yd No: 067 Loa 299.70 (BB) Br ex - Dght 18.230 Lbp 291.75 Br md 50.00 Dpth 25.00 Welded, 1 dk	**(A21A2BC) Bulk Carrier** Double Bottom Entire Compartment Length Grain: 218,790 Compartments: 9 Ho, ER 9 Ha: ER	**1 oil engine** driving 1 FP propeller Total Power: 16,610kW (22,583hp) 14.0kn MAN-B&W 6S70MC-C 1 x 2 Stroke 6 Cy. 700 x 2800 16610kW (22583bhp) Mitsui Engineering & Shipbuilding CLtd-Japan Fuel: 5240.0
9483310 *3FGV6* -	**SG EXPRESS** **China Jupiter Shipping Inc** Vision Ship Management Ltd SatCom: Inmarsat C 435177211 *Panama* *Panama* MMSI: 351772000 Official number: 4108310	**94,863** 59,675 180,157 T/cm 124.3	Class: LR ✠ **100A1** SS 11/2009 bulk carrier CSR BC-A GRAB (25) Nos. 2, 4, 6 & 8 holds may be empty ESP **ShipRight** (CM) *IWS LI ✠ **LMC** **UMS** Eq.Ltr: B*; Cable: 742.5/107.0 U3 (a)	**2009-11 Dalian Shipbuilding Industry Co Ltd — Dalian LN (No 2 Yard)** Yd No: BC1800-26 Loa 294.91 (BB) Br ex 46.05 Dght 18.100 Lbp 285.00 Br md 46.00 Dpth 24.80 Welded, 1 dk	**(A21A2BC) Bulk Carrier** Grain: 201,953 Compartments: 9 Ho, ER 9 Ha: ER	**1 oil engine** driving 1 FP propeller Total Power: 18,660kW (25,370hp) 14.5kn MAN-B&W 6S70MC-C 1 x 2 Stroke 6 Cy. 700 x 2800 18660kW (25370bhp) Dalian Marine Diesel Co Ltd-China AuxGen: 3 x 900kW 450V 60Hz a.c Boilers: AuxB (Comp) 9.1kgf/cm² (8.9bar)
9483293 *3FTC* -	**SG FOUNDATION** **China Saturn Shipping Inc** Vision Ship Management Ltd SatCom: Inmarsat C 435697710 *Panama* *Panama* MMSI: 356977000 Official number: 4103010	**94,863** 59,646 180,403 T/cm 124.3	Class: NK (LR) ✠ Classed LR until 1/2/10	**2009-09 Dalian Shipbuilding Industry Co Ltd — Dalian LN (No 2 Yard)** Yd No: BC1800-25 Loa 294.91 (BB) Br ex 46.05 Dght 18.120 Lbp 285.00 Br md 46.00 Dpth 24.80 Welded, 1 dk	**(A21A2BC) Bulk Carrier** Grain: 201,953 Compartments: 9 Ho, ER 9 Ha: ER	**1 oil engine** driving 1 FP propeller Total Power: 18,660kW (25,370hp) 14.5kn MAN-B&W 6S70MC-C 1 x 2 Stroke 6 Cy. 700 x 2800 18660kW (25370bhp) Dalian Marine Diesel Co Ltd-China AuxGen: 3 x 900kW 450V 60Hz a.c Boilers: AuxB (Comp) 9.1kgf/cm² (8.9bar) Fuel: 5550.0
9288576 *HPOP* -	**SG FRIENDSHIP** *ex* Fairchem Friendship *-2014* *ex* Golden Friendship *-2012* **SG Line SA** MTM Ship Management Pte Ltd *Panama* *Panama* MMSI: 351322000 Official number: 31460PEXT5	**11,594** 6,301 19,772 T/cm 29.8	Class: NK	**2003-10 Fukuoka Shipbuilding Co Ltd — Fukuoka FO** Yd No: 1231 Loa 144.03 (BB) Br ex 24.23 Dght 9.570 Lbp 136.00 Br md 24.19 Dpth 12.80 Welded, 1 dk	**(A12B2TR) Chemical/Products Tanker** Double Hull (13F) Liq: 21,651; Liq (Oil): 21,651 Cargo Heating Coils Compartments: 26 Wing Ta, 2 Wing Slop Ta, ER 26 Cargo Pump (s): 14x200m³/hr, 12x300m³/hr Manifold: Bow/CM: 71.9m	**1 oil engine** driving 1 FP propeller Total Power: 6,230kW (8,470hp) 14.5kn Mitsubishi 7UEC45LA 1 x 2 Stroke 7 Cy. 450 x 1350 6230kW (8470bhp) Akasaka Tekkosho KK (Akasaka DieselLtd)-Japan AuxGen: 3 x 400kW a.c Thrusters: 1 Tunnel thruster (f) Fuel: 126.0 (d.f.) 938.0 (r.f.)
9499981 *9V7406* -	**SG GLORY** *ex* Crest Radiant 2 *-2011* **Star Global Marine Pte Ltd** - *Singapore* *Singapore* MMSI: 563286000 Official number: 394082	**764** 229 1,000	Class: BV	**2008-09 Guangdong Jiangmen Shipyard Co Ltd — Jiangmen GD** Yd No: GMG0633 Loa 53.00 Br ex - Dght 3.800 Lbp 48.00 Br md 12.00 Dpth 4.80 Welded, 1 dk	**(B21B20A) Anchor Handling Tug Supply** Passengers: berths: 22	**2 oil engines** reduction geared to sc. shafts driving 2 FP propellers Total Power: 2,354kW (3,200hp) 12.0kn Cummins KTA-50-M2 2 x Vee 4 Stroke 16 Cy. 159 x 159 each-1177kW (1600bhp) Cummins Engine Co Inc-USA AuxGen: 3 x 240kW 415V 50Hz a.c Thrusters: 1 Thwart. FP thruster (f) Fuel: 605.0 (d.f.)
9494876 *3FZE* -	**SG PEGASUS** *ex* Golden Pegasus *-2011* **SG Line SA** MTM Ship Management Pte Ltd SatCom: Inmarsat C 435720110 *Panama* *Panama* MMSI: 357201000 Official number: 4273611A	**8,195** 4,001 13,086 T/cm 22.9	Class: NK	**2011-03 K.K. Miura Zosensho — Saiki** Yd No: 1358 Loa 132.07 (BB) Br ex - Dght 8.664 Lbp 123.25 Br md 20.00 Dpth 11.40 Welded, 1 dk	**(A12B2TR) Chemical/Products Tanker** Double Hull (13F) Liq: 14,108; Liq (Oil): 14,000 Cargo Heating Coils Compartments: 8 Wing Ta, 8 Wing Ta, ER	**1 oil engine** driving 1 FP propeller Total Power: 4,200kW (5,710hp) 13.9kn MAN-B&W 6S35MC 1 x 2 Stroke 6 Cy. 350 x 1400 4200kW (5710bhp) The Hanshin Diesel Works Ltd-Japan Thrusters: 1 Tunnel thruster (f) Fuel: 933.0 (r.f.)

9632222 *9V9554* -	**SG SPLENDOUR** **Star Global Alliance Pte Ltd** - *Singapore* *Singapore* Official number: 397261	131 40 110	Class: NK	**2011-10 Tuong Aik Shipyard Sdn Bhd — Sibu** Yd No: 2926 Loa 23.50 Br ex - Dght 2.412 Lbp 21.30 Br md 7.00 Dpth 3.00 Welded, 1 dk	**(B32A2ST) Tug**	**2 oil engines** reduction geared to sc. shafts driving 2 FP propellers Total Power: 894kW (1,216hp) Cummins KTA-19-M3 2 x 4 Stroke 6 Cy. 159 x 159 each-447kW (608bhp) Cummins Engine Co Ltd-United Kingdom Fuel: 95.0 (d.f.)
9614919 *3EWE7* -	**SG UNITED** **Ocean Hope Maritime SA** NS United Kaiun Kaisha Ltd *Panama* *Panama* MMSI: 373693000 Official number: 4415112	92,752 60,504 181,415 T/cm 125.0	Class: NK	**2012-07 Koyo Dockyard Co Ltd — Mihara HS** Yd No: 2358 Loa 291.98 (BB) Br ex - Dght 18.214 Lbp 283.80 Br md 45.00 Dpth 24.70 Welded, 1 dk	**(A21A2BC) Bulk Carrier** Grain: 201,243 Compartments: 9 Ho, ER 9 Ha: ER	**1 oil engine** driving 1 FP propeller Total Power: 18,660kW (25,370hp) 14.0kn MAN-B&W 6S70MC-C 1 x 2 Stroke 6 Cy. 700 x 2800 18660kW (25370bhp) Hitachi Zosen Corp-Japan Fuel: 5800.0
9491276 *9V7437* -	**SG VICTORY** **Star Global Marine Pte Ltd** - *Singapore* *Singapore* MMSI: 565940000 Official number: 393750	261 78 -	Class: GL	**2008-04 Eastern Marine Shipbuilding Sdn Bhd — Sibu** Yd No: 72 Loa 30.00 Br ex - Dght 3.500 Lbp 27.73 Br md 8.60 Dpth 4.12 Welded, 1 dk	**(B32A2ST) Tug**	**2 oil engines** reverse reduction geared to sc. shafts driving 2 FP propellers Total Power: 1,790kW (2,434hp) Cummins KTA-38-M2 2 x Vee 4 Stroke 12 Cy. 159 x 159 each-895kW (1217bhp) Cummins Engine Co Inc-USA AuxGen: 2 x 80kW a.c
8115174 - - - - -	**SGF-21** *ex* Kapriz *-2007* *ex* Celeste *-2004* *ex* Celeste VII *-1996* *ex* Daiki Maru No. 25 *-1995* *ex* Dairin Maru No. 25 *-1993* *ex* Mito Maru No. 23 *-1984* - -	316 121 210	Class: (RS)	**1981-09 K.K. Yoshida Zosen Tekko — Kesennuma** Yd No: 303 Loa 35.72 Br ex 7.02 Dght 3.640 Lbp 34.29 Br md 7.00 Dpth - Welded, 1 dk	**(B11B2FV) Fishing Vessel**	**1 oil engine** reduction geared to sc. shaft driving 1 FP propeller 9.0kn Fuji 6S26NH 1 x 4 Stroke 6 Cy. 260 x 410 Fuji Diesel Co Ltd-Japan Fuel: 136.0 (d.f.)
9236121 - -	**SGS 1** *ex* Dk. No. 1 *-2008* *ex* Chang Hung No. 8 *-2003* **Nakahara Shipping Panama SA** Korea Ship Management Co Ltd *South Korea* MMSI: 440123020	5,264 1,579 10,300	Class: (BV)	**2002-12 Jiangsu Xinhua Shipyard Co Ltd — Nanjing JS** Yd No: H407 Loa 103.80 Br ex - Dght 5.650 Lbp 100.40 Br md 25.00 Dpth 7.50 Welded, 1 dk	**(A31C2GD) Deck Cargo Ship**	**2 oil engines** geared to sc. shafts driving 2 FP propellers Total Power: 3,386kW (4,604hp) 11.0kn Daihatsu 6DLM-28 2 x 4 Stroke 6 Cy. 280 x 360 each-1693kW (2302bhp) Daihatsu Diesel Manufacturing Co Lt-Japan
8033089 *UBSB* -	**SGV-FLOT** *ex* Nefterudovoz-40m *-2009* **Seaboard Universal Corp** LLC 'Samarashipping' ('Samarashipping' Ltd) *St Petersburg* *Russia* MMSI: 273458830	2,615 1,144 3,345	Class: RS	**1981-07 Sudostroitelnyy Zavod "Kama" — Perm** Yd No: 839 Loa 118.93 Br ex 13.47 Dght 3.800 Lbp 112.84 Br md - Dpth 5.82 Welded, 1 dk	**(A22B2BR) Ore/Oil Carrier** Grain: 1,821; Liq: 3,556; Liq (Oil): 3,556 Compartments: 1 Ho, 8 Wing Ta, ER 1 Ha: (70.4 x 4.9)ER Ice Capable	**2 oil engines** driving 2 FP propellers Total Power: 970kW (1,318hp) 11.0kn S.K.L. 6NVD48A-U 2 x 4 Stroke 6 Cy. 320 x 480 each-485kW (659bhp) VEB Schwermaschinenbau "KarlLiebknecht" (SKL)-Magdeburg AuxGen: 3 x 100kW a.c Fuel: 77.0 (d.f.)
9466843 *TCWW4* -	**SH-BEYKOZ** **Istanbul Buyuksehir Belediye Baskanligi** Istanbul Sehir Hatlari Turizm Sanayi ve Ticaret AS *Istanbul* *Turkey* MMSI: 271040153 Official number: TUGS 1760	747 359 250	Class: TL	**2009-07 Celiktrans Deniz Insaat Kizaklari Ltd. Sti — Tuzla,Ist** Yd No: 37 Loa 67.96 Br ex - Dght 2.500 Lbp 63.38 Br md 13.00 Dpth 3.70 Welded, 1 dk	**(A37B2PS) Passenger Ship** Passengers: 1800	**4 oil engines** reduction geared to sc. shafts driving 2 Propellers Total Power: 2,208kW (3,000hp) Volvo Penta D16MG 4 x 4 Stroke 6 Cy. 144 x 165 each-552kW (750bhp) AB Volvo Penta-Sweden
9466831 *TCTQ5* -	**SH-BEYOGLU** **Istanbul Buyuksehir Belediye Baskanligi** Istanbul Sehir Hatlari Turizm Sanayi ve Ticaret AS *Istanbul* *Turkey* MMSI: 271002736	747 359 250	Class: TL	**2009-05 Celiktrans Deniz Insaat Kizaklari Ltd. Sti — Tuzla,Ist** Yd No: 36 Loa 67.96 Br ex - Dght 2.500 Lbp 63.38 Br md 13.00 Dpth 3.90 Welded, 1 dk	**(A37B2PS) Passenger Ship** Passengers: 1800	**4 oil engines** reduction geared to sc. shaft driving 2 Propellers Total Power: 2,208kW (3,000hp) Volvo Penta D16MG 4 x 4 Stroke 6 Cy. 144 x 165 each-552kW (750bhp) AB Volvo Penta-Sweden
9466788 *TCA3009* -	**SH-FATIH** *ex* Celiktrans 34 *-2008* **Istanbul Buyuksehir Belediye Baskanligi** Istanbul Sehir Hatlari Turizm Sanayi ve Ticaret AS *Istanbul* *Turkey* MMSI: 271002699	747 359 250	Class: TL	**2008-12 Celiktrans Deniz Insaat Kizaklari Ltd. Sti — Tuzla,Ist** Yd No: 34 Loa 67.95 Br ex - Dght 2.500 Lbp 63.38 Br md 13.00 Dpth 3.70 Welded, 1 dk	**(A37B2PS) Passenger Ship** Passengers: 1800	**4 diesel electric oil engines** driving 2 Propellers Total Power: 1,656kW (2,252hp) Volvo Penta D16MG 4 x 4 Stroke 6 Cy. 144 x 165 each-414kW (563bhp) AB Volvo Penta-Sweden AuxGen: 1 x 116kW a.c Thrusters: 1 Tunnel thruster (f)
9316957 *3EFB9* -	**SH GRACE** **East Bulk Shipping SA** Toshin Kisen Co Ltd *Panama* *Panama* MMSI: 371993000 Official number: 3163806A	17,944 10,748 29,828 T/cm 40.5	Class: NK	**2006-04 Shikoku Dockyard Co. Ltd. — Takamatsu** Yd No: 1026 Loa 170.70 (BB) Br ex - Dght 9.716 Lbp 163.50 Br md 27.00 Dpth 13.80 Welded, 1 dk	**(A21A2BC) Bulk Carrier** Grain: 40,031; Bale: 38,422 Compartments: 5 Ho, ER 5 Ha: 4 (20.0 x 17.8)ER (12.8 x 16.2) Cranes: 4x30.5t	**1 oil engine** driving 1 FP propeller Total Power: 6,150kW (8,362hp) 14.3kn MAN-B&W 6S42MC 1 x 2 Stroke 6 Cy. 420 x 1764 6150kW (8362bhp) Mitsui Engineering & Shipbuilding CLtd-Japan Fuel: 1680.0
9564023 *TCYA6* -	**SH-HASKOY** **Istanbul Buyuksehir Belediye Baskanligi** Istanbul Sehir Hatlari Turizm Sanayi ve Ticaret AS *Istanbul* *Turkey* MMSI: 271040573 Official number: TUGS 1841	*175* 71 100	Class: TL	**2010-02 Almar Atlas Is Ortakligi — Istanbul** Yd No: 03 Loa 41.90 Br ex 8.80 Dght 1.800 Lbp 38.32 Br md 8.50 Dpth 2.80 Welded, 1 dk	**(A37B2PS) Passenger Ship** Passengers: unberthed: 600	**2 oil engines** reduction geared to sc. shafts driving 2 Propellers Total Power: 956kW (1,300hp) 12.0kn Volvo Penta D16MH 2 x 4 Stroke 6 Cy. 144 x 165 each-478kW (650bhp) AB Volvo Penta-Sweden
9466829 *TCTT2* -	**SH-KADIKOY** **Istanbul Buyuksehir Belediye Baskanligi** Istanbul Sehir Hatlari Turizm Sanayi ve Ticaret AS *Istanbul* *Turkey* MMSI: 271002711	747 359 250	Class: TL	**2009-03 Celiktrans Deniz Insaat Kizaklari Ltd. Sti — Tuzla,Ist** Yd No: 35 Loa 67.96 Br ex - Dght 2.500 Lbp 63.38 Br md 13.00 Dpth 3.70 Welded, 1 dk	**(A37B2PS) Passenger Ship** Passengers: 1800	**4 diesel electric oil engines** driving 2 Propellers Total Power: 1,656kW (2,252hp) 14.0kn Volvo Penta D16MG 4 x 4 Stroke 6 Cy. 144 x 165 each-414kW (563bhp) AB Volvo Penta-Sweden
9563990 *TCXH9* -	**SH-KASIMPASA** **Istanbul Buyuksehir Belediye Baskanligi** Istanbul Sehir Hatlari Turizm Sanayi ve Ticaret AS *Istanbul* *Turkey* Official number: TUGS 1800	*175* 69 100	Class: TL	**2009-12 Almar Atlas Is Ortakligi — Istanbul** Yd No: 01 Loa 41.90 Br ex 8.80 Dght 1.800 Lbp 38.32 Br md 8.50 Dpth 2.80 Welded, 1 dk	**(A37B2PS) Passenger Ship** Passengers: unberthed: 600	**2 oil engines** reduction geared to sc. shafts driving 2 Propellers Total Power: 956kW (1,300hp) 12.0kn Volvo Penta D16MH 2 x 4 Stroke 6 Cy. 144 x 165 each-478kW (650bhp) AB Volvo Penta-Sweden
9466855 *TCWO8* -	**SH-SARIYER** **Istanbul Buyuksehir Belediye Baskanligi** Istanbul Sehir Hatlari Turizm Sanayi ve Ticaret AS *Istanbul* *Turkey* MMSI: 271040027	741 382 250	Class: TL	**2009-10 Celiktrans Deniz Insaat Kizaklari Ltd. Sti — Tuzla,Ist** Yd No: 38 Loa 67.96 Br ex - Dght 2.500 Lbp 63.38 Br md 13.00 Dpth 3.90 Welded, 1 dk	**(A37B2PS) Passenger Ship** Passengers: 1800	**4 oil engines** reduction geared to sc. shafts driving 2 Propellers Total Power: 2,208kW (3,000hp) Volvo Penta D16MG 4 x 4 Stroke 6 Cy. 144 x 165 each-552kW (750bhp) AB Volvo Penta-Sweden Thrusters: 1 Tunnel thruster (f)
9564009 *TCXU7* -	**SH-SUTLUCE** **Istanbul Buyuksehir Belediye Baskanligi** Istanbul Sehir Hatlari Turizm Sanayi ve Ticaret AS *Istanbul* *Turkey* MMSI: 271040378 Official number: TUGS 1828	*175* 71 100	Class: TL	**2010-01 Almar Atlas Is Ortakligi — Istanbul** Yd No: 02 Loa 41.90 Br ex 8.80 Dght 1.800 Lbp 38.32 Br md 8.50 Dpth 2.80 Welded, 1 dk	**(A37B2PS) Passenger Ship** Passengers: unberthed: 600	**2 oil engines** reduction geared to sc.shafts driving 2 Propellers Total Power: 956kW (1,300hp) 12.0kn Volvo Penta D16MH 2 x 4 Stroke 6 Cy. 144 x 165 each-478kW (650bhp) AB Volvo Penta-Sweden
9265615 *VRYD4* -	**SHA CHAU** **Hongkong United Dockyards Ltd** The Hongkong Salvage & Towage Co Ltd *Hong Kong* *Hong Kong* MMSI: 477042000 Official number: HK-0929	295 88 170	Class: LR ✠ **100A1** SS 10/2012 tug ✠ **LMC** Eq.Ltr: F; Cable: 275.0/19.0 U2 (a)	**2002-10 Kegoya Dock K.K. — Kure** Yd No: 1075 Loa 29.00 Br ex - Dght 3.500 Lbp 23.50 Br md 9.50 Dpth 4.70 Welded, 1 dk	**(B32A2ST) Tug**	**2 oil engines** gearing integral to driving 2 Z propellers Total Power: 2,942kW (4,000hp) 13.3kn Yanmar 6N260-EN 2 x 4 Stroke 6 Cy. 260 x 360 each-1471kW (2000bhp) Yanmar Diesel Engine Co Ltd-Japan AuxGen: 2 x 80kW 385V 50Hz a.c

9323730 *VRAP2* -	**SHA TIN** **Hongkong United Dockyards Ltd** The Hongkong Salvage & Towage Co Ltd *Hong Kong* *Hong Kong* MMSI: 477990500 Official number: HK-1438	**297** 89 170	Class: LR ✠**100A1** SS 05/2010 tug ✠**LMC** Eq.Ltr: F; Cable: 302.5/22.0 U2 (a)	**2005-05 Hin Lee (Zhuhai) Shipyard Co Ltd — Zhuhai GD** (Hull) Yd No: 079 **2005-05 Cheoy Lee Shipyards Ltd — Hong Kong** Yd No: 4847 Loa 29.07 Br ex 11.12 Dght 3.500 Lbp 23.50 Br md 9.50 Dpth 4.70 Welded, 1 dk	**(B32A2ST) Tug**	**2 oil engines** gearing integral to driving 2 Z propellers Total Power: 2,942kW (4,000hp) 11.5kn Niigata 6L26HLX 2 x 4 Stroke 6 Cy. 260 x 350 each-1471kW (2000bbhp) Niigata Engineering Co Ltd-Japan AuxGen: 2 x 80kW 385V 50Hz a.c
9040390 -	**SHA TIN PRINCE** -	*1,042* 375 1,200		**1990-11 Runzhou Shipyard — Zhenjiang JS** Loa - Br ex - Dght 3.627 Lbp 61.12 Br md 12.00 Dpth 4.80 Welded	**(B34E2SW) Waste Disposal Vessel**	**2 oil engines** driving 2 FP propellers
7229227 *SUKT* -	**SHABAR** **Suez Canal Authority** *Port Said* *Egypt*	*143* - 67	Class: (GL)	**1958 L Smit & Zoon's Scheeps- & Werktuigbouw NV — Kinderdijk** Yd No: C0366 Loa 27.39 Br ex 7.83 Dght 3.074 Lbp 25.00 Br md 7.26 Dpth 3.81 Welded, 1 dk	**(B32A2ST) Tug**	**1 oil engine** reverse reduction geared to sc. shaft driving 1 FP propeller Total Power: 1,206kW (1,640hp) General Motors 16-278-A 1 x Vee 2 Stroke 16 Cy. 222 x 267 1206kW (1640bhp) General Motors Corp-USA
6608696 *9GCW* -	**SHABDA** *ex Akwadu -1985* **Amptrade Enterprise Ltd** *Takoradi* *Ghana* Official number: 316547	*1,083* 443 -	Class: (LR) ✠ Classed LR until 23/6/82	**1969-02 Newport SB. & Eng. Ltd. — Newport, Mon.** Yd No: 93 Loa 72.90 Br ex 11.61 Dght 5.030 Lbp 63.56 Br md 11.59 Dpth 7.85 Welded, 2 dks	**(B11A2FS) Stern Trawler** Ins: 1,001	**1 oil engine** with flexible coupling driving 1 CP propeller Total Power: 1,698kW (2,309hp) 15.0kn Mirrlees ALSSDM6 1 x 4 Stroke 6 Cy. 483 x 686 1698kW (2309bhp) Mirrlees National Ltd.-Stockport AuxGen: 3 x 160kW 440V 50Hz a.c
9349588 *EPBQ7* -	**SHABDIS** *ex Riona -2012 ex Second Ocean -2012* **Oghiaanous Khoroushan Shipping Lines Co of Kish** Rahbaran Omid Darya Ship Management Co *Qeshm Island* *Iran* MMSI: 422031200 Official number: 1070	**74,175** 42,558 86,018	Class: IN (GL)	**2009-12 Hanjin Heavy Industries & Construction Co Ltd — Busan** Yd No: 181 Loa 299.32 (BB) Br ex - Dght 14.523 Lbp 286.70 Br md 40.00 Dpth 24.60 Welded, 1 dk	**(A33A2CC) Container Ship (Fully Cellular)** Double Bottom Entire Compartment Length TEU 6572 incl 500 ref C. Ice Capable	**1 oil engine** driving 1 FP propeller Total Power: 57,200kW (77,769hp) 25.6kn Wartsila 10RTA96C 1 x 2 Stroke 10 Cy. 960 x 2500 57200kW (77769bhp) Doosan Engine Co Ltd-South Korea AuxGen: 4 x 2100kW a.c Thrusters: 1 Tunnel thruster (f)
9346524 *EPBR9* -	**SHABGOUN** *ex Alva -2012 ex Sabalan -2011* *completed as Iran Sabalan -2008* **Mosakhar Darya Shipping Co PJS** Rahbaran Omid Darya Ship Management Co *Qeshm Island* *Iran* MMSI: 422032300	**54,851** 34,827 66,488	Class: (LR) (BV) ✠ Classed LR until 9/2/12	**2008-07 Hyundai Heavy Industries Co Ltd — Ulsan** Yd No: 1819 Loa 294.10 (BB) Br ex 32.25 Dght 13.500 Lbp 283.20 Br md 32.20 Dpth 21.80 Welded, 1 dk	**(A33A2CC) Container Ship (Fully Cellular)** TEU 4795 C Ho 2299 TEU C Dk 2496 TEU incl. 330 ref C. Compartments: 6 Cell Ho, ER	**1 oil engine** driving 1 FP propeller Total Power: 41,040kW (55,798hp) 23.5kn MAN-B&W 9K90MC-C 1 x 2 Stroke 9 Cy. 900 x 2300 41040kW (55798bhp) Hyundai Heavy Industries Co Ltd-South Korea AuxGen: 4 x 1700kW 450V 60Hz a.c Boilers: e (ex.g.) 11.2kgf/cm² (11.0bar), WTAuxB (o.f.) 8.2kgf/cm² (8.0bar) Thrusters: 1 Thwart. CP thruster (f)
8610540 - -	**SHABNAM II** *ex Kesinee Marine 1 -2007* *ex Kyosei Maru No. 2 -2001* *ex Hiyoshi Maru No. 6 -1989* **Shabnam Vegetable Oil Industries Ltd** - *Bangladesh*	**691** 207 1,230		**1986-10 Murakami Hide Zosen K.K. — Imabari** Yd No: 258 Converted From: Products Tanker-2007 Loa 64.50 Br ex - Dght 4.500 Lbp 60.00 Br md 10.00 Dpth 4.50 Welded, 1 dk	**(A12D2LV) Vegetable Oil Tanker** Liq: 1,326; Liq (Oil): 1,326 2 Cargo Pump (s): 2x500m³/hr	**1 oil engine** driving 1 FP propeller Total Power: 736kW (1,001hp) 10.5kn Niigata 6M28AGTE 1 x 4 Stroke 6 Cy. 280 x 480 736kW (1001bhp) Niigata Engineering Co Ltd-Japan Fuel: 81.5 (d.f.) 4.0pd
9059236 -	**SHABWA** **Hodeidah Port Authority** *Hodeidah* *Yemen*	**140** - -	Class: (LR) ✠ Classed LR until 22/6/05	**1995-12 Stocznia Tczew Sp z oo — Tczew** (Hull) **1995-12 B.V. Scheepswerf Damen — Gorinchem** Yd No: 6511 Loa 22.55 Br ex 7.45 Dght 3.180 Lbp 19.82 Br md 7.20 Dpth 3.74 Welded, 1 dk	**(B32A2ST) Tug**	**2 oil engines** with clutches, flexible couplings & sr reverse geared to sc. shafts driving 2 FP propellers Total Power: 1,910kW (2,596hp) Caterpillar 3512TA 2 x Vee 4 Stroke 12 Cy. 170 x 190 each-955kW (1298bhp) Caterpillar Inc-USA AuxGen: 2 x 50kW 380V 50Hz a.c
8519899 *7OQI* -	**SHABWAH** **The Yemen Ports & Shipping Corp** *Aden* *Yemen* Official number: 0071	**212** 63 77 T/cm 1.8	Class: (LR) ✠ Classed LR until 2/12/98	**1987-04 McTay Marine Ltd. — Bromborough** Yd No: 69 Loa 28.38 Br ex 8.67 Dght 3.512 Lbp 26.52 Br md 8.01 Dpth 3.31 Welded, 1 dk	**(B32A2ST) Tug**	**2 oil engines** with flexible couplings & dr gearedto sc. shafts driving 2 Directional propellers Total Power: 1,000kW (1,360hp) 10.8kn MAN 6L20/27 2 x 4 Stroke 6 Cy. 200 x 270 each-500kW (680bhp) MAN B&W Diesel GmbH-Augsburg AuxGen: 2 x 80kW 415V 50Hz a.c, 1 x 38kW 415V 50Hz a.c
7932874 *JI3016* -	**SHACHI MARU** **Kansai Harbour Service Co Ltd (Kansai Kowan Service KK)** - *Sakai, Osaka* *Japan* Official number: 119725	*100* - -		**1979-07 Edogawa Shipbuilding Co. Ltd. — Tokyo** Yd No: 247 Loa 20.70 Br ex - Dght 1.750 Lbp 18.70 Br md 7.00 Dpth 2.80 Welded	**(B34G2SE) Pollution Control Vessel**	**2 oil engines** reduction geared to sc. shafts driving 2 FP propellers Total Power: 750kW (1,020hp) G.M. (Detroit Diesel) 12V-71-TI 2 x Vee 2 Stroke 12 Cy. 108 x 127 each-375kW (510bhp) General Motors Detroit DieselAllison Divn-USA
9558854 *EIIW9* -	**SHACKLETON** **Dublin Port Co** *Dublin* *Irish Republic* MMSI: 250002011 Official number: 404625	**284** 85 137	Class: BV	**2010-01 Astilleros Zamakona SA — Santurtzi** Yd No: 681 Loa 24.50 Br ex - Dght 5.000 Lbp 22.75 Br md 11.00 Dpth - Welded, 1 dk	**(B32A2ST) Tug**	**2 oil engines** reduction geared to sc. shafts driving 2 Voith-Schneider propellers Total Power: 3,788kW (5,150hp) 11.5kn Caterpillar 3516B-HD 2 x Vee 4 Stroke 16 Cy. 170 x 215 each-1894kW (2575bhp) Caterpillar Inc-USA
6622202 *EPQR* -	**SHAD 1** *ex Ernest I -1991 ex Ernest T -1989* *ex Heleen C -1989 ex Apricity -1982* **Denver Shipping Ltd** Seawaves Shipping Services Co Ltd *Bandar Imam Khomeini* *Iran* MMSI: 422003400 Official number: 20355	*691* 496 1,183	Class: AS (LR) ✠ Classed LR until 11/1/95	**1967-06 Clelands Shipbuilding Co. Ltd. — Wallsend** Yd No: 292 Loa 68.23 Br ex 10.60 Dght 3.722 Lbp 64.01 Br md 10.54 Dpth 4.74 Riveted\Welded, 1 dk	**(A31A2GX) General Cargo Ship** Grain: 1,666; Bale: 1,506 Compartments: 2 Ho, ER 2 Ha: 2 (15.2 x 6.4)ER	**1 oil engine** reverse reduction geared to sc. shaft driving 1 FP propeller Total Power: 662kW (900hp) 9.5kn Blackstone ETS8 1 x 4 Stroke 8 Cy. 222 x 292 662kW (900bhp) (Re-engined ,made 1967, Reconditioned & fitted 1989) Lister Blackstone Marine Ltd.-Dursley AuxGen: 2 x 50kW 220V d.c, 1 x 30kW 220V d.c, 1 x 25kW 220V d.c Fuel: 37.5 (d.f.) 2.5pd
8869775 *EPBD5* -	**SHADAB** *ex Shabtab 1 -2012 ex Yaoki Maru -2011* **Abbas Mahmoud Nezhad & Hossein Mahmood Nezhad** - *Iran* MMSI: 422019300	*199* 100 609	Class: IS	**1993-02 Sokooshi Zosen K.K. — Osakikamijima** Yd No: 316 Loa 56.00 Br ex - Dght 3.300 Lbp 49.50 Br md 9.20 Dpth 5.50 Welded, 1 dk	**(A31A2GX) General Cargo Ship**	**1 oil engine** driving 1 FP propeller Total Power: 515kW (700hp) 11.0kn Yanmar MF26-ST 1 x 4 Stroke 6 Cy. 260 x 500 515kW (700bhp) Yanmar Diesel Engine Co Ltd-Japan
7416167 - -	**SHADAD** *ex Shanak -1984* **Al-Kulaib International Trading & Construction Co WLL (A K Lines)** - *Kuwait* *Kuwait*	*200* 49 129	Class: (BV)	**1976-04 Astilleros Zamakona SA — Santurtzi** Yd No: 110 Loa 31.40 Br ex - Dght 3.301 Lbp 27.31 Br md 7.50 Dpth 3.81 Welded, 1 dk	**(B11A2FT) Trawler**	**1 oil engine** geared to sc. shaft driving 1 FP propeller Total Power: 416kW (566hp) 10.5kn Caterpillar D379SCAC 1 x Vee 4 Stroke 8 Cy. 159 x 203 416kW (566bhp) Caterpillar Tractor Co-USA Fuel: 70.5 (d.f.)
7217925 *VRVC5* -	**SHADDAD** **Chevron Hong Kong Ltd** - *Hong Kong* *Hong Kong* Official number: 343842	*298* 104 -	Class: AB	**1972 Jakobson Shipyard, Inc. — Oyster Bay, NY** Yd No: 450 Loa 32.34 Br ex 9.68 Dght 3.947 Lbp 30.94 Br md 9.15 Dpth 4.88 Welded, 1 dk	**(B32A2ST) Tug**	**2 oil engines** driving 2 FP propellers Total Power: 2,206kW (3,000hp) 12.0kn EMD (Electro-Motive) 12-645-E5 2 x Vee 2 Stroke 12 Cy. 230 x 254 each-1103kW (1500bhp) General Motors Corp-USA
9399143 *A7MS* -	**SHADDAD** **Halul Offshore Services Co WLL** - *Doha* *Qatar* MMSI: 466083000 Official number: 338/13	**5,782** 1,735 1,500	Class: NV	**2014-02 ABG Shipyard Ltd — Surat** Yd No: 382 Loa 91.10 Br ex - Dght 5.500 Lbp 83.41 Br md 18.20 Dpth 7.80 Welded, 1 dk	**(B22A2OV) Diving Support Vessel**	**5 oil engines** reduction geared to sc. shafts driving 2 Directional propellers Caterpillar 5 x 4 Stroke Caterpillar Inc-USA Thrusters: 1 Tunnel thruster (f); 1 Retract. directional thruster (f)

8605789 *A6E2238* -	**SHADEED** **P&O Maritime FZE** - *Dubai* *United Arab Emirates* Official number: UAE/D/556	**239** 71 110	Class: LR ✠ **100A1** SS 10/2012 tug Arabian Gulf and Gulf of Oman west of a line Ras al Hadd to Gwadar ✠ **LMC** Eq.Ltr: F; Cable: 332.0/19.0 U2	**1987**-02 **Bodewes Binnenvaart B.V. — Millingen a/d Rijn** Yd No: 790 Loa 28.50 Br ex 9.12 Dght 3.261 Lbp 26.19 Br md 8.81 Dpth 4.27 Welded, 1 dk	**(B32A2ST) Tug**	**2 oil engines** with clutches, flexible couplings & sr reverse geared to sc. shafts driving 2 FP propellers Total Power: 2,864kW (3,894hp) Caterpillar 3516TA 2 x Vee 4 Stroke 16 Cy. 170 x 190 each-1432kW (1947bhp) Caterpillar Inc-USA AuxGen: 2 x 125kW 380V 50Hz a.c Fuel: 94.0 (d.f.) 7.5pd
8309696 *EPBX7* -	**SHADFAR** *ex* Admiral *-2012* *ex* Dais *-2009* *ex* Iran Shariati *-2008* **Key Charter Development Ltd** Rahbaran Omid Darya Ship Management Co *Iran* MMSI: 422037500	**25,768** 14,253 43,406 T/cm 50.0	Class: (BV) (NV)	**1985**-11 **Daewoo Shipbuilding & Heavy Machinery Ltd — Geoje** Yd No: 1018 Loa 191.01 (BB) Br ex 30.03 Dght 11.618 Lbp 181.01 Br md 30.01 Dpth 16.31 Welded, 1 dk	**(A21A2BC) Bulk Carrier** Grain: 52,560; Bale: 50,134 Compartments: 5 Ho, ER 5 Ha: (17.6 x 11.0)4 (17.6 x 14.5)ER Cranes: 4x25t	**1 oil engine** driving 1 FP propeller Total Power: 8,458kW (11,499hp) 14.5kn B&W 6L60MC 1 x 2 Stroke 6 Cy. 600 x 1944 8458kW (11499bhp) Hitachi Zosen Corp-Japan AuxGen: 4 x 500kW 450V 60Hz a.c Fuel: 268.5 (d.f.) 2073.0 (r.f.)
8320121 *EPBX9* -	**SHADROKH** *ex* Aerolite *-2012* *ex* Delegate *-2009* *ex* Iran Sadr *-2008* **Great Equity Investments Ltd** Rahbaran Omid Darya Ship Management Co *Iran* MMSI: 422037700	**25,768** 14,253 43,265 T/cm 50.0	Class: (BV) (NV)	**1985**-01 **Daewoo Shipbuilding & Heavy Machinery Ltd — Geoje** Yd No: 1020 Loa 190.00 (BB) Br ex 30.03 Dght 11.618 Lbp 181.01 Br md 30.01 Dpth 16.31 Welded, 1 dk	**(A21A2BC) Bulk Carrier** Grain: 52,560; Bale: 50,765 Compartments: 5 Ho, ER 5 Ha: (17.6 x 11.0)4 (17.6 x 14.5)ER Cranes: 4x25t	**1 oil engine** driving 1 FP propeller Total Power: 8,458kW (11,499hp) 14.5kn B&W 6L60MCE 1 x 2 Stroke 6 Cy. 600 x 1944 8458kW (11499bhp) Korea Heavy Industries & ConstrCo Ltd (HANJUNG)-South Korea AuxGen: 4 x 500kW 450V 60Hz a.c Fuel: 268.5 (d.f.) 2073.0 (r.f.)
8985878 *GCLN* -	**SHAF** *ex* Akitou *-2008* **Euroka Ltd** - *London* *United Kingdom* MMSI: 235536000 Official number: 399006	**638** 191 168	Class: BV	**1981** **C.R.N. Cant. Nav. Ancona S.r.l. — Ancona** Yd No: 180 Loa 52.80 Br ex - Dght 2.570 Lbp 46.05 Br md 8.40 Dpth 5.03 Welded, 1 dk	**(X11A2YP) Yacht**	**2 oil engines** geared to sc. shafts driving 2 FP propellers Total Power: 4,698kW (6,388hp) 24.0kn M.T.U. 16V396TB94 2 x Vee 4 Stroke 16 Cy. 165 x 185 each-2349kW (3194bhp) MTU Friedrichshafen GmbH-Friedrichshafen AuxGen: 3 x 360kW 228/380V
8857186 - -	**SHAFAG** *ex* Zarya *-1993* **Baku International Sea Trade Port** *Baku* *Azerbaijan* Official number: DGR-0222	**235** 120 455	Class: RS	**1985** **Bakinskiy Sudostroitelnyy Zavod im Vano Sturua — Baku** Yd No: 381 Loa 35.17 Br ex 8.01 Dght 3.120 Lbp 33.25 Br md 7.58 Dpth 3.60 Welded, 1 dk	**(B34G2SE) Pollution Control Vessel** Liq: 468; Liq (Oil): 468 Cargo Heating Coils Compartments: 10 Ta Ice Capable	**1 oil engine** geared to sc. shaft driving 1 FP propeller Total Power: 166kW (226hp) 8.1kn Daldizel 6CHNSP18/22 1 x 4 Stroke 6 Cy. 180 x 220 166kW (226bhp) Daldizel-Khabarovsk AuxGen: 1 x 50kW, 1 x 30kW Fuel: 11.0 (d.f.)
9645322 *4JOQ* -	**SHAFAG** *ex* Safak *-2011* **Government of The Republic of Azerbaijan (The Seaside Boulevard Office Under the Cabinet of Minister of the Republic of Azerbaijan)** - *Baku* *Azerbaijan* Official number: DGR-0572	**155** 46 135	Class: TL	**2012**-03 **Bogazici Denizcilik Sanayi ve Ticaret AS — Altinova** Yd No: 1017 Loa 28.00 Br ex - Dght 1.500 Lbp 26.02 Br md 7.00 Dpth 2.90 Welded, 1 dk	**(A37B2PS) Passenger Ship**	**2 oil engines** reduction geared to sc. shafts driving 2 Propellers Total Power: 1,060kW (1,442hp) 15.0kn Daewoo V222TIH 2 x Vee 4 Stroke 12 Cy. 128 x 142 each-530kW (721bhp) Doosan Infracore Co Ltd-South Korea
6717978 - -	**SHAFICO-1** *ex* Ciclon *-1981* **Sharjah Fishing Co (Shafico)** - *Sharjah* *United Arab Emirates*	*999* 417 -	Class: (LR) ✠ Classed LR until 14/5/82	**1967**-11 **Hijos de J. Barreras S.A. — Vigo** Yd No: 1359 Loa 65.77 Br ex 11.43 Dght 4.801 Lbp 56.01 Br md 11.41 Dpth 7.24 Riveted\Welded, 2 dks	**(B11A2FS) Stern Trawler** Ice Capable	**1 oil engine** driving 1 FP propeller Total Power: 1,471kW (2,000hp) 13.0kn Werkspoor TMABS398 1 x 4 Stroke 8 Cy. 390 x 680 1471kW (2000bhp) Hijos de J Barreras SA-Spain AuxGen: 3 x 197kW 400V 50Hz a.c
9079664 *POFL* -	**SHAFIYAH** *ex* Mitsu Maru No. 21 *-2011* - - *Indonesia* MMSI: 525006108	*699* - 1,900		**1994**-06 **Kyoei Zosen KK — Mihara HS** Yd No: 261 Loa 74.45 Br ex - Dght - Lbp 70.00 Br md 11.20 Dpth 5.30 Welded, 1 dk	**(A13B2TP) Products Tanker** 3 Cargo Pump (s): 2x750m³/hr, 1x300m³/hr	**1 oil engine** geared to sc. shaft driving 1 FP propeller Total Power: 736kW (1,001hp) 11.0kn Hanshin LH31G 1 x 4 Stroke 6 Cy. 310 x 530 736kW (1001bhp) The Hanshin Diesel Works Ltd-Japan
9521980 *D5BR4* -	**SHAGANG FAITH** **Bargel Shipping (No 2) Inc** Zodiac Maritime Agencies Ltd *Monrovia* *Liberia* MMSI: 636015590 Official number: 15590	**152,306** 55,601 298,085	Class: NK	**2013**-01 **Dalian COSCO KHI Ship Engineering Co Ltd (DACKS) — Dalian LN** Yd No: NE108 Loa 327.00 (BB) Br ex - Dght 21.430 Lbp 321.50 Br md 55.00 Dpth 29.00 Welded, 1 dk	**(A21B2BO) Ore Carrier** Grain: 184,102 Compartments: 6 Ho, ER 6 Ha: ER	**1 oil engine** driving 1 FP propeller Total Power: 22,360kW (30,401hp) 14.5kn MAN-B&W 6S80MC-C 1 x 2 Stroke 6 Cy. 800 x 3200 22360kW (30401bhp) CSSC MES Diesel Co Ltd-China Fuel: 8480.0
9311440 *3EFF5* -	**SHAGANG FIRST** **Nikko Kisen Co Ltd & Sun Lanes Shipping SA** Nissen Kaiun Co Ltd (Nissen Kaiun KK) SatCom: Inmarsat C 435367610 *Panama* *Panama* MMSI: 353676000 Official number: 3185006A	**88,490** 58,950 177,656 T/cm 119.0	Class: NK	**2006**-05 **Mitsui Eng. & SB. Co. Ltd., Chiba Works — Ichihara** Yd No: 1611 Loa 289.00 (BB) Br ex 45.00 Dght 17.975 Lbp 279.00 Br md 45.00 Dpth 24.40 Welded, 1 dk	**(A21A2BC) Bulk Carrier** Grain: 197,050 Compartments: 9 Ho, ER 9 Ha: 7 (15.5 x 20.6)ER 2 (15.5 x 15.0)	**1 oil engine** driving 1 FP propeller Total Power: 16,860kW (22,923hp) 15.0kn MAN-B&W 6S70MC 1 x 2 Stroke 6 Cy. 700 x 2674 16860kW (22923bhp) Mitsui Engineering & Shipbuilding CLtd-Japan Fuel: 4950.0
9002738 *A8CN4* -	**SHAGANG GIANT** *ex* Starlight Jewel *-2008* *ex* Front Tartar *-2001* *ex* Tartar *-2000* **Bart Maritime (No 2) Inc** Zodiac Maritime Agencies Ltd SatCom: Inmarsat C 463704080 *Monrovia* *Liberia* MMSI: 636011949 Official number: 11949	**157,402** 47,220 306,902 T/cm 169.7	Class: LR (NV) **100A1** SS 08/2013 ore carrier ESP LI **LMC** **UMS** Eq.Ltr: C*; Cable: 111.0/77.0 U3 (a)	**1993**-01 **Sumitomo Heavy Industries Ltd. — Oppama Shipyard, Yokosuka** Yd No: 1179 Converted From: Crude Oil Tanker-2008 Conv to DH-2008 Loa 332.05 (BB) Br ex 60.04 Dght 22.030 Lbp 317.00 Br md 60.00 Dpth 30.60 Welded, 1 dk	**(A21B2BO) Ore Carrier** Grain: 143,713 Compartments: 10 Ho, ER 10 Ha: ER	**1 oil engine** driving 1 FP propeller Total Power: 20,158kW (27,407hp) 14.9kn Sulzer 7RTA84M 1 x 2 Stroke 7 Cy. 840 x 2900 20158kW (27407bhp) Diesel United Ltd.-Aioi AuxGen: 1 x 800kW 450V 60Hz a.c, 3 x 800kW 450V 60Hz a.c Boilers: AuxB (ex.g.) 6.4kgf/cm² (6.3bar), AuxB (o.f.) 18.0kgf/cm² (17.7bar) Fuel: 473.1 (d.f.) (Heating Coils) 4183.2 (r.f.) 59.8pd
9595424 *A8ZX5* -	**SHAGANG HAILI** **Seno Kisen Co Ltd & Erica Navigation SA** Toyo Sangyo Co Ltd (Toyo Sangyo KK) *Monrovia* *Liberia* MMSI: 636015314 Official number: 15314	**106,372** 64,038 207,725	Class: NK	**2011**-08 **Universal Shipbuilding Corp — Tsu ME** Yd No: 166 Loa 299.70 (BB) Br ex - Dght 18.230 Lbp 291.75 Br md 50.00 Dpth 25.00 Welded, 1 dk	**(A21A2BC) Bulk Carrier** Double Hull Grain: 218,790 Compartments: 9 Ho, ER 9 Ha: ER	**1 oil engine** driving 1 FP propeller Total Power: 16,610kW (22,583hp) 14.0kn MAN-B&W 6S70MC-C 1 x 2 Stroke 6 Cy. 700 x 2800 16610kW (22583bhp) Mitsui Engineering & Shipbuilding CLtd-Japan Fuel: 5200.0
9595606 *9V9139* -	**SHAGANG HONGCHANG** **PST Management Pte Ltd** Pacific International Lines (Pte) Ltd SatCom: Inmarsat C 456618010 *Singapore* *Singapore* MMSI: 566180000 Official number: 396674	**93,228** 60,051 179,469 T/cm 124.7	Class: NK	**2011**-09 **Hyundai Heavy Industries Co Ltd — Gunsan** Yd No: 2409 Loa 291.97 (BB) Br ex - Dght 18.220 Lbp 283.50 Br md 45.00 Dpth 24.70 Welded, 1 dk	**(A21A2BC) Bulk Carrier** Grain: 200,170; Bale: 181,000 Compartments: 9 Ho, ER 9 Ha: ER	**1 oil engine** driving 1 FP propeller Total Power: 18,660kW (25,370hp) 14.5kn MAN-B&W 6S70MC-C8 1 x 2 Stroke 6 Cy. 700 x 2800 18660kW (25370bhp) Hyundai Heavy Industries Co Ltd-South Korea Fuel: 5860.0
9595591 *9V9138* -	**SHAGANG HONGFA** **PST Management Pte Ltd** Pacific International Lines (Pte) Ltd SatCom: Inmarsat C 456617810 *Singapore* *Singapore* MMSI: 566178000 Official number: 396673	**93,228** 60,051 179,461 T/cm 124.7	Class: NK	**2011**-09 **Hyundai Heavy Industries Co Ltd — Gunsan** Yd No: 2408 Loa 291.97 (BB) Br ex - Dght 18.221 Lbp 283.50 Br md 45.00 Dpth 24.70 Welded, 1 dk	**(A21A2BC) Bulk Carrier** Grain: 200,170; Bale: 181,000 Compartments: 9 Ho, ER 9 Ha: ER	**1 oil engine** driving 1 FP propeller Total Power: 18,660kW (25,370hp) 14.5kn MAN-B&W 6S70MC-C8 1 x 2 Stroke 6 Cy. 700 x 2800 18660kW (25370bhp) Hyundai Heavy Industries Co Ltd-South Korea Fuel: 5860.0
9519573 *D5BR2* -	**SHAGANG VOLITION** **Nogam Shipping Inc** Zodiac Maritime Agencies Ltd *Monrovia* *Liberia* MMSI: 636015588 Official number: 15588	**152,306** 55,601 298,004	Class: NK	**2012**-09 **Dalian COSCO KHI Ship Engineering Co Ltd (DACKS) — Dalian LN** Yd No: NE107 Loa 327.00 (BB) Br ex - Dght 21.427 Lbp 321.50 Br md 55.00 Dpth 29.00 Welded, 1 dk	**(A21B2BO) Ore Carrier** Grain: 184,102 Compartments: 6 Ho, ER 6 Ha: ER	**1 oil engine** driving 1 FP propeller Total Power: 22,360kW (30,401hp) 14.5kn MAN-B&W 6S80MC-C 1 x 2 Stroke 6 Cy. 800 x 3200 22360kW (30401bhp) CSSC MES Diesel Co Ltd-China Fuel: 8480.0

9573737 *3FMN9* -	**SHAGANGFIRST ERA** **Osprey Maritime Co SA** Daiichi Chuo Kisen Kaisha SatCom: Inmarsat C 435107910 *Panama* *Panama* MMSI: 351079000 Official number: 40978PEXT1	**92,758** 60,504 181,447 T/cm 125.0	Class: NK	**2010-09 Koyo Dockyard Co Ltd — Mihara HS** Yd No: 2300 Loa 291.98 (BB) Br ex - Dght 18.237 Lbp 283.80 Br md 45.00 Dpth 24.70 Welded, 1 dk	**(A21A2BC) Bulk Carrier** Grain: 201,243 Compartments: 9 Ho, ER 9 Ha: ER	**1 oil engine** driving 1 FP propeller Total Power: 18,660kW (25,370hp) 14.0kn MAN-B&W 6S70MC-C 1 x 2 Stroke 6 Cy. 700 x 2800 18660kW (25370bhp) Mitsui Engineering & Shipbuilding CLtd-Japan Fuel: 5432.0 (r.f.)
9520716 *3FDQ6* -	**SHAGANGFIRST POWER** **Long Glory SA** Doun Kisen KK (Doun Kisen Co Ltd) SatCom: Inmarsat C 437192213 *Panama* *Panama* MMSI: 371922000 Official number: 4247411	**93,228** 60,051 179,527 T/cm 124.7	Class: NK	**2011-02 Hyundai Heavy Industries Co Ltd — Gunsan** Yd No: 2284 Loa 291.97 (BB) Br ex - Dght 18.221 Lbp 283.50 Br md 45.00 Dpth 24.70 Welded, 1 dk	**(A21A2BC) Bulk Carrier** Grain: 200,170; Bale: 181,000 Compartments: 9 Ho, ER 9 Ha: ER	**1 oil engine** driving 1 FP propeller Total Power: 18,660kW (25,370hp) 14.5kn MAN-B&W 6S70MC-C 1 x 2 Stroke 6 Cy. 700 x 2800 18660kW (25370bhp) Hyundai Heavy Industries Co Ltd-South Korea Fuel: 5868.0 (r.f.)
9520728 *3FXL* -	**SHAGANGFIRST STAR** **Long Unity SA** Doun Kisen KK (Doun Kisen Co Ltd) SatCom: Inmarsat C 435450913 *Panama* *Panama* MMSI: 354509000 Official number: 4267311	**93,228** 60,051 179,488 T/cm 124.7	Class: NK	**2011-04 Hyundai Heavy Industries Co Ltd — Gunsan** Yd No: 2285 Loa 291.97 (BB) Br ex - Dght 18.222 Lbp 283.50 Br md 45.00 Dpth 24.70 Welded, 1 dk	**(A21A2BC) Bulk Carrier** Grain: 200,170; Bale: 181,000 Compartments: 9 Ho, ER 9 Ha: ER	**1 oil engine** driving 1 FP propeller Total Power: 18,660kW (25,370hp) 14.5kn MAN-B&W 6S70MC-C 1 x 2 Stroke 6 Cy. 700 x 2800 18660kW (25370bhp) Hyundai Heavy Industries Co Ltd-South Korea Fuel: 5860.0
7375909 *S2XH* -	**SHAGAR KANNYA** *ex* Sanyo Maru No. 18 *-1987* **Mariners Navigation Co Ltd** - *Chittagong* *Bangladesh* Official number: C.594	*499* 325 1,016	Class: (NK)	**1973 Shin Nikko Zosen K.K. — Onomichi** Yd No: 88 Loa - Br ex 10.04 Dght 4.090 Lbp 52.02 Br md 10.01 Dpth 4.35 Riveted\Welded, 1 dk	**(A13B2TU) Tanker (unspecified)** Liq: 1,144; Liq (Oil): 1,144	**1 oil engine** driving 1 FP propeller Total Power: 883kW (1,201hp) Yanmar 6GL-ET 1 x 4 Stroke 6 Cy. 240 x 290 883kW (1201bhp) Yanmar Diesel Engine Co Ltd-Japan AuxGen: 2 x 40kW a.c
7114381 *9BOS* -	**SHAGHAYEGH** *ex* Shirin *-2004* *ex* Sharjah Flower *-1996* *ex* Phoenix *-1995* *ex* Pine No. 65 *-1988* *ex* Yuko Maru No. 18 *-1980* **Seyed Mohammad Rezagamaroonipour** - *Bushehr* *Iran* MMSI: 422685000	**619** 362 -	Class: AS (KR)	**1971 Niigata Engineering Co Ltd — Niigata NI** Yd No: 1033 Converted From: Fishing Vessel-2002 Loa 54.26 (BB) Br ex 8.51 Dght 3.353 Lbp 47.66 Br md 8.49 Dpth 6.00 Welded, 1 dk	**(A31A2GX) General Cargo Ship** Ins: 446 4 Ha: (1.3 x 0.9) (1.6 x 1.6)2 (1.4 x 0.9)ER	**1 oil engine** driving 1 FP propeller Total Power: 708kW (963hp) MaK 6M451AK 1 x 4 Stroke 6 Cy. 320 x 450 708kW (963bhp) (new engine 1989) MaK Motoren GmbH & Co. KG-Kiel AuxGen: 2 x 200kW 225V a.c
9418365 *V7OF4* -	**SHAGRA** **Nakilat SHI 1751 Inc** Qatar Liquefied Gas Co Ltd SatCom: Inmarsat C 453834749 *Majuro* *Marshall Islands* MMSI: 538003348 Official number: 3348	**163,922** 51,596 130,102 T/cm 163.1	Class: AB	**2009-11 Samsung Heavy Industries Co Ltd — Geoje** Yd No: 1751 Loa 345.32 (BB) Br ex 53.83 Dght 12.200 Lbp 332.00 Br md 53.80 Dpth 27.00 Welded, 1 dk	**(A11A2TN) LNG Tanker** Double Hull Liq (Gas): 261,988 5 x Gas Tank (s); 5 membrane (s.stl) pri horizontal 10 Cargo Pump (s): 10x1400m³/hr Manifold: Bow/CM: 170.4m	**2 oil engines** driving 2 FP propellers Total Power: 37,880kW (51,502hp) 19.0kn MAN-B&W 7S70ME-C 2 x 2 Stroke 7 Cy. 700 x 2800 each-18940kW (25751bhp) Doosan Engine Co Ltd-South Korea AuxGen: 4 x 4300kW 6600V 60Hz a.c Fuel: 582.0 (d.f.) 8125.0 (r.f.)
9522910 *A8XI8* -	**SHAH** **Shah Shipping Co Inc** Abu Dhabi National Tanker Co (ADNATCO) SatCom: Inmarsat C 463708957 *Monrovia* *Liberia* MMSI: 636014904 Official number: 14904	**22,668** 12,334 36,490 T/cm 46.1	Class: NV	**2010-10 Hyundai Mipo Dockyard Co Ltd — Ulsan** Yd No: 6006 Loa 187.00 (BB) Br ex 27.83 Dght 10.900 Lbp 178.00 Br md 27.80 Dpth 15.60 Welded, 1 dk	**(A21A2BC) Bulk Carrier** Grain: 47,922; Bale: 47,692 Compartments: 5 Ho, ER 5 Ha: ER Cranes: 4x30t	**1 oil engine** driving 1 FP propeller Total Power: 7,860kW (10,686hp) 14.8kn MAN-B&W 6S46MC-C 1 x 2 Stroke 6 Cy. 460 x 1932 7860kW (10686bhp) Hyundai Heavy Industries Co Ltd-South Korea AuxGen: 3 x a.c
8911243 - -	**SHAH AMANAT** *ex* Eiko Maru *-1999* **Shah Amanat Petroleum Carrier** - *Chittagong* *Bangladesh* Official number: C.1345	*499* 309 1,227	Class: NK	**1989-12 KK Ura Kyodo Zosensho — Awaji HG** Yd No: 278 Loa 64.70 Br ex - Dght 3.960 Lbp 60.03 Br md 10.01 Dpth 4.53 Welded, 1 dk	**(A13B2TP) Products Tanker** Liq: 1,128; Liq (Oil): 1,128 Compartments: 8 Ta, ER	**1 oil engine** geared to sc. shaft driving 1 FP propeller Total Power: 736kW (1,001hp) 12.0kn Hanshin LH28G 1 x 4 Stroke 6 Cy. 280 x 460 736kW (1001bhp) The Hanshin Diesel Works Ltd-Japan Fuel: 45.0 (d.f.)
9063536 - -	**SHAH AMANAT-2** *ex* Mogami Maru *-2011* **Shah Amanat Petroleum Carrier** - *Chittagong* *Bangladesh* Official number: C-1746	*592* 402 1,550	Class: NK	**1993-04 K.K. Miura Zosensho — Saiki** Yd No: 1065 Loa 74.15 Br ex - Dght 4.320 Lbp 68.00 Br md 11.00 Dpth 5.00 Welded, 1 dk	**(A13B2TP) Products Tanker** Liq: 1,814; Liq (Oil): 1,814	**1 oil engine** driving 1 FP propeller Total Power: 1,324kW (1,800hp) Hanshin LH30LG 1 x 4 Stroke 6 Cy. 300 x 600 1324kW (1800bhp) The Hanshin Diesel Works Ltd-Japan Fuel: 67.0
9420617 *9HA2528* -	**SHAH DENIZ** *ex* Solea *-2010* **Ocean Navigation 5 Co Ltd** Palmali Gemicilik ve Acentelik AS (Palmali Shipping & Agency) SatCom: Inmarsat C 424882110 *Valletta* *Malta* MMSI: 248821000 Official number: 9420617	**60,379** 32,114 107,507 T/cm 95.2	Class: LR **✠ 100A1** SS 07/2010 Double Hull oil tanker CSR ESP **ShipRight** (CM) *IWS LI **✠ LMC** **UMS IGS** Eq.Ltr: S†; Cable: 687.5/87.0 U3 (a)	**2010-07 Tsuneishi Holdings Corp Tsuneishi Shipbuilding Co — Tadotsu KG** Yd No: 1420 Loa 243.80 (BB) Br ex 42.03 Dght 14.550 Lbp 237.00 Br md 42.00 Dpth 21.30 Welded, 1 dk	**(A13A2TV) Crude Oil Tanker** Double Hull (13F) Liq: 121,560; Liq (Oil): 123,970 Cargo Heating Coils Compartments: 12 Wing Ta, 2 Wing Slop Ta, ER 3 Cargo Pump (s): 3x3000m³/hr Manifold: Bow/CM: 121.3m	**1 oil engine** driving 1 FP propeller Total Power: 13,560kW (18,436hp) 15.4kn MAN-B&W 6S60MC-C 1 x 2 Stroke 6 Cy. 600 x 2400 13560kW (18436bhp) Mitsui Engineering & Shipbuilding CLtd-Japan AuxGen: 3 x 640kW 450V 60Hz a.c Boilers: e (ex.g.) 22.4kgf/cm² (22.0bar), AuxB (o.f.) 18.6kgf/cm² (18.2bar) Fuel: 250.0 (d.f.) 3500.0 (r.f.)
9284116 *4JMW* -	**SHAH ISMAYIL KHATAI** **Azerbaijan State Caspian Shipping Co (ASCSS)** Meridian Shipping & Management LLC *Baku* *Azerbaijan* MMSI: 423205100 Official number: DGR-0450	**7,833** 3,521 13,470 T/cm 25.0	Class: RS	**2005-10 Sudostroitelnyy Zavod "Krasnoye Sormovo" — Nizhniy Novgorod** Yd No: 19619/3 Loa 149.90 (BB) Br ex - Dght 7.140 Lbp 143.11 Br md 17.30 Dpth 10.50 Welded, 1 dk	**(A13B2TP) Products Tanker** Double Hull (13F) Liq: 14,475; Liq (Oil): 14,475 Cargo Heating Coils Compartments: 2 Wing Slop Ta, 12 Wing Ta, ER 4 Cargo Pump (s): 4x350m³/hr Manifold: Bow/CM: 76.2m Ice Capable	**2 oil engines** geared to sc. shafts driving 2 FP propellers Total Power: 3,236kW (4,400hp) 10.9kn Wartsila 9L20 2 x 4 Stroke 9 Cy. 200 x 280 each-1618kW (2200bhp) Wartsila Finland Oy-Finland AuxGen: 3 x 400kW 380/220V 50Hz a.c Thrusters: 1 Thwart. FP thruster (f) Fuel: 70.0 (d.f.) 289.0 (r.f.)
6908931 *5VBG9* -	**SHAHAAN** *ex* Lesse *-2012* **MEW (Pvt) Ltd** - *Lome* *Togo* MMSI: 671220000	**1,520** 456 1,945	Class: (BV)	**1956 L Smit & Zoon's Scheeps- & Werktuigbouw NV — Kinderdijk** Yd No: C0323 Loa 70.87 Br ex 13.31 Dght 4.500 Lbp 70.00 Br md 13.00 Dpth 5.49 Welded, 1 dk	**(B33A2DS) Suction Dredger** Liq: 1,304; Hopper: 2,542	**2 oil engines** driving 2 FP propellers Total Power: 1,324kW (1,800hp) 10.3kn MAN RBL666 2 x 4 Stroke 6 Cy. 450 x 660 each-662kW (900bhp) J & K Smit's Machinehandel NV-Netherlands
7856240 *HO2672* -	**SHAHAB** *ex* Shabab *-2001* *ex* Hamriya 12 *-2001* *ex* Al Budoor *-2001* *ex* Captain Omar *-1997* *ex* Uco VII *-1993* *ex* Fuji Maru No. 2 *-1980* **White Ocean General Trading LLC** - *Panama* *Panama* MMSI: 353330000 Official number: 30015PEXT1	**198** 60 383	Class: (BV) (NK)	**1972 Iguchi Zosen Y.K. — Onomichi** Yd No: 302 Loa 29.01 Br ex - Dght 3.025 Lbp 27.67 Br md 8.40 Dpth 3.80 Welded, 1 dk	**(B32A2ST) Tug**	**2 oil engines** driving 2 FP propellers Total Power: 1,766kW (2,402hp) 10.5kn Yanmar 6GAL-UT 2 x 4 Stroke 6 Cy. 240 x 290 each-883kW (1201bhp) Yanmar Diesel Engine Co Ltd-Japan AuxGen: 2 x 24kW
9443188 *9BQX* -	**SHAHAB 1** *ex* Xing Long Zhou 115 *-1980* **Pour Yaghoubi V** - *Bushehr* *Iran* MMSI: 422748000 Official number: 17607	**472** 315 951	Class: AS	**2007-03 Wenling Henghe Shiprepair & Building Yard — Wenling ZJ** Yd No: 115 Loa 52.80 Br ex - Dght 3.450 Lbp 48.00 Br md 8.80 Dpth 4.05 Welded, 1 dk	**(A31A2GX) General Cargo Ship**	**1 oil engine** driving 1 Propeller Total Power: 986kW (1,341hp) M.T.U. 8V396TE74 1 x Vee 4 Stroke 8 Cy. 165 x 185 986kW (1341bhp) Zibo Diesel Engine Factory-China

7905584 *EPAN9* -	**SHAHAB 14** *ex* Shaheen *ex* Giswee *-2009* *ex* Ana del Mar *-1995* *ex* WEC Canarias *-1992* *ex* Ana del Mar *-1985* **Seyyed Ahmad Pourmatouri** - *Khorramshahr* *Iran* MMSI: 422006300 Official number: 20729	**2,063** 909 3,120	Class: AS (GL)	**1980**-04 **Maritima del Musel S.A. — Gijon** Yd No: 209 Loa 94.09 Br ex 13.21 Dght 5.161 Lbp 86.19 Br md 13.20 Dpth 7.45 Welded, 1 dk	**(A31A2GX) General Cargo Ship** Grain: 4,790; Bale: 4,520 TEU 185 C. 185/20' incl 66 ref C. Compartments: 2 Ho, ER 2 Ha: ER Ice Capable	**1 oil engine** geared to sc. shaft driving 1 FP propeller Total Power: 1,618kW (2,200hp) 13.0kn Deutz RBV6M358 1 x 4 Stroke 6 Cy. 400 x 580 1618kW (2200bhp) Hijos de J Barreras SA-Spain AuxGen: 3 x 380kW a.c Fuel: 47.0 (d.f.) 159.0 (r.f.) 9.5pd
9655963 *EPAM8*	**SHAHAB 110** **Mr Salehi** Shenavaran Ziba Shipbuilding Co *Khorramshahr* *Iran* MMSI: 422005400 Official number: 10180	**498** 151 950	Class: AS (Class contemplated)	**2012**-10 **Shenavaran Ziba Shipbuilding Co — Khorramshahr** Yd No: SH-A02 Loa 50.08 Br ex - Dght 2.510 Lbp 48.50 Br md 14.50 Dpth 3.00 Welded, 1 dk	**(A35D2RL) Landing Craft** Bow ramp (centre)	**2 oil engines** reduction geared to sc. shafts driving 2 Propellers Total Power: 1,342kW (1,824hp) Yanmar 6AYP-WGT 2 x 4 Stroke 6 Cy. 155 x 180 each-671kW (912bhp) Yanmar Diesel Engine Co Ltd-Japan
9035852 *ELQX7*	**SHAHAMAH** - **Shahamah Inc** National Gas Shipping Co Ltd (NGSCO) SatCom: Inmarsat C 463649710 *Monrovia* *Liberia* MMSI: 636010085 Official number: 10085	**110,895** 33,269 71,931 T/cm 108.2	Class: NV	**1994**-10 **Kawasaki Heavy Industries Ltd — Sakaide KG** (Hull) Yd No: 1438 **1994**-10 **Mitsui Eng. & SB. Co. Ltd., Chiba Works — Ichihara** Yd No: 1391 Loa 293.00 (BB) Br ex 45.84 Dght 11.270 Lbp 280.00 Br md 45.75 Dpth 25.50 Welded, 1 dk	**(A11A2TN) LNG Tanker** Double Hull Liq (Gas): 137,756 5 x Gas Tank (s); 5 independent Kvaerner-Moss (alu) sph 10 Cargo Pump (s): 10x1100m³/hr Manifold: Bow/CM: 151m	**1 Steam Turb** reduction geared to sc. shaft driving 1 FP propeller Total Power: 28,709kW (39,033hp) 19.5kn Kawasaki UA-400 1 x steam Turb 28709kW (39033shp) Kawasaki Heavy Industries Ltd-Japan AuxGen: 2 x 2700kW a.c, 1 x 2700kW a.c Fuel: 130.0 (d.f.) 5490.0 (r.f.)
6912736 - -	**SHAHAR** - **United Petroleum Corp Ltd** - *Ashdod* *Israel* Official number: MS.288	*184* 135 326	Class: (LR) ✠ Classed LR until 1/70	**1968**-11 **Israel Shipyards Ltd. — Haifa** Yd No: 16 Loa 25.61 Br ex 8.46 Dght - Lbp 24.01 Br md 8.01 Dpth 2.90 Welded, 1 dk	**(A13B2TU) Tanker (unspecified)**	**1 oil engine** reverse reduction geared to sc. shaft driving 1 FP propeller Total Power: 113kW (154hp) Scania D11 1 x 4 Stroke 6 Cy. 127 x 145 113kW (154bhp) AB Scania Vabis-Sweden AuxGen: 1 x 6kW 28V d.c, 1 x 1kW 28V d.c
7820590 *5AOS*	**SHAHAT** - **Mr El Naji Qwaidr** - *Tripoli* *Libya* Official number: 57	*128* 33	Class: (LR) ✠ Classed LR until 4/2/87	**1981**-08 **Khalkis Shipyard S.A. — Khalkis** Yd No: 926 Loa 24.57 (BB) Br ex 7.01 Dght 2.501 Lbp 19.56 Br md 7.00 Dpth 3.51 Welded, 1 dk	**(B11A2FS) Stern Trawler**	**1 oil engine** driving 1 CP propeller Total Power: 368kW (500hp) Alpha 405-26VO 1 x 2 Stroke 5 Cy. 260 x 400 368kW (500bhp) B&W Alpha Diesel A/S-Denmark AuxGen: 2 x 32kW 380V 50Hz a.c Fuel: 21.5 (d.f.)
7431143 *9LB2339* -	**SHAHD 1** *ex* Nagham F *-2009* *ex* Loire *-2002* *ex* Atlantic Trader *-1995* *ex* Pep Regulus *-1984* *ex* Mercandian Prince *-1981* **Feast Maritime Shipping & Trading Co Ltd** Feast Marine Shipping Agency SatCom: Inmarsat C 466700533 *Freetown* *Sierra Leone* MMSI: 667002193 Official number: SL102193	**2,920** 1,795 5,584	Class: IS MG (RI) (NV)	**1977**-07 **Frederikshavn Vaerft A/S — Frederikshavn** Yd No: 371 Loa 96.53 Br ex 16.08 Dght 5.648 Lbp 87.08 Br md 16.01 Dpth 8.82 Welded, 2 dks	**(A31A2GX) General Cargo Ship** Grain: 7,704; Bale: 7,234 TEU 90 C.Ho 90/20' Compartments: 2 Ho, ER, 2 Tw Dk 2 Ha: 2 (25.3 x 10.6)ER Cranes: 1x100t,2x5t Ice Capable	**1 oil engine** driving 1 CP propeller Total Power: 1,912kW (2,600hp) 12.5kn MaK 8M453AK 1 x 4 Stroke 8 Cy. 320 x 420 1912kW (2600bhp) MaK Maschinenbau GmbH-Kiel AuxGen: 2 x 144kW 440V 60Hz a.c, 1 x 48kW 440V 60Hz a.c Fuel: 244.0 (r.f.) 8.0pd
7046821 *3ESJ6* -	**SHAHD CLEOPATRA** *ex* Hoggar *-2005* *ex* Hibiscus *-1976* **Mohamed Abd Alla Hassan Saleh** - *Panama* *Panama* MMSI: 370318000 Official number: 37555PEXT	**9,420** 5,071 1,981	Class: (PR) (BV)	**1971**-04 **Mitsubishi Heavy Industries Ltd. — Kobe** Yd No: 1022 Loa 118.01 Br ex 20.48 Dght 6.120 Lbp 106.03 Br md 20.43 Dpth 12.70 Riveted\Welded, 2 dks	**(A36A2PR) Passenger/Ro-Ro Ship (Vehicles)** Passengers: unberthed: 825; berths: 320 Bow door & ramp Stern door/ramp Side door/ramp (p) Lane-Len: 380 Cars: 190	**2 oil engines** sr geared to sc. shafts driving 2 CP propellers Total Power: 8,208kW (11,160hp) 19.0kn Pielstick 12PC2V-400 2 x Vee 4 Stroke 12 Cy. 400 x 460 each-4104kW (5580bhp) Nippon Kokan KK (NKK Corp)-Japan AuxGen: 3 x 570kW 450V a.c Fuel: 172.5 36.5pd
9297802 *4JOL* -	**SHAHDAG** *ex* Makhachkala-1 *-2011* **Azerbaijan State Caspian Shipping Co (ASCSS)** - *Baku* *Azerbaijan* MMSI: 423359100 Official number: 040205	**8,547** 3,134 5,985 T/cm 24.0	Class: RS	**2005**-07 **'Uljanik' Brodogradiliste dd — Pula** Yd No: 459 Loa 154.50 Br ex 18.30 Dght 4.700 Lbp 144.92 Br md 17.50 Dpth 7.50 Welded, 2 dks	**(A35A2RT) Rail Vehicles Carrier** Passengers: driver berths: 12 Lane-Len: 960 Rail Wagons: 52	**2 oil engines** driving 2 CP propellers Total Power: 4,000kW (5,438hp) 14.0kn MAN-B&W 5S26MC 2 x 2 Stroke 5 Cy. 260 x 980 each-2000kW (2719bhp) 'Uljanik' Strojogradnja dd-Croatia Thrusters: 1 Tunnel thruster (f)
9381548 - -	**SHAHEED ALI** - **Government of The Republic of The Maldives (Ministry of Defence & National Security)** - *Male* *Maldives*	**300** - -		**2007**-03 **Colombo Dockyard Ltd. — Colombo** Yd No: 200 Loa 35.00 Br ex - Dght - Lbp - Br md - Dpth - Welded, 1 dk	**(B12D2FP) Fishery Patrol Vessel**	**2 oil engines** reduction geared to sc. shafts driving 2 Water jets Total Power: 2,690kW (3,658hp) Cummins KTA-50-M2 2 x Vee 4 Stroke 16 Cy. 159 x 159 each-1345kW (1829bhp) Cummins Engine Co Inc-USA
9519274 *HP2846* -	**SHAHEED SAGAR** - **Global Cambay Marine Services Pte Ltd** - *Panama* *Panama* MMSI: 355201000 Official number: 42978PEXT	**763** 254 1,147	Class: RI (IR)	**2007**-05 **Gujarat Marine Engineering Works — Jamnagar** Yd No: 152 Loa 48.60 Br ex - Dght 3.500 Lbp - Br md 12.50 Dpth 4.90 Welded, 1 dk	**(A14A2LO) Water Tanker** Single Hull	**2 oil engines** reduction geared to sc. shafts driving 2 Propellers Total Power: 596kW (810hp) 10.0kn Cummins NTA-855-M 2 x 4 Stroke 6 Cy. 140 x 152 each-298kW (405bhp) Cummins India Ltd-India
8857605 - -	**SHAHEEN 1** - **Shaheen Shipping Ltd** - *Chittagong* *Bangladesh* Official number: C.911	**463** 333 598	Class: (NK)	**1990** **Green Star Dockyard & Engineering Works — Bangladesh** Yd No: 101 L reg 47.70 Br ex - Dght 3.258 Lbp - Br md 9.00 Dpth 3.80 Welded, 1 dk	**(A31A2GX) General Cargo Ship** 2 Ha: 2 (12.6 x 7.5)ER	**2 oil engines** reduction geared to sc. shafts driving 2 FP propellers Total Power: 368kW (500hp) 9.0kn Chinese Std. Type 6160A 2 x 4 Stroke 6 Cy. 160 x 225 each-184kW (250bhp) Weifang Diesel Engine Factory-China
9178965 *EQYI* -	**SHAHID HAGHGOO** - **Government of The Islamic Republic of Iran (Ports & Maritime Organisation)** - *Tehran* *Iran* MMSI: 422239000	**300** 80 -	Class: (BV)	**2001**-06 **at Bandar Abbas** (Hull) **2001**-06 **B.V. Scheepswerf Damen — Gorinchem** Yd No: 7921 Loa 30.70 Br ex - Dght 4.300 Lbp 29.80 Br md 9.40 Dpth 4.80 Welded, 1 dk	**(B32A2ST) Tug**	**2 oil engines** geared to sc. shafts driving 2 Directional propellers Total Power: 3,240kW (4,406hp) Wartsila 6L26 2 x 4 Stroke 6 Cy. 260 x 320 each-1620kW (2203bhp) Wartsila Nederland BV-Netherlands
8859548 *9LB2354* -	**SHAHIN** *ex* Hisayoshi Maru *-2011* **Island Sky Trading (LLC)** - *Freetown* *Sierra Leone* MMSI: 667002223 Official number: SL102223	*199* 60 699		**1991**-12 **YK Furumoto Tekko Zosensho — Osakikamijima** Yd No: 587 Loa 58.24 Br ex - Dght 3.300 Lbp 53.00 Br md 9.40 Dpth 5.55 Welded, 1 dk	**(A31A2GX) General Cargo Ship** Grain: 1,345; Bale: 1,161	**1 oil engine** driving 1 FP propeller Total Power: 625kW (850hp) Matsui ML626GSC-3 1 x 4 Stroke 6 Cy. 260 x 480 625kW (850bhp) Matsui Iron Works Co Ltd-Japan
7026314 - -	**SHAHIN** *ex* Salvixen *-2011* *ex* Ryusho Maru *-1969* **Iran America Line Co Ltd** - *Khorramshahr* *Iran*	*130* 38 259	Class: (BV)	**1966** **Ishibashi Kogyo — Kitakyushu** Loa 25.71 Br ex 7.85 Dght 3.810 Lbp 22.86 Br md 7.47 Dpth 4.20 Welded, 1 dk	**(B32A2ST) Tug**	**2 oil engines** driving 2 CP propellers Total Power: 810kW (1,102hp) 11.0kn Makita 2 x 4 Stroke 6 Cy. 260 x 400 each-405kW (551bhp) Makita Tekkosho-Japan AuxGen: 2 x 60kW 110V a.c Fuel: 26.5 (d.f.)
8009612 *S2SK* -	**SHAHJALAL 1** - **Strajul Islam Chowdhury Trawlers Ltd** - *Chittagong* *Bangladesh* Official number: 373475	*120* 43 69	Class: (NK)	**1979**-12 **ShinA Shipbuilding Co Ltd — Tongyeong** Yd No: 231 Loa 23.40 Br ex 6.43 Dght 3.015 Lbp 21.04 Br md 6.41 Dpth 3.51 Welded, 1 dk	**(B11B2FV) Fishing Vessel**	**1 oil engine** geared to sc. shaft driving 1 FP propeller Total Power: 294kW (400hp) Yanmar 6AL-UT 1 x 4 Stroke 6 Cy. 165 x 200 294kW (400bhp) Yanmar Diesel Engine Co Ltd-Japan

8009624 **SHAHJALAL 2** *S2SL* - **Strajul Islam Chowdhury Trawlers Ltd** - *Chittagong* *Bangladesh* Official number: 373476	*120* 43 69	Class: (NK)	**1979-12 ShinA Shipbuilding Co Ltd — Tongyeong** Yd No: 232 Loa 23.40 Br ex 6.43 Dght 3.015 Lbp 21.04 Br md 6.41 Dpth 3.51 Welded, 1 dk	**(B11B2FV) Fishing Vessel**	**1 oil engine** geared to sc. shaft driving 1 FP propeller Total Power: 294kW (400hp) Yanmar 6AL-UT 1 x 4 Stroke 6 Cy. 165 x 200 294kW (400bhp) Yanmar Diesel Engine Co Ltd-Japan
5321629 **SHAHM** *SUXK* - **Government of The Arab Republic of Egypt (Ministry of War - Port of Alexandria General Organisation)** - *Alexandria* *Egypt*	*120* 31 -	Class: (LR) ✠ Classed LR until 9/68	**1962-02 Angyalfold Shipyard, Hungarian Ship & Crane Works — Budapest** Yd No: 1915 Loa 29.06 Br ex 6.91 Dght 2.763 Lbp 26.12 Br md 6.51 Dpth 3.26 Welded, 1 dk	**(B32A2ST) Tug**	**1 oil engine** with flexible coupling driving 1 FP propeller Total Power: 636kW (865hp) Lang 8LD315RF 1 x 4 Stroke 8 Cy. 315 x 450 636kW (865bhp) Lang Gepgyar-Budapest
1001544 **SHAHNAZ** *ZCCD2* - *ex* El Bravo of Cayman *-1999* *ex* El Bravo *-1995* **Coral Sands Ltd** - SatCom: Inmarsat A 1304143 *George Town* *Cayman Islands (British)* MMSI: 319908000 Official number: 726637	**1,134** 340 -	Class: LR ✠ **100A1** SS 05/2011 Yacht ✠ **LMC** Eq.Ltr: K;	**1991-05 Nuovi Cantieri Liguri SpA — Pietra Ligure** Yd No: 103 Loa 63.50 Br ex 11.00 Dght 3.200 Lbp 53.50 Br md - Dpth 5.20 Welded, 1 dk	**(X11A2YP) Yacht**	**2 oil engines** driving 2 FP propellers Total Power: 3,050kW (4,146hp) Deutz SBV8M628 2 x 4 Stroke 8 Cy. 240 x 280 each-1525kW (2073bhp) Motoren Werke Mannheim AG (MWM)-Mannheim
9270684 **SHAHR E KORD** *EPAK8* - *ex* Iran Shahr-E-Kord *-2012* **Islamic Republic of Iran Shipping Lines (IRISL)** - *Qeshm Island* *Iran* MMSI: 422905000	**23,289** - 29,870	Class: (GL)	**2012-12 Persian Gulf Shipbuilding Corp. — Bandar Abbas** Yd No: 104 Loa 187.14 (BB) Br ex - Dght 11.550 Lbp 176.48 Br md 29.80 Dpth 16.50 Welded, 1 dk	**(A33A2CC) Container Ship (Fully Cellular)** TEU 2200 Ice Capable	**1 oil engine** driving 1 FP propeller Total Power: 16,980kW (23,086hp) 20.9kn MAN-B&W 6L70MC 1 x 2 Stroke 6 Cy. 700 x 2268 16980kW (23086bhp) Hyundai Heavy Industries Co Ltd-South Korea Thrusters: 1 Tunnel thruster (f)
9349576 **SHAHRAZ** *EPBR2* - *ex* Marisol *-2012* *ex* First Ocean *-2011* **Kish Roaring Ocean Shipping Co PJS** Rahbaran Omid Darya Ship Management Co *Qeshm Island* *Iran* MMSI: 422031500 Official number: 1072	**74,175** 42,558 85,896	Class: (GL)	**2008-07 Hanjin Heavy Industries & Construction Co Ltd — Busan** Yd No: 180 Loa 299.20 (BB) Br ex - Dght 14.520 Lbp 286.70 Br md 40.00 Dpth 24.60 Welded, 1 dk	**(A33A2CC) Container Ship (Fully Cellular)** TEU 6572 incl 1200 ref C Ice Capable	**1 oil engine** driving 1 FP propeller Total Power: 57,200kW (77,769hp) 25.6kn Wartsila 10RTA96C 1 x 2 Stroke 10 Cy. 960 x 2500 57200kW (77769bhp) Doosan Engine Co Ltd-South Korea AuxGen: 4 x 2100kW 450V Thrusters: 1 Tunnel thruster (f)
7230161 **SHAHRAZAD** *J8B4693* - *ex* Tuna Service Dos *-1992* *ex* Sea Dynamic *-1990* *ex* Oil Explorer *-1989* **Divers Marine Contracting LLC** Whitesea Shipping & Supply (LLC) *Kingstown* *St Vincent & The Grenadines* MMSI: 376411000 Official number: 11166	**796** 254 1,053	Class: BV (LR) (GL) ✠ Classed LR until 22/12/92	**1972-10 Scheepsw. en Ghbw. v/h Jonker & Stans N.V. — Hendrik-Ido-Ambacht** Yd No: 326 Loa 56.44 Br ex 12.76 Dght 4.268 Lbp 51.34 Br md 12.50 Dpth 4.81 Welded, 1 dk	**(B21B20T) Offshore Tug/Supply Ship**	**2 oil engines** reverse reduction geared to sc. shafts driving 2 FP propellers Total Power: 2,942kW (4,000hp) 10.0kn Allen 12PVBCS12-F 2 x Vee 4 Stroke 12 Cy. 242 x 305 each-1471kW (2000bhp) W. H. Allen, Sons & Co. Ltd.-Bedford AuxGen: 3 x 144kW 220/440V 60Hz a.c Thrusters: 1 Thwart. FP thruster (f) Fuel: 412.5 (d.f.) 11.0pd
8323678 **SHAHRIAR JAHAN** *S2DT* - *ex* Ocean Reliance *-2009* *ex* Yare *-2009* *ex* Muirfield *-2003* *ex* Prospero *-2002* *ex* Nan An *-2000* *ex* Mei Kha Lar *-1994* *ex* Trans Pioneer *-1989* *ex* Ocean Diplomat *-1988* **SR Shipping Ltd** Brave Royal Ship Management (BD) Ltd SatCom: Inmarsat C 440500080 *Chittagong* *Bangladesh* MMSI: 405000076 Official number: 206	**22,053** 12,483 37,568 T/cm 46.6	Class: NK	**1985-02 Kurushima Dockyard Co. Ltd. — Onishi** Yd No: 2293 Loa 188.00 (BB) Br ex - Dght 10.867 Lbp 180.01 Br md 28.01 Dpth 15.40 Welded, 1 dk	**(A21A2BC) Bulk Carrier** Grain: 47,699; Bale: 45,714 Compartments: 5 Ho, ER 5 Ha: (18.4 x 14.1)3 (20.8 x 14.1) (15.2 x 14.1)ER Cranes: 4x25t	**1 oil engine** driving 1 CP propeller Total Power: 6,804kW (9,251hp) 14.0kn Sulzer 6RTA58 1 x 2 Stroke 6 Cy. 580 x 1700 6804kW (9251bhp) Sumitomo Heavy Industries Ltd-Japan AuxGen: 1 x 500kW 440V 60Hz a.c, 2 x 440kW 440V 60Hz a.c Fuel: 97.0 (d.f.) 1585.5 (r.f.) 25.0pd
6520117 **SHAHRYAR** *EPYA* - *ex* Smit-Lloyd 51 *-1969* **Bandar Abbas Supply & Service Co Inc** - *Bandar Abbas* *Iran* Official number: 138	*187* 76 -	Class: (AB)	**1965 Brooke Marine Ltd. — Lowestoft** Yd No: 331 Loa 32.87 Br ex 6.63 Dght 1.969 Lbp 30.48 Br md 6.56 Dpth 3.76 Welded, 1 dk	**(B34R2QY) Supply Tender** Passengers: 36	**2 oil engines** driving 2 FP propellers Total Power: 2,868kW (3,900hp) Maybach 2 x 4 Stroke 6 Cy. 185 x 200 each-1434kW (1950bhp) Maybach Motorenbau GmbH-Friedrichshafen AuxGen: 2 x 32kW 230V 50Hz a.c
7118105 **SHAHRYAR** *EQZB* - *ex* Sea Boutcher *-1969* *ex* Adel Star *-2000* *ex* Shahriar *-2000* *ex* Gulf Venture *-1994* *ex* Captain Jac *-1986* *ex* Sue *-1986* **Dashtinejad M S** - *Bushehr* *Iran* Official number: 16575	*198* 134 -	Class: AS (HR) (AB)	**1967 Halter Marine Services, Inc. — New Orleans, La** Yd No: 175 L reg 30.40 Br ex 8.69 Dght - Lbp 28.86 Br md 8.53 Dpth 3.66 Welded, 1 dk	**(B32A2ST) Tug**	**2 oil engines** reverse reduction geared to sc. shafts driving 2 FP propellers Total Power: 1,250kW (1,700hp) Caterpillar D398B 2 x Vee 4 Stroke 12 Cy. 153 x 203 each-625kW (850bhp) Caterpillar Tractor Co-USA AuxGen: 2 x 60kW
8741753 **SHAHRYAR 1** *EPFB* - **Mohammad Tangestani** - *Khorramshahr* *Iran* MMSI: 422526000 Official number: 20617	**395** 294 750	Class: AS	**1974-01 Arvandan Shipbuilding Co., — Iran** Converted From: Oil Storage Vessel-2005 Loa 59.90 Br ex 9.42 Dght 2.200 Lbp 56.84 Br md 9.40 Dpth 3.05 Welded, 1 dk	**(A35D2RL) Landing Craft**	**2 oil engines** reduction geared to sc. shafts driving 2 Propellers Total Power: 1,192kW (1,620hp) Cummins 2 x Vee 4 Stroke 12 Cy. each-596kW (810bhp) Cummins Engine Co Inc-USA
8110629 **SHAHZADEH** *J8B3612* - *ex* Lamnalco Snipe *-2006* *ex* Stirling Snipe *-1994* **Gide Marine Services Ltd** Whitesea Shipping & Supply (LLC) *Kingstown* *St Vincent & The Grenadines* MMSI: 376471000 Official number: 10085	**847** 358 1,175	Class: BV (LR) ✠ Classed LR until 15/10/98	**1982-07 Cochrane Shipbuilders Ltd. — Selby** Yd No: 120 Loa 61.73 Br ex 11.84 Dght 4.030 Lbp 57.21 Br md 11.60 Dpth 4.65 Welded, 1 dk	**(B21A20S) Platform Supply Ship** Cranes: 1x22t	**2 oil engines** with clutches, flexible couplings & dr reverse geared to sc. shafts driving 2 FP propellers Total Power: 2,354kW (3,200hp) 13.0kn Yanmar 6Z-ST 2 x 4 Stroke 6 Cy. 280 x 340 each-1177kW (1600bhp) Yanmar Diesel Engine Co Ltd-Japan AuxGen: 3 x 200kW 440V 60Hz a.c Thrusters: 1 Tunnel thruster (f) Fuel: 91.5 (d.f.) 4.0pd
7125720 **SHAHZAMAN** *A6E2814* - *ex* Sigiri *-2000* *ex* Bosisa *-1990* *ex* OSA Dragon *-1987* **Whitesea Shipping & Supply (LLC)** - *Sharjah* *United Arab Emirates* MMSI: 470619000 Official number: 4648	**876** 262 1,190	Class: GL (LR) ✠ Classed LR until 19/2/82	**1972-05 Vosper Thornycroft Uniteers Pte Ltd — Singapore** Yd No: B.912 Loa 56.47 Br ex 13.39 Dght 3.899 Lbp 51.87 Br md 13.11 Dpth 4.58 Welded, 1 dk	**(B21B20A) Anchor Handling Tug Supply** Cranes: 1x175t,1x5t	**2 oil engines** reverse reduction geared to sc. shafts driving 2 FP propellers Total Power: 2,574kW (3,500hp) 11.0kn Deutz SBA12M528 2 x Vee 4 Stroke 12 Cy. 220 x 280 each-1287kW (1750bhp) Kloeckner Humboldt Deutz AG-West Germany AuxGen: 2 x 180kW 440V 60Hz a.c, 1 x 96kW 440V 60Hz a.c Thrusters: 1 Thwart. FP thruster (f) Fuel: 510.0
8023711 **SHAIKAT** - - **Government of The People's Republic of Bangladesh (Ministry of Food)** - *Bangladesh*	*215* - 400		**1984-06 Highspeed Shipbuilding & Heavy Engineering Co Ltd — Dhaka** Yd No: 83 Loa - Br ex - Dght - Lbp 48.01 Br md 7.82 Dpth 2.52 Welded	**(A31A2GX) General Cargo Ship**	**1 oil engine** geared to sc. shaft driving 1 FP propeller Total Power: 287kW (390hp) Deutz SBA6M816 1 x 4 Stroke 6 Cy. 142 x 160 287kW (390bhp) Kloeckner Humboldt Deutz AG-West Germany
8743543 **SHAIKHA-1** *5IM580* - *ex* Ismail 1 *-2012* **Al Behar Shipping Agencies & Ship Oil Supply** - *Zanzibar* *Tanzania (Zanzibar)* MMSI: 677048000 Official number: 300323	**201** 60 788		**2005-01 in Iraq** Loa 30.00 Br ex - Dght - Lbp - Br md 8.00 Dpth 4.00 Welded, 1 dk	**(B32A2ST) Tug**	**1 oil engine** reduction geared to sc. shaft driving 1 Propeller 9.0kn Skoda 1 x 4 Stroke Skoda-Praha

6822577 - -	**SHAIMA** *ex* Saad 7 *ex* Gray Beaver *ex* Al Qader *-1982* *ex* Lady Howard *-1971* **Juma Abu Sheikha** -	*142* - 45	Class: (LR) (HR) ✠ Classed LR until 27/11/87	**1968**-10 **Richards (Shipbuilders) Ltd — Lowestoft** Yd No: 495 Loa 28.96 Br ex 7.62 Dght 3.125 Lbp 26.22 Br md 7.17 Dpth 3.66 Welded, 1 dk	**(B32A2ST) Tug**	**1 oil engine** reverse reduction geared to sc. shaft driving 1 FP propeller Total Power: 993kW (1,350hp) 11.5kn Ruston 6ARM 1 x 4 Stroke 6 Cy. 260 x 368 993kW (1350bhp) Ruston & Hornsby Ltd.-Lincoln AuxGen: 2 x 29kW 220V d.c Fuel: 36.5 (d.f.)
6902743 - -	**SHAIMA-2** *ex* Kanhaiya *-1993* *ex* Sea Gull *-1993* *ex* Grayotter *-1984* *ex* Al Hamed *-1981* *ex* Elizabeth Howard *-1971* **Ahmed Khalifa Mohamed Juma** -	*150* - -	Class: (LR) (HR) ✠ Classed LR until 9/3/88	**1969**-02 **Richards (Shipbuilders) Ltd — Lowestoft** Yd No: 497 Loa 28.96 Br ex 7.62 Dght 3.069 Lbp 26.22 Br md 7.17 Dpth 3.66 Welded, 1 dk	**(B32A2ST) Tug**	**1 oil engine** reverse reduction geared to sc. shaft driving 1 FP propeller Total Power: 993kW (1,350hp) 11.5kn Ruston 6ARM 1 x 4 Stroke 6 Cy. 260 x 368 993kW (1350bhp) Ruston & Hornsby Ltd.-Lincoln AuxGen: 2 x 29kW 220V d.c Fuel: 36.5 (d.f.)
7611169 *4JEJ* -	**SHAIR SABIR** *ex* Poet Sabir *-1994* **Azerbaijan State Caspian Shipping Co (ASCSS)** Meridian Shipping & Management LLC *Baku* *Azerbaijan* MMSI: 423059100 Official number: DGR-0020	**2,434** 994 3,135 T/cm 13.0	Class: RS	**1975 Sudostroitelnyy Zavod "Krasnoye Sormovo" — Gorkiy** Yd No: 50 Loa 114.03 Br ex 13.21 Dght 3.649 Lbp 108.01 Br md 12.98 Dpth 5.52 Welded, 1 dk	**(A31A2GX) General Cargo Ship** Bale: 4,287 Compartments: 4 Ho, ER 4 Ha: (17.6 x 9.3)3 (18.0 x 9.3)ER Ice Capable	**2 oil engines** driving 2 FP propellers Total Power: 970kW (1,318hp) 10.8kn S.K.L. 6NVD48A-U 2 x 4 Stroke 6 Cy. 320 x 480 each-485kW (659bhp) VEB Schwermaschinenbau "KarlLiebknecht" (SKL)-Magdeburg AuxGen: 3 x 50kW Fuel: 102.0 (d.f.)
7640732 - -	**SHAIR VIDADI** *ex* Poet Vidadi *-1994* **Azerbaijan State Caspian Shipping Co (ASCSS)** Meridian Shipping & Management LLC SatCom: Inmarsat C 442306910 *Baku* *Azerbaijan* MMSI: 423069100 Official number: DGR-0021	**2,434** 939 3,135	Class: (RS)	**1976**-08 **Sudostroitelnyy Zavod im Volodarskogo — Rybinsk** Yd No: 72 Loa 114.03 Br ex 13.21 Dght 3.649 Lbp 108.01 Br md 12.98 Dpth 5.52 Welded, 1 dk	**(A31A2GX) General Cargo Ship** Bale: 4,297 Compartments: 4 Ho, ER 4 Ha: (17.6 x 9.3)3 (18.0 x 9.3)ER Ice Capable	**2 oil engines** driving 2 FP propellers Total Power: 970kW (1,318hp) 10.8kn S.K.L. 6NVD48A-U 2 x 4 Stroke 6 Cy. 320 x 480 each-485kW (659bhp) VEB Schwermaschinenbau "KarlLiebknecht" (SKL)-Magdeburg AuxGen: 3 x 50kW Fuel: 102.0 (d.f.)
7905560 *D6DE8* -	**SHAKER** *ex* Panza *-2005* *ex* Sancho Panza *-2005* **Gulf Promotrade for Marine Service & General Trading Ltd** - SatCom: Inmarsat C 461643110 *Moroni* *Union of Comoros* MMSI: 616431000 Official number: 1200504	**4,506** 1,357 1,400	Class: (LR) (HR) ✠ Classed LR until 12/1/09	**1980**-11 **Astilleros de Murueta S.A. — Gernika-Lumo** Yd No: 141 Loa 88.22 Br ex 15.68 Dght 3.766 Lbp 78.69 Br md 15.50 Dpth 3.79 Welded, 2 dks light cargoes only 2 hoistable decks	**(A35A2RR) Ro-Ro Cargo Ship** Stern door/ramp (centre)	**1 oil engine** driving 1 CP propeller Total Power: 1,912kW (2,600hp) Deutz RBV8M358 1 x 4 Stroke 8 Cy. 400 x 580 1912kW (2600bhp) Hijos de J Barreras SA-Spain AuxGen: 3 x 168kW 380V 50Hz a.c Thrusters: 1 Thwart. FP thruster
8823434 *9BEY* -	**SHAKER** *ex* Shin Ryowa No. 5 *-2006* **Mahmodnejad A** - *Khorramshahr* *Iran* Official number: 822	**492** 199 700	Class: AS	**1988**-08 **K.K. Kamishima Zosensho — Osakikamijima** Yd No: 225 Loa 54.48 Br ex - Dght 3.800 Lbp 49.50 Br md 9.00 Dpth 5.50 Welded, 1 dk	**(A31A2GX) General Cargo Ship**	**1 oil engine** reverse geared to sc. shaft driving 1 FP propeller Total Power: 625kW (850hp) Akasaka T26SR 1 x 4 Stroke 6 Cy. 260 x 440 625kW (850bhp) Akasaka Tekkosho KK (Akasaka DieselLtd)-Japan
8879108 *T2ND4* -	**SHAKER** *ex* Fukutoku Maru No. 1 *-2013* *ex* Shosen Maru *-2011* **Mohammad Reza Raeisian & Habib Matough Pour** - *Funafuti* *Tuvalu* Official number: 29549413	*183* - 527	Class: IZ	**1994**-09 **K.K. Kamishima Zosensho — Osakikamijima** Yd No: 567 Loa 53.75 Br ex - Dght 3.160 Lbp 47.00 Br md 9.00 Dpth 5.20 Welded, 1 dk	**(A31A2GX) General Cargo Ship**	**1 oil engine** driving 1 FP propeller Total Power: 736kW (1,001hp) 12.5kn Hanshin LH26G 1 x 4 Stroke 6 Cy. 260 x 440 736kW (1001bhp) The Hanshin Diesel Works Ltd-Japan
7929102 *5VCH4* -	**SHAKER 1** *ex* Ajman Maya *-2008* *ex* Maya I *-2004* *ex* Marco V *-2001* *ex* Mario *-2000* **HOM Management Consultancy FZ LLC** - *Lome* *Togo* MMSI: 671398000	**5,841** 1,752 3,250	Class: (HR) (RI)	**1981**-07 **Cantiere Navale Visentini di Visentini F e C SAS — Porto Viro** Yd No: 139 Loa 110.85 (BB) Br ex 19.72 Dght 4.701 Lbp 97.52 Br md 19.70 Dpth 11.76 Welded, 2 dks	**(A35A2RR) Ro-Ro Cargo Ship** Passengers: cabins: 3; berths: 10; driver berths: 12 Stern door/ramp Len: 14.50 Wid: 13.20 Swl: - Lane-Len: 732 Trailers: 61 TEU 247 C RoRo Dk 117 TEU C Dk 130 TEU	**1 oil engine** driving 1 CP propeller Total Power: 2,589kW (3,520hp) 14.0kn Nohab F216V 1 x Vee 4 Stroke 16 Cy. 250 x 300 2589kW (3520bhp) Nohab Diesel AB-Sweden AuxGen: 4 x 205kW 380V 50Hz a.c Thrusters: 1 Thwart. FP thruster (f) Fuel: 431.5 (d.f.) 11.0pd
8223244 *5VCL5* -	**SHAKER 2** *ex* Kibris Yildizi *-2013* *ex* Rijeka *-2010* *ex* Lilleborg *-2003* *ex* Zohra *-2001* *ex* Vis *-1996* **Star Line Maritime Co Ltd** - *Lome* *Togo* MMSI: 671424000	**7,084** 2,125 3,979	Class: TL (RI) (BV) (CS)	**1984**-11 **Cantiere Navale Visentini di Visentini F e C SAS — Porto Viro** Yd No: 149 Loa 125.60 (BB) Br ex - Dght 4.752 Lbp 111.90 Br md 19.70 Dpth 11.75 Welded, 2 dks	**(A35A2RR) Ro-Ro Cargo Ship** Passengers: cabins: 12; driver berths: 12 Stern door/ramp Len: 12.00 Wid: 13.20 Swl: - Lane-Len: 900 Lane-clr ht: 6.10 Trailers: 75 TEU 347 incl 10 ref C.	**1 oil engine** with flexible couplings & sr gearedto sc. shaft driving 1 CP propeller Total Power: 4,089kW (5,559hp) Wartsila 12V32 1 x Vee 4 Stroke 12 Cy. 320 x 350 4089kW (5559bhp) Oy Wartsila Ab-Finland Thrusters: 1 Thwart. CP thruster (f)
9576636 *SSFF* -	**SHAKER ABD ELWAHED** **Egyptian Armaments Authority** - *Alexandria* *Egypt*	**141** 42 -	Class: BV	**2010**-07 **Brodogradiliste Novi Sad doo — Novi Sad** (Hull) Yd No: (509642) **2010**-07 **B.V. Scheepswerf Damen — Gorinchem** Yd No: 509642 Loa 26.16 Br ex 7.90 Dght 3.710 Lbp 22.57 Br md 7.80 Dpth 3.74 Welded, 1 dk	**(B32A2ST) Tug**	**2 oil engines** reduction geared to sc. shafts driving 2 FP propellers Total Power: 2,028kW (2,758hp) Caterpillar 3512B 2 x Vee 4 Stroke 12 Cy. 170 x 190 each-1014kW (1379bhp) Caterpillar Inc-USA AuxGen: 2 x 51kW 400/230V 50Hz a.c
9081485 *4JDC* -	**SHAKHRIYAR** **Caspian Fish Co** - *Baku* *Azerbaijan* Official number: DGR-0146	**189** 57 73	Class: (RS)	**1992**-09 **OAO Astrakhanskaya Sudoverf — Astrakhan** Yd No: 99 Loa 31.85 Br ex 7.08 Dght 2.100 Lbp 27.80 Br md - Dpth 3.15 Welded, 1 dk	**(B11B2FV) Fishing Vessel** Ins: 100 Ice Capable	**1 oil engine** geared to sc. shaft driving 1 FP propeller Total Power: 232kW (315hp) 10.3kn Daldizel 6CHSPN2A18-315 1 x 4 Stroke 6 Cy. 180 x 220 232kW (315bhp) Daldizel-Khabarovsk AuxGen: 2 x 25kW a.c Fuel: 14.0 (d.f.)
7023829 - -	**SHAKHTYOR** **Polus-Nord Co Ltd (OOO 'Polyus-Nord')** -	**245** 74 92	Class: (RS)	**1970**-07 **VEB Schiffswerft "Edgar Andre" — Magdeburg** Yd No: 7030 Loa 34.80 Br ex 8.51 Dght 2.921 Lbp 30.41 Br md 8.21 Dpth 3.71 Welded, 1 dk	**(B32A2ST) Tug** Ice Capable	**1 oil engine** driving 1 CP propeller Total Power: 552kW (750hp) 11.5kn S.K.L. 6NVD48A-2U 1 x 4 Stroke 6 Cy. 320 x 480 552kW (750bhp) VEB Schwermaschinenbau "KarlLiebknecht" (SKL)-Magdeburg AuxGen: 2 x 44kW Fuel: 50.0 (d.f.)
7438220 *UPOW* -	**SHAKHTYORSK** *ex* RS-300 No. 67 *-1996* **A/O 'Kazakhrybflot'** - *Bautino* *Kazakhstan* Official number: 730407	**182** 55 42	Class: (RS)	**1974 Astrakhanskaya Sudoverf im. "Kirova" — Astrakhan** Yd No: 67 Converted From: Fishing Vessel-1995 Loa 34.02 Br ex 7.12 Dght 2.640 Lbp 30.00 Br md - Dpth 3.69 Welded, 1 dk	**(B12B2FC) Fish Carrier** Compartments: 1 Ho, ER 1 Ha: (1.3 x 1.6) Derricks: 2x2t; Winches: 2 Ice Capable	**1 oil engine** driving 1 FP propeller Total Power: 224kW (305hp) 9.5kn S.K.L. 8NVD36-1U 1 x 4 Stroke 8 Cy. 240 x 360 224kW (305bhp) VEB Schwermaschinenbau "KarlLiebknecht" (SKL)-Magdeburg
8810475 *9BJV* -	**SHAKIBA** *ex* Setaysh *-2006* *ex* Fuji *-2005* **Mahmodnejad A** - *Bushehr* *Iran* Official number: 850	**605** 399 677	Class: AS	**1988**-09 **Sanuki Shipbuilding & Iron Works Co Ltd — Mitoyo KG** Yd No: 1186 Loa 57.36 (BB) Br ex - Dght 3.300 Lbp 51.90 Br md 9.30 Dpth 5.55 Welded, 2 dks	**(A31A2GX) General Cargo Ship** Bale: 1,193 Compartments: 1 Ho, ER 1 Ha: ER	**1 oil engine** driving 1 FP propeller Total Power: 625kW (850hp) 10.5kn Niigata 6M26BFT 1 x 4 Stroke 6 Cy. 260 x 460 625kW (850bhp) Niigata Engineering Co Ltd-Japan
8619211 *9BCV* -	**SHAKIL** *ex* Kinei Maru *-2003* **Mahmodnejad A** - *Bushehr* *Iran* Official number: 778	**495** 280 697	Class: AS	**1987**-02 **Taiyo Shipbuilding Co Ltd — Sanyoonoda YC** Yd No: 200 Loa 55.35 (BB) Br ex 9.43 Dght 3.280 Lbp 50.02 Br md 9.40 Dpth 5.52 Welded, 1 dk	**(A31A2GX) General Cargo Ship** Bale: 1,148 Compartments: 1 Ho, ER 1 Ha: ER	**1 oil engine** with clutches & reverse reduction geared to sc. shaft driving 1 FP propeller Total Power: 588kW (799hp) Hanshin 6LU26G 1 x 4 Stroke 6 Cy. 260 x 440 588kW (799bhp) The Hanshin Diesel Works Ltd-Japan

IMO / Call sign	Name / Owner / Port	Tonnage	Class	Builder / Dimensions	Type	Machinery
6822204 *ATCT* -	**SHAKTAN** **Prince Marine Transport Services Pvt Ltd** - *Kochi* *India* Official number: 1297	*272* - -	Class: (LR) ✠ Classed LR until 10/69	**1968-08 D.W. Kremer Sohn — Elmshorn** Yd No: 1128 Loa 33.66 Br ex 9.38 Dght 3.404 Lbp 30.26 Br md 8.91 Dpth 4.27 Welded, 1 dk	**(B32A2ST) Tug**	**2 oil engines** sr reverse geared to sc. shafts driving 2 FP propellers Total Power: 1,030kW (1,400hp) MAN G7V235/330ATL 2 x 4 Stroke 7 Cy. 235 x 330 each-515kW (700bhp) Maschinenbau Augsburg Nuernberg (MAN)-Augsburg AuxGen: 3 x 23kW 415V 50Hz a.c
8869361 *UISY* -	**SHALA** *ex* Volgo-Don 5094 *-1994* **CJSC 'Moskovskiy'** JSC Polar Shipping SatCom: Inmarsat C 427300288 *St Petersburg* *Russia* MMSI: 273338400 Official number: 865981	**2,829** 1,012 4,000	Class: RS	**1986-03 Santierul Naval Oltenita S.A. — Oltenita** Yd No: 204 Shortened-1994 Loa 105.30 Br ex 16.70 Dght 3.840 Lbp 100.24 Br md 16.50 Dpth 5.50 Welded, 1 dk	**(A31A2GX) General Cargo Ship** Grain: 3,847 Compartments: 2 Ho, ER 2 Ha: (27.6 x 13.2) (28.2 x 13.2)ER Ice Capable	**2 oil engines** driving 2 FP propellers Total Power: 1,324kW (1,800hp) 10.8kn Dvigatel Revolyutsii 6CHRN36/45 2 x 4 Stroke 6 Cy. 360 x 450 each-662kW (900bhp) Zavod "Dvigatel Revolyutsii"-Gorkiy AuxGen: 2 x 100kW a.c Thrusters: 1 Thwart. FP thruster (f)
9122502 - -	**SHALAKAMY 1** **Shalkamy Red Sea Co** - *Alexandria* *Egypt*	*200* - 50		**1995-10 Shalkami Shipyard — Giza** Yd No: 11/95 Loa 20.70 Br ex 6.30 Dght 1.500 Lbp 16.60 Br md 6.00 Dpth 3.50 Welded, 2 dks	**(A37A2PC) Passenger/Cruise** Passengers: cabins: 6; berths: 12	**2 oil engines** with clutches, flexible couplings & sr geared to sc. shafts driving 2 FP propellers Total Power: 224kW (304hp) 10.0kn Caterpillar 3208TA 2 x Vee 4 Stroke 8 Cy. 114 x 127 each-112kW (152bhp) Caterpillar Inc-USA
8127921 *GDCL* -	**SHALDER** **Shetland Islands Council Towage Operations** - *Lerwick* *United Kingdom* MMSI: 232003479 Official number: 399393	**538** 161 235	Class: LR ✠ **100A1** CS 08/2013 tug ✠ **LMC** **UMS** Eq.Ltr: I; Cable: 330.0/30.0 U2 (a)	**1983-08 Ferguson-Ailsa Ltd — Port Glasgow** Yd No: 490 Loa 37.44 Br ex 11.82 Dght 5.376 Lbp 35.01 Br md 11.31 Dpth 4.20 Welded, 1 dk	**(B32A2ST) Tug**	**2 oil engines** sr geared to sc. shafts driving 2 Voith-Schneider propellers Total Power: 2,942kW (4,000hp) Ruston 12RKCM 2 x Vee 4 Stroke 12 Cy. 254 x 305 each-1471kW (2000bhp) Ruston Diesels Ltd.-Newton-le-Willows AuxGen: 3 x 80kW 440V 50Hz a.c Fuel: 141.0 (d.f.) 14.5pd
8905191 - -	**SHALEM** *ex* New Tsushima *-2012* **PT Surya Timur Lines** - *Indonesia*	*1,776* - 733		**1989-10 Kanda Zosensho K.K. — Kawajiri** Yd No: 329 Loa 93.20 (BB) Br ex - Dght 3.930 Lbp 85.00 Br md 14.40 Dpth 5.20 Welded, 2 dks	**(A36A2PR) Passenger/Ro-Ro Ship (Vehicles)** Passengers: unberthed: 975	**2 oil engines** with clutches, flexible couplings & sr reverse geared to sc. shafts driving 2 FP propellers Total Power: 5,884kW (8,000hp) 19.5kn Niigata 8MG32CLX 2 x 4 Stroke 8 Cy. 320 x 420 each-2942kW (4000bhp) Niigata Engineering Co Ltd-Japan AuxGen: 2 x 480kW 225V 60Hz a.c Thrusters: 1 Thwart. CP thruster (f)
8933605 - -	**SHALIM** **Aliansoil LLC** - *Murmansk* *Russia*	**191** 85 323	Class: RS	**1984 Svetlovskiy Sudoremontnyy Zavod — Svetlyy** Yd No: 22 Loa 29.45 Br ex 8.15 Dght 3.120 Lbp 28.50 Br md 7.58 Dpth 3.60 Welded, 1 dk	**(B34G2SE) Pollution Control Vessel** Liq: 336; Liq (Oil): 336 Compartments: 8 Ta Ice Capable	**1 oil engine** geared to sc. shaft driving 1 FP propeller Total Power: 165kW (224hp) 7.5kn Daldizel 6CHNSP18/22 1 x 4 Stroke 6 Cy. 180 x 220 165kW (224bhp) Daldizel-Khabarovsk AuxGen: 1 x 50kW, 1 x 25kW Fuel: 11.0 (d.f.)
8990641 - -	**SHALIMAR I** *ex* Shalimar *-2010* - -	**155** 46 19		**2004 Superyachts GmbH — Saal/Donau** Yd No: 54 Loa 31.00 Br ex 6.80 Dght 1.800 Lbp 25.52 Br md 6.40 Dpth 3.29 Bonded, 1 dk	**(X11A2YP) Yacht** Hull Material: Reinforced Plastic	**2 oil engines** geared to sc. shafts driving 2 Propellers Total Power: 2,942kW (4,000hp) M.T.U. 16V2000M91 2 x Vee 4 Stroke 16 Cy. 130 x 150 each-1471kW (2000bhp) MTU Friedrichshafen GmbH-Friedrichshafen
8713005 *MJLF9* PD 303	**SHALIMAR II** *ex* Ulysses II *-2002* **Shalimar Fishing Co Ltd** Peterhead Fishermen Ltd SatCom: Inmarsat C 423325410 *Peterhead* *United Kingdom* MMSI: 235003850 Official number: A13161	**246** 74 146		**1988-07 James N. Miller & Sons Ltd. — St. Monans** Yd No: 1034 Loa 26.52 Br ex 7.42 Dght - Lbp 23.37 Br md 7.36 Dpth 3.92 Welded, 1 dk	**(B11A2FS) Stern Trawler** Ins: 180	**1 oil engine** with clutches, flexible couplings & sr geared to sc. shaft driving 1 CP propeller Total Power: 625kW (850hp) Alpha 5L23/30 1 x 4 Stroke 5 Cy. 225 x 300 625kW (850bhp) MAN B&W Diesel A/S-Denmark
9122514 - -	**SHALKAMY EXPLORER** **Shalkamy Red Sea Co** - *Alexandria* *Egypt*	**200** - 50		**1997 Shalkami Shipyard — Giza** Yd No: 12/95 Loa 23.90 Br ex - Dght 1.500 Lbp 20.00 Br md 6.00 Dpth 3.50 Welded, 1 dk	**(A37A2PC) Passenger/Cruise** Passengers: cabins: 6; berths: 12	**2 oil engines** with clutches, flexible couplings & sr geared to sc. shafts driving 2 FP propellers Total Power: 354kW (482hp) 10.0kn Caterpillar D334 2 x 4 Stroke 6 Cy. 121 x 152 each-177kW (241bhp) Caterpillar Inc-USA
9122801 - -	**SHALKAMY EXPLORER 1** **Shalkamy Red Sea Co** - *Alexandria* *Egypt*	**400** - 50		**1997-12 Shalkami Shipyard — Giza** Yd No: 15/95 Loa 36.30 Br ex - Dght 1.900 Lbp 32.20 Br md 8.00 Dpth 3.60 Welded, 1 dk	**(A37A2PC) Passenger/Cruise**	**2 oil engines** geared to sc. shafts driving 2 FP propellers Total Power: 1,822kW (2,478hp) 14.0kn Caterpillar 3412TA 2 x Vee 4 Stroke 12 Cy. 137 x 152 each-911kW (1239bhp) Caterpillar Inc-USA
9123776 - -	**SHALKAMY EXPLORER 2** **Shalkamy Red Sea Co** - *Alexandria* *Egypt*	**400** - 50		**1997-12 Shalkami Shipyard — Giza** Yd No: 14/95 Loa 36.30 Br ex - Dght 1.900 Lbp 31.40 Br md 7.00 Dpth 3.60 Welded, 1 dk	**(A37A2PC) Passenger/Cruise**	**2 oil engines** geared to sc. shafts driving 2 FP propellers Total Power: 872kW (1,186hp) Caterpillar 3408TA 2 x Vee 4 Stroke 8 Cy. 137 x 152 each-436kW (593bhp) Caterpillar Inc-USA
8422539 - -	**SHALLOW WATER '84** **Marlin Inc** - *Georgetown* *Guyana* Official number: 0000203	*101* 69 -		**1984-10 Steiner Shipyard, Inc. — Bayou La Batre, Al** Yd No: 198 Loa 22.86 Br ex - Dght - Lbp 20.12 Br md 6.71 Dpth 3.36 Welded, 1 dk	**(B11A2FT) Trawler**	**1 oil engine** geared to sc. shaft driving 1 FP propeller Total Power: 294kW (400hp) Cummins KT-19-M 1 x 4 Stroke 6 Cy. 159 x 159 294kW (400bhp) Cummins Engine Co Inc-USA
5347128 - -	**SHALOM I** *ex* Shalom *-1992* *ex* E. B. Cane *-1992* *ex* Sydney Cove *-1978* - - -	*245* 70 -	Class: (LR) ✠ Classed LR until 13/7/94	**1956-04 P K Harris & Sons Ltd — Bideford** Yd No: 101 Loa 35.26 Br ex 9.15 Dght 3.233 Lbp 31.75 Br md 8.88 Dpth 3.99 Welded, 1 dk	**(B32A2ST) Tug**	**1 oil engine** sr geared to sc. shaft driving 1 FP propeller Total Power: 1,059kW (1,440hp) 11.0kn National Gas 1 x 4 Stroke 6 Cy. 432 x 546 1059kW (1440bhp) National Gas & Oil Eng. Co.-Ashton-under-Lyne AuxGen: 3 x 20kW 220V d.c Fuel: 101.5 (d.f.)
7235692 *HO5111* -	**SHALOM I** *ex* Vos Rebel *-2008* *ex* Guardian *-2005* *ex* Jan *-1989* *ex* Vijf Gebroeders *-1987* *ex* Jurrie Sjoerd *-1981* *ex* Prins Willem Alexander *-1974* **Adonai Shipping BV** - *Panama* *Panama* MMSI: 354664000 Official number: 3422908	**263** 78 97	Class: BV	**1973-01 N.V. Scheepsbouwbedrijf v/h Th.J. Fikkers — Foxhol** Yd No: 137 Converted From: Fishing Vessel-1990 Loa 33.46 Br ex 7.57 Dght 3.600 Lbp 29.44 Br md 7.50 Dpth 4.09 Welded, 1 dk	**(B22G2OY) Standby Safety Vessel** Cranes: 2x2t	**1 oil engine** driving 1 FP propeller Total Power: 820kW (1,115hp) Deutz SBV6M545 1 x 4 Stroke 6 Cy. 320 x 450 820kW (1115bhp) Kloeckner Humboldt Deutz AG-West Germany AuxGen: 1 x 32kW 220V a.c, 1 x 30kW 220V a.c Thrusters: 1 Tunnel thruster (f) Fuel: 65.0
7211892 *HP9180* -	**SHALOM II** *ex* Vos Rover *-2009* *ex* Seabird *-2005* *ex* Maria Paulina *-1992* *ex* Johanna *-1991* *ex* Rijnmond VI *-1981* **Adonai Shipping BV** - *Panama* *Panama* MMSI: 352294000 Official number: 4111610	**372** 188 104	Class: BV	**1972-05 Scheepswerf Haak N.V. — Zaandam** Yd No: 918 Converted From: Stern Trawler-1992 Deepened-1987 Loa 35.26 Br ex 8.54 Dght 3.750 Lbp 31.85 Br md 8.49 Dpth 6.48 Welded, 2 dks	**(B22G2OY) Standby Safety Vessel**	**2 oil engines** geared to sc. shaft driving 1 CP propeller Total Power: 1,052kW (1,430hp) 11.0kn Caterpillar 3508 2 x Vee 4 Stroke 8 Cy. 170 x 190 each-526kW (715bhp) (, fitted 2003) Caterpillar Inc-USA AuxGen: 2 x 100kW 380/220V 50Hz a.c Thrusters: 1 Tunnel thruster (f)
8129474 *CPB902* -	**SHAM** *ex* Apaydin Mukafat *-2013* *ex* Nursen K *-2012* *ex* Orkan *-2012* *ex* Merve *-1995* **Sham Maritime & International Trade Ltd** Arados Bureau for Sea Services *La Paz* *Bolivia* MMSI: 720863000 Official number: 0213221015	*2,241* 1,410 3,990	Class: AD (Class contemplated) (TL) (AB) (BV)	**1983-06 Gunsin Gemi Insaat ve Ticaret Ltd. Sti. — Balat, Istanbul** Yd No: 26 Deepened-1989 Loa 82.85 Br ex 14.00 Dght 6.333 Lbp 74.73 Br md 14.00 Dpth 7.61 Welded, 1 dk	**(A31A2GX) General Cargo Ship** Grain: 4,927; Bale: 4,672 Compartments: 2 Ho, ER 2 Ha: (- x 10.3) (19.5 x 10.3)ER Derricks: 4x5t; Winches: 4	**1 oil engine** driving 1 FP propeller Total Power: 1,214kW (1,651hp) 12.5kn Skoda 9L350IIPS 1 x 4 Stroke 9 Cy. 350 x 500 1214kW (1651bhp) CKD Praha-Praha AuxGen: 2 x 128kW a.c, 1 x 70kW a.c, 2 x 40kW a.c

IMO / Call sign	Name / Owner	Tonnage	Class	Builder / Dimensions	Type	Machinery
9598892 *A6E2595* -	**SHAM** - **Liwa Marine Services LLC** - *Abu Dhabi* *United Arab Emirates* MMSI: 470481000	**457** 137 550	Class: BV	**2010-09 Piasau Slipways Sdn Bhd — Miri** Yd No: 336 Loa 47.00 Br ex - Dght 2.500 Lbp 43.21 Br md 11.00 Dpth 3.20 Welded, 1 dk	**(A35D2RL) Landing Craft** Bow ramp (centre)	**2 oil engines** reduction geared to sc. shafts driving 2 FP propellers Total Power: 942kW (1,280hp) 10.0kn Cummins KT-19-M2 2 x 4 Stroke 6 Cy. 159 x 159 each-471kW (640bhp) Cummins Engine Co Inc-USA AuxGen: 2 x 80kW 50Hz a.c
9444675 *A6E2882* -	**SHA'M** - **Mina Saqr Port Authority** - *Mina Saqr, Ras al Khaimah* *United Arab Emirates* MMSI: 470686000	**176** 52 100	Class: LR (BV) **100A1** SS 02/2013 tug **LMC** Eq.Ltr: D; Cable: 247.5/17.0 U2 (a)	**2008-02 Stocznia Tczew Sp z oo — Tczew** (Hull) Yd No: (509819) **2008-02 B.V. Scheepswerf Damen — Gorinchem** Yd No: 509819 Loa 26.16 Br ex 7.95 Dght 3.080 Lbp 23.96 Br md 7.90 Dpth 4.05 Welded, 1 dk	**(B32A2ST) Tug**	**2 oil engines** with clutches, flexible couplings & sr reverse geared to sc. shafts driving 2 FP propellers Total Power: 2,850kW (3,874hp) Caterpillar 3512B-HD 2 x Vee 4 Stroke 12 Cy. 170 x 215 each-1425kW (1937bhp) Caterpillar Inc-USA AuxGen: 2 x 51kW 400V 50Hz a.c
7515030 - -	**SHAM 105** *ex* Jaramac 70 *-1994* *ex* Ice Berg *-1994* - -	**233** 90 -		**1967 Halter Marine Services, Inc. — New Orleans, La** Yd No: 170 Loa - Br ex 7.62 Dght - Lbp 21.80 Br md - Dpth 3.51 Welded, 1 dk	**(B21A20S) Platform Supply Ship**	**2 oil engines** geared to sc. shafts driving 2 FP propellers Total Power: 1,250kW (1,700hp) Caterpillar D398TA 2 x Vee 4 Stroke 12 Cy. 159 x 203 each-625kW (850bhp) Caterpillar Tractor Co-USA
7515042 - -	**SHAM 110** *ex* Jaramac 71 *-1994* *ex* Ice Pack *-1994* - -	**133** 90 -		**1967 Halter Marine Services, Inc. — New Orleans, La** Yd No: 168 Loa - Br ex 7.62 Dght - Lbp 21.80 Br md - Dpth 3.51 Welded, 1 dk	**(B21A20S) Platform Supply Ship**	**2 oil engines** geared to sc. shafts driving 2 FP propellers Total Power: 1,250kW (1,700hp) Caterpillar D398TA 2 x Vee 4 Stroke 12 Cy. 159 x 203 each-625kW (850bhp) Caterpillar Tractor Co-USA
8725668 *4JGA* -	**SHAMAKHY** *ex* Shemakha *-1993* *ex* Stepan Shaumyan *-1990* **Azerbaijan State Caspian Shipping Co (ASCSS)** Meridian Shipping & Management LLC *Baku* *Azerbaijan* MMSI: 423061100 Official number: DGR-0071	**6,052** 2,105 7,410 T/cm 20.0	Class: RS	**1988-05 Santierul Naval Drobeta-Turnu Severin S.A. — Drobeta-Turnu S.** Yd No: 2080007 Conv to DH-2012 Loa 147.00 Br ex 17.44 Dght 5.300 Lbp 137.46 Br md 17.40 Dpth 7.50 Welded, 1 dk	**(A13B2TP) Products Tanker** Double Hull (13F) Liq: 8,011; Liq (Oil): 7,980 Compartments: 7 Ta, ER Ice Capable	**2 oil engines** driving 2 FP propellers Total Power: 3,060kW (4,160hp) 12.5kn Sulzer 8TAD36 2 x 2 Stroke 8 Cy. 360 x 600 each-1530kW (2080bhp) Zaklady Urzadzen Technicznych'Zgoda' SA-Poland AuxGen: 3 x 320kW a.c Fuel: 134.0 (d.f.) 314.0 (r.f.) 16.8pd
9319727 *A6E2414* -	**SHAMAL** - **P&O Maritime FZE** - *Dubai* *United Arab Emirates* MMSI: 470221000	**317** 95 134	Class: LR ✠ **100A1** SS 11/2009 tug, firefighting Ship 1 (2400 cubic m/hr) with water spray Arabian Gulf and Gulf or Oman service ✠ **LMC** Eq.Ltr: F; Cable: 255.0/17.5 U2 (a)	**2004-11 Dubai Drydocks — Dubai** Yd No: 28 Loa 30.66 Br ex 10.32 Dght 3.850 Lbp 26.30 Br md 10.00 Dpth 5.00 Welded, 1 dk	**(B32A2ST) Tug**	**2 oil engines** gearing integral to driving 2 Directional propellers Total Power: 3,200kW (4,350hp) 12.0kn Wartsila 9L20 2 x 4 Stroke 9 Cy. 200 x 280 each-1600kW (2175bhp) Wartsila Finland Oy-Finland AuxGen: 2 x 160kW 380V 50Hz a.c
9113769 *VTGJ* -	**SHAMBHAVI** - **New Mangalore Port Trust** - *Mumbai* *India* MMSI: 419091700 Official number: 2603	**374** 112 141	Class: IR	**1996-02 Cochin Shipyard Ltd — Ernakulam** Yd No: BY-21 Loa 32.90 Br ex 10.02 Dght 2.790 Lbp 31.50 Br md 10.00 Dpth 4.25 Welded, 1 dk	**(B32A2ST) Tug**	**2 oil engines** gearing integral to driving 2 Voith-Schneider propellers Total Power: 2,540kW (3,454hp) 12.0kn Nohab 6R25 2 x 4 Stroke 6 Cy. 250 x 300 each-1270kW (1727bhp) Wartsila Diesel AB-Sweden AuxGen: 2 x 100kW 415V 50Hz a.c Fuel: 50.0 (d.f.)
9177753 - -	**SHAMBHU SINGH** - **Government of The Republic of India (Navy Department)** - *Chennai* *India*	**290** 87 55	Class: (IR)	**1999-04 Tebma Shipyards Ltd — Chengalpattu** Yd No: 64 Loa - Br ex - Dght 3.680 Lbp - Br md - Dpth - Welded, 1 dk	**(B32A2ST) Tug**	**1 oil engine** driving 1 FP propeller Wartsila 8L20 1 x 4 Stroke 8 Cy. 200 x 280 Wartsila NSD Finland Oy-Finland
9270658 *EPBL5* -	**SHAMIM** *ex* Silver Zone *-2012* *ex* Iran Bushehr *-2008* **Kish Roaring Ocean Shipping Co PJS** Hafiz Darya Shipping Co (HDSC) *Bandar Abbas* *Iran* MMSI: 422026500	**23,285** 11,054 30,145	Class: (GL)	**2004-08 Nordseewerke GmbH — Emden** Yd No: 536 Loa 187.25 (BB) Br ex - Dght 11.550 Lbp 177.08 Br md 29.80 Dpth 16.50 Welded, 1 dk	**(A33A2CC) Container Ship (Fully Cellular)** TEU 2188 C Ho 866 TEU C Dk 1322 TEU incl 80 ref C. Ice Capable	**1 oil engine** driving 1 FP propeller Total Power: 16,946kW (23,040hp) 21.5kn B&W 6L70MC 1 x 2 Stroke 6 Cy. 700 x 2268 16946kW (23040bhp) Hyundai Heavy Industries Co Ltd-South Korea AuxGen: 3 x 970kW 450/230V 60Hz a.c Thrusters: 1 Thwart. FP thruster (f)
7610971 *4JGD* -	**SHAMKHOR** *ex* General Babayan *-1990* **Azerbaijan State Caspian Shipping Co (ASCSS)** Meridian Shipping & Management LLC SatCom: Inmarsat C 442306210 *Baku* *Azerbaijan* MMSI: 423062100 Official number: DGR-0072	**7,807** 3,612 12,335 T/cm 21.7	Class: RS	**1975-07 Astrakhanskaya Sudoverf im. "Kirova" — Astrakhan** Yd No: 1205 Loa 147.03 (BB) Br ex 17.43 Dght 8.000 Lbp 138.61 Br md 17.38 Dpth 11.21 Welded, 1 dk	**(A13B2TP) Products Tanker** Single Hull Liq: 16,929; Liq (Oil): 16,929 Cargo Heating Coils Compartments: 21 Ta, ER 3 Cargo Pump (s): 3x900m³/hr	**2 oil engines** driving 2 FP propellers Total Power: 3,678kW (5,000hp) 13.3kn Skoda 6L525IIPS 2 x 4 Stroke 6 Cy. 525 x 720 each-1839kW (2500bhp) CKD Praha-Praha Fuel: 641.0 (d.f.) 18.6pd
8648860 *V4HO2* -	**SHAMMA** *ex* Hatai 1 *-1990* *ex* VSP 101 *-1990* *ex* Sinroongroj *-1990* **Arabian Sea Shipping SA** - *Basseterre* *St Kitts & Nevis* MMSI: 341974000 Official number: SKN 1002192	**291** 168 -	Class: IS	**1988-05 Thonburi Shipyard LP — Samut Prakan** Loa 33.00 Br ex - Dght 3.500 Lbp - Br md 9.50 Dpth 4.50 Welded, 1 dk	**(B21B20T) Offshore Tug/Supply Ship**	**2 oil engines** reduction geared to sc. shafts driving 2 Propellers Total Power: 1,154kW (1,568hp) Cummins 2 x 4 Stroke each-577kW (784bhp) Cummins Engine Co Inc-USA
7023099 *5NXV* -	**SHAMMAH** *ex* Fusa *-2014* *ex* Fusa I *-1987* *ex* Stord *-1986* **Havskyss AS** - *Nigeria* MMSI: 657103900	**675** 243 -	Class: (NV)	**1970-06 Hatlo Verksted AS — Ulsteinvik** Yd No: 41 Loa 44.38 Br ex 10.62 Dght - Lbp 40.52 Br md 10.60 Dpth 4.20 Welded, 1 dk	**(A36A2PR) Passenger/Ro-Ro Ship (Vehicles)** Cars: 40	**1 oil engine** driving 1 FP propeller Total Power: 662kW (900hp) 12.5kn Wichmann 6ACA 1 x 2 Stroke 6 Cy. 280 x 420 662kW (900bhp) Wichmann Motorfabrikk AS-Norway AuxGen: 2 x 50kW 220V 50Hz a.c Thrusters: 1 Thwart. FP thruster (f)
8985880 *MZGQ5* -	**SHAMOUN** - **Shamoun Shipping Co NV** Seatrade Groningen BV *London* *United Kingdom* MMSI: 235011490 Official number: 902421	**118** 35 -	Class: BV	**1999-07 in the Netherlands** Yd No: 9612 Loa 33.05 Br ex - Dght 2.300 Lbp 24.60 Br md 7.50 Dpth 2.30 Welded, 1 dk	**(X11A2YS) Yacht (Sailing)** Hull Material: Aluminium Alloy Passengers: cabins: 4; berths: 8	**2 oil engines** reduction geared to sc. shafts driving 2 CP propellers Total Power: 468kW (636hp) 11.5kn Scania DSI944M 2 x 4 Stroke 6 Cy. 115 x 144 each-234kW (318bhp) Scania AB-Sweden AuxGen: 1 x 45kW
9208435 *8PRY* -	**SHAMROCK** - **Clarke Shipping Inc** Thien & Heyenga Bereederungs- und Befrachtungsgesellschaft mbH *Bridgetown* *Barbados* MMSI: 314190000 Official number: 733440	**4,654** 1,400 4,850	Class: BV	**2000-11 Santierul Naval Constanta S.A. — Constanta** Yd No: 533 Loa 119.99 (BB) Br ex - Dght 5.400 Lbp 113.80 Br md 18.00 Dpth 8.00 Welded	**(A35A2RR) Ro-Ro Cargo Ship** TEU 430 incl 100 ref C Compartments: 3 Ho, ER 3 Ha: 3 (12.5 x 15.3)ER Cranes: 2x40t Ice Capable	**2 oil engines** geared to sc. shafts driving 2 CP propellers Total Power: 5,760kW (7,832hp) 16.0kn MAN 6L32/40 2 x 4 Stroke 6 Cy. 320 x 400 each-2880kW (3916bhp) MAN B&W Diesel AG-Augsburg AuxGen: 1 x 750kW 220/440V 60Hz a.c, 2 x 500kW 220/440V 60Hz a.c Thrusters: 1 Tunnel thruster (f) Fuel: 501.4 (d.f.)
8950275 - -	**SHAMROCK I** *ex* Maresil II *-1998* - -	*156* 57 -		**1984 Steiner Shipyard, Inc. — Bayou La Batre, Al** Loa - Br ex - Dght - Lbp 25.06 Br md 6.06 Dpth 3.60 Welded, 1 dk	**(B11A2FT) Trawler**	**1 oil engine** driving 1 FP propeller Total Power: 313kW (426hp) Cummins 1 x 4 Stroke 313kW (426bhp) Cummins Engine Co Inc-USA

IMO / Call sign	Name / Owner / Manager	Tonnage	Class	Builder / Dimensions	Type / Cargo	Machinery
9416082 *3FXP2* -	**SHAMROCK JUPITER** **Orchid Transporte SA** Serromah Shipping BV SatCom: Inmarsat Mini-M 764883718 *Panama* *Panama* MMSI: 370999000 Official number: 4017409	**11,726** 6,138 19,837 T/cm 29.3	Class: NK	**2009-01 Fukuoka Shipbuilding Co Ltd — Fukuoka FO** Yd No: 1273 Loa 146.60 (BB) Br ex 23.73 Dght 9.622 Lbp 138.00 Br md 23.69 Dpth 13.00 Welded, 1 dk	**(A12B2TR) Chemical/Products Tanker** Double Hull (13F) Liq: 20,474; Liq (Oil): 21,617 Cargo Heating Coils Compartments: 18 Wing Ta, 2 Wing Slop Ta, ER 18 Cargo Pump (s): 12x300m³/hr, 6x200m³/hr Manifold: Bow/CM: 73.4m	**1 oil engine** driving 1 FP propeller Total Power: 6,150kW (8,362hp) 14.6kn MAN-B&W 6S42MC 1 x 2 Stroke 6 Cy. 420 x 1764 6150kW (8362bhp) Hitachi Zosen Corp-Japan AuxGen: 3 x 500kW a.c Thrusters: 1 Tunnel thruster (f) Fuel: 122.0 (d.f.) 909.0 (r.f.)
9477531 *3FPP3* -	**SHAMROCK MERCURY** **Mercury Transporte SA** Serromah Shipping BV *Panama* *Panama* MMSI: 371936000 Official number: 4481713	**11,628** 6,126 19,998 T/cm 28.8	Class: NK	**2010-10 Usuki Shipyard Co Ltd — Usuki OT** Yd No: 1725 Loa 145.53 (BB) Br ex 23.73 Dght 9.715 Lbp 137.00 Br md 23.70 Dpth 13.35 Welded, 1 dk	**(A12B2TR) Chemical/Products Tanker** Double Hull (13F) Liq: 22,204; Liq (Oil): 22,500 Cargo Heating Coils Compartments: 20 Wing Ta, ER 20 Cargo Pump (s): 12x300m³/hr, 8x200m³/hr Manifold: Bow/CM: 75m	**1 oil engine** driving 1 FP propeller Total Power: 6,150kW (8,362hp) 14.7kn MAN-B&W 6S42MC 1 x 2 Stroke 6 Cy. 420 x 1764 6150kW (8362bhp) Hitachi Zosen Corp-Japan AuxGen: 3 x 430kW a.c Thrusters: 1 Tunnel thruster (f) Fuel: 80.0 (d.f.) 1030.0 (r.f.)
7625988 *HO2324* -	**SHAMROCK PRIDE** *ex* Seabulk Pride *-2001* *ex* GMMOS Pride *-1997* *ex* Luisella *-1992* **Selat Marine Services Co Ltd** - *Panama* *Panama* MMSI: 354155000 Official number: 2855202B	**495** 157 668	Class: BV (RI)	**1977-12 Cant. Nav. M. Morini & C. — Ancona** Yd No: 158 Loa 38.01 Br ex 10.42 Dght 4.650 Lbp 33.48 Br md 10.00 Dpth 5.47 Welded, 1 dk	**(B32A2ST) Tug**	**2 oil engines** reduction geared to sc. shafts driving 2 CP propellers Total Power: 3,678kW (5,000hp) 14.0kn MaK 6M453AK 2 x 4 Stroke 6 Cy. 320 x 420 each-1839kW (2500bhp) MaK Maschinenbau GmbH-Kiel AuxGen: 3 x 130kW 380V 50Hz a.c Thrusters: 1 Thwart. FP thruster (f) Fuel: 264.0 (d.f.) 14.0pd
8027834 *3EHE5* -	**SHAMS** *ex* Khawla Bint al Azwar *-2000* *ex* Khawla *-1988* **Al Riyadh Investment Co Group** - *Panama* *Panama* MMSI: 372035000 Official number: 34913PEXT	**6,331** 2,917 3,985	Class: (LR) (RS) ✠ Classed LR until 14/5/97	**1983-06 Helsingor Vaerft A/S — Helsingor** Yd No: 428 Loa 110.67 (BB) Br ex 19.00 Dght 5.512 Lbp 96.35 Br md 18.80 Dpth 12.10 Welded, 2 dks	**(A35A2RR) Ro-Ro Cargo Ship** Side door/ramp (s) Len: - Wid: 5.00 Swl: 50 Slewing stern door/ramp (centre) Len: 35.00 Wid: 5.00 Swl: 55 Lane-Len: 880 Grain: 10,320; Bale: 8,649 TEU 170 C Ho 90 TEU C Dk 80 TEU Cranes: 1x50t	**2 oil engines** with clutches, flexible couplings & sr geared to sc. shafts driving 2 CP propellers Total Power: 4,414kW (6,002hp) 15.5kn M.T.U. 12V1163TB62 2 x Vee 4 Stroke 12 Cy. 230 x 280 each-2207kW (3001bhp) MTU Friedrichshafen GmbH-Friedrichshafen AuxGen: 4 x 292kW 380V 50Hz a.c Thrusters: 1 Thwart. CP thruster (f) Fuel: 660.5 (d.f.) 20.5pd
7928299 - -	**SHAMS** **Suez Canal Authority** - *Ismailia* *Egypt*	*125* 80 79	Class: (GL)	**1980-06 Canal Naval Construction Co. — Port Said (Port Fuad)** Yd No: 173 Loa 27.72 Br ex 6.51 Dght 2.050 Lbp 26.01 Br md 6.20 Dpth 2.49 Welded, 1 dk	**(B32A2ST) Tug**	**2 oil engines** reverse reduction geared to sc. shafts driving 2 FP propellers Total Power: 618kW (840hp) 10.0kn MAN D2542MTE 2 x Vee 4 Stroke 12 Cy. 125 x 142 each-309kW (420bhp) Maschinenbau Augsburg Nuernberg (MAN)-Augsburg
9085039 *EPAS6* -	**SHAMS 110** *ex* Rana 1 *-2011* *ex* Eiko Maru *-2010* **Yaser Moshtaghi & Partners** - *Bushehr* *Iran* Official number: 993	**498** 244 583	Class: IN (Class contemplated)	**1994-05 Taiyo Shipbuilding Co Ltd — Sanyoonoda YC** Yd No: 252 Loa 53.32 Br ex - Dght 3.250 Lbp 49.47 Br md 9.00 Dpth 5.30 Welded, 1 dk	**(A31A2GX) General Cargo Ship** Bale: 1,032 Compartments: 1 Ho, ER 1 Ha: ER	**1 oil engine** driving 1 FP propeller Total Power: 1,323kW (1,799hp) Hanshin LH26G 1 x 4 Stroke 6 Cy. 260 x 440 1323kW (1799bhp) The Hanshin Diesel Works Ltd-Japan Thrusters: 1 Thwart. FP thruster (f)
8301890 *BRSS* -	**SHAN CHA** **Guangzhou Zhenhua Shipping Co Ltd** - *Guangzhou, Guangdong* *China* MMSI: 412585000	*4,083* 1,773 1,135	Class: (CC)	**1983-12 Guangzhou Shipyard — Guangzhou GD** Yd No: 424-2 Loa 107.69 Br ex - Dght 4.420 Lbp 96.40 Br md 15.20 Dpth 8.00 Welded, 2 dks	**(A32A2GF) General Cargo/Passenger Ship**	**1 oil engine** driving 1 FP propeller Total Power: 3,310kW (4,500hp) Shanghai 12V300 1 x Vee 2 Stroke 12 Cy. 300 x 550 3310kW (4500bhp) Shanghai Shipyard-China
9362384 *3EEH9* -	**SHAN CHENG 1** **Wang Yongshan** Shancheng Shipping (HK) Co Ltd SatCom: Inmarsat C 437190310 *Panama* *Panama* MMSI: 371903000 Official number: 43313PEXTF	**2,985** 1,888 5,300	Class: IT	**2005-01 Zhejiang Dongtou Damen Shipyard — Dongtou County ZJ** Loa 98.00 Br ex - Dght 5.900 Lbp 91.50 Br md 15.80 Dpth 7.40 Welded, 1 dk	**(A31A2GX) General Cargo Ship** Grain: 6,825; Bale: 6,279	**1 oil engine** geared to sc. shaft driving 1 FP propeller Total Power: 1,765kW (2,400hp) 11.0kn Chinese Std. Type G8300ZC 1 x 4 Stroke 8 Cy. 300 x 380 1765kW (2400bhp) Wuxi Antai Power Machinery Co Ltd-China
9611694 *BPGJ* -	**SHAN CHI** **China Shipping Tanker Co Ltd** - *Shanghai* *China* MMSI: 414748000	**30,325** 12,927 48,740	Class: CC	**2013-01 Guangzhou Shipyard International Co Ltd — Guangzhou GD** Yd No: 10130020 Loa 184.88 (BB) Br ex 32.23 Dght 12.400 Lbp 176.00 Br md 32.20 Dpth 18.60 Welded, 1 dk	**(A13A2TW) Crude/Oil Products Tanker** Double Hull (13F) Liq: 50,802; Liq (Oil): 50,760 Compartments: 6 Wing Ta, 6 Wing Ta, 1 Wing Slop Ta, 1 Wing Slop Ta, 1 Slop Ta, ER Ice Capable	**1 oil engine** driving 1 FP propeller Total Power: 9,960kW (13,542hp) 14.5kn MAN-B&W 6S50MC-C8 1 x 2 Stroke 6 Cy. 500 x 2000 9960kW (13542bhp) Dalian Marine Diesel Co Ltd-China AuxGen: 3 x 750kW 450V a.c
9210787 *BYAY* -	**SHAN GANG JUN 8** **Government of The People's Republic of China (Shantou Harbour Construction Command Department)** - *Shantou, Guangdong* *China* MMSI: 412057010	**1,615** 484 2,378	Class: CC	**1999-10 Guangdong New China Shipyard Co Ltd — Dongguan GD** Yd No: 98-005 Loa 73.80 Br ex - Dght 4.200 Lbp 69.00 Br md 14.00 Dpth 5.10 Welded, 1 dk	**(B33A2DS) Suction Dredger** Hopper: 1,500	**2 oil engines** geared to sc. shafts driving 2 FP propellers Total Power: 1,426kW (1,938hp) 10.4kn Chinese Std. Type 6230ZC 2 x 4 Stroke 6 Cy. 230 x 300 each-713kW (969bhp) Guangzhou Diesel Engine Factory CoLtd-China AuxGen: 3 x 300kW 400V a.c
9279915 *BYCX* -	**SHAN GANG JUN 9** **Guang Dong Grand Ever Green Construction Co** - SatCom: Inmarsat C 441239015 *Shantou, Guangdong* *China* MMSI: 412057020 Official number: 02R4004	**1,718** 516 2,237	Class: CC	**2002-10 Guangdong New China Shipyard Co Ltd — Dongguan GD** Yd No: 01-003 Loa 73.80 Br ex - Dght 4.200 Lbp 69.00 Br md 14.00 Dpth 5.10 Welded, 1 Dk.	**(B33B2DT) Trailing Suction Hopper Dredger** Hopper: 1,546 Compartments: 1 Ho, ER 1 Ha: ER (30.0 x 8.0)	**2 oil engines** reduction geared to sc. shafts driving 2 Propellers Total Power: 1,940kW (2,638hp) 11.0kn Guangzhou 6320ZCD 2 x 4 Stroke 6 Cy. 320 x 440 each-970kW (1319bhp) Guangzhou Diesel Engine Factory CoLtd-China AuxGen: 3 x 320kW 400V a.c
8884309 - -	**SHAN GANG YIN 5** **Government of The People's Republic of China (Shantou Harbour Construction Command Department)** - *Shantou, Guangdong* *China*	**355** 107 108	Class: CC	**1993-01 Zhenjiang Shipyard — Zhenjiang JS** Loa 32.00 Br ex - Dght 3.350 Lbp 29.40 Br md 10.00 Dpth 4.50 Welded, 1 dk	**(B32A2ST) Tug**	**2 oil engines** geared to sc. shafts driving 2 FP propellers Total Power: 1,838kW (2,498hp) 12.5kn Daihatsu 6DLM-26SL 2 x 4 Stroke 6 Cy. 260 x 340 each-919kW (1249bhp) Daihatsu Diesel Manufacturing Co Lt-Japan AuxGen: 2 x 75kW 400V a.c
9069059 *BTVL* -	**SHAN GANG YIN 8** **Government of The People's Republic of China (Shantou Harbour Construction Command Department)** - *Shantou, Guangdong* *China*	**407** 122 122	Class: CC	**2005-09 Jiangsu Zhenjiang Shipyard Co Ltd — Zhenjiang JS** Loa 36.00 Br ex - Dght - Lbp 33.47 Br md 9.80 Dpth 4.50 Welded, 1 dk	**(B32A2ST) Tug**	**2 oil engines** geared to sc. shafts driving 2 Propellers Total Power: 2,500kW (3,400hp) 12.5kn Daihatsu 6DLM-26 2 x 4 Stroke 6 Cy. 260 x 340 each-1250kW (1700bhp) Daihatsu Diesel Manufacturing Co Lt-Japan
9155339 *BOHP* -	**SHAN HAI** **COSCO Bulk Carrier Co Ltd (COSCO BULK)** - SatCom: Inmarsat C 441295710 *Tianjin* *China* MMSI: 412238000 Official number: 98M3008	**27,585** 14,848 47,077 T/cm 53.0	Class: CC	**1998-09 Hudong Shipbuilding Group — Shanghai** Yd No: H1248A Loa 189.94 (BB) Br ex - Dght 11.710 Lbp 180.00 Br md 32.20 Dpth 16.60 Welded, 1 dk	**(A21A2BC) Bulk Carrier** Grain: 57,104; Bale: 55,962 Compartments: 5 Ho, ER 5 Ha: (16.0 x 15.0)4 (17.6 x 15.0)ER Cranes: 4x30t	**1 oil engine** driving 1 FP propeller Total Power: 7,336kW (9,974hp) 13.8kn B&W 6L50MC 1 x 2 Stroke 6 Cy. 500 x 1620 7336kW (9974bhp) Hudong Shipyard-China

IMO / Call sign	Name / Owner	Tonnage	Class	Build / Dimensions	Type	Machinery
9043641 *BOAZ* -	**SHAN HE** **COSCO Container Lines Co Ltd (COSCON)** - SatCom: Inmarsat C 441212211 *Shanghai* *China* MMSI: 412122000 Official number: SUI-05001358	**49,375** 29,710 51,982 T/cm 74.2	Class: CC (LR) ✠ Classed LR until 24/6/94	**1994-06 Hitachi Zosen Corp — Nagasu KM** Yd No: 4871 Loa 274.99 (BB) Br ex 32.30 Dght 12.524 Lbp 263.37 Br md 32.20 Dpth 21.40 Welded, 1 dk	**(A33A2CC) Container Ship (Fully Cellular)** TEU 3801 C Ho 2220 C Dk 1581 incl 240 ref C. Compartments: ER, 8 Cell Ho 16 Ha: (12.6 x 13.0) (12.6 x 23.2)ER (6.4 x 28.3)13 (12.6 x 28.3) Ice Capable	**1 oil engine** driving 1 FP propeller Total Power: 36,445kW (49,551hp) 24.0kn Sulzer 9RTA84C 1 x 2 Stroke 9 Cy. 840 x 2400 36445kW (49551bhp) Hitachi Zosen Corp-Japan Thrusters: 1 Thwart. CP thruster (f) Fuel: 365.8 (d.f.) 5349.5 (r.f.) 157.5pd
9435600 *BPFY* -	**SHAN HU ZUO** **China Shipping Tanker Co Ltd** - *Shanghai* *China* MMSI: 413181000	**43,718** 21,966 75,596 T/cm 68.0	Class: CC	**2010-05 Dalian Shipbuilding Industry Co Ltd — Dalian LN (No 1 Yard)** Yd No: PC760-16 Loa 228.60 (BB) Br ex 32.29 Dght 14.700 Lbp 220.00 Br md 32.26 Dpth 21.20 Welded, 1 dk	**(A13B2TP) Products Tanker** Double Hull (13F) Liq: 80,690; Liq (Oil): 83,897 Cargo Heating Coils Compartments: 12 Wing Ta, 2 Wing Slop Ta, ER 3 Cargo Pump (s): 3x2000m³/hr Manifold: Bow/CM: 113.4m Ice Capable	**1 oil engine** driving 1 FP propeller Total Power: 12,240kW (16,642hp) 15.4kn MAN-B&W 6S60MC 1 x 2 Stroke 6 Cy. 600 x 2292 12240kW (16642bhp) Dalian Marine Diesel Co Ltd-China AuxGen: 3 x 740kW 450V a.c Fuel: 175.0 (d.f.) 2530.0 (r.f.)
8972120 *BWAV* -	**SHAN LIAN HUA 1** *ex Min Hai You 2 -2003* **Guangzhou Shengshi Shipping Co Ltd** - *Guangzhou, Guangdong* *China* MMSI: 413461820	**1,093** 612 1,333	Class: (CC)	**1990-11 Mawei Shipyard — Fuzhou FJ** Loa 75.19 Br ex - Dght 4.000 Lbp 69.99 Br md 10.60 Dpth 4.60 Welded, 1 dk	**(A12A2LP) Molten Sulphur Tanker** Liq: 735 Compartments: 5 Ta, ER	**1 oil engine** driving 1 FP propeller Total Power: 661kW (899hp) 11.1kn Chinese Std. Type 6350ZC 1 x 4 Stroke 6 Cy. 350 x 500 661kW (899bhp) Shanghai Diesel Engine Co Ltd-China AuxGen: 2 x 90kW 400V a.c
9638898 *BIAR4* -	**SHAN NENG** **CSIC-IMC Shipping Co Ltd** - *Shanghai* *China* MMSI: 413376840	**4,500** 2,000 6,998 T/cm 16.0	Class: CC	**2012-01 Chongqing Chuandong Shipbuilding Industry Co Ltd — Chongqing** Yd No: HT0110 Loa 109.85 (BB) Br ex 17.52 Dght 6.000 Lbp 103.90 Br md 17.50 Dpth 8.00 Welded, 1 dk	**(A12B2TR) Chemical/Products Tanker** Double Hull (13F) Liq: 6,035; Liq (Oil): 6,035 Compartments: 8 Wing Ta, 2 Wing Slop Ta, ER 8 Cargo Pump (s): 8x200m³/hr Manifold: Bow/CM: 59m	**1 oil engine** reduction geared to sc. shaft driving 1 FP propeller Total Power: 2,500kW (3,399hp) 11.6kn Daihatsu 8DKM-28 1 x 4 Stroke 8 Cy. 280 x 390 2500kW (3399bhp) Shaanxi Diesel Heavy Industry Co Lt-China AuxGen: 3 x 320kW 400V 60Hz a.c Fuel: 115.0 (d.f.) 342.0 (r.f.)
9646376 *BIAV7* -	**SHAN SHI** **CSIC-IMC Shipping Co Ltd** - *Shanghai* *China* MMSI: 412379380 Official number: CN20109966792	**4,498** 2,000 6,998 T/cm 16.0	Class: CC	**2012-05 Chongqing Chuandong Shipbuilding Industry Co Ltd — Chongqing** Yd No: HT0117 Loa 109.85 (BB) Br ex 17.52 Dght 6.420 Lbp 103.90 Br md 17.50 Dpth 8.00 Welded, 1 dk	**(A12B2TR) Chemical/Products Tanker** Double Hull (13F) Liq: 6,031; Liq (Oil): 6,037 Cargo Heating Coils Compartments: 4 Wing Ta, 4 Wing Ta, 1 Wing Slop Ta, 1 Wing Slop Ta, ER 8 Cargo Pump (s): 8x200m³/hr Manifold: Bow/CM: 59m	**1 oil engine** reduction geared to sc. shaft driving 1 FP propeller Total Power: 2,500kW (3,399hp) 11.6kn Daihatsu 8DKM-28 1 x 4 Stroke 8 Cy. 280 x 390 2500kW (3399bhp) Shaanxi Diesel Heavy Industry Co Lt-China AuxGen: 3 x 320kW 400V a.c Thrusters: 1 Tunnel thruster (f) Fuel: 115.0 (d.f.) 440.0 (r.f.)
7381673 *BSPC* -	**SHAN TOU** *ex CO 842 -1975* **CCCC Guangzhou Dredging Co Ltd** - *Guangzhou, Guangdong* *China* MMSI: 412052570	**1,955** 586 1,769	Class: (CC) (BV)	**1975-10 Scheepsw. en Mfbk."De Biesbosch-Dordrecht" B.V. — Dordrecht** Yd No: 665 Loa 83.85 Br ex 13.11 Dght 4.509 Lbp 78.00 Br md 13.00 Dpth 5.00 Welded, 1 dk	**(B33B2DT) Trailing Suction Hopper Dredger** Hopper: 1,500	**2 oil engines** driving 2 FP propellers Total Power: 2,472kW (3,360hp) 11.8kn Smit-Bolnes 307HDK 2 x 2 Stroke 7 Cy. 300 x 550 each-1236kW (1680bhp) Motorenfabriek Smit & Bolnes NV-Netherlands Thrusters: 1 Thwart. FP thruster (f) Fuel: 262.0
8888032 - -	**SHAN WAI** - - -	*350* 220 -		**1990 in the People's Republic of China** Loa 43.00 Br ex - Dght - Lbp - Br md 6.40 Dpth 3.40 Welded, 1 dk	**(A31A2GX) General Cargo Ship**	**1 oil engine** driving 1 FP propeller
8888056 - -	**SHAN WAI LUN No. 5582** - - -	*350* 220 -		**1990 in the People's Republic of China** Loa 43.00 Br ex - Dght - Lbp - Br md 6.40 Dpth 3.40 Welded, 1 dk	**(A31A2GX) General Cargo Ship**	**1 oil engine** driving 1 FP propeller
9646388 *BIAV6* -	**SHAN YI** **CSIC-IMC Shipping Co Ltd** - *Shanghai* *China* MMSI: 412379370 Official number: CN20106296039	**4,498** 2,000 6,929 T/cm 16.0	Class: CC	**2012-06 Chongqing Chuandong Shipbuilding Industry Co Ltd — Chongqing** Yd No: HT0118 Loa 109.85 (BB) Br ex 17.52 Dght 6.420 Lbp 103.90 Br md 17.50 Dpth 8.00 Welded, 1 dk	**(A12B2TR) Chemical/Products Tanker** Double Hull (13F) Liq: 6,046; Liq (Oil): 6,046 Compartments: 5 Wing Ta, 3 Wing Ta, 1 Wing Slop Ta, 1 Wing Slop Ta, ER 8 Cargo Pump (s): 8x200m³/hr Manifold: Bow/CM: 59m	**1 oil engine** reduction geared to sc. shaft driving 1 CP propeller Total Power: 2,500kW (3,399hp) 12.0kn Daihatsu 8DKM-28 1 x 4 Stroke 8 Cy. 280 x 390 2500kW (3399bhp) Shaanxi Diesel Heavy Industry Co Lt-China AuxGen: 3 x 320kW 400V a.c Fuel: 115.0 (d.f.) 442.0 (r.f.)
9538440 *9V8980* -	**SHAN YING ZUO** **Shanyingzuo Shipping Pte Ltd** China Shipping Tanker Co Ltd SatCom: Inmarsat C 456442010 *Singapore* *Singapore* MMSI: 564420000 Official number: 396470	**43,718** 21,966 75,588 T/cm 68.0	Class: CC	**2010-11 Dalian Shipbuilding Industry Co Ltd — Dalian LN (No 1 Yard)** Yd No: PC760-24 Loa 228.60 (BB) Br ex 32.29 Dght 14.700 Lbp 220.00 Br md 32.26 Dpth 21.20 Welded, 1 dk	**(A13B2TP) Products Tanker** Double Hull (13F) Liq: 80,740; Liq (Oil): 80,740 Cargo Heating Coils Compartments: 12 Wing Ta, 2 Wing Slop Ta, ER 3 Cargo Pump (s): 3x2000m³/hr Manifold: Bow/CM: 113.4m Ice Capable	**1 oil engine** driving 1 FP propeller Total Power: 12,240kW (16,642hp) 15.4kn MAN-B&W 6S60MC 1 x 2 Stroke 6 Cy. 600 x 2292 12240kW (16642bhp) Dalian Marine Diesel Co Ltd-China AuxGen: 3 x 740kW 450V a.c Fuel: 175.0 (d.f.) 2530.0 (r.f.)
8888044 - -	**SHAN YUN No. 20185** - - -	*350* 220 -		**1990 in the People's Republic of China** Loa 43.00 Br ex - Dght - Lbp - Br md 6.40 Dpth 3.40 Welded, 1 dk	**(A31A2GX) General Cargo Ship**	**1 oil engine** driving 1 FP propeller
9628635 *BIAL7* -	**SHAN ZHI** **CSIC-IMC Shipping Co Ltd** - *Shanghai* *China* MMSI: 413376570	**4,500** 2,000 7,000 T/cm 16.0	Class: CC	**2011-09 Chongqing Chuandong Shipbuilding Industry Co Ltd — Chongqing** Yd No: HT0109 Loa 109.85 (BB) Br ex 17.52 Dght 6.420 Lbp 103.90 Br md 17.50 Dpth 8.00 Welded, 1 dk	**(A12B2TR) Chemical/Products Tanker** Double Hull (13F) Liq: 6,035; Liq (Oil): 6,035 Cargo Heating Coils Compartments: 4 Wing Ta, 4 Wing Ta, 1 Wing Slop Ta, 1 Wing Slop Ta, ER 8 Cargo Pump (s): 8x200m³/hr Manifold: Bow/CM: 59m	**1 oil engine** reduction geared to sc. shaft driving 1 FP propeller Total Power: 2,500kW (3,399hp) 11.6kn Daihatsu 8DKM-28 1 x 4 Stroke 8 Cy. 280 x 390 2500kW (3399bhp) Shaanxi Diesel Heavy Industry Co Lt-China AuxGen: 3 x 320kW 400V a.c Fuel: 115.0 (d.f.) 342.0 (r.f.)
9575539 *FFZR* -	**SHANA DES SLOPS** **Sermap Group** *Marseille* *France (FIS)* MMSI: 228003800	**386** - 550	Class: BV	**2011-02 Kocatepe Gemi Cekek ve Insa Sanayi Ltd. Sti. — Tuzla** Yd No: 8 Loa 46.80 (BB) Br ex - Dght 3.200 Lbp 45.47 Br md 7.50 Dpth 3.60 Welded, 1 dk	**(A13B2TP) Products Tanker** Double Hull (13F) Liq: 534; Liq (Oil): 532 Compartments: 4 Wing Ta, 4 Wing Ta, ER	**1 oil engine** reduction geared to sc. shaft driving 1 FP propeller Total Power: 441kW (600hp) 10.0kn Yanmar 6HYM-ETE 1 x 4 Stroke 6 Cy. 133 x 165 441kW (600bhp) Yanmar Diesel Engine Co Ltd-Japan AuxGen: 2 x 100kW 50Hz a.c Thrusters: 1 Tunnel thruster (f) Fuel: 22.0
9051002 *EQSN* -	**SHANAK** **Gasem Jamali** *Bushehr* *Iran* Official number: 17255	*181* 54 80	Class: AS (LR) ✠ Classed LR until 7/7/94	**1992-12 Sing Koon Seng Shipbuilding & Engineering Ltd — Singapore** Yd No: 702 Loa 26.00 Br ex 7.58 Dght - Lbp 22.70 Br md 7.48 Dpth 4.19 Welded, 1 dk	**(B11A2FS) Stern Trawler**	**1 oil engine** with clutches, flexible couplings & sr geared to sc. shaft driving 1 CP propeller Total Power: 459kW (624hp) Caterpillar 3412TA 1 x Vee 4 Stroke 12 Cy. 137 x 152 459kW (624bhp) Caterpillar Inc-USA AuxGen: 2 x 50kW 440V 60Hz a.c
8996700 *CFG6210* -	**SHANALEEN** **C & P Fisheries Ltd** *St John's, NL* *Canada* MMSI: 316006110 Official number: 811353	*102* 50 -		**1988-01 Glovertown Shipyards Ltd — Glovertown NL** L reg 18.78 Br ex - Dght - Lbp - Br md 6.74 Dpth 2.35 Welded, 1 dk	**(B11B2FV) Fishing Vessel**	**1 oil engine** driving 1 Propeller Total Power: 331kW (450hp) 10.0kn
7509811 - -	**SHANDHANI** **Bangladesh Inland Water Transport Authority** - *Chittagong* *Bangladesh* Official number: BIWTACP-4	*365* 84 164	Class: (NK)	**1975-09 Ito Iron Works & SB. Co. Ltd. — Sasebo** Yd No: 189 Loa 44.00 Br ex 9.02 Dght 2.134 Lbp 39.98 Br md 9.00 Dpth 3.64 Welded	**(B31A2SR) Research Survey Vessel** 1 Ha: (1.9 x 2.9)ER	**2 oil engines** sr geared to sc. shafts driving 2 FP propellers Total Power: 706kW (960hp) 11.3kn Yanmar 6MAL-HT 2 x 4 Stroke 6 Cy. 200 x 240 each-353kW (480bhp) Yanmar Diesel Engine Co Ltd-Japan AuxGen: 3 x 44kW

9592032 *VRIZ2* -	**SHANDONG CHONG WEN** *ex Xiao Xiao -2012* **Hai Kuo Shipping 1221 Ltd** Shandong Shipping Corp SatCom: Inmarsat C 447798847 *Hong Kong* *Hong Kong* MMSI: 477434600 Official number: HK-3180	**41,254** 25,658 76,098 T/cm 68.6	Class: AB	**2011-09 Hudong-Zhonghua Shipbuilding (Group) Co Ltd — Shanghai** Yd No: H1641A Loa 225.00 (BB) Br ex - Dght 14.250 Lbp 217.00 Br md 32.26 Dpth 19.70 Welded, 1 dk	**(A21A2BC) Bulk Carrier** Grain: 90,540; Bale: 89,882 Compartments: 7 Ho, ER 7 Ha: ER	**1 oil engine** driving 1 FP propeller Total Power: 11,300kW (15,363hp) 14.5kn MAN-B&W 5S60MC-C 1 x 2 Stroke 5 Cy. 600 x 2400 11300kW (15363bhp) Hudong Heavy Machinery Co Ltd-China AuxGen: 3 x 570kW a.c Fuel: 267.0 (d.f.) 2709.0 (r.f.)
9593919 *9V9131* -	**SHANDONG DA CHENG** *ex Vale Carajas -2014* **Vale Shipping Enterprise Pte Ltd** Vale SA *Singapore* *Singapore* MMSI: 566471000 Official number: 396665	**198,980** 67,993 402,285	Class: NV	**2012-05 Daewoo Shipbuilding & Marine Engineering Co Ltd — Geoje** Yd No: 1212 Loa 362.00 (BB) Br ex 65.06 Dght 23.020 Lbp 350.00 Br md 65.00 Dpth 30.40 Welded, 1 dk	**(A21B2BO) Ore Carrier** Grain: 238,000 Compartments: 7 Ho, ER 7 Ha: ER	**1 oil engine** driving 1 FP propeller Total Power: 31,500kW (42,827hp) 14.8kn MAN-B&W 7S80ME-C8 1 x 2 Stroke 7 Cy. 800 x 3200 31500kW (42827bhp) AuxGen: 3 x a.c
9572329 *9V9128* -	**SHANDONG DA DE** *ex Vale Rio De Janeiro -2013* **Vale Shipping Enterprise Pte Ltd** Vale SA *Singapore* *Singapore* MMSI: 566173000 Official number: 396662	**198,980** 67,993 402,303	Class: NV	**2011-09 Daewoo Shipbuilding & Marine Engineering Co Ltd — Geoje** Yd No: 1202 Loa 362.00 (BB) Br ex 65.06 Dght 23.000 Lbp 350.00 Br md 65.00 Dpth 30.40 Welded, 1 dk	**(A21B2BO) Ore Carrier** Grain: 238,000 Compartments: 7 Ho, ER 7 Ha: ER	**1 oil engine** driving 1 FP propeller Total Power: 31,500kW (42,827hp) 14.8kn MAN-B&W 7S80ME-C8 1 x 2 Stroke 7 Cy. 800 x 3200 31500kW (42827bhp) AuxGen: 3 x a.c
9572343 *9V9130* -	**SHANDONG DA REN** *ex Vale Malaysia -2014* **Vale Shipping Enterprise Pte Ltd** Vale SA *Singapore* *Singapore* MMSI: 566412000 Official number: 396664	**198,980** 67,993 402,285	Class: NV	**2012-03 Daewoo Shipbuilding & Marine Engineering Co Ltd — Geoje** Yd No: 1204 Loa 362.00 (BB) Br ex 65.06 Dght 23.020 Lbp 350.00 Br md 65.00 Dpth 30.40 Welded, 1 dk	**(A21B2BO) Ore Carrier** Grain: 238,000 Compartments: 7 Ho, ER 7 Ha: ER	**1 oil engine** driving 1 FP propeller Total Power: 31,500kW (42,827hp) 14.8kn MAN-B&W 7S80ME-C8 1 x 2 Stroke 7 Cy. 800 x 3200 31500kW (42827bhp) AuxGen: 3 x a.c
9593957 *9V9132* -	**SHANDONG DA ZHI** *ex Vale Minas Gerais -2013* **Vale Shipping Enterprise Pte Ltd** Vale SA SatCom: Inmarsat C 456649410 *Singapore* *Singapore* MMSI: 566494000 Official number: 396666	**198,980** 67,993 400,000	Class: NV	**2012-07 Daewoo Shipbuilding & Marine Engineering Co Ltd — Geoje** Yd No: 1213 Loa 362.00 (BB) Br ex 65.06 Dght 23.020 Lbp 350.00 Br md 65.00 Dpth 30.40 Welded, 1 dk	**(A21B2BO) Ore Carrier** Grain: 238,000 Compartments: 7 Ho, ER 7 Ha: ER	**1 oil engine** driving 1 FP propeller Total Power: 31,500kW (42,827hp) 14.8kn MAN-B&W 7S80ME-C8 1 x 2 Stroke 7 Cy. 800 x 3200 31500kW (42827bhp) AuxGen: 3 x a.c
9621144 *VRLM9* -	**SHANDONG DING SHENG** **CMBL Sea Chen Co Ltd** Shandong Shipping Corp *Hong Kong* *Hong Kong* MMSI: 477222900 Official number: HK-3711	**94,710** 59,528 179,959 T/cm 124.3	Class: CC	**2013-03 Qingdao Beihai Shipbuilding Heavy Industry Co Ltd — Qingdao SD** Yd No: BC18.0-46 Loa 295.00 (BB) Br ex 46.06 Dght 18.100 Lbp 285.00 Br md 46.00 Dpth 24.80 Welded, 1 dk	**(A21A2BC) Bulk Carrier** Grain: 201,954 Compartments: 9 Ho, ER 9 Ha: 7 (15.5 x 20.0)ER 2 (15.5 x 16.5)	**1 oil engine** driving 1 FP propeller Total Power: 17,153kW (23,321hp) 14.5kn MAN-B&W 6S70MC-C8 1 x 2 Stroke 6 Cy. 700 x 2800 17153kW (23321bhp) Dalian Marine Diesel Co Ltd-China AuxGen: 3 x 900kW 450V a.c
8712647 *3EGA7* -	**SHANDONG EXPRESS** *ex Golden Dynasty -2009 ex Milky Way -2007* **Shandong Express SA** Nova Shipping & Logistics Pte Ltd SatCom: Inmarsat A 1331344 *Panama* *Panama* MMSI: 352794000 Official number: 1844889E	**36,202** 15,851 43,661	Class: NK	**1989-03 Imabari Shipbuilding Co Ltd — Marugame KG (Marugame Shipyard)** Yd No: 1171 Loa 197.91 (BB) Br ex 32.23 Dght 10.518 Lbp 189.00 Br md 32.20 Dpth 21.60 Welded, 1 dk	**(A24B2BW) Wood Chips Carrier** Grain: 81,214 Compartments: 6 Ho, ER 6 Ha: ER	**1 oil engine** driving 1 FP propeller Total Power: 6,252kW (8,500hp) 13.8kn Sulzer 5RTA58 1 x 2 Stroke 5 Cy. 580 x 1700 6252kW (8500bhp) Nippon Kokan KK (NKK Corp)-Japan AuxGen: 3 x 310kW a.c Fuel: 2040.0 (r.f.)
9502647 *VRIZ3* -	**SHANDONG HAI CHANG** **Shandong Haiyang Shipping Co Ltd** Shandong Shipping Corp SatCom: Inmarsat C 447798873 *Hong Kong* *Hong Kong* MMSI: 477424700 Official number: HK-3181	**41,101** 25,643 75,200 T/cm 68.3	Class: BV	**2011-10 Penglai Zhongbai Jinglu Ship Industry Co Ltd — Penglai SD** Yd No: JL0026 (B) Loa 225.00 (BB) Br ex - Dght 14.200 Lbp 217.00 Br md 32.26 Dpth 19.60 Welded, 1 dk	**(A21A2BC) Bulk Carrier** Grain: 89,728 Compartments: 7 Ho, ER 7 Ha: ER	**1 oil engine** driving 1 FP propeller Total Power: 8,833kW (12,009hp) 14.5kn MAN-B&W 5S60MC-C 1 x 2 Stroke 5 Cy. 600 x 2400 8833kW (12009bhp) Hyundai Heavy Industries Co Ltd-South Korea AuxGen: 3 x 560kW 60Hz a.c
9621132 *VRLQ8* -	**SHANDONG HAI DA** **Hai Kuo Shipping 1228 Ltd** Shandong Shipping Corp *Hong Kong* *Hong Kong* MMSI: 477250300 Official number: HK3742	**32,987** 19,236 56,734 T/cm 58.8	Class: LR ✠ **100A1** SS 03/2013 bulk carrier CSR BC-A GRAB (20) Nos. 2 & 4 holds may be empty ESP **ShipRight** (ACS (B), CM) *IWS LI EP ✠ **LMC** **UMS** Cable: 632.5/73.0 U3 (a)	**2013-03 Jinling Shipyard — Nanjing JS** Yd No: JLZ9110402 Loa 189.99 (BB) Br ex 32.30 Dght 12.800 Lbp 185.00 Br md 32.26 Dpth 18.00 Welded, 1 dk	**(A21A2BC) Bulk Carrier** Grain: 71,634; Bale: 68,200 Compartments: 5 Ho, ER 5 Ha: ER Cranes: 4x30t	**1 oil engine** driving 1 FP propeller Total Power: 9,480kW (12,889hp) 14.2kn MAN-B&W 6S50MC-C8 1 x 2 Stroke 6 Cy. 500 x 2000 9480kW (12889bhp) STX Engine Co Ltd-South Korea AuxGen: 3 x 600kW 450V 60Hz a.c Boilers: AuxB (Comp) 9.2kgf/cm² (9.0bar)
9626546 *BBUA* -	**SHANDONG HAI SHENG** **Shandong Shipping Co Ltd** SatCom: Inmarsat C 441405710 *Qingdao, Shandong* *China* MMSI: 414057000	**32,960** 19,142 56,531 T/cm 58.8	Class: CC	**2011-10 Yangzhou Guoyu Shipbuilding Co Ltd — Yangzhou JS** Yd No: GY441 Loa 189.99 (BB) Br ex - Dght 12.800 Lbp 185.00 Br md 32.26 Dpth 18.00 Welded, 1 dk	**(A21A2BC) Bulk Carrier** Grain: 71,634; Bale: 68,200 Compartments: 5 Ho, ER 5 Ha: ER Cranes: 4x36t	**1 oil engine** driving 1 FP propeller Total Power: 9,480kW (12,889hp) 14.5kn Wartsila 6RT-flex50 1 x 2 Stroke 6 Cy. 500 x 2050 9480kW (12889bhp) Qingdao Qiyao Wartsila MHI LinshanMarine Diesel Co Ltd (QMD)-China AuxGen: 3 x 600kW 450V a.c Fuel: 166.0 (d.f.) 2246.0 (r.f.) 32.5pd
9621120 *VRKD3* -	**SHANDONG HAI TONG** **Hai Kuo Shipping 1220 Ltd** Shandong Shipping Corp *Hong Kong* *Hong Kong* MMSI: 477098800 Official number: HK-3421	**32,987** 19,231 56,724 T/cm 58.8	Class: LR ✠ **100A1** SS 05/2012 bulk carrier CSR BC-A GRAB (20) Nos. 2 & 4 holds may be empty ESP **ShipRight** (ACS (B),CM) *IWS LI EP ✠ **LMC** **UMS** Cable: 632.5/73.0 U3 (a)	**2012-05 Jinling Shipyard — Nanjing JS** Yd No: JLZ9110401 Loa 189.99 (BB) Br ex 32.30 Dght 12.800 Lbp 185.00 Br md 32.26 Dpth 18.00 Welded, 1 dk	**(A21A2BC) Bulk Carrier** Grain: 71,634; Bale: 68,200 Compartments: 5 Ho, ER 5 Ha: 4 (21.3 x 18.3)ER (18.9 x 18.3) Cranes: 4x30t	**1 oil engine** driving 1 FP propeller Total Power: 9,480kW (12,889hp) 14.2kn MAN-B&W 6S50MC-C 1 x 2 Stroke 6 Cy. 500 x 2000 9480kW (12889bhp) STX Engine Co Ltd-South Korea AuxGen: 3 x 600kW 450V 60Hz a.c Boilers: WTAuxB (Comp) 9.1kgf/cm² (8.9bar)
9591533 *VRNC6* -	**SHANDONG HAI YAO** **Minsheng Jiahe (Tianjin) Shipping Leasing Co Ltd** Shandong Shipping Corp *Hong Kong* *Hong Kong* MMSI: 477117300 Official number: HK-4045	**41,605** 26,095 75,750	Class: CC	**2014-01 Jiangsu Rongsheng Shipbuilding Co Ltd — Rugao JS** Yd No: 1146 Loa 224.90 (BB) Br ex 32.29 Dght 14.250 Lbp 217.00 Br md 32.25 Dpth 19.70 Welded, 1 dk	**(A21A2BC) Bulk Carrier** Grain: 92,070 Compartments: 7 Ho, ER 7 Ha: 6 (15.5 x 15.0)ER (15.5 x 13.0)	**1 oil engine** driving 1 FP propeller Total Power: 10,900kW (14,820hp) 14.5kn Wartsila 5RT-flex58T 1 x 2 Stroke 5 Cy. 580 x 2416 10900kW (14820bhp) AuxGen: 3 x a.c
9621156 *VRQM8* -	**SHANDONG HENG CHANG** **Sea 2 Leasing Co Ltd** Shandong Shipping Corp *Hong Kong* *Hong Kong* MMSI: 477219100 Official number: HK-3951	**94,710** 59,527 179,965 T/cm 124.3	Class: CC	**2013-10 Qingdao Beihai Shipbuilding Heavy Industry Co Ltd — Qingdao SD** Yd No: BC18.0-47 Loa 295.00 (BB) Br ex 46.06 Dght 18.100 Lbp 285.00 Br md 46.00 Dpth 24.80 Welded, 1 dk	**(A21A2BC) Bulk Carrier** Grain: 201,954 Compartments: 9 Ho, ER 9 Ha: 7 (15.5 x 20.0)ER 2 (15.5 x 16.5)	**1 oil engine** driving 1 FP propeller Total Power: 17,153kW (23,321hp) 14.5kn MAN-B&W 6S70MC-C8 1 x 2 Stroke 6 Cy. 700 x 2800 17153kW (23321bhp) Dalian Marine Diesel Co Ltd-China AuxGen: 3 x 900kW 450V a.c

Ship	Tonnage	Class	Build / Dimensions	Type	Machinery
9621168 **SHANDONG HUA ZHANG** *VRMU5* - **Sea 3 Leasing Co Ltd** Shandong Shipping Co Ltd *Hong Kong* *Hong Kong* MMSI: 477257600 Official number: HK-3980	**94,710** 59,528 180,000 T/cm 124.3	Class: CC	**2014-03 Qingdao Beihai Shipbuilding Heavy Industry Co Ltd — Qingdao SD** Yd No: BC18.0-48 Loa 295.00 (BB) Br ex 46.06 Dght 18.100 Lbp 285.00 Br md 46.00 Dpth 24.80 Welded, 1 dk	**(A21A2BC) Bulk Carrier** Grain: 201,900 Compartments: 9 Ho, ER 9 Ha: ER	**1 oil engine** driving 1 FP propeller Total Power: 18,660kW (25,370hp) 14.5kn MAN-B&W 6S70MC-C8 1 x 2 Stroke 6 Cy. 700 x 2800 18660kW (25370bhp) Dalian Marine Diesel Co Ltd-China AuxGen: 3 x a.c
9480552 **SHANDONG PENG CHENG** *C6YP9* - *ex Abeille -2013* **Shandong Shipping (Hong Kong) Co Ltd** Louis Dreyfus Commodities Suisse SA *Nassau* *Bahamas* MMSI: 311041500 Official number: 8001785	**43,024** 27,239 82,154 T/cm 70.2	Class: CC (NK)	**2010-07 Tsuneishi Group (Zhoushan) Shipbuilding Inc — Daishan County ZJ** Yd No: SS-059 Loa 228.99 (BB) Br ex - Dght 14.429 Lbp 222.00 Br md 32.26 Dpth 20.05 Welded, 1 dk	**(A21A2BC) Bulk Carrier** Grain: 97,381 Compartments: 7 Ho, ER 7 Ha: 6 (17.8 x 15.4)ER (14.2 x 13.8)	**1 oil engine** driving 1 FP propeller Total Power: 9,710kW (13,202hp) 14.5kn MAN-B&W 6S60MC-C 1 x 2 Stroke 6 Cy. 600 x 2400 9710kW (13202bhp) Mitsui Engineering & Shipbuilding CLtd-Japan Fuel: 3184.0 (r.f.)
8021189 **SHANDRANI** *3BIO* - *ex Hosei Maru No. 68 -1993* **Hemraz Ghina Sea Lord Fishing Ltd** - *Port Louis* *Mauritius* Official number: MR049	*397* 196 -		**1981-02 Miho Zosensho K.K. — Shimizu** Yd No: 1191 Loa 55.40 Br ex - Dght 3.501 Lbp 48.72 Br md 9.01 Dpth 3.87 Welded, 1 dk	**(B11B2FV) Fishing Vessel**	**1 oil engine** driving 1 FP propeller Total Power: 1,177kW (1,600hp) Akasaka DM33 1 x 4 Stroke 6 Cy. 330 x 500 1177kW (1600bhp) Akasaka Tekkosho KK (Akasaka DieselLtd)-Japan
8317007 **SHANDRINI** *5RSM* TM 98024 *ex Tanko Maru No. 53 -1993* *ex Ying Chin Shiang No. 16 -1998* *ex Kinsai Maru No. 28 -1998* - - *Toamasina* *Madagascar*	*289* - 291		**1983-10 Goriki Zosensho — Ise** Yd No: 863 Loa - Br ex - Dght 3.390 Lbp 42.12 Br md 8.31 Dpth 3.51 Welded, 1 dk	**(B11B2FV) Fishing Vessel** Ins: 535 Compartments: 5 Ho, ER 5 Ha: ER	**1 oil engine** driving 1 FP propeller Total Power: 736kW (1,001hp) Hanshin 6LU26G 1 x 4 Stroke 6 Cy. 260 x 440 736kW (1001bhp) The Hanshin Diesel Works Ltd-Japan
8993473 **SHANDY PAULINE II** - - **Russell's Fisheries Ltd** - *St John's, NL* *Canada* MMSI: 316006292 Official number: 826452	*138* 103 -		**2004-07 TWL Enterprises Ltd — Trinity TB NL** L reg 18.80 Br ex - Dght - Lbp - Br md 7.62 Dpth 3.66 Bonded, 1 dk	**(B11B2FV) Fishing Vessel** Hull Material: Reinforced Plastic	**1 oil engine** driving 1 Propeller Total Power: 536kW (729hp) 10.0kn
8135667 **SHANELIN K** *YGXP* - *ex Maiko -2005 ex Koei Maru No. 1 -2001* *ex Camellia Maru -1989* *ex Kannon Maru No. 8 -1989* **PT Citra Baru Adinusantara** - *Surabaya* *Indonesia*	*482* 227 750	Class: KI	**1982-04 Shin Nippon Jukogyo K.K. — Osakikamijima** Yd No: 180 Loa 47.02 Br ex - Dght 3.150 Lbp 42.54 Br md 8.01 Dpth 5.01 Welded, 1 dk	**(A31A2GX) General Cargo Ship**	**1 oil engine** geared to sc. shaft driving 1 FP propeller Total Power: 368kW (500hp) 9.0kn Yanmar 6U-UT 1 x 4 Stroke 6 Cy. 200 x 240 368kW (500bhp) Yanmar Diesel Engine Co Ltd-Japan
7918282 **SHANG DAR** - - *ex Yusho Maru -2000* *ex Junko Maru No. 38 -1992* **Shang Dar Fishery Inc** Kando Maritime Co Ltd	**643** 274 -		**1980-02 Sanuki Shipbuilding & Iron Works Co Ltd — Mitoyo KG** Yd No: 1051 Loa 55.30 Br ex 8.91 Dght 3.500 Lbp 48.31 Br md - Dpth 3.87 Welded, 1 dk	**(B11B2FV) Fishing Vessel**	**1 oil engine** reverse geared to sc. shaft driving 1 FP propeller Total Power: 1,214kW (1,651hp) Akasaka DM30R 1 x 4 Stroke 6 Cy. 300 x 480 1214kW (1651bhp) Akasaka Tekkosho KK (Akasaka DieselLtd)-Japan
9636527 **SHANG DIAN XIANG AN 5** *BPRI* - **Bank of Communications Finance Leasing Co Ltd** Shanghai Xiangan Electric Power Shipping Co SatCom: Inmarsat C 441402110 *China* MMSI: 414021000	**28,000** - 45,000	Class: ZC	**2011-07 Chengxi Shipyard Co Ltd — Jiangyin JS** Yd No: CX0405 Loa 200.00 (BB) Br ex - Dght 11.000 Lbp - Br md 32.00 Dpth 15.40 Welded, 1 dk	**(A21A2BC) Bulk Carrier** Grain: 55,500 Compartments: 5 Ho, ER 5 Ha: ER	**1 oil engine** driving 1 FP propeller 14.2kn
9636539 **SHANG DIAN XIANG AN 6** *BPRJ* - **Bank of Communications Finance Leasing Co Ltd** Shanghai Xiangan Electric Power Shipping Co *China* MMSI: 414022000	**28,000** - 45,000	Class: ZC	**2011-07 Chengxi Shipyard Co Ltd — Jiangyin JS** Yd No: CX0406 Loa 200.00 (BB) Br ex - Dght 11.000 Lbp - Br md 32.00 Dpth 15.40 Welded, 1 dk	**(A21A2BC) Bulk Carrier** Grain: 55,500 Compartments: 5 Ho, ER 5 Ha: ER	**1 oil engine** driving 1 FP propeller 14.2kn
9636541 **SHANG DIAN XIANG AN 7** *BPRK* - **Bank of Communications Finance Leasing Co Ltd** Shanghai Xiangan Electric Power Shipping Co SatCom: Inmarsat C 441403810 *China* MMSI: 414038000	**28,000** - 45,000	Class: ZC	**2011-08 Chengxi Shipyard Co Ltd — Jiangyin JS** Yd No: CX0407 Loa 200.00 (BB) Br ex - Dght 11.000 Lbp - Br md 32.00 Dpth 15.40 Welded, 1 dk	**(A21A2BC) Bulk Carrier** Grain: 55,500 Compartments: 5 Ho, ER 5 Ha: ER	**1 oil engine** driving 1 FP propeller 14.2kn
9636553 **SHANG DIAN XIANG AN 8** *BPLC* - **Bank of Communications Finance Leasing Co Ltd** Shanghai Xiangan Electric Power Shipping Co SatCom: Inmarsat C 441403910 *China* MMSI: 414039000	**28,000** - 45,000	Class: ZC	**2011-10 Chengxi Shipyard Co Ltd — Jiangyin JS** Yd No: CX0408 Loa 200.00 (BB) Br ex - Dght 11.000 Lbp - Br md 32.00 Dpth 15.40 Welded, 1 dk	**(A21A2BC) Bulk Carrier** Grain: 55,500 Compartments: 5 Ho, ER 5 Ha: ER	**1 oil engine** driving 1 FP propeller 14.2kn
8851792 **SHANG FUH No. 11** - - - -	*353* 178 -		**1985 in Chinese Taipei** Loa - Br ex - Dght 3.500 Lbp 45.60 Br md 8.60 Dpth 3.66 Welded, 1 dk	**(B11B2FV) Fishing Vessel**	**1 oil engine** driving 1 FP propeller
8851780 **SHANG FUH No. 12** - - - -	*353* 178 -		**1982 in Chinese Taipei** Loa 45.70 Br ex - Dght 2.900 Lbp 39.20 Br md 7.60 Dpth 3.30 Welded, 1 dk	**(B11B2FV) Fishing Vessel**	**1 oil engine** driving 1 FP propeller
8952443 **SHANG HE XIN** *BR3562* - *ex Calbee Potato Maru -2013* **Shangke Marine Transport Corp** - *Chinese Taipei* MMSI: 416004527	*499* - -		**1999-08 Tokuoka Zosen K.K. — Naruto** Yd No: 253 Loa 81.06 Br ex - Dght - Lbp 75.00 Br md 12.80 Dpth 6.40 Welded, 1 dk	**(A31A2GX) General Cargo Ship** Grain: 2,553 Compartments: 1 Ho, ER 1 Ha: (45.0 x 10.4)ER	**1 oil engine** driving 1 FP propeller Total Power: 1,471kW (2,000hp) 13.0kn Niigata 6M38GT 1 x 4 Stroke 6 Cy. 380 x 720 1471kW (2000bhp) Niigata Engineering Co Ltd-Japan Fuel: 140.0 (d.f.)
8977560 **SHANG JYI** - - **Shine-Year Maritime SA** -	**230** 98 -		**2002-04 in Chinese Taipei** L reg 39.00 Br ex - Dght - Lbp - Br md 7.00 Dpth 3.00 Welded, 1 dk	**(B11A2FT) Trawler**	**1 oil engine** driving 1 FP propeller Total Power: 883kW (1,201hp) Yanmar 1 x 4 Stroke 883kW (1201bhp) Yanmar Diesel Engine Co Ltd-Japan
8648602 **SHANG SHUN NO. 112** *BI2375* LL1613 *ex Hsin Cheng Hsiang No. 112 -2011* **Lung Soon Fishery Co Ltd** - *Kaohsiung* *Chinese Taipei* Official number: CT7-0375	**711** 278 -		**2005-06 Sen Koh Shipbuilding Corp — Kaohsiung** Loa 47.80 Br ex - Dght - Lbp - Br md 8.90 Dpth - Welded, 1 dk	**(B11B2FV) Fishing Vessel**	**1 oil engine** driving 1 Propeller
8648626 **SHANG SHUN NO. 168** - LL2249 **Lung Yuin Fishery Co Ltd** - *Kaohsiung* *Chinese Taipei* Official number: CT7-0527	**660** 300 -		**2000-11 San Yang Shipbuilding Co., Ltd. — Kaohsiung** Loa 51.90 Br ex 9.00 Dght - Lbp - Br md - Dpth - Welded, 1 dk	**(B11B2FV) Fishing Vessel**	**1 oil engine** driving 1 Propeller

Ship	Tonnage	Class	Build / Dimensions	Type / Cargo	Machinery
9198147 **SHANG SHUN No. 622** *BI2541* LL2314 **Shang Yuin Fishery Co Ltd** - *Kaohsiung* *Chinese Taipei* Official number: CT7-0541	**680** 296 -		**1998-08 Fong Kuo Shipbuilding Co Ltd — Kaohsiung** Yd No: 347 Loa 57.78 Br ex - Dght - Lbp 50.12 Br md 8.90 Dpth 3.85 Welded, 1 dk	**(B11B2FV) Fishing Vessel**	**1 oil engine** driving 1 FP propeller Total Power: 1,500kW (2,039hp) 13.0kn Matsui MA29GSC-3 1 x 4 Stroke 6 Cy. 290 x 540 1500kW (2039bhp) Matsui Iron Works Co Ltd-Japan
8648638 **SHANG SHUN NO. 668** *BI2510* LL964540 **Shang Shun Fishery Co Ltd** - *Kaohsiung* *Chinese Taipei* Official number: CT7-0510	**720** 301 -		**2000-11 Fong Kuo Shipbuilding Co Ltd — Kaohsiung** Yd No: 355 Loa 50.12 Br ex 8.90 Dght - Lbp - Br md - Dpth - Welded, 1 dk	**(B11B2FV) Fishing Vessel**	**1 oil engine** driving 1 Propeller
8319299 **SHANG YUN** - *ex* Kashima Maru No. 26 *-1998* - *ex* Ryoan Maru No. 18 *-1993* - *ex* Koei Maru No. 7 *-1989* - -	**619** 228 452		**1983-10 Miho Zosensho K.K. — Shimizu** Yd No: 1237 Loa 54.51 Br ex - Dght - Lbp 47.66 Br md 8.62 Dpth 3.76 Welded, 1 dk	**(B11B2FV) Fishing Vessel** Ins: 214 Compartments: 2 Ho, ER 2 Ha: ER	**1 oil engine** with clutches, flexible couplings & dr reverse geared to sc. shaft driving 1 FP propeller Total Power: 956kW (1,300hp) Akasaka A31R 1 x 4 Stroke 6 Cy. 310 x 600 956kW (1300bhp) Akasaka Tekkosho KK (Akasaka DieselLtd)-Japan
9118458 **SHANGHAI** *D5DH9* *ex* Hellespont Trinity *-2012* *ex* Marina M *-2005* - **Haven Finance Inc** Dynacom Tankers Management Ltd *Monrovia* *Liberia* MMSI: 636015885 Official number: 15885	**80,637** 45,963 148,018 T/cm 116.7	Class: AB	**1996-05 Samsung Heavy Industries Co Ltd — Geoje** Yd No: 1144 Loa 274.10 (BB) Br ex 47.84 Dght 16.022 Lbp 264.00 Br md 47.80 Dpth 22.80 Welded, 1 dk	**(A13A2TW) Crude/Oil Products Tanker** Double Hull (13F) Liq: 163,420; Liq (Oil): 163,420 Cargo Heating Coils Compartments: 12 Wing Ta, 2 Wing Slop Ta, ER 3 Cargo Pump (s): 3x3500m³/hr Manifold: Bow/CM: 136.2m Ice Capable	**1 oil engine** driving 1 FP propeller Total Power: 15,622kW (21,240hp) 14.6kn B&W 6S70MC 1 x 2 Stroke 6 Cy. 700 x 2674 15622kW (21240bhp) Hyundai Heavy Industries Co Ltd-South Korea AuxGen: 3 x 900kW 440V 60Hz a.c Fuel: 445.5 (d.f.) (Heating Coils) 4065.5 (r.f.) 60.0pd
9585364 **SHANGHAI** *VRGH2* - **South China Towing Co Ltd** - *Hong Kong* *Hong Kong*	**286** 86 172	Class: BV	**2010-05 Hin Lee (Zhuhai) Shipyard Co Ltd — Zhuhai GD** (Hull) Yd No: 182 **2010-05 Cheoy Lee Shipyards Ltd — Hong Kong** Yd No: 4977 Loa 31.00 Br ex - Dght 3.870 Lbp 29.04 Br md 9.50 Dpth 4.70 Welded, 1 dk	**(B32A2ST) Tug**	**2 oil engines** reduction geared to sc. shafts driving 2 Z propellers Total Power: 2,942kW (4,000hp) Niigata 6L26HLX 2 x 4 Stroke 6 Cy. 260 x 350 each-1471kW (2000bhp) Niigata Engineering Co Ltd-Japan AuxGen: 2 x 100kW 50Hz a.c
9599913 **SHANGHAI BULKER** *9V9911* - **Bright Ocean Pte Ltd** Soon Fong Shipping Pte Ltd SatCom: Inmarsat C 456667410 *Singapore* *Singapore* MMSI: 566674000 Official number: 397738	**32,987** 19,231 56,719 T/cm 58.8	Class: LR ✠ **100A1** SS 09/2012 bulk carrier CSR BC-A Nos. 2 & 4 holds may be empty GRAB (20) ESP **ShipRight** (CM,ACS (B)) *IWS LI EP ✠ **LMC** **UMS** Cable: 632.5/73.0 U3 (a)	**2012-09 Jinling Shipyard — Nanjing JS** Yd No: JLZ9100418 Loa 189.99 (BB) Br ex 32.30 Dght 12.800 Lbp 185.00 Br md 32.26 Dpth 18.00 Welded, 1 dk	**(A21A2BC) Bulk Carrier** Grain: 71,634; Bale: 68,200 Compartments: 5 Ho, ER 5 Ha: ER Cranes: 4x30t	**1 oil engine** driving 1 FP propeller Total Power: 9,480kW (12,889hp) 14.2kn MAN-B&W 6S50MC-C 1 x 2 Stroke 6 Cy. 500 x 2000 9480kW (12889bhp) STX (Dalian) Engine Co Ltd-China AuxGen: 3 x 600kW 450V 60Hz a.c Boilers: AuxB (Comp) 8.8kgf/cm² (8.6bar)
8915407 **SHANGHAI CARRIER** *DSPR8* *ex* Front Birch *-2007* *ex* Birch *-1999* - **Sinokor Merchant Marine Co Ltd** - SatCom: Inmarsat C 444000245 *Jeju* *South Korea* MMSI: 441431000 Official number: JJR-072115	**80,994** 46,232 156,750	Class: KR (NV)	**1991-07 Daewoo Shipbuilding & Heavy Machinery Ltd — Geoje** Yd No: 5046 Converted From: Crude Oil Tanker-2008 Loa 267.00 (BB) Br ex - Dght 17.654 Lbp 256.00 Br md 46.20 Dpth 23.80 Welded, 1 dk	**(A21A2BC) Bulk Carrier** Double Sides Entire Compartment Length Grain: 125,494 Compartments: 7 Ho, ER 7 Ha: 6 (15.8 x 14.2)ER (15.8 x 12.4)	**1 oil engine** driving 1 FP propeller Total Power: 15,401kW (20,939hp) 14.0kn MAN-B&W 6S70MC 1 x 2 Stroke 6 Cy. 700 x 2674 15401kW (20939bhp) Korea Heavy Industries & ConstrCo Ltd (HANJUNG)-South Korea AuxGen: 3 x 700kW 450V 60Hz a.c Fuel: 331.0 (d.f.) 5854.0 (r.f.) 63.0pd
9501368 **SHANGHAI EXPRESS** *DJBF2* - **Hapag-Lloyd AG** - *Hamburg* *Germany* MMSI: 218427000 Official number: 23591	**142,295** 60,481 142,022	Class: GL	**2013-03 Hyundai Heavy Industries Co Ltd — Ulsan** Yd No: 2245 Loa 366.52 (BB) Br ex - Dght 15.500 Lbp 350.00 Br md 48.20 Dpth 29.85 Welded, 1 dk	**(A33A2CC) Container Ship (Fully Cellular)** TEU 13167 incl 800 ref C	**1 oil engine** driving 1 FP propeller Total Power: 62,920kW (85,546hp) 24.7kn MAN-B&W 11K98ME 1 x 2 Stroke 11 Cy. 980 x 2660 62920kW (85546bhp) Thrusters: 2 Tunnel thruster (f)
9294343 **SHANGHAI HIGHWAY** *3ECE2* - **Skipjack Marine SA** Taiyo Nippon Kisen Co Ltd *Panama* *Panama* MMSI: 371318000 Official number: 3116605B	**48,927** 14,679 15,413	Class: NK	**2005-08 Nantong COSCO KHI Ship Engineering Co Ltd (NACKS) — Nantong JS** Yd No: 034 Loa 179.99 (BB) Br ex - Dght 9.417 Lbp 167.00 Br md 32.20 Dpth 32.21 Welded, 12 dks. incl. 3 movable dks.	**(A35B2RV) Vehicles Carrier** Side door/ramp (s) Quarter stern door/ramp (s. a.) Cars: 5,036	**1 oil engine** driving 1 FP propeller Total Power: 12,500kW (16,995hp) 20.0kn MAN-B&W 7S60ME-C 1 x 2 Stroke 7 Cy. 600 x 2400 12500kW (16995bhp) Kawasaki Heavy Industries Ltd-Japan AuxGen: 3 x 760kW 450/220V 60Hz a.c Thrusters: 1 Thwart. CP thruster (f) Fuel: 2660.0 (r.f.)
8869995 **SHANGHAI MARU No. 23** *HP7743* *ex* Kojin Maru No. 23 *-1994* - **Shanghai Trading Co SA** - *Panama* *Panama* Official number: D9021789PEXT	*499* 250 -		**1971 Shin Nippon Jukogyo K.K. — Osakikamijima** Loa 45.50 Br ex - Dght 3.800 Lbp 40.00 Br md 11.00 Dpth 4.70 Welded, 1 dk	**(A31A2GX) General Cargo Ship**	**1 oil engine** driving 1 FP propeller Total Power: 736kW (1,001hp) 9.5kn Matsui 1 x 4 Stroke 6 Cy. 736kW (1001bhp) Matsui Iron Works Co Ltd-Japan
9010785 **SHANGHAI REEFER** *HPXZ* *ex* Klajpedskij Bereg *-2004* - **Waterbeck Group Ltd** Laskaridis Shipping Co Ltd *Panama* *Panama* MMSI: 356567000 Official number: 31709PEXT3	**12,413** 5,564 13,283	Class: RS (NV)	**1990-05 VEB Mathias-Thesen-Werft — Wismar** Yd No: 243 Loa 152.14 Br ex 22.22 Dght 9.500 Lbp 142.00 Br md 22.20 Dpth 13.60 Welded, 1 dk, 2nd & 3rd dk in holds only	**(B12B2FC) Fish Carrier** Ins: 13,300 Compartments: 4 Ho, ER, 8 Tw Dk 4 Ha: 4 (6.0 x 3.9)ER Derricks: 2x10t,7x5t Ice Capable	**1 oil engine** driving 1 FP propeller Total Power: 7,599kW (10,332hp) 17.4kn MAN K5SZ70/125BL 1 x 2 Stroke 5 Cy. 700 x 1250 7599kW (10332bhp) VEB Dieselmotorenwerk Rostock-Rostock AuxGen: 4 x 588kW 390V 50Hz a.c Fuel: 633.0 (d.f.) 3902.0 (r.f.) 41.5pd
9326328 **SHANGHAI SPIRIT** *VRDO4* *ex* Western Grace *-2010* *ex* Asian Hope *-2008* - **Shanghai Spirit Shipping Ltd** OSL Shipping Ltd *Hong Kong* *Hong Kong* MMSI: 477007200 Official number: HK-2058	**11,751** 6,377 18,828 T/cm 30.7	Class: NK	**2005-11 Yamanishi Corp — Ishinomaki MG** Yd No: 1037 Loa 139.92 (BB) Br ex - Dght 8.444 Lbp 132.00 Br md 25.00 Dpth 11.50 Welded, 1 dk	**(A21A2BC) Bulk Carrier** Grain: 23,161; Bale: 22,563 4 Ha: ER 4 (17.5 x 15.0) Cranes: 3x30.5t	**1 oil engine** driving 1 FP propeller Total Power: 5,180kW (7,043hp) 13.0kn MAN-B&W 7S35MC 1 x 2 Stroke 7 Cy. 350 x 1400 5180kW (7043bhp) Makita Corp-Japan Fuel: 1010.0
9033751 **SHANGHAI SUPER EXPRESS** *HPOD* *ex* Musashi Maru *-2003* - *ex* Nissan Musashi Maru *-1995* **Jackal Shipping Navigation SA** MOL Ship Management Co Ltd (MOLSHIP) *Panama* *Panama* MMSI: 355188000 Official number: 2945503B	**16,350** 4,905 4,881	Class: NK	**1991-11 Naikai Shipbuilding & Engineering Co Ltd — Onomichi HS (Setoda Shipyard)** Yd No: 569 Loa 145.62 (BB) Br ex 24.02 Dght 6.517 Lbp 131.00 Br md 24.00 Dpth 10.00 Welded, 2 dks	**(A35A2RR) Ro-Ro Cargo Ship** Passengers: berths: 8 Stern door/ramp Len: 8.30 Wid: 5.60 Swl: - Quarter stern door/ramp (s) Len: 26.70 Wid: 5.60 Swl: - Lane-Len: 1250 Trailers: 121	**1 oil engine** driving 1 FP propeller Total Power: 10,923kW (14,851hp) 20.8kn B&W 9L50MC 1 x 2 Stroke 9 Cy. 500 x 1620 10923kW (14851bhp) Hitachi Zosen Corp-Japan AuxGen: 3 x 680kW a.c, 1 x 80kW a.c Thrusters: 1 Thwart. CP thruster (f); 1 Thwart. CP thruster (a) Fuel: 690.0 (r.f.)
8979659 **SHANGRILA** - *ex* Super Marine No. 2 *-2007* - **Eunsung Shipping Co Ltd** - *South Korea*	*181* - -		**2002-12 Setouchi Craft Co Ltd — Onomichi** Yd No: S-227 L reg 34.15 Br ex - Dght - Lbp - Br md 6.79 Dpth 2.88 Welded, 1 dk	**(A37B2PS) Passenger Ship** Hull Material: Aluminium Alloy	**2 oil engines** driving 2 Propellers Total Power: 2,898kW (3,940hp) M.T.U. 16V396TB83 2 x Vee 4 Stroke 16 Cy. 165 x 185 each-1449kW (1970bhp) MTU Friedrichshafen GmbH-Friedrichshafen
7649207 **SHANKA CHIL 2** *S2ES* *ex* Ebisu Maru *-1993* - **Unichart Navigation Ltd** - *Chittagong* *Bangladesh* Official number: C.1030	*749* 615 1,500		**1977 Takao Zosen Kogyo K.K. — Tateyama** Loa 53.50 Br ex - Dght 3.720 Lbp 47.00 Br md 11.00 Dpth 4.09 Welded, 1dk	**(A13B2TP) Products Tanker** Liq: 1,590; Liq (Oil): 1,590 Compartments: 4 Ta, ER	**1 oil engine** driving 1 FP propeller Total Power: 736kW (1,001hp) 8.0kn Daihatsu 1 x 4 Stroke 6 Cy. 736kW (1001bhp) Daihatsu Diesel Manufacturing Co Lt-Japan

7851460 - -	**SHANKAR** *ex* Gabon Lady *ex* Camus *ex* Tong Hoe *-1993* *ex* Hosei Maru *-1990* *ex* Kinsei Maru No. 20 *-1982* **Orient Glory Shipping Co Inc** - *San Lorenzo* *Honduras* Official number: L-0325664	*199* 106 559		**1968 Sagawa Zosen — Imabari** Yd No: 137 Loa 43.35 Br ex - Dght 3.310 Lbp 41.00 Br md 7.60 Dpth 5.20 Welded, 1 dk	**(A31A2GX) General Cargo Ship**	**1 oil engine** driving 1 FP propeller Total Power: 405kW (551hp) 11.0kn Makita 1 x 4 Stroke 405kW (551bhp) Makita Diesel Co Ltd-Japan
7535224 *S2HZ* -	**SHANKCHIL** *ex* Satsuki Maru *-1986* **Unichart Navigation Ltd** - *Chittagong* *Bangladesh* Official number: C.662	*663* 482 1,600		**1971 Taisei Zosen K.K. — Osakikamijima** Yd No: 157 Loa 63.71 Br ex 10.04 Dght 4.750 Lbp 57.71 Br md 10.01 Dpth 5.01 Welded, 1 dk	**(A13B2TP) Products Tanker** Liq: 1,878; Liq (Oil): 1,878 Compartments: 4 Ta, ER	**1 oil engine** driving 1 FP propeller Total Power: 1,177kW (1,600hp) 12.0kn Niigata 1 x 4 Stroke 1177kW (1600bhp) Niigata Engineering Co Ltd-Japan AuxGen: 1 x 40kW 220V Fuel: 69.0 4.0pd
9680308 *A4BB6* -	**SHANNAH** **National Ferries Co SAOC** *Oman* MMSI: 461000134	**350** - 102	Class: LR (Class contemplated) **100A1** 01/2014 Class contemplated	**2014-01 Strategic Marine (V) Co Ltd — Vung Tau** Yd No: H690 Loa 45.80 (BB) Br ex - Dght 1.500 Lbp - Br md 16.00 Dpth - Welded, 1 dk	**(A36A2PR) Passenger/Ro-Ro Ship (Vehicles)** Passengers: unberthed: 294 Bow ramp (centre) Stern door/ramp (centre) Cars: 38	**4 oil engines** reduction geared to sc. shafts driving 2 Propellers Total Power: 4,641kW (6,309hp) 15.0kn Caterpillar C18 ACERT 4 x 4 Stroke 6 Cy. 145 x 183 each-357kW (485bhp) Thrusters: 2 Tunnel thruster 1 (p) 1 (s)
8991724 *WDB6914* -	**SHANNAN C** **J Sercovich LLC** - *Buras, LA* *United States of America* MMSI: 366932780 Official number: 631579	**104** 71 -		**1981 Marine Construction, Inc. — Slidell, La** Yd No: 2 L reg 18.90 Br ex - Dght - Lbp - Br md 7.71 Dpth 2.59 Welded, 1 dk	**(B32A2ST) Tug**	**1 oil engine** driving 1 Propeller
8971669 *WYD6451* -	**SHANNON** *ex* Connewango (YTM-388) *-1977* *ex* Connewango (YTB-388) *-1977* **Gaelic Tugboat Co** - *Grosse Ile, MI* *United States of America* MMSI: 367043260 Official number: 584862	*145* 98 -		**1944-11 Consolidated Shipbuilding Corp. — New York, NY** Yd No: 3195 Loa 30.78 Br ex - Dght - Lbp - Br md 7.86 Dpth 2.49 Welded, 1 dk	**(B32A2ST) Tug**	**2 oil engines** driving 2 gen. Connecting to 1 elec. Motor of (736kW) reduction geared to sc. shaft driving 1 FP propeller 15.0kn Caterpillar 1 x 4 Stroke Caterpillar Tractor Co-USA
9016844 *PNFN* -	**SHANNON** *ex* Iyo Maru *-2009* **PT Linc Bintang Line** - *Tanjung Priok* *Indonesia* MMSI: 525019530	**1,342** 574 1,561	Class: KI	**1990-12 Yamanaka Zosen K.K. — Imabari** Yd No: 506 Loa 72.81 (BB) Br ex - Dght 4.383 Lbp 68.00 Br md 11.50 Dpth 6.90 Welded	**(A31A2GX) General Cargo Ship** Compartments: 1 Ho, ER 1 Ha: ER	**1 oil engine** reverse geared to sc. shaft driving 1 FP propeller Total Power: 1,214kW (1,651hp) Hanshin 6LU32G 1 x 4 Stroke 6 Cy. 320 x 510 1214kW (1651bhp) The Hanshin Diesel Works Ltd-Japan AuxGen: 2 x 107kW 225V a.c
8871754 *YJQC6* -	**SHANNON** **Shannon Offshore Shipping Ltd** Rederij Groen BV *Port Vila* *Vanuatu* MMSI: 576330000 Official number: 1913	**333** 99 -		**1991 Industrielle des Pecheries S.V. (IDP) — Oostende** Converted From: Trawler-1991 Loa 36.98 Br ex - Dght - Lbp - Br md 8.30 Dpth 4.40 Welded, 1 dk	**(B22G2OY) Standby Safety Vessel**	**1 oil engine** driving 1 FP propeller Total Power: 1,177kW (1,600hp) MaK 1 x 4 Stroke 1177kW (1600bhp) Krupp MaK Maschinenbau GmbH-Kiel AuxGen: 2 x 100kW 220/380V 50Hz a.c Thrusters: 1 Tunnel thruster (f)
5321784 *WCX8376* -	**SHANNON** *ex* Judi M *-2010* *ex* Shannon Foss *-2004* **Marine Works Construction Inc** - *Seattle, WA* *United States of America* MMSI: 366740920 Official number: 275963	**141** 42 -		**1957-07 Todd Shipyards Corp. — Seattle, Wa** Yd No: 14 Loa 27.70 Br ex 7.70 Dght - Lbp - Br md 7.40 Dpth 4.01 Welded, 1 dk	**(B32A2ST) Tug**	**1 oil engine** driving 1 FP propeller Total Power: 883kW (1,201hp) Nordberg FMD.138 1 x 4 Stroke 8 Cy. 330 x 419 883kW (1201bhp) Nordberg Manufacturing Co-USA
9333292 *WDB9898* -	**SHANNON** *ex* Shannon McAllister *-2006* **Suderman & Young Towing Co LP** - *Houston, TX* *United States of America* MMSI: 366984720 Official number: 1158652	**280** 84 193	Class: AB	**2004-09 Eastern Shipbuilding Group — Panama City, Fl** Yd No: 816 Loa 29.26 Br ex - Dght 3.660 Lbp 27.87 Br md 10.98 Dpth 4.54 Welded, 1 dk	**(B32A2ST) Tug**	**2 oil engines** reduction geared to sc. shafts driving 2 Z propellers Total Power: 3,752kW (5,102hp) EMD (Electro-Motive) 12-645-F7B 2 x Vee 2 Stroke 12 Cy. 230 x 254 each-1876kW (2551bhp) General Motors Corp.Electro-Motive Div.-La Grange AuxGen: 2 x 99kW a.c
7207748 *WCD6367* -	**SHANNON DANN** *ex* Alice H *-1998* *ex* Chelsea *-1998* *ex* Elmire G. Defelice *-1987* **Dann Ocean Towing Inc** - SatCom: Inmarsat C 433853310 *Tampa, FL* *United States of America* MMSI: 338533000 Official number: 531906	**246** 73 -	Class: AB	**1971-04 McDermott Shipyards Inc — Morgan City LA** Yd No: 169 Loa - Br ex - Dght 3.887 Lbp 28.33 Br md 9.15 Dpth 4.37 Welded, 1 dk	**(B32A2ST) Tug**	**2 oil engines** reverse reduction geared to sc. shafts driving 2 FP propellers Total Power: 1,434kW (1,950hp) EMD (Electro-Motive) 8-645-E5 2 x Vee 2 Stroke 8 Cy. 230 x 254 each-717kW (975bhp) General Motors Corp.Electro-Motive Div.-La Grange AuxGen: 2 x 75kW Fuel: 200.0 (d.f.)
7900625 *YHOH* -	**SHANNON EXPRESS** *ex* Sun Pulse *-1995* *ex* Nissho Maru *-1994* *ex* Kami Maru No. 5 *-1988* **PT Bahtera Citra Mandiri** PT Perusahaan Pelayaran Hanisakita Persada *Jakarta* *Indonesia* MMSI: 525019214	**1,408** 662 1,441	Class: KI (NK)	**1979-03 Mategata Zosen K.K. — Namikata** Yd No: 168 Loa 71.13 Br ex - Dght 4.045 Lbp 65.99 Br md 12.01 Dpth 6.45 Welded, 2 dks	**(A31A2GX) General Cargo Ship** Grain: 3,145; Bale: 2,925 1 Ha: (40.6 x 9.3)ER	**1 oil engine** driving 1 FP propeller Total Power: 1,618kW (2,200hp) 12.5kn Akasaka DM38AR 1 x 4 Stroke 6 Cy. 380 x 600 1618kW (2200bhp) Akasaka Tekkosho KK (Akasaka DieselLtd)-Japan AuxGen: 2 x 192kW
9320489 *C6UU7* -	**SHANNON FISHER** - **FSL-3 Inc** James Fisher (Shipping Services) Ltd *Nassau* *Bahamas* MMSI: 308539000 Official number: 8001059	**3,501** 1,444 5,420 T/cm 13.3	Class: LR ✠ **100A1** SS 01/2011 Double Hull oil tanker bottom strengthened for loading and unloading aground ESP LI *IWS ✠ **LMC** **UMS** Eq.Ltr: A†; Cable: 467.0/40.0 U3 (a)	**2006-01 Santierul Naval Damen Galati S.A. — Galati** (Hull) Yd No: 1066 **2006-01 B.V. Scheepswerf Damen Bergum — Bergum** Yd No: 9378 Loa 85.32 (BB) Br ex 17.20 Dght 6.300 Lbp 81.12 Br md 17.00 Dpth 8.95 Welded, 1 dk	**(A13B2TP) Products Tanker** Double Hull (13F) Liq: 5,730; Liq (Oil): 5,730 Compartments: 10 Wing Ta, 1 Slop Ta, ER 10 Cargo Pump (s): 10x200m³/hr Manifold: Bow/CM: 35.3m	**1 oil engine** with clutches, flexible couplings & sr geared to sc. shafts driving 1 CP propeller Total Power: 2,640kW (3,589hp) 12.2kn MaK 8M25 1 x 4 Stroke 8 Cy. 255 x 400 2640kW (3589bhp) Caterpillar Motoren GmbH & Co. KG-Germany AuxGen: 1 x 335kW 230/400V 50Hz a.c, 2 x 450kW 230/400V 50Hz a.c Boilers: TOH (ex.g.) 10.2kgf/cm² (10.0bar), TOH (o.f.) 10.2kgf/cm² (10.0bar) Thrusters: 1 Thwart. FP thruster (f) Fuel: 37.5 (d.f.) 167.4 (r.f.)
9032941 *WCC5850* -	**SHANNON MCALLISTER** *ex* Alice Winslow *-2012* **McAllister Towing & Transportation Co Inc (MT & T)** - *Wilmington, DE* *United States of America* MMSI: 367558070 Official number: 975943	**233** 70 -		**1991-05 Washburn & Doughty Associates Inc — East Boothbay ME** Yd No: 39 Loa 27.43 Br ex - Dght - Lbp 25.94 Br md 9.14 Dpth 4.42 Welded, 1 dk	**(B32A2ST) Tug**	**2 oil engines** with clutches & sr geared to sc. shafts driving 2 FP propellers Total Power: 3,100kW (4,214hp) 10.5kn Alco 12V251F 2 x Vee 4 Stroke 12 Cy. 229 x 267 each-1550kW (2107bhp) White Industrial Power Inc-USA AuxGen: 1 x 60kW 110V a.c, 1 x 40kW 110V a.c Fuel: 48.9 (d.f.) 5.9pd
8521799 *T3RD* -	**SHANNON PROSPER** *ex* M Nagoya *-2009* *ex* Toyo No. 5 *-2007* **Shannon Prosper Shipping SA** Hangli Shipping & Trading Pte Ltd *Tarawa* *Kiribati* MMSI: 529197000 Official number: K-11850866	**2,147** 830 2,530	Class: NK	**1985-11 Kinoura Zosen K.K. — Imabari** Yd No: 151 Loa 79.10 Br ex - Dght 5.211 Lbp 73.00 Br md 13.01 Dpth 8.51 Welded, 1 dk	**(A31A2GX) General Cargo Ship** Grain: 4,391; Bale: 4,037 1 Ha: (39.4 x 9.0)ER Derricks: 1x12t,1x8t	**1 oil engine** driving 1 FP propeller Total Power: 1,324kW (1,800hp) 10.8kn Akasaka A31 1 x 4 Stroke 6 Cy. 310 x 600 1324kW (1800bhp) Akasaka Tekkosho KK (Akasaka DieselLtd)-Japan Fuel: 210.0 (r.f.)

IMO / Call sign	Name / Owner	Tonnage	Class	Builder / Dimensions	Type / Capacity	Machinery
9503926 *9HA2409* -	**SHANNON STAR** *ex* Seine Star *-2010* **Rigel Bereederungs GmbH & Co KG mt 'Shannon Star'** Rigel Schiffahrts GmbH & Co KG SatCom: Inmarsat C 424855310 *Valletta* *Malta* MMSI: 248553000 Official number: 9503926	**8,581** 4,117 13,023 T/cm 23.2	Class: AB	**2010-07 21st Century Shipbuilding Co Ltd — Tongyeong** Yd No: 265 Loa 128.60 (BB) Br ex - Dght 8.714 Lbp 120.40 Br md 20.40 Dpth 11.50 Welded, 1 dk	**(A12B2TR) Chemical/Products Tanker** Double Hull (13F) Liq: 13,916; Liq (Oil): 13,916 Compartments: 12 Wing Ta, 2 Wing Slop Ta, ER 12 Cargo Pump (s): 12x300m^3/hr Manifold: Bow/CM: 61.2m	**1 oil engine** driving 1 FP propeller Total Power: 4,440kW (6,037hp) 13.4kn MAN-B&W 6S35MC 1 x 2 Stroke 6 Cy. 350 x 1400 4440kW (6037bhp) STX Engine Co Ltd-South Korea Thrusters: 1 Tunnel thruster (f) Fuel: 65.0 (d.f.) 570.0 (r.f.)
9474606 *BITY* -	**SHANREN** - **CSIC-IMC Shipping Co Ltd** MSI Ship Management (Qingdao) Co Ltd *Shanghai* *China* MMSI: 413375790	**4,289** 1,843 6,575 T/cm 16.2	Class: CC	**2010-02 Chongqing Chuandong Shipbuilding Industry Co Ltd — Chongqing** Yd No: HT0105 Loa 104.95 (BB) Br ex - Dght 6.450 Lbp 99.00 Br md 17.50 Dpth 8.00 Welded, 1 dk	**(A12B2TR) Chemical/Products Tanker** Double Hull (13F) Liq: 6,126; Liq (Oil): 6,126 Cargo Heating Coils Compartments: 10 Wing Ta, ER 10 Cargo Pump (s): 2x100m^3/hr, 8x200m^3/hr Manifold: Bow/CM: 48m	**1 oil engine** reduction geared to sc. shaft driving 1 Propeller Total Power: 2,500kW (3,399hp) 12.0kn Daihatsu 8DKM-28 1 x 4 Stroke 8 Cy. 280 x 390 2500kW (3399bhp) Shaanxi Diesel Heavy Industry Co Lt-China AuxGen: 3 x 320kW 400V a.c Fuel: 95.0 (d.f.) 320.0 (r.f.)
8933590 - -	**SHANS** - **Kerch Fishing Combine (A/O 'Kerchenskiy Rybokombinat')** - *Kerch* *Ukraine* Official number: 930495	**104** 31 58	Class: (RS)	**1994 AO Azovskaya Sudoverf — Azov** Yd No: 1073 Loa 26.50 Br ex 6.59 Dght 2.360 Lbp 22.90 Br md - Dpth 3.05 Welded, 1 dk	**(B11A2FS) Stern Trawler** Ins: 48	**1 oil engine** geared to sc. shaft driving 1 FP propeller Total Power: 165kW (224hp) 9.3kn Daldizel 6CHNSP18/22 1 x 4 Stroke 6 Cy. 180 x 220 165kW (224bhp) Daldizel-Khabarovsk AuxGen: 2 x 30kW Fuel: 9.0 (d.f.)
8815097 *UCGR* -	**SHANS 102** *ex* Yamato Maru No. 3 *-2011* **JSC Vostok-1** - *Nakhodka* *Russia* MMSI: 273359510	**540** 225 -	Class: RS	**1988-09 Niigata Engineering Co Ltd — Niigata NI** Yd No: 2103 Loa 49.42 (BB) Br ex - Dght 3.249 Lbp 43.75 Br md 8.30 Dpth 3.60 Welded, 1 dk	**(B11B2FV) Fishing Vessel** Ins: 421	**1 oil engine** with clutches, flexible couplings & sr geared to sc. shaft driving 1 CP propeller Total Power: 699kW (950hp) 15.4kn Niigata 6M28BFT 1 x 4 Stroke 6 Cy. 280 x 480 699kW (950bhp) Niigata Engineering Co Ltd-Japan Fuel: 170.0 (d.f.)
8608858 *UBDH9* -	**SHANS 103** *ex* Kaio Maru No. 88 *-2011* *ex* Habomai Maru No. 88 *-2000* **JSC Vostok-1** - *Nakhodka* *Russia* MMSI: 273358420	**678** 254 482	Class: RS	**1986-09 Miho Zosensho K.K. — Shimizu** Yd No: 1290 Loa 54.79 Br ex - Dght 3.441 Lbp 48.01 Br md 8.62 Dpth 3.81 Welded, 1 dk	**(B11B2FV) Fishing Vessel** Ins: 620	**1 oil engine** with clutches & sr geared to sc. shaft driving 1 FP propeller Total Power: 736kW (1,001hp) Akasaka DM28AFD 1 x 4 Stroke 6 Cy. 280 x 460 736kW (1001bhp) Akasaka Tekkosho KK (Akasaka DieselLtd)-Japan
9614476 *9V9710* -	**SHANSI** - **The China Navigation Co Pte Ltd** - *Singapore* *Singapore* MMSI: 566866000 Official number: 397497	**25,483** 11,814 30,700	Class: LR ✠ **100A1** SS 04/2013 container ship, holds Nos. 3 & 4 strengthened for heavy cargo, general cargo in all holds, holds Nos. 3 & 4 suitable for unloading by grab (20 tonnes) **ShipRight** ACS (B) *IWS LI EP ✠ **LMC** **UMS** Eq.Ltr: M†; Cable: 638.5/73.0 U3 (a)	**2013-04 Zhejiang Ouhua Shipbuilding Co Ltd — Zhoushan ZJ** Yd No: 637 Loa 199.90 (BB) Br ex 28.28 Dght 10.500 Lbp 188.79 Br md 28.20 Dpth 15.50 Welded, 1 dk	**(A33A2CC) Container Ship (Fully Cellular)** TEU 2082 C Ho 916 TEU C Dk 1166 TEU incl 147 ref C Compartments: 2 Ho, 2 Tw Dk, 3 Cell Ho, ER 5 Ha: ER Cranes: 4x60t	**1 oil engine** driving 1 FP propeller Total Power: 13,560kW (18,436hp) 15.5kn Wartsila 6RT-flex58T 1 x 2 Stroke 6 Cy. 580 x 2416 13560kW (18436bhp) Hudong Heavy Machinery Co Ltd-China AuxGen: 3 x 1058kW 450V 60Hz a.c Boilers: AuxB (Comp) 8.4kgf/cm^2 (8.2bar) Thrusters: 1 Tunnel thruster (f)
9640748 *AVOB* -	**SHANTAM** - **Sadhav Shipping Ltd** - *Mumbai* *India* MMSI: 419000370 Official number: 3884	**1,323** 651 2,300	Class: IR	**2012-06 Waterways Shipyard Pvt Ltd — Goa** Yd No: 150 Loa 69.26 Br ex 14.02 Dght 3.200 Lbp 67.14 Br md 13.99 Dpth 4.40 Welded, 1 dk	**(A31A2GX) General Cargo Ship** Bale: 2,584 Compartments: 1 Ho, ER 1 Ha: ER	**2 oil engines** reduction geared to sc. shaft (s) driving 2 FP propellers Total Power: 536kW (728hp) 10.4kn Cummins NT-855-M 2 x 4 Stroke 6 Cy. 140 x 152 each-268kW (364bhp) Cummins India Ltd-India
9190274 *UBNJ7* -	**SHANTAR** *ex* Morraborg *-2013* **Sakhalin Shipping Co (SASCO)** - *Kholmsk* *Russia* MMSI: 273359190	**6,540** 3,464 9,200 T/cm 19.4	Class: RS (BV)	**1999-05 Scheepswerf Bijlsma Lemmer BV — Lemmer** Yd No: 684 Loa 134.55 (BB) Br ex 16.60 Dght 7.110 Lbp 127.20 Br md 16.50 Dpth 9.80 Welded, 1 dk	**(A31A2GX) General Cargo Ship** Grain: 13,079; Bale: 13,059 TEU 604 C Ho 264 TEU C Dk 340 TEU incl 60 ref C. Compartments: 2 Ho, ER 2 Ha: (39.2 x 13.5) (52.5 x 13.5)ER Ice Capable	**1 oil engine** geared to sc. shaft driving 1 CP propeller Total Power: 5,280kW (7,179hp) 16.0kn Wartsila 8L38 1 x 4 Stroke 8 Cy. 380 x 475 5280kW (7179bhp) Wartsila NSD Nederland BV-Netherlands AuxGen: 1 x 750kW a.c, 2 x 350kW a.c Thrusters: 1 Thwart. FP thruster (f)
8728452 *UFCN* -	**SHANTAR-I** *ex* Auda *-1999* **Dalnevostochnoe Poberezhe Co Ltd** - *Sovetskaya Gavan* *Russia* MMSI: 273436440 Official number: 882205	**806** 241 316	Class: RS	**1989-05 Zavod "Leninskaya Kuznitsa" — Kiyev** Yd No: 271 Converted From: Stern Trawler-1995 Loa 53.75 Br ex 10.71 Dght 4.400 Lbp 47.93 Br md 10.50 Dpth 6.02 Welded, 1 dk	**(B11B2FV) Fishing Vessel** Ins: 218 Ice Capable	**1 oil engine** driving 1 CP propeller Total Power: 971kW (1,320hp) 12.6kn S.K.L. 8NVD48A-2U 1 x 4 Stroke 8 Cy. 320 x 480 971kW (1320bhp) VEB Schwermaschinenbau "KarlLiebknecht" (SKL)-Magdeburg AuxGen: 1 x 300kW a.c, 1 x 300kW a.c
8861905 - -	**SHANTARSKIY** - **'Voskhod' Fishing Collective (Rybolovetskiy Kolkhoz 'Voskhod')** -	**741** 222 322	Class: (RS)	**1991-08 Volgogradskiy Sudostroitelnyy Zavod — Volgograd** Yd No: 268 Loa 53.74 Br ex 10.71 Dght 4.040 Lbp 47.92 Br md - Dpth 6.00 Welded, 1 dk	**(B11A2FS) Stern Trawler** Ice Capable	**1 oil engine** driving 1 FP propeller Total Power: 969kW (1,317hp) 12.7kn S.K.L. 8NVD48A-2U 1 x 4 Stroke 8 Cy. 320 x 480 969kW (1317bhp) (made 1991) SKL Motoren u. Systemtechnik AG-Magdeburg
7047875 *WY7842* -	**SHANTELLE & NANCY** *ex* Lady Grace *-1999* **N & A Fishing Corp** - *Boston, MA* *United States of America* Official number: 522996	*135* 95 -		**1969 Marine Builders, Inc. — Mobile, Al** L reg 23.47 Br ex 6.84 Dght - Lbp - Br md - Dpth 3.38 Welded	**(B11B2FV) Fishing Vessel**	**1 oil engine** driving 1 FP propeller Total Power: 368kW (500hp)
9396610 *V2DL8* -	**SHANTI** *ex* Alianca Neuquen *-2010* *ex* Shanti *-2009* *launched as* Rickmers Japan *-2008* **Shanti Schiffahrts GmbH & Co KG** Rohden Bereederung GmbH & Co KG *Saint John's* *Antigua & Barbuda* MMSI: 305253000 Official number: 4474	**16,162** 6,128 17,350	Class: GL (BV)	**2008-05 Jiangsu Yangzijiang Shipbuilding Co Ltd — Jiangyin JS** Yd No: 2006-727C Loa 161.30 (BB) Br ex - Dght 9.500 Lbp 149.60 Br md 25.00 Dpth 14.90 Welded, 1 dk	**(A33A2CC) Container Ship (Fully Cellular)** TEU 1345 C Ho 556 TEU C Dk 789 TEU incl 449 ref C Cranes: 2x45t	**1 oil engine** driving 1 FP propeller Total Power: 12,640kW (17,185hp) 19.3kn MAN-B&W 8S50MC-C 1 x 2 Stroke 8 Cy. 500 x 2000 12640kW (17185bhp) Hudong Heavy Machinery Co Ltd-China AuxGen: 2 x 1520kW 450V a.c, 2 x 1140kW 450V a.c Thrusters: 1 Tunnel thruster (f)
7235317 - -	**SHANTI DOOT** - **Seatrans Shipping Co** - *Mormugao* *India* Official number: B7060	*230* 138 -	Class: (IR) (NV)	**1972 S.K. Dhondy & Co. — Mumbai** Yd No: 118 Converted From: Unknown Function Loa 40.04 Br ex 9.02 Dght 2.134 Lbp - Br md - Dpth 2.21 Welded, 1 dk	**(B35E2TF) Bunkering Tanker**	**2 oil engines** driving 2 FP propellers Total Power: 302kW (410hp) G.M. (Detroit Diesel) 6V-71-TI 2 x Vee 2 Stroke 6 Cy. 108 x 127 each-151kW (205bhp) Detroit Diesel Corporation-Detroit, Mi AuxGen: 1 x 24V d.c
9658604 *AVRR* -	**SHANTI SAGAR 14** - **Adani Ports & Special Economic Zone Ltd** - *Mumbai* *India* MMSI: 419000503 Official number: 3959	**774** 232 1,043	Class: IR	**2012-05 Dempo Engineering Works Ltd. — Goa** Yd No: 442 Loa 55.60 Br ex 12.02 Dght 3.000 Lbp 54.40 Br md 12.00 Dpth 3.80 Welded, 1 dk	**(B33B2DG) Grab Hopper Dredger** Liq: 650	**2 oil engines** reduction geared to sc. shafts driving 2 Propellers Total Power: 1,192kW (1,620hp) 8.2kn Cummins 2 x each-596kW (810bhp) Cummins India Ltd-India
9471147 *AUUA* -	**SHANTI SAGAR - IV** *ex* Zhe *-2008* *ex* Zhe Shui Jian 11 *-2007* **Adani Ports & Special Economic Zone Ltd** Pluto Shipping Ltd *Mumbai* *India* MMSI: 419075200 Official number: 3415	**5,292** 1,493 1,087	Class: IR	**2007-07 Zhoushan Zhaobao Shipbuilding & Repair Co Ltd — Zhoushan ZJ** Yd No: 060705 Loa 102.00 Br ex - Dght 6.600 Lbp 96.80 Br md 18.80 Dpth 8.60 Welded, 1 dk	**(B33B2DS) Suction Hopper Dredger** Hopper: 5,200	**2 oil engines** geared to sc. shafts driving 2 Propellers Total Power: 3,568kW (4,852hp) 12.0kn Chinese Std. Type G8300ZC 2 x 4 Stroke 8 Cy. 300 x 380 each-1784kW (2426bhp) Wuxi Antai Power Machinery Co Ltd-China

8657782 *AVRU* -	**SHANTINATH** **United Shippers Ltd** - *Mumbai* India MMSI: 419000506 Official number: 3962	**1,054** 513 1,700	Class: IR	**2010-03 Dempo Engineering Works Ltd. — Goa** Yd No: 381 Loa 67.10 Br ex 12.01 Dght 3.200 Lbp 64.03 Br md 12.00 Dpth 4.35 Welded, 1 dk	**(A31A2GX) General Cargo Ship** Compartments: 1 Ho, ER 1 Ha: ER	**2 oil engines** reduction geared to sc. shafts driving 2 FP propellers Total Power: 536kW (728hp) 8.6kn Cummins NT-855-M 2 x 4 Stroke 6 Cy. 140 x 152 each-268kW (364bhp) Cummins India Ltd-India
5321813 - -	**SHANTINATH No. 5** **Shantilal Khushaldas & Brothers Pvt Ltd** - *Mormugao* India	*266* - -	Class: IR	**1962 Kanagawa Zosen — Kobe** Yd No: 45 Loa - Br ex - Dght 2.032 Lbp 44.99 Br md 8.21 Dpth 2.70 Welded, 1 dk	**(A31A2GX) General Cargo Ship**	**2 oil engines** driving 2 FP propellers Total Power: 264kW (358hp) Kelvin T6 2 x 4 Stroke 6 Cy. 165 x 184 each-132kW (179bhp) Bergius Kelvin Co. Ltd.-Glasgow
5321825 - -	**SHANTINATH No. 6** **Shantilal Khushaldas & Brothers Pvt Ltd** - *Mormugao* India	*266* - -	Class: IR	**1962 Kanagawa Zosen — Kobe** Yd No: 49 Loa - Br ex - Dght 2.032 Lbp 44.99 Br md 8.21 Dpth 2.70 Welded, 1 dk	**(A31A2GX) General Cargo Ship**	**2 oil engines** driving 2 FP propellers Total Power: 236kW (320hp) Mitsubishi 2 x 4 Stroke 6 Cy. 135 x 160 each-118kW (160bhp) Mitsubishi Nippon Heavy Industry-Japan
5321837 - -	**SHANTINATH No. 7** **Shantilal Khushaldas & Brothers Pvt Ltd** - *Mormugao* India	*266* - -	Class: IR	**1962 Kanagawa Zosen — Kobe** Yd No: 50 Loa - Br ex - Dght 2.032 Lbp 44.99 Br md 8.21 Dpth 2.70 Welded, 1 dk	**(A31A2GX) General Cargo Ship**	**2 oil engines** driving 2 FP propellers Total Power: 264kW (358hp) Kelvin T6 2 x 4 Stroke 6 Cy. 165 x 184 each-132kW (179bhp) Bergius Kelvin Co. Ltd.-Glasgow
6511960 - -	**SHANTINATH No. 9** **Shantilal Khushaldas & Brothers Pvt Ltd** - *Mormugao* India	*360* - 498	Class: IR	**1965 Nagasaki Zosen K.K. — Nagasaki** Yd No: 106 Loa 47.81 Br ex 10.37 Dght 2.007 Lbp 44.99 Br md 10.30 Dpth 2.80 Welded, 1 dk	**(A31A2GX) General Cargo Ship**	**2 oil engines** driving 2 FP propellers Total Power: 264kW (358hp) Kelvin T6 2 x 4 Stroke 6 Cy. 165 x 184 each-132kW (179bhp) Bergius Kelvin Co. Ltd.-Glasgow
6511958 - -	**SHANTINATH No. 10** **Shantilal Khushaldas & Brothers Pvt Ltd** - *Mormugao* India	*360* - 498	Class: IR	**1965 Maebata Zosen Tekko K.K. — Sasebo** Yd No: 38 Loa 47.81 Br ex 10.37 Dght 2.007 Lbp 44.99 Br md 10.30 Dpth 2.80 Welded, 1 dk	**(A31A2GX) General Cargo Ship**	**2 oil engines** driving 2 FP propellers Total Power: 264kW (358hp) Kelvin T6 2 x 4 Stroke 6 Cy. 165 x 184 each-132kW (179bhp) Bergius Kelvin Co. Ltd.-Glasgow
6511946 - -	**SHANTINATH No. 11** **Shantilal Khushaldas & Brothers Pvt Ltd** - *Mormugao* India	*360* - 498	Class: IR	**1965 Nagasaki Zosen K.K. — Nagasaki** Yd No: 107 Loa 47.81 Br ex 10.37 Dght 2.007 Lbp 44.99 Br md 10.30 Dpth 2.80 Welded, 1 dk	**(A31A2GX) General Cargo Ship**	**2 oil engines** driving 2 FP propellers Total Power: 264kW (358hp) Kelvin T6 2 x 4 Stroke 6 Cy. 165 x 184 each-132kW (179bhp) Bergius Kelvin Co. Ltd.-Glasgow
6522658 - -	**SHANTINATH No. 12** **Shantilal Khushaldas & Brothers Pvt Ltd** - *Mormugao* India	*360* 193 498	Class: IR	**1965 Fukae Zosen K.K. — Etajima** Yd No: 94 Loa 48.42 Br ex 10.32 Dght 2.001 Lbp 45.01 Br md 10.30 Dpth 2.80 Welded, 1 dk	**(A31A2GX) General Cargo Ship**	**2 oil engines** driving 2 FP propellers Total Power: 354kW (482hp) Kelvin T8 2 x 4 Stroke 8 Cy. 165 x 184 each-177kW (241bhp) Bergius Kelvin Co. Ltd.-Glasgow
9178032 *VRXX6* -	**SHANTOU** **South China Towing Co Ltd** - *Hong Kong* Hong Kong MMSI: 477249000 Official number: HK-0883	**291** 87 220	Class: BV	**1998-03 Matsuura Tekko Zosen K.K. — Osakikamijima** Yd No: 505 Loa 31.00 Br ex - Dght 3.500 Lbp 25.50 Br md 9.00 Dpth 4.70 Welded, 1 dk	**(B32A2ST) Tug**	**2 oil engines** gearing integral to driving 2 Z propellers Total Power: 2,648kW (3,600hp) 13.0kn Niigata 6L25HX 2 x 4 Stroke 6 Cy. 250 x 350 each-1324kW (1800bhp) Niigata Engineering Co Ltd-Japan
9614488 *9V9711* -	**SHANTUNG** **The China Navigation Co Pte Ltd** - *Singapore* Singapore MMSI: 566908000 Official number: 397498	**25,483** 11,819 30,814	Class: LR ✠**100A1** SS 05/2013 container ship, holds Nos. 3 & 4 strengthened for heavy cargo, general cargo in all holds, holds Nos. 3 & 4 suitable for unloading by grab (20 tonnes) **ShipRight** ACS (B) *IWS LI EP ✠**LMC** **UMS** Eq.Ltr: M†; Cable: 638.5/73.0 U3 (a)	**2013-05 Zhejiang Ouhua Shipbuilding Co Ltd — Zhoushan ZJ** Yd No: 638 Loa 199.90 (BB) Br ex 28.28 Dght 10.500 Lbp 188.79 Br md 28.20 Dpth 15.50 Welded, 1 dk	**(A33A2CC) Container Ship (Fully Cellular)** TEU 2082 C Ho 916 TEU C Dk 1166 TEU incl 147 ref C Compartments: 2 Ho, 2 Tw Dk, 3 Cell Ho, ER 5 Ha: ER Cranes: 4x60t	**1 oil engine** driving 1 FP propeller Total Power: 13,560kW (18,436hp) 15.5kn Wartsila 6RT-flex58T 1 x 2 Stroke 6 Cy. 580 x 2416 13560kW (18436bhp) Hudong Heavy Machinery Co Ltd-China AuxGen: 3 x 1058kW 450V 60Hz a.c Boilers: AuxB (Comp) 8.4kgf/cm² (8.2bar) Thrusters: 1 Tunnel thruster (f)
9474591 *BITZ* -	**SHANXIN** **CSIC-IMC Shipping Co Ltd** MSI Ship Management (Qingdao) Co Ltd *Shanghai* China MMSI: 413375810	**4,289** 1,843 6,575 T/cm 16.0	Class: CC	**2010-09 Chongqing Chuandong Shipbuilding Industry Co Ltd — Chongqing** Yd No: HT0106 Loa 104.95 (BB) Br ex 17.52 Dght 6.450 Lbp 99.00 Br md 17.50 Dpth 8.00 Welded, 1 dk	**(A12B2TR) Chemical/Products Tanker** Double Hull (13F) Liq: 5,993; Liq (Oil): 5,993 Cargo Heating Coils Compartments: 8 Wing Ta, 2 Wing Slop Ta, ER 8 Cargo Pump (s): 8x200m³/hr Manifold: Bow/CM: 48m	**1 oil engine** reduction geared to sc. shaft driving 1 Propeller Total Power: 2,500kW (3,399hp) 12.0kn Daihatsu 8DKM-28 1 x 4 Stroke 8 Cy. 280 x 390 2500kW (3399bhp) Shaanxi Diesel Heavy Industry Co Lt-China AuxGen: 3 x 320kW 400V a.c Fuel: 115.0 (d.f.) 342.0 (r.f.)
9138496 *VRHO9* -	**SHAO SHAN 1** *ex* Shao Shan 2 *-2013* *ex* Chia May *-2010* **Shaoshan Two Shipping Ltd** Hunan Ocean Shipping Co (COSCO HUNAN) *Hong Kong* Hong Kong MMSI: 477961900 Official number: HK2897	**38,338** 24,681 74,009	Class: CC (BV)	**1997-06 Tsuneishi Shipbuilding Co Ltd — Fukuyama HS** Yd No: 1100 Loa 225.00 Br ex - Dght 13.850 Lbp 216.00 Br md 32.26 Dpth 19.10 Welded, 1 dk	**(A21A2BC) Bulk Carrier** Grain: 88,331 Compartments: 7 Ho, ER 7 Ha: 6 (17.0 x 15.4)ER (15.3 x 12.0)	**1 oil engine** driving 1 FP propeller Total Power: 8,899kW (12,099hp) 14.0kn B&W 6S60MC 1 x 2 Stroke 6 Cy. 600 x 2292 8899kW (12099bhp) Mitsui Engineering & Shipbuilding CLtd-Japan AuxGen: 3 x 400kW 450V 60Hz a.c
9500302 *VRKO9* -	**SHAO SHAN 5** **Tianjin CMB Sea Safety Shipping Co Ltd** Hunan Ocean Shipping Co (COSCO HUNAN) SatCom: Inmarsat C 447703993 *Hong Kong* Hong Kong MMSI: 477325700 Official number: HK-3516	**41,342** 25,325 75,700	Class: CC (BV)	**2012-06 Guangzhou Huangpu Shipbuilding Co Ltd — Guangzhou GD** Yd No: 3009 Loa 225.00 Br ex - Dght 14.200 Lbp 217.00 Br md 32.26 Dpth 19.60 Welded, 1 dk	**(A21A2BC) Bulk Carrier** Grain: 90,067; Bale: 90,066 Compartments: 7 Ho, ER 7 Ha: (14.6 x 13.2)6 (15.5 x 14.4)ER	**1 oil engine** driving 1 FP propeller Total Power: 8,833kW (12,009hp) 14.5kn MAN-B&W 5S60MC 1 x 2 Stroke 5 Cy. 600 x 2292 8833kW (12009bhp) Hudong Heavy Machinery Co Ltd-China AuxGen: 3 x 560kW 60Hz a.c Fuel: 2510.0
9500314 *VRKP2* -	**SHAO SHAN 6** **Tianjin CMB Sea Healthy Shipping Co Ltd** Hunan Ocean Shipping Co (COSCO HUNAN) *Hong Kong* Hong Kong MMSI: 477325600 Official number: HK-3517	**41,342** 25,325 75,700	Class: CC (Class contemplated) (BV)	**2012-06 Guangzhou Huangpu Shipbuilding Co Ltd — Guangzhou GD** Yd No: 3010 Loa 225.00 (BB) Br ex - Dght 14.200 Lbp 217.00 Br md 32.26 Dpth 19.60 Welded, 1 dk	**(A21A2BC) Bulk Carrier** Grain: 90,067; Bale: 90,066 Compartments: 7 Ho, ER 7 Ha: (14.6 x 13.2)6 (15.5 x 14.4)ER	**1 oil engine** driving 1 FP propeller Total Power: 8,833kW (12,009hp) 14.5kn MAN-B&W 5S60MC 1 x 2 Stroke 5 Cy. 600 x 2292 8833kW (12009bhp) Hudong Heavy Machinery Co Ltd-China AuxGen: 3 x 560kW 60Hz a.c Fuel: 2510.0
9670808 *VRMB4* -	**SHAO SHAN 7** **CMBL Sea Hua Co Ltd** Hunan Ocean Shipping Co (COSCO HUNAN) *Hong Kong* Hong Kong MMSI: 477608600 Official number: HK-3826	**40,913** 25,963 75,409 T/cm 68.2	Class: CC	**2013-10 Guangzhou Huangpu Shipbuilding Co Ltd — Guangzhou GD** Yd No: HPS3019 Loa 225.00 (BB) Br ex - Dght 14.200 Lbp 217.00 Br md 32.26 Dpth 19.60 Welded, 1 dk	**(A21A2BC) Bulk Carrier** Grain: 90,428; Bale: 90,066 Compartments: 7 Ho, ER 7 Ha: 6 (15.5 x 14.4)ER (14.6 x 13.2)	**1 oil engine** driving 1 FP propeller Total Power: 8,833kW (12,009hp) 14.5kn MAN-B&W 5S60ME-C 1 x 2 Stroke 5 Cy. 600 x 2400 8833kW (12009bhp) AuxGen: 3 x 560kW 450V a.c
8426535 - -	**SHAO YAO** *ex* Hong Wei 11 *-1983* **Guangzhou Maritime Transport (Group) Co Ltd** - *Guangzhou, Guangdong* China MMSI: 412050850	*2,671* 1,664 669		**1979 Guangzhou Wenchong Shipyard — Guangzhou GD** Loa 94.34 Br ex - Dght 3.501 Lbp 83.00 Br md 13.80 Dpth 7.50 Welded, 2 dks	**(A31A2GX) General Cargo Ship** Compartments: 2 Ho, ER 2 Ha: (6.5 x 4.4) (4.5 x 4.4) Derricks: 2x1.5t; Winches: 2	**2 oil engines** driving 1 FP propeller Total Power: 1,722kW (2,342hp) 14.0kn S.K.L. 8NVD48A-2U 2 x 4 Stroke 8 Cy. 320 x 480 each-861kW (1171bhp) VEB Schwermaschinenbau "KarlLiebknecht" (SKL)-Magdeburg AuxGen: 2 x 200kW 400V 50Hz a.c

IMO / Call sign	Name / Owner / Registry	Tonnage	Class	Builder / Dimensions	Type	Machinery
9614490 *9V9712* -	**SHAOSHING** - **The China Navigation Co Pte Ltd** - *Singapore* *Singapore* MMSI: 563091000 Official number: 397499	**25,483** 11,808 30,814	Class: LR **✠100A1** SS 07/2013 container ship, holds Nos. 3 & 4 strengthened for heavy cargo, general cargo in all holds, holds Nos. 3 & 4 suitable for unloading by grab (20 tonnes) **ShipRight** ACS (B) *IWS LI EP **✠LMC** **UMS** Eq.Ltr: M†; Cable: 638.5/73.0 U3 (a)	**2013-07 Zhejiang Ouhua Shipbuilding Co Ltd — Zhoushan ZJ** Yd No: 639 Loa 199.90 (BB) Br ex 28.28 Dght 10.500 Lbp 188.79 Br md 28.20 Dpth 15.50 Welded, 1 dk	**(A33A2CC) Container Ship (Fully Cellular)** TEU 2082 C Ho 916 TEU C Dk 1166 TEU incl 147 ref C Compartments: 2 Ho, 2 Tw Dk, 3 Cell Ho, ER 5 Ha: ER Cranes: 4x60t	**1 oil engine** driving 1 FP propeller Total Power: 13,560kW (18,436hp) 15.5kn Wartsila 6RT-flex58T 1 x 2 Stroke 6 Cy. 580 x 2416 13560kW (18436bhp) Hudong Heavy Machinery Co Ltd-China AuxGen: 3 x 1058kW 450V 60Hz a.c Boilers: AuxB (Comp) 8.4kgf/cm² (8.2bar) Thrusters: 1 Tunnel thruster (f)
7223302 *WYZ7448* -	**SHAPACY** - **Erwin W Blocker, Trustee** - *San Diego, CA* *United States of America* Official number: 539543	*199* 81 -		**1972 Campbell Industries — San Diego, Ca** Yd No: 85 L reg 27.47 Br ex 7.62 Dght - Lbp - Br md - Dpth 2.77 Welded	**(B12B2FC) Fish Carrier**	**1 oil engine** geared to sc. shaft driving 1 FP propeller Total Power: 533kW (725hp) General Motors 1 x 2 Stroke 533kW (725bhp) General Motors Corp-USA
8814184 *MHQV8* -	**SHAPINSAY** - **Orkney Islands Council** Orkney Ferries Ltd *Kirkwall* *United Kingdom* MMSI: 235019175 Official number: 710152	**219** 66 70 T/cm 2.1		**1989-07 Yorkshire D.D. Co. Ltd. — Hull** (Hull) Yd No: 321 **1989-07 Jones Buckie Shipyard Ltd. — Buckie** Yd No: 193 Loa 30.21 Br ex - Dght - Lbp - Br md 8.80 Dpth - Welded, 1 dk	**(A36B2PL) Passenger/Landing Craft** Passengers: unberthed: 91 Bow door/ramp Len: 8.50 Wid: 4.75 Swl: - Lane-Len: 22 Lane-Wid: 4.00 Cars: 12, Trailers: 1	**2 oil engines** sr tandem geared to sc. shafts driving 2 FP propellers Total Power: 560kW (762hp) 10.0kn Volvo Penta TAMD121 2 x 4 Stroke 6 Cy. 130 x 150 each-280kW (381bhp) AB Volvo Penta-Sweden AuxGen: 2 x 50kW 440V 50Hz a.c Thrusters: 1 Directional thruster (f) Fuel: 10.6 (d.f.) 1.6pd
8702599 - -	**SHAPTADINGA 2** *ex* Takafuji Maru No. 8 **Specialised Shipping & Trading Co Ltd** - *Chittagong* *Bangladesh* Official number: C-1301	**539** - 1,277	Class: NK	**1987-02 Kochi Jyuko K.K. — Kochi** Yd No: 1946 Loa 65.13 (BB) Br ex - Dght 4.103 Lbp 60.00 Br md 10.01 Dpth 4.65 Welded, 1 dk	**(A13B2TP) Products Tanker** Liq: 1,380; Liq (Oil): 1,380 Compartments: 8 Ta, ER	**1 oil engine** driving 1 FP propeller Total Power: 956kW (1,300hp) Hanshin 6LU32G 1 x 4 Stroke 6 Cy. 320 x 510 956kW (1300bhp) The Hanshin Diesel Works Ltd-Japan Fuel: 47.0 (r.f.)
9344411 *4RCH* -	**SHARAF ENERGY** - **Sharaf Shipping Agency LLC** Emarat Maritime LLC *Sri Lanka* MMSI: 417222364	**103** 36 20	Class: RI	**2005-03 Mech Marine Engineers Pvt Ltd — Vasai** Yd No: 147 Loa 23.00 Br ex 6.30 Dght 1.800 Lbp 19.90 Br md 6.00 Dpth 2.80 Welded, 1 dk	**(B21A20C) Crew/Supply Vessel**	**2 oil engines** reduction geared to sc. shafts driving 2 Propellers Total Power: 1,472kW (2,002hp) 18.0kn Caterpillar 3412E 2 x Vee 4 Stroke 12 Cy. 137 x 152 each-736kW (1001bhp) Caterpillar Inc-USA
9305269 *IBLN* -	**SHARDEN** - **Compagnia Italiana Di Navigazione Srl** - *Naples* *Italy* MMSI: 247130700	**39,798** 18,583 7,031	Class: RI	**2005-03 Fincantieri-Cant. Nav. Italiani S.p.A. — Castellammare di Stabia** Yd No: 6114 Loa 213.96 (BB) Br ex - Dght 7.300 Lbp 192.44 Br md 26.40 Dpth 9.99 Welded, 1 dk	**(A36A2PR) Passenger/Ro-Ro Ship (Vehicles)** Passengers: unberthed: 3000 Stern door/ramp (a) Lane-Len: 1900 Cars: 1,085	**4 oil engines** geared to sc. shafts driving 2 CP propellers Total Power: 51,360kW (69,828hp) 30.0kn Wartsila 12V46C 4 x Vee 4 Stroke 12 Cy. 460 x 580 each-12840kW (17457bhp) Wartsila Italia SpA-Italy
7531010 *J8HO8* -	**SHAREEN** *ex* Dimini II *-1993* *ex* Showa Maru *-1988* **Alshaz Ltd** Alba Petroleum Ltd *Kingstown* *St Vincent & The Grenadines* MMSI: 375152000 Official number: 3861	**631** 414 1,369 T/cm 5.2	Class: (NK)	**1976-04 Sasaki Shipbuilding Co Ltd — Osakikamijima HS** Yd No: 303 Loa 62.01 Br ex 10.04 Dght 4.652 Lbp 58.02 Br md 10.01 Dpth 4.73 Welded, 1 dk	**(A13B2TP) Products Tanker** Single Hull Liq: 1,694; Liq (Oil): 1,694 Compartments: 8 Ta, ER 2 Cargo Pump (s): 2x500m³/hr Manifold: Bow/CM: 34m	**1 oil engine** driving 1 FP propeller Total Power: 1,103kW (1,500hp) 11.3kn Makita GNLH630 1 x 4 Stroke 6 Cy. 300 x 480 1103kW (1500bhp) Makita Diesel Co Ltd-Japan AuxGen: 2 x 72kW a.c Fuel: 10.0 (d.f.) 57.0 (r.f.) 4.5pd
9254305 *A6E2979* -	**SHARIEF ALERT** *launched as* Golden Power *-2004* **Global Marine Services** - *Sharjah* *United Arab Emirates* MMSI: 470815000 Official number: 4998	**491** 148 455	Class: LR (GL) **100A1** SS 01/2010 escort tug **LMC** Eq.Ltr: G; Cable: 330.0/24.0 U2 (a)	**2004-12 Tai Kong Trading Co — Singapore** (Hull) Yd No: 217 **2004-12 Marinteknik Shipbuilders (S) Pte Ltd — Singapore** Yd No: 177 Loa 36.80 Br ex - Dght 4.300 Lbp 33.60 Br md 11.50 Dpth 5.60 Welded, 1 dk	**(B21B20T) Offshore Tug/Supply Ship** Passengers: berths: 18	**2 oil engines** gearing integral to driving 2 Z propellers Total Power: 4,050kW (5,506hp) 12.0kn Deutz SBV9M628 2 x 4 Stroke 9 Cy. 240 x 280 each-2025kW (2753bhp) Deutz AG-Koeln AuxGen: 3 x 120kW 380V 50Hz a.c Thrusters: 1 Tunnel thruster (f) Fuel: 430.0 (d.f.)
9508146 *A6E2412* -	**SHARIEF EXPRESS** - **Global Marine Services** - *Sharjah* *United Arab Emirates* MMSI: 470512000 Official number: 5864	**499** 149 340	Class: LR (AB) **100A1** SS 05/2013 tug, fire-fighting Ship 1 (3000m3/h) with water spray **LMC**	**2008-05 Jingjiang Nanyang Shipbuilding Co Ltd — Jingjiang JS** (Hull) Yd No: (1233) **2008-05 Pacific Ocean Engineering & Trading Pte Ltd (POET) — Singapore** Yd No: 1233 Loa 35.70 Br ex 12.00 Dght 4.100 Lbp 30.54 Br md 11.50 Dpth 5.60 Welded, 1 dk	**(B32A2ST) Tug**	**2 oil engines** reduction geared to sc. shafts driving 2 Directional propellers Total Power: 3,676kW (4,998hp) Niigata 6L28HX 2 x 4 Stroke 6 Cy. 280 x 370 each-1838kW (2499bhp) (new engine 2008) Niigata Engineering Co Ltd-Japan AuxGen: 3 x 184kW 415V 50Hz a.c Thrusters: 1 Tunnel thruster (f) Fuel: 400.0 (d.f.)
9543158 *A6E2267* -	**SHARIEF FALCON** *ex* Cyk Falcon *-2010* **Global Marine Services** - SatCom: Inmarsat C 447036010 *Sharjah* *United Arab Emirates* MMSI: 470360000	**1,092** 327 760	Class: BV	**2010-11 Guangdong Jiangmen Shipyard Co Ltd — Jiangmen GD** Yd No: GMG0744 Loa 50.00 Br ex - Dght 4.500 Lbp 43.77 Br md 13.20 Dpth 5.20 Welded, 1 dk	**(B21B20A) Anchor Handling Tug Supply**	**2 oil engines** reduction geared to sc. shafts driving 2 CP propellers Total Power: 3,678kW (5,000hp) 13.5kn Caterpillar 3516B-HD 2 x Vee 4 Stroke 16 Cy. 170 x 215 each-1839kW (2500bhp) Caterpillar Inc-USA AuxGen: 3 x 315kW 50Hz a.c
9543160 *A6E2347* -	**SHARIEF HAWK** *ex* Cyk Hawk *-2013* **Global Marine Services** - *Sharjah* *United Arab Emirates* MMSI: 470245000	**1,092** 327 760	Class: BV	**2011-06 Guangdong Jiangmen Shipyard Co Ltd — Jiangmen GD** Yd No: GMG0745 Loa 50.00 Br ex - Dght 4.500 Lbp 43.77 Br md 13.20 Dpth 5.20 Welded, 1 dk	**(B21B20A) Anchor Handling Tug Supply**	**2 oil engines** reduction geared to sc. shafts driving 2 CP propellers Total Power: 3,678kW (5,000hp) 13.5kn Caterpillar 3516B 2 x Vee 4 Stroke 16 Cy. 170 x 190 each-1839kW (2500bhp) Caterpillar Inc-USA AuxGen: 3 x 350kW 450V 50Hz a.c Fuel: 590.0 (d.f.)
9136436 *A6E2734* -	**SHARIEF LEADER** *ex* Golden Crystal Tug *-1997* **Global Marine Services** - *Sharjah* *United Arab Emirates* MMSI: 470355000 Official number: UAE/SHJ/4346	**299** 89 122	Class: LR **✠100A1** SS 11/2012 tug **✠LMC** Eq.Ltr: G; Cable: 302.5/20.5 U2	**1997-11 Tai Kong Trading Co — Singapore** Yd No: 212 Loa 31.21 Br ex 10.22 Dght 3.600 Lbp 27.40 Br md 9.90 Dpth 4.50 Welded, 1 dk	**(B32A2ST) Tug** Passengers: berths: 30	**2 oil engines** gearing integral to driving 2 Voith-Schneider propellers Total Power: 3,132kW (4,258hp) 12.5kn Caterpillar 3516TA 2 x Vee 4 Stroke 16 Cy. 170 x 190 each-1566kW (2129bhp) Caterpillar Inc-USA AuxGen: 2 x 85kW 380V 50Hz a.c
9492749 *A6E2692* -	**SHARIEF PILOT** *ex* Superior Pilot *-2008* **Global Marine Services** - *Sharjah* *United Arab Emirates* MMSI: 470535000 Official number: 5867	**499** 149 222	Class: LR (AB) **100A1** SS 01/2013 fire-fighting Ship 1 (3000m3/h) with water spray, tug **LMC**	**2008-01 Jingjiang Nanyang Shipbuilding Co Ltd — Jingjiang JS** Yd No: 1232 Loa 35.70 Br ex - Dght 4.100 Lbp 30.54 Br md 11.50 Dpth 5.60 Welded, 1 dk	**(B21B20A) Anchor Handling Tug Supply**	**2 oil engines** reduction geared to sc. shafts driving 2 Directional propellers Total Power: 3,676kW (4,998hp) Niigata 6L28HX 2 x 4 Stroke 6 Cy. 280 x 370 each-1838kW (2499bhp) Niigata Engineering Co Ltd-Japan AuxGen: 3 x 160kW 415V 50Hz a.c Thrusters: 1 Tunnel thruster (f) Fuel: 400.0 (d.f.)
9188283 *A6E2785* -	**SHARIEF PIONEER** *ex* Golden Able *-2000* **Global Marine Services** - *Sharjah* *United Arab Emirates* MMSI: 470596000 Official number: 4650	**290** 87 90	Class: LR **✠100A1** SS 05/2010 tug **✠LMC** Eq.Ltr: F; Cable: 275.0/19.0 U2	**2000-05** (Hull) Yd No: 04 **2000-05 Tai Kong Trading Co — Singapore** Yd No: 313 Loa 30.50 Br ex 9.92 Dght 3.500 Lbp 29.60 Br md 9.90 Dpth 4.50 Welded, 1 dk	**(B32A2ST) Tug** Passengers: cabins: 8; berths: 18	**2 oil engines** reduction geared to sc. shafts driving 2 Directional propellers Total Power: 3,132kW (4,258hp) Caterpillar 3516B-TA 2 x Vee 4 Stroke 16 Cy. 170 x 190 each-1566kW (2129bhp) Caterpillar Inc-USA AuxGen: 2 x 85kW 380V 50Hz a.c Fuel: 120.0 (d.f.)

IMO / Call sign	Name / Owner	Tonnage	Class	Builder / Dimensions	Type	Machinery
9254317 *A6E3012* -	**SHARIEF POWER** **Global Marine Services** - *Sharjah* *United Arab Emirates* MMSI: 470849000 Official number: 5087	**491** 148 455	Class: LR (GL) **100A1** SS 07/2010 escort tug **LMC** Eq.Ltr: G; Cable: 330.0/24.0 U2 (a)	**2005-08 Tai Kong Trading Co — Singapore** (Hull) Yd No: 218 **2005-08 Marinteknik Shipbuilders (S) Pte Ltd — Singapore** Yd No: 178 Loa 36.80 Br ex - Dght 4.100 Lbp 33.28 Br md 11.50 Dpth 5.60 Welded, 1 dk	**(B21B20T) Offshore Tug/Supply Ship** Passengers: berths: 18	**2 oil engines** gearing integral to driving 2 Z propellers Total Power: 4,050kW (5,506hp) 12.0kn Deutz SBV9M628 2 x 4 Stroke 9 Cy. 240 x 280 each-2025kW (2753bhp) Deutz AG-Koeln AuxGen: 3 x 120kW 380V 60Hz a.c Thrusters: 1 Tunnel thruster (f) Fuel: 430.0 (d.f.)
8827349 *A6E3115* -	**SHARIEF PROVIDER** *ex* Zamil 31 *-2007* *ex* Malaviya Fourteen *-2005* *ex* SKBB Kemajuan 303 *-1998* **Global Marine Services** - *Sharjah* *United Arab Emirates* MMSI: 470957000 Official number: 5654	**967** 290 885	Class: LR (AB) (IR) (BV) **100A1** SS 02/2010 **LMC**	**1989 Greenbay Marine Pte Ltd — Singapore** Yd No: 72 Loa 59.00 Br ex - Dght 2.510 Lbp 51.53 Br md 12.00 Dpth 3.80 Welded, 1 dk	**(B21A20S) Platform Supply Ship**	**2 oil engines** reduction geared to sc. shafts driving 2 FP propellers Total Power: 1,908kW (2,594hp) 10.0kn Caterpillar 3512TA 2 x Vee 4 Stroke 12 Cy. 170 x 190 each-954kW (1297bhp) Caterpillar Inc-USA AuxGen: 3 x 215kW 220V 50Hz a.c Thrusters: 1 Tunnel thruster (f) Fuel: 152.0 (d.f.)
9425435 *A6E2821* -	**SHARIEF RELIANCE** *ex* Crest Hercules *-2009* **Global Marine Services** - *Sharjah* *United Arab Emirates* MMSI: 470627000 Official number: 6077	**975** 292 757	Class: LR (BV) **100A1** SS 01/2013 tug, fire-fighting Ship 1 (2,400m3/h) with water spray **LMC** Eq.Ltr: P; Cable: 440.0/36.0 U2 (a)	**2008-01 Guangdong Jiangmen Shipyard Co Ltd — Jiangmen GD** Yd No: GMG0515 Loa 48.00 Br ex - Dght 4.500 Lbp 42.40 Br md 13.20 Dpth 5.20 Welded, 1 dk	**(B21B20A) Anchor Handling Tug Supply**	**2 oil engines** with clutches, flexible couplings & sr geared to sc. shafts driving 2 CP propellers Total Power: 3,840kW (5,220hp) Caterpillar 3516B 2 x Vee 4 Stroke 16 Cy. 170 x 190 each-1920kW (2610bhp) Caterpillar Inc-USA AuxGen: 3 x 315kW 415V 50Hz a.c Thrusters: 1 Thwart. CP thruster (f)
8023826 *J8B3710* -	**SHARIEF SUPPLIER** *ex* Ave Maria *-2010* *ex* Sem Courageous *-2007* *ex* Sea Courageous *-1993* *ex* Point Christie *-1991* **Global Marine Services** - *Kingstown* *St Vincent & The Grenadines* MMSI: 376781000 Official number: 10183	**754** 226 1,220	Class: LR (AB) **100A1** SS 06/2011 TOC contemplated	**1981-03 Halter Marine, Inc. — Moss Point, Ms** Yd No: 955 Loa - Br ex - Dght 3.664 Lbp 51.33 Br md 12.20 Dpth 4.27 Welded, 1 dk	**(B21B20A) Anchor Handling Tug Supply** Ice Capable	**2 oil engines** reverse reduction geared to sc. shafts driving 2 FP propellers Total Power: 2,942kW (4,000hp) EMD (Electro-Motive) 16-645-E6 2 x Vee 2 Stroke 16 Cy. 230 x 254 each-1471kW (2000bhp) (Reconditioned , Reconditioned & fitted 1981) General Motors Corp.Electro-Motive Div.-La Grange AuxGen: 2 x 99kW Thrusters: 1 Thwart. FP thruster (f)
8023838 *J8B3786* -	**SHARIEF SUPPORTER** *ex* Zara *-2010* *ex* Sea Endeavor *-2007* *ex* Africa Eagle *-1996* *ex* Temasek Eagle *-1993* *ex* Point Hope *-1992* **Global Marine Services** Artemiz Marine Services JLT *Kingstown* *St Vincent & The Grenadines* MMSI: 375713000 Official number: 10259	**737** 331 918	Class: LR (AB) **100A1** SS 12/2012 **LMC**	**1981-04 Halter Marine, Inc. — Moss Point, Ms** Yd No: 956 Loa 53.33 Br ex - Dght 3.664 Lbp 52.51 Br md 12.20 Dpth 4.27 Welded, 1 dk	**(B21B20A) Anchor Handling Tug Supply**	**2 oil engines** reverse reduction geared to sc. shafts driving 2 FP propellers Total Power: 3,090kW (4,202hp) 10.0kn EMD (Electro-Motive) 16-645-E6 2 x Vee 2 Stroke 16 Cy. 230 x 254 each-1545kW (2101bhp) (Reconditioned , Reconditioned & fitted 1981) General Motors Corp.Electro-Motive Div.-La Grange AuxGen: 2 x 99kW Thrusters: 1 Thwart. FP thruster (f)
9359442 *A6E2944* -	**SHARIEF VERVE** *ex* PW Beta *-2009* **Global Marine Services** - *Sharjah* *United Arab Emirates* MMSI: 470752000 Official number: 6085	**329** 98 161	Class: LR (AB) **100A1** SS 01/2012 tug **LMC**	**2007-01 Bengbu Shenzhou Machinery Co Ltd — Bengbu AH** (Hull) Yd No: (1201) **2007-01 Pacific Ocean Engineering & Trading Pte Ltd (POET) — Singapore** Yd No: 1201 Loa 27.70 Br ex - Dght 4.900 Lbp 22.94 Br md 9.80 Dpth 5.20 Welded, 1 dk	**(B32A2ST) Tug**	**2 oil engines** reduction geared to sc. shafts driving 2 Z propellers Total Power: 2,648kW (3,600hp) Yanmar 8N21A-EN 2 x 4 Stroke 8 Cy. 210 x 290 each-1324kW (1800bhp) Yanmar Diesel Engine Co Ltd-Japan AuxGen: 2 x 99kW a.c Fuel: 170.0
8651805 *EPCH2* -	**SHARIF10** *ex* Sharif 10 *-2013* *ex* Shareef *-2013* *ex* Namdar *-2011* *ex* Fukuyo Maru No. 12 *-2011* *ex* Kiku Maru *-2004* **Abdol Amir Marhounian Nezhad** - *Iran* MMSI: 422045700	**128** 38 -	Class: SL (Class contemplated)	**1988-02 Imamura Zosen — Kure** Yd No: 264 Loa 23.74 Br ex - Dght - Lbp - Br md 7.30 Dpth 3.20 Welded, 1 dk	**(B32A2ST) Tug**	**1 oil engine** reduction geared to sc. shaft driving 1 Propeller Total Power: 1,838kW (2,499hp) Niigata 6MG28HX 1 x 4 Stroke 6 Cy. 280 x 370 1838kW (2499bhp) Niigata Engineering Co Ltd-Japan
9083287 *6AGV* -	**SHARIFA 4** *ex* Falster Spirit *-2010* *ex* Bona Rover *-1999* *ex* Vendonna *-1996* **Pyramid Navigation Co ESA** International Marine Management Co Inc *Alexandria* *Egypt* MMSI: 622120921	**52,875** 28,319 95,416 T/cm 91.4	Class: LR (NV) **100A1** SS 11/2010 oil tanker ESP **LMC** **UMS**	**1995-11 Hyundai Heavy Industries Co Ltd — Ulsan** Yd No: 896 Loa 244.06 (BB) Br ex 42.04 Dght 13.617 Lbp 234.00 Br md 42.00 Dpth 19.50 Welded, 1 dk	**(A13A2TV) Crude Oil Tanker** Double Hull (13F) Liq: 103,360; Liq (Oil): 103,360 Compartments: 7 Ta, ER, 2 Wing Slop Ta 3 Cargo Pump (s): 3x2500m³/hr Manifold: Bow/CM: 121.2m	**1 oil engine** driving 1 FP propeller Total Power: 12,902kW (17,542hp) 14.5kn B&W 5S70MC 1 x 2 Stroke 5 Cy. 700 x 2674 12902kW (17542bhp) Hyundai Heavy Industries Co Ltd-South Korea AuxGen: 3 x 680kW 220/450V 60Hz a.c Fuel: 2662.8 (d.f.) 173.9 (r.f.)
8023149 *A4DJ4* -	**SHARIYAHA** **Al Majali International SAOC** - *Oman* MMSI: 461000047 Official number: 629	*145* 61 170	Class: IS (BV) (AB)	**1981-02 Sing Koon Seng Pte Ltd — Singapore** Yd No: SKS551 Loa 25.00 Br ex 8.51 Dght 1.601 Lbp 24.01 Br md 8.21 Dpth 2.37 Welded, 1 dk	**(A35D2RL) Landing Craft** Bow door/ramp	**2 oil engines** reverse reduction geared to sc. shafts driving 2 FP propellers Total Power: 230kW (312hp) 6.0kn Volvo Penta MD70C 2 x 4 Stroke 6 Cy. 105 x 130 each-115kW (156bhp) AB Volvo Penta-Sweden AuxGen: 2 x 12kW
9080807 - -	**SHARJAH 1** **Sharjah Ports Authority** - *Sharjah* *United Arab Emirates*	**134** 40 180	Class: BV (LR) ✠ Classed LR until 9/10/06	**1994-10 Stocznia Tczew Sp z oo — Tczew** (Hull) **1994-10 B.V. Scheepswerf Damen — Gorinchem** Yd No: 6514 Loa 22.50 Br ex 7.45 Dght 2.820 Lbp 20.40 Br md 7.25 Dpth 3.75 Welded, 1 dk	**(B32A2ST) Tug**	**2 oil engines** with clutches, flexible couplings & sr reverse geared to sc. shafts driving 2 FP propellers Total Power: 1,910kW (2,596hp) 11.6kn Caterpillar 3512TA 2 x Vee 4 Stroke 12 Cy. 170 x 190 each-955kW (1298bhp) Caterpillar Inc-USA AuxGen: 2 x 50kW 380V 50Hz a.c
7516503 *A6E2481* -	**SHARJAH MOON** *ex* Blue Bird *-2005* *ex* Lamnalco 18 *-1993* *ex* Lamnalco Baker Bluebird *-1982* **Alco Shipping Services LLC** - *Sharjah* *United Arab Emirates* Official number: 3260	*682* 207 387	Class: RI (LR) (BV) ✠ Classed LR until 1/3/87	**1976-09 Cheoy Lee Shipyards Ltd — Hong Kong** Yd No: 2963 Loa 56.47 Br ex 11.03 Dght 2.831 Lbp 52.10 Br md 10.66 Dpth 3.97 Welded, 1 dk	**(B22D2OZ) Production Testing Vessel** Passengers: berths: 28	**2 oil engines** reverse reduction geared to sc. shafts driving 2 FP propellers Total Power: 1,344kW (1,828hp) 11.0kn Caterpillar D398SCAC 2 x Vee 4 Stroke 12 Cy. 159 x 203 each-672kW (914bhp) Caterpillar Tractor Co-USA AuxGen: 3 x 185kW 440V 60Hz a.c Thrusters: 1 Thwart. FP thruster (f) Fuel: 199.0 (d.f.)
9138886 - -	**SHARJAH PRIDE** *ex* El Phos *-2009* **Sea Victory International Shipping Inc** Givenergy FZC	**41,401** 18,712 68,790 T/cm 71.0	Class: (NK)	**1996-09 Namura Shipbuilding Co Ltd — Imari SG** Yd No: 952 Loa 221.37 Br ex - Dght 12.526 Lbp 212.00 Br md 36.00 Dpth 19.20 Welded, 1 dk	**(A13A2TV) Crude Oil Tanker** Double Hull Liq: 83,130; Liq (Oil): 83,130 Compartments: 14 Ta, ER 3 Cargo Pump (s): 3x2000m³/hr	**1 oil engine** driving 1 FP propeller Total Power: 12,181kW (16,561hp) 15.0kn Sulzer 6RTA62 1 x 2 Stroke 6 Cy. 620 x 2150 12181kW (16561bhp) Mitsubishi Heavy Industries Ltd-Japan AuxGen: 3 x 500kW a.c Fuel: 2211.0 (r.f.) 41.4pd
9163922 - -	**SHARK** - -	**225** - -		**1997-02 B.V. Scheepswerf Damen — Gorinchem** Yd No: 6793 Loa 25.00 Br ex 10.00 Dght 1.900 Lbp - Br md - Dpth 3.35 Welded, 1 dk	**(B32B2SP) Pusher Tug**	**2 oil engines** sr geared to sc. shafts driving 2 FP propellers Total Power: 896kW (1,218hp) Caterpillar 3412TA 2 x Vee 4 Stroke 12 Cy. 137 x 152 each-448kW (609bhp) Caterpillar Inc-USA
8306060 - -	**SHARK** **M Umraow & Sons** - *Georgetown* *Guyana* Official number: 385136	*108* 48 98		**1983-06 Bender Shipbuilding & Repair Co Inc — Mobile AL** Yd No: 179 Loa - Br ex - Dght 2.590 Lbp 21.95 Br md 6.10 Dpth 3.28 Welded, 1 dk	**(B11A2FT) Trawler**	**1 oil engine** sr geared to sc. shaft driving 1 FP propeller Total Power: 268kW (364hp) 9.3kn Caterpillar 3408TA 1 x Vee 4 Stroke 8 Cy. 137 x 152 268kW (364bhp) Caterpillar Tractor Co-USA AuxGen: 2 x 3kW 32V d.c Fuel: 43.5 (d.f.) 1.0pd

9637478 *9HA3295* - **SHARK 1** - **SC Shark Srl** *Valletta* *Malta*
461 138 229 Class: AB
2014-03 **Santierul Naval Constanta S.A. — Constanta** Yd No: 3930
Loa 43.87 (BB) Br ex - Dght 3.700
Lbp 40.20 Br md 7.60 Dpth 4.60
Welded, 1 dk
(B22A2OV) Diving Support Vessel
2 oil engines reduction geared to sc. shafts driving 2 Directional propellers
Total Power: 1,270kW (1,726hp)
GUASCOR SF240TA-SP
2 x 4 Stroke 8 Cy. 152 x 165 each-635kW (863bhp)
Gutierrez Ascunce Corp (GUASCOR)-Spain
Thrusters: 1 Tunnel thruster

7930199 *A6E3065* - **SHARK 2** - **Jawar Al Khaleej Shipping (LLC)** - *Dubai* *United Arab Emirates* MMSI: 470904000
531 159 - Class: BV (AB)
1980-02 **Shikoku Dockyard Co. Ltd. — Takamatsu** Yd No: 807
Loa 40.80 Br ex - Dght 3.710
Lbp 37.01 Br md 10.01 Dpth 4.73
Welded, 1 dk
(B32A2ST) Tug
2 oil engines reverse reduction geared to sc. shafts driving 2 FP propellers
Total Power: 3,090kW (4,202hp) 13.0kn
Yanmar 8ZL-UT
2 x 4 Stroke 8 Cy. 280 x 340 each-1545kW (2101bhp)
Yanmar Diesel Engine Co Ltd-Japan
AuxGen: 2 x 160kW a.c

8727874 - - **SHARK 2** - **Spring Tours Co** - *Suez* *Egypt*
290 - 100 Class: (LR) Classed LR until 14/6/00
1991-12 **Arab Contractors Marine Workshops — Helwan** Yd No: 701
Loa 28.00 Br ex 6.75 Dght 3.250
Lbp 26.50 Br md 6.50 Dpth 3.50
Welded, 1 dk
(A37B2PS) Passenger Ship
2 oil engines sr reverse geared to sc. shafts driving 2 FP propellers
Total Power: 354kW (482hp) 8.0kn
Caterpillar 3406TA
2 x 4 Stroke 6 Cy. 137 x 165 each-177kW (241bhp)
Caterpillar Inc-USA
AuxGen: 1 x 71kW 380V 50Hz a.c

8421145 - - **SHARK 3** - **Arabian Gulf Mechanical Service & Contracting Co Ltd** - *Kuwait* *Kuwait* Official number: KT1515
217 65 102 Class: (NK)
1985-04 **Yokohama Yacht Co Ltd — Yokohama KN** Yd No: 837-1
Loa 28.00 Br ex 8.84 Dght 2.310
Lbp 27.61 Br md 8.60 Dpth 3.20
Welded, 1 dk
(B32A2ST) Tug
2 oil engines with clutches, flexible couplings & sr geared to sc. shafts driving 2 Directional propellers
Total Power: 1,912kW (2,600hp)
Yanmar T260L-ST
2 x 4 Stroke 6 Cy. 260 x 330 each-956kW (1300bhp)
Yanmar Diesel Engine Co Ltd-Japan

9314155 *9KDA* - **SHARK 5** - **Arabian Gulf Mechanical Service & Contracting Co Ltd** - *Kuwait* *Kuwait* MMSI: 447106000 Official number: KT1684
499 149 249 Class: AB
2004-09 **Guangzhou Hangtong Shipbuilding & Shipping Co Ltd — Jiangmen GD** Yd No: 032003
Loa 36.00 Br ex 11.40 Dght 3.750
Lbp 32.60 Br md 10.80 Dpth 5.40
Welded, 1 dk
(B32A2ST) Tug
2 oil engines geared to sc. shafts driving 2 FP propellers
Total Power: 3,840kW (5,220hp)
Yanmar 6EY26
2 x 4 Stroke 6 Cy. 260 x 385 each-1920kW (2610bhp)
Yanmar Diesel Engine Co Ltd-Japan
AuxGen: 2 x 150kW a.c
Thrusters: 1 Tunnel thruster (f)

8022157 *9KHU* - **SHARK-10** *ex* Shark 10 *-2006* *ex* Centaur *-1990* **Arabian Gulf Mechanical Service & Contracting Co Ltd** - *Kuwait* *Kuwait*
465 139 - Class: AB
1981-01 **Teraoka Shipyard Co Ltd — Minamiawaji HG** Yd No: 197
Loa 34.35 Br ex - Dght 3.801
Lbp 34.02 Br md 9.52 Dpth 4.53
Welded, 1 dk
(B32A2ST) Tug
2 oil engines reverse reduction geared to sc. shafts driving 2 FP propellers
Total Power: 2,388kW (3,246hp) 12.0kn
Yanmar 6ZL-UT
2 x 4 Stroke 6 Cy. 280 x 340 each-1194kW (1623bhp)
Yanmar Diesel Engine Co Ltd-Japan
AuxGen: 2 x 125kW a.c, 1 x 52kW a.c
Fuel: 300.0

9276377 *9KCK* - **SHARK 20** - **Arabian Gulf Mechanical Service & Contracting Co Ltd** - *Kuwait* *Kuwait* MMSI: 447091000 Official number: KT1671
498 150 240 Class: BV
2003-03 **Cheoy Lee Shipyards Ltd — Hong Kong** Yd No: 4791
Loa 39.79 Br ex - Dght 3.550
Lbp 35.95 Br md 10.40 Dpth 5.01
Welded, 1 dk
(B32A2ST) Tug
2 oil engines geared to sc. shafts driving 2 FP propellers
Total Power: 2,980kW (4,052hp) 12.0kn
Caterpillar 3516TA
2 x Vee 4 Stroke 16 Cy. 170 x 190 each-1490kW (2026bhp)
Caterpillar Inc-USA
AuxGen: 2 x 170kW 60Hz a.c

9528586 *9KCJ* - **SHARK 30** - **Arabian Gulf Mechanical Service & Contracting Co Ltd** - *Kuwait* *Kuwait* MMSI: 447090000 Official number: KT1741
1,196 359 1,393 Class: AB
2009-01 **Hin Lee (Zhuhai) Shipyard Co Ltd — Zhuhai GD** (Hull) Yd No: 177
2009-02 **Cheoy Lee Shipyards Ltd — Hong Kong** Yd No: 4969
Loa 58.00 Br ex - Dght 4.750
Lbp 53.82 Br md 13.80 Dpth 5.50
Welded, 1 dk
(B21B20A) Anchor Handling Tug Supply
2 oil engines reduction geared to sc. shafts driving 2 CP propellers
Total Power: 3,840kW (5,220hp) 12.0kn
Caterpillar 3516B-HD
2 x Vee 4 Stroke 16 Cy. 170 x 215 each-1920kW (2610bhp)
Caterpillar Inc-USA
AuxGen: 3 x 320kW 450V 60Hz a.c
Thrusters: 1 Tunnel thruster (f)
Fuel: 420.0 (d.f.)

9528598 *9KBK* - **SHARK 40** - **Arabian Gulf Mechanical Service & Contracting Co Ltd** - *Kuwait* *Kuwait* MMSI: 447137000 Official number: KT1742
1,197 359 1,380 Class: AB
2009-04 **Hin Lee (Zhuhai) Shipyard Co Ltd — Zhuhai GD** (Hull) Yd No: 175
2009-04 **Cheoy Lee Shipyards Ltd — Hong Kong** Yd No: 4958
Loa 58.00 Br ex - Dght 4.750
Lbp 53.82 Br md 13.80 Dpth 5.50
Welded, 1 dk
(B21B20A) Anchor Handling Tug Supply
2 oil engines reduction geared to sc. shafts driving 2 CP propellers
Total Power: 3,840kW (5,220hp) 12.0kn
Caterpillar 3516B-HD
2 x Vee 4 Stroke 16 Cy. 170 x 215 each-1920kW (2610bhp)
Caterpillar Inc-USA
AuxGen: 3 x 320kW a.c
Thrusters: 1 Tunnel thruster (f)
Fuel: 420.0

9588627 *9KCP* - **SHARK-51** - **Arabian Gulf Mechanical Service & Contracting Co Ltd** - *Kuwait* *Kuwait* MMSI: 447096000 Official number: KT-1744
1,161 348 1,100 Class: AB
2011-05 **Nanjing East Star Shipbuilding Co Ltd — Nanjing JS** Yd No: HT5501
Loa 55.00 Br ex - Dght 4.300
Lbp 47.80 Br md 13.80 Dpth 5.50
Welded, 1 dk
(B21B20A) Anchor Handling Tug Supply
2 oil engines reduction geared to sc. shafts driving 2 FP propellers
Total Power: 3,840kW (5,220hp) 12.5kn
Caterpillar 3516B-HD
2 x Vee 4 Stroke 16 Cy. 170 x 215 each-1920kW (2610bhp)
Caterpillar Inc-USA
AuxGen: 3 x 260kW a.c
Fuel: 420.0 (d.f.)

9588639 *9KCU* - **SHARK-52** - **Arabian Gulf Mechanical Service & Contracting Co Ltd** - *Kuwait* *Kuwait* MMSI: 447100000 Official number: KT-1745
1,161 348 1,078 Class: AB
2011-07 **Nanjing East Star Shipbuilding Co Ltd — Nanjing JS** Yd No: HT5502
Loa 55.00 Br ex - Dght 4.300
Lbp 47.80 Br md 13.80 Dpth 5.50
Welded, 1 dk
(B21B20A) Anchor Handling Tug Supply Cranes: 1x5t
2 oil engines reduction geared to sc. shafts driving 2 FP propellers
Total Power: 3,840kW (5,220hp) 12.5kn
Caterpillar 3516B-HD
2 x Vee 4 Stroke 16 Cy. 170 x 215 each-1920kW (2610bhp)
Caterpillar Inc-USA
AuxGen: 3 x 260kW a.c
Fuel: 420.0 (d.f.)

9588641 *9KCX* - **SHARK-53** - **Arabian Gulf Mechanical Service & Contracting Co Ltd** - *Kuwait* *Kuwait* MMSI: 447022000 Official number: KT-1746
1,161 348 1,093 Class: AB
2011-09 **Nanjing East Star Shipbuilding Co Ltd — Nanjing JS** Yd No: HT5503
Loa 55.00 Br ex - Dght 4.300
Lbp 47.80 Br md 13.80 Dpth 5.50
Welded, 1 dk
(B21B20A) Anchor Handling Tug Supply Cranes: 1x5t
2 oil engines reduction geared to sc. shafts driving 2 FP propellers
Total Power: 3,840kW (5,220hp) 12.5kn
Caterpillar 3516B-HD
2 x Vee 4 Stroke 16 Cy. 170 x 215 each-1920kW (2610bhp)
Caterpillar Inc-USA
AuxGen: 3 x 260kW a.c
Fuel: 420.0 (d.f.)

9589487 *9KDB* - **SHARK-54** - **Arabian Gulf Mechanical Service & Contracting Co Ltd** - *Kuwait* *Kuwait* MMSI: 447107000 Official number: KT-1747
1,161 348 1,105 Class: AB
2011-06 **Jiangsu Zhenjiang Shipyard Co Ltd — Zhenjiang JS** Yd No: VZJ6184-0901
Loa 55.00 Br ex - Dght 4.300
Lbp 48.10 Br md 13.80 Dpth 5.50
Welded, 1 dk
(B21B20A) Anchor Handling Tug Supply
2 oil engines reduction geared to sc. shafts driving 2 CP propellers
Total Power: 3,840kW (5,220hp) 12.5kn
Caterpillar 3516B-HD
2 x Vee 4 Stroke 16 Cy. 170 x 215 each-1920kW (2610bhp)
Caterpillar Inc-USA
AuxGen: 3 x 260kW a.c
Fuel: 420.0 (d.f.)

9589504 *9KBB* - **SHARK-55** - **Arabian Gulf Mechanical Service & Contracting Co Ltd** - *Kuwait* *Kuwait* MMSI: 447129000 Official number: KT-1748
1,161 348 1,102 Class: AB
2011-09 **Jiangsu Zhenjiang Shipyard Co Ltd — Zhenjiang JS** Yd No: VZJ6184-0903
Loa 55.00 Br ex - Dght 4.300
Lbp 48.10 Br md 13.80 Dpth 5.50
Welded, 1 dk
(B21B20A) Anchor Handling Tug Supply
2 oil engines reduction geared to sc. shafts driving 2 CP propellers
Total Power: 3,840kW (5,220hp) 12.5kn
Caterpillar 3516B-HD
2 x Vee 4 Stroke 16 Cy. 170 x 215 each-1920kW (2610bhp)
Caterpillar Inc-USA
AuxGen: 3 x 260kW a.c
Fuel: 420.0 (d.f.)

IMO / Call sign	Name / Owner / Registry	Tonnage	Class	Builder / Dimensions	Type	Machinery
9589499 *9KEI* -	**SHARK-56** **Arabian Gulf Mechanical Service & Contracting Co Ltd** - *Kuwait* *Kuwait* MMSI: 447021000 Official number: KT-1749	1,161 348 1,000	Class: AB	2011-08 **Jiangsu Zhenjiang Shipyard Co Ltd — Zhenjiang JS** Yd No: VZJ6184-0902 Loa 55.00 Br ex - Dght 4.300 Lbp 48.10 Br md 13.80 Dpth 5.50 Welded, 1 dk	**(B21B20A) Anchor Handling Tug Supply**	**2 oil engines** reduction geared to sc. shafts driving 2 CP propellers Total Power: 3,840kW (5,220hp) 12.5kn Caterpillar 3516B-HD 2 x Vee 4 Stroke 16 Cy. 170 x 215 each-1920kW (2610bhp) Caterpillar Inc-USA AuxGen: 3 x 260kW a.c Fuel: 420.0 (d.f.)
8817758 *3FPY9* -	**SHARK H** *ex* Shark C *-2010* *ex* Shark *-2009* *ex* 28 de Septiembre *-1992* **Caribbean Petroleum International Services SA** - SatCom: Inmarsat C 435766613 *Panama* *Panama* MMSI: 357666000 Official number: 28314PEXT5	3,878 1,435 4,400	Class: RC	1988-04 **Santierul Naval Braila — Braila** Loa - Br ex - Dght 6.401 Lbp 101.61 Br md 16.41 Dpth 8.20 Welded, 1 dk	**(A13B2TP) Products Tanker**	**1 oil engine** driving 1 FP propeller Total Power: 2,207kW (3,001hp) 13.5kn S.K.L. 6VDS48/42AL-1 1 x 4 Stroke 6 Cy. 420 x 480 2207kW (3001bhp)
7047710 *H02195* -	**SHARK III** *ex* Shark *-2006* *ex* Tasoulis K *-2000* *ex* Nazek *-1994* *ex* Offshore Houston *-1985* **Al Bahar Shipping Inc** - *Panama* *Panama* MMSI: 372318000 Official number: 35187PEXT	591 177 352	Class: (HR) (AB)	1969 **Mangone Shipbuilding Co. — Houston, Tx** Yd No: 87 Loa - Br ex 10.98 Dght 3.842 Lbp 50.30 Br md 10.67 Dpth 4.58 Welded, 1 dk	**(B21A20S) Platform Supply Ship**	**2 oil engines** reverse reduction geared to sc. shaft driving 2 FP propellers Total Power: 1,766kW (2,402hp) 15.0kn EMD (Electro-Motive) 12-567-BC 2 x Vee 2 Stroke 12 Cy. 216 x 254 each-883kW (1201bhp) General Motors Corp-USA AuxGen: 2 x 100kW a.c
6621648 *CY8121* -	**SHARLENE K.** - **Seamaid Fishing Ltd** - *Vancouver, BC* *Canada* MMSI: 316003449 Official number: 327223	*147* 86 -		1966 **Benson Bros Shipbuilding Co (1960) Ltd — Vancouver BC** Loa 24.39 Br ex 6.76 Dght - Lbp - Br md 6.71 Dpth 3.28 Welded, 1 dk	**(B11A2FT) Trawler**	**1 oil engine** driving 1 FP propeller Total Power: 386kW (525hp) 11.0kn
7727968 *DUA2597* -	**SHARMAINE** *ex* Suwa Maru No. 28 *-1993* **Mega Fishing Corp** - *Manila* *Philippines* Official number: MNLD002039	*216* 118 300		1978-03 **Tokushima Zosen K.K. — Fukuoka** Yd No: 1273 Loa 44.10 (BB) Br ex 7.01 Dght 3.001 Lbp 37.80 Br md 7.00 Dpth 3.28 Welded, 1 dk	**(A34A2GR) Refrigerated Cargo Ship**	**1 oil engine** geared to sc. shaft driving 1 FP propeller Total Power: 956kW (1,300hp) 13.0kn Niigata 6L25BX 1 x 4 Stroke 6 Cy. 250 x 320 956kW (1300bhp) Niigata Engineering Co Ltd-Japan
9114347 *C6SL4* -	**SHARMIN** *ex* Clipper Mandarin *-2013* *ex* CEC Morning *-2010* *ex* Angkor Star *-2001* *ex* CEC Morning *-2000* *ex* Helene Delmas *-2000* *ex* Arktis Morning *-1999* *ex* Maersk Luanda *-1999* *ex* Arktis Morning *-1998* **Sharmin Shipping Co Ltd** Okyanus Ege Denizcilik Ticaret AS *Nassau* *Bahamas* MMSI: 311377000 Official number: 8000476	6,310 3,108 8,973 T/cm 17.9	Class: LR (BV) **100A1** SS 12/2010 container cargoes in all holds, on upper deck and on all hatch covers **LMC** **UMS** Eq.Ltr: A†; Cable: 522.5/56.0 U2 (a)	1996-06 **Aarhus Flydedok A/S — Aarhus** Yd No: 218 Loa 100.85 (BB) Br ex 20.44 Dght 8.210 Lbp 93.10 Br md 20.20 Dpth 11.00 Welded, 1 dk	**(A31A2GX) General Cargo Ship** Grain: 10,296; Bale: 9,713 TEU 652 C Ho 218 TEU C Dk 434 TEU incl 84 ref C. Compartments: 1 Ho, ER 1 Ha: (62.9 x 15.3)ER Cranes: 2x70t Ice Capable	**1 oil engine** with flexible couplings & sr gearedto sc. shaft driving 1 CP propeller Total Power: 6,000kW (8,158hp) 15.0kn MaK 8M552C 1 x 4 Stroke 8 Cy. 450 x 520 6000kW (8158bhp) Krupp MaK Maschinenbau GmbH-Kiel AuxGen: 1 x 900kW 440V 60Hz a.c, 3 x 512kW 440V 60Hz a.c Boilers: TOH (ex.g.) 6.7kgf/cm² (6.6bar), TOH (o.f.) 7.1kgf/cm² (7.0bar) Thrusters: 1 Thwart. CP thruster (f) Fuel: 89.7 (d.f.) (Heating Coils) 797.7 (r.f.) 23.7pd
9187136 *PHQA* -	**SHARON** *ex* Solvi A *-2013* *ex* Claudia C *-2008* *ex* Claudia *-2008* **Miss Sharon BV** Flagship Management Co BV *Delfzijl* *Netherlands* MMSI: 245871000 Official number: 52405	2,999 1,714 5,049 T/cm 11.5	Class: GL (LR) ✠ Classed LR until 29/6/09	1999-09 **B.V. Scheepswerf Damen Hoogezand — Foxhol** Yd No: 741 1999-09 **Damen Shipyards Yichang Co Ltd — Yichang HB** (Hull) Loa 94.99 (BB) Br ex 13.20 Dght 6.200 Lbp 90.25 Br md 13.17 Dpth 7.15 Welded, 1 dk	**(A31A2GX) General Cargo Ship** Double Bottom Entire Compartment Length Grain: 6,196 TEU 224 C. Cargo Heating Coils Compartments: 1 Ho, ER 1 Ha: (67.7 x 11.0)ER Ice Capable	**1 oil engine** with clutches & sr geared to sc. shaft driving 1 CP propeller Total Power: 1,496kW (2,034hp) 12.0kn MaK 6M453C 1 x 4 Stroke 6 Cy. 320 x 420 1496kW (2034bhp) MaK Motoren GmbH & Co. KG-Kiel AuxGen: 1 x 232kW 400V 50Hz a.c, 2 x 100kW 400V 50Hz a.c Thrusters: 1 Thwart. FP thruster (f) Fuel: 38.0 (d.f.) (Heating Coils) 216.2 (r.f.) 10.0pd
9160841 *PNFU* -	**SHARON** - **PT Segara Gloria Anugrah Marine** - *Jakarta* *Indonesia* MMSI: 525015695 Official number: GT. 14.474 NO. 1233/DDA	14,474 4,626 18,294	Class: AB	1998-05 **Pan-United Shipyard Pte Ltd — Singapore** Yd No: 6120 Loa 158.00 (BB) Br ex - Dght 7.000 Lbp 151.80 Br md 27.00 Dpth 11.70 Welded, 1 dk	**(A13A2TV) Crude Oil Tanker** Double Hull (13F) Liq: 24,750; Liq (Oil): 24,750 Cargo Heating Coils Compartments: 10 Wing Ta, ER	**1 oil engine** driving 1 FP propeller Total Power: 4,901kW (6,663hp) 13.0kn B&W 7S35MC 1 x 2 Stroke 7 Cy. 350 x 1400 4901kW (6663bhp) MAN B&W Diesel A/S-Denmark AuxGen: 3 x 600kW 440V 60Hz a.c Fuel: 120.6 (d.f.) (Heating Coils) 815.5 (r.f.) 19.5pd
8932431 - -	**SHARON** *ex* Ran *-1995* - -	190 49 -		1964 **Orlogsvaerftet (Naval Dockyard) — Copenhagen** Yd No: P435 Loa 34.20 Br ex 6.75 Dght - Lbp - Br md - Dpth 3.70 Welded, 1 dk	**(B12D2FP) Fishery Patrol Vessel**	**2 oil engines** driving 2 FP propellers Total Power: 1,104kW (1,500hp) Maybach MD655 2 x Vee 4 Stroke 12 Cy. 185 x 200 each-552kW (750bhp) Maybach Motorenbau GmbH-Friedrichshafen
8302698 *XUGT5* -	**SHARON** *ex* Sea Wave *-2014* *ex* Ibinabo *-2014* *ex* Jade *-2012* *ex* Vera *-2012* *ex* Sam *-1999* *ex* Inez III *-1995* **Voilet Co Ltd** - *Phnom Penh* *Cambodia* MMSI: 514383000 Official number: 1385092	2,054 1,141 3,720 T/cm 12.0	Class: PX (LR) ✠ Classed LR until 10/4/12	1985-07 **Fulton Marine N.V. — Ruisbroek** Yd No: 151 Converted From: Chemical Tanker-1999 Loa 110.01 Br ex 11.38 Dght 4.001 Lbp 106.38 Br md 11.37 Dpth 6.25 Welded, 1 dk	**(A13B2TP) Products Tanker** Liq: 5,110; Liq (Oil): 5,110 Compartments: 15 Ta, ER 2 Cargo Pump (s): 2x550m³/hr Manifold: Bow/CM: 26m	**1 oil engine** with clutches, flexible couplings & sr reverse geared to sc. shaft driving 1 FP propeller Total Power: 1,420kW (1,931hp) 11.0kn A.B.C. 8MDZC 1 x 4 Stroke 8 Cy. 256 x 310 1420kW (1931bhp) Anglo Belgian Corp NV (ABC)-Belgium AuxGen: 2 x 64kW 380V 50Hz a.c, 1 x 40kW 380V 50Hz a.c, 1 x 29kW 380V 50Hz a.c Boilers: (TOH (fitted: 1985)) (10.2kgf/cm² (10.0bar)) Thrusters: 1 Thwart. FP thruster (f) Fuel: 95.0 (d.f.)
7531292 - -	**SHARON 1** *ex* Stadt Tug *-2013* *ex* Montado *-2006* *ex* Sun Kent *-2000* - - -	282 84 175	Class: (LR) ✠ Classed LR until 14/2/13	1977-10 **R. Dunston (Hessle) Ltd. — Hessle** Yd No: H911 Converted From: Tug-2013 Loa 32.92 Br ex 9.61 Dght 4.172 Lbp 29.01 Br md 9.15 Dpth 4.91 Welded, 1 dk	**(X11A2YP) Yacht**	**1 oil engine** dr geared to sc. shaft driving 1 CP propeller Total Power: 1,522kW (2,069hp) 12.0kn Ruston 12RKCM 1 x Vee 4 Stroke 12 Cy. 254 x 305 1522kW (2069bhp) Ruston Diesels Ltd.-Newton-le-Willows AuxGen: 3 x 60kW 440V 50Hz a.c Fuel: 92.0 (d.f.)
7321702 *E5U2741* -	**SHARON 2** *ex* Stadt Assister *-2013* *ex* Punta Tambo *-2006* **SG Finans AS** Stadt Sjotransport AS *Cook Islands* MMSI: 518794000	*194* 58 119	Class: (BV)	1974 **Astilleros de Murueta S.A. — Gernika-Lumo** Yd No: 119 Loa 28.30 Br ex 8.49 Dght 3.290 Lbp 25.02 Br md 7.90 Dpth 3.97 Welded	**(B32A2ST) Tug**	**1 oil engine** reverse reduction geared to sc. shaft driving 1 FP propeller Total Power: 1,287kW (1,750hp) Alpha 14V23L-VO 1 x Vee 4 Stroke 14 Cy. 225 x 300 1287kW (1750bhp) Construcciones Echevarria SA-Spain Thrusters: 1 Tunnel thruster (f)
7732717 *WAT5905* -	**SHARON ANN** *ex* Mabel Susan III *-2005* **Aquaharvesters Inc** - *Oceanside, NY* *United States of America* MMSI: 366136260 Official number: 584548	*134* 108 -		1977 **Deep Sea Boat Builders, Inc. — Bayou La Batre, Al** L reg 22.38 Br ex - Dght - Lbp - Br md 6.71 Dpth 3.46 Welded, 1 dk	**(B11B2FV) Fishing Vessel**	**1 oil engine** geared to sc. shaft driving 1 FP propeller Total Power: 268kW (364hp) Cummins KT-1150-M 1 x 4 Stroke 6 Cy. 159 x 159 268kW (364bhp) Cummins Engine Co Inc-USA
9069487 *WDD6191* -	**SHARON ELIZABETH** *ex* Hartford *-2007* *ex* Cape Jellison *-2000* *ex* Gordon Winslow *-1990* *ex* Hartford *-1980* *ex* William J. Tracy *-1970* **McAllister Towing & Transportation Co Inc (MT & T)** - *Wilmington, DE* *United States of America* MMSI: 367169430 Official number: 262119	*256* 7 -	Class: (AB)	1951-06 **Levingston SB. Co. — Orange, Tx** Yd No: 467 Loa - Br ex - Dght - Lbp 30.46 Br md 8.23 Dpth 4.27 Welded, 1 dk	**(B32A2ST) Tug**	**2 oil engines** reverse reduction geared to sc. shafts driving 2 Propellers Total Power: 1,206kW (1,640hp) General Motors 16-278-A 2 x Vee 2 Stroke 16 Cy. 222 x 267 each-603kW (820bhp) General Motors Corp-USA

Identification	Name / Owner	Tonnage	Classification	Build / Dimensions	Type / Cargo	Machinery
8997962 *WDD5662* -	**SHARON K** *ex* John & Nicholas *-2007* **Kenpac Fishing Corp** - *New Bedford, MA* *United States of America* MMSI: 367161650 Official number: 1178384	**257** 77 -		**2005-01 La Force Shipyard Inc — Coden AL** Yd No: 144 Loa 31.00 Br ex - Dght - Lbp - Br md 8.22 Dpth 4.26 Welded, 1 dk	**(B11B2FV) Fishing Vessel**	**1 oil engine** driving 1 Propeller
9084059 *CFP2006* -	**SHARON M I** *ex* Pacific Tempest *-2013* *ex* Mai Po *-2008* **McKeil Work Boats Ltd** McKeil Marine Ltd *St John's, NL* *Canada* MMSI: 316024256 Official number: 837315	**450** 135 359	Class: LR (BV) **100A1** SS 04/2013 fire fighting ship (2,400 cubic metre/hr) with water spray **LMC** Eq.Ltr: K; Cable: 357.0/28.0 U2	**1994-05 Imamura Zosen — Kure** Yd No: 373 Loa 34.95 Br ex 10.52 Dght 4.900 Lbp 30.00 Br md 10.50 Dpth 5.30 Welded, 1 dk	**(B32A2ST) Tug** Cranes: 1x4t	**2 oil engines** with flexible couplings & reduction geared to sc. shafts driving 2 CP propellers Total Power: 2,942kW (4,000hp) 13.9kn Niigata 6L28HX 2 x 4 Stroke 6 Cy. 280 x 370 each-1471kW (2000bhp) Niigata Engineering Co Ltd-Japan AuxGen: 1 x 225kW 385V 50Hz a.c, 2 x 144kW 385V 50Hz a.c Thrusters: 1 Thwart. CP thruster (f) Fuel: 205.4 (d.f.) 14.6pd
8961389 *WDE6865* -	**SHARON NICOLE** *ex* Dang Brothers *-2008* **Sharon Nicole LLC** - *Hobucken, NC* *United States of America* Official number: 1106603	**172** 51 -		**2000 La Force Shipyard Inc — Coden AL** Yd No: 104 L reg 26.18 Br ex - Dght - Lbp - Br md 7.62 Dpth 3.71 Welded, 1 dk	**(B11B2FV) Fishing Vessel**	**1 oil engine** driving 1 FP propeller
7323061 - -	**SHARON No. 31** *ex* Shinto Maru No. 85 *-1990* - - SatCom: Inmarsat A 1334134	*199* 111 187		**1973 Kyokuyo Shipbuilding & Iron Works Co Ltd — Shimonoseki YC** Yd No: 261 Loa 42.98 Br ex 7.04 Dght 3.277 Lbp 37.57 Br md 7.01 Dpth 3.41 Welded, 1 dk	**(B11B2FV) Fishing Vessel**	**1 oil engine** driving 1 FP propeller Total Power: 956kW (1,300hp) Niigata 6L25BX 1 x 4 Stroke 6 Cy. 250 x 320 956kW (1300bhp) Niigata Engineering Co Ltd-Japan
7824168 - -	**SHARON No. 33** *ex* Kyotoku Maru No. 28 *-1990* **Sharon Fishing Co S de RL** - *San Lorenzo* *Honduras* Official number: L-1823277	*145* - 178		**1979-02 Tokushima Zosen K.K. — Fukuoka** Yd No: 1311 Loa 38.10 (BB) Br ex 6.63 Dght 2.513 Lbp 32.11 Br md 6.61 Dpth 2.82 Welded, 1 dk	**(B12B2FC) Fish Carrier**	**1 oil engine** driving 1 FP propeller Total Power: 736kW (1,001hp) 11.3kn Hanshin 6LU26G 1 x 4 Stroke 6 Cy. 260 x 440 736kW (1001bhp) Hanshin Nainenki Kogyo-Japan
9316232 *A8XU5* -	**SHARON SEA** - **HLL Sharon Sea Shipping Inc** Harren & Partner Ship Management GmbH & Co KG SatCom: Inmarsat C 463709071 *Monrovia* *Liberia* MMSI: 636015749 Official number: 15749	**42,167** 22,451 73,870 T/cm 67.5	Class: LR ✠ **100A1** SS 11/2011 Double Hull oil tanker ESP **ShipRight** (SDA, FDA, CM) LI *IWS SPM ✠ **LMC** **UMS IGS** Eq.Ltr: P†; Cable: 679.0/81.0 U3 (a)	**2006-11 New Century Shipbuilding Co Ltd — Jingjiang JS** Yd No: 0307321 Loa 228.60 (BB) Br ex 32.29 Dght 14.518 Lbp 218.00 Br md 32.26 Dpth 20.80 Welded, 1 dk	**(A13A2TV) Crude Oil Tanker** Double Hull (13F) Liq: 83,186; Liq (Oil): 83,186 Cargo Heating Coils Compartments: 12 Wing Ta, 2 Wing Slop Ta, ER 3 Cargo Pump (s): 3x2300m³/hr Manifold: Bow/CM: 113m	**1 oil engine** driving 1 FP propeller Total Power: 11,300kW (15,363hp) 14.0kn MAN-B&W 5S60MC-C 1 x 2 Stroke 5 Cy. 600 x 2400 11300kW (15363bhp) Hudong Heavy Machinery Co Ltd-China AuxGen: 3 x 900kW 450V 60Hz a.c Boilers: AuxB (Comp) 10.2kgf/cm² (10.0bar), WTAuxB (o.f.) 18.4kgf/cm² (18.0bar) Fuel: 274.8 (d.f.) 1941.9 (r.f.)
9132595 *4XFS* -	**SHARONA 1** - **The Israel Electric Corp Ltd** - *Haifa* *Israel*	**478** 143 170	Class: LR ✠ **100A1** SS 07/2012 tug Eastern Mediterranean and Red Sea service ✠ **LMC** **UMS** Eq.Ltr: I; Cable: 330.0/24.0 U2	**1997-07 Israel Shipyards Ltd. — Haifa** Yd No: 1083 Loa 32.84 Br ex 11.12 Dght 5.025 Lbp 27.12 Br md 10.50 Dpth 5.84 Welded, 1 dk	**(B32A2ST) Tug**	**2 oil engines** reduction geared to sc. shafts driving 2 Directional propellers Total Power: 3,560kW (4,840hp) 12.5kn Normo KRM-8 2 x 4 Stroke 8 Cy. 250 x 300 each-1780kW (2420bhp) Ulstein Bergen AS-Norway AuxGen: 2 x 160kW 400V 50Hz a.c
9513919 *V7YZ5* -	**SHARP** - **Miraero SG No 4 SA** Genel Denizcilik Nakliyati AS (GEDEN LINES) *Majuro* *Marshall Islands* MMSI: 538004771 Official number: 4771	**32,795** 18,550 55,340 T/cm 57.1	Class: NV	**2013-01 Hyundai-Vinashin Shipyard Co Ltd — Ninh Hoa** Yd No: S050 Loa 188.00 Br ex - Dght 12.800 Lbp 182.50 Br md 32.24 Dpth 18.30 Welded, 1 dk	**(A21A2BC) Bulk Carrier** Grain: 67,681 Compartments: 5 Ho, ER 5 Ha: ER Cranes: 4x30t	**1 oil engine** driving 1 FP propeller Total Power: 9,960kW (13,542hp) 14.5kn MAN-B&W 6S50MC-C8 1 x 2 Stroke 6 Cy. 500 x 2000 9960kW (13542bhp) Hyundai Heavy Industries Co Ltd-South Korea AuxGen: 3 x a.c
9577044 *2EKQ4* -	**SHARP LADY** - **Blenheim Shipping UK Ltd** - SatCom: Inmarsat C 423592880 *Douglas* *Isle of Man (British)* MMSI: 235090261 Official number: 742824	**64,089** 35,252 116,619 T/cm 99.5	Class: LR ✠ **100A1** SS 04/2012 Double Hull oil tanker CSR ESP **ShipRight** (CM, ACS (B)) *IWS LI SPM ✠ **LMC** **UMS IGS** Cable: 715.0/92.0 U3 (a)	**2012-04 Sungdong Shipbuilding & Marine Engineering Co Ltd — Tongyeong** Yd No: 2038 Loa 249.90 (BB) Br ex 44.03 Dght 15.123 Lbp 239.00 Br md 44.00 Dpth 21.50 Welded, 1 dk	**(A13A2TV) Crude Oil Tanker** Double Hull (13F) Liq: 127,234; Liq (Oil): 124,140 Cargo Heating Coils Compartments: 12 Wing Ta, 2 Wing Slop Ta, ER 3 Cargo Pump (s): 3x3000m³/hr Manifold: Bow/CM: 124.6m	**1 oil engine** driving 1 FP propeller Total Power: 13,560kW (18,436hp) 15.1kn MAN-B&W 6S60MC-C 1 x 2 Stroke 6 Cy. 600 x 2400 13560kW (18436bhp) Hyundai Engine & Machinery Co Ltd-South Korea AuxGen: 3 x 740kW 450V 60Hz a.c Boilers: e (ex.g.) 21.4kgf/cm² (21.0bar), AuxB (o.f.) 18.2kgf/cm² (17.8bar) Fuel: 344.0 (d.f.) 2750.0 (r.f.) 44.5pd
9620712 *A7DR* -	**SHARQ** - **Katara Hospitality** Ritz-Carlton Hotel Co *Doha* *Qatar* MMSI: 466074000 Official number: 316/11	**488** 146 53	Class: AB	**2011-03 Overmarine SpA — Viareggio** Yd No: 165/06 Loa 49.90 Br ex - Dght 1.670 Lbp 42.80 Br md 9.20 Dpth 5.10 Bonded, 1 dk	**(X11A2YP) Yacht** Hull Material: Reinforced Plastic	**3 oil engines** reduction geared to sc. shafts driving 3 Water jets Total Power: 9,360kW (12,726hp) M.T.U. 16V4000M93 3 x Vee 4 Stroke 16 Cy. 170 x 190 each-3120kW (4242bhp) MTU Friedrichshafen GmbH-Friedrichshafen AuxGen: 2 x 99kW a.c Fuel: 40.0 (d.f.)
9187801 *3FHS8* -	**SHARROW BAY** - **Davidoff Corp Ltd** B & S Enterprise Co Ltd SatCom: Inmarsat M 635434610 *Panama* *Panama* MMSI: 354346000 Official number: 2543198CH	**4,769** 2,682 7,430	Class: NK	**1998-03 Kanawa Dockyard Co. Ltd. — Hiroshima** Yd No: 1017 Loa 98.50 (BB) Br ex - Dght 7.720 Lbp 89.95 Br md 18.00 Dpth 11.00 Welded, 2 dks	**(A31A2GX) General Cargo Ship** Grain: 10,761; Bale: 9,934 Compartments: 2 Ho, ER, 1 Tw Dk 2 Ha: (18.9 x 10.5) (32.9 x 10.5)ER Derricks: 2x30t,1x25t	**1 oil engine** driving 1 FP propeller Total Power: 2,427kW (3,300hp) 12.0kn Akasaka A41 1 x 4 Stroke 6 Cy. 410 x 800 2427kW (3300bhp) Akasaka Tekkosho KK (Akasaka DieselLtd)-Japan AuxGen: 2 x 300kW 445V 60Hz a.c Fuel: 101.4 (d.f.) (Heating Coils) 482.2 (r.f.) 9.0pd
9602045 *ZR4144* -	**SHASA** - **Transnet Ltd** - *Port Elizabeth* *South Africa* MMSI: 601119500 Official number: 40903	**460** 138 -		**2009-11 Southern African Shipyards (Pty.) Ltd. — Durban** Yd No: 306 Loa 31.00 Br ex - Dght 6.180 Lbp 29.00 Br md 11.50 Dpth - Welded, 1 dk	**(B32A2ST) Tug**	**2 oil engines** reduction geared to sc. shafts driving 2 Voith-Schneider propellers Total Power: 5,440kW (7,396hp) MAN-B&W 8L27/38 2 x 4 Stroke 8 Cy. 270 x 380 each-2720kW (3698bhp)
9512288 *9W006* -	**SHASHVADHAA 1** *ex* Sea Home Shine *-2013* **Straits Kinabalu Shipping Sdn Bhd** Borneo Bulk Carriers Sdn Bhd *Kota Kinabalu* *Malaysia* MMSI: 533849000 Official number: 332721	**2,551** 1,497 4,374	Class: (VR)	**2008-06 Dai Duong Shipbuilding Co Ltd — Haiphong** Yd No: HP703-05 Loa 90.74 Br ex 13.01 Dght 6.160 Lbp 84.90 Br md 12.98 Dpth 7.60 Welded, 1 dk	**(A31A2GX) General Cargo Ship** Grain: 4,850 Compartments: 2 Ho, ER 2 Ha: ER 2 (21.0 x 8.0)	**1 oil engine** reduction geared to sc. shaft driving 1 FP propeller Total Power: 1,500kW (2,039hp) 11.0kn Chinese Std. Type G8300ZC 1 x 4 Stroke 8 Cy. 300 x 380 1500kW (2039bhp) Wuxi Antai Power Machinery Co Ltd-China AuxGen: 2 x 170kW 400V 50Hz a.c
9134684 *D5FI2* -	**SHASTA** *ex* Coast *-2013* *ex* Vento Di Grecale *-2013* *ex* Coast *-2012* *ex* Nordcoast *-2011* *ex* Cala Puebla *-2009* *ex* Nordcoast *-2005* *ex* Safmarine Nahoon *-2002* *ex* DAL East London *-2002* *ex* Nordcoast *-2001* *ex* Alianca Parana *-2000* *ex* Nordcoast *-2000* *ex* CSAV Buenos Aires *-1999* *ex* Nordcoast *-1997* **Almond Shipping Investments LLC** Conbulk Shipping SA *Monrovia* *Liberia* MMSI: 636016271 Official number: 16271	**16,264** 8,719 22,420	Class: BV GL	**1997-11 Stocznia Szczecinska SA — Szczecin** Yd No: B186/3/14 Loa 179.58 (BB) Br ex - Dght 9.940 Lbp 167.26 Br md 25.30 Dpth 13.50 Welded, 1 dk	**(A33A2CC) Container Ship (Fully Cellular)** Grain: 29,676 TEU 1684 C Ho 630 TEU C Dk 1054 TEU incl 160 ref C. Compartments: 4 Cell Ho, ER 9 Ha: ER Cranes: 3x45t	**1 oil engine** driving 1 FP propeller Total Power: 13,328kW (18,121hp) 19.0kn Sulzer 6RTA62U 1 x 2 Stroke 6 Cy. 620 x 2150 13328kW (18121bhp) H Cegielski Poznan SA-Poland AuxGen: 1 x 1000kW 440V 60Hz a.c, 3 x 570kW 440V 60Hz a.c Thrusters: 1 Thwart. CP thruster (f) Fuel: 175.0 (d.f.) (Heating Coils) 1550.0 (r.f.) 65.0pd

8350906 - -	**SHATIROBO** *ex* Dana 8 *-2008* *ex* Shun Tong *-2008* *ex* Tenrei Maru No. 18 *-1998* -	1,249 475 1,389		**1982-11 Yamanaka Zosen K.K. — Imabari** Yd No: 267 Loa 71.60 Br ex - Dght 4.000 Lbp 66.90 Br md 11.50 Dpth 6.70 Welded, 1 dk	**(A31A2GX) General Cargo Ship** Grain: 2,740; Bale: 2,650 Compartments: 1 Ho, ER 1 Ha: (38.0 x 9.0)ER	**1 oil engine** driving 1 FP propeller Makita 1 x 4 Stroke 6 Cy. Makita Corp-Japan
9263394 *AUAN* -	**SHATIXA** *ex* Bulk Challenger *-2006* **Timblo Pvt Ltd** Bernhard Schulte Shipping (India) Pvt Ltd *Mumbai* *India* MMSI: 419031700 Official number: 2982	8,345 2,504 12,207	Class: IR (BV)	**2002-09 Jiangsu Xinhua Shipyard Co Ltd — Nanjing JS** Yd No: 518 Loa 106.00 Br ex 32.27 Dght 5.500 Lbp 100.57 Br md 32.25 Dpth 7.50 Welded, 1 dk	**(B34W2QJ) Trans Shipment Vessel** Grain: 12,500 Cranes: 2x30t	**2 diesel electric oil engines** driving 4 gen. each 1200kW 440V a.c Connecting to 2 elec. motors driving 2 Azimuth electric drive units Total Power: 2,438kW (3,314hp) 10.0kn Cummins KTA-50-M2 2 x Vee 4 Stroke 16 Cy. 159 x 159 each-1219kW (1657bhp) Cummins India Ltd-India Fuel: 384.0 (d.f.)
9322140 *HNSA* -	**SHATT AL ARAB** *ex* Mini Me *-2010* **Iraqi Oil Tankers Co** Iraqi Oil Tankers Co *Basrah* *Iraq* MMSI: 425000003	8,539 4,117 13,050 T/cm 23.2	Class: BV (AB)	**2006-01 21st Century Shipbuilding Co Ltd — Tongyeong** Yd No: 209 Loa 128.60 (BB) Br ex - Dght 8.714 Lbp 120.40 Br md 20.40 Dpth 11.50 Welded, 1 dk	**(A12B2TR) Chemical/Products Tanker** Double Hull (13F) Liq: 13,402; Liq (Oil): 13,402 Cargo Heating Coils Compartments: 12 Wing Ta, 2 Wing Slop Ta, ER 12 Cargo Pump (s): 12x300m³/hr Manifold: Bow/CM: 60.7m	**1 oil engine** driving 1 FP propeller Total Power: 4,400kW (5,982hp) 13.4kn MAN-B&W 6S35MC 1 x 2 Stroke 6 Cy. 350 x 1400 4400kW (5982bhp) STX Engine Co Ltd-South Korea AuxGen: 3 x 550kW a.c Thrusters: 1 Tunnel thruster (f) Fuel: 65.0 (d.f.) 640.0 (r.f.)
7329871 - - -	**SHATT AL BASRAH** *ex* Granter *-1975* - -	*647* 210 404	Class: (RS)	**1973 Zavod "Leninskaya Kuznitsa" — Kiyev** Yd No: 1376 Loa 54.79 Br ex 9.99 Dght 4.680 Lbp 49.41 Br md 9.81 Dpth 5.01 Welded, 2 dks	**(B11A2FS) Stern Trawler** Ins: 400 Compartments: 2 Ho, ER 3 Ha: 3 (1.5 x 1.6) Derricks: 2x1.5t; Winches: 2 Ice Capable	**1 oil engine** driving 1 CP propeller Total Power: 736kW (1,001hp) 12.0kn S.K.L. 8NVD48-2U 1 x 4 Stroke 8 Cy. 320 x 480 736kW (1001bhp) VEB Schwermaschinenbau "KarlLiebknecht" (SKL)-Magdeburg
8800004 - -	**SHATT ALARAB 1** *ex* Ghasha *-2011* *ex* Tlaloc *-2005* *ex* Aurora Prince *-2002* *ex* Bright Gulf *-2001* *ex* Tlaloc *-1997* - -	6,885 2,705 9,917 T/cm 24.4	Class: (LR) (BV) ✠ Classed LR until 6/1/11	**1995-08 Astilleros Corrientes S.A. — Buenos Aires** Yd No: 157 Loa 129.00 Br ex 20.52 Dght 6.100 Lbp 122.80 Br md 20.50 Dpth 8.95 Welded, 1 dk	**(A13B2TP) Products Tanker** Double Bottom Entire Compartment Length Liq: 10,950; Liq (Oil): 10,950 Cargo Heating Coils Compartments: 4 Ta, 8 Wing Ta, ER 14 Cargo Pump (s)	**2 oil engines** with clutches, flexible couplings & sr reverse geared to sc. shafts driving 2 FP propellers Total Power: 4,350kW (5,914hp) 12.8kn Sulzer 8ATL25H 2 x 4 Stroke 8 Cy. 250 x 300 each-2175kW (2957bhp) Ente Administrador Astilleros RioSantiago-Argentina AuxGen: 3 x 520kW 440V 60Hz a.c Boilers: AuxB (o.f.) 8.0kgf/cm² (7.8bar) Thrusters: 1 Thwart. CP thruster (f)
8746909 *9MHX9* -	**SHAULA 1** **Government of Malaysia (Director of Marine & Ministry of Transport)** - *Port Klang* *Malaysia* Official number: 333809	140 42 25		**2008-02 Kay Marine Sdn Bhd — Kuala Terengganu** (Assembled by) Yd No: J104-4 **2008-02 Inform Marine Technology — Fremantle WA** (Parts for assembly by) Loa 26.00 Br ex - Dght 1.200 Lbp - Br md 9.20 Dpth 2.55 Welded, 1 dk	**(A37B2PS) Passenger Ship** Hull Material: Aluminium Alloy	**2 oil engines** reduction geared to sc. shafts driving 2 Propellers Total Power: 2,206kW (3,000hp) M.T.U. 12V2000M91 2 x Vee 4 Stroke 12 Cy. 130 x 150 each-1103kW (1500bhp) MTU Friedrichshafen GmbH-Friedrichshafen
8729822 *H04697* -	**SHAULA I** *ex* Shaula *-2008* *ex* Ramigala *-2006* **Inter Oceanic Marine Overseas Inc** - *Panama* *Panama* Official number: 34835PEXT2	359 107 129	Class: (RS)	**1989-05 Sudostroitelnyy Zavod "Avangard" — Petrozavodsk** Yd No: 617 Loa 35.74 Br ex - Dght 3.491 Lbp 31.02 Br md 8.93 Dpth 6.08 Welded, 2 dk	**(B11A2FS) Stern Trawler**	**1 oil engine** driving 1 FP propeller Total Power: 589kW (801hp) 11.0kn S.K.L. 6NVD48A-2U 1 x 4 Stroke 6 Cy. 320 x 480 589kW (801bhp) VEB Schwermaschinenbau "KarlLiebknecht" (SKL)-Magdeburg
9210660 *EI5920* G 276	**SHAUNA ANN** **Shauna Ann Ltd** - SatCom: Inmarsat C 425024010 *Galway* *Irish Republic* MMSI: 250240000 Official number: 403296	340 102 -	Class: (LR) ✠ Classed LR until 19/8/01	**2000-05 Factoria Naval de Marin S.A. — Marin** Yd No: 128 Loa 27.64 (BB) Br ex - Dght 4.140 Lbp 23.00 Br md 8.50 Dpth 4.75 Welded, 1 dk	**(B11A2FS) Stern Trawler**	**1 oil engine** with clutches, flexible couplings & sr geared to sc. shaft driving 1 CP propeller Total Power: 696kW (946hp) Cummins KTA-50-M2 1 x Vee 4 Stroke 16 Cy. 159 x 159 696kW (946bhp) Cummins Engine Co Inc-USA AuxGen: 1 x 216kW 380V 50Hz a.c, 1 x 163kW 380V 50Hz a.c Thrusters: 1 Thwart. FP thruster (f)
7050755 *WY5117* -	**SHAWNEE** **McCall's Boat Rentals LLC** *Biloxi, MS* *United States of America* Official number: 516840	*133* 90 -		**1968 Graham Boats, Inc. — Pascagoula, Ms** L reg 21.71 Br ex 6.46 Dght - Lbp - Br md - Dpth 3.66 Welded	**(B11B2FV) Fishing Vessel**	**1 oil engine** driving 1 FP propeller Total Power: 268kW (364hp)
7207906 *WDG2740* -	**SHAWNEE** *ex* Accu X *-2012* *ex* Shawnee *-2009* **High Sierra Marine LLC** *New Orleans, LA* *United States of America* MMSI: 367518770 Official number: 531578	*232* 158 -		**1971 Halter Marine Services, Inc. — Lockport, La** Yd No: 290 Loa - Br ex 9.15 Dght - Lbp 25.91 Br md 9.14 Dpth 2.90 Welded, 1 dk	**(B32B2SP) Pusher Tug**	**2 oil engines** driving 2 FP propellers Total Power: 1,324kW (1,800hp) G.M. (Detroit Diesel) 16V-149 2 x Vee 2 Stroke 16 Cy. 146 x 146 each-662kW (900bhp) General Motors Corp-USA
9103362 *C6SL9* -	**SHAYA** *ex* Clipper Mariner *-2013* *ex* Seaboard Explorer II *-2009* *ex* CEC Mariner *-2002* *ex* P&O Nedlloyd Belem *-2000* *ex* Arktis Mariner *-2000* *ex* Melfi Halifax *-1998* *ex* Melbridge Major *-1997* *ex* Arktis Mariner *-1996* **Shaya Shipping Co Ltd** Okyanus Ege Denizcilik Ticaret AS *Nassau* *Bahamas* MMSI: 311388000 Official number: 8000486	6,285 3,108 8,972 T/cm 17.9	Class: BV (LR) Classed LR until 26/4/13	**1996-01 Aarhus Flydedok A/S — Aarhus** Yd No: 216 Loa 100.80 (BB) Br ex 20.44 Dght 8.210 Lbp 93.10 Br md 20.20 Dpth 11.00 Welded, 1 dk	**(A31A2GX) General Cargo Ship** Grain: 10,296; Bale: 9,713 TEU 652 C Ho 218 TEU C Dk 434 TEU incl 84 ref C. Compartments: 1 Ho, ER 1 Ha: (62.9 x 15.3)ER Cranes: 2x70t	**1 oil engine** with flexible couplings & sr geared to sc. shaft driving 1 CP propeller Total Power: 6,000kW (8,158hp) 15.0kn MaK 8M552C 1 x 4 Stroke 8 Cy. 450 x 520 6000kW (8158bhp) Krupp MaK Maschinenbau GmbH-Kiel AuxGen: 1 x 900kW 440V 60Hz a.c, 3 x 512kW 440V 60Hz a.c Boilers: TOH (ex.g.) 9.2kgf/cm² (9.0bar), TOH (o.f.) 9.2kgf/cm² (9.0bar) Thrusters: 1 Thwart. CP thruster (f) Fuel: 89.7 (d.f.) (Heating Coils) 797.7 (r.f.) 23.7pd
9420356 *9BTB* -	**SHAYAN 1** **Teu Feeder Ltd** Valfajre Shipping Co *Qeshm Island* *Iran* MMSI: 422813000	9,957 5,032 13,772 T/cm 28.0	Class: (GL)	**2008-11 Jinling Shipyard — Nanjing JS** Yd No: 04-0427 Loa 147.87 (BB) Br ex - Dght 8.500 Lbp 140.30 Br md 23.25 Dpth 11.50 Welded, 1 dk	**(A33A2CC) Container Ship (Fully Cellular)** Grain: 16,000; Bale: 16,000 TEU 1118 C Ho 334 TEU C Dk 784 incl 240 ref C Cranes: 2x45t Ice Capable	**1 oil engine** reduction geard to sc. shafts driving 1 CP propeller Total Power: 9,730kW (13,229hp) 19.6kn MAN-B&W 7L58/64 1 x 4 Stroke 7 Cy. 580 x 640 9730kW (13229bhp) Hudong Heavy Machinery Co Ltd-China AuxGen: 3 x 570kW 450V a.c, 1 x 1400kW 450V a.c Thrusters: 1 Retract. directional thruster (f)
9058749 *EPBF4* -	**SHAYAN 8** *ex* Shayan *-2011* *ex* Taiyo Maru No. 8 *-2011* **Abdolamir Marhoonian Nejad & Susan Kazemzadeh** - *Bushehr* *Iran* MMSI: 422020900	*499* - 1,550		**1992-10 K.K. Miura Zosensho — Saiki** Yd No: 1052 Loa 72.30 Br ex - Dght 3.840 Lbp 70.00 Br md 12.30 Dpth 6.70 Welded, 1 dk	**(A31A2GX) General Cargo Ship**	**1 oil engine** driving 1 FP propeller Total Power: 1,324kW (1,800hp) Hanshin 6EL30 1 x 4 Stroke 6 Cy. 300 x 600 1324kW (1800bhp) The Hanshin Diesel Works Ltd-Japan
9166558 *HP9598* -	**SHAYBAH** *ex* Gantu *-1999* **Arab Maritime Petroleum Transport Co (AMPTC)** - *Panama* *Panama* MMSI: 353699000 Official number: 2642399C	28,519 12,385 47,185 T/cm 50.2	Class: AB	**1998-08 Onomichi Dockyard Co Ltd — Onomichi HS** Yd No: 431 Loa 182.50 (BB) Br ex - Dght 12.650 Lbp 172.00 Br md 32.20 Dpth 19.10 Welded, 1 dk	**(A13B2TP) Products Tanker** Double Hull (13F) Liq: 50,335; Liq (Oil): 50,335 Cargo Heating Coils Compartments: 2 Ta, 12 Wing Ta, 2 Wing Slop Ta, ER 4 Cargo Pump (s): 4x1000m³/hr	**1 oil engine** driving 1 FP propeller Total Power: 8,562kW (11,641hp) 15.3kn MAN-B&W 6S50MC 1 x 2 Stroke 6 Cy. 500 x 1910 8562kW (11641bhp) Mitsui Engineering & Shipbuilding CLtd-Japan AuxGen: 3 x 420kW a.c Fuel: 107.0 (d.f.) 1369.0 (r.f.) 33.4pd
9033036 *EPAM2* -	**SHAYESTEH** *ex* Shabtab *-2011* *ex* Shayesteh *-2010* *ex* Miyayoshi Maru *-2009* **Abbas M Nezhad & Mohammad M Nejad** - *Iran* MMSI: 422004700	*176* - 450		**1991-09 Hamamoto Zosensho K.K. — Tokushima** Yd No: 755 Loa 50.30 (BB) Br ex - Dght 3.218 Lbp 45.00 Br md 8.50 Dpth 4.90 Welded	**(A31A2GX) General Cargo Ship** Compartments: 1 Ho, ER 1 Ha: ER	**1 oil engine** driving 1 FP propeller Total Power: 405kW (551hp) Matsui 6M26KGHS 1 x 4 Stroke 6 Cy. 260 x 400 405kW (551bhp) Matsui Iron Works Co Ltd-Japan

7336070 **SHCHAPINO**
UGTZ
\- **Schapino Co Ltd**
\-
Petropavlovsk-Kamchatskiy *Russia*
MMSI: 273560200

195 Class: RS
64
98

1973-09 Zavod 'Nikolayevsk-na-Amure' — Nikolayevsk-na-Amure Yd No: 86
Loa 33.96 Br ex 7.09 Dght -
Lbp 29.97 Br md - Dpth 3.66
Welded, 1 dk

(B11B2FV) Fishing Vessel
Bale: 115
Compartments: 1 Ho, ER
1 Ha: (1.6 x 1.3)
Derricks: 2x2t
Ice Capable

1 oil engine driving 1 FP propeller
Total Power: 224kW (305hp) 9.5kn
S.K.L. 8NVD36-1U
1 x 4 Stroke 8 Cy. 240 x 360 224kW (305bhp)
VEB Schwermaschinenbau "KarlLiebknecht" (SKL)-Magdeburg
Fuel: 23.0 (d.f.)

8855176 **SHE DEVIL**
WDB3589 *ex* Sherri Lynn *-2010* *ex* Lady Linda *-2005*
\- **Stanco Boat Rental Ltd**
\-
Freeport, TX *United States of America*
MMSI: 366889090
Official number: 908902

139
111
\-

1986 Kerry Huynh — Biloxi, Ms
Loa - Br ex - Dght -
Lbp 23.93 Br md 7.01 Dpth 3.51
Welded, 1 dk

(B11B2FV) Fishing Vessel

1 oil engine driving 1 FP propeller

9280093 **SHEANNE**
EIGP
SO 716 **O'Shea Fishing Co Ltd**
\-
Sligo *Irish Republic*
MMSI: 250495000
Official number: 403789

1,588 Class: NV
514
\-

2003-11 Celiktekne Sanayii ve Ticaret A.S. — Tuzla, Istanbul (Hull) Yd No: 48
2003-11 Solstrand AS — Tomrefjord Yd No: 77
Loa 61.60 (BB) Br ex - Dght 7.500
Lbp 54.60 Br md 13.32 Dpth 8.30
Welded

(B11A2FS) Stern Trawler
Ice Capable

1 oil engine geared to sc. shaft driving 1 CP propeller
Total Power: 4,500kW (6,118hp) 16.0kn
MaK 9M32C
1 x 4 Stroke 9 Cy. 320 x 480 4500kW (6118bhp)
Caterpillar Motoren GmbH & Co. KG-Germany
AuxGen: 1 x 968kW a.c, 1 x 620kW a.c
Thrusters: 1 Thwart. FP thruster (f); 1 Thwart. FP thruster (a)

9363091 **SHEARWATER**
3ESK5
\- **Olamar Navegacion SA**
Usui Kaiun KK (Usui Kaiun Co Ltd)
Panama *Panama*
MMSI: 370338000
Official number: 3437008A

49,720 Class: NK
18,358
64,533

2008-09 Sanoyas Hishino Meisho Corp — Kurashiki OY Yd No: 1260
Loa 209.99 (BB) Br ex - Dght 12.029
Lbp 204.00 Br md 37.00 Dpth 22.85
Welded, 1 dk

(A24B2BW) Wood Chips Carrier
Grain: 123,617
Compartments: 6 Ho, ER
6 Ha: ER
Cranes: 3x15.5t

1 oil engine driving 1 FP propeller
Total Power: 9,480kW (12,889hp) 14.6kn
MAN-B&W 6S50MC-C
1 x 2 Stroke 6 Cy. 500 x 2000 9480kW (12889bhp)
Mitsui Engineering & Shipbuilding CLtd-Japan
Fuel: 3050.0

9055814 **SHEARWATER**
WDD3792
\- **Marine Spill Response Corp**
\-
Seattle, WA *United States of America*
MMSI: 367136250
Official number: 978841

357 Class: (AB)
107
609

1992-03 Goudy & Stevens — East Boothbay, Me Yd No: 239
Loa - Br ex - Dght 3.255
Lbp 35.11 Br md 9.45 Dpth 4.12
Welded

(B34G2SE) Pollution Control Vessel

2 oil engines driving 2 FP propellers
Total Power: 1,412kW (1,920hp)

8993966 **SHEARWATER**
WDF5838
\- **Alpine Ocean Seismic Survey Inc**
\-
New York, NY *United States of America*
MMSI: 368528000
Official number: 641188

401
175
\-

1982-11 Bell Halter Inc. — New Orleans, La
Converted From: Patrol Vessel-2011
Loa 33.25 Br ex - Dght 2.130
Lbp - Br md 11.88 Dpth 4.87
Welded, 1 dk

(B31A2SR) Research Survey Vessel
Hull Material: Aluminium Alloy
A-frames: 1x5t,1x2t; Cranes: 1x14t

2 oil engines geared to sc. shafts driving 2 Z propellers
Total Power: 774kW (1,052hp)
John Deere 6125A-FM
2 x 4 Stroke 6 Cy. 127 x 165 each-387kW (526bhp) (new engine 2011)
AuxGen: 2 x 135kW a.c

7522057 **SHEARWATER**
S7KE *ex* Matador *-1994* *ex* Lirola *-1989*
ex Osteteam *-1986*
Shearwater Shipping Lines Ltd
HDSA Shipping Pty Ltd
SatCom: Inmarsat C 466411510
Victoria *Seychelles*
MMSI: 664115000
Official number: 50028

1,733 Class: (GL)
746
2,554

1976-07 J.J. Sietas Schiffswerft — Hamburg Yd No: 800
Loa 92.41 (BB) Br ex 11.33 Dght 3.990
Lbp 88.63 Br md 11.30 Dpth 6.02
Welded, 2 dks

(A31A2GX) General Cargo Ship
Grain: 3,253; Bale: 3,029
TEU 96 C.Ho 56/20' C.Dk 40/20'
Compartments: 1 Ho, ER
1 Ha: (58.2 x 8.8)ER
Ice Capable

1 oil engine reduction geared to sc. shaft driving 1 CP propeller
Total Power: 1,066kW (1,449hp) 11.0kn
Alpha 10V23L-VO
1 x Vee 4 Stroke 10 Cy. 225 x 300 1066kW (1449bhp)
Alpha Diesel A/S-Denmark
Thrusters: 1 Thwart. FP thruster (f)

6822216 **SHEARWATER**
\-
\- -
\-

342
124
305

1968-03 Hall, Russell & Co. Ltd. — Aberdeen Yd No: 939
Loa 36.56 Br ex 9.12 Dght 2.591
Lbp 34.14 Br md 9.00 Dpth 3.05
Welded, 1 dk

(B33A2DU) Dredger (unspecified)
Hopper: 200

2 oil engines driving 2 FP propellers
Total Power: 264kW (358hp) 9.0kn
Kelvin T6
2 x 4 Stroke 6 Cy. 165 x 184 each-132kW (179bhp)
Bergius Kelvin Co. Ltd.-Glasgow

8037487 **SHEARWATER**
WYR4071 *ex* FS-411 *-1964*
\- **Omega Protein Inc**
\-
Reedville, VA *United States of America*
MMSI: 367108930
Official number: 624092

607
446
\-

1945-04 Hickenbotham Bros. Construction Div. — Stockton, Ca
L reg 50.66 Br ex 9.78 Dght -
Lbp - Br md - Dpth 3.54
Welded, 1 dk

(B11B2FV) Fishing Vessel

1 oil engine driving 1 FP propeller
Total Power: 780kW (1,060hp)
G.M. (Detroit Diesel) 16V-149
1 x Vee 2 Stroke 16 Cy. 146 x 146 780kW (1060bhp) (new engine 1975)
General Motors Corp-USA

8028400 **SHEARWATER BAY**
\- *ex* Jan de Boer *-2001* *ex* Klaasje *-1989*
L1064 **Marco Fishing (Pty) Ltd**
\-
Luderitz *Namibia*
Official number: 2001LB005

336
100
\-

1982-06 W. Visser & Zoon B.V. Werf "De Lastdrager" — Den Helder Yd No: 97
Loa 38.77 Br ex 8.03 Dght 3.270
Lbp 34.80 Br md 8.00 Dpth 4.36
Welded, 1 dk

(B11B2FV) Fishing Vessel

1 oil engine sr geared to sc. shaft driving 1 FP propeller
Total Power: 1,103kW (1,500hp) 10.8kn
Kromhout 9F/SW240
1 x 4 Stroke 9 Cy. 240 x 260 1103kW (1500bhp)
Stork Werkspoor Diesel BV-Netherlands
AuxGen: 1 x 200kW 220V 50Hz a.c, 1 x 70kW 220V 50Hz a.c, 1 x 60kW 220V 50Hz a.c, 2 x 25kW 220V 50Hz a.c
Thrusters: 1 Thwart. FP thruster (f)

9385594 **SHEBELLE**
ETSL
\- **Ethiopian Shipping & Logistics Services Enterprise**
\-
Addis Ababa *Ethiopia*
MMSI: 624013000
Official number: 13/99

20,471 Class: AB
10,630
27,391
T/cm
41.9

2006-11 Kouan Shipbuilding Industry Co — Taizhou JS Yd No: KA301
Loa 178.80 (BB) Br ex - Dght 10.200
Lbp 169.40 Br md 27.20 Dpth 14.20
Welded, 1 dk

(A31A2GX) General Cargo Ship
Grain: 39,551
TEU 1377
Compartments: 5 Ho, ER, 5 Tw Dk
5 Ha: ER
Cranes: 2x45t,2x40t

1 oil engine driving 1 FP propeller
Total Power: 8,250kW (11,217hp) 15.1kn
Mitsubishi 6UEC50LSII
1 x 2 Stroke 6 Cy. 500 x 1950 8250kW (11217bhp)
Mitsubishi Heavy Industries Ltd-Japan
AuxGen: 3 x 700kW a.c
Thrusters: 1 Tunnel thruster (f)
Fuel: 183.0 (d.f.) 2052.0 (r.f.)

9101912 **SHEDAR**
\-
\- **OOO 'Meganom'**
\-

378 Class: (RS)
113
157

1993-07 Khabarovskiy Sudostroitelnyy Zavod im Kirova — Khabarovsk Yd No: 103
Loa 41.90 Br ex 9.07 Dght 3.180
Lbp 37.27 Br md - Dpth 4.60
Welded, 1 dk

(B11B2FV) Fishing Vessel
2 Ha: 2 (2.1 x 2.4)
Derricks: 2x1t
Ice Capable

1 oil engine driving 1 FP propeller
Total Power: 450kW (612hp) 9.5kn
S.K.L. 6VD18/15AL-2
1 x 4 Stroke 6 Cy. 150 x 180 450kW (612bhp)
SKL Motoren u. Systemtechnik AG-Magdeburg

7601346 **SHEDEED**
SULU
Government of The Arab Republic of Egypt (Ministry of Maritime Transport - Ports & Lighthouses Administration)
Ships & Boats Marine Management & Supplies
Suez *Egypt*

518 Class: (AB)
59
\-

1984-04 Egyptian Shipbuilding & Repairs Co. — Alexandria Yd No: 6/80
Loa 36.00 Br ex 9.00 Dght 4.012
Lbp 29.01 Br md 8.51 Dpth 4.65
Welded, 1 dk

(B32A2ST) Tug

2 oil engines driving 1 FP propeller
Total Power: 1,008kW (1,370hp) 10.0kn
MWM TBD440-8K
2 x 4 Stroke 8 Cy. 230 x 270 each-504kW (685bhp)
Motoren Werke Mannheim AG (MWM)-West Germany

7733759 **SHEDUVA**
\-
\- -
\-

187 Class: (RS)
48
80

1978 Sudostroitelnyy Zavod "Avangard" — Petrozavodsk Yd No: 318
Loa 31.63 Br ex 7.32 Dght 2.899
Lbp 29.15 Br md - Dpth 3.51
Welded, 1 dk

(B11B2FV) Fishing Vessel
Ins: 100
Compartments: 1 Ho, ER
1 Ha: (1.4 x 1.4)
Derricks: 1x1.5t; Winches: 1
Ice Capable

1 oil engine driving 1 FP propeller
Total Power: 221kW (300hp) 9.5kn
S.K.L. 8NVD36-1U
1 x 4 Stroke 8 Cy. 240 x 360 221kW (300bhp)
VEB Schwermaschinenbau "KarlLiebknecht" (SKL)-Magdeburg

9108790 **SHEEM**
A6E2445
\- **Abu Dhabi Petroleum Ports Operating Co (IRSHAD)**
\-
Abu Dhabi *United Arab Emirates*
MMSI: 470675000
Official number: 3878

481 Class: LR
144 ✠ **100A1** SS 06/2010
625 tug
fire fighting ship 1 (2400 cubic metre/hr) with water spray
Arabian Gulf service
✠ **LMC**
Eq.Ltr: H; Cable: 495.0/30.0 U2

1995-06 Stocznia Polnocna SA (Northern Shipyard) — Gdansk (Hull)
1995-06 B.V. Scheepswerf Damen — Gorinchem Yd No: 6772
Loa 36.67 Br ex 10.83 Dght 4.250
Lbp 33.24 Br md 10.50 Dpth 5.00
Welded, 1 dk

(B32A2ST) Tug

2 oil engines with clutches, flexible couplings & sr reverse geared to sc. shafts driving 2 CP propellers
Total Power: 4,060kW (5,520hp) 12.0kn
Caterpillar 3608TA
2 x 4 Stroke 8 Cy. 280 x 300 each-2030kW (2760bhp)
Caterpillar Inc-USA
AuxGen: 2 x 200kW 380V 50Hz a.c
Thrusters: 1 Thwart. FP thruster (f)

8508137 **SHEENA MAC II**
\-
\- **Bob McNab**
\-
Roatan *Honduras*
Official number: U-1911334

106
72
\-

1985-05 Steiner Shipyard, Inc. — Bayou La Batre, Al
Loa 22.86 Br ex - Dght -
Lbp 20.12 Br md 6.71 Dpth 3.36
Welded, 1 dk

(B11A2FT) Trawler

1 oil engine geared to sc. shaft driving 1 FP propeller
Cummins KT-1150-M
1 x 4 Stroke 6 Cy. 159 x 159
Cummins Diesel International Ltd-USA

IMO / Call sign	Name / Owner / Port	Tonnage	Class	Builder / Dimensions	Type	Machinery
9557575 - - -	**SHEERAZ** **Karachi Port Trust** - *Karachi* *Pakistan*	**455** 136 304	Class: BV	**2010-03 Uzmar Gemi Insa Sanayi ve Ticaret AS — Basiskele** Yd No: 33 Loa 30.25 Br ex 12.05 Dght 4.240 Lbp 26.60 Br md 11.75 Dpth 5.28 Welded, 1 dk	**(B32A2ST) Tug**	**2 oil engines** reduction geared to sc. shafts driving 2 Z propellers Total Power: 3,946kW (5,364hp) Caterpillar 3516B-HD 2 x Vee 4 Stroke 16 Cy. 170 x 215 each-1973kW (2682bhp) Caterpillar Inc-USA AuxGen: 2 x 80kW 50Hz a.c Fuel: 150.0
1003786 *IU8676* -	**SHEERGOLD** *ex* Serafina *-1996* *ex* Sheergold *-1996* **SISSI Ltd** Agenzia Marittima Taverna Srl SatCom: Inmarsat A 1152427 *La Spezia* *Italy* MMSI: 247007800 Official number: SP27ND	*387* 116 -	Class: (LR) (RI) ✠ Classed LR until 27/2/07	**1987-07 Amels Holland BV — Makkum** Yd No: 406 Loa 42.00 Br ex 8.30 Dght 2.500 Lbp 36.50 Br md - Dpth 4.55 Welded, 1 dk	**(X11A2YP) Yacht**	**2 oil engines** with clutches, flexible couplings & sr reverse geared to sc. shafts driving 2 FP propellers Total Power: 1,156kW (1,572hp) Caterpillar 3508TA 2 x Vee 4 Stroke 8 Cy. 170 x 190 each-578kW (786bhp) (made 1986) Caterpillar Tractor Co-USA Thrusters: 1 Thwart. FP thruster (f)
8109369 *VTFD* -	**SHEETAL** **Uni General** Unimarine Pvt Ltd *Mumbai* *India* Official number: 1942	*115* 38 81	Class: IR (LR) ✠ Classed LR until 23/2/94	**1982-02 B.V. Scheepswerf "De Hoop" — Hardinxveld-Giessendam** Yd No: 763 Loa 23.68 Br ex 6.58 Dght 2.909 Lbp 21.24 Br md 6.51 Dpth 3.43 Welded, 1 dk	**(B11A2FS) Stern Trawler** Ins: 70	**1 oil engine** with clutches, flexible couplings & sr reverse geared to sc. shaft driving 1 FP propeller Total Power: 405kW (551hp) Caterpillar 3408TA 1 x Vee 4 Stroke 8 Cy. 137 x 152 405kW (551bhp) Caterpillar Tractor Co-USA AuxGen: 2 x 12kW 380V 50Hz a.c
7623758 *BYJV* -	**SHEH HENG No. 1** **Sheh Heng Marine Products Co Ltd** - *Kaohsiung* *Chinese Taipei* Official number: 5468	*359* 189 -	Class: (CR)	**1975 Taiwan Machinery Manufacturing Corp. — Kaohsiung** Loa 43.74 Br ex 7.60 Dght 3.036 Lbp 38.61 Br md 7.50 Dpth 3.36 Welded, 1 dk	**(B11B2FV) Fishing Vessel** Compartments: 3 Ho, ER 4 Ha: 2 (1.3 x 1.3)2 (1.3 x 1.0)ER	**1 oil engine** driving 1 FP propeller Total Power: 809kW (1,100hp) 10.5kn Niigata 6L28X 1 x 4 Stroke 6 Cy. 280 x 440 809kW (1100bhp) Niigata Engineering Co Ltd-Japan AuxGen: 1 x 200kW 220V a.c, 1 x 176kW 220V a.c
6828583 *BVMD* -	**SHEH HONG No. 7** *ex* Eastuna *-1969* **Sheh Hong Fishery Co Ltd** - *Kaohsiung* *Chinese Taipei*	*289* 151 98	Class: (CR)	**1968 Taiwan Machinery Manufacturing Corp. — Kaohsiung** Loa 40.19 Br ex 7.37 Dght 2.845 Lbp 35.01 Br md 7.09 Dpth 3.20 Welded, 1 dk	**(B11A2FS) Stern Trawler** Ins: 240 Compartments: 3 Ho, ER 3 Ha: (1.9 x 1.6)2 (1.3 x 0.9)ER Derricks: 2x1t; Winches: 2	**1 oil engine** driving 1 FP propeller Total Power: 552kW (750hp) 12.5kn Niigata 1 x 4 Stroke 6 Cy. 280 x 440 552kW (750bhp) Niigata Engineering Co Ltd-Japan AuxGen: 2 x 64kW 230V a.c
7110842 *BVAS* -	**SHEH HONG No. 11** **Sheh Hong Fishery Co Ltd** - *Kaohsiung* *Chinese Taipei*	*269* 189 -	Class: (CR)	**1972 Fong Kuo Shipbuilding Co Ltd — Kaohsiung** Loa 39.22 Br ex 6.94 Dght 2.750 Lbp 33.99 Br md 6.91 Dpth 3.15 Welded, 1 dk	**(B11A2FS) Stern Trawler** Ins: 255 Compartments: 3 Ho, ER 4 Ha: 2 (1.0 x 1.0)2 (1.2 x 1.0)ER Derricks: 1x1t	**1 oil engine** driving 1 FP propeller Total Power: 478kW (650hp) 10.5kn Hanshin 6L26ASH 1 x 4 Stroke 6 Cy. 260 x 400 478kW (650bhp) Hanshin Nainenki Kogyo-Japan AuxGen: 2 x 80kW 230V a.c
7613557 *BYJU* -	**SHEH YING No. 3** **Sheh Ying Marine Products Co Ltd** - *Kaohsiung* *Chinese Taipei* Official number: 5376	*359* 189 -	Class: (CR)	**1974 Taiwan Machinery Manufacturing Corp. — Kaohsiung** Loa 43.59 Br ex 7.57 Dght 3.041 Lbp 38.61 Br md 7.50 Dpth 3.36 Welded, 1 dk	**(B11B2FV) Fishing Vessel** Ins: 384 Compartments: 3 Ho, ER 4 Ha: 2 (1.3 x 1.0)2 (1.3 x 1.3)ER	**1 oil engine** driving 1 FP propeller Total Power: 809kW (1,100hp) 10.5kn Niigata 6L28X 1 x 4 Stroke 6 Cy. 280 x 440 809kW (1100bhp) Niigata Engineering Co Ltd-Japan AuxGen: 1 x 200kW 240V, 1 x 176kW 240V
9481764 *9BRP* -	**SHEHAB 2** *ex* Xing Long Zhou 215 *-2007* **Seyyed Ahmad Pourmatouri & Masoud Khayatzade** Control Pardaz Co Ltd *Khorramshahr* *Iran* Official number: 20685	**445** 272 965	Class: AS	**2007-12 Wenling Henghe Shiprepair & Building Yard — Wenling ZJ** Loa 52.80 Br ex - Dght 3.450 Lbp 48.00 Br md 8.80 Dpth 4.80 Welded, 1 dk	**(A31A2GX) General Cargo Ship**	**1 oil engine** driving 1 Propeller Total Power: 218kW (296hp) Chinese Std. Type 1 x 4 Stroke 218kW (296bhp) Zibo Diesel Engine Factory-China
9512240 *EPAC3* -	**SHEHAB 3** *launched as* Xing Long Zhou 225 *-2009* *ex* Wengling Henghe *-2009* **Seyyed Ahmad Pourmatouri** Control Pardaz Co Ltd *Khorramshahr* *Iran* MMSI: 422083000 Official number: 20711	**498** 279 965	Class: AS	**2008-04 Wenling Henghe Shiprepair & Building Yard — Wenling ZJ** Loa 52.80 Br ex - Dght 3.450 Lbp 48.00 Br md 8.80 Dpth 4.08 Welded, 1 dk	**(A31A2GX) General Cargo Ship**	**1 oil engine** driving 1 Propeller Total Power: 218kW (296hp) 9.0kn Chinese Std. Type 1 x 4 Stroke 218kW (296bhp) Zibo Diesel Engine Factory-China
8316364 *3ERV5* -	**SHEHAB ALMUHIEDDINE** *ex* Paris Texas *-2008* *ex* Alegre I *-2004* *ex* Sanko Spruce *-1999* **Seapower Shipping Co Ltd** Judi Group JKM *Panama* *Panama* MMSI: 370178000 Official number: 3465109A	**15,786** 9,209 26,523 T/cm 37.6	Class: NK	**1985-07 KK Kanasashi Zosen — Toyohashi AI** Yd No: 3064 Loa 167.20 (BB) Br ex - Dght 9.541 Lbp 160.00 Br md 26.01 Dpth 13.31 Welded, 1 dk	**(A21A2BC) Bulk Carrier** Grain: 33,867; Bale: 32,650 Compartments: 5 Ho, ER 5 Ha: (13.8 x 13.0)4 (19.2 x 13.0)ER Cranes: 4x25t	**1 oil engine** driving 1 FP propeller Total Power: 4,314kW (5,865hp) 14.0kn B&W 6L50MCE 1 x 2 Stroke 6 Cy. 500 x 1620 4314kW (5865bhp) Mitsui Engineering & Shipbuilding CLtd-Japan AuxGen: 3 x 360kW 450V 60Hz a.c Fuel: 127.0 (d.f.) (Heating Coils) 1254.5 (r.f.) 20.0pd
7738046 *CNCF* -	**SHEHERAZADE** *ex* Kometa-37 *-1973* **Transports Touristiques Intercontinentaux SA (TRANSTOUR)** - *Tangier* *Morocco*	*136* 88 46	Class: (BV) (GL) (RS)	**1972 Feodosiyskoye Sudostroitelnoye Obyedineniye "More" — Feodosiya** Yd No: S-37 Loa 35.11 Br ex 11.00 Dght 3.601 Lbp 30.00 Br md 6.00 Dpth 1.81 Welded, 1 dk	**(A37B2PS) Passenger Ship** Hull Material: Aluminium Alloy Passengers: unberthed: 116	**2 oil engines** driving 2 FP propellers Total Power: 1,324kW (1,800hp) 30.0kn Zvezda M401 2 x Vee 4 Stroke 12 Cy. 180 x 200 each-662kW (900bhp) "Zvezda"-Leningrad
9208643 - - -	**SHEHZORE** *ex* Sanmar VII *-2000* **Karachi Port Trust** - *Karachi* *Pakistan*	**224** 72 -	Class: (AB)	**1999-09 Sahin Celik Sanayi A.S. — Tuzla** Yd No: 26 Loa 25.25 Br ex - Dght 3.000 Lbp 23.19 Br md 8.60 Dpth 4.00 Welded, 1 dk	**(B32A2ST) Tug**	**2 oil engines** reduction geared to sc. shafts driving 2 FP propellers Total Power: 2,126kW (2,890hp) 10.0kn Caterpillar 3512TA 2 x Vee 4 Stroke 12 Cy. 170 x 190 each-1063kW (1445bhp) Caterpillar Inc-USA AuxGen: 2 x 60kW 380V 50Hz a.c Fuel: 68.0 (d.f.) 8.0pd
7819254 - - -	**SHEIKH BASHIR** **Government of The Democratic Republic of Somalia** - *Mogadiscio* *Somalia*	*121* 62 103		**1979-12 Brodogradiliste Greben — Vela Luka** Yd No: 809 Loa 23.19 Br ex 7.07 Dght 3.571 Lbp 21.21 Br md 6.85 Dpth 3.71 Bonded, 1 dk	**(B11A2FS) Stern Trawler** Hull Material: Reinforced Plastic	**1 oil engine** with clutches, flexible couplings & sr reverse geared to sc. shaft driving 1 FP propeller Total Power: 265kW (360hp) Caterpillar 3408PCTA 1 x Vee 4 Stroke 8 Cy. 137 x 152 265kW (360bhp) Caterpillar Tractor Co-USA AuxGen: 1 x 20kW 231/400V 50Hz a.c
7701201 *H02549* -	**SHEIKHA II** *ex* Chuan Yi *-2000* *ex* Golden Petroleum *-1995* *ex* Ozu Maru No. 2 *-1991* **Blue Bird Shipping Co SA** Khorkalba Marine Services LLC *Panama* *Panama* Official number: 29797PEXT	**759** 434 1,200 T/cm 5.2	Class: (BV)	**1977-07 Kurinoura Dockyard Co Ltd — Yawatahama EH** Yd No: 119 Loa 61.35 Br ex - Dght 4.050 Lbp 57.03 Br md 10.51 Dpth 4.63 Welded, 1 dk	**(A13B2TP) Products Tanker** Liq: 2,000; Liq (Oil): 2,000 Compartments: 8 Ta 2 Cargo Pump (s): 2x400m³/hr	**1 oil engine** driving 1 FP propeller Total Power: 956kW (1,300hp) 11.1kn Hanshin 6LU32 1 x 4 Stroke 6 Cy. 320 x 510 956kW (1300bhp) Hanshin Nainenki Kogyo-Japan AuxGen: 2 x 44kW 225V 60Hz a.c
7742396 *WYA2267* -	**SHEILA** *ex* Cape Kennedy *-2001* **Sheila Inc** - *Brownsville, TX* *United States of America* Official number: 591885	*106* 72 -		**1978 J & S Marine Services, Inc. — Brazoria, Tx** Yd No: 17 L reg 20.06 Br ex 6.43 Dght - Lbp - Br md - Dpth 3.46 Welded, 1 dk	**(B11A2FT) Trawler**	**1 oil engine** geared to sc. shaft driving 1 FP propeller Total Power: 268kW (364hp) Cummins KT-1150-M 1 x 4 Stroke 6 Cy. 159 x 159 268kW (364bhp) Cummins Engine Co Inc-USA
9138094 *C6FD2* -	**SHEILA ANN** **Hull 2227 Shipping Ltd** CSL Americas *Nassau* *Bahamas* MMSI: 308717000 Official number: 731928	**41,428** 19,174 70,037	Class: NV	**1999-10 Jiangnan Shipyard (Group) Co Ltd — Shanghai** Yd No: H2227 Loa 224.90 (BB) Br ex 32.19 Dght 14.420 Lbp 214.99 Br md 32.18 Dpth 19.51 Welded, 1 dk	**(A23A2BD) Bulk Carrier, Self-discharging** Grain: 66,503 Compartments: 7 Ho, ER 8 Ha: 2 (12.3 x 5.8) (12.3 x 16.0)5 (14.8 x 16.0)ER	**1 oil engine** driving 1 FP propeller Total Power: 10,784kW (14,662hp) 15.0kn MAN-B&W 6S60MC 1 x 2 Stroke 6 Cy. 600 x 2292 10784kW (14662bhp) Dalian Marine Diesel Works-China AuxGen: 2 x 1200kW a.c, 2 x 625kW a.c Thrusters: 1 Thwart. FP thruster (f) Fuel: 320.0 (d.f.) 1700.0 (r.f.)

7420417 *WYN6274* -	**SHEILA MORAN** - **Moran Towing Corp** - *Wilmington, DE* *United States of America* MMSI: 366939810 Official number: 569710	*295* 200 -	Class: AB	**1975**-12 **McDermott Shipyards Inc — Morgan City LA** Yd No: 212 Loa - Br ex 10.37 Dght 4.282 Lbp 36.56 Br md 10.32 Dpth 4.91 Welded, 1 dk	**(B32A2ST) Tug**	**2 oil engines** reverse reduction geared to sc. shafts driving 2 FP propellers Total Power: 3,162kW (4,300hp) 12.0kn EMD (Electro-Motive) 12-645-E6 2 x Vee 2 Stroke 12 Cy. 230 x 254 each-1581kW (2150bhp) General Motors Corp-USA AuxGen: 2 x 75kW Fuel: 406.5 (d.f.)
7933464 *WDC8925* -	**SHEILA RENE** *ex* Gina K *-2005* *ex* Master Mike *-2001* *ex* Daddy's Girl *-2001* **Oyster Creek Seafood Inc** - *Wanchese, NC* *United States of America* MMSI: 367095140 Official number: 606114	*129* 87 -		**1979 Bayou Marine Builders, Inc. — Bayou La Batre, Al** Yd No: 3 L reg 23.69 Br ex 6.76 Dght - Lbp - Br md - Dpth 3.54 Welded, 1 dk	**(B11A2FT) Trawler**	**1 oil engine** geared to sc. shaft driving 1 FP propeller Total Power: 346kW (470hp) Cummins KTA-1150-M 1 x 4 Stroke 6 Cy. 159 x 159 346kW (470bhp) Cummins Engine Co Inc-USA
7707035 *9GYA* -	**SHEKETEH** - **State Fishing Corp** - *Takoradi* *Ghana* Official number: 316619	*1,296* 569 1,038	Class: (LR) ✠ Classed LR until 2/90	**1978**-12 **Soc. Esercizio Cant. S.p.A. — Viareggio** Yd No: 621 Loa 73.21 (BB) Br ex 12.02 Dght 5.014 Lbp 62.79 Br md 12.01 Dpth 7.90 Welded	**(B11A2FS) Stern Trawler** Ins: 1,221	**1 oil engine** sr geared to sc. shaft driving 1 CP propeller Total Power: 2,207kW (3,001hp) 14.5kn Deutz SBV6M540 1 x 4 Stroke 6 Cy. 370 x 400 2207kW (3001bhp) Kloeckner Humboldt Deutz AG-West Germany AuxGen: 3 x 440kW 380V 50Hz a.c, 1 x 64kW 380V 50Hz a.c
7722877 *5NKF2* -	**SHEKINAH** *ex* Alia *-2009* *ex* Petro Merit *-1998* *ex* Sentosa *-1992* *ex* Shosei Maru *-1986* **Pokat Nigeria Ltd** - *Lagos* *Nigeria* MMSI: 657419000 Official number: 377762	**3,334** 1,514 4,995 T/cm 13.5	Class: (NK) (BV)	**1978**-03 **Shimoda Dockyard Co. Ltd. — Shimoda** Yd No: 281 Loa 105.20 Br ex 15.52 Dght 6.261 Lbp 98.02 Br md 15.51 Dpth 7.83 Welded, 1 dk	**(A13A2TW) Crude/Oil Products Tanker** Double Bottom Entire Compartment Length Liq: 5,401; Liq (Oil): 5,511 Cargo Heating Coils Compartments: 10 Ta, ER 2 Cargo Pump (s): 2x500m³/hr Manifold: Bow/CM: 52m	**1 oil engine** driving 1 FP propeller Total Power: 3,825kW (5,200hp) 14.0kn Ito M556HUS 1 x 4 Stroke 6 Cy. 550 x 900 3825kW (5200bhp) Ito Tekkosho-Japan AuxGen: 2 x 240kW 445V 60Hz a.c Thrusters: 1 Tunnel thruster (f) Fuel: 67.0 (d.f.) (Part Heating Coils) 295.0 (r.f.) 15.0pd
7738357 *WYC4705* -	**SHEKINAH GLORY** *ex* Haley Clark *-1986* *ex* My Girl Shirl *-1986* **Goose Creek Trawlers Inc** - *New Orleans, LA* *United States of America* Official number: 588410	*156* 106 -		**1977 Gulf Coast Marine Builders, Inc. — Bayou La Batre, Al** L reg 23.75 Br ex 7.32 Dght - Lbp - Br md - Dpth 3.69 Welded, 1 dk	**(B11A2FT) Trawler**	**1 oil engine** driving 1 FP propeller Total Power: 331kW (450hp) Caterpillar 3412T 1 x Vee 4 Stroke 12 Cy. 137 x 152 331kW (450bhp) Caterpillar Tractor Co-USA
9138927 *VRAQ7* -	**SHEKOU SEA** *ex* Topyield *-1998* **First Link Shipping Ltd** COSCO (HK) Shipping Co Ltd *Hong Kong* *Hong Kong* MMSI: 477840400 Official number: HK-1451	**37,846** 23,677 72,394 T/cm 66.9	Class: CC (NK)	**1996**-12 **Sasebo Heavy Industries Co. Ltd. — Sasebo Yard, Sasebo** Yd No: 417 Loa 225.00 Br ex - Dght 13.521 Lbp 218.00 Br md 32.20 Dpth 18.70 Welded, 1 dk	**(A21A2BC) Bulk Carrier** Grain: 84,790 Compartments: 7 Ho, ER 7 Ha: (15.3 x 12.8)6 (17.0 x 14.4)ER	**1 oil engine** driving 1 FP propeller Total Power: 8,827kW (12,001hp) 14.5kn B&W 6S60MC 1 x 2 Stroke 6 Cy. 600 x 2292 8827kW (12001bhp) Mitsui Engineering & Shipbuilding CLtd-Japan AuxGen: 3 x 400kW 450V a.c
8876572 *9HA3032* -	**SHEKSNA** - **Donna Shipping Co Ltd** Aspol-Baltic Corp Ltd (Kontsern Aspol-Baltik) *Valletta* *Malta* MMSI: 229058000 Official number: 8876572	**2,052** 943 2,769	Class: RS	**1994**-07 **Gdanska Stocznia 'Remontowa' SA — Gdansk** Yd No: TS82/01 Loa 82.40 Br ex 12.70 Dght 4.950 Lbp 79.00 Br md 12.50 Dpth 6.50 Welded, 1 dk	**(A31A2GX) General Cargo Ship** Grain: 3,240 TEU 126 C. 126/20' Compartments: 1 Ho, ER 1 Ha: (50.7 x 10.6)ER	**1 oil engine** geared to sc. shaft driving 1 FP propeller Total Power: 1,700kW (2,311hp) 12.0kn Wartsila 12V22 1 x Vee 4 Stroke 12 Cy. 220 x 240 1700kW (2311bhp) Wartsila Diesel Oy-Finland AuxGen: 2 x 209kW a.c Fuel: 172.0 (d.f.)
9069475 *WCV6157* -	**SHELBY** *ex* Bill Hinton *-2000* *ex* Chad F. Hebert *-1990* **Weeks Marine Inc** - *New York, NY* *United States of America* MMSI: 366939080 Official number: 593220	*131* 89 -		**1978**-01 **Houma Shipbuilding Co Inc — Houma LA** Yd No: 68 L reg 22.10 Br ex - Dght - Lbp - Br md 7.30 Dpth 3.05 Welded, 1 dk	**(B32A2ST) Tug**	**1 oil engine** driving 1 Propeller
8227082 *WAU8898* -	**SHELBY ANN** *ex* D. E. C. O. X *-1990* **Hard Bottom Fisheries Inc** - *Wakefield, RI* *United States of America* Official number: 602895	*115* 84 -		**1979 St Augustine Trawlers, Inc. — Saint Augustine, Fl** Loa 19.77 Br ex 6.71 Dght - Lbp - Br md - Dpth 3.13 Welded, 1 dk	**(B11B2FV) Fishing Vessel**	**1 oil engine** driving 1 FP propeller Total Power: 382kW (519hp) Caterpillar 3412TA 1 x Vee 4 Stroke 12 Cy. 137 x 152 382kW (519bhp) Caterpillar Tractor Co-USA
9485930 *D5BJ6* -	**SHELDUCK** *ex* As Elysia *-2014* **Sockeye Shipping Inc** Seastar Shipmanagement Ltd *Monrovia* *Liberia* MMSI: 636015534 Official number: 15534	**23,443** 11,526 34,467	Class: NK (GL) (AB)	**2012**-03 **SPP Shipbuilding Co Ltd — Tongyeong** Yd No: H4044 Loa 180.00 (BB) Br ex - Dght 9.900 Lbp 172.00 Br md 30.00 Dpth 14.70 Welded, 1 dk	**(A21A2BC) Bulk Carrier** Single Hull Grain: 48,766; Bale: 46,815 Compartments: 5 Ho, ER 5 Ha: ER Cranes: 4x35t	**1 oil engine** driving 1 FP propeller Total Power: 7,900kW (10,741hp) 14.0kn MAN-B&W 5S50MC-C 1 x 2 Stroke 5 Cy. 500 x 2000 7900kW (10741bhp) Doosan Engine Co Ltd-South Korea AuxGen: 3 x 600kW a.c Fuel: 190.0 (d.f.) 1700.0 (r.f.)
7730094 *USJP* -	**SHELF** *ex* RS-300 No. 100 *-2002* **M N Muravlenko** - *Kerch* *Ukraine* Official number: 770688	**171** 51 88	Class: (RS)	**1977**-11 **Astrakhanskaya Sudoverf im. "Kirova" — Astrakhan** Yd No: 100 Loa 34.02 Br ex 7.09 Dght 2.901 Lbp 30.00 Br md - Dpth 3.66 Welded, 1 dk	**(B11B2FV) Fishing Vessel** Ins: 78 Compartments: 1 Ho, ER 1 Ha: (1.6 x 1.3) Derricks: 2x2t; Winches: 2 Ice Capable	**1 oil engine** driving 1 FP propeller Total Power: 224kW (305hp) 9.0kn S.K.L. 8NVD36-1U 1 x 4 Stroke 8 Cy. 240 x 360 224kW (305bhp) VEB Schwermaschinenbau "KarlLiebknecht" (SKL)-Magdeburg AuxGen: 1 x 75kW a.c, 1 x 50kW a.c, 1 x 28kW a.c Fuel: 23.0 (d.f.)
7646839 *UAUP* -	**SHELF** - **PP Shirshov Institute of Oceanology** - *Kaliningrad* *Russia* MMSI: 273415400	**179** 53 38	Class: (RS)	**1977**-09 **Sretenskiy Sudostroitelnyy Zavod — Sretensk** Yd No: 6 Loa 33.96 Br ex 7.09 Dght 2.591 Lbp 30.00 Br md - Dpth 3.69 Welded, 1 dk	**(B31A2SR) Research Survey Vessel** Derricks: 2x2t Ice Capable	**1 oil engine** driving 1 FP propeller Total Power: 224kW (305hp) 9.0kn S.K.L. 8NVD36-1U 1 x 4 Stroke 8 Cy. 240 x 360 224kW (305bhp) VEB Schwermaschinenbau "KarlLiebknecht" (SKL)-Magdeburg Fuel: 12.0 (d.f.)
8727783 *UAMF* -	**SHELF** - **Kaliningrad Fishing Port Authority** - SatCom: Inmarsat M 627707310 *Kaliningrad* *Russia* MMSI: 273246400	**674** 202 561	Class: (RS)	**1986**-05 **Khabarovskiy Sudostroitelnyy Zavod im Kirova — Khabarovsk** Yd No: 504 Loa 54.90 Br ex 9.52 Dght 4.470 Lbp 50.27 Br md - Dpth 5.17 Welded, 1 dk	**(B34G2SE) Pollution Control Vessel** Ice Capable	**1 oil engine** driving 1 FP propeller Total Power: 588kW (799hp) 11.2kn S.K.L. 6NVD48A-2U 1 x 4 Stroke 6 Cy. 320 x 480 588kW (799bhp) VEB Schwermaschinenbau "KarlLiebknecht" (SKL)-Magdeburg AuxGen: 2 x 150kW a.c
8964599 *WDA6056* -	**SHELF ACHIEVER** *ex* Gulf Runner III *-2010* **Shelf Work Boats LLC** - *Chalmette, LA* *United States of America* MMSI: 366827210 Official number: 1050721	**250** 75 -		**1997**-11 **Breaux Brothers Enterprises, Inc. — Loreauville, La** Yd No: 1242 Loa - Br ex - Dght - Lbp 36.80 Br md 8.26 Dpth 3.52 Welded, 1 dk	**(B21A2OC) Crew/Supply Vessel**	**4 oil engines** driving 4 FP propellers Total Power: 2,976kW (4,048hp)
8521531 *OUZN2* -	**SHELF EXPRESS** - **A1Offshore ApS** JMB Bjerrum & Jensen ApS *Fredericia* *Denmark (DIS)* MMSI: 219433000 Official number: D4595	**1,423** 427 1,550	Class: NV	**1986**-11 **B.V. Scheepswerf Damen Bergum — Bergum** Yd No: 4454 Loa 61.62 Br ex 14.30 Dght 4.611 Lbp 56.04 Br md 14.00 Dpth 5.90 Welded, 1 dk	**(B21A2OS) Platform Supply Ship**	**2 oil engines** with flexible couplings & sr gearedto sc. shafts driving 2 CP propellers Total Power: 3,162kW (4,300hp) 13.0kn Deutz SBV8M628 2 x 4 Stroke 8 Cy. 240 x 280 each-1581kW (2150bhp) Kloeckner Humboldt Deutz AG-West Germany AuxGen: 2 x 580kW 440V 60Hz a.c, 1 x 275kW 440V 60Hz a.c Thrusters: 1 Thwart. CP thruster (f); 1 Thwart. CP thruster (a)
8415421 - -	**SHELFORD** *ex* Tensho Maru No. 18 *-2007* **Intergrated Team Ltd** -	*499* - 1,198		**1984**-11 **Uchida Zosen — Ise** Yd No: 832 Loa - Br ex - Dght 4.001 Lbp 58.53 Br md 10.01 Dpth 4.53 Welded, 1 dk	**(B34E2SY) Effluent carrier** Liq: 1,161 Compartments: 4 Ta, ER	**1 oil engine** driving 1 CP propeller Total Power: 1,103kW (1,500hp) Akasaka A28 1 x 4 Stroke 6 Cy. 280 x 550 1103kW (1500bhp) Akasaka Tekkosho KK (Akasaka DieselLtd)-Japan

IMO / Call sign	Name / Owner	Tonnage	Class	Builder / Dimensions	Type	Machinery
7728637 - - -	**SHELIKHOV** *ex* Shelikof *-1994* *ex* State Hawk *-1994* - -	**454** 136 553	Class: (RS) (AB)	**1978-09 Blount Marine Corp. — Warren, RI** Yd No: 217 Converted From: Offshore Supply Ship-1978 Loa 45.70 Br ex 10.93 Dght 2.920 Lbp 41.92 Br md 10.69 Dpth 3.69 Welded, 1 dk	**(B11B2FV) Fishing Vessel**	**2 oil engines** reverse reduction geared to sc. shafts driving 2 FP propellers Total Power: 1,030kW (1,400hp) 11.0kn G.M. (Detroit Diesel) 12V-149 2 x Vee 2 Stroke 12 Cy. 146 x 146 each-515kW (700bhp) General Motors Detroit DieselAllison Divn-USA AuxGen: 2 x 75kW Thrusters: 1 Thwart. FP thruster (f)
7049196 *WX9276* -	**SHELL KEYS** *ex* Zapata Shell Keys *-1979* *ex* Argosy *-1979* **Omega Protein Inc** - *New Orleans, LA* *United States of America* MMSI: 366986170 Official number: 298792	*520* 353		**1965 Burton Shipyard Co., Inc. — Port Arthur, Tx** Yd No: 378 L reg 49.93 Br ex 10.11 Dght - Lbp - Br md - Dpth 3.56 Welded, 1 dk	**(B11B2FV) Fishing Vessel**	**1 oil engine** driving 1 FP propeller Total Power: 1,125kW (1,530hp)
8912792 *3EUV9* -	**SHELLEY EXPRESS** *ex* Arctic Sea *-2011* *ex* Jogaila *-2005* *ex* Torm Senegal *-2000* *ex* Alrai *-1998* *ex* Zim Venezuela *-1998* *ex* Okhotskoe *-1996* **Amber Express Cargo Inc** International Management Co *Panama* *Panama* MMSI: 373452000 Official number: 42703PEXT	**3,988** 1,618 4,706	Class: (LR) (RS) (GL) Classed LR until 11/4/05	**1991-12 Sedef Gemi Endustrisi A.S. — Gebze** Yd No: 84 Loa 97.80 Br ex 17.33 Dght 6.010 Lbp 90.00 Br md 17.30 Dpth 7.00 Welded, 1 dk	**(A31A2GX) General Cargo Ship** Grain: 5,242; Bale: 5,227 TEU 221 C Ho 111 TEU C Dk 110 TEU incl 12 ref C. Compartments: 2 Ho, ER 2 Ha: 2 (25.7 x 12.5)ER Cranes: 2x25t Ice Capable	**1 oil engine** driving 1 CP propeller Total Power: 3,360kW (4,568hp) 12.5kn B&W 6L35MC 1 x 2 Stroke 6 Cy. 350 x 1050 3360kW (4568bhp) H Cegielski Poznan SA-Poland AuxGen: 1 x 300kW 220/380V 50Hz a.c, 2 x 264kW 220/380V 50Hz a.c Thrusters: 1 Thwart. FP thruster (f) Fuel: 90.0 (d.f.) 275.0 (r.f.) 12.7pd
8960529 - -	**SHELLFISH** - - -	*214* - -	Class: (BV)	**1996 Societatea Comerciala Navol S.A. Oltenita — Oltenita** Yd No: 383 Loa 40.90 Br ex - Dght 1.600 Lbp 36.92 Br md 9.22 Dpth 2.82 Welded, 1 dk	**(B11B2FV) Fishing Vessel**	**2 oil engines** driving 2 FP propellers Total Power: 662kW (900hp) Caterpillar 2 x 4 Stroke each-331kW (450bhp) Caterpillar Inc-USA
7308774 *WDB7938* -	**SHELLFISH** **John A Dooley** SatCom: Inmarsat C 436627910 *San Francisco, CA* *United States of America* MMSI: 366950140 Official number: 506986	**196** 58 -		**1967 Pacific Fishermen, Inc. — Seattle, Wa** L reg 25.64 Br ex 7.93 Dght - Lbp - Br md - Dpth 3.08 Welded	**(B11B2FV) Fishing Vessel**	**1 oil engine** driving 1 FP propeller Total Power: 441kW (600hp)
9677868 *WDG4237* -	**SHELTER COVE** **Shelter Cove Alaska LLC** - *Cordova, AK* *United States of America* MMSI: 367534430 Official number: 1239174	**106** 85 -		**2012-06 in the United States of America** Yd No: 1 L reg 17.67 Br ex - Dght - Lbp - Br md 7.62 Dpth 3.35 Welded, 1 dk	**(B11B2FV) Fishing Vessel**	**1 oil engine** reduction geared to sc. shaft driving 1 Propeller
9198733 - -	**SHEMA** **Seri Mukali Sdn Bhd** -	**339** 101 300	Class: (LR) ✠ 28/6/02	**1999-12 Ironwoods Shipyard Sdn Bhd — Kuching** Yd No: 053 Loa 30.00 Br ex - Dght 4.200 Lbp 25.90 Br md 9.50 Dpth 5.00 Welded, 1 dk	**(B32A2ST) Tug**	**2 oil engines** reduction geared to sc. shafts driving 2 Directional propellers Total Power: 2,684kW (3,650hp) 10.0kn Yanmar 6Z280-EN 2 x 4 Stroke 6 Cy. 280 x 360 each-1342kW (1825bhp) Yanmar Diesel Engine Co Ltd-Japan
7324168 - -	**SHEMARA** **Pegasus Fishing Ltd** - *Lyttelton* *New Zealand* Official number: 349368	**133** 39 -	Class: (LR) Classed LR until 14/9/00	**1973-12 J R Hepworth & Co (Hull) Ltd — Hull** Yd No: 115 Loa 26.20 Br ex 6.87 Dght - Lbp 23.24 Br md 6.86 Dpth 3.66 Welded, 1 dk	**(B11B2FV) Fishing Vessel**	**1 oil engine** reverse reduction geared to sc. shaft driving 1 FP propeller Total Power: 469kW (638hp) Blackstone ESL6MK2 1 x 4 Stroke 6 Cy. 222 x 292 469kW (638bhp) Mirrlees Blackstone (Stamford)Ltd.-Stamford AuxGen: 1 x 135kW 440V 50Hz a.c, 1 x 25kW 440V 50Hz a.c
7904750 *OJ6077* -	**SHEMARA** *ex* Brendelen *-1997* **Holma Fisk KB** - *Dragsfjard* *Finland* MMSI: 230001770 Official number: 12424	**374** 125 -	Class: (BV)	**1980-06 Scheepswerf "De Amstel" B.V. — Ouderkerk a/d Amstel** Lengthened-1991 Lengthened-1986 Loa 38.05 Br ex 7.40 Dght 3.101 Lbp - Br md 7.31 Dpth 3.71 Welded, 1 dk	**(B11A2FS) Stern Trawler**	**1 oil engine** geared to sc. shaft driving 1 FP propeller Total Power: 827kW (1,124hp) 12.0kn Caterpillar D399SCAC 1 x Vee 4 Stroke 16 Cy. 159 x 203 827kW (1124bhp) Caterpillar Tractor Co-USA
8749717 *GMGZ* -	**SHEMARA** **Charles William Dunstone** - *London* *United Kingdom* Official number: 166799	**878** 480 -	Class: NV (Class contemplated) (LR) ✠ Classed LR until 1/75	**1938-07 John I Thornycroft & Co Ltd — Southampton** Yd No: 1175 Loa 61.38 Br ex - Dght - Lbp - Br md 9.23 Dpth 4.05 Welded, 1 dk	**(X11A2YP) Yacht**	**2 oil engines** driving 2 Propellers Total Power: 1,412kW (1,920hp) MaK 2 x each-706kW (960bhp) Atlas Werke AG-Bremen
9120889 *MVRR7* LH 65	**SHEMARAH II** **Moodie Fishing Co Ltd** Peterhead Fishermen Ltd *Leith* *United Kingdom* MMSI: 232007650 Official number: B14521	**301** 140 100		**1995-12 Campbeltown Shipyard Ltd. — Campbeltown** Yd No: 097 Loa 25.99 Br ex 8.50 Dght 4.500 Lbp 25.50 Br md - Dpth - Welded, 1 dk	**(B11A2FS) Stern Trawler**	**1 oil engine** geared to sc. shaft driving 1 FP propeller Total Power: 699kW (950hp) 10.5kn Cummins KTA-50-M 1 x Vee 4 Stroke 16 Cy. 159 x 159 699kW (950bhp) Cummins Engine Co Ltd-United Kingdom
8739401 *9BIR* -	**SHEMSHAD** **Fatemeh Dashti Nejad & Partners** - *Bandar Imam Khomeini* *Iran* Official number: 20503	**399** 272 1,000	Class: AS	**1974-01 in Iran** Loa 44.48 Br ex - Dght 3.460 Lbp - Br md 8.15 Dpth 4.22 Welded, 1 dk	**(A31A2GX) General Cargo Ship**	**3 oil engines** reduction geared to sc. shafts driving 3 FP propellers Total Power: 1,460kW (1,986hp) Caterpillar 1 x 4 Stroke 416kW (566bhp) (new engine 1974) Caterpillar Tractor Co-USA Cummins KTA-19-M4 2 x 4 Stroke 6 Cy. 159 x 159 each-522kW (710bhp) (new engine 1974) Cummins Engine Co Ltd-United Kingdom
8963533 *WDA3649* -	**SHEMYA** **Shemya Fisheries LLC** - *Kodiak, AK* *United States of America* MMSI: 366800680 Official number: 1104597	**174** 141 -		**2000 Fred Wahl Marine Construction Inc — Reedsport, Or** Yd No: 00-59-11 L reg 16.09 Br ex - Dght - Lbp - Br md 8.68 Dpth 4.05 Welded, 1 dk	**(B11B2FV) Fishing Vessel**	**1 oil engine** geared to sc. shaft driving 1 FP propeller Total Power: 449kW (610hp) Caterpillar 3412 1 x Vee 4 Stroke 12 Cy. 137 x 152 449kW (610bhp) Caterpillar Inc-USA
8877291 *BP3011* -	**SHEN AO No. 3** **CPC Corp Taiwan** - *Keelung* *Chinese Taipei* Official number: 12280	*389* 117 -	Class: CR	**1992-07 Taiwan Machinery Manufacturing Corp. — Kaohsiung** Loa 31.50 Br ex - Dght 2.750 Lbp - Br md 11.00 Dpth 4.20 Welded, 1 dk	**(B32A2ST) Tug**	**2 oil engines** driving 2 FP propellers Total Power: 2,560kW (3,480hp) Nohab 6R25 2 x 4 Stroke 6 Cy. 250 x 300 each-1280kW (1740bhp) Wartsila Diesel AB-Sweden AuxGen: 2 x 165kW 450V a.c
8877289 *BP3012* -	**SHEN AO No. 5** **CPC Corp Taiwan** - *Keelung* *Chinese Taipei* Official number: 12279	*389* 117 -	Class: CR	**1992-07 Taiwan Machinery Manufacturing Corp. — Kaohsiung** Loa 31.50 Br ex - Dght 2.750 Lbp - Br md 11.00 Dpth 4.20 Welded, 1 dk	**(B32A2ST) Tug**	**2 oil engines** driving 2 FP propellers Total Power: 2,560kW (3,480hp) Nohab 6R25 2 x 4 Stroke 6 Cy. 250 x 300 each-1280kW (1740bhp) Wartsila Diesel AB-Sweden AuxGen: 2 x 165kW 450V a.c
8746014 *BH3191* -	**SHEN FU** *ex* CHIN TANG NO. 1 *-2010* *ex* Yung Chin Fa No. 101 *-2010* **Shen Fu Fishery Co Ltd** - *Kaohsiung* *Chinese Taipei* Official number: 011482	**496** 197 -		**1989-05 in Chinese Taipei** Loa 44.95 Br ex 8.20 Dght 3.210 Lbp - Br md - Dpth - Welded, 1 dk	**(B11B2FV) Fishing Vessel**	**1 oil engine** driving 1 Propeller Sumiyoshi 1 x 4 Stroke Sumiyoshi Marine Diesel Co Ltd-Japan

IMO / Call sign	Name / Owner	Tonnage	Class	Builder / Dimensions	Type / Capacity	Machinery
8628523 *BZXD4* -	**SHEN GANG FA NO. 1** *ex* Hae Yang No. 1 *-2010* **Shengang Overseas Industrial Co Ltd** - *Shenzhen, Guangdong* *China* Official number: YQ000003	**576** 235 -		**1993-08 ShinA Shipbuilding Co Ltd — Tongyeong** Yd No: S930803 Loa 53.29 Br ex 8.70 Dght - Lbp 46.88 Br md - Dpth 3.75 Welded, 1 dk	**(B11B2FV) Fishing Vessel**	**1 oil engine** driving 1 Propeller Total Power: 882kW (1,199hp)
9583677 *VRID2* -	**SHEN HAI** **Shanghai LNG Shipping Co Ltd** China LNG Shipping (International) Co Ltd *Hong Kong* *Hong Kong* MMSI: 477413600 Official number: HK-3011	**98,068** 29,420 82,625	Class: AB CC	**2012-09 Hudong-Zhonghua Shipbuilding (Group) Co Ltd — Shanghai** Yd No: H1621A Loa 290.00 (BB) Br ex 43.38 Dght 11.430 Lbp 274.10 Br md 43.35 Dpth 26.25 Welded, 1 dk	**(A11A2TN) LNG Tanker** Double Hull Liq (Gas): 142,741 5 x Gas Tank (s); 4 membrane (36% Ni.stl) pri horizontal, ER 8 Cargo Pump (s): 8x1700m³/hr	**1 Steam Turb** reduction geared to sc. shaft driving 1 FP propeller Total Power: 27,300kW (37,117hp) 19.5kn Kawasaki UA-400 1 x steam Turb 27300kW (37117shp) Kawasaki Heavy Industries Ltd-Japan AuxGen: 2 x 1600kW 6600V a.c, 2 x 3200kW 6600V a.c Thrusters: 1 Tunnel thruster (f) Fuel: 307.0 (d.f.) 5601.0 (r.f.)
9063158 *BEMB3* -	**SHEN HE** *ex* Heng Ya *-2003* **Hua Zhong Shipping Group Ltd** Wuhan Datong Industry Co Ltd *Wuhan, Hubei* *China* MMSI: 412590480	**1,691** 1,043 2,232	Class: (CC)	**1993-12 Jiangxi Jiangzhou Shipyard — Ruichang JX** Yd No: A426 Loa 83.10 Br ex - Dght 4.500 Lbp 76.30 Br md 12.80 Dpth 5.90 Welded, 1 dk	**(A31A2GX) General Cargo Ship**	**1 oil engine** driving 1 FP propeller Total Power: 662kW (900hp) Chinese Std. Type 6350ZC 1 x 4 Stroke 6 Cy. 350 x 500 662kW (900bhp) Shanghai Diesel Engine Co Ltd-China
9321811 *BDZS* -	**SHEN HUA** **Shenhua Huanghua Harbour Administration Corp** - *Huanghua, Hebei* *China* MMSI: 412270580	**6,819** 2,045 6,348	Class: CC	**2004-10 Hudong-Zhonghua Shipbuilding (Group) Co Ltd — Shanghai** Yd No: H1325A Loa 113.80 (BB) Br ex - Dght 5.820 Lbp 105.00 Br md 22.00 Dpth 7.70 Welded, 1 dk	**(B33B2DT) Trailing Suction Hopper Dredger** Hopper: 5,000 Compartments: 1 Ho, ER 1 Ha: ER (46.2 x 14.8) Cranes: 1x17t Ice Capable	**2 oil engines** reduction geared to sc. shafts driving 2 CP propellers Total Power: 7,002kW (9,520hp) 14.3kn MAN-B&W 8L32/40 2 x 4 Stroke 8 Cy. 320 x 400 each-3501kW (4760bhp) MAN B&W Diesel AG-Augsburg AuxGen: 3 x 1225kW 400V 50Hz a.c Thrusters: 1 Tunnel thruster (f)
9651565 *BRRE* -	**SHEN HUA 501** **Shenhuazhonghai Shipping Co Ltd** SatCom: Inmarsat C 441406710 *Shanghai* *China* MMSI: 414067000	**29,152** 16,325 44,508	Class: ZC	**2011-12 Chengxi Shipyard Co Ltd — Jiangyin JS** Yd No: CX0409 Loa 189.99 (BB) Br ex - Dght 11.200 Lbp 185.00 Br md 32.26 Dpth 16.20 Welded, 1 dk	**(A21A2BC) Bulk Carrier** Grain: 59,000 Compartments: 5 Ho, ER 5 Ha: ER	**1 oil engine** driving 1 FP propeller Total Power: 8,280kW (11,257hp) 13.5kn MAN-B&W 6S50MC-C 1 x 2 Stroke 6 Cy. 500 x 2000 8280kW (11257bhp) Hudong Heavy Machinery Co Ltd-China AuxGen: 3 x 640kW Fuel: 70.0 (d.f.) 850.0 (r.f.)
9651577 *BRMA* -	**SHEN HUA 502** **Shenhuazhonghai Shipping Co Ltd** - SatCom: Inmarsat C 441224310 *China* MMSI: 412243000	**29,152** 16,325 43,376	Class: ZC (Class contemplated)	**2013-06 Chengxi Shipyard Co Ltd — Jiangyin JS** Yd No: CX0410 Loa 189.99 (BB) Br ex - Dght 11.200 Lbp 185.00 Br md 32.26 Dpth 16.20 Welded, 1 dk	**(A21A2BC) Bulk Carrier** Grain: 59,000 Compartments: 5 Ho, ER 5 Ha: ER	**1 oil engine** driving 1 FP propeller Total Power: 9,480kW (12,889hp) 13.5kn MAN-B&W 6S50MC-C 1 x 2 Stroke 6 Cy. 500 x 2000 9480kW (12889bhp)
9651589 *BRMB* -	**SHEN HUA 503** **Shenhuazhonghai Shipping Co Ltd** - SatCom: Inmarsat C 441253510 *Shanghai* *China* MMSI: 412535000	**29,152** 16,325 43,318	Class: ZC (Class contemplated)	**2013-08 Chengxi Shipyard Co Ltd — Jiangyin JS** Yd No: CX0411 Loa 189.99 (BB) Br ex - Dght 11.200 Lbp 182.36 Br md 32.26 Dpth 16.20 Welded, 1 dk	**(A21A2BC) Bulk Carrier** Grain: 59,000 Compartments: 5 Ho, ER 5 Ha: ER Ice Capable	**1 oil engine** driving 1 FP propeller Total Power: 7,440kW (10,115hp) 13.5kn MAN-B&W 6S50MC-C 1 x 2 Stroke 6 Cy. 500 x 2000 7440kW (10115bhp) Hudong Heavy Machinery Co Ltd-China AuxGen: 3 x a.c
9651591 *BRMC* -	**SHEN HUA 505** **Shenhuazhonghai Shipping Co Ltd** - *Shanghai* *China*	**29,152** 16,325 43,419	Class: CC	**2013-10 Chengxi Shipyard Co Ltd — Jiangyin JS** Yd No: CX0412 Loa 189.99 (BB) Br ex - Dght 10.500 Lbp 182.36 Br md 32.26 Dpth 16.20 Welded, 1 dk	**(A21A2BC) Bulk Carrier** Grain: 59,000 Compartments: 5 Ho, ER 5 Ha: ER Ice Capable	**1 oil engine** driving 1 FP propeller Total Power: 7,440kW (10,115hp) 13.5kn MAN-B&W 6S50MC-C 1 x 2 Stroke 6 Cy. 500 x 2000 7440kW (10115bhp) Hudong Heavy Machinery Co Ltd-China
9651606 *BRMD* -	**SHEN HUA 506** **Shenghua Management Ltd** - *Shanghai* *China*	**29,152** 16,325 43,336	Class: ZC (Class contemplated)	**2013-10 Chengxi Shipyard Co Ltd — Jiangyin JS** Yd No: CX0413 Loa 189.99 (BB) Br ex - Dght 11.200 Lbp 182.36 Br md 32.26 Dpth 16.20 Welded, 1 dk	**(A21A2BC) Bulk Carrier** Grain: 59,000 Compartments: 5 Ho, ER 5 Ha: ER	**1 oil engine** driving 1 FP propeller Total Power: 7,440kW (10,115hp) 13.5kn MAN-B&W 6S50MC-C 1 x 2 Stroke 6 Cy. 500 x 2000 7440kW (10115bhp) Hudong Heavy Machinery Co Ltd-China
9651618 *BRME* -	**SHEN HUA 508** **Shenghua Management Ltd** - *Shanghai* *China*	**29,152** 16,325 43,325	Class: ZC (Class contemplated)	**2013-10 Chengxi Shipyard Co Ltd — Jiangyin JS** Yd No: CX0414 Loa 189.99 (BB) Br ex - Dght 11.200 Lbp 182.36 Br md 32.26 Dpth 16.20 Welded, 1 dk	**(A21A2BC) Bulk Carrier** Grain: 59,000 Compartments: 5 Ho, ER 5 Ha: ER	**1 oil engine** driving 1 FP propeller Total Power: 7,440kW (10,115hp) 13.5kn MAN-B&W 6S50MC-C 1 x 2 Stroke 6 Cy. 500 x 2000 7440kW (10115bhp) Hudong Heavy Machinery Co Ltd-China
9731999 - -	**SHEN HUA 511** **Shenhuazhonghai Shipping Co Ltd** - *China*	**29,153** 16,325 46,207		**2013-12 Chengxi Shipyard Co Ltd — Jiangyin JS** Yd No: CX0421 Loa 189.99 Br ex - Dght 11.000 Lbp 182.36 Br md 32.26 Dpth 16.20 Welded, 1 dk	**(A21A2BC) Bulk Carrier**	**1 oil engine** driving 1 Propeller Total Power: 7,800kW (10,605hp) Hudong 1 x 2 Stroke 6 Cy. 500 x 2000 7800kW (10605bhp) Hudong Heavy Machinery Co Ltd-China
8306761 *BRMK* -	**SHEN HUA 511** *ex* Wan Run *-2013* *ex* Ming Cheng *-2009* **Dalian Port Wantong Logistics Co Ltd** - SatCom: Inmarsat C 441216242 *China* MMSI: 412079000	**9,683** 4,637 13,449	Class: (CC)	**1985 Dalian Shipyard Co Ltd — Dalian LN** Yd No: C120/4 Converted From: Container Ship (Fully Cellular)-2009 Loa 147.50 (BB) Br ex - Dght 8.190 Lbp 138.00 Br md 22.20 Dpth 10.90 Welded, 1 dk	**(A21A2BC) Bulk Carrier** Grain: 16,567; Bale: 15,999 Compartments: 4 Ho, ER 4 Ha: ER	**1 oil engine** driving 1 FP propeller Total Power: 5,502kW (7,481hp) 15.0kn B&W 5L55GB 1 x 2 Stroke 5 Cy. 550 x 1380 5502kW (7481bhp) Dalian Marine Diesel Works-China
7374008 *BRML* -	**SHEN HUA 512** *ex* Hua Mao *-2014* *ex* East Sunrise 6 *-2009* *ex* Hui Chang Hai *-2008* *ex* Hua Tong Hai *-1999* *ex* Vinstra *-1980* - - *China* MMSI: 412094000	**35,252** 22,894 64,444 T/cm 62.6	Class: (CC) (NV)	**1975-07 Mitsubishi Heavy Industries Ltd. — Kobe** Yd No: 1066 Loa 223.99 (BB) Br ex 31.83 Dght 13.348 Lbp 211.28 Br md 31.80 Dpth 18.35 Welded, 1 dk	**(A21A2BC) Bulk Carrier** Grain: 73,793 Compartments: 7 Ho, ER 7 Ha: (12.0 x 10.2)6 (14.4 x 13.5)ER	**1 oil engine** driving 1 FP propeller Total Power: 10,297kW (14,000hp) 11.0kn Sulzer 7RND76 1 x 2 Stroke 7 Cy. 760 x 1550 10297kW (14000bhp) Mitsubishi Heavy Industries Ltd-Japan AuxGen: 3 x 400kW 440V a.c Fuel: 3312.5 (r.f.) 46.5pd
9732008 - -	**SHEN HUA 512** **Shenhuazhonghai Shipping Co Ltd** - *China*	**29,153** 16,325 46,207		**2013-12 Chengxi Shipyard Co Ltd — Jiangyin JS** Yd No: CX0422 Loa 189.99 Br ex - Dght 11.000 Lbp 182.36 Br md 32.26 Dpth 16.20 Welded, 1 dk	**(A21A2BC) Bulk Carrier**	**1 oil engine** driving 1 Propeller Total Power: 7,800kW (10,605hp) Hudong 1 x 2 Stroke 6 Cy. 500 x 2000 7800kW (10605bhp) Hudong Heavy Machinery Co Ltd-China
9732010 - -	**SHEN HUA 513** **Shenhuazhonghai Shipping Co Ltd** - *China*	**29,153** 16,325 46,207		**2013-12 Chengxi Shipyard Co Ltd — Jiangyin JS** Yd No: CX0423 Loa 189.99 Br ex - Dght 11.000 Lbp 182.36 Br md 32.26 Dpth 16.20 Welded, 1 dk	**(A21A2BC) Bulk Carrier**	**1 oil engine** driving 1 Propeller Total Power: 7,800kW (10,605hp) Hudong 1 x 2 Stroke 6 Cy. 500 x 2000 7800kW (10605bhp) Hudong Heavy Machinery Co Ltd-China
9737620 *BRMN* -	**SHEN HUA 515** **Shenhuazhonghai Shipping Co Ltd** - *China* MMSI: 412164000	**29,153** 16,325 46,207	Class: CC	**2014-03 Chengxi Shipyard Co Ltd — Jiangyin JS** Yd No: CX0424 Loa 189.99 Br ex - Dght 11.000 Lbp 182.36 Br md 32.26 Dpth 16.20 Welded, 1 dk	**(A21A2BC) Bulk Carrier**	**1 oil engine** driving 1 Propeller Total Power: 7,800kW (10,605hp) Hudong 1 x 2 Stroke 6 Cy. 500 x 2000 7800kW (10605bhp) Hudong Heavy Machinery Co Ltd-China
9737632 *BRMO* -	**SHEN HUA 516** **Shenhuazhonghai Shipping Co Ltd** - *China* Official number: 412175000	**29,153** 16,325 46,207	Class: CC	**2014-04 Chengxi Shipyard Co Ltd — Jiangyin JS** Yd No: CX0425 Loa 189.99 Br ex - Dght 11.000 Lbp 182.36 Br md 32.26 Dpth 16.20 Welded, 1 dk	**(A21A2BC) Bulk Carrier**	**1 oil engine** driving 1 Propeller Total Power: 7,800kW (10,605hp) Hudong 1 x 2 Stroke 6 Cy. 500 x 2000 7800kW (10605bhp) Hudong Heavy Machinery Co Ltd-China

9639933 *BRRH* -	**SHEN HUA 521** **Shenhuazhonghai Shipping Co Ltd** - *Shanghai* China MMSI: 414078000	**29,152** 16,325 46,000	Class: ZC (Class contemplated) (CC)	**2012-03 China Shipping Industry (Jiangsu) Co Ltd — Jiangdu JS** Yd No: CIS46000-01 Loa 189.99 (BB) Br ex - Dght 10.700 Lbp 185.00 Br md 32.26 Dpth 16.20 Welded, 1 dk	**(A21A2BC) Bulk Carrier** Grain: 57,200 Compartments: 5 Ho, ER 5 Ha: ER	**1 oil engine** driving 1 FP propeller Total Power: 9,480kW (12,889hp) 13.0kn MAN-B&W 6S50MC-C 1 x 2 Stroke 6 Cy. 500 x 2000 9480kW (12889bhp)
9639945 *BRMF* -	**SHEN HUA 522** **Shenhuazhonghai Shipping Co Ltd** - *Shanghai* China	**29,152** 16,325 43,274	Class: CC	**2013-10 China Shipping Industry (Jiangsu) Co Ltd — Jiangdu JS** Yd No: CIS46000-02 Loa 189.99 (BB) Br ex - Dght 10.500 Lbp 185.00 Br md 32.26 Dpth 16.20 Welded, 1 dk	**(A21A2BC) Bulk Carrier** Grain: 57,200 Compartments: 5 Ho, ER 5 Ha: ER Ice Capable	**1 oil engine** driving 1 FP propeller Total Power: 7,440kW (10,115hp) 13.0kn MAN-B&W 6S50MC-C 1 x 2 Stroke 6 Cy. 500 x 2000 7440kW (10115bhp) Dalian Marine Diesel Co Ltd-China
9639957 *BRMG* -	**SHEN HUA 523** **Shenhuazhonghai Shipping Co Ltd** - *Shanghai* China MMSI: 412452000	**29,152** 16,325 46,000	Class: CC	**2013-08 China Shipping Industry (Jiangsu) Co Ltd — Jiangdu JS** Yd No: CIS46000-03 Loa 189.99 (BB) Br ex - Dght 10.700 Lbp 185.00 Br md 32.26 Dpth 16.20 Welded, 1 dk	**(A21A2BC) Bulk Carrier** Grain: 57,200 Compartments: 5 Ho, ER 5 Ha: ER	**1 oil engine** driving 1 FP propeller Total Power: 6,450kW (8,769hp) MAN-B&W 6S46MC-C 1 x 2 Stroke 6 Cy. 460 x 1932 6450kW (8769bhp)
9720548 *BRMH* -	**SHEN HUA 525** **Shenhuazhonghai Shipping Co Ltd** - *Shanghai* China	**29,152** 16,325 43,307		**2013-10 China Shipping Industry (Jiangsu) Co Ltd — Jiangdu JS** Yd No: CIS46000-06 Loa 189.99 Br ex - Dght 10.500 Lbp 185.00 Br md 32.26 Dpth 16.20 Welded, 1 dk	**(A21A2BC) Bulk Carrier** Compartments: 5 Ho, ER 5 Ha: ER	**1 oil engine** driving 1 FP propeller Total Power: 9,480kW (12,889hp) 13.0kn MAN-B&W 6S50MC-C 1 x 2 Stroke 6 Cy. 500 x 2000 9480kW (12889bhp) Dalian Marine Diesel Co Ltd-China
9604823 *BRMI* -	**SHEN HUA 526** **Shenhuazhonghai Shipping Co Ltd** - *Shanghai* China	**29,152** 16,325 43,307	Class: CC	**2013-09 China Shipping Industry (Jiangsu) Co Ltd — Jiangdu JS** Yd No: CIS46000-05 Loa 189.99 (BB) Br ex - Dght 10.700 Lbp 185.00 Br md 32.26 Dpth 16.20 Welded, 1 dk	**(A21A2BC) Bulk Carrier** Grain: 59,200 Compartments: 5 Ho, ER 5 Ha: ER Ice Capable	**1 oil engine** driving 1 FP propeller Total Power: 7,440kW (10,115hp) 13.0kn MAN-B&W 6S50ME-C8 1 x 2 Stroke 6 Cy. 500 x 2000 7440kW (10115bhp) Dalian Marine Diesel Co Ltd-China
9604330 *BRMJ* -	**SHEN HUA 528** **Shenhuazhonghai Shipping Co Ltd** - *Shanghai* China MMSI: 412566000	**29,152** 16,325 43,307		**2013-10 China Shipping Industry (Jiangsu) Co Ltd — Jiangdu JS** Yd No: CIS46000-04 Loa 189.99 (BB) Br ex - Dght 10.700 Lbp 185.00 Br md 32.26 Dpth 16.20 Welded, 1 dk	**(A21A2BC) Bulk Carrier** Grain: 59,200 Compartments: 5 Ho, ER 5 Ha: ER	**1 oil engine** driving 1 FP propeller Total Power: 9,480kW (12,889hp) 13.0kn MAN-B&W 6S50ME-C8 1 x 2 Stroke 6 Cy. 500 x 2000 9480kW (12889bhp)
9725940 *BRMQ* -	**SHEN HUA 531** **Shenhuazhonghai Shipping Co Ltd** - *Shanghai* China MMSI: 412997000	**29,141** 16,318 45,963	Class: CC	**2013-11 China Shipping Industry (Jiangsu) Co Ltd — Jiangdu JS** Yd No: CIS47700-01 Loa 189.99 Br ex - Dght 11.200 Lbp 185.00 Br md 32.26 Dpth 16.20 Welded, 1 dk	**(A21A2BC) Bulk Carrier** Grain: 57,200 Compartments: 5 Ho, ER 5 Ha: ER	**1 oil engine** driving 1 Propeller Total Power: 7,800kW (10,605hp) 13.0kn MAN-B&W 6S50ME-C8 1 x 2 Stroke 6 Cy. 500 x 2000 7800kW (10605bhp) Hudong Heavy Machinery Co Ltd-China
9725952 *BRMR* -	**SHEN HUA 532** **Shenhuazhonghai Shipping Co Ltd** - China MMSI: 412153000	**28,000** - 47,700		**2014-03 China Shipping Industry (Jiangsu) Co Ltd — Jiangdu JS** Yd No: CIS47700-02 Loa 189.99 Br ex - Dght 11.200 Lbp - Br md 32.26 Dpth 16.20 Welded, 1 dk	**(A21A2BC) Bulk Carrier** Grain: 57,200 Compartments: 5 Ho, ER 5 Ha: ER	**1 oil engine** driving 1 Propeller Total Power: 9,960kW (13,542hp) 13.0kn MAN-B&W 6S50ME-C8 1 x 2 Stroke 6 Cy. 500 x 2000 9960kW (13542bhp)
9662904 *BRLA* -	**SHEN HUA 801** **Shenhuazhonghai Shipping Co Ltd** China Shipping International Shipmanagement Co Ltd *Shanghai* China MMSI: 412084000	**40,943** 25,978 75,331 T/cm 68.2	Class: CC	**2013-10 Jiangnan Shipyard (Group) Co Ltd — Shanghai** Yd No: H2522 Loa 224.95 (BB) Br ex - Dght 14.000 Lbp 217.00 Br md 32.26 Dpth 19.60 Welded, 1 dk	**(A21A2BC) Bulk Carrier** Grain: 90,067 Compartments: 7 Ho, ER 7 Ha: 6 (15.5 x 14.4)ER (15.5 x 13.2)	**1 oil engine** driving 1 FP propeller Total Power: 8,833kW (12,009hp) 14.5kn MAN-B&W 5S60ME-C 1 x 2 Stroke 5 Cy. 600 x 2400 8833kW (12009bhp) Hudong Heavy Machinery Co Ltd-China AuxGen: 3 x 600kW 450V a.c
9662916 *BRLB* -	**SHEN HUA 802** **Shenhuazhonghai Shipping Co Ltd** China Shipping International Shipmanagement Co Ltd *Shanghai* China MMSI: 412056000	**40,943** 25,978 75,380 T/cm 68.2	Class: CC	**2013-10 Jiangnan Shipyard (Group) Co Ltd — Shanghai** Yd No: H2523 Loa 224.95 (BB) Br ex - Dght 14.000 Lbp 217.00 Br md 32.26 Dpth 19.60 Welded, 1 dk	**(A21A2BC) Bulk Carrier** Grain: 90,067 Compartments: 7 Ho, ER 7 Ha: 6 (15.5 x 14.4)ER (15.5 x 13.2)	**1 oil engine** driving 1 FP propeller Total Power: 8,833kW (12,009hp) 14.5kn MAN-B&W 5S60ME-C 1 x 2 Stroke 5 Cy. 600 x 2400 8833kW (12009bhp) Hudong Heavy Machinery Co Ltd-China AuxGen: 3 x 600kW 450V a.c
9662928 *BRLC* -	**SHEN HUA 803** **Shenhuazhonghai Shipping Co Ltd** - *Shanghai* China MMSI: 412149000	**40,913** 25,963 75,403 T/cm 68.2	Class: CC	**2013-11 Jiangnan Shipyard (Group) Co Ltd — Shanghai** Yd No: H2524 Loa 224.95 (BB) Br ex - Dght 14.000 Lbp 217.00 Br md 32.26 Dpth 19.60 Welded, 1 dk	**(A21A2BC) Bulk Carrier** Grain: 90,067 Compartments: 7 Ho, ER 7 Ha: 6 (15.5 x 14.4)ER (15.5 x 13.2)	**1 oil engine** driving 1 FP propeller Total Power: 8,833kW (12,009hp) 14.5kn MAN-B&W 5S60ME-C 1 x 2 Stroke 5 Cy. 600 x 2400 8833kW (12009bhp) Hudong Heavy Machinery Co Ltd-China AuxGen: 3 x 600kW 450V a.c
9663752 *BRLG* -	**SHEN HUA 811** **Shenhuazhonghai Shipping Co Ltd** - *Shanghai* China MMSI: 412158000	**42,203** 26,234 76,150	Class: CC	**2013-12 Shanhaiguan Shipbuilding Industry Co Ltd — Qinhuangdao HE** Yd No: BC760-05 Loa 225.00 (BB) Br ex - Dght 14.200 Lbp 219.00 Br md 32.26 Dpth 19.60 Welded, 1 dk	**(A21A2BC) Bulk Carrier** Grain: 92,000 Compartments: 7 Ho, ER 7 Ha: 6 (15.5 x 14.4)ER (14.6 x 13.2)	**1 oil engine** driving 1 FP propeller Total Power: 9,108kW (12,383hp) 14.5kn MAN-B&W 5S60ME-C8 1 x 2 Stroke 5 Cy. 600 x 2400 9108kW (12383bhp) Dalian Marine Diesel Co Ltd-China AuxGen: 3 x 600kW 450V a.c
9093749 *BDWW* -	**SHEN HUA TUO 1** **Shenhua Huanghua Harbour Administration Corp** - *Huanghua, Hebei* China	**383** 114 153	Class: CC	**2001-10 Penglai Bohai Shipyard Co Ltd — Penglai SD** Loa 34.80 Br ex - Dght 3.400 Lbp 30.53 Br md 9.80 Dpth 4.50 Welded, 1 dk	**(B32A2ST) Tug** Ice Capable	**2 oil engines** reduction geared to sc. shafts driving 2 Propellers Total Power: 2,942kW (4,000hp) Yanmar 6N260-EN 2 x 4 Stroke 6 Cy. 260 x 360 each-1471kW (2000bhp) Yanmar Diesel Engine Co Ltd-Japan AuxGen: 2 x 80kW 400V a.c
9093751 *BDWX* -	**SHEN HUA TUO 2** **Shenhua Huanghua Harbour Administration Corp** - *Huanghua, Hebei* China	**383** 114 150	Class: CC	**2001-10 Penglai Bohai Shipyard Co Ltd — Penglai SD** Loa 34.80 Br ex - Dght 3.400 Lbp 30.53 Br md 9.80 Dpth 4.50 Welded, 1 dk	**(B32A2ST) Tug** Ice Capable	**2 oil engines** reduction geared to sc. shafts driving 2 Propellers Total Power: 2,942kW (4,000hp) Yanmar 6N260-EN 2 x 4 Stroke 6 Cy. 260 x 360 each-1471kW (2000bhp) Yanmar Diesel Engine Co Ltd-Japan AuxGen: 2 x 80kW 400V a.c
9294410 *BDWY* -	**SHEN HUA TUO 3** **Shenhua Huanghua Harbour Administration Corp** - *Huanghua, Hebei* China	**359** 7 -	Class: CC	**2003-06 Penglai Bohai Shipyard Co Ltd — Penglai SD** Yd No: 02-24 Loa 40.00 Br ex - Dght 3.200 Lbp 35.50 Br md 9.30 Dpth 4.30 Welded, 1 dk	**(B32A2ST) Tug**	**2 oil engines** reduction geared to sc. shafts driving 2 Propellers Total Power: 2,648kW (3,600hp) Yanmar 8N21A-SN 2 x 4 Stroke 8 Cy. 210 x 290 each-1324kW (1800bhp) Yanmar Diesel Engine Co Ltd-Japan AuxGen: 2 x 80kW 400V a.c
9320879 *BDZP* -	**SHEN HUA TUO 5** **Shenhua Huanghua Harbour Administration Corp** - *Huanghua, Hebei* China	**417** 125 200	Class: CC	**2004-05 Jiangxi Jiangxin Shipyard — Hukou County JX** Loa 35.00 Br ex - Dght 3.300 Lbp 31.20 Br md 9.80 Dpth 4.50 Welded, 1 dk	**(B32A2ST) Tug** Ice Capable	**2 oil engines** reduction geared to sc. shafts driving 2 Propellers Total Power: 2,648kW (3,600hp) Yanmar 6N260M-EV 2 x 4 Stroke 6 Cy. 260 x 360 each-1324kW (1800bhp) Yanmar Diesel Engine Co Ltd-Japan AuxGen: 2 x 86kW 400V a.c
9320881 - -	**SHEN HUA TUO 6** **Shenhua Huanghua Harbour Administration Corp** - *Huanghua, Hebei* China	**417** 125 200	Class: CC	**2004-05 Jiangxi Jiangxin Shipyard — Hukou County JX** Loa 35.00 Br ex - Dght 3.300 Lbp 31.20 Br md 9.80 Dpth 4.50 Welded, 1 dk	**(B32A2ST) Tug** Ice Capable	**2 oil engines** reduction geared to sc. shafts driving 2 Propellers Total Power: 2,648kW (3,600hp) Yanmar 6N260M-EV 2 x 4 Stroke 6 Cy. 260 x 360 each-1324kW (1800bhp) Yanmar Diesel Engine Co Ltd-Japan AuxGen: 2 x 86kW 400V a.c

9320893 - -	**SHEN HUA TUO 7** **Shenhua Huanghua Harbour Administration Corp** - *Huanghua, Hebei* *China*	**417** 125 200	Class: CC	**2004-05 Jiangxi Jiangxin Shipyard — Hukou County JX** Loa 35.00 Br ex - Dght 3.300 Lbp 31.20 Br md 9.80 Dpth 4.50 Welded, 1 dk	**(B32A2ST) Tug** Ice Capable	**2 oil engines** reduction geared to sc. shafts driving 2 Propellers Total Power: 3,236kW (4,400hp) Yanmar 6N280M-SV 2 x 4 Stroke 6 Cy. 280 x 380 each-1618kW (2200bhp) Yanmar Diesel Engine Co Ltd-Japan AuxGen: 2 x 86kW 400V a.c
7402594 *BUVH* -	**SHEN JIANG HAI** *ex* Hui Long 7 *-2005* *ex* Dong Fang Yang *-2003* *ex* San Ya Wan *-1991* *ex* Lux Challenger *-1990* *ex* Fer Jamaica *-1987* **Shanghai Changjiang Shipping Corp** - SatCom: Inmarsat C 441280412 *Shanghai* *China* MMSI: 412079230	**9,208** 5,961 15,253 T/cm 24.0	Class: (LR) (CC) (BV) ✠ Classed LR until 21/1/88	**1978-02 EN Bazan de Construcciones Navales Militares SA — San Fernando (Sp)** Yd No: 189 Loa 144.99 (BB) Br ex 20.83 Dght 9.295 Lbp 140.83 Br md 20.52 Dpth 11.40 Welded, 1 dk	**(A21A2BC) Bulk Carrier** Grain: 20,855; Bale: 19,992 Compartments: 4 Ho, ER 4 Ha: 2 (17.0 x 11.5)2 (16.3 x 11.5)ER Derricks: 4x25t; Winches: 4 Ice Capable	**1 oil engine** geared to sc. shaft driving 1 FP propeller Total Power: 4,057kW (5,516hp) 14.8kn MAN 12V40/54A 1 x Vee 4 Stroke 12 Cy. 400 x 540 4057kW (5516bhp) EN Bazan de Construcciones NavalesMilitares SA-Spain AuxGen: 3 x 304kW 380V 50Hz a.c
8656623 *HP2918* -	**SHEN LI** *ex* Hai Guan Shan 168 *-2013* *ex* Huang Hao 128 *-2006* **Ye Cheng Co Ltd** - *Panama* *Panama* MMSI: 372863000 Official number: 4519413	**1,459** 796 2,400		**1988 Ningbo Beilun 2nd Shiprepair Yard — Ningbo ZJ** Loa 83.88 Br ex - Dght 5.100 Lbp - Br md 12.50 Dpth - Welded, 1 dk	**(A13B2TP) Products Tanker**	**1 oil engine** driving 1 Propeller Total Power: 735kW (999hp) 9.0kn Nippon Hatsudoki HS6NV238 1 x 4 Stroke 6 Cy. 380 x 580 735kW (999bhp) The Hanshin Diesel Works Ltd-Japan
8663195 *BZXC5* -	**SHEN LIAN CHENG 702** **Liancheng Overseas Fishery Co Ltd** - *Shekou, Guangdong* *China*	**112** 33 -		**1993-06 Zhoushan Putuo No 1 Shipyard — Zhoushan ZJ** Loa 25.50 Br ex - Dght - Lbp - Br md 5.40 Dpth 2.90 Welded, 1 dk	**(B11B2FV) Fishing Vessel**	**1 oil engine** driving 1 Propeller
8663080 *BZXC12* -	**SHEN LIAN CHENG 706** **Liancheng Overseas Fishery Co Ltd** - *Shekou, Guangdong* *China* Official number: YUE2005No.YQ000019	**105** 31 -		**1993-04 Qidong Fishing Vessel Shipyard — Qidong JS** Yd No: 8934650 Loa 27.17 Br ex - Dght - Lbp - Br md 5.60 Dpth 2.60 Welded, 1 dk	**(B11B2FV) Fishing Vessel**	**1 oil engine** driving 1 Propeller
8655617 *BZXC7* -	**SHEN LIAN CHENG 707** *ex* Fu Yuan Yu 386 *-2005* **Liancheng Overseas Fishery Co Ltd** - *Shekou, Guangdong* *China* MMSI: 412698170 Official number: YUE2005NOYQ000020	**105** 31 -		**1995-05 Nantong Fishing Vessel Yard — Nantong JS** Loa 27.17 Br ex 5.60 Dght - Lbp - Br md - Dpth 2.60 Welded, 1 dk	**(B11B2FV) Fishing Vessel**	**1 oil engine** driving 1 Propeller
8655629 *BZXC8* -	**SHEN LIAN CHENG 708** *ex* Fu Yuan Yu 387 *-1995* **Liancheng Overseas Fishery Co Ltd** - *Shekou, Guangdong* *China* MMSI: 412698180 Official number: YUE2005NOYQ000021	**105** 31 -		**1995-05 Nantong Fishing Vessel Yard — Nantong JS** Loa 27.17 Br ex - Dght - Lbp - Br md 5.60 Dpth 2.60 Welded, 1 dk	**(B11B2FV) Fishing Vessel**	**1 oil engine** driving 1 Propeller
8655447 *BZXC9* -	**SHEN LIAN CHENG 709** *ex* Fu Yuan Yu 382 *-2005* **Liancheng Overseas Fishery Co Ltd** - *Shekou, Guangdong* *China* MMSI: 412698190 Official number: YUE2005NOYQ000022	**105** 31 -		**1993-04 Qidong Fishing Vessel Shipyard — Qidong JS** Yd No: 8934650 Loa 27.17 Br ex - Dght - Lbp - Br md 5.60 Dpth 2.60 Welded, 1 dk	**(B11B2FV) Fishing Vessel**	**1 oil engine** driving 1 Propeller
8655344 *BZXC15* -	**SHEN LIAN CHENG 710** **Liancheng Overseas Fishery Co Ltd** - *Shekou, Guangdong* *China* MMSI: 412699440 Official number: YUE2005YQ000041	**117** 35 -		**2005-12 Fujian Guo'an Shipbuilding Industry Co Ltd — Longhai FJ** Yd No: 7652340 Loa 25.31 Br ex - Dght - Lbp - Br md 6.00 Dpth 2.70 Welded, 1 dk	**(B11B2FV) Fishing Vessel**	**1 oil engine** driving 1 Propeller
8655356 *BZXC16* -	**SHEN LIAN CHENG 711** **Liancheng Overseas Fishery Co Ltd** - *Shekou, Guangdong* *China* MMSI: 412699450 Official number: YUE2005YQ000044	**117** 35 -		**2005-12 Fujian Guo'an Shipbuilding Industry Co Ltd — Longhai FJ** Yd No: 7652655 Loa 25.31 Br ex - Dght - Lbp - Br md 6.00 Dpth 2.70 Welded, 1 dk	**(B11B2FV) Fishing Vessel**	**1 oil engine** driving 1 Propeller
8655368 *BZXC17* -	**SHEN LIAN CHENG 712** **Liancheng Overseas Fishery Co Ltd** - *Shekou, Guangdong* *China* MMSI: 412699460 Official number: YUE2005YQ000042	**117** 35 -		**2005-12 Fujian Guo'an Shipbuilding Industry Co Ltd — Longhai FJ** Yd No: 7652375 Loa 25.31 Br ex - Dght - Lbp - Br md 6.00 Dpth 2.70 Welded, 1 dk	**(B11B2FV) Fishing Vessel**	**1 oil engine** driving 1 Propeller
8655370 *BZXC18* -	**SHEN LIAN CHENG 713** **Liancheng Overseas Fishery Co Ltd** - *Shekou, Guangdong* *China* MMSI: 412699470 Official number: YUE2005YQ000043	**117** 35 -		**2005-12 Fujian Guo'an Shipbuilding Industry Co Ltd — Longhai FJ** Yd No: 7652863 Loa 25.31 Br ex - Dght - Lbp - Br md 6.00 Dpth 2.70 Welded, 1 dk	**(B11B2FV) Fishing Vessel**	**1 oil engine** driving 1 Propeller
8663171 *BZXC24* -	**SHEN LIAN CHENG 735** *ex* Fu Yuan Yu035 *-2013* **Liancheng Overseas Fishery Co Ltd** - *Shekou, Guangdong* *China* MMSI: 412699530	**107** 32 -		**1996-01 Fujian Changle Yingqian Haixing Shipbuilding Yard — Changle FJ** Loa 26.50 Br ex - Dght 2.100 Lbp - Br md 6.20 Dpth 2.65 Welded, 1 dk	**(B11B2FV) Fishing Vessel**	**1 oil engine** driving 1 Propeller
8663183 *BZXC25* -	**SHEN LIAN CHENG 736** *ex* Fu Yuan Yu036 *-2013* **Liancheng Overseas Fishery Co Ltd** - *Shekou, Guangdong* *China* MMSI: 412699540	**107** 32 -		**1996-01 Fujian Changle Yingqian Haixing Shipbuilding Yard — Changle FJ** Loa 26.50 Br ex - Dght - Lbp - Br md 6.20 Dpth 2.65 Welded, 1 dk	**(B11B2FV) Fishing Vessel**	**1 oil engine** driving 1 Propeller
8655631 *BZXC27* -	**SHEN LIAN CHENG 737** *ex* Fu Yuan Yu 037 *-2006* **Liancheng Overseas Fishery Co Ltd** - *Shekou, Guangdong* *China* Official number: YUE2006NOYD000007	**100** 30 -		**1996-04 in the People's Republic of China** Loa 26.50 Br ex - Dght - Lbp - Br md 6.20 Dpth 2.50 Welded, 1 dk	**(B11B2FV) Fishing Vessel**	**1 oil engine** driving 1 Propeller
8655643 - -	**SHEN LIAN CHENG 738** *ex* Fu Yuan Yu 038 *-2006* **Liancheng Overseas Fishery Co Ltd** - *Shekou, Guangdong* *China* Official number: YUE2006NOYQ000008	**100** 30 -		**1996-04 in the People's Republic of China** Loa 26.50 Br ex - Dght - Lbp - Br md 6.20 Dpth 2.50 Welded, 1 dk	**(B11B2FV) Fishing Vessel**	**1 oil engine** driving 1 Propeller

IMO / Call sign	Name / Owner	Tonnage	Class	Built	Type	Machinery
8655655 *BZXC28* -	**SHEN LIAN CHENG 739** *ex* Fu Yuan Yu 039 *-2006* **Liancheng Overseas Fishery Co Ltd** - *Shekou, Guangdong* *China* Official number: YUE2006NOYQ000009	**100** 30 -		**1996-04 in the People's Republic of China** Loa 26.50 Br ex - Dght - Lbp - Br md 6.20 Dpth 2.50 Welded, 1 dk	**(B11B2FV) Fishing Vessel**	**1 oil engine** driving 1 Propeller
8655150 *BZXC32* -	**SHEN LIAN CHENG 760** *ex* Fujian Guoan 7100501 *-2011* **Liancheng Overseas Fishery Co Ltd** - *Shekou, Guangdong* *China* MMSI: 412460054 Official number: YUE2011NO.YQ000005	**192** 57 -		**2011-03 Fujian Guo'an Shipbuilding Industry Co Ltd — Longhai FJ** Yd No: 7100501 Loa 34.40 Br ex - Dght - Lbp 30.24 Br md 6.60 Dpth 3.10 Welded, 1 dk	**(B11B2FV) Fishing Vessel**	**1 oil engine** driving 1 Propeller
8655162 *BZXC33* -	**SHEN LIAN CHENG 761** *ex* Fujian Guoan 7100502 *-2011* **Liancheng Overseas Fishery Co Ltd** - *Shekou, Guangdong* *China* MMSI: 412460055 Official number: YUE2011NO.YQ000006	**192** 57 -		**2011-03 Fujian Guo'an Shipbuilding Industry Co Ltd — Longhai FJ** Yd No: 7100502 Loa 34.40 Br ex - Dght - Lbp 30.24 Br md 6.60 Dpth 3.10 Welded, 1 dk	**(B11B2FV) Fishing Vessel**	**1 oil engine** driving 1 Propeller
8655435 *BZXD2* -	**SHEN LIAN CHENG 808** *ex* Zhen Long 339 *-2006* **Liancheng Overseas Fishery Co Ltd** - *Shekou, Guangdong* *China* Official number: YUE2006NOYQ000011	**123** 36 -		**1995-10 Zhanjiang Haibin Shipyard — Zhanjiang GD** Yd No: 7652875 Loa 26.50 Br ex - Dght - Lbp - Br md 6.00 Dpth 3.02 Welded, 1 dk	**(B11B2FV) Fishing Vessel**	**1 oil engine** driving 1 Propeller
8663133 *BZXD92* -	**SHEN LIAN CHENG 881** - **Liancheng Overseas Fishery Co Ltd** - *Shekou, Guangdong* *China*	**296** 141 -		**2013-04 Huanghai Shipbuilding Co Ltd — Rongcheng SD** Yd No: HC876-7 Loa 42.00 Br ex - Dght 3.000 Lbp 37.00 Br md 7.00 Dpth 3.80 Welded, 1 dk	**(B11B2FV) Fishing Vessel**	**1 oil engine** driving 1 Propeller
8663145 *BZXD93* -	**SHEN LIAN CHENG 882** - **Liancheng Overseas Fishery Co Ltd** - *Shekou, Guangdong* *China*	**296** 141 -		**2013-05 Huanghai Shipbuilding Co Ltd — Rongcheng SD** Yd No: HC876-8 Loa 42.00 Br ex - Dght 3.000 Lbp 37.00 Br md 7.00 Dpth 3.80 Welded, 1 dk	**(B11B2FV) Fishing Vessel**	**1 oil engine** driving 1 Propeller
8663157 *BZXD94* -	**SHEN LIAN CHENG 883** - **Liancheng Overseas Fishery Co Ltd** - *Shekou, Guangdong* *China*	**296** 141 -		**2013-05 Huanghai Shipbuilding Co Ltd — Rongcheng SD** Yd No: HC876-9 Loa 42.00 Br ex - Dght 3.000 Lbp 37.00 Br md 7.00 Dpth 3.80 Welded, 1 dk	**(B11B2FV) Fishing Vessel**	**1 oil engine** driving 1 Propeller
9718313 *BZXD95* -	**SHEN LIAN CHENG 884** - **Liancheng Overseas Fishery Co Ltd** - *Shekou, Guangdong* *China*	**296** 141 -		**2013-07 Huanghai Shipbuilding Co Ltd — Rongcheng SD** Yd No: HC876-10 Loa 38.15 Br ex - Dght 3.000 Lbp 37.00 Br md 7.00 Dpth 3.80 Welded, 1 dk	**(B11B2FV) Fishing Vessel**	**1 oil engine** reduction geared to sc. shaft driving 1 Propeller Chinese Std. Type
9718325 *BZXD96* -	**SHEN LIAN CHENG 885** - **Liancheng Overseas Fishery Co Ltd** - *Shekou, Guangdong* *China*	**296** 141 -		**2013-07 Huanghai Shipbuilding Co Ltd — Rongcheng SD** Yd No: HC876-11 Loa 38.15 Br ex - Dght 3.000 Lbp 37.00 Br md 7.00 Dpth 3.80 Welded, 1 dk	**(B11B2FV) Fishing Vessel**	**1 oil engine** reduction geared to sc. shaft driving 1 Propeller Chinese Std. Type
8663169 *BZXC6* -	**SHEN LIAN CHENG 901** - **Liancheng Overseas Fishery Co Ltd** - *Shekou, Guangdong* *China*	**102** 30 -		**2002-08 in the People's Republic of China** Loa 24.00 Br ex - Dght - Lbp - Br md 5.20 Dpth 2.20 Bonded, 1 dk	**(B11B2FV) Fishing Vessel** Hull Material: Reinforced Plastic	**1 oil engine** driving 1 Propeller
8103573 - -	**SHEN LONG** *ex* Teng Long *-2007* *ex* Sun Hope *-1987* *ex* Sky River *-1984* *ex* Tasman Queen *-1984* *ex* Tenmei *-1983* *ex* Ladybird *-1982* - *Shenzhen, Guangdong* *China* MMSI: 412461430	**3,128** 1,731 5,133	Class: (NK) (CC)	**1981-06 Hakata Zosen K.K. — Imabari** Yd No: 255 Loa 96.20 Br ex - Dght 6.200 Lbp 89.50 Br md 16.00 Dpth 7.50 Welded, 1 dk	**(A31A2GX) General Cargo Ship** Grain: 6,207; Bale: 5,616 Compartments: 2 Ho, ER 2 Ha: (18.8 x 8.4) (29.9 x 8.4)ER Derricks: 2x22t,1x15t; Winches: 3	**1 oil engine** driving 1 FP propeller Total Power: 2,354kW (3,200hp) 12.5kn Hanshin 6LUS46 1 x 4 Stroke 6 Cy. 460 x 740 2354kW (3200bhp) The Hanshin Diesel Works Ltd-Japan AuxGen: 2 x 132kW 445V 60Hz a.c Fuel: 483.0 (d.f.) 8.5pd
9230385 *BRUO* -	**SHEN NONG FENG** - **China Shipping Development Co Ltd Tramp Co** - *Guangzhou, Guangdong* *China* MMSI: 412518000	**39,894** 25,925 73,983 T/cm 64.0	Class: CC	**2002-08 Jiangnan Shipyard (Group) Co Ltd — Shanghai** Yd No: H2275 Loa 225.00 Br ex - Dght 14.000 Lbp 217.00 Br md 32.26 Dpth 19.20 Welded, 1 dk	**(A21A2BC) Bulk Carrier** Grain: 88,465; Bale: 86,173 Compartments: 7 Ho, ER 7 Ha: 6 (15.5 x 15.0)ER (15.5 x 13.2)	**1 oil engine** driving 1 FP propeller Total Power: 10,223kW (13,899hp) 14.7kn MAN-B&W 5S60MC 1 x 2 Stroke 5 Cy. 600 x 2292 10223kW (13899bhp) HHM Shangchuan Diesel Co Ltd-China AuxGen: 3 x 600kW 450V a.c
9648570 *BSIS* -	**SHEN QIAN HAO** *ex* Wuchang A215l *-2012* **Shanghai Salvage Co** - *Shanghai* *China* MMSI: 413046110	**10,140** 3,042 6,785	Class: CC	**2012-06 Qingdao Wuchuan Heavy Industry Co Ltd — Qingdao SD** Yd No: A215L Loa 125.70 (BB) Br ex - Dght 7.200 Lbp 108.80 Br md 25.00 Dpth 10.60 Welded, 1 dk	**(B22A20V) Diving Support Vessel** A-frames: 1x350t; Cranes: 1x140t Ice Capable	**4 diesel electric oil engines** driving 4 gen. each 3860kW 6600V Connecting to 2 elec. motors each (3500kW) driving 2 Azimuth electric drive units Total Power: 16,000kW (21,752hp) 14.5kn MAN-B&W 4 x each-4000kW (5438bhp) STX Engine Co Ltd-South Korea AuxGen: 1 x 1230kW a.c Thrusters: 1 Retract. directional thruster (f); 2 Tunnel thruster (f)
8814512 *BJTP* -	**SHEN TOU WAN** *ex* Saronikos Bridge *-2010* *ex* CMA CGM Makassar *-2007* *ex* Hanjin Felixstowe *-2003* - *Yangpu, Hainan* *China* MMSI: 413963000	**37,193** 15,205 44,044 T/cm 64.4	Class: CC (LR) (KR) (AB) Classed LR until 12/1/10	**1990-03 Samsung Shipbuilding & Heavy Industries Co Ltd — Geoje** Yd No: 1071 Loa 242.86 (BB) Br ex 32.27 Dght 11.717 Lbp 226.70 Br md 32.20 Dpth 19.00 Welded, 1 dk	**(A33A2CC) Container Ship (Fully Cellular)** TEU 2932 C Ho 1348 TEU C Dk 1584 TEU incl 153 ref C. Compartments: ER, 7 Cell Ho 14 Ha: 2 (13.0 x 8.1)2 (13.0 x 10.5)ER 10 (12.6 x 10.5) 24 Wing Ha: 2 (12.6 x 5.4)5 (13.0 x 8.0)17 (12.6 x 8.0)	**1 oil engine** driving 1 FP propeller Total Power: 23,170kW (31,502hp) 21.7kn Sulzer 7RTA84 1 x 2 Stroke 7 Cy. 840 x 2400 23170kW (31502bhp) Korea Heavy Industries & ConstrCo Ltd (HANJUNG)-South Korea AuxGen: 3 x 1000kW 450V 60Hz a.c Boilers: e (ex.g.) 7.0kgf/cm² (6.9bar), AuxB (o.f.) 9.0kgf/cm² (8.8bar) Thrusters: 1 Thwart. CP thruster (f)
9151644 *BXPZ* -	**SHEN XIAO ER HAO** - **Shenzhen Public Security Bureau, Fire Services Department** - *Shenzhen, Guangdong* *China* MMSI: 412461860 Official number: CN19966331351	**250** - 290		**1996-12 Greenbay Marine Pte Ltd — Singapore** Yd No: 116 Loa 36.00 Br ex - Dght 2.800 Lbp - Br md 7.80 Dpth 4.00 Welded, 1 dk	**(B32A2ST) Tug**	**2 oil engines** geared to sc. shafts driving 2 CP propellers Total Power: 2,236kW (3,040hp) Caterpillar 3512TA 2 x Vee 4 Stroke 12 Cy. 170 x 190 each-1118kW (1520bhp) Caterpillar Inc-USA
9151632 *BXPY* -	**SHEN XIAO YI HAO** - **Shenzhen Public Security Bureau, Fire Services Department** - *Shenzhen, Guangdong* *China* MMSI: 412461850 Official number: CN19969718935	**250** - 290		**1996-12 Greenbay Marine Pte Ltd — Singapore** Yd No: 115 Loa 36.00 Br ex - Dght 2.800 Lbp - Br md 7.80 Dpth 4.00 Welded, 1 dk	**(B32A2ST) Tug**	**2 oil engines** geared to sc. shafts driving 2 CP propellers Total Power: 2,236kW (3,040hp) Caterpillar 3512TA 2 x Vee 4 Stroke 12 Cy. 170 x 190 each-1118kW (1520bhp) Caterpillar Inc-USA

Number	Name / Owner	Tonnage	Class	Builder / Dimensions	Type	Machinery
8405359 *T3MC2* -	**SHEN YOU 12** *ex* Nan Yang No. 1 *-2014* *ex* Nissei Maru No. 21 *-1991* **PT Hengtat Samudra Bahari** - *Tarawa* *Kiribati* Official number: K-17841472	**1,335** 747 1,850	Class: CC (NK)	**1984-06 Sasaki Shipbuilding Co Ltd — Osakikamijima HS** Yd No: 380 Loa 79.58 Br ex - Dght 5.001 Lbp 74.02 Br md 12.01 Dpth 5.52 Welded, 1 dk	**(A13B2TP) Products Tanker** Liq: 2,300; Liq (Oil): 2,300 Compartments: 10 Ta, ER	**1 oil engine** driving 1 CP propeller Total Power: 1,589kW (2,160hp) 12.5kn Hanshin 6EL35 1 x 4 Stroke 6 Cy. 350 x 700 1589kW (2160bhp) The Hanshin Diesel Works Ltd-Japan AuxGen: 1 x 144kW 445V 60Hz a.c, 1 x 120kW 445V 60Hz a.c Fuel: 43.5 (d.f.) 78.5 (r.f.) 7.0pd
6928151 *BVI* -	**SHEN YU No. 12** - **San Yu Fishing Co Ltd** - *Kaohsiung* *Chinese Taipei*	*252* 99 -		**1969 Fong Kuo Shipbuilding Co Ltd — Kaohsiung** Yd No: 144 Loa 36.43 Br ex 6.53 Dght - Lbp 31.98 Br md 6.51 Dpth 2.95 Welded, 1 dk	**(B11B2FV) Fishing Vessel**	**1 oil engine** driving 1 FP propeller Total Power: 405kW (551hp) Hanshin 1 x 4 Stroke 405kW (551bhp) Hanshin Nainenki Kogyo-Japan
8660818 - -	**SHEN YUAN 2** - **Zhejiang Shen Yuan Marine Engineering Co Ltd** - *Zhoushan, Zhejiang* *China* Official number: 070310000222	**990** 554 1,399	Class: ZC (Class contemplated)	**2010-05 Ningbo Dajiang Shipbuilding Co Ltd — Xiangshan County ZJ** Yd No: DJ-0907 Loa 57.25 Br ex - Dght 3.200 Lbp 54.00 Br md 12.80 Dpth 4.30 Welded, 1 dk	**(A31A2GX) General Cargo Ship**	**2 oil engines** driving 2 Propellers Total Power: 660kW (898hp) Chinese Std. Type 2 x each-330kW (449bhp) Zibo Diesel Engine Factory-China
8660806 - -	**SHEN YUAN 8** - **Zhejiang Shen Yuan Marine Engineering Co Ltd** - *Zhoushan, Zhejiang* *China* Official number: 070310000221	**990** 554 1,399	Class: ZC (Class contemplated)	**2010-05 Ningbo Dajiang Shipbuilding Co Ltd — Xiangshan County ZJ** Yd No: DJ-0906 Loa 57.25 Br ex - Dght - Lbp 54.00 Br md 12.80 Dpth 4.30 Welded, 1 dk	**(A31A2GX) General Cargo Ship**	**2 oil engines** driving 2 Propellers Total Power: 660kW (898hp) Chinese Std. Type 2 x each-330kW (449bhp) Zibo Diesel Engine Factory-China
8897069 *BKRJ5* -	**SHEN YUAN 18** *ex* KAI TUO 3 *-2011* **Zhejiang Sunyun Offshore Engineering Co Ltd** - SatCom: Inmarsat C 441200690 *Zhoushan, Zhejiang* *China* MMSI: 413439290	**1,478** 443 1,900	Class: CC	**1993-01 Shanghai Zhenhua Port Machinery Co Ltd — Jiangyin JS** Loa 66.70 Br ex - Dght 3.600 Lbp 64.00 Br md 14.20 Dpth 4.80 Welded, 1 dk	**(B34A2SH) Hopper, Motor** Grain: 1,000	**2 oil engines** geared to sc. shafts driving 2 FP propellers Total Power: 778kW (1,058hp) 7.5kn Cummins KTA-19-M2 2 x 4 Stroke 6 Cy. 159 x 159 each-389kW (529bhp) Cummins Engine Co Inc-USA AuxGen: 3 x 64kW 400V a.c
8830358 - -	**SHEN ZHEN CHUN** - **Shenzhen Pengxing Shipping Co Ltd** - *Shenzhen, Guangdong* *China* MMSI: 412462480	**117** 35 20	Class: (CC)	**1985 Afai Engineers & Shiprepairers Ltd — Hong Kong** Loa 21.99 Br ex - Dght 1.650 Lbp 19.28 Br md 8.71 Dpth 2.72 Welded, 1 dk	**(A37B2PS) Passenger Ship**	**2 oil engines** driving 2 FP propellers Total Power: 1,294kW (1,760hp) 27.0kn Isotta Fraschini ID36SS8V 2 x Vee 4 Stroke 8 Cy. 170 x 170 each-647kW (880bhp) Isotta Fraschini SpA-Italy AuxGen: 2 x 40kW 380V a.c
9572862 *VRLY5* -	**SHEN ZHEN WAN** *ex* Hang Zhou Wan *-2013* *launched as* Captain Giorgis *-2012* **Braving Wind Shipping Co Ltd** Wealth China Shipping (HK) Ltd *Hong Kong* *Hong Kong* MMSI: 477608500 Official number: HK-3803	**4,126** 1,717 5,869 T/cm 15.9	Class: BV	**2012-04 Zhejiang Tianshi Shipbuilding Co Ltd — Wenling ZJ** Yd No: TY2 Loa 112.10 Br ex - Dght 6.000 Lbp 105.50 Br md 16.20 Dpth 8.00 Welded, 1 dk	**(A13C2LA) Asphalt/Bitumen Tanker** Double Hull (13F) Liq: 5,880; Liq (Oil): 6,001 Compartments: 5 Wing Ta, 5 Wing Ta, ER Ice Capable	**1 oil engine** reduction geared to sc. shaft driving 1 FP propeller Total Power: 2,465kW (3,351hp) 12.5kn Daihatsu 8DKM-28 1 x 4 Stroke 8 Cy. 280 x 390 2465kW (3351bhp) Shaanxi Diesel Heavy Industry Co Lt-China AuxGen: 3 x 200kW 50Hz a.c Fuel: 473.6
9624524 - -	**SHEN ZHOU 1** *ex* Zhong Fu Bo 1 *-2011* - -	**1,292** 388 -		**2011-01 in the People's Republic of China** Yd No: HG-1022 Loa 63.00 Br ex 16.20 Dght 2.850 Lbp 58.50 Br md 16.00 Dpth 3.80 Welded, 1 dk	**(A31A2GA) General Cargo Ship (with Ro-Ro facility)** Bow door/ramp (centre)	**2 oil engines** reduction geared to sc. shafts driving 2 Propellers Total Power: 522kW (710hp) 10.0kn Cummins 2 x 4 Stroke each-261kW (355bhp) Chongqing Cummins Engine Co Ltd-China
9622538 - -	**SHEN ZHOU 3** *ex* Zhong Fu Bo 3 *-2011* - -	**1,292** 338 -		**2011-01 Fujian Honggang Shipping Industry Co Ltd — Fu'an FJ** Yd No: HG-1020 Loa 63.00 Br ex 16.20 Dght 2.850 Lbp 58.50 Br md 16.00 Dpth 3.80 Welded, 1 dk	**(A35D2RL) Landing Craft**	**2 oil engines** reduction geared to sc. shafts driving 2 Propellers Total Power: 1,044kW (1,420hp) 10.0kn Cummins KTA-19-M4 2 x 4 Stroke 6 Cy. 159 x 159 each-522kW (710bhp) Chongqing Cummins Engine Co Ltd-China
9622526 - -	**SHEN ZHOU 8** *ex* Zhong Fu Bo 8 *-2011* - -	**1,800** 630 -		**2011-01 Fujian Honggang Shipping Industry Co Ltd — Fu'an FJ** Yd No: HG-1021 Loa 76.00 Br ex 16.20 Dght 3.150 Lbp 71.40 Br md 16.00 Dpth 4.30 Welded, 1 dk	**(A35D2RL) Landing Craft**	**2 oil engines** reduction geared to sc. shafts driving 2 Propellers Total Power: 1,044kW (1,420hp) 10.0kn Cummins KTA-19-M4 2 x 4 Stroke 6 Cy. 159 x 159 each-522kW (710bhp) Chongqing Cummins Engine Co Ltd-China
9629689 - -	**SHEN ZHOU 9** *completed as* Mei Shen 9 *-2011* - -	**1,464** 439 -		**2011-05 Fujian Honggang Shipping Industry Co Ltd — Fu'an FJ** Yd No: HG-1024 Loa 76.00 Br ex 16.20 Dght 3.150 Lbp 71.40 Br md 16.00 Dpth 4.30 Welded, 1 dk	**(A35D2RL) Landing Craft** Bow ramp (centre)	**2 oil engines** reduction geared to sc. shafts driving 2 Propellers Total Power: 1,044kW (1,420hp) 9.0kn Cummins KTA-19-M4 2 x 4 Stroke 6 Cy. 159 x 159 each-522kW (710bhp) Chongqing Cummins Engine Co Ltd-China
8654584 - -	**SHEN ZHOU 98** *ex* Xiang Ning Xiang Ji 0198 *-2012* - -	**2,143** 1,200 -		**2007-07 Chongqing Xiangli Shipbuilding Co Ltd — Chongqing** Loa 90.10 Br ex - Dght - Lbp - Br md 16.20 Dpth 4.30 Welded, 1 dk	**(A31A2GX) General Cargo Ship**	**1 oil engine** driving 1 Propeller 13.0kn
9711963 - -	**SHEN ZHOU 3501** - **Chongqing New Jinhang Shipping Co Ltd** - *Chongqing* *China*	**3,659** 2,049 4,500	Class: ZC	**2013-02 Chongqing Dongfeng Ship Industry Co — Chongqing** Loa 100.02 Br ex - Dght 5.000 Lbp 94.60 Br md 17.20 Dpth 6.00 Welded, 1 dk	**(A12A2TC) Chemical Tanker** Double Hull (13F)	**1 oil engine** reduction geared to sc. shaft driving 1 Propeller Total Power: 662kW (900hp) Chinese Std. Type 6210ZLC 1 x 4 Stroke 6 Cy. 210 x 300 662kW (900bhp) Ningbo CSI Power & Machinery GroupCo Ltd-China
9711987 - -	**SHEN ZHOU 3502** - **Chongqing New Jinhang Shipping Co Ltd** - *Chongqing* *China*	**3,659** 2,049 4,500	Class: ZC	**2013-05 Chongqing Dongfeng Ship Industry Co — Chongqing** Loa 100.02 Br ex - Dght 5.000 Lbp 94.60 Br md 17.20 Dpth 6.00 Welded, 1 dk	**(A12A2TC) Chemical Tanker** Double Hull (13F)	**1 oil engine** reduction geared to sc. shaft driving 1 Propeller Total Power: 662kW (900hp) Chinese Std. Type 6210ZLC 1 x 4 Stroke 6 Cy. 210 x 300 662kW (900bhp) Ningbo CSI Power & Machinery GroupCo Ltd-China
9711975 - -	**SHEN ZHOU 3505** - **Chongqing New Jinhang Shipping Co Ltd** - *Chongqing* *China*	**3,659** 2,049 4,500	Class: ZC	**2013-08 Chongqing Dongfeng Ship Industry Co — Chongqing** Loa 100.02 Br ex - Dght 5.000 Lbp 94.60 Br md 17.20 Dpth 6.00 Welded, 1 dk	**(A12A2TC) Chemical Tanker** Double Hull (13F)	**1 oil engine** reduction geared to sc.shaft driving 1 Propeller Total Power: 662kW (900hp) Chinese Std. Type 6210ZLC 1 x 4 Stroke 6 Cy. 210 x 300 662kW (900bhp) Ningbo CSI Power & Machinery GroupCo Ltd-China
9711999 - -	**SHEN ZHOU 3509** - **Chongqing New Jinhang Shipping Co Ltd** - *Chongqing* *China*	**3,659** 2,049 4,500	Class: ZC	**2013-03 Chongqing Donggang Marine Industry Co Ltd — Chongqing** Loa 100.02 Br ex - Dght 5.000 Lbp 94.60 Br md 17.20 Dpth 6.00 Welded, 1 dk	**(A12A2TC) Chemical Tanker** Double Hull (13F)	**1 oil engine** reduction geared to sc. shaft driving 1 Propeller Total Power: 662kW (900hp) Chinese Std. Type 6210ZLC 1 x 4 Stroke 6 Cy. 210 x 300 662kW (900bhp) Ningbo CSI Power & Machinery GroupCo Ltd-China
9712008 - -	**SHEN ZHOU 3512** - **Chongqing New Jinhang Shipping Co Ltd** - *Chongqing* *China*	**3,659** 2,049 4,500	Class: ZC	**2013-05 Chongqing Donggang Marine Industry Co Ltd — Chongqing** Loa 100.02 Br ex - Dght 5.000 Lbp 94.60 Br md 17.20 Dpth 6.00 Welded, 1 dk	**(A12A2TC) Chemical Tanker** Double Hull (13F)	**1 oil engine** reduction geared to sc. shaft driving 1 Propeller Total Power: 662kW (900hp) Chinese Std. Type 6210ZLC 1 x 4 Stroke 6 Cy. 210 x 300 662kW (900bhp) Ningbo CSI Power & Machinery GroupCo Ltd-China
9712010 - -	**SHEN ZHOU 3515** - **Chongqing New Jinhang Shipping Co Ltd** - *Chongqing* *China*	**3,659** 2,049 4,500	Class: ZC	**2013-04 Chongqing Donggang Marine Industry Co Ltd — Chongqing** Loa 100.02 Br ex - Dght 5.000 Lbp 94.60 Br md 17.20 Dpth 6.00 Welded, 1 dk	**(A12A2TC) Chemical Tanker** Double Hull (13F)	**1 oil engine** reduction geared to sc. shaft driving 1 Propeller Total Power: 662kW (900hp) Chinese Std. Type 6210ZLC 1 x 4 Stroke 6 Cy. 210 x 300 662kW (900bhp) Ningbo CSI Power & Machinery GroupCo Ltd-China
9712022 - -	**SHEN ZHOU 3516** - **Chongqing New Jinhang Shipping Co Ltd** - *Chongqing* *China*	**3,659** 2,049 4,500	Class: ZC	**2013-09 Chongqing Donggang Marine Industry Co Ltd — Chongqing** Loa 100.02 Br ex - Dght 5.000 Lbp 94.60 Br md 17.20 Dpth 6.00 Welded, 1 dk	**(A12A2TC) Chemical Tanker** Double Hull (13F)	**1 oil engine** reduction geared to sc. shaft driving 1 Propeller Total Power: 662kW (900hp) Chinese Std. Type 6210ZLC 1 x 4 Stroke 6 Cy. 210 x 300 662kW (900bhp) Ningbo CSI Power & Machinery GroupCo Ltd-China

9712034 - -	**SHEN ZHOU 3518** - **Chongqing New Jinhang Shipping Co Ltd** - *Chongqing* *China*	**3,659** 2,049 4,500	Class: ZC	**2013-09 Chongqing Donggang Marine Industry Co Ltd — Chongqing** Loa 100.02 Br ex - Dght 5.000 Lbp 94.60 Br md 17.20 Dpth 6.00 Welded, 1 dk	**(A12A2TC) Chemical Tanker** Double Hull (13F)	**1 oil engine** reduction geared to sc. shaft driving 1 Propeller Total Power: 662kW (900hp) Chinese Std. Type 6210ZLC 1 x 4 Stroke 6 Cy. 210 x 300 662kW (900bhp) Ningbo CSI Power & Machinery GroupCo Ltd-China
8828848 *BBLX5* -	**SHENG AN** *ex Hao Min -2009 ex Mu Dan Xiang -2006* *ex Hong Qi 177 -1999* **Weihai Sheng An Shipping Co Ltd** *Weihai, Shandong* *China* MMSI: 413322740	**4,119** 1,769 5,207	Class: (CC)	**1985-07 Wuchang Shipyard — Wuhan HB** Loa 105.32 Br ex - Dght 6.500 Lbp 98.99 Br md 16.00 Dpth 9.00 Welded, 2 dks	**(A31A2GX) General Cargo Ship** Grain: 7,655; Bale: 7,041 Compartments: 3 Ho, ER 3 Ha: (10.5 x 8.0) (16.8 x 8.0) (12.6 x 8.0)ER Derricks: 1x10t,3x5t	**1 oil engine** driving 1 FP propeller Total Power: 2,207kW (3,001hp) 13.0kn Hudong 6ESDZ43/82B 1 x 2 Stroke 6 Cy. 430 x 820 2207kW (3001bhp) Hudong Shipyard-China AuxGen: 3 x 250kW 400V a.c
9485318 *BMUQ* -	**SHENG AN DA 12** **Qinzhou Guiqin Shipping Group Co Ltd** SatCom: Inmarsat C 441300180 *Qinzhou, Guangxi* *China* MMSI: 413501960	**2,989** 1,500 4,082	Class: CC	**2008-03 Yamen Shipyard Ltd — Jiangmen GD** Yd No: YM06-001 Loa 93.80 Br ex - Dght 5.600 Lbp 86.80 Br md 15.60 Dpth 7.50 Welded, 1 dk	**(A31A2GX) General Cargo Ship** Grain: 5,579 TEU 230 Compartments: 2 Ho, ER 2 Ha: ER 2 (25.8 x 12.4)	**1 oil engine** reduction geared to sc. shaft driving 1 Propeller Total Power: 2,000kW (2,719hp) 11.0kn Chinese Std. Type G8300ZC 1 x 4 Stroke 8 Cy. 300 x 380 2000kW (2719bhp) (made 2007) Ningbo CSI Power & Machinery GroupCo Ltd-China AuxGen: 2 x 120kW 400V a.c
9204283 *BMKS* -	**SHENG AN DA 19** *ex En An -2010 ex Min Tai No. 7 -2005* **Qinzhou Guiqin Shipping Group Co Ltd** SatCom: Inmarsat C 441219361 *Quanzhou, Fujian* *China* MMSI: 412502520	**1,598** 837 2,393	Class: CC	**1998-07 Fujian Southeast Shipyard — Fuzhou FJ** Loa 79.80 Br ex 13.03 Dght 4.200 Lbp 74.80 Br md 13.00 Dpth 5.40 Welded, 1 dk	**(A33A2CC) Container Ship (Fully Cellular)** Grain: 2,724 TEU 150 Compartments: 2 Cell Ho, ER 2 Ha: (27.0 x 10.1) (25.2 x 10.1)ER	**1 oil engine** reduction geared to sc. shaft driving 1 FP propeller Total Power: 736kW (1,001hp) 11.0kn Chinese Std. Type 6230ZC 1 x 4 Stroke 6 Cy. 230 x 300 736kW (1001bhp) Guangzhou Diesel Engine Factory CoLtd-China AuxGen: 2 x 75kW 400V a.c
9586930 *BMVR* -	**SHENG AN DA 69** *launched as Hai Xiang Xing -2011* **Qinzhou Guiqin Shipping Group Co Ltd** - SatCom: Inmarsat C 441219768 *Quanzhou, Fujian* *China* MMSI: 412502890	**19,996** 11,341 32,906	Class: CC	**2011-06 No 4807 Shipyard of PLA — Fu'an FJ** Yd No: 30000T 1# Loa 178.00 (BB) Br ex 27.96 Dght 9.600 Lbp 170.80 Br md 27.60 Dpth 13.90 Welded, 1 dk	**(A21A2BC) Bulk Carrier** Grain: 40,768 Compartments: 5 Ho, ER 5 Ha: 4 (19.5 x 14.7)ER (13.9 x 14.7) Cranes: 4x30t	**1 oil engine** driving 1 FP propeller Total Power: 5,220kW (7,097hp) 11.2kn MAN-B&W 6S35ME-B9 1 x 2 Stroke 6 Cy. 350 x 1550 5220kW (7097bhp) Yichang Marine Diesel Engine Co Ltd-China AuxGen: 3 x 440kW 400V a.c
9590486 *BMXS* -	**SHENG AN DA 99** *ex Jin Cheng Zhou 118 -2013* *ex Tian Long 18 -2011 ex Tian Long 8 -2011* **Qinzhou Guiqin Shipping Group Co Ltd** - *Taizhou, Zhejiang* *China* MMSI: 412503190	**15,953** 7,738 23,294	Class: CC (BV)	**2010-07 Taizhou Yuanyang Shipbuilding Co Ltd — Linhai ZJ** Yd No: CYC07-01 Loa 159.88 Br ex - Dght 9.800 Lbp 149.80 Br md 24.40 Dpth 14.00 Welded, 1 dk	**(A21A2BC) Bulk Carrier** Grain: 30,355 Compartments: 4 Ho, ER 4 Ha: 2 (21.0 x 15.0) (21.0 x 13.0)ER (12.0 x 15.0) Cranes: 3x30t Ice Capable	**1 oil engine** driving 1 FP propeller Total Power: 5,180kW (7,043hp) 13.2kn MAN-B&W 7S35MC 1 x 2 Stroke 7 Cy. 350 x 1400 5180kW (7043bhp) STX Engine Co Ltd-South Korea AuxGen: 3 x 465kW 450V a.c
9505467 *BRNI* -	**SHENG AN HAI** **China Shipping Haisheng Co Ltd** - *Haikou, Hainan* *China* MMSI: 414727000	**32,976** 19,142 56,564 T/cm 58.8	Class: CC	**2012-11 Guangzhou Huangpu Shipbuilding Co Ltd — Guangzhou GD** Yd No: 2301 Loa 189.99 (BB) Br ex - Dght 12.500 Lbp 185.00 Br md 32.26 Dpth 18.00 Welded, 1 dk	**(A21A2BC) Bulk Carrier** Grain: 71,634; Bale: 68,200 Compartments: 5 Ho, ER 5 Ha: 4 (21.3 x 18.3)ER (18.9 x 18.3) Cranes: 4x30t	**1 oil engine** driving 1 FP propeller Total Power: 9,480kW (12,889hp) 14.2kn MAN-B&W 6S50MC-C8 1 x 2 Stroke 6 Cy. 500 x 2000 9480kW (12889bhp) Dalian Marine Diesel Co Ltd-China AuxGen: 3 x 600kW 450V a.c
7401423 *BNGY* -	**SHENG AO No. 1** **CPC Corp Taiwan** *Keelung* *Chinese Taipei* Official number: 5337	*263* 75 -	Class: (CR)	**1974-11 K.K. Miura Zosensho — Saiki** Yd No: 505 Loa 32.01 Br ex - Dght 3.988 Lbp 28.50 Br md 8.59 Dpth 4.45 Welded, 1 dk	**(B32A2ST) Tug**	**2 oil engines** driving 2 CP propellers Total Power: 1,618kW (2,200hp) Niigata 6L25BX 2 x 4 Stroke 6 Cy. 250 x 320 each-809kW (1100bhp) Niigata Engineering Co Ltd-Japan
7419767 *BNGZ* -	**SHENG AO No. 2** **CPC Corp Taiwan** *Keelung* *Chinese Taipei* Official number: 5338	*263* 75 -	Class: (CR)	**1974-12 K.K. Miura Zosensho — Saiki** Yd No: 508 Loa 32.01 Br ex - Dght 3.988 Lbp 28.50 Br md 8.59 Dpth 4.45 Welded, 1 dk	**(B32A2ST) Tug**	**2 oil engines** driving 2 CP propellers Total Power: 1,618kW (2,200hp) Niigata 6L25BX 2 x 4 Stroke 6 Cy. 250 x 320 each-809kW (1100bhp) Niigata Engineering Co Ltd-Japan
8222628 *BYZI* LL1967	**SHENG BO** *ex Yung Kuo -2011* **Sheng Bo Fishery Co Ltd** *Kaohsiung* *Chinese Taipei* Official number: CT6-000795	*350* 239 263	Class: (CR)	**1982-05 Fong Kuo Shipbuilding Co Ltd — Kaohsiung** Yd No: 176 Loa 45.70 (BB) Br ex 7.70 Dght 2.901 Lbp 39.20 Br md 7.62 Dpth 3.38 Welded, 1 dk	**(B11B2FV) Fishing Vessel** Ins: 434 Compartments: 3 Ho, ER 4 Ha: ER	**1 oil engine** reverse reduction geared to sc. shaft driving 1 FP propeller Total Power: 588kW (799hp) Akasaka 6MH25SSR 1 x 4 Stroke 6 Cy. 250 x 400 588kW (799bhp) Akasaka Tekkosho KK (Akasaka DieselLtd)-Japan AuxGen: 2 x 128kW 220V 50Hz a.c
7530547 *V3UQ8* -	**SHENG CHANG** *ex Han Wei -2003 ex Consort Justice -1996* *ex Ocean Pride -1991 ex Hokko Maru -1987* **Bai Yuh Fishery Co** Billion Star Marine Services Ltd *Belize City* *Belize* MMSI: 312898000 Official number: 119820498	**1,709** 767 2,890	Class: PD (NK)	**1976-10 Nishii Dock Co. Ltd. — Nansei** Yd No: 285 Loa 86.87 Br ex 12.73 Dght 5.243 Lbp 79.02 Br md 12.70 Dpth 6.08 Welded, 1 dk	**(A13B2TP) Products Tanker** Liq: 2,831; Liq (Oil): 2,831	**1 oil engine** driving 1 FP propeller Total Power: 1,545kW (2,101hp) 12.0kn Niigata 6M37X 1 x 4 Stroke 6 Cy. 370 x 540 1545kW (2101bhp) Niigata Engineering Co Ltd-Japan AuxGen: 2 x 96kW 445V 60Hz a.c Fuel: 33.0 (d.f.) 90.5 (r.f.) 4.5pd
9505481 *BRNH* -	**SHENG CHENG HAI** **China Shipping Haisheng Co Ltd** - *Haikou, Hainan* *China* MMSI: 414740000	**32,976** 19,142 56,633 T/cm 58.8	Class: CC	**2013-11 Guangzhou Huangpu Shipbuilding Co Ltd — Guangzhou GD** Yd No: 2302 Loa 189.99 (BB) Br ex - Dght 12.500 Lbp 185.00 Br md 32.26 Dpth 18.00 Welded, 1 dk	**(A21A2BC) Bulk Carrier** Grain: 71,634; Bale: 68,200 Compartments: 5 Ho, ER 5 Ha: 4 (21.3 x 18.3)ER (18.9 x 18.3) Cranes: 4x30t	**1 oil engine** driving 1 FP propeller Total Power: 9,480kW (12,889hp) 14.2kn MAN-B&W 6S50MC-C8 1 x 2 Stroke 6 Cy. 500 x 2000 9480kW (12889bhp) Yichang Marine Diesel Engine Co Ltd-China AuxGen: 3 x 600kW 450V a.c
9251444 *BPCV* -	**SHENG CHI** **China Shipping Tanker Co Ltd** - *Shanghai* *China* MMSI: 413062000	**27,155** 11,280 42,147 T/cm 51.5	Class: CC	**2003-12 Guangzhou Shipyard International Co Ltd — Guangzhou GD** Yd No: 0130012 Loa 187.80 Br ex - Dght 10.500 Lbp 178.00 Br md 31.50 Dpth 16.80 Welded, 1 dk	**(A13B2TP) Products Tanker** Double Hull (13F) Liq: 44,692; Liq (Oil): 44,692 Compartments: 12 Wing Ta, 2 Wing Slop Ta, ER 3 Cargo Pump (s) Ice Capable	**1 oil engine** driving 1 FP propeller Total Power: 8,561kW (11,640hp) 14.5kn MAN-B&W 6S50MC 1 x 2 Stroke 6 Cy. 500 x 1910 8561kW (11640bhp) Dalian Marine Diesel Works-China AuxGen: 3 x 664kW 450V a.c
7213735 *BVWR* -	**SHENG CHIANG No. 12** **Sing Chang Fisheries Co Ltd** - *Kaohsiung* *Chinese Taipei*	*321* 217 274	Class: (CR)	**1969 Korea Shipbuilding & Engineering Corp — Busan** Loa 43.59 Br ex 7.52 Dght 2.896 Lbp 38.61 Br md 7.50 Dpth 3.36 Welded, 1 dk	**(B11B2FV) Fishing Vessel** Compartments: 3 Ho, ER 4 Ha: 2 (1.0 x 1.0)2 (1.5 x 1.5)ER Derricks: 4x1t; Winches: 4	**1 oil engine** driving 1 FP propeller Total Power: 552kW (750hp) 11.5kn Niigata 1 x 4 Stroke 6 Cy. 280 x 440 552kW (750bhp) Niigata Engineering Co Ltd-Japan AuxGen: 2 x 80kW 230V 60Hz a.c
8113827 *BXCM* -	**SHENG CHUN** *ex Xin Shun -2011 ex Sohwa Maru -1993* **Shenzhen Haifa Shipping Co Ltd** - *Shenzhen, Guangdong* *China* MMSI: 412466620 Official number: 140009000021	**1,844** 1,033 2,756	Class: CC (NK)	**1982-02 Hakata Zosen K.K. — Imabari** Yd No: 262 Loa 88.30 Br ex - Dght 5.871 Lbp 82.00 Br md 12.50 Dpth 6.51 Welded, 1 dk	**(A13B2TP) Products Tanker** Liq: 3,250; Liq (Oil): 3,250 Compartments: 10 Ta, ER	**1 oil engine** with clutches & reverse reduction geared to sc. shaft driving 1 CP propeller Total Power: 1,624kW (2,208hp) 13.1kn Akasaka A37 1 x 4 Stroke 6 Cy. 370 x 720 1624kW (2208bhp) Akasaka Tekkosho KK (Akasaka DieselLtd)-Japan AuxGen: 1 x 200kW 450V 60Hz a.c Fuel: 53.5 (d.f.) 157.0 (r.f.) 5.0pd
7820760 *BXFP* -	**SHENG DA** *ex Sheng Tat -1996* *ex Hakusei Maru No. 31 -1994* **Hai Sheng Shipping (HK) Co Ltd** *China* MMSI: 412461870	**1,145** 395 1,041	Class: (CC) (NK)	**1979-01 Higaki Zosen K.K. — Imabari** Yd No: 217 Loa 67.90 Br ex 11.03 Dght 4.269 Lbp 62.00 Br md 11.00 Dpth 5.10 Riveted\Welded, 1 dk	**(A11B2TG) LPG Tanker** Liq (Gas): 1,506 2 x Gas Tank (s);	**1 oil engine** driving 1 FP propeller Total Power: 1,471kW (2,000hp) 12.0kn Hanshin 6LUD35 1 x 4 Stroke 6 Cy. 350 x 550 1471kW (2000bhp) The Hanshin Diesel Works Ltd-Japan AuxGen: 3 x 312kW Fuel: 112.0 6.5pd

7926069 - -	**SHENG DA 2** *ex* Poyang *-1999* *ex* Micronesian Pride *-1994* *ex* Siam Star *-1992* *ex* Swire Star *-1983* *ex* Michele *-1981* **Great Famous Shipping Ltd** -	6,764 3,958 7,546 T/cm 21.7	Class: CC (LR) ✠ Classed LR until 24/9/99	**1981-08 Mie Shipyard Co. Ltd. — Yokkaichi** Yd No: 199 Loa 120.81 (BB) Br ex 20.86 Dght 6.750 Lbp 110.90 Br md 20.81 Dpth 10.52 Welded, 1 dk	**(A33A2CC) Container Ship (Fully Cellular)** TEU 576 C Ho 228 TEU C Dk 348 TEU incl 70 ref C. Compartments: 5 Cell Ho, ER 10 Ha: 10 (12.9 x 8.3)ER	**1 oil engine** driving 1 FP propeller Total Power: 5,149kW (7,001hp) 15.6kn Mitsubishi 7UEC45/115H 1 x 2 Stroke 7 Cy. 450 x 1150 5149kW (7001bhp) Kobe Hatsudoki KK-Japan AuxGen: 3 x 400kW 450V 60Hz a.c Thrusters: 1 Thwart. FP thruster (f) Fuel: 97.5 (d.f.) 549.0 (r.f.) 18.5pd
7817971 *HP8877* -	**SHENG FA** *ex* Santai Maru *-1994* **Hainan Haifa Shipping Co** - *Panama* *Panama* Official number: 27965PEXTF	741 327 1,250		**1979-01 Hakata Zosen K.K. — Imabari** Yd No: 206 Loa - Br ex - Dght - Lbp 60.03 Br md 10.01 Dpth 4.53 Riveted\Welded, 1 dk	**(A12A2TC) Chemical Tanker**	**1 oil engine** driving 1 FP propeller Total Power: 883kW (1,201hp) 10.0kn Hanshin 6LU28G 1 x 4 Stroke 6 Cy. 280 x 440 883kW (1201bhp) Hanshin Nainenki Kogyo-Japan
8648195 *BZAU* LL1946	**SHENG FA** *ex* Chien Yu No. 3 *-2011* **Sheng Fa Fishery Co Ltd** - *Kaohsiung* *Chinese Taipei* Official number: CT6-000804	351 234 -		**1982-08 Fong Kuo Shipbuilding Co Ltd — Kaohsiung** Yd No: 180 Loa 44.65 Br ex 7.62 Dght - Lbp - Br md - Dpth - Welded, 1 dk	**(B11B2FV) Fishing Vessel**	**1 oil engine** driving 1 Propeller
9108958 *BI2481* LL1677	**SHENG FAN NO. 119** *ex* Hung Te No. 212 *-2011* **Sherng Hao Fishery Co Ltd** - SatCom: Inmarsat A 1355662 *Kaohsiung* *Chinese Taipei* Official number: CT7-0481	718 309 309		**1994-03 Fong Kuo Shipbuilding Co Ltd — Kaohsiung** Yd No: 306 Loa 57.00 (BB) Br ex 8.92 Dght - Lbp 50.00 Br md 8.90 Dpth 3.85 Welded, 1 dk	**(B11B2FV) Fishing Vessel** Ins: 650	**1 oil engine** with clutches & reverse reduction geared to sc. shaft driving 1 FP propeller Total Power: 1,177kW (1,600hp) Niigata 6M28HFT 1 x 4 Stroke 6 Cy. 280 x 480 1177kW (1600bhp) Niigata Engineering Co Ltd-Japan
8648353 *BI2406* LL0846	**SHENG FAN NO. 399** **Sherng Wang Shyang Fishery Co Ltd** - *Kaohsiung* *Chinese Taipei* Official number: CT7-0406	711 214 -		**1990-03 San Yang Shipbuilding Co., Ltd. — Kaohsiung** Loa 56.10 Br ex - Dght - Lbp - Br md 8.90 Dpth - Welded, 1 dk	**(B11B2FV) Fishing Vessel**	**1 oil engine** driving 1 Propeller
8648341 *BI2129* LL1796	**SHENG FAN NO. 699** **Yung Sheng Fishery Co Ltd** - *Kaohsiung* *Chinese Taipei* Official number: CT7-0129	740 272 -		**1987-04 San Yang Shipbuilding Co., Ltd. — Kaohsiung** Loa 55.10 Br ex - Dght - Lbp - Br md 8.60 Dpth - Welded, 1 dk	**(B11B2FV) Fishing Vessel**	**1 oil engine** driving 1 Propeller
8961999 *HQLD7* -	**SHENG FENG No. 6** **Hu Kung Fishery Co Ltd** - *San Lorenzo* *Honduras* Official number: L-1924621	*387* 188 -		**1987 San Yang Shipbuilding Co., Ltd. — Kaohsiung** L reg 41.32 Br ex - Dght 2.850 Lbp - Br md 7.40 Dpth 3.27 Welded, 1 dk	**(B11B2FV) Fishing Vessel**	**1 oil engine** driving 1 FP propeller Total Power: 883kW (1,201hp) 9.0kn Sumiyoshi 1 x 4 Stroke 6 Cy. 883kW (1201bhp) Sumiyoshi Marine Diesel Co Ltd-Japan
8327674 *BZBY* LL1044	**SHENG FU** *ex* Gwo Been *-2011* **Sheng Fu Fishery Co Ltd** - *Kaohsiung* *Chinese Taipei* Official number: CT6-000939	*352* 240 -	Class: (CR)	**1983-03 Fong Kuo Shipbuilding Co Ltd — Kaohsiung** Yd No: 190 Loa 45.65 Br ex 7.68 Dght 2.901 Lbp 39.20 Br md 7.62 Dpth 3.38 Welded, 1 dk	**(B11B2FV) Fishing Vessel** Ins: 345	**1 oil engine** driving 1 FP propeller Total Power: 588kW (799hp) 10.8kn Akasaka 6MH25SSR 1 x 4 Stroke 6 Cy. 250 x 400 588kW (799bhp) Akasaka Tekkosho KK (Akasaka DieselLtd)-Japan AuxGen: 1 x 240kW 220V a.c, 1 x 128kW 220V a.c
9731107 *BZXD52* -	**SHENG GANG FA 15** **Shengang Overseas Industrial Co Ltd** - *Shenzhen, Guangdong* *China* MMSI: 412460281 Official number: 4403992013070003	302 119 -		**2013-07 Rongcheng Yandunjiao Shipbuilding Aquatic Co Ltd — Rongcheng SD** L reg 38.85 Br ex - Dght - Lbp - Br md 7.20 Dpth 3.80 Welded, 1 dk	**(B11B2FV) Fishing Vessel**	**1 oil engine** driving 1 Propeller Total Power: 720kW (979hp) Chinese Std. Type XCW6200ZC 1 x 4 Stroke 6 Cy. 200 x 270 720kW (979bhp) in China
9731119 *BZXD53* -	**SHENG GANG FA 16** **Shengang Overseas Industrial Co Ltd** - *Shenzhen, Guangdong* *China* MMSI: 412460282 Official number: 4403992013070004	302 119 -		**2013-07 Rongcheng Yandunjiao Shipbuilding Aquatic Co Ltd — Rongcheng SD** L reg 38.85 Br ex - Dght - Lbp - Br md 7.20 Dpth 3.80 Welded, 1 dk	**(B11B2FV) Fishing Vessel**	**1 oil engine** driving 1 Propeller Total Power: 720kW (979hp) Chinese Std. Type XCW6200ZC 1 x 4 Stroke 6 Cy. 200 x 270 720kW (979bhp) in China
9731133 *BZXD54* -	**SHENG GANG FA 17** **Shengang Overseas Industrial Co Ltd** - *Shenzhen, Guangdong* *China* MMSI: 412460283 Official number: 4403992013070005	302 119 -		**2013-07 Rongcheng Yandunjiao Shipbuilding Aquatic Co Ltd — Rongcheng SD** L reg 38.85 Br ex - Dght - Lbp - Br md 7.20 Dpth 3.80 Welded, 1 dk	**(B11B2FV) Fishing Vessel**	**1 oil engine** driving 1 Propeller Total Power: 720kW (979hp) Chinese Std. Type XCW6200ZC 1 x 4 Stroke 6 Cy. 200 x 270 720kW (979bhp) in China
9731145 *BZXD55* -	**SHENG GANG FA 18** **Shengang Overseas Industrial Co Ltd** - *Shenzhen, Guangdong* *China* MMSI: 412460284 Official number: 4403992013070006	302 119 -		**2013-07 Rongcheng Yandunjiao Shipbuilding Aquatic Co Ltd — Rongcheng SD** L reg 38.85 Br ex - Dght - Lbp - Br md 7.20 Dpth 3.80 Welded, 1 dk	**(B11B2FV) Fishing Vessel**	**1 oil engine** driving 1 Propeller Total Power: 720kW (979hp) Chinese Std. Type XCW6200ZC 1 x 4 Stroke 6 Cy. 200 x 270 720kW (979bhp) in China
8823343 *XUGH7* -	**SHENG HAI** *ex* Ageshio Maru No. 2 *-2004* **Sheng Hai Shipping Co Ltd** Yantai Dahai Shipping Co Ltd SatCom: Inmarsat C 451574710 *Phnom Penh* *Cambodia* MMSI: 515747000 Official number: 0489264	1,321 685 1,750	Class: UB	**1989-02 K.K. Uno Zosensho — Imabari** Loa 73.31 Br ex - Dght 4.370 Lbp 70.66 Br md 11.50 Dpth 7.10 Welded, 1 dk	**(A31A2GX) General Cargo Ship**	**1 oil engine** reduction geared to sc. shaft driving 1 FP propeller Total Power: 1,030kW (1,400hp) Hanshin LH28G 1 x 4 Stroke 6 Cy. 280 x 460 1030kW (1400bhp) The Hanshin Diesel Works Ltd-Japan
9505493 *BRNF* -	**SHENG HENG HAI** **China Shipping Haisheng Co Ltd** - *Haikou, Hainan* *China* MMSI: 414753000	32,976 19,142 56,649 T/cm 58.8	Class: CC	**2013-11 Guangzhou Huangpu Shipbuilding Co Ltd — Guangzhou GD** Yd No: 2303 Loa 189.99 (BB) Br ex - Dght 12.500 Lbp 185.00 Br md 32.26 Dpth 18.00 Welded, 1 dk	**(A21A2BC) Bulk Carrier** Grain: 71,634; Bale: 68,200 Compartments: 5 Ho, ER 5 Ha: 4 (21.3 x 18.3)ER (18.9 x 18.3) Cranes: 4x30t	**1 oil engine** driving 1 FP propeller Total Power: 9,960kW (13,542hp) 14.2kn MAN-B&W 6S50MC-C8 1 x 2 Stroke 6 Cy. 500 x 2000 9960kW (13542bhp) Yichang Marine Diesel Engine Co Ltd-China AuxGen: 3 x 600kW 450V a.c
8611752 *BNJG* -	**SHENG HO** *ex* Kiwi Hope *-1994* *ex* Clipper Eagle *-1987* **Ta-Ho Maritime Corp** - SatCom: Inmarsat A 1346276 *Keelung* *Chinese Taipei* MMSI: 416357000	11,000 4,569 18,039 T/cm 28.3	Class: CR (NK)	**1987-11 The Hakodate Dock Co Ltd — Hakodate HK (Hull)** Yd No: 735 **1987-11 Kurushima Dockyard Co. Ltd. — Onishi** Yd No: 2476 Converted From: Bulk Carrier-1995 Loa 145.50 (BB) Br ex 23.13 Dght 9.160 Lbp 136.00 Br md 23.10 Dpth 12.40 Welded, 1 dk	**(A24A2BT) Cement Carrier** Grain: 23,590; Bale: 22,907 Compartments: 4 Ho, ER 4 Ha: 3 (12.0 x 19.3) (12.0 x 19.3)ER	**1 oil engine** driving 1 FP propeller Total Power: 3,722kW (5,060hp) 13.8kn Mitsubishi 6UEC45LA 1 x 2 Stroke 6 Cy. 450 x 1350 3722kW (5060bhp) Kobe Hatsudoki KK-Japan AuxGen: 2 x 400kW 450V a.c Fuel: 90.2 (d.f.) 757.8 (r.f.) 16.0pd
9114555 *H8NZ* -	**SHENG HONG** *ex* Pan Hope *-2011* *ex* Izumo *-2005* **Ming Wei Navigation SA** Da-Flying Navigation SA *Panama* *Panama* MMSI: 352329000 Official number: 4331111	3,782 2,159 5,626	Class: CR (KR) (NK)	**1995-02 Kurinoura Dockyard Co Ltd — Yawatahama EH** Yd No: 327 Loa 96.62 (BB) Br ex 16.02 Dght 6.722 Lbp 89.80 Br md 16.00 Dpth 9.75 Welded, 1 dk	**(A31A2GX) General Cargo Ship** Grain: 8,595; Bale: 7,555 Compartments: 2 Ho, ER 2 Ha: (15.4 x 8.5) (32.2 x 8.5)ER Cranes: 3x20t	**1 oil engine** driving 1 FP propeller Total Power: 2,059kW (2,799hp) 11.0kn Akasaka A38 1 x 4 Stroke 6 Cy. 380 x 740 2059kW (2799bhp) Akasaka Tekkosho KK (Akasaka DieselLtd)-Japan

7920869 BZLL - | **SHENG HONG NO. 806** *ex* Jih Yu No. 806 *-2003* *ex* Blue Arrow *-1989* *ex* Tohfu Maru *-1987* *ex* Takashiro Maru No. 53 *-1981* **Chern Lung Fishery Co Ltd** - SatCom: Inmarsat C 441670211 *Kaohsiung* *Chinese Taipei* MMSI: 416702000
1,866 980 1,956 Class: (NK)
1980-01 Fukuoka Shipbuilding Co Ltd — Fukuoka FO Yd No: 1076
Loa 83.06 (BB) Br ex - Dght 5.015
Lbp 77.02 Br md 13.21 Dpth 7.85
Welded, 2 dks
(A34A2GR) Refrigerated Cargo Ship
Ins: 2,755
Compartments: 3 Ho, ER
3 Ha: 3 (4.9 x 4.0)ER
Derricks: 6x4t
1 oil engine driving 1 FP propeller
Total Power: 2,207kW (3,001hp) 14.0kn
Akasaka AH40
1 x 4 Stroke 6 Cy. 400 x 600 2207kW (3001bhp)
Akasaka Tekkosho KK (Akasaka DieselLtd)-Japan
AuxGen: 2 x 350kW a.c

9378802 BXAI - | **SHENG HUA 631** **Shenzhen Rising Capital Co Ltd** Shenzhen Haifa Shipping Co Ltd *Shenzhen, Guangdong* *China* MMSI: 412469280
1,520 851 2,330 Class: CC
2005-12 Ocean Leader Shipbuilding Co Ltd — Zhongshan GD Yd No: 200407
Loa 78.60 Br ex - Dght -
Lbp 73.80 Br md 12.50 Dpth 5.20
Welded, 1 dk
(A12B2TR) Chemical/Products Tanker
Double Hull (13F)
1 oil engine reduction geared to sc. shaft driving 1 Propeller
Total Power: 1,324kW (1,800hp) 10.8kn
Guangzhou 6320ZCD
1 x 4 Stroke 6 Cy. 320 x 440 1324kW (1800bhp)
Guangzhou Diesel Engine Factory CoLtd-China

9403956 BXCT - | **SHENG HUA 632** **Shenzhen Haifa Shipping Co Ltd** - *Shenzhen, Guangdong* *China* MMSI: 412470190
1,562 875 2,303 Class: CC
2006-08 Ocean Leader Shipbuilding Co Ltd — Zhongshan GD Yd No: 2600M3
Loa 79.80 Br ex - Dght 4.300
Lbp 75.00 Br md 12.50 Dpth 5.20
Welded, 1 dk
(A12B2TR) Chemical/Products Tanker
Double Hull (13F)
Liq: 1,367; Liq (Oil): 1,367
Compartments: 10 Wing Ta, ER
1 oil engine reduction geared to sc. shaft driving 1 FP propeller
Total Power: 1,325kW (1,801hp) 10.8kn
Guangzhou 6320ZCD
1 x 4 Stroke 6 Cy. 320 x 440 1325kW (1801bhp)
Guangzhou Diesel Engine Factory CoLtd-China
AuxGen: 2 x 90kW 400V a.c

9599365 BYDJ - | **SHENG HUA 633** *ex* Sheng Hua *-2011* **Shenzhen Haifa Shipping Co Ltd** - SatCom: Inmarsat C 441301792 *Shenzhen, Guangdong* *China* MMSI: 413465320
2,947 1,243 4,421 Class: CC
2011-07 Jiangsu Sanfeng Shipbuilding Industries Co Ltd — Zhenjiang JS Yd No: SF0901
Loa 97.25 Br ex - Dght 5.800
Lbp 90.65 Br md 15.00 Dpth 7.40
Welded, 1 dk
(A12B2TR) Chemical/Products Tanker
Double Hull (13F)
Liq: 4,512; Liq (Oil): 4,512
Compartments: 4 Wing Ta, 4 Wing Ta, 1 Slop Ta, ER
Ice Capable
1 oil engine reduction geared to sc. shaft driving 1 FP propeller
Total Power: 2,060kW (2,801hp) 11.5kn
Guangzhou 8320ZC
1 x 4 Stroke 8 Cy. 320 x 440 2060kW (2801bhp)
Guangzhou Diesel Engine Factory CoLtd-China
AuxGen: 3 x 200kW 400V a.c

9605451 BYEL - | **SHENG HUA 635** **Shenzhen Haifa Shipping Co Ltd** - SatCom: Inmarsat C 441219922 *Shenzhen, Guangdong* *China* MMSI: 412474190
2,947 1,243 4,430 Class: CC
2011-12 Jiangsu Sanfeng Shipbuilding Industries Co Ltd — Zhenjiang JS Yd No: SF0902
Loa 97.25 Br ex - Dght 5.800
Lbp 90.65 Br md 15.00 Dpth 7.40
Welded, 1 dk
(A12B2TR) Chemical/Products Tanker
Double Hull (13F)
Liq: 4,326; Liq (Oil): 4,326
Compartments: 4 Wing Ta, 4 Wing Ta, 1 Slop Ta, ER
Ice Capable
1 oil engine reduction geared to sc. shaft driving 1 Propeller
Total Power: 2,060kW (2,801hp) 11.5kn
Chinese Std. Type 8320ZC
1 x 4 Stroke 8 Cy. 320 x 440 2060kW (2801bhp)
Guangzhou Diesel Engine Factory CoLtd-China
AuxGen: 3 x 200kW 400V a.c

8651142 BG3685 CT5-1685 | **SHENG I TSAI 688** **Ming-Chu Huang** - *Kaohsiung* *Chinese Taipei*
142 42 -
2009-03 Jin Jianh Lih Shipbuilding Co., Ltd. — Hsinyuan
Loa 28.60 Br ex - Dght -
Lbp - Br md 5.70 Dpth 2.20
Welded, 1 dk
(B11B2FV) Fishing Vessel
1 oil engine driving 1 FP propeller

8816493 XUGG7 - | **SHENG JIA 1** *ex* Shin Hachiryu Maru *-2002* **Yilong Shipping Co Ltd** - *Phnom Penh* *Cambodia* MMSI: 515744000 Official number: 1088604
1,340 499 1,620
1988-09 Yamanaka Zosen K.K. — Imabari Yd No: 371
Loa 72.72 (BB) Br ex - Dght 4.323
Lbp 68.00 Br md 11.50 Dpth 6.70
Welded
(A31A2GX) General Cargo Ship
Grain: 2,690; Bale: 2,485
1 oil engine with clutches & sr reverse geared to sc. shaft driving 1 CP propeller
Total Power: 1,030kW (1,400hp)
Hanshin LH28
1 x 4 Stroke 6 Cy. 280 x 460 1030kW (1400bhp)
The Hanshin Diesel Works Ltd-Japan

9633719 BKWX5 - | **SHENG JIE 1** **Zhejiang Shine Raise Marine Co Ltd** Zhejiang Bao Hong Shipping Co Ltd SatCom: Inmarsat C 441369219 *Zhoushan, Zhejiang* *China* MMSI: 413445550 Official number: 070012000008
4,696 2,601 7,161 Class: CC
2012-03 Zhoushan Haichen Marine Service & Engineering Co Ltd — Zhoushan ZJ Yd No: HC08-06
Loa 109.90 Br ex - Dght 6.450
Lbp 102.70 Br md 17.20 Dpth 8.50
Welded, 1 dk
(A31A2GX) General Cargo Ship
Grain: 8,879; Bale: 8,879
Compartments: 2 Ho, ER
2 Ha: ER 2 (30.7 x 10.4)
Ice Capable
1 oil engine reduction geared to sc. shaft driving 1 FP propeller
Total Power: 2,060kW (2,801hp) 12.0kn
Chinese Std. Type 8320ZC
1 x 4 Stroke 8 Cy. 320 x 440 2060kW (2801bhp)
Guangzhou Diesel Engine Factory CoLtd-China
AuxGen: 2 x 160kW 400V a.c

8748737 BH3380 CT6-1380 | **SHENG JYI SHYANG NO. 1** **Yu-Hung Cheng** Tri-Marine International (Pte) Ltd *Kaohsiung* *Chinese Taipei* MMSI: 416003647 Official number: 014899
225 76 -
2008-08 Shing Sheng Fa Boat Building Co — Kaohsiung
Loa 36.60 Br ex - Dght 2.500
Lbp 32.64 Br md 6.80 Dpth 2.90
Welded, 1 dk
(B11B2FV) Fishing Vessel
1 oil engine reduction geared to sc. shaft driving 1 Propeller
Total Power: 759kW (1,032hp)
Mitsubishi
1 x 759kW (1032bhp)
Mitsubishi Heavy Industries Ltd-Japan

7942532 BPPA - | **SHENG LI 2** **Shanghai Shipping Consortium Co** - *Shanghai* *China*
2,485 1,175 3,596 Class: (CC)
1977 Hudong Shipyard — Shanghai
Loa 102.10 Br ex - Dght 5.701
Lbp 92.00 Br md 13.80 Dpth 6.50
Welded, 1 dk
(A13B2TP) Products Tanker
Liq: 4,232; Liq (Oil): 4,232
Compartments: 10 Ta, ER
2 Cargo Pump (s): 2x100m³/hr
1 oil engine driving 1 FP propeller
Total Power: 2,207kW (3,001hp) 14.5kn
Hudong 6ESDZ43/82B
1 x 2 Stroke 6 Cy. 430 x 820 2207kW (3001bhp)
Hudong Shipyard-China
AuxGen: 2 x 250kW 400V 50Hz a.c

7942568 BJTK - | **SHENG LI 5** **Shanghai Shipping Consortium Co** - *Haikou, Hainan* *China*
2,464 1,175 3,387 Class: (CC)
1980 Hudong Shipyard — Shanghai
Loa 102.10 Br ex - Dght 5.701
Lbp 92.00 Br md 13.80 Dpth 6.50
Welded, 1 dk
(A13B2TP) Products Tanker
Liq: 4,236; Liq (Oil): 4,236
Compartments: 10 Ta, ER
1 oil engine driving 1 FP propeller
Total Power: 2,207kW (3,001hp) 14.5kn
Hudong 6ESDZ43/82B
1 x 2 Stroke 6 Cy. 430 x 820 2207kW (3001bhp)
Hudong Shipyard-China
AuxGen: 2 x 250kW 400V 50Hz a.c

7942570 BBCQ - | **SHENG LI 6** **China Shipping Tanker Co Ltd** - SatCom: Inmarsat A 1571622 *Shanghai* *China* MMSI: 412756000
2,485 1,175 3,596 Class: (CC)
1980-07 Hudong Shipyard — Shanghai
Loa 102.10 Br ex - Dght 5.701
Lbp 92.00 Br md 13.80 Dpth 6.50
Welded, 1 dk
(A13B2TP) Products Tanker
Liq: 4,236; Liq (Oil): 4,236
Compartments: 10 Ta, ER
2 Cargo Pump (s): 2x100m³/hr
1 oil engine driving 1 FP propeller
Total Power: 2,207kW (3,001hp) 14.5kn
Hudong 6ESDZ43/82B
1 x 2 Stroke 6 Cy. 430 x 820 2207kW (3001bhp)
Hudong Shipyard-China
AuxGen: 2 x 250kW 400V 50Hz a.c

8037994 BPXU - | **SHENG LI 10** *ex* Chuang Ye 3 *-1983* **Dalian Steam Shipping Co** - *Dalian, Liaoning* *China*
2,485 1,175 3,576 Class: (CC)
1979-07 Hudong Shipyard — Shanghai
Loa 102.10 Br ex - Dght 5.680
Lbp 92.00 Br md 13.80 Dpth 6.50
Welded, 1 dk
(A13B2TP) Products Tanker
Liq: 4,240; Liq (Oil): 4,240
Compartments: 5 Ta, ER
2 Cargo Pump (s): 2x100m³/hr
1 oil engine driving 1 FP propeller
Total Power: 2,207kW (3,001hp) 14.5kn
Hudong 6ESDZ43/82B
1 x 2 Stroke 6 Cy. 430 x 820 2207kW (3001bhp)
Hudong Shipyard-China
AuxGen: 2 x 250kW 400V 50Hz a.c

8037308 BPXV - | **SHENG LI 11** *ex* Chuang Ye 4 *-1983* **China Shipping Passenger Liner Co Ltd** - *Dalian, Liaoning* *China*
2,485 1,175 3,576 Class: (CC)
1979-07 Hudong Shipyard — Shanghai
Loa 102.00 Br ex - Dght 5.680
Lbp 92.00 Br md 13.80 Dpth 6.50
Welded, 1 dk
(A13B2TP) Products Tanker
Liq: 4,240; Liq (Oil): 4,240
Compartments: 5 Ta, ER
2 Cargo Pump (s): 2x100m³/hr
1 oil engine driving 1 FP propeller
Total Power: 2,207kW (3,001hp) 14.5kn
Hudong 6ESDZ43/82B
1 x 2 Stroke 6 Cy. 430 x 820 2207kW (3001bhp)
Hudong Shipyard-China
AuxGen: 2 x 250kW 400V 50Hz a.c

8830994 BDAX - | **SHENG LI 202** **Shengli Oil Field Offshore Drilling Co** - *Yantai, Shandong* *China*
436 - -
1979 Qingdao Shipyard — Qingdao SD
Loa 41.80 Br ex - Dght 3.500
Lbp 36.30 Br md 9.20 Dpth 4.65
Welded, 1 dk
(B32A2ST) Tug
2 oil engines driving 2 FP propellers
Total Power: 1,442kW (1,960hp) 13.0kn
Skoda 6L350IIPN
2 x 4 Stroke 6 Cy. 350 x 500 each-721kW (980bhp)
Skoda-Praha
AuxGen: 2 x 100kW 200V a.c

8831003 BDBC - | **SHENG LI 203** **Shengli Oil Field Offshore Drilling Co** - *Yantai, Shandong* *China*
151 - -
1979 Qingdao Shipyard — Qingdao SD
Loa 27.00 Br ex - Dght 2.300
Lbp 24.50 Br md 6.80 Dpth 3.20
Welded, 1 dk
(B32A2ST) Tug
1 oil engine geared to sc. shaft driving 1 FP propeller
Total Power: 294kW (400hp) 10.0kn
Chinese Std. Type 6300
1 x 4 Stroke 6 Cy. 300 x 380 294kW (400bhp)
Zibo Diesel Engine Factory-China
AuxGen: 1 x 16kW 220V a.c

8830906 BBAM5 - | **SHENG LI 211** **Shengli Oil Field Offshore Drilling Co** - *Yantai, Shandong* *China*
496 149 - Class: (CC)
1987 Qingdao Shipyard — Qingdao SD
Loa 46.22 Br ex - Dght 1.810
Lbp 42.50 Br md 9.80 Dpth 3.20
Welded, 1 dk
(B21B20T) Offshore Tug/Supply Ship
2 oil engines driving 2 FP propellers
Total Power: 740kW (1,006hp) 11.0kn
Caterpillar 3412T
2 x Vee 4 Stroke 12 Cy. 137 x 152 each-370kW (503bhp)
Caterpillar Inc-USA
AuxGen: 2 x 90kW 162V a.c

8830918 *BBBE9* -	**SHENG LI 221** - **Shengli Oil Field Offshore Drilling Co** - *Yantai, Shandong* *China* MMSI: 412320840	*821* Class: (CC) 246 577	**1987 Qingdao Shipyard — Qingdao SD** Loa 55.96 Br ex - Dght 2.460 Lbp 50.00 Br md 12.20 Dpth 3.70 Welded, 1 dk	**(B21B20T) Offshore Tug/Supply Ship**	**2 oil engines** geared to sc. shafts driving 2 FP propellers Total Power: 1,600kW (2,176hp) 12.9kn MAN 8L20/27 2 x 4 Stroke 8 Cy. 200 x 270 each-800kW (1088bhp) MAN B&W Diesel GmbH-Augsburg AuxGen: 2 x 120kW 400V a.c
8029387 - -	**SHENG LI 231** *ex Fuji Maru -1985* **Shengli Oil Field Offshore Drilling Co** - *Yantai, Shandong* *China*	*293* 107 -	**1981-06 Sagami Zosen Tekko K.K. — Yokosuka** Yd No: 210 Loa 34.85 Br ex - Dght 3.200 Lbp 30.25 Br md 9.60 Dpth 4.20 Welded, 1 dk	**(B32A2ST) Tug**	**2 oil engines** driving 2 FP propellers Total Power: 2,354kW (3,200hp) Niigata 6L28BX 2 x 4 Stroke 6 Cy. 280 x 320 each-1177kW (1600bhp) Niigata Engineering Co Ltd-Japan
8830566 *BBCA4* -	**SHENG LI 232** - **Shengli Oil Field Offshore Drilling Co** - *Yantai, Shandong* *China* MMSI: 412320860	*825* Class: (CC) 247 389	**1989 Qingdao Shipyard — Qingdao SD** Loa 58.80 Br ex - Dght 2.250 Lbp 52.20 Br md 11.60 Dpth 4.00 Welded, 1 dk	**(B21B20T) Offshore Tug/Supply Ship**	**4 oil engines** driving 2 FP propellers Total Power: 3,176kW (4,320hp) 13.5kn Caterpillar D399TA 4 x Vee 4 Stroke 16 Cy. 159 x 203 each-794kW (1080bhp) Caterpillar Inc-USA AuxGen: 3 x 840kW 600V a.c, 1 x 64kW 380V a.c, 1 x 24kW 380V a.c
9262027 *BBBX5* -	**SHENG LI 251** - **China Petroleum & Chemical Corp (Sinopec)** - SatCom: Inmarsat C 441240415 *Yantai, Shandong* *China* MMSI: 412324470	**1,281** Class: CC 384 763	**2003-05 Wuhu Shipyard — Wuhu AH** Yd No: 50011 Loa 67.20 Br ex 13.60 Dght 4.000 Lbp 60.60 Br md 13.00 Dpth 5.20 Welded, 1 dk	**(B21B20T) Offshore Tug/Supply Ship** Ice Capable	**2 oil engines** geared to sc. shafts driving 2 CP propellers Total Power: 3,846kW (5,229hp) 14.0kn Wartsila 6L26 1 x 4 Stroke 6 Cy. 260 x 320 1860kW (2529bhp) Wartsila Nederland BV-Netherlands Wartsila 6L26 1 x 4 Stroke 6 Cy. 260 x 320 1986kW (2700bhp) Wartsila Finland Oy-Finland AuxGen: 2 x 420kW 400V a.c, 2 x 211kW 400V a.c
9657911 *BBGI* -	**SHENG LI 252** - **Sinopec Shengli Oilfield Co Ltd** - *Yantai, Shandong* *China*	**1,523** Class: CC 456 675	**2011-12 Dalian Liaonan Shipyard — Dalian LN** Loa 69.50 Br ex - Dght 4.000 Lbp 60.80 Br md 12.80 Dpth 5.35 Welded, 1 dk	**(B21B20T) Offshore Tug/Supply Ship** Ice Capable	**2 oil engines** reduction geared to sc. shafts driving 2 Propellers Total Power: 4,080kW (5,548hp) 12.5kn MAN-B&W 6L27/38 2 x 4 Stroke 6 Cy. 270 x 380 each-2040kW (2774bhp) MAN Diesel A/S-Denmark AuxGen: 2 x 550kW 380V a.c, 2 x 248kW 400V a.c
9678941 *BBGJ* -	**SHENG LI 253** - **Sinopec Shengli Oilfield Co Ltd** - *Yantai, Shandong* *China*	**1,523** Class: CC 456 671	**2012-01 Dalian Liaonan Shipyard — Dalian LN** Loa 69.50 Br ex - Dght 4.000 Lbp 60.80 Br md 12.80 Dpth 5.35 Welded, 1 dk	**(B21B20T) Offshore Tug/Supply Ship** Ice Capable	**2 oil engines** reduction geared to sc. shafts driving 2 Propellers Total Power: 4,080kW (5,548hp) 14.0kn MAN-B&W 6L27/38 2 x 4 Stroke 6 Cy. 270 x 380 each-2040kW (2774bhp) MAN Diesel A/S-Denmark AuxGen: 2 x 550kW 380V a.c, 2 x 248kW 400V a.c
8831027 *BBCB2* -	**SHENG LI 261** - **Sinopec Shengli Oilfield Co Ltd** - SatCom: Inmarsat C 441207312 *Yantai, Shandong* *China* MMSI: 412320870	*1,197* Class: CC 359 1,277	**1985 Wuchang Shipyard — Wuhan HB** Loa 58.60 Br ex - Dght 5.100 Lbp 50.00 Br md 13.00 Dpth 6.50 Welded, 1 dk	**(B21B20T) Offshore Tug/Supply Ship** Ice Capable	**2 oil engines** driving 2 FP propellers Total Power: 4,804kW (6,532hp) 14.0kn MaK 12M282AK 2 x Vee 4 Stroke 12 Cy. 240 x 280 each-2402kW (3266bhp) Krupp MaK Maschinenbau GmbH-Kiel AuxGen: 2 x 560kW 440V a.c, 2 x 250kW 440V a.c
8843915 *BBCA9* -	**SHENG LI 262** - **China Petroleum & Chemical Corp (Sinopec)** - *Yantai, Shandong* *China* MMSI: 412320880	*1,197* Class: CC 359 1,276	**1984 Wuchang Shipyard — Wuhan HB** Loa 58.63 Br ex - Dght 5.100 Lbp 50.00 Br md 13.00 Dpth 6.50 Welded, 1 dk	**(B21B20T) Offshore Tug/Supply Ship** Ice Capable	**2 oil engines** driving 2 FP propellers Total Power: 4,804kW (6,532hp) 14.0kn MaK 12M282AK 2 x Vee 4 Stroke 12 Cy. 240 x 280 each-2402kW (3266bhp) Krupp MaK Maschinenbau GmbH-Kiel AuxGen: 2 x 560kW 440V a.c, 2 x 250kW 440V a.c
9642643 *BBHP* -	**SHENG LI 281** - **SINOPRL Shengli Field Offshore Oil Ship Centre** - *Yantai, Shandong* *China* MMSI: 413326790	**2,060** Class: CC 618 1,803	**2012-06 Wuchang Shipbuilding Industry Co Ltd — Wuhan HB** Yd No: A255L Loa 72.50 Br ex 15.60 Dght 4.800 Lbp 63.80 Br md 15.00 Dpth 7.00 Welded, 1 dk	**(B21B20T) Offshore Tug/Supply Ship** Ice Capable	**2 oil engines** reduction geared to sc. shafts driving 2 Propellers Total Power: 6,000kW (8,158hp) MaK 6M32C 2 x 4 Stroke 6 Cy. 320 x 480 each-3000kW (4079bhp) Caterpillar Motoren GmbH & Co. KG-Germany AuxGen: 2 x 1100kW 400V a.c, 2 x 392kW 400V a.c
9294707 *BBBX4* -	**SHENG LI 291** - **China Petroleum & Chemical Corp (Sinopec)** - *Yantai, Shandong* *China* MMSI: 412324510 Official number: 03V3001	**2,338** Class: CC 701 2,074	**2003-09 Wuchang Shipyard — Wuhan HB** Yd No: A080L Loa 74.00 Br ex - Dght - Lbp 65.00 Br md 15.60 Dpth 7.10 Welded, 1 dk	**(B21B20T) Offshore Tug/Supply Ship** Ice Capable	**2 oil engines** geared to sc. shafts driving 2 CP propellers Total Power: 7,800kW (10,604hp) Wartsila 9L32 2 x 4 Stroke 9 Cy. 320 x 400 each-3900kW (5302bhp) Wartsila Finland Oy-Finland AuxGen: 2 x 312kW 400V a.c, 2 x 1100kW 400V a.c Thrusters: 1 Tunnel thruster (f)
9570369 *BBGZ* -	**SHENG LI 292** - **China Petroleum & Chemical Corp** Shengli Offshore Oil Shipping Centre *Yantai, Shandong* *China* MMSI: 413324410	**2,074** Class: CC 622 1,893	**2009-12 Qingdao Shipyard — Qingdao SD** Yd No: QDZ469 Loa 72.50 Br ex - Dght 4.800 Lbp 63.80 Br md 15.00 Dpth 7.00 Welded, 1 dk	**(B21B20T) Offshore Tug/Supply Ship** Ice Capable	**2 oil engines** reduction geared to sc. shafts driving 2 Propellers Total Power: 6,920kW (9,408hp) 15.0kn Caterpillar C280-12 2 x Vee 4 Stroke 12 Cy. 280 x 300 each-3460kW (4704bhp) Caterpillar Inc-USA AuxGen: 2 x 1375kW 400V a.c, 2 x 392kW 400V a.c
8831039 *BDBB* -	**SHENG LI 501** - **Shengli Oil Field Offshore Drilling Co** - *Yantai, Shandong*	*368* 280 -	**1979 Dagu Shipyard — Tianjin** Loa 42.50 Br ex - Dght 1.500 Lbp 39.10 Br md 12.60 Dpth 3.10 Welded, 1 dk	**(B31A2SR) Research Survey Vessel**	**2 oil engines** geared to sc. shafts driving 2 FP propellers Total Power: 588kW (800hp) 10.0kn Chinese Std. Type 12V150C 2 x Vee 4 Stroke 12 Cy. 150 x 225 each-294kW (400bhp) Changchun Diesel Engine Works-China AuxGen: 2 x 64kW 380V a.c
8831041 *BDBI* -	**SHENG LI 502** - **Shengli Oil Field Offshore Drilling Co** - *Yantai, Shandong*	*367* - -	**1981 Dagu Shipyard — Tianjin** Loa 42.56 Br ex - Dght 1.500 Lbp 39.10 Br md 12.60 Dpth 3.10 Welded, 1 dk	**(B31A2SR) Research Survey Vessel**	**2 oil engines** geared to sc. shafts driving 2 FP propellers Total Power: 588kW (800hp) 10.0kn Chinese Std. Type 12V150C 2 x Vee 4 Stroke 12 Cy. 150 x 225 each-294kW (400bhp) Changchun Diesel Engine Works-China AuxGen: 2 x 64kW 380V a.c
8831089 *BDBE* -	**SHENG LI 610** - **Shengli Oil Field Offshore Drilling Co** - *Yantai, Shandong* *China*	*104* 35 46	**1979 Jiangsu Xinhua Shipyard Co Ltd — Nanjing JS** Loa 28.45 Br ex - Dght 1.410 Lbp 24.00 Br md 5.40 Dpth 2.70 Welded, 1 dk	**(B21B20T) Offshore Tug/Supply Ship**	**2 oil engines** geared to sc. shafts driving 2 FP propellers Total Power: 304kW (414hp) 11.0kn Chinese Std. Type 12V135C 2 x Vee 4 Stroke 12 Cy. 135 x 140 each-152kW (207bhp) Xianfeng Machinery Factory-China
8831091 *BDBF* -	**SHENG LI 611** - **Shengli Oil Field Offshore Drilling Co** - *Yantai, Shandong* *China*	*104* 35 46	**1979 Jiangsu Xinhua Shipyard Co Ltd — Nanjing JS** Loa 28.45 Br ex - Dght 1.410 Lbp 24.00 Br md 5.40 Dpth 2.70 Welded, 1 dk	**(B21B20T) Offshore Tug/Supply Ship**	**2 oil engines** geared to sc. shafts driving 2 FP propellers Total Power: 304kW (414hp) 11.0kn Chinese Std. Type 12V135C 2 x Vee 4 Stroke 12 Cy. 135 x 140 each-152kW (207bhp) Xianfeng Machinery Factory-China
8830982 - -	**SHENG LI 612** - **Shengli Oil Field Offshore Drilling Co** - *Yantai, Shandong* *China*	*337* 188 300	**1981-01 Wenzhou Shipyard — Wenzhou ZJ** Loa 43.50 Br ex - Dght 3.000 Lbp 39.00 Br md 8.20 Dpth 3.50 Welded, 1 dk	**(A13B2TU) Tanker (unspecified)** Liq: 326; Liq (Oil): 326 Compartments: 2 Ta, ER	**1 oil engine** geared to sc. shaft driving 1 FP propeller Total Power: 294kW (400hp) 9.0kn Chinese Std. Type 6300 1 x 4 Stroke 6 Cy. 300 x 380 294kW (400bhp) Guangzhou Diesel Engine Factory CoLtd-China AuxGen: 1 x 64kW 380V a.c, 1 x 40kW 380V a.c
8830970 - -	**SHENG LI 613** - **Shengli Oil Field Offshore Drilling Co** - *Yantai, Shandong* *China*	*337* 188 300	**1980 Yantai Shipyard — Yantai SD** Loa 43.50 Br ex - Dght 3.000 Lbp 39.00 Br md 8.20 Dpth 3.50 Welded, 1 dk	**(B34R2QY) Supply Tender**	**1 oil engine** geared to sc. shaft driving 1 FP propeller Total Power: 294kW (400hp) 9.0kn Chinese Std. Type 6300 1 x 4 Stroke 6 Cy. 300 x 380 294kW (400bhp) in China AuxGen: 1 x 64kW 380V a.c, 1 x 40kW 380V a.c

IMO / Call sign	Ship / Owner	Tonnage	Class	Build / Dimensions	Type	Machinery
9185205 *BBBU2* -	**SHENG LI 614** **Shengli Petroleum Administration Ocean Petroleum Shipping Co** - *Yantai, Shandong* *China* MMSI: 412322210 Official number: CN19933691211	**1,486** 832 1,721	Class: (CC)	**1998**-01 **Dalian New Shipbuilding Heavy Industries Co Ltd — Dalian LN** Yd No: PC-15 Loa - Br ex - Dght 4.400 Lbp 68.00 Br md 12.00 Dpth 5.90 Welded, 1 dk	**(A13A2TV) Crude Oil Tanker** Double Hull	**1 oil engine** driving 1 FP propeller Total Power: 1,177kW (1,600hp)
7903469 - -	**SHENG LI 619** *ex* Jing Sheng Yi Hao *-1996* *ex* King Fortune *-1994* *ex* Kaiei Maru *-1993* *ex* Kaiei Maru No. 1 *-1993* **Shengli Petroleum Administration Ocean Petroleum Shipping Co** - *Yantai, Shandong* *China*	**1,205** 674 2,080	Class: (CC) (GL)	**1979**-06 **K.K. Matsuura Zosensho — Osakikamijima** Yd No: 268 Loa 74.91 Br ex 12.53 Dght 5.311 Lbp 70.01 Br md 12.50 Dpth 5.52 Welded, 1 dk	**(A13B2TP) Products Tanker** Double Bottom Entire Compartment Length Liq: 2,684; Liq (Oil): 2,684	**1 oil engine** reverse geared to sc. shaft driving 1 FP propeller Total Power: 1,103kW (1,500hp) 11.0kn Hanshin 6LU32G 1 x 4 Stroke 6 Cy. 320 x 510 1103kW (1500bhp) Hanshin Nainenki Kogyo-Japan AuxGen: 2 x 116kW 220V a.c
8130112 - -	**SHENG LI 620** *ex* Jin Sheng Er Hao *-1996* *ex* Tamariki Maru No. 31 *-1996* **Shengli Petroleum Administration Ocean Petroleum Shipping Co** - *Yantai, Shandong* *China*	**1,337** 748 2,320	Class: (CC)	**1982**-07 **K.K. Matsuura Zosensho — Osakikamijima** Yd No: 300 Loa 79.28 (BB) Br ex - Dght 4.985 Lbp 74.02 Br md 12.01 Dpth 5.52 Welded, 1 dk	**(A13A2TV) Crude Oil Tanker**	**1 oil engine** driving 1 FP propeller Total Power: 1,618kW (2,200hp) Akasaka A34 1 x 4 Stroke 6 Cy. 340 x 660 1618kW (2200bhp) Akasaka Tekkosho KK (Akasaka DieselLtd)-Japan
9609897 *BCAU* -	**SHENG LI 705** **Sinopec Shengli Petroleum Administration Bureau** - SatCom: Inmarsat C 441301618 *Dongying, Shandong* *China* MMSI: 413325360 Official number: 2010D0000843	**491** 147 125	Class: CC	**2010**-11 **Rushan Shipbuilding Co Ltd — Rushan SD** Yd No: SRC903 Loa 48.13 Br ex - Dght 2.200 Lbp 42.07 Br md 9.50 Dpth 3.00 Welded, 1 dk	**(B31A2SR) Research Survey Vessel** Ice Capable	**2 oil engines** reduction geared to sc. shafts driving 2 FP propellers Total Power: 700kW (952hp) 10.0kn Volvo Penta D16MH 2 x 4 Stroke 6 Cy. 144 x 165 each-350kW (476bhp) AB Volvo Penta-Sweden AuxGen: 2 x 168kW 499V a.c
9109392 *H08621* -	**SHENG MING** *ex* Jag Arnav *-2013* *ex* Floral Deigo *-2001* **Sincerity Shipping Ltd** - *Panama* *Panama* MMSI: 371119000 Official number: 4499013	**38,265** 24,053 71,122 T/cm 42.2	Class: RI (LR) (IR) (NK) Classed LR until 17/5/13	**1995**-03 **Namura Shipbuilding Co Ltd — Imari SG** Yd No: 940 Loa 224.94 (BB) Br ex 32.24 Dght 13.632 Lbp 217.00 Br md 32.20 Dpth 18.80 Welded, 1 dk	**(A21A2BC) Bulk Carrier** Grain: 85,011 Compartments: 7 Ho, ER 7 Ha: (16.6 x 13.2)6 (16.6 x 14.4)ER	**1 oil engine** driving 1 FP propeller Total Power: 8,017kW (10,900hp) 14.0kn Sulzer 6RTA62 1 x 2 Stroke 6 Cy. 620 x 2150 8017kW (10900bhp) Mitsubishi Heavy Industries Ltd-Japan AuxGen: 3 x 500kW 450V 60Hz a.c Boilers: e (ex.g.), AuxB (o.f.) 5.0kgf/cm² (4.9bar) Fuel: 103.0 (d.f.) 2075.0 (r.f.)
9118264 *VRVM2* -	**SHENG MU** **Hilane Ltd** Fenwick Shipping Services Ltd *Hong Kong* *Hong Kong* MMSI: 477555000 Official number: HK-0359	**10,490** 5,268 16,860 T/cm 27.0	Class: LR ✠ **100A1** SS 02/2013 bulk carrier strengthened for heavy cargoes, Nos. 1 & 3 holds may be empty ESP timber deck cargoes LI ✠ **LMC** Eq.Ltr: C†; Cable: 550.0/54.0 U3	**1998**-03 **Tianjin Xingang Shipyard — Tianjin** Yd No: 299 Loa 143.45 (BB) Br ex 22.03 Dght 8.814 Lbp 134.00 Br md 22.00 Dpth 12.20 Welded, 1 dk	**(A21A2BC) Bulk Carrier** Grain: 19,855; Bale: 18,172 Compartments: 4 Ho, ER 4 Ha: (13.3 x 11.3)3 (14.3 x 11.3)ER Cranes: 2x25t	**1 oil engine** driving 1 FP propeller Total Power: 3,900kW (5,302hp) 13.5kn B&W 6L35MC 1 x 2 Stroke 6 Cy. 350 x 1050 3900kW (5302bhp) Yichang Marine Diesel Engine Co Ltd-China AuxGen: 3 x 456kW 450V 60Hz a.c Boilers: AuxB (Comp) 8.2kgf/cm² (8.0bar)
7632292 *HQTU5* -	**SHENG PAO No. 7** *ex* Kaisei Maru No. 25 *-1997* *ex* Kaisei Maru *-1996* *ex* Aomori Maru No. 2 *-1990* *ex* Aomori Maru *-1990* **Saint Power Fishery S de RL** - *San Lorenzo* *Honduras* Official number: L-1926927	*497* - 59		**1977**-03 **Hayashikane Shipbuilding & Engineering Co Ltd — Yokosuka KN** Yd No: 731 Loa 51.52 Br ex 8.62 Dght 3.691 Lbp 45.01 Br md 8.60 Dpth 3.92 Welded, 1 dk	**(B11B2FV) Fishing Vessel**	**1 oil engine** driving 1 FP propeller Total Power: 956kW (1,300hp) Niigata 6M28EX 1 x 4 Stroke 6 Cy. 280 x 440 956kW (1300bhp) Niigata Engineering Co Ltd-Japan
8896883 - -	**SHENG PING** *ex* Yun Long *-1990* **Shandong Province International Marine Shipping Co** - *Yantai, Shandong* *China*	**875** 409 1,300	Class: CC	**1986**-01 **Huanghai Shipbuilding Co Ltd — Rongcheng SD** Loa 65.23 Br ex - Dght 4.500 Lbp 59.23 Br md 10.80 Dpth 5.35 Welded, 1 dk	**(A21A2BC) Bulk Carrier** Grain: 1,641; Bale: 1,510 Compartments: 2 Ho, ER 2 Ha: ER Ice Capable	**1 oil engine** driving 1 FP propeller Total Power: 810kW (1,101hp) 11.2kn Chinese Std. Type 6350 1 x 4 Stroke 6 Cy. 350 x 500 810kW (1101bhp) Shanghai Diesel Engine Co Ltd-China AuxGen: 2 x 90kW 400V a.c
9505455 *BRNY* -	**SHENG PING HAI** **China Shipping Haisheng Co Ltd** - *Haikou, Hainan* *China* MMSI: 414725000	**32,976** 19,142 57,000 T/cm 58.8	Class: CC	**2012**-11 **Guangzhou Huangpu Shipbuilding Co Ltd — Guangzhou GD** Yd No: 2300 Loa 189.99 (BB) Br ex - Dght 12.500 Lbp 185.00 Br md 32.26 Dpth 18.00 Welded, 1 dk	**(A21A2BC) Bulk Carrier** Grain: 71,634; Bale: 68,200 Compartments: 5 Ho, ER 5 Ha: ER Cranes: 4x30t	**1 oil engine** driving 1 FP propeller Total Power: 9,960kW (13,542hp) 14.5kn MAN-B&W 6S50MC-C8 1 x 2 Stroke 6 Cy. 500 x 2000 9960kW (13542bhp) Dalian Marine Diesel Co Ltd-China
9144536 *VRVR8* -	**SHENG QIANG** **Victory Castle Shipping Ltd** COSCO (HK) Shipping Co Ltd SatCom: Inmarsat B 347761810 *Hong Kong* *Hong Kong* MMSI: 477618000 Official number: HK-0411	**26,062** 14,872 45,706 T/cm 49.8	Class: CC	**1998**-09 **Tsuneishi Shipbuilding Co Ltd — Fukuyama HS** Yd No: 1125 Loa 185.74 (BB) Br ex - Dght 11.620 Lbp 177.00 Br md 30.40 Dpth 16.50 Welded, 1 dk	**(A21A2BC) Bulk Carrier** Grain: 57,000; Bale: 55,564 Compartments: 5 Ho, ER 5 Ha: (20.0 x 15.3)4 (20.8 x 15.3)ER Cranes: 4x25t	**1 oil engine** driving 1 FP propeller Total Power: 7,172kW (9,751hp) 14.0kn B&W 6S50MC 1 x 2 Stroke 6 Cy. 500 x 1910 7172kW (9751bhp) Mitsui Engineering & Shipbuilding CLtd-Japan
8664785 - -	**SHENG RONG 2068** *ex* Yuan Han You 9 *-2004* **Jiangmen Xinhui Shengrong Shipping Co Ltd** - *Jiangmen, Guangdong* *China* Official number: 090712000067	**739** 413 998		**2004**-03 **in the People's Republic of China** Yd No: 65321 Loa 58.30 Br ex - Dght - Lbp - Br md 11.00 Dpth 3.80 Welded, 1 dk	**(A13B2TP) Products Tanker**	**2 oil engines** reduction geared to sc. shafts driving 2 Propellers Total Power: 440kW (598hp) Weifang R6160 2 x 4 Stroke 6 Cy. 160 x 225 each-220kW (299bhp) Weifang Diesel Engine Factory-China
8741545 *BBIS6* -	**SHENG SHENG 1** **Weihai Haida Passenger Transport Co Ltd** - *Weihai, Shandong* *China* MMSI: 412328670	**10,347** 5,380 2,541	Class: CC	**2006**-06 **Huanghai Shipbuilding Co Ltd — Rongcheng SD** Loa 120.00 (BB) Br ex - Dght 5.000 Lbp 110.50 Br md 20.40 Dpth 6.80 Welded, 1 dk	**(A36A2PR) Passenger/Ro-Ro Ship (Vehicles)** Passengers: unberthed: 1026 Vehicles: 123 Ice Capable	**2 oil engines** reduction geared to sc. shafts driving 2 Propellers Total Power: 5,000kW (6,798hp) 16.0kn Daihatsu 8DKM-28 2 x 4 Stroke 8 Cy. 280 x 390 each-2500kW (3399bhp) Shaanxi Diesel Heavy Industry Co Lt-China Thrusters: 1 Tunnel thruster (f)
8514253 - -	**SHENG SHI** *ex* Xie Chang 1 *-2002* *ex* Seiho Maru No. 3 *-1998* **Shenzhen Haifa Shipping Co Ltd** - *Shenzhen, Guangdong* *China*	**949** 531 1,735 T/cm 4.5	Class: (CC)	**1985**-08 **Sasaki Shipbuilding Co Ltd — Osakikamijima HS** Yd No: 391 Loa 77.37 (BB) Br ex - Dght 4.580 Lbp 72.00 Br md 11.20 Dpth 5.00 Welded, 1 dk	**(A13B2TP) Products Tanker** Compartments: 10 Ta, ER	**1 oil engine** with clutches & reverse reduction geared to sc. shaft driving 1 CP propeller Total Power: 1,177kW (1,600hp) 12.5kn Akasaka A31R 1 x 4 Stroke 6 Cy. 310 x 600 1177kW (1600bhp) Akasaka Tekkosho KK (Akasaka DieselLtd)-Japan AuxGen: 1 x 80kW 440V 60Hz a.c Fuel: 15.0 (d.f.) 66.0 (r.f.)
9446477 *VRDV8* -	**SHENG SHI** **Jadeway Ltd** CSC RoRo Logistics Co Ltd *Hong Kong* *Hong Kong* MMSI: 477170100 Official number: HK-2118	**43,810** 13,143 15,154	Class: NK	**2008**-11 **Mitsubishi Heavy Industries Ltd. — Shimonoseki** Yd No: 1130 Loa 180.00 (BB) Br ex 30.03 Dght 9.222 Lbp 171.70 Br md 30.00 Dpth 33.52 Welded, 10 dks. incl. 2 liftable dks.	**(A35B2RV) Vehicles Carrier** Side door/ramp (s) Len: - Wid: - Swl: 25 Quarter stern door/ramp (s. a.) Len: - Wid: - Swl: 100 Cars: 3,505	**1 oil engine** driving 1 FP propeller Total Power: 11,560kW (15,717hp) 19.9kn Mitsubishi 8UEC50LSII 1 x 2 Stroke 8 Cy. 500 x 1950 11560kW (15717bhp) Mitsubishi Heavy Industries Ltd-Japan AuxGen: 3 x 875kW 45V 60Hz a.c Thrusters: 1 Thwart. CP thruster (f) Fuel: 2290.0 (r.f.)

IMO / Call sign	Name / Owner / Manager / Flag	Tonnage	Class	Built / Dimensions	Type / Capacities	Machinery
9728459 - -	**SHENG SONG GONG 111** - **Zhang Quan Xi** - *Taizhou, Jiangsu* *China* Official number: 2013D2102794	**1,347** 754 -	Class: IZ ZC	**2013-08 Jiangsu Ping'an Shipbuilding Co Ltd — Dongtai JS** Yd No: DTPA2012003 Loa 73.80 Br ex - Dght - Lbp 68.92 Br md 15.80 Dpth 4.30 Welded, 1 dk	**(A31C2GD) Deck Cargo Ship**	**2 oil engines** reduction geared to sc. shafts driving 2 Propellers Total Power: 1,320kW (1,794hp) Chinese Std. Type 2 x each-660kW (897bhp) Weichai Power Co Ltd-China
9169304 *BUNV* -	**SHENG TAI** - **China Yangtze River Shipping Co Ltd** Shanghai Changjiang Shipping Corp *Shanghai* *China* MMSI: 412081630	**4,048** 1,836 5,210	Class: CC	**1997-05 Zhejiang Shipyard — Ningbo ZJ** Yd No: 95-58 Loa 98.50 Br ex - Dght 5.800 Lbp 92.00 Br md 16.80 Dpth 7.80 Welded, 1 dk	**(A31A2GX) General Cargo Ship** Grain: 6,233; Bale: 6,127 Compartments: 2 Ho, ER 2 Ha: (19.5 x 12.6) (37.7 x 12.6)ER	**2 oil engines** geared to sc. shafts driving 2 FP propellers Total Power: 2,000kW (2,720hp) 12.4kn Alpha 8L23/30 2 x 4 Stroke 8 Cy. 225 x 300 each-1000kW (1360bhp) Zhenjiang Marine Diesel Works-China AuxGen: 2 x 200kW 400V a.c, 1 x 100kW 400V a.c
8733926 - -	**SHENG TAI 6** - **He Gui Shipping Co Ltd** Changning Shipping Co Ltd *China*	**5,849** 3,275 9,511	Class: UB	**2007-11 in the People's Republic of China** Yd No: 2007Y4300202 Loa 127.80 Br ex - Dght 6.500 Lbp 121.10 Br md 18.80 Dpth 8.60 Welded, 1 dk	**(A31A2GX) General Cargo Ship**	**1 oil engine** reduction geared to sc. shaft driving 1 FP propeller Total Power: 2,500kW (3,399hp) 12.5kn Daihatsu 8DKM-28 1 x 4 Stroke 8 Cy. 280 x 390 2500kW (3399bhp) Shaanxi Diesel Heavy Industry Co Lt-China
9416549 *BRNJ* -	**SHENG WANG HAI** - **China Shipping Haisheng Co Ltd** - SatCom: Inmarsat C 441389610 *Haikou, Hainan* *China* MMSI: 413896000	**33,580** 18,486 57,208 T/cm 60.6	Class: CC	**2009-10 Bohai Shipbuilding Heavy Industry Co Ltd — Huludao LN** Yd No: 409-6 Loa 199.99 Br ex - Dght 12.500 Lbp 192.00 Br md 32.26 Dpth 18.00 Welded, 1 dk	**(A21A2BC) Bulk Carrier** Grain: 71,579 Compartments: 5 Ho, ER 5 Ha: 4 (22.1 x 16.8)ER (18.9 x 15.0) Cranes: 4x30t Ice Capable	**1 oil engine** driving 1 FP propeller Total Power: 8,510kW (11,570hp) 14.0kn MAN-B&W 6S50MC-C 1 x 2 Stroke 6 Cy. 500 x 2000 8510kW (11570bhp) Dalian Marine Diesel Co Ltd-China AuxGen: 3 x 645kW 450V a.c
9038426 *XUCZ3* -	**SHENG XIANG** *ex Azhou Maru -2009 ex Ashu Maru -2008* **Sheng Xiang Shipping Co Ltd** Yantai Weisheng International Shipping Co Ltd *Phnom Penh* *Cambodia* MMSI: 514047000 Official number: 0992028	**1,882** 1,172 3,700	Class: UB	**1992-03 Miho Zosensho K.K. — Shimizu** Yd No: 1414 Converted From: Stern Trawler-2009 Rebuilt & Lengthened & Deepened-2009 Loa 88.20 (BB) Br ex - Dght - Lbp - Br md 13.50 Dpth 7.20 Welded, 1 dk	**(A31A2GX) General Cargo Ship** Grain: 4,500; Bale: 4,200 Compartments: 2 Ho, ER 2 Ha: ER 2 (19.8 x 9.0)	**1 oil engine** with flexible couplings & sr geared to sc. shaft driving 1 FP propeller Total Power: 1,177kW (1,600hp) Yanmar MF29-ST 1 x 4 Stroke 6 Cy. 290 x 520 1177kW (1600bhp) Matsue Diesel KK-Japan
9416537 *BRNL* -	**SHENG XING HAI** - **China Shipping Haisheng Co Ltd** - SatCom: Inmarsat C 441219137 *Haikou, Hainan* *China* MMSI: 412523710	**33,580** 18,486 57,291 T/cm 60.6	Class: CC	**2009-08 Bohai Shipbuilding Heavy Industry Co Ltd — Huludao LN** Yd No: 409-5 Loa 199.90 Br ex - Dght 12.500 Lbp 192.00 Br md 32.26 Dpth 18.00 Welded, 1 dk	**(A21A2BC) Bulk Carrier** Grain: 71,579 Compartments: 5 Ho, ER 5 Ha: 4 (22.1 x 16.8)ER (18.9 x 15.0) Cranes: 4x30t Ice Capable	**1 oil engine** driving 1 FP propeller Total Power: 8,510kW (11,570hp) 14.0kn MAN-B&W 6S50MC-C 1 x 2 Stroke 6 Cy. 500 x 2000 8510kW (11570bhp) Dalian Marine Diesel Co Ltd-China AuxGen: 3 x 645kW 450V a.c
8847416 *BLGQ* -	**SHENG YANG** *ex Qian Tang -1998* **Sheyang Rongshen Sea Transportation Co Ltd** - *Lianyungang, Jiangsu* *China*	**1,594** 478 1,540	Class: CC	**1990-12 Qianjiang Shipyard — Hangzhou ZJ** Loa 80.90 Br ex - Dght 3.000 Lbp 75.00 Br md 13.00 Dpth 5.20 Welded, 1 dk	**(A31A2GX) General Cargo Ship** Grain: 2,055; Bale: 2,022 Compartments: 2 Ho, ER 2 Ha: 2 (9.1 x 8.0)ER Derricks: 4x4t	**1 oil engine** geared to sc. shaft driving 1 FP propeller Total Power: 588kW (799hp) 10.5kn Chinese Std. Type 6300 1 x 4 Stroke 6 Cy. 300 x 380 588kW (799bhp) Guangzhou Diesel Engine Factory CoLtd-China AuxGen: 2 x 75kW 400V a.c
9296509 - -	**SHENG YING** - **Zhejiang Changsheng Marine Shipping Co** - *China*	**198** 75 25		**2003 Wuhan Nanhua High Speed Ship Engineering Co Ltd — Wuhan HB** Loa 44.27 Br ex - Dght 1.300 Lbp 38.50 Br md 5.20 Dpth 2.60 Welded, 1 dk	**(A37B2PS) Passenger Ship** Passengers: unberthed: 200	**2 oil engines** geared to sc. shafts driving 2 FP propellers Total Power: 2,536kW (3,448hp) 29.5kn Cummins KTA-50-M2 2 x Vee 4 Stroke 16 Cy. 159 x 159 each-1268kW (1724bhp) Cummins Engine Co Inc-USA
8741557 *BKSI2* -	**SHENG YING 1** - **Zhejiang Shengsi Changsheng Shipping Co Ltd** - *Zhoushan, Zhejiang* *China*	**392** 196 34	Class: CC	**2005-03 Wuhan Nanhua High Speed Ship Engineering Co Ltd — Wuhan HB** Loa 48.30 Br ex - Dght 1.520 Lbp 43.00 Br md 7.20 Dpth 3.30 Welded, 1 dk	**(A37B2PS) Passenger Ship**	**2 oil engines** reduction geared to sc. shafts driving 2 Propellers Total Power: 3,372kW (4,584hp) 31.0kn Caterpillar 3516B-HD 2 x Vee 4 Stroke 16 Cy. 170 x 215 each-1686kW (2292bhp) Caterpillar Inc-USA
8734607 *T2BG3* -	**SHENG YONG 3** *ex Shun King 12 -2008* **Sheng Yong Marine Sdn Bhd** - *Funafuti* *Tuvalu* Official number: 18549208	**101** 59 -		**1992 Zhuhai Xiangzhou Shipyard — Zhuhai GD** Loa 23.02 Br ex - Dght - Lbp - Br md 5.20 Dpth 2.94 Welded, 1 dk	**(B32A2ST) Tug**	**1 oil engine** geared to sc. shaft driving 1 Propeller Total Power: 449kW (610hp) Caterpillar 3412 1 x Vee 4 Stroke 12 Cy. 137 x 152 449kW (610bhp) Caterpillar Inc-USA
8660519 *BYDFD* -	**SHENG YOU 222** *ex Shun Hang You 5 -2010* **Shenzhen Haifa Shipping Co Ltd** - *Shenzhen, Guangdong* *China* MMSI: 413465040 Official number: 140010000027	**2,998** 1,678 4,738	Class: ZC	**2007-04 Ningbo Dacheng Shengli Shipyard — Ninghai County ZJ** Yd No: LJX5113 Loa 105.30 Br ex - Dght 4.200 Lbp 99.80 Br md 17.60 Dpth 5.80 Welded, 1 dk	**(A13B2TP) Products Tanker**	**2 oil engines** driving 2 Propellers Total Power: 2,648kW (3,600hp) Chinese Std. Type G6300ZC 2 x 4 Stroke 6 Cy. 300 x 380 each-1324kW (1800bhp) Ningbo CSI Power & Machinery GroupCo Ltd-China
9535759 *BYGJ* -	**SHENG YOU 225** *ex Qian Li Shan 10 -2012* **Fujian Congrong Shipping Co Ltd** - *Fuzhou, Fujian* *China* MMSI: 413470530	**2,993** 1,809 4,980	Class: (CC)	**2008-09 Mindong Congmao Ship Industry Co Ltd — Fu'an FJ** Yd No: 10 Loa 98.80 Br ex 15.10 Dght 6.000 Lbp 91.60 Br md 15.00 Dpth 7.40 Welded, 1 dk	**(A13B2TP) Products Tanker** Single Hull Liq: 6,141; Liq (Oil): 6,141 Compartments: 10 Wing Ta, 2 Wing Slop Ta, ER	**1 oil engine** reduction geared to sc. shaft driving 1 FP propeller Total Power: 1,325kW (1,801hp) 11.0kn Guangzhou 6320ZCD 1 x 4 Stroke 6 Cy. 320 x 440 1325kW (1801bhp) Guangzhou Diesel Engine Factory CoLtd-China AuxGen: 3 x 180kW 400V a.c
9551167 *BYIE* -	**SHENG YOU 226** *ex Qian Li Shan 9 -2012* **Shenzhen Haifa Shipping Co Ltd** - SatCom: Inmarsat C 441338910 *Shenzhen, Guangdong* *China* MMSI: 413389000	**2,993** 1,809 4,980	Class: CC	**2009-06 Mindong Congmao Ship Industry Co Ltd — Fu'an FJ** Yd No: 09 Loa 98.80 Br ex 15.10 Dght 6.000 Lbp 91.60 Br md 15.00 Dpth 7.40 Welded, 1 dk	**(A13B2TP) Products Tanker** Double Hull (13F) Liq: 6,141; Liq (Oil): 6,141 Compartments: 10 Wing Ta, 2 Wing Slop Ta, ER	**1 oil engine** reduction geared to sc. shaft driving 1 FP propeller Total Power: 1,325kW (1,801hp) 11.0kn Guangzhou 6320ZCD 1 x 4 Stroke 6 Cy. 320 x 440 1325kW (1801bhp) Guangzhou Diesel Engine Factory CoLtd-China AuxGen: 3 x 180kW 400V a.c
9465124 *BYIP* -	**SHENG YOU 227** *ex Qian Li Shan 8 -2012* **Shenzhen Haifa Shipping Co Ltd** - SatCom: Inmarsat C 441369298 *Shenzhen, Guangdong* *China* MMSI: 413472880	**2,993** 1,809 4,980	Class: CC	**2007-12 Mindong Congmao Ship Industry Co Ltd — Fu'an FJ** Yd No: 08 Loa 98.80 Br ex - Dght 6.000 Lbp 91.60 Br md 15.00 Dpth 7.40 Welded, 1 dk	**(A13B2TP) Products Tanker** Double Hull (13F) Liq: 6,267; Liq (Oil): 6,267 Compartments: 10 Wing Ta, 2 Wing Slop Ta, ER	**1 oil engine** reduction geared to sc. shaft driving 1 FP propeller Total Power: 1,325kW (1,801hp) 11.0kn Guangzhou 6320ZCD 1 x 4 Stroke 6 Cy. 320 x 440 1325kW (1801bhp) Guangzhou Diesel Engine Factory CoLtd-China AuxGen: 3 x 150kW 400V a.c
8734437 *XUFP5* -	**SHENG YUAN** *ex Qiang Quan 168 -2012* **Sheng Tai Shipping Co Ltd** Yun Xing Shipping Co Ltd *Phnom Penh* *Cambodia* MMSI: 515895000 Official number: 1299026	**1,971** 863 1,768		**1999-12 Mindong Dongfu Shipbuilding Co Ltd — Fu'an FJ** Loa 71.80 Br ex - Dght 5.000 Lbp - Br md 11.00 Dpth 5.90 Welded, 1 dk	**(A31A2GX) General Cargo Ship**	**1 oil engine** reduction geared to sc. shaft driving 1 Propeller Total Power: 487kW (662hp) Chinese Std. Type 6350ZC 1 x 4 Stroke 6 Cy. 350 x 500 487kW (662bhp) Shaanxi Diesel Engine Factory-China
8519409 - -	**SHENG YUN** *ex Shoun Maru No. 11 -1999* - -	*199* - 682		**1985-10 Tokushima Zosen Sangyo K.K. — Komatsushima** Yd No: 1851 Loa 54.89 Br ex - Dght 3.220 Lbp 51.00 Br md 9.30 Dpth 5.48 Welded, 1 dk	**(A31A2GX) General Cargo Ship** Grain: 1,336; Bale: 1,311 Compartments: 1 Ho, ER 1 Ha: ER	**1 oil engine** driving 1 FP propeller Total Power: 588kW (799hp) Hanshin 6LU26 1 x 4 Stroke 6 Cy. 260 x 440 588kW (799bhp) The Hanshin Diesel Works Ltd-Japan
9602320 *HOEX* -	**SHENG YUN LAI** - **Plentiful Lead (Hong Kong) Ltd** Chang An Ship Management Ltd SatCom: Inmarsat C 435265711 *Panama* *Panama* MMSI: 352657000 Official number: 4301011	**13,622** 6,975 21,247	Class: BV	**2011-01 Jiangsu Huatai Shipbuilding Co Ltd — Taixing JS** Yd No: HT008 Loa 158.60 (BB) Br ex - Dght 9.300 Lbp 149.90 Br md 22.80 Dpth 13.20 Welded, 1 dk	**(A21A2BC) Bulk Carrier** Grain: 24,779 Compartments: 4 Ho, ER 4 Ha: ER Cranes: 3x25t	**1 oil engine** reduction geared to sc. shaft driving 1 FP propeller Total Power: 4,320kW (5,873hp) 12.9kn MAN-B&W 9L32/40 1 x 4 Stroke 9 Cy. 320 x 400 4320kW (5873bhp) Hyundai Heavy Industries Co Ltd-South Korea AuxGen: 3 x 372kW 50Hz a.c

IMO / Call sign	Ship / Owner / Manager / Flag	Tonnage	Class	Builder / Dimensions	Type / Cargo	Machinery
8708737 - - -	**SHENG ZHOU** *ex* Seaprodex 02 *-1992* **Global Reefer Shipping Co Ltd** Jiangsu Business Refrigeration Shipping Co	**1,287** 447 1,264	Class: (CC) (NK)	**1988-05 Hayashikane Dockyard Co Ltd — Nagasaki NS** Yd No: 955 Loa 71.23 (BB) Br ex 11.03 Dght 4.001 Lbp 64.52 Br md 11.00 Dpth 6.51 Welded, 1 dk	**(A34A2GR) Refrigerated Cargo Ship** Ins: 1,716 Compartments: 2 Ho, ER, 2 Tw Dk 2 Ha: 2 (5.2 x 4.0)ER Derricks: 4x5t	**1 oil engine** driving 1 FP propeller Total Power: 1,324kW (1,800hp) 12.0kn Yanmar MF33-UT 1 x 4 Stroke 6 Cy. 330 x 620 1324kW (1800bhp) Yanmar Diesel Engine Co Ltd-Japan AuxGen: 3 x 120kW a.c
9614505 *9V9713* - -	**SHENGKING** **The China Navigation Co Pte Ltd** - *Singapore* *Singapore* MMSI: 563324000 Official number: 397500	**25,483** 11,813 30,813	Class: LR ✠**100A1** SS 09/2013 Hold Nos. 3 & 4 holds strengthened for heavy cargoes container cargoes in all holds and on upper deck and on all hatch covers **ShipRight** ACS (B) *IWS LI EP ✠**LMC** **UMS** Eq.Ltr: M†; Cable: 638.5/73.0 U3 (a)	**2013-09 Zhejiang Ouhua Shipbuilding Co Ltd — Zhoushan ZJ** Yd No: 640 Loa 199.90 (BB) Br ex 28.28 Dght 10.500 Lbp 188.79 Br md 28.20 Dpth 15.50 Welded, 1 dk	**(A31A2GX) General Cargo Ship** TEU 2082 C Ho 916 TEU C Dk 1166 TEU incl 147 ref C Compartments: 2 Ho, 2 Tw Dk, 3 Cell Ho, ER 5 Ha: ER Cranes: 4x60t	**1 oil engine** driving 1 FP propeller Total Power: 13,560kW (18,436hp) 15.5kn Wartsila 6RT-flex58T 1 x 2 Stroke 6 Cy. 580 x 2416 13560kW (18436bhp) Hudong Heavy Machinery Co Ltd-China AuxGen: 3 x 1058kW 450V 60Hz a.c Boilers: AuxB (Comp) 8.4kgf/cm² (8.2bar) Thrusters: 1 Tunnel thruster (f)
8319483 *BTER* -	**SHENGO 38** *ex* Qin You 3 Hao *-2013* **PT Khatulistiwa Raya Energy** - *Qinhuangdao, Hebei* *China* MMSI: 412011030	**852** 355 1,000	Class: (CC)	**1984-05 K.K. Odo Zosen Tekko — Shimonoseki** Yd No: 303 Loa 62.50 Br ex 10.04 Dght 4.020 Lbp 57.50 Br md 10.00 Dpth 4.60 Welded, 1 dk	**(A13B2TP) Products Tanker** Liq: 1,332; Liq (Oil): 1,332 Compartments: 8 Ta, ER	**1 oil engine** with clutches, flexible couplings & sr geared to sc. shaft driving 1 FP propeller Total Power: 883kW (1,201hp) Niigata 6MG25BX 1 x 4 Stroke 6 Cy. 250 x 320 883kW (1201bhp) Niigata Engineering Co Ltd-Japan
8626214 *V3AW2* -	**SHENGXIANG 6** *ex* Sea Bridge *-2013* *ex* Fengshun 6 *-2006* *ex* Shin Koyo Maru *-1999* **Sheng Xiang Shipping Hong Kong Ltd** Jiade Shipping Co Ltd *Belize City* *Belize* MMSI: 312588000 Official number: 169920362	**1,263** 724 1,560		**1984-07 Kishigami Zosen K.K. — Akitsu** Loa 71.53 Br ex - Dght 4.501 Lbp 65.99 Br md 11.51 Dpth 6.71 Welded, 1 dk	**(A31A2GX) General Cargo Ship** Grain: 2,675; Bale: 2,476	**1 oil engine** driving 1 FP propeller Total Power: 883kW (1,201hp) 11.0kn Hanshin 6LUN28 1 x 4 Stroke 6 Cy. 280 x 480 883kW (1201bhp) The Hanshin Diesel Works Ltd-Japan
9682564 *VRLS7*	**SHENGYANG** **South China Towing Co Ltd** - *Hong Kong* *Hong Kong* MMSI: 477195500	**397** 119 -	Class: BV	**2013-05 Hin Lee (Zhuhai) Shipyard Co Ltd — Zhuhai GD** (Hull) Yd No: (5045) **2013-05 Cheoy Lee Shipyards Ltd — Hong Kong** Yd No: 5045 Loa 32.50 Br ex - Dght 3.800 Lbp 31.63 Br md 10.50 Dpth 5.10 Welded, 1 dk	**(B32A2ST) Tug** Hull Material: Aluminium Alloy	**2 oil engines** reduction geared to sc. shafts driving 2 Propellers Total Power: 3,676kW (4,998hp) Niigata 6L28HX 2 x 4 Stroke 6 Cy. 280 x 370 each-1838kW (2499bhp) Niigata Engineering Co Ltd-Japan
9379210 *C6XA2* -	**SHENLONG SPIRIT** **Shenlong Spirit LLC** Teekay Marine (Singapore) Pte Ltd SatCom: Inmarsat C 430950410 *Nassau* *Bahamas* MMSI: 309504000 Official number: 9000269	**85,030** 52,168 159,021 T/cm 119.1	Class: LR (CC) ✠**100A1** SS 09/2009 Double Hull oil tanker ESP **ShipRight** (SDA, FDA. CM) *IWS LI SPM ✠**LMC** **UMS IGS** Eq.Ltr: Y†; Cable: 742.5/97.0 U3 (a)	**2009-09 Bohai Shipbuilding Heavy Industry Co Ltd — Huludao LN** Yd No: 508-6 Loa 274.64 (BB) Br ex 48.03 Dght 17.300 Lbp 264.00 Br md 48.00 Dpth 24.00 Welded, 1 dk	**(A13A2TV) Crude Oil Tanker** Double Hull (13F) Liq: 176,816; Liq (Oil): 180,304 Cargo Heating Coils Compartments: 12 Wing Ta, 2 Wing Slop Ta, ER 3 Cargo Pump (s): 3x3500m³/hr Manifold: Bow/CM: 139.3m	**1 oil engine** driving 1 FP propeller Total Power: 16,860kW (22,923hp) 14.8kn MAN-B&W 6S70MC 1 x 2 Stroke 6 Cy. 700 x 2674 16860kW (22923bhp) Dalian Marine Diesel Co Ltd-China AuxGen: 3 x 900kW 450V 60Hz a.c Boilers: e (ex.g.) 20.4kgf/cm² (20.0bar), WTAuxB (o.f.) 18.4kgf/cm² (18.0bar) Fuel: 231.8 (d.f.) 3767.6 (r.f.)
8603200 - -	**SHENYANG** *ex* Chiyoda Maru *-1996* **South China Towing Co Ltd**	**264** 79 -	Class: (BV)	**1986-05 Kanagawa Zosen — Kobe** Yd No: 286 Loa 31.60 Br ex - Dght 2.701 Lbp 27.01 Br md 8.62 Dpth 3.81 Welded, 1 dk	**(B32A2ST) Tug**	**2 oil engines** sr geared to sc. shafts driving 2 FP propellers Total Power: 2,206kW (3,000hp) 13.0kn Niigata 6L25CXE 2 x 4 Stroke 6 Cy. 250 x 320 each-1103kW (1500bhp) Niigata Engineering Co Ltd-Japan
8935201 *5VAX2* -	**SHENYANG I** *ex* Seaquality *-2011* *ex* Everlastingness *-2009* *ex* Lady *-2007* *ex* Piter *-2003* *ex* Olviya *-1997* **Fagot Marine SA** *Lome* *Togo* MMSI: 671163000	**218** 101 248	Class: DR (RS)	**1959 Zavod No. 490 — Ilyichyovsk** Yd No: 331 Loa 41.10 Br ex 6.90 Dght 2.080 Lbp 38.40 Br md - Dpth 3.00 Welded, 1 dk	**(A31A2GX) General Cargo Ship** Grain: 414 Compartments: 2 Ho 2 Ha: (4.5 x 2.0) (6.5 x 2.0)	**1 oil engine** geared to sc. shaft driving 1 FP propeller Total Power: 220kW (299hp) 8.0kn Barnaultransmash 3D12A 1 x Vee 4 Stroke 12 Cy. 150 x 180 220kW (299bhp) (new engine 1977) Barnaultransmash-Barnaul AuxGen: 2 x 25kW Fuel: 32.0 (d.f.)
9533555 *YJQM9* -	**SHEPHERD TIDE** **Tidewater Marine International Inc** Tidewater Marine International Inc *Port Vila* *Vanuatu* MMSI: 576702000 Official number: 1968	**3,601** 1,429 5,154	Class: AB	**2011-04 Fujian Mawei Shipbuilding Ltd — Fuzhou FJ** Yd No: 619-1 Loa 87.20 (BB) Br ex - Dght 6.200 Lbp 83.00 Br md 18.80 Dpth 7.40 Welded, 1 dk	**(B21A20S) Platform Supply Ship**	**4 diesel electric oil engines** driving 4 gen. each 1600kW a.c Connecting to 2 elec. motors driving 2 Azimuth electric drive units Total Power: 7,300kW (9,924hp) 12.0kn Cummins QSK60-M 4 x Vee 4 Stroke 16 Cy. 159 x 190 each-1825kW (2481bhp) Cummins Engine Co Inc-USA Thrusters: 1 Thwart. CP thruster (f); 1 Retract. directional thruster (f) Fuel: 850.0
8717312 *VMTA* -	**SHEPPARTON** **Government of The Commonwealth of Australia** Government of The Commonwealth of Australia (Hydrographic Systems Program Offices) (HSPO) *Sydney, NSW* *Australia*	**468** 140 76	Class: LR ✠**100A1** SS 07/2010 Australia and environs coastal service within 300nm range to refuge ✠**LMC** **UMS** Cable: 275.0/19.0 U2	**1990-02 Eglo Engineering Pty Ltd — Port Adelaide SA** Yd No: 6 Loa 36.65 (BB) Br ex 13.13 Dght 2.270 Lbp 33.75 Br md 12.80 Dpth 3.96 Welded, 1 dk	**(B31A2SR) Research Survey Vessel**	**2 oil engines** with clutches, flexible couplings & sr reverse geared to sc. shafts driving 2 FP propellers Total Power: 810kW (1,102hp) G.M. (Detroit Diesel) 12V-92-TA 2 x Vee 2 Stroke 12 Cy. 123 x 127 each-405kW (551bhp) General Motors Detroit DieselAllison Divn-USA AuxGen: 2 x 100kW 415V 50Hz a.c
7397103 - -	**SHER-E-BANGLA** **Bangladesh Railways Board** - *Chittagong* *Bangladesh*	*450* 168	Class: (LR) ✠	**1975-10 Dockyard & Engineering Works Ltd — Narayanganj** (Assembled by) **1975-11 Friedr. Krupp GmbH Ruhrorter Schiffswerft — Duisburg** (Parts for assembly by) Yd No: 541 Loa 70.11 Br ex 13.21 Dght 1.296 Lbp 66.76 Br md 12.81 Dpth 2.65 Welded, 1 dk	**(A37B2PS) Passenger Ship**	**3 oil engines** driving 3 FP propellers Total Power: 2,427kW (3,300hp) 15.0kn MaK 6M451AK 3 x 4 Stroke 6 Cy. 320 x 450 each-809kW (1100bhp) MaK Maschinenbau GmbH-Kiel AuxGen: 2 x 80kW 380/220V 50Hz a.c, 1 x 51kW 380/220V 50Hz a.c
9523495 *A8WR3* -	**SHER-E PUNJAB** **Patriotic Services Inc** Ship Management Services Inc SatCom: Inmarsat C 463709757 *Monrovia* *Liberia* MMSI: 636014811 Official number: 14811	**43,753** 27,357 79,200 T/cm 71.9	Class: NV	**2011-05 COSCO (Dalian) Shipyard Co Ltd — Dalian LN** Yd No: N214 Loa 229.00 (BB) Br ex - Dght 14.850 Lbp 222.00 Br md 32.26 Dpth 20.25 Welded, 1 dk	**(A21A2BC) Bulk Carrier** Grain: 97,000; Bale: 90,784 Compartments: 7 Ho, ER 7 Ha: 5 (18.3 x 15.0) (15.7 x 15.1)ER (13.1 x 13.2) Cranes: 4x35t	**1 oil engine** driving 1 FP propeller Total Power: 11,060kW (15,037hp) 14.0kn MAN-B&W 7S50MC-C 1 x 2 Stroke 7 Cy. 500 x 2000 11060kW (15037bhp) Doosan Engine Co Ltd-South Korea AuxGen: 3 x a.c
6618823 *PHDD*	**SHERAKHAN** *ex* Prinses Margriet *-2004* **Unlimited Yacht Charter Beheer BV** Unlimited Yacht Charter Vof SatCom: Inmarsat C 424637010 *Rotterdam* *Netherlands* MMSI: 246370000 Official number: 238	**1,945** 583 -	Class: BV	**1966-11 A. Vuijk & Zonen's Scheepswerven N.V. — Capelle a/d IJssel** Yd No: 800 Converted From: Training Vessel-2003 Loa 69.04 Br ex 12.04 Dght 4.496 Lbp 60.00 Br md 11.99 Dpth 5.80 Welded, 3 dks	**(X11A2YP) Yacht** Passengers: berths: 22 1 Ha: (3.0 x 2.5) Derricks: 2x3t	**1 oil engine** sr geared to sc. shaft driving 1 FP propeller Total Power: 1,014kW (1,379hp) 12.0kn Caterpillar 3512B-TA 1 x Vee 4 Stroke 12 Cy. 170 x 190 1014kW (1379bhp) (new engine 2005) Caterpillar Inc-USA AuxGen: 2 x 310kW 440/230V 50Hz a.c
6704672 *HP5369* -	**SHERATON II** *ex* Toyo Maru No. 7 *-1989* - - *Panama* *Panama* Official number: 1859489A	*700* 358 640		**1966 Ujina Zosensho — Hiroshima** Yd No: 461 Loa 67.59 Br ex 10.75 Dght 3.201 Lbp 61.02 Br md 10.72 Dpth 4.50 Welded, 1 dk	**(A35A2RR) Ro-Ro Cargo Ship** Compartments: 1 Ho, ER	**1 oil engine** driving 1 FP propeller Total Power: 809kW (1,100hp) 11.8kn Hanshin Z6WS 1 x 4 Stroke 6 Cy. 350 x 500 809kW (1100bhp) Hanshin Nainenki Kogyo-Japan AuxGen: 1 x 40kW 225V a.c, 1 x 20kW 225V a.c Fuel: 50.0 4.0pd

IMO / Call sign	Name / Owner	Tonnage	Class	Built / Dimensions	Type	Machinery
9403700 - -	**SHERAZADE** **Felix Maritime Agency** - *Port Said* *Egypt* MMSI: 622171701 Official number: 1358	*263* 139 252	Class: BV	**2006-02 Port Said Marine Shipyard — Port Said** Loa 31.43 Br ex - Dght 2.200 Lbp 29.00 Br md 7.80 Dpth 4.00 Welded, 1 dk	**(X11A2YP) Yacht**	**2 oil engines** reduction geared to sc. shafts driving 2 FP propellers Total Power: 1,200kW (1,632hp) 12.0kn Caterpillar 3412B 2 x Vee 4 Stroke 12 Cy. 137 x 152 each-600kW (816bhp) Caterpillar Inc-USA
7820497 *P3ZJ8* -	**SHERBATSKIY** *ex* Oleander *-2013* *ex* P&OSL Picardy *-2001* *ex* Pride of Bruges *-1999* *ex* Pride of Free Enterprise *-1988* **Novgorod Shipping Ltd** Kajster doo *Limassol* *Cyprus* MMSI: 210422000 Official number: 7820497	**13,728** 4,538 3,810	Class: BV (LR) ✠ Classed LR until 7/6/08	**1980-11 Schichau-Unterweser AG — Bremerhaven** Yd No: 2281 Loa 131.91 Br ex 23.19 Dght 5.719 Lbp 126.52 Br md 22.70 Dpth 12.60 Welded, 3 dks	**(A36A2PR) Passenger/Ro-Ro Ship (Vehicles)** Passengers: unberthed: 1278; cabins: 25; berths: 48; driver berths: 48 Bow door & ramp (centre) Len: 4.90 Wid: 6.00 Swl: - Stern door & ramp (centre) Len: 4.90 Wid: 8.50 Swl: - Lane-Len: 660 Lane-clr ht: 4.50 Lorries: 50, Cars: 200	**3 oil engines** sr geared to sc. shafts driving 3 CP propellers Total Power: 17,652kW (24,000hp) 22.0kn Sulzer 12ZV40/48 3 x Vee 2 Stroke 12 Cy. 400 x 480 each-5884kW (8000bhp) Cie de Constructions Mecaniques (CCM), procede Sulzer-France AuxGen: 2 x 1600kW 400V 50Hz a.c, 3 x 850kW 400V 50Hz a.c Thrusters: 1 Thwart. FP thruster (f); 1 Thwart. FP thruster (f) Fuel: 63.0 (d.f.) 296.9 (r.f.)
9513945 *V7YQ8*	**SHERGAR** *completed as* SK Line 18 *-2009* **Global Offshore Services BV** Global Offshore Services Ltd *Majuro* *Marshall Islands* MMSI: 538004712 Official number: 4712	**1,960** 588 1,761	Class: AB	**2009-08 Jiangsu Zhenjiang Shipyard Co Ltd — Zhenjiang JS** Yd No: 42-ZJS200603 Loa 61.25 Br ex 16.04 Dght 5.100 Lbp 58.70 Br md 16.00 Dpth 6.00 Welded, 1 dk	**(B21B20A) Anchor Handling Tug Supply**	**2 oil engines** reduction geared to sc. shafts driving 2 CP propellers Total Power: 3,680kW (5,004hp) 12.5kn Yanmar 6EY26 2 x 4 Stroke 6 Cy. 260 x 385 each-1840kW (2502bhp) Yanmar Diesel Engine Co Ltd-Japan AuxGen: 2 x 400kW a.c, 2 x 1000kW a.c Fuel: 730.0
8107971 - -	**SHERIDAN TIDE** *ex* Marsea Nine *-1991* **Twenty Grand Marine Service LLC** Tidewater de Mexico S de RL de CV	**720** 216 1,200	Class: AB	**1981-09 Quality Shipyards Inc — Houma LA** Yd No: 170 Loa 56.29 Br ex - Dght 3.664 Lbp 51.44 Br md 12.20 Dpth 4.27 Welded, 1 dk	**(B21B20T) Offshore Tug/Supply Ship**	**2 oil engines** reverse reduction geared to sc. shafts driving 2 FP propellers Total Power: 2,868kW (3,900hp) 12.0kn EMD (Electro-Motive) 16-645-E2 2 x Vee 2 Stroke 16 Cy. 230 x 254 each-1434kW (1950bhp) General Motors Corp.Electro-Motive Div.-La Grange AuxGen: 2 x 99kW 440V 60Hz a.c Thrusters: 1 Thwart. FP thruster (f) Fuel: 298.0 (d.f.) 12.0pd
5322609 - -	**SHERIFA** **Government of The Democratic Republic of The Sudan (Railways Department)** *Sudan*	*297* 24 -	Class: (LR) ✠ Classed LR until 3/57	**1955-06 Scott & Sons — Bowling** Yd No: 404 Loa 36.76 Br ex 9.28 Dght 3.817 Lbp 33.53 Br md 9.15 Dpth 4.12 Riveted	**(B32A2ST) Tug** Derricks: 1x0.5t	**1 Steam Recip** driving 1 FP propeller Total Power: 736kW (1,001hp) 1 x Steam Recip. 736kW (1001ihp) Plenty & Son Ltd.-Newbury
8721088 *OA2787* -	**SHERIFF** *ex* Pacific Sheriff *-2010* *ex* Semiozernoye *-2009* **J Wiludi & Asociados Consultores en Pesca SAC** - *Callao* *Peru* MMSI: 760125000	**6,231** 1,869 3,166	Class: RS	**1985-08 GP Chernomorskiy Sudostroitelnyy Zavod — Nikolayev** Yd No: 549 Lengthened-2008 Loa 125.22 Br ex 16.03 Dght 6.300 Lbp 117.20 Br md 16.00 Dpth 10.20 Welded, 2 dks	**(B11A2FG) Factory Stern Trawler** Ice Capable	**2 oil engines** reduction geared to sc. shaft driving 1 CP propeller Total Power: 5,148kW (7,000hp) 16.1kn Russkiy 6CHN40/46 2 x 4 Stroke 6 Cy. 400 x 460 each-2574kW (3500bhp) Mashinostroitelnyy Zavod"Russkiy-Dizel"-Leningrad AuxGen: 2 x 1600kW 220/380V 50Hz a.c, 3 x 200kW 220/380V 50Hz a.c Fuel: 1227.0 (d.f.)
8003943 *5VBN2* -	**SHERIN** *ex* Sydland *-2012* *ex* Sydgard *-2004* *ex* Verena *-1993* *ex* Ina Lehmann *-1989* **BIA Shipping Co** - *Lome* *Togo* MMSI: 671257000	**2,225** 935 2,574	Class: DR (LR) (GL) Classed LR until 27/5/12	**1981-02 J.J. Sietas KG Schiffswerft GmbH & Co. — Hamburg** Yd No: 870 Loa 80.81 (BB) Br ex 13.44 Dght 5.061 Lbp 75.65 Br md 13.40 Dpth 7.50 Welded, 2 dks	**(A31A2GX) General Cargo Ship** Grain: 4,202; Bale: 4,138 TEU 154 C.Ho 84/20' C.Dk 70/20' Compartments: 1 Ho, ER 1 Ha: (52.2 x 10.8)ER	**1 oil engine** reduction geared to sc. shaft driving 1 FP propeller Total Power: 1,290kW (1,754hp) 13.0kn MWM TBD484-8 1 x 4 Stroke 8 Cy. 320 x 480 1290kW (1754bhp) Motoren Werke Mannheim AG (MWM)-West Germany AuxGen: 1 x 120kW 230/440V 50Hz a.c, 1 x 64kW 230/440V 50Hz a.c Thrusters: 1 Thwart. FP thruster (f)
5065366 - -	**SHERLENE** *ex* Broddon Express *-2010* *ex* Dahomey Express *-2006* *ex* Vaagvik *-2003* *ex* Bas *-1984* *ex* Casino *-1966* - -	**274** 149 450	Class: (NV)	**1962-08 Sandnessjoen Slip & Mek. Verksted — Sandnessjoen** Yd No: 5 Lengthened-1979 Loa 41.46 Br ex 7.40 Dght 3.182 Lbp 31.70 Br md 7.38 Dpth 3.41 Welded, 1 dk	**(A31A2GX) General Cargo Ship** Grain: 481; Bale: 381 Compartments: 1 Ho, ER 1 Ha: (15.7 x 5.4)ER Cranes: 1x5t; Derricks: 2x3t; Winches: 2 Ice Capable	**1 oil engine** driving 1 CP propeller Total Power: 276kW (375hp) 9.3kn Wichmann 3ACA 1 x 2 Stroke 3 Cy. 280 x 420 276kW (375bhp) (new engine 1970) Wichmann Motorfabrikk AS-Norway AuxGen: 1 x 4kW 24V, 1 x 2kW 24V Fuel: 14.0 (d.f.)
8706741 *4RCX* -	**SHERMAC** *ex* Ocean Ace No. 7 *-2013* *ex* Shosei Maru *-2002* **Interocean Energy (Pvt) Ltd** - *Colombo* *Sri Lanka* MMSI: 417222379 Official number: 1344	**1,003** 592 1,767	Class: IR KR (NK)	**1987-07 Hakata Zosen K.K. — Imabari** Yd No: 355 Loa 74.94 Br ex - Dght 4.299 Lbp 70.01 Br md 11.51 Dpth 5.01 Welded, 1 dk	**(A13B2TP) Products Tanker** Liq: 2,199; Liq (Oil): 2,199	**1 oil engine** driving 1 FP propeller Total Power: 1,177kW (1,600hp) 11.7kn Makita LN33L 1 x 4 Stroke 6 Cy. 330 x 640 1177kW (1600bhp) Makita Diesel Co Ltd-Japan AuxGen: 3 x 93kW a.c
8722331 - -	**SHERMAHI** *ex* Marzoogi 1 *-1998* *ex* MRTK-0730 *-1993* **Ahmed Mohamed El Banna** -	**117** 35 30	Class: (RS)	**1988-06 Sosnovskiy Sudostroitelnyy Zavod — Sosnovka** Yd No: 730 Loa 25.50 Br ex 7.00 Dght 2.390 Lbp 22.00 Br md - Dpth 3.30 Welded, 1 dk	**(B11A2FS) Stern Trawler** Ice Capable	**1 oil engine** driving 1 FP propeller Total Power: 221kW (300hp) 9.5kn S.K.L. 6NVD26A-2 1 x 4 Stroke 6 Cy. 180 x 260 221kW (300bhp) VEB Schwermaschinenbau "KarlLiebknecht" (SKL)-Magdeburg
7700166 *5VBX2* -	**SHERRIE ANNE** *ex* Wilhelm Kaisen *-2012* **Worldwide Procurement Services FZE** Tier One Holdings Ltd *Lome* *Togo* MMSI: 671329000 Official number: TG00395L	*284* 85 -	Class: DR	**1978-07 Fr Schweers Schiffs- und Bootswerft GmbH & Co KG — Berne** Yd No: 6430 Loa 44.00 Br ex - Dght 1.501 Lbp 42.02 Br md 7.65 Dpth 3.90 Welded	**(B34M2QS) Search & Rescue Vessel**	**2 oil engines** reduction geared to sc. shafts driving 2 FP propellers Total Power: 1,620kW (2,202hp) M.T.U. 2 x 4 Stroke each-810kW (1101bhp) MTU Friedrichshafen GmbH-Friedrichshafen
5150757 *WD3765* -	**SHERRY D** *ex* Delta Carey *-2012* *ex* Sonja V. *-2012* *ex* Hilo *-2012* *ex* Hilo Packet *-1981* *ex* Catherine Moran *-1960* *ex* Sheila Moran *-1947* *ex* YTM-732 *-1947* *ex* Canasatego *-1947* *ex* Sheila Moran *-1947* **Thomas R Decker** - *San Francisco, CA* *United States of America* Official number: 238401	*137* 60 -	Class: (AB)	**1939 Pennsylvania Shipyards Inc. — Beaumont, Tx** Yd No: 210 Loa 28.81 Br ex 6.74 Dght - Lbp 27.13 Br md 6.71 Dpth 3.28 Welded, 1 dk	**(B32A2ST) Tug**	**1 diesel electric oil engine** Connecting to 2 elec. motors driving 1 FP propeller Total Power: 662kW (900hp) EMD (Electro-Motive) 12-567-BC 1 x Vee 2 Stroke 12 Cy. 216 x 254 662kW (900bhp) General Motors Corp-USA Fuel: 72.0
7813406 *C6RV6* -	**SHETLAND CEMENT** *ex* Cem Press *-2004* *ex* Cem Express *-2004* *ex* Frima Star *-2001* *ex* Avebe Star *-1997* *ex* Star *-1985* **KGJS Cement AS** Kristian Gerhard Jebsen Skipsrederi AS (KGJS) *Nassau* *Bahamas* MMSI: 311206000 Official number: 8000319	**1,094** 328 1,150	Class: BV	**1978-07 Soby Motorfabrik og Staalskibsvaerft A/S — Soby** Yd No: 58 Converted From: Bulk Powder Carrier-2004 Converted From: General Cargo Ship-1986 Loa 62.66 Br ex 11.23 Dght 3.571 Lbp 57.00 Br md 11.21 Dpth 6.20 Welded, 1 dk & S dk	**(A24A2BT) Cement Carrier** Compartments: 2 Ho, ER 1 Ha: (34.2 x 7.7)ER Ice Capable	**1 oil engine** driving 1 CP propeller Total Power: 728kW (990hp) 10.0kn Alpha 409-26VO 1 x 2 Stroke 9 Cy. 260 x 400 728kW (990bhp) Alpha Diesel A/S-Denmark

9030486 *8PUM* -	**SHETLAND TRADER** *ex* Lass Mars *-2007* *launched as* Mars *-1992* - **Faversham Ships Ltd** - *Bridgetown* *Barbados* MMSI: 314257000 Official number: 733513	**1,512** 696 2,386	Class: GL	**1992**-07 **Rosslauer Schiffswerft GmbH — Rosslau** Yd No: 233 Loa 74.94 Br ex - Dght 4.352 Lbp 70.47 Br md 11.40 Dpth 5.50 Welded, 1 dk	**(A31A2GX) General Cargo Ship** Grain: 2,550; Bale: 2,550 Compartments: 1 Ho, ER 1 Ha: (48.0 x 9.0)ER Ice Capable	**2 oil engines** reverse reduction geared to sc. shafts driving 2 Directional propellers Total Power: 894kW (1,216hp) 11.0kn Cummins KT-19-M3 2 x 4 Stroke 6 Cy. 159 x 159 each-447kW (608bhp) Cummins Engine Co Inc-USA AuxGen: 2 x 88kW 220/440V a.c Thrusters: 1 Thwart. FP thruster (f) Fuel: 65.0
8111946 *VWCR* -	**SHETRUNJI** - **Government of The Republic of India (Gujarat Maritime Board)** - *Mumbai* *India* Official number: 2006	**232** 70 106	Class: (LR) (IR) ✠ Classed LR until 12/2/92	**1985**-05 **Chowgule & Co Pvt Ltd — Goa** Yd No: 539 Loa 29.42 Br ex 8.54 Dght 3.201 Lbp 25.99 Br md 8.03 Dpth 3.97 Welded, 1 dk	**(B32A2ST) Tug**	**2 oil engines** with clutches, flexible couplings & sr reverse geared to sc. shafts driving 2 FP propellers Total Power: 1,112kW (1,512hp) 11.5kn MAN G5V30/45ATL 2 x 4 Stroke 5 Cy. 300 x 450 each-556kW (756bhp) Garden Reach Shipbuilders &Engineers Ltd-India AuxGen: 2 x 56kW 415V 50Hz a.c, 1 x 32kW 415V 50Hz a.c Fuel: 62.0 (d.f.)
7209552 *BECD* -	**SHEY SIN No. 11** - **Shey Sin Fishery Co Ltd** - *Kaohsiung* *Chinese Taipei*	*264* 184 -	Class: (CR)	**1972 Fong Kuo Shipbuilding Co Ltd — Kaohsiung** Loa 39.22 Br ex 6.94 Dght 2.750 Lbp 33.99 Br md 6.91 Dpth 3.15 Welded, 1 dk	**(B11B2FV) Fishing Vessel** Ins: 255 Compartments: 3 Ho, ER 4 Ha: 2 (1.0 x 1.0) (1.0 x 1.2) (1.2 x 1.2)ER Derricks: 1x1t	**1 oil engine** driving 1 FP propeller Total Power: 478kW (650hp) 10.5kn Akasaka 6MH25SSR 1 x 4 Stroke 6 Cy. 250 x 400 478kW (650bhp) Akasaka Tekkosho KK (Akasaka DieselLtd)-Japan AuxGen: 2 x 80kW 230V a.c
7526807 *BODW* -	**SHI DA** *ex* Yun Cheng *-2008* *ex* Aristodikos *-1979* **Legend Shipping (Shanghai) Co Ltd** Adani Shipping (China) Co Ltd (Adani Dalian) SatCom: Inmarsat C 441276210 *Shanghai* *China* MMSI: 412154000	**11,959** 7,525 18,587	Class: (LR) (CC) ✠ Classed LR until 6/4/79	**1977**-03 **Mitsui Eng. & SB. Co. Ltd., Fujinagata Works — Osaka** Yd No: 1088 Loa 147.70 (BB) Br ex 23.02 Dght 9.634 Lbp 140.00 Br md 22.86 Dpth 13.00 Welded, 2 dks	**(A31A2GX) General Cargo Ship** Grain: 25,467; Bale: 23,819 TEU 232 C Ho 136 TEU C Dk 96 TEU incl 60 ref C. Compartments: 4 Ho, ER 7 Ha: (13.9 x 6.9)6 (15.7 x 6.9)ER Cranes: 2x25t,3x12.5t	**1 oil engine** driving 1 FP propeller Total Power: 6,914kW (9,400hp) 15.0kn B&W 7K62EF 1 x 2 Stroke 7 Cy. 620 x 1400 6914kW (9400bhp) Mitsui Engineering & Shipbuilding CLtd-Japan AuxGen: 3 x 500kW 440V 60Hz a.c Fuel: 113.0 (d.f.) 1103.5 (r.f.)
9352949 *BPDT* -	**SHI DAI 1** - **Shanghai Time Shipping Co Ltd** - *Shanghai* *China* MMSI: 413301000	**40,892** 25,841 76,611 T/cm 68.2	Class: CC	**2007**-09 **Jiangnan Shipyard (Group) Co Ltd — Shanghai** Yd No: H2347 Loa 225.00 (BB) Br ex - Dght 14.200 Lbp 217.00 Br md 32.26 Dpth 19.60 Welded, 1 dk	**(A21A2BC) Bulk Carrier** Grain: 90,100 Compartments: 7 Ho, ER 7 Ha: 6 (15.5 x 14.4)ER (14.6 x 13.2)	**1 oil engine** driving 1 FP propeller Total Power: 10,200kW (13,868hp) 14.5kn MAN-B&W 5S60MC 1 x 2 Stroke 5 Cy. 600 x 2292 10200kW (13868bhp) Hudong Heavy Machinery Co Ltd-China AuxGen: 3 x 560kW 450V a.c
9352951 *BPDU* -	**SHI DAI 2** - **Shanghai Time Shipping Co Ltd** - *Shanghai* *China* MMSI: 413302000	**40,892** 25,841 76,510 T/cm 68.2	Class: CC	**2007**-12 **Jiangnan Shipyard (Group) Co Ltd — Shanghai** Yd No: H2348 Loa 225.00 (BB) Br ex - Dght 14.200 Lbp 217.00 Br md 32.26 Dpth 19.60 Welded, 1 dk	**(A21A2BC) Bulk Carrier** Grain: 90,100 Compartments: 7 Ho, ER 7 Ha: 6 (15.5 x 14.4)ER (14.6 x 13.2)	**1 oil engine** driving 1 FP propeller Total Power: 10,200kW (13,868hp) 14.4kn MAN-B&W 5S60MC 1 x 2 Stroke 5 Cy. 600 x 2292 10200kW (13868bhp) Hudong Heavy Machinery Co Ltd-China AuxGen: 3 x 560kW 450V a.c
9104548 *BPDV* -	**SHI DAI 3** *ex* Fivos *-2007* *ex* Global Ace *-2002* *ex* Global Star *-2002* **Shanghai Time Shipping Co Ltd** - *Shanghai* *China* MMSI: 413263000	**36,561** 23,007 69,659 T/cm 65.6	Class: CC (NK)	**1994**-09 **Tsuneishi Shipbuilding Co Ltd — Fukuyama HS** Yd No: 1041 Loa 225.00 (BB) Br ex 32.24 Dght 13.257 Lbp 215.00 Br md 32.20 Dpth 18.30 Welded, 1 dk	**(A21A2BC) Bulk Carrier** Grain: 81,809 Compartments: 7 Ho, ER 7 Ha: (14.3 x 12.8)6 (16.8 x 14.4)ER	**1 oil engine** driving 1 FP propeller Total Power: 8,562kW (11,641hp) 14.1kn B&W 6S60MC 1 x 2 Stroke 6 Cy. 600 x 2292 8562kW (11641bhp) Mitsui Engineering & Shipbuilding CLtd-Japan AuxGen: 2 x 480kW a.c Fuel: 2408.0 (r.f.) 29.9pd
9086942 *BPDX* -	**SHI DAI 5** *ex* Alexandra I *-2007* *ex* Ocean Cherry *-2002* **Shanghai Time Shipping Co Ltd** - *Shanghai* *China* MMSI: 413270000	**35,886** 23,321 69,090 T/cm 64.4	Class: CC (NK)	**1994**-06 **Imabari Shipbuilding Co Ltd — Marugame KG (Marugame Shipyard)** Yd No: 1226 Loa 224.98 (BB) Br ex - Dght 13.295 Lbp 215.00 Br md 32.20 Dpth 18.30 Welded, 1 dk	**(A21A2BC) Bulk Carrier** Grain: 81,770 Compartments: 7 Ho, ER 7 Ha: (13.0 x 12.8)4 (17.9 x 14.4) (16.3 x 14.4) (14.7 x 14.4)ER	**1 oil engine** driving 1 FP propeller Total Power: 10,246kW (13,930hp) 14.5kn Sulzer 6RTA62 1 x 2 Stroke 6 Cy. 620 x 2150 10246kW (13930bhp) Mitsubishi Heavy Industries Ltd-Japan AuxGen: 3 x 440kW 450V a.c Fuel: 2552.0 38.2pd
9115224 *BPDY* -	**SHI DAI 6** *ex* Achilleas *-2007* *ex* Milky Ace *-2002* *ex* Milky Star *-2002* **Shanghai Time Shipping Co Ltd** - *Shanghai* *China* MMSI: 413271000	**35,879** 23,407 69,180 T/cm 64.4	Class: CC (NK)	**1994**-10 **Koyo Dockyard Co Ltd — Mihara HS** Yd No: 2061 Loa 224.98 (BB) Br ex 32.24 Dght 13.298 Lbp 215.00 Br md 32.20 Dpth 18.30 Welded, 1 dk	**(A21A2BC) Bulk Carrier** Grain: 82,025 Compartments: 7 Ho, ER 7 Ha: (13.0 x 12.8) (16.3 x 14.4)4 (17.9 x 14.4) (14.7 x 14.4)ER	**1 oil engine** driving 1 FP propeller Total Power: 9,930kW (13,501hp) 14.8kn Sulzer 6RTA62 1 x 2 Stroke 6 Cy. 620 x 2150 9930kW (13501bhp) Mitsubishi Heavy Industries Ltd-Japan AuxGen: 3 x 400kW a.c Fuel: 2336.0 (r.f.) 32.5pd
9063641 *BPDZ* -	**SHI DAI 7** *ex* Pelorus Island *-2007* *ex* Four Sterling *-2006* *ex* Unisterling *-2003* *ex* Lautan Star *-2000* *ex* Oceanic Star *-1998* **Shanghai Time Shipping Co Ltd** - *Shanghai* *China* MMSI: 413272000	**36,561** 23,007 69,616 T/cm 65.6	Class: CC (AB) (NK)	**1993**-09 **Tsuneishi Shipbuilding Co Ltd — Fukuyama HS** Yd No: 1023 Loa 225.00 Br ex 32.24 Dght 13.234 Lbp 215.00 Br md 32.20 Dpth 18.30 Welded, 1 dk	**(A21A2BC) Bulk Carrier** Grain: 81,809 Compartments: 7 Ho, ER 7 Ha: (14.3 x 12.8)6 (16.8 x 14.4)ER	**1 oil engine** driving 1 FP propeller Total Power: 8,562kW (11,641hp) 14.1kn B&W 6S60MC 1 x 2 Stroke 6 Cy. 600 x 2292 8562kW (11641bhp) Mitsui Engineering & Shipbuilding CLtd-Japan AuxGen: 2 x 480kW 450V 60Hz a.c
9591698 *BPJA* -	**SHI DAI 8** - **Shanghai Time Shipping Co Ltd** - *Shanghai* *China* MMSI: 414716000	**40,913** 25,963 75,458 T/cm 68.2	Class: CC	**2012**-09 **Jiangnan Shipyard (Group) Co Ltd — Shanghai** Yd No: H2482 Loa 225.00 (BB) Br ex - Dght 14.200 Lbp 217.00 Br md 32.26 Dpth 19.60 Welded, 1 dk	**(A21A2BC) Bulk Carrier** Grain: 90,070 Compartments: 7 Ho, ER 7 Ha: 6 (15.5 x 14.4)ER (15.5 x 13.2)	**1 oil engine** driving 1 FP propeller Total Power: 8,833kW (12,009hp) 14.5kn MAN-B&W 5S60ME-C 1 x 2 Stroke 5 Cy. 600 x 2400 8833kW (12009bhp) Hudong Heavy Machinery Co Ltd-China AuxGen: 3 x 560kW 450V a.c
9591703 *BPJB* -	**SHI DAI 9** - **Shanghai Time Shipping Co Ltd** - *Shanghai* *China* MMSI: 414722000	**40,913** 25,963 75,423 T/cm 68.2	Class: CC	**2012**-11 **Jiangnan Shipyard (Group) Co Ltd — Shanghai** Yd No: H2483 Loa 225.00 (BB) Br ex - Dght 14.200 Lbp 217.00 Br md 32.26 Dpth 19.60 Welded, 1 dk	**(A21A2BC) Bulk Carrier** Grain: 90,070 Compartments: 7 Ho, ER 7 Ha: 6 (15.5 x 14.4)ER (15.5 x 13.2)	**1 oil engine** driving 1 FP propeller Total Power: 8,833kW (12,009hp) 14.5kn MAN-B&W 5S60ME-C 1 x 2 Stroke 5 Cy. 600 x 2400 8833kW (12009bhp) Hudong Heavy Machinery Co Ltd-China AuxGen: 3 x 560kW 450V a.c
9591715 *BPJC* -	**SHI DAI 10** - **Shanghai Time Shipping Co Ltd** - *Shanghai* *China* MMSI: 414724000	**40,913** 25,963 75,414 T/cm 68.2	Class: CC	**2012**-12 **Jiangnan Shipyard (Group) Co Ltd — Shanghai** Yd No: H2484 Loa 225.00 (BB) Br ex - Dght 14.200 Lbp 217.00 Br md 32.26 Dpth 19.60 Welded, 1 dk	**(A21A2BC) Bulk Carrier** Grain: 90,725 Compartments: 7 Ho, ER 7 Ha: ER	**1 oil engine** driving 1 FP propeller Total Power: 11,900kW (16,179hp) 14.5kn MAN-B&W 5S60ME-C 1 x 2 Stroke 5 Cy. 600 x 2400 11900kW (16179bhp) Hudong Heavy Machinery Co Ltd-China
9591727 *BPJD* -	**SHI DAI 11** - **Shanghai Time Shipping Co Ltd** - *Shanghai* *China* MMSI: 414733000	**40,913** 25,963 75,467 T/cm 68.2	Class: CC	**2012**-12 **Jiangnan Shipyard (Group) Co Ltd — Shanghai** Yd No: H2487 Loa 225.00 (BB) Br ex - Dght 14.200 Lbp 217.00 Br md 32.26 Dpth 19.60 Welded, 1 dk	**(A21A2BC) Bulk Carrier** Grain: 90,725 Compartments: 7 Ho, ER 7 Ha: ER	**1 oil engine** driving 1 FP propeller Total Power: 11,900kW (16,179hp) 14.5kn MAN-B&W 5S60ME-C 1 x 2 Stroke 5 Cy. 600 x 2400 11900kW (16179bhp) Hudong Heavy Machinery Co Ltd-China
9493834 *BPJL* -	**SHI DAI 20** - **Shanghai Time Shipping Co Ltd** - *Shanghai* *China* MMSI: 413983000 Official number: 0010000242	**64,654** 37,347 115,664	Class: CC	**2010**-10 **Shanghai Jiangnan Changxing Heavy Industry Co Ltd — Shanghai** Yd No: H1009A Loa 254.00 (BB) Br ex 43.03 Dght 14.500 Lbp 249.80 Br md 43.00 Dpth 20.80 Welded, 1 dk	**(A21A2BC) Bulk Carrier** Grain: 132,246 Compartments: 7 Ho, ER 7 Ha: (16.5 x 21.0)4 (19.2 x 21.0) (18.3 x 21.0)ER (14.6 x 18.0)	**1 oil engine** driving 1 FP propeller Total Power: 13,080kW (17,784hp) 14.5kn Wartsila 6RT-flex58T 1 x 2 Stroke 6 Cy. 580 x 2416 13080kW (17784bhp) Hudong Heavy Machinery Co Ltd-China AuxGen: 3 x 720kW 450V a.c
9493846 *BPJM* -	**SHI DAI 21** - **Shanghai Time Shipping Co Ltd** - *Shanghai* *China* MMSI: 413984000 Official number: 0010000264	**65,125** 37,347 115,496	Class: CC	**2010**-11 **Shanghai Jiangnan Changxing Heavy Industry Co Ltd — Shanghai** Yd No: H1010A Loa 254.00 (BB) Br ex 43.30 Dght 14.500 Lbp 249.80 Br md 43.00 Dpth 20.80 Welded, 1 dk	**(A21A2BC) Bulk Carrier** Grain: 132,246 Compartments: 7 Ho, ER 7 Ha: (16.5 x 21.0)4 (19.2 x 21.0) (18.3 x 21.0)ER (14.6 x 18.0)	**1 oil engine** driving 1 FP propeller Total Power: 13,080kW (17,784hp) 14.5kn Wartsila 6RT-flex58T 1 x 2 Stroke 6 Cy. 580 x 2416 13080kW (17784bhp) Hudong Heavy Machinery Co Ltd-China

IMO / Call sign	Name / Owner	Tonnage	Class	Builder / Dimensions	Type	Machinery
8504375 *BTDQ* -	**SHI GANG JIAO 1** **Government of The People's Republic of China (Shijiu Port Authority Office)** - *Qingdao, Shandong* *China*	**157** 47 50	Class: (CC)	**1985-07 Ishii Zosen K.K. — Futtsu** Yd No: 172 Loa 32.00 Br ex - Dght 1.600 Lbp 29.60 Br md 6.50 Dpth 3.20 Welded, 1 dk	**(A37B2PS) Passenger Ship**	**2 oil engines** with clutches, flexible couplings & sr reverse geared to sc. shafts driving 2 FP propellers Total Power: 442kW (600hp) Yanmar 6HA-DTE 2 x 4 Stroke 6 Cy. 130 x 150 each-221kW (300bhp) Yanmar Diesel Engine Co Ltd-Japan
8216980 *BTCY* -	**SHI GANG TUO 1** **Government of The People's Republic of China** - *China*	*329* 98 121		**1982-12 Ishikawajima Ship & Chemical Plant Co Ltd — Tokyo** Yd No: 547 Loa 32.85 Br ex - Dght 3.301 Lbp 30.64 Br md 9.52 Dpth 4.42 Welded, 1 dk	**(B32A2ST) Tug**	**2 oil engines** dr geared to sc. shafts driving 2 FP propellers Total Power: 2,354kW (3,200hp) Daihatsu 6DSM-26 2 x 4 Stroke 6 Cy. 260 x 320 each-1177kW (1600bhp) Daihatsu Diesel Manufacturing Co Lt-Japan
8216992 *BTCZ* -	**SHI GANG TUO 2** **Government of The People's Republic of China** - *China*	*328* 98 121		**1983-01 Ishikawajima Ship & Chemical Plant Co Ltd — Tokyo** Yd No: 548 Loa 32.85 Br ex - Dght 3.301 Lbp 30.64 Br md 9.52 Dpth 4.42 Welded, 1 dk	**(B32A2ST) Tug**	**2 oil engines** dr geared to sc. shafts driving 2 FP propellers Total Power: 2,354kW (3,200hp) Daihatsu 8DSM-26 2 x 4 Stroke 8 Cy. 260 x 320 each-1177kW (1600bhp) Daihatsu Diesel Manufacturing Co Lt-Japan
8324218 - -	**SHI GANG TUO 3** **Government of The People's Republic of China (Shijiu Port Authority Office)** - *Qingdao, Shandong* *China*	*370* 111 107		**1984-09 Sagami Zosen Tekko K.K. — Yokosuka** Yd No: 223 Loa 35.00 Br ex - Dght 3.320 Lbp 30.25 Br md 9.60 Dpth 4.20 Welded, 1 dk	**(B32A2ST) Tug**	**2 oil engines** with clutches, flexible couplings & dr geared to sc. shafts driving 2 FP propellers Total Power: 2,354kW (3,200hp) Daihatsu 6DSM-28 2 x 4 Stroke 6 Cy. 280 x 340 each-1177kW (1600bhp) Daihatsu Diesel Manufacturing Co Lt-Japan
8324220 - -	**SHI GANG TUO 4** **Government of The People's Republic of China (Shijiu Port Authority Office)** - *Qingdao, Shandong* *China*	*370* 111 124		**1984-08 Sagami Zosen Tekko K.K. — Yokosuka** Yd No: 224 Loa 35.00 Br ex - Dght 3.320 Lbp 30.25 Br md 9.60 Dpth 4.22 Welded, 1 dk	**(B32A2ST) Tug**	**2 oil engines** with clutches, flexible couplings & dr geared to sc. shafts driving 2 FP propellers Total Power: 2,354kW (3,200hp) Daihatsu 6DSM-28 2 x 4 Stroke 6 Cy. 280 x 340 each-1177kW (1600bhp) Daihatsu Diesel Manufacturing Co Lt-Japan
8832538 - -	**SHI HAI JIAO 4** *ex Ling Nan Chun ex Sui Hai Jiao 4 -1983* **Guangzhou Maritime Transport (Group) Co Ltd** - *Guangzhou, Guangdong* *China*	*266* 159 -		**1981 Guangzhou Wenchong Shipyard — Guangzhou GD** Loa 40.00 Br ex - Dght 1.500 Lbp 36.00 Br md 7.40 Dpth 2.90 Welded, 1 dk	**(B12A2FF) Fish Factory Ship**	**2 oil engines** geared to sc. shafts driving 2 FP propellers Total Power: 338kW (460hp) 12.0kn Chinese Std. Type 12V135C 2 x Vee 4 Stroke 12 Cy. 135 x 140 each-169kW (230bhp) Shanghai Diesel Engine Co Ltd-China
9275086 *BPEP* -	**SHI JI KUAI HANG** *ex Lindaexpress -2004* **Yangshan Tongshang Port Construction Co Ltd** CCCC Shanghai Dredging Co Ltd *Shanghai* *China*	**499** 249 32	Class: CC (NV)	**2002-06 OAO Sudostroitelnaya Firma "Almaz" — Sankt-Peterburg** Yd No: 600 Loa 40.28 Br ex 12.40 Dght 1.200 Lbp 36.75 Br md 12.40 Dpth 3.45 Welded, 2 dks	**(A37B2PS) Passenger Ship** Hull Material: Aluminium Alloy Passengers: unberthed: 286	**4 oil engines** geared to sc. shafts driving 4 Water jets Total Power: 6,956kW (9,456hp) 55.0kn M.T.U. 12V4000M70 4 x Vee 4 Stroke 12 Cy. 165 x 190 each-1739kW (2364bhp) MTU Friedrichshafen GmbH-Friedrichshafen AuxGen: 2 x 70kW 400V a.c
9712060 *BPXF* -	**SHI LONG LING** **Dalian Marine Transport (Group) Co** - *Dalian, Liaoning* *China* MMSI: 414772000	**22,494** 11,767 34,510	Class: CC	**2013-12 Shanhaiguan Shipbuilding Industry Co Ltd — Qinhuangdao HE** Yd No: BC350-03 Loa 179.88 Br ex - Dght 10.300 Lbp 172.00 Br md 28.80 Dpth 14.60 Welded, 1 dk	**(A21A2BC) Bulk Carrier** Grain: 45,538 Compartments: 5 Ho, ER 5 Ha: 4 (20.0 x 20.0)ER (13.6 x 15.4) Cranes: 4x30t Ice Capable	**1 oil engine** driving 1 FP propeller Total Power: 6,480kW (8,810hp) 14.0kn MAN-B&W 6S42MC7 1 x 2 Stroke 6 Cy. 420 x 1764 6480kW (8810bhp) Yichang Marine Diesel Engine Co Ltd-China AuxGen: 3 x 600kW 450V a.c
9046801 *JG5104* -	**SHI SHI OH** *ex Oval LP -2003* **Matsuda Kaiun KK** - *Komatsushima, Tokushima* *Japan* MMSI: 431501864 Official number: 133138	*698* - 950	Class: NK	**1992-02 K.K. Miura Zosensho — Saiki** Yd No: 1025 Loa 65.10 (BB) Br ex - Dght 4.051 Lbp 60.00 Br md 11.00 Dpth 5.10 Welded, 1 dk	**(A11B2TG) LPG Tanker** Liq (Gas): 1,247 2 x Gas Tank (s);	**1 oil engine** geared to sc. shaft driving 1 FP propeller Total Power: 1,324kW (1,800hp) 12.5kn Hanshin 6EL30G 1 x 4 Stroke 6 Cy. 300 x 600 1324kW (1800bhp) The Hanshin Diesel Works Ltd-Japan AuxGen: 3 x 146kW a.c Fuel: 85.0 (d.f.)
8733249 - -	**SHI TAI 99** *ex Shi Tai 36 -2009* **Guangzhou Shitai Shipping Co Ltd** -	**2,616** 785 -		**2005-10 Guangzhou Panyu Xinyi Shiprepair Yard — Guangzhou GD** Loa 68.00 Br ex - Dght 2.040 Lbp 65.00 Br md 18.00 Dpth 5.60 Welded, 1 dk	**(B33A2DC) Cutter Suction Dredger**	**3 oil engines** reduction geared to sc. shafts driving 3 Propellers Total Power: 1,221kW (1,659hp) Cummins KTA-19-M3 3 x 4 Stroke 6 Cy. 159 x 159 each-407kW (553bhp) Chongqing Cummins Engine Co Ltd-China
9704568 - -	**SHI TAI 222** **Shenzhen Haibangda Shipping Co Ltd** - *Shenzhen, Guangdong* *China* Official number: 140013000096	**1,995** 1,296 -	Class: ZC	**2013-03 Dongguan Nanxiang Shipbuilding Co Ltd — Dongguan GD** Loa 59.98 (BB) Br ex - Dght - Lbp - Br md 17.30 Dpth 4.90 Welded, 1 dk	**(A33A2CC) Container Ship (Fully Cellular)**	**2 oil engines** driving 2 Propellers Total Power: 894kW (1,216hp) Chinese Std. Type 2 x each-447kW (608bhp) in China
9738557 - -	**SHI TONG 29** **Xinde Marine Engineering Pte Ltd** - *Yangzhou, Jiangsu* *China* Official number: CN20138825057	**346** 104 -	Class: BV (Class contemplated)	**2014-03 Yangzhou Topniche Shipbuilding Co Ltd — Yangzhou JS** Yd No: TG-04 Loa 32.30 Br ex - Dght - Lbp - Br md 9.50 Dpth 4.60 Welded, 1 dk	**(B32A2ST) Tug**	**2 oil engines** reduction geared to sc. shafts driving 2 Propellers Total Power: 2,354kW (3,200hp) Yanmar 2 x each-1177kW (1600bhp) Yanmar Diesel Engine Co Ltd-Japan
9405758 *BFGN* -	**SHI YAN 1** **Government of The People's Republic of China (Institute of Acoustics Chinese Academy of Sciences IACAS)** - *Tianjin* *China* MMSI: 413542000	**3,071** 921 698	Class: CC	**2009-04 Bohai Shipbuilding Heavy Industry Co Ltd — Huludao LN** Yd No: BH908 Loa 60.90 Br ex 26.26 Dght 6.500 Lbp 53.40 Br md 26.00 Dpth 10.50 Welded, 1 dk	**(B31A2SR) Research Survey Vessel**	**2 diesel electric oil engines** driving 2 Propellers Total Power: 3,400kW (4,622hp)
8832497 *BXMB* -	**SHI YAN 2** **Government of The People's Republic of China (South China Sea Geological Investigation Headquarters)** - SatCom: Inmarsat A 1571473 *Guangzhou, Guangdong* *China* MMSI: 412461040	*655* 341 -		**1980 Guangzhou Shipyard — Guangzhou GD** Loa 68.45 Br ex - Dght 3.500 Lbp 60.00 Br md 10.00 Dpth 5.40 Welded, 2 dks	**(B31A2SR) Research Survey Vessel**	**2 oil engines** geared to sc. shafts driving 2 FP propellers Total Power: 1,618kW (2,200hp) 13.0kn Chinese Std. Type 8300 2 x 4 Stroke 8 Cy. 300 x 380 each-809kW (1100bhp) Hongwei Machinery Factory-China AuxGen: 2 x 980kW 400V a.c
8427046 *BXMC* -	**SHI YAN 3** **Government of The People's Republic of China (South China Sea Institute of Oceanography of the Academic Sinica)** SatCom: Inmarsat C 441298810 *Guangzhou, Guangdong* *China* MMSI: 412988000	*2,609* 782 866	Class: CC	**1981 Hudong Shipyard — Shanghai** Loa 104.21 Br ex - Dght 4.901 Lbp 93.00 Br md 13.74 Dpth 7.80 Welded, 2 dks	**(B31A2SR) Research Survey Vessel**	**2 oil engines** driving 1 FP propeller Total Power: 7,796kW (10,600hp) 20.0kn B&W 6K45GF 2 x 2 Stroke 6 Cy. 450 x 900 each-3898kW (5300bhp) Tvornica Dizel Motora 'Uljanik'-Yugoslavia AuxGen: 3 x 400kW 400V 50Hz a.c, 1 x 90kW 400V 50Hz a.c
9052898 *BRAW7* -	**SHI YUAN** *ex Orange Sky -2012* **Zhongpu Shipping Co Ltd** Shanghai Yuhai Shipping Co *Shanghai* *China* MMSI: 412379550	**9,981** 3,492 5,184	Class: CC (NK)	**1993-01 Usuki Shipyard Co Ltd — Usuki OT** Yd No: 1618 Loa 109.60 (BB) Br ex - Dght 6.913 Lbp 100.00 Br md 21.00 Dpth 13.95 Welded, 7 dks, incl 2 hoistable	**(A35B2RV) Vehicles Carrier** Quarter stern door/ramp (s) Len: 20.00 Wid: 7.40 Swl: 50 Cars: 953	**1 oil engine** driving 1 FP propeller Total Power: 3,089kW (4,200hp) 14.3kn Mitsubishi 6UEC37LA 1 x 2 Stroke 6 Cy. 370 x 880 3089kW (4200bhp) Kobe Hatsudoki KK-Japan AuxGen: 3 x 275kW a.c Fuel: 580.0 (r.f.)
9617466 *VRIG4* -	**SHI ZI SHAN** **Yin Ying Shipping Co Ltd** China Shipping International Shipmanagement Co Ltd SatCom: Inmarsat C 447703418 *Hong Kong* *Hong Kong* MMSI: 477013400 Official number: HK-3036	**32,962** 19,142 57,000 T/cm 58.8	Class: CC	**2011-07 China Shipping Industry (Jiangsu) Co Ltd — Jiangdu JS** Yd No: CIS57000-02 Loa 189.99 (BB) Br ex 32.30 Dght 12.800 Lbp 185.00 Br md 32.26 Dpth 18.00 Welded, 1 dk	**(A21A2BC) Bulk Carrier** Grain: 71,634; Bale: 68,200 Compartments: 5 Ho, ER 5 Ha: 4 (21.3 x 18.3)ER (18.9 x 18.3) Cranes: 4x30t	**1 oil engine** driving 1 FP propeller Total Power: 9,480kW (12,889hp) 14.2kn MAN-B&W 6S50MC-C 1 x 2 Stroke 6 Cy. 500 x 2000 9480kW (12889bhp) Dalian Marine Diesel Co Ltd-China AuxGen: 3 x 600kW 450V a.c

IMO / Call sign	Name / Owner	Tonnage	Class	Builder / Dimensions	Type	Machinery
9303704 *BPFR* -	**SHI ZI ZUO** - **China Shipping Tanker Co Ltd** - *Shanghai* *China* MMSI: 413137000	**43,153** 22,236 75,447 T/cm 67.8	Class: CC	**2005-09 Dalian Shipyard Co Ltd — Dalian LN** Yd No: OT750-2 Loa 228.60 Br ex 32.26 Dght 14.700 Lbp 217.00 Br md 32.26 Dpth 21.10 Welded, 1 dk	**(A13B2TP) Products Tanker** Double Hull (13F) Liq: 80,409; Liq (Oil): 84,100 Cargo Heating Coils Compartments: 12 Wing Ta, 2 Wing Slop Ta, ER 3 Cargo Pump (s) Manifold: Bow/CM: 116m Ice Capable	**1 oil engine** driving 1 FP propeller Total Power: 12,240kW (16,642hp) 14.0kn MAN-B&W 6S60MC 1 x 2 Stroke 6 Cy. 600 x 2292 12240kW (16642bhp) Dalian Marine Diesel Works-China AuxGen: 3 x 800kW 450V a.c
8623509 - -	**SHIAN FENG CHANG 16** - **South African Sea Products Ltd** - *Cape Town* *South Africa* Official number: 19303	*150* 45 -		**1973 Taiwan Machinery Manufacturing Corp. — Kaohsiung** L reg 28.38 Br ex 6.02 Dght - Lbp - Br md - Dpth 2.62 Welded, 1 dk	**(B11A2FT) Trawler**	**1 oil engine** driving 1 FP propeller Total Power: 177kW (241hp) 8.5kn Matsui 1 x 4 Stroke 6 Cy. 260 x 470 177kW (241bhp) Matsui Iron Works Co Ltd-Japan
8623511 *ZR2298* CTA 713	**SHIAN FENG CHANG 18** - **All Hooked Up Fishing (Pty) Ltd** - SatCom: Inmarsat C 460101081 *Cape Town* *South Africa* Official number: 19302	*150* 45 -		**1973 Taiwan Machinery Manufacturing Corp. — Kaohsiung** L reg 28.38 Br ex 6.02 Dght - Lbp - Br md - Dpth 2.62 Welded, 1 dk	**(B11A2FT) Trawler**	**1 oil engine** driving 1 FP propeller Total Power: 177kW (241hp) 8.5kn Matsui 1 x 4 Stroke 6 Cy. 260 x 470 177kW (241bhp) Matsui Iron Works Co Ltd-Japan
7007849 *BVYK* -	**SHIAN FENG No. 11** - **Shian Feng Fishery Co Ltd** - *Kaohsiung* *Chinese Taipei*	*251* 170 -	Class: (CR)	**1969 Chou Mao Shipbuilding Co., Ltd. — Kaohsiung** Loa 36.33 Br ex 6.41 Dght 2.515 Lbp 31.53 Br md 6.38 Dpth 3.00 Welded, 1 dk	**(B11B2FV) Fishing Vessel** Ins: 200 Compartments: 3 Ho, ER 4 Ha: 2 (1.1 x 1.2)ER 2 (1.0 x 0.8)	**1 oil engine** driving 1 FP propeller Total Power: 405kW (551hp) 10.5kn Alpha 405-26VO 1 x 2 Stroke 5 Cy. 260 x 400 405kW (551bhp) Taiwan Machinery ManufacturingCorp.-Kaohsiung AuxGen: 2 x 64kW
8122517 - -	**SHIANG YING** *ex* Hosei Maru No. 25 *-1995* - - -	*498* 250 1,455		**1982-01 K.K. Matsuura Zosensho — Osakikamijima** Yd No: 287 Loa 70.70 (BB) Br ex 11.24 Dght 4.260 Lbp 65.00 Br md 11.00 Dpth 6.25 Welded, 1 dk	**(A31A2GX) General Cargo Ship** Compartments: 2 Ho, ER 2 Ha: ER	**1 oil engine** driving 1 FP propeller Total Power: 1,250kW (1,700hp) Hanshin 6LU35 1 x 4 Stroke 6 Cy. 350 x 550 1250kW (1700bhp) The Hanshin Diesel Works Ltd-Japan
9270646 *EPBM6* -	**SHIBA** *ex* Valili *-2012* *ex* Iran Arak *-2010* **Heliotrope Shipping Ltd** Hafiz Darya Shipping Co (HDSC) *Bandar Abbas* *Iran* MMSI: 422027500	**23,289** 11,054 30,239	Class: (GL)	**2010-05 Persian Gulf Shipbuilding Corp. — Bandar Abbas** Yd No: 101 Loa 187.25 (BB) Br ex - Dght 11.550 Lbp 176.48 Br md 29.80 Dpth 16.50 Welded, 1 dk	**(A33A2CC) Container Ship (Fully Cellular)** TEU 2200 Ice Capable	**1 oil engine** driving 1 FP propeller Total Power: 16,980kW (23,086hp) 20.9kn MAN-B&W 6L70MC 1 x 2 Stroke 6 Cy. 700 x 2268 16980kW (23086bhp) AuxGen: 3 x 816kW 400/220V a.c Thrusters: 1 Tunnel thruster (f)
9460497 *7JDB* -	**SHIBAURA** - - - *Miura, Kanagawa* *Japan* MMSI: 432643000 Official number: 140726	*499* - 603		**2008-03 Miho Zosensho K.K. — Shimizu** Yd No: 1527 Loa 64.75 Br ex - Dght 4.070 Lbp 58.00 Br md 9.30 Dpth 5.34 Welded, 1 dk	**(B12D2FP) Fishery Patrol Vessel**	**1 oil engine** reduction geared to sc. shafts driving 1 FP propeller Total Power: 1,838kW (2,499hp) 15.0kn Akasaka 6U28AK 1 x 4 Stroke 6 Cy. 280 x 380 1838kW (2499bhp) Akasaka Tekkosho KK (Akasaka DieselLtd)-Japan
7338731 - -	**SHIBAURA** *ex* Shibaura Maru *-2010* **Shibaura Tsusen KK** - *San Lorenzo* *Honduras* Official number: L-0323358	*142* 44 -	Class: (BV)	**1965 Kurushima Dockyard Co. Ltd. — Imabari** Yd No: 316 Loa 25.61 Br ex 7.83 Dght 3.161 Lbp - Br md - Dpth 3.51 Welded, 1 dk	**(B32A2ST) Tug**	**2 oil engines** geared to sc. shaft driving 1 FP propeller Total Power: 1,544kW (2,100hp) 11.8kn Nippon Hatsudoki HS6NV325 2 x 4 Stroke 6 Cy. 325 x 460 each-772kW (1050bhp) Nippon Hatsudoki-Japan AuxGen: 2 x 40kW
9078127 *JG5269* -	**SHIBAURA MARU No. 5** - **Shibaura Kaiun KK** - *Tokyo* *Japan* Official number: 134300	*139* - 468		**1993-09 Hanasaki Zosensho K.K. — Yokosuka** Yd No: 235 Loa 40.00 Br ex 8.50 Dght 2.700 Lbp 38.00 Br md 8.30 Dpth 2.90 Welded, 1 dk	**(A13B2TP) Products Tanker** Liq: 550; Liq (Oil): 550	**1 oil engine** with clutches & reverse reduction geared to sc. shaft driving 1 FP propeller Total Power: 405kW (551hp) Yanmar S165L-ST 1 x 4 Stroke 6 Cy. 165 x 210 405kW (551bhp) Yanmar Diesel Engine Co Ltd-Japan Thrusters: 1 Thwart. FP thruster (f)
8844543 *JG4956* -	**SHIBAURA MARU No. 21** - **Shibaura Kaiun KK** - *Tokyo* *Japan* Official number: 132005	*131* - 350		**1990-08 Ishibashi Sangyo K.K. — Ichihara** Loa 35.50 Br ex - Dght 2.800 Lbp 33.00 Br md 8.30 Dpth 3.00 Welded, 1 dk	**(A24A2BT) Cement Carrier**	**1 oil engine** driving 1 FP propeller Total Power: 382kW (519hp) 9.0kn Yanmar 6LAK-ST1 1 x 4 Stroke 6 Cy. 150 x 165 382kW (519bhp) Yanmar Diesel Engine Co Ltd-Japan
8859160 *JG5073* -	**SHIBAURA MARU No. 22** - **Shibaura Kaiun KK** - *Tokyo* *Japan* Official number: 133102	*122* - 297		**1991-08 Ishibashi Sangyo K.K. — Ichihara** Loa 35.00 Br ex - Dght 2.570 Lbp 32.50 Br md 8.00 Dpth 3.00 Welded, 1 dk	**(A24A2BT) Cement Carrier**	**1 oil engine** driving 1 FP propeller Total Power: 302kW (411hp) 9.0kn Yanmar 6KHK-ST 1 x 4 Stroke 6 Cy. 133 x 160 302kW (411bhp) Yanmar Diesel Engine Co Ltd-Japan
8922838 *JG5464* -	**SHIBAURA MARU No. 23** - **Shibaura Kaiun KK** - *Tokyo* *Japan* Official number: 135825	*119* - 300		**1996-03 Hanasaki Zosensho K.K. — Yokosuka** Loa 36.20 Br ex - Dght 2.700 Lbp 34.00 Br md 7.20 Dpth 3.00 Welded, 1 dk	**(A24A2BT) Cement Carrier**	**1 oil engine** driving 1 FP propeller Total Power: 302kW (411hp) 10.0kn Yanmar 6KH-ST 1 x 4 Stroke 6 Cy. 133 x 160 302kW (411bhp) Yanmar Diesel Engine Co Ltd-Japan
9108611 *JH3290* -	**SHIBAURU MARU NO. 6** *ex* Shuho Maru *-2011* **Shibaura Kaiun KK** - *Tokyo* *Japan* Official number: 134363	*497* - 1,200		**1994-11 K.K. Matsuura Zosensho — Osakikamijima** Yd No: 508 Loa - Br ex - Dght 4.200 Lbp 58.00 Br md 10.00 Dpth 4.55 Welded, 1 dk	**(A13B2TP) Products Tanker**	**1 oil engine** driving 1 FP propeller Total Power: 883kW (1,201hp) Matsui MA28GSC-35 1 x 4 Stroke 6 Cy. 280 x 540 883kW (1201bhp) Matsui Iron Works Co Ltd-Japan
9260201 - -	**SHIBSHA** - **Government of The People's Republic of Bangladesh (Navy Department)** - *Bangladesh*	**212** 63 110	Class: (LR) ✠ Classed LR until 13/7/05	**2004-04 Khulna Shipyard Ltd — Khulna** (Hull) Yd No: 622/1 **2004-04 B.V. Scheepswerf Damen — Gorinchem** Yd No: 506305 Loa 30.00 Br ex 8.43 Dght 3.500 Lbp 28.25 Br md 7.80 Dpth 4.05 Welded, 1 dk	**(B32A2ST) Tug**	**2 oil engines** with clutches & sr reverse geared to sc. shafts driving 2 FP propellers Total Power: 2,014kW (2,738hp) 12.0kn Caterpillar 3512B-TA 2 x Vee 4 Stroke 12 Cy. 170 x 190 each-1007kW (1369bhp) Caterpillar Inc-USA AuxGen: 2 x 85kW 415V 50Hz a.c
9408085 *9HA2345* -	**SHIBUMI** - **Kingswood Marine SA** TMS Dry Ltd SatCom: Inmarsat C 424838910 *Valletta* *Malta* MMSI: 248389000 Official number: 9408085	**91,373** 58,745 178,090 T/cm 120.6	Class: AB	**2010-03 Shanghai Waigaoqiao Shipbuilding Co Ltd — Shanghai** Yd No: 1106 Loa 292.00 (BB) Br ex 45.05 Dght 18.300 Lbp 282.00 Br md 45.00 Dpth 24.80 Welded, 1 dk	**(A21A2BC) Bulk Carrier** Grain: 194,486; Bale: 183,425 Compartments: 9 Ho, ER 9 Ha: 7 (15.5 x 20.0)ER 2 (15.5 x 16.5)	**1 oil engine** driving 1 FP propeller Total Power: 16,860kW (22,923hp) 14.0kn MAN-B&W 6S70MC 1 x 2 Stroke 6 Cy. 700 x 2674 16860kW (22923bhp) Mitsui Engineering & Shipbuilding CLtd-Japan AuxGen: 3 x 960kW 450V a.c Fuel: 330.0 (d.f.) 4350.0 (r.f.)
7627156 - -	**SHICHIRUI MARU No. 1** *ex* Daiei Maru No. 23 *-1986* - -	*110* - 109		**1977-03 Tokushima Zosen K.K. — Fukuoka** Yd No: 1227 Loa 38.05 (BB) Br ex 6.96 Dght 2.439 Lbp 31.55 Br md 6.95 Dpth 2.75 Welded, 1 dk	**(B11B2FV) Fishing Vessel**	**1 oil engine** driving 1 FP propeller Total Power: 883kW (1,201hp) Niigata 6L25BX 1 x 4 Stroke 6 Cy. 250 x 320 883kW (1201bhp) Niigata Engineering Co Ltd-Japan

8819158 *DSPX5* -	**SHIDAO** *ex* Huadong Pearl II *-2008* *ex* Ferry Nadeshiko No. 3 *-2005* *ex* Orange Ace *-2005* **KDB Capital Corp** Chang Myung Shipping Co Ltd SatCom: Inmarsat C 444048010 *Jeju* *South Korea* MMSI: 441480000 Official number: JJR-089394	**17,022** 5,106 2,902	Class: CC KR	**1989-07 Imabari Shipbuilding Co Ltd — Imabari EH (Imabari Shipyard)** Yd No: 478 Loa 147.22 (BB) Br ex - Dght 4.501 Lbp 136.00 Br md 23.50 Dpth 7.32 Welded	**(A36A2PR) Passenger/Ro-Ro Ship (Vehicles)** Passengers: unberthed: 400; berths: 100; driver berths: 104 Lane-Len: 800 Trailers: 107	**2 oil engines** geared to sc. shafts driving 2 CP propellers Total Power: 13,240kW (18,002hp) 21.0kn Pielstick 12PC2-6V-400 2 x Vee 4 Stroke 12 Cy. 400 x 460 each-6620kW (9001bhp) Ishikawajima Harima Heavy IndustrieCo Ltd (IHI)-Japan AuxGen: 2 x 1000kW 450V 60Hz a.c Fuel: 385.0 (d.f.) 738.0 (r.f.) 50.2pd
5322752 *GNGE* -	**SHIELDHALL** **The Solent Steam Packet Ltd** - *Glasgow* *United Kingdom* MMSI: 232003964 Official number: 185030	*1,753* 999 1,870	Class: (LR) ✠ Classed LR until 11/1/89	**1955-10 Lobnitz & Co. Ltd. — Renfrew** Yd No: 1132 Converted From: Waste Disposal Vessel-1991 Loa 81.69 Br ex 13.59 Dght 4.064 Lbp 78.64 Br md 13.11 Dpth 5.49 Riveted\Welded, 1 dk	**(B35A2QE) Exhibition Vessel** Passengers: unberthed: 80	**2 Steam Recips** driving 2 FP propellers 9.0kn Lobnitz & Co. Ltd.-Renfrew AuxGen: 1 x 25kW 220V d.c, 1 x 25kW 220V d.c Fuel: 79.3 (r.f.)
8656116 - -	**SHIENNY 03** **Sdr Suriansyah** - *Samarinda* *Indonesia*	**116** 35 -	Class: KI	**2010-12 PT Mangkupalas Mitra Makmur — Samarinda** Loa 21.75 Br ex - Dght 1.970 Lbp 20.06 Br md 6.50 Dpth 2.65 Welded, 1 dk	**(B32A2ST) Tug**	**2 oil engines** reduction geared to sc. shafts driving 2 FP propellers AuxGen: 2 x 40kW 380V a.c
8410627 - -	**SHIGE MARU** *ex* Kyodo Maru No. 17 *-1995* - - - *Philippines*	*498* - 1,611		**1984-11 K.K. Matsuura Zosensho — Osakikamijima** Yd No: 316 Loa 72.85 Br ex 11.64 Dght 4.301 Lbp 68.03 Br md 11.61 Dpth 7.01 Welded, 2 dks	**(A31A2GX) General Cargo Ship** Grain: 2,894; Bale: 2,527 Compartments: 1 Ho, ER 1 Ha: ER	**1 oil engine** with clutches, flexible couplings & sr geared to sc. shaft driving 1 FP propeller Total Power: 956kW (1,300hp) Hanshin 6LUN28A 1 x 4 Stroke 6 Cy. 280 x 480 956kW (1300bhp) The Hanshin Diesel Works Ltd-Japan
9393292 *JD2315* -	**SHIGE MARU** **Eiyu Kaiun Co Ltd** - *Tokyo* *Japan* MMSI: 431000161 Official number: 140398	*4,322* - 4,999	Class: NK	**2007-10 Niigata Shipbuilding & Repair Inc — Niigata NI** Yd No: 0015 Loa 104.90 Br ex 16.02 Dght 6.400 Lbp 92.32 Br md 16.00 Dpth 8.50 Welded, 1 dk	**(A13B2TP) Products Tanker** Double Hull (13F) Liq: 6,127; Liq (Oil): 6,127	**2 oil engines** reduction geared to sc. shafts driving 2 CP propellers Total Power: 3,300kW (4,486hp) 14.9kn Wartsila 9L20 2 x 4 Stroke 9 Cy. 200 x 280 each-1650kW (2243bhp) Wartsila Finland Oy-Finland AuxGen: 2 x 620kW a.c Fuel: 300.0
9105413 *JM6372* -	**SHIGEFUKU MARU No. 8** **Shigefuku Kaiun YK** - *Shimonoseki, Yamaguchi* *Japan* Official number: 134462	*499* - 1,200		**1994-10 K.K. Miura Zosensho — Saiki** Yd No: 1111 Loa 65.00 Br ex - Dght 4.140 Lbp 60.00 Br md 10.00 Dpth 4.40 Welded, 1 dk	**(A13B2TP) Products Tanker** 2 Cargo Pump (s): 2x500m³/hr	**1 oil engine** driving 1 FP propeller Total Power: 736kW (1,001hp) 11.8kn Hanshin LH28LG 1 x 4 Stroke 6 Cy. 280 x 530 736kW (1001bhp) The Hanshin Diesel Works Ltd-Japan
9087984 *JM6367* -	**SHIGEFUKU MARU No. 11** **Shigefuku Kaiun YK** - *Shimonoseki, Yamaguchi* *Japan* Official number: 133654	*199* - 600		**1994-05 K.K. Miura Zosensho — Saiki** Yd No: 1101 Loa - Br ex - Dght - Lbp 44.10 Br md 8.00 Dpth 3.43 Welded, 1 dk	**(A13B2TP) Products Tanker**	**1 oil engine** geared to sc. shaft driving 1 FP propeller Total Power: 588kW (799hp) Hanshin 6LC26G 1 x 4 Stroke 6 Cy. 260 x 440 588kW (799bhp) The Hanshin Diesel Works Ltd-Japan
7927477 - -	**SHIGEFUKU No. 11** *ex* Shigefuku Maru No. 11 *-1994* *ex* Kinyu Maru No. 7 *-1989* - -	*199* 117 250		**1980-03 KK Ura Kyodo Zosensho — Awaji HG** Yd No: 201 Loa - Br ex - Dght - Lbp 42.02 Br md 7.51 Dpth 3.36 Welded, 1 dk	**(A13B2TU) Tanker (unspecified)**	**1 oil engine** driving 1 FP propeller Total Power: 441kW (600hp) Yanmar 1 x 4 Stroke 6 Cy. 260 x 400 441kW (600bhp) Yanmar Diesel Engine Co Ltd-Japan
9178630 *7JCU* -	**SHIGEN** *ex* Ramform Victory *-2008* **Government of Japan (Ministry of Economy, Trade & Industry)** Japan Oil Gas & Metals National Corp (JOGMEC) *Funabashi, Chiba* *Japan* MMSI: 432638000 Official number: 140668	**10,395** 3,118 5,200	Class: NK (NV)	**1999-01 Tangen Verft AS — Kragero** (Hull launched by) Yd No: 119 **1999-01 Langsten AS — Tomrefjord** (Hull completed by) Yd No: 177 Loa 86.20 (BB) Br ex - Dght 8.500 Lbp 76.97 Br md 39.60 Dpth 8.50 Welded, 1 dk	**(B31A2SR) Research Survey Vessel** Ice Capable	**4 diesel electric oil engines** driving 4 gen. each 3220kW 4400V a.c Connecting to 4 elec. motors each (3355kW) driving 2 Directional propellers Total Power: 13,420kW (18,244hp) 13.0kn Normo BRM-8 4 x 4 Stroke 8 Cy. 320 x 360 each-3355kW (4561bhp) Ulstein Bergen AS-Norway Thrusters: 1 Retract. directional thruster (f) Fuel: 3567.2 (d.f.) 36.0pd
9523225 *9LY2099* -	**SHIH CHUAN** **Shih Chuan Construction Co Ltd** Kang Long Shipping Co Ltd SatCom: Inmarsat C 466746010 *Freetown* *Sierra Leone* MMSI: 667460000 Official number: SL100460	**3,341** 1,202 -	Class: OM	**2008-05 Changhong Ship Engineering Co Ltd — Fu'an FJ** Yd No: 08H003 Loa 89.45 Br ex - Dght 5.000 Lbp 84.60 Br md 18.00 Dpth 6.60 Welded, 1 dk	**(A31A2GX) General Cargo Ship**	**2 oil engines** reduction geared to sc. shafts driving 2 FP propellers Total Power: 2,648kW (3,600hp) Chinese Std. Type LB8250ZLC 2 x 4 Stroke 8 Cy. 250 x 320 each-1324kW (1800bhp) Zibo Diesel Engine Factory-China
8972912 *ZACU* -	**SHIJAKU** **Xhemal Balliu** - *Durres* *Albania* Official number: T-746	**284** 116 250		**1987 Kantieri Detar "Durres" — Durres** Loa 34.00 Br ex 7.25 Dght 2.740 Lbp - Br md 7.00 Dpth 3.20 Welded, 1 dk	**(A31A2GX) General Cargo Ship**	**1 oil engine** driving 1 FP propeller Total Power: 147kW (200hp) S.K.L. 6NVD36 1 x 4 Stroke 6 Cy. 240 x 360 147kW (200bhp) VEB Schwermaschinenbau "KarlLiebknecht" (SKL)-Magdeburg
8956554 *UFOG* -	**SHIKHAN** *ex* ST-1354 *-2001* **Bashkirian River Shipping Co** Neva-Hugen Ltd *Taganrog* *Russia* MMSI: 273452280 Official number: 207688	**1,456** 504 1,533	Class: RR	**1986-01 Sudostroitelnyy Zavod im. "40-aya Godovshchina Oktyabrya"-Bor** Yd No: 312 Shortened-2001 Loa 82.00 Br ex 12.30 Dght 2.600 Lbp 80.40 Br md 12.00 Dpth 3.50 Welded, 1 dk	**(A31A2GX) General Cargo Ship** Grain: 2,260	**2 oil engines** driving 2 FP propellers Total Power: 882kW (1,200hp) S.K.L. 8VDS36/24A-1 2 x 4 Stroke 8 Cy. 240 x 360 each-441kW (600bhp) VEB Schwermaschinenbau "KarlLiebknecht" (SKL)-Magdeburg AuxGen: 3 x 50kW a.c
8965103 *JG5614* -	**SHIKINAMI** **Government of Japan (Ministry of Land, Infrastructure & Transport) (The Coastguard)** - *Tokyo* *Japan* MMSI: 431301511 Official number: 136972	*116* - -		**2000-10 Ishihara Zosen — Takasago** Yd No: 9291 Loa 35.00 Br ex - Dght - Lbp - Br md 6.50 Dpth 3.43 Welded, 1 dk	**(B34H2SQ) Patrol Vessel**	**2 oil engines** geared to sc. shafts driving 2 FP propellers Total Power: 2,942kW (4,000hp) 24.0kn M.T.U. 12V396TB94 2 x Vee 4 Stroke 12 Cy. 165 x 185 each-1471kW (2000bhp) MTU Friedrichshafen GmbH-Friedrichshafen
8742472 *7JFM* -	**SHIKINE** **Government of Japan (Ministry of Land, Infrastructure & Transport) (The Coastguard)** - *Tokyo* *Japan* MMSI: 432720000 Official number: 141039	*1,324* - -		**2009-10 Mitsubishi Heavy Industries Ltd. — Shimonoseki** Loa 89.00 Br ex - Dght - Lbp 73.63 Br md 11.00 Dpth 5.00 Welded, 1 dk	**(B34H2SQ) Patrol Vessel**	**4 oil engines** reduction geared to sc. shafts driving 4 Water jets Total Power: 14,760kW (20,068hp)
9078646 *JM6252* -	**SHIKISAN** **Kotobuki Kaiun Co Ltd (Kotobuki Kaiun KK)** - *Omuta, Fukuoka* *Japan* Official number: 133531	*731* - 2,050		**1993-07 K.K. Miura Zosensho — Saiki** Yd No: 1072 Loa - Br ex - Dght - Lbp 78.50 Br md 12.80 Dpth 7.80 Welded	**(A31A2GX) General Cargo Ship**	**1 oil engine** driving 1 FP propeller Total Power: 1,471kW (2,000hp) 12.2kn Hanshin LH36LA 1 x 4 Stroke 6 Cy. 360 x 670 1471kW (2000bhp) The Hanshin Diesel Works Ltd-Japan
9009566 *JPHH* -	**SHIKISHIMA** **Government of Japan (Ministry of Land, Infrastructure & Transport) (The Coastguard)** - *Tokyo* *Japan* MMSI: 431004000 Official number: 133100	*7,175* - 3,800		**1992-04 Ishikawajima-Harima Heavy Industries Co Ltd (IHI) — Tokyo** Yd No: 3000 L reg 138.50 Br ex - Dght 5.800 Lbp 150.00 Br md 16.50 Dpth 9.00 Welded	**(B34H2SQ) Patrol Vessel**	**4 oil engines** driving 2 CP propellers Total Power: 26,480kW (36,004hp) Pielstick 12PC2-6V-400 4 x Vee 4 Stroke 12 Cy. 400 x 460 each-6620kW (9001bhp) Diesel United Ltd.-Aioi

9036404 - -	**SHIKO MARU** - - *Indonesia*	*499* - 1,326		**1992**-01 **Honda Zosen — Saiki** Yd No: 832 Loa 76.09 Br ex - Dght 4.250 Lbp 70.00 Br md 11.50 Dpth 7.00 Welded, 1 dk	**(A31A2GX) General Cargo Ship** Compartments: 1 Ho, ER 1 Ha: (40.2 x 9.1)ER	**1 oil engine** driving 1 FP propeller Total Power: 1,177kW (1,600hp) 10.5kn Niigata 6M28HFT 1 x 4 Stroke 6 Cy. 280 x 480 1177kW (1600bhp) Niigata Engineering Co Ltd-Japan
8833972 - -	**SHILALE** - **Burevestnik JSC (OOO 'Burevestnik')** -	**359** 107 129	Class: (RS)	**1990**-04 **Sudostroitelnyy Zavod "Avangard" — Petrozavodsk** Yd No: 623 Loa 35.74 Br ex 8.93 Dght 3.491 Lbp 31.00 Br md - Dpth 6.08 Welded, 1dk	**(B11A2FS) Stern Trawler** Ins: 98	**1 oil engine** driving 1 FP propeller Total Power: 588kW (799hp) 10.9kn S.K.L. 6NVD48A-2U 1 x 4 Stroke 6 Cy. 320 x 480 588kW (799bhp) VEB Schwermaschinenbau "KarlLiebknecht" (SKL)-Magdeburg AuxGen: 2 x 200kW a.c
8954908 *UBIH8* -	**SHILKA** *ex Yunlong -2005 ex Yakutsk -2005* **Tabatha Shipping Inc** Azia Shipping Holding Ltd *Vanino* *Russia* MMSI: 273352130	**3,281** 1,124 5,139	Class: RS	**1972 Krasnoyarskiy Sudostroitelnyy Zavod — Krasnoyarsk** Loa 108.61 Br ex 15.00 Dght 4.740 Lbp 102.14 Br md 14.82 Dpth 7.41 Welded, 1 dk	**(A31A2GX) General Cargo Ship** Compartments: 4 Ho, ER 4 Ha: ER 4 (10.9 x 15.6) Ice Capable	**2 oil engines** driving 2 FP propellers Total Power: 1,030kW (1,400hp) 9.0kn S.K.L. 6NVD48A-2U 2 x 4 Stroke 6 Cy. 320 x 480 each-515kW (700bhp) VEB Schwermaschinenbau "KarlLiebknecht" (SKL)-Magdeburg AuxGen: 3 x 50kW a.c
8813489 *6MET* -	**SHILLA CHALLENGER** - **Silla Co Ltd** - SatCom: Inmarsat C 444045514 *Busan* *South Korea* MMSI: 440492000 Official number: 9512410-6260004	*1,349* 611 1,916	Class: KR	**1990**-06 **Campbell Industries — San Diego, Ca** Yd No: 146 Loa 78.33 (BB) Br ex - Dght 5.586 Lbp 68.70 Br md 13.72 Dpth 7.93 Welded, 2 dks	**(B11B2FV) Fishing Vessel** Ins: 1,614	**1 oil engine** with clutches, flexible couplings & sr geared to sc. shaft driving 1 FP propeller Total Power: 2,942kW (4,000hp) 15.5kn EMD (Electro-Motive) 20-645-F7B 1 x Vee 2 Stroke 20 Cy. 230 x 254 2942kW (4000bhp) General Motors Corp.Electro-Motive Div.-La Grange AuxGen: 3 x 466kW 480V a.c Thrusters: 1 Thwart. FP thruster (f)
8812203 *6MPH* -	**SHILLA EXPLORER** - **Silla Co Ltd** - SatCom: Inmarsat C 444045412 *Busan* *South Korea* MMSI: 440450000 Official number: 9512399-6260000	*1,349* 611 1,916	Class: KR	**1990**-01 **Campbell Industries — San Diego, Ca** Yd No: 144 Loa 78.33 Br ex - Dght 5.586 Lbp 68.70 Br md 13.64 Dpth 6.29 Welded, 2 dks	**(B11B2FV) Fishing Vessel** Ins: 1,614	**1 oil engine** with clutches, flexible couplings & sr geared to sc. shaft driving 1 FP propeller Total Power: 2,942kW (4,000hp) 15.9kn EMD (Electro-Motive) 20-645-E7B 1 x Vee 2 Stroke 20 Cy. 230 x 254 2942kW (4000bhp) General Motors Corp.Electro-Motive Div.-La Grange AuxGen: 3 x 511kW 480V a.c Thrusters: 1 Thwart. FP thruster (f)
9634919 *6KCA5* -	**SHILLA HARVESTER** - **Silla Co Ltd** - *Busan* *South Korea* Official number: 1201001-6261103	**2,359** 713 2,768	Class: KR	**2012**-02 **Ching Fu Shipbuilding Co Ltd — Kaohsiung** Yd No: 090 Loa 79.90 Br ex - Dght 7.011 Lbp 73.20 Br md 15.09 Dpth 8.73 Welded, 1 dk	**(B11B2FV) Fishing Vessel**	**1 oil engine** reduction geared to sc. shaft driving 1 Propeller Total Power: 3,309kW (4,499hp) 17.5kn Daihatsu 6DKM-36 1 x 4 Stroke 6 Cy. 360 x 480 3309kW (4499bhp) Daihatsu Diesel Manufacturing Co Lt-Japan
9199220 *DTBE8* -	**SHILLA JUPITER** *ex Silla Jupiter -2003* **Silla Co Ltd** - *Busan* *South Korea* MMSI: 441066000 Official number: 0104003-6260001	**1,774** 580 2,000	Class: KR	**2001**-05 **Astilleros Marco Chilena Ltda. — Iquique** Yd No: 217 Loa 78.96 Br ex - Dght 6.100 Lbp 69.05 Br md 13.23 Dpth 8.06 Welded, 1 dk	**(B11B2FV) Fishing Vessel** Ins: 1,600	**1 oil engine** reduction geared to sc. shaft driving 1 FP propeller Total Power: 2,942kW (4,000hp) 17.5kn EMD (Electro-Motive) 20-645-F7B 1 x Vee 2 Stroke 20 Cy. 230 x 254 2942kW (4000bhp) General Motors Corp.Electro-Motive Div.-La Grange
8813477 *6MSQ* -	**SHILLA PIONEER** - **Silla Co Ltd** - SatCom: Inmarsat C 444044712 *Busan* *South Korea* MMSI: 440542000 Official number: 9512406-6260000	*1,349* 611 1,916	Class: KR	**1990**-03 **Campbell Industries — San Diego, Ca** Yd No: 145 Loa 78.33 Br ex - Dght 5.586 Lbp 68.70 Br md 13.72 Dpth 7.93 Welded	**(B11B2FV) Fishing Vessel** Ins: 1,614	**1 oil engine** with clutches, flexible couplings & sr geared to sc. shaft driving 1 FP propeller Total Power: 2,942kW (4,000hp) 15.9kn EMD (Electro-Motive) 20-645-E7B 1 x Vee 2 Stroke 20 Cy. 230 x 254 2942kW (4000bhp) General Motors Corp.Electro-Motive Div.-La Grange AuxGen: 3 x 511kW 480V a.c Thrusters: 1 Thwart. FP thruster (f)
9634945 *6KCB4* -	**SHILLA SPRINTER** - **Silla Co Ltd** - *Busan* *South Korea* Official number: 1205001-6261105	**2,359** 713 2,768	Class: KR	**2012**-06 **Ching Fu Shipbuilding Co Ltd — Kaohsiung** Yd No: 091 Loa 79.90 Br ex - Dght 7.000 Lbp 73.20 Br md 15.09 Dpth 8.82 Welded, 1 dk	**(B11B2FV) Fishing Vessel**	**1 oil engine** reduction geared to sc. shaft driving 1 Propeller Total Power: 3,309kW (4,499hp) 17.8kn Daihatsu 6DKM-36 1 x 4 Stroke 6 Cy. 360 x 480 3309kW (4499bhp) Daihatsu Diesel Manufacturing Co Lt-Japan
9069841 - -	**SHILOH** *ex LT-1973 -2003* **Buchanan Renewable Energies (Liberia) Inc**	*234* - -	Class: (AB)	**1954**-01 **Higgins Industries, Inc. — New Orleans, La** Yd No: 11654 Loa 32.60 Br ex 8.18 Dght 3.500 Lbp 30.56 Br md 8.08 Dpth 4.53 Welded, 1 dk	**(B32A2ST) Tug**	**1 oil engine** driving 1 FP propeller Enterprise 37F16 1 x 2 Stroke 10 Cy. 406 x 508 Fairbanks Morse & Co.-New Orleans, La
8709341 *VTSL* -	**SHILPA** - **Surya Sea Foods Pvt Ltd** - *Visakhapatnam* *India* Official number: VSP101	*179* 53 108	Class: (LR) (IR) ✠ Classed LR until 4/3/92	**1989**-03 **Chungmu Shipbuilding Co Inc — Tongyeong** Yd No: 191 Loa 27.40 Br ex 7.38 Dght 2.806 Lbp 23.00 Br md 7.20 Dpth 3.30 Welded, 1 dk	**(B11A2FS) Stern Trawler** Ins: 120	**1 oil engine** with clutches, flexible couplings & sr reverse geared to sc. shaft driving 1 FP propeller Total Power: 416kW (566hp) 9.5kn MAN D2842ME 1 x Vee 4 Stroke 12 Cy. 128 x 141 416kW (566bhp) MAN Nutzfahrzeuge AG-Nuernberg AuxGen: 2 x 52kW 440V 60Hz a.c
9172363 *JG5370* -	**SHIMA MARU** - **Tokyo Kisen KK & KK Nissan Marine Service** Tokyo Kisen KK *Yokohama, Kanagawa* *Japan* Official number: 136605	*166* - -		**1997**-08 **Kanagawa Zosen — Kobe** Yd No: 451 Loa 38.00 Br ex - Dght - Lbp 33.50 Br md 8.40 Dpth 3.40 Welded, 1 dk	**(B32A2ST) Tug**	**2 oil engines** Geared Integral to driving 2 Z propellers Total Power: 2,280kW (3,100hp) 15.3kn Niigata 6L25HX 2 x 4 Stroke 6 Cy. 250 x 350 each-1140kW (1550bhp) Niigata Engineering Co Ltd-Japan
8747898 *JD2942* -	**SHIMAGUMO** - **Government of Japan (Ministry of Land, Infrastructure & Transport) (The Coastguard)** - *Tokyo* *Japan* Official number: 141059	*101* - -		**2009**-08 **Sumidagawa Zosen K.K. — Tokyo** Loa 32.00 Br ex - Dght - Lbp - Br md 6.50 Dpth 3.37 Welded, 1 dk	**(B34H2SQ) Patrol Vessel** Hull Material: Aluminium Alloy	**2 oil engines** reduction geared to sc. shafts driving 2 Propellers 36.0kn
7808853 - -	**SHIMAJI** - - - *Indonesia*	*199* - 40		**1978**-06 **Kanbara Zosen K.K. — Onomichi** Yd No: 235 Loa - Br ex - Dght 1.501 Lbp 29.01 Br md 6.51 Dpth 2.52 Riveted\Welded	**(A37B2PS) Passenger Ship**	**2 oil engines** driving 2 FP propellers Total Power: 772kW (1,050hp) G.M. (Detroit Diesel) 12V-71-TI 2 x Vee 2 Stroke 12 Cy. 108 x 127 each-386kW (525bhp) General Motors Corp-USA
9624574 *7JKX* -	**SHIMAKAZE** - **Government of Japan (Okinawa Customs Office)** - *Naha, Okinawa* *Japan* Official number: 141587	*120* - -		**2012**-03 **Universal Shipbuilding Corp — Yokohama KN (Keihin Shipyard)** Yd No: 0073 Loa 38.00 Br ex - Dght 3.100 Lbp - Br md 6.70 Dpth - Welded, 1 dk	**(B34H2SQ) Patrol Vessel**	**2 oil engines** reduction geared to sc. shafts driving 2 Propellers Total Power: 4,640kW (6,308hp) M.T.U. 16V4000M70 2 x Vee 4 Stroke 16 Cy. 165 x 190 each-2320kW (3154bhp) MTU Friedrichshafen GmbH-Friedrichshafen
7856680 *JG3702* -	**SHIMANAMI** - **Government of Japan (Ministry of Land, Infrastructure & Transport) (The Coastguard)** - *Tokyo* *Japan* Official number: 121464	*123* - -		**1977**-12 **Mitsubishi Heavy Industries Ltd. — Shimonoseki** Loa 26.00 Br ex 6.30 Dght 1.130 Lbp 24.50 Br md 6.29 Dpth 3.04 Welded, 1 dk	**(B34H2SQ) Patrol Vessel** Hull Material: Aluminium Alloy	**3 oil engines** driving 3 FP propellers Total Power: 2,208kW (3,003hp) 22.0kn Mitsubishi 12DM20TK 3 x Vee 4 Stroke 12 Cy. 160 x 200 each-736kW (1001bhp) Mitsubishi Heavy Industries Ltd-Japan Fuel: 5.0 (d.f.)

IMO / Call sign / Flag	Name / Owner / Manager / Port	Tonnage	Class	Builder / Dimensions	Type / Cargo	Machinery
9589786 *3FTV* -	**SHIMANAMI QUEEN** **Seavance Shipping SA** Misuga Kaiun Co Ltd *Panama* *Panama* MMSI: 356222000 Official number: 4272411	**34,778** 20,209 61,472 T/cm 61.4	Class: NK	**2011-06 Shin Kasado Dockyard Co Ltd — Kudamatsu YC** Yd No: K-024 Loa 199.98 (BB) Br ex - Dght 13.010 Lbp 195.00 Br md 32.24 Dpth 18.60 Welded, 1 dk	**(A21A2BC) Bulk Carrier** Grain: 77,674; Bale: 73,552 Compartments: 5 Ho, ER 5 Ha: 4 (23.5 x 19.0)ER (18.7 x 19.0) Cranes: 4x30.5t	**1 oil engine** driving 1 FP propeller Total Power: 8,450kW (11,489hp) 14.5kn MAN-B&W 6S50MC-C8 1 x 2 Stroke 6 Cy. 500 x 2000 8450kW (11489bhp) Hitachi Zosen Corp-Japan
9377717 *C6VN9* -	**SHIMANAMI STAR** **Madison Marine Corp** Evalend Shipping Co SA *Nassau* *Bahamas* MMSI: 309116000 Official number: 8001216	**16,960** 10,498 28,447 T/cm 39.6	Class: NK	**2006-06 Shimanami Shipyard Co Ltd — Imabari EH** Yd No: 514 Loa 169.26 (BB) Br ex - Dght 9.780 Lbp 160.40 Br md 27.20 Dpth 13.60 Welded, 1 dk	**(A21A2BC) Bulk Carrier** Grain: 37,523; Bale: 35,762 Compartments: 5 Ho, ER 5 Ha: 4 (19.2 x 17.6)ER (13.6 x 16.0) Cranes: 4x30.5t	**1 oil engine** driving 1 FP propeller Total Power: 5,850kW (7,954hp) 13.5kn MAN-B&W 6S42MC 1 x 2 Stroke 6 Cy. 420 x 1764 5850kW (7954bhp) Makita Corp-Japan AuxGen: 3 x 440kW a.c Fuel: 115.0 (d.f.) 1100.0 (r.f.)
9308778 *H8WG* -	**SHIMANAMI SUNSHINE** **Marugame Kisen Kaisha Ltd & La Darien Navegacion SA** Thome Ship Management Pte Ltd *Panama* *Panama* MMSI: 355752000 Official number: 3010904B	**28,799** 12,962 47,999 T/cm 51.8	Class: NK	**2004-07 Koyo Dockyard Co Ltd — Mihara HS** Yd No: 2187 Loa 179.99 Br ex - Dght 12.486 Lbp 172.00 Br md 32.20 Dpth 19.05 Welded, 1 dk	**(A13B2TP) Products Tanker** Double Hull (13F) Liq: 57,240; Liq (Oil): 57,240 Cargo Heating Coils Compartments: 10 Ta, ER 4 Cargo Pump (s) Manifold: Bow/CM: 92m	**1 oil engine** driving 1 FP propeller Total Power: 9,480kW (12,889hp) 15.1kn B&W 6S50MC-C 1 x 2 Stroke 6 Cy. 500 x 2000 9480kW (12889bhp) Mitsui Engineering & Shipbuilding CLtd-Japan Fuel: 2130.0
9072953 *7LNO* -	**SHIMANE MARU** **Shimane Prefecture** Shimane Prefecture Gyogyo Kanri-ka *Matsue, Shimane* *Japan* MMSI: 431925000 Official number: 133670	*142* - 133		**1993-02 Wakamatsu Zosen K.K. — Kitakyushu** Yd No: 501 Loa 39.25 (BB) Br ex 6.92 Dght 2.600 Lbp 32.00 Br md 6.90 Dpth 2.90 Welded, 1 dk	**(B12D2FR) Fishery Research Vessel**	**1 oil engine** with clutches, flexible couplings & dr geared to sc. shaft driving 1 CP propeller Total Power: 883kW (1,201hp) Yanmar 6T240-ET 1 x 4 Stroke 6 Cy. 240 x 310 883kW (1201bhp) Yanmar Diesel Engine Co Ltd-Japan Thrusters: 1 Thwart. FP thruster (f)
9234056 *JG5641* -	**SHIMANTO** **Corporation for Advanced Transport & Technology & Sumise Kaiun KK** Sumise Kaiun KK *Tokyo* *Japan* MMSI: 431301574 Official number: 137010	*8,767* - 13,398	Class: NK	**2001-05 Shin Kochi Jyuko K.K. — Kochi** Yd No: 7137 Loa 149.53 Br ex - Dght 7.130 Lbp 142.00 Br md 20.50 Dpth 9.80 Welded, 1 dk	**(A24E2BL) Limestone Carrier** Grain: 10,448 Compartments: 4 Ho, ER 4 Ha: 2 (21.6 x 10.5)2 (22.4 x 10.5)ER	**1 oil engine** driving 1 FP propeller Total Power: 4,457kW (6,060hp) 13.0kn B&W 6S35MC 1 x 2 Stroke 6 Cy. 350 x 1400 4457kW (6060bhp) Makita Corp-Japan Fuel: 530.0
9030199 *JK5089* -	**SHIMANTO GAWA** **Setonaikai Kisen Co Ltd** *Hiroshima, Hiroshima* *Japan* MMSI: 431000477 Official number: 132535	*699* - 238		**1991-06 Kanda Zosensho K.K. — Kawajiri** Yd No: 339 Loa 60.85 Br ex - Dght 2.801 Lbp 55.00 Br md 13.60 Dpth 3.80 Welded	**(A36A2PR) Passenger/Ro-Ro Ship (Vehicles)** Lorries: 8	**2 oil engines** geared to sc. shafts driving 2 CP propellers Total Power: 2,060kW (2,800hp) 14.4kn Niigata 6MG26HX 2 x 4 Stroke 6 Cy. 260 x 275 each-1030kW (1400bhp) Niigata Engineering Co Ltd-Japan AuxGen: 2 x 180kW 445V 60Hz a.c Thrusters: 1 Thwart. CP thruster (f)
9115470 *JL6315* -	**SHIMANTO MARU** **Oki Tsutae** *Shimanto, Kochi* *Japan* MMSI: 431500288 Official number: 133967	*498* - 1,598		**1994-12 Shirahama Zosen K.K. — Honai** Yd No: 168 Loa 70.05 (BB) Br ex - Dght 3.974 Lbp 65.00 Br md 13.60 Dpth 6.76 Welded, 1 dk	**(A24D2BA) Aggregates Carrier**	**1 oil engine** geared to sc. shaft driving 1 FP propeller Total Power: 736kW (1,001hp) Hanshin 6LU35G 1 x 4 Stroke 6 Cy. 350 x 550 736kW (1001bhp) The Hanshin Diesel Works Ltd-Japan Thrusters: 1 Thwart. CP thruster (f)
8989496 *JH3516* -	**SHIMAYURI** **Meitetsu Kaijo Kankosen KK** - *Minami-chita, Aichi* *Japan* Official number: 135714	*276* - 150		**2004-02 Suzuki Shipyard Co. Ltd. — Yokkaichi** Yd No: 683 Loa 36.95 Br ex - Dght - Lbp 32.00 Br md 10.40 Dpth 3.20 Welded, 1 dk	**(A36A2PR) Passenger/Ro-Ro Ship (Vehicles)**	**1 oil engine** reduction geared to sc. shaft driving 1 Propeller Total Power: 736kW (1,001hp) Yanmar 6RY17P-GV 1 x 4 Stroke 6 Cy. 165 x 219 736kW (1001bhp) Yanmar Diesel Engine Co Ltd-Japan
8839691 - -	**SHIMIZU MARU NO. 2** *ex Ise Maru No. 2 -2010 ex Shoki Maru -1993* - -	*294* - 1,049		**1989-11 K.K. Kamishima Zosensho — Osakikamijima** Yd No: 303 Loa 54.24 Br ex - Dght 3.900 Lbp 46.00 Br md 11.50 Dpth 5.60 Welded, 1 dk	**(A24D2BA) Aggregates Carrier** 1 Ha: (15.4 x 9.0)ER	**1 oil engine** driving 1 FP propeller Total Power: 736kW (1,001hp) 11.0kn Matsui ML628GSC 1 x 4 Stroke 6 Cy. 280 x 520 736kW (1001bhp) Matsui Iron Works Co Ltd-Japan
7914705 - -	**SHIMIZU MARU No. 28** - -	*528* - 1,000		**1979-03 K.K. Kanmasu Zosensho — Imabari** Yd No: 89 Loa 50.00 Br ex - Dght 2.601 Lbp 48.10 Br md 17.00 Dpth 3.30 Welded, 1 dk	**(B34B2SC) Crane Vessel**	**1 oil engine** driving 1 FP propeller Total Power: 1,067kW (1,451hp) Akasaka AH28A 1 x 4 Stroke 6 Cy. 280 x 460 1067kW (1451bhp) Akasaka Tekkosho KK (Akasaka DieselLtd)-Japan
8742458 *7JEP* -	**SHIMOKITA** *ex Motobu -2012* **Government of Japan (Ministry of Land, Infrastructure & Transport) (The Coastguard)** *Tokyo* *Japan* MMSI: 432689000 Official number: 140914	*1,349* - -		**2009-03 Mitsui Eng. & SB. Co. Ltd. — Tamano** Yd No: 1752 Loa 89.00 Br ex - Dght - Lbp - Br md 11.00 Dpth 5.00 Welded, 1 dk	**(B34H2SQ) Patrol Vessel**	**4 oil engines** reduction geared to sc. shafts driving 4 Water jets Total Power: 14,760kW (20,068hp)
9084243 *JG5297* -	**SHIMOKITA MARU** **Shinwa Naiko Kaiun Kaisha Ltd** *Tokyo* *Japan* MMSI: 431100125 Official number: 134330	*4,483* - 5,500	Class: NK	**1994-03 Shikoku Dockyard Co. Ltd. — Takamatsu** Yd No: 869 Loa 94.00 (BB) Br ex - Dght 6.313 Lbp 88.00 Br md 17.20 Dpth 9.70 Welded, 1 dk	**(A24E2BL) Limestone Carrier** Grain: 4,065 Compartments: 2 Ho, ER 3 Ha: (15.8 x 11.2) (10.2 x 11.2) (16.5 x 11.2)ER	**1 oil engine** driving 1 FP propeller Total Power: 3,236kW (4,400hp) 12.3kn B&W 5L35MC 1 x 2 Stroke 5 Cy. 350 x 1050 3236kW (4400bhp) Mitsui Engineering & Shipbuilding CLtd-Japan Fuel: 75.0 (d.f.)
9279240 *4XJF* -	**SHIMSHON** **Ashdod Port Co Ltd** - *Ashdod* *Israel*	363 109 168	Class: LR ✠ **100A1** SS 02/2008 tug fire fighting Ship 1 (2400 cubic m/hr) with water spray ✠ **LMC** **UMS** Eq.Ltr: G; Cable: 302.5/24.0 U2 (a)	**2003-02 Union Naval Valencia SA (UNV) — Valencia** Yd No: 329 Loa 29.50 Br ex 11.62 Dght 3.450 Lbp 28.00 Br md 11.00 Dpth 4.00 Welded, 1 dk	**(B32A2ST) Tug**	**2 oil engines** gearing integral to driving 2 Voith-Schneider propellers Total Power: 3,870kW (5,262hp) Caterpillar 3606TA 2 x 4 Stroke 6 Cy. 280 x 300 each-1935kW (2631bhp) Caterpillar Inc-USA AuxGen: 2 x 145kW 380V 50Hz a.c
9635286 *JD3307* -	**SHIN AI MARU** **Shinko Butsuryu KK** - *Kobe, Hyogo* *Japan* MMSI: 431003187 Official number: 141604	*499* - 1,810		**2012-01 Yamanaka Zosen K.K. — Imabari** Yd No: 822 Loa 74.24 Br ex - Dght 4.362 Lbp 68.00 Br md 12.00 Dpth 7.37 Welded, 1 dk	**(A31A2GX) General Cargo Ship** Grain: 2,921	**1 oil engine** geared to sc. shaft driving 1 FP propeller Total Power: 1,618kW (2,200hp) Hanshin LA32G 1 x 4 Stroke 6 Cy. 320 x 680 1618kW (2200bhp) The Hanshin Diesel Works Ltd-Japan
9088756 *JJ3872* -	**SHIN ASAHI MARU** **Shinsei Kaiun YK** - *Anan, Tokushima* *Japan* MMSI: 431300114 Official number: 132403	*499* - 1,600		**1993-10 Watanabe Zosen KK — Imabari EH** Yd No: 275 Loa - Br ex - Dght 4.160 Lbp 71.50 Br md 11.70 Dpth 7.18 Welded	**(A31A2GX) General Cargo Ship**	**1 oil engine** driving 1 FP propeller Total Power: 1,471kW (2,000hp) Niigata 6M34AGT 1 x 4 Stroke 6 Cy. 340 x 620 1471kW (2000bhp) Niigata Engineering Co Ltd-Japan
9623582 *JD3184* -	**SHIN BUNGO MARU** **Oita Kaiun KK** - *Tsukumi, Oita* *Japan* Official number: 141429	*310* - 908		**2011-04 Hongawara Zosen K.K. — Fukuyama** Yd No: 651 Loa 56.18 Br ex 10.22 Dght 3.750 Lbp 52.00 Br md 10.20 Dpth 5.50 Welded, 1 dk	**(A24A2BT) Cement Carrier**	**1 oil engine** driving 1 Propeller Total Power: 736kW (1,001hp) Yanmar 1 x 4 Stroke 736kW (1001bhp) Yanmar Diesel Engine Co Ltd-Japan

IMO / Call sign	Name / Owner	Tonnage	Class	Builder / Dimensions	Type	Machinery
8109151 - -	**SHIN CHANG 1** *ex* Ebisu Maru No. 18 *-1999* *ex* Eishin Maru No. 18 *-1994* - -	*199* - 697		**1981**-02 **K.K. Saidaiji Zosensho — Okayama** Yd No: 77 Loa - Br ex - Dght 3.252 Lbp 52.02 Br md 9.01 Dpth 4.91 Welded, 1 dk	**(A31A2GX) General Cargo Ship**	**1 oil engine** driving 1 FP propeller Total Power: 662kW (900hp) Hanshin 6LU28G 1 x 4 Stroke 6 Cy. 280 x 440 662kW (900bhp) Hanshin Nainenki Kogyo-Japan
7853377 - -	**SHIN CHANG No. 9** *ex* Taihei Maru No. 11 *-1999* - -	*335* - 700		**1976 Edogawa Shipbuilding Co. Ltd. — Tokyo** Loa 42.19 Br ex - Dght 3.701 Lbp 38.99 Br md 8.60 Dpth 3.92 Welded, 1 dk	**(A13B2TU) Tanker (unspecified)**	**1 oil engine** driving 1 FP propeller Total Power: 368kW (500hp) 9.0kn Matsui 1 x 4 Stroke 368kW (500bhp) Matsui Iron Works Co Ltd-Japan
6715401 *6NMF* -	**SHIN CHANG No. 301** *ex* Shin Heung No. 301 *-1996* *ex* Cheog Yang No. 31 *-1993* *ex* Seisho Maru No. 7 *-1976* *ex* Chosho Maru No. 11 *-1976* **Shin Chang Fisheries Co Ltd** - *Busan* *South Korea* Official number: 9506032-6210005	*370* 186 433	Class: (KR)	**1967 Miho Zosensho K.K. — Shimizu** Yd No: 612 Loa 54.30 Br ex 8.23 Dght 3.395 Lbp 49.15 Br md 8.20 Dpth 3.80 Welded, 1 dk	**(B11B2FV) Fishing Vessel** Ins: 348	**1 oil engine** driving 1 FP propeller Total Power: 956kW (1,300hp) 11.5kn Niigata 6M37HS 1 x 4 Stroke 6 Cy. 370 x 540 956kW (1300bhp) Niigata Engineering Co Ltd-Japan AuxGen: 2 x 184kW 225V a.c
7426473 *6MPW*	**SHIN CHANG No. 502** *ex* Shin Heung No. 502 *-1996* *ex* Hae Nam 502 *-1995* *ex* Massur No. 2 *-1990* *ex* Clover No. 110 *-1984* **Shin Chang Fisheries Co Ltd** - *Busan* *South Korea* Official number: 9502020-6210007	*337* 160 373	Class: (KR)	**1975**-06 **Minami-Nippon Zosen KK — Ichikikushikino KS** Yd No: 226 Loa 48.32 Br ex - Dght 3.214 Lbp 41.81 Br md 8.11 Dpth 3.51 Welded, 1 dk	**(B11B2FV) Fishing Vessel** Ins: 337 3 Ha: (1.3 x 1.0) (1.6 x 1.6) (1.3 x 0.9)	**1 oil engine** driving 1 FP propeller Total Power: 625kW (850hp) 12.4kn Hanshin 6LUS24G 1 x 4 Stroke 6 Cy. 240 x 405 625kW (850bhp) The Hanshin Diesel Works Ltd-Japan AuxGen: 2 x 160kW 225V a.c
8431255 - -	**SHIN CHIEN CHUNG No. 361** - -	*322* 177 -		**1983 Taiwan Machinery Manufacturing Corp. — Kaohsiung** L reg 36.15 Br ex - Dght - Lbp - Br md 7.62 Dpth 3.38 Welded, 1 dk	**(B11B2FV) Fishing Vessel**	**1 oil engine** driving 1 FP propeller Total Power: 809kW (1,100hp) 11.0kn
8431267 - -	**SHIN CHIEN CHUNG No. 362** - -	*322* 177 -		**1983 Taiwan Machinery Manufacturing Corp. — Kaohsiung** L reg 36.15 Br ex - Dght - Lbp - Br md 7.62 Dpth 3.38 Welded, 1 dk	**(B11B2FV) Fishing Vessel**	**1 oil engine** driving 1 FP propeller Total Power: 809kW (1,100hp) 11.0kn
9272840 *7JGW* -	**SHIN CHOU MARU** *ex* Omni Taran *-2010* *ex* Shin Chou Maru *-2007* **Offshore Engineering Co Ltd** Kyoei Marine Co Ltd *Tokyo* *Japan* MMSI: 432743000 Official number: 141208	**2,475** 742 2,633	Class: NK (AB)	**2003**-05 **Niigata Shipbuilding & Repair Inc — Niigata NI** Yd No: 2506 Loa 71.15 Br ex - Dght 6.160 Lbp 63.00 Br md 16.00 Dpth 6.80 Welded, 1 dk	**(B21B20A) Anchor Handling Tug Supply**	**2 oil engines** geared to sc. shafts driving 2 CP propellers Total Power: 5,520kW (7,504hp) 13.0kn Wartsila 6L32 2 x 4 Stroke 6 Cy. 320 x 400 each-2760kW (3752bhp) Wartsila Finland Oy-Finland AuxGen: 2 x 1295kW 450V 60Hz a.c, 3 x 425kW 450V 60Hz a.c Thrusters: 2 Thwart. CP thruster (f); 1 Thwart. CP thruster (a) Fuel: 990.0
9166297 *3FPI8* -	**SHIN CHUETSU** **Superior Chip Carriers SA** Iino Marine Service Co Ltd SatCom: Inmarsat C 435292110 *Panama* *Panama* MMSI: 352921000 Official number: 2578398C	**22,601** 6,781 25,331	Class: NK	**1998**-07 **Hitachi Zosen Corp — Maizuru KY** Yd No: 4939 Loa 162.00 (BB) Br ex - Dght 9.070 Lbp 153.00 Br md 27.60 Dpth 18.20 Welded, 1 dk	**(A24B2BW) Wood Chips Carrier** Grain: 51,534 Compartments: 4 Ho, ER 4 Ha: ER Cranes: 2x12.5t	**1 oil engine** driving 1 FP propeller Total Power: 5,590kW (7,600hp) 14.0kn B&W 5S50MC 1 x 2 Stroke 5 Cy. 500 x 1910 5590kW (7600bhp) Hitachi Zosen Corp-Japan AuxGen: 3 x 600kW a.c Fuel: 1524.0 (r.f.) 19.8pd
8611790 *VRFD2* -	**SHIN CHUN** **Wan Hai Lines (Singapore) Pte Ltd** Wan Hai Lines Ltd *Hong Kong* *Hong Kong* MMSI: 477218300 Official number: HK-2383	**9,965** 4,776 14,263 T/cm 28.0	Class: CR NK (AB)	**1987**-03 **Naikai Shipbuilding & Engineering Co Ltd — Onomichi HS (Setoda Shipyard)** Yd No: 519 Loa 151.60 (BB) Br ex 23.53 Dght 8.702 Lbp 142.02 Br md 23.50 Dpth 11.61 Welded, 1 dk	**(A33A2CC) Container Ship (Fully Cellular)** TEU 640 incl 70 ref C. Compartments: 4 Cell Ho, ER 7 Ha: (6.3 x 13.6)6 (12.6 x 19.0)ER Cranes: 1x30.5t	**1 oil engine** driving 1 FP propeller Total Power: 6,222kW (8,459hp) 18.8kn B&W 7L50MC 1 x 2 Stroke 7 Cy. 500 x 1620 6222kW (8459bhp) Hitachi Zosen Corp-Japan AuxGen: 3 x 500kW a.c Thrusters: 1 Thwart. CP thruster (f) Fuel: 770.0 (r.f.)
8500446 - -	**SHIN CHUN No. 106** *ex* Hokushin Maru *-2000* **Trans Pacific Journey Fishing Corp** - *Philippines*	**1,463** 479 1,430	Class: (NK)	**1984**-10 **Kinoura Zosen K.K. — Imabari** Yd No: 123 Loa 75.77 Br ex - Dght 4.172 Lbp 70.01 Br md 11.82 Dpth 4.22 Welded, 2 dks	**(A31A2GX) General Cargo Ship** Ins: 1,841 2 Ha: 2 (5.2 x 4.6)ER Derricks: 4x2t	**1 oil engine** driving 1 FP propeller Total Power: 1,324kW (1,800hp) 12.0kn Akasaka A31 1 x 4 Stroke 6 Cy. 310 x 600 1324kW (1800bhp) Akasaka Tekkosho KK (Akasaka DieselLtd)-Japan AuxGen: 2 x 240kW a.c
8614819 - -	**SHIN CHUN YANG** *ex* Toko Maru *-2000* **Sam Kyung Co Ltd** - *Yeosu* *South Korea* MMSI: 440300280 Official number: YSR-005727	*699* - 2,050	Class: (KR)	**1987**-03 **Hakata Zosen K.K. — Imabari** Yd No: 352 Loa - Br ex - Dght 4.801 Lbp 68.51 Br md 12.01 Dpth 5.11 Welded, 1 dk	**(A13B2TP) Products Tanker** Liq: 2,149; Liq (Oil): 2,149 Compartments: 10 Ta, ER	**1 oil engine** driving 1 FP propeller Total Power: 1,103kW (1,500hp) Niigata 6M30GT 1 x 4 Stroke 6 Cy. 300 x 530 1103kW (1500bhp) Niigata Engineering Co Ltd-Japan
8609840 *3FWS5* -	**SHIN CO-OP MARU** **Kuma Shipping Corp** Kumazawa Kaiun Co Ltd SatCom: Inmarsat C 435413610 *Panama* *Panama* MMSI: 354136000 Official number: 24885PEXT2	**4,007** 1,543 5,993	Class: NK	**1986**-10 **Usuki Iron Works Co Ltd — Saiki OT** Yd No: 1332 Loa 97.69 (BB) Br ex - Dght 7.651 Lbp 90.00 Br md 17.01 Dpth 8.92 Welded, 1 dk	**(A13B2TP) Products Tanker** Double Bottom Entire Compartment Length Liq: 5,092; Liq (Oil): 5,092 Compartments: 8 Ta, ER	**1 oil engine** driving 1 CP propeller Total Power: 2,354kW (3,200hp) 12.7kn Akasaka DM40AKFD 1 x 4 Stroke 6 Cy. 400 x 640 2354kW (3200bhp) Akasaka Tekkosho KK (Akasaka DieselLtd)-Japan AuxGen: 2 x 300kW 60Hz a.c Fuel: 920.0 (r.f.)
9337145 *7JOA* -	**SHIN-EI** **NS United Kaiun Kaisha Ltd** NS United Marine Service Corp *Kimitsu, Chiba* *Japan* MMSI: 432919000 Official number: 141859	**106,384** 64,195 207,933	Class: NK	**2008**-06 **Universal Shipbuilding Corp — Tsu ME** Yd No: 054 Loa 299.70 (BB) Br ex - Dght 18.230 Lbp 291.75 Br md 50.00 Dpth 25.00 Welded, 1 dk	**(A21A2BC) Bulk Carrier** Grain: 218,790 Compartments: 9 Ho, ER 9 Ha: ER	**1 oil engine** driving 1 FP propeller Total Power: 16,610kW (22,583hp) 14.0kn MAN-B&W 6S70MC-C 1 x 2 Stroke 6 Cy. 700 x 2800 16610kW (22583bhp) Mitsui Engineering & Shipbuilding CLtd-Japan AuxGen: 3 x 560kW 450V a.c Fuel: 507.0 (d.f.) (Heating Coils) 4695.0 (r.f.)
6928163 - -	**SHIN FU TAI No. 11** - **Fu Tai Fishing Co Ltd** - *Kaohsiung* *Chinese Taipei*	*230* - -		**1969 Suao Shipbuilding Co., Ltd. — Suao** Loa 36.58 Br ex 6.94 Dght - Lbp 31.98 Br md 6.91 Dpth 3.00 Welded, 1 dk	**(B11B2FV) Fishing Vessel**	**1 oil engine** driving 1 FP propeller Total Power: 405kW (551hp) Niigata 1 x 4 Stroke 405kW (551bhp) Niigata Engineering Co Ltd-Japan
9140281 *YJQA4* -	**SHIN FUJI** **Sea Road Line Inc** Kyoei Kaiun Kaisha Ltd *Port Vila* *Vanuatu* MMSI: 576276000 Official number: 1900	**3,822** 1,561 3,966	Class: NK	**1996**-07 **Miyoshi Shipbuilding Co Ltd — Uwajima EH** Yd No: 335 Loa 99.50 (BB) Br ex - Dght 6.553 Lbp 89.50 Br md 16.40 Dpth 9.90 Welded, 1 dk	**(A34A2GR) Refrigerated Cargo Ship** Ins: 4,724 4 Ha: 4 (4.3 x 3.8) Derricks: 8x3t	**1 oil engine** driving 1 FP propeller Total Power: 2,942kW (4,000hp) 14.0kn Mitsubishi 6UEC33LSII 1 x 2 Stroke 6 Cy. 330 x 1050 2942kW (4000bhp) Akasaka Tekkosho KK (Akasaka DieselLtd)-Japan Thrusters: 1 Tunnel thruster (f) Fuel: 860.0 (r.f.)
9110030 *JI3572* -	**SHIN FUJI MARU** **KK Kansai Kowan Kogyo & Seiho Kogyo KK** - *Osaka, Osaka* *Japan* Official number: 135013	*129* - -		**1994**-07 **Kegoya Dock K.K. — Kure** Yd No: 962 Loa 27.00 Br ex - Dght 3.870 Lbp 24.50 Br md 11.00 Dpth 6.00 Welded, 1 dk	**(B32A2ST) Tug**	**2 oil engines** driving 2 FP propellers Total Power: 3,220kW (4,378hp) 11.0kn Yanmar MF33-ET 2 x 4 Stroke 6 Cy. 330 x 620 each-1610kW (2189bhp) Yanmar Diesel Engine Co Ltd-Japan AuxGen: 2 x 120kW 220V 60Hz a.c Thrusters: 1 Thwart. CP thruster (f) Fuel: 37.0 (d.f.) 19.9pd

8923806 *JL6456* -	**SHIN FUKUJU MARU** **Umemaru Kisen YK** - *Imabari, Ehime* Japan MMSI: 431500453 Official number: 135167	*199* - 689		**1996-04 K.K. Kamishima Zosensho — Osakikamijima** Yd No: 587 Loa 56.91 Br ex - Dght 3.240 Lbp 51.00 Br md 9.40 Dpth 5.43 Welded, 1 dk	**(A31A2GX) General Cargo Ship** Compartments: 1 Ho, ER 1 Ha: (29.5 x 7.4)ER	**1 oil engine** driving 1 FP propeller Total Power: 736kW (1,001hp) 11.5kn Matsui MA28GSC-33 1 x 4 Stroke 6 Cy. 280 x 540 736kW (1001bhp) Matsui Iron Works Co Ltd-Japan
8738287 *JD2699* -	**SHIN HAKUUN MARU** **Hakata Koun KK & Green Shipping KK** - *Fukuoka, Fukuoka* Japan Official number: 140782	*196* - -		**2008-05 Kotobuki Kogyo KK — Ichikikushikino KS** Yd No: 130 Loa 36.30 Br ex - Dght 2.860 Lbp 32.00 Br md 9.20 Dpth 3.98 Welded, 1 dk	**(B32A2ST) Tug**	**2 oil engines** reduction geared to sc. shafts driving 2 Propellers Total Power: 3,676kW (4,998hp) 12.0kn Niigata 6L28HX 2 x 4 Stroke 6 Cy. 280 x 370 each-1838kW (2499bhp) Niigata Engineering Co Ltd-Japan
8214839 *3FRT* -	**SHIN HANG** *ex* Glacier Bay *-2011* *ex* Cap Verde *-1995* *ex* Causewaybay *-1989* *ex* Cap Delgado *-1989* **Shin Hang Shipping Co Ltd** Dalian Transquare-line International Ship Management Co Ltd *Panama* Panama MMSI: 351763000 Official number: 4328711	**8,739** 3,973 9,746	Class: BV (NK)	**1985-02 Shikoku Dockyard Co. Ltd. — Takamatsu** Yd No: 823 Loa 143.52 (BB) Br ex 21.52 Dght 8.516 Lbp 135.01 Br md 21.51 Dpth 13.11 Welded, 4 dks	**(A34A2GR) Refrigerated Cargo Ship** Ins: 12,253 TEU 28 incl 16 ref C Compartments: 4 Ho, ER 4 Ha: 4 (7.7 x 7.7)ER Derricks: 8x7t	**1 oil engine** sr geared to sc. shaft driving 1 FP propeller Total Power: 6,620kW (9,001hp) 18.0kn Pielstick 12PC2-6V-400 1 x Vee 4 Stroke 12 Cy. 400 x 460 6620kW (9001bhp) Ishikawajima Harima Heavy IndustrieCo Ltd (IHI)-Japan AuxGen: 3 x 640kW 440/110V 60Hz a.c Fuel: 265.0 (d.f.) 1365.0 (r.f.) 25.0pd
8318659 *3FOZ2* -	**SHIN HANG 6** *ex* Atlantic Hope *-2013* *ex* Magellan Rex *-1996* **Shinhang Reefer Shipping Co Ltd** Dalian Transquare-line International Ship Management Co Ltd SatCom: Inmarsat A 1335506 *Panama* Panama MMSI: 356878000 Official number: 12353PEXT4	**7,777** 3,909 8,495	Class: NK	**1984-03 Hayashikane Shipbuilding & Engineering Co Ltd — Shimonoseki YC** Yd No: 1274 Loa 142.04 (BB) Br ex 19.84 Dght 8.516 Lbp 134.02 Br md 19.80 Dpth 12.50 Welded, 4 dks	**(A34A2GR) Refrigerated Cargo Ship** Side doors (p) Ins: 11,672 TEU 8 Compartments: 4 Ho, ER 4 Ha: 4 (9.0 x 7.0)ER Derricks: 8x5t; Winches: 8	**1 oil engine** driving 1 FP propeller Total Power: 6,708kW (9,120hp) 18.3kn Mitsubishi 6UEC52HA 1 x 2 Stroke 6 Cy. 520 x 1250 6708kW (9120bhp) Kobe Hatsudoki KK-Japan AuxGen: 3 x 700kW Fuel: 1230.0 (r.f.)
9271602 *7JIS* -	**SHIN HEIRYU** **Nippon Yusen Kabushiki Kaisha (NYK Line)** NYK Shipmanagement Pte Ltd SatCom: Inmarsat C 443279310 *Tokyo* Japan MMSI: 432793000 Official number: 141370	**102,207** 66,554 203,315 T/cm 138.0	Class: NK	**2003-06 Universal Shipbuilding Corp — Tsu ME** Yd No: 228 Loa 299.95 (BB) Br ex - Dght 17.910 Lbp 290.00 Br md 50.00 Dpth 24.10 Welded, 1 dk	**(A21A2BC) Bulk Carrier** Grain: 217,968 Compartments: 9 Ho, ER 9 Ha: ER 9 (23.4 x 15.7)	**1 oil engine** driving 1 FP propeller Total Power: 16,020kW (21,781hp) 14.5kn B&W 6S70MC 1 x 2 Stroke 6 Cy. 700 x 2674 16020kW (21781bhp) Mitsui Engineering & Shipbuilding CLtd-Japan AuxGen: 3 x 600kW 440/10V 60Hz a.c Fuel: 383.0 (d.f.) (Heating Coils) 5329.0 (r.f.) 54.9pd
9115482 *JM6425* -	**SHIN HEISEI** *ex* Shinnikko Maru *-2012* - - *Uki, Kumamoto* Japan MMSI: 431600313 Official number: 134515	*216* - 700		**1994-11 Shitanoe Shipbuilding Co Ltd — Usuki OT** Yd No: 1158 Loa - Br ex - Dght 3.120 Lbp 53.10 Br md 9.50 Dpth 5.30 Welded, 1 dk	**(A31A2GX) General Cargo Ship**	**1 oil engine** driving 1 FP propeller Total Power: 736kW (1,001hp) Niigata 6M26AGTE 1 x 4 Stroke 6 Cy. 260 x 460 736kW (1001bhp) Niigata Engineering Co Ltd-Japan
9220653 *T3LR* -	**SHIN HO CHUN No. 101** **Tunago Shipping Co Ltd** *Tarawa* Kiribati MMSI: 529089000 Official number: K-10990740	**2,495** 1,108 3,000	Class: CR	**1999-12 Lin Sheng Shipbuilding Co, Ltd — Kaohsiung** Yd No: 8801 Loa 95.20 Br ex 14.00 Dght - Lbp 86.40 Br md - Dpth 6.70 Welded, 1 dk	**(B12B2FC) Fish Carrier**	**1 oil engine** driving 1 FP propeller Total Power: 2,427kW (3,300hp) Akasaka A41 1 x 4 Stroke 6 Cy. 410 x 800 2427kW (3300bhp) Akasaka Tekkosho KK (Akasaka DieselLtd)-Japan
9262182 *T3LN* -	**SHIN HO CHUN NO. 102** **Tunago Shipping Co Ltd** *Tarawa* Kiribati MMSI: 529086000 Official number: K-10020737	**2,900** 1,473 2,500		**2002-01 Lien Cherng Shipbuilding Co, Ltd — Kaohsiung** Yd No: 106 Loa 95.20 Br ex 14.00 Dght - Lbp 85.20 Br md - Dpth 6.70 Welded, 1 dk	**(B12B2FC) Fish Carrier**	**1 oil engine** driving 1 FP propeller Total Power: 2,427kW (3,300hp) Akasaka A41 1 x 4 Stroke 6 Cy. 410 x 800 2427kW (3300bhp) Akasaka Tekkosho KK (Akasaka DieselLtd)-Japan
9220524 *JG5597* -	**SHIN HOKUO MARU** **Japan Railway Construction, Transport & Technology Agency & Hokusei Kaiun Co Ltd** Hokusei Kaiun KK *Tokyo* Japan MMSI: 431100865 Official number: 136771	*5,901* - 4,409	Class: NK	**1999-12 Imabari Shipbuilding Co Ltd — Imabari EH (Imabari Shipyard)** Yd No: 562 Loa 136.21 (BB) Br ex - Dght 6.915 Lbp 126.00 Br md 21.40 Dpth 7.55 Welded, 4 dks	**(A35A2RR) Ro-Ro Cargo Ship** Lane-Len: 1200 Trailers: 87	**1 oil engine** driving 1 FP propeller Total Power: 12,621kW (17,160hp) 20.5kn B&W 8S50MC-C 1 x 2 Stroke 8 Cy. 500 x 2000 12621kW (17160bhp) Kawasaki Heavy Industries Ltd-Japan AuxGen: 3 x 880kW a.c Fuel: 693.0 (r.f.)
9088196 - -	**SHIN HOSEI** *ex* Miho Maru No. 20 *-1999* - Indonesia	*498* - 1,599		**1994-03 Shin Kochi Jyuko K.K. — Kochi** Yd No: 7043 Loa - Br ex - Dght 3.918 Lbp 70.00 Br md 12.50 Dpth 6.80 Welded, 2 dks	**(A31A2GX) General Cargo Ship** Grain: 3,064; Bale: 2,478 Compartments: 1 Ho, ER 1 Ha: (39.0 x 9.5)ER	**1 oil engine** driving 1 FP propeller Total Power: 736kW (1,001hp) Niigata 6M31BLGT 1 x 4 Stroke 6 Cy. 310 x 600 736kW (1001bhp) Niigata Engineering Co Ltd-Japan
9370953 *JD2250* -	**SHIN HOSHU MARU** **Nishitaki Kaiun KK** *Tsukumi, Oita* Japan MMSI: 431602336 Official number: 140321	*696* - 2,160		**2006-05 Yamanaka Zosen K.K. — Imabari** Yd No: 722 Loa 80.59 Br ex - Dght 4.370 Lbp 75.00 Br md 13.40 Dpth 7.57 Welded, 2 dks	**(A31A2GX) General Cargo Ship** Grain: 2,695; Bale: 2,695 1 Ha: ER (39.4 x 10.0)	**1 oil engine** driving 1 FP propeller Total Power: 1,324kW (1,800hp) 12.0kn Hanshin LH30LG 1 x 4 Stroke 6 Cy. 300 x 600 1324kW (1800bhp) The Hanshin Diesel Works Ltd-Japan
9296652 *JK5619* -	**SHIN HOUYOSHI MARU** **Fuji Transportation Co Ltd & Komenaka Kaiun KK** Fuji Transportation Co Ltd (Fuji Unyu KK) *Kaminoseki, Yamaguchi* Japan Official number: 136184	*999* - 2,400	Class: NK	**2003-09 K.K. Miura Zosensho — Saiki** Yd No: 1267 Loa 79.78 Br ex - Dght 5.250 Lbp 76.00 Br md 12.20 Dpth 5.75 Welded, 1 dk	**(A13B2TP) Products Tanker** Liq: 2,600; Liq (Oil): 2,600	**1 oil engine** driving 1 FP propeller Total Power: 1,618kW (2,200hp) Akasaka A34C 1 x 4 Stroke 6 Cy. 340 x 620 1618kW (2200bhp) Akasaka Tekkosho KK (Akasaka DieselLtd)-Japan Fuel: 90.0 (d.f.)
8625571 - -	**SHIN HOWA MARU** **Jehan Shipping Corp** - Philippines	*199* - 692		**1986 K.K. Kamishima Zosensho — Osakikamijima** Yd No: 177 Loa 54.11 Br ex - Dght 3.450 Lbp 49.51 Br md 9.01 Dpth 5.52 Welded, 1 dk	**(A31A2GX) General Cargo Ship** Grain: 1,273; Bale: 1,228	**1 oil engine** driving 1 FP propeller Total Power: 405kW (551hp) 10.3kn Matsui 6M26KGHS 1 x 4 Stroke 6 Cy. 260 x 400 405kW (551bhp) Matsui Iron Works Co Ltd-Japan
9132715 *JM6476* -	**SHIN HOYO MARU** **Corporation for Advanced Transport & Technology & GK Nakatsuru Gumi** GK Nakatsuru Gumi *Tsukumi, Oita* Japan MMSI: 431400491 Official number: 134587	*749* - 1,753	Class: NK	**1995-10 Kambara Marine Development & Shipbuilding Co Ltd — Fukuyama HS** Yd No: OE-203 Loa 68.75 Br ex - Dght 4.611 Lbp 65.00 Br md 11.50 Dpth 5.10 Welded, 1 dk	**(A24A2BT) Cement Carrier** Grain: 1,355	**1 oil engine** reduction geared to sc. shaft driving 1 FP propeller Total Power: 1,030kW (1,400hp) 11.0kn Niigata 6M28BFT 1 x 4 Stroke 6 Cy. 280 x 480 1030kW (1400bhp) Niigata Engineering Co Ltd-Japan AuxGen: 2 x 160kW 445V 60Hz a.c Fuel: 20.0 (d.f.) 38.0 (r.f.) 4.1pd
8430055 - -	**SHIN HUAN No. 201** **Lubmain International SA** *San Lorenzo* Honduras Official number: L-1822712	**707** 238 -		**1987-01 Kaohsiung Shipbuilding Co. Ltd. — Kaohsiung** L reg 48.20 Br ex - Dght 3.440 Lbp - Br md 8.60 Dpth 4.20 Welded, 1 dk	**(B11B2FV) Fishing Vessel**	**1 oil engine** driving 1 FP propeller Total Power: 883kW (1,201hp) 13.0kn
9695468 *DSHQ3* -	**SHIN HWA HO** **Friendship Marine Co Ltd** *Yeosu* South Korea MMSI: 441981000 Official number: YSR-132821	**461** 138 -	Class: KR	**2013-05 Namyang Shipbuilding Co Ltd — Yeosu** Yd No: 1126 Loa 34.26 Br ex - Dght 3.600 Lbp 32.30 Br md 10.00 Dpth 4.60 Welded, 1 dk	**(B32A2ST) Tug**	**2 oil engines** reduction geared to sc. shafts driving 2 Propellers Total Power: 3,678kW (5,000hp) 13.9kn Niigata 2 x 4 Stroke 6 Cy. each-1839kW (2500bhp) Niigata Engineering Co Ltd-Japan

8876065 *BR3239* -	**SHIN HWA NO. 8** *ex* Nam Sun No. 3 *-2011* **Shin Hwa Navigation Co** - *Keelung* *Chinese Taipei* MMSI: 416388000	**998** - 2,511	Class: (KR)	**1994 Hanpo Shipbuilding Co Ltd — Busan** Yd No: 005 Loa 74.73 Br ex - Dght 5.310 Lbp 68.28 Br md 11.80 Dpth 5.80 Welded, 1 dk	**(A13B2TP) Products Tanker** Liq: 3,010; Liq (Oil): 3,010	**1 oil engine** driving 1 FP propeller Total Power: 1,261kW (1,714hp) 10.5kn Alpha 6L28/32A 1 x 4 Stroke 6 Cy. 280 x 320 1261kW (1714bhp) Ssangyong Heavy Industries Co Ltd-South Korea AuxGen: 2 x 104kW 225V a.c Fuel: 103.0 (d.f.)
8609060 *JI3276* -	**SHIN IBUKI MARU** - **Taiyo Shipping Co Ltd (Taiyo Kisen KK)** - *Osaka, Osaka* *Japan* MMSI: 431300569 Official number: 128657	*207* - 400		**1986-05 Sasaki Shipbuilding Co Ltd — Osakikamijima HS** Yd No: 398 Loa 41.53 Br ex - Dght 2.801 Lbp 38.51 Br md 8.21 Dpth 3.03 Welded, 1 dk	**(A24A2BT) Cement Carrier** Grain: 300	**1 oil engine** with clutches, flexible couplings & reverse reduction geared to sc. shaft driving 1 FP propeller Total Power: 515kW (700hp) Daihatsu 6DLM-20S 1 x 4 Stroke 6 Cy. 200 x 260 515kW (700bhp) Daihatsu Diesel Manufacturing Co Lt-Japan
9674452 *JD3490* -	**SHIN ITIKAWA MARU** - **Tsukiboshi Kaiun KK** - *Osaka, Osaka* *Japan* MMSI: 431004252 Official number: 141882	*749* - 2,400		**2013-02 Yamanaka Zosen K.K. — Imabari** Yd No: 833 Loa 84.60 Br ex - Dght 4.520 Lbp - Br md 13.00 Dpth 8.10 Welded, 1 dk	**(A31A2GX) General Cargo Ship** Grain: 3,978	**1 oil engine** driving 1 Propeller Total Power: 1,618kW (2,200hp) Hanshin LA32G 1 x 4 Stroke 6 Cy. 320 x 680 1618kW (2200bhp) The Hanshin Diesel Works Ltd-Japan
9186936 *YJQA5* -	**SHIN IZU** - **Sea Road Line Inc** Kyoei Kaiun Kaisha Ltd *Port Vila* *Vanuatu* MMSI: 576277000 Official number: 1901	**2,781** 1,142 2,920	Class: NK	**1998-03 Kurinoura Dockyard Co Ltd — Yawatahama EH** Yd No: 347 Loa 95.92 (BB) Br ex - Dght 5.229 Lbp 86.75 Br md 14.00 Dpth 8.25 Welded, 1 dk	**(A34A2GR) Refrigerated Cargo Ship** Ins: 3,797 Compartments: 3 Ho, ER 3 Ha: 3 (4.5 x 4.0)ER Derricks: 6x5t	**1 oil engine** driving 1 FP propeller Total Power: 2,648kW (3,600hp) 14.0kn Akasaka A41 1 x 4 Stroke 6 Cy. 410 x 800 2648kW (3600bhp) Akasaka Tekkosho KK (Akasaka DieselLtd)-Japan Fuel: 660.0
8946858 *YJRT3* -	**SHIN JAAN SHIN NO. 168** *ex* Fortuna No. 2 *-2009* **Hung Shin Fishery Co Ltd** - *Port Vila* *Vanuatu* MMSI: 576634000 Official number: 1285	**499** 163 -		**1995-11 Lien Ho Shipbuilding Co, Ltd — Kaohsiung** Yd No: 061 Loa 53.45 Br ex - Dght - Lbp 46.50 Br md 8.50 Dpth 3.65 Welded, 1 dk	**(B11B2FV) Fishing Vessel**	**1 oil engine** driving 1 FP propeller Total Power: 883kW (1,201hp) 12.0kn Matsui ML627GSC 1 x 4 Stroke 6 Cy. 270 x 480 883kW (1201bhp) Matsui Iron Works Co Ltd-Japan
7354498 *D7TY* -	**SHIN JIN** *ex* Kasagi Maru *-1985* **O Yang Shipping Co Ltd** - *Yeosu* *South Korea* Official number: YSR-736443	*195* 68 74	Class: KR	**1973-12 Ishikawajima Ship & Chemical Plant Co Ltd — Tokyo** Yd No: 453 Loa 31.70 Br ex 8.64 Dght 2.642 Lbp 26.50 Br md 8.62 Dpth 3.51 Welded, 1 dk	**(B32A2ST) Tug**	**2 oil engines** geared to sc. shafts driving 2 FP propellers Total Power: 1,912kW (2,600hp) 13.0kn Fuji 6M27.5FH 2 x 4 Stroke 6 Cy. 275 x 320 each-956kW (1300bhp) Fuji Diesel Co Ltd-Japan AuxGen: 2 x 48kW 445V a.c
8923375 *DSQE3* -	**SHIN JUNG 77** *ex* Fujitaka Maru *-1996* **Song Bok Sik** - *Busan* *South Korea* MMSI: 441546000 Official number: BSR-070323	**210** 63 -		**1996-06 Amakusa Zosen K.K. — Amakusa** Yd No: 114 Loa 26.30 Br ex - Dght 3.010 Lbp 23.73 Br md 9.00 Dpth 3.53 Welded, 1 dk	**(B32B2SP) Pusher Tug**	**1 oil engine** driving 1 FP propeller Total Power: 736kW (1,001hp) 10.0kn Niigata 6M34AGT 1 x 4 Stroke 6 Cy. 340 x 620 736kW (1001bhp) Niigata Engineering Co Ltd-Japan
9611230 *JD3177* -	**SHIN KAIHOU** - **Muneta Zosen KK (Muneta Shipbuilding Co Ltd)** - *Akashi, Hyogo* *Japan* MMSI: 431002459 Official number: 141415	*204* - -		**2011-02 Kanbara Zosen K.K. — Onomichi** Yd No: 726 Loa 34.00 Br ex - Dght 3.000 Lbp 29.50 Br md 8.60 Dpth 3.60 Welded, 1 dk	**(B32A2ST) Tug**	**2 oil engines** reduction geared to sc. shafts driving 2 Propellers Total Power: 2,352kW (3,198hp) Hanshin LH28LG 2 x 4 Stroke 6 Cy. 280 x 530 each-1176kW (1599bhp) The Hanshin Diesel Works Ltd-Japan
9181314 *JK5485* -	**SHIN KAZURYU** - **Tetsuro Nishimura** - *Hofu, Yamaguchi* *Japan* MMSI: 431400691 Official number: 135331	*499* - -		**1997-06 K.K. Kamishima Zosensho — Osakikamijima** Yd No: 612 Loa 74.51 Br ex - Dght - Lbp 71.00 Br md 12.00 Dpth 6.90 Welded, 1 dk	**(A31A2GX) General Cargo Ship** Bale: 2,516	**1 oil engine** driving 1 FP propeller Total Power: 736kW (1,001hp) 11.0kn Akasaka A34 1 x 4 Stroke 6 Cy. 340 x 660 736kW (1001bhp) Akasaka Tekkosho KK (Akasaka DieselLtd)-Japan
9254678 *HOZI* -	**SHIN KENRYU** - **Erica Navigation SA** Toyo Sangyo Co Ltd (Toyo Sangyo KK) SatCom: Inmarsat C 435767410 *Panama* *Panama* MMSI: 357674000 Official number: 2905203B	**101,953** 66,394 203,508 T/cm 138.0	Class: NK	**2003-03 Universal Shipbuilding Corp — Tsu ME** Yd No: 218 Loa 299.95 (BB) Br ex - Dght 17.910 Lbp 291.17 Br md 50.00 Dpth 24.10 Welded, 1 dk	**(A21A2BC) Bulk Carrier** Grain: 217,968 Compartments: 9 Ho, ER 9 Ha: ER 9 (15.7 x 23.4)	**1 oil engine** driving 1 FP propeller Total Power: 16,020kW (21,781hp) 14.5kn B&W 6S70MC 1 x 2 Stroke 6 Cy. 700 x 2674 16020kW (21781bhp) Mitsui Engineering & Shipbuilding CLtd-Japan Fuel: 5260.0
8915988 *JG4880* -	**SHIN KENYO MARU** - **Asia Pacific Marine Corp** - *Tokyo* *Japan* MMSI: 431100231 Official number: 131901	*4,413* - 6,564 T/cm 16.2	Class: NK	**1990-08 Kambara Marine Development & Shipbuilding Co Ltd — Fukuyama HS** Yd No: OE-167 Loa 114.13 (BB) Br ex - Dght 6.497 Lbp 107.00 Br md 17.60 Dpth 8.30 Welded, 1 dk	**(A24A2BT) Cement Carrier** Grain: 5,309; Bale: 5,309 Compartments: 2 Ho, ER 12 Ha: ER	**1 oil engine** with clutches & geared to sc. shaft driving 1 CP propeller Total Power: 3,163kW (4,300hp) 12.5kn Hanshin 6LF50A 1 x 4 Stroke 6 Cy. 500 x 800 3163kW (4300bhp) The Hanshin Diesel Works Ltd-Japan AuxGen: 1 x 450kW 450V 60Hz a.c, 1 x 400kW 450V 60Hz a.c, 1 x 300kW 450V 60Hz a.c Thrusters: 1 Thwart. CP thruster (f) Fuel: 44.6 (d.f.) 131.2 (r.f.) 10.5pd
9423358 *3FEK7* -	**SHIN KOHO** - **Magnus Line Inc** NYK Bulk & Projects Carriers Ltd *Panama* *Panama* MMSI: 371546000 Official number: 4276511	**93,031** 58,480 182,128 T/cm 125.0	Class: NK	**2011-05 Universal Shipbuilding Corp — Tsu ME** Yd No: 139 Loa 292.00 Br ex - Dght 18.180 Lbp 287.90 Br md 45.00 Dpth 24.50 Welded, 1 dk	**(A21A2BC) Bulk Carrier** Double Hull Grain: 193,396 Compartments: 9 Ho, ER 9 Ha: ER	**1 oil engine** driving 1 FP propeller Total Power: 16,580kW (22,542hp) 14.0kn MAN-B&W 7S65ME-C 1 x 2 Stroke 7 Cy. 650 x 2730 16580kW (22542bhp) Hitachi Zosen Corp-Japan Fuel: 4834.0 (r.f.)
9398149 *3FSQ3* -	**SHIN KORYU** - **Picer Marine SA** Biko Kisen Co Ltd SatCom: Inmarsat C 435684910 *Panama* *Panama* MMSI: 356849000 Official number: 4097910	**106,367** 64,038 207,991	Class: NK	**2009-10 Universal Shipbuilding Corp — Tsu ME** Yd No: 101 Loa 299.70 (BB) Br ex - Dght 18.230 Lbp 291.75 Br md 50.00 Dpth 25.00 Welded, 1 dk	**(A21A2BC) Bulk Carrier** Grain: 218,790 Compartments: 9 Ho, ER 9 Ha: ER	**1 oil engine** driving 1 FP propeller Total Power: 16,610kW (22,583hp) 14.0kn MAN-B&W 6S70MC-C 1 x 2 Stroke 6 Cy. 700 x 2800 16610kW (22583bhp) Mitsui Engineering & Shipbuilding CLtd-Japan Fuel: 5290.0 (r.f.)
9714109 *JD3448* -	**SHIN KUNISAKI MARU** - **Green Shipping Ltd** - *Oita, Oita* *Japan* Official number: 141815	*218* - -		**2012-12 Kotobuki Kogyo KK — Ichikikushikino KS** Loa - Br ex - Dght - Lbp - Br md - Dpth - Welded, 1 dk	**(B32A2ST) Tug**	**2 oil engines** gearing integral to driving 2 Z propellers Total Power: 3,676kW (4,998hp) Niigata 6L28HX 2 x 4 Stroke 6 Cy. 280 x 370 each-1838kW (2499bhp) Niigata Engineering Co Ltd-Japan
9141247 *JG5453* -	**SHIN KUSHIRO MARU** - **Kuribayashi Logistics System Co Ltd** Kuribayashi Maritime KK *Tokyo* *Japan* MMSI: 431100239 Official number: 135811	*5,310* - 5,506	Class: NK	**1996-06 Yamanishi Corp — Ishinomaki MG** Yd No: 1010 Loa 139.72 (BB) Br ex - Dght 6.315 Lbp 130.00 Br md 21.50 Dpth 14.80 Welded, 1 dk	**(A35A2RR) Ro-Ro Cargo Ship** Quarter stern door/ramp (s. f.) Lane-Len: 600 Bale: 15,299	**1 oil engine** with flexible couplings & sr gearedto sc. shaft driving 1 CP propeller Total Power: 7,944kW (10,801hp) 17.0kn Pielstick 6PC40L570 1 x 4 Stroke 6 Cy. 570 x 750 7944kW (10801bhp) Nippon Kokan KK (NKK Corp)-Japan AuxGen: 2 x 800kW a.c, 1 x 400kW a.c Thrusters: 1 Thwart. CP thruster (f); 1 Tunnel thruster (a) Fuel: 346.0 (d.f.) 28.7pd

IMO / Call sign	Name / Owner	Tonnage	Class	Builder / Dimensions	Type / Cargo	Machinery
9054688 *DSFA8* -	**SHIN KWANG** *ex Eiko Maru No. 8 -1999* **KDB Capital Corp** Shinsung Shipping Co Ltd *Jeju* *South Korea* MMSI: 440639000 Official number: JJR-990391	**3,623** 1,631 5,400	Class: KR (NK)	**1992-09 Kegoya Dock K.K. — Kure** Yd No: 936 Loa 107.82 Br ex 15.03 Dght 6.600 Lbp 99.80 Br md 15.00 Dpth 8.10 Welded, 2 dks	**(A31A2GX) General Cargo Ship** Grain: 5,625 Compartments: 2 Ho, ER 2 Ha: (28.0 x 9.6) (28.7 x 9.6)ER	**1 oil engine** driving 1 FP propeller Total Power: 2,795kW (3,800hp) 12.3kn Hanshin 6LF50 1 x 4 Stroke 6 Cy. 500 x 800 2795kW (3800bhp) The Hanshin Diesel Works Ltd-Japan AuxGen: 3 x 184kW a.c Thrusters: 1 Thwart. CP thruster (f)
8748153 *JD2990* -	**SHIN KYOEI MARU** - **Nishikyushu Kyodo Kowan KK** - *Matsuura, Nagasaki* *Japan* Official number: 141135	*198* - -		**2009-11 K.K. Odo Zosen Tekko — Shimonoseki** Yd No: 607 Loa 34.00 Br ex - Dght 3.100 Lbp 29.00 Br md 9.20 Dpth 4.15 Welded, 1 dk	**(B32A2ST) Tug**	**2 oil engines** reduction geared to sc. shafts driving 2 Propellers Total Power: 3,676kW (4,998hp) Niigata 6L28HX 2 x 4 Stroke 6 Cy. 280 x 370 each-1838kW (2499bhp) Niigata Engineering Co Ltd-Japan
9325283 *JD2017* -	**SHIN KYOKUHO MARU** - **AST Inc** - *Osaka, Osaka* *Japan* MMSI: 431301745 Official number: 140050	*324* - 660		**2004-10 Koa Sangyo KK — Takamatsu KG** Yd No: 623 Loa 52.55 Br ex 8.82 Dght 3.600 Lbp 48.00 Br md 8.80 Dpth 4.00 Welded, 1 dk	**(A12A2TC) Chemical Tanker** Double Hull (13F) Liq: 520 2 Cargo Pump (s): 2x200m³/hr	**1 oil engine** geared to sc. shaft driving 1 FP propeller Total Power: 736kW (1,001hp) Hanshin LH26G 1 x 4 Stroke 6 Cy. 260 x 440 736kW (1001bhp) The Hanshin Diesel Works Ltd-Japan
9267998 *JG5692* -	**SHIN KYOWA MARU** - **Kyowa Marine Transportation Co Ltd & Kyoma Marine Service Co Ltd** Kyowa Marine Transportation Co Ltd (Kyowa Sangyo Kaiun KK) *Tokyo* *Japan* MMSI: 431101018 Official number: 137153	*3,819* - 4,999	Class: NK	**2002-11 Sasaki Shipbuilding Co Ltd — Osakikamijima HS** Yd No: 643 Loa 103.82 Br ex - Dght 6.313 Lbp 98.00 Br md 16.00 Dpth 8.00 Welded, 1 dk	**(A13B2TP) Products Tanker** Double Hull (13F) Liq: 6,500; Liq (Oil): 6,500	**1 oil engine** driving 1 FP propeller Total Power: 3,310kW (4,500hp) 13.8kn Akasaka A45S 1 x 4 Stroke 6 Cy. 450 x 880 3310kW (4500bhp) Akasaka Tekkosho KK (Akasaka DieselLtd)-Japan Fuel: 320.0
6928175 *BVVC* -	**SHIN LUNG No. 6** - **Shin Hing Fishing Co Ltd** - *Kaohsiung* *Chinese Taipei*	*252* 99 -		**1969 Fong Kuo Shipbuilding Co Ltd — Kaohsiung** Loa 36.43 Br ex 6.53 Dght - Lbp 31.98 Br md 6.51 Dpth 2.95 Welded, 1 dk	**(B11B2FV) Fishing Vessel**	**1 oil engine** driving 1 FP propeller Total Power: 405kW (551hp) Niigata 1 x 4 Stroke 405kW (551bhp) Niigata Engineering Co Ltd-Japan
7102194 - -	**SHIN LUNG No. 11** - **Shin Lung Fishery Co Ltd** - *Kaohsiung* *Chinese Taipei*	*270* 156 -	Class: (CR)	**1971 Fong Kuo Shipbuilding Co Ltd — Kaohsiung** Yd No: S01062 Loa 39.22 Br ex 6.96 Dght 2.744 Lbp 33.99 Br md 6.91 Dpth 3.15 Welded, 1 dk	**(B11B2FV) Fishing Vessel** Ins: 250 Compartments: 3 Ho, ER 4 Ha: 2 (1.0 x 1.0)2 (1.2 x 1.0)ER Derricks: 1x1t	**1 oil engine** driving 1 FP propeller Total Power: 478kW (650hp) 10.5kn Hanshin 6L26AGSH 1 x 4 Stroke 6 Cy. 260 x 400 478kW (650bhp) Hanshin Nainenki Kogyo-Japan AuxGen: 2 x 80kW 230V a.c
8649656 *BZLW* CT7-0350	**SHIN LUNG NO. 202** - **Shin Lung Fishery Co Ltd** - *Kaohsiung* *Chinese Taipei* Official number: 11556	**709** 268 -		**1989-07 Fong Kuo Shipbuilding Co Ltd — Kaohsiung** Yd No: 279 Loa 54.85 Br ex - Dght 3.583 Lbp 47.78 Br md 8.90 Dpth 3.85 Welded, 1 dk	**(B11B2FV) Fishing Vessel**	**1 oil engine** driving 1 Propeller
8947474 *BI2296* CT7-0296	**SHIN LUNG NO. 216** *ex Victory -2002 ex Shin Lung 216 -2002* **Shin Lung Fishery Co Ltd** - *Kaohsiung* *Chinese Taipei* Official number: 11500	**718** 287 -		**1989-06 Kaohsiung Shipbuilding Co. Ltd. — Kaohsiung** Yd No: SK059 Loa 56.00 Br ex - Dght 3.792 Lbp - Br md 8.90 Dpth 3.85 Welded, 1 dk	**(B11B2FV) Fishing Vessel**	**1 oil engine** driving 1 FP propeller Total Power: 1,030kW (1,400hp) 12.0kn Sulzer 1 x 4 Stroke 1030kW (1400bhp) Akasaka Tekkosho KK (Akasaka DieselLtd)-Japan
7110737 - -	**SHIN MAO** - **Shin Mao Fishing Co Ltd** - *Kaohsiung* *Chinese Taipei*	*150* 105 81		**1971 Taiwan Machinery Manufacturing Corp. — Kaohsiung** Yd No: 468 Loa 33.91 Br ex 5.85 Dght 2.413 Lbp 29.72 Br md 5.82 Dpth 2.82 Welded, 1 dk	**(B11B2FV) Fishing Vessel**	**1 oil engine** driving 1 FP propeller Total Power: 405kW (551hp) 9.0kn Matsui 1 x 4 Stroke 6 Cy. 230 x 380 405kW (551bhp) Matsui Iron Works Co Ltd-Japan
8967175 *JM6691* -	**SHIN MASUEI** - - - *Kamiamakusa, Kumamoto* *Japan* Official number: 136439	*199* - -		**2001-03 Amakusa Zosen K.K. — Amakusa** Yd No: 137 Loa 55.51 Br ex - Dght - Lbp 51.00 Br md 9.30 Dpth 5.80 Welded, 1 dk	**(A31A2GX) General Cargo Ship**	**1 oil engine** driving 1 FP propeller Total Power: 736kW (1,001hp) 11.0kn Niigata 6M26AGTE 1 x 4 Stroke 6 Cy. 260 x 460 736kW (1001bhp) Niigata Engineering Co Ltd-Japan Fuel: 21.0 (d.f.)
8922917 - -	**SHIN MEIKO** *ex Yushin Maru -2002* - -	*352* - 823		**1996-02 Yano Zosen K.K. — Imabari** Yd No: 163 Loa 67.68 Br ex - Dght 3.370 Lbp 62.00 Br md 11.00 Dpth 6.00 Welded, 1 dk	**(A31A2GX) General Cargo Ship** Grain: 1,750; Bale: 1,647 Compartments: 1 Ho, ER 1 Ha: (34.8 x 8.7)ER	**1 oil engine** driving 1 FP propeller Total Power: 736kW (1,001hp) 11.5kn Matsui MA29GSC-31 1 x 4 Stroke 6 Cy. 290 x 540 736kW (1001bhp) Matsui Iron Works Co Ltd-Japan
8748323 *JD3031* -	**SHIN MEZURA MARU** - **KK Nagai** - *Imari, Saga* *Japan* Official number: 141197	*192* - -		**2010-04 K.K. Odo Zosen Tekko — Shimonoseki** Yd No: 608 Loa 33.50 Br ex - Dght 3.500 Lbp - Br md 9.20 Dpth 4.16 Welded, 1 dk	**(B32A2ST) Tug**	**2 oil engines** reduction geared to sc. shafts driving 2 Propellers Total Power: 3,676kW (4,998hp) 13.5kn Niigata 6L28HX 2 x 4 Stroke 6 Cy. 280 x 370 each-1838kW (2499bhp) Niigata Engineering Co Ltd-Japan
8731277 *JD2336* -	**SHIN MISAKI** - **Daiyu Kisen YK** - *Imabari, Ehime* *Japan* Official number: 140427	*259* - 750		**2006-10 Yano Zosen K.K. — Imabari** Yd No: 211 Loa 63.62 Br ex - Dght 3.120 Lbp 57.40 Br md 10.00 Dpth 5.55 Welded, 1 dk	**(A31A2GX) General Cargo Ship** Compartments: 1 Ho, ER 1 Ha: ER (34.0 x 7.8)	**1 oil engine** reduction geared to sc. shaft driving 1 Propeller Total Power: 1,177kW (1,600hp) 11.0kn Niigata 6M28NT 1 x 4 Stroke 6 Cy. 280 x 480 1177kW (1600bhp) Niigata Engineering Co Ltd-Japan
9678977 *7JQA* -	**SHIN NICHI MARU** - **Offshore Engineering Co Ltd** - *Tokyo* *Japan* MMSI: 432949000 Official number: 142013	*997* 229 1,061	Class: NK	**2013-10 Maebata Zosen Tekko K.K. — Sasebo** Yd No: 318 Loa 61.01 Br ex - Dght 4.714 Lbp 51.06 Br md 11.80 Dpth 5.45 Welded, 1 dk	**(B34T2QR) Work/Repair Vessel**	**2 oil engines** reduction geared to sc. shafts driving 2 Propellers Total Power: 2,942kW (4,000hp) Niigata 6L28HX 2 x 4 Stroke 6 Cy. 280 x 370 each-1471kW (2000bhp) Niigata Engineering Co Ltd-Japan Fuel: 560.0
9296420 *7JHG* -	**SHIN NICHIHO** - **Nippon Yusen Kabushiki Kaisha (NYK Line)** Hachiuma Steamship Co Ltd (Hachiuma Kisen KK) SatCom: Inmarsat C 443275910 *Tokyo* *Japan* MMSI: 432759000 Official number: 141256	**102,208** 66,775 203,180 T/cm 138.0	Class: NK	**2005-04 Universal Shipbuilding Corp — Tsu ME** Yd No: 242 Loa 299.95 (BB) Br ex - Dght 17.910 Lbp 290.00 Br md 50.00 Dpth 24.10 Welded, 1 dk	**(A21A2BC) Bulk Carrier** Grain: 217,968 Compartments: 9 Ho, ER 9 Ha: ER 9 (15.7 x 23.4)	**1 oil engine** driving 1 FP propeller Total Power: 16,020kW (21,781hp) 14.5kn B&W 6S70MC 1 x 2 Stroke 6 Cy. 700 x 2674 16020kW (21781bhp) Mitsui Engineering & Shipbuilding CLtd-Japan Fuel: 5285.0
9087697 *JK5300* -	**SHIN NICHIRYU MARU** - - - *Bizen, Okayama* *Japan* Official number: 134057	*179* - 266		**1994-04 Hitachi Zosen Mukaishima Marine Co Ltd — Onomichi HS** Yd No: 81 Loa 41.75 Br ex - Dght 2.900 Lbp 38.00 Br md 7.00 Dpth 3.35 Welded, 1 dk	**(A12A2TC) Chemical Tanker**	**1 oil engine** with clutches & reverse geared to sc. shaft driving 1 FP propeller Total Power: 405kW (551hp) Matsui ML624GHS 1 x 4 Stroke 6 Cy. 240 x 400 405kW (551bhp) Matsui Iron Works Co Ltd-Japan
9213832 *JG5594* -	**SHIN OH MARU** - **Japan Railway Construction, Transport & Technology Agency & Kuribayashi Logistics System Co Ltd** Kuribayashi Steamship Co Ltd *Tokyo* *Japan* MMSI: 431100859 Official number: 136762	*11,790* - 6,689 T/cm 26.8	Class: NK	**1999-11 Yamanishi Corp — Ishinomaki MG** Yd No: 1020 Loa 162.52 (BB) Br ex - Dght 7.015 Lbp 150.00 Br md 24.00 Dpth 15.80 Welded, 4 dks including 2 hoistable	**(A35A2RR) Ro-Ro Cargo Ship** Quarter bow door/ramp (p) Len: 4.30 Wid: 7.00 Swl: 50 Quarter stern door/ramp (p) Len: 4.50 Wid: 7.00 Swl: 50 Lane-Len: 1838 Lane-Wid: 7.00 Lane-clr ht: 4.50 Lorries: 132, Cars: 53	**1 oil engine** with clutches & sr reverse geared to sc. shaft driving 1 CP propeller Total Power: 15,888kW (21,601hp) 21.2kn Pielstick 12PC4-2B-570 1 x Vee 4 Stroke 12 Cy. 570 x 660 15888kW (21601bhp) Nippon Kokan KK (NKK Corp)-Japan AuxGen: 2 x 1000kW 450V a.c Thrusters: 1 Thwart. CP thruster (f); 1 Thwart. CP thruster (a) Fuel: 23.0 (d.f.) (Heating Coils) 528.0 (r.f.) 39.8pd

9331517 *A8JZ9* -	**SHIN OHGISHIMA** **Erica Navigation SA** Toyo Sangyo Co Ltd (Toyo Sangyo KK) SatCom: Inmarsat C 463791683 *Monrovia* *Liberia* MMSI: 636013011 Official number: 13011	**101,953** 66,394 203,280 T/cm 138.0	Class: NK	**2006-08 Universal Shipbuilding Corp — Nagasu KM (Ariake Shipyard)** Yd No: 024 Loa 299.95 (BB) Br ex 50.00 Dght 17.910 Lbp 291.17 Br md 50.00 Dpth 24.10 Welded, 1 dk	**(A21A2BC) Bulk Carrier** Grain: 217,968 Compartments: 9 Ho, ER 9 Ha: ER 9 (15.7 x 23.4)	**1 oil engine** driving 4 gen. driving 1 FP propeller Total Power: 16,020kW (21,781hp) 14.5kn MAN-B&W 6S70MC 1 x 2 Stroke 6 Cy. 700 x 2674 16020kW (21781bhp) Hitachi Zosen Corp-Japan AuxGen: 3 x a.c Fuel: 5265.0
9231444 *JNWI* OT-88	**SHIN OITA MARU** **Oita Prefecture** - *Usuki, Oita* *Japan* MMSI: 432106000 Official number: 136369	*499* - 368		**2000-05 Shitanoe Shipbuilding Co Ltd — Usuki OT** Yd No: 1208 Loa 56.96 Br ex 9.42 Dght 3.906 Lbp 48.50 Br md 9.40 Dpth 6.25 Welded, 1 dk	**(B11B2FV) Fishing Vessel**	**1 oil engine** reverse geared to sc. shaft driving 1 FP propeller Total Power: 1,324kW (1,800hp) 12.5kn Niigata 6M31BFT 1 x 4 Stroke 6 Cy. 310 x 530 1324kW (1800bhp) Niigata Engineering Co Ltd-Japan Thrusters: 1 Thwart. FP thruster (f)
9138874 *3FSH6* -	**SHIN ONDO** **Frontier Maritime Shipping II SA & Tsukiboshi Shipping Corp SA** Hachiuma Steamship Co Ltd (Hachiuma Kisen KK) SatCom: Inmarsat B 335257210 *Panama* *Panama* MMSI: 352572000 Official number: 2348597CH	**77,065** 49,122 151,833	Class: NK	**1996-11 Namura Shipbuilding Co Ltd — Imari SG** Yd No: 947 Loa 273.00 (BB) Br ex - Dght 17.624 Lbp 260.00 Br md 43.00 Dpth 24.00 Welded, 1 dk	**(A21A2BC) Bulk Carrier** Grain: 167,444 Compartments: 9 Ho, ER 9 Ha: (15.1 x 16.0)8 (15.1 x 19.2)ER	**1 oil engine** driving 1 FP propeller Total Power: 12,210kW (16,601hp) 14.3kn Sulzer 6RTA72 1 x 2 Stroke 6 Cy. 720 x 2500 12210kW (16601bhp) Mitsubishi Heavy Industries Ltd-Japan AuxGen: 3 x 600kW 450V 60Hz a.c Fuel: 3490.0 (r.f.) 40.1pd
9271597 *HODB* -	**SHIN ONOE** **Adrastea Maritima SA** NYK Shipmanagement Pte Ltd SatCom: Inmarsat C 435784710 *Panama* *Panama* MMSI: 357847000 Official number: 3037905B	**101,953** 66,394 203,248 T/cm 138.0	Class: NK	**2004-11 Universal Shipbuilding Corp — Tsu ME** Yd No: 235 Loa 299.95 (BB) Br ex - Dght 17.910 Lbp 290.00 Br md 50.00 Dpth 24.10 Welded	**(A21A2BC) Bulk Carrier** Grain: 217,968 Compartments: 9 Ho, ER 9 Ha: ER 9 (15.7 x 23.4)	**1 oil engine** driving 1 FP propeller Total Power: 16,020kW (21,781hp) 14.5kn B&W 6S70MC 1 x 2 Stroke 6 Cy. 700 x 2674 16020kW (21781bhp) Mitsui Engineering & Shipbuilding CLtd-Japan Fuel: 5260.0
9163116 *JG5508* -	**SHIN PROPANE MARU** **Kyowa Marine Transportation Co Ltd & Kyoma Marine Service Co Ltd** Kyowa Marine Transportation Co Ltd (Kyowa Sangyo Kaiun KK) *Tokyo* *Japan* MMSI: 431100348 Official number: 135885	*749* - 1,043	Class: NK	**1997-08 Sasaki Shipbuilding Co Ltd — Osakikamijima HS** Yd No: 612 Loa 66.11 (BB) Br ex - Dght 4.000 Lbp 61.50 Br md 11.20 Dpth 5.00 Welded, 1 dk	**(A11B2TG) LPG Tanker** Liq (Gas): 1,270 2 x Gas Tank (s); 2 cyl 2 Cargo Pump (s): 2x350m³/hr	**1 oil engine** driving 1 CP propeller Total Power: 1,471kW (2,000hp) 12.0kn Akasaka A34C 1 x 4 Stroke 6 Cy. 340 x 620 1471kW (2000bhp) Akasaka Tekkosho KK (Akasaka DieselLtd)-Japan AuxGen: 1 x 400kW a.c, 1 x 180kW a.c Thrusters: 1 Thwart. FP thruster (f) Fuel: 108.0 (d.f.) 7.0pd
8430249 *HQHT4* -	**SHIN REEFER** *ex* Shie Shing No. 11 *-1991* **Lubmain International SA** - *San Lorenzo* *Honduras* Official number: L-0323742	**303** 144 -		**1971 Fong Kuo Shipbuilding Co Ltd — Kaohsiung** L reg 37.75 Br ex - Dght - Lbp - Br md 6.90 Dpth 3.15 Welded, 1 dk	**(B11B2FV) Fishing Vessel**	**1 oil engine** driving 1 FP propeller Total Power: 478kW (650hp) 11.0kn
9337169 *3ESR2* -	**SHIN-REI** **Orchard Maritime (Panama) SA** Excel Marine Co Ltd SatCom: Inmarsat C 437040010 *Panama* *Panama* MMSI: 370400000 Official number: 3428608A	**106,367** 64,038 207,923	Class: NK	**2008-08 Universal Shipbuilding Corp — Tsu ME** Yd No: 066 Loa 299.70 (BB) Br ex - Dght 18.230 Lbp 291.75 Br md 50.00 Dpth 25.00 Welded, 1 dk	**(A21A2BC) Bulk Carrier** Double Hull Grain: 218,790 Compartments: 9 Ho, ER 9 Ha: ER	**1 oil engine** driving 1 FP propeller Total Power: 16,610kW (22,583hp) 14.0kn MAN-B&W 6S70MC-C 1 x 2 Stroke 6 Cy. 700 x 2800 16610kW (22583bhp) Mitsui Engineering & Shipbuilding CLtd-Japan AuxGen: 4 x 455kW a.c Fuel: 5240.0
9196802 *3FXV9* -	**SHIN-SAKAIDE** **Grimstad Shipping SA** Nippon Yusen Kabushiki Kaisha (NYK Line) *Panama* *Panama* MMSI: 357943000 Official number: 2683600D	**50,238** 28,900 91,443 T/cm 88.0	Class: NK	**2000-01 Oshima Shipbuilding Co Ltd — Saikai NS** Yd No: 10264 Loa 235.00 (BB) Br ex - Dght 12.860 Lbp 226.00 Br md 43.00 Dpth 18.55 Welded, 1 dk	**(A21A2BC) Bulk Carrier** Double Bottom Entire Compartment Length Grain: 110,413 Compartments: 7 Ho, ER 7 Ha: (16.5 x 18.9)5 (14.6 x 21.9) (18.3 x 21.9)ER	**1 oil engine** driving 1 FP propeller Total Power: 11,915kW (16,200hp) 14.3kn Mitsubishi 6UEC60LSII 1 x 2 Stroke 6 Cy. 600 x 2300 11915kW (16200bhp) Mitsubishi Heavy Industries Ltd-Japan AuxGen: 3 x 463kW 440V 60Hz a.c Thrusters: 1 Thwart. FP thruster (f) Fuel: 117.0 (d.f.) 3173.0 (r.f.) 43.5pd
8609113 - -	**SHIN SANKYU MARU** - - *Chinese Taipei*	*457* - 1,223		**1986-07 Shitanoe Shipbuilding Co Ltd — Usuki OT** Yd No: 1061 Loa 69.40 (BB) Br ex 11.51 Dght 3.801 Lbp 64.60 Br md 11.00 Dpth 6.33 Welded, 2 dks	**(A31A2GX) General Cargo Ship** Bale: 2,445 Compartments: 1 Ho, ER, 1 Tw Dk 1 Ha: ER	**1 oil engine** driving 1 FP propeller Total Power: 883kW (1,201hp) Niigata 6M28AFTE 1 x 4 Stroke 6 Cy. 280 x 480 883kW (1201bhp) Niigata Engineering Co Ltd-Japan
8890138 *JL6393* -	**SHIN SANTOKU MARU** **Santoku Kaiun YK** - *Anan, Tokushima* *Japan* MMSI: 431500367 Official number: 135077	*199* - -		**1995-09 Y.K. Takasago Zosensho — Naruto** Yd No: 208 Loa 59.00 Br ex - Dght 3.170 Lbp 53.00 Br md 9.50 Dpth 5.42 Welded, 1 dk	**(A31A2GX) General Cargo Ship** Grain: 1,180 Compartments: 1 Ho, ER 1 Ha: (30.3 x 7.5)ER	**1 oil engine** driving 1 FP propeller Total Power: 736kW (1,001hp) 12.0kn Hanshin LH28G 1 x 4 Stroke 6 Cy. 280 x 460 736kW (1001bhp) The Hanshin Diesel Works Ltd-Japan
9343508 *7JLI* -	**SHIN SANYO MARU** **Nippon Yusen Kabushiki Kaisha (NYK Line)** Hachiuma Steamship Co Ltd (Hachiuma Kisen KK) SatCom: Inmarsat C 443285310 *Hamada, Shimane* *Japan* MMSI: 432853000 Official number: 141621	**50,502** 28,235 91,439	Class: NK	**2007-02 Oshima Shipbuilding Co Ltd — Saikai NS** Yd No: 10472 Loa 235.00 (BB) Br ex - Dght 12.930 Lbp 226.00 Br md 43.00 Dpth 18.55 Welded, 1 dk	**(A21A2BC) Bulk Carrier** Double Hull Grain: 108,929 Compartments: 5 Ho, ER 5 Ha: 3 (24.7 x 21.0) (22.0 x 21.0)ER (22.9 x 21.0)	**1 oil engine** driving 1 FP propeller Total Power: 11,915kW (16,200hp) 14.0kn Mitsubishi 6UEC60LSII 1 x 2 Stroke 6 Cy. 600 x 2300 11915kW (16200bhp) Mitsubishi Heavy Industries Ltd-Japan AuxGen: 3 x a.c Fuel: 3095.0
9257412 *JPQG* -	**SHIN SAPPORO MARU** **Nippon Yusen Kaisha (NYK Lines) & Mitsui OSK Lines Ltd** Nippon Yusen Kabushiki Kaisha (NYK Line) *Tokyo* *Japan* MMSI: 432355000 Official number: 137140	**50,578** 28,762 91,439 T/cm 88.1	Class: NK	**2002-08 Oshima Shipbuilding Co Ltd — Saikai NS** Yd No: 10335 Loa 235.00 (BB) Br ex - Dght 12.890 Lbp 226.00 Br md 43.00 Dpth 18.55 Welded, 1 dk	**(A21A2BC) Bulk Carrier** Grain: 111,687 Compartments: 5 Ho, ER 5 Ha: (22.9 x 18.0)3 (24.7 x 21.0) (22.0 x 21.0)ER	**1 oil engine** driving 1 FP propeller Total Power: 11,916kW (16,201hp) 14.0kn Mitsubishi 6UEC60LSII 1 x 2 Stroke 6 Cy. 600 x 2300 11916kW (16201bhp) Mitsubishi Heavy Industries Ltd-Japan Fuel: 3130.0
9217113 *JM6570* -	**SHIN SATSUMA** **Kyodo Ferry Unyu YK** - *Nishinoomote, Kagoshima* *Japan* MMSI: 431601978 Official number: 136419	*2,557* - 2,300		**2000-05 K.K. Miura Zosensho — Saiki** Yd No: 1225 Loa 121.00 (BB) Br ex - Dght 5.200 Lbp 110.00 Br md 16.50 Dpth 12.30 Welded	**(A35A2RR) Ro-Ro Cargo Ship** Stern ramp Len: 17.00 Wid: 7.00 Swl: - Lane-Len: 324 Cars: 24	**1 oil engine** reduction geared to sc. shaft driving 1 FP propeller Total Power: 6,620kW (9,001hp) 19.0kn Pielstick 12PC2-6V-400 1 x Vee 4 Stroke 12 Cy. 400 x 460 6620kW (9001bhp) Niigata Engineering Co Ltd-Japan AuxGen: 2 x 600kW a.c, 1 x 105kW a.c Thrusters: 1 Thwart. FP thruster (f) Fuel: 186.0 (r.f.) 25.0pd
8629539 *HLLA* -	**SHIN SEONG NO. 101** *ex* Dong Sam No. 901 *-1986* **Dong Sam Fisheries Co Ltd** - SatCom: Inmarsat A 1660326 *Busan* *South Korea* MMSI: 440879000 Official number: 9509022-6260001	*124* - -	Class: (KR)	**1986-11 Namsung Shipyard Co Ltd — Busan** Loa 40.04 Br ex - Dght 3.090 Lbp 31.80 Br md 7.30 Dpth - Welded, 1 dk	**(B11B2FV) Fishing Vessel**	**1 oil engine** driving 1 FP propeller Total Power: 1,214kW (1,651hp) 11.2kn Akasaka DM30 1 x 4 Stroke 6 Cy. 300 x 480 1214kW (1651bhp) Akasaka Tekkosho KK (Akasaka DieselLtd)-Japan AuxGen: 1 x 144kW 225V a.c

IMO / Call sign	Name / Owner / Manager / Registry	Tonnage	Class	Builder / Dimensions	Type / Capacity	Machinery
9331426 *A8HJ3* -	**SHIN SETO** **Erica Navigation SA** Toyo Sangyo Co Ltd (Toyo Sangyo KK) SatCom: Inmarsat C 463790787 *Monrovia* *Liberia* MMSI: 636012726 Official number: 12726	**101,953** 66,394 203,264 T/cm 138.0	Class: NK	**2005**-11 **Universal Shipbuilding Corp — Nagasu KM (Ariake Shipyard)** Yd No: 023 Loa 299.95 (BB) Br ex 50.00 Dght 17.910 Lbp 291.17 Br md 50.00 Dpth 24.10 Welded, 1 dk	**(A21A2BC) Bulk Carrier** Double Hull Grain: 217,968 Compartments: 9 Ho, ER 9 Ha: ER 9 (15.7 x 23.4)	**1 oil engine** driving 1 FP propeller Total Power: 16,020kW (21,781hp) 14.5kn B&W 6S70MC 1 x 2 Stroke 6 Cy. 700 x 2674 16020kW (21781bhp) Hitachi Zosen Corp-Japan AuxGen: 3 x a.c Fuel: 5265.0
8944185 *JG5012* -	**SHIN SHIBAURA MARU** *ex* Sanei Maru No. 10 *-2007* **Shibaura Kaiun KK** *Tokyo* *Japan* Official number: 136628	*129* - -		**1998**-07 **Takao Zosen Kogyo K.K. — Tateyama** Yd No: 127 Loa 35.46 Br ex - Dght - Lbp 33.00 Br md 8.00 Dpth 3.00 Welded, 1 dk	**(A24D2BA) Aggregates Carrier**	**1 oil engine** driving 1 FP propeller Total Power: 257kW (349hp) 9.2kn Yanmar MF24-HT 1 x 4 Stroke 6 Cy. 240 x 420 257kW (349bhp) Yanmar Diesel Engine Co Ltd-Japan
9324124 *S6HB8* -	**SHIN-SHO** **Pear Libra Pte Ltd** Sandigan Ship Services Inc SatCom: Inmarsat C 456522510 *Singapore* *Singapore* MMSI: 565225000 Official number: 392116	**88,541** 58,950 177,489 T/cm 119.0	Class: NK	**2006**-09 **Mitsui Eng. & SB. Co. Ltd., Chiba Works — Ichihara** Yd No: 1624 Loa 289.00 (BB) Br ex - Dght 17.980 Lbp 279.00 Br md 45.00 Dpth 24.40 Welded, 1 dk	**(A21A2BC) Bulk Carrier** Grain: 197,050 Compartments: 9 Ho, ER 9 Ha: 7 (15.5 x 20.6)ER 2 (15.5 x 15.0)	**1 oil engine** driving 1 FP propeller Total Power: 16,858kW (22,920hp) 15.0kn MAN-B&W 6S70MC 1 x 2 Stroke 6 Cy. 700 x 2674 16858kW (22920bhp) Mitsui Engineering & Shipbuilding CLtd-Japan Fuel: 4710.0
8749547 *BG3667* -	**SHIN SHUEN FAR NO. 16** **Lien Hsiang Fishery Co Ltd** *Kaohsiung* *Chinese Taipei* Official number: 014861	**160** 48 -		**2008**-02 **Shing Sheng Fa Boat Building Co — Kaohsiung** Loa 30.12 Br ex - Dght 2.600 Lbp - Br md 5.90 Dpth 2.60 Welded, 1 dk	**(B11B2FV) Fishing Vessel**	**1 oil engine** driving 1 Propeller Yanmar 1 x 4 Stroke Yanmar Diesel Engine Co Ltd-Japan
8749561 *BG3676* -	**SHIN SHUEN FAR NO. 69** **Shin Shuen Far Fishery Co Ltd** - *Kaohsiung* *Chinese Taipei* Official number: 014939	**180** 59 -		**2009**-08 **Shing Sheng Fa Boat Building Co — Kaohsiung** Loa 30.19 Br ex - Dght 2.600 Lbp - Br md 6.20 Dpth - Welded, 1 dk	**(B11B2FV) Fishing Vessel**	**1 oil engine** driving 1 Propeller Yanmar 1 x 4 Stroke Yanmar Diesel Engine Co Ltd-Japan
9627318 *BG3694* CT5-1694	**SHIN SHUEN FAR NO. 668** **Shin Fong Fishery Co Ltd** - *Kaohsiung* *Chinese Taipei* Official number: 015069	**198** 68 -		**2011**-01 **Shing Sheng Fa Boat Building Co — Kaohsiung** Loa 36.10 Br ex - Dght 2.200 Lbp 32.89 Br md 6.40 Dpth 2.60 Bonded, 1 dk	**(B11B2FV) Fishing Vessel** Hull Material: Reinforced Plastic	**1 oil engine** driving 1 Propeller Total Power: 736kW (1,001hp) Yanmar 1 x 4 Stroke 6 Cy. 736kW (1001bhp) Yanmar Diesel Engine Co Ltd-Japan
9691993 *BG3733* CT5-1733	**SHIN SHUEN FAR NO. 688** **Lian Zhan Fishery Co Ltd** - *Kaohsiung* *Chinese Taipei* Official number: 015332	**198** 68 -		**2012**-12 **Shing Sheng Fa Boat Building Co — Kaohsiung** L reg 32.89 Br ex - Dght - Lbp - Br md 6.40 Dpth 2.60 Bonded, 1 dk	**(B11B2FV) Fishing Vessel** Hull Material: Reinforced Plastic	**1 oil engine** reduction geared to sc. shaft driving 1 FP propeller Yanmar 1 x 4 Stroke 6 Cy. Yanmar Diesel Engine Co Ltd-Japan
9607021 *7JME* -	**SHIN SUMA** **Nippon Yusen Kabushiki Kaisha (NYK Line)** - *Tokyo* *Japan* MMSI: 432875000 Official number: 141694	**106,360** 64,031 206,396	Class: NK	**2012**-08 **Universal Shipbuilding Corp — Tsu ME** Yd No: 172 Loa 299.70 (BB) Br ex - Dght 18.230 Lbp 291.75 Br md 50.00 Dpth 25.00 Welded, 1 dk	**(A21A2BC) Bulk Carrier** Double Hull Grain: 218,211 Compartments: 9 Ho, ER 9 Ha: ER	**1 oil engine** driving 1 FP propeller Total Power: 16,810kW (22,855hp) 14.0kn MAN-B&W 7S65ME-C 1 x 2 Stroke 7 Cy. 650 x 2730 16810kW (22855bhp) Mitsui Engineering & Shipbuilding CLtd-Japan Fuel: 5330.0
8216863 *DSHG* -	**SHIN SUNG** *ex* Su Hae No. 5 *-2007* *ex* Awa Maru *-1990* **New Star Marine Corp** *Boryeong* *South Korea* Official number: DSR-905124	**237** - 114	Class: KR	**1983**-08 **Hikari Kogyo K.K. — Yokosuka** Yd No: 326 Loa 36.81 Br ex 9.53 Dght 3.101 Lbp 32.52 Br md 9.50 Dpth 4.32 Welded, 1 dk	**(B32A2ST) Tug** Passengers: cabins: 12	**3 oil engines** with clutches, flexible couplings & sr geared to sc. shafts driving 3 Directional propellers Total Power: 3,750kW (5,100hp) 15.3kn Yanmar 6Z280L-ST 3 x 4 Stroke 6 Cy. 280 x 360 each-1250kW (1700bhp) Yanmar Diesel Engine Co Ltd-Japan AuxGen: 2 x 160kW 440V 60Hz a.c Fuel: 37.0 (d.f.) 18.0pd
9254666 *HOFH* -	**SHIN SURUGA** **Erica Navigation SA** Toyo Sangyo Co Ltd (Toyo Sangyo KK) SatCom: Inmarsat C 435478110 *Panama* *Panama* MMSI: 354781000 Official number: 2859802B	**88,674** 58,558 176,391 T/cm 119.5	Class: NK	**2002**-06 **Nippon Kokan KK (NKK Corp) — Tsu ME** Yd No: 217 Loa 289.00 (BB) Br ex - Dght 17.850 Lbp 280.75 Br md 45.00 Dpth 24.10 Welded, 1 dk	**(A21A2BC) Bulk Carrier** Grain: 194,291 Compartments: 9 Ho, ER 9 Ha: 9 (15.2 x 21.0)ER	**1 oil engine** driving 1 FP propeller Total Power: 16,020kW (21,781hp) 14.9kn B&W 6S70MC 1 x 2 Stroke 6 Cy. 700 x 2674 16020kW (21781bhp) Mitsui Engineering & Shipbuilding CLtd-Japan Fuel: 4710.0
8966341 - -	**SHIN TAI** - - - *Kaohsiung* *Chinese Taipei* Official number: 13198	**198** 71 42		**1997**-01 **Lien Ho Shipbuilding Co, Ltd — Kaohsiung** Loa 30.02 Br ex - Dght 1.350 Lbp 27.63 Br md 6.29 Dpth 2.70 Welded, 1 dk	**(A37B2PS) Passenger Ship**	**2 oil engines** reduction geared to sc. shafts driving 2 FP propellers Total Power: 2,942kW (4,000hp) 26.0kn M.T.U. 12V396TE74 2 x Vee 4 Stroke 12 Cy. 165 x 185 each-1471kW (2000bhp) MTU Friedrichshafen GmbH-Friedrichshafen AuxGen: 2 x 55kW 225V a.c
9254331 *JL6612* -	**SHIN TAISEI** **Taisei Kosan KK & Sanwa Kaiun KK** Taisei Kosan KK *Imabari, Ehime* *Japan* MMSI: 431501693 Official number: 136536	*498* - 1,600		**2001**-06 **Yamanaka Zosen K.K. — Imabari** Yd No: 665 Loa 76.23 (BB) Br ex - Dght 4.100 Lbp 70.00 Br md 12.00 Dpth 7.01 Welded, 1 dk	**(A31A2GX) General Cargo Ship** Grain: 2,832; Bale: 2,761	**1 oil engine** driving 1 FP propeller Total Power: 1,176kW (1,599hp) 11.0kn Hanshin LH30L 1 x 4 Stroke 6 Cy. 300 x 600 1176kW (1599bhp) The Hanshin Diesel Works Ltd-Japan AuxGen: 2 x 96kW a.c Thrusters: 1 Thwart. FP thruster (f) Fuel: 98.0 (d.f.)
8815504 *JJ3623* -	**SHIN TAISEI MARU No. 1** **Ryugo Takenaka** - *Himeji, Hyogo* *Japan* Official number: 130839	*469* - 619		**1989**-02 **K.K. Saidaiji Zosensho — Okayama** Yd No: 161 Loa 51.00 (BB) Br ex - Dght 3.220 Lbp 46.00 Br md 10.50 Dpth 5.40 Welded, 1 dk	**(B33A2DG) Grab Dredger**	**1 oil engine** driving 1 FP propeller Total Power: 552kW (750hp) 10.5kn Hanshin 6LUN28AG 1 x 4 Stroke 6 Cy. 280 x 480 552kW (750bhp) The Hanshin Diesel Works Ltd-Japan Fuel: 20.0
9672662 *JD3511* -	**SHIN TAIYO MARU** **Japan Railway Construction, Transport & Technology Agency & YK Kotobuki Shipping** YK Kotobuki Shipping *Bizen, Okayama* *Japan* MMSI: 431004516 Official number: 141914	*749* - 1,952	Class: NK	**2013**-05 **Maebata Zosen Tekko K.K. — Sasebo** Yd No: 316 Loa 74.18 (BB) Br ex - Dght 4.841 Lbp 69.00 Br md 11.40 Dpth 5.35 Welded, 1 dk	**(A13B2TP) Products Tanker** Double Hull (13F) Liq: 2,142; Liq (Oil): 2,184	**1 oil engine** reverse reduction geared to sc. shaft driving 1 Propeller Total Power: 1,323kW (1,799hp) 10.5kn Akasaka AX28R 1 x 4 Stroke 6 Cy. 280 x 600 1323kW (1799bhp) Akasaka Tekkosho KK (Akasaka DieselLtd)-Japan AuxGen: 2 x 280kW a.c Fuel: 78.0
9083976 *JM6245* -	**SHIN TANEGASHIMA MARU** **Satomura Kyodo Kisen KK** - *Nishinoomote, Kagoshima* *Japan* MMSI: 431600152 Official number: 133570	*999* - 1,200		**1993**-11 **Honda Zosen — Saiki** Yd No: 852 Loa 89.52 Br ex - Dght 4.680 Lbp 80.00 Br md 13.50 Dpth 8.08 Welded, 2 dks	**(A35A2RR) Ro-Ro Cargo Ship** Passengers: berths: 12 Stern door/ramp Len: 11.25 Wid: 6.45 Swl: - Lane-Len: 215	**1 oil engine** driving 1 CP propeller Total Power: 2,942kW (4,000hp) 16.0kn Pielstick 8PC2-6L-400 1 x 4 Stroke 8 Cy. 400 x 460 2942kW (4000bhp) Niigata Engineering Co Ltd-Japan Thrusters: 1 Thwart. FP thruster (f)
8603872 *JK4509* -	**SHIN TOMEI MARU** **Tosoh Logistics Corp (Tosoh Butsuryu KK)** - *Shunan, Yamaguchi* *Japan* MMSI: 431401171 Official number: 127994	*199* - -		**1986**-07 **Ube Dockyard Co. Ltd. — Ube** Yd No: 198 Loa - Br ex - Dght 3.252 Lbp 26.40 Br md 8.60 Dpth 3.87 Welded, 1 dk	**(B32B2SP) Pusher Tug**	**2 oil engines** driving 2 FP propellers Total Power: 2,648kW (3,600hp) Pielstick 6PA5 2 x 4 Stroke 6 Cy. 255 x 270 each-1324kW (1800bhp) Niigata Engineering Co Ltd-Japan

IMO / Call sign	Name / Owner / Registry	Tonnage	Class	Build	Type	Machinery
9159220 *JG5499* -	**SHIN TOSA MARU** - **Shinwa Naiko Kaiun Kaisha Ltd** - *Tokyo* *Japan* Official number: 135870	*130* - -		**1997**-03 **K.K. Miura Zosensho — Saiki** Yd No: 1182 Loa - Br ex - Dght - Lbp 25.00 Br md 9.50 Dpth 6.50 Welded, 1	**(B32B2SP) Pusher Tug**	**2 oil engines** driving 2 FP propellers Total Power: 2,942kW (4,000hp) Niigata 6M34BGT 2 x 4 Stroke 6 Cy. 340 x 620 each-1471kW (2000bhp) Niigata Engineering Co Ltd-Japan
8738043 *JD2566* -	**SHIN TOYOKAWA MARU** - **Kyokusen Kaiun KK** - *Osaka, Osaka* *Japan* Official number: 140694	*498* - 1,701		**2008**-01 **Fukushima Zosen Ltd. — Matsue** Yd No: 357 Loa 65.00 Br ex - Dght 4.000 Lbp 60.00 Br md 9.80 Dpth 4.65 Welded, 1 dk	**(A12A2TC) Chemical Tanker** Liq: 608	**1 oil engine** driving 1 Propeller Total Power: 735kW (999hp) 11.0kn Yanmar DY28-UN 1 x 4 Stroke 6 Cy. 280 x 530 735kW (999bhp) Yanmar Diesel Engine Co Ltd-Japan
9262247 *JM6700* -	**SHIN TSUNETOYO MARU** - **YK Seiryu Kaiun Kensetsu** Nishitaki Kaiun KK *Tsukumi, Oita* *Japan* Official number: 136814	*498* - 1,585		**2002**-06 **Shin Kochi Jyuko K.K. — Kochi** Yd No: 7151 Loa 74.40 Br ex - Dght - Lbp - Br md 12.00 Dpth 7.00 Welded, 1 dk	**(A31A2GX) General Cargo Ship**	**1 oil engine** geared to sc. shaft driving 1 FP propeller Total Power: 1,177kW (1,600hp) Hanshin LH28G 1 x 4 Stroke 6 Cy. 280 x 460 1177kW (1600bhp) The Hanshin Diesel Works Ltd-Japan
7512947 - -	**SHIN WA** *ex* Shinwa Maru *-1994* *ex* Eifuku Maru No. 3 *-1987* *ex* Shinkai Maru No. 2 *-1983* *ex* Kito Maru No. 8 *-1981* **Ta Sheng Navigation Co Ltd** -	*351* - 730		**1975**-09 **Shin Nikko Zosen K.K. — Onomichi** Yd No: 109 Loa - Br ex 10.01 Dght 3.277 Lbp 57.00 Br md 9.99 Dpth 3.38 Riveted\Welded, 1 dk	**(A31A2GX) General Cargo Ship**	**1 oil engine** driving 1 FP propeller Total Power: 809kW (1,100hp) Hanshin 6LU28 1 x 4 Stroke 6 Cy. 280 x 440 809kW (1100bhp) Hanshin Nainenki Kogyo-Japan
9204207 *HO3914* -	**SHIN WON NO. 5** *ex* Kosyu Maru No. 48 *-2004* **Shin Won Marine SA** Shin Won Marine Co Ltd *Panama* *Panama* Official number: 33178PEXT	**484** 145 -		**1998**-04 **Hongawara Zosen K.K. — Fukuyama** Yd No: 490 Loa 32.65 Br ex - Dght - Lbp - Br md 9.60 Dpth 5.80 Welded, 1 dk	**(B32A2ST) Tug**	**2 oil engines** driving 2 FP propellers Total Power: 2,942kW (4,000hp) 11.0kn Niigata 6M34BLGT 2 x 4 Stroke 6 Cy. 340 x 680 each-1471kW (2000bhp) Niigata Engineering Co Ltd-Japan
8033003 *CXOE* -	**SHIN WU No. 2** *ex* Yung Yu *-1984* **Atunera Shin Wu SA** - *Montevideo* *Uruguay*	*352* 237 -	Class: (CR)	**1981 Fong Kuo Shipbuilding Co Ltd — Kaohsiung** Loa 43.64 Br ex 7.68 Dght 2.901 Lbp 38.10 Br md 7.60 Dpth 3.38 Welded, 1 dk	**(B11B2FV) Fishing Vessel**	**1 oil engine** driving 1 FP propeller Total Power: 588kW (799hp) 10.8kn Niigata 6M24EGT 1 x 4 Stroke 6 Cy. 240 x 410 588kW (799bhp) Niigata Engineering Co Ltd-Japan AuxGen: 2 x 96kW 220V a.c
7921631 - -	**SHIN YAMAKAWA MARU** - - - *China*	*498* - 1,592	Class: (NK)	**1979**-12 **Nishi Shipbuilding Co Ltd — Imabari EH** Yd No: 206 Loa 68.92 Br ex - Dght 4.293 Lbp 64.01 Br md 11.51 Dpth 6.30 Welded, 2 dks	**(A31A2GX) General Cargo Ship** Grain: 2,551; Bale: 2,424 1 Ha: (37.7 x 8.5)ER	**1 oil engine** geared to sc. shaft driving 1 FP propeller Total Power: 1,324kW (1,800hp) 11.5kn Hanshin 6LU35G 1 x 4 Stroke 6 Cy. 350 x 550 1324kW (1800bhp) The Hanshin Diesel Works Ltd-Japan AuxGen: 2 x 144kW
9343182 *DSOL7* -	**SHIN YANG** *ex* Hyunjin Ks No. 3 *-2009* *ex* Global No. 1 *-2005* *ex* Global Young *-2005* **Ssangyong Shipping Co Ltd** - *Busan* *South Korea* MMSI: 440870000 Official number: BSR-051521	**6,422** 2,688 10,771	Class: KR	**2005**-09 **Nantong Tongshun Shiprepair & Building Co Ltd — Nantong JS** Yd No: TS040515 Loa 123.00 Br ex - Dght 7.874 Lbp 116.00 Br md 19.40 Dpth 10.35 Welded, 1 dk	**(A24A2BT) Cement Carrier**	**1 oil engine** driving 1 FP propeller Total Power: 3,900kW (5,302hp) 13.5kn B&W 6L35MC 1 x 2 Stroke 6 Cy. 350 x 1050 3900kW (5302bhp) STX Engine Co Ltd-South Korea
8649670 *BENH* -	**SHIN YEOU NO. 6** - **Shin Yeou Fishery Co Ltd** - *Kaohsiung* *Chinese Taipei* Official number: 011181	**713** 290		**1988**-11 **Fong Kuo Shipbuilding Co Ltd — Kaohsiung** Loa 56.16 Br ex - Dght 3.580 Lbp - Br md 8.90 Dpth 3.85 Welded, 1 dk	**(B11B2FV) Fishing Vessel** Ins: 789	**1 oil engine** driving 1 Propeller Total Power: 1,030kW (1,400hp)
8431372 *BEDE* CT7-000157	**SHIN YEOU No. 16** - **Shin Yeou Fishery Co Ltd** - *Kaohsiung* *Chinese Taipei* Official number: 011182	**723** 286 -		**1988**-11 **Taiwan Machinery Manufacturing Corp. — Kaohsiung** Loa 56.15 Br ex - Dght 2.370 Lbp - Br md 8.90 Dpth 3.85 Welded, 1 dk	**(B11B2FV) Fishing Vessel**	**1 oil engine** driving 1 FP propeller Total Power: 1,030kW (1,400hp) 12.0kn Akasaka 1 x 4 Stroke 6 Cy. 1030kW (1400bhp) Akasaka Tekkosho KK (Akasaka DieselLtd)-Japan
9316062 *3EEU5* -	**SHIN YO** - **Caribstar Shipping SA** Chugoku Sougyo Co Ltd *Panama* *Panama* MMSI: 371816000 Official number: 3144506A	**40,042** 25,318 76,863 T/cm 67.3	Class: NK	**2006**-02 **Sasebo Heavy Industries Co. Ltd. — Sasebo Yard, Sasebo** Yd No: 730 Loa 225.00 (BB) Br ex 32.23 Dght 14.200 Lbp 218.00 Br md 32.20 Dpth 19.80 Welded, 1 dk	**(A21A2BC) Bulk Carrier** Grain: 90,911; Bale: 88,950 Compartments: 7 Ho, ER 7 Ha: 6 (17.0 x 14.4)ER (15.3 x 12.8)	**1 oil engine** driving 1 FP propeller Total Power: 9,230kW (12,549hp) 14.5kn MAN-B&W 7S50MC-C 1 x 2 Stroke 7 Cy. 500 x 2000 9230kW (12549bhp) Mitsui Engineering & Shipbuilding CLtd-Japan Fuel: 2470.0
8971308 *JL4978* -	**SHIN YOSHI MARU No. 53** *ex* Sagamyojin Maru No. 53 *-2001* **YK Shin Yoshi** - *Kuroshio, Kochi* *Japan* Official number: 125450	*116* - -		**1981**-10 **Nishii Dock Co. Ltd. — Ise** L reg 29.00 Br ex - Dght - Lbp - Br md 5.75 Dpth 2.45 Bonded, 1 dk	**(B11B2FV) Fishing Vessel** Hull Material: Reinforced Plastic	**1 oil engine** driving 1 FP propeller Niigata 1 x 4 Stroke Niigata Engineering Co Ltd-Japan
9134945 - -	**SHIN YOUNG** *ex* Hamayu *-2009* **Young Sung Global Co Ltd** - *Busan* *South Korea* MMSI: 440134050 Official number: BSR-090831	**749** - 2,096	Class: KR (NK)	**1995**-09 **Hakata Zosen K.K. — Imabari** Yd No: 585 Loa 77.06 Br ex - Dght 4.761 Lbp 73.20 Br md 11.50 Dpth 5.33 Welded, 1 dk	**(A13B2TP) Products Tanker** Liq: 2,250; Liq (Oil): 2,250	**1 oil engine** geared to sc. shaft driving 1 FP propeller Total Power: 1,471kW (2,000hp) 11.5kn Hanshin 6LU35G 1 x 4 Stroke 6 Cy. 350 x 550 1471kW (2000bhp) The Hanshin Diesel Works Ltd-Japan Fuel: 75.0 (d.f.)
8823800 *DSNR8* -	**SHIN YOUNG NO. 8** *ex* Nam Do *-2008* *ex* Hang Lim Queen *-2006* *ex* Sennichi *-2004* *ex* Seiko Maru *-2001* **Shin Young Marine Co Ltd** - *Jeju* *South Korea* MMSI: 440243000 Official number: JJR 018856	**1,313** 629 852	Class: KR	**1988**-10 **Amakusa Zosen K.K. — Amakusa** Lengthened-2001 Loa 69.95 Br ex - Dght 3.390 Lbp 64.00 Br md 12.20 Dpth 5.60 Welded, 1 dk	**(B33A2DG) Grab Dredger** Compartments: 1 Ho, ER 1 Ha: (14.3 x 10.0)ER Cranes: 1	**1 oil engine** driving 1 FP propeller Total Power: 736kW (1,001hp) 10.6kn Hanshin LH28G 1 x 4 Stroke 6 Cy. 280 x 460 736kW (1001bhp) The Hanshin Diesel Works Ltd-Japan
8949264 *BG3348* -	**SHIN YU FA No. 68** *ex* Sheng Hua 666 *-2001* **Eng Soon Shipping Co Ltd** - *Keelung* *Chinese Taipei* Official number: 009174	*130* 50 -		**1984 Suao Shipbuilding Co., Ltd. — Suao** L reg 28.20 Br ex - Dght - Lbp - Br md 5.40 Dpth 2.60 Welded, 1 dk	**(B11B2FV) Fishing Vessel**	**1 oil engine** driving 1 FP propeller Total Power: 309kW (420hp) Matsui 1 x 4 Stroke 309kW (420bhp) Matsui Iron Works Co Ltd-Japan
9635274 *JD3290* -	**SHIN YU MARU** - **Shinko Butsuryu KK** - *Kobe, Hyogo* *Japan* MMSI: 431003256 Official number: 141583	*499* - 1,810		**2012**-02 **Yamanaka Zosen K.K. — Imabari** Yd No: 821 Loa 74.24 Br ex - Dght 4.362 Lbp 68.00 Br md 12.00 Dpth 7.37 Welded, 1 dk	**(A31A2GX) General Cargo Ship** Grain: 2,921	**1 oil engine** geared to sc. shaft driving 1 FP propeller Total Power: 1,618kW (2,200hp) Hanshin LA32G 1 x 4 Stroke 6 Cy. 320 x 680 1618kW (2200bhp) The Hanshin Diesel Works Ltd-Japan
8714231 *6LGQ* -	**SHIN YUNG No. 51** - **Silla Co Ltd** - *Busan* *South Korea* MMSI: 440604000 Official number: 9512351-6260006	**401** - 443	Class: KR	**1988**-06 **ShinA Shipbuilding Co Ltd — Tongyeong** Yd No: 329 Loa 53.50 Br ex - Dght 3.670 Lbp 48.01 Br md 8.91 Dpth 3.76 Welded, 1 dk	**(B11B2FV) Fishing Vessel** Ins: 598	**1 oil engine** sr geared to sc. shaft driving 1 FP propeller Total Power: 883kW (1,201hp) Niigata 6M28AFTE 1 x 4 Stroke 6 Cy. 280 x 480 883kW (1201bhp) Ssangyong Heavy Industries Co Ltd-South Korea

8717984 *6NJJ* -	**SHIN YUNG No. 52** - **Silla Co Ltd** - *Busan* *South Korea* MMSI: 440612000 Official number: 9512358-6260009	**401** - 439	Class: KR	**1988-08 ShinA Shipbuilding Co Ltd — Tongyeong** Yd No: 330 Loa 53.50 (BB) Br ex 8.93 Dght 3.670 Lbp 48.01 Br md 8.90 Dpth 3.76 Welded, 1 dk	**(B11B2FV) Fishing Vessel** Ins: 598	**1 oil engine** sr geared to sc. shaft driving 1 FP propeller Total Power: 883kW (1,201hp) Niigata 6M28AFTE 1 x 4 Stroke 6 Cy. 280 x 480 883kW (1201bhp) Ssangyong Heavy Industries Co Ltd-South Korea
8815712 *6MWO* -	**SHIN YUNG No. 53** - **Silla Co Ltd** - *Busan* *South Korea* MMSI: 440628000 Official number: 9512381-6260000	**424** 274 504	Class: KR	**1989-06 ShinA Shipbuilding Co Ltd — Tongyeong** Yd No: 332 Loa 55.20 Br ex 9.22 Dght 3.747 Lbp 49.50 Br md 9.20 Dpth 3.85 Welded, 1 dk	**(B11B2FV) Fishing Vessel** Ins: 574	**1 oil engine** with clutches & sr reverse geared to sc. shaft driving 1 FP propeller Total Power: 883kW (1,201hp) Niigata 6M28AFTE 1 x 4 Stroke 6 Cy. 280 x 480 883kW (1201bhp) Ssangyong Heavy Industries Co Ltd-South Korea
8815724 *6MWP* -	**SHIN YUNG No. 55** - **Silla Co Ltd** - SatCom: Inmarsat A 1660437 *Busan* *South Korea* MMSI: 440503000 Official number: 9512384-6260007	**424** 274 505	Class: KR	**1989-07 ShinA Shipbuilding Co Ltd — Tongyeong** Yd No: 333 Loa 55.20 Br ex - Dght 3.747 Lbp 49.77 Br md 9.20 Dpth 3.85 Welded, 1 dk	**(B11B2FV) Fishing Vessel** Ins: 574	**1 oil engine** driving 1 FP propeller Total Power: 883kW (1,201hp) Niigata 6M28AFTE 1 x 4 Stroke 6 Cy. 280 x 480 883kW (1201bhp) Ssangyong Heavy Industries Co Ltd-South Korea
8619326 *HLWA* -	**SHIN YUNG No. 56** *ex* O Dae Yang No. 707 *-1989* **Silla Co Ltd** - *Busan* *South Korea* MMSI: 440504000 Official number: 9512328-6260005	**384** 234 406	Class: KR	**1987-04 Dae Sun Shipbuilding & Engineering Co Ltd — Busan** Yd No: 309 Loa 53.29 Br ex - Dght 3.649 Lbp 46.89 Br md 8.70 Dpth 3.76 Welded, 1 dk	**(B11B2FV) Fishing Vessel** Ins: 605	**1 oil engine** sr reverse geared to sc. shaft driving 1 FP propeller Total Power: 736kW (1,001hp) 11.5kn Niigata 6M28AFTE 1 x 4 Stroke 6 Cy. 280 x 480 736kW (1001bhp) Ssangyong Heavy Industries Co Ltd-South Korea AuxGen: 2 x 280kW 225V a.c
9387114 *3EJW7* -	**SHIN-ZUI** - **Shoei Kisen Kaisha Ltd & Paraiso Shipping SA** Shoei Kisen Kaisha Ltd SatCom: Inmarsat C 437263410 *Panama* *Panama* MMSI: 372634000 Official number: 3266307A	**90,092** 59,287 180,201 T/cm 121.0	Class: NK	**2007-04 Koyo Dockyard Co Ltd — Mihara HS** Yd No: 2176 Loa 288.93 (BB) Br ex - Dght 18.171 Lbp 280.80 Br md 45.00 Dpth 24.70 Welded, 1 dk	**(A21A2BC) Bulk Carrier** Grain: 199,725 Compartments: 9 Ho, ER 9 Ha: ER	**1 oil engine** driving 1 FP propeller Total Power: 18,630kW (25,329hp) 14.5kn MAN-B&W 6S70MC-C 1 x 2 Stroke 6 Cy. 700 x 2800 18630kW (25329bhp) Mitsui Engineering & Shipbuilding CLtd-Japan AuxGen: 3 x a.c Fuel: 5685.0
9238935 *JG5628* -	**SHIN ZUI MARU** - **Japan Railway Construction, Transport & Technology Agency & Kuribayashi Logistics System Co Ltd** Kuribayashi Steamship Co Ltd *Tokyo* *Japan* MMSI: 431100948 Official number: 136995	*13,097* - 6,799	Class: NK	**2001-05 Yamanishi Corp — Ishinomaki MG** Yd No: 1023 Loa 160.56 (BB) Br ex - Dght 6.820 Lbp 150.00 Br md 26.60 Dpth 15.80 Welded, 4 dks	**(A35A2RR) Ro-Ro Cargo Ship** Angled stern door/ramp (s. a.) Quarter bow door/ramp (s) Lane-Len: 1574 Cars: 200, Trailers: 76 Bale: 1,049	**1 oil engine** reduction geared to sc. shaft driving 1 CP propeller Total Power: 15,888kW (21,601hp) 21.2kn Pielstick 12PC4-2B-570 1 x Vee 4 Stroke 12 Cy. 570 x 660 15888kW (21601bhp) Nippon Kokan KK (NKK Corp)-Japan AuxGen: 2 x 1560kW 450V 60Hz a.c Thrusters: 1 Thwart. FP thruster (f) Fuel: 615.0
9015084 *JI3470* -	**SHINAKI MARU** *ex* Yoshu Maru No. 3 *-2012* **Aki Kaiun Co Ltd (Aki Kaiun KK)** Aki Line Co Ltd *Osaka, Osaka* *Japan* MMSI: 431300592 Official number: 131721	*4,335* 1,548 6,167	Class: NK	**1991-09 Kanda Zosensho K.K. — Kawajiri** Yd No: 338 Loa 110.00 (BB) Br ex 16.82 Dght 6.490 Lbp 105.00 Br md 16.80 Dpth 8.50 Welded, 1 dk	**(A24A2BT) Cement Carrier** Grain: 5,597 Compartments: 6 Ho, ER	**1 oil engine** driving 1 CP propeller Total Power: 3,604kW (4,900hp) 13.3kn Mitsubishi 7UEC37LA 1 x 2 Stroke 7 Cy. 370 x 880 3604kW (4900bhp) Akasaka Tekkosho KK (Akasaka DieselLtd)-Japan AuxGen: 3 x 340kW a.c Thrusters: 1 Thwart. CP thruster (f) Fuel: 230.0 (r.f.)
9038048 - -	**SHINANO** *ex* Shinano Maru *-2006* **Yangpu Jintong Shipping Co Ltd** China Communications Import & Export Corp	*167* - -		**1991-10 Kanagawa Zosen — Kobe** Yd No: 364 Loa 38.00 Br ex - Dght 3.000 Lbp 33.50 Br md 8.40 Dpth 3.40 Welded, 1 dk	**(B32A2ST) Tug**	**2 oil engines** Geared Integral to driving 2 Z propellers Total Power: 2,280kW (3,100hp) Niigata 6L25HX 2 x 4 Stroke 6 Cy. 250 x 350 each-1140kW (1550bhp) Niigata Engineering Co Ltd-Japan
8986444 *JH3505* -	**SHINANO MARU** - **Sanyo Kaiji KK** - *Nagoya, Aichi* *Japan* Official number: 135712	*154* - -		**2003-10 Hatayama Zosen KK — Yura WK** Yd No: 241 L reg 29.18 Br ex - Dght - Lbp - Br md 8.60 Dpth 3.50 Welded, 1 dk	**(B32A2ST) Tug**	**2 oil engines** geared to sc. shafts driving 2 Propellers Total Power: 1,766kW (2,402hp) Yanmar 6N21A-SV 2 x 4 Stroke 6 Cy. 210 x 290 each-883kW (1201bhp) Yanmar Diesel Engine Co Ltd-Japan
7396989 *V4ZK* -	**SHINANO MARU** *ex* Kakuyo Maru No. 1 *-1985* **Shinano Maru Co** MFH (Maritime Fleet Handling) *Basseterre* *St Kitts & Nevis* MMSI: 341666000 Official number: SKN 1001666	**603** 180 490	Class: IS (NK) (BV)	**1974-09 Hibikinada Dock Co. Ltd. — Kitakyushu** Yd No: 138 Loa 38.00 Br ex 10.04 Dght 5.320 Lbp 34.02 Br md 10.00 Dpth 5.69 Welded, 1 dk	**(B32B2SP) Pusher Tug**	**2 oil engines** driving 2 FP propellers Total Power: 3,090kW (4,202hp) 13.8kn Daihatsu 6DSM-32 2 x 4 Stroke 6 Cy. 320 x 380 each-1545kW (2101bhp) Daihatsu Diesel Manufacturing Co Lt-Japan AuxGen: 2 x 104kW a.c
9600126 *7JJK* -	**SHINANO MARU** - **Fukushima Kisen KK** - *Iwaki, Fukushima* *Japan* Official number: 141468	**483** - 470	Class: LR NK ✠ **100A1** SS 03/2012 tug, fire-fighting Ship 1 (2400 m/h) with water spray **ShipRight** ACS (B) ✠ **LMC** **UMS** Eq.Ltr: J; Cable: 357.5/28.0 U2 (a)	**2012-03 Niigata Shipbuilding & Repair Inc — Niigata NI** Yd No: 0053 Loa 39.30 (BB) Br ex 13.62 Dght 4.800 Lbp 36.29 Br md 13.60 Dpth 5.30 Welded, 1 dk	**(B32A2ST) Tug**	**2 oil engines** gearing integral to driving 2 Voith-Schneider propellers Total Power: 5,300kW (7,206hp) Wartsila 8L26 2 x 4 Stroke 8 Cy. 260 x 320 each-2650kW (3603bhp) Wartsila Italia SpA-Italy AuxGen: 2 x 250kW 440V 60Hz a.c Fuel: 250.0
9523641 *JD2842* -	**SHINANO MARU** - **Tokyo Kisen KK** - *Yokohama, Kanagawa* *Japan* Official number: 140899	*178* - -		**2008-11 Kanagawa Zosen — Kobe** Yd No: 600 Loa 37.20 Br ex - Dght 2.900 Lbp 32.70 Br md 8.80 Dpth 3.60 Welded, 1 dk	**(B32A2ST) Tug**	**2 oil engines** reduction geared to sc. shafts driving 2 Propellers Total Power: 2,646kW (3,598hp) Niigata 6L26HLX 2 x 4 Stroke 6 Cy. 260 x 350 each-1323kW (1799bhp) Niigata Engineering Co Ltd-Japan
9396177 *A4BA2* -	**SHINAS** - **Government of The Sultanate of Oman (Ministry of Economy)** National Ferries Co SAOC *Port Sultan Qaboos* *Oman* MMSI: 461000050	**2,005** 602 146	Class: NV	**2007-12 Austal Ships Pty Ltd — Fremantle WA** Yd No: 263 Loa 64.80 (BB) Br ex - Dght 2.100 Lbp 61.10 Br md 16.70 Dpth 6.20 Welded, 1 dk	**(A36A2PR) Passenger/Ro-Ro Ship (Vehicles)** Hull Material: Aluminium Alloy Passengers: unberthed: 203 Cars: 56	**4 oil engines** reduction geared to sc. shafts driving 4 Water jets Total Power: 26,000kW (35,348hp) 50.0kn M.T.U. 20V1163TB73 4 x Vee 4 Stroke 20 Cy. 230 x 280 each-6500kW (8837bhp) MTU Friedrichshafen GmbH-Friedrichshafen AuxGen: 2 x a.c
9495739 *JD2931* -	**SHINATSU** - **Japan Railway Construction, Transport & Technology Agency & Toko Kaiun Co Ltd** Toko Kaiun Co Ltd (Toko Kaiun KK) *Kobe, Hyogo* *Japan* MMSI: 431000985 Official number: 141043	*3,575* - 5,671	Class: NK	**2009-07 Hakata Zosen K.K. — Imabari** Yd No: 710 Loa 104.20 (BB) Br ex - Dght 6.916 Lbp 98.00 Br md 16.00 Dpth 8.20 Welded, 1 dk	**(A13B2TP) Products Tanker** Double Hull (13F) Liq: 5,488; Liq (Oil): 5,488	**1 oil engine** driving 1 FP propeller Total Power: 3,309kW (4,499hp) 14.2kn Akasaka A45S 1 x 4 Stroke 6 Cy. 450 x 880 3309kW (4499bhp) Akasaka Tekkosho KK (Akasaka DieselLtd)-Japan Fuel: 270.0
8949006 *JI3656* -	**SHINBISHI** - **Tsukiboshi Kaiun KK** - *Osaka, Osaka* *Japan* Official number: 135959	*130* - -		**1998-10 Kegoya Dock K.K. — Kure** Yd No: 1021 Loa 30.01 Br ex - Dght - Lbp 28.00 Br md 9.00 Dpth 5.75 Welded, 1 dk	**(B32B2SA) Articulated Pusher Tug**	**2 oil engines** driving 2 FP propellers Total Power: 2,354kW (3,200hp) 10.0kn Yanmar DY28-SN 2 x 4 Stroke 6 Cy. 280 x 530 each-1177kW (1600bhp) Yanmar Diesel Engine Co Ltd-Japan

IMO / Call sign	Name / Owner	Tonnage	Class	Builder / Dimensions	Type	Machinery
9008081 *DSOJ4* -	**SHINCHANG** *ex* Sunjoo Kwangyang *-2006* *ex* Sider Tide *-2005* *ex* Socofl Tide *-2004* *ex* Tidenes *-2002* *ex* Socofl Tide *-1996* **Shin Chang Shipping Co Ltd** - *Jeju* *South Korea* MMSI: 440753000 Official number: JJR-059604	**4,944** 2,200 6,280 T/cm 17.8	Class: KR (LR) (BV) ✠ Classed LR until 9/1/04	**1992-07 Kyokuyo Shipyard Corp — Shimonoseki YC** Yd No: 375 Loa 111.60 (BB) Br ex 18.05 Dght 5.813 Lbp 105.00 Br md 18.00 Dpth 7.60 Welded, 1 dk	**(A31A2GX) General Cargo Ship** Grain: 7,935; Bale: 7,835 Compartments: 2 Ho, ER 2 Ha: ER Cranes: 2x25t Ice Capable	**1 oil engine** driving 1 FP propeller Total Power: 2,574kW (3,500hp) 12.8kn Hanshin 6LF46 1 x 4 Stroke 6 Cy. 460 x 740 2574kW (3500bhp) The Hanshin Diesel Works Ltd-Japan AuxGen: 3 x 270kW 450V 60Hz a.c Boilers: TOH (o.f.) 8.6kgf/cm² (8.4bar), TOH (ex.g.) 8.6kgf/cm² (8.4bar)
9114579 *JBKB* -	**SHINCHI MARU** **Nippon Yusen Kabushiki Kaisha (NYK Line)** Hachiuma Steamship Co Ltd (Hachiuma Kisen KK) SatCom: Inmarsat C 443174310 *Shinchi, Fukushima* *Japan* MMSI: 431743000 Official number: 133325	**58,098** 25,095 91,443	Class: NK	**1995-05 Mitsubishi Heavy Industries Ltd. — Nagasaki** Yd No: 2087 Loa 240.00 (BB) Br ex 43.04 Dght 12.778 Lbp 230.00 Br md 43.00 Dpth 20.50 Welded, 1 dk	**(A21A2BC) Bulk Carrier** Grain: 118,600 Compartments: 7 Ho, ER 7 Ha: (15.8 x 17.6) (15.8 x 17.6)5 (15.7 x 20.8)ER	**1 oil engine** driving 1 FP propeller Total Power: 10,813kW (14,701hp) 14.0kn Mitsubishi 7UEC60LS 1 x 2 Stroke 7 Cy. 600 x 2200 10813kW (14701bhp) Mitsubishi Heavy Industries Ltd-Japan Fuel: 3520.0 (r.f.)
9130420 - -	**SHINDAGHA-5** **Dubai Drydocks** - *Dubai* *United Arab Emirates* Official number: 4086	**322** 96 220	Class: LR ✠ **100A1** SS 09/2011 tug Arabian Gulf and Gulf of Oman service ✠ **LMC** Eq.Ltr: G; Cable: 302.5/20.5 U2	**1996-09 Dubai Drydocks — Dubai** Yd No: C719 Loa 30.85 Br ex 10.65 Dght 4.200 Lbp 26.30 Br md 10.00 Dpth 5.00 Welded, 1 dk	**(B32A2ST) Tug**	**2 oil engines** gearing integral to driving 2 Z propellers Total Power: 3,090kW (4,202hp) 13.0kn Nohab 6R25 2 x 4 Stroke 6 Cy. 250 x 300 each-1545kW (2101bhp) Wartsila Diesel AB-Sweden AuxGen: 2 x 124kW 380V 50Hz a.c Fuel: 84.0 (d.f.) 3.5pd
7912915 *JM4611* -	**SHINDOKAI MARU** **Dokai Marine Systems Ltd** - *Kitakyushu, Fukuoka* *Japan* MMSI: 431601961 Official number: 120712	*195* - -		**1979-08 Kanagawa Zosen — Kobe** Yd No: 201 Loa 33.30 Br ex - Dght 2.501 Lbp 29.52 Br md 8.21 Dpth 3.41 Welded, 1 dk	**(B32A2ST) Tug**	**2 oil engines** Geared Integral to driving 2 Z propellers Total Power: 1,912kW (2,600hp) 13.5kn Niigata 6L25BX 2 x 4 Stroke 6 Cy. 250 x 320 each-956kW (1300bhp) Niigata Engineering Co Ltd-Japan
8839861 - -	**SHINE** *ex* ELC *-2011* *ex* Yusei Maru *-2010* *ex* Osima Maru *-2007* *ex* Oshima *-2000* *ex* Taikei *-1999* *ex* Goishi Maru No. 38 *-1995* **Eastern Logistic Co** -	**193** 119 225	Class: (RS)	**1979 Sasaki Shipbuilding Co Ltd — Ofunato IW** Yd No: 166 Loa 35.80 Br ex 6.20 Dght 2.340 Lbp 29.70 Br md - Dpth 2.58 Welded, 1 dk	**(B11B2FV) Fishing Vessel**	**1 oil engine** geared to sc. shaft driving 1 FP propeller Total Power: 522kW (710hp) 11.0kn Akasaka MH23R 1 x 4 Stroke 6 Cy. 230 x 390 522kW (710bhp) Akasaka Tekkosho KK (Akasaka DieselLtd)-Japan
8317344 *HPOZ* -	**SHINE HO** *ex* Kiwi Queen *-1991* **Chi Ho Maritime SA** Ta-Ho Maritime Corp SatCom: Inmarsat C 435154810 *Panama* *Panama* MMSI: 351548000 Official number: 2967804B	**10,944** 4,756 17,071 T/cm 28.1	Class: CR (NK)	**1984-11 Shikoku Dockyard Co. Ltd. — Takamatsu** Yd No: 829 Converted From: Bulk Carrier-1992 Loa 147.00 (BB) Br ex - Dght 9.002 Lbp 136.02 Br md 22.81 Dpth 12.22 Welded, 1 dk	**(A24A2BT) Cement Carrier** Compartments: 2 Ho, ER	**1 oil engine** driving 1 FP propeller Total Power: 5,517kW (7,501hp) 13.7kn B&W 6L50MCE 1 x 2 Stroke 6 Cy. 500 x 1620 5517kW (7501bhp) Mitsui Engineering & Shipbuilding CLtd-Japan AuxGen: 2 x 360kW 450V 60Hz a.c, 1 x 260kW 450V 60Hz a.c Fuel: 118.5 (d.f.) (Heating Coils) 910.0 (r.f.) 20.0pd
8618671 *PONG* -	**SHINEI** *ex* Shinei Maru No. 18 *-2013* *ex* Heiwa Maru No. 18 *-2004* **PT Indo Shipping Operator** - *Tanjung Priok* *Indonesia* MMSI: 525022136	**1,605** 937 -	Class: KI	**1987-06 K.K. Miura Zosensho — Saiki** Yd No: 778 Converted From: Bucket Dredger-2013 Lengthened-2013 Loa 81.53 (BB) Br ex 13.24 Dght 4.540 Lbp 76.30 Br md 13.21 Dpth 5.80 Welded, 1 dk	**(A31A2GX) General Cargo Ship** Cranes: 1	**1 oil engine** reduction geared to sc. shaft driving 1 FP propeller Total Power: 662kW (900hp) Hanshin 6LU32G 1 x 4 Stroke 6 Cy. 320 x 510 662kW (900bhp) The Hanshin Diesel Works Ltd-Japan AuxGen: 2 x 107kW 220V a.c
9720835 *JD3649* -	**SHINEI** **Tahara Kaiun YK** - *Japan*	*498* - 1,187	Class: FA	**2014-02 KK Ura Kyodo Zosensho — Awaji HG** Yd No: 352 Loa 64.45 Br ex - Dght 4.114 Lbp - Br md 10.00 Dpth - Welded, 1 dk	**(A13B2TP) Products Tanker** Double Hull (13F)	**1 oil engine** reduction geared to sc. shaft driving 1 Propeller Total Power: 1,029kW (1,399hp) Niigata 6M28BGT 1 x 4 Stroke 6 Cy. 280 x 480 1029kW (1399bhp) Niigata Engineering Co Ltd-Japan
9402976 *JD2348* -	**SHINEI MARU** **Japan Railway Construction, Transport & Technology Agency & Niijima Bussan KK** Niijima Bussan KK *Niijima, Tokyo* *Japan* Official number: 140458	*492* - 663		**2007-02 Sanuki Shipbuilding & Iron Works Co Ltd — Mitoyo KG** (Hull) Yd No: 1316 **2007-02 IHI Marine United Inc — Yokohama KN** Yd No: 3241 Loa 59.20 (BB) Br ex - Dght 3.420 Lbp 55.00 Br md 9.80 Dpth 3.50 Welded, 1 dk	**(A31A2GT) General Cargo/Tanker** Cranes: 1	**3 diesel electric oil engines** driving 3 gen. each 400kW a.c Connecting to 2 elec. motors each (500kW) geared to sc. shaft driving 1 Contra-rotating propeller Total Power: 1,497kW (2,034hp) 11.9kn Yanmar 6N18AL-HV 3 x 4 Stroke 6 Cy. 180 x 280 each-499kW (678bhp) Yanmar Diesel Engine Co Ltd-Japan
8614297 *JL5554* -	**SHINEI MARU** **Hayashida Kaiun YK** - *Sakaide, Kagawa* *Japan* Official number: 129060	*129* - 250		**1987-01 Koa Sangyo KK — Takamatsu KG** Yd No: 528 Loa 33.20 Br ex - Dght 2.200 Lbp 30.00 Br md 7.20 Dpth 2.80 Welded, 1 dk	**(A12A2TC) Chemical Tanker** Liq: 210 Compartments: 4 Ta, ER	**1 oil engine** driving 1 FP propeller Total Power: 368kW (500hp) Hanshin D4T-TK 1 x 4 Stroke 4 Cy. 170 x 210 368kW (500bhp) The Hanshin Diesel Works Ltd-Japan
8001713 - -	**SHINEI MARU** **Seapower Shipping & Trading Pte Ltd** -	*489* 303 1,350		**1980-08 Mategata Zosen K.K. — Namikata** Yd No: 186 Loa - Br ex - Dght 4.501 Lbp 60.03 Br md 10.01 Dpth 6.23 Welded, 1 dk	**(A31A2GX) General Cargo Ship**	**1 oil engine** driving 1 FP propeller Total Power: 1,103kW (1,500hp) Makita GSLH630 1 x 4 Stroke 6 Cy. 300 x 480 1103kW (1500bhp) Makita Diesel Co Ltd-Japan
7220398 *JJ2795* -	**SHINEI MARU** *ex* Onohama Maru *-1989* - *Shingu, Wakayama* *Japan* Official number: 112595	*199* - 52		**1972-03 Ishikawajima Ship & Chemical Plant Co Ltd — Tokyo** Yd No: 423 Loa 28.38 Br ex 8.64 Dght 2.572 Lbp 25.00 Br md 8.62 Dpth 3.51 Welded, 1 dk	**(B32A2ST) Tug**	**2 oil engines** driving 2 FP propellers Total Power: 1,398kW (1,900hp) 12.0kn Daihatsu 8PSHTCM-26D 2 x 4 Stroke 8 Cy. 260 x 320 each-699kW (950bhp) Daihatsu Diesel Manufacturing Co Lt-Japan AuxGen: 2 x 48kW 440V a.c
8743309 *JD2899* -	**SHINEI MARU** *ex* Nichirin Maru *-2012* **Odomari Kaiun YK** - *Himeji, Hyogo* *Japan* Official number: 140996	*499* - 1,800		**2009-03 YK Nakanoshima Zosensho — Kochi KC** Yd No: 260 Loa 74.71 Br ex - Dght 4.330 Lbp 69.00 Br md 12.00 Dpth 7.35 Welded, 1 dk	**(A31A2GX) General Cargo Ship** Bale: 2,497 Compartments: 1 Ho, ER 1 Ha: ER (40.1 x 9.6)	**1 oil engine** driving 1 Propeller Total Power: 1,618kW (2,200hp) 12.5kn Niigata 6M34BGT 1 x 4 Stroke 6 Cy. 340 x 620 1618kW (2200bhp) Niigata Engineering Co Ltd-Japan
9119763 *JL6382* -	**SHINEI MARU** **Kosei Marine KK** - *Komatsushima, Tokushima* *Japan* Official number: 135066	*199* - 650		**1995-06 Hamamoto Zosensho K.K. — Tokushima** Yd No: 803 Loa 59.44 Br ex - Dght 3.230 Lbp 53.00 Br md 9.60 Dpth 5.32 Welded, 1 dk	**(A31A2GX) General Cargo Ship**	**1 oil engine** driving 1 FP propeller Total Power: 736kW (1,001hp) 10.5kn Niigata 6M28BGT 1 x 4 Stroke 6 Cy. 280 x 480 736kW (1001bhp) Niigata Engineering Co Ltd-Japan
9124952 *JM6456* -	**SHINEI MARU** *ex* Sakae Maru No. 21 *-2009* **Nakagawa Kaiun YK** - *Anan, Tokushima* *Japan* Official number: 134547	*199* - 441		**1995-06 K.K. Watanabe Zosensho — Nagasaki** Yd No: 032 Loa 45.81 Br ex - Dght - Lbp 41.00 Br md 7.50 Dpth 3.30 Welded, 1 dk	**(A13B2TP) Products Tanker**	**1 oil engine** driving 1 FP propeller Total Power: 588kW (799hp) Matsui 6M26KGHS 1 x 4 Stroke 6 Cy. 260 x 400 588kW (799bhp) Matsui Iron Works Co Ltd-Japan
9153812 *JJ3930* -	**SHINEI MARU** **Marouka Kaiun KK** - *Kakogawa, Hyogo* *Japan* Official number: 134246	*499* - 1,576		**1996-05 Hitachi Zosen Mukaishima Marine Co Ltd — Onomichi HS** Yd No: 107 Loa - Br ex - Dght 4.120 Lbp 69.00 Br md 12.00 Dpth 7.18 Welded, 1 dk	**(A31A2GX) General Cargo Ship**	**1 oil engine** driving 1 FP propeller Total Power: 1,324kW (1,800hp) 11.8kn Hanshin LH30LG 1 x 4 Stroke 6 Cy. 300 x 600 1324kW (1800bhp) The Hanshin Diesel Works Ltd-Japan
9183910 *JI3644* -	**SHINEI MARU** **Taiyo Shipping Co Ltd (Taiyo Kisen KK)** - *Osaka, Osaka* *Japan* MMSI: 431500761 Official number: 135941	*682* - 2,080		**1997-11 Yamanaka Zosen K.K. — Imabari** Yd No: 617 Loa 79.26 Br ex - Dght 4.720 Lbp 73.00 Br md 12.00 Dpth 7.30 Welded, 1 dk	**(A31A2GX) General Cargo Ship** Grain: 3,365; Bale: 2,852 Compartments: 1 Ho, ER 1 Ha: (42.0 x 9.5)ER	**1 oil engine** driving 1 FP propeller Total Power: 1,618kW (2,200hp) 12.0kn Akasaka A34C 1 x 4 Stroke 6 Cy. 340 x 620 1618kW (2200bhp) Akasaka Tekkosho KK (Akasaka DieselLtd)-Japan

IMO / Call sign	Name / Owner	Tonnage	Class	Builder / Dimensions	Type	Machinery
9003706 *JM6034* -	**SHINEI MARU** - **Ube Shipping & Logistics Ltd (Ube Kosan KK)** - *Ube, Yamaguchi* *Japan* MMSI: 431400715 Official number: 132587	*13,787* - 21,493	Class: NK	**1991-06 Kanda Zosensho K.K. — Kawajiri** Yd No: 335 Loa 159.70 (BB) Br ex - Dght 9.016 Lbp 152.50 Br md 24.20 Dpth 13.20 Welded, 1 dk	**(A24A2BT) Cement Carrier** Grain: 17,720 Compartments: 13 Ho, ER	**1 oil engine** driving 1 CP propeller Total Power: 5,119kW (6,960hp) 13.0kn B&W 6L42MC 1 x 2 Stroke 6 Cy. 420 x 1360 5119kW (6960bhp) Hitachi Zosen Corp-Japan Thrusters: 1 Thwart. CP thruster (f) Fuel: 440.0 (r.f.)
9047336 *JM6201* -	**SHINEI MARU** - **YK Shirahama Kaiun** - *Anan, Tokushima* *Japan* Official number: 133472	*199* - 655		**1992-09 Yamakawa Zosen Tekko K.K. — Kagoshima** Yd No: 711 Loa 58.30 Br ex - Dght 3.240 Lbp 52.40 Br md 9.60 Dpth 5.48 Welded, 1 dk	**(A31A2GX) General Cargo Ship**	**1 oil engine** driving 1 FP propeller Total Power: 625kW (850hp) Niigata 6M26AGTE 1 x 4 Stroke 6 Cy. 260 x 460 625kW (850bhp) Niigata Engineering Co Ltd-Japan
7104491 - -	**SHINEI MARU No. 1** *ex Kiku Maru No. 27 -1978* **Kenji Yoshizawa** -	*114* 49 -		**1970 Hayashikane Shipbuilding & Engineering Co Ltd — Nagasaki NS** Yd No: 787 Loa 34.22 Br ex 6.33 Dght 2.388 Lbp 28.78 Br md 6.30 Dpth 2.85 Welded, 1 dk	**(B11A2FT) Trawler**	**1 oil engine** driving 1 FP propeller Total Power: 515kW (700hp) Niigata 6L25BX 1 x 4 Stroke 6 Cy. 250 x 320 515kW (700bhp) Niigata Engineering Co Ltd-Japan
7104506 - -	**SHINEI MARU No. 2** *ex Kiku Maru No. 28 -1978* **Kenji Yoshizawa** -	*114* 49 -		**1970 Hayashikane Shipbuilding & Engineering Co Ltd — Nagasaki NS** Yd No: 788 Loa 34.22 Br ex 6.33 Dght 2.388 Lbp 28.78 Br md 6.30 Dpth 2.85 Welded, 1 dk	**(B11A2FT) Trawler**	**1 oil engine** driving 1 FP propeller Total Power: 515kW (700hp) Niigata 6L25BX 1 x 4 Stroke 6 Cy. 250 x 320 515kW (700bhp) Niigata Engineering Co Ltd-Japan
9088720 *JG5314* -	**SHINEI MARU No. 2** - **Shirahama Kisen YK** - *Anan, Tokushima* *Japan* Official number: 134353	*499* - 1,709	Class: NK	**1994-08 Y.K. Takasago Zosensho — Naruto** Yd No: 203 Loa 75.74 Br ex - Dght 4.271 Lbp 68.00 Br md 12.00 Dpth 7.20 Welded, 1 dk	**(A31A2GX) General Cargo Ship** Bale: 5,560 Compartments: 1 Ho, ER 1 Ha: (38.4 x 9.5)ER	**1 oil engine** driving 1 FP propeller Total Power: 1,177kW (1,600hp) 12.0kn Hanshin LH34LAG 1 x 4 Stroke 6 Cy. 340 x 640 1177kW (1600bhp) The Hanshin Diesel Works Ltd-Japan Fuel: 125.0 (d.f.) 4.8pd
9137947 *JL6338* -	**SHINEI MARU No. 3** - **YK Shimazaki Kaiun** - *Kure, Hiroshima* *Japan* Official number: 135115	*497* - 1,500		**1996-01 K.K. Miura Zosensho — Saiki** Yd No: 1153 Loa - Br ex - Dght 4.400 Lbp 61.00 Br md 13.00 Dpth 6.90 Welded, 1 dk	**(A31A2GX) General Cargo Ship**	**1 oil engine** driving 1 FP propeller Total Power: 736kW (1,001hp) 9.0kn Niigata 6M34AGT 1 x 4 Stroke 6 Cy. 340 x 620 736kW (1001bhp) Niigata Engineering Co Ltd-Japan
8963313 - -	**SHINEI MARU No. 5** *ex Sanei Maru No. 11 -1978* **Hai Thong Co** -	*150* - 210		**1963-04 Kominato Zosen K.K. — Amatsu-Kominato** Loa 31.00 Br ex - Dght 2.200 Lbp 26.00 Br md 6.50 Dpth 2.45 Welded, 1 dk	**(A31A2GX) General Cargo Ship** Compartments: 1 Ho, ER 1 Ha: (18.1 x 5.5)ER	**1 oil engine** driving 1 FP propeller Total Power: 88kW (120hp) 7.5kn Yanmar 1 x 4 Stroke 88kW (120bhp) Yanmar Diesel Engine Co Ltd-Japan
8738146 *JD2631* -	**SHINEI MARU No. 7** - **Yuji Kaiun KK** - *Tokushima, Tokushima* *Japan* Official number: 140734	*499* - 1,830		**2008-02 YK Nakanoshima Zosensho — Kochi KC** Yd No: 253 Loa 74.71 Br ex - Dght 4.320 Lbp 69.00 Br md 12.00 Dpth 7.35 Welded, 1 dk	**(A31A2GX) General Cargo Ship** Bale: 2,466 1 Ha: (40.0 x 9.5)	**1 oil engine** geared to sc. shaft driving 1 Propeller Total Power: 1,471kW (2,000hp) 12.0kn Niigata 6M34BGT 1 x 4 Stroke 6 Cy. 340 x 620 1471kW (2000bhp) Niigata Engineering Co Ltd-Japan
8824335 *JJ3622* -	**SHINEI MARU No. 8** *ex Tenjin Maru No. 22 -1994* *ex Shinei Maru No. 8 -1993* **Nakata Kensetsu KK** - *Himeji, Hyogo* *Japan* Official number: 130838	*498* - 1,382		**1989-04 K.K. Yoshida Zosen Kogyo — Arida** Yd No: 1382 Loa 68.00 Br ex - Dght 4.220 Lbp 63.00 Br md 13.00 Dpth 7.00 Welded, 1 dk	**(B33A2DG) Grab Dredger**	**1 oil engine** driving 1 FP propeller Total Power: 736kW (1,001hp) Yanmar MF33-ST 1 x 4 Stroke 6 Cy. 330 x 620 736kW (1001bhp) Matsue Diesel KK-Japan
6903890 - -	**SHINEI MARU No. 8** - **Entreposto Frigorifico de Pesca de Mocambique Ltda** *Quelimane* *Mozambique*	*345* 183 -		**1968 Yamanishi Shipbuilding Co Ltd — Ishinomaki MG** Yd No: 587 Loa 47.99 Br ex 8.41 Dght 3.302 Lbp 42.02 Br md 8.39 Dpth 3.76 Welded, 2 dks	**(B11B2FV) Fishing Vessel**	**1 oil engine** driving 1 FP propeller Total Power: 919kW (1,249hp) Akasaka 6DH35SS 1 x 4 Stroke 6 Cy. 350 x 520 919kW (1249bhp) Akasaka Tekkosho KK (Akasaka DieselLtd)-Japan
7396977 - -	**SHINEI MARU No. 8** - - - *Papua New Guinea*	*115* 61 71		**1973 K.K. Odo Zosen Tekko — Shimonoseki** Yd No: 198 Loa 32.60 Br ex 6.02 Dght 2.100 Lbp 26.00 Br md 6.00 Dpth 2.50 Welded, 1 dk	**(A37B2PS) Passenger Ship**	**1 oil engine** driving 1 FP propeller Total Power: 353kW (480hp) Yanmar 6ML-HTS 1 x 4 Stroke 6 Cy. 200 x 240 353kW (480bhp) Yanmar Diesel Engine Co Ltd-Japan
9123893 *JM6407* -	**SHINEI MARU NO. 11** *ex Shinpuku Maru No. 17 -2003* **Shinei Kaiun YK** - *Kainan, Wakayama* *Japan* Official number: 134566	*491* - 1,198		**1995-07 Honda Zosen — Saiki** Yd No: 877 Loa - Br ex - Dght - Lbp 62.00 Br md 13.20 Dpth 7.40 Welded, 1 dk	**(A31A2GX) General Cargo Ship**	**1 oil engine** driving 1 FP propeller Total Power: 1,471kW (2,000hp) Niigata 6M34AGT 1 x 4 Stroke 6 Cy. 340 x 620 1471kW (2000bhp) Niigata Engineering Co Ltd-Japan
9084437 *JJ3810* -	**SHINEI MARU No. 12** - **Nakata Kensetsu KK** - *Himeji, Hyogo* *Japan* Official number: 132312	*499* - -		**1993-09 K.K. Yoshida Zosen Kogyo — Arida** Yd No: 486 Loa 66.00 Br ex - Dght - Lbp 61.00 Br md 13.20 Dpth 7.20 Welded, 1 dk	**(A24D2BA) Aggregates Carrier**	**1 oil engine** driving 1 FP propeller Total Power: 736kW (1,001hp) 10.5kn Yanmar MF33-ST 1 x 4 Stroke 6 Cy. 330 x 620 736kW (1001bhp) Yanmar Diesel Engine Co Ltd-Japan
8743452 *JD2875* -	**SHINEI MARU NO. 15** - **KK Shinei Kaiun Kensetsu** - *Kainan, Wakayama* *Japan* Official number: 140939	*499* - 1,840		**2009-03 KS Yanase Marine — Fukuyama HS** Yd No: 105 Loa 68.76 Br ex - Dght 4.390 Lbp 63.00 Br md 13.20 Dpth 7.34 Welded, 1 dk	**(A31A2GX) General Cargo Ship** Grain: 1,464; Bale: 1,464 Compartments: 1 Ho, ER 1 Ha: ER	**1 oil engine** driving 1 Propeller Total Power: 1,618kW (2,200hp) 12.0kn Niigata 6M34BGT 1 x 4 Stroke 6 Cy. 340 x 620 1618kW (2200bhp) Niigata Engineering Co Ltd-Japan
9078397 *JE3114* MG1-1875	**SHINEI MARU No. 17** - **YK Shinei Suisan** *Kesennuma, Miyagi* *Japan* Official number: 133309	*119* - 221		**1993-09 Kidoura Shipyard Co Ltd — Kesennuma MG** Yd No: 583 Loa 39.85 (BB) Br ex 6.42 Dght 2.500 Lbp 32.56 Br md 6.40 Dpth 2.79 Welded, 1 dk	**(B11B2FV) Fishing Vessel** Ins: 159	**1 oil engine** with clutches, flexible couplings & reduction geared to sc. shaft driving 1 CP propeller Total Power: 800kW (1,088hp) 12.8kn Sumiyoshi S26RD 1 x 4 Stroke 6 Cy. 260 x 470 800kW (1088bhp) Sumiyoshi Marine Diesel Co Ltd-Japan AuxGen: 2 x 120kW a.c Fuel: 93.4 (d.f.) 3.0pd
9084176 *JL6146* -	**SHINEI MARU No. 18** - **Aono Kaiun KK (Aono Marine Co Ltd)** - *Niihama, Ehime* *Japan* Official number: 133876	*332* - 736		**1994-01 Koa Sangyo KK — Takamatsu KG** Yd No: 576 Loa 49.99 Br ex - Dght 3.660 Lbp 46.50 Br md 9.00 Dpth 4.00 Welded, 1 dk	**(A12A2TC) Chemical Tanker** Liq: 365 Compartments: 6 Ta, ER 2 Cargo Pump (s): 2x90m³/hr	**1 oil engine** driving 1 FP propeller Total Power: 736kW (1,001hp) Yanmar MF26-HT 1 x 4 Stroke 6 Cy. 260 x 500 736kW (1001bhp) Yanmar Diesel Engine Co Ltd-Japan
9054078 *JJ3788* -	**SHINEI MARU No. 18** - **Torayoshi Yamagata** - *Himeji, Hyogo* *Japan* Official number: 132287	*469* - 529		**1992-05 Masui Zosensho K.K. — Nandan** Yd No: 223 Loa 50.00 Br ex - Dght 3.370 Lbp 46.00 Br md 10.50 Dpth 5.54 Welded, 2 dks	**(A31A2GX) General Cargo Ship** Grain: 644; Bale: 433 Compartments: 1 Ho, ER 1 Ha: (16.5 x 8.3)ER	**1 oil engine** driving 1 FP propeller Total Power: 478kW (650hp) Matsui ML628GSC 1 x 4 Stroke 6 Cy. 280 x 520 478kW (650bhp) Matsui Iron Works Co Ltd-Japan
9161572 *JJ3937* -	**SHINEI MARU No. 18** - **Oishi Kaiun YK** - *Himeji, Hyogo* *Japan* Official number: 134192	*367* - 1,030		**1997-05 Ishii Zosen K.K. — Futtsu** Yd No: 372 Loa 56.00 Br ex - Dght 4.190 Lbp 52.50 Br md 11.50 Dpth 6.00 Welded, 1 dk	**(A31A2GX) General Cargo Ship** Grain: 1,000 Compartments: 1 Ho, ER 1 Ha: ER	**1 oil engine** reverse geared to sc. shaft driving 1 FP propeller Total Power: 736kW (1,001hp) Akasaka A28 1 x 4 Stroke 6 Cy. 280 x 550 736kW (1001bhp) Akasaka Tekkosho KK (Akasaka DieselLtd)-Japan Thrusters: 1 Thwart. FP thruster (f)

IMO / Call sign	Name / Owner	Tonnage	Class	Build / Dimensions	Type	Machinery
6818198 - -	**SHINEI MARU No. 26** *ex* Nikko Maru No. 26 - -	*114* 44 -		**1968 Fukuoka Shipbuilding Co Ltd — Fukuoka FO** Yd No: 920 Loa 34.09 Br ex 6.13 Dght 2.388 Lbp 29.21 Br md 6.10 Dpth 2.80 Welded, 1 dk	**(B11B2FV) Fishing Vessel**	**1 oil engine** driving 1 FP propeller Total Power: 478kW (650hp) Akasaka 6MH25SSR 1 x 4 Stroke 6 Cy. 250 x 400 478kW (650bhp) Akasaka Tekkosho KK (Akasaka DieselLtd)-Japan
6818203 - -	**SHINEI MARU No. 28** *ex* Nikko Maru No. 28 - -	*114* 43 -		**1968 Fukuoka Shipbuilding Co Ltd — Fukuoka FO** Yd No: 921 Loa 34.09 Br ex 6.13 Dght 2.388 Lbp 29.21 Br md 6.10 Dpth 2.80 Welded, 1 dk	**(B11B2FV) Fishing Vessel**	**1 oil engine** driving 1 FP propeller Total Power: 478kW (650hp) Akasaka 6MH25SSR 1 x 4 Stroke 6 Cy. 250 x 400 478kW (650bhp) Akasaka Tekkosho KK (Akasaka DieselLtd)-Japan
8301761 - -	**SHINEI MARU No. 63** - **Ishikawa Fumiaki** -	*279* - 534		**1983-07 Yamanishi Shipbuilding Co Ltd — Ishinomaki MG** Yd No: 892 Loa 58.20 (BB) Br ex 9.83 Dght 4.760 Lbp 50.25 Br md 9.81 Dpth 6.13 Welded, 2 dks	**(B11A2FS) Stern Trawler** Ins: 476 Compartments: 5 Ho, ER 5 Ha: ER	**1 oil engine** with flexible couplings & sr gearedto sc. shaft driving 1 CP propeller Total Power: 1,912kW (2,600hp) Akasaka AH40A 1 x 4 Stroke 6 Cy. 400 x 640 1912kW (2600bhp) Akasaka Tekkosho KK (Akasaka DieselLtd)-Japan AuxGen: 2 x 320kW 225V a.c
9180504 *JK5484* -	**SHINEIKAN** - **Nakano Kisen YK** - *Hofu, Yamaguchi* *Japan* MMSI: 431400637 Official number: 134800	*699* - -		**1997-03 K.K. Kamishima Zosensho — Osakikamijima** Loa 79.50 Br ex - Dght - Lbp 72.00 Br md 13.00 Dpth 8.00 Welded, 1 dk	**(A31A2GX) General Cargo Ship**	**1 oil engine** driving 1 FP propeller Total Power: 1,471kW (2,000hp) 12.0kn Hanshin 6LH38LG 1 x 4 Stroke 6 Cy. 380 x 760 1471kW (2000bhp) The Hanshin Diesel Works Ltd-Japan
8649888 *WDE8818* -	**SHINEY V. MORAN** *ex* C&G Boat Works 104 *-2009* **US Bancorp Equipment Finance Inc** Moran Towing Corp *Wilmington, DE* *United States of America* MMSI: 367409990 Official number: 1219051	**281** 84 170	Class: AB	**2009-06** Yd No: 104 Loa 26.21 Br ex - Dght 3.450 Lbp 23.79 Br md 10.97 Dpth 4.54 Welded, 1 dk	**(B32A2ST) Tug**	**2 oil engines** reduction geared to sc. shafts driving 2 Z propellers Total Power: 4,000kW (5,438hp) M.T.U. 16V4000M61 2 x Vee 4 Stroke 16 Cy. 165 x 190 each-2000kW (2719bhp) MTU Friedrichshafen GmbH-Friedrichshafen AuxGen: 2 x 99kW a.c
8963478 *JH2458* -	**SHINGI MARU** - **Masaki Ozaki** - *Nishio, Aichi* *Japan* Official number: 111197	*175* - 300		**1971-01 Masayasu Hirai — Japan** Loa 33.20 Br ex - Dght 3.080 Lbp 30.00 Br md 6.70 Dpth 3.10 Welded, 1 dk	**(A31A2GX) General Cargo Ship**	**1 oil engine** driving 1 FP propeller Total Power: 191kW (260hp) 7.0kn Sumiyoshi S6MBE 1 x 4 Stroke 6 Cy. 220 x 400 191kW (260bhp) Sumiyoshi Marine Diesel Co Ltd-Japan
8036079 *XUHG6* -	**SHINGLE** *ex* Korsun *-2013* *ex* Malabo *-2002* *ex* Geroi Perekopa *-1996* **Belmont Capital Ltd** - *Phnom Penh* *Cambodia* MMSI: 515270000 Official number: 1382258	**669** 240 497	Class: (PR) (RS)	**1982-03 Khabarovskiy Sudostroitelnyy Zavod im Kirova — Khabarovsk** Yd No: 837 Loa 55.02 Br ex 9.53 Dght 4.341 Lbp 50.04 Br md - Dpth 5.19 Welded, 1 dk	**(A31A2GX) General Cargo Ship** Ins: 632 Compartments: 2 Ho, ER 2 Ha: 2 (2.9 x 2.7) Derricks: 4x3.3t Ice Capable	**1 oil engine** driving 1 FP propeller Total Power: 441kW (600hp) 11.3kn S.K.L. 6NVD48A-2U 1 x 4 Stroke 6 Cy. 320 x 480 441kW (600bhp) VEB Schwermaschinenbau "KarlLiebknecht" (SKL)-Magdeburg
9184342 - -	**SHINHAE No. 9** - **Government of The Republic of South Korea (Ministry of Oceans & Fisheries)** Hae Kwang Transport Ltd *Mokpo* *South Korea* Official number: MPR-975080	**154** - 89	Class: KR	**1997-12 Korea Shipyard Co Ltd — Mokpo** Yd No: 9701 Loa 49.50 Br ex - Dght 1.704 Lbp 41.00 Br md 7.00 Dpth 2.20 Welded, 1 dk	**(A36A2PR) Passenger/Ro-Ro Ship (Vehicles)** Cars: 15	**2 oil engines** driving 2 FP propellers Total Power: 1,030kW (1,400hp) 15.0kn Yanmar 8LAAM-DTE 2 x Vee 4 Stroke 8 Cy. 148 x 165 each-515kW (700bhp) Kwangyang Diesel Engine Co Ltd-South Korea AuxGen: 1 x 65kW 225V a.c
9016595 *JH3231* -	**SHINHARUMI MARU** - **KK Daito Corp & Surugawan Eisen KK** Harumi Eisen Co Ltd *Shizuoka, Shizuoka* *Japan* Official number: 131553	*171* - -	Class: NK	**1991-03 Sagami Zosen Tekko K.K. — Yokosuka** Yd No: 248 Loa 33.22 Br ex 8.82 Dght 3.020 Lbp 30.89 Br md 8.80 Dpth 3.80 Welded, 1 dk	**(B32A2ST) Tug**	**2 oil engines** with clutches & reduction geared to sc. shafts driving 2 Directional propellers Total Power: 2,206kW (3,000hp) Yanmar T260-ET 2 x 4 Stroke 6 Cy. 260 x 330 each-1103kW (1500bhp) Yanmar Diesel Engine Co Ltd-Japan Fuel: 35.0 (d.f.)
9677260 *JD3452* -	**SHINHO** - **Wakisaka Kaiun KK** - *Kure, Hiroshima* *Japan* MMSI: 431004154 Official number: 141821	*749* - 2,300		**2013-01 Koike Zosen Kaiun KK — Osakikamijima** Yd No: 553 Loa 80.00 Br ex - Dght - Lbp 72.00 Br md 14.20 Dpth 8.08 Welded, 1 dk	**(A24D2BA) Aggregates Carrier**	**1 oil engine** reduction geared to sc. shaft driving 1 Propeller Total Power: 1,911kW (2,598hp) Hanshin LA34G 1 x 4 Stroke 6 Cy. 340 x 720 1911kW (2598bhp) The Hanshin Diesel Works Ltd-Japan
7914183 - -	**SHINHO MARU** - - - *Chinese Taipei*	*497* - 1,600		**1980-02 K.K. Uno Zosensho — Imabari** Yd No: 127 Loa 71.00 Br ex - Dght 4.261 Lbp 65.03 Br md 11.51 Dpth 6.02 Welded, 1 dk	**(A31A2GX) General Cargo Ship**	**1 oil engines** driving 1 FP propeller Total Power: 1,324kW (1,800hp) Hanshin 6LU35 1 x 4 Stroke 6 Cy. 350 x 550 1324kW (1800bhp) The Hanshin Diesel Works Ltd-Japan
8604876 - -	**SHINHO MARU** - - -	*198* - 540		**1986-11 Hakata Zosen K.K. — Imabari** Yd No: 333 Loa - Br ex - Dght 3.452 Lbp 43.01 Br md 8.01 Dpth 3.79 Welded, 1 dk	**(A12A2TC) Chemical Tanker**	**1 oil engine** driving 1 FP propeller Total Power: 368kW (500hp) Yanmar M200L-ST 1 x 4 Stroke 6 Cy. 200 x 260 368kW (500bhp) Yanmar Diesel Engine Co Ltd-Japan
9624251 *3FHB6* -	**SHINING DRAGON** - **Ayame Ship Holding SA** Daiichi Chuo Kisen Kaisha *Panama* *Panama* MMSI: 373668000 Official number: 4406212	**92,758** 60,504 181,365 T/cm 125.0	Class: NK	**2012-07 Imabari Shipbuilding Co Ltd — Saijo EH (Saijo Shipyard)** Yd No: 8118 Loa 291.98 (BB) Br ex - Dght 18.235 Lbp 283.80 Br md 45.00 Dpth 24.70 Welded, 1 dk	**(A21A2BC) Bulk Carrier** Grain: 201,243 Compartments: 9 Ho, ER 9 Ha: ER	**1 oil engine** driving 1 FP propeller Total Power: 18,660kW (25,370hp) 14.0kn MAN-B&W 6S70MC-C 1 x 2 Stroke 6 Cy. 700 x 2800 18660kW (25370bhp) Mitsui Engineering & Shipbuilding CLtd-Japan Fuel: 5800.0
9203382 *3FIV9* -	**SHINING PESCADORES** - **Shining Pescadores SA** Shih Wei Navigation Co Ltd *Panama* *Panama* MMSI: 357442000 Official number: 2626999C	**5,002** 3,188 8,595 T/cm 16.3	Class: NK	**1999-04 Higaki Zosen K.K. — Imabari** Yd No: 502 Loa 100.74 Br ex - Dght 7.817 Lbp 93.80 Br md 19.60 Dpth 9.80 Welded, 1 dk	**(A31A2GX) General Cargo Ship** Grain: 10,814; Bale: 9,981 Compartments: 2 Ho, ER 2 Ha: 2 (25.9 x 9.8)ER Derricks: 2x30t,2x25t	**1 oil engine** driving 1 FP propeller Total Power: 3,236kW (4,400hp) 12.5kn Mitsubishi 6UEC33LSII 1 x 2 Stroke 6 Cy. 330 x 1050 3236kW (4400bhp) Akasaka Tekkosho KK (Akasaka DieselLtd)-Japan AuxGen: 2 x 230kW a.c Fuel: 86.0 (d.f.) 501.0 (r.f.) 13.1pd
8604929 *HSB2924* -	**SHINING STAR** - **Ayudhya Development Leasing Co Ltd (ADLC)** Chemstar Shipping Co Ltd *Bangkok* *Thailand* MMSI: 567054400 Official number: 451001142	**547** 189 698	Class: (TL)	**1986-06 Mukaishima Zoki Co. Ltd. — Onomichi** Yd No: 220 Loa 51.97 Br ex 9.02 Dght 3.501 Lbp 48.01 Br md 9.01 Dpth 3.92 Welded, 1 dk	**(A12A2TC) Chemical Tanker** Liq: 695 Compartments: 6 Ta, ER	**1 oil engine** reverse reduction geared to sc. shaft driving 1 FP propeller Total Power: 662kW (900hp) Hanshin 6LU26G 1 x 4 Stroke 6 Cy. 260 x 440 662kW (900bhp) The Hanshin Diesel Works Ltd-Japan
8891118 - -	**SHINING STAR** - **The Star Ferry Co Ltd** - *Hong Kong* *Hong Kong* Official number: 317272	*164* 40 -		**1964 Hong Kong & Whampoa Dock Co Ltd — Hong Kong** Yd No: 1027 Loa 33.78 Br ex 9.22 Dght 2.430 Lbp - Br md 8.57 Dpth 2.61 Welded, 1 dk	**(A37B2PS) Passenger Ship** Passengers: unberthed: 555	**1 oil engine** driving 1 FP propeller Total Power: 352kW (479hp) Crossley HGN6 1 x 2 Stroke 6 Cy. 267 x 343 352kW (479bhp) Crossley Bros. Ltd.-Manchester
9260603 *JG5697* -	**SHINJU MARU NO. 1** - **Japan Railway Construction, Transport & Technology Agency & Shinwa Chemical Tanker Kaisha Ltd** Shinwa Chemical Tanker KK *Tokyo* *Japan* MMSI: 431101044 Official number: 137158	**2,936** - 1,781	Class: NK	**2003-07 Higaki Zosen K.K. — Imabari** (Hull) Yd No: 545 **2003-07 Kawasaki Shipbuilding Corp — Kobe HG** Yd No: 1529 Loa 86.25 (BB) Br ex - Dght 4.183 Lbp 80.30 Br md 15.10 Dpth 7.00 Welded, 1 dk	**(A11A2TN) LNG Tanker** Double Hull Liq (Gas): 2,538 3 x Gas Tank (s); 2 independent (alu) cyl horizontal, ER 4 Cargo Pump (s): 4x300m³/hr	**1 oil engine** driving 1 CP propeller Total Power: 1,912kW (2,600hp) 12.7kn Hanshin LH36LA 1 x 4 Stroke 6 Cy. 360 x 670 1912kW (2600bhp) The Hanshin Diesel Works Ltd-Japan AuxGen: 2 x 320kW a.c Thrusters: 1 Tunnel thruster (f) Fuel: 250.0

IMO / Call sign	Ship / Owner	Tonnage	Class	Build / Dimensions	Type	Machinery	
9433884 *JD2812* -	**SHINJU MARU NO. 2** **Chuo Kaiun KK & Shinwa Chemical Tanker KK** Shinwa Chemical Tanker KK *Tokyo* *Japan* MMSI: 431000767 Official number: 140863	*2,930* - 1,781	Class: NK	**2008-10 Higaki Zosen K.K. — Imabari** Yd No: 618 Loa 86.29 (BB) Br ex - Dght 4.200 Lbp 80.30 Br md 15.10 Dpth 7.00 Welded, 1 dk	**(A11A2TN) LNG Tanker** Double Hull Liq (Gas): 2,536 2 x Gas Tank (s); 2 independent (stl) cyl horizontal 2 Cargo Pump (s)	**1 oil engine** driving 1 Propeller Total Power: 1,912kW (2,600hp) Hanshin 1 x 4 Stroke 6 Cy. 360 x 670 1912kW (2600bhp) The Hanshin Diesel Works Ltd-Japan AuxGen: 3 x 300kW a.c Fuel: 250.0	13.0kn LH36LA
8924135 - -	**SHINJUNG 801** *ex* Seungchang 2 *-2010* *ex* Sae Kwang *-2008* *ex* Tae Heung 9 *-2004* *ex* Kenryu *-2004* **Park Han-Gyu** - *Busan* *South Korea* MMSI: 440109500 Official number: BSR-969221	**164** - -		**1971-05 K.K. Izutsu Zosensho — Nagasaki** Yd No: 566 Loa 33.90 Br ex - Dght 2.500 Lbp 30.70 Br md 6.90 Dpth 2.75 Welded, 1 dk	**(B32A2ST) Tug**	**1 oil engine** driving 1 FP propeller Total Power: 1,618kW (2,200hp) Yanmar 1 x 4 Stroke 1618kW (2200bhp) Yanmar Diesel Engine Co Ltd-Japan	11.0kn
9021801 *DSAK5* -	**SHINJUNG NO. 101** **Shinjung Shipping Co Ltd** - *Busan* *South Korea* MMSI: 440112480 Official number: BSR-931277	**196** 58 91	Class: KR	**1993-12 Daesung Shipbuilding Co — Busan** Loa 35.80 Br ex 7.40 Dght 2.717 Lbp 33.10 Br md 7.40 Dpth 3.40 Welded, 1 dk	**(B32A2ST) Tug**	**1 oil engine** Geared Integral to driving 1 Propeller Total Power: 1,764kW (2,398hp) Niigata 1 x 4 Stroke 6 Cy. 310 x 380 1764kW (2398bhp) Niigata Engineering Co Ltd-Japan AuxGen: 2 x 66kW 220V a.c Fuel: 63.0 (r.f.)	6L31EZ
8961511 *D7MJ* -	**SHINJUNG NO. 601** *ex* Sunyoo No. 101 *-2010* *ex* Seorin No. 101 *-2010* *ex* Eunsung No. 101 *-2010* **Shinjung Shipping Co Ltd** - *Busan* *South Korea* MMSI: 441078000 Official number: BSR-920411	**205** 61 -		**1992 Kyungnam Shipbuilding Co Ltd — Busan** Loa 36.00 Br ex - Dght 3.060 Lbp 31.80 Br md 7.40 Dpth 3.60 Welded, 1 dk	**(B32A2ST) Tug**	**1 oil engine** driving 1 FP propeller Total Power: 1,177kW (1,600hp) Akasaka 1 x 4 Stroke 1177kW (1600bhp) Akasaka Tekkosho KK (Akasaka DieselLtd)-Japan	
8740929 *DSAY4* -	**SHINJUNG NO. 901** *ex* Chang Il No. 3000 *-2011* *ex* Dolphin No. 1 *-2009* **Han Gyu Park** Shinjung Shipping Co Ltd *Busan* *South Korea* MMSI: 440007600 Official number: BSR-952013	**272** 81 61	Class: KR	**1994-12 Samkwang Shipbuilding & Engineering Co Ltd — Incheon** Yd No: 94-05 Loa 33.60 Br ex - Dght 2.700 Lbp 28.50 Br md 8.40 Dpth 3.27 Welded, 1 dk	**(B32A2ST) Tug**	**2 oil engines** reduction geared to sc. shafts driving 2 FP propellers Total Power: 2,204kW (2,996hp) Hanshin 2 x 4 Stroke 6 Cy. 320 x 510 each-1102kW (1498bhp) The Hanshin Diesel Works Ltd-Japan	12.1kn
7231763 - -	**SHINKAI** **PT Aria Indonesia Jaya** Asia Maritime Pte Ltd *Indonesia*	*165* - -		**1971-02 Aki Kogyo K.K. — Kure** Yd No: 147 Loa 28.99 Br ex 7.83 Dght 2.801 Lbp 24.01 Br md 7.80 Dpth 3.61 Welded, 1 dk	**(B32A2ST) Tug**	**2 oil engines** driving 2 FP propellers Total Power: 1,472kW (2,002hp) Hanshin 2 x 4 Stroke 6 Cy. 280 x 440 each-736kW (1001bhp) Hanshin Nainenki Kogyo-Japan AuxGen: 1 x 32kW 225V a.c Fuel: 38.5 7.0pd	9.0kn 6LU28G
7929700 *JIPK* -	**SHINKAI MARU** *ex* Seisui Maru *-2008* **Offshore Engineering Co Ltd** Fukada Salvage & Marine Works Co Ltd (Fukada Salvage Kensetsu KK) *Tokyo* *Japan* MMSI: 431402000 Official number: 122588	*329* - -		**1980-07 Mitsubishi Heavy Industries Ltd. — Shimonoseki** Yd No: 822 Converted From: Fishing Vessel-2008 Loa 47.00 Br ex - Dght 3.458 Lbp 42.02 Br md 8.41 Dpth 4.02 Welded, 1 dk	**(B22A2OR) Offshore Support Vessel**	**1 oil engine** reduction geared to sc. shaft driving 1 CP propeller Total Power: 956kW (1,300hp) Daihatsu 1 x 4 Stroke 6 Cy. 260 x 320 956kW (1300bhp) Daihatsu Diesel Manufacturing Co Lt-Japan AuxGen: 2 x 265kW a.c Thrusters: 1 Tunnel thruster (f)	11.0kn 6DSM-26
9157454 *7LOV* -	**SHINKAI MARU** **Shimane Prefecture** - SatCom: Inmarsat B 343145310 *Matsue, Shimane* *Japan* MMSI: 431453000 Official number: 133676	*499* - 396		**1997-03 Miho Zosensho K.K. — Shimizu** Yd No: 1458 Loa 57.94 (BB) Br ex 9.40 Dght 3.750 Lbp 49.00 Br md 9.00 Dpth 6.10 Welded, 1 dk	**(B11A2FS) Stern Trawler** Ins: 80	**1 oil engine** with clutches, flexible couplings & sr reverse geared to sc. shaft driving 1 CP propeller Total Power: 1,324kW (1,800hp) Akasaka 1 x 4 Stroke 6 Cy. 280 x 480 1324kW (1800bhp) Akasaka Tekkosho KK (Akasaka DieselLtd)-Japan AuxGen: 2 x 400kW 225V 60Hz a.c Thrusters: 1 Thwart. CP thruster (f) Fuel: 240.0 (d.f.) 6.1pd	12.5kn E28BD
9610274 *7JNI* -	**SHINKAI MARU** **Shimane Prefecture** - *Matsue, Shimane* *Japan* MMSI: 432899000 Official number: 141790	*695* - -		**2013-03 Yamanishi Corp — Ishinomaki MG** Yd No: 1090 Loa 67.50 Br ex - Dght 3.800 Lbp 58.00 Br md 10.00 Dpth - Welded, 1 dk	**(B11B2FV) Fishing Vessel**	**1 oil engine** reduction geared to sc. shaft driving 1 Propeller Total Power: 1,618kW (2,200hp) Niigata 1 x 4 Stroke 6 Cy. 340 x 620 1618kW (2200bhp) Niigata Engineering Co Ltd-Japan	6M34BFT
9218985 *JJ4012* -	**SHINKAI MARU** **Shinko Butsuryu KK** Kobelco Logistics Ltd *Kobe, Hyogo* *Japan* Official number: 134281	*499* - 1,600		**1999-01 Yamanaka Zosen K.K. — Imabari** Yd No: 632 Loa 76.23 Br ex - Dght - Lbp 70.00 Br md 12.00 Dpth 7.01 Welded, 1 dk	**(A31A2GX) General Cargo Ship** Grain: 2,950; Bale: 2,841 Compartments: 1 Ho, ER 1 Ha: (40.0 x 9.3)ER	**1 oil engine** driving 1 FP propeller Total Power: 1,324kW (1,800hp) Hanshin 1 x 4 Stroke 6 Cy. 300 x 600 1324kW (1800bhp) The Hanshin Diesel Works Ltd-Japan	12.7kn LH30LG
7330739 - -	**SHINKAI MARU No. 12** **Chang Shin Enterprise Co Ltd** *South Korea*	*298* 87 -		**1973-09 Daiko Dockyard Co. Ltd. — Osaka** Yd No: 79 Loa - Br ex 9.02 Dght 3.004 Lbp 28.50 Br md 9.00 Dpth 3.92 Riveted\Welded, 1 dk	**(B32B2SA) Articulated Pusher Tug**	**2 oil engines** geared to sc. shafts driving 2 FP propellers Total Power: 2,354kW (3,200hp) Hanshin 2 x 4 Stroke 6 Cy. 320 x 510 each-1177kW (1600bhp) Hanshin Nainenki Kogyo-Japan	6LUD32G
9218973 *JJ4014* -	**SHINKAI MARU No. 18** **Yorigami Ocean KK** Yorigami Maritime Construction Co Ltd (Yorigami Kensetsu KK) *Kobe, Hyogo* *Japan* Official number: 134283	*187* - -		**1999-03 K.K. Watanabe Zosensho — Nagasaki** Yd No: 074 Loa 41.02 Br ex - Dght - Lbp - Br md 10.00 Dpth 4.83 Welded, 1 dk	**(B32A2ST) Tug**	**2 oil engines** gearing integral to driving 2 Z propellers Total Power: 2,942kW (4,000hp) Yanmar 2 x 4 Stroke 6 Cy. 280 x 380 each-1471kW (2000bhp) Yanmar Diesel Engine Co Ltd-Japan AuxGen: 2 x 104kW 225V 60Hz a.c Fuel: 192.0 (d.f.)	13.0kn 6N280-UN
8817124 *JJ3633* -	**SHINKAI MARU No. 28** **Yorigami Ocean KK** Yorigami Maritime Construction Co Ltd (Yorigami Kensetsu KK) *Kobe, Hyogo* *Japan* Official number: 129211	*147* - -		**1988-09 Kanrei Zosen K.K. — Naruto** Yd No: 329 Loa 30.00 Br ex - Dght 3.210 Lbp 28.00 Br md 9.00 Dpth 4.80 Welded, 1 dk	**(B32B2SP) Pusher Tug**	**2 oil engines** driving 2 FP propellers Total Power: 2,206kW (3,000hp) Daihatsu 2 x 4 Stroke 6 Cy. 240 x 320 each-1103kW (1500bhp) Daihatsu Diesel Manufacturing Co Lt-Japan	6DLM-24S
8948959 *JM6656* -	**SHINKAI MARU No. 73** **YK Nakano Suisan** - *Nango, Miyazaki* *Japan* MMSI: 431351000 Official number: 135466	*157* - -		**1998-12 Higashi Kyushu Shipbuilding Co Ltd — Usuki OT** L reg 34.28 Br ex - Dght - Lbp - Br md 6.01 Dpth 2.80 Bonded, 1 dk	**(B11B2FV) Fishing Vessel** Hull Material: Reinforced Plastic	**1 oil engine** driving 1 FP propeller	
9143738 *JG5239* -	**SHINKANAGAWA MARU** **Ajinomoto Butsuryu KK** - *Tokyo* *Japan* MMSI: 431200113 Official number: 134947	*199* - 542		**1995-09 Iisaku Zosen K.K. — Nishi-Izu** Yd No: 95175 Loa 48.50 Br ex - Dght 3.300 Lbp 44.00 Br md 7.80 Dpth 3.50 Welded, 1 dk	**(A13B2TP) Products Tanker** Liq: 420; Liq (Oil): 420 Compartments: 4 Ta, ER	**1 oil engine** with clutches, flexible couplings & reverse geared to sc. shaft driving 1 FP propeller Total Power: 736kW (1,001hp) Hanshin 1 x 4 Stroke 6 Cy. 260 x 440 736kW (1001bhp) The Hanshin Diesel Works Ltd-Japan	LH26G

9124847 *JM6415* -	**SHINKAWA MARU** **Uyeno Chemical Unyu KK** is not printed; **Shinkawa Kaiun KK** Uyeno Chemical Unyu KK *Ube, Yamaguchi* *Japan* MMSI: 431400461 Official number: 134504	*495* - 768		**1995**-07 **Mukaishima Zoki Co. Ltd. — Onomichi** Yd No: 302 Loa 58.60 Br ex 10.02 Dght 3.587 Lbp 54.00 Br md 10.00 Dpth 4.50 Welded, 1 dk	**(A12A2TC) Chemical Tanker** Liq: 457 Compartments: 2 Ta, ER 2 Cargo Pump (s): 2x150m³/hr	**1 oil engine** with clutches & reverse geared to sc. shafts driving 1 FP propeller Total Power: 736kW (1,001hp) Hanshin LH28G 1 x 4 Stroke 6 Cy. 280 x 460 736kW (1001bhp) The Hanshin Diesel Works Ltd-Japan
9084889 - -	**SHINKEIWA MARU** *ex Shinoji Maru -2003* **Matsya Shipping Lines Corp** -	*499* - 1,000		**1994**-03 **K.K. Miura Zosensho — Saiki** Yd No: 1087 Loa - Br ex - Dght - Lbp 74.50 Br md 11.20 Dpth 6.50 Welded	**(A31A2GX) General Cargo Ship**	**1 oil engine** reverse geared to sc. shaft driving 1 FP propeller Total Power: 736kW (1,001hp) Hanshin LH34LAG 1 x 4 Stroke 6 Cy. 340 x 640 736kW (1001bhp) The Hanshin Diesel Works Ltd-Japan
9364887 *S6FP8* -	**SHINKEN ACE** **Shinken Trading Singapore Pte Ltd** Sugahara Kisen KK *Singapore* *Singapore* MMSI: 565221000 Official number: 392043	**7,454** 3,415 10,132	Class: NK	**2006**-09 **Nishi Shipbuilding Co Ltd — Imabari EH** Yd No: 447 Loa 110.67 (BB) Br ex - Dght 8.564 Lbp 102.00 Br md 19.20 Dpth 13.50 Welded, 1 dk	**(A31A2GX) General Cargo Ship** Grain: 15,504; Bale: 14,332 Compartments: 2 Ho, ER 2 Ha: ER Cranes: 1x70t,2x35.8t; Derricks: 1x30t	**1 oil engine** driving 1 FP propeller Total Power: 3,900kW (5,302hp) 15.5kn MAN-B&W 6L35MC 1 x 2 Stroke 6 Cy. 350 x 1050 3900kW (5302bhp) The Hanshin Diesel Works Ltd-Japan AuxGen: 2 x a.c Fuel: 710.0
9587776 *JD3070* -	**SHINKIMI MARU** **Nippon Steel Logistics Kimitsu KK** - *Kimitsu, Chiba* *Japan* Official number: 141249	*131* - 320		**2010**-04 **Hongawara Zosen K.K. — Fukuyama** Yd No: 642 Loa 35.00 Br ex - Dght 2.300 Lbp 33.00 Br md 8.50 Dpth 2.80 Welded, 1 dk	**(A31A2GX) General Cargo Ship**	**1 oil engine** driving 1 FP propeller Total Power: 559kW (760hp) Yanmar 1 x 4 Stroke 559kW (760bhp) Yanmar Diesel Engine Co Ltd-Japan
8979647 *JM6717* -	**SHINKISSHO** **Hirano Kaiun YK** - *Kamiamakusa, Kumamoto* *Japan* Official number: 136868	*202* - -		**2003**-01 **Yano Zosen K.K. — Imabari** Yd No: 187 L reg 54.77 (BB) Br ex - Dght - Lbp - Br md 9.60 Dpth 5.55 Welded, 1 dk	**(A31A2GX) General Cargo Ship**	**1 oil engine** driving 1 Propeller Total Power: 735kW (999hp) Niigata 6M26AGTE 1 x 4 Stroke 6 Cy. 260 x 460 735kW (999bhp) Niigata Engineering Co Ltd-Japan
9114086 *JL6378* -	**SHINKIZAN** *ex Biho Maru -2009* **KK Kansei** - *Komatsushima, Tokushima* *Japan* MMSI: 431500316 Official number: 135062	*498* - 1,405		**1995**-03 **K.K. Tachibana Senpaku Tekko — Anan** Yd No: 840 Loa 75.24 Br ex - Dght 4.170 Lbp 70.50 Br md 12.00 Dpth 7.10 Welded, 1 dk	**(A31A2GX) General Cargo Ship**	**1 oil engine** driving 1 FP propeller Total Power: 736kW (1,001hp) Niigata 6M31BGT 1 x 4 Stroke 6 Cy. 310 x 530 736kW (1001bhp) Niigata Engineering Co Ltd-Japan
9003976 - -	**SHINKO** *ex Shinko Maru -2013 ex Shourin Maru -1997* **PT Indo Shipping Operator**	*355* - 871	Class: IZ (NK)	**1990**-10 **Murakami Hide Zosen K.K. — Imabari** Yd No: 317 Loa 53.52 Br ex - Dght 3.961 Lbp 49.50 Br md 9.50 Dpth 4.20 Welded, 1 dk	**(A12A2TC) Chemical Tanker** Liq: 669	**1 oil engine** driving 1 FP propeller Total Power: 736kW (1,001hp) 10.2kn Yanmar MF28-UT 1 x 4 Stroke 6 Cy. 280 x 450 736kW (1001bhp) Matsue Diesel KK-Japan AuxGen: 3 x 64kW a.c Fuel: 45.0 (d.f.)
9011260 *T3MK2* -	**SHINKO** *ex Shinko Maru No. 15 -2014* *ex Eiho Maru No. 65 -2009* **PT Indo Shipping Operator** - *Tarawa* *Kiribati* Official number: K-17901480	*498* 389 1,199	Class: IZ	**1990**-11 **Mukaishima Zoki Co. Ltd. — Onomichi** Yd No: 265 Loa 64.33 Br ex - Dght 4.165 Lbp 60.00 Br md 10.00 Dpth 4.50 Welded, 1 dk	**(A12A2TC) Chemical Tanker** Liq: 1,299 Compartments: 8 Ta, ER 2 Cargo Pump (s): 2x300m³/hr	**1 oil engine** with clutches & reverse geared to sc. shaft driving 1 FP propeller Total Power: 736kW (1,001hp) Hanshin LH28G 1 x 4 Stroke 6 Cy. 280 x 460 736kW (1001bhp) The Hanshin Diesel Works Ltd-Japan
9019298 *JAYW* -	**SHINKO MARU** **Shinko Kaiji YK** - SatCom: Inmarsat A 1201661 *Hiroshima, Hiroshima* *Japan* MMSI: 432625000 Official number: 131740	*201* - 576		**1990**-02 **Kanawa Dockyard Co. Ltd. — Hiroshima** Yd No: 1005 Loa 35.50 Br ex 9.20 Dght 3.100 Lbp 31.00 Br md 8.80 Dpth 3.80 Welded, 1 dk	**(B32A2ST) Tug**	**2 oil engines** dr geared to sc. shaft driving 1 FP propeller Total Power: 1,618kW (2,200hp) 12.0kn Yanmar T260-ST 2 x 4 Stroke 6 Cy. 260 x 330 each-809kW (1100bhp) Yanmar Diesel Engine Co Ltd-Japan AuxGen: 2 x 80kW 445V 60Hz a.c
8980658 *JG5709* -	**SHINKO MARU** **Shinko Kaiun KK** Seibu Tanker KK (Seibu Tanker Co Ltd) *Tokyo* *Japan* Official number: 137189	**499** - 1,240		**2003**-12 **Kyoei Zosen KK — Mihara HS** Yd No: 337 Loa 65.00 Br ex 10.02 Dght - Lbp 62.00 Br md 10.00 Dpth 4.50 Welded, 1 dk	**(A12A2TC) Chemical Tanker** Double Hull (13F)	**1 oil engine** driving 1 FP propeller Total Power: 1,177kW (1,600hp) Hanshin LH28G 1 x 4 Stroke 6 Cy. 280 x 460 1177kW (1600bhp) The Hanshin Diesel Works Ltd-Japan
9066863 - -	**SHINKO MARU** - -	*496* - 470		**1993**-04 **Ishii Zosen K.K. — Futtsu** Yd No: 300 Loa 48.00 (BB) Br ex - Dght 3.320 Lbp 42.10 Br md 11.60 Dpth 3.50 Welded, 1 dk	**(A24D2BA) Aggregates Carrier** Grain: 803 Compartments: 1 Ho, ER 1 Ha: ER	**1 oil engine** with clutches & reverse geared to sc. shaft driving 1 FP propeller Total Power: 1,030kW (1,400hp) Hanshin LH28G 1 x 4 Stroke 6 Cy. 280 x 460 1030kW (1400bhp) The Hanshin Diesel Works Ltd-Japan Thrusters: 1 Thwart. FP thruster (f)
9047714 *JJ3783* -	**SHINKO MARU** *ex Myojin Maru -2012* **Wakamiya Kaiun Kensetsu KK** - *Fukuyama, Hiroshima* *Japan* Official number: 132282	*168* - -		**1992**-02 **Shin Yamamoto Shipbuilding & Engineering Co Ltd — Kochi KC** Yd No: 340 Loa 31.00 Br ex - Dght 3.800 Lbp 28.00 Br md 10.00 Dpth 7.00 Welded, 1 dk	**(B32A2ST) Tug**	**1 oil engine** geared to sc. shaft driving 1 FP propeller Total Power: 1,471kW (2,000hp) Niigata 6M38HFT 1 x 4 Stroke 6 Cy. 380 x 700 1471kW (2000bhp) Niigata Engineering Co Ltd-Japan
9113965 *JL6304* -	**SHINKO MARU** **Miyoshi Kaiun YK** - *Yawatahama, Ehime* *Japan* Official number: 134881	*260* - 600		**1995**-04 **Koa Sangyo KK — Takamatsu KG** Yd No: 585 Loa 49.90 Br ex - Dght 3.400 Lbp 46.00 Br md 8.00 Dpth 3.55 Welded, 1 dk	**(A13B2TP) Products Tanker**	**1 oil engine** driving 1 FP propeller Total Power: 736kW (1,001hp) 10.5kn Hanshin LH26G 1 x 4 Stroke 6 Cy. 260 x 440 736kW (1001bhp) The Hanshin Diesel Works Ltd-Japan
9110080 *JG5231* -	**SHINKO MARU** **Corporation for Advanced Transport & Technology & Sanko Kisen KK** Sanko Kisen KK *Yokohama, Kanagawa* *Japan* MMSI: 431100148 Official number: 134937	*919* - 2,301	Class: NK	**1994**-11 **Kurinoura Dockyard Co Ltd — Yawatahama EH** Yd No: 326 Loa 77.00 Br ex - Dght 5.262 Lbp 72.00 Br md 11.60 Dpth 5.95 Welded, 1 dk	**(A13B2TP) Products Tanker** Liq: 2,201; Liq (Oil): 2,201	**1 oil engine** driving 1 FP propeller Total Power: 1,618kW (2,200hp) 12.8kn Akasaka A34 1 x 4 Stroke 6 Cy. 340 x 660 1618kW (2200bhp) Akasaka Tekkosho KK (Akasaka DieselLtd)-Japan AuxGen: 4 x a.c Fuel: 110.0 (d.f.)
9103051 *JK5357* -	**SHINKO MARU** **Gaku Funada** - *Hiroshima, Hiroshima* *Japan* Official number: 134108	*497* - 1,300		**1993**-10 **Kimura Zosen K.K. — Kure** Yd No: 125 Loa - Br ex - Dght - Lbp - Br md - Dpth - Welded, 1 dk	**(B33A2DU) Dredger (unspecified)**	**1 oil engine** reverse geared to sc. shaft driving 1 FP propeller Total Power: 736kW (1,001hp) Hanshin LH28G 1 x 4 Stroke 6 Cy. 280 x 460 736kW (1001bhp) The Hanshin Diesel Works Ltd-Japan
9087831 *JK5360* -	**SHINKO MARU** - - *Hiroshima, Hiroshima* *Japan* Official number: 134111	*653* - 539		**1994**-01 **Kegoya Dock K.K. — Kure** Yd No: 957 Loa 54.00 Br ex 12.81 Dght 2.960 Lbp 48.00 Br md 12.50 Dpth 5.60 Welded, 2 dks	**(A31A2GX) General Cargo Ship** Compartments: 1 Ho, ER	**1 oil engine** reverse geared to sc. shaft driving 1 FP propeller Total Power: 736kW (1,001hp) Niigata 6M30BGT 1 x 4 Stroke 6 Cy. 300 x 530 736kW (1001bhp) Niigata Engineering Co Ltd-Japan
9119919 *JK5395* -	**SHINKO MARU** **Isao Shintaku** - *Hiroshima, Hiroshima* *Japan* Official number: 134749	*652* - 539		**1995**-01 **Kegoya Dock K.K. — Kure** Yd No: 966 Loa 54.00 (BB) Br ex 12.52 Dght 2.970 Lbp 48.00 Br md 12.50 Dpth 5.60 Welded, 1 dk	**(A31A2GX) General Cargo Ship** Grain: 1,079 Compartments: 1 Ho, ER 1 Ha: ER	**1 oil engine** with clutches, flexible couplings & reverse geared to sc. shaft driving 1 FP propeller Total Power: 736kW (1,001hp) Niigata 6M30BGT 1 x 4 Stroke 6 Cy. 300 x 530 736kW (1001bhp) Niigata Engineering Co Ltd-Japan Thrusters: 1 Thwart. FP thruster (f)

9128594 *JL6429* -
SHINKO MARU *499* - 1,200
Yoshioka Kaiun YK
-
Anan, Tokushima *Japan*
Official number: 135133
1995-10 Imura Zosen K.K. — Komatsushima Yd No: 276
Loa 65.05 Br ex - Dght 4.350
Lbp 60.00 Br md 10.00 Dpth 4.50
Welded, 1 dk
(A13B2TP) Products Tanker
Liq: 1,280; Liq (Oil): 1,280
2 Cargo Pump (s): 2x500m³/hr
1 oil engine driving 1 FP propeller
Total Power: 736kW (1,001hp) 10.5kn
Hanshin LH28LG
1 x 4 Stroke 6 Cy. 280 x 530 736kW (1001bhp)
The Hanshin Diesel Works Ltd-Japan
Fuel: 57.4 (d.f.) 3.6pd

8894718 *JJ3635* -
SHINKO MARU *103* - -
KK Marutatsu Shokai
-
Kobe, Hyogo *Japan*
Official number: 129213
1988-12 Shunkei Abe — Nandan, Hyogo Pref.
Loa 29.98 Br ex - Dght 3.000
Lbp 27.00 Br md 7.00 Dpth 3.10
Welded, 1 dk
(B32A2ST) Tug
1 oil engine driving 1 FP propeller
Total Power: 662kW (900hp) 10.5kn
Yanmar MF28-ST
1 x 4 Stroke 6 Cy. 280 x 450 662kW (900bhp)
Yanmar Diesel Engine Co Ltd-Japan

8743464 *JD2939* -
SHINKO MARU *498* - 1,845
Nichitoku Kisen KK
-
Higashihiroshima, Hiroshima *Japan*
Official number: 141054
2009-09 Koike Zosen Kaiun KK — Osakikamijima Yd No: 517
Loa 74.50 (BB) Br ex - Dght 4.330
Lbp 69.00 Br md 12.00 Dpth 7.35
Welded, 1 dk
(A31A2GX) General Cargo Ship
Compartments: 1 Ho, ER
1 Ha: ER
1 oil engine reduction geared to sc. shaft driving 1 FP propeller
Total Power: 1,471kW (2,000hp) 11.0kn
Niigata 6M34BGT
1 x 4 Stroke 6 Cy. 340 x 620 1471kW (2000bhp)
Niigata Engineering Co Ltd-Japan
Thrusters: 1 Tunnel thruster (f)

5323407 - -
SHINKO MARU *120* - 220
-
-
South Korea
1960 Hashihama Shipbuilding Co Ltd — Imabari EH Yd No: 104
Loa 30.00 Br ex 6.02 Dght 2.100
Lbp 25.50 Br md 6.00 Dpth 2.63
Welded, 1 dk
(A14A2LO) Water Tanker
1 oil engine driving 1 FP propeller

8015245 - -
SHINKO MARU *493* - 1,580
Amigo Shipping Corp
-
Philippines
1980-09 K.K. Uno Zosensho — Imabari Yd No: 131
Loa 70.62 Br ex - Dght 4.271
Lbp 65.82 Br md 11.00 Dpth 6.20
Welded, 2 dks
(A31A2GX) General Cargo Ship
1 oil engine driving 1 FP propeller
Total Power: 1,177kW (1,600hp)
Hanshin 6LU32
1 x 4 Stroke 6 Cy. 320 x 510 1177kW (1600bhp)
The Hanshin Diesel Works Ltd-Japan

8514497 - -
SHINKO MARU *499* - 1,600
Shanghai Maofeng Shipping Co Ltd
-
China
1985-11 K.K. Yoshida Zosen Kogyo — Arida Yd No: 411
Loa - Br ex - Dght 4.231
Lbp 65.99 Br md 11.51 Dpth 6.71
Welded, 1 dk
(A31A2GX) General Cargo Ship
Grain: 2,430; Bale: 2,090
Compartments: 1 Ho, ER
1 Ha: ER
1 oil engine driving 1 FP propeller
Total Power: 1,103kW (1,500hp)
Akasaka DM30
1 x 4 Stroke 6 Cy. 300 x 480 1103kW (1500bhp)
Akasaka Tekkosho KK (Akasaka DieselLtd)-Japan

9355094 *JD2361* -
SHINKO MARU *6,188* - 9,500 Class: NK
Shinko Butsuryu KK
Kobelco Logistics Ltd
Kobe, Hyogo *Japan*
MMSI: 431000139
Official number: 140470
2007-03 Shin Kochi Jyuko K.K. — Kochi Yd No: 7198
Loa 130.03 Br ex - Dght 6.534
Lbp 123.00 Br md 19.30 Dpth 8.50
Welded, 1 dk
(A24E2BL) Limestone Carrier
Grain: 7,653
1 oil engine driving 1 FP propeller
Total Power: 3,308kW (4,498hp) 12.5kn
Hanshin LH46LA
1 x 4 Stroke 6 Cy. 460 x 880 3308kW (4498bhp)
The Hanshin Diesel Works Ltd-Japan
AuxGen: 1 x 450kW a.c
Fuel: 340.0

9203239 *JL6636* -
SHINKO MARU *698* - 860 Class: NK
YK Kato Unyu
-
Seiyo, Ehime *Japan*
MMSI: 431501479
Official number: 135559
1998-12 Kyoei Zosen KK — Mihara HS Yd No: 301
Loa 66.00 Br ex - Dght 4.262
Lbp 60.00 Br md 11.00 Dpth 5.00
Welded, 1 dk
(A11B2TG) LPG Tanker
Liq (Gas): 1,186
2 x Gas Tank (s);
1 oil engine reverse geared to sc. shaft driving 1 FP propeller
Total Power: 1,324kW (1,800hp) 12.0kn
Akasaka A31R
1 x 4 Stroke 6 Cy. 310 x 600 1324kW (1800bhp)
Akasaka Tekkosho KK (Akasaka DieselLtd)-Japan
Fuel: 80.0 (d.f.)

9296080 *JG5706* -
SHINKO MARU *233* - -
Nippon Marine Service & Engineering Co Ltd (Nippon Kaiji Kogyo KK)
-
Tokyo *Japan*
Official number: 137182
2003-09 Kanagawa Zosen — Kobe Yd No: 516
Loa 37.50 Br ex - Dght -
Lbp 33.40 Br md 9.20 Dpth 4.10
Welded, 1 dk
(B32A2ST) Tug
2 oil engines Geared Integral to driving 2 Z propellers
Total Power: 2,942kW (4,000hp)
Niigata 6L28HX
2 x 4 Stroke 6 Cy. 280 x 370 each-1471kW (2000bhp)
Niigata Engineering Co Ltd-Japan

9401415 *JD2400* -
SHINKO MARU NO. 1 **2,114** 652 2,821 Class: NK
Seibu Tanker KK (Seibu Tanker Co Ltd)
-
Tokyo *Japan*
MMSI: 431000195
Official number: 140521
2007-05 K.K. Watanabe Zosensho — Nagasaki Yd No: 130
Loa 83.87 Br ex - Dght 5.412
Lbp 78.00 Br md 14.00 Dpth 7.00
Welded, 1 dk
(A12B2TR) Chemical/Products Tanker
Double Hull (13F)
Liq: 2,347; Liq (Oil): 2,347
1 oil engine driving 1 FP propeller
Total Power: 2,207kW (3,001hp)
Hanshin LH38L
1 x 4 Stroke 6 Cy. 380 x 760 2207kW (3001bhp)
The Hanshin Diesel Works Ltd-Japan
Fuel: 175.0

8815499 *JL5806* -
SHINKO MARU No. 3 *444* - 1,207
Shinko Kogyo KK
-
Himeji, Hyogo *Japan*
Official number: 131413
1989-03 K.K. Saidaiji Zosensho — Okayama Yd No: 160
Loa 58.00 (BB) Br ex - Dght 4.570
Lbp 53.00 Br md 12.00 Dpth 6.40
Welded, 1 dk
(B33A2DG) Grab Dredger
1 oil engine geared to sc. shaft driving 1 FP propeller
Total Power: 736kW (1,001hp) 11.3kn
Hanshin 6LU32G
1 x 4 Stroke 6 Cy. 320 x 510 736kW (1001bhp)
The Hanshin Diesel Works Ltd-Japan
Fuel: 50.0

9124330 *JJ3902* -
SHINKO MARU No. 3 *199* - 247
Yorigami Ocean KK
Yorigami Maritime Construction Co Ltd (Yorigami Kensetsu KK)
Kobe, Hyogo *Japan*
MMSI: 431300253
Official number: 132436
1995-04 K.K. Watanabe Zosensho — Nagasaki Yd No: 029
Loa - Br ex - Dght 3.550
Lbp 34.83 Br md 10.00 Dpth 4.80
Welded, 1 dk
(B32A2ST) Tug
2 oil engines geared to sc. shafts driving 2 FP propellers
Total Power: 2,942kW (4,000hp)
Yanmar 6N280-UN
2 x 4 Stroke 6 Cy. 280 x 380 each-1471kW (2000bhp)
Yanmar Diesel Engine Co Ltd-Japan

8838013 - -
SHINKO MARU No. 5 *108* - -
Solomon Pacific Co Ltd
1981 K.K. Murakami Zosensho — Ishinomaki
L reg 29.30 Br ex - Dght 2.000
Lbp - Br md 6.20 Dpth 2.50
Welded, 1 dk
(B11B2FV) Fishing Vessel
1 oil engine driving 1 FP propeller
Total Power: 294kW (400hp)
Hanshin
1 x 4 Stroke 294kW (400bhp)
The Hanshin Diesel Works Ltd-Japan

9676450 *JD3346* -
SHINKO MARU NO. 5 *499* - 1,730
Japan Railway Construction, Transport & Technology Agency & Hakuyo Kisen YK
Hakuyo Kisen YK
Anan, Tokushima *Japan*
Official number: 141659
2012-04 YK Nakanoshima Zosensho — Kochi KC
Loa 74.71 (BB) Br ex - Dght 4.220
Lbp 69.00 Br md 12.00 Dpth 7.26
Welded, 1 dk
(A31A2GX) General Cargo Ship
1 Ha: ER (40.0 x 10.0)
1 oil engine reduction geared to sc. shaft driving 1 FP propeller
Total Power: 1,618kW (2,200hp)
Niigata 6M34BGT
1 x 4 Stroke 6 Cy. 340 x 620 1618kW (2200bhp)
Niigata Engineering Co Ltd-Japan
Thrusters: 1 Thwart. FP thruster (f)

8844206 - -
SHINKO MARU No. 6 *199* - 427
-
-
1990-09 Osaki Zosen KK — Awaji HG
Loa 45.30 Br ex - Dght 3.150
Lbp 42.00 Br md 8.00 Dpth 3.60
Welded, 1 dk
(A31A2GX) General Cargo Ship
1 Ha: (20.0 x 5.0)ER
1 oil engine driving 1 FP propeller
Total Power: 405kW (551hp) 12.0kn
Sumiyoshi S25G
1 x 4 Stroke 6 Cy. 250 x 450 405kW (551bhp)
Sumiyoshi Marine Diesel Co Ltd-Japan

9037628 *JE2964* -
SHINKO MARU NO. 6 *132* - 216
ex Kinsei Maru No. 1 -2004
Nobuhiro Terada
-
Kamaishi, Iwate *Japan*
Official number: 132217
1991-08 Kidoura Shipyard Co Ltd — Kesennuma MG Yd No: 573
Loa 37.51 (BB) Br ex 6.52 Dght 2.400
Lbp 31.00 Br md 6.50 Dpth 2.72
Welded, 1 dk
(B11B2FV) Fishing Vessel
Ins: 107
1 oil engine with clutches, flexible couplings & dr geared to sc. shaft driving 1 CP propeller
Total Power: 669kW (910hp)
Pielstick 6PA5LX
1 x 4 Stroke 6 Cy. 255 x 270 669kW (910bhp)
Niigata Engineering Co Ltd-Japan

9044437 *JL5973* -
SHINKO MARU No. 8 *199* - -
YK Toda Suisan
-
Uwajima, Ehime *Japan*
Official number: 131439
1991-08 Mikami Zosen K.K. — Japan Yd No: 316
L reg 41.00 Br ex - Dght -
Lbp - Br md 7.80 Dpth 3.70
Welded, 1 dk
(B12B2FC) Fish Carrier
1 oil engine driving 1 FP propeller
Total Power: 736kW (1,001hp)
Niigata 6M28BGT
1 x 4 Stroke 6 Cy. 280 x 480 736kW (1001bhp)
Niigata Engineering Co Ltd-Japan

8738225 *JD2658* -
SHINKO MARU NO. 8 *499* - 1,800
Shinko Kaiun KK
-
Imabari, Ehime *Japan*
Official number: 140761
2008-05 Namikata Shipbuilding Co Ltd — Imabari EH Yd No: 226
Loa 74.50 Br ex - Dght 4.350
Lbp 68.00 Br md 12.00 Dpth 7.35
Welded, 1 dk
(A31A2GX) General Cargo Ship
Grain: 2,552; Bale: 2,516
1 Ha: (40.0 x 9.5)
1 oil engine driving 1 Propeller
Total Power: 1,471kW (2,000hp) 11.5kn
Akasaka A34C
1 x 4 Stroke 6 Cy. 340 x 620 1471kW (2000bhp)
Akasaka Tekkosho KK (Akasaka DieselLtd)-Japan

8620703 - -	**SHINKO MARU No. 8** *ex* Katoku Maru No. 8 *-1993* - *Chinese Taipei*	*125* - -		**1984 K.K. Watanabe Zosensho — Nagasaki** Yd No: 1032 Loa - Br ex - Dght - Lbp 30.99 Br md 7.00 Dpth 2.90 Welded, 1 dk	**(B11B2FV) Fishing Vessel**	**1 oil engine** driving 1 FP propeller
9705380 *JD3499* -	**SHINKO MARU NO. 8** - **Japan Railway Construction, Transport & Technology Agency & Shinyo Kaiun KK** - *Kitakyushu, Fukuoka* *Japan* MMSI: 431004302 Official number: 141895	*499* - 1,730		**2013-03 Koike Zosen Kaiun KK — Osakikamijima** Yd No: 555 Loa 75.60 Br ex - Dght - Lbp 70.00 Br md 12.00 Dpth 7.21 Welded, 1 dk	**(A31A2GX) General Cargo Ship**	**1 oil engine** driving 1 Propeller Total Power: 1,471kW (2,000hp) Niigata 6M34BGT 1 x 4 Stroke 6 Cy. 340 x 620 1471kW (2000bhp) Niigata Engineering Co Ltd-Japan
8923911 *JL6514* -	**SHINKO MARU No. 10** - **Iwaki Kisen KK** - *Kamijima, Ehime* *Japan* Official number: 135541	*179* - 80		**1996-06 Takuma Zosen K.K. — Mitoyo** Yd No: 101 Loa 31.65 Br ex - Dght 2.600 Lbp 28.50 Br md 8.70 Dpth 2.79 Welded, 1 dk	**(A36A2PR) Passenger/Ro-Ro Ship (Vehicles)** Passengers: unberthed: 250	**1 oil engine** driving 1 FP propeller Total Power: 471kW (640hp) 10.0kn Yanmar 1 x 4 Stroke 471kW (640bhp) Yanmar Diesel Engine Co Ltd-Japan
9643075 *JD3324* -	**SHINKO MARU NO. 11** - **Shinko Kaiun KK** - *Imabari, Ehime* *Japan* Official number: 141590	*499* - 1,650		**2012-03 Namikata Shipbuilding Co Ltd — Imabari EH** Yd No: 236 Loa 75.87 Br ex - Dght 4.090 Lbp 71.00 Br md 12.00 Dpth 7.07 Welded, 1 dk	**(A31A2GX) General Cargo Ship** Grain: 2,507; Bale: 2,487 1 Ha: ER (40.0 x 9.5)	**1 oil engine** driving 1 FP propeller Total Power: 1,620kW (2,203hp) 11.5kn Akasaka A34C 1 x 4 Stroke 6 Cy. 340 x 620 1620kW (2203bhp) Akasaka Tekkosho KK (Akasaka DieselLtd)-Japan
5413501 - -	**SHINKO MARU No. 12** *ex* Shinko Maru *-1990* *ex* Shinnunobuki Maru *-1990* - -	*159* 45 -		**1963-07 Mitsui SB. & Eng. Co. Ltd. — Tamano** Yd No: 690 Loa 27.81 Br ex - Dght 2.300 Lbp 25.00 Br md 7.30 Dpth 3.30 Welded, 1 dk	**(B32A2ST) Tug**	**2 oil engines** driving 2 FP propellers Total Power: 1,214kW (1,650hp) 12.0kn Matsui 2 x 4 Stroke each-607kW (825bhp) Mitsui Engineering & Shipbuilding CLtd-Japan
6928230 - -	**SHINKO MARU No. 18** *ex* Miyagi Maru No. 2 *-1983* *ex* Ebisu Maru No. 1 *-1980* *ex* Tosan Maru No. 8 *-1979* - -	*199* - 329		**1969 Fukuoka Shipbuilding Co Ltd — Fukuoka FO** Yd No: 961 Loa 41.36 Br ex 7.01 Dght 2.998 Lbp 37.55 Br md 6.99 Dpth 3.41 Welded, 1 dk	**(B11B2FV) Fishing Vessel**	**1 oil engine** driving 1 FP propeller Total Power: 736kW (1,001hp) Makita FSHC629 1 x 4 Stroke 6 Cy. 290 x 440 736kW (1001bhp) Makita Tekkosho-Japan
8510178 - -	**SHINKO MARU No. 18** - **Dong Sung Oil Shipping Co Ltd** - *South Korea*	*199* - 549		**1985-11 Maeno Zosen KK — Sanyoonoda YC** Yd No: 116 Loa 48.02 Br ex 8.03 Dght 3.240 Lbp 43.50 Br md 8.00 Dpth 3.45 Welded, 1 dk	**(A13A2TV) Crude Oil Tanker** Liq: 590; Liq (Oil): 590 Compartments: 6 Ta, ER	**1 oil engine** reverse reduction geared to sc. shaft driving 1 FP propeller Total Power: 478kW (650hp) Hanshin 6LU24 1 x 4 Stroke 6 Cy. 240 x 410 478kW (650bhp) The Hanshin Diesel Works Ltd-Japan
8952429 *JJ3953* -	**SHINKO MARU No. 18** - **Araoka Kensetsu Kaiun KK** - *Himeji, Hyogo* *Japan* Official number: 134208	*498* - -		**1999-07 Nagashima Zosen KK — Kihoku ME** Yd No: 525 Loa 70.63 Br ex - Dght - Lbp 62.60 Br md 13.50 Dpth 7.00 Welded, 1 dk	**(A24D2BA) Aggregates Carrier** Compartments: 1 Ho, ER 1 Ha: (22.2 x 10.0)ER Cranes: 1x18t	**1 oil engine** driving 1 FP propeller Total Power: 1,471kW (2,000hp) 12.4kn Akasaka A34S 1 x 4 Stroke 6 Cy. 340 x 660 1471kW (2000bhp) Akasaka Tekkosho KK (Akasaka DieselLtd)-Japan Fuel: 45.0 (d.f.)
9698680 *JD3625* -	**SHINKO MARU NO. 18** - **Shinko Kaiun KK** - *Japan* MMSI: 431005083	*749* - 2,250	Class: FA	**2013-12 Namikata Shipbuilding Co Ltd — Imabari EH** Yd No: 250 Loa 81.94 (BB) Br ex - Dght 4.654 Lbp - Br md 13.00 Dpth - Welded, 1 dk	**(A31A2GX) General Cargo Ship** Double Hull	**1 oil engine** driving 1 Propeller Total Power: 1,765kW (2,400hp) Akasaka AX34 1 x 4 Stroke 1765kW (2400bhp) Akasaka Tekkosho KK (Akasaka DieselLtd)-Japan
9652272 *3FCG* -	**SHINKO MARU NO. 23** - **Shinko Kaiun Co Ltd & Shinko Panama Overseas SA** SHL Maritime Co Ltd *Panama* *Panama* MMSI: 370975000 Official number: 4446213	**2,211** 664 2,456	Class: NK	**2012-12 Shitanoe Shipbuilding Co Ltd — Usuki OT** Yd No: 1316 Loa 86.20 Br ex 13.62 Dght 4.963 Lbp 80.70 Br md 13.60 Dpth 6.50 Welded, 1 dk	**(A12A2TC) Chemical Tanker** Double Hull (13F) Liq: 1,981	**1 oil engine** driving 1 FP propeller Total Power: 1,912kW (2,600hp) 12.0kn Hanshin LA34G 1 x 4 Stroke 6 Cy. 340 x 720 1912kW (2600bhp) The Hanshin Diesel Works Ltd-Japan AuxGen: 2 x 336kW a.c Fuel: 240.0
9180487 *JM6509* -	**SHINKO MARU No. 25** - **Shinko Kaiun Co Ltd** - *Tokyo* *Japan* Official number: 134613	*499* - -		**1997-03 Kyoei Zosen KK — Mihara HS** Yd No: 281 Loa 65.00 Br ex - Dght - Lbp 62.00 Br md 10.00 Dpth 4.50 Welded, 1 dk	**(A13B2TU) Tanker (unspecified)** Liq: 1,245; Liq (Oil): 1,245 2 Cargo Pump (s): 2x300m³/hr	**1 oil engine** driving 1 FP propeller Total Power: 736kW (1,001hp) 11.0kn Hanshin LH28LG 1 x 4 Stroke 6 Cy. 280 x 530 736kW (1001bhp) The Hanshin Diesel Works Ltd-Japan
9263100 *JL6676* -	**SHINKO MARU NO. 28** - **Toda Suisan KK** - *Uwajima, Ehime* *Japan* MMSI: 431649000 Official number: 136520	*324* - -		**2002-01 Nagasaki Zosen K.K. — Nagasaki** Yd No: 1178 Loa 58.31 Br ex 8.82 Dght 3.600 Lbp 51.00 Br md 8.80 Dpth 4.10 Welded, 1 dk	**(B11B2FV) Fishing Vessel**	**1 oil engine** driving 1 FP propeller Total Power: 809kW (1,100hp) Niigata 1 x 4 Stroke 809kW (1100bhp) Niigata Engineering Co Ltd-Japan
7933036 - -	**SHINKO MARU No. 30** - **Jehan Shipping Corp** - *Philippines*	*181* - 497		**1979 Kochi Jyuko K.K. — Kochi** Yd No: 1347 Loa - Br ex - Dght 3.200 Lbp 42.02 Br md 8.01 Dpth 5.01 Welded, 1 dk	**(A31A2GX) General Cargo Ship**	**1 oil engine** driving 1 FP propeller Total Power: 441kW (600hp) Hanshin 6L26AGS 1 x 4 Stroke 6 Cy. 260 x 400 441kW (600bhp) Hanshin Nainenki Kogyo-Japan
8631843 - -	**SHINKO MARU No. 31** - **Delstar Marine Corp** - *Philippines*	*109* - -		**1977-09 Sanuki Shipbuilding & Iron Works Co Ltd — Mitoyo KG** Loa - Br ex - Dght 2.000 Lbp 29.10 Br md 6.70 Dpth 2.50 Welded, 1 dk	**(B11B2FV) Fishing Vessel**	**1 oil engine** driving 1 FP propeller
8849828 *JH2854* -	**SHINKO MARU No. 31** - **YK Shinko Suisan** - *Noto, Ishikawa* *Japan* Official number: 123818	*138* - -		**1979-10 KK Toyo Zosen Tekkosho — Kamaishi IW** L reg 29.70 Br ex - Dght - Lbp - Br md 6.30 Dpth 2.50 Welded, 1 dk	**(B11B2FV) Fishing Vessel**	**1 oil engine** driving 1 FP propeller Total Power: 331kW (450hp) Yanmar 1 x 4 Stroke 331kW (450bhp) Yanmar Diesel Engine Co Ltd-Japan
8877019 - -	**SHINKO MARU No. 35** - - -	*496* - 1,520		**1994-01 Mategata Zosen K.K. — Namikata** Yd No: 1051 Loa 74.00 Br ex - Dght 4.050 Lbp 69.00 Br md 12.00 Dpth 6.90 Welded, 1 dk	**(A31A2GX) General Cargo Ship** Grain: 2,714; Bale: 2,646 Compartments: 1 Ho 1 Ha: (38.0 x 9.0)ER	**1 oil engine** driving 1 FP propeller Total Power: 736kW (1,001hp) 11.0kn Niigata 6M31AFTE 1 x 4 Stroke 6 Cy. 310 x 530 736kW (1001bhp) Niigata Engineering Co Ltd-Japan
9135133 *JG5443* -	**SHINKO MARU No. 35** - **Seibu Tanker KK (Seibu Tanker Co Ltd)** - *Tokyo* *Japan* MMSI: 431400515 Official number: 135228	*749* - 1,784		**1996-01 Kanmon Zosen K.K. — Shimonoseki** Yd No: 570 Loa 74.97 (BB) Br ex 11.02 Dght 4.812 Lbp 70.58 Br md 11.00 Dpth 5.30 Welded, 1 dk	**(A12A2TC) Chemical Tanker** Liq: 1,650 Compartments: 10 Ta, ER 2 Cargo Pump (s): 2x750m³/hr	**1 oil engine** driving 1 CP propeller Total Power: 1,912kW (2,600hp) Hanshin LH36LA 1 x 4 Stroke 6 Cy. 360 x 670 1912kW (2600bhp) The Hanshin Diesel Works Ltd-Japan
8865406 *JL5928* -	**SHINKO MARU No. 38** - **Shinko Kaiun KK** - *Imabari, Ehime* *Japan* Official number: 132950	*499* - -		**1992-10 Namikata Shipbuilding Co Ltd — Imabari EH** Yd No: 168 L reg 72.60 Br ex - Dght 6.000 Lbp - Br md 12.00 Dpth 7.00 Welded, 1 dk	**(A31A2GX) General Cargo Ship**	**1 oil engine** reverse geared to sc. shaft driving 1 FP propeller Total Power: 736kW (1,001hp) Akasaka A31R 1 x 4 Stroke 6 Cy. 310 x 600 736kW (1001bhp) Akasaka Tekkosho KK (Akasaka DieselLtd)-Japan

8865432 *JL5986* -	**SHINKO MARU No. 38** **YK Toda Suisan** - *Uwajima, Ehime* *Japan* Official number: 133014	*199* - -	**1992-11 Mikami Zosen K.K. — Japan** L reg 41.00 Br ex - Dght 3.200 Lbp - Br md 7.80 Dpth 3.70 Welded, 1 dk	**(B11B2FV) Fishing Vessel**	**1 oil engine** driving 1 FP propeller Total Power: 736kW (1,001hp) Niigata 6M28BGT 1 x 4 Stroke 6 Cy. 280 x 480 736kW (1001bhp) Niigata Engineering Co Ltd-Japan
7535808 - -	**SHINKO MARU No. 38** *ex* Ebisu Maru No. 35 *-1988* *ex* Asahi Maru No. 85 *-1985* *ex* Matsuo Maru No. 81 *-1983* **Shinko Gyogyo Seisan Kumiai** -	*155* - -	**1975-07 K.K. Yoshida Zosen Tekko — Kesennuma** Yd No: 220 Loa 39.20 Br ex - Dght 2.801 Lbp 33.60 Br md 6.60 Dpth 3.20 Welded, 1 dk	**(B12B2FC) Fish Carrier**	**1 oil engine** geared to sc. shaft driving 1 FP propeller Total Power: 736kW (1,001hp) Daihatsu 6DSM-22 1 x 4 Stroke 6 Cy. 220 x 280 736kW (1001bhp) Daihatsu Diesel Manufacturing Co Lt-Japan
8731368 *JD2353* -	**SHINKO MARU NO. 55** **Hakuyo Kisen YK** *Anan, Tokushima* *Japan* Official number: 140462	*498* - 1,750	**2006-12 Tokuoka Zosen K.K. — Naruto** Yd No: 301 Loa 76.02 Br ex - Dght 4.200 Lbp 70.20 Br md 12.10 Dpth 7.20 Welded, 1 dk	**(A31A2GX) General Cargo Ship** Compartments: 1 Ho, ER 1 Ha: ER (40.0 x 10.0)	**1 oil engine** driving 1 Propeller Total Power: 1,618kW (2,200hp) Niigata 6M34BT 1 x 4 Stroke 6 Cy. 340 x 620 1618kW (2200bhp) Niigata Engineering Co Ltd-Japan
8838362 *JL5657* -	**SHINKO MARU No. 58** *ex* Taikei Maru No. 51 *-2008* *ex* Wakayama Maru No. 51 *-2000* **YK Toda Suisan** *Uwajima, Ehime* *Japan* MMSI: 431845000 Official number: 129943	*498* - -	**1989-02 Shin Yamamoto Shipbuilding & Engineering Co Ltd — Kochi KC** L reg 55.65 (BB) Br ex - Dght 4.000 Lbp - Br md 9.60 Dpth 4.80 Welded, 1 dk	**(B11B2FV) Fishing Vessel**	**1 oil engine** driving 1 FP propeller Niigata 1 x 4 Stroke Niigata Engineering Co Ltd-Japan
9124081 - -	**SHINKO MARU No. 58** **PT Armada Contener Nusantara** -	*499* - 1,528	**1995-04 K.K. Miura Zosensho — Saiki** Yd No: 1117 Loa 72.20 Br ex - Dght 3.950 Lbp 66.40 Br md 13.20 Dpth 6.75 Welded, 1 dk	**(A31A2GX) General Cargo Ship**	**1 oil engine** driving 1 FP propeller Total Power: 1,471kW (2,000hp) Akasaka 1 x 4 Stroke 1471kW (2000bhp) Akasaka Tekkosho KK (Akasaka DieselLtd)-Japan
7535822 - -	**SHINKO MARU No. 65** *ex* Mankichi Maru No. 17 *-1993* *ex* Kinshin Maru No. 17 *-1992* *ex* Dairyo Maru No. 83 *-1984* - -	*154* - -	**1975-04 K.K. Watanabe Zosensho — Nagasaki** Yd No: 657 Loa 38.99 Br ex 6.61 Dght - Lbp 32.57 Br md 6.41 Dpth 2.93 Welded, 1 dk	**(B12B2FC) Fish Carrier**	**1 oil engine** reduction geared to sc. shaft driving 1 FP propeller Total Power: 405kW (551hp) Niigata 6L25BX 1 x 4 Stroke 6 Cy. 250 x 320 405kW (551bhp) Niigata Engineering Co Ltd-Japan
8998320 *JD2081* -	**SHINKO MARU NO. 68** **Shinko Sangyo KK** - *Nishi-izu, Shizuoka* *Japan* MMSI: 432659000 Official number: 140135	*499* - 1,600	**2005-01 Yamanaka Zosen K.K. — Imabari** Yd No: 706 Loa 71.73 (BB) Br ex - Dght 4.490 Lbp 64.00 Br md 12.50 Dpth 7.46 Welded, 1 dk	**(A31A2GX) General Cargo Ship** Grain: 1,750 2 Ha: (15.0 x 9.0)ER (14.3 x 8.2) Cranes: 1x12t	**1 oil engine** driving 1 Propeller Total Power: 1,471kW (2,000hp) 11.4kn Akasaka A34S 1 x 4 Stroke 6 Cy. 340 x 660 1471kW (2000bhp) Akasaka Tekkosho KK (Akasaka DieselLtd)-Japan Thrusters: 1 Thwart. FP thruster (f); 1 Thwart. FP thruster (a)
7396135 - -	**SHINKO MARU No. 72** *ex* Takojima Maru No. 72 *-1984* - -	*178* - -	**1974-06 Usuki Iron Works Co Ltd — Usuki OT** Yd No: 935 Loa 38.41 Br ex 6.61 Dght - Lbp 34.22 Br md 6.58 Dpth 3.05 Welded, 1 dk	**(B11B2FV) Fishing Vessel**	**1 oil engine** driving 1 FP propeller Total Power: 956kW (1,300hp) Daihatsu 6DSM-26 1 x 4 Stroke 6 Cy. 260 x 320 956kW (1300bhp) Daihatsu Diesel Manufacturing Co Lt-Japan
9597692 *JD3101* -	**SHINKO MARU NO. 78** **Shinko Sangyo KK** - *Nishi-izu, Shizuoka* *Japan* Official number: 141258	**499** - 1,640	**2010-08 Namikata Shipbuilding Co Ltd — Imabari EH** Yd No: 232 Loa 70.75 Br ex - Dght 4.340 Lbp 63.00 Br md 12.00 Dpth 7.25 Welded, 1 dk	**(A31A2GX) General Cargo Ship**	**1 oil engine** driving 1 Propeller Total Power: 1,765kW (2,400hp) Akasaka A34S 1 x 4 Stroke 6 Cy. 340 x 660 1765kW (2400bhp) Akasaka Tekkosho KK (Akasaka DieselLtd)-Japan
6419356 - -	**SHINKO No. 3** *ex* Shinsaiwai Maru No. 3 *-1994* *ex* Takao Maru *-1991* - -	*160* 45 -	**1964 Kanagawa Zosen — Kobe** Yd No: 58 Loa 24.19 Br ex 7.65 Dght 2.998 Lbp - Br md 7.60 Dpth 3.61 Riveted\Welded, 1 dk	**(B32A2ST) Tug**	**2 oil engines** driving 2 FP propellers Total Power: 1,324kW (1,800hp) 12.0kn Nippon Hatsudoki HS6NV325 2 x 4 Stroke 6 Cy. 325 x 460 each-662kW (900bhp) Nippon Hatsudoki-Japan Fuel: 22.5
9054133 *JK5195* -	**SHINKOGA MARU** **YK Okita Kisen** - *Kure, Hiroshima* *Japan* MMSI: 431400076 Official number: 133051	*199* - 539	**1992-12 Nippon Zosen Tekko K.K. — Kitakyushu** Yd No: 341 Loa 47.93 Br ex 8.05 Dght 3.285 Lbp 44.00 Br md 8.00 Dpth 3.45 Welded, 1 dk	**(A13B2TP) Products Tanker** Liq: 584; Liq (Oil): 584 Compartments: 6 Ta, ER	**1 oil engine** with clutches & reverse geared to sc. shaft driving 1 FP propeller Total Power: 736kW (1,001hp) Yanmar MF26-ST 1 x 4 Stroke 6 Cy. 260 x 500 736kW (1001bhp) Yanmar Diesel Engine Co Ltd-Japan
8895308 - -	**SHINKOSHO MARU** - - -	*103* - -	**1990-10 Abe Koma Zosensho — Nandan** Loa 31.23 Br ex - Dght 2.700 Lbp 29.23 Br md 8.50 Dpth 3.80 Welded, 1 dk	**(B32A2ST) Tug**	**2 oil engines** driving 2 FP propellers Total Power: 1,104kW (1,500hp) 10.0kn Matsui ML624GSC-2 2 x 4 Stroke 6 Cy. 240 x 400 each-552kW (750bhp) Matsui Iron Works Co Ltd-Japan
9632662 *JD3269* -	**SHINKOU MARU NO. 8** **Yoshioka Kaiun YK** - *Anan, Tokushima* *Japan* Official number: 141557	*999* Class: NK - 2,347	**2011-12 Kanrei Zosen K.K. — Naruto** Yd No: 427 Loa 79.78 (BB) Br ex - Dght 5.230 Lbp 76.00 Br md 12.20 Dpth 5.75 Welded, 1 dk	**(A13B2TP) Products Tanker** Double Hull (13F) Liq: 2,351; Liq (Oil): 2,351	**1 oil engine** reduction geared to sc. shaft driving 1 Propeller Total Power: 1,839kW (2,500hp) Hanshin LA34G 1 x 4 Stroke 6 Cy. 340 x 720 1839kW (2500bhp) The Hanshin Diesel Works Ltd-Japan Fuel: 100.0
9638343 *JD3266* -	**SHINKOU MARU NO. 28** **Shinei Kaiun YK** - *Shimonoseki, Yamaguchi* *Japan* MMSI: 431003024 Official number: 141553	*499* - 1,235	**2011-10 Suzuki Shipyard Co. Ltd. — Yokkaichi** Yd No: 731 Loa 65.98 Br ex - Dght 4.100 Lbp 61.80 Br md 10.00 Dpth 4.50 Welded, 1 dk	**(A13B2TP) Products Tanker** Double Hull (13F)	**1 oil engine** geared to sc. shaft driving 1 Propeller Total Power: 1,177kW (1,600hp) 11.5kn Hanshin LH28LG 1 x 4 Stroke 6 Cy. 280 x 530 1177kW (1600bhp) The Hanshin Diesel Works Ltd-Japan
8890059 *JK5451* -	**SHINKYO MARU** *ex* Fukuyoshi Maru No. 5 *-2004* **Shinkyo Kaiun KK** - *Kobe, Hyogo* *Japan* Official number: 134763	*196* - -	**1995-07 K.K. Saidaiji Zosensho — Okayama** Yd No: 211 Loa 55.22 Br ex - Dght - Lbp 49.50 Br md 9.30 Dpth 5.60 Welded, 1 dk	**(A31A2GX) General Cargo Ship**	**1 oil engine** driving 1 FP propeller Total Power: 736kW (1,001hp) 10.5kn Yanmar MF26-HT 1 x 4 Stroke 6 Cy. 260 x 500 736kW (1001bhp) Yanmar Diesel Engine Co Ltd-Japan
9700603 *JD3651* -	**SHINKYOKUTO MARU** **Asahi Tanker Co Ltd** Asahi Marine Ltd *Tokyo* *Japan* MMSI: 431005236 Official number: 142123	**3,637** Class: NK - 5,578	**2014-03 Shin Kurushima Dockyard Co. Ltd. — Akitsu** Yd No: 5825 Loa 104.90 (BB) Br ex - Dght 6.600 Lbp - Br md 16.00 Dpth 8.00 Welded, 1 dk	**(A13B2TP) Products Tanker** Double Hull (13F)	**1 oil engine** driving 1 Propeller Total Power: 3,309kW (4,499hp) Akasaka A45S 1 x 4 Stroke 6 Cy. 450 x 880 3309kW (4499bhp)
9124706 *JL6410* -	**SHINKYOKUYO MARU** **Umagoshi Kisen KK** *Imabari, Ehime* *Japan* MMSI: 431500357 Official number: 135089	*199* Class: NK - 700	**1995-07 Hakata Zosen K.K. — Imabari** Yd No: 578 Loa 56.12 Br ex - Dght 3.118 Lbp 52.00 Br md 9.60 Dpth 3.15 Welded, 1 dk	**(A31A2GX) General Cargo Ship** Grain: 1,251; Bale: 1,064 Compartments: 1 Ho, ER 1 Ha: (28.8 x 7.5)ER	**1 oil engine** reverse geared to sc. shaft driving 1 FP propeller Total Power: 736kW (1,001hp) 10.5kn Akasaka K28BR 1 x 4 Stroke 6 Cy. 280 x 480 736kW (1001bhp) Akasaka Tekkosho KK (Akasaka DieselLtd)-Japan Fuel: 25.0 (d.f.)
9643714 *JD3397* -	**SHINKYOU MARU NO. 3** **Shinkyo Kaiun KK** - *Kobe, Hyogo* *Japan* Official number: 141738	*199* - 720	**2012-07 Taiyo Shipbuilding Co Ltd — Sanyoonoda YC** Yd No: 331 Loa 55.90 Br ex - Dght 3.250 Lbp - Br md 9.50 Dpth 5.40 Welded, 1 dk	**(A31A2GX) General Cargo Ship**	**1 oil engine** reduction geared to sc. shaft driving 1 Propeller Total Power: 882kW (1,199hp) Hanshin LH26G 1 x 4 Stroke 6 Cy. 260 x 440 882kW (1199bhp) The Hanshin Diesel Works Ltd-Japan

IMO / Call sign / Flag	Ship name / Former names / Owner	Tonnage	Class	Build	Type / Cargo	Machinery
8303874 *JZKR* -	**SHINLINE 4** *ex* Quint Star *-1995* *ex* Sumbawa *-1991* *ex* Excelsior *-1984* **PT Pelayaran Baruna Adiprasetya** - *Jakarta* *Indonesia*	**5,708** 2,288 6,682	Class: NK	**1983-07 Kochi Jyuko K.K. — Kochi** Yd No: 2275 Loa 100.17 (BB) Br ex 18.83 Dght 7.576 Lbp 89.79 Br md 18.80 Dpth 12.90 Welded, 2 dks	**(A31A2GX) General Cargo Ship** Grain: 12,847; Bale: 11,816 2 Ha: 2 (20.3 x 10.2)ER Derricks: 2x25t,2x20t	**1 oil engine** driving 1 FP propeller Total Power: 2,501kW (3,400hp) 13.0kn B&W 5L35MC 1 x 2 Stroke 5 Cy. 350 x 1050 2501kW (3400bhp) Makita Diesel Co Ltd-Japan AuxGen: 2 x 240kW a.c Fuel: 595.0 (r.f.)
8514801 *9WDH7* -	**SHINLINE 5** *ex* Sanjose Ace *-1997* *ex* Pacific Tiger *-1990* **Shinline Sdn Bhd** - *Kuching* *Malaysia* MMSI: 533297000 Official number: 328991	**5,557** 2,307 7,059	Class: NK	**1985-12 Kochi Jyuko K.K. — Kochi** Yd No: 2453 Loa 98.17 (BB) Br ex 18.85 Dght 7.430 Lbp 89.95 Br md 18.81 Dpth 12.90 Welded, 2 dks	**(A31A2GX) General Cargo Ship** Grain: 13,560; Bale: 12,554 TEU 187 C. 187/20' Compartments: 2 Ho, ER 2 Ha: 2 (20.3 x 12.7)ER Derricks: 3x20t	**1 oil engine** driving 1 FP propeller Total Power: 2,795kW (3,800hp) 13.0kn B&W 5L35MC 1 x 2 Stroke 5 Cy. 350 x 1050 2795kW (3800bhp) Hitachi Zosen Corp-Japan AuxGen: 2 x 240kW a.c Fuel: 535.0 (r.f.)
8603248 *9WDS7* -	**SHINLINE 6** *ex* Mariana 1 *-1999* *ex* Pioneer Sebelas *-1990* **Shinline Sdn Bhd** - *Kuching* *Malaysia* MMSI: 533492000 Official number: 329234	**5,558** 2,352 7,025	Class: NK	**1986-07 Kochi Jyuko K.K. — Kochi** Yd No: 2487 Loa 98.17 (BB) Br ex - Dght 7.411 Lbp 89.95 Br md 18.81 Dpth 12.90 Welded, 2 dks	**(A31A2GX) General Cargo Ship** Grain: 13,762; Bale: 12,594 Compartments: 2 Ho, ER 2 Ha: 2 (20.3 x 12.7)ER Cranes: 2x30t,2x25t	**1 oil engine** driving 1 FP propeller Total Power: 2,243kW (3,050hp) 13.0kn B&W 5L35MCE 1 x 2 Stroke 5 Cy. 350 x 1050 2243kW (3050bhp) Hitachi Zosen Corp-Japan Fuel: 520.0 (r.f.)
8922199 *9WDW9* -	**SHINLINE 9** *ex* Oriental Hero *-2000* **Shinline Sdn Bhd** - SatCom: Inmarsat B 335566610 *Kuching* *Malaysia* MMSI: 533511000 Official number: 329315	**5,554** 2,337 7,009	Class: NK	**1990-08 Shin Kochi Jyuko K.K. — Kochi** Yd No: 7006 Loa 98.17 (BB) Br ex - Dght 7.429 Lbp 89.95 Br md 18.80 Dpth 12.90 Welded, 1 dk	**(A31A2GX) General Cargo Ship** Grain: 13,647; Bale: 12,484 Compartments: 2 Ho, ER 2 Ha: ER Derricks: 3x30t,1x25t	**1 oil engine** driving 1 FP propeller Total Power: 2,501kW (3,400hp) 12.4kn B&W 5L35MC 1 x 2 Stroke 5 Cy. 350 x 1050 2501kW (3400bhp) Makita Corp-Japan AuxGen: 3 x 164kW a.c Fuel: 510.0 (r.f.)
9559470 *9WFE4* -	**SHINLINE 10** **Shinline Sdn Bhd** - SatCom: Inmarsat C 453301476 *Kuching* *Malaysia* MMSI: 533002720 Official number: 333110	**9,799** 4,647 13,583	Class: NK	**2011-03 Shin Yang Shipyard Sdn Bhd — Miri** Yd No: 290 Loa 127.90 (BB) Br ex 20.52 Dght 9.177 Lbp 118.00 Br md 20.50 Dpth 14.30 Welded, 1 dk	**(A31A2GX) General Cargo Ship** Grain: 21,046; Bale: 19,118 Compartments: 2 Ho, ER 2 Ha: ER Cranes: 2x30t; Derricks: 2x25t	**1 oil engine** driving 1 FP propeller Total Power: 4,440kW (6,037hp) 12.5kn MAN-B&W 6S35MC 1 x 2 Stroke 6 Cy. 350 x 1400 4440kW (6037bhp) STX Engine Co Ltd-South Korea AuxGen: 3 x 450kW a.c Fuel: 660.0
9559482 *9WGF2* -	**SHINLINE 11** **Shinline Sdn Bhd** - SatCom: Inmarsat C 453301634 *Kuching* *Malaysia* MMSI: 533004410 Official number: 333111	**9,799** 4,647 13,608	Class: NK	**2011-08 Shin Yang Shipyard Sdn Bhd — Miri** Yd No: 291 Loa 127.90 (BB) Br ex 20.52 Dght 9.177 Lbp 118.00 Br md 20.50 Dpth 14.30 Welded, 1 dk	**(A31A2GX) General Cargo Ship** Grain: 21,046; Bale: 19,118 Compartments: 2 Ho, ER 2 Ha: ER Cranes: 2x30t; Derricks: 2x25t	**1 oil engine** driving 1 FP propeller Total Power: 4,440kW (6,037hp) 12.5kn MAN-B&W 6S35MC 1 x 2 Stroke 6 Cy. 350 x 1400 4440kW (6037bhp) STX Engine Co Ltd-South Korea AuxGen: 3 x 450kW a.c Fuel: 790.0
9629225 *9WLK5* -	**SHINLINE 12** **Shinline Sdn Bhd** - *Kuching* *Malaysia* MMSI: 533170047 Official number: 333380	**9,792** 4,647 13,409	Class: NK	**2012-06 Shin Yang Shipyard Sdn Bhd — Miri** Yd No: 292 Loa 127.90 (BB) Br ex 20.52 Dght 9.174 Lbp 118.27 Br md 20.50 Dpth 14.30 Welded, 1 dk	**(A31A2GX) General Cargo Ship** Grain: 21,032; Bale: 19,119 Compartments: 2 Ho, ER 2 Ha: ER Cranes: 2x30t; Derricks: 2x25t	**1 oil engine** driving 1 FP propeller Total Power: 4,440kW (6,037hp) 12.5kn MAN-B&W 6S35MC7 1 x 2 Stroke 6 Cy. 350 x 1400 4440kW (6037bhp) STX Engine Co Ltd-South Korea AuxGen: 3 x 450kW a.c Fuel: 610.0
9629237 *9WLK6* -	**SHINLINE 15** **Shinline Sdn Bhd** - *Kuching* *Malaysia* MMSI: 533170107 Official number: 333381	**9,792** 4,647 13,459	Class: NK	**2013-05 Shin Yang Shipyard Sdn Bhd — Miri** Yd No: 293 Loa 127.90 (BB) Br ex 20.52 Dght 9.174 Lbp 118.27 Br md 20.50 Dpth 14.30 Welded, 1 dk	**(A31A2GX) General Cargo Ship** Grain: 21,032; Bale: 19,119 Compartments: 2 Ho, ER 2 Ha: ER Cranes: 2x30t; Derricks: 2x25t	**1 oil engine** driving 1 FP propeller Total Power: 4,440kW (6,037hp) 12.5kn MAN-B&W 6S35MC7 1 x 2 Stroke 6 Cy. 350 x 1400 4440kW (6037bhp) STX Engine Co Ltd-South Korea AuxGen: 3 x 450kW a.c Fuel: 610.0
8865004 *JK5193* -	**SHINMARUOKA MARU** **YK Hamamoto Kaiun** - *Ondo, Hiroshima* *Japan* Official number: 133046	*173* - 350		**1992-09 Hongawara Zosen K.K. — Fukuyama** L reg 37.00 Br ex - Dght 2.700 Lbp - Br md 7.50 Dpth 3.20 Welded, 1 dk	**(A13B2TU) Tanker (unspecified)**	**1 oil engine** driving 1 FP propeller Total Power: 441kW (600hp) Yanmar MF24-HT 1 x 4 Stroke 6 Cy. 240 x 420 441kW (600bhp) Yanmar Diesel Engine Co Ltd-Japan
9234185 *JG5617* -	**SHINMEI MARU** **Corporation for Advanced Transport & Technology & Kuribayashi Steamship Co Ltd** Kuribayashi Steamship Co Ltd *Tokyo* *Japan* MMSI: 431100922 Official number: 136981	*13,091* - 7,012	Class: NK	**2000-12 Yamanishi Corp — Ishinomaki MG** Yd No: 1022 Loa 160.56 (BB) Br ex - Dght 7.015 Lbp 150.00 Br md 26.60 Dpth 10.40 Welded, 4 dks	**(A35A2RR) Ro-Ro Cargo Ship** Angled stern door/ramp (s. a.) Quarter bow door/ramp (s) Lane-Len: 1788 Cars: 200, Trailers: 76 Bale: 1,049	**1 oil engine** with flexible couplings & sr gearedto sc. shaft driving 1 CP propeller Total Power: 15,886kW (21,599hp) 21.2kn Pielstick 12PC4-2B-570 1 x Vee 4 Stroke 12 Cy. 570 x 660 15886kW (21599bhp) Nippon Kokan KK (NKK Corp)-Japan AuxGen: 2 x 1560kW a.c Thrusters: 1 Thwart. CP thruster (f); 1 Tunnel thruster (a) Fuel: 610.0
8975110 *JH2230* -	**SHINMEI MARU NO. 8** *ex* Seifuku Maru No. 3 *-2000* **Kenichi Kurachi** - *Hazu, Aichi* *Japan* Official number: 104958	*167* - 230		**1968-09 Ito Iron Works & SB. Co. Ltd. — Sasebo** Loa 35.50 Br ex - Dght 2.500 Lbp 32.00 Br md 6.00 Dpth 3.00 Welded, 1 dk	**(A31A2GX) General Cargo Ship** Compartments: 1 Ho, ER 1 Ha: ER (21.9 x 4.8)	**1 oil engine** driving 1 Propeller Total Power: 221kW (300hp) 6.0kn Yanmar 1 x 4 Stroke 221kW (300bhp) Yanmar Diesel Engine Co Ltd-Japan
8943624 - -	**SHINMEI No. 8** *ex* Sanko Maru No. 5 *-1998* *ex* Fuyo Maru No. 10 *-1998* *ex* Shigei Maru No. 2 *-1998* **-** -	*224* 141 -		**1969-05 Binan Senpaku Kogyo K.K. — Onomichi** Converted From: Vehicles Carrier-1994 Converted From: Ferry (Passenger/Vehicle)-1986 Lengthened & Widened-1981 Loa 42.00 Br ex - Dght 1.880 Lbp 39.50 Br md 12.00 Dpth 3.50 Welded, 1 dk	**(A24D2BA) Aggregates Carrier**	**1 oil engine** driving 1 FP propeller Total Power: 272kW (370hp) Hanshin 1 x 4 Stroke 272kW (370bhp) (new engine 1994) The Hanshin Diesel Works Ltd-Japan
9267730 *JM6603* -	**SHINMICHI MARU** **Eiwa Unyu KK & Showa Kaiun Co Ltd** Eiwa Unyu KK SatCom: Inmarsat C 443235610 *Shimonoseki, Yamaguchi* *Japan* MMSI: 432356000 Official number: 136822	*3,785* - 4,998	Class: (NK)	**2002-08 Murakami Hide Zosen K.K. — Imabari** Yd No: 525 Loa 104.95 Br ex - Dght 6.174 Lbp 98.50 Br md 16.00 Dpth 8.40 Welded, 1 dk	**(A13B2TP) Products Tanker** Double Hull (13F) Liq: 6,330; Liq (Oil): 6,330	**1 oil engine** driving 1 FP propeller Total Power: 4,045kW (5,500hp) 12.0kn Hanshin 6LF54 1 x 4 Stroke 6 Cy. 540 x 850 4045kW (5500bhp) The Hanshin Diesel Works Ltd-Japan
9012329 - -	**SHINMIYAGI MARU** **-** -	*450* - 450		**1991-03 Yamanishi Shipbuilding Co Ltd — Ishinomaki MG** Yd No: 996 Loa 58.50 (BB) Br ex 8.92 Dght 3.644 Lbp 49.00 Br md 8.90 Dpth 3.95 Welded	**(B11A2FS) Stern Trawler** Ins: 157	**1 oil engine** with clutches, flexible couplings & sr geared to sc. shaft driving 1 FP propeller Total Power: 1,324kW (1,800hp) 13.0kn Akasaka K31FD 1 x 4 Stroke 6 Cy. 310 x 530 1324kW (1800bhp) Akasaka Tekkosho KK (Akasaka DieselLtd)-Japan Thrusters: 1 Thwart. CP thruster (f)
8930512 *JK2729* -	**SHINMOJI No. 8** *ex* Kamiamakusa *-1999* *ex* Shinko Maru No. 8 *-1997* *ex* Habu Maru No. 7 *-1997* **Kazuhiko Fujii** - *Kasaoka, Okayama* *Japan* Official number: 100677	*153* - -		**1968-07 Binan Senpaku Kogyo K.K. — Onomichi** Loa 33.00 Br ex - Dght 2.500 Lbp 28.00 Br md 7.00 Dpth 2.70 Welded, 1 dk	**(A36A2PR) Passenger/Ro-Ro Ship (Vehicles)**	**1 oil engine** geared to sc. shaft driving 1 FP propeller Total Power: 331kW (450hp) 10.0kn Daihatsu 6PSTCM-22 1 x 4 Stroke 6 Cy. 220 x 280 331kW (450bhp) Daihatsu Diesel Manufacturing Co Lt-Japan

IMO / Call sign	Name / Owner	Tonnage	Class	Built / Dimensions	Type	Machinery
8955990 - -	**SHINN DAR** *ex* Costa Bella No. 2 *-1995* **Germane Marine SA**	*798* 340 -		**1991 Fong Kuo Shipbuilding Co Ltd — Kaohsiung** L reg 59.60 Br ex - Dght - Lbp - Br md 9.50 Dpth 4.20 Welded, 1 dk	**(B11B2FV) Fishing Vessel**	**1 oil engine** driving 1 FP propeller 13.0kn Niigata 1 x 4 Stroke Niigata Engineering Co Ltd-Japan
8947565 *S7RE* -	**SHINN MANN NO. 21** *ex* Shuenn Mann No. 21 *-2005* *ex* Shinn Mann No. 21 *-2003* **Minn Maan Marine Ltd** - *Victoria* *Seychelles*	**683** 285 -		**1998-03 Jong Shyn Shipbuilding Co., Ltd. — Kaohsiung** Yd No: 068 Loa 50.80 Br ex - Dght 3.650 Lbp - Br md 9.00 Dpth 3.95 Welded, 1 dk	**(B11B2FV) Fishing Vessel**	**1 oil engine** driving 1 FP propeller Total Power: 1,177kW (1,600hp) 13.0kn Matsui 1 x 4 Stroke 1177kW (1600bhp) Matsui Iron Works Co Ltd-Japan
6803557 - -	**SHINNECOCK** - **Jewan Singh** - *Georgetown* *Guyana* Official number: 257967	*297* 202 -		**1949 R.T.C. Shipbuilding Corp. — Camden, NJ** Yd No: 191 L reg 44.51 Br ex 6.81 Dght - Lbp - Br md - Dpth 2.98 Welded, 1 dk	**(B11B2FV) Fishing Vessel**	**1 oil engine** driving 1 FP propeller Total Power: 588kW (799hp) 10.0kn Enterprise DMG8 1 x 4 Stroke 8 Cy. 305 x 381 588kW (799bhp) Enterprise Engine & Foundry Co-USA
9159490 *JL6525*	**SHINNICHI MARU** - **Chuo Kaiun KK (Chuo Kaiun Kaisha Ltd)** Shinwa Chemical Tanker KK *Tokyo* *Japan* MMSI: 431400631 Official number: 135563	*749* - 1,707	Class: NK	**1996-12 Sasaki Shipbuilding Co Ltd — Osakikamijima HS** Yd No: 606 Loa 74.25 Br ex - Dght 4.718 Lbp 69.95 Br md 11.20 Dpth 5.20 Welded, 1 dk	**(A12B2TR) Chemical/Products Tanker** Double Hull (13F) Liq: 1,450; Liq (Oil): 1,450	**1 oil engine** driving 1 FP propeller Total Power: 1,618kW (2,200hp) 12.8kn Hanshin LH34LA 1 x 4 Stroke 6 Cy. 340 x 640 1618kW (2200bhp) The Hanshin Diesel Works Ltd-Japan Fuel: 90.0 (d.f.)
7904267 - -	**SHINNIKKAFUJI MARU** - - -	*1,960* - 2,536		**1979-07 Shimoda Dockyard Co. Ltd. — Shimoda** Yd No: 294 Loa 78.90 Br ex - Dght 5.109 Lbp 73.00 Br md 13.01 Dpth 7.22 Welded, 1 dk	**(A24E2BL) Limestone Carrier** 1 Ha: (36.0 x 9.0)ER	**1 oil engine** driving 1 FP propeller Total Power: 1,545kW (2,101hp) 13.0kn Akasaka AH36 1 x 4 Stroke 6 Cy. 360 x 540 1545kW (2101bhp) Akasaka Tekkosho KK (Akasaka DieselLtd)-Japan AuxGen: 2 x 64kW 445V 60Hz a.c Fuel: 10.0 (d.f.) 70.0 (r.f.) 4.0pd
9652351 *JD3455* -	**SHINNIKKO MARU** - **Hamaguchi Ocean Shipping Co Ltd (Hamaguchi Kaiun KK)** - *Kamiamakusa, Kumamoto* *Japan* MMSI: 431004146 Official number: 141823	*384* - 1,285		**2012-12 Taiyo Shipbuilding Co Ltd — Sanyoonoda YC** Yd No: 332 Loa 67.80 Br ex - Dght 3.770 Lbp - Br md 11.00 Dpth 6.30 Welded, 1 dk	**(A31A2GX) General Cargo Ship** Grain: 1,758	**1 oil engine** reduction geared to sc. shaft driving 1 Propeller Total Power: 1,323kW (1,799hp) Hanshin LA28G 1 x 4 Stroke 6 Cy. 280 x 590 1323kW (1799bhp) The Hanshin Diesel Works Ltd-Japan
8922773 *JG5430* -	**SHINONOME** - **Government of Japan (Ministry of Land, Infrastructure & Transport) (The Coastguard)** - *Tokyo* *Japan* MMSI: 431200131 Official number: 135214	*113* - -		**1996-02 Ishihara Zosen — Takasago** Loa 35.00 Br ex - Dght 1.250 Lbp 32.00 Br md 6.30 Dpth 3.43 Welded, 1 dk	**(B34H2SQ) Patrol Vessel**	**2 oil engines** geared to sc. shafts driving 2 FP propellers Total Power: 2,942kW (4,000hp) 25.0kn M.T.U. 12V396TB94 2 x Vee 4 Stroke 12 Cy. 165 x 185 each-1471kW (2000bhp) MTU Friedrichshafen GmbH-Friedrichshafen
9140413 - -	**SHINPO** - **PT Indo Shipping Operator** -	*497* - 1,000		**1996-03 Sasaki Shipbuilding Co Ltd — Osakikamijima HS** Yd No: 602 Loa - Br ex - Dght 4.050 Lbp 70.00 Br md 12.00 Dpth 7.00 Welded, 1 dk	**(A31A2GX) General Cargo Ship**	**1 oil engine** driving 1 FP propeller Total Power: 736kW (1,001hp) Akasaka A31 1 x 4 Stroke 6 Cy. 310 x 600 736kW (1001bhp) Akasaka Tekkosho KK (Akasaka DieselLtd)-Japan
9151450 *JL6521* -	**SHINPO** - **Koyo Marine KK** - *Yokohama, Kanagawa* *Japan* Official number: 135548	*153* - -		**1996-11 Suzuki Shipyard Co. Ltd. — Yokkaichi** Yd No: 631 Loa 28.00 Br ex - Dght 2.600 Lbp 26.00 Br md 9.50 Dpth 3.20 Welded, 1 dk	**(B34B2SC) Crane Vessel** Cranes: 1x40t	**2 oil engines** driving 2 FP propellers Total Power: 1,618kW (2,200hp) Niigata 6MG22LX 2 x 4 Stroke 6 Cy. 220 x 290 each-809kW (1100bhp) (made 1983) Niigata Engineering Co Ltd-Japan
8823812 *YGMB* -	**SHINPO 88** *ex* New Kosei *-2005* **PT Sinar Bahari Nusantara** - *Surabaya* *Indonesia*	*497* 313 422	Class: KI	**1988-09 KK Ouchi Zosensho — Matsuyama EH** Loa 50.00 Br ex - Dght 3.070 Lbp 45.00 Br md 8.20 Dpth 5.00 Welded, 1 dk	**(A31A2GX) General Cargo Ship**	**1 oil engine** driving 1 FP propeller Total Power: 368kW (500hp) Yanmar MF24-DT 1 x 4 Stroke 6 Cy. 240 x 420 368kW (500bhp) Matsue Diesel KK-Japan AuxGen: 1 x 45kW 220V a.c
7825069 *YCPZ* -	**SHINPO 89** *ex* Ning Feng *-2011* *ex* Yong Feng *-2005* *ex* North Union *-2004* *ex* Hai Xin *-2001* *ex* Trawind *-2000* *ex* Famper *-1999* *ex* Trucker *-1998* *ex* Uriah *-1998* *ex* Falco *-1998* *ex* Grandway Vesta *-1997* *ex* Kensei Maru *-1994* **PT Pelayaran Berkat Abadi Jaya Makmur** - *Tanjung Priok* *Indonesia*	**892** 428 1,101	Class: KI	**1979-02 K.K. Matsuura Zosensho — Osakikamijima** Yd No: 265 Loa 62.64 Br ex 9.83 Dght 3.852 Lbp 57.60 Br md 9.81 Dpth 5.82 Welded, 2 dks	**(A31A2GX) General Cargo Ship**	**1 oil engine** driving 1 FP propeller Total Power: 883kW (1,201hp) Hanshin 6LU28G 1 x 4 Stroke 6 Cy. 280 x 440 883kW (1201bhp) Hanshin Nainenki Kogyo-Japan
8923868 *JM6521* -	**SHINPO MARU** - **Shinpo Kaiun YK** - *Karatsu, Saga* *Japan* Official number: 135399	*378* - 1,704		**1996-06 KK Ouchi Zosensho — Matsuyama EH** Yd No: 515 Loa 59.03 Br ex - Dght 4.120 Lbp 52.00 Br md 12.00 Dpth 6.40 Welded, 1 dk	**(A31A2GX) General Cargo Ship** Compartments: 1 Ho, ER 1 Ha: (18.2 x 9.4)ER Cranes: 1x3t	**1 oil engine** Geared Integral to driving 1 Z propeller Total Power: 625kW (850hp) 10.5kn Hanshin 6LC28LG 1 x 4 Stroke 6 Cy. 280 x 530 625kW (850bhp) The Hanshin Diesel Works Ltd-Japan
8889866 *JL6358*	**SHINPO MARU** - **Takeshi Noma** - *Imabari, Ehime* *Japan* Official number: 135081	*199* - 649		**1995-04 Yano Zosen K.K. — Imabari** Loa 57.50 Br ex - Dght 3.130 Lbp 53.00 Br md 9.50 Dpth 5.34 Welded, 1 dk	**(A31A2GX) General Cargo Ship** Bale: 1,164 Compartments: 1 Ho, ER 1 Ha: (30.3 x 7.5)ER	**1 oil engine** driving 1 FP propeller Total Power: 736kW (1,001hp) 12.0kn Matsui ML627GSC 1 x 4 Stroke 6 Cy. 270 x 480 736kW (1001bhp) Matsui Iron Works Co Ltd-Japan
9233947 *JJ4027* -	**SHINPO MARU** - **Shinmei Kisen YK** - *Awaji, Hyogo* *Japan* Official number: 135971	*199* - 600		**2000-09 K.K. Matsuura Zosensho — Osakikamijima** Yd No: 536 Loa 57.13 Br ex - Dght - Lbp 52.00 Br md 9.60 Dpth 5.35 Welded, 1 dk	**(A31A2GX) General Cargo Ship** Grain: 1,065 Compartments: 1 Ho, ER 1 Ha: (28.6 x 7.7)ER	**1 oil engine** driving 1 FP propeller Total Power: 735kW (999hp) 11.5kn Hanshin LH26G 1 x 4 Stroke 6 Cy. 260 x 440 735kW (999bhp) The Hanshin Diesel Works Ltd-Japan Fuel: 28.5 (d.f.)
9562013 *JD2972* -	**SHINPO MARU** - **Kuribayashi Buturyu System** - *Tokyo* *Japan* Official number: 141107	*498* - 1,660		**2009-09 Yamanaka Zosen K.K. — Imabari** Yd No: 780 Loa 76.26 Br ex - Dght 4.080 Lbp 70.00 Br md 12.00 Dpth 7.01 Welded, 1 dk	**(A31A2GX) General Cargo Ship** Grain: 2,779; Bale: 2,815 1 Ha: ER (40.0 x 9.5)	**1 oil engine** driving 1 Propeller Total Power: 1,618kW (2,200hp) 12.7kn Niigata 6M34BGT 1 x 4 Stroke 6 Cy. 340 x 620 1618kW (2200bhp) Niigata Engineering Co Ltd-Japan
8909678 *JL5873*	**SHINPO MARU No. 5** - - - *Kamiamakusa, Kumamoto* *Japan* Official number: 131442	*199* - 480		**1989-12 Koa Sangyo KK — Takamatsu KG** Yd No: 551 Loa 49.59 Br ex - Dght 2.905 Lbp 45.00 Br md 7.80 Dpth 3.30 Welded, 1 dk	**(A12A2TC) Chemical Tanker** Liq: 400 Compartments: 6 Ta, ER 2 Cargo Pump (s): 1x120m³/hr, 1x150m³/hr	**1 oil engine** reverse geared to sc. shaft driving 1 FP propeller Total Power: 588kW (799hp) Yanmar MF24-UT 1 x 4 Stroke 6 Cy. 240 x 420 588kW (799bhp) Yanmar Diesel Engine Co Ltd-Japan

ID	Ship / Owner	Tonnage	Class	Built	Type	Machinery
9088677 *JM6365* -	**SHINPO MARU NO. 5** *ex* Shunpo Maru *-1994* **Shimazu Shoji Co Ltd** *Shimonoseki, Yamaguchi* *Japan* MMSI: 431400281 Official number: 133652	*695* - 905	Class: NK	**1994-03 Shirahama Zosen K.K. — Honai** Yd No: 163 Loa 64.95 Br ex - Dght 4.011 Lbp 60.00 Br md 11.00 Dpth 5.00 Welded, 1 dk	**(A11B2TG) LPG Tanker** Liq (Gas): 1,245 2 x Gas Tank (s); 2 cyl horizontal	**1 oil engine** with clutches & reverse geared to sc. shaft driving 1 FP propeller Total Power: 1,324kW (1,800hp) 11.5kn Hanshin LH30LG 1 x 4 Stroke 6 Cy. 300 x 600 1324kW (1800bhp) The Hanshin Diesel Works Ltd-Japan AuxGen: 2 x 2496kW a.c Thrusters: 1 Thwart. FP thruster (f) Fuel: 90.0 (d.f.)
8998459 *JD2100* -	**SHINPO MARU NO. 11** **YK Sanko Kaiun** - *Sakaide, Kagawa* *Japan* Official number: 140159	*212* - 700		**2005-04 Koa Sangyo KK — Takamatsu KG** Yd No: 125 Loa 56.50 Br ex - Dght 3.270 Lbp 52.30 Br md 9.50 Dpth 5.51 Welded, 1 dk	**(A31A2GX) General Cargo Ship**	**1 oil engine** reverse geared to sc. shaft driving 1 Propeller Total Power: 736kW (1,001hp) Hanshin LH28G 1 x 4 Stroke 6 Cy. 280 x 460 736kW (1001bhp) The Hanshin Diesel Works Ltd-Japan
7903823 - -	**SHINPO MARU No. 18** *ex* Jyunei Maru *-1992* *ex* Kuroshio Maru *-1987* **Century Product Inc** - *Indonesia*	*199* - 696		**1979-06 Nakatani Shipyard Co. Ltd. — Etajima** Yd No: 450 Loa 54.21 Br ex - Dght 3.101 Lbp 50.02 Br md 9.01 Dpth 3.41 Welded, 2 dks	**(A31A2GX) General Cargo Ship**	**1 oil engine** reduction geared to sc. shaft driving 1 FP propeller Total Power: 736kW (1,001hp) Niigata 6M26ZE 1 x 4 Stroke 6 Cy. 260 x 400 736kW (1001bhp) Niigata Engineering Co Ltd-Japan
8865353 - -	**SHINPO MARU No. 28** *ex* Yushin Maru No. 28 *-1996* - - *Philippines*	*199* - 656		**1992-12 Y.K. Akamatsu Zosen — Uwajima** Yd No: 123 L reg 54.70 Br ex - Dght 3.220 Lbp - Br md 9.60 Dpth 5.40 Welded, 1 dk	**(A31A2GX) General Cargo Ship**	**1 oil engine** driving 1 FP propeller
9677064 *JD3456*	**SHINPU MARU** - **Sanko Unyu KK** - *Matsuyama, Ehime* *Japan* MMSI: 431004247 Official number: 141824	*749* - 1,528		**2013-04 Nakatani Shipyard Co. Ltd. — Etajima** Yd No: 632 Loa 70.90 Br ex - Dght - Lbp - Br md 12.00 Dpth - Welded, 1 dk	**(A12A2TC) Chemical Tanker**	**1 oil engine** reverse geared to sc. shaft driving 1 Propeller Total Power: 1,618kW (2,200hp) Akasaka AX33BR 1 x 4 Stroke 6 Cy. 330 x 620 1618kW (2200bhp) Akasaka Tekkosho KK (Akasaka DieselLtd)-Japan
9180645 *JL6543* -	**SHINPUKU MARU** **Omaezaki Kaiun KK** - *Imabari, Ehime* *Japan* MMSI: 431500572 Official number: 135573	*691* - 2,000		**1997-04 K.K. Uno Zosensho — Imabari** Yd No: 508 Loa 78.00 Br ex - Dght - Lbp 71.70 Br md 13.50 Dpth 7.60 Welded, 1 dk	**(A31A2GX) General Cargo Ship**	**1 oil engine** driving 1 FP propeller Total Power: 1,471kW (2,000hp) 11.0kn Hanshin LH36LA 1 x 4 Stroke 6 Cy. 360 x 670 1471kW (2000bhp) The Hanshin Diesel Works Ltd-Japan
8503163 - -	**SHINPUKU MARU No. 15** **Syuki Hiramoto**	*450* - 1,050		**1985-03 K.K. Miura Zosensho — Saiki** Yd No: 722 Loa - Br ex - Dght 3.401 Lbp 55.02 Br md 12.01 Dpth 5.87 Welded, 1 dk	**(A31A2GX) General Cargo Ship**	**1 oil engine** driving 1 FP propeller Total Power: 883kW (1,201hp) Makita LN31L 1 x 4 Stroke 6 Cy. 310 x 600 883kW (1201bhp) Makita Diesel Co Ltd-Japan
9205859 *JM6680* -	**SHINPUKU MARU No. 18** **Hirata Kaiun KK** - *Karatsu, Saga* *Japan* Official number: 136427	*499* - 1,450		**1999-06 Honda Zosen — Saiki** Yd No: 1018 Loa 76.32 Br ex - Dght 3.850 Lbp 71.50 Br md 12.60 Dpth 6.85 Welded, 1 dk	**(A31A2GX) General Cargo Ship**	**1 oil engine** driving 1 FP propeller Total Power: 1,471kW (2,000hp) 13.0kn Niigata 6M34BGT 1 x 4 Stroke 6 Cy. 340 x 620 1471kW (2000bhp) Niigata Engineering Co Ltd-Japan
9250880 *JM6683* -	**SHINPUKU MARU No. 21** **Hirata Kaiun KK** - *Karatsu, Saga* *Japan* MMSI: 431602058 Official number: 136851	*734* - 2,000		**2001-05 Honda Zosen — Saiki** Yd No: 1025 Loa 79.95 Br ex - Dght 4.700 Lbp 75.00 Br md 13.00 Dpth 7.80 Welded, 1 dk	**(A31A2GX) General Cargo Ship**	**1 oil engine** driving 1 FP propeller Total Power: 2,060kW (2,801hp) 14.0kn Niigata 6M38GT 1 x 4 Stroke 6 Cy. 380 x 720 2060kW (2801bhp) Niigata Engineering Co Ltd-Japan
8997168 *JD2028* -	**SHINPUKU MARU NO. 22** **Hirata Kaiun KK** - *Karatsu, Saga* *Japan* Official number: 140064	*499* - 1,600		**2004-08 K.K. Watanabe Zosensho — Nagasaki** Yd No: 115 L reg 71.63 Br ex - Dght 4.090 Lbp 69.00 Br md 12.00 Dpth 7.38 Welded, 1 dk	**(A31A2GX) General Cargo Ship**	**1 oil engine** driving 1 Propeller Total Power: 736kW (1,001hp) Niigata 6M34BGT 1 x 4 Stroke 6 Cy. 340 x 620 736kW (1001bhp) Niigata Engineering Co Ltd-Japan
9427718 *JD2458*	**SHINPUU** **Fukuoka Prefecture** - *Fukuoka, Fukuoka* *Japan* Official number: 140581	*114* - -		**2007-09 Universal Shipbuilding Corp — Yokohama KN (Keihin Shipyard)** Yd No: 0039 Loa 34.82 Br ex - Dght 1.240 Lbp 31.53 Br md 6.50 Dpth 3.12 Welded, 1 dk	**(B12D2FP) Fishery Patrol Vessel** Hull Material: Aluminium Alloy	**2 oil engines** reduction geared to sc. shafts driving 2 Propellers Total Power: 5,440kW (7,396hp) M.T.U. 16V4000M90 2 x Vee 4 Stroke 16 Cy. 165 x 190 each-2720kW (3698bhp) MTU Friedrichshafen GmbH-Friedrichshafen
7903419 - -	**SHINRIKI** *ex* Shinriki Maru No. 11 *-1996* - -	*294* - 400		**1979-12 Masui Zosensho K.K. — Nandan** Yd No: 156 Loa - Br ex - Dght - Lbp 42.02 Br md 7.92 Dpth 3.41 Welded, 1 dk	**(A13B2TU) Tanker (unspecified)**	**1 oil engine** driving 1 FP propeller Total Power: 552kW (750hp) Niigata 6M26ZE 1 x 4 Stroke 6 Cy. 260 x 400 552kW (750bhp) Niigata Engineering Co Ltd-Japan
8879524 *JM6400* -	**SHINRIKI MARU** *ex* Shinriki Maru No. 8 *-2011* **Yotsumi Kaiun YK** - *Tonosho, Kagawa* *Japan* Official number: 134473	*499* - 1,299		**1994-11 K.K. Kamishima Zosensho — Osakikamijima** Yd No: 570 Loa 69.41 Br ex - Dght 3.960 Lbp 60.00 Br md 13.00 Dpth 6.10 Welded, 1 dk	**(A31A2GX) General Cargo Ship**	**1 oil engine** driving 1 FP propeller Total Power: 736kW (1,001hp) 10.0kn Hanshin LH34LG 1 x 4 Stroke 6 Cy. 340 x 640 736kW (1001bhp) The Hanshin Diesel Works Ltd-Japan
8609149 - -	**SHINRIKI MARU No. 8** *ex* Kyokusho Maru *-1991* - - *Madagascar*	*199* 118 699		**1986-06 K.K. Taihei Kogyo — Akitsu** Yd No: 1901 Loa 55.52 (BB) Br ex - Dght 3.020 Lbp 51.00 Br md 9.50 Dpth 5.20 Welded, 2 dks	**(A31A2GX) General Cargo Ship** Compartments: 1 Ho, ER 1 Ha: ER	**1 oil engine** driving 1 FP propeller Total Power: 588kW (799hp) 11.0kn Hanshin 6LU28G 1 x 4 Stroke 6 Cy. 280 x 440 588kW (799bhp) The Hanshin Diesel Works Ltd-Japan
8822296 *JJ3626* -	**SHINRIKI MARU No. 15** **Yoheiji Arai** - *Himeji, Hyogo* *Japan* Official number: 131832	*471* - 590		**1989-03 Shitanoe Shipbuilding Co Ltd — Usuki OT** Yd No: 1095 Loa 49.91 (BB) Br ex - Dght 3.450 Lbp 46.00 Br md 10.50 Dpth 5.68 Welded, 1 dk	**(B33A2DG) Grab Dredger** Bale: 402 Compartments: 1 Ho, ER 1 Ha: ER	**1 oil engine** reverse geared to sc. shaft driving 1 FP propeller Total Power: 552kW (750hp) Matsui ML628GSC 1 x 4 Stroke 6 Cy. 280 x 520 552kW (750bhp) Matsui Iron Works Co Ltd-Japan
9033086 *JJ3772* -	**SHINRIKI MARU No. 18** **Miyatama Kaiun KK** - *Himeji, Hyogo* *Japan* Official number: 132271	*499* - 1,237		**1991-06 Hitachi Zosen Mukaishima Marine Co Ltd — Onomichi HS** Yd No: 50 Loa 64.69 (BB) Br ex 13.30 Dght 4.211 Lbp 59.00 Br md 13.20 Dpth 6.30 Welded	**(A24D2BA) Aggregates Carrier** Grain: 2,400 Compartments: 1 Ho, ER 1 Ha: ER	**1 oil engine** driving 1 FP propeller Total Power: 736kW (1,001hp) Matsui M31M28 1 x 4 Stroke 6 Cy. 310 x 550 736kW (1001bhp) Matsui Iron Works Co Ltd-Japan
8864440 *JK5129* -	**SHINRIKI No. 5** **Fudo Kaiun YK** - *Kagoshima, Kagoshima* *Japan* Official number: 133037	*199* - 609		**1992-05 YK Furumoto Tekko Zosensho — Osakikamijima** Yd No: 600 Loa 57.21 Br ex 9.80 Dght 3.050 Lbp 52.00 Br md 9.70 Dpth 5.30 Welded, 2 dks	**(A31A2GX) General Cargo Ship** Compartments: 1 Ho, ER	**1 oil engine** reverse geared to sc. shaft driving 1 FP propeller Total Power: 552kW (750hp) 11.0kn Matsui ML627GSC 1 x 4 Stroke 6 Cy. 270 x 480 552kW (750bhp) Matsui Iron Works Co Ltd-Japan
9291341 *7JIN* -	**SHINRYO MARU** **Nippon Yusen Kabushiki Kaisha (NYK Line)** Hachiuma Steamship Co Ltd (Hachiuma Kisen KK) *Okinawa, Okinawa* *Japan* MMSI: 432800000 Official number: 141357	**50,464** 28,813 91,443 T/cm 88.1	Class: NK	**2003-08 Oshima Shipbuilding Co Ltd — Saikai NS** Yd No: 10349 Loa 235.00 (BB) Br ex - Dght 12.929 Lbp 226.00 Br md 43.00 Dpth 18.55 Welded, 1 dk	**(A21A2BC) Bulk Carrier** Grain: 111,787 Compartments: 5 Ho, ER 5 Ha: (24.7 x 21.0)2 (24.7 x 21.0) (22.0 x 21.0)ER (22.9 x 21.0)	**1 oil engine** driving 1 FP propeller Total Power: 11,915kW (16,200hp) 14.3kn Mitsubishi 6UEC60LSII 1 x 2 Stroke 6 Cy. 600 x 2300 11915kW (16200bhp) Mitsubishi Heavy Industries Ltd-Japan Fuel: 3190.0

Identity	Name / Owner	Tonnage	Class	Construction	Type	Machinery
8633425 - -	**SHINRYO MARU No. 5** - -	*121* - -		**1973-09 Kidoura Shipyard Co Ltd — Kesennuma MG** L reg 29.10 Br ex - Dght 2.100 Lbp - Br md 6.20 Dpth 2.60 Welded, 1 dk	**(B11B2FV) Fishing Vessel**	**1 oil engine** driving 1 FP propeller
9140114 *JHBF* -	**SHINRYU** **Banyo Jitsugyo KK** Shinko Senpaku KK *Tokyo* *Japan* MMSI: 431843000 Official number: 135230	*499* - -		**1996-03 KK Kanasashi — Shizuoka SZ** Yd No: 3378 Loa 62.00 (BB) Br ex - Dght 3.800 Lbp 55.00 Br md 9.00 Dpth 4.00 Welded, 1 dk	**(B12D2FP) Fishery Patrol Vessel**	**1 oil engine** with flexible couplings & sr reverse geared to sc. shaft driving 1 FP propeller Total Power: 1,839kW (2,500hp) Akasaka 6U28AK 1 x 4 Stroke 6 Cy. 280 x 380 1839kW (2500bhp) Akasaka Tekkosho KK (Akasaka DieselLtd)-Japan
9110303 *JM6289* -	**SHINRYU** **Yahata Senpaku Kyogyo Kumiai** - *Kitakyushu, Fukuoka* *Japan* MMSI: 431600251 Official number: 133562	*747* - 2,100		**1994-07 Yamanaka Zosen K.K. — Imabari** Yd No: 562 Loa - Br ex - Dght 4.470 Lbp 80.00 Br md 13.00 Dpth 7.80 Welded, 1 dk	**(A31A2GX) General Cargo Ship**	**1 oil engine** driving 1 FP propeller Total Power: 1,765kW (2,400hp) Hanshin LH36L 1 x 4 Stroke 6 Cy. 360 x 670 1765kW (2400bhp) The Hanshin Diesel Works Ltd-Japan
9048500 *JM6109* -	**SHINRYU MARU** **Kanda Senpaku Kyogyo Kumiai** - *Tsukumi, Oita* *Japan* MMSI: 431400021 Official number: 132763	*699* - 1,500	Class: NK	**1992-07 Kambara Marine Development & Shipbuilding Co Ltd — Fukuyama HS** Yd No: OE-173 Loa 68.98 (BB) Br ex 11.52 Dght 4.337 Lbp 65.00 Br md 11.50 Dpth 5.10 Welded, 1 dk	**(A24A2BT) Cement Carrier** Grain: 1,467 Compartments: 4 Ho, ER	**1 oil engine** with clutches, flexible couplings & sr geared to sc. shaft driving 1 CP propeller Total Power: 1,177kW (1,600hp) 11.0kn Yanmar MF29-ST 1 x 4 Stroke 6 Cy. 290 x 520 1177kW (1600bhp) Matsue Diesel KK-Japan AuxGen: 1 x 280kW 445V 60Hz a.c Fuel: 60.0 (d.f.)
9234197 *JPCV* -	**SHINRYU MARU** **Offshore Engineering Co Ltd** Fukada Salvage & Marine Works Co Ltd (Fukada Salvage Kensetsu KK) *Tokyo* *Japan* MMSI: 431195000 Official number: 136977	**998** 299 1,112	Class: NK	**2000-12 Niigata Engineering Co Ltd — Niigata NI** Yd No: 2378 Loa 60.98 (BB) Br ex - Dght 4.743 Lbp 54.43 Br md 11.80 Dpth 5.45 Welded, 1 dk	**(B21B20A) Anchor Handling Tug Supply**	**2 oil engines** gearing integral to driving 2 Z propellers Total Power: 2,942kW (4,000hp) 13.0kn Niigata 6L28HX 2 x 4 Stroke 6 Cy. 280 x 370 each-1471kW (2000bhp) Niigata Engineering Co Ltd-Japan AuxGen: 1 x 200kW 445V 60Hz a.c Thrusters: 1 Thwart. CP thruster (f) Fuel: 519.0 (d.f.)
8909769 *JKBT* -	**SHINRYU MARU NO. 1** *ex* Choyo Maru No. 7 *-2007* *ex* Daitoku Maru No. 55 *-1991* **KK Shinryu Suisan** SatCom: Inmarsat A 1200260 *Tokyo* *Japan* MMSI: 432508000 Official number: 130767	*379* - 445		**1989-09 Miho Zosensho K.K. — Shimizu** Yd No: 1369 Loa 54.74 (BB) Br ex 8.62 Dght 3.409 Lbp 48.00 Br md 8.60 Dpth 3.75 Welded	**(B11B2FV) Fishing Vessel** Ins: 741	**1 oil engine** with clutches & sr reverse geared to sc. shaft driving 1 FP propeller Total Power: 736kW (1,001hp) Niigata 6M28HFT 1 x 4 Stroke 6 Cy. 280 x 480 736kW (1001bhp) Niigata Engineering Co Ltd-Japan
9088706 *JL6325* -	**SHINRYU MARU No. 8** **Hamamoto Kaijo Unso YK** - *Shodoshima, Kagawa* *Japan* Official number: 134895	*198* - 550		**1994-08 Suzuki Shipyard Co. Ltd. — Yokkaichi** Yd No: 617 Loa 40.01 Br ex - Dght - Lbp 36.00 Br md 8.80 Dpth 3.80 Welded, 1 dk	**(A13B2TP) Products Tanker** 2 Cargo Pump (s): 2x400m³/hr	**1 oil engine** driving 1 FP propeller Total Power: 588kW (799hp) 10.2kn Matsui 6M26KGHS 1 x 4 Stroke 6 Cy. 260 x 400 588kW (799bhp) Matsui Iron Works Co Ltd-Japan
8915158 *JIRS* S01-1088	**SHINRYU MARU NO. 11** *ex* Fujisei Maru No. 27 *-2007* **KK Shinryu Suisan** SatCom: Inmarsat A 1204351 *Tokyo* *Japan* MMSI: 431200450 Official number: 130096	*379* - -		**1990-02 Niigata Engineering Co Ltd — Niigata NI** Yd No: 2167 Loa 54.07 (BB) Br ex - Dght 3.440 Lbp 47.91 Br md 8.70 Dpth 3.80 Welded, 1 dk	**(B11B2FV) Fishing Vessel** Ins: 468	**1 oil engine** with clutches, flexible couplings & sr reverse geared to sc. shaft driving 1 FP propeller Total Power: 699kW (950hp) Niigata 6M28BFT 1 x 4 Stroke 6 Cy. 280 x 480 699kW (950bhp) Niigata Engineering Co Ltd-Japan
8910976 *JKJQ* -	**SHINRYU MARU NO. 21** *ex* Fukuyoshi Maru No. 56 *-2008* *ex* Chidori Maru No. 20 *-1999* **KK Shinryu Suisan** SatCom: Inmarsat A 1206422 *Tokyo* *Japan* MMSI: 431704460 Official number: 130896	*379* - -		**1990-01 Niigata Engineering Co Ltd — Niigata NI** Yd No: 2136 Loa 54.58 (BB) Br ex - Dght 3.440 Lbp 47.90 Br md 8.70 Dpth 3.80 Welded, 1 dk	**(B11B2FV) Fishing Vessel** Ins: 494	**1 oil engine** with clutches, flexible couplings & sr reverse geared to sc. shaft driving 1 FP propeller Total Power: 699kW (950hp) Niigata 6M28BFT 1 x 4 Stroke 6 Cy. 280 x 480 699kW (950bhp) Niigata Engineering Co Ltd-Japan
8619168 - -	**SHINRYUSHO MARU** **Rui Feng (HK) Marine Co Ltd**	*157* - 66	Class: (NK)	**1987-03 K.K. Odo Zosen Tekko — Shimonoseki** Yd No: 327 Loa 29.05 Br ex 8.44 Dght - Lbp 26.20 Br md 8.20 Dpth 3.90 Welded, 1 dk	**(B32B2SP) Pusher Tug**	**2 oil engines** with clutches, flexible couplings & dr geared to sc. shafts driving 2 Directional propellers Total Power: 1,472kW (2,002hp) 11.0kn Yanmar T260-ST 2 x 4 Stroke 6 Cy. 260 x 330 each-736kW (1001bhp) Yanmar Diesel Engine Co Ltd-Japan Fuel: 31.0 (d.f.)
8890102 *JG5237* -	**SHINSEI** *ex* Seiwa Maru *-2011* **Yano Kaiun KK (Yano Shipping Co Ltd)** - *Kitakyushu, Fukuoka* *Japan* Official number: 134945	*243* - -		**1995-09 Keihin Dock Co Ltd — Yokohama** Yd No: 241 Loa 36.20 Br ex - Dght 3.200 Lbp 31.50 Br md 9.80 Dpth 4.38 Welded, 1 dk	**(B32A2ST) Tug**	**2 oil engines** driving 2 FP propellers Total Power: 2,942kW (4,000hp) 13.5kn Niigata 6L28HX 2 x 4 Stroke 6 Cy. 280 x 370 each-1471kW (2000bhp) Niigata Engineering Co Ltd-Japan
8889672 *JM6439* -	**SHINSEI** **Akikazu Mori** - *Kasaoka, Okayama* *Japan* Official number: 134534	*199* - 654		**1995-04 YK Furumoto Tekko Zosensho — Osakikamijima** Yd No: 615 Loa 57.45 Br ex - Dght 3.800 Lbp 51.00 Br md 9.50 Dpth 5.55 Welded, 1 dk	**(A31A2GX) General Cargo Ship** Grain: 1,170 Compartments: 1 Ho, ER 1 Ha: (30.0 x 7.5)ER	**1 oil engine** driving 1 FP propeller Total Power: 736kW (1,001hp) 11.0kn Matsui ML627GSC 1 x 4 Stroke 6 Cy. 270 x 480 736kW (1001bhp) Matsui Iron Works Co Ltd-Japan
8728141 - -	**SHINSEI** *ex* Shinsei Maru No. 18 *-2000* - - -	**193** 80 -		**1984 Higashi Kyushu Shipbuilding Co Ltd — Usuki OT** L reg 28.10 Br ex - Dght 1.700 Lbp - Br md 6.10 Dpth 2.40 Bonded, 1 dk	**(B11B2FV) Fishing Vessel** Hull Material: Reinforced Plastic	**1 oil engine** driving 1 FP propeller Total Power: 272kW (370hp) Yanmar 1 x 4 Stroke 272kW (370bhp) Yanmar Diesel Engine Co Ltd-Japan
9119880 *JGSE* TK1-1325	**SHINSEI** *ex* Hatsutaka *-2001* **Toyo Senpaku Co Ltd** - *Tokyo* *Japan* MMSI: 431728000 Official number: 135008	*449* - -		**1995-03 KK Kanasashi — Shizuoka SZ** Yd No: 3363 Loa 62.00 Br ex - Dght 3.700 Lbp 55.00 Br md 9.00 Dpth 4.00 Welded, 1 dk	**(B12D2FP) Fishery Patrol Vessel**	**1 oil engine** reduction geared to sc. shaft driving 1 FP propeller Total Power: 2,427kW (3,300hp) 17.0kn Akasaka 8U28AK 1 x 4 Stroke 8 Cy. 280 x 380 2427kW (3300bhp) Akasaka Tekkosho KK (Akasaka DieselLtd)-Japan AuxGen: 2 x 220kW a.c Thrusters: 1 Thwart. FP thruster (f) Fuel: 282.0 (d.f.) 3.0pd
9346990 *JD2214* -	**SHINSEI** **Yamanaka Kaiun YK** - *Kamiamakusa, Kumamoto* *Japan* Official number: 140286	*199* - 800		**2006-01 Yano Zosen K.K. — Imabari** Yd No: 207 Loa 55.30 Br ex - Dght 3.690 Lbp 49.50 Br md 9.20 Dpth 5.95 Welded, 1 dk	**(A31A2GX) General Cargo Ship**	**1 oil engine** geared to sc. shaft driving 1 FP propeller Total Power: 735kW (999hp) 11.0kn Niigata 6M26AGTE 1 x 4 Stroke 6 Cy. 260 x 460 735kW (999bhp) Niigata Engineering Co Ltd-Japan

IMO / Call sign	Name / Owner	Tonnage	Class	Built	Type	Machinery
9347217 *JD2188* -	**SHINSEI MARU** **Japan Railway Construction, Transport & Technology Agency & Tabuchi Kaiun Co Ltd** Tabuchi Kaiun Co Ltd *Osaka, Osaka* *Japan* MMSI: 431301775 Official number: 140256	*3,779* - 4,999	Class: NK	**2005-12 K.K. Miura Zosensho — Saiki** Yd No: 1302 Loa 104.85 Br ex 16.02 Dght 6.400 Lbp 99.20 Br md 16.00 Dpth 8.10 Welded, 1 dk	**(A13B2TP) Products Tanker** Double Hull (13F) Liq: 6,272; Liq (Oil): 6,400	**1 oil engine** driving 1 FP propeller Total Power: 3,900kW (5,302hp) 13.5kn MAN-B&W 6L35MC 1 x 2 Stroke 6 Cy. 350 x 1050 3900kW (5302bhp) Makita Corp-Japan Fuel: 270.0
9243722 *JPFQ* -	**SHINSEI MARU** **Offshore Engineering Co Ltd** Fukada Salvage & Marine Works Co Ltd (Fukada Salvage Kensetsu KK) *Tokyo* *Japan* MMSI: 432301000 Official number: 137003	**997** 299 1,121	Class: NK	**2001-05 Niigata Engineering Co Ltd — Niigata NI** Yd No: 2382 Loa 60.98 (BB) Br ex - Dght 4.743 Lbp 51.05 Br md 11.80 Dpth 5.45 Welded, 1 dk	**(B21B20A) Anchor Handling Tug Supply**	**2 oil engines** gearing integral to driving 2 Z propellers Total Power: 2,942kW (4,000hp) 13.0kn Niigata 6L28HX 2 x 4 Stroke 6 Cy. 280 x 370 each-1471kW (2000bhp) Niigata Engineering Co Ltd-Japan AuxGen: 1 x 200kW 445V 60Hz a.c Thrusters: 1 Thwart. CP thruster (f) Fuel: 519.0 (d.f.)
9279458 *JD2762* -	**SHINSEI MARU** **Otaru Kisen Gyogyo GK** - *Otaru, Hokkaido* *Japan* Official number: 135345	*160* - -		**2002-08 Narasaki Zosen KK — Muroran HK** Yd No: 1175 Loa 37.31 Br ex - Dght 3.350 Lbp 30.50 Br md 7.90 Dpth 4.70 Welded, 1 Dk.	**(B11B2FV) Fishing Vessel**	**1 oil engine** driving 1 Propeller Total Power: 1,029kW (1,399hp) Hanshin 6MUH28 1 x 4 Stroke 6 Cy. 280 x 340 1029kW (1399bhp) The Hanshin Diesel Works Ltd-Japan
9251585 *JPPE* -	**SHINSEI MARU** **JX Tanker Co Ltd & Showa Nittan Corp** JX Ocean Co Ltd *Tokyo* *Japan* MMSI: 432340000 Official number: 137115	**56,212** 32,655 106,361 T/cm 91.7	Class: NK	**2002-05 Nippon Kokan KK (NKK Corp) — Tsu ME** Yd No: 221 Loa 243.00 Br ex - Dght 14.752 Lbp 233.00 Br md 42.00 Dpth 20.70 Welded, 1 dk	**(A13A2TV) Crude Oil Tanker** Double Hull (13F) Liq: 120,142; Liq (Oil): 120,142 3 Cargo Pump (s)	**1 oil engine** driving 1 FP propeller Total Power: 12,000kW (16,315hp) 14.5kn Sulzer 6RTA58T 1 x 2 Stroke 6 Cy. 580 x 2416 12000kW (16315bhp) Diesel United Ltd.-Aioi Fuel: 2680.0
9459888 *JD2531* -	**SHINSEI MARU** **Japan Railway Construction, Transport & Technology Agency & Heisei Shoun Co Ltd** Heisei Shoun KK *Saiki, Oita* *Japan* MMSI: 431000346 Official number: 140663	*749* - 1,872	Class: NK	**2007-11 Suzuki Shipyard Co. Ltd. — Yokkaichi** Yd No: 712 Loa 70.23 Br ex - Dght 4.740 Lbp 66.00 Br md 12.00 Dpth 5.20 Welded, 1 dk	**(A13B2TP) Products Tanker** Double Hull (13F) Liq: 2,057; Liq (Oil): 2,057	**1 oil engine** reverse geared to sc. shaft driving 1 FP propeller Total Power: 1,618kW (2,200hp) Akasaka AX33 1 x 4 Stroke 6 Cy. 330 x 620 1618kW (2200bhp) Akasaka Tekkosho KK (Akasaka DieselLtd)-Japan Fuel: 47.0 (d.f.)
9666003 *JD3498* -	**SHINSEI MARU** **Fukusho Kisen KK & YK Taoyama Kaiun** Fukusho Kisen KK *Ube, Yamaguchi* *Japan* MMSI: 431004315 Official number: 141891	*749* - 2,200	Class: NK	**2013-04 K.K. Miura Zosensho — Saiki** Yd No: 1385 Loa 79.60 Br ex - Dght 4.720 Lbp 75.00 Br md 14.00 Dpth 7.80 Welded, 1 dk	**(A24D2BA) Aggregates Carrier** Double Hull Grain: 2,432	**1 oil engine** reduction geared to sc. shaft driving 1 Propeller Total Power: 1,765kW (2,400hp) Yanmar 6EY26 1 x 4 Stroke 6 Cy. 260 x 385 1765kW (2400bhp) Yanmar Diesel Engine Co Ltd-Japan Fuel: 99.0
9660425 *7JOO* -	**SHINSEI MARU** **Independent Administrative Institution Japan Agency for Marine-Earth Science & Technology (JAMSTEC)** *Otsuchi, Iwate* *Japan* MMSI: 432928000 Official number: 141890	*1,629* 488 692	Class: NK	**2013-06 Mitsubishi Heavy Industries Ltd. — Shimonoseki** Yd No: 1166 Loa 66.00 (BB) Br ex - Dght 4.514 Lbp 61.06 Br md 13.00 Dpth 6.20 Welded, 1 dk	**(B31A2SR) Research Survey Vessel**	**2 diesel electric oil engines** driving 2 gen. Connecting to 2 elec. motors each (1300kW) driving 2 Azimuth electric drive units Total Power: 2,400kW (3,264hp) 12.0kn Daihatsu 6DEM-23 2 x 4 Stroke 6 Cy. 230 x 320 each-1200kW (1632bhp) Daihatsu Diesel Manufacturing Co Lt-Japan Thrusters: 1 Tunnel thruster (f) Fuel: 344.0
9129615 *JK5240* -	**SHINSEI MARU** *ex Shosei Maru -2009* - - *Onomichi, Hiroshima* *Japan* Official number: 134733	*499* - 1,553		**1995-10 K.K. Matsuura Zosensho — Osakikamijima** Yd No: 513 Loa 76.21 (BB) Br ex 12.02 Dght 4.240 Lbp 70.00 Br md 12.00 Dpth 7.20 Welded, 1 dk	**(A31A2GX) General Cargo Ship** Grain: 2,848; Bale: 2,832 Compartments: 1 Ho, ER 1 Ha: ER	**1 oil engine** driving 1 FP propeller Total Power: 736kW (1,001hp) Hanshin LH34LAG 1 x 4 Stroke 6 Cy. 340 x 640 736kW (1001bhp) The Hanshin Diesel Works Ltd-Japan Thrusters: 1 Thwart. FP thruster (f)
9156436 *JI3623* -	**SHINSEI MARU** *ex Fuji Maru No. 7 -2008* **Sanyo Kaiun Shokai Co Ltd (KK Sanyo Kaiun Shokai)** - *Osaka, Osaka* *Japan* MMSI: 431300454 Official number: 135921	*1,594* - 3,264	Class: NK	**1996-10 Hakata Zosen K.K. — Imabari** Yd No: 607 Loa 86.45 Br ex - Dght 5.564 Lbp 81.50 Br md 14.00 Dpth 6.20 Welded, 1 dk	**(A13B2TP) Products Tanker** Liq: 3,500; Liq (Oil): 3,500	**1 oil engine** driving 1 FP propeller Total Power: 2,207kW (3,001hp) Hanshin LH38L 1 x 4 Stroke 6 Cy. 380 x 760 2207kW (3001bhp) The Hanshin Diesel Works Ltd-Japan Fuel: 110.0 (d.f.)
9037991 *JL6108* -	**SHINSEI MARU** **Yasukochi Kaiun YK** - *Kobe, Hyogo* *Japan* Official number: 133002	*269* - 740		**1992-08 Imura Zosen K.K. — Komatsushima** Yd No: 261 Loa 61.00 Br ex - Dght 3.460 Lbp 55.00 Br md 9.80 Dpth 5.60 Welded, 2 dks	**(A31A2GX) General Cargo Ship** Bale: 1,446 Compartments: 1 Ho, ER 1 Ha: ER	**1 oil engine** reverse geared to sc. shaft driving 1 FP propeller Total Power: 662kW (900hp) Hanshin LH26G 1 x 4 Stroke 6 Cy. 260 x 440 662kW (900bhp) The Hanshin Diesel Works Ltd-Japan
9038012 *JJ3697* -	**SHINSEI MARU** **Shin Marubishi Kaiun KK** - *Kobe, Hyogo* *Japan* Official number: 132337	*193* - -		**1991-06 Kanagawa Zosen — Kobe** Yd No: 359 L reg 29.90 Br ex - Dght - Lbp - Br md 9.20 Dpth 4.10 Welded	**(B32A2ST) Tug**	**2 oil engines** geared to sc. shafts driving 2 FP propellers Total Power: 2,648kW (3,600hp) Yanmar 6Z280-EN 2 x 4 Stroke 6 Cy. 280 x 360 each-1324kW (1800bhp) Yanmar Diesel Engine Co Ltd-Japan
9038086 *JK5057* -	**SHINSEI MARU** **YK Taoyama Kaiun** - *Hofu, Yamaguchi* *Japan* MMSI: 431400859 Official number: 132467	*499* - 912		**1991-10 K.K. Miura Zosensho — Saiki** Yd No: 1017 Loa - Br ex - Dght 4.010 Lbp 58.00 Br md 10.50 Dpth 4.50 Welded	**(A31A2GX) General Cargo Ship**	**1 oil engine** geared to sc. shaft driving 1 FP propeller Total Power: 736kW (1,001hp) Daihatsu 6DLM-24 1 x 4 Stroke 6 Cy. 240 x 320 736kW (1001bhp) Daihatsu Diesel Manufacturing Co Lt-Japan
8986511 *JI3713* -	**SHINSEI MARU** **Tsukiboshi Kaiun KK** - *Osaka, Osaka* *Japan* Official number: 137239	*150* - -		**2003-10 K.K. Watanabe Zosensho — Nagasaki** Yd No: 107 Loa 17.61 Br ex - Dght - Lbp - Br md 12.12 Dpth 6.34 Welded, 1 dk	**(B32B2SP) Pusher Tug**	**1 oil engine** driving 1 Propeller Total Power: 2,206kW (2,999hp) Niigata 6MG28HLX 1 x 4 Stroke 6 Cy. 280 x 400 2206kW (2999bhp) Niigata Engineering Co Ltd-Japan
8731382 *JD2360* -	**SHINSEI MARU** **YK Shinsei Kaiun** - *Kure, Hiroshima* *Japan* MMSI: 431402073 Official number: 140469	*497* - 1,780		**2007-03 Fukushima Zosen Ltd. — Matsue** Yd No: 356 Loa 74.00 Br ex - Dght 4.350 Lbp 69.00 Br md 12.00 Dpth 7.38 Welded, 1 dk	**(A31A2GX) General Cargo Ship** Grain: 2,515; Bale: 2,515 Compartments: 1 Ho, ER 1 Ha: ER (40.0 x 9.5)	**1 oil engine** driving 1 Propeller Total Power: 1,618kW (2,200hp) Niigata 6M34BGT 1 x 4 Stroke 6 Cy. 340 x 620 1618kW (2200bhp) Niigata Engineering Co Ltd-Japan
8844660 *JJ3761* -	**SHINSEI MARU** *ex Sumiyoshi Maru -1994* - - *Oita, Oita* *Japan* Official number: 131879	*485* - 534		**1990-10 Ieshima Dock K.K. — Himeji** Loa 45.00 Br ex - Dght 3.020 Lbp 41.00 Br md 11.50 Dpth 5.20 Welded, 1 dk	**(B33A2DG) Grab Dredger**	**1 oil engine** driving 1 FP propeller Total Power: 515kW (700hp) 10.0kn Matsui ML628GSC 1 x 4 Stroke 6 Cy. 280 x 520 515kW (700bhp) Matsui Iron Works Co Ltd-Japan
8747850 *JD2901* -	**SHINSEI MARU** **YK Marinos** - *Kure, Hiroshima* *Japan* Official number: 140998	*135* - 238		**2009-07 K.K. Watanabe Zosensho — Nagasaki** Yd No: 156 Loa 16.00 Br ex - Dght 4.300 Lbp 14.50 Br md 12.19 Dpth 6.00 Welded, 1 dk	**(B32B2SP) Pusher Tug**	**1 oil engine** reduction geared to sc. shaft driving 1 Propeller Total Power: 1,471kW (2,000hp) 8.5kn Niigata 6MG26HLX 1 x 4 Stroke 6 Cy. 260 x 350 1471kW (2000bhp) Niigata Engineering Co Ltd-Japan

ID	Name / Owner	Tonnage	Class	Build / Dimensions	Type	Machinery
8890695 *JM6397* -	**SHINSEI MARU** *ex* Yusei Maru *-2008* **Yoshikazu Izumi** - *Kainan, Tokushima* *Japan* Official number: 134575	*149* - -		**1995**-11 **Mikami Zosen K.K. — Japan** Yd No: 338 L reg 36.20 Br ex - Dght - Lbp - Br md 7.30 Dpth 3.10 Welded, 1 dk	**(A13B2TU) Tanker (unspecified)**	**1 oil engine** driving 1 FP propeller Total Power: 441kW (600hp) 9.6kn Yanmar MF24-HT 1 x 4 Stroke 6 Cy. 240 x 420 441kW (600bhp) Yanmar Diesel Engine Co Ltd-Japan
8923820 *JG5456*	**SHINSEI MARU** - **YK Shinsei Maru** - *Niijima, Tokyo* *Japan* Official number: 135816	*155* - 359		**1996**-04 **K.K. Tago Zosensho — Nishi-Izu** Yd No: 265 Loa 49.97 Br ex - Dght 2.870 Lbp 46.00 Br md 8.20 Dpth 4.70 Welded, 1 dk	**(A31A2GX) General Cargo Ship** Compartments: 1 Ho, ER 1 Ha: (22.0 x 5.3)ER	**1 oil engine** driving 1 FP propeller Total Power: 736kW (1,001hp) 12.0kn Yanmar MF26-SD 1 x 4 Stroke 6 Cy. 260 x 500 736kW (1001bhp) Yanmar Diesel Engine Co Ltd-Japan
8627220 - -	**SHINSEI MARU** - - - *Chinese Taipei*	*190* - 512		**1984 Shin Nippon Jukogyo K.K. — Osakikamijima** Yd No: 195 Loa 51.21 Br ex - Dght 3.350 Lbp 46.00 Br md 8.21 Dpth 5.01 Welded, 1 dk	**(A31A2GX) General Cargo Ship** Grain: 1,229; Bale: 1,152	**1 oil engine** driving 1 FP propeller Total Power: 441kW (600hp) 10.0kn Yanmar 1 x 4 Stroke 441kW (600bhp) Yanmar Diesel Engine Co Ltd-Japan
8317320 - -	**SHINSEI MARU** *ex* Sun Lake *-1989* *ex* Daiten *-1985* - - *South Korea*	**737** 221 662	Class: (NK)	**1983**-12 **Sanyo Zosen K.K. — Onomichi** Yd No: 868 Converted From: Tug-1991 Loa 49.92 Br ex 10.83 Dght 3.958 Lbp 45.17 Br md 10.80 Dpth 4.50 Welded, 1 dk	**(B32B2SP) Pusher Tug**	**2 oil engines** with clutches, flexible couplings & sr reverse geared to sc. shafts driving 2 FP propellers Total Power: 3,678kW (5,000hp) 12.0kn Daihatsu 8DSM-28 2 x 4 Stroke 8 Cy. 280 x 340 each-1839kW (2500bhp) Daihatsu Diesel Manufacturing Co Lt-Japan AuxGen: 2 x 160kW Thrusters: 1 Thwart. CP thruster (f)
8319172 - -	**SHINSEI MARU** *ex* Meiwa Maru No. 5 *-1988* - -	*499* 301 1,233	Class: (NK)	**1984**-03 **Kochi Jyuko (Kaisei Zosen) K.K. — Kochi** Yd No: 1650 Loa 64.83 (BB) Br ex - Dght 4.388 Lbp 59.01 Br md 10.00 Dpth 4.60 Welded, 1 dk	**(A12A2TC) Chemical Tanker** Liq: 1,300 Compartments: 8 Ta, ER	**1 oil engine** sr geared to sc. shaft driving 1 FP propeller Total Power: 956kW (1,300hp) Akasaka DM28A 1 x 4 Stroke 6 Cy. 280 x 460 956kW (1300bhp) Akasaka Tekkosho KK (Akasaka DieselLtd)-Japan
8220888 - -	**SHINSEI MARU** *ex* Kisei Maru *-1995* **In Sung Shipping Co Ltd** - *South Korea*	*128* 56 220		**1982 Hatayama Zosen KK — Yura WK** Yd No: 163 Loa 30.10 Br ex - Dght 2.500 Lbp 28.00 Br md 6.00 Dpth 2.60 Welded, 1 dk	**(A13B2TP) Products Tanker** Liq: 220; Liq (Oil): 220 Compartments: 6 Ta, ER	**1 oil engine** driving 1 FP propeller Total Power: 221kW (300hp) 9.0kn Niigata 6MG16S 1 x 4 Stroke 6 Cy. 160 x 200 221kW (300bhp) Niigata Engineering Co Ltd-Japan
8997156 *JD2066*	**SHINSEI MARU NO. 1** - **Shinsei Kaiun KK** - *Shikokuchuo, Ehime* *Japan* Official number: 140058	*299* - 711		**2005**-01 **Koa Sangyo KK — Takamatsu KG** L reg 48.00 Br ex - Dght 3.600 Lbp 48.00 Br md 8.80 Dpth 3.80 Welded, 1 dk	**(A12A2TC) Chemical Tanker** Double Hull (13F) Liq: 620	**1 oil engine** driving 1 Propeller
7722449 *JK3910* -	**SHINSEI MARU No. 2** *ex* Tamano Maru *-1996* **Nipponkai Koun KK** - *Takahama, Fukui* *Japan* Official number: 120372	*156* - -		**1977**-11 **Kanagawa Zosen — Kobe** Yd No: 180 Loa 29.80 Br ex - Dght 2.601 Lbp 25.51 Br md 8.62 Dpth 3.70 Welded, 1 dk	**(B32A2ST) Tug**	**2 oil engines** Geared Integral to driving 2 Z propellers Total Power: 1,912kW (2,600hp) 6L25BX Niigata 2 x 4 Stroke 6 Cy. 250 x 320 each-956kW (1300bhp) Niigata Engineering Co Ltd-Japan
8520094 *JAAL* -	**SHINSEI MARU No. 3** - **Taiyo A&F Co Ltd (Taiyo A&F KK)** - SatCom: Inmarsat A 1200520 *Yaizu, Shizuoka* *Japan* MMSI: 432521000 Official number: 128862	*495* - -		**1986**-02 **KK Kanasashi Zosen — Shizuoka SZ** Yd No: 3101 Loa 53.52 (BB) Br ex 8.74 Dght 3.401 Lbp 46.89 Br md 8.70 Dpth 3.76 Welded, 1 dk	**(B11B2FV) Fishing Vessel**	**1 oil engine** with clutches, flexible couplings & sr reverse geared to sc. shaft driving 1 FP propeller Total Power: 736kW (1,001hp) Hanshin 6LUN28AG 1 x 4 Stroke 6 Cy. 280 x 480 736kW (1001bhp) The Hanshin Diesel Works Ltd-Japan
9041538 *JK5120*	**SHINSEI MARU No. 3** - **Shinsei Kaiun KK** - *Kure, Hiroshima* *Japan* Official number: 132525	*498* - 1,285	Class: NK	**1992**-01 **Hitachi Zosen Mukaishima Marine Co Ltd — Onomichi HS** Yd No: 55 Loa 67.21 (BB) Br ex 10.02 Dght 4.243 Lbp 62.00 Br md 10.00 Dpth 4.55 Welded, 1 dk	**(A12A2TC) Chemical Tanker** Liq: 1,260 Compartments: 8 Ta, ER	**1 oil engine** with clutches & sr reverse geared to sc. shaft driving 1 FP propeller Total Power: 736kW (1,001hp) 10.0kn Niigata 6M28BFT 1 x 4 Stroke 6 Cy. 280 x 480 736kW (1001bhp) Niigata Engineering Co Ltd-Japan AuxGen: 3 x 90kW a.c Fuel: 50.0 (d.f.)
8713524 *JK4706* -	**SHINSEI MARU No. 3** - **Isshin Kisen YK** - *Bizen, Okayama* *Japan* Official number: 129528	*131* - 334		**1987**-10 **KK Ura Kyodo Zosensho — Awaji HG** Yd No: 265 Loa 38.50 Br ex - Dght 2.600 Lbp 35.00 Br md 7.00 Dpth 2.80 Welded, 1 dk	**(A13B2TP) Products Tanker** Ins: 840	**1 oil engine** driving 1 FP propeller Total Power: 257kW (349hp) Matsui ML624GA 1 x 4 Stroke 6 Cy. 240 x 400 257kW (349bhp) Matsui Iron Works Co Ltd-Japan
9058531 *JK5196* -	**SHINSEI MARU No. 5** - **Shinsei Kaiun KK** - *Kure, Hiroshima* *Japan* Official number: 133698	*498* - 1,283	Class: NK	**1993**-01 **Hitachi Zosen Mukaishima Marine Co Ltd — Onomichi HS** Yd No: 66 Loa 67.21 (BB) Br ex 10.02 Dght 4.242 Lbp 62.00 Br md 10.00 Dpth 4.55 Welded, 1 dk	**(A12A2TC) Chemical Tanker** Liq: 1,260 Cargo Heating Coils Compartments: 8 Ta, ER	**1 oil engine** with clutches & sr reverse geared to sc. shaft driving 1 FP propeller Total Power: 736kW (1,001hp) 10.0kn Niigata 6M28BFT 1 x 4 Stroke 6 Cy. 280 x 480 736kW (1001bhp) Niigata Engineering Co Ltd-Japan AuxGen: 3 x 90kW a.c Fuel: 50.0 (d.f.)
8609785 - -	**SHINSEI MARU No. 5** - - -	*379* - -		**1986**-09 **KK Kanasashi Zosen — Shizuoka SZ** Yd No: 3118 Loa 53.52 (BB) Br ex 8.74 Dght 3.401 Lbp 47.22 Br md 8.70 Dpth 3.76 Welded, 1 dk	**(B11B2FV) Fishing Vessel**	**1 oil engine** with clutches, flexible couplings & sr reverse geared to sc. shaft driving 1 FP propeller Total Power: 736kW (1,001hp) Hanshin 6LUN28AG 1 x 4 Stroke 6 Cy. 280 x 480 736kW (1001bhp) The Hanshin Diesel Works Ltd-Japan
8859483 *JJ3705* -	**SHINSEI MARU No. 8** - **Yorigami Ocean KK** - *Kobe, Hyogo* *Japan* Official number: 132349	*147* - -		**1991**-12 **Masui Zosensho K.K. — Nandan** Loa 26.50 Br ex - Dght 2.750 Lbp - Br md 8.50 Dpth 3.60 Welded, 1 dk	**(B32B2SP) Pusher Tug**	**1 oil engine** driving 1 FP propeller Total Power: 1,471kW (2,000hp) Daihatsu 6DLM-22S 1 x 4 Stroke 6 Cy. 220 x 300 1471kW (2000bhp) Daihatsu Diesel Manufacturing Co Lt-Japan
9197260 *JM6648* -	**SHINSEI MARU No. 8** - **Miyoki Kaiun KK** - *Uki, Kumamoto* *Japan* Official number: 136395	*199* - 650		**1998**-07 **Yamakawa Zosen Tekko K.K. — Kagoshima** Yd No: 760 Loa 56.58 Br ex - Dght 3.190 Lbp 51.50 Br md 9.00 Dpth 5.44 Welded, 1 dk	**(A31A2GX) General Cargo Ship** Compartments: 1 Ho, ER 1 Ha: (28.8 x 6.8)ER	**1 oil engine** driving 1 FP propeller Total Power: 736kW (1,001hp) 11.0kn Hanshin LH26G 1 x 4 Stroke 6 Cy. 260 x 440 736kW (1001bhp) The Hanshin Diesel Works Ltd-Japan
8874275 - -	**SHINSEI MARU No. 12** *ex* Ebisu Maru *-1996* *ex* Nichiei Maru *-1996* *ex* Eitoku Maru No. 8 *-1996* *ex* Sumihisa Maru No. 2 *-1996* **Seapower Shipping & Trading Pte Ltd** -	*198* 102 480		**1969 Okayama Zosen K.K. — Hinase** Loa 40.50 Br ex 7.20 Dght 3.300 Lbp 38.00 Br md - Dpth 3.40 Welded, 1 dk	**(A31A2GX) General Cargo Ship**	**1 oil engine** driving 1 FP propeller Total Power: 368kW (500hp) 9.0kn Hanshin 6L24MS 1 x 4 Stroke 6 Cy. 240 x 400 368kW (500bhp) The Hanshin Diesel Works Ltd-Japan
9183908 *JL6536* -	**SHINSEI MARU No. 18** - **Shinsei Kaiun YK** - *Ikata, Ehime* *Japan* Official number: 135554	*499* - 1,600		**1997**-09 **Yamanaka Zosen K.K. — Imabari** Yd No: 616 Loa 66.01 Br ex - Dght 4.640 Lbp 60.00 Br md 13.20 Dpth 7.60 Welded, 1 dk	**(A31A2GX) General Cargo Ship** Compartments: 1 Ho, ER 1 Ha: (22.2 x 9.6)ER	**1 oil engine** driving 1 FP propeller Total Power: 736kW (1,001hp) 11.0kn Niigata 6M34BGT 1 x 4 Stroke 6 Cy. 340 x 620 736kW (1001bhp) Niigata Engineering Co Ltd-Japan

9379088 *7JA8* -	**SHINSEI MARU NO. 26** **YK Matsushita Shinseimaru Gyogyo** - *Tosa-Shimizu, Kochi* *Japan* Official number: 140213	*119* - -		**2005-12 Miho Zosensho K.K. — Shimizu** Yd No: 1513 Loa 39.74 Br ex - Dght 2.538 Lbp 32.00 Br md 5.70 Dpth 2.84 Welded, 1 dk	**(B11B2FV) Fishing Vessel**	**1 oil engine** reduction geared to sc. shaft driving 1 Propeller Total Power: 1,471kW (2,000hp) Niigata 1 x 4 Stroke 1471kW (2000bhp) Niigata Engineering Co Ltd-Japan
8417302 *7KTN* K01-657	**SHINSEI MARU No. 36** **YK Matsushita Shinseimaru Gyogyo** - *Tosa-Shimizu, Kochi* *Japan* Official number: 126329	*143* - 191		**1983-02 Nishii Dock Co. Ltd. — Ise** Yd No: 673 Loa 40.37 Br ex - Dght 2.528 Lbp 32.11 Br md 6.01 Dpth 2.82 Bonded, 1 dk	**(B11B2FV) Fishing Vessel** Hull Material: Reinforced Plastic Ins: 109 Compartments: 3 Ho, ER 4 Ha: ER	**1 oil engine** sr geared to sc. shaft driving 1 FP propeller Total Power: 743kW (1,010hp) Yanmar 6Z280L-ET 1 x 4 Stroke 6 Cy. 280 x 360 743kW (1010bhp) Yanmar Diesel Engine Co Ltd-Japan AuxGen: 2 x 160kW 225V a.c
8630899 *JD2493* HK1-951	**SHINSEI MARU No. 58** *ex* Hoyo Maru No. 38 *-1999* *ex* Seisho Maru No. 58 *-1997* *ex* Marunaka Maru No. 38 *-1996* *ex* Hoyo Maru No. 38 *-1996* *ex* Taihei Maru No. 26 *-1992* **Terumi Shirahama** - *Niigata, Niigata* *Japan* Official number: 118670	*125* - -		**1980-02 K.K. Yoshida Zosen Tekko — Kesennuma** Loa 31.20 Br ex - Dght 2.100 Lbp - Br md 5.80 Dpth 2.60 Welded, 1 dk	**(B11B2FV) Fishing Vessel**	**1 oil engine** driving 1 FP propeller Total Power: 368kW (500hp) Niigata 1 x 4 Stroke 368kW (500bhp) Niigata Engineering Co Ltd-Japan
8406846 - -	**SHINSEI MARU No. 61** *ex* Kyoei Maru No. 31 *-1994* *ex* Tomi Maru No. 8 *-1993* **Winer Enterprise Ltd** -	*125* - -		**1983-08 Kakusei Zosen K.K. — Hachinohe** Yd No: 165 Loa 34.90 (BB) Br ex 7.12 Dght - Lbp 28.22 Br md 6.71 Dpth 2.57 Welded, 1 dk	**(B11A2FS) Stern Trawler** Ins: 96	**1 oil engine** with clutches, flexible couplings & sr geared to sc. shaft driving 1 CP propeller Total Power: 736kW (1,001hp) Akasaka DM28AR 1 x 4 Stroke 6 Cy. 280 x 460 736kW (1001bhp) Akasaka Tekkosho KK (Akasaka DieselLtd)-Japan
9152430 *JQJQ* AM1-689	**SHINSEI MARU No. 62** **Sadami Shimawaki** *Hachinohe, Aomori* *Japan* MMSI: 431700340 Official number: 133348	*144* - -		**1996-08 Niigata Engineering Co Ltd — Niigata NI** Yd No: 2307 Loa 36.00 (BB) Br ex - Dght - Lbp 29.00 Br md 7.00 Dpth 4.65 Welded, 1 dk	**(B11A2FS) Stern Trawler** Ins: 84	**1 oil engine** with clutches, flexible couplings & sr geared to sc. shaft driving 1 CP propeller Total Power: 735kW (999hp) 12.3kn Niigata 6MG26HLX 1 x 4 Stroke 6 Cy. 260 x 350 735kW (999bhp) Niigata Engineering Co Ltd-Japan AuxGen: 2 x 144kW 225V 60Hz a.c Fuel: 69.0 (d.f.)
9228502 *JE3177* AM1-705	**SHINSEI MARU No. 65** **Sadami Shimawaki** *Hachinohe, Aomori* *Japan* MMSI: 432015000 Official number: 136273	*184* - 191		**2000-04 Kidoura Shipyard Co Ltd — Kesennuma MG** Yd No: 610 Loa 43.96 (BB) Br ex 7.42 Dght 2.940 Lbp 36.20 Br md 7.40 Dpth 3.40 Welded, 1 dk	**(B11A2FS) Stern Trawler** Ins: 131	**1 oil engine** with clutches & dr geared to sc. shaft driving 1 CP propeller Total Power: 802kW (1,090hp) 13.3kn Niigata 6MG28HX 1 x 4 Stroke 6 Cy. 280 x 370 802kW (1090bhp) Niigata Engineering Co Ltd-Japan AuxGen: 1 x 320kW 225V a.c, 1 x 240kW 225V a.c Thrusters: 1 Thwart. FP thruster (f); 1 Tunnel thruster (a)
9072939 *JK5288* -	**SHINSEI No. 5** **Yabumoto Kisen YK** - *Bizen, Okayama* *Japan* Official number: 134044	*138* - 350		**1993-09 KK Ura Kyodo Zosensho — Awaji HG** Yd No: 293 Loa 39.01 Br ex - Dght 2.750 Lbp 35.01 Br md 7.00 Dpth 2.80 Welded, 1 dk	**(A13B2TP) Products Tanker**	**1 oil engine** driving 1 FP propeller Total Power: 368kW (500hp) 9.0kn Matsui ML624GS 1 x 4 Stroke 6 Cy. 240 x 400 368kW (500bhp) Matsui Iron Works Co Ltd-Japan
9599224 *JD3092* -	**SHINSEITOKU MARU** **YK Taisei Kisen** *Kure, Hiroshima* *Japan* MMSI: 431001704 Official number: 141288	*499* - 1,830		**2010-08 K.K. Matsuura Zosensho — Osakikamijima** Yd No: 573 L reg 70.06 (BB) Br ex - Dght 4.390 Lbp 68.00 Br md 12.00 Dpth 7.35 Welded, 1 dk	**(A31A2GX) General Cargo Ship** Grain: 2,495 1 Ha: ER (40.0 x 9.5)	**1 oil engine** reduction geared to sc. shaft driving 1 Propeller Total Power: 1,618kW (2,200hp) 12.5kn Hanshin LA32G 1 x 4 Stroke 6 Cy. 320 x 680 1618kW (2200bhp) The Hanshin Diesel Works Ltd-Japan
9257034 *JG5654* -	**SHINSEN MARU** **Japan Railway Construction, Transport & Technology Agency & Izumi Kisen Co Ltd** Izumi Kisen KK (Izumi Shipping Co Ltd) *Tokyo* *Japan* MMSI: 431100987 Official number: 137111	*13,089* - 7,078	Class: NK	**2002-03 Yamanishi Corp — Ishinomaki MG** Yd No: 1027 Loa 160.56 (BB) Br ex - Dght 7.015 Lbp 150.00 Br md 26.60 Dpth 20.90 Welded, 4 dks	**(A35A2RR) Ro-Ro Cargo Ship** Angled stern door/ramp (s. a.) Quarter bow door/ramp (s) Lane-Len: 1788 Cars: 200, Trailers: 76 Grain: 1,428; Bale: 1,049	**1 oil engine** geared to sc. shaft driving 1 CP propeller Total Power: 15,886kW (21,599hp) 21.2kn Pielstick 12PC4-2B-570 1 x Vee 4 Stroke 12 Cy. 570 x 660 15886kW (21599bhp) Nippon Kokan KK (NKK Corp)-Japan AuxGen: 3 x 1066kW a.c Thrusters: 1 Tunnel thruster (f); 1 Tunnel thruster (a) Fuel: 600.0
9673185 - -	**SHINSETO** **Japan Railway Construction, Transport & Technology Agency & GK Marumiya Kaiun Shokai** *Japan*	*749* - 1,800	Class: FA	**2013-09 Honda Zosen — Saiki** Yd No: 1081 Loa 85.00 Br ex - Dght 6.850 Lbp - Br md 14.00 Dpth - Welded, 1 dk	**(A33A2CC) Container Ship (Fully Cellular)** TEU 80	**1 oil engine** driving 1 Propeller Total Power: 2,207kW (3,001hp) Hanshin LH38L 1 x 4 Stroke 6 Cy. 380 x 760 2207kW (3001bhp) The Hanshin Diesel Works Ltd-Japan
8859067 *JK5111* -	**SHINSETO** **GK Marumiya Kaiun Shokai** *Omuta, Fukuoka* *Japan* MMSI: 431400712 Official number: 132515	*491* - 1,399		**1991-07 Amakusa Zosen K.K. — Amakusa** Yd No: 81 Loa 77.06 Br ex - Dght 3.920 Lbp 70.50 Br md 11.80 Dpth 6.40 Welded, 1 dk	**(A31A2GX) General Cargo Ship** Grain: 2,298; Bale: 2,252 TEU 96 C. 96/20' 1 Ha: (38.4 x 8.1)ER	**1 oil engine** driving 1 FP propeller 11.8kn Hanshin 6EL32 1 x 4 Stroke 6 Cy. 320 x 640 The Hanshin Diesel Works Ltd-Japan
9661780 *JD3332* -	**SHINSHIN MARU** **Japan Railway Construction, Transport & Technology Agency & Nichiyo Kaiun KK** Iwasaki Kisen KK (Iwasaki Kisen Co Ltd) *Bizen, Okayama* *Japan* MMSI: 431003616 Official number: 141640	*749* - 1,794	Class: NK	**2012-06 Fukushima Zosen Ltd. — Matsue** Yd No: 376 Loa 74.15 (BB) Br ex - Dght 4.710 Lbp 69.95 Br md 11.50 Dpth 5.20 Welded, 1 dk	**(A12B2TR) Chemical/Products Tanker** Double Hull (13F) Liq: 1,470; Liq (Oil): 1,470	**2 diesel electric oil engines** driving 2 gen. each 705kW Connecting to 2 elec. motors driving 2 CP propellers Total Power: 1,000kW (1,360hp) 12.0kn Thrusters: 1 Tunnel thruster (f) Fuel: 110.0
9179957 *JJ4005* -	**SHINSHO MARU** **Shinko Butsuryu KK** Kobelco Logistics Ltd *Kobe, Hyogo* *Japan* MMSI: 431300873 Official number: 134271	*3,899* - 6,154	Class: NK	**1998-04 Hitachi Zosen Mukaishima Marine Co Ltd — Onomichi HS** Yd No: 127 Loa 110.93 Br ex - Dght 6.271 Lbp 103.00 Br md 17.60 Dpth 7.70 Welded, 1 dk	**(A24E2BL) Limestone Carrier** Grain: 5,615 Compartments: 2 Ho, ER 2 Ha: (33.4 x 10.6) (21.4 x 10.6)ER	**1 oil engine** driving 1 FP propeller Total Power: 3,310kW (4,500hp) 14.5kn Hanshin LH46LA 1 x 4 Stroke 6 Cy. 460 x 880 3310kW (4500bhp) The Hanshin Diesel Works Ltd-Japan AuxGen: 2 x 300kW a.c Fuel: 230.0
8504595 *7KNM* AM1-531	**SHINSHO MARU No. 3** *ex* Narita Maru No. 35 *-1987* **YK Shinsho Gyogyo** - *Hachinohe, Aomori* *Japan* MMSI: 432203000 Official number: 126666	*160* - -		**1985-07 Narasaki Zosen KK — Muroran HK** Yd No: 1075 Loa 38.13 (BB) Br ex 7.42 Dght 3.220 Lbp - Br md 7.41 Dpth 4.63 Welded, 1 dk	**(B11A2FS) Stern Trawler** Ins: 117	**1 oil engine** with clutches, flexible couplings & sr geared to sc. shaft driving 1 CP propeller Total Power: 1,398kW (1,901hp) Daihatsu 6DSM-28 1 x 4 Stroke 6 Cy. 280 x 340 1398kW (1901bhp) Daihatsu Diesel Manufacturing Co Lt-Japan
7649465 *HQPD5* -	**SHINSHO No. 5** *ex* Shinsei Maru No. 5 *-1987* **Wakachiku Construction S de RL** - *San Lorenzo* *Honduras* Official number: L-0325642	*499* 297 495		**1971 Yoshicho Zosen — Ise** Loa 42.02 Br ex - Dght 5.001 Lbp 38.31 Br md 10.00 Dpth 5.11 Welded, 1dk	**(A31A2GX) General Cargo Ship** Grain: 330 1 Ha: ER	**1 oil engine** driving 1 FP propeller Total Power: 736kW (1,001hp) 10.0kn Matsui 1 x 4 Stroke 736kW (1001bhp) Matsui Iron Works Co Ltd-Japan

IMO / Call sign	Name, former names, owner, port	Tonnage	Class	Built	Type	Machinery
7530585 - -	**SHINSHO No. 18** *ex* Shinsho Maru No. 18 *-1994* *ex* Meitoku Maru *-1992* *ex* Shinsho Maru No. 18 *-1991* *ex* Meitoku Maru *-1983* - -	*498* 359 1,099		**1976-02 Omishima Dock K.K. — Imabari** Yd No: 1043 Loa - Br ex 11.03 Dght - Lbp 57.99 Br md 11.02 Dpth 4.37 Welded, 1 dk	**(A13B2TU) Tanker (unspecified)**	**1 oil engine** driving 1 FP propeller Total Power: 993kW (1,350hp) Akasaka AH28 1 x 4 Stroke 6 Cy. 280 x 440 993kW (1350bhp) Akasaka Tekkosho KK (Akasaka DieselLtd)-Japan
8838374 *JJRD* -	**SHINSHU MARU NO. 11** *ex* Hoyo Maru No. 38 *-2005* **YK Shinshu Suisan** - SatCom: Inmarsat A 1204163 *Tokyo* *Japan* MMSI: 431700640 Official number: 130754	*379* - -		**1989-03 Miyagi-ken Zosen Tekko K.K. — Kesennuma** Loa 48.21 (BB) Br ex - Dght 3.100 Lbp - Br md 8.70 Dpth 3.75 Welded, 1 dk	**(B11B2FV) Fishing Vessel** Ins: 496	**1 oil engine** geared to sc. shaft driving 1 FP propeller Total Power: 736kW (1,001hp) Hanshin LH28G 1 x 4 Stroke 6 Cy. 280 x 460 736kW (1001bhp) The Hanshin Diesel Works Ltd-Japan
9014468 *JRHZ* -	**SHINSHU MARU NO. 22** *ex* Hoyo Maru No. 51 *-2005* **YK Shinshu Suisan** - SatCom: Inmarsat A 1201657 *Tokyo* *Japan* MMSI: 431700480 Official number: 130901	*379* - 449		**1990-04 Miyagi-ken Zosen Tekko K.K. — Kesennuma** Loa 55.07 (BB) Br ex - Dght 3.630 Lbp 48.00 Br md 8.70 Dpth 5.15 Welded, 1 dk	**(B11B2FV) Fishing Vessel**	**1 oil engine** with clutches, flexible couplings & sr reverse geared to sc. shaft driving 1 FP propeller Total Power: 736kW (1,001hp) Hanshin LH28G 1 x 4 Stroke 6 Cy. 280 x 460 736kW (1001bhp) The Hanshin Diesel Works Ltd-Japan
9046320 *JQDW* -	**SHINSHU MARU NO. 61** *ex* Hoyo Maru No. 52 *-2005* **YK Shinshu Suisan** - SatCom: Inmarsat A 1204517 *Tokyo* *Japan* MMSI: 431700570 Official number: 132197	*379* - 456		**1991-06 Miyagi-ken Zosen Tekko K.K. — Kesennuma** Yd No: 112 Loa 55.07 Br ex 8.72 Dght 3.428 Lbp 48.00 Br md 8.70 Dpth 3.75 Welded, 1 dk	**(B11B2FV) Fishing Vessel**	**1 oil engine** with clutches, flexible couplings & sr geared to sc. shaft driving 1 FP propeller Total Power: 736kW (1,001hp) Hanshin LH28G 1 x 4 Stroke 6 Cy. 280 x 460 736kW (1001bhp) The Hanshin Diesel Works Ltd-Japan
8415902 *JGJY* -	**SHINSHU MARU NO. 62** *ex* Kyoshin Maru No. 88 *-2005* **YK Shinshu Suisan** - SatCom: Inmarsat A 1205647 *Tokyo* *Japan* MMSI: 431201150 Official number: 127809	*409* - 504		**1984-12 Miho Zosensho K.K. — Shimizu** Yd No: 1245 Loa 55.61 Br ex 8.72 Dght 3.491 Lbp 49.03 Br md 8.70 Dpth 3.87 Welded, 1 dk	**(B11B2FV) Fishing Vessel** Ins: 161	**1 oil engine** with flexible couplings & sr gearedto sc. shaft driving 1 FP propeller Total Power: 736kW (1,001hp) Hanshin 6LUN28AG 1 x 4 Stroke 6 Cy. 280 x 480 736kW (1001bhp) The Hanshin Diesel Works Ltd-Japan
8713316 *7KMC* -	**SHINSHU MARU NO. 66** *ex* Kyoshin Maru No. 1 *-2005* **YK Shinshu Suisan** - SatCom: Inmarsat A 1205265 *Tokyo* *Japan* MMSI: 431201160 Official number: 129496	*439* - 582		**1987-11 Miho Zosensho K.K. — Shimizu** Yd No: 1310 Loa 56.54 Br ex 8.92 Dght 3.704 Lbp 49.80 Br md 8.90 Dpth 4.07 Welded	**(B11B2FV) Fishing Vessel** Ins: 570	**1 oil engine** with clutches, flexible couplings & sr geared to sc. shaft driving 1 FP propeller Total Power: 1,103kW (1,500hp) Hanshin 6LUN30ARG 1 x 4 Stroke 6 Cy. 300 x 480 1103kW (1500bhp) The Hanshin Diesel Works Ltd-Japan
9195262 *JG5537* -	**SHINSUI MARU NO. 8** - **Toshin Yusosen Co Ltd (Toshin Yusosen KK)** - *Tokyo* *Japan* MMSI: 431100682 Official number: 136648	*3,317* - 4,999	Class: NK	**1998-12 K.K. Miura Zosensho — Saiki** Yd No: 1217 Loa 105.00 Br ex - Dght 6.514 Lbp 99.00 Br md 15.50 Dpth 7.85 Welded, 1 dk	**(A13B2TP) Products Tanker** Double Hull (13F) Liq: 5,800; Liq (Oil): 5,800	**1 oil engine** driving 1 FP propeller Total Power: 3,884kW (5,281hp) 14.5kn B&W 6L35MC 1 x 2 Stroke 6 Cy. 350 x 1050 3884kW (5281bhp) The Hanshin Diesel Works Ltd-Japan Fuel: 270.0
9167590 *JJ3942* -	**SHINSUMIYOSHI MARU No. 15** - **Otama Kaiun YK** - *Himeji, Hyogo* *Japan* Official number: 134197	*497* - -		**1997-06 Hamamoto Zosensho K.K. — Tokushima** Yd No: 815 Loa 77.05 Br ex - Dght - Lbp 62.00 Br md 13.50 Dpth 7.25 Welded, 1 dk	**(A24D2BA) Aggregates Carrier** Compartments: 1 Ho, ER 1 Ha: (21.6 x 10.5)ER Cranes: 1x4t	**1 oil engine** driving 1 FP propeller Total Power: 736kW (1,001hp) 12.0kn Niigata 6M34BGT 1 x 4 Stroke 6 Cy. 340 x 620 736kW (1001bhp) Niigata Engineering Co Ltd-Japan
9176187 *DSPK4* -	**SHINSUNG DREAM** *ex* Evangeli *-2013* *ex* Evangelia *-2007* *ex* Jaydee M *-2005* *ex* Cornelie Oldendorff *-2003* *ex* Maxima *-2003* *ex* Cornelie Oldendorff *-2002* *ex* Asia Melody *-2001* **KDB Capital Corp** Shinsung Shipping Co Ltd *Jeju* *South Korea* MMSI: 441155000 Official number: JJR-079906	**6,804** 3,567 11,042	Class: KR (BV) (NK)	**1998-06 K.K. Miura Zosensho — Saiki** Yd No: 1207 Loa 105.50 (BB) Br ex - Dght 9.605 Lbp 95.00 Br md 19.00 Dpth 13.50 Welded	**(A31A2GX) General Cargo Ship** Grain: 14,066; Bale: 13,825 Compartments: 2 Ho, ER 2 Ha: 2 (25.9 x 14.0)ER Cranes: 2x30.5t; Derricks: 1x30.5t	**1 oil engine** driving 1 FP propeller Total Power: 3,884kW (5,281hp) 13.0kn B&W 6L35MC 1 x 2 Stroke 6 Cy. 350 x 1050 3884kW (5281bhp) Makita Corp-Japan AuxGen: 2 x 280kW a.c Fuel: 147.0 (d.f.) 545.0 (r.f.) 11.7pd
9513206 *DSRD4*	**SHINSUNG EVER** - **Shinsung Shipping Co Ltd** - *Jeju* *South Korea* MMSI: 441783000 Official number: JJR-111028	**10,850** 4,486 14,706	Class: KR	**2011-05 Mokpo Shipbuilding & Engineering Co Ltd — Mokpo** Yd No: 07-195 Loa 126.80 Br ex - Dght 9.365 Lbp 119.69 Br md 21.50 Dpth 14.50 Welded, 1 dk	**(A31A2GX) General Cargo Ship** Grain: 20,988; Bale: 20,416 2 Ha: ER 2 (32.2 x 14.0) Cranes: 2x30t; Derricks: 2x30t	**1 oil engine** driving 1 FP propeller Total Power: 4,440kW (6,037hp) 14.2kn MAN-B&W 6S35MC 1 x 2 Stroke 6 Cy. 350 x 1400 4440kW (6037bhp) STX Engine Co Ltd-South Korea Fuel: 699.0 (r.f.)
9163075 *PMIS*	**SHINTA** - **PT Pelayaran Parnaraya Nusantara** - *Jakarta* *Indonesia* MMSI: 525011121	**2,670** 1,210 3,580	Class: NK	**1998-02 Chungmu Shipbuilding Co Inc — Tongyeong** Yd No: 249 Loa 90.00 (BB) Br ex - Dght 5.000 Lbp 85.00 Br md 15.00 Dpth 7.00 Welded, 1 dk	**(A13B2TP) Products Tanker** Double Bottom Partial Compartment Length Liq: 4,531; Liq (Oil): 4,531	**1 oil engine** driving 1 FP propeller Total Power: 1,618kW (2,200hp) 11.4kn Hanshin LH34LA 1 x 4 Stroke 6 Cy. 340 x 640 1618kW (2200bhp) The Hanshin Diesel Works Ltd-Japan Fuel: 225.0
8889892 *JJ3911*	**SHINTAIHO** - **Taiho Kaiun YK** - *Minamiawaji, Hyogo* *Japan* MMSI: 431300291 Official number: 132445	*435* - -		**1995-09 Amakusa Zosen K.K. — Amakusa** Yd No: 111 Loa 71.70 Br ex - Dght - Lbp 65.00 Br md 10.80 Dpth 6.20 Welded, 1 dk	**(A31A2GX) General Cargo Ship**	**1 oil engine** driving 1 FP propeller Total Power: 1,177kW (1,600hp) 11.0kn Hanshin LH31G 1 x 4 Stroke 6 Cy. 310 x 530 1177kW (1600bhp) The Hanshin Diesel Works Ltd-Japan
7328358 - -	**SHINTATSU MARU** *ex* Steintor *-1988* **Octraco Investments Ltd** -	**946** 284 910	Class: (NK) (GL)	**1973-12 JG Hitzler Schiffswerft und Masch GmbH & Co KG — Lauenburg** Yd No: 742 Loa 57.50 Br ex 12.02 Dght 4.513 Lbp 50.60 Br md 11.70 Dpth 5.60 Welded, 1 dk	**(B21B20T) Offshore Tug/Supply Ship** Ice Capable	**2 oil engines** reverse reduction geared to sc. shafts driving 2 CP propellers Total Power: 3,384kW (4,600hp) 14.0kn MWM TBD441V16 2 x Vee 4 Stroke 16 Cy. 230 x 270 each-1692kW (2300bhp) Motoren Werke Mannheim AG (MWM)-West Germany
8923480 *JK5501* -	**SHINTATSU MARU No. 8** - **Shintatsu Kisen YK** - *Kure, Hiroshima* *Japan* Official number: 134719	*199* - 616		**1996-06 Y.K. Okajima Zosensho — Matsuyama** Yd No: 249 Loa 56.22 Br ex - Dght 3.330 Lbp 50.00 Br md 9.30 Dpth 5.57 Welded, 1 dk	**(A31A2GX) General Cargo Ship**	**1 oil engine** driving 1 FP propeller Total Power: 736kW (1,001hp) 11.0kn Niigata 6M26AGTE 1 x 4 Stroke 6 Cy. 260 x 460 736kW (1001bhp) Niigata Engineering Co Ltd-Japan
8904642 *JM5843* -	**SHINTO MARU No. 31** - **Yukyu Gyogyo Seisan Kumiai** - *Shimonoseki, Yamaguchi* *Japan* Official number: 130500	*324* - 627		**1989-06 K.K. Izutsu Zosensho — Nagasaki** Yd No: 970 Loa 61.30 (BB) Br ex - Dght 4.280 Lbp 55.75 Br md 8.90 Dpth 4.40 Welded, 1 dk	**(B11B2FV) Fishing Vessel**	**1 oil engine** with clutches, flexible couplings & reduction geared to sc. shaft driving 1 CP propeller Total Power: 1,140kW (1,550hp) Niigata 6MG32CLX 1 x 4 Stroke 6 Cy. 320 x 420 1140kW (1550bhp) Niigata Engineering Co Ltd-Japan Thrusters: 1 Thwart. CP thruster (f)

8411346 *JM5318* -	**SHINTO MARU No. 32** - **Yukyu Gyogyo Seisan Kumiai** - *Shimonoseki, Yamaguchi* *Japan* Official number: 127035	*280* - 543		**1984-06 K.K. Izutsu Zosensho — Nagasaki** Yd No: 885 Loa 51.97 (BB) Br ex - Dght 3.501 Lbp 44.20 Br md 8.60 Dpth 3.99 Welded, 1 dk	**(B11B2FV) Fishing Vessel** Ins: 523 Compartments: 9 Ho, ER 9 Ha: ER	**1 oil engine** with clutches, flexible couplings & sr reverse geared to sc. shaft driving 1 FP propeller Total Power: 861kW (1,171hp) Yanmar 6Z280-ET 1 x 4 Stroke 6 Cy. 280 x 360 861kW (1171bhp) Yanmar Diesel Engine Co Ltd-Japan
8895425 - -	**SHINTO MARU No. 38** - **CD Trading** - *Philippines*	*147* - -		**1977 K.K. Murakami Zosensho — Ishinomaki** L reg 34.80 Br ex - Dght - Lbp - Br md 6.70 Dpth 3.20 Welded, 1 dk	**(B11B2FV) Fishing Vessel**	**1 oil engine** driving 1 FP propeller
8815164 *JM5790* -	**SHINTO No. 1** - **Saito Shipping Co Ltd (Saito Kaiun KK)** - *Fukuoka, Fukuoka* *Japan* Official number: 130489	*131* - 264		**1988-11 Nippon Zosen Tekko K.K. — Kitakyushu** Yd No: 325 Loa 32.50 Br ex - Dght 3.520 Lbp 30.00 Br md 9.60 Dpth 5.60 Welded, 1 dk	**(B32B2SP) Pusher Tug**	**2 oil engines** with clutches & dr geared to sc. shaft driving 2 FP propellers Total Power: 1,912kW (2,600hp) Daihatsu 6DLM-28S 2 x 4 Stroke 6 Cy. 280 x 360 each-956kW (1300bhp) Daihatsu Diesel Manufacturing Co Lt-Japan
5195367 - -	**SHINTOKI MARU No. 3** *ex* Kotoshiro Maru No. 30 **Toen Sangyo Co Ltd** - *South Korea*	*480* 310 -		**1960 Usuki Iron Works Co Ltd — Saiki OT** Yd No: 517 Loa 52.00 Br ex 8.67 Dght 3.709 Lbp 46.82 Br md 8.62 Dpth 4.14 Welded, 1 dk	**(B11B2FV) Fishing Vessel**	**1 oil engine** driving 1 FP propeller Total Power: 809kW (1,100hp) 12.0kn Akasaka YM6SS 1 x 4 Stroke 6 Cy. 370 x 520 809kW (1100bhp) Akasaka Tekkosho KK (Akasaka DieselLtd)-Japan Fuel: 233.5
7621190 *JI2892* -	**SHINTOKU** *ex* Iyonami *-2002* *ex* Nanyo Maru *-1995* - - *Komatsushima, Tokushima* *Japan* Official number: 119522	*103* - -		**1976-10 Shin Yamamoto Shipbuilding & Engineering Co Ltd — Kochi KC** Yd No: 193 Loa 23.25 Br ex 6.63 Dght 2.200 Lbp 22.00 Br md 6.61 Dpth 3.00 Welded, 1 dk	**(B32A2ST) Tug**	**2 oil engines** Geared Integral to driving 2 Z propellers Total Power: 558kW (758hp) Niigata 6L16X 2 x 4 Stroke 6 Cy. 160 x 200 each-279kW (379bhp) Niigata Engineering Co Ltd-Japan
5303108 - -	**SHINTOKU MARU** *ex* Shoei Maru *-1995* *ex* Ryuo Maru *-1995* **KK Fuji Salvage** -	*153* 55 -		**1960 Yokohama Zosen — Chiba** Loa 30.00 Br ex 7.83 Dght 3.201 Lbp 24.49 Br md 7.80 Dpth 3.38 Welded, 1 dk	**(B32A2ST) Tug**	**2 oil engines** driving 2 FP propellers Total Power: 1,104kW (1,500hp) 11.0kn Hanshin SR8 2 x 4 Stroke 8 Cy. 260 x 330 each-552kW (750bhp) Hanshin Nainenki Kogyo-Japan AuxGen: 1 x 45kW 225V a.c, 1 x 10kW 225V a.c Fuel: 18.5 5.0pd
9038050 *JL6007* -	**SHINTOKU MARU No. 1** - - - *Niihama, Ehime* *Japan* Official number: 132135	*191* - 365		**1991-09 Koa Sangyo KK — Takamatsu KG** Yd No: 562 Loa 45.82 Br ex - Dght - Lbp 42.00 Br md 7.50 Dpth 3.40 Welded	**(A24A2BT) Cement Carrier** Liq: 175	**1 oil engine** driving 1 FP propeller Total Power: 441kW (600hp) Matsui 6M26KGHS 1 x 4 Stroke 6 Cy. 260 x 400 441kW (600bhp) Matsui Iron Works Co Ltd-Japan
8961602 - -	**SHINTOKU MARU No. 5** *ex* Esan Maru *-1995* **KK Fuji Salvage** -	*168* - -		**1967-04 The Hakodate Dock Co Ltd — Hakodate HK** Loa 23.20 Br ex - Dght 2.500 Lbp - Br md 8.00 Dpth 3.80 Welded, 1 dk	**(B32A2ST) Tug**	**2 oil engines** driving 2 FP propellers Total Power: 1,324kW (1,800hp) 10.5kn Fuji 6S27.5CH 2 x 4 Stroke 6 Cy. 275 x 410 each-662kW (900bhp) Fuji Diesel Co Ltd-Japan
9053543 *JE3103* MG1-1867	**SHINTOKU MARU No. 28** - **YK Shintoku Maru Gyogyo** - *Kesennuma, Miyagi* *Japan* Official number: 133293	*119* - 213		**1992-07 Kidoura Shipyard Co Ltd — Kesennuma MG** Yd No: 578 Loa 37.44 (BB) Br ex 6.42 Dght 2.500 Lbp - Br md 6.40 Dpth 2.80 Welded, 1 dk	**(B11B2FV) Fishing Vessel**	**1 oil engine** with clutches, flexible couplings & dr geared to sc. shaft driving 1 CP propeller Total Power: 592kW (805hp) Sumiyoshi S26G 1 x 4 Stroke 6 Cy. 260 x 470 592kW (805bhp) Sumiyoshi Marine Diesel Co Ltd-Japan
8967307 *JK5616* -	**SHINTOKUYAMA** - **Tokuyama Unyu KK** - *Shunan, Yamaguchi* *Japan* MMSI: 431401877 Official number: 136181	*499* - -		**2001-05 K.K. Miura Zosensho — Saiki** Yd No: 1235 Loa 73.55 Br ex - Dght - Lbp 67.00 Br md 12.00 Dpth 7.78 Welded, 1 dk	**(A31A2GX) General Cargo Ship** Compartments: 1 Ho, ER 1 Ha: (37.8 x 9.1)ER	**1 oil engine** driving 1 FP propeller Total Power: 1,470kW (1,999hp) 12.5kn Niigata 6M34BGT 1 x 4 Stroke 6 Cy. 340 x 620 1470kW (1999bhp) Niigata Engineering Co Ltd-Japan Fuel: 97.0 (d.f.) 7.0pd
8351261 *JG4301* -	**SHINTOKYO MARU** - **Tokyo Harbor Construction Office (Tokyoko Kensetsu Jimusho)** - *Tokyo* *Japan* Official number: 126723	*197* - -		**1983-03 Ishikawajima-Harima Heavy Industries Co Ltd (IHI) — Tokyo** Yd No: 2814 Loa 31.89 Br ex - Dght 1.300 Lbp 29.90 Br md 7.84 Dpth 2.90 Welded, 1 dk	**(B31A2SR) Research Survey Vessel**	**2 oil engines** driving 2 FP propellers Total Power: 1,838kW (2,498hp) 14.2kn Maybach MB820DB 2 x Vee 4 Stroke 12 Cy. 175 x 205 each-919kW (1249bhp)
9015814 *YCIS* -	**SHINTOMARU** *ex* Ramah *-2009* *ex* Shinto Maru *-2007* **Nilasari Winata** - *Surabaya* *Indonesia*	**497** 193 755	Class: KI	**1990-12 Hitachi Zosen Mukaishima Marine Co Ltd — Onomichi HS** Yd No: 35 Loa 48.46 Br ex - Dght - Lbp 43.90 Br md 9.30 Dpth 4.70 Welded	**(A31A2GX) General Cargo Ship** Grain: 907; Bale: 832 Compartments: 1 Ho, ER 1 Ha: ER	**1 oil engine** with flexible couplings & reverse geared to sc. shaft driving 1 FP propeller Total Power: 736kW (1,001hp) Niigata 6M26AGTE 1 x 4 Stroke 6 Cy. 260 x 460 736kW (1001bhp) Niigata Engineering Co Ltd-Japan AuxGen: 1 x 140kW 225/130V a.c, 1 x 30kW 225/130V a.c
8982670 *JI3712* -	**SHINTSUGARU MARU** - **KK Hanshin Shipping** - *Osaka, Osaka* *Japan* MMSI: 431401957 Official number: 137237	*745* - -		**2003-07 Nakatani Shipyard Co. Ltd. — Etajima** Yd No: 596 L reg 83.51 Br ex - Dght - Lbp - Br md 12.80 Dpth 7.73 Welded, 1 dk	**(A31A2GX) General Cargo Ship**	**1 oil engine** driving 1 Propeller Total Power: 1,839kW (2,500hp) Hanshin LA34 1 x 4 Stroke 6 Cy. 340 x 720 1839kW (2500bhp) The Hanshin Diesel Works Ltd-Japan
8936504 *JM6645* -	**SHINWA MARU** - - - *Kamiamakusa, Kumamoto* *Japan* Official number: 136391	*237* - -		**1997-12 Hongawara Zosen K.K. — Fukuyama** Loa 49.97 Br ex - Dght - Lbp 46.00 Br md 8.00 Dpth 3.50 Welded, 1 dk	**(A12A2TC) Chemical Tanker** 1 Cargo Pump (s): 1x150m³/hr	**1 oil engine** driving 1 FP propeller Total Power: 736kW (1,001hp) 11.0kn Hanshin LH26G 1 x 4 Stroke 6 Cy. 260 x 440 736kW (1001bhp) The Hanshin Diesel Works Ltd-Japan
5349774 *JJLP* -	**SHINWA MARU** *ex* Taisho Maru No. 3 *-1979* *ex* Kinsei Maru No. 5 *-1962* **Sugahara Jeneralist Co Ltd** - *Marugame, Kagawa* *Japan* Official number: 82723	*199* - 530		**1959-05 Tsuneishi Shipbuilding Co Ltd — Fukuyama HS** Yd No: 25 Loa 45.50 Br ex 7.29 Dght 3.353 Lbp 41.05 Br md 7.27 Dpth 3.66 Welded, 1 dk	**(A12A2TC) Chemical Tanker** Compartments: 6 Ta, ER 1 Cargo Pump (s): 1x150m³/hr	**1 oil engine** driving 1 FP propeller Total Power: 588kW (799hp) 10.0kn Yanmar MF24-UT 1 x 4 Stroke 6 Cy. 240 x 420 588kW (799bhp) (new engine 1993) Yanmar Diesel Engine Co Ltd-Japan
9472799 *JD2518* -	**SHINWA MARU** - **Kuribayashi Logistics System Co Ltd** Kuribayashi Steamship Co Ltd *Tokyo* *Japan* Official number: 140650	*499* - 1,845		**2007-10 Yamanaka Zosen K.K. — Imabari** Yd No: 753 Loa 74.20 Br ex - Dght 4.360 Lbp 68.00 Br md 12.00 Dpth 7.37 Welded, 1 dk	**(A31A2GX) General Cargo Ship** Compartments: 1 Ho, ER 1 Ha: ER (40.0 x 9.5)	**1 oil engine** driving 1 FP propeller Total Power: 1,323kW (1,799hp) Niigata 6M31BLGT 1 x 4 Stroke 6 Cy. 310 x 600 1323kW (1799bhp) Niigata Engineering Co Ltd-Japan
9307877 *JK5640* -	**SHINWA MARU** - **YK Shinwa Kisen** - *Kure, Hiroshima* *Japan* Official number: 136205	**499** - 1,260	Class: (NK)	**2003-10 KK Ura Kyodo Zosensho — Awaji HG** Yd No: 320 Loa 64.76 Br ex - Dght 4.278 Lbp 60.00 Br md 10.00 Dpth 4.50 Welded, 1 dk	**(A12A2TC) Chemical Tanker**	**1 oil engine** driving 1 Propeller Total Power: 1,471kW (2,000hp) 12.0kn Niigata 1 x 4 Stroke 1471kW (2000bhp) Niigata Engineering Co Ltd-Japan

IMO / Call sign	Name / Owner / Manager / Port	Tonnage	Class	Builder / Dimensions	Type	Machinery
9325295 *7JPN* -	**SHINWA-MARU** *ex Shinwa Maru -2010* **NS United Kaiun Kaisha Ltd** NS United Marine Service Corp *Oita, Oita* Japan MMSI: 432946000 Official number: 141964	**150,918** 53,666 297,541	Class: NK	**2008-09 Universal Shipbuilding Corp — Nagasu KM (Ariake Shipyard)** Yd No: 070 Loa 327.00 (BB) Br ex - Dght 21.400 Lbp 318.00 Br md 55.00 Dpth 29.25 Welded, 1 dk	**(A21B2BO) Ore Carrier** Grain: 180,474 Compartments: 6 Ho, ER 6 Ha: ER	**1 oil engine** driving 1 FP propeller Total Power: 23,280kW (31,651hp) 14.3kn MAN-B&W 6S80MC-C 1 x 2 Stroke 6 Cy. 800 x 3200 23280kW (31651bhp) Hitachi Zosen Corp-Japan Fuel: 7270.0
9125310 *JL6383* -	**SHINWA MARU No. 6** - - *Anan, Tokushima* Japan Official number: 135067	*494* - 1,200		**1995-06 Imura Zosen K.K. — Komatsushima** Yd No: 275 Loa 73.00 Br ex - Dght 4.200 Lbp 65.00 Br md 11.00 Dpth 6.60 Welded, 1 dk	**(A31A2GX) General Cargo Ship**	**1 oil engine** driving 1 FP propeller Total Power: 1,000kW (1,360hp) 11.0kn Hanshin LH30LG 1 x 4 Stroke 6 Cy. 300 x 600 1000kW (1360bhp) The Hanshin Diesel Works Ltd-Japan
9202974 *JL6568* -	**SHINWA MARU No. 7** - - *Anan, Tokushima* Japan Official number: 135588	*497* - -		**1998-03 Imura Zosen K.K. — Komatsushima** Yd No: 278 Loa 75.86 Br ex - Dght - Lbp 70.00 Br md 11.70 Dpth 7.24 Welded, 1 dk	**(A31A2GX) General Cargo Ship** Compartments: 1 Ho, ER 1 Ha: (40.0 x 9.0)ER	**1 oil engine** driving 1 FP propeller Total Power: 736kW (1,001hp) 11.0kn Hanshin LH26G 1 x 4 Stroke 6 Cy. 260 x 440 736kW (1001bhp) The Hanshin Diesel Works Ltd-Japan
9066849 *JG4993* -	**SHINWA MARU No. 8** - **YK Shinwa Shoji** - *Minamiboso, Chiba* Japan Official number: 132048	*498* - 1,198		**1994-03 Iisaku Zosen K.K. — Nishi-Izu** Yd No: 94172 Loa 63.60 (BB) Br ex - Dght 4.250 Lbp 58.00 Br md 10.00 Dpth 4.50 Welded, 1 dk	**(A13B2TP) Products Tanker** Compartments: 8 Ta, ER	**1 oil engine** with clutches, flexible couplings & reverse geared to sc. shaft driving 1 FP propeller Total Power: 1,030kW (1,400hp) Sumiyoshi S27G 1 x 4 Stroke 6 Cy. 270 x 480 1030kW (1400bhp) Sumiyoshi Tekkosho-Japan
9581784 *3EUW9* -	**SHINY HALO** - **Murakami Sekiyu Co Ltd & Tradewind Navigation SA** Reitaku Kaiun Co Ltd (Reitaku Kaiun KK) SatCom: Inmarsat C 437014810 *Panama* Panama MMSI: 370148000 Official number: 4259111	**34,778** 20,209 61,496 T/cm 61.4	Class: NK	**2011-04 Shin Kasado Dockyard Co Ltd — Kudamatsu YC** Yd No: K-047 Loa 199.98 (BB) Br ex - Dght 13.010 Lbp 195.00 Br md 32.24 Dpth 18.60 Welded, 1 dk	**(A21A2BC) Bulk Carrier** Grain: 77,674; Bale: 73,552 Compartments: 5 Ho, ER 5 Ha: 4 (23.5 x 19.0)ER (18.7 x 19.0) Cranes: 4x30.5t	**1 oil engine** driving 1 FP propeller Total Power: 8,450kW (11,489hp) 14.5kn MAN-B&W 6S50MC-C8 1 x 2 Stroke 6 Cy. 500 x 2000 8450kW (11489bhp) Mitsui Engineering & Shipbuilding CLtd-Japan
6824214 - -	**SHINYA MARU** *ex Kaiko Maru No. 8 -2010* - -	*194* 70 -		**1968 Niigata Engineering Co Ltd — Niigata NI** Yd No: 765 Loa 42.35 Br ex 6.61 Dght 2.896 Lbp 34.90 Br md 6.58 Dpth 3.18 Welded, 1 dk	**(B11B2FV) Fishing Vessel**	**1 oil engine** driving 1 FP propeller Total Power: 625kW (850hp) Niigata 6M28KHS 1 x 4 Stroke 6 Cy. 280 x 440 625kW (850bhp) Niigata Engineering Co Ltd-Japan
7736567 - -	**SHINYO** *ex Shinyo Maru No. 2 -1994* *ex Kojin Maru No. 8 -1990* - -	*129* 67 302		**1978 YK Furumoto Tekko Zosensho — Osakikamijima** Yd No: 382 Loa 39.12 Br ex - Dght 2.400 Lbp 34.00 Br md 7.60 Dpth 3.90 Welded, 1 dk	**(A31A2GX) General Cargo Ship**	**1 oil engine** geared to sc. shaft driving 1 FP propeller Total Power: 441kW (600hp) Yanmar 6U-UT 1 x 4 Stroke 6 Cy. 200 x 240 441kW (600bhp) Yanmar Diesel Engine Co Ltd-Japan
9209257 *JM6635* -	**SHINYO** - **YK Hiramatsu Shokai** - *Sasebo, Nagasaki* Japan Official number: 136384	*499* - 1,558		**1999-08 Honda Zosen — Saiki** Yd No: 1020 Loa 73.00 Br ex - Dght 4.110 Lbp 67.00 Br md 13.50 Dpth 7.00 Welded, 1 dk	**(A31A2GX) General Cargo Ship** Grain: 1,005	**1 oil engine** driving 1 FP propeller Total Power: 1,471kW (2,000hp) 13.5kn Niigata 6M38GT 1 x 4 Stroke 6 Cy. 380 x 720 1471kW (2000bhp) Niigata Engineering Co Ltd-Japan Fuel: 75.0 (d.f.)
9197870 *VRAN3* -	**SHINYO KANNIKA** *ex Formosapetro Brilliance -2004* **Shinyo Kannika Ltd** Univan Ship Management Ltd SatCom: Inmarsat C 447700115 *Hong Kong* Hong Kong MMSI: 477720400 Official number: HK-1423	**149,274** 93,658 281,395 T/cm 168.8	Class: AB	**2001-04 Ishikawajima-Harima Heavy Industries Co Ltd (IHI) — Kure** Yd No: 3126 Loa 330.00 (BB) Br ex 60.04 Dght 20.428 Lbp 316.60 Br md 60.00 Dpth 28.90 Welded, 1 dk	**(A13A2TV) Crude Oil Tanker** Double Hull (13F) Liq: 321,889; Liq (Oil): 321,889 Compartments: 5 Ta, 10 Wing Ta, ER 3 Cargo Pump (s): 3x5000m³/hr Manifold: Bow/CM: 155m	**1 oil engine** driving 1 FP propeller Total Power: 22,680kW (30,836hp) 15.4kn Sulzer 7RTA84T 1 x 2 Stroke 7 Cy. 840 x 3150 22680kW (30836bhp) Diesel United Ltd.-Aioi AuxGen: 3 x 930kW 450V a.c Fuel: 6256.0 (r.f.) (Heating Coils)
9515931 *VRIO8* -	**SHINYO KIERAN** - **Shinyo Keiran Ltd** Univan Ship Management Ltd SatCom: Inmarsat C 447703548 *Hong Kong* Hong Kong MMSI: 477276400 Official number: HK-3106	**157,036** 99,050 297,066 T/cm 177.9	Class: CC NV	**2011-06 Dalian Shipbuilding Industry Co Ltd — Dalian LN (No 2 Yard)** Yd No: T3000-36 Loa 330.00 (BB) Br ex - Dght 21.500 Lbp 317.53 Br md 60.00 Dpth 29.70 Welded, 1 dk	**(A13A2TV) Crude Oil Tanker** Double Hull (13F) Liq: 324,600; Liq (Oil): 323,000 Compartments: 5 Wing Ta, 5 Ta, 5 Wing Ta, 1 Wing Slop Ta, 1 Wing Slop Ta, ER 3 Cargo Pump (s): 3x5500m³/hr	**1 oil engine** driving 1 FP propeller Total Power: 25,480kW (34,643hp) 15.5kn MAN-B&W 7S80MC 1 x 2 Stroke 7 Cy. 800 x 3056 25480kW (34643bhp) MAN Nutzfahrzeuge AG-Nuernberg AuxGen: 3 x 975kW 450V a.c
9250919 *JL6607* -	**SHINYO MARU** - **Reitaku Kaiun Co Ltd (Reitaku Kaiun KK)** - *Imabari, Ehime* Japan Official number: 136531	*199* - 500		**2001-03 Hakata Zosen K.K. — Imabari** Yd No: 632 Loa 50.04 Br ex - Dght - Lbp 47.00 Br md 8.00 Dpth 3.20 Welded, 1 dk	**(A13B2TU) Tanker (unspecified)** Double Hull (13F) Liq: 500; Liq (Oil): 500	**1 oil engine** reduction geared to sc. shaft driving 1 FP propeller Total Power: 956kW (1,300hp) 11.0kn Daihatsu 6DKM-20 1 x 4 Stroke 6 Cy. 200 x 300 956kW (1300bhp) Daihatsu Diesel Manufacturing Co Lt-Japan
9348962 *7JAO* MZ1-700	**SHINYO MARU** - **Miyazaki Prefecture Board of Education** - *Miyazaki, Miyazaki* Japan MMSI: 432511000 Official number: 140116	*646* - -		**2005-03 Nagasaki Zosen K.K. — Nagasaki** Yd No: 1200 Loa 64.21 Br ex 10.02 Dght 3.800 Lbp 55.50 Br md 10.00 Dpth 4.10 Welded, 1 dk	**(B11B2FV) Fishing Vessel**	**1 oil engine** reduction geared to sc. shaft driving 1 FP propeller Total Power: 1,471kW (2,000hp) Niigata 1 x 4 Stroke 1471kW (2000bhp) Niigata Engineering Co Ltd-Japan
9733636 *JD3650* -	**SHINYO MARU** - **Japan Railway Construction, Transport & Technology Agency & Nissen Kisen Co Ltd** Nissen Kisen KK *Onomichi, Hiroshima* Japan MMSI: 431005249 Official number: 142121	*749* - 1,692	Class: NK	**2014-03 Hongawara Zosen K.K. — Fukuyama** Yd No: 690 Loa 72.32 Br ex 11.42 Dght 4.622 Lbp 68.00 Br md 11.40 Dpth 5.30 Welded, 1 dk	**(A12B2TR) Chemical/Products Tanker** Double Hull (13F)	**1 oil engine** driving 1 Propeller Total Power: 1,417kW (1,927hp) Niigata 1 x 4 Stroke 6 Cy. 340 x 620 1417kW (1927bhp) Niigata Engineering Co Ltd-Japan AuxGen: 3 x 213kW a.c
8400593 *JFCL* -	**SHINYO MARU** *launched as Kamitaka Maru -1984* **Government of Japan (Ministry of Education, Culture, Sports, Science & Technology)** Tokyo University of Marine Science & Technology (Tokyo Kaiyo-Daigaku) SatCom: Inmarsat B 343146610 *Tokyo* Japan MMSI: 431466000 Official number: 128130	*649* - 584		**1984-12 Sumitomo Heavy Industries Ltd. — Uraga Shipyard, Yokosuka** Yd No: 1130 Loa 60.03 (BB) Br ex 10.62 Dght 4.201 Lbp 53.01 Br md 10.61 Dpth 6.81 Welded, 2 dks	**(B11A2FS) Stern Trawler**	**1 oil engine** with clutches, flexible couplings & sr geared to sc. shaft driving 1 CP propeller Total Power: 1,545kW (2,101hp) Pielstick 8PA5 1 x 4 Stroke 8 Cy. 255 x 270 1545kW (2101bhp) Niigata Engineering Co Ltd-Japan Thrusters: 1 Thwart. CP thruster (f)
8630162 - -	**SHINYO MARU** - **Dong Cheon Oil Removal & Tank Cleaning Co Ltd** - South Korea	*111* - 350		**1986-10 K.K. Tago Zosensho — Nishi-Izu** Yd No: 207 Loa 36.50 Br ex 7.87 Dght 2.450 Lbp 34.50 Br md 7.85 Dpth 2.65 Welded, 1 dk	**(A13B2TU) Tanker (unspecified)**	**1 oil engine** driving 1 FP propeller Total Power: 257kW (349hp) 8.5kn Sumiyoshi S623TS 1 x 4 Stroke 6 Cy. 230 x 400 257kW (349bhp) Sumiyoshi Marine Diesel Co Ltd-Japan
9033127 *JI3455* -	**SHINYO MARU** *ex Kanzaki Maru -2011* **Osaka Municipal Office** - *Osaka, Osaka* Japan Official number: 131705	*182* - -		**1991-03 Kanagawa Zosen — Kobe** Yd No: 356 Loa 33.40 Br ex 10.50 Dght 3.000 Lbp 29.00 Br md 9.20 Dpth 4.00 Welded	**(B32A2ST) Tug**	**2 oil engines** gearing integral to driving 2 Z propellers Total Power: 2,352kW (3,198hp) 13.7kn Yanmar 6Z280-EN 2 x 4 Stroke 6 Cy. 280 x 360 each-1176kW (1599bhp) Yanmar Diesel Engine Co Ltd-Japan AuxGen: 2 x 104kW 225V 60Hz a.c Fuel: 43.0 (d.f.) 1.9pd

IMO / Call sign / Flag	Name / Owner / Manager / Port	Tonnage	Class	Construction / Dimensions	Type / Cargo	Machinery
8975938 *JG5698* -	**SHINYO MARU** **Niijima Bussan KK** - *Niijima, Tokyo* *Japan* Official number: 137159	*438* - -		**2002-11 K.K. Watanabe Zosensho — Nagasaki** Yd No: 101 L reg 50.02 Br ex - Dght - Lbp - Br md 9.60 Dpth 3.49 Welded, 1 dk	**(A31A2GT) General Cargo/Tanker**	**1 oil engine** driving 1 Propeller Total Power: 736kW (1,001hp) Niigata 6M30BGT 1 x 4 Stroke 6 Cy. 300 x 530 736kW (1001bhp) Niigata Engineering Co Ltd-Japan
8998411 *JD2095* -	**SHINYO MARU** **Shinyo Kaiun YK** - *Kure, Hiroshima* *Japan* Official number: 140153	*199* - 700		**2005-05 Y.K. Okajima Zosensho — Matsuyama** Yd No: 260 Loa 56.27 Br ex - Dght 3.340 Lbp 50.00 Br md 9.30 Dpth 5.57 Welded, 1 dk	**(A31A2GX) General Cargo Ship** 1 Ha: ER (28.1 x 7.0)	**1 oil engine** reverse geared to sc. shaft driving 1 FP propeller Total Power: 736kW (1,001hp) Akasaka K26SR 1 x 4 Stroke 6 Cy. 260 x 480 736kW (1001bhp) Akasaka Tekkosho KK (Akasaka DieselLtd)-Japan
8998227 *JD2072* -	**SHINYO MARU** **YK Nisshin Kaiun** - *Kure, Hiroshima* *Japan* Official number: 140121	*499* - 1,600		**2005-02 K.K. Matsuura Zosensho — Osakikamijima** Yd No: 555 L reg 72.11 Br ex - Dght 4.120 Lbp 70.00 Br md 12.50 Dpth 7.00 Welded, 1 dk	**(A31A2GX) General Cargo Ship** Grain: 2,486 1 Ha: ER (40.2 x 9.5)	**1 oil engine** driving 1 Propeller Total Power: 1,471kW (2,000hp) 12.1kn Hanshin LH34LA 1 x 4 Stroke 6 Cy. 340 x 640 1471kW (2000bhp) The Hanshin Diesel Works Ltd-Japan
8864177 *JM6123* -	**SHINYO MARU** **Toyo Kaiun KK** - *Sasebo, Nagasaki* *Japan* Official number: 132689	*202* - 649		**1992-01 Y.K. Okajima Zosensho — Matsuyama** Yd No: 236 Loa 57.47 Br ex - Dght 3.200 Lbp 52.00 Br md 9.50 Dpth 5.42 Welded, 1 dk	**(A31A2GX) General Cargo Ship**	**1 oil engine** driving 1 FP propeller Total Power: 588kW (799hp) 12.0kn Matsui ML627GSC 1 x 4 Stroke 6 Cy. 270 x 480 588kW (799bhp) Matsui Iron Works Co Ltd-Japan
8824359 *JK4918* -	**SHINYO MARU** **Okayama Kaiun KK** - *Kurashiki, Okayama* *Japan* Official number: 130982	*199* - 699		**1989-04 K.K. Kawamoto Zosensho — Osakikamijima** Loa 54.74 Br ex - Dght 3.590 Lbp 49.60 Br md 9.20 Dpth 5.93 Welded, 1 dk	**(A31A2GX) General Cargo Ship**	**1 oil engine** reverse geared to sc. shaft driving 1 FP propeller Total Power: 625kW (850hp) Akasaka K26SR 1 x 4 Stroke 6 Cy. 260 x 480 625kW (850bhp) Akasaka Tekkosho KK (Akasaka DieselLtd)-Japan
8713469 *JJ3563* -	**SHINYO MARU** **Kazuo Murasumi** - *Himeji, Hyogo* *Japan* Official number: 129307	*494* - 963		**1987-12 Shitanoe Shipbuilding Co Ltd — Usuki OT** Yd No: 1075 Loa 60.00 (BB) Br ex 12.02 Dght 4.160 Lbp 54.89 Br md 12.01 Dpth 6.30 Welded, 1 dk	**(B33A2DG) Grab Dredger** Grain: 1,025 Compartments: 1 Ho, ER 1 Ha: (18.2 x 9.0)ER Cranes: 1	**1 oil engine** driving 1 FP propeller Total Power: 1,300kW (1,767hp) Fuji 6S32G 1 x 4 Stroke 6 Cy. 320 x 610 1300kW (1767bhp) Fuji Diesel Co Ltd-Japan
8730936 *JD2299* -	**SHINYO MARU** **Kanda Senpaku Kyogyo Kumiai** - *Tsukumi, Oita* *Japan* Official number: 140380	*499* - 1,600		**2006-08 YK Nakanoshima Zosensho — Kochi KC** Yd No: 233 Loa 75.52 Br ex - Dght 4.160 Lbp 70.00 Br md 12.20 Dpth 7.15 Welded, 1 dk	**(A31A2GX) General Cargo Ship** Grain: 2,585 1 Ha: ER (40.2 x 10.0)	**1 oil engine** driving 1 Propeller Total Power: 1,618kW (2,200hp) Niigata 6M34BGT 1 x 4 Stroke 6 Cy. 340 x 620 1618kW (2200bhp) Niigata Engineering Co Ltd-Japan
8823484 - -	**SHINYO MARU No. 1** - - -	*198* - 405		**1988-09 K.K. Tago Zosensho — Nishi-Izu** Yd No: 216 Loa 39.02 Br ex - Dght 2.640 Lbp 35.07 Br md 9.00 Dpth 2.90 Welded, 1 dk	**(A24D2BA) Aggregates Carrier** Compartments: 1 Ho, ER 1 Ha: (14.3 x 6.8)ER	**1 oil engine** driving 1 FP propeller Total Power: 382kW (519hp) Sumiyoshi S26G 1 x 4 Stroke 6 Cy. 260 x 470 382kW (519bhp) Sumiyoshi Marine Diesel Co Ltd-Japan
9159608 *JM6576* -	**SHINYO MARU No. 2** **Sanyo Kaiun KK** - *Kitakyushu, Fukuoka* *Japan* MMSI: 431600639 Official number: 135438	*749* - 1,730		**1996-11 Yamanaka Zosen K.K. — Imabari** Yd No: 605 Loa - Br ex - Dght 4.500 Lbp 65.00 Br md 11.50 Dpth 5.05 Welded, 1 dk	**(A24A2BT) Cement Carrier**	**1 oil engine** driving 1 FP propeller Total Power: 1,324kW (1,800hp) Hanshin LH30LG 1 x 4 Stroke 6 Cy. 300 x 600 1324kW (1800bhp) The Hanshin Diesel Works Ltd-Japan
8631063 *JK4732* -	**SHINYO MARU No. 8** *ex* Sumitoku Maru No. 11 *-1992* **Uchida Kensetsu KK** - *Himeji, Hyogo* *Japan* Official number: 129569	*496* - 1,379		**1987-07 K.K. Taihei Kogyo — Akitsu** Yd No: 1983 Loa 66.00 Br ex 13.02 Dght 4.370 Lbp 60.00 Br md 13.00 Dpth 6.80 Welded, 1 dk	**(A24D2BA) Aggregates Carrier**	**1 oil engine** geared to sc. shaft driving 1 FP propeller Total Power: 736kW (1,001hp) Hanshin 6LU35G 1 x 4 Stroke 6 Cy. 350 x 550 736kW (1001bhp) The Hanshin Diesel Works Ltd-Japan
9652466 *7JMI* -	**SHINYO MARU NO. 53** **Nemuro Gyogyo Kyodo Kumiai** Kinone Suisan KK *Nemuro, Hokkaido* *Japan* Official number: 141712	*199* - -		**2012-07 The Hakodate Dock Co Ltd — Muroran HK** Yd No: W3212 Loa 46.90 Br ex - Dght 3.350 Lbp - Br md 7.50 Dpth - Welded, 1 dk	**(B11B2FV) Fishing Vessel**	**1 oil engine** reduction geared to sc. shaft driving 1 Propeller Total Power: 1,838kW (2,499hp) Niigata 6MG28HX 1 x 4 Stroke 6 Cy. 280 x 370 1838kW (2499bhp) Niigata Engineering Co Ltd-Japan
7916765 *7JZK* -	**SHINYO MARU NO. 58** *ex* Kyoshin Maru No. 8 *-2005* **YK Shinyo Maru** - *Uwajima, Ehime* *Japan* MMSI: 431524000 Official number: 123205	*322* - -		**1979-10 Uchida Zosen — Ise** Yd No: 798 L reg 47.90 Br ex - Dght 3.501 Lbp 47.02 Br md 9.01 Dpth 4.10 Welded, 1 dk	**(B11B2FV) Fishing Vessel**	**1 oil engine** driving 1 FP propeller Total Power: 1,103kW (1,500hp) Hanshin 6LU32G 1 x 4 Stroke 6 Cy. 320 x 510 1103kW (1500bhp) Hanshin Nainenki Kogyo-Japan
8712817 - -	**SHINYO MARU No. 62** - - - *South Korea*	*306* - 580		**1987-11 K.K. Odo Zosen Tekko — Shimonoseki** Yd No: 338 Loa 47.90 Br ex 9.02 Dght 3.150 Lbp 43.50 Br md 9.00 Dpth 3.50 Welded, 1 dk	**(B34E2SW) Waste Disposal Vessel**	**1 oil engine** driving 1 FP propeller Total Power: 588kW (799hp) Yanmar MF24-UT 1 x 4 Stroke 6 Cy. 240 x 420 588kW (799bhp) Yanmar Diesel Engine Co Ltd-Japan
9246011 *JL6640* -	**SHINYO MARU No. 68** **YK Shinyo Maru** - *Uwajima, Ehime* *Japan* MMSI: 431271000 Official number: 136513	*324* - -		**2001-01 Nagasaki Zosen K.K. — Nagasaki** Yd No: 1172 Loa 58.31 Br ex 9.02 Dght 3.600 Lbp 51.00 Br md 9.00 Dpth 4.10 Welded, 1 dk	**(B11B2FV) Fishing Vessel**	**1 oil engine** geared to sc. shaft driving 1 FP propeller Total Power: 809kW (1,100hp) Niigata 6M31BFT 1 x 4 Stroke 6 Cy. 310 x 530 809kW (1100bhp) Niigata Engineering Co Ltd-Japan
9197868 *VRCN4* -	**SHINYO OCEAN** *ex* Formosapetro Ace *-2007* **Shinyo Ocean Ltd** Univan Ship Management Ltd SatCom: Inmarsat C 447700632 *Hong Kong* *Hong Kong* MMSI: 477656700 Official number: HK-1841	**149,274** 90,656 281,395 T/cm 168.8	Class: AB	**2001-03 Ishikawajima-Harima Heavy Industries Co Ltd (IHI) — Kure** Yd No: 3125 Loa 330.00 (BB) Br ex 60.04 Dght 20.428 Lbp 316.60 Br md 60.00 Dpth 28.90 Welded, 1 dk	**(A13A2TV) Crude Oil Tanker** Double Hull (13F) Liq: 321,889; Liq (Oil): 321,889 Compartments: 5 Ta, 10 Wing Ta, ER, 2 Wing Slop Ta 3 Cargo Pump (s): 3x5000m³/hr Manifold: Bow/CM: 155m	**1 oil engine** driving 1 FP propeller Total Power: 22,680kW (30,836hp) 15.4kn Sulzer 7RTA84T 1 x 2 Stroke 7 Cy. 840 x 3150 22680kW (30836bhp) Diesel United Ltd.-Aioi AuxGen: 3 x 930kW 450V a.c Fuel: 6256.0 (r.f.) (Heating Coils)
9515929 *VRHA4* -	**SHINYO SAOWALAK** **Shinyo Saowalak Ltd** Univan Ship Management Ltd SatCom: Inmarsat C 447702857 *Hong Kong* *Hong Kong* MMSI: 477786700 Official number: HK-2779	**157,039** 99,017 296,988 T/cm 177.9	Class: CC NV	**2010-06 Dalian Shipbuilding Industry Co Ltd — Dalian LN (No 2 Yard)** Yd No: T3000-35 Loa 330.00 (BB) Br ex - Dght 21.500 Lbp 317.53 Br md 60.00 Dpth 29.70 Welded, 1 dk	**(A13A2TV) Crude Oil Tanker** Double Hull (13F) Liq: 324,600; Liq (Oil): 323,000 Compartments: 5 Ta, 10 Wing Ta, 2 Wing Slop Ta, ER 3 Cargo Pump (s): 3x5500m³/hr	**1 oil engine** driving 1 FP propeller Total Power: 25,480kW (34,643hp) 15.8kn MAN-B&W 7S80MC 1 x 2 Stroke 7 Cy. 800 x 3056 25480kW (34643bhp) MAN Nutzfahrzeuge AG-Nuernberg AuxGen: 3 x 975kW a.c
9004530 *VRZP7* -	**SHINYO SPLENDOR** *ex* Shinyo Landes *-2007* *ex* Berge Stavanger *-2004* **Shinyo Loyalty Ltd** Univan Ship Management Ltd SatCom: Inmarsat C 447787910 *Hong Kong* *Hong Kong* MMSI: 477879000 Official number: HK-1236	**160,299** 98,908 306,474 T/cm 170.0	Class: AB (KR) (BV) (NV)	**1993-10 Nippon Kokan KK (NKK Corp) — Tsu ME** Yd No: 134 Loa 331.45 (BB) Br ex 58.39 Dght 22.365 Lbp 316.96 Br md 58.00 Dpth 31.40 Welded, 1 dk	**(A13A2TV) Crude Oil Tanker** Double Hull (13F) Liq: 333,334; Liq (Oil): 343,337 Compartments: 5 Ta, 10 Wing Ta, ER 3 Cargo Pump (s): 3x5500m³/hr Manifold: Bow/CM: 160m	**1 oil engine** driving 1 FP propeller Total Power: 25,745kW (35,003hp) 15.4kn Sulzer 7RTA84M 1 x 2 Stroke 7 Cy. 840 x 2900 25745kW (35003bhp) Diesel United Ltd.-Aioi AuxGen: 1 x 900kW 450V 60Hz a.c, 2 x 900kW 450V 60Hz a.c Fuel: 254.0 (d.f.) (Heating Coils) 7072.0 (r.f.) 98.0pd

IMO / Call sign	Name / Owner	Tonnage	Builder / Dimensions	Type	Machinery
8966987 *JH3498* -	**SHINYU MARU** *ex Kyokuei Maru -2001* **Toei Unyu KK** - *Nagoya, Aichi* *Japan* Official number: 133163	*102* - -	**1992-05 Iisaku Zosen K.K. — Nishi-Izu** Yd No: 92161 L reg 34.22 Br ex - Dght 2.300 Lbp - Br md 7.40 Dpth 2.50 Welded, 1 dk	**(A13B2TU) Tanker (unspecified)**	**1 oil engine** driving 1 FP propeller Total Power: 257kW (349hp) Yanmar MF24-ST 1 x 4 Stroke 6 Cy. 240 x 420 257kW (349bhp) Yanmar Diesel Engine Co Ltd-Japan
8717178 *JQLE*	**SHINYU MARU** *ex Hokusho Maru -2007* **Offshore Engineering Co Ltd** Fukada Salvage & Marine Works Co Ltd (Fukada Salvage Kensetsu KK) SatCom: Inmarsat A 1203732 *Tokyo* *Japan* MMSI: 431611000 Official number: 130217	*280* - -	**1988-03 Niigata Engineering Co Ltd — Niigata NI** Yd No: 2078 Converted From: Fishing Vessel-2008 Loa 60.69 (BB) Br ex 11.23 Dght 4.141 Lbp 54.41 Br md 11.21 Dpth 6.61 Welded, 2 dks	**(B22A2OR) Offshore Support Vessel**	**1 oil engine** with clutches, flexible couplings & sr geared to sc. shaft driving 1 CP propeller Total Power: 2,059kW (2,799hp) 11.2kn Niigata 6MG32CLX 1 x 4 Stroke 6 Cy. 320 x 420 2059kW (2799bhp) Niigata Engineering Co Ltd-Japan AuxGen: 2 x 440kW a.c Thrusters: 1 Tunnel thruster (f)
8864866 *JH3292* -	**SHINYU MARU** - **Tadataka Shimizu** - *Hazu, Aichi* *Japan* Official number: 133191	*220* - 650	**1992-07 K.K. Tago Zosensho — Nishi-Izu** Yd No: 250 L reg 38.00 Br ex - Dght 2.300 Lbp - Br md 7.80 Dpth 2.70 Welded, 1 dk	**(A31A2GX) General Cargo Ship**	**1 oil engine** geared to sc. shaft driving 1 FP propeller Total Power: 257kW (349hp) Sumiyoshi S23G 1 x 4 Stroke 6 Cy. 230 x 400 257kW (349bhp) Sumiyoshi Tekkosho-Japan
7935046 - -	**SHINYU MARU** - -	*228* - 500	**1979 Oshima Kogyo K.K. — Yokosuka** Yd No: 54-SH-5 Loa 39.50 (BB) Br ex - Dght 2.550 Lbp 37.50 Br md 8.21 Dpth 2.80 Welded, 1 dk	**(A13B2TU) Tanker (unspecified)**	**1 oil engine** driving 1 FP propeller Total Power: 250kW (340hp) Mitsubishi 4SAC-1 1 x 4 Stroke 4 Cy. 200 x 240 250kW (340bhp) Mitsubishi Heavy Industries Ltd-Japan
8998057 *JL6027* -	**SHINYU MARU NO. 8** - - *Imabari, Ehime* *Japan* Official number: 132163	*101* - -	**1991-12 Namikata Shipbuilding Co Ltd — Imabari EH** L reg 22.16 Br ex - Dght - Lbp - Br md 7.50 Dpth 2.89 Welded, 1 dk	**(B32A2ST) Tug**	**1 oil engine** driving 1 Propeller
8710883 *JG4796* -	**SHINZAN** *ex Akiyoshi -2001 ex Mihashi -1997* **Government of Japan (Ministry of Land, Infrastructure & Transport) (The Coastguard)** - *Tokyo* *Japan* Official number: 130254	*182* - -	**1988-09 Mitsubishi Heavy Industries Ltd. — Shimonoseki** Yd No: 911 Loa 43.00 Br ex 7.52 Dght 1.651 Lbp 39.00 Br md 7.50 Dpth 4.09 Welded, 1 dk	**(B34H2SQ) Patrol Vessel** Hull Material: Aluminium Alloy	**3 oil engines** geared to sc. shafts driving 2 FP propellers , 1 Water jet Total Power: 6,547kW (8,900hp) 35.0kn Mitsubishi S12U-MTK 2 x Vee 4 Stroke 12 Cy. 240 x 260 each-2354kW (3200bhp) Mitsubishi Heavy Industries Ltd-Japan Mitsubishi S8U-MTK 1 x 4 Stroke 8 Cy. 240 x 260 1839kW (2500bhp) Mitsubishi Heavy Industries Ltd-Japan
9115353 *JM6453* -	**SHINZAN MARU No. 18** - **Shoshin Kaiun GK** Kato Kaiun KK *Kamiamakusa, Kumamoto* *Japan* Official number: 134545	*497* Class: (NK) - 1,580	**1995-03 K.K. Miura Zosensho — Saiki** Yd No: 1120 Loa 66.00 (BB) Br ex - Dght 4.180 Lbp 62.00 Br md 13.00 Dpth 6.50 Welded, 1 dk	**(A31A2GX) General Cargo Ship** Grain: 1,264 Compartments: 1 Ho, ER 1 Ha: ER	**1 oil engine** driving 1 FP propeller Total Power: 736kW (1,001hp) Niigata 6M34AGT 1 x 4 Stroke 6 Cy. 340 x 620 736kW (1001bhp) Niigata Engineering Co Ltd-Japan Thrusters: 1 Thwart. FP thruster (f)
8859079 - - -	**SHINZUISHO MARU** - - - *United Arab Emirates*	*174* - 422	**1991-08 KK Ouchi Zosensho — Matsuyama EH** Loa 49.50 (BB) Br ex - Dght 3.220 Lbp 45.00 Br md 8.30 Dpth 5.00 Welded, 1 dk	**(A31A2GX) General Cargo Ship** 1 Ha: (26.5 x 6.3)ER	**1 oil engine** driving 1 FP propeller Total Power: 405kW (551hp) 10.0kn Matsui 6M26KGHS 1 x 4 Stroke 6 Cy. 260 x 400 405kW (551bhp) Matsui Iron Works Co Ltd-Japan
7395741 - -	**SHIOJI** - **KK Hashimoto Shoten** -	*167* - 28	**1974-09 Hikari Kogyo K.K. — Yokosuka** Yd No: 262 Loa 25.00 Br ex - Dght 1.340 Lbp 23.25 Br md 12.40 Dpth 2.49 Welded, 1 dk	**(B34G2SE) Pollution Control Vessel**	**2 oil engines** geared to sc. shafts driving 2 FP propellers Total Power: 1,030kW (1,400hp) 10.5kn G.M. (Detroit Diesel) 16V-71-N 2 x Vee 2 Stroke 16 Cy. 108 x 127 each-515kW (700bhp) General Motors Detroit DieselAllison Divn-USA
8608561 *JG4644* -	**SHIOJI MARU** - **Government of Japan (Ministry of Education, Culture, Sports, Science & Technology)** Tokyo University of Marine Science & Technology (Tokyo Kaiyo-Daigaku) *Tokyo* *Japan* MMSI: 431100037 Official number: 129829	*425* - 269	**1987-02 Ishikawajima-Harima Heavy Industries Co Ltd (IHI) — Tokyo** Yd No: 2957 Loa 49.94 Br ex - Dght 3.001 Lbp 46.00 Br md 10.01 Dpth 3.81 Welded	**(B34K2QT) Training Ship**	**1 oil engine** with clutches, flexible couplings & sr geared to sc. shaft driving 1 CP propeller Total Power: 1,030kW (1,400hp) 14.1kn Daihatsu 6DLM-26SL 1 x 4 Stroke 6 Cy. 260 x 340 1030kW (1400bhp) Daihatsu Diesel Manufacturing Co Lt-Japan AuxGen: 1 x 400kW 450V 60Hz a.c, 2 x 160kW 205V 50Hz a.c Thrusters: 1 Directional thruster (f); 1 Directional thruster (a)
9185138 *JH3471*	**SHIOJI MARU** - **Nagoya Kisen KK (Nagoya Kisen Kaisha Ltd)** - *Nagoya, Aichi* *Japan* Official number: 135648	*194* - -	**1998-05 Kanagawa Zosen — Kobe** Yd No: 458 Loa 33.80 Br ex - Dght - Lbp 29.50 Br md 9.20 Dpth 4.21 Welded, 1 dk	**(B32A2ST) Tug**	**2 oil engines** Geared Integral to driving 2 Z propellers Total Power: 2,574kW (3,500hp) 14.4kn Niigata 6L28HX 2 x 4 Stroke 6 Cy. 280 x 370 each-1287kW (1750bhp) Niigata Engineering Co Ltd-Japan
8922929 *JL6448*	**SHIOKAZE** - **Nippon Shio Kaiso Co Ltd** - *Sakaide, Kagawa* *Japan* Official number: 135159	*199* - 700	**1996-02 Shinwa Sangyo K.K. — Osakikamijima** Loa 58.39 Br ex - Dght 3.200 Lbp 53.00 Br md 9.40 Dpth 5.46 Welded, 1 dk	**(A31A2GX) General Cargo Ship** Grain: 1,104; Bale: 1,102 Compartments: 1 Ho, ER 1 Ha: (31.9 x 7.0)ER	**1 oil engine** driving 1 FP propeller Total Power: 736kW (1,001hp) 12.4kn Hanshin LH26G 1 x 4 Stroke 6 Cy. 260 x 440 736kW (1001bhp) The Hanshin Diesel Works Ltd-Japan
8974817 *JG5679* -	**SHIOMI MARU** - - - *Yokohama, Kanagawa* *Japan* Official number: 136958	*243* - -	**2002-03 Keihin Dock Co Ltd — Yokohama** Yd No: 255 Loa 36.20 Br ex - Dght 3.200 Lbp 31.50 Br md 9.80 Dpth 4.38 Welded, 1 dk	**(B32A2ST) Tug**	**2 oil engines** gearing integral to driving 2 Z propellers Total Power: 2,942kW (4,000hp) Yanmar 6N280-UN 2 x 4 Stroke 6 Cy. 280 x 380 each-1471kW (2000bhp) Yanmar Diesel Engine Co Ltd-Japan
9468188 *3FHW5* -	**SHIOSAI** - **Sea Green Shipping SA** Kitaura Kaiun KK SatCom: Inmarsat C 437231310 *Panama* *Panama* MMSI: 372313000 Official number: 4105410A	**89,603** Class: NK 58,437 176,827 T/cm 121.7	**2009-11 Namura Shipbuilding Co Ltd — Imari SG** Yd No: 296 Loa 288.97 (BB) Br ex - Dght 17.955 Lbp 279.00 Br md 45.00 Dpth 24.40 Welded, 1 dk	**(A21A2BC) Bulk Carrier** Grain: 198,963; Bale: 195,968 Compartments: 9 Ho, ER 9 Ha: ER	**1 oil engine** driving 1 FP propeller Total Power: 16,860kW (22,923hp) 14.8kn MAN-B&W 6S70MC 1 x 2 Stroke 6 Cy. 700 x 2674 16860kW (22923bhp) Mitsui Engineering & Shipbuilding CLtd-Japan Fuel: 4260.0 (r.f.)
9608116 *JD3239*	**SHIOTA MARU NO. 8** - **Japan Railway Construction, Transport & Technology Agency & Shiota Yusosen KK** Shiota Yusosen KK *Awaji, Hyogo* *Japan* MMSI: 431301247 Official number: 141510	*499* - 1,180	**2011-09 Imura Zosen K.K. — Komatsushima** Yd No: 336 Loa 64.99 Br ex - Dght 4.218 Lbp 59.98 Br md 10.40 Dpth 4.50 Welded, 1 dk	**(A13B2TP) Products Tanker** Double Hull (13F) Liq: 1,180; Liq (Oil): 1,180	**1 oil engine** reduction geared to sc. shaft driving 1 Propeller Total Power: 1,030kW (1,400hp) 11.5kn Hanshin LH28G 1 x 4 Stroke 6 Cy. 280 x 460 1030kW (1400bhp) The Hanshin Diesel Works Ltd-Japan
9048055 - - -	**SHIOTA MARU No. 8** - - -	*497* - 730	**1992-10 KK Ura Kyodo Zosensho — Awaji HG** Yd No: 289 Loa 64.40 (BB) Br ex - Dght - Lbp 60.00 Br md 10.00 Dpth 4.50 Welded, 1 dk	**(A13B2TU) Tanker (unspecified)** Liq: 1,350; Liq (Oil): 1,350 Compartments: 4 Ta, ER	**1 oil engine** geared to sc. shaft driving 1 FP propeller Total Power: 736kW (1,001hp) 12.0kn Hanshin LH28G 1 x 4 Stroke 6 Cy. 280 x 460 736kW (1001bhp) The Hanshin Diesel Works Ltd-Japan

Identity / Owner	Tonnage	Class	Build / Dimensions	Type / Cargo	Machinery
9137868 **SHIP-2-SHORE** *ZCPB9* - **Labadee Investments Ltd** Royal Caribbean Cruises Ltd (RCCL) *George Town* *Cayman Islands (British)* Official number: 726018	**119** 66 -	Class: NV	**1995-09 Keith Marine Inc — Palatka FL** Yd No: 31 Loa 26.00 Br ex - Dght 3.270 Lbp 24.45 Br md 7.01 Dpth 3.28 Welded, 1 dk	**(A37B2PS) Passenger Ship**	**2 oil engines** with clutches & sr reverse geared to sc. shafts driving 2 FP propellers Total Power: 1,056kW (1,436hp) 10.0kn G.M. (Detroit Diesel) 12V-71 2 x Vee 2 Stroke 12 Cy. 108 x 127 each-528kW (718bhp) General Motors Detroit DieselAllison Divn-USA AuxGen: 2 x 20kW 110/208V 50Hz a.c Fuel: 22.0 (d.f.) 2.7pd
8916243 **SHIP OCEAN I** *T2VC3* *ex Formosa Four -2011* - **PT Argopuro Maju Sukses** Timur Ship Management Pte Ltd *Funafuti* *Tuvalu* MMSI: 572240210	**19,081** 10,063 35,672 T/cm 45.1	Class: (CR) (AB)	**1991-08 Shin Kurushima Dockyard Co. Ltd. — Onishi** Yd No: 2697 Loa 174.92 (BB) Br ex 30.03 Dght 10.528 Lbp 167.00 Br md 30.00 Dpth 14.20 Welded, 1 dk	**(A12A2TC) Chemical Tanker** Double Hull Liq: 33,806 Compartments: 12 Wing Ta, 1 Slop Ta, ER 16 Cargo Pump (s) Manifold: Bow/CM: 90.3m	**1 oil engine** driving 1 FP propeller Total Power: 9,047kW (12,300hp) 15.5kn Mitsubishi 6UEC60LA 1 x 2 Stroke 6 Cy. 600 x 1900 9047kW (12300bhp) Kobe Hatsudoki KK-Japan AuxGen: 3 x 560kW a.c Fuel: 140.0 (d.f.) 1700.0 (r.f.)
8920361 **SHIP OCEAN III** - *ex Jose Bright -2011* - *ex Chembulk Rotterdam -2005 ex Fifi -1995* **PT Argopuro Maju Sukses** Timur Ship Management Pte Ltd	**21,142** 11,498 32,442 T/cm 39.9	Class: (NV) (AB)	**1993-07 OAO Khersonskiy Sudostroitelnyy Zavod — Kherson** Yd No: 1423 Conv to DH-2007 Loa 178.96 (BB) Br ex 25.33 Dght 12.320 Lbp 164.71 Br md 25.30 Dpth 15.00 Welded, 1 dk	**(A12B2TR) Chemical/Products Tanker** Double Hull (13F) Liq: 36,135; Liq (Oil): 36,135 Compartments: 14 Wing Ta, 2 Wing Slop Ta, ER 14 Cargo Pump (s): 10x425m³/hr, 4x250m³/hr Manifold: Bow/CM: 90m Ice Capable	**1 oil engine** driving 1 FP propeller Total Power: 9,370kW (12,739hp) 14.5kn B&W 6L60MC 1 x 2 Stroke 6 Cy. 600 x 1944 9370kW (12739bhp) AO Bryanskiy MashinostroitelnyyZavod (BMZ)-Bryansk AuxGen: 3 x 880kW 400V 50Hz a.c Fuel: 110.3 (d.f.) (Part Heating Coils) 1412.2 (r.f.) 32.9pd
8923935 **SHIPKA** - - **OOO Kardi** *Novorossiysk* *Russia* MMSI: 273428160	*853* 386 1,240	Class: (RS)	**1967-12 Shipbuilding & Shiprepairing Yard 'Ivan Dimitrov' — Rousse** Yd No: 64 Loa 53.28 Br ex 10.82 Dght 4.200 Lbp - Br md - Dpth 5.50 Welded, 1 dk	**(B35E2TF) Bunkering Tanker** Liq: 1,270; Liq (Oil): 1,270 Compartments: 15 Ta, ER Ice Capable	**1 oil engine** gearing integral to driving 1 Voith-Schneider propeller Total Power: 221kW (300hp) 5.6kn S.K.L. 6NVD36-1U 1 x 4 Stroke 6 Cy. 240 x 360 221kW (300bhp) VEB Schwermaschinenbau "KarlLiebknecht" (SKL)-Magdeburg AuxGen: 1 x 34kW a.c, 1 x 25kW a.c Fuel: 2.0 (d.f.)
9022166 **SHIPKA** - - - -	**205** - -	Class: (BR)	**1989-01 Ilyichyovskiy Sudoremontnyy Zavod im. "50-letiya SSSR" — Ilyichyovsk** Loa 34.01 Br ex - Dght 1.690 Lbp - Br md 6.90 Dpth 2.90 Welded, 1 dk	**(A37B2PS) Passenger Ship**	**3 oil engines** reduction geared to sc. shafts driving 3 FP propellers Total Power: 956kW (1,301hp) 16.0kn Russkiy 6CHSP15/18 2 x 4 Stroke 6 Cy. 150 x 180 each-110kW (150bhp) Barnaultransmash-Barnaul Zvezda M401A-1 1 x Vee 4 Stroke 12 Cy. 180 x 200 736kW (1001bhp) "Zvezda"-Leningrad
6622771 **SHIPMARIN 09** *XVEY* *ex Song Hau -2006 ex An Bien 06 -1993* - *ex Le Ngoc Thuy -1993 ex Charlotte -1989* **Saigon Shipbuilding & Marine Industry Co** - *Saigon* *Vietnam* Official number: VNSG-1321N-TH	**831** 526 1,064	Class: VR (GL)	**1966 J.J. Sietas Schiffswerft — Hamburg** Yd No: 581 Loa 61.90 Br ex 10.04 Dght 3.960 Lbp 56.39 Br md 10.01 Dpth 6.20 Welded, 2 dks	**(A31A2GX) General Cargo Ship** Grain: 2,027; Bale: 1,857 Compartments: 1 Ho, ER 2 Ha: (19.2 x 6.4) (10.4 x 6.4)ER Derricks: 1x3t; Winches: 1 Ice Capable	**1 oil engine** driving 1 FP propeller Total Power: 588kW (799hp) 11.0kn Deutz RV6M545 1 x 4 Stroke 6 Cy. 320 x 450 588kW (799bhp) Kloeckner Humboldt Deutz AG-West Germany AuxGen: 2 x 48kW 380V 50Hz a.c Fuel: 55.0 (d.f.)
9409716 **SHIPMARIN STAR** *3WYP* - **Saigon Shipbuilding & Marine Industry Co** SatCom: Inmarsat C 457440610 *Saigon* *Vietnam* MMSI: 574406000 Official number: VNSG-02/DD/2011	**4,318** 2,411 6,819	Class: NK VR	**2012-01 Saigon Shipbuilding & Marine Ind One Member Co Ltd — Ho Chi Minh City** Yd No: H-181/01 Loa 103.02 (BB) Br ex - Dght 7.210 Lbp 94.50 Br md 17.00 Dpth 9.10 Welded, 1 dk	**(A31A2GX) General Cargo Ship** Grain: 9,008 Compartments: 2 Ho, ER 2 Ha: ER Cranes: 1x20t,2x18t	**1 oil engine** driving 1 FP propeller Total Power: 2,648kW (3,600hp) 13.5kn Hanshin LH41LA 1 x 4 Stroke 6 Cy. 410 x 800 2648kW (3600bhp) The Hanshin Diesel Works Ltd-Japan Fuel: 430.0
9534717 **SHIPMARIN VICTORY** *3WDR9* - **Saigon Shipbuilding & Marine Industry Co** *Saigon* *Vietnam* MMSI: 574405000 Official number: VNSG-2118-TH	**4,318** 2,411 6,783	Class: NK VR	**2012-06 Saigon Shipbuilding & Marine Ind One Member Co Ltd — Ho Chi Minh City** Yd No: H-181/02 Loa 103.02 (BB) Br ex - Dght 7.210 Lbp 94.50 Br md 17.00 Dpth 9.10 Welded, 1 dk	**(A31A2GX) General Cargo Ship** Grain: 9,008 Cranes: 2x20t,1x19t	**1 oil engine** driving 1 FP propeller Total Power: 2,648kW (3,600hp) 13.5kn Hanshin LH41LA 1 x 4 Stroke 6 Cy. 410 x 800 2648kW (3600bhp) The Hanshin Diesel Works Ltd-Japan Fuel: 430.0
7106669 **SHIPMARINE 10** *XVDV* *ex Song Sai Gon -2008 ex Duyen Phat 05 -2002* - *ex Wathana -2001 ex Chang Aik -2001* *ex Chokyu Maru No. 7 -1990* **Saigon Shipbuilding & Marine Industry Co** - SatCom: Inmarsat C 457417410 *Saigon* *Vietnam* MMSI: 574174164 Official number: VNSG-1576-TH	**995** 669 1,737	Class: VR	**1971 Honda Zosen — Saiki** Yd No: 585 Loa 64.52 Br ex 11.02 Dght 4.800 Lbp 60.05 Br md 10.98 Dpth 6.20 Welded, 1 dk	**(A31A2GX) General Cargo Ship** Grain: 2,200; Bale: 2,000 Compartments: 1 Ho, ER 1 Ha: (32.0 x 7.0)ER	**1 oil engine** driving 1 FP propeller Total Power: 1,103kW (1,500hp) 12.0kn Hanshin 6LUD32 1 x 4 Stroke 6 Cy. 320 x 510 1103kW (1500bhp) Hanshin Nainenki Kogyo-Japan Fuel: 69.0
9301562 **SHIPPAN ISLAND** *V7UX7* *ex Asian Glory -2010 ex Alianca Pampas -2009* - **CV Two LLC** MTM Ship Management Pte Ltd *Majuro* *Marshall Islands* MMSI: 538004054 Official number: 4054	**9,956** 5,032 13,727 T/cm 28.0	Class: GL	**2005-11 Jiangdong Shipyard — Wuhu AH** Yd No: 1100TEU-6 Loa 147.80 (BB) Br ex - Dght 8.506 Lbp 140.30 Br md 23.25 Dpth 11.50 Welded, 1 dk	**(A33A2CC) Container Ship (Fully Cellular)** Grain: 16,000; Bale: 16,000 TEU 1118 C Ho 334 TEU C Dk 784 incl 240 ref C Cranes: 2x45t	**1 oil engine** reduction geared to sc. shaft driving 1 CP propeller Total Power: 9,737kW (13,238hp) 20.0kn MAN-B&W 7L58/64 1 x 4 Stroke 7 Cy. 580 x 640 9737kW (13238bhp) MAN B&W Diesel AG-Augsburg AuxGen: 1 x 1400kW 450/230V a.c, 3 x 570kW 450/230V a.c Thrusters: 1 Tunnel thruster (f)
8911748 **SHIPPER** *OJDM* *ex Birka Shipper -2013 ex Styrso -2002* - **Eckero Shipping AB Ltd** - SatCom: Inmarsat C 423000044 *Mariehamn* *Finland* MMSI: 230226000 Official number: 51120	**6,620** 1,986 5,387 T/cm 18.1	Class: NV	**1992-06 Brodogradiliste 'Sava' — Macvanska Mitrovica** (Hull) Yd No: 306 **1992-06 Fosen Mek. Verksteder AS — Rissa** Yd No: 47 Loa 122.00 (BB) Br ex - Dght 6.363 Lbp 112.00 Br md 19.00 Dpth 12.40 Welded, 2 dks	**(A35A2RR) Ro-Ro Cargo Ship** Stern door/ramp Lane-Len: 1278 Lane-clr ht: 5.00 Bale: 12,000 TEU 296 Compartments: 2 Ho, ER 1 Ha: ER Ice Capable	**1 oil engine** with flexible couplings & sr geared to sc. shaft driving 1 CP propeller Total Power: 4,500kW (6,118hp) 16.5kn Wartsila 16V32D 1 x Vee 4 Stroke 16 Cy. 320 x 350 4500kW (6118bhp) Wartsila Diesel Oy-Finland AuxGen: 1 x 600kW 440V 60Hz a.c, 2 x 328kW 440V 60Hz a.c Thrusters: 1 Thwart. CP thruster (f) Fuel: 47.0 (d.f.) 600.0 (r.f.) 24.0pd
9150121 **SHIQMA** - - **Eilat-Ashkelon Pipe Line Co (EAPL Co Ltd)** *Ashqelon* *Israel* Official number: MS.361	**162** - 38	Class: (LR) ✠ Classed LR until 25/6/98	**1997-04 Israel Shipyards Ltd. — Haifa** Yd No: 1086 Loa 24.92 Br ex 7.50 Dght 2.800 Lbp 22.50 Br md 7.20 Dpth 3.85 Welded, 1 dk	**(B32A2ST) Tug**	**2 oil engines** with clutches, flexible couplings & sr reverse geared to sc. shafts driving 2 FP propellers Total Power: 1,060kW (1,442hp) 10.0kn Caterpillar 3412TA 2 x Vee 4 Stroke 12 Cy. 137 x 152 each-530kW (721bhp) Caterpillar Inc-USA AuxGen: 1 x 85kW 380V 50Hz a.c
7200697 **SHIQMONA** *4XIY* *ex Julien C -1983 ex N. F. Candies -1983* - **Government of The State of Israel (Israel Oceanographic & Limnological Research Institute)** - *Haifa* *Israel* Official number: MS.270	*172* 91 -		**1963 Breaux Bay Craft, Inc. — Loreauville, La** Yd No: 640 Converted From: Crewboat-1983 L reg 25.00 Br ex 6.71 Dght - Lbp - Br md - Dpth 3.64 Welded	**(B31A2SR) Research Survey Vessel**	**2 oil engines** driving 2 FP propellers Total Power: 742kW (1,008hp) General Motors 2 x 2 Stroke each-371kW (504bhp) General Motors Corp-USA

IMO / Call sign	Name / Owner / Port	Tonnage	Class	Build / Dimensions	Type	Machinery
8705280 *4XGQ* -	**SHIRA** *ex* Abbira II *-2003* **Eilat Port Co Ltd** - *Haifa* *Israel* Official number: MS.312	**249** 74 80	Class: LR ✠**100A1** SS 02/2013 tug short international voyages ✠**LMC** **UMS** Eq.Ltr: (F) ; Cable: 275.0/22.0 U2 (a)	**1988-05 Israel Shipyards Ltd. — Haifa** Yd No: 1063 Loa 28.53 Br ex 9.30 Dght 4.701 Lbp 26.45 Br md 8.81 Dpth 3.71 Welded, 1 dk	**(B32A2ST) Tug**	**2 oil engines** with flexible couplings & reductiongeared to sc. shafts driving 2 Voith-Schneider propellers Total Power: 2,160kW (2,936hp) 12.0kn Deutz SBV6M628 2 x 4 Stroke 6 Cy. 240 x 280 each-1080kW (1468bhp) Kloeckner Humboldt Deutz AG-West Germany AuxGen: 2 x 104kW 400V 50Hz a.c Thrusters: 2 Thwart. FP thruster (a) Fuel: 61.5 (d.f.) 4.5pd
8213770 *JAXB* -	**SHIRAFUJI MARU** - **Fisheries Research Agency** - *Hatsukaichi, Hiroshima* *Japan* MMSI: 431400972 Official number: 125816	*138* - 150		**1983-03 Mitsubishi Heavy Industries Ltd. — Shimonoseki** Yd No: 856 Loa 36.50 Br ex Dght 2.971 Lbp 31.02 Br md 6.91 Dpth 2.95 Welded, 1 dk	**(B12D2FR) Fishery Research Vessel**	**1 oil engine** with clutches, flexible couplings & dr reverse geared to sc. shaft driving 1 CP propeller Total Power: 736kW (1,001hp) Daihatsu 6DSM-22 1 x 4 Stroke 6 Cy. 220 x 280 736kW (1001bhp) Daihatsu Diesel Manufacturing Co Lt-Japan
9088055 *JGGF* -	**SHIRAHAGI MARU** - **Government of Japan (Ministry of Agriculture & Forestry - Fisheries Agency)** - SatCom: Inmarsat A 1206161 *Tokyo* *Japan* MMSI: 431622000 Official number: 134329	*499* - -		**1994-03 Nagasaki Zosen K.K. — Nagasaki** Yd No: 1121 Loa 63.35 Br ex - Dght 4.000 Lbp 57.00 Br md 9.60 Dpth 5.59 Welded, 1 dk	**(B12D2FP) Fishery Patrol Vessel**	**2 oil engines** driving 2 FP propellers Total Power: 2,942kW (4,000hp) Niigata 6MG28HX 2 x 4 Stroke 6 Cy. 280 x 370 each-1471kW (2000bhp) Niigata Engineering Co Ltd-Japan
8909161 *JG4872* -	**SHIRAHAMA MARU** - **Tokyowan Ferry KK** - *Yokosuka, Kanagawa* *Japan* MMSI: 431000239 Official number: 131115	*3,351* - 600		**1989-12 Sumitomo Heavy Industries Ltd. — Oppama Shipyard, Yokosuka** Yd No: 1164 Loa 79.09 Br ex - Dght 3.500 Lbp 72.90 Br md 16.00 Dpth 4.80 Welded, 2 dks	**(A36A2PR) Passenger/Ro-Ro Ship (Vehicles)** Passengers: 722	**2 oil engines** driving 2 CP propellers Total Power: 3,236kW (4,400hp) 13.5kn Niigata 6M34AET 2 x 4 Stroke 6 Cy. 340 x 620 each-1618kW (2200bhp) Niigata Engineering Co Ltd-Japan Thrusters: 1 Thwart. CP thruster (f)
7929413 *JK4188* -	**SHIRAISHI** *ex* Toyoura Maru *-1997* **Sanyo Kisen KK** - *Kasaoka, Okayama* *Japan* Official number: 122236	*172* - 40		**1980-05 Kanbara Zosen K.K. — Onomichi** Yd No: 247 Loa 37.50 Br ex 8.62 Dght 1.748 Lbp 28.00 Br md 8.21 Dpth 2.54 Welded, 2 dks	**(A37B2PS) Passenger Ship**	**1 oil engine** driving 1 FP propeller Yanmar 6ML-T 1 x 4 Stroke 6 Cy. 200 x 240 Yanmar Diesel Engine Co Ltd-Japan
8704250 - -	**SHIRAKABA** *ex* Kuko No. 1 *-2004* *ex* Matsu Maru *-1999* - - *China*	*143* - 94		**1987-08 Imamura Zosen — Kure** Yd No: 313 Loa 32.52 Br ex 8.74 Dght 3.001 Lbp 28.02 Br md 8.51 Dpth 3.61 Welded, 1 dk	**(B34H2SQ) Patrol Vessel**	**2 oil engines** with clutches, flexible couplings & sr geared to sc. shafts driving 2 CP propellers Total Power: 1,760kW (2,392hp) Niigata 6MG22LX 2 x 4 Stroke 6 Cy. 220 x 290 each-880kW (1196bhp) Niigata Engineering Co Ltd-Japan
9363675 *3ERX4* -	**SHIRAKAMI** - **Yutoku Shipping Corp SA** SeoYang Shipping Co Ltd *Panama* *Panama* MMSI: 370191000 Official number: 3423008A	**29,761** 16,187 52,224 T/cm 54.8	Class: NK	**2008-07 Oshima Shipbuilding Co Ltd — Saikai NS** Yd No: 10503 Loa 188.50 Br ex - Dght 12.173 Lbp 179.00 Br md 32.26 Dpth 17.15 Welded, 1 dk	**(A21A2BC) Bulk Carrier** Double Hull Grain: 61,214; Bale: 60,783 Compartments: 5 Ho, ER 5 Ha: ER Cranes: 4x30t	**1 oil engine** driving 1 FP propeller Total Power: 8,045kW (10,938hp) 14.5kn Mitsubishi 6UEC50LSII 1 x 2 Stroke 6 Cy. 500 x 1950 8045kW (10938bhp) Mitsubishi Heavy Industries Ltd-Japan AuxGen: 3 x 440kW a.c Fuel: 2700.0
9644809 *JD3279* -	**SHIRAKAMI** - **Tohoku Port Service KK** - *Noshiro, Akita* *Japan* MMSI: 431003186 Official number: 141573	*230* - -		**2011-12 Kanagawa Zosen — Kobe** Yd No: 632 Loa 36.00 Br ex - Dght 3.200 Lbp 31.50 Br md 10.00 Dpth 4.17 Welded, 1 dk	**(B32A2ST) Tug**	**2 oil engines** reduction geared to sc. shafts driving 2 Propellers Total Power: 3,676kW (4,998hp) Niigata 6L28HX 2 x 4 Stroke 6 Cy. 280 x 370 each-1838kW (2499bhp) Niigata Engineering Co Ltd-Japan
9523304 *JD2787* -	**SHIRAKAMISAN** - **Japan Railway Construction, Transport & Technology Agency & Yutoku Kinkai Kisen KK** Yutoku Kinkai Kisen KK *Omuta, Fukuoka* *Japan* Official number: 140832	*499* - 1,795		**2008-07 Yamanaka Zosen K.K. — Imabari** Yd No: 765 Loa 74.24 Br ex - Dght 4.360 Lbp 68.00 Br md 12.00 Dpth 7.37 Welded, 1 dk	**(A31A2GX) General Cargo Ship** Grain: 2,451 1 Ha: ER (40.0 x 9.5)	**1 oil engine** driving 1 FP propeller Total Power: 1,471kW (2,000hp) Hanshin LH34LA 1 x 4 Stroke 6 Cy. 340 x 640 1471kW (2000bhp) The Hanshin Diesel Works Ltd-Japan
9296482 *JK5620* -	**SHIRAKISAN** - **Iwakuni Matsuyama Kosoku Co Ltd** - *Suo-Oshima, Yamaguchi* *Japan* Official number: 136185	*443* - 295		**2004-03 Naikai Zosen Corp — Onomichi HS (Setoda Shipyard)** Yd No: 689 Loa 62.97 Br ex - Dght 2.860 Lbp 55.00 Br md 11.00 Dpth 3.80 Welded	**(A36A2PR) Passenger/Ro-Ro Ship (Vehicles)** Passengers: unberthed: 150 Bow door/ramp (centre) Stern door/ramp (centre)	**2 oil engines** geared to sc. shafts driving 2 FP propellers Total Power: 2,500kW (3,400hp) 15.8kn Daihatsu 8DKM-20 2 x 4 Stroke 8 Cy. 200 x 300 each-1250kW (1700bhp) Daihatsu Diesel Manufacturing Co Lt-Japan
9317822 *9VAG3* -	**SHIRAKUMO** - **Papaya Lepus Pte Ltd** Nippon Yusen Kabushiki Kaisha (NYK Line) *Singapore* *Singapore* MMSI: 565188000 Official number: 392172	**47,051** 27,005 87,144 T/cm 79.7	Class: NK	**2006-07 IHI Marine United Inc — Yokohama KN** Yd No: 3213 Loa 229.00 (BB) Br ex 36.50 Dght 14.130 Lbp 219.90 Br md 36.50 Dpth 19.90 Welded, 1 dk	**(A21A2BC) Bulk Carrier** Double Hull Grain: 98,961; Bale: 94,844 Compartments: 7 Ho, ER 7 Ha: ER	**1 oil engine** driving 1 FP propeller Total Power: 10,300kW (14,004hp) 14.5kn Sulzer 6RTA58T 1 x 2 Stroke 6 Cy. 580 x 2416 10300kW (14004bhp) Diesel United Ltd.-Aioi AuxGen: 3 x 520kW 450V 60Hz a.c Fuel: 279.0 (d.f.) 3048.0 (r.f.)
7501467 *JI2834* -	**SHIRANE MARU** - **KK Tomac** - *Tokyo* *Japan* Official number: 115822	*107* - -		**1975-02 Naikai Shipbuilding & Engineering Co Ltd — Onomichi HS (Taguma Shipyard)** Yd No: 398 Loa 23.50 Br ex 8.22 Dght 1.550 Lbp 21.50 Br md 8.20 Dpth 2.20 Riveted\Welded, 1 dk	**(B34X2QA) Anchor Handling Vessel**	**2 oil engines** driving 2 FP propellers Total Power: 206kW (280hp) Yanmar 6KFL 2 x 4 Stroke 6 Cy. 145 x 170 each-103kW (140bhp) Yanmar Diesel Engine Co Ltd-Japan
8839873 - -	**SHIRANUI NO. 2** *ex* Kanon No. 2 *-1999* **Daima Shipping Corp** - *Philippines*	*282* - -		**1989-07 K.K. Kawamoto Zosensho — Osakikamijima** Yd No: 116 Loa 42.70 Br ex - Dght 2.200 Lbp 35.07 Br md 9.50 Dpth 3.10 Welded, 1 dk	**(A37B2PS) Passenger Ship** Passengers: unberthed: 350	**1 oil engine** driving 1 FP propeller Total Power: 883kW (1,201hp) Yanmar T240-ET 1 x 4 Stroke 6 Cy. 240 x 310 883kW (1201bhp) Yanmar Diesel Engine Co Ltd-Japan
9513816 *3FMO4* -	**SHIRARA** - **Catalina Shipping SA & Imabari Sangyo Kaisha Ltd** Shoei Kisen Kaisha Ltd SatCom: Inmarsat C 435683712 *Panama* *Panama* MMSI: 356837000 Official number: 4088509	**90,111** 59,287 180,188 T/cm 121.0	Class: NK (BV)	**2009-09 Imabari Shipbuilding Co Ltd — Saijo EH (Saijo Shipyard)** Yd No: 8116 Loa 288.93 (BB) Br ex - Dght 18.170 Lbp 280.90 Br md 45.00 Dpth 24.70 Welded, 1 dk	**(A21A2BC) Bulk Carrier** Grain: 199,724 Compartments: 9 Ho, ER 9 Ha: ER	**1 oil engine** driving 1 FP propeller Total Power: 18,660kW (25,370hp) 14.5kn MAN-B&W 6S70MC-C 1 x 2 Stroke 6 Cy. 700 x 2800 18660kW (25370bhp) Mitsui Engineering & Shipbuilding CLtd-Japan Fuel: 5400.0
9145762 *JG5482* -	**SHIRASAGI** - - - *Kagoshima, Kagoshima* *Japan* Official number: 135847	*104* - -		**1996-07 Kanagawa Zosen — Kobe** Yd No: 432 Loa 24.65 Br ex - Dght - Lbp 22.05 Br md 8.00 Dpth 3.20 Welded, 1 dk	**(B34G2SE) Pollution Control Vessel**	**2 oil engines** Geared Integral to driving 2 Z propellers Total Power: 588kW (800hp) 10.0kn Niigata 6NSF-Z 2 x 4 Stroke 6 Cy. 190 x 260 each-294kW (400bhp) Niigata Engineering Co Ltd-Japan
8998382 *7JAS* -	**SHIRASAGI** - **Government of Japan (Ministry of Agriculture & Forestry - Fisheries Agency)** - *Tokyo* *Japan* Official number: 140149	*149* - -		**2005-03 Mitsubishi Heavy Industries Ltd. — Shimonoseki** Loa 42.50 Br ex - Dght - Lbp 39.00 Br md 6.70 Dpth 3.30 Welded, 1 dk	**(B12D2FP) Fishery Patrol Vessel** Hull Material: Aluminium Alloy	**2 oil engines** reduction geared to sc. shafts driving 2 Propellers Total Power: 4,766kW (6,480hp) 35.0kn M.T.U. 16V4000M90 2 x Vee 4 Stroke 16 Cy. 165 x 190 each-2383kW (3240bhp) MTU Friedrichshafen GmbH-Friedrichshafen

IMO / Call sign	Name / Owner / Port	Tonnage	Class	Built / Builder / Dimensions	Type	Machinery
8989628 *JL6731* -	**SHIRASAGI** - **Seiun Kisen KK** - *Uwajima, Ehime* *Japan* Official number: 136576	*182* - 44		**2003-10 Kurinoura Dockyard Co Ltd — Yawatahama EH** Yd No: 376 Loa 37.07 Br ex - Dght - Lbp - Br md 7.40 Dpth 2.78 Welded, 1 dk	**(A31A2GX) General Cargo Ship**	**1 oil engine** reduction geared to sc. shaft driving 1 Propeller Total Power: 1,029kW (1,399hp) 12.5kn Niigata 6MG22HX 1 x 4 Stroke 6 Cy. 220 x 280 1029kW (1399bhp) Niigata Engineering Co Ltd-Japan
8864567 *JM6136* -	**SHIRATAKA MARU** - **Kowa Kogyo KK** - *Nagasaki, Nagasaki* *Japan* Official number: 132716	*168* - -		**1992-03 K.K. Watanabe Zosensho — Nagasaki** Yd No: 1206 Loa 30.88 Br ex - Dght 2.800 Lbp 26.00 Br md 8.80 Dpth 3.77 Welded, 1 dk	**(B32A2ST) Tug**	**2 oil engines** Geared Integral to driving 2 Z propellers Total Power: 2,206kW (3,000hp) Niigata 6L25HX 2 x 4 Stroke 6 Cy. 250 x 350 each-1103kW (1500bhp) Niigata Engineering Co Ltd-Japan
5324762 - -	**SHIRAYURI MARU** - **YK Koei Sangyo** -	*152* - 28		**1962 Osaka Shipbuilding Co Ltd — Osaka OS** Yd No: 210 Loa 32.70 Br ex 6.02 Dght 1.750 Lbp 29.50 Br md 6.00 Dpth 2.60 Welded, 1 dk	**(A37B2PS) Passenger Ship**	**1 oil engine** driving 1 FP propeller Kinoshita 1 x 4 Stroke 6 Cy. 300 x 420 Kinoshita Tekkosho-Japan
7823346 *ZR6500* -	**SHIRAZ** *ex* Ben Schoeman **Transnet Ltd** Portnet Dredging Services *Cape Town* *South Africa* MMSI: 601055000 Official number: 351178	*429* 126 -	Class: (LR) ✠ Classed LR until 10/4/81	**1980-02 Dorman Long Vanderbijl Corp. Ltd. (DORBYL) — Durban** Yd No: 5800 Loa 36.40 Br ex 11.61 Dght 3.563 Lbp 33.28 Br md 11.00 Dpth 4.12 Welded, 1 dk	**(B32A2ST) Tug**	**2 oil engines** sr geared to sc. shafts driving 2 Voith-Schneider propellers Total Power: 2,942kW (4,000hp) 11.0kn MAN 8L25/30 2 x 4 Stroke 8 Cy. 250 x 300 each-1471kW (2000bhp) Maschinenbau Augsburg Nuernberg (MAN)-Augsburg AuxGen: 3 x 92kW 400V 50Hz a.c Fuel: 75.5 (d.f.)
8742460 *7JEQ* -	**SHIRETOKO** *ex* Kunigami *-2012* **Government of Japan (Ministry of Land, Infrastructure & Transport) (The Coastguard)** - *Tokyo* *Japan* MMSI: 432690000 Official number: 140915	*1,349* - -		**2009-03 Mitsui Eng. & SB. Co. Ltd. — Tamano** Yd No: 1753 Loa 89.00 Br ex - Dght - Lbp - Br md 11.00 Dpth 5.00 Welded, 1 dk	**(B34H2SQ) Patrol Vessel**	**4 oil engines** reduction geared to sc. shafts driving 4 Water jets Total Power: 14,760kW (20,068hp)
9587336 *EZHD* -	**SHIRIN** *ex* AHT Provider *-2011* **GAC Marine Holdings Ltd** GAC Marine SA *Turkmenbashy* *Turkmenistan* MMSI: 434122000	**573** 172 330	Class: BV (AB)	**2010-09 Jiangsu Wuxi Shipyard Co Ltd — Wuxi JS** (Hull) Yd No: (1355) **2010-09 Pacific Ocean Engineering & Trading Pte Ltd (POET) — Singapore** Yd No: 1355 Loa 41.80 Br ex 10.05 Dght 3.200 Lbp 37.40 Br md 10.00 Dpth 4.60 Welded, 1 dk	**(B21B20A) Anchor Handling Tug Supply**	**2 oil engines** reverse reduction geared to sc. shafts driving 2 FP propellers Total Power: 2,684kW (3,650hp) 11.0kn Yanmar 8N21A-EN 2 x 4 Stroke 8 Cy. 210 x 290 each-1342kW (1825bhp) Yanmar Diesel Engine Co Ltd-Japan AuxGen: 3 x 225kW a.c Thrusters: 1 Tunnel thruster (f)
9644457 *JD3351* -	**SHIRIUCHI MARU** - **Japan Railway Construction, Transport & Technology Agency, Asahi Tanker Co Ltd & Eiyu Kaiun Co Ltd** Eiyu Kaiun Co Ltd *Tokyo* *Japan* MMSI: 431003595 Official number: 141666	**3,587** - 5,631	Class: NK	**2012-06 Shin Kurushima Dockyard Co. Ltd. — Akitsu** Yd No: 5748 Loa 104.93 (BB) Br ex - Dght 6.610 Lbp 98.00 Br md 16.00 Dpth 8.00 Welded, 1 dk	**(A13B2TP) Products Tanker** Double Hull (13F) Liq: 5,391; Liq (Oil): 5,391	**1 oil engine** driving 1 FP propeller Total Power: 3,309kW (4,499hp) 14.0kn Akasaka A45S 1 x 4 Stroke 6 Cy. 450 x 880 3309kW (4499bhp) Akasaka Tekkosho KK (Akasaka DieselLtd)-Japan Fuel: 310.0
9391024 *V2DC6* -	**SHIRKAN C** - **ms 'Shirkan' Shipping GmbH & Co KG** Rohden Bereederung GmbH & Co KG *Saint John's* *Antigua & Barbuda* MMSI: 305169000 Official number: 4400	**5,629** 2,877 8,046 T/cm 17.8	Class: GL	**2007-12 Jiangsu Yangzijiang Shipbuilding Co Ltd — Jiangyin JS** Yd No: 2005-701C Loa 108.20 (BB) Br ex 18.48 Dght 7.057 Lbp 103.90 Br md 18.20 Dpth 9.00 Welded, 1 dk	**(A31A2GX) General Cargo Ship** Grain: 10,210; Bale: 10,210 Compartments: 3 Ho, ER 3 Ha: 2 (25.9 x 15.2)ER (17.5 x 15.2) Cranes: 2x25t Ice Capable	**1 oil engine** driving 1 CP propeller Total Power: 2,800kW (3,807hp) 12.4kn MAN-B&W 7S26MC 1 x 2 Stroke 7 Cy. 260 x 980 2800kW (3807bhp) STX Engine Co Ltd-South Korea AuxGen: 2 x 365kW 450V a.c Thrusters: 1 Tunnel thruster (f)
7629099 - -	**SHIRLEY ANN** - - -	*126* 81 -		**1974 Nick Wowcerk Boat Building Co. — Los Angeles, Ca** L reg 19.60 Br ex 5.80 Dght - Lbp - Br md - Dpth 3.15 Welded, 1 dk	**(B11B2FV) Fishing Vessel**	**1 oil engine** driving 1 FP propeller Total Power: 331kW (450hp)
8970316 *WDG2136* -	**SHIRLEY B** *ex* Orchid Lady II *-2011* *ex* Marie III *-2007* **Charca Fish IV LLC** - *San Diego, CA* *United States of America* Official number: 1110940	**164** 49 -		**2001 Ocean Marine, Inc. — Bayou La Batre, Al** Yd No: 393 L reg 25.35 Br ex - Dght - Lbp - Br md 7.62 Dpth 4.05 Welded, 1 dk	**(B11B2FV) Fishing Vessel**	**1 oil engine** driving 1 FP propeller
8618982 - -	**SHIRLEY SMITH** - **Sydney Ports Corp** - *Sydney, NSW* *Australia* Official number: 852857	**156** 46 -		**1987-11 Carrington Slipways Pty Ltd — Newcastle NSW** Yd No: 202 Loa 24.52 Br ex - Dght 3.001 Lbp 22.00 Br md 8.01 Dpth 4.02 Welded, 1 dk	**(B32A2ST) Tug**	**2 oil engines** with clutches & dr reverse geared to sc. shafts driving 2 CP propellers Total Power: 1,030kW (1,400hp) G.M. (Detroit Diesel) 12V-92-TA 2 x Vee 2 Stroke 12 Cy. 123 x 127 each-515kW (700bhp) General Motors Detroit DieselAllison Divn-USA Thrusters: 1 Thwart. FP thruster (f)
9218258 *JHQA* -	**SHIROCHIDORI** - **Mie Prefecture** - *Shima, Mie* *Japan* MMSI: 431729000 Official number: 135645	*499* - 741		**2000-03 Kanasashi Heavy Industries Co Ltd — Shizuoka SZ** Yd No: 8001 Loa 59.15 Br ex - Dght - Lbp 53.00 Br md 9.40 Dpth 3.95 Welded, 1 dk	**(B11B2FV) Fishing Vessel**	**1 oil engine** driving 1 CP propeller Total Power: 1,545kW (2,101hp) Yanmar 6N280-EN 1 x 4 Stroke 6 Cy. 280 x 380 1545kW (2101bhp) Yanmar Diesel Engine Co Ltd-Japan Thrusters: 1 Thwart. FP thruster (f)
8922840 *JG5243* -	**SHIROGANE MARU** - **Higashi Nippon Tug Boat KK** - *Hachinohe, Aomori* *Japan* MMSI: 431100215 Official number: 134951	*177* - -		**1996-01 Keihin Dock Co Ltd — Yokohama** Yd No: 243 Loa 30.80 Br ex - Dght 2.700 Lbp 27.00 Br md 9.00 Dpth 3.60 Welded, 1 dk	**(B32A2ST) Tug**	**2 oil engines** driving 2 FP propellers Total Power: 2,354kW (3,200hp) 13.0kn Niigata 6L25HX 2 x 4 Stroke 6 Cy. 250 x 350 each-1177kW (1600bhp) Niigata Engineering Co Ltd-Japan
9181895 *3FPX8* -	**SHIROUMA** *ex* North Fortune *-2000* **Erica Navigation SA** Toyo Sangyo Co Ltd (Toyo Sangyo KK) SatCom: Inmarsat B 335359510 *Panama* *Panama* Official number: 2580598C	**43,434** 23,683 77,739 T/cm 75.4	Class: (NK)	**1998-07 Sasebo Heavy Industries Co. Ltd. — Sasebo Yard, Sasebo** Yd No: 441 Loa 229.00 (BB) Br ex - Dght 12.820 Lbp 218.00 Br md 36.50 Dpth 18.50 Welded, 1 dk	**(A21A2BC) Bulk Carrier** Grain: 92,608 Compartments: 5 Ho, ER 5 Ha: (27.5 x 16.0)4 (24.3 x 16.0)ER	**1 oil engine** driving 1 FP propeller Total Power: 7,249kW (9,856hp) 14.3kn B&W 5S60MC 1 x 2 Stroke 5 Cy. 600 x 2292 7249kW (9856bhp) Mitsui Engineering & Shipbuilding CLtd-Japan AuxGen: 3 x 460kW a.c Fuel: 2823.0 (r.f.) 33.5pd
8748062 *JD3007* -	**SHIROYAMA** - **Kosoku Ieshima KK** - *Himeji, Hyogo* *Japan* Official number: 141076	*113* - -		**2009-09 Katahara Zosen K.K. — Gamagori** Yd No: 428 Loa 32.95 Br ex - Dght 1.000 Lbp 29.50 Br md 6.30 Dpth 2.61 Welded, 1 dk	**(A37B2PS) Passenger Ship** Hull Material: Aluminium Alloy Passengers: unberthed: 141	**2 oil engines** reduction geared to sc. shafts driving 2 Propellers Total Power: 1,518kW (2,064hp) 20.0kn Mitsubishi S6R2-MTK3L 2 x 4 Stroke 6 Cy. 170 x 220 each-759kW (1032bhp) Mitsubishi Heavy Industries Ltd-Japan
7912173 *4JHU* -	**SHIRVAN** - **Specialized Sea Oil Fleet Organisation, Caspian Sea Oil Fleet, State Oil Co of the Republic of Azerbaijan** - *Baku* *Azerbaijan* MMSI: 423169100 Official number: DGR-0204	*2,700* 943 1,392	Class: RS	**1982-08 Brodogradiliste '3 Maj' — Rijeka** Yd No: 618 Loa 98.99 Br ex 17.43 Dght 3.201 Lbp 91.17 Br md 17.01 Dpth 6.10 Welded, 1 dk	**(B34B2SC) Crane Vessel** Cranes: 1x100t Ice Capable	**2 diesel electric oil engines** driving 2 FP propellers Total Power: 3,178kW (4,320hp) Sulzer 8ASL25/30 2 x 4 Stroke 8 Cy. 250 x 300 each-1589kW (2160bhp) Tvornica Dizel Motora 'Jugoturbina'-Yugoslavia Thrusters: 1 Thwart. FP thruster (f) Fuel: 479.0 (d.f.)

IMO / Call sign	Name / Owner / Manager	Tonnage	Class	Builder / Dimensions	Type / Capacity	Machinery
7643904 *4JEZ* -	**SHIRVAN** *ex* Kosta Khetagurov **Azerbaijan State Caspian Shipping Co (ASCSS)** Meridian Shipping & Management LLC *Baku* *Azerbaijan* MMSI: 423058100 Official number: DGR-0022	**3,714** 1,715 4,150 T/cm 15.2	Class: RS	**1977-04 Navashinskiy Sudostroitelnyy Zavod 'Oka' — Navashino** Yd No: 1285 Loa 123.50 Br ex 15.02 Dght 4.500 Lbp 117.00 Br md - Dpth 6.51 Welded, 1 dk	**(A31A2GX) General Cargo Ship** Grain: 6,070; Bale: 5,800 Compartments: 4 Ho, ER 4 Ha: 2 (11.8 x 8.0)2 (13.4 x 8.0)ER Cranes: 2x8t Ice Capable	**2 oil engines** driving 2 FP propellers Total Power: 1,472kW (2,002hp) 11.8kn Russkiy 8DR30/50-4 2 x 2 Stroke 8 Cy. 300 x 500 each-736kW (1001bhp) Mashinostroitelnyy Zavod"Russkiy-Dizel"-Leningrad Fuel: 202.0 (d.f.)
9368596 *9HXW8* -	**SHIRVAN** *ex* Paltrader-3 *-2007* **Paltrading-3 Co Ltd** Palmali Gemicilik ve Acentelik AS (Palmali Shipping & Agency) *Valletta* *Malta* MMSI: 256583000 Official number: 9368596	**4,922** 2,841 6,354	Class: RS	**2007-05 Sudostroitelnyy Zavod "Krasnoye Sormovo" — Nizhniy Novgorod** Yd No: 03003 Loa 121.70 (BB) Br ex 16.70 Dght 5.060 Lbp 117.06 Br md 16.50 Dpth 6.20 Welded, 1 dk	**(A31A2GX) General Cargo Ship** Grain: 9,370; Bale: 9,370 TEU 234 Compartments: 3 Ho, ER 2 Ha: ER	**1 oil engine** reduction geared to sc. shaft driving 1 CP propeller Total Power: 2,450kW (3,331hp) 11.5kn Wartsila 6R32LN 1 x 4 Stroke 6 Cy. 320 x 350 2450kW (3331bhp) Wartsila Finland Oy-Finland AuxGen: 2 x 294kW a.c, 1 x 160kW a.c Thrusters: 1 Tunnel thruster (f) Fuel: 316.0
8207197 *4JIP* -	**SHIRVAN 2** - **Specialized Sea Oil Fleet Organisation, Caspian Sea Oil Fleet, State Oil Co of the Republic of Azerbaijan** - *Baku* *Azerbaijan* MMSI: 423134100 Official number: DGR-0212	**2,971** 891 1,326	Class: RS	**1985-10 Brodogradiliste 'Uljanik' — Pula** Yd No: 314 Loa 98.98 Br ex 17.43 Dght 3.200 Lbp 92.40 Br md 17.00 Dpth 6.10 Welded, 1 dk	**(B34B2SC) Crane Vessel** Cranes: 1x100t	**2 diesel electric oil engines** driving 4 gen. each 200kW a.c Connecting to 2 elec. motors each (1100kW) driving 2 FP propellers Total Power: 3,200kW (4,350hp) 11.3kn Sulzer 8ASL25/30 2 x 4 Stroke 8 Cy. 250 x 300 each-1600kW (2175bhp) Tvornica Dizel Motora 'Jugoturbina'-Yugoslavia Fuel: 479.0 (d.f.)
8207202 *4JCG* -	**SHIRVAN 3** - **Specialized Sea Oil Fleet Organisation, Caspian Sea Oil Fleet, State Oil Co of the Republic of Azerbaijan** - *Baku* *Azerbaijan* MMSI: 423135100 Official number: DGR-0288	**2,971** 891 1,326	Class: (RS)	**1986-04 Brodogradiliste 'Titovo' — Kraljevica** Yd No: 462 Loa 98.99 Br ex 17.43 Dght 3.201 Lbp 92.40 Br md 17.01 Dpth 6.13 Welded, 1 dk	**(B34B2SC) Crane Vessel** Cranes: 1x100t	**2 diesel electric oil engines** driving 4 gen. each 200kW a.c Connecting to 2 elec. motors each (1100kW) driving 2 FP propellers Total Power: 3,178kW (4,320hp) Sulzer 8ASL25/30 2 x 4 Stroke 8 Cy. 250 x 300 each-1589kW (2160bhp) Tvornica Dizel Motora 'Jugoturbina'-Yugoslavia Thrusters: 1 Thwart. FP thruster (f) Fuel: 479.0 (d.f.)
9061916 *JL6136* -	**SHIRYU MARU** - **JFE Logistics Corp & Koike Kisen KK** Koike Kisen KK *Imabari, Ehime* *Japan* MMSI: 431500067 Official number: 133891	*5,137* - 2,790	Class: NK	**1993-03 Nippon Kokan KK (NKK Corp) — Yokohama KN (Tsurumi Shipyard)** Yd No: 1055 Loa 111.50 (BB) Br ex 18.04 Dght 3.420 Lbp 106.50 Br md 18.00 Dpth 8.90 Welded, 1 dk	**(A31B2GP) Palletised Cargo Ship** Bale: 4,240 Compartments: 1 Ho, ER 1 Ha: ER	**1 oil engine** driving 1 CP propeller Total Power: 1,471kW (2,000hp) 10.0kn Hanshin 6LU40 1 x 4 Stroke 6 Cy. 400 x 640 1471kW (2000bhp) The Hanshin Diesel Works Ltd-Japan AuxGen: 3 x 300kW a.c Thrusters: 1 Thwart. CP thruster (f) Fuel: 95.0 (r.f.)
8840274 *JK5013* -	**SHISAKA MARU** - **YK Shisaka Kaiun** - *Kure, Hiroshima* *Japan* MMSI: 431400933 Official number: 131747	*194* - 315		**1990-02 Kyoei Zosen KK — Mihara HS** Loa 41.80 Br ex - Dght 3.100 Lbp 38.00 Br md 7.80 Dpth 3.45 Welded, 1 dk	**(A12A2TC) Chemical Tanker**	**1 oil engine** driving 1 FP propeller Total Power: 441kW (600hp) Yanmar MF24-HT 1 x 4 Stroke 6 Cy. 240 x 420 441kW (600bhp) Yanmar Diesel Engine Co Ltd-Japan
9596404 *JD2936* -	**SHISEI MARU** - **Ebina Hisami** - *Imabari, Ehime* *Japan* Official number: 141051	*498* - 1,830		**2009-08 Fujiwara Zosensho — Imabari** Loa 73.45 (BB) Br ex - Dght 4.410 Lbp 68.50 Br md 11.80 Dpth 7.45 Welded, 1 dk	**(A31A2GX) General Cargo Ship** Grain: 2,447	**1 oil engine** driving 1 Propeller Total Power: 736kW (1,001hp) Niigata 1 x 4 Stroke 736kW (1001bhp) Niigata Engineering Co Ltd-Japan Thrusters: 1 Thwart. FP thruster (f)
8879287 - -	**SHISSIWANI-2** *ex* Jaeggevarre I *-2005* *ex* Jaeggevarre *-2002* **Sourette Misbahou** - *Mutsamudu* *Union of Comoros*	**518** 149 -	Class: (NV)	**1960 Kaarbos Mek. Verksted AS — Harstad** Yd No: 29 Loa 43.68 Br ex 9.80 Dght - Lbp - Br md - Dpth 4.00 Welded, 1 dk	**(A36A2PR) Passenger/Ro-Ro Ship (Vehicles)** Passengers: unberthed: 250 Cars: 23	**1 oil engine** driving 1 FP propeller Total Power: 643kW (874hp) Wichmann 1 x 643kW (874bhp) Wichmann Motorfabrikk AS-Norway
8501282 - -	**SHIV I** - - - *Nigeria*	*139* 89 -		**1984-12 Quality Shipyards Inc — Houma LA** Yd No: 172 Loa 27.21 Br ex - Dght - Lbp - Br md - Dpth - Welded, 1 dk	**(B11A2FT) Trawler**	**1 oil engine** driving 1 FP propeller Total Power: 460kW (625hp) Caterpillar 3412PCTA 1 x Vee 4 Stroke 12 Cy. 137 x 152 460kW (625bhp) Caterpillar Tractor Co-USA
9678173 *AWAE* -	**SHIV SHAKTI** - **m/s Shiv Shipping Services** Proactive Ship Management Pvt Ltd *Mumbai* *India* MMSI: 419000726 Official number: 4077	**1,583** 529 2,440	Class: IR	**2013-09 Dosti Fabricators — Jamnagar** Yd No: DF-101 Loa 72.40 Br ex - Dght 3.500 Lbp - Br md 14.00 Dpth 5.20 Welded, 1 dk	**(A31A2GX) General Cargo Ship**	**2 oil engines** reduction geared to sc. shafts driving 2 Propellers Total Power: 894kW (1,216hp) Cummins KTA-19-M3 2 x 4 Stroke 6 Cy. 159 x 159 each-447kW (608bhp) Cummins India Ltd-India
7045451 - -	**SHIVA** *ex* Americana *-2002* *ex* La Liberte *-1997* *ex* Ural *-1995* - -	*1,361* 473 526	Class: (RS)	**1970 Zelenodolskiy Sudostroitelnyy Zavod im. "Gorkogo" — Zelenodolsk** Yd No: 506 Loa 72.07 Br ex 10.83 Dght 3.620 Lbp 64.80 Br md - Dpth 5.72 Welded, 1 dk	**(B11A2FT) Trawler** Ins: 677 Compartments: 2 Ho, ER 2 Ha: 2 (2.5 x 2.5) Derricks: 4x3t; Winches: 4 Ice Capable	**1 oil engine** driving 1 FP propeller Total Power: 736kW (1,001hp) 12.3kn S.K.L. 8NVD48AU 1 x 4 Stroke 8 Cy. 320 x 480 736kW (1001bhp) VEB Schwermaschinenbau "KarlLiebknecht" (SKL)-Magdeburg AuxGen: 2 x 300kW a.c, 1 x 50kW a.c Fuel: 113.0 (d.f.)
9121962 *AUNF* -	**SHIVA** *ex* Keasin 29 *-2006* **i-Marine Infratech (India) Pvt Ltd** - *Mumbai* *India* Official number: 3239	**108** 32 98	Class: IR (BV)	**1994-01 Nga Chai Shipyard Sdn Bhd — Sibu** Yd No: 9401 Loa 23.17 Br ex 6.71 Dght 2.400 Lbp 21.03 Br md 6.70 Dpth 2.90 Welded, 1 dk	**(B32A2ST) Tug**	**2 oil engines** geared to sc. shafts driving 2 FP propellers Total Power: 744kW (1,012hp) Cummins KTA-19-M 2 x 4 Stroke 6 Cy. 159 x 159 each-372kW (506bhp) Chongqing Automotive Engine Factory-China AuxGen: 2 x 16kW 415V 50Hz a.c Fuel: 73.0 (d.f.)
8717336 - -	**SHIVA-1** - **High Sea Foods Ltd** - *Visakhapatnam* *India* Official number: 2325	*150* - 48	Class: (IR)	**1988-07 K Shipyard Construction Co — Fremantle WA** Yd No: 105 Loa 25.33 Br ex - Dght 3.101 Lbp 23.93 Br md 7.41 Dpth 3.74 Welded, 1 dk	**(B11A2FS) Stern Trawler** Ins: 120	**1 oil engine** with clutches & sr reverse geared to sc. shaft driving 1 FP propeller Total Power: 370kW (503hp) Caterpillar 3412TA 1 x Vee 4 Stroke 12 Cy. 137 x 152 370kW (503bhp) Caterpillar Inc-USA
8115411 - -	**SHIVA PRIYA** - **D B Bandodkar & Sons Pvt Ltd** - *Panaji* *India* Official number: PNJ125	*640* 435 925	Class: (BV)	**1982-05 Shivam Engineers Pvt. Ltd. — Goa** Yd No: 013 Loa 55.50 Br ex - Dght 2.501 Lbp 53.52 Br md 10.01 Dpth 3.20 Welded, 1 dk	**(A31A2GX) General Cargo Ship** Compartments: 1 Ho, ER 1 Ha: (34.8 x 7.0)ER	**2 oil engines** sr geared to sc. shafts driving 2 FP propellers Total Power: 376kW (512hp) MAN W8V175/22M 2 x 4 Stroke 8 Cy. 175 x 220 each-188kW (256bhp) Kirloskar Oil Engines Ltd-India
9226217 *VWWH* -	**SHIVALI** **Bhoir Offshore Pvt Ltd** Amba Shipping & Logistics Pvt Ltd *Mumbai* *India* MMSI: 419010200 Official number: 2864	**214** 64 121	Class: IR (RI)	**2001-04 Mech Marine Engineers Pvt Ltd — Vasai** Yd No: 140 Loa 27.50 Br ex 9.03 Dght 3.200 Lbp 25.50 Br md 9.00 Dpth 4.00 Welded, 1 dk	**(B32A2ST) Tug**	**2 oil engines** reduction geared to sc. shafts driving 2 FP propellers Total Power: 1,404kW (1,908hp) 8.0kn Cummins KTA-2300-M 2 x Vee 4 Stroke 12 Cy. 159 x 159 each-702kW (954bhp) Cummins India Ltd-India AuxGen: 2 x 60kW 415V 50Hz a.c

IMO / Call sign	Name / Owner / Registry	Tonnage	Class	Builder / Dimensions	Type	Machinery
9207297 *AUVE* -	**SHIVALI II** *ex* Epsom Odin *-2010* *ex* Deity Jaya *-2008* *ex* Jaya Eagle *-2001* *ex* Radhit Jaya *-2000* *ex* Jaya Eagle *-1999* **Bhoir Dredging Co Pvt Ltd** Amba Shipping & Logistics Pvt Ltd *Mumbai* *India* MMSI: 419075800 Official number: 3445	**247** 74 184	Class: IR (AB)	**1999-06 Jiangdu Yuehai Shipbuilding Co Ltd — Jiangdu JS** Yd No: JD9729-03 Loa 29.00 Br ex 9.03 Dght 3.900 Lbp 26.50 Br md 9.00 Dpth 4.25 Welded, 1 dk	**(B32A2ST) Tug**	**2 oil engines** geared to sc. shafts driving 2 FP propellers Total Power: 1,472kW (2,002hp) 11.0kn Wartsila UD25V12M5D 2 x Vee 4 Stroke 12 Cy. 150 x 180 each-736kW (1001bhp) Wartsila NSD France SA-France AuxGen: 2 x 85kW 415V 50Hz a.c Fuel: 130.0 (d.f.)
8901951 *VWVH* -	**SHIVAM** *ex* Atco Hebah *-1999* **Shiv Vani Oil & Gas Exploration Services Ltd** Modest Maritime Services Pvt Ltd *Mumbai* *India* MMSI: 419071900 Official number: 2858	**122** 36 30	Class: IR (AB)	**1988 Halter Marine, Inc. — New Orleans, La** Yd No: 1121 Loa 30.99 Br ex 6.48 Dght 1.520 Lbp 29.07 Br md 6.40 Dpth 2.90 Welded	**(B21A20C) Crew/Supply Vessel** Hull Material: Aluminium Alloy	**3 oil engines** reverse reduction geared to sc. shafts driving 3 FP propellers Total Power: 1,125kW (1,530hp) 15.0kn G.M. (Detroit Diesel) 12V-71-TI 3 x Vee 2 Stroke 12 Cy. 108 x 127 each-375kW (510bhp) General Motors Detroit DieselAllison Divn-USA AuxGen: 2 x 30kW 220V 60Hz a.c Fuel: 14.0 (d.f.)
9260108 *UEAH* -	**SHIVELUCH** - **Shiveluch Co Ltd** - *Petropavlovsk-Kamchatskiy* *Russia* Official number: 010125	**276** 82 142	Class: RS	**2001-11 Dalian Fishing Vessel Co — Dalian LN** Yd No: 1024 Loa 38.50 Br ex - Dght 2.920 Lbp 33.00 Br md 7.60 Dpth 3.60 Welded, 1 dk	**(B11B2FV) Fishing Vessel** Ice Capable	**1 oil engine** reduction geared to sc. shaft driving 1 FP propeller Total Power: 407kW (553hp) Cummins KTA-19-M 1 x 4 Stroke 6 Cy. 159 x 159 407kW (553bhp) Chongqing Cummins Engine Co Ltd-China
8663640 *JD3222* -	**SHIWAKU MARU** - **Marugame City** - *Marugame, Kagawa* *Japan* Official number: 141484	*269* - -		**2011-08 Ishida Zosen KK — Onomichi HS** Yd No: 807 Loa 47.81 Br ex - Dght 2.400 Lbp 35.00 Br md 10.50 Dpth 3.19 Welded, 1 dk	**(A36A2PR) Passenger/Ro-Ro Ship (Vehicles)** Passengers: unberthed: 150 Bow ramp (centre)	**2 oil engines** reduction geared to sc. shafts driving 2 Propellers Total Power: 1,472kW (2,002hp) 10.5kn Yanmar 6N18A-DV 2 x 4 Stroke 6 Cy. 180 x 280 each-736kW (1001bhp) Yanmar Diesel Engine Co Ltd-Japan
7852658 - -	**SHIWAKU MARU** *ex* Kokusai Maru No. 11 *-1982* **Glory Shipping S de RL** Daelim Marine Co Ltd *San Lorenzo* *Honduras* Official number: L-0124072	*493* 298 112		**1972 Shinhama Dockyard Co. Ltd. — Anan** Yd No: 136 Loa 52.51 Br ex - Dght 2.801 Lbp 46.00 Br md 10.00 Dpth 3.31 Welded, 1 dk	**(A36A2PR) Passenger/Ro-Ro Ship (Vehicles)** Passengers: 421	**2 oil engines** driving 2 FP propellers Total Power: 1,472kW (2,002hp) 13.5kn Niigata 2 x 4 Stroke each-736kW (1001bhp) Niigata Engineering Co Ltd-Japan
9233533 *H9EC* -	**SHIYO** - **Forward Gloria Navigation SA** Daiwa Kisen KK (Daiwa Kisen Co Ltd) *Panama* *Panama* MMSI: 355008000 Official number: 2794601B	**43,462** 23,683 77,514 T/cm 75.4	Class: NK	**2001-05 Sasebo Heavy Industries Co. Ltd. — Sasebo Yard, Sasebo** Yd No: 474 Loa 229.00 Br ex - Dght 12.820 Lbp 218.00 Br md 36.50 Dpth 18.50 Welded, 1 dk	**(A21A2BC) Bulk Carrier** Double Bottom Entire Compartment Length Grain: 92,608 Compartments: 5 Ho, ER 5 Ha: (27.5 x 11.2)Tappered 4 (27.5 x 16.0)ER	**1 oil engine** driving 1 FP propeller Total Power: 9,857kW (13,402hp) 14.3kn B&W 5S60MC 1 x 2 Stroke 5 Cy. 600 x 2292 9857kW (13402bhp) Mitsui Engineering & Shipbuilding CLtd-Japan Fuel: 2800.0 (d.f.) (Heating Coils) 140.0 (r.f.)
8979661 *JL6494* -	**SHIYODOSHIMA MARU NO. 2** - **Shikoku Ferry KK** - *Takamatsu, Kagawa* *Japan* Official number: 137046	*994* - -		**2003-03 Sanuki Shipbuilding & Iron Works Co Ltd — Mitoyo KG** Yd No: 1308 L reg 68.26 Br ex - Dght - Lbp - Br md 14.30 Dpth 3.64 Welded, 1 dk	**(A36A2PR) Passenger/Ro-Ro Ship (Vehicles)**	**2 oil engines** driving 2 Propellers Total Power: 2,648kW (3,600hp) Niigata 6M31BFT 2 x 4 Stroke 6 Cy. 310 x 530 each-1324kW (1800bhp) Niigata Engineering Co Ltd-Japan
8871572 *UIPI* -	**SHIZHNYA** *ex* Volgo-Don 5098 *-1994* **Highland Shipping Ltd** Albros Shipping & Trading Ltd Co (Albros Denizcilik ve Ticaret Ltd Sti) *Astrakhan* *Russia* MMSI: 273339100	**2,829** 1,012 3,997	Class: RS	**1987-12 Santierul Naval Oltenita S.A. — Oltenita** Yd No: 204 Shortened-1994 Loa 105.30 Br ex 16.70 Dght 3.850 Lbp 99.60 Br md 16.50 Dpth 5.50 Welded, 1 dk	**(A31A2GX) General Cargo Ship** Grain: 5,250	**2 oil engines** driving 2 FP propellers Total Power: 1,324kW (1,800hp) 10.0kn Dvigatel Revolyutsii 6CHRNP36/45 2 x 4 Stroke 6 Cy. 360 x 450 each-662kW (900bhp) Zavod "Dvigatel Revolyutsii"-Gorkiy
9084011 *DSQL2* -	**SHIZKA** *ex* Shoyo Maru No. 18 *-2009* **Yu Jin Shipping Co Ltd** - *Jeju* *South Korea* MMSI: 441613000 Official number: JJR-092159	**1,510** 851 2,544	Class: KR	**1994-02 Honda Zosen — Saiki** Yd No: 861 Loa 75.52 Br ex - Dght 5.388 Lbp 70.00 Br md 12.20 Dpth 7.15 Welded	**(A31A2GX) General Cargo Ship** Grain: 2,709; Bale: 2,584 Compartments: 1 Ho, ER 1 Ha: (40.2 x 10.0)ER	**1 oil engine** driving 1 FP propeller Total Power: 1,324kW (1,800hp) 13.6kn Niigata 6M31BLGT 1 x 4 Stroke 6 Cy. 310 x 600 1324kW (1800bhp) Niigata Engineering Co Ltd-Japan
9339997 *7JFB* -	**SHIZUKISAN** - **Silver Lining Maritime Inc** Mitsui OSK Lines Ltd (MOL) SatCom: Inmarsat C 443270110 *Tokyo* *Japan* MMSI: 432701000 Official number: 141008	**160,078** 103,974 310,984 T/cm 183.9	Class: NK	**2009-04 Mitsui Eng. & SB. Co. Ltd., Chiba Works — Ichihara** Yd No: 1679 Loa 333.00 (BB) Br ex 60.04 Dght 20.943 Lbp 324.00 Br md 60.00 Dpth 28.80 Welded, 1 dk	**(A13A2TV) Crude Oil Tanker** Double Hull (13F) Liq: 339,586; Liq (Oil): 339,900 Compartments: 5 Ta, 10 Wing Ta, 2 Wing Slop Ta, ER 3 Cargo Pump (s): 3x5500m³/hr Manifold: Bow/CM: 167.3m	**1 oil engine** driving 1 FP propeller Total Power: 27,184kW (36,959hp) 15.9kn MAN-B&W 7S80MC-C 1 x 2 Stroke 7 Cy. 800 x 3200 27184kW (36959bhp) Mitsui Engineering & Shipbuilding CLtd-Japan AuxGen: 3 x 1050kW 440V 60Hz a.c Fuel: 466.0 (d.f.) 7900.0 (r.f.)
8883460 - -	**SHIZUNAMI** - **Kamara Co** -	*199* 114 -		**1973 Oto Zosen — Japan** Loa 33.00 Br ex - Dght 1.310 Lbp 30.30 Br md 6.20 Dpth 2.69 Welded, 1 dk	**(A37B2PS) Passenger Ship** Passengers: unberthed: 180	**2 oil engines** driving 2 FP propellers Total Power: 736kW (1,000hp) 13.8kn Kubota M6D20BCS 2 x 4 Stroke 6 Cy. 200 x 240 each-368kW (500bhp) Kubota Corp-Japan
7742736 *LLCP* -	**SHJANDY** *ex* Kjerringoy II *-1997* *ex* Kjerringoy *-1991* *ex* Gisle *-1986* **Skyssbaatservice Torgeir Vareberg** - *Bergen* *Norway* MMSI: 257072600	*221* 66 -		**1956 Gravdal Skipsbyggeri — Sunde i Sunnhordland** Yd No: 40 Loa 38.18 Br ex 8.87 Dght - Lbp - Br md - Dpth - Welded, 1 dk	**(A36A2PR) Passenger/Ro-Ro Ship (Vehicles)** Passengers: unberthed: 146 Lane-clr ht: 4.50 Cars: 23	**1 oil engine** driving 1 FP propeller Total Power: 441kW (600hp) Wichmann 6ACA 1 x 2 Stroke 6 Cy. 280 x 420 441kW (600bhp) (made 1955, fitted 1971) Wichmann Motorfabrikk AS-Norway
8721870 *UCXG* -	**SHKIPER** *ex* Basargin *-2011* *ex* Morning Star 1 *-2008* *ex* Muravjova *-1998* *ex* Muravyovo *-1992* **Sigma Marine Technology Co Ltd (OOO 'Sigma Marin Tekhnolodzhi')** - *Sovetskaya Gavan* *Russia* MMSI: 273435700	**928** 278 355	Class: RS	**1986-05 Zavod "Leninskaya Kuznitsa" — Kiyev** Yd No: 262 Loa 53.74 Br ex 10.71 Dght 4.400 Lbp 47.92 Br md 10.50 Dpth 6.00 Welded, 1 dk	**(B11A2FS) Stern Trawler** Ice Capable	**1 oil engine** driving 1 CP propeller Total Power: 971kW (1,320hp) 12.6kn S.K.L. 8NVD48A-2U 1 x 4 Stroke 8 Cy. 320 x 480 971kW (1320bhp) VEB Schwermaschinenbau "KarlLiebknecht" (SKL)-Magdeburg AuxGen: 3 x 160kW a.c
8924848 - -	**SHKVAL** *ex* MRTK-3286 *-1992* **National JSC 'Chernomorneftegaz'** - *Chernomorskiy* *Ukraine*	**120** 36 36	Class: (RS)	**1979-08 Sosnovskiy Sudostroitelnyy Zavod — Sosnovka** Yd No: 3286 Loa 25.50 Br ex 7.00 Dght 2.390 Lbp 22.00 Br md - Dpth 3.30 Welded, 1 dk	**(B11B2FV) Fishing Vessel** Ins: 64 Ice Capable	**1 oil engine** driving 1 FP propeller Total Power: 287kW (390hp) 9.5kn S.K.L. 6NVD26A-3 1 x 4 Stroke 6 Cy. 180 x 260 287kW (390bhp) VEB Schwermaschinenbau "KarlLiebknecht" (SKL)-Magdeburg AuxGen: 1 x 25kW a.c, 2 x 12kW a.c Fuel: 12.0 (d.f.)
6873411 - -	**SHKVAL** - **Azerbaijan State Caspian Shipping Co (ASCSS)** -	*368* 25 155	Class: (RS)	**1958-06 Bakinskiy Sudostroitelnyy Zavod im Vano Sturua — Baku** Yd No: 42 Converted From: Tug Loa 44.40 Br ex 9.48 Dght 3.341 Lbp 41.00 Br md 9.02 Dpth 4.42 Welded, 1 dk	**(B31A2SR) Research Survey Vessel** Derricks: 1x1.5t Ice Capable	**2 oil engines** driving 2 FP propellers Total Power: 882kW (1,200hp) 12.3kn Russkiy 6DR30/50 2 x 2 Stroke 6 Cy. 300 x 500 each-441kW (600bhp) Mashinostroitelnyy Zavod"Russkiy-Dizel"-Leningrad AuxGen: 2 x 100kW Fuel: 86.0 (d.f.)
8737415 *YB6365* -	**SHM 15** - **PT Karya Samudera Mandiri** - *Samarinda* *Indonesia*	**204** 70 -	Class: KI	**2008-12 C.V. Karya Lestari Industri — Samarinda** Loa 37.50 Br ex - Dght - Lbp 36.05 Br md 8.00 Dpth 2.40 Welded, 1 dk	**(A35D2RL) Landing Craft**	**2 oil engines** driving 2 Propellers Total Power: 478kW (650hp) Nissan RE8 2 x Vee 4 Stroke 8 Cy. 135 x 132 each-239kW (325bhp) Nissan Diesel Motor Co. Ltd.-Ageo AuxGen: 2 x 400V 50Hz a.c

IMO / Call sign	Name / Owner / Port	Tonnage	Class	Builder / Dimensions	Type	Machinery
9358785 *VNW5796* -	**SHOAL CAPE** **MacKenzie Marine & Towage Pty Ltd (MacKenzie's Tug Service)** - *Fremantle, WA* *Australia* Official number: 857916	*249* 74 -	Class: BV	**2006-08 Damen Shipyards Changde Co Ltd — Changde HN** (Hull) **2006-08 B.V. Scheepswerf Damen — Gorinchem** Yd No: 512206 Loa 24.47 Br ex - Dght 5.310 Lbp 22.16 Br md 11.33 Dpth 4.60 Welded, 1 dk	**(B32A2ST) Tug**	**2 oil engines** reduction geared to sc. shafts driving 2 Z propellers Total Power: 4,200kW (5,710hp) Caterpillar 3516B-HD 2 x Vee 4 Stroke 16 Cy. 170 x 215 each-2100kW (2855bhp) Caterpillar Inc-USA AuxGen: 1 x 52kW 230/400V 50Hz a.c
7647742 *WYL8687* -	**SHOALS** - *Tampa, FL* *United States of America* Official number: 580958	*113* 76 -		**1977 Steiner Shipyard, Inc. — Bayou La Batre, Al** L reg 20.18 Br ex 6.71 Dght - Lbp - Br md - Dpth 3.46 Welded, 1dk	**(B11B2FV) Fishing Vessel**	**1 oil engine** driving 1 FP propeller Total Power: 268kW (364hp)
8852289 - -	**SHOALS '86** **Noble House Seafoods Co Ltd** - *Georgetown* *Guyana* Official number: 0000370	*101* 69 -		**1986 Steiner Shipyard, Inc. — Bayou La Batre, Al** Loa 24.39 Br ex 6.71 Dght 1.520 Lbp 20.33 Br md 6.71 Dpth 3.35 Welded, 1 dk	**(B11A2FT) Trawler**	**1 oil engine** driving 1 FP propeller
9556337 *5BYP2* -	**SHOALWAY** **Boskalis Westminster Shipping BV** Baggermaatschappij Boskalis BV SatCom: Inmarsat C 421211511 *Limassol* *Cyprus* MMSI: 212115000	**4,088** 1,229 5,490	Class: BV	**2010-04 in Poland** (Hull) Yd No: (221) **2010-04 Intervak BV — Harlingen** Yd No: 221 Loa 90.00 (BB) Br ex - Dght 5.930 Lbp 83.09 Br md 19.00 Dpth 7.25 Welded, 1 dk	**(B33B2DT) Trailing Suction Hopper Dredger** Hopper: 5,600	**2 oil engines** reduction geared to sc. shafts driving 2 Directional propellers Total Power: 2,984kW (4,058hp) 11.0kn Caterpillar 3516C 2 x Vee 4 Stroke 16 Cy. 170 x 190 each-1492kW (2029bhp) Caterpillar Inc-USA Thrusters: 1 Tunnel thruster (f) Fuel: 340.0 (r.f.)
9233909 *JG5631* -	**SHOAN MARU** **Corporation for Advanced Transport & Technology & Daiichi Kaiun Co Ltd** Daiichi Kaiun Co Ltd (Daiichi Kaiun KK) *Tokyo* *Japan* MMSI: 431100938 Official number: 136998	*699* - 963	Class: NK	**2001-03 Shin Kurushima Dockyard Co. Ltd. — Hashihama, Imabari** Yd No: 5100 Loa 64.52 (BB) Br ex - Dght 4.062 Lbp 60.00 Br md 11.20 Dpth 4.90 Welded, 1 dk	**(A11B2TG) LPG Tanker** Single Hull Liq (Gas): 1,190 2 x Gas Tank (s); 2 Cargo Pump (s): 2x200m³/hr	**1 oil engine** reverse geared to sc. shaft driving 1 FP propeller Total Power: 1,323kW (1,799hp) 12.0kn Akasaka A31R 1 x 4 Stroke 6 Cy. 310 x 600 1323kW (1799bhp) Akasaka Tekkosho KK (Akasaka DieselLtd)-Japan AuxGen: 2 x 240kW a.c, 1 x 64kW a.c Thrusters: 1 Thwart. FP thruster (f) Fuel: 94.0 (d.f.)
7823774 - -	**SHOAN MARU No. 2** - -	*600* - 623	Class: (NK)	**1979-07 Sanyo Zosen K.K. — Onomichi** Yd No: 776 Loa 57.26 Br ex - Dght 3.712 Lbp 52.02 Br md 9.42 Dpth 4.47 Welded, 1 dk	**(A11B2TG) LPG Tanker** Liq (Gas): 684 2 x Gas Tank (s);	**1 oil engine** driving 1 FP propeller Total Power: 956kW (1,300hp) 11.0kn Hanshin 6LUN28AG 1 x 4 Stroke 6 Cy. 280 x 480 956kW (1300bhp) The Hanshin Diesel Works Ltd-Japan AuxGen: 2 x 192kW
8616685 - -	**SHOAN MARU No. 3** - -	**710** 213 503	Class: (NK)	**1987-02 Minami-Kyushu Zosen KK — Ichikikushikino KS** Yd No: 517 Loa 55.03 Br ex - Dght 3.010 Lbp 50.02 Br md 10.01 Dpth 4.32 Welded, 1 dk	**(A11B2TG) LPG Tanker** Liq (Gas): 543 1 x Gas Tank (s);	**1 oil engine** with clutches & reverse reduction geared to sc. shaft driving 1 FP propeller Total Power: 588kW (799hp) 10.3kn Hanshin 6LU24G 1 x 4 Stroke 6 Cy. 240 x 410 588kW (799bhp) The Hanshin Diesel Works Ltd-Japan Fuel: 65.0 (d.f.)
8911205 *JI3383* -	**SHOAN MARU No. 5** **Yokota Kaiun YK** *Kainan, Wakayama* *Japan* Official number: 128776	*315* - 351	Class: NK	**1990-01 Shitanoe Shipbuilding Co Ltd — Usuki OT** Yd No: 1106 Loa 47.23 (BB) Br ex 9.32 Dght 2.960 Lbp 43.00 Br md 9.30 Dpth 3.80 Welded, 1 dk	**(A11B2TG) LPG Tanker** Liq (Gas): 400 1 x Gas Tank (s);	**1 oil engine** sr reverse geared to sc. shaft driving 1 FP propeller Total Power: 736kW (1,001hp) Yanmar T240-ST 1 x 4 Stroke 6 Cy. 240 x 310 736kW (1001bhp) Yanmar Diesel Engine Co Ltd-Japan Fuel: 45.0 (d.f.)
9539028 *JD2952* -	**SHOAN MARU NO. 8** **Daiichi Kaiun Co Ltd (Daiichi Kaiun KK)** *Tokyo* *Japan* Official number: 141071	*493* - 752		**2009-09 Imura Zosen K.K. — Komatsushima** Yd No: 327 Loa 58.80 Br ex - Dght 3.620 Lbp 55.00 Br md 10.00 Dpth 4.50 Welded, 1 dk	**(A11B2TG) LPG Tanker** Single Hull Liq (Gas): 900	**1 oil engine** reverse geared to sc. shaft driving 1 FP propeller Total Power: 1,030kW (1,400hp) Akasaka K28BR 1 x 4 Stroke 6 Cy. 280 x 480 1030kW (1400bhp) Akasaka Tekkosho KK (Akasaka DieselLtd)-Japan
7506613 - -	**SHOBAIR** *ex* Al-Hather *-2008* **Abduljabbar & Abdulsattar & Khazaal**	*474* 142 368	Class: (LR) ✠ Classed LR until 29/1/92	**1976-03 K.K. Odo Zosen Tekko — Shimonoseki** Yd No: 211 Loa 42.02 Br ex 10.24 Dght 4.152 Lbp 37.17 Br md 10.00 Dpth 4.70 Welded, 1 dk	**(B32A2ST) Tug**	**1 oil engine** driving 1 CP propeller Total Power: 1,839kW (2,500hp) Niigata 6M40X 1 x 4 Stroke 6 Cy. 400 x 600 1839kW (2500bhp) Niigata Engineering Co Ltd-Japan AuxGen: 2 x 176kW 385V 50Hz a.c, 1 x 100kW 385V 50Hz a.c Fuel: 180.0 (d.f.)
9233612 *JL6626* -	**SHODOSHIMA MARU No. 1** **Shikoku Ferry KK** *Takamatsu, Kagawa* *Japan* Official number: 136486	*999* - 349		**2000-09 Sanuki Shipbuilding & Iron Works Co Ltd — Mitoyo KG** Yd No: 1302 Loa 66.60 Br ex - Dght - Lbp - Br md 14.30 Dpth 3.70 Welded	**(A36A2PR) Passenger/Ro-Ro Ship (Vehicles)** Passengers: berths: 492 Bow door/ramp (centre) Stern door/ramp (centre) Cars: 52	**2 oil engines** geared to sc. shafts driving 2 FP propellers Total Power: 2,648kW (3,600hp) 13.5kn Niigata 6M31BFT 2 x 4 Stroke 6 Cy. 310 x 530 each-1324kW (1800bhp) Niigata Engineering Co Ltd-Japan
9250311 *JL6630* -	**SHODOSHIMA MARU No. 7** **Shikoku Ferry KK** *Takamatsu, Kagawa* *Japan* Official number: 136490	*993* - 350		**2001-10 Sanuki Shipbuilding & Iron Works Co Ltd — Mitoyo KG** Yd No: 1303 Loa 68.26 Br ex - Dght - Lbp - Br md 14.30 Dpth 3.65 Welded	**(A37B2PS) Passenger Ship**	**2 oil engines** geared to sc. shafts driving 2 FP propellers Total Power: 2,648kW (3,600hp) Niigata 6M31BFT 2 x 4 Stroke 6 Cy. 310 x 530 each-1324kW (1800bhp) Niigata Engineering Co Ltd-Japan
7918309 - -	**SHODOSHIMA MARU No. 8** *ex* Tamataka Maru No. 75 *-1989* **Government of The People's Republic of China** - *China*	*642* - 100		**1979-11 Shikoku Dockyard Co. Ltd. — Takamatsu** Yd No: 806 Loa - Br ex - Dght 2.501 Lbp 55.02 Br md 14.01 Dpth 3.51 Welded	**(A36A2PR) Passenger/Ro-Ro Ship (Vehicles)** Passengers: unberthed: 480 Cars: 22	**2 oil engines** driving 2 FP propellers Total Power: 1,912kW (2,600hp) 12.0kn Makita GNLH630 2 x 4 Stroke 6 Cy. 300 x 480 each-956kW (1300bhp) Makita Diesel Co Ltd-Japan
8217582 - -	**SHODOSHIMA MARU No. 8** *ex* Tamataka Maru No. 78 *-1992* **Ever Green Management Inc** Hinode Shoji YK	*680* - 150		**1982-11 Sanuki Shipbuilding & Iron Works Co Ltd — Mitoyo KG** Yd No: 1113 Loa 59.90 Br ex - Dght 2.501 Lbp 55.02 Br md 11.02 Dpth 3.51 Welded, 1 dk	**(A36A2PR) Passenger/Ro-Ro Ship (Vehicles)** Passengers: unberthed: 480 Trailers: 22	**2 oil engines** sr geared to sc. shafts driving 2 FP propellers Total Power: 1,472kW (2,002hp) 12.0kn Makita GNLH630 2 x 4 Stroke 6 Cy. 300 x 480 each-736kW (1001bhp) Makita Diesel Co Ltd-Japan
8961913 *JI3679* -	**SHOEI MARU** **Taiyo Shipping Co Ltd (Taiyo Kisen KK)** *Osaka, Osaka* *Japan* MMSI: 431301503 Official number: 136807	*697* - -		**2000-09 Yamanaka Zosen K.K. — Imabari** Yd No: 657 Loa 79.30 Br ex - Dght - Lbp 73.00 Br md 12.60 Dpth 8.20 Welded, 1 dk	**(A31A2GX) General Cargo Ship** Compartments: 1 Ho, ER 1 Ha: (41.4 x 9.8)ER	**1 oil engine** driving 1 FP propeller Total Power: 1,618kW (2,200hp) 12.5kn Hanshin LH34L 1 x 4 Stroke 6 Cy. 340 x 640 1618kW (2200bhp) The Hanshin Diesel Works Ltd-Japan Fuel: 103.0 (d.f.)
8870190 *JL6084* -	**SHOEI MARU** *ex* Hanei Maru *-2009* *ex* Keiwa Maru *-2008* *ex* Myoetsu Maru No. 18 *-2005* *ex* Hanei Maru No. 18 *-1999* **Hanei Kaiun YK** - *Otaru, Hokkaido* *Japan* Official number: 132974	*613* - 1,448		**1993-05 Nagashima Zosen KK — Kihoku ME** Loa 71.30 Br ex - Dght 4.100 Lbp 65.00 Br md 13.50 Dpth 6.94 Welded, 1 dk	**(A24D2BA) Aggregates Carrier**	**1 oil engine** driving 1 FP propeller Total Power: 736kW (1,001hp) 11.0kn Niigata 6M34AGT 1 x 4 Stroke 6 Cy. 340 x 620 736kW (1001bhp) Niigata Engineering Co Ltd-Japan
8876986 *JM6346* -	**SHOEI MARU** **Shoei Kaiun YK** *Karatsu, Saga* *Japan* Official number: 133630	*199* - 649		**1994-03 YK Furumoto Tekko Zosensho — Osakikamijima** Loa 59.31 Br ex - Dght 3.300 Lbp 53.00 Br md 9.40 Dpth 5.55 Welded, 1 dk	**(A31A2GX) General Cargo Ship**	**1 oil engine** driving 1 FP propeller Total Power: 736kW (1,001hp) 11.0kn Matsui ML627GSC 1 x 4 Stroke 6 Cy. 270 x 480 736kW (1001bhp) Matsui Iron Works Co Ltd-Japan

9047738 *V4PE2* -	**SHOEI MARU** *ex* Hoei Maru *-2011* **Jenvey Ltd** - *Basseterre* *St Kitts & Nevis* MMSI: 341368000 Official number: SKN 1002405	723 396 1,220		**1992-07 KK Ura Kyodo Zosensho — Awaji HG** Yd No: 288 Loa 64.40 (BB) Br ex - Dght - Lbp 60.00 Br md 10.00 Dpth 4.50 Welded, 1 dk	**(A13B2TP) Products Tanker** Liq: 1,350; Liq (Oil): 1,350 Compartments: 4 Ta, ER	**1 oil engine** geared to sc. shaft driving 1 FP propeller Total Power: 736kW (1,001hp) 12.0kn Hanshin LH28G 1 x 4 Stroke 6 Cy. 280 x 460 736kW (1001bhp) The Hanshin Diesel Works Ltd-Japan
9020857 *JG5125* -	**SHOEI MARU** - **Sea Grove Co Ltd** Ikous Co Ltd *Shunan, Yamaguchi* *Japan* MMSI: 431600827 Official number: 133160	*995* - 1,362	Class: NK	**1992-06 Shirahama Zosen K.K. — Honai** Yd No: 156 Loa 70.00 (BB) Br ex - Dght 4.583 Lbp 65.00 Br md 12.20 Dpth 5.50 Welded, 1 dk	**(A11B2TG) LPG Tanker** Liq (Gas): 1,643 3 x Gas Tank (s); 2 horizontal, ER	**1 oil engine** driving 1 FP propeller Total Power: 1,618kW (2,200hp) 12.0kn Hanshin 6EL35 1 x 4 Stroke 6 Cy. 350 x 700 1618kW (2200bhp) The Hanshin Diesel Works Ltd-Japan Fuel: 160.0 (r.f.)
9128752 *JM6311* -	**SHOEI MARU** - **Abe Kisen KK** - *Imabari, Ehime* *Japan* Official number: 134585	*499* - 1,501	Class: NK	**1995-09 K.K. Miura Zosensho — Saiki** Yd No: 1130 Loa 75.50 Br ex - Dght 3.982 Lbp 70.00 Br md 12.30 Dpth 6.87 Welded, 1 dk	**(A31A2GX) General Cargo Ship** Bale: 2,466 Compartments: 1 Ho, ER 1 Ha: (39.0 x 10.0)ER	**1 oil engine** driving 1 FP propeller Total Power: 736kW (1,001hp) 12.0kn Hanshin LH30LG 1 x 4 Stroke 6 Cy. 300 x 600 736kW (1001bhp) The Hanshin Diesel Works Ltd-Japan Fuel: 83.4 (d.f.)
9103427 - -	**SHOEI MARU** - - -	*199* - 686		**1993-04 YK Furumoto Tekko Zosensho — Osakikamijima** Yd No: 605 Loa 57.20 Br ex - Dght - Lbp 52.00 Br md 9.70 Dpth 5.30 Welded, 1 dk	**(A31A2GX) General Cargo Ship**	**1 oil engine** geared to sc. shaft driving 1 FP propeller Total Power: 736kW (1,001hp) 12.2kn Hanshin LH26G 1 x 4 Stroke 6 Cy. 260 x 440 736kW (1001bhp) The Hanshin Diesel Works Ltd-Japan
9151503 *JI3552* -	**SHOEI MARU** *ex* Seiun Maru *-2006* *ex* Yamataka Maru No. 5 *-2001* **Shoei KK** - *Kitakyushu, Fukuoka* *Japan* Official number: 135031	*497* - 1,500		**1997-01 K.K. Yoshida Zosen Kogyo — Arida** Yd No: 505 Loa 70.32 Br ex - Dght - Lbp 65.00 Br md 13.00 Dpth 7.00 Welded, 1 dk	**(A31A2GX) General Cargo Ship**	**1 oil engine** driving 1 FP propeller Total Power: 1,618kW (2,200hp) 12.0kn Niigata 6M34BGT 1 x 4 Stroke 6 Cy. 340 x 620 1618kW (2200bhp) Niigata Engineering Co Ltd-Japan
9207156 *JM6652* -	**SHOEI MARU** - **Kyowa Kisen KK (Kyowa Steamship Co Ltd)** - *Fukuoka, Fukuoka* *Japan* Official number: 136433	*499* - 1,600		**1999-05 K.K. Miura Zosensho — Saiki** Yd No: 1221 Loa 75.50 Br ex - Dght 4.000 Lbp 70.00 Br md 12.50 Dpth 6.90 Welded, 1 dk	**(A31A2GX) General Cargo Ship** Compartments: 1 Ho, ER 1 Ha: (40.2 x 10.0)ER	**1 oil engine** driving 1 FP propeller Total Power: 1,471kW (2,000hp) 12.5kn Hanshin LH34LAG 1 x 4 Stroke 6 Cy. 340 x 640 1471kW (2000bhp) The Hanshin Diesel Works Ltd-Japan
9588861 *JD3054* -	**SHOEI MARU** - **Showa Nittan Corp** - *Tokyo* *Japan* MMSI: 431001401 Official number: 141227	*3,763* 1,800 4,999	Class: NK	**2010-05 Kumamoto Dock K.K. — Yatsushiro** Yd No: 453 Loa 104.97 (BB) Br ex - Dght 6.250 Lbp 98.80 Br md 16.00 Dpth 8.30 Welded, 1 dk	**(A12B2TR) Chemical/Products Tanker** Double Hull (13F) Liq: 6,075; Liq (Oil): 6,075	**1 oil engine** driving 1 FP propeller Total Power: 2,950kW (4,011hp) MAN-B&W 5L35MC 1 x 2 Stroke 5 Cy. 350 x 1050 2950kW (4011bhp) Hitachi Zosen Corp-Japan Thrusters: 1 Thwart. FP thruster (f) Fuel: 200.0 (r.f.)
9304564 *JFGJ* -	**SHOEI MARU NO. 1** - **Katsukura Gyogyo KK** - *Tokyo* *Japan* MMSI: 432448000 Official number: 137195	*439* - -		**2004-02 Niigata Shipbuilding & Repair Inc — Niigata NI** Yd No: 0002 Loa 56.77 (BB) Br ex - Dght 3.830 Lbp - Br md 9.00 Dpth 3.90 Welded, 1 dk	**(B11B2FV) Fishing Vessel**	**1 oil engine** geared to sc. shaft driving 1 FP propeller Total Power: 736kW (1,001hp) Niigata 6M28BFT 1 x 4 Stroke 6 Cy. 280 x 480 736kW (1001bhp) Niigata Engineering Co Ltd-Japan
9120023 *JQTN* MG1-1917	**SHOEI MARU No. 7** - **Katsukura Gyogyo KK** - SatCom: Inmarsat B 343176210 *Kesennuma, Miyagi* *Japan* MMSI: 431700260 Official number: 133315	*410* - -		**1995-06 Niigata Engineering Co Ltd — Niigata NI** Yd No: 2277 Loa 57.43 (BB) Br ex - Dght - Lbp 49.00 Br md 9.00 Dpth 3.90 Welded, 1 dk	**(B11B2FV) Fishing Vessel** Ins: 510	**1 oil engine** with clutches, flexible couplings & sr geared to sc. shaft driving 1 CP propeller Total Power: 699kW (950hp) Niigata 6M28HFT 1 x 4 Stroke 6 Cy. 280 x 480 699kW (950bhp) Niigata Engineering Co Ltd-Japan
7914729 *JM4595* -	**SHOEI MARU No. 7** - **Shoei Kaiun KK** - *Ube, Yamaguchi* *Japan* Official number: 122739	*198* - 200		**1979-01 Maeno Zosen KK — Sanyoonoda YC** Yd No: 38 Loa 38.54 Br ex 7.83 Dght 2.800 Lbp 34.19 Br md 7.80 Dpth 3.00 Welded, 1 dk	**(A12A2TC) Chemical Tanker**	**1 oil engine** driving 1 FP propeller Matsui MU623CS 1 x 4 Stroke 6 Cy. 230 x 380 Matsui Iron Works Co Ltd-Japan
6610273 - -	**SHOEI MARU No. 8** *ex* Fukuichi Maru No. 33 *-1970* **Seishin Suisan** - *South Korea*	*190* 65 -		**1965 Miho Zosensho K.K. — Shimizu** Yd No: 568 L reg 34.90 Br ex 6.61 Dght - Lbp 34.42 Br md 6.58 Dpth 3.20 Welded, 1 dk	**(B11B2FV) Fishing Vessel**	**1 oil engine** driving 1 FP propeller Total Power: 552kW (750hp) Niigata 1 x 4 Stroke 6 Cy. 280 x 440 552kW (750bhp) Niigata Engineering Co Ltd-Japan
9115274 *JFFX* -	**SHOEI MARU NO. 8** *ex* Shoyo Maru No. 2 *-2011* **KK Shoei Maru** - SatCom: Inmarsat B 343169310 *Yaizu, Shizuoka* *Japan* MMSI: 431693000 Official number: 134380	*499* 303 708		**1995-01 Miho Zosensho K.K. — Shimizu** Yd No: 1451 Loa 66.00 (BB) Br ex - Dght 3.964 Lbp 56.77 Br md 9.50 Dpth 4.45 Welded, 1 dk	**(B11B2FV) Fishing Vessel** Ins: 828	**1 oil engine** with flexible couplings & sr geared to sc. shaft driving 1 FP propeller Total Power: 1,471kW (2,000hp) Yanmar 6N280-EN 1 x 4 Stroke 6 Cy. 280 x 380 1471kW (2000bhp) Yanmar Diesel Engine Co Ltd-Japan
9020869 *JM6037* -	**SHOEI MARU No. 8** - **Shoei Kaiun KK** - *Ube, Yamaguchi* *Japan* Official number: 132699	*220* - 435		**1991-06 Taiyo Shipbuilding Co Ltd — Sanyoonoda YC** Yd No: 226 Loa 47.43 Br ex - Dght 2.940 Lbp 43.00 Br md 7.80 Dpth 3.35 Welded, 1 dk	**(A12A2TC) Chemical Tanker** Liq: 342 Compartments: 6 Ta, ER	**1 oil engine** with clutches & geared to sc. shaft driving 1 FP propeller Total Power: 625kW (850hp) Hanshin 6LC26G 1 x 4 Stroke 6 Cy. 260 x 440 625kW (850bhp) Hanshin Nainenki Kogyo-Japan
9078139 *JL5999* -	**SHOEI MARU No. 8** - **Goda Kisen KK** - *Shikokuchuo, Ehime* *Japan* Official number: 133874	*499* - 1,300	Class: NK	**1993-06 Hakata Zosen K.K. — Imabari** Yd No: 551 Loa 64.99 Br ex - Dght 4.249 Lbp 60.90 Br md 10.00 Dpth 4.50 Welded, 1 dk	**(A12A2TC) Chemical Tanker** Liq: 1,230	**1 oil engine** reverse geared to sc. shaft driving 1 FP propeller Total Power: 735kW (999hp) 11.0kn Hanshin LH28G 1 x 4 Stroke 6 Cy. 280 x 460 735kW (999bhp) The Hanshin Diesel Works Ltd-Japan Fuel: 50.0 (d.f.)
8515752 *JM5334* -	**SHOEI MARU No. 11** - **Shoei Kaiun KK** - *Ube, Yamaguchi* *Japan* Official number: 127891	*334* - 725		**1985-12 Maeno Zosen KK — Sanyoonoda YC** Yd No: 118 Loa 55.00 Br ex 8.64 Dght 3.501 Lbp 50.02 Br md 8.60 Dpth 4.02 Welded, 1 dk	**(A12A2TC) Chemical Tanker** 2 Cargo Pump (s): 2x100m³/hr	**1 oil engine** reverse reduction geared to sc. shaft driving 1 FP propeller Total Power: 736kW (1,001hp) Hanshin 6LU26G 1 x 4 Stroke 6 Cy. 260 x 440 736kW (1001bhp) The Hanshin Diesel Works Ltd-Japan
8967333 *JD3000* -	**SHOEI MARU NO. 18** *ex* Suikoumaru No. 1 *-2010* *ex* Wakaei Maru No. 1 *-2005* **Nihon Kotsuzai KK** - *Shimonoseki, Yamaguchi* *Japan* Official number: 141152	*413* 147 -		**2001-05 Nagashima Zosen KK — Kihoku ME** Yd No: 557 Loa 29.97 Br ex - Dght - Lbp 26.67 Br md 17.65 Dpth 7.53 Welded, 1 dk	**(B32B2SP) Pusher Tug**	**2 oil engines** driving 2 FP propellers Total Power: 2,942kW (4,000hp) Niigata 6M37GT 2 x 4 Stroke 6 Cy. 370 x 720 each-1471kW (2000bhp) Niigata Engineering Co Ltd-Japan
8815061 *JJOS* -	**SHOEI MARU No. 18** - **KK Shoei Maru** - SatCom: Inmarsat A 1204410 *Yaizu, Shizuoka* *Japan* MMSI: 431523000 Official number: 130751	*463* - 590		**1988-12 Miho Zosensho K.K. — Shimizu** Yd No: 1344 Loa 61.68 (BB) Br ex - Dght 3.743 Lbp 52.30 Br md 8.90 Dpth 4.15 Welded, 1 dk	**(B11B2FV) Fishing Vessel** Ins: 563	**1 oil engine** with clutches, flexible couplings & sr geared to sc. shaft driving 1 FP propeller Total Power: 1,324kW (1,800hp) Akasaka K31FD 1 x 4 Stroke 6 Cy. 310 x 530 1324kW (1800bhp) Akasaka Tekkosho KK (Akasaka DieselLtd)-Japan AuxGen: 2 x 560kW 445V a.c

8804880 - -	**SHOEI MARU NO. 18** *ex* Take Maru No. 18 *-2002* *ex* Tsuru Maru No. 18 *-1990* -	*498* - 1,594		**1988-09 Honda Zosen — Saiki** Yd No: 773 Loa 68.18 (BB) Br ex 13.03 Dght 4.271 Lbp 63.00 Br md 13.01 Dpth 6.81 Welded, 1 dk	**(B33A2DG) Grab Dredger**	**1 oil engine** reverse reduction geared to sc. shaft driving 1 FP propeller Total Power: 1,177kW (1,600hp) Niigata 6M30GT 1 x 4 Stroke 6 Cy. 300 x 530 1177kW (1600bhp) Niigata Engineering Co Ltd-Japan Thrusters: 1 Thwart. FP thruster (f)
8916164 *JKIL* MG1-1737	**SHOEI MARU No. 28** - **Katsukura Gyogyo KK** - SatCom: Inmarsat A 1200555 *Kesennuma, Miyagi* *Japan* MMSI: 431701110 Official number: 130779	*379* - -		**1990-03 Niigata Engineering Co Ltd — Niigata NI** Yd No: 2153 Loa 54.56 (BB) Br ex - Dght 3.440 Lbp 47.90 Br md 8.70 Dpth 3.80 Welded, 1 dk	**(B11B2FV) Fishing Vessel** Ins: 477	**1 oil engine** with clutches, flexible couplings & sr geared to sc. shaft driving 1 CP propeller Total Power: 736kW (1,001hp) Niigata 6M28BFT 1 x 4 Stroke 6 Cy. 280 x 480 736kW (1001bhp) Niigata Engineering Co Ltd-Japan
7603033 - -	**SHOEI MARU No. 38** *ex* Shoei Maru No. 8 *-1986* *ex* Nissho Maru No. 23 *-1984* *ex* Kaiei Maru No. 31 *-1980* **Shoei Gyogyo KK** -	*116* 32 -		**1976-03 Minami-Nippon Zosen KK — Ichikikushikino KS** Yd No: 252 Loa 37.19 Br ex 7.55 Dght 2.482 Lbp 31.12 Br md 6.96 Dpth 2.80 Welded, 1 dk	**(B11B2FV) Fishing Vessel**	**1 oil engine** driving 1 FP propeller Total Power: 883kW (1,201hp) Niigata 6L28BX 1 x 4 Stroke 6 Cy. 280 x 320 883kW (1201bhp) Niigata Engineering Co Ltd-Japan
8704339 *JL5627* -	**SHOEI MARU No. 51** - **Shoei Kaiun KK** - *Tokushima, Tokushima* *Japan* MMSI: 431500532 Official number: 129899	*694* - 2,050		**1987-06 Kasado Dockyard Co Ltd — Kudamatsu YC** Yd No: 367 Loa 75.01 (BB) Br ex 14.64 Dght 4.522 Lbp 69.02 Br md 14.61 Dpth 7.40 Welded, 2 dks	**(B33A2DG) Grab Dredger** Grain: 1,545; Hopper: 1,320 Compartments: 1 Ho, ER 1 Ha: ER	**1 oil engine** with clutches, flexible couplings & sr geared to sc. shaft driving 1 CP propeller Total Power: 1,471kW (2,000hp) 12.0kn Fuji 6H32 1 x 4 Stroke 6 Cy. 320 x 470 1471kW (2000bhp) Fuji Diesel Co Ltd-Japan Thrusters: 1 Thwart. CP thruster (f) Fuel: 57.0
9162332 *JL6485* -	**SHOEI MARU No. 55** - **Shoei Kaiun KK** - *Tokushima, Tokushima* *Japan* MMSI: 431500583 Official number: 135520	*749* - 2,015		**1997-03 Hitachi Zosen Mukaishima Marine Co Ltd — Onomichi HS** Yd No: 112 Loa 75.85 (BB) Br ex - Dght 4.510 Lbp 71.00 Br md 14.70 Dpth 7.64 Welded, 1 dk	**(B33A2DG) Grab Dredger** Cranes: 1	**1 oil engine** driving 1 FP propeller Total Power: 1,471kW (2,000hp) 13.0kn B&W 6S26MC 1 x 2 Stroke 6 Cy. 260 x 980 1471kW (2000bhp) The Hanshin Diesel Works Ltd-Japan Thrusters: 1 Tunnel thruster (f)
9221736 *JL6654* -	**SHOEI MARU No. 58** - **Shoei Kaiun KK** - *Tokushima, Tokushima* *Japan* MMSI: 431501632 Official number: 136545	*2,774* - 5,495	Class: NK	**2000-03 Kegoya Dock K.K. — Kure** Yd No: 1036 Loa 103.11 (BB) Br ex - Dght 5.574 Lbp 94.00 Br md 20.00 Dpth 9.50 Welded, 1 dk	**(A31A2GX) General Cargo Ship** Grain: 6,500; Bale: 6,500 Compartments: 2 Ho, ER 2 Ha: (23.8 x 14.0) (24.4 x 14.0)ER Cranes: 1x40t	**1 oil engine** driving 1 FP propeller Total Power: 3,883kW (5,279hp) 11.0kn B&W 6L35MC 1 x 2 Stroke 6 Cy. 350 x 1050 3883kW (5279bhp) The Hanshin Diesel Works Ltd-Japan Thrusters: 1 Tunnel thruster (f) Fuel: 390.0
8310475 - -	**SHOEI MARU No. 72** *ex* Koei Maru No. 12 *-1991* *ex* Yae Maru No. 12 *-1985* - -	*119* - -		**1983-07 Sanuki Shipbuilding & Iron Works Co Ltd — Mitoyo KG** Yd No: 1118 Loa 36.76 (BB) Br ex - Dght 2.340 Lbp 30.03 Br md 6.16 Dpth 2.62 Welded, 1 dk	**(B11B2FV) Fishing Vessel** Ins: 115 Compartments: 9 Ho, ER 12 Ha: ER	**1 oil engine** driving 1 FP propeller Total Power: 588kW (799hp) Akasaka DM26K 1 x 4 Stroke 6 Cy. 260 x 440 588kW (799bhp) Akasaka Tekkosho KK (Akasaka DieselLtd)-Japan
9036715 *JQFE* MG1-1838	**SHOEI MARU No. 88** *ex* Shoei Maru No. 8 *-2009* **Katsukura Gyogyo KK** - SatCom: Inmarsat A 1204525 *Kesennuma, Miyagi* *Japan* MMSI: 431700970 Official number: 132200	*409* - 495		**1991-10 Miho Zosensho K.K. — Shimizu** Yd No: 1397 Loa 56.90 (BB) Br ex 9.02 Dght 3.500 Lbp 49.90 Br md 9.00 Dpth 3.85 Welded	**(B11B2FV) Fishing Vessel** Ins: 660	**1 oil engine** with flexible couplings & sr geared to sc. shaft driving 1 FP propeller Total Power: 736kW (1,001hp) Akasaka K28SFD 1 x 4 Stroke 6 Cy. 280 x 500 736kW (1001bhp) Akasaka Tekkosho KK (Akasaka DieselLtd)-Japan
8936396 *JK5544* -	**SHOEI MARU No. 88** - **KK Sunagawa Gumi** - *Kure, Hiroshima* *Japan* Official number: 135263	*197* - -		**1997-12 Kanbara Zosen K.K. — Onomichi** Yd No: 497 Loa 29.75 Br ex - Dght - Lbp 27.00 Br md 9.00 Dpth 3.79 Welded, 1 dk	**(B32A2ST) Tug**	**2 oil engines** driving 2 FP propellers Total Power: 1,472kW (2,002hp) 10.0kn Hanshin LH34LG 2 x 4 Stroke 6 Cy. 340 x 640 each-736kW (1001bhp) The Hanshin Diesel Works Ltd-Japan
9599810 *3EYI4* -	**SHOEI PROSPERITY** - **Los Halillos Shipping Co SA** Nippon Yusen Kabushiki Kaisha (NYK Line) *Panama* *Panama* MMSI: 373903000 Official number: 42807TJ	**92,752** 60,504 181,403 T/cm 125.0	Class: NK	**2012-01 Imabari Shipbuilding Co Ltd — Saijo EH (Saijo Shipyard)** Yd No: 8115 Loa 291.98 (BB) Br ex - Dght 18.200 Lbp 283.80 Br md 45.00 Dpth 24.70 Welded, 1 dk	**(A21A2BC) Bulk Carrier** Grain: 201,243 Compartments: 9 Ho, ER 9 Ha: ER	**1 oil engine** driving 1 FP propeller Total Power: 18,660kW (25,370hp) 14.0kn MAN-B&W 6S70MC-C 1 x 2 Stroke 6 Cy. 700 x 2800 18660kW (25370bhp) Mitsui Engineering & Shipbuilding CLtd-Japan Fuel: 5800.0
9011179 *JRUL* MG1-1776	**SHOFUKU MARU No. 1** - **KK Usufuku Honten** - SatCom: Inmarsat A 1201777 *Kesennuma, Miyagi* *Japan* MMSI: 431700550 Official number: 130913	*454* - -		**1990-09 KK Kanasashi Zosen — Shizuoka SZ** Yd No: 3233 Loa 58.01 (BB) Br ex - Dght 3.600 Lbp 51.00 Br md 9.00 Dpth 3.95 Welded	**(B11B2FV) Fishing Vessel**	**1 oil engine** with clutches, flexible couplings & sr reverse geared to sc. shaft driving 1 FP propeller Total Power: 1,250kW (1,700hp) Akasaka K31FD 1 x 4 Stroke 6 Cy. 310 x 530 1250kW (1700bhp) Akasaka Tekkosho KK (Akasaka DieselLtd)-Japan
8933992 *JL6465* -	**SHOFUKU MARU No. 3** - **Shofuku Kisen KK** - *Imabari, Ehime* *Japan* Official number: 135537	*199* - 627		**1996-07 Yano Zosen K.K. — Imabari** Yd No: 166 Loa 58.80 Br ex - Dght 3.230 Lbp 52.80 Br md 9.50 Dpth 5.45 Welded, 1 dk	**(A31A2GX) General Cargo Ship** Compartments: 1 Ho, ER 1 Ha: (30.2 x 7.5)ER	**1 oil engine** reverse geared to sc. shaft driving 1 FP propeller Total Power: 736kW (1,001hp) 11.2kn Akasaka T26SKR 1 x 4 Stroke 6 Cy. 260 x 440 736kW (1001bhp) Akasaka Tekkosho KK (Akasaka DieselLtd)-Japan
9254123 *JCNJ* MG1-1980	**SHOFUKU MARU No. 8** - **KK Usufuku Honten** - *Kesennuma, Miyagi* *Japan* MMSI: 432282000 Official number: 136285	*409* - -		**2002-01 Kanasashi Heavy Industries Co Ltd — Shizuoka SZ** Yd No: 8008 Loa 56.17 Br ex - Dght - Lbp 49.20 Br md 8.80 Dpth 3.85 Welded, 1 dk	**(B11B2FV) Fishing Vessel**	**1 oil engine** geared to sc. shaft driving 1 FP propeller Total Power: 736kW (1,001hp) Akasaka K28SFD 1 x 4 Stroke 6 Cy. 280 x 500 736kW (1001bhp) Akasaka Tekkosho KK (Akasaka DieselLtd)-Japan
9009621 *JRLX* MG1-1762	**SHOFUKU MARU No. 28** **KK Usufuku Honten** - SatCom: Inmarsat A 1203115 *Kesennuma, Miyagi* *Japan* MMSI: 431702620 Official number: 130908	*392* - -		**1990-06 KK Kanasashi Zosen — Shizuoka SZ** Yd No: 3226 Loa 54.71 (BB) Br ex 8.73 Dght 3.401 Lbp 48.10 Br md 8.70 Dpth 3.75 Welded, 1 dk	**(B11B2FV) Fishing Vessel** Ins: 491	**1 oil engine** with clutches, flexible couplings & sr reverse geared to sc. shaft driving 1 FP propeller Total Power: 736kW (1,001hp) Akasaka K28FD 1 x 4 Stroke 6 Cy. 280 x 480 736kW (1001bhp) Akasaka Tekkosho KK (Akasaka DieselLtd)-Japan
9037549 *JQGA* MG1-1850	**SHOFUKU MARU No. 38** - **KK Usufuku Honten** - SatCom: Inmarsat A 1204612 *Kesennuma, Miyagi* *Japan* MMSI: 431700560 Official number: 132223	*418* - -		**1991-09 KK Kanasashi — Shizuoka SZ** Yd No: 3273 Loa 56.70 (BB) Br ex 8.83 Dght 3.450 Lbp 49.60 Br md 8.80 Dpth 3.84 Welded	**(B11B2FV) Fishing Vessel** Ins: 517	**1 oil engine** with clutches, flexible couplings & sr reverse geared to sc. shaft driving 1 FP propeller Total Power: 736kW (1,001hp) Akasaka K28SFD 1 x 4 Stroke 6 Cy. 280 x 500 736kW (1001bhp) Akasaka Tekkosho KK (Akasaka DieselLtd)-Japan

9135080 **SHOFUKU MARU No. 58**
JBPQ
MG1-1920 **KK Usufuku Honten**
-
SatCom: Inmarsat C 443179110
Kesennuma, Miyagi *Japan*
MMSI: 431791000
Official number: 133338

423
-
-

1995-09 **KK Kanasashi — Shizuoka SZ**
Yd No: 3368
Loa 56.00 (BB) Br ex - Dght -
Lbp 49.00 Br md 8.00 Dpth 3.00
Welded, 1 dk

(B11B2FV) Fishing Vessel
Ins: 492

1 oil engine with flexible couplings & sr reverse geared to sc. shaft driving 1 FP propeller
Total Power: 736kW (1,001hp)
Akasaka K28SFD
1 x 4 Stroke 6 Cy. 280 x 500 736kW (1001bhp)
Akasaka Tekkosho KK (Akasaka DieselLtd)-Japan

9115145 **SHOFUKU MARU No. 78**
JQRJ
MG1-1908 **KK Usufuku Honten**
-
SatCom: Inmarsat A 1206247
Kesennuma, Miyagi *Japan*
MMSI: 431700210
Official number: 133314

395
231
-

1994-12 **KK Kanasashi — Shizuoka SZ**
Yd No: 3346
Loa 56.00 (BB) Br ex - Dght 3.450
Lbp 49.20 Br md 8.80 Dpth 3.85
Welded, 1 dk

(B11B2FV) Fishing Vessel
Ins: 541

1 oil engine with clutches, flexible couplings & sr reverse geared to sc. shaft driving 1 FP propeller
Total Power: 736kW (1,001hp) 13.0kn
Akasaka K28BFD
1 x 4 Stroke 6 Cy. 280 x 480 736kW (1001bhp)
Akasaka Tekkosho KK (Akasaka DieselLtd)-Japan
AuxGen: 2 x 320kW a.c
Fuel: 289.0 (d.f.) 3.0pd

6706474 **SHOFUKU MARU No. 78**
-
- -
-

196
106
-

1967 K.K. Izutsu Zosensho — Nagasaki Yd No: 472
Loa 36.78 Br ex 6.63 Dght -
Lbp 36.00 Br md 6.61 Dpth 3.26
Welded, 1 dk

(B12B2FC) Fish Carrier

1 oil engine driving 1 FP propeller
Total Power: 537kW (730hp)
Nippon Hatsudoki HS6NV325
1 x 4 Stroke 6 Cy. 325 x 460 537kW (730bhp)
Nippon Hatsudoki-Japan

8921121 **SHOFUKU MARU No. 88**
JRGW
MG1-1752 **KK Usufuku Honten**
-
SatCom: Inmarsat A 1202130
Kesennuma, Miyagi *Japan*
MMSI: 431702580
Official number: 130900

391
-
-

1990-02 **KK Kanasashi Zosen — Shizuoka SZ**
Yd No: 3216
Loa 54.71 (BB) Br ex 8.73 Dght 3.400
Lbp 48.10 Br md 8.70 Dpth 3.75
Welded, 1 dk

(B11B2FV) Fishing Vessel
Ins: 493

1 oil engine with clutches, flexible couplings & sr reverse geared to sc. shaft driving 1 FP propeller
Total Power: 736kW (1,001hp)
Akasaka K28FD
1 x 4 Stroke 6 Cy. 280 x 480 736kW (1001bhp)
Akasaka Tekkosho KK (Akasaka DieselLtd)-Japan

9110092 **SHOGI MARU**
JM6411 *ex* Ogi Maru *-2009*
- **Shogi Kisen KK**
-
Karatsu, Saga *Japan*
MMSI: 431400389
Official number: 134499

698 Class: NK
-
943

1994-12 **Kyoei Zosen KK — Mihara HS** Yd No: 266
Loa 66.50 (BB) Br ex - Dght 4.100
Lbp 60.00 Br md 11.00 Dpth 5.00
Welded, 1 dk

(A11B2TG) LPG Tanker
Liq (Gas): 1,246
2 x Gas Tank (s); 2 independent cyl horizontal
2 Cargo Pump (s): 2x370m³/hr

1 oil engine driving 1 FP propeller
Total Power: 1,324kW (1,800hp) 11.5kn
Hanshin LH30LG
1 x 4 Stroke 6 Cy. 300 x 600 1324kW (1800bhp)
The Hanshin Diesel Works Ltd-Japan
AuxGen: 1 x 320kW a.c
Fuel: 121.7 (d.f.) 5.4pd

7909138 **SHOGI NO. 8**
- *ex* Shogi Maru No. 8 *-1999*
- -
-

699 Class: (NK)
503
770

1979-11 **Setouchi Zosen K.K. — Osakikamijima**
Yd No: 483
Loa 60.30 Br ex 10.04 Dght 4.090
Lbp 55.50 Br md 10.00 Dpth 4.63
Welded, 1 dk

(A11B2TG) LPG Tanker
Liq (Gas): 1,189
2 x Gas Tank (s);

1 oil engine driving 1 FP propeller
Total Power: 1,214kW (1,651hp) 12.0kn
Hanshin 6LUD32
1 x 4 Stroke 6 Cy. 320 x 510 1214kW (1651bhp)
The Hanshin Diesel Works Ltd-Japan
AuxGen: 2 x 360kW
Fuel: 99.5 (d.f.) 5.5pd

7626542 **SHOGUN**
DUA3002 *ex* Kitagami Maru *-1990*
- **International Tankers Corp**
-
Manila *Philippines*
MMSI: 548515000
Official number: 00-0000022

717 Class: (BV) (NK)
301
1,115

1977-12 **Mukaishima Zoki Co. Ltd. — Onomichi**
Yd No: 161
Loa 58.15 Br ex - Dght 3.971
Lbp 53.50 Br md 10.41 Dpth 4.86
Riveted\Welded, 1 dk

(A12A2TC) Chemical Tanker
Liq: 1,146
Cargo Heating Coils

1 oil engine driving 1 FP propeller
Total Power: 736kW (1,001hp) 10.8kn
Otsuka SOD6-29C
1 x 4 Stroke 6 Cy. 290 x 420 736kW (1001bhp)
KK Otsuka Diesel-Japan
AuxGen: 2 x 192kW

9242443 **SHOGUN**
IBZO
- **Mediterranea di Navigazione SpA**
-
Ravenna *Italy*
MMSI: 247064200

24,997 Class: AB RI
8,727
44,485
T/cm
49.9

2002-06 **Hyundai Mipo Dockyard Co Ltd — Ulsan**
Yd No: 0020
Loa 176.00 (BB) Br ex 31.03 Dght 12.000
Lbp 168.00 Br md 31.00 Dpth 17.00
Welded, 1 dk

(A12B2TR) Chemical/Products Tanker
Double Hull (13F)
Liq: 42,855; Liq (Oil): 42,855
Cargo Heating Coils
Compartments: 14 Wing Ta, 2 Wing Slop Ta, ER
14 Cargo Pump (s): 14x500m³/hr
Manifold: Bow/CM: 89.4m

1 oil engine driving 1 FP propeller
Total Power: 8,580kW (11,665hp) 14.5kn
B&W 6S50MC
1 x 2 Stroke 6 Cy. 500 x 1910 8580kW (11665bhp)
Hyundai Heavy Industries Co Ltd-South Korea
AuxGen: 3 x 740kW 450V 60Hz a.c
Thrusters: 1 Tunnel thruster (f)
Fuel: 293.0 (d.f.) 1469.0 (r.f.)

9658927 **SHOHAKU**
7JPW
Tsubaki Ship Holding LLC
Hachiuma Steamship Co Ltd (Hachiuma Kisen KK)
Iwaki, Fukushima *Japan*
MMSI: 432940000
Official number: 141995

50,668 Class: NK
29,023
91,073

2013-09 **Oshima Shipbuilding Co Ltd — Saikai NS**
Yd No: 10702
Loa 234.99 (BB) Br ex - Dght 13.073
Lbp 230.00 Br md 43.00 Dpth 18.55
Welded, 1 dk

(A21A2BC) Bulk Carrier
Double Sides Partial, Double Bottom Partial
Grain: 109,210
Compartments: 7 Ho, ER
7 Ha: ER

1 oil engine driving 1 FP propeller
Total Power: 10,335kW (14,051hp) 15.0kn
Mitsubishi 7UEC60LSII
1 x 2 Stroke 7 Cy. 600 x 2300 10335kW (14051bhp)
Mitsubishi Heavy Industries Ltd-Japan
AuxGen: 3 x 560kW a.c
Fuel: 3739.0

8865468 **SHOHEI MARU**
JJ3799 *ex* Shotoku Maru *-2005*
- *ex* Matsuo Maru No. 21 *-1995*
Oshima Kaiun KK
-
Kurashiki, Okayama *Japan*
Official number: 132301

199
-
530

1993-01 **Shimazaki Zosen — Nandan**
Loa 48.27 Br ex - Dght 2.900
Lbp 39.00 Br md 8.00 Dpth 3.40
Welded, 1 dk

(A13B2TU) Tanker (unspecified)
Liq: 590; Liq (Oil): 590
1 Cargo Pump (s): 1x500m³/hr

1 oil engine geared to sc. shaft driving 1 FP propeller
Total Power: 625kW (850hp) 10.5kn
Hanshin 6LC26G
1 x 4 Stroke 6 Cy. 260 x 440 625kW (850bhp)
The Hanshin Diesel Works Ltd-Japan

8823161 **SHOHEI MARU**
JM5777
Yoshidome Kaiun KK
-
Kagoshima, Kagoshima *Japan*
MMSI: 431601146
Official number: 131218

108
-
-

1989-02 **Kanbara Zosen K.K. — Onomichi**
Yd No: 376
Loa 25.00 Br ex - Dght 2.100
Lbp 23.00 Br md 8.50 Dpth 2.99
Welded, 1 dk

(B32A2ST) Tug

2 oil engines driving 2 FP propellers
Total Power: 736kW (1,000hp)
Niigata 6NSE-M
2 x 4 Stroke 6 Cy. 150 x 165 each-368kW (500bhp)
Niigata Engineering Co Ltd-Japan

8513924 **SHOHEI MARU No. 28**
-
- -
-

115
-
430

1985-10 **Iisaku Zosen K.K. — Nishi-Izu**
Yd No: 85124
Loa 37.06 Br ex - Dght 2.600
Lbp 35.00 Br md 7.85 Dpth 2.70
Welded, 1 dk

(A13B2TP) Products Tanker

1 oil engine with clutches & reverse reduction geared to sc. shaft driving 1 FP propeller
Total Power: 257kW (349hp)
Matsui MU323DGSC
1 x 4 Stroke 3 Cy. 230 x 380 257kW (349bhp)
Matsui Iron Works Co Ltd-Japan

9073701 **SHOHJIN**
3FUX9 *ex* Green Cove *-2012* *ex* Shohjin *-2000*
Frazer Shipholding SA
Nippon Yusen Kabushiki Kaisha (NYK Line)
SatCom: Inmarsat C 435529711
Panama *Panama*
MMSI: 355297000
Official number: 43887TJ

50,308 Class: NK (AB)
15,093
16,178
T/cm
45.0

1994-03 **KK Kanasashi — Toyohashi AI**
Yd No: 3315
Loa 179.03 (BB) Br ex 32.29 Dght 9.222
Lbp 170.00 Br md 32.26 Dpth 14.88
Welded, 12 dks

(A35B2RV) Vehicles Carrier
Side door/ramp (p)
Len: - Wid: - Swl: 10
Side door/ramp (s)
Len: - Wid: - Swl: 10
Quarter stern door/ramp (s. a.)
Len: - Wid: - Swl: 80
Cars: 4,148

1 oil engine driving 1 FP propeller
Total Power: 11,620kW (15,799hp) 19.0kn
Mitsubishi 7UEC60LS
1 x 2 Stroke 7 Cy. 600 x 2200 11620kW (15799bhp)
Kobe Hatsudoki KK-Japan
Thrusters: 1 Tunnel thruster (f)
Fuel: 2910.0

9062403 **SHOHO MARU**
JK5206
YK Shinwa Kisen
-
Bizen, Okayama *Japan*
Official number: 133680

452 Class: (NK)
-
1,043

1992-11 **Kyoei Zosen KK — Mihara HS** Yd No: 252
Loa 59.90 Br ex - Dght 4.261
Lbp 54.80 Br md 9.40 Dpth 4.40
Welded, 1 dk

(A12A2TC) Chemical Tanker
Liq: 725
Compartments: 6 Ta, ER

1 oil engine with clutches, flexible couplings & reverse geared to sc. shaft driving 1 FP propeller
Total Power: 736kW (1,001hp) 10.8kn
Hanshin LH26G
1 x 4 Stroke 6 Cy. 260 x 440 736kW (1001bhp)
The Hanshin Diesel Works Ltd-Japan
AuxGen: 2 x 120kW a.c
Fuel: 85.0 (d.f.)

9154634 **SHOHO MARU**
JL6463
Oura Kisen KK
-
Imabari, Ehime *Japan*
MMSI: 431500511
Official number: 135534

698
-
2,100

1996-08 **Yamanaka Zosen K.K. — Imabari**
Yd No: 601
Loa - Br ex - Dght 4.410
Lbp 77.30 Br md 12.90 Dpth 7.69
Welded, 2 dks

(A31A2GX) General Cargo Ship
Grain: 3,652

1 oil engine driving 1 FP propeller
Total Power: 736kW (1,001hp)
Hanshin LH34LG
1 x 4 Stroke 6 Cy. 340 x 640 736kW (1001bhp)
The Hanshin Diesel Works Ltd-Japan

7920936 **SHOHO MARU**
-
- -
-

198
-
77

1980-02 **K.K. Odo Zosen Tekko — Shimonoseki**
Yd No: 261
Loa 30.60 Br ex - Dght 2.810
Lbp 27.01 Br md 8.81 Dpth 3.51
Welded, 1 dk

(B34G2SE) Pollution Control Vessel

2 oil engines Geared Integral to driving 2 Z propellers
Total Power: 1,912kW (2,600hp) 13.5kn
Niigata 6L25BX
2 x 4 Stroke 6 Cy. 250 x 320 each-956kW (1300bhp)
Niigata Engineering Co Ltd-Japan

IMO / Call sign / Flag	Name / Owner / Port	Tonnage	Builder / Dimensions	Type	Machinery
8106355 - -	**SHOHO MARU** - - *China*	*499* - 1,126	**1981**-06 **Omishima Dock K.K. — Imabari** Yd No: 1101 Loa - Br ex - Dght 4.150 Lbp 55.00 Br md 9.61 Dpth 4.40 Welded, 1 dk	**(A13B2TP) Products Tanker**	**1 oil engine** driving 1 FP propeller Total Power: 883kW (1,201hp) Akasaka DM28AR 1 x 4 Stroke 6 Cy. 280 x 460 883kW (1201bhp) Akasaka Tekkosho KK (Akasaka DieselLtd)-Japan
7501716 *JM3958* -	**SHOHO MARU** **Nishi Nippon Kaiun KK** - *Kitakyushu, Fukuoka* *Japan* Official number: 118223	*199* - -	**1976**-03 **Towa Zosen K.K. — Shimonoseki** Yd No: 493 Loa 30.61 Br ex 8.82 Dght 2.947 Lbp 27.01 Br md 8.81 Dpth 3.51 Welded, 1 dk	**(B32A2ST) Tug**	**2 oil engines** Geared Integral to driving 2 Z propellers Total Power: 2,294kW (3,118hp) Niigata 6L25BX 2 x 4 Stroke 6 Cy. 250 x 320 each-1147kW (1559bhp) Niigata Engineering Co Ltd-Japan
9325623 *JD2043* -	**SHOHO MARU** **Tofuku Kisen KK** Taiheiyo Enkai Kisen KK (Pacific Coastal Shipping Co Ltd) *Onomichi, Hiroshima* *Japan* MMSI: 431401999 Official number: 140086	*696* - 1,299	**2004**-11 **Nichizo Iron Works & Marine Corp — Onomichi HS** Yd No: 177 Loa 67.92 Br ex - Dght 4.030 Lbp 64.00 Br md 11.20 Dpth 5.00 Welded, 1 dk	**(A12A2TC) Chemical Tanker** Double Hull (13F) Liq: 1,499	**1 oil engine** driving 1 FP propeller Total Power: 1,177kW (1,600hp) 10.8kn Hanshin LH28LG 1 x 4 Stroke 6 Cy. 280 x 530 1177kW (1600bhp) The Hanshin Diesel Works Ltd-Japan
9330173 *JD2007* -	**SHOHO MARU** **Showa Nittan Corp** Showa Nittan Maritime Co Ltd *Tokyo* *Japan* MMSI: 431800677 Official number: 140038	**3,541** Class: NK 1,707 4,999	**2004**-10 **Kanrei Zosen K.K. — Naruto** Yd No: 397 Loa 104.95 Br ex - Dght 6.256 Lbp 98.00 Br md 15.38 Dpth 8.10 Welded, 1 dk	**(A12B2TR) Chemical/Products Tanker** Double Hull (13F) Liq: 6,100; Liq (Oil): 6,100	**1 oil engine** driving 1 FP propeller Total Power: 2,950kW (4,011hp) 13.7kn MAN-B&W 5L35MC 1 x 2 Stroke 5 Cy. 350 x 1050 2950kW (4011bhp) The Hanshin Diesel Works Ltd-Japan Fuel: 230.0
9388998 *JD2244* -	**SHOHO MARU** **Nitto Tugboat KK** - *Kurashiki, Okayama* *Japan* Official number: 140313	*158* - -	**2006**-03 **Kanagawa Zosen — Kobe** Yd No: 551 Loa 30.80 Br ex - Dght 2.700 Lbp 26.40 Br md 8.60 Dpth 3.78 Welded, 1 dk	**(B32A2ST) Tug**	**2 oil engines** reduction geared to sc. shafts driving 2 Propellers Total Power: 1,912kW (2,600hp) Yanmar 6N21A-EV 2 x 4 Stroke 6 Cy. 210 x 290 each-956kW (1300bhp) Yanmar Diesel Engine Co Ltd-Japan
8603822 *7JHJ* MG1-1981	**SHOHO MARU NO. 1** *ex Seifuku Maru No. 55 -2002* **YK Nakayama Shoji** - SatCom: Inmarsat A 1201155 *Kesennuma, Miyagi* *Japan* MMSI: 432568000 Official number: 125056	*289* - 303	**1986**-03 **Niigata Engineering Co Ltd — Niigata NI** Yd No: 1882 Loa 47.33 (BB) Br ex 8.23 Dght 3.156 Lbp 42.02 Br md 8.21 Dpth 3.51 Welded, 1 dk	**(B11B2FV) Fishing Vessel** Ins: 356	**1 oil engine** with clutches, flexible couplings & sr geared to sc. shaft driving 1 CP propeller Total Power: 699kW (950hp) Niigata 6M28AFTE 1 x 4 Stroke 6 Cy. 280 x 480 699kW (950bhp) Niigata Engineering Co Ltd-Japan
9047130 *JK5142* -	**SHOHO MARU No. 2** **YK Shinyu Kaiun** - *Bizen, Okayama* *Japan* MMSI: 431400035 Official number: 132548	*498* - 1,199	**1992**-09 **Mukaishima Zoki Co. Ltd. — Onomichi** Yd No: 277 Loa 66.02 Br ex 10.02 Dght 4.128 Lbp 61.80 Br md 10.00 Dpth 4.50 Welded, 1 dk	**(A12A2TC) Chemical Tanker** Liq: 1,230 Compartments: 8 Ta, ER 2 Cargo Pump (s): 2x300m³/hr	**1 oil engine** with clutches, flexible couplings & sr reverse geared to sc. shaft driving 1 FP propeller Total Power: 836kW (1,137hp) Niigata 6M28BFT 1 x 4 Stroke 6 Cy. 280 x 480 836kW (1137bhp) Niigata Engineering Co Ltd-Japan
9073490 *JK5289* -	**SHOHO MARU No. 3** **YK Shinyu Kaiun** - *Bizen, Okayama* *Japan* MMSI: 431400211 Official number: 134045	*498* - 1,199	**1993**-09 **Mukaishima Zoki Co. Ltd. — Onomichi** Yd No: 285 Loa 65.99 Br ex 10.20 Dght 4.014 Lbp 61.80 Br md 10.00 Dpth 4.50 Welded, 1 dk	**(A13B2TP) Products Tanker** Liq: 1,230; Liq (Oil): 1,230 Compartments: 8 Ta, ER	**1 oil engine** with clutches, flexible couplings & sr geared to sc. shaft driving 1 FP propeller Total Power: 735kW (999hp) Niigata 6M28BFT 1 x 4 Stroke 6 Cy. 280 x 480 735kW (999bhp) Niigata Engineering Co Ltd-Japan
9004750 *JK5051* -	**SHOHO MARU No. 3** **Shoho Kisen YK** - *Kaminoseki, Yamaguchi* *Japan* Official number: 132461	*199* - 530	**1990**-11 **Taiyo Shipbuilding Co Ltd — Sanyoonoda YC** Yd No: 222 Loa 48.03 Br ex 8.05 Dght 3.150 Lbp 44.15 Br md 8.00 Dpth 3.45 Welded, 1 dk	**(A13B2TU) Tanker (unspecified)** Liq: 572; Liq (Oil): 572 Compartments: 6 Ta, ER	**1 oil engine** with clutches & geared to sc. shaft driving 1 FP propeller Total Power: 625kW (850hp) Hanshin 6LC26G 1 x 4 Stroke 6 Cy. 260 x 440 625kW (850bhp) The Hanshin Diesel Works Ltd-Japan
8820690 - -	**SHOHO MARU No. 8** *ex Koei Maru -1998* - - *Bangladesh*	*495* - 1,198	**1989**-01 **Sasaki Shipbuilding Co Ltd — Osakikamijima HS** Yd No: 526 Loa 64.22 Br ex - Dght 4.164 Lbp 60.00 Br md 10.00 Dpth 4.50 Welded, 1 dk	**(A12A2TC) Chemical Tanker** Compartments: 8 Ta, ER	**1 oil engine** with clutches, flexible couplings & sr geared to sc. shaft driving 1 FP propeller Total Power: 736kW (1,001hp) Niigata 6M28BFT 1 x 4 Stroke 6 Cy. 280 x 480 736kW (1001bhp) (made 1988) Niigata Engineering Co Ltd-Japan
9615365 *JD3231* -	**SHOHO NO. 1** **Masatoshi Yamashita** - *Tottori, Tottori* *Japan* MMSI: 431002893 Official number: 141497	*199* - 725	**2011**-08 **Taiyo Shipbuilding Co Ltd — Sanyoonoda YC** Yd No: 327 Loa 55.63 Br ex - Dght 3.230 Lbp 51.00 Br md 9.50 Dpth 5.45 Welded, 1 dk	**(A31A2GX) General Cargo Ship** Single Hull Grain: 1,195	**1 oil engine** reduction geared to sc. shaft driving 1 Propeller Total Power: 735kW (999hp) Hanshin LH26G 1 x 4 Stroke 6 Cy. 260 x 440 735kW (999bhp) The Hanshin Diesel Works Ltd-Japan
7236610 - -	**SHOICHI MARU No. 3** *ex Shoichi Maru No. 2 -1981* *ex Nikko Maru No. 18 -1980* - -	*284* 141 373	**1972 Miho Zosensho K.K. — Shimizu** Yd No: 842 Loa 49.41 Br ex 8.23 Dght 3.347 Lbp 43.01 Br md 8.21 Dpth 3.56 Welded, 1 dk	**(B11B2FV) Fishing Vessel**	**1 oil engine** driving 1 FP propeller Total Power: 736kW (1,001hp) Niigata 6M28KHS 1 x 4 Stroke 6 Cy. 280 x 440 736kW (1001bhp) Niigata Engineering Co Ltd-Japan
8217439 - -	**SHOICHI MARU No. 18** **NFH Fishing Enterprises** - *Philippines*	*135* - 129	**1982**-11 **K.K. Murakami Zosensho — Ishinomaki** Yd No: 1118 Loa 38.28 (BB) Br ex 7.60 Dght 2.400 Lbp 30.94 Br md 7.00 Dpth 2.80 Welded, 1 dk	**(B11B2FV) Fishing Vessel**	**1 oil engine** driving 1 FP propeller Total Power: 772kW (1,050hp) Yanmar 6Z280L-ET 1 x 4 Stroke 6 Cy. 280 x 360 772kW (1050bhp) Yanmar Diesel Engine Co Ltd-Japan
7018719 - -	**SHOICHI MARU No. 87** *ex Nadayoshi Maru No. 1 -1980* - -	*332* 166 -	**1969 Miho Zosensho K.K. — Shimizu** Yd No: 711 Loa 51.77 Br ex 8.03 Dght 3.048 Lbp 46.11 Br md 8.01 Dpth 3.61 Welded, 1 dk	**(B11B2FV) Fishing Vessel**	**1 oil engine** driving 1 FP propeller Total Power: 736kW (1,001hp) Hanshin 6LU28 1 x 4 Stroke 6 Cy. 280 x 440 736kW (1001bhp) Hanshin Nainenki Kogyo-Japan
8318075 *EPBY5* -	**SHOJA 2** *ex Just Mariam -2012 ex Hanne Christine -2009* *ex Caribbean Breeze -1997 ex Grimsnis -1993* *ex Blue Caribe Carrier -1993 ex Grimsnis -1991* *ex Ville du Mistral -1985 ex Grimsnis -1984* - - *Iran* MMSI: 422038200	**2,970** Class: MG (BV) (GL) 1,407 2,876	**1984**-10 **Kroegerwerft Rendsburg GmbH — Schacht-Audorf** Yd No: 1509 Loa 89.79 (BB) Br ex 16.03 Dght 4.852 Lbp 83.39 Br md 16.00 Dpth 8.00 Welded, 2 dks	**(A31A2GX) General Cargo Ship** Grain: 4,982; Bale: 4,940 TEU 221 C.Ho 106/20' (40') C.Dk 115/20' (40') incl. 20 ref C. Compartments: 1 Ho, ER 1 Ha: (50.8 x 12.6)ER Cranes: 1x35t Ice Capable	**1 oil engine** with flexible couplings & sr gearedto sc. shaft driving 1 CP propeller Total Power: 1,470kW (1,999hp) 13.0kn MWM TBD510-6 1 x 4 Stroke 6 Cy. 330 x 360 1470kW (1999bhp) (new engine 1998) Motoren Werke Mannheim AG (MWM)-West Germany AuxGen: 2 x 280kW 380V 50Hz a.c, 1 x 155kW 380V 50Hz a.c Thrusters: 1 Thwart. FP thruster (f)
9279501 *JPQT* TK1-1365	**SHOJIN MARU NO. 38** **Shojin Fishery Co Ltd (Shojin Fishery YK)** - *Tokyo* *Japan* MMSI: 432365000 Official number: 137148	*439* - -	**2002**-08 **Kanasashi Heavy Industries Co Ltd — Shizuoka SZ** Yd No: 8018 Loa 56.17 Br ex - Dght 3.450 Lbp 49.00 Br md 8.80 Dpth 3.85 Welded, 1 Dk.	**(B11B2FV) Fishing Vessel**	**1 oil engine** driving 1 FP propeller Total Power: 736kW (1,001hp) Hanshin LH28LG 1 x 4 Stroke 6 Cy. 280 x 530 736kW (1001bhp) The Hanshin Diesel Works Ltd-Japan
9084396 *JM6334* -	**SHOJU MARU No. 5** **Sanki Kisen KK** - *Imabari, Ehime* *Japan* Official number: 133615	*199* - 700	**1994**-03 **K.K. Watanabe Zosensho — Nagasaki** Yd No: 011 Loa - Br ex - Dght - Lbp 54.60 Br md 9.60 Dpth 5.40 Welded	**(A31A2GX) General Cargo Ship**	**1 oil engine** reverse geared to sc. shaft driving 1 FP propeller Total Power: 736kW (1,001hp) Hanshin LH26G 1 x 4 Stroke 6 Cy. 260 x 440 736kW (1001bhp) The Hanshin Diesel Works Ltd-Japan

IMO / Call sign	Name / Owner / Manager / Port	GT / DWT	Class	Build / Dimensions	Type / Cargo	Machinery
9124976 *JM6396* -	**SHOJU MARU No. 7** **YK Matsuo Kaiun** Kyowa Kisen KK (Kyowa Steamship Co Ltd) *Shimabara, Nagasaki* *Japan* Official number: 134574	*199* - 660		**1995**-08 **Yamakawa Zosen Tekko K.K. — Kagoshima** Yd No: 728 Loa 58.30 (BB) Br ex - Dght 3.208 Lbp 52.40 Br md 9.60 Dpth 5.43 Welded, 1 dk	**(A31A2GX) General Cargo Ship** Bale: 1,145 Compartments: 1 Ho, ER 1 Ha: ER	**1 oil engine** driving 1 FP propeller Total Power: 736kW (1,001hp) Niigata 6M26AGTE 1 x 4 Stroke 6 Cy. 260 x 460 736kW (1001bhp) Niigata Engineering Co Ltd-Japan Thrusters: 1 Thwart. FP thruster (f)
9048615 *JM6192* -	**SHOKA MARU** - **Shoei Kaiun KK** - *Ube, Yamaguchi* *Japan* MMSI: 431400037 Official number: 133465	*396* - 1,081		**1992**-09 **Taiyo Shipbuilding Co Ltd — Sanyoonoda YC** Yd No: 232 Loa 67.87 (BB) Br ex - Dght 3.650 Lbp - Br md 11.00 Dpth 6.00 Welded, 2 dks	**(A31A2GX) General Cargo Ship** Compartments: 1 Ho, ER 1 Ha: ER	**1 oil engine** with clutches & reverse geared to sc. shaft driving 1 FP propeller Total Power: 736kW (1,001hp) Hanshin LH28G 1 x 4 Stroke 6 Cy. 280 x 460 736kW (1001bhp) The Hanshin Diesel Works Ltd-Japan
9128726 *JL6395* -	**SHOKAI MARU** - **YK Rokko Senpaku** - *Kobe, Hyogo* *Japan* Official number: 135079	*499* - 1,512		**1995**-09 **Miho Zosensho K.K. — Shimizu** Yd No: 1465 Loa 71.00 (BB) Br ex - Dght - Lbp 70.00 Br md 11.00 Dpth 4.00 Welded, 1 dk	**(A31A2GX) General Cargo Ship** Grain: 2,575 Compartments: 1 Ho, ER 1 Ha: ER	**1 oil engine** with clutches & reverse geared to sc. shaft driving 1 FP propeller Total Power: 736kW (1,001hp) Hanshin LH30LG 1 x 4 Stroke 6 Cy. 300 x 600 736kW (1001bhp) The Hanshin Diesel Works Ltd-Japan Thrusters: 1 Thwart. FP thruster (f)
8150746 *JH2529* -	**SHOKAI MARU** - **Kazuo Yamashita** - *Minami-chita, Aichi* *Japan* Official number: 112279	*199* - 366		**1972**-05 **Hamajima Zosen K.K. — Japan** Loa 37.50 Br ex - Dght 2.801 Lbp 34.29 Br md 7.00 Dpth 3.20 Welded, 1 dk	**(A31A2GX) General Cargo Ship**	**1 oil engine** driving 1 FP propeller Total Power: 368kW (500hp) 9.0kn
8974726 *JM6631* -	**SHOKAKU** - **Toyotsuru Shipping Co Ltd** Tsurumaru Shipping Co Ltd *Kitakyushu, Fukuoka* *Japan* Official number: 136839	*499* - 1,600		**2002**-03 **Yamanaka Zosen K.K. — Imabari** Yd No: 671 Loa 76.23 Br ex - Dght 4.080 Lbp 70.00 Br md 12.00 Dpth 7.01 Welded, 1 dk	**(A31A2GX) General Cargo Ship** Grain: 2,736; Bale: 2,692 Compartments: 1 Ho, ER 1 Ha: ER (40.0 x 9.5)	**1 oil engine** reverse geared to sc. shaft driving 1 FP propeller Total Power: 1,373kW (1,867hp) 12.7kn Akasaka A31R 1 x 4 Stroke 6 Cy. 310 x 600 1373kW (1867bhp) Akasaka Tekkosho KK (Akasaka DieselLtd)-Japan
9700110 - -	**SHOKAKU** - **Syouei Co Ltd (Syouei KK)** - *Japan*	*499* - -	Class: FA	**2014**-02 **Miho Zosensho K.K. — Shimizu** Yd No: 1564 Loa 59.70 Br ex - Dght 5.340 Lbp - Br md 9.30 Dpth - Welded, 1 dk	**(B12D2FP) Fishery Patrol Vessel**	**1 oil engine** reduction geared to sc. shaft driving 1 Propeller Total Power: 1,838kW (2,499hp) Niigata 6MG28HX 1 x 4 Stroke 6 Cy. 280 x 370 1838kW (2499bhp) Niigata Engineering Co Ltd-Japan
8948973 *JL6556* -	**SHOKEI MARU** - **Tokei Kaiun KK** - *Imabari, Ehime* *Japan* Official number: 135607	*498* - -		**1998**-10 **K.K. Uno Zosensho — Imabari** Yd No: 510 L reg 72.51 Br ex - Dght - Lbp - Br md 12.00 Dpth 7.10 Welded, 1 dk	**(A31A2GX) General Cargo Ship**	**1 oil engine** driving 1 FP propeller
9140499 *JH3375* -	**SHOKEI MARU No. 3** *ex Toyu Maru -1998* **Odomari Kaiun YK** - *Anan, Tokushima* *Japan* Official number: 134368	*498* - 1,472		**1996**-01 **Shitanoe Shipbuilding Co Ltd — Usuki OT** Yd No: 1173 Loa 75.40 (BB) Br ex 12.02 Dght 4.150 Lbp 70.50 Br md 12.00 Dpth 7.10 Welded, 1 dk	**(A31A2GX) General Cargo Ship** Bale: 2,428 Compartments: 1 Ho, ER 1 Ha: ER	**1 oil engine** reverse geared to sc. shaft driving 1 FP propeller Total Power: 1,324kW (1,800hp) Akasaka A31R 1 x 4 Stroke 6 Cy. 310 x 600 1324kW (1800bhp) Akasaka Tekkosho KK (Akasaka DieselLtd)-Japan
9204219 - -	**SHOKEI MARU No. 8** - **Shin Chang Maritime Co Ltd** - *South Korea*	*953* - -		**1998**-05 **Namikata Shipbuilding Co Ltd — Imabari EH** Yd No: 208 Loa 76.02 Br ex - Dght - Lbp 70.00 Br md 15.20 Dpth 7.80 Welded, 1 dk	**(A31A2GX) General Cargo Ship**	**1 oil engine** driving 1 FP propeller Total Power: 1,471kW (2,000hp) 11.8kn Niigata 6M34BLGT 1 x 4 Stroke 6 Cy. 340 x 680 1471kW (2000bhp) Niigata Engineering Co Ltd-Japan
9375458 *JD2179* -	**SHOKEN MARU** - **Showa Nittan Corp** Showa Nittan Maritime Co Ltd *Tokyo* *Japan* MMSI: 431800699 Official number: 140248	**3,785** - 4,999	Class: NK	**2006**-01 **Kanrei Zosen K.K. — Naruto** Yd No: 399 Loa 104.97 Br ex 16.02 Dght 6.266 Lbp 98.80 Br md 16.00 Dpth 8.30 Welded, 1 dk	**(A12B2TR) Chemical/Products Tanker** Double Hull (13F) Liq: 6,200; Liq (Oil): 6,200	**1 oil engine** driving 1 FP propeller Total Power: 2,950kW (4,011hp) 13.7kn MAN-B&W 5L35MC 1 x 2 Stroke 5 Cy. 350 x 1050 2950kW (4011bhp) The Hanshin Diesel Works Ltd-Japan Fuel: 200.0
8990146 *JI3720* -	**SHOKI MARU** - **Taiyo Shipping Co Ltd (Taiyo Kisen KK)** - *Osaka, Osaka* *Japan* Official number: 137246	*499* - 1,680		**2004**-01 **Yamanaka Zosen K.K. — Imabari** Yd No: 686 L reg 69.96 Br ex - Dght 4.400 Lbp 68.00 Br md 11.80 Dpth 7.43 Welded, 1 dk	**(A31A2GX) General Cargo Ship** Grain: 2,570	**1 oil engine** driving 1 Propeller Total Power: 1,471kW (2,000hp) Hanshin LH34LAG 1 x 4 Stroke 6 Cy. 340 x 640 1471kW (2000bhp) The Hanshin Diesel Works Ltd-Japan
8877746 *JM6348* -	**SHOKI MARU** - **Yotsumi Kaiun YK** - *Tonosho, Kagawa* *Japan* Official number: 134469	*483* - 1,198		**1994**-04 **K.K. Kamishima Zosensho — Osakikamijima** Yd No: 558 Loa 65.92 Br ex - Dght 4.000 Lbp 56.00 Br md 13.00 Dpth 5.90 Welded, 1 dk	**(A31A2GX) General Cargo Ship** Grain: 1,243 Compartments: 1 Ho, ER 1 Ha: (20.9 x 10.7)ER Cranes: 1	**1 oil engine** driving 1 FP propeller Total Power: 736kW (1,001hp) 11.0kn Niigata 6M34AGT 1 x 4 Stroke 6 Cy. 340 x 620 736kW (1001bhp) Niigata Engineering Co Ltd-Japan
8844270 *JD2450* -	**SHOKI MARU** - **YK Matsuzaki Kaiun** - *Shimabara, Nagasaki* *Japan* Official number: 128596	*198* - 699		**1990**-07 **K.K. Kamishima Zosensho — Osakikamijima** Yd No: 500 Loa 51.89 Br ex - Dght 3.250 Lbp 45.00 Br md 10.50 Dpth 5.30 Welded, 1 dk	**(B33A2DG) Grab Dredger** Grain: 480 Compartments: 1 Ho, ER 1 Ha: (14.3 x 7.8)ER Cranes: 1x2.5t	**1 oil engine** driving 1 FP propeller Total Power: 662kW (900hp) 9.2kn Matsui ML628GSC 1 x 4 Stroke 6 Cy. 280 x 520 662kW (900bhp) Matsui Iron Works Co Ltd-Japan
8628066 - -	**SHOKI MARU** - - -	*422* - 700		**1986**-05 **K.K. Kamishima Zosensho — Osakikamijima** Yd No: 180 Loa - Br ex - Dght 3.320 Lbp 45.01 Br md 10.00 Dpth 5.31 Welded, 1 dk	**(B33A2DG) Grab Dredger**	**1 oil engine** driving 1 FP propeller Total Power: 662kW (900hp) 10.0kn Matsui MS25GSC 1 x 4 Stroke 6 Cy. 250 x 470 662kW (900bhp) Matsui Iron Works Co Ltd-Japan
9061514 *JL6196* -	**SHOKO** - **Ishizaki Kisen KK** - *Matsuyama, Ehime* *Japan* MMSI: 431500504 Official number: 133973	*189* - 22		**1994**-03 **Hitachi Zosen Corp — Kawasaki KN** Yd No: 117311 Loa 31.00 Br ex - Dght 1.950 Lbp 27.00 Br md 9.00 Dpth 3.00 Welded, 1 dk	**(A37B2PS) Passenger Ship** Hull Material: Aluminium Alloy Passengers: unberthed: 200	**2 oil engines** sr geared to sc. shafts driving 2 Water jets Total Power: 3,678kW (5,000hp) 34.0kn Niigata 16V16FX 2 x Vee 4 Stroke 16 Cy. 165 x 185 each-1839kW (2500bhp) Niigata Engineering Co Ltd-Japan
9124861 *JG4999* -	**SHOKO MARU** *ex Yoshie Maru No. 7 -2003* **Shoho Kaiun KK** - *Osakikamijima, Hiroshima* *Japan* MMSI: 431400494 Official number: 132787	*998* - 2,242	Class: NK	**1995**-12 **Nakatani Shipyard Co. Ltd. — Etajima** Yd No: 568 Loa 81.02 (BB) Br ex - Dght 5.060 Lbp 75.00 Br md 11.80 Dpth 5.60 Welded, 1 dk	**(A13A2TV) Crude Oil Tanker** Liq: 2,250; Liq (Oil): 2,250 2 Cargo Pump (s): 2x750m³/hr	**1 oil engine** driving 1 CP propeller Total Power: 1,912kW (2,600hp) 12.5kn Hanshin LH36LA 1 x 4 Stroke 6 Cy. 360 x 670 1912kW (2600bhp) The Hanshin Diesel Works Ltd-Japan AuxGen: 2 x 240kW 450V a.c Thrusters: 1 Thwart. FP thruster (f) Fuel: 118.0 (d.f.) 6.8pd
9088017 *JG5221* -	**SHOKO MARU** - **Sanko Unyu KK (Sanko Unyu Co Ltd)** - *Yokohama, Kanagawa* *Japan* MMSI: 431100122 Official number: 134019	*922* - 2,300	Class: NK	**1994**-02 **Miyoshi Shipbuilding Co Ltd — Uwajima EH** Yd No: 318 Loa 77.02 Br ex - Dght 5.262 Lbp 72.00 Br md 11.60 Dpth 5.95 Welded, 1 dk	**(A13B2TP) Products Tanker** Liq: 2,203; Liq (Oil): 2,203	**1 oil engine** driving 1 FP propeller Total Power: 1,618kW (2,200hp) 12.5kn Akasaka A34 1 x 4 Stroke 6 Cy. 340 x 660 1618kW (2200bhp) Akasaka Tekkosho KK (Akasaka DieselLtd)-Japan Fuel: 115.0 (d.f.)

8703775 *JJXE* FS1-521
SHOKO MARU No. 1
ex Kumano Maru No. 53 *-2001*
GK Tashichi Shoten
-
Iwaki, Fukushima *Japan*
MMSI: 432213000
Official number: 130116
174 / - / -
1987-05 Yamanishi Shipbuilding Co Ltd — Ishinomaki MG Yd No: 931
Loa 39.83 (BB) Br ex 8.08 Dght 2.550
Lbp 31.91 Br md 6.81 Dpth 2.87
Welded, 1 dk
(B11B2FV) Fishing Vessel
Ins: 117
1 oil engine with clutches, flexible couplings & sr geared to sc. shaft driving 1 FP propeller
Total Power: 699kW (950hp)
Akasaka K28FD
1 x 4 Stroke 6 Cy. 280 x 480 699kW (950bhp)
Akasaka Tekkosho KK (Akasaka DieselLtd)-Japan
Thrusters: 1 Thwart. FP thruster (f); 1 Tunnel thruster (a)

8706791 *JL5643* -
SHOKO MARU No. 18
-
Shoko Suisan YK
-
SatCom: Inmarsat B 343181910
Uwajima, Ehime *Japan*
MMSI: 431819000
Official number: 129038
323 / - / -
1987-09 Ishii Zosen K.K. — Futtsu Yd No: 208
Loa 57.20 Br ex 8.74 Dght 3.990
Lbp 51.01 Br md 8.70 Dpth 4.22
Welded
(B12B2FC) Fish Carrier
Grain: 665
1 oil engine with clutches & sr reverse geared to sc. shaft driving 1 FP propeller
Total Power: 736kW (1,001hp)
Matsui MS25GTSC-3
1 x 4 Stroke 6 Cy. 250 x 470 736kW (1001bhp)
Matsui Iron Works Co Ltd-Japan
Thrusters: 1 Thwart. FP thruster (f)

8520006 *JL5503* -
SHOKO MARU No. 88
-
Shoko Suisan YK
-
Uwajima, Ehime *Japan*
Official number: 128322
199 / - / 452
1986-02 Ishii Zosen K.K. — Futtsu Yd No: 188
Loa 49.60 Br ex - Dght 3.350
Lbp 43.90 Br md 7.82 Dpth 3.81
Welded, 1 dk
(B12B2FC) Fish Carrier
1 oil engine geared to sc. shaft driving 1 FP propeller
Total Power: 736kW (1,001hp)
Matsui MS25GSC-3
1 x 4 Stroke 6 Cy. 250 x 470 736kW (1001bhp)
Matsui Iron Works Co Ltd-Japan
Thrusters: 1 Thwart. FP thruster (f)

9125528 *S7WO* -
SHOKO NO. 18
ex Shoko Maru No. 18 *-2009*
ex Shoyo Maru No. 18 *-2007*
ex Ito Maru No. 58 *-1999*
Shoko Fishery Inc
-
Victoria *Seychelles*
MMSI: 664525000
Official number: 50191
492 / 188 / 370
1995-06 K.K. Yoshida Zosen Tekko — Kesennuma Yd No: 388
Loa 53.86 (BB) Br ex - Dght 3.240
Lbp 45.70 Br md 8.60 Dpth 3.60
Welded, 1 dk
(B11B2FV) Fishing Vessel
Ins: 428
1 oil engine with clutches & sr geared to sc. shaft driving 1 CP propeller
Total Power: 736kW (1,001hp)
Niigata 6M28BFT
1 x 4 Stroke 6 Cy. 280 x 480 736kW (1001bhp)
Niigata Engineering Co Ltd-Japan

9067104 *EPAL5* -
SHOKOH
ex Bahr Alnoor *-2010* *ex* Misaki Maru *-2009*
-
-
Iran
MMSI: 422908000
199 / 60 / 700
1993-09 Shinhama Dockyard Co. Ltd. — Tamano Yd No: 260
Loa 57.57 (BB) Br ex - Dght 3.310
Lbp 53.00 Br md 9.50 Dpth 5.58
Welded, 2 dks
(A31A2GX) General Cargo Ship
Grain: 1,353; Bale: 1,317
Compartments: 1 Ho, ER
1 Ha: ER
1 oil engine driving 1 FP propeller
Total Power: 625kW (850hp)
Hanshin LH26G
1 x 4 Stroke 6 Cy. 260 x 440 625kW (850bhp)
The Hanshin Diesel Works Ltd-Japan

8866668 *V3QZ5* -
SHOKSHA
ex Volgo-Don 5103 *-1994*
Volgodon LLC
Sailtrade Denizcilik ve Ticaret Ltd Sti
SatCom: Inmarsat C 431236510
Belize City *Belize*
MMSI: 312365000
Official number: 141220220D
3,952 / 1,395 / 5,150
Class: IV (RS) (RR)
1989-03 Santierul Naval Oltenita S.A. — Oltenita
Loa 138.80 Br ex 16.70 Dght 3.650
Lbp - Br md 16.50 Dpth 5.50
Welded, 1 dk
(A31A2GX) General Cargo Ship
Grain: 6,270
2 oil engines driving 2 FP propellers
Total Power: 1,324kW (1,800hp) 11.0kn
Dvigatel Revolyutsii 6CHRNP36/45
2 x 4 Stroke 6 Cy. 360 x 450 each-662kW (900bhp)
Zavod "Dvigatel Revolyutsii"-Gorkiy

9079755 *JG5288* -
SHOKYU MARU
-
Showa Nittan Corp
Showa Nittan Maritime Co Ltd
Tokyo *Japan*
MMSI: 431000253
Official number: 134320
2,593 / - / 3,950
Class: NK
1994-02 Usuki Shipyard Co Ltd — Usuki OT Yd No: 1624
Loa 91.00 Br ex - Dght 5.320
Lbp 86.00 Br md 15.80 Dpth 7.50
Welded, 1 dk
(A13B2TP) Products Tanker
Liq: 5,050; Liq (Oil): 5,050
1 oil engine driving 1 FP propeller
Total Power: 1,765kW (2,400hp) 11.5kn
Hanshin LH36L
1 x 4 Stroke 6 Cy. 360 x 670 1765kW (2400bhp)
The Hanshin Diesel Works Ltd-Japan
Fuel: 85.0 (d.f.)

7427180 *4JMG* -
SHOLLAR
ex Delta Tank *-2004* *ex* Gardyloo *-2001*
Azerbaijan State Caspian Shipping Co (ASCSS)
Meridian Shipping & Management LLC
Baku *Azerbaijan*
MMSI: 423105100
Official number: DGR-0091
1,876 / 624 / 2,695
Class: RS (LR)
✠ Classed LR until 25/9/02
1976-08 Ferguson Bros (Port Glasgow) Ltd — Port Glasgow Yd No: 471
Converted From: Waste Disposal Vessel-2004
Loa 85.88 Br ex 14.23 Dght 4.719
Lbp 80.02 Br md 13.71 Dpth 6.41
Welded, 1 dk
(A14A2LO) Water Tanker
Liq: 2,425
Compartments: 4 Ta, ER
1 oil engine sr geared to sc. shaft driving 1 CP propeller
Total Power: 1,396kW (1,898hp) 12.0kn
Blackstone ESL16MK2
1 x Vee 4 Stroke 16 Cy. 222 x 292 1396kW (1898bhp)
Mirrlees Blackstone (Stamford)Ltd.-Stamford
Thrusters: 1 Water jet (f)
Fuel: 54.0 (d.f.)

9519602 *JD2716* -
SHOMEI
-
Shoho Kaiun KK
-
Osakikamijima, Hiroshima *Japan*
MMSI: 431000635
Official number: 140784
749 / - / 2,030
2008-06 Koike Zosen Kaiun KK — Osakikamijima Yd No: 505
Loa 74.62 Br ex - Dght 4.830
Lbp 69.95 Br md 11.60 Dpth 5.50
Welded, 1 dk
(A13B2TP) Products Tanker
Double Hull (13F)
Liq: 2,515; Liq (Oil): 2,515
1 oil engine reduction geared to sc. shaft driving 1 FP propeller
Total Power: 1,618kW (2,200hp) 1.8kn
Daihatsu 6DKM-26
1 x 4 Stroke 6 Cy. 260 x 380 1618kW (2200bhp)
Daihatsu Diesel Manufacturing Co Lt-Japan

8985373 *VVYI* -
SHOMPEN
-
Government of The Republic of India (Andaman & Nicobar Administration)
The Shipping Corporation of India Ltd (SCI)
Mumbai *India*
MMSI: 419019200
Official number: 2906
430 / 129 / 168
Class: IR
2001-08 Alcock Ashdown (Gujarat) Ltd. — Bhavnagar Yd No: 227
Loa 40.40 Br ex 8.42 Dght 2.650
Lbp 36.50 Br md 8.40 Dpth 4.00
Welded, 1 dk
(A37B2PS) Passenger Ship
2 oil engines reduction geared to sc. shafts driving 2 FP propellers
Total Power: 1,324kW (1,800hp) 12.5kn
Yanmar M200-EN
2 x 4 Stroke 6 Cy. 200 x 260 each-662kW (900bhp)
Yanmar Diesel Engine Co Ltd-Japan
Fuel: 36.0 (d.f.)

9195092 *JG5377* -
SHONAI MARU
ex Ibuki Maru *-2012*
Wing Maritime Service Corp
-
Sakata, Yamagata *Japan*
Official number: 136619
167 / - / -
1998-11 Sagami Zosen Tekko K.K. — Yokosuka Yd No: 269
Loa 30.80 Br ex - Dght 2.700
Lbp 27.00 Br md 8.80 Dpth 3.58
Welded, 1 dk
(B32A2ST) Tug
2 oil engines Geared Integral to driving 2 Z propellers
Total Power: 2,280kW (3,100hp) 14.0kn
Niigata 6L25HX
2 x 4 Stroke 6 Cy. 250 x 350 each-1140kW (1550bhp)
Niigata Engineering Co Ltd-Japan

7426552 - -
SHONAN
ex Shonan Maru *-1992*
Galaxy Nine Ltd
-
492 / 122 / -
1976-05 Miho Zosensho K.K. — Shimizu Yd No: 1017
Loa 52.30 Br ex 8.64 Dght 3.683
Lbp 45.19 Br md 8.62 Dpth 3.92
Welded, 1 dk
(B11B2FV) Fishing Vessel
1 oil engine driving 1 FP propeller
Total Power: 993kW (1,350hp)
Akasaka AH28
1 x 4 Stroke 6 Cy. 280 x 440 993kW (1350bhp)
Akasaka Tekkosho KK (Akasaka DieselLtd)-Japan

8731394 *JD2362* -
SHONAN MARU
-
Toyo Kaiun Sangyo KK
-
Yokohama, Kanagawa *Japan*
Official number: 140471
162 / - / -
2007-03 Kanagawa Zosen — Kobe Yd No: 560
Loa 38.00 Br ex - Dght -
Lbp 33.50 Br md 8.40 Dpth 3.40
Welded, 1 dk
(B32A2ST) Tug
2 oil engines geared to sc. shafts driving 2 Propellers
Total Power: 2,942kW (4,000hp) 15.2kn
Niigata 6L26HLX
2 x 4 Stroke 6 Cy. 260 x 350 each-1471kW (2000bhp)
Niigata Engineering Co Ltd-Japan

9195016 *JDAI* -
SHONAN MARU
-
Kanagawa Prefecture
-
Miura, Kanagawa *Japan*
MMSI: 431254000
Official number: 136621
646 / - / 485
1999-02 Niigata Engineering Co Ltd — Niigata NI Yd No: 2363
Loa 64.23 (BB) Br ex - Dght 3.928
Lbp 56.00 Br md 9.80 Dpth 6.38
Welded, 1 dk
(B11B2FV) Fishing Vessel
Compartments: 1 Ho, ER
1 Ha: ER
1 oil engine with clutches, flexible couplings & sr geared to sc. shaft driving 1 CP propeller
Total Power: 1,471kW (2,000hp) 13.0kn
Niigata 6M34BGT
1 x 4 Stroke 6 Cy. 340 x 620 1471kW (2000bhp)
Niigata Engineering Co Ltd-Japan
Thrusters: 1 Thwart. FP thruster (f)

7225166 *JFCF* TK1-844
SHONAN MARU No. 2
Kyodo Senpaku Kaisha Ltd
-
SatCom: Inmarsat A 1205445
Tokyo *Japan*
MMSI: 431934000
Official number: 112872
1,015 / 304 / 628
Class: NK
1972-10 Hitachi Zosen Corp — Onomichi HS (Mukaishima Shipyard) Yd No: 4392
Converted From: Whale-catcher-1988
Loa 70.55 Br ex 10.24 Dght 4.763
Lbp 63.51 Br md 10.19 Dpth 5.20
Riveted\Welded, 1 dk
(B12F2FW) Whale Catcher
1 oil engine driving 1 FP propeller
Total Power: 4,045kW (5,500hp) 15.0kn
B&W 9-50VBF-90
1 x 2 Stroke 9 Cy. 500 x 900 4045kW (5500bhp)
Hitachi Zosen Corp-Japan
Fuel: 440.0 13.0pd

9243552 *JL6663* -
SHONAN MARU No. 13
-
Shonan Kaiun KK
-
Komatsushima, Tokushima *Japan*
Official number: 136554
196 / - / -
2001-03 Kanagawa Zosen — Kobe Yd No: 493
Loa 32.30 Br ex - Dght -
Lbp 28.50 Br md 9.40 Dpth 3.88
Welded, 1 dk
(B32A2ST) Tug
2 oil engines Geared Integral to driving 2 Z propellers
Total Power: 2,648kW (3,600hp) 14.4kn
Niigata 6L28HX
2 x 4 Stroke 6 Cy. 280 x 370 each-1324kW (1800bhp)
Niigata Engineering Co Ltd-Japan

7308815 *WA9378* -	**SHOOTING STAR** **Olympic Offshore Boats Inc** *Morgan City, LA* *United States of America* Official number: 501391	*129* 88 -		**1965 St Charles Steel Works Inc — Thibodaux, La** Yd No: 62 L reg 23.72 Br ex - Dght - Lbp - Br md 7.32 Dpth 3.20 Welded	**(B31A2SR) Research Survey Vessel**	**2 oil engines** geared to sc. shafts driving 2 FP propellers Total Power: 552kW (750hp) G.M. (Detroit Diesel) 12V-71 2 x Vee 2 Stroke 12 Cy. 108 x 127 each-276kW (375bhp) General Motors Corp-USA
8886656 - -	**SHOOTING STAR** *ex* Nha Trang **Gessler Dave Bennett & James D Wattler** - *New Orleans, LA* *United States of America* Official number: 658788	*150* 102 -		**1983 Master Boat Builders, Inc. — Coden, Al** Yd No: 54 L reg 23.26 Br ex - Dght - Lbp - Br md 7.31 Dpth 3.70 Welded, 1 dk	**(B11B2FV) Fishing Vessel**	**1 oil engine** driving 1 FP propeller
9429651 *VRDM7* -	**SHOPPES COTAI CENTRAL** *ex* The Gondolier *-2012* **Cotaijet 314 Ltd** Chu Kong High-Speed Ferry Co Ltd *Hong Kong* *Hong Kong* MMSI: 477937500 Official number: HK-2045	**700** 240 84	Class: NV	**2008-01 Austal Ships Pty Ltd — Fremantle WA** Yd No: 314 Loa 47.50 (BB) Br ex 12.10 Dght 1.660 Lbp 43.80 Br md 11.80 Dpth 3.80 Welded, 1 dk	**(A37B2PS) Passenger Ship** Hull Material: Aluminium Alloy Passengers: 417	**4 oil engines** reduction geared to sc. shafts driving 4 Water jets Total Power: 9,148kW (12,436hp) M.T.U. 16V4000M70 4 x Vee 4 Stroke 16 Cy. 165 x 190 each-2287kW (3109bhp) MTU Friedrichshafen GmbH-Friedrichshafen AuxGen: 2 x a.c
9429675 *VRDV4* -	**SHOPPES FOUR SEASONS** *ex* San Luca *-2012* *ex* The Shoppes At 4 Seasons *-2009* **Cotaijet 316 Ltd** Chu Kong High-Speed Ferry Co Ltd *Hong Kong* *Hong Kong* MMSI: 477937600 Official number: HK-2114	**700** 210 84	Class: NV	**2008-03 Austal Ships Pty Ltd — Fremantle WA** Yd No: 316 Loa 47.50 Br ex 12.10 Dght 1.640 Lbp 44.11 Br md 11.80 Dpth 3.80 Welded, 1 dk	**(A37B2PS) Passenger Ship** Hull Material: Aluminium Alloy Passengers: 417	**4 oil engines** reduction geared to sc. shafts driving 4 Water jets Total Power: 9,148kW (12,436hp) M.T.U. 16V4000M70 4 x Vee 4 Stroke 16 Cy. 165 x 190 each-2287kW (3109bhp) MTU Friedrichshafen GmbH-Friedrichshafen AuxGen: 2 x a.c
7936894 - -	**SHOQRAH** **Yemen Fishing Corp** - *Aden* *Yemen* Official number: 022	*330* 100 -		**1974 Nichiro Zosen K.K. — Ishinomaki** Yd No: 352 Loa 45.42 Br ex - Dght - Lbp 39.98 Br md 8.30 Dpth 4.09 Welded, 1 dk	**(B11A2FS) Stern Trawler**	**1 oil engine** driving 1 FP propeller Total Power: 809kW (1,100hp) Akasaka AH27 1 x 4 Stroke 6 Cy. 270 x 420 809kW (1100bhp) Akasaka Tekkosho KK (Akasaka DieselLtd)-Japan
9257486 *H9NI* -	**SHOREKI** **TKC Panama SA** Dojima Marine Co Ltd *Panama* *Panama* MMSI: 351535000 Official number: 2815401C	**1,999** 600 2,309 T/cm 7.2	Class: NK	**2001-10 K.K. Miura Zosensho — Saiki** Yd No: 1251 Loa 79.99 Br ex - Dght 5.013 Lbp 74.00 Br md 13.20 Dpth 6.40 Welded, 1 dk	**(A13C2LA) Asphalt/Bitumen Tanker** Double Bottom Entire Compartment Length Liq: 2,148; Liq (Oil): 2,148; Asphalt: 2,148 Compartments: 8 Wing Ta, ER 2 Cargo Pump (s): 2x300m³/hr Manifold: Bow/CM: 35m	**1 oil engine** driving 1 FP propeller Total Power: 1,618kW (2,200hp) 12.0kn Akasaka A34C 1 x 4 Stroke 6 Cy. 340 x 620 1618kW (2200bhp) Akasaka Tekkosho KK (Akasaka DieselLtd)-Japan AuxGen: 2 x 240kW 100/450V 60Hz a.c Thrusters: 1 Thwart. FP thruster (f) Fuel: 42.9 (d.f.) (Heating Coils) 107.7 (r.f.) 5.8pd
9420344 *5BLH2* -	**SHOREWAY** **Boskalis Westminster Shipping BV** Koninklijke Boskalis Westminster NV (Royal Boskalis Westminster NV) *Limassol* *Cyprus* MMSI: 210921000	**5,005** 1,501 8,362	Class: BV	**2009-04 IHC Beaver Dredgers BV — Sliedrecht** Yd No: C01251 Loa 97.50 (BB) Br ex - Dght 7.100 Lbp 84.95 Br md 21.60 Dpth 7.60 Welded, 1 dk	**(B33B2DT) Trailing Suction Hopper Dredger** Hopper: 5,600	**2 oil engines** geared to sc. shafts driving 2 CP propellers Total Power: 4,046kW (5,500hp) 12.8kn Wartsila 6L26 2 x 4 Stroke 6 Cy. 260 x 320 each-2023kW (2750bhp) Wartsila Italia SpA-Italy AuxGen: 1 x 528kW 60Hz a.c, 1 x 1000kW 450V a.c Thrusters: 1 Tunnel thruster (f)
9118733 *JL6348* -	**SHORI MARU** **Yoshida Kaiun KK** - *Imabari, Ehime* *Japan* MMSI: 431500286 Official number: 134918	*749* - 1,305	Class: NK	**1995-01 Asakawa Zosen K.K. — Imabari** Yd No: 385 Loa 67.95 (BB) Br ex 11.22 Dght 4.223 Lbp 64.00 Br md 11.20 Dpth 4.65 Welded, 1 dk	**(A13C2LA) Asphalt/Bitumen Tanker** Liq: 1,263; Liq (Oil): 1,263; Asphalt: 1,263 Compartments: 8 Ta, ER	**1 oil engine** driving 1 FP propeller Total Power: 1,471kW (2,000hp) 12.0kn Akasaka A34 1 x 4 Stroke 6 Cy. 340 x 660 1471kW (2000bhp) Akasaka Tekkosho KK (Akasaka DieselLtd)-Japan AuxGen: 2 x 200kW 450V 60Hz a.c Thrusters: 1 Thwart. FP thruster (f) Fuel: 100.0 (d.f.)
9593581 - -	**SHOROK 1** **Government of The Arab Republic of Egypt (Ministry of Public Works & Water Resources)** - *Cairo* *Egypt*	**200** - -		**2012-11 General Egyptian Co. — Cairo** Yd No: 1091 Loa 30.00 Br ex - Dght 1.050 Lbp 26.67 Br md 7.50 Dpth 2.50 Welded, 1 dk	**(A31A2GX) General Cargo Ship**	**2 oil engines** reduction geared to sc. shafts driving 2 Propellers Total Power: 198kW (270hp) Caterpillar 3056 2 x 4 Stroke 6 Cy. 100 x 127 each-99kW (135bhp) Caterpillar Inc-USA
9593593 - -	**SHOROK 2** **Government of The Arab Republic of Egypt (Ministry of Public Works & Water Resources)** - *Cairo* *Egypt*	**200** - -		**2012-11 General Egyptian Co. — Cairo** Yd No: 1092 Loa 30.00 Br ex - Dght 1.050 Lbp 26.67 Br md 7.50 Dpth 2.50 Welded, 1 dk	**(A31A2GX) General Cargo Ship**	**2 oil engines** reduction geared to sc. shafts driving 2 Propellers Total Power: 198kW (270hp) Caterpillar 3056 2 x 4 Stroke 6 Cy. 100 x 127 each-99kW (135bhp) Caterpillar Inc-USA
9593608 - -	**SHOROK 3** **Government of The Arab Republic of Egypt (Ministry of Public Works & Water Resources)** - *Cairo* *Egypt*	**200** - -		**2012-11 General Egyptian Co. — Cairo** Yd No: 1093 Loa 30.00 Br ex - Dght 1.050 Lbp 26.67 Br md 7.50 Dpth 2.50 Welded, 1 dk	**(A31A2GX) General Cargo Ship**	**2 oil engines** reduction geared to sc. shafts driving 2 Propellers Total Power: 198kW (270hp) Caterpillar 3056 2 x 4 Stroke 6 Cy. 100 x 127 each-99kW (135bhp) Caterpillar Inc-USA
9593610 - -	**SHOROK 4** **Government of The Arab Republic of Egypt (Ministry of Public Works & Water Resources)** - *Cairo* *Egypt*	**200** - -		**2012-11 General Egyptian Co. — Cairo** Yd No: 1094 Loa 30.00 Br ex - Dght 1.050 Lbp 26.67 Br md 7.50 Dpth 2.50 Welded, 1 dk	**(A31A2GX) General Cargo Ship**	**2 oil engines** reduction geared to sc. shafts driving 2 Propellers Total Power: 198kW (270hp) Caterpillar 3056 2 x 4 Stroke 6 Cy. 100 x 127 each-99kW (135bhp) Caterpillar Inc-USA
9167318 *DXPF* -	**SHORTHORN EXPRESS** **August International Navigation Inc** Livestock Express BV SatCom: Inmarsat B 354809413 *Manila* *Philippines* MMSI: 548392000 Official number: MNLA000443	**6,872** 2,102 4,422 T/cm 15.0	Class: BV	**1998-05 Scheepswerf van Diepen B.V. — Waterhuizen** Yd No: 1043 Loa 116.60 (BB) Br ex - Dght 6.010 Lbp 109.80 Br md 15.85 Dpth 11.50 Welded, 5 dks	**(A38A2GL) Livestock Carrier** Grain: 3,841 Compartments: 2 Ho, ER 2 Ha: ER	**1 oil engine** with flexible couplings & sr gearedto sc. shaft driving 1 CP propeller Total Power: 4,046kW (5,501hp) 16.0kn MaK 6M552C 1 x 4 Stroke 6 Cy. 450 x 520 4046kW (5501bhp) MaK Motoren GmbH & Co. KG-Kiel AuxGen: 1 x 848kW 450/230V 60Hz a.c, 2 x 450kW 450/230V 60Hz a.c, 1 x 440kW 450/230V 60Hz a.c Thrusters: 1 Thwart. FP thruster (f) Fuel: 126.0 (d.f.) (Heating Coils) 697.0 (r.f.) 19.0pd
8511550 - -	**SHORTLAND** **State Transit - Sydney Ferries** - *Newcastle, NSW* *Australia*	**174** - 76	Class: (LR) ✠ Classed LR until 7/87	**1986-04 Carrington Slipways Pty Ltd — Newcastle NSW** Yd No: 187 Loa 18.62 Br ex 9.30 Dght 1.501 Lbp 17.00 Br md 8.84 Dpth 2.49 Welded, 1 dk	**(A37B2PS) Passenger Ship** Passengers: unberthed: 200	**2 oil engines** with clutches & sr reverse geared to sc. shafts driving 2 FP propellers Total Power: 282kW (384hp) 8.0kn Gardner 8LXB 2 x 4 Stroke 8 Cy. 121 x 152 each-141kW (192bhp) L. Gardner & Sons Ltd.-Manchester AuxGen: 1 x 6kW 415V 50Hz a.c, 2 x 3kW 24V d.c Fuel: 1.5 (d.f.)
7856446 *JG2789* -	**SHORYU** **Government of Japan (Ministry of Land, Infrastructure & Transport) (The Coastguard)** - *Tokyo* *Japan* Official number: 107244	*200* - -		**1970-03 Nippon Kokan KK (NKK Corp) — Yokohama KN (Asano Dockyard)** Yd No: 149 Loa 27.50 Br ex 10.41 Dght 2.240 Lbp 25.50 Br md 10.39 Dpth 3.79 Welded, 1 dk	**(B34F2SF) Fire Fighting Vessel**	**2 oil engines** driving 2 FP propellers Total Power: 1,618kW (2,200hp) 13.2kn Maybach MB820DB 2 x Vee 4 Stroke 12 Cy. 175 x 205 each-809kW (1100bhp) Ikegai Tekkosho-Japan

IMO / Call sign	Name / Owner / Port	Tonnage	Class	Builder / Dimensions	Type / Capacity	Machinery
8998540 *JD2116* -	**SHORYU** - **Daisen Butsuryu KK** - *Osaka, Osaka* *Japan* Official number: 140175	*498* - 1,750		**2005-06 Tokuoka Zosen K.K. — Naruto** Yd No: 285 Loa 74.90 Br ex - Dght 4.470 Lbp 69.00 Br md 11.80 Dpth 7.55 Welded, 1 dk	**(A31A2GX) General Cargo Ship**	**1 oil engine** driving 1 Propeller Total Power: 1,471kW (2,000hp) 11.5kn Niigata 6M34BGT 1 x 4 Stroke 6 Cy. 340 x 620 1471kW (2000bhp) Niigata Engineering Co Ltd-Japan
9011090 - -	**SHORYU** - **Jiangyan Yuduo Transport Co** -	*181* - -		**1990-09 Kanagawa Zosen — Kobe** Yd No: 348 Loa 33.20 Br ex - Dght - Lbp 29.00 Br md 8.80 Dpth 3.80 Welded, 1 dk	**(B32A2ST) Tug**	**2 oil engines** driving 2 FP propellers Total Power: 2,206kW (3,000hp) Niigata 6L25CXE 2 x 4 Stroke 6 Cy. 250 x 320 each-1103kW (1500bhp) Niigata Engineering Co Ltd-Japan
9477206 *3FVC5* -	**SHORYU** - **Olamar Navegacion SA** Usui Kaiun KK (Usui Kaiun Co Ltd) *Panama* *Panama* MMSI: 351897000 Official number: 4183310	**50,888** 29,493 92,418	Class: NK	**2010-07 Oshima Shipbuilding Co Ltd — Saikai NS** Yd No: 10590 Loa 235.00 (BB) Br ex - Dght 13.059 Lbp 230.00 Br md 43.00 Dpth 18.55 Welded, 1 dk	**(A21A2BC) Bulk Carrier** Grain: 111,714 Compartments: 5 Ho, ER 5 Ha: ER	**1 oil engine** driving 1 FP propeller Total Power: 11,106kW (15,100hp) 14.5kn MAN-B&W 6S60MC-C 1 x 2 Stroke 6 Cy. 600 x 2400 11106kW (15100bhp) Mitsui Engineering & Shipbuilding CLtd-Japan Fuel: 3772.0 (r.f.)
9133020 - -	**SHORYU 79** *ex* Waka Maru No. 12 *-2013* - - *Indonesia*	*499* - 1,550		**1996-01 Yamakawa Zosen Tekko K.K. — Kagoshima** Yd No: 732 Loa 75.81 (BB) Br ex - Dght 4.128 Lbp 70.00 Br md 12.00 Dpth 7.10 Welded, 2 dks	**(A31A2GX) General Cargo Ship** Bale: 2,427 Compartments: 1 Ho, ER 1 Ha: ER	**1 oil engine** with clutches, flexible couplings & reverse geared to sc. shaft driving 1 FP propeller Total Power: 736kW (1,001hp) Niigata 6M31BLGT 1 x 4 Stroke 6 Cy. 310 x 600 736kW (1001bhp) Niigata Engineering Co Ltd-Japan Thrusters: 1 Thwart. FP thruster (f)
7853107 *YFDY* -	**SHORYU I** *ex* Shikishima Maru No. 21 *-1992* **PT Sari Ampenan** - *Surabaya* *Indonesia*	**866** 511 1,150	Class: (KI)	**1974-07 Sokooshi Zosen K.K. — Osakikamijima** Loa 58.50 Br ex - Dght 3.750 Lbp 54.01 Br md 10.00 Dpth 5.80 Welded, 1 dk	**(A31A2GX) General Cargo Ship**	**1 oil engine** driving 1 FP propeller Total Power: 1,103kW (1,500hp) 12.0kn Sumiyoshi S6HBSS 1 x 4 Stroke 6 Cy. 330 x 520 1103kW (1500bhp) Sumiyoshi Tekkosho-Japan
8890645 *YFMN* -	**SHORYU IX** *ex* Mitsu Maru *-1996* **PT Sari Ampenan** - *Surabaya* *Indonesia*	**582** 323 672	Class: KI	**1977-04 Tonoura Dock Co. Ltd. — Miyazaki** Loa 51.20 Br ex - Dght 3.220 Lbp 49.80 Br md 9.30 Dpth 5.00 Welded, 1 dk	**(A31A2GX) General Cargo Ship** Compartments: 1 Ho, ER 1 Ha: (27.5 x 7.0)ER	**1 oil engine** driving 1 FP propeller Total Power: 736kW (1,001hp) 10.5kn Niigata 1 x 4 Stroke 736kW (1001bhp) Niigata Engineering Co Ltd-Japan
8736485 *JD2467* -	**SHORYU MARU** - **Asuka Kisen YK (Asuka Kisen Co Ltd)** - *Imabari, Ehime* *Japan* Official number: 140598	*498* - 1,700		**2007-08 Namikata Shipbuilding Co Ltd — Imabari EH** Yd No: 223 Loa 74.50 Br ex - Dght 4.320 Lbp 68.00 Br md 12.00 Dpth 7.35 Welded, 1 dk	**(A31A2GX) General Cargo Ship** Compartments: 1 Ho, ER 1 Ha: ER (40.0 x 9.5)	**1 oil engine** driving 1 Propeller Total Power: 1,618kW (2,200hp) 11.5kn Hanshin LH34LA 1 x 4 Stroke 6 Cy. 340 x 640 1618kW (2200bhp) The Hanshin Diesel Works Ltd-Japan
9166584 *JM6554* -	**SHORYU MARU** - **Oita Kaiun KK** - *Tsukumi, Oita* *Japan* Official number: 135418	*749* - 1,600		**1998-09 K.K. Miura Zosensho — Saiki** Yd No: 1200 Loa 69.50 Br ex - Dght - Lbp 65.00 Br md 11.50 Dpth 5.10 Welded, 1 dk	**(A31A2GX) General Cargo Ship**	**1 oil engine** driving 1 FP propeller Total Power: 1,177kW (1,600hp) 11.5kn Hanshin LH28L 1 x 4 Stroke 6 Cy. 280 x 530 1177kW (1600bhp) The Hanshin Diesel Works Ltd-Japan
7203390 - -	**SHORYU MARU** *ex* Ryusei Maru *-1995* **PT Aria Indonesia Jaya** -	*189* - -		**1970 Towa Zosen K.K. — Shimonoseki** Yd No: 408 Loa 30.51 Br ex 8.84 Dght 2.515 Lbp 27.01 Br md 8.82 Dpth 3.51 Welded, 1 dk	**(B32A2ST) Tug**	**2 oil engines** driving 2 FP propellers Total Power: 1,766kW (2,402hp) 13.5kn Niigata 6L25BX 2 x 4 Stroke 6 Cy. 250 x 320 each-883kW (1201bhp) Niigata Engineering Co Ltd-Japan AuxGen: 2 x 70kW 225V a.c
9512836 *JD2864* -	**SHORYU MARU** - **Japan Railway Construction, Transport & Technology Agency, Shosei Kisen KK & Kaisei Sangyo KK** Shosei Kisen Co Ltd (Shosei Kisen KK) *Saiki, Oita* *Japan* MMSI: 431000689 Official number: 140927	*748* - 986	Class: NK	**2008-12 K.K. Miura Zosensho — Saiki** Yd No: 1351 Loa 67.79 Br ex - Dght 3.990 Lbp 63.50 Br md 11.50 Dpth 4.70 Welded, 1 dk	**(A11B2TG) LPG Tanker** Liq (Gas): 1,510 3 x Gas Tank (s); , ER	**1 oil engine** geared to sc. shaft driving 1 FP propeller Total Power: 1,325kW (1,801hp) 11.5kn Akasaka A31R 1 x 4 Stroke 6 Cy. 310 x 600 1325kW (1801bhp) Akasaka Tekkosho KK (Akasaka DieselLtd)-Japan AuxGen: 3 x 544kW a.c Fuel: 116.0
8135227 - -	**SHORYU MARU No. 31** *ex* Koyo Maru No. 3 *-1999* - -	*179* - -		**1982-08 Muneta Zosen K.K. — Akashi** Yd No: 888 Loa 31.50 Br ex - Dght - Lbp 28.00 Br md 7.51 Dpth 3.31 Welded, 1 dk	**(B32A2ST) Tug**	**1 oil engine** driving 1 FP propeller Total Power: 1,471kW (2,000hp) 12.0kn Niigata 1 x 4 Stroke 1471kW (2000bhp) Niigata Engineering Co Ltd-Japan
8869672 - -	**SHORYU PERMAI** *ex* Shoryu Maru *-2013* *ex* Koho No. 3 *-2007* *ex* Hayanami Maru No. 3 *-2006* - - *Indonesia*	*199* - 622		**1993-01 YK Furumoto Tekko Zosensho — Osakikamijima** Loa 57.10 Br ex - Dght 3.900 Lbp 51.00 Br md 9.50 Dpth 5.55 Welded, 1 dk	**(A31A2GX) General Cargo Ship**	**1 oil engine** driving 1 FP propeller Total Power: 736kW (1,001hp) 10.5kn Matsui ML626GSC-4 1 x 4 Stroke 6 Cy. 260 x 480 736kW (1001bhp) Matsui Iron Works Co Ltd-Japan
7700843 *YGJU* -	**SHORYU XI** *ex* Eagle V *-2000* *ex* Kobe Maru No. 2 *-2000* **PT Sari Ampenan** - *Surabaya* *Indonesia*	**1,388** 882 2,079	Class: KI (NK)	**1977-08 Higaki Zosen K.K. — Imabari** Yd No: 197 Loa 72.90 Br ex - Dght 5.014 Lbp 67.01 Br md 11.41 Dpth 5.11 Welded, 1 dk	**(A31A2GX) General Cargo Ship** Grain: 3,118; Bale: 2,717 Compartments: 1 Ho, ER 1 Ha: (39.5 x 8.9)ER Derricks: 2x5t	**1 oil engine** geared to sc. shaft driving 1 FP propeller Total Power: 1,324kW (1,800hp) 12.0kn Hanshin 6LU35G 1 x 4 Stroke 6 Cy. 350 x 550 1324kW (1800bhp) Hanshin Nainenki Kogyo-Japan AuxGen: 2 x 120kW 225V 60Hz a.c Fuel: 9.5 (d.f.) 84.0 (r.f.) 6.0pd
8852148 - -	**SHORYU XIX** *ex* Hokusei Maru *-2011* - - *Indonesia*	*699* - 2,092		**1991-03 Yamanaka Zosen K.K. — Imabari** Yd No: 511 Loa 81.20 Br ex - Dght 4.750 Lbp 75.00 Br md 12.50 Dpth 7.50 Welded, 1 dk	**(A31A2GX) General Cargo Ship**	**1 oil engine** reduction geared to sc. shaft driving 1 FP propeller Total Power: 1,471kW (2,000hp) Hanshin 6LU38G 1 x 4 Stroke 6 Cy. 380 x 580 1471kW (2000bhp) The Hanshin Diesel Works Ltd-Japan
9041887 *PMUG* -	**SHORYU XXVII** *ex* Seiun Maru No. 28 *-2009* **PT Sari Ampenan** *Surabaya* *Indonesia*	**1,360** 514 1,600	Class: KI	**1991-08 Yamanaka Zosen K.K. — Imabari** Yd No: 516 Loa 72.72 (BB) Br ex - Dght 4.293 Lbp 68.00 Br md 11.50 Dpth 6.80 Welded	**(A31A2GX) General Cargo Ship** Grain: 2,548; Bale: 2,498 Compartments: 1 Ho, ER 1 Ha: ER	**1 oil engine** sr reverse geared to sc. shaft driving 1 FP propeller Total Power: 736kW (1,001hp) Hanshin LH31G 1 x 4 Stroke 6 Cy. 310 x 530 736kW (1001bhp) The Hanshin Diesel Works Ltd-Japan AuxGen: 1 x 137kW 225V a.c, 1 x 40kW 225V a.c
8202252 *YGSK* -	**SHORYU XXXIII** *ex* Teiho Maru *-2000* **PT Sari Ampenan** - *Surabaya* *Indonesia*	**571** 336 850	Class: KI	**1982-04 Kogushi Zosen K.K. — Okayama** Yd No: 235 Loa 52.61 Br ex - Dght 3.830 Lbp 48.01 Br md 8.51 Dpth 5.11 Welded, 1 dk	**(A31A2GX) General Cargo Ship** Grain: 1,033; Bale: 795 Compartments: 1 Ho, ER 1 Ha: ER	**1 oil engine** driving 1 FP propeller Total Power: 441kW (600hp) Akasaka MH23FD 1 x 4 Stroke 6 Cy. 230 x 390 441kW (600bhp) Akasaka Tekkosho KK (Akasaka DieselLtd)-Japan
9411472 *JD2296* -	**SHOSEI** *ex* Kyokushou Maru *-2009* **Shoho Kaiun KK** - *Osakikamijima, Hiroshima* *Japan* MMSI: 431101162 Official number: 140375	*999* - 2,429	Class: NK	**2006-10 ISB Co Ltd — Futtsu CH** Yd No: 509 Loa 79.00 Br ex 12.00 Dght 5.149 Lbp 75.00 Br md 12.00 Dpth 5.60 Welded, 1 dk	**(A13B2TP) Products Tanker** Double Hull (13F) Liq: 2,400; Liq (Oil): 2,400	**1 oil engine** driving 1 FP propeller Total Power: 1,618kW (2,200hp) Hanshin LH34LA 1 x 4 Stroke 6 Cy. 340 x 640 1618kW (2200bhp) The Hanshin Diesel Works Ltd-Japan AuxGen: 3 x a.c Fuel: 133.0 (r.f.)
9578426 *JD2993* -	**SHOSEI MARU** - **Mineo Matsuda** - *Onomichi, Hiroshima* *Japan* Official number: 141141	*499* - 1,820		**2009-11 K.K. Matsuura Zosensho — Osakikamijima** Yd No: 571 Loa 73.00 (BB) Br ex - Dght 4.390 Lbp 68.00 Br md 12.00 Dpth 7.35 Welded, 1 dk	**(A31A2GX) General Cargo Ship** Grain: 2,495 1 Ha: ER (40.0 x 9.5)	**1 oil engine** reverse geared to sc. shaft driving 1 Propeller Total Power: 1,618kW (2,200hp) 13.6kn Akasaka AX33 1 x 4 Stroke 6 Cy. 330 x 620 1618kW (2200bhp) Akasaka Tekkosho KK (Akasaka DieselLtd)-Japan

IMO / Call sign / Fishing no.	Name / Owner / Manager / Port / Flag	Tonnage	Class	Builder / Dimensions	Type / Cargo	Machinery
9268007 *JJ4047* -	**SHOSEI MARU** **Taiyo Kaihatsu KK & Satokuni Kisen Kaisha Ltd & Chiyoda Naiko Kisen Kaisha** Satokuni Kisen Kaisha Ltd *Kobe, Hyogo* *Japan* MMSI: 431301658 Official number: 135995	*3,753* - 4,999	Class: NK	**2002**-11 **Shin Kochi Jyuko K.K. — Kochi** Yd No: 7153 Loa 104.93 Br ex - Dght 6.147 Lbp 98.00 Br md 16.00 Dpth 8.30 Welded, 1 dk	**(A13B2TP) Products Tanker** Double Hull (13F) Liq: 6,300; Liq (Oil): 6,300	**1 oil engine** driving 1 FP propeller Total Power: 3,883kW (5,279hp) 14.4kn B&W 6L35MC 1 x 2 Stroke 6 Cy. 350 x 1050 3883kW (5279bhp) Kawasaki Heavy Industries Ltd-Japan Fuel: 300.0
8631207 - -	**SHOSEI MARU** *ex* Shinei Maru *-2001* **Bukwang Marine Bunkering Co Ltd** - *South Korea*	*132* - 290		**1987**-12 **Kimura Zosen K.K. — Kure** Loa 35.82 Br ex 7.02 Dght 2.250 Lbp 32.00 Br md 7.00 Dpth 3.20 Welded, 1 dk	**(A13B2TU) Tanker (unspecified)**	**1 oil engine** driving 1 FP propeller Total Power: 280kW (381hp) Yanmar 6MAL-HTS 1 x 4 Stroke 6 Cy. 200 x 240 280kW (381bhp) Yanmar Diesel Engine Co Ltd-Japan
7613234 - -	**SHOSEI MARU** *ex* Shosei Maru No. 8 *-1994* - -	*499* 267 1,100		**1976**-08 **Tokushima Zosen Sangyo K.K. — Komatsushima** Yd No: 515 Loa - Br ex 9.45 Dght 4.401 Lbp 53.01 Br md 9.42 Dpth 4.60 Welded, 1 dk	**(A13B2TU) Tanker (unspecified)**	**1 oil engine** geared to sc. shaft driving 1 FP propeller Total Power: 883kW (1,201hp) Hanshin 6LU28G 1 x 4 Stroke 6 Cy. 280 x 440 883kW (1201bhp) Hanshin Nainenki Kogyo-Japan
9066942 *JG5261* -	**SHOSEI MARU** *ex* Sensho Maru *-2002* **Showa Nittan Corp** Showa Nittan Maritime Co Ltd *Tokyo* *Japan* MMSI: 431400216 Official number: 134290	*2,983* - 4,991	Class: NK	**1993**-10 **Kanrei Zosen K.K. — Naruto** Yd No: 362 Loa 105.04 Br ex - Dght 6.366 Lbp 98.00 Br md 15.38 Dpth 7.50 Welded, 1 dk	**(A13B2TP) Products Tanker** Liq: 5,400; Liq (Oil): 5,400 Compartments: 10 Ta, ER	**1 oil engine** driving 1 FP propeller Total Power: 3,089kW (4,200hp) 14.0kn Mitsubishi 6UEC37LA 1 x 2 Stroke 6 Cy. 370 x 880 3089kW (4200bhp) Akasaka Tekkosho KK (Akasaka DieselLtd)-Japan Fuel: 240.0 (r.f.)
9115157 *JM6426* -	**SHOSEI MARU** **Shinko Kaiun Co Ltd** *Kamiamakusa, Kumamoto* *Japan* Official number: 134516	*199* - 541		**1994**-12 **Kanmon Zosen K.K. — Shimonoseki** Yd No: 566 Loa 47.61 (BB) Br ex 8.02 Dght 3.281 Lbp 44.00 Br md 8.00 Dpth 3.50 Welded, 1 dk	**(A13B2TP) Products Tanker** Liq: 570; Liq (Oil): 570 Compartments: 6 Ta, ER	**1 oil engine** with clutches & reverse geared to sc. shaft driving 1 FP propeller Total Power: 736kW (1,001hp) Hanshin LH26G 1 x 4 Stroke 6 Cy. 260 x 440 736kW (1001bhp) The Hanshin Diesel Works Ltd-Japan
6808985 - -	**SHOSEI MARU No. 1** *ex* Shotoku Maru No. 11 *-2002* - -	*113* 47 -		**1967 Tokushima Zosen K.K. — Fukuoka** Yd No: 708 Loa 34.22 Br ex 5.64 Dght 2.363 Lbp 29.39 Br md 5.62 Dpth 2.72 Welded, 1 dk	**(B11B2FV) Fishing Vessel**	**1 oil engine** driving 1 FP propeller Total Power: 397kW (540hp) Daihatsu 1 x 4 Stroke 6 Cy. 250 x 320 397kW (540bhp) Daihatsu Kogyo-Japan
6808997 - -	**SHOSEI MARU No. 2** *ex* Shotoku Maru No. 12 *-2002* - -	*114* 47 -		**1967 Tokushima Zosen K.K. — Fukuoka** Yd No: 710 Loa 34.22 Br ex 5.64 Dght 2.363 Lbp 29.39 Br md 5.62 Dpth 2.70 Welded, 1 dk	**(B11B2FV) Fishing Vessel**	**1 oil engine** driving 1 FP propeller Total Power: 397kW (540hp) Daihatsu 1 x 4 Stroke 6 Cy. 250 x 320 397kW (540bhp) Daihatsu Kogyo-Japan
9115561 *JM6352* -	**SHOSEN MARU** **Shosen Kaiun KK** *Sasebo, Nagasaki* *Japan* Official number: 133633	*498* - 1,200		**1994**-12 **K.K. Watanabe Zosensho — Nagasaki** Yd No: 022 Loa - Br ex - Dght 4.100 Lbp 60.18 Br md 10.00 Dpth 4.50 Welded, 1 dk	**(A13B2TP) Products Tanker**	**1 oil engine** driving 1 FP propeller Total Power: 736kW (1,001hp) Niigata 6M30BGT 1 x 4 Stroke 6 Cy. 300 x 530 736kW (1001bhp) Niigata Engineering Co Ltd-Japan
9084695 *JI3571* -	**SHOSEN MARU** *ex* Kiyo Maru *-2006* **Showa Nittan Corp & Asahi Tanker Co Ltd** Showa Nittan Maritime Co Ltd *Tokyo* *Japan* MMSI: 431300218 Official number: 135012	**5,944** 3,048 9,999	Class: NK	**1994**-09 **Asakawa Zosen K.K. — Imabari** Yd No: 381 Loa 123.00 Br ex - Dght 7.839 Lbp 116.00 Br md 18.80 Dpth 9.60 Welded, 1 dk	**(A13B2TP) Products Tanker** Double Bottom Entire Compartment Length Liq: 10,767; Liq (Oil): 10,767	**1 oil engine** driving 1 FP propeller Total Power: 4,472kW (6,080hp) 13.6kn B&W 8L35MC 1 x 2 Stroke 8 Cy. 350 x 1050 4472kW (6080bhp) Hitachi Zosen Corp-Japan AuxGen: 5 x 302kW a.c Fuel: 440.0 (r.f.)
8922735 *JK5474* -	**SHOSEN MARU** *ex* Eiwa Maru No. 8 *-2011* **YK Koho Kaiun** - *Komatsushima, Tokushima* *Japan* Official number: 134787	*199* - 679		**1996**-02 **Y.K. Okajima Zosensho — Matsuyama** Yd No: 248 Loa 58.03 Br ex - Dght 3.210 Lbp 52.00 Br md 9.50 Dpth 5.42 Welded, 1 dk	**(A31A2GX) General Cargo Ship**	**1 oil engine** reverse geared to sc. shaft driving 1 FP propeller Total Power: 736kW (1,001hp) 11.5kn Akasaka T26SKR 1 x 4 Stroke 6 Cy. 260 x 440 736kW (1001bhp) Akasaka Tekkosho KK (Akasaka DieselLtd)-Japan
9134452 *JL6441* -	**SHOSEN MARU NO. 3** *ex* Tomoyoshi Maru No. 3 *-2012* **YK Koho Kaiun** - *Komatsushima, Tokushima* *Japan* Official number: 135145	*498* - 1,500		**1996**-03 **K.K. Yoshida Zosen Kogyo — Arida** Yd No: 500 Loa 75.97 Br ex - Dght - Lbp 72.00 Br md 11.50 Dpth 7.20 Welded, 1 dk	**(A31A2GX) General Cargo Ship**	**1 oil engine** driving 1 FP propeller Total Power: 1,324kW (1,800hp) 11.5kn Niigata 6M31BLGT 1 x 4 Stroke 6 Cy. 310 x 600 1324kW (1800bhp) Niigata Engineering Co Ltd-Japan
8870669 *JK5260* -	**SHOSEN MARU NO. 5** *ex* Akishima *-2012* **YK Koho Kaiun** - *Komatsushima, Tokushima* *Japan* MMSI: 431400218 Official number: 134065	*199* - 600		**1993**-09 **YK Furumoto Tekko Zosensho — Osakikamijima** Loa 59.24 Br ex - Dght - Lbp 53.00 Br md 9.40 Dpth 5.55 Welded, 1 dk	**(A31A2GX) General Cargo Ship**	**1 oil engine** driving 1 FP propeller Total Power: 736kW (1,001hp) 11.0kn Niigata 6M26AGTE 1 x 4 Stroke 6 Cy. 260 x 460 736kW (1001bhp) Niigata Engineering Co Ltd-Japan
8922682 *JM6517* -	**SHOSHIN MARU** **Showa Butsuryu KK** - *Uki, Kumamoto* *Japan* Official number: 134632	*198* - 421		**1996**-03 **Hongawara Zosen K.K. — Fukuyama** Yd No: 448 Loa 47.64 Br ex - Dght 2.950 Lbp 42.50 Br md 7.80 Dpth 3.40 Welded, 1 dk	**(A12A2TC) Chemical Tanker** 2 Cargo Pump (s): 2x90m³/hr	**1 oil engine** driving 1 FP propeller Total Power: 478kW (650hp) 10.0kn Niigata 6M26BGT 1 x 4 Stroke 6 Cy. 260 x 460 478kW (650bhp) Niigata Engineering Co Ltd-Japan
8604943 - -	**SHOSHIN MARU No. 3** - -	*339* - 698		**1986**-09 **Mukaishima Zoki Co. Ltd. — Onomichi** Yd No: 222 Loa 51.97 Br ex 9.20 Dght 3.550 Lbp 48.01 Br md 9.02 Dpth 3.92 Welded, 1 dk	**(A12A2TC) Chemical Tanker** Liq: 695 Compartments: 6 Ta, ER	**1 oil engine** with clutches & reverse reduction geared to sc. shaft driving 1 FP propeller Total Power: 662kW (900hp) Hanshin 6LU26G 1 x 4 Stroke 6 Cy. 260 x 440 662kW (900bhp) The Hanshin Diesel Works Ltd-Japan
8510257 *JE2847* AM1-482	**SHOSHIN MARU No. 8** **KK Marukichi** - *Hachinohe, Aomori* *Japan* Official number: 126667	*125* - 165		**1985**-08 **Niigata Engineering Co Ltd — Niigata NI** Yd No: 1857 Loa 37.62 (BB) Br ex 7.42 Dght - Lbp 30.99 Br md 7.00 Dpth 3.15 Welded, 1 dk	**(B11A2FS) Stern Trawler** Ins: 118 Compartments: 2 Ho, ER 2 Ha: ER	**1 oil engine** with clutches, flexible couplings & sr geared to sc. shaft driving 1 CP propeller Total Power: 736kW (1,001hp) Pielstick 6PA5 1 x 4 Stroke 6 Cy. 255 x 270 736kW (1001bhp) Niigata Engineering Co Ltd-Japan
9063548 *JL5997* -	**SHOSHIN MARU NO. 8** **Toyo Kisen KK** Shinsen Kaiun KK *Kasaoka, Okayama* *Japan* Official number: 133872	*499* - 1,563		**1993**-05 **K.K. Miura Zosensho — Saiki** Yd No: 1066 Loa - Br ex - Dght 3.990 Lbp 70.00 Br md 12.50 Dpth 6.90 Welded, 1 dk	**(A31A2GX) General Cargo Ship**	**1 oil engine** driving 1 FP propeller Total Power: 736kW (1,001hp) Hanshin LH34LAG 1 x 4 Stroke 6 Cy. 340 x 640 736kW (1001bhp) The Hanshin Diesel Works Ltd-Japan
8980634 *JL2552* -	**SHOSHIN MARU NO. 8** *ex* Shiryo Maru *-2012* **Nobuo Ozaki** - *Gamagori, Aichi* *Japan* Official number: 101391	*193* - 336		**1966**-11 **S. Wakayama — Naruto** Loa 36.20 Br ex - Dght 2.700 Lbp 32.00 Br md 7.00 Dpth 2.82 Welded, 1 dk	**(A31A2GX) General Cargo Ship**	**1 oil engine** driving 1 Propeller Total Power: 368kW (500hp) 11.0kn Kubota 1 x 4 Stroke 368kW (500bhp) Kubota Tekkosho-Japan
8909848 *JJIJ* -	**SHOSHIN MARU No. 11** **KK Marukichi** - *Hachinohe, Aomori* *Japan* MMSI: 431700317 Official number: 130856	*149* - -		**1989**-08 **Niigata Engineering Co Ltd — Niigata NI** Yd No: 2151 Loa 36.29 (BB) Br ex - Dght 2.501 Lbp 30.00 Br md 7.20 Dpth 4.68 Welded	**(B11A2FS) Stern Trawler** Ins: 103	**1 oil engine** with clutches, flexible couplings & sr geared to sc. shaft driving 1 CP propeller Total Power: 713kW (969hp) Pielstick 6PA5 1 x 4 Stroke 6 Cy. 255 x 270 713kW (969bhp) Niigata Engineering Co Ltd-Japan

9659048 *7JNK* -	**SHOSHIN MARU NO. 21** - **Hachinohe Kisen Gyogyo KK** KK Marukichi *Hachinohe, Aomori* *Japan* Official number: 141797	*184* - -	**2013-03 Niigata Shipbuilding & Repair Inc — Niigata NI** Yd No: 0065 Loa 41.70 Br ex - Dght 2.850 Lbp - Br md 7.10 Dpth - Welded, 1 dk	**(B11B2FV) Fishing Vessel**	**1 oil engine** reduction geared to sc. shaft driving 1 Propeller Total Power: 1,029kW (1,399hp) Niigata 6MG22HX 1 x 4 Stroke 6 Cy. 220 x 280 1029kW (1399bhp) Niigata Engineering Co Ltd-Japan
8850126 *JE2366* AM1-550	**SHOSHIN MARU No. 31** - **KK Marukichi** - *Hachinohe, Aomori* *Japan* Official number: 121290	*154* - -	**1977-07 Niigata Engineering Co Ltd — Niigata NI** L reg 29.30 Br ex - Dght - Lbp - Br md 6.40 Dpth 2.50 Welded, 1 dk	**(B11B2FV) Fishing Vessel**	**1 oil engine** driving 1 FP propeller Total Power: 346kW (470hp) Niigata 1 x 4 Stroke 346kW (470bhp) Niigata Engineering Co Ltd-Japan
8821371 *JMZB* AM1-636	**SHOSHIN MARU No. 38** - **KK Marukichi** - SatCom: Inmarsat A 1202373 *Hachinohe, Aomori* *Japan* MMSI: 431701010 Official number: 130730	*439* - -	**1989-05 Niigata Engineering Co Ltd — Niigata NI** Yd No: 2122 Loa 49.32 (BB) Br ex - Dght 3.486 Lbp 49.15 Br md 8.90 Dpth 3.85 Welded, 1 dk	**(B11B2FV) Fishing Vessel** Ins: 565	**1 oil engine** with clutches, flexible couplings & sr geared to sc. shaft driving 1 CP propeller Total Power: 1,177kW (1,600hp) Niigata 6M31AFTE 1 x 4 Stroke 6 Cy. 310 x 530 1177kW (1600bhp) Niigata Engineering Co Ltd-Japan
9135391 *JQJP* AM1-683	**SHOSHIN MARU No. 80** - **KK Marukichi** - SatCom: Inmarsat C 443180210 *Hachinohe, Aomori* *Japan* MMSI: 431802000 Official number: 132243	*379* - -	**1995-11 Niigata Engineering Co Ltd — Niigata NI** Yd No: 2301 Loa 56.00 (BB) Br ex - Dght - Lbp 49.00 Br md 8.00 Dpth 3.00 Welded, 1 dk	**(B11B2FV) Fishing Vessel** Ins: 468	**1 oil engine** with clutches, flexible couplings & sr geared to sc. shaft driving 1 CP propeller Total Power: 699kW (950hp) Niigata 6M28HFT 1 x 4 Stroke 6 Cy. 280 x 480 699kW (950bhp) Niigata Engineering Co Ltd-Japan
8821369 *JMYN* AM1-635	**SHOSHIN MARU No. 82** - **KK Marukichi** - SatCom: Inmarsat A 1200475 *Hachinohe, Aomori* *Japan* MMSI: 431701040 Official number: 130729	*419* - -	**1989-05 Niigata Engineering Co Ltd — Niigata NI** Yd No: 2121 Loa 49.32 (BB) Br ex - Dght 3.486 Lbp 49.15 Br md 8.90 Dpth 3.85 Welded, 1 dk	**(B11B2FV) Fishing Vessel** Ins: 565	**1 oil engine** with clutches, flexible couplings & sr geared to sc. shaft driving 1 CP propeller Total Power: 1,177kW (1,600hp) Niigata 6M31AFTE 1 x 4 Stroke 6 Cy. 310 x 530 1177kW (1600bhp) Niigata Engineering Co Ltd-Japan
9167813 *JQKC* AM1-694	**SHOSHIN MARU No. 83** - **KK Marukichi** - SatCom: Inmarsat B 343103810 *Hachinohe, Aomori* *Japan* MMSI: 431038000 Official number: 133353	**431** 260 443	**1997-07 Niigata Engineering Co Ltd — Niigata NI** Yd No: 2327 Loa 56.00 (BB) Br ex 9.00 Dght - Lbp 49.99 Br md - Dpth 3.90 Welded, 1 dk	**(B11B2FV) Fishing Vessel** Ins: 529	**1 oil engine** with clutches, flexible couplings & sr reverse geared to sc. shaft driving 1 FP propeller Total Power: 883kW (1,201hp) 13.3kn Niigata 6M31BFT 1 x 4 Stroke 6 Cy. 310 x 530 883kW (1201bhp) Niigata Engineering Co Ltd-Japan AuxGen: 2 x 308kW 225V a.c
8510283 *JFQN* -	**SHOSHIN MARU No. 88** *ex Sumiyoshi Maru No. 86 -1997* **KK Marukichi** - SatCom: Inmarsat A 1204563 *Hachinohe, Aomori* *Japan* MMSI: 431701440 Official number: 128912	*494* - 510	**1985-09 Niigata Engineering Co Ltd — Niigata NI** Yd No: 1865 Loa 58.15 (BB) Br ex 9.12 Dght 3.823 Lbp 51.57 Br md 9.11 Dpth 4.02 Welded, 1 dk	**(B11B2FV) Fishing Vessel** Ins: 557	**1 oil engine** with clutches, flexible couplings & sr reverse geared to sc. shaft driving 1 FP propeller Total Power: 1,103kW (1,500hp) Niigata 6M31AFTE 1 x 4 Stroke 6 Cy. 310 x 530 1103kW (1500bhp) Niigata Engineering Co Ltd-Japan
7933737 *WRC8541* -	**SHOSHONE** - **Trinity Resources Corp** - *Juneau, AK* *United States of America* Official number: 603871	*118* 82 -	**1979-04 Freeman Howard, Inc. — Gold Beach, Or** L reg 19.91 Br ex 6.84 Dght - Lbp - Br md - Dpth 3.43 Welded, 1 dk	**(B11B2FV) Fishing Vessel** Hull Material: Aluminium Alloy	**1 oil engine** driving 1 FP propeller Total Power: 349kW (475hp) Caterpillar D353SCAC 1 x 4 Stroke 6 Cy. 159 x 203 349kW (475bhp) Caterpillar Tractor Co-USA
8731667 *JD2406* -	**SHOSHUN** - **Shoho Kaiun KK** - *Osakikamijima, Hiroshima* *Japan* Official number: 140530	*499* - 1,820	**2007-05 Koike Zosen Kaiun KK — Osakikamijima** Yd No: 500 Loa 74.30 Br ex - Dght 4.230 Lbp 69.00 Br md 12.00 Dpth 7.20 Welded, 1 dk	**(A31A2GX) General Cargo Ship**	**1 oil engine** driving 1 Propeller Total Power: 1,618kW (2,200hp) 13.6kn Niigata 6M34BGT 1 x 4 Stroke 6 Cy. 340 x 620 1618kW (2200bhp) Niigata Engineering Co Ltd-Japan
9194892 *YJQP4* -	**SHOTA MARU** *ex Tunastates -2012* **Panama TRL SA** Toei Reefer Line Ltd *Port Vila* *Vanuatu* MMSI: 576732000 Official number: 1975	**3,936** Class: NK 1,564 4,250	**1998-10 KK Kanasashi — Shizuoka SZ** Yd No: 3498 Loa 100.98 (BB) Br ex - Dght 6.624 Lbp 93.00 Br md 16.60 Dpth 9.90 Welded, 1 dk	**(A34A2GR) Refrigerated Cargo Ship** Ins: 5,007 Compartments: 4 Ho, ER 4 Ha: 4 (3.6 x 3.6)ER Derricks: 8x5t	**1 oil engine** driving 1 FP propeller Total Power: 2,942kW (4,000hp) 15.0kn Mitsubishi 6UEC33LSII 1 x 2 Stroke 6 Cy. 330 x 1050 2942kW (4000bhp) Akasaka Tekkosho KK (Akasaka DieselLtd)-Japan Thrusters: 1 Thwart. FP thruster (f) Fuel: 910.0
6816451 - -	**SHOTEN MARU** *ex Ise Maru No. 2 -2012* - -	*192* 62 -	**1967 Miho Zosensho K.K. — Shimizu** Yd No: 635 Loa 41.71 Br ex 6.61 Dght - Lbp 35.01 Br md 6.58 Dpth 3.18 Welded, 1 dk	**(B11B2FV) Fishing Vessel**	**1 oil engine** driving 1 FP propeller Total Power: 603kW (820hp) Akasaka TM6SS 1 x 4 Stroke 6 Cy. 300 x 440 603kW (820bhp) Akasaka Tekkosho KK (Akasaka DieselLtd)-Japan
9058153 *JG5250* -	**SHOTO MARU** - **YK Murakinao Kaiun** - *Tokyo* *Japan* Official number: 133995	*497* - 1,350	**1993-05 KK Ura Kyodo Zosensho — Awaji HG** Yd No: 291 Loa 58.60 (BB) Br ex - Dght 4.200 Lbp 55.00 Br md 11.00 Dpth 4.50 Welded, 1 dk	**(A13B2TP) Products Tanker** Liq: 1,580; Liq (Oil): 1,580 Compartments: 8 Ta, ER	**1 oil engine** driving 1 FP propeller Total Power: 736kW (1,001hp) Matsui ML628GSC 1 x 4 Stroke 6 Cy. 280 x 520 736kW (1001bhp) Matsui Iron Works Co Ltd-Japan
9658824 *JD3410* -	**SHOTO MARU** - **Japan Railway Construction, Transport & Technology Agency & Shinwa Naiko Kaiun KK** Shinwa Naiko Kaiun Kaisha Ltd *Tokyo* *Japan* MMSI: 431003928 Official number: 141763	*748* - 2,150	**2012-10 Yamanaka Zosen K.K. — Imabari** Yd No: 825 Loa 75.20 (BB) Br ex - Dght 4.692 Lbp - Br md 13.80 Dpth 8.00 Welded, 1 dk	**(A24A2BT) Cement Carrier** Grain: 3,978	**3 diesel electric oil engines** driving 3 gen. each 800kW a.c Connecting to 2 elec. motors driving 2 CP propellers Total Power: 2,640kW (3,588hp) Yanmar 6N21AL-SW 3 x 4 Stroke 6 Cy. 210 x 290 each-880kW (1196bhp) Yanmar Diesel Engine Co Ltd-Japan Thrusters: 1 Retract. directional thruster (f)
9607368 *JD3166* -	**SHOTO MARU NO. 1** - **KK Shotomaru** - *Tottori, Tottori* *Japan* Official number: 141400	*118* - -	**2011-07 Fukushima Zosen Ltd. — Matsue** Loa 37.70 Br ex - Dght - Lbp 29.48 Br md 6.25 Dpth 2.58 Welded, 1 dk	**(B11B2FV) Fishing Vessel**	**1 oil engine** driving 1 Propeller Total Power: 1,029kW (1,399hp) Niigata 6MG22HX 1 x 4 Stroke 6 Cy. 220 x 280 1029kW (1399bhp) Niigata Engineering Co Ltd-Japan
7506132 - -	**SHOTO MARU No. 1** - **Arekay Inc** Venture Shipping (Managers) Ltd *San Lorenzo* *Honduras* Official number: L-1324983	*488* 319 1,149	**1975-04 Hanasaki Zosensho K.K. — Yokosuka** Yd No: 163 Loa 52.24 Br ex 9.02 Dght 4.000 Lbp 48.66 Br md 9.00 Dpth 4.35 Welded, 1 dk	**(A13B2TU) Tanker (unspecified)**	**1 oil engine** driving 1 FP propeller Total Power: 515kW (700hp) Niigata 6M26ZE 1 x 4 Stroke 6 Cy. 260 x 400 515kW (700bhp) Niigata Engineering Co Ltd-Japan
9021289 *JM6059* -	**SHOTOKU MARU No. 7** - **Tomiei Kaiun YK** - *Nagasaki, Nagasaki* *Japan* Official number: 132621	*338* - 576	**1991-08 K.K. Mukai Zosensho — Nagasaki** Yd No: 631 Loa - Br ex - Dght 3.960 Lbp 53.30 Br md 8.90 Dpth 4.40 Welded, 1 dk	**(B11B2FV) Fishing Vessel**	**1 oil engine** with clutches & sr reverse geared to sc. shaft driving 1 CP propeller Total Power: 1,140kW (1,550hp) Niigata 6MG32CLX 1 x 4 Stroke 6 Cy. 320 x 420 1140kW (1550bhp) Niigata Engineering Co Ltd-Japan Thrusters: 1 Thwart. FP thruster (f)

8820377 *JM5805* -	**SHOTOKU MARU No. 18** - **Shotoku Suisan KK** - *Nagasaki, Nagasaki* *Japan* MMSI: 431599000 Official number: 131220	*135* - 120	**1989**-02 **K.K. Izutsu Zosensho — Nagasaki** Yd No: 962 Loa 47.75 (BB) Br ex 8.75 Dght 2.900 Lbp 38.00 Br md 8.10 Dpth 3.31 Welded, 1 dk	**(B11B2FV) Fishing Vessel**	**1 oil engine** driving 1 CP propeller Total Power: 861kW (1,171hp) Niigata 6MG28HX 1 x 4 Stroke 6 Cy. 280 x 370 861kW (1171bhp) Niigata Engineering Co Ltd-Japan
8713184 *JM5700* NS1-1024	**SHOTOKU MARU No. 21** - **Shotoku Suisan KK** - *Nagasaki, Nagasaki* *Japan* MMSI: 431492000 Official number: 130343	*135* - 122	**1987**-12 **K.K. Izutsu Zosensho — Nagasaki** Yd No: 938 Loa 46.41 (BB) Br ex 8.77 Dght 2.801 Lbp 37.01 Br md 7.90 Dpth 3.23 Welded, 1 dk	**(B11B2FV) Fishing Vessel**	**1 oil engine** driving 1 CP propeller Total Power: 861kW (1,171hp) Niigata 6MG28CX 1 x 4 Stroke 6 Cy. 280 x 350 861kW (1171bhp) Niigata Engineering Co Ltd-Japan
9033385 *JM5990* NS1-1078	**SHOTOKU MARU No. 23** - **Shotoku Suisan KK** - *Nagasaki, Nagasaki* *Japan* Official number: 132615	*338* - 577	**1991**-04 **K.K. Mukai Zosensho — Nagasaki** Yd No: 633 Loa 62.14 (BB) Br ex 8.97 Dght 3.961 Lbp 53.30 Br md 8.90 Dpth 4.40 Welded	**(B12B2FC) Fish Carrier** Ins: 497	**1 oil engine** with clutches & sr reverse geared to sc. shaft driving 1 CP propeller Total Power: 1,140kW (1,550hp) Niigata 6MG32CLX 1 x 4 Stroke 6 Cy. 320 x 420 1140kW (1550bhp) Niigata Engineering Co Ltd-Japan Thrusters: 1 Thwart. FP thruster (f)
9036595 *JM6036* -	**SHOTOKU MARU No. 31** *ex* Sumiei Maru No. 37 *-1995* **Tomiei Kaiun YK** - *Nagasaki, Nagasaki* *Japan* MMSI: 431606000 Official number: 132589	*135* - -	**1991**-07 **K.K. Izutsu Zosensho — Nagasaki** Yd No: 1015 Loa - Br ex - Dght 2.950 Lbp 38.70 Br md 8.30 Dpth 3.37 Welded, 1 dk	**(B11B2FV) Fishing Vessel**	**1 oil engine** driving 1 FP propeller Total Power: 853kW (1,160hp) Yanmar 6N280-EN 1 x 4 Stroke 6 Cy. 280 x 380 853kW (1160bhp) Yanmar Diesel Engine Co Ltd-Japan
7627053 - -	**SHOTOKU MARU No. 31** - **Feng Pang Yuyeh Co Ltd** - *Chinese Taipei*	*116* 21 150	**1976**-12 **Nagasaki Zosen K.K. — Nagasaki** Yd No: 580 Loa 37.32 Br ex 7.01 Dght 2.363 Lbp 30.94 Br md 6.99 Dpth 2.80 Welded, 1 dk	**(B12B2FC) Fish Carrier**	**1 oil engine** driving 1 FP propeller Total Power: 368kW (500hp) Niigata 6L25BX 1 x 4 Stroke 6 Cy. 250 x 320 368kW (500bhp) Niigata Engineering Co Ltd-Japan
7238735 - -	**SHOTOKU MARU No. 35** - **Junten Gyogyo Co Ltd** - *Chinese Taipei*	*361* 204 -	**1972**-12 **Shimoda Dockyard Co. Ltd. — Shimoda** Yd No: 217 Loa - Br ex 8.03 Dght 3.398 Lbp 47.53 Br md 8.01 Dpth 3.87 Welded, 1 dk	**(B11B2FV) Fishing Vessel**	**1 oil engine** driving 1 FP propeller Total Power: 1,471kW (2,000hp) Niigata 6L31EZ 1 x 4 Stroke 6 Cy. 310 x 380 1471kW (2000bhp) Niigata Engineering Co Ltd-Japan
8132110 - -	**SHOTOKU MARU No. 35** - - - *South Korea*	*258* - 418	**1982**-05 **K.K. Mukai Zosensho — Nagasaki** Yd No: 515 Loa 49.05 (BB) Br ex - Dght 3.069 Lbp 42.80 Br md 7.70 Dpth 3.41 Welded, 1 dk	**(B11B2FV) Fishing Vessel** Ins: 336 Compartments: 8 Ho, ER 8 Ha: ER	**1 oil engine** with clutches & sr geared to sc. shaft driving 1 FP propeller Total Power: 1,030kW (1,400hp) Niigata 6MG28BX 1 x 4 Stroke 6 Cy. 280 x 320 1030kW (1400bhp) Niigata Engineering Co Ltd-Japan
9003677 *JD2653* -	**SHOTOKU MARU NO. 37** *ex* Eikyu Maru No. 88 *-2003* **Tomiei Kaiun YK** - *Nagasaki, Nagasaki* *Japan* Official number: 128545	*328* - 648	**1990**-06 **K.K. Izutsu Zosensho — Nagasaki** Yd No: 986 Loa 60.30 Br ex - Dght 3.900 Lbp 51.90 Br md 9.00 Dpth 4.40 Welded, 1 dk	**(B11B2FV) Fishing Vessel**	**1 oil engine** driving 1 CP propeller Total Power: 1,140kW (1,550hp) Niigata 6MG32CLX 1 x 4 Stroke 6 Cy. 320 x 420 1140kW (1550bhp) Niigata Engineering Co Ltd-Japan Thrusters: 1 Thwart. FP thruster (f)
9037587 *JE3051* -	**SHOTOKU MARU NO. 38** *ex* Shutoku Maru No. 38 *-2011* *ex* Choju Maru No. 35 *-1996* **Momoe Satoe** - *Tsuruoka, Yamagata* *Japan* Official number: 132206	*136* - -	**1991**-05 **Kesennuma Tekko — Kesennuma** Yd No: 278 L reg 31.60 (BB) Br ex - Dght - Lbp 31.50 Br md 6.40 Dpth 2.80 Welded	**(B11B2FV) Fishing Vessel**	**1 oil engine** with clutches, flexible couplings & sr geared to sc. shaft driving 1 CP propeller Total Power: 592kW (805hp) Niigata 6M26AFTE 1 x 4 Stroke 6 Cy. 260 x 460 592kW (805bhp) Niigata Engineering Co Ltd-Japan
8621056 - -	**SHOTOKU MARU No. 38** *ex* Shofuku Maru No. 75 *-1998* - -	*311* - -	**1986**-09 **K.K. Watanabe Zosensho — Nagasaki** Yd No: 1100 Loa - Br ex - Dght - Lbp 48.01 Br md 8.31 Dpth 4.22 Welded, 1 dk	**(B11B2FV) Fishing Vessel**	**1 oil engine** driving 1 FP propeller Total Power: 1,147kW (1,559hp) Daihatsu 6DLM-32 1 x 4 Stroke 6 Cy. 320 x 400 1147kW (1559bhp) Daihatsu Diesel Manufacturing Co Lt-Japan
7238747 - -	**SHOTOKU MARU No. 38** - **Junten Gyogyo Co Ltd** - *Chinese Taipei*	*362* 206 -	**1972**-12 **Shimoda Dockyard Co. Ltd. — Shimoda** Yd No: 218 Loa - Br ex 8.03 Dght - Lbp 47.53 Br md 8.01 Dpth 3.87 Welded, 1 dk	**(B11B2FV) Fishing Vessel**	**1 oil engine** driving 1 FP propeller Total Power: 1,471kW (2,000hp) Niigata 6L31EZ 1 x 4 Stroke 6 Cy. 310 x 380 1471kW (2000bhp) Niigata Engineering Co Ltd-Japan
8916700 *JM5930* -	**SHOTOKU MARU No. 52** - **Fuei Kaiun YK** - *Nagasaki, Nagasaki* *Japan* Official number: 131319	*339* - 576	**1989**-12 **K.K. Mukai Zosensho — Nagasaki** Yd No: 618 Loa 53.30 Br ex - Dght 3.960 Lbp 47.00 Br md 8.90 Dpth 4.40 Welded, 1 dk	**(B12B2FC) Fish Carrier**	**1 oil engine** sr geared to sc. shaft driving 1 CP propeller Total Power: 1,140kW (1,550hp) Niigata 6MG32CLX 1 x 4 Stroke 6 Cy. 320 x 420 1140kW (1550bhp) Niigata Engineering Co Ltd-Japan Thrusters: 1 Thwart. CP thruster (f)
7823827 - -	**SHOTOKU MARU No. 53** *ex* Meisho Maru No. 87 *-1981* **Kemuning Perudana Co Ltd** -	*314* - -	**1979**-03 **Uchida Zosen — Ise** Yd No: 793 Loa - Br ex - Dght 3.280 Lbp 44.96 Br md 8.60 Dpth 3.61 Riveted\Welded, 1 dk	**(B11B2FV) Fishing Vessel**	**1 oil engine** driving 1 FP propeller Total Power: 956kW (1,300hp) Hanshin 6LUN28AG 1 x 4 Stroke 6 Cy. 280 x 480 956kW (1300bhp) Hanshin Nainenki Kogyo-Japan
8633504 - -	**SHOTOKU MARU No. 55** - - -	*199* - -	**1982**-02 **Sasaki Shipbuilding Co Ltd — Osakikamijima HS** L reg 34.60 Br ex - Dght 2.700 Lbp - Br md 6.20 Dpth 3.20 Welded, 1 dk	**(B11B2FV) Fishing Vessel**	**1 oil engine** driving 1 FP propeller Total Power: 346kW (470hp) Fuji 1 x 4 Stroke 346kW (470bhp) Fuji Diesel Co Ltd-Japan
8916712 *JM5933* NS1-1096	**SHOTOKU MARU No. 56** - **Shotoku Suisan KK** - *Nagasaki, Nagasaki* *Japan* Official number: 131322	*339* - 576	**1990**-02 **K.K. Mukai Zosensho — Nagasaki** Yd No: 620 Loa 61.76 (BB) Br ex - Dght 3.960 Lbp 53.30 Br md 8.90 Dpth 4.40 Welded, 1 dk	**(B12B2FC) Fish Carrier** Ins: 496	**1 oil engine** with flexible couplings & sr geared to sc. shaft driving 1 CP propeller Total Power: 1,140kW (1,550hp) Niigata 6MG32CLX 1 x 4 Stroke 6 Cy. 320 x 420 1140kW (1550bhp) Niigata Engineering Co Ltd-Japan Thrusters: 1 Thwart. FP thruster (f)
8114625 - -	**SHOTOKU MARU No. 57** - **Feng Hsin Shui Chan Co Ltd** - *Chinese Taipei*	*208* - -	**1981**-09 **Nagasaki Zosen K.K. — Nagasaki** Yd No: 786 Loa 41.03 Br ex - Dght 2.752 Lbp 38.51 Br md 7.41 Dpth 3.18 Welded, 1 dk	**(B11B2FV) Fishing Vessel**	**1 oil engine** driving 1 FP propeller Total Power: 883kW (1,201hp) Niigata 6MG25CX 1 x 4 Stroke 6 Cy. 250 x 320 883kW (1201bhp) Niigata Engineering Co Ltd-Japan
8712740 - -	**SHOTOKU MARU No. 61** - - -	*349* - 919	**1987**-11 **K.K. Mukai Zosensho — Nagasaki** Yd No: 582 Loa 70.82 (BB) Br ex 10.62 Dght 4.192 Lbp 63.51 Br md 10.61 Dpth 7.01 Welded, 2 dks	**(B11B2FV) Fishing Vessel** Ins: 323	**1 oil engine** with flexible couplings & sr gearedto sc. shaft driving 1 CP propeller Total Power: 1,177kW (1,600hp) Niigata 6MG28CX 1 x 4 Stroke 6 Cy. 280 x 350 1177kW (1600bhp) Niigata Engineering Co Ltd-Japan Thrusters: 1 Thwart. CP thruster (f)
6809264 - L909	**SHOTOKU MARU No. 71** *ex* Yusei Maru No. 76 *-1981* **Namibia Marine Products** - *Namibia*	*198* 105 -	**1967 Fukuoka Shipbuilding Co Ltd — Fukuoka FO** Yd No: 908 Loa 40.95 Br ex 6.91 Dght 2.896 Lbp 35.18 Br md 6.61 Dpth 3.33 Welded, 1 dk	**(B11B2FV) Fishing Vessel**	**1 oil engine** driving 1 FP propeller Total Power: 588kW (799hp) Usuki 6MRS32HC 1 x 4 Stroke 6 Cy. 320 x 460 588kW (799bhp) Usuki Tekkosho-Usuki

8921585 *JH3156* -
SHOTOKU MARU NO. 85
ex Daishi Maru No. 16 *-2011*
Tomiei Kaiun YK
-
Nagasaki, Nagasaki *Japan*
Official number: 131543
300 - 513
1990-02 **K.K. Watanabe Zosensho — Nagasaki** Yd No: 1167
Loa 59.56 (BB) Br ex - Dght 4.000
Lbp 49.90 Br md 8.50 Dpth 4.30
Welded, 1 dk
(B11B2FV) Fishing Vessel
Ins: 444
1 oil engine driving 1 CP propeller
Total Power: 1,155kW (1,570hp)
Niigata 8MG28HX
1 x 4 Stroke 8 Cy. 280 x 370 1155kW (1570bhp)
Niigata Engineering Co Ltd-Japan
Thrusters: 1 Thwart. FP thruster (f)

8716540 *JM5619* -
SHOTOKU MARU NO. 86
ex Kaiko Maru No. 38 *-2008*
Fuei Kaiun YK
-
Nagasaki, Nagasaki *Japan*
Official number: 129444
255 - 400
1987-06 **K.K. Watanabe Zosensho — Nagasaki** Yd No: 1118
Loa 51.41 (BB) Br ex 8.03 Dght -
Lbp 45.50 Br md 8.01 Dpth 3.92
Welded
(B12B2FC) Fish Carrier
Ins: 381
Compartments: 8 Ho, ER
8 Ha:
1 oil engine with clutches & sr reverse geared to sc. shaft driving 1 FP propeller
Total Power: 1,710kW (2,325hp)
Yanmar 6Z280-GN
1 x 4 Stroke 6 Cy. 280 x 360 1710kW (2325bhp)
Yanmar Diesel Engine Co Ltd-Japan

8320858 - -
SHOTOKU MARU No. 86
-
-
South Korea
276 - 386
1983-07 **K.K. Mukai Zosensho — Nagasaki** Yd No: 525
Loa 52.00 (BB) Br ex 8.08 Dght 3.161
Lbp 45.00 Br md 8.01 Dpth 4.00
Welded, 1 dk
(B11B2FV) Fishing Vessel
Ins: 334
Compartments: 8 Ho, ER
8 Ha: ER
1 oil engine with clutches & sr reverse geared to sc. shaft driving 1 FP propeller
Total Power: 861kW (1,171hp)
Niigata 6MG28BXE
1 x 4 Stroke 6 Cy. 280 x 320 861kW (1171bhp)
Niigata Engineering Co Ltd-Japan

9033440 *JM6058* -
SHOTOKU MARU No. 87
Tomiei Kaiun YK
-
Nagasaki, Nagasaki *Japan*
Official number: 132619
340 - -
1991-08 **Nagasaki Zosen K.K. — Nagasaki** Yd No: 1086
Loa - Br ex - Dght 3.850
Lbp 53.50 Br md 9.00 Dpth 4.45
Welded, 1 dk
(B11B2FV) Fishing Vessel
1 oil engine driving 1 FP propeller
Total Power: 1,140kW (1,550hp)
Niigata 6MG32CLX
1 x 4 Stroke 6 Cy. 320 x 420 1140kW (1550bhp)
Niigata Engineering Co Ltd-Japan

9632296 *VRMH9* -
SHOU CHEN SHAN
Yin He Shipping Co Ltd
China Shipping International Shipmanagement Co Ltd
Hong Kong *Hong Kong*
MMSI: 477767300
Official number: HK-3880
32,962 19,142 56,621 T/cm 58.8
Class: CC
2013-11 **China Shipping Industry (Jiangsu) Co Ltd — Jiangdu JS** Yd No: CIS57000-06
Loa 189.99 (BB) Br ex 32.30 Dght 12.800
Lbp 185.00 Br md 32.26 Dpth 18.00
Welded, 1 dk
(A21A2BC) Bulk Carrier
Grain: 71,634; Bale: 68,200
Compartments: 5 Ho, ER
5 Ha: 4 (21.3 x 18.3)ER (18.9 x 18.3)
Cranes: 4x30t
1 oil engine driving 1 FP propeller
Total Power: 9,480kW (12,889hp) 14.2kn
MAN-B&W 6S50MC-C
1 x 2 Stroke 6 Cy. 500 x 2000 9480kW (12889bhp)
Yichang Marine Diesel Engine Co Ltd-China
AuxGen: 3 x 600kW 450V a.c

8032906 - -
SHOU FENG
Hualien Harbor Bureau
-
Hualien *Chinese Taipei*
195 39 -
Class: (CR)
1980 Taiwan Machinery Manufacturing Corp. — Kaohsiung
Loa 32.01 Br ex 8.82 Dght 2.901
Lbp 30.82 Br md 8.81 Dpth 3.92
Welded, 1 dk
(B32A2ST) Tug
2 oil engines driving 2 FP propellers
Total Power: 1,766kW (2,402hp) 12.0kn
Niigata 6MG25BX
2 x 4 Stroke 6 Cy. 250 x 320 each-883kW (1201bhp)
Niigata Engineering Co Ltd-Japan
AuxGen: 2 x 64kW 225V a.c

8316510 *BOHK* -
SHOU NING HAI
COSCO Bulk Carrier Co Ltd (COSCO BULK)
-
Tianjin *China*
MMSI: 412226000
27,766 14,290 45,130
Class: CC
1985-03 **Namura Shipbuilding Co Ltd — Imari SG** Yd No: 879
Loa 189.00 (BB) Br ex 32.24 Dght 11.240
Lbp 182.00 Br md 32.20 Dpth 16.60
Welded, 1 dk
(A21A2BC) Bulk Carrier
Grain: 57,724
Compartments: 5 Ho, ER
5 Ha: (12.0 x 16.0)4 (14.4 x 16.0)ER
Cranes: 4x25t
Ice Capable
1 oil engine driving 1 FP propeller
Total Power: 7,024kW (9,550hp) 14.5kn
B&W 6L60MCE
1 x 2 Stroke 6 Cy. 600 x 1944 7024kW (9550bhp)
Hitachi Zosen Corp-Japan
AuxGen: 3 x 480kW 450V 60Hz a.c
Fuel: 1823.0 (r.f.) 25.5pd

9469508 *VRFR3* -
SHOU SHAN
Shoushan Shipping Ltd
Tianjin Cosbulk Ship Management Co Ltd
Hong Kong *Hong Kong*
MMSI: 477826300
Official number: HK-2494
43,717 26,433 79,775
Class: LR
✠ **100A1** SS 06/2010
bulk carrier
BC-A
strengthened for heavy cargoes, Nos. 2, 4 & 6 holds amy be empty
ESP
ESN
ShipRight (SDA, FDA, CM)
*IWS
LI
Ice Class 1D at a draught of 14.599m
Max/min draughts fwd 14.745/4.714m
Max/min draughts aft not applicable
Required power 11620kw, installed power 11620kw
✠ **LMC** **UMS**
Eq.Ltr: Q†;
Cable: 687.5/81.0 U3 (a)
2010-06 **Fujian Crown Ocean Shipbuilding Industry Co Ltd — Lianjiang County FJ** Yd No: GH402B
Loa 229.00 (BB) Br ex 32.31 Dght 14.580
Lbp 222.00 Br md 32.26 Dpth 20.25
Welded, 1 dk
(A21A2BC) Bulk Carrier
Double Hull
Grain: 97,000
Compartments: 7 Ho, ER
7 Ha: ER
Ice Capable
1 oil engine driving 1 FP propeller
Total Power: 11,620kW (15,799hp) 14.0kn
Wartsila 7RT-flex50
1 x 2 Stroke 7 Cy. 500 x 2050 11620kW (15799bhp)
Yichang Marine Diesel Engine Co Ltd-China
AuxGen: 3 x 700kW 450V 60Hz a.c
Boilers: AuxB (Comp) 7.6kgf/cm² (7.5bar)

8702898 *BR3363* -
SHOU SHAN No. 3
CPC Corp Taiwan
-
Kaohsiung *Chinese Taipei*
MMSI: 416003692
492 252 980
Class: CR
1988-02 **China Shipbuilding Corp (CSBC) — Kaohsiung** Yd No: 347
Loa 40.00 Br ex 10.22 Dght 4.000
Lbp 38.80 Br md 10.00 Dpth 4.70
Welded, 1 dk
(A13B2TP) Products Tanker
Liq: 1,000; Liq (Oil): 1,000
2 oil engines dr geared to sc. shafts driving 2 FP propellers
Total Power: 364kW (494hp)
Cummins VTA-28-M
2 x Vee 4 Stroke 12 Cy. 140 x 152 each-182kW (247bhp)
Cummins Engine Co Inc-USA

9671735 *7JOL* -
SHOUEI MARU NO. 123
Katsukura Gyogyo KK
-
Kesennuma, Miyagi *Japan*
MMSI: 432918000
Official number: 141883
439 - -
2013-05 **Niigata Shipbuilding & Repair Inc — Niigata NI** Yd No: 0067
Loa 57.10 Br ex - Dght 3.500
Lbp - Br md 9.00 Dpth -
Welded, 1 dk
(B11B2FV) Fishing Vessel
1 oil engine reverse reduction geared to sc. shaft driving 1 Propeller
Total Power: 1,029kW (1,399hp)
Niigata 6M28BFT
1 x 4 Stroke 6 Cy. 280 x 480 1029kW (1399bhp)
Niigata Engineering Co Ltd-Japan

8419324 *4JDT* -
SHOULAN
Specialized Sea Oil Fleet Organisation, Caspian Sea Oil Fleet, State Oil Co of the Republic of Azerbaijan
-
Baku *Azerbaijan*
MMSI: 423142100
Official number: DGR-0269
997 299 707
Class: (RS)
1987-11 **Rauma-Repola Oy — Savonlinna** Yd No: 472
Loa 56.11 Br ex 11.21 Dght 3.652
Lbp 47.43 Br md 11.02 Dpth 4.81
Welded, 1 dk
(A12A2TC) Chemical Tanker
Liq: 740
Compartments: 5 Ta, ER
Ice Capable
2 oil engines driving 2 Directional propellers
Total Power: 1,472kW (2,002hp) 10.5kn
Zvezda M401A-1
2 x Vee 4 Stroke 12 Cy. 180 x 200 each-736kW (1001bhp)
"Zvezda"-Leningrad
AuxGen: 2 x 200kW a.c
Thrusters: 2 Thwart. FP thruster (a)
Fuel: 166.0 (d.f.)

8859524 *JK5117* -
SHOUN MARU
Shizue Terachi
-
Kure, Hiroshima *Japan*
Official number: 132522
189 - 420
1991-10 **Hongawara Zosen K.K. — Fukuyama**
Loa 44.40 Br ex - Dght 3.050
Lbp 40.00 Br md 7.60 Dpth 3.25
Welded, 1 dk
(A12A2TC) Chemical Tanker
Liq: 289
1 Cargo Pump (s): 1x125m³/hr
1 oil engine driving 1 FP propeller
Total Power: 588kW (799hp) 9.5kn
Yanmar MF24-UT
1 x 4 Stroke 6 Cy. 240 x 420 588kW (799bhp)
Yanmar Diesel Engine Co Ltd-Japan

9063550 *JL6103* -
SHOUN MARU No. 1
Seiun Kaiun YK
-
Kochi, Kochi *Japan*
Official number: 133882
499 - 1,502
1993-03 **K.K. Miura Zosensho — Saiki** Yd No: 1067
Loa 74.50 Br ex - Dght 4.190
Lbp 69.00 Br md 12.00 Dpth 7.15
Welded, 1 dk
(A31A2GX) General Cargo Ship
1 oil engine geared to sc. shaft driving 1 FP propeller
Total Power: 736kW (1,001hp)
Hanshin LH30LG
1 x 4 Stroke 6 Cy. 300 x 600 736kW (1001bhp)
The Hanshin Diesel Works Ltd-Japan

8844737 *JM5978* -
SHOUN MARU No. 2
Kiyohide Kawasaki
-
Hiroshima, Hiroshima *Japan*
Official number: 130480
498 - 411
1990-12 **Amakusa Zosen K.K. — Amakusa**
Loa 47.00 Br ex - Dght 2.750
Lbp 42.00 Br md 12.00 Dpth 5.50
Welded, 1 dk
(A24D2BA) Aggregates Carrier
1 oil engine driving 1 FP propeller
Total Power: 736kW (1,001hp)
Niigata 6M28BGT
1 x 4 Stroke 6 Cy. 280 x 480 736kW (1001bhp)
Niigata Engineering Co Ltd-Japan

8965270 - -
SHOUN MARU No. 5
Shin Fa Marine Co Ltd
-
Chinese Taipei
106 - 250
1993-06 **Hashimoto Zosen — Japan**
Loa 26.90 Br ex - Dght 2.400
Lbp - Br md 7.50 Dpth 2.80
Welded, 1 dk
(A24D2BA) Aggregates Carrier
Compartments: 1 Ho, ER
1 Ha: (10.0 x 5.5)ER
Cranes: 1
1 oil engine geared to sc. shaft driving 1 FP propeller
Total Power: 250kW (340hp) 7.5kn
Yanmar 6M-T
1 x 4 Stroke 6 Cy. 200 x 240 250kW (340bhp)
Yanmar Diesel Engine Co Ltd-Japan

Identity	Ship / Owner	Tonnage / Class	Builder / Dimensions	Type / Capacity	Machinery
9036674 *JG5113* -	**SHOUN MARU NO. 8** *ex* Daiwa Maru No. 2 *-2005* *ex* Koyu Maru *-2003* *ex* Sanko Maru No. 16 *-2000* **YK Tsukushi Sangyo** - *Yokohama, Kanagawa* *Japan* Official number: 133090	*104* - 330	**1991-09 Kominato Zosen K.K. — Amatsu-Kominato** Yd No: 1018 Loa 37.50 Br ex - Dght 2.300 Lbp 35.50 Br md 7.80 Dpth 2.60 Welded, 1 dk	**(A13B2TP) Products Tanker** Liq: 380; Liq (Oil): 380 Compartments: 3 Ta, ER	**1 oil engine** with clutches & reverse geared to sc. shaft driving 1 FP propeller Total Power: 294kW (400hp) Sumiyoshi S623TS 1 x 4 Stroke 6 Cy. 230 x 400 294kW (400bhp) Sumiyoshi Marine Diesel Co Ltd-Japan
8135332 *JG4252* -	**SHOUN MARU NO. 11** *ex* Koei Maru No. 1 *-2009* **Mihachiro Ito** - *Yokohama, Kanagawa* *Japan* Official number: 126689	*147* - 263	**1982-07 K.K. Takagi Zosensho — Matsuzaki** Yd No: 205 Loa 31.78 Br ex - Dght 2.500 Lbp 29.90 Br md 6.71 Dpth 2.70 Welded, 1 dk	**(A13B2TU) Tanker (unspecified)**	**1 oil engine** driving 1 FP propeller Total Power: 228kW (310hp) 8.9kn Sumiyoshi S623TE 1 x 4 Stroke 6 Cy. 230 x 400 228kW (310bhp) Sumiyoshi Marine Diesel Co Ltd-Japan
7922958 - -	**SHOUN MARU NO. 11-1** *ex* Shoun Maru No. 11 *-1998* *ex* Shinki Maru *-1991* **Blue Mountain S de RL** -	*498* - -	**1979-05 Muneta Zosen K.K. — Akashi** Yd No: 820 Loa - Br ex - Dght - Lbp 46.00 Br md 16.01 Dpth 3.00 Welded, 1 dk	**(B34B2SC) Crane Vessel**	**1 oil engine** driving 1 FP propeller Total Power: 588kW (799hp) Yanmar MF28-HT 1 x 4 Stroke 6 Cy. 280 x 450 588kW (799bhp) Yanmar Diesel Engine Co Ltd-Japan
7818597 - -	**SHOUN MARU No. 20** - - *China*	*183* 84 252	**1978-12 Niigata Engineering Co Ltd — Niigata NI** Yd No: 1613 Loa 42.02 Br ex 7.42 Dght 2.820 Lbp 36.40 Br md 7.41 Dpth 3.15 Welded, 1 dk	**(B11B2FV) Fishing Vessel**	**1 oil engine** driving 1 FP propeller Total Power: 625kW (850hp) Niigata 6M26ZG 1 x 4 Stroke 6 Cy. 260 x 400 625kW (850bhp) Niigata Engineering Co Ltd-Japan
7036436 - -	**SHOUN MARU No. 27** *ex* Yoshi Maru No. 38 *-1979* **Hemei Fishing Co Ltd** *Chinese Taipei*	*284* 139 656	**1970 Niigata Engineering Co Ltd — Niigata NI** Yd No: 1002 Loa 47.66 Br ex 8.23 Dght 3.201 Lbp 42.55 Br md 8.21 Dpth 3.61 Welded, 1 dk	**(B11B2FV) Fishing Vessel**	**1 oil engine** driving 1 FP propeller Total Power: 736kW (1,001hp) Niigata 1 x 4 Stroke 6 Cy. 280 x 440 736kW (1001bhp) Niigata Engineering Co Ltd-Japan
9011325 *JRMX* IT1-280	**SHOUN MARU No. 51** **Kanazawa Gyogyo KK** SatCom: Inmarsat A 1201757 *Miyako, Iwate* *Japan* MMSI: 432008000 Official number: 130927	*319* - -	**1990-09 Niigata Engineering Co Ltd — Niigata NI** Yd No: 2183 Loa 49.75 (BB) Br ex - Dght 3.249 Lbp 43.75 Br md 8.30 Dpth 3.60 Welded	**(B11B2FV) Fishing Vessel** Ins: 408	**1 oil engine** with clutches, flexible couplings & sr geared to sc. shaft driving 1 CP propeller Total Power: 699kW (950hp) Niigata 6M28BFT 1 x 4 Stroke 6 Cy. 280 x 480 699kW (950bhp) Niigata Engineering Co Ltd-Japan
8850190 *JE2538* AM1-597	**SHOUN MARU NO. 55** *ex* Kyoshin Maru No. 5 *-2010* *ex* Shoun Maru *-2004* *ex* Kyoshin Maru No. 5 *-2003* **YK Kyoshin Gyogyo** - *Hachinohe, Aomori* *Japan* Official number: 123131	*138* - -	**1979-07 Kakusei Zosen K.K. — Hachinohe** L reg 29.40 Br ex - Dght - Lbp - Br md 6.20 Dpth 2.50 Welded, 1 dk	**(B11B2FV) Fishing Vessel**	**1 oil engine** driving 1 FP propeller Total Power: 346kW (470hp) Sumiyoshi 1 x 4 Stroke 346kW (470bhp) Sumiyoshi Marine Diesel Co Ltd-Japan
9109469 *JPYK* IT1-320	**SHOUN MARU No. 151** **Kanazawa Gyogyo KK** SatCom: Inmarsat A 1204457 *Miyako, Iwate* *Japan* MMSI: 432007000 Official number: 132190	*319* - -	**1994-09 Niigata Engineering Co Ltd — Niigata NI** Yd No: 2273 Loa 51.00 (BB) Br ex - Dght 3.249 Lbp 44.00 Br md 8.00 Dpth 3.60 Welded, 1 dk	**(B11B2FV) Fishing Vessel** Ins: 391	**1 oil engine** with clutches, flexible couplings & sr geared to sc. shaft driving 1 CP propeller Total Power: 699kW (950hp) Niigata 6M28BFT 1 x 4 Stroke 6 Cy. 280 x 480 699kW (950bhp) Niigata Engineering Co Ltd-Japan
9578610 *3EDB9* -	**SHOURONG HARMONY** **China Mercury Shipping Inc** Vision Ship Management Ltd SatCom: Inmarsat C 437144411 *Panama* *Panama* MMSI: 371444000 Official number: 4214110	**94,710** Class: CC 59,527 180,323 T/cm 124.3	**2010-09 Dalian Shipbuilding Industry Co Ltd — Dalian LN (No 2 Yard)** Yd No: BC1800-30 Loa 295.00 (BB) Br ex - Dght 18.100 Lbp 285.00 Br md 46.00 Dpth 24.80 Welded, 1 dk	**(A21A2BC) Bulk Carrier** Grain: 201,953 Compartments: 9 Ho, ER 9 Ha: 7 (15.5 x 20.0)ER 2 (15.5 x 16.5)	**1 oil engine** driving 1 FP propeller Total Power: 18,660kW (25,370hp) 14.5kn MAN-B&W 6S70MC-C 1 x 2 Stroke 6 Cy. 700 x 2800 18660kW (25370bhp) Dalian Marine Diesel Co Ltd-China AuxGen: 3 x 900kW 450V a.c
9668477 *JD3432* -	**SHOURYU NO. 2** **YK Kaifuku** - *Kasaoka, Okayama* *Japan* Official number: 141793	*267* - 800	**2012-10 Yano Zosen K.K. — Imabari** Yd No: 262 Loa 61.00 Br ex - Dght 3.440 Lbp - Br md 9.80 Dpth 6.00 Welded, 1 dk	**(A31A2GX) General Cargo Ship** Double Hull Grain: 1,371; Bale: 1,328	**1 oil engine** reduction geared to sc. shaft driving 1 FP propeller Total Power: 1,029kW (1,399hp) Niigata 6M28BGT 1 x 4 Stroke 6 Cy. 280 x 480 1029kW (1399bhp) Niigata Engineering Co Ltd-Japan
9608075 *JD3224* -	**SHOUSEI MARU** **Showa Butsuryu KK** - *Uki, Kumamoto* *Japan* Official number: 141489	*499* - 1,830	**2011-07 Yano Zosen K.K. — Imabari** Yd No: 251 Loa 74.50 Br ex - Dght 4.444 Lbp 68.30 Br md 12.00 Dpth 7.50 Welded, 1 dk	**(A31A2GX) General Cargo Ship** Double Hull Grain: 2,583	**1 oil engine** driving 1 FP propeller Total Power: 1,471kW (2,000hp) 12.0kn Niigata 6M34BGT 1 x 4 Stroke 6 Cy. 340 x 620 1471kW (2000bhp) Niigata Engineering Co Ltd-Japan
9459979 *5BMD2* -	**SHOVELER** **Rewako Investments BV** Navarone SA SatCom: Inmarsat C 420918210 *Limassol* *Cyprus* MMSI: 209182000 Official number: 9459979	**19,814** Class: GL 10,208 30,928	**2009-05 Shandong Weihai Shipyard — Weihai SD** Yd No: SN326 Loa 185.02 (BB) Br ex - Dght 10.400 Lbp 178.00 Br md 23.70 Dpth 14.60 Welded, 1 dk	**(A21A2BC) Bulk Carrier** Grain: 38,635; Bale: 37,476 Compartments: 6 Ho, ER 6 Ha: (16.0 x 17.4)3 (19.2 x 17.4) (13.6 x 17.4)ER (10.4 x 13.2) Cranes: 3x30t Ice Capable	**1 oil engine** driving 1 FP propeller Total Power: 7,200kW (9,789hp) 13.5kn MAN-B&W 6S46MC-C 1 x 2 Stroke 6 Cy. 460 x 1932 7200kW (9789bhp) STX Engine Co Ltd-South Korea AuxGen: 3 x 680kW 450/230V 60Hz a.c Thrusters: 1 Tunnel thruster (f) Fuel: 350.0 (d.f.) 1300.0 (r.f.)
7341518 - -	**SHOVETTE** *ex* Grey Lash *-1983* **Deans Tugs & Workboats Ltd** - *Rochester* *United Kingdom*	*157* 19 -	**1974-12 London & Rochester Trading Co. Ltd. — Strood** Loa 24.29 Br ex - Dght 2.591 Lbp - Br md 8.54 Dpth 2.77 Welded	**(B32B2SP) Pusher Tug**	**2 oil engines** driving 2 Directional propellers Total Power: 536kW (728hp) 8.0kn Caterpillar D343TA 2 x 4 Stroke 6 Cy. 137 x 165 each-268kW (364bhp) Caterpillar Tractor Co-USA
9046655 - -	**SHOWA** *ex* Showa Maru *-2013* *ex* Eiryo Maru No. 5 *-1995* **Asia Automotive Pte Ltd** -	*460* Class: IZ - 1,140	**1992-03 Hitachi Zosen Mukaishima Marine Co Ltd — Onomichi HS** Yd No: 61 Loa 66.02 (BB) Br ex 9.62 Dght 4.320 Lbp 61.00 Br md 9.60 Dpth 4.50 Welded, 1 dk	**(A12A2TC) Chemical Tanker** Liq: 834 Compartments: 8 Ta, ER 2 Cargo Pump (s): 2x200m³/hr	**1 oil engine** with clutches & reverse geared to sc. shaft driving 1 FP propeller Total Power: 736kW (1,001hp) Hanshin LH28G 1 x 4 Stroke 6 Cy. 280 x 460 736kW (1001bhp) The Hanshin Diesel Works Ltd-Japan
9063574 *JG5215* -	**SHOWA MARU** **Chiyoda Kaihatsu KK** - *Tokyo* *Japan* MMSI: 431400179 Official number: 133990	*495* - 999	**1993-07 Mukaishima Zoki Co. Ltd. — Onomichi** Yd No: 283 Loa 62.95 Br ex 10.02 Dght 3.950 Lbp 58.80 Br md 10.00 Dpth 4.50 Welded, 1 dk	**(A12A2TC) Chemical Tanker** Liq: 1,100 Compartments: 8 Ta, ER 3 Cargo Pump (s): 1x300m³/hr, 2x200m³/hr	**1 oil engine** with clutches & reverse geared to sc. shaft driving 1 FP propeller Total Power: 735kW (999hp) Hanshin LH28G 1 x 4 Stroke 6 Cy. 280 x 460 735kW (999bhp) The Hanshin Diesel Works Ltd-Japan Thrusters: 1 Thwart. FP thruster (f)
8844373 *5VAM2* -	**SHOWA MARU** *ex* Kosei Maru *-2006* *ex* Kisho Maru *-2001* **Sunny Line Corp Ltd** Dalian Heyang Shipping Agency Co Ltd *Lome* *Togo* MMSI: 671097000	*498* Class: UM - 1,581	**1990-09 K.K. Uno Zosensho — Imabari** Yd No: 217 Loa 75.18 Br ex - Dght 4.140 Lbp 70.50 Br md 12.00 Dpth 7.10 Welded, 1 dk	**(A31A2GX) General Cargo Ship** Grain: 2,952; Bale: 2,728 Compartments: 1 Ho, ER 1 Ha: (39.0 x 9.6)ER	**1 oil engine** reverse geared to sc. shaft driving 1 FP propeller Total Power: 1,324kW (1,800hp) 11.5kn Akasaka K31R 1 x 4 Stroke 6 Cy. 310 x 530 1324kW (1800bhp) Akasaka Tekkosho KK (Akasaka DieselLtd)-Japan
8743218 *JD2867* -	**SHOWA MARU** **KK Hiramatsu Kaiun** - *Sasebo, Nagasaki* *Japan* Official number: 140931	*498* - 1,640	**2008-12 Shinnagashima Shipyard Co Ltd — Kihoku ME** L reg 65.15 Br ex - Dght 4.370 Lbp 63.00 Br md 13.20 Dpth 7.30 Welded, 1 dk	**(A24D2BA) Aggregates Carrier** 1 Ha: ER (21.0 x 10.7)	**1 oil engine** driving 1 Propeller Total Power: 1,471kW (2,000hp) 12.0kn Niigata 1 x 4 Stroke 1471kW (2000bhp) Niigata Engineering Co Ltd-Japan

IMO / Call sign	Name / Owner / Port	Tonnage	Class	Builder / Dimensions	Type	Machinery
7426344 - -	**SHOWA MARU** *ex Seiwa Maru -1981* **Bright Star Marine SA** SatCom: Inmarsat C 433406010 *San Lorenzo* *Honduras* Official number: L-1323834	*199* 119 541		**1975-02 Shin Nikko Zosen K.K. — Onomichi** Yd No: 104 Loa 43.69 Br ex 7.52 Dght - Lbp 40.04 Br md 7.50 Dpth 3.38 Riveted\Welded, 1 dk	**(A13B2TU) Tanker (unspecified)**	**1 oil engine** driving 1 FP propeller Total Power: 478kW (650hp) Hanshin 6L26AGSH 1 x 4 Stroke 6 Cy. 260 x 400 478kW (650bhp) Hanshin Nainenki Kogyo-Japan
8220864 *JM5048* -	**SHOWA MARU** *ex Shin Puku Maru No. 13 -1985* **Sendai Kawa Jari Seisan** - *Satsumasendai, Kagoshima* *Japan* Official number: 124769	*192* - 300		**1982-03 Y.K. Tokai Zosensho — Tsukumi** Yd No: 610 Loa - Br ex - Dght - Lbp 46.61 Br md 10.01 Dpth 5.01 Welded, 1 dk	**(A31A2GX) General Cargo Ship**	**1 oil engine** driving 1 FP propeller Total Power: 736kW (1,001hp) 10.0kn Niigata 6M26AGT 1 x 4 Stroke 6 Cy. 260 x 460 736kW (1001bhp) Niigata Engineering Co Ltd-Japan
9479761 *JD2514* -	**SHOWA MARU** **Showa Nittan Corp** Showa Nittan Maritime Co Ltd *Tokyo* *Japan* MMSI: 431000359 Official number: 140647	**3,535** - 5,676	Class: NK	**2007-12 Kanasashi Heavy Industries Co Ltd — Shizuoka SZ** Yd No: 8203 Loa 104.95 Br ex - Dght 6.616 Lbp 98.00 Br md 16.00 Dpth 7.90 Welded, 1 dk	**(A13B2TP) Products Tanker** Double Hull (13F) Liq: 5,600; Liq (Oil): 5,600	**1 oil engine** driving 1 FP propeller Total Power: 3,309kW (4,499hp) 12.5kn Hanshin LH46LA 1 x 4 Stroke 6 Cy. 460 x 880 3309kW (4499bhp) AuxGen: 2 x a.c
6911744 - -	**SHOWA MARU No. 3** *ex Taisei Maru No. 1 -1979* **Elevas Shipping SA** Tae Kyung Deep Sea Co	*294* 135 -		**1968 KK Kanasashi Zosen — Shizuoka SZ** Yd No: 912 Loa 50.14 Br ex 8.41 Dght 3.099 Lbp 43.19 Br md 8.39 Dpth 3.48 Welded, 1 dk	**(B11B2FV) Fishing Vessel**	**1 oil engine** driving 1 FP propeller Total Power: 736kW (1,001hp) Niigata 1 x 4 Stroke 6 Cy. 280 x 440 736kW (1001bhp) Niigata Engineering Co Ltd-Japan
9124316 - -	**SHOWA MARU No. 3** *ex Akaboshi No. 3 -2007* -	*499* - 1,600	Class: (NK)	**1995-07 K.K. Tachibana Senpaku Tekko — Anan** Yd No: 843 Loa 75.22 Br ex - Dght 4.142 Lbp 70.00 Br md 12.00 Dpth 7.10 Welded, 1 dk	**(A31A2GX) General Cargo Ship** Grain: 2,825; Bale: 2,522 Compartments: 1 Ho, ER 1 Ha: (40.2 x 9.5)ER	**1 oil engine** reverse geared to sc. shaft driving 1 FP propeller Total Power: 736kW (1,001hp) 11.5kn Akasaka A31R 1 x 4 Stroke 6 Cy. 310 x 600 736kW (1001bhp) Akasaka Tekkosho KK (Akasaka DieselLtd)-Japan
8135526 *JK4373* -	**SHOWA MARU No. 5** **YK Sanko Kisen** *Kure, Hiroshima* *Japan* Official number: 125783	*184* - 395		**1982-04 YK Furumoto Tekko Zosensho — Osakikamijima** Yd No: 516 Loa - Br ex - Dght 3.800 Lbp 39.40 Br md 7.60 Dpth 4.60 Welded, 1 dk	**(A31A2GX) General Cargo Ship**	**1 oil engine** driving 1 FP propeller Total Power: 331kW (450hp) 8.0kn Yanmar 1 x 4 Stroke 331kW (450bhp) Yanmar Diesel Engine Co Ltd-Japan
9104354 *JL6217* -	**SHOWA MARU No. 8** **Sanyo Kaiun Shokai Co Ltd (KK Sanyo Kaiun Shokai)** *Osaka, Osaka* *Japan* Official number: 133942	*297* - 600		**1993-09 Nagato Zosen K.K. — Shimonoseki** Yd No: 510 Loa - Br ex - Dght - Lbp - Br md - Dpth - Welded, 1 dk	**(A13B2TP) Products Tanker**	**1 oil engine** reverse geared to sc. shaft driving 1 FP propeller Total Power: 736kW (1,001hp) Hanshin LH26G 1 x 4 Stroke 6 Cy. 260 x 440 736kW (1001bhp) The Hanshin Diesel Works Ltd-Japan
8925103 *JJ3835* -	**SHOWA MARU No. 25** **YK Showa Kaiun Kogyo** *Himeji, Hyogo* *Japan* Official number: 134180	*499* - 1,449		**1996-07 Nagashima Zosen KK — Kihoku ME** Yd No: 501 Loa 73.03 Br ex - Dght 4.110 Lbp 65.00 Br md 13.50 Dpth 6.90 Welded, 1 dk	**(A24D2BA) Aggregates Carrier**	**1 oil engine** driving 1 FP propeller Total Power: 1,471kW (2,000hp) 12.9kn Akasaka A37 1 x 4 Stroke 6 Cy. 370 x 720 1471kW (2000bhp) Akasaka Tekkosho KK (Akasaka DieselLtd)-Japan
6609913 *LGHL* -	**SHOWTIME** *ex Forsand -2009 ex Fugloysund -1998* *ex Eidssund -1991 ex Strand -1982* **Showboat AS** - *Bergen* *Norway* MMSI: 257259400	**547** 189 -	Class: (NV)	**1966 Loland Motorverkstad AS — Leirvik i Sogn** Yd No: 23 Converted From: Ferry (Passenger/Vehicle) Loa 45.55 Br ex 9.28 Dght 3.750 Lbp 41.99 Br md 9.00 Dpth 3.74 Welded, 1 dk	**(A37B2PS) Passenger Ship** Passengers: unberthed: 200	**2 oil engines** driving 2 CP propellers Total Power: 1,104kW (1,500hp) Wichmann 5ACA 2 x 2 Stroke 5 Cy. 280 x 420 each-552kW (750bhp) Wichmann Motorfabrikk AS-Norway AuxGen: 2 x 44kW 220V 50Hz a.c Fuel: 21.5 (d.f.) 5.5pd
8861917 - -	**SHOYNA** **Pacific Union Ltd**	**742** 223 386	Class: (RS)	**1991-10 Zavod "Leninskaya Kuznitsa" — Kiyev** Yd No: 1644 Loa 54.82 Br ex 10.15 Dght 4.140 Lbp 50.30 Br md - Dpth 5.00 Welded, 1 dk	**(B11A2FS) Stern Trawler** Ice Capable	**1 oil engine** driving 1 FP propeller Total Power: 852kW (1,158hp) 12.0kn S.K.L. 8NVD48A-2U 1 x 4 Stroke 8 Cy. 320 x 480 852kW (1158bhp) SKL Motoren u. Systemtechnik AG-Magdeburg
9203019 *JLPT* -	**SHOYO** **Government of Japan (Ministry of Land, Infrastructure & Transport) (The Coastguard)** - *Tokyo* *Japan* MMSI: 431130000 Official number: 135889	*3,128* - -		**1998-03 Mitsui Eng. & SB. Co. Ltd. — Tamano** Yd No: 1440 Loa 98.00 Br ex - Dght 5.300 Lbp 92.00 Br md 15.20 Dpth 7.80 Welded	**(B31A2SR) Research Survey Vessel**	**2 oil engines** geared to sc. shafts driving 2 FP propellers Total Power: 5,958kW (8,100hp) 16.5kn ADD 6ADD30V 2 x Vee 4 Stroke 6 Cy. 300 x 480 each-2979kW (4050bhp) Mitsui Engineering & Shipbuilding CLtd-Japan AuxGen: 2 x 2800kW a.c, 2 x 360kW a.c
9362982 *3ESL5* -	**SHOYO** *ex Energy Pyxis -2013* **Morning Daedalus Navigation SA** Universal Marine Corp *Panama* *Panama* MMSI: 370347000 Official number: 37585PEXT1	**40,690** 25,762 77,008	Class: NK	**2008-08 Namura Shipbuilding Co Ltd — Imari SG** Yd No: 285 Loa 224.99 (BB) Br ex - Dght 14.078 Lbp 217.00 Br md 32.26 Dpth 19.50 Welded, 1 dk	**(A21A2BC) Bulk Carrier** Grain: 92,128 Compartments: 7 Ho, ER 7 Ha: ER	**1 oil engine** driving 1 FP propeller Total Power: 9,930kW (13,501hp) 14.1kn MAN-B&W 6S60MC 1 x 2 Stroke 6 Cy. 600 x 2292 9930kW (13501bhp) Mitsui Engineering & Shipbuilding CLtd-Japan AuxGen: 3 x a.c Fuel: 2264.0
9370898 *JD2149* 	**SHOYO MARU** **Shinwa Naiko Kaiun Kaisha Ltd** EPDC Coal Tech & Marine Co Ltd *Tokyo* *Japan* MMSI: 431101122 Official number: 140210	*749* - 1,400		**2005-10 Yamanaka Zosen K.K. — Imabari** Yd No: 713 Loa 69.19 Br ex - Dght 2.100 Lbp 65.00 Br md 11.50 Dpth 4.65 Welded, 1 dk	**(A24A2BT) Cement Carrier**	**1 oil engine** driving 1 FP propeller Total Power: 1,324kW (1,800hp) Hanshin LH30LG 1 x 4 Stroke 6 Cy. 300 x 600 1324kW (1800bhp) The Hanshin Diesel Works Ltd-Japan
9380958 *JD2209* 	**SHOYO MARU** **Shoyo Kisen Kaisha Ltd** - *Osaka, Osaka* *Japan* MMSI: 432543000 Official number: 140282	**434** 130 282	Class: NK	**2006-02 Keihin Dock Co Ltd — Yokohama** Yd No: 275 Loa 38.00 Br ex - Dght 3.869 Lbp 35.25 Br md 9.50 Dpth 4.50 Welded, 1 dk	**(B32A2ST) Tug**	**2 oil engines** reduction geared to sc. shafts driving 2 Propellers Total Power: 2,942kW (4,000hp) 14.0kn Niigata 6L28HX 2 x 4 Stroke 6 Cy. 280 x 370 each-1471kW (2000bhp) Niigata Engineering Co Ltd-Japan Fuel: 185.0 (d.f.)
9523316 *JD2807* -	**SHOYO MARU** *ex Mitsuhiro No. 3 -2008* **YK Mihara Kisen** Nittetsu Butsuryu KK *Kanonji, Kagawa* *Japan* MMSI: 431000706 Official number: 140857	*498* - 1,410		**2008-08 Yamanaka Zosen K.K. — Imabari** Yd No: 766 Loa 77.10 Br ex - Dght 3.760 Lbp 71.30 Br md 13.00 Dpth 6.62 Welded, 1 dk	**(A31A2GX) General Cargo Ship** Grain: 2,916; Bale: 2,882	**1 oil engine** driving 1 FP propeller Total Power: 1,471kW (2,000hp) Niigata 6M34BGT 1 x 4 Stroke 6 Cy. 340 x 620 1471kW (2000bhp) Niigata Engineering Co Ltd-Japan
9462457 *JD2564* -	**SHOYO MARU** **Hakko Kaiun YK** - *Bizen, Okayama* *Japan* Official number: 140692	*498* - 1,274		**2008-01 KK Ura Kyodo Zosensho — Awaji HG** Yd No: 331 Loa 64.46 Br ex - Dght 4.210 Lbp 60.00 Br md 10.00 Dpth 4.50 Welded, 1 dk	**(A13B2TP) Products Tanker** Double Hull (13F) Liq: 1,230; Liq (Oil): 1,230	**1 oil engine** reduction geared to sc. shafts driving 1 FP propeller Total Power: 1,029kW (1,399hp) 11.0kn Niigata 6M28BGT 1 x 4 Stroke 6 Cy. 280 x 480 1029kW (1399bhp) Niigata Engineering Co Ltd-Japan
9629275 *JD3356* -	**SHOYO MARU** **Showa Nittan Corp** Showa Nittan Maritime Co Ltd *Tokyo* *Japan* MMSI: 431003521 Official number: 141674	*3,673* - 5,476	Class: NK	**2012-05 Kumamoto Dock K.K. — Yatsushiro** Yd No: 460 Loa 104.95 (BB) Br ex - Dght 6.616 Lbp 98.50 Br md 16.00 Dpth 8.30 Welded, 1 dk	**(A13B2TP) Products Tanker** Double Hull (13F) Liq: 5,488; Liq (Oil): 5,600	**1 oil engine** reduction geared to sc. shaft driving 1 FP propeller Total Power: 3,250kW (4,419hp) 13.3kn MAN-B&W 5L35MC 1 x 2 Stroke 5 Cy. 350 x 1050 3250kW (4419bhp) Hitachi Zosen Corp-Japan Fuel: 230.0

Number / Call sign / Flag	Name / Owner / Port	Tonnage	Class	Build / Dimensions	Type	Machinery
8920804 *JL5862* -	**SHOYO MARU** - **Ishizaki Kisen KK** - *Matsuyama, Ehime* *Japan* MMSI: 431000526 Official number: 130640	*696* - 245		**1990**-07 **Kanda Zosensho K.K. — Kawajiri** Yd No: 334 Loa 55.90 Br ex 14.08 Dght 2.800 Lbp 50.00 Br md 13.60 Dpth 3.81 Welded, 1 dk	**(A36A2PR) Passenger/Ro-Ro Ship (Vehicles)**	**2 oil engines** reverse geared to sc. shafts driving 2 FP propellers Total Power: 1,912kW (2,600hp) 14.2kn Daihatsu 6DLM-26 2 x 4 Stroke 6 Cy. 260 x 340 each-956kW (1300bhp) Daihatsu Diesel Manufacturing Co Lt-Japan AuxGen: 2 x 180kW a.c
8910809 *JG4790* -	**SHOYO MARU** *ex* Soshu Maru *-2008* - *Hakodate, Hokkaido* *Japan* MMSI: 431100660 Official number: 131110	*166* - 143		**1989**-12 **K.K. Murakami Zosensho — Ishinomaki** Yd No: 1228 Loa 39.44 (BB) Br ex - Dght 2.900 Lbp 33.96 Br md 7.40 Dpth 3.20 Welded, 1 dk	**(B11B2FV) Fishing Vessel** Ins: 115	**1 oil engine** sr geared to sc. shaft driving 1 FP propeller Total Power: 736kW (1,001hp) Sumiyoshi S25RD 1 x 4 Stroke 6 Cy. 250 x 450 736kW (1001bhp) Sumiyoshi Marine Diesel Co Ltd-Japan
8910677 *JRMQ* MG1-1785	**SHOYO MARU** - **Murata Gyogyo KK** - SatCom: Inmarsat A 1203124 *Kesennuma, Miyagi* *Japan* MMSI: 431703830 Official number: 130912	*469* - 510		**1990**-09 **Miho Zosensho K.K. — Shimizu** Yd No: 1359 Loa 56.49 (BB) Br ex - Dght 3.611 Lbp 49.80 Br md 8.90 Dpth 3.97 Welded	**(B11B2FV) Fishing Vessel** Ins: 721	**1 oil engine** with clutches, flexible couplings & sr reverse geared to sc. shaft driving 1 FP propeller Total Power: 1,177kW (1,600hp) Niigata 6M31AFTE 1 x 4 Stroke 6 Cy. 310 x 530 1177kW (1600bhp) Niigata Engineering Co Ltd-Japan
8944070 *JJ4007* -	**SHOYO MARU** - **Meiwa Kaiun KK** - *Kobe, Hyogo* *Japan* Official number: 134274	*199* - -		**1998**-07 **K.K. Yoshida Zosen Kogyo — Arida** Yd No: 511 Loa 56.52 Br ex - Dght - Lbp 52.00 Br md 9.20 Dpth 5.60 Welded, 1 dk	**(A31A2GX) General Cargo Ship**	**1 oil engine** driving 1 FP propeller Total Power: 736kW (1,001hp) 10.0kn Hanshin LH26G 1 x 4 Stroke 6 Cy. 260 x 440 736kW (1001bhp) The Hanshin Diesel Works Ltd-Japan
9103661 - -	**SHOYO MARU** - **PT Berlian Samudra Pacific** - *Indonesia*	*199* - 658		**1994**-04 **Yano Zosen K.K. — Imabari** Yd No: 151 Loa 57.50 Br ex - Dght - Lbp 53.00 Br md 9.50 Dpth 5.30 Welded, 1 dk	**(A31A2GX) General Cargo Ship** Bale: 1,146 Compartments: 1 Ho 1 Ha: (30.3 x 7.4)	**1 oil engine** geared to sc. shaft driving 1 FP propeller Total Power: 736kW (1,001hp) 12.2kn Hanshin LH26G 1 x 4 Stroke 6 Cy. 260 x 440 736kW (1001bhp) The Hanshin Diesel Works Ltd-Japan
9149782 *JLOJ* -	**SHOYO MARU** - **Government of Japan (Ministry of Agriculture & Forestry - Fisheries Agency)** - SatCom: Inmarsat B 343146513 *Tokyo* *Japan* MMSI: 431465000 Official number: 135883	*2,214* - 1,079		**1998**-05 **Nippon Kokan KK (NKK Corp) — Yokohama KN (Tsurumi Shipyard)** Yd No: 1069 Loa 87.60 Br ex - Dght 5.422 Lbp 76.00 Br md 14.00 Dpth 7.30 Welded, 1 dk	**(B11A2FS) Stern Trawler**	**2 oil engines** reduction geared to sc. shaft driving 1 CP propeller Total Power: 4,414kW (6,002hp) 16.0kn Yanmar 6N330-EN 2 x 4 Stroke 6 Cy. 330 x 440 each-2207kW (3001bhp) Yanmar Diesel Engine Co Ltd-Japan AuxGen: 3 x 650kW a.c Thrusters: 1 Thwart. CP thruster (f) Fuel: 561.0 (d.f.)
9153939 *JJ3931* -	**SHOYO MARU** *ex* Taiyo Maru No. 16 *-2005* - *Kitakyushu, Fukuoka* *Japan* Official number: 134186	*498* - 1,350		**1996**-11 **Kegoya Dock K.K. — Kure** Yd No: 990 Loa - Br ex - Dght 4.300 Lbp 63.00 Br md 13.50 Dpth 7.17 Welded, 1 dk	**(A31A2GX) General Cargo Ship**	**1 oil engine** driving 1 FP propeller Total Power: 736kW (1,001hp) Niigata 6M28BGT 1 x 4 Stroke 6 Cy. 280 x 480 736kW (1001bhp) Niigata Engineering Co Ltd-Japan
9162734 *JG5356* -	**SHOYO MARU** - **JFE Logistics Corp** - *Tokyo* *Japan* MMSI: 431100299 Official number: 135244	*497* - 1,595		**1997**-01 **Nakatani Shipyard Co. Ltd. — Etajima** Yd No: 576 Loa 76.22 (BB) Br ex - Dght 4.140 Lbp 70.00 Br md 12.00 Dpth 7.12 Welded, 1 dk	**(A31A2GX) General Cargo Ship** Grain: 2,796; Bale: 2,312 Compartments: 1 Ho, ER 1 Ha: (40.2 x 9.2)ER	**1 oil engine** driving 1 CP propeller Total Power: 1,324kW (1,800hp) 12.5kn Hanshin LH30L 1 x 4 Stroke 6 Cy. 300 x 600 1324kW (1800bhp) The Hanshin Diesel Works Ltd-Japan AuxGen: 2 x 144kW 445V a.c Thrusters: 1 Thwart. FP thruster (f) Fuel: 86.0 (d.f.) 5.3pd
9021435 - -	**SHOYO MARU** - **Chuwa Bussan Co Ltd** - *China*	*271* - -		**1991**-06 **Shin Yamamoto Shipbuilding & Engineering Co Ltd — Kochi KC** Yd No: 332 L reg 34.20 Br ex - Dght - Lbp - Br md 9.50 Dpth 4.30 Welded	**(B32A2ST) Tug**	**2 oil engines** driving 2 FP propellers Total Power: 3,090kW (4,202hp) Niigata 6L28HX 2 x 4 Stroke 6 Cy. 280 x 370 each-1545kW (2101bhp) Niigata Engineering Co Ltd-Japan
9016064 *JNWJ* -	**SHOYO MARU** *ex* Gem Star *-2004* **Shosei Kisen KK & Ryusei Kisen Kabushiki Kaisha** Shosei Kisen Co Ltd (Shosei Kisen KK) *Saiki, Oita* *Japan* MMSI: 432464000 Official number: 136817	**3,004** 901 2,890 T/cm 11.0	Class: NK (RI)	**1992**-06 **Cant. Nav. de Poli S.p.A. — Pellestrina** Yd No: 140 Loa 89.40 (BB) Br ex 14.65 Dght 5.758 Lbp 82.00 Br md 14.63 Dpth 7.20 Welded, 1 dk	**(A11B2TG) LPG Tanker** Liq (Gas): 2,940 2 x Gas Tank (s); 2 independent (Ni.stl) cyl horizontal 2 Cargo Pump (s): 2x300m³/hr Manifold: Bow/CM: 39m	**1 oil engine** sr geared to sc. shaft driving 1 CP propeller Total Power: 2,460kW (3,345hp) 13.0kn Wartsila 6R32E 1 x 4 Stroke 6 Cy. 320 x 350 2460kW (3345bhp) Wartsila Diesel Oy-Finland AuxGen: 4 x 511kW 440V 60Hz a.c Fuel: 105.0 (d.f.) 310.0 (r.f.)
6804159 - -	**SHOYO MARU** - **Societe de Peche Mitsu** - *Guinea*	*184* 65 213		**1967** **Wakamatsu Zosen K.K. — Kitakyushu** Yd No: 170 Loa 37.90 Br ex 6.84 Dght - Lbp 31.88 Br md 6.81 Dpth 3.18 Welded, 1 dk	**(B11B2FV) Fishing Vessel**	**1 oil engine** driving 1 FP propeller Total Power: 625kW (850hp) Niigata 6M28KHS 1 x 4 Stroke 6 Cy. 280 x 440 625kW (850bhp) Niigata Engineering Co Ltd-Japan
9499527 *JD2788* -	**SHOYO MARU NO. 3** - **Syoyo Kaiun YK** - *Kasaoka, Okayama* *Japan* MMSI: 431000725 Official number: 140833	*299* - 1,050		**2008**-08 **Taiyo Shipbuilding Co Ltd — Sanyoonoda YC** Yd No: 317 Loa 63.30 Br ex - Dght 3.640 Lbp 58.00 Br md 10.20 Dpth 6.15 Welded, 1 dk	**(A31A2GX) General Cargo Ship** Grain: 1,545; Bale: 1,545 Compartments: 1 Ho, ER 1 Ha: ER (33.5 x 7.8)	**1 oil engine** reverse reduction geared to sc. shaft driving 1 FP propeller Total Power: 736kW (1,001hp) Niigata 6M28BGT 1 x 4 Stroke 6 Cy. 280 x 480 736kW (1001bhp) Niigata Engineering Co Ltd-Japan
9304552 *JD2715* -	**SHOYO MARU NO. 8** - **KK Maruriki Asakura Shoten** - *Abashiri, Hokkaido* *Japan* MMSI: 431800671 Official number: 135383	*160* - -		**2004**-02 **Narasaki Zosen KK — Muroran HK** Yd No: 1180 Loa 38.38 Br ex - Dght 3.830 Lbp - Br md 7.80 Dpth 4.61 Welded, 1 dk	**(B11B2FV) Fishing Vessel**	**1 oil engine** geared to sc. shaft driving 1 FP propeller Total Power: 1,030kW (1,400hp) Akasaka 6U28AK 1 x 4 Stroke 6 Cy. 280 x 380 1030kW (1400bhp) Akasaka Tekkosho KK (Akasaka DieselLtd)-Japan
7118363 - -	**SHOYO MARU No. 8** - - -	*124* 42 -		**1971** **Narasaki Zosen KK — Muroran HK** Yd No: 772 Loa 34.90 Br ex 7.12 Dght - Lbp 29.93 Br md 7.09 Dpth 2.67 Welded, 1 dk	**(B11B2FV) Fishing Vessel**	**1 oil engine** driving 1 FP propeller Total Power: 956kW (1,300hp) Akasaka AH28 1 x 4 Stroke 6 Cy. 280 x 440 956kW (1300bhp) Akasaka Tekkosho KK (Akasaka DieselLtd)-Japan
7233802 - -	**SHOYO MARU No. 18** - - -	*374* 177 -		**1972** **Mie Shipyard Co. Ltd. — Yokkaichi** Yd No: 70 Loa 55.10 Br ex 8.41 Dght - Lbp 46.41 Br md 8.39 Dpth 3.79 Welded, 1 dk	**(B11B2FV) Fishing Vessel**	**1 oil engine** driving 1 FP propeller Total Power: 1,250kW (1,700hp) Niigata 6M37AHS 1 x 4 Stroke 6 Cy. 370 x 540 1250kW (1700bhp) Niigata Engineering Co Ltd-Japan
8926200 *JM6536* -	**SHOYO MARU No. 18** - **Sakamoto Kaiun KK** - *Sado, Niigata* *Japan* Official number: 134651	*499* - -		**1996**-12 **Y.K. Takasago Zosensho — Naruto** Loa 73.60 Br ex - Dght - Lbp 65.00 Br md 13.20 Dpth 7.00 Welded, 1 dk	**(A31A2GX) General Cargo Ship**	**1 oil engine** driving 1 FP propeller Total Power: 736kW (1,001hp) 10.7kn Niigata 6M34BGT 1 x 4 Stroke 6 Cy. 340 x 620 736kW (1001bhp) Niigata Engineering Co Ltd-Japan
8889660 *JM6379* -	**SHOYO MARU No. 18** - **Kawaguchi Kaiun YK** - *Kitakyushu, Fukuoka* *Japan* MMSI: 431600345 Official number: 134478	*653* - 1,303		**1995**-03 **Amakusa Zosen K.K. — Amakusa** Loa 70.00 Br ex - Dght 3.930 Lbp 62.00 Br md 13.50 Dpth 6.30 Welded, 1 dk	**(A24D2BA) Aggregates Carrier**	**1 oil engine** driving 1 FP propeller Total Power: 736kW (1,001hp) 10.5kn Hanshin 6LU35 1 x 4 Stroke 6 Cy. 350 x 550 736kW (1001bhp) The Hanshin Diesel Works Ltd-Japan

IMO / Call sign	Name / Owner / Port	Tonnage	Class	Construction / Dimensions	Type / Cargo	Machinery
9641376 *3FZH2* -	**SHOYOH** **TDC Shipping SA** Daiichi Chuo Kisen Kaisha *Panama* Panama MMSI: 352055000 Official number: 4509013	**60,876** 25,481 97,114	Class: NK	**2013**-07 **Japan Marine United Corp (JMU) — Kure HS** Yd No: 3336 Loa 239.90 (BB) Br ex - Dght 13.053 Lbp 234.50 Br md 43.00 Dpth 20.50 Welded, 1 dk	**(A21A2BC) Bulk Carrier** Grain: 115,826 Compartments: 5 Ho, ER 5 Ha: ER	**1 oil engine** driving 1 FP propeller Total Power: 9,680kW (13,161hp) 14.2kn Wartsila 6RT-flex58T 1 x 2 Stroke 6 Cy. 580 x 2416 9680kW (13161bhp) Diesel United Ltd.-Aioi AuxGen: 4 x 500kW a.c Fuel: 3720.0
9638458 *JD3303* -	**SHOYU** **Shoho Kaiun KK** - *Osakikamijima, Hiroshima* Japan Official number: 141599	*749* - 2,550		**2012**-01 **Koike Zosen Kaiun KK — Osakikamijima** Yd No: 538 Loa 79.10 (BB) Br ex - Dght 4.770 Lbp 71.00 Br md 13.40 Dpth 8.10 Welded, 1 dk	**(A31A2GX) General Cargo Ship** Compartments: 1 Ho, ER 1 Ha: ER Cranes: 1	**1 oil engine** driving 1 FP propeller Total Power: 1,914kW (2,602hp) Daihatsu 6DKM-28 1 x 4 Stroke 6 Cy. 280 x 390 1914kW (2602bhp) Daihatsu Diesel Manufacturing Co Lt-Japan Thrusters: 1 Thwart. FP thruster (f)
6720523 *H06932* -	**SHOYU** *ex* Shoyu Maru *-1983* **Max Line Co Ltd Inc** - *Panama* Panama Official number: 1315183	*198* 69 170		**1967 Hayashikane Shipbuilding & Engineering Co Ltd — Yokosuka KN** Yd No: 659 Loa 35.79 Br ex 7.17 Dght - Lbp 31.60 Br md 7.14 Dpth 3.33 Welded, 1 dk	**(B11B2FV) Fishing Vessel**	**1 oil engine** driving 1 FP propeller Total Power: 699kW (950hp) Niigata 6M31HS 1 x 4 Stroke 6 Cy. 310 x 460 699kW (950bhp) Niigata Engineering Co Ltd-Japan
8630540 *JH2970* IK1-228	**SHOYU MARU** *ex* Suei Maru No. 31 *-2008* *ex* Eiho Maru No. 28 *-2002* *ex* Kitsushin Maru No. 58 *-1992* - - *Hakodate, Hokkaido* Japan Official number: 125705	*166* - -		**1984**-01 **Ishimura Zosen — Kimaishi** Loa 29.10 Br ex - Dght 2.400 Lbp - Br md 6.20 Dpth 2.90 Welded, 1 dk	**(B11B2FV) Fishing Vessel**	**1 oil engine** driving 1 FP propeller Total Power: 592kW (805hp) Pielstick 5PA5 1 x 4 Stroke 5 Cy. 225 x 270 592kW (805bhp) Niigata Engineering Co Ltd-Japan
8805119 *JL5676* -	**SHOYU MARU** **Sanei Unyu Kiko KK** Tabuchi Kaiun Co Ltd *Anan, Tokushima* Japan Official number: 129925	*294* - 495		**1988**-08 **Mukaishima Zoki Co. Ltd. — Onomichi** Yd No: 250 Loa - Br ex 8.62 Dght 3.140 Lbp 46.00 Br md 8.60 Dpth 3.60 Welded, 1 dk	**(A11B2TG) LPG Tanker** Liq (Gas): 350 2 Cargo Pump (s): 2x140m³/hr	**1 oil engine** with clutches & reverse reduction geared to sc. shaft driving 1 FP propeller Total Power: 900kW (1,224hp) Daihatsu 6DLM-22 1 x 4 Stroke 6 Cy. 220 x 300 900kW (1224bhp) Daihatsu Diesel Manufacturing Co Lt-Japan
9072458 *JL6222* -	**SHOYU MARU** **Miyazaki Kaiun Co Ltd** - *Imabari, Ehime* Japan MMSI: 431500144 Official number: 133947	*2,997* - 4,999	Class: NK	**1993**-10 **Asakawa Zosen K.K. — Imabari** Yd No: 377 Loa 104.97 Br ex - Dght 6.413 Lbp 98.00 Br md 15.40 Dpth 7.60 Welded, 1 dk	**(A13B2TP) Products Tanker** Liq: 5,628; Liq (Oil): 5,628	**1 oil engine** driving 1 CP propeller Total Power: 2,942kW (4,000hp) 13.9kn Hanshin 6LF50 1 x 4 Stroke 6 Cy. 500 x 800 2942kW (4000bhp) The Hanshin Diesel Works Ltd-Japan AuxGen: 2 x 320kW a.c Fuel: 300.0 (r.f.)
9020182 *JIUP* S01-1092	**SHOYU MARU No. 18** **KK Ichimaru** - SatCom: Inmarsat B 343118710 *Yaizu, Shizuoka* Japan MMSI: 431187000 Official number: 131551	*349* - 857		**1991**-04 **Miho Zosensho K.K. — Shimizu** Yd No: 1398 Loa 63.51 (BB) Br ex - Dght 4.453 Lbp 55.65 Br md 12.00 Dpth 7.24 Welded, 2 dks	**(B11B2FV) Fishing Vessel** Ins: 1,231	**1 oil engine** with clutches, flexible couplings & sr geared to sc. shaft driving 1 FP propeller Total Power: 1,986kW (2,700hp) Akasaka DM40AKD 1 x 4 Stroke 6 Cy. 400 x 640 1986kW (2700bhp) Akasaka Tekkosho KK (Akasaka DieselLtd)-Japan Thrusters: 1 Thwart. FP thruster
7217286 - -	**SHOYU MARU No. 25** **Shoei Suisan KK** -	*383* 176 491		**1971 Miho Zosensho K.K. — Shimizu** Yd No: 800 Loa 54.95 Br ex 9.76 Dght 3.556 Lbp 46.49 Br md 8.49 Dpth 3.94 Welded, 1 dk	**(B11B2FV) Fishing Vessel**	**1 oil engine** driving 1 FP propeller Total Power: 1,214kW (1,651hp) Akasaka 6DH36SS 1 x 4 Stroke 6 Cy. 360 x 540 1214kW (1651bhp) Akasaka Tekkosho KK (Akasaka DieselLtd)-Japan
7302615 - -	**SHOYU MARU No. 35** - -	*432* 216 562		**1973 Miho Zosensho K.K. — Shimizu** Yd No: 878 Loa 57.41 Br ex 9.02 Dght 3.836 Lbp 49.00 Br md 9.00 Dpth 4.09 Welded, 1 dk	**(B11B2FV) Fishing Vessel**	**1 oil engine** driving 1 FP propeller Total Power: 1,214kW (1,651hp) Akasaka 6DH36SS 1 x 4 Stroke 6 Cy. 360 x 540 1214kW (1651bhp) Akasaka Tekkosho KK (Akasaka DieselLtd)-Japan
9078402 *JM6263* -	**SHOZAN** *ex* Shinpo Maru No. 3 *-2002* **Koyo Yusosen KK** - *Nagoya, Aichi* Japan Official number: 133601	*180* - 410		**1993**-09 **Kurinoura Dockyard Co Ltd — Yawatahama EH** Yd No: 317 Loa 42.32 Br ex 7.62 Dght 3.270 Lbp 38.00 Br md 7.60 Dpth 3.30 Welded, 1 dk	**(A13B2TP) Products Tanker** Compartments: 6 Ta, ER	**1 oil engine** reverse geared to sc. shaft driving 1 FP propeller Total Power: 588kW (799hp) Yanmar MF26-SD 1 x 4 Stroke 6 Cy. 260 x 500 588kW (799bhp) Yanmar Diesel Engine Co Ltd-Japan
9481673 *5BNW3* -	**SHRAVAN** **Essar Shipping (Cyprus) Ltd** Essar Shipping Ltd *Limassol* Cyprus MMSI: 209922000 Official number: 9481673	**62,271** 34,753 106,438	Class: AB	**2012**-04 **STX (Dalian) Shipbuilding Co Ltd — Wafangdian LN** Yd No: D2045 Loa 253.50 Br ex - Dght 13.600 Lbp 249.20 Br md 43.00 Dpth 19.80 Welded, 1 dk	**(A21A2BC) Bulk Carrier** Grain: 133,971 Compartments: 7 Ho, ER 7 Ha: ER	**1 oil engine** driving 1 FP propeller Total Power: 13,560kW (18,436hp) 14.5kn MAN-B&W 6S60MC-C8 1 x 2 Stroke 6 Cy. 600 x 2400 13560kW (18436bhp) STX (Dalian) Engine Co Ltd-China AuxGen: 3 x 625kW a.c Fuel: 190.0 (d.f.) 2836.0 (r.f.)
8662191 *AVPQ* -	**SHREE KRISHNA-16** *ex* Ag 19287 *-2009* **Shree Krishna Stevedores Pvt Ltd** - *Mumbai* India MMSI: 419000412 Official number: 3918	**1,256** 608 1,809		**2009**-01 **in Vietnam** Yd No: V67-19931 Loa 61.67 Br ex - Dght 4.000 Lbp - Br md 11.20 Dpth 4.40 Welded, 1 dk	**(A31A2GX) General Cargo Ship**	**2 oil engines** reduction geared to sc. shafts driving 2 Propellers Total Power: 588kW (800hp) Cummins 2 x each-294kW (400bhp) Cummins India Ltd-India
8662220 - -	**SHREE KRISHNA-17** *ex* BTR-5383 *-2009* **Shree Krishna Stevedores Pvt Ltd** - Vietnam Official number: 5363/DK	**1,537** 730 2,200		**2009**-10 **in Vietnam** Yd No: V 71-07302 Loa 65.00 Br ex - Dght - Lbp - Br md 12.80 Dpth 4.50 Welded, 1 dk	**(A31A2GX) General Cargo Ship**	**2 oil engines** reduction geared to sc. shafts driving 2 Propellers Total Power: 1,176kW (1,598hp) Cummins 2 x each-588kW (799bhp) Cummins Engine Co Inc-USA
8652988 *AVPK* -	**SHREE KRISHNA-IX** **Shree Krishna Stevedores Pvt Ltd** - *Mumbai* India MMSI: 419000406 Official number: 3912	**1,518** 488 2,450	Class: (IR)	**2009**-01 **Khattar Shipyard — Jamnagar** Yd No: 104 Loa 70.00 Br ex - Dght 3.200 Lbp 66.77 Br md 16.00 Dpth 4.50 Welded, 1 dk	**(A31A2GX) General Cargo Ship**	**2 oil engines** reduction geared to sc. shafts driving 2 Propellers Total Power: 736kW (1,000hp) 8.0kn Cummins 2 x each-368kW (500bhp) Cummins India Ltd-India
8652976 *AVPG* -	**SHREE KRISHNA VII** **Shree Krishna Stevedores Pvt Ltd** - *Mumbai* India MMSI: 419000401 Official number: 3908	**1,520** 632 2,450	Class: IR	**2010**-02 **Padhiar Hi Tech Engineering Services — Jamnagar** Yd No: 105 Loa 70.00 Br ex - Dght 3.200 Lbp 66.77 Br md 16.00 Dpth 4.50 Welded, 1 dk	**(A31A2GX) General Cargo Ship**	**2 oil engines** reduction geared to sc. shafts driving 2 Propellers Total Power: 736kW (1,000hp) 8.0kn Cummins 2 x each-368kW (500bhp) Cummins India Ltd-India
8652990 *AVPF* -	**SHREE KRISHNA-VIII** **Shree Krishna Stevedores Pvt Ltd** - *Mumbai* India MMSI: 419000403 Official number: 3907	**1,520** 632 2,450	Class: IR	**2010**-01 **Gujarat Marine Engineering Works — Jamnagar** Yd No: 107 Loa 70.00 Br ex - Dght 3.200 Lbp 66.77 Br md 16.00 Dpth 4.50 Welded, 1 dk	**(A31A2GX) General Cargo Ship**	**2 oil engines** reduction geared to sc. shafts driving 2 Propellers Total Power: 736kW (1,000hp) 8.0kn Cummins 2 x each-368kW (500bhp) Cummins India Ltd-India
8653009 *AVPE* -	**SHREE KRISHNA-X** **Shree Krishna Stevedores Pvt Ltd** - *Mumbai* India MMSI: 419000399 Official number: 3906	**1,529** 785 -	Class: IR	**2010**-05 **Timblo Drydocks Pvt Ltd — Goa** Yd No: 120 Loa 75.00 Br ex - Dght 3.500 Lbp 72.50 Br md 14.00 Dpth - Welded, 1 dk	**(A31A2GX) General Cargo Ship**	**2 oil engines** reduction geared to sc. shafts driving 2 Propellers Total Power: 588kW (800hp) Cummins 2 x each-294kW (400bhp) Cummins India Ltd-India

IMO No. / Call sign	Name / Owners	Tonnage	Class	Builder / Dimensions	Type	Machinery
8653011 *AVPD* -	**SHREE KRISHNA-XI** - **Shree Krishna Stevedores Pvt Ltd** - *Mumbai* India MMSI: 419000398 Official number: 3905	**1,672** 489 -	Class: IR	**2010-03 Timblo Drydocks Pvt Ltd — Goa** Yd No: 121 Loa 75.00 Br ex - Dght 3.500 Lbp 72.50 Br md 14.00 Dpth - Welded, 1 dk	**(A31A2GX) General Cargo Ship**	**2 oil engines** reduction geared to sc. shafts driving 2 Propellers Total Power: 588kW (800hp) Cummins 2 x each-294kW (400bhp) Cummins India Ltd-India
9596208 *AVLH* -	**SHREE KRISHNA-XV** *ex* Champa *-2011* **Shree Krishna Quarry Pvt Ltd** Doehle Danautic India Pvt Ltd SatCom: Inmarsat C 441923081 *Mumbai* India MMSI: 419000293 Official number: 3833	**708** 264 1,084	Class: IR (RI) (BV)	**2010-12 Zhejiang Chengzhou Shipbuilding Co Ltd — Sanmen County ZJ** Yd No: CZ1002 Loa 48.02 (BB) Br ex 11.52 Dght 3.300 Lbp 44.50 Br md 11.50 Dpth 4.60 Welded, 1 dk	**(A13B2TP) Products Tanker** Double Hull (13F) Liq: 1,106; Liq (Oil): 871 Compartments: 3 Wing Ta, 3 Wing Ta, ER	**2 oil engines** reduction geared to sc. shafts driving 2 Z propellers Total Power: 596kW (810hp) 9.0kn Cummins NTA-855-M 2 x 4 Stroke 6 Cy. 140 x 152 each-298kW (405bhp) Chongqing Cummins Engine Co Ltd-China AuxGen: 2 x 150kW 50Hz a.c Fuel: 27.0
8304971 *VWCF* -	**SHREE KRISHNA XVIII** *ex* Garware V *-2012* **Shree Krishna Stevedores Pvt Ltd** New Horizons Shipmanagement Pvt Ltd *Mumbai* India MMSI: 419002300 Official number: 1998	**867** 260 1,047	Class: IR (AB)	**1984-03 Maroil Engineers & Shipbuilders Pte Ltd — Singapore** Yd No: 1032 Loa 56.39 Br ex - Dght 4.431 Lbp 51.57 Br md 12.01 Dpth 5.01 Welded, 1 dk	**(B21A20S) Platform Supply Ship**	**2 oil engines** sr reverse geared to sc. shafts driving 2 FP propellers Total Power: 3,530kW (4,800hp) 12.3kn Wartsila 12V22HF 2 x Vee 4 Stroke 12 Cy. 220 x 240 each-1765kW (2400bhp) Oy Wartsila Ab-Finland AuxGen: 3 x 125kW 440V 60Hz a.c Thrusters: 1 Thwart. CP thruster (f) Fuel: 415.0 (d.f.) 8.5pd
8663391 - -	**SHREYA** - **Agencia Ultramarina Pvt Ltd** - *Panaji* India Official number: PNJ 511	**1,407** 1,241 2,178	Class: IR (Class contemplated)	**2010-11 Timblo Drydocks Pvt Ltd — Goa** Yd No: 122 Loa 70.00 Br ex 13.02 Dght - Lbp 67.40 Br md 13.00 Dpth 4.45 Welded, 1 dk	**(A31A2GX) General Cargo Ship**	**2 oil engines** reduction geared to sc. shafts driving 2 Propellers Total Power: 536kW (728hp) Cummins NT-855-M 2 x 4 Stroke 6 Cy. 140 x 152 each-268kW (364bhp) Cummins India Ltd-India
8827193 *VVRV* -	**SHREYAS I** - **Shreyas Seafoods Pvt Ltd** - *Mumbai* India Official number: 2287	*116* 35 105	Class: (AB) (IR)	**1988-11 Alcock, Ashdown & Co. Ltd. — Bhavnagar** Yd No: 171 Loa 23.50 (BB) Br ex 7.50 Dght 2.830 Lbp 20.35 Br md 7.30 Dpth 3.23 Welded, 1 dk	**(B11A2FT) Trawler**	**1 oil engine** driving 1 FP propeller Total Power: 296kW (402hp) 9.5kn Caterpillar 1 x 4 Stroke 8 Cy. 296kW (402bhp) Caterpillar Inc-USA AuxGen: 2 x 42kW 415V 50Hz a.c Fuel: 50.0 (d.f.)
8827208 *VVRW* -	**SHRI SHABARI I** - **Shri Shabari Fisheries Ltd** - *Mumbai* India Official number: 2288	*116* 35 105	Class: (IR)	**1988-08 Alcock, Ashdown & Co. Ltd. — Bhavnagar** Loa 23.50 (BB) Br ex 7.50 Dght 2.830 Lbp 20.35 Br md 7.30 Dpth 3.23 Welded, 1 dk	**(B11A2FT) Trawler** Ins: 70	**1 oil engine** driving 1 FP propeller Total Power: 296kW (402hp) 9.5kn Caterpillar 1 x 4 Stroke 8 Cy. 296kW (402bhp) Caterpillar Inc-USA AuxGen: 2 x 42kW 415V 50Hz a.c Fuel: 50.0 (d.f.)
9130494 - -	**SHRI SHAKTI** - - - *Kakinada* India	*296* - 170	Class: (LR) ✠	**1996-09 Tebma Engineering Ltd — Chengalpattu** Yd No: 046 Loa 30.50 Br ex 11.02 Dght 1.608 Lbp 29.00 Br md 10.50 Dpth 2.60 Welded, 1 dk	**(A11B2TG) LPG Tanker** Liq (Gas): 294 2 x Gas Tank (s);	**2 oil engines** with clutches & sr reverse geared to sc. shafts driving 2 FP propellers Total Power: 334kW (454hp) 7.7kn Cummins NT-743-M 2 x 4 Stroke 6 Cy. 130 x 152 each-167kW (227bhp) Kirloskar Oil Engines Ltd-India AuxGen: 2 x 24kW 415V 50Hz a.c
9237187 *V7MN5* -	**SHRIKE** *ex* Fortune Bright *-2007* **Shrike Shipping LLC** Eagle Shipping International (USA) LLC *Majuro* *Marshall Islands* MMSI: 538002876 Official number: 2876	**29,862** 18,434 53,343	Class: AB (KR)	**2003-03 Toyohashi Shipbuilding Co Ltd — Toyohashi AI** Yd No: 3547 Loa 189.99 (BB) Br ex - Dght 12.170 Lbp 182.00 Br md 32.26 Dpth 17.00 Welded, 1 dk	**(A21A2BC) Bulk Carrier** Grain: 68,259; Bale: 65,617 Compartments: 5 Ho, ER 5 Ha: ER 4 (20.8 x 17.6) (16.8 x 17.6) Cranes: 4x30t	**1 oil engine** driving 1 FP propeller Total Power: 8,580kW (11,665hp) 14.3kn MAN-B&W 6S50MC 1 x 2 Stroke 6 Cy. 500 x 1910 8580kW (11665bhp) Mitsui Engineering & Shipbuilding CLtd-Japan AuxGen: 3 x 400kW 450V a.c Fuel: 1742.0 (r.f.)
9670183 *AVRO* -	**SHRIMANGAL** - **Asianol Shipping Ltd** - *Mumbai* India MMSI: 419000499 Official number: 3956	**1,624** 760 2,808	Class: IR	**2012-10 Waterways Shipyard Pvt Ltd — Goa** Yd No: 153 Loa 78.37 Br ex - Dght 3.510 Lbp 75.98 Br md 14.50 Dpth 4.82 Welded, 1 dk	**(A31A2GX) General Cargo Ship** Compartments: 1 Ho, ER 1 Ha: ER	**2 oil engines** reduction geared to sc. shafts driving 2 FP propellers Total Power: 596kW (810hp) 9.9kn Cummins NTA-855-M 2 x 4 Stroke 6 Cy. 140 x 152 each-298kW (405bhp) Cummins India Ltd-India
5427978 - -	**SHRIMPER** *ex* Fatima *-2003* *ex* Asmak-Mother *-1999* *ex* Dubai Dolphin *-1999* *ex* Reinier Casper *-1990* *ex* Kommandor Ellen *-1990* *ex* Oil Hunter *-1984* *ex* Lofottral I *-1974* **Saad Abdul Aziz Al-Sullami** -	**929** 253 242	Class: (HR) (BV) (NV)	**1963-10 AS Trondhjems Mekaniske Verksted — Trondheim** Yd No: 545 Converted From: Research Vessel-1987 Converted From: Stern Trawler-1974 Loa 57.90 Br ex 9.80 Dght 4.407 Lbp 49.00 Br md 9.78 Dpth 6.35 Welded, 2 dks	**(B11A2FS) Stern Trawler** Ins: 320 Ice Capable	**1 oil engine** driving 1 CP propeller Total Power: 1,030kW (1,400hp) 10.0kn Deutz SBV6M358 1 x 4 Stroke 6 Cy. 400 x 580 1030kW (1400bhp) Kloeckner Humboldt Deutz AG-West Germany AuxGen: 2 x 137kW 380V 50Hz a.c, 1 x 75kW 380V 50Hz a.c Fuel: 223.5 (d.f.) 4.5pd
7236646 - -	**SHRIMVEN 1** *ex* Kaho Maru No. 36 *-1988* - -	*299* 153 392	Class: (KR)	**1972 Miho Zosensho K.K. — Shimizu** Yd No: 845 Loa 50.40 Br ex 8.23 Dght 3.379 Lbp 44.20 Br md 8.21 Dpth 3.61 Welded, 1 dk	**(B11B2FV) Fishing Vessel**	**1 oil engine** driving 1 FP propeller Total Power: 736kW (1,001hp) Hanshin 6LU28 1 x 4 Stroke 6 Cy. 280 x 440 736kW (1001bhp) Hanshin Nainenki Kogyo-Japan
9497115 *9HYB9*	**SHROPSHIRE** - **Bibby Navigation Ltd** ICAP Shipping Ltd SatCom: Inmarsat C 424968810 *Valletta* Malta MMSI: 249688000 Official number: 9497115	**32,957** 19,231 56,812 T/cm 58.8	Class: LR (BV) **100A1** SS 07/2009 bulk carrier CSR BC-A Nos. 2 & 4 holds may be empty ESP *IWS LI **LMC** **UMS**	**2009-07 Yangzhou Guoyu Shipbuilding Co Ltd — Yangzhou JS** Yd No: GY409 Loa 189.99 (BB) Br ex - Dght 12.800 Lbp 185.00 Br md 32.26 Dpth 18.00 Welded, 1 dk	**(A21A2BC) Bulk Carrier** Grain: 71,634; Bale: 68,200 Compartments: 5 Ho, ER 5 Ha: ER Cranes: 4x36t	**1 oil engine** driving 1 FP propeller Total Power: 9,480kW (12,889hp) 14.5kn Wartsila 6RT-flex50 1 x 2 Stroke 6 Cy. 500 x 2050 9480kW (12889bhp) Yichang Marine Diesel Engine Co Ltd-China AuxGen: 3 x 600kW 60Hz a.c Fuel: 2000.0
9221293 *MCNJ9* -	**SHROVE** *ex* Bergslep *-2003* **Londonderry Port & Harbour Commissioners (Foyle Port) (Foyle Marine Services) (Foyle Consulting Engineers)** - *Londonderry* *United Kingdom* MMSI: 235013522 Official number: 908410	**112** 44 -		**2000-05 Longva Mek. Verksted AS — Gursken** Yd No: 26 Loa 17.00 Br ex - Dght - Lbp 15.00 Br md 8.00 Dpth 4.45 Welded, 1 dk	**(B32A2ST) Tug**	**2 oil engines** geared to sc. shafts driving 2 Directional propellers Total Power: 1,940kW (2,638hp) Caterpillar 3512TA 2 x Vee 4 Stroke 12 Cy. 170 x 190 each-970kW (1319bhp) Caterpillar Inc-USA
8897540 - -	**SHS-32** - **Turkmen Shipping Co (Turkmenistanyn Denyiz Paroxodjylygy)** - *Turkmenbashy* *Turkmenistan* Official number: 804189	*297* - 374	Class: (RS)	**1985 Chkalovskiy Sudostroitelnyy Zavod im. "Lenina" — Chkalovsk** Yd No: 18 Loa 47.90 Br ex 8.22 Dght 1.900 Lbp 47.34 Br md - Dpth 2.40 Welded, 1 dk	**(B34A2SH) Hopper, Motor**	**1 oil engine** geared to sc. shaft driving 1 FP propeller Total Power: 165kW (224hp) 5.8kn Daldizel 6CHSPN2A18-225 1 x 4 Stroke 6 Cy. 180 x 220 165kW (224bhp) Daldizel-Khabarovsk Fuel: 8.0 (d.f.)
8897538 - -	**SHS-65** - **Turkmen Shipping Co (Turkmenistanyn Denyiz Paroxodjylygy)** - *Turkmenbashy* *Turkmenistan* Official number: 941117	**297** - 374	Class: (RS)	**1994 AO Chkalovskaya Sudoverf — Chkalovsk** Yd No: 65 Loa 47.90 Br ex 8.22 Dght 1.900 Lbp 47.34 Br md - Dpth 2.40 Welded, 1 dk	**(B34A2SH) Hopper, Motor**	**1 oil engine** geared to sc. shaft driving 1 FP propeller Total Power: 165kW (224hp) 5.8kn Daldizel 6CHSPN2A18-225 1 x 4 Stroke 6 Cy. 180 x 220 165kW (224bhp) Daldizel-Khabarovsk AuxGen: 1 x 12kW a.c Fuel: 8.0 (d.f.)

No. / Call sign	Name / Owner	Tonnage	Class	Builder / Dimensions	Type	Machinery
8211801 ERRE -	**SHT HUSEYIN AKIL** ex Ephesus -2012 ex Orka -2007 ex Ork -2006 ex Orka -2005 ex Storm -2001 ex Maas -1997 ex Stern -1995 ex Maas -1993 **Vegamar Denizcilik ve Ticaret Sti** - Giurgiulesti Moldova MMSI: 214181805	**1,316** 749 2,175	Class: IC (GL)	**1983-04 Machinefabriek en Scheepswerf Vervako B.V. — Heusden** Yd No: 2859 Lengthened-1988 Loa 73.70 Br ex 11.41 Dght 4.192 Lbp 69.86 Br md 11.31 Dpth 5.21 Welded, 1 dk	**(A31A2GX) General Cargo Ship** Double Bottom Partial Compartment Length Grain: 2,180; Bale: 2,820 Compartments: 1 Ho, ER 1 Ha: ER (47.1 x 8.5)	**1 oil engine** with clutches, flexible couplings & sr reverse geared to sc. shaft driving 1 FP propeller Total Power: 777kW (1,056hp) 9.0kn G.M. (Detroit Diesel) 12V-149-TI 1 x Vee 2 Stroke 12 Cy. 146 x 146 777kW (1056bhp) General Motors Detroit DieselAllison Divn-USA AuxGen: 2 x 64kW 380/220V a.c Thrusters: 1 Tunnel thruster (f)
7334632 UETE -	**SHTIL** ex Pluton -2004 **E V Trusova** Flotservice Co Ltd (OOO 'Flotservis') Taganrog Russia MMSI: 273316060	*140* 42 47	Class: RS (BR)	**1966-11 VEB Schiffswerft "Edgar Andre" — Magdeburg** Yd No: 2826 Loa 26.43 Br ex 8.03 Dght 3.000 Lbp 23.33 Br md 7.60 Dpth 3.51 Welded, 1 dk	**(B32A2ST) Tug** Ice Capable	**1 oil engine** driving 1 CP propeller Total Power: 552kW (750hp) 11.5kn S.K.L. 6NVD48A-U 1 x 4 Stroke 6 Cy. 320 x 480 552kW (750bhp) VEB Schwermaschinenbau "KarlLiebknecht" (SKL)-Magdeburg AuxGen: 2 x 64kW 380V a.c Fuel: 25.0 (d.f.)
8727795 - -	**SHTIL** - **State Enterprise Makhachkala International Sea Commercial Port** - Makhachkala Russia Official number: 851264	**235** 120 455		**1985-12 Bakinskiy Sudostroitelnyy Zavod im Vano Sturua — Baku** Yd No: 380 Loa 35.17 Br ex 8.01 Dght 3.120 Lbp 33.25 Br md - Dpth 3.60 Welded, 1 dk	**(B34G2SE) Pollution Control Vessel** Liq: 468; Liq (Oil): 468 Compartments: 10 Ta Ice Capable	**1 oil engine** geared to sc. shaft driving 1 FP propeller Total Power: 166kW (226hp) 8.1kn Daldizel 6CHNSP18/22 1 x 4 Stroke 6 Cy. 180 x 220 166kW (226bhp) Daldizel-Khabarovsk AuxGen: 1 x 50kW, 1 x 30kW Fuel: 11.0 (d.f.)
8933241 UFKH -	**SHTORM** ex Valeriy Ostapeyev -1998 **Sotsialisticheskiy Put Fishing Collective (Rybolovetskiy Kolkhoz 'Sotsialisticheskiy Put')** - Taganrog Russia	**104** 31 58	Class: RS	**1994-10 AO Azovskaya Sudoverf — Azov** Yd No: 1063 Loa 26.50 Br ex 6.59 Dght 2.360 Lbp 22.90 Br md 6.50 Dpth 3.05 Welded, 1 dk	**(B11A2FS) Stern Trawler** Ins: 48	**1 oil engine** geared to sc. shaft driving 1 FP propeller Total Power: 165kW (224hp) 9.3kn Daldizel 6CHNSP18/22 1 x 4 Stroke 6 Cy. 180 x 220 165kW (224bhp) Daldizel-Khabarovsk AuxGen: 2 x 30kW Fuel: 9.0 (d.f.)
8227032 - -	**SHTORM** - **Trading House Mortrans Co Ltd** Mortrans Co Ltd Vladivostok Russia MMSI: 273446450 Official number: 832422	*124* 37 16	Class: RS	**1983-12 Ilyichyovskiy Sudoremontnyy Zavod im. "50-letiya SSSR" — Ilyichyovsk** Yd No: 24 Loa 28.71 Br ex 6.35 Dght 1.600 Lbp 27.00 Br md - Dpth 2.49 Welded, 1 dk	**(A37B2PS) Passenger Ship** Passengers: unberthed: 116	**2 oil engines** driving 2 FP propellers Total Power: 220kW (300hp) 10.4kn Barnaultransmash 3D6C 2 x 4 Stroke 6 Cy. 150 x 180 each-110kW (150bhp) Barnaultransmash-Barnaul AuxGen: 2 x 1kW Fuel: 2.0 (d.f.)
8933796 - -	**SHTURMAN** - **SRZ Ltd** - Mariupol Ukraine Official number: 721821	**192** 57 68	Class: (RS)	**1972 "Petrozavod" — Leningrad** Yd No: 812 Loa 29.30 Br ex 8.49 Dght 3.250 Lbp 27.00 Br md - Dpth 4.35 Welded, 1 dk	**(B21A2OC) Crew/Supply Vessel** Ice Capable	**2 oil engines** driving 2 CP propellers Total Power: 882kW (1,200hp) 11.4kn Russkiy 6D30/50-4-2 2 x 2 Stroke 6 Cy. 300 x 500 each-441kW (600bhp) Mashinostroitelnyy Zavod"Russkiy-Dizel"-Leningrad AuxGen: 1 x 50kW, 1 x 25kW Fuel: 43.0 (d.f.)
1005942 ZCRL -	**SHU SHE II** ex Pestifer I -2012 ex Pestifer -2009 **Red Eagle Yachting** - SatCom: Inmarsat M 631944115 George Town Cayman Islands (British) MMSI: 319441000 Official number: 731910	**620** 186 -	Class: LR ✠ **100A1** SS 08/2008 Yacht ✠ **LMC** **UMS** Cable: 440.0/22.0 U2 (a)	**1998-08 Italam '86 Srl. — Ancona** Yd No: 114 Loa 49.75 (BB) Br ex - Dght 3.350 Lbp 47.33 Br md 9.18 Dpth 5.15 Welded, 1 dk	**(X11A2YP) Yacht**	**2 oil engines** with clutches, flexible couplings & sr reverse geared to sc. shafts driving 2 FP propellers Total Power: 2,984kW (4,058hp) 17.0kn Caterpillar 3516B-TA 2 x Vee 4 Stroke 16 Cy. 170 x 190 each-1492kW (2029bhp) Caterpillar Inc-USA AuxGen: 2 x 155kW 380V 50Hz a.c, 1 x 88kW 380V 50Hz a.c Thrusters: 1 Thwart. FP thruster (f)
6720535 HZQF -	**SHUAIBA** - **Bakri Navigation Co Ltd** Red Sea Marine Services Dammam Saudi Arabia MMSI: 403536000 Official number: 859	**373** 114 -	Class: (LR) (GL) ✠ Classed LR until 16/12/99	**1967-06 Tokushima Zosen Sangyo K.K. — Komatsushima** Yd No: 257 Loa 37.83 Br ex 9.28 Dght 3.817 Lbp 34.22 Br md 9.15 Dpth 4.55 Riveted\Welded	**(B32A2ST) Tug**	**1 oil engine** driving 1 CP propeller Total Power: 1,545kW (2,101hp) Hanshin 6L46SH 1 x 4 Stroke 6 Cy. 460 x 680 1545kW (2101bhp) Hanshin Nainenki Kogyo-Japan AuxGen: 2 x 88kW 225V 50Hz a.c
8202783 A7D4008 -	**SHUAIBA** - **Qatar Petroleum** - Doha Qatar Official number: 066/83	**144** 43 -	Class: (LR) ✠ Classed LR until 1/7/07	**1982-11 Fritimco B.V. — Bergum** (Hull) **1982-11 B.V. Scheepswerf Damen — Gorinchem** Yd No: 4630 Loa 30.89 Br ex 6.74 Dght 1.650 Lbp 27.64 Br md 6.53 Dpth 3.59 Welded, 1 dk	**(B21A2OC) Crew/Supply Vessel** Passengers: unberthed: 12	**2 oil engines** with clutches, flexible couplings & sr reverse geared to sc. shafts driving 2 FP propellers Total Power: 2,088kW (2,838hp) 22.0kn M.T.U. 12V396TB83 2 x Vee 4 Stroke 12 Cy. 165 x 185 each-1044kW (1419bhp) MTU Friedrichshafen GmbH-Friedrichshafen AuxGen: 2 x 60kW 400V 50Hz a.c Fuel: 14.0 (d.f.) 6.0pd
8847387 BWFT -	**SHUANG FENG SHAN** - **Fujian Shipping Co (FUSCO)** - Fuzhou, Fujian China MMSI: 412906000	*2,255* 1,231 3,244	Class: (CC)	**1991 Tianjin Xingang Shipyard — Tianjin** Loa 81.15 Br ex - Dght 5.200 Lbp 76.00 Br md 15.00 Dpth 6.80 Welded, 1 dk	**(A33A2CC) Container Ship (Fully Cellular)** TEU 100 C Ho 54 TEU C Dk 46 TEU Compartments: 2 Cell Ho, ER 2 Ha: 2 (19.2 x 10.8)ER	**1 oil engine** geared to sc. shaft driving 1 FP propeller Total Power: 971kW (1,320hp) Chinese Std. Type 6320ZCD 1 x 4 Stroke 6 Cy. 320 x 440 971kW (1320bhp) Guangzhou Diesel Engine Factory CoLtd-China AuxGen: 3 x 120kW 400V a.c
8749066 BH2963 -	**SHUANG LIAN** ex Yung Chuan No. 2 -2011 **Shen Lian Fishery Co** - Kaohsiung Chinese Taipei Official number: 8564	**420** 143 -		**1983-08 Shin Tien Erh Shipbuilding Co, Ltd — Kaohsiung** Loa 48.60 Br ex - Dght 3.150 Lbp - Br md 7.80 Dpth 3.52 Welded, 1 dk	**(B11B2FV) Fishing Vessel**	**1 oil engine** driving 1 Propeller Sumiyoshi 1 x 4 Stroke Sumiyoshi Marine Diesel Co Ltd-Japan
9406740 BPLR -	**SHUANG LONG HAI** ex Wan Lin 1 Hao -2010 ex Wan Lin No. 1 -2006 **CSIC-IMC Shipping Co Ltd** - SatCom: Inmarsat C 441203519 Shanghai China MMSI: 412373530	**2,974** 1,269 4,172 T/cm 11.9	Class: CC	**2006-09 East China Shipbuilding Co Ltd — Taixing JS** Yd No: 3500-01 Loa 90.00 (BB) Br ex 15.22 Dght 5.600 Lbp 84.00 Br md 15.20 Dpth 7.20 Welded, 1 dk	**(A12B2TR) Chemical/Products Tanker** Double Hull (13F) Liq: 4,339; Liq (Oil): 4,350 Cargo Heating Coils Compartments: 12 Wing Ta, 2 Wing Slop Ta, ER 14 Cargo Pump (s): 14x120m³/hr Manifold: Bow/CM: 44.1m	**2 oil engines** reduction geared to sc. shafts driving 2 FP propellers Total Power: 2,160kW (2,936hp) 11.5kn Wartsila 6L20C 2 x 4 Stroke 6 Cy. 200 x 280 each-1080kW (1468bhp) Wartsila Finland Oy-Finland AuxGen: 2 x 500kW a.c Fuel: 68.0 (d.f.) 137.0 (r.f.)
9291872 - -	**SHUANG TAI 8** - **Guangdong Shuangtai Transport Group Co Ltd** - Hai'an, Guangdong China MMSI: 412466570 Official number: 03R2008	**4,504** 2,342 1,043	Class: (CC)	**2003-04 Kouan Shipbuilding Industry Co — Taizhou JS** Yd No: KA201 Loa 90.75 Br ex - Dght - Lbp 80.00 Br md 18.00 Dpth 5.40 Welded	**(A36A2PR) Passenger/Ro-Ro Ship (Vehicles)**	**2 oil engines** geared to sc. shafts driving 2 Propellers Total Power: 2,648kW (3,600hp)
9302346 BTQI -	**SHUANG TAI 9** - **Guangdong Shuangtai Transport Group Co Ltd** - Hai'an, Guangdong China MMSI: 412466710	**4,504** 2,342 1,043	Class: CC	**2003-09 Kouan Shipbuilding Industry Co — Taizhou JS** Yd No: KA202 Loa 90.75 Br ex - Dght - Lbp 83.00 Br md 18.00 Dpth 5.40 Welded, 1 dk	**(A36A2PR) Passenger/Ro-Ro Ship (Vehicles)**	**2 oil engines** driving 1 FP propeller Total Power: 2,650kW (3,602hp) Chinese Std. Type LB8250ZLC 2 x 4 Stroke 8 Cy. 250 x 320 each-1325kW (1801bhp) Zibo Diesel Engine Factory-China
9663685 - -	**SHUANG TAI 11** - **Guangdong Shuangtai Transport Group Co Ltd** - Hai'an, Guangdong China MMSI: 413718000	**5,195** - 600		**2009-04 Taizhou Kouan Shipbuilding Co Ltd — Taizhou JS** Loa 93.96 Br ex - Dght 3.650 Lbp - Br md 19.00 Dpth 5.40 Welded, 1 dk	**(A36A2PR) Passenger/Ro-Ro Ship (Vehicles)** Passengers: unberthed: 650 Vehicles: 36	**1 oil engine** driving 1 Propeller
9663697 - -	**SHUANG TAI 12** - **Guangdong Shuangtai Transport Group Co Ltd** - Hai'an, Guangdong China MMSI: 413719000	**5,195** - 600		**2009-04 Taizhou Kouan Shipbuilding Co Ltd — Taizhou JS** Loa 93.96 Br ex - Dght 3.650 Lbp - Br md 19.00 Dpth 5.40 Welded, 1 dk	**(A36A2PR) Passenger/Ro-Ro Ship (Vehicles)** Passengers: unberthed: 650 Vehicles: 36	**1 oil engine** driving 1 Propeller

IMO / Call sign	Name / Owner / Registry	Tonnage	Class	Build / Dimensions	Type / Cargo	Machinery
9663659 - -	**SHUANG TAI 16** - **Guangdong Shuangtai Transportation (Group) Co Ltd** - *Zhanjiang, Guangdong* *China*	**8,410** 4,541 2,000	Class: CC	**2012-11 Taizhou Kouan Shipbuilding Co Ltd — Taizhou JS** Yd No: TK0410 Loa 111.98 Br ex - Dght 4.600 Lbp 103.00 Br md 20.50 Dpth 6.10 Welded, 1 dk	**(A36A2PR) Passenger/Ro-Ro Ship (Vehicles)** Passengers: unberthed: 680 Vehicles: 40	**2 oil engines** reduction geared to sc. shafts driving 2 CP propellers Total Power: 2,940kW (3,998hp) 13.0kn Chinese Std. Type LB8250ZLC 1 x 4 Stroke 8 Cy. 250 x 320 1470kW (1999bhp)
9640267 - -	**SHUANG TAI 18** - **Guangdong Shuangtai Transport Group Co Ltd** - *Hai'an, Guangdong* *China* MMSI: 413469140	**3,000** - 500	Class: CC (Class contemplated)	**2011-08 Taizhou Kouan Shipbuilding Co Ltd — Taizhou JS** Yd No: TK0406 Loa 110.00 Br ex - Dght 6.000 Lbp - Br md 20.30 Dpth - Welded, 1 dk	**(A36A2PR) Passenger/Ro-Ro Ship (Vehicles)** Passengers: unberthed: 960 Cars: 42	**1 oil engine** driving 1 Propeller
9663661 - -	**SHUANG TAI 19** - **Guangdong Shuangtai Transport Group Co Ltd** - *Hai'an, Guangdong* *China* MMSI: 413469150	**3,000** - 500	Class: CC (Class contemplated)	**2011-10 Taizhou Kouan Shipbuilding Co Ltd — Taizhou JS** Yd No: TK0408 Loa - Br ex - Dght - Lbp 110.00 Br md 20.30 Dpth 6.00 Welded, 1 dk	**(A36A2PR) Passenger/Ro-Ro Ship (Vehicles)** Passengers: unberthed: 960 Vehicles: 42	**1 oil engine** driving 1 Propeller
9256145 - -	**SHUANG TAI YI HAO** - **Guangdong Shuangtai Transport Group Co Ltd** - *Hai'an, Guangdong* *China* MMSI: 412468110 Official number: 95K4026	**278** 84 26		**2000 Guangxi Wuzhou Shipyard — Wuzhou GX** Loa 30.00 Br ex - Dght - Lbp 27.35 Br md 9.50 Dpth 3.00 Welded, 1 dk	**(A37B2PS) Passenger Ship**	**1 oil engine** driving 1 FP propeller M.T.U. 1 x 4 Stroke MTU Friedrichshafen GmbH-Friedrichshafen
8972443 *V7QC3* -	**SHUBRA II** *ex* Nira *-2008* *ex* Beluga *-2008* *ex* Frequency *-2008* *ex* La Baronessa *-1999* **Phoenix Global Ltd** - *Jaluit* *Marshall Islands* MMSI: 538070567 Official number: 70567	**987** 296 -	Class: LR (AB) **100A1** SS 08/2012 SSC Yacht, mono, G6 **LMC**	**1998-11 Palmer Johnson Yachts LLC — Sturgeon Bay WI** Yd No: 228 Loa 59.40 Br ex 10.52 Dght 4.130 Lbp 51.56 Br md 10.50 Dpth 5.55 Welded, 1 dk	**(X11A2YP) Yacht** Hull Material: Aluminium Alloy	**2 oil engines** sr geared to sc. shafts driving 2 CP propellers Total Power: 3,044kW (4,138hp) Caterpillar 3512B 2 x Vee 4 Stroke 12 Cy. 170 x 190 each-1522kW (2069bhp) (new engine 1998) Caterpillar Inc-USA AuxGen: 3 x 160kW 380V 50Hz a.c
7110725 - -	**SHUE CHI** - **Shue Chi Fishing Co Ltd** - *Kaohsiung* *Chinese Taipei*	*150* 105 81		**1971 Taiwan Machinery Manufacturing Corp. — Kaohsiung** Yd No: 499 Loa 33.91 Br ex 5.85 Dght 2.413 Lbp 29.72 Br md 5.82 Dpth 2.82 Welded, 1 dk	**(B11B2FV) Fishing Vessel**	**1 oil engine** driving 1 FP propeller Total Power: 368kW (500hp) 9.0kn Niigata 6M26HS 1 x 4 Stroke 6 Cy. 260 x 400 368kW (500bhp) Niigata Engineering Co Ltd-Japan
7110804 - -	**SHUE CHI No. 2** - **Shue Chi Fishing Co Ltd** - *Kaohsiung* *Chinese Taipei*	*150* 105 81		**1971 Taiwan Machinery Manufacturing Corp. — Kaohsiung** Yd No: 500 Loa 33.91 Br ex 5.85 Dght 2.413 Lbp 29.72 Br md 5.82 Dpth 2.82 Welded, 1 dk	**(B11B2FV) Fishing Vessel**	**1 oil engine** driving 1 FP propeller Total Power: 368kW (500hp) 9.0kn Niigata 6M26HS 1 x 4 Stroke 6 Cy. 260 x 400 368kW (500bhp) Niigata Engineering Co Ltd-Japan
9363194 *JD2128* -	**SHUEI** - **Nobutani Kisen YK** - *Bizen, Okayama* *Japan* Official number: 140184	*499* - 1,199		**2005-07 KK Ura Kyodo Zosensho — Awaji HG** Yd No: 324 Loa 64.46 Br ex - Dght 4.270 Lbp 60.00 Br md 10.00 Dpth 4.50 Welded, 1 dk	**(A12A2TC) Chemical Tanker** Double Hull (13F) Liq: 1,230	**1 oil engine** reverse geared to sc. shaft driving 1 FP propeller Total Power: 736kW (1,001hp) 12.0kn Akasaka K28BR 1 x 4 Stroke 6 Cy. 280 x 480 736kW (1001bhp) Akasaka Tekkosho KK (Akasaka DieselLtd)-Japan
9614347 *3EXY7* -	**SHUEI** - **Coll's Maritime SA** YK Seiko Kaiun (Seiko Shipping Co Ltd) *Panama* *Panama* MMSI: 373185000 Official number: 4374912	**12,825** 6,403 19,968	Class: NK	**2012-04 Shin Kochi Jyuko K.K. — Kochi** Yd No: 7263 Loa 149.53 Br ex - Dght 8.730 Lbp 142.00 Br md 24.00 Dpth 12.40 Welded, 1 dk	**(A21A2BC) Bulk Carrier** Grain: 25,393; Bale: 24,733 Compartments: 4 Ho, ER 4 Ha: ER Cranes: 3x30.5t	**1 oil engine** driving 1 FP propeller Total Power: 5,180kW (7,043hp) 13.8kn MAN-B&W 7S35MC 1 x 2 Stroke 7 Cy. 350 x 1400 5180kW (7043bhp) Makita Corp-Japan Fuel: 1160.0
9544798 *JD2935* -	**SHUEI MARU** - **Japan Railway Construction, Transport & Technology Agency & Masunaga Kaiun Co Ltd** Fuji Transportation Co Ltd (Fuji Unyu KK) *Saiki, Oita* *Japan* MMSI: 431000972 Official number: 141050	*934* - 2,291	Class: NK	**2009-06 Suzuki Shipyard Co. Ltd. — Yokkaichi** Yd No: 723 Loa 78.75 Br ex - Dght 5.092 Lbp 74.00 Br md 12.00 Dpth 5.60 Welded, 1 dk	**(A13B2TP) Products Tanker** Double Hull (13F) Liq: 2,205; Liq (Oil): 2,205	**1 oil engine** driving 1 Propeller Total Power: 1,618kW (2,200hp) Hanshin LA32G 1 x 4 Stroke 6 Cy. 320 x 680 1618kW (2200bhp) The Hanshin Diesel Works Ltd-Japan Fuel: 70.0
8923856 *JK5467* -	**SHUEI MARU NO. 5** - **Nobutani Kisen YK** - *Bizen, Okayama* *Japan* Official number: 135303	*343* - 680		**1996-06 Hongawara Zosen K.K. — Fukuyama** Yd No: 455 Loa 52.90 Br ex - Dght 3.650 Lbp 47.60 Br md 9.00 Dpth 4.00 Welded, 1 dk	**(A12A2TC) Chemical Tanker** Liq: 683 2 Cargo Pump (s): 2x200m³/hr	**1 oil engine** driving 1 FP propeller Total Power: 736kW (1,001hp) 10.5kn Yanmar MF26-ST 1 x 4 Stroke 6 Cy. 260 x 500 736kW (1001bhp) Yanmar Diesel Engine Co Ltd-Japan
9114830 *V3GR3* -	**SHUEN FAR 168** *ex* Angel 125 *-2013* *ex* Alpha Prestige *-2012* **Thrive Most Ltd** Gold Advance Corp *Belize City* *Belize* MMSI: 312982000 Official number: 281230179	**5,537** 2,261 8,420 T/cm 18.0	Class: (NV)	**1995-09 Atlantis Shipyard Pte Ltd — Singapore** Yd No: 1016 Loa 109.79 (BB) Br ex 18.02 Dght 7.410 Lbp 102.80 Br md 18.00 Dpth 10.30 Welded, 1 dk	**(A13B2TP) Products Tanker** Double Hull (13F) Liq: 8,431; Liq (Oil): 8,909 Compartments: 12 Wing Ta, 2 Wing Slop Ta, ER 3 Cargo Pump (s): 3x700m³/hr Manifold: Bow/CM: 51.2m	**1 oil engine** driving 1 FP propeller Total Power: 2,460kW (3,345hp) 12.5kn Wartsila 6R32E 1 x 4 Stroke 6 Cy. 320 x 350 2460kW (3345bhp) Wartsila Diesel Oy-Finland AuxGen: 2 x 300kW 60Hz a.c, 1 x 300kW 60Hz a.c Fuel: 83.0 (d.f.) 331.0 (r.f.)
8947187 *S7SO* -	**SHUENN PERNG NO. 202** *ex* Jain Yung No. 202 *-2004* *ex* Jain Horn No. 202 *-1998* **Jain Yung Fishery SA** - *Victoria* *Seychelles* Official number: 50139	**599** 252 -		**1997 San Yang Shipbuilding Co., Ltd. — Kaohsiung** L reg 55.10 Br ex - Dght - Lbp 48.60 Br md 8.60 Dpth 3.75 Welded, 1 dk	**(B11B2FV) Fishing Vessel**	**1 oil engine** driving 1 FP propeller Total Power: 1,030kW (1,400hp) 12.5kn Matsui 1 x 4 Stroke 1030kW (1400bhp) Matsui Iron Works Co Ltd-Japan
7426514 - -	**SHUHAIR** - - -	*147* 51 -		**1975-06 Minami-Nippon Zosen KK — Ichikikushikino KS** Yd No: 231 Loa 28.73 Br ex 6.51 Dght - Lbp 24.52 Br md - Dpth 3.10 Welded, 1 dk	**(B11A2FT) Trawler**	**1 oil engine** driving 1 FP propeller Total Power: 368kW (500hp) Daihatsu 6DSM-18A 1 x 4 Stroke 6 Cy. 180 x 230 368kW (500bhp) Daihatsu Diesel Manufacturing Co Lt-Japan
9634878 *JD3366* -	**SHUHO** - **Shiraishi Kaiun, Ast Inc & Japan Railway Construction, Transport & Technology Agency** Shiraishi Kaiun KK *Bizen, Okayama* *Japan* MMSI: 431003635 Official number: 141684	*499* - 963	Class: NK	**2012-06 Sasaki Shipbuilding Co Ltd — Osakikamijima HS** Yd No: 676 Loa 59.37 (BB) Br ex - Dght 3.861 Lbp 56.00 Br md 10.80 Dpth 4.50 Welded, 1 dk	**(A11B2TG) LPG Tanker** Liq (Gas): 855 1 Cargo Pump (s): 1x200m³/hr	**1 oil engine** geared to sc. shaft driving 1 Propeller Total Power: 735kW (999hp) 12.0kn Hanshin LH28G 1 x 4 Stroke 6 Cy. 280 x 460 735kW (999bhp) The Hanshin Diesel Works Ltd-Japan Thrusters: 1 Tunnel thruster (f) Fuel: 89.0
9250335 *JG5652* -	**SHUHO** - **Corporation for Advanced Transport & Technology & Sumise Kaiun KK** Sumise Kaiun KK *Tokyo* *Japan* MMSI: 431301608 Official number: 137109	*8,766* - 13,399	Class: NK	**2002-01 Shin Kochi Jyuko K.K. — Kochi** Yd No: 7138 Loa 149.53 Br ex - Dght 7.135 Lbp - Br md 20.50 Dpth 9.80 Welded, 1 dk	**(A24E2BL) Limestone Carrier** Grain: 10,448 Compartments: 4 Ho, ER 4 Ha: 2 (21.6 x 10.5)2 (22.4 x 10.5)ER	**1 oil engine** driving 1 FP propeller Total Power: 4,201kW (5,712hp) 13.0kn B&W 6S35MC 1 x 2 Stroke 6 Cy. 350 x 1400 4201kW (5712bhp) Makita Corp-Japan Fuel: 530.0
9296951 *JI3614* -	**SHUHO MARU** - **Ajiro Marine Business** - *Kainan, Wakayama* *Japan* Official number: 135038	*199* - 479		**2003-06 Koa Sangyo KK — Takamatsu KG** Yd No: 618 Loa 46.84 Br ex 7.82 Dght 3.140 Lbp 43.00 Br md 7.80 Dpth 3.30 Welded, 1 dk	**(A13B2TP) Products Tanker**	**1 oil engine** geared to sc. shaft driving 1 FP propeller Total Power: 735kW (999hp) Yanmar 1 x 4 Stroke 735kW (999bhp) Yanmar Diesel Engine Co Ltd-Japan

IMO / Call sign / Flag	Name / Owner	Tonnage	Class	Construction / Dimensions	Type / Capacity	Machinery
9392200 *7JBX* -	**SHUHO MARU** **Shinomiya Tanker Co Ltd & Yoshitoshi Kaiun YK** Shinomiya Tanker KK (Shinomiya Tanker Co Ltd) *Anan, Tokushima* *Japan* MMSI: 432584000 Official number: 140473	**1,358** 484 1,445	Class: NK	**2007-03 K.K. Miura Zosensho — Saiki** Yd No: 1311 Loa 69.90 Br ex - Dght 4.548 Lbp 66.00 Br md 12.50 Dpth 5.55 Welded, 1 dk	**(A11B2TG) LPG Tanker** Liq (Gas): 1,828	**1 oil engine** driving 1 FP propeller Total Power: 1,471kW (2,000hp) Akasaka A37 1 x 4 Stroke 6 Cy. 370 x 720 1471kW (2000bhp) Akasaka Tekkosho KK (Akasaka DieselLtd)-Japan Fuel: 210.0
9084736 *XUPJ3* -	**SHUHO MARU** **Rich International Shipping Co Ltd** Dalian Heyang Shipping Agency Co Ltd *Phnom Penh* *Cambodia* MMSI: 515163000 Official number: 0993287	**1,481** 854 1,600	Class: UM (NK)	**1993-10 Hakata Zosen K.K. — Imabari** Yd No: 560 Loa 74.10 Br ex - Dght 4.071 Lbp 69.00 Br md 12.00 Dpth 6.90 Welded, 1 dk	**(A31A2GX) General Cargo Ship** Grain: 2,709; Bale: 2,640 Compartments: 1 Ho, ER 1 Ha: (40.2 x 9.1)ER	**1 oil engine** reverse geared to sc. shaft driving 1 FP propeller Total Power: 736kW (1,001hp) 11.5kn Hanshin LH30LG 1 x 4 Stroke 6 Cy. 300 x 600 736kW (1001bhp) The Hanshin Diesel Works Ltd-Japan
9057783 - -	**SHUHO MARU** - - *South Korea*	*263* - 709		**1993-01 Fujishin Zosen K.K. — Kamo** Yd No: 580 Loa 49.11 (BB) Br ex - Dght 3.700 Lbp 44.65 Br md 9.00 Dpth 4.00 Welded, 1 dk	**(A12A2TC) Chemical Tanker** Liq: 699 Compartments: 6 Ta, ER	**1 oil engine** with clutches & sr reverse geared to sc. shaft driving 1 FP propeller Total Power: 588kW (799hp) Yanmar M200-SN 1 x 4 Stroke 6 Cy. 200 x 260 588kW (799bhp) Yanmar Diesel Engine Co Ltd-Japan
9066203 *JM6198* -	**SHUHO MARU No. 25** **Shoei Kaiun KK** - *Shimonoseki, Yamaguchi* *Japan* Official number: 133534	*499* - 1,295		**1993-02 Kanmon Zosen K.K. — Shimonoseki** Yd No: 550 Loa 66.01 (BB) Br ex 10.02 Dght 4.000 Lbp 62.00 Br md 10.00 Dpth 4.50 Welded, 1 dk	**(A13B2TP) Products Tanker** Liq: 1,260; Liq (Oil): 1,260 Compartments: 8 Ta, ER	**1 oil engine** driving 1 FP propeller Total Power: 736kW (1,001hp) Yanmar MF29-UT 1 x 4 Stroke 6 Cy. 290 x 520 736kW (1001bhp) Yanmar Diesel Engine Co Ltd-Japan
9110028 *JM6373* -	**SHUHO MARU No. 31** **Shoei Kaiun KK** - *Shimonoseki, Yamaguchi* *Japan* MMSI: 431400366 Official number: 134463	*749* - 1,870		**1994-11 Kanmon Zosen K.K. — Shimonoseki** Yd No: 563 Loa 75.51 (BB) Br ex 11.42 Dght 4.550 Lbp 72.00 Br md 11.40 Dpth 5.30 Welded, 1 dk	**(A13B2TP) Products Tanker** Liq: 2,190; Liq (Oil): 2,190 Compartments: 10 Ta, ER	**1 oil engine** with clutches, flexible couplings & sr geared to sc. shaft driving 1 CP propeller Total Power: 1,839kW (2,500hp) Yanmar 6N280-EN 1 x 4 Stroke 6 Cy. 280 x 380 1839kW (2500bhp) Yanmar Diesel Engine Co Ltd-Japan Thrusters: 1 Thwart. CP thruster (f)
7735056 *BOZJ* -	**SHUI CHENG** *ex Colombo Star -1998 ex Shui Cheng -1998* *ex Shao Xing -1987* **COSCO Angang Shipping Co Ltd** - SatCom: Inmarsat A 1570705 *Dalian, Liaoning* *China* MMSI: 412186000	**10,610** 5,953 13,720	Class: (CC)	**1978-09 Shanghai Shipyard — Shanghai** Loa 161.90 (BB) Br ex - Dght 9.220 Lbp 148.00 Br md 21.20 Dpth 12.50 Welded, 2 dks	**(A31A2GX) General Cargo Ship** Grain: 19,925; Bale: 19,925; Ins: 2,600 Compartments: ER, 5 Ho 5 Ha: (12.7 x 8.0)2 (15.0 x 9.0) (9.8 x 9.0)ER (9.0 x 8.0) Derricks: 1x60t,8x10t,6x5t; Winches: 14 Ice Capable	**1 oil engine** driving 1 FP propeller Total Power: 6,620kW (9,001hp) 18.5kn Shanghai 6ESDZ76/160 1 x 2 Stroke 6 Cy. 760 x 1600 6620kW (9001bhp) Shanghai Diesel Engine Co Ltd-China AuxGen: 3 x 400kW 400V 50Hz a.c
8667957 *T3NB2* -	**SHUI YANG JIANG 2558** **Jiangsu Haisheng Municipal Engineering Construction Co Ltd** - *Tarawa* *Kiribati* Official number: K-18061405	**265** 80 -		**2006-06 Xinghua Taozhuang Tongda Shipyard — Xinghua JS** Loa 40.04 Br ex - Dght - Lbp 38.20 Br md 7.85 Dpth 2.80 Welded, 1 dk	**(A31A2GX) General Cargo Ship**	**1 oil engine** driving 1 Propeller Total Power: 131kW (178hp) Chinese Std. Type 1 x 131kW (178bhp) Shanghai Diesel Engine Co Ltd-China
9133123 *5ZNN* -	**SHUJAA** **Government of The Republic of Kenya (Kenya Navy)** - *Mombasa* *Kenya* Official number: P3130	**661** 198 144	Class: (LR) ✠ Classed LR until 20/10/99	**1996-12 Astilleros Gondan SA — Castropol** Yd No: 371 Loa 60.00 Br ex 9.91 Dght 2.612 Lbp 54.00 Br md 9.90 Dpth 6.00 Welded, 2 dks	**(B31A2SR) Research Survey Vessel**	**2 oil engines** with clutches, flexible couplings & sr geared to sc. shafts driving 2 FP propellers Total Power: 6,000kW (8,158hp) 23.0kn M.T.U. 16V956 2 x Vee 4 Stroke 16 Cy. 230 x 230 each-3000kW (4079bhp) EN Bazan de Construcciones NavalesMilitares SA-Spain AuxGen: 2 x 170kW 440V 60Hz a.c
9487392 *JD2605* -	**SHUKA MARU NO. 2** **Iwai Kaiun YK** - *Tokyo* *Japan* MMSI: 431000529 Official number: 140723	*498* - 1,287		**2008-03 Suzuki Shipyard Co. Ltd. — Yokkaichi** Yd No: 716 Loa 64.98 Br ex - Dght 4.030 Lbp 61.80 Br md 10.00 Dpth 4.50 Welded, 1 dk	**(A12B2TR) Chemical/Products Tanker** Double Hull (13F) Liq (Gas): 1,229	**1 oil engine** geared to sc. shaft driving 1 FP propeller Total Power: 1,030kW (1,400hp) 12.0kn Hanshin LH28G 1 x 4 Stroke 6 Cy. 280 x 460 1030kW (1400bhp) The Hanshin Diesel Works Ltd-Japan
9459450 *JD2480* -	**SHUKO MARU** **Seagate Corp** - *Shunan, Yamaguchi* *Japan* Official number: 140609	*221* - -		**2007-09 Kanagawa Zosen — Kobe** Yd No: 566 Loa 35.00 Br ex - Dght 3.100 Lbp 30.50 Br md 9.60 Dpth 4.17 Welded, 1 dk	**(B32A2ST) Tug**	**2 oil engines** reduction geared to sc. shafts driving 2 Propellers Total Power: 3,676kW (4,998hp) 14.5kn Niigata 6L28HX 2 x 4 Stroke 6 Cy. 280 x 370 each-1838kW (2499bhp) Niigata Engineering Co Ltd-Japan
8228115 - -	**SHUMNYY** **Preobrazheniye Trawler Fleet Base (Preobrazhenskaya Baza Tralovogo Flota)** - *Nakhodka* *Russia*	**228** - 86	Class: RS	**1984-06 Brodogradiliste 'Tito' — Belgrade** Yd No: 1095 Loa 35.84 Br ex 9.30 Dght 3.150 Lbp 30.00 Br md 9.01 Dpth 4.50 Welded, 1 dk	**(B32A2ST) Tug**	**2 oil engines** geared to sc. shafts driving 2 FP propellers Total Power: 1,854kW (2,520hp) 11.5kn Sulzer 6ASL25/30 2 x 4 Stroke 6 Cy. 250 x 300 each-927kW (1260bhp) Tvornica Dizel Motora 'Jugoturbina'-Yugoslavia Fuel: 61.0 (r.f.)
9081502 *UBMK* -	**SHUMSHU** *ex Dapkor-01 -1992* **Akvatoriya Co Ltd** - *Petropavlovsk-Kamchatskiy* *Russia* MMSI: 273813800	**190** 57 70	Class: (RS)	**1992-07 OAO Astrakhanskaya Sudoverf — Astrakhan** Yd No: 100 Loa 31.85 Br ex 7.08 Dght 2.100 Lbp 27.80 Br md 6.90 Dpth 3.15 Welded, 1 dk	**(B12B2FC) Fish Carrier** Ins: 100 Ice Capable	**1 oil engine** geared to sc. shaft driving 1 FP propeller Total Power: 232kW (315hp) 10.3kn Daldizel 6CHSPN2A18-315 1 x 4 Stroke 6 Cy. 180 x 220 232kW (315bhp) Daldizel-Khabarovsk AuxGen: 2 x 25kW a.c Fuel: 14.0 (d.f.)
7701457 *UASZ* -	**SHUMSHU 107** *ex Kyoshin Maru No. 58 -1996* **Atlantica Co Ltd** - SatCom: Inmarsat C 427320884 *Kholmsk* *Russia* MMSI: 273457700 Official number: 763735	**498** 216 260	Class: RS	**1977-04 Miho Zosensho K.K. — Shimizu** Yd No: 1059 Loa 50.60 Br ex 8.54 Dght 3.190 Lbp 44.20 Br md 8.51 Dpth 3.51 Welded, 1 dk	**(B11B2FV) Fishing Vessel** Ins: 508	**1 oil engine** driving 1 FP propeller Total Power: 809kW (1,100hp) 13.0kn Niigata 6M28GX 1 x 4 Stroke 6 Cy. 280 x 440 809kW (1100bhp) Niigata Engineering Co Ltd-Japan AuxGen: 2 x 224kW a.c Fuel: 222.0 (d.f.)
9520364 - -	**SHUN AN 09** **Anqing Shun'an Shipping Co Ltd** An Da International Shipping Co Ltd *Anqing, Anhui* *China* MMSI: 413551180	**2,880** 1,613 4,300	Class: ZC	**2008-05 Anqing Ningjiang Shipbuilding Co Ltd — Anqing AH** Yd No: 0803 Loa 95.30 Br ex - Dght 5.200 Lbp 88.78 Br md 14.80 Dpth 6.80 Welded, 1 dk	**(A21A2BC) Bulk Carrier**	**1 oil engine** reduction geared to sc. shaft driving 1 FP propeller Total Power: 735kW (999hp) Chinese Std. Type LB6250ZLC 1 x 4 Stroke 6 Cy. 250 x 320 735kW (999bhp) Zibo Diesel Engine Factory-China
8648688 *BH3290* LL964777	**SHUN AN NO. 6** **Yu Song Fishery Co Ltd** - *Kaohsiung* *Chinese Taipei* Official number: CT6-1290	**368** 160 -		**1993-04 Lin Sheng Shipbuilding Co, Ltd — Kaohsiung** Loa 40.58 Br ex 7.60 Dght - Lbp - Br md - Dpth - Welded, 1 dk	**(B11B2FV) Fishing Vessel**	**1 oil engine** driving 1 Propeller
8408064 - -	**SHUN CHANG** *ex Tian Long 15 -2008 ex Cheng Gong 15 -2008* *ex Tokin Maru No. 1 -2001* - -	**997** 558 1,600		**1984-09 K.K. Miura Zosensho — Saiki** Yd No: 711 Loa 70.57 Br ex - Dght 4.401 Lbp 67.47 Br md 11.51 Dpth 6.51 Welded, 1 dk	**(A31A2GX) General Cargo Ship**	**1 oil engine** driving 1 FP propeller Total Power: 883kW (1,201hp) Hanshin 6LUN28A 1 x 4 Stroke 6 Cy. 280 x 480 883kW (1201bhp) The Hanshin Diesel Works Ltd-Japan

No.	Name / Owners	Tonnage	Class	Construction	Type	Machinery
8514356 *BZYF5* -	**SHUN CHANG NO. 4** *ex* Hatsukei Maru No. 2 *-2013* *ex* Shiriasu Maru *-2000* **China National Fisheries Corp** - *Qinhuangdao, Hebei* *China* MMSI: 412689760 Official number: 1300001986030020	**703** 296 -		**1986-03 Tohoku Shipbuilding Co Ltd — Shiogama MG** Yd No: 216 Converted From: Stern Trawler-2001 Loa 56.32 Br ex 9.12 Dght 3.601 Lbp 49.03 Br md 9.10 Dpth 3.92 Welded, 1 dk	**(B11B2FV) Fishing Vessel**	**1 oil engine** with clutches, flexible couplings & dr reverse geared to sc. shaft driving 1 FP propeller Total Power: 1,030kW (1,400hp) Akasaka DM28AKFD 1 x 4 Stroke 6 Cy. 280 x 460 1030kW (1400bhp) Akasaka Tekkosho KK (Akasaka DieselLtd)-Japan Thrusters: 1 Thwart. CP thruster (f)
8021438 *3CM2089* -	**SHUN CHAO** *ex* Kyuho Maru No. 31 *-1998* *ex* Zuiho Maru No. 31 *-1992* **Chin Fu Fishery Co Ltd SA** - *Malabo* *Equatorial Guinea* Official number: EQ-968898	*329* 150 -		**1981-02 Niigata Engineering Co Ltd — Niigata NI** Yd No: 1703 Loa 51.57 (BB) Br ex 8.62 Dght 3.298 Lbp 45.67 Br md 8.60 Dpth 3.66 Welded, 1 dk	**(B11B2FV) Fishing Vessel**	**1 oil engine** reduction geared to sc. shaft driving 1 FP propeller Total Power: 809kW (1,100hp) Niigata 6M28AFT 1 x 4 Stroke 6 Cy. 280 x 480 809kW (1100bhp) Niigata Engineering Co Ltd-Japan
9152806 *BBUL* -	**SHUN CHENG** *ex* Shuncheng *-2011* **Qingdao Shipping Co Ltd** Qingdao Marine Shipping Co Ltd SatCom: Inmarsat B 341294910 *Qingdao, Shandong* *China* MMSI: 412949000	**6,568** 3,420 10,094	Class: CC	**1998-06 Husumer Schiffswerft Inh. Gebr. Kroeger GmbH & Co. KG — Husum** Yd No: 1526 Loa 128.00 Br ex - Dght 8.180 Lbp 119.04 Br md 18.60 Dpth 10.90 Welded, 1 dk	**(A31A2GX) General Cargo Ship** Grain: 11,927 TEU 598 C.Ho 258/20' (40') C.Dk 340/20' (40') incl. 60 ref C. Compartments: 3 Ho, ER 3 Ha: (12.5 x 10.2) (25.2 x 15.3) (37.8 x 15.3)ER	**1 oil engine** with flexible couplings & reductiongeared to sc. shaft driving 1 CP propeller Total Power: 5,400kW (7,342hp) 16.9kn MaK 8M552C 1 x 4 Stroke 8 Cy. 450 x 520 5400kW (7342bhp) MaK Motoren GmbH & Co. KG-Kiel AuxGen: 1 x 900kW 220/440V 60Hz a.c, 2 x 375kW 220/440V 60Hz a.c Thrusters: 1 Thwart. FP thruster (f)
7903108 - -	**SHUN CHUAN No. 6** *ex* Fukutoku Maru No. 1 *-1995* **Chin Hsiang Fishery Sde RL** - SatCom: Inmarsat B 333449010 *San Lorenzo* *Honduras* Official number: L-1925983	**611** 223 -		**1979-05 KK Kanasashi Zosen — Shizuoka SZ** Yd No: 2021 Loa 49.79 Br ex - Dght 3.301 Lbp 43.79 Br md 8.60 Dpth 3.66 Welded, 1 dk	**(B11B2FV) Fishing Vessel**	**1 oil engine** driving 1 FP propeller Total Power: 736kW (1,001hp) Niigata 6M28ZG 1 x 4 Stroke 6 Cy. 280 x 440 736kW (1001bhp) Niigata Engineering Co Ltd-Japan
8630241 *3FTI* -	**SHUN DA** *ex* Shun Chao *-2011* *ex* Jing An *-2011* *ex* Sumiyoshi Maru *-2003* **Shantou Shunhai Shipping Co Ltd** Sun Rising Shipmanagement Co Ltd *Panama* *Panama* MMSI: 355495000 Official number: 45196PEXTF	**2,363** 1,364 -	Class: OM (CC) (NK)	**1986-10 K.K. Miura Zosensho — Saiki** Yd No: 770 Converted From: Bulk Aggregates Carrier-2003 Lengthened-2003 Loa 89.44 Br ex 13.02 Dght 5.400 Lbp 83.79 Br md 13.00 Dpth 7.00 Welded, 1 dk	**(A33A2CC) Container Ship (Fully Cellular)** Compartments: ER	**1 oil engine** geared to sc. shaft driving 1 FP propeller Total Power: 736kW (1,001hp) 10.0kn Hanshin 6LU35G 1 x 4 Stroke 6 Cy. 350 x 550 736kW (1001bhp) The Hanshin Diesel Works Ltd-Japan
8316998 *9LY2609* -	**SHUN DA** *ex* Yong Win 9 *-2013* *ex* Hui Tong 56 *-2013* *ex* Chun Feng *-2010* *ex* Zhong Hua 1 *-2008* *ex* Arce *-1994* *ex* Tomoe 8 *-1985* **Jumbo Sino Investment Development Ltd** - *Sierra Leone* MMSI: 667003412 Official number: SL103412	**4,462** 2,405 7,327	Class: CC (NK)	**1984-03 Asakawa Zosen K.K. — Imabari** Yd No: 321 Loa 114.10 (BB) Br ex - Dght 7.022 Lbp 105.42 Br md 16.51 Dpth 8.21 Welded, 1 dk	**(A12B2TR) Chemical/Products Tanker** Double Bottom Entire Compartment Length Liq: 8,332; Liq (Oil): 8,332 Cargo Heating Coils Compartments: 12 Ta, ER 6 Cargo Pump (s) Manifold: Bow/CM: 45m	**1 oil engine** driving 1 FP propeller Total Power: 2,850kW (3,875hp) 12.5kn Mitsubishi 6UEC37/88H 1 x 2 Stroke 6 Cy. 370 x 880 2850kW (3875bhp) Akasaka Tekkosho KK (Akasaka DieselLtd)-Japan AuxGen: 3 x 220kW 445V a.c
9078543 *XUCY4* -	**SHUN DA** *ex* Lofty Peace *-2011* *ex* Erimo Maru *-2010* **The Sisters Ltd** Palace Rose Ltd *Phnom Penh* *Cambodia* MMSI: 515104000 Official number: 1194744	**1,470** 627 1,558	Class: UM	**1994-01 K.K. Matsuura Zosensho — Osakikamijima** Yd No: 505 Loa 75.88 (BB) Br ex 12.02 Dght 4.210 Lbp 70.00 Br md 12.00 Dpth 7.20 Welded, 2 dks	**(A31A2GX) General Cargo Ship** Compartments: 1 Ho, ER	**1 oil engine** driving 1 FP propeller Total Power: 735kW (999hp) 9.5kn Hanshin LH30L 1 x 4 Stroke 6 Cy. 300 x 600 735kW (999bhp) The Hanshin Diesel Works Ltd-Japan Thrusters: 1 Thwart. FP thruster (f)
9122772 *BXAP* -	**SHUN DE** - **Shun Gang Passenger Corp** Chu Kong Shipping Enterprises (Holdings) Co Ltd *Shunde, Guangdong* *China* MMSI: 412460910	**543** 179 46	Class: CC	**1995-09 Austal Ships Pty Ltd — Fremantle WA** Yd No: 116 Loa 40.10 (BB) Br ex 11.81 Dght 1.266 Lbp 38.00 Br md 11.50 Dpth 3.80 Welded, 1 dk	**(A37B2PS) Passenger Ship** Hull Material: Aluminium Alloy Passengers: unberthed: 332	**2 oil engines** reduction geared to sc. shafts driving 2 Water jets Total Power: 4,000kW (5,438hp) 39.5kn M.T.U. 16V396TE74L 2 x Vee 4 Stroke 16 Cy. 165 x 185 each-2000kW (2719bhp) (new engine 2002) MTU Friedrichshafen GmbH-Friedrichshafen AuxGen: 2 x 108kW 380V a.c
8011598 *JVME4* -	**SHUN FA** *ex* An Da You 3 *-2009* *ex* Koyu Maru No. 8 *-1994* **Shun Fa (HK) Marine Co Ltd** - *Ulaanbaatar* *Mongolia* MMSI: 457418000 Official number: 29011180	**1,336** 824 2,233	Class: (CC)	**1980-07 Yamanaka Zosen K.K. — Imabari** Yd No: 226 Loa - Br ex - Dght 4.800 Lbp 74.02 Br md 12.01 Dpth 5.52 Welded, 1 dk	**(A13B2TP) Products Tanker**	**1 oil engine** driving 1 FP propeller Total Power: 1,618kW (2,200hp) Hanshin 6LU38 1 x 4 Stroke 6 Cy. 380 x 580 1618kW (2200bhp) The Hanshin Diesel Works Ltd-Japan
7725099 - -	**SHUN FA** *ex* Ze Zhan *-2001* *ex* Shi Fa *-2001* *ex* Haifa 18 *-1998* *ex* Taisei Maru *-1998* **Shantou Xiangji Water Transportation Ltd**	**975** 546 1,053		**1978-01 Yamanaka Zosen K.K. — Imabari** Yd No: 171 Loa - Br ex - Dght - Lbp 60.03 Br md 11.02 Dpth 6.02 Riveted\Welded, 1 dk	**(A31A2GX) General Cargo Ship**	**1 oil engine** driving 1 FP propeller Total Power: 1,177kW (1,600hp) Hanshin 6LU32 1 x 4 Stroke 6 Cy. 320 x 510 1177kW (1600bhp) Hanshin Nainenki Kogyo-Japan
8956736 *BAMQ* -	**SHUN FA 1** - **Dalian Haixing Shipping Co Ltd** - *Dalian, Liaoning* *China* Official number: 030010000009	**218** 65 145	Class: CC	**1991-04 Huanghai Shipbuilding Co Ltd — Rongcheng SD** Loa 41.00 Br ex - Dght 2.790 Lbp 35.00 Br md 7.20 Dpth 3.70 Welded, 1 dk	**(B12B2FC) Fish Carrier**	**1 oil engine** geared to sc. shaft driving 1 FP propeller Total Power: 294kW (400hp) Chinese Std. Type 6300 1 x 4 Stroke 6 Cy. 300 x 380 294kW (400bhp) Zibo Diesel Engine Factory-China
8956748 - -	**SHUN FA 2** - **Dalian Haixing Shipping Co Ltd** - *Dalian, Liaoning* *China*	**298** 94 173	Class: (CC)	**1995-12 Yantai Fishing Vessel Shipyard — Yantai SD** Loa 44.98 Br ex - Dght 2.950 Lbp 38.60 Br md 7.80 Dpth 3.90 Welded, 1 dk	**(B12B2FC) Fish Carrier**	**1 oil engine** geared to sc. shaft driving 1 FP propeller Total Power: 662kW (900hp) Chinese Std. Type 8300 1 x 4 Stroke 8 Cy. 300 x 380 662kW (900bhp) Zibo Diesel Engine Factory-China
8964886 *BASQ* -	**SHUN FA 6** - **Zhang Renyu** Dalian Hualong Group Aquatic Product Co Ltd SatCom: Inmarsat C 451561210 *Dalian, Liaoning* *China*	**140** 42 -	Class: (CC)	**1997 Changhai Zhangzidao Shiprepair & Building Yard — Changhai County LN** Loa 34.27 Br ex - Dght 2.200 Lbp 28.50 Br md 6.20 Dpth 2.90 Welded, 1 dk	**(B11B2FV) Fishing Vessel**	**1 oil engine** geared to sc. shaft driving 1 FP propeller Total Power: 260kW (353hp) Chinese Std. Type Z6170ZL 1 x 4 Stroke 6 Cy. 170 x 200 260kW (353bhp) Zibo Diesel Engine Factory-China
8622127 *9LY2399* -	**SHUN FA 6** *ex* Sea Plain No. 1 *-2008* *ex* Jin Sheng *-2006* *ex* Hoei Maru *-2002* **Shanghai Jinduo Shipping Co Ltd** Shandong Jinghai Industrial Group Co Ltd *Freetown* *Sierra Leone* MMSI: 667003202 Official number: SL103202	**1,186** 598 1,599	Class: IS	**1983-07 Y.K. Tokai Zosensho — Tsukumi** Yd No: 625 Loa 70.31 Br ex - Dght 4.420 Lbp 65.99 Br md 11.51 Dpth 6.51 Welded, 1 dk	**(A31A2GX) General Cargo Ship**	**1 oil engine** driving 1 FP propeller Total Power: 956kW (1,300hp) 11.0kn Hanshin 6LUN28A 1 x 4 Stroke 6 Cy. 280 x 480 956kW (1300bhp) The Hanshin Diesel Works Ltd-Japan
8964898 *BASR* -	**SHUN FA 7** - **Dalian Zhangzi Island Aquatic Product Refrigerating & Transportation Co** Dalian Jinzhou Shipping Co *Dalian, Liaoning* *China*	**140** 42 -	Class: CC	**1997 Changhai Zhangzidao Shiprepair & Building Yard — Changhai County LN** Loa 34.27 Br ex - Dght 2.200 Lbp 28.50 Br md 6.20 Dpth 2.90 Welded, 1 dk	**(B11B2FV) Fishing Vessel**	**1 oil engine** geared to sc. shaft driving 1 FP propeller Total Power: 260kW (353hp) Chinese Std. Type Z6170ZL 1 x 4 Stroke 6 Cy. 170 x 200 260kW (353bhp) Zibo Diesel Engine Factory-China
8720319 - -	**SHUN FA 8** *ex* Chang Jiang No. 7 *-2011* *ex* Kaijin Maru No. 1 *-2005* - -	**1,376** 524 1,591		**1988-04 Mategata Zosen K.K. — Namikata** Yd No: 1018 Loa 73.25 Br ex 11.52 Dght 4.270 Lbp 68.50 Br md 11.50 Dpth 7.10 Welded, 1 dk	**(A31A2GX) General Cargo Ship**	**1 oil engine** driving 1 FP propeller Total Power: 1,177kW (1,600hp) 11.5kn Hanshin 6LUN30ARG 1 x 4 Stroke 6 Cy. 300 x 480 1177kW (1600bhp) (made 1988) The Hanshin Diesel Works Ltd-Japan

8975964 *BZZJ5* -	**SHUN FA 8** *ex Jin Fa -2009* **Dalian Haixing Shipping Co Ltd** - *Dalian, Liaoning* *China* Official number: 030010000011	**280** 84 189	Class: CC	**1990-08 Dalian Fishing Vessel Co — Dalian LN** Loa 47.90 Br ex - Dght 2.800 Lbp 41.10 Br md 7.60 Dpth 3.80 Welded, 1 dk	**(A31A2GX) General Cargo Ship** Grain: 279 Compartments: 2 Ho, ER 2 Ha: ER 2 (2.2 x 2.0)	**1 oil engine** driving 1 Propeller Total Power: 441kW (600hp) Chinese Std. Type DY8300ZC 1 x 4 Stroke 8 Cy. 300 x 380 441kW (600bhp) Dalian Fishing Vessel Co-China
9234460 *BAJA* -	**SHUN FA 8** **Dalian Haixing Shipping Co Ltd** - *Dalian, Liaoning* *China* Official number: 00L2011	**137** 48 87	Class: (CC)	**2000-06 Rongcheng Haida Shipbuilding Co Ltd — Rongcheng SD** Yd No: HD89979 Loa 36.00 Br ex - Dght 2.180 Lbp 29.00 Br md 6.30 Dpth 2.85 Welded, 1 dk	**(B12C2FL) Live Fish Carrier (Well Boat)** Compartments: 3 Ho 2 Ha: (1.5 x 1.4) (2.5 x 1.4)	**1 oil engine** geared to sc. shaft driving 1 FP propeller Total Power: 220kW (299hp) 11.0kn Chinese Std. Type G6190ZLC 1 x 4 Stroke 6 Cy. 190 x 210 220kW (299bhp) Jinan Diesel Engine Co Ltd-China AuxGen: 1 x 24kW 400V a.c, 1 x 16kW 400V a.c
9093892 *XUGR2* -	**SHUN FA 11** *ex Shun Fa 10 -2013 ex Daniel No. 11 -2012* *ex Sun Yard -2011 ex Cheng Gong 28 -2007* **Hong Kong Shun Fa International Shipping Ltd (China)** - *Phnom Penh* *Cambodia* MMSI: 514056000 Official number: 1387201	**1,483** 929 -	Class: IS	**1987-01 Zhoushan Putuo Yaofeng Shipbuilding Co Ltd — Zhoushan ZJ** Loa 73.20 Br ex - Dght 5.000 Lbp 68.00 Br md 11.50 Dpth 6.70 Welded, 1 dk	**(A31A2GX) General Cargo Ship**	**1 oil engine** driving 1 Propeller Total Power: 735kW (999hp) Hanshin 6LUN28ARG 1 x 4 Stroke 6 Cy. 280 x 480 735kW (999bhp) The Hanshin Diesel Works Ltd-Japan
8820157 *9LY2598* -	**SHUN FA 16** *ex Chang Jiang No. 8 -2013* *ex Tatsuhiro Maru No. 5 -1998* **Hong Kong Shun Fa International Shipping Ltd (China)** - *Freetown* *Sierra Leone* MMSI: 667003401	**1,349** 538 1,600	Class: IS	**1988-10 Higaki Zosen K.K. — Imabari** Yd No: 362 Loa 74.43 (BB) Br ex 11.72 Dght 4.150 Lbp 69.50 Br md 11.70 Dpth 7.13 Welded, 2 dks	**(A31A2GX) General Cargo Ship** Bale: 2,982 Compartments: 1 Ho, ER 1 Ha: ER	**1 oil engine** with clutches & sr reverse geared to sc. shaft driving 1 FP propeller Total Power: 1,030kW (1,400hp) Hanshin LH28G 1 x 4 Stroke 6 Cy. 280 x 460 1030kW (1400bhp) (made 1988) The Hanshin Diesel Works Ltd-Japan
8510128 *XUSR8* -	**SHUN FA 19** *ex New Century 1 -2013 ex Taiyo Maru -2004* **Wealth Ocean Ltd** - *Phnom Penh* *Cambodia* MMSI: 514008000 Official number: 0885018	**1,491** 645 1,599	Class: (CC)	**1985-10 Kochi Jyuko (Kaisei Zosen) K.K. — Kochi** Yd No: 1831 Loa 73.03 Br ex - Dght 4.052 Lbp 68.03 Br md 12.41 Dpth 7.01 Welded, 2 dks	**(A31A2GX) General Cargo Ship** Grain: 3,063; Bale: 3,002 TEU 70 C. 70/20' Compartments: 2 Ho, ER 2 Ha: 2 (38.5 x 10.0)ER	**1 oil engine** sr geared to sc. shaft driving 1 FP propeller Total Power: 883kW (1,201hp) 10.9kn Hanshin LH28 1 x 4 Stroke 6 Cy. 280 x 460 883kW (1201bhp) The Hanshin Diesel Works Ltd-Japan
9289221 *YJST7* -	**SHUN FA NO. 8** **Shun Fa Fishery Co Ltd** - *Port Vila* *Vanuatu* MMSI: 576829000 Official number: 1465	**1,280** 406 -		**2003-05 Jong Shyn Shipbuilding Co., Ltd. — Kaohsiung** Yd No: 112 Loa - Br ex - Dght - Lbp - Br md - Dpth - Welded, 1 dk	**(B11B2FV) Fishing Vessel**	**1 oil engine** geared to sc. shaft driving 1 Propeller
7950620 *H03728* -	**SHUN FENG** *ex Dong Chang Shun -2004* *ex Matsuo Maru No. 72 -1995* *ex Hakko Maru No. 22 -1982* *ex Sada Maru No. 8 -1981* **Hongkong Sunshine Shipping Co Ltd** - *Panama* *Panama* MMSI: 351519000 Official number: 3184306	**397** 126 -	Class: (CC)	**1974-08 K.K. Murakami Zosensho — Ishinomaki** Loa 52.91 Br ex - Dght 3.240 Lbp 44.74 Br md 8.01 Dpth 3.69 Welded, 1 dk	**(B11B2FV) Fishing Vessel**	**1 oil engine** driving 1 FP propeller Total Power: 1,103kW (1,500hp) Akasaka AH30 1 x 4 Stroke 6 Cy. 300 x 480 1103kW (1500bhp) Akasaka Tekkosho KK (Akasaka DieselLtd)-Japan
8657550 *HP3788* -	**SHUN FENG NO. 6** *ex Yan Hang 1 -2012 ex Hai Biao 0514 -2012* **Yantai Yu'an Shipyard Co Ltd** - *Panama* *Panama* MMSI: 356592000	**457** 137 -		**1986-01 Wenzhou Dongfang Shipyard — Yueqing ZJ** Converted From: Lighthouse Tender-1986 Loa 49.98 Br ex 9.40 Dght - Lbp 44.16 Br md - Dpth 3.85 Welded, 1 dk	**(B34T2QR) Work/Repair Vessel**	**2 oil engines** reduction geared to sc. shafts driving 2 Propellers Total Power: 1,176kW (1,598hp) Guangzhou 2 x each-588kW (799bhp) Guangzhou Diesel Engine Factory CoLtd-China
8806503 *3FDE3* -	**SHUN FU** *ex B Asia -2012 ex Spar Carina -2006* *ex Maersk Taikung -2001* **Shunfu Shipping (Hong Kong) Ltd** Greatsources Shipping Consultants Ltd *Panama* *Panama* MMSI: 373264000 Official number: 4404612	**38,337** 23,174 70,424 T/cm 68.7	Class: RI (LR) ✠ Classed LR until 11/1/10	**1990-04 Hyundai Heavy Industries Co Ltd — Ulsan** Yd No: 646 Loa 229.98 (BB) Br ex 32.24 Dght 13.200 Lbp 219.70 Br md 32.20 Dpth 18.30 Welded, 1 dk	**(A21A2BC) Bulk Carrier** Grain: 82,975 Compartments: 7 Ho, ER 7 Ha: (14.9 x 11.0)6 (14.9 x 14.9)ER Cranes: 4x25t	**1 oil engine** driving 1 FP propeller Total Power: 7,848kW (10,670hp) 15.0kn B&W 5S60MC 1 x 2 Stroke 5 Cy. 600 x 2292 7848kW (10670bhp) Hyundai Heavy Industries Co Ltd-South Korea AuxGen: 3 x 580kW 450V 60Hz a.c Boilers: e (ex.g.) 8.1kgf/cm² (7.9bar), AuxB (o.f.) 8.1kgf/cm² (7.9bar)
7815399 - -	**SHUN HAI** *ex An Shun -2007 ex Jin Qiang 338 -2005* *ex Zhong An 809 -2005 ex Voronica -2003* *ex Zhong An -1998* *ex Niihama Maru No. 24 -1998* -	**1,293** 724 2,000		**1979-06 K.K. Miura Zosensho — Saiki** Yd No: 565 Loa 70.23 (BB) Br ex - Dght 5.150 Lbp 65.00 Br md 11.20 Dpth 6.27 Welded, 1 dk	**(A31A2GX) General Cargo Ship**	**1 oil engine** driving 1 FP propeller Total Power: 736kW (1,001hp) Hanshin 1 x 4 Stroke 736kW (1001bhp) The Hanshin Diesel Works Ltd-Japan
9540704 *BCDS2* -	**SHUN HAI 6** *ex Shun Hai -2013* **Weifang Zhenbei International Marine Co Ltd** Shandong Tongda International Shipping Management Co Ltd *China* MMSI: 413328710	**5,715** 3,200 8,500	Class: OM	**2009-05 Huajie Shipbuilding Co Ltd — Linhai ZJ** Yd No: 544 Loa 125.00 Br ex - Dght 6.680 Lbp 116.00 Br md 18.20 Dpth 9.00 Welded, 1 dk	**(A31A2GX) General Cargo Ship**	**1 oil engine** reduction geared to sc. shaft driving 1 CP propeller Total Power: 1,192kW (1,621hp) 12.0kn Chinese Std. Type GN8320ZC 1 x 4 Stroke 8 Cy. 320 x 380 1192kW (1621bhp) Guangzhou Diesel Engine Factory CoLtd-China
8106381 *3CM2088* -	**SHUN HE** *ex Taishin Maru -1998* *ex Taisei Maru No. 21 -1998* **Pesquera Shun He SA** - SatCom: Inmarsat A 1633115 *Malabo* *Equatorial Guinea* Official number: EGF-968897	**712** 285 -		**1981-03 Sanuki Shipbuilding & Iron Works Co Ltd — Mitoyo KG** Yd No: 1082 Loa - Br ex - Dght - Lbp 47.30 Br md 8.70 Dpth 3.71 Welded, 1 dk	**(B11B2FV) Fishing Vessel**	**1 oil engine** driving 1 FP propeller Total Power: 1,177kW (1,600hp) Akasaka DM33 1 x 4 Stroke 6 Cy. 330 x 500 1177kW (1600bhp) Akasaka Tekkosho KK (Akasaka DieselLtd)-Japan
8747874 *3EXW7* -	**SHUN HENG** *ex Bao Zhong 26 -2011 ex Hang Feng -2010* **Shantou Shunhai Shipping Co Ltd** Sun Rising Shipmanagement Co Ltd *Panama* *Panama* MMSI: 372921000 Official number: 41826PEXTF	**1,720** 890 1,920	Class: OM (CC)	**1997-01 Chongqing Shipyard — Chongqing** Loa 81.64 (BB) Br ex - Dght 4.280 Lbp 75.80 Br md 13.00 Dpth 5.20 Welded, 1 dk	**(A33A2CC) Container Ship (Fully Cellular)** Cranes: 4; Derricks: 1	**1 oil engine** driving 1 Propeller Total Power: 1,103kW (1,500hp) 9.0kn Chinese Std. Type 6320ZCD 1 x 4 Stroke 6 Cy. 320 x 440 1103kW (1500bhp) Guangzhou Diesel Engine Factory CoLtd-China
8748232 *H9QD* -	**SHUN HONG** *ex Jin Sheng Hai 18 -2011 ex Heng Yi -1994* **Shantou Shunhai Shipping Co Ltd** - *Panama* *Panama* MMSI: 356485000 Official number: 41985PEXTF2	**2,388** 1,419 4,063	Class: OM (CC)	**1994-01 Zhejiang Yueqing Qiligang Ship Industry Co Ltd — Yueqing ZJ** Loa 83.00 Br ex - Dght 5.800 Lbp 74.20 Br md 14.00 Dpth 7.20 Welded, 1 dk	**(A31A2GX) General Cargo Ship**	**1 oil engine** driving 1 Propeller Total Power: 735kW (999hp) 10.0kn Niigata 6M28KGHS 1 x 4 Stroke 6 Cy. 280 x 440 735kW (999bhp) Niigata Engineering Co Ltd-Japan
8883599 - -	**SHUN HU No. 1** **Government of Taiwan** - *Kaohsiung* *Chinese Taipei* Official number: 12365	**785** 236 490	Class: (CR)	**1992 Lien Ho Shipbuilding Co, Ltd — Kaohsiung** Loa 59.95 Br ex - Dght 4.330 Lbp 51.40 Br md 9.60 Dpth 4.50 Welded, 1 dk	**(B12D2FP) Fishery Patrol Vessel**	**2 oil engines** geared to sc. shafts driving 2 FP propellers Total Power: 1,104kW (1,500hp) 12.0kn Yanmar T260-ET 2 x 4 Stroke 6 Cy. 260 x 330 each-552kW (750bhp) Yanmar Diesel Engine Co Ltd-Japan AuxGen: 2 x 44kW a.c

IMO / Call sign	Name / Owner / Port / Flag	Tonnage	Class	Builder / Dimensions	Type / Details	Machinery
8883604 *BEBY* -	**SHUN HU No. 2** - **Government of Taiwan** - *Kaohsiung* *Chinese Taipei* Official number: 12371	**496** 149 327	Class: (CR) (NV)	**1992 Jong Shyn Shipbuilding Co., Ltd. — Kaohsiung** Loa 51.55 Br ex - Dght 3.700 Lbp 45.20 Br md 8.40 Dpth 4.00 Welded, 1 dk	**(B12D2FP) Fishery Patrol Vessel**	**1 oil engine** driving 1 FP propeller Total Power: 1,839kW (2,500hp) 16.0kn Daihatsu 6DLM-32F 1 x 4 Stroke 6 Cy. 320 x 400 1839kW (2500bhp) Daihatsu Diesel Manufacturing Co Lt-Japan AuxGen: 2 x 200kW 450V a.c
8883616 *BEBW* -	**SHUN HU No. 3** - **Government of Taiwan** - SatCom: Inmarsat C 441690210 *Kaohsiung* *Chinese Taipei* Official number: 12370	**496** 149 327	Class: (CR) (NV)	**1992 Jong Shyn Shipbuilding Co., Ltd. — Kaohsiung** Loa 51.55 Br ex - Dght 3.700 Lbp 45.20 Br md 8.40 Dpth 4.00 Welded, 1 dk	**(B12D2FP) Fishery Patrol Vessel**	**1 oil engine** driving 1 FP propeller Total Power: 1,839kW (2,500hp) 16.0kn Daihatsu 6DLM-32F 1 x 4 Stroke 6 Cy. 320 x 400 1839kW (2500bhp) Daihatsu Diesel Manufacturing Co Lt-Japan AuxGen: 2 x 200kW 450V a.c
8883628 *BEBZ* -	**SHUN HU No. 5** - **Government of Taiwan** - *Kaohsiung* *Chinese Taipei* Official number: 12369	**131** 39 -	Class: (CR)	**1992 Fong Kuo Shipbuilding Co Ltd — Kaohsiung** Loa 31.55 Br ex 6.21 Dght 1.150 Lbp 29.00 Br md 6.20 Dpth 3.10 Welded, 1 dk	**(B12D2FP) Fishery Patrol Vessel**	**2 oil engines** geared to sc. shafts driving 2 FP propellers Total Power: 904kW (1,230hp) M.T.U. 12V331TC92 2 x Vee 4 Stroke 12 Cy. 165 x 155 each-452kW (615bhp) MTU Friedrichshafen GmbH-Friedrichshafen AuxGen: 2 x 55kW 220V a.c
8883630 *BECB* -	**SHUN HU No. 6** - **Government of Taiwan** - *Kaohsiung* *Chinese Taipei* Official number: 12386	**228** 68 -	Class: (CR)	**1993 Fong Kuo Shipbuilding Co Ltd — Kaohsiung** Loa 38.16 Br ex 7.01 Dght 1.250 Lbp 35.20 Br md 7.00 Dpth 3.40 Welded, 1 dk	**(B12D2FP) Fishery Patrol Vessel**	**2 oil engines** geared to sc. shafts driving 2 FP propellers Total Power: 2,400kW (3,264hp) M.T.U. 12V396TE84 2 x Vee 4 Stroke 12 Cy. 165 x 185 each-1200kW (1632bhp) MTU Friedrichshafen GmbH-Friedrichshafen AuxGen: 2 x 200kW 450V a.c
8426901 *BZTH* -	**SHUN JI** *ex* Ling Shui Ba Hao *-2005* *ex* Zhe Leng 2 *-1994* *ex* Bo Leng Er Hao *-1994* **Dalian Shunfa Fishery Co Ltd** - *Dalian, Liaoning* *China* MMSI: 412202420	**1,289** 412 500	Class: (CC)	**1979 Bohai Shipyard — Huludao LN** Loa 66.75 Br ex - Dght 3.950 Lbp 61.50 Br md 11.50 Dpth 6.50 Welded, 1 dk	**(A34A2GR) Refrigerated Cargo Ship** Ins: 396 Compartments: 4 Ho, ER 4 Ha: 2 (2.2 x 3.3)2 (1.2 x 1.9) Cranes: 2x2t	**1 oil engine** driving 1 FP propeller Total Power: 971kW (1,320hp) 13.0kn S.K.L. 8NVD48A-2U 1 x 4 Stroke 8 Cy. 320 x 480 971kW (1320bhp) VEB Schwermaschinenbau "KarlLiebknecht" (SKL)-Magdeburg AuxGen: 3 x 120kW 400V 50Hz a.c
7432678 *3FSH8* -	**SHUN JIANG** *ex* American Career *-1980* *ex* American Venture *-1978* **Shantou Ocean Transport Co** - SatCom: Inmarsat C 435727310 *Panama* *Panama* MMSI: 357273000 Official number: 27434PEXTF	**4,666** 2,305 6,699	Class: (CC) (AB) (NK)	**1976-06 Okayama Zosen K.K. — Hinase** Yd No: 255 Loa 108.50 (BB) Br ex - Dght 6.501 Lbp 99.00 Br md 18.80 Dpth 8.60 Welded, 1 dk	**(A33A2CC) Container Ship (Fully Cellular)** TEU 270 C Ho 126 TEU C Dk 144 TEU incl 18 ref C Compartments: 5 Cell Ho, ER 5 Ha: ER Cranes: 1x38t	**1 oil engine** driving 1 FP propeller Total Power: 3,825kW (5,200hp) 13.0kn Makita KSLH654 1 x 4 Stroke 6 Cy. 540 x 850 3825kW (5200bhp) Makita Diesel Co Ltd-Japan AuxGen: 3 x 200kW 445V 60Hz a.c
9080443 *BXOJ* -	**SHUN JING** - **Shun Gang Passenger Corp** Yuet Hing Marine Supplies Co Ltd *Shunde, Guangdong* *China* MMSI: 412882000	**484** 168 48	Class: CC	**1994-03 Austal Ships Pty Ltd — Fremantle WA** Yd No: 105 Loa 40.10 Br ex 11.81 Dght 1.250 Lbp 38.00 Br md 11.50 Dpth 3.80 Welded, 1 dk	**(A37B2PS) Passenger Ship** Hull Material: Aluminium Alloy Passengers: unberthed: 354	**2 oil engines** reduction geared to sc. shafts driving 2 Water jets Total Power: 4,000kW (5,438hp) 39.5kn M.T.U. 16V396TE74L 2 x Vee 4 Stroke 16 Cy. 165 x 185 each-2000kW (2719bhp) (new engine 1998) MTU Friedrichshafen GmbH-Friedrichshafen AuxGen: 2 x 80kW 380V a.c
8811376 *HOZJ* -	**SHUN KANG** *ex* Shun Fa 1 *-2013* *ex* B Indonesia *-2012* *ex* Spar Capella *-2006* *ex* Maersk Tukang *-2001* **Shunkang Shipping (Hong Kong) Ltd** Chengyi International Ship Management Co Ltd *Panama* *Panama* MMSI: 373106000 Official number: 4402212A	**38,337** 23,174 70,424 T/cm 68.7	Class: RI (LR) ✠ Classed LR until 1/5/10	**1990-09 Hyundai Heavy Industries Co Ltd — Ulsan** Yd No: 649 Loa 229.98 (BB) Br ex 32.24 Dght 13.320 Lbp 219.70 Br md 32.20 Dpth 18.30 Welded, 1 dk	**(A21A2BC) Bulk Carrier** Grain: 82,975 Compartments: 7 Ho, ER 7 Ha: (14.9 x 11.0)6 (14.9 x 14.9)ER Cranes: 4x25t	**1 oil engine** driving 1 FP propeller Total Power: 7,848kW (10,670hp) 15.0kn B&W 5S60MC 1 x 2 Stroke 5 Cy. 600 x 2292 7848kW (10670bhp) Hyundai Heavy Industries Co Ltd-South Korea AuxGen: 3 x 580kW 450V 60Hz a.c Boilers: e (ex.g.) 8.1kgf/cm² (7.9bar), AuxB (o.f.) 8.1kgf/cm² (7.9bar)
7805368 *3CM2064* -	**SHUN LIEN** *ex* Shun Lien No. 2 *-1999* *ex* Shun Lien *-1998* *ex* Yoshi Maru No. 83 *-1996* *ex* Shinmei Maru No. 8 *-1990* **Chin Fu Fishery Co Ltd SA** - SatCom: Inmarsat A 1633131 *Malabo* *Equatorial Guinea* Official number: EG-968873	**575** 243 370		**1978-07 Niigata Engineering Co Ltd — Niigata NI** Yd No: 1602 Loa 46.38 (BB) Br ex - Dght 3.260 Lbp 42.80 Br md 8.51 Dpth 3.61 Welded, 1 dk	**(B11B2FV) Fishing Vessel**	**1 oil engine** driving 1 FP propeller Total Power: 809kW (1,100hp) Niigata 6L28X 1 x 4 Stroke 6 Cy. 280 x 440 809kW (1100bhp) Niigata Engineering Co Ltd-Japan
9625633 *BKXC5* -	**SHUN LONG 68** *ex* Zhejiang Chengzhou Cz1001 *-2014* **Zhejiang Shunlong Shipping Co Ltd** - *Zhoushan, Zhejiang* *China*	**2,997** 1,678 4,645	Class: CC (Class contemplated)	**2014-02 Zhejiang Chengzhou Shipbuilding Co Ltd — Sanmen County ZJ** Yd No: CZ1001 Loa 96.09 Br ex - Dght 5.780 Lbp 89.80 Br md 15.80 Dpth 6.80 Welded, 1 dk	**(A13B2TP) Products Tanker** Double Hull (13F)	**1 oil engine** driving 1 FP propeller
7903043 - -	**SHUN LU** *ex* Delos Courier *-1997* *ex* Ro-Ro Imia *-1997* *ex* Andes Express *-1996* *ex* Ro-Ro Sprinter *-1995* *ex* Ohkoh Maru *-1988* - - *Yantai, Shandong* *China* MMSI: 412202410	**7,315** 2,195 3,390	Class: (NV) (NK)	**1979-08 Imabari Shipbuilding Co Ltd — Imabari EH (Imabari Shipyard)** Yd No: 385 Loa 114.86 Br ex - Dght 5.628 Lbp 105.01 Br md 19.02 Dpth 5.64 Welded, 3 dks	**(A36A2PR) Passenger/Ro-Ro Ship (Vehicles)** Stern door/ramp Quarter bow door/ramp (p) Lane-Len: 300	**1 oil engine** driving 1 FP propeller Total Power: 6,694kW (9,101hp) 17.0kn Pielstick 14PC2-5V-400 1 x Vee 4 Stroke 14 Cy. 400 x 460 6694kW (9101bhp) Niigata Engineering Co Ltd-Japan AuxGen: 2 x 450kW 450V 60Hz a.c Fuel: 67.0 (d.f.) 347.0 (r.f.) 20.0pd
9192961 *YJSV9* -	**SHUN MENG** *ex* Shin Kai No. 6 *-2004* **Shun Meng Fishery Co Ltd** - *Port Vila* *Vanuatu* MMSI: 576847000 Official number: 1483	**498** 222 -		**1998 Fuzhou Zhongyi Shipbuilding Co Ltd — Fuzhou FJ** Loa - Br ex - Dght 3.500 Lbp 46.75 Br md 8.50 Dpth 3.75 Welded, 1 dk	**(B11B2FV) Fishing Vessel**	**1 oil engine** driving 1 FP propeller Total Power: 956kW (1,300hp) Matsui 1 x 4 Stroke 956kW (1300bhp) Matsui Iron Works Co Ltd-Japan
8974130 *BAJQ* -	**SHUN PENG 6** *ex* Li Da *-2004* *ex* Shun Peng 6 *-2004* *ex* Yun Zhong *-2004* **Dalian Jianghaida Shipping Co Ltd** - *Dalian, Liaoning* *China* Official number: 030111000187	**952** 533 -		**2002-08 in the People's Republic of China** Yd No: 455 Loa 66.65 Br ex 9.80 Dght - Lbp - Br md - Dpth 5.60 Welded, 1 dk	**(A31A2GX) General Cargo Ship**	**1 oil engine** driving 1 FP propeller Total Power: 736kW (1,001hp) Chinese Std. Type 8300 1 x 4 Stroke 8 Cy. 300 x 380 736kW (1001bhp) Zibo Diesel Engine Factory-China
8660870 *BHQK4* -	**SHUN QIANG 19** *ex* Hua Shun 69 *-2013* **Jiangsu Quanqiang Shipping Co Ltd** - *China* MMSI: 413363270	**2,996** 1,678 -		**2008-01 Viva Vessel Group Co Ltd — Yueqing ZJ** Loa 97.00 Br ex - Dght 5.900 Lbp 89.80 Br md 15.80 Dpth 7.40 Welded, 1 dk	**(A31A2GX) General Cargo Ship**	**1 oil engine** reduction geared to sc. shaft driving 1 FP propeller Total Power: 2,000kW (2,719hp) Chinese Std. Type G8300ZC 1 x 4 Stroke 8 Cy. 300 x 380 2000kW (2719bhp) Wuxi Antai Power Machinery Co Ltd-China
9531014 *BHMF* -	**SHUN QIANG 58** *completed as* Irbis *-2011* *launched as* Bi Sheng Long 12 *-2011* - *China* MMSI: 413356320	**9,076** 5,083 14,315		**2011-01 Yueqing Yuanhang Shipbuilding Co Ltd — Yueqing ZJ** Yd No: XSY-07-02 Loa 145.50 (BB) Br ex - Dght 7.800 Lbp 138.00 Br md 20.20 Dpth 10.80 Welded, 1 dk	**(A31A2GX) General Cargo Ship** Grain: 19,439	**1 oil engine** reduction geared to sc. shaft driving 1 CP propeller Total Power: 3,840kW (5,221hp) 13.0kn MAN-B&W 8L32/40 1 x 4 Stroke 8 Cy. 320 x 400 3840kW (5221bhp) MAN B&W Diesel AG-Augsburg
8942852 - -	**SHUN RONG** *ex* Chang Tong *-1996* **Shantou Shunhai Shipping Co Ltd** - *Shantou, Guangdong* *China* MMSI: 412460060 Official number: 370300331	**998** 559 -		**1996-09 Hubei Jingsha Shipyard — Jingzhou HB** Loa 65.99 Br ex 11.40 Dght - Lbp 59.90 Br md - Dpth 5.20 Welded, 1 dk	**(A31A2GX) General Cargo Ship**	**1 oil engine** driving 1 FP propeller Total Power: 662kW (900hp) Alpha 6T23LU 1 x 4 Stroke 6 Cy. 225 x 300 662kW (900bhp) Guangzhou Diesel Engine Factory CoLtd-China

8307571 *3FVS6* -	**SHUN RU** *ex* Shun An *-2013* *ex* Shun Tai *-2012* *ex* Cypria *-2009* *ex* Spring Swift *-1996* *ex* Sanko Swift *-1986* **Shunru Shipping (Hong Kong) Ltd** Chengyi International Ship Management Co Ltd SatCom: Inmarsat A 1241540 *Panama* *Panama* MMSI: 354544000 Official number: 2358997H	**24,643** 13,377 40,572 T/cm 48.7	Class: (RI) (NK)	**1984-11 Mitsui Eng. & SB. Co. Ltd. — Tamano** Yd No: 1286 Loa 182.80 (BB) Br ex - Dght 11.015 Lbp 174.02 Br md 30.51 Dpth 15.78 Welded, 1 dk	**(A21A2BC) Bulk Carrier** Grain: 51,025; Bale: 50,025 Compartments: 5 Ho, ER 5 Ha: (16.7 x 15.6)3 (19.2 x 15.6) (18.4 x 15.6)ER Cranes: 4x25t	**1 oil engine** driving 1 FP propeller Total Power: 6,192kW (8,419hp) 14.0kn B&W 6L60MCE 1 x 2 Stroke 6 Cy. 600 x 1944 6192kW (8419bhp) Mitsui Engineering & Shipbuilding CLtd-Japan AuxGen: 3 x 400kW 450V 60Hz a.c Fuel: 167.5 (d.f.) (Heating Coils) 1695.0 (r.f.) 23.5pd
9279692 *VRMV2* -	**SHUN SHENG** *ex* Stolt Orchid *-2013* **Xiangyuan International Shipping Ltd** Taihua Ship Management (Shanghai) Ltd *Hong Kong* *Hong Kong* MMSI: 477904400 Official number: HK-3985	**5,376** 2,621 8,811 T/cm 17.8	Class: NK	**2003-08 Shin Kurushima Dockyard Co. Ltd. — Hashihama, Imabari** Yd No: 5227 Loa 113.98 (BB) Br ex 18.23 Dght 7.478 Lbp 108.50 Br md 18.20 Dpth 9.65 Welded, 1 Dk.	**(A12B2TR) Chemical/Products Tanker** Double Hull (13F) Liq: 9,175; Liq (Oil): 9,362 Cargo Heating Coils Compartments: 16 Wing Ta (s.stl), 1 Wing Slop Ta, 1 Wing Slop Ta (s.stl), ER (s.stl) 16 Cargo Pump (s): 16x200m³/hr Manifold: Bow/CM: 56.7m	**1 oil engine** driving 1 FP propeller Total Power: 3,900kW (5,302hp) 13.8kn B&W 6L35MC 1 x 2 Stroke 6 Cy. 350 x 1050 3900kW (5302bhp) Makita Corp-Japan AuxGen: 2 x 455kW 450/105V 60Hz a.c Fuel: 49.0 (d.f.) (Heating Coils) 567.0 (r.f.) 15.5pd
9082520 *BXCD* -	**SHUN SHUI** *ex* Gui Feng *-2005* **Shun Gang Passenger Corp** Chu Kong Shipping Enterprises (Holdings) Co Ltd *Shunde, Guangdong* *China* MMSI: 412878000	**457** 155 37	Class: CC	**1993-11 Austal Ships Pty Ltd — Fremantle WA** Yd No: 109 Loa 39.90 (BB) Br ex 10.31 Dght 1.275 Lbp 35.00 Br md 10.00 Dpth 3.80 Welded, 1 dk	**(A37B2PS) Passenger Ship** Hull Material: Aluminium Alloy Passengers: unberthed: 354	**2 oil engines** with clutches, flexible couplings & sr geared to sc. shafts driving 2 Water jets Total Power: 3,840kW (5,220hp) 33.0kn M.T.U. 16V396TE74L 2 x Vee 4 Stroke 16 Cy. 165 x 185 each-1920kW (2610bhp) MTU Friedrichshafen GmbH-Friedrichshafen AuxGen: 2 x 100kW 380V a.c
8977558 - -	**SHUN SING NO. 1** *ex* Chin Jui Yng No. 11 *-2007* *ex* Yeast *-2004* *ex* Hai Min No. 2 *-2004* **Macalluns SA** Wang Chang Yi	**276** 90 -		**1984 Higashi Kyushu Shipbuilding Co Ltd — Usuki OT** L reg 32.06 Br ex - Dght - Lbp - Br md 6.30 Dpth 2.53 Welded, 1 dk	**(B11A2FT) Trawler**	**1 oil engine** driving 1 Propeller Total Power: 1,177kW (1,600hp)
9158783 *3EYA2* -	**SHUN TAI 98** *ex* Yi Shun 86 *-2014* *ex* Da Xin Hua Qiu Shun *-2013* *ex* Tong Xin Quan *-2008* **Xingyun International Shipping Co** Sun Rising Shipmanagement Co Ltd *Panama* *Panama* MMSI: 354253000 Official number: 45127PEXT1	**4,165** 1,616 5,480	Class: (CC) (BV)	**1998-06 Huanghai Shipbuilding Co Ltd — Rongcheng SD** Yd No: Y15 Loa 100.93 Br ex - Dght 6.300 Lbp 91.00 Br md 18.00 Dpth 8.20 Welded, 1 dk	**(A31A2GX) General Cargo Ship** Grain: 5,853; Bale: 5,600 TEU 398 C.Ho 126/20' C.Dk 272/20' incl. 40 ref C Compartments: 2 Ho, ER 2 Ha: (25.2 x 15.2)Tappered (25.2 x 15.2)ER Ice Capable	**1 oil engine** with flexible couplings & sr reverse geared to sc. shaft driving 1 CP propeller Total Power: 3,960kW (5,384hp) 13.5kn MaK 9M32 1 x 4 Stroke 9 Cy. 320 x 480 3960kW (5384bhp) MaK Motoren GmbH & Co. KG-Kiel AuxGen: 2 x 350kW 400V a.c Fuel: 58.6 (d.f.) (Heating Coils) 434.6 (r.f.) 18.0pd
9056727 *XUMN3* -	**SHUN TAI NO. 1** *ex* Hoan *-2006* *ex* Hoan Maru *-2002* **Run Sheng Shipping Co Ltd** Yantai Runhai International Shipping Management Co Ltd *Phnom Penh* *Cambodia* MMSI: 515124000 Official number: 0692355	**1,490** 875 1,400	Class: UB	**1992-10 Shinhama Dockyard Co. Ltd. — Anan** Yd No: 817 Loa 74.93 (BB) Br ex 12.02 Dght 4.130 Lbp 70.50 Br md 12.00 Dpth 7.10 Welded, 1 dk	**(A31A2GX) General Cargo Ship** Bale: 2,697 Compartments: 1 Ho, ER 1 Ha: ER	**1 oil engine** with clutches & reverse geared to sc. shaft driving 1 FP propeller Total Power: 735kW (999hp) Hanshin LH31G 1 x 4 Stroke 6 Cy. 310 x 530 735kW (999bhp) The Hanshin Diesel Works Ltd-Japan
8921729 *XUVG3* -	**SHUN TAI NO. 6** *ex* Shin Choei Maru No. 8 *-2009* **Shun Tai Shipping Co Ltd** Yantai Runhai International Shipping Management Co Ltd SatCom: Inmarsat C 451422110 *Phnom Penh* *Cambodia* MMSI: 514221000 Official number: 0990340	**1,467** 670 1,400	Class: UB	**1990-07 Honda Zosen — Saiki** Yd No: 813 L reg 72.50 Br ex - Dght 4.052 Lbp 70.00 Br md 12.00 Dpth 7.00 Welded, 1 dk	**(A31A2GX) General Cargo Ship** Compartments: 1 Ho, ER 1 Ha: ER	**1 oil engine** with clutches, flexible couplings & sr geared to sc. shaft driving 1 FP propeller Total Power: 1,177kW (1,600hp) Niigata 6M28HFT 1 x 4 Stroke 6 Cy. 280 x 480 1177kW (1600bhp) Niigata Engineering Co Ltd-Japan Thrusters: 1 Thwart. FP thruster (f)
8150796 *HQPX9* -	**SHUN TAK** *ex* Oi Fung *-1994* *ex* Sol *-1992* *ex* Aoi Maru *-1992* **Kam Fap Shipping Trading Co SA** SatCom: Inmarsat A 1334364 *San Lorenzo* *Honduras* Official number: L-0325845	**721** 396 715		**1975-08 K.K. Yoshida Zosen Kogyo — Arida** Loa 59.47 Br ex - Dght 3.850 Lbp 55.00 Br md 9.30 Dpth 5.52 Welded, 1 dk	**(A31A2GX) General Cargo Ship**	**1 oil engine** driving 1 FP propeller Total Power: 736kW (1,001hp) 10.5kn Makita 1 x 4 Stroke 736kW (1001bhp) Makita Diesel Co Ltd-Japan
7323396 *BZEJ* -	**SHUN TIAN FA 168** *ex* Win Yeong Tai No. 136 *-2008* *ex* Sinda No. 136 *-1989* *ex* Ching Haue No. 101 *-1989* *ex* Nikko Maru *-1986* *ex* Ryutoku *-1978* *ex* Satsu Maru No. 27 *-1978* - - *Chinese Taipei* MMSI: 416602000	*1,095* 617 1,861	Class: CR (NK)	**1973-04 Yamanishi Shipbuilding Co Ltd — Ishinomaki MG** Yd No: 727 Loa 76.82 Br ex 12.02 Dght 4.760 Lbp 70.01 Br md 11.99 Dpth 7.40 Welded, 1 dk, pt 2nd dk	**(A34A2GR) Refrigerated Cargo Ship** Ins: 2,336 Compartments: 2 Ho, ER 2 Ha: 2 (8.2 x 3.9)ER Derricks: 4x3t	**1 oil engine** driving 1 FP propeller Total Power: 1,986kW (2,700hp) 12.5kn Niigata 6M40X 1 x 4 Stroke 6 Cy. 400 x 600 1986kW (2700bhp) Niigata Engineering Co Ltd-Japan AuxGen: 2 x 528kW Fuel: 501.0 12.0pd
8748531 *BZMX* -	**SHUN TIEN NO. 606** **Shuenn Tian Fishery Co Ltd** *Kaohsiung* *Chinese Taipei* Official number: 011908	**995** 571 -		**1990-07 Lien Ho Shipbuilding Co, Ltd — Kaohsiung** Loa 66.40 Br ex - Dght 4.510 Lbp 58.90 Br md 11.80 Dpth 4.55 Welded, 1 dk	**(B11B2FV) Fishing Vessel**	**1 oil engine** reduction geared to sc. shaft driving 1 Propeller Total Power: 2,206kW (2,999hp) Daihatsu 8DLM-32 1 x 4 Stroke 8 Cy. 320 x 400 2206kW (2999bhp) Daihatsu Diesel Manufacturing Co Lt-Japan
8910380 *3EYU2* -	**SHUN TONG** *ex* Cemtex Orient *-2010* **Tong Yun Shipping SA** Qingdao Da Tong International Shipping Management Co Ltd SatCom: Inmarsat C 437124010 *Panama* *Panama* MMSI: 371240000 Official number: 4167810A	**38,203** 24,135 71,435 T/cm 65.8	Class: IB (CC) (AB) (CR)	**1990-07 Hitachi Zosen Corp — Maizuru KY** Yd No: 4849 Loa 223.64 (BB) Br ex 32.23 Dght 13.453 Lbp 215.00 Br md 32.20 Dpth 18.60 Welded, 1 dk	**(A21A2BC) Bulk Carrier** Grain: 85,107; Bale: 82,337 Compartments: 7 Ho, ER 7 Ha: (16.2 x 13.0)6 (17.0 x 14.6)ER Cranes: 4	**1 oil engine** driving 1 FP propeller Total Power: 7,620kW (10,360hp) 14.0kn B&W 6S60MCE 1 x 2 Stroke 6 Cy. 600 x 2292 7620kW (10360bhp) Hitachi Zosen Corp-Japan AuxGen: 3 x 560kW a.c, 1 x 82kW a.c
8890542 - -	**SHUN UN** - -	*306* 107 -		**1995-07 Shantou Shipyard — Shantou GD** Loa 47.00 Br ex - Dght - Lbp - Br md 6.40 Dpth 3.50 Welded, 1 dk	**(A31A2GX) General Cargo Ship**	**1 oil engine** driving 1 FP propeller
9036806 *3FRQ8* -	**SHUN WANG** *ex* Maritime Queen *-2011* **Easy Grand Shipping Ltd** Chengyi International Ship Management Co Ltd *Panama* *Panama* MMSI: 370085000 Official number: 4308111	**38,481** 24,924 73,350 T/cm 65.2	Class: NK	**1994-01 Oshima Shipbuilding Co Ltd — Saikai NS** Yd No: 10155 Loa 225.00 (BB) Br ex - Dght 13.874 Lbp 217.00 Br md 32.26 Dpth 19.00 Welded, 1 dk	**(A21A2BC) Bulk Carrier** Grain: 88,234; Bale: 86,527 Compartments: 7 Ho, ER 7 Ha: (16.6 x 12.3)6 (16.6 x 15.4)ER Cranes: 4x30t	**1 oil engine** driving 1 FP propeller Total Power: 9,047kW (12,300hp) 14.8kn Sulzer 6RTA62 1 x 2 Stroke 6 Cy. 620 x 2150 9047kW (12300bhp) Diesel United Ltd.-Aioi AuxGen: 3 x 480kW a.c Fuel: 2053.0 (r.f.) 33.6pd
8510398 - -	**SHUN XIN** *ex* Silver Moon No. 1 *-2004* *ex* Jin Ze No. 6 *-2000* *ex* Taiyo Maru No. 3 *-1999* - - *Indonesia*	**1,279** 486 1,600		**1985-11 Shitanoe Shipbuilding Co Ltd — Usuki OT** Yd No: 1053 Loa 67.01 Br ex 11.51 Dght - Lbp - Br md - Dpth 6.71 Welded	**(A31A2GX) General Cargo Ship**	**1 oil engine** driving 1 FP propeller Total Power: 1,030kW (1,400hp) Niigata 6M28AFTE 1 x 4 Stroke 6 Cy. 280 x 480 1030kW (1400bhp) Niigata Engineering Co Ltd-Japan

Ship / Owner	Tonnage	Class	Build / Dimensions	Type / Capacity	Machinery
9454656 **SHUN XIN** *VRGG3* - **Top Harvest Shipping Ltd** COSCO (HK) Shipping Co Ltd *Hong Kong* *Hong Kong* MMSI: 477685700 Official number: HK-2616	**32,983** 19,191 56,933 T/cm 58.8	Class: NK	**2010-02 COSCO (Zhoushan) Shipyard Co Ltd — Zhoushan ZJ** Yd No: ZS07005 Loa 189.99 (BB) Br ex - Dght 12.818 Lbp 185.00 Br md 32.26 Dpth 18.00 Welded, 1 dk	**(A21A2BC) Bulk Carrier** Grain: 71,634; Bale: 68,200 Compartments: 5 Ho, ER 5 Ha: ER Cranes: 4x30t	**1 oil engine** driving 1 FP propeller Total Power: 9,960kW (13,542hp) 14.2kn MAN-B&W 6S50MC-C 1 x 2 Stroke 6 Cy. 500 x 2000 9960kW (13542bhp) STX Engine Co Ltd-South Korea Fuel: 2170.0
9155286 **SHUN XING** *T3KK2* - *ex* Bao Jia *-2013* *ex* Sheng Feng *-2013* **Green Prosperous Shipping Co Ltd** Hua Heng Shipping Ltd *Tarawa* *Kiribati* MMSI: 529660000 Official number: K17961318	**2,772** 1,144 2,823	Class: CC IZ	**1996-09 Shandong Weihai Shipyard — Weihai SD** Yd No: Z92 Loa 84.57 (BB) Br ex - Dght 4.940 Lbp 79.00 Br md 15.00 Dpth 7.30 Welded, 1 dk	**(A33A2CC) Container Ship (Fully Cellular)** TEU 226 C.Ho 88 TEU C.Dk 138 TEU	**1 oil engine** geared to sc. shaft driving 1 FP propeller Total Power: 956kW (1,300hp) Alpha 6L28/32 1 x 4 Stroke 6 Cy. 280 x 320 956kW (1300bhp) Zhenjiang Marine Diesel Works-China
9631826 **SHUN YING** *3FSU2* - **Da Shun Shipping SA** Qingdao Da Tong International Shipping Management Co Ltd *Panama* *Panama* MMSI: 354281000 Official number: 43933PEXT1	**43,990** 27,662 81,108 T/cm 71.9	Class: BV	**2012-11 New Century Shipbuilding Co Ltd — Jingjiang JS** Yd No: 0108220 Loa 229.00 (BB) Br ex 32.30 Dght 14.450 Lbp 225.50 Br md 32.26 Dpth 20.05 Welded, 1 dk	**(A21A2BC) Bulk Carrier** Grain: 97,883; Bale: 90,784 Compartments: 7 Ho, ER 7 Ha: 5 (18.3 x 15.0) (15.7 x 15.1)ER (13.1 x 13.2)	**1 oil engine** driving 1 FP propeller Total Power: 9,800kW (13,324hp) 14.0kn MAN-B&W 5S60MC-C8 1 x 2 Stroke 5 Cy. 600 x 2400 9800kW (13324bhp) Wuxi Antai Power Machinery Co Ltd-China AuxGen: 3 x 710kW 60Hz a.c Fuel: 3260.0
9266815 **SHUN YO MARU** *JI3707* - **Corporation for Advanced Transport & Technology & Shoei Kaiun KK** Ikous Co Ltd *Osaka, Osaka* *Japan* MMSI: 431301663 Official number: 137233	*749* - 1,899	Class: NK	**2003-01 K.K. Miura Zosensho — Saiki** Yd No: 1260 Loa 69.98 Br ex - Dght 4.754 Lbp 66.00 Br md 12.00 Dpth 5.20 Welded, 1 dk	**(A13B2TP) Products Tanker** Double Hull (13F) Liq: 2,200; Liq (Oil): 2,200	**1 oil engine** driving 1 FP propeller Total Power: 1,471kW (2,000hp) 12.0kn Akasaka A34C 1 x 4 Stroke 6 Cy. 340 x 620 1471kW (2000bhp) Akasaka Tekkosho KK (Akasaka DieselLtd)-Japan Fuel: 80.0
8621070 **SHUN YOU** - WK1-182 *ex* Yachiyo Maru No. 1 *-1998* - -	**492** 231 -		**1986-02 Katsuura Dockyard Co. Ltd. — Nachi-Katsuura** Yd No: 282 Loa - (BB) Br ex - Dght - Lbp 44.12 Br md 8.50 Dpth 3.56 Welded, 1 dk	**(B11B2FV) Fishing Vessel** Ins: 428	**1 oil engine** driving 1 FP propeller Hanshin 1 x 4 Stroke The Hanshin Diesel Works Ltd-Japan
8947577 **SHUN YU** *BI2548* LL2306 **Shun Yu Ocean Enterprise Co Ltd** - *Kaohsiung* *Chinese Taipei* MMSI: 416111600 Official number: 014137	**530** 238 -		**1998-05 Jong Shyn Shipbuilding Co., Ltd. — Kaohsiung** Yd No: 067 L reg 47.30 Br ex - Dght - Lbp - Br md 8.60 Dpth 3.70 Welded, 1 dk	**(B11B2FV) Fishing Vessel**	**1 oil engine** driving 1 FP propeller Total Power: 1,030kW (1,400hp) 11.0kn Niigata 1 x 4 Stroke 1030kW (1400bhp) Niigata Engineering Co Ltd-Japan
9220158 **SHUN YUAN 15** *BWIF* - *ex* Jin Sheng 98 *-2011* **Fujian Shunyuan Shipping Co Ltd** Min An Shipping & Enterprise Co Ltd *Fuzhou, Fujian* *China* MMSI: 412441760	**1,616** 855 2,380	Class: CC	**1999-08 Fujian Southeast Shipyard — Fuzhou FJ** Loa 79.80 Br ex 13.03 Dght 4.200 Lbp 74.80 Br md 13.00 Dpth 5.40 Welded, 1 dk	**(A33A2CC) Container Ship (Fully Cellular)** Grain: 2,481; Bale: 2,481 TEU 112 C Ho 62 TEU C Dk 50 TEU. Compartments: 2 Ho, ER 2 Ha: ER 2 (25.2 x 10.0)	**1 oil engine** reduction geared to sc. shaft driving 1 FP propeller Total Power: 1,103kW (1,500hp) 12.0kn Chinese Std. Type LB8250ZLC 1 x 4 Stroke 8 Cy. 250 x 320 1103kW (1500bhp) Zibo Diesel Engine Factory-China
8313154 **SHUN YUAN 107** *BYJT* - *ex* Yan Hai *-2013* *ex* Euronavigator *-1996* **Hainan Shunyuan Maritime Shipping Development Co Ltd** - SatCom: Inmarsat C 441329410 *Shantou, Guangdong* *China* MMSI: 413475020 Official number: CN19832173305	**2,688** 806 3,126	Class: CC (NK)	**1983-12 Sanyo Zosen K.K. — Onomichi** Yd No: 867 Loa 92.51 Br ex 14.64 Dght 5.100 Lbp 84.92 Br md 14.61 Dpth 6.51 Welded, 1 dk	**(A11B2TG) LPG Tanker** Liq (Gas): 2,503 2 x Gas Tank (s);	**1 oil engine** driving 1 FP propeller Total Power: 2,354kW (3,200hp) 12.8kn Akasaka A41 1 x 4 Stroke 6 Cy. 410 x 800 2354kW (3200bhp) Akasaka Tekkosho KK (Akasaka DieselLtd)-Japan AuxGen: 2 x 240kW Thrusters: 1 Thwart. CP thruster (f)
8905830 **SHUN YUAN 108** *BJKE* - *ex* Kun Peng *-2004* *ex* Hua Yue *-1991* **Hainan Shunyuan Maritime Shipping Development Co Ltd** - *Yangpu, Hainan* *China* MMSI: 413520420	**2,771** 1,551 2,404	Class: CC	**1991-02 Jiangnan Shipyard — Shanghai** Yd No: 2187 Loa 96.95 Br ex - Dght 5.000 Lbp 89.60 Br md 14.60 Dpth 6.60 Welded, 1 dk	**(A11B2TG) LPG Tanker** Liq (Gas): 3,002 2 x Gas Tank (s); 2 independent (stl) cyl 2 Cargo Pump (s): 2x150m³/hr Ice Capable	**1 oil engine** driving 1 FP propeller Total Power: 1,214kW (1,651hp) 14.0kn Hudong 6ESDZ43/82C 1 x 2 Stroke 6 Cy. 430 x 820 1214kW (1651bhp) Hudong Shipyard-China AuxGen: 2 x 312kW 400V a.c
9647344 **SHUN YUE 13** *6YRM7* - **Dalian Shunyue Shipping Freight Co Ltd** Dalian Sincere Nice International Ship Management Co Ltd *Jamaica* MMSI: 339300610	**3,692** 1,865 5,436	Class: IB	**2011-11 Zhoushan Honglisheng Ship Engineering Co Ltd — Zhoushan ZJ** Yd No: ZCJ09066 Loa 99.98 Br ex 15.80 Dght - Lbp - Br md - Dpth - Welded, 1 dk	**(A31A2GX) General Cargo Ship**	**1 oil engine** driving 1 Propeller 11.0kn
8649723 **SHUN YUE 18** *6YRM5* - **Dalian Shunyue Shipping Freight Co Ltd** Dalian Sincere Nice International Ship Management Co Ltd *Jamaica* MMSI: 339300590	**3,542** 1,815 5,040	Class: IB ZC	**2009-06 Wenling Xingyuan Shipbuilding & Repair Co Ltd — Wenling ZJ** Yd No: ZTZ08199 Loa 99.98 Br ex - Dght 6.060 Lbp 92.40 Br md 15.80 Dpth 7.60 Welded, 1 dk	**(A31A2GX) General Cargo Ship**	**1 oil engine** driving 1 Propeller 12.2kn
9634050 **SHUN YUE 19** *6YRM3* - **Dalian Shunyue Shipping Freight Co Ltd** Dalian Sincere Nice International Ship Management Co Ltd *Jamaica* MMSI: 339300580	**6,752** 3,781 8,085	Class: IB ZC	**2011-06 Zhoushan Honglisheng Ship Engineering Co Ltd — Zhoushan ZJ** Loa 126.00 Br ex - Dght 6.700 Lbp 116.00 Br md 18.20 Dpth 10.00 Welded, 1 dk	**(A31A2GX) General Cargo Ship**	**1 oil engine** reduction geared to sc. shaft driving 1 FP propeller Total Power: 2,500kW (3,399hp) 12.0kn Chinese Std. Type GN8320ZC 1 x 4 Stroke 8 Cy. 320 x 380 2500kW (3399bhp) Ningbo CSI Power & Machinery GroupCo Ltd-China
8805755 **SHUN ZE** *3EXK7* - *ex* Xin Hua Tai 6 *-2013* *ex* Jin Rong *-2008* *ex* Shinei Maru No. 10 *-2002* **La Payse Trading Ltd** - *Panama* *Panama* MMSI: 352324000 Official number: 4512313	**2,283** 1,258 -	Class: ZC	**1988-02 Kurinoura Dockyard Co Ltd — Yawatahama EH** Yd No: 246 Converted From: Grab Dredger-2003 Lengthened-2003 Loa 88.19 Br ex 12.62 Dght 5.200 Lbp 83.20 Br md 12.60 Dpth 6.60 Welded, 1 dk	**(A31A2GX) General Cargo Ship**	**1 oil engine** driving 1 FP propeller Total Power: 736kW (1,001hp) 9.0kn Hanshin 6LU32G 1 x 4 Stroke 6 Cy. 320 x 510 736kW (1001bhp) (made 1987) The Hanshin Diesel Works Ltd-Japan
5261972 **SHUNA** - - *ex* Sound of Shuna *-2003* *ex* Olandssund IV *-1973* - -	*244* 85 137 T/cm 2.9		**1962 AB Asi-Verken — Amal** Yd No: 65 Loa 41.92 Br ex 9.02 Dght 2.540 Lbp 40.04 Br md 9.00 Dpth 3.51 Welded, 1 dk	**(A36A2PR) Passenger/Ro-Ro Ship (Vehicles)** Passengers: unberthed: 200 Bow door/ramp Len: 1.20 Wid: 3.58 Swl: - Stern door/ramp Len: 1.20 Wid: 3.58 Swl: - Lane-Len: 108 Lane-Wid: 2.70 Lane-clr ht: 4.20 Lorries: 3, Cars: 26 Ice Capable	**4 oil engines** with clutches, flexible couplings & sr geared to sc. shafts driving 2 CP propellers 1 fwd and 1 aft Total Power: 448kW (608hp) 7.0kn Scania DS11 4 x 4 Stroke 6 Cy. 127 x 145 each-112kW (152bhp) (new engine 1980) Scania AB-Sweden AuxGen: 1 x 30kW 240V 50Hz a.c Fuel: 10.9 (d.f.) 1.5pd
9278997 **SHUNDE** *VRXZ9* - **South China Towing Co Ltd** - *Hong Kong* *Hong Kong* MMSI: 477331000 Official number: HK-0902	**298** 89 196	Class: BV	**2002-11 K.K. Odo Zosen Tekko — Shimonoseki** Yd No: 586 Loa 31.00 Br ex 9.52 Dght 3.800 Lbp 25.50 Br md 9.50 Dpth 4.70 Welded, 1 Dk.	**(B32A2ST) Tug**	**2 oil engines** geared to sc. shafts driving 2 Z propellers Total Power: 2,942kW (4,000hp) Niigata 6MG26HLX 1 x 4 Stroke 6 Cy. 260 x 350 1471kW (2000bhp) Niigata Engineering Co Ltd-Japan

8743440 JD2809 -	**SHUNEI** - **Muneta Zosen KK (Muneta Shipbuilding Co Ltd)** - *Akashi, Hyogo* *Japan* Official number: 140858	*293* - 999		**2008-12 KS Yanase Marine — Fukuyama HS** Yd No: 102 Loa 62.00 Br ex - Dght 3.670 Lbp 56.80 Br md 10.40 Dpth 6.10 Welded, 1 dk	**(A31A2GX) General Cargo Ship** Compartments: 1 Ho, ER 1 Ha: ER	**1 oil engine** reduction geared to sc. shaft driving 1 Propeller Total Power: 736kW (1,001hp) 10.5kn Yanmar 6RY17P-GV 1 x 4 Stroke 6 Cy. 165 x 219 736kW (1001bhp) Yanmar Diesel Engine Co Ltd-Japan
8870592 JL6206 -	**SHUNEI MARU** - **YK Doei Kisen** YK Taisei Kaiun *Imabari, Ehime* *Japan* Official number: 133901	*498* - 1,210		**1993-07 K.K. Uno Zosensho — Imabari** Yd No: 231 Loa 64.48 Br ex - Dght 4.160 Lbp 59.98 Br md 10.00 Dpth 4.38 Welded, 1 dk	**(A13B2TP) Products Tanker** Liq: 1,279; Liq (Oil): 1,279 2 Cargo Pump (s): 2x500m³/hr	**1 oil engine** driving 1 FP propeller Total Power: 736kW (1,001hp) 11.0kn Niigata 6M28BGT 1 x 4 Stroke 6 Cy. 280 x 480 736kW (1001bhp) Niigata Engineering Co Ltd-Japan Fuel: 93.0 (d.f.)
9240586 JJ4022 -	**SHUNEI MARU** *ex Kansai Maru No. 38 -2009* **Muneta Zosen KK (Muneta Shipbuilding Co Ltd)** - *Akashi, Hyogo* *Japan* Official number: 135965	*197* - -		**2000-06 KK Yanase Dock — Onomichi HS** Yd No: 361 Loa 31.00 Br ex - Dght - Lbp - Br md 9.00 Dpth 4.00 Welded, 1 dk	**(B32B2SP) Pusher Tug**	**2 oil engines** geared to sc. shafts driving 2 FP propellers Total Power: 2,354kW (3,200hp) 12.8kn Yanmar 6N260-EN 2 x 4 Stroke 6 Cy. 260 x 360 each-1177kW (1600bhp) Yanmar Diesel Engine Co Ltd-Japan
8956877 - -	**SHUNEI MARU No. 1** - -	*157* - -		**1975-12 Muneta Zosen K.K. — Akashi** Loa 29.80 Br ex - Dght 2.800 Lbp 26.00 Br md 7.80 Dpth 3.19 Welded, 1 dk	**(B32A2ST) Tug**	**1 oil engine** driving 1 FP propeller Total Power: 2,207kW (3,001hp) 12.0kn
8844672 JK4908 -	**SHUNEI MARU NO. 2** *ex Sanyo Maru -2008* **Muneta Zosen KK (Muneta Shipbuilding Co Ltd)** - *Akashi, Hyogo* *Japan* Official number: 132473	*177* - -		**1990-11 Hongawara Zosen K.K. — Fukuyama** Yd No: 330 Loa 33.40 Br ex - Dght 2.500 Lbp 29.00 Br md 8.20 Dpth 3.48 Welded, 1 dk	**(B32A2ST) Tug**	**2 oil engines** driving 2 FP propellers Total Power: 1,766kW (2,402hp) Niigata 2 x 4 Stroke each-883kW (1201bhp) Niigata Engineering Co Ltd-Japan
7731074 - -	**SHUNEI MARU No. 28** *ex Shintoku Maru No. 1 -2008* -	*192* 46 -		**1971 Y.K. Tokai Zosensho — Tsukumi** Loa 28.00 Br ex - Dght 2.801 Lbp 22.70 Br md 8.00 Dpth 3.80 Welded, 1 dk	**(B32B2SP) Pusher Tug**	**1 oil engine** driving 1 FP propeller Total Power: 1,103kW (1,500hp) 12.0kn
9314416 JMXQ -	**SHUNHO MARU** - **Iino Gas Transport Co Ltd** - *Kobe, Hyogo* *Japan* MMSI: 432477000 Official number: 136011	**1,357** 484 1,405	Class: NK	**2004-06 Shitanoe Shipbuilding Co Ltd — Usuki OT** Yd No: 1237 Loa 69.90 (BB) Br ex 12.52 Dght 4.518 Lbp 66.00 Br md 12.50 Dpth 5.55 Welded, 1 dk	**(A11B2TG) LPG Tanker** Double Sides Entire Compartment Length Liq (Gas): 1,830 2 x Gas Tank (s); 2 independent cyl horizontal 2 Cargo Pump (s): 2x400m³/hr Manifold: Bow/CM: 29.6m	**1 oil engine** driving 1 FP propeller Total Power: 1,912kW (2,600hp) 13.0kn Hanshin LH36LA 1 x 4 Stroke 6 Cy. 360 x 670 1912kW (2600bhp) The Hanshin Diesel Works Ltd-Japan AuxGen: 2 x 310kW 440/110V 60Hz a.c Thrusters: 1 Tunnel thruster (f) Fuel: 37.0 (d.f.) 175.0 (r.f.)
9715012 JD3505 -	**SHUNKO** - **Harukaze Kaiun KK** - *Kitakyushu, Fukuoka* *Japan* Official number: 141906	*285* - -		**2013-04 K.K. Odo Zosen Tekko — Shimonoseki** Yd No: 615 Loa 34.51 Br ex - Dght 3.200 Lbp 31.06 Br md 9.00 Dpth 4.00 Welded, 1 dk	**(B32A2ST) Tug**	**2 oil engines** gearing integral to driving 2 Z propellers Total Power: 2,648kW (3,600hp) Niigata 6L26LX 2 x each-1324kW (1800bhp) Niigata Engineering Co Ltd-Japan
8840042 JK5002 -	**SHUNKO MARU** - **Teruo Nakayama** - *Kisaradu, Chiba* *Japan* Official number: 131736	*496* - 828		**1989-09 Kyoei Zosen KK — Mihara HS** Loa 44.00 Br ex - Dght 3.850 Lbp 40.00 Br md 11.50 Dpth 5.50 Welded, 1 dk	**(A24D2BA) Aggregates Carrier**	**1 oil engine** driving 1 FP propeller Total Power: 736kW (1,001hp) Niigata 6M26AGTE 1 x 4 Stroke 6 Cy. 260 x 460 736kW (1001bhp) Niigata Engineering Co Ltd-Japan
8629266 BG3671 2247	**SHUNN SHING NO. 626** - **Chen Ying-Ren** - *Kaohsiung* *Chinese Taipei* Official number: 014911	**184** 64 -		**2008-06 Chien Yuan Shipbuilding Co., Ltd. — Xinyuan** Loa 30.20 Br ex 6.20 Dght - Lbp - Br md - Dpth 2.60 Bonded, 1 dk	**(B11B2FV) Fishing Vessel** Hull Material: Reinforced Plastic	**1 oil engine** driving 1 Propeller
7416301 - -	**SHUNSEI** *ex Kariyushi 1 -2008* **Sea Lion Shipping Lines Inc** - *Philippines*	*129* - 12		**1975-07 Hitachi Zosen Corp — Kawasaki KN** Yd No: 117064 Loa 27.54 Br ex 10.80 Dght 1.372 Lbp 26.34 Br md 5.84 Dpth 3.56 Welded, 1 dk	**(A37B2PS) Passenger Ship** Hull Material: Aluminium Alloy Passengers: unberthed: 105	**2 oil engines** driving 2 FP propellers Total Power: 1,618kW (2,200hp) 38.0kn Maybach MB820DB 2 x Vee 4 Stroke 12 Cy. 175 x 205 each-809kW (1100bhp) Ikegai Tekkosho-Japan
9020041 XUTJ7 -	**SHUNTAI NO. 9** *ex Shun Tai No. 9 -2011 ex Shinei Maru -2009* **Run Jia Shipping Co Ltd** Yantai Runhai International Shipping Management Co Ltd *Phnom Penh* *Cambodia* MMSI: 514209000 Official number: 0991266	**1,498** 729 1,551	Class: UB	**1991-07 Honda Zosen — Saiki** Yd No: 821 Loa - Br ex - Dght 4.180 Lbp 70.00 Br md 11.50 Dpth 7.00 Welded, 1 dk	**(A31A2GX) General Cargo Ship** Compartments: 1 Ho, ER 1 Ha: ER	**1 oil engine** with clutches, flexible couplings & sr reverse geared to sc. shaft driving 1 FP propeller Total Power: 883kW (1,201hp) Niigata 6M31AFTE 1 x 4 Stroke 6 Cy. 310 x 530 883kW (1201bhp) Niigata Engineering Co Ltd-Japan
8201741 HO4479 -	**SHUNTER** *ex CS Safe -2011 ex Smit-Lloyd Safe -2006* *ex TS 51 Safe -1993* **Newbury Holdings Two Ltd** Focus Energy Ltd *Panama* *Panama* MMSI: 354515000 Official number: 3303807C	**1,521** 456 1,866	Class: LR (AB) (GL) **100A1** SS 12/2007 offshore tug/supply ship **LMC** **UMS** Eq.Ltr: U; Cable: 907.5/32.0 U2 (a)	**1983-04 Elsflether Werft AG — Elsfleth** Yd No: 404 Loa 67.60 Br ex 14.33 Dght 5.971 Lbp 58.81 Br md 14.00 Dpth 6.91 Welded, 1 dk	**(B21B20A) Anchor Handling Tug Supply** Grain: 256 Compartments: 4 Ta, ER	**2 oil engines** with clutches, flexible couplings & sr geared to sc. shafts driving 2 CP propellers Total Power: 5,884kW (8,000hp) 11.0kn MWM TBD510-8 2 x 4 Stroke 8 Cy. 330 x 360 each-2942kW (4000bhp) Motoren Werke Mannheim AG (MWM)-West Germany AuxGen: 2 x 550kW 440V 60Hz a.c, 2 x 275kW 440V 60Hz a.c Thrusters: 1 Thwart. CP thruster (f) Fuel: 834.5 (d.f.) 17.0pd
9614517 9V9714 -	**SHUNTIEN** - **The China Navigation Co Pte Ltd** - *Singapore* *Singapore* MMSI: 563709000 Official number: 397501	**25,483** 11,810 30,852	Class: LR ✠ **100A1** SS 11/2013 container ship, Nos. 3 & 4 holds strengthened for heavy cargoes **ShipRight** ACS (B) *IWS LI EP ✠ **LMC** **UMS** Eq.Ltr: Mt; Cable: 638.5/73.0 U3 (a)	**2013-11 Zhejiang Ouhua Shipbuilding Co Ltd — Zhoushan ZJ** Yd No: 641 Loa 199.90 (BB) Br ex 28.28 Dght 10.500 Lbp 188.79 Br md 28.20 Dpth 15.50 Welded, 1 dk	**(A33A2CC) Container Ship (Fully Cellular)** TEU 2082 C Ho 916 TEU C Dk 1166 TEU incl 147 ref C Compartments: 2 Ho, 2 Tw Dk, 3 Cell Ho, ER 5 Ha: ER Cranes: 4x60t	**1 oil engine** driving 1 FP propeller Total Power: 13,560kW (18,436hp) 15.5kn Wartsila 6RT-flex58T 1 x 2 Stroke 6 Cy. 580 x 2416 13560kW (18436bhp) Hudong Heavy Machinery Co Ltd-China AuxGen: 3 x 1058kW 450V 60Hz a.c Boilers: AuxB (Comp) 8.4kgf/cm² (8.2bar) Thrusters: 1 Tunnel thruster (f)
9573816 3FIT3 -	**SHUNWA** - **Wakoh Panama SA** Kasuga Shipping Co Ltd SatCom: Inmarsat C 435605011 *Panama* *Panama* MMSI: 356050000 Official number: 4181910	**17,025** 10,108 28,351 T/cm 39.6	Class: NK	**2010-08 Shimanami Shipyard Co Ltd — Imabari EH** Yd No: 528 Loa 169.37 (BB) Br ex - Dght 9.819 Lbp 160.40 Br md 27.20 Dpth 13.60 Welded, 1 dk	**(A21A2BC) Bulk Carrier** Grain: 37,320; Bale: 35,742 Compartments: 5 Ho, ER 5 Ha: ER Cranes: 4x30.7t	**1 oil engine** driving 1 FP propeller Total Power: 5,850kW (7,954hp) 14.0kn MAN-B&W 6S42MC 1 x 2 Stroke 6 Cy. 420 x 1764 5850kW (7954bhp) Makita Corp-Japan Fuel: 1538.0 (r.f.)
7929360 - -	**SHUNWA MARU** - **PT Teguh Permata Nusantara** - *Indonesia*	*299* - 670		**1980-06 Jyonan Zosen K.K. — Ube** Yd No: 136 Loa 52.18 Br ex 8.62 Dght 3.385 Lbp 48.01 Br md 8.60 Dpth 3.81 Welded, 1 dk	**(A12A2TC) Chemical Tanker**	**1 oil engine** driving 1 FP propeller Total Power: 588kW (799hp) 10.3kn Yanmar MF24-UT 1 x 4 Stroke 6 Cy. 240 x 420 588kW (799bhp) Matsue Diesel KK-Japan
7935096 HP7328 -	**SHUNYO MARU** - **Sea Power Pte Ltd** - *Panama* *Panama* Official number: D7191789PEXT	*199* 108 546		**1979 K.K. Watanabe Zosensho — Nagasaki** Yd No: 811 Loa 46.00 Br ex 7.95 Dght - Lbp 41.20 Br md 7.80 Dpth 3.31 Welded, 1 dk	**(A13B2TU) Tanker (unspecified)**	**1 oil engine** driving 1 FP propeller Total Power: 441kW (600hp) Hanshin 1 x 4 Stroke 6 Cy. 230 x 280 441kW (600bhp) The Hanshin Diesel Works Ltd-Japan

8997352 **SHUNYO MARU**
JD2040
-
Shunzan Kaiun KK (Shunzan Kaiun Co Ltd)
-
Imabari, Ehime *Japan*
Official number: 140078

499
-
1,760

2004-09 **Yamanaka Zosen K.K. — Imabari**
Loa 74.20 Br ex - Dght 4.310
Lbp 68.00 Br md 12.30 Dpth 7.30
Welded, 1 dk

(A31A2GX) General Cargo Ship

1 oil engine reduction geared to sc. shaft driving 1 Propeller
Total Power: 1,324kW (1,800hp) 12.0kn
Daihatsu 6DKM-26
1 x 4 Stroke 6 Cy. 260 x 380 1324kW (1800bhp)
Daihatsu Diesel Manufacturing Co Lt-Japan

8922943 **SHUNYO MARU**
JL6452
-
Shiraishi Kaiun KK
-
Imabari, Ehime *Japan*
Official number: 135163

199
-
649

1996-03 **K.K. Kamishima Zosensho — Osakikamijima** Yd No: 586
Loa 57.00 Br ex - Dght 3.300
Lbp 52.50 Br md 9.40 Dpth 5.40
Welded, 1 dk

(A31A2GX) General Cargo Ship
Grain: 1,304; Bale: 1,160
Compartments: 1 Ho, ER
1 Ha: (30.5 x 7.3)ER

1 oil engine driving 1 FP propeller
Total Power: 1,030kW (1,400hp) 11.0kn
Hanshin LH28G
1 x 4 Stroke 6 Cy. 280 x 460 1030kW (1400bhp)
The Hanshin Diesel Works Ltd-Japan

9223239 **SHUNYO MARU**
JETM
-
Government of Japan (Ministry of Agriculture & Forestry - Fisheries Agency)
-
Shizuoka, Shizuoka *Japan*
MMSI: 431494000
Official number: 135624

887
-
-

2001-04 **Niigata Engineering Co Ltd — Niigata NI** Yd No: 2375
Loa 66.31 Br ex - Dght 4.750
Lbp 58.80 Br md 11.40 Dpth 7.10
Welded, 1 dk

(B12D2FR) Fishery Research Vessel

2 oil engines reduction geared to sc. shaft driving 1 CP propeller
Total Power: 2,942kW (4,000hp) 17.5kn
Niigata 6MG28HX
2 x 4 Stroke 6 Cy. 280 x 370 each-1471kW (2000bhp)
Niigata Engineering Co Ltd-Japan
AuxGen: 1 x 400kW 450V 60Hz a.c, 2 x 400kW 450V 60Hz a.c
Fuel: 259.0 (d.f.)

9281188 **SHUNYO MARU**
JM6666
-
Kowa Kogyo KK
-
Nagasaki, Nagasaki *Japan*
Official number: 136410

145
-
-

2002-05 **K.K. Watanabe Zosensho — Nagasaki** Yd No: 097
Loa 34.02 Br ex - Dght -
Lbp 28.50 Br md 9.20 Dpth 4.19
Welded, 1 dk

(B32A2ST) Tug

2 oil engines Geared Integral to driving 2 Z propellers
Total Power: 2,942kW (4,000hp)
Niigata 6L28HX
2 x 4 Stroke 6 Cy. 280 x 370 each-1471kW (2000bhp)
Niigata Engineering Co Ltd-Japan

9054652 **SHUNYO MARU No. 8**
JK5145
-
Niihama Shipping Co Ltd (Niihama Kaiun KK)
YK Shunyo
Niihama, Ehime *Japan*
MMSI: 431400039
Official number: 132551

432 Class: NK
-
999

1992-10 **Hitachi Zosen Mukaishima Marine Co Ltd — Onomichi HS** Yd No: 63
Loa 59.22 Br ex 9.67 Dght 4.061
Lbp 54.50 Br md 9.60 Dpth 4.30
Welded, 1 dk

(A12B2TR) Chemical/Products Tanker
Liq: 650; Liq (Oil): 650

1 oil engine driving 1 FP propeller
Total Power: 735kW (999hp) 10.5kn
Niigata 6M26AGTE
1 x 4 Stroke 6 Cy. 260 x 460 735kW (999bhp)
Niigata Engineering Co Ltd-Japan
AuxGen: 2 x 120kW a.c
Fuel: 51.0 (d.f.)

8620739 **SHUNYO MARU No. 38**
JBDH
HK1-923
ex Hoken Maru No. 18 *-1991*
Kanefuji Gyogyo KK
-
Hakodate, Hokkaido *Japan*
Official number: 124434

127
-
-

1980-04 **Narasaki Zosen KK — Muroran HK** Yd No: 990
Lengthened-1985
Loa - Br ex - Dght -
Lbp 32.01 Br md 6.00 Dpth 2.60
Welded, 1 dk

(B11A2FS) Stern Trawler

1 oil engine driving 1 FP propeller
Total Power: 382kW (519hp)
Akasaka DM28R
1 x 4 Stroke 6 Cy. 280 x 460 382kW (519bhp)
Akasaka Tekkosho KK (Akasaka DieselLtd)-Japan

8895396 **SHUNYO MARU No. 68**
-
-
ex Kosei Maru No. 7 *-1999*
ex Koei Maru No. 68 *-1999*
-
-

117
-
-

1984-04 **K.K. Honma Zosensho — Niigata**
L reg 29.00 Br ex - Dght -
Lbp - Br md 6.00 Dpth 2.48
Welded, 1 dk

(B11B2FV) Fishing Vessel

1 oil engine driving 1 FP propeller
Niigata
1 x 4 Stroke
Niigata Engineering Co Ltd-Japan

7433672 **SHUO HAI**
BUUX
-
ex Lucky Sun *-2004* *ex* Mega S *-2002*
ex M. Aksu *-2001* *ex* Aramis *-1994*
launched as Almirante Aniceto *-1988*
Shanghai Changjiang Shipping Corp
-
SatCom: Inmarsat C 441271815
China
MMSI: 412079280

22,354 Class: (CC) (NV) (AB)
13,706
38,281

1988-03 **Engenharia e Maquinas S.A. (EMAQ) — Rio de Janeiro** Yd No: 311
Loa 193.86 (BB) Br ex - Dght 10.910
Lbp 183.01 Br md 27.61 Dpth 14.81
Welded, 1 dk

(A21A2BC) Bulk Carrier
Grain: 45,840; Bale: 42,500
Compartments: 7 Ho, ER
7 Ha: (11.8 x 13.5)2 (15.2 x 13.5)4 (9.3 x 13.5)ER
Cranes: 2x35t,2x25t

1 oil engine driving 1 FP propeller
Total Power: 8,826kW (12,000hp) 15.0kn
Sulzer 6RND76
1 x 2 Stroke 6 Cy. 760 x 1550 8826kW (12000bhp)
Ishikawajima do Brasil Estaleiros S (ISHIBRAS)-Brazil
AuxGen: 3 x 480kW 450V 60Hz a.c

9677272 **SHUO MARU**
-
-
YK Hamayu Kaiun
-
Shimonoseki, Yamaguchi *Japan*

749 Class: FA
-
1,604

2013-07 **Shinosaki Zosen — Kumamoto** Yd No: 130
Loa 72.00 Br ex - Dght 4.700
Lbp - Br md 11.00 Dpth -
Welded, 1 dk

(A12A2TC) Chemical Tanker
Double Hull (13F)

1 oil engine reduction geared to sc. shaft driving 1 Propeller
Total Power: 1,839kW (2,500hp) 12.0kn
Hanshin LA34G
1 x 4 Stroke 6 Cy. 340 x 720 1839kW (2500bhp)
The Hanshin Diesel Works Ltd-Japan

9133135 **SHUPAVU**
5ZNO
-
Government of The Republic of Kenya (Kenya Navy)
-
Mombasa *Kenya*
Official number: P3131

661 Class: (LR)
198 ✠ Classed LR until 20/10/99
144

1997-03 **Astilleros Gondan SA — Castropol** Yd No: 372
Loa 60.00 Br ex 9.91 Dght 2.612
Lbp 54.00 Br md 9.90 Dpth 6.00
Welded, 2 dks

(B31A2SR) Research Survey Vessel

2 oil engines with clutches, flexible couplings & sr geared to sc. shafts driving 2 FP propellers
Total Power: 6,000kW (8,158hp) 23.0kn
M.T.U. 16V956
2 x Vee 4 Stroke 16 Cy. 230 x 230 each-3000kW (4079bhp)
EN Bazan de Construcciones NavalesMilitares SA-Spain
AuxGen: 2 x 170kW 440V 60Hz a.c

9217606 **SHUREI**
JM4167
-
Ryukyu Kaiun Kaisha ('The Ryukyu Line')
-
Naha, Okinawa *Japan*
MMSI: 431680175
Official number: 133763

6,562 Class: NK
-
5,376

2000-01 **Saiki Heavy Industries Co Ltd — Saiki OT** Yd No: 1100
Loa 149.57 (BB) Br ex - Dght 6.714
Lbp 138.00 Br md 23.00 Dpth 7.35
Welded, 4 dks

(A35A2RR) Ro-Ro Cargo Ship
Angled bow door/ramp (s. f.)
Angled stern door/ramp (s. a.)
Lorries: 9, Cars: 121, Trailers: 88

1 oil engine reduction geared to sc. shaft driving 1 FP propeller
Total Power: 16,991kW (23,101hp) 22.3kn
Pielstick 14PC4-2V-570
1 x Vee 4 Stroke 14 Cy. 570 x 620 16991kW (23101bhp)
Nippon Kokan KK (NKK Corp)-Japan
AuxGen: 3 x 1040kW a.c
Thrusters: 1 Thwart. FP thruster (f); 1 Tunnel thruster (a)
Fuel: 720.0

9276274 **SHURI**
JL6688
-
Japan Railway Construction, Transport & Technology Agency & Seno Kisen Co Ltd & Shikoku Kaihatsu Ferry Co Ltd
Seno Kisen KK (Seno Kisen Co Ltd)
Imabari, Ehime *Japan*
MMSI: 431501723
Official number: 137018

9,813 Class: NK
-
6,566

2002-07 **Imabari Shipbuilding Co Ltd — Imabari EH (Imabari Shipyard)** Yd No: 578
Loa 167.72 (BB) Br ex - Dght 7.215
Lbp 156.00 Br md 24.00 Dpth 10.70
Welded

(A35A2RR) Ro-Ro Cargo Ship
Quarter stern door & ramp (s. f.)
Len: 23.50 Wid: 7.00 Swl: -
Quarter stern door/ramp (s. a.)
Len: 31.50 Wid: 7.00 Swl: -
Lane-Len: 1900
Cars: 100, Trailers: 125

1 oil engine driving 1 FP propeller
Total Power: 12,621kW (17,160hp) 21.0kn
B&W 8S50MC-C
1 x 2 Stroke 8 Cy. 500 x 2000 12621kW (17160bhp)
Mitsui Engineering & Shipbuilding CLtd-Japan
AuxGen: 3 x 980kW a.c
Thrusters: 1 Tunnel thruster (f); 2 Tunnel thruster (a)
Fuel: 891.0 (r.f.)

8727678 **SHURSHA**
UGDJ
-
JSC Vostok-1
-
SatCom: Inmarsat C 427320199
Nakhodka *Russia*
MMSI: 273819400

836 Class: RS (Class contemplated)
223
414

1985-05 **Zavod "Leninskaya Kuznitsa" — Kiyev** Yd No: 1556
Loa 54.82 Br ex 9.95 Dght 4.140
Lbp 50.30 Br md 9.80 Dpth 5.00
Welded, 1 dk

(B11A2FS) Stern Trawler
Ice Capable

1 oil engine driving 1 CP propeller
Total Power: 853kW (1,160hp) 12.0kn
S.K.L. 8NVD48A-2U
1 x 4 Stroke 8 Cy. 320 x 480 853kW (1160bhp)
VEB Schwermaschinenbau "KarlLiebknecht" (SKL)-Magdeburg
AuxGen: 4 x 160kW a.c

9564633 **SHUSHA**
4JNT
-
Azerbaijan State Caspian Shipping Co (ASCSS)
-
SatCom: Inmarsat C 442332710
Baku *Azerbaijan*
MMSI: 423327100
Official number: DGR-0540

7,834 Class: RS
3,521
13,008
T/cm
25.0

2009-07 **Sudostroitelnyy Zavod "Krasnoye Sormovo" — Nizhniy Novgorod** Yd No: 19619/13
Loa 149.90 (BB) Br ex 17.30 Dght 7.140
Lbp 147.60 Br md - Dpth 10.50
Welded, 1 dk

(A13B2TP) Products Tanker
Double Hull (13F)
Liq: 14,770; Liq (Oil): 14,770
Cargo Heating Coils
Compartments: 12 Wing Ta, ER
4 Cargo Pump (s): 4x350m³/hr
Manifold: Bow/CM: 76.2m
Ice Capable

2 oil engines reduction geared to sc.shafts driving 2 FP propellers
Total Power: 3,240kW (4,406hp) 10.0kn
Wartsila 9L20
2 x 4 Stroke 9 Cy. 200 x 280 each-1620kW (2203bhp)
Wartsila Finland Oy-Finland
AuxGen: 3 x 384kW a.c
Thrusters: 1 Thwart. FP thruster (f)
Fuel: 300.0 (d.f.)

9458054 **SHUSHA**
9HA2401
-
completed as Thera *-2010*
Titan Shipping-4 Co Ltd
Palmali Gemicilik ve Acentelik AS (Palmali Shipping & Agency)
SatCom: Inmarsat C 424853310
Valletta *Malta*
MMSI: 248533000
Official number: 9458054

8,995 Class: RS (BV)
4,523
14,355
T/cm
25.7

2010-05 **Celiktekne Sanayii ve Ticaret A.S. — Tuzla, Istanbul** Yd No: 73
Loa 142.98 (BB) Br ex 21.70 Dght 8.695
Lbp 134.00 Br md 21.70 Dpth 11.10
Welded, 1 dk

(A12B2TR) Chemical/Products Tanker
Double Hull (13F)
Liq: 15,105; Liq (Oil): 15,850
Cargo Heating Coils
Compartments: 12 Wing Ta, 2 Wing Slop Ta, ER
14 Cargo Pump (s): 14x330m³/hr
Manifold: Bow/CM: 72m
Ice Capable

1 oil engine driving 1 CP propeller
Total Power: 4,440kW (6,037hp) 14.0kn
MAN-B&W 6S35MC
1 x 2 Stroke 6 Cy. 350 x 1400 4440kW (6037bhp)
AuxGen: 3 x 715kW a.c, 1 x 850kW a.c
Thrusters: 1 Tunnel thruster (f)
Fuel: 753.0 (r.f.)

IMO / Call sign	Name / Owner	Tonnage	Class	Builder / Dimensions	Type	Machinery
9632650 - -	**SHUSWAP** **Samson Tug Boats Inc** *Vancouver, BC* *Canada* MMSI: 316020067 Official number: 835426	**114** 85 -		**2011-07 Sylte Shipyard Ltd — Maple Ridge BC** L reg 17.68 Br ex - Dght - Lbp - Br md 8.61 Dpth 3.91 Welded, 1 dk	**(B32A2ST) Tug**	**2 oil engines** reduction geared to sc. shafts driving 2 Directional propellers Total Power: 2,280kW (3,100hp) M.T.U. 2 x 4 Stroke each-1140kW (1550bhp) MTU Friedrichshafen GmbH-Friedrichshafen
7722023 *YYV3458* -	**SHUT OUT** *ex* H. O. S. Shut Out *-1996* *ex* Joseph J. Orgeron *-1993* **Tidewater Marine Service CA (SEMARCA)** *Maracaibo* *Venezuela* Official number: AJZL - 30.823	**497** 149 450	Class: (AB)	**1977-10 Halter Marine, Inc. — Lockport, La** Yd No: 641 Loa 50.60 Br ex 11.89 Dght 3.341 Lbp 47.33 Br md 11.59 Dpth 3.97 Welded, 1 dk	**(B21A2OS) Platform Supply Ship**	**2 oil engines** reverse reduction geared to sc. shafts driving 2 FP propellers Total Power: 1,648kW (2,240hp) 12.0kn G.M. (Detroit Diesel) 16V-149-TI 2 x Vee 2 Stroke 16 Cy. 146 x 146 each-824kW (1120bhp) General Motors Detroit DieselAllison Divn-USA AuxGen: 2 x 75kW Thrusters: 1 Thwart. FP thruster (f)
9039602 *JG5247* -	**SHUTTLE ACE** **Mitsui Muromachi Shipping Co Ltd (Mitsui Muromachi Kaiun KK)** - *Tokyo* *Japan* MMSI: 431100499 Official number: 133992	*8,280* - 5,271	Class: NK	**1993-07 Shin Kurushima Dockyard Co. Ltd. — Onishi** Yd No: 2767 Loa 161.52 (BB) Br ex - Dght 6.715 Lbp 150.00 Br md 26.00 Dpth 9.60 Welded, 3 dks	**(A35B2RV) Vehicles Carrier** Quarter bow door/ramp (s) Len: 27.50 Wid: 7.00 Swl: 38 Quarter stern door/ramp (s. a.) Len: 20.00 Wid: 8.50 Swl: 38 Lorries: 120, Cars: 210	**1 oil engine** reduction geared to sc. shaft driving 1 CP propeller Total Power: 11,916kW (16,201hp) 20.2kn Pielstick 9PC40L570 1 x 4 Stroke 9 Cy. 570 x 750 11916kW (16201bhp) Diesel United Ltd.-Aioi AuxGen: 1 x 720kW a.c Thrusters: 1 Thwart. CP thruster (f) Fuel: 759.0 (r.f.) 142.0 (d.f.)
9245201 *V8V3091* -	**SHUTTLE HOPE** *ex* Shirakisan *-2004* **PKL Jaya Sdn Bhd** Sanyang Marine Pte Ltd *Muara* *Brunei* MMSI: 508111130 Official number: 21500109	*482* 146 360	Class: LR **100A1** SS 12/2009 roll on-roll off passenger/vehicle ferry Muara, Brunei to Menumbok, Malaysia service **LMC**	**2001-06 Naikai Zosen Corp — Onomichi HS (Setoda Shipyard)** Yd No: 671 Loa 49.90 Br ex - Dght - Lbp 43.00 Br md 11.00 Dpth 3.59 Welded	**(A36A2PR) Passenger/Ro-Ro Ship (Vehicles)** Passengers: unberthed: 200 Bow door/ramp (centre) Stern door/ramp (centre) Vehicles: 45	**2 oil engines** reduction geared to sc. shafts driving 2 FP propellers Total Power: 1,544kW (2,100hp) 13.8kn Daihatsu 6DKM-20 2 x 4 Stroke 6 Cy. 200 x 300 each-772kW (1050bhp) Daihatsu Diesel Manufacturing Co Lt-Japan AuxGen: 2 x 96kW a.c Thrusters: 1 Thwart. FP thruster (f)
9603831 *JD3256* -	**SHUTTLE HOYO** **Kokudo Kyushi Ferry KK** *Oita, Oita* *Japan* MMSI: 431003061 Official number: 141538	*999* - 750		**2012-02 Usuki Shipyard Co Ltd — Usuki OT** Yd No: 1732 Loa 78.50 (BB) Br ex - Dght 3.500 Lbp 70.00 Br md 13.40 Dpth 9.45 Welded, 1 dk	**(A36A2PR) Passenger/Ro-Ro Ship (Vehicles)** Passengers: unberthed: 292	**2 oil engines** reduction geared to sc. shafts driving 2 Propellers Total Power: 3,680kW (5,004hp) 18.5kn Yanmar 6EY26 2 x 4 Stroke 6 Cy. 260 x 385 each-1840kW (2502bhp) Yanmar Diesel Engine Co Ltd-Japan
8882832 - -	**SHUTTLE II** *ex* Taishu Maru No. 16 *-2004* *ex* Hino Maru *-2004* *ex* Hino Maru No. 3 *-2004* - -	*175* 91 426		**1976 Hayashi Zosen — Osakikamijima** Loa 40.00 Br ex - Dght 3.200 Lbp 36.00 Br md 7.50 Dpth 4.80 Welded, 1 dk	**(A31A2GX) General Cargo Ship** 1 Ha: (19.5 x 5.5)	**1 oil engine** driving 1 FP propeller Total Power: 405kW (551hp) 9.5kn Matsui 1 x 4 Stroke 405kW (551bhp) Matsui Iron Works Co Ltd-Japan
8926212 *JK5483* -	**SHUTTLE No. 5** **KK Ezaki Kairiku Unso** *Saikai, Nagasaki* *Japan* Official number: 134798	*346* - -		**1996-11 Naikai Zosen Corp — Onomichi HS (Setoda Shipyard)** Yd No: 622 Loa 49.90 Br ex - Dght 2.600 Lbp 38.90 Br md 10.00 Dpth 3.60 Welded, 1 dk	**(A36A2PR) Passenger/Ro-Ro Ship (Vehicles)** Passengers: unberthed: 350 Bow ramp Stern ramp Cars: 10	**1 oil engine** driving 1 FP propeller Total Power: 1,177kW (1,600hp) 11.6kn Daihatsu 6DLM-26FSL 1 x 4 Stroke 6 Cy. 260 x 340 1177kW (1600bhp) Daihatsu Diesel Manufacturing Co Lt-Japan AuxGen: 2 x 80kW 220V 60Hz a.c Fuel: 31.0 (d.f.) 6.3pd
9105841 *UIWD* -	**SHUYA** **Baltasar Shipping SA** CJSC 'Onegoship' SatCom: Inmarsat C 427321774 *St Petersburg* *Russia* MMSI: 273417060	**2,889** 1,034 3,148	Class: RS	**1994-07 Schiffswerft und Maschinenfabrik Cassens GmbH — Emden** Yd No: 200 Loa 96.00 Br ex 13.40 Dght 4.300 Lbp 93.00 Br md 13.20 Dpth 6.90 Welded, 1 dk	**(A31A2GX) General Cargo Ship** Grain: 5,250 TEU 160 C. 160/20' Compartments: 1 Ho, ER 1 Ha: ER	**1 oil engine** with flexible couplings & sr reverse geared to sc. shaft driving 1 FP propeller Total Power: 1,600kW (2,175hp) 11.0kn MaK 8M332C 1 x 4 Stroke 8 Cy. 240 x 330 1600kW (2175bhp) Krupp MaK Maschinenbau GmbH-Kiel AuxGen: 2 x 200kW a.c, 1 x 103kW a.c Thrusters: 1 Thwart. FP thruster (f) Fuel: 204.0 (d.f.)
8129589 *UAXZ* -	**SHUYA** **'Arktikmorneftegazrazvedka' OJSC** - SatCom: Inmarsat C 427321774 *Murmansk* *Russia* MMSI: 273412200	**5,082** 1,796 5,834	Class: (RS)	**1983-05 Rauma-Repola Oy — Rauma** Yd No: 278 Loa 115.80 Br ex 17.05 Dght 7.001 Lbp 105.01 Br md 17.01 Dpth 8.51 Welded, 1 dk	**(A13B2TP) Products Tanker** Single Hull Bale: 121; Liq: 6,308; Liq (Oil): 6,308 Part Cargo Heating Coils Compartments: 1 Ho, 8 Ta, ER 1 Ha: (2.5 x 3.2)ER Ice Capable	**1 oil engine** driving 1 CP propeller Total Power: 2,465kW (3,351hp) 14.0kn B&W 5DKRN50/110-2 1 x 2 Stroke 5 Cy. 500 x 1100 2465kW (3351bhp) Bryanskiy Mashinostroitelnyy Zavod (BMZ)-Bryansk AuxGen: 3 x 264kW 380V 50Hz a.c Fuel: 88.0 (d.f.) (Part Heating Coils) 400.0 (r.f.) 16.5pd
8035142 *UITQ* -	**SHUYA** **Russian Inspector's & Marine Surveyor's Corp (RIMSCO)** *Sovetskaya Gavan* *Russia* MMSI: 273420530 Official number: 812397	**1,166** 349 404	Class: (RS)	**1982-06 Yaroslavskiy Sudostroitelnyy Zavod — Yaroslavl** Yd No: 220 Loa 58.58 Br ex 12.68 Dght 4.680 Lbp 51.62 Br md 12.64 Dpth 5.92 Welded, 1 dk	**(B32A2ST) Tug** Ice Capable	**2 diesel electric oil engines** driving 2 gen. each 1000kW 900V Connecting to 2 elec. motors each (950kW) driving 1 FP propeller Total Power: 2,208kW (3,002hp) 13.2kn Kolomna 6CHN30/38 2 x 4 Stroke 6 Cy. 300 x 380 each-1104kW (1501bhp) Kolomenskiy Zavod-Kolomna AuxGen: 2 x 300kW 400V a.c, 2 x 160kW 400V a.c Fuel: 346.0 (d.f.)
7810234 *XYBZ* -	**SHWAY PALEI** *ex* 701 *-1981* - - *Yangon* *Myanmar* MMSI: 506081000	*363* 204 357	Class: (NV)	**1979-07 AS Storviks Mek. Verksted — Kristiansund** Yd No: 93 Loa 35.90 Br ex - Dght 3.201 Lbp 33.15 Br md 8.50 Dpth 5.16 Welded, 1 dk	**(A34A2GR) Refrigerated Cargo Ship** Ins: 593 Compartments: 2 Ho, ER 2 Ha: 2 (2.5 x 2.5) Derricks: 1x5t,1x5t	**1 oil engine** reduction geared to sc. shaft driving 1 CP propeller Total Power: 357kW (485hp) 10.0kn Caterpillar D379TA 1 x Vee 4 Stroke 8 Cy. 159 x 203 357kW (485bhp) Caterpillar Tractor Co-USA Fuel: 92.0 (d.f.) 2.5pd
8002614 - -	**SHWE LUN PYAN** **Government of The Union of Myanmar (People's Pearl & Fishery Board)** - *Yangon* *Myanmar* Official number: 1804	*118* 48 101	Class: (LR) ✠	**1982-09 Lewis Offshore Ltd. — Stornoway** Yd No: 7903 Loa 28.40 Br ex 8.18 Dght 1.574 Lbp 25.13 Br md 8.01 Dpth 1.86 Welded, 1 dk	**(A35D2RL) Landing Craft** Bow door/ramp	**2 oil engines** with clutches, flexible couplings & sr reverse geared to sc. shafts driving 2 FP propellers Total Power: 640kW (870hp) Caterpillar 3406TA 2 x 4 Stroke 6 Cy. 137 x 165 each-320kW (435bhp) Caterpillar Tractor Co-USA AuxGen: 1 x 19kW 415V 50Hz a.c
8327791 *XYNN* -	**SHWE PYI THA** *ex* Huttaw *-1981* **Myanma Petroleum Enterprises** - *Yangon* *Myanmar*	*498* 330 1,125		**1978 Burma Dockyard Corp. — Rangoon** Loa 66.30 Br ex 10.22 Dght 3.801 Lbp - Br md - Dpth 4.02 Welded, 1 dk	**(A13B2TU) Tanker (unspecified)**	**1 oil engine** driving 1 FP propeller 12.0kn
8988040 *XYTI* -	**SHWE THARA PHU** **P I Transportation Co Ltd** Dr Khin Maung Kyaing *Yangon* *Myanmar* Official number: 5458	**497** 330 1,400		**2003-08 P.I. Co. Ltd. — Myanmar** Yd No: 056 Loa 62.20 Br ex 11.00 Dght 4.680 Lbp 57.02 Br md 10.85 Dpth 5.50 Welded, 1 dk	**(A31A2GX) General Cargo Ship**	**3 oil engines** driving 3 Propellers Total Power: 906kW (1,233hp) Nissan RF10 3 x Vee 4 Stroke 10 Cy. 138 x 142 each-302kW (411bhp) Nissan Diesel Motor Co. Ltd.-Ageo
8988052 *XYTP* -	**SHWE ZAY YAR AUNG** **P I Transportation Co Ltd** Dr Khin Maung Kyaing *Yangon* *Myanmar* Official number: 4807	**489** 264 800		**1998-12 P.I. Co. Ltd. — Myanmar** Yd No: 045 Loa 56.40 Br ex 7.65 Dght 3.960 Lbp 52.80 Br md 7.60 Dpth 4.25 Welded, 1 dk	**(A31A2GX) General Cargo Ship**	**3 oil engines** driving 3 Propellers Total Power: 552kW (750hp) Hino 3 x 4 Stroke each-184kW (250bhp) Hino Motors Ltd.-Tokyo

IMO / Call sign	Name / Owner / Port	Tonnage	Class	Built / Dimensions	Type	Machinery
8332693 *S2FI* -	**SHYAMA** *ex* Nisshin No. 5 *-1986* *ex* Myoei Maru No. 5 *-1985* **Navigation Ltd** - *Chittagong* *Bangladesh* Official number: C.673	*303* 193 541	Class: (KR)	**1971 YK Furumoto Tekko Zosensho — Osakikamijima** Loa 43.52 Br ex - Dght 3.001 Lbp 39.22 Br md 7.00 Dpth 3.31 Welded, 1 dk	**(A13B2TU) Tanker (unspecified)** Liq: 603; Liq (Oil): 603 Compartments: 3 Ta, ER	**1 oil engine** driving 1 FP propeller Total Power: 405kW (551hp) 9.5kn Hanshin 6L26AGSH 1 x 4 Stroke 6 Cy. 260 x 400 405kW (551bhp) The Hanshin Diesel Works Ltd-Japan AuxGen: 1 x 12kW 225V a.c
7616834 - -	**SHYAMA RANI** - **Shyama Coastal Shipping Pvt Co Ltd** - *Mormugao* *India*	*432* 298 500	Class: IR (BV)	**1976-11 Goa Shipyard Ltd. — Goa** Yd No: 1052 Loa 49.13 Br ex 9.15 Dght 1.831 Lbp 47.00 Br md 8.74 Dpth 2.49 Welded, 1 dk	**(A31A2GX) General Cargo Ship** Grain: 352 Compartments: 1 Ho, ER 1 Ha: (27.9 x 7.0)ER	**2 oil engines** reverse reduction geared to sc. shafts driving 2 FP propellers Total Power: 320kW (436hp) 8.8kn Cummins NT-743-M 2 x 4 Stroke 6 Cy. 130 x 152 each-160kW (218bhp) Kirloskar Oil Engines Ltd-India AuxGen: 1 x 415kW 24V 50Hz a.c
8749042 *BH3058* -	**SHYANG CHYANG NO. 8** *ex* Hung I No. 221 *-2011* **Wei Der Fishery Co Ltd** - *Kaohsiung* *Chinese Taipei* Official number: 010301	**447** 181 -		**1987-06 Taiwan Machinery Manufacturing Corp. — Kaohsiung** Loa 49.68 Br ex - Dght 3.520 Lbp 43.28 Br md 8.00 Dpth - Welded, 1 dk	**(B11B2FV) Fishing Vessel**	**1 oil engine** driving 1 Propeller
8749054 *BH2983* -	**SHYANG CHYANG NO. 88** - **Shang Qiang Fishery Co Ltd** - *Kaohsiung* *Chinese Taipei* Official number: 018897	**437** 203 -		**1984-05 Fong Kuo Shipbuilding Co Ltd — Kaohsiung** Loa 41.80 Br ex - Dght 3.500 Lbp - Br md 8.00 Dpth - Welded, 1 dk	**(B11B2FV) Fishing Vessel**	**1 oil engine** driving 1 Propeller
8649046 *BI2475* CT7-0475	**SHYANG CHYANG NO. 888** - **Shang Qiang Fishery Co Ltd** - *Kaohsiung* *Chinese Taipei* Official number: 012400	**674** 296 -		**1993-01 Fong Kuo Shipbuilding Co Ltd — Kaohsiung** Loa 50.00 Br ex - Dght 3.850 Lbp - Br md 8.90 Dpth - Welded, 1 dk	**(B11B2FV) Fishing Vessel**	**1 oil engine** driving 1 Propeller
7825215 *S7UP* -	**SHYANG CHYANG NO. 889** *ex* Jetmark No. 31 *-2012* *ex* Fu Yuan No. 31 *-2001* *ex* Chi Hao No. 66 *-1998* *ex* Chi Fuw No. 6 *-1998* *ex* Fuku Maru *-1998* *ex* Fukutoku Maru No. 28 *-1994* *ex* Koshin Maru No. 38 *-1988* **Sunshine Fishery Co Ltd** - *Victoria* *Seychelles* MMSI: 664641000 Official number: 50217	**554** 239 -		**1979-03 KK Kanasashi Zosen — Shizuoka SZ** Yd No: 2016 Loa 53.68 Br ex - Dght 3.401 Lbp 47.00 Br md 8.81 Dpth 3.76 Welded, 1 dk	**(B11B2FV) Fishing Vessel**	**1 oil engine** driving 1 FP propeller Total Power: 883kW (1,201hp) Akasaka DM28AR 1 x 4 Stroke 6 Cy. 280 x 460 883kW (1201bhp) Akasaka Tekkosho KK (Akasaka DieselLtd)-Japan
8748866 *BH3268* -	**SHYANG MAAN NO. 11** - **Jia Yih Fishery Co Ltd** - *Kaohsiung* *Chinese Taipei* Official number: 011972	**497** 193 -		**1990-11 Chung Yi Shipbuilding Corp. — Kaohsiung** Loa 45.61 Br ex - Dght 3.280 Lbp - Br md 8.30 Dpth - Welded, 1 dk	**(B11B2FV) Fishing Vessel**	**1 oil engine** driving 1 Propeller
8748878 *BH3341* -	**SHYANG MAAN NO. 368** - **Shyang Shin Fishery Co Ltd** - *Kaohsiung* *Chinese Taipei* Official number: 013749	**496** 242 -		**2000-01 Kaohsiung Shipbuilding Co. Ltd. — Kaohsiung** Loa 47.30 Br ex - Dght 3.288 Lbp - Br md 8.60 Dpth 3.70 Welded, 1 dk	**(B11B2FV) Fishing Vessel**	**1 oil engine** reduction geared to sc. shaft driving 1 FP propeller Niigata Niigata Engineering Co Ltd-Japan
7613569 *BYMT* -	**SHYANG MOU No. 11** - **Shyang Mou Ocean Enterprise Co Ltd** - *Kaohsiung* *Chinese Taipei*	*351* 178 -	Class: (CR)	**1974 Taiwan Machinery Manufacturing Corp. — Kaohsiung** Loa 43.59 Br ex 7.57 Dght 3.041 Lbp 38.61 Br md 7.50 Dpth 3.36 Welded, 1 dk	**(B11B2FV) Fishing Vessel** Ins: 384 Compartments: 3 Ho, ER 4 Ha: 2 (1.3 x 1.0)2 (1.3 x 1.3)ER	**1 oil engine** driving 1 FP propeller Total Power: 809kW (1,100hp) 11.5kn Niigata 6L28X 1 x 4 Stroke 6 Cy. 280 x 440 809kW (1100bhp) Niigata Engineering Co Ltd-Japan AuxGen: 1 x 170kW 220V a.c, 1 x 144kW 220V a.c
7623784 *BYON* -	**SHYANG MOU No. 12** - **Shyang Mou Ocean Enterprise Co Ltd** - *Kaohsiung* *Chinese Taipei* Official number: 5391	*356* 181 -	Class: (CR)	**1974 Taiwan Machinery Manufacturing Corp. — Kaohsiung** Loa 43.59 Br ex 7.57 Dght 3.041 Lbp 38.61 Br md 7.50 Dpth 3.36 Welded, 1 dk	**(B11B2FV) Fishing Vessel** Ins: 384 Compartments: 3 Ho, ER 4 Ha: 2 (1.3 x 1.3)2 (1.3 x 1.0)ER	**1 oil engine** driving 1 FP propeller Total Power: 809kW (1,100hp) 11.5kn Niigata 6L28X 1 x 4 Stroke 6 Cy. 280 x 440 809kW (1100bhp) Niigata Engineering Co Ltd-Japan
8822739 - -	**SHYE JIN No. 1** - **Lubmain International SA** - *San Lorenzo* *Honduras* Official number: L-1822851	*426* 203 -		**1985 Fong Kuo Shipbuilding Co Ltd — Kaohsiung** Loa 48.80 Br ex 8.02 Dght 2.510 Lbp - Br md 8.00 Dpth 3.15 Welded, 1 dk	**(B11B2FV) Fishing Vessel**	**1 oil engine** driving 1 FP propeller Total Power: 736kW (1,001hp) Sumiyoshi S26T 1 x 4 Stroke 6 Cy. 260 x 470 736kW (1001bhp) Sumiyoshi Marine Diesel Co Ltd-Japan
8947448 - -	**SHYE SIN No. 1** - - -	**598** 261 -		**1997 Fong Kuo Shipbuilding Co Ltd — Kaohsiung** L reg 48.60 Br ex - Dght - Lbp - Br md 8.70 Dpth 3.75 Welded, 1 dk	**(B11B2FV) Fishing Vessel**	**1 oil engine** driving 1 FP propeller Total Power: 1,030kW (1,400hp) 13.0kn Niigata 6M28HFT 1 x 4 Stroke 6 Cy. 280 x 480 1030kW (1400bhp) Niigata Engineering Co Ltd-Japan
8700199 - -	**SI** *ex* Alpha *-2012* *ex* Shkotovo *-2007* **UBI Energy Ghana Ltd** - *Takoradi* *Ghana* Official number: GSR 0131	**2,966** 918 3,086 T/cm 11.7	Class: RS	**1990-12 Hollming Oy — Rauma** Yd No: 286 Loa 97.40 Br ex 14.23 Dght 5.100 Lbp 90.44 Br md 14.20 Dpth 6.50 Welded, 1 dk	**(A13B2TP) Products Tanker** Single Hull Liq: 3,258; Liq (Oil): 3,258 Compartments: 4 Ta, 4 Wing Ta, ER, 1 Slop Ta, 2 Wing Slop Ta 4 Cargo Pump (s): 4x130m³/hr Manifold: Bow/CM: 46m Ice Capable	**1 oil engine** with clutches, flexible couplings & sr geared to sc. shaft driving 1 CP propeller Total Power: 2,576kW (3,502hp) 13.5kn Russkiy 6CHN40/46 1 x 4 Stroke 6 Cy. 400 x 460 2576kW (3502bhp) Mashinostroitelnyy Zavod"Russkiy-Dizel"-Leningrad AuxGen: 1 x 400kW 50Hz a.c, 2 x 300kW 50Hz a.c Fuel: 59.0 (d.f.) 228.0 (r.f.) 13.2pd
9034365 *FGYP* AC 768588	**SI...** - **Francis Favroul** - SatCom: Inmarsat C 422744210 *Arcachon* *France* MMSI: 227442000 Official number: 768588	*112* 42 46		**1991-12 OCEA SA — Les Sables-d'Olonne** Loa 21.00 (BB) Br ex - Dght 1.810 Lbp 20.07 Br md 9.61 Dpth 3.25 Welded, 1 dk	**(B11B2FV) Fishing Vessel** Hull Material: Aluminium Alloy Ins: 70	**2 oil engines** with clutches, flexible couplings & sr reverse geared to sc. shafts driving 2 FP propellers Total Power: 360kW (490hp) 13.0kn MAN D2866LE 2 x 4 Stroke 6 Cy. 128 x 155 each-180kW (245bhp) MAN Nutzfahrzeuge AG-Nuernberg
8648781 *BH3248* LL0835	**SI CHUEN NO. 212** *ex* Hui Chuan No. 3 *-2011* **Si Chuen Fishery Co Ltd** - *Kaohsiung* *Chinese Taipei* Official number: CT6-001248	**497** 198 -		**1979-02 San Yang Shipbuilding Co., Ltd. — Kaohsiung** Yd No: 771 Loa 50.80 Br ex 8.20 Dght - Lbp - Br md - Dpth - Welded, 1 dk	**(B11B2FV) Fishing Vessel**	**1 oil engine** driving 1 Propeller
9615717 *7TBU* -	**SI EL HOUAS** - **Entreprise Portuaire d'Alger (EPA)** - *Alger* *Algeria* MMSI: 605026425	**437** 131 -	Class: BV	**2012-04 Chantiers Piriou — Concarneau** Yd No: C307 Loa 32.00 Br ex - Dght 4.990 Lbp 30.40 Br md 11.00 Dpth 5.05 Welded, 1 dk	**(B32A2ST) Tug**	**2 oil engines** reduction geared to sc. shafts driving 2 Directional propellers Total Power: 5,280kW (7,178hp) MaK 8M25C 2 x 4 Stroke 8 Cy. 255 x 400 each-2640kW (3589bhp) Caterpillar Motoren GmbH & Co. KG-Germany AuxGen: 2 x 112kW 50Hz a.c Fuel: 180.0

IMO / Call sign	Name / Owner	Tonnage	Class	Builder / Dimensions	Type	Machinery
8605698 *3FWX3* -	**SI HANG CAI SHA 1** *ex* Tokai Maru *-2012* *ex* Tokai Maru No. 8 *-2011* **The First Engineering Co of CCCC Fourth Harbor Engineering Co Ltd** - *Panama* *Panama* MMSI: 371547000 Official number: 4467013	**1,986** 673 2,998		**1986-07 Kanrei Zosen K.K. — Naruto** Yd No: 319 Loa 81.01 Br ex - Dght 5.101 Lbp 75.01 Br md 15.02 Dpth 7.80 Welded, 2 dks	**(B33A2DG) Grab Dredger** Compartments: 1 Ho, ER 1 Ha: ER	**1 oil engine** with clutches, flexible couplings & reverse reduction geared to sc. shaft driving 1 FP propeller Total Power: 1,471kW (2,000hp) 11.5kn Niigata 6M34AGT 1 x 4 Stroke 6 Cy. 340 x 620 1471kW (2000bhp) Niigata Engineering Co Ltd-Japan Thrusters: 1 Thwart. CP thruster (f)
9715139 *H06880* -	**SI HANG YUN 1** *ex* De Xing 1 *-2013* **The Second Engineering Company of CCCC Fourth Harbor Engineering Co Ltd** - *Panama* *Panama* Official number: 45292PEXT	**1,129** 340 -	Class: ZC	**2013-07 Zhejiang Tianshi Shipbuilding Co Ltd — Wenling ZJ** Yd No: TS074 Loa 67.10 Br ex - Dght - Lbp 63.80 Br md 16.20 Dpth 3.68 Welded, 1 dk	**(A31C2GD) Deck Cargo Ship** Bow ramp (centre)	**2 oil engines** reduction geared to sc. shafts driving 2 Propellers Total Power: 900kW (1,224hp) 9.0kn Chinese Std. Type Z6170ZLC 2 x 4 Stroke 6 Cy. 170 x 200 each-450kW (612bhp) Zibo Diesel Engine Factory-China
9715141 *H07402* -	**SI HANG YUN 2** *ex* De Xing 3 *-2013* **The Second Engineering Company of CCCC Fourth Harbor Engineering Co Ltd** - *Panama* *Panama* Official number: 45293PEXT	**1,129** 339 -	Class: ZC	**2013-07 Zhejiang Tianshi Shipbuilding Co Ltd — Wenling ZJ** Yd No: TS076 Loa 67.10 Br ex - Dght - Lbp 63.80 Br md 16.20 Dpth 3.68 Welded, 1 dk	**(A31C2GD) Deck Cargo Ship** Bow ramp (centre)	**2 oil engines** reduction geared to sc. shafts driving 2 Propellers Total Power: 900kW (1,224hp) 9.0kn Chinese Std. Type Z6170ZLC 2 x 4 Stroke 6 Cy. 170 x 200 each-450kW (612bhp) Zibo Diesel Engine Factory-China
9715127 *H07534* -	**SI HANG YUN 3** *ex* Fu Ri Yun 158 *-2013* **The Second Engineering Company of CCCC Fourth Harbor Engineering Co Ltd** - *Panama* *Panama* Official number: 45294PEXT	**1,129** 339 -	Class: ZC	**2013-05 Zhejiang Tianshi Shipbuilding Co Ltd — Wenling ZJ** Yd No: TS073 Loa 67.10 Br ex - Dght - Lbp 63.80 Br md 16.20 Dpth 3.68 Welded, 1 dk	**(A31C2GD) Deck Cargo Ship** Bow ramp (centre)	**2 oil engines** reduction geared to sc. shafts driving 2 Propellers Total Power: 900kW (1,224hp) 9.0kn Chinese Std. Type Z6170ZLC 2 x 4 Stroke 6 Cy. 170 x 200 each-450kW (612bhp) Zibo Diesel Engine Factory-China
8626941 - -	**SI-HONG No. 126** *ex* Shin Yuk No. 10 *-2013* **Si-Tai Fishery Co Ltd** - *Kaohsiung* *Chinese Taipei* Official number: CT6-0690	*200* - -		**1980 Fong Kuo Shipbuilding Co Ltd — Kaohsiung** Loa - Br ex - Dght - Lbp - Br md - Dpth - Welded, 1 dk	**(B11B2FV) Fishing Vessel**	**1 oil engine** driving 1 FP propeller
8974532 *BI2584* LL965016	**SI HONG NO. 128** **Si-Tai Fishery Co Ltd** - *Kaohsiung* *Chinese Taipei* Official number: CT7-0584	**598** 261 -		**1987-12 Fong Kuo Shipbuilding Co Ltd — Kaohsiung** Yd No: 351 Loa 55.75 Br ex - Dght - Lbp 48.60 Br md 8.70 Dpth 3.75 Welded, 1 dk	**(B11B2FV) Fishing Vessel**	**1 oil engine** driving 1 Propeller Total Power: 1,030kW (1,400hp) Sumiyoshi S27G 1 x 4 Stroke 6 Cy. 270 x 480 1030kW (1400bhp) Sumiyoshi Tekkosho-Japan
7937549 *WDE2787* -	**SI SE PUEDE** *ex* Palmito Hill *-2001* *ex* Cape Camaron *-2000* **Si Se Puede Inc** - *Brownsville, TX* *United States of America* Official number: 597508	*106* 72 -		**1978 J & S Marine Services, Inc. — Brazoria, Tx** Yd No: 18 L reg 20.06 Br ex 6.43 Dght - Lbp - Br md - Dpth 3.46 Welded, 1 dk	**(B11A2FT) Trawler**	**1 oil engine** geared to sc. shaft driving 1 FP propeller Total Power: 268kW (364hp) Cummins KT-1150-M 1 x 4 Stroke 6 Cy. 159 x 159 268kW (364bhp) Cummins Engine Co Inc-USA
8947450 *BI2557* LL2308	**SI TAI No. 326** **Si Union Fishery Corp** - *Kaohsiung* *Chinese Taipei* Official number: CT7-0557	**598** 261 -		**1987-10 Fong Kuo Shipbuilding Co Ltd — Kaohsiung** Yd No: 348 Loa 55.75 Br ex - Dght - Lbp - Br md 8.70 Dpth 3.75 Welded, 1 dk	**(B11B2FV) Fishing Vessel**	**1 oil engine** driving 1 FP propeller 13.0kn Sumiyoshi 1 x 4 Stroke Sumiyoshi Marine Diesel Co Ltd-Japan
7715434 *OWFI2* -	**SIA** *ex* Claymore *-2010* **CT Offshore AS** - *Klintebjerg* *Denmark (DIS)* MMSI: 219013938 Official number: D4448	**2,525** 758 1,000	Class: LR ✠ **100A1** SS 05/2010 ✠ **LMC** **UMS** Eq.Ltr: (Q) ; Cable: 440.0/38.0 U2	**1978-12 Robb Caledon Shipbuilders Ltd. — Leith** Yd No: 522 Converted From: Ro-Ro Cargo Ship-2010 Converted From: Ferry (Passenger/Vehicle)-2006 Loa 77.20 Br ex 16.26 Dght 2.800 Lbp 70.08 Br md 15.50 Dpth 4.80 Welded, 1 dk	**(B34D2SL) Cable Layer** Stern ramp Len: 5.82 Wid: 4.05 Swl: - Side ramp (p) Len: 4.20 Wid: 6.40 Swl: 28 Side ramp (s) Len: 4.20 Wid: 6.40 Swl: 28 Lane-Len: 230 Lane-Wid: 6.40 Lane-clr ht: 3.80 Cars: 47 A-frames: 1x20t	**2 oil engines** reduction geared to sc. shafts driving 2 CP propellers Total Power: 2,500kW (3,400hp) 12.5kn Blackstone ESL16MK2 2 x Vee 4 Stroke 16 Cy. 222 x 292 each-1250kW (1700bhp) Mirrlees Blackstone (Stamford)Ltd.-Stamford AuxGen: 4 x a.c Thrusters: 4 Thwart. FP thruster (f); 1 Thwart. CP thruster (f); 3 Thwart. FP thruster (a) Fuel: 233.0
9662863 *ZGCJ3*	**SIA** **Ocean Sunshine Ltd** *George Town* *Cayman Islands (British)* MMSI: 319042600 Official number: 743718	**236** 70 34	Class: RI	**2012-04 Sunseeker International Ltd — Poole** Loa 34.65 Br ex - Dght 2.485 Lbp 26.60 Br md 7.28 Dpth 3.79 Bonded, 1 dk	**(X11A2YP) Yacht** Hull Material: Reinforced Plastic	**2 oil engines** reduction geared to sc. shafts driving 2 FP propellers Total Power: 3,878kW (5,272hp) 20.0kn M.T.U. 16V2000M94 2 x Vee 4 Stroke 16 Cy. 135 x 156 each-1939kW (2636bhp) MTU Friedrichshafen GmbH-Friedrichshafen AuxGen: 2 x 65kW a.c
7634692 - -	**SIAC I** *ex* Diama *-1981* *ex* Ryoun Maru No. 7 *-1975* **Inter-Arika SA** - *Nouadhibou* *Mauritania*	*390* 184 -	Class: (RI) (BV)	**1968 Yamanishi Shipbuilding Co Ltd — Ishinomaki MG** L reg 50.60 Br ex 8.82 Dght - Lbp 46.11 Br md 8.81 Dpth 3.81 Welded, 2 dks	**(B11A2FT) Trawler**	**1 oil engine** driving 1 CP propeller Total Power: 1,324kW (1,800hp) 12.8kn Akasaka 6DM38SS 1 x 4 Stroke 6 Cy. 380 x 560 1324kW (1800bhp) Akasaka Tekkosho KK (Akasaka DieselLtd)-Japan Fuel: 278.0 (d.f.)
8825042 - -	**SIAG** *ex* Pellworm II *-1975* **Norwegian Maritime Group A/S** - *Conakry* *Guinea*	*149* 62 -	Class: (GL)	**1972-01 Husumer Schiffswerft — Husum** Loa - Br ex 9.62 Dght 1.300 Lbp 29.62 Br md - Dpth 2.32 Welded	**(A36A2PR) Passenger/Ro-Ro Ship (Vehicles)** Passengers: unberthed: 47 Ice Capable	**1 oil engine** reverse reduction geared to sc. shaft driving 1 FP propeller Total Power: 1,103kW (1,500hp) 9.0kn MWM RHS618V12 1 x Vee 4 Stroke 12 Cy. 140 x 180 1103kW (1500bhp) Motoren Werke Mannheim AG (MWM)-West Germany AuxGen: 1 x 22kW 220/380V a.c
7014816 *YBLJ*	**SIAK** **PT Gelora Insan Samudera** - *Jakarta* *Indonesia*	*136* 9 121	Class: KI (BV)	**1970-03 Robin Shipyard Pte Ltd — Singapore** Yd No: 26 Loa 29.11 Br ex 7.47 Dght 2.848 Lbp 26.83 Br md 7.42 Dpth 3.36 Welded, 1 dk	**(B32A2ST) Tug**	**2 oil engines** reverse reduction geared to sc. shafts driving 2 FP propellers Total Power: 634kW (862hp) 11.0kn Caterpillar D353 2 x 4 Stroke 6 Cy. 159 x 203 each-317kW (431bhp) Caterpillar Tractor Co-USA AuxGen: 1 x 24kW, 1 x 10kW Fuel: 78.0 (d.f.)
9550888 *YDA4478* -	**SIAK SELAMAT** *ex* Jasa Selamat *-2009* **PT Jasatama Kemasindo** PACC Ship Managers Pte Ltd *Jakarta* *Indonesia* MMSI: 525011128 Official number: GT180	**180** 54 114	Class: AB KI (NK)	**2009-03 Fulsail Sdn Bhd — Sibu** (Hull) Yd No: 7511 **2009-03 Pacific Ocean Engineering & Trading Pte Ltd (POET) — Singapore** Loa 27.00 Br ex 8.25 Dght 2.807 Lbp 24.95 Br md 8.20 Dpth 3.60 Welded, 1 dk	**(B32A2ST) Tug**	**2 oil engines** reduction geared to sc. shafts driving 2 FP propellers Total Power: 1,790kW (2,434hp) Cummins KTA-38-M2 2 x Vee 4 Stroke 12 Cy. 159 x 159 each-895kW (1217bhp) Cummins Engine Co Inc-USA AuxGen: 2 x a.c Fuel: 110.0
9539432 *3FAN* -	**SIAM FORTUNE** **Polar Bear SA** Seiwa Navigation Corp Ltd SatCom: Inmarsat C 435577410 *Panama* *Panama* MMSI: 355774000 Official number: 4316311	**7,404** 3,747 12,440	Class: NK	**2011-10 Shin Kochi Jyuko K.K. — Kochi** Yd No: 7256 Loa 115.33 Br ex - Dght 8.787 Lbp 109.00 Br md 19.60 Dpth 11.40 Welded, 1 dk	**(A21A2BC) Bulk Carrier** Double Bottom Partial Compartment Length Grain: 13,201; Bale: 12,900 Compartments: 3 Ho, ER 3 Ha: ER Cranes: 2x30.5t,1x30t	**1 oil engine** driving 1 FP propeller Total Power: 3,900kW (5,302hp) 13.3kn MAN-B&W 6L35MC 1 x 2 Stroke 6 Cy. 350 x 1050 3900kW (5302bhp) Makita Corp-Japan Fuel: 810.0

7505712 - -	**SIAM LAKJOONG 2** *ex* Thong Noppa Khun *-2000* *ex* Salveto *-1987* *ex* Asiatic Drive *-1981* **Thai International Shipbreakers** - *Bangkok* *Thailand* Official number: 301041565	*177* 11 -	Class: (AB)	**1976-05 Sea Services Pte Ltd — Singapore** Yd No: Y106 Loa - Br ex - Dght 2.950 Lbp 26.55 Br md 7.66 Dpth 3.51 Welded, 1 dk	**(B32A2ST) Tug**	**1 oil engine** reverse reduction geared to sc. shaft driving 1 FP propeller Total Power: 713kW (969hp) 11.5kn Caterpillar D349TA 1 x Vee 4 Stroke 16 Cy. 137 x 165 713kW (969bhp) Caterpillar Tractor Co-USA AuxGen: 2 x 32kW a.c
9123934 *3FFE5* -	**SIAM OCEAN** **Ocean Woodland Shipping Co Ltd** MMS Co Ltd SatCom: Inmarsat C 435519210 *Panama* *Panama* MMSI: 355192000 Official number: 2237295D	**30,153** 11,718 33,800	Class: NK	**1995-06 Imabari Shipbuilding Co Ltd — Marugame KG (Marugame Shipyard)** Yd No: 1243 Loa 175.17 (BB) Br ex 31.03 Dght 10.050 Lbp 164.00 Br md 31.00 Dpth 21.40 Welded, 1 dk	**(A24B2BW) Wood Chips Carrier** Grain: 74,152 Compartments: 4 Ho, ER 4 Ha: 3 (17.6 x 17.6) (14.4 x 17.6)ER Cranes: 2x14t	**1 oil engine** driving 1 FP propeller Total Power: 5,149kW (7,001hp) 13.5kn Mitsubishi 6UEC52LA 1 x 2 Stroke 6 Cy. 520 x 1600 5149kW (7001bhp) Akasaka Tekkosho KK (Akasaka Diesel Ltd)-Japan Fuel: 1340.0 (r.f.)
8916061 *HSB2792* -	**SIAM RAPEEPARN** *ex* Hassho Maru No. 3 *-2001* **Siam Mongkol Marine Co Ltd** - *Thailand* MMSI: 567031900 Official number: 441001043	*1,012* 476 1,969 T/cm 6.7		**1989-11 Kurinoura Dockyard Co Ltd — Yawatahama EH** Yd No: 278 Loa 74.80 Br ex 11.22 Dght 4.820 Lbp 70.00 Br md 11.20 Dpth 5.30 Welded, 1 dk	**(A13B2TP) Products Tanker** Liq: 2,158; Liq (Oil): 2,158 Compartments: 10 Ta, ER 2 Cargo Pump (s)	**1 oil engine** geared to sc. shaft driving 1 FP propeller Total Power: 1,471kW (2,000hp) Hanshin 6EL32G 1 x 4 Stroke 6 Cy. 320 x 640 1471kW (2000bhp) The Hanshin Diesel Works Ltd-Japan
9539339 *3FLW3* -	**SIAM SUCCESS** **Polar Bear SA** Kansai Steamship Co Ltd *Panama* *Panama* MMSI: 351840000 Official number: 4163410	**7,404** 3,747 12,427	Class: NK	**2010-05 Shin Kochi Jyuko K.K. — Kochi** Yd No: 7240 Loa 115.33 (BB) Br ex - Dght 8.787 Lbp 109.00 Br md 19.60 Dpth 11.40 Welded, 1 dk	**(A21A2BC) Bulk Carrier** Double Hull Grain: 13,201; Bale: 12,900 Compartments: 3 Ho, ER 3 Ha: ER Cranes: 2x30.5t,1x30t	**1 oil engine** driving 1 FP propeller Total Power: 3,900kW (5,302hp) 13.3kn MAN-B&W 6L35MC 1 x 2 Stroke 6 Cy. 350 x 1050 3900kW (5302bhp) Makita Corp-Japan AuxGen: 2 x 380kW a.c Fuel: 610.0 (r.f.)
7709332 *HSBZ2* -	**SIAM SUPHA** *ex* Ahimsa *-1998* *ex* Golden Ocean *-1997* *ex* Oxalis Sakura *-1995* *ex* Sakura Maru *-1988* - - *Thailand* MMSI: 567001900	**2,487** 1,420 4,232 T/cm 10.6	Class: (NK)	**1977-09 Imamura Zosen — Kure** Yd No: 233 Loa 93.35 Br ex 13.82 Dght 6.393 Lbp 86.72 Br md 13.81 Dpth 7.42 Welded, 1 dk	**(A13A2TW) Crude/Oil Products Tanker** Liq: 4,455; Liq (Oil): 4,455 Cargo Heating Coils Compartments: 10 Ta, ER 2 Cargo Pump (s): 2x1000m³/hr Manifold: Bow/CM: 32m	**1 oil engine** driving 1 FP propeller Total Power: 2,354kW (3,200hp) 13.0kn Hanshin 6LU46A 1 x 4 Stroke 6 Cy. 460 x 740 2354kW (3200bhp) Hanshin Nainenki Kogyo-Japan AuxGen: 2 x 160kW 445V 60Hz a.c Fuel: 43.0 (d.f.) (Part Heating Coils) 182.5 (r.f.) 10.5pd
8608535 *HSB2888* -	**SIAM THANANYA** *ex* Tomowa Maru *-2002* **Siam Mongkol Marine Co Ltd** - *Thailand* MMSI: 567036200 Official number: 451000497	*1,386* 808 2,495		**1986-11 Hakata Zosen K.K. — Imabari** Yd No: 337 Loa - Br ex - Dght 5.101 Lbp 76.51 Br md 12.01 Dpth 5.77 Welded, 1 dk	**(A13B2TP) Products Tanker** Liq: 2,500; Liq (Oil): 2,500 Compartments: 10 Ta, ER	**1 oil engine** driving 1 FP propeller Total Power: 1,471kW (2,000hp) Hanshin 6EL32 1 x 4 Stroke 6 Cy. 320 x 640 1471kW (2000bhp) The Hanshin Diesel Works Ltd-Japan
9392107 *3FWZ5* -	**SIAM TRIUMPH** **New Shipcarrier SA** Seiwa Navigation Corp Ltd *Panama* *Panama* MMSI: 354054000 Official number: 4026809	**7,404** 3,884 12,497	Class: NK	**2009-04 Shin Kochi Jyuko K.K. — Kochi** Yd No: 7228 Loa 115.33 (BB) Br ex - Dght 8.787 Lbp 109.00 Br md 19.60 Dpth 11.40 Welded	**(A21A2BC) Bulk Carrier** Grain: 13,666; Bale: 12,900 Compartments: 3 Ho, ER 3 Ha: ER Cranes: 1x60t,2x30.5t,1x30t	**1 oil engine** driving 1 FP propeller Total Power: 3,641kW (4,950hp) 13.3kn Mitsubishi 7UEC37LA 1 x 2 Stroke 7 Cy. 370 x 880 3641kW (4950bhp) Akasaka Tekkosho KK (Akasaka Diesel Ltd)-Japan Fuel: 700.0
7631808 - -	**SIAM VANICH 2** **Siam Merchant Marine Co Ltd** - *Bangkok* *Thailand*	*469* 386 600		**1980-10 Bangkok Shipbuilding Co. — Bangkok** Yd No: 029 Loa 49.03 Br ex 9.00 Dght 3.752 Lbp 46.00 Br md - Dpth 4.27 Welded, 1 dk	**(A31A2GX) General Cargo Ship**	**1 oil engine** geared to sc. shaft driving 1 FP propeller Total Power: 405kW (551hp) Yanmar 6MA-DT 1 x 4 Stroke 6 Cy. 200 x 240 405kW (551bhp) Yanmar Diesel Engine Co Ltd-Japan
7534440 *5IM526* -	**SIAM VARICH** *ex* Ehime Maru No. 2 *-1982* *ex* Koho Maru *-1982* **Hong Ye Global Pte Ltd** *Zanzibar* *Tanzania (Zanzibar)* MMSI: 677042600 Official number: 300267	*794* 590 2,031		**1972 Shirahama Zosen K.K. — Honai** Yd No: 48 Loa 77.50 Br ex 10.83 Dght 4.573 Lbp 71.51 Br md 10.80 Dpth 5.00 Welded, 1 dk	**(A13B2TP) Products Tanker** Single Hull Liq: 2,341; Liq (Oil): 2,341 Compartments: 5 Ta, ER	**1 oil engine** driving 1 FP propeller Total Power: 1,177kW (1,600hp) 12.5kn Niigata 6M34EX 1 x 4 Stroke 6 Cy. 340 x 520 1177kW (1600bhp) Niigata Engineering Co Ltd-Japan
9355111 *3EKI8* -	**SIAM VICTORY** **New Shipcarrier SA** Seiwa Navigation Corp Ltd *Panama* *Panama* MMSI: 372734000 Official number: 3276907A	**7,404** 3,884 12,509	Class: NK	**2007-05 Shin Kochi Jyuko K.K. — Kochi** Yd No: 7203 Loa 115.30 (BB) Br ex - Dght 8.787 Lbp 109.00 Br md 19.60 Dpth 11.40 Welded, 1 dk	**(A21A2BC) Bulk Carrier** Grain: 13,667; Bale: 13,353 Compartments: 3 Ho, ER 3 Ha: ER Cranes: 2x30.5t,1x30t	**1 oil engine** driving 1 FP propeller Total Power: 3,640kW (4,949hp) 13.3kn Mitsubishi 7UEC37LA 1 x 2 Stroke 7 Cy. 370 x 880 3640kW (4949bhp) Akasaka Tekkosho KK (Akasaka Diesel Ltd)-Japan Fuel: 700.0
7025322 *HSOG* -	**SIAM WANICH 3** *ex* Chatchawal *-1982* *ex* Kofuku Maru *-1977* **Siam Merchant Marine Co Ltd** - *Bangkok* *Thailand* Official number: 191011516	*1,475* 824 2,435	Class: (NK)	**1969-09 Fukushima Zosen Ltd. — Matsue** Yd No: 227 Loa 74.99 Br ex 11.84 Dght 5.411 Lbp 68.03 Br md 11.82 Dpth 6.20 Welded, 1 dk	**(A31A2GX) General Cargo Ship** Grain: 2,880; Bale: 2,706 Compartments: 2 Ho, ER 2 Ha: (12.1 x 6.2) (21.4 x 6.2)ER Derricks: 1x15t,2x7.5t	**1 oil engine** driving 1 FP propeller Total Power: 1,324kW (1,800hp) 12.5kn Nippon Hatsudoki HS6NV238 1 x 4 Stroke 6 Cy. 380 x 580 1324kW (1800bhp) Nippon Hatsudoki-Japan AuxGen: 2 x 96kW 445V a.c Fuel: 208.5 6.5pd
7123954 *HSB2100* -	**SIAM WARIN** *ex* Fuji Maru No. 17 *-1983* **Thavorn Marine Co Ltd** - *Bangkok* *Thailand* Official number: 261031854	**1,225** 753 2,462		**1971-10 Hashihama Shipbuilding Co Ltd — Imabari EH** Yd No: 319 Loa 78.00 Br ex 12.04 Dght 5.004 Lbp 72.01 Br md 11.99 Dpth 5.49 Riveted\Welded, 1 dk	**(A13B2TP) Products Tanker** Compartments: 5 Ta, ER	**1 oil engine** driving 1 FP propeller Total Power: 1,545kW (2,101hp) 11.0kn Akasaka AH38 1 x 4 Stroke 6 Cy. 380 x 560 1545kW (2101bhp) Akasaka Tekkosho KK (Akasaka Diesel Ltd)-Japan AuxGen: 2 x 80kW 445V a.c Fuel: 86.5 6.0pd
9355082 *3EHZ4* -	**SIAM WIN** **Dynawin Maritime Inc** Seiwa Navigation Corp Ltd *Panama* *Panama* MMSI: 372039000 Official number: 3228907A	**7,404** 3,884 12,519	Class: NK	**2006-10 Shin Kochi Jyuko K.K. — Kochi** Yd No: 7196 Loa 115.33 (BB) Br ex 19.60 Dght 8.790 Lbp 109.00 Br md 19.60 Dpth 11.40 Welded, 1 dk	**(A21A2BC) Bulk Carrier** Grain: 13,666; Bale: 12,900 Compartments: 3 Ho, ER 3 Ha: ER Cranes: 1x60t,3x30t	**1 oil engine** driving 1 FP propeller Total Power: 3,640kW (4,949hp) 13.3kn Mitsubishi 7UEC37LA 1 x 2 Stroke 7 Cy. 370 x 880 3640kW (4949bhp) Akasaka Tekkosho KK (Akasaka Diesel Ltd)-Japan AuxGen: 3 x 347kW a.c Fuel: 700.0
7006170 - -	**SIAMAK** **Iran Brothers** - *Khorramshahr* *Iran*	*210* 144 457		**1969 Yorkshire D.D. Co. Ltd. — Hull** Yd No: 145 Loa 39.63 Br ex 7.12 Dght 2.439 Lbp 38.56 Br md 7.01 Dpth 2.75 Welded, 1 dk	**(A31A2GX) General Cargo Ship**	**2 oil engines** geared to sc. shafts driving 2 FP propellers Total Power: 294kW (400hp) Gardner 8L3B 2 x 4 Stroke 8 Cy. 140 x 197 each-147kW (200bhp) L. Gardner & Sons Ltd.-Manchester
7937795 *HSB2194* -	**SIAMSASIRATCH** *ex* Harin Transport 12 *-2012* *ex* Eiho Maru No. 26 *-1990* **Commonwealth Co Ltd** - *Bangkok* *Thailand* Official number: 331002143	*495* 343 1,500		**1980-03 YK Furumoto Tekko Zosensho — Osakikamijima** Yd No: 505 Loa 63.00 Br ex - Dght 4.900 Lbp 58.00 Br md 10.50 Dpth 6.40 Welded, 1dk	**(A31A2GX) General Cargo Ship** 1 Ha: (34.0 x 7.8)	**1 oil engine** driving 1 FP propeller
9338149 *MPJD7* -	**SIAN C** **Lucia SA** Carisbrooke Shipping Ltd *Cowes* *United Kingdom* MMSI: 232910000 Official number: 3230907A	**9,177** 4,751 13,479 T/cm 24.1	Class: LR (BV) **100A1** SS 12/2011 *IWS LI **LMC** **UMS** Cable: U3 (a)	**2006-12 Kyokuyo Shipyard Corp — Shimonoseki YC** Yd No: 467 Loa 136.43 (BB) Br ex - Dght 8.350 Lbp 126.88 Br md 21.20 Dpth 11.30 Welded, 1 dk	**(A31A2GX) General Cargo Ship** Double Sides Entire Compartment Length Grain: 17,092; Bale: 16,870 TEU 172 Compartments: 4 Ho, ER 4 Ha: (24.9 x 17.6) (24.8 x 17.6) (15.8 x 17.6)ER (16.1 x 12.6) Cranes: 2x30t	**1 oil engine** driving 1 FP propeller Total Power: 5,180kW (7,043hp) 14.6kn MAN-B&W 7S35MC 1 x 2 Stroke 7 Cy. 350 x 1400 5180kW (7043bhp) Makita Corp-Japan AuxGen: 3 x 400kW 450/220V 60Hz a.c Boilers: TOH (o.f.) 10.0kgf/cm² (9.8bar), TOH (o.f.) 10.0kgf/cm² (9.8bar) Thrusters: 1 Tunnel thruster (f) Fuel: 93.5 (d.f.) 969.0 (r.f.) 19.5pd

IMO / Call sign / Flag	Name / Owners / Registry	Tonnage	Classification	Builder / Dimensions	Type / Capacity	Machinery
7106712 - - -	**SIANG HING** *ex* Hoe Hing *-1981* *ex* Kashima Maru *-1979* **Ethid (Malaysia) Sdn Bhd** Kudrat Maritime Malaysia Sdn Bhd	*499* 319 1,021	Class: (BV)	**1970 Usuki Iron Works Co Ltd — Usuki OT** Yd No: 772 Lengthened-1973 Loa 56.11 Br ex 8.84 Dght 4.201 Lbp 52.00 Br md 8.79 Dpth 4.40 Welded, 1 dk	**(A13B2TU) Tanker (unspecified)** Liq: 866; Liq (Oil): 866 Compartments: 5 Ta, ER	**1 oil engine** driving 1 FP propeller Total Power: 993kW (1,350hp) 12.0kn Usuki 6MRS35HC 1 x 4 Stroke 6 Cy. 350 x 500 993kW (1350bhp) Usuki Tekkosho-Usuki AuxGen: 2 x 40kW 225V a.c Fuel: 45.5
8866577 *9WCE6* -	**SIANG PING No. 1** *ex* Island No. 1 *-1996* **Siang Ping Shipping** *Labuan* *Malaysia* Official number: 327132	**494** 149 492	Class: (NK)	**1980 Hai Lee Engineering Works — Singapore** Yd No: 5188 Loa 45.76 Br ex - Dght 2.207 Lbp 44.80 Br md 12.20 Dpth 3.05 Welded, 1 dk	**(A35D2RL) Landing Craft**	**2 oil engines** reduction geared to sc. shafts driving 2 FP propellers Total Power: 426kW (580hp) 8.2kn Volvo Penta TMD121 2 x 4 Stroke 6 Cy. 130 x 150 each-213kW (290bhp) AB Volvo Penta-Sweden AuxGen: 2 x 8kW a.c
9614529 *9V9832*	**SIANGTAN** **The China Navigation Co Pte Ltd** - *Singapore* *Singapore* MMSI: 563991000 Official number: 397640	**25,483** 11,805 31,756	Class: LR ✠ **100A1** SS 12/2013 Holds Nos. 3 & 4 strengthened for heavy cargoes container cargoes in all holds and on upper deck and on all hatch covers **ShipRight** (ACS (B)) *IWS LI IP ✠ **LMC** **UMS** Eq.Ltr: M†; Cable: 638.5/73.0 U3 (a)	**2013-12 Zhejiang Ouhua Shipbuilding Co Ltd — Zhoushan ZJ** Yd No: 642 Loa 199.90 (BB) Br ex 28.28 Dght 10.500 Lbp 188.79 Br md 28.20 Dpth 15.50 Welded, 1 dk	**(A31A2GX) General Cargo Ship** TEU 2082 C Ho 916 TEU C Dk 1166 TEU incl 147 ref C Compartments: 2 Ho, 2 Tw Dk, 3 Cell Ho, ER 5 Ha: ER Cranes: 4x60t	**1 oil engine** driving 1 FP propeller Total Power: 13,560kW (18,436hp) 15.5kn Wartsila 6RT-flex58T 1 x 2 Stroke 6 Cy. 580 x 2416 13560kW (18436bhp) Hudong Heavy Machinery Co Ltd-China AuxGen: 3 x 1058kW 450V 60Hz a.c Boilers: AuxB (Comp) 8.4kgf/cm² (8.2bar) Thrusters: 1 Tunnel thruster (f)
7607302 *PLXS* -	**SIANIRI** **PT Reksa Sarana Sagara** PT Pelayaran Nasional Indonesia (PELNI) *Jakarta* *Indonesia* MMSI: 525018282	**1,689** 622 1,700	Class: KI (NV)	**1978-06 AS Storviks Mek. Verksted — Kristiansund** Yd No: 82 Loa 71.51 Br ex 12.93 Dght 4.420 Lbp 65.41 Br md 12.70 Dpth 7.12 Welded, 2 dks	**(A31A2GX) General Cargo Ship** Grain: 3,570; Bale: 2,987 Compartments: 2 Ho, ER 2 Ha: (13.2 x 7.0) (18.9 x 7.0)ER	**1 oil engine** driving 1 FP propeller Total Power: 1,195kW (1,625hp) 12.0kn Kromhout 9FDHD240 1 x 4 Stroke 9 Cy. 240 x 260 1195kW (1625bhp) Stork Werkspoor Diesel BV-Netherlands AuxGen: 3 x 96kW 220/380V 50Hz a.c
7810765 - -	**SIANTEK** *ex* Best One *-1997* *ex* Eiko Maru *-1994* **Sentek Marine & Trading Pte Ltd**	**468** 224 752	Class: GL	**1978-08 Takebe Zosen — Takamatsu** Yd No: 75 Loa 51.60 Br ex - Dght 3.496 Lbp 47.00 Br md 8.31 Dpth 3.92 Riveted\Welded, 1 dk	**(A13B2TU) Tanker (unspecified)**	**1 oil engine** driving 1 FP propeller Total Power: 552kW (750hp) 10.0kn Niigata 6M26ZG 1 x 4 Stroke 6 Cy. 260 x 400 552kW (750bhp) Niigata Engineering Co Ltd-Japan AuxGen: 2 x 40kW 220V a.c
8626496 *9BAX* -	**SIAVASH** *ex* Shinryowa *-2004* **Abdolreza Ravian** Bushehr Atlas Co *Bushehr* *Iran* MMSI: 422326000 Official number: 782	**492** 355 695	Class: AS	**1985-06 Y.K. Kaneko Zosensho — Hojo** Loa 54.00 Br ex - Dght 3.410 Lbp 49.50 Br md 9.00 Dpth 5.73 Welded, 1 dk	**(A31A2GX) General Cargo Ship**	**1 oil engine** reverse geared to sc. shaft driving 1 FP propeller Total Power: 405kW (551hp) 10.0kn Akasaka A24R 1 x 4 Stroke 6 Cy. 240 x 450 405kW (551bhp) Akasaka Tekkosho KK (Akasaka DieselLtd)-Japan
8627828 *9BCC* -	**SIAVASH 2** *ex* Taiyo Maru No. 8 *-2003* **Mehdi Maigoli** Bushehr Atlas Co *Bushehr* *Iran* MMSI: 422513000 Official number: 795	**453** 164 440	Class: AS	**1985 Nagashima Zosen KK — Kihoku ME** Loa 43.04 Br ex - Dght 3.020 Lbp 38.00 Br md 10.00 Dpth 4.65 Welded, 1 dk	**(A31A2GX) General Cargo Ship**	**1 oil engine** driving 1 FP propeller Total Power: 405kW (551hp) 8.5kn Niigata 6M26BGT 1 x 4 Stroke 6 Cy. 260 x 460 405kW (551bhp) Niigata Engineering Co Ltd-Japan
8999738 *9BQN* -	**SIAVASH 3** *ex* Galaxy 1 *-2009* *ex* LCT 888 *-1998* **Zahedi Aliakbar** *Iran* MMSI: 422192000	*388* 255 -		**1990-01 Santiago Shipyard — Consolacion** L reg 67.98 Br ex - Dght - Lbp - Br md 12.80 Dpth 2.65 Welded, 1 dk	**(A35D2RL) Landing Craft**	**2 oil engines** driving 2 Propellers Total Power: 736kW (1,000hp) Cummins 2 x 4 Stroke 6 Cy. each-368kW (500bhp) Cummins Engine Co Inc-USA
7607326 *PLXM* -	**SIBAYAK** **PT Perusahaan Pelayaran Dalam Negeri Juli Rahayu** *Jakarta* *Indonesia* MMSI: 525020091	**1,748** 621 1,650	Class: KI (NV)	**1977-11 Ulstein Hatlo AS — Ulsteinvik** Yd No: 149 Loa 71.91 Br ex - Dght 4.380 Lbp 65.41 Br md 12.70 Dpth 7.12 Welded, 2 dks	**(A32A2GF) General Cargo/Passenger Ship** Passengers: 198 Grain: 3,390 Compartments: 2 Ho, ER 2 Ha: (13.2 x 8.0) (18.9 x 8.0)ER Derricks: 2x20t,2x5t	**1 oil engine** driving 1 FP propeller Total Power: 1,195kW (1,625hp) 12.0kn Kromhout 9FDHD240 1 x 4 Stroke 9 Cy. 240 x 260 1195kW (1625bhp) Stork Werkspoor Diesel BV-Netherlands AuxGen: 3 x 96kW 220/380V 50Hz a.c, 1 x 48kW 220/380V 50Hz a.c
7900091 *5IM270* -	**SIBEL J** *ex* Opus *-2012* *ex* Nadine *-2002* *ex* Canopus I *-2000* *ex* Canopus *-1994* **Noor Shipping Co** Arados Shipping Co Srl *Zanzibar* *Tanzania (Zanzibar)* MMSI: 677017000 Official number: 300031	**2,862** 1,518 3,128	Class: (RS) (GL)	**1979-12 Elsflether Werft AG — Elsfleth** Yd No: 400 Loa 98.71 (BB) Br ex 15.96 Dght 4.220 Lbp 91.88 Br md 15.91 Dpth 5.82 Welded, 2 dks	**(A31A2GX) General Cargo Ship** Grain: 5,097; Bale: 4,814 TEU 204 C.Ho 88/20' C.Dk 116/20' incl. 10 ref C. Compartments: 1 Ho, ER 1 Ha: (57.1 x 10.2)Tappered ER Ice Capable	**1 oil engine** geared to sc. shaft driving 1 FP propeller Total Power: 1,100kW (1,496hp) 12.5kn MaK 6M453AK 1 x 4 Stroke 6 Cy. 320 x 420 1100kW (1496bhp) MaK Maschinenbau GmbH-Kiel Thrusters: 1 Tunnel thruster (f)
9508237 *ZCTR* -	**SIBELLE** **Earnest Investments Ltd** Schroder Trust SA *George Town* *Cayman Islands (British)* MMSI: 319355000 Official number: 740237	**458** 137 200	Class: AB	**2008-06 Heesen Shipyards B.V. — Oss** Yd No: 13944 Loa 44.17 Br ex 9.00 Dght 1.925 Lbp 36.30 Br md 8.50 Dpth 3.90 Welded, 1 dk	**(X11A2YP) Yacht** Hull Material: Aluminium Alloy	**2 oil engines** reverse reduction geared to sc. shafts driving 2 Propellers Total Power: 5,440kW (7,396hp) M.T.U. 16V4000M90 2 x Vee 4 Stroke 16 Cy. 165 x 190 each-2720kW (3698bhp) MTU Friedrichshafen GmbH-Friedrichshafen AuxGen: 2 x 65kW a.c
8944862 - -	**SIBERIA DRAGON 8** *ex* James *-1994* **Siberia Dragon Inc** *Cebu* *Philippines* Official number: CEB1000302	*239* 144 -		**1970 at Cebu** L reg 45.97 Br ex - Dght - Lbp - Br md 10.66 Dpth 1.95 Welded, 1 dk	**(A35D2RL) Landing Craft**	**1 oil engine** driving 1 FP propeller Total Power: 419kW (570hp) Isuzu 1 x 4 Stroke 419kW (570bhp) Isuzu Marine Engine Inc-Japan
9498717 *ZDKY2* -	**SIBERIAN EXPRESS** **Bulk Express I BV** Vroon BV *Gibraltar* *Gibraltar (British)* MMSI: 236111844	**51,209** 31,192 92,974 T/cm 80.9	Class: LR ✠ **100A1** SS 08/2012 bulk carrier CSR BC-A GRAB (20) Nos. 2, 4 and 6 holds may be empty ESP **ShipRight** (CM,ACS (B) *IWS LI ✠ **LMC** **UMS** Eq.Ltr: S†; Cable: 687.5/87.0 U3 (a)	**2012-08 COSCO (Dalian) Shipyard Co Ltd — Dalian LN** Yd No: N252 Loa 229.26 (BB) Br ex 38.04 Dght 14.900 Lbp 222.05 Br md 38.00 Dpth 20.70 Welded, 1 dk	**(A21A2BC) Bulk Carrier** Grain: 110,330 Compartments: 7 Ho, ER 7 Ha: ER	**1 oil engine** driving 1 FP propeller Total Power: 12,240kW (16,642hp) 14.1kn MAN-B&W 6S60MC 1 x 2 Stroke 6 Cy. 600 x 2292 12240kW (16642bhp) Mitsui Engineering & Shipbuilding CLtd-Japan AuxGen: 3 x 730kW 450V 60Hz a.c Boilers: WTAuxB (Comp) 9.2kgf/cm² (9.0bar)
9054377 *WDB9466* -	**SIBERIAN SEA** **Siberian Sea Fisheries LLC** *Seattle, WA* *United States of America* MMSI: 366433000 Official number: 975853	**741** 427 -		**1991 Mid-Coast Marine Oregon Corp. — Coos Bay, Or** Yd No: 9930 Loa 42.00 Br ex - Dght 3.962 Lbp - Br md 10.35 Dpth 4.27 Welded	**(B11B2FV) Fishing Vessel** Ins: 340	**2 oil engines** geared to sc. shafts driving 2 FP propellers Total Power: 992kW (1,348hp) Cummins VTA-28-M 2 x Vee 4 Stroke 12 Cy. 140 x 152 each-496kW (674bhp) Cummins Engine Co Inc-USA

IMO / Call sign	Name / Owner	Tonnage	Class	Builder / Dimensions	Type	Machinery
7823358 *WDE5028* -	**SIBERIAN SEA** *ex* Heidi E. Roehrig *-2008* *ex* Matthew *-2004* *ex* Star Avjet *-2004* *ex* Texaco Avjet *-1990* **Kirby Offshore Marine Operating LLC** - *New York, NY* *United States of America* MMSI: 367361040 Official number: 620541	**338** 193 -	Class: (AB)	**1980-05 Jakobson Shipyard, Inc. — Oyster Bay, NY** Yd No: 462 Loa 32.01 Br ex - Dght 3.917 Lbp 29.88 Br md 9.76 Dpth 4.86 Welded, 1 dk	**(B32A2ST) Tug**	**2 oil engines** reverse reduction geared to sc. shafts driving 2 FP propellers Total Power: 2,206kW (3,000hp) 12.0kn EMD (Electro-Motive) 12-645-E6 2 x Vee 2 Stroke 12 Cy. 230 x 254 each-1103kW (1500bhp) General Motors Corp.Electro-Motive Div.-La Grange AuxGen: 2 x 75kW
9519224 *AQQH* -	**SIBI** *ex* Panarrow *-2011* *ex* Tri Arrows *-2010* **Sibi Shipping Pvt Ltd** Pakistan National Shipping Corp *Karachi* *Pakistan* MMSI: 463043101 Official number: 368044	**17,018** 10,109 28,442 T/cm 39.7	Class: NK	**2009-09 Imabari Shipbuilding Co Ltd — Marugame KG (Marugame Shipyard)** Yd No: 1550 Loa 169.37 (BB) Br ex - Dght 9.820 Lbp 160.40 Br md 27.20 Dpth 13.60 Welded, 1 dk	**(A21A2BC) Bulk Carrier** Grain: 37,320; Bale: 35,742 Compartments: 5 Ho, ER 5 Ha: 4 (19.2 x 17.6)ER (13.6 x 16.0) Cranes: 4x30.5t	**1 oil engine** driving 1 FP propeller Total Power: 5,850kW (7,954hp) 14.0kn MAN-B&W 6S42MC 1 x 2 Stroke 6 Cy. 420 x 1764 5850kW (7954bhp) Makita Corp-Japan AuxGen: 3 x 440kW 60Hz a.c Fuel: 1230.0 (r.f.)
7717250 *IPNM* -	**SIBILLA** **Sardegna Regionale Marittima SpA (SAREMAR)** - *Cagliari* *Italy* MMSI: 247045300 Official number: 578	*1,397* 761 613	Class: RI	**1979-07 Cant. Nav. "Luigi Orlando" — Livorno** Yd No: 147 Loa 69.59 (BB) Br ex 14.03 Dght 3.610 Lbp 64.29 Br md 14.00 Dpth 4.81 Welded, 2 dks	**(A36A2PR) Passenger/Ro-Ro Ship (Vehicles)** Passengers: unberthed: 1250 Bow door/ramp Stern door/ramp Lane-Len: 160 Vehicles: 60	**2 oil engines** reverse reduction geared to sc. shaft driving 2 CP propellers Total Power: 3,706kW (5,038hp) 16.5kn GMT B230.12V 2 x Vee 4 Stroke 12 Cy. 230 x 270 each-1853kW (2519bhp) Grandi Motori Trieste-Italy Thrusters: 1 Thwart. FP thruster (f) Fuel: 95.5 (d.f.) 15.0pd
7604491 - -	**SIBIR** **Government of The Russian Federation** Federal State Unitary Enterprise 'Atomflot' *Murmansk* *Russia*	**20,665** 6,199 4,096	Class: (RS)	**1977 Baltiyskiy Zavod — Leningrad** Yd No: 701 Loa 147.99 Br ex 30.00 Dght 11.000 Lbp 136.00 Br md 28.01 Dpth 17.20 Welded, 4 dks	**(B34C2SI) Icebreaker** Bale: 1,092 Compartments: 1 Ho, ER 2 Ha: 2 (1.9 x 2.3) Cranes: 2x3.3t Ice Capable	**4 turbo electric Steam Turbs** driving 4 gen. each 27500kW Connecting to 3 elec. motors driving 3 FP propellers Total Power: 55,168kW (75,008hp) 21.0kn 4 x steam Turb each-13792kW (18752shp) in the U.S.S.R. Boilers: (NR), (NR)
8974350 *UAHM* -	**SIBIR** **Sudoverfryba CJSC** - *Petropavlovsk-Kamchatskiy* *Russia* Official number: 000091	**196** 58 87	Class: RS	**2001-01 Dalian Fishing Vessel Co — Dalian LN** Yd No: 2000-1202 Loa 33.20 Br ex 7.00 Dght 2.600 Lbp 28.00 Br md - Dpth 3.40 Welded, 1 dk	**(B11A2FS) Stern Trawler** Ice Capable	**1 oil engine** reduction geared to sc. shaft driving 1 FP propeller Total Power: 339kW (461hp) 10.5kn Cummins KTA-19-M 1 x 4 Stroke 6 Cy. 159 x 159 339kW (461bhp) Chongqing Cummins Engine Co Ltd-China AuxGen: 1 x 250kW, 1 x 50kW Fuel: 49.0 (d.f.)
7808308 *UDDE* -	**SIBIRSKIY** **Federal State Financed Institution 'Far-Eastern Expeditionary Division of Emergency & Rescue Operations'** - *Vladivostok* *Russia* MMSI: 273814200 Official number: 802478	**3,121** 936 1,474	Class: RS	**1980-07 Oy Wartsila Ab — Helsinki** Yd No: 427 Lengthened Loa 74.41 Br ex 18.32 Dght 6.700 Lbp 65.00 Br md 18.00 Dpth 9.02 Welded, 1 dk	**(B32A2ST) Tug** Compartments: 2 Ho, ER 2 Ha: ER 2 (2.2 x 2.2) Cranes: 2x5t,2x3t Ice Capable	**2 oil engines** driving 2 CP propellers Total Power: 5,738kW (7,802hp) 15.0kn Pielstick 6PC2-5L-400 2 x 4 Stroke 6 Cy. 400 x 460 each-2869kW (3901bhp) Oy Wartsila Ab-Finland AuxGen: 3 x 508kW Thrusters: 1 Thwart. FP thruster (f) Fuel: 1400.0 (r.f.)
8862284 *V4KB2* -	**SIBIRSKIY-2101** **Seastar Maritime Ltd** Vestra Ltd *Basseterre* *St Kitts & Nevis* MMSI: 341106000	**3,409** 1,021 3,172	Class: RS (RR)	**1980-08 Valmet Oy — Helsinki** Yd No: 370 Loa 128.43 Br ex 15.65 Dght 3.000 Lbp 125.00 Br md 15.50 Dpth 5.45 Welded, 1 dk	**(A31A2GX) General Cargo Ship** Bale: 4,700 TEU 48 C. 48/20' (40')	**2 oil engines** driving 2 FP propellers Total Power: 1,324kW (1,800hp) 10.5kn Dvigatel Revolyutsii 6CHRNP36/45 2 x 4 Stroke 6 Cy. 360 x 450 each-662kW (900bhp) Zavod "Dvigatel Revolyutsii"-Gorkiy Thrusters: 1 Thwart. FP thruster (f) Fuel: 251.0 (d.f.)
7801843 - -	**SIBIRSKIY-2102** **Martek Internacional Srl** - *Asuncion* *Paraguay*	**3,415** 1,024 3,052	Class: (RS)	**1980-10 Valmet Oy — Helsinki** Yd No: 371 Loa 128.20 Br ex 15.63 Dght 3.030 Lbp 125.00 Br md 15.40 Dpth 5.45 Welded, 1 dk	**(A31A2GX) General Cargo Ship** Grain: 4,813; Bale: 4,700 TEU 142 C Compartments: 4 Ho, ER 4 Ha: 4 (20.0 x 11.0)ER Ice Capable	**2 oil engines** driving 2 CP propellers Total Power: 1,324kW (1,800hp) 10.0kn Dvigatel Revolyutsii 6CHRN36/45 2 x 4 Stroke 6 Cy. 360 x 450 each-662kW (900bhp) Zavod "Dvigatel Revolyutsii"-Gorkiy AuxGen: 3 x 122kW a.c Thrusters: 1 Thwart. FP thruster (f) Fuel: 183.0 (d.f.)
7811044 *UBXE8* -	**SIBIRSKIY-2112** *ex* Tasey *-2009* *ex* Sibirskiy-2112 *-2007* *ex* Pan Julia *-1994* *ex* Sibirskiy-2112 *-1992* **Don River Shipping JSC (OAO 'Donrechflot')** LLC Rosshipcom SatCom: Inmarsat C 427301920 *Taganrog* *Russia* MMSI: 273342420	**3,743** 1,122 3,507	Class: RS	**1980-11 Hollming Oy — Rauma** Yd No: 227 Loa 129.52 Br ex 15.80 Dght 3.200 Lbp 123.02 Br md 15.60 Dpth 6.02 Welded, 1 dk	**(A31A2GX) General Cargo Ship** Bale: 5,400 TEU 144 C. 144/20'	**2 oil engines** driving 2 FP propellers Total Power: 1,324kW (1,800hp) 10.2kn Dvigatel Revolyutsii 6CHRN36/45 2 x 4 Stroke 6 Cy. 360 x 450 each-662kW (900bhp) Zavod "Dvigatel Revolyutsii"-Gorkiy AuxGen: 2 x 126kW a.c Thrusters: 1 Thwart. FP thruster (f) Fuel: 210.0 (r.f.)
7911478 *UHNT* -	**SIBIRSKIY-2115** *ex* Nercha *-2009* *ex* Sibirskiy-2115 *-2007* **Don River Shipping JSC (OAO 'Donrechflot')** - *Taganrog* *Russia* MMSI: 273387100	**3,743** 1,122 4,376	Class: RS	**1981-07 Hollming Oy — Rauma** Yd No: 232 Loa 129.52 Br ex 15.80 Dght 3.720 Lbp 123.02 Br md 15.60 Dpth 6.02 Welded, 1 dk	**(A31A2GX) General Cargo Ship** Bale: 5,400	**2 oil engines** driving 2 FP propellers Total Power: 1,324kW (1,800hp) 10.2kn Dvigatel Revolyutsii 6CHRN36/45 2 x 4 Stroke 6 Cy. 360 x 450 each-662kW (900bhp) Zavod "Dvigatel Revolyutsii"-Gorkiy AuxGen: 3 x 122kW a.c Thrusters: 1 Thwart. FP thruster (f) Fuel: 210.0 (r.f.)
7911480 *UBXE3* -	**SIBIRSKIY-2116** *ex* Arey *-2009* *ex* Sibirskiy-2116 *-2007* **Don River Shipping JSC (OAO 'Donrechflot')** *Taganrog* *Russia* MMSI: 273347320	**3,743** 1,122 4,409	Class: RS	**1981-08 Hollming Oy — Rauma** Yd No: 233 Loa 129.52 Br ex 15.80 Dght 3.720 Lbp 123.02 Br md 15.60 Dpth 6.02 Welded, 1 dk	**(A31A2GX) General Cargo Ship** Bale: 5,400	**2 oil engines** driving 2 FP propellers Total Power: 1,324kW (1,800hp) 10.2kn Dvigatel Revolyutsii 6CHRN36/45 2 x 4 Stroke 6 Cy. 360 x 450 each-662kW (900bhp) Zavod "Dvigatel Revolyutsii"-Gorkiy AuxGen: 3 x 122kW a.c Thrusters: 1 Thwart. FP thruster (f) Fuel: 210.0 (r.f.)
7911507 *UBHZ* -	**SIBIRSKIY-2118** *ex* Torey *-2009* *ex* Sibirskiy-2118 *-2007* *ex* Pan Dina *-1994* *ex* Sibirskiy-2118 *-1992* **Don River Shipping JSC (OAO 'Donrechflot')** - *Taganrog* *Russia* MMSI: 273385100	**3,743** 1,122 4,068	Class: RS	**1982-04 Hollming Oy — Rauma** Yd No: 235 Loa 129.52 Br ex 15.80 Dght 3.540 Lbp 125.71 Br md 15.60 Dpth 6.02 Welded, 1 dk	**(A31A2GX) General Cargo Ship** Bale: 5,400 TEU 144 C. 144/20'	**2 oil engines** driving 2 FP propellers Total Power: 1,324kW (1,800hp) 10.2kn Dvigatel Revolyutsii 6CHRN36/45 2 x 4 Stroke 6 Cy. 360 x 450 each-662kW (900bhp) Zavod "Dvigatel Revolyutsii"-Gorkiy AuxGen: 2 x 126kW a.c Thrusters: 1 Thwart. FP thruster (f) Fuel: 210.0 (d.f.)
7911519 *UIAM* -	**SIBIRSKIY-2119** *ex* Dauria *-2010* *ex* Sibirskiy-2119 *-2007* **Don River Shipping JSC (OAO 'Donrechflot')** - *Taganrog* *Russia* MMSI: 273381200	**3,743** 1,122 3,505	Class: RS	**1982-05 Hollming Oy — Rauma** Yd No: 236 Loa 129.52 Br ex 15.80 Dght 3.720 Lbp 125.71 Br md 15.60 Dpth 6.02 Welded, 1 dk	**(A31A2GX) General Cargo Ship** Bale: 5,400	**2 oil engines** driving 2 FP propellers Total Power: 1,324kW (1,800hp) 10.2kn Dvigatel Revolyutsii 6CHRN36/45 2 x 4 Stroke 6 Cy. 360 x 450 each-662kW (900bhp) Zavod "Dvigatel Revolyutsii"-Gorkiy AuxGen: 3 x 122kW a.c Thrusters: 1 Thwart. FP thruster (f) Fuel: 210.0 (r.f.)
8100416 *UBEX* -	**SIBIRSKIY-2128** **North-Western Fleet (A/O 'Severo-Zapadnyy Flot')** - *St Petersburg* *Russia* MMSI: 273312900	**3,409** 1,021 3,480	Class: RS RR	**1982-11 Valmet Oy — Turku** Yd No: 391 Loa 127.70 Br ex 15.40 Dght 3.170 Lbp 123.55 Br md - Dpth 5.45 Welded, 1 dk	**(A31A2GX) General Cargo Ship** Bale: 4,700 TEU 142 C.Ho 94/20' C.Dk 48/20'	**2 oil engines** driving 2 FP propellers Total Power: 1,324kW (1,800hp) 10.0kn Dvigatel Revolyutsii 6CHRN36/45 2 x 4 Stroke 6 Cy. 360 x 450 each-662kW (900bhp) Zavod "Dvigatel Revolyutsii"-Gorkiy AuxGen: 3 x 100kW a.c, 1 x 50kW a.c Thrusters: 1 Thwart. FP thruster (f) Fuel: 226.0 (r.f.)

8100428 *UFDD* -	**SIBIRSKIY-2129** **VF International Transportation Ltd Co (OOO 'VF Zagranperevozki')** JSC Volga Shipping (OAO Sudokhodnaya Kompaniya 'Volzhskoye Parokhodstvo') *St Petersburg* *Russia* MMSI: 273327500 Official number: 822793	**3,415** 1,024 3,052	Class: RS (RR)	**1983-05 Valmet Oy — Turku** Yd No: 392 Loa 128.43 Br ex 15.65 Dght 3.170 Lbp 125.00 Br md 15.40 Dpth 5.45 Welded, 1 dk	**(A31A2GX) General Cargo Ship** Bale: 4,700 TEU 190 Compartments: 4 Ho, ER 4 Ha: ER 4 (18.9 x 10.9) Ice Capable	**2 oil engines** driving 2 FP propellers Total Power: 1,324kW (1,800hp) 11.0kn Dvigatel Revolyutsii 6CHRN36/45 2 x 4 Stroke 6 Cy. 360 x 450 each-662kW (900bhp) Zavod "Dvigatel Revolyutsii"-Gorkiy AuxGen: 3 x 100kW a.c, 1 x 50kW a.c Thrusters: 1 Thwart. FP thruster (f) Fuel: 267.0 (r.f.)
8104187 *UBEF* -	**SIBIRSKIY-2131** **North-Western Fleet (A/O 'Severo-Zapadnyy Flot')** - SatCom: Inmarsat B 327327710 *St Petersburg* *Russia* MMSI: 273312800	**3,978** 1,194 4,130	Class: RS (RR)	**1982-10 Hollming Oy — Rauma** Yd No: 248 Loa 129.50 Br ex 15.80 Dght 3.550 Lbp 125.75 Br md 15.60 Dpth 6.00 Welded, 1 dk	**(A31A2GX) General Cargo Ship** Bale: 5,400 Compartments: 4 Ho, ER	**2 oil engines** driving 2 FP propellers Total Power: 1,324kW (1,800hp) 10.0kn Dvigatel Revolyutsii 6CHRN36/45 2 x 4 Stroke 6 Cy. 360 x 450 each-662kW (900bhp) Zavod "Dvigatel Revolyutsii"-Gorkiy AuxGen: 3 x 110kW a.c Thrusters: 1 Thwart. FP thruster (f) Fuel: 226.0 (d.f.)
8211136 *UBEG* -	**SIBIRSKIY-2132** **North-Western Fleet (A/O 'Severo-Zapadnyy Flot')** - *St Petersburg* *Russia* MMSI: 273313800 Official number: 820374	**3,978** 1,021 4,477	Class: RS (RR)	**1983-09 Hollming Oy — Rauma** Yd No: 249 Loa 129.50 Br ex 15.80 Dght 3.720 Lbp 123.00 Br md 15.60 Dpth 6.00 Welded, 1 dk	**(A31A2GX) General Cargo Ship** Bale: 5,400 Compartments: 4 Ho, ER 4 Ha: 2 (19.2 x 10.9)ER 2 (19.7 x 10.9)	**2 oil engines** driving 2 FP propellers Total Power: 1,324kW (1,800hp) 10.0kn Dvigatel Revolyutsii 6CHRN36/45 2 x 4 Stroke 6 Cy. 360 x 450 each-662kW (900bhp) Zavod "Dvigatel Revolyutsii"-Gorkiy AuxGen: 3 x 110kW a.c, 1 x 58kW a.c Thrusters: 1 Thwart. FP thruster (f) Fuel: 226.0 (d.f.)
8211148 *UBEH* -	**SIBIRSKIY-2133** **North-Western Fleet (A/O 'Severo-Zapadnyy Flot')** - *St Petersburg* *Russia* MMSI: 273329300 Official number: 821292	**3,978** 1,194 4,447	Class: RS (RR)	**1983-11 Hollming Oy — Rauma** Yd No: 250 Loa 129.50 Br ex 15.80 Dght 3.720 Lbp 125.75 Br md 15.60 Dpth 6.00 Welded, 1 dk	**(A31A2GX) General Cargo Ship** Bale: 5,400 Compartments: 4 Ho, ER 4 Ha: 2 (19.7 x 10.9)2 (19.2 x 10.9)ER	**2 oil engines** driving 2 FP propellers Total Power: 1,324kW (1,800hp) 10.0kn Dvigatel Revolyutsii 6CHRN36/45 2 x 4 Stroke 6 Cy. 360 x 450 each-662kW (900bhp) Zavod "Dvigatel Revolyutsii"-Gorkiy AuxGen: 3 x 110kW a.c, 1 x 58kW a.c Thrusters: 1 Thwart. FP thruster (f) Fuel: 226.0 (d.f.)
8725876 *UFSN* -	**SIBIRTSEVO** **Kometa Joint Stock Co (A/O 'Kometa')** - SatCom: Inmarsat C 427321045 *Nakhodka* *Russia* MMSI: 273815110	**528** 158 134	Class: RS	**1986-07 Zavod 'Nikolayevsk-na-Amure' — Nikolayevsk-na-Amure** Yd No: 1242 Loa 44.88 Br ex 9.47 Dght 3.770 Lbp 39.37 Br md 9.30 Dpth 5.15 Welded, 1 dk	**(B11A2FS) Stern Trawler** Ice Capable	**1 oil engine** driving 1 FP propeller Total Power: 588kW (799hp) 11.5kn S.K.L. 6NVD48A-2U 1 x 4 Stroke 6 Cy. 320 x 480 588kW (799bhp) VEB Schwermaschinenbau "KarlLiebknecht" (SKL)-Magdeburg AuxGen: 3 x 150kW a.c
7701196 *YFTN* -	**SIBOGAT** *ex* Ardiona *-2011* *ex* Puteri Tiga *-2010* *ex* Ocean Hero *-1998* *ex* Hakko Maru No. 5 *-1987* **PT Kreasi Mas Marine** - *Surabaya* *Indonesia*	**1,288** 648 2,310	Class: KI (NK)	**1977-04 Kurinoura Dockyard Co Ltd — Yawatahama EH** Yd No: 111 Loa 78.70 Br ex 12.04 Dght 5.020 Lbp 72.00 Br md 12.00 Dpth 5.52 Welded, 1 dk	**(A13B2TP) Products Tanker** Liq: 2,393; Liq (Oil): 2,393	**1 oil engine** driving 1 FP propeller Total Power: 1,545kW (2,101hp) Hanshin 6LU38 1 x 4 Stroke 6 Cy. 380 x 580 1545kW (2101bhp) The Hanshin Diesel Works Ltd-Japan AuxGen: 2 x 96kW a.c
8324024 *XUHY7* -	**SIBOR** *ex* Wishes *-2008* *ex* Fukuriki Maru No. 8 *-2002* **Rich Win International Group Ltd** Golden Lake Ship Management Pte Ltd *Phnom Penh* *Cambodia* MMSI: 515834000 Official number: 0584086	**1,194** 545 1,600	Class: (NK)	**1984-05 K.K. Miura Zosensho — Saiki** Yd No: 703 Loa 72.01 Br ex - Dght 4.201 Lbp 67.01 Br md 11.51 Dpth 6.51 Welded, 2 dks	**(A31A2GX) General Cargo Ship** Grain: 2,375; Bale: 2,206 1 Ha: ER	**1 oil engine** driving 1 FP propeller Total Power: 883kW (1,201hp) Hanshin 6LUN28A 1 x 4 Stroke 6 Cy. 280 x 480 883kW (1201bhp) The Hanshin Diesel Works Ltd-Japan
8203505 *S2VQ* -	**SIBSA** **Chalna Port Authority** - *Chittagong* *Bangladesh* Official number: C.282	**256** 76 91	Class: (LR) ✠ Classed LR until 7/84	**1983-04 Detlef Hegemann Rolandwerft GmbH & Co. KG — Berne** Yd No: 121 Loa 31.40 Br ex 9.38 Dght 3.322 Lbp 28.00 Br md 9.16 Dpth 3.92 Welded, 1 dk	**(B32A2ST) Tug**	**2 oil engines** with clutches, flexible couplings & sr reverse geared to sc. shafts driving 2 FP propellers Total Power: 1,838kW (2,498hp) Deutz SBA8M528 2 x 4 Stroke 8 Cy. 220 x 280 each-919kW (1249bhp) Kloeckner Humboldt Deutz AG-West Germany AuxGen: 2 x 80kW 400V 50Hz a.c, 1 x 25kW 400V 50Hz a.c Fuel: 40.0 (d.f.)
8958722 *9WDR6* -	**SIBU GLORY** **Grolite Shipping Sdn Bhd** - *Kuching* *Malaysia* MMSI: 533479000 Official number: 329208	**673** 380 1,200	Class: MY	**1999 Pao Hing Shipyard Sdn Bhd — Sibu** Loa 57.75 Br ex - Dght 2.965 Lbp 54.74 Br md 11.58 Dpth 3.65 Welded, 1 dk	**(A13B2TP) Products Tanker**	**2 oil engines** geared to sc. shafts driving 2 FP propellers Total Power: 736kW (1,000hp) Cummins KTA-19-M 2 x 4 Stroke 6 Cy. 159 x 159 each-368kW (500bhp) Cummins Engine Co Inc-USA
8815592 *9MLJ5* -	**SIBU SATU** *ex* Eastern Pearl *-2010* *ex* Eiho Maru *-2009* *ex* Shinsei *-2004* **Zone Arctic Sdn Bhd** - *Port Klang* *Malaysia* MMSI: 533045500 Official number: 334244	**220** 131 290		**1988-11 KK Ura Kyodo Zosensho — Awaji HG** Yd No: 271 Loa 39.00 Br ex - Dght 2.600 Lbp 35.00 Br md 7.00 Dpth 2.80 Welded, 1 dk	**(A13B2TP) Products Tanker**	**1 oil engine** driving 1 FP propeller Total Power: 257kW (349hp) Matsui ML624GA 1 x 4 Stroke 6 Cy. 240 x 400 257kW (349bhp) Matsui Iron Works Co Ltd-Japan
9655511 *D5CM8* -	**SIBUR TOBOL** **NS Vanino Shipping Inc** Unicom Management Services (Cyprus) Ltd *Monrovia* *Liberia* MMSI: 636015737 Official number: 15737	**18,425** 5,527 22,765 T/cm 35.9	Class: RS (LR) ✠ Classed LR until 30/9/13	**2013-09 Hyundai Mipo Dockyard Co Ltd — Ulsan** Yd No: 8107 Loa 159.97 (BB) Br ex 25.64 Dght 10.900 Lbp 152.21 Br md 25.60 Dpth 16.40 Welded, 1 dk	**(A11B2TG) LPG Tanker** Double Hull (13F) Liq (Gas): 20,311 4 x Gas Tank (s); 4 independent dcy horizontal 8 Cargo Pump (s): 8x250m³/hr Manifold: Bow/CM: 81m Ice Capable	**1 oil engine** driving 1 FP propeller Total Power: 7,780kW (10,578hp) 16.0kn MAN-B&W 6S46MC-C8 1 x 2 Stroke 6 Cy. 460 x 1932 7780kW (10578bhp) Hyundai Heavy Industries Co Ltd-South Korea AuxGen: 2 x 1250kW 450V 60Hz a.c, 1 x 800kW 450V 60Hz a.c Boilers: e (ex.g.) 9.2kgf/cm² (9.0bar), AuxB (o.f.) 9.2kgf/cm² (9.0bar) Fuel: 497.0 (d.f.) 1584.0 (r.f.)

Ship	Tonnage	Class	Builder / Dimensions	Type	Machinery
9655509 **SIBUR VORONEZH** *D5CM7* - **NS Ust Luga Shipping Inc** Sovcomflot (UK) Ltd *Monrovia* *Liberia* MMSI: 636015736 Official number: 15736	**18,425** 5,527 22,780 T/cm 35.9	Class: LR RS ✠ **100A1** SS 07/2013 liquified gas carrier, Ship type 2G Anhydrous ammonia, butadiene, butane, butane and propane mixture, butylenes, diethyl ether, dimethylamine, isoprene, isopropylamine, monoethylamine, propane, propylene, VCM and vinyl ethyl ether in independent tank Type C, maximim SG 0.972, maximum vapour pressure 5.3 bar g, minimum cargo temp. minus 48 degree C **ShipRight** (ACS (B), SDA, FDA, CM), ECO (P, IHM, BWT), *IWS LI SPM4 Ice Class 1B FS at draught of 10.90m Max/min draught fwd 12.12/5.77m Max/min draught aft 10.26/6.23m Power required 4812kw, power installed 7780kw ✠ **LMC UMS +Lloyd's RMC (LG)** Eq.Ltr: I†; Cable: 605.0/64.0 U3 (a)	**2013-07 Hyundai Mipo Dockyard Co Ltd — Ulsan** Yd No: 8106 Loa 159.97 (BB) Br ex 25.64 Dght 10.916 Lbp 152.20 Br md 25.60 Dpth 16.40 Welded, 1 dk	**(A11B2TG) LPG Tanker** Double Hull (13F) Liq (Gas): 20,311 4 x Gas Tank (s); 4 horizontal 8 Cargo Pump (s): 8x250m³/hr Manifold: Bow/CM: 81m Ice Capable	**1 oil engine** driving 1 FP propeller Total Power: 7,780kW (10,578hp) 16.0kn MAN-B&W 6S46MC-C8 1 x 2 Stroke 6 Cy. 460 x 1932 7780kW (10578bhp) Hyundai Heavy Industries Co Ltd-South Korea AuxGen: 2 x 1250kW 450V 60Hz a.c, 1 x 800kW 450V 60Hz a.c Boilers: e (ex.g.) 9.2kgf/cm² (9.0bar), AuxB (o.f.) 9.2kgf/cm² (9.0bar) Fuel: 497.0 (d.f.) 1584.0 (r.f.)
7310521 **SIBYL W** - *ex Imperial Tofino -1992* - **Honduras Aero Marine S de RL de CV** - SatCom: Inmarsat C 433477310 *Honduras* Official number: L-1328335	**763** 353 752	Class: (LR) ✠ Classed LR until 16/3/09	**1973-06 McKenzie Barge & Marine Ways Ltd — North Vancouver BC** Yd No: 70 Converted From: Chemical Tanker-1994 Lengthened-1979 Loa 52.13 (BB) Br ex 10.65 Dght 4.185 Lbp 49.84 Br md 10.29 Dpth 4.57 Welded, 1 dk	**(A13B2TU) Tanker (unspecified)** Liq: 875; Liq (Oil): 875 Compartments: 10 Ta, ER	**1 oil engine** sr geared to sc. shaft driving 1 CP propeller Total Power: 736kW (1,001hp) 10.5kn Polar SF18VS-D 1 x Vee 4 Stroke 8 Cy. 250 x 300 736kW (1001bhp) AB NOHAB-Sweden AuxGen: 1 x 250kW 480V 60Hz a.c, 1 x 150kW 480V 60Hz a.c Thrusters: 1 Water jet (f) Fuel: 52.0 (d.f.) 5.0pd
9099200 **SICAL PERUGIA** - *ex Duo Jun -2007* - - - -	**139** 41 -		**2006-06 Shanghai Zhongzhou Shipping Co Ltd — Shanghai** Yd No: DS910 Loa 26.20 Br ex - Dght 1.800 Lbp 22.03 Br md 8.00 Dpth 3.20 Welded, 1 dk	**(B34L2QU) Utility Vessel**	**2 oil engines** geared to sc. shafts driving 2 Propellers Total Power: 660kW (898hp) Weifang X6170ZC 2 x 4 Stroke 6 Cy. 170 x 200 each-330kW (449bhp) Weifang Diesel Engine Factory-China
9014341 **SICAN** *OA2412* *ex Pangui -2011* - **Petrolera Transoceanica SA** - *Callao* *Peru*	*238* 71 165	Class: LR ✠ **100A1** SS 04/2011 tug ✠ **LMC** Eq.Ltr: (G) ; Cable: 388.0/20.5 U2	**1991-04 Astilleros y Servicios Navales S.A. (ASENAV) — Valdivia** Yd No: 083 Loa 30.50 Br ex 9.44 Dght 3.250 Lbp 26.76 Br md 9.00 Dpth 4.02 Welded, 1 dk	**(B32A2ST) Tug**	**2 oil engines** with clutches, flexible couplings & sr geared to sc. shafts driving 2 CP propellers Total Power: 1,558kW (2,118hp) 13.6kn Caterpillar 3512TA 2 x Vee 4 Stroke 12 Cy. 170 x 190 each-779kW (1059bhp) Caterpillar Inc-USA AuxGen: 2 x 42kW 220/380V 50Hz a.c Fuel: 90.5 (d.f.)
9354571 **SICHEM AMETHYST** *3EGQ6* *ex Songa Amethyst -2007* - **New Victory Line SA** Bernhard Schulte Shipmanagement (India) Pvt Ltd SatCom: Inmarsat C 437201611 *Panama* *Panama* MMSI: 372016000 Official number: 3216306B	**5,303** 2,631 8,817 T/cm 17.3	Class: NK	**2006-10 Murakami Hide Zosen K.K. — Imabari** Yd No: 548 Loa 114.99 (BB) Br ex - Dght 7.770 Lbp 108.50 Br md 18.20 Dpth 9.65 Welded, 1 dk	**(A12B2TR) Chemical/Products Tanker** Double Hull (13F) Liq: 9,204; Liq (Oil): 9,204 Cargo Heating Coils Compartments: 12 Wing Ta, ER 12 Cargo Pump (s): 12x220m³/hr Manifold: Bow/CM: 60.3m	**1 oil engine** driving 1 FP propeller Total Power: 3,900kW (5,302hp) 13.4kn MAN-B&W 6L35MC 1 x 2 Stroke 6 Cy. 350 x 1050 3900kW (5302bhp) Hitachi Zosen Corp-Japan AuxGen: 2 x 450kW a.c Thrusters: 1 Tunnel thruster (f) Fuel: 110.0 (d.f.) 450.0 (r.f.)
9171735 **SICHEM ANELINE** *V7HV3* *ex Songa Aneline -2007 ex Gironde -2004* - *ex Garonne -2004 ex Alexander -2003* **OIF (Panama) SA** Eitzen Chemical (Singapore) Pte Ltd *Majuro* *Marshall Islands* MMSI: 538002315 Official number: 2315	**6,206** 2,746 8,941 T/cm 18.3	Class: NV (BV)	**1998-11 Hijos de J. Barreras S.A. — Vigo** Yd No: 1568 Loa 115.30 (BB) Br ex 18.63 Dght 7.987 Lbp 108.00 Br md 18.60 Dpth 10.25 Welded, 1 dk	**(A12B2TR) Chemical/Products Tanker** Double Hull (13F) Liq: 9,421; Liq (Oil): 9,384 Cargo Heating Coils Compartments: 10 Wing Ta, 2 Wing Slop Ta, ER 10 Cargo Pump (s): 10x290m³/hr Manifold: Bow/CM: 57.4m Ice Capable	**1 oil engine** reduction geared to sc. shaft driving 1 CP propeller Total Power: 3,962kW (5,387hp) 14.0kn MAN 9L32/40 1 x 4 Stroke 9 Cy. 320 x 400 3962kW (5387bhp) MAN B&W Diesel AG-Augsburg AuxGen: 3 x 448kW 380V 50Hz a.c, 1 x a.c Thrusters: 1 Tunnel thruster (f) Fuel: 97.0 (d.f.) 445.0 (r.f.)
9397042 **SICHEM BEIJING** *9VHK4* - **Eitzen Chemical (Singapore) Pte Ltd** Eitzen Chemical A/S SatCom: Inmarsat Mini-M 761138040 *Singapore* *Singapore* MMSI: 565585000 Official number: 393442	**8,581** 4,117 13,068 T/cm 23.3	Class: AB	**2007-10 21st Century Shipbuilding Co Ltd — Tongyeong** Yd No: 238 Loa 128.60 (BB) Br ex 20.42 Dght 8.714 Lbp 120.40 Br md 20.40 Dpth 11.50 Welded, 1 dk	**(A12B2TR) Chemical/Products Tanker** Double Hull (13F) Liq: 13,403; Liq (Oil): 13,403 Cargo Heating Coils Compartments: 12 Wing Ta, 1 Slop Ta, 2 Wing Slop Ta, ER 12 Cargo Pump (s): 12x300m³/hr Manifold: Bow/CM: 60.8m	**1 oil engine** driving 1 FP propeller Total Power: 4,440kW (6,037hp) 13.4kn MAN-B&W 6S35MC 1 x 2 Stroke 6 Cy. 350 x 1400 4440kW (6037bhp) STX Engine Co Ltd-South Korea AuxGen: 3 x 550kW 450V 60Hz a.c Thrusters: 1 Tunnel thruster (f) Fuel: 121.0 (d.f.) 657.0 (r.f.)
8916504 **SICHEM CASABLANCA** *MFMR8* *ex Ievoli Gold -2013 ex Gold -2003* - **Napoli Chemical KS** Eitzen Chemical A/S *London* *United Kingdom* MMSI: 232107000 Official number: 909205	**4,556** 2,217 6,999 T/cm 17.4	Class: NV (BV) (RI)	**1993-11 Soc. Esercizio Cant. S.p.A. — Viareggio** Yd No: 769 Loa 117.07 (BB) Br ex 17.53 Dght 6.390 Lbp 108.50 Br md 17.50 Dpth 8.00 Welded, 1 dk	**(A12A2TC) Chemical Tanker** Double Hull Liq: 7,766 Cargo Heating Coils Compartments: 22 Wing Ta, ER 22 Cargo Pump (s): 18x175m³/hr, 4x80m³/hr Manifold: Bow/CM: 57m	**1 oil engine** with clutches, flexible couplings & sr geared to sc. shaft driving 1 CP propeller Total Power: 3,380kW (4,595hp) 14.2kn Wartsila 9R32D 1 x 4 Stroke 9 Cy. 320 x 350 3380kW (4595bhp) Wartsila Diesel Oy-Finland AuxGen: 2 x 975kW 380V 50Hz a.c Thrusters: 1 Directional thruster (f) Fuel: 107.0 (d.f.) 267.0 (r.f.) 15.0pd
9196448 **SICHEM CHALLENGE** *9VAA5* *ex Songa Challenge -2007* - *ex North Challenge -2006* *ex Queen of Montreux -1999* **Eitzen Chemical (Singapore) Pte Ltd** Eitzen Chemical (USA) LLC SatCom: Inmarsat C 456532710 *Singapore* *Singapore* MMSI: 565327000 Official number: 392636	**7,179** 3,846 12,181 T/cm 21.0	Class: NK	**1998-12 Watanabe Zosen KK — Imabari EH** Yd No: 310 Loa 124.02 (BB) Br ex 20.62 Dght 8.564 Lbp 116.00 Br md 20.60 Dpth 11.20 Welded, 1 dk	**(A12B2TR) Chemical/Products Tanker** Double Hull (13F) Liq: 13,265; Liq (Oil): 13,265 Cargo Heating Coils Compartments: 20 Wing Ta, 2 Wing Slop Ta, ER 20 Cargo Pump (s): 20x200m³/hr Manifold: Bow/CM: 62m	**1 oil engine** driving 1 FP propeller Total Power: 4,891kW (6,650hp) 13.8kn B&W 7S35MC 1 x 2 Stroke 7 Cy. 350 x 1400 4891kW (6650bhp) Makita Corp-Japan AuxGen: 3 x 400kW a.c Thrusters: 1 Thwart. FP thruster (f) Fuel: 108.0 (d.f.) 681.0 (r.f.) 19.5pd
9216042 **SICHEM COLIBRI** *9HHB8* *ex Colibri -2005* - **Eitzen Chemical (Singapore) Pte Ltd** Eitzen Chemical (Spain) SA *Valletta* *Malta* MMSI: 215975000 Official number: 9789	**2,764** 1,042 3,592 T/cm 10.9	Class: LR ✠ **100A1** SS 04/2011 Double Hull oil and chemical tanker, MARPOL 21.2.2, Ship Type 2 CR (s.stl), SG 1.90 in all tanks, ESP *IWS LI ✠ **LMC** **UMS** Eq.Ltr: S; Cable: 467.5/42.0 U2 (a)	**2001-04 Ilheung Shipbuilding & Engineering Co Ltd — Mokpo** Yd No: 99-93 Loa 92.90 (BB) Br ex 14.46 Dght 5.942 Lbp 83.50 Br md 14.40 Dpth 7.00 Welded, 1 dk	**(A12B2TR) Chemical/Products Tanker** Double Hull (13F) Liq: 3,684; Liq (Oil): 3,751 Cargo Heating Coils Compartments: 10 Wing Ta, 2 Wing Slop Ta, ER 10 Cargo Pump (s): 10x200m³/hr Manifold: Bow/CM: 39.1m	**1 oil engine** driving 1 CP propeller Total Power: 2,400kW (3,263hp) 13.2kn MAN-B&W 6S26MC 1 x 2 Stroke 6 Cy. 260 x 980 2400kW (3263bhp) Ssangyong Heavy Industries Co Ltd-South Korea AuxGen: 3 x 320kW 450V 60Hz a.c Thrusters: 1 Tunnel thruster (f) Fuel: 88.0 (d.f.) (Heating Coils) 301.0 (r.f.) 10.0pd

9416020 **SICHEM CONTESTER**
9VFQ4
\- **United Sky Shipping Pte Ltd**
Eitzen Chemical A/S
SatCom: Inmarsat Mini-M 764806256
Singapore *Singapore*
MMSI: 565621000
Official number: 393389

11,757 Class: NK
6,127
19,822
T/cm
29.4

2007-10 Fukuoka Shipbuilding Co Ltd — Fukuoka FO Yd No: 1267
Loa 146.60 (BB) Br ex 23.73 Dght 9.622
Lbp 138.00 Br md 23.70 Dpth 13.00
Welded, 1 dk

(A12B2TR) Chemical/Products Tanker
Double Hull (13F)
Liq: 21,620; Liq (Oil): 22,061
Cargo Heating Coils
Compartments: 18 Wing Ta, 2 Wing Slop Ta, ER
18 Cargo Pump (s): 12x300m^3/hr, 6x200m^3/hr
Manifold: Bow/CM: 73.3m

1 oil engine driving 1 FP propeller
Total Power: 6,150kW (8,362hp) 14.6kn
MAN-B&W 6S42MC
1 x 2 Stroke 6 Cy. 420 x 1764 6150kW (8362bhp)
Imex Co Ltd-Japan
AuxGen: 3 x 530kW a.c
Thrusters: 1 Tunnel thruster (f)
Fuel: 122.0 (d.f.) 932.0 (r.f.)

9216470 **SICHEM CROISIC**
9HYL9 *ex Pointe Du Croisic -2008*
\- **Sichem Pearl Shipping Co Pte Ltd**
Eitzen Chemical (Spain) SA
Valletta *Malta*
MMSI: 249704000
Official number: 9216470

5,214 Class: AB (BV)
2,043
7,721
T/cm
17.0

2001-01 Kleven Floro AS — Floro Yd No: 145
Loa 112.00 (BB) Br ex - Dght 7.350
Lbp 105.90 Br md 17.00 Dpth 9.15
Welded, 1 dk

(A12B2TR) Chemical/Products Tanker
Double Hull (13F)
Liq: 6,903; Liq (Oil): 6,903
Compartments: 18 Wing Ta, ER
18 Cargo Pump (s): 18x200m^3/hr
Manifold: Bow/CM: 54m

1 oil engine with flexible couplings & sr gearedto sc. shaft driving 1 FP propeller
Total Power: 4,320kW (5,873hp) 14.0kn
MaK 9M32
1 x 4 Stroke 9 Cy. 320 x 480 4320kW (5873bhp)
MaK Motoren GmbH & Co. KG-Kiel
AuxGen: 3 x 500kW 230/440V 60Hz a.c
Thrusters: 1 Thwart. CP thruster (f)
Fuel: 92.3 (d.f.) (Heating Coils) 513.4 (r.f.) 18.0pd

9244374 **SICHEM DEFIANCE**
V7JQ3 *ex Songa Defiance -2007*
\- *ex North Defiance -2006*
Eitzen Chemical (Singapore) Pte Ltd
\-
Majuro *Marshall Islands*
MMSI: 538002559
Official number: 2559

9,900 Class: NK
5,335
17,396
T/cm
26.6

2001-03 Fukuoka Shipbuilding Co Ltd — Fukuoka FO Yd No: 1213
Loa 135.33 (BB) Br ex 22.83 Dght 9.665
Lbp 127.70 Br md 22.80 Dpth 12.50
Welded, 1 dk

(A12B2TR) Chemical/Products Tanker
Double Hull (13F)
Liq: 17,424; Liq (Oil): 17,424
Cargo Heating Coils
Compartments: 18 Wing Ta (s.stl), 2 Wing Slop Ta (s.stl), ER
18 Cargo Pump (s): 8x200m^3/hr, 10x300m^3/hr
Manifold: Bow/CM: 65.8m
Ice Capable

1 oil engine driving 1 FP propeller
Total Power: 5,980kW (8,130hp) 14.0kn
B&W 6L42MC
1 x 2 Stroke 6 Cy. 420 x 1360 5980kW (8130bhp)
Hitachi Zosen Corp-Japan
AuxGen: 3 x 400kW a.c
Thrusters: 1 Tunnel thruster (f)
Fuel: 126.0 (d.f.) 868.0 (r.f.)

9376933 **SICHEM DUBAI**
9HOJ9
\- **Eitzen Chemical (Singapore) Pte Ltd**
Eitzen Chemical A/S
Valletta *Malta*
MMSI: 249276000
Official number: 9376933

8,455 Class: NV (KR)
4,031
12,936
T/cm
22.9

2007-12 Samho Shipbuilding Co Ltd — Tongyeong Yd No: 1074
Loa 127.08 (BB) Br ex 20.42 Dght 8.700
Lbp 119.00 Br md 20.40 Dpth 11.50
Welded, 1 dk

(A12B2TR) Chemical/Products Tanker
Double Hull (13F)
Liq: 14,054; Liq (Oil): 14,054
Cargo Heating Coils
Compartments: 12 Wing Ta, 2 Wing Slop Ta, ER
12 Cargo Pump (s): 12x300m^3/hr
Manifold: Bow/CM: 46m

1 oil engine driving 1 FP propeller
Total Power: 4,200kW (5,710hp) 13.4kn
MAN-B&W 6S35MC
1 x 2 Stroke 6 Cy. 350 x 1400 4200kW (5710bhp)
STX Engine Co Ltd-South Korea
AuxGen: 3 x 480kW a.c
Thrusters: 1 Tunnel thruster (f)
Fuel: 74.0 (d.f.) 677.0 (r.f.)

9388704 **SICHEM EAGLE**
9VNR6
\- **Eitzen Chemical (Singapore) Pte Ltd**
\-
Singapore *Singapore*
MMSI: 565913000
Official number: 394287

17,789 Class: AB
6,662
25,421
T/cm
37.4

2008-07 Dae Sun Shipbuilding & Engineering Co Ltd — Busan Yd No: 472
Loa 170.11 (BB) Br ex 26.24 Dght 10.016
Lbp 161.00 Br md 26.20 Dpth 15.60
Welded, 1 dk

(A12B2TR) Chemical/Products Tanker
Double Hull (13F)
Liq: 29,121; Liq (Oil): 29,121
Compartments: 12 Wing Ta, 2 Wing Slop Ta, ER
12 Cargo Pump (s): 12x380m^3/hr
Manifold: Bow/CM: 87m
Ice Capable

1 oil engine driving 1 FP propeller
Total Power: 7,860kW (10,686hp) 14.3kn
MAN-B&W 6S46MC-C
1 x 2 Stroke 6 Cy. 460 x 1932 7860kW (10686bhp)
STX Engine Co Ltd-South Korea
AuxGen: 3 x 850kW a.c
Thrusters: 1 Tunnel thruster (f)
Fuel: 176.0 (d.f.) 1395.0 (r.f.)

9352066 **SICHEM EDINBURGH**
S6AT8
\- **Eitzen Chemical (Singapore) Pte Ltd**
Eitzen Chemical A/S
SatCom: Inmarsat C 456543910
Singapore *Singapore*
MMSI: 565439000
Official number: 392846

8,589 Class: AB
4,117
13,153
T/cm
23.3

2007-05 21st Century Shipbuilding Co Ltd — Tongyeong Yd No: 227
Loa 128.60 (BB) Br ex 20.42 Dght 8.714
Lbp 120.40 Br md 20.40 Dpth 11.50
Welded, 1 dk

(A12B2TR) Chemical/Products Tanker
Double Hull (13F)
Liq: 13,403; Liq (Oil): 13,403
Cargo Heating Coils
Compartments: 12 Wing Ta, 3 Wing Slop Ta, ER
12 Cargo Pump (s): 12x300m^3/hr
Manifold: Bow/CM: 60.8m

1 oil engine driving 1 FP propeller
Total Power: 4,400kW (5,982hp) 13.4kn
MAN-B&W 6S35MC
1 x 2 Stroke 6 Cy. 350 x 1400 4400kW (5982bhp)
STX Engine Co Ltd-South Korea
AuxGen: 3 x 550kW a.c
Thrusters: 1 Tunnel thruster (f)
Fuel: 93.0 (d.f.) 657.0 (r.f.)

9396012 **SICHEM FALCON**
9HT09
\- **Eitzen Chemical (Singapore) Pte Ltd**
Eitzen Chemical A/S
SatCom: Inmarsat Mini-M 764888387
Valletta *Malta*
MMSI: 249533000
Official number: 9396012

17,822 Class: AB
6,662
25,419
T/cm
37.3

2009-01 Dae Sun Shipbuilding & Engineering Co Ltd — Busan Yd No: 474
Loa 170.11 (BB) Br ex 26.23 Dght 10.016
Lbp 161.00 Br md 26.20 Dpth 15.60
Welded, 1 dk

(A12B2TR) Chemical/Products Tanker
Double Hull (13F)
Liq: 29,136; Liq (Oil): 29,136
Compartments: 12 Wing Ta, 2 Wing Slop Ta, ER
12 Cargo Pump (s): 12x380m^3/hr
Manifold: Bow/CM: 60.8m

1 oil engine driving 1 FP propeller
Total Power: 7,860kW (10,686hp) 14.3kn
MAN-B&W 6S46MC-C
1 x 2 Stroke 6 Cy. 460 x 1932 7860kW (10686bhp)
STX Engine Co Ltd-South Korea
AuxGen: 3 x 850kW 450V 60Hz a.c
Thrusters: 1 Tunnel thruster (f)
Fuel: 180.0 (d.f.) 1423.0 (r.f.)

8510489 **SICHEM FENOL I**
9LB2351 *ex Sichem Fenol -2010 ex Fenol -2005*
\- *ex Sunrise Fair -1997 ex Unix Fair -1994*
ex Southern Fair -1990 ex Kyokuho Iris -1987
Black Sea Shipping & Trading Co Ltd
Overseas Shipping & Stevedoring Co (OSSCO)
Freetown *Sierra Leone*
MMSI: 667002217
Official number: SL102217

4,441 Class: (NK)
2,242
7,158
T/cm
16.0

1985-12 Towa Zosen K.K. — Shimonoseki Yd No: 566
Loa 107.00 (BB) Br ex - Dght 6.813
Lbp 99.00 Br md 18.20 Dpth 8.10
Welded, 1 dk

(A12B2TR) Chemical/Products Tanker
Double Bottom Entire Compartment Length
Liq: 7,969; Liq (Oil): 7,969
Part Cargo Heating Coils
Compartments: 14 Ta, ER
9 Cargo Pump (s): 8x250m^3/hr, 1x400m^3/hr
Manifold: Bow/CM: 43m

1 oil engine driving 1 FP propeller
Total Power: 2,438kW (3,315hp) 12.5kn
Mitsubishi 6UEC37/88H
1 x 2 Stroke 6 Cy. 370 x 880 2438kW (3315bhp)
Kobe Hatsudoki KK-Japan
AuxGen: 2 x 300kW a.c
Fuel: 67.0 (d.f.) 511.0 (r.f.)

9141895 **SICHEM FUMI**
3FNC6 *ex Golden Fumi -2011*
\- **Eitzen Chemical (Singapore) Pte Ltd**
Thome Ship Management Pte Ltd
SatCom: Inmarsat C 435680210
Panama *Panama*
MMSI: 356802000
Official number: 2337896F

6,275 Class: NK
3,563
11,674
T/cm
19.7

1996-09 Fukuoka Shipbuilding Co Ltd — Fukuoka FO Yd No: 1192
Loa 117.00 (BB) Br ex 20.02 Dght 8.766
Lbp 110.00 Br md 20.00 Dpth 11.20
Welded, 1 dk

(A12B2TR) Chemical/Products Tanker
Double Hull (13F)
Liq: 12,543; Liq (Oil): 12,543
Cargo Heating Coils
Compartments: 18 Wing Ta, 2 Wing Slop Ta, ER
18 Cargo Pump (s): 4x100m^3/hr, 6x200m^3/hr, 8x250m^3/hr
Manifold: Bow/CM: 53.6m

1 oil engine driving 1 FP propeller
Total Power: 3,604kW (4,900hp) 13.0kn
Mitsubishi 7UEC37LA
1 x 2 Stroke 7 Cy. 370 x 880 3604kW (4900bhp)
Kobe Hatsudoki KK-Japan
AuxGen: 2 x 400kW a.c
Thrusters: 1 Thwart. CP thruster (f)
Fuel: 102.0 (d.f.) 706.0 (r.f.)

9396000 **SICHEM HAWK**
9HSE9
\- **Eitzen Chemical (Singapore) Pte Ltd**
Eitzen Chemical A/S
SatCom: Inmarsat Mini-M 764866893
Valletta *Malta*
MMSI: 249445000
Official number: 9396000

17,822 Class: AB
6,662
25,385
T/cm
37.4

2008-10 Dae Sun Shipbuilding & Engineering Co Ltd — Busan Yd No: 473
Loa 170.11 (BB) Br ex 26.23 Dght 10.016
Lbp 161.94 Br md 26.20 Dpth 15.60
Welded, 1 dk

(A12B2TR) Chemical/Products Tanker
Double Hull (13F)
Liq: 29,129; Liq (Oil): 30,661
Compartments: 12 Wing Ta, 2 Wing Slop Ta, ER
12 Cargo Pump (s): 12x380m^3/hr
Manifold: Bow/CM: 85.7m
Ice Capable

1 oil engine driving 1 FP propeller
Total Power: 7,860kW (10,686hp) 14.3kn
MAN-B&W 6S46MC-C
1 x 2 Stroke 6 Cy. 460 x 1932 7860kW (10686bhp)
STX Engine Co Ltd-South Korea
AuxGen: 3 x 850kW a.c
Thrusters: 1 Tunnel thruster (f)
Fuel: 180.0 (d.f.) 1423.0 (r.f.)

9361483 **SICHEM HIROSHIMA**
9VJD6
\- **Southern Breeze Navigation Pte Ltd**
Eitzen Chemical (USA) LLC
SatCom: Inmarsat Mini-M 764839462
Singapore *Singapore*
MMSI: 565592000
Official number: 393474

8,582 Class: AB
4,117
13,119
T/cm
23.2

2008-05 Sekwang Heavy Industries Co Ltd — Ulsan Yd No: 1156
Loa 128.60 (BB) Br ex 20.43 Dght 8.714
Lbp 120.40 Br md 20.40 Dpth 11.51
Welded, 1 dk

(A12B2TR) Chemical/Products Tanker
Double Hull (13F)
Liq: 13,394; Liq (Oil): 13,335
Cargo Heating Coils
Compartments: 12 Wing Ta, 2 Wing Slop Ta, Wing ER
12 Cargo Pump (s): 12x300m^3/hr
Manifold: Bow/CM: 61.7m

1 oil engine driving 1 FP propeller
Total Power: 4,457kW (6,060hp) 13.4kn
MAN-B&W 6S35MC
1 x 2 Stroke 6 Cy. 350 x 1400 4457kW (6060bhp)
STX Engine Co Ltd-South Korea
AuxGen: 3 x 480kW a.c
Thrusters: 1 Tunnel thruster (f)
Fuel: 77.0 (d.f.) 675.0 (r.f.)

9397054 **SICHEM HONG KONG**
9VVK7
\- **Eitzen Chemical (Singapore) Pte Ltd**
Eitzen Chemical A/S
Singapore *Singapore*
MMSI: 565637000
Official number: 393565

8,581 Class: AB
4,117
13,069
T/cm
23.2

2007-10 21st Century Shipbuilding Co Ltd — Tongyeong Yd No: 240
Loa 128.60 (BB) Br ex 20.42 Dght 8.700
Lbp 120.40 Br md 20.40 Dpth 11.50
Welded, 1 dk

(A12B2TR) Chemical/Products Tanker
Double Hull (13F)
Liq: 13,407; Liq (Oil): 13,403
Cargo Heating Coils
Compartments: 12 Wing Ta, 1 Slop Ta, 2 Wing Slop Ta, ER
12 Cargo Pump (s): 12x300m^3/hr
Manifold: Bow/CM: 60.8m

1 oil engine driving 1 FP propeller
Total Power: 4,440kW (6,037hp) 13.4kn
MAN-B&W 6S35MC
1 x 2 Stroke 6 Cy. 350 x 1400 4440kW (6037bhp)
STX Engine Co Ltd-South Korea
AuxGen: 3 x 550kW a.c
Thrusters: 1 Tunnel thruster (f)
Fuel: 76.0 (d.f.) 644.0 (r.f.)

9104873 **SICHEM HOUSTON**
MFML7 *ex Attilio Ievoli -2013*
\- **Napoli Chemical KS**
Eitzen Chemical A/S
SatCom: Inmarsat C 424706620
London *United Kingdom*
MMSI: 232119000
Official number: 909010

4,450 Class: NV (RI) (BV)
1,982
6,239
T/cm
15.9

1995-09 Cant. Nav. Mario Morini S.p.A. — Ancona Yd No: 244
Loa 115.50 (BB) Br ex 16.03 Dght 6.343
Lbp 103.90 Br md 16.00 Dpth 7.98
Welded, 1 dk

(A12A2TC) Chemical Tanker
Double Hull
Liq: 5,851
Cargo Heating Coils
Compartments: 18 Wing Ta, 2 Wing Slop Ta, ER
26 Cargo Pump (s): 18x175m^3/hr, 2x50m^3/hr, 6x80m^3/hr
Manifold: Bow/CM: 51.7m

1 oil engine with clutches, flexible couplings & sr geared to sc. shaft driving 1 CP propeller
Total Power: 3,375kW (4,589hp) 13.0kn
Wartsila 9R32D
1 x 4 Stroke 9 Cy. 320 x 350 3375kW (4589bhp)
Wartsila Diesel Oy-Finland
AuxGen: 1 x 850kW 220/380V 50Hz a.c, 3 x 675kW 220/380V 50Hz a.c
Thrusters: 1 Thwart. FP thruster (f)
Fuel: 63.0 (d.f.) (Heating Coils) 331.0 (r.f.) 14.5pd

9392183 *9HND9* -	**SICHEM IRIS** **Eitzen Chemical (Singapore) Pte Ltd** Thome Ship Management Pte Ltd *Valletta* *Malta* MMSI: 249210000 Official number: 9392183	**5,744** 2,551 8,139 T/cm 18.0	Class: NV	**2008-08 Sekwang Heavy Industries Co Ltd — Ulsan** Yd No: 1168 Loa 115.00 (BB) Br ex - Dght 7.450 Lbp 107.00 Br md 18.20 Dpth 9.60 Welded, 1 dk	**(A12B2TR) Chemical/Products Tanker** Double Hull (13F) Liq: 8,499; Liq (Oil): 8,499 Cargo Heating Coils Compartments: 10 Wing Ta, ER, 2 Wing Slop Ta 10 Cargo Pump (s): 10x200m³/hr Manifold: Bow/CM: 58.3m	**1 oil engine** driving 1 FP propeller Total Power: 3,900kW (5,302hp) 14.0kn MAN-B&W 6L35MC 1 x 2 Stroke 6 Cy. 350 x 1050 3900kW (5302bhp) Hyundai Heavy Industries Co Ltd-South Korea AuxGen: 3 x a.c Thrusters: 1 Tunnel thruster (f) Fuel: 95.0 (d.f.) 440.0 (r.f.)
9393395 *9HNE9* -	**SICHEM LILY** **Eitzen Chemical (Singapore) Pte Ltd** Thome Ship Management Pte Ltd *Valletta* *Malta* MMSI: 249209000 Official number: 9393395	**5,744** 2,551 8,110 T/cm 18.0	Class: NV	**2009-01 Sekwang Heavy Industries Co Ltd — Ulsan** Yd No: 1170 Loa 115.26 (BB) Br ex 18.22 Dght 7.450 Lbp 107.00 Br md 18.20 Dpth 9.60 Welded, 1 dk	**(A12B2TR) Chemical/Products Tanker** Double Hull (13F) Liq: 8,500; Liq (Oil): 8,500 Cargo Heating Coils Compartments: 10 Wing Ta (s.stl), 2 Wing Slop Ta (s.stl), ER 10 Cargo Pump (s): 10x200m³/hr Manifold: Bow/CM: 61.6m	**1 oil engine** driving 1 FP propeller Total Power: 4,200kW (5,710hp) 14.0kn MAN-B&W 6L35MC 1 x 2 Stroke 6 Cy. 350 x 1050 4200kW (5710bhp) Hyundai Heavy Industries Co Ltd-South Korea AuxGen: 3 x 615kW 450V 60Hz a.c Thrusters: 1 Tunnel thruster (f) Fuel: 95.0 (d.f.) 463.0 (r.f.)
9322097 *9VEZ6* -	**SICHEM MANILA** **Eitzen Chemical (Singapore) Pte Ltd** Eitzen Chemical A/S SatCom: Inmarsat Mini-M 764685941 *Singapore* *Singapore* MMSI: 565341000 Official number: 392385	**8,562** 4,095 13,125 T/cm 23.3	Class: NV (KR)	**2007-01 21st Century Shipbuilding Co Ltd — Tongyeong** Yd No: 216 Loa 128.60 (BB) Br ex 20.43 Dght 8.714 Lbp 120.85 Br md 20.40 Dpth 11.50 Welded, 1 dk	**(A12B2TR) Chemical/Products Tanker** Double Hull (13F) Liq: 13,416; Liq (Oil): 13,416 Compartments: 12 Wing Ta, 2 Wing Slop Ta, ER 12 Cargo Pump (s): 12x300m³/hr Manifold: Bow/CM: 60.8m	**1 oil engine** driving 1 FP propeller Total Power: 4,440kW (6,037hp) 13.4kn MAN-B&W 6S35MC 1 x 2 Stroke 6 Cy. 350 x 1400 4440kW (6037bhp) STX Engine Co Ltd-South Korea AuxGen: 3 x 480kW 445V a.c Thrusters: 1 Tunnel thruster (f) Fuel: 93.0 (d.f.) 657.0 (r.f.)
9378199 *9VNX6* -	**SICHEM MARSEILLE** *launched as* Sichem Marseilles *-2007* **Eitzen Chemical (Singapore) Pte Ltd** Eitzen Chemical A/S SatCom: Inmarsat Mini-M 761137927 *Singapore* *Singapore* MMSI: 565474000 Official number: 393088	**8,455** 4,031 12,927 T/cm 22.9	Class: NV (KR)	**2007-06 Samho Shipbuilding Co Ltd — Tongyeong** Yd No: 1080 Loa 127.20 (BB) Br ex 20.43 Dght 8.714 Lbp 119.00 Br md 20.40 Dpth 11.50 Welded, 1 dk	**(A12B2TR) Chemical/Products Tanker** Double Hull (13F) Liq: 13,077; Liq (Oil): 13,077 Cargo Heating Coils Compartments: 12 Wing Ta, 2 Wing Slop Ta, ER 12 Cargo Pump (s): 12x300m³/hr Manifold: Bow/CM: 62.3m	**1 oil engine** driving 1 FP propeller Total Power: 4,457kW (6,060hp) 13.4kn MAN-B&W 6S35MC 1 x 2 Stroke 6 Cy. 350 x 1400 4457kW (6060bhp) MAN Diesel A/S-Denmark AuxGen: 3 x 490kW 440/220V 50Hz a.c Thrusters: 1 Tunnel thruster (f) Fuel: 74.0 (d.f.) 677.0 (r.f.)
9376921 *9VDR8* -	**SICHEM MELBOURNE** **Eitzen Chemical (Singapore) Pte Ltd** Eitzen Chemical A/S SatCom: Inmarsat Mini-M 761137957 *Singapore* *Singapore* MMSI: 565507000 Official number: 393263	**8,455** 4,031 12,936 T/cm 22.9	Class: NV (KR)	**2007-07 Samho Shipbuilding Co Ltd — Tongyeong** Yd No: 1073 Loa 127.20 (BB) Br ex 20.43 Dght 8.714 Lbp 119.00 Br md 20.40 Dpth 11.50 Welded, 1 dk	**(A12B2TR) Chemical/Products Tanker** Double Hull (13F) Liq: 13,079; Liq (Oil): 13,079 Cargo Heating Coils Compartments: 12 Wing Ta, 2 Wing Slop Ta, ER 12 Cargo Pump (s): 12x300m³/hr Manifold: Bow/CM: 60.6m	**1 oil engine** driving 1 FP propeller Total Power: 4,457kW (6,060hp) 13.4kn MAN-B&W 6S35MC 1 x 2 Stroke 6 Cy. 350 x 1400 4457kW (6060bhp) MAN Diesel A/S-Denmark AuxGen: 3 x 490kW 445V 50Hz a.c Thrusters: 1 Tunnel thruster (f) Fuel: 74.0 (d.f.) 677.0 (r.f.)
9376658 *3FZR9* -	**SICHEM MISSISSIPPI** **Trio Happiness SA** Eitzen Chemical A/S *Panama* *Panama* MMSI: 372464000 Official number: 4006309A	**7,598** 3,760 12,273 T/cm 21.1	Class: AB (BV)	**2008-12 Sasaki Shipbuilding Co Ltd — Osakikamijima HS** Yd No: 664 Loa 123.85 (BB) Br ex 20.03 Dght 8.915 Lbp 116.00 Br md 20.00 Dpth 11.50 Welded, 1 dk	**(A12B2TR) Chemical/Products Tanker** Double Hull (13F) Liq: 12,320; Liq (Oil): 12,320 Cargo Heating Coils Compartments: 18 Wing Ta, 2 Wing Slop Ta, ER 18 Cargo Pump (s): 18x200m³/hr Manifold: Bow/CM: 65.3m	**1 oil engine** driving 1 FP propeller Total Power: 3,900kW (5,302hp) 13.5kn MAN-B&W 6L35MC 1 x 2 Stroke 6 Cy. 350 x 1050 3900kW (5302bhp) The Hanshin Diesel Works Ltd-Japan AuxGen: 2 x 400kW 450V 60Hz a.c Thrusters: 1 Tunnel thruster (f) Fuel: 89.0 (d.f.) 643.0 (r.f.)
9404900 *9VLS2* -	**SICHEM MONTREAL** **Eitzen Chemical (Singapore) Pte Ltd** Eitzen Chemical A/S *Singapore* *Singapore* MMSI: 565884000 Official number: 394207	**8,581** 4,117 13,069 T/cm 23.2	Class: AB	**2008-10 21st Century Shipbuilding Co Ltd — Tongyeong** Yd No: 243 Loa 128.60 (BB) Br ex - Dght 8.700 Lbp 120.40 Br md 20.40 Dpth 11.50 Welded, 1 dk	**(A12B2TR) Chemical/Products Tanker** Double Hull (13F) Liq: 13,407; Liq (Oil): 13,407 Cargo Heating Coils Compartments: 14 Wing Ta, 2 Wing Slop Ta, ER 14 Cargo Pump (s): 12x300m³/hr, 2x100m³/hr Manifold: Bow/CM: 60.8m	**1 oil engine** driving 1 FP propeller Total Power: 4,440kW (6,037hp) 13.4kn MAN-B&W 6S35MC 1 x 2 Stroke 6 Cy. 350 x 1400 4440kW (6037bhp) STX Engine Co Ltd-South Korea AuxGen: 3 x 550kW a.c Thrusters: 1 Tunnel thruster (f) Fuel: 65.0 (d.f.) 586.0 (r.f.)
9322085 *3EHA7* -	**SICHEM MUMBAI** **Trio Happiness SA** Toda Kisen KK SatCom: Inmarsat Mini-M 764661563 *Panama* *Panama* MMSI: 356100000 Official number: 3234707B	**8,562** 4,095 13,085 T/cm 23.2	Class: NK (KR)	**2006-10 21st Century Shipbuilding Co Ltd — Tongyeong** Yd No: 214 Loa 128.60 (BB) Br ex 20.40 Dght 8.714 Lbp 120.40 Br md 20.40 Dpth 11.50 Welded, 1 dk	**(A12B2TR) Chemical/Products Tanker** Double Hull (13F) Liq: 13,416; Liq (Oil): 13,416 Cargo Heating Coils Compartments: 12 Wing Ta, 2 Wing Slop Ta, ER 12 Cargo Pump (s): 12x300m³/hr Manifold: Bow/CM: 60.8m	**1 oil engine** driving 1 FP propeller Total Power: 4,440kW (6,037hp) 13.5kn MAN-B&W 6S35MC 1 x 2 Stroke 6 Cy. 350 x 1400 4440kW (6037bhp) STX Engine Co Ltd-South Korea AuxGen: 4 x 480kW 445V a.c Thrusters: 1 Tunnel thruster (f) Fuel: 93.0 (d.f.) 957.0 (r.f.)
9337834 *S6BQ4* -	**SICHEM NEW YORK** **Eitzen Chemical (Singapore) Pte Ltd** Eitzen Chemical A/S SatCom: Inmarsat Mini-M 764360122 *Singapore* *Singapore* MMSI: 565404000 Official number: 392863	**8,455** 4,031 12,945 T/cm 22.9	Class: NV (KR)	**2007-04 Samho Shipbuilding Co Ltd — Tongyeong** Yd No: 1057 Loa 127.20 (BB) Br ex 20.43 Dght 8.714 Lbp 119.00 Br md 20.40 Dpth 11.50 Welded, 1 dk	**(A12B2TR) Chemical/Products Tanker** Double Hull (13F) Liq: 13,075; Liq (Oil): 13,075 Cargo Heating Coils Compartments: 12 Wing Ta, 2 Wing Slop Ta, ER 12 Cargo Pump (s): 12x300m³/hr Manifold: Bow/CM: 60.6m	**1 oil engine** driving 1 FP propeller Total Power: 4,457kW (6,060hp) 13.4kn MAN-B&W 6S35MC 1 x 2 Stroke 6 Cy. 350 x 1400 4457kW (6060bhp) STX Engine Co Ltd-South Korea AuxGen: 3 x 475kW a.c Thrusters: 1 Tunnel thruster (f) Fuel: 74.0 (d.f.) 677.0 (r.f.)
9361471 *9VJD5* -	**SICHEM ONOMICHI** **Southern Breeze Navigation Pte Ltd** Eitzen Chemical (USA) LLC SatCom: Inmarsat Mini-M 764831990 *Singapore* *Singapore* MMSI: 565591000 Official number: 393473	**8,582** 4,117 13,105 T/cm 23.2	Class: AB	**2008-02 Sekwang Heavy Industries Co Ltd — Ulsan** Yd No: 1155 Loa 128.60 (BB) Br ex 20.43 Dght 8.714 Lbp 120.40 Br md 20.40 Dpth 11.50 Welded, 1 dk	**(A12B2TR) Chemical/Products Tanker** Double Hull (13F) Liq: 13,399; Liq (Oil): 13,335 Cargo Heating Coils Compartments: 12 Wing Ta, 2 Wing Slop Ta, ER 12 Cargo Pump (s): 12x300m³/hr Manifold: Bow/CM: 61.7m	**1 oil engine** driving 1 FP propeller Total Power: 4,457kW (6,060hp) 13.4kn MAN-B&W 6S35MC 1 x 2 Stroke 6 Cy. 350 x 1400 4457kW (6060bhp) STX Engine Co Ltd-South Korea AuxGen: 3 x 480kW a.c Thrusters: 1 Tunnel thruster (f) Fuel: 86.0 (d.f.) 580.0 (r.f.)
9393383 *9HNC9* -	**SICHEM ORCHID** **Eitzen Chemical (Singapore) Pte Ltd** Thome Ship Management Pte Ltd *Valletta* *Malta* MMSI: 249213000 Official number: 9393383	**5,744** 2,551 8,139 T/cm 18.0	Class: NV	**2008-11 Sekwang Heavy Industries Co Ltd — Ulsan** Yd No: 1169 Loa 115.00 (BB) Br ex 18.23 Dght 7.460 Lbp 107.00 Br md 18.20 Dpth 9.60 Welded, 1 dk	**(A12B2TR) Chemical/Products Tanker** Double Hull (13F) Liq: 8,487; Liq (Oil): 8,487 Cargo Heating Coils Compartments: 10 Wing Ta, 2 Wing Slop Ta, ER 10 Cargo Pump (s): 10x200m³/hr Manifold: Bow/CM: 59.3m	**1 oil engine** driving 1 FP propeller Total Power: 3,900kW (5,302hp) 14.0kn MAN-B&W 6L35MC 1 x 2 Stroke 6 Cy. 350 x 1050 3900kW (5302bhp) Hyundai Heavy Industries Co Ltd-South Korea AuxGen: 3 x 460kW a.c Thrusters: 1 Tunnel thruster (f) Fuel: 109.0 (d.f.) 487.0 (r.f.)
9396024 *9HTP9* -	**SICHEM OSPREY** **Eitzen Chemical (Singapore) Pte Ltd** Eitzen Chemical A/S SatCom: Inmarsat Mini-M 764903595 *Valletta* *Malta* MMSI: 249534000 Official number: 9396024	**17,822** 6,662 25,432 T/cm 37.4	Class: AB	**2009-04 Dae Sun Shipbuilding & Engineering Co Ltd — Busan** Yd No: 475 Loa 170.00 (BB) Br ex 26.23 Dght 10.000 Lbp 161.00 Br md 26.20 Dpth 15.60 Welded, 1 dk	**(A12B2TR) Chemical/Products Tanker** Double Hull (13F) Liq: 29,130; Liq (Oil): 29,130 Compartments: 12 Wing Ta, 2 Wing Slop Ta, ER 12 Cargo Pump (s): 12x380m³/hr Manifold: Bow/CM: 83.6m	**1 oil engine** driving 1 FP propeller Total Power: 7,860kW (10,686hp) 14.3kn MAN-B&W 6S46MC-C 1 x 2 Stroke 6 Cy. 460 x 1932 7860kW (10686bhp) STX Engine Co Ltd-South Korea AuxGen: 3 x 850kW 60Hz a.c Thrusters: 1 Tunnel thruster (f) Fuel: 180.0 (d.f.) 1423.0 (r.f.)
9304318 *S6AV8* -	**SICHEM PALACE** **Eitzen Chemical (Singapore) Pte Ltd** Thome Ship Management Pte Ltd *Singapore* *Singapore* MMSI: 564823000 Official number: 390810	**5,451** 2,640 8,807 T/cm 17.7	Class: NK	**2004-09 Usuki Shipyard Co Ltd — Usuki OT** Yd No: 1688 Loa 112.02 (BB) Br ex 19.03 Dght 7.564 Lbp 105.00 Br md 19.00 Dpth 10.00 Welded, 1 dk	**(A12B2TR) Chemical/Products Tanker** Double Hull (13F) Liq: 9,245; Liq (Oil): 9,433 Cargo Heating Coils Compartments: 10 Wing Ta, 2 Wing Slop Ta, ER 10 Cargo Pump (s): 10x250m³/hr Manifold: Bow/CM: 47.7m	**1 oil engine** driving 1 FP propeller Total Power: 3,900kW (5,302hp) 14.0kn MAN-B&W 6L35MC 1 x 2 Stroke 6 Cy. 350 x 1050 3900kW (5302bhp) Makita Corp-Japan AuxGen: 2 x 400kW 450V 60Hz a.c Thrusters: 1 Tunnel thruster (f) Fuel: 75.0 (d.f.) 560.0 (r.f.)
9404895 *9VLS3* -	**SICHEM PARIS** **Eitzen Chemical (Singapore) Pte Ltd** Eitzen Chemical A/S SatCom: Inmarsat Mini-M 764851756 *Singapore* *Singapore* MMSI: 565885000 Official number: 394208	**8,581** 4,117 13,079 T/cm 23.3	Class: AB	**2008-07 21st Century Shipbuilding Co Ltd — Tongyeong** Yd No: 242 Loa 128.60 (BB) Br ex 20.42 Dght 8.714 Lbp 120.40 Br md 20.40 Dpth 11.50 Welded, 1 dk	**(A12B2TR) Chemical/Products Tanker** Double Hull (13F) Liq: 13,403; Liq (Oil): 13,403 Cargo Heating Coils Compartments: 12 Wing Ta, ER, 2 Wing Slop Ta 12 Cargo Pump (s): 12x300m³/hr Manifold: Bow/CM: 60.8m	**1 oil engine** driving 1 FP propeller Total Power: 4,440kW (6,037hp) 13.4kn MAN-B&W 6S35MC 1 x 2 Stroke 6 Cy. 350 x 1400 4440kW (6037bhp) STX Engine Co Ltd-South Korea AuxGen: 3 x 550kW a.c Thrusters: 1 Tunnel thruster (f) Fuel: 122.0 (d.f.) 448.0 (r.f.)

9322073 *ICJD* -	**SICHEM RIO** **Eitzen Chemical (Singapore) Pte Ltd** Eitzen Chemical A/S SatCom: Inmarsat Mini-M 764836491 *Palermo* *Italy* MMSI: 247229300	**8,562** 4,095 13,162 T/cm 23.2	Class: NV RI (KR)	**2006-06 21st Century Shipbuilding Co Ltd — Tongyeong** Yd No: 212 Loa 128.60 (BB) Br ex 20.43 Dght 8.714 Lbp 120.40 Br md 20.40 Dpth 11.50 Welded, 1 dk	**(A12B2TR) Chemical/Products Tanker** Double Hull (13F) Liq: 13,426; Liq (Oil): 13,426 Cargo Heating Coils Compartments: 12 Wing Ta, 2 Wing Slop Ta, ER 12 Cargo Pump (s): 12x300m^3/hr Manifold: Bow/CM: 60.8m	**1 oil engine** driving 1 FP propeller Total Power: 4,200kW (5,710hp) 13.4kn MAN-B&W 6S35MC 1 x 2 Stroke 6 Cy. 350 x 1400 4200kW (5710bhp) MAN B&W Diesel A/S-Denmark AuxGen: 3 x 550kW a.c Thrusters: 1 Tunnel thruster (f) Fuel: 93.0 (d.f.) 657.0 (r.f.)
9344174 *3EGI7* -	**SICHEM RUBY** *ex* Songa Ruby *-2007* **Fresh South Shipping SA** Bernhard Schulte Shipmanagement (India) Pvt Ltd *Panama* *Panama* MMSI: 356826000 Official number: 3203306B	**5,303** 2,631 8,824 T/cm 17.3	Class: NK	**2006-08 Murakami Hide Zosen K.K. — Imabari** Yd No: 547 Loa 114.99 (BB) Br ex 18.20 Dght 7.770 Lbp 108.50 Br md 18.20 Dpth 9.65 Welded, 1 dk	**(A12B2TR) Chemical/Products Tanker** Double Hull (13F) Liq: 9,394; Liq (Oil): 9,394 Cargo Heating Coils Compartments: 12 Wing Ta, ER 12 Cargo Pump (s): 12x220m^3/hr Manifold: Bow/CM: 60.3m	**1 oil engine** driving 1 FP propeller Total Power: 3,900kW (5,302hp) 13.8kn MAN-B&W 6L35MC 1 x 2 Stroke 6 Cy. 350 x 1050 3900kW (5302bhp) Imex Co Ltd-Japan AuxGen: 3 x 1040kW a.c Thrusters: 1 Tunnel thruster (f) Fuel: 96.0 (d.f.) 410.0 (r.f.)
9322061 *ICGO* -	**SICHEM SINGAPORE** **Eitzen Chemical (Singapore) Pte Ltd** Eitzen Chemical A/S SatCom: Inmarsat Mini-M 764861761 *Palermo* *Italy* MMSI: 247216100	**8,562** 4,095 13,141 T/cm 23.2	Class: NV RI (KR)	**2006-03 21st Century Shipbuilding Co Ltd — Tongyeong** Yd No: 210 Loa 128.60 (BB) Br ex 20.65 Dght 8.714 Lbp 120.40 Br md 20.40 Dpth 11.50 Welded, 1 dk	**(A12B2TR) Chemical/Products Tanker** Double Hull (13F) Liq: 13,416; Liq (Oil): 13,416 Compartments: 12 Wing Ta, 2 Wing Slop Ta, ER 12 Cargo Pump (s): 12x300m^3/hr Manifold: Bow/CM: 60.8m	**1 oil engine** driving 1 FP propeller Total Power: 4,440kW (6,037hp) 13.4kn MAN-B&W 6S35MC 1 x 2 Stroke 6 Cy. 350 x 1400 4440kW (6037bhp) STX Engine Co Ltd-South Korea AuxGen: 3 x 550kW a.c Thrusters: 1 Thwart. FP thruster (f) Fuel: 93.0 (d.f.) 657.0 (r.f.)
9216054 *9HHA8* -	**SICHEM SPARROW** *ex* Sparrow *-2005* **Eitzen Chemical (Singapore) Pte Ltd** Eitzen Chemical (Spain) SA *Valletta* *Malta* MMSI: 215974000 Official number: 9788	**2,764** 1,042 3,596 T/cm 10.9	Class: LR ✠ **100A1** SS 06/2011 Double Hull oil and chemical tanker, MARPOL 21.2.2, Ship Type 2 CR (s.stl), SG 1.90 in all tanks, ESP *IWS LI ✠ **LMC** **UMS** Eq.Ltr: S; Cable: 467.5/42.0 U2 (a)	**2001-06 Ilheung Shipbuilding & Engineering Co Ltd — Mokpo** Yd No: 99-94 Loa 92.90 (BB) Br ex 14.46 Dght 5.942 Lbp 83.50 Br md 14.40 Dpth 7.00 Welded, 1 dk	**(A12B2TR) Chemical/Products Tanker** Double Hull (13F) Liq: 3,751; Liq (Oil): 3,751 Cargo Heating Coils Compartments: 10 Wing Ta, 2 Wing Slop Ta, ER 10 Cargo Pump (s): 10x200m^3/hr Manifold: Bow/CM: 39.1m	**1 oil engine** driving 1 CP propeller Total Power: 2,400kW (3,263hp) 13.2kn B&W 6S26MC 1 x 2 Stroke 6 Cy. 260 x 980 2400kW (3263bhp) STX Corp-South Korea AuxGen: 3 x 400kW 450V 60Hz a.c Boilers: 2 AuxB (o.f.) 10.2kgf/cm^2 (10.0bar), sg 6.1kgf/cm^2 (6.0bar), e (ex.g.) 12.2kgf/cm^2 (12.0bar) Thrusters: 1 Thwart. FP thruster (f) Fuel: 93.0 (d.f.) (Heating Coils) 302.0 (r.f.) 10.0pd
8033106 *UYNQ* -	**SICHESLAV-YUG** *ex* Poiskovik *-2005* **Zvezda Rybaka Co Ltd (OOO 'Zvezda Rybaka')** - *Sevastopol* *Ukraine* MMSI: 272007500	**748** 224 308	Class: (RS)	**1981-10 Zavod "Leninskaya Kuznitsa" — Kiyev** Yd No: 1500 Loa 54.84 Br ex 9.96 Dght 3.980 Lbp 50.29 Br md 9.80 Dpth 5.23 Welded, 1 dk	**(B11A2FS) Stern Trawler** Ins: 414 Compartments: 2 Ho, ER 3 Ha: 3 (1.5 x 1.6) Derricks: 2x1.3t Ice Capable	**1 oil engine** driving 1 FP propeller Total Power: 736kW (1,001hp) 12.0kn S.K.L. 8NVD48-2U 1 x 4 Stroke 8 Cy. 320 x 480 736kW (1001bhp) VEB Schwermaschinenbau "KarlLiebknecht" (SKL)-Magdeburg Fuel: 182.0 (d.f.)
9430935 *A8PF5* -	**SICILIA** *launched as* Montreal Strait *-2008* **ms 'Sicilia' GmbH & Co KG** Ahrenkiel Shipmanagement GmbH & Co KG *Monrovia* *Liberia* MMSI: 636091542 Official number: 91542	**21,018** 9,156 25,927	Class: GL	**2008-04 Taizhou Kouan Shipbuilding Co Ltd — Taizhou JS** Yd No: KA507 Loa 179.74 (BB) Br ex - Dght 10.700 Lbp 167.20 Br md 27.60 Dpth 15.90 Welded, 1 dk	**(A33A2CC) Container Ship (Fully Cellular)** TEU 1794 C Ho 740 TEU C Dk 1054 TEU incl 319 ref C Cranes: 2x40t	**1 oil engine** driving 1 FP propeller Total Power: 16,664kW (22,656hp) 20.5kn MAN-B&W 7S60MC-C 1 x 2 Stroke 7 Cy. 600 x 2400 16664kW (22656bhp) Hudong Heavy Machinery Co Ltd-China AuxGen: 2 x 1709kW 450V a.c, 1 x 1330kW 450V a.c Thrusters: 1 Tunnel thruster (f)
9498729 *ZDNF8* -	**SICILIAN EXPRESS** **Bulk Express II BV** Vroon BV *Gibraltar* *Gibraltar (British)* MMSI: 236111913	**51,209** 31,195 93,076 T/cm 80.9	Class: LR ✠ **100A1** SS 01/2013 bulk carrier CSR BC-A GRAB (20) Nos. 2, 4 & 6 holds may be empty ESP **ShipRight** (CM, ACS (B)) *IWS LI ✠ **LMC** **UMS** Eq.Ltr: St; Cable: 687.5/87.0 U3 (a)	**2013-01 COSCO (Dalian) Shipyard Co Ltd — Dalian LN** Yd No: N253 Loa 229.20 (BB) Br ex 38.04 Dght 14.900 Lbp 222.00 Br md 38.00 Dpth 20.70 Welded, 1 dk	**(A21A2BC) Bulk Carrier** Grain: 110,330 Compartments: 7 Ho, ER 7 Ha: ER	**1 oil engine** driving 1 CP propeller Total Power: 12,240kW (16,642hp) 14.1kn MAN-B&W 6S60MC 1 x 2 Stroke 6 Cy. 600 x 2292 12240kW (16642bhp) Hyundai Heavy Industries Co Ltd-South Korea AuxGen: 3 x 730kW 450V 60Hz a.c Boilers: WTAuxB (Comp) 9.2kgf/cm^2 (9.0bar)
7021144 *TUN2141* AN 739	**SICRUS 1** **Societe Ivoirienne de Crustaces (SICRUS)** - *Abidjan* *Cote d'Ivoire*	*131* 63 -	Class: (BV)	**1970 Soc Nouvelle des Ats et Chs de La Rochelle-Pallice — La Rochelle** Yd No: 52/039 Loa 25.20 Br ex 6.81 Dght 2.302 Lbp 21.72 Br md 6.71 Dpth 3.61 Welded, 1 dk	**(B11B2FV) Fishing Vessel** Ins: 148 Compartments: 1 Ho, ER 1 Ha: (1.1 x 1.6)	**1 oil engine** reverse reduction geared to sc. shaft driving 1 FP propeller Total Power: 291kW (396hp) 9.0kn Caterpillar D353SCAC 1 x 4 Stroke 6 Cy. 159 x 203 291kW (396bhp) Caterpillar Tractor Co-USA Fuel: 48.5 (d.f.)
7014830 *TUN2142* AN 740	**SICRUS 2** *ex* Khobat I *-1972* **Societe Ivoirienne de Crustaces (SICRUS)** - *Abidjan* *Cote d'Ivoire*	*131* 63 -	Class: (BV)	**1970 Ch. Normands Reunis — Courseulles-sur-Mer** Yd No: 14 Loa 24.80 Br ex 6.81 Dght 2.490 Lbp 22.31 Br md 6.71 Dpth 3.51 Welded, 1 dk	**(B11B2FV) Fishing Vessel** Ins: 142 Compartments: 1 Ho, ER 1 Ha: (1.1 x 1.6)	**1 oil engine** sr geared to sc. shaft driving 1 FP propeller Total Power: 279kW (379hp) Caterpillar D353SCAC 1 x 4 Stroke 6 Cy. 159 x 203 279kW (379bhp) Caterpillar Tractor Co-USA Fuel: 48.5 (d.f.)
7022930 *TUN2143* AN 741	**SICRUS 3** *ex* Khobat VIII *-1971* **Societe Ivoirienne de Crustaces (SICRUS)** - *Abidjan* *Cote d'Ivoire*	*131* 63 -	Class: (BV)	**1970 Ch. Normands Reunis — Courseulles-sur-Mer** Yd No: 15 Loa 25.20 Br ex 6.81 Dght 2.490 Lbp 21.72 Br md 6.71 Dpth 3.51 Welded, 1 dk	**(B11B2FV) Fishing Vessel** Ins: 142 Compartments: 1 Ho, ER 1 Ha: (1.1 x 1.6)	**1 oil engine** driving 1 FP propeller Total Power: 279kW (379hp) 9.0kn Caterpillar D353SCAC 1 x 4 Stroke 6 Cy. 159 x 203 279kW (379bhp) Caterpillar Tractor Co-USA Fuel: 48.5 (d.f.)
7021156 *TUN2145* AN 743	**SICRUS 5** *ex* Nagroor V *-1971* **Societe Ivoirienne de Crustaces (SICRUS)** - *Abidjan* *Cote d'Ivoire*	*131* 63 -	Class: (BV)	**1970 Soc Nouvelle des Ats et Chs de La Rochelle-Pallice — La Rochelle** Yd No: 52/040 Loa 25.20 Br ex 6.81 Dght 2.302 Lbp 21.72 Br md 6.71 Dpth 3.61 Welded, 1 dk	**(B11B2FV) Fishing Vessel** Ins: 148 Compartments: 1 Ho, ER 1 Ha: (1.1 x 1.6)	**1 oil engine** reverse reduction geared to sc. shaft driving 1 FP propeller Total Power: 291kW (396hp) 9.0kn Caterpillar D353SCAC 1 x 4 Stroke 6 Cy. 159 x 203 291kW (396bhp) Caterpillar Tractor Co-USA Fuel: 48.5 (d.f.)
7021168 *TUN2146* AN 744	**SICRUS 6** *ex* Nagroor VI *-1971* **Societe Ivoirienne de Crustaces (SICRUS)** - *Abidjan* *Cote d'Ivoire*	*131* 63 -	Class: (BV)	**1970 Soc Nouvelle des Ats et Chs de La Rochelle-Pallice — La Rochelle** Yd No: 52/041 Loa 25.20 Br ex 6.81 Dght 2.302 Lbp 21.72 Br md 6.71 Dpth 3.61 Welded, 1 dk	**(B11B2FV) Fishing Vessel** Ins: 148 Compartments: 1 Ho, ER 1 Ha: (1.1 x 1.6)	**1 oil engine** reverse reduction geared to sc. shaft driving 1 FP propeller Total Power: 291kW (396hp) 9.0kn Caterpillar D353SCAC 1 x 4 Stroke 6 Cy. 159 x 203 291kW (396bhp) Caterpillar Tractor Co-USA Fuel: 48.5 (d.f.)
7022992 *TUN2147* AN 745	**SICRUS 7** *ex* Nagroor VII *-1971* **Societe Ivoirienne de Crustaces (SICRUS)** - *Abidjan* *Cote d'Ivoire*	*131* 66 -	Class: (BV)	**1970 Soc Nouvelle des Ats et Chs de La Rochelle-Pallice — La Rochelle** Yd No: 52/042 Loa 25.20 Br ex 6.81 Dght 2.302 Lbp 21.72 Br md 6.71 Dpth 3.61 Welded, 1 dk	**(B11B2FV) Fishing Vessel** Ins: 148 Compartments: 1 Ho, ER 1 Ha: (1.1 x 1.6)	**1 oil engine** reverse reduction geared to sc. shaft driving 1 FP propeller Total Power: 291kW (396hp) 9.0kn Caterpillar D353SCAC 1 x 4 Stroke 6 Cy. 159 x 203 291kW (396bhp) Caterpillar Tractor Co-USA Fuel: 48.5 (d.f.)
8128054 - -	**SICULA PESCA** - **International Fishing Co Ltd** -	*150* - -		**1981-09 G. De Vincenzi — Trapani** Loa 29.49 Br ex 6.63 Dght - Lbp 22.59 Br md 6.61 Dpth 3.20 Welded, 1 dk	**(B11A2FS) Stern Trawler**	**1 oil engine** geared to sc. shaft driving 1 FP propeller Total Power: 402kW (547hp) Blackstone E8 1 x 4 Stroke 8 Cy. 222 x 292 402kW (547bhp) Mirrlees Blackstone (Stamford)Ltd.-Stamford

IMO / Call sign / Flag	Name / Owner / Port	Tonnage	Class	Builder / Dimensions	Type	Machinery
6719524 *CNRY* -	**SID TAJANI** *ex* Tarzan *-1983* **Societe Pecatlan SA** - *Agadir* Morocco Official number: 8-635	*239* 84 364	Class: (BV)	**1967 Construcciones Navales Santodomingo SA — Vigo** Yd No: 333 Loa 32.01 Br ex 7.14 Dght 3.271 Lbp 27.51 Br md 7.12 Dpth 3.66 Welded, 1 dk	**(B11A2FT) Trawler** Ins: 155 Compartments: 1 Ho, ER 1 Ha: (1.4 x 1.1)	**1 oil engine** reduction geared to sc. shaft driving 1 FP propeller Total Power: 360kW (489hp) 10.6kn MWM 1 x 4 Stroke 8 Cy. 180 x 260 360kW (489bhp) Motoren Werke Mannheim AG (MWM)-West Germany AuxGen: 2 x 105kW 220/380V d.c, 1 x 30kW 220/380V d.c Fuel: 63.0 (d.f.)
8874823 - -	**SIDANGOLI I** **PT Tunggal Agathis Indah Wood Industries** - *Jakarta* Indonesia	**126** 75 -	Class: KI	**1994-02 P.T. Tunggal Agathis Indah Wood Industries — Ternate** Loa 23.75 Br ex - Dght - Lbp 20.75 Br md 6.70 Dpth 3.40 Welded, 1 dk	**(B32A2ST) Tug**	**2 oil engines** geared to sc. shafts driving 2 FP propellers Total Power: 736kW (1,000hp) 10.0kn Cummins KTA-19-M 2 x 4 Stroke 6 Cy. 159 x 159 each-368kW (500bhp) Cummins Engine Co Inc-USA AuxGen: 2 x 12kW 220/380V a.c
9116436 *YFBK* -	**SIDANGOLI SUKSES** **PT Tunggal Agathis Indah Wood Industries** - *Jakarta* Indonesia	**294** 89 83	Class: (KI)	**1994-01 Lingco Marine Sdn Bhd — Sibu** Yd No: 192 Loa - Br ex - Dght 1.800 Lbp 35.80 Br md 9.75 Dpth 2.75 Welded, 1 dk	**(A35D2RL) Landing Craft** Bow door/ramp (centre)	**2 oil engines** geared to sc. shafts driving 2 FP propellers Total Power: 514kW (698hp) Cummins NTA-855-M 2 x 4 Stroke 6 Cy. 140 x 152 each-257kW (349bhp) (made 1993) Cummins Engine Co Ltd-United Kingdom
9363053 *9HGG9* -	**SIDARI** **Thunder Navigation Corp** TMS Dry Ltd *Valletta* Malta MMSI: 256944000 Official number: 9363053	**40,170** 25,603 75,204	Class: AB	**2007-12 Hudong-Zhonghua Shipbuilding (Group) Co Ltd — Shanghai** Yd No: H1397A Loa 225.00 (BB) Br ex 32.30 Dght 14.250 Lbp 217.00 Br md 32.26 Dpth 19.60 Welded, 1 dk	**(A21A2BC) Bulk Carrier** Grain: 91,717; Bale: 89,882 Compartments: 7 Ho, ER 7 Ha: 6 (14.6 x 15.0)ER (14.6 x 13.2)	**1 oil engine** driving 1 FP propeller Total Power: 8,990kW (12,223hp) 14.0kn MAN-B&W 5S60MC-C 1 x 2 Stroke 5 Cy. 600 x 2400 8990kW (12223bhp) Hudong Heavy Machinery Co Ltd-China AuxGen: 3 x 570kW a.c
1003889 *HP4564* -	**SIDARTA I** **Nogara Shipping Inc** - *Panama* Panama Official number: 1745087J	**307** 92 -	Class: LR ✠ **100A1** SS 05/2011 Yacht ✠ **LMC** **UMS**	**1987-06 Scheepswerf Haak B.V. — Zaandam** Loa 38.00 Br ex 7.50 Dght 3.300 Lbp 33.57 Br md - Dpth 4.40 Welded, 1 dk	**(X11A2YP) Yacht**	**2 oil engines** driving 2 FP propellers Total Power: 1,302kW (1,770hp) Caterpillar 3512TA 2 x Vee 4 Stroke 12 Cy. 170 x 190 each-651kW (885bhp) Caterpillar Inc-USA
9091715 - -	**SIDDHI** **R & D Engineers** - India	**250** 75 115	Class: IR	**1998-08 Shiva Engineering Works — Dhamra** Yd No: 01 Loa 34.00 Br ex 8.00 Dght 1.220 Lbp - Br md 7.98 Dpth 3.00 Welded, 1 dk	**(A31A2GX) General Cargo Ship**	**1 oil engine** geared to sc. shaft driving 1 FP propeller Total Power: 176kW (239hp) 9.0kn Cummins NT-743-M 1 x 4 Stroke 6 Cy. 130 x 152 176kW (239bhp) Cummins India Ltd-India AuxGen: 2 x 12kW 450V 50Hz a.c Fuel: 10.0 (d.f.)
8709236 *AVLP* -	**SIDDHIDHATA** *ex* Shivaji *-2012* **Glory Shipmanagement Pvt Ltd** *Mumbai* India MMSI: 419000301 Official number: 3840	**320** 96 145	Class: IR (LR) ✠ Classed LR until 1/4/99	**1989-06 Hyundai Heavy Industries Co Ltd — Ulsan** Yd No: 282 Loa 33.00 Br ex 9.82 Dght 2.900 Lbp 30.50 Br md 9.50 Dpth 4.02 Welded, 1 dk	**(B32A2ST) Tug**	**2 oil engines** gearing integral to driving 2 Voith-Schneider propellers Total Power: 2,000kW (2,720hp) MAN 12V20/27 2 x Vee 4 Stroke 12 Cy. 200 x 270 each-1000kW (1360bhp) MAN B&W Diesel GmbH-Augsburg AuxGen: 2 x 90kW 415V 50Hz a.c
8709224 *AVOT* -	**SIDDHIPRIYA** *ex* Elephanta *-2013* **Glory Shipmanagement Pvt Ltd** *Mumbai* India MMSI: 419000388 Official number: 3897	**320** 96 165	Class: IR (LR) ✠ Classed LR until 1/4/99	**1989-06 Hyundai Heavy Industries Co Ltd — Ulsan** Yd No: 281 Loa 33.00 Br ex 9.82 Dght 2.900 Lbp 30.50 Br md 9.50 Dpth 4.02 Welded, 1 dk	**(B32A2ST) Tug**	**2 oil engines** gearing integral to driving 2 Voith-Schneider propellers Total Power: 2,000kW (2,720hp) 11.0kn MAN-B&W 12V20/27 2 x Vee 4 Stroke 12 Cy. 200 x 270 each-1000kW (1360bhp) MAN B&W Diesel GmbH-Augsburg AuxGen: 2 x 90kW 415V 50Hz a.c
9475181 *LGOU* -	**SIDDIS MARINER** *launched as* Siem Pilot *-2011* **Siem Meling Offshore DA** O H Meling & Co AS SatCom: Inmarsat C 425979510 *Stavanger* Norway MMSI: 259795000	**5,106** 1,531 4,800	Class: NV	**2011-03 Umo Gemi Sanayi ve Ticaret Ltd — Karadeniz Eregli** (Hull) Yd No: 05 **2011-03 Myklebust Mek. Verksted AS — Gursken** Yd No: 348 Loa 88.30 (BB) Br ex - Dght 7.200 Lbp 77.70 Br md 20.00 Dpth 8.60 Welded, 1 dk	**(B21A20S) Platform Supply Ship** Cranes: 1x70t Ice Capable	**4 diesel electric oil engines** driving 4 gen. each 2188kW a.c Connecting to 2 elec. motors each (2200kW) driving 2 Azimuth electric drive units Total Power: 10,100kW (13,732hp) 12.5kn Caterpillar 3516C 4 x Vee 4 Stroke 16 Cy. 170 x 215 each-2525kW (3433bhp) Caterpillar Inc-USA Thrusters: 2 Thwart. CP thruster (f); 1 Retract. directional thruster (f)
9307114 *LMLU* -	**SIDDIS SKIPPER** **Clearwater Seafoods Ltd Partnership** - *Stavanger* Norway MMSI: 258431000 Official number: 3089	**2,604** 1,138 3,600	Class: NV	**2004-01 Malta Shipbuilding Co. Ltd. — Marsa** (Hull) Yd No: 187 **2004-01 Kleven Verft AS — Ulsteinvik** Yd No: 297 Loa 73.40 (BB) Br ex 16.61 Dght 6.420 Lbp 64.00 Br md 16.60 Dpth 7.60 Welded, 1 dk	**(B21A20S) Platform Supply Ship**	**2 oil engines** reduction geared to sc. shafts driving 2 CP propellers Total Power: 4,060kW (5,520hp) 11.5kn Caterpillar 3606 2 x 4 Stroke 6 Cy. 280 x 300 each-2030kW (2760bhp) Caterpillar Inc-USA AuxGen: 2 x 410kW a.c, 2 x 1300kW a.c Thrusters: 2 Tunnel thruster (f); 2 Tunnel thruster (a)
9546605 *3YTJ* -	**SIDDIS SUPPLIER** **Siddis Supplier AS** O H Meling & Co AS *Stavanger* Norway MMSI: 257608000	**2,656** 898 3,350	Class: NV	**2010-09 OAO Sudostroitelnyy Zavod "Severnaya Verf" — St.-Peterburg** Yd No: 797 Loa 73.40 (BB) Br ex 16.88 Dght 6.420 Lbp 64.00 Br md 16.60 Dpth 7.60 Welded, 1 dk	**(B21A20S) Platform Supply Ship**	**2 oil engines** reduction geared to sc. shafts driving 2 CP propellers Total Power: 5,268kW (7,162hp) MaK 8M25 2 x 4 Stroke 8 Cy. 255 x 400 each-2634kW (3581bhp) Caterpillar Motoren GmbH & Co. KG-Germany AuxGen: 2 x 345kW 450V 60Hz a.c, 2 x 1600kW 450V 60Hz a.c Thrusters: 2 Tunnel thruster (f); 2 Tunnel thruster (a)
8876338 *P2V5249* -	**SIDDY** *ex* Jodo Ferry *-2009* **Lutheran Shipping (LUSHIP)** - *Papua New Guinea*	**166** - 83	Class: (KR)	**1994-09 Mokpo Shipbuilding & Engineering Co Ltd — Mokpo** Yd No: 94-097 Loa 43.00 Br ex - Dght 1.385 Lbp 36.50 Br md 8.50 Dpth 2.50 Welded, 1 dk	**(A36A2PR) Passenger/Ro-Ro Ship (Vehicles)**	**2 oil engines** reduction geared to sc. shafts driving 2 FP propellers Total Power: 420kW (572hp) 12.6kn Yanmar 2 x 4 Stroke 6 Cy. 120 x 150 each-210kW (286bhp) Kwangyang Diesel Engine Co Ltd-South Korea AuxGen: 2 x 69kW 225V a.c Fuel: 12.0
7434846 *TC6566* -	**SIDE** **Port Akdeniz (Ortadogu Antalya Liman Isletmeleri AS)** - *Antalya* Turkey MMSI: 271010670	*126* 37 -	Class: TL	**1979-10 Denizcilik Bankasi T.A.O. — Alaybey, Izmir** Yd No: 29 Loa 26.17 Br ex 7.12 Dght 2.500 Lbp 24.00 Br md 6.70 Dpth 3.10 Welded, 1 dk	**(B32A2ST) Tug**	**1 oil engine** geared to sc. shaft driving 1 FP propeller Total Power: 662kW (900hp) A.B.C. 6MDXC 1 x 4 Stroke 6 Cy. 242 x 320 662kW (900bhp) Anglo Belgian Co NV (ABC)-Belgium
6907468 *DUH2518* -	**SIDE ARM** *ex* Soma Maru *-2003* *ex* Daishin Maru No. 26 *-1991* *ex* Soma Maru *-1988* *ex* Katsura Maru *-1986* **Assist Tow Marine Services** - *Cebu* Philippines Official number: CEB1006204	*168* 139 -		**1969-02 Osaka Shipbuilding Co Ltd — Osaka OS** Yd No: 295 Loa 25.51 Br ex 8.64 Dght 2.515 Lbp 22.20 Br md 8.62 Dpth 3.79 Riveted\Welded, 1 dk	**(B32A2ST) Tug**	**2 oil engines** driving 2 Directional propellers Total Power: 1,398kW (1,900hp) Daihatsu 8PSHTBM-26D 2 x 4 Stroke 8 Cy. 260 x 320 each-699kW (950bhp) Daihatsu Kogyo-Japan AuxGen: 1 x 40kW 225V a.c, 1 x 20kW 225V a.c Fuel: 28.5 (d.f.)
5407588 *DUA2481* -	**SIDE MATE** *ex* Fukuho Maru No. 7 *-1995* *ex* Takasago Maru *-1987* *ex* Obako Maru *-1987* **Julius Quano** - *Cebu* Philippines Official number: CEB1001464	*125* 84 -		**1963-05 Nipponkai Heavy Ind. Co. Ltd. — Toyama** Yd No: 109 Loa 25.94 Br ex 7.32 Dght 2.300 Lbp 23.00 Br md 7.30 Dpth 3.10 Riveted\Welded, 1 dk	**(B32A2ST) Tug**	**2 oil engines** driving 2 FP propellers 11.0kn Matsui 2 x 4 Stroke 6 Cy. 270 x 400 Matsui Iron Works Co Ltd-Japan Fuel: 6.0

IMO / Name / Owner	Tonnage	Class	Built / Dimensions	Type / Capacity	Machinery
9586435 *9HA2559* - **SIDER ALICUDI** **Lona Shipping SA** Argenmar SA SatCom: Inmarsat C 424887510 *Valletta* *Malta* MMSI: 248875000 Official number: 9586435	**5,235** 2,913 8,100 T/cm 17.5	Class: RI (BV)	**2011-01 Ningbo Xinle Shipbuilding Co Ltd — Ningbo ZJ** Yd No: XL-127 Loa 119.95 (BB) Br ex 16.84 Dght 6.713 Lbp 111.97 Br md 16.80 Dpth 8.20 Welded, 1 dk	**(A21A2BC) Bulk Carrier** Grain: 10,106; Bale: 9,904 Compartments: 2 Ho, ER 2 Ha: ER 2 (29.9 x 12.6) Cranes: 2x25t	**1 oil engine** reduction geared to sc. shaft driving 1 FP propeller Total Power: 2,500kW (3,399hp) 12.0kn Daihatsu 8DKM-28 1 x 4 Stroke 8 Cy. 280 x 390 2500kW (3399bhp) Daihatsu Diesel Manufacturing Co Lt-Japan Thrusters: 1 Tunnel thruster (f)
9618795 *9HA2856* - **SIDER ATLANTIC** *ex* Sider Queen *-2014* **Norschif Transportes e Servicos Maritimos Lda** Sider Navi SpA *Valletta* *Malta* MMSI: 256410000 Official number: 9618795	**15,545** 8,149 24,252	Class: RI (BV)	**2011-09 Ningbo Xinle Shipbuilding Co Ltd — Ningbo ZJ** Yd No: XL-134 Loa 157.00 (BB) Br ex - Dght 9.582 Lbp 149.80 Br md 24.80 Dpth 13.70 Welded, 1 dk	**(A21A2BC) Bulk Carrier** Double Hull Grain: 30,915; Bale: 30,298 Compartments: 4 Ho, ER 4 Ha: ER Cranes: 3x30t	**1 oil engine** driving 1 FP propeller Total Power: 5,180kW (7,043hp) 13.0kn MAN-B&W 7S35MC 1 x 2 Stroke 7 Cy. 350 x 1400 5180kW (7043bhp) STX Engine Co Ltd-South Korea AuxGen: 3 x 515kW 50Hz a.c Fuel: 1150.0
9143403 *9HA2175* - **SIDER CAPRI** *ex* Henny *-2009* **Pol-Euro Shipping Lines Plc-SA** - *Valletta* *Malta* MMSI: 248098000 Official number: 9143403	**3,415** 1,661 4,834	Class: PR (Class contemplated) (RI) (BV) (GL)	**1997-09 Kroeger Werft GmbH & Co. KG — Schacht-Audorf** Yd No: 1542 Loa 99.56 (BB) Br ex - Dght 5.910 Lbp 91.45 Br md 16.90 Dpth 7.55 Welded, 1 dk	**(A31A2GX) General Cargo Ship** Double Hull TEU 366 C Ho 80 TEU C Dk 286 TEU incl 40 ref C. Compartments: 1 Cell Ho, ER 3 Ha: 2 (25.6 x 13.2) (6.2 x 10.6)ER Ice Capable	**1 oil engine** geared to sc. shaft driving 1 CP propeller Total Power: 2,940kW (3,997hp) 14.5kn Alpha 12V28/32A 1 x Vee 4 Stroke 12 Cy. 280 x 320 2940kW (3997bhp) MAN B&W Diesel AG-Augsburg AuxGen: 2 x 276kW 440V a.c Thrusters: 1 Thwart. FP thruster (f) Fuel: 38.8 (d.f.) 212.0 (r.f.)
9656541 *3FLP8* - **SIDER COLOMBIA** *ex* Xinle No. 26 *-2013* **Nano Shipping Inc** Navigest Trust Services & Ship Management SA SatCom: Inmarsat C 437363610 *Panama* *Panama* MMSI: 373636000 Official number: 43527PEXT1	**9,989** 4,388 13,166	Class: RI (BV)	**2012-06 Ningbo Xinle Shipbuilding Co Ltd — Ningbo ZJ** Yd No: XL-151 Loa 138.90 (BB) Br ex 21.03 Dght 8.620 Lbp 130.00 Br md 21.00 Dpth 11.40 Welded, 1 dk	**(A31A2GX) General Cargo Ship** Grain: 17,630 Compartments: 3 Ho, ER 3 Ha: ER	**1 oil engine** reduction geared to sc. shaft driving 1 FP propeller Total Power: 3,300kW (4,487hp) 12.5kn Daihatsu 6DKM-36 1 x 4 Stroke 6 Cy. 360 x 480 3300kW (4487bhp) Daihatsu Diesel Manufacturing Co Lt-Japan AuxGen: 3 x 400kW 50Hz a.c Fuel: 700.0
9615860 *9HA3281* - **SIDER ITACA** **Haminford Shipping Inc** Navigest Trust Services & Ship Management SA *Valletta* *Malta* MMSI: 229375000	**5,256** 2,913 8,100	Class: BV	**2012-06 Ningbo Xinle Shipbuilding Co Ltd — Ningbo ZJ** Yd No: XL-130 Loa 119.95 (BB) Br ex 16.84 Dght 6.680 Lbp 111.97 Br md 16.80 Dpth 8.20 Welded, 1 dk	**(A21A2BC) Bulk Carrier** Grain: 10,029 Compartments: 2 Ho, ER 2 Ha: ER	**1 oil engine** reduction geared to sc. shaft driving 1 FP propeller Total Power: 2,500kW (3,399hp) 12.0kn Daihatsu 8DKM-28 1 x 4 Stroke 8 Cy. 280 x 390 2500kW (3399bhp) Daihatsu Diesel Manufacturing Co Lt-Japan AuxGen: 1 x 64kW 50Hz a.c, 2 x 275kW 50Hz a.c Fuel: 330.0
9427586 *ICRF* - **SIDER JOY** **Romeo Invest SpA** Sider Navi SpA SatCom: Inmarsat C 424703482 *Naples* *Italy* MMSI: 247305200	**15,861** 7,520 25,026 T/cm 36.3	Class: RI (NK) (KR)	**2011-10 Yamanishi Corp — Ishinomaki MG** Yd No: 1064 Loa 157.23 (BB) Br ex - Dght 9.114 Lbp 150.60 Br md 26.80 Dpth 13.20 Welded, 1 dk	**(A21A2BC) Bulk Carrier** Double Hull Grain: 30,736; Bale: 29,325 Compartments: 4 Ho, ER 4 Ha: ER Cranes: 3x30t	**1 oil engine** driving 1 FP propeller Total Power: 5,850kW (7,954hp) 14.6kn MAN-B&W 6S42MC 1 x 2 Stroke 6 Cy. 420 x 1764 5850kW (7954bhp) Makita Corp-Japan Fuel: 1120.0
9615913 *ICSF* - **SIDER KING** **Sider Navi SpA** *Naples* *Italy* MMSI: 247311300	**15,545** 8,204 25,013	Class: RI (BV)	**2011-06 Ningbo Xinle Shipbuilding Co Ltd — Ningbo ZJ** Yd No: XL-133 Loa 157.00 (BB) Br ex 24.83 Dght 9.800 Lbp 149.80 Br md 24.80 Dpth 13.70 Welded, 1 dk	**(A21A2BC) Bulk Carrier** Grain: 30,800; Bale: 30,297 Compartments: 4 Ho, ER 4 Ha: ER Cranes: 3x30t	**1 oil engine** driving 1 FP propeller Total Power: 5,180kW (7,043hp) 13.0kn MAN-B&W 7S35MC 1 x 2 Stroke 7 Cy. 350 x 1400 5180kW (7043bhp) STX Engine Co Ltd-South Korea
9119907 *9HA2446* - **SIDER LIPARI** *ex* Yujin *-2007* *ex* Chuo Maru No. 7 *-2003* **Pol-Euro Shipping Lines Plc-SA** - *Valletta* *Malta* MMSI: 248631000 Official number: 9119907	**5,352** 2,069 4,999	Class: PR (BV) (KR)	**1994-10 Kegoya Dock K.K. — Kure** Yd No: 963 Loa 106.71 Br ex - Dght 6.460 Lbp 99.80 Br md 20.00 Dpth 9.60 Welded, 1 dk	**(A24D2BA) Aggregates Carrier**	**1 oil engine** geared to sc. shaft driving 1 FP propeller Total Power: 2,501kW (3,400hp) 11.2kn Yanmar 8N330-EN 1 x 4 Stroke 8 Cy. 330 x 440 2501kW (3400bhp) Yanmar Diesel Engine Co Ltd-Japan
9495595 *3EVA6* - **SIDER LUCK** **Valoa Shipping SA** Navigest Trust Services & Ship Management SA *Panama* *Panama* MMSI: 373571000 Official number: 4431812	**15,561** 7,520 25,056 T/cm 36.3	Class: BV (NK)	**2012-06 Kanasashi Heavy Industries Co Ltd — Shizuoka SZ** (Hull) Yd No: (1072) **2012-06 Yamanishi Corp — Ishinomaki MG** Yd No: 1072 Loa 157.23 (BB) Br ex - Dght 9.114 Lbp 150.60 Br md 26.80 Dpth 13.20 Welded, 1 dk	**(A21A2BC) Bulk Carrier** Double Hull Grain: 30,736; Bale: 29,325 Compartments: 4 Ho, ER 4 Ha: ER Cranes: 3x30t	**1 oil engine** driving 1 FP propeller Total Power: 5,850kW (7,954hp) 14.0kn MAN-B&W 6S42MC 1 x 2 Stroke 6 Cy. 420 x 1764 5850kW (7954bhp) Makita Corp-Japan AuxGen: 3 x 400kW 60Hz a.c Fuel: 1120.0
9243899 *IBSF* - **SIDER MARLEEN** **Sider Navi SpA** Italtech Srl *Naples* *Italy* MMSI: 247113900	**3,289** 1,879 5,751	Class: BV	**2002-03 Bodewes Scheepswerf "Volharding" Foxhol B.V. — Foxhol** Yd No: 507 Loa 104.55 (BB) Br ex - Dght 6.180 Lbp 99.78 Br md 13.60 Dpth 7.20 Welded, 1 dk	**(A31A2GX) General Cargo Ship** Grain: 6,794 TEU 310 C. 310/20' Compartments: 2 Ho, ER 2 Ha: ER 2 (37.7 x 11.0) Ice Capable	**1 oil engine** reduction geared to sc. shaft driving 1 CP propeller Total Power: 1,800kW (2,447hp) 12.2kn MaK 6M25 1 x 4 Stroke 6 Cy. 255 x 400 1800kW (2447bhp) Caterpillar Motoren GmbH & Co. KG-Germany AuxGen: 2 x 336kW 400/230V 50Hz a.c, 1 x 240kW 400/230V 50Hz a.c
9519377 *9HRK9* - **SIDER PAMINA** *ex* Marti Princess *-2013* *completed as* Jin Cheng Zhou 131 *-2008* **Lavey Shipping SA** Navigest Trust Services & Ship Management SA *Valletta* *Malta* MMSI: 249413000 Official number: 9519377	**6,019** 3,502 8,637	Class: BV (CC)	**2008-08 Linhai Hongsheng Shipbuilding Co Ltd — Linhai ZJ** Yd No: 0601 Loa 128.60 Br ex 18.40 Dght 6.500 Lbp 119.80 Br md 18.00 Dpth 8.80 Welded, 1 dk	**(A31A2GX) General Cargo Ship** Grain: 12,321 Compartments: 3 Ho, ER 3 Ha: 2 (22.4 x 11.0)ER (18.2 x 11.0) Cranes: 2x20t Ice Capable	**1 oil engine** reduction geared to sc. shafts driving 1 CP propeller Total Power: 2,970kW (4,038hp) 12.0kn MaK 9M25 1 x 4 Stroke 9 Cy. 255 x 400 2970kW (4038bhp) Caterpillar Motoren (Guangdong) CoLtd-China AuxGen: 3 x 256kW 400V a.c
9173446 *9HA2176* - **SIDER PANAREA** *ex* Heike *-2009* **Sider Navi SpA** - *Valletta* *Malta* MMSI: 248099000 Official number: 9173446	**3,415** 1,661 5,001 T/cm 24.4	Class: RI (BV) (GL)	**1998-11 Kroeger Werft GmbH & Co. KG — Schacht-Audorf** Yd No: 1544 Loa 99.51 (BB) Br ex - Dght 6.185 Lbp - Br md 16.90 Dpth 7.55 Welded, 1 dk	**(A31A2GX) General Cargo Ship** Double Hull Grain: 5,841; Bale: 5,841 TEU 366 C Ho 80 TEU C Dk 286 TEU incl 40 ref C. Compartments: 2 Ho, ER 3 Ha: (16.7 x 13.2) (25.4 x 13.2) (6.8 x 10.6)ER Ice Capable	**1 oil engine** reduction geared to sc. shaft driving 1 CP propeller Total Power: 2,940kW (3,997hp) 14.8kn MAN-B&W 12V28/32A 1 x Vee 4 Stroke 12 Cy. 280 x 320 2940kW (3997bhp) MAN B&W Diesel A/S-Denmark AuxGen: 1 x 625kW 220/440V a.c, 2 x 256kW 220/440V a.c Thrusters: 1 Thwart. FP thruster (f) Fuel: 254.0 (d.f.)
9363883 *A8LM6* - **SIDER PINK** **Shine Navigation Ltd** International Maritime Advisors & Management Corp *Monrovia* *Liberia* MMSI: 636013224 Official number: 13224	**11,674** 6,457 19,101 T/cm 30.7	Class: NK (RI)	**2006-10 Yamanishi Corp — Ishinomaki MG** Yd No: 1044 Loa 139.90 (BB) Br ex - Dght 8.480 Lbp 132.00 Br md 25.00 Dpth 11.50 Welded, 1 dk	**(A21A2BC) Bulk Carrier** Grain: 23,161; Bale: 22,563 Compartments: 4 Ho, ER 4 Ha: ER 4 (17.5 x 15.0) Cranes: 3x30t	**1 oil engine** reduction geared to sc. shaft driving 1 FP propeller Total Power: 6,000kW (8,158hp) 13.0kn Wartsila 12V32 1 x Vee 4 Stroke 12 Cy. 320 x 400 6000kW (8158bhp) Wartsila Finland Oy-Finland AuxGen: 3 x 442kW a.c Fuel: 46.0 (d.f.) 811.0 (r.f.)
9143398 *9HA2174* - **SIDER PONZA** *ex* Betsy S *-2009* *ex* Betsy *-2003* **Sider Navi SpA** - *Valletta* *Malta* MMSI: 248097000 Official number: 9143398	**3,415** 1,661 5,001 T/cm 14.0	Class: RI (BV) (GL)	**1998-06 Societatea Comerciala Navol S.A. Oltenita — Oltenita** (Hull launched by) Yd No: 361 **1998-06 Kroeger Werft GmbH & Co. KG — Schacht-Audorf** (Hull completed by) Yd No: 1541 Loa 99.51 (BB) Br ex - Dght 6.185 Lbp - Br md 16.90 Dpth 7.55 Welded, 1 dk	**(A31A2GX) General Cargo Ship** Double Hull Grain: 5,841; Bale: 5,841 TEU 366 C Ho 80 TEU C Dk 286 TEU incl 60 ref C. Compartments: 2 Ho, ER 3 Ha: (16.7 x 13.2) (25.4 x 13.2) (6.8 x 10.6)ER Ice Capable	**1 oil engine** with flexible couplings & reductiongeared to sc. shaft driving 1 CP propeller Total Power: 2,940kW (3,997hp) 14.8kn Alpha 12V28/32A 1 x Vee 4 Stroke 12 Cy. 280 x 320 2940kW (3997bhp) MAN B&W Diesel A/S-Denmark AuxGen: 1 x 520kW 220/440V 60Hz a.c, 2 x 256kW 220/440V 60Hz a.c Thrusters: 1 Thwart. FP thruster (f)

9600592 **SIDER POROS**
3EUI4
-
Kenton Shipping Inc
Navigest Trust Services & Ship Management SA
Panama *Panama*
MMSI: 354187000
Official number: 4416112

5,214 2,913 8,107 — Class: BV

2012-06 Ningbo Xinle Shipbuilding Co Ltd — Ningbo ZJ Yd No: XL-129
Loa 119.95 (BB) Br ex 16.84 Dght 6.680
Lbp 111.97 Br md 16.80 Dpth 8.20
Welded, 1 dk

(A21A2BC) Bulk Carrier
Grain: 10,029
Compartments: 2 Ho, ER
2 Ha: ER 2 (29.9 x 12.6)

1 oil engine reduction geared to sc. shaft driving 1 FP propeller
Total Power: 2,500kW (3,399hp) 11.5kn
Daihatsu 8DKM-28
1 x 4 Stroke 8 Cy. 280 x 390 2500kW (3399bhp)
Daihatsu Diesel Manufacturing Co Lt-Japan
AuxGen: 3 x 275kW 50Hz a.c
Fuel: 330.0

9634062 **SIDER PROCIDA**
DUEO
-
Denton Shipping Inc
Navigest Trust Services & Ship Management SA
Manila *Philippines*
MMSI: 548866000

5,214 2,913 8,100 — Class: BV

2012-06 Ningbo Xinle Shipbuilding Co Ltd — Ningbo ZJ Yd No: XL-136
Loa 119.95 Br ex 16.84 Dght 6.680
Lbp 111.97 Br md 16.80 Dpth 8.20
Welded, 1 dk

(A21A2BC) Bulk Carrier
Grain: 10,106
Compartments: 2 Ho, ER
2 Ha: ER

1 oil engine reduction geared to sc. shaft driving 1 FP propeller
Total Power: 2,500kW (3,399hp) 11.5kn
Daihatsu 8DKM-28
1 x 4 Stroke 8 Cy. 280 x 390 2500kW (3399bhp)
Daihatsu Diesel Manufacturing Co Lt-Japan
AuxGen: 3 x 275kW 50Hz a.c
Fuel: 330.0

9486324 **SIDER STAR**
ICPU
ex Star *-2010*
-
Sider Navi SpA
-
Naples *Italy*
MMSI: 247302200

5,214 2,913 8,100 — Class: RI (BV)

2009-12 Ningbo Xinle Shipbuilding Co Ltd — Ningbo ZJ Yd No: XL-125
Loa 119.95 (BB) Br ex 16.84 Dght 6.680
Lbp 111.97 Br md 16.80 Dpth 8.20
Welded, 1 dk

(A21A2BC) Bulk Carrier
Grain: 9,904
Compartments: 2 Ho, ER
2 Ha: ER 2 (29.9 x 12.6)

1 oil engine Reduction geared to sc shaft driving 1 FP propeller
Total Power: 2,500kW (3,399hp) 11.5kn
Daihatsu 8DKM-28
1 x 4 Stroke 8 Cy. 280 x 390 2500kW (3399bhp)
Daihatsu Diesel Manufacturing Co Lt-Japan
AuxGen: 3 x 304kW 50Hz a.c

9343065 **SIDER SUN**
9HBM8
launched as Xinle 1 *-2005*
-
Canbrook Shipping SA
Navigest Trust Services & Ship Management SA
Valletta *Malta*
MMSI: 215807000
Official number: 9343065

5,029 3,002 7,491 T/cm 17.5 — Class: RI (NK)

2005-02 Ningbo Xinle Shipbuilding Co Ltd — Ningbo ZJ Yd No: 04/001
Loa 118.90 (BB) Br ex 16.84 Dght 6.590
Lbp 115.44 Br md 16.80 Dpth 8.20
Welded, 1 dk

(A21A2BC) Bulk Carrier
Double Hull
Grain: 10,106; Bale: 9,903
Compartments: 2 Ho, ER
2 Ha: ER 2 (31.2 x 12.6)

1 oil engine geared to sc. shaft driving 1 FP propeller
Total Power: 2,500kW (3,399hp) 12.0kn
Daihatsu 8DKM-28
1 x 4 Stroke 8 Cy. 280 x 390 2500kW (3399bhp)
Shaanxi Diesel Heavy Industry Co Lt-China
AuxGen: 3 x 190kW 450/230V 60Hz a.c

9651541 **SIDER TIS**
9HA3279
ex BBT Ocean *-2013*
-
launched as Montelema *-2013*
Foxton Shipping Inc
Italtech Srl
Valletta *Malta*
MMSI: 229372000

7,875 3,350 10,396 — Class: GL RI

2013-02 Shandong Baibuting Shipbuilding Co Ltd — Rongcheng SD Yd No: BBTZ812
Loa 119.80 Br ex - Dght 8.000
Lbp 115.00 Br md 18.20 Dpth 10.60
Welded, 1 dk

(A31A2GX) General Cargo Ship
Grain: 14,330
Compartments: 3 Ho, ER
3 Ha: ER
Cranes: 2x40t
Ice Capable

1 oil engine reduction geared to sc. shaft driving 1 CP propeller
Total Power: 4,000kW (5,438hp) 13.0kn
MaK 8M32C
1 x 4 Stroke 8 Cy. 320 x 480 4000kW (5438bhp)
Caterpillar Motoren (Guangdong) CoLtd-China

9486336 **SIDER VEGA**
ICOH
-
Sider Navi SpA
-
Naples *Italy*
MMSI: 247292100

5,214 2,913 8,108 — Class: RI (BV)

2010-05 Ningbo Xinle Shipbuilding Co Ltd — Ningbo ZJ Yd No: XL-126
Loa 119.95 (BB) Br ex - Dght 6.680
Lbp 111.97 Br md 16.80 Dpth 8.20
Welded, 1 dk

(A21A2BC) Bulk Carrier
Grain: 9,904
Compartments: 2 Ho, ER
2 Ha: ER 2 (29.9 x 12.6)

1 oil engine reduction geared to sc. shaft driving 1 FP propeller
Total Power: 2,970kW (4,038hp) 12.0kn
MaK 9M25C
1 x 4 Stroke 9 Cy. 255 x 400 2970kW (4038bhp)
Caterpillar Motoren GmbH & Co. KG-Germany

9629847 **SIDER VIVARA**
3FJJ6
-
Yortel Shipping Inc
Navigest Trust Services & Ship Management SA
SatCom: Inmarsat C 437361610
Panama *Panama*
MMSI: 373616000
Official number: 43506PEXT

5,214 2,913 7,489 — Class: BV RI

2012-06 Ningbo Xinle Shipbuilding Co Ltd — Ningbo ZJ Yd No: XL-135
Converted From: Bulk Carrier-2014
Loa 119.95 (BB) Br ex - Dght 6.200
Lbp 111.97 Br md 16.80 Dpth 8.20
Welded, 1 dk

(A24A2BT) Cement Carrier

1 oil engine reduction geared to sc. shaft driving 1 FP propeller
Total Power: 2,500kW (3,399hp) 13.0kn
Daihatsu 8DKM-28
1 x 4 Stroke 8 Cy. 280 x 390 2500kW (3399bhp)
Daihatsu Diesel Manufacturing Co Lt-Japan
AuxGen: 3 x 275kW 50Hz a.c
Thrusters: 1 Tunnel thruster (f)
Fuel: 330.0

9486312 **SIDER VULCANO**
ICRJ
launched as Seiwakaluo *-2010*
-
Sider Navi SpA
-
SatCom: Inmarsat C 424703542
Naples *Italy*
MMSI: 247306300

5,214 2,913 8,108 — Class: RI (BV)

2010-09 Ningbo Xinle Shipbuilding Co Ltd — Ningbo ZJ Yd No: XL-124
Loa 119.95 (BB) Br ex 16.84 Dght 6.680
Lbp 111.97 Br md 16.80 Dpth 8.20
Welded, 1 dk

(A21A2BC) Bulk Carrier
Grain: 9,904
Compartments: 2 Ho, ER
2 Ha: ER 2 (29.9 x 12.6)

1 oil engine reduction geared to sc. shafts driving 1 Propeller
Total Power: 2,970kW (4,038hp) 13.0kn
MaK 9M25C
1 x 4 Stroke 9 Cy. 255 x 400 2970kW (4038bhp)
Caterpillar Motoren GmbH & Co. KG-Germany

9353022 **SIDER WARRIOR**
9HBN8
ex Ocean Sirius *-2014* *ex* Global Hebe *-2013*
-
ex Leonore *-2008* *ex* Sider Sky *-2005*
Kolmar Shipping Ltd
Navigest Trust Services & Ship Management SA
Valletta *Malta*
MMSI: 229676000
Official number: 9353022

5,029 3,002 7,486 T/cm 17.5 — Class: RI (BV) (GL) (NK)

2005-06 Ningbo Xinle Shipbuilding Co Ltd — Ningbo ZJ Yd No: 04/002
Loa 119.60 (BB) Br ex 16.84 Dght 6.270
Lbp 112.98 Br md 16.80 Dpth 8.20
Welded, 2 dks

(A31A2GX) General Cargo Ship
Grain: 10,106; Bale: 9,903
Compartments: 2 Ho, ER
2 Ha: (42.6 x 12.6)ER (41.9 x 12.6)

1 oil engine reduction geared to sc. shaft driving 1 FP propeller
Total Power: 2,500kW (3,399hp) 11.0kn
Daihatsu 8DKM-28
1 x 4 Stroke 8 Cy. 280 x 390 2500kW (3399bhp)
Daihatsu Diesel Manufacturing Co Lt-Japan
AuxGen: 2 x 200kW 400/220V 60Hz a.c
Fuel: 200.0

9254628 **SIDERAKI**
HOQJ
ex Ancash Queen *-2013* *ex* Bright Queen *-2002*
-
Sideraki Shipping SA
Thalkat Shipping SA
Panama *Panama*
MMSI: 355953000
Official number: 30696PEXT2

26,195 15,577 46,673 T/cm 50.2 — Class: NK

2002-11 Kanasashi Heavy Industries Co Ltd — Toyohashi AI Yd No: 3543
Loa 183.04 (BB) Br ex - Dght 11.670
Lbp 174.30 Br md 31.00 Dpth 16.47
Welded, 1 dk

(A21A2BC) Bulk Carrier
Double Bottom Entire Compartment Length
Grain: 59,077; Bale: 58,014
Compartments: 5 Ho, ER
5 Ha: 4 (20.0 x 15.6)ER (14.4 x 15.6)
Cranes: 4x30t

1 oil engine driving 1 FP propeller
Total Power: 7,980kW (10,850hp) 14.4kn
Mitsubishi 6UEC52LS
1 x 2 Stroke 6 Cy. 520 x 1850 7980kW (10850bhp)
Kobe Hatsudoki KK-Japan
AuxGen: 3 x 440kW 450V 60Hz a.c
Fuel: 1944.0 (r.f.) (Heating Coils) 30.2pd

8806929 **SIDERAL**
EHWI
ex Polaris *-1989*
GI-4-2163
Gude Gonzalez Hermanos SC
-
SatCom: Inmarsat C 422452810
Gijon *Spain*
MMSI: 224528000
Official number: 3-2163/

632 190 271 — Class: BV

1988-08 Astilleros Armon SA — Navia Yd No: 158
Loa 37.00 Br ex - Dght 4.200
Lbp 31.50 Br md 8.11 Dpth 4.20
Welded, 1 dk

(B11B2FV) Fishing Vessel
Ins: 304

1 oil engine with clutches, flexible couplings & reverse reduction geared to sc. shaft driving 1 FP propeller
Total Power: 588kW (799hp)
Caterpillar 3512TA
1 x Vee 4 Stroke 12 Cy. 170 x 190 588kW (799bhp)
Caterpillar Inc-USA

9406881 **SIDERIS GS**
V7LE4
-
Jaluit Shipping Co Inc
Diana Shipping Services SA
SatCom: Inmarsat C 453847159
Majuro *Marshall Islands*
MMSI: 538002731
Official number: 2731

88,955 58,078 174,187 T/cm 119.0 — Class: BV (AB)

2006-11 Shanghai Waigaoqiao Shipbuilding Co Ltd — Shanghai Yd No: 1026
Loa 288.92 (BB) Br ex 45.05 Dght 18.120
Lbp 278.20 Br md 45.00 Dpth 24.50
Welded, 1 dk

(A21A2BC) Bulk Carrier
Grain: 193,247; Bale: 183,425
Compartments: 9 Ho, ER
9 Ha: 7 (15.4 x 20.0)ER 2 (15.4 x 16.5)

1 oil engine driving 1 FP propeller
Total Power: 16,860kW (22,923hp) 14.5kn
MAN-B&W 6S70MC
1 x 2 Stroke 6 Cy. 700 x 2674 16860kW (22923bhp)
Hudong Heavy Machinery Co Ltd-China
AuxGen: 3 x 750kW 450/110V 60Hz a.c
Fuel: 343.0 (d.f.) 4466.0 (r.f.)

7319797 **SIDHARTA**
-
-
PT Fajar Lines
-
Dumai *Indonesia*

235 - - — Class: (LR) (KI) ✠ Classed LR until 15/1/82

1973-09 Kaohsiung Prov. Junior College of Marine Tech. SY — Kaohsiung
Loa 29.49 Br ex 8.18 Dght -
Lbp 26.01 Br md 8.04 Dpth 3.61
Welded, 1 dk

(B32A2ST) Tug

2 oil engines driving 2 CP propellers
Total Power: 736kW (1,000hp) 10.0kn
Alpha 405-26VO
2 x 2 Stroke 5 Cy. 260 x 400 each-368kW (500bhp)
Alpha Diesel A/S-Denmark
AuxGen: 2 x 30kW 380V 50Hz a.c

9278363 **SIDI ABDERRAHMANE**
7TAX
-
Entreprise Portuaire d'Alger (EPA)
-
Alger *Algeria*

313 93 245 — Class: (BV)

2003-03 PO SevMash Predpriyatiye — Severodvinsk (Hull) Yd No: (511715)
2003-03 B.V. Scheepswerf Damen — Gorinchem Yd No: 511715
Loa 30.82 Br ex 10.20 Dght 4.500
Lbp 29.80 Br md 9.40 Dpth 4.80
Welded, 1 dk

(B32A2ST) Tug

2 oil engines geared to sc. shafts driving 2 Directional propellers
Total Power: 2,160kW (2,936hp)
MaK 6M20
2 x 4 Stroke 6 Cy. 200 x 300 each-1080kW (1468bhp)
Caterpillar Motoren GmbH & Co. KG-Germany

7500906 **SIDI ABOU EL ABBAS EL MOURSY**
-
-
Alexandria Port Authority
-
Alexandria *Egypt*

378 31 - — Class: (AB)

1976-12 Robin Shipyard Pte Ltd — Singapore Yd No: 235
Loa - Br ex - Dght 4.141
Lbp 36.02 Br md 9.01 Dpth 4.53
Welded, 1 dk

(B32A2ST) Tug

2 oil engines reverse reduction geared to sc. shafts driving 2 FP propellers
Total Power: 2,162kW (2,940hp) 12.0kn
MAN 6L25/30
2 x 4 Stroke 6 Cy. 250 x 300 each-1081kW (1470bhp)
Maschinenbau Augsburg Nuernberg (MAN)-Augsburg
AuxGen: 2 x 80kW
Fuel: 249.0 (d.f.)

IMO / Call sign	Name / Owner	Tonnage	Class	Builder / Dimensions	Type	Machinery
8224248 *CNOA* -	**SIDI BANNOUR** **Government of The Kingdom of Morocco (Ministere de l'Equipment & de la Promotion Nationale)** Royaume Du Maroc (Societe d'Exploitation des Ports (SODEP) - Marsa Maroc) *Jorf Lasfar* *Morocco*	*162* 62 -	Class: (BV)	**1984-12 Scheepsbouw Alblas B.V. — Krimpen a/d IJssel** (Hull) **1984-12 B.V. Scheepswerf Damen — Gorinchem** Yd No: 3145 Loa 26.01 Br ex 8.23 Dght 3.250 Lbp 23.86 Br md 7.80 Dpth 4.05 Welded, 1 dk	**(B32A2ST) Tug**	**2 oil engines** with clutches & sr reverse geared to sc. shafts driving 2 FP propellers Total Power: 1,176kW (1,598hp) Deutz SBA16M816 2 x Vee 4 Stroke 16 Cy. 142 x 160 each-588kW (799bhp) Kloeckner Humboldt Deutz AG-West Germany AuxGen: 2 x 50kW 380/220V a.c
9163805 *TSBJ* -	**SIDI BOU SAID** **Government of The Republic of Tunisia (Ministry of Defence)** *Tunis* *Tunisia*	**368** 110 300	Class: (BV)	**1998-02 'Crist' Sp z oo — Gdansk** (Hull) **1998-02 B.V. Scheepswerf Damen — Gorinchem** Yd No: 3707 Loa 38.80 Br ex 10.25 Dght 1.800 Lbp 37.16 Br md 10.00 Dpth 2.80 Welded, 1 dk	**(B34Q2QB) Buoy Tender** A-frames: 1x50t; Cranes: 1x20t	**2 oil engines** reduction geared to sc. shafts driving 2 FP propellers Total Power: 596kW (810hp) 10.4kn Caterpillar 3406TA 2 x 4 Stroke 6 Cy. 137 x 165 each-298kW (405bhp) Caterpillar Inc-USA AuxGen: 2 x 85kW 220/380V 50Hz a.c
8812124 - -	**SIDI BOUBACAR II** *ex* Messoud II *-2004* *ex* Tichitt IV *-2001* *ex* Ribat 1 *-1989* *ex* Loto *-1988* **Santamar** - *Nouadhibou* *Mauritania*	**220** 70 146	Class: (BV) (RI)	**1988-06 Astilleros Armon SA — Navia** Yd No: 195 Loa 29.50 Br ex - Dght 3.150 Lbp 25.51 Br md 7.76 Dpth 4.22 Welded, 1 dk	**(B11A2FS) Stern Trawler** Ins: 187	**1 oil engine** with clutches, flexible couplings & reverse reduction geared to sc. shaft driving 1 FP propeller Total Power: 570kW (775hp) 11.3kn Caterpillar 3508TA 1 x Vee 4 Stroke 8 Cy. 170 x 190 570kW (775bhp) Caterpillar Inc-USA
9366770 *7TCD* -	**SIDI BRAHIM** **Entreprise Portuaire de Annaba (EPA)** - *Annaba* *Algeria* MMSI: 605036464	**309** 92 -	Class: BV	**2006-10 Stal-Rem SA — Gdansk** (Hull) Yd No: (511730) **2006-10 B.V. Scheepswerf Damen — Gorinchem** Yd No: 511730 Loa 30.82 Br ex - Dght 4.080 Lbp 28.03 Br md 9.40 Dpth 4.80 Welded, 1 dk	**(B32A2ST) Tug**	**2 oil engines** reduction geared to sc. shafts driving 2 Directional propellers Total Power: 3,040kW (4,134hp) 12.3kn MaK 8M20 2 x 4 Stroke 8 Cy. 200 x 300 each-1520kW (2067bhp) Caterpillar Motoren GmbH & Co. KG-Germany AuxGen: 2 x 90kW 400/230V 50Hz a.c
9393979 *PHFM* -	**SIDI C** *ex* Neptunus 295 *-2006* **Stemat BV** - *Rotterdam* *Netherlands* MMSI: 246522000 Official number: 47686	**314** 94 235	Class: BV	**2006-05 Scheepswerf Wout Liezen BV — Meppel** (Hull) **2006-05 Neptune Shipyards BV — Aalst (Nl)** Yd No: 295 Loa 31.85 Br ex - Dght 2.100 Lbp 25.85 Br md 11.05 Dpth 3.60 Welded, 1 dk	**(B34T2QR) Work/Repair Vessel** Cranes: 1	**2 oil engines** reduction geared to sc. shafts driving 2 FP propellers Total Power: 1,940kW (2,638hp) Cummins KTA-38-M2 2 x Vee 4 Stroke 12 Cy. 159 x 159 each-970kW (1319bhp) Cummins Engine Co Inc-USA Thrusters: 1 Tunnel thruster (f) Fuel: 126.7 (d.f.)
8224250 *CNFK* -	**SIDI ISMAIL** **Royaume Du Maroc (Direction de l'exploitation au Port de Tanger-Marsa Maroc)** - *Casablanca* *Morocco*	*162* 62 -	Class: BV	**1984-12 Scheepsbouw Alblas B.V. — Krimpen a/d IJssel** (Hull) **1984-12 B.V. Scheepswerf Damen — Gorinchem** Yd No: 3146 Loa 26.01 Br ex 8.23 Dght 3.250 Lbp 23.86 Br md 7.80 Dpth 4.50 Welded, 1 dk	**(B32A2ST) Tug**	**2 oil engines** with clutches & sr reverse geared to sc. shafts driving 2 FP propellers Total Power: 1,176kW (1,598hp) 12.4kn Deutz SBA16M816 2 x Vee 4 Stroke 16 Cy. 142 x 160 each-588kW (799bhp) Kloeckner Humboldt Deutz AG-West Germany
9220691 *CNA3931* -	**SIDI MOUSSA** **Societe Cherifienne de Remorquage et d'Assistance** - *Casablanca* *Morocco*	**119** 36 62	Class: BV (LR) ✠ Classed LR until 27/2/12	**2000-06 Stocznia Tczew Sp z oo — Tczew** (Hull) **2000-06 B.V. Scheepswerf Damen — Gorinchem** Yd No: 6560 Loa 22.50 Br ex 7.25 Dght 3.180 Lbp 20.42 Br md 7.25 Dpth 3.75 Welded, 1 dk	**(B32A2ST) Tug**	**2 oil engines** with clutches, flexible couplings & sr reverse geared to sc. shafts driving 2 FP propellers Total Power: 1,432kW (1,946hp) 11.3kn Caterpillar 3508TA 2 x Vee 4 Stroke 8 Cy. 170 x 190 each-716kW (973bhp) Caterpillar Inc-USA AuxGen: 2 x 50kW 380V 50Hz a.c
7500982 - -	**SIDI YAQUT EL ARSH** **Alexandria Port Authority** - *Alexandria* *Egypt*	*128* 1 57	Class: (AB)	**1977-12 Robin Shipyard Pte Ltd — Singapore** Yd No: 243 Loa 29.11 Br ex 7.45 Dght 2.850 Lbp 26.83 Br md 7.42 Dpth 3.36 Welded, 1 dk	**(B32A2ST) Tug**	**2 oil engines** geared to sc. shafts driving 2 FP propellers Total Power: 1,324kW (1,800hp) 12.0kn MWM TBD440-6 2 x 4 Stroke 6 Cy. 230 x 270 each-662kW (900bhp) Motoren Werke Mannheim AG (MWM)-West Germany AuxGen: 2 x 24kW
8501414 *V3NL8* -	**SIDIMI** *ex* QC Teal *-2007* *ex* Transport Schelde *-1996* *ex* C. U. R. Benjamin *-1989* *ex* L. Delwaide *-1988* **Inderton Ltd SA** Natie Shipping Co Ltd *Belize City* *Belize* MMSI: 312207000 Official number: 571130004	**5,608** 3,088 7,130	Class: IB (GL)	**1987-04 N.V. Boelwerf S.A. — Temse** Yd No: 1524 Loa 116.85 (BB) Br ex 20.27 Dght 6.133 Lbp 106.86 Br md 19.61 Dpth 8.01 Welded, 1 dk	**(A31A2GA) General Cargo Ship (with Ro-Ro facility)** Stern door/ramp (centre) Len: 11.00 Wid: 6.50 Swl: - Grain: 9,150 TEU 574 C.Ho 206/20' C.Dk 368/20' incl. 30 ref C. Compartments: 1 Ho, ER 1 Ha: (76.5 x 15.2)ER Cranes: 2x35t Ice Capable	**1 oil engine** with flexible couplings & sr gearedto sc. shaft driving 1 CP propeller Total Power: 3,199kW (4,349hp) 13.0kn MaK 6M551AK 1 x 4 Stroke 6 Cy. 450 x 550 3199kW (4349bhp) Krupp MaK Maschinenbau GmbH-Kiel AuxGen: 2 x 320kW 440V 60Hz a.c Thrusters: 1 Thwart. FP thruster (f)
8425660 *DUA2994* -	**SIDNEY** *ex* Stephanie *-2006* *ex* Carlos I *-1994* **Landing Craft Transport Inc** - *Manila* *Philippines* Official number: 00-0001133	*118* 51 -		**1969 Cebu Shipyard & Engineering Works Inc — Lapu-Lapu** L reg 24.03 Br ex 6.91 Dght 1.520 Lbp - Br md 6.87 Dpth 2.54 Welded, 1 dk	**(B32A2ST) Tug**	**2 oil engines** reduction geared to sc. shafts Total Power: 1,022kW (1,390hp) 5.0kn Cummins 2 x 4 Stroke each-511kW (695bhp) Cummins Engine Co Inc-USA
8958629 *WCZ2397* -	**SIDNEY** **Sidney Fisheries Inc** - *Brownsville, TX* *United States of America* Official number: 1079074	**140** 42 -		**1999 Russell Portier, Inc. — Chauvin, La** Yd No: 101 L reg 24.59 Br ex - Dght - Lbp - Br md 7.62 Dpth 3.62 Welded, 1 dk	**(B11B2FV) Fishing Vessel**	**1 oil engine** driving 1 FP propeller
9231341 *WCZ8883* -	**SIDNEY CANDIES** **Otto Candies LLC** - *New Orleans, LA* *United States of America* MMSI: 338765000 Official number: 1096764	**1,020** 306 2,500	Class: AB	**2000-06 Bender Shipbuilding & Repair Co Inc — Mobile AL** Yd No: 6930 Loa 44.81 Br ex 15.24 Dght 4.880 Lbp 42.10 Br md 14.76 Dpth 6.40 Welded, 1 dk	**(B21B20A) Anchor Handling Tug Supply**	**3 oil engines** gearing integral to driving 1 FP propeller , 2 Z propellers Total Power: 6,914kW (9,401hp) 12.0kn EMD (Electro-Motive) 16-645-E6 2 x Vee 2 Stroke 16 Cy. 230 x 254 each-1618kW (2200bhp) General Motors Corp.Electro-Motive Div.-La Grange EMD (Electro-Motive) 20-710-G7B 1 x Vee 2 Stroke 20 Cy. 230 x 279 3678kW (5001bhp) General Motors Corp.Electro-Motive Div.-La Grange AuxGen: 2 x 175kW a.c
7626190 *WYL5445* -	**SIDNEY FOSS** **Foss Maritime Co** - *Seattle, WA* *United States of America* MMSI: 366934310 Official number: 578098	*198* 134 -	Class: (AB)	**1976 McDermott Shipyards Inc — New Iberia LA** Yd No: 106 Loa 38.41 Br ex - Dght 4.166 Lbp 34.65 Br md 10.37 Dpth 4.88 Welded, 1 dk	**(B32A2ST) Tug**	**2 oil engines** reverse reduction geared to sc. shafts driving 2 FP propellers Total Power: 2,206kW (3,000hp) 10.0kn EMD (Electro-Motive) 12-645-E6 2 x Vee 2 Stroke 12 Cy. 230 x 254 each-1103kW (1500bhp) General Motors Corp.Electro-Motive Div.-La Grange AuxGen: 2 x 115kW
9007893 *ELRS2* -	**SIDRA AL KHALEEJ** *ex* Matarah *-2006* *ex* Natalia *-1996* **Sidra Al Khaleej Shipping Co** Woqod Marine Services Co *Monrovia* *Liberia* MMSI: 636010221 Official number: 10221	**2,204** 1,053 3,573	Class: LR ✠ **100A1** SS 07/2011 oil tanker carriage of oils with a FP exceeding 60~C ESP Ice Class 1D ✠ **LMC** **UMS** Eq.Ltr: Q; Cable: 461.2/38.0 U2	**1996-07 Rousse Shipyard Ltd — Rousse** Yd No: 602 Loa 84.93 Br ex 14.56 Dght 5.380 Lbp 80.23 Br md 14.00 Dpth 6.50 Welded, 1 dk	**(A13B2TP) Products Tanker** Double Bottom Entire Compartment Length Liq: 3,835; Liq (Oil): 3,835 Compartments: 8 Wing Ta, ER Ice Capable	**1 oil engine** driving 1 FP propeller Total Power: 883kW (1,201hp) 10.0kn S.K.L. 8NVD48A-2U 1 x 4 Stroke 8 Cy. 320 x 480 883kW (1201bhp) SKL Motoren u. Systemtechnik AG-Magdeburg AuxGen: 3 x 160kW 400V 50Hz a.c Boilers: AuxB (o.f.) 7.1kgf/cm² (7.0bar) Thrusters: 1 Thwart. FP thruster (f)
9481178 *A8NH2* -	**SIDRA AL WAJBAH** *ex* Hao Xiang 66 *-2007* **Sidra Al Wajbah Shipping Co** Woqod Marine Services Co *Monrovia* *Liberia* MMSI: 636013478 Official number: 13478	**2,684** 1,211 4,173	Class: CC	**2007-12 Zhoushan Haichen Marine Service & Engineering Co Ltd — Zhoushan ZJ** Yd No: HC06-03 Loa 99.90 Br ex - Dght 5.650 Lbp 93.20 Br md 14.00 Dpth 6.90 Welded, 1 dk	**(A13C2LA) Asphalt/Bitumen Tanker** Double Hull (13F) Liq: 4,265; Liq (Oil): 4,349 Compartments: 10 Wing Ta, ER	**1 oil engine** reduction geared to sc. shaft driving 1 Propeller Total Power: 1,765kW (2,400hp) 11.0kn Chinese Std. Type 8320ZC 1 x 4 Stroke 8 Cy. 320 x 440 1765kW (2400bhp) Guangzhou Diesel Engine Factory CoLtd-China AuxGen: 3 x 160kW 400V a.c

9007881 *ELRR9* -	**SIDRA DOHA** *ex* Al Barriyab *-2006* *ex* Ekaterina *-1996* **Sidra Doha Shipping Co** Woqod Marine Services Co *Monrovia* *Liberia* MMSI: 636010220 Official number: 10220	**2,204** 1,053 3,573	Class: LR ✠**100A1** SS 07/2011 oil tanker ESP FP exceeding 60~C Ice Class 1D ✠**LMC** **UMS** Eq.Ltr: Q; Cable: 462.8/38.0 U2	**1996-07 Rousse Shipyard Ltd — Rousse** Yd No: 601 Loa 84.93 Br ex 14.56 Dght 5.376 Lbp 80.23 Br md 14.00 Dpth 6.50 Welded, 1 dk	**(A13B2TP) Products Tanker** Double Bottom Entire Compartment Length Liq: 3,835; Liq (Oil): 3,835 Compartments: 8 Wing Ta, ER Ice Capable	**1 oil engine** driving 1 FP propeller Total Power: 883kW (1,201hp) 10.0kn S.K.L. 8NVD48A-2U 1 x 4 Stroke 8 Cy. 320 x 480 883kW (1201bhp) SKL Motoren u. Systemtechnik AG-Magdeburg AuxGen: 3 x 160kW 400V 50Hz a.c Thrusters: 1 Thwart. FP thruster (f)
9462990 *A8PQ2* -	**SIDRA MESSAIED** *ex* Sj Ace *-2008* **Sidra Messaied Shipping Co** Woqod Marine Services Co *Monrovia* *Liberia* MMSI: 636013811 Official number: 13811	**3,691** 1,265 4,999	Class: CC	**2008-04 Linhai Huipu Shipbuilding Co Ltd — Linhai ZJ** Yd No: HP0605 Loa 101.90 (BB) Br ex - Dght 5.930 Lbp 96.00 Br md 16.00 Dpth 8.00 Welded, 1 dk	**(A13A2TV) Crude Oil Tanker** Double Hull (13F) Liq: 4,467; Liq (Oil): 4,467 Compartments: 10 Wing Ta, 2 Wing Slop Ta, ER Ice Capable	**1 oil engine** reduction geared to sc. shaft driving 1 FP propeller Total Power: 2,060kW (2,801hp) 11.5kn Guangzhou 8320ZC 1 x 4 Stroke 8 Cy. 320 x 440 2060kW (2801bhp) Guangzhou Diesel Engine Factory CoLtd-China AuxGen: 2 x 250kW 400V a.c
9339648 *A8OT6* -	**SIDRA RAS LAFFAN** *ex* Alam Cergas *-2007* **Sidra Raslaffan Shipping Co** Woqod Marine Services Co *Monrovia* *Liberia* MMSI: 636013705 Official number: 13705	**22,184** 9,431 34,671 T/cm 41.5	Class: LR ✠**100A1** SS 06/2012 Double Hull oil and chemical tanker, Type 3 vegetable oils only ESP **ShipRight** (SDA, FDA, CM) *IWS SPM LI ✠**LMC** **UMS IGS** Eq.Ltr: J†; Cable: 605.0/66.0 U3 (a)	**2007-06 Dalian Shipbuilding Industry Co Ltd — Dalian LN (No 1 Yard)** Yd No: PC350-13 Loa 171.20 (BB) Br ex 27.44 Dght 11.815 Lbp 162.00 Br md 27.40 Dpth 17.30 Welded, 1 dk	**(A12B2TR) Chemical/Products Tanker** Double Hull (13F) Liq: 36,800; Liq (Oil): 36,800 Compartments: 12 Wing Ta, 2 Wing Slop Ta, ER 12 Cargo Pump (s): 10x500m^3/hr, 2x300m^3/hr Manifold: Bow/CM: 83.3m	**1 oil engine** driving 1 FP propeller Total Power: 7,150kW (9,721hp) 14.5kn MAN-B&W 5S50MC 1 x 2 Stroke 5 Cy. 500 x 1910 7150kW (9721bhp) Dalian Marine Diesel Works-China AuxGen: 3 x 910kW 450V 60Hz a.c Boilers: AuxB (ex.g.) 8.7kgf/cm^2 (8.5bar), WTAuxB (o.f.) 8.7kgf/cm^2 (8.5bar) Fuel: 110.0 (d.f.) 1150.0 (r.f.)
9001899 *DCYE* HOO 70	**SIEBENNUS GERJETS** **David de Leeuw Muschelzucht GmbH** - *Hooksiel* *Germany* MMSI: 211363300 Official number: 370	**221** 66 110	Class: (GL)	**1990-12 Constructie en Scheepsbouw van Santen B.V. — Sliedrecht** (Hull) Yd No: 278 **1990-12 Machinefabriek Padmos Stellendam B.V. — Stellendam** Yd No: 136 Loa 32.26 Br ex - Dght 1.800 Lbp 25.15 Br md 9.00 Dpth 2.40 Welded, 1 dk	**(B11B2FV) Fishing Vessel**	**2 oil engines** sr reverse geared to sc. shafts driving 2 FP propellers Total Power: 600kW (816hp) 10.0kn Volvo Penta TAMD162A 2 x 4 Stroke 6 Cy. 144 x 165 each-300kW (408bhp) AB Volvo Penta-Sweden
9349447 *PCBC* -	**SIEGEDIJK** *launched as* Weserdijk *-2010* **Beheermaatschappij ms Siegedijk BV** Navigia Shipmanagement BV *Groningen* *Netherlands* MMSI: 246706000 Official number: 53933	**6,668** 3,350 9,640	Class: GL	**2010-07 Penglai Bohai Shipyard Co Ltd — Penglai SD** Yd No: PBZ04-38A Loa 106.99 (BB) Br ex - Dght 8.220 Lbp 103.00 Br md 18.20 Dpth 10.50 Welded, 1 dk	**(A31A2GX) General Cargo Ship** Grain: 11,770; Bale: 11,770 TEU 132 Compartments: 3 Ho, ER 3 Ha: 2 (25.9 x 15.2)ER (16.2 x 15.2) Cranes: 2x35t Ice Capable	**1 oil engine** reduction geared to sc. shaft driving 1 CP propeller Total Power: 3,840kW (5,221hp) 13.0kn MaK 8M32C 1 x 4 Stroke 8 Cy. 320 x 480 3840kW (5221bhp) Caterpillar Motoren GmbH & Co. KG-Germany AuxGen: 1 x 500kW 400/220V 50Hz a.c, 2 x 425kW 400/220V 50Hz a.c Thrusters: 1 Tunnel thruster (f) Fuel: 100.0 (d.f.) 500.0 (r.f.)
9325142 *V2GL5* -	**SIEGFRIED LEHMANN** *ex* Skarpoe *-2013* **ms 'Siegfried Lehmann' Schifffahrts GmbH & Co KG** Reederei Lehmann GmbH & Co KG *Saint John's* *Antigua & Barbuda* MMSI: 305982000	**3,183** 1,765 4,508	Class: GL	**2005-04 Societatea Comerciala Severnav S.A. — Drobeta-Turnu Severin** (Hull) Yd No: (634) **2005-04 Bodewes' Scheepswerven B.V. — Hoogezand** Yd No: 634 Loa 89.94 Br ex - Dght 5.250 Lbp 84.98 Br md 15.20 Dpth 6.90 Welded, 1 dk	**(A31A2GX) General Cargo Ship** Grain: 6,393 TEU 218 Compartments: 1 Ho, ER Ice Capable	**1 oil engine** reduction geared to sc. shafts driving 1 CP propeller Total Power: 1,850kW (2,515hp) 12.0kn MaK 6M25 1 x 4 Stroke 6 Cy. 255 x 400 1850kW (2515bhp) Caterpillar Motoren GmbH & Co. KG-Germany AuxGen: 1 x 400/220V a.c, 1 x 400/220V a.c Thrusters: 1 Tunnel thruster (f)
9442433 *LCBM* -	**SIEM AMETHYST** **Siem Offshore Rederi AS** Siem Offshore AS *Kristiansand* *Norway* MMSI: 259801000	**7,473** 2,241 4,250	Class: NV	**2011-04 OAO Khersonskiy Sudostroitelnyy Zavod — Kherson** (Hull) Yd No: (336) **2011-04 Kleven Verft AS — Ulsteinvik** Yd No: 336 Loa 91.00 (BB) Br ex 22.04 Dght 7.900 Lbp 79.35 Br md 22.00 Dpth 9.60 Welded, 1 dk	**(B21B20A) Anchor Handling Tug Supply** Cranes: 1x27.5t; Gantry cranes: 1x42t Ice Capable	**4 diesel electric oil engines** driving 2 gen. each 2100kW 690V a.c Connecting to 2 elec. motors each (2400kW) reduction geared to sc. shafts driving 2 CP propellers Total Power: 20,096kW (27,322hp) 10.0kn Caterpillar 3516C 2 x Vee 4 Stroke 16 Cy. 170 x 215 each-2158kW (2934bhp) Caterpillar Inc-USA Wartsila 16V32 2 x Vee 4 Stroke 16 Cy. 320 x 400 each-7890kW (10727bhp) Wartsila Finland Oy-Finland AuxGen: 2 x 3400kW 690V 60Hz a.c Thrusters: 2 Tunnel thruster (f); 1 Retract. directional thruster (f); 2 Tunnel thruster (a) Fuel: 1020.0 (d.f.)
9417725 *LARB* -	**SIEM AQUAMARINE** **Siem Offshore Rederi AS** Siem Offshore AS *Kristiansand* *Norway* MMSI: 257662000	**7,473** 2,241 4,250	Class: NV	**2010-05 'Crist' Sp z oo — Gdansk** (Hull) **2010-05 Kleven Verft AS — Ulsteinvik** Yd No: 333 Loa 91.00 (BB) Br ex 22.04 Dght 7.900 Lbp 79.35 Br md 22.00 Dpth 9.60 Welded, 1 dk	**(B21B20A) Anchor Handling Tug Supply** A-frames: 1; Cranes: 1 Ice Capable	**4 diesel electric oil engines** driving 2 gen. each 2100kW 690V a.c Connecting to 2 elec. motors each (2400kW) reduction geared to sc. shafts driving 2 CP propellers Total Power: 18,954kW (25,770hp) 10.0kn Caterpillar 3516C 2 x Vee 4 Stroke 16 Cy. 170 x 190 each-1587kW (2158bhp) Caterpillar Inc-USA Wartsila 16V32 2 x Vee 4 Stroke 16 Cy. 320 x 400 each-7890kW (10727bhp) Wartsila Finland Oy-Finland Thrusters: 2 Tunnel thruster (f); 1 Retract. directional thruster (f); 2 Tunnel thruster (a) Fuel: 1020.0 (d.f.)
9578660 *PYYI* -	**SIEM ATLAS** **Siem Offshore do Brasil SA** - *Rio de Janeiro* *Brazil* MMSI: 710000563	**3,933** 1,180 4,700	Class: NV	**2013-05 Vard Niteroi SA — Niteroi** Yd No: PRO-29 Loa 87.90 (BB) Br ex 19.24 Dght 6.600 Lbp 79.38 Br md 19.00 Dpth 8.00 Welded, 1 dk	**(B21A20S) Platform Supply Ship**	**4 diesel electric oil engines** driving 4 gen. Connecting to 2 elec. motors driving 2 Azimuth electric drive units Total Power: 7,060kW (9,600hp) 11.0kn Caterpillar 3512C 4 x Vee 4 Stroke 12 Cy. 170 x 215 each-1765kW (2400bhp) Caterpillar Inc-USA Thrusters: 2 Tunnel thruster (f)
9604873 *PYYK* -	**SIEM CAETES** **Siem Offshore do Brasil SA** - *Rio de Janeiro* *Brazil* MMSI: 710000373 Official number: 30467	**492** 147 354	Class: AB	**2011-09 Industria Naval do Ceara S.A. (INACE) — Fortaleza** Yd No: 580 Loa 50.00 Br ex 10.00 Dght 2.700 Lbp - Br md 9.75 Dpth 4.00 Welded, 1 dk	**(B21A20C) Crew/Supply Vessel** Hull Material: Aluminium Alloy	**4 oil engines** reduction geared to sc. shafts driving 4 FP propellers Total Power: 5,296kW (7,200hp) 15.0kn Cummins KTA-50-M2 4 x Vee 4 Stroke 16 Cy. 159 x 159 each-1324kW (1800bhp) Cummins Engine Co Inc-USA AuxGen: 2 x 90kW a.c, 2 x 165kW a.c Thrusters: 2 Tunnel thruster (f) Fuel: 22.0
9604885 *PY2002* -	**SIEM CARAJAS** **Siem Offshore do Brasil SA** - *Rio de Janeiro* *Brazil* MMSI: 710000445 Official number: 30473	**492** 147 350	Class: AB	**2012-03 Industria Naval do Ceara S.A. (INACE) — Fortaleza** Yd No: 581 Loa 50.00 Br ex 10.00 Dght 2.700 Lbp - Br md 9.75 Dpth 4.00 Welded, 1 dk	**(B21A20C) Crew/Supply Vessel** Hull Material: Aluminium Alloy	**4 oil engines** reduction geared to sc. shafts driving 4 FP propellers Total Power: 5,968kW (8,116hp) 15.0kn Cummins KTA-50-M2 4 x Vee 4 Stroke 16 Cy. 159 x 159 each-1492kW (2029bhp) Cummins Engine Co Inc-USA AuxGen: 2 x 90kW a.c, 2 x 165kW a.c Thrusters: 2 Tunnel thruster (f) Fuel: 110.0 (d.f.)

9121845 *LNJD3* -	**SIEM CARRIER** *ex Ocean Carrier -2006 ex Inverclyde -2005* *ex Stirling Clyde -2002* **Siem Offshore Rederi AS** Siem Offshore do Brasil SA *Aalesund* *Norway (NIS)* MMSI: 259672000	**3,017** 1,462 4,688 T/cm 13.0	Class: LR ✠ **100A1** SS 09/2011 offshore supply ship ✠ **LMC** **UMS** Eq.Ltr: (V) ; Cable: 1210.0/45.0 U3	**1996**-09 **Ferguson Shipbuilders Ltd — Port Glasgow** Yd No: 612 Converted From: Offshore Supply Ship-2007 Loa 83.00 (BB) Br ex 19.29 Dght 6.310 Lbp 75.80 Br md 19.00 Dpth 7.60 Welded, 1 dk	**(B34D2SL) Cable Layer**	**2 oil engines** with clutches, flexible couplings & sr geared to sc. shafts driving 2 CP propellers Total Power: 4,920kW (6,690hp) 11.0kn Wartsila 6R32E 2 x 4 Stroke 6 Cy. 320 x 350 each-2460kW (3345bhp) Wartsila Diesel Oy-Finland AuxGen: 2 x 1800kW 440V 60Hz a.c, 1 x 335kW 440V 60Hz a.c Thrusters: 1 Retract. directional thruster (f); 1 Thwart. CP thruster (f); 2 Thwart. CP thruster (a) Fuel: 250.0 (r.f.) (Part Heating Coils) 930.0 (d.f.) 12.0pd
9660102 *5BXQ3* -	**SIEM DAYA 1** **Siem Offshore Rederi AS** Siem Offshore AS *Limassol* *Cyprus* MMSI: 210708000 Official number: 9660102	**8,594** 2,579 5,000	Class: NV	**2013**-08 **Vard Tulcea SA — Tulcea** (Hull) Yd No: (793) **2013**-08 **Vard Brattvaag — Brattvaag** Yd No: 793 Loa 120.80 (BB) Br ex 25.90 Dght 6.600 Lbp 110.80 Br md 22.00 Dpth 9.00 Welded, 1 dk	**(B22A2OR) Offshore Support Vessel** Cranes: 1x250t,1x50t Ice Capable	**4 diesel electric oil engines** driving 4 gen. Connecting to 2 elec. motors driving 2 Azimuth electric drive units Total Power: 12,000kW (16,316hp) Wartsila 6L32 2 x each-3000kW (4079bhp) Wartsila Finland Oy-Finland Wartsila 6L32 2 x 4 Stroke 6 Cy. 320 x 400 each-3000kW (4079bhp) Wartsila Finland Oy-Finland Thrusters: 2 Tunnel thruster (f); 1 Retract. directional thruster (f)
9660114 *5BZQ3* -	**SIEM DAYA 2** **Siem Offshore Rederi AS** Siem Offshore AS *Cyprus* MMSI: 212253000	**8,594** 2,579 5,000	Class: NV	**2013**-12 **Vard Tulcea SA — Tulcea** (Hull) Yd No: (794) **2013**-12 **Vard Brattvaag — Brattvaag** Yd No: 794 Loa 120.80 (BB) Br ex - Dght 6.600 Lbp 110.80 Br md 22.00 Dpth 9.00 Welded, 1 dk	**(B22A2OR) Offshore Support Vessel** Cranes: 1x250t Ice Capable	**4 diesel electric oil engines** driving 4 gen. Connecting to 2 elec. motors driving 2 Azimuth electric drive units Total Power: 12,000kW (16,316hp) Wartsila 6L32 4 x 4 Stroke 6 Cy. 320 x 400 each-3000kW (4079bhp) Wartsila Finland Oy-Finland Thrusters: 2 Tunnel thruster (f); 1 Retract. directional thruster (f)
9417749 *LAXK3* -	**SIEM DIAMOND** **Siem Offshore Rederi AS** Siem Offshore AS *Kristiansand* *Norway (NIS)* MMSI: 259029000	**7,473** 2,241 4,250	Class: NV	**2010**-10 **'Crist' SA — Gdansk** (Hull) **2010**-10 **Kleven Verft AS — Ulsteinvik** Yd No: 335 Loa 91.00 (BB) Br ex 22.04 Dght 7.950 Lbp 79.35 Br md 22.00 Dpth 9.60 Welded, 1 dk	**(B21B20A) Anchor Handling Tug Supply** Double Hull Ice Capable	**4 diesel electric oil engines** driving 2 gen. each 2100kW 690V a.c Connecting to 2 elec. motors each (2400kW) reduction geared to sc. shafts driving 2 CP propellers Total Power: 20,096kW (27,322hp) 10.0kn Caterpillar 3516C 2 x Vee 4 Stroke 16 Cy. 170 x 215 each-2158kW (2934bhp) Caterpillar Inc-USA Wartsila 16V32 2 x Vee 4 Stroke 16 Cy. 320 x 400 each-7890kW (10727bhp) Wartsila Finland Oy-Finland AuxGen: 2 x 3400kW 690V 60Hz a.c Thrusters: 2 Tunnel thruster (f); 1 Retract. directional thruster (f); 2 Tunnel thruster (a) Fuel: 1020.0 (d.f.)
9417701 *LARH3* -	**SIEM EMERALD** **Siem Offshore Rederi AS** Siem Offshore AS *Kristiansand* *Norway (NIS)* MMSI: 257434000	**7,473** 2,241 4,250	Class: NV	**2009**-12 **Kleven Verft AS — Ulsteinvik** Yd No: 329 Loa 91.00 (BB) Br ex 22.04 Dght 7.950 Lbp 79.35 Br md 22.00 Dpth 9.60 Welded, 1 dk	**(B21B20A) Anchor Handling Tug Supply** Double Hull Cranes: 1x10t Ice Capable	**4 diesel electric oil engines** driving 2 gen. each 2100kW 690V a.c Connecting to 2 elec. motors each (2400kW) reduction geared to sc. shafts driving 2 CP propellers Total Power: 20,096kW (27,322hp) 10.0kn Caterpillar 3516C 2 x Vee 4 Stroke 16 Cy. 170 x 215 each-2158kW (2934bhp) Caterpillar Inc-USA Wartsila 16V32 2 x Vee 4 Stroke 16 Cy. 320 x 400 each-7890kW (10727bhp) Wartsila Finland Oy-Finland AuxGen: 2 x 3400kW 690V 60Hz a.c Thrusters: 2 Tunnel thruster (f); 1 Retract. directional thruster (f); 2 Tunnel thruster (a) Fuel: 1020.0 (d.f.)
9442421 *LCBN* -	**SIEM GARNET** **Zenith Energy Pte Ltd** Siem Offshore AS SatCom: Inmarsat C 425908310 *Kristiansand* *Norway* MMSI: 259083000	**7,473** 2,241 4,250	Class: NV	**2010**-11 **Kleven Verft AS — Ulsteinvik** Yd No: 335 Loa 91.00 (BB) Br ex 22.04 Dght 7.950 Lbp 79.35 Br md 22.00 Dpth 9.60 Welded, 1 dk	**(B21B20A) Anchor Handling Tug Supply** Ice Capable	**4 diesel electric oil engines** driving 2 gen. each 2100kW 690V a.c Connecting to 2 elec. motors each (2400kW) driving 2 CP propellers Total Power: 20,096kW (27,322hp) 10.0kn Caterpillar 3516C 2 x Vee 4 Stroke 16 Cy. 170 x 215 each-2158kW (2934bhp) Caterpillar Inc-USA Wartsila 16V32 2 x Vee 4 Stroke 16 Cy. 320 x 400 each-7890kW (10727bhp) Wartsila Finland Oy-Finland AuxGen: 2 x 3400kW 690V 60Hz a.c Thrusters: 2 Tunnel thruster (f); 1 Retract. directional thruster (f); 2 Tunnel thruster (a) Fuel: 1020.0 (d.f.)
9384461 *LASX3* -	**SIEM HANNE** **Siem Offshore Rederi AS** Siem Offshore AS SatCom: Inmarsat C 425894110 *Aalesund* *Norway (NIS)* MMSI: 258941000	**2,615** 794 3,750	Class: NV	**2007**-10 **SC Aker Tulcea SA — Tulcea** (Hull) Yd No: 359 **2007**-10 **Aker Yards AS Aukra — Aukra** Yd No: 126 Loa 73.40 (BB) Br ex - Dght 6.500 Lbp 64.00 Br md 16.60 Dpth 7.60 Welded, 1 dk	**(B21A20S) Platform Supply Ship**	**2 oil engines** reduction geared to sc. shafts driving 2 CP propellers Total Power: 3,800kW (5,166hp) 12.0kn Caterpillar 3606 2 x 4 Stroke 6 Cy. 280 x 300 each-1900kW (2583bhp) Caterpillar Inc-USA AuxGen: 2 x a.c, 2 x a.c Thrusters: 1 Tunnel thruster (f); 1 Retract. directional thruster (f); 2 Tunnel thruster (a)
9355977 *LARA7* -	**SIEM LOUISA** **Siem Offshore Rederi AS** Siem Offshore AS *Aalesund* *Norway (NIS)* MMSI: 258666000	**2,465** 859 3,570	Class: NV	**2006**-09 **OAO Vyborgskiy Sudostroitelnyy Zavod — Vyborg** (Hull) Yd No: 043 **2006**-09 **Aker Yards AS Aukra — Aukra** Yd No: 119 Loa 73.40 (BB) Br ex 16.63 Dght 6.500 Lbp 64.00 Br md 16.60 Dpth 7.60 Welded, 1 dk	**(B21A20S) Platform Supply Ship**	**2 oil engines** geared to sc. shafts driving 2 CP propellers Total Power: 4,060kW (5,520hp) 14.0kn Caterpillar 3606 2 x 4 Stroke 6 Cy. 280 x 300 each-2030kW (2760bhp) Caterpillar Inc-USA AuxGen: 2 x 320kW a.c, 2 x 1300kW a.c Thrusters: 2 Tunnel thruster (f); 2 Tunnel thruster (a) Fuel: 1016.5 (r.f.)
9408994 *LAQQ3* -	**SIEM MARLIN** **Siem Offshore Rederi AS** Siem Offshore AS *Aalesund* *Norway (NIS)* MMSI: 259628000	**4,869** 1,616 4,214	Class: NV	**2009**-02 **Kleven Verft AS — Ulsteinvik** Yd No: 323 Loa 93.60 (BB) Br ex 19.74 Dght 6.300 Lbp 86.60 Br md 19.70 Dpth 7.85 Welded, 1 dk	**(B21A20S) Platform Supply Ship** Cranes: 1x100t Ice Capable	**4 diesel electric oil engines** driving 4 gen. each 2188kW a.c Connecting to 2 elec. motors each (2200kW) driving 2 Azimuth electric drive units Total Power: 8,999kW (12,235hp) 12.0kn Caterpillar 3516C 4 x Vee 4 Stroke 16 Cy. 170 x 215 each-2158kW (2934bhp) Caterpillar Inc-USA AuxGen: 2 x 550kW a.c Thrusters: 1 Retract. directional thruster (f); 2 Thwart. CP thruster (f) Fuel: 1150.0 (d.f.)
9676216 *LARE7* -	**SIEM MOXIE** **Siem Offshore Rederi AS** Siem Offshore AS *Kristiansand* *Norway* MMSI: 258704000	**4,367** 1,311 2,835	Class: NV	**2014**-04 **Fjellstrand AS — Omastrand** Yd No: 1697 **2014**-04 **Ada Denizcilik ve Tersane Isletmeciligi AS — Istanbul (Tuzla)** (Hull) Loa 74.00 Br ex - Dght 6.000 Lbp 67.90 Br md 17.00 Dpth 8.00 Welded, 1 dk	**(B22A2OR) Offshore Support Vessel**	**2 oil engines** Connecting to 2 elec. motors each (1850kW) reduction geared to sc. shaft (s) driving 2 Voith-Schneider propellers M.T.U. 2 x 4 Stroke Thrusters: 2 Tunnel thruster (f); 1 Retract. directional thruster (f)

IMO / Call sign	Name / Owner / Manager	Tonnage	Class	Builder / Dimensions	Type	Machinery
9442419 *LAXM* -	**SIEM OPAL** **Neptune Energy Pte Ltd** Siem Offshore AS SatCom: Inmarsat C 425970410 *Kristiansand* *Norway* MMSI: 259704000	**7,473** 2,241 4,250	Class: NV	**2011**-01 **OAO Khersonskiy Sudostroitelnyy Zavod — Kherson** (Hull) Yd No: (334) **2011**-01 **Kleven Verft AS — Ulsteinvik** Yd No: 334 Loa 91.00 (BB) Br ex 22.04 Dght 7.950 Lbp 79.35 Br md 22.00 Dpth 9.60 Welded, 1 dk	**(B21B20A) Anchor Handling Tug Supply** Cranes: 1x27.5t; Gantry cranes: 42x1t Ice Capable	**4 diesel electric oil engines** driving 2 gen. each 2100kW 690V a.c Connecting to 2 elec. motors each (2400kW) reduction geared to ssc. shafts driving 2 CP propellers Total Power: 20,096kW (27,322hp) 10.0kn Caterpillar 3516C 2 x Vee 4 Stroke 16 Cy. 170 x 215 each-2158kW (2934bhp) Caterpillar Inc-USA Wartsila 16V32 2 x Vee 4 Stroke 16 Cy. 320 x 400 each-7890kW (10727bhp) Wartsila Finland Oy-Finland AuxGen: 2 x 3400kW 690V 60Hz a.c Thrusters: 2 Tunnel thruster (f); 1 Retract. directional thruster (f); 2 Tunnel thruster (a) Fuel: 1020.0 (d.f.)
9417684 *LAQW3* -	**SIEM PEARL** **Siem Offshore Rederi AS** Siem Offshore AS SatCom: Inmarsat C 425728610 *Kristiansand* *Norway (NIS)* MMSI: 257286000	**7,473** 2,241 4,250	Class: NV	**2009**-09 **Kleven Verft AS — Ulsteinvik** Yd No: 327 Loa 91.00 (BB) Br ex 22.04 Dght 7.950 Lbp 79.35 Br md 22.00 Dpth 9.60 Welded, 1 dk	**(B21B20A) Anchor Handling Tug Supply** Double Hull Passengers: cabins: 40 Ice Capable	**4 diesel electric oil engines** driving 2 gen. each 2100kW 690V a.c Connecting to 2 elec. motors each (2400kW) reduction geared to sc. shafts driving 2 CP propellers Total Power: 20,096kW (27,322hp) 10.0kn Caterpillar 3516C 2 x Vee 4 Stroke 16 Cy. 170 x 215 each-2158kW (2934bhp) Caterpillar Inc-USA Wartsila 16V32 2 x Vee 4 Stroke 16 Cy. 320 x 400 each-7890kW (10727bhp) Wartsila Finland Oy-Finland AuxGen: 2 x 3400kW 690V 60Hz a.c Thrusters: 2 Tunnel thruster (f); 1 Retract. directional thruster (f); 2 Tunnel thruster (a) Fuel: 1020.0 (d.f.)
9604902 *PY2017* -	**SIEM PENDOTIBA** **Siem Offshore do Brasil SA** - *Rio de Janeiro* *Brazil* MMSI: 710007010 Official number: 30622	**247** 74 117	Class: BV	**2011**-02 **ETP Engenharia Ltda — Niteroi** Yd No: 019/09 Loa 36.00 Br ex - Dght 1.500 Lbp 32.90 Br md 7.50 Dpth 3.50 Welded, 1 dk	**(B34J2SD) Crew Boat** Hull Material: Aluminium Alloy	**3 oil engines** reduction geared to sc. shafts driving 3 Propellers Total Power: 2,460kW (3,345hp) 20.0kn Caterpillar C32 3 x Vee 4 Stroke 12 Cy. 145 x 162 each-820kW (1115bhp) Caterpillar Inc-USA AuxGen: 2 x 99kW a.c Thrusters: 1 Tunnel thruster (f)
9604897 *PQAG* -	**SIEM PIATA** **Siem Offshore do Brasil SA** - *Aracaju* *Brazil* MMSI: 710006470 Official number: 30621	**247** 74 117	Class: BV	**2011**-02 **ETP Engenharia Ltda — Niteroi** Yd No: 018/09 Loa 36.00 Br ex - Dght 3.000 Lbp 32.90 Br md 7.50 Dpth 5.60 Welded, 1 dk	**(B34J2SD) Crew Boat** Hull Material: Aluminium Alloy Passengers: unberthed: 60	**3 oil engines** reduction geared to sc. shafts driving 3 Water jets Total Power: 2,460kW (3,345hp) 20.0kn Caterpillar C32 3 x Vee 4 Stroke 12 Cy. 145 x 162 each-820kW (1115bhp) Caterpillar Inc-USA AuxGen: 2 x 99kW 60Hz a.c Thrusters: 1 Tunnel thruster (f)
9510307 *LCPF* -	**SIEM PILOT** **Siem Meling Offshore DA** O H Meling & Co AS *Stavanger* *Norway* MMSI: 257458000	**5,106** 1,531 4,800	Class: NV	**2010**-03 **Umo Gemi Sanayi ve Ticaret Ltd — Karadeniz Eregli** (Hull) Yd No: 09 **2010**-03 **Eidsvik Skipsbyggeri AS — Uskedalen** Yd No: 75 Loa 88.30 (BB) Br ex - Dght 7.210 Lbp 77.70 Br md 20.00 Dpth 8.60 Welded, 1 dk	**(B21A20S) Platform Supply Ship** Cranes: 1x70t Ice Capable	**4 diesel electric oil engines** driving 4 gen. each 2188kW a.c Connecting to 2 elec. motors each (2200kW) driving 2 Azimuth electric drive units Total Power: 10,100kW (13,732hp) 12.5kn Caterpillar 3516C 4 x Vee 4 Stroke 16 Cy. 170 x 215 each-2525kW (3433bhp) Caterpillar Inc-USA Thrusters: 2 Thwart. CP thruster (f); 1 Retract. directional thruster (f)
9413444 *LKJV3* -	**SIEM RUBY** *launched as* Normand Prosper *-2010* **Siem Offshore Rederi AS** Siem Offshore AS *Kristiansund* *Norway (NIS)* MMSI: 257733000	**7,558** 2,267 5,250	Class: NV	**2010**-06 **'Crist' Sp z oo — Gdansk** (Hull) **2010**-06 **Kleven Verft AS — Ulsteinvik** Yd No: 332 Loa 91.00 (BB) Br ex 22.04 Dght 7.950 Lbp 79.35 Br md 22.00 Dpth 9.60 Welded, 1 dk	**(B21B20A) Anchor Handling Tug Supply** Ice Capable	**2 oil engines** reduction geared to sc. shafts driving 2 CP propellers Total Power: 16,000kW (21,754hp) 18.5kn Wartsila 16V32 2 x Vee 4 Stroke 16 Cy. 320 x 400 each-8000kW (10877bhp) Wartsila Finland Oy-Finland AuxGen: 2 x 60Hz a.c Thrusters: 1 Retract. directional thruster (f); 2 Tunnel thruster (f); 2 Tunnel thruster (a)
9370070 *LNVG* -	**SIEM SAILOR** **Siem Meling Offshore DA** O H Meling & Co AS SatCom: Inmarsat C 425826810 *Stavanger* *Norway* MMSI: 258268000	**4,601** 1,380 4,800	Class: NV	**2007**-12 **Societatea Comerciala Severnav S.A. — Drobeta-Turnu Severin** (Hull) Yd No: 0260006 **2007**-12 **Karmsund Maritime Service AS — Kopervik** Yd No: 26 Loa 85.00 (BB) Br ex 20.03 Dght 7.200 Lbp 77.70 Br md 20.00 Dpth 8.60 Welded, 1 dk	**(B21A20S) Platform Supply Ship** Ice Capable	**4 diesel electric oil engines** driving 4 gen. each 1901kW a.c Connecting to 2 elec. motors driving 2 Azimuth electric drive units Total Power: 7,604kW (10,340hp) 12.0kn Caterpillar 3516B-TA 4 x Vee 4 Stroke 16 Cy. 170 x 190 each-1901kW (2585bhp) Caterpillar Inc-USA Thrusters: 2 Tunnel thruster (f); 1 Retract. directional thruster (f) Fuel: 950.0 (d.f.)
9417696 *LARG3* -	**SIEM SAPPHIRE** **Siem Offshore Rederi AS** Siem Offshore AS *Kristiansand* *Norway (NIS)* MMSI: 257544000	**7,473** 2,241 4,250	Class: NV	**2010**-03 **OAO Khersonskiy Sudostroitelnyy Zavod — Kherson** (Hull) Yd No: (331) **2010**-03 **Myklebust Mek. Verksted AS — Gursken** (Hull completed by) Yd No: 331 **2010**-03 **Kleven Verft AS — Ulsteinvik** Yd No: 331 Loa 91.00 (BB) Br ex 22.04 Dght 7.900 Lbp 79.35 Br md 22.00 Dpth 9.60 Welded, 1 dk	**(B21B20A) Anchor Handling Tug Supply** Double Hull Ice Capable	**4 diesel electric oil engines** driving 2 gen. each 2100kW 690V a.c Connecting to 2 elec. motors each (2400kW) reduction geared to sc. shafts driving 2 CP propellers Total Power: 20,096kW (27,322hp) 10.0kn Caterpillar 3516C 2 x Vee 4 Stroke 16 Cy. 170 x 215 each-2158kW (2934bhp) Caterpillar Inc-USA Wartsila 16V32 2 x Vee 4 Stroke 16 Cy. 320 x 400 each-7890kW (10727bhp) Wartsila Finland Oy-Finland AuxGen: 2 x 3400kW 690V 60Hz a.c Thrusters: 2 Tunnel thruster (f); 1 Retract. directional thruster (f); 2 Tunnel thruster (a) Fuel: 1020.0 (d.f.)
9334533 *LFW3* -	**SIEM SASHA** *ex* Sasha *-2007* **Siem Offshore Rederi AS** Siem Offshore AS *Aalesund* *Norway (NIS)* MMSI: 257117000	**2,465** 859 3,555	Class: NV (IR)	**2005**-10 **SC Aker Braila SA — Braila** (Hull) Yd No: 1078 **2005**-10 **Aker Langsten AS — Tomrefjord** Yd No: 204 Loa 73.40 (BB) Br ex 16.62 Dght 6.500 Lbp 64.00 Br md 16.60 Dpth 7.60 Welded, 1 dk	**(B21A20S) Platform Supply Ship**	**2 oil engines** geared to sc. shafts driving 2 CP propellers Total Power: 4,060kW (5,520hp) 14.5kn Caterpillar 3606 2 x 4 Stroke 6 Cy. 280 x 300 each-2030kW (2760bhp) Caterpillar Inc-USA AuxGen: 2 x 320kW 440V 60Hz a.c, 2 x 1300kW 440V 60Hz a.c Thrusters: 2 Tunnel thruster (f); 2 Tunnel thruster (a)
9424508 *C6YG5* -	**SIEM STORK** *ex* Adams Vision *-2013* *ex* Siem Dorado *-2010* **Siem Offshore Rederi AS** Siem Offshore AS SatCom: Inmarsat C 431100681 *Nassau* *Bahamas* MMSI: 311031800 Official number: 8001727	**4,869** 1,616 4,257	Class: AB (LR) (NV) Classed LR until 9/2/10	**2009**-06 **Kleven Verft AS — Ulsteinvik** Yd No: 326 Loa 93.60 (BB) Br ex - Dght 6.290 Lbp 86.60 Br md 19.69 Dpth 7.85 Welded, 1 dk	**(B21A20S) Platform Supply Ship** Double Hull Cranes: 1x100t Ice Capable	**4 diesel electric oil engines** Connecting to 2 elec. motors each (2200kW) driving 2 Azimuth electric drive units Total Power: 8,632kW (11,736hp) 12.0kn Caterpillar 3516C 4 x Vee 4 Stroke 16 Cy. 170 x 215 each-2158kW (2934bhp) Caterpillar Inc-USA AuxGen: 2 x 550kW a.c Thrusters: 2 Tunnel thruster (f); 1 Retract. directional thruster (f)

Identity	Name / Owner	Tonnage / Class	Builder / Dimensions	Type	Machinery
9186601 *LJKB3* -	**SIEM SUPPLIER** *ex* Stril Supplier *-2007* **Siem Offshore Rederi AS** Aracaju Servicos Auxiliares Ltda SatCom: Inmarsat C 425958310 *Aalesund* *Norway (NIS)* MMSI: 259583000	**3,200** Class: NV 1,422 4,308	**1999**-04 **"De Hoop" Heusden B.V. — Heusden** (Hull) Yd No: 1032 **1999**-04 **Dok- en Werf-Mij. Wilton-Fijenoord B.V. — Schiedam** (Hull completed by) **1999**-04 **YVC Ysselwerf B.V. — Capelle a/d IJssel** Yd No: 273 Loa 83.70 (BB) Br ex - Dght 6.100 Lbp 76.20 Br md 19.70 Dpth 7.45 Welded, 1 dk	**(B21A2OP) Pipe Carrier**	**4 diesel electric oil engines** driving 2 gen. each 1360kW 690V a.c 2 gen. each 1825kW 690V a.c Connecting to 2 elec. motors each (2200kW) driving 2 Directional propellers contra-rotating propellers Total Power: 6,650kW (9,040hp) 12.0kn Caterpillar 3512B 2 x Vee 4 Stroke 12 Cy. 170 x 190 each-1425kW (1937bhp) Caterpillar Inc-USA Caterpillar 3516B 2 x Vee 4 Stroke 16 Cy. 170 x 190 each-1900kW (2583bhp) Caterpillar Inc-USA Thrusters: 1 Thwart. CP thruster (f); 1 Retract. directional thruster (f) Fuel: 1363.0 (d.f.) 8.5pd
9417713 *LARI* -	**SIEM TOPAZ** **Siem Offshore Rederi AS** Siem Offshore AS *Kristiansund* *Norway* MMSI: 257709000	**7,473** Class: NV 2,241 4,250	**2010**-07 **OAO Khersonskiy Sudostroitelnyy Zavod — Kherson** (Hull launched by) Yd No: (334) **2010**-07 **Myklebust Mek. Verksted AS — Gursken** (Hull completed by) Yd No: (334) **2010**-07 **Kleven Verft AS — Ulsteinvik** Yd No: 334 Loa 91.00 (BB) Br ex 22.04 Dght 7.900 Lbp 79.35 Br md 22.00 Dpth 9.60 Welded, 1 dk	**(B21B20A) Anchor Handling Tug Supply** Ice Capable	**2 diesel electric oil engines** Connecting to 2 elec. motors each (2400kW) reduction geared to sc shafts driving 2 CP propellers Total Power: 15,780kW (21,454hp) Wartsila 16V32 2 x Vee 4 Stroke 16 Cy. 320 x 400 each-7890kW (10727bhp) Wartsila Finland Oy-Finland AuxGen: 2 x 3400kW 690V 60Hz a.c, 2 x 2000kW 690V 60Hz a.c Thrusters: 2 Tunnel thruster (f); 1 Retract. directional thruster (f); 2 Tunnel thruster (a) Fuel: 1020.0 (d.f.)
8740046 *EBYG* 3-ST-36-01	**SIEMPRE AL ALBA** **San Felicisimo Martir SL** - *Santona* *Spain* Official number: 3-6/2001	**121** 36 -	**2002**-04 **in Spain** Loa 27.40 Br ex - Dght - Lbp 22.56 Br md - Dpth - Bonded, 1 dk	**(B11B2FV) Fishing Vessel** Hull Material: Reinforced Plastic	**1 oil engine** driving 1 Propeller Total Power: 294kW (400hp)
8731875 *EBYX* 3-VI-53-02	**SIEMPRE ANTARES** **Antares Pesca SL** - *Burela* *Spain* MMSI: 224055240 Official number: 3-3/2002	**335** 100 -	**2002**-01 **Montajes Cies S.L. — Vigo** Loa 33.00 (BB) Br ex - Dght - Lbp 26.00 Br md - Dpth - Welded, 1 dk	**(B11B2FV) Fishing Vessel**	**1 oil engine** driving 1 Propeller Total Power: 367kW (499hp)
8734982 *EA2342* 3-GI-82-94	**SIEMPRE BALUARTE** **Luanco Pesquerias SL** - *Luarca* *Spain* Official number: 3-2/1994	**108** 32 -	**1994**-01 **Astilleros Armon SA — Navia** Loa 22.00 Br ex - Dght 2.420 Lbp 18.00 Br md 6.50 Dpth 2.70 Welded, 1 dk	**(B11B2FV) Fishing Vessel**	**1 oil engine** driving 1 Propeller Total Power: 183kW (249hp)
9166089 *EAPI* 3-FE-26-97	**SIEMPRE BELLA VISTA** **Justo Eijo Eijo & Jose Leal Castro** - *Viveiro* *Spain* MMSI: 224028000 Official number: 3-6/1997	**206** 62 -	**1997**-06 **Astilleros Armon Burela SA — Burela** Yd No: 99 Loa - Br ex - Dght 3.000 Lbp 23.50 Br md 6.70 Dpth 3.40 Welded, 1 dk	**(B11A2FS) Stern Trawler**	**1 oil engine** geared to sc. shaft driving 1 FP propeller Total Power: 199kW (271hp) 10.0kn Caterpillar 3508TA 1 x Vee 4 Stroke 8 Cy. 170 x 190 199kW (271bhp) Caterpillar Inc-USA
8733380 *EBRM* 3-VI-521-0	**SIEMPRE BELUSO** **Jose Perez Balseiro & Antonio Maya Fernandez** - *San Cibrao* *Spain* Official number: 3-21/2000	**371** - -	**2001**-01 **Montajes Cies S.L. — Vigo** Loa 39.00 (BB) Br ex - Dght - Lbp 32.00 Br md 8.10 Dpth 3.65 Welded, 1 dk	**(B11B2FV) Fishing Vessel** Ins: 300	**1 oil engine** geared to sc. shaft driving 1 Propeller Total Power: 451kW (613hp) 10.0kn
8733835 *EAOF* 3-GI-63-99	**SIEMPRE CAMPO EDER** **Miguel Angel Renteria Larranaga** - *Aviles* *Spain* Official number: 3-3/1999	**217** - -	**1999** **Astilleros Ria de Aviles SL — Nieva** Loa 27.50 Br ex - Dght - Lbp 22.00 Br md 7.50 Dpth 3.40 Welded, 1 dk	**(B11A2FS) Stern Trawler**	**1 oil engine** driving 1 Propeller Total Power: 294kW (400hp)
8810865 *LW8552* -	**SIEMPRE DON JOSE MOSCUZZA** *ex* Crevillente *-2003* **Frescomar Argentina SA** - SatCom: Inmarsat C 470181159 *Mar del Plata* *Argentina* MMSI: 701000588 Official number: 02257	*421* Class: (RI) (BV) 136 300	**1990**-05 **Astilleros de Santander SA (ASTANDER) — El Astillero** Yd No: 182 Loa 39.40 (BB) Br ex 9.02 Dght 4.260 Lbp 32.97 Br md 9.01 Dpth 6.18 Welded	**(B11A2FS) Stern Trawler** Ins: 390	**1 oil engine** sr geared to sc. shaft driving 1 CP propeller Total Power: 840kW (1,142hp) 11.0kn Wartsila 6R22 1 x 4 Stroke 6 Cy. 220 x 240 840kW (1142bhp) Construcciones Echevarria SA-Spain
9265299 *EBYT* 3-FE-21-02	**SIEMPRE ELIFE** **Lestao SL** - *La Coruna* *Spain* Official number: 3-1/2002	**344** 132	**2002**-10 **Astilleros Armon Burela SA — Burela** Yd No: 204 Loa 34.20 Br ex - Dght 3.000 Lbp 28.00 Br md 8.00 Dpth 3.60 Welded, 1 dk	**(B11A2FT) Trawler** Ins: 48	**1 oil engine** reduction geared to sc. shaft driving 1 FP propeller Total Power: 419kW (570hp) 10.0kn Caterpillar 1 x 4 Stroke 419kW (570bhp) Caterpillar Inc-USA
8735871 *EA3060* 3-ST-11-97	**SIEMPRE FELICIDAD MADRE** *ex* Abeluche *-2005* *ex* Nuevo Anlu *-2000* **Manuel Angel & Federico Andres Toca Llata** - *Castro-Urdiales* *Spain* Official number: 3-1/1997	**103** 30 -	**1997**-06 **Andres Cajeao Alonso (Gestinaval S.L.) — Cudillero** Loa 25.00 Br ex - Dght 2.720 Lbp 19.85 Br md 6.50 Dpth 3.20 Welded, 1 dk	**(B11B2FV) Fishing Vessel**	**1 oil engine** driving 1 Propeller Total Power: 159kW (216hp) 9.0kn
8733407 *EA3663* 3-VI-714-9	**SIEMPRE JUAN LUIS** *ex* Marivi Dos *-2000* **Perquera Juan Luis** - *La Guardia* *Spain* Official number: 3-14/1999	**235** - -	**1999**-01 **Astilleros Armon Burela SA — Burela** Loa 27.30 (BB) Br ex - Dght - Lbp 23.40 Br md 7.00 Dpth 3.30 Welded, 1 dk	**(B11B2FV) Fishing Vessel**	**1 oil engine** driving 1 Propeller Total Power: 306kW (416hp) 10.4kn
8737609 *EA3951* 3-CT-41-98	**SIEMPRE KALIMA** **Manu Bea SL** - *Cartagena* *Spain* Official number: 3-1/1998	**146** 43 -	**1999**-06 **Nicolas Casas SL — Adra** Loa 25.68 Br ex - Dght - Lbp 22.06 Br md 6.48 Dpth 3.24 Bonded, 1 dk	**(B11B2FV) Fishing Vessel** Hull Material: Reinforced Plastic	**1 oil engine** driving 1 Propeller Total Power: 174kW (237hp) 11.0kn
9221504 *EAXQ* 3-VI-53-00	**SIEMPRE NUEVO ANGEL** **Juan Jose Otero Fernandez & Manuel Sanchez Otero** - *Vigo* *Spain* MMSI: 224452000 Official number: 3-3/2000	**236** 71 -	**2000**-03 **Astilleros Armon Burela SA — Burela** Yd No: 105 Loa - Br ex - Dght 3.250 Lbp 24.05 Br md 7.00 Dpth 3.50 Welded, 1 dk	**(B11B2FV) Fishing Vessel**	**1 oil engine** geared to sc. shaft driving 1 FP propeller Total Power: 250kW (340hp) 9.0kn Caterpillar 3508TA 1 x Vee 4 Stroke 8 Cy. 170 x 190 250kW (340bhp) Caterpillar Inc-USA
8735302 *EA2630* 3-ST-31-96	**SIEMPRE PECO** **Siempre Peco CB** - *Santona* *Spain* Official number: 3-1/1996	**111** 35 -	**1996** **Andres Cajeao Alonso (Gestinaval S.L.) — Cudillero** Loa 27.00 Br ex - Dght 3.110 Lbp 22.00 Br md 6.50 Dpth 3.15 Welded, 1 dk	**(B11B2FV) Fishing Vessel**	**1 oil engine** driving 1 Propeller Total Power: 294kW (400hp) 8.5kn

Identity	Name / Owner / Port	Tonnage	Classification	Construction	Type	Machinery
9266736 *EBZI* 3-VI-57-02	**SIEMPRE PERLA** **Maria Silvia & Rosana Miguez Lopez, Ana Maria Lopez Fernandez, Maria del Carmen Ben Balseiro & Antonio Gomez Diaz** - *Vigo* *Spain* Official number: 3-7/2002	**182** 69 -		**2003**-01 **Montajes Cies S.L. — Vigo** Yd No: 41 Loa 28.00 Br ex - Dght - Lbp 22.40 Br md 6.50 Dpth 3.30 Welded, 1 dk	**(B11B2FV) Fishing Vessel**	**1 oil engine** reduction geared to sc. shaft driving 1 FP propeller GUASCOR 1 x 4 Stroke Gutierrez Ascunce Corp (GUASCOR)-Spain
8739774 *EADY* 3-GI-61-00	**SIEMPRE RATONERO** *ex* Siempre Arca Noe *-2008* **Jose Perez Suarez** - *Aviles* *Spain* Official number: 3-1/2000	**124** - -		**2000**-04 **Astilleros Pineiro, S.L. — Moana** Loa 25.75 (BB) Br ex - Dght 2.530 Lbp 20.90 Br md 6.50 Dpth 3.10 Welded, 1 dk	**(B11B2FV) Fishing Vessel**	**1 oil engine** driving 1 Propeller Total Power: 420kW (571hp)
9344904 *ECDS* 3-LU-24-06	**SIEMPRE REVUELTA** **Sombriza SL** - *Burela* *Spain* MMSI: 224936000 Official number: 3-4/2006	**321** 96 120		**2007**-07 **Montajes Cies S.L. — Vigo** Yd No: 126 Loa 33.50 Br ex - Dght 3.250 Lbp 27.50 Br md 7.50 Dpth 3.65 Welded, 1 dk	**(B11B2FV) Fishing Vessel**	**1 oil engine** reduction geared to sc. shaft driving 1 FP propeller Total Power: 496kW (674hp) A.B.C. 6DXC 1 x 4 Stroke 6 Cy. 242 x 320 496kW (674bhp) Anglo Belgian Corp NV (ABC)-Belgium
9194206 *EA3208* 3-VI-723-9	**SIEMPRE SAN BENITO** **Pesquera Alonso Martinez SL** - *La Guardia* *Spain* MMSI: 224029760 Official number: 3-23/1997	**196** 61 -		**1998**-02 **Montajes Cies S.L. — Vigo** Yd No: 53 Loa 28.00 Br ex - Dght 4.550 Lbp - Br md 6.50 Dpth 3.30 Welded, 1 dk	**(B11A2FS) Stern Trawler**	**1 oil engine** driving 1 FP propeller Total Power: 530kW (721hp) Mitsubishi S6R2-MPTK 1 x 4 Stroke 6 Cy. 170 x 220 530kW (721bhp) Mitsubishi Heavy Industries Ltd-Japan
9163386 *EA2815* 3-FE-24-96	**SIEMPRE SAN PRUDENCIO** **Iberia Lopez Baltar y otros** - *Burela* *Spain* Official number: 3-4/1996	**168** 50 -		**1996**-12 **Montajes Cies S.L. — Vigo** Yd No: 33 Loa - Br ex - Dght - Lbp - Br md - Dpth - Welded, 1 dk	**(B11B2FV) Fishing Vessel**	**1 oil engine** geared to sc. shaft driving 1 FP propeller Caterpillar 1 x 4 Stroke Caterpillar Inc-USA
8600715 *LW6398* -	**SIEMPRE SANTA ROSA** **Frigorifico Mellino SA** - *Puerto Deseado* *Argentina* MMSI: 701006055 Official number: 0494	**119** 94 130	Class: (AB)	**1986**-08 **SANYM S.A. — Buenos Aires** Yd No: 37 Loa 25.51 Br ex - Dght 2.890 Lbp 22.92 Br md 6.51 Dpth 3.31 Welded, 1 dk	**(B11A2FT) Trawler** Ins: 145	**1 oil engine** reverse reduction geared to sc. shaft driving 1 FP propeller Total Power: 397kW (540hp) 10.0kn Caterpillar 3412T 1 x Vee 4 Stroke 12 Cy. 137 x 152 397kW (540bhp) Caterpillar Tractor Co-USA AuxGen: 2 x 60kW a.c
9329150 *EAJH* 3-VI-54-05	**SIEMPRE SANTA TECLA** **Pesquera Santa Tecla SA** - *Vigo* *Spain* MMSI: 224900000 Official number: 3-4/2005	**440** 132 434	Class: (BV)	**2006**-09 **Montajes Cies S.L. — Vigo** Yd No: 62 Loa 40.50 Br ex - Dght 3.700 Lbp 31.90 Br md 8.80 Dpth 5.85 Welded, 1 dk	**(B11B2FV) Fishing Vessel**	**1 oil engine** geared to sc. shaft driving 1 FP propeller Total Power: 956kW (1,300hp) 10.0kn Yanmar 6N21A-SV 1 x 4 Stroke 6 Cy. 210 x 290 956kW (1300bhp) Yanmar Diesel Engine Co Ltd-Japan
9245976 *EBWQ* 3-VI-512-0	**SIEMPRE SOCIO** **Pesquera Aguadoce SL** - *Vigo* *Spain* MMSI: 224445000 Official number: 3-12/2001	**442** 133 248		**2002**-01 **Astilleros Armon Burela SA — Burela** Yd No: 144 Loa 37.50 Br ex - Dght 3.310 Lbp 31.25 Br md 8.10 Dpth 3.80 Welded, 1 dk	**(B11A2FS) Stern Trawler**	**1 oil engine** reduction geared to sc. shaft driving 1 FP propeller Total Power: 451kW (613hp) 10.0kn Caterpillar 3512B-HD 1 x Vee 4 Stroke 12 Cy. 170 x 215 451kW (613bhp) Caterpillar Inc-USA
8706052 *EDVL* -	**SIEMPRE TERIN** **Jose Antonio & Manuel Francisco Marinas Mendez & Arcadia Mendez Rivas** - *Gijon* *Spain* Official number: 3-2138/	*200* 60 105		**1987**-06 **Astilleros Armon SA — Navia** Yd No: 152 Loa 27.31 Br ex - Dght 3.001 Lbp 22.51 Br md 6.51 Dpth 3.51 Welded, 1 dk	**(B11B2FV) Fishing Vessel** Ins: 126	**1 oil engine** with clutches, flexible couplings & reverse reduction geared to sc. shaft driving 1 FP propeller Total Power: 316kW (430hp) Baudouin 1 x 4 Stroke 6 Cy. 160 x 190 316kW (430bhp) Societe des Moteurs Baudouin SA-France
8731825 *ECDN* 3-GI-62-03	**SIEMPRE VIRIATO** **Fernando Iglesias Marques, Dario Iglesias Menendez & Maria Luiz & Anselmo Menendez Martinez** - *Aviles* *Spain* Official number: 3-2/2003	**195** 34 -		**2003**-01 **Andres Cajeao Alonso (Gestinaval S.L.) — Cudillero** Loa 26.00 Br ex - Dght - Lbp 20.68 Br md - Dpth - Welded, 1 dk	**(B11B2FV) Fishing Vessel**	**1 oil engine** driving 1 Propeller Total Power: 367kW (499hp)
9239939 *SYMT* -	**SIENA** **Siena Transportation Special Maritime Enterprise (ENE)** Neda Maritime Agency Co Ltd *Piraeus* *Greece* MMSI: 239914000 Official number: 11040	**56,899** 31,164 105,357 T/cm 95.1	Class: LR ✠ **100A1** SS 07/2012 Double Hull oil tanker ESP *IWS LI SPM **ShipRight** (SDA, FDA, CM) ✠ **LMC** **UMS IGS** Eq.Ltr: U†; Cable: 715.0/90.0 U3 (a)	**2002**-08 **Daewoo Shipbuilding & Marine Engineering Co Ltd — Geoje** Yd No: 5216 Loa 248.00 (BB) Br ex 43.04 Dght 14.300 Lbp 238.00 Br md 43.00 Dpth 21.00 Welded, 1 dk	**(A13A2TV) Crude Oil Tanker** Double Hull (13F) Liq: 122,700; Liq (Oil): 122,700 Compartments: 12 Wing Ta, Wing ER 3 Cargo Pump (s)	**1 oil engine** driving 1 FP propeller Total Power: 15,550kW (21,142hp) 15.2kn MAN-B&W 5S70MC-C 1 x 2 Stroke 5 Cy. 700 x 2800 15550kW (21142bhp) Doosan Engine Co Ltd-South Korea AuxGen: 3 x 700kW 450V 60Hz a.c Boilers: e (ex.g.) 24.0kgf/cm² (23.5bar), WTAuxB (o.f.) 18.9kgf/cm² (18.5bar)
9357640 *3FKN4* -	**SIENE** **Siene SA** Akron Trade & Transport SatCom: Inmarsat C 435595810 *Panama* *Panama* MMSI: 355958000 Official number: 4235211	**8,251** 2,997 11,020	Class: NV (CC)	**2010**-11 **Haidong Shipyard — Taizhou ZJ** Yd No: DBD-2005-032 Loa 129.60 Br ex 20.02 Dght 7.600 Lbp 123.00 Br md 20.00 Dpth 11.50 Welded, 1 dk	**(A12B2TR) Chemical/Products Tanker** Double Hull (13F) Liq: 12,976; Liq (Oil): 12,716 Compartments: 6 Wing Ta, 6 Wing Ta, 1 Wing Slop Ta, 1 Wing Slop Ta, ER	**2 oil engines** reduction geared to sc. shafts driving 2 FP propellers Total Power: 4,000kW (5,438hp) 12.5kn Chinese Std. Type G8300ZC 2 x 4 Stroke 8 Cy. 300 x 380 each-2000kW (2719bhp) Ningbo CSI Power & Machinery GroupCo Ltd-China AuxGen: 3 x 320kW 400V a.c
8823965 - -	**SIENKIEWICZ** *ex* Sin Fat *-1991* *ex* Coral Sea I *-1990* *ex* Ringo *-1990* *ex* Tenei Maru No. 20 *-1989* **Anstel Shipping Corp** - *Panama* *Panama* Official number: 20586HK	*199* 100 401		**1970** **K.K. Yoshida Zosen Kogyo — Arida** Loa 39.30 Br ex - Dght 3.300 Lbp 35.00 Br md 7.98 Dpth 3.60 Welded, 1 dk	**(A24D2BA) Aggregates Carrier**	**1 oil engine** driving 1 FP propeller
9075761 *PG6257* -	**SIER** **Wagenborg Passagiersdiensten BV** Wagenborg Shipping BV *Ameland* *Netherlands* MMSI: 244710741 Official number: 28098	**2,286** 792 1,164	Class: BV	**1995**-02 **Scheepswerf Bijlsma BV — Wartena** Yd No: 666 Loa 73.20 Br ex 15.90 Dght 1.700 Lbp 69.31 Br md 15.10 Dpth 4.45 Welded	**(A36A2PR) Passenger/Ro-Ro Ship (Vehicles)** Passengers: unberthed: 1463 Bow ramp Stern ramp Cars: 72	**4 oil engines** reverse reduction geared to sc. shafts driving 4 Directional propellers 2 fwd and 2 aft Total Power: 2,700kW (3,672hp) 10.8kn Caterpillar 3508TA 4 x Vee 4 Stroke 8 Cy. 170 x 190 each-675kW (918bhp) Caterpillar Inc-USA AuxGen: 2 x 250kW a.c Fuel: 40.0 (d.f.)
6606844 - -	**SIERO 1** *ex* Mestre Costeiro *-2006* *ex* Margie Barry *-1973* *ex* Margie B. *-1967* **Nelson Lucio Pais Quaresma**	*147* 82 295	Class: RP (LR) ✠ Classed LR until 13/10/78	**1965**-11 **Les Chantiers Maritimes de Paspebiac Inc — Paspebiac QC** (Hull) Yd No: 13 **1965**-11 **Marine Industries Ltee (MIL) — Sorel QC** Yd No: 331 Loa 27.00 Br ex 6.62 Dght 2.760 Lbp 23.98 Br md 6.60 Dpth 3.17 Welded, 1 dk	**(B11A2FT) Trawler**	**1 oil engine** sr reverse geared to sc. shaft driving 1 FP propeller Total Power: 515kW (700hp) G.M. (Detroit Diesel) 16V-71 1 x Vee 2 Stroke 16 Cy. 108 x 127 515kW (700bhp) General Motors Corp-USA

7408093 *WSNB* -	**SIERRA** *ex Kenai -2006* **SeaRiver Maritime Inc** - *Wilmington, DE* *United States of America* MMSI: 366238000 Official number: 586127	**64,329** 39,583 125,133 T/cm 97.8	Class: AB	**1979-01 Sun Shipbuilding & Dry Dock Co — Chester PA** Yd No: 669 Loa 264.88 (BB) Br ex 41.51 Dght 16.770 Lbp 251.47 Br md 41.46 Dpth 21.85 Welded, 1 dk	**(A13A2TV) Crude Oil Tanker** Double Hull (13F) Liq: 124,893; Liq (Oil): 127,837 Compartments: 12 Wing Ta, 1 Slop Ta, ER 4 Cargo Pump (s): 3x2964m³/hr, 1x1465m³/hr Manifold: Bow/CM: 130.8m	**1 Steam Turb** dr geared to sc. shaft driving 1 FP propeller Total Power: 22,065kW (30,000hp) 17.0kn General Electric 1 x steam Turb 22065kW (30000shp) General Electric Co.-Lynn, Ma AuxGen: 2 x 1250kW Fuel: 130.0 (d.f.) (Heating Coils) 4800.0 (r.f.) 160.0pd
8419532 *DUC9104* -	**SIERRA** *ex Ketherine A -2004 ex Kazu Maru No. 8 -1999* **Starcki Ventures Corp** - SatCom: Inmarsat A 1363267 *Manila* *Philippines* Official number: MNLD010269	**1,490** 1,080 1,828	Class: (NK)	**1985-03 Kochi Jyuko (Kaisei Zosen) K.K. — Kochi** Yd No: 1782 Loa 81.62 (BB) Br ex - Dght 4.601 Lbp 75.52 Br md 13.61 Dpth 4.65 Welded, 2 dks	**(A34A2GR) Refrigerated Cargo Ship** Ins: 2,550 Compartments: 2 Ho, ER 2 Ha: 2 (3.5 x 3.6)ER Derricks: 4x5t	**1 oil engine** driving 1 FP propeller Total Power: 1,324kW (1,800hp) 12.8kn Akasaka A31 1 x 4 Stroke 6 Cy. 310 x 600 1324kW (1800bhp) Akasaka Tekkosho KK (Akasaka DieselLtd)-Japan AuxGen: 2 x 360kW a.c
8216198 *UAID* -	**SIERRA** *ex Sierra Cazorla -2010* **Eastwad Co Ltd** Ostshipping Co Ltd (OOO 'Ostshipping') *Nakhodka* *Russia* MMSI: 273358510	**2,618** 1,009 2,725	Class: RS (LR) ✠ Classed LR until 8/4/10	**1984-10 Maritima del Musel S.A. — Gijon** Yd No: 249 Loa 91.85 (BB) Br ex 14.25 Dght 5.071 Lbp 84.26 Br md 14.20 Dpth 7.70 Welded, 2 dks	**(A34A2GR) Refrigerated Cargo Ship** Ins: 3,942 Compartments: 4 Ho, ER, 4 Tw Dk 4 Ha: 4 (4.9 x 5.4)ER Cranes: 3	**1 oil engine** with flexible couplings & sr geared to sc. shaft driving 1 CP propeller Total Power: 2,400kW (3,263hp) 13.0kn MaK 8M453AK 1 x 4 Stroke 8 Cy. 320 x 420 2400kW (3263bhp) Krupp MaK Maschinenbau GmbH-Kiel AuxGen: 1 x 520kW 380V 50Hz a.c, 2 x 360kW 380V 50Hz a.c Boilers: AuxB (Comp) 7.5kgf/cm² (7.4bar) Fuel: 78.0 (d.f.) 437.0 (r.f.) 9.0pd
9383778 *T2MN2* -	**SIERRA 3** - **Safe Sea Services FZC** - *Funafuti* *Tuvalu* MMSI: 572314000 Official number: 13380606	**182** 54 175	Class: BV	**2006-05 Albwardy Marine Engineering LLC — Dubai** Yd No: 005 Loa 26.00 Br ex - Dght 2.000 Lbp 23.18 Br md 10.00 Dpth 3.00 Welded, 1 dk	**(B34L2QU) Utility Vessel**	**2 oil engines** reduction geared to sc. shafts driving 2 Z propellers Total Power: 220kW (300hp) 6.0kn G.M. (Detroit Diesel) 6-71-N 2 x 2 Stroke 6 Cy. 108 x 127 each-110kW (150bhp) (made 1980, fitted 1995) Detroit Diesel Corporation-Detroit, Mi
8218770 - -	**SIERRA 6** - - -	*110* - -		**1982-05 Bender Shipbuilding & Repair Co Inc — Mobile AL** Yd No: 163 Loa - Br ex - Dght - Lbp 23.78 Br md 6.71 Dpth 3.51 Welded, 1 dk	**(B11A2FT) Trawler**	**1 oil engine** geared to sc. shaft driving 1 FP propeller Total Power: 305kW (415hp) Caterpillar 3412TA 1 x Vee 4 Stroke 12 Cy. 137 x 152 305kW (415bhp) Caterpillar Tractor Co-USA
8218782 - -	**SIERRA 7** - - -	*110* - -		**1982-05 Bender Shipbuilding & Repair Co Inc — Mobile AL** Yd No: 164 Loa - Br ex - Dght - Lbp 23.78 Br md 6.71 Dpth 3.51 Welded, 1 dk	**(B11A2FT) Trawler**	**1 oil engine** geared to sc. shaft driving 1 FP propeller Total Power: 305kW (415hp) Caterpillar 3412TA 1 x Vee 4 Stroke 12 Cy. 137 x 152 305kW (415bhp) Caterpillar Tractor Co-USA
8218794 - -	**SIERRA 8** - - -	*110* - -		**1982-07 Bender Shipbuilding & Repair Co Inc — Mobile AL** Yd No: 165 Loa - Br ex - Dght - Lbp 23.78 Br md 6.71 Dpth 3.51 Welded, 1 dk	**(B11A2FT) Trawler**	**1 oil engine** geared to sc. shaft driving 1 FP propeller Total Power: 305kW (415hp) Caterpillar 3412TA 1 x Vee 4 Stroke 12 Cy. 137 x 152 305kW (415bhp) Caterpillar Tractor Co-USA
8218809 - -	**SIERRA 9** - - -	*110* - -		**1982-07 Bender Shipbuilding & Repair Co Inc — Mobile AL** Yd No: 166 Loa - Br ex - Dght - Lbp 23.78 Br md 6.71 Dpth 3.51 Welded, 1 dk	**(B11A2FT) Trawler**	**1 oil engine** geared to sc. shaft driving 1 FP propeller Total Power: 305kW (415hp) Caterpillar 3412TA 1 x Vee 4 Stroke 12 Cy. 137 x 152 305kW (415bhp) Caterpillar Tractor Co-USA
8218811 - -	**SIERRA 10** - - -	*110* - -		**1982-09 Bender Shipbuilding & Repair Co Inc — Mobile AL** Yd No: 167 Loa - Br ex - Dght - Lbp 23.78 Br md 6.71 Dpth 3.51 Welded, 1 dk	**(B11A2FT) Trawler**	**1 oil engine** geared to sc. shaft driving 1 FP propeller Total Power: 305kW (415hp) Caterpillar D348TA 1 x Vee 4 Stroke 12 Cy. 137 x 165 305kW (415bhp) Caterpillar Tractor Co-USA
8218823 - -	**SIERRA 11** - - -	*110* - -		**1982-09 Bender Shipbuilding & Repair Co Inc — Mobile AL** Yd No: 168 Loa - Br ex - Dght - Lbp 23.78 Br md 6.71 Dpth 3.51 Welded, 1 dk	**(B11A2FT) Trawler**	**1 oil engine** geared to sc. shaft driving 1 FP propeller Total Power: 305kW (415hp) Caterpillar D348TA 1 x Vee 4 Stroke 12 Cy. 137 x 165 305kW (415bhp) Caterpillar Tractor Co-USA
8218835 - -	**SIERRA 12** - - -	*110* - -		**1982-09 Bender Shipbuilding & Repair Co Inc — Mobile AL** Yd No: 169 Loa - Br ex - Dght - Lbp 23.78 Br md 6.71 Dpth 3.51 Welded, 1 dk	**(B11A2FT) Trawler**	**1 oil engine** geared to sc. shaft driving 1 FP propeller Total Power: 305kW (415hp) Caterpillar D348TA 1 x Vee 4 Stroke 12 Cy. 137 x 165 305kW (415bhp) Caterpillar Tractor Co-USA
8416669 - -	**SIERRA 18** - - -	*177* 53 107		**1985-03 Chungmu Shipbuilding Co Inc — Tongyeong** Yd No: 140 Loa 29.39 Br ex 7.17 Dght 2.518 Lbp 24.01 Br md 7.00 Dpth 3.31 Welded, 1 dk	**(B11A2FS) Stern Trawler**	**1 oil engine** with clutches, flexible couplings & sr reverse geared to sc. shaft driving 1 FP propeller Total Power: 504kW (685hp) Caterpillar 3412T 1 x Vee 4 Stroke 12 Cy. 137 x 152 504kW (685bhp) Caterpillar Tractor Co-USA
8416671 - -	**SIERRA 19** - - -	*177* 53 107		**1985-03 Chungmu Shipbuilding Co Inc — Tongyeong** Yd No: 141 Loa 29.39 Br ex 7.17 Dght 2.493 Lbp 24.01 Br md 7.00 Dpth 3.31 Welded, 1 dk	**(B11A2FS) Stern Trawler**	**1 oil engine** with clutches, flexible couplings & sr reverse geared to sc. shaft driving 1 FP propeller Total Power: 504kW (685hp) Caterpillar 3412T 1 x Vee 4 Stroke 12 Cy. 137 x 152 504kW (685bhp) Caterpillar Tractor Co-USA
8416683 - -	**SIERRA 20** - - -	**177** 53 107		**1985-05 Chungmu Shipbuilding Co Inc — Tongyeong** Yd No: 142 Loa 29.39 Br ex 7.17 Dght 2.518 Lbp 24.01 Br md 7.00 Dpth 3.31 Welded, 1 dk	**(B11A2FS) Stern Trawler** Ins: 133	**1 oil engine** with clutches, flexible couplings & sr reverse geared to sc. shaft driving 1 FP propeller Total Power: 504kW (685hp) Caterpillar 3412T 1 x Vee 4 Stroke 12 Cy. 137 x 152 504kW (685bhp) Caterpillar Tractor Co-USA
8416695 - -	**SIERRA 21** - - -	**177** 53 107		**1985-05 Chungmu Shipbuilding Co Inc — Tongyeong** Yd No: 143 Loa 29.39 Br ex 7.17 Dght 2.518 Lbp 24.01 Br md 7.00 Dpth 3.31 Welded, 1 dk	**(B11A2FS) Stern Trawler** Ins: 133	**1 oil engine** with clutches, flexible couplings & sr reverse geared to sc. shaft driving 1 FP propeller Total Power: 504kW (685hp) Caterpillar 3412T 1 x Vee 4 Stroke 12 Cy. 137 x 152 504kW (685bhp) Caterpillar Tractor Co-USA
9144627 *EAUC* 3-HU-314-9	**SIERRA DE HUELVA** - **Baltimar SA** - *Huelva* *Spain* Official number: 3-14/1998	*305* 91 157	Class: BV	**1998-12 Ast. de Huelva S.A. — Huelva** Yd No: 459 Loa 27.68 (BB) Br ex - Dght 3.350 Lbp 26.70 Br md 7.90 Dpth 5.40 Welded, 1 dk	**(B11B2FV) Fishing Vessel** Ins: 179	**1 oil engine** with flexible couplings & reverse reduction geared to sc. shaft driving 1 FP propeller Total Power: 451kW (613hp) 10.0kn Caterpillar 3512TA 1 x Vee 4 Stroke 12 Cy. 170 x 190 451kW (613bhp) Caterpillar Inc-USA
8810786 *PESF* -	**SIERRA KING** *ex Holland Klipper -2013* **Holland Klipper Shipping Co BV** Seatrade Groningen BV SatCom: Inmarsat C 424454210 *Scheveningen* *Netherlands* MMSI: 244542000 Official number: 4886	**3,999** 2,619 5,450	Class: BV	**1989-09 YVC Ysselwerf B.V. — Capelle a/d IJssel** Yd No: 247 Loa 107.70 (BB) Br ex - Dght 7.560 Lbp 99.95 Br md 16.20 Dpth 9.30 Welded, 1 dk	**(A34A2GR) Refrigerated Cargo Ship** Ins: 7,398 TEU 16 incl 6 ref C Compartments: 3 Ho, ER 4 Ha: 4 (8.8 x 8.5)ER Cranes: 4x5t	**1 oil engine** sr geared to sc. shaft driving 1 CP propeller Total Power: 4,197kW (5,706hp) 16.0kn MaK 8M551AK 1 x 4 Stroke 8 Cy. 450 x 550 4197kW (5706bhp) Krupp MaK Maschinenbau GmbH-Kiel AuxGen: 1 x 1042kW 380V 50Hz a.c, 3 x 480kW 380V 50Hz a.c Thrusters: 1 Tunnel thruster (f) Fuel: 65.0 (d.f.) 520.0 (r.f.) 16.0pd

Ship	Tonnage	Class	Build / Dimensions	Type / Cargo	Machinery
9120205 **SIERRA LARA** *9HA3420* - **Sierra Lara Shipping Co BV** Seatrade Groningen BV *Valletta* *Malta* MMSI: 229575000 Official number: 9120205	**5,110** 2,314 5,970	Class: LR ✠ **100A1** SS 09/2011 *IWS ✠ **LMC** **UMS +Lloyd's RMC** Eq.Ltr: W; Cable: 495.0/44.0 U3	**1996**-09 **Construcciones Navales P Freire SA — Vigo** Yd No: 392 Loa 117.27 (BB) Br ex 17.53 Dght 6.700 Lbp 108.50 Br md 17.50 Dpth 9.75 Welded, 1 dk, 2nd dk in Nos. 1 - 4 holds, 3rd dk in Nos 2 - 4 holds	**(A34A2GR) Refrigerated Cargo Ship** Ins: 7,364 TEU 41 incl 41 ref C. Compartments: 4 Ho, ER, 1 Tw Dk in Fo'c's'l, 3 Tw Dk 4 Ha: (7.7 x 8.0)3 (7.8 x 8.0)ER Cranes: 4x5t	**1 oil engine** driving 1 CP propeller Total Power: 4,902kW (6,665hp) 16.8kn B&W 7S35MC 1 x 2 Stroke 7 Cy. 350 x 1400 4902kW (6665bhp) Manises Diesel Engine Co. S.A.-Valencia AuxGen: 1 x 650kW 380V 50Hz a.c, 2 x 650kW 380V 50Hz a.c, 1 x 350kW 380V 50Hz a.c Boilers: AuxB (Comp) 7.1kgf/cm² (7.0bar) Thrusters: 1 Thwart. FP thruster (f) Fuel: 1079.5 (d.f.)
9163403 **SIERRA LAUREL** *9HA3533* - **Sierra Laurel Shipping Co BV** Seatrade Shipmanagement BV *Valletta* *Malta* Official number: 9163403	**5,100** 2,314 5,937	Class: LR ✠ **100A1** SS 02/2013 ✠ **LMC** **UMS +Lloyd's RMC** Eq.Ltr: W; Cable: 495.0/44.0 U3	**1998**-01 **Construcciones Navales P Freire SA — Vigo** Yd No: 395 Loa 117.27 (BB) Br ex 17.53 Dght 6.500 Lbp 108.50 Br md 17.50 Dpth 9.75 Welded, 1 dk, 2nd dk in Nos. 1 - 4 holds, 3rd dk in Nos 2 - 4 holds	**(A34A2GR) Refrigerated Cargo Ship** Ins: 7,420 TEU 41 incl 41 ref C Compartments: 4 Ho, ER, 1 Tw Dk in Fo'c's'l, 3 Tw Dk 4 Ha: (7.7 x 8.0)3 (7.8 x 8.0)ER Cranes: 4x5t	**1 oil engine** driving 1 CP propeller Total Power: 4,900kW (6,662hp) 16.0kn B&W 7S35MC 1 x 2 Stroke 7 Cy. 350 x 1400 4900kW (6662bhp) MAN B&W Diesel A/S-Denmark AuxGen: 1 x 650kW 380V 50Hz a.c, 2 x 650kW 380V 50Hz a.c, 1 x 350kW 380V 50Hz a.c Boilers: AuxB (Comp) 7.1kgf/cm² (7.0bar) Thrusters: 1 Thwart. FP thruster (f) Fuel: 825.0 (d.f.) 715.0 (r.f.)
9135822 **SIERRA LEYRE** *PCPM* - **Sierra Leyre Shipping Co BV** Seatrade Groningen BV *Groningen* *Netherlands* MMSI: 245973000	**5,100** 2,314 5,937	Class: LR ✠ **100A1** SS 07/2012 ✠ **LMC** **UMS +Lloyd's RMC** Eq.Ltr: W; Cable: 495.0/44.0 U3	**1997**-07 **Construcciones Navales P Freire SA — Vigo** Yd No: 394 Loa 117.27 (BB) Br ex 17.53 Dght 6.500 Lbp 108.50 Br md 17.50 Dpth 9.75 Welded, 3 dks	**(A34A2GR) Refrigerated Cargo Ship** Ins: 7,364 TEU 41 incl 41 ref C Compartments: 4 Ho, ER, 4 Tw Dk 4 Ha: ER Cranes: 4x5t	**1 oil engine** driving 1 CP propeller Total Power: 4,900kW (6,662hp) 16.8kn B&W 7S35MC 1 x 2 Stroke 7 Cy. 350 x 1400 4900kW (6662bhp) MAN B&W Diesel A/S-Denmark AuxGen: 1 x 650kW 380V 50Hz a.c, 2 x 650kW 380V 50Hz a.c, 1 x 350kW 380V 50Hz a.c Boilers: AuxB (Comp) 7.1kgf/cm² (7.0bar) Thrusters: 1 Thwart. CP thruster (f)
9120217 **SIERRA LOBA** *PJYS* - **Sierra Loba Shipping Co BV** Seatrade Groningen BV SatCom: Inmarsat C 430687211 *Willemstad* *Curacao* MMSI: 306872000 Official number: 2008-C-1962	**5,100** 2,314 5,970	Class: LR ✠ **100A1** SS 10/2011 ✠ **LMC** **UMS +Lloyd's RMC** Eq.Ltr: W; Cable: 495.0/44.0 U3	**1997**-02 **Construcciones Navales P Freire SA — Vigo** Yd No: 393 Loa 117.27 (BB) Br ex 17.53 Dght 6.700 Lbp 108.50 Br md 17.50 Dpth 9.75 Welded, 1 dk, 2nd dk in Nos. 1 - 4 holds, 3rd dk in Nos 2 - 4 holds	**(A34A2GR) Refrigerated Cargo Ship** Ins: 7,420 TEU 41 incl 41 ref C Compartments: 4 Ho, ER, 1 Tw Dk in Fo'c's'l, 3 Tw Dk 4 Ha: (7.7 x 8.0)3 (7.8 x 8.0)ER Cranes: 4x5t	**1 oil engine** driving 1 CP propeller Total Power: 4,902kW (6,665hp) 16.0kn B&W 7S35MC 1 x 2 Stroke 7 Cy. 350 x 1400 4902kW (6665bhp) Manises Diesel Engine Co. S.A.-Valencia AuxGen: 1 x 650kW 380V 50Hz a.c, 3 x 650kW 380V 50Hz a.c Boilers: AuxB (Comp) 7.1kgf/cm² (7.0bar) Thrusters: 1 Thwart. CP thruster (f)
9076246 **SIERRA MEDOC** *9HA3287* *ex* Sierra Modoc *-2013* *ex* FRIO Poseidon *-2012* - **Pareefers KS** Seatrade Shipmanagement BV *Valletta* *Malta* MMSI: 229382000 Official number: 9076246	**6,964** 2,804 6,620 T/cm 50.0	Class: BV (GL)	**1994**-10 **DP Sudnobudivnyi Zavod im. "61 Kommunara" — Mykolayiv** Yd No: 1139 Loa 133.90 (BB) Br ex - Dght 7.500 Lbp 120.00 Br md 18.00 Dpth 10.70 Welded	**(A34A2GR) Refrigerated Cargo Ship** Ins: 7,615 TEU 89 C Ho 48 TEU C Dk 41 TEU Compartments: 4 Ho, ER, 4 Tw Dk 4 Ha: (6.5 x 7.8)ER Derricks: 8x5t Ice Capable	**1 oil engine** driving 1 FP propeller Total Power: 5,100kW (6,934hp) 16.5kn B&W 6L42MC 1 x 2 Stroke 6 Cy. 420 x 1360 5100kW (6934bhp) AO Bryanskiy MashinostroitelnyyZavod (BMZ)-Bryansk
9093048 **SIERRA NEGRA** *HC4656* - **Parque Nacional Galapagos** - *Puerto Ayora* *Ecuador* MMSI: 735059055 Official number: TN-01-0193	**209** 62 -		**2004**-01 **Logistica y Servicios del Golfo SA (LOGSESA) — Guayaquil** Loa 33.87 Br ex - Dght 2.030 Lbp - Br md 8.00 Dpth 3.40 Welded, 1 dk	**(B31A2SR) Research Survey Vessel**	**2 oil engines** geared to sc. shafts driving 2 Propellers Total Power: 404kW (550hp) Caterpillar 2 x 4 Stroke each-202kW (275bhp) Caterpillar Inc-USA
9675224 **SIERRA NEVADA** - - **Coltugs SAS** -	**455** 136 285	Class: AB	**2013**-10 **SIMA Serv. Ind. de la Marina Callao (SIMAC) — Callao** Yd No: 1250 Loa 30.00 Br ex - Dght 3.800 Lbp 28.00 Br md 12.00 Dpth 5.50 Welded, 1 dk	**(B32A2ST) Tug**	**2 oil engines** reduction geared to sc. shafts driving 2 Propellers Total Power: 3,840kW (5,220hp) 12.0kn Caterpillar 3516C-HD 2 x Vee 4 Stroke 16 Cy. 170 x 215 each-1920kW (2610bhp) Caterpillar Inc-USA AuxGen: 2 x 86kW a.c Fuel: 200.0 (d.f.)
9325439 **SIERRA NEVADA HIGHWAY** *3EIO4* - **Rabell Navigation Corp** Taiyo Nippon Kisen Co Ltd *Panama* *Panama* MMSI: 372346000 Official number: 3241107A	**44,364** 13,310 12,851	Class: NK	**2007**-01 **Naikai Zosen Corp — Onomichi HS (Setoda Shipyard)** Yd No: 697 Loa 183.00 (BB) Br ex 30.20 Dght 8.722 Lbp 170.40 Br md 30.20 Dpth 28.80 Welded, 1 dk	**(A35B2RV) Vehicles Carrier** Side door/ramp1 (p) 1 (s) Quarter stern door/ramp (s. a.) Cars: 4,318	**1 oil engine** driving 1 FP propeller Total Power: 11,620kW (15,799hp) 20.0kn MAN-B&W 6S60MC-C 1 x 2 Stroke 6 Cy. 600 x 2400 11620kW (15799bhp) Kawasaki Heavy Industries Ltd-Japan AuxGen: 3 x a.c Thrusters: 1 Tunnel thruster (f) Fuel: 2350.0
8738744 **SIERRA ROMEO** *9HA2191* - **Sierra Romeo Yachting Ltd** - *Valletta* *Malta* MMSI: 248129000 Official number: 8738744	**349** 104 -		**2007**-07 **Mondo Marine SpA — Savona** Yd No: 18/3 Loa 41.56 Br ex 8.50 Dght 2.500 Lbp - Br md 8.10 Dpth 4.10 Welded, 1 dk	**(X11A2YP) Yacht** Hull Material: Aluminium Alloy Passengers: berths: 12	**2 oil engines** reduction geared to sc. shafts driving 2 FP propellers Total Power: 3,360kW (4,568hp) 19.0kn M.T.U. 12V396TE94 2 x Vee 4 Stroke 12 Cy. 165 x 185 each-1680kW (2284bhp) MTU Friedrichshafen GmbH-Friedrichshafen
7807495 **SIETE MARES** *XCIM5* *ex* Global Warrior *-2007* *ex* Gallant Man *-2006* - *ex* H. O. S. Gallant Man *-1996* *ex* Kudu *-1993* **Intermar Carmen SA de CV** - *Campeche* *Mexico* MMSI: 345070199	**717** 215 1,000	Class: AB	**1979**-01 **Halter Marine, Inc. — New Orleans, La** Yd No: 710 Loa 56.39 Br ex - Dght 3.671 Lbp 54.87 Br md 12.20 Dpth 4.27 Welded, 1 dk	**(B21A2OS) Platform Supply Ship**	**2 oil engines** reverse reduction geared to sc. shafts driving 2 FP propellers Total Power: 1,654kW (2,248hp) 12.0kn Caterpillar D399SCAC 2 x Vee 4 Stroke 16 Cy. 159 x 203 each-827kW (1124bhp) Caterpillar Tractor Co-USA AuxGen: 2 x 125kW Thrusters: 1 Thwart. FP thruster (f)
7424358 **SIF R** *PIVA* *ex* Zaanstad *-1999* *ex* H. E. V. 1 *-1991* - *ex* La Nive *-1988* **RN Dredging BV** Rohde Nielsen A/S *Zeist* *Netherlands* MMSI: 246058000 Official number: 4184	**1,693** 508 2,700	Class: GL (BV)	**1974**-07 **Soc. Ind. des Forges de Strasbourg — Strasbourg** Rebuilt-1989 Loa 80.00 Br ex - Dght 3.360 Lbp 76.74 Br md 13.80 Dpth 5.59 Welded, 1 dk	**(B33B2DT) Trailing Suction Hopper Dredger** Hopper: 2,173	**2 oil engines** reduction geared to sc. shafts driving 2 FP propellers Total Power: 1,382kW (1,878hp) 8.0kn Cummins KTA-38-M 2 x Vee 4 Stroke 12 Cy. 159 x 159 each-691kW (939bhp) (new engine 1989) Cummins Engine Co Ltd-United Kingdom Thrusters: 1 Tunnel thruster (f)
9441245 **SIFA** *V7YD6* *launched as* Qurayyat *-2011* - **SIFA Maritime Transportation Co Ltd** Oman Ship Management Co SAOC *Majuro* *Marshall Islands* MMSI: 538004634 Official number: 4634	**163,066** 107,929 316,373 T/cm 178.1	Class: LR ✠ **100A1** SS 01/2011 Double Hull oil tanker CSR ESP **ShipRight** (CM, ACS (B)) *IWS LI DSPM4 EP (B,I,P,Vc) ✠ **LMC** **UMS IGS** Cable: 770.0/122.0 U3 (a)	**2011**-01 **Hyundai Heavy Industries Co Ltd — Ulsan** Yd No: 2247 Loa 333.14 (BB) Br ex 60.05 Dght 22.600 Lbp 319.00 Br md 60.00 Dpth 30.40 Welded, 1 dk	**(A13A2TV) Crude Oil Tanker** Double Hull (13F) Liq: 338,000; Liq (Oil): 317,000 Compartments: 5 Ta, 10 Wing Ta, 2 Wing Slop Ta, ER 3 Cargo Pump (s): 3x5000m³/hr Manifold: Bow/CM: 166m	**1 oil engine** driving 1 FP propeller Total Power: 31,640kW (43,018hp) 15.5kn Wartsila 7RT-flex82T 1 x 2 Stroke 7 Cy. 820 x 3375 31640kW (43018bhp) Hyundai Heavy Industries Co Ltd-South Korea AuxGen: 3 x 1400kW 450V 60Hz a.c Boilers: e (ex.g.) 24.0kgf/cm² (23.5bar), WTAuxB (o.f.) 20.0kgf/cm² (19.6bar) Fuel: 340.0 (d.f.) 7885.0 (r.f.)
9456379 **SIFNOS** *A8TH9* - **Valaam Inc** Goldenport Shipmanagement Ltd SatCom: Inmarsat C 463708780 *Monrovia* *Liberia* MMSI: 636014359 Official number: 14359	**32,983** 19,191 57,050 T/cm 58.8	Class: NK	**2010**-11 **COSCO (Zhoushan) Shipyard Co Ltd — Zhoushan ZJ** Yd No: ZS07037 Loa 189.99 (BB) Br ex - Dght 12.818 Lbp 185.00 Br md 32.26 Dpth 18.00 Welded, 1 dk	**(A21A2BC) Bulk Carrier** Grain: 71,634; Bale: 68,200 Compartments: 5 Ho, ER 5 Ha: ER Cranes: 4x30t	**1 oil engine** driving 1 FP propeller Total Power: 9,480kW (12,889hp) 14.2kn MAN-B&W 6S50MC-C 1 x 2 Stroke 6 Cy. 500 x 2000 9480kW (12889bhp) Kawasaki Heavy Industries Ltd-Japan

IMO / Call sign	Name / Owner	Tonnage	Class	Builder / Dimensions	Type / Cargo	Machinery
9191711 *SXPM* -	**SIFNOS** **Sea Coral Enterprises Corp** Kyklades Maritime Corp (Kyklades Naftiki Eteria) SatCom: Inmarsat C 423964710 *Piraeus* *Greece* MMSI: 239647000 Official number: 10676	**78,845** 47,271 150,875 T/cm 118.0	Class: LR ✠ **100A1** SS 10/2009 Double Hull oil tanker ESP *IWS LI **ShipRight** (SDA, FDA, CM) ✠ **LMC** **UMS IGS**	**1999-10 Nippon Kokan KK (NKK Corp) — Tsu ME** Yd No: 196 Loa 274.20 (BB) Br ex 48.04 Dght 16.022 Lbp 263.00 Br md 48.00 Dpth 22.40 Welded, 1 dk	**(A13A2TW) Crude/Oil Products Tanker** Double Hull (13F) Liq: 166,710; Liq (Oil): 166,710 Cargo Heating Coils Compartments: 12 Wing Ta, 2 Wing Slop Ta, ER 3 Cargo Pump (s): 3x3500m^3/hr Manifold: Bow/CM: 134m	**1 oil engine** driving 1 FP propeller Total Power: 15,810kW (21,495hp) 15.4kn Sulzer 6RTA72 1 x 2 Stroke 6 Cy. 720 x 2500 15810kW (21495bhp) Diesel United Ltd.-Aioi AuxGen: 3 x 750kW 440V 60Hz a.c Fuel: 300.0 (d.f.) (Heating Coils) 3857.0 (r.f.) 58.4pd
8319550 *3FXZ5* -	**SIFNOS MARE** *ex* Spar Jade *-2011* *ex* Federal Aalesund *-1997* *ex* Fiona Mary *-1993* **Shark Maritime SA** Sifnos Navigation SA *Panama* *Panama* MMSI: 373002000 Official number: 4356112	**18,011** 9,816 30,674	Class: NV (NK)	**1985-02 Sasebo Heavy Industries Co. Ltd. — Sasebo Yard, Sasebo** Yd No: 341 Loa 179.81 (BB) Br ex - Dght 10.975 Lbp 170.01 Br md 23.11 Dpth 15.52 Welded, 1 dk	**(A21A2BC) Bulk Carrier** Grain: 37,765 TEU 112 Compartments: 5 Ho, ER 5 Ha: (12.8 x 11.2)4 (20.0 x 11.2)ER Cranes: 4x25t Ice Capable	**1 oil engine** driving 1 FP propeller Total Power: 6,002kW (8,160hp) 14.0kn Mitsubishi 6UE52LA 1 x 2 Stroke 6 Cy. 520 x 1600 6002kW (8160bhp) Kobe Hatsudoki KK-Japan AuxGen: 3 x 400kW 440V 60Hz a.c
8932027 - -	**SIGAL-1** *ex* Zund *-2012* *ex* Nikolay Levin *-2010* **L N Terentyeva** Sochi Shipping Co Ltd (Sudokhodnaya Kompania Sochi) *Sochi* *Russia*	*111* 39 24	Class: RS	**1974-06 "Petrozavod" — Leningrad** Yd No: 563 Loa 24.20 Br ex 7.25 Dght 2.260 Lbp 22.55 Br md 6.94 Dpth 2.96 Welded, 1 dk	**(B32A2ST) Tug** Ice Capable	**2 oil engines** gearing integral to driving 2 Voith-Schneider propellers Total Power: 662kW (900hp) 9.8kn Pervomaysk 6CHN25/34 2 x 4 Stroke 6 Cy. 250 x 340 each-331kW (450bhp) Pervomaydizelmash (PDM)-Pervomaysk AuxGen: 1 x 30kW a.c, 1 x 25kW a.c Fuel: 17.0 (d.f.)
9379234 *VRCO6* -	**SIGAS INGRID** *launched as* Songa River *-2007* **Eight River Shipping SA** Evergas A/S *Hong Kong* *Hong Kong* MMSI: 477658800 Official number: HK-1867	**4,279** 1,373 5,073 T/cm 15.2	Class: NK	**2007-02 K.K. Miura Zosensho — Saiki** Yd No: 1307 Loa 99.98 (BB) Br ex 17.53 Dght 6.113 Lbp 94.00 Br md 17.50 Dpth 8.00 Welded, 1 dk	**(A11B2TG) LPG Tanker** Double Bottom Entire Compartment Length Liq (Gas): 4,919 2 x Gas Tank (s); 2 independent (C.mn.stl) cyl 2 Cargo Pump (s): 2x300m^3/hr Manifold: Bow/CM: 45.9m	**1 oil engine** driving 1 FP propeller Total Power: 3,309kW (4,499hp) 12.0kn Hanshin LH46LA 1 x 4 Stroke 6 Cy. 460 x 880 3309kW (4499bhp) The Hanshin Diesel Works Ltd-Japan AuxGen: 2 x 300kW a.c Thrusters: 1 Tunnel thruster (f) Fuel: 140.0 (d.f.) 599.0 (r.f.)
9346407 *3EFY* -	**SIGAS MARGRETHE** **Asuka Kisen Co Ltd & Jolly Fellow Shipping SA** Evergas A/S *Panama* *Panama* MMSI: 355122000 Official number: 3204106A	**4,253** 1,374 4,970 T/cm 14.7	Class: BV	**2006-08 Sasaki Shipbuilding Co Ltd — Osakikamijima HS** Yd No: 657 Loa 99.98 (BB) Br ex 17.22 Dght 6.050 Lbp 93.50 Br md 17.20 Dpth 7.80 Welded, 1 dk	**(A11B2TG) LPG Tanker** Double Sides Entire Compartment Length Liq (Gas): 5,018 2 x Gas Tank (s); 2 independent (stl) cyl horizontal 2 Cargo Pump (s): 2x300m^3/hr Manifold: Bow/CM: 45.5m	**1 oil engine** driving 1 FP propeller Total Power: 3,900kW (5,302hp) 16.0kn MAN-B&W 6L35MC 1 x 2 Stroke 6 Cy. 350 x 1050 3900kW (5302bhp) The Hanshin Diesel Works Ltd-Japan AuxGen: 2 x 400kW 440/100V 60Hz a.c Thrusters: 1 Tunnel thruster (f) Fuel: 107.0 (d.f.) 503.0 (r.f.)
9363522 *3EGE3* -	**SIGAS MAUD** *ex* Songa Stream *-2006* **STK Line SA** Evergas A/S *Panama* *Panama* MMSI: 357426000 Official number: 3187106C	**4,279** 1,373 5,073 T/cm 15.2	Class: NK	**2006-06 K.K. Miura Zosensho — Saiki** Yd No: 1306 Loa 99.98 (BB) Br ex 17.53 Dght 6.113 Lbp 94.00 Br md 17.50 Dpth 8.00 Welded, 1 dk	**(A11B2TG) LPG Tanker** Double Sides Entire Compartment Length Liq (Gas): 5,018 3 x Gas Tank (s); 2 independent (C.mn.stl) cyl horizontal, ER 2 Cargo Pump (s): 2x300m^3/hr Manifold: Bow/CM: 45.9m	**1 oil engine** driving 1 FP propeller Total Power: 3,309kW (4,499hp) 12.0kn Hanshin LH46LA 1 x 4 Stroke 6 Cy. 460 x 880 3309kW (4499bhp) The Hanshin Diesel Works Ltd-Japan AuxGen: 3 x 950kW a.c Thrusters: 1 Tunnel thruster (f) Fuel: 140.0 (d.f.) 595.0 (r.f.)
9355135 *S6ES6* -	**SIGAS SILVIA** **Windansea Shipping Pte Ltd** Evergas A/S *Singapore* *Singapore* MMSI: 565494000 Official number: 393215	**4,224** 1,372 4,867 T/cm 13.7	Class: NK (BV)	**2007-07 Murakami Hide Zosen K.K. — Imabari** Yd No: 556 Loa 99.98 (BB) Br ex 17.53 Dght 6.163 Lbp 93.50 Br md 17.50 Dpth 7.80 Welded, 1 dk	**(A11B2TG) LPG Tanker** Double Hull Liq (Gas): 5,032 2 x Gas Tank (s); 2 independent (stl) cyl horizontal 2 Cargo Pump (s): 2x300m^3/hr Manifold: Bow/CM: 46.8m	**1 oil engine** driving 1 FP propeller Total Power: 3,120kW (4,242hp) 14.3kn Mitsubishi 6UEC37LA 1 x 2 Stroke 6 Cy. 370 x 880 3120kW (4242bhp) Hitachi Zosen Corp-Japan AuxGen: 2 x 360kW 445/100V 60Hz a.c Thrusters: 1 Tunnel thruster (f) Fuel: 116.0 (d.f.) 450.0 (r.f.)
9355123 *3EKI9* -	**SIGAS SONJA** **Yaoki Shipping SA** Evergas A/S *Panama* *Panama* MMSI: 372735000 Official number: 3278707A	**4,224** 1,372 4,866 T/cm 13.7	Class: NK (BV)	**2007-05 Murakami Hide Zosen K.K. — Imabari** Yd No: 553 Loa 99.98 (BB) Br ex 17.53 Dght 6.163 Lbp 93.53 Br md 17.50 Dpth 7.80 Welded, 1 dk	**(A11B2TG) LPG Tanker** Double Hull Liq (Gas): 4,934 2 x Gas Tank (s); 2 independent (stl) cyl 2 Cargo Pump (s): 2x300m^3/hr Manifold: Bow/CM: 46.8m	**1 oil engine** driving 1 FP propeller Total Power: 3,120kW (4,242hp) 14.3kn Mitsubishi 6UEC37LA 1 x 2 Stroke 6 Cy. 370 x 880 3120kW (4242bhp) Akasaka Tekkosho KK (Akasaka DieselLtd)-Japan AuxGen: 2 x 360kW 445/100V 60Hz a.c Thrusters: 1 Tunnel thruster (f) Fuel: 116.0 (d.f.) 458.0 (r.f.)
9644639 *3DPJ* -	**SIGAVOU** **Government of The Republic of The Fiji Islands (Government Shipping Service - Ministry of Works, Transport & Public Utilities)** - *Suva* *Fiji* MMSI: 520263000 Official number: 001506	**495** 149 2,000	Class: NK	**2014-01 Eastern Marine Shipbuilding Sdn Bhd — Sibu** Yd No: 100 Loa 47.00 Br ex - Dght 2.500 Lbp 43.21 Br md 11.00 Dpth 3.20 Welded, 1 dk	**(A35D2RL) Landing Craft**	**2 oil engines** reduction geared to sc. shafts driving 2 Propellers Total Power: 970kW (1,318hp) Yanmar 6AYM-WST 2 x 4 Stroke 6 Cy. 155 x 180 each-485kW (659bhp) Yanmar Diesel Engine Co Ltd-Japan
8423492 *LFHE*	**SIGFART** *ex* Bomlo *-1996* *ex* Kopervik *-1985* *ex* Oklandsnes *-1985* *ex* Musca *-1985* *ex* Vulcanus *-1985* **Lokeland Eiendom AS** *Haugesund* *Norway* MMSI: 257026600	*158* 69 203		**1914 AS Mjellem & Karlsen — Bergen** Loa 31.09 Br ex 6.71 Dght 2.744 Lbp - Br md - Dpth - Welded, 1 dk	**(A31A2GX) General Cargo Ship** Bale: 255 Compartments: 1 Ho, ER 1 Ha: (8.5 x 3.6)ER Derricks: 1x2t; Winches: 1	**1 oil engine** driving 1 FP propeller Total Power: 169kW (230hp) G.M. (Detroit Diesel) 8V-71-N 1 x Vee 2 Stroke 8 Cy. 108 x 127 169kW (230bhp) General Motors Corp-USA
8645131 *DJCK* -	**SIGGI** *ex* Liselotte *-1989* *ex* Harmke *-1928* **Hans-Werner Weihs** - *Flensburg* *Germany* Official number: 2360	*116* 45 -	Class: (BV)	**1927 W. Mulder — Stadskanaal** Converted From: General Cargo Ship L reg 29.73 Br ex - Dght 2.088 Lbp - Br md 5.02 Dpth 2.43 Riveted, 1 dk	**(B33A2DS) Suction Dredger**	**1 oil engine** geared to sc. shaft driving 1 Propeller 9.0kn Volvo Penta 1 x 4 Stroke AB Volvo Penta-Sweden
9224221 *TFUR* GK 005	**SIGGI BJARNA** *ex* Ymir *-2003* **Dori Ehf** - *Gardur* *Iceland* MMSI: 251037110 Official number: 2454	**116** 35 61	Class: NV	**2001-04 Dalian Fishing Vessel Co — Dalian LN** Yd No: 99-200-6 Loa 21.50 Br ex - Dght 2.000 Lbp 19.50 Br md 6.40 Dpth 3.20 Welded, 1 dk	**(B11B2FV) Fishing Vessel** Ice Capable	**1 oil engine** reduction geared to sc. shaft driving 1 CP propeller Total Power: 440kW (598hp) 11.3kn Cummins KTA-19-M3 1 x 4 Stroke 6 Cy. 159 x 159 440kW (598bhp) Cummins Engine Co Inc-USA
6617946 *TFGT* GK 057	**SIGHVATUR** *ex* Bjartur *-2003* *ex* Vikurberg *-1981* *ex* Grimseyingur *-1976* *ex* Bjartur *-1972* **Visir hf** - *Grindavik* *Iceland* MMSI: 251330110 Official number: 0975	**436** 118 -		**1965 VEB Elbewerft — Boizenburg** Loa 33.94 Br ex 7.22 Dght - Lbp 31.63 Br md 7.19 Dpth 3.59 Welded, 1 dk	**(B11B2FV) Fishing Vessel**	**1 oil engine** geared to sc. shaft driving 1 FP propeller Total Power: 485kW (659hp) Blackstone ERS8M 1 x 4 Stroke 8 Cy. 222 x 292 485kW (659bhp) Lister Blackstone Marine Ltd.-Dursley
7382914 *TFVH* VE 081	**SIGHVATUR BJARNASON** *ex* Gunnar Langva *-1996* **Vinnslustodin hf** - *Vestmannaeyjar* *Iceland* MMSI: 251391000 Official number: 2281	**1,153** 431 666	Class: NV	**1975-01 Vaagland Baatbyggeri AS — Vaagland** Yd No: 87 Lengthened-1990 Lengthened-1978 Loa 69.10 Br ex 9.83 Dght 6.025 Lbp 61.50 Br md 9.80 Dpth 7.50 Welded, 1 dk	**(B11A2FT) Trawler** Ice Capable	**1 oil engine** driving 1 CP propeller Total Power: 809kW (1,100hp) MWM TD484-6 1 x 4 Stroke 6 Cy. 320 x 480 809kW (1100bhp) (made 1968, fitted 1975) Motoren Werke Mannheim AG (MWM)-West Germany AuxGen: 1 x 220V 50Hz a.c, 1 x 220V 50Hz a.c Thrusters: 1 Thwart. FP thruster (f); 1 Tunnel thruster (a) Fuel: 93.0 (d.f.) 4.0pd

IMO / Call sign	Name / Owner	Tonnage	Class	Builder / Dimensions	Type	Machinery
8661159 *PODM* -	**SIGINJAI** **PT ASDP Indonesia Ferry (Persero) - Angkutan Sungai Danau & Penyeberangan** - *Jakarta* *Indonesia* MMSI: 525004108 Official number: 7098	**616** 185 -		**2012-03 PT Dumas — Surabaya** Yd No: 103 Loa 47.73 Br ex - Dght 2.150 Lbp 40.92 Br md 12.00 Dpth 3.20 Welded, 1 dk	**(A36A2PR) Passenger/Ro-Ro Ship (Vehicles)**	**2 oil engines** reduction geared to sc. shafts driving 2 Propellers Total Power: 1,220kW (1,658hp) Yanmar 6AYM-WET 2 x 4 Stroke 6 Cy. 155 x 180 each-610kW (829bhp) Yanmar Diesel Engine Co Ltd-Japan
8116312 *UFOM* -	**SIGLAN** *ex* Nikolay Kuropatkin *-1999* **JSC Dalryba (A/O 'Dalryba')** - SatCom: Inmarsat M 627332910 *Vladivostok* *Russia* MMSI: 273219500 Official number: 820942	**3,834** 1,150 1,796	Class: RS	**1982-12 Stocznia Gdanska im Lenina — Gdansk** Yd No: B408/23 Loa 93.91 Br ex - Dght 5.671 Lbp 85.02 Br md 15.91 Dpth 10.01 Welded, 2 dks	**(B11A2FG) Factory Stern Trawler** Ins: 1,947 Compartments: 3 Ho, ER 4 Ha: (0.6 x 0.6)3 (2.4 x 2.1) Derricks: 6x3t Ice Capable	**1 oil engine** geared to sc. shaft driving 1 FP propeller Total Power: 3,825kW (5,200hp) 15.8kn Sulzer 8ZL40/48 1 x 4 Stroke 8 Cy. 400 x 480 3825kW (5200bhp) Zaklady Urzadzen Technicznych'Zgoda' SA-Poland AuxGen: 1 x 1200kW 400V 50Hz a.c, 1 x 760kW 400V 50Hz a.c, 2 x 350kW 320V 50Hz a.c Fuel: 1319.0 (r.f.)
7638375 *LCIJ* M-35-F	**SIGLAR** *ex* Stalegg *-2010* *ex* Dicada *-2008* *ex* Havbas *-2007* *ex* Nordsjobas *-2006* **Maron AS** - *Bergen* *Norway* MMSI: 259682000	**891** 333 827	Class: NV	**1978-04 Smedvik Mek. Verksted AS — Tjorvaag** Yd No: 59 Loa 52.05 Br ex 10.01 Dght 6.545 Lbp 44.75 Br md 10.00 Dpth 7.59 Welded, 1 dk & S dk	**(B11A2FT) Trawler** Compartments: 1 Ho, 9 Ta, ER 10 Ha: ER Cranes: 1x3.5t,1x2t Ice Capable	**1 oil engine** sr geared to sc. shaft driving 1 CP propeller Total Power: 1,765kW (2,400hp) 13.5kn MaK 6M453AK 1 x 4 Stroke 6 Cy. 320 x 420 1765kW (2400bhp) MaK Maschinenbau GmbH-Kiel AuxGen: 1 x 380V 50Hz a.c, 1 x 380V 50Hz a.c, 1 x a.c Thrusters: 1 Thwart. FP thruster (f); 1 Tunnel thruster (a) Fuel: 180.0 (d.f.) 7.0pd
8715883 *LAXT4* -	**SIGLOO HAV** *ex* Igloo Hav *-2004* *ex* Gudrun Maersk *-1995* **Evergas A/S** Thome Ship Management Pte Ltd SatCom: Inmarsat C 425972910 *Oslo* *Norway (NIS)* MMSI: 259729000	**11,191** 3,357 14,520 T/cm 28.7	Class: NV (LR) ✠ Classed LR until 17/4/96	**1989-06 Thyssen Nordseewerke GmbH — Emden** Yd No: 495 Loa 153.05 (BB) Br ex 22.04 Dght 9.011 Lbp 142.25 Br md 22.00 Dpth 12.20 Welded, 1 dk	**(A11B2TH) LPG/Chemical Tanker** Double Hull (13F) Liq: 11,628; Liq (Gas): 11,646 7 x Gas Tank (s); 7 independent (s.stl) cyl horizontal 7 Cargo Pump (s): 7x160m³/hr Manifold: Bow/CM: 76.2m Ice Capable	**1 oil engine** driving 1 FP propeller Total Power: 7,290kW (9,911hp) 16.5kn B&W 6L50MC 1 x 2 Stroke 6 Cy. 500 x 1620 7290kW (9911bhp) Hyundai Heavy Industries Co Ltd-South Korea AuxGen: 1 x 1368kW 440V 60Hz a.c, 3 x 900kW 440V 60Hz a.c Fuel: 322.0 (d.f.) 972.0 (r.f.)
7102534 *TFYS* SH 036	**SIGLUNES** *ex* Danski Petur *-1995* **TC Offshore Ehf** - *Grundarfjordur* *Iceland* MMSI: 251018000 Official number: 1146	**187** 56 132		**1971 Skipasmidastod Thorgeir & Ellert h/f — Akranes** Yd No: 23 Loa 27.64 Br ex 6.63 Dght 3.048 Lbp 25.56 Br md 6.61 Dpth 4.96 Welded, 1 dk	**(B11B2FV) Fishing Vessel** Compartments: 1 Ho, ER 1 Ha: (2.2 x 1.5)ER	**1 oil engine** driving 1 CP propeller Total Power: 368kW (500hp) 11.8kn Alpha 405-26VO 1 x 2 Stroke 5 Cy. 260 x 400 368kW (500bhp) Alpha Diesel A/S-Denmark AuxGen: 1 x 30kW 220V a.c, 1 x 24kW 220V a.c Fuel: 16.5 (d.f.)
7207463 *LAKT6* -	**SIGMA** *ex* Geco Sigma *-2000* *ex* Svalbard *-1982* *ex* Gadus III *-1977* *ex* Seafridge Osprey *-1975* **Maritim Research I AS** Maritim Management AS *Aalesund* *Norway (NIS)* MMSI: 258821000	**1,467** 441 600	Class: NV (LR) Classed LR until 10/10/75	**1972-04 A.M. Liaaen AS — Aalesund** Yd No: 117 Converted From: Fishing Vessel-1982 Loa 60.00 (BB) Br ex 11.03 Dght 6.300 Lbp 52.50 Br md 11.00 Dpth 7.35 Welded, 2 dks	**(B31A2SR) Research Survey Vessel** Ice Capable	**1 oil engine** sr geared to sc. shaft driving 1 CP propeller Total Power: 2,001kW (2,721hp) 13.8kn Wartsila 8R32 1 x 4 Stroke 8 Cy. 320 x 350 2001kW (2721bhp) (new engine 1981) Oy Wartsila Ab-Finland AuxGen: 2 x 1125kW 380V 50Hz a.c, 1 x 400kW 380V 50Hz a.c Thrusters: 1 Thwart. FP thruster (f) Fuel: 391.0 (d.f.)
5266398 *HQQN7* -	**SIGMA** *ex* Gannet *-1998* *ex* Pax I *-1990* *ex* Pax *-1984* *ex* Stephenson *-1978* *ex* Harma *-1977* *ex* Oster Till *-1973* **Flotta SA** - *San Lorenzo* *Honduras* Official number: L-0326016	**462** 269 690	Class: (HR) (GL)	**1962 Schiffbau Gesellschaft Unterweser AG — Bremerhaven** Yd No: 432 Loa 49.51 Br ex 8.84 Dght 3.110 Lbp 46.00 Br md 8.79 Dpth 3.61 Welded, 1 dk	**(A31A2GX) General Cargo Ship** Grain: 967; Bale: 903 Compartments: 2 Ho, ER 2 Ha: (10.0 x 5.0) (12.5 x 5.0)ER	**1 oil engine** driving 1 FP propeller Total Power: 257kW (349hp) 9.0kn Deutz RV6M545 1 x 4 Stroke 6 Cy. 320 x 450 257kW (349bhp) Kloeckner Humboldt Deutz AG-West Germany AuxGen: 2 x 7kW 230V Fuel: 20.5 (d.f.)
9018440 - -	**SIGMA** *ex* Kifuku Maru No. 5 *-2004* **Trans Cargo Ocean Co Ltd**	*176* - -		**1990-04 Katsuura Dockyard Co. Ltd. — Nachi-Katsuura** Yd No: 306 L reg 31.20 Br ex - Dght - Lbp - Br md 6.50 Dpth 2.70 Welded	**(B11B2FV) Fishing Vessel**	**1 oil engine** driving 1 FP propeller
9227168 *AUAP* -	**SIGMA** **Sea Sparkle Harbour Services Pvt Ltd** Ocean Sparkle Ltd *Chennai* *India* MMSI: 419027500 Official number: 2984	**290** 87 110	Class: IR (LR) ✠ Classed LR until 9/8/08	**2000-12 ASL Shipyard Pte Ltd — Singapore** Yd No: 188 Loa 29.95 Br ex 10.20 Dght 3.800 Lbp 26.27 Br md 9.80 Dpth 4.80 Welded, 1 dk	**(B32A2ST) Tug**	**2 oil engines** reduction geared to sc. shafts driving 2 Directional propellers Total Power: 2,648kW (3,600hp) 12.0kn Yanmar 8N21AL-EN 2 x 4 Stroke 8 Cy. 210 x 290 each-1324kW (1800bhp) Yanmar Diesel Engine Co Ltd-Japan AuxGen: 2 x 83kW 415V 50Hz a.c Fuel: 61.0 (d.f.)
7122924 *HQEN3* -	**SIGMA 01** *ex* Cool Liner 01 *-1997* *ex* Rima Bueno *-1997* *ex* Jufuku Maru No. 15 *-1989* *ex* Misaki Maru No. 28 *-1981* *ex* Ryoei Maru No. 28 *-1979* **Sigma Overseas Holding SA** - SatCom: Inmarsat A 1334114 *San Lorenzo* *Honduras* Official number: L-1922830	*299* 154 -		**1971 KK Kanasashi Zosen — Shizuoka SZ** Yd No: 1082 Loa 49.51 Br ex 8.26 Dght 3.302 Lbp 44.00 Br md 8.23 Dpth 3.66 Welded, 1 dk	**(B11B2FV) Fishing Vessel**	**1 oil engine** driving 1 FP propeller Total Power: 736kW (1,001hp) Hanshin 6LU28 1 x 4 Stroke 6 Cy. 280 x 440 736kW (1001bhp) Hanshin Nainenki Kogyo-Japan
9381471 *HP4706* -	**SIGMA I** *ex* PW Sigma *-2013* **PW International SA** Safe Spring Marine SA *Panama* *Panama* MMSI: 357356000 Official number: 44239PEXT3	**318** 95 161	Class: AB	**2006-12 Jiangsu Wuxi Shipyard Co Ltd — Wuxi JS** (Hull) Yd No: (1214) **2006-12 Pacific Ocean Engineering & Trading Pte Ltd (POET) — Singapore** Yd No: 1214 Loa 27.70 Br ex - Dght 4.000 Lbp 22.94 Br md 9.80 Dpth 4.90 Welded, 1 dk	**(B32A2ST) Tug**	**2 oil engines** reduction geared to sc. shafts driving 2 Z propellers Total Power: 2,648kW (3,600hp) 10.2kn Yanmar 8N21A-EN 2 x 4 Stroke 8 Cy. 210 x 290 each-1324kW (1800bhp) Yanmar Diesel Engine Co Ltd-Japan AuxGen: 2 x 99kW 415V 50Hz a.c Fuel: 148.3 (r.f.)
9410648 *A8RO4* -	**SIGMA INTEGRITY** *ex* Alpine Alaska *-2014* **Conti 161 Schifffahrts GmbH & Co KG mt 'Conti Alaska'** Conti Reederei Management GmbH SatCom: Inmarsat Mini-M 764895220 *Monrovia* *Liberia* MMSI: 636091685 Official number: 91685	**57,221** 32,953 105,291 T/cm 92.1	Class: LR ✠ **100A1** SS 02/2009 Double Hull oil tanker CSR ESP **ShipRight** (CM) *IWS LI SPM ✠ **LMC** **UMS IGS** Eq.Ltr: T†; Cable: 715.0/87.0 U3 (a)	**2009-02 Hyundai Heavy Industries Co Ltd — Ulsan** Yd No: 1965 Loa 244.00 (BB) Br ex 42.04 Dght 15.021 Lbp 234.00 Br md 42.00 Dpth 21.00 Welded, 1 dk	**(A13A2TW) Crude/Oil Products Tanker** Double Hull (13F) Liq: 114,610; Liq (Oil): 105,000 Cargo Heating Coils Compartments: 12 Wing Ta, 2 Wing Slop Ta, ER 3 Cargo Pump (s): 3x3000m³/hr Manifold: Bow/CM: 123.2m	**1 oil engine** driving 1 FP propeller Total Power: 13,560kW (18,436hp) 14.8kn MAN-B&W 6S60MC-C 1 x 2 Stroke 6 Cy. 600 x 2400 13560kW (18436bhp) Hyundai Heavy Industries Co Ltd-South Korea AuxGen: 3 x 710kW 450V 60Hz a.c Boilers: e (ex.g.) 21.4kgf/cm² (21.0bar), WTAuxB (o.f.) 18.4kgf/cm² (18.0bar) Fuel: 147.0 (d.f.) 2867.0 (r.f.)
9183568 *V2MQ* -	**SIGMAGAS** *ex* Tarquin Forth *-2002* **Partenreederei mt 'Sigmagas'** Sloman Neptun Schiffahrts-Aktiengesellschaft SatCom: Inmarsat C 430441320 *Saint John's* *Antigua & Barbuda* MMSI: 304413000	**6,051** 2,398 7,876 T/cm 18.3	Class: GL (BV)	**1998-09 Hyundai Heavy Industries Co Ltd — Ulsan** Yd No: 1092 Loa 118.88 (BB) Br ex 17.23 Dght 7.750 Lbp 110.94 Br md 17.20 Dpth 8.90 Welded, 1 dk	**(A11B2TG) LPG Tanker** Double Bottom Entire Compartment Length Liq (Gas): 8,636 2 x Gas Tank (s); 2 independent (stl) cyl horizontal 4 Cargo Pump (s): 4x260m³/hr Manifold: Bow/CM: 57.1m Ice Capable	**1 oil engine** driving 1 CP propeller Total Power: 4,891kW (6,650hp) 16.0kn B&W 7S35MC 1 x 2 Stroke 7 Cy. 350 x 1400 4891kW (6650bhp) Hyundai Heavy Industries Co Ltd-South Korea AuxGen: 3 x 472kW 440V a.c, 1 x 400kW 440V 60Hz a.c Thrusters: 1 Tunnel thruster (f) Fuel: 313.0 (d.f.) 822.0 (r.f.)

7616937 *OW2147* FD 581	**SIGMUND** *ex* Vadhorn *-1995* **P/F Eysturoy** Johannus M Olsen *Nordskali* *Faeroe Islands (Danish)* MMSI: 231176000 Official number: D2371	**266** 80 -	Class: NV	**1976**-02 **Szczecinska Stocznia Remontowa 'Gryfia' SA — Szczecin** Yd No: B30/01 Loa 32.69 (BB) Br ex - Dght 3.531 Lbp 28.12 Br md 7.62 Dpth 5.72 Welded, 1 dk & S dk	**(B11B2FV) Fishing Vessel** Compartments: 1 Ho, ER 1 Ha: (1.9 x 1.9)ER Ice Capable	**1 oil engine** driving 1 FP propeller Total Power: 596kW (810hp) MWM TBD440-6 1 x 4 Stroke 6 Cy. 230 x 270 596kW (810bhp) Motoren Werke Mannheim AG (MWM)-West Germany AuxGen: 2 x 56kW 380V 50Hz a.c
9497165 *3EWX5* -	**SIGNE BULKER** - **Lauritzen Bulkers A/S** - *Panama* *Panama* MMSI: 353381000 Official number: 4122510CH	**20,809** 11,689 32,688 T/cm 46.0	Class: NV (BV)	**2010**-01 **Jiangmen Nanyang Ship Engineering Co Ltd — Jiangmen GD** Yd No: 115 Loa 179.90 (BB) Br ex - Dght 10.150 Lbp 171.50 Br md 28.40 Dpth 14.10 Welded, 1 dk	**(A21A2BC) Bulk Carrier** Grain: 42,565; Bale: 40,558 Compartments: 5 Ho, ER 5 Ha: 3 (16.0 x 15.2) (14.7 x 15.4)ER (11.4 x 13.8) Cranes: 4x30.5t	**1 oil engine** driving 1 FP propeller Total Power: 6,480kW (8,810hp) 13.7kn MAN-B&W 6S42MC 1 x 2 Stroke 6 Cy. 420 x 1764 6480kW (8810bhp) STX Engine Co Ltd-South Korea AuxGen: 3 x a.c Fuel: 108.0 (d.f.) 1560.0 (r.f.)
6904179 *OVSO* HG 410	**SIGNET** *ex* Wicki Alex *-1999* *ex* Galway *-1992* *ex* Loch Ness *-1989* *ex* Andromeda *-1968* **Tonny Christian Esperen** - *Hirtshals* *Denmark* MMSI: 219738000 Official number: H1049	**210** 124 -	Class: (BV)	**1968 VEB Rosslauer Schiffswerft — Rosslau** Yd No: D.561/43 Loa 33.58 Br ex 6.61 Dght 2.699 Lbp 29.57 Br md 6.58 Dpth 3.31 Welded, 1 dk	**(B11A2FT) Trawler** Ins: 180 Compartments: 2 Ho, ER 2 Ha: 2 (1.5 x 1.2)ER Derricks: 1x0.5t; Winches: 1 Ice Capable	**1 oil engine** driving 1 CP propeller Total Power: 425kW (578hp) 11.0kn S.K.L. 8NVD36A-1U 1 x 4 Stroke 8 Cy. 240 x 360 425kW (578bhp) VEB Schwermaschinenbau "KarlLiebknecht" (SKL)-Magdeburg AuxGen: 2 x 16kW 220V d.c Fuel: 16.5 (d.f.)
9499199 *ZJL8034* -	**SIGNET ATLANTIC** *ex* OP Spirit *-2010* **Atlantic Shipping Ltd** Signet Maritime Corp *Road Harbour* *British Virgin Islands* MMSI: 378289000 Official number: 742022	**478** 143 -	Class: LR ✠ **100A1** SS 04/2014 tug, fire fighting Ship 1 (2400 m3/h) with water spray ✠ **LMC** Eq.Ltr: I; Cable: 330.0/24.0 U2 (a)	**2009**-04 **Guangzhou Panyu Lingnan Shipbuilding Co Ltd — Guangzhou GD** Yd No: HY2153 Loa 30.98 Br ex 11.50 Dght 4.600 Lbp 26.21 Br md 11.00 Dpth 5.60 Welded, 1 dk	**(B32A2ST) Tug**	**2 oil engines** gearing integral to driving 2 Z propellers Total Power: 3,840kW (5,220hp) 12.0kn Caterpillar 3516B-HD 2 x Vee 4 Stroke 16 Cy. 170 x 215 each-1920kW (2610bhp) Caterpillar Inc-USA AuxGen: 2 x 136kW 380V 50Hz a.c Thrusters: 1 Thwart. FP thruster (f)
8983090 *WDC5854* -	**SIGNET CHALLENGER** *ex* HMS Frontier *-2005* **GATX Corp** Signet Maritime Corp *Ingleside, TX* *United States of America* MMSI: 367047370 Official number: 1145058	**379** 113 4		**2003**-09 **Thoma-Sea Boatbuilders Inc — Houma LA** Yd No: 121 Loa 31.70 Br ex - Dght - Lbp 28.04 Br md 10.98 Dpth 5.06 Welded, 1 dk	**(B32A2ST) Tug**	**2 oil engines** gearing integral to driving 2 Z propellers Total Power: 3,090kW (4,202hp) Cummins QSK60-M 2 x Vee 4 Stroke 16 Cy. 159 x 190 each-1545kW (2101bhp) Cummins Engine Co Inc-USA AuxGen: 2 x 95kW 200V 60Hz a.c
9593139 *WDF9663* -	**SIGNET CONSTELLATION** - **Signet Maritime Corp** - *United States of America* MMSI: 367507520 Official number: 1236472	**484** 145 -	Class: AB	**2011**-12 **Trinity Offshore LLC — Gulfport MS** Yd No: TO-22 Loa 30.48 Br ex - Dght - Lbp - Br md 12.20 Dpth 5.50 Welded, 1 dk	**(B32A2ST) Tug**	**2 oil engines** reduction geared to sc. shafts driving 2 Z propellers Total Power: 5,160kW (7,016hp) Caterpillar C175-16 2 x Vee 4 Stroke 16 Cy. 175 x 220 each-2580kW (3508bhp) Caterpillar Inc-USA AuxGen: 3 x 99kW 480V 60Hz a.c
7434028 *WDB7918* -	**SIGNET COURAGEOUS** *ex* Coastal Butucu *-2003* *ex* Coastal Dade *-1997* *ex* Coastal Butucu *-1995* *ex* Coastal Dade *-1990* *ex* Mary Belcher *-1989* **Signet Maritime Corp** - *Dover, DE* *United States of America* MMSI: 366949850 Official number: 568354	**230** 103 103	Class: (AB)	**1975 Marine Industries of Morgan City, Inc. — Morgan City, La** (Hull launched by) Yd No: 10 **1975 Main Iron Works, Inc. — Houma, La** (Hull completed by) Loa 29.06 Br ex 8.39 Dght 3.658 Lbp 20.09 Br md 8.34 Dpth 4.30 Welded, 1 dk	**(B32A2ST) Tug**	**2 oil engines** reverse reduction geared to sc. shafts driving 2 FP propellers Total Power: 2,206kW (3,000hp) 12.0kn EMD (Electro-Motive) 12-645-E6 2 x Vee 2 Stroke 12 Cy. 230 x 254 each-1103kW (1500bhp) General Motors Corp.Electro-Motive Div.-La Grange AuxGen: 2 x 75kW 480V 60Hz a.c Fuel: 96.5 (d.f.)
9201982 *WDF8136* -	**SIGNET DEFENDER** *ex* Kimberly Colle *-2012* **Signet Maritime Corp** - *Pascagoula, MS* *United States of America* MMSI: 367441380 Official number: 1070115	**385** 115 499	Class: AB	**1998**-09 **Main Iron Works, Inc. — Houma, La** Yd No: 403 Loa 32.90 Br ex - Dght 4.570 Lbp 31.10 Br md 10.50 Dpth 5.49 Welded, 1 dk	**(B32A2ST) Tug**	**2 oil engines** reduction geared to sc. shafts driving 2 FP propellers Total Power: 2,240kW (3,046hp) 12.5kn EMD (Electro-Motive) 12-645-E6 2 x Vee 2 Stroke 12 Cy. 230 x 254 each-1120kW (1523bhp) General Motors Corp.Electro-Motive Div.-La Grange AuxGen: 2 x 75kW 240V 60Hz a.c Fuel: 315.0 (d.f.)
9204403 *WCZ2977* -	**SIGNET ENTERPRISE** *ex* Delta Deanna *-2009* **Signet Maritime Corp** - *Ingleside, TX* *United States of America* MMSI: 366998410 Official number: 1078814	**366** 109 -		**1999**-06 **MARCO Shipyard, Inc. — Seattle, Wa** Yd No: 483 Loa 32.00 Br ex - Dght 4.870 Lbp - Br md 10.36 Dpth 5.02 Welded, 1 dk	**(B32A2ST) Tug**	**2 oil engines** gearing integral to driving 2 Z propellers Total Power: 3,236kW (4,400hp) Caterpillar 3516B 2 x Vee 4 Stroke 16 Cy. 170 x 190 each-1618kW (2200bhp) Caterpillar Inc-USA AuxGen: 2 x 99kW 200V 60Hz a.c
9204398 *WCZ2547* -	**SIGNET INTREPID** *ex* Delta Linda *-2009* **Signet Maritime Corp** - *Ingleside, TX* *United States of America* MMSI: 366998420 Official number: 1078815	**366** 109 -		**1999**-04 **MARCO Shipyard, Inc. — Seattle, Wa** Yd No: 482 Loa 32.00 Br ex - Dght 4.870 Lbp - Br md 11.20 Dpth 5.02 Welded, 1 dk	**(B32A2ST) Tug**	**2 oil engines** gearing integral to driving 2 Z propellers Total Power: 3,236kW (4,400hp) Caterpillar 3516B 2 x Vee 4 Stroke 16 Cy. 170 x 190 each-1618kW (2200bhp) Caterpillar Inc-USA AuxGen: 2 x 99kW 200V 60Hz a.c
9706853 *WDG8427* -	**SIGNET MAGIC** - **Signet Maritime Corp** - *Pascagoula, MS* *United States of America* MMSI: 367577390 Official number: 1247231	**393** 117 -	Class: AB (Class contemplated)	**2013**-07 **Signet Shipbuilding & Repair — Pascagoula MS** Yd No: 106 Loa 24.38 Br ex - Dght - Lbp - Br md 10.97 Dpth 4.85 Welded, 1 dk	**(B32A2ST) Tug**	**2 oil engines** gearing integral to driving 2 Z propellers Total Power: 3,840kW (5,220hp) Caterpillar 3516C-HD 2 x Vee 4 Stroke 16 Cy. 170 x 190 each-1920kW (2610bhp) Caterpillar Inc-USA AuxGen: 2 x 125kW 480V 60Hz a.c
9499204 *ZJL8037* -	**SIGNET PACIFIC** *ex* OP Sprite *-2010* **Regent Shipping Ltd** Signet Maritime Corp *Road Harbour* *British Virgin Islands* MMSI: 378291000 Official number: 742036	**478** 136 -	Class: LR ✠ **100A1** SS 05/2009 tug, fire fighting Ship 1 (2400 m3/h) with water spray ✠ **LMC** Eq.Ltr: I; Cable: 330.0/24.0 U2 (a)	**2009**-05 **Guangzhou Panyu Lingnan Shipbuilding Co Ltd — Guangzhou GD** Yd No: HY2154 Loa 31.02 Br ex 11.50 Dght 4.600 Lbp 26.21 Br md 11.00 Dpth 5.59 Welded, 1 dk	**(B32A2ST) Tug**	**2 oil engines** gearing integral to driving 2 Z propellers Total Power: 3,840kW (5,220hp) Caterpillar 3516B-HD 2 x Vee 4 Stroke 16 Cy. 170 x 215 each-1920kW (2610bhp) Caterpillar Inc-USA AuxGen: 2 x 136kW 380V 50Hz a.c Thrusters: 1 Tunnel thruster (f) Fuel: 120.0
8654273 *WDG2313* -	**SIGNET PURITAN** *ex* Jim Colle *-2013* *ex* Mr. Cav *-1974* **Signet Maritime Corp** - *Pascagoula, MS* *United States of America* MMSI: 367514370 Official number: 502616	*145* 98 -		**1966**-01 **Main Iron Works, Inc. — Houma, La** Yd No: 164 Loa 23.80 Br ex - Dght - Lbp - Br md 8.23 Dpth 2.57 Welded, 1 dk	**(B32A2ST) Tug**	**2 oil engines** reduction geared to sc. shafts driving 2 Propellers Total Power: 2,460kW (3,344hp) Caterpillar 3512B 2 x Vee 4 Stroke 12 Cy. 170 x 190 each-1230kW (1672bhp) (new engine 2000) Caterpillar Inc-USA AuxGen: 1 x 55kW a.c, 1 x 40kW 60Hz a.c
9548677 *WDF8126* -	**SIGNET RELIANCE** *ex* John Colle *-2012* **Signet Maritime Corp** - *Pascagoula, MS* *United States of America* MMSI: 367491660 Official number: 1205626	**393** 117 -		**2008**-03 **Colle Towing Co Inc — Pascagoula MS** Yd No: 104 Loa - Br ex - Dght 4.570 Lbp 24.53 Br md 10.97 Dpth 5.23 Welded, 1 dk	**(B32A2ST) Tug**	**2 oil engines** gearing integral to driving 2 Z propellers Total Power: 3,282kW (4,462hp) Caterpillar 3516B 2 x Vee 4 Stroke 16 Cy. 170 x 190 each-1641kW (2231bhp) Caterpillar Inc-USA AuxGen: 2 x 125kW 480V 60Hz a.c
7626229 *WDF8125* -	**SIGNET RESOLUTE** *ex* Janet Colle *-2013* **Signet Maritime Corp** - *Pascagoula, MS* *United States of America* MMSI: 367491650 Official number: 578417	*154* 105 -	Class: (AB)	**1976**-12 **Main Iron Works, Inc. — Houma, La** Yd No: 310 Loa - Br ex - Dght 3.823 Lbp 26.34 Br md 9.76 Dpth 4.37 Welded, 1 dk	**(B32A2ST) Tug**	**2 oil engines** reverse reduction geared to sc. shafts driving 2 FP propellers Total Power: 2,206kW (3,000hp) EMD (Electro-Motive) 12-645-E6 2 x Vee 2 Stroke 12 Cy. 230 x 254 each-1103kW (1500bhp) General Motors Corp.Electro-Motive Div.-La Grange AuxGen: 2 x 75kW 60Hz a.c

9593141 *WDF9652* -	**SIGNET STARS & STRIPES** **General Electric Credit Corp of Tennessee** Signet Maritime Corp *United States of America* MMSI: 367507390 Official number: 1236478	**484** 145 -	Class: AB	**2011-12 Trinity Offshore LLC — Gulfport MS** Yd No: T0-23 Loa 30.50 Br ex - Dght - Lbp - Br md 12.20 Dpth 5.50 Welded, 1 dk	**(B32A2ST) Tug**	**2 oil engines** reduction geared to sc. shafts driving 2 Z propellers Total Power: 5,160kW (7,016hp) Caterpillar C175-16 2 x Vee 4 Stroke 16 Cy. 175 x 220 each-2580kW (3508bhp) Caterpillar Inc-USA AuxGen: 3 x 99kW 480V 60Hz a.c
8964551 *WDF9598* -	**SIGNET VALIANT** *ex* Natalie Colle *-2012* **Signet Maritime Corp** - *Pascagoula, MS* *United States of America* MMSI: 367506840 Official number: 1027362	**215** 64 -		**1995-06 Colle Towing Co Inc — Pascagoula MS** Yd No: 101 Loa 25.00 Br ex - Dght - Lbp - Br md 9.75 Dpth 4.90 Welded, 1 dk	**(B32A2ST) Tug**	**2 oil engines** gearing integral to driving 2 Z propellers Total Power: 2,942kW (4,000hp) EMD (Electro-Motive) 12-645-E6 2 x Vee 2 Stroke 12 Cy. 230 x 254 each-1471kW (2000bhp) General Motors Corp.Electro-Motive Div.-La Grange AuxGen: 2 x 50kW 60Hz a.c
8968208 *WDF9599* -	**SIGNET VICTORY** *ex* Daniel Colle *-2010* **Signet Maritime Corp** - *Pascagoula, MS* *United States of America* MMSI: 367506850 Official number: 1115336	**215** 64 -		**2001 Colle Towing Co Inc — Pascagoula MS** Yd No: 103 Loa 25.00 Br ex - Dght - Lbp - Br md 9.75 Dpth 3.99 Welded, 1 dk	**(B32A2ST) Tug**	**2 oil engines** gearing integral to driving 2 Z propellers Total Power: 2,942kW (4,000hp) EMD (Electro-Motive) 12-645-E6 2 x Vee 2 Stroke 12 Cy. 230 x 254 each-1471kW (2000bhp) General Motors Corp.Electro-Motive Div.-La Grange AuxGen: 2 x 50kW 60Hz a.c
8963208 *WDC7377* -	**SIGNET VOLUNTEER** *ex* Belle Watling *-2005* **Signet Maritime Corp** - *Ingleside, TX* *United States of America* MMSI: 367070480 Official number: 1106302	*146* 117 -		**2000 Horizon Shipbuilding, Inc. — Bayou La Batre, Al** Yd No: 044 Loa 21.33 Br ex - Dght - Lbp - Br md 7.92 Dpth 3.65 Welded, 1 dk	**(B32A2ST) Tug**	**2 oil engines** gearing integral to driving 2 Z propellers Total Power: 736kW (1,000hp) 9.5kn Cummins KTA-19-M3 2 x 4 Stroke 6 Cy. 159 x 159 each-368kW (500bhp) Cummins Engine Co Inc-USA AuxGen: 2 x 35kW 200V 60Hz a.c
9581124 *WDG2023* -	**SIGNET WEATHERLY** - **Signet Maritime Corp** - *United States of America* MMSI: 367511340 Official number: 1236838	**250** - -		**2012-03 Signet Shipbuilding & Repair — Pascagoula MS** Yd No: 105 Loa 32.92 Br ex - Dght - Lbp - Br md 11.58 Dpth 5.39 Welded, 1 dk	**(B32A2ST) Tug**	**2 oil engines** gearing integral to driving 2 Z propellers Total Power: 3,520kW (4,786hp) M.T.U. 16V4000M60 2 x Vee 4 Stroke 16 Cy. 165 x 190 each-1760kW (2393bhp) MTU Friedrichshafen GmbH-Friedrichshafen AuxGen: 2 x 99kW 480V 60Hz a.c
5133589 *IFZC2* -	**SIGNORA DEL VENTO** *ex* Peace *-2008* *ex* Goplo *-1993* **M AR TE International Rent - Mare Aria Terra Srl** - SatCom: Inmarsat C 424701248 *Rome* *Italy* MMSI: 247216500	**818** 245 514	Class: RI (HR) (PR)	**1962 Stocznia im Komuny Paryskiej — Gdynia** Yd No: B20/13 Converted From: Trawler-1994 Loa 79.80 Br ex 9.83 Dght 4.420 Lbp 57.92 Br md 9.81 Dpth 5.19 Welded, 1 dk	**(A37A2PC) Passenger/Cruise** Passengers: cabins: 28; berths: 56 Ice Capable	**1 oil engine** driving 1 FP propeller Total Power: 1,011kW (1,375hp) 12.5kn Deutz RBV6M358 1 x 4 Stroke 6 Cy. 400 x 580 1011kW (1375bhp) Kloeckner Humboldt Deutz AG-West Germany AuxGen: 1 x 184kW 230V d.c, 1 x 160kW 230V d.c, 1 x 100kW 230V d.c, 1 x 22kW 230V d.c
9147552 *EAVL* 3-CO-22-98	**SIGRAS** - **Pesqueras Patino SA** - *La Coruna* *Spain* MMSI: 224093750 Official number: 3-2/1998	**259** 78 129		**1999-02 Jose Valina Lavandeira — La Coruna** Yd No: 124 Loa - Br ex - Dght 3.400 Lbp 24.25 Br md 7.40 Dpth 5.65 Welded, 1 dk	**(B11A2FS) Stern Trawler** Bale: 133	**1 oil engine** reduction geared to sc. shaft driving 1 FP propeller Total Power: 293kW (398hp) 11.0kn A.B.C. 6MDXS 1 x 4 Stroke 6 Cy. 242 x 320 293kW (398bhp) Anglo Belgian Corp NV (ABC)-Belgium AuxGen: 2 x 100kW 220V 50Hz a.c
9030369 *LEMT* -	**SIGRID** - **Boreal Transport Nord AS** - *Sandnessjoen* *Norway* MMSI: 257243500	**2,490** 1,110 460	Class: (NV)	**1992-03 Voldnes Skipsverft AS — Fosnavaag** (Hull) **1992-03 Tronderverftet AS — Hommelvik** Yd No: 70 Loa 69.24 Br ex 13.70 Dght 3.800 Lbp 56.40 Br md 13.20 Dpth 5.00 Welded	**(A36A2PR) Passenger/Ro-Ro Ship (Vehicles)** Passengers: unberthed: 299 Bow door Stern door Cars: 50	**2 oil engines** with clutches, flexible couplings & sr geared to sc. shafts driving 2 CP propellers Total Power: 1,770kW (2,406hp) Caterpillar 3606TA 2 x 4 Stroke 6 Cy. 280 x 300 each-885kW (1203bhp) Caterpillar Inc-USA AuxGen: 2 x 136kW 230V 50Hz a.c
9631840 *SBPY* -	**SIGRID** - **Svensk Karnbranslehantering AB** Furetank Rederi AB *Oskarshamn* *Sweden* MMSI: 266416000	**7,329** 5,875 1,600	Class: LR ✠ **100A1** SS 10/2013 roll on - roll off cargo ship *IWS LI EP Ice Class 1A FS at a draught of 5.0m Max/min draughts fwd 5.0/3.7m Max/min draughts aft 5.5/3.7m Power required 2494kw, power installed 3300kw ✠ **LMC** **UMS CCS** Eq.Ltr: X; Cable: 495.0/46.0 U3 (a)	**2013-10 Santierul Naval Damen Galati S.A. — Galati** (Hull) Yd No: 1226 **2013-10 B.V. Scheepswerf Damen — Gorinchem** Yd No: 551017 Loa 99.50 Br ex - Dght 4.500 Lbp 90.97 Br md 18.00 Dpth 6.50 Welded, 1 dk	**(A38D2GZ) Nuclear Fuel Carrier (with Ro-Ro facility)** Stern door/ramp (a) Lane-Len: 180 Lane-clr ht: 5.60 Ice Capable	**4 oil engines** with clutches, flexible couplings & sr geared to sc. shafts driving 2 CP propellers Total Power: 3,300kW (4,488hp) 12.0kn MaK 6M20C 4 x 4 Stroke 6 Cy. 200 x 300 each-825kW (1122bhp) Caterpillar Motoren GmbH & Co. KG-Germany AuxGen: 2 x 412kW 400V 50Hz a.c, 2 x 680kW 400V 50Hz a.c Boilers: HWH (o.f.) 6.1kgf/cm² (6.0bar) Thrusters: 2 Thwart. FP thruster (f)
9149665 *A8CL2* -	**SIGRUN BOLTEN** *ex* Cielo di Savona *-2001* *ex* Sigrun Bolten *-1997* **ms 'Sigrun Bolten' GmbH & Co KG** Aug Bolten Wm Miller's Nachfolger (GmbH & Co) KG SatCom: Inmarsat B 363666410 *Monrovia* *Liberia* MMSI: 636090664 Official number: 90664	**19,354** 9,614 29,534 T/cm 41.0	Class: NK (AB)	**1997-10 Dalian Shipyard Co Ltd — Dalian LN** Yd No: MC280-8 Loa 181.00 (BB) Br ex 26.06 Dght 10.040 Lbp 172.00 Br md 26.00 Dpth 14.40 Welded, 1 dk	**(A31A2GX) General Cargo Ship** Double Hull Grain: 36,311; Bale: 35,452 TEU 1130 C Ho 680 TEU C Dk 450 TEU incl 12 ref C. Compartments: 5 Ho, ER 5 Ha: (19.2 x 15.2)Tappered 2 (25.2 x 22.5) (19.3 x 22.5) (19.2 x 12.8)Tappered ER Cranes: 5x30t	**1 oil engine** driving 1 FP propeller Total Power: 6,400kW (8,701hp) 14.5kn B&W 5S50MC 1 x 2 Stroke 5 Cy. 500 x 1910 6400kW (8701bhp) Dalian Marine Diesel Works-China AuxGen: 1 x 500kW 440V 60Hz a.c, 2 x 500kW 440V 60Hz a.c Fuel: 152.6 (d.f.) 1328.5 (r.f.) 26.0pd
8228361 *UBPF5* -	**SIGULDA** - **ZAO 'Kamak'** - *St Petersburg* *Russia* MMSI: 273332420	**949** 284 1,068	Class: RS	**1984 Santierul Naval Drobeta-Turnu Severin S.A. — Drobeta-Turnu S.** Yd No: 110-001 Loa 56.19 Br ex 11.21 Dght 3.701 Lbp 53.20 Br md 11.19 Dpth 4.45 Welded, 1 dk	**(B34A2SH) Hopper, Motor** Ice Capable	**2 oil engines** driving 2 FP propellers Total Power: 544kW (740hp) 8.9kn S.K.L. 6NVD26A-3 2 x 4 Stroke 6 Cy. 180 x 260 each-272kW (370bhp) VEB Schwermaschinenbau "KarlLiebknecht" (SKL)-Magdeburg AuxGen: 2 x 100kW Fuel: 123.0 (d.f.)
7702669 *TFMO* OF 001	**SIGURBJORG** - **Rammi hf** - SatCom: Inmarsat C 425101510 *Olafsfjordur* *Iceland* MMSI: 251015000 Official number: 1530	**893** 268 445	Class: NV	**1979-05 Slippstodin h/f — Akureyri** Yd No: 60 Loa 55.00 Br ex 10.29 Dght 4.446 Lbp 48.27 Br md 10.28 Dpth 6.91 Welded, 2 dks	**(B11A2FS) Stern Trawler** Ice Capable	**1 oil engine** driving 1 FP propeller Total Power: 1,978kW (2,689hp) Nohab 12V25 1 x Vee 4 Stroke 12 Cy. 250 x 300 1978kW (2689bhp) (new engine 1986) Wartsila Diesel AB-Sweden
6705963 *TFOO* SH 012	**SIGURBORG** *ex* Freyja *-1980* *ex* Sveinbjornsson *-1977* **Soffanias Cecilsson hf** - *Grundarfjordur* *Iceland* MMSI: 251368110 Official number: 1019	**317** 95 -	Class: (NV)	**1966 AS Hommelvik Mek. Verksted — Hommelvik** Yd No: 108 Loa 34.60 Br ex 7.22 Dght 3.722 Lbp 30.43 Br md 7.19 Dpth 5.69 Welded, 1 dk	**(B11B2FV) Fishing Vessel** Compartments: 1 Ho, ER 2 Ha: (1.9 x 1.4) (2.5 x 1.4)ER Derricks: 1x2.5t; Winches: 1 Ice Capable	**1 oil engine** geared to sc. shaft driving 1 FP propeller Total Power: 485kW (659hp) Blackstone ERS8M 1 x 4 Stroke 8 Cy. 222 x 292 485kW (659bhp) Lister Blackstone Marine Ltd.-Dursley AuxGen: 2 x 50kW 220V 50Hz a.c
5302257 *TFVX* SF 044	**SIGURDUR OLAFSSON** *ex* Sigurdur Sveinsson *-1979* *ex* Sigurvon *-1978* *ex* Runolfur *-1971* **Sigurdur Olafsson hf** - *Hornafjordur* *Iceland* MMSI: 251065110 Official number: 0173	**188** 56 -	Class: (NV)	**1960 Lindstols Skips- & Baatbyggeri AS — Risor** Yd No: 255 Loa 31.76 Br ex 6.15 Dght - Lbp - Br md 6.10 Dpth 3.26 Welded, 1 dk	**(B11B2FV) Fishing Vessel** Compartments: 1 Ho, ER 1 Ha: (2.4 x 1.5)ER Derricks: 1x2.5t; Winches: 1 Ice Capable	**1 oil engine** driving 1 FP propeller Total Power: 221kW (300hp) Wichmann 3ACA 1 x 2 Stroke 3 Cy. 280 x 420 221kW (300bhp) Wichmann Motorfabrikk AS-Norway AuxGen: 1 x 18kW 220V 50Hz a.c

IMO / Call sign	Name / Owner	Tonnage	Class	Build / Dimensions	Type / Cargo	Machinery
8500886 *TFEB* GK 138	**SIGURFARI** *ex Glomfjord -1986* **Nesfiskur Ehf** - *Gardur* *Iceland* MMSI: 251283110 Official number: 1743	**225** 69 -	Class: NV	**1984**-05 **Strandby Skibsvaerft I/S — Strandby** Yd No: 79 Lengthened-1999 Loa 28.96 (BB) Br ex - Dght 3.400 Lbp 23.30 Br md 6.80 Dpth 5.85 Welded, 2 dks	**(B11A2FS) Stern Trawler**	**1 oil engine** geared to sc. shaft driving 1 FP propeller Total Power: 526kW (715hp) Caterpillar 3508TA 1 x Vee 4 Stroke 8 Cy. 170 x 190 526kW (715bhp) (new engine 1994) Caterpillar Inc-USA AuxGen: 1 x 68kW 380V 50Hz a.c, 1 x 14kW 380V 50Hz a.c Thrusters: 1 Thwart. FP thruster (f)
6407535 - -	**SIGURVON** *ex Faxaborg -2003 ex Sigurvon -2003* *ex Budafell -1972 ex Sigurvon -1970* - -	**276** 83 -	Class: (NV)	**1964 Lindstols Skips- & Baatbyggeri AS — Risor** Yd No: 259 Loa 35.06 Br ex 7.07 Dght - Lbp 30.99 Br md 7.01 Dpth 3.66 Welded, 1 dk	**(B11B2FV) Fishing Vessel** Compartments: 1 Ho, ER 2 Ha: (1.4 x 1.4) (2.5 x 1.4)ER Derricks: 1x2.5t; Winches: 1	**1 oil engine** driving 1 FP propeller Total Power: 441kW (600hp) Wichmann 4ACA 1 x 2 Stroke 4 Cy. 280 x 420 441kW (600bhp) Wichmann Motorfabrikk AS-Norway AuxGen: 2 x 25kW 220V d.c, 1 x 5kW 220V d.c
6606260 *JXKM*	**SIGYN** *ex Stabben Junior -1996 ex Askita -1994* *ex Hokland -1986 ex Lundevaag -1986* *ex Froland -1976 ex Tobiclipper -1975* **Alutrans AS** Torhus Shipping AS *Drammen* *Norway* MMSI: 257271500	**741** 316 748	Class: (LR) (BV) (NV) Classed LR until 10/6/85	**1966**-03 **Oy Laivateollisuus Ab — Turku** Yd No: 242 Loa 54.82 Br ex 9.78 Dght 3.309 Lbp 49.89 Br md 9.76 Dpth 5.69 Welded, 1 dk & S dk	**(A31A2GX) General Cargo Ship** Grain: 1,726; Bale: 1,527 Compartments: 1 Ho, ER, 2 Tw Dk 2 Ha: (5.9 x 5.9) (27.2 x 5.9)ER Derricks: 1x5t,1x3t; Winches: 2 Ice Capable	**1 oil engine** driving 1 CP propeller Total Power: 588kW (799hp) 12.0kn Alpha 408-26VO 1 x 2 Stroke 8 Cy. 260 x 400 588kW (799bhp) (made 1974, fitted 1982) Alpha Diesel A/S-Denmark AuxGen: 2 x 24kW 380V 50Hz a.c Fuel: 45.0 (d.f.) 2.0pd
8025941 *SLGW* -	**SIGYN** - **Svensk Karnbranslehantering AB** Furetank Rederi AB SatCom: Inmarsat C 426504310 *Oskarshamn* *Sweden* MMSI: 265043000	**4,166** 1,249 2,044 T/cm 14.2	Class: LR (BV) ✠ **100A1** SS 08/2009 Ice Class 1B Max draught amidships 4.116m Max/min draught aft 4.116/3.775m Max/min draught fwd 4.116/3.455m Installed power 2338kw, reqired power 1412kw ✠ **LMC** **UMS** Eq.Ltr: U; Cable: 467.5/46.0 U2	**1982**-10 **Societe Nouvelle des Ateliers et Chantiers du Havre — Le Havre** Yd No: 260 Loa 90.33 Br ex 18.04 Dght 4.011 Lbp 81.97 Br md 18.00 Dpth 6.66 Welded, 1 dk	**(A38D2GZ) Nuclear Fuel Carrier (with Ro-Ro facility)** Stern door/ramp (centre) Len: 12.00 Wid: 10.00 Swl: 380 Lane-Len: 100 Lane-Wid: 9.00 Lane-clr ht: 5.65 Compartments: 1 Ho, ER 1 Ha: ER Cranes: 2x11t Ice Capable	**2 oil engines** with clutches, flexible couplings & sr geared to sc. shafts driving 2 CP propellers Total Power: 2,338kW (3,178hp) 11.0kn Alpha 6SL28L-VO 2 x 4 Stroke 6 Cy. 280 x 320 each-1169kW (1589bhp) B&W Alpha Diesel A/S-Denmark AuxGen: 2 x 440kW 380V 50Hz a.c, 1 x 346kW 380V 50Hz a.c Boilers: AuxB (o.f.) 8.1kgf/cm² (7.9bar) Thrusters: 2 Thwart. CP thruster (f) Fuel: 136.0 (d.f.) (Heating Coils) 250.0 (r.f.) 11.0pd
9114361 *OZHB2*	**SIGYN** - **Danbor Service A/S** Svitzer Sverige AB SatCom: Inmarsat C 421967910 *Kalundborg* *Denmark (DIS)* MMSI: 219679000 Official number: D3617	**485** 145 311	Class: LR ✠ **100A1** SS 01/2011 tug Ice Class 1B at a maximum draught 5.025m amidship Max/min draughts fwd 4.850/3.370m Max/min draughts aft 5.275/3.955m Power required 1000kw, power installed 2940kw ✠ **LMC** **UMS** Eq.Ltr: H; Cable: 302.5/22.0 U2	**1996**-01 **Svendborg Vaerft A/S — Svendborg** Yd No: 207 Loa 33.80 Br ex 10.75 Dght 5.125 Lbp 28.80 Br md 10.20 Dpth 5.50 Welded, 1 dk	**(B32A2ST) Tug** Ice Capable	**2 oil engines** gearing integral to driving 2 Z propellers Total Power: 2,940kW (3,998hp) 10.5kn Alpha 6L28/32A 2 x 4 Stroke 6 Cy. 280 x 320 each-1470kW (1999bhp) MAN B&W Diesel A/S-Denmark AuxGen: 2 x 240kW 380V 50Hz a.c Thrusters: 1 Thwart. CP thruster (f) Fuel: 243.0 (d.f.) 4.5pd
8308721 - -	**SIHAM** - **Waha Oil Co of Libya Inc** - *Es Sider* *Libya*	*300* - 370	Class: (LR) ✠ Classed LR until 1/6/02	**1984**-09 **Fleet International (U.K.) Ltd. — Chatham** Yd No: W1084 Loa 39.53 Br ex 8.51 Dght 2.101 Lbp 39.20 Br md 8.21 Dpth 2.60 Welded, 1 dk	**(B34A2SH) Hopper, Motor**	**1 oil engine** with clutches, flexible couplings & sr geared to sc. shaft driving 1 Directional propeller Total Power: 320kW (435hp) Caterpillar 3406TA 1 x 4 Stroke 6 Cy. 137 x 165 320kW (435bhp) Caterpillar Tractor Co-USA AuxGen: 2 x 13kW 220V 50Hz a.c Fuel: 8.0 (d.f.)
9644196 *9HA3159* -	**SIIRT** - **Siirt Maritime Ltd** Ciner Gemi Acente Isletmeleri Sanayi ve Ticaret AS (Ciner Ship Management) *Valletta* *Malta* MMSI: 229221000 Official number: 9644196	**35,812** 21,224 63,500 T/cm 62.1	Class: LR (BV) **100A1** SS 03/2013 bulk carrier CSR BC-A GRAB (20) Nos. 2 & 4 holds may be empty ESP **ShipRight** (ACS (B)) *IWS LI **LMC** **UMS**	**2013**-03 **Yangzhou Dayang Shipbuilding Co Ltd — Yangzhou JS** Yd No: DY4025 Loa 199.99 (BB) Br ex - Dght 13.300 Lbp 195.90 Br md 32.26 Dpth 18.50 Welded, 1 dk	**(A21A2BC) Bulk Carrier** Grain: 77,493; Bale: 75,555 Compartments: 5 Ho, ER 5 Ha: ER Cranes: 4x35t	**1 oil engine** driving 1 FP propeller Total Power: 8,300kW (11,285hp) 14.5kn MAN-B&W 5S60ME-C8 1 x 2 Stroke 5 Cy. 600 x 2400 8300kW (11285bhp) Doosan Engine Co Ltd-South Korea AuxGen: 3 x 620kW a.c
8427838 *DUA2358* -	**SIKAD** *ex Ray Patrick G-III -1975* **Paros Maritime Inc** Batangas Bay Carriers Inc *Manila* *Philippines* Official number: 00-0000179	*270* 148 -		**1978 Sandoval Shipyards Inc. — Manila** Loa - Br ex 8.72 Dght - Lbp 37.80 Br md 8.70 Dpth 2.60 Welded, 1 dk	**(B35X2XX) Vessel (function unknown)**	**1 oil engine** driving 1 FP propeller Total Power: 169kW (230hp)
8922058 *VTZQ* -	**SIKANDER** - **Kandla Port Trust** - *Mumbai* *India* Official number: 2502	*294* 87 130	Class: (IR)	**1993**-02 **Bharati Shipyard Ltd — Ratnagiri** Yd No: 227 Loa 29.45 Br ex 9.22 Dght 3.100 Lbp 26.50 Br md 9.20 Dpth 4.00 Welded, 1 dk	**(B32A2ST) Tug**	**2 oil engines** with clutches & sr geared to sc. shafts driving 2 Directional propellers Total Power: 1,176kW (1,598hp) 11.0kn Cummins KT-2300-M 2 x Vee 4 Stroke 12 Cy. 159 x 159 each-588kW (799bhp) Kirloskar Cummins Ltd-India AuxGen: 3 x 66kW 415V 50Hz a.c Fuel: 32.4 (d.f.) 3.3pd
7416571 *DUA2548* -	**SIKATUNA** *ex Atami Maru No. 2 -1995* **Malayan Towage & Salvage Corp (SALVTUG)** - *Manila* *Philippines* Official number: 00-0001228	*197* 71 91	Class: (NK)	**1974**-09 **Sagami Zosen Tekko K.K. — Yokosuka** Yd No: 174 Loa 28.43 Br ex 8.82 Dght 2.711 Lbp 26.98 Br md 8.79 Dpth 3.48 Welded, 1 dk	**(B32A2ST) Tug**	**2 oil engines** gearing integral to driving 2 Z propellers Total Power: 1,912kW (2,600hp) Niigata 6L25BX 2 x 4 Stroke 6 Cy. 250 x 320 each-956kW (1300bhp) Niigata Engineering Co Ltd-Japan
9403633 *ZR7289* -	**SIKHULULEKILE** - **Robben Island Museum** - *Cape Town* *South Africa* Official number: 10736	**268** 80 80	Class: LR ✠ **100A1** SS 02/2013 SSC passenger A catamaran HSC G3 (Between Cape Town and Robben Island) ✠ **LMC** Cable: 130.0/24.0 U2 (a)	**2008**-02 **Farocean Marine Pty Ltd — Cape Town** (Hull) Yd No: 450 **2008**-02 **B.V. Scheepswerf Damen — Gorinchem** Yd No: 538401 Loa 31.30 Br ex 9.30 Dght 2.590 Lbp 29.95 Br md 9.00 Dpth 3.30 Welded, 1 dk	**(A37B2PS) Passenger Ship** Hull Material: Aluminium Alloy Passengers: unberthed: 297	**2 oil engines** with clutches, flexible couplings & reverse reduction geared to sc. shafts driving 2 FP propellers Total Power: 2,100kW (2,856hp) M.T.U. 16V2000M70 2 x Vee 4 Stroke 16 Cy. 130 x 150 each-1050kW (1428bhp) MTU Friedrichshafen GmbH-Friedrichshafen AuxGen: 2 x 40kW 380V 50Hz a.c
9043495 - -	**SIKIN** - **Abu Dhabi Petroleum Ports Operating Co (IRSHAD)** - *United Arab Emirates*	*120* - -	Class: (LR) ✠ Classed LR until 15/4/93	**1992**-04 **Scheepswerf Bijlholt B.V. — Foxhol** (Hull) **1992**-04 **B.V. Scheepswerf Damen — Gorinchem** Yd No: 3211 Loa 19.55 Br ex 6.62 Dght 2.601 Lbp 17.35 Br md 6.40 Dpth 3.06 Welded, 1 dk	**(B32A2ST) Tug**	**2 oil engines** with clutches, flexible couplings & sr reverse geared to sc. shafts driving 2 FP propellers Total Power: 600kW (816hp) Caterpillar 3408TA 2 x Vee 4 Stroke 8 Cy. 137 x 152 each-300kW (408bhp) Caterpillar Inc-USA AuxGen: 2 x 22kW 220/380V 50Hz a.c
9191723 *SXYK* -	**SIKINOS** - **Sea Diamond Enterprises Corp** Kyklades Maritime Corp (Kyklades Naftiki Eteria) SatCom: Inmarsat C 423972010 *Piraeus* *Greece* MMSI: 239720000 Official number: 10752	**78,845** 47,271 150,709 T/cm 118.0	Class: LR ✠ **100A1** SS 06/2010 Double Hull oil tanker ESP *IWS LI **ShipRight** (SDA, FDA, CM) ✠ **LMC** **UMS IGS** Eq.Ltr: 0†; Cable: 742.5/97.0 U3	**2000**-06 **Nippon Kokan KK (NKK Corp) — Tsu ME** Yd No: 201 Loa 274.20 (BB) Br ex 48.04 Dght 16.022 Lbp 263.00 Br md 48.00 Dpth 22.40 Welded, 1 dk	**(A13A2TW) Crude/Oil Products Tanker** Double Hull (13F) Liq: 166,700; Liq (Oil): 170,112 Cargo Heating Coils Compartments: 12 Wing Ta, ER, 2 Wing Slop Ta 3 Cargo Pump (s): 3x3500m³/hr Manifold: Bow/CM: 134m	**1 oil engine** driving 1 FP propeller Total Power: 16,460kW (22,379hp) 15.4kn Sulzer 6RTA72 1 x 2 Stroke 6 Cy. 720 x 2500 16460kW (22379bhp) Diesel United Ltd.-Aioi AuxGen: 3 x 750kW 450V 60Hz a.c Boilers: 2 AuxB (o.f.) 18.1kgf/cm² (17.8bar), e (ex.g.) 23.0kgf/cm² (22.6bar) Fuel: 300.0 (d.f.) (Heating Coils) 3857.0 (r.f.)

9460851 *9HA2865* -	**SIKINOS** *launched as* Tinos *-2011* **Aegean VII Shipping Ltd** Aegean Bunkering Services Inc *Valletta* *Malta* MMSI: 256462000 Official number: 9460851	**3,212** 1,294 4,595	Class: AB	**2011-08 Fujian Southeast Shipyard — Fuzhou FJ** Yd No: 3800-15 Loa 90.22 (BB) Br ex - Dght 6.009 Lbp 85.00 Br md 15.60 Dpth 7.80 Welded, 1 dk	**(A13B2TP) Products Tanker** Double Hull (13F) Liq: 4,216; Liq (Oil): 4,216 Cargo Heating Coils Compartments: 5 Wing Ta, 5 Wing Ta, ER 3 Cargo Pump (s): 2x500m^3/hr, 1x300m^3/hr	**1 oil engine** reduction geared to sc. shaft driving 1 FP propeller Total Power: 2,480kW (3,372hp) 12.5kn Wartsila 8L26 1 x 4 Stroke 8 Cy. 260 x 320 2480kW (3372bhp) Wartsila Italia SpA-Italy AuxGen: 3 x 500kW a.c Thrusters: 1 Tunnel thruster (f) Fuel: 128.0 (d.f.) 312.6 (r.f.)
7356044 - -	**SIKOR I** - -	*122* 98 -	Class: (AB)	**1973-12 Ingenieria y Maq. Especializada S.A. (IMESA) — Salina Cruz** Yd No: 89 Loa - Br ex - Dght - Lbp 20.50 Br md 6.10 Dpth 3.43 Welded, 1 dk	**(B11B2FV) Fishing Vessel** Compartments: 1 Ho, ER 1 Ha:	**1 oil engine** reverse reduction geared to sc. shaft driving 1 FP propeller Total Power: 368kW (500hp) 8.0kn MWM RHHS618V16 1 x Vee 4 Stroke 16 Cy. 140 x 180 368kW (500bhp) Motoren Werke Mannheim AG (MWM)-West Germany AuxGen: 2 x 2kW d.c Fuel: 34.5 (d.f.)
7356068 - -	**SIKOR III** - -	*122* 98 -	Class: (AB)	**1973-12 Ingenieria y Maq. Especializada S.A. (IMESA) — Salina Cruz** Yd No: 91 Loa - Br ex - Dght - Lbp 20.50 Br md 6.10 Dpth 3.43 Welded, 1 dk	**(B11B2FV) Fishing Vessel** Compartments: 1 Ho, ER 1 Ha:	**1 oil engine** reverse reduction geared to sc. shaft driving 1 FP propeller Total Power: 368kW (500hp) 8.0kn MWM RHHS618V16 1 x Vee 4 Stroke 16 Cy. 140 x 180 368kW (500bhp) Motoren Werke Mannheim AG (MWM)-West Germany AuxGen: 2 x 2kW d.c
9107837 *WCQ6174* -	**SIKU** **Crowley Marine Services Inc** *San Francisco, CA* *United States of America* MMSI: 366888910 Official number: 1029298	**210** 63 120	Class: AB	**1995-04 McDermott Shipyards Inc — Amelia LA** Yd No: 298 Loa 24.38 Br ex - Dght 2.740 Lbp - Br md 8.65 Dpth 3.05 Welded, 1 dk	**(B32A2ST) Tug**	**2 oil engines** reverse reduction geared to sc. shafts driving 2 FP propellers Total Power: 932kW (1,268hp) Caterpillar 3412TA 2 x Vee 4 Stroke 12 Cy. 137 x 152 each-466kW (634bhp) Caterpillar Inc-USA AuxGen: 2 x 105kW a.c
7637436 - -	**SIKUVUT** *ex* Oujukoaq *-2011* *ex* Gissur Hviti *-2006* *ex* Vigdis Helga *-2000* *ex* Klettur *-2000* *ex* Hersir *-2000* *ex* Hafrenningur *-1984* *ex* Michelle-Cherie *-1982* **Oujukoaq Fisheries Ltd** Nataaqnaq Fisheries *Iqaluit, NU* *Canada* MMSI: 316013110 Official number: 818887	**485** 145 -	Class: (NV)	**1976-11 Sakskobing Maskinfabrik og Skibsvaerft ApS — Sakskobing** Yd No: 20 Converted From: Trawler-1980 Loa 41.66 Br ex 8.21 Dght - Lbp 38.66 Br md 8.18 Dpth 6.30 Welded	**(B11B2FV) Fishing Vessel**	**1 oil engine** driving 1 FP propeller Total Power: 588kW (799hp) Alpha 408-26VO 1 x 2 Stroke 8 Cy. 260 x 400 588kW (799bhp) Alpha Diesel A/S-Denmark
9379650 *V7UG2* -	**SIKYON** *ex* Palawan *-2010* **Sikyon LLC** Maritime Equity Management LLC *Majuro* *Marshall Islands* MMSI: 538002149 Official number: 2149	**19,846** 10,514 32,029 T/cm 45.1	Class: NV (GL) (NK)	**2007-06 The Hakodate Dock Co Ltd — Hakodate HK** Yd No: 812 Loa 175.50 (BB) Br ex - Dght 9.620 Lbp 167.00 Br md 29.40 Dpth 13.70 Welded, 1 dk	**(A31A2GX) General Cargo Ship** Double Hull Grain: 40,904; Bale: 39,618 Compartments: 5 Ho, ER 5 Ha: 4 (20.0 x 19.5)ER (13.6 x 15.0) Cranes: 4x30t	**1 oil engine** driving 1 FP propeller Total Power: 6,840kW (9,300hp) 14.5kn Mitsubishi 6UEC52LA 1 x 2 Stroke 6 Cy. 520 x 1600 6840kW (9300bhp) Akasaka Tekkosho KK (Akasaka DieselLtd)-Japan AuxGen: 2 x 400kW 450V a.c
6515021 *H02650* -	**SIL** *ex* Emir *-2006* *ex* Greenland *-2003* *ex* Landaverde *-1982* **Galicia Fishing Corp** - *Panama* *Panama* Official number: 019091789PE	**219** 81 110	Class: (BV)	**1965 Astilleros de Murueta S.A. — Gernika-Lumo** Yd No: 66 Loa 32.92 Br ex 6.48 Dght 3.226 Lbp 28.66 Br md 6.41 Dpth 3.66 Riveted\Welded, 1 dk	**(B11A2FT) Trawler** Ins: 149 Compartments: 2 Ho, ER 2 Ha: 2 (1.0 x 1.0)ER Derricks: 1x2t	**1 oil engine** driving 1 FP propeller Total Power: 552kW (750hp) 12.0kn Deutz 1 x 2 Stroke 6 Cy. 276 x 360 552kW (750bhp) Kloeckner Humboldt Deutz AG-West Germany Fuel: 73.5 (d.f.)
8521347 *ZDLR1* 3 9904	**SIL** **Polar Ltd** Lafonia Sea Foods SA SatCom: Inmarsat M 650397314 *Stanley* *Falkland Islands (British)* MMSI: 740356000 Official number: 730450	**2,156** 647 2,497	Class: BV	**1987-05 Construcciones Navales Santodomingo SA — Vigo** Yd No: 470 Loa 78.52 (BB) Br ex 14.33 Dght 5.071 Lbp 70.01 Br md 14.01 Dpth 6.02 Welded, 2 dks	**(B11A2FG) Factory Stern Trawler** Ins: 1,600 Ice Capable	**2 oil engines** with flexible couplings & sr gearedto sc. shaft driving 1 CP propeller Total Power: 2,832kW (3,850hp) 14.0kn Deutz SBV8M628 2 x 4 Stroke 8 Cy. 240 x 280 each-1416kW (1925bhp) Hijos de J Barreras SA-Spain AuxGen: 2 x 680kW 380V 50Hz a.c, 1 x 360kW 380V 50Hz a.c Fuel: 120.0 (d.f.) 650.0 (r.f.) 14.0pd
9062594 *PNDZ* -	**SIL EXPRESS** *ex* Eishin Maru No. 3 *-2001* **PT Gurita Lintas Samudera** - *Jakarta* *Indonesia* MMSI: 525016563	**1,083** 390 1,691	Class: KI	**1993-01 Nakatani Shipyard Co. Ltd. — Etajima** Yd No: 550 Loa 70.94 (BB) Br ex - Dght 4.720 Lbp 65.00 Br md 11.30 Dpth 5.15 Welded, 1 dk	**(A12A2TC) Chemical Tanker** Compartments: 8 Ta, ER	**1 oil engine** reverse geared to sc. shaft driving 1 FP propeller Total Power: 1,471kW (2,000hp) Hanshin 6EL32G 1 x 4 Stroke 6 Cy. 320 x 640 1471kW (2000bhp) The Hanshin Diesel Works Ltd-Japan
8311601 - -	**SIL TIDE** **Multiplan Nigeria Ltd**	**359** 107 -	Class: AB	**1983-05 Service Machine & Shipbuilding Co — Amelia LA** Yd No: 147 Loa 39.02 Br ex 9.17 Dght 2.598 Lbp 37.34 Br md 9.15 Dpth 3.51 Welded, 1 dk	**(B21B20A) Anchor Handling Tug Supply**	**2 oil engines** reverse reduction geared to sc. shafts driving 2 FP propellers Total Power: 832kW (1,132hp) 10.0kn Caterpillar D379SCAC 2 x Vee 4 Stroke 8 Cy. 159 x 203 each-416kW (566bhp) Caterpillar Tractor Co-USA AuxGen: 2 x 62kW
9521887 *A8ZZ2* -	**SILA** *ex* African Coastal One *-2011* **Sila Shipping Ltd** International Maritime Advisors & Management Corp *Monrovia* *Liberia* MMSI: 636015322 Official number: 15322	**5,688** 3,144 7,608	Class: NK (BV)	**2009-11 Jiangsu Shenghua Shipbuilding Co Ltd — Zhenjiang JS** Yd No: 536 Loa 110.80 (BB) Br ex - Dght 6.970 Lbp 104.66 Br md 18.20 Dpth 9.00 Welded, 1 dk	**(A31A2GX) General Cargo Ship** Grain: 10,282 TEU 294 Compartments: 3 Ho, ER 3 Ha: ER Cranes: 2x45t Ice Capable	**1 oil engine** reduction geared to sc. shafts driving 1 FP propeller Total Power: 3,089kW (4,200hp) 12.4kn Chinese Std. Type GN8320ZC 1 x 4 Stroke 8 Cy. 320 x 380 3089kW (4200bhp) Ningbo CSI Power & Machinery GroupCo Ltd-China AuxGen: 2 x 424kW 50Hz a.c Fuel: 460.0
8929537 - -	**SILACH** **JSC Nakhodka Commercial Sea Port (A/O 'Nakhodkinskiy Morskoy Torgovyy Port')** - *Nakhodka* *Russia*	**269** 80 83	Class: RS	**1971-03 Brodogradiliste 'Tito' Beograd - Brod 'Tito' — Belgrade** Yd No: 241 Loa 35.43 Br ex 9.21 Dght 3.210 Lbp 30.00 Br md 9.00 Dpth 4.50 Welded, 1 dk	**(B32A2ST) Tug** Ice Capable	**2 oil engines** geared to sc. shaft driving 1 CP propeller Total Power: 1,704kW (2,316hp) 13.5kn B&W 7-26MTBF-40 2 x 4 Stroke 7 Cy. 260 x 400 each-852kW (1158bhp) Titovi Zavodi 'Litostroj'-Yugoslavia AuxGen: 2 x 100kW a.c Fuel: 60.0 (d.f.)
8929549 - -	**SILACH** **'Arktikmorneftegazrazvedka' OJSC** - *Murmansk* *Russia*	*182* 54 46	Class: RS	**1981-05 Gorokhovetskiy Sudostroitelnyy Zavod — Gorokhovets** Yd No: 399 Loa 29.30 Br ex 8.49 Dght 3.090 Lbp 27.00 Br md 8.20 Dpth 4.35 Welded, 1 dk	**(B32A2ST) Tug** Ice Capable	**2 oil engines** driving 2 CP propellers Total Power: 882kW (1,200hp) 11.4kn Russkiy 6D30/50-4-3 2 x 2 Stroke 6 Cy. 300 x 500 each-441kW (600bhp) Mashinostroitelnyy Zavod"Russkiy-Dizel"-Leningrad AuxGen: 2 x 30kW a.c Fuel: 42.0 (d.f.)
8843927 *9A6281* -	**SILBA** *ex* Zhen Xing Hu *-1998* **Jadrolinija** - *Rijeka* *Croatia* MMSI: 238112340	*363* 108 39	Class: CS (CC)	**1990-03 WaveMaster International Pty Ltd — Fremantle WA** Loa 36.52 Br ex - Dght 1.190 Lbp 31.99 Br md 9.80 Dpth 3.70 Welded, 1 dk	**(A37B2PS) Passenger Ship** Passengers: unberthed: 310	**2 oil engines** driving 2 Water jets Total Power: 3,048kW (4,144hp) 30.0kn Deutz TBD620V12 2 x Vee 4 Stroke 12 Cy. 170 x 195 each-1524kW (2072bhp) Deutz AG-Koeln AuxGen: 2 x 80kW 380V a.c
7635579 - -	**SILBERMOWE** - -	*117* 38 59	Class: (DS)	**1977-10 Stocznia Ustka SA — Ustka** Yd No: B403/02 Loa 26.24 Br ex 7.27 Dght 3.050 Lbp 22.99 Br md 7.22 Dpth 3.48 Welded	**(B11A2FS) Stern Trawler** Ins: 98	**1 oil engine** geared to sc. shaft driving 1 FP propeller Total Power: 419kW (570hp) 10.5kn Sulzer 6AL20/24 1 x 4 Stroke 6 Cy. 200 x 240 419kW (570bhp) Puckie Zaklady Mechaniczne Ltd-Puck

IMO / Call sign	Name / Owner / Flag	Tonnage	Class	Builder / Dimensions	Type	Machinery
9600956 *XVLP* -	**SILCO SKY** **Song Nguyen JSC** - *Haiphong* *Vietnam*	171 52 96	Class: VR	**2010-06 An Phu Works — Ho Chi Minh City** Loa 25.60 Br ex 8.30 Dght 2.800 Lbp 22.66 Br md 8.00 Dpth 3.90 Welded, 1 dk	**(B32A2ST) Tug**	**2 oil engines** reduction geared to sc. shafts driving 2 FP propellers Total Power: 882kW (1,200hp) 7.0kn Niigata L6FH18HS 2 x 4 Stroke 6 Cy. 180 x 200 each-441kW (600bhp) (made 1998, fitted 2010) Niigata Engineering Co Ltd-Japan AuxGen: 2 x 32kW 380V a.c Fuel: 50.0 (d.f.)
8738859 - -	**SILCO STAR** *ex* PTSC - Binh An 19 *-2012* *ex* Binh An 19 *-2010* **Binh An Trading & Transport Service Agency Co Ltd** - SatCom: Inmarsat C 457495610 *Saigon* *Vietnam* Official number: VNSG-1784-TK	100 32 -	Class: VR	**2006-10 An Phu Works — Ho Chi Minh City** Yd No: HA-0501 Loa 24.20 Br ex 7.62 Dght 3.050 Lbp 21.08 Br md 7.42 Dpth 4.19 Welded, 1 dk	**(B32A2ST) Tug**	**2 oil engines** reduction geared to sc. shafts driving 2 Propellers Total Power: 1,324kW (1,800hp) Caterpillar D398 2 x Vee 4 Stroke 12 Cy. 159 x 203 each-662kW (900bhp) Caterpillar Inc-USA
9025895 *LMMF* SF-1-V	**SILDSKJAER** **Sildskjaer AS** - *Maaloy* *Norway* MMSI: 257594600	456 153 -		**2004-03 Stalkon Sp z oo — Szczecin** (Hull) **2004-03 Havyard Eid AS — Nordfjordeid** Yd No: 062 Loa 27.99 Br ex - Dght - Lbp - Br md 8.50 Dpth 4.79 Welded, 1 dk	**(B11B2FV) Fishing Vessel**	**1 oil engine** driving 1 Propeller
8309294 *D5FF7* -	**SILEB** *ex* Fountain 5 *-2014* *ex* Taviland *-2009* *ex* Tawe *-2009* *ex* Hansa Merchant *-2000* *launched as* Sanko Jupiter *-1987* **Golondrina Marine SA** TST International SA *Monrovia* *Liberia* MMSI: 636016251 Official number: 16251	24,646 13,377 41,574 T/cm 48.6	Class: RI (NK)	**1987-01 Mitsui Eng. & SB. Co. Ltd., Chiba Works — Ichihara** Yd No: 1295 Loa 182.80 (BB) Br ex - Dght 11.015 Lbp 174.02 Br md 30.51 Dpth 15.78 Welded, 1 dk	**(A21A2BC) Bulk Carrier** Grain: 51,025; Bale: 50,025 Compartments: 5 Ho, ER 5 Ha: (16.8 x 15.6)4 (19.2 x 15.6)ER Cranes: 4x25t	**1 oil engine** driving 1 FP propeller Total Power: 6,192kW (8,419hp) 14.0kn B&W 6L60MCE 1 x 2 Stroke 6 Cy. 600 x 1944 6192kW (8419bhp) Mitsui Engineering & Shipbuilding CLtd-Japan AuxGen: 3 x 400kW 450V 60Hz a.c Fuel: 164.0 (d.f.) 1539.5 (r.f.) 22.0pd
8996803 *MLGX2* -	**SILENCIO** *ex* Perseus *-2012* **Five Stars Sailing Ltd** Camper & Nicholsons France SARL *Douglas* *Isle of Man (British)* MMSI: 232747000 Official number: 734924	422 126 -	Class: AB	**2001-11 Perini Navi SpA (Divisione Picchiotti) — Viareggio** Yd No: 2031 Loa 49.80 Br ex - Dght 3.200 Lbp 46.20 Br md 10.27 Dpth 5.85 Welded, 1 dk	**(X11A2YS) Yacht (Sailing)**	**2 oil engines** geared to sc. shafts driving 2 Propellers Total Power: 1,392kW (1,892hp) 15.0kn Deutz TBD616V12 2 x Vee 4 Stroke 12 Cy. 132 x 160 each-696kW (946bhp) Deutz AG-Koeln
9377652 *9HBF9* -	**SILENT** *ex* Carry *-2013* **Silent Shipping LLC** Norient Product Pool ApS *Valletta* *Malta* MMSI: 256716000 Official number: 9377652	23,248 9,915 37,847 T/cm 45.2	Class: NV (AB)	**2007-10 Hyundai Mipo Dockyard Co Ltd — Ulsan** Yd No: 2023 Loa 184.32 (BB) Br ex 27.45 Dght 11.515 Lbp 176.00 Br md 27.40 Dpth 17.20 Welded, 1 dk	**(A12B2TR) Chemical/Products Tanker** Double Hull (13F) Liq: 40,781; Liq (Oil): 42,687 Cargo Heating Coils Compartments: 12 Wing Ta, 2 Wing Slop Ta, ER 12 Cargo Pump (s): 2x300m^3/hr, 10x500m^3/hr Manifold: Bow/CM: 92.6m Ice Capable	**1 oil engine** driving 1 FP propeller Total Power: 9,480kW (12,889hp) 15.0kn MAN-B&W 6S50MC-C 1 x 2 Stroke 6 Cy. 500 x 2000 9480kW (12889bhp) Hyundai Heavy Industries Co Ltd-South Korea AuxGen: 3 x 900kW a.c Thrusters: 1 Tunnel thruster (f)
7112357 *WDE2881* -	**SILENT LADY** *ex* Shaylen Nicholas *-1990* *ex* Flying Diamond I *-1986* **Silent Lady Inc** - *Cape May, NJ* *United States of America* MMSI: 367330880 Official number: 529872	*632* 189 -		**1971-05 Zigler Shipyards Inc — Jennings LA** Yd No: 212 Converted From: Offshore Supply Ship-1986 Loa 45.72 Br ex 10.98 Dght 3.836 Lbp 42.12 Br md 10.96 Dpth 4.58 Welded, 1 dk	**(B11A2FT) Trawler**	**2 oil engines** driving 1 FP propeller Total Power: 1,250kW (1,700hp) Caterpillar D398B 2 x Vee 4 Stroke 12 Cy. 153 x 203 each-625kW (850bhp) Caterpillar Tractor Co-USA
7738254 - -	**SILENT ONE** *ex* Slieve Donard *-1986* **Pacific Coast Fisheries Pty Ltd** - *Brisbane, Qld* *Australia* Official number: 385319	*173* 145 -		**1978 R Miller — Gold Coast QLD** Loa - Br ex - Dght - Lbp 21.70 Br md 7.35 Dpth 2.49 Welded, 1 dk	**(B11A2FS) Stern Trawler**	**1 oil engine** driving 1 FP propeller Total Power: 291kW (396hp) 10.0kn Caterpillar 3406TA 1 x 4 Stroke 6 Cy. 137 x 165 291kW (396bhp) Caterpillar Tractor Co-USA
9085194 *LAHW* -	**SILEX** **Bugsertjeneste II AS KS** Ostensjo Rederi AS *Haugesund* *Norway* MMSI: 258568000	543 163 430	Class: NV (RI)	**1994-07 SIMEK AS — Flekkefjord** Yd No: 79 Loa 35.11 Br ex 10.84 Dght 5.020 Lbp 32.50 Br md 10.80 Dpth 5.70 Welded, 1 dk	**(B32A2ST) Tug** Passengers: cabins: 7	**2 oil engines** geared to sc. shafts driving 2 Directional propellers Total Power: 3,600kW (4,894hp) 11.0kn Wichmann 6L28B 2 x 2 Stroke 6 Cy. 280 x 360 each-1800kW (2447bhp) Wartsila Wichmann Diesel AS-Norway AuxGen: 2 x 207kW 400V 50Hz a.c Thrusters: 1 Thwart. FP thruster (f) Fuel: 120.8 (d.f.) 12.0pd
7932317 *WDB8095* -	**SILI** *ex* Cameron Seahorse *-2004* **Government of American Samoa** - *Pago Pago, AS* *United States of America* MMSI: 338038000 Official number: 632330	558 167 450	Class: (AB)	**1981-02 Houma Fabricators Inc — Houma LA** Yd No: 68 Loa 48.77 Br ex - Dght 3.752 Lbp 47.55 Br md 11.60 Dpth 4.35 Welded, 1 dk	**(B21A20S) Platform Supply Ship**	**2 oil engines** reverse reduction geared to sc. shafts driving 2 FP propellers Total Power: 1,214kW (1,650hp) 12.0kn Caterpillar D398TA 2 x Vee 4 Stroke 12 Cy. 159 x 203 each-607kW (825bhp) Caterpillar Tractor Co-USA AuxGen: 2 x 75kW 120/440V 60Hz a.c Thrusters: 1 Thwart. FP thruster (f)
9229374 *A8RW7* -	**SILIA T.** **Romeo Shipping Co Ltd** Tsakos Columbia Shipmanagement (TCM) SA SatCom: Inmarsat C 463704324 *Monrovia* *Liberia* MMSI: 636014171 Official number: 14171	84,586 53,710 164,286 T/cm 123.1	Class: AB	**2002-06 Samho Heavy Industries Co Ltd — Samho** Yd No: 137 Loa 274.19 (BB) Br ex 50.04 Dght 17.022 Lbp 264.00 Br md 50.00 Dpth 23.10 Welded, 1 dk	**(A13A2TV) Crude Oil Tanker** Double Hull (13F) Liq: 173,947; Liq (Oil): 173,947 Cargo Heating Coils Compartments: 12 Wing Ta, 2 Wing Slop Ta, ER 3 Cargo Pump (s): 3x4000m^3/hr Manifold: Bow/CM: 135.8m Ice Capable	**1 oil engine** driving 1 FP propeller Total Power: 18,624kW (25,321hp) 15.5kn B&W 6S70MC-C 1 x 2 Stroke 6 Cy. 700 x 2800 18624kW (25321bhp) Hyundai Heavy Industries Co Ltd-South Korea AuxGen: 3 x 850kW a.c Fuel: 156.0 (d.f.) (Heating Coils) 3780.0 (r.f.)
8605208 *3EZZ6* -	**SILICA II** *ex* A. V. Kastner *-2010* **Grey Land Shipping & Trading Inc** Gulf of Aden Shipping LLC *Panama* *Panama* MMSI: 352538000 Official number: 4235911	12,702 4,947 19,075 T/cm 29.0	Class: NV (LR) ✠ Classed LR until 14/7/10	**1987-11 Hyundai Heavy Industries Co Ltd — Ulsan** Yd No: P044 Loa 158.63 Br ex 23.04 Dght 9.637 Lbp 147.00 Br md 23.02 Dpth 13.29 Welded, 1 dk	**(A23A2BD) Bulk Carrier, Self-discharging** Double Sides Entire Compartment Length Grain: 17,107 Compartments: 5 Ho, ER 5 Ha: (9.7 x 15.0)3 (13.5 x 15.0) (12.0 x 15.0)ER Ice Capable	**1 oil engine** driving 1 CP propeller Total Power: 5,649kW (7,680hp) 15.0kn Sulzer 4RTA58 1 x 2 Stroke 4 Cy. 580 x 1700 5649kW (7680bhp) Hyundai Engine & Machinery Co Ltd-South Korea AuxGen: 3 x 600kW 440V 60Hz a.c, 1 x 570kW 440V 60Hz a.c Boilers: e 11.7kgf/cm^2 (11.5bar), AuxB (o.f.) 9.1kgf/cm^2 (8.9bar) Thrusters: 1 Tunnel thruster (f) Fuel: 155.0 (d.f.) 695.0 (r.f.) 22.0pd
9229506 - -	**SILIN** **Government of Libya (Socialist Ports Co)** - *Homs* *Libya*	176 52 176	Class: (LR) ✠ Classed LR until 1/2/11	**2005-12 FGUP Mashinostroitelnoye Predp 'Zvyozdochka' — Severodvinsk** (Hull) Yd No: (509802) **2005-12 Damen (Stock Hull) — Gorinchem** Yd No: 509802 Loa 26.09 Br ex 7.95 Dght 3.443 Lbp 23.98 Br md 7.95 Dpth 4.05 Welded, 1 dk	**(B32A2ST) Tug**	**2 oil engines** with clutches, flexible couplings & sr reverse geared to sc. shafts driving 2 FP propellers Total Power: 2,612kW (3,552hp) 11.7kn Caterpillar 3512B-TA 2 x Vee 4 Stroke 12 Cy. 170 x 190 each-1306kW (1776bhp) Caterpillar Inc-USA AuxGen: 2 x 50kW 400V 50Hz a.c
7906784 - -	**SILISTEA 2** *ex* 6279 *-2010* **Administratia Fluviala a Dunarii de Jos (AFDJ) (River Administration of the Lower Danube)** Aras Gemi Kurtarma ve Deniz Insaat Ticaret Ltd Sti *Romania*	746 734 1,500	Class: (RN)	**1979-06 Santierul Naval Drobeta-Turnu Severin S.A. — Drobeta-Turnu S.** Yd No: 18346005 Loa 60.30 Br ex - Dght 3.420 Lbp 59.70 Br md 11.30 Dpth 4.00 Welded, 1 dk	**(B34A2SH) Hopper, Motor** Hopper: 940 Compartments: 1 Ho, ER 1 Ha: ER	**2 oil engines** driving 2 FP propellers Total Power: 500kW (680hp) 5.5kn Maybach MB836BB 2 x 4 Stroke 8 Cy. 175 x 205 each-250kW (340bhp) Uzina 23 August Bucuresti-Bucuresti AuxGen: 2 x 1kW 24V d.c

IMO / Call sign	Name / Owner	Tonnage	Class	Builder / Dimensions	Type	Machinery
8741818 *OXUX2* -	**SILJA** *ex* Wavecat One *-2011* *ex* KBV 020 *-2010* **JD Crafts A/S** JD-Contractor A/S *Struer* *Denmark (DIS)* MMSI: 219014412 Official number: H1691	**173** 44 -		**1982-01 Djupviks Batvarv — Fagerfjall** Yd No: 317 Converted From: Patrol Vessel-2010 Loa 27.32 Br ex - Dght 1.700 Lbp 25.40 Br md 9.20 Dpth 3.50 Welded, 1 dk	**(B34R2QY) Supply Tender** Hull Material: Aluminium Alloy	**2 oil engines** reduction geared to sc. shafts driving 2 Propellers Total Power: 3,360kW (4,568hp) M.T.U. 12V396TC82 2 x Vee 4 Stroke 12 Cy. 165 x 185 each-1680kW (2284bhp) MTU Friedrichshafen GmbH-Friedrichshafen
8919805 *ESUJ* -	**SILJA EUROPA** *launched as* Europa *-1993* **Tallink Group Ltd (AS Tallink Grupp)** Silja Line Oyj *Tallinn* *Estonia* MMSI: 276807000 Official number: 5P13A01	**59,912** 41,309 4,650	Class: BV	**1993-03 Jos L Meyer GmbH & Co — Papenburg** (Fwd & aft sections) Yd No: 627 **1993-03 Neptun Reparaturwerft GmbH — Rostock** (Cargo section) Loa 201.78 (BB) Br ex 32.60 Dght 6.800 Lbp 171.60 Br md 32.00 Dpth 14.70 Welded, 6 dks	**(A36A2PR) Passenger/Ro-Ro Ship (Vehicles)** Passengers: cabins: 1194; berths: 3746; driver berths: 52 Bow door/ramp (f) Stern door/ramp (p) Stern door/ramp (s) Lane-Len: 926 Lane-clr ht: 4.80 Lorries: 60, Cars: 350 Ice Capable	**4 oil engines** with clutches, flexible couplings & dr geared to sc. shafts driving 2 CP propellers Total Power: 31,800kW (43,236hp) 21.5kn MAN 6L58/64 4 x 4 Stroke 6 Cy. 580 x 640 each-7950kW (10809bhp) MAN B&W Diesel AG-Augsburg Thrusters: 2 Thwart. CP thruster (f); 1 Tunnel thruster (a) Fuel: 800.0 (r.f.) 64.0pd
8306498 *YLBS* -	**SILJA FESTIVAL** *ex* Wellamo *-1991* **Tallinn Swedish Line Ltd** Tallink Silja Oy *Riga* *Latvia* MMSI: 275380000	**34,414** 19,646 3,720	Class: NV	**1986-01 Oy Wartsila Ab — Helsinki** Yd No: 471 Loa 168.03 (BB) Br ex 31.60 Dght 6.514 Lbp 152.71 Br md 27.61 Dpth 14.46 Welded, 7 dks	**(A36A2PR) Passenger/Ro-Ro Ship (Vehicles)** Passengers: unberthed: 63; cabins: 588; berths: 1937 Bow door/ramp (f) Len: 16.50 Wid: 7.00 Swl: - Stern door/ramp (p) Len: 7.70 Wid: 9.00 Swl: - Stern door/ramp (s) Len: 7.70 Wid: 6.00 Swl: - Lane-Len: 1200 Lane-clr ht: 4.60 Cars: 350, Trailers: 60 Ice Capable	**4 oil engines** with clutches, flexible couplings & sr geared to sc. shafts driving 2 CP propellers Total Power: 26,408kW (35,904hp) 22.0kn Pielstick 12PC2-6V-400 4 x Vee 4 Stroke 12 Cy. 400 x 460 each-6602kW (8976bhp) Oy Wartsila Ab-Finland AuxGen: 4 x 2000kW 380V 50Hz a.c, 1 x 400kW 380V 50Hz a.c Thrusters: 2 Thwart. CP thruster (f); 1 Thwart. CP thruster (a) Fuel: 210.6 (d.f.) 877.7 (r.f.)
8715259 *OJCS* -	**SILJA SERENADE** **Tallink Silja Oy** Silja Line Oyj *Mariehamn* *Finland* MMSI: 230184000 Official number: 50772	**58,376** 38,970 5,100 T/cm 49.3	Class: AB (LR) ✠ Classed LR until 22/11/12	**1990-11 Masa-Yards Inc — Turku** Yd No: 1301 Loa 203.03 (BB) Br ex 31.93 Dght 7.116 Lbp 180.66 Br md 31.50 Dpth 21.00 Welded, 5 dks	**(A36A2PR) Passenger/Ro-Ro Ship (Vehicles)** Passengers: cabins: 986; berths: 2841; driver berths: 30 Bow door & ramp Len: 4.90 Wid: 6.00 Swl: - Stern door/ramp Len: 4.90 Wid: 12.50 Swl: - Lane-Len: 1775 Lane-clr ht: 4.60 Cars: 450	**4 oil engines** with clutches, flexible couplings & sr geared to sc. shafts driving 2 CP propellers Total Power: 32,580kW (44,296hp) 21.0kn Wartsila 9R46 4 x 4 Stroke 9 Cy. 460 x 580 each-8145kW (11074bhp) Wartsila Diesel Oy-Finland AuxGen: 2 x 3200kW 660V 50Hz a.c, 2 x 2400kW 660V 50Hz a.c Boilers: 8 e (ex.g.) 11.2kgf/cm² (11.0bar), 2 AuxB (o.f.) 8.7kgf/cm² (8.5bar) Thrusters: 2 Thwart. CP thruster (f); 1 Thwart. CP thruster (a) Fuel: 142.4 (d.f.) 1501.6 (r.f.) 80.0pd
8803769 *SCGB* -	**SILJA SYMPHONY** **Tallinn Swedish Line Ltd** Silja Line Oyj *Stockholm* *Sweden* MMSI: 265004000	**58,377** 35,961 5,340 T/cm 49.3	Class: LR ✠ **100A1** SS 05/2011 passenger/vehicle ferry, movable decks Ice Class 1A Super Max draught midship 7.116m Max/min draught forward 7.116/6.0m Max/min draught aft 7.116/6.0m ✠ **LMC** Eq.Ltr: Q†; Cable: 687.5/81.0 U3	**1991-05 Kvaerner Masa-Yards Inc — Turku** Yd No: 1309 Loa 203.03 (BB) Br ex 31.93 Dght 7.101 Lbp 180.66 Br md 31.50 Dpth 21.00 Welded, 7 dks	**(A36A2PR) Passenger/Ro-Ro Ship (Vehicles)** Passengers: cabins: 986; berths: 2841; driver berths: 30 Bow door/ramp Stern door/ramp Lane-Len: 1775 Cars: 470, Trailers: 60 Ice Capable	**4 oil engines** with clutches, flexible couplings & sr geared to sc. shafts driving 2 CP propellers Total Power: 32,580kW (44,296hp) 21.0kn Wartsila 9R46 4 x 4 Stroke 9 Cy. 460 x 580 each-8145kW (11074bhp) Wartsila Diesel Oy-Finland AuxGen: 2 x 3280kW 660V 50Hz a.c, 2 x 2460kW 660V 50Hz a.c Boilers: 8 e (ex.g.) 11.2kgf/cm² (11.0bar), 2 AuxB (o.f.) 8.7kgf/cm² (8.5bar) Thrusters: 2 Thwart. CP thruster (f); 1 Thwart. CP thruster (a) Fuel: 142.4 (d.f.) 1501.6 (r.f.) 80.0pd
9222390 *LCPE* -	**SILLE MARIE** *ex* Lovon *-2011* **Sille Marie AS** - *Kristiansand* *Norway* MMSI: 259893000 Official number: 03543	**457** 145 -	Class: NV	**2001-04 AS Rigas Kugu Buvetava (Riga Shipyard) — Riga** (Hull) Yd No: 1014 **2001-04 Tjornvarvet AB Ronnang — Ronnang** Yd No: 125 Loa 37.30 Br ex - Dght 5.630 Lbp 30.20 Br md 9.00 Dpth 6.60 Welded, 1 dk	**(B11B2FV) Fishing Vessel**	**1 oil engine** driving 1 FP propeller Total Power: 730kW (993hp) Wartsila 9L20 1 x 4 Stroke 9 Cy. 200 x 280 730kW (993bhp) Wartsila Finland Oy-Finland AuxGen: 1 x a.c
7606528 *ILEK* -	**SILM III** *ex* Tazzoli *-1987* *ex* Tora *-1986* *ex* Esco 11 *-1982* *ex* Asiatic Hunter *-1982* **AG Operae Srl** - *Naples* *Italy* Official number: 1680	*125* 42 -	Class: RI (AB) (GL)	**1974 Sea Services Pte Ltd — Singapore** Yd No: Y42 Loa 25.30 Br ex 7.24 Dght 2.820 Lbp 23.50 Br md 7.21 Dpth 3.38 Welded, 1 dk	**(B32A2ST) Tug**	**2 oil engines** reduction geared to sc. shafts driving 2 FP propellers Total Power: 540kW (734hp) 10.0kn Caterpillar D343 2 x 4 Stroke 6 Cy. 137 x 165 each-270kW (367bhp) Caterpillar Tractor Co-USA Fuel: 42.5 (d.f.)
9424584 *9AA4565* -	**SILNI** **'Brodospas' dd Split** *Split* *Croatia*	**168** - 80	Class: BV CS	**2007-01 van Noorloos Lasbedrijf B.V. — Sliedrecht** (Hull) Yd No: 544803 **2007-01 B.V. Scheepswerf Damen — Gorinchem** Yd No: 544803 Loa 35.80 Br ex 7.40 Dght 1.650 Lbp 34.45 Br md 7.36 Dpth 3.30 Welded, 1 dk	**(B21A20C) Crew/Supply Vessel** Hull Material: Aluminium Alloy Passengers: unberthed: 30	**3 oil engines** reduction geared to sc. shafts driving 3 FP propellers Total Power: 3,132kW (4,257hp) 26.0kn Caterpillar C32 3 x Vee 4 Stroke 12 Cy. 145 x 162 each-1044kW (1419bhp) Caterpillar Inc-USA AuxGen: 2 x 60kW 400/220V 50Hz a.c Thrusters: 1 Tunnel thruster (f)
8868056 *UECZ* -	**SILNIY** *ex* Sarmat-1 *-2011* *ex* Ruza-3 *-2002* *ex* ST-1314 *-2002* **Sovfracht JSC (A/O 'Sovfrakht')** SatCom: Inmarsat C 427310536 *Taganrog* *Russia* MMSI: 273329600 Official number: 855000	**1,785** 639 2,063	Class: RS	**1986-09 Sudostroitelnyy Zavod im Volodarskogo — Rybinsk** Yd No: 04907 Loa 86.70 Br ex 12.30 Dght 3.400 Lbp 82.55 Br md 12.00 Dpth 3.50 Welded, 1 dk	**(A31A2GX) General Cargo Ship** Grain: 2,230 TEU 54 C.Ho 36/20' C.Dk 18/20' Compartments: 1 Ho, ER 2 Ha: 2 (19.8 x 9.0)ER Ice Capable	**2 oil engines** driving 2 FP propellers Total Power: 1,030kW (1,400hp) S.K.L. 6NVDS48A-2U 2 x 4 Stroke 6 Cy. 320 x 480 each-515kW (700bhp) VEB Schwermaschinenbau "KarlLiebknecht" (SKL)-Magdeburg
8892588 *YFAJ* -	**SILOK** **Government of The Republic of Indonesia (Direktorat Jenderal Perhubungan Darat - Ministry of Land Communications)** PT ASDP Indonesia Ferry (Persero) - Angkutan Sungai Danau & Penyeberangan *Jakarta* *Indonesia*	*132* 79 -	Class: KI	**1994-10 P.T. Dok & Perkapalan Kodja Bahari — Palembang** Loa 21.50 Br ex - Dght - Lbp 19.50 Br md 8.09 Dpth 2.50 Welded, 1 dk	**(A37B2PS) Passenger Ship**	**2 oil engines** driving 2 FP propellers Total Power: 354kW (482hp) 9.6kn Yanmar 6HAL-HTE 2 x 4 Stroke 6 Cy. 130 x 150 each-177kW (241bhp) (made 1991) Yanmar Diesel Engine Co Ltd-Japan
8700694 *TC5014* -	**SILOPI** **BOTAS Boru Hatlari Ile Petrol Tasima AS (Botas Petroleum Pipeline Corp)** - *Istanbul* *Turkey* Official number: 271	**325** 98 127	Class: TL (LR) ✠ Classed LR until 20/10/89	**1988-06 Sedef Gemi Endustrisi A.S. — Gebze** Yd No: 58 Loa 32.42 Br ex - Dght 2.890 Lbp 31.02 Br md 9.31 Dpth 3.89 Welded, 1 dk	**(B32A2ST) Tug**	**2 oil engines** with flexible couplings & dr gearedto sc. shafts driving 2 Directional propellers Total Power: 2,354kW (3,200hp) 12.0kn Deutz SBV6M628 2 x 4 Stroke 6 Cy. 240 x 280 each-1177kW (1600bhp) Kloeckner Humboldt Deutz AG-West Germany AuxGen: 2 x 104kW 400V 50Hz a.c Fuel: 55.0 (d.f.) 12.0pd
9253002 *HBDF* -	**SILS** *ex* Norasia Sils *-2006* *launched as* Sils *-2003* **Oceana Shipping AG** Suisse-Atlantique Societe de Navigation Maritime SA *Basel* *Switzerland* MMSI: 269016000 Official number: 167	**27,779** 14,769 39,425 T/cm 56.7	Class: GL	**2003-07 Hyundai Mipo Dockyard Co Ltd — Ulsan** Yd No: 0114 Loa 222.16 (BB) Br ex - Dght 12.000 Lbp 210.00 Br md 30.00 Dpth 16.80 Welded, 1 dk	**(A33A2CC) Container Ship (Fully Cellular)** TEU 2824 C Ho 1026 C Dk 1798 incl 554 ref C.	**1 oil engine** driving 1 FP propeller Total Power: 25,230kW (34,303hp) 22.5kn B&W 7K80MC-C 1 x 2 Stroke 7 Cy. 800 x 2300 25230kW (34303bhp) Hyundai Heavy Industries Co Ltd-South Korea AuxGen: 4 x 1500kW 440/220V 60Hz a.c Thrusters: 1 Tunnel thruster (f) Fuel: 215.0 (d.f.) 3241.0 (r.f.)

Ship / Owner	Tonnage	Class	Builder / Dimensions	Type / Capacity	Machinery
7038862 **SILUET** *UEJW* - **AOZT 'Vostoktransservis' Marine Shipping Co** - *Vladivostok* *Russia* MMSI: 273836100 Official number: 682034	**1,614** 540 1,531	Class: (RS)	**1969-04 Sudostroitelnyy Zavod "Zaliv" — Kerch** Yd No: 428 Loa 83.55 Br ex 12.03 Dght 4.650 Lbp 74.00 Br md 12.00 Dpth 5.30 Welded, 1 dk	**(A13B2TP) Products Tanker** Liq: 2,034; Liq (Oil): 2,034 Cargo Heating Coils Compartments: 12 Ta, ER Ice Capable	**1 oil engine** driving 1 FP propeller Total Power: 1,471kW (2,000hp) 13.8kn Skoda 8DR43/61-V1 1 x 2 Stroke 8 Cy. 430 x 610 1471kW (2000bhp) CKD Praha-Praha Fuel: 126.0 (d.f.) (Heating Coils) 7.5pd
7606968 **SILUMBA** *PLXL* - **PT Tirta Kerta Abadi** - *Jakarta* *Indonesia*	**1,783** 631 1,650	Class: KI (NV)	**1978-02 Aukra Bruk AS — Aukra** Yd No: 63 Loa 71.91 Br ex - Dght 4.301 Lbp 65.41 Br md 12.70 Dpth 7.12 Welded, 2 dks	**(A32A2GF) General Cargo/Passenger Ship** Passengers: 198 Grain: 3,570 Compartments: 2 Ho, ER 2 Ha: (13.2 x 8.0) (18.9 x 8.0)ER Derricks: 2x20t,2x5t	**1 oil engine** driving 1 FP propeller Total Power: 1,177kW (1,600hp) 12.0kn Kromhout 9FDHD240 1 x 4 Stroke 9 Cy. 240 x 260 1177kW (1600bhp) Stork Werkspoor Diesel BV-Netherlands AuxGen: 3 x 96kW 220/380V 50Hz a.c, 1 x 48kW 220/380V 50Hz a.c
8328795 **SILURE** *FULX* *ex* Lekuine *ex* Freres Jacques LS 554922 **Silure Armement** - SatCom: Inmarsat C 422822110 *Les Sables-d'Olonne* *France* MMSI: 228221000	*127* 54 -	Class: (BV)	**1982 Ateliers du Bastion SA — Les Sables-d'Olonne** Loa 26.09 Br ex 6.91 Dght 3.280 Lbp 22.43 Br md - Dpth 4.09 Welded, 1 dk	**(B11B2FV) Fishing Vessel**	**1 oil engine** sr geared to sc. shaft driving 1 CP propeller Total Power: 423kW (575hp) 11.0kn Duvant 6VJS 1 x 4 Stroke 6 Cy. 255 x 300 423kW (575bhp) Moteurs Duvant-France AuxGen: 2 x 36kW 380V 50Hz a.c
8325561 **SILVA** *ELFE8* *ex* Silba *-2005* - **Melinda Holdings SA** Delfi SA SatCom: Inmarsat B 363682910 *Monrovia* *Liberia* MMSI: 636007879 Official number: 7879	**46,632** 26,702 82,424 T/cm 88.0	Class: BV (CS)	**1986-04 Brodogradiliste 'Uljanik' — Pula** Yd No: 356 Loa 210.50 Br ex - Dght 12.640 Lbp 203.03 Br md 48.01 Dpth 18.01 Welded, 1 dk	**(A13A2TV) Crude Oil Tanker** Double Sides Entire Compartment Length Liq: 101,633; Liq (Oil): 101,633 Cargo Heating Coils Compartments: 11 Ta, ER 3 Cargo Pump (s): 3x2400m³/hr Manifold: Bow/CM: 103m	**1 oil engine** driving 1 FP propeller Total Power: 10,300kW (14,004hp) 14.5kn B&W 4L80MC 1 x 2 Stroke 4 Cy. 800 x 2592 10300kW (14004bhp) Tvornica Dizel Motora 'Uljanik'-Yugoslavia AuxGen: 4 x 780kW 440V 60Hz a.c Fuel: 2936.0 (r.f.) (Heating Coils) 40.5pd
8614467 **SILVA** *5IM609* *ex* Kirsten *-2012* *ex* Torm Kirsten *-2000* *ex* Tempera *-1994* *ex* Georgia *-1990* **AR Shipping (HK) Ltd** Atlas Ships Management Est SatCom: Inmarsat C 467400479 *Zanzibar* *Tanzania (Zanzibar)* MMSI: 677050900 Official number: 300354	**44,322** 20,402 83,651 T/cm 68.0	Class: (BV) (NV)	**1988-07 Brodogradiliste '3 Maj' — Rijeka** Yd No: 650 Loa 228.28 (BB) Br ex 32.21 Dght 16.020 Lbp 220.50 Br md 32.20 Dpth 21.66 Welded, 1 dk	**(A13B2TP) Products Tanker** Double Hull (13F) Liq: 86,603; Liq (Oil): 89,180 Compartments: 12 Wing Ta, 2 Wing Slop Ta, ER 12 Cargo Pump (s): 12x950m³/hr Manifold: Bow/CM: 117.8m	**1 oil engine** driving 1 FP propeller Total Power: 8,330kW (11,325hp) 14.0kn Sulzer 6RTA62 1 x 2 Stroke 6 Cy. 620 x 2150 8330kW (11325bhp) Tvornica Dizel Motora '3 Maj'-Yugoslavia AuxGen: 3 x 875kW 440V 60Hz a.c Fuel: 262.0 (d.f.) 1997.0 (r.f.) 36.5pd
9237010 **SILVA** *MGXL8* - **Navalis Shipping GmbH & Co KG** Schiffahrtskontor tom Worden GmbH & Co KG *Douglas* *Isle of Man (British)* MMSI: 235008610 Official number: DR122	**3,978** 1,757 5,021	Class: GL (BV)	**2001-05 Jiangdong Shipyard — Wuhu AH** Yd No: JD2000-1 Loa 99.95 (BB) Br ex - Dght 5.200 Lbp 96.00 Br md 16.50 Dpth 7.35 Welded, 1 dk	**(A31A2GX) General Cargo Ship** Grain: 5,077; Bale: 5,051 TEU 210 C Ho 150 TEU C Dk 60 TEU Compartments: 1 Ho, ER 1 Ha: (63.9 x 12.9)ER Ice Capable	**1 oil engine** reduction geared to sc. shaft driving 1 CP propeller Total Power: 2,700kW (3,671hp) 12.0kn MaK 9M25 1 x 4 Stroke 9 Cy. 255 x 400 2700kW (3671bhp) MaK Motoren GmbH & Co. KG-Kiel AuxGen: 1 x 300kW 380/220V 50Hz a.c, 2 x 216kW 380/220V 50Hz a.c Thrusters: 1 Thwart. FP thruster (f)
9357573 **SILVA** *3FVU2* - **Silvan SA** Akron Trade & Transport *Panama* *Panama* MMSI: 371502000 Official number: 4045809A	**8,251** 2,997 11,028	Class: CC	**2009-04 Haidong Shipyard — Taizhou ZJ** Yd No: DBD-2005-030 Loa 129.60 Br ex 20.02 Dght 7.600 Lbp 123.00 Br md 20.00 Dpth 11.50 Welded, 1 dk	**(A12B2TR) Chemical/Products Tanker** Double Hull (13F) Liq: 12,976; Liq (Oil): 13,520 Compartments: 12 Wing Ta, 2 Wing Slop Ta, ER	**2 oil engines** reduction geared to sc. shafts driving 2 FP propellers Total Power: 4,000kW (5,438hp) 10.5kn Chinese Std. Type G8300ZC 2 x 4 Stroke 8 Cy. 300 x 380 each-2000kW (2719bhp) Ningbo CSI Power & Machinery GroupCo Ltd-China AuxGen: 3 x 320kW 400V a.c Thrusters: 1 Tunnel thruster (f)
5327996 **SILVA OF HALIFAX** - *ex* Silva *-2002* - **Tall Ship Silva Inc** - *Halifax, NS* *Canada* Official number: 824280	**167** 61 297	Class: (BV)	**1939-01 Karlstads Varv AB — Karlstad** Yd No: 113 Converted From: General Cargo Ship-2002 Loa 33.13 Br ex 7.35 Dght 3.302 Lbp - Br md 7.32 Dpth 3.36 Riveted, 1 dk	**(B35Y2XV) Sailing Vessel** Passengers: unberthed: 80 Grain: 453 Compartments: 1 Ho, ER 1 Ha: (14.8 x 5.1)ER Derricks: 2x1.5t; Winches: 2	**1 oil engine** reduction geared to sc. shaft driving 1 CP propeller Total Power: 213kW (290hp) 9.5kn Volvo Penta TMD121 1 x 4 Stroke 6 Cy. 130 x 150 213kW (290bhp) (made 1978, fitted 1980) AB Volvo Penta-Sweden
9240172 **SILVAPLANA** *SYLY* *ex* Apanemo *-2006* - **Silvaplana Transportation Special Maritime Enterprise (ENE)** Neda Maritime Agency Co Ltd SatCom: Inmarsat C 423787710 *Piraeus* *Greece* MMSI: 237877000 Official number: 11089	**62,216** 34,702 109,250 T/cm 99.2	Class: AB	**2003-01 Daewoo Shipbuilding & Marine Engineering Co Ltd — Geoje** Yd No: 5221 Loa 249.90 (BB) Br ex 44.04 Dght 14.260 Lbp 239.00 Br md 44.00 Dpth 21.00 Welded, 1 dk	**(A13A2TW) Crude/Oil Products Tanker** Double Hull (13F) Liq: 122,183; Liq (Oil): 127,414 Cargo Heating Coils Compartments: 12 Wing Ta, ER, 2 Wing Slop Ta 3 Cargo Pump (s): 3x3000m³/hr Manifold: Bow/CM: 125.6m	**1 oil engine** driving 1 FP propeller Total Power: 14,342kW (19,499hp) 15.0kn MAN-B&W 5S70MC-C 1 x 2 Stroke 5 Cy. 700 x 2800 14342kW (19499bhp) Doosan Engine Co Ltd-South Korea AuxGen: 3 x 750kW 450V 60Hz a.c Fuel: 190.0 (d.f.) (Heating Coils) 3477.0 (r.f.) 53.0pd
9276743 **SILVAPLANA** *HBFB* *ex* F. D. Clara d'Amato *-2007* - *ex* Benedetta d'Amato *-2006* **Oceana Shipping AG** Suisse-Atlantique Societe de Navigation Maritime SA *Basel* *Switzerland* MMSI: 269696000 Official number: 186	**17,951** 10,748 29,721 T/cm 40.5	Class: AB (RI) (NK)	**2003-04 Shikoku Dockyard Co. Ltd. — Takamatsu** Yd No: 1007 Loa 170.70 Br ex - Dght 9.500 Lbp 163.50 Br md 27.00 Dpth 13.80 Welded, 1 dk	**(A21A2BC) Bulk Carrier** Grain: 40,031; Bale: 38,422 Compartments: 5 Ho, ER 5 Ha: (20.0 x 17.8)3 (20.0 x 17.8)ER (12.8 x 16.2) Cranes: 4x30.5t	**1 oil engine** driving 1 FP propeller Total Power: 6,156kW (8,370hp) 14.3kn B&W 6S42MC 1 x 2 Stroke 6 Cy. 420 x 1764 6156kW (8370bhp) Mitsui Engineering & Shipbuilding CLtd-Japan
9236303 **SILVER** *CNCS* *ex* Adrar *-2013* *ex* Mar Carmen *-2013* - *ex* Mar Cristina *-2012* **MARCAB Sarl La Marocaine de Cabotage** - SatCom: Inmarsat C 424213711 *Laayoune* *Morocco* MMSI: 242137100	**4,401** 2,063 6,672 T/cm 16.1	Class: LR (BV) **100A1** SS 10/2011 Double Hull oil & chemical tanker, Ship Type 2 ESP LI Ice Class 1D at a draught of 6.8m Max/min draughts fwd 6.8/3.1m Max/min draughts aft 6.8/4.7m **LMC** **UMS**	**2001-10 Selah Makina Sanayi ve Ticaret A.S. — Tuzla, Istanbul** Yd No: 32 Loa 114.00 (BB) Br ex 16.90 Dght 6.802 Lbp 106.00 Br md 16.90 Dpth 8.40 Welded, 1 dk	**(A12B2TR) Chemical/Products Tanker** Double Hull (13F) Liq: 7,134; Liq (Oil): 7,134 Cargo Heating Coils Compartments: 12 Wing Ta, ER, 1 Slop Ta 13 Cargo Pump (s): 12x200m³/hr, 1x120m³/hr Manifold: Bow/CM: 59m Ice Capable	**1 oil engine** reduction geared to sc. shaft driving 1 CP propeller Total Power: 3,750kW (5,099hp) 15.0kn MaK 8M32 1 x 4 Stroke 8 Cy. 320 x 480 3750kW (5099bhp) Caterpillar Motoren GmbH & Co. KG-Germany AuxGen: 3 x 400kW 380/220V 50Hz a.c, 1 x 640kW 380/220V 50Hz a.c Thrusters: 1 Thwart. CP thruster (f) Fuel: 80.0 (d.f.) 370.0 (r.f.)
9594468 **SILVER** *5BNC3* - **Almi Navigation Ltd** Navarone SA *Limassol* *Cyprus* MMSI: 209666000	**19,943** 11,325 32,956	Class: GL	**2013-01 Yangfan Group Co Ltd — Zhoushan ZJ** Yd No: 2172 Loa 177.39 (BB) Br ex - Dght 10.200 Lbp 168.00 Br md 28.20 Dpth 14.20 Welded, 1 dk	**(A21A2BC) Bulk Carrier** Grain: 42,700 Compartments: 5 Ho, ER 5 Ha: ER Cranes: 4x30t Ice Capable	**1 oil engine** driving 1 FP propeller Total Power: 6,480kW (8,810hp) 14.2kn MAN-B&W 6S42MC 1 x 2 Stroke 6 Cy. 420 x 1764 6480kW (8810bhp) STX (Dalian) Engine Co Ltd-China
5328081 **SILVER** - - **Joseph Yambode & Co Ltd** - *Lagos* *Nigeria* Official number: 184228	*120* 82 224		**1952-12 Wm. Weatherhead & Sons Ltd. — Berwick** Yd No: 633 L reg 25.91 Br ex 6.13 Dght - Lbp - Br md - Dpth - Welded, 1 dk	**(A31A2GX) General Cargo Ship** Compartments: 1 Ho, ER 1 Ha: (14.4 x 4.1)ER	**1 oil engine** driving 1 FP propeller Total Power: 74kW (101hp) Foden FD4 1 x 4 Stroke 4 Cy. 92 x 120 74kW (101bhp) (made 1954, fitted 1974) Fodens Ltd.-Sandbach
8725321 **SILVER** - *ex* PTR-50 No. 7 *-1992* - -	**187** 56 77	Class: (RS)	**1985-11 Astrakhanskaya Sudoverf im. "Kirova" — Astrakhan** Yd No: 7 Loa 31.85 Br ex 7.08 Dght 2.130 Lbp 27.80 Br md - Dpth 3.15 Welded, 1 dk	**(B12B2FC) Fish Carrier** Ins: 100	**1 oil engine** geared to sc. shaft driving 1 FP propeller Total Power: 221kW (300hp) 10.2kn Daldizel 6CHNSP18/22-300 1 x 4 Stroke 6 Cy. 180 x 220 221kW (300bhp) Daldizel-Khabarovsk AuxGen: 2 x 25kW Fuel: 14.0 (d.f.)

7912484 *HQRC6* -	**SILVER 9** *ex* Atago Maru *-2013* *ex* Atago Maru No. 3 *-1997* **Joaquim International Ltd** Success Blossom Trading Pte Ltd *San Lorenzo* *Honduras* Official number: L-1326143	**924** 587 1,841 T/cm 6.2		1979-08 **Hakata Zosen K.K. — Imabari** Yd No: 218 Loa - Br ex - Dght 3.788 Lbp 65.21 Br md 11.02 Dpth 5.06 Welded, 1 dk	**(A13B2TP) Products Tanker** Liq: 2,203; Liq (Oil): 2,203 Compartments: 10 Ta, ER 2 Cargo Pump (s): 2x500m^3/hr Manifold: Bow/CM: 33m	**1 oil engine** geared to sc. shaft driving 1 FP propeller Total Power: 1,324kW (1,800hp) 12.0kn Hanshin 6LU35G 1 x 4 Stroke 6 Cy. 350 x 550 1324kW (1800bhp) The Hanshin Diesel Works Ltd-Japan Fuel: 10.5 (d.f.) (Part Heating Coils) 52.5 (r.f.)
1009522 *2BZX4* -	**SILVER ANGEL** - **Westhurst Partners SA** Camper & Nicholsons France SARL SatCom: Inmarsat C 423591671 *Douglas* *Isle of Man (British)* MMSI: 235070865 Official number: 740827	**1,407** 422 250	Class: LR **✠100A1** SS 06/2009 SSC Yacht (P), mono, G6 **LMC** **UMS** Cable: 385.0/26.0 U3 (a)	2009-06 **Azimut-Benetti SpA — Livorno** Yd No: FB247 Loa 64.50 Br ex 12.34 Dght 3.550 Lbp 54.40 Br md 12.10 Dpth 6.20 Welded, 1 dk	**(X11A2YP) Yacht**	**2 oil engines** with clutches, flexible couplings & sr reverse geared to sc. shafts driving 2 FP propellers Total Power: 3,370kW (4,582hp) Caterpillar 3516B 2 x Vee 4 Stroke 16 Cy. 170 x 215 each-1685kW (2291bhp) Caterpillar Inc-USA AuxGen: 2 x 200kW 400V 50Hz a.c, 1 x 85kW 400V 50Hz a.c, 1 x 348kW 400V 50Hz a.c Thrusters: 1 Thwart. FP thruster (f)
7506455 *DUG6244* -	**SILVER BASS** *ex* Kinsei Maru No. 55 *-1990* *ex* Myoken Maru No. 55 *-1986* *ex* Ontake Maru No. 55 *-1982* **Jumbo Fishing Corp** - *Iloilo* *Philippines* Official number: 06-0000479	*163* 96 -		1975-07 **Minami-Nippon Zosen KK — Ichikikushikino KS** Yd No: 236 Loa 37.17 Br ex 6.81 Dght 2.439 Lbp 31.96 Br md 6.41 Dpth 2.87 Welded, 1 dk	**(B11B2FV) Fishing Vessel**	**1 oil engine** driving 1 FP propeller Total Power: 441kW (600hp) Niigata 6L25BX 1 x 4 Stroke 6 Cy. 250 x 320 441kW (600bhp) Niigata Engineering Co Ltd-Japan
7309302 - -	**SILVER BAY** *ex* Tugidak *-2013* *ex* Pacific Star *-2011* *ex* North Star *-2005* *ex* Teejin II *-1979* *ex* Tugidak *-1979* **Stikine Holdings LLC** - *Naknek, AK* *United States of America* Official number: 512076	**277** 83 -		1967 **Pacific Fishermen, Inc. — Seattle, Wa** L reg 25.18 Br ex 7.93 Dght - Lbp - Br md - Dpth 3.08 Welded	**(B11B2FV) Fishing Vessel**	**1 oil engine** driving 1 FP propeller Total Power: 360kW (489hp)
8863109 *LIHW* H-95-B	**SILVER BAY** *ex* Stattvaering *-2000* *ex* Tanja III *-1996* *ex* Flid *-1986* **Eivind Waage AS** - *Maaloy* *Norway* MMSI: 259377000	**126** 50		1968-01 **Kystvaagen Slip & Baatbyggeri — Kristiansund** Loa 23.43 Br ex 6.57 Dght - Lbp - Br md 6.51 Dpth 3.35 Welded, 1 dk	**(B11B2FV) Fishing Vessel**	**1 oil engine** geared to sc. shaft driving 1 FP propeller Total Power: 441kW (600hp) 10.0kn Caterpillar 1 x 4 Stroke 441kW (600bhp) (new engine 1997) Caterpillar Inc-USA
6609896 *H05274* -	**SILVER BEACH** *ex* Helgard *-1981* *ex* Heli *-1979* *ex* Westervik *-1979* *ex* Selstein *-1975* *ex* Sine Bres *-1974* *ex* Cowes *-1974* *ex* Sine Bres *-1972* **Panmarine Inc** - *Panama* *Panama* Official number: 1196882	*298* 171 832	Class: (BV) (NV)	1966 **Batservice Verft AS — Mandal** Yd No: 526 Loa 55.00 Br ex 9.33 Dght 3.506 Lbp 50.02 Br md 9.30 Dpth 3.56 Welded, 2 dks	**(A31A2GX) General Cargo Ship** Grain: 1,566; Bale: 1,344 Compartments: 1 Ho, ER 2 Ha: 2 (13.3 x 6.0)ER Derricks: 2x5t; Winches: 4 Ice Capable	**1 oil engine** driving 1 CP propeller Total Power: 375kW (510hp) 9.5kn Alpha 406-24VO 1 x 2 Stroke 6 Cy. 240 x 400 375kW (510bhp) Alpha Diesel A/S-Denmark AuxGen: 2 x 18kW 220V d.c, 1 x 9kW 220V d.c, 1 x 8kW 220V d.c Fuel: 37.5 (d.f.) 2.5pd
8405945 *DSEF3* -	**SILVER BELL** *ex* Ryozui Maru *-1995* **Dong Won Shipping Co Ltd** - *Busan* *South Korea* MMSI: 440119900 Official number: BSR-951579	*3,578* - 4,250	Class: (KR) (NK)	1984-07 **Higaki Zosen K.K. — Imabari** Yd No: 316 Loa 105.87 (BB) Br ex 16.03 Dght 6.771 Lbp 98.61 Br md 16.01 Dpth 8.41 Welded, 1 dk	**(A31A2GX) General Cargo Ship** Grain: 7,625; Bale: 7,316 Compartments: 3 Ho, ER 3 Ha: (17.6 x 9.6) (22.1 x 9.6) (16.9 x 9.6)ER	**1 oil engine** sr geared to sc. shaft driving 1 CP propeller Total Power: 2,059kW (2,799hp) 12.0kn Hanshin 6EL38 1 x 4 Stroke 6 Cy. 380 x 760 2059kW (2799bhp) The Hanshin Diesel Works Ltd-Japan AuxGen: 4 x 183kW a.c Thrusters: 1 Thwart. CP thruster (f)
8716033 *3FMV* -	**SILVER BELL** - **Tiger United SA** Korea Line Corp SatCom: Inmarsat C 435691011 *Panama* *Panama* MMSI: 356910000 Official number: 4066009	**110,352** 64,853 207,672	Class: KR (NK)	1989-12 **Samsung Shipbuilding & Heavy Industries Co Ltd — Geoje** Yd No: 1065 Loa 311.92 (BB) Br ex - Dght 18.020 Lbp 300.00 Br md 50.00 Dpth 25.70 Welded, 1 dk	**(A21A2BC) Bulk Carrier** Grain: 238,784 Compartments: 9 Ho, ER 9 Ha: (15.8 x 17.0)8 (15.8 x 23.0)ER	**1 oil engine** driving 1 FP propeller Total Power: 12,122kW (16,481hp) 12.8kn B&W 6L80MCE 1 x 2 Stroke 6 Cy. 800 x 2592 12122kW (16481bhp) Korea Heavy Industries & ConstrCo Ltd (HANJUNG)-South Korea AuxGen: 5 x 530kW a.c
7426394 *DUA6539* -	**SILVER BELL 2** *ex* Yusei Maru No. 81 *-2008* **Frabelle Fishing Corp** - *Zamboanga* *Philippines* Official number: MNLD002927	*253* 136 386		1975-02 **Tokushima Zosen K.K. — Fukuoka** Yd No: 1160 Loa 47.20 Br ex 7.62 Dght 3.226 Lbp 41.48 Br md 7.60 Dpth 3.61 Welded, 1 dk	**(B11B2FV) Fishing Vessel**	**1 oil engine** geared to sc. shaft driving 1 FP propeller Total Power: 956kW (1,300hp) Daihatsu 6DSM-26 1 x 4 Stroke 6 Cy. 260 x 320 956kW (1300bhp) Daihatsu Diesel Manufacturing Co Lt-Japan
9140944 *LAH06* -	**SILVER BERGEN** *ex* Frio Athens *-2005* *ex* Andromeda *-1999* **Silver Bergen II AS** Fjord Shipping AS *Bergen* *Norway (NIS)* MMSI: 257951000	**3,817** 1,446 4,240 T/cm 12.9	Class: LR **✠100A1** SS 03/2012 Ice Class 1B **✠LMC** **UMS +Lloyd's RMC** Eq.Ltr: U; Cable: 467.5/46.0 U2	1997-03 **Aarhus Flydedok A/S — Aarhus** Yd No: 206 Loa 97.60 (BB) Br ex 15.73 Dght 6.000 Lbp 91.50 Br md 15.70 Dpth 10.10 Welded, 3 dks	**(A34A2GR) Refrigerated Cargo Ship** Ins: 5,512 TEU 54 C. 54/20' Compartments: 2 Ho, ER, 2 Tw Dk 2 Ha: 2 (6.5 x 5.4)ER Cranes: 2x8t Ice Capable	**1 oil engine** with clutches, flexible couplings & sr geared to sc. shaft driving 1 CP propeller Total Power: 3,251kW (4,420hp) 15.5kn MaK 8M32 1 x 4 Stroke 8 Cy. 320 x 480 3251kW (4420bhp) MaK Motoren GmbH & Co. KG-Kiel AuxGen: 1 x 648kW 380V 50Hz a.c, 3 x 420kW 380V 50Hz a.c Boilers: TOH (o.f.) 10.2kgf/cm^2 (10.0bar), TOH (ex.g.) 10.2kgf/cm^2 (10.0bar) Thrusters: 1 Thwart. FP thruster (f) Fuel: 400.0 (r.f.)
7901033 *ZR5390* -	**SILVER BOUNTY** *ex* Khalf 2 *-1993* **West Point Fishing Corp Pty Ltd** - *Cape Town* *South Africa* Official number: 19308	*271* 81 321	Class: (LR) ✠ Classed LR until 5/11/86	1979-09 **Maebata Zosen Tekko K.K. — Sasebo** Yd No: 132 Loa 30.23 Br ex 8.21 Dght 4.160 Lbp 26.50 Br md 8.01 Dpth 4.35 Welded, 2 dks	**(B11B2FV) Fishing Vessel**	**1 oil engine** sr geared to sc. shaft driving 1 CP propeller Total Power: 588kW (799hp) Yanmar T220-UT 1 x 4 Stroke 6 Cy. 220 x 280 588kW (799bhp) Yanmar Diesel Engine Co Ltd-Japan AuxGen: 2 x 52kW 380V 50Hz a.c
9200756 *V7XO2* -	**SILVER BRIDGE** *ex* Century River *-2011* **Kamco No 32 Shipping Co SA** Sinokor Merchant Marine Co Ltd *Majuro* *Marshall Islands* MMSI: 538004526 Official number: 4526	**57,944** 31,829 107,212 T/cm 91.0	Class: KR (NK)	1999-08 **Koyo Dockyard Co Ltd — Mihara HS** Yd No: 2106 Loa 246.80 (BB) Br ex 42.03 Dght 14.798 Lbp 235.00 Br md 42.00 Dpth 21.30 Welded, 1 dk	**(A13A2TW) Crude/Oil Products Tanker** Double Hull (13F) Liq: 116,684; Liq (Oil): 122,814 Cargo Heating Coils Compartments: 14 Wing Ta, ER, 2 Wing Slop Ta 3 Cargo Pump (s): 3x2500m^3/hr Manifold: Bow/CM: 123.7m	**1 oil engine** driving 1 FP propeller Total Power: 12,797kW (17,399hp) 14.5kn Sulzer 7RTA62 1 x 2 Stroke 7 Cy. 620 x 2150 12797kW (17399bhp) Diesel United Ltd.-Aioi AuxGen: 3 x 680kW a.c Fuel: 294.0 (d.f.) 3677.0 (r.f.)
7901069 *ZR2932* -	**SILVER CHALLENGER** *ex* Seatas 5 *-1996* *ex* Khalf 5 *-1996* **Saldanha Bay Canning Co (Pty) Ltd** - *Cape Town* *South Africa* Official number: 19605	*271* 81 321	Class: (LR) ✠ Classed LR until 18/2/87	1980-02 **Maebata Zosen Tekko K.K. — Sasebo** Yd No: 135 Loa 30.23 Br ex 8.21 Dght 3.701 Lbp 26.50 Br md 8.01 Dpth 4.37 Welded, 1 dk	**(B11B2FV) Fishing Vessel**	**1 oil engine** sr geared to sc. shaft driving 1 CP propeller Total Power: 588kW (799hp) 10.0kn Yanmar T220-UT 1 x 4 Stroke 6 Cy. 220 x 280 588kW (799bhp) Yanmar Diesel Engine Co Ltd-Japan AuxGen: 2 x 52kW 380V 50Hz a.c
8744456 *ZR6589* -	**SILVER CHAMPION** - **Talhado Fishing Enterprises (Pty) Ltd** - *Port Elizabeth* *South Africa* MMSI: 601782000 Official number: 40401	**108** - -		2004-03 **Tallie Marine Pty Ltd — St Helena Bay** Loa 25.40 Br ex - Dght 2.400 Lbp - Br md 7.20 Dpth - Bonded, 1 dk	**(B11B2FV) Fishing Vessel** Hull Material: Reinforced Plastic	**1 oil engine** driving 1 Propeller 9.5kn Scania 1 x Vee 4 Stroke 8 Cy. Scania AB-Sweden

IMO / Call sign	Name / Owner	Tonnage	Class	Build / Dimensions	Type	Machinery
8903923 *C6MQ5* -	**SILVER CLOUD** - **Silver Cloud Shipping Co Ltd** Silversea Cruises Ltd SatCom: Inmarsat C 430902710 *Nassau* *Bahamas* MMSI: 309027000 Official number: 725348	**16,927** 5,302 1,564	Class: RI (LR) ✠ Classed LR until 1/4/97	**1994-03 Cantiere Navale Visentini Srl — Porto Viro** (Hull launched by) **1994-03 T. Mariotti SpA — Genova** (Hull completed by) **1994-03 Soc. Esercizio Cant. S.p.A. — Viareggio** Yd No: 775 Loa 155.81 (BB) Br ex 21.42 Dght 5.350 Lbp 134.84 Br md 21.40 Dpth 13.20 Welded, 3 dks	**(A37A2PC) Passenger/Cruise** Passengers: cabins: 148; berths: 296	**2 oil engines** with clutches, flexible couplings & sr geared to sc. shafts driving 2 CP propellers Total Power: 11,700kW (15,908hp) 17.5kn Wartsila 6R46 2 x 4 Stroke 6 Cy. 460 x 580 each-5850kW (7954bhp) Wartsila Diesel Oy-Finland AuxGen: 2 x 2700kW 440V 60Hz a.c, 2 x 2700kW 440V 60Hz a.c Thrusters: 2 Thwart. CP thruster (f) Fuel: 989.0 (r.f.)
9187667 *5ISD33* -	**SILVER CLOUD** *ex Christina -2013 ex Castor -2012* *ex Amol -2012 ex Iran Amol -2008* **NITC** - *Zanzibar* *Tanzania (Zanzibar)* MMSI: 677003200	**56,068** 29,042 99,094 T/cm 94.5	Class: KR (LR) ✠ Classed LR until 7/4/12	**2000-11 Daewoo Shipbuilding & Marine Engineering Co Ltd — Geoje** Yd No: 5149 Loa 248.00 (BB) Br ex 43.03 Dght 13.520 Lbp 238.00 Br md 43.00 Dpth 19.80 Welded, 1 dk	**(A13A2TW) Crude/Oil Products Tanker** Double Hull (13F) Liq: 111,556; Liq (Oil): 111,556 Compartments: 12 Wing Ta, 2 Wing Slop Ta, ER 3 Cargo Pump (s): 3x2500m³/hr Manifold: Bow/CM: 62m	**1 oil engine** driving 1 FP propeller Total Power: 14,312kW (19,459hp) 15.0kn Sulzer 7RTA58T 1 x 2 Stroke 7 Cy. 580 x 2416 14312kW (19459bhp) HSD Engine Co Ltd-South Korea AuxGen: 3 x 860kW 450V 60Hz a.c Boilers: 2 AuxB (o.f.) 18.7kgf/cm² (18.3bar), e (ex.g.) 22.0kgf/cm² (21.6bar) Fuel: 207.0 (d.f.) (Heating Coils) 3246.0 (r.f.) 59.0pd
9514860 *ZCXJ8* -	**SILVER CLOUD** - **Silver Cloud Investments Inc** - *George Town* *Cayman Islands (British)* MMSI: 319440000 Official number: 740660	**498** 350 90	Class: (GL)	**2008-09 AO Pribaltiyskiy Sudostroitelnyy Zavod "Yantar" — Kaliningrad** (Hull) Yd No: (6480) **2008-09 Schiffs- u. Yachtwerft Abeking & Rasmussen GmbH & Co. — Lemwerder** Yd No: 6480 Loa 40.50 (BB) Br ex - Dght 4.500 Lbp 38.00 Br md 17.80 Dpth 7.30 Welded, 1 dk	**(X11A2YP) Yacht**	**2 oil engines** reduction geared to sc. shafts driving 2 FP propellers Total Power: 1,640kW (2,230hp) 12.5kn Caterpillar C32 2 x Vee 4 Stroke 12 Cy. 145 x 162 each-820kW (1115bhp) Caterpillar Inc-USA AuxGen: 2 x 176kW 400V a.c Thrusters: 1 Tunnel thruster (f)
8663834 - -	**SILVER CONDOR** - **Andrew Lavallee** - *Quebec, QC* *Canada* Official number: 802583	**111** 83 -		**1983 Les Ateliers Maritimes de Tilly — St-Antoine-de-Tilly QC** Lengthened-2005 Loa 18.53 Br ex - Dght - Lbp - Br md 6.00 Dpth 3.05 Bonded, 1 dk	**(B11B2FV) Fishing Vessel** Hull Material: Reinforced Plastic	**1 oil engine** driving 1 Propeller Total Power: 272kW (370hp) 10.0kn
9143386 *LAHD6* -	**SILVER COPENHAGEN** *ex Frio London -2004* *launched as Centavr -1999* **Silver Copenhagen II AS** Fjord Shipping AS *Bergen* *Norway (NIS)* MMSI: 257859000	**3,817** 1,446 4,230	Class: LR ✠ **100A1** SS 08/2009 Ice Class 1B ✠ **LMC** **UMS +Lloyd's RMC** Eq.Ltr: U; Cable: 467.5/46.0 U2	**1998-07 Aarhus Flydedok A/S — Aarhus** Yd No: 224 Loa 97.60 (BB) Br ex 15.73 Dght 6.000 Lbp 91.50 Br md 15.70 Dpth 10.10 Welded, 3 dks	**(A34A2GR) Refrigerated Cargo Ship** Ins: 5,512 TEU 52 C.Ho 12/20' C.Dk 40/20' Compartments: 2 Ho, ER, 2 Tw Dk 2 Ha: ER Cranes: 2x8t Ice Capable	**1 oil engine** with clutches, flexible couplings & sr geared to sc. shaft driving 1 FP propeller Total Power: 3,250kW (4,419hp) 15.5kn MaK 8M32 1 x 4 Stroke 8 Cy. 320 x 480 3250kW (4419bhp) MaK Motoren GmbH & Co. KG-Kiel AuxGen: 1 x 648kW 380V 50Hz a.c, 3 x 420kW 380V 50Hz a.c Boilers: TOH (o.f.) 12.8kgf/cm² (12.6bar), TOH (ex.g.) 12.8kgf/cm² (12.6bar) Thrusters: 1 Thwart. CP thruster (f)
8993942 *VQGG6* PZ 1196	**SILVER DAWN** - **Silver Dawn Fishing Ltd** - *Penzance* *United Kingdom* MMSI: 235005150 Official number: C17466	*118* 36 -		**2002-01 Riverside Fabrications Ltd. — Falmouth** Loa 17.93 Br ex - Dght - Lbp - Br md 6.25 Dpth 2.25 Welded, 1 dk	**(B11B2FV) Fishing Vessel**	**1 oil engine** reduction geared to sc. shaft driving 1 Propeller Total Power: 200kW (272hp) 10.5kn Baudouin 8M26SR 1 x 4 Stroke 8 Cy. 150 x 150 200kW (272bhp) Societe des Moteurs Baudouin SA-France
8800195 *C6OZ3* -	**SILVER DISCOVERER** *ex Clipper Odyssey -2013* *ex Oceanic Odyssey -1998* *ex Oceanic Grace -1997* **Odyssey Owner Ltd** FleetPro Ocean Inc SatCom: Inmarsat A 1307675 *Nassau* *Bahamas* MMSI: 309913000 Official number: 730526	**5,218** 1,565 938 T/cm 11.9	Class: BV (NK)	**1989-04 Nippon Kokan KK (NKK Corp) — Tsu ME** Yd No: 112 Loa 102.97 (BB) Br ex 15.42 Dght 4.312 Lbp 92.00 Br md 15.40 Dpth 6.20 Welded	**(A37A2PC) Passenger/Cruise** Passengers: cabins: 64; berths: 128	**2 oil engines** sr geared to sc. shafts driving 2 CP propellers Total Power: 5,194kW (7,062hp) 18.0kn Wartsila 16V22HF 2 x Vee 4 Stroke 16 Cy. 220 x 240 each-2597kW (3531bhp) Wartsila Diesel Oy-Finland AuxGen: 3 x 500kW 440/220V 60Hz a.c Thrusters: 1 Thwart. FP thruster (f) Fuel: 394.0 (d.f.)
7437721 *WCI6929* -	**SILVER DOLPHIN** - **Brekkaa Fisheries Inc** - *Seattle, WA* *United States of America* MMSI: 367609000 Official number: 547726	**237** 71 -		**1973 Marine Construction & Design Co. (MARCO) — Seattle, Wa** L reg 27.99 Br ex 8.34 Dght - Lbp - Br md - Dpth 2.82 Welded, 1 dk	**(B11B2FV) Fishing Vessel**	**1 oil engine** driving 1 FP propeller Total Power: 625kW (850hp) Caterpillar D398SCAC 1 x Vee 4 Stroke 12 Cy. 159 x 203 625kW (850bhp) Caterpillar Tractor Co-USA
6515825 - -	**SILVER DOLPHIN** *ex Frederick K -2002 ex Silver Dolphin -2001* **Branden Fisheries Ltd** - *St John's, NL* *Canada* Official number: 320898	*190* 130 -		**1965 Benson Bros Shipbuilding Co (1960) Ltd — Vancouver BC** Yd No: 12 L reg 27.74 Br ex 7.47 Dght - Lbp - Br md 7.42 Dpth 3.84 Welded	**(B11A2FT) Trawler**	**1 oil engine** driving 1 FP propeller Total Power: 496kW (674hp) Caterpillar D379SCAC 1 x Vee 4 Stroke 8 Cy. 159 x 203 496kW (674bhp) Caterpillar Tractor Co-USA
9364447 *VRCA6* -	**SILVER DRAGON** - **Allied Shipping Ltd** Valles Steamship (Canada) Inc *Hong Kong* *Hong Kong* MMSI: 477415800 Official number: HK-1739	**40,492** 25,884 74,748 T/cm 67.0	Class: AB	**2006-10 Hudong-Zhonghua Shipbuilding (Group) Co Ltd — Shanghai** Yd No: H1386A Loa 225.00 (BB) Br ex - Dght 14.250 Lbp 217.00 Br md 32.26 Dpth 19.60 Welded, 1 dk	**(A21A2BC) Bulk Carrier** Grain: 91,717; Bale: 89,883 Compartments: 7 Ho, ER 7 Ha: 6 (14.6 x 15.0)ER (14.6 x 13.2)	**1 oil engine** driving 1 FP propeller Total Power: 11,299kW (15,362hp) 14.0kn MAN-B&W 5S60MC-C 1 x 2 Stroke 5 Cy. 600 x 2400 11299kW (15362bhp) Hudong Heavy Machinery Co Ltd-China Fuel: 137.4 (d.f.) 2656.7 (r.f.)
9359222 *XUJM8* -	**SILVER DREAM** *ex Sunshine 21 -2012* **East Line Shipping (Hong Kong) Ltd** East Line Shipping Co Ltd *Phnom Penh* *Cambodia* MMSI: 515864000 Official number: 0505134	**2,039** 974 2,987 T/cm 9.8	Class: GM	**2005-06 Nanjing Sanxing Shipyard — Nanjing JS** Loa 83.00 (BB) Br ex - Dght 4.870 Lbp 77.18 Br md 13.20 Dpth 6.00 Welded, 1 dk	**(A31A2GX) General Cargo Ship**	**1 oil engine** reduction geared to sc. shaft driving 1 FP propeller Total Power: 882kW (1,199hp) 12.0kn Chinese Std. Type LB8250ZLC 1 x 4 Stroke 8 Cy. 250 x 320 882kW (1199bhp) Zibo Diesel Engine Factory-China AuxGen: 2 x 120kW 380/220V 50Hz a.c Fuel: 35.0 (d.f.) 135.0 (r.f.) 6.0pd
9462988 *ZCFZ8* -	**SILVER DREAM** *ex Slipstream -2009* **Mikaroo Pty Ltd** Nigel Burgess Ltd (BURGESS) *George Town* *Cayman Islands (British)* MMSI: 319634000 Official number: 734579	**395** 118 51	Class: AB	**2001-03 Dave Warren Yachts — Kincumber NSW** Yd No: 135 Loa 43.30 Br ex 8.50 Dght 2.100 Lbp 37.00 Br md 8.25 Dpth 4.24 Welded, 1 dk	**(X11A2YP) Yacht**	**2 oil engines** reduction geared to sc. shafts driving 2 Propellers Total Power: 999kW (1,358hp) Caterpillar 3412E 2 x Vee 4 Stroke 12 Cy. 137 x 152 each-499kW (678bhp) Caterpillar Inc-USA
8503450 *WDC3612* -	**SILVER EAGLE** *ex Rio La Plata -1987* *launched as Rio Del Plata -1984* **Oscar Niemeth Towing Inc** - *San Francisco, CA* *United States of America* MMSI: 367011160 Official number: 662137	*185* 68 -		**1984 Sanchez Marine Services Corp. — Fall River, Ma** Yd No: 8210 Loa 32.47 Br ex - Dght 4.879 Lbp 31.17 Br md 10.22 Dpth 5.21 Welded, 1 dk	**(B32A2ST) Tug**	**1 oil engine** gearing integral to driving 2 Z propellers EMD (Electro-Motive) 16-645 1 x Vee 2 Stroke 16 Cy. 230 x 254 General Motors Corp.Electro-Motive Div.-La Grange
8744585 *ZR8126* -	**SILVER EAGLE** - **Talhado Fishing Enterprises (Pty) Ltd** - *Port Elizabeth* *South Africa* MMSI: 601116700 Official number: 40904	**126** - -		**2009-01 in the Republic of South Africa** Loa 19.63 Br ex - Dght - Lbp - Br md - Dpth - Bonded, 1 dk	**(B11B2FV) Fishing Vessel** Hull Material: Reinforced Plastic	**2 oil engines** reduction geared to sc. shafts driving 2 Propellers 9.0kn

IMO / Call sign	Name / Owner	Tonnage	Class	Builder / Dimensions	Type / Cargo	Machinery
9667265 *JD3491* -	**SILVER EIGHT** **Japan Railway Construction, Transport & Technology Agency & Tsugarukaikyo Ferry Co Ltd** Tsugarukaikyo Ferry Co Ltd *Hachinohe, Aomori* *Japan* MMSI: 431004622 Official number: 141878	*9,483* - 3,250	Class: FA (Class contemplated)	**2013-06 Naikai Zosen Corp — Onomichi HS (Setoda Shipyard)** Yd No: 760 Loa 142.59 (BB) Br ex - Dght 5.600 Lbp - Br md 23.40 Dpth 14.10 Welded, 1 dk	**(A36A2PR) Passenger/Ro-Ro Ship (Vehicles)** Passengers: 600 Bow door/ramp (centre) Stern door/ramp (centre) Vehicles: 68	**2 oil engines** driving 2 Propellers Total Power: 13,930kW (18,940hp) 20.5kn MAN-B&W 7L42MC 1 x 2 Stroke 7 Cy. 420 x 1360 6965kW (9470bhp) Hitachi Zosen Corp-Japan
8806747 *C6TA8* -	**SILVER EXPLORER** *ex* Prince Albert II *-2011* *ex* World Discoverer *-2008* *ex* Dream 21 *-2002* *ex* Delfin Star *-1997* *ex* Baltic Clipper *-1992* *ex* Sally Clipper *-1992* *ex* Delfin Clipper *-1990* **Silversea Discoverer Shipping Co Ltd** V Ships Leisure SAM *Nassau* *Bahamas* MMSI: 311562000 Official number: 8000671	**6,130** 1,839 635	Class: LR (KR) ✠ **100A1** SS 06/2009 passenger ship Ice Class 1A at a draught of 4.511m Max/min draughts fwd 4.511/3.511m Max/min draughts aft 4.511/3.511m Power required 2442kw, power installed 4500kw ✠ **LMC** Eq.Ltr: T; Cable: 467.5/38.0 U3	**1989-06 Rauma-Repola Oy — Rauma** Yd No: 304 Loa 108.11 (BB) Br ex 15.83 Dght 4.380 Lbp 95.95 Br md 15.60 Dpth 9.60 Welded, 3 dks	**(A37A2PC) Passenger/Cruise** Passengers: cabins: 68; berths: 158 Ice Capable	**2 oil engines** with clutches, flexible couplings & sr geared to sc. shafts driving 2 CP propellers Total Power: 4,500kW (6,118hp) 15.0kn Wartsila 6R32D 2 x 4 Stroke 6 Cy. 320 x 350 each-2250kW (3059bhp) Wartsila Diesel Oy-Finland AuxGen: 2 x 1000kW 440V 60Hz a.c, 2 x 840kW 440V 60Hz a.c Boilers: 2 TOH (o.f.) 10.2kgf/cm² (10.0bar), 2 TOH (ex.g.) 10.2kgf/cm² (10.0bar) Thrusters: 1 Thwart. CP thruster (f)
9077355 *D8CA* -	**SILVER EXPRESS** *ex* Aquabella *-2013* *ex* Merchant Prestige *-1998* **Sinokor Merchant Marine Co Ltd** - *Jeju* *South Korea* MMSI: 441974000 Official number: JJR-131038	**81,273** 53,173 161,010 T/cm 113.8	Class: KR (LR) (AB) ✠ Classed LR until 28/12/99	**1995-01 Hyundai Heavy Industries Co Ltd — Ulsan** Yd No: 874 Loa 280.07 (BB) Br ex 45.05 Dght 17.519 Lbp 270.00 Br md 45.00 Dpth 23.80 Welded, 1 dk	**(A21A2BC) Bulk Carrier** Grain: 175,753 Compartments: 9 Ho, ER 9 Ha: 7 (14.5 x 20.0)2 (14.5 x 15.2)ER	**1 oil engine** driving 1 FP propeller Total Power: 17,098kW (23,246hp) 14.5kn B&W 6S70MC 1 x 2 Stroke 6 Cy. 700 x 2674 17098kW (23246bhp) Hyundai Heavy Industries Co Ltd-South Korea AuxGen: 3 x 650kW 450V 60Hz a.c Fuel: 253.0 (d.f.) 3251.4 (r.f.) 55.3pd
8410483 *S2EX* -	**SILVER EXPRESS** *ex* Keiyo Maru No. 25 *-1996* *ex* Shinko Maru No. 25 *-1992* **Tripple A Carriers Ltd** - *Chittagong* *Bangladesh* Official number: C.1158	*705* - 1,110	Class: (NK)	**1984-10 Kanmon Zosen K.K. — Shimonoseki** Yd No: 369 Loa 61.35 Br ex - Dght 3.963 Lbp 56.52 Br md 10.22 Dpth 4.53 Welded, 1 dk	**(A13A2TV) Crude Oil Tanker** Liq: 1,097; Liq (Oil): 1,097 Compartments: 6 Ta, ER	**1 oil engine** driving 1 CP propeller Total Power: 883kW (1,201hp) Hanshin 6LUN28A 1 x 4 Stroke 6 Cy. 280 x 480 883kW (1201bhp) The Hanshin Diesel Works Ltd-Japan
9380099 *3FNL4* -	**SILVER EXPRESS** **Mi-Das Line SA** MTM Ship Management Pte Ltd SatCom: Inmarsat C 435522110 *Panama* *Panama* MMSI: 355221000 Official number: 4074809	**26,900** 13,660 47,401 T/cm 50.3	Class: NK	**2009-08 Onomichi Dockyard Co Ltd — Onomichi HS** Yd No: 544 Loa 182.50 (BB) Br ex - Dght 12.600 Lbp 172.00 Br md 32.20 Dpth 18.10 Welded, 1 dk	**(A13B2TP) Products Tanker** Double Hull (13F) Liq: 50,560; Liq (Oil): 50,560 Compartments: 12 Wing Ta, 2 Wing Slop Ta, ER 4 Cargo Pump (s): 4x1000m³/hr Manifold: Bow/CM: 93.1m	**1 oil engine** driving 1 FP propeller Total Power: 8,580kW (11,665hp) 14.0kn MAN-B&W 6S50MC 1 x 2 Stroke 6 Cy. 500 x 1910 8580kW (11665bhp) Mitsui Engineering & Shipbuilding CLtd-Japan AuxGen: 3 x a.c Fuel: 1580.0 (r.f.)
9136591 *3FIB6* -	**SILVER FERN** *ex* MOL Silver Fern 2 *-2011* *ex* MOL Silver Fern *-2010* *ex* Ocean Lemon *-2000* **Seabright Shipping Inc** Bernhard Schulte Shipmanagement (China) Co Ltd SatCom: Inmarsat B 335654010 *Panama* *Panama* MMSI: 356540000 Official number: 2312796E	**13,310** 7,546 17,429	Class: NK	**1996-06 Iwagi Zosen Co Ltd — Kamijima EH** Yd No: 160 Loa 161.85 (BB) Br ex - Dght 8.926 Lbp 150.00 Br md 25.60 Dpth 12.90 Welded, 1 dk	**(A33A2CC) Container Ship (Fully Cellular)** TEU 1133 incl 100 ref C. Compartments: 5 Cell Ho, ER 16 Ha: 2 (12.8 x 5.7)14 (12.8 x 10.9)ER Cranes: 2x35t	**1 oil engine** driving 1 FP propeller Total Power: 9,989kW (13,581hp) 18.1kn B&W 7S50MC 1 x 2 Stroke 7 Cy. 500 x 1910 9989kW (13581bhp) Hitachi Zosen Corp-Japan AuxGen: 3 x a.c Thrusters: 1 Tunnel thruster (f) Fuel: 1050.0 (r.f.)
8963131 - -	**SILVER FIN** *ex* Dong Chang No. 89 *-2000* **Ostrov Co Ltd** -	**184** 71 124	Class: (RS)	**1989-12 Banguhjin Engineering & Shipbuilding Co Ltd — Ulsan** Yd No: 78 Loa 38.30 Br ex 6.45 Dght 2.670 Lbp 33.10 Br md - Dpth 3.30 Welded, 1 dk	**(B11A2FS) Stern Trawler** Ins: 262 2 Ha: 2 (1.0 x 1.0)ER	**1 oil engine** driving 1 FP propeller Total Power: 625kW (850hp) 11.5kn Niigata 6M26ZG 1 x 4 Stroke 6 Cy. 260 x 400 625kW (850bhp) (made 1973) Niigata Engineering Co Ltd-Japan AuxGen: 1 x 148kW a.c, 1 x 104kW a.c Fuel: 89.0 (d.f.)
8300327 *3FWE9* -	**SILVER FJORD** *ex* Ludvig Andersen *-2007* *ex* Saga *-1997* *ex* Star Saga *-1992* **Silver Fjord AS** Fjord Shipping AS *Panama* *Panama* MMSI: 357903000 Official number: 2713600CH	**2,462** 738 1,700	Class: NV	**1984-03 p/f Skala Skipasmidja — Skali** Yd No: 41 Converted From: Ro-Ro Cargo Ship-2007 Loa 77.63 (BB) Br ex 13.03 Dght 4.360 Lbp 69.60 Br md 13.01 Dpth 9.80 Welded, 3 dks	**(A34A2GR) Refrigerated Cargo Ship** Side door/ramp (s) Len: 6.00 Wid: 7.00 Swl: - Ins: 1,376 1 Ha: (10.2 x 5.1)ER Ice Capable	**1 oil engine** reduction geared to sc. shaft driving 1 CP propeller Total Power: 2,340kW (3,181hp) 14.3kn Alpha 12U28L-VO 1 x Vee 4 Stroke 12 Cy. 280 x 320 2340kW (3181bhp) B&W Alpha Diesel A/S-Denmark AuxGen: 1 x 450kW 380V 50Hz a.c, 2 x 184kW 380V 50Hz a.c Thrusters: 1 Thwart. FP thruster (f) Fuel: 48.5 (d.f.) 155.5 (r.f.) 9.0pd
9427445 *PCLZ* -	**SILVER FREYA** *ex* Global River *-2012* **Silverburn Shipping Isle of Man Ltd** Marin Ship Management BV *Delfzijl* *Netherlands* MMSI: 245092000	**5,424** 2,444 7,519 T/cm 17.6	Class: BV	**2011-03 Taixing Ganghua Ship Industry Co Ltd — Taixing JS** Yd No: GHCY 1002 Loa 112.70 (BB) Br ex 17.63 Dght 7.200 Lbp 106.47 Br md 17.60 Dpth 9.40 Welded, 1 dk	**(A12B2TR) Chemical/Products Tanker** Double Hull (13F) Liq: 8,341; Liq (Oil): 8,500 Cargo Heating Coils Compartments: 18 Wing Ta, 2 Wing Slop Ta, ER 18 Cargo Pump (s): 2x100m³/hr, 16x150m³/hr Manifold: Bow/CM: 51.4m Ice Capable	**2 oil engines** reduction geared to sc. shafts driving 2 CP propellers Total Power: 3,440kW (4,678hp) 14.0kn MAN-B&W 8L21/31 2 x 4 Stroke 8 Cy. 210 x 310 each-1720kW (2339bhp) Shanghai Xinzhong Power MachinePlant-China AuxGen: 2 x 500kW 450V 60Hz a.c, 3 x 400kW 450V 60Hz a.c Thrusters: 1 Tunnel thruster (f) Fuel: 89.0 (d.f.) 264.0 (r.f.)
7901071 *ZR6288* -	**SILVER GALAXY** *ex* Seatas 6 *-2012* *ex* Khalf 6 *-2012* **Saldanha Bay Canning Co (Pty) Ltd** - *Cape Town* *South Africa* Official number: 19604	*271* 81 321	Class: (LR) ✠ Classed LR until 18/2/87	**1980-03 Maebata Zosen Tekko K.K. — Sasebo** Yd No: 136 Loa 30.23 Br ex 8.18 Dght 3.701 Lbp 26.50 Br md 7.99 Dpth 4.35 Welded, 1 dk	**(B11B2FV) Fishing Vessel**	**1 oil engine** sr geared to sc. shaft driving 1 CP propeller Total Power: 588kW (799hp) Yanmar T220L-UT 1 x 4 Stroke 6 Cy. 220 x 280 588kW (799bhp) Yanmar Diesel Engine Co Ltd-Japan AuxGen: 2 x 52kW 380V 50Hz a.c
9183336 *D7MI* -	**SILVER GENEVA** *ex* Yangtze Marvel *-2013* *ex* Star Fortune *-2013* *ex* Shinrei *-2008* **Sinokor Merchant Marine Co Ltd** - *Jeju* *South Korea* MMSI: 440118000 Official number: JJR-131063	**84,335** 56,021 170,974 T/cm 114.9	Class: KR (NK)	**1999-02 Ishikawajima-Harima Heavy Industries Co Ltd (IHI) — Kure** Yd No: 3098 Loa 289.00 (BB) Br ex - Dght 17.625 Lbp 277.00 Br md 45.00 Dpth 23.80 Welded, 1 dk	**(A21A2BC) Bulk Carrier** Grain: 186,650 Compartments: 9 Ho, ER 9 Ha: (18.4 x 17.0)2 (17.6 x 20.4)5 (13.6 x 20.4) (16.8 x 17.0)ER	**1 oil engine** driving 1 FP propeller Total Power: 16,040kW (21,808hp) 14.5kn Sulzer 6RTA72 1 x 2 Stroke 6 Cy. 720 x 2500 16040kW (21808bhp) Diesel United Ltd.-Aioi AuxGen: 3 x 630kW 440V 60Hz a.c Fuel: 273.6 (d.f.) (Heating Coils) 4858.9 (r.f.) 61.1pd
9682318 *V7EE6* -	**SILVER GINNY** **Silver No 1 SA** Sinokor Maritime Co Ltd *Majuro* *Marshall Islands* MMSI: 538005462 Official number: 5462	**29,460** 13,632 49,780	Class: AB KR	**2014-03 Hyundai Mipo Dockyard Co Ltd — Ulsan** Yd No: 2393 Loa 183.00 (BB) Br ex 32.21 Dght 11.000 Lbp 174.00 Br md 32.20 Dpth 19.10 Welded, 1 dk	**(A12B2TR) Chemical/Products Tanker** Double Hull (13F)	**1 oil engine** driving 1 FP propeller 15.0kn
9206035 *V7EK9* -	**SILVER GLORY** *ex* Kumanogawa *-2014* **Ocean Glory SA** Sinokor Merchant Marine Co Ltd *Majuro* *Marshall Islands* MMSI: 538005486 Official number: 5486	**159,566** 95,425 302,203 T/cm 184.0	Class: KR (Class contemplated) NK	**2001-04 Kawasaki Heavy Industries Ltd — Sakaide KG** Yd No: 1496 Loa 333.00 (BB) Br ex 60.04 Dght 20.880 Lbp 320.00 Br md 60.00 Dpth 29.30 Welded, 1 dk	**(A13A2TV) Crude Oil Tanker** Double Hull (13F) Liq: 342,400; Liq (Oil): 342,400 Compartments: 5 Ta, 10 Wing Ta, ER, 2 Wing Slop Ta 3 Cargo Pump (s): 3x5500m³/hr	**1 oil engine** driving 1 FP propeller Total Power: 25,480kW (34,643hp) 15.3kn B&W 7S80MC 1 x 2 Stroke 7 Cy. 800 x 3056 25480kW (34643bhp) Kawasaki Heavy Industries Ltd-Japan Fuel: 319.0 (d.f.) 7495.0 (r.f.)

IMO / Call sign	Ship / Owner	Tonnage	Class	Build / Dimensions	Type / Cargo	Machinery
6820103 *DUNL* -	**SILVER GLORY** *ex* Lady Janelle *-2000* *ex* Ricsan 5 *-2000* *ex* Chokyu Maru No. 15 *-1978* **Jumbo Fishing Corp** - *Cebu* *Philippines* Official number: CEB1001365	*349* 218 -		**1968**-08 **Kochiken Zosen — Kochi** Yd No: 350 L reg 42.10 Br ex 7.95 Dght 3.277 Lbp - Br md 7.93 Dpth 3.64 Welded, 1 dk	**(B11B2FV) Fishing Vessel**	**1 oil engine** driving 1 FP propeller Total Power: 625kW (850hp) Daihatsu 1 x 4 Stroke 6 Cy. 320 x 450 625kW (850bhp) Daihatsu Kogyo-Japan
6911421 *DUAM3* -	**SILVER HARVEST** *ex* Dona Elena 1 *-1978* *ex* Kotobuki Maru *-1979* *ex* Kotobuki Maru No. 28 *-1979* **Jumbo Fishing Corp** - *Iloilo* *Philippines* Official number: 06-0000202	*232* 93 -		**1968**-12 **Niigata Engineering Co Ltd — Niigata NI** Yd No: 805 Loa 42.75 Br ex 7.24 Dght - Lbp 37.42 Br md 7.22 Dpth 3.15 Welded, 1 dk	**(B11B2FV) Fishing Vessel**	**1 oil engine** driving 1 FP propeller Total Power: 478kW (650hp) Niigata 6M26KCHS 1 x 4 Stroke 6 Cy. 260 x 400 478kW (650bhp) Niigata Engineering Co Ltd-Japan
9279616 *HPBU* -	**SILVER HAWK** *ex* Golden Glory *-2012* **Asahiya Investors SA** Wooil Marine Co Ltd *Panama* *Panama* MMSI: 351723000 Official number: 2926903C	**5,203** 2,636 8,829 T/cm 17.3	Class: NK	**2003**-06 **Murakami Hide Zosen K.K. — Imabari** Yd No: 528 Loa 114.99 (BB) Br ex 18.22 Dght 7.770 Lbp 108.50 Br md 18.20 Dpth 9.65 Welded, 1 Dk.	**(A12B2TR) Chemical/Products Tanker** Double Hull (13F) Liq: 8,845; Liq (Oil): 8,845 Cargo Heating Coils Compartments: 1 Wing Ta, 15 Wing Ta (s.stl), 1 Wing Slop Ta, 1 Wing Slop Ta (s.stl), ER (s.stl) 16 Cargo Pump (s): 16x200m³/hr Manifold: Bow/CM: 59.9m	**1 oil engine** driving 1 FP propeller Total Power: 3,900kW (5,302hp) 13.4kn B&W 6L35MC 1 x 2 Stroke 6 Cy. 350 x 1050 3900kW (5302bhp) Hitachi Zosen Corp-Japan AuxGen: 2 x 480kW 445/110V 60Hz a.c Fuel: 119.0 (d.f.) (Heating Coils) 476.6 (r.f.)
7367873 *XUEY9* -	**SILVER HOPE** *ex* Maasborg *-2004* **Arnedo Finance Inc** East Marine Co Ltd *Phnom Penh* *Cambodia* MMSI: 515673000 Official number: 0474173	**2,905** 1,358 1,820	Class: IV (IS) (BV)	**1974**-10 **Scheepswerf 'Friesland' BV — Lemmer** Yd No: 69 Loa 81.82 Br ex 15.27 Dght 5.950 Lbp 75.00 Br md 14.99 Dpth 8.72 Welded, 1 dk & S dk	**(A31A2GX) General Cargo Ship** Grain: 5,380 Compartments: 1 Ho, ER 3 Ha: (13.4 x 12.5) (15.5 x 12.5) (13.1 x 12.5)ER Cranes: 3x8t Ice Capable	**2 oil engines** geared to sc. shaft driving 1 FP propeller Total Power: 1,942kW (2,640hp) 12.0kn Polar SF18VS-E 2 x Vee 4 Stroke 8 Cy. 250 x 300 each-971kW (1320bhp) AB NOHAB-Sweden
8907204 *LAKU6* -	**SILVER HORN** *ex* Cape Palmas *-2006* *ex* Blue Crest *-1999* **Silver Horn II AS** Fjord Shipping AS *Bergen* *Norway (NIS)* MMSI: 258818000	**6,419** 3,588 6,807	Class: GL RI	**1991**-11 **Shanghai Shipyard — Shanghai** Yd No: 143 Loa 120.50 Br ex - Dght 7.908 Lbp 111.60 Br md 18.55 Dpth 10.17 Welded, 1 dk, 2nd & 3rd dk in Nos. 1 - 4 holds, 4th dk in Nos. 2 - 4 holds	**(A34A2GR) Refrigerated Cargo Ship** Ins: 8,498 TEU 228 C Ho 84 TEU C Dk 144 TEU incl 36 ref C Compartments: 4 Ho, ER, 11 Tw Dk 4 Ha: 4 (12.4 x 8.0)ER Derricks: 8x10t Ice Capable	**1 oil engine** driving 1 FP propeller Total Power: 7,723kW (10,500hp) 15.0kn Sulzer 5RTA52 1 x 2 Stroke 5 Cy. 520 x 1800 7723kW (10500bhp) Shanghai Diesel Engine Co Ltd-China AuxGen: 3 x 600kW 220/440V a.c, 1 x 92kW 220/440V a.c Thrusters: 1 Thwart. FP thruster (f)
7819759 *D6DA5* -	**SILVER ICE** *ex* Ice Queen *-2005* *ex* Reefer Empress *-2000* *ex* Pacific Empress *-1990* *launched as* Gomba Reefer II *-1979* **Fishing & Cargo Services SA** - *Moroni* *Union of Comoros* MMSI: 616401000 Official number: 1200469	**1,753** 851 2,225	Class: (LR) (RS) ✠ Classed LR until 27/9/00	**1979**-04 **Frederikshavn Vaerft A/S — Frederikshavn** Yd No: 383 Loa 75.21 (BB) Br ex 13.29 Dght 5.011 Lbp 67.09 Br md 13.21 Dpth 7.27 Welded, 1 dk	**(A34A2GR) Refrigerated Cargo Ship** Ins: 2,570 TEU 12 C.Dk 12/20' Compartments: 3 Ho, ER 3 Ha: (8.7 x 4.7)2 (7.0 x 4.7)ER Derricks: 3x3t	**1 oil engine** sr geared to sc. shaft driving 1 CP propeller Total Power: 1,368kW (1,860hp) 11.5kn Alpha 12V23L-VO 1 x Vee 4 Stroke 12 Cy. 225 x 300 1368kW (1860bhp) Alpha Diesel A/S-Denmark AuxGen: 3 x 280kW 440V 60Hz a.c, 1 x 44kW 440V 60Hz a.c
9427524 *PCRP* -	**SILVER KENNA** *ex* Global Sun *-2012* **Silverburn Shipping Isle of Man Ltd** Marin Ship Management BV *Delfzijl* *Netherlands* MMSI: 246893000	**3,166** 1,318 4,393 T/cm 12.4	Class: BV	**2011**-04 **Yizheng Yangzi Shipbuilding Co Ltd — Yizheng JS** Yd No: 006-3600-III Loa 93.15 (BB) Br ex 15.23 Dght 5.800 Lbp 86.35 Br md 15.20 Dpth 7.20 Welded, 1 dk	**(A12B2TR) Chemical/Products Tanker** Double Hull (13F) Liq: 4,548; Liq (Oil): 4,500 Cargo Heating Coils Compartments: 6 Wing Ta, 6 Wing Ta, 1 Wing Slop Ta, 1 Wing Slop Ta, ER 12 Cargo Pump (s): 12x150m³/hr Manifold: Bow/CM: 42m Ice Capable	**2 oil engines** reduction geared to sc. shafts driving 2 CP propellers Total Power: 2,560kW (3,480hp) 12.5kn MAN-B&W 8L23/30A 2 x 4 Stroke 8 Cy. 225 x 300 each-1280kW (1740bhp) Zhenjiang Marine Diesel Works-China AuxGen: 2 x 400kW 450V 60Hz a.c Thrusters: 1 Tunnel thruster (f) Fuel: 63.0 (d.f.) 197.0 (r.f.)
7922491 *9H8638* -	**SILVER KING** *ex* Domenico *-2008* *ex* Silver King *-2007* *launched as* King Fisher *-1980* **Silver King Ltd** - *Valletta* *Malta* Official number: 7922491	*277* 77 -		**1980**-11 **W. Visser & Zoon B.V. Werf "De Lastdrager" — Den Helder** Yd No: 92 Loa 27.26 Br ex - Dght 3.150 Lbp 24.10 Br md 7.50 Dpth 4.20 Welded	**(B11A2FT) Trawler**	**1 oil engine** sr geared to sc. shaft driving 1 CP propeller Total Power: 699kW (950hp) Kromhout 6F/SW240 1 x 4 Stroke 6 Cy. 240 x 260 699kW (950bhp) Stork Werkspoor Diesel BV-Netherlands
9377963 *VRDN6* -	**SILVER LAKE** **Lake Stevens Ltd** Pacific Basin Shipping (HK) Ltd *Hong Kong* *Hong Kong* MMSI: 477003800 Official number: HK-2052	**20,987** 11,524 33,171 T/cm 46.1	Class: LR ✠ **100A1** SS 01/2013 bulk carrier BC-A strengthened for heavy cargoes, Nos. 2, 4 holds may be empty **ShipRight** (SDA, FDA, CM) timber deck cargo ESP ESN LI *IWS ✠ **LMC** **CCS** Eq.Ltr: It; Cable: 605.0/73.0 U2 (a)	**2008**-01 **Jiangmen Nanyang Ship Engineering Co Ltd — Jiangmen GD** Yd No: 101 Loa 179.90 (BB) Br ex 28.44 Dght 10.150 Lbp 171.50 Br md 28.40 Dpth 14.10 Welded, 1 dk	**(A21A2BC) Bulk Carrier** Grain: 42,565; Bale: 40,558 Compartments: 5 Ho, ER 5 Ha: 3 (20.0 x 19.2) (18.4 x 19.2)ER (14.4 x 17.6) Cranes: 4x30.5t	**1 oil engine** driving 1 FP propeller Total Power: 6,480kW (8,810hp) 13.7kn MAN-B&W 6S42MC 1 x 2 Stroke 6 Cy. 420 x 1764 6480kW (8810bhp) STX Engine Co Ltd-South Korea AuxGen: 3 x 440kW 450V 60Hz a.c Boilers: AuxB (Comp) 7.9kgf/cm² (7.7bar) Fuel: 125.0 (d.f.) 1230.0 (r.f.) 29.0pd
9359648 *V2PH6* -	**SILVER LAKE** *ex* Dalfoss *-2009* **Atlantic Frost Co Ltd** Silver Liner AS SatCom: Inmarsat C 430413310 *Saint John's* *Antigua & Barbuda* MMSI: 304133000 Official number: 2870	**3,538** 1,062 2,532	Class: NV	**2007**-05 **OAO Khersonskiy Sudostroitelnyy Zavod — Kherson** (Hull) **2007**-05 **Myklebust Mek. Verksted AS — Gursken** Yd No: 43 Loa 81.55 (BB) Br ex 16.02 Dght 6.100 Lbp 78.15 Br md 16.00 Dpth 12.10 Welded, 1 dk	**(A34A2GR) Refrigerated Cargo Ship** Ins: 5,500 FEU 14 ref C Ice Capable	**1 oil engine** reduction geared to sc. shaft driving 1 CP propeller Total Power: 3,000kW (4,079hp) 14.0kn MaK 6M32C 1 x 4 Stroke 6 Cy. 320 x 480 3000kW (4079bhp) Caterpillar Motoren GmbH & Co. KG-Germany AuxGen: 2 x 590kW a.c, 1 x a.c Thrusters: 1 Tunnel thruster (f); 1 Tunnel thruster (a) Fuel: 60.0 (d.f.) 320.0 (r.f.)
9266475 *HOWS* -	**SILVER LINING** **Melodia Maritime Pte Ltd** MMS Co Ltd SatCom: Inmarsat C 435731610 *Panama* *Panama* MMSI: 357316000 Official number: 2911103A	**28,059** 11,645 46,013 T/cm 50.6	Class: NK	**2003**-02 **Shin Kurushima Dockyard Co. Ltd. — Onishi** Yd No: 5156 Loa 179.88 (BB) Br ex 32.23 Dght 12.022 Lbp 172.00 Br md 32.20 Dpth 18.70 Welded, 1 dk	**(A13B2TP) Products Tanker** Double Hull (13F) Liq: 50,753; Liq (Oil): 53,000 Cargo Heating Coils Compartments: 14 Wing Ta, ER, 2 Wing Slop Ta 4 Cargo Pump (s): 4x1000m³/hr Manifold: Bow/CM: 91.3m	**1 oil engine** driving 1 FP propeller Total Power: 9,267kW (12,599hp) 14.6kn Mitsubishi 6UEC60LA 1 x 2 Stroke 6 Cy. 600 x 1900 9267kW (12599bhp) Kobe Hatsudoki KK-Japan AuxGen: 3 x a.c Fuel: 156.0 (d.f.) 1761.0 (r.f.)
9594676 *VRHT4* -	**SILVER LUCKY** **Silver Lucky Shipping Ltd** Yantai Golden Ocean Shipping Co Ltd SatCom: Inmarsat C 447702962 *Hong Kong* *Hong Kong* MMSI: 477746300 Official number: HK-2932	**9,129** 4,009 12,258	Class: CC	**2011**-01 **Wuchang Shipbuilding Industry Co Ltd — Wuhan HB** Yd No: A190M Loa 120.00 (BB) Br ex 20.83 Dght 8.600 Lbp 112.00 Br md 20.80 Dpth 13.00 Welded, 1 dk	**(A31A2GX) General Cargo Ship** Grain: 16,805; Bale: 14,461 Compartments: 2 Ho, ER 2 Ha: (39.9 x 18.2)ER (38.5 x 18.2) Cranes: 2x30t Ice Capable	**1 oil engine** driving 1 FP propeller Total Power: 3,309kW (4,499hp) 11.8kn Hanshin LH46LA 1 x 4 Stroke 6 Cy. 460 x 880 3309kW (4499bhp) The Hanshin Diesel Works Ltd-Japan AuxGen: 3 x 250kW 400V a.c
7900508 - -	**SILVER MAC** *ex* Showa Maru No. 25 *-1992* **Taito Panama SA** Taito Seiko Co Ltd	**629** 234 434	Class: (NK)	**1979**-05 **Kochi Jyuko (Kaisei Zosen) K.K. — Kochi** Yd No: 1298 Loa 53.66 Br ex - Dght 3.301 Lbp 46.51 Br md 8.81 Dpth 3.71 Welded, 1 dk	**(B11B2FV) Fishing Vessel** Ins: 584	**1 oil engine** driving 1 FP propeller Total Power: 736kW (1,001hp) 11.5kn Akasaka DM28A 1 x 4 Stroke 6 Cy. 280 x 460 736kW (1001bhp) Akasaka Tekkosho KK (Akasaka DieselLtd)-Japan

9073488 *V7XQ6* -	**SILVER MARINER** *ex* New Brisk *-2011* *ex* Bungo *-2001* *ex* Bungo Maru *-1999* **Silver Mariner SA** Sinokor Merchant Marine Co Ltd SatCom: Inmarsat C 453837291 *Majuro* *Marshall Islands* MMSI: 538004545 Official number: 4545	**85,629** 53,906 168,421	Class: KR (NK)	**1995**-01 **Mitsui Eng. & SB. Co. Ltd., Chiba Works — Ichihara** Yd No: 1404 Loa 290.00 (BB) Br ex - Dght 17.025 Lbp 278.00 Br md 46.00 Dpth 23.25 Welded, 1 dk	**(A21A2BC) Bulk Carrier** Grain: 183,321 Compartments: 9 Ho, ER 9 Ha: (17.1 x 14.6)7 (15.4 x 21.2) (17.1 x 21.2)Tappered ER	**1 oil engine** driving 1 FP propeller Total Power: 16,859kW (22,921hp) 14.7kn B&W 6S70MC 1 x 2 Stroke 6 Cy. 700 x 2674 16859kW (22921bhp) Mitsui Engineering & Shipbuilding CLtd-Japan AuxGen: 3 x 600kW a.c Fuel: 3808.0 (r.f.) 59.1pd
7641750 *YD4687* -	**SILVER MAS I** *ex* Silver Mas *-2000* **PT Karimata Asia** - *Jakarta* *Indonesia*	*138* 82 449	Class: KI (NK)	**1976**-09 **Nam Cheong Dockyard Sdn Bhd — Miri** Yd No: 274 Loa 23.19 Br ex 7.40 Dght 2.431 Lbp 21.80 Br md 7.01 Dpth 2.87 Welded, 1 dk	**(B32A2ST) Tug**	**2 oil engines** geared to sc. shafts driving 2 FP propellers Total Power: 536kW (728hp) 10.0kn Caterpillar D343TA 2 x 4 Stroke 6 Cy. 137 x 165 each-268kW (364bhp) Caterpillar Tractor Co-USA AuxGen: 2 x 22kW a.c
9120035 *V7XM6* -	**SILVER MASTER** *ex* Santa Isabel *-2011* **Silver Master SA** Sinokor Merchant Marine Co Ltd *Majuro* *Marshall Islands* MMSI: 538004517 Official number: 4517	**79,855** 52,253 158,387 T/cm 106.0	Class: KR (NK)	**1996**-07 **Sasebo Heavy Industries Co. Ltd. — Sasebo Yard, Sasebo** Yd No: 405 Loa 280.00 (BB) Br ex - Dght 17.645 Lbp 271.00 Br md 43.00 Dpth 24.00 Welded, 1 dk	**(A21A2BC) Bulk Carrier** Grain: 176,294 Compartments: 9 Ho, ER 9 Ha: (13.8 x 15.3)8 (14.9 x 20.4)ER	**1 oil engine** driving 1 FP propeller Total Power: 13,498kW (18,352hp) 13.5kn B&W 6S70MC 1 x 2 Stroke 6 Cy. 700 x 2674 13498kW (18352bhp) Mitsui Engineering & Shipbuilding CLtd-Japan AuxGen: 3 x 580kW 450V a.c Fuel: 120.0 (d.f.) (Heating Coils) 3800.0 (r.f.) 48.0pd
9106223 *V7XD2* -	**SILVER MERCHANT** *ex* Brisbane *-2011* *ex* Spring Brave *-2007* *ex* Dyna Gemini *-2002* **Silver Merchant SA** Sinokor Merchant Marine Co Ltd *Majuro* *Marshall Islands* MMSI: 538004450 Official number: 4450	**77,298** 48,787 151,066 T/cm 106.0	Class: KR (BV) (NK)	**1995**-05 **Nippon Kokan KK (NKK Corp) — Tsu ME** Yd No: 148 Loa 273.00 Br ex - Dght 17.419 Lbp 260.00 Br md 43.00 Dpth 23.90 Welded, 1 dk	**(A21A2BC) Bulk Carrier** Grain: 167,715 Compartments: 9 Ho, ER 9 Ha: ER	**1 oil engine** driving 1 FP propeller Total Power: 15,400kW (20,938hp) 15.8kn B&W 6S70MC 1 x 2 Stroke 6 Cy. 700 x 2674 15400kW (20938bhp) Mitsui Engineering & Shipbuilding CLtd-Japan
8912675 *9MBD5* -	**SILVER MOON** *ex* Nepline Redang *-2012* *ex* Tuah Tankers Lima *-2005* *ex* Nur Marina *-2002* **Silverline Maritime Sdn Bhd** - *Port Klang* *Malaysia* MMSI: 533000700 Official number: 326090	**2,298** 1,354 4,295 T/cm 11.3	Class: BV (AB)	**1990**-03 **Malaysia Shipyard & Engineering Sdn Bhd — Pasir Gudang** Yd No: 038 Loa 84.50 Br ex - Dght 6.060 Lbp 80.00 Br md 15.80 Dpth 6.80 Welded, 1 dk	**(A13B2TP) Products Tanker** Single Hull Liq: 4,830; Liq (Oil): 4,830 Cargo Heating Coils 6 Cargo Pump (s): 6x400m³/hr	**1 oil engine** reverse reduction geared to sc. shaft driving 1 FP propeller Total Power: 1,217kW (1,655hp) Stork-Werkspoor 6SW280 1 x 4 Stroke 6 Cy. 280 x 300 1217kW (1655bhp) Stork Wartsila Diesel BV-Netherlands AuxGen: 2 x 175kW a.c
9613769 *V7WI3* -	**SILVER NAVIGATOR** **Sailing Shipholding Inc** Silver Lake Shipping Co SA *Majuro* *Marshall Islands* MMSI: 538004305 Official number: 4305	**43,884** 26,623 80,312 T/cm 71.9	Class: RI	**2011**-07 **STX Offshore & Shipbuilding Co Ltd — Changwon (Jinhae Shipyard)** Yd No: 1526 Loa 229.00 (BB) Br ex - Dght 14.450 Lbp 222.00 Br md 32.24 Dpth 20.10 Welded, 1 dk	**(A21A2BC) Bulk Carrier** Grain: 95,172 Compartments: 7 Ho, ER 7 Ha: ER	**1 oil engine** driving 1 FP propeller Total Power: 11,060kW (15,037hp) 14.4kn MAN-B&W 7S50MC-C 1 x 2 Stroke 7 Cy. 500 x 2000 11060kW (15037bhp) STX Engine Co Ltd-South Korea
9298430 *V3GA3* -	**SILVER OCEAN** **Belize Silver Ocean Shipping SA** Yantai Golden Ocean Shipping Co Ltd *Belize City* *Belize* MMSI: 312730000 Official number: 440320024	**1,997** 1,106 2,846	Class: CC	**2003**-11 **Qingdao Lingshan Ship Engineering Co Ltd — Jiaonan SD** Yd No: 101 Loa 79.99 (BB) Br ex - Dght 5.200 Lbp 74.00 Br md 13.60 Dpth 7.00 Welded, 1 dk	**(A21A2BC) Bulk Carrier** Grain: 4,127; Bale: 3,893 Compartments: 1 Ho, ER 1 Ha: ER (38.4 x 10.0) Ice Capable	**1 oil engine** geared to sc. shaft driving 1 CP propeller Total Power: 1,080kW (1,468hp) 11.7kn MAN-B&W 8L23/30 1 x 4 Stroke 8 Cy. 225 x 300 1080kW (1468bhp) Zhenjiang Marine Diesel Works-China AuxGen: 3 x 90kW 400V a.c
9140932 *LAHP6* -	**SILVER OCEAN** *ex* Frio Vladivostok *-2005* *ex* Alexandra *-1999* **Silver Ocean AS** Fjord Shipping AS *Bergen* *Norway (NIS)* MMSI: 257962000	**3,817** 1,446 4,260 T/cm 12.9	Class: LR ✠ **100A1** SS 01/2012 refrigerated cargo ship Ice Class 1B ✠ **LMC** **UMS +Lloyd's RMC** Eq.Ltr: U; Cable: 467.5/46.0	**1997**-01 **Aarhus Flydedok A/S — Aarhus** Yd No: 205 Loa 97.60 (BB) Br ex 15.73 Dght 6.000 Lbp 91.50 Br md 15.70 Dpth 10.10 Welded, 3 dks	**(A34A2GR) Refrigerated Cargo Ship** Ins: 5,512 TEU 52 C.Ho 12/20' C.Dk 40/20' Compartments: 2 Ho, ER, 2 Tw Dk 2 Ha: 2 (6.5 x 5.4)ER Cranes: 2x8t Ice Capable	**1 oil engine** with clutches, flexible couplings & sr geared to sc. shaft driving 1 CP propeller Total Power: 3,251kW (4,420hp) 15.5kn MaK 8M32 1 x 4 Stroke 8 Cy. 320 x 480 3251kW (4420bhp) MaK Motoren GmbH & Co. KG-Kiel AuxGen: 1 x 648kW 380V 50Hz a.c, 3 x 420kW 380V 50Hz a.c Boilers: TOH (o.f.) 10.2kgf/cm² (10.0bar), TOH (ex.g.) 10.2kgf/cm² (10.0bar) Thrusters: 1 Thwart. FP thruster (f) Fuel: 400.0 (r.f.) 16.1pd
9050307 *V7XQ4* -	**SILVER OCEAN** *ex* Kamisu Maru *-2011* **Silver Ocean Maritime SA** Sinokor Merchant Marine Co Ltd SatCom: Inmarsat C 453837273 *Majuro* *Marshall Islands* MMSI: 538004543 Official number: 4543	**74,843** 48,918 151,102 T/cm 104.1	Class: KR (NK)	**1994**-03 **Shin Kurushima Dockyard Co. Ltd. — Onishi** Yd No: 2768 Loa 269.04 (BB) Br ex 43.05 Dght 17.701 Lbp 259.00 Br md 43.00 Dpth 24.10 Welded, 1 dk	**(A21A2BC) Bulk Carrier** Grain: 165,733 Compartments: 9 Ho, ER 9 Ha: (12.8 x 15.8)7 (14.4 x 19.0)ER	**1 oil engine** driving 1 FP propeller Total Power: 12,944kW (17,599hp) 14.2kn B&W 6S70MC 1 x 2 Stroke 6 Cy. 700 x 2674 12944kW (17599bhp) Mitsui Engineering & Shipbuilding CLtd-Japan AuxGen: 3 x 560kW 450V 60Hz a.c Fuel: 190.0 (d.f.) 3775.0 (r.f.) 50.0pd
7303190 *H04129* -	**SILVER OCEAN** *ex* Hector *-2005* *ex* Al Mohamadia *-1986* *ex* Saudi Rastanura *-1985* *ex* Marjan 3 *-1983* **Silver Ocean Shipping SA** - *Panama* *Panama* Official number: 33657PEXT	*445* - -	Class: (AB)	**1973**-04 **B.V. Scheepswerven v/h H.H. Bodewes — Millingen a/d Rijn** Yd No: 707 Loa 40.75 Br ex 11.13 Dght 5.614 Lbp 35.13 Br md 10.52 Dpth 6.86 Welded, 1 dk	**(B32A2ST) Tug**	**1 oil engine** sr geared to sc. shaft driving 1 CP propeller Total Power: 2,868kW (3,899hp) 14.0kn MAN R7V40/54 1 x 4 Stroke 7 Cy. 400 x 540 2868kW (3899bhp) Maschinenbau Augsburg Nuernberg (MAN)-Augsburg AuxGen: 2 x 250kW Fuel: 199.0
9208502 *A8OY3* -	**SILVER ONE** *ex* Silverstone *-2003* **Sea Breeze HH Schiff Verwaltungs GmbH & Co KG** KG Reederei Roth GmbH & Co *Monrovia* *Liberia* MMSI: 636091510 Official number: 91510	**38,684** 24,591 72,917 T/cm 65.8	Class: GL (LR) ✠ Classed LR until 17/1/07	**2000**-01 **Daedong Shipbuilding Co Ltd — Changwon (Jinhae Shipyard)** Yd No: 1038 Loa 225.00 (BB) Br ex 32.25 Dght 13.913 Lbp 216.55 Br md 32.24 Dpth 19.10 Welded, 1 dk	**(A21A2BC) Bulk Carrier** Grain: 85,592 Compartments: 7 Ho, ER 7 Ha: (16.6 x 11.3)6 (16.6 x 14.1)ER	**1 oil engine** driving 1 FP propeller Total Power: 10,412kW (14,156hp) 15.0kn B&W 6S60MC 1 x 2 Stroke 6 Cy. 600 x 2292 10412kW (14156bhp) Hyundai Heavy Industries Co Ltd-South Korea AuxGen: 3 x 500kW 450V 60Hz a.c Boilers: AuxB (Comp) 7.1kgf/cm² (7.0bar)
9607655 *VRIN9* -	**SILVER PEACE** **Silver Peace Shipping Ltd** Yantai Golden Ocean Shipping Co Ltd *Hong Kong* *Hong Kong* MMSI: 477276100 Official number: HK-3099	**9,129** 4,009 12,267	Class: CC	**2011**-07 **Wuchang Shipbuilding Industry Co Ltd — Wuhan HB** Yd No: A191M Loa 120.00 Br ex 20.83 Dght 8.600 Lbp 112.00 Br md 20.80 Dpth 13.00 Welded, 1 dk	**(A31A2GX) General Cargo Ship** Grain: 16,805; Bale: 15,965 Compartments: 2 Ho, ER 2 Ha: (39.9 x 18.2)ER (38.5 x 18.2) Cranes: 2x30t Ice Capable	**1 oil engine** driving 1 FP propeller Total Power: 3,309kW (4,499hp) 11.8kn Hanshin LH46LA 1 x 4 Stroke 6 Cy. 460 x 880 3309kW (4499bhp) The Hanshin Diesel Works Ltd-Japan AuxGen: 3 x 250kW 400V a.c
9343455 *3ENT4* -	**SILVER PEGASUS** **Satsuki Maritime SA** Kitaura Kaiun KK *Panama* *Panama* MMSI: 352293000 Official number: 3340608A	**43,621** 19,125 54,347	Class: NK	**2007**-12 **Oshima Shipbuilding Co Ltd — Saikai NS** Yd No: 10463 Loa 210.00 (BB) Br ex 32.26 Dght 11.526 Lbp 203.58 Br md 32.20 Dpth 22.98 Welded, 1 dk	**(A24B2BW) Wood Chips Carrier** Double Hull Grain: 109,043 Compartments: 6 Ho, ER 6 Ha: ER Cranes: 3x14.7t	**1 oil engine** driving 1 FP propeller Total Power: 9,194kW (12,500hp) 14.0kn Mitsubishi 7UEC50LSII 1 x 2 Stroke 7 Cy. 500 x 1950 9194kW (12500bhp) Mitsubishi Heavy Industries Ltd-Japan AuxGen: 3 x a.c Fuel: 3100.0
9363455 *VRCA5* -	**SILVER PHOENIX** **Oceanlink Inc** Valles Steamship (Canada) Inc *Hong Kong* *Hong Kong* MMSI: 477265800 Official number: HK-1738	**40,489** 25,884 74,759 T/cm 67.0	Class: AB	**2006**-08 **Hudong-Zhonghua Shipbuilding (Group) Co Ltd — Shanghai** Yd No: H1369A Loa 225.00 (BB) Br ex - Dght 14.250 Lbp 217.00 Br md 32.26 Dpth 19.60 Welded, 1 dk	**(A21A2BC) Bulk Carrier** Grain: 91,717; Bale: 89,883 Compartments: 7 Ho, ER 7 Ha: ER	**1 oil engine** driving 1 FP propeller Total Power: 8,990kW (12,223hp) 14.0kn MAN-B&W 5S60MC-C 1 x 2 Stroke 5 Cy. 600 x 2400 8990kW (12223bhp) Hudong Heavy Machinery Co Ltd-China AuxGen: 3 x 530kW a.c Fuel: 137.8 (d.f.) 2555.0 (r.f.)

8713689 - -	**SILVER PHOENIX** *ex Megisti Star F -2008* **Joseph & Marcia Bronwyn Valente Pty Ltd** - *Port Adelaide, SA* *Australia* Official number: 851397	*245* 74 -	Class: (NV)	**1988-10 K Shipyard Construction & Repairs Pty Ltd — Port Adelaide SA** Yd No: 7 Loa 29.76 (BB) Br ex 7.81 Dght - Lbp 28.00 Br md 7.66 Dpth 3.87 Welded, 1 dk	**(B11A2FS) Stern Trawler** Ins: 167	**1 oil engine** with flexible couplings & sr gearedto sc. shaft driving 1 FP propeller Total Power: 640kW (870hp) Yanmar M220-UN 1 x 4 Stroke 6 Cy. 220 x 300 640kW (870bhp) Yanmar Diesel Engine Co Ltd-Japan AuxGen: 2 x 120kW 415V 50Hz a.c Thrusters: 1 Thwart. FP thruster (f)
9218832 *DSRL6* -	**SILVER PIONEER** *ex Cape Salvia -2013* **Sinokor Merchant Marine Co Ltd** - *Jeju* *South Korea* MMSI: 441904000 Official number: JJR-131007	**87,430** 57,570 172,559 T/cm 119.0	Class: KR (NK)	**2002-02 Nippon Kokan KK (NKK Corp) — Tsu ME** Yd No: 206 Loa 289.00 (BB) Br ex - Dght 17.810 Lbp 279.00 Br md 45.00 Dpth 24.10 Welded, 1 dk	**(A21A2BC) Bulk Carrier** Grain: 191,720 Compartments: 9 Ho, ER 9 Ha: (15.2 x 18.8)7 (15.2 x 20.6) (15.2 x 17.5)ER	**1 oil engine** driving 1 FP propeller Total Power: 14,710kW (20,000hp) 14.6kn B&W 6S70MC 1 x 2 Stroke 6 Cy. 700 x 2674 14710kW (20000bhp) Mitsui Engineering & Shipbuilding CLtd-Japan AuxGen: 3 x 570kW 440/220V 60Hz a.c Fuel: 3740.0
9510462 *9HA2668* -	**SILVER POINT** - **PB Tankers SpA** - *Valletta* *Malta* MMSI: 215182000 Official number: 9510462	**29,717** 13,609 51,063 T/cm 52.1	Class: RI	**2011-04 STX Offshore & Shipbuilding Co Ltd — Changwon (Jinhae Shipyard)** Yd No: 1313 Loa 183.00 (BB) Br ex - Dght 13.165 Lbp 173.90 Br md 32.20 Dpth 19.10 Welded, 1 dk	**(A12B2TR) Chemical/Products Tanker** Double Hull (13F) Liq: 53,627; Liq (Oil): 53,627 Cargo Heating Coils	**1 oil engine** driving 1 FP propeller Total Power: 9,480kW (12,889hp) 14.5kn MAN-B&W 6S50MC-C 1 x 2 Stroke 6 Cy. 500 x 2000 9480kW (12889bhp) STX Engine Co Ltd-South Korea Thrusters: 1 Tunnel thruster (f)
9597616 *JD3309* -	**SILVER PRINCESS** - **Kawasaki Kinkai Kisen KK (Kawasaki Kinkai Kisen Kaisha Ltd)** - *Hachinohe, Aomori* *Japan* MMSI: 431003381 Official number: 141608	*10,536* - 4,315		**2012-04 Mitsubishi Heavy Industries Ltd. — Shimonoseki** Yd No: 1158 Loa 150.00 (BB) Br ex - Dght 5.700 Lbp 137.50 Br md 25.00 Dpth 8.00 Welded, 1 dk	**(A36A2PR) Passenger/Ro-Ro Ship (Vehicles)** Passengers: 500 Stern door/ramp (s. a.) Len: 8.80 Wid: 6.80 Swl: - Quarter bow door/ramp (s. f.) Len: 18.00 Wid: 5.70 Swl: - Lane-Len: 1104 Lane-clr ht: 4.20 Cars: 30	**2 oil engines** reduction geared to sc. shafts driving 2 CP propellers Total Power: 18,000kW (24,472hp) 20.5kn Pielstick 12PC2.6B 2 x Vee 4 Stroke 12 Cy. 400 x 500 each-9000kW (12236bhp) AuxGen: 3 x 800kW a.c Fuel: 737.0 (r.f.)
9279630 *3FDY6* -	**SILVER QUEEN** *ex Queenie -2011* **Asahiya Investors SA** Asahi Shosen Co Ltd *Panama* *Panama* MMSI: 372424000 Official number: 4274411	**5,201** 2,636 8,831 T/cm 17.3	Class: NK	**2003-11 Murakami Hide Zosen K.K. — Imabari** Yd No: 531 Loa 114.99 (BB) Br ex - Dght 7.770 Lbp 108.50 Br md 18.20 Dpth 9.65 Welded, 1 dk	**(A12B2TR) Chemical/Products Tanker** Double Hull (13F) Liq: 9,214; Liq (Oil): 9,214 Cargo Heating Coils Compartments: 16 Wing Ta (s.stl), ER 16 Cargo Pump (s): 16x200m³/hr Manifold: Bow/CM: 57.8m	**1 oil engine** driving 1 FP propeller Total Power: 3,900kW (5,302hp) 13.4kn MAN-B&W 6L35MC 1 x 2 Stroke 6 Cy. 350 x 1050 3900kW (5302bhp) Imex Co Ltd-Japan AuxGen: 2 x 450kW a.c Fuel: 97.0 (d.f.) 476.0 (r.f.)
9166223 *JE3161* -	**SILVER QUEEN** - **Kawasaki Kinkai Kisen KK (Kawasaki Kinkai Kisen Kaisha Ltd)** - *Hachinohe, Aomori* *Japan* MMSI: 431700169 Official number: 133355	*7,005* - 3,455		**1998-03 Mitsubishi Heavy Industries Ltd. — Shimonoseki** Yd No: 1041 Loa 134.00 (BB) Br ex 21.03 Dght 5.700 Lbp 125.00 Br md 21.00 Dpth 7.03 Welded, 2 dks	**(A36A2PR) Passenger/Ro-Ro Ship (Vehicles)** Passengers: unberthed: 600 Stern door/ramp Len: 8.80 Wid: 6.77 Swl: - Quarter bow door/ramp (s) Len: 13.45 Wid: 5.70 Swl: - Lane-clr ht: 4.20 Lorries: 92	**2 oil engines** with flexible couplings & sr gearedto sc. shafts driving 2 CP propellers Total Power: 17,594kW (23,920hp) 20.8kn Pielstick 16PC2-6V-400 2 x Vee 4 Stroke 16 Cy. 400 x 460 each-8797kW (11960bhp) Diesel United Ltd.-Aioi AuxGen: 3 x 850kW a.c Thrusters: 1 Thwart. CP thruster (f) Fuel: 408.0 (r.f.) 64.0pd
8327715 *DUA6088* -	**SILVER QUEEN** *ex Polaris II -1995 ex Woo Jin No. 9 -1987* *ex Puertorico -1984* **Frabelle Fishing Corp** - *Manila* *Philippines* Official number: MNLD001461	*960* 517 894	Class: (KR)	**1975 Tacoma Boatbuilding Co., Inc. — Tacoma, Wa** Yd No: 258 Loa 57.16 Br ex - Dght 5.800 Lbp 53.73 Br md 10.98 Dpth 6.33 Welded, 1 dk	**(B11B2FV) Fishing Vessel** Ins: 1,106 5 Ha: 4 (1.8 x 1.8) (1.2 x 1.7) Derricks: 1x20t,2x7t	**1 oil engine** driving 1 FP propeller Total Power: 2,648kW (3,600hp) 13.5kn EMD (Electro-Motive) 20-645-E7B 1 x Vee 2 Stroke 20 Cy. 230 x 254 2648kW (3600bhp) General Motors Corp.Electro-Motive Div.-La Grange AuxGen: 3 x 173kW 450V a.c
9493133 *D5DR6* -	**SILVER RAY** *ex Kenton Park -2014* **Evtor Shipping Inc** Eastern Pacific Shipping Pte Ltd *Monrovia* *Liberia* MMSI: 636015953 Official number: 15953	**11,733** 6,115 19,801 T/cm 29.3	Class: NK	**2013-02 Kitanihon Zosen K.K. — Hachinohe** Yd No: 531 Loa 141.00 (BB) Br ex 24.23 Dght 9.714 Lbp 133.00 Br md 24.20 Dpth 13.20 Welded, 1 dk	**(A12B2TR) Chemical/Products Tanker** Double Hull (13F) Liq: 21,687; Liq (Oil): 21,560 Cargo Heating Coils Compartments: 16 Wing Ta, ER 16 Cargo Pump (s): 16x250m³/hr Manifold: Bow/CM: 72.5m	**1 oil engine** driving 1 FP propeller Total Power: 6,230kW (8,470hp) 14.5kn Mitsubishi 6UEC43LSII 1 x 2 Stroke 6 Cy. 430 x 1500 6230kW (8470bhp) Akasaka Tekkosho KK (Akasaka DieselLtd)-Japan AuxGen: 3 x 500kW a.c Thrusters: 1 Tunnel thruster (f) Fuel: 140.0 (d.f.) 899.0 (r.f.)
9359650 *V2PI* -	**SILVER RIVER** *ex Langfoss -2009* **Atlantic Ice Co Ltd** Silver Liner AS SatCom: Inmarsat C 430413510 *Saint John's* *Antigua & Barbuda* MMSI: 304135000 Official number: 2508	**3,538** 1,062 2,500	Class: NV	**2007-09 OAO Khersonskiy Sudostroitelnyy Zavod — Kherson** (Hull) **2007-09 Myklebust Mek. Verksted AS — Gursken** Yd No: 44 Loa 81.80 (BB) Br ex 16.02 Dght 5.995 Lbp 78.15 Br md 16.00 Dpth 12.10 Welded, 1 dk	**(A34A2GR) Refrigerated Cargo Ship** Ins: 5,500 TEU 31 Ice Capable	**1 oil engine** reduction geared to sc. shaft driving 1 CP propeller Total Power: 3,000kW (4,079hp) 14.0kn MaK 6M32C 1 x 4 Stroke 6 Cy. 320 x 480 3000kW (4079bhp) Caterpillar Motoren GmbH & Co. KG-Germany AuxGen: 1 x a.c, 2 x 590kW a.c Thrusters: 1 Tunnel thruster (f); 1 Tunnel thruster (a) Fuel: 60.0 (d.f.) 320.0 (r.f.)
7826972 - -	**SILVER RIVER** *ex Yvonne Bailey -2009* **Laborde Marine Brazil LLC** Laborde Marine LLC	**251** 75 500	Class: (AB)	**1978 Swiftships Inc — Morgan City LA** Yd No: 185 Loa 38.10 Br ex - Dght 3.398 Lbp 36.58 Br md 8.53 Dpth 3.62 Welded, 1 dk	**(B21A2OS) Platform Supply Ship**	**2 oil engines** reduction geared to sc. shafts driving 2 FP propellers Total Power: 1,030kW (1,400hp) 12.0kn G.M. (Detroit Diesel) 12V-149 2 x Vee 2 Stroke 12 Cy. 146 x 146 each-515kW (700bhp) General Motors Corp-USA AuxGen: 2 x 40kW a.c Fuel: 105.0 (d.f.)
6825218 *MEVM4* -	**SILVER RIVER** *ex Nathurn -1986 ex Sea Trent -1982* *ex Seacon -1971* **Mezeron Ltd** - *Ramsey* *Isle of Man (British)* MMSI: 232003561 Official number: 335848	**277** 138 373	Class: GL (LR) ✠ Classed LR until 14/8/82	**1968-07 Schiffswerft Gebr Schloemer Oldersum — Moormerland** Yd No: 185 Loa 44.66 Br ex 7.35 Dght 2.674 Lbp 40.01 Br md 7.18 Dpth 3.08 Welded, 1 dk	**(A31A2GX) General Cargo Ship** Grain: 522; Bale: 483 Compartments: 1 Ho, ER 1 Ha: (24.4 x 5.1)ER Ice Capable	**1 oil engine** reverse reduction geared to sc. shaft driving 1 FP propeller Total Power: 349kW (475hp) 9.0kn Caterpillar 3412TA 1 x Vee 4 Stroke 12 Cy. 137 x 152 349kW (475bhp) (new engine 1990) Caterpillar Inc-USA AuxGen: 2 x 8kW 400V 50Hz a.c Fuel: 10.5 (d.f.)
9241657 *DSRL2* -	**SILVER ROAD** *ex Cape Future -2013* **Sinokor Merchant Marine Co Ltd** - *Jeju* *South Korea* MMSI: 441897000 Official number: JJR-131001	**93,030** 61,566 185,820 T/cm 125.6	Class: KR (NK)	**2002-07 Kawasaki Heavy Industries Ltd — Sakaide KG** Yd No: 1512 Loa 290.00 (BB) Br ex - Dght 17.973 Lbp 280.00 Br md 47.00 Dpth 24.40 Welded, 1 dk	**(A21A2BC) Bulk Carrier** Double Bottom Entire Compartment Length Grain: 202,500 Compartments: 9 Ho, ER 9 Ha: (15.5 x 16.5)7 (15.5 x 22.6) (15.5 x 15.0)ER	**1 oil engine** driving 1 FP propeller Total Power: 16,860kW (22,923hp) 14.7kn B&W 6S70MC 1 x 2 Stroke 6 Cy. 700 x 2674 16860kW (22923bhp) Kawasaki Heavy Industries Ltd-Japan AuxGen: 3 x 600kW 450/230V 60Hz a.c Fuel: 4600.0
9571349 *VRGJ4* -	**SILVER SAFETY** - **Silver Safety Shipping Ltd** Yantai Golden Ocean Shipping Co Ltd *Hong Kong* *Hong Kong* MMSI: 477711400	**7,243** 2,881 8,500	Class: CC	**2010-01 Wuchang Shipbuilding Industry Co Ltd — Wuhan HB** Yd No: A186L Loa 110.40 (BB) Br ex - Dght 7.600 Lbp 100.90 Br md 19.60 Dpth 11.80 Welded, 1 dk	**(A31A2GX) General Cargo Ship** Grain: 12,644; Bale: 12,644 Compartments: 2 Ho, ER 2 Ha: ER 2 (25.2 x 15.0) Cranes: 2x30t Ice Capable	**1 oil engine** driving 1 Propeller Total Power: 2,648kW (3,600hp) 11.5kn Hanshin LH41LA 1 x 4 Stroke 6 Cy. 410 x 800 2648kW (3600bhp) The Hanshin Diesel Works Ltd-Japan AuxGen: 3 x 250kW 400V a.c
9598763 *VRIH8* -	**SILVER SAILING** - **Silver Sailing Shipping Ltd** Yantai Golden Ocean Shipping Co Ltd *Hong Kong* *Hong Kong* MMSI: 477861300 Official number: HK-3048	**7,243** 2,881 8,551	Class: CC	**2011-06 Qingdao Wuchuan Heavy Industry Co Ltd — Qingdao SD** Yd No: A187L Loa 110.40 Br ex - Dght 7.600 Lbp 100.90 Br md 19.60 Dpth 11.80 Welded, 1 dk	**(A31A2GX) General Cargo Ship** Grain: 12,644; Bale: 12,644 Compartments: 2 Ho, ER 2 Ha: ER 2 (25.2 x 15.0) Cranes: 2x30t Ice Capable	**1 oil engine** driving 1 Propeller Total Power: 2,648kW (3,600hp) 11.5kn Hanshin LH41LA 1 x 4 Stroke 6 Cy. 410 x 800 2648kW (3600bhp) The Hanshin Diesel Works Ltd-Japan AuxGen: 3 x 250kW 400V a.c

IMO / Call sign	Name / Owner	Tonnage	Class	Builder / Dimensions	Type	Machinery
8132691 *WDB6632* -	**SILVER SEA** *ex* Venturer *-2005* *ex* Linda Ann *-1992* **FV Silver Sea LLC** - *Cape May, NJ* *United States of America* Official number: 601595	*154* 46 -		**1980 Bayou Shipyards, Inc. — Seabrook, Tx** Yd No: 40 L reg 24.60 Br ex 7.32 Dght - Lbp - Br md - Dpth 3.74 Welded, 1 dk	**(B11B2FV) Fishing Vessel**	**1 oil engine** driving 1 FP propeller Total Power: 500kW (680hp)
7727102 *HSB2700* -	**SILVER SEA 1** *ex* Silver Sea *-2000* *ex* Celtic Ice *-2000* *ex* Celtic *-1989* **Silver Sea Reefer Co Ltd** - SatCom: Inmarsat C 430608920 *Bangkok* *Thailand* MMSI: 567175000 Official number: 437400120	**2,285** 1,229 2,468	Class: LR (BV) ✠**100A1** SS 05/2012 ✠**LMC** **UMS RMC** Eq.Ltr: Q; Cable: U2 (a)	**1979-04 Scheepswerf 'Friesland' BV — Lemmer** Yd No: 366 Lengthened-1982 Loa 81.74 (BB) Br ex 13.21 Dght 5.650 Lbp 74.99 Br md 13.01 Dpth 7.65 Welded, 2 dks	**(A34A2GR) Refrigerated Cargo Ship** Ins: 3,806 Compartments: 3 Ho, ER, 3 Tw Dk 3 Ha: (8.4 x 7.5)2 (11.9 x 7.5)ER Cranes: 1x5t; Derricks: 4x3t	**1 oil engine** sr geared to sc. shaft driving 1 CP propeller Total Power: 1,839kW (2,500hp) Deutz SBV6M540 1 x 4 Stroke 6 Cy. 370 x 400 1839kW (2500bhp) Kloeckner Humboldt Deutz AG-West Germany AuxGen: 3 x 168kW 440V 60Hz a.c Thrusters: 1 Thwart. FP thruster (f) Fuel: 305.0 (d.f.)
7727097 *HSB2719* -	**SILVER SEA 2** *ex* Atlantic Ice *-2000* *ex* Atlantic *-1989* **Silver Sea Reefer Co Ltd** - SatCom: Inmarsat C 430614520 *Bangkok* *Thailand* MMSI: 567183000 Official number: 437401215	**2,285** 1,198 2,448	Class: LR (BV) ✠**100A1** SS 01/2012 Ice Class 2, with main engine ouput restricted to 1900BHP ✠**LMC** **UMS +Lloyd's RMC** Eq.Ltr: Q; Cable: U2 (a)	**1979-05 Tille Scheepsbouw B.V. — Kootstertille** Yd No: 210 Lengthened-1982 Loa 81.01 (BB) Br ex 13.19 Dght 5.630 Lbp 74.55 Br md 13.01 Dpth 7.65 Welded, 2 dks	**(A34A2GR) Refrigerated Cargo Ship** Ins: 3,806 Compartments: 3 Ho, ER, 3 Tw Dk 3 Ha: (8.4 x 7.5)2 (11.9 x 7.5)ER Cranes: 1x5t; Derricks: 4x3t Ice Capable	**1 oil engine** sr geared to sc. shaft driving 1 CP propeller Total Power: 1,839kW (2,500hp) 12.0kn Deutz SBV6M540 1 x 4 Stroke 6 Cy. 370 x 400 1839kW (2500bhp) Kloeckner Humboldt Deutz AG-West Germany AuxGen: 1 x 400kW 220/440V 60Hz a.c, 3 x 168kW 220/440V 60Hz a.c Thrusters: 1 Thwart. FP thruster (f) Fuel: 305.0 (d.f.)
7006376 *HSB2233* -	**SILVER SEA 3** *ex* Img 3 *-2010* *ex* Polly Polaris *-1992* *ex* Diamond Despina *-1988* *ex* Leo Polaris *-1984* **Silver Sea Reefer Co Ltd** - SatCom: Inmarsat C 456723610 *Bangkok* *Thailand* MMSI: 567006700 Official number: 357400335	**1,812** 620 1,835	Class: (LR) ✠ Classed LR until 3/11/09	**1970-01 N.V. Nieuwe Noord Nederlandse Scheepswerven — Groningen** Yd No: 355 Loa 82.83 Br ex 12.02 Dght 4.915 Lbp 74.25 Br md 11.80 Dpth 7.01 Welded, 2 dks	**(A34A2GR) Refrigerated Cargo Ship** Ins: 2,568 Compartments: 3 Ho, ER, 3 Tw Dk 3 Ha: 3 (10.0 x 4.8)ER Derricks: 3x3t; Winches: 3	**1 oil engine** driving 1 FP propeller Total Power: 2,184kW (2,969hp) 15.0kn Deutz RBV12M350 1 x Vee 4 Stroke 12 Cy. 400 x 500 2184kW (2969bhp) Kloeckner Humboldt Deutz AG-West Germany AuxGen: 3 x 144kW 380V 50Hz a.c
7804900 *HSBX* -	**SILVER SEA LINE** *ex* TTV Star *-2004* *ex* Scorff *-2001* *ex* Icelandic Klipper *-1991* *ex* Icelandic *-1987* **Silver Sea Line Co Ltd** Dech Reefer Co Ltd *Bangkok* *Thailand* MMSI: 567046600 Official number: 470004272	**2,966** 1,437 3,514	Class: BV	**1979-05 B.V. v/h Scheepswerven Gebr. van Diepen — Waterhuizen** Yd No: 1015 **1983 Boele's Scheepswerven en Machinefabriek B.V. — Bolnes** (Additional cargo section) Lengthened-1983 Loa 101.28 (BB) Br ex 13.70 Dght 5.258 Lbp 92.66 Br md 13.50 Dpth 8.11 Welded, 2 dks	**(A34A2GR) Refrigerated Cargo Ship** Ins: 5,339 Compartments: 4 Ho, ER, 4 Tw Dk 4 Ha: 4 (10.3 x 8.0)ER Cranes: 1x3t; Derricks: 6x5t	**1 oil engine** reduction geared to sc. shaft driving 1 CP propeller Total Power: 2,427kW (3,300hp) 13.6kn Deutz SBV6M540 1 x 4 Stroke 6 Cy. 370 x 400 2427kW (3300bhp) Kloeckner Humboldt Deutz AG-West Germany AuxGen: 1 x 480kW 220/380V 50Hz a.c, 4 x 166kW 220/380V 50Hz a.c Fuel: 651.0 (d.f.)
7727114 *HSCY2* -	**SILVER SEA LINE 2** *ex* Silver Sea Line *-2011* *ex* IMG 6 *-2010* *ex* Baltic Ice *-1999* *ex* Baltic *-1988* - - SatCom: Inmarsat C 456700098 *Bangkok* *Thailand* MMSI: 567011500 Official number: 427400039	**2,285** 1,229 2,468	Class: (LR) (BV) ✠ Classed LR until 20/5/09	**1979-10 Scheepswerf 'Friesland' BV — Lemmer** Yd No: 367 Lengthened-1981 Loa 81.74 (BB) Br ex 13.21 Dght 5.050 Lbp 74.99 Br md 13.01 Dpth 7.65 Welded, 2 dks	**(A34A2GR) Refrigerated Cargo Ship** Ins: 3,806 Compartments: 3 Ho, ER, 3 Tw Dk 3 Ha: (8.4 x 7.5)2 (11.9 x 7.5)ER Cranes: 1x5t; Derricks: 4x3t Ice Capable	**1 oil engine** sr geared to sc. shaft driving 1 CP propeller Total Power: 1,839kW (2,500hp) 12.5kn Deutz SBV6M540 1 x 4 Stroke 6 Cy. 370 x 400 1839kW (2500bhp) Kloeckner Humboldt Deutz AG-West Germany AuxGen: 1 x 500kW 440V 60Hz a.c, 3 x 168kW 440V 60Hz a.c Thrusters: 1 Thwart. FP thruster (f) Fuel: 305.0 (d.f.)
8002119 *HQTL7* -	**SILVER SEAS** *ex* Kosei Maru *-2013* *ex* Marine Empire *-1997* *ex* Kosei Maru *-1993* **Seatrout Management Ltd** Success Blossom Trading Pte Ltd *San Lorenzo* *Honduras* Official number: L-1326802	**946** 573 1,776	Class: (BV)	**1980-01 Sasaki Shipbuilding Co Ltd — Osakikamijima HS** Yd No: 336 Loa 69.80 Br ex 11.03 Dght 4.628 Lbp 65.03 Br md 11.00 Dpth 5.01 Welded, 1 dk	**(A13B2TP) Products Tanker**	**1 oil engine** driving 1 FP propeller Total Power: 1,324kW (1,800hp) Hanshin 6LU35 1 x 4 Stroke 6 Cy. 350 x 550 1324kW (1800bhp) The Hanshin Diesel Works Ltd-Japan
9192167 *C6FN6* -	**SILVER SHADOW** - **Hai Xing 1201 Ltd** V Ships Leisure SAM *Nassau* *Bahamas* MMSI: 308628000 Official number: 732045	**28,258** 9,144 2,980	Class: RI	**2000-08 Cantiere Navale Visentini Srl — Porto Viro** (Hull) **2000-08 T. Mariotti SpA — Genova** Yd No: 981 Loa 186.00 (BB) Br ex - Dght 6.120 Lbp 161.80 Br md 24.80 Dpth 11.30 Welded	**(A37A2PC) Passenger/Cruise** Passengers: cabins: 194; berths: 388	**2 oil engines** reduction geared to sc. shafts driving 2 CP propellers Total Power: 11,474kW (15,600hp) 17.5kn Wartsila 8L46B 2 x 4 Stroke 8 Cy. 460 x 580 each-5737kW (7800bhp) Wartsila NSD Finland Oy-Finland AuxGen: 3 x 2340kW a.c Thrusters: 2 Thwart. FP thruster (f)
1010557 *V7TW8* -	**SILVER SHALIS** - **KS Properties Ltd** - *Jaluit* *Marshall Islands* MMSI: 538070721 Official number: 70721	**846** 253 -	Class: LR ✠**100A1** SS 05/2010 SSC Yacht, G6 **LMC** Eq.Ltr: O; Cable: 304.8/24.0 U2 (a)	**2010-05 Kvichak Marine Industries — Seattle, Wa** (Hull) Yd No: (175038) **2010-05 Delta Marine Industries, Inc. — Seattle, Wa** Yd No: 175038 Loa 53.30 Br ex 9.96 Dght 2.290 Lbp 45.90 Br md 9.96 Dpth 4.74 Welded, 1 dk	**(X11A2YP) Yacht** Hull Material: Aluminium Alloy	**2 oil engines** with clutches, flexible couplings & reverse reduction geared to sc. shafts driving 2 FP propellers Total Power: 4,946kW (6,724hp) 18.5kn M.T.U. 16V4000M90 2 x Vee 4 Stroke 16 Cy. 165 x 190 each-2473kW (3362bhp) MTU Friedrichshafen GmbH-Friedrichshafen AuxGen: 2 x 185kW 120V 60Hz a.c Thrusters: 1 Thwart. FP thruster (f)
7948237 *HQEW5* -	**SILVER SHORE** *ex* Miss Janet *-1991* **Irwin & Valjean Elwin Dixon** - *Roatan* *Honduras* Official number: U-1822133	*111* 76 -		**1979 Steiner Shipyard, Inc. — Bayou La Batre, Al** L reg 20.46 Br ex 6.71 Dght - Lbp - Br md - Dpth 3.43 Welded, 1 dk	**(B11B2FV) Fishing Vessel**	**1 oil engine** driving 1 FP propeller Total Power: 268kW (364hp)
8519722 *3EZX8* -	**SILVER SKY** *ex* DYVI Baltic *-2012* *ex* Hannover *-2002* **PCTC Holding I AS** Maritime Management Services Sarl *Panama* *Panama* MMSI: 373206000 Official number: 4410512	**39,043** 11,712 9,772 T/cm 41.0	Class: BV (NV) (GL)	**1989-02 Jiangnan Shipyard — Shanghai** Yd No: 2174 Loa 182.50 (BB) Br ex - Dght 7.702 Lbp 170.89 Br md 29.60 Dpth 14.10 Welded, 9 dks	**(A35B2RV) Vehicles Carrier** Side door/ramp (s) Len: 19.90 Wid: 5.10 Swl: 10 Quarter stern door/ramp (s) Len: 32.00 Wid: 8.10 Swl: 70 Cars: 4,049 Bale: 32,400 TEU 362	**1 oil engine** driving 1 FP propeller Total Power: 7,944kW (10,801hp) 17.5kn B&W 6L60MCE 1 x 2 Stroke 6 Cy. 600 x 1944 7944kW (10801bhp) Hitachi Zosen Corp-Japan AuxGen: 2 x 840kW 220/440V 60Hz a.c, 1 x a.c Thrusters: 1 Thwart. FP thruster (f) Fuel: 220.2 (d.f.)
9563029 *VRFP8* -	**SILVER SMOOTH** - **Silver Smooth Shipping Ltd** Yantai Golden Ocean Shipping Co Ltd *Hong Kong* *Hong Kong* MMSI: 477595200	**7,243** 2,881 8,500	Class: CC	**2009-12 Wuchang Shipbuilding Industry Co Ltd — Wuhan HB** Yd No: A185L Loa 110.40 (BB) Br ex - Dght 7.600 Lbp 100.90 Br md 19.60 Dpth 11.80 Welded, 1 dk	**(A31A2GX) General Cargo Ship** Grain: 12,557; Bale: 12,557 Compartments: 2 Ho, ER 2 Ha: ER 2 (25.2 x 15.0) Cranes: 2x30t Ice Capable	**1 oil engine** driving 1 Propeller Total Power: 2,648kW (3,600hp) 11.5kn Hanshin LH41LA 1 x 4 Stroke 6 Cy. 410 x 800 2648kW (3600bhp) The Hanshin Diesel Works Ltd-Japan AuxGen: 3 x 250kW 400V a.c
8718706 *HP3446* -	**SILVER SOUL** *ex* NOCC Caribbean *-2012* *ex* Cypress Pass *-2011* **Sasco Line SA** - *Panama* *Panama* MMSI: 351852000 Official number: 4461713	**42,447** 12,734 12,763	Class: AB (KR)	**1988-03 Hyundai Heavy Industries Co Ltd — Ulsan** Yd No: 612 Loa 183.90 (BB) Br ex 30.64 Dght 8.214 Lbp 174.00 Br md 30.60 Dpth 30.23 Welded, 12 dks	**(A35B2RV) Vehicles Carrier** Side door/ramp (s) Len: 19.00 Wid: 5.00 Swl: - Quarter stern door/ramp (s. a.) Len: 35.00 Wid: 7.25 Swl: - Lane-Wid: 7.25 Lane-clr ht: 4.30 Cars: 4,800	**1 oil engine** driving 1 FP propeller Total Power: 10,592kW (14,401hp) 18.0kn B&W 8L60MCE 1 x 2 Stroke 8 Cy. 600 x 1944 10592kW (14401bhp) Hyundai Engine & Machinery Co Ltd-South Korea AuxGen: 3 x 650kW a.c Thrusters: 1 Thwart. CP thruster (f)
9437866 *C6XU6* -	**SILVER SPIRIT** - **Silver Spirit Shipping Co Ltd** Silversea Cruises Ltd *Nassau* *Bahamas* MMSI: 311022500 Official number: 8001647	**36,009** 12,314 3,882	Class: RI	**2009-12 Fincantieri-Cant. Nav. Italiani S.p.A. — Ancona** Yd No: 6178 Loa 195.80 (BB) Br ex - Dght 6.400 Lbp 167.50 Br md 26.50 Dpth 11.50 Welded, 1 dk	**(A37A2PC) Passenger/Cruise** Passengers: cabins: 270; berths: 576	**4 diesel electric oil engines** driving 4 gen. each 6250kW a.c Connecting to 2 elec. motors each (8500kW) driving 2 FP propellers Total Power: 26,100kW (35,484hp) 20.3kn Wartsila 9L38 4 x 4 Stroke 9 Cy. 380 x 475 each-6525kW (8871bhp) Wartsila Finland Oy-Finland Thrusters: 2 Tunnel thruster (f) Fuel: 150.0 (d.f.) 1450.0 (r.f.) 88.0pd

8855970 *WDC8162* -	**SILVER SPRAY** **Silver Spray Seafoods LLC** - *Kodiak, AK* *United States of America* MMSI: 367082610 Official number: 964016	*320* 110 -		**1990 Master Boat Builders, Inc. — Coden, Al** Yd No: 144 Loa - Br ex - Dght - Lbp 30.36 Br md 9.14 Dpth 4.42 Welded, 1 dk	**(B11B2FV) Fishing Vessel**	**1 oil engine** driving 1 FP propeller
8857045 *4JP0* -	**SILVER STAR** *ex* Amur-2540 *-2014* **'Samaya Co Ltd' LLC** - *Baku* *Azerbaijan* MMSI: 423401100	**3,086** 999 3,332	Class: RS (RR)	**1991-03 Slovenske Lodenice a.s. — Komarno** Yd No: 2340 Loa 116.03 Br ex 13.43 Dght 4.130 Lbp 110.20 Br md 13.00 Dpth 6.00 Welded, 1 dk	**(A31A2GX) General Cargo Ship** Grain: 4,064 TEU 102 C.Ho 62/20' (40') C.Dk 40/20' (40') Compartments: 3 Ho, ER 3 Ha: (11.6 x 10.1) (23.0 x 10.1) (24.0 x 10.1)ER	**2 oil engines** sr geared to sc. shafts driving 2 FP propellers Total Power: 1,030kW (1,400hp) 10.0kn Skoda 6L275A2 2 x 4 Stroke 6 Cy. 275 x 350 each-515kW (700bhp) CKD Praha-Praha AuxGen: 3 x 138kW a.c, 1 x 25kW a.c Thrusters: 1 Thwart. FP thruster (f) Fuel: 157.0 (d.f.) 7.5pd
8891156 - -	**SILVER STAR** **The Star Ferry Co Ltd** - *Hong Kong* *Hong Kong* Official number: 317706	*164* 40 72		**1965 Hong Kong & Whampoa Dock Co Ltd — Hong Kong** Yd No: 1046 Loa 33.78 Br ex 9.22 Dght 2.430 Lbp - Br md 8.57 Dpth 2.61 Welded, 1 dk	**(A37B2PS) Passenger Ship** Passengers: unberthed: 555	**1 oil engine** driving 1 FP propeller Total Power: 352kW (479hp) Crossley HGN6 1 x 2 Stroke 6 Cy. 267 x 343 352kW (479bhp) Crossley Bros. Ltd.-Manchester
8959817 *MLAS2* FR 821	**SILVER STAR** *ex* Froybas *-2005* *ex* Melbuvaering *-2004* *ex* Boen Jr. *-2002* *ex* Vassoybuen *-1995* **Silver Star (Fraserburgh) LLP** - *Fraserburgh* *United Kingdom* MMSI: 235010380 Official number: C18608	*128* 78		**1990 Aas Mek. Verksted AS — Vestnes** Yd No: 131 Loa 18.21 Br ex - Dght - Lbp - Br md 6.00 Dpth 3.60 Welded, 1 dk	**(B11B2FV) Fishing Vessel** Bale: 95	**1 oil engine** driving 1 FP propeller Total Power: 346kW (470hp) 10.0kn Volvo Penta TAMD162A 1 x 4 Stroke 6 Cy. 144 x 165 346kW (470bhp) AB Volvo Penta-Sweden Thrusters: 1 Thwart. FP thruster (f)
9085663 *3WOK* -	**SILVER STAR** *ex* Crane Pacific *-2002* **Vietnam Ocean Shipping JSC (VOSCO) (Cong Ty Co Phan Van Tai Bien Viet Nam)** - *Haiphong* *Vietnam* MMSI: 574207000 Official number: VN-2453-VT	**13,865** 7,738 21,967	Class: NK VR	**1995-01 Saiki Heavy Industries Co Ltd — Saiki OT** (Hull) Yd No: 1037 **1995-01 Onomichi Dockyard Co Ltd — Onomichi HS** Yd No: 383 Loa 157.70 (BB) Br ex - Dght 9.115 Lbp 148.00 Br md 25.00 Dpth 12.70 Welded, 1 dk	**(A21A2BC) Bulk Carrier** Grain: 29,254; Bale: 28,299 Compartments: 4 Ho, ER 4 Ha: (20.0 x 11.7)3 (20.8 x 17.5)ER Cranes: 4x30t	**1 oil engine** driving 1 FP propeller Total Power: 5,296kW (7,200hp) 14.0kn Mitsubishi 6UEC45LA 1 x 2 Stroke 6 Cy. 450 x 1350 5296kW (7200bhp) Kobe Hatsudoki KK-Japan Fuel: 1265.0 (r.f.)
8114417 *JVLV4* -	**SILVER STAR** *ex* Calypso N *-2011* *ex* Seahope *-1991* *ex* Chantara Pearl *-1986* *ex* Seahope *-1985* *ex* Celtic Venture *-1985* **Tuan Huy Shipping Co Ltd** International Transportation & Trading JSC (ITC Corp) *Ulaanbaatar* *Mongolia* MMSI: 457412000 Official number: 28901183	**20,366** 11,502 33,009 T/cm 41.5	Class: VR (LR) ✠ Classed LR until 1/7/11	**1983-04 Minaminippon Shipbuilding Co Ltd — Usuki OT** Yd No: 555 Loa 183.50 (BB) Br ex 26.67 Dght 10.769 Lbp 172.02 Br md 26.61 Dpth 15.02 Welded, 1 dk	**(A21A2BC) Bulk Carrier** Grain: 41,584; Bale: 39,788 Compartments: 5 Ho, ER 5 Ha: (16.8 x 12.8) (12.8 x 15.0)3 (16.8 x 15.0)ER Cranes: 5x25t	**1 oil engine** driving 1 FP propeller Total Power: 7,723kW (10,500hp) 14.0kn B&W 7L55GFCA 1 x 2 Stroke 7 Cy. 550 x 1380 7723kW (10500bhp) Mitsui Engineering & Shipbuilding CLtd-Japan AuxGen: 3 x 680kW 450V 60Hz a.c Boilers: e 11.0kgf/cm² (10.8bar), AuxB (o.f.) 8.0kgf/cm² (7.8bar) Fuel: 190.5 (d.f.) 2072.5 (r.f.)
6703472 *OIQZ* -	**SILVER STAR** *ex* Nordstrand II *-1983* *ex* Moby Dick *-1979* *launched as* Frisia XI *-1966* **Suomen Hopealinja Oy (Finnish Silverline Ltd)** - *Hameenlinna* *Finland* Official number: 10036	**123** 55 -	Class: (GL)	**1966 C Cassens Schiffswerft — Emden** Yd No: 83 Loa 30.05 Br ex 5.82 Dght 0.931 Lbp 28.61 Br md 5.80 Dpth 1.66 Welded, 1 dk	**(A37B2PS) Passenger Ship** Passengers: unberthed: 160 Ice Capable	**2 oil engines** driving 2 FP propellers Total Power: 236kW (320hp) 14.5kn Daimler MB846AB 2 x 4 Stroke 6 Cy. 150 x 190 each-118kW (160bhp) Daimler Benz AG-West Germany
7205893 - -	**SILVER STAR** *ex* Nourstar *-1966* *ex* Jenstar *-1992* *ex* Dejro *-1988* *ex* Lillan Coast *-1981* **Bassam J Hadi** -	*299* 162 710	Class: (BV)	**1972 A/S Nordsovaerftet — Ringkobing** Yd No: 64 Loa 49.76 Br ex 8.34 Dght 3.474 Lbp 44.43 Br md 8.30 Dpth 5.49 Riveted\Welded, 2 dks	**(A31A2GX) General Cargo Ship** Grain: 1,312; Bale: 1,159 Compartments: 1 Ho, ER 1 Ha: (24.5 x 5.0)ER Derricks: 2x5t; Winches: 2 Ice Capable	**1 oil engine** driving 1 CP propeller Total Power: 441kW (600hp) 11.0kn Alpha 406-26VO 1 x 2 Stroke 6 Cy. 260 x 400 441kW (600bhp) Alpha Diesel A/S-Denmark AuxGen: 2 x 48kW 380V 50Hz a.c Fuel: 100.5 (d.f.)
9512214 *3FF04* -	**SILVER STAR** **Action Partner Ltd** Stellar Ocean Transport LLC *Panama* *Panama* MMSI: 352050000 Official number: 43002114	**43,830** 27,811 79,200 T/cm 71.9	Class: LR ✠**100A1** SS 06/2011 bulk carrier CSR BC-A GRAB (25) Nos. 2, 4 & 6 holds may be empty ESP **ShipRight** (CM) *IWS LI ✠**LMC** **UMS** Eq.Ltr: Q†; Cable: 687.5/81.0 U3 (a)	**2011-06 COSCO (Dalian) Shipyard Co Ltd — Dalian LN** Yd No: N243 Loa 229.00 (BB) Br ex 32.30 Dght 14.600 Lbp 222.00 Br md 32.26 Dpth 20.25 Welded, 1 dk	**(A21A2BC) Bulk Carrier** Grain: 97,000; Bale: 90,784 Compartments: 7 Ho, ER 7 Ha: ER Cranes: 4x35t	**1 oil engine** driving 1 FP propeller Total Power: 11,060kW (15,037hp) 14.0kn MAN-B&W 7S50MC-C 1 x 2 Stroke 7 Cy. 500 x 2000 11060kW (15037bhp) Hyundai Heavy Industries Co Ltd-South Korea AuxGen: 3 x 730kW 450V 60Hz a.c Boilers: AuxB (Comp) 9.2kgf/cm² (9.0bar)
9542257 *T3SE* -	**SILVER STAR** **She Ji Min** Ningbo Shanglun Ship Management Co Ltd *Tarawa* *Kiribati* MMSI: 529222000 Official number: K-11080992	**2,953** 1,758 5,280	Class: IZ (CC)	**2008-10 Nanjing Doumen Fufeng Shiprepair & Building Yard — Nanjing JS** Yd No: 070920 Loa 96.90 Br ex 15.83 Dght 5.820 Lbp - Br md 15.80 Dpth 7.40 Welded, 1 dk	**(A31A2GX) General Cargo Ship**	**1 oil engine** reduction geared to sc. shaft driving 1 FP propeller Total Power: 1,765kW (2,400hp) 11.0kn Chinese Std. Type 1 x 4 Stroke 1765kW (2400bhp) in China
5014769 *HQNN* -	**SILVER STAR II** *ex* Tasos *-2000* *ex* Faith *-1985* *ex* Amethyst *-1980* **Gulf Development Marine Services Co Ltd** - *San Lorenzo* *Honduras* MMSI: 334119000 Official number: L-0331214	*1,547* 810 2,356	Class: (LR) (HR) ✠ Classed LR until 28/7/92	**1958-07 Ailsa Shipbuilding Co Ltd — Troon** Yd No: 502 Loa 78.64 Br ex 12.04 Dght 5.214 Lbp 74.07 Br md 11.59 Dpth 6.02 Riveted\Welded, 1 dk	**(A31A2GX) General Cargo Ship** Grain: 3,007; Bale: 2,903 Compartments: 3 Ho, ER 3 Ha: 3 (9.7 x 7.0)ER Derricks: 3x3t; Winches: 3	**1 oil engine** driving 1 FP propeller Total Power: 1,030kW (1,400hp) 12.0kn Deutz RBV6M366 1 x 4 Stroke 6 Cy. 420 x 660 1030kW (1400bhp) Kloeckner Humboldt Deutz AG-West Germany AuxGen: 3 x 48kW 220V d.c Fuel: 159.5 (d.f.)
8001608 *3BHJ* -	**SILVER STAR NO. 2** *ex* Noor Star No. 2 *-2011* *ex* Showa Maru No. 26 *-1992* **Max Fishing Co Ltd** - *Port Louis* *Mauritius* Official number: MR031	*299* 151 -		**1980-04 Kochi Jyuko (Kaisei Zosen) K.K. — Kochi** Yd No: 1386 Loa - Br ex - Dght 3.201 Lbp 43.62 Br md 8.51 Dpth 3.56 Welded, 1 dk	**(B11B2FV) Fishing Vessel**	**1 oil engine** reverse geared to sc. shaft driving 1 FP propeller Total Power: 1,214kW (1,651hp) Akasaka DM30R 1 x 4 Stroke 6 Cy. 300 x 480 1214kW (1651bhp) Akasaka Tekkosho KK (Akasaka DieselLtd)-Japan
8519710 *3FAU2* -	**SILVER SUN** *ex* DYVI Adriatic *-2012* *ex* Wolfsburg *-2003* **PCTC Holding I AS** Maritime Management Services Sarl *Panama* *Panama* MMSI: 373207000 Official number: 4410612	**39,187** 11,756 9,772 T/cm 41.0	Class: NV (GL)	**1988-10 Jiangnan Shipyard — Shanghai** Yd No: 2173 Loa 182.71 (BB) Br ex - Dght 9.020 Lbp 170.52 Br md 29.61 Dpth 14.13 Welded, 9 dks	**(A35B2RV) Vehicles Carrier** Side door/ramp (s) Len: 19.90 Wid: 5.10 Swl: 10 Quarter stern door/ramp (s. a.) Len: 32.00 Wid: 8.10 Swl: 70 Cars: 4,049 Bale: 32,400 TEU 362	**1 oil engine** driving 1 FP propeller Total Power: 7,920kW (10,768hp) 17.5kn B&W 6L60MCE 1 x 2 Stroke 6 Cy. 600 x 1944 7920kW (10768bhp) Hitachi Zosen Corp-Japan AuxGen: 2 x 800kW 220/440V a.c, 1 x a.c Thrusters: 1 Thwart. FP thruster (f)
9482940 *V7BF6* -	**SILVER SURFER** **Marina Celsie Shipping Ltd** Sinokor Maritime Co Ltd *Majuro* *Marshall Islands* MMSI: 538005131 Official number: 5131	**92,921** 59,331 180,000	Class: KR	**2013-07 Sungdong Shipbuilding & Marine Engineering Co Ltd — Tongyeong** Yd No: 1111 Loa 292.00 (BB) Br ex - Dght 18.300 Lbp 279.40 Br md 45.00 Dpth 24.80 Welded, 1 dk	**(A21A2BC) Bulk Carrier** Grain: 199,500; Bale: 187,719 Compartments: 9 Ho, ER 9 Ha: 7 (15.5 x 20.6)ER 2 (15.5 x 17.2)	**1 oil engine** driving 1 FP propeller Total Power: 18,660kW (25,370hp) 14.3kn MAN-B&W 6S70MC-C 1 x 2 Stroke 6 Cy. 700 x 2800 18660kW (25370bhp) Hyundai Heavy Industries Co Ltd-South Korea AuxGen: 3 x a.c

9107916 *3FRL2* -	**SILVER TRADE** *ex* Samsara *-2011* *ex* Cape Venture *-2007* *ex* Mineral Venture *-2004* **Silver Trade Maritime SA** Sinokor Merchant Marine Co Ltd SatCom: Inmarsat C 435421410 *Panama* *Panama* MMSI: 354214000 Official number: 4318411	**77,255** 48,714 150,393 T/cm 106.3	Class: KR (BV) (NV)	**1996**-01 **Kawasaki Heavy Industries Ltd — Sakaide KG** Yd No: 1454 Loa 273.00 (BB) Br ex - Dght 17.400 Lbp 260.00 Br md 43.00 Dpth 23.90 Welded, 1 dk	**(A21A2BC) Bulk Carrier** Grain: 167,886 Compartments: 9 Ho, ER 9 Ha: (14.2 x 18.4)7 (14.2 x 19.8) (14.2 x 14.0)ER	**1 oil engine** driving 1 FP propeller Total Power: 12,725kW (17,301hp) 14.5kn B&W 6S70MC 1 x 2 Stroke 6 Cy. 700 x 2674 12725kW (17301bhp) Kawasaki Heavy Industries Ltd-Japan AuxGen: 3 x 560kW 450V 60Hz a.c Fuel: 366.0 (d.f.) (Heating Coils) 3226.0 (r.f.) 54.0pd
8724872 *DUG6053* -	**SILVER TUNA B** *ex* Catherine I *-2004* *ex* Koyo Maru No. 2 *-1989* *ex* Mashima Maru No. 2 *-1986* *ex* Konpira Maru No. 18 *-1981* **Jumbo Fishing Corp** - *Iloilo* *Philippines* Official number: ILO3000164	*155* 102 -		**1973**-09 **K.K. Izutsu Zosensho — Nagasaki** L reg 31.90 Br ex 5.82 Dght 2.500 Lbp - Br md 5.80 Dpth 2.80 Welded, 1 dk	**(B11B2FV) Fishing Vessel**	**2 oil engines** driving 2 FP propellers Total Power: 504kW (686hp) MWM 2 x Vee 4 Stroke 12 Cy. each-252kW (343bhp) Motoren Werke Mannheim AG (MWM)-West Germany Thrusters: 1 Thwart. FP thruster (f)
5328263 *CY5089* -	**SILVER VIKING** *ex* Silver Viking II *-1959* **Jim Pattison Enterprises Ltd** *Vancouver, BC* *Canada* Official number: 310395	*138* 67 152		**1958 Yarrows Ltd — Victoria BC** Yd No: 169 Loa 21.70 Br ex 6.74 Dght 3.048 Lbp - Br md - Dpth - Welded, 1 dk	**(B11B2FV) Fishing Vessel**	**1 oil engine** driving 1 FP propeller Total Power: 399kW (542hp) Caterpillar D353SCAC 1 x 4 Stroke 6 Cy. 159 x 203 399kW (542bhp) Caterpillar Tractor Co-USA
9187576 *3FNO9* -	**SILVER VOYAGER** *ex* Rubin Hope *-2012* **Atlantic Dragon SA** Sinokor Maritime Co Ltd *Panama* *Panama* MMSI: 357591000 Official number: 28230PEXT1	**84,482** 56,059 170,409 T/cm 114.9	Class: KR (NK)	**1999**-07 **Ishikawajima-Harima Heavy Industries Co Ltd (IHI) — Kure** Yd No: 3116 Loa 289.00 (BB) Br ex - Dght 17.625 Lbp 277.00 Br md 45.00 Dpth 23.80 Welded, 1 dk	**(A21A2BC) Bulk Carrier** Grain: 186,667 Compartments: 9 Ho, ER 9 Ha: 2 (17.6 x 20.4)5 (13.6 x 20.4) (16.8 x 20.4) (18.4 x 17.0)ER	**1 oil engine** driving 1 FP propeller Total Power: 16,043kW (21,812hp) 14.8kn Sulzer 6RTA72 1 x 2 Stroke 6 Cy. 720 x 2500 16043kW (21812bhp) Diesel United Ltd.-Aioi AuxGen: 3 x 725kW 450V a.c Fuel: 4595.0
8605155 *JVCN2* -	**SILVER WATER 18** *ex* Nissho Maru No. 2 *-2004* **Silver Water Holding Ltd** - *Ulaanbaatar* *Mongolia* MMSI: 457047000 Official number: 10620386	*449* 177 849		**1986**-02 **Sasaki Shipbuilding Co Ltd — Osakikamijima HS** Yd No: 397 Loa 52.20 Br ex - Dght 3.952 Lbp 48.01 Br md 9.01 Dpth 4.12 Welded, 1 dk	**(A12A2TC) Chemical Tanker** Compartments: 6 Ta, ER	**1 oil engine** with clutches, flexible couplings & reverse reduction geared to sc. shaft driving 1 FP propeller Total Power: 625kW (850hp) Niigata 6M26BGT 1 x 4 Stroke 6 Cy. 260 x 460 625kW (850bhp) Niigata Engineering Co Ltd-Japan
8862193 *YFEJ* -	**SILVER WHALE** *ex* Chung Pao Ocean *-1994* *ex* Oriental Harvest No. 1 *-1993* *ex* Koei Maru No. 5 *-1993* *ex* Konpira Maru No. 5 *-1993* **PT Inti Samudera Abdi Nusantara** - *Jakarta* *Indonesia*	**259** 105 420	Class: KI	**1968**-07 **Kogushi Zosen K.K. — Okayama** Loa 40.40 Br ex - Dght 3.010 Lbp 35.00 Br md 7.20 Dpth 3.23 Welded, 1 dk	**(A31A2GX) General Cargo Ship**	**1 oil engine** driving 1 FP propeller Total Power: 368kW (500hp) 9.5kn Hanshin Z627ASH 1 x 4 Stroke 6 Cy. 270 x 400 368kW (500bhp) The Hanshin Diesel Works Ltd-Japan
9192179 *C6FN7* -	**SILVER WHISPER** **UniCredit Leasing SpA** Silversea Cruises Ltd *Nassau* *Bahamas* MMSI: 308322000 Official number: 732046	**28,258** 9,144 2,980	Class: RI	**2001**-06 **Cantiere Navale Visentini Srl — Porto Viro** (Hull) **2001**-06 **T. Mariotti SpA — Genova** Yd No: 982 Loa 186.00 Br ex - Dght 6.120 Lbp 161.80 Br md 24.80 Dpth 11.30 Welded	**(A37A2PC) Passenger/Cruise** Passengers: cabins: 194; berths: 388	**2 oil engines** reduction geared to sc. shafts driving 2 CP propellers Total Power: 11,474kW (15,600hp) 21.0kn Wartsila 8L46B 2 x 4 Stroke 8 Cy. 460 x 580 each-5737kW (7800bhp) Wartsila Finland Oy-Finland AuxGen: 3 x 2340kW 220/440V 60Hz a.c, 2 x 220/440V 60Hz a.c
8903935 *C6FG2* -	**SILVER WIND** **Silver Wind Shipping Ltd** Silversea Cruises Ltd SatCom: Inmarsat C 424707630 *Nassau* *Bahamas* MMSI: 308814000 Official number: 731985	**17,235** 5,350 1,790	Class: RI (LR) ✠ Classed LR until 1/4/97	**1995**-01 **Cantiere Navale Visentini Srl — Porto Viro** (Hull launched by) **1995**-01 **T. Mariotti SpA — Genova** (Hull completed by) **1995**-01 **Soc. Esercizio Cant. S.p.A. — Viareggio** Yd No: 776 Loa 155.81 (BB) Br ex 21.42 Dght 5.350 Lbp 134.84 Br md 21.40 Dpth 13.20 Welded, 3 dks	**(A37A2PC) Passenger/Cruise** Passengers: cabins: 148; berths: 296	**2 oil engines** with clutches, flexible couplings & sr geared to sc. shafts driving 2 CP propellers Total Power: 11,700kW (15,908hp) 17.0kn Wartsila 6R46 2 x 4 Stroke 6 Cy. 460 x 580 each-5850kW (7954bhp) Wartsila Diesel Oy-Finland AuxGen: 2 x 2700kW 440V 60Hz a.c, 2 x 2700kW 440V 60Hz a.c Thrusters: 1 Thwart. CP thruster (f); 1 Tunnel thruster (a) Fuel: 832.0 (d.f.) 43.0pd
8630289 *XUTY9* -	**SILVER WIND** *ex* Glorious Grace *-2013* *ex* Jin Chen *-2008* *ex* Fu Shen *-2005* *ex* Fukujin Maru No. 21 *-2003* *ex* Taisei Maru No. 62 *-1996* **'Shell World' Trading Co Inc** East Line Shipping Co Ltd *Phnom Penh* *Cambodia* MMSI: 515429000 Official number: 0786711	**1,809** 1,272 1,175		**1986**-10 **K.K. Yoshida Zosen Kogyo — Arida** Loa 65.00 (BB) Br ex 13.22 Dght 3.870 Lbp 58.00 Br md 13.20 Dpth 6.00 Welded, 1 dk	**(B33A2DG) Grab Dredger**	**1 oil engine** driving 1 FP propeller Total Power: 1,030kW (1,400hp) 10.5kn Hanshin 6LU32G 1 x 4 Stroke 6 Cy. 320 x 510 1030kW (1400bhp) The Hanshin Diesel Works Ltd-Japan
6519156 - -	**SILVERFORS** *ex* Amazon *-2008* *ex* Silversjo *-2006* *ex* Silverfors *-2005* *ex* Crescent *-1991* *ex* Pelago *-1988* *ex* Westero av Hono *-1981* *ex* Shamrock *-1979* *ex* Rattvik *-1970* **Keskikala Oy** - *Finland*	**270** 81 577	Class: (NV)	**1965**-10 **AB Nya Marstrandsverken — Marstrand** Yd No: 2 Lengthened-1971 Loa 37.70 Br ex 6.84 Dght 4.040 Lbp 33.91 Br md 6.74 Dpth 4.90 Welded, 1 dk	**(B11B2FV) Fishing Vessel** Compartments: 2 Ho, ER 4 Ha: (0.9 x 1.3) (1.4 x 1.4) (1.4 x 1.1) (0.9 x 1.0)ER Derricks: 1x2.5t,1x0.3t; Winches: 1 Ice Capable	**1 oil engine** driving 1 FP propeller Total Power: 736kW (1,001hp) Deutz RBV6M545 1 x 4 Stroke 6 Cy. 320 x 450 736kW (1001bhp) Kloeckner Humboldt Deutz AG-West Germany AuxGen: 1 x 14kW 110V d.c, 1 x 6kW 110V d.c
8882583 - LA 558	**SILVERMERMAID I** **Atlantic Shrimpers Ltd** - *Lagos* *Nigeria*	*139* 89 -		**1989 Ocean Marine, Inc. — Bayou La Batre, Al** Yd No: 226 Loa - Br ex - Dght - Lbp - Br md - Dpth - Welded, 1 dk	**(B11B2FV) Fishing Vessel**	**1 oil engine** driving 1 FP propeller
8882595 - LA 557	**SILVERMERMAID II** **Atlantic Shrimpers Ltd** - *Lagos* *Nigeria*	*139* 89 -		**1989 Ocean Marine, Inc. — Bayou La Batre, Al** Yd No: 227 Loa - Br ex - Dght - Lbp - Br md - Dpth - Welded, 1 dk	**(B11B2FV) Fishing Vessel**	**1 oil engine** driving 1 FP propeller
8621393 *SEJW* -	**SILVERPILEN** **Kent Krusell Fartygsservice AB** Uto Rederi AB *Stockholm* *Sweden* MMSI: 265317000	**220** 93 -		**1974 Boghammar Marin AB — Lidingo** Yd No: 1057 Loa 35.08 Br ex - Dght 1.501 Lbp 33.61 Br md 7.01 Dpth 3.03 Welded, 1 dk	**(A37B2PS) Passenger Ship** Hull Material: Aluminium Alloy Passengers: unberthed: 300	**3 oil engines** with flexible couplings & sr reverse geared to sc. shafts driving 3 Propellers Total Power: 1,398kW (1,902hp) 21.0kn Volvo Penta TAMD121 3 x 4 Stroke 6 Cy. 130 x 150 each-466kW (634bhp) AB Volvo Penta-Sweden
8306216 - -	**SILVERSIDE** **Guyana Fisheries Ltd** - *Georgetown* *Guyana* Official number: 708107	*108* 48 98		**1984**-02 **Bender Shipbuilding & Repair Co Inc — Mobile AL** Yd No: 192 Loa - Br ex - Dght 2.590 Lbp 21.95 Br md 6.11 Dpth 3.28 Welded, 1 dk	**(B11A2FT) Trawler**	**1 oil engine** sr geared to sc. shaft driving 1 FP propeller Total Power: 268kW (364hp) 9.3kn Caterpillar 3408TA 1 x Vee 4 Stroke 8 Cy. 137 x 152 268kW (364bhp) Caterpillar Tractor Co-USA AuxGen: 2 x 3kW 32V d.c Fuel: 43.5 (d.f.) 1.0pd
9351220 *VMQ8974* -	**SILVERSONIC** **Quicksilver Connections Ltd** - *Port Douglas, Qld* *Australia* Official number: 857923	**156** 52 21		**2005**-09 **North West Bay Ships Pty Ltd — Margate TAS** Yd No: 014 Loa 29.50 Br ex - Dght 1.500 Lbp 27.10 Br md 8.30 Dpth 2.71 Welded, 1 dk	**(A37B2PS) Passenger Ship** Passengers: unberthed: 130	**2 oil engines** geared to sc. shafts driving 2 FP propellers Total Power: 1,846kW (2,510hp) 33.0kn Deutz TBD616V16 2 x Vee 4 Stroke 16 Cy. 132 x 160 each-923kW (1255bhp) Deutz AG-Koeln

9194880 *C4MH2* -	**SILVERSTAR** *ex Century Forest -2006* **Oceanbond Shipping Co Ltd** Seastar Chartering Ltd *Limassol* *Cyprus* MMSI: 210219000 Official number: 9194880	**19,731** 11,389 31,762 T/cm 45.4	Class: NK	**1999-02 The Hakodate Dock Co Ltd — Hakodate HK** Yd No: 773 Loa 176.75 (BB) Br ex - Dght 9.562 Lbp 168.00 Br md 29.40 Dpth 13.50 Welded, 1 dk	**(A21A2BC) Bulk Carrier** Grain: 42,178; Bale: 40,657 Compartments: 5 Ho, ER 5 Ha: (13.6 x 15.0)4 (20.0 x 19.6)ER Cranes: 4x30.5t	**1 oil engine** driving 1 FP propeller Total Power: 7,061kW (9,600hp) 14.2kn Mitsubishi 6UEC52LA 1 x 2 Stroke 6 Cy. 520 x 1600 7061kW (9600bhp) Akasaka Tekkosho KK (Akasaka DieselLtd)-Japan AuxGen: 2 x a.c Fuel: 1370.0
9434319 *DUAR* -	**SILVERSTONE EXPRESS** **PCTC Express I BV** Vroon BV SatCom: Inmarsat C 454880710 *Manila* *Philippines* MMSI: 548807000 Official number: MNLA000730	**43,810** 13,143 15,154	Class: NK	**2009-05 Mitsubishi Heavy Industries Ltd. — Shimonoseki** Yd No: 1132 Loa 180.00 (BB) Br ex 30.03 Dght 9.222 Lbp 171.70 Br md 30.00 Dpth 33.52 Welded, 10 dks. incl. 2 liftable dks.	**(A35B2RV) Vehicles Carrier** Side door/ramp (s) Len: - Wid: - Swl: 25 Quarter stern door/ramp (s. a.) Len: - Wid: - Swl: 100 Cars: 3,205	**1 oil engine** driving 1 FP propeller Total Power: 11,560kW (15,717hp) 19.9kn Mitsubishi 8UEC50LSII 1 x 2 Stroke 8 Cy. 500 x 1950 11560kW (15717bhp) Mitsubishi Heavy Industries Ltd-Japan AuxGen: 3 x 875kW 450V 60Hz a.c Thrusters: 1 Thwart. CP thruster (f) Fuel: 2320.0 (r.f.)
8612562 *SLHW* -	**SILVERTARNAN** **A/B Goteborg-Styrso Skargardstrafik** - *Gothenburg* *Sweden* MMSI: 265547260	**230** 96 -		**1986-02 Djupviks Batvarv — Fagerfjall** Yd No: 332 Loa 30.23 Br ex - Dght 2.220 Lbp 26.90 Br md 7.73 Dpth 3.10 Welded, 1 dk	**(A37B2PS) Passenger Ship** Hull Material: Aluminium Alloy Passengers: unberthed: 389	**2 oil engines** sr geared to sc. shafts driving 2 CP propellers Total Power: 1,052kW (1,430hp) 13.0kn Volvo Penta D12 2 x 4 Stroke 6 Cy. 131 x 150 each-526kW (715bhp) (new engine 2003) AB Volvo Penta-Sweden
9568079 *LCYH* R-734-K	**SILVERVAG** *ex Anders Nees -2011* **Najaden Fiskeri AS** - *Skudeneshavn* *Norway*	**168** 67 -		**2010-05 AS Rigas Kugu Buvetava (Riga Shipyard) — Riga** (Hull) Yd No: 126 **2010-06 Vestvaerftet ApS — Hvide Sande** Yd No: 285 Loa 23.10 (BB) Br ex - Dght 3.250 Lbp - Br md 7.00 Dpth 5.74 Welded, 1 dk	**(B11B2FV) Fishing Vessel**	**1 oil engine** reduction geared to sc. shaft driving 1 CP propeller Total Power: 610kW (829hp) 10.0kn Mitsubishi S6R2-MPTK 1 x 4 Stroke 6 Cy. 170 x 220 610kW (829bhp) Mitsubishi Heavy Industries Ltd-Japan AuxGen: 2 x 57kW 415V 50Hz a.c Thrusters: 1 Tunnel thruster (f)
9212670 *OZUE* FN 384	**SILVERVAG** *ex Silvervag Av Hono -2009 ex Raytheon -2007* **Alice Snebang & Soren Trolle Godtliebsen** - *Strandby* *Denmark* Official number: H1679	**158** 65 -		**1999-09 AS Rigas Kugu Buvetava (Riga Shipyard) — Riga** (Hull) Yd No: 003 **1999-09 Vestvaerftet ApS — Hvide Sande** Yd No: 216 Loa 22.92 Br ex - Dght 3.390 Lbp 19.59 Br md 6.60 Dpth 5.59 Welded, 1 dk	**(B11B2FV) Fishing Vessel**	**1 oil engine** geared to sc. shaft driving 1 CP propeller Yanmar 1 x 4 Stroke Yanmar Diesel Engine Co Ltd-Japan
9360489 *V2GE4* -	**SILVES** **NAVEIRO-Transportes Maritimos SA** Naveiro Transportes Maritimos (Madeira) Lda *Saint John's* *Antigua & Barbuda* MMSI: 305912000	**2,956** 1,558 4,671	Class: GL (LR) ✠ Classed LR until 22/12/12	**2008-10 DP Sudnobudivnyi Zavod im. "61 Kommunara" — Mykolayiv** (Hull) Yd No: (150) **2008-10 Factoria Naval de Marin S.A. — Marin** Yd No: 150 Loa 89.50 (BB) Br ex 13.70 Dght 6.000 Lbp 83.40 Br md 13.70 Dpth 8.00 Welded, 1 dk	**(A31A2GX) General Cargo Ship** Grain: 5,578 TEU 111 Compartments: 1 Ho, ER 1 Ha: ER (60.5 x 11.0)	**1 oil engine** with clutches, flexible couplings & dr reverse geared to sc. shaft driving 1 CP propeller Total Power: 1,850kW (2,515hp) 12.0kn MaK 6M25 1 x 4 Stroke 6 Cy. 255 x 400 1850kW (2515bhp) Caterpillar Motoren GmbH & Co. KG-Germany AuxGen: 2 x 184kW 380V 50Hz a.c, 1 x 448kW 380V 50Hz a.c Boilers: HWH (o.f.) 6.1kgf/cm² (6.0bar), HWH (ex.g.) 6.1kgf/cm² (6.0bar) Thrusters: 1 Thwart. FP thruster (f)
7609350 *WYU8918* -	**SILVESTRE** *ex Deco I -2005 ex Fox Fire -2001* **Silmen Trawlers Inc** - *Aransas Pass, TX* *United States of America* Official number: 558592	*120* 82 -		**1974 Master Marine, Inc. — Bayou La Batre, Al** Yd No: 164 L reg 22.59 Br ex - Dght - Lbp - Br md 6.72 Dpth 3.43 Welded, 1 dk	**(B11A2FT) Trawler**	**1 oil engine** driving 1 FP propeller Total Power: 239kW (325hp) Caterpillar D353TA 1 x 4 Stroke 6 Cy. 159 x 203 239kW (325bhp) Caterpillar Tractor Co-USA
8107000 *LZSI* -	**SILVIA** *ex Storrington -2011* **Silvia SA** 'VM International' Ltd SatCom: Inmarsat C 420735410 *Varna* *Bulgaria* MMSI: 207354000 Official number: 1	**7,788** 4,025 11,990 T/cm 22.2	Class: LR ✠ **100A1** SS 04/2012 strengthened for heavy cargoes Ice Class 3 ✠ **LMC** **UMS** Eq.Ltr: Y; Cable: 522.5/52.0 U2	**1982-03 Verolme Scheepswerf Heusden B.V. — Heusden** Yd No: 992 Loa 137.60 (BB) Br ex 18.67 Dght 7.924 Lbp 129.93 Br md 18.61 Dpth 10.70 Welded, 1 dk	**(A31A2GX) General Cargo Ship** Grain: 14,166 Compartments: 3 Ho, ER 3 Ha: (25.1 x 11.0)2 (26.6 x 13.6)ER Ice Capable	**1 oil engine** with flexible couplings & sr gearedto sc. shaft driving 1 CP propeller Total Power: 4,781kW (6,500hp) 14.0kn Werkspoor 9TM410 1 x 4 Stroke 9 Cy. 410 x 470 4781kW (6500bhp) Stork Werkspoor Diesel BV-Netherlands AuxGen: 3 x 294kW 440V 60Hz a.c Boilers: TOH (o.f.) 10.0kgf/cm² (9.8bar), TOH (ex.g.) 10.0kgf/cm² (9.8bar) Thrusters: 1 Thwart. FP thruster (f) Fuel: 80.0 (d.f.) 590.0 (r.f.) 14.5pd
9622930 *VRJG4* -	**SILVIA AMBITION** **Best Soar Ltd** Farenco Shipping Pte Ltd *Hong Kong* *Hong Kong* MMSI: 477424500 Official number: HK-3240	**33,042** 19,132 56,880 T/cm 58.8	Class: NK (GL)	**2011-11 Yangfan Group Co Ltd — Zhoushan ZJ** Yd No: 2196 Loa 189.99 (BB) Br ex - Dght 12.800 Lbp 185.00 Br md 32.26 Dpth 18.00 Welded, 1 dk	**(A21A2BC) Bulk Carrier** Grain: 71,634; Bale: 68,200 Compartments: 5 Ho, ER 5 Ha: 4 (21.3 x 18.3)ER (18.9 x 18.3) Cranes: 4x36t	**1 oil engine** driving 1 FP propeller Total Power: 9,480kW (12,889hp) 14.2kn MAN-B&W 6S50MC-C 1 x 2 Stroke 6 Cy. 500 x 2000 9480kW (12889bhp) STX Engine Co Ltd-South Korea Fuel: 2400.0
9119385 *CXQZ* -	**SILVIA ANA L** **Los Cipreses SA (BUQUEBUS)** - *Montevideo* *Uruguay* MMSI: 770576231 Official number: P808	**7,895** 2,369 466	Class: NV	**1996-11 EN Bazan de Construcciones Navales Militares SA — San Fernando (Sp)** Yd No: 327 Loa 125.00 Br ex 18.70 Dght 2.524 Lbp 110.00 Br md 14.70 Dpth 11.20 Welded, 2 dks	**(A36A2PR) Passenger/Ro-Ro Ship (Vehicles)** Hull Material: Aluminium Alloy Passengers: unberthed: 1250 Stern door/ramp (p) Len: 6.50 Wid: 5.50 Swl: - Stern door/ramp (s) Len: 6.50 Wid: 5.50 Swl: - Lorries: 4, Cars: 238	**6 oil engines** reduction geared to sc. shafts driving 5 Water jets , booster unit Total Power: 33,900kW (46,092hp) 38.0kn Caterpillar 3616TA 6 x Vee 4 Stroke 16 Cy. 280 x 300 each-5650kW (7682bhp) Caterpillar Inc-USA AuxGen: 3 x 280kW 220/380V 60Hz a.c, 1 x 160kW 220/380V 60Hz a.c Thrusters: 2 Thwart. FP thruster (f)
9622942 *VRJZ4* -	**SILVIA GLORY** **Best Excellence Corp Ltd** Farenco Shipping Pte Ltd *Hong Kong* *Hong Kong* MMSI: 477739800 Official number: HK-3390	**33,042** 19,132 56,797 T/cm 58.8	Class: NK (GL)	**2012-04 Yangfan Group Co Ltd — Zhoushan ZJ** Yd No: 2197 Loa 189.98 (BB) Br ex - Dght 12.800 Lbp 185.00 Br md 32.26 Dpth 18.00 Welded, 1 dk	**(A21A2BC) Bulk Carrier** Grain: 71,634; Bale: 68,200 Compartments: 5 Ho, ER 5 Ha: 4 (21.3 x 18.3)ER (18.9 x 18.3) Cranes: 4x36t	**1 oil engine** driving 1 FP propeller Total Power: 9,480kW (12,889hp) 14.2kn MAN-B&W 6S50MC-C 1 x 2 Stroke 6 Cy. 500 x 2000 9480kW (12889bhp) STX Engine Co Ltd-South Korea Fuel: 2400.0
8714906 *IXSX* -	**SILVIA ONORATO** **San Cataldo SpA** - SatCom: Inmarsat C 424758730 *Naples* *Italy* MMSI: 247429000 Official number: 1608	**275** 82 117	Class: RI	**1987-08 Cantiere Navale di Pesaro SpA (CNP) — Pesaro** Yd No: 62 Loa 32.41 Br ex 9.28 Dght 3.899 Lbp 29.01 Br md 8.60 Dpth 4.27 Welded, 1 dk	**(B32A2ST) Tug**	**1 oil engine** with clutches, flexible couplings & sr geared to sc. shaft driving 1 CP propeller Total Power: 2,250kW (3,059hp) 13.5kn Nohab F312V 1 x Vee 4 Stroke 12 Cy. 250 x 300 2250kW (3059bhp) Wartsila Diesel AB-Sweden AuxGen: 3 x 104kW 380V 50Hz a.c Thrusters: 1 Thwart. FP thruster (f) Fuel: 95.0 (d.f.) 11.0pd
8414415 *YGGM* -	**SILVIA XII** *ex Suwa Maru -1999* **PT Sukses Osean Khatulistiwa Line** - *Jakarta* *Indonesia* MMSI: 525016028	**1,846** 908 3,302	Class: KI (NK)	**1984-07 Sasaki Shipbuilding Co Ltd — Osakikamijima HS** Yd No: 379 Loa 88.83 Br ex - Dght 5.952 Lbp 82.02 Br md 12.62 Dpth 6.41 Welded, 1 dk	**(A13B2TP) Products Tanker** Liq: 3,399; Liq (Oil): 3,399 Compartments: 8 Ta, ER	**1 oil engine** driving 1 FP propeller Total Power: 1,765kW (2,400hp) 12.5kn Hanshin 6EL35 1 x 4 Stroke 6 Cy. 350 x 700 1765kW (2400bhp) The Hanshin Diesel Works Ltd-Japan AuxGen: 2 x 160kW a.c
9238595 *HOCC* -	**SILVICULTURE** **Cygnet Bulk Carriers SA** Philippine MT Shipmanagement Corp *Panama* *Panama* MMSI: 353707000 Official number: 2856602C	**46,515** 14,561 54,086	Class: NK	**2002-05 Sanoyas Hishino Meisho Corp — Kurashiki OY** Yd No: 1196 Loa 203.50 Br ex - Dght 10.818 Lbp 196.00 Br md 37.20 Dpth 22.30 Welded, 1 dk	**(A24B2BW) Wood Chips Carrier** Grain: 115,699 Compartments: 6 Ho, ER 6 Ha: 2 (14.6 x 22.5)2 (16.2 x 22.5)2 (15.4 x 22.5)ER Cranes: 3x14.7t	**1 oil engine** driving 1 FP propeller Total Power: 9,120kW (12,400hp) 14.5kn B&W 6S50MC-C 1 x 2 Stroke 6 Cy. 500 x 2000 9120kW (12400bhp) Mitsui Engineering & Shipbuilding CLtd-Japan Fuel: 3030.0

IMO / Call sign	Name, owners, manager, port, flag	Tonnage	Class	Construction & dimensions	Type	Machinery
9276779 *HBFT* -	**SILVRETTA** *ex* F. D. Umberto d'Amato *-2007* *ex* Umberto d'Amato *-2006* **Oceana Shipping AG** Suisse-Atlantique Societe de Navigation Maritime SA *Basel* *Switzerland* MMSI: 269019000 Official number: 185	**17,951** 10,748 29,721 T/cm 40.5	Class: RI (NK)	**2003-11 Shikoku Dockyard Co. Ltd. — Takamatsu** Yd No: 1011 Loa 170.70 Br ex - Dght 9.716 Lbp 163.50 Br md 27.00 Dpth 13.80 Welded, 1 dk	**(A21A2BC) Bulk Carrier** Grain: 40,031; Bale: 38,422 Compartments: 5 Ho, ER 5 Ha: (20.0 x 17.8)3 (20.0 x 17.8)ER (12.8 x 16.2) Cranes: 4x30.5t	**1 oil engine** driving 1 FP propeller Total Power: 6,156kW (8,370hp) 14.3kn B&W 6S42MC 1 x 2 Stroke 6 Cy. 420 x 1764 6156kW (8370bhp) Mitsui Engineering & Shipbuilding CLtd-Japan
8504935 *3EOF6* -	**SILVY** *ex* Pemba *-2007* *ex* Jetty *-1996* *ex* Karola-S *-1992* **World Neptune SA** World Shipping Management Corp SA *Panama* *Panama* MMSI: 355617000 Official number: 3480109	**2,726** 1,117 2,958	Class: IT (GL)	**1986-06 Buesumer Werft GmbH — Buesum** Yd No: 2034 Loa 92.56 (BB) Br ex 13.85 Dght 4.422 Lbp 86.85 Br md 13.81 Dpth 6.81 Welded, 1 dk	**(A31A2GX) General Cargo Ship** Grain: 5,214; Bale: 5,141 TEU 204 C.Ho 108/20' C.Dk 96/20' incl.10 ref C. Compartments: 1 Ho, ER 1 Ha: (57.9 x 11.0)ER Cranes: 2x25t	**1 oil engine** with flexible couplings & sr gearedto sc. shaft driving 1 CP propeller Total Power: 879kW (1,195hp) 12.2kn MaK 6M453B 1 x 4 Stroke 6 Cy. 320 x 420 879kW (1195bhp) Krupp MaK Maschinenbau GmbH-Kiel AuxGen: 1 x 440kW, 1 x 220kW Thrusters: 1 Thwart. FP thruster (f)
7023324 - -	**SILY** **Office d'Amenagement de Boke (OFAB)** Halco (Mining) Inc *Conakry* *Guinea*	*148* 14 134	Class: (BV)	**1970 Gutehoffnungshuette Sterkrade AG Rheinwerft Walsum — Duisburg** Loa 28.02 Br ex 8.56 Dght 2.801 Lbp 25.25 Br md 8.16 Dpth 3.41 Welded, 1 dk	**(B32A2ST) Tug**	**1 oil engine** driving 1 FP propeller Total Power: 610kW (829hp) 10.0kn Deutz SBA8M528 1 x 4 Stroke 8 Cy. 220 x 280 610kW (829bhp) Kloeckner Humboldt Deutz AG-West Germany AuxGen: 1 x 23kW 110V d.c, 1 x 11kW 110V d.c Fuel: 56.0 (d.f.)
8101501 *S7TO* -	**SIM KWAN 1** *ex* J. C. Marine 32 *-2005* *ex* Na Tai *-2005* **Sim Kwan Holdings Ltd** QSA Marine & Logistics Pte Ltd *Victoria* *Seychelles* MMSI: 664383000 Official number: 50162	**360** 108 -	Class: (BV)	**1980-02 Sing Koon Seng Pte Ltd — Singapore** Yd No: SKS521 Loa 35.00 Br ex - Dght 3.001 Lbp 32.32 Br md 9.50 Dpth 4.63 Welded, 1 dk	**(B32A2ST) Tug**	**2 oil engines** geared to sc. shafts driving 2 FP propellers Total Power: 1,654kW (2,248hp) 11.5kn Caterpillar D399SCAC 2 x Vee 4 Stroke 16 Cy. 159 x 203 each-827kW (1124bhp) Caterpillar Tractor Co-USA
9601845 *9MLM9*	**SIM MERCURY** **Simgood Pte Ltd** PT Indoliziz Marine *Port Klang* *Malaysia* MMSI: 533057600 Official number: 334279	**251** 75 -	Class: BV	**2010-04 P.T. Batam Expressindo Shipyard — Batam** Yd No: 838 Loa 40.50 Br ex - Dght 1.800 Lbp 38.00 Br md 7.50 Dpth 3.65 Welded, 1 dk	**(B34J2SD) Crew Boat** Hull Material: Aluminium Alloy	**3 oil engines** reduction geared to sc. shafts driving 3 FP propellers Total Power: 2,430kW (3,303hp) 25.0kn Caterpillar 3412E 3 x Vee 4 Stroke 12 Cy. 137 x 152 each-810kW (1101bhp) Caterpillar Inc-USA AuxGen: 2 x 80kW 50Hz a.c
7395648 *A6E2797*	**SIM SIM** *ex* Chieftain Service *-1997* *ex* Bushford *-1980* *ex* Bruinford *-1978* *ex* Sea Bruin *-1978* **National Shipping Service LLC** Whitesea Shipping & Supply (LLC) *Sharjah* *United Arab Emirates* MMSI: 470542000 Official number: 4658	**1,114** 334 1,571	Class: GL (AB)	**1976-03 Mangone Shipbuilding Co. — Houston, Tx** Yd No: 117 Loa 66.65 Br ex 12.86 Dght 4.893 Lbp 59.97 Br md 12.82 Dpth 5.80 Welded, 1 dk	**(B21B20T) Offshore Tug/Supply Ship** Cranes: 1x7t	**2 oil engines** sr geared to sc. shafts driving 2 CP propellers Total Power: 5,296kW (7,200hp) 10.0kn EMD (Electro-Motive) 20-645-E5 2 x Vee 2 Stroke 20 Cy. 230 x 254 each-2648kW (3600bhp) General Motors Corp.Electro-Motive Div.-La Grange AuxGen: 2 x 160kW 450V 60Hz a.c Thrusters: 1 Thwart. FP thruster (f) Fuel: 564.0 (d.f.)
8418564 *OUXR2* -	**SIMA** *ex* Neftegaz-66 *-2012* **JD Crafts A/S** JD-Contractor A/S *Struer* *Denmark (DIS)* MMSI: 219017151 Official number: D4582	**2,881** 817 1,393	Class: RI (RS)	**1990-03 Stocznia Szczecinska im A Warskiego — Szczecin** Yd No: B92/216 Loa 81.37 Br ex 16.30 Dght 4.900 Lbp 71.45 Br md 15.96 Dpth 7.20 Welded, 2 dks	**(B21B20A) Anchor Handling Tug Supply** Cranes: 1x12.5t Ice Capable	**2 oil engines** reduction geared to sc. shafts driving 2 CP propellers Total Power: 5,300kW (7,206hp) 12.0kn Sulzer 6ZL40/48 2 x 4 Stroke 6 Cy. 400 x 480 each-2650kW (3603bhp) Zaklady Urzadzen Technicznych'Zgoda' SA-Poland AuxGen: 3 x 400kW 400V 50Hz a.c Thrusters: 1 Tunnel thruster (f); 1 Retract. directional thruster (f) Fuel: 659.0
9400045 *ZJL7715* -	**SIMA** **Sima Pty Ltd** - *Road Harbour* *British Virgin Islands* MMSI: 378259000 Official number: 740150	**328** 98 33	Class: BV	**2007-07 C.R.N. Cant. Nav. Ancona S.r.l. — Ancona** Yd No: 128/04 Loa 39.30 Br ex - Dght 2.780 Lbp 35.87 Br md 7.60 Dpth 3.71 Bonded, 1 dk	**(X11A2YP) Yacht** Hull Material: Reinforced Plastic	**2 oil engines** reduction geared to sc. shafts driving 2 FP propellers Total Power: 4,082kW (5,550hp) 28.0kn M.T.U. 12V4000M90 2 x Vee 4 Stroke 12 Cy. 165 x 190 each-2041kW (2775bhp) MTU Friedrichshafen GmbH-Friedrichshafen
9292450 *S6BC8* -	**SIMA PERFECT** *ex* Sima Pars *-2012* **Perfect Navigation Pte Ltd** Simatech Shipping & Forwarding LLC *Singapore* *Singapore* MMSI: 564481000 Official number: 390881	**14,036** 4,959 17,281	Class: BV (GL)	**2005-01 Peene-Werft GmbH — Wolgast** (Hull) Yd No: 515 **2005-01 Detlef Hegemann Rolandwerft GmbH & Co. KG — Berne** Yd No: 220 Loa 154.59 (BB) Br ex - Dght 9.000 Lbp 146.70 Br md 24.50 Dpth 14.20 Welded, 1 dk	**(A33A2CC) Container Ship (Fully Cellular)** TEU 1223 C Ho 476 TEU C Dk 747 TEU incl 178 ref C. Ice Capable	**1 oil engine** driving 1 CP propeller Total Power: 11,059kW (15,036hp) 18.3kn MAN-B&W 7S50MC-C 1 x 2 Stroke 7 Cy. 500 x 2000 11059kW (15036bhp) MAN B&W Diesel A/S-Denmark AuxGen: 3 x 740kW 440/220V a.c, 1 x 900kW 440/220V a.c Thrusters: 1 Thwart. CP thruster (f)
9292462 *S6BC9* -	**SIMA PRESTIGE** *ex* St. John Peace *-2014* *ex* Sima Paya *-2013* **Prime Navigation Pte Ltd** Simatech Shipping & Forwarding LLC *Singapore* *Singapore* MMSI: 563202000 Official number: 390882	**14,036** 4,959 17,266	Class: BV (GL)	**2005-03 Peene-Werft GmbH — Wolgast** (Hull) Yd No: 516 **2005-03 Detlef Hegemann Rolandwerft GmbH & Co. KG — Berne** Yd No: 221 Loa 154.59 (BB) Br ex - Dght 9.000 Lbp 147.44 Br md 24.50 Dpth 14.20 Welded, 1 dk	**(A33A2CC) Container Ship (Fully Cellular)** TEU 1223 C Ho 476 TEU C Dk 747 TEU incl 178 ref C. Ice Capable	**1 oil engine** driving 1 CP propeller Total Power: 11,059kW (15,036hp) 19.3kn MAN-B&W 7S50MC-C 1 x 2 Stroke 7 Cy. 500 x 2000 11059kW (15036bhp) MAN B&W Diesel A/S-Denmark AuxGen: 3 x 740kW 440/230V 60Hz a.c, 1 x 900kW 440/230V 60Hz a.c Thrusters: 1 Thwart. CP thruster (f)
9292436 *S6AF9* -	**SIMA PRIDE** **Pride Navigation Pte Ltd** Simatech Shipping Pte Ltd *Singapore* *Singapore* MMSI: 563676000 Official number: 390570	**14,067** 4,959 17,266	Class: BV (GL)	**2004-03 Peene-Werft GmbH — Wolgast** Yd No: 513 Loa 154.54 (BB) Br ex - Dght 9.500 Lbp 146.70 Br md 24.50 Dpth 14.20 Welded, 1 dk	**(A33A2CC) Container Ship (Fully Cellular)** TEU 1223 C Ho 476 TEU C Dk 747 TEU incl 178 ref C. Cranes: 2x45t Ice Capable	**1 oil engine** driving 1 CP propeller Total Power: 11,059kW (15,036hp) 18.3kn MAN-B&W 7S50MC-C 1 x 2 Stroke 7 Cy. 500 x 2000 11059kW (15036bhp) MAN B&W Diesel A/S-Denmark AuxGen: 3 x 740kW 450/230V a.c, 1 x 900kW 450/230V a.c Thrusters: 1 Tunnel thruster (f)
7322897 - -	**SIMA QIAN BARU 22** *ex* Corvus *-2010* *ex* Galaxy *-2008* *ex* Cetan *-2008* *ex* Ina Maka *-2008* *ex* Black Moon *-2007* *ex* Eolo *-2006* *ex* Thule *-2004* *ex* Magnus *-2004* *ex* Dorita *-2004* *ex* Viarsa II *-2004* *ex* Koshin Maru No. 8 *-1984* - -	**656** 197 -	Class: (BV)	**1973-05 KK Kanasashi Zosen — Shizuoka SZ** Yd No: 1112 Loa 48.21 Br ex 8.23 Dght 3.252 Lbp 42.30 Br md 8.21 Dpth 3.61 Welded, 1 dk	**(B11B2FV) Fishing Vessel**	**1 oil engine** driving 1 FP propeller Total Power: 809kW (1,100hp) Yanmar 6GL-ST 1 x 4 Stroke 6 Cy. 240 x 290 809kW (1100bhp) Yanmar Diesel Engine Co Ltd-Japan
9330939 *S6HK6* -	**SIMA SADAF** **Great Lakes Navigation Pte Ltd** Simatech Shipping Pte Ltd *Singapore* *Singapore* MMSI: 565608000 Official number: 392082	**15,995** 6,251 20,335	Class: GL	**2007-09 Peene-Werft GmbH — Wolgast** Yd No: 541 Loa 170.05 (BB) Br ex - Dght 9.500 Lbp 160.70 Br md 25.00 Dpth 14.20 Welded, 1 dk	**(A33A2CC) Container Ship (Fully Cellular)** TEU 1440 C.Ho 532 TEU C.Dk 908 TEU incl 124 ref C.	**1 oil engine** driving 1 FP propeller Total Power: 12,640kW (17,185hp) 19.8kn MAN-B&W 8S50MC-C 1 x 2 Stroke 8 Cy. 500 x 2000 12640kW (17185bhp) MAN Diesel A/S-Denmark AuxGen: 3 x 865kW a.c Thrusters: 1 Tunnel thruster (f)
9330903 *S6HK3* -	**SIMA SAPPHIRE** *ex* Sima Saman *-2012* **Sapphire Navigation Pte Ltd** Simatech Shipping & Forwarding LLC *Singapore* *Singapore* MMSI: 565229000 Official number: 392080	**15,995** 6,251 20,291	Class: GL	**2006-09 Peene-Werft GmbH — Wolgast** Yd No: 538 Loa 170.05 (BB) Br ex - Dght 9.500 Lbp 160.70 Br md 25.00 Dpth 14.20 Welded, 1 dk	**(A33A2CC) Container Ship (Fully Cellular)** TEU 1440 C Ho 532 TEU C Dk 908 TEU incl 174 ref C.	**1 oil engine** driving 1 FP propeller Total Power: 12,640kW (17,185hp) 19.0kn MAN-B&W 8S50MC-C 1 x 2 Stroke 8 Cy. 500 x 2000 12640kW (17185bhp) MAN B&W Diesel A/S-Denmark AuxGen: 3 x 865kW 450V 60Hz a.c Thrusters: 1 Tunnel thruster (f)

Ship	Tonnage	Class	Build / Dimensions	Type / Cargo	Machinery
9320386 **SIMAISMA** *SWSP* - **Greenwell Corp** Maran Gas Maritime Inc SatCom: Inmarsat C 424048610 *Piraeus* *Greece* MMSI: 240486000 Official number: 11504	**97,496** 29,249 84,863 T/cm 104.3	Class: AB	**2006**-07 **Daewoo Shipbuilding & Marine Engineering Co Ltd — Geoje** Yd No: 2235 Loa 285.40 (BB) Br ex 43.44 Dght 12.521 Lbp 274.40 Br md 43.40 Dpth 26.00 Welded, 1 dk	**(A11A2TN) LNG Tanker** Double Bottom Entire Compartment Length Liq (Gas): 142,971 4 x Gas Tank (s); 4 membrane (36% Ni.stl) pri horizontal 8 Cargo Pump (s): 8x1700m³/hr Manifold: Bow/CM: 144.6m	**1 Steam Turb** reduction geared to sc. shaft driving 1 FP propeller Total Power: 27,400kW (37,253hp) 19.1kn Kawasaki UA-400 1 x steam Turb 27400kW (37253shp) Kawasaki Heavy Industries Ltd-Japan AuxGen: 2 x 3500kW 6600V a.c, 1 x 3500kW 6600V a.c Thrusters: 1 Tunnel thruster (f) Fuel: 435.0 (d.f.) 6915.0 (r.f.)
5246001 **SIMALI 1** *HSKG* *ex* Siam Queen *-1976* *ex* Nikitas II *-1974* - *ex* Nordhaff *-1971* *ex* Naguilan *-1969* *ex* Atlas *-1959* **Siam Maritime Lines Co Ltd** - *Bangkok* *Thailand* Official number: 191000793	*2,742* 1,437 5,080	Class: (GL)	**1951**-05 **Flensburger Schiffbau-Ges. mbH — Flensburg** Yd No: 530 Loa 116.29 Br ex 15.07 Dght 7.332 Lbp 107.22 Br md 15.02 Dpth 9.25 Riveted\Welded, 2 dks	**(A31A2GX) General Cargo Ship** Grain: 8,883; Bale: 8,254 Compartments: 4 Ho, ER 4 Ha: (7.0 x 5.9)2 (16.0 x 5.9) (9.0 x 5.9) Derricks: 1x54t,1x15t,8x5t,2x3t,2x1t; Winches: 10	**2 oil engines** geared to sc. shaft driving 1 FP propeller Total Power: 2,648kW (3,600hp) 13.0kn MAN M9V40/46MA 2 x 4 Stroke 9 Cy. 400 x 460 each-1324kW (1800bhp) Maschinenbau Augsburg Nuernberg (MAN)-Augsburg AuxGen: 3 x 80kW 230V d.c Fuel: 508.0 (d.f.)
9506409 **SIMANO** *9HUD9* - **Massatlantic (Malta) Ltd** Massoel Ltd *Valletta* *Malta* MMSI: 249538000 Official number: 9506409	**5,087** 2,625 7,300	Class: BV	**2008**-11 **Universe Shipbuilding (Yangzhou) Co Ltd — Yizheng JS** Yd No: 06-005 Loa 112.80 Br ex - Dght 6.900 Lbp 106.00 Br md 17.20 Dpth 9.10 Welded, 1 dk	**(A21A2BC) Bulk Carrier** Grain: 9,394 Compartments: 3 Ho, ER 3 Ha: ER Cranes: 2x25t	**1 oil engine** reduction geared to sc. shaft driving 1 FP propeller Total Power: 2,500kW (3,399hp) 12.0kn Daihatsu 8DKM-28 1 x 4 Stroke 8 Cy. 280 x 390 2500kW (3399bhp) Shaanxi Diesel Heavy Industry Co Lt-China AuxGen: 3 x 250kW 50Hz a.c
5289601 **SIMAR** *YDEB* *ex* Asian Sapphire *-1959* *ex* Wave Ruler *-1982* - *ex* Lotus Greeta *-1981* *ex* Kuwa Mariya *-1981* *ex* Otori Maru *-1981* *ex* Rakuyo Maru No. 11 *-1971* **PT Damai Kurnia Lines** - *Jakarta* *Indonesia*	*473* 278 680	Class: (KI) (NK)	**1960**-11 **Kurushima Dockyard Co. Ltd. — Imabari** Yd No: 65 Loa 50.65 Br ex 8.06 Dght 3.571 Lbp 46.00 Br md 8.01 Dpth 4.02 Riveted\Welded, 1 dk	**(A31A2GX) General Cargo Ship** Grain: 916; Bale: 863 Compartments: 1 Ho, ER 1 Ha: (22.4 x 4.9)ER Derricks: 4x3t; Winches: 4	**1 oil engine** driving 1 FP propeller Total Power: 478kW (650hp) 10.5kn Nippon Hatsudoki S6NV32 1 x 4 Stroke 6 Cy. 320 x 460 478kW (650bhp) Nippon Hatsudoki-Japan AuxGen: 1 x 5kW 110V d.c Fuel: 27.5
9390604 **SIMAR ESPERANCA** *C6AA4* *ex* Seven Sisters *-2013* - **Subsea 7 Offshore Resources (UK) Ltd** Subsea 7 International Contracting Ltd *Nassau* *Bahamas* MMSI: 311073700	**5,275** 1,582 4,665	Class: NV	**2008**-06 **'Crist' Sp z oo — Gdansk** (Hull) **2008**-06 **Kleven Verft AS — Ulsteinvik** Yd No: 319 Loa 103.70 (BB) Br ex 19.74 Dght 6.145 Lbp 96.80 Br md 19.70 Dpth 7.70 Welded, 1 dk	**(B21A2OS) Platform Supply Ship** Cranes: 1x150t Ice Capable	**4 diesel electric oil engines** driving 4 gen. Connecting to 2 elec. motors each (2200kW) driving 2 Azimuth electric drive units Total Power: 8,632kW (11,736hp) 12.0kn Caterpillar 3516C 4 x Vee 4 Stroke 16 Cy. 170 x 215 each-2158kW (2934bhp) Caterpillar Inc-USA AuxGen: 1 x 910kW a.c Thrusters: 1 Retract. directional thruster (f); 2 Tunnel thruster (f)
9502661 **SIMAY G** *TCWA9* *launched as* Lara Y *-2013* - **Dearsan Gemi Insaat Sanayii AS** - *Istanbul* *Turkey* MMSI: 271043467	**4,825** 2,290 6,913 T/cm 16.9	Class: BV	**2013**-02 **Dearsan Gemi Insaat ve Sanayii Koll. Sti. — Tuzla** Yd No: 2050 Loa 119.10 (BB) Br ex - Dght 6.763 Lbp 111.60 Br md 16.90 Dpth 8.40 Welded, 1 dk	**(A12B2TR) Chemical/Products Tanker** Double Hull (13F) Liq: 7,854; Liq (Oil): 7,854 Cargo Heating Coils Compartments: 12 Wing Ta, 2 Wing Slop Ta, ER 12 Cargo Pump (s): 12x200m³/hr Manifold: Bow/CM: 57m Ice Capable	**1 oil engine** reduction geared to sc. shaft driving 1 FP propeller Total Power: 3,060kW (4,160hp) 14.0kn MAN-B&W 9L27/38 1 x 4 Stroke 9 Cy. 270 x 380 3060kW (4160bhp) MAN Diesel A/S-Denmark AuxGen: 3 x 430kW 50Hz a.c, 1 x 800kW 50Hz a.c Thrusters: 1 Tunnel thruster (f) Fuel: 67.0 (d.f.) 422.0 (r.f.)
8205462 **SIMBA** - - **Tanzania Ports Authority** - *Dar es Salaam* *Tanzania*	**208** 62 109	Class: (LR) (BV) ✠ Classed LR until 12/12/07	**1983**-04 **Tille Scheepsbouw B.V. — Kootstertille** (Hull) Yd No: 233 **1983**-04 **B.V. Scheepswerf Damen — Gorinchem** Yd No: 3143 Loa 30.21 Br ex 8.06 Dght 3.310 Lbp 26.95 Br md 7.80 Dpth 4.04 Welded, 1 dk	**(B32A2ST) Tug**	**2 oil engines** with clutches, flexible couplings & sr reverse geared to sc. shafts driving 2 FP propellers Total Power: 2,284kW (3,106hp) Deutz SBV8M628 2 x 4 Stroke 8 Cy. 240 x 280 each-1142kW (1553bhp) Kloeckner Humboldt Deutz AG-West Germany AuxGen: 2 x 60kW 415V 50Hz a.c, 1 x 26kW 415V 50Hz a.c Fuel: 78.0 (d.f.)
9288112 **SIMBA III** *5ZXJ* - **Kenya Ports Authority (KPA)** *Mombasa* *Kenya* Official number: 10173	**313** 93 248	Class: LR ✠ **100A1** SS 01/2009 tug **LMC** **UMS** Eq.Ltr: F; Cable: 275.0/19.0 U2 (a)	**2004**-01 **B.V. Scheepswerf Damen — Gorinchem** Yd No: 511721 Loa 30.82 Br ex 10.20 Dght 4.080 Lbp 29.80 Br md 9.40 Dpth 4.80 Welded, 1 dk	**(B32A2ST) Tug**	**2 oil engines** reduction geared to sc. shafts driving 2 Directional propellers Total Power: 3,542kW (4,816hp) 12.5kn Caterpillar 3516B-HD 2 x Vee 4 Stroke 16 Cy. 170 x 215 each-1771kW (2408bhp) Caterpillar Inc-USA AuxGen: 2 x 85kW 400V 50Hz a.c Fuel: 118.0 (r.f.)
6722040 **SIMBAD** *CNRF* *ex* Semla *-1970* - **Omnium Marocain Commercial et Industrial (OMACI)** - *Agadir* *Morocco*	*249* 85 -	Class: (LR) ✠ Classed LR until 10/10/80	**1967**-07 **Verolme Scheepswerf Heusden N.V. — Heusden** (Hull launched by) Yd No: 681 **1967**-07 **T. van Duijvendijk's Scheepswerf N.V. — Lekkerkerk** (Hull completed by) Yd No: Z82 Loa 36.71 Br ex 7.35 Dght - Lbp 32.14 Br md 7.21 Dpth 4.02 Welded	**(B11A2FT) Trawler** Derricks: 1x5t	**1 oil engine** sr geared to sc. shaft driving 1 CP propeller Total Power: 555kW (755hp) 11.0kn Ruston 6AP2 1 x 4 Stroke 6 Cy. 203 x 273 555kW (755bhp) Ruston & Hornsby Ltd.-Lincoln AuxGen: 1 x 80kW 380V 50Hz a.c, 1 x 24kW 380V 50Hz a.c Thrusters: 1 Thwart. FP thruster (f) Fuel: 34.5 (d.f.)
8841333 **SIME** *9AA4768* *ex* Dupin MR-36 *-1991* - **Tihana Kustura** - *Split* *Croatia* Official number: 5R-181	*221* 66 -	Class: CS	**1955**-01 **Brodogradiliste Split (Brodosplit) — Split** Converted From: Tug-1991 Loa 32.79 Br ex 7.93 Dght 3.160 Lbp - Br md - Dpth 4.13 Welded, 1 dk	**(B11B2FV) Fishing Vessel**	**1 oil engine** driving 1 FP propeller Total Power: 956kW (1,300hp) 10.5kn MAN W8V30/38 1 x Vee 4 Stroke 8 Cy. 300 x 380 956kW (1300bhp) (, fitted 1973) Maschinenbau Augsburg Nuernberg (MAN)-Augsburg
9247912 **SIMEIZ** *URBX* *ex* Nantai *-2003* *ex* Florence *-2003* - **Fishing Co Foros Ltd** Chuan-Chuan Yoo International Trade Ltd *Sevastopol* *Ukraine* MMSI: 272364000 Official number: 226	**871** 292 788		**2001**-06 **Lien Cherng Shipbuilding Co, Ltd — Kaohsiung** Yd No: LC-102 Loa 63.15 Br ex - Dght 3.900 Lbp 55.00 Br md 10.00 Dpth 4.20 Welded, 1 dk	**(B11B2FV) Fishing Vessel**	**1 oil engine** geared to sc. shaft driving 1 FP propeller Total Power: 1,177kW (1,600hp) Hanshin LH28G 1 x 4 Stroke 6 Cy. 280 x 460 1177kW (1600bhp) The Hanshin Diesel Works Ltd-Japan
8944757 **SIMENT 1** *DXLT* - **Siment Transport Inc** - *Cebu* *Philippines* Official number: CEB1000242	*422* 258 -		**1987 at Cebu** L reg 42.54 Br ex - Dght - Lbp - Br md 8.90 Dpth 3.04 Welded, 1 dk	**(A31A2GX) General Cargo Ship**	**1 oil engine** driving 1 FP propeller Total Power: 515kW (700hp) Isuzu 1 x 4 Stroke 515kW (700bhp) Isuzu Marine Engine Inc-Japan
9049384 **SIMEULUE** *YHWQ* - **Government of The Republic of Indonesia (Direktorat Jenderal Perhubungan Laut - Ministry of Sea Communications)** PT ASDP Indonesia Ferry (Persero) - Angkutan Sungai Danau & Penyeberangan *Jakarta* *Indonesia*	**330** 100 35	Class: KI	**2004**-01 **PT Bayu Bahari Sentosa — Jakarta** Loa 40.00 Br ex - Dght 1.990 Lbp 34.50 Br md 10.50 Dpth 2.80 Welded, 1 dk	**(A36A2PR) Passenger/Ro-Ro Ship (Vehicles)** Bow ramp (centre) Stern ramp (centre)	**2 oil engines** geared to sc. shafts driving 2 Propellers Total Power: 999kW (1,358hp) 9.0kn MAN D2848LE 2 x Vee 4 Stroke 8 Cy. 128 x 142 each-499kW (678bhp) (made 2003) MAN Nutzfahrzeuge AG-Nuernberg AuxGen: 2 x 52kW 380V a.c
9466881 **SIMFEROPOL** *V7VC7* *ex* Fesco Simferopol *-2013* - **Diomid Maritime Ltd** Far-Eastern Shipping Co (FESCO) (Dalnevostochnoye Morskoye Parokhodstvo) *Majuro* *Marshall Islands* MMSI: 538004088 Official number: 4088	**33,044** 19,231 56,742 T/cm 58.8	Class: BV	**2011**-11 **Qingshan Shipyard — Wuhan HB** Yd No: 20060372 Loa 189.99 (BB) Br ex - Dght 12.800 Lbp 185.00 Br md 32.26 Dpth 18.00 Welded, 1 dk	**(A21A2BC) Bulk Carrier** Grain: 71,634; Bale: 68,200 Compartments: 5 Ho, ER 5 Ha: ER Cranes: 4x30t	**1 oil engine** driving 1 FP propeller Total Power: 9,480kW (12,889hp) 14.2kn MAN-B&W 6S50MC-C 1 x 2 Stroke 6 Cy. 500 x 2000 9480kW (12889bhp) STX Engine Co Ltd-South Korea AuxGen: 3 x 600kW 60Hz a.c Fuel: 2400.0

IMO / Call sign	Name / Owner	Tonnage	Class	Builder / Dimensions	Type	Machinery
9197612 *PNHS* -	**SIMFONI SEJATI** *ex* Pacific Falcon *-2010* **PT Pelayaran Putra Sejati** PT Pelayaran Nusantara Sejati *Jakarta* *Indonesia* MMSI: 525016614	**8,132** 2,841 8,477	Class: KI (NK)	**1998-09 Kegoya Dock K.K. — Kure** Yd No: 1025 Loa 115.40 (BB) Br ex - Dght 7.455 Lbp 105.40 Br md 20.00 Dpth 13.30 Welded, 2 dks	**(A31A2GA) General Cargo Ship (with Ro-Ro facility)** Quarter stern door/ramp (s. a.) Len: - Wid: - Swl: 40 Cars: 288 Grain: 17,049; Bale: 15,180 TEU 381 Compartments: 2 Ho, ER 2 Ha: (19.6 x 12.6) (37.1 x 12.6)ER Cranes: 2x30t; Derricks: 1x25t	**1 oil engine** driving 1 FP propeller Total Power: 4,193kW (5,701hp) 14.1kn B&W 6S35MC 1 x 2 Stroke 6 Cy. 350 x 1400 4193kW (5701bhp) The Hanshin Diesel Works Ltd-Japan AuxGen: 2 x 492kW a.c Fuel: 950.0
8516627 *UFEF* -	**SIMFONIYA** *ex* Slavyanka *-2006* **Alioth Shipping Co Ltd** Peta Chemical Co Ltd *Vladivostok* *Russia* MMSI: 273313270	**4,298** 1,305 3,750	Class: RS (NV)	**1989-06 Hellenic Shipyards — Skaramanga** Yd No: 1162 Loa 103.00 (BB) Br ex - Dght 7.200 Lbp 93.40 Br md 17.00 Dpth 9.65 Welded, 1 dk	**(A34A2GR) Refrigerated Cargo Ship** Ins: 4,879 TEU 62 C. 62/20' incl. 20 ref C. Compartments: 3 Ho, ER, 2 Tw Dk 3 Ha: ER Cranes: 3x8t Ice Capable	**1 oil engine** driving 1 FP propeller Total Power: 5,701kW (7,751hp) 16.8kn B&W 5L50MC 1 x 2 Stroke 5 Cy. 500 x 1620 5701kW (7751bhp) Zaklady Przemyslu Metalowego 'HCegielski' SA-Poznan AuxGen: 4 x 500kW 380V 50Hz a.c
9373618 *9HBV9* -	**SIMGE AKSOY** *ex* Nord Mariner *-2007* **Lightwave Marine Co Ltd** Akmar Shipping & Trading SA (Akmar Denizcilik ve Ticaret AS) *Valletta* *Malta* MMSI: 256761000 Official number: 9373618	**32,474** 17,790 53,399 T/cm 57.3	Class: NK (NV)	**2006-08 Chengxi Shipyard — Jiangyin JS** Yd No: 4219 Loa 190.00 (BB) Br ex - Dght 12.556 Lbp 183.05 Br md 32.26 Dpth 17.50 Welded, 1 dk	**(A21A2BC) Bulk Carrier** Double Hull Grain: 65,752; Bale: 64,000 Compartments: 5 Ho, ER 5 Ha: 4 (21.6 x 22.4)ER (19.2 x 20.8) Cranes: 4x36t	**1 oil engine** driving 1 FP propeller Total Power: 9,480kW (12,889hp) 14.2kn MAN-B&W 6S50MC-C 1 x 2 Stroke 6 Cy. 500 x 2000 9480kW (12889bhp) Hudong Heavy Machinery Co Ltd-China AuxGen: 3 x 680kW 440V 60Hz a.c Fuel: 200.0 (d.f.) 2000.0 (r.f.) 34.5pd
9535319 *9MIC9* -	**SIMGOOD 12** - **Simgaz Pte Ltd** PT Indoliziz Marine *Port Klang* *Malaysia* MMSI: 533882000 Official number: 333961	**1,159** 347 1,021	Class: AB	**2009-02 Nantong MLC Tongbao Shipbuilding Co Ltd — Rugao JS** Yd No: MLC5284 Loa 52.80 Br ex - Dght 4.500 Lbp 47.20 Br md 13.20 Dpth 5.20 Welded, 1 dk	**(B21B20A) Anchor Handling Tug Supply**	**2 oil engines** reduction geared to sc. shafts driving 2 FP propellers Total Power: 2,942kW (4,000hp) 11.0kn Cummins QSK60-M 2 x Vee 4 Stroke 16 Cy. 159 x 190 each-1471kW (2000bhp) Cummins Engine Co Inc-USA AuxGen: 3 x 400kW a.c
8984678 *YDA4810* -	**SIMGOOD 21** *ex* Bestlink-II *-2011* *ex* Sabang Marindo *-2011* **PT Indoliziz Marine** - *Batam* *Indonesia*	**142** 43 46	Class: BV (Class contemplated) KI	**1997-12 P.T. Batam Expressindo Shipyard — Batam** Yd No: 829 Loa 34.00 Br ex 6.12 Dght 3.230 Lbp 31.34 Br md 6.10 Dpth 3.23 Welded, 1 dk	**(B21A20C) Crew/Supply Vessel** Hull Material: Aluminium Alloy	**4 oil engines** geared to sc. shafts driving 4 FP propellers Total Power: 3,236kW (4,400hp) Caterpillar 3412 4 x Vee 4 Stroke 12 Cy. 137 x 152 each-809kW (1100bhp) Caterpillar Inc-USA AuxGen: 2 x 66kW 400/200V a.c
8900220 *SW5620* -	**SIMI II** *ex* Symi II *-2001* **Anonymos Naftiliaki Eteria Symis (ANES)** - *Piraeus* *Greece* MMSI: 237015400 Official number: 9208	**486** 208 105	Class: (HR)	**1990-08 L Glynos SA — Greece** Yd No: 11 Loa - Br ex - Dght 2.890 Lbp 36.61 Br md 12.41 Dpth - Welded, 1 dk	**(A36A2PR) Passenger/Ro-Ro Ship (Vehicles)**	**2 oil engines** with clutches & dr geared to sc. shafts driving 2 FP propellers Total Power: 2,520kW (3,426hp) MWM TBD604BV12 2 x Vee 4 Stroke 12 Cy. 170 x 195 each-1260kW (1713bhp) Motoren Werke Mannheim AG (MWM)-West Germany
9248978 *D3N2058* -	**SIMIONE** - **Government of The People's Republic of Angola (Missao de Estudos Bioceanologicos e de Pesca de Angola)** Inter-Burgo SA *Luanda* *Angola*	**222** - 334	Class: (KR)	**2001-04 Yongsung Shipbuilding Co Ltd — Geoje** Yd No: 170 Loa 45.59 Br ex - Dght - Lbp 37.50 Br md 7.20 Dpth 4.20 Welded, 1 dk	**(B11B2FV) Fishing Vessel**	**1 oil engine** geared to sc. shaft driving 1 FP propeller Total Power: 883kW (1,201hp) Yanmar M220-EN 1 x 4 Stroke 6 Cy. 220 x 300 883kW (1201bhp) Yanmar Diesel Engine Co Ltd-Japan
8132885 - -	**SIMMENTAL** - - *Nigeria*	*133* 90 -		**1981 Henry's Boatbuilding, Inc. — Morgan City, La** Yd No: 81-026 Loa 19.82 Br ex 7.93 Dght - Lbp - Br md - Dpth 2.60 Welded, 1 dk	**(B32A2ST) Tug**	**1 oil engine** driving 1 FP propeller Total Power: 503kW (684hp) G.M. (Detroit Diesel) 8V-71-N 1 x Vee 2 Stroke 8 Cy. 108 x 127 503kW (684bhp) General Motors Detroit DieselAllison Divn-USA
9288916 *V7QT3* -	**SIMOA** *ex* Gagarmayang *-2012* *ex* Cape Bauld *-2005* **Seminyak AS** Klaveness Marine Holding AS *Majuro* *Marshall Islands* MMSI: 538003432 Official number: 3432	**25,108** 10,181 40,354 T/cm 49.3	Class: NV (GL)	**2004-10 Hyundai Mipo Dockyard Co Ltd — Ulsan** Yd No: 0256 Loa 176.00 (BB) Br ex 31.04 Dght 11.120 Lbp 168.00 Br md 31.00 Dpth 17.00 Welded, 1 dk	**(A12B2TR) Chemical/Products Tanker** Double Hull (13F) Liq: 42,682; Liq (Oil): 42,682 Compartments: 12 Wing Ta, ER, 2 Wing Slop Ta 12 Cargo Pump (s): 12x500m³/hr Manifold: Bow/CM: 89.8m	**1 oil engine** driving 1 FP propeller Total Power: 8,580kW (11,665hp) 14.5kn B&W 6S50MC 1 x 2 Stroke 6 Cy. 500 x 1910 8580kW (11665bhp) Hyundai Heavy Industries Co Ltd-South Korea AuxGen: 3 x a.c Thrusters: 1 Tunnel thruster (f)
9182241 - -	**SIMON** - **Austral Group SAA** - *Callao* *Peru* Official number: CO-18517-PM	**287** 110 473	Class: (GL)	**1998-03 Remesa Astilleros S.A. — Callao** Yd No: 098 Loa 41.90 Br ex - Dght 4.050 Lbp 36.08 Br md 8.80 Dpth 4.40 Welded, 1 dk	**(B11B2FV) Fishing Vessel** Ins: 434	**1 oil engine** reduction geared to sc. shaft driving 1 FP propeller Total Power: 895kW (1,217hp) 11.0kn Caterpillar 3512TA 1 x Vee 4 Stroke 12 Cy. 170 x 190 895kW (1217bhp) Caterpillar Inc-USA
8981523 *DLXQ* WYK-9	**SIMON ALEXANDER** - **FK Zeeland Muscheln GmbH** - *Wyk auf Foehr* *Germany* MMSI: 211413470 Official number: 2581	**406** 121 -		**2003 B.V. Scheepswerf Maaskant — Stellendam** Yd No: 571 Loa 43.59 (BB) Br ex - Dght - Lbp - Br md 10.00 Dpth 3.27 Welded, 1 dk	**(B11B2FV) Fishing Vessel**	**1 oil engine** driving 1 Propeller Thrusters: 2 Tunnel thruster (f)
7903902 - -	**SIMON ALFONS 5** *ex* Ryoun Maru No. 1 *-2012* **Irma Fishing & Trading Inc** -	*179* - 126		**1979-08 Narasaki Senpaku Kogyo K.K. — Muroran** Yd No: 152 Loa 37.90 (BB) Br ex - Dght 2.420 Lbp 30.97 Br md 7.38 Dpth 4.63 Welded, 2 dks	**(B11B2FV) Fishing Vessel**	**1 oil engine** reduction geared to sc. shaft driving 1 FP propeller Total Power: 552kW (750hp) Akasaka 6U28 1 x 4 Stroke 6 Cy. 280 x 340 552kW (750bhp) Akasaka Tekkosho KK (Akasaka DieselLtd)-Japan
8511029 *V2GJ4* -	**SIMON B** *ex* Perseas *-2013* *ex* Viper *-2008* *ex* Lisa *-2001* *ex* Edith *-1990* *ex* Echo Lisa *-1990* *ex* Edith *-1989* **mv 'Simon B' GmbH & Co KG** GBS-Shipmanagement GmbH & Co KG *Saint John's* *Antigua & Barbuda* MMSI: 305306000	**1,587** 843 2,380	Class: GL	**1986-01 Husumer Schiffswerft Inh. Gebr. Kroeger GmbH & Co. KG — Husum** Yd No: 1500 Loa 82.02 Br ex - Dght 4.220 Lbp 77.50 Br md 11.50 Dpth 5.41 Welded, 2 dks	**(A31A2GX) General Cargo Ship** Grain: 2,662 Compartments: 1 Ho, ER 1 Ha: (50.3 x 9.0)ER Ice Capable	**1 oil engine** with flexible couplings & sr gearedto sc. shaft driving 1 CP propeller Total Power: 599kW (814hp) 10.0kn MAN 8L20/27 1 x 4 Stroke 8 Cy. 200 x 270 599kW (814bhp) MAN B&W Diesel GmbH-Augsburg Thrusters: 1 Thwart. FP thruster (f)
8607127 *CLDN* -	**SIMON BOLIVAR** *ex* Angara *-2010* *ex* Milan *-1998* *ex* Kapitan Orlikova *-1997* **Empresa Mixta Socialista Pesquera Industrial del Alba SA** - *Cuba* MMSI: 323102000	**7,765** 2,329 3,365	Class: RC (RS)	**1988-03 VEB Volkswerft Stralsund — Stralsund** Yd No: 803 Loa 120.71 Br ex 19.02 Dght 6.401 Lbp 107.02 Br md 19.00 Dpth 12.25 Welded, 3 dks	**(B11A2FG) Factory Stern Trawler** Ins: 3,900	**2 oil engines** with clutches, flexible couplings & reduction geared to sc. shaft driving 1 CP propeller Total Power: 5,298kW (7,204hp) 15.5kn S.K.L. 6VDS48/42AL-2 2 x 4 Stroke 6 Cy. 420 x 480 each-2649kW (3602bhp) VEB Schwermaschinenbau "KarlLiebknecht" (SKL)-Magdeburg AuxGen: 2 x 1500kW a.c, 2 x 760kW a.c Fuel: 1838.0
5328732 - -	**SIMON FRASER** *ex* 2001-07 *-2006* *ex* Simon Fraser *-2001* **Quay Marine Associates Inc** - *Livorno* *Italy*	*1,353* 431 484	Class: (LR) (BV) ✠ Classed LR until 23/6/78	**1960-02 Burrard Dry Dock Co Ltd — North Vancouver BC** Yd No: 306 Converted From: Buoy Tender-2011 Loa 62.26 Br ex 12.86 Dght 4.268 Lbp 56.16 Br md 12.81 Dpth 5.57 Welded, 1 dk	**(X11A2YP) Yacht** Compartments: 1 Ho, ER 1 Ha: (5.2 x 4.2) Derricks: 1x15t,1x1t Ice Capable	**2 diesel electric oil engines** driving 2 gen. each 1150kW 750V d.c Connecting to 2 elec. motors driving 2 FP propellers Total Power: 2,450kW (3,332hp) 13.5kn Alco 12V251E 2 x Vee 4 Stroke 12 Cy. 229 x 267 each-1225kW (1666bhp) Dominion Engineering Works Ltd-Canada AuxGen: 2 x 240kW 230V d.c Fuel: 178.0 (d.f.)

Identity / Owner	Tonnage	Class	Builder / Dimensions	Type	Machinery
8978382 **SIMON JR** *WDC8941* *ex* Sallie McCall *-2005* - **Abe's Boat Rentals Inc** - *Empire, LA* *United States of America* MMSI: 367095420 Official number: 629684	**194** 68 -		**1980 A.W. Covacevich Shipyard, Inc. — Biloxi, Ms** Yd No: 52 Loa 33.52 Br ex - Dght - Lbp 29.87 Br md 7.31 Dpth 3.65 Welded, 1 dk	**(B34L2QU) Utility Vessel**	**2 oil engines** with clutches, flexible couplings & sr reverse geared to sc. shafts driving 2 FP propellers Total Power: 662kW (900hp) 10.0kn G.M. (Detroit Diesel) 12V-71 2 x Vee 2 Stroke 12 Cy. 108 x 127 each-331kW (450bhp) Detroit Diesel Corporation-Detroit, Mi AuxGen: 2 x 40kW Fuel: 59.0 (d.f.) 2.3pd
7230276 **SIMON KEGHIAN** - *ex* Thierry Pascal *-1995* - **Upul Devasurendra** - *Sri Lanka*	*592* 247 411	Class: (BV)	**1972 Stocznia im Komuny Paryskiej — Gdynia** Yd No: B423/10 Loa 54.26 Br ex 11.03 Dght 4.601 Lbp 46.21 Br md 11.00 Dpth 5.19 Welded, 2 dks	**(B11A2FS) Stern Trawler** Ins: 516 Compartments: 1 Ho, ER	**1 oil engine** reduction geared to sc. shaft driving 1 FP propeller Total Power: 1,471kW (2,000hp) 14.5kn Crepelle 12PSN 1 x Vee 4 Stroke 12 Cy. 260 x 280 1471kW (2000bhp) Moteurs Duvant Crepelle-France Fuel: 205.5 (d.f.)
9132868 **SIMON SCHULTE** *A8FZ2* *ex* Alfred Oldendorff *-2009* - *ex* Diamond Halo *-2004* **ms 'Simon Schulte' Schiffahrtsgesellschaft mbH & Co KG** Bernhard Schulte Shipmanagement (Deutschland) GmbH & Co KG *Monrovia* *Liberia* MMSI: 636090819 Official number: 90819	**25,074** 15,145 46,489 T/cm 50.6	Class: GL (NK)	**1996-04 Oshima Shipbuilding Co Ltd — Saikai NS** Yd No: 10183 Loa 189.60 (BB) Br ex - Dght 11.276 Lbp 181.60 Br md 30.50 Dpth 15.80 Welded, 1 dk	**(A21A2BC) Bulk Carrier** Grain: 56,457; Bale: 55,364 Compartments: 5 Ho, ER 5 Ha: 4 (20.0 x 15.3) (16.0 x 15.3)ER Cranes: 4x30t	**1 oil engine** driving 1 FP propeller Total Power: 7,392kW (10,050hp) 14.3kn Mitsubishi 6UEC50LSII 1 x 2 Stroke 6 Cy. 500 x 1950 7392kW (10050bhp) Mitsubishi Heavy Industries Ltd-Japan AuxGen: 3 x 480kW 450V 60Hz a.c Fuel: 116.0 (d.f.) (Heating Coils) 1460.0 (r.f.) 25.8pd
9622681 **SIMON STEVIN** *ORBS* - **DAB Vloot** - *Ostend* *Belgium* MMSI: 205180219 Official number: 556055	**458** 137 -	Class: BV	**2012-05 Santierul Naval Damen Galati S.A. — Galati** (Hull launched by) Yd No: (556055) **2012-05 B.V. Scheepswerf Maaskant — Stellendam** (Hull completed by) Yd No: 607 **2012-05 B.V. Scheepswerf Damen — Gorinchem** Yd No: 556055 Loa 36.31 (BB) Br ex 9.56 Dght 3.100 Lbp 32.12 Br md 9.40 Dpth 4.50 Welded, 1 dk	**(B31A2SR) Research Survey Vessel** A-frames: 1x6t	**3 diesel electric oil engines** driving 3 gen. Connecting to 2 elec. motors each (765kW) driving 2 FP propellers 12.0kn Thrusters: 1 Tunnel thruster (f)
9464807 **SIMON STEVIN** *LXUB* - **Dredging & Maritime Management SA** - *Luxembourg* *Luxembourg* MMSI: 253309000	**35,034** 10,510 35,930	Class: BV	**2010-02 Construcciones Navales del Norte SL — Sestao** Yd No: 333 Loa 191.50 (BB) Br ex 40.30 Dght 9.250 Lbp 175.00 Br md 40.00 Dpth 13.20 Welded, 1 dk	**(B22K2OB) Pipe Burying Vessel** Hopper: 16,000	**5 diesel electric oil engines** driving 4 gen. each 4500kW a.c Connecting to 4 elec. motors each (3300kW) driving 4 Directional propellers Total Power: 22,505kW (30,600hp) 15.5kn MAN-B&W 9L32/40 5 x 4 Stroke 9 Cy. 320 x 400 each-4501kW (6120bhp) STX Engine Co Ltd-South Korea Thrusters: 2 Tunnel thruster (f); 1 Tunnel thruster amid
8607220 **SIMONAS DAUKANTAS** *LYAH* *ex* Beta I *-2014* *ex* Beta *-2005* - *ex* Simonas Daukantas *-1998* *ex* Karolis Pozhela *-1992* **JSC 'Baltlanta' (UAB 'Baltlanta')** - *Klaipeda* *Lithuania* MMSI: 277510000	**7,765** 2,330 3,372	Class: NV (RS)	**1989-04 VEB Volkswerft Stralsund — Stralsund** Yd No: 813 Loa 120.47 Br ex 19.03 Dght 6.632 Lbp 108.12 Br md 19.00 Dpth 12.22 Welded, 1 dk	**(B11A2FG) Factory Stern Trawler** Ins: 3,900 Ice Capable	**2 oil engines** with clutches, flexible couplings & reduction geared to sc. shaft driving 1 CP propeller Total Power: 5,298kW (7,204hp) 14.9kn S.K.L. 6VDS48/42AL-2 2 x 4 Stroke 6 Cy. 420 x 480 each-2649kW (3602bhp) VEB Schwermaschinenbau "KarlLiebknecht" (SKL)-Magdeburg AuxGen: 2 x 1500kW a.c
6810031 **SIMONE** - *ex* Destinee *-2011* *ex* Safe Carrier *-1998* - *ex* Seatruck 1 *-1990* *ex* Adamsturm *-1986* - - *Sao Tome & Principe*	**676** 203 714	Class: (GL)	**1968-07 JG Hitzler Schiffswerft und Masch GmbH & Co KG — Lauenburg** Yd No: 700 Converted From: Offshore Supply Ship Converted From: Offshore Tug/Supply Ship-1990 Loa 53.55 Br ex 11.26 Dght 3.341 Lbp 49.18 Br md 11.00 Dpth 3.97 Welded, 1 dk	**(A31C2GD) Deck Cargo Ship** Stern ramp (centre) Grain: 100 Derricks: 1x5t; Winches: 1 Ice Capable	**2 oil engines** driving 2 FP propellers Total Power: 2,016kW (2,740hp) 12.5kn MWM TB16RS18/22 2 x Vee 4 Stroke 16 Cy. 180 x 220 each-1008kW (1370bhp) Motoren Werke Mannheim AG (MWM)-West Germany Thrusters: 1 Thwart. FP thruster (f)
7029548 **SIMONE** *WDD4939* *ex* Leslie Foss *-2013* *ex* Caribe Pioneer *-2012* - *ex* Leslie Foss *-1989* **Marigny Tug LLC** TradeWinds Towing LLC *St Augustine, FL* *United States of America* MMSI: 367546250 Official number: 525754	**347** 104 307	Class: (AB)	**1970 McDermott Shipyards Inc — Morgan City LA** Yd No: 162 Loa 36.58 Br ex 9.66 Dght 3.871 Lbp 34.88 Br md 9.45 Dpth 4.55 Welded, 1 dk	**(B32A2ST) Tug**	**2 oil engines** reverse reduction geared to sc. shafts driving 2 FP propellers Total Power: 2,206kW (3,000hp) 12.5kn EMD (Electro-Motive) 12-645-E6 2 x Vee 2 Stroke 12 Cy. 230 x 254 each-1103kW (1500bhp) General Motors Corp-USA AuxGen: 2 x 98kW 216V 60Hz a.c Fuel: 284.5
7393755 **SIMONE CHRISTINA** - *ex* Marianne Holm *-2009* - *ex* Poul Henrik Nordfisk *-1982* - -	**439** 153 300	Class: (NV)	**1975-06 Bolsones Verft AS — Molde** Yd No: 239 Loa 41.15 Br ex 8.08 Dght 4.122 Lbp 36.99 Br md 8.06 Dpth 4.14 Welded, 1 dk	**(B11A2FT) Trawler** Compartments: 2 Ho, 6 Ta, ER 3 Ha: 2 (0.9 x 1.2) (1.5 x 1.2) Ice Capable	**1 oil engine** driving 1 CP propeller Total Power: 662kW (900hp) 9.5kn Alpha 409-26VO 1 x 2 Stroke 9 Cy. 260 x 400 662kW (900bhp) Alpha Diesel A/S-Denmark AuxGen: 2 x 40kW 380V 50Hz a.c Fuel: 82.0 (d.f.) 4.5pd
9199919 **SIMONE K** *5NIU* - **Rangk Ltd** - *Lagos* *Nigeria* MMSI: 657152000 Official number: SSR195	**242** 72 -	Class: AB	**1998-07 Swiftships Inc — Morgan City LA** Yd No: 491 Loa 44.19 Br ex 8.15 Dght 1.580 Lbp 42.79 Br md 8.07 Dpth 3.60 Welded, 1 dk	**(B21A2OC) Crew/Supply Vessel** Hull Material: Aluminium Alloy	**3 oil engines** reverse reduction geared to sc. shafts driving 3 Water jets Total Power: 1,821kW (2,475hp) 21.0kn Caterpillar 3412TA 3 x Vee 4 Stroke 12 Cy. 137 x 152 each-607kW (825bhp) Caterpillar Inc-USA AuxGen: 2 x 50kW
8411293 **SIMONE MARTINI** *IKCX* - **Compagnia delle Isole SpA** - *Palermo* *Italy* MMSI: 247003800 Official number: 1045	*1,493* 724 513	Class: RI	**1985-04 Nuovi Cantieri Apuania SpA — Carrara** Yd No: 1124 Loa 71.15 (BB) Br ex 14.03 Dght 3.610 Lbp 64.29 Br md 14.03 Dpth 4.81 Welded, 1 dk	**(A36A2PR) Passenger/Ro-Ro Ship (Vehicles)** Passengers: unberthed: 1250 Lane-Len: 160	**2 oil engines** with clutches, flexible couplings & sr geared to sc. shafts driving 2 CP propellers Total Power: 3,706kW (5,038hp) GMT BL230.12V 2 x Vee 4 Stroke 12 Cy. 230 x 310 each-1853kW (2519bhp) SA Fiat SGM-Torino Thrusters: 1 Thwart. CP thruster (f)
8987797 **SIMORGH DARYA** *9BHG* *ex* Sea Dragon *-2005* *ex* Sea Dragon 1 *-2005* - *ex* Sea Dragon *-2004* *ex* Queen Josephine *-2004* **Bushehr Atlas Co** - *Bushehr* *Iran* MMSI: 422515000 Official number: 832	**1,512** 758 -	Class: AS	**1988 Cochico Shipyard — Cotabato** Loa 71.57 Br ex - Dght - Lbp 67.60 Br md 14.63 Dpth 4.20 Welded, 1 dk	**(A31A2GX) General Cargo Ship**	**3 oil engines** reduction geared to sc. shafts driving 3 FP propellers Total Power: 993kW (1,350hp) Niigata 3 x 4 Stroke 6 Cy. each-331kW (450bhp) Niigata Engineering Co Ltd-Japan
8216681 **SIMPHONY** *3FSM9* *ex* Simphony M *-2007* *ex* Grace A *-2005* - *ex* Grace II *-2003* *ex* Caliope *-2003* *ex* Seletar *-1999* *ex* Aditya Vaibhav *-1993* *ex* Tomoe 135 *-1988* **Cooperative & Agricultural Credit Bank** Overseas Shipping & Stevedoring Co (OSSCO) *Panama* *Panama* MMSI: 357748000 Official number: 28402PEXT5	**6,481** 3,624 10,885 T/cm 19.5	Class: PX (NK)	**1983-04 Asakawa Zosen K.K. — Imabari** Yd No: 316 Loa 123.63 (BB) Br ex - Dght 8.187 Lbp 115.60 Br md 18.20 Dpth 9.80 Welded, 1 dk	**(A12B2TR) Chemical/Products Tanker** Double Bottom Entire Compartment Length Liq: 12,056; Liq (Oil): 12,056 Cargo Heating Coils Compartments: 12 Ta, ER 6 Cargo Pump (s) Manifold: Bow/CM: 57m	**1 oil engine** driving 1 FP propeller Total Power: 4,413kW (6,000hp) 13.5kn Mitsubishi 6UEC45HA 1 x 2 Stroke 6 Cy. 450 x 1150 4413kW (6000bhp) Akasaka Tekkosho KK (Akasaka DieselLtd)-Japan AuxGen: 2 x 320kW 445V 60Hz a.c, 1 x 240kW 445V 60Hz a.c Fuel: 135.0 (d.f.) 826.0 (r.f.) 19.5pd
8517059 **SIMPLE** - *ex* Simple Ii *-2013* *ex* Avana Ii *-2010* - *ex* Silver Wind *-2010* *ex* Sichem Maya *-2007* *ex* Songa Maya *-2006* *ex* Lake Maya *-2006* *ex* Kapitan Rudnev *-2003* **Shine Crystal Navigation Co** Donbasspecgeologia LLC	**10,948** 5,140 17,060 T/cm 27.9	Class: BV (NV) (RS)	**1988-04 Brodogradiliste 'Uljanik' — Pula** Yd No: 373 Converted From: Products Tanker-2008 Conv to DH-2008 Loa 151.30 (BB) Br ex - Dght 9.451 Lbp 142.60 Br md 22.40 Dpth 12.15 Welded, 1 dk	**(A12B2TR) Chemical/Products Tanker** Double Hull (13F) Liq: 17,280; Liq (Oil): 20,062 Cargo Heating Coils Compartments: 6 Ta, 10 Wing Ta, 2 Wing Slop Ta, ER 16 Cargo Pump (s): 16x250m³/hr Manifold: Bow/CM: 73m Ice Capable	**1 oil engine** driving 1 CP propeller Total Power: 5,700kW (7,750hp) 12.0kn MAN-B&W 5L50MC 1 x 2 Stroke 5 Cy. 500 x 1620 5700kW (7750bhp) Tvornica Dizel Motora 'Uljanik'-Yugoslavia AuxGen: 1 x 900kW a.c, 2 x 700kW a.c, 1 x 100kW a.c Thrusters: 1 Thwart. CP thruster (f) Fuel: 143.2 (d.f.) 1549.3 (r.f.)

8036512 *WDB2544* -
SIMPLE MAN
ex Quang Minh I *-2004* *ex* Timmy D II *-1993*
ex Star II *-1992* *ex* Lady Nina *-1992*
B&B Boats Inc
-
Pascagoula, MS *United States of America*
MMSI: 366877090
Official number: 620974
108 74 -
1980 Collier Shipbuilding, Inc. — Bayou La Batre, Al Yd No: 5
L reg 22.65 Br ex 6.71 Dght -
Lbp - Br md - Dpth 3.38
Welded, 1 dk
(B11B2FV) Fishing Vessel
1 oil engine driving 1 FP propeller
Total Power: 268kW (364hp)

8108688 *PCFG* SCH 65
SIMPLON
Jaczon Visserij Maatschappij Bravo BV
Jaczon BV
Scheveningen *Netherlands*
MMSI: 246742000
Official number: 53528
310 93 300
Class: BV
1982-05 Con. Mec. de Normandie — Cherbourg Yd No: 34/07
Loa 34.02 Br ex 8.31 Dght 3.720
Lbp 31.02 Br md 7.92 Dpth 4.27
Welded, 1 dk
(B11A2FS) Stern Trawler
Ins: 180
Compartments: 1 Ho, ER
2 Ha:
1 oil engine with clutches, flexible couplings & sr geared to sc. shaft driving 1 CP propeller
Total Power: 588kW (799hp) 12.3kn
Crepelle 6PSN3
1 x 4 Stroke 6 Cy. 260 x 280 588kW (799bhp)
Crepelle et Cie-France
AuxGen: 1 x 72kW 380V 50Hz a.c, 1 x 59kW 380V 50Hz a.c
Thrusters: 1 Thwart. FP thruster (f)
Fuel: 50.0 (d.f.) 3.0pd

7048491 *JXHE* -
SIMRAD ECHO
ex Simrad *-1999* *ex* Kobboy *-1992*
Kongsberg Maritime AS
Kongsberg Gruppen AS
Horten *Norway*
MMSI: 258584000
138 55 20
1970 Flekkefjord Slipp & Maskinfabrikk AS AS — Flekkefjord Yd No: 106
Converted From: Ferry (Passenger/Vehicle)-1995
Loa 26.04 Br ex 7.01 Dght 2.439
Lbp 24.26 Br md 6.99 Dpth -
Welded, 1 dk
(B22A20R) Offshore Support Vessel
1 oil engine driving 1 FP propeller
Total Power: 268kW (364hp) 11.0kn
Caterpillar D343TA
1 x 4 Stroke 6 Cy. 137 x 165 268kW (364bhp)
Caterpillar Tractor Co-USA
Fuel: 11.0 (d.f.)

9136644 *H04359* -
SIMRAN
ex Nichiasu Maru No. 10 *-2006*
Great Eastern Investments Inc
Prime Tankers LLC
Panama *Panama*
MMSI: 356762000
Official number: 3327007A
1,043 374 1,312
Class: IR IS (RI)
1995-10 Kurinoura Dockyard Co Ltd — Yawatahama EH Yd No: 331
Loa 71.00 (BB) Br ex 10.82 Dght 4.140
Lbp 65.00 Br md 10.80 Dpth 4.60
Welded, 1 dk
(A13C2LA) Asphalt/Bitumen Tanker
Liq: 1,423; Liq (Oil): 1,423; Asphalt: 1,423
Compartments: 8 Ta, ER
2 Cargo Pump (s): 2x400m³/hr
1 oil engine with clutches & reverse geared to sc. shaft driving 1 FP propeller
Total Power: 1,471kW (2,000hp) 13.0kn
Akasaka K31SR
1 x 4 Stroke 6 Cy. 310 x 550 1471kW (2000bhp)
Akasaka Tekkosho KK (Akasaka DieselLtd)-Japan
AuxGen: 2 x 140kW 445V 60Hz a.c

9054365 *PHHN* -
SIMSON
Svitzer Amsterdam BV
Svitzer Europe Holding BV
IJmuiden *Netherlands*
MMSI: 245285000
Official number: 23829
314 94 180
Class: BV
1993-09 Construcciones Navales Santodomingo SA — Vigo Yd No: 701
Loa 30.52 Br ex 10.00 Dght 4.100
Lbp 28.11 Br md 9.50 Dpth 4.95
Welded, 1 dk
(B32A2ST) Tug
2 oil engines with flexible couplings & sr geared to sc. shafts driving 2 CP propellers
Total Power: 3,192kW (4,340hp) 12.8kn
A.B.C. 8DZC
2 x 4 Stroke 8 Cy. 256 x 310 each-1596kW (2170bhp)
Anglo Belgian Corp NV (ABC)-Belgium
AuxGen: 2 x 240kW 380V 50Hz a.c, 2 x 70kW 380/220V 50Hz a.c
Thrusters: 1 Thwart. FP thruster (f)
Fuel: 93.2 (d.f.)

6610651 *OJGP* -
SIMSON
ex Sim *-1994* *ex* Simson *-1994*
Oy Kraftline AB
-
Pietarsaari *Finland*
Official number: 11759
234 70 -
Class: (LR)
✠ Classed LR until 17/5/95
1966-04 AB Asi-Verken — Amal Yd No: 76
Loa 30.87 Br ex 8.44 Dght 4.115
Lbp 27.89 Br md 8.41 Dpth 4.81
Welded, 1 dk
(B32A2ST) Tug
Cranes: 1x1t
Ice Capable
1 oil engine driving 1 CP propeller
Total Power: 1,236kW (1,680hp) 12.5kn
Polar MN18
1 x 2 Stroke 8 Cy. 340 x 570 1236kW (1680bhp)
Nydqvist & Holm AB-Sweden
AuxGen: 2 x 72kW 380V 50Hz a.c
Fuel: 51.0 (d.f.) 7.0pd

9552965 *V7BJ6* -
SIMURGH
Irvington Navigation Inc
Escobal Japan Ltd
Majuro *Marshall Islands*
MMSI: 538005152
Official number: 5152
31,864 16,746 55,861
Class: NK
2013-09 Oshima Shipbuilding Co Ltd — Saikai NS Yd No: 10642
Loa 189.99 Br ex - Dght 12.568
Lbp 185.79 Br md 32.26 Dpth 17.87
Welded, 1 dk
(A21A2BC) Bulk Carrier
Double Hull
Grain: 64,364; Bale: 64,064
TEU 306
Compartments: 8 Ho, ER
8 Ha: ER
Cranes: 4x40t
1 oil engine driving 1 FP propeller
Total Power: 7,615kW (10,353hp) 14.5kn
MAN-B&W 6S50ME-C
1 x 2 Stroke 6 Cy. 500 x 2000 7615kW (10353bhp)
Kawasaki Heavy Industries Ltd-Japan
AuxGen: 3 x 470kW a.c
Fuel: 2162.0

9179385 *UBRI5* -
SIMUSHIR
ex Munteborg *-2012* *ex* MSC Baltic *-2004*
ex Munteborg *-2000*
Sakhalin Shipping Co (SASCO)
-
Kholmsk *Russia*
MMSI: 273356170
6,540 3,464 9,405 T/cm 19.4
Class: RS (BV)
1998-10 Scheepswerf Bijlsma Lemmer BV — Lemmer Yd No: 682
Loa 134.55 (BB) Br ex 16.60 Dght 7.110
Lbp 127.20 Br md 16.50 Dpth 9.80
Welded, 1 dk
(A31A2GX) General Cargo Ship
Grain: 13,059; Bale: 13,059
TEU 604 C Ho 264 TEU C Dk 340 TEU incl 60 ref C.
Compartments: 2 Ho, ER
2 Ha: (39.2 x 10.5) (52.5 x 13.5)ER
Ice Capable
1 oil engine with flexible couplings & sr gearedto sc. shaft driving 1 CP propeller
Total Power: 5,280kW (7,179hp) 16.0kn
Wartsila 8L38
1 x 4 Stroke 8 Cy. 380 x 475 5280kW (7179bhp)
Wartsila NSD Nederland BV-Netherlands
AuxGen: 2 x 305kW 440V 60Hz a.c
Thrusters: 1 Thwart. CP thruster (f)
Fuel: 98.4 (d.f.) (Heating Coils) 639.1 (r.f.) 25.0pd

8332344 *9WPM* -
SIN BEE I
Ajang Shipping Sdn Bhd
-
Kuching *Malaysia*
MMSI: 533267000
Official number: 325228
1,131 339 1,251
Class: BV (GL)
1983-03 Indonesia Onshore/Offshore Pte Ltd — Singapore Yd No: 29
Loa 54.87 Br ex 15.24 Dght 2.523
Lbp 54.74 Br md 15.23 Dpth 3.05
Welded, 1 dk
(B21A20S) Platform Supply Ship
2 oil engines reverse reduction geared to sc. shafts driving 2 FP propellers
Total Power: 514kW (698hp) 9.0kn
Caterpillar 3412T
2 x Vee 4 Stroke 12 Cy. 137 x 152 each-257kW (349bhp)
Caterpillar Tractor Co-USA

9075113 *9WBJ8* -
SIN BEE II
Ajang Shipping Sdn Bhd
-
SatCom: Inmarsat A 1710624
Kuching *Malaysia*
MMSI: 533268000
Official number: 326541
1,383 415 1,355
Class: NK
1992-11 Kian Juan Dockyard Sdn Bhd — Miri Yd No: 7190
Loa 65.00 Br ex - Dght 2.769
Lbp 59.09 Br md 15.24 Dpth 3.66
Welded
(B34T2QR) Work/Repair Vessel
Cranes: 1x25t
2 oil engines geared to sc. shafts driving 2 FP propellers
Total Power: 1,254kW (1,704hp) 8.0kn
G.M. (Detroit Diesel) 16V-92-TA
2 x Vee 2 Stroke 16 Cy. 123 x 127 each-627kW (852bhp)
General Motors Detroit DieselAllison Divn-USA
AuxGen: 2 x 120kW a.c
Fuel: 185.0 (d.f.)

6503133 *6MKY* -
SIN BO No. 27
ex Sin Bo No. 73 *-1989* *ex* Sam Boo No. 3 *-1988*
ex Dae Won No. 33 *-1984*
ex Takatori Maru No. 11 *-1972*
Sin Bo Fisheries Co Ltd
-
Busan *South Korea*
Official number: BS02-A582
229 109 -
Class: (KR)
1964 KK Kanasashi Zosen — Shizuoka SZ Yd No: 583
Loa 43.72 Br ex 7.57 Dght 3.052
Lbp 38.54 Br md 7.50 Dpth 3.31
Welded, 1 dk
(B11B2FV) Fishing Vessel
Ins: 307
4 Ha: 2 (1.0 x 1.0)2 (1.2 x 1.2)ER
1 oil engine driving 1 FP propeller
Total Power: 478kW (650hp) 10.5kn
Hanshin V6
1 x 4 Stroke 6 Cy. 320 x 450 478kW (650bhp)
Hanshin Nainenki Kogyo-Japan
AuxGen: 2 x 72kW 230V a.c

6408383 *6MNX* -
SIN BO No. 63
ex Sam Song No. 17 *-1988*
ex Shinmei Maru No. 31 *-1973*
ex Hokushu Maru No. 21 *-1968*
Bae Jong-Tae
-
Busan *South Korea*
Official number: BS-A-657
176 74 -
Class: (KR)
1963 Miho Zosensho K.K. — Shimizu Yd No: 374
Loa 38.64 Br ex 6.91 Dght 2.881
Lbp 33.38 Br md 6.90 Dpth 3.15
Welded, 1 dk
(B11B2FV) Fishing Vessel
Ins: 229
3 Ha: (1.1 x 0.8)2 (1.1 x 1.3)ER
1 oil engine driving 1 FP propeller
Total Power: 478kW (650hp) 11.0kn
Fuji
1 x 4 Stroke 6 Cy. 300 x 420 478kW (650bhp)
Fuji Diesel Co Ltd-Japan
AuxGen: 2 x 96kW 225V a.c

5123883 *6NVL* -
SIN BO No. 71
ex Se Yang No. 35 *-1986* *ex* Sam In No. 6 *-1986*
ex Gojyo Maru No. 8 *-1973*
ex Fukyu Maru No. 25 *-1973*
Sin Bo Fisheries Co Ltd
-
Busan *South Korea*
Official number: BS-A-1187
222 111 -
Class: (KR)
1962 KK Kanasashi Zosen — Shizuoka SZ Yd No: 451
Loa 41.51 Br ex 7.35 Dght -
Lbp 36.58 Br md 7.31 Dpth 3.41
Welded, 1 dk
(B11B2FV) Fishing Vessel
Ins: 270
4 Ha: 3 (1.3 x 1.3) (0.7 x 1.3)ER
1 oil engine driving 1 FP propeller
Total Power: 478kW (650hp) 11.0kn
Niigata M6F31S
1 x 4 Stroke 6 Cy. 310 x 440 478kW (650bhp)
Niigata Engineering Co Ltd-Japan
AuxGen: 2 x 54kW 230V a.c

6408137 *DTBX* -
SIN BO No. 72
ex Dai Ho No. 11 *-1985*
ex Lucky Star No. 101 *-1979*
ex Ohzuru Maru No. 2 *-1972*
Sin Bo Fisheries Co Ltd
-
Busan *South Korea*
Official number: BS-A-1653
183 88 211
Class: (KR)
1963 Niigata Engineering Co Ltd — Niigata NI Yd No: 563
Loa 38.94 Br ex 6.96 Dght 2.801
Lbp 34.50 Br md 6.91 Dpth 3.10
Welded, 1 dk
(B11B2FV) Fishing Vessel
Ins: 216
Compartments: 2 Ho, ER
2 Ha: (1.3 x 1.0) (1.5 x 1.5)ER
1 oil engine driving 1 FP propeller
Total Power: 405kW (551hp) 10.0kn
Niigata 6M28DHS
1 x 4 Stroke 6 Cy. 280 x 440 405kW (551bhp)
Niigata Engineering Co Ltd-Japan
AuxGen: 2 x 48kW 225V 60Hz a.c

IMO / Call sign	Name / Owner / Port	Tonnage	Class	Builder / Dimensions	Type	Machinery
8934908 - -	**SIN DOK** - -	**1,069** 641 1,350		**1989**-12 **Kimchaek Ship Factory — Kimchaek** Yd No: 1197 Loa 58.06 Br ex - Dght 3.270 Lbp 50.06 Br md 12.40 Dpth 3.84 Welded, 1 dk	**(A13B2TP) Products Tanker**	**2 oil engines** driving 2 FP propellers Total Power: 588kW (800hp)
7213747 *BVWK* -	**SIN HAI No. 3** **Sin Ho Sing Ocean Enterprise Co Ltd** *Kaohsiung* *Chinese Taipei*	*321* 217 274	Class: (CR)	**1969 Korea Shipbuilding & Engineering Corp — Busan** Loa 43.59 Br ex 7.52 Dght 2.896 Lbp 38.61 Br md 7.50 Dpth 3.36 Welded, 1 dk	**(B11B2FV) Fishing Vessel** Compartments: 3 Ho, ER 4 Ha: 2 (1.0 x 1.0)2 (1.5 x 1.5)ER Derricks: 4x1t; Winches: 4	**1 oil engine** driving 1 FP propeller Total Power: 552kW (750hp) 11.5kn Niigata 1 x 4 Stroke 6 Cy. 280 x 440 552kW (750bhp) Niigata Engineering Co Ltd-Japan AuxGen: 2 x 80kW 230V 60Hz a.c
9727754 *BG3734* CT5-1734	**SIN HUA FONG NO. 16** **Sin Hua Fong Fishery Co Ltd** - *Kaohsiung* *Chinese Taipei* Official number: 015341	**198** 73 -		**2013**-01 **Shing Sheng Fa Boat Building Co — Kaohsiung** L reg 32.89 Br ex - Dght - Lbp - Br md 6.42 Dpth 2.60 Bonded, 1 dk	**(B11B2FV) Fishing Vessel** Hull Material: Reinforced Plastic	**1 oil engine** reduction geared to sc. shaft driving 1 FP propeller Yanmar Yanmar Diesel Engine Co Ltd-Japan
8217477 *9WDC3* -	**SIN HUAT** *ex* Thai Kheng *-2000* *ex* Senyo Maru *-1996* **Aswanijaya Sdn Bhd** Apollo Agencies (1980) Sdn Bhd *Kuching* *Malaysia* MMSI: 533498000 Official number: 328720	**1,539** 669 2,080	Class: (NK)	**1983**-04 **Narasaki Zosen KK — Muroran HK** Yd No: 1044 Loa 76.51 (BB) Br ex 12.63 Dght 4.739 Lbp 72.01 Br md 12.60 Dpth 4.83 Welded, 2 dks	**(A31A2GX) General Cargo Ship** Bale: 2,230; Liq: 2,300 Compartments: 1 Ho, ER 1 Ha: (38.4 x 8.6)ER	**1 oil engine** with clutches, flexible couplings & sr geared to sc. shaft driving 1 CP propeller Total Power: 1,140kW (1,550hp) 11.0kn Pielstick 6PA6L280 1 x 4 Stroke 6 Cy. 280 x 290 1140kW (1550bhp) Nippon Kokan KK (NKK Corp)-Japan AuxGen: 3 x 72kW Fuel: 117.0 (d.f.) 5.0pd
9518531 *YDA4852* -	**SIN HUAT HUAT 1** *launched as* Energy Bravo *-2009* **PT Widhi Satria Jaya Lines** *Batam* *Indonesia*	**163** 49 137	Class: GL KI	**2009**-10 **PT Cahaya Fortuna Bahari — Batam** Yd No: 169 Loa 25.00 Br ex - Dght 2.800 Lbp 22.68 Br md 7.32 Dpth 3.35 Welded, 1 dk	**(B32A2ST) Tug**	**2 oil engines** reverse reduction geared to sc. shafts driving 2 FP propellers Total Power: 882kW (1,200hp) Mitsubishi S6A3-MPTK 2 x 4 Stroke 6 Cy. 150 x 175 each-441kW (600bhp) Mitsubishi Heavy Industries Ltd-Japan AuxGen: 2 x 37kW 415V a.c
9712436 *9V2296* -	**SIN HUAT HUAT 8** **Sin Huat Huat Marine Transportation Pte Ltd** - *Singapore* *Singapore* Official number: 398858	**147** 45 91	Class: NK	**2013**-11 **Nga Chai Shipyard Sdn Bhd — Sibu** Yd No: 33/18 Loa 23.50 Br ex - Dght 2.512 Lbp 21.90 Br md 7.32 Dpth 3.10 Welded, 1 dk	**(B32A2ST) Tug**	**2 oil engines** reduction geared to sc. shafts driving 2 FP propellers Total Power: 970kW (1,318hp) Yanmar 6AYM-WST 2 x 4 Stroke 6 Cy. 155 x 180 each-485kW (659bhp) Yanmar Diesel Engine Co Ltd-Japan Fuel: 90.0 (d.f.)
9252321 *9V6021* -	**SIN HUAT HUAT 88** **Sin Huat Huat Marine Transportation Pte Ltd** - *Singapore* *Singapore* Official number: 389206	**125** 38 -	Class: NV	**2001**-04 **Kiong Nguong Shipbuilding Contractor Co — Sibu** Yd No: 2003 Loa 23.00 Br ex 7.33 Dght 2.512 Lbp 21.05 Br md 7.30 Dpth 3.00 Welded, 1 dk	**(B32A2ST) Tug**	**2 oil engines** Reduction geared to sc. shafts driving 2 FP propellers Total Power: 924kW (1,256hp) Yanmar 6LAHM-STE3 2 x 4 Stroke 6 Cy. 150 x 165 each-462kW (628bhp) Yanmar Diesel Engine Co Ltd-Japan AuxGen: 2 x 25kW 380V 60Hz a.c
8647995 *BH3325* LL1710	**SIN JIN NO. 36** *ex* Dong Yih No. 668 *-2009* **Jin Yu Enterprise Co Ltd** - *Kaohsiung* *Chinese Taipei* Official number: CT6-1325	**493** 252 -		**1997**-07 **San Yang Shipbuilding Co., Ltd. — Kaohsiung** Loa 55.10 Br ex 8.60 Dght - Lbp - Br md - Dpth - Welded, 1 dk	**(B11B2FV) Fishing Vessel**	**1 oil engine** driving 1 Propeller
9537393 *9AA6099* -	**SIN KALI I** **Kali Tuna doo** - *Zadar* *Croatia* MMSI: 238882640 Official number: 3R-184	**328** 98 134	Class: CS	**2008**-09 **Tehnomont Brodogradiliste Pula doo — Pula** Yd No: 58 Loa 40.15 Br ex 8.65 Dght 2.700 Lbp 32.40 Br md 8.64 Dpth 4.20 Welded, 1 dk	**(B11B2FV) Fishing Vessel**	**1 oil engine** geared to sc. shaft driving 1 FP propeller Total Power: 1,250kW (1,700hp) 14.0kn Mitsubishi S16R-MPTA 1 x Vee 4 Stroke 16 Cy. 170 x 180 1250kW (1700bhp) Mitsubishi Heavy Industries Ltd-Japan AuxGen: 1 x 240kW a.c, 1 x 88kW a.c Thrusters: 2 Thwart. FP thruster 1 (p) 1 (s)
8875736 *DSJC* -	**SIN KWANG EXPRESS FERRY** *ex* Wando Car Ferry No. 2 *-2003* **Cosmo Marine** - *Mokpo* *South Korea* MMSI: 440300386 Official number: MPR-894488	**171** - 137	Class: (KR)	**1989**-07 **Ilheung Shipbuilding & Engineering Co Ltd — Mokpo** Yd No: 88-06 Loa 49.50 Br ex - Dght 1.609 Lbp 43.00 Br md 7.00 Dpth 2.00 Welded, 1 dk	**(A36A2PR) Passenger/Ro-Ro Ship (Vehicles)**	**2 oil engines** reduction geared to sc. shafts driving 2 FP propellers Total Power: 750kW (1,020hp) 14.4kn MAN D2542MLE 2 x Vee 4 Stroke 12 Cy. 125 x 142 each-375kW (510bhp) Daewoo Heavy Industries Ltd-South Korea AuxGen: 1 x 18kW 225V a.c Fuel: 3.0 (d.f.)
8925000 *DSAS650* -	**SIN KWANG FERRY NO. 2** **Cosmo Marine** - *Mokpo* *South Korea* MMSI: 440300356 Official number: MPR-944427	**186** - 104	Class: (KR)	**1994**-12 **Korea Shipyard Co Ltd — Mokpo** Yd No: 94-18001 Loa 49.00 Br ex - Dght 1.609 Lbp 41.00 Br md 9.00 Dpth 2.30 Welded, 1 dk	**(A36A2PR) Passenger/Ro-Ro Ship (Vehicles)**	**2 oil engines** reduction geared to sc. shafts driving 1 FP propeller Total Power: 822kW (1,118hp) 14.2kn M.T.U. 12V183 2 x Vee 4 Stroke 12 Cy. 128 x 142 each-411kW (559bhp) Daewoo Heavy Industries Ltd-South Korea AuxGen: 1 x 69kW 225V a.c
9073763 *9WBI4* -	**SIN MATU 12** **Sin Matu Sdn Bhd** - *Kuching* *Malaysia* Official number: 326522	**109** 33 -	Class: (NK)	**1992**-11 **Sin Matu Shipyard Sdn Bhd — Limbang** Yd No: 001 Loa - Br ex - Dght 2.212 Lbp 21.78 Br md 6.70 Dpth 2.90 Welded, 1 dk	**(B32A2ST) Tug**	**2 oil engines** reduction geared to sc. shafts driving 2 FP propellers Total Power: 746kW (1,014hp) 10.0kn Cummins KTA-19-M 2 x 4 Stroke 6 Cy. 159 x 159 each-373kW (507bhp) Cummins Engine Co Inc-USA AuxGen: 2 x 16kW a.c
7802469 *9WCW3* -	**SIN MATU 23** *ex* Golden Lion *-2003* **Sin Matu Sdn Bhd** - *Kuching* *Malaysia* Official number: 328030	**135** 63 -	Class: (AB)	**1978**-06 **Tech 4 Marine Pte Ltd — Singapore** Yd No: 102 Loa - Br ex - Dght 2.263 Lbp 21.52 Br md 7.41 Dpth 2.87 Welded, 1 dk	**(B32A2ST) Tug**	**2 oil engines** reverse reduction geared to sc. shafts driving 2 FP propellers Total Power: 706kW (960hp) 10.0kn Caterpillar D346TA 2 x Vee 4 Stroke 8 Cy. 137 x 165 each-353kW (480bhp) Caterpillar Tractor Co-USA AuxGen: 2 x 40kW
6422884 *6MAK* -	**SIN NAM No. 11** *ex* Pioneer No. 8 *-1988* *ex* Matsuei Maru No. 5 *-1970* **Sin Nam Industrial Co Ltd** - *Busan* *South Korea* Official number: BS-A-9	*228* 112 -	Class: (KR)	**1964 KK Kanasashi Zosen — Shizuoka SZ** Yd No: 607 Loa 43.21 Br ex 7.52 Dght 2.896 Lbp 37.98 Br md 7.50 Dpth 3.38 Welded, 1 dk	**(B11B2FV) Fishing Vessel** Ins: 298	**1 oil engine** driving 1 FP propeller Total Power: 515kW (700hp) 11.0kn Niigata 1 x 4 Stroke 6 Cy. 280 x 440 515kW (700bhp) Niigata Engineering Co Ltd-Japan AuxGen: 2 x 92kW 230V a.c
5411278 *6LWY* -	**SIN NAM No. 31** *ex* Jinam No. 218 *-1982* *ex* Genryo Maru No. 21 *-1970* **Sin Nam Industrial Co Ltd** - *Busan* *South Korea* Official number: BS-A-96	*230* 116 -	Class: (KR)	**1962 KK Kanasashi Zosen — Shizuoka SZ** Yd No: 488 Loa 42.35 Br ex 7.35 Dght 2.998 Lbp 37.14 Br md 7.29 Dpth 3.41 Welded, 1 dk	**(B11B2FV) Fishing Vessel** Ins: 292	**1 oil engine** driving 1 FP propeller Total Power: 515kW (700hp) 11.0kn Akasaka MK6SS 1 x 4 Stroke 6 Cy. 300 x 420 515kW (700bhp) Akasaka Tekkosho KK (Akasaka DieselLtd)-Japan AuxGen: 2 x 60kW 230V a.c
7743778 *6KXN* -	**SIN NAM No. 101** *ex* Sam In No. 1 *-1979* *ex* Okiya Maru No. 15 *-1967* **Sin Nam Industrial Co Ltd** - *Busan* *South Korea* Official number: BS-A-290	*346* 189 -	Class: (KR)	**1962 Usuki Iron Works Co Ltd — Saiki OT** Loa 48.93 Br ex - Dght 3.432 Lbp 42.75 Br md 7.90 Dpth 3.81 Welded, 1 dk	**(B11B2FV) Fishing Vessel** Ins: 460 4 Ha: 2 (1.1 x 1.4)2 (1.6 x 1.6)	**1 oil engine** driving 1 FP propeller Total Power: 552kW (750hp) 10.0kn Niigata M6DR 1 x 4 Stroke 6 Cy. 370 x 520 552kW (750bhp) Niigata Engineering Co Ltd-Japan AuxGen: 2 x 80kW 230V a.c Fuel: 175.0

IMO / Call sign	Name / Owner	Tonnage	Class	Builder / Dimensions	Type	Machinery
8730998 *P5DL* -	**SIN PHO** **Sinpo Fishery Co** Korea Kunhae Co Ltd *Sinpo* *North Korea* MMSI: 445050000 Official number: 4902784	**2,778** 1,555 4,428	Class: KC	**1999**-12 **Wonsan Shipyard — Wonsan** Yd No: 98-07 Loa 83.10 Br ex - Dght 7.250 Lbp 78.20 Br md 14.60 Dpth 9.75 Welded, 1 dk	**(A31A2GX) General Cargo Ship**	**1 oil engine** driving 1 Propeller
5349621 - -	**SIN PUNG** *ex* Jang Hyong Je *-2008* *ex* Shosei Maru No. 12 *-1974* *ex* Taisen Maru No. 8 *-1969* - -	*298* 132 500	Class: KC	**1960 Yamanishi Shipbuilding Co Ltd — Ishinomaki MG** Yd No: 375 Loa 48.39 Br ex 7.37 Dght 3.300 Lbp 42.52 Br md 7.32 Dpth 3.79 Welded, 1 dk	**(B11B2FV) Fishing Vessel**	**1 oil engine** driving 1 FP propeller Total Power: 736kW (1,001hp) Akasaka SR6SS 1 x 4 Stroke 6 Cy. 350 x 500 736kW (1001bhp) Akasaka Tekkosho KK (Akasaka DieselLtd)-Japan
8032918 *BYUD* -	**SIN SHIH HANG No. 22** **Sin Shih Hang Fishery Co Ltd** - *Kaohsiung* *Chinese Taipei*	*436* 280 -	Class: (CR)	**1979 Fong Kuo Shipbuilding Co Ltd — Kaohsiung** Loa 47.30 Br ex 8.39 Dght 3.110 Lbp 41.05 Br md 8.31 Dpth 3.61 Welded, 1 dk	**(B11B2FV) Fishing Vessel** Ins: 538 Compartments: 4 Ho, ER 5 Ha: 2 (1.0 x 1.0)2 (1.5 x 1.6) (1.3 x 0.9)	**1 oil engine** driving 1 FP propeller Total Power: 736kW (1,001hp) 10.5kn Niigata 6M28KGHS 1 x 4 Stroke 6 Cy. 280 x 440 736kW (1001bhp) Niigata Engineering Co Ltd-Japan AuxGen: 2 x 200kW 130/200V a.c, 1 x 120kW 130/200V a.c
8430029 - -	**SIN SHIH HANG No. 22** **Geniuswise Ltd** - *San Lorenzo* *Honduras* Official number: L-1924152	**437** 281 -		**1979 Kaohsiung Shipbuilding Co. Ltd. — Kaohsiung** L reg 41.69 Br ex - Dght - Lbp - Br md 8.32 Dpth 2.89 Welded, 1 dk	**(B11B2FV) Fishing Vessel**	**1 oil engine** driving 1 FP propeller Total Power: 736kW (1,001hp) 11.0kn
9106704 *VRYU6* -	**SIN SHUN** *ex* Pacific Id *-2012* *ex* Patagonia *-2007* *ex* Tauroa Point *-2004* *ex* Atlantic Bulker *-2003* **Jin Shun Maritime Ltd** Jacksoon Shipping Safety Management Consultant Co Ltd *Hong Kong* *Hong Kong* MMSI: 477502000 Official number: HK-1068	**17,075** 9,896 27,860 T/cm 39.5	Class: NK	**1995**-02 **KK Kanasashi — Toyohashi AI** Yd No: 3375 Loa 176.60 (BB) Br ex 26.05 Dght 9.415 Lbp 169.40 Br md 26.00 Dpth 13.30 Welded, 1 dk	**(A21A2BC) Bulk Carrier** Grain: 38,240; Bale: 37,313 Compartments: 5 Ho, ER 5 Ha: (17.9 x 12.8)4 (19.5 x 17.8)ER Cranes: 4x30.5t	**1 oil engine** driving 1 FP propeller Total Power: 5,149kW (7,001hp) 13.5kn Mitsubishi 5UEC52LA 1 x 2 Stroke 5 Cy. 520 x 1600 5149kW (7001bhp) Kobe Hatsudoki KK-Japan AuxGen: 2 x 400kW 450V 60Hz a.c Fuel: 77.0 (d.f.) 1008.0 (r.f.) 20.8pd
9081590 *JYA529* -	**SINA** *ex* Volcan De Tejeda *-2012* **Arab Bridge Maritime Co** - *Aqaba* *Jordan* MMSI: 438031028 Official number: 7	**9,807** 2,942 4,226	Class: BV	**1995**-09 **Hijos de J. Barreras S.A. — Vigo** Yd No: 1545 Loa 120.00 (BB) Br ex 19.52 Dght 5.300 Lbp 107.00 Br md 19.50 Dpth 6.80 Welded, 3 dks	**(A36A2PR) Passenger/Ro-Ro Ship (Vehicles)** Passengers: unberthed: 174; cabins: 19; berths: 76 Stern door/ramp Lane-Len: 1023 Lane-clr ht: 4.50 Trailers: 62 Bale: 1,205 Compartments: 3 Ho, ER	**2 oil engines** reduction geared to sc. shafts driving 2 CP propellers Total Power: 6,800kW (9,246hp) 18.0kn MWM TBD645L6 2 x 4 Stroke 6 Cy. 330 x 450 each-3400kW (4623bhp) Hijos de J Barreras SA-Spain AuxGen: 2 x 500kW a.c, 2 x 500kW a.c Thrusters: 2 Thwart. FP thruster (f) Fuel: 138.0 (d.f.) 1196.0 (r.f.)
7517844 *D6DI9* -	**SINA** *ex* Sea Leader *-2006* *ex* Stonington *-1987* **Gulf Glory Marine Services (LLC)** Whitesea Shipping & Supply (LLC) *Moroni* *Union of Comoros* MMSI: 616464000	**658** 197 701	Class: BV (AB)	**1976**-09 **Wall Shipyard, Inc. — Harvey, La** Yd No: 1975-37 Loa 53.65 Br ex - Dght 3.972 Lbp 49.00 Br md 11.89 Dpth 4.58 Welded, 1 dk	**(B21B20A) Anchor Handling Tug Supply** Cranes: 1x5t	**2 oil engines** reverse reduction geared to sc. shafts driving 2 FP propellers Total Power: 2,538kW (3,450hp) 10.0kn Nohab F28V 2 x Vee 4 Stroke 8 Cy. 250 x 300 each-1269kW (1725bhp) AB Bofors NOHAB-Sweden AuxGen: 2 x 99kW 440V 60Hz a.c, 1 x 60kW a.c Thrusters: 1 Thwart. FP thruster (f)
7702463 *J8B4796* -	**SINA** *ex* Nima *-1999* *ex* Ocean Amber *-1993* *ex* Al Zora 1 *-1990* **Tariq Star Shipping & Trading Ltd** Seawaves Shipping Co LLC *Kingstown* *St Vincent & The Grenadines* MMSI: 375809000 Official number: 11269	*171* 52 -	Class: GL (AB)	**1978**-01 **Arab Heavy Industries Ltd SA — Ajman** Yd No: AS001 Loa 25.20 Br ex - Dght 2.831 Lbp 24.01 Br md 7.82 Dpth 3.51 Welded, 1 dk	**(B32A2ST) Tug**	**2 oil engines** reverse reduction geared to sc. shafts driving 2 FP propellers Total Power: 992kW (1,348hp) G.M. (Detroit Diesel) 12V-149 2 x Vee 2 Stroke 12 Cy. 146 x 146 each-496kW (674bhp) General Motors Detroit DieselAllison Divn-USA AuxGen: 2 x 65kW 220/380V a.c
9410026 *9BIF* -	**SINA 10** - **Aziz Hamidavi & Partners** Reza Shamsimehr *Bandar Imam Khomeini* *Iran* MMSI: 422533000 Official number: 20610	**388** 260 860	Class: AS	**2006**-01 **Arshia Sahel Karoun — Khorramshahr** Loa 45.30 Br ex - Dght 3.600 Lbp - Br md 9.00 Dpth 4.15 Welded, 1 dk	**(A31A2GX) General Cargo Ship**	**2 oil engines** driving 2 Propellers Total Power: 840kW (1,142hp) Yanmar 2 x 4 Stroke each-420kW (571bhp)
9139672 *YFOY* -	**SINABUNG** **Government of The Republic of Indonesia (Direktorat Jenderal Perhubungan Laut - Ministry of Sea Communications)** PT Pelayaran Nasional Indonesia (PELNI) SatCom: Inmarsat B 352502510 *Belawan* *Indonesia* MMSI: 525005031	**14,716** 5,680 3,485	Class: (GL) (KI)	**1997**-12 **Jos L Meyer GmbH & Co — Papenburg** Yd No: 644 Loa 146.50 (BB) Br ex 23.70 Dght 5.888 Lbp 130.00 Br md 23.40 Dpth 13.40 Welded, 8 dks	**(A37B2PS) Passenger Ship** Passengers: unberthed: 1398; cabins: 88; berths: 508 Grain: 1,400; Bale: 1,200	**2 oil engines** reduction geared to sc. shafts driving 2 CP propellers Total Power: 17,040kW (23,168hp) 22.4kn MaK 8M601C 2 x 4 Stroke 8 Cy. 580 x 600 each-8520kW (11584bhp) MaK Motoren GmbH & Co. KG-Kiel AuxGen: 4 x 800kW 220/380V a.c Thrusters: 1 Thwart. CP thruster (f)
5018844 - -	**SINAH** *ex* Nourberg *-2006* *ex* Nourberg Mofarrij *-1994* *ex* Skala *-1993* *ex* Taladi *-1993* *ex* Rikke Grenius *-1983* *ex* Mette Jensen *-1981* *ex* Asvig *-1977* *ex* Skala *-1974* *ex* Varmland *-1969* *ex* Annchen Felter *-1964* *ex* Eike Knudsen *-1953* - -	*285* 127 508	Class: (BV)	**1950**-01 **Werft Nobiskrug GmbH — Rendsburg** Yd No: 538 Loa 47.05 Br ex 8.11 Dght 3.048 Lbp 47.00 Br md 8.08 Dpth 4.96 Riveted\Welded, 1 dk & S dk H5.8m	**(A31A2GX) General Cargo Ship** Grain: 1,047; Bale: 994 Compartments: 1 Ho, ER 2 Ha: (10.3 x 5.0) (11.4 x 5.0)ER Derricks: 2x2t; Winches: 2 Ice Capable	**1 oil engine** driving 1 FP propeller Total Power: 368kW (500hp) 9.0kn Alpha 407-24VO 1 x 2 Stroke 7 Cy. 240 x 400 368kW (500bhp) (new engine 1962) Alpha Diesel A/S-Denmark AuxGen: 2 x 13kW 110V d.c, 1 x 5kW 110V d.c
7912393 - -	**SINAI** - -	*1,192* 456 1,286	Class: (LR) ✠ Classed LR until 29/1/92	**1980**-05 **IHC Smit BV — Kinderdijk** Yd No: C01132 Loa 66.81 Br ex 12.45 Dght 3.501 Lbp 61.50 Br md 12.43 Dpth 4.40 Welded, 1 dk	**(B33B2DT) Trailing Suction Hopper Dredger** Hopper: 600	**2 oil engines** reverse reduction geared to sc. shafts driving 2 FP propellers Total Power: 750kW (1,020hp) 9.5kn MWM TBD440-6 2 x 4 Stroke 6 Cy. 230 x 270 each-375kW (510bhp) Motoren Werke Mannheim AG (MWM)-West Germany AuxGen: 2 x 202kW 380V 50Hz a.c, 1 x 136kW 380V 50Hz a.c
7122895 - -	**SINAMAICA** *ex* Chitose Maru *-1977* **Government of The Republic of Venezuela (Ministerio de Comunicaciones)** - *Maracaibo* *Venezuela* Official number: AJZL-10039	*196* 67 57	Class: (NK)	**1971 Ishikawajima Ship & Chemical Plant Co Ltd — Tokyo** Yd No: 421 Loa 28.35 Br ex 8.67 Dght 3.090 Lbp 25.00 Br md 8.62 Dpth 3.48 Welded, 1 dk	**(B32A2ST) Tug**	**2 oil engines** driving 2 FP propellers Total Power: 1,398kW (1,900hp) 11.0kn Daihatsu 8PSHTCM-26 2 x 4 Stroke 8 Cy. 260 x 320 each-699kW (950bhp) Daihatsu Diesel Manufacturing Co Lt-Japan AuxGen: 2 x 72kW
7520700 *TCBX6* -	**SINAN** **Butoni Denizcilik ve Ticaret AS** Sinan Gemisi Donatma Istiraki *Istanbul* *Turkey* MMSI: 271002024 Official number: TUGS 1519	**962** 591 1,882	Class: (TL) (BV) (GL)	**1977**-08 **Gunsin Gemi Insaat ve Ticaret Ltd. Sti. — Balat, Istanbul** Yd No: 16 Loa 74.05 Br ex 11.20 Dght 3.650 Lbp 70.68 Br md 11.00 Dpth 6.00 Welded, 2 dks	**(A31A2GX) General Cargo Ship** Grain: 2,575; Bale: 2,343 Compartments: 2 Ho, ER 2 Ha: (11.9 x 5.8) (19.2 x 5.8)ER Cranes: 1x5t,2x3t	**1 oil engine** dr geared to sc. shaft driving 1 FP propeller Total Power: 364kW (495hp) 12.3kn S.K.L. 8NVD48-2U 1 x 4 Stroke 8 Cy. 320 x 480 364kW (495bhp) VEB Schwermaschinenbau "KarlLiebknecht" (SKL)-Magdeburg

IMO / Call sign	Name / Owner / Manager	Tonnage	Class	Builder / Dimensions	Type / Cargo	Machinery
9174787 *TCEA* -	**SINAN ATASOY** **Mumcuoglu Gemicilik Insaat Trz Ticaret Sanayi Ltd Sti** Atasoy Group of Shipping Companies (Atasoy Grup Denizcilik Ticaret Ltd Sti) *Istanbul* *Turkey* MMSI: 271000501 Official number: 7091	**2,491** 1,611 4,448	Class: BV	**1997-07 Anadolu Deniz Insaat Kizaklari San. ve Tic. Ltd. Sti. — Tuzla** Yd No: 172 Loa 94.56 Br ex - Dght 5.990 Lbp 84.58 Br md 14.30 Dpth 7.40 Welded, 1 dk	**(A31A2GX) General Cargo Ship** Grain: 5,852; Bale: 5,294 Compartments: 2 Ho, ER 2 Ha: (18.9 x 10.2) (25.2 x 10.2)ER	**1 oil engine** reduction geared to sc. shaft driving 1 FP propeller Total Power: 1,103kW (1,500hp) 11.0kn S.K.L. 8NVD48A-2U 1 x 4 Stroke 8 Cy. 320 x 480 1103kW (1500bhp) SKL Motoren u. Systemtechnik AG-Magdeburg AuxGen: 1 x 60kW 380V 50Hz a.c
7721976 *TCCW2* -	**SINAN NAIBOGLU** *ex* Papila I *-1998* **Berem Denizcilik Sanayi ve Ticaret Ltd Sti** Albedo Denizcilik ve Nakliyat Sanayi Ticaret Ltd Sti (Albedo Shipping Co Ltd) *Istanbul* *Turkey* MMSI: 271002341 Official number: TUGS 563	*972* 528 897	Class: BR (TL) (AB)	**1979-11 Profilo Sanayi Ve Ticaret A.S. — Istanbul** Yd No: 5 Converted From: Stern Trawler-1997 Loa 60.08 Br ex 10.04 Dght 3.680 Lbp 56.22 Br md 10.00 Dpth 5.31 Welded, 1 dk & S dk	**(A31A2GX) General Cargo Ship** Compartments: 2 Ho, ER 2 Ha: ER Derricks: 2	**1 oil engine** reverse reduction geared to sc. shaft driving 1 FP propeller Total Power: 416kW (566hp) 10.0kn Caterpillar D379SCAC 1 x Vee 4 Stroke 8 Cy. 159 x 203 416kW (566bhp) Caterpillar Tractor Co-USA AuxGen: 1 x 210kW a.c, 1 x 85kW a.c Thrusters: 1 Thwart. FP thruster (f)
9321627 - -	**SINAN NONG HYUP FERRY** *ex* Song Lim Ferry *-2006* **Sinan Agricultural Cooperative** - *Mokpo* *South Korea* MMSI: 440307870 Official number: MPR-044892	**254** - 272	Class: KR	**2004-05 Moonchang Shipbuilding Dockyard Co Ltd — Mokpo** Yd No: 03-21 Loa 49.35 Br ex 11.60 Dght 1.800 Lbp 40.00 Br md 10.00 Dpth 2.30 Welded, 1 dk	**(A36A2PR) Passenger/Ro-Ro Ship (Vehicles)**	**2 oil engines** geared to sc. shafts driving 2 FP propellers Total Power: 1,060kW (1,442hp) 12.3kn Caterpillar 3412C 2 x Vee 4 Stroke 12 Cy. 137 x 152 each-530kW (721bhp) Caterpillar Inc-USA
8875205 - -	**SINAN NONG HYUP FERRY NO. 2** *ex* Dae Heung Ferry No. 5 *-2011* **Sinan Agricultural Cooperative** - *Mokpo* *South Korea* MMSI: 440304060 Official number: MPR-934536	**254** - 149	Class: KR	**1994-02 Ilheung Shipbuilding & Engineering Co Ltd — Mokpo** Yd No: 92-43 Loa 49.95 Br ex - Dght 1.310 Lbp 46.00 Br md 9.60 Dpth 2.20 Welded, 1 dk	**(A36A2PR) Passenger/Ro-Ro Ship (Vehicles)**	**2 oil engines** geared to sc. shafts driving 2 FP propellers Total Power: 1,100kW (1,496hp) 13.9kn M.T.U. 12V183TE72 2 x Vee 4 Stroke 12 Cy. 128 x 142 each-550kW (748bhp) MTU Friedrichshafen GmbH-Friedrichshafen AuxGen: 2 x 72kW 220V a.c
9150262 *TCBZ9* -	**SINAN PASA** **Istanbul Deniz Otobusleri Sanayi ve Ticaret AS (IDO)** - *Istanbul* *Turkey* MMSI: 271002308 Official number: TUGS 590	**516** 188 48	Class: TL (BV)	**1996-11 Austal Ships Pty Ltd — Fremantle WA** Yd No: 56 Loa 40.10 (BB) Br ex 10.80 Dght 1.200 Lbp 35.00 Br md 10.50 Dpth 3.80 Welded, 1 dk	**(A37B2PS) Passenger Ship** Hull Material: Aluminium Alloy Passengers: unberthed: 450	**2 oil engines** with clutches, flexible couplings & sr geared to sc. shafts driving 2 Water jets Total Power: 3,960kW (5,384hp) 33.5kn M.T.U. 16V396TE74L 2 x Vee 4 Stroke 16 Cy. 165 x 185 each-1980kW (2692bhp) MTU Friedrichshafen GmbH-Friedrichshafen AuxGen: 2 x 112kW a.c
9340867 *YD8014* -	**SINAR 77** **PT Sinar Jaya Wijaya** - *Bitung* *Indonesia*	**121** 37 113	Class: KI NK	**2004-12 Tang Tiew Hee & Sons Sdn Bhd — Sibu** Yd No: 21 Loa 23.17 Br ex - Dght 2.388 Lbp 21.39 Br md 7.00 Dpth 2.90 Welded, 1 dk	**(B32A2ST) Tug**	**2 oil engines** geared to sc. shafts driving 2 FP propellers Total Power: 882kW (1,200hp) Cummins KTA-19-M3 2 x 4 Stroke 6 Cy. 159 x 159 each-441kW (600bhp) Cummins Engine Co Inc-USA
9349124 *PNJK* -	**SINAR AGRA** **Foremost Maritime Pte Ltd** Samudera Shipping Line Ltd *Jakarta* *Indonesia* MMSI: 525019521 Official number: 2985/PST	**7,687** 3,266 11,244 T/cm 20.6	Class: AB KI	**2006-11 STX Shipbuilding Co Ltd — Busan** Yd No: 5015 Loa 116.50 (BB) Br ex 20.00 Dght 8.400 Lbp 109.00 Br md 20.00 Dpth 11.70 Welded, 1 dk	**(A12B2TR) Chemical/Products Tanker** Double Hull (13F) Liq: 11,594; Liq (Oil): 11,594 Cargo Heating Coils Compartments: 12 Wing Ta, 2 Wing Slop Ta, ER 10 Cargo Pump (s): 10x300m³/hr Manifold: Bow/CM: 52.7m	**1 oil engine** driving 1 FP propeller Total Power: 4,440kW (6,037hp) 13.6kn MAN-B&W 6S35MC 1 x 2 Stroke 6 Cy. 350 x 1400 4440kW (6037bhp) STX Engine Co Ltd-South Korea AuxGen: 3 x 450kW 450V a.c Thrusters: 1 Thwart. FP thruster (f) Fuel: 99.6 (d.f.) 834.1 (r.f.)
9420382 *YCFR* -	**SINAR AMBON** *ex* Sejahtera Dua *-2009* *ex* Jian Gong 88 *-2006* **PT Samudera Shipping Services** PT Samudera Indonesia Ship Management (PT SISM) *Jakarta* *Indonesia* MMSI: 525009051 Official number: 1932	**3,430** 2,053 4,888	Class: KI	**2006-11 Wenling Kaili Shiprepair & Building Co Ltd — Wenling ZJ** Loa 92.00 Br ex - Dght 5.800 Lbp 90.00 Br md 15.60 Dpth 7.50 Welded, 1 dk	**(A31A2GX) General Cargo Ship**	**1 oil engine** geared to sc. shaft driving 1 FP propeller Total Power: 2,000kW (2,719hp) 11.0kn Chinese Std. Type G8300ZC 1 x 4 Stroke 8 Cy. 300 x 380 2000kW (2719bhp) Wuxi Antai Power Machinery Co Ltd-China AuxGen: 3 x 160kW 400V a.c
9136515 *YDPV* -	**SINAR ANYER** *ex* Eastern Fellow *-2000* **PT Samudera Shipping Services** PT Samudera Indonesia Ship Management (PT SISM) *Jakarta* *Indonesia* MMSI: 525009039 Official number: 4060/L	**1,772** 695 2,780 T/cm 8.8	Class: KI NK	**1996-01 Hitachi Zosen Mukaishima Marine Co Ltd — Onomichi HS** Yd No: 103 Loa 84.35 (BB) Br ex 13.02 Dght 5.290 Lbp 78.50 Br md 13.00 Dpth 6.20 Welded, 1 dk	**(A12B2TR) Chemical/Products Tanker** Double Bottom Entire Compartment Length Liq: 2,531; Liq (Oil): 2,531 Compartments: 8 Wing Ta, 1 Slop Ta, Wing ER 8 Cargo Pump (s): 6x250m³/hr, 2x100m³/hr Manifold: Bow/CM: 35.5m	**1 oil engine** driving 1 FP propeller Total Power: 2,405kW (3,270hp) 13.5kn B&W 6S26MC 1 x 2 Stroke 6 Cy. 260 x 980 2405kW (3270bhp) The Hanshin Diesel Works Ltd-Japan Fuel: 50.0 (d.f.) 220.0 (r.f.)
8010295 *YHEX* -	**SINAR ARROW** *ex* Charlotte Sif *-2002* *ex* Salif Bay *-1994* *ex* Lotte Sif *-1993* *ex* C.R. Kourou *-1992* *ex* Lotte Sif *-1990* *ex* Lotte Scheel *-1989* **PT Salam Pacific Indonesia Lines** - *Jakarta* *Indonesia* MMSI: 525017036	**4,317** 1,730 4,486	Class: KI (NV)	**1981-12 Orskov Christensens Staalskibsvaerft A/S — Frederikshavn** Yd No: 120 Loa 102.49 (BB) Br ex 17.04 Dght 5.411 Lbp 92.61 Br md 17.01 Dpth 9.02 Welded, 2 dks	**(A31A2GX) General Cargo Ship** Grain: 9,466; Bale: 8,614 TEU 352 C.Ho 140/20' C.Dk 212/20' incl. 40 ref C. Compartments: 2 Ho, ER, 2 Tw Dk 2 Ha: (25.9 x 12.8) (39.0 x 12.8)ER Cranes: 2x80t Ice Capable	**1 oil engine** with flexible couplings & sr gearedto sc. shaft driving 1 CP propeller Total Power: 2,700kW (3,671hp) 13.5kn MaK 9M453AK 1 x 4 Stroke 9 Cy. 320 x 420 2700kW (3671bhp) Krupp MaK Maschinenbau GmbH-Kiel AuxGen: 1 x 304kW 380V 50Hz a.c, 3 x 264kW 380V 50Hz a.c Thrusters: 1 Thwart. CP thruster (f)
9052422 - -	**SINAR BAHAGIA 01** *ex* Rimba Megah XXIV *-2002* *ex* Ewis Dynamic *-1999* **PT Mustika Bahari** - *Pontianak* *Indonesia*	**150** 90 167	Class: KI (NK)	**1992-01 Nam Cheong Dockyard Sdn Bhd — Miri** Yd No: 376 L reg 25.00 Br ex Dght 2.850 Lbp 23.35 Br md 7.30 Dpth 3.55 Welded	**(B32A2ST) Tug**	**2 oil engines** geared to sc. shafts driving 2 FP propellers Total Power: 736kW (1,000hp) Cummins KTA-19-M 2 x 4 Stroke 6 Cy. 159 x 159 each-368kW (500bhp) Cummins Engine Co Inc-USA AuxGen: 2 x 30kW a.c
9352432 *9V9470* -	**SINAR BANDUNG** **Samudera Shipping Line Ltd** Apex Ship Management Pte Ltd *Singapore* *Singapore* MMSI: 566127000 Official number: 397130	**12,584** 5,618 14,984 T/cm 28.7	Class: NK (BV)	**2005-06 Hakata Zosen K.K. — Imabari** Yd No: 668 Loa 147.00 (BB) Br ex - Dght 8.960 Lbp 135.45 Br md 25.00 Dpth 13.70 Welded, 1 dk	**(A33A2CC) Container Ship (Fully Cellular)** TEU 1060 C Ho 444 TEU C Dk 616 TEU incl 104 ref C. Cranes: 2x40t	**1 oil engine** driving 1 FP propeller Total Power: 9,988kW (13,580hp) 18.0kn B&W 7S50MC 1 x 2 Stroke 7 Cy. 500 x 1910 9988kW (13580bhp) Mitsui Engineering & Shipbuilding CLtd-Japan AuxGen: 3 x a.c Thrusters: 1 Tunnel thruster (f) Fuel: 1320.0
9220304 *9V9093* -	**SINAR BANGKA** **Iseaco Pte Ltd** Iseaco Shipmanagement Pte Ltd *Singapore* *Singapore* MMSI: 564820000 Official number: 396622	**12,563** 5,336 15,236 T/cm 28.7	Class: BV	**2000-02 Hakata Zosen K.K. — Imabari** Yd No: 616 Loa 147.00 (BB) Br ex - Dght 8.960 Lbp 135.00 Br md 25.00 Dpth 13.70 Welded, 1 dk	**(A33A2CC) Container Ship (Fully Cellular)** TEU 1060 C Ho 444 TEU C Dk 616 TEU incl 104 ref C. Compartments: 4 Cell Ho Cranes: 2	**1 oil engine** driving 1 FP propeller Total Power: 9,989kW (13,581hp) 18.0kn B&W 7S50MC 1 x 2 Stroke 7 Cy. 500 x 1910 9989kW (13581bhp) Mitsui Engineering & Shipbuilding CLtd-Japan AuxGen: 3 x 560kW 440/100V 60Hz a.c Thrusters: 1 Tunnel thruster (f)
9441740 *3EQD5* -	**SINAR BANTEN** **Asian Shipping SA** Meiho Kaiun KK (Meiho Kaiun Co Ltd) *Panama* *Panama* MMSI: 351325000 Official number: 3377708A	**12,598** 5,614 14,978 T/cm 28.7	Class: NK	**2008-04 Hakata Zosen K.K. — Imabari** Yd No: 682 Loa 147.00 (BB) Br ex - Dght 8.965 Lbp 135.45 Br md 25.00 Dpth 13.70 Welded, 1 dk	**(A33A2CC) Container Ship (Fully Cellular)** TEU 1060 C Ho 444 TEU C Dk 616 TEU incl 104 ref C. Cranes: 2x40t	**1 oil engine** driving 1 FP propeller Total Power: 9,988kW (13,580hp) 19.3kn MAN-B&W 7S50MC-C 1 x 2 Stroke 7 Cy. 500 x 2000 9988kW (13580bhp) Mitsui Engineering & Shipbuilding CLtd-Japan AuxGen: 3 x a.c Thrusters: 1 Tunnel thruster (f) Fuel: 1320.0
9101560 *3FEG5* -	**SINAR BIAK** *ex* Kuo Lih *-2006* **Evershine Shipping SA** Samudera Shipping Line Ltd *Panama* *Panama* MMSI: 355136000 Official number: 2215895E	**15,184** 6,261 18,421 T/cm 35.9	Class: NK (LR) Classed LR until 16/9/03	**1995-06 Imabari Shipbuilding Co Ltd — Imabari EH (Imabari Shipyard)** Yd No: 513 Loa 166.67 (BB) Br ex 27.25 Dght 8.350 Lbp 158.00 Br md 27.20 Dpth 13.60 Welded, 1 dk	**(A33A2CC) Container Ship (Fully Cellular)** TEU 1441 C Ho 566 TEU C Dk 875 TEU incl 42 ref C. Compartments: 4 Cell Ho, ER 4 Ha: ER	**1 oil engine** driving 1 FP propeller Total Power: 8,128kW (11,051hp) 17.0kn B&W 7S50MC 1 x 2 Stroke 7 Cy. 500 x 1910 8128kW (11051bhp) Hitachi Zosen Corp-Japan AuxGen: 3 x 460kW 440V 60Hz a.c Fuel: 174.4 (d.f.) 1520.8 (r.f.) 33.1pd

9397107 *9VFV7* -	**SINAR BIMA** *launched as* Trinity Bay *-2008* **Samudera Shipping Line Ltd** - - *Singapore* *Singapore* MMSI: 564437000 Official number: 393843	**9,957** 5,020 13,632 T/cm 28.0	Class: GL NK	**2008-01 Taizhou Kouan Shipbuilding Co Ltd — Taizhou JS** Yd No: KA408 Loa 147.87 (BB) Br ex 23.45 Dght 8.510 Lbp 140.30 Br md 23.25 Dpth 11.50 Welded, 1 dk	**(A33A2CC) Container Ship (Fully Cellular)** Grain: 16,067; Bale: 15,745 TEU 1118 C Ho 334 TEU C Dk 784 incl 240 ref C Compartments: 5 Ho, ER 7 Ha: ER Cranes: 2x45t Ice Capable	**1 oil engine** reduction geared to sc. shaft driving 1 CP propeller Total Power: 9,730kW (13,229hp) 19.6kn MAN-B&W 7L58/64 1 x 4 Stroke 7 Cy. 580 x 640 9730kW (13229bhp) MAN B&W Diesel AG-Augsburg AuxGen: 2 x 400kW 440V a.c, 1 x 1400kW 440V a.c Thrusters: 1 Tunnel thruster (f) Fuel: 1640.0
9250957 *9V9257* -	**SINAR BINTAN** **Samudera Shipping Line Ltd** - *Singapore* *Singapore* MMSI: 563984000 Official number: 396843	**12,563** 5,336 14,971 T/cm 28.7	Class: BV	**2002-03 Hakata Zosen K.K. — Imabari** Yd No: 633 Loa 144.00 (BB) Br ex - Dght 8.960 Lbp 135.00 Br md 25.00 Dpth 13.70 Welded, 1 dk	**(A33A2CC) Container Ship (Fully Cellular)** TEU 1060 C Ho 444 TEU C Dk 616 TEU incl 104 ref C. Cranes: 2x40t	**1 oil engine** driving 1 FP propeller Total Power: 9,988kW (13,580hp) 18.0kn B&W 7S50MC 1 x 2 Stroke 7 Cy. 500 x 1910 9988kW (13580bhp) Mitsui Engineering & Shipbuilding CLtd-Japan AuxGen: 3 x 560kW 440/100V 60Hz a.c Thrusters: 1 Tunnel thruster (f) Fuel: 1343.0
9052434 *YD4933* -	**SINAR BINTANG SAKTI** *ex* Ocean Star *-2003* *ex* Sarana Dua *-2000* **PT Sinar Bintang Sakti** - *Jakarta* *Indonesia*	**115** 69 -	Class: KI (GL) (NK)	**1992-01 Zarah Sdn Bhd — Tawau** Yd No: 040 Loa 22.70 Br ex - Dght 2.250 Lbp 21.34 Br md 7.50 Dpth 3.20 Welded, 1 dk	**(B32A2ST) Tug**	**2 oil engines** reduction geared to sc. shafts driving 2 FP propellers Total Power: 514kW (698hp) 9.0kn Caterpillar 3408TA 2 x Vee 4 Stroke 8 Cy. 137 x 152 each-257kW (349bhp) Caterpillar Inc-USA
9412799 *3ELD8* -	**SINAR BITUNG** **Twin Bright Shipping Co SA** Soki Kisen KK *Panama* *Panama* MMSI: 372925000 Official number: 3288907A	**13,596** 7,536 17,815 T/cm 32.0	Class: NK	**2007-07 Imabari Shipbuilding Co Ltd — Imabari EH (Imabari Shipyard)** Yd No: 647 Loa 161.85 (BB) Br ex - Dght 9.065 Lbp 150.00 Br md 25.60 Dpth 12.90 Welded, 1 dk	**(A33A2CC) Container Ship (Fully Cellular)** TEU 1032 C Ho 496 TEU C Dk 536 TEU incl 100 ref C Compartments: 4 Cell Ho, ER 8 Ha: ER	**1 oil engine** driving 1 FP propeller Total Power: 12,640kW (17,185hp) 19.4kn MAN-B&W 8S50MC-C 1 x 2 Stroke 8 Cy. 500 x 2000 12640kW (17185bhp) Mitsui Engineering & Shipbuilding CLtd-Japan AuxGen: 3 x a.c Thrusters: 1 Tunnel thruster (f) Fuel: 1392.0
9065118 *PMNJ* -	**SINAR BONTANG** *ex* Joo Yang *-2002* **PT Samudera Shipping Services** PT Samudera Indonesia Ship Management (PT SISM) *Jakarta* *Indonesia* MMSI: 525009050	**1,990** 1,035 3,786 T/cm 9.8	Class: KI KR	**1992-06 Cheunggu Marine Industry Co Ltd — Ulsan** Yd No: 1078 Loa 86.50 (BB) Br ex 14.00 Dght 5.912 Lbp 78.30 Br md 14.00 Dpth 6.70 Welded, 1 dk	**(A12B2TR) Chemical/Products Tanker** Double Bottom Entire Compartment Length Liq: 3,755; Liq (Oil): 3,755 Compartments: 10 Wing Ta, ER, 2 Wing Slop Ta 10 Cargo Pump (s): 10x100m³/hr Manifold: Bow/CM: 43.8m	**1 oil engine** geared to sc. shaft driving 1 FP propeller Total Power: 1,681kW (2,285hp) 12.0kn Alpha 8L28/32 1 x 4 Stroke 8 Cy. 280 x 320 1681kW (2285bhp) (made 1991) Ssangyong Heavy Industries Co Ltd-South Korea AuxGen: 3 x 206kW 450V a.c Fuel: 30.0 (d.f.) 100.0 (r.f.)
9522788 *3FWZ7* -	**SINAR BRANI** **Hiro Shipping (Panama) SA** Fukusei Sangyo KK *Panama* *Panama* MMSI: 357200000 Official number: 4161710	**12,559** 5,618 15,204 T/cm 28.7	Class: BV	**2010-06 Hakata Zosen K.K. — Imabari** Yd No: 711 Loa 147.00 (BB) Br ex - Dght 8.960 Lbp 135.00 Br md 25.00 Dpth 13.70 Welded, 1 dk	**(A33A2CC) Container Ship (Fully Cellular)** TEU 1060 C Ho 444 TEU C Dk 616 TEU incl 104 ref C.	**1 oil engine** driving 1 FP propeller Total Power: 9,988kW (13,580hp) 18.0kn MAN-B&W 7S50MC 1 x 2 Stroke 7 Cy. 500 x 1910 9988kW (13580bhp) Mitsui Engineering & Shipbuilding CLtd-Japan AuxGen: 3 x 560kW 60Hz a.c Thrusters: 1 Tunnel thruster (f)
9441764 *3FQO7* -	**SINAR BROMO** *ex* Hakata 685 *-2009* **Seiun Shipping SA & Tsurumi Kisen Co Ltd** Tsurumi Kisen Co Ltd *Panama* *Panama* MMSI: 355732000 Official number: 38441KJ	**12,545** 5,614 15,208 T/cm 28.7	Class: NK	**2009-01 Hakata Zosen K.K. — Imabari** Yd No: 685 Loa 147.00 (BB) Br ex - Dght 8.960 Lbp 135.45 Br md 25.00 Dpth 13.70 Welded, 1 dk	**(A33A2CC) Container Ship (Fully Cellular)** TEU 1060 C Ho 444 TEU C Dk 616 TEU incl 104 ref C.	**1 oil engine** driving 1 FP propeller Total Power: 9,988kW (13,580hp) 18.0kn MAN-B&W 7S50MC 1 x 2 Stroke 7 Cy. 500 x 1910 9988kW (13580bhp) Mitsui Engineering & Shipbuilding CLtd-Japan AuxGen: 3 x a.c Thrusters: 1 Tunnel thruster (f)
9010113 *PMMZ* -	**SINAR BUKOM** *ex* Miyuki *-2003* **PT Samudera Shipping Services** PT Samudera Indonesia Ship Management (PT SISM) *Jakarta* *Indonesia* MMSI: 525009048 Official number: 2008 PST NO.5308/L	**2,025** 959 3,097 T/cm 9.4	Class: KI NK	**1990-09 Yamanaka Zosen K.K. — Imabari** Yd No: 503 Loa 84.30 (BB) Br ex - Dght 5.616 Lbp 79.00 Br md 14.00 Dpth 6.70 Welded, 1dk	**(A12B2TR) Chemical/Products Tanker** Double Bottom Entire Compartment Length Liq: 3,611; Liq (Oil): 3,611 Cargo Heating Coils Compartments: 4 Ta, 12 Wing Ta, ER 6 Cargo Pump (s): 6x200m³/hr Manifold: Bow/CM: 40.5m	**1 oil engine** driving 1 FP propeller Total Power: 1,912kW (2,600hp) 12.0kn Akasaka A37 1 x 4 Stroke 6 Cy. 370 x 720 1912kW (2600bhp) Akasaka Tekkosho KK (Akasaka DieselLtd)-Japan AuxGen: 3 x 176kW 445V 60Hz a.c Fuel: 41.0 (d.f.) 185.0 (r.f.)
9346483 *POEL* -	**SINAR BUSAN** *completed as* Clipper Kikki *-2006* **PT Samudera Shipping Services** - *Jakarta* *Indonesia* MMSI: 525009075	**7,687** 3,266 11,277 T/cm 20.6	Class: AB KI	**2006-07 STX Shipbuilding Co Ltd — Busan** Yd No: 5014 Loa 116.50 (BB) Br ex - Dght 8.400 Lbp 109.00 Br md 20.00 Dpth 11.70 Welded, 1 dk	**(A12B2TR) Chemical/Products Tanker** Double Hull (13F) Liq: 12,250; Liq (Oil): 12,250 Cargo Heating Coils Compartments: 10 Wing Ta, ER, 2 Wing Slop Ta 10 Cargo Pump (s): 10x300m³/hr Manifold: Bow/CM: 52.7m	**1 oil engine** driving 1 FP propeller Total Power: 4,440kW (6,037hp) 13.6kn MAN-B&W 6S35MC 1 x 2 Stroke 6 Cy. 350 x 1400 4440kW (6037bhp) STX Engine Co Ltd-South Korea AuxGen: 3 x 450kW 450V a.c Thrusters: 1 Tunnel thruster (f) Fuel: 91.0 (d.f.) 829.0 (r.f.)
9441752 *3FRF4* -	**SINAR BUTON** **Southern Route Maritime SA** Nissen Kaiun Co Ltd (Nissen Kaiun KK) *Panama* *Panama* MMSI: 370700000 Official number: 4001108	**12,545** 5,614 15,210 T/cm 28.7	Class: NK	**2008-10 Hakata Zosen K.K. — Imabari** Yd No: 683 Loa 147.00 (BB) Br ex - Dght 8.960 Lbp 135.45 Br md 25.00 Dpth 13.70 Welded, 1 dk	**(A33A2CC) Container Ship (Fully Cellular)** TEU 1060 C Ho 444 TEU C Dk 616 TEU incl 104 ref C.	**1 oil engine** driving 1 FP propeller Total Power: 9,988kW (13,580hp) 17.5kn MAN-B&W 7S50MC 1 x 2 Stroke 7 Cy. 500 x 1910 9988kW (13580bhp) Mitsui Engineering & Shipbuilding CLtd-Japan AuxGen: 4 x 440kW a.c Thrusters: 1 Tunnel thruster (f) Fuel: 1320.0
7649398 *YDAD* -	**SINAR DELI** *ex* Susanna *-2001* *ex* Susana *-1982* *ex* Daifuku Maru *-1981* **PT Pelayaran Dillah Laut Pasifik** - *Jakarta* *Indonesia*	**936** 527 1,770	Class: (KI)	**1970-08 Yamanaka Zosen K.K. — Imabari** Loa 62.75 Br ex - Dght 4.471 Lbp 57.00 Br md 10.00 Dpth 6.10 Welded, 2dks	**(A31A2GX) General Cargo Ship** Grain: 2,040; Bale: 1,877 1 Ha: (33.0 x 6.4)ER	**1 oil engine** driving 1 FP propeller Total Power: 883kW (1,201hp) 11.8kn Niigata 6MG28DHS 1 x 4 Stroke 6 Cy. 280 x 440 883kW (1201bhp) Niigata Engineering Co Ltd-Japan
9382011 *YEPL* -	**SINAR DEMAK** **PT Samudera Shipping Services** PT Samudera Indonesia Ship Management (PT SISM) *Jakarta* *Indonesia* MMSI: 525009041 Official number: 2346/BA	**2,656** 797 4,370	Class: KI (AB)	**2006-05 PT Dok dan Perkapalan Surabaya (Persero) — Surabaya** Yd No: 05595 Loa 86.03 Br ex - Dght 3.980 Lbp 82.74 Br md 20.00 Dpth 5.67 Welded, 1 dk	**(A31C2GD) Deck Cargo Ship** TEU 265	**2 oil engines** driving 3 gen. each 100kW a.c reduction geared to sc. shafts driving 2 Directional propellers Total Power: 2,206kW (3,000hp) 14.0kn Caterpillar 3512B 2 x Vee 4 Stroke 12 Cy. 170 x 190 each-1103kW (1500bhp) Caterpillar Inc-USA AuxGen: 3 x 120kW 380V a.c Fuel: 248.5 (d.f.)
9178238 *PNMR* -	**SINAR EMAS** **PT Samudera Shipping Services** PT Samudera Indonesia Ship Management (PT SISM) *Jakarta* *Indonesia* MMSI: 525009063	**13,960** 4,722 18,010 T/cm 39.2	Class: KI LR ✠ **100A1** SS 04/2010 Double Hull oil tanker ESP LI ✠ **LMC** Eq.Ltr: G†; Cable: 577.5/68.0 U2	**2000-04 Jiangdu Yuehai Shipbuilding Co Ltd — Jiangdu JS** Yd No: 17500-001 Loa 160.00 (BB) Br ex 27.02 Dght 7.000 Lbp 153.00 Br md 27.00 Dpth 11.70 Welded, 1 dk	**(A13B2TP) Products Tanker** Double Hull (13F) Liq: 17,418; Liq (Oil): 17,418 Compartments: 12 Wing Ta, ER, 2 Wing Slop Ta 3 Cargo Pump (s): 3x600m³/hr	**1 oil engine** driving 1 FP propeller Total Power: 4,900kW (6,662hp) 13.0kn B&W 7S35MC 1 x 2 Stroke 7 Cy. 350 x 1400 4900kW (6662bhp) Yichang Marine Diesel Engine Co Ltd-China AuxGen: 3 x 510kW 400V 50Hz a.c Boilers: AuxB (Comp) 9.0kgf/cm² (8.8bar) Fuel: 860.0 (r.f.)
7703728 *YHWP* -	**SINAR ENDE** *ex* Sejahtera Satu *-2009* *ex* Gigi *-2003* *ex* Castor *-1995* *ex* Fuensanta del Mar *-1994* **PT Mitra Lautan Nusantara** - *Jakarta* *Indonesia*	**1,766** 814 2,600	Class: (GL) (KI)	**1979-03 Ast. y Talleres Celaya S.A. — Bilbao** Yd No: 163 Loa 85.71 Br ex 13.24 Dght 5.161 Lbp 78.01 Br md 13.21 Dpth 6.38 Welded, 1 dk	**(A31A2GX) General Cargo Ship** TEU 85 C. 85/20' incl. 56 ref C. Compartments: 1 Ho, ER 1 Ha: (58.6 x 10.4)	**1 oil engine** geared to sc. shaft driving 1 FP propeller Total Power: 1,471kW (2,000hp) 14.5kn Deutz RBV6M358 1 x 4 Stroke 6 Cy. 400 x 580 1471kW (2000bhp) Hijos de J Barreras SA-Spain AuxGen: 1 x 623kW 380/220V
7852983 - -	**SINAR FAJAR 7** *ex* Sinar Mustika *-2006* *ex* Sungai Musi *-2005* *ex* Toyo Maru No. 17 *-1992* *ex* Kasuga Maru No. 2 *-1983* **PT Sarana Bahari Prima** - *Jakarta* *Indonesia*	*877* 427 1,350	Class: KI	**1977-03 K.K. Yoshida Zosen Kogyo — Arida** Loa 60.30 Br ex - Dght 3.760 Lbp 55.00 Br md 10.41 Dpth 5.69 Welded, 1 dk	**(A31A2GX) General Cargo Ship**	**1 oil engine** driving 1 FP propeller Total Power: 883kW (1,201hp) 11.0kn Makita 1 x 4 Stroke 883kW (1201bhp) Makita Diesel Co Ltd-Japan

8113839 *YGZX* -	**SINAR HARAPAN 78** *ex* Amami Fortuna *-2008* *ex* Manbo No. 1 *-2001* *ex* Big Eight *-1999* **Tuan Andi Kangnata** - *Surabaya* *Indonesia* MMSI: 525019114	**3,274** 1,391 3,973	Class: KI (NK)	**1982**-04 **Hakata Zosen K.K. — Imabari** Yd No: 263 Loa 87.28 Br ex - Dght 5.900 Lbp 81.01 Br md 14.51 Dpth 9.90 Welded, 2 dks	**(A31A2GX) General Cargo Ship** Grain: 7,625; Bale: 7,084 Compartments: 2 Ho, ER 2 Ha: ER Derricks: 1x15t,2x10t	**1 oil engine** driving 1 FP propeller Total Power: 1,471kW (2,000hp) 11.0kn Hanshin 6EL32 1 x 4 Stroke 6 Cy. 320 x 640 1471kW (2000bhp) The Hanshin Diesel Works Ltd-Japan AuxGen: 2 x 120kW 440V 60Hz a.c Fuel: 42.0 (d.f.) 259.5 (r.f.) 6.5pd
8842820 - -	**SINAR INTAN** - **PT Pelayaran Mustika Andalas** - *Indonesia*	*386* 198 -		**1989** Loa - Br ex - Dght - Lbp - Br md - Dpth - Welded, 1 dk	**(A31A2GX) General Cargo Ship**	**1 oil engine** driving 1 FP propeller
9382023 *YEBN* -	**SINAR JAMBI** **PT Samudera Shipping Services** PT Samudera Indonesia Ship Management (PT SISM) *Jakarta* *Indonesia* MMSI: 525009040 Official number: 2338/BA	**2,656** 797 4,353	Class: KI (AB)	**2006**-04 **PT Dok dan Perkapalan Surabaya (Persero) — Surabaya** Yd No: 05596 Loa 86.03 Br ex - Dght 3.980 Lbp 82.74 Br md 20.00 Dpth 5.70 Welded, 1 dk	**(A31C2GD) Deck Cargo Ship** TEU 265	**2 oil engines** reduction geared to sc. shafts driving 2 Directional propellers Total Power: 2,206kW (3,000hp) 13.0kn Caterpillar 3512B 2 x Vee 4 Stroke 12 Cy. 170 x 190 each-1103kW (1500bhp) Caterpillar Inc-USA AuxGen: 3 x 120kW 380V a.c Fuel: 248.5 (d.f.)
8987993 - -	**SINAR JAYA** - **Sutopo** - *Samarinda* *Indonesia*	**121** 72 -	Class: KI	**2002 C.V. Teknik Jaya Industri — Samarinda** Loa 23.50 Br ex - Dght - Lbp 20.20 Br md 6.50 Dpth 3.10 Welded, 1 dk	**(B32A2ST) Tug**	**2 oil engines** geared to sc. shafts driving 2 Propellers Total Power: 736kW (1,000hp) Mitsubishi 10DC11-1A 2 x Vee 4 Stroke 10 Cy. 141 x 152 each-368kW (500bhp) Mitsubishi Heavy Industries Ltd-Japan AuxGen: 2 x 60kW 400/200V a.c
9387669 *POBC* -	**SINAR JEPARA** *ex* SITC Busan *-2011* **PT Samudera Shipping Services** - *Jakarta* *Indonesia* MMSI: 525009573	**4,632** 2,306 6,300	Class: KI (IZ)	**2006**-06 **Zhejiang Shenzhou Shipbuilding Co Ltd — Xiangshan County ZJ** Loa 118.60 (BB) Br ex - Dght 6.150 Lbp 109.19 Br md 16.20 Dpth 7.80 Welded, 1 dk	**(A33A2CC) Container Ship (Fully Cellular)** TEU 378	**1 oil engine** reduction geared to sc. shaft driving 1 FP propeller Total Power: 2,500kW (3,399hp) 12.0kn Daihatsu 8DKM-28 1 x 4 Stroke 8 Cy. 280 x 390 2500kW (3399bhp) Shaanxi Diesel Heavy Industry Co Lt-China AuxGen: 3 x 240kW 55V a.c
9378010 *POBD* -	**SINAR JIMBARAN** *ex* SITC Yantai *-2011* *completed as* Yan Tai *-2006* **PT Samudera Shipping Services** - *Jakarta* *Indonesia* MMSI: 525009074	**4,632** 2,306 6,300	Class: IZ KI	**2006**-02 **Ningbo Boda Shipbuilding Co Ltd — Xiangshan County ZJ** Yd No: SJ05-401 Loa 118.60 (BB) Br ex - Dght 6.150 Lbp 109.19 Br md 16.20 Dpth 7.80 Welded, 1 dk	**(A33A2CC) Container Ship (Fully Cellular)** TEU 378 incl 60 ref C	**1 oil engine** reduction geared to sc. shaft driving 1 FP propeller Total Power: 2,500kW (3,399hp) 12.0kn Daihatsu 8DKM-28 1 x 4 Stroke 8 Cy. 280 x 390 2500kW (3399bhp) Shaanxi Diesel Heavy Industry Co Lt-China AuxGen: 3 x 240kW 400V a.c
9178240 *PNTC* -	**SINAR JOGYA** - **PT Samudera Shipping Services** PT Samudera Indonesia Ship Management (PT SISM) *Jakarta* *Indonesia* MMSI: 525009064	**13,960** 4,722 18,050 T/cm 39.2	Class: KI LR ✠ **100A1** SS 01/2011 Double Hull oil tanker ESP LI ✠ **LMC** Eq.Ltr: G†; Cable: 577.5/68.0 U2	**2001**-01 **Jiangdu Yuehai Shipbuilding Co Ltd — Jiangdu JS** Yd No: 17500-002 Loa 160.00 (BB) Br ex 27.02 Dght 7.000 Lbp 153.00 Br md 27.00 Dpth 11.70 Welded, 1 dk	**(A13B2TP) Products Tanker** Double Hull (13F) Liq: 24,685; Liq (Oil): 24,685 Compartments: 12 Wing Ta, ER, 2 Wing Slop Ta 3 Cargo Pump (s): 3x600m³/hr	**1 oil engine** driving 1 FP propeller Total Power: 4,670kW (6,349hp) 13.0kn B&W 7S35MC 1 x 2 Stroke 7 Cy. 350 x 1400 4670kW (6349bhp) Yichang Marine Diesel Engine Co Ltd-China AuxGen: 3 x 510kW 400V 50Hz a.c Boilers: AuxB (Comp) 9.1kgf/cm² (8.9bar) Fuel: 133.0 (d.f.) 957.0 (r.f.)
9036870 *PMMS* -	**SINAR JOHOR** *ex* Eastern Bliss *-2006* **PT Samudera Shipping Services** PT Samudera Indonesia Ship Management (PT SISM) *Jakarta* *Indonesia* MMSI: 525009047 Official number: 2008 PST NO.5307/L	**2,025** 959 3,098 T/cm 9.4	Class: KI NK	**1991**-07 **Yamanaka Zosen K.K. — Imabari** Yd No: 512 Loa 84.30 (BB) Br ex 14.00 Dght 5.597 Lbp 79.00 Br md 14.00 Dpth 6.70 Welded, 1 dk	**(A12B2TR) Chemical/Products Tanker** Double Bottom Entire Compartment Length Liq: 3,538; Liq (Oil): 3,538 Compartments: 4 Ta, 12 Wing Ta, ER 6 Cargo Pump (s): 6x200m³/hr Manifold: Bow/CM: 40.5m	**1 oil engine** driving 1 FP propeller Total Power: 1,912kW (2,600hp) 12.0kn Akasaka A37 1 x 4 Stroke 6 Cy. 370 x 720 1912kW (2600bhp) Akasaka Tekkosho KK (Akasaka DieselLtd)-Japan AuxGen: 2 x a.c Fuel: 12.8 (d.f.) 163.0 (r.f.)
9494151 *9V9264* -	**SINAR KAPUAS** - **Foremost Maritime Pte Ltd** PT Samudera Indonesia Ship Management (PT SISM) *Singapore* *Singapore* MMSI: 564136000 Official number: 396850	**33,348** 19,342 57,374 T/cm 57.3	Class: LR ✠ **100A1** SS 04/2011 bulk carrier CSR BC-A GRAB (20) Nos. 2 & 4 holds may be empty ESP **ShipRight** (CM,ACS (B) *IWS LI ✠ **LMC** **UMS** Eq.Ltr: N†; Cable: 660.0/76.0 U3 (a)	**2011**-03 **STX Offshore & Shipbuilding Co Ltd — Changwon (Jinhae Shipyard)** Yd No: 1339 Loa 190.00 (BB) Br ex 32.26 Dght 13.000 Lbp 183.30 Br md 32.26 Dpth 18.50 Welded, 1 dk	**(A21A2BC) Bulk Carrier** Grain: 71,850 Compartments: 5 Ho, ER 5 Ha: ER Cranes: 4x30t	**1 oil engine** driving 1 FP propeller Total Power: 9,480kW (12,889hp) 14.5kn MAN-B&W 6S50MC-C 1 x 2 Stroke 6 Cy. 500 x 2000 9480kW (12889bhp) STX Engine Co Ltd-South Korea AuxGen: 3 x 625kW 450V 60Hz a.c Boilers: AuxB (Comp) 9.2kgf/cm² (9.0bar)
9172507 *YGFH* -	**SINAR KUDUS** - **PT Samudera Indonesia Tbk** - SatCom: Inmarsat C 435722510 *Jakarta* *Indonesia* MMSI: 525009027 Official number: 2000-PST1953/L	**7,717** 2,697 8,911	Class: KI NK	**1999**-02 **Shin Kochi Jyuko K.K. — Kochi** Yd No: 7110 Loa 113.22 (BB) Br ex - Dght 7.290 Lbp 105.40 Br md 19.60 Dpth 13.20 Welded, 2 dks	**(A31A2GX) General Cargo Ship** Grain: 16,822; Bale: 15,176 Compartments: 2 Ho, ER 2 Ha: (33.6 x 14.8) (20.3 x 14.8)ER Cranes: 2x30t; Derricks: 1x25t	**1 oil engine** driving 1 FP propeller Total Power: 3,883kW (5,279hp) 13.5kn B&W 6L35MC 1 x 2 Stroke 6 Cy. 350 x 1050 3883kW (5279bhp) Makita Corp-Japan Fuel: 780.0
9699490 *YDB4497* -	**SINAR KUMALA 138** - **PT Sinar Tanjung** - *Pontianak* *Indonesia*	**138** 42 72	Class: NK	**2014**-02 **Rajang Maju Shipbuilding Sdn Bhd — Sibu** Yd No: RMM0061 Loa 23.50 Br ex - Dght 2.400 Lbp 21.17 Br md 7.32 Dpth 3.05 Welded, 1 dk	**(B32A2ST) Tug**	**2 oil engines** reduction geared to sc. shafts driving 2 Propellers Total Power: 970kW (1,318hp) Yanmar 6AYM-WST 2 x 4 Stroke 6 Cy. 155 x 180 each-485kW (659bhp) Yanmar Diesel Engine Co Ltd-Japan
9494149 *9V9263* -	**SINAR KUTAI** - **Foremost Maritime Pte Ltd** PT Samudera Indonesia Ship Management (PT SISM) SatCom: Inmarsat C 456413210 *Singapore* *Singapore* MMSI: 564132000 Official number: 396849	**33,348** 19,342 57,334 T/cm 57.3	Class: LR ✠ **100A1** SS 03/2011 bulk carrier CSR BC-A GRAB (20) Nos. 2 & 4 holds may be empty ESP **ShipRight** (ACS (B),CM) *IWS LI ✠ **LMC** **UMS** Eq.Ltr: N†; Cable: 660.0/76.0 U3 (a)	**2011**-02 **STX Offshore & Shipbuilding Co Ltd — Changwon (Jinhae Shipyard)** Yd No: 1334 Loa 190.00 (BB) Br ex 32.26 Dght 13.000 Lbp 183.30 Br md 32.26 Dpth 18.50 Welded, 1 dk	**(A21A2BC) Bulk Carrier** Grain: 71,850 Compartments: 5 Ho, ER 5 Ha: ER Cranes: 4x30t	**1 oil engine** driving 1 FP propeller Total Power: 9,480kW (12,889hp) 14.5kn MAN-B&W 6S50MC-C 1 x 2 Stroke 6 Cy. 500 x 2000 9480kW (12889bhp) STX Engine Co Ltd-South Korea AuxGen: 3 x 625kW 450V 60Hz a.c Boilers: AuxB (Comp) 9.3kgf/cm² (9.1bar)
9085156 *PMST* -	**SINAR LABUAN** *ex* Unam Poseidon *-2003* **PT Samudera Shipping Services** PT Samudera Indonesia Ship Management (PT SISM) *Jakarta* *Indonesia* MMSI: 525009052	**1,994** 1,078 3,519 T/cm 9.8	Class: KI KR	**1994**-05 **Cheunggu Marine Industry Co Ltd — Ulsan** Yd No: 1086 Loa 85.30 (BB) Br ex - Dght 5.613 Lbp 78.61 Br md 14.00 Dpth 6.60 Welded, 1 dk	**(A12B2TR) Chemical/Products Tanker** Double Bottom Entire Compartment Length Liq: 3,927; Liq (Oil): 3,927 Cargo Heating Coils Compartments: 10 Wing Ta, 1 Slop Ta, ER 2 Cargo Pump (s): 2x400m³/hr Manifold: Bow/CM: 44.6m	**1 oil engine** driving 3 gen. each 250kW 480V a.c driving 1 FP propeller Total Power: 1,618kW (2,200hp) 12.0kn Akasaka A34 1 x 4 Stroke 6 Cy. 340 x 660 1618kW (2200bhp) Hyundai Heavy Industries Co Ltd-South Korea AuxGen: 3 x 227kW 480V a.c Fuel: 32.6 (d.f.) 131.0 (r.f.)
8738794 - -	**SINAR LANCAR 1** - **PT Guna Karya Samudera** - *Pontianak* *Indonesia*	**165** 50 -	Class: KI	**2008 CV Bina Citra — Pontianak** Loa 23.00 Br ex - Dght - Lbp 21.66 Br md 7.30 Dpth 3.60 Welded, 1 dk	**(B32A2ST) Tug**	**2 oil engines** driving 2 Propellers Total Power: 728kW (990hp) Mitsubishi S6N-MPTK 2 x 4 Stroke 6 Cy. 160 x 180 each-364kW (495bhp) Mitsubishi Heavy Industries Ltd-Japan

Ship / Owner	Tonnage	Class	Builder / Dimensions	Type	Machinery
9646596 **SINAR LESTARI 9** - - **PT Pelayaran Sinar Gratia Nusantara** - *Batam* *Indonesia*	**185** 56 -	Class: BV	**2011**-12 **PT Bandar Abadi — Batam** Yd No: 133 Loa 26.00 Br ex - Dght 3.000 Lbp 23.68 Br md 8.00 Dpth 3.65 Welded, 1 dk	**(B32A2ST) Tug**	**2 oil engines** reduction geared to sc. shafts driving 2 FP propellers Total Power: 1,104kW (1,500hp) Chinese Std. Type 6190ZLC 2 x 4 Stroke 6 Cy. 190 x 210 each-552kW (750bhp) Jinan Diesel Engine Co Ltd-China AuxGen: 2 x 58kW 50Hz a.c
8837693 **SINAR MAS** - - **PT Pelayaran Mulyono Santoso** - *Samarinda* *Indonesia*	*261* 151 -	Class: (KI)	**1981 PT Menumbar Kaltim — Samarinda** Loa 36.65 Br ex - Dght 1.900 Lbp 33.65 Br md 8.50 Dpth 2.70 Welded, 1 dk	**(A35D2RL) Landing Craft** Bow door/ramp	**2 oil engines** geared to sc. shafts driving 2 FP propellers Total Power: 280kW (380hp) 8.0kn Caterpillar 3306TA 2 x 4 Stroke 6 Cy. 121 x 152 each-140kW (190bhp) Caterpillar Tractor Co-USA
8810621 **SINAR MAS** *PMWK* *ex* Lani No. 2 *-2009* *ex* Chokyu Maru *-2009* - **PT Sinar Lautan Mas** - *Tanjung Priok* *Indonesia*	*655* 403 900	Class: KI	**1988**-12 **Taiyo Shipbuilding Co Ltd — Sanyoonoda YC** Yd No: 211 Loa 56.72 Br ex - Dght 3.930 Lbp 52.51 Br md 9.50 Dpth 5.15 Welded	**(A31A2GX) General Cargo Ship** Bale: 1,198 Compartments: 1 Ho, ER 1 Ha: ER	**1 oil engine** epicyclic geared to sc. shaft driving 1 FP propeller Total Power: 588kW (799hp) Hanshin 6LU26G 1 x 4 Stroke 6 Cy. 260 x 440 588kW (799bhp) The Hanshin Diesel Works Ltd-Japan AuxGen: 1 x 74kW 225V a.c
9545390 **SINAR MATARAM** *POTN* *ex* Spring Mistral *-2012* - **PT Samudera Energi Tangguh** PT Samudera Indonesia Ship Management (PT SISM) *Jakarta* *Indonesia* MMSI: 525009077	**2,888** 1,295 3,818 T/cm 10.9	Class: NK	**2009**-05 **KK Onishigumi Zosensho — Mihara HS** Yd No: 362 Loa 88.60 (BB) Br ex - Dght 6.112 Lbp 84.99 Br md 14.60 Dpth 7.55 Welded, 1 dk	**(A12B2TR) Chemical/Products Tanker** Double Hull (13F) Liq: 4,458; Liq (Oil): 4,460 Cargo Heating Coils Compartments: 8 Wing Ta, ER 8 Cargo Pump (s): 8x150m³/hr Manifold: Bow/CM: 44.4m	**1 oil engine** driving 1 Propeller Total Power: 2,647kW (3,599hp) 12.5kn Akasaka A41S 1 x 4 Stroke 6 Cy. 410 x 800 2647kW (3599bhp) Akasaka Tekkosho KK (Akasaka DieselLtd)-Japan Thrusters: 1 Tunnel thruster (f) Fuel: 71.0 (d.f.) 255.0 (r.f.)
8114170 **SINAR MINANG** *YDAX* *ex* Sinar Sambas *-2004* - *ex* Darpo Duabelas *-1998* *ex* Bahari Prasetya *-1992* *ex* Kaiho *-1981* **PT Joesoef Shipping Lines** - *Jakarta* *Indonesia* MMSI: 525016489 Official number: BA5674/1	**2,323** 1,227 3,277	Class: KI (NK)	**1981**-07 **Kinoura Zosen K.K. — Imabari** Yd No: 72 Loa 80.20 Br ex - Dght 5.536 Lbp 75.01 Br md 13.50 Dpth 8.15 Welded, 2 dks	**(A31A2GX) General Cargo Ship** Grain: 5,345; Bale: 4,765 2 Ha: (9.8 x 8.9) (24.4 x 8.9)ER Derricks: 1x15t,2x10t	**1 oil engine** driving 1 FP propeller Total Power: 1,618kW (2,200hp) 11.0kn Akasaka DM38A 1 x 4 Stroke 6 Cy. 380 x 600 1618kW (2200bhp) Akasaka Tekkosho KK (Akasaka DieselLtd)-Japan AuxGen: 2 x 96kW
9033438 **SINAR MULIA 1** *PMVZ* *ex* Teratai *-2013* *ex* Seifuku Maru No. 6 *-2009* - *ex* Nangoku Maru No. 8 *-2005* **Kwee Kong Hwee** - *Surabaya* *Indonesia*	**1,500** 478 1,599	Class: KI	**1992**-02 **K.K. Murakami Zosensho — Naruto** Yd No: 203 Loa 75.42 Br ex 12.02 Dght 4.073 Lbp 70.60 Br md 12.00 Dpth 7.00 Welded, 1 dk	**(A31A2GX) General Cargo Ship** Bale: 2,363 Compartments: 1 Ho, ER 1 Ha: ER	**1 oil engine** with clutches, flexible couplings & dr geared to sc. shaft driving 1 FP propeller Total Power: 736kW (1,001hp) Akasaka K31FD 1 x 4 Stroke 6 Cy. 310 x 530 736kW (1001bhp) Akasaka Tekkosho KK (Akasaka DieselLtd)-Japan AuxGen: 1 x 137kW 225V a.c, 1 x 37kW 225V a.c
9295907 **SINAR MUTIARA 1** *YD9006* *ex* Osmaru 1 *-2007* - **PT Sinar Jaya Wijaya** - *Ambon* *Indonesia* Official number: MMA 735/L	**230** 69 275	Class: KI NK	**2003**-07 **C E Ling Shipbuilding Sdn Bhd — Miri** Yd No: 036 Loa 27.67 Br ex - Dght 3.312 Lbp 25.50 Br md 8.23 Dpth 4.00 Welded, 1 dk	**(B32A2ST) Tug**	**2 oil engines** geared to sc. shafts driving 2 FP propellers Total Power: 1,516kW (2,062hp) 10.0kn Mitsubishi S6R2-MPTK2 2 x 4 Stroke 6 Cy. 170 x 220 each-758kW (1031bhp) Mitsubishi Heavy Industries Ltd-Japan Fuel: 220.0 (d.f.)
9089152 **SINAR NUSANTARA 1** *YD3282* - **PT Sinar Jaya Wijaya** - *Batam* *Indonesia*	**155** 47 -	Class: KI	**2005**-01 **Berjaya Dockyard Sdn Bhd — Miri** Loa 24.00 Br ex - Dght 2.990 Lbp 22.53 Br md 7.30 Dpth 3.50 Welded, 1 dk	**(B32A2ST) Tug**	**2 oil engines** geared to sc. shafts driving 2 FP propellers Total Power: 1,043kW (1,418hp) Cummins KTA-19-M3 2 x 4 Stroke 6 Cy. 159 x 159 each-521kW (708bhp) Cummins Engine Co Ltd-United Kingdom
9412244 **SINAR PADANG** *YBMK* - **PT Samudera Shipping Services** - *Jakarta* *Indonesia* MMSI: 525009046	**2,705** 812 4,181	Class: KI (AB)	**2007**-03 **PT Dok dan Perkapalan Surabaya (Persero) — Surabaya** Yd No: 05598 Loa 86.01 Br ex - Dght 4.000 Lbp 82.74 Br md 20.00 Dpth 5.70 Welded, 1 dk	**(A31C2GD) Deck Cargo Ship** TEU 241 Cranes: 2x40t	**2 oil engines** driving 1 gen. of 100kW a.c 2 gen. each 83kW a.c Connecting to 1 elec. Motor of (100kW) 2 elec. motors each (83kW) reduction geared to sc. shafts driving 2 Directional propellers Total Power: 2,236kW (3,040hp) 10.0kn Caterpillar 3512B 2 x Vee 4 Stroke 12 Cy. 170 x 190 each-1118kW (1520bhp) Caterpillar Inc-USA AuxGen: 2 x 300kW 380V a.c, 1 x 140kW 380V a.c Fuel: 248.0 (d.f.)
9094042 **SINAR PAGI 01** *YCCA* - **PT Bunga Nusa Mahakam** - *Samarinda* *Indonesia*	**315** 95 -	Class: KI	**2004**-12 **PT Cahaya Pagi — Indonesia** Yd No: 03 Loa 47.00 Br ex - Dght - Lbp 45.70 Br md 9.00 Dpth 2.60 Welded, 1 dk	**(A35D2RL) Landing Craft**	**2 oil engines** geared to sc. shafts driving 2 Propellers Total Power: 662kW (900hp) Nissan RH10 2 x Vee 4 Stroke 10 Cy. 135 x 125 each-331kW (450bhp) Nissan Diesel Motor Co. Ltd.-Ageo
7622728 **SINAR PALEMBANG II** - - **PT Pelayaran Lokal 'Sriguna'** - *Palembang* *Indonesia* Official number: 33	*172* 93 -	Class: (KI)	**1959 at Palembang** Loa - Br ex - Dght - Lbp 34.19 Br md 7.01 Dpth 2.19 Welded, 1 dk	**(A31A2GX) General Cargo Ship**	**1 oil engine** driving 1 FP propeller Total Power: 368kW (500hp) General Motors 8-268A 1 x 2 Stroke 8 Cy. 165 x 178 368kW (500bhp) (made 1942, fitted 1959) General Motors Corp-USA AuxGen: 1 x 5kW 115V
9412232 **SINAR PANJANG** *YCCE* *ex* Sinar Bintan *-2011* - **PT Samudera Shipping Services** PT Samudera Indonesia Ship Management (PT SISM) *Jakarta* *Indonesia* MMSI: 525009045	**2,705** 812 4,373	Class: KI (AB)	**2007**-01 **PT Dok dan Perkapalan Surabaya (Persero) — Surabaya** Yd No: 05597 Loa 86.01 Br ex - Dght 3.980 Lbp 82.74 Br md 20.00 Dpth 5.70 Welded, 1 dk	**(A31C2GD) Deck Cargo Ship** TEU 241 Cranes: 2x40t	**2 oil engines** driving 1 gen. of 100kW a.c 2 gen. each 83kW a.c Connecting to 1 elec. Motor of (100kW) 2 elec. motors each (83kW) reduction geared to sc. shafts driving 2 Directional propellers Total Power: 2,236kW (3,040hp) 10.0kn Caterpillar 3512B 2 x Vee 4 Stroke 12 Cy. 170 x 190 each-1118kW (1520bhp) Caterpillar Inc-USA AuxGen: 2 x 300kW 380V a.c, 1 x 100kW 380V a.c Fuel: 248.0 (d.f.)
8100569 **SINAR PAPUA** *YHKK* *ex* Dolphin Ace *-2003* *ex* Silver Ying *-1995* - *ex* Theodor Fontane *-1994* *ex* Dhaulagiri *-1992* *ex* Tiger Bay *-1989* *ex* Theodor Fontane *-1988* **PT Pelayaran Mana Lagi** PT Salam Pacific Indonesia Lines *Jakarta* *Indonesia* MMSI: 525017033	**4,473** 2,387 6,500	Class: KI (NK) (GL)	**1981**-10 **Husumer Schiffswerft Inh. Gebr. Kroeger GmbH & Co. KG — Husum** Yd No: 1466 Loa 110.27 (BB) Br ex 17.96 Dght 6.541 Lbp 99.64 Br md 17.81 Dpth 8.46 Welded, 2 dks	**(A31A2GX) General Cargo Ship** Grain: 8,326; Bale: 7,553 TEU 343 C.Ho 146/20' C.Dk 197/20' Compartments: 2 Ho, ER, 2 Tw Dk 2 Ha: (25.1 x 12.7) (37.8 x 12.7)ER Cranes: 2x35t Ice Capable	**1 oil engine** with flexible couplings & sr gearedto sc. shaft driving 1 CP propeller Total Power: 2,942kW (4,000hp) 13.5kn MaK 6M551AK 1 x 4 Stroke 6 Cy. 450 x 550 2942kW (4000bhp) Krupp MaK Maschinenbau GmbH-Kiel AuxGen: 1 x 384kW 220/380V 50Hz a.c, 2 x 318kW 220/380V 50Hz a.c Thrusters: 1 Thwart. FP thruster (f) Fuel: 96.0 (d.f.) 540.0 (r.f.) 12.5pd
8974283 **SINAR PAWAN I** *YD5051* *ex* Toshi Maru No. 8 *-1999* - **PT Suri Adidjaya Kapuas** - *Semarang* *Indonesia*	**108** 64 -	Class: KI	**1969**-01 **Toyo Zosen Tekko KK — Kitakyushu FO** L reg 20.99 Br ex - Dght 1.800 Lbp 20.50 Br md 5.50 Dpth 2.60 Welded, 1 dk	**(B32A2ST) Tug**	**1 oil engine** reverse geared to sc. shaft driving 1 FP propeller Total Power: 736kW (1,001hp) Akasaka AH25 1 x 4 Stroke 6 Cy. 250 x 410 736kW (1001bhp) Akasaka Tekkosho KK (Akasaka DieselLtd)-Japan AuxGen: 1 x 20kW 230V a.c
9278478 **SINAR PELUTAN 1** *9WFG9* - **Woodman Avenue Sdn Bhd** Woodman Sdn Bhd *Kuching* *Malaysia* MMSI: 533000897 Official number: 329463	**256** 77 255	Class: NK	**2002**-09 **C E Ling Shipbuilding Sdn Bhd — Miri** Yd No: 033 Loa 28.05 Br ex - Dght 3.312 Lbp 25.77 Br md 8.60 Dpth 4.30 Welded	**(B32A2ST) Tug**	**2 oil engines** reduction geared to sc. shaft (s) driving 1 Propeller Total Power: 1,204kW (1,636hp) 10.0kn Mitsubishi S6R2-MPTK 2 x 4 Stroke 6 Cy. 170 x 220 each-602kW (818bhp) Mitsubishi Heavy Industries Ltd-Japan AuxGen: 2 x a.c Fuel: 200.0 (d.f.)
8701856 **SINAR PERMATASARI** *PMPN* *ex* Shunsho Maru No. 7 *-2012* - **PT Samudra Intim Perkasa** - *Surabaya* *Indonesia*	**683** 241 700	Class: KI	**1987**-01 **Shitanoe Shipbuilding Co Ltd — Usuki OT** Yd No: 1065 Loa 56.70 (BB) Br ex 9.53 Dght 4.000 Lbp 53.30 Br md 9.30 Dpth 5.55 Welded, 1 dk	**(A31A2GX) General Cargo Ship** Compartments: 2 Ho, ER 2 Ha: ER	**1 oil engine** geared to sc. shaft driving 1 FP propeller Total Power: 552kW (750hp) Hanshin 6LB26RG 1 x 4 Stroke 6 Cy. 260 x 440 552kW (750bhp) The Hanshin Diesel Works Ltd-Japan

8820523 *PKYG* -	**SINAR PRIMA 1** *ex* Bangkit *-2010* *ex* Nissho Maru *-2007* **PT Akita Putera Lines** - *Surabaya* *Indonesia*	**680** 225 650	Class: KI	**1989-02 K.K. Miura Zosensho — Saiki** Yd No: 833 Loa 57.14 (BB) Br ex - Dght 2.900 Lbp 53.00 Br md 9.80 Dpth 5.10 Welded, 2 dks	**(A31A2GX) General Cargo Ship** Compartments: 1 Ho, ER 1 Ha: ER	**1 oil engine** reverse geared to sc. shaft driving 1 FP propeller Total Power: 588kW (799hp) Hanshin 6LU26G 1 x 4 Stroke 6 Cy. 260 x 440 588kW (799bhp) The Hanshin Diesel Works Ltd-Japan
8658487 - -	**SINAR PUTRA I** **PT Sinar Putra Kapuas** - *Tanjung Priok* *Indonesia*	**127** 39 -	Class: KI	**2011-02 PT Karya Docking Nusantara — Samarinda** Loa 23.00 Br ex - Dght 2.740 Lbp 21.74 Br md 6.50 Dpth 3.20 Welded, 1 dk	**(B32A2ST) Tug**	**2 oil engines** reduction geared to sc. shafts driving 2 Propellers AuxGen: 2 x 30kW 400V a.c
9633678 *YDA 3346* -	**SINAR PUTRA VII** *ex* Capricorn 90 *-2013* **PT Sinar Putra Kapuas** - *Jakarta* *Indonesia*	**140** 42 107	Class: NK	**2013-02 Capricorn Central Shipbuilding Sdn Bhd — Sibu** Yd No: 016 Loa 23.50 Br ex - Dght 2.712 Lbp 21.99 Br md 7.32 Dpth 3.20 Welded, 1 dk	**(B32A2ST) Tug**	**2 oil engines** reduction geared to sc. shafts driving 2 FP propellers Total Power: 894kW (1,216hp) Cummins KTA-19-M3 2 x 4 Stroke 6 Cy. 159 x 159 each-447kW (608bhp) Cummins Engine Co Inc-USA Fuel: 90.0 (d.f.)
9435234 *9V7718* -	**SINAR SABANG** **Samudera Shipping Line Ltd** - *Singapore* *Singapore* MMSI: 563516000 Official number: 394694	**18,321** 10,392 23,350 T/cm 38.0	Class: GL NK	**2008-10 Guangzhou Wenchong Shipyard Co Ltd — Guangzhou GD** Yd No: 340 Loa 175.50 (BB) Br ex - Dght 10.920 Lbp 165.00 Br md 27.40 Dpth 14.30 Welded, 1 dk	**(A33A2CC) Container Ship (Fully Cellular)** TEU 1740 C Ho 700 TEU C Dk 1040 TEU incl 300 ref C. Compartments: 5 Cell Ho, ER Cranes: 2x45t,1x26t	**1 oil engine** driving 1 FP propeller Total Power: 16,660kW (22,651hp) 19.5kn MAN-B&W 7S60MC-C8 1 x 2 Stroke 7 Cy. 600 x 2400 16660kW (22651bhp) Hudong Heavy Machinery Co Ltd-China AuxGen: 3 x 1180kW 60Hz a.c Thrusters: 1 Tunnel thruster (f) Fuel: 170.0 (d.f.) 1700.0 (r.f.)
8975146 *YD4645* -	**SINAR SAKTI I** *ex* Mitra Kencana II *-2008* *ex* Meiko Maru *-1999* **PT Taruna Cipta Kencana** - *Jakarta* *Indonesia*	*130* 39 -	Class: KI	**1986-09 Sakamoto Zosensho — Nandan** Loa 25.00 Br ex - Dght - Lbp 22.50 Br md 6.50 Dpth 3.00 Welded, 1 dk	**(B32A2ST) Tug**	**2 oil engines** geared to sc. shafts driving 2 Propellers Total Power: 1,104kW (1,500hp) Niigata 6MG20AX 2 x 4 Stroke 6 Cy. 200 x 260 each-552kW (750bhp) Niigata Engineering Co Ltd-Japan AuxGen: 1 x 50kW 225V a.c
8801694 *YHGV* -	**SINAR SALJU** *ex* Taisetsusan Maru *-2002* **PT Pelayaran Mana Lagi** PT Salam Pacific Indonesia Lines *Jakarta* *Indonesia* MMSI: 525017032	**5,042** 1,711 3,872	Class: (KI) (NK)	**1988-04 Nishi Shipbuilding Co Ltd — Imabari EH** Yd No: 347 Loa 110.34 (BB) Br ex - Dght 6.219 Lbp 101.91 Br md 18.70 Dpth 10.20 Welded, 1 dk	**(A33A2CC) Container Ship (Fully Cellular)** TEU 190 incl 35 ref C. Compartments: 2 Cell Ho, ER 2 Ha: ER Gantry cranes: 1	**1 oil engine** driving 1 CP propeller Total Power: 7,282kW (9,901hp) B&W 6L50MC 1 x 2 Stroke 6 Cy. 500 x 1620 7282kW (9901bhp) Mitsui Engineering & Shipbuilding CLtd-Japan Thrusters: 1 Tunnel thruster (f)
9049839 - -	**SINAR SAMUDERA** **Thio Rahayu Thiowati** - *Samarinda* *Indonesia*	**354** 107 -	Class: KI	**2005-10 Galangan Kapal Tunas Harapan — Samarinda** Loa 49.50 Br ex - Dght - Lbp 48.30 Br md 9.15 Dpth 2.72 Welded, 1 dk	**(A35D2RL) Landing Craft** Bow ramp (centre)	**2 oil engines** geared to sc. shafts driving 2 Propellers Total Power: 592kW (804hp) Caterpillar 3406 1 x 4 Stroke 6 Cy. 137 x 165 296kW (402bhp) Caterpillar Inc-USA Caterpillar 3406C-TA 1 x 4 Stroke 6 Cy. 137 x 165 296kW (402bhp) Caterpillar Inc-USA AuxGen: 1 x 140kW 380/220V a.c, 1 x 100kW 380/220V a.c
9444962 *3ERD9* -	**SINAR SANGIR** **Sun Lanes Shipping SA** Nissen Kaiun Co Ltd (Nissen Kaiun KK) *Panama* *Panama* MMSI: 370017000 Official number: 3382908A	**17,515** 8,074 21,937	Class: NK	**2008-05 Imabari Shipbuilding Co Ltd — Imabari EH (Imabari Shipyard)** Yd No: 653 Loa 171.99 (BB) Br ex - Dght 9.517 Lbp 160.00 Br md 27.60 Dpth 14.00 Welded, 1 dk	**(A33A2CC) Container Ship (Fully Cellular)** TEU 1708 C Ho 610 TEU C Dk 1098 incl 172 ref C	**1 oil engine** driving 1 FP propeller Total Power: 15,820kW (21,509hp) 19.8kn MAN-B&W 7S60MC-C 1 x 2 Stroke 7 Cy. 600 x 2400 15820kW (21509bhp) Mitsui Engineering & Shipbuilding CLtd-Japan AuxGen: 3 x a.c Thrusters: 1 Tunnel thruster (f) Fuel: 2180.0
8985347 - -	**SINAR SEJAHTERA** - -	**263** 129 -		**1987 Sinandaman Co. Ltd. — Phuket** Loa 36.00 Br ex - Dght - Lbp - Br md 7.15 Dpth 2.36 Welded, 1 dk	**(A31A2GX) General Cargo Ship**	**1 oil engine** driving 1 Propeller Total Power: 261kW (355hp) Cummins NTA-350-M 1 x 4 Stroke 6 Cy. 117 x 140 261kW (355bhp) Cummins Engine Co Inc-USA
9154153 *POGP* -	**SINAR SEJATI 2** *ex* Megah Lima *-2011* *ex* Jurong *-2005* *ex* Woo Jin *-2001* **PT Pelayaran Putra Sejati** - *Jakarta* *Indonesia* MMSI: 525014065	**6,388** 3,891 8,680	Class: KI (NK)	**1997-01 Shin Kurushima Dockyard Co. Ltd. — Hashihama, Imabari** Yd No: 2920 Loa 100.59 Br ex - Dght 8.219 Lbp 93.50 Br md 18.80 Dpth 13.00 Welded, 1 dk	**(A31A2GX) General Cargo Ship** Grain: 13,941; Bale: 13,096 Compartments: 4 Ho, ER 4 Ha: ER Cranes: 2x30t; Derricks: 2x25t	**1 oil engine** driving 1 FP propeller Total Power: 3,236kW (4,400hp) 12.4kn B&W 5L35MC 1 x 2 Stroke 5 Cy. 350 x 1050 3236kW (4400bhp) Makita Corp-Japan AuxGen: 2 x 487kW a.c Fuel: 650.0
9091246 - -	**SINAR SENTOSA** **Wecoy Marine (Hong Kong) Ltd**	**155** 47 -		**2006-01 PT Natwell Shipyard — Batam** L reg 25.00 Br ex - Dght - Lbp - Br md 7.50 Dpth 3.50 Welded, 1 dk	**(B32A2ST) Tug**	**2 oil engines** driving 2 Propellers Total Power: 1,388kW (1,888hp) Mitsubishi 2 x 4 Stroke each-694kW (944bhp) Mitsubishi Heavy Industries Ltd-Japan
9202792 *9V7837* -	**SINAR SOLO** **Samudera Shipping Line Ltd** PT Samudera Indonesia Ship Management (PT SISM) *Singapore* *Singapore* MMSI: 565953000	**12,531** 5,336 15,218 T/cm 28.7	Class: BV	**1999-01 Hakata Zosen K.K. — Imabari** Yd No: 613 Loa 144.50 (BB) Br ex - Dght 8.960 Lbp 135.00 Br md 25.00 Dpth 13.70 Welded, 1 dk	**(A33A2CC) Container Ship (Fully Cellular)** TEU 1060 C Ho 444 TEU C Dk 616 TEU incl 104 ref C. Compartments: 7 Cell Ho, ER 7 Ha: ER	**1 oil engine** driving 1 FP propeller Total Power: 9,994kW (13,588hp) 18.0kn B&W 7S50MC 1 x 2 Stroke 7 Cy. 500 x 1910 9994kW (13588bhp) Mitsui Engineering & Shipbuilding CLtd-Japan AuxGen: 3 x 560kW 450V a.c Thrusters: 1 Tunnel thruster (f)
7641463 - -	**SINAR SONA** *ex* Sona *-2001* *ex* Xiamen Bridge *-1997* *ex* Korean Bridge *-1993* **PT Pelayaran Laut Baru** - *Jakarta* *Indonesia* MMSI: 525015207	**2,151** 1,186 2,928	Class: (KI) (KR)	**1977-03 Daedong Shipbuilding Co Ltd — Busan** Yd No: 167 Loa 79.20 Br ex - Dght 5.514 Lbp 72.80 Br md 13.86 Dpth 7.60 Welded, 1 dk	**(A33A2CC) Container Ship (Fully Cellular)** TEU 126 incl 15 ref C. Compartments: 4 Cell Ho, ER 8 Ha: 2 (6.6 x 2.9)6 (12.6 x 5.5)ER	**1 oil engine** driving 1 FP propeller Total Power: 1,692kW (2,300hp) 14.6kn Hanshin 6LUS38 1 x 4 Stroke 6 Cy. 380 x 580 1692kW (2300bhp) Hanshin Nainenki Kogyo-Japan AuxGen: 2 x 200kW 445V 60Hz a.c Fuel: 222.5 (d.f.) 8.5pd
7707413 *YDCK* -	**SINAR SORONG** *ex* Anshun *-2006* *ex* Epos *-2003* *ex* MSC Poti *-1999* *ex* Luck *-1997* *ex* Trade Luck *-1996* *ex* Nordheide *-1991* *launched as* Multicon *-1979* **PT Pelayaran Mana Lagi** PT Salam Pacific Indonesia Lines *Jakarta* *Indonesia* MMSI: 525015098	**5,202** 3,290 7,415	Class: KI (GL)	**1979-12 Singapore Shipbuilding & Engineering Pte Ltd — Singapore** Yd No: 134 Loa 120.40 (BB) Br ex 17.84 Dght 6.490 Lbp 112.02 Br md 17.81 Dpth 8.82 Welded, 2 dks	**(A31A2GX) General Cargo Ship** Grain: 11,295; Bale: 10,176 TEU 431 C Ho 176 TEU C Dk 255 TEU incl 30 ref C. Compartments: 2 Ho, ER 2 Ha: 2 (37.8 x 12.9)ER Ice Capable	**1 oil engine** driving 1 CP propeller Total Power: 2,942kW (4,000hp) 13.5kn Mitsubishi 6UET45/80D 1 x 2 Stroke 6 Cy. 450 x 800 2942kW (4000bhp) Akasaka Tekkosho KK (Akasaka DieselLtd)-Japan AuxGen: 1 x 480kW 220/440V 60Hz a.c, 3 x 240kW 220/440V 60Hz a.c Thrusters: 1 Thwart. CP thruster (f) Fuel: 60.0 (d.f.) 490.0 (r.f.) 14.0pd
9444974 *3ESP9* -	**SINAR SUBANG** **Green Spanker Shipping SA** Philsynergy Maritime Inc *Panama* *Panama* MMSI: 370390000 Official number: 3416308A	**17,515** 8,074 21,935	Class: NK	**2008-08 Imabari Shipbuilding Co Ltd — Imabari EH (Imabari Shipyard)** Yd No: 654 Loa 171.99 (BB) Br ex - Dght 9.510 Lbp 160.00 Br md 27.60 Dpth 14.00 Welded, 1 dk	**(A33A2CC) Container Ship (Fully Cellular)** TEU 1708 C Ho 610 TEU C Dk 1098 incl 172 ref C	**1 oil engine** driving 1 FP propeller Total Power: 15,820kW (21,509hp) 19.7kn MAN-B&W 7S60MC-C 1 x 2 Stroke 7 Cy. 600 x 2400 15820kW (21509bhp) Mitsui Engineering & Shipbuilding CLtd-Japan AuxGen: 3 x a.c Thrusters: 1 Tunnel thruster (f) Fuel: 2180.0
9435222 *9VLH6* -	**SINAR SUMBA** **Samudera Shipping Line Ltd** - *Singapore* *Singapore* MMSI: 565891000 Official number: 394161	**18,321** 10,392 23,350 T/cm 38.0	Class: GL NK	**2008-06 Guangzhou Wenchong Shipyard Co Ltd — Guangzhou GD** Yd No: 339 Loa 175.50 (BB) Br ex - Dght 10.900 Lbp 165.00 Br md 27.40 Dpth 14.30 Welded, 1 dk	**(A33A2CC) Container Ship (Fully Cellular)** TEU 1740 C Ho 700 TEU C Dk 1040 TEU incl 300 ref C. Compartments: 5 Cell Ho, ER Cranes: 2x45t	**1 oil engine** driving 1 FP propeller Total Power: 16,660kW (22,651hp) 19.5kn MAN-B&W 7S60MC-C 1 x 2 Stroke 7 Cy. 600 x 2400 16660kW (22651bhp) (new engine 2008) Hudong Heavy Machinery Co Ltd-China AuxGen: 3 x 1195kW 450V a.c Thrusters: 1 Tunnel thruster (f) Fuel: 170.0 (d.f.) 1700.0 (r.f.)

IMO / Call sign	Name, former names, owner, port	Tonnage	Classification	Builder and dimensions	Ship type	Machinery
9120920 *9VJJ* -	**SINAR TANJUNG** *ex* Gallant Wave *-2013* *ex* Royal Container *-1996* **Soon Fong Shipping Pte Ltd** - SatCom: Inmarsat C 456401710 *Singapore* *Singapore* MMSI: 564017000 Official number: 387033	**17,613** 8,215 23,650	Class: LR (AB) **100A1** SS 06/2011 container ship **LMC** Eq.Ltr: I†; Cable: 605.0/64.0 U3 (a)	**1996-06 Shin Kurushima Dockyard Co. Ltd. — Onishi** Yd No: 2878 Loa 182.83 (BB) Br ex - Dght 9.500 Lbp 170.00 Br md 28.00 Dpth 14.00 Welded, 1 dk	**(A33A2CC) Container Ship (Fully Cellular)** TEU 1510 C Ho 558 TEU C Dk 952 TEU incl 60 ref C. Compartments: ER, 6 Cell Ho 9 Ha: ER	**1 oil engine** driving 1 FP propeller Total Power: 11,680kW (15,880hp) 19.0kn B&W 6S60MC 1 x 2 Stroke 6 Cy. 600 x 2292 11680kW (15880bhp) Mitsui Engineering & Shipbuilding CLtd-Japan AuxGen: 3 x 560kW 450V 60Hz a.c Boilers: e (ex.g.) 10.7kgf/cm² (10.5bar), AuxB (o.f.) 7.1kgf/cm² (7.0bar) Thrusters: 1 Thwart. FP thruster (f)
8870267 - - -	**SINAR TERANG ABADI 2** *ex* Kaisei Maru *-2013* *ex* Hosho Maru *-1997* - -	*199* - 685	Class: IZ	**1993-06 Sokooshi Zosen K.K. — Osakikamijima** Yd No: 317 Loa 57.15 Br ex - Dght 3.190 Lbp 52.50 Br md 9.50 Dpth 5.40 Welded, 1 dk	**(A31A2GX) General Cargo Ship**	**1 oil engine** reverse geared to sc. shaft driving 1 FP propeller Total Power: 736kW (1,001hp) 10.5kn Akasaka T26SR 1 x 4 Stroke 6 Cy. 260 x 440 736kW (1001bhp) Akasaka Tekkosho KK (Akasaka DieselLtd)-Japan
9297709 *S6AP6* -	**SINAR TOKYO** - **Foremost Maritime Pte Ltd** PT Samudera Indonesia Ship Management (PT SISM) *Singapore* *Singapore* MMSI: 564571000 Official number: 390703	**1,942** 774 2,949 T/cm 9.1	Class: NK	**2004-08 Shitanoe Shipbuilding Co Ltd — Usuki OT** Yd No: 1232 Loa 81.00 (BB) Br ex 13.62 Dght 5.462 Lbp 75.50 Br md 13.60 Dpth 6.50 Welded, 1 dk	**(A12B2TR) Chemical/Products Tanker** Double Hull (13F) Liq: 2,883; Liq (Oil): 2,883 Cargo Heating Coils Compartments: 6 Wing Ta, 1 Ta, ER 7 Cargo Pump (s): 7x150m³/hr Manifold: Bow/CM: 39.8m	**1 oil engine** driving 1 FP propeller Total Power: 2,059kW (2,799hp) 12.8kn Akasaka A38 1 x 4 Stroke 6 Cy. 380 x 740 2059kW (2799bhp) Akasaka Tekkosho KK (Akasaka DieselLtd)-Japan AuxGen: 2 x 250kW 450V 60Hz a.c Fuel: 45.0 (d.f.) 196.0 (r.f.)
8825846 *YEEX* -	**SINAR USAHA JAYA** *ex* Pembangunan *-2003* **PT Samudra Usaha Jaya Lines** - *Pontianak* *Indonesia*	**376** 177 -	Class: (KI)	**1983 P.T. Karya Teknik Kapuas Maju — Pontianak** Loa 48.23 Br ex 8.00 Dght 2.700 Lbp 44.50 Br md - Dpth 3.20 Welded, 1 dk	**(A31A2GX) General Cargo Ship**	**1 oil engine** geared to sc. shaft driving 1 FP propeller Total Power: 294kW (400hp) Yanmar 6LA-DTE 1 x 4 Stroke 6 Cy. 148 x 165 294kW (400bhp) Yanmar Diesel Engine Co Ltd-Japan AuxGen: 1 x 115V a.c
8843173 *YB4198* -	**SINAR USAHA JAYA 1** *ex* Nita III *-1997* *ex* Intan 11 *-1996* *ex* Kotoku Maru *-1990* **PT Samudra Usaha Jaya Lines** - *Jakarta* *Indonesia*	*357* 152 530	Class: (KI)	**1971-03 KK Kushikino Zosensho — Ichikikushikino KS** Loa 44.00 Br ex - Dght 3.200 Lbp 39.00 Br md 8.00 Dpth 4.73 Welded, 1 dk	**(A31A2GX) General Cargo Ship** Compartments: 1 Ho, ER	**1 oil engine** driving 1 FP propeller Total Power: 309kW (420hp) Nissan RF10 1 x Vee 4 Stroke 10 Cy. 138 x 142 309kW (420bhp) Nissan Diesel Motor Co. Ltd.-Ageo
8625856 *YGHH* -	**SINAR USAHA JAYA 2** *ex* Koei 11 *-2001* *ex* Koei Maru No. 11 *-1999* **PT Samudra Usaha Jaya Lines** - *Jakarta* *Indonesia*	*398* 268 700	Class: KI	**1985-12 Tokuoka Zosen K.K. — Naruto** Loa 54.50 Br ex - Dght 3.410 Lbp 49.50 Br md 9.00 Dpth 5.50 Welded, 1 dk	**(A31A2GX) General Cargo Ship**	**1 oil engine** driving 1 FP propeller Total Power: 405kW (551hp) 10.0kn Niigata 6M26AGTE 1 x 4 Stroke 6 Cy. 260 x 460 405kW (551bhp) Niigata Engineering Co Ltd-Japan
9182875 *YD3188* -	**SINAR WIJAYA** *ex* Promex 22 *-2002* *ex* Celiyanto 1 *-2000* *ex* Midbest 1 *-2000* **PT Sinar Jaya Wijaya** - *Tanjungpinang* *Indonesia* MMSI: 525015168	**172** 103 178	Class: KI (NK)	**1997-04 C E Ling Shipbuilding Sdn Bhd — Miri** Yd No: 8 Loa 26.00 Br ex - Dght 3.012 Lbp 23.50 Br md 7.92 Dpth 3.65 Welded, 1 dk	**(B32A2ST) Tug**	**2 oil engines** reduction geared to sc. shafts driving 2 FP propellers Total Power: 1,060kW (1,442hp) 6.0kn Mitsubishi S6R2-MTK 2 x 4 Stroke 6 Cy. 170 x 220 each-530kW (721bhp) Mitsubishi Heavy Industries Ltd-Japan AuxGen: 2 x 40kW a.c
8654998 *XUEV6* -	**SINARAN ANDAMAN** *ex* Xiang Xiangtan Huo 0082 *-2012* **Andaman Unik Sdn Bhd** - *Phnom Penh* *Cambodia* MMSI: 515227000 Official number: 1204911	**793** 345 1,591		**2005-04 Jiangdu Xinhua Shipyard — Yangzhou JS** Loa 67.60 Br ex 11.80 Dght 2.500 Lbp 64.80 Br md 11.60 Dpth 3.30 Welded, 1 dk	**(A33A2CC) Container Ship (Fully Cellular)**	**2 oil engines** reduction geared to sc. shafts driving 2 Propellers Total Power: 352kW (478hp) Steyr WD615.67C 2 x 4 Stroke 6 Cy. 126 x 130 each-176kW (239bhp) Weifang Diesel Engine Factory-China AuxGen: 1 x 50kW 400V a.c
9559717 *V3MA6* -	**SINARAN BULAN** *ex* Sp-Power Iii *-2011* **KIMSAR Corporation Pte Ltd** - *Belize City* *Belize* MMSI: 312456000 Official number: 130910798	**183** 55 -		**2009-02 Kiong Nguong Shipbuilding Contractor Co — Sibu** Yd No: 2058 Loa 26.00 Br ex - Dght - Lbp - Br md 7.93 Dpth 3.65 Welded, 1 dk	**(B32A2ST) Tug**	**2 oil engines** reduction geared to sc. shafts driving 2 Propellers Total Power: 1,716kW (2,334hp) 10.0kn Mitsubishi S12A2-MPTK 2 x Vee 4 Stroke 12 Cy. 150 x 160 each-858kW (1167bhp) Mitsubishi Heavy Industries Ltd-Japan
9095967 - -	**SINARAN GUOHENG** *ex* Efilya *-2007* **Sinaran Ushawan Sdn Bhd** -	**286** 86 -	Class: (KI)	**2002-06 C.V. Jaya Terang — Sorong** Yd No: 11 Loa 42.00 Br ex - Dght 2.490 Lbp 39.70 Br md 9.00 Dpth 3.30 Welded, 1 dk	**(A35D2RL) Landing Craft**	**2 oil engines** geared to sc. shaft driving 2 Propellers Total Power: 514kW (698hp) Hyundai Himsen D6AC-G1 2 x 4 Stroke 6 Cy. 130 x 140 each-257kW (349bhp) Hyundai Heavy Industries Co Ltd-South Korea AuxGen: 2 x 24kW 380/220V a.c
9049334 *YD9507* -	**SINARAN JAYA** - **PT Sinar Jaya Wijaya** - *Sorong* *Indonesia* MMSI: 525015689	**111** 66 -	Class: KI	**2004-06 Celtug Service Shipyard Sdn Bhd — Sibu** Loa 23.17 Br ex - Dght 2.360 Lbp 21.03 Br md 6.70 Dpth 2.90 Welded, 1 dk	**(B32A2ST) Tug**	**2 oil engines** geared to sc. shafts driving 2 Propellers Total Power: 894kW (1,216hp) Cummins KTA-19-M 2 x 4 Stroke 6 Cy. 159 x 159 each-447kW (608bhp) Chongqing Cummins Engine Co Ltd-China AuxGen: 2 x 28kW 220V a.c
9736494 - -	**SINARAN LANGIT** - **Kangsar Corp Pte Ltd** - *Singapore* *Singapore*	**207** 63 -	Class: RI (Class contemplated)	**2014-03 PT Karya Teknik Utama — Batam** Yd No: KTU-967 Loa 27.00 Br ex - Dght 3.000 Lbp 24.97 Br md 8.20 Dpth 4.00 Welded, 1 dk	**(B32A2ST) Tug**	**2 oil engines** reduction geared to sc. shafts driving 2 Propellers Total Power: 1,492kW (2,028hp) Caterpillar C32 ACERT 2 x Vee 4 Stroke 12 Cy. 145 x 162 each-746kW (1014bhp) Caterpillar Inc-USA
9165372 *9WDJ5* -	**SINARAN LAUT** - **Government of Malaysia (Director of Marine - Sarawak)** - SatCom: Inmarsat C 453330010 *Kuching* *Malaysia* MMSI: 533260000 Official number: 329064	**1,083** 324 459	Class: (LR) ✠ Classed LR until 13/11/13	**1998-12 Brooke Dockyard & Engineering Works Corp — Kuching** Yd No: 146 Loa 52.60 Br ex 13.30 Dght 3.300 Lbp 46.40 Br md 13.00 Dpth 5.00 Welded, 1 dk	**(B34Q2QB) Buoy Tender**	**2 oil engines** geared to sc. shafts driving 2 Directional propellers Total Power: 2,500kW (3,400hp) 13.3kn Yanmar 6Z280-EN 2 x 4 Stroke 6 Cy. 280 x 360 each-1250kW (1700bhp) Yanmar Diesel Engine Co Ltd-Japan AuxGen: 3 x 200kW 400V 50Hz a.c Thrusters: 1 Thwart. FP thruster (f)
9564334 *9V7599* -	**SINARAN MENTARI** *ex* Dragonet VIII *-2011* **Hansar Corp Pte Ltd** - *Singapore* *Singapore* Official number: 394490	**277** 84 310	Class: NK	**2009-08 Sapor Shipbuilding Industries Sdn Bhd — Sibu** Yd No: SAPOR 55 Loa 30.20 Br ex - Dght 3.800 Lbp 27.20 Br md 9.00 Dpth 4.60 Welded, 1 dk	**(B32A2ST) Tug**	**2 oil engines** reduction geared to sc. shafts driving 2 Propellers Total Power: 1,518kW (2,064hp) Mitsubishi S6R2-MTK3L 2 x 4 Stroke 6 Cy. 170 x 220 each-759kW (1032bhp) Mitsubishi Heavy Industries Ltd-Japan Fuel: 215.0 (d.f.)
9685281 *9V2106* -	**SINARAN SETIA** - **Bursar Corp Pte Ltd** - *Singapore* *Singapore* MMSI: 563204760 Official number: 398623	**217** 65 164	Class: RI	**2013-01 PT Karya Teknik Utama — Batam** Yd No: KTU-718 Loa 28.05 Br ex - Dght 3.310 Lbp 24.97 Br md 8.20 Dpth 4.31 Welded, 1 dk	**(B32A2ST) Tug**	**2 oil engines** reduction geared to sc. shafts driving 2 FP propellers Total Power: 1,492kW (2,028hp) 10.0kn Caterpillar C32 ACERT 2 x Vee 4 Stroke 12 Cy. 145 x 162 each-746kW (1014bhp) Caterpillar Inc-USA
9685293 *9V2221* -	**SINARAN WARNA** - **Macassar Corp Pte Ltd** - *Singapore* *Singapore* MMSI: 563025470 Official number: 398762	**217** 65 164	Class: RI	**2013-01 PT Karya Teknik Utama — Batam** Yd No: KTU-752 Loa 28.00 Br ex - Dght 3.310 Lbp 24.97 Br md 8.20 Dpth 4.31 Welded, 1 dk	**(B32A2ST) Tug**	**2 oil engines** reduction geared to sc. shafts driving 2 FP propellers Total Power: 1,492kW (2,028hp) 10.0kn Caterpillar C32 ACERT 2 x Vee 4 Stroke 12 Cy. 145 x 162 each-746kW (1014bhp) Caterpillar Inc-USA

IMO / Call sign	Name / Owner	Tonnage	Class	Builder / Dimensions	Type	Machinery
7900431 *A4DL2* -	**SINAW 8** *ex* Atun Uno *-2008* *ex* Cristobal *-1986* *launched as* Hai Wang No. 21 *-1979* **Century Star LLC** - *Oman* MMSI: 461000061 Official number: 196	**663** 227 530	Class: (KR)	**1979-06 KK Kanasashi Zosen — Toyohashi AI** Yd No: 1290 Loa 55.94 Br ex 8.82 Dght 3.501 Lbp 49.51 Br md 8.81 Dpth 4.04 Welded, 1 dk	**(B11B2FV) Fishing Vessel**	**1 oil engine** driving 1 FP propeller Total Power: 883kW (1,201hp) 11.5kn Hanshin 6LUN28AG 1 x 4 Stroke 6 Cy. 280 x 480 883kW (1201bhp) Hanshin Nainenki Kogyo-Japan
7900429 *A4DL3* -	**SINAW 16** *ex* Atun Dos *-2008* *ex* Kingstar No. 81 *-1986* **Century Star LLC** - *Port Sultan Qaboos* *Oman* Official number: 252	**665** 269 530	Class: (KR) (NK)	**1979-05 KK Kanasashi Zosen — Toyohashi AI** Yd No: 1289 Loa 55.94 Br ex - Dght 3.750 Lbp 49.51 Br md 8.81 Dpth 4.07 Welded, 1 dk	**(B11B2FV) Fishing Vessel**	**1 oil engine** driving 1 FP propeller Total Power: 993kW (1,350hp) 11.5kn Hanshin 6LUN28AG 1 x 4 Stroke 6 Cy. 280 x 480 993kW (1350bhp) The Hanshin Diesel Works Ltd-Japan AuxGen: 2 x 200kW 225V a.c
7932006 *JVMX4*	**SINBAD** *ex* Skredsvik *-2012* *ex* M 70 *-1995* *ex* KBV 172 *-1992* *ex* TV 172 *-1992* - *Ulaanbaatar* *Mongolia* MMSI: 457432000 Official number: 29221181	*250* - -		**1981-10 Karlskronavarvet AB — Karlskrona** Yd No: 394 Loa 49.92 Br ex 8.64 Dght 2.610 Lbp 46.00 Br md 8.53 Dpth 4.55 Bonded, 1 dk	**(B12D2FP) Fishery Patrol Vessel** Hull Material: Reinforced Plastic	**2 oil engines** sr geared to sc. shafts driving 2 CP propellers Total Power: 3,296kW (4,482hp) 18.8kn Hedemora V16A/15 2 x Vee 4 Stroke 16 Cy. 185 x 210 each-1648kW (2241bhp) Hedemora Diesel AB-Sweden AuxGen: 2 x 170kW 380V 50Hz a.c Thrusters: 1 Thwart. FP thruster (f) Fuel: 73.0 (d.f.) 15.0pd
8978344 - -	**SINBAD** - **Dream Destinations** McDonalds Restaurants Pte Ltd	**468** 140 -		**2002-06 Delta Marine Industries, Inc. — Seattle, Wa** Yd No: 126001 Loa 38.18 Br ex 8.65 Dght 3.200 Lbp 34.05 Br md 8.63 Dpth 4.67 Bonded, 1 dk	**(X11A2YP) Yacht** Hull Material: Reinforced Plastic	**2 oil engines** geared to sc. shafts driving 2 Propellers 12.0kn Caterpillar 3508B 2 x Vee 4 Stroke 8 Cy. 170 x 190 Caterpillar Inc-USA
9233569 *H9HT* -	**SINCERE PISCES** - **Sincere Pisces SA** Mitsubishi Ore Transport Co Ltd (Mitsubishi Koseki Yuso KK) SatCom: Inmarsat C 435451010 *Panama* *Panama* MMSI: 354510000 Official number: 2803101C	**73,427** 24,641 105,716	Class: NK	**2001-08 Imabari Shipbuilding Co Ltd — Marugame KG (Marugame Shipyard)** Yd No: 1353 Loa 234.93 (BB) Br ex - Dght 15.268 Lbp 226.00 Br md 43.00 Dpth 25.40 Welded, 1 dk	**(A21A2BC) Bulk Carrier** Double Hull Grain: 126,189 Compartments: 6 Ho, ER 6 Ha: 6 (26.4 x 28.8)ER Gantry cranes: 2x49t	**1 oil engine** driving 1 FP propeller Total Power: 15,151kW (20,599hp) 15.0kn Mitsubishi 8UEC60LSII 1 x 2 Stroke 8 Cy. 600 x 2300 15151kW (20599bhp) Kobe Hatsudoki KK-Japan Fuel: 4270.0
9326122 *7JNA* -	**SINCERE SALUTE** - **Nippon Yusen Kabushiki Kaisha (NYK Line)** - *Matsuura, Nagasaki* *Japan* MMSI: 432883000 Official number: 141761	**46,466** 25,867 85,778	Class: NK	**2004-12 Oshima Shipbuilding Co Ltd — Saikai NS** Yd No: 10407 Loa 228.05 (BB) Br ex - Dght 13.869 Lbp 223.00 Br md 36.50 Dpth 19.89 Welded, 1 dk	**(A21A2BC) Bulk Carrier** Double Hull Grain: 103,482; Bale: 101,794 Compartments: 5 Ho, ER 5 Ha: (24.7 x 16.9)3 (26.6 x 16.9)ER (25.7 x 15.4)	**1 oil engine** driving 1 FP propeller Total Power: 10,223kW (13,899hp) 14.0kn MAN-B&W 5S60MC-C 1 x 2 Stroke 5 Cy. 600 x 2400 10223kW (13899bhp) Kawasaki Heavy Industries Ltd-Japan Fuel: 2970.0
9593270 *9V9153* -	**SINCERITY** - **United Maritime Pte Ltd** - SatCom: Inmarsat C 456601911 *Singapore* *Singapore* MMSI: 566019000 Official number: 396707	**3,828** 1,765 5,683	Class: NK	**2011-07 Yangzhou Kejin Shipyard Co Ltd — Jiangdu JS** Yd No: 08090 Loa 88.90 Br ex - Dght 7.214 Lbp 83.50 Br md 17.30 Dpth 9.60 Welded, 1 dk	**(A13B2TP) Products Tanker** Double Hull (13F) Liq: 6,147; Liq (Oil): 6,147	**2 oil engines** reduction geared to sc. shafts driving 2 Propellers Total Power: 2,942kW (4,000hp) 12.4kn Yanmar 6EY26 2 x 4 Stroke 6 Cy. 260 x 385 each-1471kW (2000bhp) Yanmar Diesel Engine Co Ltd-Japan Fuel: 290.0
9519092 *3FFD7* -	**SINCERITY ACE** - **Cypress Maritime (Panama) SA** Shoei Kisen Kaisha Ltd SatCom: Inmarsat C 435169010 *Panama* *Panama* MMSI: 351690000 Official number: 4042209	**59,408** 19,152 19,265	Class: NK	**2009-06 Imabari Shipbuilding Co Ltd — Marugame KG (Marugame Shipyard)** Yd No: 1501 Loa 199.97 (BB) Br ex - Dght 10.017 Lbp 192.00 Br md 32.26 Dpth 34.80 Welded, 10 dks plus 2 movable dks	**(A35B2RV) Vehicles Carrier** Side door/ramp (s) Quarter stern door/ramp (s. a.) Cars: 6,237	**1 oil engine** driving 1 FP propeller Total Power: 15,100kW (20,530hp) 20.0kn Mitsubishi 8UEC60LSII 1 x 2 Stroke 8 Cy. 600 x 2300 15100kW (20530bhp) Kobe Hatsudoki KK-Japan Thrusters: 1 Tunnel thruster (f) Fuel: 2700.0
5080093 *IRIR* -	**SINDACO MALVITO V** *ex* Rusbel *-1979* *ex* Cornelis Broere *-1973* *ex* Cornelis B *-1960* **Vetor Srl** - *Naples* *Italy* MMSI: 247223300 Official number: 1871	*490* 248 774	Class: RI (LR) ✠ Classed LR until 4/1/74	**1958-08 D.W. Kremer Sohn — Elmshorn** Yd No: 1064 Loa 58.67 Br ex 8.69 Dght 3.513 Lbp 54.34 Br md 8.60 Dpth 3.74 Riveted\Welded, 1 dk	**(A14A2LO) Water Tanker** Liq: 914 Compartments: 10 Ta, ER	**1 oil engine** driving 1 FP propeller Total Power: 478kW (650hp) 10.5kn Deutz RBV6M545 1 x 4 Stroke 6 Cy. 320 x 450 478kW (650bhp) Kloeckner Humboldt Deutz AG-West Germany AuxGen: 1 x 10kW 110V d.c, 2 x 8kW 110V d.c Fuel: 56.0 (d.f.) 2.5pd
8121161 *YDXQ* -	**SINDANG/PERTAMINA 3010** - **PT PERTAMINA (PERSERO)** - *Jakarta* *Indonesia* MMSI: 525008027	**22,156** 11,477 29,996 T/cm 45.0	Class: (LR) (KI) ✠ Classed LR until 14/12/07	**1982-12 Korea Shipbuilding & Engineering Corp — Busan** Yd No: 2009 Loa 179.97 (BB) Br ex 30.03 Dght 9.119 Lbp 171.10 Br md 30.01 Dpth 15.02 Welded, 1 dk	**(A13B2TP) Products Tanker** Single Hull Liq: 38,786; Liq (Oil): 38,786 Compartments: 11 Ta, ER 3 Cargo Pump (s): 3x1000m³/hr Manifold: Bow/CM: 92m	**1 oil engine** driving 1 FP propeller Total Power: 9,731kW (13,230hp) 15.5kn Sulzer 6RLB66 1 x 2 Stroke 6 Cy. 660 x 1400 9731kW (13230bhp) Mitsubishi Heavy Industries Ltd-Japan AuxGen: 3 x 500kW 450V 60Hz a.c Boilers: e 22.0kgf/cm² (21.6bar), AuxB (o.f.) 16.0kgf/cm² (15.7bar) Fuel: 173.0 (d.f.) (Part Heating Coils) 1333.0 (r.f.) 35.0pd
8417522 - -	**SINDBAD** - **Karachi Port Trust** - *Karachi* *Pakistan*	*344* 106 242	Class: (LR) ✠ Classed LR until 29/3/93	**1985-11 Neue Jadewerft GmbH — Wilhelmshaven** Yd No: 165 Loa 34.35 Br ex 10.14 Dght 3.504 Lbp 32.26 Br md 9.53 Dpth 4.09 Welded, 1 dk	**(B32A2ST) Tug**	**2 oil engines** with flexible couplings & dr gearedto sc. shafts driving 2 Directional propellers Total Power: 2,350kW (3,196hp) 12.0kn MAN 8L25/30 2 x 4 Stroke 8 Cy. 250 x 300 each-1175kW (1598bhp) MAN B&W Diesel GmbH-Augsburg AuxGen: 2 x 88kW 400V 50Hz a.c, 1 x 36kW 400V 50Hz a.c
5173814 - -	**SINDBAD GLORY** *ex* John Herbert *-1981* **Sindbad Shipping Co** -	*137* - -	Class: (LR) ✠ Classed LR until 19/10/79	**1955-08 Henry Robb Ltd. — Leith** Yd No: 444 Loa 28.25 Br ex 7.52 Dght 2.985 Lbp 26.22 Br md 7.01 Dpth 3.51 Riveted\Welded, 1 dk	**(B32A2ST) Tug** Passengers: 20	**2 oil engines** driving 2 FP propellers Total Power: 530kW (720hp) 10.0kn Crossley HRN5 2 x 2 Stroke 5 Cy. 267 x 343 each-265kW (360bhp) Crossley Bros. Ltd.-Manchester Fuel: 20.5
8429458 *AUUM* -	**SINDH** *ex* Borcos 106 *-2008* *ex* Amal *-1989* **ARC Marine Pvt Ltd** - *Mumbai* *India* MMSI: 419076200 Official number: 3427	**122** 36 20	Class: IR (GL)	**1986 Marinteknik Shipbuilders (S) Pte Ltd — Singapore** Yd No: 106 Loa 30.80 Br ex - Dght 0.850 Lbp 28.06 Br md 6.41 Dpth 2.57 Welded, 1 dk	**(B21A2OC) Crew/Supply Vessel** Passengers: unberthed: 50	**2 oil engines** geared to sc. shafts driving 2 Water jets Total Power: 876kW (1,192hp) 16.0kn MWM TBD234V12 2 x Vee 4 Stroke 12 Cy. 128 x 140 each-438kW (596bhp) Motoren Werke Mannheim AG (MWM)-West Germany AuxGen: 2 x 30kW 220/380V 50Hz a.c
9608855 *AVCO* -	**SINDHU SADHANA** - **National Institute of Oceanography Goa** - *Mumbai* *India* MMSI: 419091900 Official number: 3635	**4,154** 1,246 1,200	Class: IR	**2013-12 ABG Shipyard Ltd — Surat** Yd No: 353 Loa 80.00 (BB) Br ex - Dght 5.000 Lbp 70.80 Br md 17.60 Dpth 7.80 Welded, 1 dk	**(B31A2SR) Research Survey Vessel**	**4 oil engines** reduction geared to sc. shafts driving 2 Propellers Total Power: 4,920kW (6,688hp) Caterpillar 3512B 4 x Vee 4 Stroke 12 Cy. 170 x 190 each-1230kW (1672bhp) Caterpillar Inc-USA
8810308 *AUYB* -	**SINDHU SANKALP** *ex* Pacific Spirit *-2010* *ex* Chishio Maru *-2006* **Government of The Republic of India (National Institute of Oceanography)** Seaport Shipping Pvt Ltd *Mumbai* *India* MMSI: 419751000 Official number: 3520	**709** 213 103	Class: IR	**1989-03 KK Kanasashi Zosen — Shizuoka SZ** Yd No: 3186 Converted From: Stern Trawler-2006 Loa 56.30 (BB) Br ex 9.13 Dght 3.500 Lbp 49.00 Br md 9.10 Dpth 3.90 Welded	**(X11A2YP) Yacht**	**1 oil engine** with clutches & sr reverse geared to sc. shaft driving 1 FP propeller Total Power: 1,103kW (1,500hp) 11.5kn Fuji 6S32G 1 x 4 Stroke 6 Cy. 320 x 610 1103kW (1500bhp) Fuji Diesel Co Ltd-Japan Thrusters: 1 Thwart. FP thruster (f)

ID	Ship / Owner	Tonnage	Class	Built	Type	Machinery
7410228 - -	**SINDIBAD I** *ex* Dong Soo No. 110 *-1979* **La Societe Maroco Coreene de Peche** - *Agadir* *Morocco* Official number: 8-526	*675* 324 -	Class: (KR)	**1974**-07 **Miho Zosensho K.K. — Shimizu** Yd No: 998 Loa 57.79 Br ex 10.34 Dght 3.836 Lbp 51.52 Br md 10.30 Dpth 6.66 Welded, 1 dk	**(B11A2FS) Stern Trawler** Ins: 596 2 Ha: 2 (2.2 x 2.2)ER	**1 oil engine** driving 1 FP propeller Total Power: 1,750kW (2,379hp) 13.0kn Akasaka AH40 1 x 4 Stroke 6 Cy. 400 x 600 1750kW (2379bhp) Akasaka Tekkosho KK (Akasaka DieselLtd)-Japan AuxGen: 2 x 200kW 440V a.c
7416507 *CNHN* -	**SINDIBAD II** *ex* Dong Soo No. 111 *-1979* **La Societe Maroco Coreene de Peche** - SatCom: Inmarsat C 424244310 *Agadir* *Morocco* MMSI: 242443000 Official number: 8-522	*656* 309 315	Class: (KR)	**1975**-04 **Miho Zosensho K.K. — Shimizu** Yd No: 1006 Loa 57.79 Br ex 10.34 Dght 3.836 Lbp 51.52 Br md 10.29 Dpth 6.66 Welded, 1 dk	**(B11A2FS) Stern Trawler** Ins: 596 2 Ha: 2 (2.2 x 2.2)	**1 oil engine** driving 1 FP propeller Total Power: 1,750kW (2,379hp) 14.3kn Akasaka AH40 1 x 4 Stroke 6 Cy. 400 x 600 1750kW (2379bhp) Akasaka Tekkosho KK (Akasaka DieselLtd)-Japan AuxGen: 2 x 200kW 445V a.c
9043964 *9V3665* -	**SINDO 1** *ex* Penguin 1 *-2012* *ex* Auto Batam 1 *-2000* *ex* Sing Batam 1 *-1994* **Sindo Ferry Pte Ltd** Sanyang Marine Pte Ltd *Singapore* *Singapore* MMSI: 563917000 Official number: 385071	**144** 63 50	Class: (BV)	**1991**-12 **SBF Shipbuilders (1977) Pty Ltd — Fremantle WA** Yd No: SB30 Loa 30.00 Br ex - Dght 1.900 Lbp 24.60 Br md 6.50 Dpth - Welded	**(A37B2PS) Passenger Ship** Hull Material: Aluminium Alloy Passengers: unberthed: 200	**3 oil engines** reduction geared to sc. shafts driving 3 FP propellers Total Power: 1,650kW (2,244hp) 28.0kn M.T.U. 12V183TE62 3 x Vee 4 Stroke 12 Cy. 128 x 142 each-550kW (748bhp) MTU Friedrichshafen GmbH-Friedrichshafen AuxGen: 2 x 60kW 240V 50Hz a.c
8928466 *9V3472* -	**SINDO 6** *ex* Penguin 6 *-2012* *ex* Auto Batam 6 *-2001* **Sindo Ferry Pte Ltd** Sanyang Marine Pte Ltd *Singapore* *Singapore* MMSI: 563000660 Official number: 384427	**121** 55 -	Class: (BV)	**1990 SBF Shipbuilders (1977) Pty Ltd — Fremantle WA** Loa 29.16 Br ex - Dght - Lbp 23.63 Br md 6.34 Dpth - Welded, 1 dk	**(A37B2PS) Passenger Ship** Passengers: unberthed: 200	**3 oil engines** reduction geared to sc. shafts driving 3 FP propellers Total Power: 1,650kW (2,244hp) 28.0kn M.T.U. 12V183TE62 3 x Vee 4 Stroke 12 Cy. 128 x 142 each-550kW (748bhp) MTU Friedrichshafen GmbH-Friedrichshafen Fuel: 4.8 (d.f.)
9042166 *9V3424* -	**SINDO 7** *ex* Penguin 7 *-2012* *ex* Auto Batam 7 *-2000* **Sindo Ferry Pte Ltd** - *Singapore* *Singapore* MMSI: 563921000 Official number: 384707	*121* 55 40	Class: (BV)	**1991**-03 **SBF Shipbuilders (1977) Pty Ltd — Fremantle WA** Loa 30.00 Br ex 6.50 Dght 1.900 Lbp 24.60 Br md - Dpth - Welded	**(A37B2PS) Passenger Ship** Passengers: unberthed: 200	**3 oil engines** reduction geared to sc. shafts driving 3 FP propellers Total Power: 1,650kW (2,244hp) 27.0kn M.T.U. 12V183TE62 3 x Vee 4 Stroke 12 Cy. 128 x 142 each-550kW (748bhp) MTU Friedrichshafen GmbH-Friedrichshafen Fuel: 4.8 (d.f.)
9105700 *9V3923* -	**SINDO 9** *ex* Penguin 9 *-2013* *ex* Auto Batam 9 *-2000* **Sindo Ferry Pte Ltd** - *Singapore* *Singapore* MMSI: 563923000 Official number: 385877	*183* 71 -		**1993**-10 **Greenbay Marine Pte Ltd — Singapore** Yd No: 89 Loa - Br ex - Dght 1.900 Lbp 30.00 Br md 6.50 Dpth - Welded, 1 dk	**(A37B2PS) Passenger Ship** Hull Material: Aluminium Alloy Passengers: unberthed: 200	**3 oil engines** reduction geared to sc. shafts driving 3 FP propellers Total Power: 1,650kW (2,244hp) 30.0kn M.T.U. 12V183TE62 3 x Vee 4 Stroke 12 Cy. 128 x 142 each-550kW (748bhp) MTU Friedrichshafen GmbH-Friedrichshafen
8879330 *9V5119* -	**SINDO 10** *ex* Penguin 10 *-2012* *ex* Auto Batam 10 *-2000* **Sindo Ferry Pte Ltd** Sanyang Marine Pte Ltd *Singapore* *Singapore* MMSI: 563008450	**177** 69 -		**1994 Greenbay Marine Pte Ltd — Singapore** Yd No: 93 Loa 32.00 Br ex 6.40 Dght - Lbp - Br md - Dpth 3.00 Welded, 1 dk	**(A37B2PS) Passenger Ship** Passengers: unberthed: 200	**3 oil engines** reduction geared to sc. shafts driving 2 FP propellers , 1 Water jet Total Power: 1,830kW (2,487hp) 26.0kn M.T.U. 12V183TE72 3 x Vee 4 Stroke 12 Cy. 128 x 142 each-610kW (829bhp) MTU Friedrichshafen GmbH-Friedrichshafen AuxGen: 2 x 40kW 220/415V 50Hz a.c
9140839 *9V5175* -	**SINDO 12** *ex* Penguin 12 *-2012* *ex* Auto Batam 12 *-2000* **Sindo Ferry Pte Ltd** - *Singapore* *Singapore* MMSI: 563780000 Official number: 386687	**174** 68 -		**1995 Greenbay Marine Pte Ltd — Singapore** Yd No: 109 Loa 32.00 Br ex 6.40 Dght - Lbp - Br md - Dpth 3.00 Welded, 1 dk	**(A37B2PS) Passenger Ship** Passengers: unberthed: 200	**3 oil engines** reduction geared to sc. shafts driving 2 FP propellers , 1 Water jet Total Power: 1,830kW (2,487hp) 26.0kn M.T.U. 12V183TE72 3 x Vee 4 Stroke 12 Cy. 128 x 142 each-610kW (829bhp) MTU Friedrichshafen GmbH-Friedrichshafen AuxGen: 2 x 40kW 220/415V 50Hz a.c
8888173 *9V5176* -	**SINDO 31** *ex* Penguin 31 *-2012* *ex* Auto Batam 13 *-2001* **Sindo Ferry Pte Ltd** Sanyang Marine Pte Ltd *Singapore* *Singapore* MMSI: 563781000 Official number: 386688	**174** 68 -		**1995**-11 **Greenbay Marine Pte Ltd — Singapore** Yd No: 111 Loa 32.00 Br ex 6.40 Dght 1.370 Lbp - Br md - Dpth 3.00 Welded, 1 dk	**(A37B2PS) Passenger Ship** Hull Material: Aluminium Alloy Passengers: unberthed: 200	**3 oil engines** reduction geared to sc. shafts driving 2 FP propellers , 1 Water jet Total Power: 1,830kW (2,487hp) 26.0kn M.T.U. 12V183TE72 3 x Vee 4 Stroke 12 Cy. 128 x 142 each-610kW (829bhp) MTU Friedrichshafen GmbH-Friedrichshafen AuxGen: 2 x 40kW 220/415V 50Hz a.c
7233826 *9GPO* -	**SINDO 901** *ex* Abeto *-2011* *ex* Goshen No. 603 *-1991* *ex* Toyohata Maru No. 23 *-1987* **Sidon Fisheries Ltd** - *Takoradi* *Ghana* Official number: 316717	*374* 170 486	Class: (KR)	**1972 K.K. Ichikawa Zosensho — Ise** Yd No: 1304 Loa 54.40 Br ex 8.54 Dght - Lbp 47.25 Br md 8.51 Dpth 3.94 Riveted\Welded, 1 dk	**(B11B2FV) Fishing Vessel**	**1 oil engine** driving 1 FP propeller Total Power: 1,324kW (1,800hp) Hanshin 6LUD35 1 x 4 Stroke 6 Cy. 350 x 550 1324kW (1800bhp) Hanshin Nainenki Kogyo-Japan
9070876 *9V3894* -	**SINDO EMPRESS** *ex* Penguin Empress *-2012* **Sindo Ferry Pte Ltd** - *Singapore* *Singapore* MMSI: 563665000 Official number: 385798	**190** 66 100		**1993**-10 **Aluminium Craft (88) Pte Ltd — Singapore** Yd No: 22 Loa 27.95 Br ex 7.00 Dght - Lbp 26.00 Br md 6.80 Dpth 2.85 Welded, 1 dk	**(A37B2PS) Passenger Ship** Hull Material: Aluminium Alloy Passengers: unberthed: 150	**2 oil engines** reduction geared to sc. shafts driving 2 FP propellers Total Power: 1,208kW (1,642hp) 24.0kn M.T.U. 12V183TE72 2 x Vee 4 Stroke 12 Cy. 128 x 142 each-604kW (821bhp) MTU Friedrichshafen GmbH-Friedrichshafen AuxGen: 2 x 40kW 550V 50Hz a.c Fuel: 5.0 (d.f.)
8718328 *PNOZ* -	**SINDO JAYA** *ex* Timor Laut *-2010* *ex* We Fong *-2009* *ex* Hakushu Maru *-2002* **PT Sindo Utama Jaya** Singmalloyd Marine (S) Pte Ltd *Indonesia*	*298* 156 700		**1988**-03 **Hakata Zosen K.K. — Imabari** Yd No: 365 Loa - Br ex - Dght 3.052 Lbp 53.01 Br md 9.61 Dpth 5.21 Welded	**(A31A2GX) General Cargo Ship**	**1 oil engine** driving 1 FP propeller Total Power: 625kW (850hp) Niigata 6M26BGT 1 x 4 Stroke 6 Cy. 260 x 460 625kW (850bhp) Niigata Engineering Co Ltd-Japan
8734176 *YD3376* -	**SINDO OCEAN I** **PT Usda Seroja Jaya** - *Dumai* *Indonesia*	**227** 69 -	Class: KI	**2006 PT Usda Seroja Jaya — Rengat** Loa 30.00 Br ex - Dght 2.790 Lbp 26.00 Br md 9.00 Dpth 3.40 Welded, 1 dk	**(B32A2ST) Tug**	**2 oil engines** geared to sc. shafts driving 2 FP propellers Total Power: 1,766kW (2,402hp) Hanshin 6LU28G 1 x 4 Stroke 6 Cy. 280 x 440 883kW (1201bhp) (made 1990, fitted 2006) The Hanshin Diesel Works Ltd-Japan Hanshin 6LU28G 1 x 4 Stroke 6 Cy. 280 x 440 883kW (1201bhp) (made 1999, fitted 2006) The Hanshin Diesel Works Ltd-Japan AuxGen: 2 x 50kW 220V a.c
8735596 *YD3383* -	**SINDO OCEAN III** **PT Usda Seroja Jaya** - *Dumai* *Indonesia*	**110** 33 -	Class: KI	**2007**-09 **PT Usda Seroja Jaya — Rengat** Loa 25.25 Br ex - Dght 2.300 Lbp 22.00 Br md 6.00 Dpth 3.00 Welded, 1 dk	**(B32A2ST) Tug**	**1 oil engine** driving 1 Propeller Total Power: 883kW (1,201hp) 8.0kn Niigata 6M28GX 1 x 4 Stroke 6 Cy. 280 x 440 883kW (1201bhp) (made 1998, fitted 2007) Niigata Engineering Co Ltd-Japan AuxGen: 2 x 96kW 220V a.c
8743062 *YD3507* -	**SINDO PERKASA 8** *ex* Chu Maru No. 28 *-2009* **Pan Orient Pacific** - *Dumai* *Indonesia*	**161** 49 -	Class: KI	**1993**-08 **Mikami Zosen K.K. — Japan** Loa 23.55 Br ex - Dght 2.550 Lbp 21.55 Br md 8.00 Dpth 3.00 Welded, 1 dk	**(B32B2SP) Pusher Tug**	**2 oil engines** reduction geared to sc. shaft driving 2 FP propellers Total Power: 1,472kW (2,002hp) Niigata 6M26GX 2 x 4 Stroke 6 Cy. 260 x 440 each-736kW (1001bhp) Niigata Engineering Co Ltd-Japan AuxGen: 1 x 24kW 225V a.c

IMO / Call sign	Name / Owner / Port	Tonnage	Class	Builder / Dimensions	Type	Machinery
7330911 *YD3252* -	**SINDO PERKASA I** *ex* Aoki Maru No. 15 *-2004* *ex* Sumi Maru No. 88 *-2004* **Pan Orient Pacific** - *Dumai* *Indonesia*	*263* 79 470	Class: KI (NK)	**1973-08 Imura Zosen K.K. — Komatsushima** Yd No: 167 Loa 31.73 Br ex 8.54 Dght 3.190 Lbp 29.70 Br md 8.51 Dpth 3.69 Riveted\Welded, 1 dk	**(B32A2ST) Tug**	**2 oil engines** driving 2 FP propellers Total Power: 2,206kW (3,000hp) 12.5kn Hanshin 6LU32 2 x 4 Stroke 6 Cy. 320 x 510 each-1103kW (1500bhp) Hanshin Nainenki Kogyo-Japan Fuel: 64.0 5.5pd
8223933 *YD3261* -	**SINDO PERKASA II** *ex* Sachi Maru *-2005* *ex* Eishin Maru No. 10 *-2001* **Pan Orient Pacific** - *Dumai* *Indonesia*	*296* 89 350	Class: KI	**1983-03 Shirahama Zosen K.K. — Honai** Yd No: 112 Loa 27.21 Br ex - Dght 3.590 Lbp 25.02 Br md 9.80 Dpth 4.30 Welded, 1 dk	**(B32A2ST) Tug**	**1 oil engine** driving 1 FP propeller Total Power: 1,471kW (2,000hp) Niigata 6M34AFT 1 x 4 Stroke 6 Cy. 340 x 620 1471kW (2000bhp) Niigata Engineering Co Ltd-Japan
8973291 *YD3302* -	**SINDO PERKASA III** *ex* Sumiyoshi Maru No. 58 *-2005* *ex* Ryusho Maru No. 3 *-2005* **Pan Orient Pacific** - *Dumai* *Indonesia*	*159* 48 -	Class: (KI)	**1971-04 Toyo Zosen Tekko KK — Kitakyushu FO** Loa 27.50 Br ex - Dght 3.100 Lbp 24.63 Br md 6.20 Dpth 3.80 Welded, 1 dk	**(B32A2ST) Tug**	**1 oil engine** driving 1 FP propeller Total Power: 1,471kW (2,000hp) 13.0kn Niigata 6M34AFT 1 x 4 Stroke 6 Cy. 340 x 620 1471kW (2000bhp) Niigata Engineering Co Ltd-Japan AuxGen: 1 x 28kW 225V a.c
8626226 *PNSI* -	**SINDO PERMAI** *ex* Sindo 1 *-2010* *ex* Cygnus *-2010* *ex* Harmony *-2007* *ex* Too Maru No. 28 *-1999* **PT Sindo Utama Jaya** - *Jakarta* *Indonesia*	**1,283** 675 2,068	Class: KI (BV)	**1984 Shitanoe Shipbuilding Co Ltd — Usuki OT** Loa 71.81 Br ex - Dght 5.090 Lbp 67.01 Br md 11.51 Dpth 6.71 Welded, 1 dk	**(A31A2GX) General Cargo Ship**	**1 oil engine** driving 1 FP propeller Total Power: 956kW (1,300hp) 10.0kn Akasaka DM28AFD 1 x 4 Stroke 6 Cy. 280 x 460 956kW (1300bhp) Akasaka Tekkosho KK (Akasaka DieselLtd)-Japan
9070888 *9V3893* -	**SINDO PRINCESS** *ex* Penguin Princess *-2012* **Sindo Ferry Pte Ltd** Sanyang Marine Pte Ltd *Singapore* *Singapore* MMSI: 563869000 Official number: 385797	**190** 66 100		**1993-11 Aluminium Craft (88) Pte Ltd — Singapore** Yd No: 23 Loa 27.95 Br ex 7.00 Dght - Lbp 26.00 Br md 6.80 Dpth 2.85 Welded, 1 dk	**(A37B2PS) Passenger Ship** Hull Material: Aluminium Alloy Passengers: unberthed: 150	**2 oil engines** reduction geared to sc. shafts driving 2 FP propellers Total Power: 1,208kW (1,642hp) 24.0kn M.T.U. 12V183TE72 2 x Vee 4 Stroke 12 Cy. 128 x 142 each-604kW (821bhp) MTU Friedrichshafen GmbH-Friedrichshafen AuxGen: 2 x 40kW 550V 50Hz a.c Fuel: 5.0 (d.f.)
9152155 *PMWV* -	**SINDU DWITAMA** *ex* Aki *-2009* **PT Sindutama Bahari** - *Surabaya* *Indonesia* MMSI: 525016445	**818** 246 305	Class: KI	**1997-02 Kanda Zosensho K.K. — Kawajiri** Yd No: 383 Loa 59.69 Br ex 14.00 Dght 2.830 Lbp 55.00 Br md 12.80 Dpth 3.10 Welded, 1 dk	**(A36A2PR) Passenger/Ro-Ro Ship (Vehicles)** Passengers: unberthed: 430 Bow door/ramp (centre) Stern door/ramp (centre) Cars: 8	**2 oil engines** reduction geared to sc. shafts driving 2 FP propellers Total Power: 2,648kW (3,600hp) 15.2kn Daihatsu 6DKM-26 2 x 4 Stroke 6 Cy. 260 x 380 each-1324kW (1800bhp) Daihatsu Diesel Manufacturing Co Lt-Japan AuxGen: 2 x 400kW a.c Fuel: 51.0 (d.f.) 10.7pd
9287015 *POWX* -	**SINDU TRITAMA** *ex* Shuttle Star *-2013* **PT Sindutama Bahari** - *Indonesia*	*388* - 180		**2005-03 Naikai Zosen Corp — Onomichi HS (Setoda Shipyard)** Yd No: 679 Loa 49.82 Br ex - Dght 2.660 Lbp 43.00 Br md 11.00 Dpth 3.59 Welded, 1 dk	**(A37B2PS) Passenger Ship** Passengers: unberthed: 230	**2 oil engines** geared to sc. shafts driving 2 FP propellers Total Power: 2,500kW (3,400hp) Daihatsu 8DKM-20 2 x 4 Stroke 8 Cy. 200 x 300 each-1250kW (1700bhp) Daihatsu Diesel Manufacturing Co Lt-Japan
9364150 *OXFL2* -	**SINE BRES** **Rederiet Nielsen og Bresling A/S (Bres-Line)** - *Faaborg* *Denmark (DIS)* MMSI: 220487000 Official number: D4153	**2,658** 1,195 3,750	Class: LR ✠ **100A1** SS 10/2011 strengthened for heavy cargoes, container cargoes in holds and on upper deck hatch covers LI Ice Class 1A FS at 5.428m draught Max/min draught fwd 5.428/2.78m Max/min draught aft 5.428/3.52m Power required 1876kw, installed power 1880kw ✠ **LMC** **UMS** Eq.Ltr: P; Cable: 440.0/32.0 U3 (a)	**2006-10 Marine Projects Ltd Sp z oo — Gdansk** (Hull) Yd No: (674) **2006-10 Bodewes' Scheepswerven B.V. — Hoogezand** Yd No: 674 Loa 87.90 (BB) Br ex 12.60 Dght 5.300 Lbp 84.94 Br md 12.50 Dpth 6.80 Welded, 1 dk	**(A31A2GX) General Cargo Ship** Grain: 5,819 TEU 184 C Ho 146 TEU C Dk 38 TEU Compartments: 1 Ho, ER 1 Ha: ER (64.5 x 10.3) Ice Capable	**1 oil engine** with flexible couplings & sr geared to sc. shaft driving 1 CP propeller Total Power: 1,880kW (2,556hp) 12.5kn MaK 6M25 1 x 4 Stroke 6 Cy. 255 x 400 1880kW (2556bhp) Caterpillar Motoren GmbH & Co. KG-Germany AuxGen: 2 x 140kW 400V 50Hz a.c, 1 x 264kW 400V 50Hz a.c Thrusters: 1 Water jet (f)
9146455 *OZOK2* -	**SINE MAERSK** **A P Moller - Maersk A/S** A P Moller SatCom: Inmarsat B 321953720 *Kerteminde* *Denmark (DIS)* MMSI: 219537000 Official number: D3658	**92,198** 53,625 110,381 T/cm 124.0	Class: AB	**1998-06 Odense Staalskibsvaerft A/S — Munkebo (Lindo Shipyard)** Yd No: 163 Loa 346.98 (BB) Br ex - Dght 14.940 Lbp 331.54 Br md 42.80 Dpth 24.10 Welded, 1 dk	**(A33A2CC) Container Ship (Fully Cellular)** TEU 9578 incl 817 ref C Compartments: ER, 20 Cell Ho 20 Ha: ER	**1 oil engine** driving 1 FP propeller Total Power: 54,840kW (74,560hp) 25.0kn B&W 12K90MC 1 x 2 Stroke 12 Cy. 900 x 2550 54840kW (74560bhp) Hitachi Zosen Corp-Japan AuxGen: 5 x 3000kW 6600V 60Hz a.c Thrusters: 1 Thwart. FP thruster (f); 2 Thwart. FP thruster (a)
8718603 *HSB3851* -	**SINEE** *ex* Seiwa Maru *-2008* **Praramsarm Khonsong Co Ltd** Trans Ocean Supply (1992) Co Ltd *Bangkok* *Thailand* Official number: 510083186	**324** 107 458		**1988-03 Shitanoe Shipbuilding Co Ltd — Usuki OT** Yd No: 1078 Loa 43.00 (BB) Br ex 7.52 Dght 3.210 Lbp 39.04 Br md 7.50 Dpth 3.50 Welded, 1 dk	**(A12E2LE) Edible Oil Tanker**	**1 oil engine** sr geared to sc. shaft driving 1 FP propeller Total Power: 599kW (814hp) 11.0kn Yanmar MF24-MT 1 x 4 Stroke 6 Cy. 240 x 440 599kW (814bhp) Yanmar Diesel Engine Co Ltd-Japan
8711291 *YJRC5* -	**SINEGORSK** *ex* Fesco Sinegorsk *-2012* *ex* Sinegorsk *-2011* **Mintaka Overseas Ltd** Standard Shipping Co *Port Vila* *Vanuatu* MMSI: 576292000 Official number: 2042	**7,095** 2,936 7,365 T/cm 20.2	Class: RS	**1991-06 Ast. Reunidos del Nervion S.A. — Bilbao** Yd No: 562 Loa 132.76 Br ex 19.86 Dght 6.881 Lbp 122.06 Br md - Dpth 8.80 Welded, 1 dk	**(A31A2GX) General Cargo Ship** Grain: 10,600; Bale: 10,022 TEU 318 Compartments: 4 Ho, ER 4 Ha: (12.6 x 10.2) (19.2 x 15.4)2 (18.8 x 15.4)ER Cranes: 4x20t Ice Capable	**1 oil engine** driving 1 CP propeller Total Power: 5,100kW (6,934hp) 15.5kn B&W 6DKRN42/136 1 x 2 Stroke 6 Cy. 420 x 1360 5100kW (6934bhp) Bryanskiy Mashinostroitelnyy Zavod (BMZ)-Bryansk AuxGen: 2 x 440kW 380V 50Hz a.c, 1 x 400kW 380V 50Hz a.c
7534127 *UGGO* -	**SINEGORYE** *ex* Gc-21 *-2008* *ex* Dolinsk *-2006* *ex* Sinegorye *-2005* **Vekha Co Ltd** OOO 'Etel' *Nevelsk* *Russia*	**739** 221 358	Class: (RS)	**1975 Volgogradskiy Sudostroitelnyy Zavod — Volgograd** Yd No: 862 Loa 53.73 (BB) Br ex 10.52 Dght 4.290 Lbp 47.92 Br md 10.50 Dpth 6.00 Welded, 1 dk	**(B11A2FS) Stern Trawler** Ins: 218 Ice Capable	**1 oil engine** driving 1 CP propeller Total Power: 971kW (1,320hp) 12.5kn S.K.L. 8NVD48A-2U 1 x 4 Stroke 8 Cy. 320 x 480 971kW (1320bhp) VEB Schwermaschinenbau "KarlLiebknecht" (SKL)-Magdeburg Thrusters: 1 Thwart. FP thruster (f); 1 Tunnel thruster (a) Fuel: 192.0 (d.f.)
9066875 *UBKH3* -	**SINEKURA-1** *ex* Hisayoshi Maru *-2011* **Midglen Logistics Sakhalin LLC** - *Korsakov* *Russia* MMSI: 273357230	**825** 247 544	Class: RS	**1993-08 Ishii Zosen K.K. — Futtsu** Yd No: 301 Loa 51.00 Br ex - Dght 3.123 Lbp 46.00 Br md 12.00 Dpth 5.00 Welded, 1 dk	**(A24D2BA) Aggregates Carrier** Grain: 317 Compartments: 1 Ho, ER 1 Ha: ER	**1 oil engine** with clutches & reverse geared to sc. shaft driving 1 FP propeller Total Power: 1,030kW (1,400hp) Niigata 6M28BGT 1 x 4 Stroke 6 Cy. 280 x 480 1030kW (1400bhp) Niigata Engineering Co Ltd-Japan Thrusters: 1 Thwart. FP thruster (f)
8805884 *UBKH4* -	**SINEKURA-2** *ex* Myoho Maru *-2011* **Hydro Mechanized Enterprise 'Onega' LLC** - *Arkhangelsk* *Russia* MMSI: 273358230	**724** 215 987	Class: RS	**1988-06 Nakatani Shipyard Co. Ltd. — Etajima** Yd No: 518 Loa - Br ex - Dght 3.911 Lbp 50.02 Br md 12.01 Dpth 5.11 Welded	**(A31A2GX) General Cargo Ship**	**1 oil engine** driving 1 FP propeller Total Power: 736kW (1,001hp) Yanmar MF33-DT 1 x 4 Stroke 6 Cy. 330 x 620 736kW (1001bhp) Matsue Nainenki Kogyo-Japan
9478468 *3FLL4* -	**SINFONIA** **Adoramar Shipping Inc** World Marine Co Ltd *Panama* *Panama* MMSI: 372062000 Official number: 4208510	**21,483** 10,828 33,174 T/cm 46.5	Class: NK	**2010-10 Kanda Zosensho K.K. — Kawajiri** Yd No: 513 Loa 177.00 (BB) Br ex - Dght 10.034 Lbp 170.00 Br md 28.60 Dpth 14.35 Welded, 1 dk	**(A31A2GO) Open Hatch Cargo Ship** Double Hull Grain: 42,630; Bale: 41,207 Compartments: 5 Ho, ER 5 Ha: 3 (21.3 x 24.2) (19.7 x 24.2)ER (16.4 x 16.4) Cranes: 4x30.5t	**1 oil engine** driving 1 FP propeller Total Power: 6,550kW (8,905hp) 14.5kn Mitsubishi 6UEC45LSE 1 x 2 Stroke 6 Cy. 450 x 1840 6550kW (8905bhp) Kobe Hatsudoki KK-Japan Fuel: 130.0 (d.f.) 1290.0 (r.f.)

Number / Call sign / Flag	Name / Owner / Port	Tonnage	Class	Builder / Dimensions	Type / Cargo	Machinery
5427124 *TUN2199* AN 925	**SINFRA** *ex* Fridrika *-1977* **Ivoirgel** - *Abidjan* *Cote d'Ivoire*	*175* 60 111	Class: (BV)	**1963 Haarlemsche Scheepsbouw Mij. N.V. — Haarlem** Yd No: 579 Loa 28.00 Br ex 6.81 Dght - Lbp 25.25 Br md 6.71 Dpth 3.61 Welded, 1 dk	**(B11A2FT) Trawler** 2 Ha: 2 (1.0 x 1.3) Derricks: 1x2t	**1 oil engine** geared to sc. shaft driving 1 FP propeller Total Power: 588kW (799hp) Crepelle 8SN1 1 x 4 Stroke 8 Cy. 260 x 280 588kW (799bhp) Crepelle et Cie-France Fuel: 26.0 (d.f.)
9645255 *9WOH2* -	**SING HONG JAYA 5** **Sing Hong Jaya Shipping Sdn Bhd** - *Kuching* *Malaysia* Official number: 334697	**149** 45 138	Class: NK	**2011-11 Rantau Megajaya Shipbuilding Sdn Bhd — Sibu** Yd No: RMJ08/09 Loa 23.90 Br ex - Dght 2.850 Lbp 21.47 Br md 7.32 Dpth 3.35 Welded, 1 dk	**(B32A2ST) Tug**	**2 oil engines** reduction geared to sc. shafts driving 2 FP propellers Total Power: 894kW (1,216hp) Cummins KTA-19-M3 2 x 4 Stroke 6 Cy. 159 x 159 each-447kW (608bhp) Cummins Engine Co Inc-USA Fuel: 90.0
9062439 *9MKQ2* -	**SINGA BERLIAN** *ex* Toa Maru No. 18 *-2010* **Sin Soon Hock Sdn Bhd** - SatCom: Inmarsat C 453301193 *Penang* *Malaysia* MMSI: 533004300 Official number: 333429	**998** 586 1,940	Class: (NK)	**1993-09 Kyoei Zosen KK — Mihara HS** Yd No: 256 Loa 71.78 (BB) Br ex 11.82 Dght 4.806 Lbp 66.00 Br md 11.80 Dpth 5.35 Welded, 1 dk	**(A13B2TP) Products Tanker** Liq: 2,200; Liq (Oil): 2,200	**1 oil engine** driving 1 FP propeller Total Power: 736kW (1,001hp) 10.0kn Hanshin LH34L 1 x 4 Stroke 6 Cy. 340 x 640 736kW (1001bhp) The Hanshin Diesel Works Ltd-Japan Fuel: 70.0 (d.f.)
9087829 *9MKS3* -	**SINGA INTAN** *ex* Sankyo Maru No. 2 *-2013* **Sin Soon Hock Sdn Bhd** - *Malaysia* MMSI: 533054600	*609* 424 1,301	Class: MY	**1994-02 Kegoya Dock K.K. — Kure** Yd No: 953 Loa 68.04 (BB) Br ex 10.42 Dght 4.150 Lbp 62.00 Br md 10.40 Dpth 4.60 Welded, 1 dk	**(A13B2TP) Products Tanker** Liq: 1,200; Liq (Oil): 1,200 Cargo Heating Coils Compartments: 8 Ta, ER 2 Cargo Pump (s): 2x400m³/hr Manifold: Bow/CM: 31m	**1 oil engine** driving 1 CP propeller Total Power: 736kW (1,001hp) 10.5kn Hanshin LH31G 1 x 4 Stroke 6 Cy. 310 x 530 736kW (1001bhp) The Hanshin Diesel Works Ltd-Japan AuxGen: 1 x 120kW 220V 60Hz a.c Fuel: 69.7 (d.f.) 4.6pd
8735778 - -	**SINGA MAJU** *ex* Noknannam 15 *-2009* **Singa Tanker Sdn Bhd** Sin Soon Hock Sdn Bhd	**205** 114 300		**2000-12 PSP Marine Co Ltd — Samut Sakhon** Loa 33.00 Br ex - Dght 3.127 Lbp - Br md 7.00 Dpth 3.90 Welded, 1 dk	**(A13B2TP) Products Tanker**	**1 oil engine** geared to sc. schaft driving 1 FP propeller Total Power: 746kW (1,014hp) Cummins KT-2300-M 1 x Vee 4 Stroke 12 Cy. 159 x 159 746kW (1014bhp) Cummins Engine Co Inc-USA
8744353 - -	**SINGA MEWAH** *ex* Paong II *-2010* *ex* Sarawak *-2000* **Singa Marine Sdn Bhd** Brantas Sdn Bhd	**199** 60 -		**1988-12 Sarawak Slipways Sdn Bhd — Miri** Loa 34.89 Br ex - Dght - Lbp - Br md 9.72 Dpth 2.40 Welded, 1 dk	**(A35D2RL) Landing Craft**	**2 oil engines** reduction geared to sc. shafts driving 2 FP propellers Total Power: 596kW (810hp) Cummins NTA-855-M 2 x 4 Stroke 6 Cy. 140 x 152 each-298kW (405bhp) Cummins Engine Co Inc-USA
6402200 *HO7669* -	**SINGA RAJA** *ex* Ote Maru No. 6 *-2000* **Compania de Navegacion Sofia SA** Tunas (Pte) Ltd *Panama* *Panama* Official number: 0319373A	*361* 189 540	Class: (NK)	**1963 K.K. Taihei Kogyo — Akitsu** Yd No: 121 Loa 45.88 Br ex 7.42 Dght 3.404 Lbp 41.79 Br md 7.40 Dpth 3.71 Welded, 1 dk	**(A13B2TU) Tanker (unspecified)** Liq: 608; Liq (Oil): 608 Compartments: 6 Ta, ER	**1 oil engine** driving 1 FP propeller Total Power: 368kW (500hp) 10.0kn Kanegafuchi 1 x 4 Stroke 6 Cy. 275 x 400 368kW (500bhp) Kanegafuchi Diesel-Japan AuxGen: 1 x 7kW 105V d.c, 1 x 5kW 105V d.c Fuel: 25.5 1.5pd
9143063 *VRVL2* -	**SINGAPORE** *ex* OOCL Singapore *-2011* **Rea Marine LLC** Technomar Shipping Inc SatCom: Inmarsat B 347754410 *Hong Kong* *Hong Kong* MMSI: 477544000 Official number: HK-0350	**66,086** 30,853 67,473 T/cm 92.0	Class: RI (AB)	**1997-08 Mitsubishi Heavy Industries Ltd. — Nagasaki** Yd No: 2129 Loa 276.02 (BB) Br ex - Dght 14.000 Lbp 262.00 Br md 40.90 Dpth 24.30 Welded, 1 dk	**(A33A2CC) Container Ship (Fully Cellular)** TEU 5390 C Ho 2538 TEU C Dk 2852 TEU incl 442 ref C. Compartments: ER, 8 Cell Ho 15 Ha: ER	**1 oil engine** driving 1 FP propeller Total Power: 48,635kW (66,124hp) 24.9kn Sulzer 12RTA84C 1 x 2 Stroke 12 Cy. 840 x 2400 48635kW (66124bhp) Mitsubishi Heavy Industries Ltd-Japan AuxGen: 1 x 2100kW 450V 60Hz a.c, 3 x 2100kW 450V 60Hz a.c Thrusters: 1 Thwart. CP thruster (f) Fuel: 303.0 (d.f.) (Heating Coils) 7965.0 (r.f.)
9181742 *3FQZ8* -	**SINGAPORE BRIDGE** **Oak Shipmanagement SA** Shinyo Kaiun Co Ltd SatCom: Inmarsat B 335524810 *Panama* *Panama* MMSI: 355248000 Official number: 2580398C	**14,855** 5,397 16,563	Class: NK	**1998-08 Naikai Zosen Corp — Onomichi HS (Setoda Shipyard)** Yd No: 635 Loa 162.00 (BB) Br ex - Dght 8.272 Lbp 152.00 Br md 26.20 Dpth 13.20 Welded, 1 dk	**(A33A2CC) Container Ship (Fully Cellular)** TEU 1064 C Ho 500 TEU C Dk 564 TEU incl 150 ref C 8 Ha:	**1 oil engine** driving 1 FP propeller Total Power: 12,240kW (16,642hp) 19.0kn MAN-B&W 6S60MC 1 x 2 Stroke 6 Cy. 600 x 2292 12240kW (16642bhp) Hitachi Zosen Corp-Japan AuxGen: 3 x 720kW 450V 60Hz a.c Thrusters: 1 Tunnel thruster (f) Fuel: 1500.0
9599901 *9V9910* -	**SINGAPORE BULKER** **Brilliant Ocean Shipping Pte Ltd** Soon Fong Shipping Pte Ltd SatCom: Inmarsat C 456660610 *Singapore* *Singapore* MMSI: 566606000 Official number: 397737	**32,987** 19,231 56,719 T/cm 58.8	Class: LR ✠ **100A1** SS 07/2012 bulk carrier CSR BC-A Nos. 2 & 4 holds may be empty GRAB (20) ESP **ShipRight** (ACS (B),CM) *IWS LI EP ✠ **LMC** **UMS** Cable: 632.5/73.0 U3 (a)	**2012-07 Jinling Shipyard — Nanjing JS** Yd No: JLZ9100417 Loa 189.99 (BB) Br ex 32.30 Dght 12.800 Lbp 185.00 Br md 32.26 Dpth 18.00 Welded, 1 dk	**(A21A2BC) Bulk Carrier** Grain: 71,634; Bale: 68,200 Compartments: 5 Ho, ER 5 Ha: ER Cranes: 4x30t	**1 oil engine** driving 1 FP propeller Total Power: 9,480kW (12,889hp) 14.2kn MAN-B&W 6S50MC-C 1 x 2 Stroke 6 Cy. 500 x 2000 9480kW (12889bhp) STX Engine Co Ltd-South Korea AuxGen: 3 x 600kW 450V 60Hz a.c Boilers: WTAuxB (Comp) 8.7kgf/cm² (8.5bar)
9200809 *SYHB* -	**SINGAPORE EXPRESS** **Takoulis Maritime Corp** Costamare Shipping Co SA *Piraeus* *Greece* MMSI: 239730000 Official number: 10783	**54,401** 23,872 66,793 T/cm 83.0	Class: GL	**2000-08 Hyundai Heavy Industries Co Ltd — Ulsan** Yd No: 1229 Loa 294.06 (BB) Br ex - Dght 13.550 Lbp 283.30 Br md 32.20 Dpth 21.80 Welded, 1 dk	**(A33A2CC) Container Ship (Fully Cellular)** TEU 4843 C Ho 2326 TEU C Dk 2564 TEU incl 350 ref C 17 Ha:	**1 oil engine** driving 1 FP propeller Total Power: 40,040kW (54,438hp) 24.0kn MAN-B&W 7K98MC 1 x 2 Stroke 7 Cy. 980 x 2660 40040kW (54438bhp) Hyundai Heavy Industries Co Ltd-South Korea AuxGen: 2 x 2280kW 220/440V a.c, 1 x 1710kW 220/440V a.c, 1 x 2665kW 220/440V a.c Thrusters: 1 Thwart. CP thruster (f)
7606308 *5NTX* -	**SINGAPORE INSPECTOR** *ex* Noordhoek Singapore *-2010* *ex* Serviceman *-2000* *ex* Smit Marlin *-1997* *ex* Smit-Lloyd 61 *-1985* **Euroflow Designs Ltd** - *Lagos* *Nigeria* MMSI: 657608000 Official number: SR 1579	**1,803** 540 2,270	Class: LR (AB) **100A1** SS 04/2012 offshore supply ship **LMC** Eq.Ltr: N; Cable: 990.0/46.0 U2	**1977-06 Scheepswerf "De Waal" B.V. — Zaltbommel** Yd No: 710 Converted From: Maintenance Vessel, Offshore-1989 Converted From: Offshore Supply Ship-1985 Loa 65.65 (BB) Br ex 14.05 Dght 5.950 Lbp 60.03 Br md 14.01 Dpth 7.22 Welded, 1 dk	**(B21A20S) Platform Supply Ship** Cranes: 1x25t	**2 oil engines** sr geared to sc. shafts driving 2 CP propellers Total Power: 4,474kW (6,082hp) 12.0kn Bolnes 14VDNL150/600 2 x Vee 2 Stroke 14 Cy. 190 x 350 each-2237kW (3041bhp) 'Bolnes' Motorenfabriek BV-Netherlands AuxGen: 2 x 260kW 440V 60Hz a.c, 3 x 160kW 440V 60Hz a.c, 1 x 64kW 440V 60Hz a.c Thrusters: 1 Thwart. FP thruster (f); 1 Retract. directional thruster (f); 1 Thwart. FP thruster (a) Fuel: 750.0 (d.f.) 10.0pd
9478262 *9V7906* -	**SINGAPORE PIONEER** **Orange Maritime Pte Ltd** Wooil Marine Co Ltd SatCom: Inmarsat C 456446610 *Singapore* *Singapore* MMSI: 564466000 Official number: 395030	**6,961** 3,471 11,543 T/cm 21.1	Class: NK	**2009-07 Murakami Hide Zosen K.K. — Imabari** Yd No: 565 Loa 119.58 (BB) Br ex 20.82 Dght 7.813 Lbp 112.60 Br md 20.80 Dpth 10.60 Welded, 1 dk	**(A12B2TR) Chemical/Products Tanker** Double Hull (13F) Liq: 12,428; Liq (Oil): 12,428 Cargo Heating Coils Compartments: 14 Wing Ta, ER 14 Cargo Pump (s): 14x300m³/hr Manifold: Bow/CM: 59.9m	**1 oil engine** driving 1 FP propeller Total Power: 3,900kW (5,302hp) 13.0kn MAN-B&W 6L35MC 1 x 2 Stroke 6 Cy. 350 x 1050 3900kW (5302bhp) Hitachi Zosen Corp-Japan AuxGen: 3 x 315kW a.c Thrusters: 1 Tunnel thruster (f) Fuel: 74.2 (d.f.) 710.0 (r.f.)
9402263 *9VLV8* -	**SINGAPORE RIVER** *ex* Oasis River *-2013* **'K' Line Pte Ltd (KLPL)** - SatCom: Inmarsat Mini-M 764884243 *Singapore* *Singapore* MMSI: 563366000 Official number: 394120	**59,258** 36,052 115,126 T/cm 92.4	Class: AB	**2009-03 Sasebo Heavy Industries Co. Ltd. — Sasebo Yard, Sasebo** Yd No: 762 Loa 243.80 (BB) Br ex 42.03 Dght 15.630 Lbp 234.00 Br md 42.00 Dpth 21.50 Welded, 1 dk	**(A13A2TV) Crude Oil Tanker** Double Hull (13F) Liq: 124,078; Liq (Oil): 126,606 Cargo Heating Coils Compartments: 12 Wing Ta, 2 Wing Slop Ta, ER 3 Cargo Pump (s): 3x2500m³/hr Manifold: Bow/CM: 119.6m	**1 oil engine** driving 1 FP propeller Total Power: 12,450kW (16,927hp) 15.0kn MAN-B&W 6S60MC-C 1 x 2 Stroke 6 Cy. 600 x 2400 12450kW (16927bhp) Mitsui Engineering & Shipbuilding CLtd-Japan AuxGen: 3 x 700kW a.c Fuel: 75.0 (d.f.) 3100.0 (r.f.)

IMO / Call sign	Ship / Owner	Tonnage	Class	Builder / Dimensions	Type / Cargo	Machinery
9362372 *3EJX5* -	**SINGAPORE STAR** **South Melody Shipping Inc** Star Maritime Pte Ltd *Panama* *Panama* MMSI: 372639000 Official number: 3265807A	**30,042** 13,312 50,605 T/cm 52.0	Class: NV	**2007-03 SPP Shipbuilding Co Ltd — Tongyeong** Yd No: H1005 Loa 183.00 (BB) Br ex 32.24 Dght 13.000 Lbp 174.00 Br md 32.20 Dpth 19.10 Welded, 1 dk	**(A12B2TR) Chemical/Products Tanker** Double Hull (13F) Liq: 52,141; Liq (Oil): 52,151 Cargo Heating Coils Compartments: 12 Wing Ta, 2 Wing Slop Ta, ER 12 Cargo Pump (s): 12x600m^3/hr Manifold: Bow/CM: 92m	**1 oil engine** driving 1 FP propeller Total Power: 8,061kW (10,960hp) 14.9kn Sulzer 7RTA48T-B 1 x 2 Stroke 7 Cy. 480 x 2000 8061kW (10960bhp) Brodosplit Tvornica Dizel Motoradoo-Croatia AuxGen: 3 x 900kW 440/220V 60Hz a.c Fuel: 181.0 (d.f.) 1635.0 (r.f.)
9273052 *3EUJ4* -	**SINGAPORE VOYAGER** **MK Centennial Maritime BV** - *Panama* *Panama* MMSI: 372919000 Official number: 4237811	**56,365** 32,506 105,850 T/cm 90.4	Class: AB	**2003-01 Namura Shipbuilding Co Ltd — Imari SG** Yd No: 232 Loa 241.03 (BB) Br ex - Dght 14.923 Lbp 232.00 Br md 42.00 Dpth 21.20 Welded, 1 dk	**(A13A2TV) Crude Oil Tanker** Double Hull (13F) Liq: 119,670; Liq (Oil): 119,670 Cargo Heating Coils Compartments: 12 Wing Ta, ER 3 Cargo Pump (s): 3x2500m^3/hr Manifold: Bow/CM: 119m	**1 oil engine** driving 1 FP propeller Total Power: 11,770kW (16,002hp) 15.0kn MAN-B&W 6S60MC 1 x 2 Stroke 6 Cy. 600 x 2292 11770kW (16002bhp) Mitsui Engineering & Shipbuilding CLtd-Japan AuxGen: 3 x 500kW 440/110V 60Hz a.c Fuel: 200.0 (d.f.) (Heating Coils) 2700.0 (r.f.) 51.0pd
9188116 *S6TG* -	**SINGAPURA SELATAN** **Odyssey Maritime Pte Ltd** Nissho Odyssey Ship Management Pte Ltd SatCom: Inmarsat Mini-M 763238191 *Singapore* *Singapore* MMSI: 564577000 Official number: 388198	**2,502** 751 2,915 T/cm 10.9	Class: NK	**1998-03 Kurinoura Dockyard Co Ltd — Yawatahama EH** Yd No: 348 Loa 95.50 (BB) Br ex - Dght 4.802 Lbp 89.50 Br md 13.80 Dpth 6.40 Welded, 1 dk	**(A13C2LA) Asphalt/Bitumen Tanker** Double Hull Liq: 2,589; Liq (Oil): 2,642; Asphalt: 2,642 Cargo Heating Coils Compartments: 8 Wing Ta, ER 2 Cargo Pump (s): 2x400m^3/hr Manifold: Bow/CM: 45m	**1 oil engine** driving 1 FP propeller Total Power: 1,912kW (2,600hp) 12.5kn Akasaka A37 1 x 4 Stroke 6 Cy. 370 x 720 1912kW (2600bhp) Akasaka Tekkosho KK (Akasaka DieselLtd)-Japan AuxGen: 2 x a.c Thrusters: 1 Tunnel thruster (f) Fuel: 75.0 175.0 (r.f.)
9033945 *VTDR* -	**SINGARAVELAR** **Chennai Port Trust** - *Chennai* *India* Official number: 2601	**379** 114 90	Class: (IR)	**1996-06 Bharati Shipyard Ltd — Ratnagiri** Yd No: 233 Loa 32.00 Br ex 10.72 Dght 4.200 Lbp 31.00 Br md 10.70 Dpth 3.70 Welded, 1 dk	**(B32A2ST) Tug**	**2 oil engines** reduction geared integral to 'VS' units driving 2 Voith-Schneider propellers Total Power: 2,500kW (3,400hp) 12.0kn Normo KRM-8 2 x 4 Stroke 8 Cy. 250 x 300 each-1250kW (1700bhp) Garden Reach Shipbuilders &Engineers Ltd-India AuxGen: 2 x 60kW 415V 50Hz a.c Fuel: 40.0 (d.f.)
9710218 *9WQ02* -	**SINGAWAN ANGGUN** *ex* Lighthouse LMS101 *-2013* **Shing Liang Shipping Sdn Bhd** - *Kuching* *Malaysia* Official number: 334828	**146** 44 148	Class: NK	**2013-11 Lighthouse Marine Shipbuilding Sdn Bhd — Sibu** Yd No: LMS101 Loa 23.50 Br ex 7.33 Dght 2.700 Lbp 21.32 Br md 7.32 Dpth 3.20 Welded, 1 dk	**(B32A2ST) Tug**	**2 oil engines** reduction geared to sc. shafts driving 2 Propellers Total Power: 882kW (1,200hp) Cummins KTA-19-M3 2 x 4 Stroke 6 Cy. 159 x 159 each-441kW (600bhp) Cummins Engine Co Ltd-United Kingdom Fuel: 108.0
9197375 *PCGM* -	**SINGELGRACHT** **Rederij Singelgracht** Spliethoff's Bevrachtingskantoor BV *Amsterdam* *Netherlands* MMSI: 245546000 Official number: 36733	**16,641** 6,700 21,402 T/cm 35.1	Class: LR ✠ **100A1** SS 10/2009 strengthened for heavy cargoes, container cargoes in holds, on upper deck and upper deck hatches, timber deck cargoes tank top suitable for regular discharge by grabs LA LI *IWS Ice Class 1A (Finnish-Swedish Ice Class Rules 1985) Max draught midship 10.943m Max/min draught aft 11.47/6.6m Max/min draught forward 11.47/4.2m ✠ **LMC** **UMS** Eq.Ltr: O†; Cable: 605.0/70.0 U2	**2000-02 Mitsubishi Heavy Industries Ltd. — Shimonoseki** Yd No: 1061 Loa 168.14 (BB) Br ex 25.37 Dght 10.740 Lbp 162.08 Br md 25.20 Dpth 14.62 Welded, 1 dk	**(A31A2GX) General Cargo Ship** Grain: 23,786; Bale: 23,786 TEU 1127 C Ho 478 TEU C Dk 649 TEU incl 120 ref C. Compartments: 3 Ho, ER 3 Ha: (26.6 x 15.2)Tappered (38.4 x 17.8) (31.9 x 20.4)ER Cranes: 3x120t Ice Capable	**1 oil engine** reverse reduction geared to sc. shaft driving 1 CP propeller Total Power: 12,060kW (16,397hp) 19.5kn Wartsila 6L64 1 x 4 Stroke 6 Cy. 640 x 900 12060kW (16397bhp) Wartsila Italia SpA-Italy AuxGen: 1 x 1000kW 445V 60Hz a.c, 3 x 450kW 445V 60Hz a.c Boilers: TOH (o.f.) 10.2kgf/cm² (10.0bar), TOH (ex.g.) 10.2kgf/cm² (10.0bar) Thrusters: 1 Thwart. CP thruster (f) Fuel: 275.0 (d.f.) (Heating Coils) 1750.0 (r.f.) 45.0pd
8647268 - -	**SINGGASANA LAUT** **PT Barokah Gemilang Perkasa** - *Samarinda* *Indonesia* Official number: 4352/IIK	**399** 120 -	Class: KI	**2010-06 PT Barokah Galangan Perkasa — Samarinda** Yd No: H-001 Loa 36.00 Br ex - Dght 3.390 Lbp 32.92 Br md 9.60 Dpth 4.00 Welded, 1 dk	**(B34L2QU) Utility Vessel**	**2 oil engines** reduction geared to sc. shafts driving 2 FP propellers Total Power: 1,220kW (1,658hp) Yanmar 6AYM-ETE 2 x 4 Stroke 6 Cy. 155 x 180 each-610kW (829bhp) Yanmar Diesel Engine Co Ltd-Japan AuxGen: 2 x 120kW 400V a.c
9051404 - -	**SINGINI** **Government of The Democratic Republic of Congo (Regie des Voies Maritime de Congo)** - *Boma* *Congo (Democratic Republic)*	**184** 55 -	Class: (BV)	**1992-12 Bodewes Binnenvaart B.V. — Millingen a/d Rijn** (Hull) **1992-12 B.V. Scheepswerf Damen — Gorinchem** Yd No: 6736 Loa 30.00 Br ex - Dght - Lbp - Br md 8.00 Dpth - Welded	**(B34Q2QB) Buoy Tender**	**2 oil engines** reduction geared to sc. shafts driving 2 FP propellers Total Power: 810kW (1,102hp) Caterpillar 3408TA 2 x Vee 4 Stroke 8 Cy. 137 x 152 each-405kW (551bhp) Caterpillar Inc-USA
9377664 *9HBC9* -	**SINGLE** *ex* Rova *-2013* **Single Shipping LLC** Norient Product Pool ApS *Valletta* *Malta* MMSI: 256711000 Official number: 9377664	**23,248** 9,915 37,824 T/cm 45.2	Class: NV (AB)	**2007-10 Hyundai Mipo Dockyard Co Ltd — Ulsan** Yd No: 2024 Loa 184.32 (BB) Br ex 27.45 Dght 11.515 Lbp 175.00 Br md 27.40 Dpth 17.20 Welded, 1 dk	**(A12B2TR) Chemical/Products Tanker** Double Hull (13F) Liq: 40,781; Liq (Oil): 41,836 Compartments: 12 Wing Ta, 2 Wing Slop Ta, ER 12 Cargo Pump (s): 10x500m^3/hr, 2x300m^3/hr Manifold: Bow/CM: 92.6m Ice Capable	**1 oil engine** driving 1 FP propeller Total Power: 9,480kW (12,889hp) 15.0kn MAN-B&W 6S50MC-C 1 x 2 Stroke 6 Cy. 500 x 2000 9480kW (12889bhp) Hyundai Heavy Industries Co Ltd-South Korea AuxGen: 3 x 900kW a.c
8617732 *JVEK5* -	**SINGMA TRADER** *ex* He Xi Hao *-2013* *ex* Ping Yang No. 8 *-2007* *ex* Tenrei Maru No. 28 *-2001* **Singma Trader SA** Singmalloyd Marine (S) Pte Ltd *Ulaanbaatar* *Mongolia* MMSI: 457825000	**1,660** 667 1,453	Class: UB	**1987-03 Namikata Shipbuilding Co Ltd — Imabari EH** Yd No: 150 Loa 73.40 Br ex 11.60 Dght 4.201 Lbp 68.03 Br md - Dpth 7.32 Welded, 2 dks	**(A31A2GX) General Cargo Ship** Grain: 2,849; Bale: 2,464 Compartments: 1 Ho, ER 1 Ha: ER	**1 oil engine** driving 1 FP propeller Total Power: 883kW (1,201hp) Makita MNL28M 1 x 4 Stroke 6 Cy. 280 x 480 883kW (1201bhp) Makita Diesel Co Ltd-Japan
8514069 - -	**SINGO 88** *ex* Lu Zrong You 39 *-2012* *ex* Kiryu Maru No. 2 *-2012* **Trump Glory Enterprise Ltd** -	**992** 554 1,850		**1985-10 Kurinoura Dockyard Co Ltd — Yawatahama EH** Yd No: 215 Loa 74.50 (BB) Br ex 11.23 Dght 4.679 Lbp 70.01 Br md 11.21 Dpth 5.11 Welded, 1 dk	**(A13B2TU) Tanker (unspecified)** Liq: 2,150; Liq (Oil): 2,150 Compartments: 10 Ta, ER	**1 oil engine** with clutches, flexible couplings & sr reverse geared to sc. shaft driving 1 FP propeller Total Power: 1,177kW (1,600hp) 10.0kn Makita LS31L 1 x 4 Stroke 6 Cy. 310 x 600 1177kW (1600bhp) Makita Diesel Co Ltd-Japan
7851018 *HQSY5* -	**SINGOON 6** *ex* Sandd Marine No. 10 *-2012* *ex* Tuck Lee Hang No. 3 *-1999* *ex* Doun Maru No. 503 *-1998* **Singoon Marine Pte Ltd** - *San Lorenzo* *Honduras* Official number: L-0326675	*368* 128 650		**1967-02 Government of Japan — Shimonoseki** Loa 47.50 Br ex - Dght 3.301 Lbp 43.52 Br md 8.81 Dpth 4.02 Welded, 1 dk	**(B34A2SH) Hopper, Motor**	**1 oil engine** geared to sc. shaft driving 1 FP propeller Total Power: 441kW (600hp) 8.5kn Daihatsu 6PSHT-26D 1 x 4 Stroke 6 Cy. 260 x 320 441kW (600bhp) Daihatsu Diesel Manufacturing Co Lt-Japan
7326142 - -	**SINGSAMUT** *ex* Singhasamut *-2000* **Bangkok Sea Transport Co Ltd** - *Bangkok* *Thailand* Official number: 161008957	*232* 58 -	Class: (AB)	**1973 Neramit Kansong — Thailand** Yd No: 7 Loa 29.27 Br ex 8.54 Dght - Lbp - Br md - Dpth - Welded, 1 dk	**(B32A2ST) Tug**	**2 oil engines** geared to sc. shafts driving 2 FP propellers Total Power: 2,206kW (3,000hp)
9025912 - -	**SINGSING 18** **PT Setiakawan Makmur Bersama** - *Pontianak* *Indonesia*	**118** 70 -	Class: KI	**2003-03 in Indonesia** Loa 23.15 Br ex - Dght 2.490 Lbp 21.05 Br md 7.30 Dpth 3.00 Welded, 1 dk	**(B32A2ST) Tug**	**2 oil engines** geared to sc. shafts driving 2 Propellers Total Power: 706kW (960hp) Caterpillar 3408C 2 x Vee 4 Stroke 8 Cy. 137 x 152 each-353kW (480bhp) Caterpillar Inc-USA AuxGen: 2 x 88kW 380V a.c

IMO / Call sign	Name / Owner / Manager / Port	Tonnage	Class	Builder / Dimensions	Type / Cargo	Machinery
7610050 *XUMF8* -	**SINGULARITY** *ex* Singolarita *-1996* *ex* Singularity *-1987* **Transatlantic Shipping Service Ltd** Golden Pride Co Ltd SatCom: Inmarsat C 451528410 *Phnom Penh* *Cambodia* MMSI: 515284000 Official number: 0277320	**2,803** 1,710 4,156	Class: GM (LR) (RI) ✠ Classed LR until 14/4/87	**1977-06 Swan Hunter Shipbuilders Ltd. — Readhead Shipyard, S. Shields** Yd No: 594 Loa 89.72 Br ex 14.28 Dght 6.379 Lbp 83.19 Br md 14.20 Dpth 8.56 Welded, 2 dks	**(A31A2GX) General Cargo Ship** Grain: 5,917; Bale: 5,556 TEU 122 C.Ho 90/20' (40') C.Dk 32/20' (40') Compartments: 2 Ho, ER, 2 Tw Dk 2 Ha: 2 (24.9 x 10.1)ER Cranes: 1x20t; Derricks: 2x5t Ice Capable	**1 oil engine** sr geared to sc. shaft driving 1 FP propeller Total Power: 2,052kW (2,790hp) 12.5kn Alpha 18V23L-VO 1 x Vee 4 Stroke 18 Cy. 225 x 300 2052kW (2790bhp) Alpha Diesel A/S-Denmark AuxGen: 3 x 129kW 415V 50Hz a.c Thrusters: 1 Thwart. CP thruster Fuel: 322.0 (d.f.) 9.5pd
7603514 - -	**SINGYI-6** **Petrochemical Industries Corp** - *Yangon* *Myanmar*	*130* - 25	Class: (BV)	**1976-09 Yokohama Yacht Co Ltd — Yokohama KN** Yd No: 728-1 Loa 26.98 Br ex 7.60 Dght 1.401 Lbp 24.49 Br md 7.17 Dpth 2.11 Welded, 1 dk	**(B32B2SP) Pusher Tug**	**2 oil engines** driving 2 FP propellers Total Power: 530kW (720hp) 10.0kn Kubota M6D20BS 2 x 4 Stroke 6 Cy. 200 x 240 each-265kW (360bhp) Kubota Tekkosho-Japan
7603526 - -	**SINGYI-7** **Petrochemical Industries Corp** - *Yangon* *Myanmar*	*130* - 25	Class: (BV)	**1976-09 Yokohama Yacht Co Ltd — Yokohama KN** Yd No: 728-2 Loa 26.98 Br ex 7.60 Dght 1.401 Lbp 24.49 Br md 7.17 Dpth 2.11 Welded, 1 dk	**(B32B2SP) Pusher Tug**	**2 oil engines** driving 2 FP propellers Total Power: 530kW (720hp) 10.0kn Kubota M6D20BS 2 x 4 Stroke 6 Cy. 200 x 240 each-265kW (360bhp) Kubota Tekkosho-Japan
7603538 - -	**SINGYI-8** **Petrochemical Industries Corp** - *Yangon* *Myanmar*	*130* - 25	Class: (BV)	**1976-09 Yokohama Yacht Co Ltd — Yokohama KN** Yd No: 728-3 Loa 26.98 Br ex 7.60 Dght 1.401 Lbp 24.49 Br md 7.17 Dpth 2.11 Welded, 1 dk	**(B32B2SP) Pusher Tug**	**2 oil engines** driving 2 FP propellers Total Power: 530kW (720hp) 10.0kn Kubota M6D20BS 2 x 4 Stroke 6 Cy. 200 x 240 each-265kW (360bhp) Kubota Tekkosho-Japan
7603540 - -	**SINGYI-9** **Petrochemical Industries Corp** - *Yangon* *Myanmar*	*130* - 25	Class: (BV)	**1976-09 Yokohama Yacht Co Ltd — Yokohama KN** Yd No: 728-4 Loa 26.98 Br ex 7.60 Dght 1.401 Lbp 24.49 Br md 7.17 Dpth 2.11 Welded, 1 dk	**(B32B2SP) Pusher Tug**	**2 oil engines** driving 2 FP propellers Total Power: 530kW (720hp) 10.0kn Kubota M6D20BS 2 x 4 Stroke 6 Cy. 200 x 240 each-265kW (360bhp) Kubota Tekkosho-Japan
7603552 - -	**SINGYI-10** **Petrochemical Industries Corp** - *Yangon* *Myanmar*	*130* - 25	Class: (BV)	**1976-09 Yokohama Yacht Co Ltd — Yokohama KN** Yd No: 728-5 Loa 26.98 Br ex 7.60 Dght 1.401 Lbp 24.49 Br md 7.17 Dpth 2.11 Welded, 1 dk	**(B32B2SP) Pusher Tug**	**2 oil engines** driving 2 FP propellers Total Power: 530kW (720hp) 10.0kn Kubota M6D20BS 2 x 4 Stroke 6 Cy. 200 x 240 each-265kW (360bhp) Kubota Tekkosho-Japan
8000678 - -	**SINHABAHU II** **Government of The Democratic Socialist Republic of Sri Lanka (Ports Authority)** - *Colombo* *Sri Lanka*	*265* - 109	Class: (LR) ✠ Classed LR until 7/7/10	**1980-07 Yokohama Yacht Co Ltd — Yokohama KN** Yd No: 773 Loa 33.71 Br ex 8.89 Dght 3.412 Lbp 29.16 Br md 8.41 Dpth 3.99 Welded, 1 dk	**(B32A2ST) Tug**	**2 oil engines** driving 2 CP propellers Total Power: 1,912kW (2,600hp) 12.0kn Akasaka DM28A 2 x 4 Stroke 6 Cy. 280 x 460 each-956kW (1300bhp) Akasaka Tekkosho KK (Akasaka DieselLtd)-Japan AuxGen: 2 x 96kW 410V 50Hz a.c
9148831 - -	**SINHAE No. 5** **Government of The Republic of South Korea (Ministry of Oceans & Fisheries)** Hae Kwang Transport Ltd *Mokpo* *South Korea* MMSI: 440300013 Official number: MPR-964347	**101** - 48	Class: KR	**1996-05 Korea Shipyard Co Ltd — Mokpo** Yd No: 9501 Loa 35.00 Br ex 8.40 Dght 1.499 Lbp 30.12 Br md 7.60 Dpth 1.90 Welded, 1 dk	**(A36A2PR) Passenger/Ro-Ro Ship (Vehicles)**	**2 oil engines** geared to sc. shafts driving 2 FP propellers Total Power: 1,000kW (1,360hp) 13.8kn Caterpillar 3412TA 2 x Vee 4 Stroke 12 Cy. 137 x 152 each-500kW (680bhp) Caterpillar Inc-USA
9401207 - -	**SINHAN EXPRESS FERRY** **Shinhan Shipping Co Ltd** - *Boryeong* *South Korea* MMSI: 440500260 Official number: DSR-069014	**344** - 255	Class: KR	**2006-07 Yeunsoo Shipbuilding Co Ltd — Janghang** Yd No: 124 Loa 66.86 Br ex 10.40 Dght 1.856 Lbp 55.00 Br md 10.40 Dpth 2.75 Welded, 1 dk	**(A36A2PR) Passenger/Ro-Ro Ship (Vehicles)**	**2 oil engines** reduction geared to sc. shafts driving 2 Propellers Total Power: 1,640kW (2,230hp) 12.0kn Cummins KTA-38-M1 2 x Vee 4 Stroke 12 Cy. 159 x 159 each-820kW (1115bhp) Cummins Engine Co Inc-USA AuxGen: 2 x 100kW 225V a.c
9155640 - -	**SINHAN FERRY NO. 3** *ex* Hwawon Renaissance *-2000* **Shinhan Shipping Co Ltd** - *Boryeong* *South Korea* Official number: DSR-964461	**102** - 27	Class: (KR)	**1996-09 Han-Il Shipbuilding & Engineering Co Ltd — Mokpo** Yd No: 96-01 Loa 36.30 Br ex - Dght 1.688 Lbp 29.23 Br md 6.80 Dpth 2.10 Welded, 1 dk	**(A36A2PR) Passenger/Ro-Ro Ship (Vehicles)** Bow ramp Cars: 5	**2 diesel electric oil engines** driving 2 gen. Connecting to 2 elec. motors driving 2 FP propellers Total Power: 662kW (900hp) Yanmar 6LA-DTE 2 x 4 Stroke 6 Cy. 148 x 165 each-331kW (450bhp) Kwangyang Diesel Engine Co Ltd-South Korea
8739451 *9WHQ5* -	**SINHIN 5** **Teck Sing Hing Shipping Sdn Bhd** - *Kuching* *Malaysia* Official number: 332955	**145** 44 -		**2008-08 Kim Huak Trading Sdn Bhd — Sibu** Yd No: KHT033 Loa 23.00 Br ex - Dght - Lbp 21.47 Br md 7.32 Dpth 3.35 Welded, 1 dk	**(B32A2ST) Tug**	**2 oil engines** reduction geared to sc. shafts driving 2 Propellers Total Power: 1,002kW (1,362hp) Yanmar 6LAH-STE3 2 x 4 Stroke 6 Cy. 150 x 165 each-501kW (681bhp) Yanmar Diesel Engine Co Ltd-Japan AuxGen: 2 x 24kW a.c
7328152 - -	**SINIKURT** **Sofis Holdings Ltd** Marinetrade (Singapore) Pte Ltd	*198* 123 -		**1972 Metalock (S) Pte Ltd — Singapore** Converted From: General Cargo Barge, Non-propelled-1972 Loa 26.27 Br ex 5.52 Dght 2.134 Lbp - Br md 5.49 Dpth - Welded, 1 dk	**(A31A2GX) General Cargo Ship** Compartments: 1 Ho, ER 1 Ha: (2.4 x 3.6)ER Cranes: 1x3t	**1 oil engine** geared to sc. shaft driving 1 FP propeller Total Power: 150kW (204hp) 8.5kn Gardner 8L3B 1 x 4 Stroke 8 Cy. 140 x 197 150kW (204bhp) (made 1951, added 1972) L. Gardner & Sons Ltd.-Manchester Fuel: 10.0 (d.f.) 0.5pd
9274941 *5VCN8* -	**SININ** *ex* Laurinda *-2006* **Alicia Marine Co Ltd** IranoHind Shipping Co Ltd *Lome* *Togo* MMSI: 671442000	**30,064** 17,802 52,466 T/cm 55.5	Class: BV (AB)	**2005-05 Tsuneishi Heavy Industries (Cebu) Inc — Balamban** Yd No: SC-049 Loa 189.99 (BB) Br ex - Dght 12.020 Lbp 182.87 Br md 32.26 Dpth 17.00 Welded, 1 dk	**(A21A2BC) Bulk Carrier** Double Bottom Entire Compartment Length Grain: 67,756; Bale: 65,601 Compartments: 5 Ho, ER 5 Ha: 4 (21.3 x 18.4)ER (20.4 x 18.4) Cranes: 4x30t	**1 oil engine** driving 1 FP propeller Total Power: 7,800kW (10,605hp) 14.3kn B&W 6S50MC 1 x 2 Stroke 6 Cy. 500 x 1910 7800kW (10605bhp) Mitsui Engineering & Shipbuilding CLtd-Japan AuxGen: 3 x 480kW 450/230V 60Hz a.c Fuel: 172.0 (d.f.) 2472.0 (r.f.) 33.1pd
9153692 - -	**SINJIN FERRY No. 2** **Sinjin Shipping Ltd** - *Mokpo* *South Korea* MMSI: 440304510 Official number: MPR-964421	**108** 66 241	Class: (KR)	**1996-08 Haewoon Shipbuilding Co Ltd — Mokpo** Yd No: 95-53 Loa 29.23 Br ex 7.00 Dght 1.649 Lbp 28.50 Br md - Dpth 2.00 Welded, 1 dk	**(A37B2PS) Passenger Ship**	**1 oil engine** geared to sc. shaft driving 1 FP propeller Total Power: 350kW (476hp) Caterpillar 3408C 1 x Vee 4 Stroke 8 Cy. 137 x 152 350kW (476bhp) Caterpillar Inc-USA
6901531 - -	**SINKAT** **Government of The Democratic Republic of The Sudan (Railways Department)** - *Port Sudan* *Sudan*	*220* 70	Class: (LR) ✠ Classed LR until 5/70	**1969-04 Martin Jansen GmbH & Co. KG Schiffsw. u. Masch. — Leer** Yd No: 91 Loa 34.32 Br ex 8.36 Dght 3.887 Lbp 31.02 Br md 8.23 Dpth 3.97 Welded, 1 dk	**(B32A2ST) Tug**	**1 oil engine** reverse reduction geared to sc. shaft driving 1 FP propeller Total Power: 964kW (1,311hp) MAN G9V30/45ATL 1 x 4 Stroke 9 Cy. 300 x 450 964kW (1311bhp) Maschinenbau Augsburg Nuernberg (MAN)-Augsburg AuxGen: 2 x 22kW 115V d.c, 1 x 10kW 115V d.c
8942814 - -	**SINNAMCHAI** **Nava Pattana Shipyard Co Ltd** - *Bangkok* *Thailand* Official number: 391001199	*841* 795 -		**1996 Nava Pattana Shipyard Co., Ltd. — Bangkok** Loa 64.05 Br ex - Dght - Lbp 61.00 Br md 14.00 Dpth 5.00 Welded, 1 dk	**(A31A2GX) General Cargo Ship**	**3 oil engines** driving 3 FP propellers Total Power: 939kW (1,278hp) Nissan RD10TA 3 x Vee 4 Stroke 10 Cy. 135 x 125 each-313kW (426bhp) Nissan Diesel Motor Co. Ltd.-Ageo
8812722 *3FBC4* -	**SINO 3** *ex* Sea Hope *-2012* *ex* Cedar Forest *-1995* **Hongkong Sino 3 Shipping Ltd** Guangzhou Kuifenghang Shipping Co Ltd *Panama* *Panama* MMSI: 373433000 Official number: 4422212	**17,061** 9,904 27,939	Class: NK	**1989-02 Shin Kurushima Dockyard Co. Ltd. — Onishi** Yd No: 2608 Loa 176.60 (BB) Br ex 26.05 Dght 9.414 Lbp 169.40 Br md 26.00 Dpth 13.30 Welded, 1 dk	**(A21A2BC) Bulk Carrier** Grain: 38,239; Bale: 37,313 Compartments: 5 Ho, ER 5 Ha: (17.9 x 12.8)4 (19.5 x 17.8)ER Cranes: 4x30t	**1 oil engine** driving 1 FP propeller Total Power: 5,149kW (7,001hp) 14.2kn Mitsubishi 5UEC52LA 1 x 2 Stroke 5 Cy. 520 x 1600 5149kW (7001bhp) Kobe Hatsudoki KK-Japan AuxGen: 2 x 400kW 450V 60Hz a.c Fuel: 106.2 (d.f.) 976.9 (r.f.) 18.6pd

9488126 *VRLA8* -	**SINO 5** *ex* Liangzhou *-2013* **Hongkong Sino 5 Shipping Ltd** Guangzhou Kuifenghang Shipping Co Ltd *Hong Kong* *Hong Kong* MMSI: 477638500 Official number: HK-3614	**5,566** 3,198 7,573	Class: RI	**2012-06 Zhejiang Hexing Shipyard — Wenling ZJ** Yd No: 0702 Loa 122.58 (BB) Br ex - Dght 6.350 Lbp 115.20 Br md 17.60 Dpth 8.50 Welded, 1 dk	**(A31A2GX) General Cargo Ship** Grain: 10,172 TEU 160 Compartments: 3 Ho, ER 3 Ha: ER Cranes: 2x45t	**1 oil engine** reduction geared to sc. shaft driving 1 FP propeller Total Power: 2,500kW (3,399hp) 11.8kn Daihatsu 8DKM-28 1 x 4 Stroke 8 Cy. 280 x 390 2500kW (3399bhp) Shaanxi Diesel Heavy Industry Co Lt-China AuxGen: 2 x 283kW 50Hz a.c Thrusters: 1 Tunnel thruster (f)
9174622 *VRLN9* -	**SINO ENERGY 1** *ex* High Wind *-2012* **Sino Energy Shipping (Hong Kong) Ltd** Sinochem Shipping Co Ltd (Hainan) *Hong Kong* *Hong Kong* MMSI: 477017500 Official number: HK-3719	**28,238** 12,462 46,475 T/cm 51.9	Class: CC (RI) (AB)	**1999-04 Daedong Shipbuilding Co Ltd — Changwon (Jinhae Shipyard)** Yd No: 1022 Loa 183.00 (BB) Br ex 32.46 Dght 12.215 Lbp 173.90 Br md 32.17 Dpth 18.00 Welded, 1 dk	**(A12B2TR) Chemical/Products Tanker** Double Hull (13F) Liq: 51,690; Liq (Oil): 51,690 Cargo Heating Coils Compartments: 12 Wing Ta, ER, 2 Wing Slop Ta 12 Cargo Pump (s): 12x600m³/hr Manifold: Bow/CM: 91.6m	**1 oil engine** driving 1 FP propeller Total Power: 7,466kW (10,151hp) 14.5kn B&W 6S50MC 1 x 2 Stroke 6 Cy. 500 x 1910 7466kW (10151bhp) Samsung Heavy Industries Co Ltd-South Korea AuxGen: 3 x 740kW 440V 60Hz a.c Fuel: 203.0 (d.f.) (Heating Coils) 1410.0 (r.f.) 32.2pd
8807454 *3FZQ9* -	**SINO GRACE** *ex* Emerald Isle *-2011* *ex* Prestige *-1999* **Huajun International Shipping Ltd** Brother Marine Co Ltd SatCom: Inmarsat C 437001313 *Panama* *Panama* MMSI: 370013000 Official number: 4269511	**40,988** 19,666 68,337 T/cm 66.2	Class: RI (NV)	**1989-08 Namura Shipbuilding Co Ltd — Imari SG** Yd No: 898 Converted From: Crude Oil/Products Tanker-2011 Loa 228.66 (BB) Br ex 32.48 Dght 13.321 Lbp 219.60 Br md 32.20 Dpth 19.60 Welded, 1 dk	**(A21A2BC) Bulk Carrier** Grain: 75,390; Bale: 74,259	**1 oil engine** driving 1 FP propeller Total Power: 7,768kW (10,561hp) 13.6kn B&W 6S60MC 1 x 2 Stroke 6 Cy. 600 x 2292 7768kW (10561bhp) Hitachi Zosen Corp-Japan AuxGen: 3 x 610kW 450V 60Hz a.c Fuel: 109.4 (d.f.) 1981.5 (r.f.) 31.7pd
8605650 *HP5675* -	**SINO NEW** *ex* Kumjung Spirit *-2010* *ex* Comodo *-2000* *ex* Shingu Maru No. 3 *-1993* **Sino New shipping Co Ltd** Sino Far East Ship Management Co Ltd SatCom: Inmarsat C 437222713 *Panama* *Panama* MMSI: 372227000 Official number: 40253PEXT	**741** 357 1,050 T/cm 4.3	Class: (KR)	**1986-07 Kochi Jyuko (Eiho Zosen) K.K. — Kochi** Yd No: 1920 Loa 65.00 (BB) Br ex - Dght 3.866 Lbp 60.09 Br md 10.01 Dpth 4.50 Welded, 1 dk	**(A12B2TR) Chemical/Products Tanker** Liq: 1,284; Liq (Oil): 1,284 Compartments: 8 Ta, ER 2 Cargo Pump (s)	**1 oil engine** geared to sc. shaft driving 1 FP propeller Total Power: 736kW (1,001hp) 10.3kn Akasaka K28FD 1 x 4 Stroke 6 Cy. 280 x 480 736kW (1001bhp) Akasaka Tekkosho KK (Akasaka DieselLtd)-Japan
9335367 *T3UQ* -	**SINO-OCEAN NO. 1** *ex* Hua Hai 2 Hao *-2009* *ex* Richsky *-2009* *completed as* Cheng Lu 5 *-2004* **Sino Ocean Shipping Co Ltd** Raiser Shipping Co Ltd *Tarawa* *Kiribati* MMSI: 529280000 Official number: K-12041065	**2,389** 1,337 4,150	Class: IZ	**2004-10 Zhoushan Jinzhou Shipyard — Zhoushan ZJ** Loa 87.00 Br ex - Dght 6.150 Lbp 79.95 Br md 13.80 Dpth 7.45 Welded, 1 dk	**(A31A2GX) General Cargo Ship** Grain: 5,355 Compartments: 2 Ho, ER 2 Ha: ER	**1 oil engine** geared to sc. shaft driving 1 FP propeller Total Power: 1,765kW (2,400hp) 12.0kn Chinese Std. Type G8300ZC 1 x 4 Stroke 8 Cy. 300 x 380 1765kW (2400bhp) Wuxi Antai Power Machinery Co Ltd-China AuxGen: 2 x 138kW a.c
8217362 *3FSF6* -	**SINO PEACE** *ex* Paschalis *-2010* *ex* Paschalis D *-2001* *ex* Alessandra d'Amato *-1997* *ex* Century Hope *-1990* **Longda Shipping Co Ltd** Brother Marine Co Ltd *Panama* *Panama* MMSI: 351951000 Official number: 4131310A	**36,803** 23,053 69,171 T/cm 64.5	Class: PD (LR) (RI) (NK) ✠ Classed LR until 10/12/90	**1984-02 Mitsui Eng. & SB. Co. Ltd. — Tamano** Yd No: 1277 Loa 222.73 (BB) Br ex 32.26 Dght 13.258 Lbp 213.01 Br md 32.21 Dpth 18.32 Welded, 1 dk	**(A21A2BC) Bulk Carrier** Grain: 80,119; Bale: 78,048 Compartments: 7 Ho, ER 7 Ha: (15.2 x 12.8)6 (16.3 x 14.4)ER	**1 oil engine** driving 1 FP propeller Total Power: 9,562kW (13,000hp) 15.0kn B&W 6L67GBE 1 x 2 Stroke 6 Cy. 670 x 1700 9562kW (13000bhp) Mitsui Engineering & Shipbuilding CLtd-Japan AuxGen: 3 x 480kW 450V 60Hz a.c Fuel: 187.0 (d.f.) 2701.5 (r.f.)
9012252 *DSRM6* -	**SINOCARRIER** *ex* Bright Artemis *-2007* *ex* Cosmo Artemis *-2004* **Sinokor Merchant Marine Co Ltd** - *Jeju* *South Korea* MMSI: 441916000 Official number: JJR-131015	**147,303** 44,190 266,307	Class: KR (NK)	**1992-08 Sasebo Heavy Industries Co. Ltd. — Sasebo Yard, Sasebo** Yd No: 384 Converted From: Crude Oil Tanker-2008 Loa 324.00 (BB) Br ex - Dght 20.962 Lbp 315.00 Br md 56.00 Dpth 29.40 Welded, 1 dk	**(A21B2BO) Ore Carrier** Grain: 138,384 Compartments: 6 Ho, ER 6 Ha: ER 6 (12.8 x 13.0)	**1 oil engine** driving 1 FP propeller Total Power: 21,770kW (29,598hp) 13.5kn B&W 7L90MC 1 x 2 Stroke 7 Cy. 900 x 2916 21770kW (29598bhp) Mitsui Engineering & Shipbuilding CLtd-Japan AuxGen: 3 x 740kW 450V a.c, 1 x 740kW 450V a.c, 1 x 800kW 450V a.c Fuel: 176.0 (d.f.) 5906.0 (r.f.) 77.5pd
9617947 *VRJN5* -	**SINOCHART BEIJING** **Xingxin Shipping Ltd** Fortune Ocean Shipping Ltd *Hong Kong* *Hong Kong* MMSI: 477016800 Official number: HK-3297	**45,263** 26,562 82,000 T/cm 72.2	Class: CC	**2012-12 Guangzhou Longxue Shipbuilding Co Ltd — Guangzhou GD** Yd No: L0043 Loa 229.00 (BB) Br ex - Dght 14.450 Lbp 223.50 Br md 32.26 Dpth 20.20 Welded, 1 dk	**(A21A2BC) Bulk Carrier** Grain: 97,000 Compartments: 7 Ho, ER 7 Ha: ER	**1 oil engine** driving 1 FP propeller Total Power: 11,300kW (15,363hp) 14.5kn MAN-B&W 5S60MC-C 1 x 2 Stroke 5 Cy. 600 x 2400 11300kW (15363bhp)
9041198 *DSPN4* -	**SINOGLORY** *ex* Ardeshir H Bhiwandiwalla *-2007* *ex* Seaking *-2004* *ex* Izusan Maru *-2000* **Sinokor Merchant Marine Co Ltd** - SatCom: Inmarsat C 444000183 *Jeju* *South Korea* MMSI: 441296000 Official number: JJR-071830	**148,257** 44,778 265,816 T/cm 165.3	Class: KR (LR) (IR) (NK) **IGS** Classed LR until 1/10/07	**1992-12 Mitsubishi Heavy Industries Ltd. — Nagasaki** Yd No: 2068 Converted From: Crude Oil Tanker-2008 Loa 321.95 (BB) Br ex 58.04 Dght 20.321 Lbp 310.00 Br md 58.00 Dpth 29.50 Welded, 1 dk	**(A21B2BO) Ore Carrier** Grain: 142,418 Compartments: 6 Ho, ER 10 Ha: ER 10 (14.9 x 15.0) Cranes: 2x20t	**1 oil engine** driving 1 FP propeller Total Power: 21,917kW (29,798hp) 15.2kn Mitsubishi 6UEC85LSII 1 x 2 Stroke 6 Cy. 850 x 3150 21917kW (29798bhp) Mitsubishi Heavy Industries Ltd-Japan AuxGen: 2 x 1050kW 450V 60Hz a.c, 1 x 900kW 450V 60Hz a.c, 1 x 200kW 450V 60Hz a.c Boilers: e (ex.g.) 24.0kgf/cm² (23.5bar), AuxB (o.f.) 17.9kgf/cm² (17.6bar) Fuel: 330.0 (d.f.) (Part Heating Coils) 6321.0 (r.f.) 71.4pd
9179440 *V7BA9* -	**SINOKOR AKITA** *ex* Cape Charles *-2013* *ex* YM Doha *-2009* *ex* Cape Charles *-2008* *ex* Tiger Sea *-2000* *launched as* Cape Charles *-1998* **Sinokor Akita SA** Sinokor Merchant Marine Co Ltd *Majuro* *Marshall Islands* MMSI: 538005106 Official number: 5106	**9,038** 4,221 11,031 T/cm 25.2	Class: KR (GL)	**1998-12 Shandong Weihai Shipyard — Weihai SD** Yd No: CZ004 Loa 135.68 (BB) Br ex 22.70 Dght 8.635 Lbp 125.00 Br md 22.50 Dpth 11.20 Welded, 1 dk	**(A33A2CC) Container Ship (Fully Cellular)** Grain: 15,554 TEU 834 C Ho 286 TEU C Dk 548 TEU incl 80 ref C. Compartments: 5 Cell Ho, ER 5 Ha: ER Ice Capable	**1 oil engine** driving 1 FP propeller Total Power: 7,900kW (10,741hp) 18.0kn B&W 5S50MC-C 1 x 2 Stroke 5 Cy. 500 x 2000 7900kW (10741bhp) Hudong Shipyard-China AuxGen: 3 x 488kW 220/440V 60Hz a.c Thrusters: 1 Thwart. FP thruster (f) Fuel: 88.2 (d.f.) (Heating Coils) 813.4 (r.f.) 32.0pd
9146663 *DSRA4* -	**SINOKOR HONGKONG** *ex* Oriental Bright *-2010* **Sinokor Merchant Marine Co Ltd** STX Marine Service Co Ltd *Jeju* *South Korea* MMSI: 441777000 Official number: JJR-103006	**13,196** 7,546 17,468	Class: KR (NK)	**1996-12 Imabari Shipbuilding Co Ltd — Imabari EH (Imabari Shipyard)** Yd No: 530 Loa 162.00 (BB) Br ex - Dght 8.915 Lbp 150.00 Br md 25.60 Dpth 12.90 Welded, 1 dk	**(A33A2CC) Container Ship (Fully Cellular)** TEU 1228 C Ho 426 TEU C Dk 802 TEU incl 160 ref C. Compartments: 5 Cell Ho, ER 16 Ha: 2 (12.8 x 5.7)14 (12.8 x 10.9)ER Cranes: 2x35t	**1 oil engine** driving 1 FP propeller Total Power: 9,989kW (13,581hp) 18.1kn B&W 7S50MC 1 x 2 Stroke 7 Cy. 500 x 1910 9989kW (13581bhp) Mitsui Engineering & Shipbuilding CLtd-Japan AuxGen: 4 x 680kW 450V a.c Thrusters: 1 Tunnel thruster (f) Fuel: 1060.0 (r.f.)
8706650 *DSFR9* -	**SINOKOR INCHEON** *ex* Sinokor Pyongtaek *-2005* *ex* Shinyufutsu Maru *-2001* **Sinokor Merchant Marine Co Ltd** - *Jeju* *South Korea* MMSI: 441150000 Official number: JJR-020020	**3,625** 1,468 3,016	Class: KR (NK)	**1987-09 Naikai Shipbuilding & Engineering Co Ltd — Onomichi HS (Setoda Shipyard)** Yd No: 522 Loa 108.31 (BB) Br ex 18.04 Dght 5.825 Lbp 101.02 Br md 18.01 Dpth 7.52 Welded, 1 dk	**(A33A2CC) Container Ship (Fully Cellular)** TEU 155 7 Ha:	**1 oil engine** driving 1 CP propeller Total Power: 5,656kW (7,690hp) 17.6kn Mitsubishi 7UEC45LA 1 x 2 Stroke 7 Cy. 450 x 1350 5656kW (7690bhp) Akasaka Tekkosho KK (Akasaka DieselLtd)-Japan AuxGen: 2 x 450kW 445V 60Hz a.c Thrusters: 1 Thwart. CP thruster (a)
8213562 *DSND5* -	**SINOKOR MASAN** *ex* Akashia Baru *-2003* *ex* Shin Akashia Maru *-2001* **Sinokor Merchant Marine Co Ltd** Fair Shipmanagement Co Ltd *Jeju* *South Korea* MMSI: 441306000 Official number: JJR-039235	**3,597** - 3,033	Class: KR (KI) (NK)	**1983-02 Fukuoka Shipbuilding Co Ltd — Fukuoka FO** Yd No: 1102 Loa 110.80 (BB) Br ex 17.25 Dght 5.881 Lbp 101.81 Br md 17.21 Dpth 7.37 Welded, 1 dk	**(A33A2CC) Container Ship (Fully Cellular)** TEU 236 Compartments: 2 Cell Ho, ER 7 Ha: (7.6 x 10.6)6 (7.6 x 13.2)ER	**1 oil engine** driving 1 FP propeller Total Power: 5,149kW (7,001hp) 17.0kn Mitsubishi 7UEC45/115H 1 x 2 Stroke 7 Cy. 450 x 1150 5149kW (7001bhp) Kobe Hatsudoki KK-Japan AuxGen: 2 x 400kW 445V 60Hz a.c Fuel: 53.5 (d.f.) 214.0 (r.f.) 20.0pd

9209908 *DSRA2* -
SINOKOR NIIGATA
ex Vsico Promote *-2010* *ex* Kaido *-2009*
Sinokor Merchant Marine Co Ltd
-
Jeju *South Korea*
MMSI: 441772000
Official number: JJR103005
6,490 3,506 8,516
Class: KR VR (NK)
1999-10 Murakami Hide Zosen K.K. — Imabari Yd No: 506
Loa 119.16 (BB) Br ex - Dght 7.850
Lbp 110.00 Br md 18.20 Dpth 11.00
Welded, 1 dk
(A33A2CC) Container Ship (Fully Cellular)
TEU 550 C Ho 244 TEU C Dk 306 TEU incl 100 ref C
6 Ha: (12.6 x 10.6)5 (12.6 x 16.0)ER
Cranes: 2x36t
1 oil engine driving 1 FP propeller
Total Power: 5,178kW (7,040hp) 15.0kn
B&W 8L35MC
1 x 2 Stroke 8 Cy. 350 x 1050 5178kW (7040bhp)
Hitachi Zosen Corp-Japan
Thrusters: 1 Tunnel thruster (f)

9105578 *D8BZ* -
SINOKOR PIONEER
ex Powhatan *-2013*
Sinokor Merchant Marine Co Ltd
-
Jeju *South Korea*
MMSI: 441973000
Official number: JJR-131037
36,617 23,344 69,045
Class: KR (AB)
1995-04 Sumitomo Heavy Industries Ltd. — Oppama Shipyard, Yokosuka Yd No: 1204
Loa 225.00 (BB) Br ex 32.30 Dght 13.271
Lbp 217.00 Br md 32.26 Dpth 18.30
Welded, 1 dk
(A21A2BC) Bulk Carrier
Grain: 81,839; Bale: 78,529
Compartments: 7 Ho, ER
7 Ha: (16.7 x 13.4)6 (16.7 x 15.0)ER
1 oil engine driving 1 FP propeller
Total Power: 7,723kW (10,500hp) 14.5kn
Sulzer 6RTA62
1 x 2 Stroke 6 Cy. 620 x 2150 7723kW (10500bhp)
Diesel United Ltd.-Aioi

9160906 *V7YZ9* -
SINOKOR QINGDAO
ex Emilia Schulte *-2012*
ex Cape Canaveral *-2008* *ex* Tiger Sea *-2001*
ex Cape Canaveral *-2001*
Sinokor Qingdao SA
Sinokor Merchant Marine Co Ltd
Majuro *Marshall Islands*
MMSI: 538004775
Official number: 4775
9,030 4,222 11,031 T/cm 25.2
Class: KR (GL)
1999-01 Mawei Shipyard — Fuzhou FJ Yd No: MX438B
Loa 135.60 (BB) Br ex 22.70 Dght 8.635
Lbp 125.00 Br md 22.50 Dpth 11.20
Welded, 1 dk
(A33A2CC) Container Ship (Fully Cellular)
Grain: 15,554
TEU 834 C Ho 286 TEU C Dk 548 TEU incl 80 ref C.
Compartments: 5 Cell Ho, ER
6 Ha: ER
Ice Capable
1 oil engine driving 1 FP propeller
Total Power: 7,900kW (10,741hp) 18.0kn
B&W 5S50MC-C
1 x 2 Stroke 5 Cy. 500 x 2000 7900kW (10741bhp)
Hudong Heavy Machinery Co Ltd-China
AuxGen: 3 x 610kW 450V 60Hz a.c
Thrusters: 1 Thwart. FP thruster (f)
Fuel: 88.2 (d.f.) 813.4 (r.f.) 32.0pd

9602148 *V7WD2* -
SINOKOR SUNRISE
Marina Aventurine Shipping Ltd
Sinokor Maritime Co Ltd
Majuro *Marshall Islands*
MMSI: 538004269
Official number: 4269
43,537 26,550 79,393 T/cm 71.9
Class: KR
2011-06 Jiangsu Eastern Heavy Industry Co Ltd — Jingjiang JS Yd No: 06C-072
Loa 229.00 (BB) Br ex - Dght 14.639
Lbp 222.00 Br md 32.26 Dpth 20.25
Welded, 1 dk
(A21A2BC) Bulk Carrier
Grain: 97,000; Bale: 90,784
Compartments: 7 Ho, ER
7 Ha: 5 (18.3 x 15.0) (15.7 x 15.0)ER (13.1 x 13.2)
1 oil engine driving 1 FP propeller
Total Power: 11,620kW (15,799hp) 14.0kn
MAN-B&W 7S50MC-C8
1 x 2 Stroke 7 Cy. 500 x 2000 11620kW (15799bhp)

9160891 *V7BA4* -
SINOKOR TIANJIN
ex Cape Campbell *-2013* *ex* Tiger Pearl *-1999*
launched as Cape Campbell *-1998*
Sinokor Tianjin SA
Sinokor Merchant Marine Co Ltd
Majuro *Marshall Islands*
MMSI: 538005104
Official number: 5104
9,038 4,221 11,031 T/cm 25.2
Class: KR (GL)
1998-10 Mawei Shipyard — Fuzhou FJ Yd No: MX438A
Loa 135.68 (BB) Br ex - Dght 8.635
Lbp 125.00 Br md 22.50 Dpth 11.20
Welded, 1 dk
(A33A2CC) Container Ship (Fully Cellular)
TEU 834 C Ho 286 TEU C Dk 548 TEU incl 80 ref C.
6 Ha: (12.6 x 15.3)5 (12.6 x 17.9)ER
Ice Capable
1 oil engine driving 1 FP propeller
Total Power: 7,900kW (10,741hp) 18.5kn
B&W 5S50MC-C
1 x 2 Stroke 5 Cy. 500 x 2000 7900kW (10741bhp)
Hudong Shipyard-China
AuxGen: 3 x 610kW 450V 60Hz a.c
Thrusters: 1 Thwart. FP thruster (f)
Fuel: 81.0 (d.f.) 830.0 (r.f.) 32.0pd

9179464 *DSRC3* -
SINOKOR TOKYO
ex Carolin Schulte *-2011* *ex* Cape Canet *-2010*
ex YM Faha *-2009* *ex* Cape Canet *-2009*
Sinokor Merchant Marine Co Ltd
-
Jeju *South Korea*
MMSI: 440075000
Official number: JJR-111018
9,030 4,222 10,935 T/cm 25.1
Class: GL KR
1999-07 Shandong Weihai Shipyard — Weihai SD Yd No: CZ006
Loa 135.60 (BB) Br ex - Dght 8.640
Lbp 125.00 Br md 22.50 Dpth 11.20
Welded, 1 dk
(A33A2CC) Container Ship (Fully Cellular)
Grain: 15,554
TEU 834 C Ho 286 TEU C Dk 548 TEU incl 80 ref C.
Compartments: 6 Cell Ho, ER
6 Ha: ER
1 oil engine driving 1 FP propeller
Total Power: 7,900kW (10,741hp) 18.5kn
B&W 5S50MC-C
1 x 2 Stroke 5 Cy. 500 x 2000 7900kW (10741bhp)
Hudong Heavy Machinery Co Ltd-China
AuxGen: 3 x 610kW 220/440V a.c
Thrusters: 1 Thwart. FP thruster (f)
Fuel: 961.0 (r.f.) 33.0pd

9000261 *DSOB5* -
SINOKOR ULSAN
ex Rekio *-2005* *ex* Kuroshio Maru *-2004*
Sinokor Merchant Marine Co Ltd
-
Jeju *South Korea*
MMSI: 440497000
Official number: JJR-059148
5,356 - 4,130
Class: KR (NK)
1990-09 Fukuoka Shipbuilding Co Ltd — Fukuoka FO Yd No: 1157
Loa 119.62 (BB) Br ex - Dght 6.380
Lbp 110.00 Br md 18.40 Dpth 8.40
Welded, 1 dk
(A35A2RR) Ro-Ro Cargo Ship
Lane-Len: 180
TEU 200
Compartments: 2 Ho, ER
6 Ha: ER
1 oil engine driving 1 FP propeller
Total Power: 7,061kW (9,600hp) 18.5kn
Mitsubishi 8UEC45LA
1 x 2 Stroke 8 Cy. 450 x 1350 7061kW (9600bhp)
Kobe Hatsudoki KK-Japan
AuxGen: 2 x 500kW 450V 60Hz a.c, 1 x 360kW 450V 60Hz a.c, 1 x 346kW a.c
Thrusters: 1 Thwart. CP thruster (a)

9179452 *V7BH6* -
SINOKOR VLADIVOSTOK
ex Cadiz *-2013* *ex* Cape Cook *-2011*
ex SITC Philippines *-2009* *ex* Cape Cook *-2007*
ex MOL Accuracy *-2006* *ex* Cape Cook *-2005*
Sinokor Vladivostok SA
Sinokor Merchant Marine Co Ltd
Majuro *Marshall Islands*
MMSI: 538005143
Official number: 5143
9,038 4,221 11,400 T/cm 25.1
Class: KR (GL)
1998-12 Shandong Weihai Shipyard — Weihai SD Yd No: CZ005
Loa 135.60 (BB) Br ex - Dght 8.630
Lbp 125.00 Br md 22.50 Dpth 11.20
Welded, 1 dk
(A33A2CC) Container Ship (Fully Cellular)
Grain: 15,554
TEU 834 C Ho 286 TEU C Dk 548 TEU incl 80 ref C.
Compartments: 6 Cell Ho, ER
6 Ha: ER
Ice Capable
1 oil engine driving 1 FP propeller
Total Power: 7,900kW (10,741hp) 18.5kn
B&W 5S50MC-C
1 x 2 Stroke 5 Cy. 500 x 2000 7900kW (10741bhp)
Hudong Shipyard-China
AuxGen: 3 x 610kW 450V 60Hz a.c
Thrusters: 1 Thwart. FP thruster (f)
Fuel: 88.2 (d.f.) 813.4 (r.f.) 32.0pd

9192052 *DSRD3* -
SINOKOR YOKOHAMA
ex Henry Schulte *-2011* *ex* Cape Creus *-2010*
ex MSC Caledonien *-2008* *ex* Cape Creus *-2006*
Sinokor Merchant Marine Co Ltd
Fair Shipmanagement Co Ltd
Jeju *South Korea*
MMSI: 441782000
Official number: JJR-111025
9,030 4,222 11,031 T/cm 25.1
Class: KR (GL)
2000-01 Xiamen Shipyard — Xiamen FJ Yd No: MX438H
Loa 135.52 (BB) Br ex - Dght 8.635
Lbp 125.00 Br md 22.50 Dpth 11.20
Welded, 1 dk
(A33A2CC) Container Ship (Fully Cellular)
Double Bottom Entire Compartment Length
Grain: 15,554
TEU 834 C Ho 286 TEU C Dk 548 TEU incl 80 ref C.
Compartments: 5 Cell Ho, ER
6 Ha: 6 (12.6 x 18.0)ER
Ice Capable
1 oil engine driving 1 FP propeller
Total Power: 7,900kW (10,741hp) 18.0kn
B&W 5S50MC-C
1 x 2 Stroke 5 Cy. 500 x 2000 7900kW (10741bhp)
Hudong Heavy Machinery Co Ltd-China
AuxGen: 3 x 610kW 450V 60Hz a.c
Thrusters: 1 Thwart. FP thruster (f)
Fuel: 88.2 (d.f.) 813.4 (r.f.) 32.0pd

9149809 *DSRK3* -
SINOMERCHANT
ex Amy N *-2012* *ex* Neckar Ore *-2001*
Sinokor Merchant Marine Co Ltd
-
Jeju *South Korea*
MMSI: 441889000
Official number: JJR-121063
155,051 55,785 322,457 T/cm 172.0
Class: KR (NV) (AB)
1997-11 Daewoo Heavy Industries Ltd — Geoje Yd No: 1117
Loa 332.00 (BB) Br ex - Dght 23.021
Lbp 320.00 Br md 58.00 Dpth 30.20
Welded, 1 dk
(A21B2BO) Ore Carrier
Double Hull
Grain: 179,139
Compartments: 7 Ho, ER
7 Ha: (26.0 x 12.3)6 (26.0 x 17.6)ER
1 oil engine driving 1 FP propeller
Total Power: 25,480kW (34,643hp) 14.7kn
B&W 7S80MC
1 x 2 Stroke 7 Cy. 800 x 3056 25480kW (34643bhp)
Korea Heavy Industries & ConstrCo Ltd (HANJUNG)-South Korea
AuxGen: 3 x 1040kW 450V 60Hz a.c
Fuel: 329.0 (d.f.) (Heating Coils) 7163.0 (r.f.) 95.6pd

9644184 *9HA3115* -
SINOP
Sinop Maritime Ltd
Ciner Gemi Acente Isletmeleri Sanayi ve Ticaret AS (Ciner Ship Management)
Valletta *Malta*
MMSI: 229159000
Official number: 9644184
35,812 21,224 63,500 T/cm 62.1
Class: LR (BV)
100A1 SS 01/2013
bulk carrier
CSR
BC-A
GRAB (20)
Nos. 2 & 4 holds may be empty
ESP
ShipRight (ACS (B))
*IWS
LI
LMC **UMS**
2013-01 Yangzhou Dayang Shipbuilding Co Ltd — Yangzhou JS Yd No: DY4024
Loa 199.99 (BB) Br ex - Dght 13.300
Lbp 195.90 Br md 32.26 Dpth 18.50
Welded, 1 dk
(A21A2BC) Bulk Carrier
Grain: 77,493; Bale: 75,555
Compartments: 5 Ho, ER
5 Ha: ER
Cranes: 4x35t
1 oil engine driving 1 FP propeller
Total Power: 8,300kW (11,285hp) 14.5kn
MAN-B&W 5S60ME-C8
1 x 2 Stroke 5 Cy. 600 x 2400 8300kW (11285bhp)
Doosan Engine Co Ltd-South Korea
AuxGen: 3 x a.c

7607338 *PLXN* -
SINOPA
PT Pelayaran Fajar Sribahari Sakti
Foong Sun Shipping (Pte) Ltd
Jakarta *Indonesia*
MMSI: 525005050
1,748 621 1,650
Class: KI (NV)
1977-12 Molde Verft AS — Hjelset (Hull) Yd No: 150
1977-12 Ulstein Hatlo AS — Ulsteinvik Yd No: 150
Loa 71.51 Br ex - Dght 4.380
Lbp 65.41 Br md 12.70 Dpth 7.12
Welded, 2 dks
(A32A2GF) General Cargo/Passenger Ship
Passengers: 198
Grain: 3,390
Compartments: 2 Ho, ER
2 Ha: (13.2 x 8.0) (18.9 x 8.0)ER
Derricks: 2x20t,2x5t
1 oil engine driving 1 FP propeller
Total Power: 1,195kW (1,625hp) 12.0kn
Kromhout 9FDHD240
1 x 4 Stroke 9 Cy. 240 x 260 1195kW (1625bhp)
Stork Werkspoor Diesel BV-Netherlands
AuxGen: 3 x 96kW 220/380V 50Hz a.c, 1 x 48kW 220/380V 50Hz a.c

---

8121915 *HO3544* -
SINOPEC 381
ex BOA Princess *-2007* *ex* Smit-Lloyd 90 *-2006*
ex Atlas *-1985* *launched as* Atlantic Atlas *-1985*
Shanghai Offshore Petroleum Exploration & Development Corp (SINOPEC)
-
Panama *Panama*
MMSI: 356045000
Official number: 3353708A
1,330 472 1,487
Class: NV (BV)
1985-04 Brodogradiliste 'Titovo' — Kraljevica Yd No: 438
Loa 64.42 Br ex 14.13 Dght 5.401
Lbp 56.42 Br md 13.81 Dpth 6.91
Welded, 1 dk
(B21B20A) Anchor Handling Tug Supply
2 oil engines with clutches, flexible couplings & sr geared to sc. shafts driving 2 CP propellers
Total Power: 6,370kW (8,660hp) 12.0kn
Sulzer 16ASV25/30
2 x Vee 4 Stroke 16 Cy. 250 x 300 each-3185kW (4330bhp)
Tvornica Dizel Motora 'Jugoturbina'-Yugoslavia
AuxGen: 2 x 137kW 440V 60Hz a.c, 2 x 60Hz a.c
Thrusters: 1 Thwart. CP thruster (f)
Fuel: 659.0 (d.f.) 11.0pd

IMO / Call sign	Name / Owner / Flag	GT / NT / DWT	Class	Built / Dimensions	Type	Machinery
9038672 *DSPL5* -	**SINOTRADER** *ex* Shinyo Guardian *-2007* *ex* Navix Adventure *-2003* **Sinokor Merchant Marine Co Ltd** - SatCom: Inmarsat C 444000151 *Jeju* *South Korea* MMSI: 441189000 Official number: JJR-079821	**148,619** 44,586 267,906	Class: KR (NK)	**1993-10 Ishikawajima-Harima Heavy Industries Co Ltd (IHI) — Kure** Yd No: 3028 Converted From: Crude Oil Tanker-2008 Loa 333.00 (BB) Br ex - Dght 21.637 Lbp 319.00 Br md 60.00 Dpth 28.65 Welded, 1 dk	**(A21B2B0) Ore Carrier** Single Hull Grain: 124,210 Compartments: 10 Ho, ER 10 Ha: ER 10 (14.1 x 13.0)	**1 oil engine** driving 1 FP propeller Total Power: 20,081kW (27,302hp) 15.4kn Sulzer 7RTA84M 1 x 2 Stroke 7 Cy. 840 x 2900 20081kW (27302bhp) Diesel United Ltd.-Aioi AuxGen: 5 x 782kW 450V a.c
9367920 *VRDL9* -	**SINOTRANS BEIJING** **Trade Integrity Shipping Ltd** Sinotrans Ship Management Ltd *Hong Kong* *Hong Kong* MMSI: 477003200 Official number: HK-2039	**9,587** 5,531 12,597	Class: NK	**2008-02 Kyokuyo Shipyard Corp — Shimonoseki YC** Yd No: 475 Loa 144.83 (BB) Br ex - Dght 8.215 Lbp 134.00 Br md 22.40 Dpth 11.00 Welded, 1 dk	**(A33A2CC) Container Ship (Fully Cellular)** TEU 831 incl 120 ref C.	**1 oil engine** driving 1 FP propeller Total Power: 7,988kW (10,860hp) 18.0kn MAN-B&W 6L50MC 1 x 2 Stroke 6 Cy. 500 x 1620 7988kW (10860bhp) Hitachi Zosen Corp-Japan Thrusters: 1 Tunnel thruster (f) Fuel: 1070.0
9631644 *VRMG7* -	**SINOTRANS DALIAN** **Yunhua Shipping Co Ltd** Sinotrans Container Lines Co Ltd *Hong Kong* *Hong Kong* MMSI: 477767600 Official number: HK-3870	**9,944** 5,031 13,481	Class: NK	**2013-08 Qingshan Shipyard — Wuhan HB** Yd No: QS1100-20 Loa 147.90 (BB) Br ex - Dght 8.514 Lbp 139.60 Br md 23.25 Dpth 11.50 Welded, 1 dk	**(A33A2CC) Container Ship (Fully Cellular)** TEU 1106 incl 145 ref C.	**1 oil engine** driving 1 FP propeller Total Power: 7,200kW (9,789hp) 19.6kn MAN-B&W 6S46ME-B8 1 x 2 Stroke 6 Cy. 460 x 1932 7200kW (9789bhp) Jiangsu Antai Power Machinery Co Lt-China AuxGen: 3 x 720kW a.c Fuel: 1090.0
9642069 *BIBH2* -	**SINOTRANS FUZHOU** **Sinotrans Sunnyexpress Co Ltd** - *Shanghai* *China* MMSI: 413377720	**19,309** 10,813 27,000	Class: CC	**2013-09 Qingshan Shipyard — Wuhan HB** Yd No: QS1800-2 Loa 179.70 (BB) Br ex - Dght 10.200 Lbp 170.00 Br md 27.60 Dpth 14.20 Welded, 1 dk	**(A33A2CC) Container Ship (Fully Cellular)** TEU 1800	**1 oil engine** driving 1 FP propeller Total Power: 6,480kW (8,810hp) 15.0kn MAN-B&W 6S46MC-C 1 x 2 Stroke 6 Cy. 460 x 1932 6480kW (8810bhp)
9330769 *VRBV5* -	**SINOTRANS HONG KONG** *ex* Sunrise Express *-2010* *ex* YM Putian *-2007* *launched as* Sunrise Express *-2006* **Bright Sincere Ltd** Sinotrans Ship Management Ltd *Hong Kong* *Hong Kong* MMSI: 477109800 Official number: HK-1698	**9,590** 4,748 12,829	Class: NK	**2006-05 Dae Sun Shipbuilding & Engineering Co Ltd — Busan** Yd No: 455 Loa 142.70 (BB) Br ex - Dght 8.363 Lbp 133.50 Br md 22.60 Dpth 11.20 Welded, 1 dk	**(A33A2CC) Container Ship (Fully Cellular)** Double Hull Grain: 17,487 TEU 1049 C Ho 325 TEU C Dk 724 TEU incl 180 ref C	**1 oil engine** driving 1 FP propeller Total Power: 7,860kW (10,686hp) 18.0kn MAN-B&W 6S46MC-C 1 x 2 Stroke 6 Cy. 460 x 1932 7860kW (10686bhp) STX Engine Co Ltd-South Korea AuxGen: 3 x 615kW 445V a.c Thrusters: 1 Tunnel thruster (f) Fuel: 720.0
9301110 *C6UJ4* -	**SINOTRANS NAGOYA** *completed as* Renown *-2005* **Continent Maritime SA** Kotoku Kaiun Co Ltd (Kotoku Kaiun KK) *Nassau* *Bahamas* MMSI: 311935000 Official number: 8000974	**9,443** 4,705 11,179	Class: NK	**2005-06 Shimanami Shipyard Co Ltd — Imabari EH** Yd No: 342 Loa 139.72 (BB) Br ex - Dght 8.015 Lbp 130.00 Br md 23.00 Dpth 11.00 Welded, 1 dk	**(A33A2CC) Container Ship (Fully Cellular)** TEU 915 incl 100 ref C, Cranes: 2x40t	**1 oil engine** driving 1 FP propeller Total Power: 8,670kW (11,788hp) 18.0kn Mitsubishi 6UEC50LSII 1 x 2 Stroke 6 Cy. 500 x 1950 8670kW (11788bhp) Akasaka Tekkosho KK (Akasaka DieselLtd)-Japan Thrusters: 1 Tunnel thruster (f) Fuel: 1290.0
9367956 *VRDM3* -	**SINOTRANS NINGBO** **Trade Elegancy Shipping Ltd** Sinotrans Ship Management Ltd *Hong Kong* *Hong Kong* MMSI: 477081100 Official number: HK-2041	**9,587** 5,531 12,569	Class: NK	**2008-05 Kyokuyo Shipyard Corp — Shimonoseki YC** Yd No: 478 Loa 144.83 (BB) Br ex - Dght 8.215 Lbp 134.00 Br md 22.40 Dpth 11.00 Welded, 1 dk	**(A33A2CC) Container Ship (Fully Cellular)** TEU 847 incl 120 ref C.	**1 oil engine** driving 1 FP propeller Total Power: 7,980kW (10,850hp) 18.0kn MAN-B&W 6L50MC 1 x 2 Stroke 6 Cy. 500 x 1620 7980kW (10850bhp) Hitachi Zosen Corp-Japan AuxGen: 4 x a.c Thrusters: 1 Tunnel thruster (f) Fuel: 1070.0
9631632 *VRMG8* -	**SINOTRANS QINGDAO** **Yunrong Shipping Co Ltd** Sinotrans Container Lines Co Ltd *Hong Kong* *Hong Kong* MMSI: 477767500 Official number: HK-3871	**9,944** 5,031 13,474	Class: NK	**2013-07 Qingshan Shipyard — Wuhan HB** Yd No: QS1100-19 Loa 147.90 (BB) Br ex - Dght 8.514 Lbp 139.60 Br md 23.25 Dpth 11.50 Welded, 1 dk	**(A33A2CC) Container Ship (Fully Cellular)** TEU 1106 incl 145 ref C	**1 oil engine** driving 1 FP propeller Total Power: 7,200kW (9,789hp) 19.6kn MAN-B&W 6S46ME-B8 1 x 2 Stroke 6 Cy. 460 x 1932 7200kW (9789bhp) Jiangsu Antai Power Machinery Co Lt-China AuxGen: 3 x 720kW a.c Fuel: 1090.0
9633745 *VRMK8* -	**SINOTRANS SHANGHAI** **Yunfu Shipping Co Ltd** Sinotrans Container Lines Co Ltd *Hong Kong* *Hong Kong* MMSI: 477242600 Official number: HK-3903	**9,930** 4,756 12,968	Class: NK	**2013-08 Dae Sun Shipbuilding & Engineering Co Ltd — Busan** Yd No: 550 Loa 143.90 (BB) Br ex - Dght 8.214 Lbp 134.70 Br md 22.60 Dpth 11.20 Welded, 1 dk	**(A33A2CC) Container Ship (Fully Cellular)** TEU 1040 incl 56 ref C	**1 oil engine** driving 1 FP propeller Total Power: 8,280kW (11,257hp) 18.0kn MAN-B&W 6S46MC-C8 1 x 2 Stroke 6 Cy. 460 x 1932 8280kW (11257bhp) STX Engine Co Ltd-South Korea AuxGen: 3 x 615kW 445V a.c Fuel: 846.0
9367932 *VRDM2* -	**SINOTRANS SHENZHEN** **Trade Sincerity Shipping Ltd** Sinotrans Ship Management Ltd *Hong Kong* *Hong Kong* MMSI: 477056100 Official number: HK-2040	**9,587** 5,531 12,568	Class: NK	**2008-04 Kyokuyo Shipyard Corp — Shimonoseki YC** Yd No: 476 Loa 144.83 (BB) Br ex - Dght 8.215 Lbp 134.00 Br md 22.40 Dpth 11.00 Welded, 1 dk	**(A33A2CC) Container Ship (Fully Cellular)** TEU 847 incl 120 ref C.	**1 oil engine** driving 1 FP propeller Total Power: 7,988kW (10,860hp) 18.0kn MAN-B&W 6L50MC 1 x 2 Stroke 6 Cy. 500 x 1620 7988kW (10860bhp) Hitachi Zosen Corp-Japan AuxGen: 4 x 440kW a.c Thrusters: 1 Tunnel thruster (f) Fuel: 1070.0
9633757 *VRMK9* -	**SINOTRANS TIANJIN** **Yungui Shipping Co Ltd** Sinotrans Container Lines Co Ltd *Hong Kong* *Hong Kong* MMSI: 477219400 Official number: HK-3904	**9,930** 4,756 12,975	Class: NK	**2013-10 Dae Sun Shipbuilding & Engineering Co Ltd — Busan** Yd No: 551 Loa 143.90 (BB) Br ex - Dght 8.214 Lbp 134.70 Br md 22.60 Dpth 11.20 Welded, 1 dk	**(A33A2CC) Container Ship (Fully Cellular)** TEU 1040 incl 56 ref C.	**1 oil engine** driving 1 FP propeller Total Power: 8,280kW (11,257hp) 18.0kn MAN-B&W 6S46MC-C8 1 x 2 Stroke 6 Cy. 460 x 1932 8280kW (11257bhp) STX Engine Co Ltd-South Korea AuxGen: 3 x 750kW a.c Fuel: 840.0
9367968 *VRDM4* -	**SINOTRANS XIAMEN** **Trade Endeavor Shipping Ltd** Sinotrans Ship Management Ltd *Hong Kong* *Hong Kong* MMSI: 477107900 Official number: HK-2042	**9,587** 5,531 12,550	Class: NK	**2008-07 Kyokuyo Shipyard Corp — Shimonoseki YC** Yd No: 480 Loa 144.83 (BB) Br ex - Dght 8.215 Lbp 134.00 Br md 22.40 Dpth 11.00 Welded, 1 dk	**(A33A2CC) Container Ship (Fully Cellular)** TEU 831 incl 120 ref C.	**1 oil engine** driving 1 FP propeller Total Power: 7,988kW (10,860hp) 18.0kn MAN-B&W 6L50MC 1 x 2 Stroke 6 Cy. 500 x 1620 7988kW (10860bhp) Hitachi Zosen Corp-Japan Thrusters: 1 Tunnel thruster (f) Fuel: 1070.0
5329267 *XYUJ* -	**SINPYAUNG** **Board of Management for The Port of Yangon** - *Yangon* *Myanmar* Official number: 1110	*743* 206 579	Class: (LR) ✠ Classed LR until 3/61	**1959-05 Pacific Islands Shipbuilding Co. Ltd. — Hong Kong** Yd No: 202 Loa 59.19 Br ex 11.97 Dght 3.677 Lbp 49.18 Br md 11.28 Dpth 4.88 Riveted\Welded, 1 dk	**(B34Q2QB) Buoy Tender**	**2 oil engines** with hydraulic couplings driving 2 CP propellers Total Power: 882kW (1,200hp) Alpha 495-VO 2 x 2 Stroke 5 Cy. 290 x 490 each-441kW (600bhp) Alpha Diesel A/S-Denmark
9677105 *JD3486* -	**SINRIKI MARU** **Shinriki Kaiun YK** *Ikata, Ehime* *Japan* Official number: 141873	*267* - 800		**2013-03 Yano Zosen K.K. — Imabari** Yd No: 265 Loa 61.00 Br ex - Dght 3.440 Lbp - Br md 9.80 Dpth 6.00 Welded, 1 dk	**(A31A2GX) General Cargo Ship** Double Hull Grain: 1,371; Bale: 1,328 1 Ha: ER (31.0 x 7.5)	**1 oil engine** reduction geared to sc. shaft driving 1 Propeller Total Power: 1,029kW (1,399hp) Niigata 6M28BGT 1 x 4 Stroke 6 Cy. 280 x 480 1029kW (1399bhp) Niigata Engineering Co Ltd-Japan
7206031 *3DYI* -	**SINU-I-WASA** *ex* Straitsman *-2004* **Venu Shipping Ltd** *Suva* *Fiji* Official number: 000425	**1,481** 444 1,053	Class: (LR) ✠ Classed LR until 31/7/04	**1972-03 North Queensland Engineers & Agents Pty Ltd — Cairns QLD** Yd No: 39 Loa 62.59 Br ex 11.84 Dght 3.830 Lbp 55.00 Br md 11.59 Dpth 8.08 Welded, 2 dks	**(A35A2RR) Ro-Ro Cargo Ship** TEU 6 C.Dk 6/20'	**2 oil engines** with clutches, flexible couplings & sr reverse geared to sc. shafts driving 2 FP propellers Total Power: 1,176kW (1,598hp) 12.0kn Blackstone ESL8MK2 2 x 4 Stroke 8 Cy. 222 x 292 each-588kW (799bhp) Lister Blackstone MirrleesMarine Ltd.-Dursley AuxGen: 2 x 125kW 415V 50Hz a.c Thrusters: 1 Thwart. FP thruster (f)

Ship	Tonnage	Class	Builder / Dimensions	Type	Machinery
5423661 **SINU-I-WASA TOLU** *3DVA* *ex* Adi Savusavu *-2006* *ex* Dana Star *-1996* - *ex* Dana Scarlett *-1994* **Venu Shipping Ltd** - *Suva* *Fiji* Official number: 000054	*1,721* 757 500	Class: (LR) ✠ Classed LR until 23/3/98	**1964**-02 **Oresundsvarvet AB — Landskrona** Yd No: 190 Loa 65.31 Br ex 16.46 Dght 3.214 Lbp 59.42 Br md 16.01 Dpth 4.70 Welded, 1 dk	**(A36A2PR) Passenger/Ro-Ro Ship (Vehicles)** Passengers: unberthed: 694; berths: 6 Bow door Stern door Lane-Len: 180 Lane-clr ht: 4.20 Cars: 65 Ice Capable	**2 oil engines** driving 2 CP propellers Total Power: 1,942kW (2,640hp) 14.8kn Deutz RBV8M545 2 x 4 Stroke 8 Cy. 320 x 450 each-971kW (1320bhp) Kloeckner Humboldt Deutz AG-West Germany AuxGen: 3 x 200kW 380V 50Hz a.c Thrusters: 1 Thwart. FP thruster (f)
7109893 **SINULOG** *DUA2451* *ex* Toyofuku Maru *-1989* - **Loadstar Shipping Co Inc** - *Manila* *Philippines* Official number: 00-0000457	*1,599* 1,029 1,513	Class: (NK)	**1971**-02 **Kanda Zosensho K.K. — Kure** Yd No: 158 Loa 94.90 Br ex 16.06 Dght 4.553 Lbp 86.90 Br md 16.01 Dpth 7.85 Welded, 1 dk	**(A35B2RV) Vehicles Carrier** Quarter stern door/ramp (p) Quarter stern door/ramp (s)	**1 oil engine** driving 1 FP propeller Total Power: 2,207kW (3,001hp) 13.0kn Hanshin 6L50BSH 1 x 4 Stroke 6 Cy. 500 x 700 2207kW (3001bhp) Hanshin Nainenki Kogyo-Japan AuxGen: 2 x 136kW Fuel: 236.5 (d.f.) 7.5pd
8877215 **SINVITCO I** *HQIN2* *ex* Hama 1 *-1991* *ex* Kainan Maru *-1991* - **Sinvitco Pte Ltd** - *San Lorenzo* *Honduras* Official number: L-0323936	*197* 117 700		**1972**-05 **Hakata Zosen K.K. — Imabari** Loa 48.50 Br ex - Dght 3.010 Lbp 45.00 Br md 9.00 Dpth 4.70 Welded, 1 dk	**(A31A2GX) General Cargo Ship** Grain: 1,174; Bale: 1,062	**1 oil engine** driving 1 FP propeller Total Power: 515kW (700hp) 10.0kn Makita 1 x 4 Stroke 515kW (700bhp) Makita Corp-Japan
7701392 **SINWAN** *9WAW4* *ex* Genkai No. 8 *-1994* *ex* Shintetsu Maru *-1989* - **Super Rim Sdn Bhd** Apollo Shipping & Trading Sdn Bhd *Kuching* *Malaysia* MMSI: 533440000 Official number: 327617	**1,477** 1,035 2,512	Class: (NK)	**1977**-05 **K.K. Matsuura Zosensho — Osakikamijima** Yd No: 251 Loa 81.06 Br ex 12.04 Dght 5.164 Lbp 75.01 Br md 12.01 Dpth 6.02 Welded, 1 dk	**(A31A2GX) General Cargo Ship** Grain: 3,513; Bale: 3,347 1 Ha: (40.8 x 8.0)ER	**1 oil engine** driving 1 FP propeller Total Power: 1,471kW (2,000hp) 11.5kn Makita KSLH633 1 x 4 Stroke 6 Cy. 330 x 530 1471kW (2000bhp) Makita Diesel Co Ltd-Japan AuxGen: 2 x 96kW 220V a.c Fuel: 103.0 (d.f.) 27.0 (r.f.) 6.0pd
9358967 **SINYAR** *A6E3059* - **P&O Maritime FZE** - *Dubai* *United Arab Emirates* MMSI: 470327000 Official number: 5256	**317** 95 134	Class: LR ✠ **100A1** SS 06/2011 tug, restricted service to Arabian Gulf and Gulf of Oman ✠ **LMC** Eq.Ltr: F; Cable: 255.0/17.5 U2 (a)	**2006**-06 **Dubai Drydocks — Dubai** Yd No: NB45 Loa 30.66 Br ex 10.32 Dght 4.342 Lbp 26.30 Br md 10.00 Dpth 5.00 Welded, 1 dk	**(B32A2ST) Tug**	**2 oil engines** gearing integral to driving 2 Z propellers Total Power: 3,200kW (4,350hp) Wartsila 9L20 2 x 4 Stroke 9 Cy. 200 x 280 each-1600kW (2175bhp) Wartsila Finland Oy-Finland AuxGen: 2 x 150kW 380V 50Hz a.c
9119373 **SIOUX** *9HRW4* *ex* Mikela *-2001* *ex* Seabreeze *-1999* - *ex* Vernal *-1995* **Ocean Wind Shipping Ltd** Misha Shipping Agency & Trade Ltd SatCom: Inmarsat C 424935310 *Valletta* *Malta* MMSI: 249353000 Official number: 4520	**4,976** 2,310 5,177	Class: RS (GL)	**1994 OAO Navashinskiy Sudostroitelnyy Zavod 'Oka' — Navashino** Yd No: 1057 Lengthened-2001 Loa 139.20 Br ex 16.70 Dght 3.770 Lbp 131.20 Br md 16.50 Dpth 5.50 Welded, 1 dk	**(A31A2GX) General Cargo Ship** Grain: 6,440 TEU 109 C. 109/20' Compartments: 4 Ho, ER 4 Ha: (25.2 x 12.6)3 (18.6 x 12.6)ER	**2 oil engines** driving 2 FP propellers Total Power: 1,766kW (2,402hp) 10.0kn Dvigatel Revolyutsii 6CHRNP36/45 2 x 4 Stroke 6 Cy. 360 x 450 each-883kW (1201bhp) Zavod "Dvigatel Revolyutsii"-Nizhniy Novgorod AuxGen: 2 x 160kW 220/380V a.c, 3 x 50kW 220/380V a.c Thrusters: 1 Thwart. FP thruster (f) Fuel: 309.0 (d.f.)
8901133 **SIOUX MAIDEN** *DYND* *ex* Ikan Tuxpan *-2005* *ex* New Ample *-2004* - *ex* Angel Feather *-1997* **Birnam Maritime Corp** Roymar Ship Management Inc *Manila* *Philippines* MMSI: 548730000 Official number: MNLA000660	**23,270** 13,807 42,248 T/cm 47.6	Class: AB (NK)	**1989**-09 **Oshima Shipbuilding Co Ltd — Saikai NS** Yd No: 10119 Loa 180.00 (BB) Br ex - Dght 11.228 Lbp 172.00 Br md 30.50 Dpth 15.80 Welded, 1 dk	**(A21A2BC) Bulk Carrier** Grain: 52,125; Bale: 51,118 Compartments: 5 Ho, ER 5 Ha: (14.4 x 15.3)4 (19.2 x 15.3)ER Cranes: 4x25t	**1 oil engine** driving 1 FP propeller Total Power: 8,102kW (11,015hp) 14.0kn Sulzer 6RTA52 1 x 2 Stroke 6 Cy. 520 x 1800 8102kW (11015bhp) Sumitomo Heavy Industries Ltd-Japan AuxGen: 4 x 324kW a.c
8808898 **SIP 2** *CNA2616* - **Societe de Peche Marona SA** - SatCom: Inmarsat C 424218010 *Agadir* *Morocco*	**486** 146 330	Class: BV	**1990**-04 **IMC — Tonnay-Charente** Yd No: 318 Loa 39.71 Br ex 9.63 Dght 3.801 Lbp 34.42 Br md 9.52 Dpth 4.02 Welded	**(B11A2FS) Stern Trawler** Ins: 295	**1 oil engine** with clutches, flexible couplings & sr reverse geared to sc. shaft driving 1 FP propeller Total Power: 772kW (1,050hp) 12.0kn Deutz SBA16M816 1 x Vee 4 Stroke 16 Cy. 142 x 160 772kW (1050bhp) Kloeckner Humboldt Deutz AG-West Germany AuxGen: 2 x 128kW 380V a.c
8808927 **SIP 5** *CNA2619* - **Societe de Peche Marona SA** - SatCom: Inmarsat C 424218510 *Agadir* *Morocco*	**486** 146 330	Class: BV	**1990**-12 **IMC — Tonnay-Charente** Yd No: 321 Loa 39.71 Br ex - Dght 3.801 Lbp 34.42 Br md 9.52 Dpth 4.02 Welded	**(B11A2FS) Stern Trawler**	**1 oil engine** geared to sc. shaft driving 1 FP propeller Total Power: 774kW (1,052hp) Deutz SBA16M816 1 x Vee 4 Stroke 16 Cy. 142 x 160 774kW (1052bhp) Kloeckner Humboldt Deutz AG-West Germany
8951671 **SIPA 212** - - -	**398** 170 -		**1997 Varaderos y Talleres Duran SA (VATADUR) — Duran** L reg 47.30 Br ex - Dght - Lbp - Br md 8.40 Dpth 3.80 Welded, 1 dk	**(B11B2FV) Fishing Vessel**	**1 oil engine** driving 1 FP propeller Total Power: 809kW (1,100hp) 10.0kn Caterpillar 3512TA 1 x Vee 4 Stroke 12 Cy. 170 x 190 809kW (1100bhp) Caterpillar Inc-USA
9204673 **SIPAN** *OAAR* - **Trabajos Maritima SA (TRAMARSA)** - *Callao* *Peru* Official number: CO-18669-EM	**163** - -	Class: (AB) (GL)	**1998**-12 **Jiangsu Wuxi Shipyard Co Ltd — Wuxi JS** Yd No: 1098 Loa 25.00 Br ex - Dght 3.199 Lbp 22.00 Br md 7.60 Dpth 3.50 Welded, 1 dk	**(B32A2ST) Tug**	**2 oil engines** reverse reduction geared to sc. shafts driving 2 FP propellers Total Power: 1,060kW (1,442hp) 11.0kn Mitsubishi S6R2-MPTK 2 x 4 Stroke 6 Cy. 170 x 220 each-530kW (721bhp) Mitsubishi Heavy Industries Ltd-Japan AuxGen: 2 x 48kW
9323807 **SIPEA** *IBXU* *ex* Aurora *-2009* - **Carichi Liquidi Societa Armatoriale SpA (CALISA)** - SatCom: Inmarsat Mini-M 764678480 *Palermo* *Italy* MMSI: 247184900 Official number: RI182PA	**25,651** 9,111 37,320 T/cm 50.9	Class: RI (AB)	**2007**-01 **STX Shipbuilding Co Ltd — Changwon (Jinhae Shipyard)** Yd No: 2008 Loa 180.00 (BB) Br ex 32.00 Dght 10.016 Lbp 171.20 Br md 32.00 Dpth 16.20 Welded, 1 dk	**(A12B2TR) Chemical/Products Tanker** Double Hull (13F) Liq: 43,427; Liq (Oil): 43,427 Cargo Heating Coils Compartments: 12 Wing Ta, 2 Wing Slop Ta, ER 12 Cargo Pump (s): 12x450m³/hr Manifold: Bow/CM: 88.9m	**1 oil engine** driving 1 FP propeller Total Power: 9,488kW (12,900hp) 14.5kn MAN-B&W 6S50MC-C 1 x 2 Stroke 6 Cy. 500 x 2000 9488kW (12900bhp) STX Engine Co Ltd-South Korea AuxGen: 3 x a.c Thrusters: 1 Tunnel thruster (f) Fuel: 115.1 (d.f.) 1454.2 (r.f.)
8700852 **SIPECHE I** - - **Sipeche SA** - *Nouadhibou* *Mauritania* Official number: 614	**285** 85 187	Class: (BV) (RI)	**1987**-03 **Astilleros Armon SA — Navia** Yd No: 163 Loa 32.52 Br ex - Dght 3.901 Lbp 28.45 Br md 8.50 Dpth 4.60 Welded, 1 dk	**(B11A2FT) Trawler** Ins: 230	**1 oil engine** with clutches & reverse reduction geared to sc. shaft driving 1 FP propeller Total Power: 780kW (1,060hp) 12.0kn Caterpillar 3512TA 1 x Vee 4 Stroke 12 Cy. 170 x 190 780kW (1060bhp) Caterpillar Inc-USA AuxGen: 2 x 124kW 220/380V a.c
8812148 **SIPECHE II** - *ex* Barakat 1 *-2000* *ex* Derraman III *-1989* - *ex* Lirio *-1988* **Sipeche SA** - *Nouadhibou* *Mauritania* Official number: 642	**222** 62 164	Class: (BV) (RI)	**1988**-10 **Astilleros Armon SA — Navia** Yd No: 197 Loa 29.50 Br ex - Dght 3.150 Lbp 25.50 Br md 7.76 Dpth 4.20 Welded, 1 dk	**(B11A2FS) Stern Trawler** Ins: 187	**1 oil engine** with clutches, flexible couplings & reverse reduction geared to sc. shaft driving 1 FP propeller Total Power: 570kW (775hp) Caterpillar 3508TA 1 x Vee 4 Stroke 8 Cy. 170 x 190 570kW (775bhp) Caterpillar Inc-USA
7313030 **SIQUIJOR ISLAND 2** *DUH2490* *ex* Bantayan *-1988* *ex* Dona Isabel 2 *-2000* - *ex* Ferry Ieshima *-1988* **Orlines Sea-Land Transport Inc** - *Cebu* *Philippines* Official number: ZAM2D00303	*488* 186 145	Class: (KR)	**1973 Matsuura Tekko Zosen K.K. — Osakikamijima** Yd No: 227 Loa 47.53 Br ex 11.28 Dght 2.901 Lbp 41.51 Br md 10.80 Dpth 3.61 Welded, 1 dk	**(A36A2PR) Passenger/Ro-Ro Ship (Vehicles)** Passengers: 100	**2 oil engines** driving 2 FP propellers Total Power: 1,472kW (2,002hp) 12.8kn Niigata 6L25BX 2 x 4 Stroke 6 Cy. 250 x 320 each-736kW (1001bhp) Niigata Engineering Co Ltd-Japan Fuel: 26.5 1.5pd

IMO / Call sign	Name / Owner / Manager / Port / Flag	Tonnage	Class	Build / Dimensions	Type / Cargo	Machinery
7015157 - -	**SIR ALAN** - -	*281* 144 248	Class: (AB)	**1970 Universal Dockyard Ltd. — Hong Kong** Yd No: 65 Loa 38.87 Br ex 9.48 Dght 1.718 Lbp 36.58 Br md 9.15 Dpth 2.14 Welded, 1 dk	**(A35D2RL) Landing Craft** Bow door/ramp Compartments: 1 Ho, ER 1 Ha: (2.9 x 1.8)ER	**3 oil engines** driving 3 FP propellers Total Power: 420kW (570hp) Caterpillar D334 3 x 4 Stroke 6 Cy. 121 x 152 each-140kW (190bhp) Caterpillar Tractor Co-USA AuxGen: 1 x 50kW, 1 x 16kW Fuel: 287.5
9173355 *9HA2536*	**SIR ALBERT** *ex* Love Me Tender *-2004* **Albert Shipping Co Ltd** Hellas Marine Services Ltd *Valletta* *Malta* MMSI: 248832000 Official number: 9173355	**9,973** 4,781 15,962	Class: NK	**1997-12 Tianjin Xingang Shipyard — Tianjin** Yd No: 317 Loa 135.80 Br ex - Dght 8.800 Lbp 128.00 Br md 22.00 Dpth 12.20 Welded, 1 dk	**(A21A2BC) Bulk Carrier** Grain: 17,605 Compartments: 4 Ho, ER 4 Ha: (13.3 x 11.3)3 (14.3 x 15.4)ER Cranes: 3x30t	**1 oil engine** reduction geared to sc. shaft driving 1 FP propeller Total Power: 2,993kW (4,069hp) 13.8kn B&W 6L35MC 1 x 2 Stroke 6 Cy. 350 x 1050 2993kW (4069bhp) Fuel: 800.0
8873415 - -	**SIR BANIYAS SEAWING** - **Delma Co-Operative Society** -	**130** 39 -	Class: (BV)	**1991 Zavod im. "Ordzhonikidze" — Poti** Loa 34.50 Br ex - Dght - Lbp 30.15 Br md 5.80 Dpth 1.80 Welded, 1 dk	**(A37B2PS) Passenger Ship**	**2 oil engines** reduction geared to sc. shafts driving 2 FP propellers Total Power: 2,100kW (2,856hp) M.T.U. 12V396 2 x Vee 4 Stroke 12 Cy. 165 x 185 each-1050kW (1428bhp) MTU Friedrichshafen GmbH-Friedrichshafen AuxGen: 2 x 16kW a.c
9318735 *A6PM* -	**SIR BU'NUER** - - *Abu Dhabi* *United Arab Emirates* MMSI: 470778000	**1,687** 800 2,400	Class: (BV)	**2004-10 Shin Yang Shipyard Sdn Bhd — Miri** Yd No: 156 Loa 78.10 Br ex - Dght 3.500 Lbp 72.70 Br md 16.00 Dpth 4.80 Welded, 1 dk	**(A35D2RL) Landing Craft** Passengers: 20 Bow ramp (centre) Len: - Wid: - Swl: 70	**2 oil engines** reduction geared to sc. shafts driving 2 FP propellers Total Power: 2,000kW (2,720hp) 12.0kn Caterpillar 3512B 2 x Vee 4 Stroke 12 Cy. 170 x 190 each-1000kW (1360bhp) Caterpillar Inc-USA AuxGen: 2 x 164kW Thrusters: 1 Tunnel thruster (f)
6418613 - -	**SIR CEDRIC** *ex* Pen Arun *-1974* *ex* Lantyan *-1964* *ex* Roselyne *-1953* *ex* Empire Townsman *-1947* - -	*311* 141 -		**1943-08 R. Dunston Ltd. — Thorne** Yd No: T394 Converted From: General Cargo Ship-1943 Loa 43.16 Br ex 6.56 Dght 2.286 Lbp - Br md 6.53 Dpth - Riveted\Welded, 1 dk	**(B33A2DS) Suction Dredger** Compartments: 1 Ho, ER 1 Ha: ER	**1 oil engine** driving 1 FP propeller Total Power: 202kW (275hp) Crossley HRN5 1 x 2 Stroke 5 Cy. 267 x 343 202kW (275bhp) Crossley Bros. Ltd.-Manchester AuxGen: 1 x 6kW 110V d.c, 1 x 5kW 110V d.c
8810736 *9GEQ* -	**SIR EMMANUEL QUIST** - **Government of The Republic of Ghana (Ports & Harbours Authority)** - *Takoradi* *Ghana* Official number: 316728	**209** 62 -	Class: (GL)	**1989-04 Machinefabriek D.E. Gorter B.V. — Hoogezand** (Hull) **1989-04 B.V. Scheepswerf Damen — Gorinchem** Yd No: 3150 L reg 27.78 Br ex 8.03 Dght 3.350 Lbp - Br md 7.80 Dpth 4.05 Welded, 1 dk	**(B32A2ST) Tug**	**2 oil engines** with clutches, flexible couplings & sr reverse geared to sc. shafts driving 2 FP propellers Total Power: 1,840kW (2,502hp) 10.3kn Cummins KTA-50-M 2 x Vee 4 Stroke 16 Cy. 159 x 159 each-920kW (1251bhp) Cummins Engine Co Ltd-United Kingdom AuxGen: 1 x 52kW 220/380V a.c
5329504 - -	**SIR FRANCIS SPRING** - **Chennai Port Trust** - *Kolkata* *India* Official number: 172585	*233* - -	Class: IR (LR) ✠ Classed LR until 10/42	**1938-12 Hooghly Docking & Engineering Co. Ltd. — Howrah** Yd No: 172 Loa 27.64 Br ex 9.20 Dght 3.810 Lbp - Br md 9.15 Dpth - Riveted	**(B32A2ST) Tug**	**2 Steam Recips** driving 2 FP propellers 9.0kn Plenty Plenty & Son Ltd.-Newbury Fuel: 55.0 (r.f.)
9065340 *3BIM* -	**SIR GAETAN DUVAL** *ex* Sea Queen *-2006* **Mauritius Port Authority** - *Port Louis* *Mauritius* Official number: MR048	**275** 82 85	Class: (LR) ✠ Classed LR until 28/10/08	**1993-10 Husumer Schiffswerft Inh. Gebr. Kroeger GmbH & Co. KG — Husum** Yd No: 1511 Loa 26.70 Br ex 10.06 Dght 2.720 Lbp 25.00 Br md 10.00 Dpth 3.70 Welded, 1 dk	**(B32A2ST) Tug**	**2 oil engines** gearing integral to driving 2 Voith-Schneider propellers Total Power: 2,000kW (2,720hp) 12.0kn Alpha 6L23/30 2 x 4 Stroke 6 Cy. 225 x 300 each-1000kW (1360bhp) MAN B&W Diesel A/S-Denmark AuxGen: 2 x 80kW 400V 50Hz a.c
9151383 *DYIL*	**SIR HENRY** *ex* Rubin Lark *-2005* **Revenge Shipping Corp** Hellas Marine Services Ltd *Manila* *Philippines* MMSI: 548718000 Official number: MNLA000652	**11,194** 6,784 18,315 T/cm 28.1	Class: NK	**1997-01 Shikoku Dockyard Co. Ltd. — Takamatsu** Yd No: 882 Loa 148.17 Br ex - Dght 9.120 Lbp 135.95 Br md 22.80 Dpth 12.20 Welded, 1 dk	**(A21A2BC) Bulk Carrier** Grain: 23,212; Bale: 22,337 Compartments: 4 Ho, ER 4 Ha: (16.3 x 12.0)3 (19.5 x 12.0)ER Cranes: 3x30t	**1 oil engine** driving 1 FP propeller Total Power: 4,983kW (6,775hp) 13.5kn B&W 5L42MC 1 x 2 Stroke 5 Cy. 420 x 1360 4983kW (6775bhp) Mitsui Engineering & Shipbuilding CLtd-Japan Fuel: 1000.0
8428715 - -	**SIR HENRY MORGAN** *ex* Aulemic *-1985* - -	*128* 58 -		**1979 in Venezuela** L reg 23.99 Br ex 6.10 Dght - Lbp - Br md - Dpth 3.20 Welded, 1 dk	**(B34R2QY) Supply Tender**	**1 oil engine** driving 1 FP propeller Total Power: 405kW (551hp) 17.0kn Caterpillar D379TA 1 x Vee 4 Stroke 8 Cy. 159 x 203 405kW (551bhp) Caterpillar Tractor Co-USA
7008037 - -	**SIR IAN** *ex* Coleraine *-2008* **Greenlink Maritime Services Ltd** - *Nigeria*	**245** 73 -	Class: (LR) ✠ Classed LR until 1/3/12	**1970-03 Appledore Shipbuilders Ltd — Bideford** Yd No: A.S. 70 Loa 32.19 Br ex 8.87 Dght 3.614 Lbp 28.96 Br md 8.54 Dpth 4.12 Welded, 1 dk	**(B32A2ST) Tug**	**1 oil engine** sr geared to sc. shaft driving 1 CP propeller Total Power: 1,912kW (2,600hp) 16.0kn MWM TBRHS345AU 1 x 4 Stroke 8 Cy. 360 x 450 1912kW (2600bhp) Motoren Werke Mannheim AG (MWM)-West Germany AuxGen: 2 x 75kW 415V 50Hz a.c
9263966 *VRYS7* -	**SIR IVOR** - **Energetic Peninsula Ltd** Petredec Services (Asia) Pte Ltd *Hong Kong* *Hong Kong* MMSI: 477391000 Official number: HK-1053	**4,508** 1,352 3,633 T/cm 13.7	Class: LR ✠ **100A1** SS 04/2013 liquefied gas carrier, Ship Type 2G Type C independent tanks max. vapour pressure 18kg/cm sq min. cargo temp. 0 *IWS LI ✠ **LMC** Eq.Ltr: W; Cable: 495.0/46.0 U3 (a)	**2003-04 Zhejiang Shipbuilding Co Ltd — Ningbo ZJ** Yd No: 00-094 Loa 99.50 (BB) Br ex 18.22 Dght 5.600 Lbp 92.90 Br md 18.20 Dpth 7.80 Welded, 1 dk	**(A11B2TG) LPG Tanker** Liq (Gas): 4,930 3 x Gas Tank (s); 2 independent (stl) cyl horizontal, ER 2 Cargo Pump (s): 2x300m³/hr Manifold: Bow/CM: 49.7m	**1 oil engine** driving 1 FP propeller Total Power: 3,700kW (5,031hp) 13.0kn MAN-B&W 5S35MC 1 x 2 Stroke 5 Cy. 350 x 1400 3700kW (5031bhp) STX Corp-South Korea AuxGen: 3 x 415kW 450V 60Hz a.c Boilers: AuxB (Comp) 7.7kgf/cm² (7.6bar) Thrusters: 1 Tunnel thruster (f) Fuel: 540.0 (r.f.) 16.0pd
8969587 - -	**SIR LAWRENCE** *ex* Miss Diane IV *-2005* **Gulf Finest Investments Co** - *New Orleans, LA* *United States of America* Official number: 1119661	**178** 53 -		**2001** Yd No: 207 L reg 26.94 Br ex - Dght - Lbp - Br md 7.92 Dpth 3.81 Welded, 1 dk	**(B11B2FV) Fishing Vessel**	**1 oil engine** driving 1 FP propeller
6706955 - -	**SIR MICHAEL** *ex* Talisman *-2011* *ex* Sea-Aker Husky *-2001* *ex* Alaska Husky *-1998* **Hydrostar Ghana Ltd** - *Takoradi* *Ghana* Official number: GSR 0098	**654** 196 951	Class: (AB)	**1966 Todd Shipyards Corp. (Houston Div.) — Houston, Tx** Yd No: 495 Loa 52.70 Br ex 11.03 Dght 4.176 Lbp 51.80 Br md 10.98 Dpth 4.88 Welded, 1 dk	**(B21A20S) Platform Supply Ship** Ice Capable	**4 oil engines** reverse reduction geared to sc. shafts driving 2 FP propellers Total Power: 2,352kW (3,196hp) Caterpillar D398SCAC 4 x Vee 4 Stroke 12 Cy. 159 x 203 each-588kW (799bhp) Caterpillar Tractor Co-USA AuxGen: 2 x 98kW a.c Fuel: 190.0 (d.f.)
7320306 *HQCL5*	**SIR MICHAEL** *ex* Abu Samir *-1995* *ex* Cherdas *-1985* *ex* Bever *-1981* **Yale Invest & Finance SA** United Cement Co Bscc SatCom: Inmarsat C 433479510 *San Lorenzo* *Honduras* MMSI: 334768000 Official number: L-1721986	*475* 7 335	Class: BV (Class contemplated) RS (NV)	**1973-10 D.W. Kremer Sohn — Elmshorn** Yd No: 1157 Loa 42.30 Br ex 11.16 Dght 4.649 Lbp 36.35 Br md 10.83 Dpth 5.57 Welded, 1 dk	**(B32A2ST) Tug** Ice Capable	**2 oil engines** driving 2 CP propellers Total Power: 3,162kW (4,300hp) 13.5kn MaK 8M452AK 2 x 4 Stroke 8 Cy. 320 x 450 each-1581kW (2150bhp) MaK Maschinenbau GmbH-Kiel AuxGen: 2 x 150kW 220V 50Hz a.c Thrusters: 1 Thwart. FP thruster (f) Fuel: 30.5 (d.f.) 14.0pd

IMO / Call sign	Name / Owner	Tonnage	Class	Builder / Dimensions	Type	Machinery
9212096 *ZMR7108* -	**SIR ROBERT** **Port of Tauranga Ltd** *Tauranga* *New Zealand*	**338** - -	Class: LR ✠ **100A1** SS 11/2010 SSC mono, workboat G3 **LMC** Cable: 110.0/16.0 U2 (a)	**2000**-11 **North Port Engineering Ltd — Whangarei** Yd No: 132 Loa 22.20 Br ex 9.22 Dght 3.150 Lbp 20.80 Br md 9.20 Dpth 4.15 Welded, 1 dk	**(B32A2ST) Tug**	**2 oil engines** reduction geared to sc. shafts driving 2 Directional propellers Total Power: 3,282kW (4,462hp) 12.0kn Caterpillar 3516TA 2 x Vee 4 Stroke 16 Cy. 170 x 190 each-1641kW (2231bhp) Caterpillar Inc-USA Fuel: 98.0 (d.f.)
5297414 *PBMP* -	**SIR ROBERT BADEN POWELL** *ex* Robert *-1993* **Sir Robert Baden Powell** - *Lemmer* *Netherlands* MMSI: 245540000 Official number: 23470	**111** 53 -	Class: (PR)	**1958**-01 **VEB Schiffswerft "Edgar Andre" — Magdeburg** Yd No: 6046 Converted From: Tug-1993 Loa 42.00 Br ex 6.50 Dght 2.250 Lbp - Br md - Dpth 3.00 Welded, 1 dk	**(A37B2PS) Passenger Ship** Passengers: cabins: 7; berths: 18 Ice Capable	**1 oil engine** driving 1 FP propeller Total Power: 221kW (300hp) Mitsubishi 6DE10-TA 1 x 4 Stroke 6 Cy. 150 x 200 221kW (300bhp) (new engine 1993) Mitsubishi Heavy Industries Ltd-Japan
7391903 *VGSS* -	**SIR ROBERT BOND** **Government of Newfoundland & Labrador (Department of Works, Services & Transportation)** - *St John's, NL* *Canada* MMSI: 316003370 Official number: 347522	*11,197* 7,324 3,726	Class: LR ✠ **100A1** CS 05/2013 Ice Class 2 ✠ **LMC** Eq.Ltr: Z; Cable: U2	**1975**-10 **Port Weller Dry Docks — St Catharines ON** Yd No: 59 Converted From: Ro-Ro Cargo Ship-1978 Loa 135.34 Br ex 21.72 Dght 5.106 Lbp 122.66 Br md 21.33 Dpth 13.42 Welded, 2 dks	**(A36A2PT) Passenger/Ro-Ro Ship (Vehicles/Rail)** Passengers: unberthed: 260; cabins: 47 Stern door/ramp Len: 6.09 Wid: 7.92 Swl: - Side door (p) Lane-Len: 659 Lorries: 42, Cars: 120, Trailers: 34, Vehicles: 34 Bale: 11,575 Ice Capable	**4 oil engines** sr geared to sc. shafts driving 2 CP propellers Total Power: 6,472kW (8,800hp) 15.0kn Ruston 12RKCM 4 x Vee 4 Stroke 12 Cy. 254 x 305 each-1618kW (2200bhp) Ruston Paxman Diesels Ltd.-Colchester AuxGen: 3 x 400kW 460V 60Hz a.c Thrusters: 1 Thwart. FP thruster (f); 1 Tunnel thruster (a) Fuel: 244.0 (d.f.) 25.5pd
8608432 *3BFT* -	**SIR SEEWOOSAGUR** **Mauritius Port Authority** - *Port Louis* *Mauritius* Official number: 710810	*254* 86 174	Class: BV (LR) ✠ Classed LR until 9/4/07	**1987**-04 **Martin Jansen GmbH & Co. KG Schiffsw. u. Masch. — Leer** Yd No: 198 Loa 29.25 Br ex 9.64 Dght 4.770 Lbp 27.00 Br md 9.00 Dpth - Welded, 1 dk	**(B32A2ST) Tug**	**2 oil engines** with flexible couplings & sr gearedto sc. shafts driving 2 Directional propellers Total Power: 2,000kW (2,720hp) 11.8kn Deutz SBV6M628 2 x 4 Stroke 6 Cy. 240 x 280 each-1000kW (1360bhp) Kloeckner Humboldt Deutz AG-West Germany AuxGen: 2 x 68kW 400V 50Hz a.c
5329700 *VTFV* -	**SIR SHANMUKHAM** **Cochin Port Trust** - *Kochi* *India* Official number: 159614	*685* 356 -	Class: IR (LR) ✠	**1937**-07 **Wm. Simons & Co. Ltd. — Renfrew** Yd No: 716 Loa 50.60 Br ex 10.11 Dght 3.887 Lbp 48.90 Br md 10.06 Dpth - Riveted, 1 dk	**(B33B2DS) Suction Hopper Dredger** Hopper: 685 Compartments: 1 Ho, ER 1 Ha: (0.9 x 1.0)ER	**2 Steam Recips** driving 2 FP propellers 10.0kn Wm. Simons & Co. Ltd.-Renfrew Fuel: 69.0 (r.f.)
6618445 *2CG06* -	**SIR SILAS** *ex* Albatros *-1993* *ex* Bugsier 24 *-1986* - - *United Kingdom* MMSI: 235072606	**113** 34 -	Class: (GL)	**1959 F Schichau GmbH — Bremerhaven** Yd No: 1699 Widened-1965 Loa 26.70 Br ex 7.01 Dght 2.833 Lbp 24.01 Br md 6.46 Dpth 3.10 Welded, 1 dk	**(B32A2ST) Tug** Ice Capable	**1 oil engine** driving 1 FP propeller Total Power: 971kW (1,320hp) 10.0kn Deutz RBV8M545 1 x 4 Stroke 8 Cy. 320 x 450 971kW (1320bhp) Kloeckner Humboldt Deutz AG-West Germany
7408512 *SSHV* -	**SIR TAREK** *ex* ODS Murena *-1993* *ex* Miriam I *-1986* *ex* Cod Truck *-1981* **Rashied Maritime Services** - *Port Said* *Egypt* MMSI: 622122003 Official number: 4153	*481* 172 737	Class: RI (AB) (GL)	**1975**-05 **JG Hitzler Schiffswerft und Masch GmbH & Co KG — Lauenburg** Yd No: 749 Loa 52.88 Br ex 11.03 Dght 3.436 Lbp 49.23 Br md 11.00 Dpth 3.99 Welded, 1 dk	**(B21B20T) Offshore Tug/Supply Ship**	**2 oil engines** reverse reduction geared to sc. shafts driving 2 FP propellers Total Power: 1,692kW (2,300hp) 13.0kn MWM TBD440-8 2 x 4 Stroke 8 Cy. 230 x 270 each-846kW (1150bhp) Motoren Werke Mannheim AG (MWM)-West Germany AuxGen: 3 x 112kW 220/380V 50Hz a.c Thrusters: 1 Thwart. FP thruster (f) Fuel: 382.0 (d.f.) 7.5pd
7402520 *5NJM* -	**SIR VINCENT** *ex* Seabulk Martin II *-2007* *ex* Red Martin II *-1998* *ex* Cecilie Viking *-1996* *ex* Sealion Transporter *-1991* *ex* Sea Transporter *-1990* *ex* Stril Supplier *-1987* *ex* Seaforth Scotia *-1987* *ex* Stad Scotia *-1983* **Phenix Associates Ltd** - *Nigeria* Official number: SR600	**1,329** 399 1,930	Class: (NV)	**1976**-08 **James Brown & Hamer Ltd. — Durban** Yd No: 33 Loa 63.02 Br ex 13.85 Dght 5.171 Lbp 58.02 Br md 13.80 Dpth 6.13 Welded, 1 dk	**(B21A20P) Pipe Carrier**	**2 oil engines** geared to sc. shafts driving 2 CP propellers Total Power: 3,090kW (4,202hp) 14.0kn MaK 6M453AK 2 x 4 Stroke 6 Cy. 320 x 420 each-1545kW (2101bhp) MaK Maschinenbau GmbH-Kiel AuxGen: 3 x 120kW 440V 60Hz a.c Thrusters: 1 Thwart. FP thruster (f) Fuel: 695.0 25.0pd
9109550 *DYLO* -	**SIR WALTER** *ex* Rubin Stork *-2003* **Walter Shipping Navigation SA** Hellas Marine Services Ltd SatCom: Inmarsat B 335680810 *Manila* *Philippines* MMSI: 548667000 Official number: MNLA000595	**11,193** 6,784 18,315 T/cm 28.1	Class: NK	**1996**-04 **Shikoku Dockyard Co. Ltd. — Takamatsu** Yd No: 879 Loa 148.17 (BB) Br ex - Dght 9.104 Lbp 135.95 Br md 22.80 Dpth 12.20 Welded, 1 dk	**(A21A2BC) Bulk Carrier** Grain: 23,212; Bale: 22,337 Compartments: 4 Ho, ER 4 Ha: (16.3 x 12.0)3 (19.5 x 12.0)ER Cranes: 3x30t	**1 oil engine** driving 1 FP propeller Total Power: 4,983kW (6,775hp) 13.5kn B&W 5L42MC 1 x 2 Stroke 5 Cy. 420 x 1360 4983kW (6775bhp) Mitsui Engineering & Shipbuilding CLtd-Japan Fuel: 995.0 (r.f.)
8415495 *CGJY* -	**SIR WILFRED GRENFELL** **Government of Canada (Canadian Coast Guard)** - SatCom: Inmarsat A 1560122 *Ottawa, ON* *Canada* MMSI: 316051000 Official number: 809762	*2,404* 664 1,265	Class: (LR) ✠ Classed LR until 6/88	**1987**-12 **Marystown Shipyard Ltd — Marystown NL** Yd No: 37 Loa 68.41 Br ex 15.30 Dght 5.501 Lbp 59.59 Br md 14.99 Dpth 7.29 Welded, 1 dk	**(B34H2SQ) Patrol Vessel** Ice Capable	**4 oil engines** with clutches, flexible couplings & sr geared to sc. shafts driving 2 CP propellers Total Power: 9,460kW (12,860hp) 16.0kn Deutz SBV16M628 2 x Vee 4 Stroke 16 Cy. 240 x 280 each-3052kW (4149bhp) Kloeckner Humboldt Deutz AG-West Germany Deutz SBV9M628 2 x 4 Stroke 9 Cy. 240 x 280 each-1678kW (2281bhp) Kloeckner Humboldt Deutz AG-West Germany AuxGen: 2 x 1120kW 440V 60Hz a.c, 2 x 440kW 440V 60Hz a.c Thrusters: 1 Thwart. CP thruster (f); 1 Tunnel thruster (a) Fuel: 900.0 (d.f.)
8320456 *CGJK* -	**SIR WILFRID LAURIER** **Government of Canada (Transport Canada)** Government of Canada (Canadian Coast Guard) SatCom: Inmarsat C 431605240 *Ottawa, ON* *Canada* MMSI: 316052000 Official number: 807038	**3,812** 1,533 1,585	Class: (LR) ✠ Classed LR until 11/87	**1986**-11 **Collingwood Shipyards Ltd — Collingwood ON** Yd No: 230 Loa 82.96 Br ex 16.24 Dght 6.081 Lbp 75.01 Br md 16.20 Dpth 7.75 Welded, 1 dk	**(B34Q2QB) Buoy Tender** Compartments: 1 Ho, ER 1 Ha: (5.4 x 4.6)ER Cranes: 1x28t Ice Capable	**3 diesel electric oil engines** driving 3 gen. each 2100kW 600V a.c Connecting to 2 elec. motors driving 2 FP propellers Total Power: 7,833kW (10,650hp) 15.3kn Alco 16V251F 3 x Vee 4 Stroke 16 Cy. 229 x 267 each-2611kW (3550bhp) Bombardier Inc-Canada AuxGen: 1 x 500kW 600V 60Hz a.c Thrusters: 1 Thwart. FP thruster (f) Fuel: 726.5 (r.f.)
8320482 *CGUM* -	**SIR WILLIAM ALEXANDER** **Government of Canada (Canadian Coast Guard)** - SatCom: Inmarsat A 1560116 *Ottawa, ON* *Canada* MMSI: 316053000 Official number: 807685	*3,728* 1,503 1,660	Class: (LR) ✠ Classed LR until 6/88	**1987**-03 **Marine Industries Ltee (MIL) — Sorel QC** Yd No: 451 Loa 83.01 Br ex 16.26 Dght 6.001 Lbp 75.67 Br md 16.21 Dpth 7.75 Welded, 1 dk	**(B34Q2QB) Buoy Tender** Ice Capable	**3 diesel electric oil engines** driving 3 gen. each 2100kW 600V a.c Connecting to 2 elec. motors driving 2 FP propellers Total Power: 6,600kW (8,973hp) 15.5kn Alco 16V251E 3 x Vee 4 Stroke 16 Cy. 229 x 267 each-2200kW (2991bhp) Bombardier Inc-Canada AuxGen: 1 x 500kW 600V 60Hz a.c Thrusters: 1 Thwart. FP thruster (f) Fuel: 783.7 (d.f.)
1003968 *SY2675* -	**SIR WINSTON CHURCHILL** **Epsilon Yachting Services Maritime Ltd** - *Piraeus* *Greece* MMSI: 239970000 Official number: 11027	**205** 61 -	Class: (LR) ✠ Classed LR until 19/6/02	**1966**-03 **R. Dunston (Hessle) Ltd. — Hessle** Yd No: H802 Loa 41.17 Br ex 7.62 Dght 4.810 Lbp 32.02 Br md - Dpth 4.94 Welded, 1 dk	**(X11A2YS) Yacht (Sailing)**	**2 oil engines** driving 2 FP propellers Total Power: 198kW (270hp) Perkins 2 x 4 Stroke 6 Cy. each-99kW (135bhp) Perkins Engines Ltd.-Peterborough

8848317 *P2V5254* -	**SIR ZIBANG** *ex* Armada Cinta *-2008* **Kambang Holding Ltd** - *Papua New Guinea*	*387* 124 -	Class: (BV) (AB)	**1989-01 Far East Shipyard Co Sdn Bhd — Sibu** Yd No: 389 Loa 38.72 Br ex 9.76 Dght 2.000 Lbp - Br md - Dpth 2.90 Welded, 1 dk	**(A35D2RL) Landing Craft** Bow door/ramp	**2 oil engines** reverse reduction geared to sc. shafts driving 2 FP propellers Total Power: 626kW (852hp) 10.0kn Cummins KT-19-M 2 x 4 Stroke 6 Cy. 159 x 159 each-313kW (426bhp) Cummins Engine Co Inc-USA AuxGen: 2 x 64kW 230/415V 50Hz a.c
9408803 *V7QT5* -	**SIRA** *ex* Pramoni *-2012* **Seminyak AS** PT Berlian Laju Tanker Tbk (BLT) *Majuro* *Marshall Islands* MMSI: 538003434 Official number: 3434	**12,105** 6,438 20,832 T/cm 30.3	Class: NK	**2008-05 Shin Kurushima Dockyard Co. Ltd. — Akitsu** Yd No: 5461 Loa 147.83 (BB) Br ex 24.23 Dght 9.772 Lbp 141.00 Br md 24.20 Dpth 12.85 Welded, 1 dk	**(A12B2TR) Chemical/Products Tanker** Double Hull (13F) Liq: 18,868; Liq (Oil): 21,800 Cargo Heating Coils Compartments: 18 Wing Ta, 2 Wing Slop Ta, ER 18 Cargo Pump (s): 14x330m³/hr, 4x200m³/hr Manifold: Bow/CM: 76.6m	**1 oil engine** driving 1 FP propeller Total Power: 6,150kW (8,362hp) 15.1kn MAN-B&W 6S42MC 1 x 2 Stroke 6 Cy. 420 x 1764 6150kW (8362bhp) Makita Corp-Japan AuxGen: 3 x 450kW a.c Thrusters: 1 Tunnel thruster (f) Fuel: 38.0 (d.f.) 1101.0 (r.f.)
8601850 *EPBQ* 3GI-4-2141	**SIRAF** *ex* Costa de Normandia *-1990* **Industrial Fishing Co** Neptune Sayd Fishing Co *Bushehr* *Iran* MMSI: 422607000 Official number: 644	**860** 440 1,311	Class: AS (BV)	**1987-08 Astilleros Gondan SA — Castropol** Yd No: 273 Loa 68.00 (BB) Br ex - Dght 5.070 Lbp 60.00 Br md 11.81 Dpth 7.00 Welded, 2 dks	**(B11A2FS) Stern Trawler** Ins: 1,613	**1 oil engine** with clutches, flexible couplings & sr geared to sc. shaft driving 1 CP propeller Total Power: 1,466kW (1,993hp) 13.4kn MaK 6M453AK 1 x 4 Stroke 6 Cy. 320 x 420 1466kW (1993bhp) Krupp MaK Maschinenbau GmbH-Kiel AuxGen: 3 x 232kW a.c Fuel: 517.5 (r.f.)
8948832 *MXXB9*	**SIRAHMY** *ex* Lady In Blue *-2004* *ex* Charlie's Angels III *-2004* *ex* Idyll *-1994* *ex* Giamin II *-1990* **Fruitful Ltd** Floating Life International SA *London* *United Kingdom* MMSI: 232716000 Official number: 708982	**352** 105 107	Class: BV	**1981 Cantiere Navale M & B Benetti — Viareggio** Yd No: 136 Loa 45.32 Br ex - Dght 2.830 Lbp 35.42 Br md 7.27 Dpth 4.00 Welded, 1 dk	**(X11A2YP) Yacht**	**2 oil engines** reduction geared to sc. shafts driving 2 FP propellers Total Power: 1,104kW (1,500hp) 13.0kn Caterpillar D348TA 2 x Vee 4 Stroke 12 Cy. 137 x 165 each-552kW (750bhp) Caterpillar Tractor Co-USA Fuel: 89.0 (d.f.)
8813790 *CNRB* -	**SIRAJ** - **Peche Hauturiere Industrielle de l'atlantique Sud PHIASUD SA** - SatCom: Inmarsat C 424240510 *Agadir* *Morocco*	*433* 130 268	Class: BV	**1991-01 Hijos de J. Barreras S.A. — Vigo** Yd No: 1538 Loa 36.50 (BB) Br ex 8.43 Dght 4.310 Lbp 31.50 Br md 8.30 Dpth 6.18 Welded	**(B11A2FS) Stern Trawler** Ins: 234	**1 oil engine** with flexible couplings & dr geared to sc. shaft driving 1 FP propeller Total Power: 603kW (820hp) 10.8kn Deutz SBA8M528 1 x 4 Stroke 8 Cy. 220 x 280 603kW (820bhp) Hijos de J Barreras SA-Spain
7517545 *5IM295* -	**SIRAJ** *ex* Petsamo *-2006* *ex* DFL Helsinki *-1992* *ex* Cimbria *-1989* *ex* Aros Freighter *-1985* *ex* Frat I *-1983* *ex* Voline *-1982* **Siraj Maritime Ltd SA** United Marine Co Srl *Zanzibar* *Tanzania (Zanzibar)* MMSI: 677019500 Official number: 300052	**2,356** 1,084 2,650	Class: IS (GL)	**1976-10 Husumer Schiffswerft — Husum** Yd No: 1441 Loa 84.28 Br ex 13.52 Dght 4.961 Lbp 76.03 Br md 13.50 Dpth 5.11 Welded, 2 dks	**(A31A2GX) General Cargo Ship** Grain: 5,034; Bale: 4,601 TEU 172 C. 172/20' incl. 15 ref C. Compartments: 1 Ho, ER 1 Ha: (49.8 x 10.2)ER Ice Capable	**1 oil engine** reduction geared to sc. shaft driving 1 CP propeller Total Power: 2,207kW (3,001hp) 14.0kn MaK 8M453AK 1 x 4 Stroke 8 Cy. 320 x 420 2207kW (3001bhp) MaK Maschinenbau GmbH-Kiel Thrusters: 1 Thwart. FP thruster (f)
1003932 *ZHBA4*	**SIRAN** - **Horwath Alfa GmbH** Catalano Shipping Services SAM SatCom: Inmarsat A 1756337 *George Town* *Cayman Islands (British)* MMSI: 319512000 Official number: 715909	**1,098** 329 -	Class: LR ✠ **100A1** SS 02/2012 Yacht ✠ **LMC** **UMS**	**1992-02 de Vries Scheepsbouw B.V. — Aalsmeer** Yd No: 643 Lengthened-2006 Loa 67.01 Br ex 10.30 Dght 4.130 Lbp 58.31 Br md - Dpth 5.50 Welded, 1 dk	**(X11A2YP) Yacht**	**2 oil engines** driving 2 FP propellers Total Power: 2,342kW (3,184hp) Caterpillar 3516TA 2 x Vee 4 Stroke 16 Cy. 170 x 190 each-1171kW (1592bhp) Caterpillar Inc-USA AuxGen: 3 x 189kW
9043275 - -	**SIRAN** *ex* Chefalu 20 *-2007* *ex* Aker Tulcea 7937 *-2007* **Neven Skoljarev Ribarski Obrt** - *Zadar* *Croatia*	*152* - 31		**2005 SC Aker Tulcea SA — Tulcea** Yd No: 7937 Loa - Br ex - Dght - Lbp - Br md - Dpth - Welded	**(B11B2FV) Fishing Vessel**	**1 oil engine** driving 1 FP propeller Total Power: 450kW (612hp) S.K.L. 6VD18/15AL-2 1 x 4 Stroke 6 Cy. 150 x 180 450kW (612bhp) SKL Motoren u. Systemtechnik AG-Magdeburg
9403841 *3EMJ4* -	**SIRAYA WISDOM** - **Siraya Wisdom SA** Wisdom Marine Lines SA *Panama* *Panama* MMSI: 371693000 Official number: 3321607A	**12,655** 7,392 20,000	Class: BV (CR)	**2007-09 Murakami Hide Zosen K.K. — Imabari** Yd No: 557 Loa 153.09 (BB) Br ex - Dght 9.350 Lbp 145.19 Br md 23.00 Dpth 12.50 Welded, 1 dk	**(A21A2BC) Bulk Carrier** Grain: 25,893 Compartments: 4 Ho, ER 4 Ha: ER Cranes: 3	**1 oil engine** driving 1 FP propeller Total Power: 5,180kW (7,043hp) 14.0kn MAN-B&W 7S35MC 1 x 2 Stroke 7 Cy. 350 x 1400 5180kW (7043bhp) The Hanshin Diesel Works Ltd-Japan AuxGen: 3 x 400kW 60Hz a.c
8872057 - -	**SIRE** *ex* Beech *-2007* *ex* RPA 30 *-2005* *ex* Havendienst 17 *-2002* **Labrador Shipping Ltd** - *Terneuzen* *Netherlands*	**168** 50 -	Class: (BV)	**1966 N.V. Scheepswerf Gebr. van der Werf — Deest** Yd No: 327 Loa 33.26 Br ex - Dght 2.630 Lbp 30.27 Br md 6.80 Dpth 3.50 Welded, 1 dk	**(B32A2ST) Tug**	**2 oil engines** geared to sc. shaft driving 1 FP propeller Bolnes 8DNL190/600 2 x 2 Stroke 8 Cy. 190 x 350 NV Machinefabriek 'Bolnes' v/h JHvan Cappellen-Netherlands
8214906 *J8B4325* -	**SIREEN B** *ex* Zenobia *-2010* *ex* Eco Champion *-2005* *ex* Mar Grande *-1997* *ex* Planica *-1995* *ex* Pacific Auk *-1985* **Sireen B Shipping Co SA** Bayazid Shipping Co *Kingstown* *St Vincent & The Grenadines* MMSI: 377045000 Official number: 10798	**12,859** 7,880 21,339	Class: NK (CS)	**1984-02 Watanabe Zosen KK — Imabari EH** Yd No: 221 Loa 152.65 (BB) Br ex - Dght 9.602 Lbp 142.02 Br md 24.01 Dpth 13.21 Welded, 1 dk	**(A21A2BC) Bulk Carrier** Grain: 28,349; Bale: 27,021 Compartments: 4 Ho, ER 4 Ha: (17.6 x 12.7)3 (20.0 x 12.7)ER Cranes: 3x25t; Derricks: 1x25t	**1 oil engine** driving 1 FP propeller Total Power: 5,958kW (8,100hp) 13.5kn B&W 6L55GF 1 x 2 Stroke 6 Cy. 550 x 1380 5958kW (8100bhp) Hitachi Zosen Corp-Japan AuxGen: 3 x 360kW Fuel: 1180.0 (r.f.)
4906214 *H02796* -	**SIREN** *ex* West Wind *-2002* *ex* Cromarty *-1994* **Three Graces Maritime SA** - *Panama* *Panama* Official number: 30365PEXT	*111* 36 -		**1970 J. Lewis & Sons Ltd. — Aberdeen** Yd No: 362 Loa 24.38 Br ex 6.40 Dght - Lbp 22.86 Br md - Dpth 1.98 Welded, 1 dk	**(B34R2QY) Supply Tender**	**1 oil engine** reduction geared to sc. shaft driving 1 FP propeller Total Power: 243kW (330hp) 10.5kn Blackstone ERS4M 1 x 4 Stroke 4 Cy. 222 x 292 243kW (330bhp) Lister Blackstone Marine Ltd.-Dursley
5329918 - -	**SIREN** - - -	**1,475** 443 479	Class: (LR) (BR) ✠ Classed LR until 12/5/04	**1960-02 J. Samuel White & Co. Ltd. — Cowes** Yd No: 2003 Loa 67.36 Br ex 11.56 Dght 3.920 Lbp 62.61 Br md 11.43 Dpth 7.16 Riveted\Welded, 2 dks, 3rd dk except in mchy. space	**(B34Q2QX) Lighthouse Tender** Compartments: 1 Ho, ER 1 Ha: (3.4 x 3.4) Derricks: 1x15t	**4 diesel electric oil engines** driving 4 gen. each 292kW 230V d.c Connecting to 2 elec. motors each (533kW) driving 2 FP propellers Total Power: 1,584kW (2,152hp) 13.5kn English Electric 6RKC 4 x 4 Stroke 6 Cy. 254 x 305 each-396kW (538bhp) English Electric Co. Ltd.-Stafford
9417438 *ZCTF6*	**SIREN** - **Elboi International Ltd** Camper & Nicholsons France SARL *George Town* *Cayman Islands (British)* MMSI: 319060000 Official number: 740043	**1,585** 414 253	Class: GL	**2006-05 Nobiskrug GmbH — Rendsburg** Yd No: 778 Loa 73.15 Br ex 12.78 Dght 3.650 Lbp 58.70 Br md 12.00 Dpth 4.00 Welded, 1 dk	**(X11A2YP) Yacht**	**2 oil engines** reduction geared to sc. shafts driving 2 Propellers Total Power: 3,520kW (4,786hp) M.T.U. 16V4000M60 2 x Vee 4 Stroke 16 Cy. 165 x 190 each-1760kW (2393bhp) MTU Friedrichshafen GmbH-Friedrichshafen
9491824 *CQMD* -	**SIRENA** - **Societe de Manutention et de Materiaux Industriels Sarl (SMMI)** - *Madeira* *Portugal (MAR)* MMSI: 255803280 Official number: 07500E	**797** 239 500	Class: BV	**2009-11 P.T. Jasa Marina Indah — Semarang** Yd No: 055 Loa 55.00 Br ex - Dght 2.500 Lbp 47.25 Br md 13.50 Dpth 4.20 Welded, 1 dk	**(A35D2RL) Landing Craft** Grain: 547 Compartments: 1 Ho, ER 1 Ha: ER	**2 oil engines** greared to sc. shafts driving 2 Propellers Total Power: 1,060kW (1,442hp) Caterpillar 3412C 2 x Vee 4 Stroke 12 Cy. 137 x 152 each-530kW (721bhp) Caterpillar Inc-USA AuxGen: 2 x 84kW 380V 50Hz a.c Fuel: 111.0

IMO / Call sign / Flag	Name / Owner	GT / NT / DWT	Class	Built / Dimensions	Type	Machinery
8861254 *YQZN* -	**SIRENA** *ex* NR 8004 *-1999* **Daewoo Mangalia Heavy Industries SA** - *Mangalia* *Romania* Official number: 116	**333** - -	Class: (RN)	**1988-10 Santierul Naval Drobeta-Turnu Severin S.A. — Drobeta-Turnu S.** Loa 35.69 Br ex - Dght 3.350 Lbp 32.89 Br md 9.71 Dpth 4.70 Welded, 1 dk	**(B32A2ST) Tug** Ice Capable	**2 oil engines** reduction geared to sc. shafts driving 2 FP propellers Total Power: 1,766kW (2,402hp) 12.5kn MAN 6LDSR-28K 2 x 4 Stroke 6 Cy. 280 x 360 each-883kW (1201bhp) (made 1987) U.C.M. Resita S.A.-Resita AuxGen: 3 x 56kW 400V 50Hz a.c
8969173 - -	**SIRENA 2** *ex* 5774 *-1999* - -	**120** 45	Class: (RN)	**1979-02 Santierul Naval Oltenita S.A. — Oltenita** Loa 23.30 Br ex - Dght 2.350 Lbp 20.59 Br md 6.95 Dpth 3.30 Welded, 1 dk	**(B33B2DU) Hopper/Dredger (unspecified)**	**2 oil engines** geared to sc. shafts driving 2 FP propellers Total Power: 410kW (558hp) Maybach MB836BB 2 x 4 Stroke 8 Cy. 175 x 205 each-205kW (279bhp) Uzina 23 August Bucuresti-Bucuresti AuxGen: 2 x 35kW 400V 50Hz a.c
8969185 - -	**SIRENA 3** *ex* 5775 *-1999* - -	**111** 45	Class: (RN)	**1979-04 Santierul Naval Drobeta-Turnu Severin S.A. — Drobeta-Turnu S.** Loa 23.30 Br ex - Dght 2.350 Lbp 20.61 Br md 6.96 Dpth 3.30 Welded, 1 dk	**(B32A2ST) Tug**	**2 oil engines** reduction geared to sc. shafts driving 2 FP propellers Total Power: 410kW (558hp) Maybach MB836BB 2 x 4 Stroke 8 Cy. 175 x 205 each-205kW (279bhp) Uzina 23 August Bucuresti-Bucuresti AuxGen: 2 x 35kW 400V 50Hz a.c
8969197 - -	**SIRENA 4** - -	**111** 45 -	Class: (RN)	**1979-06 Santierul Naval Drobeta-Turnu Severin S.A. — Drobeta-Turnu S.** Loa 23.29 Br ex - Dght 2.350 Lbp 20.61 Br md 6.96 Dpth 3.30 Welded, 1 dk	**(B32A2ST) Tug**	**2 oil engines** reduction geared to sc. shafts driving 2 FP propellers Total Power: 410kW (558hp) Maybach MB836BB 2 x 4 Stroke 8 Cy. 175 x 205 each-205kW (279bhp) Uzina 23 August Bucuresti-Bucuresti AuxGen: 2 x 35kW 400V 50Hz a.c
8969202 - -	**SIRENA 5** - -	**120** 45 -	Class: (RN)	**1980-10 Santierul Naval Drobeta-Turnu Severin S.A. — Drobeta-Turnu S.** Loa 23.31 Br ex - Dght 2.350 Lbp 20.61 Br md 6.96 Dpth 3.30 Welded, 1 dk	**(B32A2ST) Tug**	**2 oil engines** reduction geared to sc. shafts driving 2 FP propellers Total Power: 410kW (558hp) Maybach MB836BB 2 x 4 Stroke 8 Cy. 175 x 205 each-205kW (279bhp) Uzina 23 August Bucuresti-Bucuresti AuxGen: 2 x 35kW 400V 50Hz a.c
8969214 - -	**SIRENA 6** **Daewoo Mangalia Heavy Industries SA** - *Mangalia* *Romania* Official number: 3	**112** 45 -	Class: (RN)	**1980-11 Santierul Naval Drobeta-Turnu Severin S.A. — Drobeta-Turnu S.** Loa 23.31 Br ex - Dght 2.350 Lbp 20.61 Br md 6.96 Dpth 3.30 Welded, 1 dk	**(B32A2ST) Tug**	**2 oil engines** geared to sc. shafts driving 2 Propellers Total Power: 410kW (558hp) Maybach MB836BB 2 x 4 Stroke 8 Cy. 175 x 205 each-205kW (279bhp) Uzina 23 August Bucuresti-Bucuresti AuxGen: 2 x 35kW 400V 50Hz a.c
8969226 *YQZI* -	**SIRENA 7** **SC Santierul Naval Orsova SA** - *Constanta* *Romania* MMSI: 264900123 Official number: 645	**111** 45 -	Class: (RN)	**1980-12 Santierul Naval Drobeta-Turnu Severin S.A. — Drobeta-Turnu S.** Loa 23.31 Br ex - Dght 2.350 Lbp 20.61 Br md 6.96 Dpth 3.30 Welded, 1 dk	**(B32A2ST) Tug**	**2 oil engines** reduction geared to sc. shafts driving 2 Propellers Total Power: 410kW (558hp) Maybach MB836BB 2 x 4 Stroke 8 Cy. 175 x 205 each-205kW (279bhp) Uzina 23 August Bucuresti-Bucuresti AuxGen: 2 x 35kW 400V 50Hz a.c
8969238 - -	**SIRENA 8** - -	**111** 45 -	Class: (RN)	**1980-12 Santierul Naval Drobeta-Turnu Severin S.A. — Drobeta-Turnu S.** Loa 23.31 Br ex - Dght 2.350 Lbp 20.61 Br md 6.96 Dpth 3.30 Welded, 1 dk	**(B32A2ST) Tug**	**2 oil engines** reduction geared to sc. shafts driving 2 Propellers Total Power: 410kW (558hp) Maybach MB836BB 2 x 4 Stroke 8 Cy. 175 x 205 each-205kW (279bhp) Uzina 23 August Bucuresti-Bucuresti AuxGen: 2 x 35kW 400V 50Hz a.c
8969240 *YQLT* -	**SIRENA 9** **SC Santierul Naval Orsova SA** - *Constanta* *Romania* MMSI: 264900124 Official number: 650	**111** 45 -	Class: (RN)	**1981-01 Santierul Naval Drobeta-Turnu Severin S.A. — Drobeta-Turnu S.** Loa 23.31 Br ex - Dght 2.350 Lbp 20.61 Br md 6.96 Dpth 3.30 Welded, 1 dk	**(B32A2ST) Tug**	**2 oil engines** reduction geared to sc. shafts driving 2 Propellers Total Power: 410kW (558hp) Maybach MB836BB 2 x 4 Stroke 8 Cy. 175 x 205 each-205kW (279bhp) Uzina 23 August Bucuresti-Bucuresti AuxGen: 2 x 35kW 400V 50Hz a.c
7024093 - -	**SIRENA BLUE** *ex* Julia IV *-2003* *ex* Kabir *-1999* *ex* Ro-Lo Carrier *-1998* *ex* Ionian Korti *-1998* *ex* Apollonia Banner *-1992* *ex* Platak *-1990* *ex* Bard *-1975* **Sirena Navigation Co Inc** Maritima del Golfo SL	**3,113** 1,274 2,828	Class: IB (NV) (JR)	**1970-06 AS Trondhjems Mekaniske Verksted — Trondheim** Yd No: 642 Loa 87.00 (BB) Br ex 15.04 Dght 6.152 Lbp 76.71 Br md 14.99 Dpth 10.85 Welded, 3 dks	**(A35A2RR) Ro-Ro Cargo Ship** Stern door/ramp Side door (s) Bale: 6,351 Compartments: 1 Ho, ER 4 Ha: 2 (18.4 x 5.3)2 (25.1 x 5.3)ER Cranes: 1x5t; Derricks: 1x20t,1x6.5t; Winches: 2 Ice Capable	**1 oil engine** geared to sc. shaft driving 1 CP propeller Total Power: 3,236kW (4,400hp) 14.8kn Werkspoor 8TM410 1 x 4 Stroke 8 Cy. 410 x 470 3236kW (4400bhp) Stork Werkspoor Diesel BV-Netherlands AuxGen: 3 x 130kW 440V 60Hz a.c Thrusters: 1 Thwart. FP thruster (f) Fuel: 254.0 (r.f.) 19.5pd
8880212 *ECHQ* -	**SIRENA REAL** *ex* Geola *-2008* *ex* Nagu *-2008* **Geola Maritime Ltd** - *Algeciras* *Spain* MMSI: 224321540 Official number: 5-2/2007	**304** 92 150		**1955 A Ahlstrom Oy — Varkaus** Yd No: 727 Converted From: Research Vessel-2008 Lengthened-1966 Loa 40.02 Br ex - Dght - Lbp 38.28 Br md 8.02 Dpth 2.80 Welded, 1 dk	**(B22A20V) Diving Support Vessel**	**2 oil engines** driving 2 FP propellers Total Power: 482kW (656hp) 7.0kn
9212163 *OULA2* -	**SIRENA SEAWAYS** *ex* Dana Sirena *-2013* *launched as* Golfo dei Delfini *-2002* **DFDS A/S** - *Esbjerg* *Denmark (DIS)* MMSI: 220174000 Official number: A509	**22,382** 8,064 5,625	Class: AB (RI)	**2003-06 Stocznia Szczecinska Nowa Sp z oo — Szczecin** Yd No: B591/I/2 Loa 199.40 (BB) Br ex 25.00 Dght 6.080 Lbp 176.80 Br md 23.40 Dpth 14.20 Welded	**(A36A2PR) Passenger/Ro-Ro Ship (Vehicles)** Passengers: cabins: 188; berths: 623 Lane-Len: 1800 Lane-Wid: 3.00 Trailers: 155	**2 oil engines** geared to sc. shafts driving 2 CP propellers Total Power: 18,900kW (25,696hp) 22.0kn Wartsila 9L46C 2 x 4 Stroke 9 Cy. 460 x 580 each-9450kW (12848bhp) Wartsila Finland Oy-Finland AuxGen: 3 x 1440kW a.c Thrusters: 2 Thwart. FP thruster (f) Fuel: 68.0 (d.f.) 1127.0 (r.f.)
8033974 *WDB2428* -	**SIRENE** *ex* Dr. K *-2005* *ex* Silver Bay *-1998* *ex* Quest-Heron *-1990* *ex* Clearwater-Heron *-1989* *ex* Donna Denise *-1989* **K H Colburn Inc** - *Dutch Harbor, AK* *United States of America* MMSI: 369221000 Official number: 615699	*185* 129 -		**1979 Marine Construction, Inc. — Slidell, La** Yd No: 92 L reg 28.05 Br ex 8.87 Dght - Lbp - Br md - Dpth 3.76 Welded, 1 dk	**(B11B2FV) Fishing Vessel**	**1 oil engine** driving 1 FP propeller Total Power: 662kW (900hp)
7210642 - -	**SIRENIAN** *ex* Cynthia Walker *-1989* *ex* Elsie Janis *-1989* **Orcaforce Foundation** -	*138* 34 -		**1955 F.B. Walker & Sons, Inc. — Pascagoula, Ms** Yd No: 155 Loa - Br ex 6.71 Dght - Lbp 27.59 Br md 6.66 Dpth 2.75 Welded, 1 dk	**(B31A2SR) Research Survey Vessel** Compartments: 1 Ho, ER 1 Ha: (1.2 x 2.4)ER	**2 oil engines** driving 2 FP propellers Total Power: 442kW (600hp) 10.0kn General Motors 2 x 2 Stroke each-221kW (300bhp) General Motors Corp-USA
9013074 *OW2363* -	**SIRI** **P/F J & K Petersen** - *Torshavn* *Faeroe Islands (Danish)*	**264** 79 435	Class: BV	**1989-05 N.E. Larsen AS, Ekstrand Verksted — Stathelle** Yd No: 78 Loa 48.60 Br ex 7.80 Dght 2.220 Lbp 46.90 Br md 7.50 Dpth 2.90 Welded, 1 dk	**(B34A2SH) Hopper, Motor** Grain: 300 Compartments: 1 Ho	**1 oil engine** with clutches, flexible couplings & sr geared to sc. shaft driving 1 FP propeller Total Power: 221kW (300hp) Volvo Penta TMD122A 1 x 4 Stroke 6 Cy. 130 x 150 221kW (300bhp) AB Volvo Penta-Sweden
9491719 *HSB4762* -	**SIRI BHUM** **Regional Container Lines Public Co Ltd** RCL Shipmanagement Pte Ltd *Bangkok* *Thailand* MMSI: 567477000	**9,757** - 13,017	Class: GL	**2013-02 Dae Sun Shipbuilding & Engineering Co Ltd — Busan** Yd No: 521 Loa 143.90 (BB) Br ex - Dght 8.200 Lbp 134.71 Br md 22.60 Dpth 11.20 Welded, 1 dk	**(A33A2CC) Container Ship (Fully Cellular)** TEU 1006 incl 180 ref	**1 oil engine** driving 1 FP propeller Total Power: 7,860kW (10,686hp) 18.0kn MAN-B&W 6S46MC-C 1 x 2 Stroke 6 Cy. 460 x 1932 7860kW (10686bhp) STX Engine Co Ltd-South Korea Thrusters: 1 Tunnel thruster (f)

8817239 *HSB2980* -	**SIRI KAMOL** *ex* Shoyu Maru No. 5 *-2003* *ex* Taiko Maru *-1999* **United Tankers Co Ltd** Nathalin Management Co Ltd *Bangkok* *Thailand* MMSI: 567040200 Official number: 460000690	*1,379* 813 2,499	Class: (NK)	**1988-12 Nakatani Shipyard Co. Ltd. — Etajima** Yd No: 525 Loa 84.00 Br ex - Dght 5.000 Lbp 78.00 Br md 12.40 Dpth 5.80 Welded, 1 dk	**(A13B2TP) Products Tanker** Liq: 2,955; Liq (Oil): 2,955	**1 oil engine** driving 1 FP propeller Total Power: 2,060kW (2,801hp) Hanshin 6EL38 1 x 4 Stroke 6 Cy. 380 x 760 2060kW (2801bhp) The Hanshin Diesel Works Ltd-Japan AuxGen: 3 x 105kW a.c
9247168 *MFCZ7* -	**SIRI KNUTSEN** **Knutsen Shuttle Tankers 3 AS** Knutsen OAS Shipping AS SatCom: Inmarsat M 600406644 *Aberdeen* *United Kingdom* MMSI: 235007690 Official number: 908880	**24,916** 10,125 35,309 T/cm 46.6	Class: NV (GL)	**2004-07 Naval Gijon S.A. (NAGISA) — Gijon** Yd No: 604 Converted From: Shuttle Tanker-2013 Converted From: Crude Oil Tanker-2004 Loa 186.93 (BB) Br ex - Dght 11.515 Lbp 174.00 Br md 27.40 Dpth 16.90 Welded, 1 dk	**(B22F2OW) Well Stimulation Vessel** Double Hull (13F) Liq: 39,787; Liq (Oil): 39,787 Compartments: 12 Wing Ta, ER, 2 Wing Slop Ta 12 Cargo Pump (s): 12x600m³/hr Manifold: Bow/CM: 93m	**1 oil engine** driving 1 CP propeller Total Power: 8,562kW (11,641hp) 15.0kn B&W 6S50MC 1 x 2 Stroke 6 Cy. 500 x 1910 8562kW (11641bhp) Manises Diesel Engine Co. S.A.-Valencia Thrusters: 1 Tunnel thruster (f); 1 Tunnel thruster (a); 1 Directional thruster (f) Fuel: 326.8 (d.f.) 1514.0 (r.f.)
8618578 *HSB2766* -	**SIRI PALA** *ex* Nippo Maru No. 87 *-2001* **United Tankers Co Ltd** Nathalin Management Co Ltd *Bangkok* *Thailand* MMSI: 567031500 Official number: 441000534	*1,025* 587 1,932	Class: (NK)	**1987-05 Kurinoura Dockyard Co Ltd — Yawatahama EH** Yd No: 236 Loa 74.55 (BB) Br ex 11.23 Dght 4.766 Lbp 70.01 Br md 11.21 Dpth 5.31 Welded, 1 dk	**(A13B2TP) Products Tanker** Double Bottom Entire Compartment Length Liq: 2,150; Liq (Oil): 2,150 Compartments: 10 Ta, ER	**1 oil engine** with clutches, flexible couplings & reverse reduction geared to sc. shaft driving 1 FP propeller Total Power: 1,250kW (1,700hp) Hanshin 6EL30G 1 x 4 Stroke 6 Cy. 300 x 600 1250kW (1700bhp) The Hanshin Diesel Works Ltd-Japan
8508814 *HSB2985* -	**SIRI THANA** *ex* Woo Joo *-2003* *ex* Eishin Maru No. 3 *-2000* **NTL Marine Co Ltd** Nathalin Co Ltd SatCom: Inmarsat C 456700518 *Bangkok* *Thailand* MMSI: 567228000 Official number: 460000991	*3,104* 1,541 4,999	Class: (BV) (KR) (NK)	**1985-09 K.K. Taihei Kogyo — Akitsu** Yd No: 1810 Loa 100.92 (BB) Br ex - Dght 6.695 Lbp 94.01 Br md 15.02 Dpth 8.01 Welded, 1 dk	**(A13B2TP) Products Tanker** Single Hull Liq: 5,549; Liq (Oil): 5,549	**1 oil engine** with clutches & dr geared to sc. shaft driving 1 CP propeller Total Power: 2,427kW (3,300hp) 13.3kn Akasaka A41 1 x 4 Stroke 6 Cy. 410 x 800 2427kW (3300bhp) Akasaka Tekkosho KK (Akasaka DieselLtd)-Japan AuxGen: 4 x 185kW a.c
7818042 *HQPB4* -	**SIRICHAI CHALLENGER** *ex* Kokai Maru *-1993* **Sirichai Fisheries Co Ltd (Sirichai Fisheries Group)** *San Lorenzo* *Honduras* Official number: L-0324968	*474* 292 1,048		**1979-06 Iwagi Zosen Co Ltd — Kamijima EH** Yd No: 10 Loa 65.03 Br ex 11.51 Dght 3.601 Lbp 57.99 Br md 11.00 Dpth 6.00 Welded, 1 dk	**(A31A2GX) General Cargo Ship**	**1 oil engine** driving 1 FP propeller Total Power: 1,324kW (1,800hp) Hanshin 6MUH28 1 x 4 Stroke 6 Cy. 280 x 340 1324kW (1800bhp) The Hanshin Diesel Works Ltd-Japan
7313212 - -	**SIRICHAI DISCOVERY** *ex* Kaiho Maru No. 3 *-1993* *ex* Koyo Maru No. 31 *-1985* - -	*391* 146 686		**1973 Miho Zosensho K.K. — Shimizu** Yd No: 886 Loa 50.40 Br ex 8.22 Dght 3.380 Lbp 44.00 Br md 8.20 Dpth 3.60 Welded, 1 dk	**(B11A2FT) Trawler**	**1 oil engine** driving 1 FP propeller Total Power: 883kW (1,201hp) Niigata 6L25BX 1 x 4 Stroke 6 Cy. 250 x 320 883kW (1201bhp) Niigata Engineering Co Ltd-Japan
7615139 *HQPB2* -	**SIRICHAI FORTUNA** *ex* Kairyu Maru *-1993* **Sirichai Fisheries Co Ltd (Sirichai Fisheries Group)** - *San Lorenzo* *Honduras* Official number: L-1925019	*149* 38 -		**1976-11 Nagasaki Zosen K.K. — Nagasaki** Yd No: 578 Loa 40.11 Br ex 6.23 Dght 2.598 Lbp 35.01 Br md 6.20 Dpth 3.20 Welded, 1 dk	**(B12D2FP) Fishery Patrol Vessel**	**1 oil engine** driving 1 FP propeller Total Power: 1,177kW (1,600hp) Niigata 6L28BX 1 x 4 Stroke 6 Cy. 280 x 320 1177kW (1600bhp) Niigata Engineering Co Ltd-Japan
7220362 *HQGQ2* -	**SIRICHAI PATTANA** *ex* Sirichai Reefer *-1998* *ex* Choyo Maru No. 25 *-1990* *ex* Fukuyoshi Maru No. 35 *-1985* **Sirichai Marine Fisheries S de RL** Sirichai Fisheries Co Ltd (Sirichai Fisheries Group) *San Lorenzo* *Honduras* Official number: L-0323443	**566** 169 521		**1972 KK Kanasashi Zosen — Shizuoka SZ** Yd No: 1066 Loa 55.30 Br ex 8.64 Dght 3.404 Lbp 49.00 Br md 8.62 Dpth 3.89 Welded, 1 dk	**(B11B2FV) Fishing Vessel**	**1 oil engine** driving 1 FP propeller Total Power: 956kW (1,300hp) Niigata 6M31X 1 x 4 Stroke 6 Cy. 310 x 460 956kW (1300bhp) Niigata Engineering Co Ltd-Japan
7123033 - -	**SIRICHAI PATTANA 2** *ex* Sirichai Reefer 2 *-2003* *ex* Shoshin Maru No. 51 *-1991* *ex* Zenko Maru No. 51 *-1991* - -	**628** 188 -		**1971 KK Kanasashi Zosen — Shizuoka SZ** Yd No: 1032 Converted From: Fishing Vessel Loa 55.94 Br ex 8.84 Dght 3.499 Lbp 49.51 Br md 8.82 Dpth 4.04 Welded, 1 dk	**(B12B2FC) Fish Carrier**	**1 oil engine** driving 1 FP propeller Total Power: 1,214kW (1,651hp) Akasaka 6DH36SS 1 x 4 Stroke 6 Cy. 360 x 540 1214kW (1651bhp) Akasaka Tekkosho KK (Akasaka DieselLtd)-Japan
8211837 *HSB2797* -	**SIRICHAI REEFER** *ex* Reefer Cliff *-2002* *ex* Klipper 3 *-1989* **Sirichai Shipping Lines Co Ltd** - *Bangkok* *Thailand* MMSI: 567196000 Official number: 447400203	**2,732** 1,587 3,357	Class: LR ✠ **100A1** SS 11/2007 Ice Class 3 ✠ **LMC** **UMS +Lloyd's RMC** Eq.Ltr: R; Cable: 440.0/40.0 U2	**1983-02 Scheepswerf en Mfbk. Ysselwerf B.V. — Capelle a/d IJssel** Yd No: 207 Loa 80.75 (BB) Br ex 15.09 Dght 6.101 Lbp 73.77 Br md 15.00 Dpth 9.00 Welded, 2 dks	**(A34A2GR) Refrigerated Cargo Ship** Ins: 4,914 Compartments: 3 Ho, ER, 3 Tw Dk 3 Ha: 3 (9.2 x 9.3)ER Cranes: 2x3t Ice Capable	**1 oil engine** sr geared to sc. shaft driving 1 CP propeller Total Power: 2,940kW (3,997hp) 14.0kn MaK 8M453AK 1 x 4 Stroke 8 Cy. 320 x 420 2940kW (3997bhp) Krupp MaK Maschinenbau GmbH-Kiel AuxGen: 1 x 416kW 380V 50Hz a.c, 2 x 224kW 380V 50Hz a.c Boilers: TOH (o.f.) 10.0kgf/cm² (9.8bar), TOH (ex.g.) 10.0kgf/cm² (9.8bar) Fuel: 83.0 (d.f.) 282.5 (r.f.) 11.0pd
7322732 *HQIQ9* -	**SIRICHAI SOVEREIGN** *ex* Nikko Maru No. 65 *-1991* *ex* Chidori Maru No. 71 *-1991* **Sirichai Fisheries Co Ltd (Sirichai Fisheries Group)** - *San Lorenzo* *Honduras* Official number: L-1923990	*284* 139 -		**1973 Mie Shipyard Co. Ltd. — Yokkaichi** Yd No: 83 Loa 49.79 Br ex 8.03 Dght 3.328 Lbp 43.49 Br md 8.01 Dpth 3.56 Riveted\Welded, 1 dk	**(B11B2FV) Fishing Vessel**	**1 oil engine** driving 1 FP propeller Total Power: 809kW (1,100hp) Akasaka AH27 1 x 4 Stroke 6 Cy. 270 x 420 809kW (1100bhp) Akasaka Tekkosho KK (Akasaka DieselLtd)-Japan
8610497 *JVPG4* -	**SIRIMA 1** *ex* Orion Achievers *-2012* *ex* Meiyo Maru *-1999* **Centaurea International Pte Ltd** - *Ulaanbaatar* *Mongolia* MMSI: 457450000 Official number: 29601186	**755** 319 1,150		**1986-11 Kurinoura Dockyard Co Ltd — Yawatahama EH** Yd No: 227 Loa - (BB) Br ex - Dght 4.201 Lbp 66.02 Br md 10.01 Dpth 4.53 Welded, 1 dk	**(A13B2TP) Products Tanker**	**1 oil engine** reverse geared to sc. shaft driving 1 FP propeller Total Power: 736kW (1,001hp) 11.0kn Akasaka K28R 1 x 4 Stroke 6 Cy. 280 x 480 736kW (1001bhp) Akasaka Tekkosho KK (Akasaka DieselLtd)-Japan
8915641 *YEIU* -	**SIRIMAU** **Government of The Republic of Indonesia (Direktorat Jenderal Perhubungan Laut - Ministry of Sea Communications)** PT Pelayaran Nasional Indonesia (PELNI) *Ambon* *Indonesia* MMSI: 525005013	**6,022** 1,806 1,400	Class: KI (GL)	**1991-03 Jos L Meyer GmbH & Co — Papenburg** Yd No: 629 Loa 99.80 (BB) Br ex 18.30 Dght 4.200 Lbp 90.50 Br md 18.00 Dpth 9.40 Welded, 3 dks	**(A37B2PS) Passenger Ship** Passengers: unberthed: 915; cabins: 17; berths: 54 Grain: 530; Bale: 490 Compartments: 1 Ho 1 Ha: (7.0 x 5.5) Cranes: 2x5t	**2 oil engines** with flexible couplings & sr geared to sc. shafts driving 2 FP propellers Total Power: 3,200kW (4,350hp) 15.0kn MaK 6M453C 2 x 4 Stroke 6 Cy. 320 x 420 each-1600kW (2175bhp) Krupp MaK Maschinenbau GmbH-Kiel AuxGen: 4 x 420kW 220/380V a.c, 1 x 168kW 220/380V a.c Thrusters: 1 Thwart. CP thruster (f) Fuel: 310.7 (d.f.)
9050955 *HSB3665* -	**SIRINUN NAVA** *ex* Srichiangthong *-2010* *ex* SS Busan *-2007* *ex* Han In *-2003* **Vescon-Thai Shipping Co Ltd** - *Thailand* MMSI: 567052600 Official number: 500053448	**1,912** 1,070 2,792	Class: (KR)	**1991-05 Hanjin Heavy Industries Co Ltd — Ulsan** Yd No: 9064 Loa 82.80 (BB) Br ex - Dght 4.650 Lbp 77.30 Br md 14.80 Dpth 5.90 Welded, 1 dk	**(A33A2CC) Container Ship (Fully Cellular)** TEU 144 C Ho 68 TEU C Dk 76 TEU Compartments: 2 Cell Ho, ER 4 Ha: ER	**1 oil engine** driving 1 FP propeller Total Power: 2,189kW (2,976hp) 12.5kn B&W 6S26MC 1 x 2 Stroke 6 Cy. 260 x 980 2189kW (2976bhp) Ssangyong Heavy Industries Co Ltd-South Korea
8825420 *D3N2013* -	**SIRIO Q** **Oceanpesca Srl di Giuseppe Quinci** - *Luanda* *Angola* Official number: C-611	**445** 133 -	Class: (RI)	**1988 SINAM s.r.l. — Mazara del Vallo** Yd No: 3 Loa 41.40 Br ex - Dght 3.290 Lbp 32.50 Br md 8.80 Dpth 6.18 Welded, 1 dk	**(B11B2FV) Fishing Vessel**	**1 oil engine** geared to sc. shaft driving 1 FP propeller Total Power: 990kW (1,346hp) Blackstone ESL8MK2 1 x 4 Stroke 8 Cy. 222 x 292 990kW (1346bhp) Mirrlees Blackstone (Stamford)Ltd.-Stamford

IMO / Call sign / Flag	Name / Former names / Owner / Manager / Port	Tonnage	Class	Built / Dimensions	Type / Cargo	Machinery
8009545 *9HA2399* -	**SIRIOS CEMENT I** *ex* Aldoha I *-2011* *ex* Elefsina *-2010* *ex* Dhan *-1993* **Sirios Cement Ltd** - *Valletta* *Malta* MMSI: 248542000 Official number: 8009545	**8,180** 2,813 13,550	Class: RI (LR) (NK) ✠ Classed LR until 11/6/93	**1981-10 Shikoku Dockyard Co. Ltd. — Takamatsu** Yd No: 814 Loa 138.00 (BB) Br ex 21.04 Dght 8.102 Lbp 130.03 Br md 21.00 Dpth 11.50 Welded, 1 dk	**(A24A2BT) Cement Carrier** Grain: 11,269 Compartments: 8 Wing Ho, ER	**2 oil engines** sr geared to sc. shafts driving 2 FP propellers Total Power: 3,024kW (4,112hp) 10.5kn MaK 6M453AK 2 x 4 Stroke 6 Cy. 320 x 420 each-1512kW (2056bhp) Ube Industries Ltd-Japan AuxGen: 3 x 220kW 450V 50Hz a.c Fuel: 70.5 (d.f.) (Part Heating Coils) 286.0 (r.f.) 12.5pd
7813561 *SVBN5* -	**SIRIOS CEMENT II** *ex* Indalo *-2012* **Sirios II Maritime Co** Sirios Shipmanagement Co Ltd *Chalkis* *Greece* MMSI: 241191000 Official number: 44	**3,375** 1,512 5,946	Class: LR ✠ **100A1** SS 12/2012 ✠ **LMC** **UMS** Eq.Ltr: S; Cable: 467.5/42.0 U2	**1980-02 Ast. del Cantabrico y de Riera — Factoria de G. Riera, Gijon** Yd No: R.139 Loa 106.33 (BB) Br ex 15.93 Dght 6.668 Lbp 99.01 Br md 15.91 Dpth 8.16 Welded, 1 dk	**(A24A2BT) Cement Carrier** Grain: 5,504 Compartments: 4 Ho, ER	**1 oil engine** sr geared to sc. shaft driving 1 FP propeller Total Power: 2,942kW (4,000hp) 15.5kn Deutz RBV12M350 1 x Vee 4 Stroke 12 Cy. 400 x 500 2942kW (4000bhp) Hijos de J Barreras SA-Spain AuxGen: 3 x 250kW 380V 50Hz a.c
9331830 *9HQE8* -	**SIRIOS CEMENT IV** *ex* Cement Explorer *-2014* *ex* Naftocement XI *-2011* **DB II SA** Sirios Shipmanagement Co Ltd *Valletta* *Malta* MMSI: 256278000 Official number: 9331830	**9,299** 3,244 12,500	Class: RI	**2006-11 Selah Makina Sanayi ve Ticaret A.S. — Tuzla, Istanbul** Yd No: 45 Loa 133.93 Br ex - Dght 8.280 Lbp 122.30 Br md 20.06 Dpth 10.50 Welded, 1 dk	**(A24A2BT) Cement Carrier**	**1 oil engine** reduction geared to sc. shaft driving 1 CP propeller Total Power: 5,800kW (7,886hp) 14.5kn Wartsila 8L38B 1 x 4 Stroke 8 Cy. 380 x 475 5800kW (7886bhp) Wartsila Finland Oy-Finland
9286425 - -	**SIRIPORNWATANA 1** - **Boonchuay Lhaosiripornwatana** -	**302** 205 -		**2002-02 Mits Decisions Co., Ltd. — Samut Sakhon** Loa 36.00 Br ex 8.00 Dght - Lbp - Br md - Dpth 4.65 Welded, 1 dk	**(B11B2FV) Fishing Vessel**	**1 oil engine** geared to sc. shaft driving 1 FP propeller Total Power: 527kW (717hp) Caterpillar 3508 1 x Vee 4 Stroke 8 Cy. 170 x 190 527kW (717bhp) Caterpillar Inc-USA
9283772 *VKSI* -	**SIRIUS** *ex* Delos *-2006* **Government of The Commonwealth of Australia** Government of The Commonwealth of Australia (Amphibious & Afloat Support System Program Office) *Sydney, NSW* *Australia* MMSI: 503170000 Official number: 857599	**25,382** 7,622 37,432 T/cm 49.6	Class: LR ✠ **100A1** SS 06/2009 Double Hull oil tanker ESP **ShipRight** (SDA, FDA, CM) LI *IWS SPM ✠ **LMC** **UMS IGS** Eq.Ltr: K†; Cable: 632.5/70.0 U3 (a)	**2004-06 Hyundai Mipo Dockyard Co Ltd — Ulsan** Yd No: 0228 Converted From: Chemical/Products Tanker-2006 Loa 175.93 (BB) Br ex 31.03 Dght 10.500 Lbp 168.00 Br md 31.00 Dpth 17.00 Welded, 1 dk	**(A13B2TP) Products Tanker** Double Hull (13F) Liq: 42,671; Liq (Oil): 35,761 Compartments: 12 Wing Ta, 2 Wing Slop Ta, ER 12 Cargo Pump (s): 12x500m³/hr Manifold: Bow/CM: 88m	**1 oil engine** driving 1 FP propeller Total Power: 8,661kW (11,775hp) 15.0kn B&W 6S50MC 1 x 2 Stroke 6 Cy. 500 x 1910 8661kW (11775bhp) Hyundai Heavy Industries Co Ltd-South Korea AuxGen: 1 x 990kW 450V 60Hz a.c, 1 x 740kW 450V 60Hz a.c Boilers: e (ex.g.) 12.0kgf/cm² (11.8bar), WTAuxB (o.f.) 9.0kgf/cm² (8.8bar), WTAuxB (o.f.) 9.0kgf/cm² (8.8bar) Thrusters: 1 Tunnel thruster (f) Fuel: 191.0 (d.f.) 1304.0 (r.f.)
9218208 *V2QB3* -	**SIRIUS** *ex* Auriga *-2009* **Sirius Maritime Ltd** Mestex Shipping & Trading Ltd *Saint John's* *Antigua & Barbuda* MMSI: 304995000 Official number: 3045	**5,381** 2,626 7,567	Class: GL	**2001-09 Santierul Naval Constanta S.A. — Constanta** (Hull) Yd No: 545 **2001-09 Muetzelfeldtwerft GmbH — Cuxhaven** Yd No: 235 Loa 107.58 (BB) Br ex - Dght 6.630 Lbp 103.00 Br md 18.20 Dpth 9.00 Welded, 1 dk	**(A21A2BC) Bulk Carrier** Double Hull Grain: 9,910; Bale: 9,797 Compartments: 3 Ho, ER 3 Ha: (17.5 x 15.2) (25.9 x 15.2) (25.1 x 15.2)ER Ice Capable	**1 oil engine** driving 1 CP propeller Total Power: 2,806kW (3,815hp) 12.0kn B&W 7S26MC 1 x 2 Stroke 7 Cy. 260 x 980 2806kW (3815bhp) MAN B&W Diesel A/S-Denmark AuxGen: 3 x 279kW 440V 60Hz a.c Thrusters: 1 Thwart. FP thruster (f) Fuel: 67.5 (d.f.) 324.0 (r.f.) 9.5pd
9370874 *AUVC* -	**SIRIUS** *ex* Bula Z13 *-2008* **Kei-Rsos Maritime Ltd** - *Visakhapatnam* *India* MMSI: 419075700 Official number: 3443	**333** 100 157	Class: IR (AB)	**2006-05 Bengbu Shenzhou Machinery Co Ltd — Bengbu AH** (Hull) Yd No: (1169) **2006-05 Pacific Ocean Engineering & Trading Pte Ltd (POET) — Singapore** Yd No: 1169 Loa 28.00 Br ex 9.82 Dght 4.000 Lbp 22.94 Br md 9.80 Dpth 4.90 Welded, 1 dk	**(B32A2ST) Tug**	**2 oil engines** reduction geared to sc. shafts driving 2 Directional propellers Total Power: 2,648kW (3,600hp) Yanmar 8N21A-EN 2 x 4 Stroke 8 Cy. 210 x 290 each-1324kW (1800bhp) Yanmar Diesel Engine Co Ltd-Japan AuxGen: 2 x 99kW 415V 50Hz a.c Fuel: 151.0
9459498 *JD2507* -	**SIRIUS** *ex* Kanagawa 569 *-2007* **Naikai Eisen KK & Nippon Eisen KK** - *Sakai, Osaka* *Japan* Official number: 140641	*117* - -		**2007-11 Kanagawa Zosen — Kobe** Yd No: 569 Loa 38.00 Br ex - Dght - Lbp 37.00 Br md 6.20 Dpth 3.34 Welded, 1 dk	**(B32A2ST) Tug**	**2 oil engines** reduction geared to sc. shafts driving 2 Propellers Total Power: 3,310kW (4,500hp) Mitsubishi S16R-MTK 2 x Vee 4 Stroke 16 Cy. 170 x 180 each-1655kW (2250bhp) Mitsubishi Heavy Industries Ltd-Japan
9541887 *5BCT3* -	**SIRIUS** - **Syracuse Shipping Ltd** S Frangoulis (Ship Management) Ltd SatCom: Inmarsat C 420953310 *Limassol* *Cyprus* MMSI: 209533000 Official number: 9541887	**23,456** 11,522 34,537	Class: NK (AB) (BV)	**2011-01 SPP Shipbuilding Co Ltd — Tongyeong** Yd No: H4058 Loa 180.00 (BB) Br ex - Dght 9.920 Lbp 172.00 Br md 30.00 Dpth 14.70 Welded, 1 dk	**(A21A2BC) Bulk Carrier** Grain: 48,620; Bale: 46,815 Compartments: 5 Ho, ER 5 Ha: ER Cranes: 4x35t	**1 oil engine** driving 1 FP propeller Total Power: 7,900kW (10,741hp) 14.0kn MAN-B&W 5S50MC-C 1 x 2 Stroke 5 Cy. 500 x 2000 7900kW (10741bhp)
9671319 *D5GD7* -	**SIRIUS** *ex* Bintang Kenyalang *-2014* **Bulanel Invest Corp** OSM Ship Management Pte Ltd *Monrovia* *Liberia* MMSI: 636016426 Official number: 16426	**2,638** 984 3,200	Class: NV	**2013-11 Fujian Southeast Shipyard — Fuzhou FJ** Yd No: NC704 Loa 78.70 (BB) Br ex - Dght 5.800 Lbp 70.10 Br md 16.00 Dpth 7.00 Welded, 1 dk	**(B21A2OS) Platform Supply Ship**	**4 diesel electric oil engines** driving 4 gen. Connecting to 2 elec. motors each (1470kW) driving 2 Azimuth electric drive units Total Power: 3,280kW (4,460hp) 12.0kn Caterpillar C32 4 x Vee 4 Stroke 12 Cy. 145 x 162 each-820kW (1115bhp) Caterpillar Inc-USA Thrusters: 2 Thwart. CP thruster (f)
7815595 *HCUR* -	**SIRIUS** - **Government of The Republic of Ecuador (Instituto Nacional de Pesca)** - *Manta* *Ecuador* Official number: P-04-0246	*141* 55 98	Class: (NK)	**1979-01 Uchida Zosen — Ise** Yd No: 784 Loa 33.20 Br ex 7.22 Dght 2.801 Lbp 30.10 Br md 7.21 Dpth 3.20 Welded, 1 dk	**(B11A2FS) Stern Trawler** Ins: 36	**1 oil engine** sr geared to sc. shaft driving 1 FP propeller Total Power: 405kW (551hp) 10.8kn Yanmar 6ML-DT 1 x 4 Stroke 6 Cy. 200 x 240 405kW (551bhp) Yanmar Diesel Engine Co Ltd-Japan AuxGen: 2 x 112kW
7945223 *OJ2715* -	**SIRIUS** *ex* Sirius 660 *-2004* **Terramare Oy** - *Helsinki* *Finland* MMSI: 230985750 Official number: 12326	**472** 142 1,320	Class: (RI)	**1972 IHC Smit NV — Kinderdijk** Loa 59.09 Br ex 9.53 Dght 3.241 Lbp 57.99 Br md 9.50 Dpth 3.36 Welded, 1 dk	**(B34A2SH) Hopper, Motor**	**2 oil engines** driving 2 Directional propellers Total Power: 368kW (500hp) Deutz BF12L714 2 x Vee 4 Stroke 12 Cy. 120 x 140 each-184kW (250bhp) Kloeckner Humboldt Deutz AG-West Germany
8124503 *DFLX* -	**SIRIUS** *ex* Gudrun *-2008* **BOT Broering Oil Transport GmbH** Empting Mineralole GmbH *Cuxhaven* *Germany* MMSI: 211228200 Official number: 780	**676** 203 801	Class: GL	**1982-06 C. Luehring Schiffswerft GmbH & Co. KG — Brake** Yd No: 8201 Loa 58.22 Br ex 10.11 Dght 3.058 Lbp 54.00 Br md 10.00 Dpth 4.65 Welded, 2 dks	**(A13B2TP) Products Tanker** Liq: 1,020; Liq (Oil): 1,020 Cargo Heating Coils Compartments: 8 Wing Ta, ER 2 Cargo Pump (s): 2x200m³/hr Manifold: Bow/CM: 40m Ice Capable	**1 oil engine** driving 1 CP propeller Total Power: 441kW (600hp) 10.5kn Callesen 6-427-FOT 1 x 4 Stroke 6 Cy. 270 x 400 441kW (600bhp) Aabenraa Motorfabrik, HeinrichCallesen A/S-Denmark Thrusters: 1 Thwart. CP thruster (f)
8139041 - -	**SIRIUS** - **Sevastopol Port Authority**	*124* 101 20	Class: (RS)	**1983 Ilyichyovskiy Sudoremontnyy Zavod im. "50-letiya SSSR" — Ilyichyovsk** Yd No: 22 Loa 28.71 Br ex 6.35 Dght 1.480 Lbp - Br md - Dpth 2.49 Welded, 1 dk	**(A37B2PS) Passenger Ship** Passengers: unberthed: 250	**2 oil engines** driving 2 FP propellers Total Power: 220kW (300hp) 10.4kn Barnaultransmash 3D6C 2 x 4 Stroke 6 Cy. 150 x 180 each-110kW (150bhp) Barnaultransmash-Barnaul AuxGen: 2 x 1kW Fuel: 2.0 (d.f.)
8112342 *HCKJ* -	**SIRIUS** - **Superintendencia del Terminal Petrolero de Balao (SUINBA)** - *Esmeraldas* *Ecuador* Official number: R-02-0809	**211** 7 -	Class: (BV)	**1981-09 Deltawerf BV — Sliedrecht** Yd No: 618 Loa 24.03 Br ex - Dght - Lbp 21.95 Br md 6.82 Dpth 2.75 Welded, 1 dk	**(B32A2ST) Tug**	**2 oil engines** sr reverse geared to sc. shafts driving 2 FP propellers Total Power: 1,060kW (1,442hp) G.M. (Detroit Diesel) 12V-71-TI 2 x Vee 2 Stroke 12 Cy. 108 x 127 each-530kW (721bhp) General Motors Corp-USA

IMO / Call sign	Name / Owner / Port	Tonnage	Class	Builder / Dimensions	Type	Machinery
8604046 - -	**SIRIUS** - **Government of The Oriental Republic of Uruguay (Armada Nacional del Uruguay - Servicio de Buques Auxiliares) (SEBAX)** - *Uruguay*	*150* - -	Class: (LR) ✠	**1989-04 Svc de Constr, Repar y Armamento de La Armada (SCRA) — Montevideo** Yd No: 21 Loa - Br ex - Dght 1.901 Lbp 33.56 Br md 10.01 Dpth 2.82 Welded, 1 dk	**(B34Q2QB) Buoy Tender**	**2 oil engines** geared to sc. shafts driving 2 FP propellers General Motors General Motors Corp-USA
8612108 *YL2771* -	**SIRIUS** *ex* Fru Thomsen *-2012* *ex* Katrine Alberte *-2009* *ex* Karina-Martin *-2003* *ex* Alloka *-1997* **Fishing Company 'Grifs' Ltd (SIA Zvejnieku Kompanija 'Grifs')** - *Riga* *Latvia* Official number: 0842	**246** 92 -		**1985-12 Alustaal af 1980 ApS — Rudkobing** Yd No: 108 Loa 33.50 Br ex - Dght - Lbp 27.11 Br md 6.51 Dpth 3.46 Welded, 1 dk	**(B11B2FV) Fishing Vessel**	**1 oil engine** geared to sc. shaft driving 1 FP propeller Total Power: 552kW (750hp) Grenaa 6FR24TK 1 x 4 Stroke 6 Cy. 240 x 300 552kW (750bhp) A/S Grenaa Motorfabrik-Denmark
8317899 - -	**SIRIUS** - **Christopher John Keys, Susan Jane Keys** - *Sydney, NSW* *Australia*	*186* 78 200	Class: (LR) ✠ Classed LR until 3/1/86	**1984-10 Carrington Slipways Pty Ltd — Newcastle NSW** Yd No: 163 Loa 25.38 Br ex 10.04 Dght - Lbp 23.40 Br md 9.61 Dpth 2.04 Welded, 1 dk	**(A37B2PS) Passenger Ship** Hull Material: Aluminium Alloy	**2 oil engines** with clutches, flexible couplings & sr reverse geared to sc. shafts driving 2 FP propellers Total Power: 900kW (1,224hp) M.T.U. 6V396TC62 2 x Vee 4 Stroke 6 Cy. 165 x 185 each-450kW (612bhp) MTU Friedrichshafen GmbH-Friedrichshafen Fuel: 8.5 (d.f.)
7331599 *DURZ2* -	**SIRIUS** *ex* Iris Maru *-1998* **Harbor Star Shipping Services Inc** - *Manila* *Philippines* Official number: 00-0000351	*189* 107 68		**1973-08 Towa Zosen K.K. — Shimonoseki** Yd No: 448 Loa 30.48 Br ex 8.82 Dght 2.598 Lbp 27.00 Br md 8.79 Dpth 3.51 Welded, 1 dk	**(B32A2ST) Tug**	**2 oil engines** driving 2 FP propellers Total Power: 1,766kW (2,402hp) Niigata 6L25BX 2 x 4 Stroke 6 Cy. 250 x 320 each-883kW (1201bhp) Niigata Engineering Co Ltd-Japan
7308906 *WN5182* -	**SIRIUS** - **Karl J Sjodin & Gene O Higgins** - *Seattle, WA* *United States of America* Official number: 290517	*144* 107 -		**1963 Bellinger Shipyards, Inc. — Jacksonville, Fl** L reg 22.13 Br ex 7.01 Dght - Lbp - Br md - Dpth 3.31 Welded, 1 dk	**(B11B2FV) Fishing Vessel**	**1 oil engine** driving 1 FP propeller Total Power: 257kW (349hp) Caterpillar 1 x 4 Stroke 257kW (349bhp) Caterpillar Tractor Co-USA
7367225 *WDD9272* -	**SIRIUS** *ex* Sea Valiant *-2004* *ex* Pacific Victory *-1993* *ex* Cecile B *-1992* *ex* Cecile *-1989* *ex* Cecile B *-1984* **Kirby Offshore Marine Pacific LLC** Kirby Offshore Marine LLC SatCom: Inmarsat M 630359610 *Seattle, WA* *United States of America* MMSI: 367309260 Official number: 558877	**726** 217 -	Class: AB	**1974-08 Main Iron Works, Inc. — Houma, La** Yd No: 279 Loa 39.15 Br ex - Dght 5.652 Lbp - Br md 11.56 Dpth 6.08 Welded, 1 dk	**(B32A2ST) Tug** Ice Capable	**2 oil engines** reverse reduction geared to sc. shafts driving 2 FP propellers Total Power: 4,230kW (5,752hp) 13.0kn EMD (Electro-Motive) 16-645-E5 2 x Vee 2 Stroke 16 Cy. 230 x 254 each-2115kW (2876bhp) General Motors Corp.Electro-Motive Div.-La Grange AuxGen: 2 x 99kW a.c Fuel: 508.0 (d.f.)
7612632 *S5ER9* -	**SIRIUS** *ex* Sirius I *-2005* *ex* Sirius *-2001* **Adria Tow doo** - *Koper* *Slovenia* MMSI: 278046000 Official number: 135	**213** 64 65	Class: RI (GL)	**1977-06 Jadewerft Wilhelmshaven GmbH — Wilhelmshaven** Yd No: 139 Loa 28.50 Br ex 8.44 Dght 4.450 Lbp 26.52 Br md 8.41 Dpth 3.43 Welded, 1 dk	**(B32A2ST) Tug** Ice Capable	**2 oil engines** reduction geared to sc. shafts driving 2 Voith-Schneider propellers Total Power: 1,148kW (1,560hp) Deutz SBA8M528 2 x 4 Stroke 8 Cy. 220 x 280 each-574kW (780bhp) Kloeckner Humboldt Deutz AG-West Germany
7700180 *PBRW* -	**SIRIUS** *ex* Bugsier 12 *-2009* **Amsterdam Tugs BV** Sleepdienst B Iskes & Zoon BV *IJmuiden* *Netherlands* MMSI: 246538000 Official number: 52996	**189** 56 108	Class: GL	**1977-06 Schiffswerft u. Maschinenfabrik Max Sieghold — Bremerhaven** Yd No: 178 Loa 26.62 Br ex 8.84 Dght 2.798 Lbp 23.80 Br md 8.81 Dpth 3.61 Welded, 1 dk	**(B32A2ST) Tug** Ice Capable	**2 oil engines** geared to sc. shafts driving 2 Directional propellers Total Power: 1,280kW (1,740hp) Deutz SBA6M528 2 x 4 Stroke 6 Cy. 220 x 280 each-640kW (870bhp) Kloeckner Humboldt Deutz AG-West Germany
7700099 *UHVP* -	**SIRIUS** *ex* Grootsand *-2006* **Karelian Shipping Co Ltd (OOO 'Karelskaya Sudokhodnaya Kompaniya')** - *Murmansk* *Russia* MMSI: 273313950	**1,727** 942 2,175	Class: RS (GL)	**1978-04 Buesumer Werft GmbH — Buesum** (Hull) Yd No: 268 **1978-04 Schlichting-Werft GmbH — Luebeck** Yd No: 1395 Loa 78.11 (BB) Br ex 12.76 Dght 5.750 Lbp 70.82 Br md 12.51 Dpth 7.52 Welded, 2 dks	**(A34A2GR) Refrigerated Cargo Ship** Ins: 2,553 Compartments: 3 Ho, ER, 3 Tw Dk 3 Ha: 3 (8.5 x 3.9)ER Derricks: 6x3t; Winches: 6 Ice Capable	**1 oil engine** sr geared to sc. shaft driving 1 FP propeller Total Power: 1,655kW (2,250hp) 13.5kn MaK 6M453AK 1 x 4 Stroke 6 Cy. 320 x 420 1655kW (2250bhp) MaK Maschinenbau GmbH-Kiel AuxGen: 2 x 444kW 380V 50Hz a.c Thrusters: 1 Thwart. FP thruster (f) Fuel: 274.0 (d.f.) 7.0pd
7632175 *ERPL*	**SIRIUS** - **Serena Sea Navigation Co** Tech Project LLC *Giurgiulesti* *Moldova*	*208* - -	Class: (CS) (JR)	**1976 Cant. Nav. Dante Castracani Srl — Ancona** Yd No: 108 Loa 29.85 Br ex 8.56 Dght 4.001 Lbp 25.61 Br md 8.01 Dpth 4.09 Welded, 1 dk	**(B32A2ST) Tug**	**1 oil engine** reverse reduction geared to sc. shaft driving 1 FP propeller Total Power: 1,596kW (2,170hp) 13.0kn Alpha 14V23L-VO 1 x Vee 4 Stroke 14 Cy. 225 x 300 1596kW (2170bhp) Alpha Diesel A/S-Denmark AuxGen: 3 x 42kW 380V a.c Fuel: 57.0
5330175 *IUJW* -	**SIRIUS** *ex* ST-677 *-2006* **Rimorchiatori Riuniti Panfido e Compagnia Srl** - *Venice* *Italy* Official number: 508	*139* 43 -	Class: (RI) (AB)	**1944 American Machinery Corp. — Beresford, Fl** Yd No: 27 Loa 26.19 Br ex 7.07 Dght 2.998 Lbp 25.00 Br md 7.04 Dpth 3.15 Welded, 1 dk	**(B32A2ST) Tug**	**1 oil engine** driving 1 FP propeller Total Power: 515kW (700hp) 10.5kn AuxGen: 2 x 30kW Fuel: 24.0 (d.f.)
6523236 *LW4156* -	**SIRIUS** *ex* G. T. O. I *-1975* **Loba Pesquera SA** - *Mar del Plata* *Argentina* MMSI: 701006063 Official number: 0905	**507** 284 629	Class: (RI)	**1965 Soc. Esercizio Cant. S.p.A. — Viareggio** Yd No: 548 Loa 59.77 Br ex 9.17 Dght 3.709 Lbp 52.86 Br md 9.16 Dpth 4.60 Welded, 1 dk	**(B11A2FT) Trawler** Compartments: 2 Ho, ER 2 Ha: 2 (1.5 x 1.5)ER Derricks: 1x3t,1x1.5t	**1 oil engine** driving 1 FP propeller Total Power: 956kW (1,300hp) 13.3kn Ansaldo Q320/8 1 x 4 Stroke 8 Cy. 320 x 420 956kW (1300bhp) SA Ansaldo Stabilimento Meccaniche-Italy AuxGen: 3 x 220V 50Hz a.c Fuel: 223.5 (d.f.)
8826242 *LCUQ* -	**SIRIUS** *ex* Priitta *-2011* *ex* Sirius *-2009* *ex* Gerakl *-1999* **Matre Shipping Reidar Matre** - *Haugesund* *Norway* MMSI: 257098000	**155** 62 27	Class: (RS)	**1989-09 RO Brodogradiliste Novi Sad — Novi Sad** Yd No: 272 Loa 23.50 Br ex 9.00 Dght 3.250 Lbp 21.01 Br md - Dpth 3.50 Welded, 1 dk	**(B32B2SP) Pusher Tug** Ice Capable	**2 oil engines** geared to sc. shafts driving 2 Directional propellers Total Power: 598kW (814hp) 10.0kn MAN D2840LE 2 x Vee 4 Stroke 10 Cy. 128 x 142 each-299kW (407bhp) MAN Nutzfahrzeuge AG-Nuernberg
8746870 *9MFC9* -	**SIRIUS** - **Government of Malaysia (Director of Marine & Ministry of Transport)** - *Port Klang* *Malaysia* MMSI: 533015200 Official number: 332363	**140** 42 25		**2007-07 Kay Marine Sdn Bhd — Kuala Terengganu** (Assembled by) Yd No: J104-1 **2007-07 Inform Marine Technology — Fremantle WA** (Parts for assembly by) Loa 26.00 Br ex - Dght 1.200 Lbp - Br md 9.20 Dpth 2.55 Welded, 1 dk	**(A37B2PS) Passenger Ship** Hull Material: Aluminium Alloy	**2 oil engines** reduction geared to sc. shafts driving 2 Propellers Total Power: 2,206kW (3,000hp) M.T.U. 12V2000M91 2 x Vee 4 Stroke 12 Cy. 130 x 150 each-1103kW (1500bhp) MTU Friedrichshafen GmbH-Friedrichshafen
8703658 *UFYJ* -	**SIRIUS** *ex* Ostrov Simushir *-2014* *ex* Pogranichnik Petrov *-2000* *ex* Meisho Maru No. 128 *-2000* **Podolie Co Ltd** - *Nevelsk* *Russia* MMSI: 273450760 Official number: 876666	**863** 290 622	Class: RS	**1987-08 Narasaki Zosen KK — Muroran HK** Yd No: 1090 Loa 58.76 (BB) Br ex 10.24 Dght 3.890 Lbp 51.01 Br md 10.20 Dpth 3.97 Welded, 1 dk	**(B11A2FS) Stern Trawler** Ins: 830	**1 oil engine** with clutches, flexible couplings & sr geared to sc. shaft driving 1 CP propeller Total Power: 1,912kW (2,600hp) Daihatsu 6DLM-40 1 x 4 Stroke 6 Cy. 400 x 480 1912kW (2600bhp) Daihatsu Diesel Manufacturing Co Lt-Japan Fuel: 252.0 (d.f.)

8725785 - -	**SIRIUS** - **Ukrainian Danube Shipping Co** -	**106** 32 14	Class: (RS)	**1985-10 Zavod "Krasnyy Moryak" — Rostov-na-Donu** Yd No: 21 Loa 23.15 Br ex 6.24 Dght 1.850 Lbp 20.00 Br md - Dpth 2.80 Welded, 1 dk	**(A37B2PS) Passenger Ship** Passengers: unberthed: 70 Ice Capable	**1 oil engine** geared to sc. shaft driving 1 FP propeller Total Power: 221kW (300hp) 9.6kn Daldizel 6CHNSP18/22-300 1 x 4 Stroke 6 Cy. 180 x 220 221kW (300bhp) Daldizel-Khabarovsk AuxGen: 1 x 16kW Fuel: 6.0 (d.f.)
8932314 *SW7893* -	**SIRIUS** - **Ajax Yachting Enterprises Co Ltd** - *Piraeus* *Greece* MMSI: 237311100 Official number: 9600	**267** 75 -	Class: HR RS (Class contemplated) (AB)	**1992-08 in Greece** Yd No: 226 Loa 33.78 Br ex 7.20 Dght 2.070 Lbp 32.25 Br md - Dpth 3.60 Welded, 1 dk	**(X11A2YP) Yacht**	**2 oil engines** reduction geared to sc. shafts driving 2 FP propellers Total Power: 1,198kW (1,628hp) 14.0kn M.T.U. 6V396TB93 2 x Vee 4 Stroke 6 Cy. 165 x 185 each-599kW (814bhp) MTU Friedrichshafen GmbH-Friedrichshafen AuxGen: 2 x 80kW a.c
9060625 *JZIT* -	**SIRIUS** *ex* Sun Sirius *-2013* *ex* Xing Hua *-2010* *ex* Sun Queen *-1997* **PT Usda Seroja Jaya** - *Batam* *Indonesia* MMSI: 525023202	**2,029** 808 2,999	Class: KI (NK) (CC)	**1993-07 Daedong Shipbuilding Co Ltd — Busan** Yd No: 385 Converted From: Chemical Tanker-2010 Loa 85.80 (BB) Br ex 14.02 Dght 5.200 Lbp 79.80 Br md 14.00 Dpth 6.50 Welded, 1 dk	**(A12B2TR) Chemical/Products Tanker** Liq: 2,965; Liq (Oil): 2,965 Cargo Heating Coils Compartments: 10 Ta, ER	**1 oil engine** driving 1 FP propeller Total Power: 1,912kW (2,600hp) 12.6kn Akasaka A37 1 x 4 Stroke 6 Cy. 370 x 720 1912kW (2600bhp) Akasaka Tekkosho KK (Akasaka DieselLtd)-Japan AuxGen: 2 x 320kW a.c Fuel: 255.0 (r.f.)
9101833 *UGRR* -	**SIRIUS** - **Fishery Plant Co Ltd (OOO 'Rybnyy Zavod')** - *Astrakhan* *Russia* Official number: 920750	**190** 57 70	Class: RR (RS)	**1993-04 OAO Astrakhanskaya Sudoverf — Astrakhan** Yd No: 106 Converted From: Fish Carrier Loa 31.85 Br ex 7.08 Dght 2.100 Lbp 27.80 Br md - Dpth 3.15 Welded, 1 dk	**(B11A2FT) Trawler** Ins: 100 Compartments: 2 Ho 2 Ha: 2 (2.1 x 2.4) Derricks: 2x1t Ice Capable	**1 oil engine** geared to sc. shaft driving 1 FP propeller Total Power: 232kW (315hp) 10.2kn Daldizel 6CHSPN2A18-315 1 x 4 Stroke 6 Cy. 180 x 220 232kW (315bhp) Daldizel-Khabarovsk AuxGen: 2 x 25kW Fuel: 14.0 (d.f.)
9127801 *V7KI6* -	**SIRIUS** - **Alpha Ship GmbH & Co KG ms 'Sirius'** Alpha Shipmanagement GmbH & Co KG *Majuro* *Marshall Islands* MMSI: 538090245 Official number: 90245	**21,199** 8,574 25,049 T/cm 40.5	Class: GL	**1998-06 Stocznia Gdynia SA — Gdynia** Yd No: 8138/3 Loa 178.05 (BB) Br ex - Dght 11.500 Lbp 164.20 Br md 28.20 Dpth 16.75 Welded, 1 dk	**(A33A2CC) Container Ship (Fully Cellular)** TEU 1617 C Ho 676 TEU C Dk 941 TEU incl 353 ref C Compartments: 4 Cell Ho, ER 8 Ha: (12.8 x 18.5)Tappered 7 (12.8 x 23.6)ER Cranes: 3x45t	**1 oil engine** driving 1 FP propeller Total Power: 17,200kW (23,385hp) 21.0kn B&W 6L70MC 1 x 2 Stroke 6 Cy. 700 x 2268 17200kW (23385bhp) H Cegielski Poznan SA-Poland AuxGen: 2 x 1180kW 440/220V 60Hz a.c, 1 x 880kW 440/220V 60Hz a.c Thrusters: 1 Thwart. FP thruster (f) Fuel: 228.0 (d.f.) (Heating Coils) 2066.0 (r.f.) 72.0pd
9075515 - -	**SIRIUS-1** *ex* MFYS *-1998* **JSC 'Port Ecosystems'** LLC Transneft-Service *Novorossiysk* *Russia*	**235** 120 455	Class: RS	**1992-06 Bakinskiy Sudostroitelnyy Zavod im Vano Sturua — Baku** Yd No: 416 Loa 35.17 Br ex 8.01 Dght 3.120 Lbp 33.25 Br md - Dpth 3.60 Welded, 1 dk	**(B34G2SE) Pollution Control Vessel** Liq: 468; Liq (Oil): 468 Cargo Heating Coils Compartments: 10 Ta Ice Capable	**1 oil engine** geared to sc. shaft driving 1 FP propeller Total Power: 166kW (226hp) 8.0kn Daldizel 6CHNSP18/22 1 x 4 Stroke 6 Cy. 180 x 220 166kW (226bhp) Daldizel-Khabarovsk AuxGen: 1 x 50kW, 1 x 30kW Fuel: 11.0 (d.f.)
9003146 *UBHH7* -	**SIRIUS-1** *ex* New Hirotsuki *-2011* **OOO 'Polluks' (Polluks Co Ltd)** - *Kholmsk* *Russia* MMSI: 273354920	**4,288** 2,027 5,178	Class: RS (NK)	**1990-10 Miyoshi Shipbuilding Co Ltd — Uwajima EH** Yd No: 280 Loa 116.20 (BB) Br ex - Dght 6.864 Lbp 105.00 Br md 16.20 Dpth 9.75 Welded	**(A34A2GR) Refrigerated Cargo Ship** Ins: 5,097 Compartments: 3 Ho, ER 3 Ha: 3 (7.4 x 6.2)ER Derricks: 6x5t	**1 oil engine** driving 1 FP propeller Total Power: 4,472kW (6,080hp) 16.0kn B&W 8L35MC 1 x 2 Stroke 8 Cy. 350 x 1050 4472kW (6080bhp) Makita Diesel Co Ltd-Japan AuxGen: 3 x 408kW a.c Thrusters: 1 Thwart. CP thruster (f) Fuel: 880.0 (r.f.)
8201260 *J8B3002* -	**SIRIUS B** *ex* Digicon Definition *-1995* **ShallSeis Ltd** - *Kingstown* *St Vincent & The Grenadines* MMSI: 377706000 Official number: 9474	**393** 118 278	Class: (AB)	**1982-04 Newpark Shipbuilding & Repair, Inc. — Houston, Tx** Yd No: 9511 Lengthened-2005 Loa - Br ex 11.13 Dght 1.677 Lbp 38.60 Br md 10.98 Dpth 2.44 Welded, 1 dk	**(B31A2SR) Research Survey Vessel**	**2 oil engines** with clutches & sr reverse geared to sc. shaft driving 2 FP propellers Total Power: 530kW (720hp) 8.5kn G.M. (Detroit Diesel) 12V-71 2 x Vee 2 Stroke 12 Cy. 108 x 127 each-265kW (360bhp) General Motors Detroit DieselAllison Divn-USA AuxGen: 2 x 175kW a.c Thrusters: 1 Directional thruster (f)
7418933 *VKSQ* -	**SIRIUS COVE** - **Tasmanian Ports Corporation Pty Ltd (TasPorts)** - *Sydney, NSW* *Australia* MMSI: 503330000 Official number: 355748	*231* 13 -	Class: LR ✠ **100A1** SS 08/2010 tug ✠ **LMC** Eq.Ltr: G; Cable: U2	**1975-08 Carrington Slipways Pty Ltd — Newcastle NSW** Yd No: 110 Loa 28.73 Br ex 9.73 Dght 3.480 Lbp 24.82 Br md 9.40 Dpth 3.92 Welded, 1 dk	**(B32A2ST) Tug**	**2 oil engines** reverse reduction geared to sc. shafts driving 2 FP propellers Total Power: 1,838kW (2,498hp) 12.0kn Blackstone ESL8MK2 2 x 4 Stroke 8 Cy. 222 x 292 each-919kW (1249bhp) Mirrlees Blackstone (Stamford)Ltd.-Stamford AuxGen: 2 x 72kW 415V 50Hz a.c
7032375 *OWLX2* -	**SIRIUS HOJ** *ex* Sirius *-1998* *ex* Shamix *-1987* *ex* Slusen *-1986* **Sirius Hoj ApS** - *Horsens* *Denmark (DIS)* MMSI: 219001724 Official number: H 1217	*109* 66 119	Class: (BV)	**1970 A/S Nordsovaerftet — Ringkobing** Yd No: 66 Converted From: Bulk Cement Carrier-1987 Loa 23.83 Br ex 6.61 Dght 2.083 Lbp 22.28 Br md 6.58 Dpth 2.67 Welded, 1 dk	**(B33B2DG) Grab Hopper Dredger** Grain: 96 Compartments: 2 Ta, ER	**1 oil engine** driving 1 FP propeller Total Power: 169kW (230hp) 8.0kn Scania DSI11 1 x 4 Stroke 6 Cy. 127 x 145 169kW (230bhp) Saab Scania AB-Sweden Thrusters: 1 Thwart. FP thruster (f) Fuel: 1.5 (d.f.) 1.0pd
7207114 *HO7190* -	**SIRIUS I** *ex* Sirius *-2011* *ex* Anne Sofie *-2000* *ex* Bremer Roland *-1984* **Betelgeuze BV** Geuze Shipping BV *Panama* *Panama* MMSI: 371049000 Official number: 42006PEXT	**823** 378 941	Class: (BV) (GL) (NV)	**1972 Hjorungavaag Verksted AS — Hjorungavaag** Yd No: 16 Loa 60.71 Br ex 9.53 Dght 3.767 Lbp 55.00 Br md 9.50 Dpth 5.26 Welded, 2 dks	**(A31A2GX) General Cargo Ship** Grain: 1,798 TEU 36 Compartments: 2 Ho, ER 2 Ha: (17.9 x 7.3) (16.8 x 7.3)ER Derricks: 2x5t; Winches: 2 Ice Capable	**1 oil engine** reduction geared to sc. shaft driving 1 CP propeller Total Power: 794kW (1,080hp) 9.5kn Deutz SBA8M528 1 x 4 Stroke 8 Cy. 220 x 280 794kW (1080bhp) Kloeckner Humboldt Deutz AG-West Germany AuxGen: 2 x 50kW 220V 50Hz a.c Thrusters: 1 Thwart. FP thruster (f) Fuel: 112.0 (d.f.)
9111175 *C6TT7* -	**SIRIUS I** - **Emerald Star Shipping Inc** Super-Eco Tankers Management Inc *Nassau* *Bahamas* MMSI: 311774000 Official number: 8000844	**28,341** 13,418 46,341 T/cm 51.8	Class: LR RI ✠ **100A1** SS 01/2011 oil tanker (Double Hull) ESP SPM ✠ **LMC** **UMS IGS** Eq.Ltr: M†; Cable: 632.5/73.0 U3	**1996-01 Astilleros Espanoles SA (AESA) — Sestao** Yd No: 299 Loa 182.85 (BB) Br ex 32.23 Dght 12.250 Lbp 173.00 Br md 32.20 Dpth 17.80 Welded, 1 dk	**(A13B2TP) Products Tanker** Double Hull (13F) Liq: 51,435; Liq (Oil): 51,435 Cargo Heating Coils Compartments: 8 Ta, ER, 2 Wing Slop Ta 8 Cargo Pump (s): 8x850m³/hr Manifold: Bow/CM: 92m	**1 oil engine** driving 1 FP propeller Total Power: 8,561kW (11,640hp) 14.0kn B&W 6S50MC 1 x 2 Stroke 6 Cy. 500 x 1910 8561kW (11640bhp) Manises Diesel Engine Co. S.A.-Valencia AuxGen: 3 x 740kW 440V 60Hz a.c Boilers: e (ex.g.) 8.6kgf/cm² (8.4bar), AuxB (o.f.) 8.2kgf/cm² (8.0bar) Fuel: 299.0 (d.f.) (Heating Coils) 1378.0 (r.f.) 30.0pd
6608139 *LW4797* -	**SIRIUS II** *ex* G. T. O. II *-1984* **El Marisco SACI** - *Mar del Plata* *Argentina* MMSI: 701000765 Official number: 0936	**506** 304 629	Class: (RI)	**1966 Soc. Esercizio Cant. S.p.A. — Viareggio** Yd No: 563 Loa 59.77 Br ex 9.17 Dght 3.709 Lbp 52.86 Br md 9.16 Dpth 4.60 Riveted\Welded, 1 dk	**(B11A2FT) Trawler** Compartments: 2 Ho, ER 2 Ha: 2 (1.5 x 1.5)ER Derricks: 1x3t,1x1.5t	**1 oil engine** driving 1 FP propeller Total Power: 956kW (1,300hp) 13.3kn Ansaldo Q320/8 1 x 4 Stroke 8 Cy. 320 x 420 956kW (1300bhp) SA Ansaldo Stabilimento Meccaniche-Italy AuxGen: 3 x 220V 50Hz a.c
6726450 *LW4803* -	**SIRIUS III** *ex* G. T. O. III *-1984* **El Marisco SACI** - SatCom: Inmarsat C 470134910 *Mar del Plata* *Argentina* MMSI: 701000529 Official number: 0937	**506** 304 624	Class: (RI)	**1967 Soc. Esercizio Cant. S.p.A. — Viareggio** Yd No: 560 Loa 59.77 Br ex 9.17 Dght 3.709 Lbp 52.86 Br md 9.16 Dpth 4.60 Riveted\Welded, 1 dk	**(B11A2FT) Trawler** Compartments: 2 Ho, ER 2 Ha: 2 (1.5 x 1.5)ER Derricks: 1x3t,1x1.5t	**1 oil engine** driving 1 FP propeller Total Power: 956kW (1,300hp) 13.3kn Ansaldo Q320/8 1 x 4 Stroke 8 Cy. 320 x 420 956kW (1300bhp) SA Ansaldo Stabilimento Meccaniche-Italy AuxGen: 3 x 220V 50Hz a.c

9213806 **SIRIUS LEADER** *9V9171* - **SSC Sirius Leader Pte Ltd** SSC Ship Management Pte Ltd *Singapore* *Singapore* MMSI: 564561000 Official number: 396729	**51,496** 15,449 16,451 T/cm 47.2	Class: NK	**2000-07 Sumitomo Heavy Industries Ltd. — Yokosuka Shipyard, Yokosuka** Yd No: 1261 Loa 180.00 (BB) Br ex - Dght 9.625 Lbp 170.00 Br md 32.26 Dpth 34.60 Welded, 12 dks, incl.3 dks hoistable	**(A35B2RV) Vehicles Carrier** Side door/ramp (s) Len: 20.00 Wid: 4.20 Swl: 15 Quarter stern door/ramp (s. a.) Len: 35.00 Wid: 8.00 Swl: 100 Cars: 4,323	**1 oil engine** driving 1 FP propeller Total Power: 13,540kW (18,409hp) 19.3kn Sulzer 7RTA62 1 x 2 Stroke 7 Cy. 620 x 2150 13540kW (18409bhp) Diesel United Ltd.-Aioi AuxGen: 3 x 1200kW 440V 60Hz a.c Thrusters: 1 Thwart. CP thruster (f); 1 Thwart. CP thruster (a) Fuel: 250.0 (d.f.) 2735.0 (r.f.)
9384198 **SIRIUS STAR** *A8NA7* - **Vela International Marine Ltd** - SatCom: Inmarsat C 463701934 *Monrovia* *Liberia* MMSI: 636013447 Official number: 13447	**162,252** 111,896 319,427 T/cm 178.7	Class: LR ✠ **100A1** SS 04/2013 Double Hull oil tanker ESP **ShipRight** (SDA, FDA plus, CM) *IWS LI SPM ✠ **LMC** **UMS IGS** Eq.Ltr: E*; Cable: 770.0/117.0 U3 (a)	**2008-04 Daewoo Shipbuilding & Marine Engineering Co Ltd — Geoje** Yd No: 5302 Loa 333.00 (BB) Br ex 60.04 Dght 22.500 Lbp 320.00 Br md 60.00 Dpth 30.50 Welded, 1 dk	**(A13A2TV) Crude Oil Tanker** Double Hull (13F) Liq: 340,584; Liq (Oil): 285,764 Compartments: 5 Ta, 10 Wing Ta, 2 Wing Slop Ta, ER 3 Cargo Pump (s): 3x5500m^3/hr Manifold: Bow/CM: 164.2m	**1 oil engine** driving 1 FP propeller Total Power: 29,340kW (39,891hp) 15.3kn MAN-B&W 6S90MC-C 1 x 2 Stroke 6 Cy. 900 x 3188 29340kW (39891bhp) Doosan Engine Co Ltd-South Korea AuxGen: 2 x 1600kW 450V 60Hz a.c, 1 x 1400kW 450V 60Hz a.c Boilers: e (ex.g.) 23.5kgf/cm^2 (23.0bar), WTAuxB (o.f.) 18.6kgf/cm^2 (18.2bar) Fuel: 354.0 (d.f.) 7680.0 (r.f.)
9051612 **SIRIUS VOYAGER** *C6FG9* *ex* Chevron Mariner *-2002* - **CalPetro Tankers (IOM) Ltd** Chevron Shipping Co LLC SatCom: Inmarsat B 336623910 *Nassau* *Bahamas* MMSI: 308927000 Official number: 731992	**88,886** 46,899 155,681 T/cm 118.2	Class: AB	**1994-10 Ind. Verolme-Ishibras S.A. (IVI) (Est. Ishibras) — Rio** Yd No: 167 Loa 274.50 (BB) Br ex 50.04 Dght 17.205 Lbp 261.00 Br md 50.00 Dpth 25.10 Welded, 1 dk	**(A13A2TV) Crude Oil Tanker** Double Hull (13F) Liq: 168,745; Liq (Oil): 183,000 Cargo Heating Coils Compartments: 12 Wing Ta, ER, 2 Wing Slop Ta 3 Cargo Pump (s): 3x3500m^3/hr Manifold: Bow/CM: 129.7m	**1 oil engine** driving 1 CP propeller Total Power: 15,447kW (21,002hp) 15.5kn Sulzer 6RTA72 1 x 2 Stroke 6 Cy. 720 x 2500 15447kW (21002bhp) Ishikawajima do Brasil Estaleiros S (ISHIBRAS)-Brazil Fuel: 416.4 (d.f.) 4808.0 (r.f.)
9397626 **SIROCCO** *MMPY9* - **Prestige Charters Ltd** Titan Fleet Management Sarl *Douglas* *Isle of Man (British)* MMSI: 235011110 Official number: 911012	**495** 148 -	Class: AB	**2006-06 Heesen Shipyards B.V. — Oss** Yd No: 12947 Loa 47.00 Br ex 9.00 Dght 2.500 Lbp 34.00 Br md 8.50 Dpth 3.92 Welded, 1 dk	**(X11A2YP) Yacht** Hull Material: Aluminium Alloy	**2 oil engines** reduction geared to sc. shafts driving 2 FP propellers Total Power: 5,440kW (7,396hp) M.T.U. 16V4000M90 2 x Vee 4 Stroke 16 Cy. 165 x 190 each-2720kW (3698bhp) MTU Friedrichshafen GmbH-Friedrichshafen
9268849 **SIROCCO** *PCBN* - **De Meer G Tilma** Wagenborg Shipping BV SatCom: Inmarsat C 4244518100 *Oostmahorn* *Netherlands* MMSI: 244518000 Official number: 41975	**3,991** 1,559 6,033	Class: LR ✠ **100A1** SS 06/2009 strengthened for heavy cargoes, containers in holds and on hatch covers Ice Class 1B FS at a draught of 5.884m Max/min draught fwd 5.884/2.40m Max/min draught aft 5.884/3.315m ✠ **LMC** **UMS** Eq.Ltr: T; Cable: 469.2/38.0 U3 (a)	**2004-06 Scheepswerf Peters B.V. — Kampen** Yd No: 806 Loa 111.40 (BB) Br ex 13.40 Dght 5.740 Lbp 107.99 Br md 13.35 Dpth 9.40 Welded, 1 dk	**(A31A2GX) General Cargo Ship** TEU 252 C.Ho 144 TEU C.Dk 108 TEU Compartments: 2 Ho, ER 2 Ha: ER Ice Capable	**1 oil engine** with flexible couplings & sr geared to sc. shaft driving 1 FP propeller Total Power: 2,040kW (2,774hp) 12.6kn Wartsila 6L26 1 x 4 Stroke 6 Cy. 260 x 320 2040kW (2774bhp) Wartsila Finland Oy-Finland AuxGen: 1 x 348kW 400V 50Hz a.c, 2 x 140kW 400V 50Hz a.c Thrusters: 1 Thwart. FP thruster (f)
9562544 **SIROCCO** *HO8233* - **Waves Razor Inc** - *Panama* *Panama* MMSI: 355582000 Official number: 45057PEXT	**416** 124 136	Class: LR ✠ **100A1** SS 10/2013 tug ✠ **LMC** Eq.Ltr: H†; Cable: 605.0/22.0 U2 (a)	**2013-10 Guangxi Guijiang Shipyard — Wuzhou GX** Yd No: 01-2008-20 Loa 28.20 Br ex 11.52 Dght 3.750 Lbp 25.90 Br md 11.50 Dpth 5.30 Welded, 1 dk	**(B32A2ST) Tug**	**2 oil engines** gearing integral to driving 2 Z propellers Total Power: 3,676kW (4,998hp) Niigata 6L28HX 2 x 4 Stroke 6 Cy. 280 x 370 each-1838kW (2499bhp) Niigata Engineering Co Ltd-Japan AuxGen: 2 x 86kW 415V 50Hz a.c
7419016 **SIROCCO II** *FZYR* *ex* Chambon Sirocco *-2013* *ex* Sirroco *-2004* *ex* Abeille No. 9 *-2004* - **Ports Normands Associes (Port of Normandy Authority) (PNA)** - *Marseille* *France* MMSI: 227007700 Official number: 188876A	**458** 137 750	Class: BV (GL)	**1975-12 Ziegler Freres — Dunkerque** Yd No: 190 Loa 37.29 Br ex 11.59 Dght 3.610 Lbp 35.01 Br md 11.00 Dpth 4.30 Welded, 1 dk	**(B32A2ST) Tug**	**2 oil engines** geared to sc. shafts driving 2 Voith-Schneider propellers Total Power: 2,884kW (3,922hp) 12.3kn AGO 240G12VS 2 x Vee 4 Stroke 12 Cy. 240 x 220 each-1442kW (1961bhp) Societe Alsacienne de ConstructionsMecaniques (SACM)-France
8523307 **SIROKO** *UFKA* *ex* Galati 2 *-2000* - **OOO 'Transship-Yug'** - *Temryuk* *Russia* MMSI: 273442990	**333** 99 133	Class: RS (RN)	**1984 Santierul Naval Drobeta-Turnu Severin S.A. — Drobeta-Turnu S.** Yd No: 11483002 Loa 35.82 Br ex 9.92 Dght 3.350 Lbp 33.00 Br md 9.72 Dpth 4.70 Welded, 1 dk	**(B32A2ST) Tug** Ice Capable	**2 oil engines** geared to sc. shafts driving 2 CP propellers Total Power: 2,236kW (3,040hp) 10.0kn Caterpillar 3512B 2 x Vee 4 Stroke 12 Cy. 170 x 190 each-1118kW (1520bhp) (new engine 2008) Caterpillar Inc-USA AuxGen: 3 x 70kW 400V 50Hz a.c
6912310 **SIROLO** *IKCI* *ex* Saint Quay *-1970* *ex* ST-699 *-1970* - **Salvatore Palermo e C - Ricuperi di Bordo SNC** *Naples* *Italy* Official number: 1655	*139* 23 -	Class: (RI) (BV)	**1944 Equitable Equipment Co. — Madisonville, La** Yd No: 390 Loa 26.42 Br ex 7.24 Dght 2.871 Lbp 24.69 Br md 7.00 Dpth 3.26 Welded, 1 dk	**(B32A2ST) Tug**	**1 oil engine** driving 1 FP propeller Total Power: 515kW (700hp) 10.0kn Enterprise DMG8 1 x 4 Stroke 8 Cy. 305 x 381 515kW (700bhp) Enterprise Engine & Foundry Co-USA Fuel: 51.0 (d.f.)
1007718 **SIRONA III** *V7JQ8* *ex* Sycara III *-2006* - **Nickel Corp Cayman Ltd** Fraser Yachts Florida Inc *Bikini* *Marshall Islands* MMSI: 538070201 Official number: 70201	**917** 275 152	Class: LR ✠ **100A1** SS 01/2014 SSC Yacht, mono, G6 ✠ **LMC** **UMS** Cable: 165.0/24.0 U2 (a)	**2004-01 Oceanfast Pty Ltd — Fremantle WA** Yd No: 77 Loa 56.50 Br ex 10.75 Dght 3.000 Lbp 47.17 Br md 10.26 Dpth 5.58 Welded, 1 dk	**(X11A2YP) Yacht**	**2 oil engines** with clutches, flexible couplings & sr reverse geared to sc. shafts driving 2 FP propellers Total Power: 2,610kW (3,548hp) 15.0kn Caterpillar 3512B 2 x Vee 4 Stroke 12 Cy. 170 x 190 each-1305kW (1774bhp) Caterpillar Inc-USA AuxGen: 2 x 210kW 240V 60Hz a.c Thrusters: 1 Thwart. FP thruster (f)
6400343 **SIROS** *SX2878* *ex* Sara Ghawar *-1995* *ex* Splendid *-1982* *ex* Thuntank 11 *-1981* - **Sekavin Tria Shipping Co** Sekavin SA *Piraeus* *Greece* MMSI: 237017200 Official number: 10292	**925** 600 2,030 T/cm 9.2	Class: (LR) (HR) Cable: SQ ✠ Classed LR until 2/2/05	**1964-01 Falkenbergs Varv AB — Falkenberg** Yd No: 136 Lengthened & Deepened-1972 Loa 74.94 Br ex 9.56 Dght 5.087 Lbp 69.42 Br md 9.45 Dpth 5.97 Welded, 1 dk	**(A13B2TP) Products Tanker** Liq: 2,260; Liq (Oil): 2,260 Cargo Heating Coils Compartments: 10 Ta, ER 3 Cargo Pump (s): 1x470m^3/hr, 1x340m^3/hr, 1x250m^3/hr Ice Capable	**1 oil engine** driving 1 FP propeller Total Power: 780kW (1,060hp) 11.5kn Deutz RBV8M545 1 x 4 Stroke 8 Cy. 320 x 450 780kW (1060bhp) Kloeckner Humboldt Deutz AG-West Germany AuxGen: 1 x 85kW 380V 50Hz a.c, 1 x 55kW 380V 50Hz a.c Boilers: AuxB 9.8kgf/cm^2 (9.6bar) Fuel: 40.0 (d.f.) 4.0pd
8626111 **SIROUS** *9BCS* *ex* Eliya I *-2004* *ex* Myoho Maru *-2003* - **Sirous Abdola Badrain** - *Bushehr* *Iran* MMSI: 422609000 Official number: 800	**286** 196 350	Class: AS	**1984 KK Ouchi Zosensho — Matsuyama EH** Loa 42.40 Br ex - Dght 3.110 Lbp 38.00 Br md 7.60 Dpth 4.70 Welded, 1 dk	**(A31A2GX) General Cargo Ship**	**1 oil engine** driving 1 FP propeller Total Power: 294kW (400hp) 9.0kn Yanmar 6M-HTS 1 x 4 Stroke 6 Cy. 200 x 240 294kW (400bhp) Yanmar Diesel Engine Co Ltd-Japan
8946418 **SIRPIFJORD** *HP9463* *ex* Zuiderzee *-1998* - **BJ Services International SA** - *Panama* *Panama* MMSI: 357095000 Official number: 27707PEXT3	**595** 178 -	Class: (BV)	**1978 A. Vuijk & Zonen's Scheepswerven B.V. — Capelle a/d IJssel** Converted From: Stone Carrier-1991 Loa 52.04 Br ex 11.60 Dght 2.410 Lbp 51.58 Br md 11.30 Dpth 3.20 Welded, 1 dk	**(A31C2GD) Deck Cargo Ship**	**2 oil engines** reduction geared to sc. shafts driving 2 FP propellers Total Power: 460kW (626hp) 7.5kn G.M. (Detroit Diesel) 8V-92 2 x Vee 2 Stroke 8 Cy. 123 x 127 each-230kW (313bhp) General Motors Corp-USA AuxGen: 2 x 32kW 220/380V 50Hz a.c Fuel: 11.2 (d.f.)

IMO / Call sign	Ship name / Owner / Manager	GT / NT / DWT	Class	Builder / Dimensions	Ship type	Machinery
9255402 *PBFR* -	**SIRRAH** **Beheermaatschappij ms Sirrah II BV** Navigia Shipmanagement BV *Groningen* *Netherlands* MMSI: 244371000 Official number: 40087	**6,386** 3,240 8,446	Class: GL	**2002-05 Detlef Hegemann Rolandwerft GmbH & Co. KG — Berne** Yd No: 205 Loa 132.23 (BB) Br ex - Dght 7.340 Lbp 125.50 Br md 19.40 Dpth 9.45 Welded, 1 dk	**(A33A2CC) Container Ship (Fully Cellular)** TEU 707 C Ho 204 TEU C Dk 503 TEU incl 150 ref C. Ice Capable	**1 oil engine** reduction geared to sc. shaft driving 1 CP propeller Total Power: 7,195kW (9,782hp) 17.0kn MaK 8M43 1 x 4 Stroke 8 Cy. 430 x 610 7195kW (9782bhp) Caterpillar Motoren GmbH & Co. KG-Germany Thrusters: 1 Thwart. FP thruster (f)
8666563 - -	**SIRSAIM** **Sesa Sterlite Ltd** - *Panaji* *India* Official number: PNJ-520	**1,451** 1,259 2,300	Class: IR	**2010-12 Sesa Goa Ltd. — Goa** Yd No: 69 Loa 70.00 Br ex - Dght 3.300 Lbp - Br md 14.00 Dpth 4.55 Welded, 1 dk	**(A31A2GX) General Cargo Ship**	**2 oil engines** reduction geared to sc. shafts driving 2 Propellers Total Power: 1,052kW (1,430hp) Volvo Penta D12 2 x 4 Stroke 6 Cy. 131 x 150 each-526kW (715bhp) AB Volvo Penta-Sweden
7364352 *5AVZ* -	**SIRTE STAR** *ex* Deniz Yildizi *-2005* *ex* Fikret Atasoy *-2002* *ex* Ozge Atasoy *-1997* *ex* Elgiz *-1995* *ex* Ufuk Aksoy *-1993* *ex* Nas *-1989* *ex* Hulya 1 *-1980* - - *Libya* MMSI: 642160050	**1,455** 857 2,952	Class: (BV) (AB)	**1976-03 Celiktekne Sanayii ve Ticaret A.S. — Tuzla, Istanbul** Yd No: 2 Loa 75.01 (BB) Br ex 11.51 Dght 5.549 Lbp 65.99 Br md 11.50 Dpth 6.51 Welded, 2 dks	**(A31A2GX) General Cargo Ship** Grain: 2,872; Bale: 2,663 Compartments: 2 Ho, ER 2 Ha: (11.9 x 7.0) (17.9 x 7.0)ER Derricks: 6x3t; Winches: 6	**1 oil engine** driving 1 FP propeller Total Power: 1,229kW (1,671hp) 12.0kn Skoda 9L350IIPS 1 x 4 Stroke 9 Cy. 350 x 500 1229kW (1671bhp) CKD Praha-Praha AuxGen: 2 x 64kW 220/280V a.c, 1 x 32kW 220/280V a.c
7341219 *9A4185* -	**SIS** *ex* Netley Castle *-1997* **Jadrolinija** *Rijeka* *Croatia* MMSI: 238114840	**1,858** 557 300	Class: CS (LR) ✠ Classed LR until 27/10/78	**1974-06 Ryton Marine Ltd. — Wallsend** Yd No: 531 Loa 73.82 Br ex 15.22 Dght 2.750 Lbp 67.11 Br md 14.64 Dpth 3.66 Welded, 1 dk	**(A36A2PR) Passenger/Ro-Ro Ship (Vehicles)** Passengers: unberthed: 782 Bow door/ramp Stern door/ramp	**4 oil engines** driving 4 Directional propellers 2 fwd and 2 aft Total Power: 1,984kW (2,696hp) 14.0kn Caterpillar D379SCAC 4 x Vee 4 Stroke 8 Cy. 159 x 203 each-496kW (674bhp) Caterpillar Tractor Co-USA AuxGen: 3 x 72kW 415V 50Hz a.c Thrusters: 1 Thwart. FP thruster (f)
8327753 *TCBJ5* -	**SIS** *ex* Kemerli *-2012* **Sis Marine Servis ve Gemi Isletmeciligi Ticaret Ltd Sti** Derin Gemi Acenteligi ve Gemi Isletmeciligi Sanayi ve Ticaret Ltd Sti (Derin Shipping Agency & Shipping Management Trade Ltd Co) *Istanbul* *Turkey* MMSI: 271002169 Official number: 5017	**745** 427 1,185	Class: TL (BV)	**1983-01 Celiktrans Deniz Insaat Kizaklari Ltd. Sti — Tuzla,Ist** Yd No: 3 Loa 63.28 Br ex - Dght 4.450 Lbp 55.15 Br md 9.20 Dpth 5.10 Welded, 1 dk	**(A31A2GX) General Cargo Ship** Grain: 1,312; Bale: 1,231 Compartments: 2 Ho, ER 2 Ha: (10.9 x 6.0) (14.7 x 6.0)ER Derricks: 2x3t	**1 oil engine** driving 1 FP propeller Total Power: 397kW (540hp) 11.0kn S.K.L. 6NVD48-2U 1 x 4 Stroke 6 Cy. 320 x 480 397kW (540bhp) VEB Schwermaschinenbau "KarlLiebknecht" (SKL)-Magdeburg
9400021 *YM9797* -	**SIS** **Milta Turizm Isletmeleri AS** *Izmir* *Turkey* MMSI: 271001046	**213** 63 21	Class: RI	**2006-05 C.R.N. Cant. Nav. Ancona S.r.l. — Ancona** Yd No: 112/12 Loa 34.09 Br ex - Dght 1.400 Lbp 29.20 Br md 7.10 Dpth 3.50 Bonded, 1 dk	**(X11A2YP) Yacht** Hull Material: Reinforced Plastic	**2 oil engines** reduction geared to sc. shafts driving 2 FP propellers Total Power: 4,080kW (5,548hp) 28.0kn M.T.U. 12V4000M90 2 x Vee 4 Stroke 12 Cy. 165 x 190 each-2040kW (2774bhp) MTU Friedrichshafen GmbH-Friedrichshafen
8111611 *HO3384* -	**SIS CHAMP** *ex* Far Sun *-2003* *ex* Far Sovereign *-1993* *ex* Seaforth Sovereign *-1989* **Humaid Badir Marine Shipping Establishment** Seaport International Shipping Co LLC *Panama* *Panama* MMSI: 356421000 Official number: 3233407A	**1,216** 379 1,540	Class: BV (LR) (NV) ✠ Classed LR until 23/12/93	**1982-10 Henry Robb Ltd. — Leith** Yd No: 531 Converted From: Offshore Supply Ship-1993 Loa 62.54 Br ex 13.67 Dght 5.012 Lbp 55.20 Br md 13.15 Dpth 6.15 Welded, 1 dk	**(B21A2OS) Platform Supply Ship** Ice Capable	**2 oil engines** with clutches, flexible couplings & sr geared to sc. shafts driving 2 CP propellers Total Power: 2,500kW (3,400hp) 10.0kn Ruston 6RKCM 2 x 4 Stroke 6 Cy. 254 x 305 each-1250kW (1700bhp) Ruston Diesels Ltd.-Newton-le-Willows AuxGen: 3 x 230kW 440V 60Hz a.c Thrusters: 1 Thwart. CP thruster (f) Fuel: 1026.0 (d.f.) 5.5pd
8107165 *3EMD9* -	**SIS PIONEER** *ex* Troms Tjeld *-2004* *ex* Odin Viking *-1997* **Seaport International Shipping Co LLC** - *Panama* *Panama* MMSI: 355210000 Official number: 3459309A	**1,345** 403 1,185	Class: (NV)	**1982-03 Ulstein Hatlo AS — Ulsteinvik** (Hull launched by) Yd No: 177 **1982-03 Ulstein Smedvik AS — Tjorvaag** (Hull completed by) Yd No: 177 Loa 64.67 Br ex - Dght 4.720 Lbp 56.39 Br md 13.81 Dpth 6.91 Welded, 2 dks	**(B21B20A) Anchor Handling Tug Supply**	**2 oil engines** geared to sc. shafts driving 2 FP propellers Total Power: 6,002kW (8,160hp) 10.0kn Nohab F316V 2 x Vee 4 Stroke 16 Cy. 250 x 300 each-3001kW (4080bhp) Nohab Diesel AB-Sweden AuxGen: 2 x 664kW 440V 60Hz a.c, 2 x 172kW 440V 60Hz a.c Thrusters: 1 Thwart. FP thruster (f)
9207376 *D6C09* -	**SIS PRINCESS** *ex* Swissco 88 *-2004* **Seaport International Shipping Co LLC** - *Moroni* *Union of Comoros* MMSI: 616314000 Official number: 1200366	**270** 81 -	Class: BV	**1998-11 Tuong Aik (Sarawak) Sdn Bhd — Sibu** Yd No: 9713 Loa 36.00 Br ex - Dght 2.824 Lbp 32.64 Br md 8.60 Dpth 3.50 Welded, 1 dk	**(B21B20T) Offshore Tug/Supply Ship**	**2 oil engines** reduction geared to sc. shafts driving 2 FP propellers Total Power: 1,250kW (1,700hp) 10.0kn Caterpillar D398TA 2 x Vee 4 Stroke 12 Cy. 159 x 203 each-625kW (850bhp) Caterpillar Inc-USA AuxGen: 2 x 80kW 410V 50Hz a.c Thrusters: 1 Tunnel thruster (f)
7420546 *D6CZ7* -	**SIS SEEKER** *ex* Northern Seeker *-2005* *ex* Jane Viking *-1997* *ex* Sea Garnet *-1990* *ex* Sea Piper *-1982* **Seaport International Shipping Co LLC** - *Moroni* *Union of Comoros* MMSI: 616396000 Official number: 1200463	**1,378** 414 2,033	Class: PR (NV)	**1975-06 Teraoka Shipyard Co Ltd — Minamiawaji HG** Yd No: 153 Converted From: Pipe Carrier-2003 Converted From: Standby Safety Vessel-1980 Converted From: Pipe Carrier-1977 Loa 63.30 Br ex 13.82 Dght 5.462 Lbp 58.81 Br md 13.80 Dpth 6.41 Welded, 1 dk	**(B22F20W) Well Stimulation Vessel**	**2 oil engines** driving 2 CP propellers Total Power: 3,090kW (4,202hp) 10.0kn Wichmann 7AXA 2 x 2 Stroke 7 Cy. 300 x 450 each-1545kW (2101bhp) Wichmann Motorfabrikk AS-Norway AuxGen: 1 x 145kW 380V 50Hz a.c, 2 x 100kW 380V 50Hz a.c Thrusters: 1 Thwart. FP thruster (f) Fuel: 813.0 (d.f.)
7910321 *FNNS* -	**SISA NE NANA** *ex* Sissa *-2000* *ex* Carole T *-2000* *ex* Emily PG *-1993* **Societe Loyaute Investissements Service SA** - *Noumea* *France* MMSI: 540005100	**613** 403 1,120	Class: LR ✠ **100A1** SS 04/2000 U.K., Eire & between River Elbe & Brest ✠ **LMC** Eq.Ltr: H; Cable: 302.0/26.0 U1	**1980-03 Yorkshire D.D. Co. Ltd. — Hull** Yd No: 266 Lengthened-1980 Loa 49.59 Br ex 9.50 Dght 3.879 Lbp 45.90 Br md 9.40 Dpth 4.75 Welded, 1 dk	**(A31A2GX) General Cargo Ship** Grain: 1,417; Bale: 1,312 Compartments: 1 Ho, ER 1 Ha: (24.1 x 6.5)ER	**2 oil engines** geared to sc. shafts driving 2 Directional propellers Total Power: 634kW (862hp) 9.0kn Cummins KT-19-M 2 x 4 Stroke 6 Cy. 159 x 159 each-317kW (431bhp) (new engine 2007) Cummins Engine Co Inc-USA AuxGen: 1 x 2kW 24V d.c, 2 x 2kW 24V d.c
8915562 *OXYW* -	**SISAK** **Government of The Kingdom of Denmark (Den Danske Stat - Justitsministeriet)** - *Nuuk* *Denmark* MMSI: 331000056 Official number: D3203	*161* 48 -	Class: (NV)	**1989-05 Soby Motorfabrik og Staalskibsvaerft A/S — Soby** Yd No: 72 Loa 27.58 Br ex 6.50 Dght 2.800 Lbp 23.00 Br md 6.30 Dpth 3.33 Welded, 1 dk	**(B34H2SQ) Patrol Vessel** Ice Capable	**1 oil engine** with clutches, flexible couplings & sr geared to sc. shaft driving 1 FP propeller Total Power: 597kW (812hp) 12.0kn Cummins KT-38-M 1 x Vee 4 Stroke 12 Cy. 159 x 159 597kW (812bhp) Cummins Engine Co Ltd-United Kingdom AuxGen: 2 x 52kW 380V 50Hz a.c
9188491 *OZOM* -	**SISAK II** **Government of The Kingdom of Denmark (Rigspolitichefen) (Commissioner of Police)** Government of The Kingdom of Denmark (Politimesteren i Gronland) (Chief Constable of Greenland) *Nuuk* *Denmark* MMSI: 331000004 Official number: D3717	**139** 42 32	Class: (NV)	**1998-04 p/f Torshavnar Skipasmidja — Torshavn** Yd No: 38 Loa 24.35 Br ex 6.32 Dght 2.300 Lbp 21.50 Br md 6.30 Dpth 3.00 Welded, 1 dk	**(B34H2SQ) Patrol Vessel**	**1 oil engine** reduction geared to sc. shaft driving 1 FP propeller 11.5kn Caterpillar 3508TA 1 x Vee 4 Stroke 8 Cy. 170 x 190 Caterpillar Inc-USA AuxGen: 1 x 52kW 220/380V 50Hz a.c, 1 x 57kW 220/380V 50Hz a.c
9199488 *OZQT* -	**SISAK III** **Government of The Kingdom of Denmark (Rigspolitichefen) (Commissioner of Police)** Government of The Kingdom of Denmark (Politimesteren i Gronland) (Chief Constable of Greenland) *Nuuk* *Denmark* MMSI: 331095100 Official number: D3718	**139** 41 32	Class: (NV)	**1998-10 p/f Torshavnar Skipasmidja — Torshavn** Yd No: 39 Loa 24.15 Br ex 6.32 Dght 2.300 Lbp 21.50 Br md 6.30 Dpth 3.00 Welded, 1 dk	**(B34H2SQ) Patrol Vessel**	**1 oil engine** geared to sc. shaft driving 1 FP propeller Total Power: 570kW (775hp) 11.5kn Caterpillar 3508TA 1 x Vee 4 Stroke 8 Cy. 170 x 190 570kW (775bhp) Caterpillar Inc-USA AuxGen: 1 x 65kW 220/380V 60Hz a.c, 1 x 57kW 220/380V 50Hz a.c

9206346 **SISAK IV** 139 Class: (NV)
OZVC 41
\- 32
Government of The Kingdom of Denmark (Rigspolitichefen) (Commissioner of Police)
Government of The Kingdom of Denmark (Politimesteren i Gronland) (Chief Constable of Greenland)
Nuuk *Denmark*
MMSI: 331099000
Official number: D3719

1999-04 p/f Torshavnar Skipasmidja — Torshavn Yd No: 40
Loa 24.15 Br ex 6.32 Dght 2.300
Lbp 21.50 Br md 6.30 Dpth 3.00
Welded, 1 dk

(B34H2SQ) Patrol Vessel

1 oil engine geared to sc. shaft driving 1 FP propeller
Total Power: 570kW (775hp)
Caterpillar 3508TA
1 x Vee 4 Stroke 8 Cy. 170 x 190 570kW (775bhp)
Caterpillar Inc-USA
AuxGen: 1 x 52kW 220V 50Hz a.c, 1 x 62kW 220V 50Hz a.c

9039779 **SISIMIUT** 2,373 Class: NV
OZIA *ex* Arnar *-1995* 712
\- **Royal Greenland AS** 1,138
\-
SatCom: Inmarsat C 433107210
Nuuk *Denmark*
MMSI: 331072000
Official number: D3631

1992-12 Stocznia Remontowa 'Nauta' SA — Gdynia (Hull) Yd No: TN65/2
1992-12 Mjellem & Karlsen Verft AS — Bergen Yd No: 148
Loa 66.88 Br ex - Dght 5.850
Lbp 52.80 Br md 14.00 Dpth 5.85
Welded, 2 dks

(B11A2FG) Factory Stern Trawler
Ice Capable

1 oil engine reduction geared to sc. shaft driving 1 FP propeller
Total Power: 3,001kW (4,080hp)
Wartsila 8R32
1 x 4 Stroke 8 Cy. 320 x 350 3001kW (4080bhp)
Wartsila Diesel Oy-Finland
AuxGen: 1 x 1600kW 440V 60Hz a.c, 2 x 720kW 440V 60Hz a.c
Thrusters: 1 Thwart. FP thruster (f)

9607095 **SISKIN ARROW** 46,295 Class: NK
V7CY6 21,763
\- **Misuga SA** 72,927
Misuga Kaiun Co Ltd
Majuro *Marshall Islands*
MMSI: 538005349
Official number: 5349

2014-01 Mitsui Eng. & SB. Co. Ltd., Chiba Works — Ichihara Yd No: 1839
Loa 210.00 (BB) Br ex - Dght 13.835
Lbp 202.00 Br md 36.00 Dpth 20.20
Welded, 1 dk

(A31A2GO) Open Hatch Cargo Ship
Grain: 87,462
Compartments: 8 Ho, ER
8 Ha: ER
Cranes: 4x45t

1 oil engine driving 1 FP propeller
Total Power: 9,450kW (12,848hp) 14.5kn
MAN-B&W 5S60ME-C8
1 x 2 Stroke 5 Cy. 600 x 2400 9450kW (12848bhp)
Mitsui Engineering & Shipbuilding CLtd-Japan
AuxGen: 2 x 1100kW 60Hz a.c, 1 x 835kW 60Hz a.c
Thrusters: 1 Tunnel thruster (f)

5154806 **SISMIK-1** 667 Class: TL (LR)
TCVR *ex* Mta Sismik I *-2012* *ex* Hora *-1976* 200 Classed LR until 19/11/01
\- *ex* Hercules *-1954* *ex* Agir *-1949* 353
Istanbul Teknik Universitesi Denizcilik Fakultesi (ITU)
\-
Istanbul *Turkey*
MMSI: 271002205
Official number: 796

1943-02 Deschimag — Mannheim Yd No: 595
1976 Denizcilik Bankasi T.A.O. — Istinye, Istanbul
Converted From: Accommodation Vessel, Stationary-1976
Converted From: Salvage Vessel-1971
Rebuilt-1976
Loa 56.70 Br ex 8.87 Dght 3.940
Lbp 52.00 Br md 8.82 Dpth 4.70
Riveted\Welded, 1 dk

(B31A2SR) Research Survey Vessel

1 oil engine driving 1 FP propeller
Total Power: 772kW (1,050hp) 13.0kn
Polar MN15
1 x 2 Stroke 5 Cy. 340 x 570 772kW (1050bhp) (new engine 1976)
AB Bofors NOHAB-Sweden
AuxGen: 2 x 90kW 380V 50Hz a.c, 1 x 27kW 380V 50Hz a.c
Fuel: 178.0 (d.f.)

8657433 **SISOL** 149 Class: CS
9A8516 *ex* Recep Cinar *-2003* 44
\- **Ribarstvo i Trgovina Gira** -
\-
Rijeka *Croatia*
Official number: 2R-131

1997 Surmene Tersanesi — Trabzon
Loa 28.65 Br ex - Dght 1.920
Lbp 25.56 Br md 9.00 Dpth 2.85
Welded, 1 dk

(B11B2FV) Fishing Vessel

1 oil engine reduction geared to sc. shaft driving 1 FP propeller
Total Power: 375kW (510hp) 10.0kn
Volvo Penta TAMD162C
1 x 4 Stroke 6 Cy. 144 x 165 375kW (510bhp)
AB Volvo Penta-Sweden

9041655 **SISOULI PREM** 44,704 Class: IR LR (KR) (NK)
AVOU *ex* Maharshi Vishwamitra *-2014* 13,411 **100A1** SS 06/2011
\- *ex* Gas Miracle *-2011* 50,400 liquefied gas carrier, Ship Type 2G
Mercator Ltd T/cm
Fleet Management India Pvt Ltd 69.5
SatCom: Inmarsat C 441923128
Mumbai *India*
MMSI: 419000389
Official number: 3898

Butane, propane, propane-butane mixture, in independent tanks Type A, maximum SG 0.61, maximum vapour pressure 0.28 bar, minimum temperature minus 46 degree C
*IWS
LI
LMC **UMS Lloyd's RMC (LG)**
Cable: 330.0/78.0 U3 (a)

1992-12 Mitsubishi Heavy Industries Ltd. — Nagasaki Yd No: 2070
Loa 230.00 (BB) Br ex 36.63 Dght 10.819
Lbp 219.00 Br md 36.60 Dpth 20.40
Welded, 1 dk

(A11B2TG) LPG Tanker
Double Bottom Entire Compartment Length
Liq (Gas): 78,503
4 x Gas Tank (s); 4 independent (C.mn.stl) pri vertical
8 Cargo Pump (s): 8x550m³/hr
Manifold: Bow/CM: 113.1m

1 oil engine driving 1 FP propeller
Total Power: 12,348kW (16,788hp) 16.7kn
Mitsubishi 7UEC60LS
1 x 2 Stroke 7 Cy. 600 x 2200 12348kW (16788bhp)
Mitsubishi Heavy Industries Ltd-Japan
AuxGen: 3 x 880kW 450V 60Hz a.c
Boilers: e (ex.g.) 12.2kgf/cm² (12.0bar), WTAuxB (o.f.) 6.1kgf/cm² (6.0bar)
Fuel: 130.0 (d.f.) (Heating Coils) 1960.0 (r.f.) 48.8pd

8927046 **SISSY** 164 Class: (HR) (RN)
\- *ex* Chefalu 5 *-1999* 101
\- **Corvette Shipping Ltd** 38
Trimimar Shipping & Trading Co Ltd

1985 Santierul Naval Tulcea — Tulcea Yd No: N89
Loa 25.65 Br ex - Dght 2.400
Lbp 23.51 Br md 7.20 Dpth 3.38
Welded, 1 dk

(B11B2FV) Fishing Vessel

1 oil engine reduction geared to sc. shaft driving 1 FP propeller
Total Power: 220kW (299hp) 9.5kn
S.K.L. 6VD18/15AL-1
1 x 4 Stroke 6 Cy. 150 x 180 220kW (299bhp)
VEB Elbe Werk-Rosslau
AuxGen: 2 x 28kW 400V 50Hz a.c
Fuel: 12.0 (d.f.)

8975031 **SISTER ACT** 409 Class: AB
ZGBD5 *ex* Sedation *-2010* *ex* New Century *-2008* 122
\- **Sister Act Yachting Ltd** -
Unique Yachting Monaco Sarl
George Town *Cayman Islands (British)*
MMSI: 319023600

1997-04 Heesen Shipyards B.V. — Oss Yd No: 9743
Loa 43.25 Br ex - Dght 2.760
Lbp 39.27 Br md 8.50 Dpth 3.68
Welded, 1 dk

(X11A2YP) Yacht
Hull Material: Aluminium Alloy
Passengers: cabins: 5; berths: 10

2 oil engines reverse reduction geared to sc. shafts driving 2 Propellers
Total Power: 4,406kW (5,990hp) 16.0kn
M.T.U. 16V396TB94
2 x Vee 4 Stroke 16 Cy. 165 x 185 each-2203kW (2995bhp)
MTU Friedrichshafen GmbH-Friedrichshafen
AuxGen: 2 x 80kW a.c

7367861 **SISTERS** 242
ZR5696 *ex* Five Sisters *-2006* *ex* Alma C *-2005* 73
\- *ex* Sola Gratia *-1991* *ex* Batavia *-1984* -
ex Eben Haezer *-1980*
Viking Inshore Fishing Pty Ltd
\-
Cape Town *South Africa*
Official number: 10601

1974-06 Scheepswerf Vooruit B.V. — Zaandam Yd No: 346
Loa 33.70 Br ex 7.55 Dght 3.798
Lbp - Br md 7.52 Dpth 4.70
Welded, 1 dk

(B11A2FT) Trawler

1 oil engine driving 1 FP propeller
Total Power: 912kW (1,240hp)
De Industrie 8D7HD
1 x 4 Stroke 8 Cy. 305 x 460 912kW (1240bhp)
"Welgelegen" Scheepswerf enMachinefabriek B.V.-Harlingen

8008412 **SISTRAUM** 1,881 Class: RS (NV)
UBUF2 *ex* Sydstraum *-2009* 885
\- **Skadar LLC** 2,550
\- T/cm
Kaliningrad *Russia* 8.5
MMSI: 273333130

1981-08 Bolsones Verft AS — Molde Yd No: 270
Loa 80.22 (BB) Br ex 13.20 Dght 5.187
Lbp 74.91 Br md 13.01 Dpth 7.37
Welded, 1 dk.

(A12B2TR) Chemical/Products Tanker
Double Hull (13F)
Liq: 2,562; Liq (Oil): 2,562
Cargo Heating Coils
Compartments: 1 Ta, 5 Ta (s.stl), 10 Wing Ta, ER, 2 Wing Slop Ta
14 Cargo Pump (s): 14x175m³/hr
Manifold: Bow/CM: 40m
Ice Capable

1 oil engine sr geared to sc. shaft driving 1 CP propeller
Total Power: 1,655kW (2,250hp) 12.8kn
Normo KVM-12
1 x Vee 4 Stroke 12 Cy. 250 x 300 1655kW (2250bhp)
AS Bergens Mek Verksteder-Norway
AuxGen: 1 x 160kW 380V 50Hz a.c, 3 x 132kW 380V 50Hz a.c
Thrusters: 1 Tunnel thruster (f)
Fuel: 34.0 (d.f.) (Part Heating Coils) 133.0 (r.f.) 7.0pd

7615361 **SISTRO** *526* Class: (BV) (GL)
ZR5420 *ex* Manuel Nores *-2009* 158
CTA 198 **Sistro Trawling Pty Ltd** 170
\-
SatCom: Inmarsat M 660100213
Cape Town *South Africa*
MMSI: 601087000
Official number: 19403

1978-01 Construcciones Navales Santodomingo SA — Vigo Yd No: 417
Lengthened-1981
Loa 49.00 Br ex - Dght 4.311
Lbp 39.65 Br md 8.51 Dpth 6.15
Welded, 2 dks

(B11A2FS) Stern Trawler

1 oil engine geared to sc. shaft driving 1 FP propeller
Total Power: 736kW (1,001hp) 12.0kn
Deutz SBA8M528
1 x 4 Stroke 8 Cy. 220 x 280 736kW (1001bhp)
Hijos de J Barreras SA-Spain
AuxGen: 2 x 488kW 380V a.c
Fuel: 242.0 (d.f.)

7359656 **SISU** 7,525
OHMW 2,258
\- **Arctia Icebreaking Oy** 9,815
\-
Helsinki *Finland*
MMSI: 230289000
Official number: 12301

1976-01 Oy Wartsila Ab — Helsinki Yd No: 403
Loa 104.60 Br ex 23.80 Dght 8.308
Lbp 95.81 Br md 22.51 Dpth 12.12
Welded

(B34C2SI) Icebreaker
Ice Capable

5 diesel electric oil engines driving 5 gen. Connecting to 4 elec. motors driving 2 CP propellers , 2 fwd
Total Power: 17,100kW (23,250hp) 18.5kn
Pielstick 12PC2-5V-400
5 x Vee 4 Stroke 12 Cy. 400 x 460 each-3420kW (4650bhp)
Oy Wartsila Ab-Finland
Fuel: 2032.0 (r.f.) 101.5pd

9581277 **SISUAQ** 3,912 Class: AB
WDG2721 *ex* Harvey Hauler *-2012* 1,173
\- **Harvey Hauler LLC** 5,450
Harvey Gulf International Marine LLC
Galliano, LA *United States of America*
MMSI: 367518570
Official number: 1230060

2012-04 Eastern Shipbuilding Group — Panama City, Fl Yd No: 162
Loa 89.00 Br ex - Dght 5.120
Lbp 85.37 Br md 19.50 Dpth 7.46
Welded, 1 dk

(B21A2OS) Platform Supply Ship

4 diesel electric oil engines driving 4 gen. each 1825kW a.c Connecting to 2 elec. motors each (2500kW) driving 2 Z propellers
Total Power: 7,300kW (9,924hp) 12.0kn
Cummins QSK60-M
4 x Vee 4 Stroke 16 Cy. 159 x 190 each-1825kW (2481bhp)
Cummins Engine Co Inc-USA
Thrusters: 2 Thwart. FP thruster (f)
Fuel: 710.0 (d.f.)

9266114 *VRMI3* -	**SITC BANGKOK** *ex* YM Earth *-2013* *ex* Ming Earth *-2004* **SITC Bangkok Shipping Co Ltd** SITC Ships Management Co Ltd *Hong Kong* *Hong Kong* MMSI: 477188700 Official number: HK-3882	**17,153** 7,533 22,078	Class: CC (NK)	**2003-07 Imabari Shipbuilding Co Ltd — Imabari EH (Imabari Shipyard)** Yd No: 582 Loa 171.99 (BB) Br ex - Dght 9.516 Lbp 160.00 Br md 27.60 Dpth 14.00 Welded, 1 dk	**(A33A2CC) Container Ship (Fully Cellular)** TEU 1620 incl 145 ref C.	**1 oil engine** driving 1 FP propeller Total Power: 15,785kW (21,461hp) 19.7kn B&W 7S60MC-C 1 x 2 Stroke 7 Cy. 600 x 2400 15785kW (21461bhp) Mitsui Engineering & Shipbuilding CLtd-Japan AuxGen: 3 x a.c Thrusters: 1 Tunnel thruster (f) Fuel: 2180.0
9610559 *VRLQY* -	**SITC BUSAN** **SITC Busan Shipping Co Ltd** SITC Ships Management Co Ltd *Hong Kong* *Hong Kong* MMSI: 477250600 Official number: HK-3741	**9,977** 4,606 13,009	Class: AB	**2013-02 Dae Sun Shipbuilding & Engineering Co Ltd — Busan** Yd No: 547 Loa 143.90 (BB) Br ex - Dght 8.200 Lbp 134.70 Br md 22.60 Dpth 11.20 Welded, 1 dk	**(A33A2CC) Container Ship (Fully Cellular)** TEU 1040 incl 160 ref C	**1 oil engine** driving 1 FP propeller Total Power: 8,280kW (11,257hp) 18.0kn MAN-B&W 6S46MC-C8 1 x 2 Stroke 6 Cy. 460 x 1932 8280kW (11257bhp) STX Engine Co Ltd-South Korea AuxGen: 3 x 730kW 445V a.c Thrusters: 1 Tunnel thruster (f) Fuel: 110.0 (d.f.) 730.0 (r.f.)
9639610 *VRLI2* -	**SITC DALIAN** **SITC Dalian Shipping Co Ltd** SITC Ships Management Co Ltd *Hong Kong* *Hong Kong* MMSI: 477444600 Official number: HK-3672	**9,734** 4,597 12,698	Class: GL	**2012-11 Yangfan Group Co Ltd — Zhoushan ZJ** Yd No: 2206 Loa 143.17 (BB) Br ex - Dght 8.300 Lbp 133.40 Br md 22.60 Dpth 11.30 Welded, 1 dk	**(A33A2CC) Container Ship (Fully Cellular)** TEU 1100 incl 120 ref C	**1 oil engine** driving 1 FP propeller Total Power: 8,730kW (11,869hp) 17.8kn Wartsila 6RT-flex48T 1 x 2 Stroke 6 Cy. 480 x 2000 8730kW (11869bhp) Qingdao Qiyao Wartsila MHI LinshanMarine Diesel Co Ltd (QMD)-China Thrusters: 1 Tunnel thruster (f)
9639660 *VRLG3* -	**SITC FANGCHENG** **SITC Fangcheng Shipping Co Ltd** SITC Ships Management Co Ltd *Hong Kong* *Hong Kong* MMSI: 477182500	**9,734** 4,597 12,697	Class: GL	**2012-10 Yangfan Group Co Ltd — Zhoushan ZJ** Yd No: 2221 Loa 143.17 (BB) Br ex - Dght 8.300 Lbp 133.38 Br md 22.60 Dpth 11.30 Welded, 1 dk	**(A33A2CC) Container Ship (Fully Cellular)** TEU 1100 incl 120 ref C	**1 oil engine** driving 1 FP propeller Total Power: 8,730kW (11,869hp) 17.8kn Wartsila 6RT-flex48T 1 x 2 Stroke 6 Cy. 480 x 2000 8730kW (11869bhp) Hudong Heavy Machinery Co Ltd-China Thrusters: 1 Tunnel thruster (f)
9261384 *VRJQ8* -	**SITC HAIPHONG** *ex* Chiangmai Bridge *-2011* **SITC Haiphong Shipping Co Ltd** SITC Shipping Management (Shanghai) Co Ltd *Hong Kong* *Hong Kong* MMSI: 477167800 Official number: HK-3322	**13,267** 7,391 18,053	Class: NK	**2002-01 Iwagi Zosen Co Ltd — Kamijima EH** Yd No: 201 Loa 161.85 (BB) Br ex - Dght 9.065 Lbp 150.00 Br md 25.60 Dpth 12.90 Welded, 1 dk	**(A33A2CC) Container Ship (Fully Cellular)** TEU 1032 incl 156 ref C. Compartments: 8 Cell Ho, ER ER 16 Wing Ha: 2 (12.6 x 5.6)14 (12.6 x 10.7)	**1 oil engine** driving 1 FP propeller Total Power: 11,440kW (15,554hp) 19.0kn B&W 8S50MC 1 x 2 Stroke 8 Cy. 500 x 1910 11440kW (15554bhp) Mitsui Engineering & Shipbuilding CLtd-Japan AuxGen: 4 x 687kW a.c Thrusters: 1 Tunnel thruster (f) Fuel: 1315.0
9253179 *VRLN2* -	**SITC HAKATA** *ex* Mactan Bridge *-2012* **SITC Hakata Shipping Co Ltd** SITC Shipping Management (Shanghai) Co Ltd *Hong Kong* *Hong Kong* MMSI: 477016900 Official number: HK-3712	**13,267** 7,391 18,069	Class: NK	**2001-08 Iwagi Zosen Co Ltd — Kamijima EH** Yd No: 200 Loa 161.85 (BB) Br ex - Dght 9.065 Lbp 150.00 Br md 25.60 Dpth 12.90 Welded, 1 dk	**(A33A2CC) Container Ship (Fully Cellular)** TEU 1098 incl 150 ref C. 8 Ha: (12.6 x 11.1)7 (12.6 x 21.5)	**1 oil engine** driving 1 FP propeller Total Power: 11,440kW (15,554hp) 18.5kn B&W 8S50MC 1 x 2 Stroke 8 Cy. 500 x 1910 11440kW (15554bhp) Mitsui Engineering & Shipbuilding CLtd-Japan AuxGen: 3 x a.c Thrusters: 1 Tunnel thruster (f) Fuel: 1315.0
9661091 *VRNC2* -	**SITC HENGSHAN** *ex* Chengyang Pioneer *-2014* *ex* Lan Hai Tong Qing *-2013* **SITC Hengshan Shipping Co Ltd** SITC Ships Management Co Ltd *Hong Kong* *Hong Kong* MMSI: 477407700 Official number: HK-3909	**41,612** 25,922 76,202	Class: CC	**2013-07 Yangfan Group Co Ltd — Zhoushan ZJ** Yd No: 2241 Loa 225.00 (BB) Br ex - Dght 14.200 Lbp 218.50 Br md 32.26 Dpth 19.60 Welded, 1 dk	**(A21A2BC) Bulk Carrier** Grain: 91,172 Compartments: 6 Ho, ER 7 Ha: 6 (15.5 x 14.4)ER (14.6 x 13.2)	**1 oil engine** driving 1 FP propeller Total Power: 8,753kW (11,901hp) 14.2kn MAN-B&W 5S60ME-C8 1 x 2 Stroke 5 Cy. 600 x 2400 8753kW (11901bhp) Hudong Heavy Machinery Co Ltd-China AuxGen: 3 x 605kW 450V a.c
9639608 *VRLI3* -	**SITC HOCHIMINH** **SITC Hochiminh Shipping Co Ltd** SITC Ships Management Co Ltd *Hong Kong* *Hong Kong* MMSI: 477203300	**9,734** 4,597 12,695	Class: GL	**2012-12 Yangfan Group Co Ltd — Zhoushan ZJ** Yd No: 2205 Loa 143.16 (BB) Br ex - Dght 8.300 Lbp 133.34 Br md 22.60 Dpth 11.30 Welded, 1 dk	**(A33A2CC) Container Ship (Fully Cellular)** TEU 1100 incl 120 ref C	**1 oil engine** driving 1 FP propeller Total Power: 8,730kW (11,869hp) 17.8kn Wartsila 6RT-flex48T 1 x 2 Stroke 6 Cy. 480 x 2000 8730kW (11869bhp) Qingdao Qiyao Wartsila MHI LinshanMarine Diesel Co Ltd (QMD)-China Thrusters: 1 Retract. directional thruster (f)
9331115 *3EKM7* -	**SITC HONGKONG** **SITC HongKong Shipping Enterprises Inc** SITC Ships Management Co Ltd *Panama* *Panama* MMSI: 372765000 Official number: 3310507A	**9,531** 5,657 12,621	Class: AB	**2007-06 Kyokuyo Shipyard Corp — Shimonoseki YC** Yd No: 470 Loa 144.83 (BB) Br ex - Dght 8.200 Lbp 134.00 Br md 22.40 Dpth 11.00 Welded, 1 dk	**(A33A2CC) Container Ship (Fully Cellular)** TEU 831 incl 120 ref C.	**1 oil engine** driving 1 FP propeller Total Power: 7,980kW (10,850hp) 17.3kn MAN-B&W 6L50MC 1 x 2 Stroke 6 Cy. 500 x 1620 7980kW (10850bhp) Hitachi Zosen Corp-Japan AuxGen: 3 x 560kW a.c Thrusters: 1 Tunnel thruster (f) Fuel: 106.2 (d.f.) 1049.5 (r.f.)
9642497 *VRLK4* -	**SITC HUANGSHAN** **SITC Huangshan Shipping Co Ltd** SITC Ships Management Co Ltd *Hong Kong* *Hong Kong* MMSI: 477017200 Official number: HK-3690	**41,684** 25,928 76,155	Class: AB	**2012-11 Yangfan Group Co Ltd — Zhoushan ZJ** Yd No: 2186 Loa 225.00 (BB) Br ex - Dght 14.200 Lbp 218.50 Br md 32.26 Dpth 19.60 Welded, 1 dk	**(A21A2BC) Bulk Carrier** Grain: 91,282 Compartments: 7 Ho, ER 7 Ha: ER	**1 oil engine** driving 1 FP propeller Total Power: 8,753kW (11,901hp) 14.2kn MAN-B&W 5S60MC-C 1 x 2 Stroke 5 Cy. 600 x 2400 8753kW (11901bhp) Hyundai Heavy Industries Co Ltd-South Korea AuxGen: 3 x 605kW a.c Fuel: 160.0 (d.f.) 2520.0 (r.f.)
9642485 *VRKJ5* -	**SITC HUASHAN** **SITC Huashan Shipping Co Ltd** SITC Steamships Co Ltd SatCom: Inmarsat C 447704219 *Hong Kong* *Hong Kong* MMSI: 477065100 Official number: HK-3471	**41,684** 25,928 76,249	Class: CC (AB)	**2012-05 Yangfan Group Co Ltd — Zhoushan ZJ** Yd No: 2185 Loa 225.00 (BB) Br ex - Dght 14.200 Lbp 218.50 Br md 32.26 Dpth 19.60 Welded, 1 dk	**(A21A2BC) Bulk Carrier** Grain: 91,171 Compartments: 7 Ho, ER 7 Ha: 6 (15.5 x 14.4)ER (14.6 x 13.2)	**1 oil engine** driving 1 FP propeller Total Power: 8,753kW (11,901hp) 14.2kn MAN-B&W 5S60MC-C 1 x 2 Stroke 5 Cy. 600 x 2400 8753kW (11901bhp) Hyundai Heavy Industries Co Ltd-South Korea AuxGen: 3 x 605kW 450V a.c
9258856 *VRIJ5* -	**SITC INCHON** *ex* Phuket Bridge *-2011* **SITC Inchon Shipping Co Ltd** SITC Ships Management Co Ltd *Hong Kong* *Hong Kong* MMSI: 477493600 Official number: HK-3061	**13,267** 7,391 18,061	Class: NK	**2001-11 Iwagi Zosen Co Ltd — Kamijima EH** Yd No: 202 Loa 161.85 (BB) Br ex - Dght 9.065 Lbp 150.00 Br md 25.60 Dpth 12.90 Welded, 1 dk	**(A33A2CC) Container Ship (Fully Cellular)** TEU 1098 incl 150 ref C. 16 Ha: 2 (12.6 x 5.6)14 (12.6 x 10.7)ER	**1 oil engine** driving 1 FP propeller Total Power: 11,440kW (15,554hp) 18.5kn MAN-B&W 8S50MC 1 x 2 Stroke 8 Cy. 500 x 1910 11440kW (15554bhp) Mitsui Engineering & Shipbuilding CLtd-Japan AuxGen: 4 x 687kW a.c Thrusters: 1 Tunnel thruster (f) Fuel: 1320.0
9266126 *VRML7* -	**SITC JAKARTA** *ex* YM People *-2013* *ex* Ming People *-2004* **SITC Jakarta Shipping Co Ltd** SITC Shipping Management (Shanghai) Co Ltd *Hong Kong* *Hong Kong* MMSI: 477652500	**17,153** 7,533 22,052	Class: CC (NK)	**2003-09 Imabari Shipbuilding Co Ltd — Imabari EH (Imabari Shipyard)** Yd No: 583 Loa 171.99 (BB) Br ex - Dght 9.516 Lbp 160.00 Br md 27.60 Dpth 14.00 Welded, 1 dk	**(A33A2CC) Container Ship (Fully Cellular)** TEU 1620 incl 145 ref C.	**1 oil engine** driving 1 FP propeller Total Power: 15,785kW (21,461hp) 19.7kn B&W 7S60MC-C 1 x 2 Stroke 7 Cy. 600 x 2400 15785kW (21461bhp) Mitsui Engineering & Shipbuilding CLtd-Japan AuxGen: 3 x a.c Thrusters: 1 Tunnel thruster (f) Fuel: 2180.0
9404510 *3EKK6* -	**SITC KAOHSIUNG** **SITC Kaohsiung Shipping Enterprises Inc** SITC Ships Management Co Ltd *Panama* *Panama* MMSI: 372748000 Official number: 3310207A	**9,280** 4,796 11,936	Class: NK	**2007-04 Nantong Yahua Shipbuilding Co Ltd — Nantong JS** (Hull) Yd No: 2006-12 **2007-04 Hangzhou Dongfeng Shipbuilding Co Ltd — Hangzhou ZJ** Yd No: 686 Loa 139.72 (BB) Br ex 23.05 Dght 8.115 Lbp 130.00 Br md 23.00 Dpth 11.00 Welded, 1 dk	**(A33A2CC) Container Ship (Fully Cellular)** TEU 915 TEU incl 100 ref C	**1 oil engine** driving 1 FP propeller Total Power: 7,980kW (10,850hp) 18.0kn MAN-B&W 6L50MC 1 x 2 Stroke 6 Cy. 500 x 1620 7980kW (10850bhp) Hitachi Zosen Corp-Japan AuxGen: 3 x 560kW a.c Thrusters: 1 Tunnel thruster (f) Fuel: 1233.0

9088902 *VRGF9* -	**SITC KEELUNG** *ex* Kapitan Byankin *-2009* **SITC Keelung Shipping Co Ltd** SITC Ships Management Co Ltd *Hong Kong* *Hong Kong* MMSI: 477682800 Official number: HK-2614	**9,530** 5,088 12,713 T/cm 26.6	Class: NK (GL)	**1994-11 Stocznia Szczecinska SA — Szczecin** Yd No: B183/217 Loa 149.60 (BB) Br ex - Dght 8.250 Lbp 140.10 Br md 22.30 Dpth 11.10 Welded, 1 dk	**(A33A2CC) Container Ship (Fully Cellular)** Grain: 16,624 TEU 1012 C Ho 334 TEU C Dk 678 TEU incl 90 ref C. 7 Ha: Ice Capable	**1 oil engine** driving 1 CP propeller Total Power: 6,930kW (9,422hp) 17.3kn B&W 6L50MC 1 x 2 Stroke 6 Cy. 500 x 1620 6930kW (9422bhp) H Cegielski Poznan SA-Poland AuxGen: 5 x 525kW 220/380V a.c Thrusters: 1 Thwart. FP thruster (f)
9293557 *H3PB* -	**SITC KOBE** **Xin Lian Shipping Enterprises Inc** SITC Ships Management Co Ltd *Panama* *Panama* MMSI: 353346000 Official number: 3001004B	**9,571** 5,531 12,645	Class: NK	**2004-03 Kyokuyo Shipyard Corp — Shimonoseki YC** Yd No: 451 Loa 144.83 (BB) Br ex - Dght 8.215 Lbp 134.00 Br md 22.40 Dpth 11.00 Welded, 1 dk	**(A33A2CC) Container Ship (Fully Cellular)** TEU 831 incl 150 ref C.	**1 oil engine** driving 1 FP propeller Total Power: 7,980kW (10,850hp) 17.3kn B&W 6L50MC 1 x 2 Stroke 6 Cy. 500 x 1620 7980kW (10850bhp) Hitachi Zosen Corp-Japan AuxGen: 3 x 560kW 440/220V 60Hz a.c Thrusters: 1 Tunnel thruster (f) Fuel: 1070.0
9610535 *VRJQ9* -	**SITC KWANGYANG** **SITC Kwangyang Shipping Co Ltd** SITC Container Lines Co Ltd *Hong Kong* *Hong Kong* MMSI: 477274900 Official number: HK-3323	**9,520** 4,820 12,868	Class: CC (KR)	**2012-01 Dae Sun Shipbuilding & Engineering Co Ltd — Busan** Yd No: 545 Loa 142.70 (BB) Br ex - Dght 8.214 Lbp 133.50 Br md 22.60 Dpth 11.20 Welded, 1 dk	**(A33A2CC) Container Ship (Fully Cellular)** Grain: 17,448; Bale: 17,448 TEU 953 C Ho 316 TEU C Dk 637 TEU Compartments: 5 Cell Ho, ER	**1 oil engine** driving 1 FP propeller Total Power: 7,860kW (10,686hp) 18.0kn MAN-B&W 6S46MC-C 1 x 2 Stroke 6 Cy. 460 x 1932 7860kW (10686bhp) STX Engine Co Ltd-South Korea AuxGen: 3 x 615kW 445V a.c Thrusters: 1 Tunnel thruster (f)
9266102 *VRMB7* -	**SITC LAEM CHABANG** *ex* YM Sky *-2013* *ex* Ming Sky *-2004* **SITC Laem Chabang Shipping Co Ltd** SITC Ships Management Co Ltd *Hong Kong* *Hong Kong* MMSI: 477631900 Official number: HK-3829	**17,153** 7,533 22,077	Class: NK	**2003-06 Imabari Shipbuilding Co Ltd — Imabari EH (Imabari Shipyard)** Yd No: 581 Loa 171.99 (BB) Br ex - Dght 9.516 Lbp 160.00 Br md 27.60 Dpth 14.00 Welded, 1 dk	**(A33A2CC) Container Ship (Fully Cellular)** TEU 1620 incl 145 ref C. 8 Ha: 7 (12.6 x 23.4)ER (12.6 x 13.2)	**1 oil engine** driving 1 FP propeller Total Power: 15,785kW (21,461hp) 19.7kn MAN-B&W 7S60MC-C 1 x 2 Stroke 7 Cy. 600 x 2400 15785kW (21461bhp) Mitsui Engineering & Shipbuilding CLtd-Japan AuxGen: 3 x a.c Thrusters: 1 Tunnel thruster (f) Fuel: 2180.0
9639634 *VRKS6* -	**SITC LIANYUNGANG** **SITC Lianyungang Shipping Co Ltd** SITC Ships Management Co Ltd *Hong Kong* *Hong Kong* MMSI: 477024800 Official number: HK-3545	**9,734** 4,660 12,715	Class: GL	**2012-07 Yangfan Group Co Ltd — Zhoushan ZJ** Yd No: 2218 Loa 143.14 (BB) Br ex - Dght 8.300 Lbp 133.38 Br md 22.60 Dpth 11.30 Welded, 1 dk	**(A33A2CC) Container Ship (Fully Cellular)** TEU 1100 incl 120 ref C	**1 oil engine** driving 1 FP propeller Total Power: 8,730kW (11,869hp) 17.8kn Wartsila 6RT-flex48T 1 x 2 Stroke 6 Cy. 480 x 2000 8730kW (11869bhp) Hudong Heavy Machinery Co Ltd-China Thrusters: 1 Tunnel thruster (f)
9642514 *VRMT9* -	**SITC LUSHAN** **SITC Huashan Shipping Co Ltd** SITC Ships Management Co Ltd *Hong Kong* *Hong Kong* MMSI: 477942900 Official number: HK-3976	**41,684** 25,928 76,132	Class: AB	**2013-11 Yangfan Group Co Ltd — Zhoushan ZJ** Yd No: 2188 Loa 225.00 (BB) Br ex - Dght 14.200 Lbp 218.50 Br md 32.26 Dpth 19.60 Welded, 1 dk	**(A21A2BC) Bulk Carrier** Grain: 91,171 Compartments: 7 Ho, ER 7 Ha: 6 (15.5 x 14.4)ER (14.6 x 13.2)	**1 oil engine** driving 1 FP propeller Total Power: 8,753kW (11,901hp) 14.2kn MAN-B&W 5S60MC-C 1 x 2 Stroke 5 Cy. 600 x 2400 8753kW (11901bhp) Hyundai Heavy Industries Co Ltd-South Korea AuxGen: 3 x 600kW a.c Fuel: 160.0 (d.f.) 2500.0 (r.f.)
9207572 *VRMT4* -	**SITC MANILA** *ex* Esm Silvana *-2013* *ex* Sitc Dalian *-2011* **SITC Manila Shipping Co Ltd** SITC Ships Management Co Ltd *Hong Kong* *Hong Kong* MMSI: 477942700 Official number: HK-3971	**9,413** 5,421 12,649	Class: AB	**2000-04 Kyokuyo Shipyard Corp — Shimonoseki YC** Yd No: 430 Loa 144.83 (BB) Br ex - Dght 8.200 Lbp 134.00 Br md 22.40 Dpth 11.00 Welded, 1 dk	**(A33A2CC) Container Ship (Fully Cellular)** TEU 787 C Ho 318 TEU C Dk 469 TEU incl 80 ref C Compartments: 7 Cell Ho, ER 7 Ha: ER	**1 oil engine** driving 1 FP propeller Total Power: 7,988kW (10,860hp) 17.3kn B&W 6L50MC 1 x 2 Stroke 6 Cy. 500 x 1620 7988kW (10860bhp) Hitachi Zosen Corp-Japan AuxGen: 2 x 560kW a.c, 1 x 440kW a.c Thrusters: 1 Thwart. FP thruster (f) Fuel: 1131.0 (r.f.)
9639593 *VRKS5* -	**SITC MOJI** **SITC Moji Shipping Co Ltd** SITC Ships Management Co Ltd *Hong Kong* *Hong Kong* MMSI: 477813700 Official number: HK-3544	**9,734** 4,660 12,737	Class: GL	**2012-07 Yangfan Group Co Ltd — Zhoushan ZJ** Yd No: 2204 Loa 143.18 (BB) Br ex - Dght 8.300 Lbp 133.40 Br md 22.60 Dpth 11.30 Welded, 1 dk	**(A33A2CC) Container Ship (Fully Cellular)** TEU 1100 incl 120 ref C	**1 oil engine** driving 1 FP propeller Total Power: 8,730kW (11,869hp) 17.8kn Wartsila 6RT-flex48T 1 x 2 Stroke 6 Cy. 480 x 2000 8730kW (11869bhp) Qingdao Zichai Boyang Diesel EngineCo Ltd-China Thrusters: 1 Tunnel thruster (f)
9308053 *3EGD6* -	**SITC NAGOYA** **SITC Nagoya Shipping Enterprises Inc** SITC Ships Management Co Ltd *Panama* *Panama* MMSI: 357368000 Official number: 3213506A	**9,531** 5,657 12,601	Class: AB	**2006-07 Kyokuyo Shipyard Corp — Shimonoseki YC** Yd No: 465 Loa 145.12 (BB) Br ex - Dght 8.200 Lbp 134.00 Br md 22.40 Dpth 11.00 Welded, 1 dk	**(A33A2CC) Container Ship (Fully Cellular)** TEU 907 C Ho 318 TEU C Dk 589 TEU incl 120 ref C	**1 oil engine** driving 1 FP propeller Total Power: 7,988kW (10,860hp) 17.3kn MAN-B&W 6L50MC 1 x 2 Stroke 6 Cy. 500 x 1620 7988kW (10860bhp) Hitachi Zosen Corp-Japan Thrusters: 1 Tunnel thruster (f)
9293569 *VRFF3* -	**SITC NINGBO** **Hai Lian Shipping Enterprises Inc** SITC Ships Management Co Ltd *Hong Kong* *Hong Kong* MMSI: 477218900 Official number: HK-2399	**9,571** 5,531 12,613	Class: NK	**2004-05 Kyokuyo Shipyard Corp — Shimonoseki YC** Yd No: 452 Loa 144.83 (BB) Br ex - Dght 8.215 Lbp 134.00 Br md 22.40 Dpth 11.00 Welded, 1 dk	**(A33A2CC) Container Ship (Fully Cellular)** TEU 831 incl 120 ref C.	**1 oil engine** driving 1 FP propeller Total Power: 7,980kW (10,850hp) 17.3kn B&W 6L50MC 1 x 2 Stroke 6 Cy. 500 x 1620 7980kW (10850bhp) Hitachi Zosen Corp-Japan AuxGen: 3 x 560kW 440/220V 60Hz a.c Thrusters: 1 Tunnel thruster (f) Fuel: 1070.0
9638329 *VRLD6* -	**SITC OSAKA** **SITC Osaka Shipping Co Ltd** SITC Ships Management Co Ltd *Hong Kong* *Hong Kong* MMSI: 477464800 Official number: HK-3636	**9,566** 4,527 11,913	Class: NK	**2012-09 Kyokuyo Shipyard Corp — Shimonoseki YC** Yd No: 505 Loa 141.03 (BB) Br ex - Dght 8.214 Lbp 133.00 Br md 22.50 Dpth 11.40 Welded, 1 dk	**(A33A2CC) Container Ship (Fully Cellular)** Grain: 17,000 TEU 1103 incl 120 ref C	**1 oil engine** driving 1 FP propeller Total Power: 8,280kW (11,257hp) 18.0kn MAN-B&W 6S46MC-C8 1 x 2 Stroke 6 Cy. 460 x 1932 8280kW (11257bhp) Hitachi Zosen Corp-Japan AuxGen: 3 x 600kW a.c Thrusters: 1 Thwart. CP thruster (f) Fuel: 910.0
9101792 *VRGG2* -	**SITC PYEONGTAEK** *ex* Yuriy Ostrovskiy *-2009* **SITC Pyeongtaek Shipping Co Ltd** SITC Ships Management Co Ltd *Hong Kong* *Hong Kong* MMSI: 477682900 Official number: HK-2615	**9,530** 5,088 12,708 T/cm 26.6	Class: NK (GL)	**1994-12 Stocznia Szczecinska SA — Szczecin** Yd No: B183/218 Loa 149.72 (BB) Br ex - Dght 8.255 Lbp 140.10 Br md 22.30 Dpth 11.10 Welded, 1 dk	**(A33A2CC) Container Ship (Fully Cellular)** TEU 1012 C Ho 334 TEU C Dk 678 TEU incl 90 ref C. 7 Ha: Ice Capable	**1 oil engine** driving 1 CP propeller Total Power: 6,930kW (9,422hp) 18.7kn B&W 6L50MC 1 x 2 Stroke 6 Cy. 500 x 1620 6930kW (9422bhp) H Cegielski Poznan SA-Poland AuxGen: 1 x 1000kW 220/380V a.c, 3 x 504kW 220/380V a.c, 1 x 116kW 220/380V a.c Thrusters: 1 Thwart. FP thruster (f)
9610547 *VRLI4* -	**SITC QINGDAO** **SITC Qingdao Shipping Co Ltd** SITC Ships Management Co Ltd *Hong Kong* *Hong Kong* MMSI: 477190600 Official number: HK-3674	**9,977** 4,606 12,998	Class: AB	**2012-11 Dae Sun Shipbuilding & Engineering Co Ltd — Busan** Yd No: 546 Loa 143.90 (BB) Br ex - Dght 8.200 Lbp 134.70 Br md 22.60 Dpth 11.20 Welded, 1 dk	**(A33A2CC) Container Ship (Fully Cellular)** TEU 1040 incl 160 ref C	**1 oil engine** driving 1 FP propeller Total Power: 8,280kW (11,257hp) 18.0kn MAN-B&W 6S46MC-C8 1 x 2 Stroke 6 Cy. 460 x 1932 8280kW (11257bhp) STX Engine Co Ltd-South Korea AuxGen: 3 x 730kW 445V a.c Thrusters: 1 Tunnel thruster (f) Fuel: 110.0 (d.f.) 730.0 (r.f.)
9258715 *HOHZ* -	**SITC SHANGHAI** **Sheng Lian Shipping Enterprises Inc** SITC Ships Management Co Ltd *Panama* *Panama* MMSI: 354936000 Official number: 2874202B	**9,413** 5,421 12,696	Class: AB	**2002-06 Kyokuyo Shipyard Corp — Shimonoseki YC** Yd No: 440 Loa 144.83 (BB) Br ex - Dght 8.200 Lbp 134.00 Br md 22.40 Dpth 11.00 Welded, 1 dk	**(A33A2CC) Container Ship (Fully Cellular)** TEU 847 incl 100 ref C.	**1 oil engine** driving 1 FP propeller Total Power: 7,988kW (10,860hp) 17.3kn B&W 6L50MC 1 x 2 Stroke 6 Cy. 500 x 1620 7988kW (10860bhp) Hitachi Zosen Corp-Japan Thrusters: 1 Tunnel thruster (f)
9639646 *VRKS7* -	**SITC SHENZHEN** **SITC Shenzhen Shipping Co Ltd** SITC Ships Management Co Ltd *Hong Kong* *Hong Kong* MMSI: 477024900 Official number: HK-3546	**9,734** 4,660 12,691	Class: GL	**2012-08 Yangfan Group Co Ltd — Zhoushan ZJ** Yd No: 2219 Loa 143.19 (BB) Br ex - Dght 8.300 Lbp 133.40 Br md 22.60 Dpth 11.30 Welded, 1 dk	**(A33A2CC) Container Ship (Fully Cellular)** TEU 1100 incl 120 ref C	**1 oil engine** driving 1 FP propeller Total Power: 8,730kW (11,869hp) 17.8kn Wartsila 6RT-flex48T 1 x 2 Stroke 6 Cy. 480 x 2000 8730kW (11869bhp) Hudong Heavy Machinery Co Ltd-China Thrusters: 1 Tunnel thruster (f)

9639658 *VRLG2* -	**SITC SHIMIZU** **SITC Shimizu Shipping Co Ltd** SITC Ships Management Co Ltd *Hong Kong* *Hong Kong* MMSI: 477335600 Official number: HK-3656	**9,734** 4,597 12,693	Class: GL	**2012-09 Yangfan Group Co Ltd — Zhoushan ZJ** Yd No: 2220 Loa 143.18 (BB) Br ex - Dght 8.300 Lbp 133.39 Br md 22.60 Dpth 11.30 Welded, 1 dk	**(A33A2CC) Container Ship (Fully Cellular)** TEU 1100 incl 120 ref C	**1 oil engine** driving 1 FP propeller Total Power: 8,730kW (11,869hp) 17.8kn Wartsila 6RT-flex48T 1 x 2 Stroke 6 Cy. 480 x 2000 8730kW (11869bhp) Hudong Heavy Machinery Co Ltd-China Thrusters: 1 Tunnel thruster (f)
9520780 *VRHJ7* -	**SITC TAISHAN** **SITC Taishan Shipping Co Ltd** SITC Steamships Co Ltd *Hong Kong* *Hong Kong* MMSI: 477925300 Official number: HK-2855	**32,315** 19,458 58,107 T/cm 57.4	Class: NK	**2010-09 Tsuneishi Group (Zhoushan) Shipbuilding Inc — Daishan County ZJ** Yd No: SS-085 Loa 189.99 (BB) Br ex - Dght 12.826 Lbp 185.60 Br md 32.26 Dpth 18.00 Welded, 1 dk	**(A21A2BC) Bulk Carrier** Grain: 72,689; Bale: 70,122 Compartments: 5 Ho, ER 5 Ha: ER Cranes: 4x30t	**1 oil engine** driving 1 FP propeller Total Power: 8,400kW (11,421hp) 14.5kn MAN-B&W 6S50MC-C 1 x 2 Stroke 6 Cy. 500 x 2000 8400kW (11421bhp) Mitsui Engineering & Shipbuilding CLtd-Japan Fuel: 2388.0 (r.f.)
9330575 *3EGN* -	**SITC TIANJIN** **SITC Tianjin Shipping Enterprises Inc** SITC Ships Management Co Ltd *Panama* *Panama* MMSI: 355898000 Official number: 3228807A	**9,531** 5,657 12,598	Class: AB	**2006-09 Kyokuyo Shipyard Corp — Shimonoseki YC** Yd No: 466 Loa 145.12 (BB) Br ex - Dght 8.200 Lbp 134.00 Br md 22.40 Dpth 11.00 Welded, 1 dk	**(A33A2CC) Container Ship (Fully Cellular)** TEU 907 C Ho 318 TEU C Dk 589 TEU incl 120 ref C	**1 oil engine** driving 1 FP propeller Total Power: 7,988kW (10,860hp) 17.4kn MAN-B&W 6L50MC 1 x 2 Stroke 6 Cy. 500 x 1620 7988kW (10860bhp) Hitachi Zosen Corp-Japan AuxGen: 3 x 560kW a.c Thrusters: 1 Tunnel thruster (f) Fuel: 106.2 (d.f.) 1049.5 (r.f.)
9258727 *HONH* -	**SITC TOKYO** **Ken Link Shipping Enterprises Inc** SITC Steamships Co Ltd *Panama* *Panama* MMSI: 355449000 Official number: 2888903B	**9,413** 5,421 12,694	Class: CC (AB)	**2002-09 Kyokuyo Shipyard Corp — Shimonoseki YC** Yd No: 441 Loa 144.83 (BB) Br ex - Dght 8.200 Lbp 134.00 Br md 22.40 Dpth 11.00 Welded, 1 dk	**(A33A2CC) Container Ship (Fully Cellular)** TEU 847 incl 100 ref C.	**1 oil engine** driving 1 FP propeller Total Power: 7,988kW (10,860hp) 17.3kn B&W 6L50MC 1 x 2 Stroke 6 Cy. 500 x 1620 7988kW (10860bhp) Hitachi Zosen Corp-Japan Thrusters: 1 Tunnel thruster (f)
9331127 *3ELU* -	**SITC XIAMEN** **SITC Xiamen Shipping Enterprises Inc** SITC Ships Management Co Ltd *Panama* *Panama* MMSI: 355090000 Official number: 3333807A	**9,531** 5,657 12,628	Class: AB	**2007-08 Kyokuyo Shipyard Corp — Shimonoseki YC** Yd No: 471 Loa 144.83 (BB) Br ex - Dght 8.200 Lbp 134.00 Br md 22.40 Dpth 11.00 Welded, 1 dk	**(A33A2CC) Container Ship (Fully Cellular)** TEU 831 incl 120 ref C.	**1 oil engine** driving 1 FP propeller Total Power: 7,980kW (10,850hp) 17.3kn MAN-B&W 6L50MC 1 x 2 Stroke 6 Cy. 500 x 1620 7980kW (10850bhp) Hitachi Zosen Corp-Japan AuxGen: 3 x 560kW a.c Thrusters: 1 Tunnel thruster (f) Fuel: 106.2 (d.f.) 1049.5 (r.f.)
9639622 *VRLI5* -	**SITC YANTAI** **SITC Yantai Shipping Co Ltd** SITC Ships Management Co Ltd *Hong Kong* *Hong Kong* MMSI: 477203700	**9,734** 4,597 12,691	Class: GL	**2012-12 Yangfan Group Co Ltd — Zhoushan ZJ** Yd No: 2207 Loa 143.17 (BB) Br ex - Dght 8.300 Lbp 133.37 Br md 22.60 Dpth 11.30 Welded, 1 dk	**(A33A2CC) Container Ship (Fully Cellular)** TEU 1100 incl 120 ref C	**1 oil engine** driving 1 FP propeller Total Power: 8,730kW (11,869hp) 17.8kn Wartsila 6RT-flex48T 1 x 2 Stroke 6 Cy. 480 x 2000 8730kW (11869bhp) Qingdao Qiyao Wartsila MHI LinshanMarine Diesel Co Ltd (QMD)-China Thrusters: 1 Tunnel thruster (f)
9638331 *VRLI6* -	**SITC YOKKAICHI** **SITC Yokkaichi Shipping Co Ltd** SITC Ships Management Co Ltd *Hong Kong* *Hong Kong* MMSI: 477190700 Official number: HK-3676	**9,566** 4,527 11,874	Class: NK	**2012-11 Kyokuyo Shipyard Corp — Shimonoseki YC** Yd No: 506 Loa 141.03 (BB) Br ex - Dght 8.214 Lbp 133.00 Br md 22.50 Dpth 11.40 Welded, 1 dk	**(A33A2CC) Container Ship (Fully Cellular)** Grain: 17,000 TEU 1103 incl 120 ref C	**1 oil engine** driving 1 FP propeller Total Power: 8,280kW (11,257hp) 18.0kn MAN-B&W 6S46MC-C8 1 x 2 Stroke 6 Cy. 460 x 1932 8280kW (11257bhp) Hitachi Zosen Corp-Japan AuxGen: 3 x 600kW a.c Thrusters: 1 Thwart. CP thruster (f) Fuel: 910.0
9308041 *H8YB* -	**SITC YOKOHAMA** **Jia Lian Shipping Enterprises Inc** SITC Ships Management Co Ltd *Panama* *Panama* MMSI: 356985000 Official number: 3038705BA	**9,549** 5,553 12,612	Class: AB	**2004-08 Kyokuyo Shipyard Corp — Shimonoseki YC** Yd No: 453 Loa 144.83 (BB) Br ex - Dght 8.200 Lbp 134.00 Br md 22.40 Dpth 11.00 Welded, 1 dk	**(A33A2CC) Container Ship (Fully Cellular)** TEU 831 incl 120 ref C.	**1 oil engine** driving 1 FP propeller Total Power: 7,988kW (10,860hp) 17.3kn B&W 6L50MC 1 x 2 Stroke 6 Cy. 500 x 1620 7988kW (10860bhp) Hitachi Zosen Corp-Japan AuxGen: 3 x 560kW 440/220V 60Hz a.c Thrusters: 1 Tunnel thruster (f)
9642502 *VRML9* -	**SITC ZHOUSHAN** **SITC Zhoushan Shipping Co Ltd** SITC Ships Management Co Ltd *Hong Kong* *Hong Kong* MMSI: 477652600 Official number: HK-3912	**41,614** 25,484 76,195	Class: AB	**2013-09 Yangfan Group Co Ltd — Zhoushan ZJ** Yd No: 2187 Loa 225.00 (BB) Br ex - Dght 14.200 Lbp 218.50 Br md 32.26 Dpth 19.60 Welded, 1 dk	**(A21A2BC) Bulk Carrier** Grain: 91,171 Compartments: 7 Ho, ER 7 Ha: 6 (15.5 x 14.4)ER (14.6 x 13.2)	**1 oil engine** driving 1 FP propeller Total Power: 8,753kW (11,901hp) 13.2kn MAN-B&W 5S60MC-C 1 x 2 Stroke 5 Cy. 600 x 2400 8753kW (11901bhp) Hyundai Heavy Industries Co Ltd-South Korea AuxGen: 3 x 605kW a.c Fuel: 165.0 (d.f.) 2525.0 (r.f.)
9326914 *9VFJ2* -	**SITEAM ADVENTURER** **Eitzen Chemical (Singapore) Pte Ltd** Thome Ship Management Pte Ltd *Singapore* *Singapore* MMSI: 565568000 Official number: 393408	**26,751** 14,137 46,099 T/cm 52.8	Class: LR ✠ **100A1** SS 11/2012 Double Hull oil and chemical tanker, Ship Type 2 SG 1.55t/m3, ESP **ShipRight** (SDA, FDA, CM) *IWS LI SPM (EP (A,B,G,N,O,P,R,S,Vc,Vp)) ✠ **LMC** **UMS** Eq.Ltr: M†; Cable: 632.5/73.0 U3 (a)	**2007-11 Brodotrogir dd - Shipyard Trogir — Trogir** Yd No: 316 Loa 182.90 (BB) Br ex 32.22 Dght 12.200 Lbp 176.00 Br md 32.20 Dpth 17.20 Welded, 1 dk	**(A12B2TR) Chemical/Products Tanker** Double Hull (13F) Liq: 51,396; Liq (Oil): 51,396 Compartments: 20 Wing Ta, 2 Wing Slop Ta, ER 20 Cargo Pump (s): 16x500m³/hr, 4x250m³/hr Manifold: Bow/CM: 94.4m	**1 oil engine** driving 1 FP propeller Total Power: 8,580kW (11,665hp) 14.5kn MAN-B&W 6S50MC 1 x 2 Stroke 6 Cy. 500 x 1910 8580kW (11665bhp) 'Uljanik' Strojogradnja dd-Croatia AuxGen: 3 x 1111kW 440V 60Hz a.c Boilers: e (ex.g.) 12.2kgf/cm² (12.0bar), WTAuxB (o.f.) 12.2kgf/cm² (12.0bar) Fuel: 104.0 (d.f.) 2086.0 (r.f.)
9111058 *V7OW7* -	**SITEAM ANJA** *ex* Team Anja *-2007* *ex* Simunye *-2005* *ex* Engen Simunye *-2000* **Eitzen Chemical (Singapore) Pte Ltd** Thome Ship Management Pte Ltd *Majuro* *Marshall Islands* MMSI: 538003176 Official number: 3176	**28,027** 12,320 44,651 T/cm 51.6	Class: LR ✠ **100A1** SS 02/2012 oil & chemical tanker (Double Hull), Ship Type 3 ESP LI **ShipRight** (SDA, FDA, CM) ✠ **LMC** **UMS IGS** Eq.Ltr: M†; Cable: 632.5/73.0 U3	**1997-02 Stocznia Szczecinska SA — Szczecin** Yd No: B573/2/1 Loa 182.97 (BB) Br ex 32.23 Dght 12.024 Lbp 171.90 Br md 32.20 Dpth 17.60 Welded, 1 dk	**(A12B2TR) Chemical/Products Tanker** Double Hull (13F) Liq: 49,324; Liq (Oil): 49,323 Compartments: 18 Wing Ta, 2 Wing Slop Ta, ER 18 Cargo Pump (s): 18x550m³/hr Manifold: Bow/CM: 92.1m	**1 oil engine** driving 1 FP propeller Total Power: 8,500kW (11,557hp) 14.5kn Sulzer 6RTA52U 1 x 2 Stroke 6 Cy. 520 x 1800 8500kW (11557bhp) H Cegielski Poznan SA-Poland AuxGen: 3 x 824kW 440V 60Hz a.c Boilers: AuxB (Comp) 8.2kgf/cm² (8.0bar), AuxB (o.f.) 8.2kgf/cm² (8.0bar) Thrusters: 1 Thwart. FP thruster (f) Fuel: 206.0 (d.f.) 1852.0 (r.f.) 34.0pd
9326938 *9VLG3* -	**SITEAM DISCOVERER** **Eitzen Chemical (Singapore) Pte Ltd** Thome Ship Management Pte Ltd *Singapore* *Singapore* MMSI: 565865000 Official number: 394140	**26,751** 14,159 46,043 T/cm 50.5	Class: LR ✠ **100A1** SS 09/2013 Double Hull oil and chemical tanker, Ship Type 2 SG 1.55 ESP **ShipRight** (SDA, FDA, CM) *IWS LI SPM (EP (A,B,G,N,O,P,R,S,Vc)) ✠ **LMC** **UMS IGS** Eq.Ltr: M†; Cable: 632.5/73.0 U3 (a)	**2008-09 Brodotrogir dd - Shipyard Trogir — Trogir** Yd No: 318 Loa 182.90 (BB) Br ex 32.22 Dght 12.216 Lbp 176.00 Br md 32.20 Dpth 17.20 Welded, 1 dk	**(A12B2TR) Chemical/Products Tanker** Double Hull (13F) Liq: 51,446; Liq (Oil): 51,446 Compartments: 20 Wing Ta, 2 Wing Slop Ta, ER 22 Cargo Pump (s): 16x500m³/hr, 6x205m³/hr Manifold: Bow/CM: 94.4m	**1 oil engine** driving 1 FP propeller Total Power: 8,200kW (11,149hp) 14.5kn MAN-B&W 6S50MC 1 x 2 Stroke 6 Cy. 500 x 1910 8200kW (11149bhp) 'Uljanik' Strojogradnja dd-Croatia AuxGen: 3 x 1111kW 440V 60Hz a.c Boilers: e (ex.g.) 12.2kgf/cm² (12.0bar), WTAuxB (o.f.) 12.2kgf/cm² (12.0bar) Fuel: 173.0 (d.f.) 2090.0 (r.f.)

9326902 **SITEAM EXPLORER** *S6AT9* - **Eitzen Chemical (Singapore) Pte Ltd** Thome Ship Management Pte Ltd SatCom: Inmarsat Mini-M 761115130 *Singapore* *Singapore* MMSI: 565389000 Official number: 392850	**26,751** 14,145 46,042 T/cm 51.5	Class: LR ✠**100A1** SS 07/2012 Double Hull oil and chemical tanker, Ship Type 2 ESP **ShipRight** (SDA, FDA, CM) SG 1.55 t/m3 *IWS LI SPM ✠**LMC** **UMS** Eq.Ltr: M†; Cable: 632.5/73.0 U3 (a)	**2007-07 Brodotrogir dd - Shipyard Trogir — Trogir** Yd No: 315 Loa 182.90 (BB) Br ex 32.22 Dght 12.216 Lbp 176.00 Br md 32.20 Dpth 17.20 Welded, 1 dk	**(A12B2TR) Chemical/Products Tanker** Double Hull (13F) Liq: 51,445; Liq (Oil): 51,329 Compartments: 18 Wing Ta, 2 Wing Slop Ta, ER 18 Cargo Pump (s): 16x500m^3/hr, 2x250m^3/hr Manifold: Bow/CM: 88.6m	**1 oil engine** driving 1 FP propeller Total Power: 8,580kW (11,665hp) 14.5kn MAN-B&W 6S50MC 1 x 2 Stroke 6 Cy. 500 x 1910 8580kW (11665bhp) 'Uljanik' Strojogradnja dd-Croatia AuxGen: 3 x 1111kW 440V 60Hz a.c Boilers: e (ex.g.) 12.5kgf/cm^2 (12.3bar), WTAuxB (o.f.) 12.5kgf/cm^2 (12.3bar) Fuel: 173.0 (d.f.) 2070.0 (r.f.)
9185487 **SITEAM JUPITER** *A8JA6* - *ex* Team Jupiter *-2008* **mt 'Team Jupiter' Schiffahrts GmbH & Co KG** Chemikalien Seetransport GmbH *Monrovia* *Liberia* MMSI: 636091062 Official number: 91062	**27,185** 14,085 48,330 T/cm 51.4	Class: AB (NV)	**2000-02 Sanoyas Hishino Meisho Corp — Kurashiki OY** Yd No: 1175 Loa 182.00 (BB) Br ex 32.23 Dght 12.672 Lbp 174.00 Br md 32.20 Dpth 17.80 Welded, 1 dk	**(A12B2TR) Chemical/Products Tanker** Double Hull (13F) Liq: 48,240; Liq (Oil): 48,240 Cargo Heating Coils Compartments: 18 Wing Ta, 3 Slop Ta, ER 21 Cargo Pump (s): 14x600m^3/hr, 6x300m^3/hr, 1x150m^3/hr Manifold: Bow/CM: 89m	**1 oil engine** driving 1 FP propeller Total Power: 7,465kW (10,149hp) 14.3kn Sulzer 6RTA48T 1 x 2 Stroke 6 Cy. 480 x 2000 7465kW (10149bhp) Diesel United Ltd.-Aioi AuxGen: 2 x 860kW 450V 60Hz a.c, 1 x 520kW 450V 60Hz a.c Thrusters: 1 Thwart. FP thruster (f) Fuel: 198.0 (d.f.) (Heating Coils) 1999.0 (r.f.)
9343194 **SITEAM LEADER** *9VNR2* - **Eitzen Chemical (Singapore) Pte Ltd** Eitzen Chemical A/S *Singapore* *Singapore* MMSI: 565917000 Official number: 394283	**26,751** 14,177 46,070 T/cm 52.7	Class: LR ✠**100A1** SS 03/2009 Double Hull oil and chemical tanker, Ship Type 2 SG 1.55t/m3 ESP **ShipRight** (SDA, FDA, CM) *IWS LI SPM EP (A,B,G,N,O,P,R,S,Vc) ✠**LMC** **UMS IGS** Eq.Ltr: M†; Cable: 632.5/73.0 U3 (a)	**2009-03 Brodotrogir dd - Shipyard Trogir — Trogir** Yd No: 319 Loa 182.90 (BB) Br ex 32.22 Dght 12.216 Lbp 176.00 Br md 32.20 Dpth 17.20 Welded, 1 dk	**(A12B2TR) Chemical/Products Tanker** Double Hull (13F) Liq: 51,445; Liq (Oil): 51,396 Compartments: 20 Wing Ta, 2 Wing Slop Ta, ER 22 Cargo Pump (s): 6x250m^3/hr, 16x500m^3/hr Manifold: Bow/CM: 89.5m	**1 oil engine** driving 1 FP propeller Total Power: 8,580kW (11,665hp) 14.5kn MAN-B&W 6S50MC 1 x 2 Stroke 6 Cy. 500 x 1910 8580kW (11665bhp) 'Uljanik' Strojogradnja dd-Croatia AuxGen: 3 x 1111kW 440V 60Hz a.c Boilers: e (ex.g.) 12.2kgf/cm^2 (12.0bar), WTAuxB (o.f.) 12.2kgf/cm^2 (12.0bar) Fuel: 150.0 (d.f.) 2086.0 (r.f.)
9185499 **SITEAM NEPTUN** *A8JC2* - *ex* Team Neptun *-2008* **mt 'Team Neptun' Schiffahrts GmbH & Co KG** Chemikalien Seetransport GmbH *Monrovia* *Liberia* MMSI: 636091067 Official number: 91067	**27,185** 14,085 48,309 T/cm 51.4	Class: AB (NV)	**2000-03 Sanoyas Hishino Meisho Corp — Kurashiki OY** Yd No: 1176 Loa 182.00 (BB) Br ex 32.23 Dght 12.672 Lbp 174.00 Br md 32.20 Dpth 17.80 Welded, 1 dk	**(A12B2TR) Chemical/Products Tanker** Double Hull (13F) Liq: 48,241; Liq (Oil): 48,241 Cargo Heating Coils Compartments: 18 Wing Ta, 3 Slop Ta, ER 18 Cargo Pump (s): 12x600m^3/hr, 6x300m^3/hr Manifold: Bow/CM: 89m	**1 oil engine** driving 1 FP propeller Total Power: 8,165kW (11,101hp) 14.3kn Sulzer 6RTA48T 1 x 2 Stroke 6 Cy. 480 x 2000 8165kW (11101bhp) Diesel United Ltd.-Aioi AuxGen: 2 x 860kW 450V 60Hz a.c, 1 x 520kW 450V 60Hz a.c Thrusters: 1 Thwart. FP thruster (f) Fuel: 198.0 (d.f.) (Heating Coils) 2088.0 (r.f.) 30.1pd
9326926 **SITEAM VOYAGER** *9VCN3* - **Eitzen Chemical (Singapore) Pte Ltd** Thome Ship Management Pte Ltd *Singapore* *Singapore* MMSI: 565812000 Official number: 393649	**26,751** 14,147 46,026 T/cm 51.5	Class: LR ✠**100A1** SS 04/2013 Double Hull oil and chemical tanker, Ship Type 2 SG 1.55t/m3 ESP **ShipRight** (SDA, FDA, CM) *IWS LI SPM (EP (A,B,G,N,O,P,R,S,Vc)) ✠**LMC** **UMS** Eq.Ltr: M†; Cable: 632.5/73.0 U3 (a)	**2008-04 Brodotrogir dd - Shipyard Trogir — Trogir** Yd No: 317 Loa 182.90 (BB) Br ex 32.22 Dght 12.200 Lbp 176.00 Br md 32.20 Dpth 17.20 Welded, 1 dk	**(A12B2TR) Chemical/Products Tanker** Double Hull (13F) Liq: 51,446; Liq (Oil): 51,446 Compartments: 20 Wing Ta, 2 Wing Slop Ta, ER 20 Cargo Pump (s): 16x500m^3/hr, 4x250m^3/hr Manifold: Bow/CM: 88.6m	**1 oil engine** driving 1 FP propeller Total Power: 8,200kW (11,149hp) 14.4kn MAN-B&W 6S50MC 1 x 2 Stroke 6 Cy. 500 x 1910 8200kW (11149bhp) 'Uljanik' Strojogradnja dd-Croatia AuxGen: 3 x 1111kW 440V 60Hz a.c Boilers: e (ex.g.) 12.2kgf/cm^2 (12.0bar), WTAuxB (o.f.) 12.2kgf/cm^2 (12.0bar) Fuel: 173.0 (d.f.) 2070.0 (r.f.)
8130851 **SITHONIA** *J8B4242* - *ex* Feluka I *-2009* *ex* Atrotos *-2000* *ex* Apollonia Nomad *-1995* *ex* Aditya Jyoti *-1993* *ex* Speco Baron *-1987* *ex* Lae *-1986* *launched as* Luise L *-1982* **Sithonia Maritime Shipping SA** Thalatta Shipping Management SA *Kingstown* *St Vincent & The Grenadines* MMSI: 377768000 Official number: 10715	**4,134** 2,369 6,607	Class: BV (NK) (IR)	**1982-09 Shinhama Dockyard Co. Ltd. — Anan** Yd No: 736 Loa 107.43 Br ex 16.44 Dght 6.862 Lbp 99.00 Br md 16.40 Dpth 8.40 Welded, 1 dk	**(A31A2GX) General Cargo Ship** Grain: 8,507; Bale: 8,009 Compartments: 2 Ho, ER 2 Ha: (27.3 x 10.0) (28.6 x 10.0)ER Derricks: 2x25t,2x15t	**1 oil engine** driving 1 FP propeller Total Power: 2,942kW (4,000hp) 12.0kn Hanshin 6EL44 1 x 4 Stroke 6 Cy. 440 x 880 2942kW (4000bhp) The Hanshin Diesel Works Ltd-Japan AuxGen: 3 x 165kW
9190937 **SITI HALIMAH** *3FKR8* - **Doman Shipping SA** Daiichi Chuo Marine Co Ltd (DC Marine) SatCom: Inmarsat B 335606810 *Panama* *Panama* MMSI: 356068000 Official number: 2573598C	**6,448** 3,114 8,746	Class: (NK)	**1998-05 Higaki Zosen K.K. — Imabari** Yd No: 492 Loa 100.33 Br ex - Dght 8.264 Lbp 93.50 Br md 19.60 Dpth 13.00 Welded, 1 dk	**(A31A2GX) General Cargo Ship** Grain: 14,755; Bale: 13,389 Compartments: 2 Ho, ER 2 Ha: (29.4 x 14.0) (19.6 x 14.0)ER Cranes: 3x25t	**1 oil engine** driving 1 FP propeller Total Power: 3,900kW (5,302hp) 13.0kn MAN-B&W 6L35MC 1 x 2 Stroke 6 Cy. 350 x 1050 3900kW (5302bhp) The Hanshin Diesel Works Ltd-Japan Fuel: 670.0
5330424 **SITKA** *A3CS4* - **Roslyndale Shipping Co Pty Ltd** Malcolm Burns Reid (Lord Howe Island Shipping Co) *Nuku'alofa* *Tonga*	*288* 138 400	Class: (BV)	**1963 H C Christensens Staalskibsvaerft af 1949 — Marstal** Yd No: 83 Loa 42.96 Br ex 7.62 Dght 2.836 Lbp 38.41 Br md 7.60 Dpth 3.10 Riveted\Welded, 1 dk	**(A31A2GX) General Cargo Ship** Grain: 561; Bale: 530 Compartments: 1 Ho, ER 1 Ha: (19.2 x 5.0)ER Derricks: 2x2t; Winches: 2 Ice Capable	**1 oil engine** driving 1 FP propeller Total Power: 313kW (426hp) 9.0kn Alpha 405-24VO 1 x 2 Stroke 5 Cy. 240 x 400 313kW (426bhp) Alpha Diesel A/S-Denmark Fuel: 15.5 (d.f.)
7308798 **SITKIN ISLAND** *WAP8870* - *ex* Kona *-1990* *ex* Shishaldin *-1977* *ex* Sentinel (AMCU-39) *-1960* *ex* LSI (L)-1052 *-1952* **Sitkin Island Inc** - *Seattle, WA* *United States of America* Official number: 289317	*369* 288 -		**1944-03 Defoe Shipbuilding Co. — Bay City, Mi** Yd No: 305 Loa 46.46 Br ex 7.12 Dght 3.460 Lbp - Br md - Dpth 3.46 Welded, 1 dk	**(B11B2FV) Fishing Vessel**	**2 oil engines** driving 2 FP propellers Total Power: 1,324kW (1,800hp) Cooper Bessemer 2 x 4 Stroke each-662kW (900bhp) Cooper Bessemer Corp-USA
8228763 **SITNIKOVO** - - *ex* Susanino *-1952* **FRL JSC (A/O 'FRL')** -	**448** 134 207	Class: (RS)	**1984-10 Zavod 'Nikolayevsk-na-Amure' — Nikolayevsk-na-Amure** Yd No: 1228 Loa 44.88 Br ex 9.47 Dght 3.770 Lbp 39.37 Br md - Dpth 5.10 Welded, 1 dk	**(B11B2FV) Fishing Vessel** Ice Capable	**1 oil engine** driving 1 FP propeller Total Power: 589kW (801hp) 11.5kn S.K.L. 6NVD48A-2U 1 x 4 Stroke 6 Cy. 320 x 480 589kW (801bhp) VEB Schwermaschinenbau "KarlLiebknecht" (SKL)-Magdeburg AuxGen: 3 x 150kW Fuel: 105.0 (d.f.)
8201545 **SITRA** *5ALD* - *ex* Satra *-2010* *ex* Sitra *-2010* *ex* Mersey V *-2008* *ex* Mersey Venture *-2007* **Amwaaj Elkhair Oil Services Co** - *Tripoli* *Libya* MMSI: 642167060	**2,647** 794 3,166	Class: (LR) ✠ Classed LR until 18/8/11	**1983-05 Appledore Shipbuilders Ltd — Bideford** Yd No: A.S.136 Loa 82.40 Br ex 16.41 Dght 5.201 Lbp 76.99 Br md 16.01 Dpth 6.51 Welded, 1 dk	**(B33B2DT) Trailing Suction Hopper Dredger** Hopper: 2,200 Compartments: 1 Ho, ER	**2 oil engines** with clutches, flexible couplings & sr reverse geared to sc. shafts driving 2 FP propellers Total Power: 3,090kW (4,202hp) Ruston 6ATCM 2 x 4 Stroke 6 Cy. 318 x 368 each-1545kW (2101bhp) Ruston Diesels Ltd.-Newton-le-Willows AuxGen: 3 x 168kW 415V 50Hz a.c Thrusters: 1 Thwart. FP thruster (f) Fuel: 156.5 (d.f.)
7720867 **SITTWE** *XYNM* - *ex* Sit Tway *-1989* **Myanma Five Star Line** - *Yangon* *Myanmar* MMSI: 506070000	**7,783** 5,092 11,660	Class: (LR) (GL) Classed LR until 5/11/09	**1980-06 Flensburger Schiffbau-Ges. mbH — Flensburg** Yd No: 651 Loa 133.81 (BB) Br ex 21.04 Dght 8.270 Lbp 124.01 Br md 21.01 Dpth 11.03 Welded, 2 dks	**(A31A2GX) General Cargo Ship** Grain: 16,300; Bale: 14,985 TEU 400 C Ho 224 TEU C Dk 176 TEU incl 24 ref C. Compartments: 3 Ho, ER, 3 Tw Dk 3 Ha: (19.2 x 10.5)2 (25.6 x 15.4)ER Derricks: 2x50t,3x24t; Winches: 5	**1 oil engine** reduction geared to sc. shaft driving 1 FP propeller Total Power: 3,972kW (5,400hp) 15.0kn MaK 8MU551AK 1 x 4 Stroke 8 Cy. 450 x 550 3972kW (5400bhp) Krupp MaK Maschinenbau GmbH-Kiel AuxGen: 3 x 320kW 440V 50Hz a.c Fuel: 96.5 (d.f.) 770.0 (r.f.) 20.5pd

6505325 *5NMN* -	**SITULA** *ex* Neptun *-1968* **Upstream Shipping Ltd** - *Nigeria*	**1,049** 573 2,000 T/cm 6.6	Class: (LR) ✠ Classed LR until 8/9/08	**1965-03 Rolandwerft GmbH — Bremen** Yd No: 923 Lengthened-1992 Loa 69.80 Br ex 10.44 Dght 3.760 Lbp 64.00 Br md 10.42 Dpth 6.01 Welded, 1 dk	**(A12B2TR) Chemical/Products Tanker** Double Hull (13F) Liq: 1,441; Liq (Oil): 1,441 Cargo Heating Coils Compartments: 10 Ta, 1 Slop Ta, ER 2 Cargo Pump (s) Ice Capable	**1 oil engine** driving 1 FP propeller Total Power: 662kW (900hp) 11.5kn Deutz RBV6M545 1 x 4 Stroke 6 Cy. 320 x 450 662kW (900bhp) Kloeckner Humboldt Deutz AG-West Germany AuxGen: 1 x 89kW 380V 50Hz a.c, 1 x 48kW 380V 50Hz a.c Boilers: AuxB 10.4kgf/cm^2 (10.2bar) Fuel: 43.0 5.0pd
9519523 *V7FE6* -	**SIVA CORAL** **ICON Siva Coral LLC** Siva Shipping Oslo AS *Majuro* *Marshall Islands* MMSI: 538005586 Official number: 5586	**5,296** 1,995 6,022 T/cm 17.6	Class: NK	**2010-08 Kyokuyo Shipyard Corp — Shimonoseki YC** Yd No: 496 Loa 117.02 (BB) Br ex 18.23 Dght 6.814 Lbp 110.00 Br md 18.20 Dpth 8.90 Welded, 1 dk	**(A11B2TG) LPG Tanker** Double Sides Entire Compartment Length Liq (Gas): 7,210 2 x Gas Tank (s); 2 independent cyl horizontal 2 Cargo Pump (s): 2x400m^3/hr Manifold: Bow/CM: 54.4m	**1 oil engine** driving 1 FP propeller Total Power: 3,900kW (5,302hp) 14.8kn MAN-B&W 6L35MC 1 x 2 Stroke 6 Cy. 350 x 1050 3900kW (5302bhp) Makita Corp-Japan AuxGen: 2 x 350kW a.c Thrusters: 1 Tunnel thruster (f) Fuel: 75.0 (d.f.) 517.0 (r.f.)
9573933 *3FLJ9* -	**SIVA EMERALD** **Wealth Line Inc** Fukujin Kisen KK (Fukujin Kisen Co Ltd) SatCom: Inmarsat C 435688011 *Panama* *Panama* MMSI: 356880000 Official number: 4209710	**17,025** 10,108 28,193 T/cm 39.7	Class: NK	**2010-09 Imabari Shipbuilding Co Ltd — Imabari EH (Imabari Shipyard)** Yd No: 730 Loa 169.37 (BB) Br ex - Dght 9.819 Lbp 160.40 Br md 27.20 Dpth 13.60 Welded, 1 dk	**(A21A2BC) Bulk Carrier** Grain: 37,320; Bale: 35,742 Compartments: 5 Ho, ER 5 Ha: ER Cranes: 4x30.5t	**1 oil engine** driving 1 FP propeller Total Power: 5,850kW (7,954hp) 14.0kn MAN-B&W 6S42MC 1 x 2 Stroke 6 Cy. 420 x 1764 5850kW (7954bhp) Makita Corp-Japan Fuel: 1538.0 (r.f.)
9519535 *9V8979* -	**SIVA PEARL** **Ocean Pearl Group SA** Siva Shipping Oslo AS *Singapore* *Singapore* MMSI: 564507000 Official number: 396469	**5,296** 1,995 6,028 T/cm 17.6	Class: NK	**2010-09 Kyokuyo Shipyard Corp — Shimonoseki YC** Yd No: 497 Loa 117.02 (BB) Br ex 18.23 Dght 6.814 Lbp 110.00 Br md 18.20 Dpth 8.90 Welded, 1 dk	**(A11B2TG) LPG Tanker** Double Sides Entire Compartment Length Liq (Gas): 7,211 2 x Gas Tank (s); 2 independent (stl) cyl horizontal 2 Cargo Pump (s): 2x400m^3/hr Manifold: Bow/CM: 54.4m	**1 oil engine** driving 1 FP propeller Total Power: 3,900kW (5,302hp) 14.8kn MAN-B&W 6L35MC 1 x 2 Stroke 6 Cy. 350 x 1050 3900kW (5302bhp) Makita Corp-Japan AuxGen: 2 x 400kW 440V 60Hz a.c Thrusters: 1 Tunnel thruster (f) Fuel: 74.0 (d.f.) 517.0 (r.f.)
9485863 *3EYW9* -	**SIVA ROTTERDAM** **Latin King SA** Nordic Tankers A/S SatCom: Inmarsat C 437347410 *Panama* *Panama* MMSI: 373474000 Official number: 4396112	**11,640** 6,126 19,995 T/cm 28.8	Class: NK	**2012-06 Usuki Shipyard Co Ltd — Usuki OT** Yd No: 1731 Loa 145.53 (BB) Br ex 23.73 Dght 9.715 Lbp 137.00 Br md 23.70 Dpth 13.35 Welded, 1 dk	**(A12B2TR) Chemical/Products Tanker** Double Hull (13F) Liq: 20,847; Liq (Oil): 20,847 Cargo Heating Coils Compartments: 9 Wing Ta, 9 Wing Ta, 1 Wing Slop Ta, 1 Wing Slop Ta, ER 18 Cargo Pump (s): 18x200m^3/hr Manifold: Bow/CM: 75m	**1 oil engine** driving 1 FP propeller Total Power: 6,150kW (8,362hp) 14.5kn MAN-B&W 6S42MC 1 x 2 Stroke 6 Cy. 420 x 1764 6150kW (8362bhp) Hitachi Zosen Corp-Japan AuxGen: 3 x 500kW 450V 60Hz a.c Thrusters: 1 Tunnel thruster (f) Fuel: 81.5 (d.f.) 1029.9 (r.f.)
9098270 *WDA4629* -	**SIVAIMOANA** **Tuna Ventures Inc** - *Pago Pago, AS* *United States of America* Official number: 1107782	*108* 86 -		**1985-01** L reg 21.33 Br ex - Dght - Lbp - Br md 6.40 Dpth 3.35 Bonded, 1 dk	**(B11B2FV) Fishing Vessel** Hull Material: Reinforced Plastic	**1 oil engine** driving 1 Propeller
9673587 *UHEF* -	**SIVER** **OOO 'Port Vysotskiy'** - *St Petersburg* *Russia* MMSI: 273335380 Official number: 12046	**294** 88 124	Class: LR RS ✠ **100A1** SS 06/2013 escort tug Ice Class 1A FS Max/min draughts fwd 4.6/2.8m Max/min draughts aft 5.2/4.0m Power required 2800kw, power installed 3132kw **LMC** **UMS** Eq.Ltr: H; Cable: 275.0/19.0 U2 (a)	**2013-06 Song Cam Shipyard — Haiphong** (Hull) Yd No: (512312) **2013-06 B.V. Scheepswerf Damen — Gorinchem** Yd No: 512312 Loa 28.67 Br ex 10.43 Dght 3.000 Lbp 23.67 Br md 9.80 Dpth 4.60 Welded, 1 dk	**(B32A2ST) Tug** Ice Capable	**2 oil engines** gearing integral to driving 2 Directional propellers Total Power: 3,132kW (4,258hp) 13.5kn Caterpillar 3516C 2 x Vee 4 Stroke 16 Cy. 170 x 215 each-1566kW (2129bhp) Caterpillar Inc-USA AuxGen: 2 x 86kW 400V 50Hz a.c
7901942 *UADJ* -	**SIVIND** *ex* Seawind *-1998* *ex* Imco 3 *-1987* **Feniks JSC (A/O 'Feniks')** - *Petropavlovsk-Kamchatskiy* *Russia* MMSI: 273840810 Official number: 793980	**889** 267 1,200	Class: RS (AB)	**1979-08 Halter Marine, Inc. — Lockport, La** Yd No: 817 Converted From: Offshore Supply Ship-1987 Loa 49.13 Br ex 11.59 Dght 3.360 Lbp 47.33 Br md 11.57 Dpth 3.97 Welded, 1 dk	**(B11B2FV) Fishing Vessel**	**2 oil engines** reverse reduction geared to sc. shafts driving 2 FP propellers Total Power: 1,250kW (1,700hp) 12.0kn Caterpillar D398SCAC 2 x Vee 4 Stroke 12 Cy. 159 x 203 each-625kW (850bhp) Caterpillar Tractor Co-USA AuxGen: 2 x 150kW Thrusters: 1 Thwart. FP thruster (f) Fuel: 224.0 (d.f.)
9541289 *V7VU8* -	**SIVIU** *ex* Samho Crystal *-2011* **White Flag Ventures I LLC** Trafigura Beheer BV *Majuro* *Marshall Islands* MMSI: 538004219 Official number: 4219	**11,290** 5,263 17,567 T/cm 28.7	Class: BV (KR)	**2009-08 Samho Shipbuilding Co Ltd — Tongyeong** Yd No: 1111 Loa 144.00 (BB) Br ex - Dght 9.210 Lbp 136.00 Br md 22.60 Dpth 12.50 Welded, 1 dk	**(A12B2TR) Chemical/Products Tanker** Double Hull (13F) Liq: 18,623; Liq (Oil): 18,623 Cargo Heating Coils Compartments: 14 Wing Ta, 2 Wing Slop Ta, ER 14 Cargo Pump (s): 14x300m^3/hr Manifold: Bow/CM: 72.3m	**1 oil engine** driving 1 FP propeller Total Power: 5,349kW (7,273hp) 15.0kn MAN-B&W 8S35MC 1 x 2 Stroke 8 Cy. 350 x 1400 5349kW (7273bhp) STX Engine Co Ltd-South Korea AuxGen: 4 x 750kW 450V a.c Thrusters: 1 Tunnel thruster (f) Fuel: 100.0 (d.f.) 835.0 (r.f.)
9363039 *9HLV9* -	**SIVOTA** **Elva Shipping Inc** TMS Dry Ltd SatCom: Inmarsat C 424915310 *Valletta* *Malta* MMSI: 249153000 Official number: 9363039	**91,407** 57,770 177,804 T/cm 120.6	Class: BV	**2008-06 Shanghai Waigaoqiao Shipbuilding Co Ltd — Shanghai** Yd No: 1062 Loa 291.95 (BB) Br ex 45.05 Dght 18.300 Lbp 278.20 Br md 45.00 Dpth 24.80 Welded, 1 dk	**(A21A2BC) Bulk Carrier** Grain: 194,000; Bale: 183,425 Compartments: 9 Ho, ER 9 Ha: 7 (15.5 x 20.0)ER 2 (15.5 x 16.5)	**1 oil engine** driving 1 FP propeller Total Power: 16,860kW (22,923hp) 14.0kn MAN-B&W 6S70MC 1 x 2 Stroke 6 Cy. 700 x 2674 16860kW (22923bhp) Dalian Marine Diesel Works-China AuxGen: 3 x 900kW a.c
7723027 *UBMG8* -	**SIVUCH** *ex* Nord *-2010* *ex* King *-2006* *ex* Yang Xho *-2005* *ex* Vasu *-2002* *ex* Shota Maru *-1988* **STK Co Ltd (Kompaniy STK)** - *Nevelsk* *Russia* MMSI: 273356010	**1,077** 351 1,070	Class: RS (NK)	**1978-01 Wakamatsu Zosen K.K. — Kitakyushu** Yd No: 280 Loa 68.35 Br ex 11.03 Dght 3.796 Lbp 64.00 Br md 11.00 Dpth 4.10 Welded, 2 dks	**(A34A2GR) Refrigerated Cargo Ship** Grain: 1,525; Bale: 1,293; Ins: 1,293 4 Ha: 4 (3.3 x 3.3)ER Derricks: 2x2t	**1 oil engine** driving 1 FP propeller Total Power: 1,324kW (1,800hp) 12.0kn Akasaka AH33 1 x 4 Stroke 6 Cy. 330 x 500 1324kW (1800bhp) Akasaka Tekkosho KK (Akasaka DieselLtd)-Japan AuxGen: 3 x 432kW
8928234 - -	**SIVUCH** *ex* Reydovyy *-2005* - -	**179** 53 46	Class: (RS)	**1977-01 Gorokhovetskiy Sudostroitelnyy Zavod — Gorokhovets** Yd No: 359 Loa 29.30 Br ex 8.49 Dght 3.090 Lbp 27.00 Br md 8.30 Dpth 4.34 Welded, 1 dk	**(B32A2ST) Tug** Ice Capable	**2 oil engines** driving 2 CP propellers Total Power: 882kW (1,200hp) 11.4kn Russkiy 6D30/50-4-3 2 x 2 Stroke 6 Cy. 300 x 500 each-441kW (600bhp) Mashinostroitelnyy Zavod"Russkiy-Dizel"-Leningrad AuxGen: 2 x 30kW a.c Fuel: 42.0 (d.f.)
7919913 - -	**SIWALEE 2** *ex* Faifah Khanom No. 1 *-2000* **Laem Chabang Marine Oil & Supply Ltd** - *Bangkok* *Thailand* Official number: 231113642	*694* 320 1,065 T/cm 5.4	Class: (NK)	**1980-07 Uchida Zosen — Ise** Yd No: 803 Loa 55.81 Br ex 10.04 Dght 4.012 Lbp 52.00 Br md 10.00 Dpth 4.60 Welded, 1 dk	**(A13B2TU) Tanker (unspecified)** Single Hull Liq: 1,109; Liq (Oil): 1,109 Cargo Heating Coils	**1 oil engine** sr geared to sc. shaft driving 1 FP propeller Total Power: 883kW (1,201hp) 11.0kn Daihatsu 6PSHTCM-26D 1 x 4 Stroke 6 Cy. 260 x 320 883kW (1201bhp) Daihatsu Diesel Manufacturing Co Lt-Japan AuxGen: 2 x 72kW
1003138 *2BFC4* -	**SIX PLUS TWO** *ex* Fivea *-2010* *ex* Magistral *-2006* *ex* Orejona *-2003* **Globebay Ltd** - *London* *United Kingdom* MMSI: 235065596 Official number: 911204	**147** 44 -	Class: BV (LR) Classed LR until 8/3/00	**1972 Cammenga Jachtbouw B.V. — Wormerveer** Loa 35.97 Br ex 8.00 Dght 3.600 Lbp 26.11 Br md - Dpth 4.65 Welded, 1 dk	**(X11A2YS) Yacht (Sailing)**	**1 oil engine** driving 1 FP propeller Total Power: 442kW (601hp) 11.0kn MAN 1 x 4 Stroke 442kW (601bhp) MAN B&W Diesel AG-Augsburg

6725509 *DTBA6* -	**SIX STAR** *ex* Akebono Maru No. 18 *-1989* **Seokyung Corp** - *Busan* *South Korea* MMSI: 440284000 Official number: 0107001-6260007	**713** 168 431	Class: KR	**1967 Narasaki Zosen KK — Muroran HK** Yd No: 611 Loa 52.48 Br ex 9.53 Dght 3.905 Lbp 47.48 Br md 9.50 Dpth 4.09 Welded, 1 dk	**(B11A2FT) Trawler**	**1 oil engine** driving 1 FP propeller Total Power: 1,177kW (1,600hp) 11.0kn Akasaka UZ6SS 1 x 4 Stroke 6 Cy. 420 x 600 1177kW (1600bhp) Akasaka Tekkosho KK (Akasaka DieselLtd)-Japan AuxGen: 2 x 320kW 445V a.c
9551557 *HP3355* -	**SIXAOLA** *ex* Cheoy Lee 4989 *-2010* **Panama Canal Authority** - *Balboa* *Panama* Official number: 4324711	**359** 107 134	Class: (LR) ✠ Classed LR until 2/3/12	**2010-12 Hin Lee (Zhuhai) Shipyard Co Ltd — Zhuhai GD** (Hull) Yd No: 201 **2010-12 Cheoy Lee Shipyards Ltd — Hong Kong** Yd No: 4989 Loa 27.40 Br ex - Dght 3.740 Lbp 25.20 Br md 12.20 Dpth 5.05 Welded, 1 dk	**(B32A2ST) Tug**	**2 oil engines** gearing integral to driving 2 Z propellers Total Power: 3,924kW (5,336hp) GE Marine 12V228 2 x Vee 4 Stroke 12 Cy. 229 x 267 each-1962kW (2668bhp) General Electric Co.-Lynn, Ma AuxGen: 2 x 103kW 208V 60Hz a.c Fuel: 110.0 (d.f.)
9442108 *3FFB2* -	**SIYA** *ex* Hiltrup *-2013* *ex* Maritza *-2010* *ex* Ning Da 28 *-2008* **Siya Shipping & Trading Corp** Akar Deniz Tasimaciligi ve Ticaret AS *Panama* *Panama* MMSI: 357434000 Official number: 4457113A	**7,180** 3,728 10,475	Class: BV (RI) (CC)	**2007-09 Ningbo Dongfang Shipyard Co Ltd — Ningbo ZJ** Yd No: C05-002 Loa 131.55 Br ex - Dght 6.870 Lbp 122.00 Br md 18.80 Dpth 9.40 Welded, 1 dk	**(A31A2GX) General Cargo Ship** TEU 529 Ice Capable	**1 oil engine** reduction geared to sc. shaft driving 1 FP propeller Total Power: 3,824kW (5,199hp) 13.5kn Pielstick 8PC2-5L 1 x 4 Stroke 8 Cy. 400 x 460 3824kW (5199bhp) Shaanxi Diesel Heavy Industry Co Lt-China
9653056 *TCVS9* -	**SIYA** - **Siya Denizcilik Ticaret** Elit Denizcilik Sanayi ve Ticaret Ltd Sti *Istanbul* *Turkey* MMSI: 271043404 Official number: TUGS2213	**1,224** - -	Class: KR (Class contemplated)	**2013-03 in Turkey** (Hull) Yd No: 125 **2013-03 Hidrodinamik Gemi Sanayi ve Ticaret A.S. — Tuzla, Istanbul** Yd No: 33 Loa 80.00 Br ex - Dght 3.500 Lbp 72.87 Br md 16.10 Dpth 3.50 Welded, 1 dk	**(A36A2PR) Passenger/Ro-Ro Ship (Vehicles)**	**2 oil engines** reduction geared to sc. shafts driving 2 Propellers Total Power: 1,616kW (2,198hp) 11.4kn Baudouin 12M26.2P2 2 x Vee 4 Stroke 12 Cy. 150 x 150 each-808kW (1099bhp) Societe des Moteurs Baudouin SA-France
7727243 *D6FB3* -	**SIYABULELA** *ex* Neptune Sea *-2012* *ex* Shamrock Belle *-2005* *ex* Seabulk Isabelle *-2001* *ex* Ocean Knight *-1998* *ex* Imsalv Lynx *-1995* *ex* Miss Safa *-1987* **Nareser-KCSL Cameroon Ltd** - *Moroni* *Union of Comoros* Official number: 1200917	**261** 78 200	Class: BV (Class contemplated) (AB)	**1978-05 Sing Koon Seng Pte Ltd — Singapore** Yd No: SKS437 Loa 29.37 Br ex - Dght 3.074 Lbp 28.06 Br md 9.15 Dpth 3.79 Welded, 1 dk	**(B32A2ST) Tug** Passengers: berths: 14	**2 oil engines** reverse reduction geared to sc. shafts driving 2 FP propellers Total Power: 832kW (1,132hp) 11.0kn Caterpillar D379SCAC 2 x Vee 4 Stroke 8 Cy. 159 x 203 each-416kW (566bhp) Caterpillar Tractor Co-USA AuxGen: 2 x 85kW 380/220V 50Hz a.c Fuel: 170.0 (d.f.) 4.0pd
9501409 *ZR9040* -	**SIYAKHULA** *ex* Kst 54 *-2011* **Smit Amandla Marine Pty Ltd** - *Durban* *South Africa* MMSI: 601159800 Official number: 21125	**469** 140 240	Class: BV (LR) (AB) ✠ Classed LR until 8/4/11	**2009-11 Keppel Nantong Shipyard Co Ltd — Nantong JS** Yd No: 017 Loa 32.00 Br ex - Dght 3.900 Lbp 26.79 Br md 11.50 Dpth 5.20 Welded, 1 dk	**(B32A2ST) Tug**	**2 oil engines** gearing integral to driving 2 Z propellers Total Power: 3,676kW (4,998hp) Niigata 6L28HX 2 x 4 Stroke 6 Cy. 280 x 370 each-1838kW (2499bhp) Niigata Engineering Co Ltd-Japan AuxGen: 3 x 120kW 415V 50Hz a.c
5330565 - -	**SIYANAH** - **Al-Zaabi Transport & General Contracting Co** - *Saudi Arabia*	*216* 59 -	Class: (LR) Classed LR until 23/4/76	**1963-06 J. Bolson & Son Ltd. — Poole** Yd No: 542 Loa 30.13 Br ex 7.50 Dght 2.521 Lbp 27.74 Br md 7.32 Dpth 3.59 Welded, 1 dk	**(B34R2QY) Supply Tender** 1 Ha: Derricks: 1x1t	**2 oil engines** sr reverse geared to sc. shafts driving 2 FP propellers Total Power: 292kW (398hp) Paxman 4RPHXM 2 x Vee 4 Stroke 4 Cy. 178 x 197 each-146kW (199bhp) Davey, Paxman & Co. Ltd.-Colchester AuxGen: 2 x 50kW 220V d.c
8711875 *UBWF3* -	**SIZIMAN** *ex* Mamola Trader *-2007* *ex* FS Kazet *-2006* *ex* FS Marion *-2002* *ex* Bistritza *-2000* **Bussola Management Inc** Far Eastern Tanker Co Ltd (OOO 'Dalnevostochnaya Tankernaya Kompaniya') SatCom: Inmarsat C 427302668 *Vanino* *Russia* MMSI: 273334330	**1,905** 844 3,389 T/cm 9.0	Class: RS (BV) (BR)	**1989-09 Shipbuilding & Shiprepairing Yard 'Ivan Dimitrov' — Rousse** Yd No: 471 Loa 77.55 Br ex 14.54 Dght 5.401 Lbp 73.21 Br md 14.01 Dpth 6.51 Welded, 1 dk	**(A13B2TP) Products Tanker** Single Hull Liq: 3,513; Liq (Oil): 3,513 Compartments: 12 Ta, ER 3 Cargo Pump (s) Ice Capable	**1 oil engine** sr geared to sc. shaft driving 1 FP propeller Total Power: 885kW (1,203hp) S.K.L. 8NVD48A-2U 1 x 4 Stroke 8 Cy. 320 x 480 885kW (1203bhp) VEB Schwermaschinenbau "KarlLiebknecht" (SKL)-Magdeburg Thrusters: 1 Thwart. CP thruster (f)
9234575 *UFKT* -	**SIZIMAN** - **Vanino Marine Trading Port JSC (Vaninskiy Morskoy Torgovyy Port OAO)** - *Vanino* *Russia* MMSI: 273429130 Official number: 000161	**188** 56 111	Class: RS (LR) ✠ Classed LR until 21/6/02	**2001-03 Stocznia Tczew Sp z oo — Tczew** (Hull) **2001-03 B.V. Scheepswerf Damen — Gorinchem** Yd No: 510801 Loa 25.86 Br ex - Dght 3.900 Lbp 22.25 Br md 8.94 Dpth 4.30 Welded, 1 dk	**(B32A2ST) Tug** Ice Capable	**2 oil engines** reduction geared to sc. shafts driving 2 Directional propellers Total Power: 1,014kW (1,378hp) 12.7kn Caterpillar 3512TA 2 x Vee 4 Stroke 12 Cy. 170 x 190 each-507kW (689bhp) Caterpillar Inc-USA AuxGen: 2 x 85kW 380V 50Hz a.c Fuel: 62.1 (d.f.)
9278210 *YDA6767* -	**SJ 01** *ex* Modalwan 1023 *-2011* **PT Bahar Budi Raya** - *Balikpapan* *Indonesia*	**115** 35 83	Class: KI (NK)	**2002-12 Bonafile Shipbuilders & Repairs Sdn Bhd — Sandakan** Yd No: 2313T Loa 23.00 Br ex - Dght 2.879 Lbp 21.29 Br md 6.80 Dpth 3.43 Welded, 1 dk	**(B32A2ST) Tug**	**2 oil engines** reverse reduction geared to sc. shaft driving 2 FP propellers Total Power: 746kW (1,014hp) Cummins KTA-19-M 1 x 4 Stroke 6 Cy. 159 x 159 373kW (507bhp) Cummins Engine Co Inc-USA AuxGen: 2 x 35kW 415/240V a.c Fuel: 90.0 (d.f.)
8014954 *5VCD4* -	**SJ AFRICAN** *ex* African Fern *-2013* **Ayan Navigation Ltd** BIA Shipping Co *Lome* *Togo* MMSI: 671372000 Official number: TG-00445L	**6,509** 3,338 9,124 T/cm 21.2	Class: (AB)	**1981-07 Shimoda Dockyard Co. Ltd. — Shimoda** Yd No: 316 Loa 135.01 Br ex 19.05 Dght 6.316 Lbp 128.02 Br md 19.00 Dpth 8.51 Welded, 1 dk	**(A21A2BC) Bulk Carrier** Grain: 11,326; Bale: 11,071 Compartments: 4 Ho, ER 4 Ha: (13.3 x 8.9)3 (12.5 x 8.9)ER Cranes: 3x5t	**1 oil engine** driving 1 FP propeller Total Power: 3,825kW (5,200hp) 15.0kn Mitsubishi 8UEC37/88H 1 x 2 Stroke 8 Cy. 370 x 880 3825kW (5200bhp) Akasaka Tekkosho KK (Akasaka DieselLtd)-Japan AuxGen: 2 x 320kW a.c
9403889 *DSRB5* -	**SJ ANGEL** *ex* Sun Angel *-2011* **Sean Shipping Co Ltd** Sung Kyung Maritime Co Ltd (SK Maritime) *Jeju* *South Korea* MMSI: 440051000 Official number: JJR-111010	**1,945** 1,078 2,909	Class: KR (CC)	**2006-09 Weihai Donghai Shipyard Co Ltd — Weihai SD** Yd No: 5C-02 Loa 79.40 Br ex - Dght 5.300 Lbp 73.40 Br md 13.60 Dpth 7.00 Welded, 1 dk	**(A31A2GX) General Cargo Ship** Grain: 4,036; Bale: 3,630 Compartments: 1 Ho, ER 1 Ha: ER (38.4 x 9.0) Ice Capable	**1 oil engine** reverse reduction geared to sc. shaft driving 1 FP propeller Total Power: 1,323kW (1,799hp) 11.7kn Hanshin LH31G 1 x 4 Stroke 6 Cy. 310 x 530 1323kW (1799bhp) (made 2005) The Hanshin Diesel Works Ltd-Japan AuxGen: 3 x 90kW 400V a.c
9415868 *DSFA* -	**SJ GLORY** *ex* Sun Glory *-2010* **SJ Marine Co Ltd** Sung Kyung Maritime Co Ltd (SK Maritime) *Jeju* *South Korea* MMSI: 440026000 Official number: JJR-103007	**1,945** 1,078 2,909	Class: KR (CC)	**2007-01 Weihai Donghai Shipyard Co Ltd — Weihai SD** Yd No: 5C-03 Loa 79.40 Br ex - Dght 5.300 Lbp 73.40 Br md 13.60 Dpth 7.00 Welded, 1 dk	**(A31A2GX) General Cargo Ship** Grain: 4,036; Bale: 3,630 Compartments: 1 Ho, ER 1 Ha: ER (38.4 x 9.0)	**1 oil engine** reduction geared to sc. shaft driving 1 FP propeller Total Power: 1,323kW (1,799hp) 12.1kn Hanshin LH31G 1 x 4 Stroke 6 Cy. 310 x 530 1323kW (1799bhp) The Hanshin Diesel Works Ltd-Japan AuxGen: 3 x 90kW 400V a.c
9390202 *DSRB4* -	**SJ HONOR** *ex* Sun Honor *-2011* **SJ Marine Co Ltd** Sung Kyung Maritime Co Ltd (SK Maritime) *Jeju* *South Korea* MMSI: 440043000 Official number: JJR-111003	**1,945** 1,078 2,909	Class: KR (CC)	**2006-06 Weihai Donghai Shipyard Co Ltd — Weihai SD** Yd No: 5C-01 Loa 79.40 Br ex - Dght 5.300 Lbp 73.40 Br md 13.60 Dpth 7.00 Welded, 1 dk	**(A31A2GX) General Cargo Ship** Grain: 4,036; Bale: 3,700 Compartments: 1 Ho, ER 1 Ha: ER (38.4 x 9.0) Ice Capable	**1 oil engine** reduction geared to sc. shaft driving 1 FP propeller Total Power: 1,323kW (1,799hp) 11.7kn Hanshin LH31G 1 x 4 Stroke 6 Cy. 310 x 530 1323kW (1799bhp) The Hanshin Diesel Works Ltd-Japan AuxGen: 3 x 90kW 400V a.c

9137454 *OW2306* -	**SJAGAKLETTUR** *ex* Ivan Shankov *-2012* **Jokin P/F** Mikkjal Hammer *Hvalba* *Faeroe Islands (Danish)* MMSI: 231216000	**837** 262 401	Class: NV (RS)	**1996-12 Peene-Werft GmbH — Wolgast** Yd No: 466 Loa 40.80 (BB) Br ex - Dght 5.200 Lbp 34.80 Br md 11.00 Dpth 7.25 Welded, 1 dk	**(B11A2FG) Factory Stern Trawler** Ins: 440 Compartments: 1 Ho 1 Ha: (2.3 x 2.3)	**1 oil engine** with clutches, flexible couplings & sr geared to sc. shaft driving 1 CP propeller Total Power: 1,920kW (2,610hp) 12.0kn Alpha 12V23/30A 1 x Vee 4 Stroke 12 Cy. 225 x 300 1920kW (2610bhp) MAN B&W Diesel A/S-Denmark AuxGen: 1 x 1000kW 380V 50Hz a.c, 2 x 380V 50Hz a.c Fuel: 200.0 (d.f.) 8.0pd
9303314 *V2CV8* -	**SJARD** - **Briese Schiffahrts GmbH & Co KG ms 'Sjard'** Briese Schiffahrts GmbH & Co KG *Saint John's* *Antigua & Barbuda* MMSI: 305121000 Official number: 4353	**12,936** 5,824 17,305	Class: GL	**2007-09 Tianjin Xingang Shipyard — Tianjin** Yd No: 355-6 Loa 143.17 (BB) Br ex 23.13 Dght 9.700 Lbp 133.00 Br md 22.80 Dpth 13.30 Welded, 1 dk	**(A31A2GX) General Cargo Ship** Grain: 21,697; Bale: 21,697 TEU 958 C Ho 408 TEU C Dk 550 TEU incl 60 ref C. Compartments: 3 Ho, ER 3 Ha: ER Cranes: 3x80t Ice Capable	**1 oil engine** driving 1 FP propeller Total Power: 7,074kW (9,618hp) 15.0kn MAN-B&W 6S46MC-C 1 x 2 Stroke 6 Cy. 460 x 1932 7074kW (9618bhp) Yichang Marine Diesel Engine Co Ltd-China AuxGen: 3 x 600kW 450/230V a.c Thrusters: 1 Tunnel thruster (f)
5330620 *JWYL* M-472-SM	**SJARM** - **Norsk Skipsbrukt Tom Martin Sjuve** - *Kristiansund* *Norway* MMSI: 258283000	**323** 98 -		**1958-07 Kjode & Kjode Georgernes Vaerft — Bergen** Yd No: 1 Lengthened-1963 Loa 40.57 Br ex 7.07 Dght - Lbp - Br md 7.01 Dpth 3.66 Welded, 1 dk	**(B11B2FV) Fishing Vessel**	**1 oil engine** driving 1 FP propeller Total Power: 500kW (680hp) Alpha 408-24VO 1 x 2 Stroke 8 Cy. 240 x 400 500kW (680bhp) (new engine 1966) Alpha Diesel A/S-Denmark
9056870 *LCGM* SF-17-SU	**SJARMOR** *ex* Themis *-2008* *ex* Martina af Roro *-2000* **Nord Solund Fiskeriselskap AS** - *Bergen* *Norway* MMSI: 257302140	**582** 174 -		**1993 'Colod' - Polsko-Kanadyjska Sp z oo — Szczecin** (Hull) Yd No: 2 **1993 Strandby Skibsvaerft I/S — Strandby** Yd No: 110 Converted From: Stern Trawler-2009 Lengthened-1993 Loa 35.28 (BB) Br ex - Dght - Lbp - Br md 8.29 Dpth 6.10 Welded	**(B11B2FV) Fishing Vessel**	**1 oil engine** geared to sc. shaft driving 1 FP propeller Alpha 6L23/30 1 x 4 Stroke 6 Cy. 225 x 300 MAN B&W Diesel A/S-Denmark Thrusters: 1 Thwart. FP thruster (f); 1 Thwart. FP thruster (a)
9192480 *LJTM* -	**SJERNAROY** - **Norled AS** - *Stavanger* *Norway* MMSI: 259593000	**1,656** 496 405	Class: (NV)	**1999-08 Gdanska Stocznia 'Remontowa' SA — Gdansk** Yd No: 438/1 Loa 65.30 Br ex 13.70 Dght 3.250 Lbp 60.00 Br md 13.40 Dpth 5.20 Welded, 1 dk	**(A36A2PR) Passenger/Ro-Ro Ship (Vehicles)** Passengers: unberthed: 200 Bow door/ramp Len: 1.50 Wid: 7.50 Swl: - Stern door/ramp Len: 1.50 Wid: 7.50 Swl: - Cars: 45	**4 diesel electric oil engines** driving 4 gen. each 400kW 690V a.c Connecting to 2 elec. motors each (700kW) driving 2 Directional propellers 1 fwd and 1 aft Total Power: 2,560kW (3,480hp) 12.0kn Mitsubishi S6R2-MTK 4 x 4 Stroke 6 Cy. 170 x 220 each-640kW (870bhp) Mitsubishi Heavy Industries Ltd-Japan
6500131 *H02986* -	**SJERP II** *ex* Telco Solent *-2007* *ex* Jannetje *-1990* *ex* Samenwerking *-1987* *ex* Adriana *-1979* *ex* Gerretje *-1970* **Dennis Lawrence Sjerp** - *Panama* *Panama* MMSI: 372832000 Official number: 3353908B	**175** 53 -	Class: (BV)	**1964 Scheepswerf Vooruit B.V. — Zaandam** Yd No: 296 Converted From: Trawler-1991 Loa 32.92 Br ex 6.76 Dght 3.250 Lbp - Br md 6.10 Dpth 3.41 Welded	**(B22G2OY) Standby Safety Vessel**	**1 oil engine** driving 1 FP propeller Total Power: 716kW (973hp) 10.0kn Kromhout 8FHD240 1 x 4 Stroke 8 Cy. 240 x 260 716kW (973bhp) (new engine 1975) Stork Werkspoor Diesel BV-Netherlands
8100624 - -	**SJIMMIE** *ex* Cedar *-2012* *ex* Aqua Pioneer *-2005* *ex* Poseldorf *-1993* **Russell Ventures Ltd** Dick van der Kamp Shipsales BV *Basseterre* *St Kitts & Nevis* Official number: SKN1002432	**1,499** 781 1,766	Class: (LR) (RS) (AB) (GL) Classed LR until 7/9/10	**1981-05 Schiffs. Hugo Peters Wewelsfleth Peters & Co. GmbH — Wewelsfleth** Yd No: 582 Loa 82.45 Br ex 11.38 Dght 4.100 Lbp 76.80 Br md 11.30 Dpth 5.40 Welded, 2 dks	**(A31A2GX) General Cargo Ship** Grain: 2,902; Bale: 2,898 TEU 48 C. 48/20' Compartments: 1 Ho, ER 1 Ha: (49.8 x 9.0)ER	**1 oil engine** with clutches, flexible couplings & sr reverse geared to sc. shaft driving 1 FP propeller Total Power: 600kW (816hp) 10.5kn Deutz SBA8M528 1 x 4 Stroke 8 Cy. 220 x 280 600kW (816bhp) Kloeckner Humboldt Deutz AG-West Germany AuxGen: 1 x 45kW 400V 50Hz a.c, 1 x 92kW 400V 50Hz a.c Thrusters: 1 Thwart. FP thruster (f)
8876546 *JXTC* -	**SJOBAS** *ex* Polar Tug *-2010* *ex* Bora Tug *-2008* *ex* Mammut Tug *-2005* *ex* Olsen *-1980* *ex* Tofte *-1980* **Stord Cruise Service AS** - *Haugesund* *Norway* MMSI: 257142400	**103** 41 -	Class: (NV)	**1956-01 A.M. Liaaen Skipsverft & Mek. Verksted — Aalesund** Yd No: 93 Loa 24.44 Br ex - Dght - Lbp - Br md 6.00 Dpth 3.37 Welded, 1 dk	**(B32A2ST) Tug**	**1 oil engine** driving 1 FP propeller Total Power: 552kW (750hp) MaK MA423 1 x 4 Stroke 8 Cy. 290 x 420 552kW (750bhp) Maschinenbau Kiel AG (MaK)-Kiel
9591923 *OZ2075* -	**SJOBORG** - **P/F 6 September 2006** P/F Skansi Offshore *Leirvik* *Faeroe Islands (Danish)* MMSI: 231065000	**3,942** 1,507 4,700	Class: NV	**2012-03 Cemre Muhendislik Gemi Insaat Sanayi ve Ticaret Ltd Sti — Altinova** (Hull) Yd No: (106) **2012-03 Havyard Leirvik AS — Leirvik i Sogn** Yd No: 106 Loa 86.00 (BB) Br ex 20.20 Dght 8.000 Lbp 75.60 Br md 19.60 Dpth 8.00 Welded, 1 dk	**(B21A2OS) Platform Supply Ship** Ice Capable	**4 diesel electric oil engines** driving 4 gen. Connecting to 2 elec. motors each (1900kW) driving 2 Azimuth electric drive units Total Power: 6,800kW (9,246hp) 15.0kn M.T.U. 12V4000M33S 2 x Vee 4 Stroke 12 Cy. 170 x 210 each-1560kW (2121bhp) MTU Friedrichshafen GmbH-Friedrichshafen M.T.U. 16V4000M23S 2 x Vee 4 Stroke 16 Cy. 170 x 210 each-1840kW (2502bhp) MTU Friedrichshafen GmbH-Friedrichshafen Thrusters: 2 Tunnel thruster (f); 1 Retract. directional thruster (f)
8506828 *JWSG* M-122-HO	**SJOBRIS** *ex* Teigenes 1 *-2006* *ex* Teigenes *-2005* **Teigebris AS** Sigurd Teige SatCom: Inmarsat B 325830310 *Fosnavaag* *Norway* MMSI: 258303000 Official number: 20141	**1,559** 604 1,394	Class: NV	**1985-11 Drammen Slip & Verksted — Drammen** Yd No: 100 Loa 70.40 Br ex - Dght 6.893 Lbp 60.19 Br md 12.01 Dpth 7.90 Welded, 2 dks	**(B11B2FV) Fishing Vessel** Ice Capable	**1 oil engine** driving 1 FP propeller Total Power: 2,207kW (3,001hp) 14.8kn Normo KVMB-12 1 x Vee 4 Stroke 12 Cy. 250 x 300 2207kW (3001bhp) AS Bergens Mek Verksteder-Norway AuxGen: 1 x 613kW 440V 60Hz a.c, 1 x 302kW 440V 60Hz a.c Thrusters: 1 Thwart. FP thruster (f); 1 Tunnel thruster (a)
8614443 *SLXP* -	**SJOBRIS** - **Blidosundsbolaget AB** - *Stockholm* *Sweden* MMSI: 265522700	**231** 102 50		**1987-04 Marinteknik Verkstads AB — Oregrund** Yd No: B63 Loa 38.21 Br ex 6.79 Dght 1.191 Lbp 36.66 Br md 6.76 Dpth 2.44 Welded, 1 dk	**(A37B2PS) Passenger Ship** Hull Material: Aluminium Alloy	**3 oil engines** with clutches & sr reverse geared to sc. shafts driving 3 FP propellers Total Power: 837kW (1,137hp) Scania DS1440M 3 x Vee 4 Stroke 8 Cy. 127 x 140 each-279kW (379bhp) Saab Scania AB-Sweden
9396995 *LIKQ* SF-2-A	**SJOGLANS** - **Heggoy AS** - *Floro* *Norway* MMSI: 258098000	**495** 157 -	Class: (NV)	**2006-09 Safe Co Ltd Sp z oo — Gdynia** (Hull) **2006-09 Larsnes Mek. Verksted AS — Larsnes** Yd No: 43 Loa 27.48 (BB) Br ex - Dght 5.200 Lbp - Br md 9.25 Dpth 6.20 Welded, 1 dk	**(B11A2FT) Trawler**	**1 oil engine** reduction geared to sc. shaft driving 1 CP propeller Total Power: 1,324kW (1,800hp) 10.5kn Yanmar 8N21A-EN 1 x 4 Stroke 8 Cy. 210 x 290 1324kW (1800bhp) Yanmar Diesel Engine Co Ltd-Japan AuxGen: 1 x 318kW a.c Thrusters: 1 Tunnel thruster (f); 1 Tunnel thruster (a)
8129424 *SKLJ* -	**SJOGULL** - **Blidosundsbolaget AB** - *Stockholm* *Sweden* MMSI: 265522690	**209** 101 50		**1982-05 Marinteknik Verkstads AB — Oregrund** Yd No: B49 Loa 38.33 Br ex 6.79 Dght 1.170 Lbp 33.46 Br md 6.76 Dpth 2.27 Welded, 1 dk	**(A37B2PS) Passenger Ship** Hull Material: Aluminium Alloy Passengers: unberthed: 300	**3 oil engines** with clutches, flexible couplings & sr reverse geared to sc. shafts driving 3 FP propellers Total Power: 783kW (1,065hp) Scania DSI1402M 3 x Vee 4 Stroke 8 Cy. 127 x 140 each-261kW (355bhp) Saab Scania AB-Sweden
8650344 *LLGI* H-4-K	**SJOHAV** - **Partrederiet Onar Og Odd Emil Sjo ANS** - *Bergen* *Norway*	**162** 64 -		**2000-01 Brodrene Langset AS — Lyngstad** Yd No: 54 Loa 21.30 Br ex - Dght - Lbp - Br md 7.20 Dpth 3.93 Welded, 1 dk	**(B11B2FV) Fishing Vessel**	**1 oil engine** reduction geared to sc. shaft driving 1 FP propeller

5336753 **SJOKRAFT**
JWTP
-
ex Seut *-2009* *ex* Katland *-1994*
ex Fru Olsen *-1988* *ex* Michael I *-1985*
ex Spiekeroog *-1974*
Fram Tugs AS
-
Fredrikstad *Norway*
MMSI: 258173000

141 / 42 / - — Class: (GL)

1958 Schulte & Bruns Schiffswerft — Emden
Yd No: 200
Loa 28.20 Br ex 6.91 Dght 3.501
Lbp 25.00 Br md 6.90 Dpth 3.74
Riveted\Welded, 1 dk

(B32A2ST) Tug
Ice Capable

1 oil engine reverse reduction geared to sc. shaft driving 1 FP propeller
Total Power: 1,020kW (1,387hp) 12.5kn
MWM TRH348AU
1 x 4 Stroke 8 Cy. 320 x 480 1020kW (1387bhp)
Motoren Werke Mannheim AG (MWM)-West Germany
AuxGen: 1 x 16kW 220V d.c

5289247 **SJOKURS**
LAVN
-
ex Gann *-2007* *ex* Ragnvald Jarl *-1995*
Sorlandet Seilende Skoleskibs Institution
-
Kristiansand *Norway*
MMSI: 258321000
Official number: 14396

2,191 / 795 / 579 — Class: NV

1956-06 Blohm & Voss AG — Hamburg Yd No: 789
Loa 81.26 Br ex 12.65 Dght 4.509
Lbp 74.99 Br md 12.60 Dpth 7.17
Riveted\Welded, 2 dks, pt 3rd dk

(A32A2GF) General Cargo/Passenger Ship
Passengers: unberthed: 281; berths: 144
Ins: 680
Compartments: 2 Ho, ER
2 Ha: (4.2 x 3.0) (3.6 x 3.0)ER
Cranes: 1x3t,2x1.5t
Ice Capable

1 oil engine driving 1 CP propeller
Total Power: 2,177kW (2,960hp) 16.0kn
MAN G10V52/74
1 x 4 Stroke 10 Cy. 520 x 740 2177kW (2960bhp)
Maschinenbau Augsburg Nuernberg (MAN)-Augsburg
AuxGen: 2 x 156kW 380V 50Hz a.c
Thrusters: 1 Tunnel thruster
Fuel: 127.0 (r.f.) 12.0pd

5131579 **SJOSERVICE 1**
LEWV
-
ex Nordive 1 *-2011* *ex* Edoy *-2009*
ex Lofotferje II *-1981* *ex* Gjemnes *-1978*
Holmgrens Sjoservice AS
-
Hammerfest *Norway*
MMSI: 257223700

168 / 50 / 73 — Class: (NV)

1949 AS Stord Verft — Stord Yd No: 7
Loa 34.60 Br ex 7.98 Dght 2.439
Lbp - Br md 7.93 Dpth 3.36
Welded, 1 dk

(A37B2PS) Passenger Ship
Passengers: unberthed: 150

1 oil engine driving 1 FP propeller
Total Power: 338kW (460hp) 11.0kn
Callesen 4-427-DOT
1 x 4 Stroke 4 Cy. 270 x 400 338kW (460bhp) (new engine 1972)
Aabenraa Motorfabrik, HeinrichCallesen A/S-Denmark
Fuel: 14.0 (d.f.)

7207047 **SJOSERVICE 2**
LEXH
-
ex Loppatind *-2011* *ex* Rognsund *-2007*
Holmgrens Sjoservice AS
-
Hammerfest *Norway*
MMSI: 257353400

175 / 52 / - — Class: (NV)

1972 AS Tromso Skipsverft & Mek. Verksted — Tromso Yd No: 39
Loa 31.60 Br ex 9.53 Dght 2.674
Lbp 29.01 Br md 9.50 Dpth 3.51
Welded, 1 dk

(A36A2PR) Passenger/Ro-Ro Ship (Vehicles)
Passengers: unberthed: 115
Bow door & ramp
Stern ramp

1 oil engine driving 2 Propellers aft, 1 fwd
Total Power: 349kW (475hp)
Caterpillar D379TA
1 x Vee 4 Stroke 8 Cy. 159 x 203 349kW (475bhp)
Caterpillar Tractor Co-USA
AuxGen: 2 x 25kW 220V 50Hz a.c

8619510 **SJOVAER**
LALK
SF-6-A
Sjovaer Havfiske AS
Jostein Sandoy Mfl
Floro *Norway*
MMSI: 259244000

562 / 233 / -

1988-09 Eidsvik Skipsbyggeri AS — Uskedalen
Yd No: 79
Loa 39.30 Br ex - Dght -
Lbp 34.02 Br md 8.50 Dpth 4.17
Welded, 1 dk

(B11B2FV) Fishing Vessel
Ins: 157

1 oil engine sr geared to sc. shaft driving 1 CP propeller
Total Power: 647kW (880hp)
Mitsubishi S12N-MPTA
1 x Vee 4 Stroke 12 Cy. 160 x 180 647kW (880bhp)
Mitsubishi Heavy Industries Ltd-Japan

7739777 **SJOVEIEN**
LIKA
-
ex Olaf Scheel *-1979*
Indre Nordhordland Dampbaatlag AS
-
Oslo *Norway*
MMSI: 258463000

331 / 99 / - — Class: (NV)

1964 AS Mjellem & Karlsen — Bergen Yd No: 84
Loa 40.67 Br ex 8.11 Dght -
Lbp 34.80 Br md - Dpth 4.35
Welded, 1 dk

(B35A2QZ) Mission Ship

1 oil engine driving 1 FP propeller
Total Power: 441kW (600hp)
Wichmann 6ACA
1 x 2 Stroke 6 Cy. 280 x 420 441kW (600bhp)
Wichmann Motorfabrikk AS-Norway
AuxGen: 3 x 24kW 230V 50Hz a.c

5198656 **SJOVIK**
HP4696
-
ex Deep Diver *-1985* *ex* Seiko *-1976*
ex Kvitfjell *-1972* *ex* Tottan *-1960*
ex Morris Dance *-1951*
Nordic Fishing Management Inc
-
Panama *Panama*
Official number: 14014PEXT

490 / 193 / 610 — Class: (LR) (NV) ✠

1940-10 Goole SB. & Repairing Co. Ltd. — Goole
Yd No: 351
Converted From: Seal-catcher-1976
Converted From: Trawler-1951
Converted From: Escort
Loa 49.87 Br ex 8.44 Dght 3.810
Lbp 46.18 Br md 8.39 Dpth 4.58
Riveted\Welded, 1 dk

(B34P2QV) Salvage Ship
Compartments: 2 Ho, ER
2 Ha: (1.6 x 2.8) (2.5 x 3.4)
Derricks: 1x3t
Ice Capable

1 oil engine driving 1 CP propeller
Total Power: 1,030kW (1,400hp) 14.0kn
MaK 8M451AK
1 x 4 Stroke 8 Cy. 320 x 450 1030kW (1400bhp) (new engine 1964)
Maschinenbau Kiel AG (MaK)-Kiel
AuxGen: 2 x 45kW 220V d.c
Thrusters: 1 Thwart. FP thruster (f)

8849206 **SJOVIK**
JWLQ
VA-122-K
ex Elvira *-2009* *ex* Solholm Senior *-2005*
ex Skudetral *-1998* *ex* Sander *-1996*
ex Jamalito *-1989*
Flekkeroyfisk AS
-
Kopervik *Norway*
MMSI: 259118000

160 / 76 / -

1985-01 Elvestad Mek. Verksted — Skien
Yd No: 24
Lengthened-1987
Loa 26.25 Br ex - Dght -
Lbp - Br md 6.50 Dpth 3.05
Welded, 1 dk

(B11B2FV) Fishing Vessel

1 oil engine driving 1 FP propeller
Total Power: 500kW (680hp) 9.0kn
Cummins
1 x 4 Stroke 500kW (680bhp)
Cummins Engine Co Inc-USA
AuxGen: 1 x 32kW, 1 x 16kW

7717092 **SJOVIND**
UIPL
-
ex Termination *-1991* *ex* Sybil Freeman *-1990*
Sjovind Enterprises Inc
JSC Kamchatimpex
SatCom: Inmarsat A 1506742
Petropavlovsk-Kamchatskiy *Russia*
MMSI: 273810080
Official number: 774138

1,076 / 322 / 997 — Class: RS (AB)

1977-11 Quality Equipment Inc — Houma LA
Yd No: 142
Converted From: Offshore Tug/Supply Ship-1991
Loa 54.90 Br ex 11.61 Dght 4.220
Lbp 54.87 Br md 11.59 Dpth 4.27
Welded, 1 dk

(B11B2FV) Fishing Vessel

2 oil engines reverse reduction geared to sc. shafts driving 2 FP propellers
Total Power: 2,206kW (3,000hp) 11.0kn
EMD (Electro-Motive) 12-645-E6
2 x Vee 2 Stroke 12 Cy. 230 x 254 each-1103kW (1500bhp)
General Motors Corp.Electro-Motive Div.-La Grange
AuxGen: 3 x 300kW a.c
Thrusters: 1 Thwart. FP thruster (f)
Fuel: 364.0 (d.f.)

8660894 **SJP 88**
YDA6551
-
PT Perusahaan Pelayaran Rusianto Bersaudara
-
Samarinda *Indonesia*
Official number: 5138

202 / 61 / - — Class: KI

2010-03 PT Menumbar Kaltim — Samarinda
Yd No: 08087
Loa 29.00 Br ex - Dght 2.860
Lbp 26.70 Br md 8.00 Dpth 3.50
Welded, 1 dk

(B32A2ST) Tug

2 oil engines reduction geared to sc. shafts driving 2 FP propellers
Total Power: 1,766kW (2,402hp)
Cummins KTA-38-M2
2 x Vee 4 Stroke 12 Cy. 159 x 159 each-883kW (1201bhp)
Cummins Engine Co Inc-USA
AuxGen: 2 x 35kW a.c

8740606 **SJP 99**
-
-
Aspul Anwar Zubair
-
Samarinda *Indonesia*

205 / 62 / - — Class: KI

2009-05 PT Candi Pasifik — Samarinda
Loa 29.00 Br ex - Dght -
Lbp 26.88 Br md 8.00 Dpth 3.50
Welded, 1 dk

(B32A2ST) Tug

2 oil engines driving 2 Propellers
Total Power: 1,716kW (2,334hp)
Mitsubishi S12A2-MPTK
2 x Vee 4 Stroke 12 Cy. 150 x 160 each-858kW (1167bhp)
Mitsubishi Heavy Industries Ltd-Japan

8739140 **SJP 168-A**
YB6316
-
Andy H
-
Samarinda *Indonesia*

209 / 63 / - — Class: KI

2006-12 C.V. Karya Lestari Industri — Samarinda
Loa - Br ex - Dght -
Lbp 36.00 Br md 8.00 Dpth 2.15
Welded, 1 dk

(A35D2RL) Landing Craft

2 oil engines driving 2 Propellers
Total Power: 486kW (660hp)
Mitsubishi 6D22
2 x 4 Stroke 6 Cy. 130 x 140 each-243kW (330bhp)
Mitsubishi Heavy Industries Ltd-Japan

8411035 **SJURDABERG**
OW2408
-
ex Haki *-2013* *ex* Salleq *-2007*
ex Polar Nanoq *-2005* *ex* Fuglberg *-2002*
ex Polar Nanoq *-2001* *ex* Qipoqqaq *-1995*
P/F J F K Trol
-
23112420
Faeroe Islands (Danish)
MMSI: 231124000

1,856 / 556 / - — Class: NV

1985-03 AS Tangen Verft Kragero — Kragero
Yd No: 110
Loa 60.00 (BB) Br ex 13.03 Dght 5.620
Lbp 51.75 Br md 13.00 Dpth 7.80
Welded, 1 dk

(B11A2FS) Stern Trawler
Ice Capable

1 oil engine geared to sc. shaft driving 1 FP propeller
Total Power: 1,978kW (2,689hp)
Alpha 9L28/32
1 x 4 Stroke 9 Cy. 280 x 320 1978kW (2689bhp)
MAN B&W Diesel A/S-Denmark
AuxGen: 1 x 1200kW 400V 50Hz a.c, 2 x 368kW 400V 50Hz a.c

9672777 **SJW PACIFIC**
JZIW
-
PT Sinar Jaya Wijaya
-
Jakarta *Indonesia*
MMSI: 525009245

872 / 262 / 1,075 — Class: NK

2013-10 Gimhwak Shipyard Sdn Bhd — Sibu
Yd No: GSY 018
Loa 64.00 Br ex 14.02 Dght 2.550
Lbp 59.35 Br md 14.00 Dpth 3.65
Welded, 1 dk

(A35D2RL) Landing Craft
Bow ramp (centre)

2 oil engines reduction geared to sc. shafts driving 2 Propellers
Total Power: 1,518kW (2,064hp)
Mitsubishi S6R2-MTK3L
2 x 4 Stroke 6 Cy. 170 x 220 each-759kW (1032bhp)
Mitsubishi Heavy Industries Ltd-Japan
Fuel: 680.0

8913875 **SJW TRANS**
POMC
-
ex Thor Blue *-2012* *ex* CEC Blue *-2008*
ex Arktis Blue *-1999*
PT Sinar Jaya Wijaya
-
Tanjung Priok *Indonesia*
MMSI: 525003134

2,815 / 1,532 / 4,110 / T/cm 11.2 — Class: BV (LR) ✠ Classed LR until 11/2/99

1992-03 A/S Nordsovaerftet — Ringkobing
Yd No: 208
Loa 88.42 (BB) Br ex 15.15 Dght 6.010
Lbp 80.30 Br md 15.00 Dpth 7.50
Welded, 1 dk, 2nd portable deck in hold

(A31A2GX) General Cargo Ship
Grain: 5,270; Bale: 4,907
TEU 247 C.Ho 93/20' (40') C.Dk 154/20' (40') incl. 25 ref C.
Compartments: 1 Ho, ER, 1 Tw Dk
1 Ha: (50.0 x 11.8)ER
Cranes: 2x50t
Ice Capable

1 oil engine with flexible couplings & sr geared to sc. shaft driving 1 FP propeller
Total Power: 1,980kW (2,692hp) 13.5kn
MaK 6M453C
1 x 4 Stroke 6 Cy. 320 x 420 1980kW (2692bhp)
Krupp MaK Maschinenbau GmbH-Kiel
AuxGen: 3 x 223kW 380V 50Hz a.c, 1 x 208kW 380V 50Hz a.c
Thrusters: 1 Thwart. FP thruster (f)
Fuel: 338.8 (d.f.) 8.0pd

IMO / Call sign	Name / Owner	Tonnage	Class	Build / Dimensions	Type	Machinery
9605229 *YD3795* -	**SK-01** **PT Bintang Laju Samudra** - *Batam* *Indonesia*	**254** 77 195	Class: NK	**2010**-10 **PT Palma Progress Shipyard — Batam** Yd No: 424 Loa 28.05 Br ex - Dght 3.312 Lbp 25.06 Br md 8.60 Dpth 4.30 Welded, 1 dk	**(B32A2ST) Tug**	**2 oil engines** reduction geared to sc.shafts driving 2 FP propellers Total Power: 1,518kW (2,064hp) Mitsubishi S6R2-MTK3L 2 x 4 Stroke 6 Cy. 170 x 220 each-759kW (1032bhp) Mitsubishi Heavy Industries Ltd-Japan AuxGen: 2 x 60kW a.c Fuel: 196.0
9609873 *YD3796* -	**SK-02** **PT Bintang Laju Samudra** - *Batam* *Indonesia*	**254** 77 193	Class: NK	**2010**-12 **PT Palma Progress Shipyard — Batam** Yd No: 434 Loa 28.05 Br ex - Dght 3.300 Lbp 25.76 Br md 8.60 Dpth 4.30 Welded, 1 dk	**(B32A2ST) Tug**	**2 oil engines** reduction geared to sc. shafts driving 2 FP propellers Total Power: 1,518kW (2,064hp) Mitsubishi S6R2-MTK3L 2 x 4 Stroke 6 Cy. 170 x 220 each-759kW (1032bhp) Mitsubishi Heavy Industries Ltd-Japan
8013900 *DTAM5* -	**SK 7** *ex* West Bay No. 8 *-2011* *ex* Oryong No. 352 *-2007* *ex* Dragon No. 21 *-1997* *ex* Fukuseki Maru No. 28 *-1997* **GOGO Fishery Co Ltd** - SatCom: Inmarsat A 1705256 *Busan* *South Korea* MMSI: 440281000 Official number: 9701003-6260006	**392** 127 378	Class: KR	**1980**-07 **KK Kanasashi Zosen — Shizuoka SZ** Yd No: 2050 Loa 48.90 Br ex - Dght 3.427 Lbp 42.96 Br md 8.51 Dpth 3.64 Welded, 1 dk	**(B11B2FV) Fishing Vessel**	**1 oil engine** driving 1 FP propeller Total Power: 956kW (1,300hp) Niigata 6M28AGT 1 x 4 Stroke 6 Cy. 280 x 480 956kW (1300bhp) Niigata Engineering Co Ltd-Japan
8518247 *6LVN* -	**SK 8** *ex* West Bay No. 18 *-2011* *ex* Oryong No. 333 *-2007* *ex* Sam Song No. 601 *-1995* **GOGO Fishery Co Ltd** - *Busan* *South Korea* MMSI: 440950000 Official number: 9503023-6210002	**398** - 425	Class: KR	**1986**-04 **Daedong Shipbuilding Co Ltd — Busan** Yd No: 283 Loa 53.29 (BB) Br ex - Dght - Lbp 46.89 Br md 8.70 Dpth 3.76 Welded, 1 dk	**(B11B2FV) Fishing Vessel**	**1 oil engine** dr reverse geared to sc. shaft driving 1 FP propeller Total Power: 883kW (1,201hp) 11.5kn Niigata 6M28AFTE 1 x 4 Stroke 6 Cy. 280 x 480 883kW (1201bhp) Ssangyong Heavy Industries Co Ltd-South Korea AuxGen: 1 x 280kW 225V a.c
8827480 *6LJT* -	**SK 9** *ex* Westbay No. 28 *-2011* *ex* Oryong No. 321 *-1993* *ex* Acacia No. 9 *-1993* **GOGO Fishery Co Ltd** - *Busan* *South Korea* MMSI: 440796000 Official number: 9512362-6260003	*385* - 419	Class: KR	**1988**-08 **Namyang Shipbuilding Co Ltd — Busan** Yd No: 115 Loa 54.00 Br ex - Dght 3.519 Lbp 48.10 Br md 8.90 Dpth 3.75 Welded, 1 dk	**(B11B2FV) Fishing Vessel**	**1 oil engine** driving 1 FP propeller Total Power: 883kW (1,201hp) 13.2kn Niigata 6M28AFTE 1 x 4 Stroke 6 Cy. 280 x 480 883kW (1201bhp) Ssangyong Heavy Industries Co Ltd-South Korea AuxGen: 2 x 608kW 225V a.c
9697208 *JZVO* -	**SK CAPELLA** **PT Bahtera Niaga Internasional** - *Jakarta* *Indonesia* MMSI: 525018275	**1,679** 503 1,340	Class: AB KI (Class contemplated)	**2013**-12 **Fujian Southeast Shipyard — Fuzhou FJ** Yd No: SK83 Loa 59.25 Br ex - Dght 4.950 Lbp 52.20 Br md 14.95 Dpth 6.10 Welded, 1 dk	**(B21B20A) Anchor Handling Tug Supply**	**2 oil engines** reduction geared to sc. shafts driving 2 CP propellers Total Power: 3,840kW (5,220hp) 11.0kn Caterpillar 3516C-HD 2 x Vee 4 Stroke 16 Cy. 170 x 215 each-1920kW (2610bhp) Caterpillar Inc-USA AuxGen: 2 x 350kW a.c, 2 x 800kW a.c
9507570 *9MLU4* -	**SK DEEP SEA** **Synergy Kenyalang Offshore Sdn Bhd** - *Port Klang* *Malaysia* MMSI: 533061900 Official number: 334351	**3,719** 1,115 2,851	Class: AB	**2011**-09 **Nam Cheong Dockyard Sdn Bhd — Miri** Yd No: 601 Loa 75.00 Br ex - Dght 5.200 Lbp 72.50 Br md 20.00 Dpth 7.20 Welded, 1 dk	**(B22A20R) Offshore Support Vessel** Cranes: 1x25t	**2 oil engines** reduction geared to sc. shafts driving 2 CP propellers Total Power: 3,200kW (4,350hp) 11.0kn Wartsila 8L20 2 x 4 Stroke 8 Cy. 200 x 280 each-1600kW (2175bhp) Wartsila Finland Oy-Finland
9633903 *9WPP8* -	**SK FALCON** *launched as* SK LINE 15 *-2012* **Nam Cheong Dockyard Sdn Bhd** - *Kuching* *Malaysia* MMSI: 533170149 Official number: 334707	**499** 150 475	Class: NK	**2013**-09 **Nam Cheong Dockyard Sdn Bhd — Miri** Yd No: SKL 15 Loa 47.00 Br ex - Dght 2.512 Lbp 43.32 Br md 11.00 Dpth 3.20 Welded, 1 dk	**(A35D2RL) Landing Craft** Bow ramp (centre) Liq: 359	**2 oil engines** driving 2 Propellers Total Power: 1,074kW (1,460hp) Caterpillar 3412C 2 x Vee 4 Stroke 12 Cy. 137 x 152 each-537kW (730bhp) Caterpillar Inc-USA Fuel: 380.0
9705940 *9V2048* -	**SK LINE 1** **SK Line Pte Ltd** AMMships Pte Ltd *Singapore* *Singapore* Official number: 398541	**3,200** 1,497 5,641	Class: AB	**2013**-12 **PT Samudra Marine Indonesia — Cilegon** Yd No: SM30 Loa 91.00 (BB) Br ex - Dght 4.500 Lbp 87.37 Br md 21.00 Dpth 6.30 Welded, 1 dk	**(A12A2TC) Chemical Tanker** Double Hull (13F)	**2 oil engines** reduction geared to sc. shafts driving 2 FP propellers Total Power: 2,386kW (3,244hp) Cummins KTA-50-M2 2 x Vee 4 Stroke 16 Cy. 159 x 159 each-1193kW (1622bhp) Cummins Engine Co Ltd-United Kingdom
9466087 *9WHH2* -	**SK LINE 10** *ex* S. K Line 10 *-2009* **Nam Cheong Dockyard Sdn Bhd** - *Kuching* *Malaysia* MMSI: 533000698 Official number: 330942	**217** 65 103	Class: LR ✠**100A1** SS 04/2013 ✠**LMC** Eq.Ltr: D; Cable: 330.0/17.5 U2 (a)	**2008**-04 **Nam Cheong Dockyard Sdn Bhd — Miri** Yd No: 551 Loa 34.00 Br ex 8.23 Dght 1.880 Lbp 32.30 Br md 8.00 Dpth 3.31 Welded, 1 dk	**(B22G20Y) Standby Safety Vessel**	**2 oil engines** with clutches, flexible couplings & reverse reduction geared to sc. shafts driving 2 FP propellers Total Power: 1,074kW (1,460hp) Caterpillar 3412D 2 x Vee 4 Stroke 12 Cy. 145 x 162 each-537kW (730bhp) Caterpillar Inc-USA AuxGen: 2 x 84kW 415V 50Hz a.c Thrusters: 1 Thwart. FP thruster (f) Fuel: 530.0
9469704 *9WHI3* -	**SK LINE 11** **SK Marine Sdn Bhd** - *Kuching* *Malaysia* MMSI: 533003430 Official number: 330961	**488** 146 436	Class: NK (LR) ✠Classed LR until 17/11/12	**2008**-07 **Kian Juan Dockyard Sdn Bhd — Miri** Yd No: 118 Loa 45.50 Br ex 10.95 Dght 2.410 Lbp 42.23 Br md 10.90 Dpth 3.20 Welded, 1 dk	**(A35D2RL) Landing Craft** Bow ramp (centre)	**2 oil engines** with clutches & sr reverse geared to sc. shafts driving 2 FP propellers Total Power: 954kW (1,298hp) 11.0kn Cummins KTA-19-M3 2 x 4 Stroke 6 Cy. 159 x 159 each-477kW (649bhp) Cummins Engine Co Inc-USA AuxGen: 2 x 80kW 415V 50Hz a.c
9469716 *9WHI4* -	**SK LINE 12** **Nam Cheong Dockyard Sdn Bhd** SK Marine Sdn Bhd *Kuching* *Malaysia* MMSI: 533003440 Official number: 330962	**488** 146 436	Class: NK (LR) ✠**100A1** SS 11/2008 ✠**LMC** Eq.Ltr: J; Cable: 357.0/26.0 U2 (a) ✠Classed LR until 17/11/12	**2008**-11 **Kian Juan Dockyard Sdn Bhd — Miri** Yd No: 119 Loa 45.50 Br ex 10.95 Dght 2.410 Lbp 42.23 Br md 10.90 Dpth 3.20 Welded, 1 dk	**(A35D2RL) Landing Craft** Bow ramp (centre)	**2 oil engines** with clutches & sr reverse geared to sc. shafts driving 2 FP propellers Total Power: 954kW (1,298hp) 11.0kn Cummins KTA-19-M3 2 x 4 Stroke 6 Cy. 159 x 159 each-477kW (649bhp) Cummins Engine Co Inc-USA AuxGen: 2 x 80kW 415V 50Hz a.c
9635250 *9MPV3* -	**SK LINE 65** *ex* Able Sentinel *-2012* **Nam Cheong (Labuan) Ltd** Nam Cheong International Ltd *Port Klang* *Malaysia* MMSI: 533130894 Official number: 334447	**1,678** 503 1,305	Class: AB	**2012**-06 **Fujian Southeast Shipyard — Fuzhou FJ** Yd No: SK65 Loa 59.25 Br ex - Dght 4.950 Lbp 52.20 Br md 14.95 Dpth 6.10 Welded, 1 dk	**(B21B20A) Anchor Handling Tug Supply**	**2 oil engines** reduction geared to sc. shafts driving 2 Propellers Total Power: 3,840kW (5,220hp) 11.0kn Caterpillar 3516C-HD 2 x Vee 4 Stroke 16 Cy. 170 x 215 each-1920kW (2610bhp) Caterpillar Inc-USA AuxGen: 2 x 800kW a.c, 2 x 350kW a.c Thrusters: 2 Tunnel thruster (f) Fuel: 540.0
9671383 *9MQI8* -	**SK LINE 77** **Icon Zara (L) Inc** Icon Ship Management Sdn Bhd SatCom: Inmarsat C 453302259 *Port Klang* *Malaysia* MMSI: 533130987 Official number: 334554	**1,679** 503 1,352	Class: AB	**2013**-06 **Fujian Southeast Shipyard — Fuzhou FJ** Yd No: SK77 Loa 59.25 Br ex - Dght 4.950 Lbp 52.20 Br md 14.95 Dpth 6.10 Welded, 1 dk	**(B21B20A) Anchor Handling Tug Supply**	**2 oil engines** reduction geared to sc. shafts driving 2 CP propellers Total Power: 3,840kW (5,220hp) 11.0kn Caterpillar 3516C-HD 2 x Vee 4 Stroke 16 Cy. 170 x 215 each-1920kW (2610bhp) Caterpillar Inc-USA AuxGen: 3 x 350kW a.c, 2 x 800kW a.c Fuel: 520.0

IMO / Call sign	Name / Owner / Manager / Port	Tonnage	Class	Built / Dimensions	Type	Machinery
9680229 *9MQL8* -	**SK LINE 80** *ex* Heroic Sentinel *-2013* **Nam Cheong International Ltd** Icon Ship Management Sdn Bhd *Port Klang* *Malaysia* MMSI: 533180013 Official number: 334581	**1,683** 504 1,331	Class: BV (AB)	**2013-11 Fujian Southeast Shipyard — Fuzhou FJ** Yd No: SK80 Loa 59.24 Br ex - Dght 4.950 Lbp 52.21 Br md 14.95 Dpth 6.10 Welded, 1 dk	**(B21B20A) Anchor Handling Tug Supply**	**2 oil engines** reduction geared to sc. shafts driving 2 CP propellers Total Power: 2,984kW (4,058hp) 11.0kn Caterpillar 3516C 2 x Vee 4 Stroke 16 Cy. 170 x 190 each-1492kW (2029bhp) Caterpillar Inc-USA AuxGen: 2 x 800kW 50Hz a.c, 2 x 350kW 50Hz a.c Thrusters: 1 Tunnel thruster (f); 1 Tunnel thruster (a) Fuel: 520.0
9534121 *9MIQ9* -	**SK LINE 106** **Yinson Indah Ltd** Regulus Offshore Sdn Bhd *Port Klang* *Malaysia* MMSI: 533640000 Official number: 334099	**2,534** 760 2,487	Class: LR (AB) **100A1** SS 07/2010 anchor handler, tug, fire-fighting Ship 1 (3300m3/h) with water spray **LMC** **UMS**	**2010-07 Fujian Crown Ocean Shipbuilding Industry Co Ltd — Lianjiang County FJ** Yd No: SK106 Loa 70.70 Br ex - Dght 6.000 Lbp 63.00 Br md 16.00 Dpth 7.20 Welded, 1 dk	**(B21B20A) Anchor Handling Tug Supply**	**2 oil engines** reduction geared to sc. shafts driving 2 CP propellers Total Power: 8,000kW (10,876hp) Bergens B32: 40L8P 2 x 4 Stroke 8 Cy. 320 x 400 each-4000kW (5438bhp) Rolls Royce Marine AS-Norway AuxGen: 2 x 1730kW 440V 60Hz a.c, 2 x 590kW 440V 50Hz a.c Thrusters: 1 Tunnel thruster (f); 1 Retract. directional thruster (f); 1 Tunnel thruster (a) Fuel: 960.0 (d.f.)
9648283 *9MQD7* -	**SK LINE 702** **Nam Cheong International Ltd** *Port Klang* *Malaysia* MMSI: 533130949 Official number: 334513	**2,901** 870 3,307	Class: AB	**2012-12 Fujian Southeast Shipyard — Fuzhou FJ** Yd No: SK702 Loa 75.00 (BB) Br ex - Dght 5.700 Lbp 67.85 Br md 17.25 Dpth 8.00 Welded, 1 dk	**(B21A20S) Platform Supply Ship**	**2 oil engines** reduction geared to sc. shafts driving 2 Z propellers Total Power: 4,412kW (5,998hp) 14.5kn Niigata 8L28HX 2 x 4 Stroke 8 Cy. 280 x 370 each-2206kW (2999bhp) Niigata Engineering Co Ltd-Japan AuxGen: 2 x 1000kW a.c, 3 x 450kW a.c Thrusters: 2 Thwart. CP thruster (f) Fuel: 1040.0 (d.f.)
9486764 *9WHO4* -	**SK LINE 800** **Nam Cheong Dockyard Sdn Bhd** - *Kuching* *Malaysia* MMSI: 533003410 Official number: 332939	**217** 65 75	Class: LR ✠**100A1** SS 06/2013 ✠**LMC** Eq.Ltr: D; Cable: 330.0/17.5 U2 (a)	**2008-06 Nam Cheong Dockyard Sdn Bhd — Miri** Yd No: 552 Loa 34.00 Br ex 8.23 Dght 1.880 Lbp 32.30 Br md 8.00 Dpth 3.30 Welded, 1 dk	**(B22G20Y) Standby Safety Vessel**	**2 oil engines** with clutches, flexible couplings & sr reverse geared to sc. shafts driving 2 FP propellers Total Power: 1,074kW (1,460hp) Caterpillar 3412TA 2 x Vee 4 Stroke 12 Cy. 137 x 152 each-537kW (730bhp) Caterpillar Inc-USA AuxGen: 2 x 80kW 415V 50Hz a.c Thrusters: 1 Thwart. FP thruster (f) Fuel: 51.4 (r.f.)
9486776 *9WHS6* -	**SK LINE 801** *ex* S. K. Line 801 *-2011* **Nam Cheong Dockyard Sdn Bhd** - *Kuching* *Malaysia* MMSI: 533003420 Official number: 332969	**217** 65 119	Class: LR ✠**100A1** SS 08/2013 ✠**LMC** Eq.Ltr: D; Cable: 330.0/17.5 U2 (a)	**2008-08 Nam Cheong Dockyard Sdn Bhd — Miri** Yd No: 553 Loa 34.00 Br ex 8.23 Dght 1.880 Lbp 32.30 Br md 8.00 Dpth 3.30 Welded, 1 dk	**(B22G20Y) Standby Safety Vessel**	**2 oil engines** with clutches, flexible couplings & reverse reduction geared to sc. shafts driving 2 FP propellers Total Power: 1,074kW (1,460hp) Caterpillar 3412D 2 x Vee 4 Stroke 12 Cy. 145 x 162 each-537kW (730bhp) Caterpillar Inc-USA AuxGen: 2 x 80kW 416V 50Hz a.c Thrusters: 1 Thwart. FP thruster (f)
9495894 *9WHW9* -	**SK LINE 803** **Nam Cheong Dockyard Sdn Bhd** - *Kuching* *Malaysia* MMSI: 533000747 Official number: 333024	**217** 65 103	Class: LR ✠**100A1** SS 03/2012 ✠**LMC** Eq.Ltr: D; Cable: 247.5/17.5 U2 (a)	**2012-03 Nam Cheong Dockyard Sdn Bhd — Miri** Yd No: 555 Loa 34.00 Br ex 8.23 Dght 1.800 Lbp 32.30 Br md 8.00 Dpth 3.30 Welded, 1 dk	**(B22G20Y) Standby Safety Vessel**	**2 oil engines** with clutches, flexible couplings & reverse reduction geared to sc. shafts driving 2 FP propellers Total Power: 1,074kW (1,460hp) 12.0kn Caterpillar 3412C 2 x Vee 4 Stroke 12 Cy. 137 x 152 each-537kW (730bhp) Caterpillar Inc-USA AuxGen: 2 x 84kW 415V 50Hz a.c Thrusters: 1 Thwart. FP thruster (f)
9495909 *9WEA7* -	**SK LINE 804** **Nam Cheong Dockyard Sdn Bhd** - *Kuching* *Malaysia* MMSI: 533004670 Official number: 333054	**217** - 103	Class: LR ✠**100A1** SS 01/2012 ✠**LMC** Eq.Ltr: D; Cable: 247.5/17.5 U2 (a)	**2012-01 Nam Cheong Dockyard Sdn Bhd — Miri** Yd No: 556 Loa 34.00 Br ex 8.23 Dght 1.800 Lbp 32.30 Br md 8.00 Dpth 3.30 Welded, 1 dk	**(B22G20Y) Standby Safety Vessel**	**2 oil engines** with clutches, flexible couplings & reverse reduction geared to sc. shafts driving 2 FP propellers Total Power: 1,074kW (1,460hp) 12.0kn Caterpillar 3412C 2 x Vee 4 Stroke 12 Cy. 137 x 152 each-537kW (730bhp) Caterpillar Inc-USA AuxGen: 2 x 84kW 416V 50Hz a.c Thrusters: 1 Thwart. FP thruster (f)
9498078 *9WPN2* -	**SK LINE 805** **Nam Cheong Dockyard Sdn Bhd** - *Kuching* *Malaysia* MMSI: 533170033 Official number: 333056	**217** 65 74	Class: LR ✠**100A1** SS 05/2012 ✠**LMC** Eq.Ltr: D; Cable: 247.5/17.5 U2 (a)	**2012-05 Nam Cheong Dockyard Sdn Bhd — Miri** Yd No: 557 Loa 34.00 Br ex 8.23 Dght 1.800 Lbp 32.20 Br md 8.00 Dpth 3.31 Welded, 1 dk	**(B22G20Y) Standby Safety Vessel**	**2 oil engines** with clutches, flexible couplings & reverse reduction geared to sc. shafts driving 2 FP propellers Total Power: 1,074kW (1,460hp) 12.0kn Caterpillar 3412C 2 x Vee 4 Stroke 12 Cy. 137 x 152 each-537kW (730bhp) Caterpillar Inc-USA AuxGen: 2 x 84kW 415V 50Hz a.c Thrusters: 1 Thwart. FP thruster (f)
9669988 *9MQL9* -	**SK LINE 810** **CS Offshore DMCCO** - *Port Klang* *Malaysia* MMSI: 533180012 Official number: 334582	**3,601** 1,429 5,188	Class: AB	**2014-04 Fujian Mawei Shipbuilding Ltd — Fuzhou FJ** Yd No: 619-47 Loa 87.08 Br ex - Dght 5.900 Lbp 83.00 Br md 18.80 Dpth 7.40 Welded, 1 dk	**(B21A20S) Platform Supply Ship**	**4 diesel electric oil engines** driving 4 gen. Connecting to 2 elec. motors driving 2 Azimuth electric drive units Total Power: 6,864kW (9,332hp) 12.0kn Cummins QSK60-M 4 x Vee 4 Stroke 16 Cy. 159 x 190 each-1716kW (2333bhp) Cummins Diesel International Ltd-USA Thrusters: 1 Tunnel thruster (f); 1 Retract. directional thruster (f)
9736482 *T3MS2* -	**SK LINE II** *launched as* Ya Jia Da 5 *-2013* **United Oil Co Pte Ltd** *Tarawa* *Kiribati* MMSI: 529715000 Official number: K-17131492	**2,554** 1,430 -	Class: IZ	**2013-12 Yangzhou Guangjin Shipyard Co Ltd — Yangzhou JS** Yd No: GJ1201 Loa 83.90 Br ex - Dght - Lbp - Br md 18.00 Dpth 5.50 Welded, 1 dk	**(A13B2TP) Products Tanker**	**2 oil engines** reduction geared to sc. shafts driving 2 Propellers Total Power: 2,640kW (3,590hp) Chinese Std. Type 6320ZC 2 x 4 Stroke 6 Cy. 320 x 440 each-1320kW (1795bhp) Guangzhou Diesel Engine Factory CoLtd-China
8848264 *DSHS* -	**SK NO. 1** *ex* Kangjin *-2005* *ex* Cheon Yong No. 92 *-1999* **Kum-Young Industry Co Ltd** - *Mokpo* *South Korea* Official number: MPR-915284	**1,493** - 3,206	Class: KR	**1991-12 Ilheung Shipbuilding & Engineering Co Ltd — Mokpo** Yd No: 90-34 Loa 76.50 Br ex 14.40 Dght 5.687 Lbp 70.00 Br md 14.00 Dpth 6.50 Welded, 1 dk	**(A24D2BA) Aggregates Carrier** Grain: 2,200 1 Ha: (27.6 x 11.4)ER	**1 oil engine** geared to sc. shaft driving 1 FP propeller Total Power: 1,681kW (2,285hp) 12.4kn Alpha 6L28/32 1 x 4 Stroke 6 Cy. 280 x 320 1681kW (2285bhp) Ssangyong Heavy Industries Co Ltd-South Korea AuxGen: 2 x 184kW 445V a.c
8704327 - -	**SK NO. 3** *ex* Shoei Maru No. 38 *-2005* *ex* S. S. 1 *-2000* *ex* Shoei Maru No. 38 *-2000* **Shin Kwang Shipping Co Ltd** - *Jeju* *South Korea* MMSI: 440114070 Official number: JJR-056543	**1,868** - 4,031	Class: KR	**1987-06 Kasado Dockyard Co Ltd — Kudamatsu YC** Yd No: 366 Lengthened-2005 Loa 82.80 (BB) Br ex 14.64 Dght 5.513 Lbp 78.20 Br md 14.61 Dpth 7.40 Welded, 2 dks	**(A31A2GX) General Cargo Ship** Grain: 1,545 Compartments: 1 Ho, ER 1 Ha: ER	**1 oil engine** with clutches, flexible couplings & dr geared to sc. shaft driving 1 CP propeller Total Power: 1,471kW (2,000hp) 13.7kn Fuji 6H32 1 x 4 Stroke 6 Cy. 320 x 470 1471kW (2000bhp) Fuji Diesel Co Ltd-Japan Thrusters: 1 Thwart. CP thruster (f)
9538000 *9MQ06* -	**SK PRIDE** *launched as* Seri Kenyalang *-2014* **Nam Cheong International Ltd** - *Port Klang* *Malaysia* MMSI: 533180033 Official number: 335503	**2,638** 984 3,200	Class: NV	**2014-03 Nam Cheong Dockyard Sdn Bhd — Miri** Yd No: 702 Loa 78.70 Br ex - Dght 5.910 Lbp 74.97 Br md 16.00 Dpth 7.00 Welded, 1 dk	**(B21A20S) Platform Supply Ship**	**4 diesel electric oil engines** driving 4 gen. each 1470kW a.c Connecting to 2 elec. motors driving 2 Azimuth electric drive units Total Power: 3,280kW (4,460hp) Caterpillar C32 4 x Vee 4 Stroke 12 Cy. 145 x 162 each-820kW (1115bhp) Caterpillar Inc-USA Thrusters: 2 Tunnel thruster (f)

Ship	Tonnage	Class	Builder / Dimensions	Type	Machinery
9648271 **SK PROACTIVE** *9MQC9* - **Nam Cheong (Labuan) Ltd** OSM Ship Management Pte Ltd *Port Klang* *Malaysia* MMSI: 533130945 Official number: 334506	**3,594** 1,078 3,358	Class: AB	**2013-01 Fujian Southeast Shipyard — Fuzhou FJ** Yd No: SK203 Loa 78.20 Br ex - Dght 6.000 Lbp 69.00 Br md 18.50 Dpth 8.00 Welded, 1 dk	**(B21B20A) Anchor Handling Tug Supply**	**2 oil engines** reduction geared to sc. shafts driving 2 CP propellers Total Power: 9,000kW (12,236hp) Bergens B32: 40L9P 2 x 4 Stroke 9 Cy. 320 x 400 each-4500kW (6118bhp) Rolls Royce Marine AS-Norway AuxGen: 2 x 1732kW a.c, 2 x 590kW a.c Fuel: 1180.0
9633898 **SK SEAHAWK** *9WPQ2* - **Nam Cheong Dockyard Sdn Bhd** - *Kuching* *Malaysia* MMSI: 533170034 Official number: 334708	**499** 150 482	Class: NK	**2012-09 Nam Cheong Dockyard Sdn Bhd — Miri** Yd No: SKL 13 Loa 47.00 Br ex - Dght 2.512 Lbp 43.31 Br md 10.90 Dpth 3.20 Welded, 1 dk	**(A35D2RL) Landing Craft** Bow ramp (centre)	**2 oil engines** reduction geared to sc. shafts driving 2 Propellers Total Power: 896kW (1,218hp) Caterpillar 3412C 2 x Vee 4 Stroke 12 Cy. 137 x 152 each-448kW (609bhp) Caterpillar Inc-USA Fuel: 380.0
9180231 **SK SPLENDOR** *3FXE9* - **Optima Leasing SA** SK Shipping Co Ltd SatCom: Inmarsat C 435793111 *Panama* *Panama* MMSI: 357931000 Official number: 2705600D	**92,866** 27,859 75,154 T/cm 98.4	Class: AB KR	**2000-03 Samsung Heavy Industries Co Ltd — Geoje** Yd No: 1258 Loa 278.40 (BB) Br ex - Dght 12.022 Lbp 266.00 Br md 42.60 Dpth 26.00 Welded, 1 dk	**(A11A2TN) LNG Tanker** Double Bottom Entire Compartment Length Liq (Gas): 135,540 4 x Gas Tank (s); 4 membrane (s.stl) pri horizontal 8 Cargo Pump (s): 8x1700m³/hr Manifold: Bow/CM: 132m	**1 Steam Turb** reverse reduction geared to sc. shaft driving 1 FP propeller Total Power: 29,467kW (40,063hp) 20.3kn Kawasaki UA-400 1 x steam Turb 29467kW (40063shp) Kawasaki Heavy Industries Ltd-Japan AuxGen: 2 x 3450kW 6600/220V 60Hz a.c, 1 x 3450kW 6600/220V 60Hz a.c Thrusters: 1 Thwart. FP thruster (f) Fuel: 386.0 (d.f.) 6670.0 (r.f.) 200.0pd
9180243 **SK STELLAR** *H3OM* - **Stellar Shipholding SA** SK Shipping Co Ltd SatCom: Inmarsat C 435611810 *Panama* *Panama* MMSI: 356118000 Official number: 2768801C	**92,866** 27,859 75,135 T/cm 98.4	Class: AB KR	**2000-12 Samsung Heavy Industries Co Ltd — Geoje** Yd No: 1259 Loa 278.85 (BB) Br ex 42.63 Dght 12.020 Lbp 266.00 Br md 42.60 Dpth 26.00 Welded, 1 dk	**(A11A2TN) LNG Tanker** Double Bottom Entire Compartment Length Liq (Gas): 135,540 4 x Gas Tank (s); 4 membrane (s.stl) pri horizontal 8 Cargo Pump (s): 8x1700m³/hr Manifold: Bow/CM: 135m	**1 Steam Turb** dr reverse geared to sc. shaft driving 1 FP propeller Total Power: 29,467kW (40,063hp) 20.8kn Kawasaki UA-400 1 x steam Turb 29467kW (40063shp) Kawasaki Heavy Industries Ltd-Japan AuxGen: 2 x 3450kW 6600/220V 60Hz a.c, 1 x 3450kW 6600/220V 60Hz a.c Thrusters: 1 Thwart. CP thruster (f) Fuel: 475.7 (d.f.) (Heating Coils) 5751.6 (r.f.)
9157624 **SK SUMMIT** *3FHD9* - **Omnia Enterprises SA** SK Shipping Co Ltd SatCom: Inmarsat C 435735710 *Panama* *Panama* MMSI: 357357000 Official number: 2650399C	**95,378** 27,761 76,064 T/cm 99.7	Class: KR NV	**1999-08 Daewoo Heavy Industries Ltd — Geoje** Yd No: 2202 Loa 277.00 (BB) Br ex - Dght 12.020 Lbp 266.00 Br md 43.40 Dpth 26.00 Welded, 1 dk	**(A11A2TN) LNG Tanker** Double Hull Liq (Gas): 135,933 4 x Gas Tank (s); 4 membrane Gas Transport (stl) pri horizontal 8 Cargo Pump (s): 8x1700m³/hr Manifold: Bow/CM: 135.3m	**1 Steam Turb** reduction geared to sc. shaft driving 1 FP propeller Total Power: 29,422kW (40,002hp) 20.5kn Kawasaki UA-400 1 x steam Turb 29422kW (40002shp) Kawasaki Heavy Industries Ltd-Japan AuxGen: 2 x 3450kW 220/450V 60Hz a.c, 1 x 3450kW 220/450V 60Hz a.c Thrusters: 1 Thwart. CP thruster (f) Fuel: 480.0 (d.f.) (Heating Coils) 6130.0 (r.f.) 202.6pd
9247194 **SK SUNRISE** *HPIY* - **Methane Navigation SA** Iino Marine Service Co Ltd SatCom: Inmarsat C 435415910 *Panama* *Panama* MMSI: 354159000 Official number: 2943803A	**92,927** 27,878 75,248 T/cm 98.3	Class: AB KR	**2003-09 Samsung Heavy Industries Co Ltd — Geoje** Yd No: 1405 Loa 278.85 (BB) Br ex 42.63 Dght 12.020 Lbp 266.00 Br md 42.60 Dpth 26.00 Welded, 1 dk	**(A11A2TN) LNG Tanker** Double Bottom Entire Compartment Length Liq (Gas): 135,505 4 x Gas Tank (s); 4 membrane (s.stl) pri horizontal 8 Cargo Pump (s): 8x1700m³/hr Manifold: Bow/CM: 139.7m	**1 Steam Turb** reduction geared to sc. shaft driving 1 FP propeller Total Power: 29,500kW (40,108hp) 20.6kn Kawasaki UA-400 1 x steam Turb 29500kW (40108shp) Kawasaki Heavy Industries Ltd-Japan AuxGen: 1 x 3630kW 6600/220V 60Hz a.c, 2 x 3450kW 6600/220V 60Hz a.c Thrusters: 1 Thwart. CP thruster (f) Fuel: 594.6 (d.f.) 6803.0 (r.f.)
9157739 **SK SUPREME** *3FOB9* - **Celeste Maritime SA** SK Shipping Co Ltd SatCom: Inmarsat C 435761210 *Panama* *Panama* MMSI: 357612000 Official number: 2684400C	**92,866** 27,859 75,320 T/cm 98.2	Class: AB KR	**2000-01 Samsung Heavy Industries Co Ltd — Geoje** Yd No: 1207 Loa 278.85 (BB) Br ex 42.63 Dght 12.022 Lbp 266.00 Br md 42.60 Dpth 26.00 Welded, 1 dk	**(A11A2TN) LNG Tanker** Double Hull Liq (Gas): 136,320 4 x Gas Tank (s); 4 membrane (s.stl) pri horizontal 8 Cargo Pump (s): 8x1700m³/hr Manifold: Bow/CM: 139.7m	**1 Steam Turb** reverse reduction geared to sc. shaft driving 1 FP propeller Total Power: 29,467kW (40,063hp) 20.8kn Kawasaki UA-400 1 x steam Turb 29467kW (40063shp) Kawasaki Heavy Industries Ltd-Japan AuxGen: 2 x 3450kW 6600/220V 60Hz a.c, 1 x 3450kW 6600/220V 60Hz a.c Thrusters: 1 Thwart. CP thruster (f) Fuel: 600.0 (d.f.) 6805.0 (r.f.)
8737324 **SKA 18** *PMOW* - **PT Barokah Bersama Perkasa** - *Samarinda* *Indonesia*	**360** 108 -	Class: KI	**2008-04 C.V. Swadaya Utama — Samarinda** Loa 33.00 Br ex - Dght 3.390 Lbp 30.91 Br md 9.60 Dpth 4.00 Welded, 1 dk	**(B32A2ST) Tug**	**2 oil engines** reduction geared to sc. shafts driving 2 Propellers Total Power: 1,766kW (2,402hp) Yanmar 6RY17P-GV 2 x 4 Stroke 6 Cy. 165 x 219 each-883kW (1201bhp) Yanmar Diesel Engine Co Ltd-Japan
9137741 **SKAFTAFELL** *ZDFR5* - *ex* BBC Brazil *-2004* *ex* Brake *-2003* *ex* BBC Brazil *-2003* *ex* Industrial Harmony *-2000* *launched as* Torum *-1997* **Briese Schiffahrts GmbH & Co KG ms 'Neuwerk'** Briese Schiffahrts GmbH & Co KG *Gibraltar* *Gibraltar (British)* MMSI: 236201000	**4,078** 2,009 4,900	Class: GL	**1997-05 Stocznia Polnocna SA (Northern Shipyard) — Gdansk** Yd No: B196/2/3 Loa 101.32 (BB) Br ex 16.78 Dght 6.397 Lbp 93.80 Br md 16.60 Dpth 8.10 Welded, 1 dk	**(A31A2GX) General Cargo Ship** Grain: 6,800 TEU 390 C Ho 127 C Dk 263 TEU incl 30 ref C. Compartments: 1 Ho, ER 1 Ha: (57.8 x 13.4)ER Cranes: 2x60t Ice Capable	**1 oil engine** with flexible couplings & sr gearedto sc. shaft driving 1 CP propeller Total Power: 3,950kW (5,370hp) 15.0kn MAN 9L32/40 1 x 4 Stroke 9 Cy. 320 x 400 3950kW (5370bhp) MAN B&W Diesel AG-Augsburg AuxGen: 1 x 640kW 400V 50Hz a.c, 2 x 378kW 400V 50Hz a.c Thrusters: 1 Thwart. FP thruster (f) Fuel: 103.0 (d.f.) 442.0 (r.f.) 15.5pd
7024146 **SKAGASTOL** *LNKR* - **Fjord1 AS** - *Floro* *Norway* MMSI: 257368400	**683** 258 -	Class: (NV)	**1970 Loland Verft AS — Leirvik i Sogn** Yd No: 30 Loa 44.66 Br ex 10.62 Dght 2.858 Lbp 40.52 Br md 10.60 Dpth 4.20 Welded, 1 dk	**(A36A2PR) Passenger/Ro-Ro Ship (Vehicles)** Passengers: 300 Bow door & ramp Len: - Wid: 4.00 Swl: - Stern door & ramp Len: - Wid: 4.50 Swl: - Lane-Len: 126 Lane-Wid: 8.00 Lane-clr ht: 4.20 Cars: 32, Trailers: 1	**1 oil engine** driving 1 FP propeller Total Power: 662kW (900hp) Wichmann 6ACA 1 x 2 Stroke 6 Cy. 280 x 420 662kW (900bhp) Wichmann Motorfabrikk AS-Norway AuxGen: 2 x 52kW 220V 50Hz a.c Thrusters: 1 Thwart. FP thruster (f)
9537472 **SKAGEN** *3FXE2* - **Skagen Shipping Ltd** Ahilleos Ship Management Ltd *Panama* *Panama* MMSI: 370798000 Official number: 4138610	**11,927** 5,507 16,807	Class: GL (BV)	**2009-10 Linhai Chengzhou Shipbuilding Industry Co Ltd — Linhai ZJ** Yd No: HC0702 Loa 147.55 (BB) Br ex - Dght 8.250 Lbp 138.20 Br md 23.00 Dpth 11.80 Welded, 1 dk	**(A31A2GX) General Cargo Ship** Grain: 21,649 Compartments: 4 Ho, ER 4 Ha: ER Cranes: 3x25t Ice Capable	**1 oil engine** reduction geared to sc. shaft driving 1 FP propeller Total Power: 4,320kW (5,873hp) 12.5kn MAN-B&W 9L32/40 1 x 4 Stroke 9 Cy. 320 x 400 4320kW (5873bhp) Shaanxi Diesel Heavy Industry Co Lt-China AuxGen: 2 x 403kW 50Hz a.c, 1 x 350kW 50Hz a.c Fuel: 315.0
9166792 **SKAGEN MAERSK** *OYOS2* - **A P Moller - Maersk A/S** A P Moller SatCom: Inmarsat C 421982110 *Skagen* *Denmark (DIS)* MMSI: 219821000 Official number: D3734	**92,198** 53,625 110,387 T/cm 124.0	Class: AB	**1999-09 Odense Staalskibsvaerft A/S — Munkebo (Lindo Shipyard)** Yd No: 168 Loa 346.98 (BB) Br ex - Dght 14.941 Lbp 331.98 Br md 42.80 Dpth 24.10 Welded, 1 dk	**(A33A2CC) Container Ship (Fully Cellular)** TEU 9578 incl 817 ref C Compartments: ER, 20 Cell Ho 20 Ha: ER	**1 oil engine** driving 1 FP propeller Total Power: 54,835kW (74,554hp) 25.0kn B&W 12K90MC 1 x 2 Stroke 12 Cy. 900 x 2550 54835kW (74554bhp) Hitachi Zosen Corp-Japan AuxGen: 5 x 3000kW 6600V 60Hz a.c Thrusters: 1 Thwart. FP thruster (f); 2 Thwart. FP thruster (a)

9313864 **SKAGENBANK**
PHMB
- **Bankship IV BV**
Pot Scheepvaart BV
Delfzijl *Netherlands*
MMSI: 245306000
Official number: 42934

2,999 1,643 4,500

Class: BV

2005-02 Ferus Smit Leer GmbH — Leer Yd No: 354
Loa 89.78 (BB) Br ex - Dght 5.950
Lbp 84.99 Br md 14.00 Dpth 7.50
Welded, 1 dk

(A31A2GX) General Cargo Ship
Grain: 5,976
TEU 144 C Ho 102 TEU C Dk 42
Compartments: 1 Ho, ER (s.stl)
1 Ha: ER (59.4 x 11.5)
Ice Capable

1 oil engine geared to sc. shaft driving 1 CP propeller
Total Power: 2,640kW (3,589hp) 13.0kn
MaK 8M25
1 x 4 Stroke 8 Cy. 255 x 400 2640kW (3589bhp)
Caterpillar Motoren GmbH & Co. KG-Germany
AuxGen: 1 x 340kW 400/230V 50Hz a.c, 2 x 188kW 400/230V 50Hz a.c
Thrusters: 1 Tunnel thruster (f)

7642170 **SKAGERAK**
SGCD
ex Stril Explorer -1993
- *ex Friedrich Heincke -1990*
Goteborgs Universitet

Hono *Sweden*
MMSI: 265280000

390 117 -

Class: (GL)

1968 August Pahl Schiffswerft — Hamburg
Yd No: 328
Loa 38.10 (BB) Br ex 9.02 Dght 3.442
Lbp 34.45 Br md 9.00 Dpth 4.02
Welded, 1 dk

(B12D2FR) Fishery Research Vessel
Ice Capable

1 oil engine driving 1 CP propeller
Total Power: 677kW (920hp) 12.5kn
MWM TB12RS18/22
1 x Vee 4 Stroke 12 Cy. 180 x 220 677kW (920bhp)
Motoren Werke Mannheim AG (MWM)-West Germany
AuxGen: 1 x 120kW 220V 50Hz a.c

9197791 **SKAGERN**
PHHL
ex Scharhorn -2006
- **MF Ship BV**
Marin Ship Management BV
Delfzijl *Netherlands*
MMSI: 246558000
Official number: 49728

2,301 1,289 3,171 T/cm 9.0

Class: GL

2000-09 Daewoo-Mangalia Heavy Industries S.A. — Mangalia (Hull) Yd No: 1006
2000-09 Scheepswerf Pattje B.V. — Waterhuizen Yd No: 415
Loa 82.50 (BB) Br ex - Dght 5.300
Lbp 78.90 Br md 12.40 Dpth 6.80
Welded, 1 dk

(A31A2GX) General Cargo Ship
Double Hull
Grain: 4,782; Bale: 4,782
TEU 132 C.Ho 96/20' (40') C. Dk 36/20' (40')
Compartments: 1 Ho, ER
1 Ha: (56.3 x 10.2)ER
Ice Capable

1 oil engine reduction geared to sc. shaft driving 1 CP propeller
Total Power: 1,800kW (2,447hp) 12.0kn
MaK 6M25
1 x 4 Stroke 6 Cy. 255 x 400 1800kW (2447bhp)
MaK Motoren GmbH & Co. KG-Kiel
AuxGen: 1 x 240kW 220/380V a.c, 2 x 90kW 220/380V a.c
Thrusters: 1 Thwart. FP thruster (f)
Fuel: 16.2 (d.f.) 168.2 (r.f.)

9187825 **SKAGET**
LJDZ
- **Altafjord Oppdrett AS**

Hammerfest *Norway*
MMSI: 257440900

111 44 -

1998-06 Saltdalsverftet AS — Rognan Yd No: 188
Loa 23.00 Br ex 8.50 Dght -
Lbp - Br md - Dpth 2.90
Welded

(A36A2PR) Passenger/Ro-Ro Ship (Vehicles)

2 oil engines driving 2 FP propellers
Total Power: 368kW (500hp)
Scania DS9
2 x 4 Stroke 6 Cy. 115 x 136 each-184kW (250bhp)
Scania AB-Sweden
Thrusters: 1 Thwart. FP thruster (f)

9029255 **SKAGOYSUND**
LMUR
T-23-T **Skagoysund AS**

Tromso *Norway*
MMSI: 258553000

498 178 -

2004-09 in Lithuania (Hull launched by)
2004-09 Vaagland Baatbyggeri AS — Vaagland (Hull completed by) Yd No: 135
Lengthened-2011
Loa 38.06 Br ex - Dght 4.660
Lbp - Br md 9.00 Dpth 4.86
Welded, 1 dk

(B11B2FV) Fishing Vessel

1 oil engine reduction geared to sc. shaft driving 1 CP propeller
Total Power: 1,000kW (1,360hp)
Mitsubishi S12R-MPTK
1 x Vee 4 Stroke 12 Cy. 170 x 180 1000kW (1360bhp)
Mitsubishi Heavy Industries Ltd-Japan
Thrusters: 1 Tunnel thruster (f)

8034928 **SKALA**
-
- **UTRF-Holding JSC (OAO 'UTRF-Holding')**
-

773 231 287

Class: (RS)

1982 Zavod "Leninskaya Kuznitsa" — Kiyev Yd No: 254
Loa 53.75 (BB) Br ex 10.72 Dght 4.330
Lbp 47.92 Br md - Dpth 6.00
Welded, 1 dk

(B11A2FS) Stern Trawler
Ins: 218
Compartments: 1 Ho, ER
1 Ha: (1.6 x 1.6)
Derricks: 2x1.5t
Ice Capable

1 oil engine driving 1 FP propeller
Total Power: 971kW (1,320hp) 12.8kn
S.K.L. 8NVD48A-2U
1 x 4 Stroke 8 Cy. 320 x 480 971kW (1320bhp)
VEB Schwermaschinenbau "KarlLiebknecht" (SKL)-Magdeburg

9256676 **SKALABERG**
TFKV
ex Esperanza Del Sur -2012 ex Skalaberg -2010
RE 307 **Brim hf**
-
Reykjavik *Iceland*
MMSI: 251424000

3,695 1,109 -

Class: NV (LR)
Classed LR until 29/12/08

2002-10 DP Sudnobudivnyi Zavod im. "61 Kommunara" — Mykolayiv (Hull) Yd No: 3103
2002-10 Kimek AS — Kirkenes Yd No: (3103)
Loa 74.50 Br ex 16.20 Dght 6.500
Lbp 65.40 Br md 16.00 Dpth 9.50
Welded, 1 dk

(B11A2FG) Factory Stern Trawler
Ice Capable

1 oil engine geared to sc. shaft driving 1 FP propeller
Total Power: 8,000kW (10,877hp)
Wartsila 16V32
1 x Vee 4 Stroke 16 Cy. 320 x 400 8000kW (10877bhp)
Wartsila Finland Oy-Finland

8996918 **SKALAFOSSUR**
XPYC
VN 559 **Dugvuberg Sp/f**
-
Vestmanna *Faeroe Islands (Danish)*
MMSI: 231371000

113 30 40

2005-04 'Crist' Sp z oo — Gdansk (Hull launched by)
2005-04 p/f Torshavnar Skipasmidja — Torshavn (Hull completed by) Yd No: 45
Loa 19.35 (BB) Br ex - Dght 2.750
Lbp 16.00 Br md 5.75 Dpth 4.65
Welded, 1 dk

(B11A2FS) Stern Trawler

1 oil engine geared to sc. shaft driving 1 Propeller
Total Power: 370kW (503hp) 10.0kn
Caterpillar 3412E
1 x Vee 4 Stroke 12 Cy. 137 x 152 370kW (503bhp)
Caterpillar Inc-USA

7833092 **SKALAT**
UGEI
- **DV Ryboprodukt Co Ltd (OOO DV Ryboprodukt)**

Khasanskiy *Russia*
MMSI: 273818500
Official number: 791330

904 271 331

Class: (RS)

1980-09 Volgogradskiy Sudostroitelnyy Zavod — Volgograd Yd No: 891
Loa 53.75 Br ex 10.72 Dght 4.290
Lbp 47.92 Br md 10.50 Dpth 6.00
Welded, 1 dk

(B11A2FS) Stern Trawler
Ins: 218
Compartments: 1 Ho, ER
1 Ha: (1.6 x 1.6)
Derricks: 2x1.5t
Ice Capable

1 oil engine driving 1 FP propeller
Total Power: 971kW (1,320hp) 12.8kn
S.K.L. 8NVD48A-2U
1 x 4 Stroke 8 Cy. 320 x 480 971kW (1320bhp)
VEB Schwermaschinenbau "KarlLiebknecht" (SKL)-Magdeburg
Fuel: 185.0 (d.f.)

7524598 **SKALNY**
HQJY4
- **Aspac Marine Pte Ltd**
-
San Lorenzo *Honduras*
Official number: L-1924351

163 39 94

Class: (RS)

1975 Sretenskiy Sudostroitelnyy Zavod — Sretensk Yd No: 78
Loa 33.96 Br ex 7.09 Dght 2.899
Lbp 30.00 Br md - Dpth 3.69
Welded, 1 dk

(B11B2FV) Fishing Vessel
Bale: 115
Compartments: 1 Ho, ER
1 Ha: (1.3 x 1.6)
Derricks: 2x2t; Winches: 2

1 oil engine driving 1 FP propeller
Total Power: 224kW (305hp) 9.5kn
S.K.L. 8NVD36-1U
1 x 4 Stroke 8 Cy. 240 x 360 224kW (305bhp)
VEB Schwermaschinenbau "KarlLiebknecht" (SKL)-Magdeburg

9533995 **SKAMANDROS**
A8ZU7
- **Staples Services Ltd**
Westgate Tankships Inc
SatCom: Inmarsat C 463712357
Monrovia *Liberia*
MMSI: 636015304
Official number: 15304

81,299 51,978 158,491 T/cm 120.0

Class: LR
✠ **100A1** SS 05/2012
Double Hull oil tanker
CSR
ESP
ShipRight (CM, ACS (B))
*IWS
LI
SPM4
✠ **LMC** **UMS IGS**
Cable: 742.5/97.0 U3 (a)

2012-05 Sungdong Shipbuilding & Marine Engineering Co Ltd — Tongyeong Yd No: 2021
Loa 274.20 (BB) Br ex 48.03 Dght 17.150
Lbp 264.00 Br md 48.00 Dpth 23.10
Welded, 1 dk

(A13A2TV) Crude Oil Tanker
Double Hull (13F)
Liq: 165,700; Liq (Oil): 165,700
Compartments: 12 Wing Ta, 2 Wing Slop Ta, ER
3 Cargo Pump (s): 3x4000m³/hr

1 oil engine driving 1 FP propeller
Total Power: 18,660kW (25,370hp) 15.5kn
MAN-B&W 6S70MC-C
1 x 2 Stroke 6 Cy. 700 x 2800 18660kW (25370bhp)
Hyundai Engine & Machinery Co Ltd-South Korea
AuxGen: 3 x 987kW 450V 60Hz a.c
Boilers: e (ex.g.) 22.4kgf/cm² (22.0bar), AuxB (o.f.) 18.4kgf/cm² (18.0bar)

7725154 **SKANDERBORG**
3FPN3
ex Dana Arabia -1984
Nordana Shipping (Singapore) Pte Ltd
Jutha Maritime Public Co Ltd
Panama *Panama*
MMSI: 354681000
Official number: 4333112

14,805 4,441 10,470 T/cm 26.1

Class: RI (LR)
✠ Classed LR until 12/11/02

1979-10 Nippon Kokan KK (NKK Corp) — Shizuoka SZ Yd No: 377
2002 Cindemir Makina Gemi Onarim ve Tersanecilik AS — Istanbul (Tuzla) (Additional cargo section)
Lengthened-2002
Loa 161.40 (BB) Br ex 24.29 Dght 6.413
Lbp 150.40 Br md 24.01 Dpth 14.36
Welded, 2 dks, Upr intermediate hoistable dk fwd & Lwr hoistable dk aft light cargoes only

(A35A2RR) Ro-Ro Cargo Ship
Stern door & ramp
Len: 14.50 Wid: 8.50 Swl: 200
Lane-Len: 1884
Lane-Wid: 6.00
Lane-clr ht: 6.30
Trailers: 149
Bale: 18,569
TEU 654 C Ho 280 TEU C Dk 374 TEU incl 12 ref C.
Compartments: 1 Ho, ER
2 Ha: (26.6 x 8.0) (21.3 x 9.0)ER
Cranes: 1x36t; Derricks: 1x120t

1 oil engine driving 1 FP propeller
Total Power: 5,913kW (8,039hp) 14.5kn
B&W 6L55GF
1 x 2 Stroke 6 Cy. 550 x 1380 5913kW (8039bhp)
Mitsui Engineering & Shipbuilding CLtd-Japan
AuxGen: 3 x 920kW 220/390V 50Hz a.c
Boilers: AuxB (o.f.) 8.0kgf/cm² (7.8bar), AuxB (ex.g.) 8.0kgf/cm² (7.8bar)
Thrusters: 1 Thwart. CP thruster (f)
Fuel: 72.0 (d.f.) (Heating Coils) 1735.0 (r.f.) 24.5pd

9387217 **SKANDI ACERGY**
2BEJ5
- **DOF Subsea Rederi AS**
DOF Management AS
SatCom: Inmarsat C 423591020
Douglas *Isle of Man (British)*
MMSI: 235065411
Official number: 740807

16,500 4,951 11,500

Class: NV

2008-07 SC Aker Tulcea SA — Tulcea (Hull) Yd No: 372
2008-07 Aker Yards AS Soviknes — Sovik Yd No: 154
Loa 156.90 (BB) Br ex 27.20 Dght 8.500
Lbp 137.70 Br md 27.00 Dpth 12.00
Welded, 1 dk

(B22A2OR) Offshore Support Vessel
Passengers: cabins: 99; berths: 140
Cranes: 1x400t,1x100t
Ice Capable

6 diesel electric oil engines driving 2 gen. each 3432kW a.c 4 gen. each 2576kW a.c driving 2 Azimuth electric drive units contra-rotating propellers, 1 CP propeller
Total Power: 19,290kW (26,226hp) 16.0kn
MAN-B&W 6L32/40CD
4 x 4 Stroke 6 Cy. 320 x 400 each-2892kW (3932bhp)
STX Engine Co Ltd-South Korea
MAN-B&W 8L32/40CD
2 x 4 Stroke 8 Cy. 320 x 400 each-3861kW (5249bhp)
STX Engine Co Ltd-South Korea
Thrusters: 2 Tunnel thruster (f); 2 Retract. directional thruster (f)
Fuel: 1900.0

IMO / Call sign	Name / Owner / Manager / Port / Flag	Tonnage	Class	Builder / Dimensions	Type	Machinery
9413810 *C6WC7* -	**SKANDI ACHIEVER** **DOF Subsea Rederi AS** DOF (UK) Ltd SatCom: Inmarsat C 430996910 *Nassau* *Bahamas* MMSI: 309969000 Official number: 8001353	**7,617** 2,286 4,000	Class: NV	**2007-08 SC Aker Tulcea SA — Tulcea** (Hull) **2007-08 Aker Yards AS Soviknes — Sovik** Yd No: 701 Loa 105.90 (BB) Br ex 21.03 Dght 6.600 Lbp 94.70 Br md 21.00 Dpth 8.50 Welded, 1 dk	**(B22A20R) Offshore Support Vessel** Cranes: 1x140t Ice Capable	**6 diesel electric oil engines** driving 2 gen. each 1900kW 690V a.c 4 gen. each 1580kW 690V a.c Connecting to 2 elec. motors each (2300kW) driving 2 Azimuth electric drive units contra-rotating propellers Total Power: 9,880kW (13,432hp) 15.5kn MAN-B&W 9L28/32A 2 x 4 Stroke 9 Cy. 280 x 320 each-1880kW (2556bhp) Wartsila 9L20 4 x 4 Stroke 9 Cy. 200 x 280 each-1530kW (2080bhp) Wartsila Finland Oy-Finland AuxGen: 2 x 370kW a.c Thrusters: 2 Tunnel thruster (f); 1 Retract. directional thruster (f) Fuel: 1035.0
9185023 *C6YY7* -	**SKANDI ADMIRAL** *ex Northern Admiral -2003* **DOF Rederi AS** Norskan Offshore Ltda *Nassau* *Bahamas* MMSI: 311049500 Official number: 8001863	**4,370** 1,715 4,400	Class: NV	**1999-07 Th Hellesoy Skipsbyggeri AS — Lofallstrand** Yd No: 135 Loa 83.30 Br ex - Dght 7.800 Lbp 75.93 Br md 20.50 Dpth 9.50 Welded, 1 dk	**(B21B20A) Anchor Handling Tug Supply** A-frames: 1x250t Ice Capable	**4 oil engines** reduction geared to sc. shafts driving 2 CP propellers Total Power: 15,876kW (21,584hp) 12.0kn Normo BRM-9 4 x 4 Stroke 9 Cy. 320 x 360 each-3969kW (5396bhp) Ulstein Bergen AS-Norway AuxGen: 2 x 2400kW 230/440V 60Hz a.c, 2 x 750kW 230/440V 60Hz a.c Thrusters: 1 Thwart. FP thruster (f); 1 Retract. directional thruster (f); 2 Thwart. CP thruster (a)
9387229 *5BXH2* -	**SKANDI AKER** *launched as Skandi Newvile -2010* **DOF Subsea Rederi AS** DOF Management AS *Limassol* *Cyprus* MMSI: 212341000	**16,942** 5,083 11,000	Class: NV	**2010-01 STX RO Offshore Tulcea SA — Tulcea** (Hull) **2010-01 STX Norway Offshore AS Soviknes — Sovik** Yd No: 705 Loa 156.90 (BB) Br ex 31.20 Dght 8.500 Lbp 137.70 Br md 27.00 Dpth 12.00 Welded, 1 dk	**(B22A20R) Offshore Support Vessel** Passengers: berths: 140 Cranes: 1x400t,1x100t Ice Capable	**6 diesel electric oil engines** driving 2 gen. 4 gen. each 2700kW a.c Connecting to 2 elec. motors each (3000kW) 1 elec. Motor driving 1 CP propeller , 2 Z propellers contra-rotating propellers Total Power: 18,700kW (25,426hp) 16.0kn MAN-B&W 6L32/40CD 4 x 4 Stroke 6 Cy. 320 x 400 each-2805kW (3814bhp) STX Engine Co Ltd-South Korea MAN-B&W 8L32/40CD 2 x 4 Stroke 8 Cy. 320 x 400 each-3740kW (5085bhp) STX Engine Co Ltd-South Korea Thrusters: 2 Tunnel thruster (f); 2 Retract. directional thruster (f)
9528328 *PQ4630* -	**SKANDI AMAZONAS** **DOF Navegacao Ltda** Norskan Offshore Ltda *Rio de Janeiro* *Brazil* MMSI: 710008890	**7,099** 2,130 4,700	Class: NV	**2011-10 STX OSV Niteroi SA — Niteroi** Yd No: PRO-26 Loa 95.00 (BB) Br ex 24.05 Dght 7.800 Lbp 84.80 Br md 24.00 Dpth 9.80 Welded, 1 dk	**(B21B20A) Anchor Handling Tug Supply** Passengers: 60	**2 oil engines** reduction geared to sc. shafts driving 2 CP propellers Total Power: 15,360kW (20,884hp) 17.0kn Wartsila 16V32 2 x Vee 4 Stroke 16 Cy. 320 x 400 each-7680kW (10442bhp) Wartsila Finland Oy-Finland AuxGen: 4 x a.c Thrusters: 2 Tunnel thruster (f); 1 Tunnel thruster (a); 1 Retract. directional thruster (f); 1 Retract. directional thruster (a)
9413822 *C6XW3* -	**SKANDI ARCTIC** **Doftech DA** DOF Management AS SatCom: Inmarsat C 431100536 *Nassau* *Bahamas* MMSI: 311023800 Official number: 8001658	**18,640** 5,593 13,000	Class: NV	**2009-03 STX RO Offshore Tulcea SA — Tulcea** (Hull) **2009-03 STX Norway Offshore AS Soviknes — Sovik** Yd No: 702 Loa 156.90 (BB) Br ex 31.20 Dght 8.500 Lbp 137.70 Br md 27.00 Dpth 12.00 Welded, 1 dk	**(B22A20V) Diving Support Vessel** Passengers: cabins: 99; berths: 140 Cranes: 1x400t,1x50t Ice Capable	**6 diesel electric oil engines** driving 6 gen. each 2845kW a.c Connecting to 2 elec. motors each (3000kW) 1 elec. Motor driving 2 Azimuth electric drive units , 1 CP propeller Total Power: 20,160kW (27,408hp) 16.0kn Wartsila 7L32 6 x 4 Stroke 7 Cy. 320 x 400 each-3360kW (4568bhp) Wartsila Finland Oy-Finland Thrusters: 2 Tunnel thruster (f); 2 Retract. directional thruster (f) Fuel: 3243.0
9447665 *LAQT7* -	**SKANDI ATLANTIC** **Aker DOF Deepwater AS** DOF ASA (District Offshore ASA) *Bergen* *Norway (NIS)* MMSI: 258004000	**3,181** 1,129 3,000	Class: NV	**2012-03 STX OSV Vung Tau Ltd — Vung Tau** Yd No: 006 Loa 74.40 (BB) Br ex - Dght 7.000 Lbp 68.01 Br md 17.40 Dpth 8.50 Welded, 1 dk	**(B21B20A) Anchor Handling Tug Supply**	**2 oil engines** reduction geared to sc. shafts driving 2 CP propellers Total Power: 12,000kW (16,316hp) 15.0kn Bergens B32: 40V12P 2 x Vee 4 Stroke 12 Cy. 320 x 400 each-6000kW (8158bhp) Rolls Royce Marine AS-Norway AuxGen: 2 x a.c Thrusters: 2 Tunnel thruster (f); 2 Tunnel thruster (a)
9625425 *LAOP7* -	**SKANDI AUKRA** **PSV Invest II AS** - *Bergen* *Norway (NIS)* MMSI: 257823000	**3,966** 1,581 4,574	Class: NV	**2012-07 STX OSV Tulcea SA — Tulcea** (Hull) **2012-07 STX OSV Aukra — Aukra** Yd No: 775 Loa 87.83 (BB) Br ex - Dght 6.600 Lbp 79.32 Br md 19.00 Dpth 8.00 Welded, 1 dk	**(B21A20S) Platform Supply Ship**	**4 diesel electric oil engines** driving 4 gen. Connecting to 2 elec. motors each (2200kW) driving 2 Azimuth electric drive units Total Power: 7,200kW (9,788hp) 11.0kn Wartsila 9L20 4 x 4 Stroke 9 Cy. 200 x 280 each-1800kW (2447bhp) Wartsila Finland Oy-Finland Thrusters: 1 Retract. directional thruster (f); 1 Tunnel thruster (f)
9330680 *LALG7* -	**SKANDI BARRA** **DOF (UK) Ltd** - *Bergen* *Norway (NIS)* MMSI: 257679000	**3,350** 1,287 4,150	Class: NV	**2005-07 SC Aker Tulcea SA — Tulcea** (Hull) Yd No: 324 **2005-07 Soviknes Verft AS — Sovik** Yd No: 144 Loa 86.65 (BB) Br ex 19.73 Dght 6.100 Lbp 77.94 Br md 19.70 Dpth 7.45 Welded, 1 dk	**(B21A20S) Platform Supply Ship** Passengers: berths: 24	**4 diesel electric oil engines** driving 4 gen. each 1480kW 690V a.c Connecting to 2 elec. motors each (2200kW) driving 2 Azimuth electric drive units contra rotating propellers Total Power: 6,120kW (8,320hp) 12.0kn Wartsila 9L20 4 x 4 Stroke 9 Cy. 200 x 280 each-1530kW (2080bhp) Wartsila Finland Oy-Finland Thrusters: 1 Thwart. CP thruster (f); 1 Retract. directional thruster (f) Fuel: 850.0
9339131 *PPTM* -	**SKANDI BOTAFOGO** *ex Norskan Botafogo -2009* **Skannor Offshore Ltda** Norskan Offshore Ltda *Rio de Janeiro* *Brazil* MMSI: 710002480 Official number: 3810516546	**3,519** 1,056 2,600	Class: NV	**2006-09 Aker Promar SA — Niteroi** Yd No: PRO-17 Loa 80.50 Br ex 18.05 Dght 6.600 Lbp 69.30 Br md 18.00 Dpth 8.00 Welded, 1 dk	**(B21B20A) Anchor Handling Tug Supply** Cranes: 1x10t	**4 oil engines** reduction geared to sc. shafts driving 2 CP propellers Total Power: 12,356kW (16,798hp) 17.0kn Bergens BRM-6 2 x 4 Stroke 6 Cy. 320 x 360 each-2648kW (3600bhp) Rolls Royce Marine AS-Norway Bergens BRM-8 2 x 4 Stroke 8 Cy. 320 x 360 each-3530kW (4799bhp) Rolls Royce Marine AS-Norway AuxGen: 2 x a.c, 2 x a.c Thrusters: 1 Thwart. CP thruster (f); 2 Thwart. CP thruster (a); 1 Retract. directional thruster (f)
9263514 *LAWP5* -	**SKANDI BUCHAN** **DOF Rederi AS** DOF (UK) Ltd *Bergen* *Norway (NIS)* MMSI: 258753000	**3,360** 1,263 4,195	Class: NV	**2002-09 DP Sudnobudivnyi Zavod im. "61 Kommunara" — Mykolayiv** (Hull) Yd No: 3002 **2002-09 Fitjar Mek. Verksted AS — Fitjar** Yd No: 18 Loa 83.85 (BB) Br ex 20.00 Dght 6.100 Lbp 75.36 Br md 19.70 Dpth 7.45 Welded, 1 dk	**(B21A20S) Platform Supply Ship** Liq: 1,200	**4 diesel electric oil engines** driving 4 gen. Connecting to 2 elec. motors each (2200kW) driving 2 Azimuth electric drive units Total Power: 6,120kW (8,320hp) 16.0kn Wartsila 9L20 4 x 4 Stroke 9 Cy. 200 x 280 each-1530kW (2080bhp) Wartsila Finland Oy-Finland Thrusters: 1 Thwart. FP thruster (f); 1 Retract. directional thruster (f)
9281657 *LALA7* -	**SKANDI CALEDONIA** **DOF ASA (District Offshore ASA)** DOF Management AS *Bergen* *Norway (NIS)* MMSI: 258765000	**3,285** 1,251 4,100	Class: NV	**2003-11 DP Sudnobudivnyi Zavod im. "61 Kommunara" — Mykolayiv** (Hull) Yd No: 3003 **2003-11 Fitjar Mek. Verksted AS — Fitjar** Yd No: 19 Loa 83.70 (BB) Br ex 20.00 Dght 6.100 Lbp 75.36 Br md 19.70 Dpth 7.45 Welded, 1 dk	**(B21A20S) Platform Supply Ship** Passengers: berths: 24	**4 diesel electric oil engines** driving 4 gen. each 1460kW a.c Connecting to 2 elec. motors each (2200kW) driving 2 Azimuth electric drive units contra rotating propellers Total Power: 6,120kW (8,320hp) 12.0kn Wartsila 9L20 4 x 4 Stroke 9 Cy. 200 x 280 each-1530kW (2080bhp) Wartsila Finland Oy-Finland Thrusters: 1 Tunnel thruster (f); 1 Retract. directional thruster (f)

IMO / Call sign	Name / Owner / Manager / Flag	Tonnage	Classification	Builder / Dimensions	Type	Machinery
9284324 *LMHJ3* -	**SKANDI CAPTAIN** **DOF Rederi II AS** DOF Management AS *Bergen* *Norway (NIS)* MMSI: 258345000	**2,592** 855 3,333	Class: NV	**2004-03 Societatea Comerciala Severnav S.A. — Drobeta-Turnu Severin** (Hull) Yd No: (37) **2004-03 Myklebust Mek. Verksted AS — Gursken** Yd No: 37 Loa 74.30 (BB) Br ex - Dght 6.225 Lbp 66.36 Br md 16.40 Dpth 7.45 Welded, 1 dk	**(B21A2OS) Platform Supply Ship** Passengers: berths: 22	**4 diesel electric oil engines** driving 4 gen. each 1016kW 690V a.c Connecting to 2 elec. motors each (1470kW) driving 2 Azimuth electric drive units contra-rotating propellers Total Power: 4,572kW (6,216hp) 12.0kn Mitsubishi S12R-MPTA 4 x Vee 4 Stroke 12 Cy. 170 x 180 each-1143kW (1554bhp) Mitsubishi Heavy Industries Ltd-Japan AuxGen: 4 x 1200kW 690V 60Hz a.c Thrusters: 2 Thwart. FP thruster (f) Fuel: 921.0 15.5pd
9239446 *C6RX4* -	**SKANDI CARLA** **DOF Subsea Rederi AS** DOF Management AS *Nassau* *Bahamas* MMSI: 311222000 Official number: 8000333	**4,456** 1,336 4,400	Class: NV	**2001-06 Aukra Industrier AS — Aukra** Yd No: 102 Loa 83.85 (BB) Br ex 20.00 Dght 6.200 Lbp 76.80 Br md 19.70 Dpth 7.45 Welded, 1 dk	**(B22A2OV) Diving Support Vessel** Passengers: berths: 80 Cranes: 1x50t	**4 diesel electric oil engines** driving 4 gen. each 2425kW Connecting to 2 elec. motors each (2200kW) driving 2 Azimuth electric drive units Total Power: 10,120kW (13,760hp) 13.0kn Caterpillar 3608TA 4 x 4 Stroke 8 Cy. 280 x 300 each-2530kW (3440bhp) Caterpillar Inc-USA Thrusters: 2 Tunnel thruster (f); 1 Retract. directional thruster (f)
9330692 *LAEP6* -	**SKANDI CHIEFTAIN** **Norskan Norway AS** Norskan Offshore Ltda *Bergen* *Norway (NIS)* MMSI: 257584000	**3,187** 957 3,355	Class: NV	**2005-10 SC Aker Tulcea SA — Tulcea** (Hull) Yd No: 325 **2005-10 Brattvaag Skipsverft AS — Brattvaag** Yd No: 108 Converted From: Offshore Supply Ship-2009 Loa 74.20 (BB) Br ex - Dght 6.225 Lbp 67.20 Br md 16.40 Dpth 7.45 Welded, 1 dk	**(B22A2OV) Diving Support Vessel** Passengers: 8 Cranes: 1x22t	**4 diesel electric oil engines** driving 4 gen. each 1200kW 690V a.c Connecting to 2 elec. motors each (1470kW) driving 2 Azimuth electric drive units Total Power: 4,760kW (6,472hp) 12.0kn Mitsubishi S12R-MPTA 4 x Vee 4 Stroke 12 Cy. 170 x 180 each-1190kW (1618bhp) Mitsubishi Heavy Industries Ltd-Japan AuxGen: 4 x 1200kW 690V 60Hz a.c Thrusters: 2 Tunnel thruster (f) Fuel: 1063.0 (r.f.) 15.5pd
9382774 *LACA7* -	**SKANDI COMMANDER** **DOF Rederi AS** Norskan Offshore Ltda *Bergen* *Norway (NIS)* MMSI: 258847000	**3,203** 961 3,224	Class: NV	**2007-05 OAO Vyborgskiy Sudostroitelnyy Zavod — Vyborg** (Hull) Yd No: 931 **2007-05 Fitjar Mek. Verksted AS — Fitjar** Yd No: 29 Converted From: Offshore Supply Ship-2011 Loa 74.30 (BB) Br ex 16.44 Dght 6.220 Lbp 67.20 Br md 16.40 Dpth 7.45 Welded, 1 dk	**(B22A2OV) Diving Support Vessel** Passengers: cabins: 8; berths: 22 A-frames: 1x30t; Cranes: 1x10t	**4 diesel electric oil engines** driving 2 gen. each 1330kW 690V a.c 2 gen. each 1140kW 690V a.c Connecting to 2 elec. motors each (1470kW) driving 2 Azimuth electric drive units Total Power: 5,589kW (7,599hp) 12.0kn MAN-B&W 6L21/31 2 x 4 Stroke 6 Cy. 210 x 310 each-1289kW (1753bhp) MAN Diesel A/S-Denmark MAN-B&W 7L21/31 2 x 4 Stroke 7 Cy. 210 x 310 each-1505kW (2046bhp) MAN Diesel A/S-Denmark AuxGen: 4 x 1016kW 690V 60Hz a.c Thrusters: 2 Tunnel thruster (f) Fuel: 1085.0
9431642 *C6ZH8* -	**SKANDI CONSTRUCTOR** *ex* Sarah *-2011* *ex* African Sarah *-2009* *completed as* Sarah *-2009* **DOF Subsea Rederi AS** DOF Management AS SatCom: Inmarsat C 431101226 *Nassau* *Bahamas* Official number: 8001918	**11,572** 3,472 8,588	Class: NV	**2009-07 ATVT Sudnobudivnyi Zavod "Zaliv" — Kerch** (Hull) Yd No: 01283 **2009-07 Ulstein Verft AS — Ulsteinvik** Yd No: 283 Loa 120.20 Br ex - Dght 8.000 Lbp 112.30 Br md 25.00 Dpth 10.00 Welded, 1 dk	**(B22F2OW) Well Stimulation Vessel** Cranes: 1x150t	**4 diesel electric oil engines** driving 2 gen. each 4145kW a.c 2 gen. each 2765kW a.c Connecting to 2 elec. motors each (3500kW) driving 2 Azimuth electric drive units Total Power: 15,000kW (20,394hp) 14.5kn Bergens B32: 40L6P 2 x 4 Stroke 6 Cy. 320 x 400 each-3000kW (4079bhp) Rolls Royce Marine AS-Norway Bergens B32: 40L9P 2 x 4 Stroke 9 Cy. 320 x 400 each-4500kW (6118bhp) Rolls Royce Marine AS-Norway Thrusters: 2 Thwart. CP thruster (f); 1 Retract. directional thruster (f); 1 Retract. directional thruster (a)
9283435 *PPQM* -	**SKANDI COPACABANA** *ex* Norskan Copacabana *-2008* **DOF Navegacao Ltda** Norskan Offshore Ltda SatCom: Inmarsat C 471000130 *Rio de Janeiro* *Brazil* MMSI: 710000840 Official number: 3810513555	**3,678** 1,104 2,400	Class: NV	**2005-06 Estaleiro Ilha S.A. (EISA) — Rio de Janeiro** Yd No: 479 Loa 80.50 Br ex 18.46 Dght 6.600 Lbp 69.30 Br md 18.00 Dpth 8.00 Welded, 1 dk	**(B21B20A) Anchor Handling Tug Supply**	**4 oil engines** reduction geared to sc. shafts driving 2 CP propellers Total Power: 12,370kW (16,818hp) 13.5kn Bergens BRM-6 2 x 4 Stroke 6 Cy. 320 x 360 each-2650kW (3603bhp) Rolls Royce Marine AS-Norway Bergens BRM-8 2 x 4 Stroke 8 Cy. 320 x 360 each-3535kW (4806bhp) Rolls Royce Marine AS-Norway AuxGen: 2 x a.c, 2 x 2240kW a.c Thrusters: 1 Tunnel thruster (f); 1 Retract. directional thruster (f); 1 Tunnel thruster (a)
9447639 *C6ZC7* -	**SKANDI EMERALD** *launched as* Sea Emerald *-2011* **Aker DOF Deepwater AS** DOF ASA (District Offshore ASA) SatCom: Inmarsat C 431101122 *Nassau* *Bahamas* MMSI: 311052400 Official number: 8001877	**3,181** 1,129 3,195	Class: NV	**2011-03 STX OSV Vung Tau Ltd — Vung Tau** Yd No: 003 Loa 75.01 (BB) Br ex 17.41 Dght 7.000 Lbp 68.03 Br md 17.40 Dpth 8.50 Welded, 1 dk	**(B21B20A) Anchor Handling Tug Supply**	**2 oil engines** reduction geared to sc. shafts driving 2 CP propellers Total Power: 12,000kW (16,316hp) 15.0kn Bergens B32: 40V12P 2 x Vee 4 Stroke 12 Cy. 320 x 400 each-6000kW (8158bhp) Rolls Royce Marine AS-Norway AuxGen: 2 x 2400kW a.c, 2 x 370kW a.c Thrusters: 2 Tunnel thruster (f); 2 Tunnel thruster (a)
8912338 *C6ZW6* -	**SKANDI FALCON** **DOF Rederi AS** DOF Management AS *Nassau* *Bahamas* MMSI: 311068200 Official number: 8002018	**2,637** 791 3,118	Class: NV (IR)	**1990-04 Kvaerner Rosenberg AS — Stavanger** (Hull) **1990-04 Brattvaag Skipsverft AS — Brattvaag** Yd No: 41 Loa 81.90 Br ex 18.03 Dght 4.980 Lbp 76.20 Br md 18.00 Dpth 7.10 Welded, 2 dks	**(B21A2OS) Platform Supply Ship** Passengers: berths: 23	**2 oil engines** reduction geared to sc. shafts driving 2 CP propellers Total Power: 4,856kW (6,602hp) 12.0kn Normo BRM-6 2 x 4 Stroke 6 Cy. 320 x 360 each-2428kW (3301bhp) Bergen Diesel AS-Norway AuxGen: 2 x 1680kW 440/220V 60Hz a.c, 2 x 300kW 440/220V 60Hz a.c Thrusters: 1 Thwart. FP thruster (f); 1 Retract. directional thruster (f); 2 Tunnel thruster (a) Fuel: 1084.0 (r.f.) 21.0pd
9607693 *LADC* -	**SKANDI FEISTEIN** **PSV Invest I AS** DOF Management AS *Bergen* *Norway* MMSI: 257007000	**3,959** 1,598 4,700	Class: NV	**2011-11 STX OSV Tulcea SA — Tulcea** (Hull) **2011-11 STX OSV Aukra — Aukra** Yd No: 752 Loa 87.90 (BB) Br ex - Dght 6.060 Lbp 79.38 Br md 19.00 Dpth 8.00 Welded, 1 dk	**(B21A2OS) Platform Supply Ship**	**4 diesel electric oil engines** driving 4 gen. each 1580kW 690V a.c Connecting to 2 elec. motors driving 2 Azimuth electric drive units contra rotating propellers Total Power: 6,660kW (9,056hp) 11.0kn Wartsila 9L20 2 x 4 Stroke 9 Cy. 200 x 280 each-1665kW (2264bhp) Wartsila Finland Oy-Finland Thrusters: 1 Tunnel thruster (f); 1 Retract. directional thruster (f)
8211863 *C6OW4* -	**SKANDI FJORD** **DOF ASA (District Offshore ASA)** DOF (UK) Ltd SatCom: Inmarsat C 425832920 *Nassau* *Bahamas* MMSI: 308073000 Official number: 732709	**3,254** 976 1,951	Class: LR (NV) **100A1** CS 02/2013 offshore well stimulation ship **LMC** **UMS** Eq.Ltr: T; Cable: 467.5/44.0 U2	**1983-03 Kaldnes Mek. Verksted AS — Tonsberg** Yd No: 216 Converted From: Pipe Carrier-1985 Loa 88.10 Br ex 18.65 Dght 4.970 Lbp 80.02 Br md 18.46 Dpth 7.12 Welded, 1 dk	**(B22F2OW) Well Stimulation Vessel** Passengers: cabins: 21	**2 oil engines** with clutches, flexible couplings & sr geared to sc. shafts driving 2 CP propellers Total Power: 5,296kW (7,200hp) 12.0kn Wichmann 9AXAG 2 x 2 Stroke 9 Cy. 300 x 450 each-2648kW (3600bhp) Wichmann Motorfabrikk AS-Norway AuxGen: 2 x 1400kW 440V 60Hz a.c, 2 x 250kW 440V 60Hz a.c Thrusters: 2 Thwart. CP thruster (f); 2 Tunnel thruster (a)
9271755 *PPPD* -	**SKANDI FLAMENGO** *ex* Norskan Flamengo *-2009* **Norskan Offshore Ltda** - *Rio de Janeiro* *Brazil* MMSI: 710000520 Official number: 3810508764	**2,151** 1,064 3,350	Class: NV	**2003-07 Aker Promar SA — Niteroi** Yd No: PRO-06 Loa 71.90 Br ex 16.04 Dght 5.900 Lbp 66.80 Br md 16.00 Dpth 7.00 Welded, 1 dk	**(B21A2OS) Platform Supply Ship**	**2 oil engines** reduction geared to sc. shafts driving 2 CP propellers Total Power: 4,016kW (5,460hp) 12.5kn Normo KRMB-9 2 x 4 Stroke 9 Cy. 250 x 300 each-2008kW (2730bhp) Rolls Royce Marine AS-Norway AuxGen: 2 x a.c, 2 x a.c Thrusters: 2 Thwart. CP thruster (f); 1 Thwart. CP thruster (a)

Ship	Tonnage / Class	Builder / Dimensions	Type	Machinery
9372896 **SKANDI FLORA** *JWLI* - **DOF Rederi AS** DOF Management AS SatCom: Inmarsat C 425823910 *Bergen* *Norway* MMSI: 258239000	**4,469** Class: NV 1,379 5,005	**2009**-02 **STX RO Offshore Tulcea SA — Tulcea** (Hull launched by) Yd No: 353 **2009**-02 **STX Norway Offshore AS Soviknes — Sovik** (Hull completed by) Yd No: 739 **2009**-02 **STX Norway Offshore AS Aukra — Aukra** Yd No: 124 Loa 94.90 (BB) Br ex - Dght 6.600 Lbp 84.99 Br md 20.00 Dpth 8.00 Welded, 1 dk	**(B21A20S) Platform Supply Ship** Passengers: berths: 25	**4 diesel electric oil engines** driving 4 gen. Connecting to 2 elec. motors each (2200kW) driving 2 Azimuth electric drive units Total Power: 7,740kW (10,524hp) 16.0kn MAN-B&W 9L21/31 4 x 4 Stroke 9 Cy. 210 x 310 each-1935kW (2631bhp) MAN B&W Diesel AG-Augsburg Thrusters: 2 Thwart. FP thruster (f); 1 Retract. directional thruster (f)
9365582 **SKANDI FLUMINENSE** *PPUS* *launched as* Norskan Fluminense *-2007* - **DOF Navegacao Ltda** Norskan Offshore Ltda SatCom: Inmarsat C 471000232 *Rio de Janeiro* *Brazil* MMSI: 710003160 Official number: 3810519103	**3,519** Class: NV 1,056 2,600	**2007**-07 **Aker Promar SA — Niteroi** Yd No: PRO-20 Loa 80.50 (BB) Br ex 18.46 Dght 6.600 Lbp 69.30 Br md 18.00 Dpth 8.00 Welded, 1 dk	**(B21B20A) Anchor Handling Tug Supply**	**4 oil engines** reduction geared to sc. shafts driving 2 CP propellers Total Power: 12,370kW (16,818hp) 17.0kn Bergens BRM-6 2 x 4 Stroke 6 Cy. 320 x 360 each-2650kW (3603bhp) Rolls Royce Marine AS-Norway Bergens BRM-8 2 x 4 Stroke 8 Cy. 320 x 360 each-3535kW (4806bhp) Rolls Royce Marine AS-Norway AuxGen: 1 x 350kW 440V a.c, 1 x 1300kW 440V a.c, 2 x 2400kW 440V a.c Thrusters: 1 Tunnel thruster (f); 2 Tunnel thruster (a); 1 Retract. directional thruster (f)
9250749 **SKANDI FOULA** *LNJF3* - **DOF Rederi AS** DOF (UK) Ltd *Bergen* *Norway (NIS)* MMSI: 259408000	**3,252** Class: NV 1,339 4,200	**2002**-04 **DP Sudnobudivnyi Zavod im. "61 Kommunara" — Mykolayiv** (Hull) Yd No: 3001 **2002**-04 **Fitjar Mek. Verksted AS — Fitjar** Yd No: 17 Loa 83.85 (BB) Br ex 20.00 Dght 6.100 Lbp 75.36 Br md 19.70 Dpth 7.45 Welded, 1 dk	**(B21A20S) Platform Supply Ship**	**4 diesel electric oil engines** driving 4 gen. each 1480kW 690V a.c Connecting to 2 elec. motors each (2200kW) reduction geared to sc. shafts driving 2 Azimuth electric drive units contra rotating propellers Total Power: 6,120kW (8,320hp) 12.0kn Wartsila 9L20 4 x 4 Stroke 9 Cy. 200 x 280 each-1530kW (2080bhp) Wartsila Finland Oy-Finland AuxGen: 1 x 344kW, 4 x 1480kW Thrusters: 1 Thwart. FP thruster (f); 1 Retract. directional thruster (f) Fuel: 1074.0 (r.f.) 22.0pd
9508067 **SKANDI GAMMA** *LCML* - **DOF Rederi AS** DOF Management AS SatCom: Inmarsat C 425969910 *Bergen* *Norway* MMSI: 259699000	**5,054** Class: NV 1,574 5,054	**2011**-02 **STX OSV Tulcea SA — Tulcea** (Hull) **2011**-02 **STX OSV Soviknes — Sovik** Yd No: 738 Loa 94.90 (BB) Br ex - Dght 6.700 Lbp 84.90 Br md 20.00 Dpth 8.00 Welded, 1 dk	**(B21A20S) Platform Supply Ship**	**3 diesel electric oil engines** driving 3 gen. Connecting to 2 elec. motors each (2200kW) driving 2 Azimuth electric drive units Total Power: 7,830kW (10,647hp) 15.3kn Wartsila 6L34DF 3 x 4 Stroke 6 Cy. 340 x 400 each-2610kW (3549bhp) Wartsila Finland Oy-Finland Thrusters: 2 Tunnel thruster (f); 1 Retract. directional thruster (f)
9226437 **SKANDI GIANT** *ZCGM5* *ex* Skandi Pms I *-2008* *ex* Boa Giant *-2004* - **Norskan Norway AS** DOF Management AS *George Town* *Cayman Islands (British)* MMSI: 319702000 Official number: 734984	**4,820** Class: NV 1,446 4,197	**2002**-05 **Dalian Shipyard Co Ltd — Dalian LN** Yd No: AH48-1 Loa 81.00 (BB) Br ex 20.04 Dght 8.200 Lbp 69.00 Br md 20.00 Dpth 9.00 Welded, 1 dk	**(B21B20A) Anchor Handling Tug Supply** Cranes: 1x15t	**2 oil engines** reduction geared to sc. shafts driving 2 FP propellers Total Power: 12,000kW (16,316hp) 12.5kn Caterpillar 3616TA 2 x Vee 4 Stroke 16 Cy. 280 x 300 each-6000kW (8158bhp) Caterpillar Inc-USA AuxGen: 2 x 2000kW 440V 60Hz a.c, 1 x 1424kW 440V 60Hz a.c, 1 x 968kW 440V 60Hz a.c Thrusters: 1 Tunnel thruster (f); 1 Retract. directional thruster (f); 1 Tunnel thruster (a)
8202824 **SKANDI HAV** *3FEX2* - **Norskan Norway AS** Norskan Offshore Ltda *Panama* *Panama* MMSI: 351242000 Official number: 4127810	**3,188** Class: NV 957 3,550	**1983**-03 **AS Trondhjems Mekaniske Verksted — Trondheim** Yd No: 839 Converted From: Cable-layer-1996 Converted From: Pipe Carrier-1993 Loa 87.69 Br ex - Dght 5.260 Lbp 80.02 Br md 18.46 Dpth 7.12 Welded, 2 dks	**(B21A20P) Pipe Carrier** Passengers: 22; cabins: 22 Cranes: 1x15t	**2 oil engines** with clutches, flexible couplings & sr geared to sc. shafts driving 2 CP propellers Total Power: 5,296kW (7,200hp) 12.0kn Wichmann 9AXAG 2 x 2 Stroke 9 Cy. 300 x 450 each-2648kW (3600bhp) Wichmann Motorfabrikk AS-Norway AuxGen: 2 x 1400kW 440V 60Hz a.c, 2 x 252kW 440V 60Hz a.c Thrusters: 2 Thwart. CP thruster (f); 2 Tunnel thruster (a); 1 Retract. directional thruster (f) Fuel: 830.0 (r.f.)
9480734 **SKANDI HAWK** *LALL7* - **DOF Rederi AS** DOF Management AS *Bergen* *Norway (NIS)* MMSI: 259028000	**4,508** Class: NV 1,606 4,400	**2012**-01 **Cochin Shipyard Ltd — Ernakulam** Yd No: BY-82 Loa 86.60 (BB) Br ex - Dght 6.600 Lbp 78.10 Br md 19.00 Dpth 8.00 Welded, 1 dk	**(B21A20S) Platform Supply Ship**	**4 diesel electric oil engines** driving 4 gen. each 1242kW a.c Connecting to 2 elec. motors driving 2 Azimuth electric drive units Total Power: 6,480kW (8,812hp) 11.0kn Wartsila 9L20 4 x 4 Stroke 9 Cy. 200 x 280 each-1620kW (2203bhp) Wartsila Finland Oy-Finland Thrusters: 1 Retract. directional thruster (f); 1 Tunnel thruster (f)
9435739 **SKANDI HERCULES** *C6YY2* - **DOF Installer ASA** DOF Management AS SatCom: Inmarsat C 431101045 *Nassau* *Bahamas* Official number: 8001857	**8,246** Class: NV 2,474 5,750	**2010**-12 **STX OSV Tulcea SA — Tulcea** (Hull) **2010**-12 **STX OSV Aukra — Aukra** Yd No: 722 Loa 109.42 (BB) Br ex - Dght 7.800 Lbp 96.20 Br md 24.00 Dpth 9.80 Welded, 1 dk	**(B21B20A) Anchor Handling Tug Supply** Passengers: 90 Cranes: 1x140t	**6 diesel electric oil engines** driving 4 gen. each 2250kW a.c reduction geared to sc. shaft (s) driving 2 CP propellers Total Power: 26,400kW (35,894hp) 12.0kn Wartsila 16V32 2 x Vee 4 Stroke 16 Cy. 320 x 400 each-8000kW (10877bhp) Wartsila Finland Oy-Finland Wartsila 8L26 4 x 4 Stroke 8 Cy. 260 x 320 each-2600kW (3535bhp) Wartsila Italia SpA-Italy Thrusters: 2 Tunnel thruster (f); 1 Retract. directional thruster (f); 2 Tunnel thruster (a)
9625011 **SKANDI HUGEN** *LEJI* - **DOF Rederi AS** DOF Management AS *Bergen* *Norway* MMSI: 257958000	**4,365** Class: NV 1,310 2,896	**2013**-01 **STX OSV Tulcea SA — Tulcea** (Hull) **2013**-01 **STX OSV Aukra — Aukra** Yd No: 780 Loa 82.20 (BB) Br ex - Dght 6.100 Lbp 74.50 Br md 17.00 Dpth 7.60 Welded, 1 dk	**(B22A20R) Offshore Support Vessel** Cranes: 2x15t	**3 diesel electric oil engines** driving 1 gen. of 1800kW a.c 2 gen. each 2700kW a.c Connecting to 2 elec. motors each (2200kW) driving 2 Azimuth electric drive units Total Power: 6,860kW (9,327hp) Wartsila 8L26 2 x 4 Stroke 8 Cy. 260 x 320 each-2600kW (3535bhp) Wartsila Italia SpA-Italy Wartsila 9L20 1 x 4 Stroke 9 Cy. 200 x 280 1660kW (2257bhp) Wartsila Finland Oy-Finland Thrusters: 2 Tunnel thruster (f); 1 Retract. directional thruster (f) Fuel: 850.0
9660073 **SKANDI ICEMAN** *LFMY* - **Iceman AS** DOF Management AS *Bergen* *Norway* MMSI: 258738000	**8,269** Class: NV 2,481 4,000	**2013**-10 **Vard Tulcea SA — Tulcea** (Hull) Yd No: (799) **2013**-10 **Vard Soviknes — Sovik** Yd No: 799 Loa 93.50 (BB) Br ex - Dght 6.500 Lbp 89.60 Br md 24.00 Dpth 9.80 Welded, 1 dk	**(B21B20A) Anchor Handling Tug Supply** Ice Capable	**2 oil engines** reduction geared to sc. shaft (s) driving 2 CP propellers Total Power: 12,000kW (16,316hp) Bergens B32: 40V12P 2 x Vee 4 Stroke 12 Cy. 320 x 400 each-6000kW (8158bhp) Rolls Royce Marine AS-Norway AuxGen: 2 x a.c, 3 x a.c Thrusters: 2 Tunnel thruster (f); 1 Retract. directional thruster (f); 2 Tunnel thruster (a)

IMO / Call sign	Name / Owner / Manager / Flag	Tonnage	Class	Build / Dimensions	Type	Machinery
9528354 *PY2026* -	**SKANDI IGUACU** *completed as* Skandi Amazonas *-2012* **DOF Navegacao Ltda** Norskan Offshore Ltda *Rio de Janeiro* *Brazil* MMSI: 710010110	**7,099** 2,130 4,700	Class: NV	**2012**-08 **STX OSV Niteroi SA — Niteroi** Yd No: PRO-27 Loa 95.00 (BB) Br ex 24.05 Dght 7.800 Lbp 85.00 Br md 24.00 Dpth 9.80 Welded, 1 dk	**(B21B20A) Anchor Handling Tug Supply** Passengers: 38	**2 oil engines** reduction geared to sc. shafts driving 2 CP propellers Total Power: 15,360kW (20,884hp) 17.0kn Wartsila 16V32 2 x Vee 4 Stroke 16 Cy. 320 x 400 each-7680kW (10442bhp) Wartsila Finland Oy-Finland AuxGen: 4 x a.c Thrusters: 2 Tunnel thruster (f); 1 Tunnel thruster (a); 1 Retract. directional thruster (a); 1 Retract. directional thruster (f)
7905285 *C6QW5* -	**SKANDI INSPECTOR** *ex* Skandi Captain *-1999* *ex* Far Captain *-1989* *ex* Tender Captain *-1986* **DOF Subsea Rederi II AS** DOF Management AS *Nassau* *Bahamas* MMSI: 308941000 Official number: 732710	**3,345** 1,003 2,413	Class: NV	**1979**-12 **Ulstein Hatlo AS — Ulsteinvik** Yd No: 165 Converted From: Standby Safety Vessel-1999 Converted From: Pipe Carrier-1981 Loa 81.10 Br ex 18.04 Dght 4.980 Lbp 76.20 Br md 18.01 Dpth 7.12 Welded, 2 dks	**(B22A20V) Diving Support Vessel** Passengers: 63; cabins: 40 Cranes: 1x50t	**2 oil engines** sr geared to sc. shafts driving 2 CP propellers Total Power: 3,530kW (4,800hp) 10.5kn MaK 6M453AK 2 x 4 Stroke 6 Cy. 320 x 420 each-1765kW (2400bhp) MaK Maschinenbau GmbH-Kiel AuxGen: 2 x 1200kW 440V 60Hz a.c, 1 x 310kW 440V 60Hz a.c, 1 x 244kW 440V 60Hz a.c Thrusters: 2 Tunnel thruster (f); 2 Tunnel thruster (a); 1 Tunnel thruster (f)
9528249 *PY2038* -	**SKANDI IPANEMA** **DOF Navegacao Ltda** Norskan Offshore Ltda *Rio de Janeiro* *Brazil* MMSI: 710005230	**2,771** 985 2,250	Class: NV	**2010**-10 **STX Brazil Offshore SA — Niteroi** Yd No: PRO-25 Loa 74.30 (BB) Br ex 17.44 Dght 6.000 Lbp 68.00 Br md 17.00 Dpth 7.20 Welded, 1 dk	**(B21B20A) Anchor Handling Tug Supply** Passengers: 60	**2 oil engines** reduction geared to sc. shafts driving 2 CP propellers Total Power: 9,000kW (12,236hp) Bergens B32: 40L9P 2 x 4 Stroke 9 Cy. 320 x 400 each-4500kW (6118bhp) Rolls Royce Marine AS-Norway AuxGen: 2 x a.c, 2 x a.c Thrusters: 1 Retract. directional thruster (f); 1 Tunnel thruster (f); 1 Tunnel thruster (a)
9613824 *LCDJ* -	**SKANDI KVITSOY** **PSV Invest I AS** DOF ASA (District Offshore ASA) *Bergen* *Norway* MMSI: 257006000	**3,958** 1,578 4,700	Class: NV	**2012**-04 **STX OSV Tulcea SA — Tulcea** (Hull) **2012**-04 **STX OSV Aukra — Aukra** Yd No: 759 Loa 87.90 (BB) Br ex - Dght 6.600 Lbp 79.40 Br md 19.00 Dpth 8.00 Welded, 1 dk	**(B21A20S) Platform Supply Ship**	**4 diesel electric oil engines** driving 4 gen. each 2000kW 690V a.c Connecting to 2 elec. motors each (2200kW) driving 2 Azimuth electric drive units Total Power: 5,968kW (8,116hp) 11.0kn Caterpillar 3516C 4 x Vee 4 Stroke 16 Cy. 170 x 190 each-1492kW (2029bhp) Caterpillar Inc-USA Thrusters: 1 Retract. directional thruster (f); 2 Tunnel thruster (f)
9273349 *PPPO* -	**SKANDI LEBLON** *ex* Norskan Leblon *-2008* **Norskan Offshore Ltda** *Rio de Janeiro* *Brazil* MMSI: 710022000 Official number: 3810510483	**2,151** 1,064 3,250	Class: NV	**2004**-02 **Aker Promar SA — Niteroi** Yd No: PRO-08 Loa 71.90 Br ex 16.04 Dght 5.820 Lbp 66.80 Br md 16.00 Dpth 7.00 Welded, 1 dk	**(B21A20S) Platform Supply Ship**	**2 oil engines** reduction geared to sc. shafts driving 2 CP propellers Total Power: 4,010kW (5,452hp) Bergens KRMB-9 2 x 4 Stroke 9 Cy. 250 x 300 each-2005kW (2726bhp) Rolls Royce Marine AS-Norway AuxGen: 2 x a.c, 2 x a.c Thrusters: 2 Tunnel thruster (f); 1 Tunnel thruster (a)
9625023 *LDWW* -	**SKANDI MAROY** *ex* Skandi Nova *-2012* **DOF Rederi AS** DOF Management AS *Bergen* *Norway* MMSI: 257957000	**3,588** 1,324 3,594	Class: NV	**2012**-11 **STX OSV Tulcea SA — Tulcea** (Hull) **2012**-11 **STX OSV Brattvaag — Brattvaag** Yd No: 779 Loa 82.20 (BB) Br ex - Dght 6.300 Lbp 74.50 Br md 17.00 Dpth 7.60 Welded, 1 dk	**(B22A20R) Offshore Support Vessel**	**3 diesel electric oil engines** driving 2 gen. each 2700kW a.c 1 gen. of 1800kW a.c Connecting to 2 elec. motors each (2200kW) driving 2 Azimuth electric drive units Total Power: 7,240kW (9,843hp) 15.0kn Wartsila 8L26 2 x 4 Stroke 8 Cy. 260 x 320 each-2720kW (3698bhp) Wartsila Italia SpA-Italy Wartsila 9L20 1 x 4 Stroke 9 Cy. 200 x 280 1800kW (2447bhp) Wartsila Finland Oy-Finland Thrusters: 2 Tunnel thruster (f); 1 Retract. directional thruster (f)
9122978 *LAKZ7* -	**SKANDI MARSTEIN** *launched as* Rem Therese *-1996* **DOF Rederi AS** DOF (UK) Ltd *Bergen* *Norway (NIS)* MMSI: 259357000	**3,171** 1,551 4,170	Class: NV	**1996**-08 **SC Santierul Naval Tulcea SA — Tulcea** (Hull) Yd No: E108 **1996**-08 **Brattvaag Skipsverft AS — Brattvaag** Yd No: 87 Loa 83.70 (BB) Br ex 19.70 Dght 6.014 Lbp 75.36 Br md 19.70 Dpth 7.45 Welded, 1 dk	**(B21A20S) Platform Supply Ship**	**4 diesel electric oil engines** driving 4 gen. each 1416kW Connecting to 2 elec. motors each (2200kW) driving 1 Contra-rotating propeller contra rotating propellers, 1 Directional propeller contra rotating propellers Total Power: 5,880kW (7,996hp) 12.0kn Wartsila 9L20 4 x 4 Stroke 9 Cy. 200 x 280 each-1470kW (1999bhp) Wartsila Propulsion AS-Norway Thrusters: 1 Retract. directional thruster (f); 1 Thwart. FP thruster (f) Fuel: 863.0 (d.f.) 21.0pd
9166613 *LMVP3* -	**SKANDI MOGSTER** **DOF Rederi II AS** Norskan Offshore Ltda *Bergen* *Norway (NIS)* MMSI: 259495000	**2,598** 870 2,752	Class: NV	**1998**-06 **Kvaerner Kleven AS — Ulsteinvik** Yd No: 274 Loa 73.60 Br ex - Dght 6.880 Lbp 66.68 Br md 16.40 Dpth 8.00 Welded, 1 dk	**(B21B20A) Anchor Handling Tug Supply**	**2 oil engines** with clutches & sr reverse geared to sc. shafts driving 2 CP propellers Total Power: 11,040kW (15,010hp) 14.0kn Wartsila 12V32 2 x Vee 4 Stroke 12 Cy. 320 x 400 each-5520kW (7505bhp) Wartsila NSD Finland Oy-Finland AuxGen: 2 x 1920kW 440V 60Hz a.c, 1 x 1070kW 440V 60Hz a.c Thrusters: 1 Retract. directional thruster (f); 1 Thwart. FP thruster (f); 1 Tunnel thruster (a) Fuel: 711.1 (d.f.) 17.0pd
9383871 *LALP* -	**SKANDI MONGSTAD** **DOF Rederi AS** DOF Management AS SatCom: Inmarsat C 425923910 *Bergen* *Norway* MMSI: 259239000	**4,859** 1,457 4,423	Class: NV	**2008**-01 **Kleven Verft AS — Ulsteinvik** Yd No: 317 Loa 96.90 (BB) Br ex 21.05 Dght 7.000 Lbp 84.96 Br md 21.00 Dpth 9.10 Welded, 1 dk	**(B21B20T) Offshore Tug/Supply Ship** Passengers: berths: 24 Cranes: 2x10t	**2 oil engines** geared to sc. shaft driving 1 CP propeller Total Power: 6,000kW (8,158hp) 12.0kn MAN-B&W 6L32/40 2 x 4 Stroke 6 Cy. 320 x 400 each-3000kW (4079bhp) MAN Diesel A/S-Denmark AuxGen: 2 x 1294kW 690V 60Hz a.c Thrusters: 2 Tunnel thruster (f); 1 Tunnel thruster (a); 1 Retract. directional thruster (f); 2 Retract. directional thruster (a)
9205720 *LASG5* -	**SKANDI NEPTUNE** **DOF Subsea Rederi AS** DOF Management AS *Bergen* *Norway (NIS)* MMSI: 258142000	**7,941** 2,383 5,090	Class: NV	**2001**-06 **SC Aker Tulcea SA — Tulcea** (Hull) Yd No: 273 **2001**-06 **Brattvaag Skipsverft AS — Brattvaag** Yd No: 92 Converted From: Cable-layer-2005 Loa 108.36 (BB) Br ex - Dght 6.300 Lbp 96.60 Br md 24.00 Dpth 10.45 Welded, 1 dk	**(B22A20R) Offshore Support Vessel** Passengers: berths: 117 A-frames: 1x60t; Cranes: 1x250t	**4 diesel electric oil engines** driving 2 gen. each 1320kW 690V a.c 2 gen. each 3056kW 690V a.c Connecting to 2 elec. motors each (3700kW) driving 2 Azimuth electric drive units Total Power: 10,260kW (13,950hp) 13.0kn Wartsila 8L32 2 x 4 Stroke 8 Cy. 320 x 400 each-3600kW (4895bhp) Wartsila Finland Oy-Finland Wartsila 9L20 2 x 4 Stroke 9 Cy. 200 x 280 each-1530kW (2080bhp) Wartsila Finland Oy-Finland Thrusters: 2 Thwart. FP thruster (f); 1 Retract. directional thruster (f) Fuel: 1511.1 (r.f.) 35.0pd
9387243 *PPZZ* -	**SKANDI NITEROI** **DOFCON do Brasil Navegacao Ltda** Norskan Offshore Ltda SatCom: Inmarsat C 471011275 *Rio de Janeiro* *Brazil* MMSI: 710006260	**15,183** 4,555 9,000	Class: NV	**2011**-01 **Estaleiro Ilha S.A. (EISA) — Rio de Janeiro** (Hull) Yd No: PRO-24 **2011**-01 **STX OSV Niteroi SA — Niteroi** Yd No: PRO-24 Loa 142.20 (BB) Br ex 27.04 Dght 8.500 Lbp 123.00 Br md 27.00 Dpth 12.00 Welded, 1 dk	**(B22A20R) Offshore Support Vessel** Cranes: 1x250t,1x50t	**6 diesel electric oil engines** driving 2 gen. 4 gen. Connecting to 2 elec. motors driving 2 Z propellers Total Power: 19,300kW (26,240hp) 16.5kn MAN-B&W 6L32/40 4 x 4 Stroke 6 Cy. 320 x 400 each-2895kW (3936bhp) MAN-B&W 8L32/40 2 x 4 Stroke 8 Cy. 320 x 400 each-3860kW (5248bhp) Thrusters: 2 Tunnel thruster (f); 2 Retract. directional thruster (f)

9625009 *LDWL* -	**SKANDI NOVA** **DOF Rederi AS** DOF Management AS *Bergen* *Norway* MMSI: 257875000	**3,788** 1,326 3,100	Class: NV	**2012-10 STX OSV Tulcea SA — Tulcea** (Hull) **2012-09 STX OSV Aukra — Aukra** Yd No: 778 Loa 82.20 (BB) Br ex - Dght 6.100 Lbp 74.50 Br md 17.00 Dpth 7.60 Welded, 1 dk	**(B21A20S) Platform Supply Ship**	**3 diesel electric oil engines** driving 2 gen. each 2600kW a.c 1 gen. of 1600kW a.c Connecting to 2 elec. motors each (2200kW) driving 2 Azimuth electric drive units Total Power: 6,860kW (9,327hp) Wartsila 8L26 1 x 4 Stroke 8 Cy. 260 x 320 2600kW (3535bhp) Wartsila Italia SpA-Italy Wartsila 9L20 1 x 4 Stroke 9 Cy. 200 x 280 1660kW (2257bhp) Wartsila Finland Oy-Finland Thrusters: 2 Tunnel thruster (f); 1 Retract. directional thruster (f)
9417359 *C6XY8* -	**SKANDI OLYMPIA** **DOF Rederi AS** DOF Management AS SatCom: Inmarsat C 431100584 *Nassau* *Bahamas* MMSI: 311026300 Official number: 8001679	**3,131** 1,167 3,550	Class: NV	**2009-07 VAT Sevastopolskyi Morskyi Zavod — Sevastopol** (Hull) Yd No: (31) **2009-07 Fitjar Mek. Verksted AS — Fitjar** Yd No: 31 Loa 79.67 (BB) Br ex - Dght 6.220 Lbp 72.00 Br md 16.40 Dpth 7.45 Welded, 1 dk	**(B21A20S) Platform Supply Ship** Passengers: cabins: 26; berths: 40	**4 diesel electric oil engines** driving 4 gen. Connecting to 2 elec. motors each (1470kW) driving 2 Azimuth electric drive units Total Power: 5,696kW (7,744hp) 12.0kn Caterpillar 3512B-TA 4 x Vee 4 Stroke 12 Cy. 170 x 190 each-1424kW (1936bhp) Caterpillar Inc-USA Thrusters: 2 Tunnel thruster (f)
9447653 *C6ZO8* -	**SKANDI PACIFIC** **Aker DOF Deepwater AS** DOF ASA (District Offshore ASA) *Nassau* *Bahamas* MMSI: 311061700 Official number: 8001966	**3,181** 1,129 3,195	Class: NV	**2011-11 STX OSV Vung Tau Ltd — Vung Tau** Yd No: 005 Loa 74.70 (BB) Br ex - Dght 7.000 Lbp 68.00 Br md 17.40 Dpth 8.50 Welded, 1 dk	**(B21B20A) Anchor Handling Tug Supply**	**2 oil engines** reduction geared to sc. shafts driving 2 CP propellers Total Power: 12,000kW (16,316hp) 15.0kn Bergens B32: 40V12P 2 x Vee 4 Stroke 12 Cy. 320 x 400 each-6000kW (8158bhp) Rolls Royce Marine AS-Norway AuxGen: 2 x a.c Thrusters: 2 Tunnel thruster (f); 2 Tunnel thruster (a)
9182203 *LLFR3* -	**SKANDI PATAGONIA** **DOF Subsea Rederi AS** DOF Management AS *Bergen* *Norway (NIS)* MMSI: 257118000	**4,641** 1,392 3,722	Class: NV	**2000-10 SC Aker Tulcea SA — Tulcea** (Hull) Yd No: 242 **2000-10 Brattvaag Skipsverft AS — Brattvaag** Yd No: 91 Loa 93.30 (BB) Br ex 19.73 Dght 6.090 Lbp 83.40 Br md 19.70 Dpth 7.45 Welded, 1 dk	**(B21B20T) Offshore Tug/Supply Ship** Passengers: cabins: 40; berths: 62 Cranes: 1x50t	**4 diesel electric oil engines** driving 2 gen. each 3056kW 2 gen. each 1320kW Connecting to 2 elec. motors each (3700kW) driving 2 Azimuth electric drive units Total Power: 10,260kW (13,950hp) 15.0kn Wartsila 8L32 2 x 4 Stroke 8 Cy. 320 x 400 each-3600kW (4895bhp) Wartsila Finland Oy-Finland Wartsila 9L20 2 x 4 Stroke 9 Cy. 200 x 280 each-1530kW (2080bhp) Wartsila Finland Oy-Finland Thrusters: 1 Retract. directional thruster (f); 2 Tunnel thruster (f) Fuel: 1380.0
9447627 *LAID7* -	**SKANDI PEREGRINO** **Aker DOF Deepwater AS** DOF ASA (District Offshore ASA) SatCom: Inmarsat C 425906910 *Bergen* *Norway (NIS)* MMSI: 259069000	**3,181** 1,129 3,195	Class: NV	**2010-11 STX Vietnam Offshore Ltd — Vung Tau** Yd No: 002 Loa 75.02 (BB) Br ex - Dght 7.000 Lbp 68.02 Br md 17.40 Dpth 8.51 Welded, 1 dk	**(B21B20A) Anchor Handling Tug Supply** Cranes: 1x5t	**2 oil engines** reduction geared to sc. shafts driving 2 CP propellers Total Power: 12,000kW (16,316hp) 15.0kn Bergens B32: 40V12P 2 x Vee 4 Stroke 12 Cy. 320 x 400 each-6000kW (8158bhp) Rolls Royce Marine AS-Norway AuxGen: 2 x a.c, 2 x a.c Thrusters: 1 Tunnel thruster (f); 1 Retract. directional thruster (f); 2 Tunnel thruster (a)
9353204 *PPTU* -	**SKANDI RIO** **DOF Navegacao Ltda** Norskan Offshore Ltda SatCom: Inmarsat C 471000211 *Rio de Janeiro* *Brazil* MMSI: 710002860 Official number: 3810517968	**3,519** 1,056 2,600	Class: NV	**2007-02 Aker Promar SA — Niteroi** Yd No: PRO-18 Loa 80.50 Br ex 18.46 Dght 6.600 Lbp 69.30 Br md 18.00 Dpth 8.00 Welded, 1 dk	**(B21B20A) Anchor Handling Tug Supply** Cranes: 1x10t	**4 oil engines** reduction geared to sc. shafts driving 2 CP propellers Total Power: 12,370kW (16,818hp) 17.0kn Bergens BRM-6 2 x 4 Stroke 6 Cy. 320 x 360 each-2650kW (3603bhp) Rolls Royce Marine AS-Norway Bergens BRM-8 2 x 4 Stroke 8 Cy. 320 x 360 each-3535kW (4806bhp) Rolls Royce Marine AS-Norway AuxGen: 1 x 1300kW 440V a.c, 1 x 350kW 440V a.c, 2 x 2400kW 440V a.c Thrusters: 1 Tunnel thruster (f); 2 Tunnel thruster (a); 1 Retract. directional thruster (f)
9249635 *LNFK3* -	**SKANDI RONA** **DOF Rederi AS** DOF (UK) Ltd *Bergen* *Norway (NIS)* MMSI: 259504000	**3,252** 1,339 4,263	Class: NV	**2002-04 Societatea Comerciala Severnav S.A. — Drobeta-Turnu Severin** (Hull) Yd No: 145 **2002-04 Myklebust Mek. Verksted AS — Gursken** Yd No: 31 Loa 83.85 (BB) Br ex 19.70 Dght 6.100 Lbp 75.54 Br md 18.00 Dpth 7.45 Welded, 1 dk	**(B21A20S) Platform Supply Ship**	**4 diesel electric oil engines** driving 4 gen. Connecting to 2 elec. motors each (2200kW) driving 2 Azimuth electric drive units Total Power: 6,120kW (8,320hp) 12.0kn Wartsila 9L20 4 x 4 Stroke 9 Cy. 200 x 280 each-1530kW (2080bhp) Wartsila Finland Oy-Finland AuxGen: 4 x 1480kW 690V 60Hz a.c, 1 x 344kW 60Hz a.c Thrusters: 1 Thwart. FP thruster (f); 1 Retract. directional thruster (f) Fuel: 900.0 (d.f.) 21.0pd
9447641 *LDFR* -	**SKANDI SAIGON** **Aker DOF Deepwater AS** DOF ASA (District Offshore ASA) *Bergen* *Norway*	**3,181** 1,129 3,195	Class: NV	**2011-08 STX OSV Vung Tau Ltd — Vung Tau** Yd No: 004 Loa 75.00 (BB) Br ex - Dght 7.000 Lbp 68.00 Br md 17.40 Dpth 8.50 Welded, 1 dk	**(B21B20A) Anchor Handling Tug Supply**	**2 oil engines** reduction geared to sc. shafts driving 2 CP propellers Total Power: 12,000kW (16,316hp) 15.0kn Bergens B32: 40V12P 2 x Vee 4 Stroke 12 Cy. 320 x 400 each-6000kW (8158bhp) Rolls Royce Marine AS-Norway AuxGen: 2 x 2400kW a.c, 2 x 370kW a.c Thrusters: 2 Tunnel thruster (f); 2 Tunnel thruster (a)
9389576 *PPQP* -	**SKANDI SALVADOR** **DOF Subsea Brasil Servicos Ltda** Norskan Offshore Ltda *Rio de Janeiro* *Brazil* MMSI: 710000110 Official number: 3813869865	**6,802** 2,041 3,600	Class: NV	**2009-01 STX Brazil Offshore SA — Niteroi** Yd No: PRO-22 Loa 105.90 (BB) Br ex 21.03 Dght 6.600 Lbp 94.70 Br md 21.00 Dpth 8.50 Welded, 1 dk	**(B22A20V) Diving Support Vessel** Cranes: 1x140t Ice Capable	**4 diesel electric oil engines** driving 4 gen. Connecting to 2 elec. motors driving 2 Azimuth electric drive units contra-rotating propellers Total Power: 10,800kW (14,684hp) 15.5kn MaK 9M25 2 x 4 Stroke 9 Cy. 255 x 400 each-2700kW (3671bhp) Caterpillar Motoren GmbH & Co. KG-Germany MaK 9M25C 2 x 4 Stroke 9 Cy. 255 x 400 each-2700kW (3671bhp) Caterpillar Motoren GmbH & Co. KG-Germany Thrusters: 2 Tunnel thruster (f); 1 Retract. directional thruster (f)
9423437 *LAGX7* -	**SKANDI SANTOS** **DOF Subsea Rederi AS** Norskan Offshore Ltda *Bergen* *Norway (NIS)* MMSI: 257420000	**9,074** 2,723 5,109	Class: NV	**2009-12 STX RO Offshore Tulcea SA — Tulcea** (Hull) **2009-12 STX Norway Offshore AS Aukra — Aukra** Yd No: 716 Loa 120.70 (BB) Br ex - Dght 7.000 Lbp 105.20 Br md 23.00 Dpth 9.00 Welded, 1 dk	**(B22A20R) Offshore Support Vessel** Cranes: 1x250t Ice Capable	**4 diesel electric oil engines** driving 4 gen. each 2880kW 690V a.c Connecting to 2 elec. motors each (3000kW) driving 2 Azimuth electric drive units Total Power: 11,880kW (16,152hp) 14.0kn MAN-B&W 9L27/38 4 x 4 Stroke 9 Cy. 270 x 380 each-2970kW (4038bhp) MAN B&W Diesel AG-Augsburg Thrusters: 2 Retract. directional thruster (f); 2 Thwart. FP thruster (f)
9408671 *2BLN8* -	**SKANDI SEVEN** **DOF Subsea Rederi AS** DOF Management AS SatCom: Inmarsat C 423591142 *Douglas* *Isle of Man (British)* MMSI: 235067199 Official number: 9408671	**9,074** 2,723 6,000	Class: NV	**2008-09 SC Aker Tulcea SA — Tulcea** (Hull) **2008-09 Aker Yards AS Soviknes — Sovik** Yd No: 703 Loa 120.70 (BB) Br ex - Dght 7.000 Lbp 105.20 Br md 23.00 Dpth 9.00 Welded, 1 dk	**(B22A20R) Offshore Support Vessel** Passengers: cabins: 73; berths: 119 Cranes: 1x250t Ice Capable	**4 diesel electric oil engines** driving 4 gen. each 2560kW a.c Connecting to 2 elec. motors reduction geared to sc. shafts driving 2 Azimuth electric drive units contra-rotating propellers Total Power: 11,880kW (16,152hp) 14.0kn MAN-B&W 9L27/38 4 x 4 Stroke 9 Cy. 270 x 380 each-2970kW (4038bhp) MAN B&W Diesel AG-Augsburg Thrusters: 2 Tunnel thruster (f); 2 Retract. directional thruster (f) Fuel: 1680.0

Identity / Owner	Tonnage / Class	Build	Type	Machinery
9429857 **SKANDI SINGAPORE** *LAEQ7* - **DOF Subsea Rederi AS** DOF Management AS *Bergen* *Norway (NIS)* MMSI: 259003000	**7,386** Class: NV 2,216 3,729	**2011-09 Singapore Technologies Marine Ltd — Singapore** Yd No: 621 Loa 107.10 (BB) Br ex - Dght 6.600 Lbp 94.70 Br md 21.00 Dpth 8.50 Welded, 1 dk	**(B22A2OR) Offshore Support Vessel** Passengers: 100; cabins: 64 Cranes: 1x140t Ice Capable	**4 diesel electric oil engines** driving 4 gen. each 3150kW 690V a.c Connecting to 2 elec. motors each (3000kW) driving 2 Azimuth electric drive units contra rotating propellers Total Power: 12,600kW (17,132hp) 15.5kn MAN-B&W 9L27/38 4 x 4 Stroke 9 Cy. 270 x 380 each-3150kW (4283bhp) Thrusters: 2 Thwart. CP thruster (f); 1 Retract. directional thruster (f)
9459759 **SKANDI SKANSEN** *C6ZK9* *ex Skandi Bergen -2011* - **DOF Installer ASA** DOF (UK) Ltd *Nassau* *Bahamas* MMSI: 311058200 Official number: 8001928	**8,222** Class: NV 2,467 4,982	**2011-07 STX OSV Tulcea SA — Tulcea** (Hull) **2011-07 STX OSV Aukra — Aukra** Yd No: 723 Loa 107.20 (BB) Br ex - Dght 7.800 Lbp 97.90 Br md 24.00 Dpth 9.80 Welded, 1 dk	**(B21B20A) Anchor Handling Tug Supply** Cranes: 1x250t	**6 diesel electric oil engines** driving 4 gen. Connecting to 2 elec. motors reduction geared to sc. shafts driving 2 CP propellers Total Power: 26,400kW (35,894hp) 12.0kn Wartsila 16V32 2 x Vee 4 Stroke 16 Cy. 320 x 400 each-8000kW (10877bhp) Wartsila Finland Oy-Finland Wartsila 8L26 4 x 4 Stroke 8 Cy. 260 x 320 each-2600kW (3535bhp) Wartsila Italia SpA-Italy Thrusters: 2 Tunnel thruster (f); 2 Tunnel thruster (a); 1 Retract. directional thruster (f)
9435727 **SKANDI SKOLTEN** *C6YQ6* - **DOF Installer ASA** DOF Management AS *Nassau* *Bahamas* MMSI: 311042100 Official number: 8001791	**8,252** Class: NV 2,476 5,750	**2010-07 STX RO Offshore Tulcea SA — Tulcea** (Hull) **2010-07 STX Norway Offshore AS Aukra — Aukra** Yd No: 707 Loa 109.40 (BB) Br ex - Dght 6.500 Lbp 96.20 Br md 24.00 Dpth 9.80 Welded, 1 dk	**(B21B20A) Anchor Handling Tug Supply** Passengers: 90 Cranes: 1x250t	**6 diesel electric oil engines** driving 4 gen. each 2250kW a.c reduction geared to sc. shafts driving 2 CP propellers Total Power: 26,400kW (35,894hp) 12.0kn Wartsila 16V32 2 x Vee 4 Stroke 16 Cy. 320 x 400 each-8000kW (10877bhp) Wartsila Finland Oy-Finland Wartsila 8L26 4 x 4 Stroke 8 Cy. 260 x 320 each-2600kW (3535bhp) Wartsila Italia SpA-Italy AuxGen: 2 x a.c Thrusters: 2 Tunnel thruster (f); 2 Tunnel thruster (a); 1 Retract. directional thruster (f) Fuel: 1200.0 (d.f.)
9276391 **SKANDI SOTRA** *LLYV* - **DOF Rederi AS** DOF Management AS *Bergen* *Norway* MMSI: 259452000	**3,482** Class: NV 1,198 3,933	**2003-01 Societatea Comerciala Severnav S.A. — Drobeta-Turnu Severin** (Hull) Yd No: 153 **2003-01 Myklebust Mek. Verksted AS — Gursken** Yd No: 33 Loa 83.85 (BB) Br ex 19.75 Dght 6.100 Lbp 76.80 Br md 19.70 Dpth 7.45 Welded, 1 dk	**(B21A20S) Platform Supply Ship**	**4 diesel electric oil engines** driving 4 gen. Connecting to 2 elec. motors each (2200kW) driving 2 Azimuth electric drive units contra-rotating Total Power: 7,280kW (9,896hp) 12.0kn Caterpillar 3516B-TA 4 x Vee 4 Stroke 16 Cy. 170 x 190 each-1820kW (2474bhp) Caterpillar Inc-USA AuxGen: 4 x 1825kW Thrusters: 2 Thwart. CP thruster (f); 1 Directional thruster (f) Fuel: 900.0 (d.f.) 15.8pd
9165970 **SKANDI STOLMEN** *LIPM3* - **DOF Rederi II AS** DOF Management AS *Bergen* *Norway (NIS)*	**1,968** Class: NV 845 3,100	**1997-07 Soviknes Verft AS — Sovik** Yd No: 119 Loa 67.00 Br ex - Dght 5.922 Lbp 61.80 Br md 16.00 Dpth 7.00 Welded, 1 dk	**(B21A20S) Platform Supply Ship**	**2 oil engines** reduction geared to sc. shafts driving 2 CP propellers Total Power: 4,010kW (5,452hp) 12.0kn Normo KRMB-9 2 x 4 Stroke 9 Cy. 250 x 300 each-2005kW (2726bhp) Ulstein Bergen AS-Norway AuxGen: 2 x 1280kW 230/440V 60Hz a.c, 2 x 248kW 230/440V 60Hz a.c Thrusters: 1 Retract. directional thruster (f); 1 Thwart. CP thruster (f); 1 Thwart. CP thruster (a) Fuel: 900.0 (d.f.)
9198484 **SKANDI STORD** *LJLD* - **DOF Rederi AS** DOF Management AS SatCom: Inmarsat B 325954210 *Bergen* *Norway* MMSI: 259542000	**2,656** Class: NV 796 2,900	**1999-02 Astilleros y Servicios Navales S.A. (ASENAV) — Valdivia** Yd No: 122 Loa 73.50 Br ex - Dght 6.900 Lbp 63.60 Br md 16.40 Dpth 8.00 Welded, 1 dk	**(B21B20A) Anchor Handling Tug Supply**	**2 oil engines** reduction geared to sc. shafts driving 2 CP propellers Total Power: 11,034kW (15,002hp) 14.0kn Wartsila 12V32 2 x Vee 4 Stroke 12 Cy. 320 x 400 each-5517kW (7501bhp) Wartsila NSD Finland Oy-Finland AuxGen: 2 x 2400kW 220/440V 60Hz a.c, 1 x 1070kW 220/440V 60Hz a.c, 1 x 324kW 220/440V 60Hz a.c Thrusters: 1 Thwart. FP thruster (f); 1 Retract. directional thruster (f); 1 Tunnel thruster (a)
9283473 **SKANDI TEXEL** *LAGP6* - **DOF Rederi AS** DOF Management AS *Bergen* *Norway (NIS)* MMSI: 258610000	**2,447** Class: NV 735 3,500	**2006-06 OAO Vyborgskiy Sudostroitelnyy Zavod — Vyborg** (Hull) Yd No: 930 **2006-06 Fitjar Mek. Verksted AS — Fitjar** Yd No: 20 Loa 69.50 (BB) Br ex 16.43 Dght 6.230 Lbp 62.40 Br md 16.40 Dpth 7.45 Welded, 1 dk	**(B21A20S) Platform Supply Ship**	**4 diesel electric oil engines** driving 2 gen. each 945kW 2 gen. each 1160kW Connecting to 2 elec. motors each (1500kW) driving 2 Azimuth electric drive units Total Power: 4,760kW (6,472hp) 12.0kn Wartsila 6L20 2 x 4 Stroke 6 Cy. 200 x 280 each-1020kW (1387bhp) Wartsila Finland Oy-Finland Wartsila 8L20 2 x 4 Stroke 8 Cy. 200 x 280 each-1360kW (1849bhp) Wartsila Finland Oy-Finland Thrusters: 2 Tunnel thruster (f) Fuel: 1050.0
9435715 **SKANDI VEGA** *3YLA* - **DOF ASA (District Offshore ASA)** DOF Management AS *Bergen* *Norway* MMSI: 257403000	**8,164** Class: NV 2,450 5,750	**2010-05 STX RO Offshore Tulcea SA — Tulcea** (Hull) **2010-05 STX Norway Offshore AS Aukra — Aukra** Yd No: 706 Loa 109.40 (BB) Br ex - Dght 7.800 Lbp 96.20 Br md 24.00 Dpth 9.80 Welded, 1 dk	**(B21B20A) Anchor Handling Tug Supply** Passengers: 90 Cranes: 1x15t,2x10t	**6 diesel electric oil engines** driving 4 gen. Connecting to 2 elec. motors reduction geared to sc. shafts driving 2 CP propellers Total Power: 26,400kW (35,894hp) 12.0kn Wartsila 16V32 2 x Vee 4 Stroke 16 Cy. 320 x 400 each-8000kW (10877bhp) Wartsila Finland Oy-Finland Wartsila 8L26 4 x 4 Stroke 8 Cy. 260 x 320 each-2600kW (3535bhp) Wartsila Italia SpA-Italy AuxGen: 2 x a.c Thrusters: 2 Tunnel thruster (f); 2 Tunnel thruster (a); 1 Retract. directional thruster (f)
9387231 **SKANDI VITORIA** *PPZK* - **DOFCON do Brasil Navegacao Ltda** Norskan Offshore Ltda *Rio de Janeiro* *Brazil* MMSI: 710005570	**15,183** Class: NV 4,555 9,000	**2010-08 Estaleiro Ilha S.A. (EISA) — Rio de Janeiro** (Hull) **2010-08 STX Brazil Offshore SA — Niteroi** Yd No: PRO-23 Loa 142.20 (BB) Br ex 27.46 Dght 8.500 Lbp 123.00 Br md 27.00 Dpth 12.00 Welded, 1 dk	**(B22A2OR) Offshore Support Vessel** Cranes: 1x250t,1x50t	**6 diesel electric oil engines** driving 2 gen. 4 gen. Connecting to 2 elec. motors driving 2 Azimuth electric drive units Total Power: 18,940kW (25,750hp) 16.5kn MAN-B&W 6L32/40 4 x 4 Stroke 6 Cy. 320 x 400 each-2895kW (3936bhp) MAN-B&W 8L32/40 2 x 4 Stroke 8 Cy. 320 x 400 each-3680kW (5003bhp) Thrusters: 2 Tunnel thruster (f); 2 Retract. directional thruster (f)
9239604 **SKANDI WAVENEY** *C6YE9* - **Waveney AS** DOF Management AS SatCom: Inmarsat C 431100662 *Nassau* *Bahamas* MMSI: 311030400 Official number: 8001714	**2,164** Class: NV 1,086 3,246	**2001-11 SC Aker Tulcea SA — Tulcea** (Hull) Yd No: 277 **2001-11 Brevik Construction AS — Brevik** Yd No: 20 Loa 71.99 Br ex 16.01 Dght 6.300 Lbp 66.74 Br md 15.98 Dpth 7.00 Welded, 1 dk	**(B21A20S) Platform Supply Ship**	**2 oil engines** reduction geared to sc. shafts driving 2 CP propellers Total Power: 4,016kW (5,460hp) 12.5kn Normo KRMB-9 2 x 4 Stroke 9 Cy. 250 x 300 each-2008kW (2730bhp) Rolls Royce Marine AS-Norway AuxGen: 2 x 1280kW 450V 60Hz a.c, 2 x 280kW 450V 60Hz a.c Thrusters: 2 Thwart. FP thruster (f); 1 Thwart. FP thruster (a)

9255098 *PPVC* -	**SKANDI YARE** **Norskan Norway AS** Norskan Offshore Ltda SatCom: Inmarsat C 471000256 *Rio de Janeiro* *Brazil* MMSI: 710003750 Official number: 381E005143	**1,970** 848 3,000	Class: NV	**2001-12 Aukra Industrier AS — Aukra** Yd No: 103 Loa 67.00 Br ex - Dght 5.900 Lbp 61.80 Br md 16.00 Dpth 7.00 Welded, 1 dk	**(B21A20S) Platform Supply Ship**	**2 oil engines** with clutches, flexible couplings & sr reverse geared to sc. shafts driving 2 CP propellers Total Power: 4,010kW (5,452hp) 13.0kn Normo KRMB-9 2 x 4 Stroke 9 Cy. 250 x 300 each-2005kW (2726bhp) Rolls Royce Marine AS-Norway AuxGen: 2 x 250kW 440V 60Hz a.c, 2 x 1280kW 440V 60Hz a.c Thrusters: 2 Thwart. FP thruster (f); 1 Tunnel thruster (a) Fuel: 746.3 (d.f.) 8.0pd
9133915 *SIEB* -	**SKANE** **Stena Rederi AB** Stena Line Scandinavia AB SatCom: Inmarsat B 326546310 *Trelleborg* *Sweden* MMSI: 265463000	**42,705** 21,731 7,290	Class: LR (NV) **100A1** SS 04/2013 passenger, vehicle and train ferry Ice Class 1B at a minimum draft 5.20M (fwd and aft) and the maximum draught not to exceed summer loadline **LMC UMS** Cable: 632.5/73.0 U3	**1998-06 Astilleros de Puerto Real SRL — Puerto Real** Yd No: 77 Loa 200.20 (BB) Br ex 29.60 Dght 6.500 Lbp 186.20 Br md 29.00 Dpth 15.30 Welded, 11 dks	**(A36A2PT) Passenger/Ro-Ro Ship (Vehicles/Rail)** Passengers: cabins: 150; berths: 600; driver berths: 80 Stern door Len: 5.10 Wid: 10.00 Swl: - Side doors (s) Len: 5.20 Wid: 6.50 Swl: - Lane-Len: 3295 Lane-Wid: 6.50 Lane-clr ht: 4.80 Lorries: 110, Cars: 500, Rail Wagons: 55 Ice Capable	**4 oil engines** reduction geared to sc. shafts driving 2 CP propellers Total Power: 28,980kW (39,400hp) 21.0kn MAN 8L48/60 4 x 4 Stroke 8 Cy. 480 x 600 each-7245kW (9850bhp) MAN B&W Diesel AG-Augsburg AuxGen: 1 x 3000kW 440/660V 50Hz a.c, 3 x 2150kW 440/660V 50Hz a.c Boilers: 2 HWH (o.f.), 2 HWH (ex.g.) Thrusters: 3 Thwart. FP thruster (f) Fuel: 86.3 (d.f.) 923.9 (r.f.) 90.0pd
6714823 *LLVX* -	**SKANEVIK** **Ferjelaget Skaanevik** Det Midthordlandske Dampskibsselskab AS *Bergen* *Norway* MMSI: 257370400	**566** 169 -	Class: (NV)	**1967-06 Molde Verft AS — Hjelset** (Hull) Yd No: (47) **1967-06 Ulstein Mek. Verksted AS — Ulsteinvik** Yd No: 47 Loa 44.33 Br ex 9.94 Dght 2.833 Lbp 39.50 Br md 9.20 Dpth 3.66 Welded, 1 dk	**(A36A2PR) Passenger/Ro-Ro Ship (Vehicles)** Passengers: 348 Cars: 30	**2 oil engines** driving 2 FP propellers Total Power: 662kW (900hp) Wichmann 3ACA 2 x 2 Stroke 3 Cy. 280 x 420 each-331kW (450bhp) Wichmann Motorfabrikk AS-Norway Fuel: 18.5 (d.f.) 3.0pd
9086588 *C6XF4* -	**SKANIA** *ex* Eurostar Roma *-2008* *ex* Superfast I *-2004* **Scania Line Ltd** Polska Zegluga Morska PP (POLSTEAM) *Nassau* *Bahamas* MMSI: 311007200 Official number: 8001532	**23,933** 8,939 5,717	Class: NV (RI) (AB) (HR)	**1995-03 Schichau Seebeckwerft AG — Bremerhaven** Yd No: 1087 Loa 173.70 (BB) Br ex 28.70 Dght 6.420 Lbp 158.00 Br md 24.00 Dpth 14.10 Welded, 2 dks	**(A36A2PR) Passenger/Ro-Ro Ship (Vehicles)** Passengers: unberthed: 780; cabins: 200; berths: 626 Bow door/ramp Len: 14.00 Wid: 5.00 Swl: - Stern door/ramp (p) Len: 7.00 Wid: 4.00 Swl: - Stern door/ramp (s) Len: 7.00 Wid: 4.00 Swl: - Lane-Len: 2135 Lane-clr ht: 4.50 Lorries: 100, Cars: 95	**4 oil engines** with clutches, flexible couplings & sr geared to sc. shafts driving 2 CP propellers Total Power: 31,680kW (43,072hp) 27.0kn Sulzer 12ZAV40S 4 x Vee 4 Stroke 12 Cy. 400 x 560 each-7920kW (10768bhp) Zaklady Urzadzen Technicznych'Zgoda' SA-Poland AuxGen: 2 x 1120kW 230/440V 60Hz a.c, 3 x 1200kW 230/440V 60Hz a.c Thrusters: 2 Thwart. CP thruster (f) Fuel: 90.0 (d.f.) 1350.0 (r.f.) 144.0pd
8417259 *OZ2063* -	**SKANSANES** *ex* Hav Sund *-2013* *ex* Sandfelli *-2008* *ex* Myras *-2007* *ex* Alko *-1996* **Sekstant Sp/f** - *Runavik* *Faeroe Islands (Danish)* MMSI: 231523000 Official number: 311079297	**1,209** 505 1,140	Class: BV (GL) (NV)	**1985-06 Kroeger Werft Kroeger GmbH & Co. Werft KG — Schacht-Audorf** Yd No: 1514 Loa 63.02 (BB) Br ex 11.46 Dght 3.371 Lbp 58.53 Br md 11.31 Dpth 5.72 Welded, 2 dks	**(A31A2GX) General Cargo Ship** Grain: 2,303; Bale: 2,282 TEU 52 C. 52/20' (40') Compartments: 1 Ho, ER 1 Ha: (37.1 x 9.0)ER Ice Capable	**1 oil engine** driving 1 CP propeller Total Power: 588kW (799hp) 10.0kn Callesen 6-427C-FOTK 1 x 4 Stroke 6 Cy. 270 x 400 588kW (799bhp) Aabenraa Motorfabrik, HeinrichCallesen A/S-Denmark Thrusters: 1 Thwart. FP thruster (f)
9028469 *LMCU* F-175-BD	**SKARBERG** *ex* Oybuen 1 *-2013* *ex* Bernt Oskar *-2010* **Ostbas AS** - *Tromso* *Norway* MMSI: 257586600	**310** 118 -		**2003-01 Klevset Mek. Verksted — Halsanaustan** Yd No: 79 Loa 24.54 (BB) Br ex - Dght - Lbp - Br md 7.40 Dpth 4.50 Welded, 1 dk	**(B11A2FS) Stern Trawler**	**1 oil engine** driving 1 Propeller Thrusters: 1 Thwart. FP thruster (f)
7727310 *SFTJ* -	**SKARGARDEN** **Waxholms Angfartygs AB** - *Vaxholm* *Sweden* MMSI: 265522480	**296** 112 60		**1978-12 Marinteknik Verkstads AB — Oregrund** Yd No: B38 Loa 35.01 Br ex 7.42 Dght 1.401 Lbp 32.11 Br md 7.23 Dpth 2.47 Welded, 2 dks	**(A37B2PS) Passenger Ship** Hull Material: Aluminium Alloy Passengers: unberthed: 399	**4 oil engines** reverse reduction geared to sc. shafts driving 4 FP propellers Total Power: 796kW (1,084hp) 18.5kn Scania DS1140M 4 x 4 Stroke 6 Cy. 127 x 145 each-199kW (271bhp) Saab Scania AB-Sweden
8512621 *LNQL* N-110-RT	**SKARHOLMEN** *ex* Notbas *-1999* *ex* Eva Marina *-1998* *ex* Johan Kr. Rokstad *-1987* **Skarholmen AS** - *Svolvaer* *Norway* MMSI: 259200000	**236** 94 -		**1985-01 Solstrand Slip & Baatbyggeri AS — Tomrefjord** Yd No: 39 Loa - Br ex - Dght - Lbp 26.22 Br md 8.01 Dpth 3.92 Welded, 1 dk	**(B11B2FV) Fishing Vessel**	**1 oil engine** driving 1 FP propeller Total Power: 515kW (700hp) 11.0kn G.M. (Detroit Diesel) 12V-149 1 x Vee 2 Stroke 12 Cy. 146 x 146 515kW (700bhp) General Motors Detroit DieselAllison Divn-USA Thrusters: 1 Thwart. FP thruster (f) Fuel: 50.0 (d.f.) 2.0pd
6415881 *SLEI* -	**SKARNAS** *ex* De Geer *-2004* **Skarnas Terminal AB** - *Iggesund* *Sweden* MMSI: 265554120	**239** 71 -	Class: (LR) ✠ Classed LR until 7/6/00	**1964-12 AB Asi-Verken — Amal** Yd No: 69 Loa 30.05 Br ex 8.64 Dght 4.600 Lbp 27.89 Br md 8.41 Dpth 4.81 Welded, 1 dk	**(B32A2ST) Tug** Ice Capable	**1 oil engine** driving 1 CP propeller Total Power: 1,236kW (1,680hp) 12.0kn Polar MN18 1 x 2 Stroke 8 Cy. 340 x 570 1236kW (1680bhp) Nydqvist & Holm AB-Sweden AuxGen: 1 x 106kW 380V 50Hz a.c, 1 x 72kW 380V 50Hz a.c Fuel: 56.0 (d.f.) 6.0pd
6501769 *SLZE* -	**SKARPO** **Waxholms Angfartygs AB** - *Runmaro* *Sweden* MMSI: 265522470	**181** 73 -		**1965 Broderna Larsson Varv & Mekaniska Verkstads — Kristinehamn** Yd No: 412 Loa 28.91 Br ex 6.84 Dght 2.661 Lbp 25.48 Br md 6.81 Dpth 2.90 Welded, 1 dk	**(A37B2PS) Passenger Ship** Passengers: 233	**1 oil engine** driving 1 FP propeller Total Power: 412kW (560hp) 12.0kn Alpha 407-24VO 1 x 2 Stroke 7 Cy. 240 x 400 412kW (560bhp) Alpha Diesel A/S-Denmark AuxGen: 2 x 20kW 220V d.c Fuel: 9.0 (d.f.) 2.0pd
6409870 *JXKF* -	**SKARSTEIN JUNIOR** *ex* Bergstral *-1999* *ex* Vea Junior *-1993* *ex* Aphrodite *-1974* **Sjomann Havfiske AS** Harry Ytroy *Farsund* *Norway*	**248** 74 186	Class: (BV)	**1964 Soc Industrielle et Commerciale de Consts Navales (SICCNa) — St-Malo** Yd No: 62 Loa 31.86 Br ex 7.27 Dght 3.671 Lbp 27.36 Br md 7.21 Dpth - Welded, 2 dks	**(B11A2FT) Trawler** Grain: 220 Derricks: 1x2t; Winches: 1	**1 oil engine** geared to sc. shaft driving 1 FP propeller Total Power: 662kW (900hp) 11.0kn Grenaa 6FR24TK 1 x 4 Stroke 6 Cy. 240 x 300 662kW (900bhp) (new engine 1985) A/S Grenaa Motorfabrik-Denmark
7947192 *SJOL* -	**SKARVEN** **A/B Goteborg-Styrso Skargardstrafik** - *Gothenburg* *Sweden* MMSI: 265547250	**197** 87 -		**1981 Djupviks Batvarv — Fagerfjall** Yd No: 309 Loa 28.81 Br ex 7.50 Dght 1.870 Lbp - Br md - Dpth - Welded	**(A37B2PS) Passenger Ship** Passengers: 300	**2 oil engines** driving 2 FP propellers Total Power: 482kW (656hp) 14.0kn Volvo Penta TMD121 2 x 4 Stroke 6 Cy. 130 x 150 each-241kW (328bhp) AB Volvo Penta-Sweden Thrusters: 1 Thwart. FP thruster (f)
9436630 *OJNT* -	**SKARVEN** **Alands Landskapsregering** - *Mariehamn* *Finland* MMSI: 230610000 Official number: 55238	**2,285** 686 350	Class: LR ✠ **100A1** SS 10/2009 passenger and vehicle ferry EU (D) Ice Class 1A FS at a draught of 4.100/3.600m Max/min draughts fwd 4.100/3.600m Max/min draughts aft 4.100/3.600m Power required 3050kw, power installed 3600kw ✠ **LMC** **UMS** Eq.Ltr: P; Cable: 275.0/38.0 U2 (a)	**2009-10 UAB Vakaru Laivu Remontas (JSC Western Shiprepair) — Klaipeda** (Hull) Yd No: (12/35) **2009-08 BLRT Laevaehitus OU — Tallinn** Yd No: 12/35 Loa 65.29 Br ex 13.41 Dght 4.100 Lbp 57.60 Br md 13.00 Dpth 5.90 Welded, 1 dk	**(A36A2PR) Passenger/Ro-Ro Ship (Vehicles)** Single Hull Passengers: unberthed: 250 Bow door/ramp (centre) Len: 5.20 Wid: 6.20 Swl: - Stern door/ramp (centre) Len: 5.20 Wid: 6.20 Swl: - Lane-clr ht: 4.40 Cars: 62 Ice Capable	**2 oil engines** reduction geared to sc. shafts driving 2 Directional propellers Total Power: 3,600kW (4,894hp) 14.0kn Wartsila 9L20 2 x 4 Stroke 9 Cy. 200 x 280 each-1800kW (2447bhp) Wartsila Finland Oy-Finland AuxGen: 2 x 140kW 400V 50Hz a.c Fuel: 105.0 (d.f.) 10.0pd

IMO / Call sign	Name / Owner	Tonnage	Class	Builder / Dimensions	Type	Machinery
8330748 - -	**SKAT** *ex* Stevns Surveyor *-2009* *ex* Solea *-1993* **Sevmorneftegeofizika-center JSC Co** *Murmansk* *Russia*	**172** 50 73	Class: RS (BV) (GL)	**1982-03 Motorenwerk Bremerhaven GmbH (MWB) — Bremerhaven** Yd No: 915 Loa 29.37 Br ex 8.06 Dght 1.201 Lbp 28.02 Br md 8.02 Dpth 2.06 Welded, 1 dk	**(B31A2SR) Research Survey Vessel**	**2 oil engines** sr geared to sc. shafts driving 2 Directional propellers Total Power: 414kW (562hp) 9.0kn MAN D2542ME 2 x Vee 4 Stroke 12 Cy. 125 x 142 each-207kW (281bhp) Maschinenbau Augsburg Nuernberg (MAN)-Augsburg AuxGen: 2 x 60kW 220/380V 50Hz a.c
1007287 *ZCGS3* -	**SKAT** **9906 Ltd** Fraser Yachts Florida Inc *George Town* *Cayman Islands (British)* MMSI: 319741000 Official number: 735479	**1,998** 599 285	Class: LR ✠ **100A1** SS 06/2012 SSC Yacht (P), mono G6 ✠ **LMC** **UMS** Cable: 387.0/28.0 U3 (a)	**2002-06 Fr. Luerssen Werft GmbH & Co. — Bremen** Yd No: 13621 Loa 70.70 (BB) Br ex 13.65 Dght 3.800 Lbp 60.55 Br md 13.20 Dpth 7.20 Welded, 1 dk	**(X11A2YP) Yacht**	**2 oil engines** with clutches & sr geared to sc. shafts driving 2 FP propellers Total Power: 4,000kW (5,438hp) 17.0kn M.T.U. 16V4000M70 2 x Vee 4 Stroke 16 Cy. 165 x 190 each-2000kW (2719bhp) MTU Friedrichshafen GmbH-Friedrichshafen AuxGen: 2 x 300kW 400V 50Hz a.c, 1 x 228kW 400V 50Hz a.c Thrusters: 1 Thwart. FP thruster (f)
8726026 - -	**SKAT** **Alfa Ltd** *Petropavlovsk-Kamchatskiy* *Russia*	**237** 113 455	Class: RS	**1987-09 Bakinskiy Sudostroitelnyy Zavod im Vano Sturua — Baku** Yd No: 393 Loa 35.17 Br ex 8.01 Dght 3.120 Lbp 33.25 Br md 7.58 Dpth 3.60 Welded, 1 dk	**(B34G2SE) Pollution Control Vessel** Liq: 468; Liq (Oil): 468 Compartments: 10 Ta Ice Capable	**1 oil engine** geared to sc. shaft driving 1 FP propeller Total Power: 166kW (226hp) 8.1kn Daldizel 6CHNSP18/22 1 x 4 Stroke 6 Cy. 180 x 220 166kW (226bhp) Daldizel-Khabarovsk AuxGen: 1 x 50kW, 1 x 30kW Fuel: 11.0 (d.f.)
8726038 - -	**SKAT** **State Enterprise Kerch Sea Fishing Port** *Kerch* *Ukraine* Official number: 850929	**191** 85 323	Class: (RS)	**1986-02 Svetlovskiy Sudoremontnyy Zavod — Svetlyy** Yd No: 28 Loa 29.45 Br ex 8.15 Dght 3.120 Lbp 28.50 Br md 7.58 Dpth 3.60 Welded, 1 dk	**(B34G2SE) Pollution Control Vessel** Liq: 332; Liq (Oil): 332 Compartments: 8 Ta Ice Capable	**1 oil engine** geared to sc. shaft driving 1 FP propeller Total Power: 165kW (224hp) 7.5kn Daldizel 6CHNSP18/22 1 x 4 Stroke 6 Cy. 180 x 220 165kW (224bhp) Daldizel-Khabarovsk AuxGen: 1 x 50kW, 1 x 25kW Fuel: 13.0 (d.f.)
8107103 *3FZK3* -	**SKAUBRYN** *ex* Skeena *-1991* **Kingston Shipping SA** Doriko Ltd *Panama* *Panama* MMSI: 371084000 Official number: 4211410	**43,312** 12,994 41,668	Class: NV	**1982-11 AS Nye Fredrikstad Mek. Verksted — Fredrikstad** Yd No: 441 Loa 182.51 Br ex 32.29 Dght 12.020 Lbp 173.23 Br md 32.26 Dpth 26.80 Welded, 3 dks	**(A35B2RV) Vehicles Carrier** Angled stern door/ramp (centre) Len: 45.15 Wid: 12.50 Swl: 208 Lane-Len: 19085 Lane-clr ht: 6.70 Cars: 4,033 Bale: 69,445 TEU 1061	**1 oil engine** driving 1 FP propeller Total Power: 11,180kW (15,200hp) 14.8kn B&W 7L67GFCA 1 x 2 Stroke 7 Cy. 670 x 1700 11180kW (15200bhp) AS Nye Fredrikstad Mek Verksted-Norway AuxGen: 3 x 1400kW 440V 60Hz a.c Thrusters: 1 Thwart. FP thruster (f) Fuel: 442.0 (d.f.) 3503.0 (r.f.) 51.0pd
9521863 *A8ZR3*	**SKAWA** **Hermione Seven Maritime Ltd** Polska Zegluga Morska PP (POLSTEAM) *Monrovia* *Liberia* MMSI: 636015278 Official number: 15278	**13,579** 5,247 16,600	Class: AB PR	**2012-06 Taizhou Sanfu Ship Engineering Co Ltd — Taizhou JS** Yd No: SF080107 Loa 149.96 (BB) Br ex - Dght 8.250 Lbp 140.80 Br md 23.60 Dpth 12.50 Welded, 1 dk	**(A21A2BC) Bulk Carrier** Grain: 23,800 Compartments: 5 Ho, ER 5 Ha: ER Cranes: 3x30t Ice Capable	**1 oil engine** driving 1 CP propeller Total Power: 6,570kW (8,933hp) 14.0kn MAN-B&W 5S50MC-C 1 x 2 Stroke 5 Cy. 500 x 2000 6570kW (8933bhp) STX (Dalian) Engine Co Ltd-China AuxGen: 1 x 645kW a.c, 2 x 520kW a.c
9707429 *OURT2* -	**SKAWLINK IV** **Rederiet Skawlink IV A/S** - *Skagen* *Denmark (DIS)* Official number: H1719	**140** 42 -		**2013-03 A/S Hvide Sande Skibs- og Baadebyggeri — Hvide Sande** Yd No: 128 Loa 23.53 Br ex - Dght - Lbp - Br md 7.50 Dpth 4.04 Welded, 1 dk	**(B21B2OT) Offshore Tug/Supply Ship**	**1 oil engine** driving 1 Propeller
9096313 *J8Y4450* -	**SKAZKA** *ex* Leonardo *-2008* **Tanela Ventures Ltd** Vitera LLC *Kingstown* *St Vincent & The Grenadines* MMSI: 376574000 Official number: 40920	**163** 48 -	Class: RI	**2002-01 Azimut-Benetti SpA — Viareggio** Yd No: 98/11 Loa 29.83 Br ex - Dght - Lbp - Br md 6.80 Dpth 3.35 Bonded, 1 dk	**(X11A2YP) Yacht** Hull Material: Reinforced Plastic	**2 oil engines** geared to sc. shafts driving 2 Propellers Total Power: 2,942kW (4,000hp) M.T.U. 16V2000M91 2 x Vee 4 Stroke 16 Cy. 130 x 150 each-1471kW (2000bhp) MTU Friedrichshafen GmbH-Friedrichshafen
9137090 *CFL8497* -	**SKEENA QUEEN** **British Columbia Ferry Services Inc** *Victoria, BC* *Canada* MMSI: 316001267 Official number: 819521	**2,453** 795 1,012	Class: LR ✠ **100A1** SS 04/2012 ro-ro cargo/ferry, Strait of Georgia service ✠ **LMC** Cable: 247.5/44.0 U2	**1997-04 Allied Shipbuilders Ltd — North Vancouver BC** Yd No: 257 Loa 110.00 Br ex 24.00 Dght 2.800 Lbp 105.00 Br md 23.45 Dpth 5.25 Welded, 1 dk	**(A36A2PR) Passenger/Ro-Ro Ship (Vehicles)** Passengers: unberthed: 600 Bow door & ramp Stern door & ramp Cars: 100	**4 oil engines** gearing integral to driving 4 Z propellers 2 fwd and 2 aft Total Power: 4,476kW (6,084hp) 14.5kn Mitsubishi S6U-MPTK 4 x 4 Stroke 6 Cy. 240 x 260 each-1119kW (1521bhp) (new engine 2000) Mitsubishi Heavy Industries Ltd-Japan AuxGen: 2 x 300kW 440V 60Hz a.c Fuel: 102.0 (d.f.)
7615505 *TFSM* -	**SKEIDFAXI** **Sementsverksmidjan hf (Cement Works Ltd Co)** *Akranes* *Iceland* MMSI: 251238110 Official number: 1483	**415** 179 650		**1977-05 Skipasmidastod Thorgeir & Ellert h/f — Akranes** Yd No: 33 Loa 46.82 Br ex - Dght - Lbp - Br md 8.75 Dpth 3.71 Welded, 1 dk	**(A24A2BT) Cement Carrier**	**1 oil engine** driving 1 FP propeller Total Power: 372kW (506hp) Caterpillar D379TA 1 x Vee 4 Stroke 8 Cy. 159 x 203 372kW (506bhp) Caterpillar Tractor Co-USA
6718099 *EI2212* D 115	**SKELLIG DAWN** *ex* Monte Marin *-1993* **Skellig Fish Ltd** - SatCom: Inmarsat C 425004920 *Dublin* *Irish Republic* MMSI: 250000872 Official number: 402137	*220* 94 184		**1967 Construcciones Navales P Freire SA — Vigo** Yd No: 46 Loa 33.56 Br ex 6.68 Dght - Lbp 30.00 Br md 6.66 Dpth 3.20 Welded, 1 dk	**(B11A2FT) Trawler**	**1 oil engine** driving 1 FP propeller Total Power: 662kW (900hp) Deutz RBV6M545 1 x 4 Stroke 6 Cy. 320 x 450 662kW (900bhp) Kloeckner Humboldt Deutz AG-West Germany
9265263 *EIBH* T 456	**SKELLIG LIGHT II** **Skellig Fish Ltd** Roberto Fontan Dominguez *Tralee* *Irish Republic* MMSI: 250486000 Official number: 403512	**325** 97 151	Class: BV	**2002-08 Astilleros Armon Burela SA — Burela** Yd No: 199 Loa 33.20 Br ex - Dght 3.370 Lbp 27.00 Br md 8.00 Dpth 3.50 Welded, 1 dk	**(B11A2FS) Stern Trawler**	**1 oil engine** reduction geared to sc. shaft driving 1 CP propeller Total Power: 834kW (1,134hp) 11.0kn Wartsila 6L20 1 x 4 Stroke 6 Cy. 200 x 280 834kW (1134bhp) Wartsila Diesel S.A.-Bermeo
9481958 *9V8731*	**SKELT** *ex* Stella Alnilam *-2013* **Skelt Marine Pte Ltd** Wellard Ships Pte Ltd SatCom: Inmarsat C 456424010 *Singapore* *Singapore* MMSI: 564240000 Official number: 396166	**22,988** 11,574 34,529 T/cm 48.9	Class: RI	**2010-11 SPP Shipbuilding Co Ltd — Tongyeong** Yd No: H4030 Loa 180.00 (BB) Br ex - Dght 9.917 Lbp 172.00 Br md 30.00 Dpth 14.70 Welded, 1 dk	**(A21A2BC) Bulk Carrier** Double Hull Grain: 48,766; Bale: 46,655 Compartments: 5 Ho, ER 5 Ha: 4 (19.2 x 20.2)ER (16.4 x 18.4) Cranes: 4x35t	**1 oil engine** driving 1 FP propeller Total Power: 10,750kW (14,616hp) 14.0kn MAN-B&W 5S50MC-C 1 x 2 Stroke 5 Cy. 500 x 2000 10750kW (14616bhp) Doosan Engine Co Ltd-South Korea AuxGen: 3 x 590kW 440V 60Hz a.c
7211127 *SX4111* -	**SKIATHOS** *ex* Eva S *-2004* *ex* Emanuela Seconda *-1995* *ex* Karen Bech *-1977* **Sporades Naftiki Eteria** - *Volos* *Greece* MMSI: 237148000 Official number: 62	**1,355** 550 1,379	Class: (RI) (BV)	**1972-07 Sonderborg Skibsvaerft A/S — Sonderborg** Yd No: 66 Loa 70.77 Br ex 13.01 Dght 3.571 Lbp 65.99 Br md 12.98 Dpth 6.30 Welded, 2 dks	**(A31A2GX) General Cargo Ship** Grain: 3,200; Bale: 2,832 Compartments: 1 Ho, ER 2 Ha: 2 (19.2 x 8.5)ER Derricks: 4x5t; Winches: 4	**1 oil engine** driving 1 CP propeller Total Power: 897kW (1,220hp) 12.0kn Alpha 10V23L-VO 1 x Vee 4 Stroke 10 Cy. 225 x 300 897kW (1220bhp) Alpha Diesel A/S-Denmark AuxGen: 3 x 80kW 380V 50Hz a.c Fuel: 128.0 (d.f.)
7726330 - -	**SKIF** *ex* Seacor Fortitude *-2005* *ex* Bigorange 30 *-2000* *ex* Veesea Diamond *-1997* *ex* Subsea *-1991* *ex* Nicor Subsea *-1990* *ex* Acadian Seafarer *-1985* **Reserved Capital Enterprises Corp** Anship LLC	**1,195** 358 1,334	Class: (AB)	**1979-06 Halter Marine, Inc. — New Orleans, La** Yd No: 653 Converted From: Diving Support Vessel-1991 Converted From: Research Vessel-1985 Converted From: Offshore Tug/Supply Ship-1979 Loa 66.10 Br ex - Dght 4.300 Lbp 65.84 Br md 13.42 Dpth 4.88 Welded, 1 dk	**(B22G2OY) Standby Safety Vessel** Ice Capable	**5 diesel electric oil engines** driving 5 gen. each 900kW 600V a.c Connecting to 4 elec. motors driving 2 FP propellers Total Power: 4,260kW (5,790hp) 12.0kn G.M. (Detroit Diesel) 16V-149-NA 5 x Vee 2 Stroke 16 Cy. 146 x 146 each-852kW (1158bhp) General Motors Detroit DieselAllison Divn-USA AuxGen: 1 x 150kW 480V 60Hz a.c Thrusters: 1 Thwart. FP thruster (f) Fuel: 938.0

8930122 - -
SKIF
-
State Enterprise Kerch Sea Fishing Port
-
Kerch *Ukraine*
MMSI: 272061600
Official number: 700832
181 54 46
Class: (RS)
1970 "Petrozavod" — Leningrad Yd No: 392
Loa 29.30 Br ex 8.49 Dght 3.090
Lbp 27.00 Br md 8.30 Dpth 4.35
Welded, 1 dk
(B32A2ST) Tug
Ice Capable
2 oil engines driving 2 CP propellers
Total Power: 882kW (1,200hp) 11.4kn
Russkiy 6D30/50-3-3
2 x 2 Stroke 6 Cy. 300 x 500 each-441kW (600bhp)
Mashinostroitelnyy Zavod"Russkiy-Dizel"-Leningrad
AuxGen: 2 x 25kW a.c
Fuel: 42.0 (d.f.)

8862894 *UCID* -
SKIF
ex ST-1311 *-2003*
Navigator Shipping Co Ltd (A/O 'Navigator')
-
Taganrog *Russia*
MMSI: 273459230
Official number: 845846
1,781 639 1,729
Class: (RS)
1985-06 Volgogradskiy Sudostroitelnyy Zavod — Volgograd Yd No: 126
Loa 86.70 Br ex 12.30 Dght 3.000
Lbp 81.52 Br md 12.00 Dpth 3.50
Welded, 1 dk
(A31A2GX) General Cargo Ship
Grain: 2,230
TEU 54 C.Ho 36/20' C.Dk 18/20'
Compartments: 1 Ho, ER
2 Ha: 2 (19.8 x 9.0)ER
Ice Capable
2 oil engines driving 2 FP propellers
Total Power: 1,176kW (1,598hp)
S.K.L. 6NVD48A-2U
2 x 4 Stroke 6 Cy. 320 x 480 each-588kW (799bhp)
VEB Schwermaschinenbau "KarlLiebknecht" (SKL)-Magdeburg
Thrusters: 1 Thwart. FP thruster (f)

9365271 *UADB* -
SKIF
-
JSC 'Sovfracht-Primorsk'
JSC 'Marine Port Service' (ZAO 'Morskoy Portovyy Servis')
SatCom: Inmarsat C 427311127
St Petersburg *Russia*
MMSI: 273319230
272 81 159
Class: RS
2005-09 OAO Leningradskiy Sudostroitelnyy Zavod 'Pella' — Otradnoye Yd No: 603
Loa 28.50 Br ex 9.50 Dght 3.500
Lbp 26.66 Br md 9.28 Dpth 4.80
Welded, 1 dk
(B32A2ST) Tug
2 oil engines reduction geared to sc. shafts driving 2 Z propellers
Total Power: 2,610kW (3,548hp) 12.0kn
Caterpillar 3512B-HD
2 x Vee 4 Stroke 12 Cy. 170 x 215 each-1305kW (1774bhp)
Caterpillar Inc-USA
AuxGen: 2 x 80kW a.c
Fuel: 82.0 (d.f.)

8858087 *UBRK6* -
SKIF-V
ex Sail *-2012* *ex* Petka *-2002*
ex City of Chios *-2000* *ex* Omskiy-29 *-1992*
Ladoga Shipping Co Ltd (OOO Sudokhodnaya Kompaniya 'Ladoga')
-
Astrakhan *Russia*
MMSI: 273336790
2,463 949 3,060
Class: RS
1984 Krasnoyarskiy Sudostroitelnyy Zavod — Krasnoyarsk Yd No: 33
Loa 108.40 Br ex 15.00 Dght 3.000
Lbp - Br md 14.80 Dpth 5.00
Welded, 1 dk
(A31A2GX) General Cargo Ship
2 oil engines driving 2 FP propellers
Total Power: 522kW (710hp) 8.0kn
S.K.L. 6NVD48A-2U
2 x 4 Stroke 6 Cy. 320 x 480 each-261kW (355bhp)
VEB Schwermaschinenbau "KarlLiebknecht" (SKL)-Magdeburg

7510884 *5VCS7* -
SKIFF
ex Alga *-2014* *ex* Thor Heidi *-2001*
ex Bolmen *-1997* *ex* Fenris *-1996*
ex Marie Lehmann *-1986*
Algamar Maritime SA
GMZ Ship Management Co SA
Lome *Togo*
MMSI: 671480000
1,864 1,238 2,991
Class: RS (LR) (GL)
Classed LR until 25/5/05
1976-10 J.J. Sietas Schiffswerft — Hamburg Yd No: 789
Lengthened-1979
Loa 83.57 (BB) Br ex 11.84 Dght 5.230
Lbp 78.30 Br md 11.82 Dpth 6.01
Welded, 2 dks
(A31A2GX) General Cargo Ship
Grain: 4,356; Bale: 4,219
TEU 91 C. 91/20'
Compartments: 1 Ho, ER
1 Ha: (44.9 x 9.3)ER
Ice Capable
1 oil engine driving 1 FP propeller
Total Power: 1,067kW (1,451hp) 11.0kn
MWM TBD484-8
1 x 4 Stroke 8 Cy. 320 x 480 1067kW (1451bhp)
Motoren Werke Mannheim AG (MWM)-West Germany
AuxGen: 2 x 63kW 380V 50Hz a.c
Boilers: db 3.1kgf/cm² (3.0bar)
Fuel: 131.0 (d.f.)

8412807 *OIRS* -
SKIFTET
-
Alands Landskapsregering
-
Mariehamn *Finland*
MMSI: 230992740
Official number: 50821
961 363 240
1985-05 Valmetin Laivateollisuus Oy — Turku Yd No: 360
Loa 48.52 Br ex 10.72 Dght 3.901
Lbp 42.91 Br md 10.51 Dpth 5.26
Welded
(A36A2PR) Passenger/Ro-Ro Ship (Vehicles)
Passengers: unberthed: 250
Cars: 47
Ice Capable
1 oil engine with clutches, flexible couplings & sr geared to sc. shaft driving 1 CP propeller
Total Power: 1,604kW (2,181hp) 13.0kn
Wartsila 12V22HF
1 x Vee 4 Stroke 12 Cy. 220 x 240 1604kW (2181bhp)
Oy Wartsila Ab-Finland
Thrusters: 1 Thwart. FP thruster (f)

9366782 *7TAD* -
SKIKDA
-
Entreprise Portuaire de Skikda (EPS)
-
Skikda *Algeria*
309 92 -
Class: BV
2007-01 Stal-Rem SA — Gdansk (Hull) Yd No: (511731)
2007-01 B.V. Scheepswerf Damen — Gorinchem Yd No: 511731
Loa 30.76 Br ex - Dght 3.760
Lbp 28.03 Br md 9.40 Dpth 4.80
Welded, 1 dk
(B32A2ST) Tug
2 oil engines reduction geared to sc. shafts driving 2 Directional propellers
Total Power: 3,040kW (4,134hp) 12.9kn
MaK 8M20
2 x 4 Stroke 8 Cy. 200 x 300 each-1520kW (2067bhp)
Caterpillar Motoren GmbH & Co. KG-Germany
AuxGen: 2 x 90kW 400/230V 50Hz a.c

8953629 *9V5848* -
SKILLFUL
-
PSA Marine Pte Ltd
-
Singapore *Singapore*
Official number: 388744
296 88 450
Class: BV
1999-12 ASL Shipyard Pte Ltd — Singapore Yd No: 167
Loa 30.00 Br ex - Dght 5.300
Lbp 28.03 Br md 9.50 Dpth -
Welded, 1 dk
(B32A2ST) Tug
Passengers: berths: 8
2 oil engines reduction geared to sc. shafts driving 2 Directional propellers
Total Power: 2,464kW (3,350hp) 12.0kn
Deutz SBV6M628
2 x 4 Stroke 6 Cy. 240 x 280 each-1232kW (1675bhp)
Deutz AG-Koeln
AuxGen: 2 x 91kW a.c

5362219 *JXBP* -
SKILSO
ex Ursus *-2004* *ex* Titan *-1989*
Morland & Karlsen AS
-
Arendal *Norway*
MMSI: 257269500
148 44 -
Class: (NV)
1958 Bolsones Verft AS — Molde Yd No: 168
Loa 27.89 Br ex 7.01 Dght -
Lbp 24.49 Br md 6.99 Dpth 3.66
Welded, 1 dk
(B32A2ST) Tug
1 oil engine driving 1 FP propeller
Total Power: 706kW (960hp)
Alpha 498-VO
1 x 2 Stroke 8 Cy. 290 x 490 706kW (960bhp)
Alpha Diesel A/S-Denmark
AuxGen: 1 x 40kW 220V d.c, 1 x 22kW 220V d.c
Fuel: 31.5 (d.f.) 4.5pd

9563213 *PBYL* -
SKINFAXE R
ex Tarka 3 *-2012*
RN Shipping A/S
Rohde Nielsen A/S
SatCom: Inmarsat C 424540412
Zwijndrecht *Netherlands*
MMSI: 245404000
Official number: 53450
221 66 200
Class: BV
2010-04 Damen Shipyards Kozle Sp z oo — Kedzierzyn-Kozle (Hull) Yd No: 1140
2010-04 B.V. Scheepswerf Damen Hardinxveld — Hardinxveld-Giessendam Yd No: 571620
Loa 27.02 Br ex 9.70 Dght 3.200
Lbp 23.84 Br md 9.10 Dpth 3.60
Welded, 1 dk
(B32A2ST) Tug
Cranes: 1x5.5t
2 oil engines geared to sc. shafts driving 2 FP propellers
Total Power: 2,236kW (3,040hp)
Caterpillar 3512B-TA
2 x Vee 4 Stroke 12 Cy. 170 x 190 each-1118kW (1520bhp)
Caterpillar Inc-USA
AuxGen: 2 x 78kW 50Hz a.c
Thrusters: 1 Tunnel thruster (f)

9395898 *TFAL* SF 20
SKINNEY
-
Skinney-Thinganes hf
-
Hornafjordur *Iceland*
MMSI: 251086000
Official number: 2732
383 115 82
Class: NV
2009-01 Ching Fu Shipbuilding Co Ltd — Kaohsiung Yd No: 061
Loa 28.90 (BB) Br ex 9.21 Dght 4.100
Lbp 27.20 Br md 9.20 Dpth 4.30
Welded, 1 dk
(B11A2FS) Stern Trawler
1 oil engine reduction geared to sc. shaft driving 1 CP propeller
Total Power: 1,103kW (1,500hp)
Mitsubishi S6U-MPTK
1 x 4 Stroke 6 Cy. 240 x 260 1103kW (1500bhp)
Mitsubishi Heavy Industries Ltd-Japan
AuxGen: 1 x a.c, 1 x a.c
Thrusters: 1 Tunnel thruster (f)

6924076 *5BKP* -
SKIP
ex Dicky Bonzo *-1992* *ex* Skip *-1989*
ex Dickybonzo *-1989*
Dropsea Shipping Ltd
-
Limassol *Cyprus*
Official number: 321170
366 220 369
1943 in Egypt (Assembled by)
1943 Vulcan Iron Works — India (Parts for assembly by)
Converted From: Naval Type
Loa 40.85 Br ex 9.35 Dght 1.982
Lbp 39.93 Br md 9.15 Dpth 2.14
Riveted, 1 dk
(B34P2QV) Salvage Ship
Compartments: 3 Ho, ER
2 oil engines driving 2 FP propellers
Total Power: 330kW (448hp) 9.0kn
National Gas
2 x 4 Stroke 6 Cy. 152 x 216 each-165kW (224bhp)
(Re-engined ,made 1969, Reconditioned & fitted 1975)
National Gas & Oil Eng. Co.-Ashton-under-Lyne
AuxGen: 1 x 27kW 220V 50Hz a.c, 1 x 10kW 220V 50Hz a.c
Fuel: 6.0 (d.f.)

8999764 *H04538* -
SKIP
ex En Ji 8 *-2006* *ex* Xie Chang 8 *-2006*
Fortune Ocean Co Ltd
Dalian East Ocean Maritime Consulting Services Co Ltd
Panama *Panama*
MMSI: 356733000
Official number: 3204706
1,436 927 -
1986-01 Zhejiang Shunhang Ship Manufacturing Co Ltd — Yueqing ZJ
Loa 74.20 Br ex - Dght 5.300
Lbp 68.31 Br md 12.00 Dpth 7.00
Welded, 1 dk
(A31A2GX) General Cargo Ship
1 oil engine driving 1 Propeller
Total Power: 736kW (1,001hp) 10.0kn
Chinese Std. Type
1 x 4 Stroke 736kW (1001bhp)
in China

9382657 *AULG* -
SKIP JACK
-
Government of The Republic of India (Administration of Union Territory of Lakshadweep)
The Shipping Corporation of India Ltd (SCI)
Kochi *India*
MMSI: 419066600
Official number: 3192
164 49 68
Class: IR (BV)
2007-07 NGV Tech Sdn Bhd — Telok Panglima Garang Yd No: 1035
Loa 32.27 Br ex - Dght 1.200
Lbp 29.30 Br md 9.00 Dpth 2.98
Welded, 1 dk
(A37B2PS) Passenger Ship
Hull Material: Aluminium Alloy
Passengers: unberthed: 50
2 oil engines reduction geared to sc. shafts driving 2 Water jets
Total Power: 1,490kW (2,026hp) 16.0kn
Caterpillar 3412E
2 x Vee 4 Stroke 12 Cy. 137 x 152 each-745kW (1013bhp)
Caterpillar Inc-USA
AuxGen: 2 x 55kW 380V 50Hz a.c
Fuel: 10.5 (d.f.)

IMO / Call sign	Name / Owner	Tonnage	Class	Builder / Dimensions	Type	Machinery
9503847 *WDE3251* -	**SKIPJACK** **Penn Maritime Inc** *Philadelphia, PA* *United States of America* MMSI: 367336380 Official number: 1208426	**499** 149 428	Class: AB	**2008**-07 **Thoma-Sea Shipbuilders LLC — Lockport LA** Yd No: 107 Loa 35.46 (BB) Br ex - Dght 4.730 Lbp 34.15 Br md 11.00 Dpth 5.13 Welded, 1 dk	**(B32B2SA) Articulated Pusher Tug**	**2 oil engines** reduction geared to sc. shafts driving 2 FP propellers Total Power: 2,984kW (4,058hp) 12.0kn Cummins QSK60-M 2 x Vee 4 Stroke 16 Cy. 159 x 190 each-1492kW (2029bhp) (new engine 2008) Cummins Engine Co Inc-USA AuxGen: 3 x 99kW a.c Fuel: 345.7 (d.f.)
6922315 *DVHC* -	**SKIPJACK** **Luzon Stevedoring Corp** - *Manila* *Philippines* Official number: 212832	*271* 163 -	Class: (AB)	**1969 Iloilo Dock & Engineering Co. — Iloilo** Yd No: 99 Loa 32.31 Br ex 8.49 Dght 3.214 Lbp 28.66 Br md 8.08 Dpth 4.12 Welded, 1 dk	**(B32A2ST) Tug**	**1 oil engine** sr geared to sc. shaft driving 1 FP propeller Total Power: 809kW (1,100hp) MWM 1 x 4 Stroke 6 Cy. 320 x 480 809kW (1100bhp) Motoren Werke Mannheim AG (MWM)-West Germany AuxGen: 1 x 98kW, 1 x 65kW Fuel: 203.0 (d.f.)
7613399 *ATVO*	**SKIPJACK** **Government of The Republic of India (Director of Central Institute of Fisheries Nautical Engineering & Training - CIFNET)** - *Kolkata* *India* Official number: 1881	*192* 114 119	Class: (LR) Classed LR until 10/1/89	**1982**-11 **Garden Reach Shipbuilders & Engineers Ltd. — Kolkata** Yd No: 1048 Loa 32.62 Br ex 7.50 Dght 3.201 Lbp 28.25 Br md 7.41 Dpth 3.74 Welded, 1 dk	**(B11A2FS) Stern Trawler** Compartments: 1 Ho, ER 2 Ha:	**1 oil engine** with clutches, flexible couplings & dr geared to sc. shaft driving 1 CP propeller Total Power: 519kW (706hp) MAN R8V16/18TL 1 x 4 Stroke 8 Cy. 160 x 180 519kW (706bhp) Garden Reach Shipbuilders &Engineers Ltd-India AuxGen: 2 x 128kW 415V 50Hz a.c
1006831 *PF9040* -	**SKIPPER** *ex* Skippur *-2003* **Authur H del Prado** Soren Christensen *Amsterdam* *Netherlands* MMSI: 244100722 Official number: 41741	**111** 33 -	Class: (LR) ✠ Classed LR until 10/9/05	**2000**-09 **Holland Jachtbouw B.V. — Zaandam** Yd No: 228 Loa 30.50 Br ex 7.21 Dght 1.800 Lbp 26.20 Br md 7.20 Dpth 3.50 Bonded, 1 dk	**(X11A2YS) Yacht (Sailing)** Hull Material: Aluminium Alloy	**1 oil engine** with clutches, flexible couplings & sr reverse geared to sc. shaft driving 1 CP propeller Total Power: 275kW (374hp) 11.0kn M.T.U. 6R183TE93 1 x 4 Stroke 6 Cy. 128 x 142 275kW (374bhp) MTU Friedrichshafen GmbH-Friedrichshafen AuxGen: 2 x 35kW 400V 50Hz a.c Thrusters: 1 Thwart. FP thruster (f); 1 Tunnel thruster (a)
8319811 *EI7060* DA.59	**SKIPPER** *ex* General Drouot *-1985* **Craig Byrne** - *Drogheda* *Irish Republic* MMSI: 250126460 Official number: 403619	*159* 47 194		**1984**-06 **Forges Caloin — Etaples** Yd No: 38 Loa 25.00 Br ex 6.86 Dght 3.015 Lbp 21.49 Br md 6.80 Dpth 3.61 Welded, 1 dk	**(B11A2FS) Stern Trawler** Compartments: 1 Ho, ER 1 Ha: ER	**1 oil engine** with clutches, flexible couplings & sr geared to sc. shaft driving 1 CP propeller Total Power: 441kW (600hp) MGO 12V175ASHR 1 x Vee 4 Stroke 12 Cy. 175 x 180 441kW (600bhp) Societe Alsacienne de ConstructionsMecaniques (SACM)-France
9234264 *9V7027*	**SKIPPER** *ex* Scorpio *-2002* **PSA Marine Pte Ltd** - *Singapore* *Singapore* MMSI: 563005290 Official number: 392564	**292** 87 110	Class: LR ✠ **100A1** SS 05/2011 tug ✠ **LMC** Eq.Ltr: F†; Cable: 275.0/19.0 U2 (a)	**2001**-05 **ASL Shipyard Pte Ltd — Singapore** Yd No: 208 Loa 29.95 Br ex - Dght 4.710 Lbp 26.10 Br md 9.80 Dpth 4.80 Welded, 1 dk	**(B32A2ST) Tug**	**2 oil engines** reduction geared to sc. shafts driving 2 Directional propellers Total Power: 3,326kW (4,522hp) 12.0kn Deutz SBV8M628 2 x 4 Stroke 8 Cy. 240 x 280 each-1663kW (2261bhp) Deutz AG-Koeln AuxGen: 2 x 83kW 415V 50Hz a.c
7636456 *ATZP*	**SKIPPER I** **Government of The Republic of India (Central Institute of Fisheries - Madras Unit)** - *Kochi* *India*	*264* 163 -	Class: IR (NV)	**1980**-10 **Goa Shipyard Ltd. — Goa** Yd No: 1075 Loa 33.51 Br ex 8.36 Dght 3.974 Lbp 28.05 Br md 8.01 Dpth 4.40 Welded, 1 dk	**(B11A2FS) Stern Trawler**	**1 oil engine** geared to sc. shaft driving 1 FP propeller Total Power: 552kW (750hp) Caterpillar D398TA 1 x Vee 4 Stroke 12 Cy. 159 x 203 552kW (750bhp) Caterpillar Tractor Co-USA AuxGen: 2 x 82kW 440V 60Hz a.c, 1 x 42kW 440V 60Hz a.c
7818133 - -	**SKIPPER II** **Government of The Republic of India (Central Institute of Fisheries - Madras Unit)** - *Kochi* *India*	*175* 65 -	Class: IR (BV)	**1979**-07 **A/S Svendborg Skibsvaerft — Svendborg** Yd No: 160 Loa 28.33 Br ex 7.62 Dght 3.031 Lbp 25.02 Br md 7.60 Dpth 3.61 Welded, 1 dk	**(B11A2FS) Stern Trawler**	**1 oil engine** driving 1 FP propeller Total Power: 441kW (600hp) 10.3kn Alpha 406-26VO 1 x 2 Stroke 6 Cy. 260 x 400 441kW (600bhp) Alpha Diesel A/S-Denmark Fuel: 30.0 (d.f.)
8315255 - -	**SKIPPER1** *ex* Rich Land *-2011* *ex* Meisho Maru *-2002* **Haiyou Shipping Co Ltd** Weihai Huayang International Ship Management Co Ltd	**1,400** 814 2,098	Class: UB (NK)	**1983**-03 **Sasaki Shipbuilding Co Ltd — Osakikamijima HS** Yd No: 368 Loa 73.08 Br ex - Dght 5.023 Lbp 68.03 Br md 11.41 Dpth 6.81 Welded, 2 dks	**(A31A2GX) General Cargo Ship** Grain: 3,065; Bale: 2,801 Compartments: 1 Ho, ER 1 Ha: ER	**1 oil engine** driving 1 FP propeller Total Power: 1,177kW (1,600hp) 12.0kn Akasaka A31 1 x 4 Stroke 6 Cy. 310 x 600 1177kW (1600bhp) Akasaka Tekkosho KK (Akasaka DieselLtd)-Japan AuxGen: 3 x 72kW
8622660 *3FUK6*	**SKIPPER2** *ex* Orient Star No. 5 *-2011* *ex* Ishikari Maru *-1998* **Haiyi Shipping International Co Ltd** Global Enterprise Corp *Panama* *Panama* MMSI: 370925000 Official number: 4010809A	**1,923** 787 2,092	Class: OM	**1984**-02 **Yamanaka Zosen K.K. — Imabari** Yd No: 273 Loa 80.83 Br ex - Dght 4.480 Lbp 75.01 Br md 13.20 Dpth 7.75 Welded, 1 dk	**(A31A2GX) General Cargo Ship**	**1 oil engine** driving 1 FP propeller Total Power: 1,471kW (2,000hp) 10.5kn Hanshin 1 x 4 Stroke 1471kW (2000bhp) The Hanshin Diesel Works Ltd-Japan
8312095 *9LD2576* -	**SKIPPERS Y** *ex* Island Skipper *-2014* **Shippers Ship-Trade Ltd** - *Freetown* *Sierra Leone* MMSI: 667085000	**17,065** 10,334 28,031 T/cm 36.0	Class: DR (AB)	**1984**-07 **Hitachi Zosen Corp — Maizuru KY** Yd No: 4771 Loa 178.21 (BB) Br ex 23.22 Dght 10.608 Lbp 167.21 Br md 23.11 Dpth 14.76 Welded, 1 dk	**(A21A2BC) Bulk Carrier** Grain: 38,555; Bale: 33,607 Compartments: 5 Ho, ER 5 Ha: (12.0 x 11.4)3 (19.2 x 11.4) (17.6 x 11.4)ER Cranes: 4x25t	**1 oil engine** driving 1 FP propeller Total Power: 7,061kW (9,600hp) 14.5kn Sulzer 6RTA58 1 x 2 Stroke 6 Cy. 580 x 1700 7061kW (9600bhp) Hitachi Zosen Corp-Japan AuxGen: 3 x 440kW 450V 60Hz a.c
9404687 *YJTC4* -	**SKIPSEY TIDE** *ex* F. D. Reliable *-2012* **Tidewater Marine International Inc** Tidewater Marine International Inc *Port Vila* *Vanuatu* MMSI: 577114000 Official number: 2177	**2,305** 848 3,105	Class: NV (RI)	**2007**-10 **Cant. Nav. Rosetti — Ravenna** Yd No: 88 Loa 72.00 Br ex - Dght 5.900 Lbp 66.80 Br md 16.00 Dpth 7.00 Welded, 1 dk	**(B21A2OS) Platform Supply Ship**	**2 oil engines** reduction geared to sc. shafts driving 2 CP propellers Total Power: 5,580kW (7,586hp) 14.0kn Wartsila 9L26A 2 x 4 Stroke 9 Cy. 260 x 320 each-2790kW (3793bhp) Wartsila Finland Oy-Finland AuxGen: 2 x 1800kW a.c, 2 x 300kW a.c Thrusters: 2 Tunnel thruster (f); 2 Tunnel thruster (a)
9328039 *5BQG2*	**SKIRNER** **ms 'Skirner' J Kahrs Schiffahrts GmbH & Co KG** J Kahrs Bereederungs GmbH & Co KG *Limassol* *Cyprus* MMSI: 212831000	**7,852** 3,363 9,350	Class: BV GL	**2006**-11 **B.V. Scheepswerf Damen Hoogezand — Foxhol** Yd No: 861 **2006**-10 **Santierul Naval Damen Galati S.A. — Galati** (Hull) Yd No: 1073 Loa 140.64 (BB) Br ex - Dght 7.330 Lbp 130.00 Br md 21.80 Dpth 9.50 Welded, 1 dk	**(A33A2CC) Container Ship (Fully Cellular)** Double Bottom Entire Compartment Length TEU 803 C Ho 206 TEU C Dk 597 TEU incl 180 ref C. Ice Capable	**1 oil engine** reduction geared to sc. shaft driving 1 CP propeller Total Power: 8,400kW (11,421hp) 18.0kn MaK 9M43 1 x 4 Stroke 9 Cy. 430 x 610 8400kW (11421bhp) Caterpillar Motoren GmbH & Co. KG-Germany AuxGen: 2 x 465kW 440V 60Hz a.c, 1 x 1600kW 440V 60Hz a.c Thrusters: 1 Thwart. CP thruster (f); 1 Thwart. CP thruster (a) Fuel: 105.0 (d.f.) 894.0 (r.f.)
5148302 *SV4691* -	**SKIRON** *ex* Chryssi Ammos *-2009* *ex* Argo Digger *-2003* *ex* Heortnesse *-1974* **Nafsipous Naftiki Eteria** - *Iraklion* *Greece* MMSI: 237098200 Official number: 29	*417* 321 819	Class: (LR) ✠ Classed LR until 27/4/79	**1959**-06 **Lobnitz & Co. Ltd. — Renfrew** Yd No: 1145 Loa 47.71 Br ex 13.26 Dght 3.703 Lbp 45.55 Br md 10.67 Dpth 4.27 Welded, 1 dk	**(B33B2DU) Hopper/Dredger (unspecified)**	**2 oil engines** with flexible couplings & reverse reduction geared to sc. shafts driving 2 FP propellers Total Power: 300kW (408hp) Mirrlees TLADM4 2 x 4 Stroke 4 Cy. 216 x 349 each-150kW (204bhp) Mirrlees, Bickerton & Day-Stockport AuxGen: 2 x 30kW 220V d.c
9068201 - -	**SKJ V** **PT Samudra Kencana Jaya** - *Jambi* *Indonesia*	**217** 66 -	Class: KI	**2002**-06 **PT Mitra Liga Mandiri Sukses — Jambi** Loa 27.90 Br ex - Dght - Lbp 25.00 Br md 8.50 Dpth 4.15 Welded, 1 dk	**(B32A2ST) Tug**	**2 oil engines** geared to sc. shafts driving 2 Propellers Total Power: 1,692kW (2,300hp) Caterpillar D399 2 x Vee 4 Stroke 16 Cy. 159 x 203 each-846kW (1150bhp) Caterpillar Inc-USA

7925649 **SKJOLDNAES** **986** Class: BV
OXDV *ex* Sam-Sine *-2009* 295
\- **AEro Kommune** 125
AErofaergerne
Soby *Denmark*
MMSI: 219000733
Official number: A354

1979-07 **Carl B Hoffmanns Maskinfabrik A/S — Esbjerg** (Hull) Yd No: 20
1979-07 **Soren Larsen & Sonners Skibsvaerft A/S — Nykobing Mors** Yd No: 137
Lengthened & Widened-2001
Loa 47.10 Br ex 11.70 Dght 2.250
Lbp 41.75 Br md - Dpth 6.81
Welded, 2 dks

(A36A2PR) Passenger/Ro-Ro Ship (Vehicles)
Passengers: unberthed: 248
Lane-Len: 41
Lane-Wid: 2.50
Lane-clr ht: 4.10
Lorries: 3, Cars: 36
Ice Capable

2 oil engines reduction geared to sc. shafts driving 2 FP propellers
Total Power: 650kW (884hp) 10.5kn
Cummins N14-M
2 x 4 Stroke 6 Cy. 140 x 152 each-325kW (442bhp) (new engine 2001)
Cummins Engine Co Inc-USA
AuxGen: 2 x 74kW 380V a.c
Thrusters: 1 Thwart. FP thruster (f)
Fuel: 10.0 (d.f.)

8304830 **SKJONGHOLM** **469** Class: (NV)
LHSQ *ex* Veidar *-2010* *ex* Jonina Jonsdottir *-1995* 140
SF-7-F *ex* Stefan Thor *-1992* *ex* Ljosfaxi *-1990* 116
ex Gunnjon *-1988*
P/R Skjongholm ANS
\-
SatCom: Inmarsat C 425932910
Floro *Norway*
MMSI: 259329000

1982-05 **Vaagland Baatbyggeri AS — Vaagland** Yd No: 103
Loa 34.02 Br ex - Dght 5.222
Lbp 29.55 Br md 8.51 Dpth 6.33
Welded, 2 dks

(B11A2FT) Trawler
Ice Capable

1 oil engine driving 1 FP propeller
Total Power: 508kW (691hp)
Callesen 6-427-FOT
1 x 4 Stroke 6 Cy. 270 x 400 508kW (691bhp)
Aabenraa Motorfabrik, HeinrichCallesen A/S-Denmark
AuxGen: 2 x 132kW 220V 50Hz a.c

9212175 **SKLINNABANKEN** **326**
LJQM *ex* Hege Cathrine *-2006* 106
N-250-BR **Bronnoy Havfiske AS** 200
\-
Hammerfest *Norway*
MMSI: 259648000

1999-12 **Stocznia Ustka SA — Ustka** (Hull) Yd No: N75/1
1999-12 **Norrona Verft AS — Hommelvik** Yd No: 75
Loa 27.33 Br ex - Dght 4.000
Lbp - Br md 8.50 Dpth 4.20
Welded, 1 dk

(B11A2FS) Stern Trawler

1 oil engine geared to sc. shaft driving 1 FP propeller
Total Power: 783kW (1,065hp)
Caterpillar 3508B
1 x Vee 4 Stroke 8 Cy. 170 x 190 783kW (1065bhp)
Caterpillar Inc-USA

9635248 **SKM AMBITION** **21,203** Class: NK
3FJN5 11,419
\- **SKM Shipping SA** 33,328
Fairmont Shipping (Canada) Ltd
Panama *Panama*
MMSI: 351123000
Official number: 44682TJ

2013-06 **Shin Kurushima Dockyard Co. Ltd. — Onishi** Yd No: 5755
Loa 179.99 (BB) Br ex - Dght 10.100
Lbp 172.00 Br md 28.20 Dpth 14.30
Welded, 1 dk

(A21A2BC) Bulk Carrier
Double Hull
Grain: 44,075; Bale: 43,118
Compartments: 5 Ho, ER
5 Ha: 3 (20.8 x 23.8) (19.2 x 23.8)ER (16.8 x 17.2)
Cranes: 4x30t

1 oil engine driving 1 FP propeller
Total Power: 6,000kW (8,158hp) 14.3kn
Mitsubishi 6UEC45LSE
1 x 2 Stroke 6 Cy. 450 x 1840 6000kW (8158bhp)
Kobe Hatsudoki KK-Japan
Fuel: 1604.0

8983741 **SKODA** **171** Class: CS
9AA6388 *ex* Kien Giang *-2007* 51
\- **Milivoj Blaslov** -
\-
Zadar *Croatia*
Official number: 3R-165

2002 Yd No: 222
Loa 30.90 Br ex - Dght 2.950
Lbp 26.00 Br md 7.62 Dpth 3.96
Welded, 1 dk

(B11B2FV) Fishing Vessel

1 oil engine reduction geared to sc. shaft driving 1 Propeller
Total Power: 449kW (610hp) 9.0kn
Caterpillar 3412
1 x Vee 4 Stroke 12 Cy. 137 x 152 449kW (610bhp)
Caterpillar Inc-USA

7725142 **SKODSBORG** **14,805** Class: RI (LR)
3FXP *ex* Dana Africa *-1984* 4,441 ✠ Classed LR until 21/2/03
\- **Vittorio Bogazzi & Figli SpA** 10,470
BNavi Ship Management Srl T/cm
SatCom: Inmarsat C 435230413 26.1
Panama *Panama*
MMSI: 352304000
Official number: 4346112

1979-07 **Nippon Kokan KK (NKK Corp) — Shizuoka SZ** Yd No: 376
2002 **Cindemir Makina Gemi Onarim ve Tersanecilik AS — Istanbul (Tuzla)**
(Additional cargo section)
Lengthened-2002
Loa 161.40 (BB) Br ex 24.29 Dght 6.413
Lbp 150.40 Br md 24.01 Dpth 14.36
Welded, 2 dks, Upr intermediate hoistable dk fwd & Lwr hoistable dk aft light cargoes only

(A35A2RR) Ro-Ro Cargo Ship
Stern door & ramp (centre)
Len: 14.50 Wid: 8.50 Swl: 200
Lane-Len: 1884
Lane-Wid: 6.00
Lane-clr ht: 6.30
Trailers: 149
Bale: 18,569
TEU 654 C Ho 280 TEU C Dk 374 TEU incl 12 ref C.
Compartments: 1 Ho, ER
2 Ha: (26.6 x 8.0) (21.3 x 9.0)ER
Cranes: 1x36t; Derricks: 1x120t

1 oil engine driving 1 FP propeller
Total Power: 5,913kW (8,039hp) 14.5kn
B&W 6L55GF
1 x 2 Stroke 6 Cy. 550 x 1380 5913kW (8039bhp)
Mitsui Engineering & Shipbuilding CLtd-Japan
AuxGen: 3 x 920kW 220/390V 50Hz a.c
Boilers: AuxB (o.f.) 8.0kgf/cm² (7.8bar), AuxB (ex.g.) 8.0kgf/cm² (7.8bar)
Thrusters: 1 Thwart. CP thruster (f)
Fuel: 72.0 (d.f.) (Heating Coils) 1735.0 (r.f.) 27.0pd

8912039 **SKOG** **4,462** Class: NV
5BPF3 *ex* Lys-Skog *-2009* 1,513
\- **Lorentzens Rederi AS** 3,728
DFDS Logistics AS
Limassol *Cyprus*
MMSI: 210488000
Official number: 8912039

1991-01 **Brodogradiliste 'Titovo' — Kraljevica** Yd No: 487
Lengthened-1999
Loa 99.43 (BB) Br ex 17.03 Dght 5.850
Lbp 94.50 Br md 17.00 Dpth 10.60
Welded, 1 dk

(A31B2GP) Palletised Cargo Ship
Side door (s)
Bale: 205
TEU 56
Compartments: 1 Ho, ER
2 Ha: ER
Ice Capable

1 oil engine sr geared to sc. shaft driving 1 CP propeller
Total Power: 2,460kW (3,345hp) 14.0kn
Wartsila 6R32E
1 x 4 Stroke 6 Cy. 320 x 350 2460kW (3345bhp)
Wartsila Diesel Oy-Finland
AuxGen: 1 x 545kW 380V 50Hz a.c, 2 x 250kW 380V 50Hz a.c
Thrusters: 1 Thwart. FP thruster (f)

9375252 **SKOGAFOSS** **7,545** Class: GL
V2EF3 *ex* Ice Bird *-2011* 3,165
\- **W Bockstiegel GmbH & Co Reederei KG ms 'Pacific Carrier'** 8,209
The Iceland Steamship Co Ltd (Eimskip Island Ehf) (Eimskip Ehf)
Saint John's *Antigua & Barbuda*
MMSI: 305411000
Official number: 4606

2007-07 **Sainty Shipbuilding (Yangzhou) Corp Ltd — Yizheng JS** Yd No: 05STIG012
Loa 129.66 (BB) Br ex - Dght 7.400
Lbp 120.34 Br md 20.60 Dpth 10.80
Welded, 1 dk

(A33A2CC) Container Ship (Fully Cellular)
Double Bottom Entire Compartment Length
Grain: 12,643; Bale: 12,643
TEU 698 C Ho 226 TEU C Dk 472 TEU incl 120 ref C.
Compartments: 4 Cell Ho, ER
4 Ha: (12.5 x 15.8)2 (25.4 x 15.8)ER (6.4 x 10.7)
Ice Capable

1 oil engine reduction geared to sc. shafts driving 1 CP propeller
Total Power: 7,200kW (9,789hp) 16.0kn
MaK 8M43C
1 x 4 Stroke 8 Cy. 430 x 610 7200kW (9789bhp)
Caterpillar Motoren GmbH & Co. KG-Germany
AuxGen: 3 x 550kW 450/230V a.c, 1 x 1000kW 450/230V a.c
Thrusters: 1 Tunnel thruster (f)

9015175 **SKOGOY** **225** Class: (NV)
LDUK 72
\- **Torghatten Nord AS** 100
\-
Narvik *Norway*
MMSI: 257361500

1991-04 **Harding Verft AS — Rosendal** Yd No: 259
Loa - Br ex - Dght 1.473
Lbp 28.76 Br md 8.01 Dpth 3.19
Welded, 1 dk

(A37B2PS) Passenger Ship
Passengers: unberthed: 130

2 oil engines reduction geared to sc. shafts driving 2 FP propellers
Total Power: 2,682kW (3,646hp)
G.M. (Detroit Diesel) 16V-149-TI
2 x Vee 2 Stroke 16 Cy. 146 x 146 each-1341kW (1823bhp)
General Motors Detroit DieselAllison Divn-USA
AuxGen: 2 x 53kW

8950108 **SKOLMEN** *340*
LJOB 107
N-25-W **Steinfjordfisk AS** -
\-
Svolvaer *Norway*
MMSI: 259563000

1998-12 **Devonport Engineering Consortium Ltd — Plymouth** (Hull)
1998-12 **O. Ulvan Baatbyggeri AS — Sandstad** Yd No: 422
Loa 27.42 Br ex - Dght -
Lbp 24.00 Br md 8.50 Dpth 6.65
Welded, 1 dk

(B11B2FV) Fishing Vessel

1 oil engine geared to sc. shaft driving 1 FP propeller
Total Power: 1,103kW (1,500hp)
Cummins KTA-38-M2
1 x Vee 4 Stroke 12 Cy. 159 x 159 1103kW (1500bhp)
Cummins Engine Co Ltd-United Kingdom

9490765 **SKOMVAER** **32,839** Class: BV
V7UV9 19,559
\- **Skomvaer Bulker AS** 58,000
Scantank AS T/cm
Majuro *Marshall Islands* 59.2
MMSI: 538004044
Official number: 4044

2010-09 **Yangzhou Dayang Shipbuilding Co Ltd — Yangzhou JS** Yd No: DY3025
Loa 189.99 (BB) Br ex - Dght 12.950
Lbp 185.00 Br md 32.26 Dpth 18.00
Welded, 1 dk

(A21A2BC) Bulk Carrier
Grain: 71,549; Bale: 69,760
Compartments: 5 Ho, ER
5 Ha: ER
Cranes: 4x35t

1 oil engine driving 1 FP propeller
Total Power: 8,700kW (11,829hp) 14.3kn
MAN-B&W 6S50MC-C
1 x 2 Stroke 6 Cy. 500 x 2000 8700kW (11829bhp)
Doosan Engine Co Ltd-South Korea
AuxGen: 3 x 645kW 60Hz a.c

5115111 **SKONNERTEN JYLLAND** **157** Class: (BV)
OXDO2 *ex* Anne El II *-2006* *ex* Elida af Tonsberg *-2003* 47
\- *ex* Victoria af Stockholm *-1999* *ex* Elida *-1995* 218
ex Elida av Kungshamn *-1988* *ex* Elida *-1985*
ex Stornes *-1984* *ex* Morild *-1974*
ex Findal *-1971* *ex* Finn *-1970*
Rederiet Jylland ApS
\-
Thisted *Denmark (DIS)*
MMSI: 220276000
Official number: H1409

1951-07 **Karlstads Varv AB — Karlstad** Yd No: 129
Converted From: Fish Carrier-1982
Loa 31.11 Br ex 6.46 Dght 2.998
Lbp 27.49 Br md 6.40 Dpth 3.10
Welded, 1 dk

(A37A2PC) Passenger/Cruise
Passengers: berths: 60
Compartments: 1 Ho, ER
1 Ha: (12.6 x 3.5)ER
Derricks: 1x1.5t; Winches: 1
Ice Capable

1 oil engine driving 1 FP propeller
Total Power: 221kW (300hp) 10.0kn
Wichmann 3ACA
1 x 2 Stroke 3 Cy. 280 x 420 221kW (300bhp) (new engine 1955)
Wichmann Motorfabrikk AS-Norway
Fuel: 6.0 (d.f.) 1.0pd

5234321 **SKOPELOS** *492* Class: (BV) (RI)
\- *ex* Panagis K *-1985* *ex* Aeolis *-1984* 216
\- *ex* Brave Enterprise *-1982* 750
ex Happy Event *-1977*
ex Brave Enterprise *-1976* *ex* Mirasol *-1973*
ex Midas *-1967*
\-
\-

1948 **Cant. del Tirreno — Genova** Yd No: 207
Loa 61.19 Br ex 9.94 Dght 3.531
Lbp 56.29 Br md 9.91 Dpth -
Riveted\Welded, 1 dk & S dk

(A31A2GX) General Cargo Ship
Grain: 1,756; Bale: 1,671
Compartments: 2 Ho, ER
2 Ha: 2 (10.0 x 3.9)ER
Derricks: 1x10t,4x3t; Winches: 4

1 oil engine driving 1 FP propeller
Total Power: 507kW (689hp) 10.5kn
Fiat
1 x 2 Stroke 4 Cy. 360 x 650 507kW (689bhp)
SA Fiat SGM-Torino
AuxGen: 1 x 45kW 220V d.c, 2 x 12kW 220V d.c
Fuel: 148.5 (d.f.)

9235737 *SVBM5* -	**SKOPELOS** *ex* Samho Dream *-2012* *ex* Neptune *-2008* *ex* World Progress *-2004* **ENE Skopelos I Ltd** Aeolos Management SA SatCom: Inmarsat C 424116510 *Piraeus* *Greece* MMSI: 241165000 Official number: 12093	**161,135** 110,526 319,360 T/cm 180.8	Class: LR (KR) **✠100A1** SS 03/2012 Double Hull oil tanker ESP *IWS SPM LI **ShipRight** (SDA, FDA, CM) **✠LMC** **UMS IGS** Eq.Ltr: A†; Cable: 770.0/114.0 U3 (a)	**2002-12 Samho Heavy Industries Co Ltd — Samho** Yd No: 136 Loa 332.99 (BB) Br ex 60.05 Dght 22.524 Lbp 319.00 Br md 60.00 Dpth 30.40 Welded, 1 dk	**(A13A2TV) Crude Oil Tanker** Double Hull (13F) Liq: 339,055; Liq (Oil): 346,270 Compartments: 5 Ta, 10 Wing Ta, 2 Wing Slop Ta, ER 3 Cargo Pump (s)	**1 oil engine** driving 1 FP propeller Total Power: 29,340kW (39,891hp) 16.1kn B&W 6S90MC-C 1 x 2 Stroke 6 Cy. 900 x 3188 29340kW (39891bhp) Hyundai Heavy Industries Co Ltd-South Korea AuxGen: 3 x 1100kW 450V 60Hz a.c Boilers: e (ex.g.) 22.9kgf/cm^2 (22.5bar), WTAuxB (o.f.) 17.9kgf/cm^2 (17.6bar) Fuel: 363.0 (d.f.) (Heating Coils) 7850.0 (r.f.)
9254862 *SYHL* -	**SKOPELOS** **Skopelos II Special Maritime Enterprise (ENE)** Eletson Corp *Piraeus* *Greece* MMSI: 240031000 Official number: 11159	**41,679** 19,343 70,146 T/cm 67.0	Class: LR **✠100A1** SS 05/2013 Double Hull oil tanker ESP *IWS LI **ShipRight** (SDA, FDA plus, CM) **✠LMC** **UMS IGS** Eq.Ltr: Q†; Cable: 687.5/81.0 U3 (a)	**2003-05 Hyundai Heavy Industries Co Ltd — Ulsan** Yd No: 1447 Loa 228.08 (BB) Br ex 32.23 Dght 13.719 Lbp 219.00 Br md 32.20 Dpth 20.40 Welded, 1 dk	**(A13B2TP) Products Tanker** Double Hull (13F) Liq: 76,397; Liq (Oil): 76,397 Cargo Heating Coils Compartments: 12 Wing Ta, 2 Wing Slop Ta, ER 3 Cargo Pump (s): 3x2000m^3/hr Manifold: Bow/CM: 114.1m	**1 oil engine** driving 1 FP propeller Total Power: 11,444kW (15,559hp) 14.7kn MAN-B&W 6S60MC-C 1 x 2 Stroke 6 Cy. 600 x 2400 11444kW (15559bhp) Hyundai Heavy Industries Co Ltd-South Korea AuxGen: 3 x 700kW 450V 60Hz a.c Boilers: e (ex.g.) 22.1kgf/cm^2 (21.7bar), AuxB (o.f.) 18.4kgf/cm^2 (18.0bar) Fuel: 133.0 (d.f.) (Heating Coils) 2232.0 (r.f.) 47.8pd
7533862 *UEFF* -	**SKOPIN** **Shtil Co Ltd** - *Nakhodka* *Russia* Official number: 752891	**172** 51 94	Class: RS	**1975-10 Sretenskiy Sudostroitelnyy Zavod — Sretensk** Yd No: 82 Loa 33.96 Br ex 7.09 Dght 2.902 Lbp 30.00 Br md 7.00 Dpth 3.69 Welded, 1 dk	**(B11B2FV) Fishing Vessel** Bale: 96 Compartments: 1 Ho, ER 1 Ha: (1.3 x 1.6) Derricks: 2x2t; Winches: 2 Ice Capable	**1 oil engine** driving 1 FP propeller Total Power: 224kW (305hp) 9.0kn S.K.L. 8NVD36-1U 1 x 4 Stroke 8 Cy. 240 x 360 224kW (305bhp) VEB Schwermaschinenbau "KarlLiebknecht" (SKL)-Magdeburg Fuel: 20.0 (d.f.)
7004342 *ESRE* -	**SKORPION** *ex* Sirius *-2001* *ex* Picasso *-1996* *ex* Sivona *-1993* *ex* Ekfjord *-1976* *launched as* Tankfjord *-1970* **Bominship OU** AS Bominflot Estonia *Tallinn* *Estonia* MMSI: 276462000 Official number: 1T01E01	**1,660** 771 2,999 T/cm 8.4	Class: RS (NV)	**1970-04 Flekkefjord Slipp & Maskinfabrikk AS AS — Flekkefjord** Yd No: 101 Lengthened-1971 Loa 86.46 Br ex 12.02 Dght 4.611 Lbp 79.48 Br md 12.01 Dpth 6.75 Welded, 1 dk	**(A13B2TP) Products Tanker** Liq: 3,300; Liq (Oil): 3,300 Part Cargo Heating Coils Compartments: 13 Ta, ER 2 Cargo Pump (s): 2x275m^3/hr Manifold: Bow/CM: 54m Ice Capable	**1 oil engine** driving 1 FP propeller Total Power: 1,839kW (2,500hp) Nohab 8V25 1 x Vee 4 Stroke 8 Cy. 250 x 300 1839kW (2500bhp) (new engine 1988) Wartsila Diesel AB-Sweden AuxGen: 3 x 68kW 380V 50Hz a.c, 1 x 40kW 380V 50Hz a.c
9266281 *IJGS2* -	**SKORPION** *ex* Express 20 *-2013* *ex* Kaltim Makmur *-2006* **Crismare Societa di Navigazione Srl** - *Genoa* *Italy* MMSI: 247340500	**162** 48 39	Class: BV	**2002-04 Strategic Marine Pty Ltd — Fremantle WA** Yd No: H102 Loa 29.80 Br ex - Dght 2.220 Lbp 26.79 Br md 7.50 Dpth 2.60 Welded, 1 dk	**(B21A2OC) Crew/Supply Vessel** Hull Material: Aluminium Alloy Passengers: unberthed: 80	**3 oil engines** geared to sc. shafts driving 3 FP propellers Total Power: 2,040kW (2,775hp) 20.0kn Caterpillar 3412E 3 x Vee 4 Stroke 12 Cy. 137 x 152 each-680kW (925bhp) Caterpillar Inc-USA AuxGen: 2 x 62kW 380V 50Hz a.c
8006397 *CBKP* -	**SKORPIOS II** **Naviera y Turismo Skorpios SA** - SatCom: Inmarsat M 672520091 *Valparaiso* *Chile* MMSI: 725002200 Official number: 2567	*1,523* 379 286	Class: AB	**1988-10 Kochifas Shipyard — Puerto Montt** Yd No: 1 Loa 70.00 Br ex - Dght 2.870 Lbp 64.80 Br md 10.01 Dpth 4.22 Welded	**(A37A2PC) Passenger/Cruise** Passengers: cabins: 64; berths: 160	**1 oil engine** reverse reduction geared to sc. shaft driving 1 FP propeller Total Power: 1,064kW (1,447hp) 12.0kn Deutz SBV6M628 1 x 4 Stroke 6 Cy. 240 x 280 1064kW (1447bhp) Kloeckner Humboldt Deutz AG-West Germany AuxGen: 2 x 300kW a.c
9143908 *CBSK* -	**SKORPIOS III** **Naviera y Turismo Skorpios SA** - SatCom: Inmarsat M 672510085 *Valparaiso* *Chile* MMSI: 725001100 Official number: 2869	**1,597** 549 450	Class: AB	**1995-12 Kochifas Shipyard — Puerto Montt** Yd No: 2 Loa 69.00 Br ex - Dght 3.299 Lbp 59.69 Br md 10.00 Dpth 4.48 Welded, 1 dk	**(A37A2PC) Passenger/Cruise** Passengers: cabins: 48; berths: 125	**1 oil engine** geared to sc. shaft driving 1 FP propeller Total Power: 1,280kW (1,740hp) 13.0kn Alpha 8L23/30 1 x 4 Stroke 8 Cy. 225 x 300 1280kW (1740bhp) MAN B&W Diesel A/S-Denmark
8871936 *LFRX* -	**SKOTTNINGEN** *ex* Kaura *-2008* *ex* Lakstrans *-2006* *ex* Laksfrakt *-1994* *ex* Skottingen *-1990* *ex* Skotningen *-1985* *ex* Kranich *-1954* **Fonnes Invest SA** Fonnes Shipping AS *Namsos* *Norway* MMSI: 257082400	**136** 40 -	Class: (BV)	**1916 G.H. Thyen — Brake** Loa - Br ex - Dght - Lbp 25.94 Br md 6.44 Dpth 3.34 Welded, 1 dk	**(B12C2FL) Live Fish Carrier (Well Boat)**	**1 oil engine** geared to sc. shaft driving 1 FP propeller Total Power: 368kW (500hp) 12.0kn Grenaa 6F24T 1 x 4 Stroke 6 Cy. 240 x 300 368kW (500bhp) (new engine 1916) A/S Grenaa Motorfabrik-Denmark
6611368 *LGER* -	**SKRUE** *ex* Nordvik *-1988* *ex* Langsteigen *-1981* *ex* Tommelise *-1975* **Skagen ANS** - *Haugesund* *Norway* MMSI: 258413000	**237** 105 406	Class: (NV)	**1966 Salthammer Baatbyggeri AS — Vestnes** Yd No: 98 Loa 37.60 Br ex 7.42 Dght 3.163 Lbp 33.71 Br md 7.41 Dpth 3.41 Welded, 1 dk	**(A31A2GX) General Cargo Ship** Grain: 497; Bale: 442 Compartments: 1 Ho, ER 1 Ha: (18.6 x 4.5)ER Derricks: 2x3t; Winches: 2 Ice Capable	**1 oil engine** sr geared to sc. shaft driving 1 CP propeller Total Power: 268kW (364hp) 9.5kn Caterpillar D343TA 1 x 4 Stroke 6 Cy. 137 x 165 268kW (364bhp) (new engine 1973) Caterpillar Tractor Co-USA Fuel: 17.5 (d.f.) 1.5pd
8826761 *UBPF6* -	**SKRUNDA** **ZAO 'Kamak'** - *St Petersburg* *Russia* MMSI: 273333420	**745** 223 1,068	Class: RS	**1990-01 Santierul Naval Drobeta-Turnu Severin S.A. — Drobeta-Turnu S.** Yd No: 1440006 Loa 56.19 Br ex 11.21 Dght 3.700 Lbp 53.20 Br md 11.19 Dpth 4.44 Welded	**(B34A2SH) Hopper, Motor** Hopper: 600 Ice Capable	**2 oil engines** driving 2 FP propellers Total Power: 574kW (780hp) 8.9kn S.K.L. 6NVD26A-3 2 x 4 Stroke 6 Cy. 180 x 260 each-287kW (390bhp) VEB Schwermaschinenbau "KarlLiebknecht" (SKL)-Magdeburg AuxGen: 2 x 100kW a.c
8514667 *XUFX6* -	**SKS** *ex* Shunei Maru *-2013* - - *Phnom Penh* *Cambodia*	*192* - 149		**1986-03 Ishikawajima Ship & Chemical Plant Co Ltd — Tokyo** Yd No: 569 Loa 31.50 Br ex - Dght 2.701 Lbp 28.00 Br md 9.50 Dpth 3.51 Welded, 1 dk	**(B34L2QU) Utility Vessel**	**2 oil engines** driving 2 CP propellers Total Power: 882kW (1,200hp) 9.0kn Daihatsu 6DSM-18A 2 x 4 Stroke 6 Cy. 180 x 230 each-441kW (600bhp) Daihatsu Diesel Manufacturing Co Lt-Japan Thrusters: 1 Thwart. CP thruster (f)
9461843 *C6ZC8* -	**SKS DARENT** **SKS OBO & Tankers AS** KGJ OBO & Tankers Fleet Management AS 773207644 *Nassau* *Bahamas* MMSI: 311052500 Official number: 8001878	**65,830** 37,162 119,456 T/cm 99.8	Class: NV	**2011-02 Hyundai Samho Heavy Industries Co Ltd — Samho** Yd No: S428 Loa 250.00 (BB) Br ex 45.04 Dght 15.200 Lbp 239.00 Br md 45.00 Dpth 21.50 Welded, 1 dk	**(A13B2TP) Products Tanker** Double Hull (13F) Liq: 131,355; Liq (Oil): 131,355 Compartments: 12 Wing Ta, 2 Wing Slop Ta, ER Manifold: Bow/CM: 122.8m	**1 oil engine** driving 1 FP propeller Total Power: 16,350kW (22,229hp) 15.2kn MAN-B&W 6S70ME-C 1 x 2 Stroke 6 Cy. 700 x 2800 16350kW (22229bhp) Hyundai Heavy Industries Co Ltd-South Korea AuxGen: 3 x 1045kW a.c
9428994 *LAIX7* -	**SKS DEE** **SKS OBO & Tankers AS** KGJ OBO & Tankers Fleet Management AS SatCom: Inmarsat C 425772210 *Bergen* *Norway (NIS)* MMSI: 257722000	**65,830** 37,162 119,456 T/cm 99.8	Class: NV	**2010-07 Hyundai Samho Heavy Industries Co Ltd — Samho** Yd No: S383 Loa 249.99 (BB) Br ex 45.04 Dght 15.200 Lbp 239.00 Br md 45.00 Dpth 21.50 Welded, 1 dk	**(A13B2TP) Products Tanker** Double Hull (13F) Liq: 131,355; Liq (Oil): 131,355 Compartments: 12 Wing Ta, 2 Wing Slop Ta, ER Manifold: Bow/CM: 122.8m	**1 oil engine** driving 1 FP propeller Total Power: 16,350kW (22,229hp) 15.2kn MAN-B&W 6S70ME-C 1 x 2 Stroke 6 Cy. 700 x 2800 16350kW (22229bhp) Hyundai Heavy Industries Co Ltd-South Korea AuxGen: 3 x 1045kW a.c
9426312 *LAIU7* -	**SKS DELTA** **SKS OBO & Tankers AS** KGJ OBO & Tankers Fleet Management AS SatCom: Inmarsat Mini-M 764915919 *Bergen* *Norway (NIS)* MMSI: 257464000	**65,830** 37,162 119,456 T/cm 99.8	Class: NV	**2010-01 Hyundai Samho Heavy Industries Co Ltd — Samho** Yd No: S380 Loa 249.99 (BB) Br ex 45.04 Dght 15.200 Lbp 239.00 Br md 45.00 Dpth 21.50 Welded, 1 dk	**(A13B2TP) Products Tanker** Double Hull (13F) Liq: 131,355; Liq (Oil): 131,355 Compartments: 12 Wing Ta, 2 Wing Slop Ta, ER Manifold: Bow/CM: 122.8m	**1 oil engine** driving 1 FP propeller Total Power: 16,350kW (22,229hp) 15.2kn MAN-B&W 6S70ME-C 1 x 2 Stroke 6 Cy. 700 x 2800 16350kW (22229bhp) Hyundai Heavy Industries Co Ltd-South Korea AuxGen: 3 x 1045kW a.c

9531636 *LAND7* -	**SKS DEMINI** **SKS OBO & Tankers AS** KGJ OBO & Tankers Fleet Management AS *Bergen* *Norway (NIS)* MMSI: 259985000	**65,830** 37,162 119,456 T/cm 99.6	Class: NV	**2012-02 Hyundai Samho Heavy Industries Co Ltd — Samho** Yd No: S503 Loa 249.99 (BB) Br ex 45.04 Dght 15.220 Lbp 239.00 Br md 45.00 Dpth 21.50 Welded, 1 dk	**(A13B2TP) Products Tanker** Double Hull (13F) Liq: 131,355; Liq (Oil): 131,355 Compartments: 12 Wing Ta, 2 Wing Slop Ta, ER 12 Cargo Pump (s): 12x1500m³/hr Manifold: Bow/CM: 122.8m	**1 oil engine** driving 1 FP propeller Total Power: 16,350kW (22,229hp) 15.2kn MAN-B&W 6S70ME-C 1 x 2 Stroke 6 Cy. 700 x 2800 16350kW (22229bhp) Hyundai Heavy Industries Co Ltd-South Korea AuxGen: 3 x 1045kW 450V 60Hz a.c
9531648 *LANE7* -	**SKS DODA** **SKS OBO & Tankers AS** KGJ OBO & Tankers Fleet Management AS *Bergen* *Norway (NIS)* MMSI: 259984000	**65,830** 37,162 119,456 T/cm 99.6	Class: NV	**2012-04 Hyundai Samho Heavy Industries Co Ltd — Samho** Yd No: S504 Loa 249.99 (BB) Br ex 45.04 Dght 15.200 Lbp 239.00 Br md 45.00 Dpth 21.50 Welded, 1 dk	**(A13B2TP) Products Tanker** Double Hull (13F) Liq: 131,355; Liq (Oil): 131,355 Compartments: 6 Wing Ta, 6 Wing Ta, 1 Wing Slop Ta, 1 Wing Slop Ta, ER 12 Cargo Pump (s): 12x1500m³/hr Manifold: Bow/CM: 122.8m	**1 oil engine** driving 1 FP propeller Total Power: 16,350kW (22,229hp) 15.2kn MAN-B&W 6S70ME-C 1 x 2 Stroke 6 Cy. 700 x 2800 16350kW (22229bhp) Hyundai Heavy Industries Co Ltd-South Korea AuxGen: 3 x 1045kW a.c
9461831 *LAKD7* -	**SKS DOKKA** **SKS OBO & Tankers AS** KGJ OBO & Tankers Fleet Management AS 773209060 *Bergen* *Norway (NIS)* MMSI: 259084000	**65,830** 37,162 119,950 T/cm 99.8	Class: NV	**2010-11 Hyundai Samho Heavy Industries Co Ltd — Samho** Yd No: S427 Loa 250.00 (BB) Br ex 45.04 Dght 15.200 Lbp 239.00 Br md 45.00 Dpth 21.50 Welded, 1 dk	**(A13B2TP) Products Tanker** Double Hull (13F) Liq: 131,355; Liq (Oil): 131,355 Compartments: 12 Wing Ta, 2 Wing Slop Ta, ER 12 Cargo Pump (s): 12x1500m³/hr Manifold: Bow/CM: 122.8m	**1 oil engine** driving 1 FP propeller Total Power: 16,350kW (22,229hp) 15.2kn MAN-B&W 6S70ME-C 1 x 2 Stroke 6 Cy. 700 x 2800 16350kW (22229bhp) Hyundai Heavy Industries Co Ltd-South Korea
9461855 *C6ZE4* -	**SKS DONGGANG** **SKS OBO & Tankers AS** KGJ OBO & Tankers Fleet Management AS 773207146 *Nassau* *Bahamas* MMSI: 311053800 Official number: 8001891	**65,830** 37,160 119,456 T/cm 99.8	Class: NV	**2011-04 Hyundai Samho Heavy Industries Co Ltd — Samho** Yd No: S429 Loa 249.99 (BB) Br ex 45.04 Dght 15.200 Lbp 239.00 Br md 45.00 Dpth 21.50 Welded, 1 dk	**(A13B2TP) Products Tanker** Double Hull (13F) Liq: 131,356; Liq (Oil): 131,355 Compartments: 12 Wing Ta, 2 Wing Slop Ta, ER 12 Cargo Pump (s): 12x1500m³/hr Manifold: Bow/CM: 122.9m	**1 oil engine** driving 1 FP propeller Total Power: 16,350kW (22,229hp) 15.2kn MAN-B&W 6S70ME-C 1 x 2 Stroke 6 Cy. 700 x 2800 16350kW (22229bhp) Hyundai Heavy Industries Co Ltd-South Korea AuxGen: 3 x 1045kW 50Hz a.c Fuel: 480.0 (d.f.) 3785.0 (r.f.)
9428982 *LAIW7* -	**SKS DOURO** **SKS OBO & Tankers AS** KGJ OBO & Tankers Fleet Management AS SatCom: Inmarsat Mini-M 764916046 *Bergen* *Norway (NIS)* MMSI: 257664000	**65,830** 37,162 119,456 T/cm 99.8	Class: NV	**2010-05 Hyundai Samho Heavy Industries Co Ltd — Samho** Yd No: S382 Loa 249.99 (BB) Br ex 45.04 Dght 15.200 Lbp 239.00 Br md 45.00 Dpth 21.50 Welded, 1 dk	**(A13B2TP) Products Tanker** Double Hull (13F) Liq: 131,355; Liq (Oil): 131,355 Compartments: 12 Wing Ta, 2 Wing Slop Ta, ER 12 Cargo Pump (s) Manifold: Bow/CM: 122.8m	**1 oil engine** driving 1 FP propeller Total Power: 16,350kW (22,229hp) 15.2kn MAN-B&W 6S70ME-C 1 x 2 Stroke 6 Cy. 700 x 2800 16350kW (22229bhp) Hyundai Heavy Industries Co Ltd-South Korea AuxGen: 3 x 1045kW a.c
9429003 *LAKC7* -	**SKS DOYLES** **SKS OBO & Tankers AS** KGJ OBO & Tankers Fleet Management AS SatCom: Inmarsat C 425900410 *Bergen* *Norway (NIS)* MMSI: 259004000	**65,830** 37,162 119,456 T/cm 99.8	Class: NV	**2010-09 Hyundai Samho Heavy Industries Co Ltd — Samho** Yd No: S426 Loa 249.99 (BB) Br ex 45.04 Dght 15.200 Lbp 239.00 Br md 45.00 Dpth 21.50 Welded, 1 dk	**(A13B2TP) Products Tanker** Double Hull (13F) Liq: 131,355; Liq (Oil): 131,355 Compartments: 12 Wing Ta, 2 Wing Slop Ta, ER 12 Cargo Pump (s): 12x500m³/hr Manifold: Bow/CM: 122.8m	**1 oil engine** driving 1 FP propeller Total Power: 16,350kW (22,229hp) 15.2kn MAN-B&W 6S70ME-C 1 x 2 Stroke 6 Cy. 700 x 2800 16350kW (22229bhp) Hyundai Heavy Industries Co Ltd-South Korea AuxGen: 3 x 1045kW a.c
9428970 *LAIV7* -	**SKS DRIVA** **SKS OBO & Tankers AS** KGJ OBO & Tankers Fleet Management AS SatCom: Inmarsat C 425757210 *Bergen* *Norway (NIS)* MMSI: 257572000	**65,830** 37,162 119,456 T/cm 99.9	Class: NV	**2010-03 Hyundai Samho Heavy Industries Co Ltd — Samho** Yd No: S381 Loa 249.99 (BB) Br ex 45.04 Dght 15.200 Lbp 239.00 Br md 45.00 Dpth 21.50 Welded, 1 dk	**(A13B2TP) Products Tanker** Double Hull (13F) Liq: 131,355; Liq (Oil): 131,355 Compartments: 12 Wing Ta, 2 Wing Slop Ta, ER 12 Cargo Pump (s) Manifold: Bow/CM: 122.8m	**1 oil engine** driving 1 FP propeller Total Power: 16,350kW (22,229hp) 15.2kn MAN-B&W 6S70ME-C 1 x 2 Stroke 6 Cy. 700 x 2800 16350kW (22229bhp) Hyundai Heavy Industries Co Ltd-South Korea AuxGen: 3 x 1045kW a.c
9240445 *LAXA5* -	**SKS MERSEY** **SKS OBO & Tankers AS** KGJ OBO & Tankers Fleet Management AS SatCom: Inmarsat B 325878610 *Bergen* *Norway (NIS)* MMSI: 258786000	**70,933** 33,583 120,499 T/cm 99.2	Class: NV	**2003-07 Hyundai Heavy Industries Co Ltd — Ulsan** Yd No: 1425 Loa 249.97 (BB) Br ex 44.04 Dght 15.720 Lbp 239.00 Br md 44.00 Dpth 23.20 Welded, 1 dk	**(A22A2BB) Bulk/Oil Carrier (OBO)** Double Hull (13F) Grain: 135,736; Liq: 132,168; Liq (Oil): 134,000 Compartments: 9 Ho/Ta, ER 9 Ha: ER 9 Cargo Pump (s): 9x1800m³/hr Manifold: Bow/CM: 122.9m	**1 oil engine** driving 1 FP propeller Total Power: 15,519kW (21,100hp) 15.2kn MAN-B&W 5S70MC-C 1 x 2 Stroke 5 Cy. 700 x 2800 15519kW (21100bhp) Hyundai Heavy Industries Co Ltd-South Korea AuxGen: 3 x 980kW a.c Fuel: 220.0 (d.f.) 3500.0 (r.f.)
9240433 *LAXB5* -	**SKS MOSEL** **SKS OBO & Tankers AS** KGJ OBO & Tankers Fleet Management AS SatCom: Inmarsat B 325879210 *Bergen* *Norway (NIS)* MMSI: 258792000 Official number: LAXB	**70,933** 33,583 120,670 T/cm 99.0	Class: NV	**2003-06 Hyundai Heavy Industries Co Ltd — Ulsan** Yd No: 1424 Loa 249.90 (BB) Br ex 44.04 Dght 14.800 Lbp 239.00 Br md 44.00 Dpth 23.20 Welded, 1 dk	**(A22A2BB) Bulk/Oil Carrier (OBO)** Double Hull Grain: 135,736; Liq: 134,000; Liq (Oil): 134,000 Compartments: 9 Ho/Ta, ER 9 Ha: ER 7 Cargo Pump (s): 7x1800m³/hr Manifold: Bow/CM: 123m	**1 oil engine** driving 1 FP propeller Total Power: 15,519kW (21,100hp) 15.2kn MAN-B&W 5S70MC-C 1 x 2 Stroke 5 Cy. 700 x 2800 15519kW (21100bhp) Hyundai Heavy Industries Co Ltd-South Korea AuxGen: 3 x 980kW a.c
9248813 *LAGW7* -	**SKS SALUDA** **SKS OBO & Tankers AS** SKS Tankers Holding AS SatCom: Inmarsat C 425984710 *Bergen* *Norway (NIS)* MMSI: 259847000	**81,270** 52,045 159,437 T/cm 118.2	Class: NV	**2003-04 Hyundai Samho Heavy Industries Co Ltd — Samho** Yd No: S155 Loa 274.20 (BB) Br ex 48.04 Dght 17.100 Lbp 264.00 Br md 48.00 Dpth 23.10 Welded, 1 dk	**(A13A2TV) Crude Oil Tanker** Double Hull (13F) Liq: 167,532; Liq (Oil): 167,532 Cargo Heating Coils Compartments: 12 Wing Ta, ER, 2 Wing Slop Ta 3 Cargo Pump (s): 3x4000m³/hr Manifold: Bow/CM: 137.9m	**1 oil engine** driving 1 FP propeller Total Power: 18,623kW (25,320hp) 15.7kn MAN-B&W 6S70MC-C 1 x 2 Stroke 6 Cy. 700 x 2800 18623kW (25320bhp) Hyundai Heavy Industries Co Ltd-South Korea AuxGen: 3 x 730kW 440V 60Hz a.c Fuel: 187.0 (d.f.) 4405.0 (r.f.)
9301524 *LAIX6* -	**SKS SATILLA** **SKS OBO & Tankers AS** KGJ OBO & Tankers Fleet Management AS SatCom: Inmarsat Mini-M 764564150 *Bergen* *Norway (NIS)* MMSI: 258676000 Official number: LAIX	**81,380** 51,942 158,843 T/cm 118.2	Class: NV	**2006-07 Hyundai Samho Heavy Industries Co Ltd — Samho** Yd No: S262 Loa 274.27 (BB) Br ex - Dght 17.050 Lbp 264.01 Br md 48.01 Dpth 23.10 Welded, 1 dk	**(A13A2TV) Crude Oil Tanker** Double Hull (13F) Liq: 167,531; Liq (Oil): 167,531 Cargo Heating Coils Compartments: 12 Wing Ta, 2 Wing Slop Ta, ER 3 Cargo Pump (s): 3x4000m³/hr Manifold: Bow/CM: 138.5m	**1 oil engine** driving 1 FP propeller Total Power: 18,623kW (25,320hp) 15.7kn MAN-B&W 6S70MC-C 1 x 2 Stroke 6 Cy. 700 x 2800 18623kW (25320bhp) Hyundai Heavy Industries Co Ltd-South Korea AuxGen: 3 x 730kW a.c Fuel: 150.0 (d.f.) 4364.0 (r.f.)
9326718 *LACH7* -	**SKS SEGURA** **SKS OBO & Tankers AS** SKS Tankers Holding AS SatCom: Inmarsat C 425888410 *Bergen* *Norway (NIS)* MMSI: 258884000	**81,380** 51,942 159,999 T/cm 118.2	Class: NV	**2007-09 Hyundai Samho Heavy Industries Co Ltd — Samho** Yd No: S286 Loa 274.27 (BB) Br ex 48.05 Dght 17.050 Lbp 264.00 Br md 48.00 Dpth 23.10 Welded, 1 dk	**(A13A2TV) Crude Oil Tanker** Double Hull (13F) Liq: 167,531; Liq (Oil): 174,500 Cargo Heating Coils Compartments: 12 Wing Ta, 2 Wing Slop Ta, ER 3 Cargo Pump (s): 3x4000m³/hr Manifold: Bow/CM: 138.5m	**1 oil engine** driving 1 FP propeller Total Power: 18,623kW (25,320hp) 15.7kn MAN-B&W 6S70MC-C 1 x 2 Stroke 6 Cy. 700 x 2800 18623kW (25320bhp) Hyundai Heavy Industries Co Ltd-South Korea AuxGen: 3 x 730kW a.c Fuel: 150.0 (d.f.) 4364.0 (r.f.)
9232931 *LAGV7* -	**SKS SINNI** **SKS OBO & Tankers AS** SKS Tankers Holding AS SatCom: Inmarsat C 425983310 *Bergen* *Norway (NIS)* MMSI: 259833000	**81,270** 52,045 159,385 T/cm 118.3	Class: NV	**2003-02 Hyundai Heavy Industries Co Ltd — Ulsan** Yd No: 1406 Loa 274.20 (BB) Br ex 48.04 Dght 17.071 Lbp 264.00 Br md 48.00 Dpth 23.10 Welded, 1 dk	**(A13A2TV) Crude Oil Tanker** Double Hull (13F) Liq: 167,532; Liq (Oil): 167,532 Cargo Heating Coils Compartments: 12 Wing Ta, 2 Wing Slop Ta, ER 3 Cargo Pump (s): 3x4000m³/hr Manifold: Bow/CM: 137.9m	**1 oil engine** driving 1 FP propeller Total Power: 18,623kW (25,320hp) 15.7kn B&W 6S70MC-C 1 x 2 Stroke 6 Cy. 700 x 2800 18623kW (25320bhp) Hyundai Heavy Industries Co Ltd-South Korea AuxGen: 3 x 730kW a.c Fuel: 190.0 (d.f.) 3900.0 (r.f.)
9301536 *LAIY6* -	**SKS SKEENA** **SKS OBO & Tankers AS** KGJ OBO & Tankers Fleet Management AS SatCom: Inmarsat Mini-M 7645564191 *Bergen* *Norway (NIS)* MMSI: 258722000	**81,380** 51,942 159,385 T/cm 118.2	Class: NV	**2006-08 Hyundai Samho Heavy Industries Co Ltd — Samho** Yd No: S263 Loa 274.27 (BB) Br ex - Dght 17.072 Lbp 264.00 Br md 48.00 Dpth 23.10 Welded, 1 dk	**(A13A2TV) Crude Oil Tanker** Double Hull (13F) Liq: 167,531; Liq (Oil): 167,531 Cargo Heating Coils Compartments: 12 Wing Ta, 2 Wing Slop Ta, ER 3 Cargo Pump (s): 3x4000m³/hr Manifold: Bow/CM: 138.5m	**1 oil engine** driving 1 FP propeller Total Power: 18,623kW (25,320hp) 15.7kn MAN-B&W 6S70MC-C 1 x 2 Stroke 6 Cy. 700 x 2800 18623kW (25320bhp) Hyundai Heavy Industries Co Ltd-South Korea AuxGen: 3 x 730kW a.c Fuel: 150.0 (d.f.) 4364.0 (r.f.)

Ship	Tonnage	Class	Builder / Dimensions	Type	Machinery
9326720 **SKS SPEY** *LACI7* - **SKS OBO & Tankers AS** SKS Tankers Holding AS SatCom: Inmarsat Mini-M 764683474 *Bergen* *Norway (NIS)* MMSI: 258881000	**81,380** 51,942 159,999 T/cm 116.5	Class: NV	**2007**-11 **Hyundai Samho Heavy Industries Co Ltd — Samho** Yd No: S287 Loa 274.26 (BB) Br ex 48.05 Dght 17.050 Lbp 264.00 Br md 48.00 Dpth 23.10 Welded, 1 dk	**(A13A2TV) Crude Oil Tanker** Double Hull (13F) Liq: 167,531; Liq (Oil): 174,500 Cargo Heating Coils Compartments: 12 Wing Ta, 2 Wing Slop Ta, Wing ER 3 Cargo Pump (s): 3x4000m³/hr Manifold: Bow/CM: 137.9m	**1 oil engine** driving 1 FP propeller Total Power: 18,623kW (25,320hp) 15.7kn MAN-B&W 6S70MC-C 1 x 2 Stroke 6 Cy. 700 x 2800 18623kW (25320bhp) Hyundai Heavy Industries Co Ltd-South Korea AuxGen: 3 x 730kW a.c
9133458 **SKS TAGUS** *LADI5* - **SKS OBO & Tankers AS** KGJ OBO & Tankers Fleet Management AS SatCom: Inmarsat B 325982110 *Bergen* *Norway (NIS)* MMSI: 259821000	**63,515** 30,821 109,933 T/cm 90.0	Class: NV	**1997**-03 **Hyundai Heavy Industries Co Ltd — Ulsan** Yd No: 958 Loa 243.61 (BB) Br ex 42.04 Dght 15.723 Lbp 234.00 Br md 42.00 Dpth 23.20 Welded, 1 dk	**(A22A2BB) Bulk/Oil Carrier (OBO)** Double Hull Grain: 122,043; Liq: 119,602; Liq (Oil): 121,038; Ore: 122,043 Compartments: 7 Ho/Ta, ER 7 Ha: (13.7 x 13.2)6 (15.4 x 18.1)ER 7 Cargo Pump (s): 7x1800m³/hr Manifold: Bow/CM: 120.6m	**1 oil engine** driving 1 FP propeller Total Power: 14,049kW (19,101hp) 15.2kn B&W 5S70MC 1 x 2 Stroke 5 Cy. 700 x 2674 14049kW (19101bhp) Hyundai Heavy Industries Co Ltd-South Korea AuxGen: 2 x 1215kW 220/450V 60Hz a.c, 1 x 910kW 220/450V 60Hz a.c Fuel: 229.0 (d.f.) (Heating Coils) 3529.0 (r.f.) 53.0pd
9116967 **SKS TANA** *LAZI4* - **SKS OBO & Tankers AS** KGJ OBO & Tankers Fleet Management AS SatCom: Inmarsat Mini-M 764683025 *Bergen* *Norway (NIS)* MMSI: 259764000	**63,515** 30,821 109,906 T/cm 90.9	Class: NV	**1996**-06 **Hyundai Heavy Industries Co Ltd — Ulsan** Yd No: 955 Loa 243.80 (BB) Br ex 42.04 Dght 15.723 Lbp 234.00 Br md 42.00 Dpth 23.20 Welded, 1 dk	**(A22A2BB) Bulk/Oil Carrier (OBO)** Double Hull Grain: 122,043; Liq: 119,602; Liq (Oil): 121,038 Compartments: 7 Ho/Ta, ER 7 Ha: (13.7 x 13.2)6 (15.4 x 18.1)ER 7 Cargo Pump (s): 7x1800m³/hr Manifold: Bow/CM: 120.6m	**1 oil engine** driving 1 FP propeller Total Power: 14,049kW (19,101hp) 15.2kn B&W 5S70MC 1 x 2 Stroke 5 Cy. 700 x 2674 14049kW (19101bhp) Hyundai Heavy Industries Co Ltd-South Korea AuxGen: 2 x 1215kW 450V 60Hz a.c, 1 x 910kW 450V 60Hz a.c Fuel: 229.0 (d.f.) (Heating Coils) 3529.0 (r.f.) 53.0pd
9172662 **SKS TANARO** *LAKV5* - **SKS OBO & Tankers AS** KGJ OBO & Tankers Fleet Management AS SatCom: Inmarsat Mini-M 763595890 *Bergen* *Norway (NIS)* MMSI: 257604000 Official number: LAKV	**63,515** 30,821 109,786 T/cm 90.9	Class: NV	**1999**-09 **Hyundai Heavy Industries Co Ltd — Ulsan** Yd No: 1084 Loa 243.80 (BB) Br ex 42.04 Dght 15.723 Lbp 234.00 Br md 42.00 Dpth 23.20 Welded, 1 dk	**(A22A2BB) Bulk/Oil Carrier (OBO)** Double Hull Grain: 122,043; Liq: 119,602; Liq (Oil): 122,500 Compartments: 7 Ho/Ta, ER 7 Ha: (13.7 x 13.2)6 (15.4 x 18.1)ER 7 Cargo Pump (s): 7x1800m³/hr Manifold: Bow/CM: 120.6m	**1 oil engine** driving 1 FP propeller Total Power: 14,049kW (19,101hp) 15.2kn B&W 5S70MC 1 x 2 Stroke 5 Cy. 700 x 2674 14049kW (19101bhp) Hyundai Heavy Industries Co Ltd-South Korea AuxGen: 2 x 1215kW 450V 60Hz a.c, 1 x 910kW 450V 60Hz a.c Fuel: 229.0 (d.f.) (Heating Coils) 3529.0 (r.f.) 53.0pd
9172650 **SKS TIETE** *LAKU5* - **SKS OBO & Tankers AS** KGJ OBO & Tankers Fleet Management AS SatCom: Inmarsat B 325757410 *Bergen* *Norway (NIS)* MMSI: 257578000	**63,515** 30,821 109,773 T/cm 90.9	Class: NV	**1999**-06 **Hyundai Heavy Industries Co Ltd — Ulsan** Yd No: 1083 Loa 243.80 (BB) Br ex 42.04 Dght 15.723 Lbp 234.00 Br md 42.00 Dpth 23.30 Welded, 1 dk	**(A22A2BB) Bulk/Oil Carrier (OBO)** Double Hull Grain: 122,043; Liq: 119,602; Liq (Oil): 121,038 Compartments: 7 Ho/Ta, ER 7 Ha: (13.7 x 13.2)6 (15.4 x 18.1)ER 7 Cargo Pump (s): 7x1800m³/hr Manifold: Bow/CM: 120.6m	**1 oil engine** driving 1 FP propeller Total Power: 14,049kW (19,101hp) 15.2kn B&W 5S70MC 1 x 2 Stroke 5 Cy. 700 x 2674 14049kW (19101bhp) Hyundai Heavy Industries Co Ltd-South Korea AuxGen: 2 x 1215kW 450V 60Hz a.c, 1 x 910kW 450V 60Hz a.c Fuel: 229.0 (d.f.) (Heating Coils) 3529.0 (r.f.) 53.0pd
9161273 **SKS TORRENS** *LAJM5* - **SKS OBO & Tankers AS** KGJ OBO & Tankers Fleet Management AS SatCom: Inmarsat B 325995610 *Bergen* *Norway (NIS)* MMSI: 259956000	**63,515** 30,821 109,846 T/cm 90.9	Class: NV	**1999**-01 **Hyundai Heavy Industries Co Ltd — Ulsan** Yd No: 1081 Loa 243.80 (BB) Br ex 42.04 Dght 15.723 Lbp 234.00 Br md 42.00 Dpth 23.20 Welded, 1 dk	**(A22A2BB) Bulk/Oil Carrier (OBO)** Double Hull Grain: 122,043; Liq: 119,602; Liq (Oil): 121,038; Ore: 122,500 Compartments: 7 Ho/Ta, ER 7 Ha: (13.7 x 13.2)6 (15.4 x 18.1)ER 7 Cargo Pump (s): 7x1800m³/hr Manifold: Bow/CM: 120.6m	**1 oil engine** driving 1 FP propeller Total Power: 14,049kW (19,101hp) 15.2kn B&W 5S70MC 1 x 2 Stroke 5 Cy. 700 x 2674 14049kW (19101bhp) Hyundai Heavy Industries Co Ltd-South Korea AuxGen: 2 x 1215kW 220/450V 60Hz a.c, 1 x 910kW 220/450V 60Hz a.c Fuel: 229.0 (d.f.) (Heating Coils) 3529.0 (r.f.) 53.0pd
9133446 **SKS TRENT** *LACP5* - **SKS OBO & Tankers AS** KGJ OBO & Tankers Fleet Management AS SatCom: Inmarsat B 325980310 *Bergen* *Norway (NIS)* MMSI: 259803000	**63,515** 30,821 109,832 T/cm 90.9	Class: NV	**1997**-01 **Hyundai Heavy Industries Co Ltd — Ulsan** Yd No: 957 Loa 243.80 (BB) Br ex 42.04 Dght 15.723 Lbp 234.00 Br md 42.00 Dpth 23.20 Welded, 1 dk	**(A22A2BB) Bulk/Oil Carrier (OBO)** Double Hull Grain: 122,043; Liq: 119,602; Liq (Oil): 121,038 Compartments: 7 Ho/Ta, ER 7 Ha: (13.7 x 13.2)6 (15.4 x 18.1)ER 7 Cargo Pump (s): 7x1800m³/hr Manifold: Bow/CM: 120.6m	**1 oil engine** driving 1 FP propeller Total Power: 14,049kW (19,101hp) 15.2kn B&W 5S70MC 1 x 2 Stroke 5 Cy. 700 x 2674 14049kW (19101bhp) Hyundai Heavy Industries Co Ltd-South Korea AuxGen: 2 x 1215kW 220/450V 60Hz a.c, 1 x 910kW 220/450V 60Hz a.c Fuel: 220.0 (d.f.) (Heating Coils) 3110.0 (r.f.) 53.0pd
9161285 **SKS TRINITY** *LAJN5* - **SKS OBO & Tankers AS** KGJ OBO & Tankers Fleet Management AS SatCom: Inmarsat B 325995710 *Bergen* *Norway (NIS)* MMSI: 259957000	**63,515** 30,821 109,779 T/cm 90.9	Class: NV	**1999**-01 **Hyundai Heavy Industries Co Ltd — Ulsan** Yd No: 1082 Loa 243.80 (BB) Br ex 42.04 Dght 15.723 Lbp 234.00 Br md 42.00 Dpth 23.20 Welded, 1 dk	**(A22A2BB) Bulk/Oil Carrier (OBO)** Double Hull Grain: 122,043; Liq: 119,602; Liq (Oil): 121,038; Ore: 122,500 Compartments: 7 Ho/Ta, ER 7 Ha: (13.7 x 13.2)6 (15.4 x 18.1)ER 7 Cargo Pump (s): 7x1800m³/hr Manifold: Bow/CM: 120.6m	**1 oil engine** driving 1 FP propeller Total Power: 14,049kW (19,101hp) 15.2kn B&W 5S70MC 1 x 2 Stroke 5 Cy. 700 x 2674 14049kW (19101bhp) Hyundai Heavy Industries Co Ltd-South Korea AuxGen: 2 x 1215kW 220/450V 60Hz a.c, 1 x 910kW 220/450V 60Hz a.c Fuel: 229.0 (d.f.) (Heating Coils) 3529.0 (r.f.) 53.0pd
9133460 **SKS TUGELA** *LACN5* - **SKS OBO & Tankers AS** KGJ OBO & Tankers Fleet Management AS SatCom: Inmarsat B 325980210 *Bergen* *Norway (NIS)* MMSI: 259802000	**63,515** 30,821 109,891 T/cm 90.0	Class: NV	**1997**-04 **Hyundai Heavy Industries Co Ltd — Ulsan** Yd No: 959 Loa 243.61 (BB) Br ex 42.04 Dght 15.723 Lbp 234.00 Br md 42.00 Dpth 23.20 Welded, 1 dk	**(A22A2BB) Bulk/Oil Carrier (OBO)** Double Hull Grain: 122,043; Liq: 119,602; Liq (Oil): 121,038; Ore: 122,043 Compartments: 7 Ho/Ta, ER 7 Ha: (13.7 x 13.2)6 (15.4 x 18.1)ER 7 Cargo Pump (s): 7x1800m³/hr Manifold: Bow/CM: 120.6m	**1 oil engine** driving 1 FP propeller Total Power: 14,049kW (19,101hp) 15.2kn B&W 5S70MC 1 x 2 Stroke 5 Cy. 700 x 2674 14049kW (19101bhp) Hyundai Heavy Industries Co Ltd-South Korea AuxGen: 2 x 1215kW 220/450V 60Hz a.c, 1 x 910kW 220/450V 60Hz a.c Fuel: 229.0 (d.f.) (Heating Coils) 3529.0 (r.f.) 53.0pd
9122928 **SKS TWEED** *LACO5* - **SKS OBO & Tankers AS** KGJ OBO & Tankers Fleet Management AS SatCom: Inmarsat B 325979710 *Bergen* *Norway (NIS)* MMSI: 259797000	**63,515** 30,821 109,832 T/cm 90.9	Class: NV	**1996**-12 **Hyundai Heavy Industries Co Ltd — Ulsan** Yd No: 956 Loa 243.80 (BB) Br ex 42.04 Dght 15.723 Lbp 234.00 Br md 42.00 Dpth 23.20 Welded, 1 dk	**(A22A2BB) Bulk/Oil Carrier (OBO)** Double Hull Grain: 122,043; Liq: 119,602; Liq (Oil): 121,038 Compartments: 7 Ho/Ta, ER 7 Ha: (13.7 x 13.2)6 (15.4 x 18.1)ER 7 Cargo Pump (s): 7x1800m³/hr Manifold: Bow/CM: 120.6m	**1 oil engine** driving 1 FP propeller Total Power: 14,049kW (19,101hp) 15.2kn B&W 5S70MC 1 x 2 Stroke 5 Cy. 700 x 2674 14049kW (19101bhp) Hyundai Heavy Industries Co Ltd-South Korea AuxGen: 2 x 1215kW 220/450V 60Hz a.c, 1 x 910kW 220/450V 60Hz a.c Fuel: 229.0 (d.f.) (Heating Coils) 3529.0 (r.f.) 53.0pd
9116955 **SKS TYNE** *LAZE4* - **SKS OBO & Tankers AS** KGJ OBO & Tankers Fleet Management AS SatCom: Inmarsat C 425976210 *Bergen* *Norway (NIS)* MMSI: 259762000	**63,515** 30,821 109,891 T/cm 90.9	Class: NV	**1996**-05 **Hyundai Heavy Industries Co Ltd — Ulsan** Yd No: 954 Loa 243.80 (BB) Br ex 42.04 Dght 15.723 Lbp 234.00 Br md 42.00 Dpth 23.20 Welded, 1 dk	**(A22A2BB) Bulk/Oil Carrier (OBO)** Double Hull Grain: 122,043; Liq: 119,602; Liq (Oil): 121,038 Compartments: 7 Ho/Ta, ER 7 Ha: (13.7 x 13.2)6 (15.4 x 18.1)ER 7 Cargo Pump (s): 7x1800m³/hr Manifold: Bow/CM: 120.6m	**1 oil engine** driving 1 FP propeller Total Power: 14,049kW (19,101hp) 15.2kn B&W 5S70MC 1 x 2 Stroke 5 Cy. 700 x 2674 14049kW (19101bhp) Hyundai Heavy Industries Co Ltd-South Korea AuxGen: 2 x 1215kW 220/450V 60Hz a.c, 1 x 910kW 220/450V 60Hz a.c Fuel: 229.0 (d.f.) (Heating Coils) 3529.0 (r.f.) 53.0pd
9361287 **SKUA** *CB9135* - **Transbordadora Austral Broom SA** - *Valparaiso* *Chile* MMSI: 725003680 Official number: 3152	**167** - -		**2006**-06 **Ast. Naval Federico Contessi y Cia. S.A. — Mar del Plata** Yd No: 101 Loa 30.80 Br ex - Dght 3.500 Lbp - Br md 6.05 Dpth - Welded, 1 dk	**(B34N2QP) Pilot Vessel**	**2 oil engines** geared to sc shafts driving 2 FP propellers Total Power: 2,060kW (2,800hp) Caterpillar C32 2 x Vee 4 Stroke 12 Cy. 145 x 162 each-1030kW (1400bhp) Caterpillar Inc-USA
9237199 **SKUA** *V7MP6* *ex Fortune Glory -2007* - **Skua Shipping LLC** Navig8 Bulk Asia Pte Ltd *Majuro* *Marshall Islands* MMSI: 538002885 Official number: 2885	**29,862** 18,434 53,350	Class: AB (KR)	**2003**-05 **Toyohashi Shipbuilding Co Ltd — Toyohashi AI** Yd No: 3548 Loa 189.99 (BB) Br ex - Dght 12.166 Lbp 182.00 Br md 32.26 Dpth 17.00 Welded, 1 dk	**(A21A2BC) Bulk Carrier** Double Bottom Entire Compartment Length Grain: 68,259; Bale: 65,617 Compartments: 5 Ho, ER 5 Ha: 4 (20.8 x 17.6)ER (16.8 x 17.6) Cranes: 4x30.5t	**1 oil engine** driving 1 FP propeller Total Power: 8,580kW (11,665hp) 14.3kn MAN-B&W 6S50MC 1 x 2 Stroke 6 Cy. 500 x 1910 8580kW (11665bhp) Mitsui Engineering & Shipbuilding CLtd-Japan AuxGen: 3 x 400kW 450V a.c
9440681 **SKUA** *PPXV* - **Magallanes Navegacao Brasileira SA** Wilson Sons Offshore SA SatCom: Inmarsat C 471011143 *Rio de Janeiro* *Brazil* MMSI: 710002370 Official number: 3813872122	**2,429** 728 3,100	Class: LR ✠**100A1** SS 07/2009 offshore supply ship LI **LMC** **UMS** Eq.Ltr: T; Cable: 495.0/42.0 U3 (a)	**2009**-07 **Wilson, Sons SA — Guaruja** (Hull) Yd No: 105 **2009**-07 **B.V. Scheepswerf Damen — Gorinchem** Yd No: 552014 Loa 71.50 (BB) Br ex 16.04 Dght 6.200 Lbp 64.80 Br md 16.00 Dpth 7.50 Welded, 1 dk	**(B21A2OS) Platform Supply Ship**	**4 diesel electric oil engines** driving 4 gen. each 1100kW 690V a.c Connecting to 2 elec. motors each (1500kW) driving 2 Directional propellers Total Power: 4,960kW (6,744hp) 11.8kn Caterpillar 3512B-TA 4 x Vee 4 Stroke 12 Cy. 170 x 190 each-1240kW (1686bhp) Caterpillar Inc-USA Thrusters: 2 Thwart. FP thruster (f)

9381055 *CA2449* -	**SKUA I** *ex* Chanul *-2008* **Sudamericana Agencias Aereas y Maritimas SA (SAAM)** - *Valparaiso* *Chile* MMSI: 725000657 Official number: 3215	**267** 80 -	Class: LR ✠**100A1** SS 11/2011 tug ✠**LMC** Eq.Ltr: F; Cable: 275.0/19.0 U2 (a)	**2006**-11 **Guangdong Hope Yue Shipbuilding Industry Ltd — Guangzhou GD** Yd No: 2144 Loa 26.00 Br ex 9.85 Dght 3.500 Lbp 25.35 Br md 9.80 Dpth 4.50 Welded, 1 dk	**(B32A2ST) Tug**	**2 oil engines** gearing integral to driving 2 Z propellers Total Power: 3,132kW (4,258hp) 12.0kn Caterpillar 3516B 2 x Vee 4 Stroke 16 Cy. 170 x 190 each-1566kW (2129bhp) Caterpillar Inc-USA AuxGen: 2 x 99kW 440V 60Hz a.c
7617022 *LEDH* -	**SKUDE** *ex* Berlevagfisk II *-2003* *ex* Polarhav *-1998* *ex* Valanes *-1997* *ex* Storskjaer *-1991* *ex* Kibergvaeringen *-1986* *ex* Mehamnfjord *-1985* *ex* Furnes *-1980* **P/R Najaden ANS** Jostein Knutsvik *Skudeneshavn* *Norway* MMSI: 258358000	*291* 87 -		**1976**-12 **Th Hellesoy Skipsbyggeri AS — Lofallstrand** Yd No: 95 Loa 30.41 Br ex - Dght - Lbp 27.03 Br md 7.62 Dpth 6.33 Welded, 1 dk	**(B11A2FT) Trawler**	**1 oil engine** driving 1 CP propeller Total Power: 736kW (1,001hp) Wichmann 5AXA 1 x 2 Stroke 5 Cy. 300 x 450 736kW (1001bhp) Wichmann Motorfabrikk AS-Norway
6826212 *LCGU* R-4-K	**SKUDE SENIOR** *ex* Pernille From *-2008* *ex* Stromboli II *-2005* *ex* Stromboli *-2004* *ex* Bente Loth *-1979* *ex* Stromboli *-1975* *ex* Fano *-1972* *launched as* Stella Polaris *-1968* **P/R Najaden ANS** - *Skudeneshavn* *Norway*	**405** 121 -	Class: (BV) (NV)	**1968 Bolsones Verft AS — Molde** Yd No: 219 Loa 40.31 Br ex 7.65 Dght 3.690 Lbp 35.34 Br md 7.62 Dpth 6.20 Welded, 1 dk	**(B11A2FT) Trawler** Compartments: 2 Ho, ER 3 Ha: (0.9 x 1.2)2 (1.5 x 1.2)ER Ice Capable	**1 oil engine** driving 1 CP propeller Total Power: 736kW (1,001hp) 11.0kn Wichmann 4AXA 1 x 2 Stroke 4 Cy. 300 x 450 736kW (1001bhp) (new engine 1976) Wichmann Motorfabrikk AS-Norway Fuel: 64.0 (d.f.)
7023556 - -	**SKUGVUR** *ex* Cutter III *-1974* - -	**386** 212 236	Class: (NV)	**1970 VEB Rosslauer Schiffswerft — Rosslau** Yd No: 3288 Loa 37.70 Br ex 8.21 Dght 3.468 Lbp 33.00 Br md 8.18 Dpth 5.49 Welded, 1 dk	**(B11A2FS) Stern Trawler** Ins: 332 Compartments: 1 Ho, ER 1 Ha: ER	**1 oil engine** reduction geared to sc. shaft driving 1 FP propeller Total Power: 883kW (1,201hp) 9.5kn Wichmann 4AXA 1 x 2 Stroke 4 Cy. 300 x 450 883kW (1201bhp) (new engine 1978) Wichmann Motorfabrikk AS-Norway AuxGen: 1 x 112kW 380V 50Hz a.c, 1 x 96kW 380V 50Hz a.c Fuel: 162.5 (d.f.)
8812021 *XPWP* TG 7	**SKUGVUR** *ex* Vagfelli *-2012* *ex* Nesborg I *-2009* *ex* Brodd *-2004* *ex* Haukafell *-1995* **P/F Faroe Origin** - *Vagur* *Faeroe Islands (Danish)* MMSI: 231321000	**364** 109 -	Class: NV	**1990**-07 **Estaleiros Navais S.A. (CARNAVE) — Aveiro** Yd No: 133 Lengthened-1995 Loa 33.96 (BB) Br ex - Dght 3.800 Lbp 29.68 Br md 7.90 Dpth 6.20 Welded, 2 dks	**(B11A2FS) Stern Trawler** Ice Capable	**1 oil engine** driving 1 CP propeller Total Power: 729kW (991hp) 9.0kn Kromhout 6FEHD240 1 x 4 Stroke 6 Cy. 240 x 260 729kW (991bhp) Stork Wartsila Diesel BV-Netherlands AuxGen: 1 x 224kW 380V 50Hz a.c, 1 x 160kW 380V 50Hz a.c
9379090 *JWLH* T-111-T	**SKULBAREN** - **Skulbaren Rederi AS** - *Tromso* *Norway* MMSI: 259225000	**498** 178 1		**2007**-03 **AS Rigas Kugu Buvetava (Riga Shipyard) — Riga** (Hull) Yd No: 012 **2007**-03 **Vaagland Baatbyggeri AS — Vaagland** Yd No: 138 Lengthened-2011 Loa 37.90 Br ex - Dght 4.660 Lbp 34.30 Br md 9.00 Dpth 4.86 Welded, 1 dk	**(B11B2FV) Fishing Vessel**	**1 oil engine** reductuion geared to sc. shaft. driving 1 Propeller Total Power: 1,210kW (1,645hp) Mitsubishi S12R-MPTK 1 x Vee 4 Stroke 12 Cy. 170 x 180 1210kW (1645bhp) Mitsubishi Heavy Industries Ltd-Japan Thrusters: 1 Tunnel thruster (f); 1 Tunnel thruster (a)
9114359 *OZ2143* -	**SKULD** - **P/F Svitzer Faroe Islands** Svitzer Sverige AB *Torshavn* *Faeroes (FAS)*	**485** 145 311	Class: LR ✠**100A1** SS 01/2011 tug Ice Class 1B at a maximum draught 5.025m amidship Max/min draughts fwd 4.850/3.370m Max/min draughts aft 5.275/3.955m Power required 1000kw, power installed 2940kw ✠**LMC** **UMS** Eq.Ltr: H; Cable: 302.5/22.0 U2	**1996**-01 **Svendborg Vaerft A/S — Svendborg** Yd No: 206 Loa 33.80 Br ex 10.75 Dght 5.250 Lbp 28.80 Br md 10.20 Dpth 5.50 Welded, 1 dk	**(B32A2ST) Tug** Ice Capable	**2 oil engines** with clutches, flexible couplings & reduction geared to sc. shafts driving 2 Directional propellers Total Power: 2,940kW (3,998hp) 10.5kn Alpha 6L28/32A 2 x 4 Stroke 6 Cy. 280 x 320 each-1470kW (1999bhp) MAN B&W Diesel A/S-Denmark AuxGen: 2 x 240kW 380V 50Hz a.c, 1 x 108kW 380V 50Hz a.c Thrusters: 1 Thwart. CP thruster (f) Fuel: 243.0 (d.f.) 4.5pd
7368695 *LFXK* SF-30-S	**SKULEBAS** *ex* Royrbuen *-2004* *ex* Sandvaer Senior *-1979* *ex* Kallur *-1977* **Opplaeringsfartoy AS** - *Maaloy* *Norway* MMSI: 259131000 Official number: 19036	**386** 115 152	Class: NV	**1974**-06 **Frostad Verft AS — Tomrefjord** Yd No: 37 Loa 34.35 (BB) Br ex 7.52 Dght 3.800 Lbp 28.00 Br md 7.51 Dpth 6.08 Welded, 2 dks	**(B11B2FV) Fishing Vessel** Compartments: 1 Ho, ER 2 Ha: 2 (1.9 x 1.6)ER Derricks: 1x1.5t; Winches: 1 Ice Capable	**1 oil engine** driving 1 CP propeller Total Power: 507kW (689hp) Callesen 6-427-FOT 1 x 4 Stroke 6 Cy. 270 x 400 507kW (689bhp) Aabenraa Motorfabrik, HeinrichCallesen A/S-Denmark AuxGen: 2 x 68kW 380V 50Hz a.c
8402204 *V3MI4* -	**SKULPTOR TOMSKIY** *ex* Skulptors Tomskis *-2008* *ex* Skulptor Tomskiy *-1991* **Skulptor Tomskiy Shipping Co Ltd** Fairwind Shipmanagement Ltd *Belize City* *Belize* MMSI: 312906000 Official number: 370830039	**9,552** 3,201 7,673	Class: RS (NV)	**1986**-02 **Aalborg Vaerft A/S — Aalborg** Yd No: 248 Loa 138.20 (BB) Br ex 23.02 Dght 8.200 Lbp 126.32 Br md 21.51 Dpth 13.10 Welded, 3 dks, 4th dk in Nos. 2 & 3 holds	**(A34A2GR) Refrigerated Cargo Ship** Side doors (p) Side doors (s) Ins: 10,723 TEU 142 C Ho 84 TEU C Dk 58 TEU incl 20 ref C Compartments: ER, 4 Ho, 9 Tw Dk 4 Ha: 3 (12.5 x 10.5)ER (8.4 x 10.5) Cranes: 4x8t Ice Capable	**1 oil engine** driving 1 FP propeller Total Power: 9,598kW (13,049hp) 20.3kn B&W 6DKRN67/170 1 x 2 Stroke 6 Cy. 670 x 1700 9598kW (13049bhp) Bryanskiy Mashinostroitelnyy Zavod (BMZ)-Bryansk AuxGen: 4 x 720kW 380V 50Hz a.c Thrusters: 1 Thwart. CP thruster (f) Fuel: 163.0 (d.f.) 1420.0 (r.f.)
7434755 *UAET* -	**SKUMUR** *ex* Ingimundur *-2006* *ex* Heidrun *-2001* **Lodfish Co Ltd** - *Murmansk* *Russia*	**472** 141 230	Class: (BV)	**1978**-01 **Bernhardsson Skipasmidastod h/f — Isafjordur** Yd No: 50 Loa 40.98 Br ex - Dght 4.350 Lbp 36.33 Br md 8.61 Dpth 5.37 Welded, 2 dks	**(B11A2FS) Stern Trawler** Ice Capable	**1 oil engine** geared to sc. shaft driving 1 CP propeller Total Power: 1,370kW (1,863hp) 12.0kn Alpha 12V23LU 1 x Vee 4 Stroke 12 Cy. 225 x 300 1370kW (1863bhp) Alpha Diesel A/S-Denmark Fuel: 77.5 (d.f.)
8842533 *UHYG* -	**SKUTUM** *ex* Algaza *-2009* **Rusryba Co Ltd** - *Murmansk* *Russia* MMSI: 273449510	**2,342** 702 901	Class: RS	**1991**-03 **Sudostroitelnyy Zavod "Baltiya" — Klaypeda** Yd No: 808 Converted From: Fishing Vessel-1992 Loa 85.06 Br ex 13.04 Dght 4.040 Lbp 76.95 Br md - Dpth 6.50 Welded, 1 dk	**(A34A2GR) Refrigerated Cargo Ship** Ins: 1,245 Compartments: 2 Ho, ER 2 Ha: 2 (3.4 x 2.2)ER Cranes: 1x3t	**1 oil engine** driving 1 FP propeller Total Power: 852kW (1,158hp) 11.3kn S.K.L. 8NVD48A-2U 1 x 4 Stroke 8 Cy. 320 x 480 852kW (1158bhp) SKL Motoren u. Systemtechnik AG-Magdeburg AuxGen: 2 x 534kW a.c, 1 x 220kW a.c Fuel: 229.0 (d.f.)
7214583 *LGFU* -	**SKUTVIK** *ex* Lodingen *-2012* **Torghatten Nord AS** - *Narvik* *Norway* MMSI: 257262500	**1,476** 644 344	Class: (NV)	**1972**-07 **Kaarbos Mek. Verksted AS — Harstad** Yd No: 73 Loa 61.27 Br ex 11.18 Dght 3.250 Lbp 55.50 Br md 11.16 Dpth 4.37 Welded, 2 dks	**(A36A2PR) Passenger/Ro-Ro Ship (Vehicles)** Passengers: 350 Lane-Len: 57 Lane-Wid: 2.50 Lane-clr ht: 4.50 Cars: 43, Trailers: 5 Ice Capable	**2 oil engines** driving 2 FP propellers Total Power: 1,618kW (2,200hp) 13.0kn Normo LDMC-8 2 x 4 Stroke 8 Cy. 250 x 300 each-809kW (1100bhp) AS Bergens Mek Verksteder-Norway AuxGen: 2 x 96kW 220V 50Hz a.c Thrusters: 1 Thwart. FP thruster (f) Fuel: 34.0 (d.f.) 5.5pd
5262756 *HQAF5* -	**SKY** *ex* Stilianos *-1985* *ex* Olna Firth *-1975* **Theodor S Koulokas** - *Honduras*	*499* 295 787	Class: (LR) ✠ Classed LR until 13/3/87	**1957**-02 **Bodewes' Scheepswerven N.V. — Hoogezand** Yd No: 426 Loa 53.80 Br ex 8.77 Dght 3.671 Lbp 49.99 Br md 8.70 Dpth 3.74 Riveted\Welded, 1 dk	**(A31A2GX) General Cargo Ship** Grain: 1,106; Bale: 1,034 Compartments: 2 Ho, ER 2 Ha: (11.5 x 5.1) (12.1 x 5.1)ER Derricks: 2x2t; Winches: 2	**1 oil engine** driving 1 FP propeller Total Power: 368kW (500hp) 10.8kn Werkspoor 1 x 4 Stroke 8 Cy. 270 x 500 368kW (500bhp) NV Werkspoor-Netherlands AuxGen: 1 x 10kW 110V d.c Fuel: 45.5 (d.f.)

Number / Call sign	Name / Owner	Tonnage	Class	Builder / Dimensions	Type	Machinery
1010806 *ZGAJ5* -	**SKY** **Emberg Enterprise Ltd** Catalano Shipping Services SAM *George Town* *Cayman Islands (British)* MMSI: 319253000 Official number: 742414	**668** 200 -	Class: LR ✠ **100A1** SS 04/2010 SSC Yacht, mono, G6 **LMC** **UMS** Cable: 200.0/19.0 U2 (a)	**2010-04 Heesen Shipyards B.V. — Oss** Yd No: 14750 Loa 49.92 (BB) Br ex 9.60 Dght 4.750 Lbp 42.22 Br md 9.10 Dpth 4.75 Welded, 1 dk	**(X11A2YP) Yacht**	**2 oil engines** with clutches, flexible couplings & sr geared to sc. shafts driving 2 FP propellers Total Power: 2,320kW (3,154hp) 15.0kn M.T.U. 8V4000M70 2 x Vee 4 Stroke 8 Cy. 165 x 190 each-1160kW (1577bhp) MTU Friedrichshafen GmbH-Friedrichshafen AuxGen: 2 x 150kW 400V 50Hz a.c Thrusters: 1 Tunnel thruster (f) Fuel: 69.0
7950280 - -	**SKY** *ex* Mountain *-2010* *ex* Sasna *-2010* *ex* Cosmos No. 1 *-2009* *ex* Murmansk *-2009* *ex* Bezdna *-2007* *ex* Kolvi *-2004* *ex* Bezdna *-2004* *ex* Lobo *-1992* *ex* Sea Shell *-1991* *ex* Eiryo Maru No. 88 *-1990* *ex* Tokuju Maru No. 27 *-1986* **Inwoo Shipping Co Ltd** -	**472** 169 271	Class: (RS) (KR)	**1972-03 Kochi Jyuko K.K. — Kochi** Yd No: 1172 Loa 50.83 Br ex - Dght 3.440 Lbp 43.81 Br md 8.30 Dpth 3.60 Welded, 1 dk	**(A34A2GR) Refrigerated Cargo Ship** Ins: 360	**1 oil engine** driving 1 FP propeller Total Power: 1,067kW (1,451hp) 12.0kn Akasaka AH30 1 x 4 Stroke 6 Cy. 300 x 480 1067kW (1451bhp) Akasaka Tekkosho KK (Akasaka DieselLtd)-Japan AuxGen: 2 x 160kW 220V a.c Fuel: 188.0 (d.f.)
9380350 *9HBD9* -	**SKY** *ex* Cotton *-2013* **Sky Shipping LLC** Norient Product Pool ApS SatCom: Inmarsat C 425671210 *Valletta* *Malta* MMSI: 256712000 Official number: 9380350	**23,248** 9,915 37,879 T/cm 45.2	Class: NV (AB)	**2007-12 Hyundai Mipo Dockyard Co Ltd — Ulsan** Yd No: 2029 Loa 184.32 (BB) Br ex 27.45 Dght 11.515 Lbp 176.00 Br md 27.40 Dpth 17.20 Welded, 1 dk	**(A12B2TR) Chemical/Products Tanker** Double Hull (13F) Liq: 40,781; Liq (Oil): 39,985 Compartments: 12 Wing Ta, 2 Wing Slop Ta, ER 12 Cargo Pump (s): 10x500m³/hr, 2x300m³/hr Manifold: Bow/CM: 92.6m Ice Capable	**1 oil engine** driving 1 FP propeller Total Power: 9,480kW (12,889hp) 15.0kn MAN-B&W 6S50MC-C 1 x 2 Stroke 6 Cy. 500 x 2000 9480kW (12889bhp) Hyundai Heavy Industries Co Ltd-South Korea AuxGen: 3 x 900kW a.c Thrusters: 1 Tunnel thruster (f) Fuel: 172.6 (d.f.) 1116.3 (r.f.)
8609022 - -	**SKY 1** *ex* Twins *-2007* *ex* Hinode Maru No. 38 *-2004* - -	**496** 205 345	Class: (RS)	**1986-06 Niigata Engineering Co Ltd — Niigata NI** Yd No: 1887 Loa 49.48 (BB) Br ex - Dght 3.202 Lbp 43.77 Br md 8.31 Dpth 3.56 Welded, 1 dk	**(B11B2FV) Fishing Vessel** Ins: 441	**1 oil engine** with clutches, flexible couplings & sr reverse geared to sc. shaft driving 1 FP propeller Total Power: 699kW (950hp) Niigata 6M28AFTE 1 x 4 Stroke 6 Cy. 280 x 480 699kW (950bhp) Niigata Engineering Co Ltd-Japan
8966327 *BP3030* -	**SKY 111** *ex* Kee 1283 *-2009* **Smit Kueen Yang Harbour Services Co Ltd** - *Keelung* *Chinese Taipei* Official number: 13349	**331** 99 93	Class: CR	**1997-05 Jong Shyn Shipbuilding Co., Ltd. — Kaohsiung** Loa 34.30 Br ex 9.72 Dght 3.000 Lbp 33.00 Br md 9.60 Dpth 4.30 Welded, 1 dk	**(B32A2ST) Tug**	**2 oil engines** reduction geared to sc. shafts driving 2 FP propellers Total Power: 2,060kW (2,800hp) 11.0kn Niigata 6L22HX 2 x 4 Stroke 6 Cy. 220 x 280 each-1030kW (1400bhp) Niigata Engineering Co Ltd-Japan AuxGen: 2 x 105kW 440V a.c
8835839 - -	**SKY 211** *ex* Kee 1164 *-2009* **Smit Kueen Yang Harbour Services Co Ltd** - *Keelung* *Chinese Taipei*	*228* 68 -	Class: (CR)	**1987 Keelung Harbour Ship & Machinery Repair Works — Keelung** Loa 27.20 Br ex 9.02 Dght 3.300 Lbp 23.30 Br md 9.00 Dpth 4.50 Welded, 1 dk	**(B32A2ST) Tug**	**1 oil engine** driving 1 FP propeller Total Power: 1,250kW (1,700hp) 9.0kn Wartsila 6R22 1 x 4 Stroke 6 Cy. 220 x 240 1250kW (1700bhp) Taiwan Machinery ManufacturingCorp.-Kaohsiung AuxGen: 2 x 48kW 220V a.c
8835889 - -	**SKY 311** *ex* Kee 1320 *-2009* **Smit Kueen Yang Harbour Services Co Ltd** - *Keelung* *Chinese Taipei*	*340* 102 -	Class: (CR)	**1989-10 Keelung Harbour Ship & Machinery Repair Works — Keelung** Loa 34.60 Br ex - Dght 3.150 Lbp 33.00 Br md 9.60 Dpth 4.30 Welded, 1 dk	**(B32A2ST) Tug**	**2 oil engines** driving 2 FP propellers Total Power: 2,428kW (3,302hp) Kromhout 8FHD240 2 x 4 Stroke 8 Cy. 240 x 260 each-1214kW (1651bhp) Stork Werkspoor Diesel BV-Netherlands AuxGen: 2 x 90kW 225V a.c
9387853 *BP3260* -	**SKY 312** *ex* Kst Super *-2011* **Smit Kueen Yang Harbour Services Co Ltd** - *Chinese Taipei* MMSI: 416004327	**246** 73 90	Class: CR (Class contemplated) (LR) ✠ Classed LR until 15/12/11	**2008-01 Keppel Batangas Shipyard Inc — Bauan** Yd No: H84 Loa 27.90 Br ex 9.58 Dght 3.800 Lbp 23.34 Br md 9.00 Dpth 4.70 Welded, 1 dk	**(B32A2ST) Tug**	**2 oil engines** gearing integral to driving 2 Z propellers Total Power: 2,646kW (3,598hp) 12.0kn Niigata 6L25HX 2 x 4 Stroke 6 Cy. 250 x 350 each-1323kW (1799bhp) Niigata Engineering Co Ltd-Japan AuxGen: 2 x 95kW 380V 50Hz a.c Fuel: 100.0 (r.f.)
9120188 *BP3240* -	**SKY 401** *ex* Union 9 *-2009* **Smit Kueen Yang Harbour Services Co Ltd** - *Chinese Taipei* MMSI: 416433000	**398** 119 256	Class: CR (LR) ✠ Classed LR until 12/2/09	**1997-04 Astilleros Armon SA — Navia** Yd No: 372 Loa 30.60 Br ex 11.04 Dght 3.337 Lbp 28.50 Br md 11.00 Dpth 4.50 Welded, 1 dk	**(B32A2ST) Tug**	**2 oil engines** gearing integral to driving 2 Voith-Schneider propellers Total Power: 3,000kW (4,078hp) 12.5kn Deutz SBV8M628 2 x 4 Stroke 8 Cy. 240 x 280 each-1500kW (2039bhp) Motoren Werke Mannheim AG (MWM)-Mannheim AuxGen: 2 x 144kW 380V 50Hz a.c, 1 x 72kW 380V 50Hz a.c Fuel: 162.0 (d.f.) 13.0pd
9174593 *BP3242* -	**SKY 501** *ex* Smit Trafalgar *-2009* *ex* Trafalgar *-2007* **Smit Kueen Yang Harbour Services Co Ltd** - *Keelung* *Chinese Taipei* MMSI: 416003893	**369** 110 320	Class: CR (Class contemplated) (LR) ✠ Classed LR until 26/8/09	**1998-05 McTay Marine — Bromborough** Yd No: 119 Loa 29.31 Br ex 11.88 Dght 3.400 Lbp 28.50 Br md 11.00 Dpth 4.30 Welded, 1 dk	**(B32A2ST) Tug**	**2 oil engines** gearing integral to driving 2 Voith-Schneider propellers Total Power: 4,064kW (5,526hp) 12.8kn Ruston 6RK270M 2 x 4 Stroke 6 Cy. 270 x 305 each-2032kW (2763bhp) Ruston Paxman Diesels Ltd.-United Kingdom AuxGen: 2 x 70kW 415V 50Hz a.c
9146247 *DSPQ9* -	**SKY ACE 1** *ex* Sky Ace *-2008* **Shinhan Capital Co Ltd** Shintoku Marine Co Ltd *Jeju* *South Korea* MMSI: 441424000 Official number: JJR-072070	**5,342** 2,635 8,765 T/cm 17.6	Class: KR (NK)	**1997-02 Usuki Shipyard Co Ltd — Usuki OT** Yd No: 1645 Loa 112.00 (BB) Br ex - Dght 7.514 Lbp 105.00 Br md 19.00 Dpth 10.00 Welded, 1 dk	**(A12B2TR) Chemical/Products Tanker** Double Hull (13F) Liq: 9,426; Liq (Oil): 9,426 Compartments: 10 Wing Ta, ER 12 Cargo Pump (s): 10x330m³/hr, 2x100m³/hr Manifold: Bow/CM: 57m	**1 oil engine** driving 1 FP propeller Total Power: 3,604kW (4,900hp) 14.9kn Mitsubishi 7UEC37LA 1 x 2 Stroke 7 Cy. 370 x 880 3604kW (4900bhp) Akasaka Tekkosho KK (Akasaka DieselLtd)-Japan AuxGen: 3 x 450kW 450V 60Hz a.c Thrusters: 1 Tunnel thruster (f) Fuel: 71.6 (d.f.) (Heating Coils) 591.0 (r.f.) 16.5pd
9062192 *DSQN8* -	**SKY ACE 3** *ex* Kikuei Maru *-2009* **KYS Co Ltd** Keo Young Shipping Co Ltd *Jeju* *South Korea* MMSI: 441638000 Official number: JJR-094262	**741** 325 1,145	Class: KR	**1992-09 Hakata Zosen K.K. — Imabari** Yd No: 501 Loa 64.30 Br ex - Dght 3.948 Lbp 60.90 Br md 10.00 Dpth 4.50 Welded, 1 dk	**(A12A2TC) Chemical Tanker** Double Hull (13F) Liq: 1,230 Compartments: 8 Ta, ER 1 Cargo Pump (s): 1x300m³/hr	**1 oil engine** driving 1 FP propeller Total Power: 736kW (1,001hp) 11.5kn Hanshin LH28G 1 x 4 Stroke 6 Cy. 280 x 460 736kW (1001bhp) The Hanshin Diesel Works Ltd-Japan AuxGen: 3 x 95kW 225V 60Hz a.c
9550175 *DSQN2* -	**SKY AURORA** **CK Line Co Ltd** - *Jeju* *South Korea* MMSI: 441632000 Official number: JJR-094188	**5,500** 2,101 6,420	Class: KR	**2009-09 Nanjing Wujiazui Shipbuilding Co Ltd — Nanjing JS** Yd No: WJZ027 Loa 101.50 Br ex - Dght 7.213 Lbp 93.50 Br md 17.60 Dpth 11.10 Welded, 1 dk	**(A31A2GX) General Cargo Ship** Compartments: 2 Ho, ER 2 Ha: (25.2 x 12.4)ER (19.6 x 12.4) Cranes: 2x30.7t; Derricks: 1x25t	**1 oil engine** driving 1 Propeller Total Power: 2,648kW (3,600hp) 12.5kn Hanshin LH41LA 1 x 4 Stroke 6 Cy. 410 x 800 2648kW (3600bhp) The Hanshin Diesel Works Ltd-Japan
9196462 *DSRI6* -	**SKY BEAUTY** *ex* Asian Fortune *-2012* **CK Line Co Ltd** - *Jeju* *South Korea* MMSI: 441874000 Official number: JJR-121048	**4,346** 1,846 5,820	Class: KR (NK)	**1998-08 Imamura Zosen — Kure** Yd No: 402 Loa 91.68 Br ex - Dght 7.114 Lbp 84.40 Br md 17.20 Dpth 11.00 Welded, 1 dk	**(A31A2GX) General Cargo Ship** Grain: 8,883; Bale: 8,643 Compartments: 2 Ho, ER 2 Ha: (18.9 x 12.1) (24.5 x 12.1)ER Cranes: 2x30t	**1 oil engine** driving 1 FP propeller Total Power: 2,648kW (3,600hp) 12.2kn Hanshin LH41LA 1 x 4 Stroke 6 Cy. 410 x 800 2648kW (3600bhp) The Hanshin Diesel Works Ltd-Japan Fuel: 490.0
8979075 *HC4379* -	**SKY DANCER** - **Ecoventura SA** - *Guayaquil* *Ecuador* Official number: TN-00-0422	*205* 67 -		**2001 Astilleros Navales Ecuatorianos (ASTINAVE) — Guayaquil** Loa 30.80 Br ex - Dght - Lbp - Br md 7.30 Dpth - Welded, 1 dk	**(A37A2PC) Passenger/Cruise** Passengers: cabins: 8; berths: 16	**1 oil engine** driving 1 Propeller 12.0kn

9505948 *3FAJ6* -	**SKY DREAM** **Shintoku Panama SA** Shintoku Marine Co Ltd *Panama* *Panama* MMSI: 357227000 Official number: 4130410	**11,752** 6,373 19,807 T/cm 29.9	Class: NK	**2010-02 Fukuoka Shipbuilding Co Ltd — Fukuoka FO** Yd No: 1282 Loa 146.03 (BB) Br ex 24.23 Dght 9.622 Lbp 136.00 Br md 24.23 Dpth 12.80 Welded, 1 dk	**(A12B2TR) Chemical/Products Tanker** Double Hull (13F) Liq: 20,477; Liq (Oil): 20,477 Cargo Heating Coils Compartments: 16 Wing Ta, 2 Wing Slop Ta, Wing ER 16 Cargo Pump (s): 6x200m^3/hr, 10x300m^3/hr Manifold: Bow/CM: 73.1m	**1 oil engine** driving 1 FP propeller Total Power: 6,150kW (8,362hp) 14.5kn MAN-B&W 6S42MC 1 x 2 Stroke 6 Cy. 420 x 1764 6150kW (8362bhp) Hitachi Zosen Corp-Japan AuxGen: 3 x 450kW a.c Fuel: 125.0 (d.f.) 1213.0 (r.f.)
9154751 *DSNV4* -	**SKY DUKE** - **CK Line Co Ltd** - *Jeju* *South Korea* MMSI: 440337000 Official number: JJR-041357	**3,992** 2,008 5,962	Class: KR	**1996-09 Dae Sun Shipbuilding & Engineering Co Ltd — Busan** Yd No: 426 Loa 107.00 (BB) Br ex 17.41 Dght 6.530 Lbp 97.50 Br md 17.20 Dpth 8.30 Welded, 1 dk	**(A33A2CC) Container Ship (Fully Cellular)** TEU 342 C Ho 132 TEU C Dk 210 TEU incl 25 ref C. Compartments: 5 Cell Ho, ER 5 Ha: ER	**1 oil engine** driving 1 FP propeller Total Power: 3,913kW (5,320hp) 14.8kn B&W 7L35MC 1 x 2 Stroke 7 Cy. 350 x 1050 3913kW (5320bhp) Ssangyong Heavy Industries Co Ltd-South Korea AuxGen: 2 x 280kW 445V 60Hz a.c
8035697 *JVXX3* -	**SKY EAGLE T-1** *ex* Choyo Maru No. 27 *-2008* *ex* Hayabusa *-1985* **Hong Kong Marine Construction Ltd** - *Ulaanbaatar* *Mongolia* MMSI: 457185000 Official number: 24430881	*143* 43 -		**1981-01 Shitanoe Shipbuilding Co Ltd — Usuki OT** Yd No: 1018 Loa 33.75 Br ex - Dght - Lbp - Br md 8.60 Dpth 3.41 Welded, 1 dk	**(B32A2ST) Tug**	**2 oil engines** Geared Integral to driving 2 Z propellers Total Power: 1,912kW (2,600hp)
9119048 *DSQX9* -	**SKY EVER** *ex* Sky Angela *-2010* *ex* Senryu Maru *-2006* **M Star Shipping Co Ltd** - SatCom: Inmarsat C 444075110 *Jeju* *South Korea* MMSI: 441751000 Official number: JJR-106157	**1,384** 749 2,676	Class: KR	**1995-02 Nakatani Shipyard Co. Ltd. — Etajima** Yd No: 563 Loa 76.16 (BB) Br ex - Dght 5.411 Lbp 70.00 Br md 12.50 Dpth 6.80 Welded, 1 dk	**(A31A2GX) General Cargo Ship** Bale: 2,572	**1 oil engine** driving 1 FP propeller Total Power: 1,323kW (1,799hp) 12.0kn Hanshin LH30LG 1 x 4 Stroke 6 Cy. 300 x 600 1323kW (1799bhp) The Hanshin Diesel Works Ltd-Japan Thrusters: 1 Thwart. FP thruster (f)
9146649 *DSQU6* -	**SKY EVOLUTION** *ex* MOL Evolution *-2010* *ex* Silver Island *-2003* *ex* Choyang Progress *-2001* **CK Line Co Ltd** - *Jeju* *South Korea* MMSI: 441707000 Official number: JJR-102061	**13,156** 7,592 17,781	Class: KR (NK)	**1996-10 Imabari Shipbuilding Co Ltd — Imabari EH (Imabari Shipyard)** Yd No: 528 Loa 162.40 (BB) Br ex - Dght 8.915 Lbp 150.00 Br md 25.60 Dpth 12.90 Welded, 1 dk	**(A33A2CC) Container Ship (Fully Cellular)** TEU 1032 incl 100 ref C. Compartments: 5 Cell Ho, ER 16 Ha: 2 (12.8 x 5.7)14 (12.8 x 10.9)ER	**1 oil engine** driving 1 FP propeller Total Power: 9,989kW (13,581hp) 18.1kn B&W 7S50MC 1 x 2 Stroke 7 Cy. 500 x 1910 9989kW (13581bhp) Mitsui Engineering & Shipbuilding CLtd-Japan AuxGen: 4 x 680kW 450V a.c Thrusters: 1 Tunnel thruster (f) Fuel: 1060.0 (r.f.)
9595802 *3EUE6* -	**SKY FLOWER** - **CKLine International Shipping SA** CK Line Co Ltd *Panama* *Panama* MMSI: 373126000 Official number: 4401112	**9,742** 4,328 11,891	Class: KR	**2012-04 Hyundai Mipo Dockyard Co Ltd — Ulsan** Yd No: 4053 Loa 146.00 (BB) Br ex - Dght 8.215 Lbp 137.48 Br md 22.70 Dpth 11.20 Welded, 1 dk	**(A33A2CC) Container Ship (Fully Cellular)** TEU 1060 incl 100 ref C	**1 oil engine** driving 1 FP propeller Total Power: 8,280kW (11,257hp) 17.0kn MAN-B&W 6S46MC-C8 1 x 2 Stroke 6 Cy. 460 x 1932 8280kW (11257bhp) Hyundai Heavy Industries Co Ltd-South Korea AuxGen: 4 x 640kW 450V a.c Thrusters: 1 Tunnel thruster (f) Fuel: 770.0
9006784 *DSPF7* -	**SKY GINI** *ex* Yuzan *-2011* *ex* Yuzan Maru *-2007* **M Star Shipping Co Ltd** - *Jeju* *South Korea* MMSI: 440910000 Official number: JJR-070684	**1,559** - 2,773	Class: KR	**1990-05 Yamanaka Zosen K.K. — Imabari** Yd No: 502 Loa 72.50 (BB) Br ex - Dght 5.813 Lbp 68.00 Br md 12.00 Dpth 7.30 Welded, 2 dks	**(A31A2GX) General Cargo Ship** Grain: 2,238 Compartments: 1 Ho, ER 1 Ha: ER	**1 oil engine** with clutches, flexible couplings & reverse geared to sc. shaft driving 1 FP propeller Total Power: 1,471kW (2,000hp) 11.0kn Hanshin 6EL32G 1 x 4 Stroke 6 Cy. 320 x 640 1471kW (2000bhp) The Hanshin Diesel Works Ltd-Japan
9463748 *V7UH2* -	**SKY GLOBE** *ex* Theresa Shandong *-2010* *launched as* Glory Wisdom *-2009* **Domina Maritime Ltd** Globus Shipmanagement Corp *Majuro* *Marshall Islands* MMSI: 538003949 Official number: 3949	**32,929** 19,132 56,854 T/cm 58.8	Class: GL	**2009-11 Taizhou Kouan Shipbuilding Co Ltd — Taizhou JS** Yd No: TK0109 Loa 189.98 (BB) Br ex - Dght 12.800 Lbp 185.00 Br md 32.26 Dpth 18.00 Welded, 1 dk	**(A21A2BC) Bulk Carrier** Grain: 71,634; Bale: 68,200 Compartments: 5 Ho, ER 5 Ha: ER Cranes: 4x36t	**1 oil engine** driving 1 FP propeller Total Power: 9,480kW (12,889hp) 14.2kn MAN-B&W 6S50MC-C 1 x 2 Stroke 6 Cy. 500 x 2000 9480kW (12889bhp) STX (Dalian) Engine Co Ltd-China AuxGen: 3 x 600kW 450V a.c
9550187 *DSQP3* -	**SKY GLORY** - **CK Line Co Ltd** - *Jeju* *South Korea* MMSI: 441654000	**5,534** 2,118 6,459	Class: KR	**2010-02 Nanjing Wujiazui Shipbuilding Co Ltd — Nanjing JS** Yd No: WJZ028 Loa 101.50 (BB) Br ex - Dght 7.213 Lbp 93.50 Br md 17.60 Dpth 11.10 Welded, 1 dk	**(A31A2GX) General Cargo Ship** Cranes: 2x30.7t; Derricks: 1x25t	**1 oil engine** driving 1 FP propeller Total Power: 2,648kW (3,600hp) 12.3kn Hanshin LH41LA 1 x 4 Stroke 6 Cy. 410 x 800 2648kW (3600bhp) The Hanshin Diesel Works Ltd-Japan AuxGen: 3 x 360kW 450V a.c Thrusters: 1 Tunnel thruster (f) Fuel: 380.0 (r.f.)
9140190 *XUBZ3* -	**SKY HARMONY** *ex* Shoyo Maru *-2009* **Sky Harmony Shipping Ltd** Yantai Sky Harmony Shipping Management Co Ltd *Phnom Penh* *Cambodia* MMSI: 515177000 Official number: 0996246	**1,422** 690 1,512	Class: UB	**1996-01 Miho Zosensho K.K. — Shimizu** Yd No: 1467 Loa 75.00 (BB) Br ex - Dght 4.230 Lbp 70.50 Br md 11.80 Dpth 7.20 Welded, 1 dk	**(A31A2GX) General Cargo Ship** Grain: 2,572 Compartments: 1 Ho, ER 1 Ha: ER	**1 oil engine** driving 1 FP propeller Total Power: 736kW (1,001hp) Hanshin LH30LG 1 x 4 Stroke 6 Cy. 300 x 600 736kW (1001bhp) The Hanshin Diesel Works Ltd-Japan Thrusters: 1 Thwart. FP thruster (f)
8501323 - -	**SKY HAWK** - - - *Nigeria*	*139* 89 -		**1984-12 Quality Shipyards Inc — Houma LA** Yd No: 176 Loa 27.21 Br ex - Dght - Lbp - Br md - Dpth - Welded, 1 dk	**(B11A2FT) Trawler**	**1 oil engine** driving 1 FP propeller Total Power: 460kW (625hp) Caterpillar 3412PCTA 1 x Vee 4 Stroke 12 Cy. 137 x 152 460kW (625bhp) Caterpillar Tractor Co-USA
9565405 *3FRP* -	**SKY HEIGHT** *launched as* Smart Snail *-2010* **Sky Height Maritime Ltd** Ningbo FTZ Cosnavi International Shipping Management Co Ltd SatCom: Inmarsat C 435373010 *Panama* *Panama* MMSI: 353730000 Official number: 4333012A	**15,899** 7,794 23,113	Class: CC	**2010-07 Taizhou Haibin Shipbuilding & Repairing Co Ltd — Sanmen County ZJ** Yd No: HBCCS-07-05 Loa 159.40 Br ex - Dght 9.800 Lbp 149.80 Br md 24.40 Dpth 14.00 Welded, 1 dk	**(A21A2BC) Bulk Carrier** Grain: 29,579 Compartments: 5 Ho, ER 5 Ha: ER Cranes: 3x25t Ice Capable	**1 oil engine** driving 1 FP propeller Total Power: 5,180kW (7,043hp) 15.0kn MAN-B&W 7S35MC 1 x 2 Stroke 7 Cy. 350 x 1400 5180kW (7043bhp) STX Engine Co Ltd-South Korea
9595797 *3EVC9* -	**SKY HOPE** - **CK International Shipping SA** CK Line Co Ltd *Panama* *Panama* MMSI: 373128000 Official number: 4401012	**9,742** 4,328 11,884	Class: KR	**2012-03 Hyundai Mipo Dockyard Co Ltd — Ulsan** Yd No: 4052 Loa 146.00 (BB) Br ex - Dght 8.215 Lbp 139.37 Br md 22.70 Dpth 11.20 Welded, 1 dk	**(A33A2CC) Container Ship (Fully Cellular)** TEU 1060 incl 100 ref C	**1 oil engine** driving 1 FP propeller Total Power: 8,280kW (11,257hp) 17.0kn MAN-B&W 6S46MC-C8 1 x 2 Stroke 6 Cy. 460 x 1932 8280kW (11257bhp) Hyundai Heavy Industries Co Ltd-South Korea AuxGen: 4 x 640kW 450V a.c Thrusters: 1 Tunnel thruster (f) Fuel: 770.0
7702920 *ERNM* -	**SKY HOPE** *ex* Lady Maga *-2005* *ex* Lady Rea *-2000* *ex* Ortrud *-1990* *ex* Carib Sun *-1988* *ex* Reggeland *-1987* *ex* Sylvia Delta *-1985* **Crest Shipping & Trading SA** Uni-marine Management Co *Giurgiulesti* *Moldova* MMSI: 214181413	**1,954** 1,095 3,214	Class: DR IM IS (LR) (GL) ✠ Classed LR until 3/8/98	**1978-02 Scheepswerf Bijlholt B.V. — Foxhol** Yd No: 603 Loa 81.72 Br ex 14.08 Dght 5.501 Lbp 74.58 Br md 14.00 Dpth 6.61 Welded, 1 dk	**(A31A2GX) General Cargo Ship** Grain: 3,859; Bale: 3,534 Compartments: 2 Ho, ER 2 Ha: 2 (21.4 x 10.2)ER	**1 oil engine** sr geared to sc. shaft driving 1 FP propeller Total Power: 1,765kW (2,400hp) 12.5kn Brons 12TD200 1 x Vee 2 Stroke 12 Cy. 220 x 380 1765kW (2400bhp) B.V. Motorenfabriek "De Industrie"-Alphen a/d Rijn AuxGen: 3 x 92kW 380V 50Hz a.c Fuel: 143.5 (d.f.) 9.0pd

9399088 *3EUT3* -	**SKY JADE** *ex* RBD Think Positive *-2012* **Diamond Camellia SA** Daiichi Chuo Marine Co Ltd (DC Marine) *Panama* *Panama* MMSI: 353947000 Official number: 4153710B	**42,604** 26,602 81,487 T/cm 69.7	Class: LR ✠ **100A1** SS 04/2010 bulk carrier BC-A strengthened for heavy cargoes, Nos. 2, 4 & 6 holds may be empty **ShipRight** (SDA, FDA, CM) ESP ESN *IWS LI ✠ **LMC** **UMS** Cable: 687.5/81.0 U3 (a)	**2010-04 Universal Shipbuilding Corp — Maizuru KY** Yd No: 117 Loa 225.00 (BB) Br ex 32.64 Dght 14.400 Lbp 222.00 Br md 32.26 Dpth 20.00 Welded, 1 dk	**(A21A2BC) Bulk Carrier** Grain: 96,030 Compartments: 7 Ho, ER 7 Ha: ER	**1 oil engine** driving 1 FP propeller Total Power: 9,700kW (13,188hp) 14.6kn MAN-B&W 7S50MC-C 1 x 2 Stroke 7 Cy. 500 x 2000 9700kW (13188bhp) Hitachi Zosen Corp-Japan AuxGen: 3 x 400kW 450V 60Hz a.c Boilers: AuxB (Comp) 7.1kgf/cm² (7.0bar)
9561942 *3FWH2* -	**SKY KNIGHT** **Ocean Hope Navigation SA** KT Marine Co Ltd *Panama* *Panama* MMSI: 373733000 Official number: 4424512	**32,714** 19,015 58,078	Class: NK	**2012-08 Shin Kurushima Dockyard Co. Ltd. — Onishi** Yd No: 5665 Loa 189.93 (BB) Br ex - Dght 12.925 Lbp 185.50 Br md 32.26 Dpth 18.40 Welded, 1 dk	**(A21A2BC) Bulk Carrier** Double Hull Grain: 73,142; Bale: 70,183 Compartments: 5 Ho, ER 5 Ha: ER Cranes: 4x30.5t	**1 oil engine** driving 1 FP propeller Total Power: 8,100kW (11,013hp) 14.2kn MAN-B&W 6S50MC-C 1 x 2 Stroke 6 Cy. 500 x 2000 8100kW (11013bhp) Mitsui Engineering & Shipbuilding CLtd-Japan Fuel: 2280.0
9364215 *2ANV9* -	**SKY LADY** **Blenheim Shipping UK Ltd** - SatCom: Inmarsat Mini-M 764840880 *Douglas* *Isle of Man (British)* MMSI: 235061402 Official number: 739360	**55,894** 29,810 105,370 T/cm 88.9	Class: LR ✠ **100A1** SS 04/2013 Double Hull oil tanker ESP **ShipRight** (SDA, FDA, CM) *IWS LI ✠ **LMC** **UMS IGS** Eq.Ltr: R†; Cable: 690.5/84.0 U3 (a)	**2008-04 Sumitomo Heavy Industries Marine & Engineering Co., Ltd. — Yokosuka** Yd No: 1337 Loa 228.60 (BB) Br ex 42.03 Dght 14.780 Lbp 217.80 Br md 42.00 Dpth 21.50 Welded, 1 dk	**(A13A2TV) Crude Oil Tanker** Double Hull (13F) Liq: 113,797; Liq (Oil): 122,000 Cargo Heating Coils Compartments: 10 Wing Ta, 2 Wing Slop Ta, ER 3 Cargo Pump (s): 3x2500m³/hr Manifold: Bow/CM: 116.6m	**1 oil engine** driving 1 FP propeller Total Power: 12,350kW (16,791hp) 14.8kn MAN-B&W 6S60MC-C 1 x 2 Stroke 6 Cy. 600 x 2400 12350kW (16791bhp) Mitsui Engineering & Shipbuilding CLtd-Japan AuxGen: 3 x 800kW 450V 60Hz a.c Boilers: e (ex.g.) 22.4kgf/cm² (22.0bar), WTAuxB (o.f.) 18.4kgf/cm² (18.0bar) Fuel: 223.0 (d.f.) 1156.0 (r.f.)
8934051 *3ENW8* -	**SKY LADY** *ex* Geiyo Maru *-2004* **Sky Ocean Shipping Co Ltd** Dalian Sky Ocean International Shipping Agency Co Ltd *Panama* *Panama* MMSI: 352326000 Official number: 3379508A	**1,995** 1,129 3,700	Class: KR	**1997-07 Nagashima Zosen KK — Kihoku ME** Yd No: 512 Converted From: Bulk Aggregates Carrier-2005 Lengthened-2005 Loa 89.78 Br ex - Dght 5.214 Lbp 85.71 Br md 13.50 Dpth 7.00 Welded, 1 dk	**(A31A2GX) General Cargo Ship** Grain: 4,762; Bale: 4,428 Compartments: 2 Ho, ER 2 Ha: 2 (20.4 x 9.5)ER Cranes: 1x18t,1x4t	**1 oil engine** driving 1 FP propeller Total Power: 1,471kW (2,000hp) 12.0kn Niigata 6M34BLGT 1 x 4 Stroke 6 Cy. 340 x 680 1471kW (2000bhp) Niigata Engineering Co Ltd-Japan
9046667 *HO5837* -	**SKY LILY** *ex* Showa Maru No. 8 *-2008* **Sky Lily Shipping Co Ltd** Dalian Sky Ocean International Shipping Agency Co Ltd *Panama* *Panama* MMSI: 357199000 Official number: 4048609A	**1,994** 1,184 4,144	Class: KR	**1992-04 Honda Zosen — Saiki** Yd No: 840 Lengthened-2009 Loa 90.60 Br ex - Dght 5.750 Lbp 84.97 Br md 13.20 Dpth 7.40 Welded	**(A31A2GX) General Cargo Ship**	**1 oil engine** driving 1 FP propeller Total Power: 736kW (1,001hp) 11.7kn Niigata 6M31AGTE 1 x 4 Stroke 6 Cy. 310 x 530 736kW (1001bhp) Niigata Engineering Co Ltd-Japan
9158862 *DSPM6* -	**SKY LOVE** **CK Line Co Ltd** - *Jeju* *South Korea* MMSI: 441238000 Official number: JJR-079984	**4,647** 2,408 7,262	Class: KR	**1997-08 Dae Sun Shipbuilding & Engineering Co Ltd — Busan** Yd No: 429 Loa 115.00 (BB) Br ex - Dght 6.763 Lbp 103.70 Br md 19.00 Dpth 8.50 Welded, 1 dk	**(A33A2CC) Container Ship (Fully Cellular)** TEU 446 C Ho 151 TEU C Dk 295 TEU incl 46 ref C. Compartments: 6 Cell Ho, ER 6 Ha: (12.6 x 8.0)5 (12.6 x 13.0)ER	**1 oil engine** driving 1 FP propeller Total Power: 4,193kW (5,701hp) 14.9kn B&W 6S35MC 1 x 2 Stroke 6 Cy. 350 x 1400 4193kW (5701bhp) Ssangyong Heavy Industries Co Ltd-South Korea AuxGen: 3 x 320kW 445V 60Hz a.c Fuel: 69.0 (d.f.) 469.0 (r.f.) 16.7pd
9562879 *YDA3601* -	**SKY MARINE 01** **PT Sky Marine** - *Batam* *Indonesia* MMSI: 525003049	**254** 77 194	Class: NK	**2009-06 PT Palma Progress Shipyard — Batam** Yd No: 362 Loa 28.05 Br ex - Dght 3.312 Lbp 25.77 Br md 8.60 Dpth 4.30 Welded, 1 dk	**(B32A2ST) Tug**	**2 oil engines** reduction geared to sc. shafts driving 2 FP propellers Total Power: 1,518kW (2,064hp) Mitsubishi S6R2-MTK3L 2 x 4 Stroke 6 Cy. 170 x 220 each-759kW (1032bhp) Mitsubishi Heavy Industries Ltd-Japan Fuel: 200.0
9322774 *3EAJ5* -	**SKY MARINER V** *ex* Sky Mariner *-2013* *ex* Nord Mariner *-2012* *ex* Santa Rita *-2008* **Marinero SA** Murad Shipmanagement Inc *Panama* *Panama* MMSI: 356908000 Official number: 3368905C	**30,002** 18,486 53,459	Class: NK	**2005-04 Imabari Shipbuilding Co Ltd — Imabari EH (Imabari Shipyard)** Yd No: 612 Loa 189.94 (BB) Br ex - Dght 12.300 Lbp 182.00 Br md 32.26 Dpth 17.30 Welded, 1 dk	**(A21A2BC) Bulk Carrier** Grain: 68,927; Bale: 65,526 Compartments: 5 Ho, ER 5 Ha: ER 5 (21.1 x 17.6) Cranes: 4x30.5t	**1 oil engine** driving 1 FP propeller Total Power: 9,480kW (12,889hp) 14.5kn MAN-B&W 6S50MC-C 1 x 2 Stroke 6 Cy. 500 x 2000 9480kW (12889bhp) Mitsui Engineering & Shipbuilding CLtd-Japan Fuel: 2090.0
7609506 *WDB7145* -	**SKY MOON** *ex* Daeinho III *-2006* *ex* Corsair *-2001* *ex* Kimberly Ann *-1993* *ex* Madam Denim Itch *-1992* *ex* Angel Marie *-1992* *ex* Miss Barbara *-1992* **Mini Corp** - *Honolulu, HI* *United States of America* Official number: 559024	*112* 78 -		**1974 Quality Marine, Inc. — Theodore, Al** L reg 21.71 Br ex - Dght - Lbp - Br md 6.71 Dpth 3.26 Welded, 1 dk	**(B11B2FV) Fishing Vessel**	**1 oil engine** driving 1 FP propeller Total Power: 386kW (525hp) G.M. (Detroit Diesel) 12V-71-TI 1 x Vee 2 Stroke 12 Cy. 108 x 127 386kW (525bhp) General Motors Detroit DieselAllison Divn-USA
8946925 - -	**SKY OCEAN 3** **Pradit Charoenpornlerd** *Thailand* Official number: 380900267	**131** 89 -		**1996 Samran Klansakul — Thailand** Loa 32.00 Br ex - Dght - Lbp 28.00 Br md 6.00 Dpth 2.50 Welded, 1 dk	**(A13B2TU) Tanker (unspecified)**	**1 oil engine** driving 1 FP propeller Total Power: 872kW (1,186hp) MAN 1 x 872kW (1186bhp) Nissan Diesel Motor Co. Ltd.-Ageo
7716476 *3FYN2* -	**SKY OCEANUS** *ex* Dock Express 10 *-2009* *ex* Dock Express France *-1994* *ex* Dock Express 10 *-1987* **Pisces Shipping Co Ltd** Tianjin Centrans Shipping Management Co Ltd *Panama* *Panama* MMSI: 356220000 Official number: 4044309A	**13,110** 3,933 12,928	Class: LR ✠ **100A1** SS 12/2008 non-perishable cargoes only at a mean draught of 7.75m when hatch covers omitted ✠ **LMC** **UMS** Eq.Ltr: E†; Cable: 577.5/64.0 U2	**1979-02 Verolme Scheepswerf Heusden B.V. — Heusden** Yd No: 966 Loa 153.78 (BB) Br ex 26.83 Dght 8.880 Lbp 117.20 Br md 24.21 Dpth 15.02 Welded, 1 dk	**(A38C2GH) Heavy Load Carrier** Stern door/ramp (centre) Grain: 17,560; Bale: 17,000 TEU 858 C. 858/20' (40') Compartments: 1 Ho, ER 1 Ha: (102.8 x 20.1) Gantry cranes: 2x500t	**2 oil engines** sr geared to sc. shafts driving 2 CP propellers Total Power: 6,252kW (8,500hp) 15.0kn Werkspoor 6TM410 2 x 4 Stroke 6 Cy. 410 x 470 each-3126kW (4250bhp) Stork Werkspoor Diesel BV-Netherlands AuxGen: 2 x 600kW 440V 60Hz a.c, 2 x 240kW 440V 60Hz a.c Boilers: TOH (o.f.), TOH (ex.g.) Thrusters: 1 Thwart. FP thruster (f)
9267986 *HOJK* -	**SKY PHOENIX** **Hope Line SA** Kaisei Tsusho KK (Kaisei Tsusho Co Ltd) *Panama* *Panama* MMSI: 354218000 Official number: 2869702B	**2,690** 1,147 3,604 T/cm 10.6	Class: BV	**2002-08 Sasaki Shipbuilding Co Ltd — Osakikamijima HS** Yd No: 641 Loa 89.80 (BB) Br ex 14.62 Dght 5.812 Lbp 83.00 Br md 14.60 Dpth 7.20 Welded, 1 dk	**(A12B2TR) Chemical/Products Tanker** Double Hull (13F) Liq: 3,986; Liq (Oil): 4,100 Cargo Heating Coils Compartments: 8 Wing Ta, 2 Wing Slop Ta, ER 8 Cargo Pump (s): 8x150m³/hr Manifold: Bow/CM: 44m	**1 oil engine** driving 1 FP propeller Total Power: 3,120kW (4,242hp) 14.7kn Mitsubishi 6UEC37LA 1 x 2 Stroke 6 Cy. 370 x 880 3120kW (4242bhp) Akasaka Tekkosho KK (Akasaka DieselLtd)-Japan AuxGen: 1 x 272kW 440/100V 60Hz a.c, 1 x 280kW 440/100V a.c Thrusters: 1 Tunnel thruster (f) Fuel: 76.0 (d.f.) (Heating Coils) 212.0 (r.f.) 12.5pd
9312468 *DSOH9* -	**SKY PRIDE** **CK Line Co Ltd** - *Jeju* *South Korea* MMSI: 440702000 Official number: JJR-059505	**9,520** 4,960 13,000	Class: KR	**2005-07 Dae Sun Shipbuilding & Engineering Co Ltd — Busan** Yd No: 451 Loa 142.70 (BB) Br ex 22.63 Dght 8.200 Lbp 133.50 Br md 22.60 Dpth 11.20 Welded, 1 dk	**(A33A2CC) Container Ship (Fully Cellular)** Double Hull TEU 962 incl 150 ref C	**1 oil engine** driving 1 FP propeller Total Power: 7,089kW (9,638hp) 18.0kn MAN-B&W 6S46MC-C 1 x 2 Stroke 6 Cy. 460 x 1932 7089kW (9638bhp) (made 2005) STX Engine Co Ltd-South Korea AuxGen: 3 x 615kW 445V a.c Thrusters: 1 Tunnel thruster (f)

IMO / Call sign	Name / Owner	Tonnage	Class	Builder / Dimensions	Type	Machinery
9016090 *3EHV9* -	**SKY QUEEN** *ex* Sky Bird *-2006* *ex* Nichiei Maru *-2006* *ex* Yoshu Maru *-1998* **Sky Bird Shipping Co Ltd** Dalian Sky Ocean International Shipping Agency Co Ltd *Panama* *Panama* MMSI: 372259000 Official number: 3259307A	**1,955** 1,083 3,883	Class: KR	**1991-04 Hamamoto Zosensho K.K. — Tokushima** Yd No: 750 Converted From: Bulk Aggregates Carrier-2006 Loa 89.90 (BB) Br ex - Dght 5.250 Lbp 83.30 Br md 13.50 Dpth 7.15 Welded, 1 dk	**(A31A2GX) General Cargo Ship** Bale: 1,039 Compartments: 1 Ho, ER 1 Ha: ER	**1 oil engine** driving 1 FP propeller Total Power: 1,470kW (1,999hp) 11.9kn Niigata 6M34AGT 1 x 4 Stroke 6 Cy. 340 x 620 1470kW (1999bhp) Niigata Engineering Co Ltd-Japan Thrusters: 1 Thwart. FP thruster (f)
9651876 *9V9858* -	**SKY QUEST** **Seaquest Tanker Pte Ltd** - *Singapore* *Singapore* MMSI: 566540000 Official number: 397665	**2,979** 1,330 4,784	Class: CC	**2013-05 Qinhuangdao China Harbour Shbldg Industry Co Ltd — Qinhuangdao HE** Yd No: 2010/38-09 Loa 89.78 Br ex - Dght 5.800 Lbp 85.40 Br md 15.80 Dpth 7.60 Welded, 1 dk	**(A13B2TP) Products Tanker** Double Hull (13F) Liq: 4,526; Liq (Oil): 4,526 Compartments: 4 Wing Ta, 4 Wing Ta, 1 Wing Slop Ta, 1 Wing Slop Ta, ER	**2 oil engines** reduction geared to sc. shafts driving 2 Propellers Total Power: 1,912kW (2,600hp) 12.5kn Daihatsu 6DKM-20 2 x 4 Stroke 6 Cy. 200 x 300 each-956kW (1300bhp) Anqing Marine Diesel Engine Works-China AuxGen: 3 x 250kW 440V a.c
8304141 *9LY2528* -	**SKY RIVER** *ex* Sun River *-2000* *ex* Daio Maru No. 8 *-1999* **PT Armada Contener Nusantara** - *Freetown* *Sierra Leone* MMSI: 667003331 Official number: SL103331	**1,479** 600 1,549		**1984-03 Nakatani Shipyard Co. Ltd. — Etajima** Yd No: 488 Loa 73.51 Br ex - Dght 4.323 Lbp 68.03 Br md 11.61 Dpth 7.01 Welded, 1 dk	**(A31A2GX) General Cargo Ship** Compartments: 1 Ho, ER 1 Ha: ER	**1 oil engine** with clutches & sr reverse geared to sc. shaft driving 1 FP propeller Total Power: 956kW (1,300hp) Hanshin 6LUN28AG 1 x 4 Stroke 6 Cy. 280 x 480 956kW (1300bhp) The Hanshin Diesel Works Ltd-Japan
7802691 *HP5736* -	**SKY SEAL** *ex* Black Seal *-1990* **CCM Transportation Ltd** Star Shipping Ltd *Panama* *Panama* MMSI: 356534000 Official number: 1950291CH	**658** 197 664	Class: (AB)	**1978-11 RYSCO Shipyard Inc. — Blountstown, Fl** Yd No: 34 Converted From: Research Vessel-1990 Loa 56.39 Br ex - Dght 3.644 Lbp 54.36 Br md 11.60 Dpth 4.27 Welded, 1 dk	**(A31C2GD) Deck Cargo Ship**	**2 oil engines** reverse reduction geared to sc. shafts driving 2 FP propellers Total Power: 1,838kW (2,498hp) 12.0kn Caterpillar D399SCAC 2 x Vee 4 Stroke 16 Cy. 159 x 203 each-919kW (1249bhp) Caterpillar Tractor Co-USA AuxGen: 2 x 210kW Thrusters: 1 Thwart. FP thruster (f)
8909135 *E5U2504* -	**SKY STAR** *ex* VTC Star *-2011* *ex* Beteigeuze *-2003* *ex* Pino Gloria *-2000* *ex* Woody Duke *-1994* **Kayia Trade & Invest Ltd** CFD Shipping Ltd *Avatiu* *Cook Islands* MMSI: 518554000 Official number: 1593	**13,705** 7,738 22,273 T/cm 32.9	Class: (RS) (NK) (VR)	**1990-04 Saiki Heavy Industries Co Ltd — Saiki OT** Yd No: 1008 Loa 157.50 (BB) Br ex - Dght 9.115 Lbp 148.00 Br md 25.00 Dpth 12.70 Welded, 1 dk	**(A21A2BC) Bulk Carrier** Grain: 29,301; Bale: 28,299 Compartments: 4 Ho, ER 4 Ha: (20.0 x 11.7)Tappered 3 (20.8 x 17.5)ER Cranes: 4x30t	**1 oil engine** driving 1 FP propeller Total Power: 4,590kW (6,241hp) 13.5kn Mitsubishi 6UEC45LA 1 x 2 Stroke 6 Cy. 450 x 1350 4590kW (6241bhp) Akasaka Tekkosho KK (Akasaka DieselLtd)-Japan AuxGen: 2 x 400kW 445V 60Hz a.c Fuel: 80.6 (d.f.) 804.9 (r.f.) 16.0pd
7716529 *3FRV7* -	**SKY TETHYS** *ex* Dock Express 12 *-2009* **Monoceros Shipping Co Ltd** Tianjin Centrans Shipping Management Co Ltd *Panama* *Panama* MMSI: 354867000 Official number: 38819PEXT	**12,124** 3,637 7,071	Class: LR ✠ **100A1** SS 11/2009 non-perishable cargoes only at a mean draught of 7.75m when hatch covers omitted ✠ **LMC** **UMS** Eq.Ltr: E†; Cable: 577.5/64.0 U2	**1979-10 Verolme Scheepswerf Heusden B.V. — Heusden** Yd No: 968 Lengthened-1987 Loa 159.49 (BB) Br ex 26.90 Dght 8.880 Lbp 116.01 Br md 24.21 Dpth 15.02 Welded, 1 dk	**(A38C2GH) Heavy Load Carrier** Stern door/ramp (centre) Grain: 17,560; Bale: 17,000 TEU 858 C. 858/20' (40') Compartments: 1 Ho, ER 1 Ha: (102.8 x 20.1) Gantry cranes: 2x500t	**2 oil engines** sr geared to sc. shafts driving 2 CP propellers Total Power: 6,252kW (8,500hp) 15.0kn Werkspoor 6TM410 2 x 4 Stroke 6 Cy. 410 x 470 each-3126kW (4250bhp) Stork Werkspoor Diesel BV-Netherlands AuxGen: 2 x 600kW 440V 60Hz a.c, 2 x 240kW 440V 60Hz a.c Boilers: TOH (o.f.), TOH (ex.g.) Thrusters: 1 Thwart. FP thruster (f)
9103489 *3ESF6* -	**SKY VENUS** *ex* Sando Maru No. 3 *-2007* **Sky Venus Shipping Co Ltd** Dalian Sky Ocean International Shipping Agency Co Ltd *Panama* *Panama* MMSI: 370285000 Official number: 3429008A	**3,606** 2,084 5,813	Class: KR	**1994-03 K.K. Imai Seisakusho — Kamijima** Yd No: 265 Lengthened-2008 Loa 106.03 (BB) Br ex - Dght 6.129 Lbp 98.35 Br md 15.00 Dpth 8.20 Welded, 1 dk	**(A31A2GX) General Cargo Ship** Single Hull Compartments: 2 Ho, ER 2 Ha: (29.3 x 11.5)ER (27.3 x 11.5)	**1 oil engine** geared to sc. shaft driving 1 FP propeller Total Power: 2,059kW (2,799hp) 12.4kn Hanshin 6EL38G 1 x 4 Stroke 6 Cy. 380 x 760 2059kW (2799bhp) The Hanshin Diesel Works Ltd-Japan AuxGen: 2 x 160kW 225V a.c
9014949 *V2PU8* -	**SKY VITA** *ex* Flevo *-2005* *ex* Waltraud *-1992* *ex* Kirsten *-1991* **Sagittarius Shipping Co Ltd** Alpha Shipping Co SIA *Saint John's* *Antigua & Barbuda* MMSI: 304768000 Official number: 2989	**2,497** 1,547 4,195 T/cm 10.6	Class: BV (Class contemplated) LR (GL) ✠ **100A1** SS 12/2011 Ice Class 1B (when engine set to 1690kw) ✠ **LMC** **UMS** Eq.Ltr: P; Cable: 440.0/32.0 U3 (a)	**1991-12 Scheepswerf Ferus Smit BV — Westerbroek** Yd No: 289 Loa 88.29 (BB) Br ex 13.21 Dght 5.448 Lbp 84.90 Br md 13.17 Dpth 7.00 Welded, 1 dk	**(A31A2GX) General Cargo Ship** Grain: 5,663 Compartments: 1 Ho, ER 2 Ha: 2 (26.0 x 10.2)ER Ice Capable	**1 oil engine** with flexible couplings & sr geared to sc. shaft driving 1 CP propeller Total Power: 1,690kW (2,298hp) 11.0kn Nohab 8V25 1 x Vee 4 Stroke 8 Cy. 250 x 300 1690kW (2298bhp) Wartsila Diesel AB-Sweden AuxGen: 1 x 176kW 220/380V 50Hz a.c, 1 x 140kW 220/380V 50Hz a.c Thrusters: 1 Water jet (f) Fuel: 23.1 (d.f.) 127.3 (r.f.) 27.4pd
8809270 *XUMH8* -	**SKY WIND** *ex* Chance *-2012* *ex* Onix *-2012* *ex* Astro *-2012* *ex* Chance *-2012* *ex* Nota *-2011* *ex* Pride No. 7 *-2011* *ex* Sunde *-2011* *ex* Onix *-2010* *ex* Bird *-2009* *ex* Daisei *-2008* *ex* Ryoyo Maru No. 1 *-2006* *ex* Tenyu Maru No. 3 *-2005* **Skywave International Group Ltd** - *Phnom Penh* *Cambodia* MMSI: 514901000 Official number: 0688421	**496** 259 -	Class: GM	**1988-07 Niigata Engineering Co Ltd — Niigata NI** Yd No: 2088 Loa 55.78 (BB) Br ex - Dght 3.490 Lbp 49.15 Br md 8.90 Dpth 3.85 Welded, 1 dk	**(B11B2FV) Fishing Vessel** Ins: 533	**1 oil engine** with clutches, flexible couplings & sr geared to sc. shaft driving 1 CP propeller Total Power: 699kW (950hp) Niigata 6M28BFT 1 x 4 Stroke 6 Cy. 280 x 480 699kW (950bhp) Niigata Engineering Co Ltd-Japan
8938966 - -	**SKYANGEL** *ex* Miss Julie *-2003* *ex* Four Stars *-2001* **Lynam, Joseph & Ella Jackson** - *Roatan* *Honduras* Official number: U-1827893	**135** 41 -		**1995 J & J Marine, Inc. — Bayou La Batre, Al** Yd No: 111 L reg 23.35 Br ex - Dght - Lbp - Br md 7.32 Dpth 3.84 Welded, 1 dk	**(B11B2FV) Fishing Vessel**	**1 oil engine** driving 1 FP propeller
8915720 *SVBU3* -	**SKYE** *ex* Rogue *-2012* *ex* Mary *-2007* *ex* Oceanic Success *-1999* **Samsara Shipping Corp** Albamar Shipping Co SA *Piraeus* *Greece* MMSI: 241268000 Official number: 12171	**23,275** 13,807 42,223 T/cm 47.6	Class: NK	**1991-02 Oshima Shipbuilding Co Ltd — Saikai NS** Yd No: 10135 Loa 180.00 (BB) Br ex - Dght 11.228 Lbp 172.00 Br md 30.50 Dpth 15.80 Welded, 1 dk	**(A21A2BC) Bulk Carrier** Grain: 52,125; Bale: 51,118 Compartments: 5 Ho, ER 5 Ha: (14.4 x 15.3)4 (19.2 x 15.3)ER Cranes: 4x25t	**1 oil engine** driving 1 FP propeller Total Power: 6,230kW (8,470hp) 14.6kn Sulzer 6RTA52 1 x 2 Stroke 6 Cy. 520 x 1800 6230kW (8470bhp) Diesel United Ltd.-Aioi AuxGen: 3 x 480kW 440V 60Hz a.c Fuel: 106.0 (d.f.) 1422.0 (r.f.) 24.2pd
8428583 *WDF3199* -	**SKYE FALGOUT** *ex* Emily Adams *-2009* *ex* Eddie Chouest *-2001* **Falgout Offshore LLC** Global Towing Service LLC SatCom: Inmarsat C 430327910 *New Orleans, LA* *United States of America* MMSI: 367567000 Official number: 652225	**977** 293 1,402	Class: (AB)	**1982-03 North American Shipbuilding Inc — Larose LA** Yd No: 125 Loa - Br ex - Dght 3.663 Lbp 59.75 Br md 13.42 Dpth 4.27 Welded, 1 dk	**(B21A20S) Platform Supply Ship**	**2 oil engines** reverse reduction geared to sc. shafts driving 2 FP propellers Total Power: 1,656kW (2,252hp) 15.0kn Caterpillar D399SCAC 2 x Vee 4 Stroke 16 Cy. 159 x 203 each-828kW (1126bhp) Caterpillar Tractor Co-USA AuxGen: 2 x 75kW a.c
1009601 *ZCTE8* -	**SKYFALL II** *ex* O'khalila *-2014* **Goldfinger Charters Ltd** Ariadne Yacht Management Ltd *George Town* *Cayman Islands (British)* MMSI: 319826000 Official number: 740036	**380** 114 49	Class: LR ✠ **100A1** SS 05/2012 SSC Yacht, mono HSC G6 Cable: 137.5/17.5 U2 (a)	**2007-05 Palmer Johnson Yachts LLC — Sturgeon Bay WI** Yd No: 243 Loa 45.70 Br ex 8.70 Dght 1.800 Lbp 38.10 Br md 8.40 Dpth 4.10 Welded, 1 dk	**(X11A2YP) Yacht** Hull Material: Aluminium Alloy	**3 oil engines** with clutches, flexible couplings & sr reverse geared to sc. shafts driving 3 FP propellers Total Power: 8,160kW (11,094hp) M.T.U. 16V4000M90 3 x Vee 4 Stroke 16 Cy. 165 x 190 each-2720kW (3698bhp) MTU Friedrichshafen GmbH-Friedrichshafen AuxGen: 2 x 70kW 400V 50Hz a.c Thrusters: 1 Thwart. FP thruster (f)

8521830 **SKYFROST**
3FTR9 *ex* Yu Shan *-2009* *ex* Hermann Matern *-1999*
\- **Berwick Group Ltd**
Laskaridis Shipping Co Ltd
SatCom: Inmarsat C 421206211
Panama *Panama*
MMSI: 357805000
Official number: 28444PEXT3

12,383 / 4,056 / 9,360
Class: RS (BV) (NV)

1985-11 VEB Mathias-Thesen-Werft — Wismar
Yd No: 233
Loa 152.94 Br ex 22.25 Dght 8.306
Lbp 142.00 Br md 22.01 Dpth 13.60
Welded, 1 dk, 2nd & 3rd dk in holds only

(B12B2FC) Fish Carrier
Ins: 13,306
Compartments: 4 Ho, ER, 8 Tw Dk
4 Ha: 4 (6.0 x 3.9)ER
Derricks: 2x10t,7x5t
Ice Capable

1 oil engine driving 1 FP propeller
Total Power: 7,600kW (10,333hp) 17.7kn
MAN K5SZ70/125BL
1 x 2 Stroke 5 Cy. 700 x 1250 7600kW (10333bhp)
VEB Dieselmotorenwerk Rostock-Rostock
AuxGen: 4 x 588kW 390V 50Hz a.c
Fuel: 633.0 (d.f.) 3902.0 (r.f.) 41.5pd

9001722 **SKYGLORY**
3FLW6 *ex* Tasman Chief *-2010*
\- *ex* Seaboard Adventurer *-2008*
ex Tasman Adventurer *-2007*
ex Helga Oldendorff *-1999*
ex FMG Mexico *-1999*
ex Helga Oldendorff *-1996* *ex* POL Europe *-1995*
Skyglory Shipping SA
Sinotrans Navigation Co Ltd
Panama *Panama*
MMSI: 353680000
Official number: 4218311

15,901 / 8,082 / 21,679
Class: CC (GL) (PR)

1991-12 Flensburger Schiffbau-Ges. mbH & Co. KG — Flensburg Yd No: 677
Loa 165.00 (BB) Br ex - Dght 9.850
Lbp 155.00 Br md 26.00 Dpth 13.50
Welded, 1 dk, 2nd dk except in hold no. 5

(A31A2GX) General Cargo Ship
Grain: 26,285; Bale: 25,000
TEU 1308 incl 80 ref C.
Compartments: 5 Ho, ER, 4 Tw Dk
9 Ha: (19.4 x 15.4)4 (25.8 x 10.3)2 (12.9 x 10.3)2 (12.8 x 5.4)ER
Cranes: 3x36t
Ice Capable

1 oil engine driving 1 FP propeller
Total Power: 7,100kW (9,653hp) 16.0kn
Sulzer 5RTA52
1 x 2 Stroke 5 Cy. 520 x 1800 7100kW (9653bhp)
Shanghai Diesel Engine Co Ltd-China
AuxGen: 3 x 1016kW 220/380V 50Hz a.c
Thrusters: 1 Thwart. CP thruster (f)

9606663 **SKYHIGH SW**
3FAT8
\- **Skyhigh Pescadores SA Panama**
Shih Wei Navigation Co Ltd
SatCom: Inmarsat C 435282810
Panama *Panama*
MMSI: 352828000
Official number: 4287711

9,963 / 4,544 / 14,260 / T/cm / 22.0
Class: CR NK

2011-06 Higaki Zosen K.K. — Imabari Yd No: 657
Loa 127.67 (BB) Br ex - Dght 9.446
Lbp 119.50 Br md 19.60 Dpth 14.50
Welded, 1 dk

(A31A2GX) General Cargo Ship
Grain: 19,930; Bale: 18,598
Compartments: 2 Ho, 2 Tw Dk, ER
2 Ha: ER
Cranes: 2x30.7t; Derricks: 2x30t

1 oil engine driving 1 FP propeller
Total Power: 4,200kW (5,710hp) 13.5kn
MAN-B&W 6S35MC
1 x 2 Stroke 6 Cy. 350 x 1400 4200kW (5710bhp)
Makita Corp-Japan

9295048 **SKYLARK**
A8FH9 *completed as* Gerhard Schulte *-2004*
\- **Skylark International Shipping Corp**
Marwave Shipmanagement BV
SatCom: Inmarsat Mini-M 764085599
Monrovia *Liberia*
MMSI: 636012414
Official number: 12414

22,184 / 9,434 / 34,620 / T/cm / 41.5
Class: LR
✠ **100A1** SS 11/2009
Double Hull oil tanker
ESP
*IWS
SPM
LI
ShipRight (SDA, FDA, CM)
✠ **LMC** **UMS IGS**
Eq.Ltr: J†;
Cable: 639.0/68.0 U3 (a)

2004-11 Dalian Shipyard Co Ltd — Dalian LN
Yd No: PC350-5
Loa 171.22 (BB) Br ex 27.42 Dght 11.815
Lbp 161.99 Br md 27.39 Dpth 17.30
Welded, 1 dk

(A13B2TP) Products Tanker
Double Hull (13F)
Liq: 36,911; Liq (Oil): 38,316
Cargo Heating Coils
Compartments: 12 Wing Ta, 2 Wing Slop Ta, ER
12 Cargo Pump (s): 10x500m³/hr, 2x300m³/hr
Manifold: Bow/CM: 83.3m

1 oil engine driving 1 FP propeller
Total Power: 7,150kW (9,721hp) 14.5kn
MAN-B&W 5S50MC
1 x 2 Stroke 5 Cy. 500 x 1910 7150kW (9721bhp)
Dalian Marine Diesel Works-China
AuxGen: 3 x 910kW 450V 60Hz a.c
Boilers: AuxB (ex.g.) 8.8kgf/cm² (8.6bar), WTAuxB (o.f.) 8.8kgf/cm² (8.6bar)
Thrusters: 1 Thwart. CP thruster (f); 1 Thwart. CP thruster (a)
Fuel: 149.8 (d.f.) 1250.0 (r.f.)

7416040 **SKYLARK**
J8QG9 *ex* Valzell *-1996*
\- **West Anatolia Shipping & Trading SA**
Anadolu Denizcilik Tasimacilik Sanayi ve Ticaret Ltd Sti
Kingstown *St Vincent & The Grenadines*
MMSI: 376659000
Official number: 6839

999 / 488 / 1,608
Class: IV (LR)
✠ Classed LR until 15/3/08

1976-06 Verolme Cork Dockyard Ltd — Cobh
Yd No: 907
Loa 61.52 Br ex 10.42 Dght 4.776
Lbp 56.49 Br md 10.25 Dpth 5.64
Welded, 1 dk

(A31A2GX) General Cargo Ship
Grain: 1,822
Compartments: 1 Ho, ER
1 Ha: (36.7 x 8.4)ER
Ice Capable

1 oil engine reverse reduction geared to sc. shaft driving 1 FP propeller
Total Power: 883kW (1,201hp) 9.8kn
Brons 6TD200
1 x 2 Stroke 6 Cy. 220 x 380 883kW (1201bhp)
NV Appingedammer Bronsmotorenfabrie-Netherlands
AuxGen: 2 x 52kW 380V 50Hz a.c, 1 x 40kW 380V 50Hz a.c
Fuel: 60.0 (d.f.)

8746002 **SKYLGE**
PHLS *ex* Rival *-1986* *ex* Alberdina *-1986*
\- **Oostzeeklipper Skylge**
Enkhuizen *Netherlands*
MMSI: 245103000
Official number: 17934ZR1989

108 / 59 / -

1910-08 Scheepswerf v/h P. & A. Ruijtenberg B.V. — Raamsdonksveer
Loa 31.65 Br ex - Dght -
Lbp - Br md 6.08 Dpth 1.50
Welded, 1 dk

(X11A2YS) Yacht (Sailing)

1 oil engine reduction geared to sc. shaft driving 1 Propeller
Total Power: 129kW (175hp)
MWM
1 x 4 Stroke 6 Cy. 129kW (175bhp)
MWM Motores Diesel Ltda-Brazil

9508809 **SKYLGE**
PBVJ
\- **SVO Skylge CV**
Skylge Shipping BV
Harlingen *Netherlands*
MMSI: 246630000
Official number: 52248

6,046 / 2,718 / 7,616
Class: GL

2010-03 Zhejiang Hongxin Shipbuilding Co Ltd — Taizhou ZJ Yd No: 2007-16
Loa 122.11 (BB) Br ex 16.50 Dght 7.200
Lbp 115.42 Br md 16.30 Dpth 10.00
Welded, 1 dk

(A31A2GX) General Cargo Ship
Grain: 10,279
TEU 414 C Ho 222 TEU C Dk 192 TEU
Compartments: 2 Ho, ER
2 Ha: (50.4 x 13.5)ER (27.3 x 13.5)
Ice Capable

1 oil engine reduction geared to sc. shaft driving 1 CP propeller
Total Power: 4,000kW (5,438hp) 14.0kn
MaK 8M32C
1 x 4 Stroke 8 Cy. 320 x 480 4000kW (5438bhp)
Caterpillar Motoren GmbH & Co. KG-Germany
AuxGen: 1 x 650kW 400V a.c, 2 x 380kW 400V a.c
Thrusters: 1 Tunnel thruster (f)

9202259 **SKYLINE**
V2QJ3 *ex* Werder Bremen *-2012*
\- **Admiral Sky Shipping Co Ltd**
Midocean (IOM) Ltd
Saint John's *Antigua & Barbuda*
MMSI: 305834000
Official number: 3108

6,378 / 3,998 / 7,144 / T/cm / 15.0
Class: GL

1999-10 J.J. Sietas KG Schiffswerft GmbH & Co. — Hamburg Yd No: 1124
Loa 121.89 (BB) Br ex 18.45 Dght 6.690
Lbp 114.90 Br md 18.20 Dpth 8.30
Welded, 1 dk

(A33A2CC) Container Ship (Fully Cellular)
Double Bottom Entire Compartment Length
Grain: 13,852; Bale: 12,536
TEU 700 C Ho 432 TEU C Dk 268 TEU incl 144 ref C.
Compartments: 4 Cell Ho, ER
4 Ha: (12.4 x 12.9) (12.4 x 15.6) (38.9 x 15.6) (12.6 x 15.6)ER
Ice Capable

1 oil engine with flexible couplings & sr geared to sc. shaft driving 1 CP propeller
Total Power: 5,300kW (7,206hp) 16.5kn
MAN 8L40/54
1 x 4 Stroke 8 Cy. 400 x 540 5300kW (7206bhp)
MAN B&W Diesel AG-Augsburg
AuxGen: 1 x 880kW 380/220V 50Hz a.c, 2 x 305kW 380/220V 50Hz a.c
Thrusters: 1 Thwart. FP thruster (f)
Fuel: 132.5 (d.f.) (Heating Coils) 606.3 (r.f.) 18.9pd

8230431 **SKYLINE**
XUAC6 *ex* Volgo-Balt 225 *-2009*
\- **Skyline Shipping Ltd**
Private Enterprise 'Valship'
SatCom: Inmarsat C 451430310
Phnom Penh *Cambodia*
MMSI: 514303000
Official number: 0980381

2,457 / 1,191 / 2,893
Class: RR (RS)

1980-07 Zavody Tazkeho Strojarstva (ZTS) — Komarno Yd No: 1956
Loa 114.00 Br ex 13.23 Dght 3.600
Lbp 110.52 Br md 13.01 Dpth 5.50
Welded, 1 dk

(A31A2GX) General Cargo Ship
Grain: 4,720
Compartments: 4 Ho, ER
4 Ha: (18.6 x 11.2)2 (18.8 x 11.2) (20.3 x 11.2)ER

2 oil engines driving 2 FP propellers
Total Power: 1,030kW (1,400hp) 10.8kn
Skoda 6L275A2
2 x 4 Stroke 6 Cy. 275 x 350 each-515kW (700bhp)
Skoda-Praha
Fuel: 110.0 (d.f.)

8121197 **SKYMAR**
\- *ex* Abdullah 3 *-2008* *ex* Guang De *-2006*
\- *ex* Sek Wang 1 *-2003*
ex Hwa Pyung Nam Jin *-1997*
Hebo Shipping Ltd
Skymar Shipping Co

3,768 / 1,958 / 5,865
Class: GM (TL) (KR)

1982-02 ShinA Shipbuilding Co Ltd — Tongyeong
Yd No: 255
Loa 104.76 Br ex 16.03 Dght 6.852
Lbp 97.01 Br md 16.01 Dpth 8.36
Welded, 1 dk

(A31A2GX) General Cargo Ship
Grain: 7,166; Bale: 6,485
Compartments: 2 Ho, ER
2 Ha: 2 (25.4 x 10.8)ER
Derricks: 3x20t,1x15t

1 oil engine driving 1 FP propeller
Total Power: 2,648kW (3,600hp) 14.3kn
Hanshin 6LU46A
1 x 4 Stroke 6 Cy. 460 x 740 2648kW (3600bhp)
Ssangyong Heavy Industries Co Ltd-South Korea
AuxGen: 2 x 220kW 445V a.c

8662828 **SKYMAX 101**
6KCC6
\- **Top Fisheries Co Ltd**
\-
Busan *South Korea*
MMSI: 440038000
Official number: 1307001-6261403

1,402 / 598 / 1,077
Class: KT

2012-10 San Yang Shipbuilding Co., Ltd. — Kaohsiung Yd No: 862
Loa 73.13 Br ex - Dght 4.500
Lbp 65.23 Br md 10.80 Dpth 4.80
Welded, 1 dk

(B11B2FV) Fishing Vessel

1 oil engine reduction geared to sc. shaft driving 1 Propeller
Total Power: 1,618kW (2,200hp)
Niigata
1 x 1618kW (2200bhp)
Niigata Engineering Co Ltd-Japan

9434022 **SKYRING**
CA2033
\- **Remolcadores Ultratug Ltda**
Administradora de Naves Humboldt Ltda
Valparaiso *Chile*
MMSI: 725004430
Official number: 3201

375 / - / 250
Class: LR
✠ **100A1** SS 06/2013
tug
✠ **LMC**
Eq.Ltr: G;
Cable: 302.5/20.0 U2 (a)

2008-06 Astilleros y Servicios Navales S.A. (ASENAV) — Valdivia Yd No: 153
Loa 32.50 Br ex 10.82 Dght 4.200
Lbp 26.97 Br md 10.50 Dpth 4.90
Welded, 1 dk

(B32A2ST) Tug

2 oil engines gearing integral to driving 2 Directional propellers
Total Power: 3,840kW (5,220hp) 11.0kn
Caterpillar 3516B
2 x Vee 4 Stroke 16 Cy. 170 x 190 each-1920kW (2610bhp)
Caterpillar Inc-USA
AuxGen: 2 x 175kW 380V 50Hz a.c

9177985 **SKYROS**
V7W03 *ex* Diamond Star *-2003*
\- **Ritena Maritime Co Ltd**
Lydia Mar Shipping Co SA
Majuro *Marshall Islands*
MMSI: 538004351
Official number: 4351

14,781 / 8,325 / 24,351 / T/cm / 34.2
Class: NK (GL)

1998-09 Saiki Heavy Industries Co Ltd — Saiki OT
Yd No: 1080
Loa 154.35 (BB) Br ex - Dght 9.730
Lbp 146.00 Br md 26.00 Dpth 13.35
Welded, 1 dk

(A21A2BC) Bulk Carrier
Grain: 30,978; Bale: 30,225
Compartments: 4 Ho, ER
4 Ha: (19.2 x 12.7)2 (20.0 x 17.5) (20.8 x 17.5)ER
Cranes: 4x30t

1 oil engine driving 1 FP propeller
Total Power: 5,296kW (7,200hp) 14.1kn
Mitsubishi 6UEC45LA
1 x 2 Stroke 6 Cy. 450 x 1350 5296kW (7200bhp)
Kobe Hatsudoki KK-Japan
Fuel: 278.0 (d.f.) 974.0 (r.f.)

Ship	Tonnage	Class	Construction	Type	Machinery
9001734 **SKYROYAL** *3FIR8* *ex* Pacific Chief *-2010* - *ex* Seaboard Discoverer *-2008* *ex* Tasman Discoverer *-2007* *ex* Henriette Oldendorff *-1999* *ex* FMG Santiago *-1999* *ex* Henriette Oldendorff *-1996* *ex* POL Asia *-1995* **Skyroyal Shipping SA** Sinotrans Navigation Co Ltd *Panama* *Panama* MMSI: 353600000 Official number: 4212510	**15,900** 8,069 21,679	Class: CC (GL) (PR)	**1992**-06 **Flensburger Schiffbau-Ges. mbH & Co. KG — Flensburg** Yd No: 678 Loa 165.10 (BB) Br ex - Dght 9.833 Lbp 156.55 Br md 26.00 Dpth 13.51 Welded, 1 dk, 2nd dk except in hold no. 5	**(A31A2GX) General Cargo Ship** Grain: 26,285; Bale: 25,000 TEU 1308 incl 80 ref C. Compartments: 5 Ho, ER, 4 Tw Dk 9 Ha: (19.4 x 15.4)4 (25.8 x 10.3)2 (12.9 x 10.3)2 (12.8 x 5.4)ER Cranes: 3x36t Ice Capable	**1 oil engine** driving 1 FP propeller Total Power: 7,100kW (9,653hp) 16.0kn Sulzer 5RTA52 1 x 2 Stroke 5 Cy. 520 x 1800 7100kW (9653bhp) Dalian Marine Diesel Works-China Thrusters: 1 Thwart. CP thruster (f)
9316701 **SKYSAN** *C6VS3* *ex* Asian Progress IV *-2013* - **Griffin Tankers SA** Mitsui OSK Lines Ltd (MOL) SatCom: Inmarsat C 430907610 *Nassau* *Bahamas* MMSI: 309076000 Official number: 8001187	**160,292** 102,497 313,992 T/cm 185.0	Class: NK	**2006**-09 **Kawasaki Shipbuilding Corp — Sakaide KG** Yd No: 1574 Loa 333.00 (BB) Br ex 60.00 Dght 21.035 Lbp 324.00 Br md 60.00 Dpth 29.00 Welded, 1 dk	**(A13A2TV) Crude Oil Tanker** Double Hull (13F) Liq: 337,157; Liq (Oil): 337,157 Compartments: 5 Ta, 10 Wing Ta, 2 Wing Slop Ta, ER 3 Cargo Pump (s): 3x5500m³/hr Manifold: Bow/CM: 166.5m	**1 oil engine** driving 1 FP propeller Total Power: 27,160kW (36,927hp) 15.6kn MAN-B&W 7S80MC-C 1 x 2 Stroke 7 Cy. 800 x 3200 27160kW (36927bhp) Kawasaki Heavy Industries Ltd-Japan AuxGen: 3 x 1325kW a.c Fuel: 279.1 (d.f.) 7204.1 (r.f.)
9423920 **SKYTHIA** *9HA2168* - **Sharman Holdings SA** Alpha Tankers & Freighters International Ltd SatCom: Inmarsat Mini-M 764945037 *Valletta* *Malta* MMSI: 248087000 Official number: 9423920	**89,990** 59,147 177,830 T/cm 120.6	Class: BV	**2010**-01 **Shanghai Waigaoqiao Shipbuilding Co Ltd — Shanghai** Yd No: 1099 Loa 292.00 (BB) Br ex 45.05 Dght 18.320 Lbp 282.00 Br md 45.00 Dpth 24.80 Welded, 1 dk	**(A21A2BC) Bulk Carrier** Grain: 194,000; Bale: 183,425 Compartments: 9 Ho, ER 9 Ha: 7 (15.5 x 20.0)ER 2 (15.5 x 16.5)	**1 oil engine** driving 1 FP propeller Total Power: 16,858kW (22,920hp) 14.0kn MAN-B&W 6S70MC 1 x 2 Stroke 6 Cy. 700 x 2674 16858kW (22920bhp) CSSC MES Diesel Co Ltd-China
8833984 **SL-2 PROFESSOR PAVLOVSKIY** - - **Krylov Scientific Research Institute (TSNII imeni Krylova)** - *Vyborg* *Russia* Official number: 886189	*155* 46 21	Class: (RS)	**1989**-11 **Sudostroitelnyy Zavod 'Pella' — Otradnoye** Yd No: 1 Loa 28.80 Br ex 6.12 Dght 2.050 Lbp 25.25 Br md - Dpth 3.66 Welded, 1 dk	**(B31A2SR) Research Survey Vessel** Ice Capable	**2 oil engines** driving 2 FP propellers Total Power: 440kW (598hp) 12.0kn Barnaultransmash 3D12A 2 x Vee 4 Stroke 12 Cy. 150 x 180 each-220kW (299bhp) Barnaultransmash-Barnaul AuxGen: 2 x 30kW a.c Fuel: 6.0 (d.f.)
8712398 **SL ARCHI** *DSOR5* *ex* Honai Maru *-2006* - **Shinhan Capital Co Ltd** Seoil Agency Co Ltd *Jeju* *South Korea* MMSI: 441240000 Official number: JJR-069304	**1,488** 656 1,751	Class: KR (NK)	**1987**-09 **Kurinoura Dockyard Co Ltd — Yawatahama EH** Yd No: 247 Loa 84.36 (BB) Br ex 13.03 Dght 4.372 Lbp 77.73 Br md 13.01 Dpth 4.40 Welded, 2 dks	**(A34A2GR) Refrigerated Cargo Ship** Ins: 2,617 Compartments: 3 Ho, ER 3 Ha: (3.8 x 3.8)2 (4.3 x 3.8)ER Derricks: 6x3t	**1 oil engine** driving 1 FP propeller Total Power: 1,471kW (2,000hp) 14.0kn Akasaka A34 1 x 4 Stroke 6 Cy. 340 x 660 1471kW (2000bhp) Akasaka Tekkosho KK (Akasaka DieselLtd)-Japan AuxGen: 2 x 450kW a.c
9607227 **SL BANABA** *DUA3134* - **SMC Shipping & Lighterage Corp** - *La Union* *Philippines* Official number: 01-0000088	**665** 545	Class: (BV)	**2010**-10 **Dansyco Marine Works & Shipbuilding Corp — Manila** Yd No: 0902 Loa 62.90 Br ex - Dght 2.590 Lbp - Br md 12.80 Dpth 3.51 Welded, 1 dk	**(A12A2TC) Chemical Tanker** Double Hull (13F)	**2 oil engines** reduction geared to sc. shafts driving 2 FP propellers Total Power: 1,060kW (1,442hp) Mitsubishi 2 x 4 Stroke each-530kW (721bhp) Mitsubishi Heavy Industries Ltd-Japan
9622722 **SL BELUGA** - - **SMC Shipping & Lighterage Corp** Swan Shipping Corp *La Union* *Philippines* Official number: 01-0000371	**1,362** 488 1,312	Class: NK	**2012**-03 **Kegoya Dock K.K. — Kure** Yd No: 1141 Loa 67.95 Br ex - Dght 4.616 Lbp 64.00 Br md 12.80 Dpth 5.50 Welded, 1 dk	**(A11B2TG) LPG Tanker** Liq (Gas): 1,837	**1 oil engine** driving 1 FP propeller Total Power: 1,765kW (2,400hp) 14.4kn Akasaka A34S 1 x 4 Stroke 6 Cy. 340 x 660 1765kW (2400bhp) Akasaka Tekkosho KK (Akasaka DieselLtd)-Japan Fuel: 180.0
9634153 **SL BIGNAY** *DUA3149* - **SMC Shipping & Lighterage Corp** - *La Union* *Philippines* Official number: 01-0000179	**665** 545 1,415		**2011**-05 **Dansyco Marine Works & Shipbuilding Corp — Manila** Yd No: 1001 Loa 62.90 Br ex - Dght 2.590 Lbp 57.58 Br md 12.80 Dpth 3.51 Welded, 1 dk	**(A12A2TC) Chemical Tanker** Double Hull (13F)	**2 oil engines** reduction geared to sc. shafts driving 2 FP propellers Total Power: 1,220kW (1,658hp) Mitsubishi S6R2-MPTK 2 x 4 Stroke 6 Cy. 170 x 220 each-610kW (829bhp) Mitsubishi Heavy Industries Ltd-Japan
8815009 **SL BOGO** *DSOZ2* *ex* Tunabridge *-2006* - **Seoil Agency Co Ltd** - *Jeju* *South Korea* MMSI: 440664000 Official number: JJR-078811	**3,483** 1,731 4,232	Class: KR (NK)	**1989**-03 **Kitanihon Zosen K.K. — Hachinohe** Yd No: 236 Loa 99.98 (BB) Br ex 16.32 Dght 7.014 Lbp 90.00 Br md 16.30 Dpth 9.80 Welded	**(A34A2GR) Refrigerated Cargo Ship** Ins: 4,261 Compartments: 1 Wing Ho	**1 oil engine** driving 1 FP propeller Total Power: 2,942kW (4,000hp) 15.3kn Mitsubishi 6UEC37LA 1 x 2 Stroke 6 Cy. 370 x 880 2942kW (4000bhp) Akasaka Tekkosho KK (Akasaka DieselLtd)-Japan AuxGen: 2 x 600kW a.c Thrusters: 1 Thwart. CP thruster (f)
9154177 **SL BUTANDING** *DUB2019* *ex* Ellen Kosan *-2011* *ex* Lady Anne *-2006* - *ex* Pegasus Gas *-2004* **SMC Shipping & Lighterage Corp** - *La Union* *Philippines* MMSI: 548058200 Official number: 010000232	**3,050** 915 3,163 T/cm 11.6	Class: NK	**1996**-11 **Shitanoe Shipbuilding Co Ltd — Usuki OT** Yd No: 1182 Loa 96.60 (BB) Br ex 15.04 Dght 5.214 Lbp 89.50 Br md 15.00 Dpth 7.00 Welded, 1 dk	**(A11B2TG) LPG Tanker** Double Bottom Entire Compartment Length Liq (Gas): 3,215 2 x Gas Tank (s); 2 independent (C.mn.stl) cyl horizontal 2 Cargo Pump (s): 2x300m³/hr Manifold: Bow/CM: 44.4m	**1 oil engine** driving 1 FP propeller Total Power: 2,427kW (3,300hp) 13.0kn Akasaka A41 1 x 4 Stroke 6 Cy. 410 x 800 2427kW (3300bhp) Akasaka Tekkosho KK (Akasaka DieselLtd)-Japan AuxGen: 2 x 200kW 450V 60Hz a.c Fuel: 53.0 (d.f.) 310.0 (r.f.)
8741600 **SL-D1** *V3NK8* *ex* Yue Dong Guan Chui 0091 *-2010* - **S L Ocean Ltd** - *Belize City* *Belize* MMSI: 312053000 Official number: 031020196	**1,203** 361 -		**1987**-09 **Jiangdu Shipyard — Jiangdu JS** Converted From: Deck-Cargo Pontoon, Non-propelled-2002 Loa 47.80 Br ex - Dght - Lbp - Br md 16.80 Dpth 4.90 Welded, 1 dk	**(B33A2DU) Dredger (unspecified)**	**4 oil engines** geared to sc. shafts driving 4 Propellers 10.0kn Cummins 4 x 4 Stroke
9636498 **SL GABON** *HP4109* *ex* Smit Gabon *-2012* - **Smit Lamnalco Ltd** Smit International (Gabon) SA *Panama* *Panama* MMSI: 373686000 Official number: 44135PEXT	**613** 183 500	Class: BV	**2012**-12 **Santierul Naval Damen Galati S.A. — Galati** (Hull) Yd No: 1228 **2012**-12 **B.V. Scheepswerf Damen — Gorinchem** Yd No: 512012 Loa 40.75 Br ex - Dght 4.250 Lbp 34.98 Br md 11.00 Dpth 4.90 Welded, 1 dk	**(B32A2ST) Tug**	**2 oil engines** reverse reduction geared to sc. shafts driving 2 FP propellers Total Power: 2,742kW (3,728hp) Caterpillar 3516B-HD 2 x Vee 4 Stroke 16 Cy. 170 x 215 each-1371kW (1864bhp) Caterpillar Inc-USA AuxGen: 3 x 175kW 50Hz a.c Thrusters: 1 Tunnel thruster (f) Fuel: 220.0 (d.f.)
9490272 **SL GRIFFIN** *9V7098* *ex* Lamnalco Griffin *-2013* - **Smit Lamnalco Singapore Pte Ltd** Smit Singapore Pte Ltd *Singapore* *Singapore* MMSI: 566875000 Official number: 398455	**1,314** 394 -	Class: BV	**2009**-10 **Guangdong Jiangmen Shipyard Co Ltd — Jiangmen GD** (Hull) Yd No: GMG0626 **2009**-10 **Greenbay Marine Pte Ltd — Singapore** Yd No: 168 Loa 49.50 Br ex - Dght 4.750 Lbp 41.60 Br md 15.00 Dpth 6.75 Welded, 1 dk	**(B32A2ST) Tug**	**2 oil engines** geared to sc. shafts driving 2 CP propellers Total Power: 4,800kW (6,526hp) Niigata 8L28HX 2 x 4 Stroke 8 Cy. 280 x 370 each-2400kW (3263bhp) Niigata Engineering Co Ltd-Japan AuxGen: 2 x 245kW a.c Thrusters: 1 Thwart. CP thruster (f) Fuel: 610.0
9362803 **SL JAMAL** - *ex* Lamnalco Jamal *-2012* - *ex* Swissco Swift *-2009* **Smit Lamnalco Ltd** - *Sharjah* *United Arab Emirates* Official number: 6292	**298** 89 -	Class: BV	**2005**-11 **Tuong Aik Shipyard Sdn Bhd — Sibu** Yd No: 2416 Loa 32.10 Br ex - Dght 3.500 Lbp 29.57 Br md 9.00 Dpth 4.20 Welded, 1 dk	**(B32A2ST) Tug**	**2 oil engines** reduction geared to sc. shafts driving 2 FP propellers Total Power: 1,766kW (2,402hp) 11.0kn Cummins KTA-38-M2 2 x Vee 4 Stroke 12 Cy. 159 x 159 each-883kW (1201bhp) Cummins Engine Co Inc-USA AuxGen: 2 x 156kW 415/230V 50Hz a.c Thrusters: 1 Tunnel thruster (f) Fuel: 200.0 (r.f.)

IMO / Call sign	Name / Owner / Port	Tonnage	Class	Builder / Dimensions	Type	Machinery
9670121 *P2V5578* -	**SL JAMBA** **Smit Lamnalco Singapore Pte Ltd** Smit Lamnalco Ltd *Port Moresby* Papua New Guinea MMSI: 553111710	**495** - 275	Class: LR (Class contemplated) **100A1** 12/2013	**2013-12 Hin Lee (Zhuhai) Shipyard Co Ltd — Zhuhai GD** (Hull) Yd No: 271 **2013-12 Cheoy Lee Shipyards Ltd — Hong Kong** Yd No: 5056 Loa 32.00 Br ex 13.20 Dght 5.680 Lbp 30.95 Br md 13.20 Dpth - Welded, 1 dk	**(B32A2ST) Tug**	**2 oil engines** reduction geared to sc. shaft (s) driving 2 Z propellers Total Power: 4,480kW (6,092hp) Caterpillar 3516C-HD 2 x Vee 4 Stroke 16 Cy. 170 x 215 each-2240kW (3046bhp) Caterpillar Inc-USA AuxGen: 2 x 270kW a.c
9638599 *5BTR3* -	**SL KESTREL** *ex* Dt Horizon *-2012* **Pacific Ocean Engineering & Trading Pte Ltd** *Limassol* Cyprus MMSI: 210198000	**168** 50 127	Class: LR (AB) **100A1** SS 09/2012 TOC contemplated	**2012-09 Bengbu Shenzhou Machinery Co Ltd — Bengbu AH** (Hull) Yd No: (1410) **2012-09 Pacific Ocean Engineering & Trading Pte Ltd (POET) — Singapore** Yd No: 1410 Loa 23.00 Br ex 8.60 Dght 3.290 Lbp 20.00 Br md 8.00 Dpth 4.25 Welded, 1 dk	**(B32A2ST) Tug**	**2 oil engines** reduction geared to sc. shafts driving 2 FP propellers Total Power: 1,264kW (1,718hp) Caterpillar 3412D 2 x Vee 4 Stroke 12 Cy. 145 x 162 each-632kW (859bhp) Caterpillar Inc-USA AuxGen: 2 x 82kW a.c Fuel: 80.0 (d.f.)
9638587 *5BTQ3* -	**SL KITE** *ex* DT Highway *-2013* **Smit Lamnalco Ltd** Lamnalco Sharjah Ltd *Limassol* Cyprus MMSI: 210195000	**168** 50 100	Class: LR (AB) **100A1** SS 06/2012 TOC contemplated	**2012-06 Bengbu Shenzhou Machinery Co Ltd — Bengbu AH** (Hull) Yd No: (1409) **2012-06 Pacific Ocean Engineering & Trading Pte Ltd (POET) — Singapore** Yd No: 1409 Loa 23.00 Br ex 8.60 Dght 3.300 Lbp 20.00 Br md 8.00 Dpth 4.25 Welded, 1 dk	**(B32A2ST) Tug**	**2 oil engines** reduction geared to sc. shafts driving 2 FP propellers Total Power: 1,264kW (1,718hp) Caterpillar 3412D 2 x Vee 4 Stroke 12 Cy. 145 x 162 each-632kW (859bhp) Caterpillar Inc-USA AuxGen: 2 x 82kW a.c
9588067 *5BTL3* -	**SL KITTIWAKE** - **Smit Lamnalco Ltd** - Cyprus MMSI: 210303000	**140** - 70	Class: BV	**2012-09 Damen Shipyards Cape Town — Cape Town** (Hull) Yd No: 509656 **2012-09 B.V. Scheepswerf Damen — Gorinchem** Yd No: 509656 Loa 22.57 Br ex - Dght 2.800 Lbp 20.42 Br md 7.84 Dpth 3.74 Welded, 1 dk	**(B32A2ST) Tug**	**2 oil engines** reduction geared to sc. shafts driving 2 FP propellers Total Power: 2,028kW (2,758hp) Caterpillar 3512B 2 x Vee 4 Stroke 12 Cy. 170 x 190 each-1014kW (1379bhp) Caterpillar Inc-USA AuxGen: 2 x 48kW 50Hz a.c Fuel: 36.0 (r.f.)
9679476 *5BAU4* -	**SL KIWI** **Smit Lamnalco Onshore Services Ltd** - *Limassol* Cyprus MMSI: 212298000	**121** 36 65	Class: BV	**2014-01 Brodogradiliste Novi Sad doo — Novi Sad** (Hull) Yd No: (509657) **2014-02 B.V. Scheepswerf Damen — Gorinchem** Yd No: 509657 Loa 22.57 Br ex 7.84 Dght 2.800 Lbp 22.00 Br md 7.80 Dpth 3.74 Welded, 1 dk	**(B32A2ST) Tug**	**2 oil engines** reduction geared to sc. shafts driving 2 Propellers Total Power: 3,530kW (4,800hp) Caterpillar 3512C 2 x Vee 4 Stroke 12 Cy. 170 x 215 each-1765kW (2400bhp) Caterpillar Inc-USA
9670133 *9V2685* -	**SL KOROWI** **Smit Lamnalco Singapore Pte Ltd** Smit Lamnalco Ltd *Singapore* Singapore MMSI: 564624000 Official number: 399318	**492** 147 275	Class: LR (Class contemplated) **100A1** 04/2014	**2014-04 Hin Lee (Zhuhai) Shipyard Co Ltd — Zhuhai GD** (Hull) Yd No: 272 **2014-04 Cheoy Lee Shipyards Ltd — Hong Kong** Yd No: 5057 Loa 32.00 Br ex 13.20 Dght 5.680 Lbp 30.95 Br md 13.20 Dpth - Welded, 1 dk	**(B32A2ST) Tug**	**2 oil engines** reduction geared to sc. shaft (s) driving 2 Z propellers Total Power: 4,480kW (6,092hp) Caterpillar 3516C-HD 2 x Vee 4 Stroke 16 Cy. 170 x 215 each-2240kW (3046bhp) Caterpillar Inc-USA AuxGen: 2 x 100kW a.c Fuel: 193.0
9596480 *9V9108* -	**SL LABUAN** *ex* Smit Labuan *-2013* *ex* Ocean Dahab *-2011* **Smit Lamnalco Labuan Pte Ltd** Smit Lamnalco Netherlands BV *Singapore* Singapore MMSI: 566031000 Official number: 396641	**1,696** 509 1,550	Class: LR (AB) **100A1** SS 06/2011 TOC contemplated	**2011-06 Guangxi Guijiang Shipyard — Wuzhou GX** Yd No: 01-2008-06 Loa 60.00 Br ex - Dght 4.200 Lbp 56.54 Br md 16.00 Dpth 6.00 Welded, 1 dk	**(B21B20A) Anchor Handling Tug Supply**	**2 oil engines** reduction geared to sc. shafts driving 2 FP propellers Total Power: 4,414kW (6,002hp) 12.5kn Yanmar 8N280M-SV 2 x 4 Stroke 8 Cy. 280 x 380 each-2207kW (3001bhp) Yanmar Diesel Engine Co Ltd-Japan AuxGen: 3 x 590kW a.c Thrusters: 2 Retract. directional thruster (f) Fuel: 520.0
9636503 *HP5726* -	**SL LIBREVILLE** *ex* Smit Libreville *-2013* **Smit Lamnalco Ltd** - *Panama* Panama MMSI: 355844000 Official number: 4473513	**613** 183 500	Class: BV	**2013-02 Santierul Naval Damen Galati S.A. — Galati** (Hull) Yd No: 1229 **2013-02 B.V. Scheepswerf Damen — Gorinchem** Yd No: 512013 Loa 40.75 Br ex 11.62 Dght 4.250 Lbp 34.98 Br md 11.00 Dpth 4.90 Welded, 1 dk	**(B32A2ST) Tug**	**2 oil engines** reduction geared to sc. shafts driving 2 FP propellers Total Power: 3,730kW (5,072hp) Caterpillar 3516B-HD 2 x Vee 4 Stroke 16 Cy. 170 x 215 each-1865kW (2536bhp) Caterpillar Inc-USA AuxGen: 3 x 218kW 50Hz a.c Thrusters: 1 Tunnel thruster (f) Fuel: 229.0
8217049 - -	**SL LIMAY 1** *ex* Limay. 1 *-2013* *ex* Soei Maru *-2011* **SMC Shipping & Lighterage Corp** - *La Union* Philippines Official number: 01-0000187	*160* 48 -		**1982-11 Kanagawa Zosen — Kobe** Yd No: 244 Loa 30.85 Br ex - Dght 2.701 Lbp 26.00 Br md 8.80 Dpth 3.80 Welded, 1 dk	**(B32A2ST) Tug**	**2 oil engines** Geared Integral to driving 2 Z propellers Total Power: 1,912kW (2,600hp) 12.9kn Fuji 6L27.5X 2 x 4 Stroke 6 Cy. 275 x 320 each-956kW (1300bhp) Fuji Diesel Co Ltd-Japan
8513986 *DUB2017* -	**SL LIMAY 2** *ex* Yawata Maru *-2011* *ex* Mineshima Maru *-2008* **SMC Shipping & Lighterage Corp** - *La Union* Philippines Official number: 01-0000203	*181* 55 -		**1985-08 Kanagawa Zosen — Kobe** Yd No: 277 Loa 35.01 Br ex - Dght 2.701 Lbp 31.00 Br md 8.60 Dpth 3.58 Welded, 1 dk	**(B32A2ST) Tug**	**2 oil engines** geared integral to driving 1 FP propeller , 1 Z propeller Total Power: 2,206kW (3,000hp) 12.5kn Niigata 6L25BX 2 x 4 Stroke 6 Cy. 250 x 320 each-1103kW (1500bhp) Niigata Engineering Co Ltd-Japan
8824555 - -	**SL LIMAY 3** *ex* Heiyo Maru *-2008* **SMC Shipping & Lighterage Corp** - *La Union* Philippines Official number: 01-0000213	*153* 46 -		**1989-01 Shin Yamamoto Shipbuilding & Engineering Co Ltd — Kochi KC** Yd No: 313 Loa 31.49 Br ex - Dght 2.000 Lbp 28.36 Br md 8.60 Dpth 3.75 Welded, 1 dk	**(B32A2ST) Tug**	**2 oil engines** geared integral to driving 2 Z propellers Total Power: 1,912kW (2,600hp) 11.7kn Niigata 6L25CXE 2 x 4 Stroke 6 Cy. 250 x 320 each-956kW (1300bhp) Niigata Engineering Co Ltd-Japan
8122921 - -	**SL LIMAY 4** *ex* Eiko Maru *-2012* *ex* Kiire Maru No. 2 *-1997* **SMC Shipping & Lighterage Corp** - *La Union* Philippines Official number: 01-0000323	*292* 88 -		**1982-09 Sanyo Zosen K.K. — Onomichi** Yd No: 830 Loa 33.63 Br ex 9.63 Dght 3.212 Lbp 29.11 Br md 9.61 Dpth 4.30 Welded, 1 dk	**(B32A2ST) Tug** Passengers: unberthed: 9	**2 oil engines** Geared Integral to driving 2 Z propellers Total Power: 2,354kW (3,200hp) 12.3kn Niigata 6L28BX 2 x 4 Stroke 6 Cy. 280 x 320 each-1177kW (1600bhp) Niigata Engineering Co Ltd-Japan AuxGen: 2 x 100kW 225V 60Hz a.c Fuel: 50.5 (d.f.) 11.0pd
9670145 *9V2744* -	**SL LOGOHU** **Smit Lamnalco Singapore Pte Ltd** Smit Lamnalco Ltd *Singapore* Singapore Official number: 399384	**492** 147 275	Class: LR (Class contemplated) **100A1** 04/2014	**2014-04 Hin Lee (Zhuhai) Shipyard Co Ltd — Zhuhai GD** (Hull) Yd No: 273 **2014-04 Cheoy Lee Shipyards Ltd — Hong Kong** Yd No: 5058 Loa 32.00 Br ex 13.20 Dght 5.680 Lbp 30.95 Br md 13.20 Dpth - Welded, 1 dk	**(B32A2ST) Tug**	**2 oil engines** reduction geared to sc. shaft (s) driving 2 Z propellers Total Power: 2,984kW (4,058hp) Caterpillar 3516C 2 x Vee 4 Stroke 16 Cy. 170 x 190 each-1492kW (2029bhp) Caterpillar Inc-USA
9337858 *DUO2013* -	**SL MAHOGANY** *ex* Samho Snipe *-2009* **SMC Shipping & Lighterage Corp** Swan Shipping Corp *La Union* Philippines MMSI: 548336100 Official number: 010000120	**2,479** 1,078 3,414 T/cm 10.1	Class: NK (KR)	**2006-02 Samho Shipbuilding Co Ltd — Tongyeong** Yd No: 1059 Loa 87.91 (BB) Br ex - Dght 5.813 Lbp 80.40 Br md 14.00 Dpth 7.30 Welded, 1 dk	**(A12B2TR) Chemical/Products Tanker** Double Hull (13F) Liq: 3,719; Liq (Oil): 3,937 Cargo Heating Coils Compartments: 1 Ta, 8 Wing Ta, 1 Slop Ta, ER 10 Cargo Pump (s): 10x200m³/hr Manifold: Bow/CM: 46.1m	**1 oil engine** driving 1 CP propeller Total Power: 2,206kW (2,999hp) 12.7kn Hanshin LH38L 1 x 4 Stroke 6 Cy. 380 x 760 2206kW (2999bhp) The Hanshin Diesel Works Ltd-Japan AuxGen: 3 x 260kW Thrusters: 1 Tunnel thruster (f) Fuel: 44.0 (d.f.) 151.0 (r.f.)
9383182 *VHMQ* -	**SL MALLARD** *ex* Lamnalco Mallard *-2013* **Smit Lamnalco Australia Pty Ltd** Lamnalco Sharjah Ltd *Dampier, WA* Australia MMSI: 503658000 Official number: 859396	**1,290** 386 941	Class: BV (AB)	**2008-02 ABG Shipyard Ltd — Surat** Yd No: 265 Loa 53.00 Br ex 13.82 Dght 4.800 Lbp 45.00 Br md 13.80 Dpth 6.00 Welded, 1 dk	**(B21B20A) Anchor Handling Tug Supply**	**2 oil engines** reduction geared to sc. shafts driving 2 Directional propellers Total Power: 5,364kW (7,292hp) 11.0kn Wartsila 8L26 2 x 4 Stroke 8 Cy. 260 x 320 each-2682kW (3646bhp) Wartsila Finland Oy-Finland AuxGen: 2 x 350kW a.c, 2 x 650kW a.c Thrusters: 1 Tunnel thruster (f)

8912716 *DUA2364* -	**SL MALUNGGAY** *ex* Kathrina **SMC Shipping & Lighterage Corp** - *La Union* *Philippines* Official number: 01-0000231	**993** 817 2,302	Class: (AB)	**1990-03 Keppel Philippines Shipyard Inc — Bauan** Yd No: 60 Loa 73.20 Br ex 13.62 Dght 2.960 Lbp 69.30 Br md 13.40 Dpth 3.96 Welded, 1 dk	**(A13B2TP) Products Tanker** Double Bottom Entire Compartment Length Liq: 3,656; Liq (Oil): 3,656	**2 oil engines** sr reverse geared to sc. shafts driving 2 FP propellers Total Power: 736kW (1,000hp) Cummins KTA-19-M 2 x 4 Stroke 6 Cy. 159 x 159 each-368kW (500bhp) Cummins Engine Co Inc-USA
9414113 *DUB2009* -	**SL MAPLE** *ex* Isle Grace *-2010* **SMC Shipping & Lighterage Corp** Swan Shipping Corp *La Union* *Philippines* MMSI: 548051200 Official number: 01-0000065	**3,999** 1,813 5,667 T/cm 13.6	Class: NK	**2008-01 Nakatani Shipyard Co. Ltd. — Etajima** Yd No: 612 Loa 99.91 (BB) Br ex - Dght 6.515 Lbp 94.00 Br md 16.30 Dpth 8.50 Welded, 1 dk	**(A12B2TR) Chemical/Products Tanker** Double Hull (13F) Liq: 6,342; Liq (Oil): 6,342 Cargo Heating Coils Compartments: 10 Wing Ta, ER, 1 Wing Slop Ta 10 Cargo Pump (s): 10x200m³/hr Manifold: Bow/CM: 42.1m	**1 oil engine** driving 1 FP propeller Total Power: 2,427kW (3,300hp) 12.5kn Hanshin LH41L 1 x 4 Stroke 6 Cy. 410 x 800 2427kW (3300bhp) The Hanshin Diesel Works Ltd-Japan AuxGen: 3 x a.c Thrusters: 1 Tunnel thruster (f) Fuel: 10.0 (d.f.) 200.0 (r.f.)
9688893 *H06248* -	**SL MBISSI** - **Smit Lamnalco Ltd** Smit International (Gabon) SA *Panama* *Panama* MMSI: 355273000 Official number: 45281PEXT	**140** 42 -	Class: BV	**2014-02 Damen Shipyards Kozle Sp z oo — Kedzierzyn-Kozle** (Hull) Yd No: (571702) **2014-02 B.V. Scheepswerf Damen Hardinxveld — Hardinxveld-Giessendam** Yd No: 571702 Loa 24.82 Br ex - Dght 1.800 Lbp 23.35 Br md 8.60 Dpth 2.99 Welded, 1 dk	**(B32A2ST) Tug**	**2 oil engines** reduction geared to sc. shafts driving 2 FP propellers Total Power: 1,000kW (1,360hp) Caterpillar C18 ACERT 2 x 4 Stroke 6 Cy. 145 x 183 each-500kW (680bhp) Caterpillar Inc-USA AuxGen: 3 x 55kW 400/230V 50Hz a.c Thrusters: 1 Tunnel thruster (f) Fuel: 46.0 (d.f.)
9572496 *5BFU3* -	**SL MESITE** *ex* Lamnalco Mesite *-2013* **Lamnalco Sharjah Ltd** - *Limassol* *Cyprus* MMSI: 209483000	**1,290** 387 853	Class: BV (AB)	**2011-04 ABG Shipyard Ltd — Surat** Yd No: 352 Loa 53.00 Br ex - Dght 4.800 Lbp 45.00 Br md 13.80 Dpth 6.00 Welded, 1 dk	**(B21B20A) Anchor Handling Tug Supply**	**2 oil engines** reduction geared to sc. shafts driving 2 Propellers Total Power: 6,120kW (8,320hp) 11.0kn Wartsila 9L26 2 x 4 Stroke 9 Cy. 260 x 320 each-3060kW (4160bhp) Wartsila Italia SpA-Italy AuxGen: 2 x 350kW a.c, 2 x 600kW a.c
9301706 *DUB2005* -	**SL MOLAVE** *ex* Alios Triton *-2009* **Carnelian Maritime SA** Swan Shipping Corp *La Union* *Philippines* Official number: 01-0000001	**3,997** 1,437 5,552 T/cm 14.2	Class: NK (LR) ✠ Classed LR until 10/2/12	**2005-11 K.K. Miura Zosensho — Saiki** Yd No: 1283 Loa 105.07 (BB) Br ex 17.02 Dght 6.300 Lbp 98.50 Br md 17.00 Dpth 9.00 Welded, 1 dk	**(A12B2TR) Chemical/Products Tanker** Double Hull (13F) Liq: 5,770; Liq (Oil): 5,769 Compartments: 10 Wing Ta, 2 Wing Slop Ta, ER 11 Cargo Pump (s): 10x200m³/hr, 1x100m³/hr Manifold: Bow/CM: 46.4m	**1 oil engine** with clutches, flexible couplings & sr reverse geared to sc. shaft driving 1 FP propeller Total Power: 2,500kW (3,399hp) 13.0kn Daihatsu 8DKM-28 1 x 4 Stroke 8 Cy. 280 x 390 2500kW (3399bhp) Daihatsu Diesel Manufacturing Co Lt-Japan AuxGen: 3 x 360kW 445V 60Hz a.c Boilers: TOH (o.f.) Thrusters: 1 Thwart. CP thruster (f) Fuel: 43.3 (d.f.) 180.0 (r.f.)
9216755 *DUB2012* -	**SL NARRA** *ex* DK Mogua *-2010* *ex* Jo Mogua *-2006* *ex* Eastern Phoenix *-2002* **El Ilustrado Shipping Corp** Swan Shipping Corp *La Union* *Philippines* MMSI: 548060200 Official number: 01-0000115	**2,166** 845 3,246 T/cm 9.9	Class: NK (KR) (NV) (BV)	**1999-09 Sasaki Shipbuilding Co Ltd — Osakikamijima HS** Yd No: 623 Loa 88.40 (BB) Br ex 14.02 Dght 5.512 Lbp 82.00 Br md 14.00 Dpth 6.51 Welded, 1 dk	**(A12B2TR) Chemical/Products Tanker** Double Hull (13F) Liq: 3,167; Liq (Oil): 2,968 Cargo Heating Coils Compartments: 1 Slop Ta (s.stl), 8 Wing Ta (s.stl), ER 8 Cargo Pump (s): 8x150m³/hr Manifold: Bow/CM: 44m	**1 oil engine** driving 1 FP propeller Total Power: 2,405kW (3,270hp) 13.0kn MAN-B&W 6S26MC 1 x 2 Stroke 6 Cy. 260 x 980 2405kW (3270bhp) The Hanshin Diesel Works Ltd-Japan AuxGen: 3 x 280kW 445V a.c Fuel: 55.0 (d.f.) 180.0 (r.f.)
8318154 *A8YC8* -	**SL SCHELDE 10** *ex* Schelde 10 *-2013* **Smit Lamnalco Netherlands BV** - *Monrovia* *Liberia* MMSI: 636015025 Official number: 15025	**235** 70 109	Class: LR ✠ **100A1** SS 05/2012 tug the area bounded by the lines, Hamburg to Hull & Brest to Lands End to Baltic Sea, North Sea, Irish Sea & English Channel, service between 61~N & 48~N ✠ **LMC** Eq.Ltr: F; Cable: 330.0/19.0 U2	**1987-05 Bodewes Binnenvaart B.V. — Millingen a/d Rijn** Yd No: 772 Loa 28.50 Br ex 9.15 Dght 3.252 Lbp 24.90 Br md 8.81 Dpth 4.27 Welded, 1 dk	**(B32A2ST) Tug**	**2 oil engines** with clutches, flexible couplings & sr reverse geared to sc. shafts driving 2 FP propellers Total Power: 1,800kW (2,448hp) 12.0kn MWM TBD440-6K 2 x 4 Stroke 6 Cy. 230 x 270 each-900kW (1224bhp) Motoren Werke Mannheim AG (MWM)-West Germany AuxGen: 2 x 70kW 380V 50Hz a.c Fuel: 84.0 (d.f.)
8325274 *A8YC9* -	**SL SCHELDE 12** *ex* Schelde 12 *-2013* **Smit Lamnalco Netherlands BV** - *Monrovia* *Liberia* MMSI: 636015026 Official number: 15026	*236* 70 143	Class: LR ✠ **100A1** SS 05/2013 tug for service in Baltic Sea, North Sea, Irish Sea and English Channel between 61~N and 48~N ✠ **LMC** Eq.Ltr: F; Cable: 332.5/19.0 U2	**1988-05 N.V. Scheepswerf van Rupelmonde — Rupelmonde** Yd No: 458 Loa 28.46 Br ex 9.13 Dght 3.261 Lbp 24.90 Br md 8.81 Dpth 4.25 Welded, 1 dk	**(B32A2ST) Tug**	**2 oil engines** with clutches, flexible couplings & sr reverse geared to sc. shafts driving 2 FP propellers Total Power: 2,040kW (2,774hp) 12.0kn Deutz SBV6M628 2 x 4 Stroke 6 Cy. 240 x 280 each-1020kW (1387bhp) Kloeckner Humboldt Deutz AG-West Germany AuxGen: 2 x 92kW 220/380V 50Hz a.c Thrusters: 1 Thwart. CP thruster (f) Fuel: 80.4 (d.f.) 9.1pd
9631060 *5BTS3* -	**SL SERVAL** - **Smit Lamnalco Netherlands BV** - *Limassol* *Cyprus* MMSI: 210578000	**453** 135 264	Class: LR ✠ **100A1** SS 11/2012 escort tug, fire-fighting Ship 1 (2400m3/h) **LMC** **UMS** Eq.Ltr: H; Cable: 302.5/22.0 U2 (a)	**2012-11 Santierul Naval Damen Galati S.A. — Galati** (Hull) Yd No: 1223 **2012-11 B.V. Scheepswerf Damen — Gorinchem** Yd No: 512512 Loa 32.70 Br ex 12.84 Dght 4.100 Lbp - Br md 12.82 Dpth 5.35 Welded, 1 dk	**(B32A2ST) Tug**	**2 oil engines** reduction geared to sc. shafts driving 2 Directional propellers Total Power: 5,050kW (6,866hp) Caterpillar 3516C-HD 2 x Vee 4 Stroke 16 Cy. 170 x 215 each-2525kW (3433bhp) Caterpillar Inc-USA AuxGen: 2 x 100kW 400V 50Hz a.c
9432452 *3EJN9* -	**SL STAR** *ex* Gold Stone *-2011* *ex* Kish Star *-2010* *ex* Ali 16 *-2009* *launched as* Xin Yong Qian 16 *-2007* **TTA Holding Corp** Sea Link Shipping LLC *Panama* *Panama* MMSI: 372575000 Official number: 3287407D	**2,827** 1,822 4,210	Class: IB	**2007-02 Zhejiang Dongfang Shipbuilding Co Ltd — Yueqing ZJ** Converted From: Container Ship (Fully Cellular)-2011 Loa 91.10 (BB) Br ex - Dght 6.000 Lbp 83.00 Br md 15.00 Dpth 7.30 Welded, 1 dk	**(A31A2GX) General Cargo Ship** TEU 198 Compartments: 2 Ho, ER 2 Ha: ER 2 (25.2 x -)	**1 oil engine** reduction geared to sc. shaft driving 1 Propeller Total Power: 1,325kW (1,801hp) 14.0kn Guangzhou 6320ZCD 1 x 4 Stroke 6 Cy. 320 x 440 1325kW (1801bhp) Guangzhou Diesel Engine Factory CoLtd-China AuxGen: 2 x 175kW a.c
8415720 - -	**SL SUAL 1** *ex* Tsukuba *-2011* **SMC Shipping & Lighterage Corp** - *La Union* *Philippines* Official number: 01-0000180	*161* 48 56		**1985-01 Keihin Dock Co Ltd — Yokohama** Yd No: 196 Loa 31.50 Br ex 9.02 Dght 2.701 Lbp 28.35 Br md 8.81 Dpth 3.61 Welded, 1 dk	**(B32A2ST) Tug**	**2 oil engines** Geared Integral to driving 2 Z propellers Total Power: 2,206kW (3,000hp) 12.5kn Niigata 6L25CXE 2 x 4 Stroke 6 Cy. 250 x 320 each-1103kW (1500bhp) Niigata Engineering Co Ltd-Japan
8402979 - -	**SL SUAL 2** *ex* Hanyo Maru *-2011* *ex* Hosyun Maru *-2003* *ex* Mitsui Maru *-1999* *ex* Buyou Maru *-1996* *ex* Miyuki Maru *-1994* **SMC Shipping & Lighterage Corp** - *La Union* *Philippines* Official number: 01-0000136	*158* 47 -		**1984-03 Kanagawa Zosen — Kobe** Yd No: 261 Loa 32.47 Br ex - Dght 2.701 Lbp 27.11 Br md 8.60 Dpth 3.77 Welded, 1 dk	**(B32A2ST) Tug**	**2 oil engines** geared integral to driving 2 Z propellers Total Power: 2,206kW (3,000hp) 12.9kn Niigata 6L25CXE 2 x 4 Stroke 6 Cy. 250 x 320 each-1103kW (1500bhp) Niigata Engineering Co Ltd-Japan
8741143 *9V2077* -	**SL-T1** *ex* Shun Yang 017 *-2010* *ex* Nan Gui Ji 017 *-2004* **STL II Marine Pte Ltd** - *Singapore* *Singapore* MMSI: 563024850 Official number: 398592	**1,484** 445 -	Class: RI	**2004-05 Shantang Navigation Shipyard Co Ltd — Qingyuan GD** Loa 75.16 Br ex - Dght 3.510 Lbp - Br md 15.20 Dpth 4.50 Welded, 1 dk	**(A24D2BA) Aggregates Carrier**	**2 oil engines** reduction geared to sc. shafts driving 2 Propellers Total Power: 880kW (1,196hp) 10.0kn Chinese Std. Type Z8170ZL 2 x 4 Stroke 8 Cy. 170 x 200 each-440kW (598bhp) Zibo Diesel Engine Factory-China
8741234 *V3NB8* -	**SL-T2** *ex* Shun Yang 018 *-2010* *ex* Nan Gui Ji 018 *-2003* **S L Ocean Ltd** - *Belize City* *Belize* MMSI: 312011000 Official number: 031020195	**1,465** 439 -		**2003-10 Shantang Navigation Shipyard Co Ltd — Qingyuan GD** Loa 73.03 Br ex - Dght - Lbp - Br md 15.20 Dpth 4.60 Welded, 1 dk	**(A24D2BA) Aggregates Carrier**	**2 oil engines** reduction geared to sc. shafts driving 2 Propellers Total Power: 880kW (1,196hp) 10.0kn Chinese Std. Type Z8170ZL 2 x 4 Stroke 8 Cy. 170 x 200 each-440kW (598bhp) Zibo Diesel Engine Factory-China

IMO / Call sign / Flag	Name / Former names / Owner / Port	Tonnage	Class	Build / Dimensions	Type	Machinery
8741246 *V3NQ8* -	**SL-T3** *ex* Shun Hong Hai 131 *-2010* *ex* Yue Xin Hui Huo 8082 *-2008* **S L Ocean Ltd** *Belize City* *Belize* MMSI: 312263000 Official number: 031020197	**683** 205 -		**2001-10 Lingshan Shipyard — Guangzhou GD** Loa 54.00 Br ex - Dght - Lbp - Br md 11.50 Dpth 3.84 Welded, 1 dk	**(A24D2BA) Aggregates Carrier**	**2 oil engines** reduction geared to sc. shafts driving 2 Propellers Total Power: 427kW (580hp)
9521617 *9V9805* -	**SL-T11** *ex* Winton T88 *-2011* *ex* Sui Dong Fang 098 *-2008* **STL I Marine Pte Ltd** - *Singapore* *Singapore* Official number: 398363	**687** 206 989	Class: RI	**2004-04 Guangzhou Panyu Lingshan Shipyard Ltd — Guangzhou GD** Yd No: 077 Loa 56.80 Br ex 13.20 Dght 3.190 Lbp 52.72 Br md 12.80 Dpth 3.80 Welded, 1 dk	**(A31A2GX) General Cargo Ship**	**2 oil engines** geared to sc. shafts driving 2 FP propellers Total Power: 576kW (784hp) 9.0kn Cummins NT-855-M 2 x 4 Stroke 6 Cy. 140 x 152 each-288kW (392bhp) Cummins Engine Co Inc-USA
9521605 *HP6737* -	**SL-T12** *ex* Winton T38 *-2011* *ex* Yue Guangzhou Huo 0228 *-2008* **S L Ocean Ltd** - *Panama* *Panama* Official number: 4057909A	**687** 206 989		**2003-12 Guangzhou Panyu Lingshan Shipyard Ltd — Guangzhou GD** Yd No: 132 Loa 56.80 Br ex 13.20 Dght 2.700 Lbp 52.72 Br md 12.80 Dpth 3.80 Welded, 1 dk	**(A31A2GX) General Cargo Ship**	**2 oil engines** geared to sc. shafts driving 2 FP propellers Total Power: 400kW (544hp) 9.0kn Cummins NT-855-M 2 x 4 Stroke 6 Cy. 140 x 152 each-200kW (272bhp) Cummins Engine Co Inc-USA
9511911 *HP7977* -	**SL-T13** *ex* Winton T68 *-2011* *ex* Yue Hui Zhou Huo 8292 *-2003* **S L Ocean Ltd** - *Panama* *Panama* Official number: 4056809A	**838** 251 1,474		**2003-12 Dongguan Dongsheng Shipyard Co Ltd — Dongguan GD** Loa 60.10 Br ex - Dght 3.350 Lbp 57.00 Br md 13.58 Dpth 4.05 Welded, 1 dk	**(A24D2BA) Aggregates Carrier**	**2 oil engines** geared to sc. shaft driving 2 FP propellers Total Power: 440kW (598hp) 9.0kn Weifang X6170ZC 2 x 4 Stroke 6 Cy. 170 x 200 each-220kW (299bhp) Weifang Diesel Engine Factory-China
8733419 *9VLD5* -	**SL-T14** *ex* Winton T168 *-2011* *ex* Zhengdong 128 *-2008* **STL I Marine Pte Ltd** - *Singapore* *Singapore* MMSI: 563022620 Official number: 398201	*1,645* 493 -	Class: RI	**2005-11 Dongguan Zhongtang Dongzhi Building Co Ltd — Dongguan GD** Loa 73.98 Br ex 17.30 Dght 3.690 Lbp 71.50 Br md 16.80 Dpth 4.90 Welded, 1 dk	**(A24D2BA) Aggregates Carrier**	**2 oil engines** geared to sc. shafts driving 2 Propellers Total Power: 1,086kW (1,476hp) 8.0kn Cummins KT-38-M 2 x Vee 4 Stroke 12 Cy. 159 x 159 each-543kW (738bhp) Chongqing Cummins Engine Co Ltd-China
9607215 *DUA3126* -	**SL TANGLAD** - **SMC Shipping & Lighterage Corp** - *La Union* *Philippines* Official number: 01-0000069	**665** 545 -	Class: (BV)	**2010-08 Dansyco Marine Works & Shipbuilding Corp — Manila** Yd No: 0901 Loa 62.90 Br ex - Dght 2.590 Lbp - Br md 12.80 Dpth 3.51 Welded, 1 dk	**(A12A2TC) Chemical Tanker** Double Hull (13F)	**2 oil engines** reduction geared to sc. shafts driving 2 FP propellers Total Power: 1,060kW (1,442hp) Mitsubishi 2 x 4 Stroke each-530kW (721bhp) Mitsubishi Heavy Industries Ltd-Japan
9631058 *5BTB3* -	**SL TIGER** - **Smit Lamnalco Netherlands BV** - *Limassol* *Cyprus* MMSI: 210211000	**453** 135 264	Class: LR ✠ **100A1** SS 10/2012 escort tug, fire-fighting Ship 1 (2400m3/h) **LMC** **UMS** Eq.Ltr: H; Cable: 302.5/22.0 U2 (a)	**2012-10 Santierul Naval Damen Galati S.A. — Galati** (Hull) Yd No: 1222 **2012-10 B.V. Scheepswerf Damen — Gorinchem** Yd No: 512511 Loa 32.70 Br ex 12.84 Dght 4.100 Lbp - Br md 12.82 Dpth 5.35 Welded, 1 dk	**(B32A2ST) Tug**	**2 oil engines** reduction geared to sc. shaft (s) driving 2 Directional propellers Total Power: 5,050kW (6,866hp) Caterpillar 3516C-HD 2 x Vee 4 Stroke 16 Cy. 170 x 215 each-2525kW (3433bhp) Caterpillar Inc-USA AuxGen: 2 x 100kW 400V 50Hz a.c
9375202 *C4QU2* -	**SL TROGON** *ex* Sl Tercel *-2013* *ex* Lamnalco Tercel *-2013* **Smit Lamnalco Netherlands BV** - *Limassol* *Cyprus* MMSI: 212936000	**454** 136 284	Class: BV (LR) ✠ Classed LR until 21/2/14	**2007-01 Guangdong Hope Yue Shipbuilding Industry Ltd — Guangzhou GD** Yd No: 2143 Loa 31.00 Br ex 11.54 Dght 4.600 Lbp 26.21 Br md 11.00 Dpth 5.60 Welded, 1 dk	**(B32A2ST) Tug**	**2 oil engines** gearing integral to driving 2 Z propellers Total Power: 4,000kW (5,438hp) 12.0kn Caterpillar 3516B 2 x Vee 4 Stroke 16 Cy. 170 x 215 each-2000kW (2719bhp) Caterpillar Inc-USA AuxGen: 2 x 136kW 380V 50Hz a.c Thrusters: 1 Directional thruster (f)
9375173 *C4QS2* -	**SL TWITE** *ex* Sl Tern *-2013* *ex* Lamnalco Tern *-2013* **Smit Lamnalco Ltd** - *Limassol* *Cyprus* MMSI: 210956000	**454** 136 294	Class: BV (LR) ✠ Classed LR until 17/2/09	**2006-12 Guangdong Hope Yue Shipbuilding Industry Ltd — Guangzhou GD** Yd No: 2140 Loa 31.00 Br ex 11.53 Dght 4.600 Lbp 26.21 Br md 11.00 Dpth 5.60 Welded, 1 dk	**(B32A2ST) Tug**	**2 oil engines** gearing integral to driving 2 Z propellers Total Power: 4,000kW (5,438hp) 12.0kn Caterpillar 3516B 2 x Vee 4 Stroke 16 Cy. 170 x 215 each-2000kW (2719bhp) Caterpillar Inc-USA AuxGen: 2 x 136kW 380V 50Hz a.c Thrusters: 1 Directional thruster (f)
9263007 - -	**SL VENUS 8** *ex* Venus Eight *-2013* **SMC Shipping & Lighterage Corp** - *La Union* *Philippines* Official number: 01-0000545	**2,987** 1,373 3,826	Class: NK	**2002-04 Kegoya Dock K.K. — Kure** Yd No: 1070 Loa 84.75 (BB) Br ex - Dght 5.952 Lbp 79.00 Br md 14.70 Dpth 9.20 Welded, 1 dk	**(A31A2GX) General Cargo Ship** Grain: 6,576 Compartments: 2 Ho, ER 2 Ha: (11.2 x 10.4)ER (25.2 x 10.4) Cranes: 2x30t; Derricks: 1x30t	**1 oil engine** driving 1 FP propeller Total Power: 2,059kW (2,799hp) 12.0kn Hanshin LH38L 1 x 4 Stroke 6 Cy. 380 x 760 2059kW (2799bhp) The Hanshin Diesel Works Ltd-Japan AuxGen: 2 x a.c Fuel: 310.0
9298349 *DUB2020* -	**SL YAKAL** *ex* MMM Ashton *-2011* *ex* Samho Family *-2006* **SMC Shipping & Lighterage Corp** Aboitiz Jebsens Shipmanagement Inc *La Union* *Philippines* MMSI: 548059200 Official number: 01-0000237	**2,479** 1,078 3,442 T/cm 10.2	Class: LR (KR) **100A1** SS 10/2009 Double Hull oil tanker ESP LI **LMC** Eq.Ltr: S; Cable: 467.5/42.0 U2 (a)	**2004-10 Samho Shipbuilding Co Ltd — Tongyeong** Yd No: 1045 Converted From: Chemical/Products Tanker-2008 Loa 87.90 (BB) Br ex - Dght 5.800 Lbp 80.40 Br md 14.00 Dpth 7.30 Welded, 1 dk	**(A13B2TP) Products Tanker** Double Hull (13F) Liq: 3,719; Liq (Oil): 3,938 Compartments: 1 Ta, 8 Wing Ta, 1 Slop Ta, ER 10 Cargo Pump (s): 10x200m³/hr Manifold: Bow/CM: 44m	**1 oil engine** with clutches, flexible couplings & reverse geared to sc. shaft driving 1 CP propeller Total Power: 2,205kW (2,998hp) 12.7kn MAN-B&W 9L28/32A 1 x 4 Stroke 9 Cy. 280 x 320 2205kW (2998bhp) STX Engine Co Ltd-South Korea AuxGen: 3 x 260kW 445V 60Hz a.c Boilers: e (ex.g.) 11.7kgf/cm² (11.5bar), WTAuxB (o.f.) 9.2kgf/cm² (9.0bar) Thrusters: 1 Tunnel thruster (f) Fuel: 50.0 (d.f.) 171.0 (r.f.)
9147174 *LMMS* H-10-AV	**SLAATTEROY** *ex* Research W *-2004* **K Halstensen AS** - *Bergen* *Norway* MMSI: 258547000	**1,821** 546 2,500	Class: NV	**1997-01 Slipen Mek. Verksted AS — Sandnessjoen** Yd No: 58 Loa 67.40 (BB) Br ex - Dght 5.800 Lbp 60.60 Br md 13.00 Dpth 5.80 Welded, 1 dk	**(B11A2FS) Stern Trawler** Ins: 1,800	**1 oil engine** geared to sc. shaft driving 1 FP propeller Total Power: 6,560kW (8,919hp) Wartsila 16V32E 1 x Vee 4 Stroke 16 Cy. 320 x 350 6560kW (8919bhp) Wartsila Propulsion AS-Norway AuxGen: 1 x 169kW 230/440V 60Hz a.c, 2 x 515kW 230/440V 60Hz a.c Thrusters: 1 Thwart. FP thruster (f); 1 Tunnel thruster (a)
9382293 *WDE2559* -	**SLAM DUNK** - **GulfMark Americas Inc** - *New Orleans, LA* *United States of America* MMSI: 367326530 Official number: 1204681	**1,691** 507 2,129	Class: AB	**2007-12 Bollinger Machine Shop & Shipyard, Inc. — Lockport, La** Yd No: 525 Loa 68.23 Br ex - Dght 4.900 Lbp 65.27 Br md 14.02 Dpth 5.50 Welded, 1 dk	**(B21A2OS) Platform Supply Ship** Passengers: cabins: 6	**3 diesel electric oil engines** driving 2 gen. each 1235kW 480V a.c 1 gen. of 435kW 480V a.c Connecting to 3 elec. motors each (843kW) driving 3 Z propellers Fixed unit Total Power: 2,905kW (3,949hp) 10.5kn Cummins KTA-19-M 1 x 4 Stroke 6 Cy. 159 x 159 435kW (591bhp) Cummins Engine Co Inc-USA Cummins KTA-50-M2 2 x Vee 4 Stroke 16 Cy. 159 x 159 each-1235kW (1679bhp) Cummins Engine Co Inc-USA Thrusters: 2 Tunnel thruster (f) Fuel: 513.0 (r.f.)
7409425 - -	**SLAMET VIII** - **PT PERTAMINA (PERSERO)** - *Jakarta* *Indonesia*	*647* 281 700 T/cm 4.1	Class: (KI)	**1977-06 P.T. Adiguna Shipbuilding & Engineering — Jakarta** Yd No: 54 Loa 57.26 Br ex - Dght 3.101 Lbp 52.02 Br md 9.01 Dpth 4.02 Welded, 1 dk	**(A13B2TP) Products Tanker** Liq: 1,050; Liq (Oil): 1,050 Compartments: 8 Ta, ER 2 Cargo Pump (s): 2x150m³/hr Manifold: Bow/CM: 38m	**1 oil engine** driving 1 FP propeller Total Power: 515kW (700hp) Niigata 6MG20AX 1 x 4 Stroke 6 Cy. 200 x 260 515kW (700bhp) Niigata Engineering Co Ltd-Japan Fuel: 36.5 (d.f.)
7431454 - -	**SLAMET XX** *ex* Slamet XVIII *-2004* *ex* Kalimambang *-2004* **PT PERTAMINA (PERSERO)** - *Jakarta* *Indonesia*	*116* 68 137	Class: (KI)	**1967 P.T. Indomarine — Jakarta** Loa - Br ex - Dght - Lbp 26.95 Br md 6.00 Dpth 2.06 Welded, 1 dk	**(A13B2TU) Tanker (unspecified)**	**1 oil engine** driving 1 FP propeller Total Power: 107kW (145hp) 7.0kn MAN D2146HM 1 x 4 Stroke 6 Cy. 121 x 140 107kW (145bhp) Maschinenbau Augsburg Nuernberg (MAN)-Augsburg AuxGen: 1 x 1kW

7941760 *UHIL* -	**SLANTSY** **JSC 'Fishery Kolkhoz Primorets'** - *Nakhodka* *Russia* MMSI: 273826600 Official number: 802145	**775** 221 327	Class: RS	**1980 Volgogradskiy Sudostroitelnyy Zavod — Volgograd** Yd No: 894 Loa 53.73 (BB) Br ex 10.72 Dght 4.290 Lbp 47.92 Br md 10.50 Dpth 6.00 Welded, 1 dk	**(B11A2FS) Stern Trawler** Ins: 218 Compartments: 1 Ho, ER 2 Ha: 2 (1.6 x 1.6) Derricks: 2x3.3t Ice Capable	**1 oil engine** driving 1 CP propeller Total Power: 971kW (1,320hp) 12.8kn S.K.L. 8NVD48A-2U 1 x 4 Stroke 8 Cy. 320 x 480 971kW (1320bhp) VEB Schwermaschinenbau "KarlLiebknecht" (SKL)-Magdeburg Thrusters: 1 Thwart. FP thruster (f); 1 Tunnel thruster (a) Fuel: 182.0 (d.f.)
9131591 *OW2333* -	**SLATTABERG** *ex* Kanstadfjord *-2012* *ex* Solvar Viking *-2006* *ex* Gunnar Langva *-2004* *ex* Serene *-1997* **P/F Naeraberg** P/F J F K Trol SatCom: Inmarsat C 423107810 *Faeroes (FAS)* MMSI: 231078000	**1,428** 429 -	Class: NV	**1995-06 Flekkefjord Slipp & Maskinfabrikk AS AS — Flekkefjord** Yd No: 159 Loa 57.20 (BB) Br ex - Dght 7.000 Lbp 50.40 Br md 12.00 Dpth 8.20 Welded, 1 dk	**(B11A2FS) Stern Trawler** Ins: 1,000	**1 oil engine** reduction geared to sc. shaft driving 1 CP propeller Total Power: 2,206kW (2,999hp) 16.0kn Wichmann 12V28B 1 x Vee 2 Stroke 12 Cy. 280 x 360 2206kW (2999bhp) Wartsila Propulsion AS-Norway AuxGen: 1 x 1520kW 230/440V 60Hz a.c, 2 x 450kW 230/440V 60Hz a.c Thrusters: 1 Thwart. CP thruster (f); 1 Tunnel thruster (a) Fuel: 380.0 (d.f.) 15.0pd
9144043 *9HA3175* -	**SLAVNIK** *ex* Glen Mooar *-2009* *ex* Antuco *-2005* **Genshipping Corp** Splosna Plovba doo (Splosna plovba International Shipping & Chartering Ltd) *Valletta* *Malta* MMSI: 229251000 Official number: 9144043	**25,537** 15,927 46,570 T/cm 49.9	Class: AB	**1998-11 Oshima Shipbuilding Co Ltd — Saikai NS** Yd No: 10228 Loa 183.00 (BB) Br ex - Dght 11.788 Lbp 174.30 Br md 30.95 Dpth 16.40 Welded, 1 dk	**(A21A2BC) Bulk Carrier** Double Bottom Entire Compartment Length Grain: 58,209; Bale: 57,083 Compartments: 5 Ho, ER 5 Ha: (17.1 x 15.6)4 (19.8 x 15.6)ER Cranes: 4x30t	**1 oil engine** driving 1 FP propeller Total Power: 7,595kW (10,326hp) 14.3kn Sulzer 6RTA48T 1 x 2 Stroke 6 Cy. 480 x 2000 7595kW (10326bhp) Diesel United Ltd.-Aioi AuxGen: 3 x 440kW 450V 60Hz a.c Fuel: 125.0 (d.f.) (Heating Coils) 1727.0 (r.f.) 29.2pd
8138504 *UGPZ* -	**SLAVNYY** *ex* Bologoe *-2000* *ex* Bambene *-1996* *ex* Bologoye *-1984* **Fishmarine-DV LLC** - *Vladivostok* *Russia* MMSI: 273890400	**806** 217 405	Class: (LR) (RS) Classed LR until 26/3/97	**1983-08 Zavod "Leninskaya Kuznitsa" — Kiyev** Yd No: 1526 Loa 54.80 Br ex 9.95 Dght 4.090 Lbp 49.40 Br md 9.77 Dpth 4.99 Welded, 1 dk	**(B11A2FS) Stern Trawler** Ice Capable	**1 oil engine** driving 1 CP propeller Total Power: 736kW (1,001hp) 12.0kn S.K.L. 8NVD48A-2U 1 x 4 Stroke 8 Cy. 320 x 480 736kW (1001bhp) VEB Schwermaschinenbau "KarlLiebknecht" (SKL)-Magdeburg AuxGen: 4 x 150kW 400V 50Hz a.c Fuel: 180.0 (d.f.)
7533874 *UHBG* -	**SLAVSK** **OOO 'Nemusco'** - *Nakhodka* *Russia* MMSI: 273412070	**175** 52 101	Class: (RS)	**1975-10 Sretenskiy Sudostroitelnyy Zavod — Sretensk** Yd No: 83 Loa 33.96 Br ex 7.09 Dght 2.900 Lbp 30.00 Br md 7.00 Dpth 3.69 Welded, 1 dk	**(B11B2FV) Fishing Vessel** Bale: 96 Compartments: 1 Ho, ER 1 Ha: (1.3 x 1.6) Derricks: 2x2t; Winches: 2 Ice Capable	**1 oil engine** driving 1 FP propeller Total Power: 224kW (305hp) 9.0kn S.K.L. 8NVD36-1U 1 x 4 Stroke 8 Cy. 240 x 360 224kW (305bhp) VEB Schwermaschinenbau "KarlLiebknecht" (SKL)-Magdeburg Fuel: 20.0 (d.f.)
8857942 *UTHL* -	**SLAVUTICH-9** **'Ukrrichflot' Joint Stock Shipping Co** - *Kherson* *Ukraine* MMSI: 272040000	**2,193** 658 3,221	Class: RR	**1988-08 Kiyevskiy Sudostroitelnyy Sudoremontnyy Zavod — Kiyev** Yd No: 9 Loa 109.00 Br ex 16.22 Dght 3.200 Lbp 105.20 Br md 16.00 Dpth 4.00 Welded, 1 dk	**(A31A2GX) General Cargo Ship**	**2 oil engines** driving 2 FP propellers Total Power: 1,294kW (1,760hp) S.K.L. 8NVD48-2U 2 x 4 Stroke 8 Cy. 320 x 480 each-647kW (880bhp) VEB Schwermaschinenbau "KarlLiebknecht" (SKL)-Magdeburg
8841527 *C4LR2* -	**SLAVUTICH 13** **Impresa di Costruzioni Ing E Mantovani SpA** Nova Mar Srl *Limassol* *Cyprus* MMSI: 209761000 Official number: 8841527	**2,193** 658 3,221	Class: RS	**1988 Kiyevskiy Sudostroitelnyy Sudoremontnyy Zavod — Kiyev** Yd No: 13 Loa 109.00 Br ex 16.22 Dght 3.200 Lbp 105.20 Br md 16.00 Dpth 4.00 Welded, 1 dk	**(A31A2GX) General Cargo Ship**	**2 oil engines** driving 2 FP propellers Total Power: 1,294kW (1,760hp) S.K.L. 8NVD48-2U 2 x 4 Stroke 8 Cy. 320 x 480 each-647kW (880bhp) VEB Schwermaschinenbau "KarlLiebknecht" (SKL)-Magdeburg
8841541 *UVZL* -	**SLAVUTICH-15** *ex* Sunrise III *-2008* *ex* Sunrise *-2001* *ex* Slavutich-15 *-2000* *ex* Nattem VIII *-2000* *ex* Slavutich-15 *-1993* **Delta Shipping Agency** - *Nikolayev* *Ukraine* MMSI: 272231000	**2,193** 658 3,111	Class: UA	**1990-06 Kiyevskiy Sudostroitelnyy Sudoremontnyy Zavod — Kiyev** Yd No: 15 Loa 109.00 Br ex 16.22 Dght 3.300 Lbp 105.20 Br md 16.00 Dpth 4.00 Welded, 1 dk	**(A31A2GX) General Cargo Ship** Compartments: 1 Ho	**2 oil engines** driving 2 FP propellers Total Power: 1,294kW (1,760hp) 10.0kn S.K.L. 8NVD48-2U 2 x 4 Stroke 8 Cy. 320 x 480 each-647kW (880bhp) VEB Schwermaschinenbau "KarlLiebknecht" (SKL)-Magdeburg
8848783 *ENYT* -	**SLAVUTICH-16** **'Ukrrichflot' Joint Stock Shipping Co** - SatCom: Inmarsat C 427204610 *Kherson* *Ukraine* MMSI: 272046000	**2,193** 658 3,221	Class: RR UA	**1991-08 Kiyevskiy Sudostroitelnyy Sudoremontnyy Zavod — Kiyev** Yd No: 16 Loa 109.00 Br ex 16.22 Dght 3.200 Lbp 105.20 Br md 16.00 Dpth 4.00 Welded, 1 dk	**(A31A2GX) General Cargo Ship**	**2 oil engines** driving 2 FP propellers Total Power: 1,294kW (1,760hp) S.K.L. 8NVD48-2U 2 x 4 Stroke 8 Cy. 320 x 480 each-647kW (880bhp) SKL Motoren u. Systemtechnik AG-Magdeburg
8892136 *ENYR* -	**SLAVUTICH-17** **'Ukrrichflot' Joint Stock Shipping Co** - *Kherson* *Ukraine* MMSI: 272064000	**2,193** 658 3,221	Class: RR	**1991-12 Kiyevskiy Sudostroitelnyy Sudoremontnyy Zavod — Kiyev** Yd No: 17 Loa 109.00 Br ex 16.22 Dght 3.200 Lbp 105.20 Br md 16.00 Dpth 4.00 Welded, 1 dk	**(A31A2GX) General Cargo Ship**	**2 oil engines** driving 2 FP propellers Total Power: 1,294kW (1,760hp) S.K.L. 8NVD48-2U 2 x 4 Stroke 8 Cy. 320 x 480 each-647kW (880bhp) SKL Motoren u. Systemtechnik AG-Magdeburg
8826840 *UBLH7* -	**SLAVYANETS** **JSC Slavyanka Shipyard (JSC 'Slavyanskiy Sudoremontnyy)** - *Vladivostok* *Russia*	**270** 81 89	Class: RS	**1990-01 Brodogradiliste 'Tito' — Belgrade** Yd No: 1128 Loa 35.78 Br ex 9.49 Dght 3.282 Lbp 30.23 Br md 9.00 Dpth 4.50 Welded, 1 dk	**(B32A2ST) Tug**	**2 oil engines** driving 1 CP propeller Total Power: 1,854kW (2,520hp) 13.5kn Sulzer 6ASL25D 2 x 4 Stroke 6 Cy. 250 x 300 each-927kW (1260bhp) Tvornica Dizel Motora 'Jugoturbina'-Yugoslavia AuxGen: 1 x 150kW a.c
8300169 - -	**SLAVYANIN** *ex* Asrar *-2007* *ex* Pacific *-2006* *ex* Scan Baltic *-2005* *ex* Baltic *-2003* *ex* Baltic Link *-2003* **Starway Management Property Ltd** Anship LLC *Zanzibar* *Tanzania (Zanzibar)*	**6,327** 1,898 6,258	Class: UA (LR) ✠ Classed LR until 1/4/08	**1984-06 Rauma-Repola Oy — Rauma** Yd No: 285 Converted From: Ro-Ro Cargo Ship-2009 Lengthened & Rebuilt-2009 Loa 150.20 Br ex - Dght 4.500 Lbp 139.94 Br md 22.00 Dpth 8.00 Welded, 2 dks	**(A35A2RT) Rail Vehicles Carrier** Stern door/ramp Side doors (s) Rail Wagons: 50 Bale: 13,264 Compartments: 1 Ho, ER Ice Capable	**1 oil engine** with clutches, flexible couplings & sr geared to sc. shaft driving 1 CP propeller Total Power: 5,500kW (7,478hp) 12.0kn Pielstick 10PC2-6V-400 1 x Vee 4 Stroke 10 Cy. 400 x 460 5500kW (7478bhp) Oy Wartsila Ab-Finland AuxGen: 1 x 480kW 450V 60Hz a.c, 3 x 275kW 450V 60Hz a.c Thrusters: 1 Tunnel thruster (f); 1 Tunnel thruster (a) Fuel: 119.5 (d.f.) 456.5 (r.f.) 21.5pd
8136324 *UGHO* -	**SLAVYANKA** **Gold Fish Co Ltd (OOO 'Gold Fish')** - *Petropavlovsk-Kamchatskiy* *Russia* MMSI: 273567800 Official number: 821636	**779** 233 332	Class: (RS)	**1983-05 Volgogradskiy Sudostroitelnyy Zavod — Volgograd** Yd No: 209 Loa 53.75 (BB) Br ex 10.72 Dght 4.290 Lbp 47.92 Br md - Dpth 6.02 Welded, 1 dk	**(B11A2FS) Stern Trawler** Ins: 218 Compartments: 1 Ho, ER 1 Ha: (1.6 x 1.6) Derricks: 2x1.5t Ice Capable	**1 oil engine** driving 1 FP propeller Total Power: 971kW (1,320hp) 12.8kn S.K.L. 8NVD48A-2U 1 x 4 Stroke 8 Cy. 320 x 480 971kW (1320bhp) VEB Schwermaschinenbau "KarlLiebknecht" (SKL)-Magdeburg Fuel: 182.0 (d.f.)
8869969 *UHVR* -	**SLAVYANKA** *ex* Omskiy-110 *-1993* **High River Shipping Ltd** Dimar-Freight Co Ltd (OOO 'Dimar-Frakht') *Taganrog* *Russia* MMSI: 273415410	**2,426** 966 3,174	Class: RS	**1982-09 Santierul Naval Oltenita S.A. — Oltenita** Yd No: 135 Loa 108.40 Br ex 15.00 Dght 3.260 Lbp 105.00 Br md - Dpth 5.00 Welded, 1 dk	**(A31A2GX) General Cargo Ship**	**2 oil engines** driving 2 FP propellers Total Power: 1,030kW (1,400hp) S.K.L. 6NVD48A-2U 2 x 4 Stroke 6 Cy. 320 x 480 each-515kW (700bhp) VEB Schwermaschinenbau "KarlLiebknecht" (SKL)-Magdeburg
8726002 *UHPL* -	**SLAVYANSKAYA** **Nafta Technologes Co Ltd** Maritime Technologies Co Ltd (OOO Morskiye Tekhnologii) *Nakhodka* *Russia* MMSI: 273457820	**745** 223 1,068	Class: RS	**1988-07 Santierul Naval Drobeta-Turnu Severin S.A. — Drobeta-Turnu S.** Yd No: 1340001 Loa 56.19 Br ex 11.21 Dght 3.700 Lbp 53.20 Br md 11.19 Dpth 4.44 Welded, 1 dk	**(B34A2SH) Hopper, Motor** Ice Capable	**2 oil engines** driving 2 FP propellers Total Power: 574kW (780hp) 8.9kn S.K.L. 6NVD26A-3 2 x 4 Stroke 6 Cy. 180 x 260 each-287kW (390bhp) VEB Schwermaschinenbau "KarlLiebknecht" (SKL)-Magdeburg AuxGen: 2 x 100kW a.c

IMO / Call sign	Name / Owner / Flag	Tonnage	Class	Builder / Dimensions	Type	Machinery
8744872 - -	**SLC 721** *ex* Shen Lian Cheng 721 *-2007* **Luen Thai Fishing Venture Ltd** Marshall Islands Fishing Venture Inc	**129** 39 99		**2007-01 Longhai Xingming Shipbuilding Industry Co Ltd — Longhai FJ** Yd No: 702 Loa 29.90 Br ex - Dght - Lbp - Br md 5.80 Dpth 2.85 Welded, 1 dk	**(B11B2FV) Fishing Vessel**	**2 oil engines** reduction geared to sc. shafts driving 2 Propellers Total Power: 596kW (810hp) Cummins NTA-855-M 2 x 4 Stroke 6 Cy. 140 x 152 each-298kW (405bhp) Chongqing Cummins Engine Co Ltd-China
8744884 - -	**SLC 722** *ex* Shen Lian Cheng 722 *-2007* **Luen Thai Fishing Venture Ltd** Marshall Islands Fishing Venture Inc	**129** 39 99		**2007-01 Longhai Xingming Shipbuilding Industry Co Ltd — Longhai FJ** Yd No: 703 Loa 29.90 Br ex - Dght - Lbp - Br md 5.80 Dpth 2.85 Welded, 1 dk	**(B11B2FV) Fishing Vessel**	**2 oil engines** reduction geared to sc. shafts driving 2 Propellers Total Power: 596kW (810hp) Cummins NTA-855-M 2 x 4 Stroke 6 Cy. 140 x 152 each-298kW (405bhp) Chongqing Cummins Engine Co Ltd-China
8744896 - -	**SLC 723** *ex* Shen Lian Cheng 723 *-2007* **Luen Thai Fishing Venture Ltd** Marshall Islands Fishing Venture Inc	**129** 39 99		**2007-01 Longhai Zishun Shipbuilding Industry Co Ltd — Longhai FJ** Yd No: 692 Loa 29.90 Br ex - Dght - Lbp - Br md 5.80 Dpth 2.85 Welded, 1 dk	**(B11B2FV) Fishing Vessel**	**2 oil engines** reduction geared to sc. shafts driving 2 Propellers Total Power: 596kW (810hp) Cummins NTA-855-M 2 x 4 Stroke 6 Cy. 140 x 152 each-298kW (405bhp) Chongqing Cummins Engine Co Ltd-China
8744901 - -	**SLC 725** *ex* Shen Lian Cheng 725 *-2007* - - *Micronesia*	**129** 39 99		**2007-01 Longhai Zishun Shipbuilding Industry Co Ltd — Longhai FJ** Yd No: 693 Loa 29.90 Br ex - Dght - Lbp - Br md 5.80 Dpth 2.85 Welded, 1 dk	**(B11B2FV) Fishing Vessel**	**2 oil engines** reduction geared to sc. shafts driving 2 Propellers Total Power: 596kW (810hp) Cummins NTA-855-M 2 x 4 Stroke 6 Cy. 140 x 152 each-298kW (405bhp) Chongqing Cummins Engine Co Ltd-China
8626989 *MKLU5* -	**SLEAT** *ex* Sound of Sleat *-2004* *ex* De Hoorn *-1988* **Shearwater Marine Services Ltd** - *Glasgow United Kingdom* MMSI: 235008071 Official number: 711873	*466* 155 266 T/cm 4.0		**1961-03 NV Scheepswerf & Mfbk 'De Merwede' v/h van Vliet & Co — Hardinxveld** Loa 40.82 Br ex 15.32 Dght 3.330 Lbp 37.39 Br md 15.21 Dpth 4.86 Welded, 1 dk	**(A36A2PR) Passenger/Ro-Ro Ship (Vehicles)** Passengers: unberthed: 220 Bow door/ramp Len: 1.20 Wid: 4.00 Swl: - Stern door/ramp Len: 1.20 Wid: 4.00 Swl: - Side ramp1 (p) 1 (s) Lane-Len: 131 Lane-Wid: 2.70 Lane-clr ht: 4.00 Lorries: 4, Cars: 30	**2 oil engines** gearing integral to driving 2 Voith-Schneider propellers 1 fwd and 1 aft Total Power: 478kW (650hp) 8.0kn Stork DR0218K 2 x 4 Stroke 8 Cy. 210 x 300 each-239kW (325bhp) Koninklijke Machinefabriek GebrStork & Co NV-Netherlands AuxGen: 2 x 55kW 110/380V d.c Thrusters: 2 Thwart. CP thruster (f) Fuel: 120.7 (d.f.) 25.0pd
7320588 - -	**SLEBECH** *ex* Beti Donosti *-1981* - -	*207* 108 -	Class: (BV)	**1974-02 Astilleros del Atlantico S.A. — Santander** Yd No: 161 Loa 35.82 Br ex 6.81 Dght - Lbp 30.03 Br md 6.79 Dpth 3.71 Welded, 1 dk	**(B11B2FV) Fishing Vessel**	**1 oil engine** driving 1 FP propeller Total Power: 765kW (1,040hp) 11.0kn MaK 6M452AK 1 x 4 Stroke 6 Cy. 320 x 450 765kW (1040bhp) MaK Maschinenbau GmbH-Kiel Fuel: 90.5 (d.f.)
8882739 - LA 568	**SLEE II** - **First City Fishing Co Ltd** - *Lagos Nigeria*	*148* 99 -		**1990 Ocean Marine, Inc. — Bayou La Batre, Al** Yd No: 246 Loa - Br ex - Dght - Lbp - Br md - Dpth - Welded, 1 dk	**(B11B2FV) Fishing Vessel**	**1 oil engine** driving 1 FP propeller
7908108 *WYD2401* -	**SLEEP ROBBER** - **Dynatrax Inc** - *Honolulu, HI United States of America* Official number: 591482	*144* 111 -		**1978-06 Hillstrom Shipbuilding Co., Inc. — Coos Bay, Or** Yd No: 35 Loa - Br ex - Dght - Lbp 23.50 Br md 6.72 Dpth 3.36 Welded, 1 dk	**(B11A2FS) Stern Trawler**	**1 oil engine** driving 1 FP propeller Total Power: 268kW (364hp) Caterpillar 3412T 1 x Vee 4 Stroke 12 Cy. 137 x 152 268kW (364bhp) Caterpillar Tractor Co-USA
7825552 *J8B4172* -	**SLEIPNER** *ex* Ardal *-1992* **Arctic Resource Norge AS** Triton Shipping AB *Kingstown St Vincent & The Grenadines* MMSI: 377294000 Official number: 10645	*753* 418 825	Class: NV	**1980-01 AS Mjellem & Karlsen — Bergen** Yd No: 127 Loa 49.66 Br ex 11.03 Dght 3.550 Lbp 45.12 Br md 11.00 Dpth 7.24 Welded, 1 dk	**(A31B2GP) Palletised Cargo Ship** Lane-Len: 45 Lane-Wid: 8.00 Lane-clr ht: 2.30 Bale: 1,130; Ins: 70 TEU 754 C. 754/20' Compartments: 1 Ho, ER 1 Ha: (6.4 x 2.9)ER Cranes: 1x10t; Derricks: 1x20t; Winches: 1 Ice Capable	**1 oil engine** geared to sc. shaft driving 1 FP propeller Total Power: 956kW (1,300hp) 12.0kn Normo LDM-8 1 x 4 Stroke 8 Cy. 250 x 300 956kW (1300bhp) AS Bergens Mek Verksteder-Norway AuxGen: 2 x 118kW 380V 50Hz a.c Thrusters: 1 Thwart. FP thruster (f)
6816358 *E5U2695* -	**SLEIPNER** *ex* Deirdre *-2012* **Pilot Sp/F** - *Cook Islands* MMSI: 518748000 Official number: 332523	**122** 36 298	Class: (LR) ✠ Classed LR until 1/7/12	**1968-06 N.V. Scheepswerf van Rupelmonde — Rupelmonde** Yd No: 396 Loa 28.02 Br ex 7.62 Dght 2.817 Lbp 25.13 Br md 7.01 Dpth 3.05 Welded, 1 dk	**(B32A2ST) Tug**	**1 oil engine** driving 1 FP propeller Total Power: 1,103kW (1,500hp) 12.0kn Deutz RBV8M545 1 x 4 Stroke 8 Cy. 320 x 450 1103kW (1500bhp) Kloeckner Humboldt Deutz AG-West Germany AuxGen: 2 x 60kW 400V 50Hz a.c
9322554 *C4FB2* -	**SLEIPNER** *ex* Halland *-2007* **ms 'Sleipner' J Kahrs GmbH & Co KG** J Kahrs Bereederungs GmbH & Co KG *Limassol Cyprus* MMSI: 209629000 Official number: P515	**7,852** 3,363 9,322	Class: BV (GL)	**2005-10 B.V. Scheepswerf Damen Hoogezand — Foxhol** Yd No: 847 **2005-10 Santierul Naval Damen Galati S.A. — Galati** (Hull) Yd No: 1041 Loa 140.64 (BB) Br ex - Dght 7.327 Lbp 130.00 Br md 21.80 Dpth 9.50 Welded, 1 dk	**(A33A2CC) Container Ship (Fully Cellular)** TEU 803 C Ho 206 TEU C Dk 597 TEU incl 180 ref C. Ice Capable	**1 oil engine** geared to sc. shaft driving 1 CP propeller Total Power: 8,100kW (11,013hp) 18.0kn MaK 9M43 1 x 4 Stroke 9 Cy. 430 x 610 8100kW (11013bhp) Caterpillar Motoren GmbH & Co. KG-Germany AuxGen: 1 x 60Hz a.c, 2 x 60Hz a.c Thrusters: 1 Thwart. CP thruster (f); 1 Thwart. CP thruster (a) Fuel: 105.0 (d.f.) 880.0 (r.f.)
9280562 *LMCC* -	**SLEIPNER** *ex* Boa Sleipner *-2005* **Fosvarets Logistikkorganisasjon** Government of The Kingdom of Norway (Sjoforsvarets Forsyningskommando) (Royal Norwegian Navy Materiel Command) *Trondheim Norway*	**247** - -	Class: (NV)	**2002-12 Vaagland Baatbyggeri AS — Vaagland** Yd No: 131 Loa 23.99 Br ex - Dght 3.530 Lbp 21.00 Br md 9.00 Dpth 4.50 Welded, 1 Dk.	**(B32A2ST) Tug**	**2 oil engines** geared to sc. shafts driving 2 Directional propellers Total Power: 2,238kW (3,042hp) 12.5kn Caterpillar 3512 2 x Vee 4 Stroke 12 Cy. 170 x 190 each-1119kW (1521bhp) Caterpillar Inc-USA AuxGen: 1 x 440V 60Hz a.c Thrusters: 1 Thwart. FP thruster (f)
9139854 *OZJK* -	**SLEIPNER-FUR** - **Skive Kommune** - *Fur Denmark* MMSI: 219000859 Official number: B315	**362** 109 286	Class: (NV) (BV)	**1996 Morso Vaerft A/S — Nykobing Mors** Yd No: 199 Loa 55.00 Br ex - Dght - Lbp 42.00 Br md 11.00 Dpth 7.80 Welded, 1dk	**(A36A2PR) Passenger/Ro-Ro Ship (Vehicles)** Passengers: unberthed: 148 Cars: 30 Ice Capable	**2 oil engines** geared to sc. shafts driving 2 Directional propellers Total Power: 458kW (622hp) 9.5kn Scania DSI11 2 x 4 Stroke 6 Cy. 127 x 145 each-229kW (311bhp) Scania AB-Sweden Fuel: 23.0 (d.f.)
9052666 *J8B3396* -	**SLETRINGEN** *ex* Vega *-2006* **Berge Rederi AS** - *Kingstown St Vincent & The Grenadines* MMSI: 375258000 Official number: 9868	**1,598** 819 2,500	Class: NV (BV)	**1992-11 Scheepswerf Bijlsma BV — Wartena** Yd No: 661 Loa 81.70 Br ex 11.10 Dght 4.500 Lbp 76.95 Br md 11.00 Dpth 5.20 Welded, 1 dk	**(A31A2GX) General Cargo Ship** Grain: 3,240 TEU 128 C. 128/20' Compartments: 1 Ho, ER 2 Ha: (26.8 x 10.3) (25.5 x 10.3)ER Ice Capable	**1 oil engine** driving 1 FP propeller Total Power: 883kW (1,201hp) 10.5kn Caterpillar 3512TA 1 x Vee 4 Stroke 12 Cy. 170 x 190 883kW (1201bhp) Caterpillar Inc-USA AuxGen: 1 x a.c, 1 x a.c
8650291 *LLHL* T-61-L	**SLETTENBERG** - **Granli Fiskeri AS** - *Tromso Norway*	**162** 64 -		**2000 Brodrene Langset AS — Lyngstad** Yd No: 6 Loa 21.30 Br ex - Dght - Lbp - Br md 7.20 Dpth 3.80 Welded, 1 dk	**(B11B2FV) Fishing Vessel**	**1 oil engine** reduction geared to sc. shaft driving 1 FP propeller

IMO / Call sign	Name / Owner	Tonnage	Class	Build / Dimensions	Type	Machinery
8996401 *OUPH* HM 654	**SLETTESTRAND** *ex* August *-2010* *ex* Pia Glanz *-2009* **August A/S** - SatCom: Inmarsat C 422018210 *Hanstholm* *Denmark* MMSI: 220182000 Official number: H1375	**118** 39 -		**2003-01 Vestvaerftet ApS — Hvide Sande** Yd No: 233 Loa 18.50 Br ex - Dght 3.300 Lbp - Br md 6.30 Dpth 5.50 Welded, 1 dk	**(B11A2FS) Stern Trawler**	**1 oil engine** reduction geared to sc. shaft driving 1 Propeller Total Power: 221kW (300hp) Mitsubishi 1 x 4 Stroke 221kW (300bhp) Mitsubishi Heavy Industries Ltd-Japan Thrusters: 1 Tunnel thruster (f)
9485875 *LAVF* N-110-L	**SLETTHOLMEN** **Luroyveiding AS** - *Sandnessjoen* *Norway* MMSI: 258228000	**466** 139 -		**2008-07 'Crist' Sp z oo — Gdansk** (Hull) Yd No: B34/01 **2008-07 Larsnes Mek. Verksted AS — Larsnes** Yd No: 46 Loa 33.99 Br ex - Dght 4.870 Lbp 28.70 Br md 9.25 Dpth 6.20 Welded, 1 dk	**(B11B2FV) Fishing Vessel**	**1 oil engine** reduction geared to sc. shaft driving 1 CP propeller Total Power: 1,324kW (1,800hp) 13.0kn Yanmar 8N21A-EN 1 x 4 Stroke 8 Cy. 210 x 290 1324kW (1800bhp) Yanmar Diesel Engine Co Ltd-Japan Thrusters: 1 Tunnel thruster (f); 1 Tunnel thruster (a)
9490739 *V7RM3* -	**SLETTNES** **Marfactor Shipping Co Ltd** Scantank AS *Majuro* *Marshall Islands* MMSI: 538003539 Official number: 3539	**32,837** 19,559 58,018 T/cm 59.2	Class: BV	**2010-07 Yangzhou Dayang Shipbuilding Co Ltd — Yangzhou JS** Yd No: DY3019 Loa 189.99 (BB) Br ex - Dght 12.950 Lbp 185.00 Br md 32.26 Dpth 18.00 Welded, 1 dk	**(A21A2BC) Bulk Carrier** Grain: 71,549; Bale: 69,760 Compartments: 5 Ho, ER 5 Ha: ER Cranes: 4x35t	**1 oil engine** driving 1 FP propeller Total Power: 9,960kW (13,542hp) 14.3kn MAN-B&W 6S50MC-C 1 x 2 Stroke 6 Cy. 500 x 2000 9960kW (13542bhp)
5331973 *YBML* -	**SLEVIK** **PT PERTAMINA (PERSERO)** - *Jakarta* *Indonesia*	*298* 147 549	Class: (GL)	**1960-05 Buesumer Schiffswerft W. & E. Sielaff — Buesum** Yd No: 196 Loa 46.64 Br ex 8.16 Dght 2.877 Lbp 42.14 Br md 8.11 Dpth 3.00 Riveted\Welded, 1 dk	**(A31A2GX) General Cargo Ship** Grain: 855; Bale: 794 Compartments: 1 Ho (comb), ER 2 Ha: (7.9 x 5.1) (11.8 x 5.1)ER Derricks: 1x10t,4x3t; Winches: 4	**1 oil engine** driving 1 FP propeller Total Power: 412kW (560hp) 10.0kn MaK MSU423A 1 x 4 Stroke 6 Cy. 290 x 420 412kW (560bhp) Maschinenbau Kiel AG (MaK)-Kiel AuxGen: 1 x 18kW 220V d.c, 1 x 15kW 220V d.c, 1 x 10kW 220V d.c Fuel: 35.5 (d.f.)
7704071 *SQIT* -	**SLEZA** **Ship-Service SA** - *Szczecin* *Poland* MMSI: 261000420 Official number: 7704071	**695** 313 1,000	Class: (PR)	**1977-12 Wroclawska Stocznia Rzeczna — Wroclaw** Yd No: B443/05 Loa 60.97 Br ex 9.63 Dght 3.640 Lbp 58.50 Br md 9.30 Dpth 4.09 Welded, 1 dk	**(A13B2TU) Tanker (unspecified)** Liq: 1,182; Liq (Oil): 1,182 Compartments: 8 Ta, ER	**1 oil engine** geared to sc. shaft driving 1 FP propeller Total Power: 691kW (939hp) 12.3kn Sulzer 6ASL25/30 1 x 4 Stroke 6 Cy. 250 x 300 691kW (939bhp) Zaklady Przemyslu Metalowego 'HCegielski' SA-Poznan AuxGen: 2 x 160kW 400V, 1 x 48kW 400V
7235367 - -	**SLI 200** *ex* Kohma VI *-2000* *ex* Shoho Maru No. 2 *-1980* **PT Salju Langgeng Indah** - *Jakarta* *Indonesia*	*122* 73 -	Class: KI	**1971-06 Yokohama Zosen — Chiba** Yd No: 1281 Loa 26.70 Br ex - Dght 2.400 Lbp 24.01 Br md 7.21 Dpth 3.08 Welded, 1 dk	**(B32A2ST) Tug**	**1 oil engine** geared to sc. shaft driving 1 FP propeller Total Power: 883kW (1,201hp) 11.0kn Caterpillar D399 1 x Vee 4 Stroke 16 Cy. 159 x 203 883kW (1201bhp) (made 1977, fitted 1980) Caterpillar Tractor Co-USA
9328053 *V2CH4* -	**SLIDUR** *ex* BG Dublin *-2010* *launched as* Slidur *-2007* **ms 'Slidur' J Kahrs Schiffahrts GmbH & Co KG** J Kahrs Bereederungs GmbH & Co KG SatCom: Inmarsat C 430500110 *Saint John's* *Antigua & Barbuda* MMSI: 305001000	**7,852** 3,363 9,322	Class: BV (GL)	**2007-01 B.V. Scheepswerf Damen Hoogezand — Foxhol** Yd No: 863 **2007-01 Santierul Naval Damen Galati S.A. — Galati** (Hull) Yd No: 1075 Loa 140.64 (BB) Br ex - Dght 7.330 Lbp 130.00 Br md 21.80 Dpth 9.50 Welded, 1 dk	**(A33A2CC) Container Ship (Fully Cellular)** TEU 803 C Ho 206 TEU C Dk 597 TEU incl 180 ref C Ice Capable	**1 oil engine** reduction geared to sc. shaft driving 1 FP propeller Total Power: 8,400kW (11,421hp) 18.0kn MaK 9M43 1 x 4 Stroke 9 Cy. 430 x 610 8400kW (11421bhp) Caterpillar Motoren GmbH & Co. KG-Germany AuxGen: 2 x 465kW 440V 60Hz a.c, 1 x 1600kW 440V 60Hz a.c Thrusters: 1 Tunnel thruster (f); 1 Tunnel thruster (a) Fuel: 105.0 (d.f.) 894.0 (r.f.)
9188245 *PCHB* -	**SLINGEBORG** **K/S UL 678** Wagenborg Shipping BV *Delfzijl* *Netherlands* MMSI: 245745000 Official number: 36245	**21,005** 10,601 12,502 T/cm 38.6	Class: BV	**2000-10 Flender Werft AG — Luebeck** Yd No: 678 Loa 183.29 (BB) Br ex - Dght 7.500 Lbp 173.60 Br md 25.20 Dpth 15.30 Welded, 2 dks	**(A35A2RR) Ro-Ro Cargo Ship** Passengers: driver berths: 12 Stern door/ramp (a) Len: 16.00 Wid: 22.70 Swl: 100 Lane-Len: 2475 Lane-clr ht: 5.30 Trailers: 136	**1 oil engine** driving 1 CP propeller Total Power: 10,920kW (14,847hp) 18.0kn Sulzer 7RTA52U 1 x 2 Stroke 7 Cy. 520 x 1800 10920kW (14847bhp) HSD Engine Co Ltd-South Korea AuxGen: 2 x 990kW a.c Thrusters: 2 Thwart. FP thruster (f); 1 Tunnel thruster (a)
9444560 *ZCYI2* -	**SLIPSTREAM** **Mikaroo Pty Ltd** Nigel Burgess Ltd (BURGESS) SatCom: Inmarsat C 431900132 *George Town* *Cayman Islands (British)* MMSI: 319005400 Official number: 741408	**1,076** 322 252	Class: BV	**2009-05 Con. Mec. de Normandie — Cherbourg** Yd No: 801 Loa 60.00 Br ex 11.20 Dght 3.450 Lbp 47.30 Br md 10.80 Dpth 5.90 Welded, 1 dk	**(X11A2YP) Yacht**	**2 oil engines** reduction geared to sc. shafts driving 2 FP propellers Total Power: 3,282kW (4,462hp) 14.5kn Caterpillar 3516B 2 x Vee 4 Stroke 16 Cy. 170 x 190 each-1641kW (2231bhp) Caterpillar Inc-USA
9640724 *YDA4969* -	**SLM 1** **PT Sentosa Laju Maritime** - *Jakarta* *Indonesia*	**190** 57 165	Class: NK	**2012-03 Tuong Aik Shipyard Sdn Bhd — Sibu** Yd No: 21107 Loa 26.00 Br ex - Dght 3.010 Lbp 23.99 Br md 8.00 Dpth 3.65 Welded, 1 dk	**(B32A2ST) Tug**	**2 oil engines** reduction geared to sc. shafts driving 2 FP propellers Total Power: 1,220kW (1,658hp) Yanmar 6AYM-WET 2 x 4 Stroke 6 Cy. 155 x 180 each-610kW (829bhp) Yanmar Diesel Engine Co Ltd-Japan Fuel: 150.0 (d.f.)
9683192 - -	**SLM 202** **PT Sentosa Laju Maritime** - *Jakarta* *Indonesia*	**192** 58 171	Class: NK	**2013-01 PT Palma Progress Shipyard — Batam** Yd No: 522 Loa 26.00 Br ex - Dght 3.012 Lbp 24.29 Br md 8.00 Dpth 3.65 Welded, 1 dk	**(B32A2ST) Tug**	**2 oil engines** reduction geared to sc. shafts driving 2 Propellers Total Power: 1,220kW (1,658hp) Yanmar 6AYM-WET 2 x 4 Stroke 6 Cy. 155 x 180 each-610kW (829bhp) Yanmar Diesel Engine Co Ltd-Japan Fuel: 140.0 (d.f.)
9713868 - -	**SLM 303** **PT Sentosa Laju Maritime** - *Jakarta* *Indonesia*	**192** 58 170	Class: NK	**2014-02 PT Palma Progress Shipyard — Batam** Yd No: 541 Loa 26.00 Br ex - Dght 3.012 Lbp 23.69 Br md 8.00 Dpth 3.65 Welded, 1 dk	**(B32A2ST) Tug**	**2 oil engines** reduction geared to sc. shaft (s) driving 2 Propellers Total Power: 1,220kW (1,658hp)
9723605 - -	**SLM 304** **PT Sentosa Laju Maritime** - *Jakarta* *Indonesia*	**192** 58 171	Class: NK	**2014-02 PT Palma Progress Shipyard — Batam** Yd No: 555 Loa 26.00 Br ex - Dght 3.012 Lbp 24.29 Br md 8.00 Dpth 3.65 Welded, 1 dk	**(B32A2ST) Tug**	**2 oil engines** reduction geared to sc. shaft (s) driving 2 Propellers
9383663 *WDH3033* -	**SLNC PAX** *ex* Bomar Eris *-2014* *ex* Ruth Theresa *-2012* **Schuyler Line Navigation Corp** Patriot Contract Services LLC *Annapolis, MD* *United States of America* MMSI: 338164000 Official number: 1251485	**5,713** 2,419 7,985 T/cm 16.9	Class: NK (Class contemplated) (BV)	**2008-04 Nantong Mingde Heavy Industry Co Ltd — Tongzhou JS** Yd No: MD004 Loa 101.39 (BB) Br ex - Dght 7.613 Lbp 94.96 Br md 19.05 Dpth 10.50 Welded, 1 dk	**(A12B2TR) Chemical/Products Tanker** Double Hull (13F) Liq: 8,963; Liq (Oil): 8,970 Cargo Heating Coils Compartments: 8 Wing Ta, 2 Wing Slop Ta, ER 4 Cargo Pump (s): 3x677m³/hr, 1x100m³/hr Manifold: Bow/CM: 48.1m	**1 oil engine** reduction geared to sc. shaft driving 1 FP propeller Total Power: 2,970kW (4,038hp) 12.6kn MaK 9M25 1 x 4 Stroke 9 Cy. 255 x 400 2970kW (4038bhp) (new engine 2008) Caterpillar Motoren GmbH & Co. KG-Germany AuxGen: 3 x 420kW 50Hz a.c, 1 x 600kW a.c Thrusters: 1 Tunnel thruster (f) Fuel: 251.0 (d.f.) 313.0 (r.f.)
9521461 *J8B3994* -	**SLOEBER** **Baggerwerken Decloedt en Zoon NV** - *Kingstown* *St Vincent & The Grenadines* MMSI: 377578000 Official number: 10467	**2,427** 728 4,580	Class: BV	**2010-02 PT ASL Shipyard Indonesia — Batam** Yd No: 894 Loa 91.15 Br ex 16.82 Dght 5.000 Lbp 85.30 Br md 16.80 Dpth 5.40 Welded, 1 dk	**(B34A2SH) Hopper, Motor** Hopper: 2,750	**2 oil engines** reduction geared to sc. shafts driving 2 Directional propellers Total Power: 1,640kW (2,230hp) 9.6kn Cummins KTA-38-M1 2 x Vee 4 Stroke 12 Cy. 159 x 159 each-820kW (1115bhp) Cummins India Ltd-India AuxGen: 2 x 98kW a.c

9586679 *V2FO7* -	**SLOMAN ARIADNE** **mt 'Sloman Ariadne' Schifffahrtsgesellschaft mbH & Co KG** Sloman Neptun Schiffahrts-Aktiengesellschaft *Saint John's* *Antigua & Barbuda* MMSI: 305759000 Official number: 4903	**18,320** 5,496 23,276 T/cm 35.8	Class: LR ✠**100A1** SS 12/2011 liquified gas carrier, Ship Type 2G Anhydrous ammonia, butane, butane and propane mixtures, butylenes, butadiene, dietyle ether, dimethylamine, isoprene, isopropylamine, monoethylamine, propane, propylene, VCM and vinyle ethyle ether in independent tanks Type C, maximum SG 0.972, maximum vapour pressure 5.3 bar g, minimum cargo temperature minus 48 degree C **ShipRight** ACS (B) LI *IWS SPM4 ✠ **LMC UMS +Lloyd's RMC (LG)** Eq.Ltr: H†; Cable: 605.0/62.0 U3 (a)	**2011-12 Hyundai Mipo Dockyard Co Ltd — Ulsan** Yd No: 8073 Loa 159.97 (BB) Br ex 25.64 Dght 10.910 Lbp 152.23 Br md 25.60 Dpth 16.40 Welded, 1 dk	**(A11B2TG) LPG Tanker** Double Sides Entire Compartment Length Liq (Gas): 20,600 4 x Gas Tank (s); 1 independent (stl) dcc horizontal, 3 independent (stl) dcy horizontal 8 Cargo Pump (s): 6x250m^3/hr, 2x1785m^3/hr Manifold: Bow/CM: 82.1m	**1 oil engine** driving 1 FP propeller Total Power: 7,860kW (10,686hp) 15.0kn MAN-B&W 6S46MC-C 1 x 2 Stroke 6 Cy. 460 x 1932 7860kW (10686bhp) Hyundai Engine & Machinery Co Ltd-South Korea AuxGen: 3 x 820kW 450V 60Hz a.c Boilers: AuxB (o.f.) 9.2kgf/cm^2 (9.0bar) Fuel: 249.0 (d.f.) 1995.0 (r.f.)
9620669 *V2FO2* -	**SLOMAN DISCOVERER** **Partenreederei mn'Sloman Discoverer'** Sloman Neptun Schiffahrts-Aktiengesellschaft *Saint John's* *Antigua & Barbuda* MMSI: 305737000 Official number: 4481	**9,611** 4,260 12,641	Class: GL	**2012-01 Jiangzhou Union Shipbuilding Co Ltd — Ruichang JX** Yd No: JZ1040 Loa 138.01 (BB) Br ex - Dght 8.000 Lbp 130.71 Br md 21.00 Dpth 11.00 Welded, 1 dk	**(A31A2GX) General Cargo Ship** Grain: 15,952; Bale: 14,856 TEU 665 incl 25 ref C. Compartments: 3 Ho, ER 3 Ha: ER Cranes: 2x150t Ice Capable	**1 oil engine** reduction geared to sc. shaft driving 1 CP propeller Total Power: 5,400kW (7,342hp) 15.0kn MaK 6M43C 1 x 4 Stroke 6 Cy. 430 x 610 5400kW (7342bhp) Caterpillar Motoren GmbH & Co. KG-Germany AuxGen: 1 x 700kW 400V a.c, 3 x 395kW 400V a.c Thrusters: 1 Tunnel thruster (f)
9620657 *V2FO3* -	**SLOMAN DISPATCHER** **Partenreederei ms Sloman Dispatcher** Sloman Neptun Schiffahrts-Aktiengesellschaft *Saint John's* *Antigua & Barbuda* MMSI: 305738000 Official number: 4882	**9,611** 4,260 12,634	Class: GL	**2012-04 Jiangzhou Union Shipbuilding Co Ltd — Ruichang JX** Yd No: JZ1041 Loa 138.10 (BB) Br ex - Dght 8.000 Lbp 130.71 Br md 21.00 Dpth 11.00 Welded, 1 dk	**(A31A2GX) General Cargo Ship** Grain: 15,952; Bale: 14,856 TEU 665 incl 25 ref C. Compartments: 3 Ho, ER 3 Ha: ER Cranes: 2x150t Ice Capable	**1 oil engine** reduction geared to sc. shaft driving 1 CP propeller Total Power: 6,000kW (8,158hp) 14.0kn MaK 6M43C 1 x 4 Stroke 6 Cy. 430 x 610 6000kW (8158bhp) Caterpillar Motoren GmbH & Co. KG-Germany
9466714 *V2FY3* -	**SLOMAN HERA** **mt 'Sloman Hera' Schifffahrtsgesellschaft mbH & Co KG** Sloman Neptun Schiffahrts-Aktiengesellschaft *Saint John's* *Antigua & Barbuda* MMSI: 305850000 Official number: 4965	**11,246** 4,961 16,426 T/cm 28.1	Class: AB	**2012-06 Jiangzhou Union Shipbuilding Co Ltd — Ruichang JX** Yd No: JZ1022 Loa 145.15 (BB) Br ex 23.03 Dght 8.810 Lbp 135.60 Br md 23.00 Dpth 12.50 Welded, 1 dk	**(A12B2TR) Chemical/Products Tanker** Double Hull (13F) Liq: 18,706; Liq (Oil): 19,088 Compartments: 6 Wing Ta, 6 Wing Ta, 1 Wing Slop Ta, 1 Wing Slop Ta, ER 12 Cargo Pump (s): 12x300m^3/hr Manifold: Bow/CM: 74m	**1 oil engine** driving 1 FP propeller Total Power: 4,440kW (6,037hp) 13.5kn MAN-B&W 6S35MC7 1 x 2 Stroke 6 Cy. 350 x 1400 4440kW (6037bhp) STX Engine Co Ltd-South Korea AuxGen: 3 x 600kW a.c Thrusters: 1 Tunnel thruster (f) Fuel: 92.0 (d.f.) 687.0 (r.f.)
9466726 *V2FY4* -	**SLOMAN HERAKLES** **mt 'Sloman Herakles' Schifffahrtsgesellschaft mbH & Co KG** Sloman Neptun Schiffahrts-Aktiengesellschaft *Saint John's* *Antigua & Barbuda* MMSI: 305851000 Official number: 4966	**11,246** 4,961 16,417 T/cm 28.1	Class: AB	**2012-06 Jiangzhou Union Shipbuilding Co Ltd — Ruichang JX** Yd No: JZ1023 Loa 145.15 (BB) Br ex 23.03 Dght 8.810 Lbp 135.60 Br md 23.00 Dpth 12.50 Welded, 1 dk	**(A12B2TR) Chemical/Products Tanker** Double Hull (13F) Liq: 18,715; Liq (Oil): 19,000 Compartments: 6 Wing Ta, 6 Wing Ta, 1 Wing Slop Ta, 1 Wing Slop Ta, ER 12 Cargo Pump (s): 12x300m^3/hr Manifold: Bow/CM: 74m	**1 oil engine** driving 1 FP propeller Total Power: 4,440kW (6,037hp) 13.5kn MAN-B&W 6S35MC 1 x 2 Stroke 6 Cy. 350 x 1400 4440kW (6037bhp) STX Engine Co Ltd-South Korea AuxGen: 3 x 600kW a.c Thrusters: 1 Tunnel thruster (f) Fuel: 92.1 (d.f.) 687.0 (r.f.)
9466738 *V2FY5* -	**SLOMAN HERMES** **mt 'Sloman Hermes' Schifffahrtsgesellschaft mbH & Co KG** Sloman Neptun Schiffahrts-Aktiengesellschaft *Saint John's* *Antigua & Barbuda* MMSI: 305852000 Official number: 4967	**11,246** 4,961 16,418 T/cm 28.1	Class: AB	**2012-06 Jiangzhou Union Shipbuilding Co Ltd — Ruichang JX** Yd No: JZ1024 Loa 145.15 (BB) Br ex 23.03 Dght 8.810 Lbp 135.60 Br md 23.00 Dpth 12.50 Welded, 1 dk	**(A12B2TR) Chemical/Products Tanker** Double Hull (13F) Liq: 19,000; Liq (Oil): 19,000 Compartments: 6 Wing Ta, 6 Wing Ta, 1 Wing Slop Ta, 1 Wing Slop Ta, ER 12 Cargo Pump (s): 12x300m^3/hr Manifold: Bow/CM: 74m	**1 oil engine** driving 1 FP propeller Total Power: 4,440kW (6,037hp) 13.5kn MAN-B&W 6S35MC 1 x 2 Stroke 6 Cy. 350 x 1400 4440kW (6037bhp) STX Engine Co Ltd-South Korea AuxGen: 3 x 600kW a.c Thrusters: 1 Tunnel thruster (f) Fuel: 92.0 (d.f.) 687.0 (r.f.)
9161003 *V2OT9* -	**SLOMAN PRODUCER** **Sloman Neptun Shipping & Transport GmbH** Sloman Neptun Schiffahrts-Aktiengesellschaft *Saint John's* *Antigua & Barbuda* MMSI: 304700000 Official number: 3894	**7,260** 3,565 7,630	Class: GL	**2004-08 Turkiye Gemi Sanayii A.S. — Camialti, Istanbul** (Hull launched by) Yd No: 244 **2004-08 Rota Denizcilik Ticaret A.S. — Tuzla, Istanbul** (Hull completed by) Yd No: (244) Loa 120.90 (BB) Br ex - Dght 6.850 Lbp 114.05 Br md 18.70 Dpth 10.15 Welded, 1 dk	**(A35A2RR) Ro-Ro Cargo Ship** Stern door/ramp (centre) Lane-Len: 1150 Bale: 10,600 TEU 783 Cranes: 2x60t Ice Capable	**1 oil engine** geared to sc. shaft driving 1 CP propeller Total Power: 4,236kW (5,759hp) 15.5kn MAN 9L32/40 1 x 4 Stroke 9 Cy. 320 x 400 4236kW (5759bhp) MAN B&W Diesel AG-Augsburg Thrusters: 1 Tunnel thruster (f)
9160994 *V2BK8* -	**SLOMAN PROVIDER** **Partenreederei ms 'Sloman Provider'** Sloman Neptun Schiffahrts-Aktiengesellschaft SatCom: Inmarsat C 430485110 *Saint John's* *Antigua & Barbuda* MMSI: 304851000	**7,260** 3,565 7,630	Class: GL	**2000-11 Turkiye Gemi Sanayii A.S. — Pendik** Yd No: 022 Loa 120.90 (BB) Br ex - Dght 6.850 Lbp 114.05 Br md 18.70 Dpth 10.15 Welded, 1 dk	**(A35A2RR) Ro-Ro Cargo Ship** Double Bottom Entire Compartment Length Stern door/ramp (centre) Lane-Len: 1150 Grain: 14,300; Bale: 10,600 TEU 783 1 Ha: Cranes: 2x60t Ice Capable	**1 oil engine** reduction geared to sc. shaft driving 1 CP propeller Total Power: 5,760kW (7,831hp) 16.0kn MAN 12V32/40 1 x Vee 4 Stroke 12 Cy. 320 x 400 5760kW (7831bhp) MAN B&W Diesel AG-Augsburg AuxGen: 1 x 544kW 220/440V a.c, 1 x 275kW 220/440V a.c, 2 x 260kW 220/440V a.c Thrusters: 1 Thwart. FP thruster (f) Fuel: 596.0 (r.f.)
7812919 *3FHO9* -	**SLOMAN ROVER** *ex* Karam Meru *-2006* *ex* Sea Crest *-2003* *ex* Karam Meru *-2003* *ex* Sea Crest *-2001* *ex* Barcelona I *-2000* *ex* Rawan 1 *-1999* *ex* Hipomar *-1993* *ex* Sloman Rover *-1989* **World Shipping Line Inc** World Shipping Management Corp SA SatCom: Inmarsat C 435766910 *Panama* *Panama* MMSI: 357669000 Official number: 3154506A	**3,910** 1,173 2,560	Class: (AB) (GL)	**1979-05 Howaldtswerke-Deutsche Werft AG (HDW) — Hamburg** Yd No: 149 Loa 91.90 (BB) Br ex 18.14 Dght 3.655 Lbp 79.20 Br md 18.01 Dpth 7.90 Welded, 2 dks	**(A35A2RR) Ro-Ro Cargo Ship** Stern door/ramp (centre) Len: 10.00 Wid: 8.74 Swl: 192 Lane-Len: 344 Lane-Wid: 7.65 Lane-clr ht: 5.50 Trailers: 30 Grain: 5,600; Bale: 6,182; Liq: 904 TEU 319 C Ho 132 TEU C Dk 187 TEU incl 20 ref C Compartments: 1 Ho, ER 1 Ha: (68.2 x 15.0) Cranes: 2x25t Ice Capable	**2 oil engines** sr reverse geared to sc. shafts driving 2 FP propellers Total Power: 2,118kW (2,880hp) 12.5kn Deutz SBA12M528 2 x Vee 4 Stroke 12 Cy. 220 x 280 each-1059kW (1440bhp) Kloeckner Humboldt Deutz AG-West Germany AuxGen: 3 x 184kW 440V 60Hz a.c Thrusters: 1 Thwart. FP thruster (f) Fuel: 90.5 (d.f.) 336.5 (r.f.) 12.0pd
9306677 *V7JD5* -	**SLOMAN THEMIS** *ex* Handytankers Unity *-2011* *ex* Sloman Themis *-2006* **mt 'Sloman Themis' Schiffahrtsgesellschaft mbH & Co KG** Sloman Neptun Schiffahrts-Aktiengesellschaft *Majuro* *Marshall Islands* MMSI: 538090195 Official number: 90195	**22,184** 9,434 34,628 T/cm 41.5	Class: GL (LR) ✠ Classed LR until 25/7/08	**2006-02 Dalian Shipbuilding Industry Co Ltd — Dalian LN (No 1 Yard)** Yd No: PC350-8 Loa 171.22 (BB) Br ex 27.44 Dght 11.815 Lbp 161.99 Br md 27.40 Dpth 17.30 Welded, 1 dk	**(A13B2TP) Products Tanker** Double Hull (13F) Liq: 36,767; Liq (Oil): 36,767 Cargo Heating Coils Compartments: 12 Wing Ta, 2 Wing Slop Ta, ER 14 Cargo Pump (s): 10x500m^3/hr, 4x300m^3/hr Manifold: Bow/CM: 84.8m	**1 oil engine** driving 1 FP propeller Total Power: 7,150kW (9,721hp) 14.5kn MAN-B&W 5S50MC 1 x 2 Stroke 5 Cy. 500 x 1910 7150kW (9721bhp) Dalian Marine Diesel Works-China AuxGen: 3 x 960kW 450/220V 60Hz a.c Boilers: AuxB (ex.g.) 8.8kgf/cm^2 (8.6bar), WTAuxB (o.f.) 8.7kgf/cm^2 (8.5bar) Thrusters: 1 Thwart. CP thruster (f); 1 Thwart. CP thruster (a) Fuel: 176.2 (d.f.) (Heating Coils) 1450.6 (r.f.) 29.0pd
9306653 *V7JQ5* -	**SLOMAN THETIS** *ex* Handytankers Liberty *-2011* *launched as* Sloman Thetis *-2006* **mt 'Sloman Thetis' Schiffahrtsgesellschaft mbH & Co KG** Sloman Neptun Schiffahrts-Aktiengesellschaft SatCom: Inmarsat Mini-M 764678278 *Majuro* *Marshall Islands* MMSI: 538090211 Official number: 90211	**22,184** 9,434 34,662 T/cm 41.5	Class: GL (LR) ✠ Classed LR until 8/5/09	**2006-12 Dalian Shipbuilding Industry Co Ltd — Dalian LN (No 1 Yard)** Yd No: PC350-10 Loa 171.22 (BB) Br ex 27.42 Dght 11.815 Lbp 161.99 Br md 27.40 Dpth 17.29 Welded, 1 dk	**(A13B2TP) Products Tanker** Double Hull (13F) Liq: 36,767; Liq (Oil): 36,767 Cargo Heating Coils Compartments: 12 Wing Ta, 2 Wing Slop Ta, ER 12 Cargo Pump (s): 10x500m^3/hr, 2x300m^3/hr Manifold: Bow/CM: 84.9m	**1 oil engine** driving 1 FP propeller Total Power: 7,150kW (9,721hp) 14.5kn MAN-B&W 5S50MC 1 x 2 Stroke 5 Cy. 500 x 1910 7150kW (9721bhp) Dalian Marine Diesel Works-China AuxGen: 3 x 910kW 450V 60Hz a.c Boilers: AuxB (ex.g.) 8.9kgf/cm^2 (8.7bar), WTAuxB (o.f.) 8.7kgf/cm^2 (8.5bar) Thrusters: 1 Thwart. CP thruster (f); 1 Thwart. CP thruster (a) Fuel: 128.0 (d.f.) 1186.0 (r.f.)

7629025 *SPG2371* -	**SLON** **'WUZ' Port & Maritime Services Co Ltd ('WUZ' Sp z oo Przedsiebiorstwo Uslug Portowych i Morskich)** - *Gdansk* *Poland*	*111* - -	Class: PR	**1975 "Petrozavod" — Leningrad** Yd No: 579 Loa 24.21 Br ex 6.94 Dght 2.240 Lbp - Br md - Dpth 2.98 Welded, 1 dk	**(B32A2ST) Tug**	**2 oil engines** driving 2 FP propellers Total Power: 662kW (900hp) 10.0kn Pervomaysk 6CH25/34 2 x 4 Stroke 6 Cy. 250 x 340 each-331kW (450bhp) Pervomaydizelmash (PDM)-Pervomaysk AuxGen: 2 x 24kW 380V a.c
9197947 *PDBP* -	**SLOTERGRACHT** **Rederij Slotergracht** Spliethoff's Bevrachtingskantoor BV *Amsterdam* *Netherlands* MMSI: 246456000 Official number: 36730	**16,641** 6,700 21,402 T/cm 35.1	Class: LR ✠ **100A1** SS 06/2009 strengthened for heavy cargoes container cargoes in holds, on upper deck and upper deck hatch covers timber deck cargoes tanktop suitable for regular discharge by grabs LA LI *IWS Ice Class 1A (Finnish-Swedish Ice Class Rules) Max draught midship 10.943m Max/min draught aft 11.47/6.6m Max/min draught forward 11.47/4.2m ✠ **LMC** **UMS** Eq.Ltr: H†; Cable: 605.0/70.0 U2 (a)	**2000-06 Tsuneishi Shipbuilding Co Ltd — Fukuyama HS** Yd No: 1173 Loa 168.14 (BB) Br ex 25.42 Dght 10.730 Lbp 159.14 Br md 25.20 Dpth 14.60 Welded, 1 dk	**(A31A2GX) General Cargo Ship** Grain: 23,786; Bale: 23,786 TEU 1127 C Ho 478 TEU C Dk 649 TEU incl 120 ref C. Cargo Heating Coils Compartments: 3 Ho, ER 3 Ha: (26.6 x 15.2)Tappered (38.4 x 17.8) (31.9 x 20.4)ER Cranes: 3x120t Ice Capable	**1 oil engine** with flexible couplings & sr reverse geared to sc. shaft driving 1 CP propeller Total Power: 12,060kW (16,397hp) 19.5kn Wartsila 6L64 1 x 4 Stroke 6 Cy. 640 x 900 12060kW (16397bhp) Wartsila Italia SpA-Italy AuxGen: 1 x 1000kW 445V 60Hz a.c, 3 x 450kW 445V 60Hz a.c Boilers: TOH (o.f.) 10.2kgf/cm² (10.0bar), TOH (ex.g.) 10.2kgf/cm² (10.0bar) Thrusters: 1 Thwart. CP thruster (f) Fuel: 275.0 (d.f.) (Heating Coils) 1750.0 (r.f.) 45.0pd
8872368 *JWUP* -	**SLOTTHEIM** - **Rederiet Fagertun AS** - *Haugesund* *Norway* MMSI: 257111400	**113** 66 153		**1958 Elektrosveis — Sagvaag** Yd No: 2 Lengthened-1976 Loa 30.11 Br ex 6.12 Dght - Lbp - Br md - Dpth 3.03 Welded, 1 dk	**(A31A2GX) General Cargo Ship** Compartments: 1 Ho, ER 1 Ha: (3.5 x 0.9)ER Derricks: 1x2t; Winches: 1	**1 oil engine** driving 1 FP propeller Total Power: 147kW (200hp) Alpha 344-F 1 x 2 Stroke 4 Cy. 200 x 340 147kW (200bhp) (new engine 1965) Alpha Diesel A/S-Denmark
8934324 - -	**SLTH 03** *ex* TH 03 **Vietnam Waterway Construction Corp (VINAWACO)** - *Haiphong* *Vietnam* Official number: VN-827-VT	**372** 113 300	Class: VR	**1988-01 Song Cam Shipyard — Haiphong** Loa 42.80 Br ex 10.02 Dght 2.400 Lbp 41.00 Br md 10.00 Dpth 3.00 Welded, 1 dk	**(B34A2SH) Hopper, Motor** Hopper: 300 Compartments: 1 Ho, ER 1 Ha: (24.0 x 6.0)ER	**1 oil engine** driving 1 FP propeller Total Power: 224kW (305hp) 6.0kn S.K.L. 6NVD36-1U 1 x 4 Stroke 6 Cy. 240 x 360 224kW (305bhp) VEB Schwermaschinenbau "KarlLiebknecht" (SKL)-Magdeburg AuxGen: 1 x 37kW a.c
9202522 *PFBE* -	**SLUISGRACHT** **Rederij Sluisgracht** Spliethoff's Bevrachtingskantoor BV *Amsterdam* *Netherlands* MMSI: 244903000 Official number: 38772	**16,639** 6,730 21,250 T/cm 35.1	Class: LR ✠ **100A1** SS 07/2010 strengthened for heavy cargoes, container cargoes in holds, on upper deck and upper deck hatch covers timber deck cargoes tank top suitable for regular discharge by grabs *IWS LI Ice Class 1A (Finnish-Swedish Ice Class Rules 1985) Max draught midship 10.959m Max/min draught aft 11.47/6.6m Max/min draught fwd 11.47/4.2m ✠ **LMC** **UMS** Eq.Ltr: I†; Cable: 618.4/64.0 U3 (a)	**2001-02 Stocznia Szczecinska Porta Holding SA — Szczecin** Yd No: B587/IV/3 Loa 172.00 (BB) Br ex 25.50 Dght 10.600 Lbp 160.29 Br md 25.30 Dpth 14.60 Welded, 1 dk	**(A31A2GX) General Cargo Ship** Grain: 22,200 TEU 1127 C Ho 478 TEU C Dk 649 TEU incl 120 ref C. Cargo Heating Coils Compartments: 3 Ho, ER 4 Ha: (6.4 x 7.5) (25.6 x 15.2)Tappered (38.4 x 17.8) (32.0 x 20.4)ER Cranes: 3x120t Ice Capable	**1 oil engine** with flexible couplings & sr gearedto sc. shaft driving 1 CP propeller Total Power: 12,060kW (16,397hp) 19.1kn Wartsila 6L64 1 x 4 Stroke 6 Cy. 640 x 900 12060kW (16397bhp) Wartsila Italia SpA-Italy AuxGen: 1 x 1000kW 445V 60Hz a.c, 3 x 450kW 445V 60Hz a.c Boilers: TOH (o.f.) 10.2kgf/cm² (10.0bar), TOH (ex.g.) 10.2kgf/cm² (10.0bar) Thrusters: 1 Thwart. CP thruster (f) Fuel: 275.0 (d.f.) (Heating Coils) 1750.0 (r.f.) 45.0pd
8930861 - -	**SLV-201** - **Vostokbunker Co Ltd** - *Nakhodka* *Russia* Official number: 722398	*209* 74 260	Class: RS	**1974-11 Sudoremontnyy Zavod "Yakor" — Sovetskaya Gavan** Yd No: 1582S/1 Loa 29.30 Br ex 7.80 Dght 2.780 Lbp 27.00 Br md 7.58 Dpth 3.60 Welded, 1 dk	**(B34G2SE) Pollution Control Vessel** Liq: 239; Liq (Oil): 239 Compartments: 7 Ta Ice Capable	**1 oil engine** geared to sc. shaft driving 1 FP propeller Total Power: 165kW (224hp) 7.9kn Daldizel 6CHNSP18/22 1 x 4 Stroke 6 Cy. 180 x 220 165kW (224bhp) Daldizel-Khabarovsk AuxGen: 1 x 50kW a.c, 1 x 30kW a.c Fuel: 24.0 (d.f.)
8930885 - -	**SLV-203** - **Aquilon LLC** OOO 'Grand-Altair' *Nakhodka* *Russia* Official number: 732718	*191* 74 258	Class: RS	**1975-10 Sudoremontnyy Zavod "Yakor" — Sovetskaya Gavan** Yd No: 1582S/3 Loa 29.30 Br ex 7.80 Dght 2.790 Lbp 28.50 Br md - Dpth 3.60 Welded, 1 dk	**(B34G2SE) Pollution Control Vessel** Liq: 238; Liq (Oil): 238 Compartments: 7 Ta Ice Capable	**1 oil engine** geared to sc. shaft driving 1 FP propeller Total Power: 166kW (226hp) 7.9kn Daldizel 6CHNSP18/22 1 x 4 Stroke 6 Cy. 180 x 220 166kW (226bhp) (new engine 1987) Daldizel-Khabarovsk AuxGen: 1 x 50kW a.c, 1 x 30kW a.c Fuel: 12.0 (d.f.)
8930897 - -	**SLV-204** - **Alfa-Marin Co Ltd** - *Vladivostok* *Russia* Official number: 742796	*209* 74 260	Class: RS	**1975-12 Sudoremontnyy Zavod "Yakor" — Sovetskaya Gavan** Yd No: 1582S/4 Loa 29.30 Br ex 7.80 Dght 2.790 Lbp 27.00 Br md 7.50 Dpth 3.60 Welded, 1 dk	**(B34G2SE) Pollution Control Vessel** Liq: 238; Liq (Oil): 238 Compartments: 7 Ta Ice Capable	**1 oil engine** geared to sc. shaft driving 1 FP propeller Total Power: 165kW (224hp) 7.9kn Daldizel 6CHNSP18/22 1 x 4 Stroke 6 Cy. 180 x 220 165kW (224bhp) Daldizel-Khabarovsk AuxGen: 1 x 50kW a.c, 1 x 30kW a.c Fuel: 12.0 (d.f.)
8985232 - -	**SLV-207** - **OOO 'Trans-Eko'** - *Vladivostok* *Russia* Official number: 772486	**209** 74 236	Class: RS	**1977-10 Sudoremontnyy Zavod "Yakor" — Sovetskaya Gavan** Yd No: 1582S/7 Loa 29.30 Br ex 7.80 Dght 2.770 Lbp 27.00 Br md 7.50 Dpth 3.60 Welded, 1 dk	**(B34G2SE) Pollution Control Vessel**	**1 oil engine** geared to sc. shaft driving 1 Propeller Total Power: 121kW (165hp) Daldizel 6CHNSP18/22 1 x 4 Stroke 6 Cy. 180 x 220 121kW (165bhp) (Re-engined ,made 1983) Daldizel-Khabarovsk
8930926 - -	**SLV-303** - **SE Sea Commercial Port of Illichivsk** - *Illichevsk* *Ukraine* Official number: 752016	*205* 77 326	Class: (RS)	**1975 Bakinskiy Sudostroitelnyy Zavod im Vano Sturua — Baku** Yd No: 303 Loa 29.17 Br ex 8.01 Dght 3.120 Lbp 28.50 Br md - Dpth 3.60 Welded, 1 dk	**(B34G2SE) Pollution Control Vessel** Liq: 330; Liq (Oil): 330 Compartments: 8 Ta Ice Capable	**1 oil engine** geared to sc. shaft driving 1 FP propeller Total Power: 166kW (226hp) 7.5kn Daldizel 6CHNSP18/22 1 x 4 Stroke 6 Cy. 180 x 220 166kW (226bhp) Daldizel-Khabarovsk AuxGen: 1 x 50kW a.c, 1 x 25kW a.c Fuel: 10.0 (d.f.)
8726117 - -	**SLV-308** - **Vladivostok Sea Fishing Port (OAO 'Vladivostokskiy Morskoy Rybnyy Port')** - *Vladivostok* *Russia*	*201* 74 325	Class: (RS)	**1980-11 Sudoremontnyy Zavod "Yakor" — Sovetskaya Gavan** Yd No: 1582U/1 Loa 29.17 Br ex 7.80 Dght 3.120 Lbp 28.50 Br md 7.58 Dpth 3.60 Welded, 1 dk	**(B34G2SE) Pollution Control Vessel** Liq: 346; Liq (Oil): 346 Compartments: 8 Ta Ice Capable	**1 oil engine** geared to sc. shaft driving 1 FP propeller Total Power: 165kW (224hp) 7.5kn Daldizel 6CHNSP18/22 1 x 4 Stroke 6 Cy. 180 x 220 165kW (224bhp) Daldizel-Khabarovsk AuxGen: 1 x 50kW a.c, 1 x 30kW a.c Fuel: 12.0 (d.f.)
8930938 - -	**SLV-309** - **Ecologia DV Co Ltd** - *Vladivostok* *Russia*	*201* 74 326	Class: RS	**1981-12 Sudoremontnyy Zavod "Yakor" — Sovetskaya Gavan** Yd No: 1582U/9 Loa 29.17 Br ex 8.01 Dght 3.120 Lbp 28.50 Br md 7.58 Dpth 3.60 Welded, 1 dk	**(B34G2SE) Pollution Control Vessel** Liq: 336; Liq (Oil): 336 Compartments: 8 Ta Ice Capable	**1 oil engine** geared to sc. shaft driving 1 FP propeller Total Power: 165kW (224hp) 7.5kn Daldizel 6CHNSP18/22 1 x 4 Stroke 6 Cy. 180 x 220 165kW (224bhp) Daldizel-Khabarovsk AuxGen: 1 x 50kW a.c, 1 x 30kW a.c Fuel: 12.0 (d.f.)

Ship / Owner	Tonnage / Class	Builder / Dimensions	Type / Capacity	Machinery
8930940 **SLV-310** *UGRU* - **Eastern Shipping Co Ltd (Vostochnaya Sudokhodnaya Kompaniya OOO)** - *Sovetskaya Gavan* *Russia* Official number: 812236	*201* Class: RS 74 326	**1982**-11 **Sudoremontnyy Zavod "Yakor" — Sovetskaya Gavan** Yd No: 1582U/10 Loa 29.17 Br ex 7.80 Dght 3.120 Lbp 28.50 Br md - Dpth 3.60 Welded, 1 dk	**(B34G2SE) Pollution Control Vessel** Liq: 346; Liq (Oil): 346 Compartments: 8 Ta Ice Capable	**1 oil engine** geared to sc. shaft driving 1 FP propeller Total Power: 165kW (224hp) 7.5kn Daldizel 6CHNSP18/22 1 x 4 Stroke 6 Cy. 180 x 220 165kW (224bhp) Daldizel-Khabarovsk AuxGen: 1 x 50kW a.c, 1 x 30kW a.c Fuel: 12.0 (d.f.)
8227159 **SLV-311** - - **Alfa-Marin Co Ltd** - *Nakhodka* *Russia*	*201* Class: RS 74 326	**1983**-12 **Sudoremontnyy Zavod "Yakor" — Sovetskaya Gavan** Yd No: 1582U/4 Loa 29.16 Br ex 7.80 Dght 3.120 Lbp 28.50 Br md 7.58 Dpth 3.61 Welded	**(B34G2SE) Pollution Control Vessel** Liq: 346; Liq (Oil): 346 Compartments: 8 Ta	**1 oil engine** geared to sc. shaft driving 1 FP propeller Total Power: 165kW (224hp) 7.5kn Daldizel 6CHNSP18/22 1 x 4 Stroke 6 Cy. 180 x 220 165kW (224bhp) Daldizel-Khabarovsk AuxGen: 1 x 50kW a.c, 1 x 30kW a.c Fuel: 12.0 (d.f.)
8726090 **SLV-313** - - **Meriko Shipping Co Ltd (Meriko Sudokhodnaya Kompaniya OOO)** - *Nakhodka* *Russia* Official number: 853128	**191** Class: RS 85 309	**1986**-08 **Sudoremontnyy Zavod "Yakor" — Sovetskaya Gavan** Yd No: 1582U/6 Converted From: Pollution Control Vessel-2005 Loa 29.23 Br ex 7.80 Dght 3.120 Lbp 28.50 Br md - Dpth 3.60 Welded, 1 dk	**(A13B2TP) Products Tanker** Liq: 346; Liq (Oil): 346 Compartments: 8 Ta Ice Capable	**1 oil engine** geared to sc. shaft driving 1 FP propeller Total Power: 165kW (224hp) 7.5kn Daldizel 6CHNSP18/22 1 x 4 Stroke 6 Cy. 180 x 220 165kW (224bhp) Daldizel-Khabarovsk AuxGen: 1 x 50kW a.c, 1 x 30kW a.c Fuel: 12.0 (d.f.)
8726088 **SLV-314** - - **Kamagro Co Ltd** - *Petropavlovsk-Kamchatskiy* *Russia* Official number: 862635	**191** Class: RS 85 326	**1987**-12 **Sudoremontnyy Zavod "Yakor" — Sovetskaya Gavan** Yd No: 1582U/7 Loa 29.17 Br ex 7.80 Dght 3.120 Lbp 28.50 Br md 7.58 Dpth 3.60 Welded, 1 dk	**(B34G2SE) Pollution Control Vessel** Liq: 346; Liq (Oil): 346 Compartments: 8 Ta Ice Capable	**1 oil engine** geared to sc. shaft driving 1 FP propeller Total Power: 166kW (226hp) 7.5kn Daldizel 6CHNSP18/22 1 x 4 Stroke 6 Cy. 180 x 220 166kW (226bhp) Daldizel-Khabarovsk AuxGen: 1 x 50kW a.c, 1 x 30kW a.c Fuel: 12.0 (d.f.)
8730340 **SLV-315** - - **Vladivostok Sea Fishing Port (OAO 'Vladivostokskiy Morskoy Rybnyy Port')** - *Vladivostok* *Russia*	**191** Class: (RS) 85 326	**1989**-07 **Sudoremontnyy Zavod "Yakor" — Sovetskaya Gavan** Yd No: 1582U/8 Loa 29.19 Br ex 7.80 Dght 3.122 Lbp 28.53 Br md 7.58 Dpth 3.61 Welded	**(B34G2SE) Pollution Control Vessel** Liq: 346; Liq (Oil): 346 Compartments: 8 Ta Ice Capable	**1 oil engine** geared to sc. shaft driving 1 FP propeller Total Power: 165kW (224hp) 7.5kn Daldizel 6CHNSP18/22 1 x 4 Stroke 6 Cy. 180 x 220 165kW (224bhp) Daldizel-Khabarovsk AuxGen: 1 x 50kW a.c, 1 x 30kW a.c Fuel: 12.0 (d.f.)
8860717 **SLV-316** - - **Okhotsk Fishing Port (Okhotskiy MRP)** -	**191** Class: (RS) 85 326	**1991**-09 **Sudoremontnyy Zavod "Yakor" — Sovetskaya Gavan** Yd No: 1582U/9 Loa 29.17 Br ex 7.80 Dght 3.120 Lbp 28.50 Br md - Dpth 3.60 Welded, 1 dk	**(B34G2SE) Pollution Control Vessel** Liq: 346; Liq (Oil): 346 Compartments: 8 Ta Ice Capable	**1 oil engine** geared to sc. shaft driving 1 FP propeller Total Power: 165kW (224hp) 7.5kn Daldizel 6CHNSP18/22 1 x 4 Stroke 6 Cy. 180 x 220 165kW (224bhp) Daldizel-Khabarovsk AuxGen: 1 x 50kW a.c, 1 x 30kW a.c Fuel: 12.0 (d.f.)
8930952 **SLV-359** - - *launched as* PS-359 *-1982* **SE Sea Commercial Port of Illichivsk** - *Illichevsk* *Ukraine* Official number: 821803	**235** Class: (RS) 120 445	**1982 Bakinskiy Sudostroitelnyy Zavod im Vano Sturua — Baku** Yd No: 359 Loa 35.17 Br ex 8.01 Dght 3.120 Lbp 33.25 Br md - Dpth 3.60 Welded, 1 dk	**(B34G2SE) Pollution Control Vessel** Liq: 468; Liq (Oil): 468 Compartments: 10 Ta Ice Capable	**1 oil engine** geared to sc. shaft driving 1 FP propeller Total Power: 166kW (226hp) 8.1kn Daldizel 6CHNSP18/22 1 x 4 Stroke 6 Cy. 180 x 220 166kW (226bhp) Daldizel-Khabarovsk AuxGen: 1 x 50kW a.c, 1 x 30kW a.c Fuel: 11.0 (d.f.)
8226416 **SLV-363** - - **Absheron Regional Sea Oil Fleet Organisation (Caspian Sea Oil Fleet, State Oil Co of the Republic of Azerbaijan)** - *Baku* *Azerbaijan* MMSI: 423251100 Official number: DGR-0166	**235** Class: RS 120 445	**1983**-09 **Bakinskiy Sudostroitelnyy Zavod im Vano Sturua — Baku** Yd No: 363 Loa 35.18 Br ex 8.01 Dght 3.120 Lbp 33.25 Br md 7.58 Dpth 3.61 Welded	**(B34G2SE) Pollution Control Vessel** Liq: 468; Liq (Oil): 468 Compartments: 10 Ta Ice Capable	**1 oil engine** geared to sc. shaft driving 1 FP propeller Total Power: 166kW (226hp) 8.0kn Daldizel 6CHNSP18/22 1 x 4 Stroke 6 Cy. 180 x 220 166kW (226bhp) Daldizel-Khabarovsk AuxGen: 1 x 50kW a.c, 1 x 30kW a.c Fuel: 11.0 (d.f.)
8228555 **SLV-370** - - **Apsheron Oil Industry Fleet Administration (Apsheronskoye Upravleniye Neftyanogo Morskogo Flota)** - *Baku* *Azerbaijan* MMSI: 423253100 Official number: DGR-0362	**235** Class: RS 120 455	**1984 Bakinskiy Sudostroitelnyy Zavod im Vano Sturua — Baku** Yd No: 370 Loa 35.18 Br ex 8.01 Dght 3.120 Lbp 33.25 Br md 7.58 Dpth 3.61 Welded, 1 dk	**(B34G2SE) Pollution Control Vessel** Liq: 468; Liq (Oil): 468 Compartments: 10 Ta Ice Capable	**1 oil engine** geared to sc. shaft driving 1 FP propeller Total Power: 165kW (224hp) 8.0kn Daldizel 6CHNSP18/22 1 x 4 Stroke 6 Cy. 180 x 220 165kW (224bhp) Daldizel-Khabarovsk AuxGen: 1 x 50kW a.c, 1 x 30kW a.c Fuel: 11.0 (d.f.)
8726076 **SLV-397** - - **Alisa Co Ltd** - *Vladivostok* *Russia* Official number: 881062	**228** Class: RS 104 426	**1988**-07 **Bakinskiy Sudostroitelnyy Zavod im Vano Sturua — Baku** Yd No: 397 Loa 35.17 Br ex 8.01 Dght 3.120 Lbp 33.25 Br md 7.99 Dpth 3.60 Welded, 1 dk	**(B34G2SE) Pollution Control Vessel** Liq: 428; Liq (Oil): 428 Compartments: 9 Ta Ice Capable	**1 oil engine** geared to sc. shaft driving 1 FP propeller Total Power: 166kW (226hp) 8.1kn Daldizel 6CHNSP18/22 1 x 4 Stroke 6 Cy. 180 x 220 166kW (226bhp) Daldizel-Khabarovsk AuxGen: 1 x 50kW a.c, 1 x 30kW a.c Fuel: 11.0 (d.f.)
8834744 **SLV-410** - - **Specialized Sea Oil Fleet Organisation, Caspian Sea Oil Fleet, State Oil Co of the Republic of Azerbaijan** - *Baku* *Azerbaijan* Official number: DGR-0102	**235** Class: (RS) 120 455	**1990**-11 **Bakinskiy Sudostroitelnyy Zavod im Vano Sturua — Baku** Yd No: 410 Converted From: Pollution Control Vessel-1999 Loa 35.18 Br ex 8.00 Dght 3.122 Lbp 33.28 Br md 7.58 Dpth 3.60 Welded, 1 dk	**(A13B2TU) Tanker (unspecified)** Liq: 468; Liq (Oil): 468 Compartments: 10 Ta Ice Capable	**1 oil engine** geared to sc. shaft driving 1 FP propeller Total Power: 166kW (226hp) 8.0kn Daldizel 6CHNSP18/22 1 x 4 Stroke 6 Cy. 180 x 220 166kW (226bhp) Daldizel-Khabarovsk AuxGen: 1 x 50kW a.c, 1 x 30kW a.c Fuel: 11.0 (d.f.)
8838570 **SLV-411** - - **Specialized Sea Oil Fleet Organisation, Caspian Sea Oil Fleet, State Oil Co of the Republic of Azerbaijan** - *Baku* *Azerbaijan* MMSI: 423194100 Official number: DGR-0283	**235** Class: (RS) 120 455	**1991**-01 **Bakinskiy Sudostroitelnyy Zavod im Vano Sturua — Baku** Yd No: 411 Loa 35.18 Br ex 8.02 Dght 3.122 Lbp 33.28 Br md 7.58 Dpth 3.61 Welded, 1 dk	**(B34G2SE) Pollution Control Vessel** Liq: 468; Liq (Oil): 468 Compartments: 10 Ta Ice Capable	**1 oil engine** geared to sc. shaft driving 1 FP propeller Total Power: 166kW (226hp) 8.0kn Daldizel 6CHNSP18/22 1 x 4 Stroke 6 Cy. 180 x 220 166kW (226bhp) Daldizel-Khabarovsk AuxGen: 1 x 50kW a.c, 1 x 30kW a.c Fuel: 11.0 (d.f.)
8860729 **SLV-414** - - **Turkmennefteflot** - *Turkmenbashy* *Turkmenistan* Official number: 912913	**235** Class: (RS) 120 455	**1992**-03 **Bakinskiy Sudostroitelnyy Zavod im Vano Sturua — Baku** Yd No: 414 Loa 35.17 Br ex 8.00 Dght 3.120 Lbp 33.25 Br md - Dpth 3.60 Welded, 1 dk	**(B34G2SE) Pollution Control Vessel** Liq: 468; Liq (Oil): 468 Compartments: 10 Ta Ice Capable	**1 oil engine** geared to sc. shaft driving 1 FP propeller Total Power: 166kW (226hp) 8.0kn Daldizel 6CHNSP18/22 1 x 4 Stroke 6 Cy. 180 x 220 166kW (226bhp) Daldizel-Khabarovsk AuxGen: 1 x 50kW a.c, 1 x 30kW a.c Fuel: 11.0 (d.f.)
8737051 **SM** *YB6384* - **PT Lumas Unggul Jaya** - *Samarinda* *Indonesia* MMSI: 525003055	**211** Class: KI 64 -	**2007 C.V. Karya Lestari Industri — Samarinda** Loa - Br ex - Dght - Lbp 37.50 Br md 8.00 Dpth 2.40 Welded, 1 dk	**(A35D2RL) Landing Craft**	**2 oil engines** driving 2 Propellers Total Power: 514kW (698hp) Yanmar 6HA2M-HTE 2 x 4 Stroke 6 Cy. 130 x 165 each-257kW (349bhp) Yanmar Diesel Engine Co Ltd-Japan
9536131 **SM 2 RAMEE** *A6E3125* - *ex* VSA 2 Ramee *-2009* **Seamaster Maritime LLC** - *Dubai* *United Arab Emirates* MMSI: 470977000	**104** Class: BV 31 -	**2008**-04 **Seaspray Marine Services & Engineering FZC — Sharjah** Yd No: 1351 Loa 23.80 Br ex - Dght 1.600 Lbp 21.50 Br md 6.80 Dpth 3.25 Welded, 1 dk	**(B21A2OC) Crew/Supply Vessel** Hull Material: Aluminium Alloy Passengers: unberthed: 45	**2 oil engines** reduction geared to sc. shafts driving 2 FP propellers Total Power: 1,140kW (1,550hp) 16.5kn Caterpillar 3412D 1 x Vee 4 Stroke 12 Cy. 145 x 162 570kW (775bhp) Caterpillar Inc-USA AuxGen: 2 x 36kW 50Hz a.c

9041899 *DSQZ9* -
SM 3
ex Komatsushima Maru *-2009*
Semyung Shipping Co Ltd
-
Jeju *South Korea*
MMSI: 441774000
Official number: JJR-105185
1,493 710 2,616
Class: KR
1991-10 Yamanaka Zosen K.K. — Imabari Yd No: 517
Loa 74.02 (BB) Br ex - Dght 5.613
Lbp 69.75 Br md 11.70 Dpth 7.20
Welded
(A31A2GX) General Cargo Ship
Compartments: 1 Ho, ER
1 Ha: ER
1 oil engine sr reverse geared to sc. shaft driving 1 FP propeller
Total Power: 736kW (1,001hp) 12.2kn
Hanshin LH31G
1 x 4 Stroke 6 Cy. 310 x 530 736kW (1001bhp)
The Hanshin Diesel Works Ltd-Japan
Thrusters: 1 Thwart. FP thruster (f)

9072692 *DSRB6* -
SM 5
ex Taisei Maru *-2011*
ASTK Co Ltd
Sung Kyung Maritime Co Ltd (SK Maritime)
Jeju *South Korea*
MMSI: 440054000
Official number: JJR-111009
1,356 698 1,600
Class: KR
1993-06 K.K. Miura Zosensho — Saiki Yd No: 1076
Loa 71.00 Br ex - Dght 4.540
Lbp 66.00 Br md 11.50 Dpth 7.10
Welded, 1 dk
(A31A2GX) General Cargo Ship
Liq: 1,230
1 oil engine reverse geared to sc. shaft driving 1 FP propeller
Total Power: 736kW (1,001hp) 11.5kn
Niigata 6M31BFT
1 x 4 Stroke 6 Cy. 310 x 530 736kW (1001bhp)
Niigata Engineering Co Ltd-Japan

9583316 - -
SM 5-MAITHA
ex Dcs Falcon *-2012*
Seamaster Maritime LLC
-
Dubai *United Arab Emirates*
102 - 47
Class: NV
2009-11 Seaspray Marine Services & Engineering FZC — Sharjah Yd No: 1733
Loa 23.80 Br ex 6.81 Dght 1.350
Lbp 22.80 Br md 6.80 Dpth 3.25
Welded, 1 dk
(B21A20C) Crew/Supply Vessel
Hull Material: Aluminium Alloy
2 oil engines reduction geared to sc. shafts driving 2 FP propellers
Total Power: 898kW (1,220hp)
Caterpillar 3412
2 x Vee 4 Stroke 12 Cy. 137 x 152 each-449kW (610bhp)
Caterpillar Inc-USA
AuxGen: 2 x 90kW a.c

8811003 *HSB4392* -
SM 19
ex Taiyo Maru No. 8 *-2009*
Siam Mongkol Marine Co Ltd
-
Thailand
MMSI: 567060200
Official number: 520084794
1,041 587 1,950
1988-11 Hakata Zosen K.K. — Imabari Yd No: 382
Loa - Br ex - Dght 4.500
Lbp 65.99 Br md 12.02 Dpth 5.31
Welded, 1 dk
(A13B2TP) Products Tanker
1 oil engine geared to sc. shaft driving 1 FP propeller
Total Power: 1,324kW (1,800hp)
Hanshin 6EL30G
1 x 4 Stroke 6 Cy. 300 x 600 1324kW (1800bhp)
The Hanshin Diesel Works Ltd-Japan

8900880 *HSOF* -
SM 20
ex Thaioil 1 *-2010*
Siam Mongkol Marine Co Ltd
-
Bangkok *Thailand*
MMSI: 567026000
Official number: 321002751
3,073 1,266 4,998 T/cm 14.0
Class: AB
1989-09 Singapore Slipway & Engineering Co. Pte Ltd — Singapore Yd No: 168
Loa 98.50 (BB) Br ex - Dght 5.071
Lbp 92.00 Br md 15.50 Dpth 7.50
Welded, 1 dk
(A13B2TP) Products Tanker
Single Hull
Liq: 5,169; Liq (Oil): 5,169
Compartments: 12 Wing Ta, ER
3 Cargo Pump (s): 3x400m³/hr
Manifold: Bow/CM: 52m
2 oil engines with flexible couplings & sr geared to sc. shafts driving 2 FP propellers
Total Power: 1,766kW (2,402hp) 11.0kn
Daihatsu 6DLM-24FL
2 x 4 Stroke 6 Cy. 240 x 320 each-883kW (1201bhp)
Daihatsu Diesel Manufacturing Co Lt-Japan
AuxGen: 2 x 200kW 380V 50Hz a.c
Fuel: 52.7 (d.f.) 112.3 (r.f.) 8.0pd

9021564 *HSB4547* -
SM 21
ex Donam Pioneer *-2011*
ex Tokyo Pioneer *-1995*
Siam Thananya Marine Co Ltd
Siam Mongkol Marine Co Ltd
SatCom: Inmarsat C 456700425
Bangkok *Thailand*
MMSI: 567417000
Official number: 540001805
1,479 715 2,489 T/cm 7.6
Class: KR
1991-06 Daedong Shipbuilding Co Ltd — Busan Yd No: 364
Loa 74.22 (BB) Br ex 12.20 Dght 5.389
Lbp 67.80 Br md 12.00 Dpth 6.20
Welded, 1 dk
(A12A2TC) Chemical Tanker
Double Bottom Entire Compartment Length
Liq: 2,489
Compartments: 4 Ta, 8 Wing Ta, 2 Wing Slop Ta, ER
3 Cargo Pump (s): 1x300m³/hr, 2x200m³/hr
Manifold: Bow/CM: 37.6m
1 oil engine driving 1 FP propeller
Total Power: 1,324kW (1,800hp)
Akasaka A31
1 x 4 Stroke 6 Cy. 310 x 600 1324kW (1800bhp)
Akasaka Tekkosho KK (Akasaka DieselLtd)-Japan
AuxGen: 2 x 104kW 445V a.c
Fuel: 30.5 (d.f.) 110.5 (r.f.)

9367499 *HSB4913* -
SM 22
ex Fengshengyou 2 *-2014*
Siam Mongkol Marine Co Ltd
-
Bangkok *Thailand*
MMSI: 567063400
3,466 1,872 6,078 T/cm 12.7
Class: CC
2005-09 Duchang Shipbuilding General Yard — Duchang County JX Yd No: 4800
Loa 103.82 (BB) Br ex - Dght 6.120
Lbp 95.91 Br md 15.50 Dpth 8.20
Welded, 1 dk
(A13B2TP) Products Tanker
Double Hull (13F)
Liq: 5,898; Liq (Oil): 5,898
Compartments: 4 Ta, 8 Wing Ta, 1 Slop Ta, ER
1 oil engine geared to sc. shaft driving 1 FP propeller
Total Power: 2,040kW (2,774hp) 12.5kn
MAN-B&W 6L27/38
1 x 4 Stroke 6 Cy. 270 x 380 2040kW (2774bhp)
MAN B&W Diesel AG-Augsburg
AuxGen: 2 x 150kW 380/220V 50Hz a.c
Fuel: 47.0 (d.f.) (Heating Coils) 185.0 (r.f.) 8.0pd

9211626 *YD6910* -
SM 88
PT Kencana Gloria Marine
-
Balikpapan *Indonesia*
216 66 195
Class: GL
1998-11 PT Nanindah Mutiara Shipyard — Batam Yd No: T52
Loa 26.30 Br ex - Dght 3.400
Lbp 24.15 Br md 8.40 Dpth 3.80
Welded, 1 dk
(B32A2ST) Tug
2 oil engines reduction geared to sc. shafts driving 2 FP propellers
Total Power: 1,176kW (1,598hp) 12.0kn
Yanmar 6N165-EN
2 x 4 Stroke 6 Cy. 165 x 232 each-588kW (799bhp)
Yanmar Diesel Engine Co Ltd-Japan
AuxGen: 2 x 32kW 220/380V a.c

9604653 *3FYS9* -
SM AURORA
SMA Marine Ltd SA
Sammok Shipping Co Ltd
Panama *Panama*
MMSI: 373229000
Official number: 4425512
44,737 27,694 81,970 T/cm 71.9
Class: GL KR (BV)
2012-08 Jiangsu Eastern Heavy Industry Co Ltd — Jingjiang JS Yd No: JEHIC10-202
Loa 228.98 (BB) Br ex - Dght 14.450
Lbp 225.50 Br md 32.26 Dpth 20.25
Welded, 1 dk
(A21A2BC) Bulk Carrier
Grain: 97,000; Bale: 90,784
Compartments: 7 Ho, ER
7 Ha: ER
1 oil engine driving 1 FP propeller
Total Power: 14,280kW (19,415hp) 14.0kn
MAN-B&W 6S60MC-C8
1 x 2 Stroke 6 Cy. 600 x 2400 14280kW (19415bhp)

8877590 *YDA4411* -
SM. GOLDEN
ex Seki Maru No. 8 *-2008*
PT Saga Mas Asia
-
Cirebon *Indonesia*
320 96 -
Class: KI
1994-04 Osaki Zosen KK — Awaji HG
Loa 33.50 Br ex - Dght -
Lbp 29.30 Br md 9.00 Dpth 3.50
Welded, 1 dk
(B32A2ST) Tug
2 oil engines reverse geared to sc. shafts driving 2 FP propellers
Total Power: 736kW (1,000hp)
Hanshin 6LC26G
2 x 4 Stroke 6 Cy. 260 x 440 each-368kW (500bhp)
The Hanshin Diesel Works Ltd-Japan
AuxGen: 2 x 120kW a.c

9025924 - -
SM III
PT Pelayaran Nasional Fajar Marindo Raya
-
Jambi *Indonesia*
154 47 -
Class: KI
1997-08 PT Pelayaran Nasional Sabang — Jambi
Loa 26.00 Br ex - Dght 3.020
Lbp 23.65 Br md 7.00 Dpth 3.50
Welded, 1 dk
(B32A2ST) Tug
2 oil engines geared to sc. shafts driving 2 FP propellers
Total Power: 988kW (1,344hp)
Caterpillar 3412
2 x Vee 4 Stroke 12 Cy. 137 x 152 each-494kW (672bhp)
Caterpillar Inc-USA
AuxGen: 2 x 52kW 380V a.c

8821230 *YD3560* -
SM. JAYA
ex Muko Maru *-2010*
PT Saga Mas Asia
-
Batam *Indonesia*
325 98 -
Class: KI
1989-03 Kanrei Zosen K.K. — Naruto Yd No: 334
Loa 30.00 Br ex - Dght 3.250
Lbp 28.00 Br md 9.00 Dpth 4.80
Welded, 1 dk
(B32B2SP) Pusher Tug
2 oil engines geared to sc. shafts driving 2 FP propellers
Total Power: 2,206kW (3,000hp) 11.0kn
Daihatsu 6DLM-26
2 x 4 Stroke 6 Cy. 260 x 340 each-1103kW (1500bhp)
Daihatsu Diesel Manufacturing Co Lt-Japan
AuxGen: 2 x 99kW 225V a.c

9549906 *YDA4453* -
SM KARYA
PT Saga Mas Asia
-
Tanjung Priok *Indonesia*
249 75 197
Class: KI (NK)
2008-12 PT Palma Progress Shipyard — Batam Yd No: 346
Loa 28.05 Br ex - Dght 3.312
Lbp 26.03 Br md 8.60 Dpth 4.30
Welded, 1 dk
(B32A2ST) Tug
2 oil engines reduction geared to sc. shafts driving 2 FP propellers
Total Power: 1,472kW (2,002hp)
Yanmar 6RY17P-GV
2 x 4 Stroke 6 Cy. 165 x 219 each-736kW (1001bhp)
Yanmar Diesel Engine Co Ltd-Japan
AuxGen: 2 x 57kW 415V a.c
Fuel: 170.0

9263019 *PNET* -
SM LIBERTY
ex Nagato *-2009*
PT Saga Mas Asia
-
Batam *Indonesia*
368 111 -
Class: KI
2002-03 Kegoya Dock K.K. — Kure Yd No: 1072
Loa 30.00 Br ex - Dght -
Lbp - Br md 9.00 Dpth 5.90
Welded, 1 dk
(B32B2SP) Pusher Tug
2 oil engines reduction geared to sc. shafts driving 2 FP propellers
Total Power: 2,942kW (4,000hp)
Daihatsu 6DKM-26
2 x 4 Stroke 6 Cy. 260 x 380 each-1471kW (2000bhp)
Daihatsu Diesel Manufacturing Co Lt-Japan
AuxGen: 2 x 135kW 225V a.c

8664553 *POOI* -
SM MANDIRI
PT Sumber Makmur Marine
-
Samarinda *Indonesia*
Official number: GT.347No.4876/lik
347 105 -
Class: KI (Class contemplated)
2011 C.V. Karya Lestari Industri — Samarinda Yd No: 5966
Loa 43.50 Br ex - Dght -
Lbp - Br md 9.00 Dpth 3.00
Welded, 1 dk
(A35D2RL) Landing Craft
2 oil engines reduction geared to sc. shafts driving 2 Propellers
Total Power: 596kW (810hp)
Yanmar
2 x each-298kW (405bhp)
Yanmar Diesel Engine Co Ltd-Japan

IMO / Call sign / Flag	Name / Former names / Owner / Manager / Port / MMSI	Tonnage (GT / NT / DWT)	Class	Build / Dimensions	Type	Machinery
8864725 *SPS2490* -	**SM-MB-1** *ex* MC 38 *-2004* *ex* Iglicioara 13 *-2004* *ex* INC 4270 *-2004* **STRABAG Wasserbau GmbH** STRABAG Hydrotech Sp z oo *Szczecin* *Poland* MMSI: 261006470	**812** 243 1,536	Class: GL (RN)	**1980-05 Santierul Naval Drobeta-Turnu Severin S.A. — Drobeta-Turnu S.** Loa 60.30 Br ex - Dght 3.551 Lbp 59.70 Br md 11.30 Dpth 4.00 Welded, 1 dk	**(B34A2SH) Hopper, Motor** Hopper: 940 Compartments: 1 Ho, ER 1 Ha: ER	**2 oil engines** reverse reduction geared to sc. shafts driving 2 Directional propellers Total Power: 1,074kW (1,460hp) Caterpillar 3412TA 2 x Vee 4 Stroke 12 Cy. 137 x 152 each-537kW (730bhp) (new engine 1998) Caterpillar Inc-USA AuxGen: 2 x 24kW 220/380V a.c
8954659 *SPS2493* -	**SM-MB-2** *ex* MC 39 *-2004* *ex* Silesia 5 *-1997* **STRABAG Wasserbau GmbH** STRABAG Hydrotech Sp z oo *Szczecin* *Poland* MMSI: 261006710	**812** 243 1,536	Class: GL	**1980-09 Santierul Naval Drobeta-Turnu Severin S.A. — Drobeta-Turnu S.** Loa 60.67 Br ex - Dght 3.090 Lbp 59.70 Br md 11.00 Dpth 4.00 Welded, 1 dk	**(B34A2SH) Hopper, Motor**	**2 oil engines** reduction geared to sc. shafts driving 2 FP propellers Total Power: 1,074kW (1,460hp) Caterpillar 3412TA 2 x Vee 4 Stroke 12 Cy. 137 x 152 each-537kW (730bhp) (new engine 1980) Caterpillar Inc-USA AuxGen: 2 x 30kW 380V a.c
8954647 *SPS2494* -	**SM-MB-3** *ex* MC 40 *-2004* *ex* Silestia 6 *-2004* **STRABAG Wasserbau GmbH** STRABAG Hydrotech Sp z oo *Szczecin* *Poland* MMSI: 261006720	**812** 243 1,534	Class: GL	**1980-11 Santierul Naval Drobeta-Turnu Severin S.A. — Drobeta-Turnu S.** Yd No: 10367004 Loa 60.67 Br ex - Dght 3.090 Lbp 59.70 Br md 11.00 Dpth 4.00 Welded, 1 dk	**(B34A2SH) Hopper, Motor**	**2 oil engines** reduction geared to SC. shafts driving 2 FP propellers Total Power: 536kW (728hp) Caterpillar 3412TA 2 x Vee 4 Stroke 12 Cy. 137 x 152 each-268kW (364bhp) (new engine 1998) Caterpillar Inc-USA
8824139 *SPS2495* -	**SM-MB-4** *ex* MC 41 *-2004* *ex* Silistea 7 *-1999* **STRABAG Wasserbau GmbH** STRABAG Hydrotech Sp z oo *Szczecin* *Poland* MMSI: 261006690	**812** 734 1,531	Class: GL (RN)	**1981-03 Santierul Naval Drobeta-Turnu Severin S.A. — Drobeta-Turnu S.** Yd No: 10371008 Loa 60.25 Br ex - Dght 3.090 Lbp 59.75 Br md 11.30 Dpth 4.00 Welded, 1 dk	**(B34A2SH) Hopper, Motor** Hopper: 940 Compartments: 1 Ho, ER 1 Ha: ER	**2 oil engines** driving 2 Directional propellers Total Power: 1,074kW (1,460hp) Caterpillar 3412TA 1 x Vee 4 Stroke 12 Cy. 137 x 152 537kW (730bhp) Caterpillar Inc-USA Caterpillar 3412TA 1 x Vee 4 Stroke 12 Cy. 137 x 152 537kW (730bhp) (new engine 1998) Caterpillar Inc-USA AuxGen: 2 x 1kW 24V d.c
8899081 *SPG2878* -	**SM-PRC-101** **Przedsiebiorstwo Robot Czerpalnych I Podwodnych - 'Dragmor' Sp z oo** - *Szczecin* *Poland* MMSI: 261011140	**539** 171 1,104	Class: PR	**1973 Plocka Stocznia Rzeczna — Plock** Yd No: SM660/613 Loa 58.96 Br ex 9.50 Dght 3.250 Lbp 57.77 Br md - Dpth 3.35 Welded, 1 dk	**(A31A2GX) General Cargo Ship**	**2 oil engines** reduction geared to sc. shafts driving 2 FP propellers Total Power: 382kW (520hp) 7.8kn Deutz BF12L714 2 x Vee 4 Stroke 12 Cy. 120 x 140 each-191kW (260bhp) Kloeckner Humboldt Deutz AG-West Germany AuxGen: 2 x 36kW 400V a.c
8937534 *SPG2914* -	**SM-PRC-102** **Przedsiebiorstwo Robot Czerpalnych I Podwodnych Sp z oo (Dredging & Underwater Works Co Ltd)** - *Gdansk* *Poland* MMSI: 261002060	*579* 555 1,068	Class: PR	**1973-09 Plocka Stocznia Rzeczna — Plock** Yd No: SM660/614 Loa 58.94 Br ex 9.53 Dght 3.250 Lbp 58.63 Br md - Dpth 3.35 Welded, 1 dk	**(B34A2SH) Hopper, Motor**	**2 oil engines** reduction geared to sc. shafts driving 2 FP propellers Total Power: 460kW (626hp) 7.8kn Deutz BF12L714 2 x Vee 4 Stroke 12 Cy. 120 x 140 each-230kW (313bhp) Kloeckner Humboldt Deutz AG-West Germany AuxGen: 1 x 30kW 400V a.c, 1 x 28kW 400V a.c
8899093 *SPG2821* -	**SM-PRC-103** **Przedsiebiorstwo Robot Czerpalnych I Podwodnych - 'Dragmor' Sp z oo** - *Szczecin* *Poland* MMSI: 261010170	**539** 171 1,104	Class: PR	**1973-12 Plocka Stocznia Rzeczna — Plock** Yd No: SM660/615 Loa 58.96 Br ex 9.50 Dght 2.910 Lbp 57.77 Br md - Dpth 3.35 Welded, 1 dk	**(A31A2GX) General Cargo Ship**	**2 oil engines** reduction geared to sc. shafts driving 2 FP propellers Total Power: 382kW (520hp) 7.8kn Deutz BF12L714 2 x Vee 4 Stroke 12 Cy. 120 x 140 each-191kW (260bhp) Kloeckner Humboldt Deutz AG-West Germany AuxGen: 2 x 36kW 400V a.c
8937558 *SPG2916* -	**SM-PRC-105** **Przedsiebiorstwo Robot Czerpalnych I Podwodnych Sp z oo (Dredging & Underwater Works Co Ltd)** - *Gdansk* *Poland* MMSI: 261002080	*580* 555 1,084	Class: PR	**1974-07 Plocka Stocznia Rzeczna — Plock** Yd No: SM660/617 Loa 59.06 Br ex 9.54 Dght 3.250 Lbp 58.99 Br md - Dpth 3.35 Welded, 1 dk	**(B34A2SH) Hopper, Motor**	**2 oil engines** reduction geared to sc. shafts driving 2 FP propellers Total Power: 460kW (626hp) 7.8kn Deutz BF12L714 2 x Vee 4 Stroke 12 Cy. 120 x 140 each-230kW (313bhp) Kloeckner Humboldt Deutz AG-West Germany AuxGen: 1 x 30kW 400V a.c, 1 x 28kW 400V a.c
8937560 *SPG2917* -	**SM-PRC-106** **Przedsiebiorstwo Robot Czerpalnych I Podwodnych Sp z oo (Dredging & Underwater Works Co Ltd)** - *Gdansk* *Poland* MMSI: 261002090 Official number: ROG2362	*579* 555 1,056	Class: PR	**1974-07 Plocka Stocznia Rzeczna — Plock** Yd No: SM660/618 Loa 58.92 Br ex 9.53 Dght 3.000 Lbp 58.63 Br md - Dpth 3.35 Welded, 1 dk	**(B34A2SH) Hopper, Motor**	**2 oil engines** reduction geared to sc. shafts driving 2 FP propellers Total Power: 460kW (626hp) 7.8kn Deutz BF12L714 2 x Vee 4 Stroke 12 Cy. 120 x 140 each-230kW (313bhp) Kloeckner Humboldt Deutz AG-West Germany AuxGen: 2 x 36kW 400V a.c
8899108 *SPG2879* -	**SM-PRC-107** **Przedsiebiorstwo Robot Czerpalnych I Podwodnych - 'Dragmor' Sp z oo** - *Szczecin* *Poland* MMSI: 261011150	**539** 170 1,104	Class: PR	**1974-09 Plocka Stocznia Rzeczna — Plock** Yd No: SM660/619 Loa 58.96 Br ex 9.50 Dght 3.250 Lbp 57.77 Br md - Dpth 3.35 Welded, 1 dk	**(A31A2GX) General Cargo Ship**	**2 oil engines** reduction geared to sc. shafts driving 2 FP propellers Total Power: 382kW (520hp) 7.8kn Deutz BF12L714 2 x Vee 4 Stroke 12 Cy. 120 x 140 each-191kW (260bhp) Kloeckner Humboldt Deutz AG-West Germany AuxGen: 2 x 36kW 380V a.c
8937572 *SPG2918* -	**SM-PRC-108** **Przedsiebiorstwo Robot Czerpalnych I Podwodnych Sp z oo (Dredging & Underwater Works Co Ltd)** - *Gdansk* *Poland* MMSI: 261002100 Official number: ROG2040	*576* 554 1,084	Class: PR	**1974-09 Plocka Stocznia Rzeczna — Plock** Yd No: SM660/620 Loa 58.55 Br ex 9.52 Dght 3.250 Lbp 57.77 Br md - Dpth 3.35 Welded, 1 dk	**(B34A2SH) Hopper, Motor**	**2 oil engines** reduction geared to sc. shafts driving 2 FP propellers Total Power: 460kW (626hp) 7.8kn Deutz BF12L714 2 x Vee 4 Stroke 12 Cy. 120 x 140 each-230kW (313bhp) Kloeckner Humboldt Deutz AG-West Germany AuxGen: 2 x 36kW 400V a.c
8937584 *SPG2919* -	**SM-PRC-110** **Przedsiebiorstwo Robot Czerpalnych I Podwodnych Sp z oo (Dredging & Underwater Works Co Ltd)** - *Gdansk* *Poland* MMSI: 261002110	*579* 555 1,068	Class: PR	**1976-01 Plocka Stocznia Rzeczna — Plock** Yd No: SM660/630 Loa 58.91 Br ex 9.53 Dght 3.250 Lbp - Br md - Dpth 3.35 Welded, 1 dk	**(B34A2SH) Hopper, Motor**	**2 oil engines** reduction geared to sc. shafts driving 2 FP propellers Total Power: 460kW (626hp) 7.8kn Deutz BF12L714 2 x Vee 4 Stroke 12 Cy. 120 x 140 each-230kW (313bhp) Kloeckner Humboldt Deutz AG-West Germany AuxGen: 2 x 28kW 380V a.c
8937596 *SPG2920* -	**SM-PRC-112** **Przedsiebiorstwo Robot Czerpalnych I Podwodnych Sp z oo (Dredging & Underwater Works Co Ltd)** - *Gdansk* *Poland* MMSI: 261002050	*580* 556 1,069	Class: (PR)	**1976-04 Plocka Stocznia Rzeczna — Plock** Yd No: SM660/632 Loa 58.96 Br ex 9.56 Dght 3.000 Lbp - Br md - Dpth 3.40 Welded, 1 dk	**(B34A2SH) Hopper, Motor**	**2 oil engines** reduction geared to sc. shafts driving 2 FP propellers Total Power: 460kW (626hp) 7.8kn Deutz BF12L714 2 x Vee 4 Stroke 12 Cy. 120 x 140 each-230kW (313bhp) Kloeckner Humboldt Deutz AG-West Germany AuxGen: 1 x 28kW 380V a.c, 1 x 11kW 380V a.c
8864244 *YD3586* -	**SM. SEDAYU** *ex* Bingo Maru *-2009* **PT Saga Mas Asia** - *Batam* *Indonesia*	**331** 100 -	Class: KI	**1992-03 Hongawara Zosen K.K. — Fukuyama** Yd No: 360 Loa 30.25 Br ex - Dght 3.300 Lbp 28.00 Br md 9.00 Dpth 4.79 Welded, 1 dk	**(B32B2SP) Pusher Tug**	**2 oil engines** driving 2 FP propellers Total Power: 1,472kW (2,002hp) Niigata 6MG25CXE 2 x 4 Stroke 6 Cy. 250 x 320 each-736kW (1001bhp) Niigata Engineering Co Ltd-Japan AuxGen: 2 x 88kW 220V a.c

IMO / Call sign	Name / Owner	Tonnage	Class	Builder / Dimensions	Type	Machinery
9025936 - -	**SM V** **PT Pelayaran Nasional Fajar Marindo Raya** - *Jambi* *Indonesia*	**154** 47 -	Class: KI	**1997**-09 **P.T. Sabang Raya Indah — Jambi** Loa 26.00 Br ex - Dght 3.000 Lbp 23.65 Br md 7.00 Dpth 3.50 Welded, 1 dk	**(B32A2ST) Tug**	**2 oil engines** reduction geared to sc. shafts driving 2 FP propellers Total Power: 988kW (1,344hp) Caterpillar 3412 2 x Vee 4 Stroke 12 Cy. 137 x 152 each-494kW (672bhp) (made 1996) Caterpillar Inc-USA AuxGen: 2 x 54kW 380/220V a.c
9025948 - -	**SM VII** **PT Pelayaran Nasional Fajar Marindo Raya** - *Jambi* *Indonesia*	**112** 67 -	Class: (KI)	**1999**-03 **P.T. Sabang Raya Indah — Jambi** L reg 23.00 Br ex - Dght 2.500 Lbp 20.50 Br md 6.50 Dpth 3.00 Welded, 1 dk	**(B32A2ST) Tug**	**2 oil engines** geared to sc. shafts driving 2 Propellers Total Power: 536kW (728hp) 12.0kn Caterpillar D343 2 x 4 Stroke 6 Cy. 137 x 165 each-268kW (364bhp) (made 1993) Caterpillar Inc-USA
9589035 *YDA3202* -	**SM XI** **PT Pelnas Fajar Marindo Raya** - *Batam* *Indonesia* MMSI: 525020080	**276** 83 -	Class: KI RI	**2012**-05 **P.T. Batam Expressindo Shipyard — Batam** Yd No: 832 Loa 29.00 Br ex - Dght 3.500 Lbp 27.42 Br md 9.00 Dpth 4.25 Welded, 1 dk	**(B32A2ST) Tug**	**2 oil engines** reduction geared to sc. shafts driving 2 FP propellers Total Power: 1,472kW (2,002hp) Caterpillar C32 ACERT 2 x Vee 4 Stroke 12 Cy. 145 x 162 each-736kW (1001bhp) Caterpillar Inc-USA AuxGen: 2 x 93kW 380V a.c
9678953 *YDA3248* -	**SM-XV** **PT Pelnas Fajar Marindo Raya** - *Batam* *Indonesia* Official number: 2012PPM No.2550/L	**154** 47 -	Class: KI	**2012**-10 **P.T. Batam Expressindo Shipyard — Batam** Yd No: 844 Loa 23.50 Br ex - Dght - Lbp - Br md 7.32 Dpth 3.20 Welded, 1 dk	**(B32A2ST) Tug**	**2 oil engines** reduction geared to sc. shafts driving 2 FP propellers Total Power: 894kW (1,216hp) Cummins KTA-19-M3 2 x 4 Stroke 6 Cy. 159 x 159 each-447kW (608bhp) Cummins Engine Co Inc-USA
9267704 *PBKD* -	**SMARAGD** **Smaragd BV** De Bock Maritiem BV *Alkmaar* *Netherlands* MMSI: 244967000 Official number: 41120	**2,339** 1,294 3,195	Class: BV	**2003**-06 **Barkmeijer Stroobos B.V. — Stroobos** Yd No: 298 Loa 89.99 Br ex - Dght 4.640 Lbp 84.99 Br md 12.50 Dpth 6.00 Welded, 1 dk	**(A31A2GX) General Cargo Ship** Double Hull Grain: 4,723 Compartments: 1 Ho, ER	**1 oil engine** geared to sc. shaft driving 1 FP propeller Total Power: 999kW (1,358hp) 11.0kn Caterpillar 3516B 1 x Vee 4 Stroke 16 Cy. 170 x 190 999kW (1358bhp) Caterpillar Inc-USA AuxGen: 2 x 96kW a.c Thrusters: 1 Tunnel thruster (f) Fuel: 270.0 (d.f.)
9175573 *V2QH5* -	**SMARAGD** *ex* MTC Jaguar *-2003* *ex* Smaragd *-2002* *ex* SJ Glory *-2001* *ex* Signet Glory *-2000* *ex* Seafreight Glory *-1999* *ex* Smaragd *-1998* **Scrambler Shipping Co Ltd** MarConsult Schiffahrt (GmbH & Co) KG *Saint John's* *Antigua & Barbuda* MMSI: 304482000 Official number: 3095	**4,028** 2,118 5,095 T/cm 13.5	Class: GL (BV)	**1998**-10 **Jinling Shipyard — Nanjing JS** Yd No: 95-7027 Loa 100.55 (BB) Br ex - Dght 6.470 Lbp 95.40 Br md 18.50 Dpth 8.25 Welded, 2 dks	**(A31A2GX) General Cargo Ship** Grain: 7,624 TEU 519 C Ho 143 TEU C Dk 376 TEU incl 60 ref C. Compartments: 3 Ho, ER, 3 Tw Dk 3 Ha: ER Cranes: 2x40t Ice Capable	**1 oil engine** with clutches, flexible couplings & sr geared to sc. shaft driving 1 CP propeller Total Power: 3,960kW (5,384hp) 15.0kn MaK 9M32 1 x 4 Stroke 9 Cy. 320 x 480 3960kW (5384bhp) MaK Motoren GmbH & Co. KG-Kiel AuxGen: 1 x 624kW 400V 50Hz a.c, 3 x 340kW 400V 50Hz a.c Thrusters: 1 Thwart. FP thruster (f) Fuel: 77.9 (d.f.) 427.8 (r.f.) 22.5pd
9171034 *LJXV* -	**SMARAGD** **Smaragd AS** - SatCom: Inmarsat C 425962410 *Aalesund* *Norway* MMSI: 259624000	**1,775** 532 850	Class: NV	**1999**-07 **Stocznia Gdanska - Grupa Stoczni Gdynia SA — Gdansk** (Hull) Yd No: 200/1 **1999**-07 **Solstrand AS — Tomrefjord** Yd No: 66 Loa 68.10 Br ex - Dght 5.800 Lbp 60.00 Br md 12.60 Dpth 8.40 Welded, 1 dk	**(B11B2FV) Fishing Vessel** Ins: 400 Ice Capable	**1 oil engine** reduction geared to sc. shaft driving 1 CP propeller Total Power: 4,320kW (5,873hp) 16.5kn MaK 9M32 1 x 4 Stroke 9 Cy. 320 x 480 4320kW (5873bhp) MaK Motoren GmbH & Co. KG-Kiel AuxGen: 1 x 1800kW 230/440V 60Hz a.c, 1 x 910kW 230/440V 60Hz a.c Thrusters: 1 Thwart. FP thruster (f); 1 Thwart. FP thruster (a)
7905041 *OW2289* FD 1000	**SMARAGD** *ex* Hvannholmur *-2002* **P/F J F K Trol** - *Skopun* *Faeroe Islands (Danish)* MMSI: 231189000 Official number: D2711	**275** 82 110	Class: NV	**1980**-01 **Johs Kristensen Skibsbyggeri A/S — Hvide Sande** Yd No: 144 Lengthened-1984 Loa 31.91 Br ex 7.60 Dght 3.900 Lbp 28.55 Br md 7.51 Dpth 6.15 Welded, 2 dks	**(B11A2FS) Stern Trawler** Ice Capable	**1 oil engine** geared to sc. shaft driving 1 FP propeller Total Power: 827kW (1,124hp) Caterpillar D399SCAC 1 x Vee 4 Stroke 16 Cy. 159 x 203 827kW (1124bhp) Caterpillar Tractor Co-USA AuxGen: 2 x 82kW 380V 50Hz a.c
8024870 *SY3839* -	**SMARAGDI** *ex* Panagia Kannala *-2009* *ex* Averity *-2003* *ex* Natalie *-1988* **Smaragdi Maritime Co** - *Piraeus* *Greece* MMSI: 240140000 Official number: 11232	*799* - 1,777 T/cm 6.5	Class: (RI) (BV) (NK)	**1981**-04 **Fukuoka Shipbuilding Co Ltd — Fukuoka FO** Yd No: 1087 Loa 69.53 Br ex 11.82 Dght 4.314 Lbp 64.01 Br md 11.80 Dpth 5.16 Welded, 1 dk	**(A13B2TP) Products Tanker** Liq: 2,117; Liq (Oil): 2,117 Compartments: 8 Ta, ER 3 Cargo Pump (s)	**1 oil engine** reverse reduction geared to sc. shaft driving 1 FP propeller Total Power: 1,030kW (1,400hp) 11.5kn Yanmar 6Z-DT 1 x 4 Stroke 6 Cy. 280 x 340 1030kW (1400bhp) Yanmar Diesel Engine Co Ltd-Japan AuxGen: 3 x 245kW 440/220V 60Hz a.c Fuel: 93.0 (d.f.) 4.5pd
5360778 *HKD08* -	**SMART** *ex* Kongsvik *-2010* *ex* Fjelltun *-1996* *ex* Skudebu *-1973* *ex* Thurosund *-1967* **Smart Shipping Ltd** - *Isla de San Andres* *Colombia* Official number: MC-07-0178	**450** 224 640	Class: (BV)	**1960**-07 **Husumer Schiffswerft — Husum** Yd No: 1163 Lengthened-1988 Loa 49.48 Br ex 7.90 Dght - Lbp 44.68 Br md 7.85 Dpth 5.02 Riveted, 1 dk	**(A31A2GX) General Cargo Ship** Grain: 970 Compartments: 1 Ho, ER 1 Ha: ER Derricks: 1x3t	**1 oil engine** driving 1 FP propeller Total Power: 682kW (928hp) 10.5kn Alpha 405-26VO 1 x 2 Stroke 5 Cy. 260 x 400 369kW (502bhp) (new engine 1974) Alpha Diesel A/S-Denmark Fuel: 25.0 (d.f.)
8943428 *XUFJ3* -	**SMART** *ex* Kapitan Surnin *-2009* *ex* Ciulman *-2009* **Delta Streamline Ltd** Blue Wave Shipping Inc *Phnom Penh* *Cambodia* MMSI: 514271000 Official number: 0987339	**2,597** 1,033 3,038	Class: RS RR	**1987**-12 **Santierul Naval Oltenita S.A. — Oltenita** Yd No: 266 Loa 108.40 Br ex 15.30 Dght 3.260 Lbp 105.00 Br md 14.80 Dpth 5.00 Welded, 1 dk	**(A31A2GX) General Cargo Ship** Grain: 4,340 Compartments: 4 Ho, ER 4 Ha: 4 (18.0 x 14.4)ER	**2 oil engines** driving 2 FP propellers Total Power: 1,030kW (1,400hp) 10.2kn S.K.L. 6NVD48A-2U 2 x 4 Stroke 6 Cy. 320 x 480 each-515kW (700bhp) VEB Schwermaschinenbau "KarlLiebknecht" (SKL)-Magdeburg AuxGen: 3 x 50kW Fuel: 89.0 (d.f.)
8666393 *VRS4520* -	**SMART GENIUS 3** **Pacific Energy Marine Transport Ltd** Chuang Xin Ship Management Co Ltd *Hong Kong* *Hong Kong* MMSI: 477995167 Official number: BM21618Y	**221** 155 337		**1999**-01 **Guangzhou Fishing Vessel Shipyard — Guangzhou GD** Loa 23.55 Br ex - Dght 1.600 Lbp 22.61 Br md 9.00 Dpth 4.10 Welded, 1 dk	**(B35E2TF) Bunkering Tanker** Single Hull	**2 oil engines** reduction geared to sc. shafts driving 2 Propellers Total Power: 536kW (728hp) Cummins NT-855-M 2 x 4 Stroke 6 Cy. 140 x 152 each-268kW (364bhp) Cummins Engine Co Inc-USA
8666381 *VRS4521* -	**SMART GENIUS 8** **Able Progress International Ltd** Chuang Xin Ship Management Co Ltd *Hong Kong* *Hong Kong* MMSI: 477995166 Official number: BM21604Y	**166** 116 201		**1998**-02 **Guangzhou Panyu Lingshan Shipyard Ltd — Guangzhou GD** Loa 23.55 Br ex - Dght 1.500 Lbp 22.61 Br md 9.00 Dpth 4.00 Welded, 1 dk	**(B35E2TF) Bunkering Tanker** Single Hull	**2 oil engines** reduction geared to sc. shafts driving 2 Propellers Total Power: 522kW (710hp) Caterpillar 2 x each-261kW (355bhp) Caterpillar Inc-USA
8419013 *T8XL* -	**SMART HASSAN** *ex* Joud 1 *-2014* *ex* Wr I *-2013* *ex* Gulf Crown *-2011* *ex* Crown A *-2006* *ex* Seacrown *-2001* *ex* Petrobulk Pilot *-1993* **Hibatallah Petroleum Inc** Joud Energy Co *Malakal Harbour* *Palau* MMSI: 511011030	**25,429** 8,959 39,008 T/cm 47.5	Class: (LR) (RI) (AB) Classed LR until 17/3/07	**1985**-09 **Onomichi Dockyard Co Ltd — Onomichi HS** Yd No: 320 Loa 182.30 (BB) Br ex 31.42 Dght 10.970 Lbp 172.02 Br md 31.40 Dpth 17.23 Welded, 1 dk	**(A13A2TW) Crude/Oil Products Tanker** Double Sides Entire Compartment Length Liq: 44,744; Liq (Oil): 44,744 Cargo Heating Coils Compartments: 7 Ta, ER, 2 Wing Slop Ta 3 Cargo Pump (s) Manifold: Bow/CM: 84m	**1 oil engine** driving 1 FP propeller Total Power: 6,767kW (9,200hp) 14.0kn Sulzer 5RTA58 1 x 2 Stroke 5 Cy. 580 x 1700 6767kW (9200bhp) Hitachi Zosen Corp-Japan AuxGen: 3 x 520kW 450V 60Hz a.c Boilers: AuxB (ex.g.) 22.4kgf/cm² (22.0bar), WTAuxB (o.f.) 16.0kgf/cm² (15.7bar) Fuel: 193.5 (d.f.) 1768.9 (r.f.)

IMO / Call sign	Name / Owner	Tonnage	Class	Builder / Dimensions	Type	Machinery
9577032 *2EKQ2* -	**SMART LADY** - **Blenheim Shipping UK Ltd** - SatCom: Inmarsat C 423592877 *Douglas* *Isle of Man (British)* MMSI: 235086622 Official number: 742823	**64,089** 35,252 116,715 T/cm 99.5	Class: LR ✠ **100A1** SS 10/2011 Double Hull oil tanker CSR ESP **ShipRight** (CM,ACS (B) *IWS LI SPM ✠ **LMC** **UMS IGS** Cable: 715.0/92.0 U3 (a)	**2011-10 Sungdong Shipbuilding & Marine Engineering Co Ltd — Tongyeong** Yd No: 2037 Loa 249.90 (BB) Br ex 44.03 Dght 15.123 Lbp 239.00 Br md 44.00 Dpth 21.50 Welded, 1 dk	**(A13A2TW) Crude/Oil Products Tanker** Double Hull (13F) Liq: 127,234; Liq (Oil): 124,140 Cargo Heating Coils Compartments: 12 Wing Ta, 2 Wing Slop Ta, ER 3 Cargo Pump (s): 3x3000m³/hr Manifold: Bow/CM: 124.6m	**1 oil engine** driving 1 FP propeller Total Power: 13,560kW (18,436hp) 15.1kn MAN-B&W 6S60MC-C 1 x 2 Stroke 6 Cy. 600 x 2400 13560kW (18436bhp) Hyundai Engine & Machinery Co Ltd-South Korea AuxGen: 3 x 740kW 450V 60Hz a.c Boilers: e (ex.g.) 21.4kgf/cm² (21.0bar), AuxB (o.f.) 18.4kgf/cm² (18.0bar) Fuel: 344.0 (d.f.) 2750.0 (r.f.) 44.5pd
8315152 *J8B4216* -	**SMART SAIL** *ex* Gant Star *-2010* *ex* Maria Bonita *-1999* **Smart Sail Ltd** Tranglory Shipping Co Ltd SatCom: Inmarsat C 437724910 *Kingstown* *St Vincent & The Grenadines* MMSI: 377249000 Official number: 10689	**13,982** 8,462 22,233	Class: RI (LR) (NV) (NK) ✠ Classed LR until 3/6/88	**1986-11 Mitsubishi Heavy Industries Ltd. — Kobe** Yd No: 1148 Loa 155.50 (BB) Br ex 25.04 Dght 9.768 Lbp 149.00 Br md 25.00 Dpth 13.60 Welded, 1 dk, 2nd dk in way of Nos. 2, 3 & 4 holds	**(A31A2GX) General Cargo Ship** Grain: 31,001; Bale: 28,979 TEU 674 C Ho 338 TEU C Dk 336 TEU incl 50 ref C. Compartments: 4 Ho, ER, 3 Tw Dk 7 Ha: (19.8 x 10.6)4 (25.6 x 8.0)2 (12.8 x 8.0)ER Cranes: 4x25t	**1 oil engine** driving 1 FP propeller Total Power: 6,540kW (8,892hp) 15.3kn Sulzer 6RTA48 1 x 2 Stroke 6 Cy. 480 x 1400 6540kW (8892bhp) Mitsubishi Heavy Industries Ltd-Japan AuxGen: 3 x 490kW 450V 60Hz a.c
9217682 *C6WB8* -	**SMARTY** *ex* Oceanthi *-2007* *ex* Nicon Frontier *-2005* **Smarty Shipping Co Ltd** Petrofin Ship Management Inc *Nassau* *Bahamas* MMSI: 309159000 Official number: 8001346	**26,067** 14,651 45,499 T/cm 50.5	Class: NK (LR) Classed LR until 13/4/07	**2000-06 Imabari Shipbuilding Co Ltd — Marugame KG (Marugame Shipyard)** Yd No: 1335 Loa 189.83 (BB) Br ex 31.03 Dght 11.659 Lbp 179.80 Br md 31.00 Dpth 16.50 Welded, 1 dk	**(A21A2BC) Bulk Carrier** Grain: 55,906; Bale: 54,360 Compartments: 5 Ho, ER 5 Ha: (20.0 x 16.0)4 (20.8 x 17.6)ER Cranes: 4x30.5t	**1 oil engine** driving 1 FP propeller Total Power: 7,281kW (9,899hp) 14.0kn MAN-B&W 6S50MC 1 x 2 Stroke 6 Cy. 500 x 1910 7281kW (9899bhp) Mitsui Engineering & Shipbuilding CLtd-Japan AuxGen: 3 x 400kW 450V 60Hz a.c Boilers: WTAuxB (Comp) 8.2kgf/cm² (8.0bar) Fuel: 1870.0
9411862 *9HZT9* -	**SMAT** - **Black Sea Ferries Shipping Ltd** IP Mikhail Melnikov *Valletta* *Malta* MMSI: 249755000 Official number: 9411862	**5,775** 1,732 6,698	Class: RS (RR)	**2007-04 OAO Khersonskiy Sudostroitelnyy Zavod — Kherson** Yd No: 18007 Loa 150.32 (BB) Br ex 22.00 Dght 3.800 Lbp 140.31 Br md 21.00 Dpth 7.15 Welded, 1 dk	**(A35A2RT) Rail Vehicles Carrier** Rail Wagons: 50	**3 diesel electric oil engines** driving 6 gen. each 450kW a.c Connecting to 2 elec. motors each (1325kW) driving 2 FP propellers Total Power: 2,700kW (3,672hp) 10.0kn G.M. (Detroit Diesel) 16V-149-TI 3 x Vee 2 Stroke 16 Cy. 146 x 146 each-900kW (1224bhp) Detroit Diesel Corporation-Detroit, Mi Thrusters: 1 Tunnel thruster (f); 1 Tunnel thruster (a) Fuel: 587.0 (d.f.)
9456812 *XCKU2* -	**SMBC MEXICALI** *ex* UNV 469 *-2009* **Servicios Maritimos de Baja California S de RL de CV** - *Ensenada* *Mexico* MMSI: 345020020 Official number: 0201304822-3	**495** 149 275	Class: AB	**2009-06 Union Naval Valencia SA (UNV) — Valencia** Yd No: 469 Loa 32.00 Br ex - Dght 5.680 Lbp 30.95 Br md 13.20 Dpth 5.55 Welded, 1 dk	**(B32A2ST) Tug**	**2 oil engines** reduction geared to sc. shafts driving 2 Z propellers Total Power: 4,930kW (6,702hp) 13.0kn M.T.U. 16V4000M71 2 x Vee 4 Stroke 16 Cy. 165 x 190 each-2465kW (3351bhp) (made 2009) MTU Friedrichshafen GmbH-Friedrichshafen AuxGen: 2 x 129kW 460V 60Hz a.c Fuel: 197.0 (d.f.)
9456795 *XCKS9* -	**SMBC MONTERREY** - **Servicios Maritimos de Baja California S de RL de CV** - *Ensenada* *Mexico* MMSI: 345020017 Official number: 0201297732-1	**495** 149 219	Class: AB	**2009-02 Union Naval Valencia SA (UNV) — Valencia** Yd No: 467 Loa 32.00 Br ex - Dght 5.660 Lbp 31.01 Br md 13.20 Dpth 5.55 Welded, 1 dk	**(B32A2ST) Tug**	**2 oil engines** reduction geared to sc. shafts driving 2 Z propellers Total Power: 4,930kW (6,702hp) 13.0kn M.T.U. 16V4000M71 2 x Vee 4 Stroke 16 Cy. 165 x 190 each-2465kW (3351bhp) MTU Friedrichshafen GmbH-Friedrichshafen AuxGen: 2 x 148kW 460V 60Hz a.c Fuel: 197.0 (d.f.)
9456824 *XCKV3* -	**SMBC ROSARITO** - **Servicios Maritimos de Baja California S de RL de CV** - SatCom: Inmarsat C 434502010 *Ensenada* *Mexico* MMSI: 345020019 Official number: 0201304922-2	**495** 149 219	Class: AB	**2009-07 Union Naval Valencia SA (UNV) — Valencia** Yd No: 470 Loa 32.00 Br ex - Dght 5.000 Lbp 30.95 Br md 13.20 Dpth 5.55 Welded, 1 dk	**(B32A2ST) Tug**	**2 oil engines** reduction geared to sc. shafts driving 2 Z propellers Total Power: 4,930kW (6,702hp) 13.0kn M.T.U. 16V4000M71 2 x Vee 4 Stroke 16 Cy. 165 x 190 each-2465kW (3351bhp) MTU Friedrichshafen GmbH-Friedrichshafen AuxGen: 2 x 148kW 460V 60Hz a.c Fuel: 197.0 (d.f.)
9456800 *XCKT1* -	**SMBC TIJUANA** - **Servicios Maritimos de Baja California S de RL de CV** - *Ensenada* *Mexico* MMSI: 345020018 Official number: 020130722-4	**495** 149 275	Class: AB	**2009-04 Union Naval Valencia SA (UNV) — Valencia** Yd No: 468 Loa 32.00 Br ex - Dght 5.680 Lbp 30.95 Br md 13.20 Dpth 5.55 Welded, 1 dk	**(B32A2ST) Tug**	**2 oil engines** gearing integral to driving 2 Z propellers Total Power: 4,930kW (6,702hp) 13.0kn M.T.U. 16V4000M71 2 x Vee 4 Stroke 16 Cy. 165 x 190 each-2465kW (3351bhp) MTU Friedrichshafen GmbH-Friedrichshafen AuxGen: 2 x 148kW 460V 60Hz a.c Fuel: 197.0 (d.f.)
8619118 *HSB3927* -	**SMC MONTRI** *ex* STT 3 *-2012* *ex* Sukho Thai Star *-2010* *ex* Morning Ventures *-2008* *ex* Andres Bonifacio *-2008* *ex* Jiogasa Star *-2000* **Ayudhya Development Leasing Co Ltd (ADLC)** - *Bangkok* *Thailand* Official number: 510084603	**2,518** 1,174 3,911	Class: (NK)	**1987-03 Kyokuyo Shipyard Corp — Shimonoseki YC** Yd No: 2521 Loa 89.97 (BB) Br ex - Dght 4.875 Lbp 84.99 Br md 17.00 Dpth 6.60 Welded, 1 dk	**(A13B2TP) Products Tanker** Liq: 5,017; Liq (Oil): 5,017 Compartments: 10 Ta, ER	**1 oil engine** reverse reduction geared to sc. shaft driving 1 FP propeller Total Power: 1,765kW (2,400hp) 11.5kn Hanshin 6EL35 1 x 4 Stroke 6 Cy. 350 x 700 1765kW (2400bhp) The Hanshin Diesel Works Ltd-Japan
8881591 - -	**SMELLINGEN** *ex* Eira *-1999* - -	**379** 146 -		**1954-07 Glommens Mek Verksted — Fredrikstad** Yd No: 148 Loa 40.31 Br ex - Dght - Lbp - Br md 9.80 Dpth - Welded, 1 dk	**(A36A2PR) Passenger/Ro-Ro Ship (Vehicles)** Passengers: unberthed: 150 Cars: 22	**1 oil engine** driving 1 FP propeller Total Power: 353kW (480hp) 11.0kn Wichmann 1 x 353kW (480bhp) Wichmann Motorfabrikk AS-Norway
7504081 - -	**SMENA** *ex* Gambero *-1988* *ex* Uyu *-1985* *launched as* Vissia *-1980* **Robert Ocram (Fishing) Ltd** - *Takoradi* *Ghana* Official number: 316833	**196** 64 103	Class: (BV) (RI)	**1980-07 Cant. Nav. Fratelli Maccioni — Viareggio** Yd No: 12 Lengthened-1986 Loa 39.64 Br ex 6.46 Dght 3.133 Lbp 33.06 Br md 6.43 Dpth 3.56 Welded, 1 dk	**(B11A2FT) Trawler**	**1 oil engine** geared to sc. shaft driving 1 CP propeller Total Power: 441kW (600hp) 12.0kn Blackstone ESL6MK2 1 x 4 Stroke 6 Cy. 222 x 292 441kW (600bhp) (made 1974, fitted 1980) Mirrlees Blackstone (Stamford)Ltd.-Stamford AuxGen: 2 x 203kW 440V a.c
5406728 - -	**SMEP 1** *ex* Manuel G. Amado *-2005* *ex* M. Gonzalez Amado *-2000* **Smep SA** - *Nouadhibou* *Mauritania*	*245* 112 -	Class: (BV) (RI)	**1963 Astilleros Santodomingo — Vigo** Yd No: 312 Loa 36.20 Br ex 6.86 Dght 3.585 Lbp 31.50 Br md 6.81 Dpth 3.89 Riveted\Welded	**(B11A2FS) Stern Trawler**	**1 oil engine** driving 1 FP propeller Total Power: 900kW (1,224hp) 12.0kn Deutz RBV6M545 1 x 4 Stroke 6 Cy. 320 x 450 900kW (1224bhp) (new engine 1984) Kloeckner Humboldt Deutz AG-West Germany
7332402 - -	**SMEP 2** *ex* Santa Marta *-2005* **Smep SA** - *Nouadhibou* *Mauritania*	*279* 110 213	Class: (BV) (RI)	**1973 Astilleros Gondan SA — Castropol** Yd No: 95 Loa 38.99 Br ex 7.52 Dght 3.607 Lbp 33.48 Br md 7.50 Dpth 4.02 Welded, 1 dk	**(B11A2FT) Trawler**	**1 oil engine** driving 1 FP propeller Total Power: 1,030kW (1,400hp) 11.5kn MWM TD500-6 1 x 4 Stroke 6 Cy. 360 x 450 1030kW (1400bhp) Motoren Werke Mannheim AG (MWM)-West Germany Fuel: 97.0 (d.f.)
1011898 *ZGCH8* -	**SMERALDA** *launched as* Silver Drei *-2012* **Government of Dubai (Royal Family)** - *George Town* *Cayman Islands (British)* MMSI: 319039800 Official number: 743708	**952** 285 250	Class: LR ✠ **100A1** SS 06/2012 SSC Yacht, mono, G6 ✠ **LMC** **UMS** Cable: 192.5/22.0 U3 (a)	**2012-06 Hanseatic Marine Pty Ltd — Fremantle WA** Yd No: 03 Loa 77.00 Br ex 10.50 Dght 2.530 Lbp 66.17 Br md 9.90 Dpth 3.05 Welded, 1 dk	**(X11A2YP) Yacht**	**2 oil engines** with clutches, flexible couplings & sr reverse geared to sc. shafts driving 2 FP propellers Total Power: 5,440kW (7,396hp) M.T.U. 16V4000M90 2 x Vee 4 Stroke 16 Cy. 165 x 190 each-2720kW (3698bhp) MTU Friedrichshafen GmbH-Friedrichshafen AuxGen: 3 x 129kW 400V 50Hz a.c Thrusters: 1 Thwart. FP thruster (f)

9148570 *IBPE* -	**SMERALDO** **Finbeta SpA** - SatCom: Inmarsat B 324798145 *Ancona* Italy MMSI: 247697000	**4,896** 1,976 7,014 T/cm 17.0	Class: RI (BV)	**1998-02 Cant. Nav. Mario Morini S.p.A. — Ancona** Yd No: 258 Loa 118.62 (BB) Br ex - Dght 6.760 Lbp 108.80 Br md 16.40 Dpth 8.40 Welded, 1 dk	**(A12B2TR) Chemical/Products Tanker** Double Hull (13F) Liq: 6,931; Liq (Oil): 6,931 Cargo Heating Coils Compartments: 1 Ta (s.stl), 10 Wing Ta (s.stl), ER 13 Cargo Pump (s): 11x170m^3/hr, 2x50m^3/hr Manifold: Bow/CM: 58.5m Ice Capable	**1 oil engine** reduction geared to sc. shaft driving 1 CP propeller Total Power: 3,960kW (5,384hp) 14.0kn Wartsila 6R38 1 x 4 Stroke 6 Cy. 380 x 475 3960kW (5384bhp) Wartsila NSD Nederland BV-Netherlands AuxGen: 1 x 1000kW 220/440V 60Hz a.c, 3 x 615kW 220/440V 60Hz a.c Thrusters: 1 Thwart. FP thruster (f) Fuel: 62.0 (d.f.) 385.0 (r.f.)
6863442 - -	**SMERCH** - -	**398** 119 157	Class: (RS)	**1958-06 Bakinskiy Sudostroitelnyy Zavod im Vano Sturua — Baku** Yd No: 41 Loa 44.51 Br ex 9.40 Dght 3.361 Lbp 40.87 Br md - Dpth 4.42 Welded, 1 dk	**(B32A2ST) Tug** Ice Capable	**2 oil engines** driving 2 FP propellers Total Power: 882kW (1,200hp) 11.0kn Russkiy 6DR30/50-3-3 2 x 2 Stroke 6 Cy. 300 x 500 each-441kW (600bhp) (new engine 1973) Mashinostroitelnyy Zavod"Russkiy-Dizel"-Leningrad AuxGen: 2 x 100kW Fuel: 72.0 (d.f.)
8801670 - -	**SMI III** *ex* Takara Maru No. 5 *-2011* **PT Samudra Marine Indonesia** - Indonesia	*496* - 1,000		**1988-01 Nakatani Shipyard Co. Ltd. — Etajima** Yd No: 515 Loa - Br ex - Dght 3.101 Lbp 56.01 Br md 17.01 Dpth 5.01 Welded	**(A31A2GX) General Cargo Ship**	**2 oil engines** driving 2 FP propellers Total Power: 1,472kW (2,002hp) Niigata 6M28BGT 2 x 4 Stroke 6 Cy. 280 x 480 each-736kW (1001bhp) Niigata Engineering Co Ltd-Japan
8408698 *XUED2* -	**SMILE** *ex* J&K *-2011* *ex* Dongjin Nagoya *-2010* *ex* Jasmine II *-1990* **Linton Consulting Ltd** MV-Line Co Ltd SatCom: Inmarsat C 451542610 *Phnom Penh* Cambodia MMSI: 515426000 Official number: 1184889	**3,255** - 4,378	Class: (KR) (NK)	**1984-10 Kochi Jyuko K.K. — Kochi** Yd No: 2398 Loa 89.65 (BB) Br ex 15.02 Dght 6.460 Lbp 81.50 Br md 15.00 Dpth 9.65 Welded	**(A31A2GX) General Cargo Ship** Grain: 7,835; Bale: 7,431 TEU 102 C. 102/20' Compartments: 2 Ho, ER 2 Ha: (14.0 x 10.2) (26.6 x 10.2)ER Derricks: 1x25t,2x22t	**1 oil engine** driving 1 FP propeller Total Power: 1,692kW (2,300hp) 11.8kn Akasaka A37 1 x 4 Stroke 6 Cy. 370 x 720 1692kW (2300bhp) Akasaka Tekkosho KK (Akasaka DieselLtd)-Japan AuxGen: 2 x 180kW a.c
9150406 *9HA3259* -	**SMILEY LADY** *ex* E.R. Durban *-2013* *ex* Maersk Verona *-2006* *ex* E. R. Durban *-2004* *ex* Direct Falcon *-2003* *ex* Griffin Clio *-1999* *launched as* E.R. Durban *-1999* **Feliz Navigation SA** Aims Shipping Corp *Valletta* Malta MMSI: 229352000 Official number: 9150406	**16,803** 8,648 23,075 T/cm 37.1	Class: GL RI (LR) ✠ Classed LR until 12/3/99	**1999-03 Stocznia Szczecinska SA — Szczecin** Yd No: B170/2/2 Loa 184.10 (BB) Br ex 25.52 Dght 9.889 Lbp 170.00 Br md 25.30 Dpth 13.50 Welded, 1 dk	**(A33A2CC) Container Ship (Fully Cellular)** TEU 1730 C Ho 634 TEU C Dk 1096 TEU incl 200 ref C. Compartments: 4 Cell Ho, ER 9 Ha: (12.5 x 13.0)8 (12.5 x 20.6)ER Cranes: 3x40t	**1 oil engine** driving 1 FP propeller Total Power: 13,320kW (18,110hp) 19.9kn Sulzer 6RTA62U 1 x 2 Stroke 6 Cy. 620 x 2150 13320kW (18110bhp) H Cegielski Poznan SA-Poland AuxGen: 3 x 1096kW 450V 60Hz a.c Thrusters: 1 Thwart. CP thruster (f) Fuel: 113.9 (d.f.) (Heating Coils) 2150.7 (r.f.) 51.0pd
9649017 *9HB2583* -	**SMILING T** **Slowwave Charter Ltd** Ocean Management GmbH *Valletta* Malta Official number: 9649017	**267** 184 186	Class: BV	**2012-02 Jade Yachts Inc — Kaohsiung** Yd No: 116 Loa 28.22 Br ex 7.65 Dght 2.500 Lbp 23.88 Br md 7.50 Dpth 3.80 Welded, 1 dk	**(X11A2YP) Yacht**	**2 oil engines** reduction geared to sc. shafts driving 2 FP propellers Total Power: 1,618kW (2,200hp) 11.0kn MAN D2842LE 2 x Vee 4 Stroke 12 Cy. 128 x 142 each-809kW (1100bhp) MAN Nutzfahrzeuge AG-Nuernberg AuxGen: 2 x 50kW 50Hz a.c
9396232 *C6WO6* -	**SMIT AFRICA** *launched as* Bogazici 2 *-2007* **Smit Lamnalco Ltd** Smit Terminals Europe Ltd *Nassau* Bahamas MMSI: 308466000 Official number: 8001425	**465** 135 -	Class: BV	**2007-11 Ge-Ta Corp. — Istanbul** Yd No: 007 Loa 32.50 Br ex - Dght 4.300 Lbp 27.60 Br md 11.70 Dpth 5.60 Welded, 1 dk	**(B32A2ST) Tug**	**2 oil engines** reduction geared to sc. shafts driving 2 FP propellers Total Power: 3,840kW (5,220hp) 13.0kn Caterpillar 3516B 2 x Vee 4 Stroke 16 Cy. 170 x 190 each-1920kW (2610bhp) Caterpillar Inc-USA Thrusters: 1 Directional thruster (f)
9532305 *C6XL3* -	**SMIT AL KOUT** **Smit Lamnalco Ltd** Smit Terminals Europe Ltd *Nassau* Bahamas MMSI: 311013100 Official number: 8001585	**255** 76 -	Class: BV	**2008-10 Neptune Shipyards BV — Aalst (Nl)** Yd No: 327 Loa 30.10 Br ex - Dght 2.200 Lbp 28.52 Br md 9.90 Dpth 3.30 Welded, 1 dk	**(B34L2QU) Utility Vessel**	**2 oil engines** reduction geared to sc. shafts driving 2 FP propellers Total Power: 1,940kW (2,638hp) 12.0kn Caterpillar C32 ACERT 2 x Vee 4 Stroke 12 Cy. 145 x 162 each-970kW (1319bhp) Caterpillar Inc-USA
7385215 *ZTUG* -	**SMIT AMANDLA** *ex* John Ross *-2003* *ex* S. A. John Ross *-1977* **Smit Amandla Marine Pty Ltd** *Cape Town* South Africa MMSI: 601524000 Official number: 350744	**2,899** 870 2,055	Class: BV (LR) ✠ Classed LR until 27/11/08	**1976-11 James Brown & Hamer Ltd. — Durban** Yd No: 29 Loa 94.65 (BB) Br ex 15.85 Dght 7.520 Lbp 85.65 Br md 15.21 Dpth 8.62 Welded, 1 dk, 2nd dk in fwd and after salvage holds	**(B32A2ST) Tug** Derricks: 1x30t	**2 oil engines** sr geared to sc. shaft driving 1 CP propeller Total Power: 14,122kW (19,200hp) 20.0kn Mirrlees KVMR16 2 x Vee 4 Stroke 16 Cy. 381 x 457 each-7061kW (9600bhp) Mirrlees Blackstone (Stockport)Ltd.-Stockport AuxGen: 2 x 740kW 440V 60Hz a.c, 2 x 308kW 440V 60Hz a.c Boilers: e 7.6kgf/cm^2 (7.5bar), AuxB (o.f.) 10.5kgf/cm^2 (10.3bar) Thrusters: 1 Thwart. CP thruster (f)
9479694 *ORQP* -	**SMIT ANGOLA** **Smit Shipping Singapore Pte Ltd** Unie van Redding - en Sleepdienst NV (Union de Remorquage et de Sauvetage SA) (Towage & Salvage Union Ltd) *Antwerpen* Belgium MMSI: 205634000 Official number: 02 00044 2012	**1,438** 431 1,127	Class: BV	**2010-06 Keppel Nantong Shipyard Co Ltd — Nantong JS** Yd No: 026 Loa 49.50 Br ex - Dght 5.200 Lbp 47.00 Br md 15.00 Dpth 6.75 Welded, 1 dk	**(B32A2ST) Tug** Cranes: 1	**2 oil engines** reduction geared to sc. shafts driving 2 Z propellers Total Power: 5,440kW (7,396hp) 16.0kn Wartsila 8L26 2 x 4 Stroke 8 Cy. 260 x 320 each-2720kW (3698bhp) Wartsila Italia SpA-Italy AuxGen: 2 x 700kW 440V 60Hz a.c, 2 x 260kW 440V 60Hz a.c Thrusters: 1 Tunnel thruster (f) Fuel: 534.0 (r.f.)
9366706 *HP4367* -	**SMIT ARUBA** **Smit International (Curacao) NV** Smit Harbour Towage Panama Inc *Panama* Panama MMSI: 356639000 Official number: 39852PEXTF1	**294** 88 153	Class: LR ✠ **100A1** SS 10/2011 tug **LMC** **UMS** Eq.Ltr: F; Cable: 275.0/19.0 U2 (a)	**2006-10 Santierul Naval Damen Galati S.A. — Galati (Hull)** Yd No: 1089 **2006-10 B.V. Scheepswerf Damen — Gorinchem** Yd No: 511523 Loa 28.75 Br ex 10.42 Dght 3.910 Lbp 25.79 Br md 9.80 Dpth 4.60 Welded, 1 dk	**(B32A2ST) Tug**	**2 oil engines** reduction geared to sc. shafts driving 2 Directional propellers Total Power: 3,730kW (5,072hp) Caterpillar 3516B-HD 2 x Vee 4 Stroke 16 Cy. 170 x 215 each-1865kW (2536bhp) Caterpillar Inc-USA AuxGen: 2 x 83kW 400V 50Hz a.c
9578490 *VHID* -	**SMIT AWOONGA** **Smit Shipping Singapore Pte Ltd** Smit Marine Australia Pty Ltd *Gladstone, Qld* Australia MMSI: 503646000 Official number: 859688	**455** 136 304	Class: BV	**2010-10 Uzmar Gemi Insa Sanayi ve Ticaret AS — Basiskele** Yd No: 55 Loa 30.25 Br ex 12.05 Dght 4.240 Lbp 26.60 Br md 11.75 Dpth 5.28 Welded, 1 dk	**(B32A2ST) Tug**	**2 oil engines** reduction geared to sc. shafts driving 2 Z propellers Total Power: 3,946kW (5,364hp) Caterpillar 3516B-HD 2 x Vee 4 Stroke 16 Cy. 170 x 215 each-1973kW (2682bhp) Caterpillar Inc-USA AuxGen: 2 x 80kW 50Hz a.c
9276834 *HO4091* -	**SMIT BALBOA** **Smit International (Curacao) NV** Smit Harbour Towage Panama Inc *Panama* Panama Official number: 33358PEXTF6	**294** 88 166	Class: LR ✠ **100A1** SS 04/2010 tug **LMC** **UMS** Eq.Ltr: F; Cable: 275.0/19.0 U2 (a)	**2005-04 Santierul Naval Damen Galati S.A. — Galati (Hull)** Yd No: 977 **2005-04 B.V. Scheepswerf Damen — Gorinchem** Yd No: 511506 Loa 28.75 Br ex 10.43 Dght 3.708 Lbp 25.79 Br md 9.80 Dpth 4.60 Welded, 1 dk	**(B32A2ST) Tug**	**2 oil engines** gearing integral to driving 2 Directional propellers Total Power: 3,524kW (4,792hp) Caterpillar 3516B-HD 2 x Vee 4 Stroke 16 Cy. 170 x 215 each-1762kW (2396bhp) Caterpillar Inc-USA AuxGen: 2 x 85kW 400V 50Hz a.c Thrusters: 1 Thwart. FP thruster (f)
7505736 - -	**SMIT BALI** *ex* Asiatic Flame *-1981* - -	*177* 11 -	Class: (AB)	**1976-05 Sea Services Pte Ltd — Singapore** Yd No: Y108 Loa - Br ex - Dght 2.931 Lbp 26.57 Br md 7.66 Dpth 3.56 Welded, 1 dk	**(B32A2ST) Tug**	**2 oil engines** driving 2 FP propellers Total Power: 882kW (1,200hp) 11.5kn Yanmar 6G-ST 2 x 4 Stroke 6 Cy. 240 x 290 each-441kW (600bhp) Yanmar Diesel Engine Co Ltd-Japan AuxGen: 2 x 32kW a.c

IMO / Call sign	Name / Owner / Manager / Port / Flag	Tonnage	Class	Builder / Dimensions	Type	Machinery
9370173 *MSDU8* -	**SMIT BARBADOS** **Smit Harbour Towage (UK) Ltd (Smit Harbour Towage Liverpool)** - *Liverpool* *United Kingdom* MMSI: 235055303 Official number: 913043	**294** 88 -	Class: LR ✠ **100A1** SS 06/2012 tug **LMC** **UMS** Eq.Ltr: F; Cable: 275.0/19.0 U2 (a)	**2007-06 Santierul Naval Damen Galati S.A. — Galati** (Hull) Yd No: 1092 **2007-06 B.V. Scheepswerf Damen — Gorinchem** Yd No: 511526 Loa 28.75 Br ex 10.59 Dght 3.708 Lbp 25.79 Br md 9.80 Dpth 4.60 Welded, 1 dk	**(B32A2ST) Tug**	**2 oil engines** gearing integral to driving 2 Directional propellers Total Power: 3,730kW (5,072hp) Caterpillar 3516B-HD 2 x Vee 4 Stroke 16 Cy. 170 x 215 each-1865kW (2536bhp) Caterpillar Inc-USA AuxGen: 2 x 85kW 400V 50Hz a.c
9345506 *5BAB4* -	**SMIT BARRACUDA** **Boskalis Offshore Marine Services BV** Smit Vessel Management Services BV *Limassol* *Cyprus* MMSI: 210667000	**230** 69 129	Class: BV	**2006-08 IHC DeltaShipyard BV — Sliedrecht** Yd No: 11017 Loa 25.80 Br ex - Dght 2.720 Lbp 23.66 Br md 10.00 Dpth 3.45 Welded, 1 dk	**(B32A2ST) Tug** Cranes: 1x26t Ice Capable	**2 oil engines** reduction geared to sc. shafts driving 2 FP propellers Total Power: 1,492kW (2,028hp) 10.0kn Caterpillar 3508B 2 x Vee 4 Stroke 8 Cy. 170 x 190 each-746kW (1014bhp) Caterpillar Inc-USA AuxGen: 2 x 78kW 50Hz a.c Thrusters: 1 Tunnel thruster (f)
9178991 *ORQI*	**SMIT BELGIE** *ex Smit Ahoada -2012* **Smit Shipping Singapore Pte Ltd** URS Belgie NV *Antwerpen* *Belgium* MMSI: 205621000 Official number: 02 00039 2012	**305** 91 223	Class: LR ✠ **100A1** SS 06/2009 tug ✠ **LMC** **UMS** Eq.Ltr: F; Cable: 275.0/19.0 U2	**1999-06 PO SevMash Predpriyatiye — Severodvinsk** (Hull) **1999-06 B.V. Scheepswerf Damen — Gorinchem** Yd No: 7925 Loa 30.82 Br ex 10.20 Dght 3.758 Lbp 26.00 Br md 9.40 Dpth 4.80 Welded, 1 dk	**(B32A2ST) Tug**	**2 oil engines** with clutches, flexible couplings & sr geared to sc. shafts driving 2 Directional propellers Total Power: 3,132kW (4,258hp) 10.5kn Caterpillar 3516B-TA 2 x Vee 4 Stroke 16 Cy. 170 x 190 each-1566kW (2129bhp) Caterpillar Inc-USA AuxGen: 2 x 85kW 380V 50Hz a.c Fuel: 115.0 (d.f.) 8.0pd
9528316 *PCBJ* -	**SMIT BELUGA** **Boskalis Offshore Marine Services BV** Smit Vessel Management Services BV *Rotterdam* *Netherlands* MMSI: 246710000 Official number: 52507	**230** 69 -	Class: BV	**2010-03 ZPUH Magra — Gdynia** (Hull) Yd No: (571613) **2010-03 B.V. Scheepswerf Damen Hardinxveld — Hardinxveld-Giessendam** Yd No: 571613 Loa 25.80 Br ex 10.05 Dght 2.720 Lbp 23.60 Br md 10.00 Dpth - Welded, 1 dk	**(B32A2ST) Tug** Cranes: 1x26t Ice Capable	**2 oil engines** reduction geared to sc. shafts driving 2 FP propellers Total Power: 1,492kW (2,028hp) Caterpillar 3508B 2 x Vee 4 Stroke 8 Cy. 170 x 190 each-746kW (1014bhp) Caterpillar Inc-USA AuxGen: 2 x 78kW 50Hz a.c Thrusters: 1 Tunnel thruster (f)
9394167 *C6WP6* -	**SMIT BIOKO** **Smit Lamnalco Netherlands BV** - *Nassau* *Bahamas* MMSI: 308756000 Official number: 8001433	**374** 112 296	Class: LR ✠ **100A1** SS 11/2012 escort tug, restricted services Port of Malabo, Equatorial Guinea, fire fighting Ship 1 (2400 m3/h with water spray) **LMC** **UMS** Eq.Ltr: H; Cable: 302.5/22.0 U2 (a)	**2007-11 Damen Shipyards Gdynia SA — Gdynia** (Hull) Yd No: 511213 **2007-11 B.V. Scheepswerf Damen — Gorinchem** Yd No: 511213 Loa 32.50 Br ex 10.64 Dght 4.270 Lbp 29.01 Br md 10.60 Dpth 5.00 Welded, 1 dk	**(B32A2ST) Tug**	**2 oil engines** reduction geared to sc. shafts driving 2 Directional propellers Total Power: 4,180kW (5,684hp) Caterpillar 3516B-HD 2 x Vee 4 Stroke 16 Cy. 170 x 215 each-2090kW (2842bhp) Caterpillar Inc-USA AuxGen: 2 x 80kW 400V 50Hz a.c Fuel: 125.0 (d.f.)
9345518 *5BZZ3* -	**SMIT BISON** **Boskalis Offshore Marine Services BV** Smit Vessel Management Services BV *Limassol* *Cyprus* MMSI: 210444000 Official number: 9345518	**230** 69 129	Class: BV	**2006-12 IHC DeltaShipyard BV — Sliedrecht** Yd No: 11018 Loa 25.40 Br ex - Dght 2.720 Lbp 23.66 Br md 10.00 Dpth 3.45 Welded, 1 dk	**(B32A2ST) Tug** Ice Capable	**2 oil engines** reduction geared to sc. shafts driving 2 FP propellers Total Power: 1,492kW (2,028hp) 10.0kn Caterpillar 3508B 2 x Vee 4 Stroke 8 Cy. 170 x 190 each-746kW (1014bhp) Caterpillar Inc-USA AuxGen: 2 x 78kW 50Hz a.c Thrusters: 1 Tunnel thruster (f)
9343247 *HO2028* -	**SMIT BONAIRE** **Smit International (Curacao) NV** Smit Harbour Towage Panama Inc *Panama* *Panama* Official number: 34998PEXTF4	**294** 88 153	Class: LR ✠ **100A1** SS 09/2011 tug **LMC** **UMS** Eq.Ltr: F; Cable: 275.0/19.0 U2 (a)	**2006-09 Santierul Naval Damen Galati S.A. — Galati** (Hull) Yd No: 1077 **2006-09 B.V. Scheepswerf Damen — Gorinchem** Yd No: 511513 Loa 28.75 Br ex 10.42 Dght 3.910 Lbp 25.79 Br md 9.80 Dpth 4.60 Welded, 1 dk	**(B32A2ST) Tug**	**2 oil engines** reduction geared to sc. shafts driving 2 Directional propellers Total Power: 3,730kW (5,072hp) Caterpillar 3516B-HD 2 x Vee 4 Stroke 16 Cy. 170 x 215 each-1865kW (2536bhp) Caterpillar Inc-USA AuxGen: 2 x 83kW 400V 50Hz a.c
8735895 *ZSSB*	**SMIT BONGANI** *ex Smit Dudula -2008 ex Dudula -2002* *ex Windbuild -2001 ex Winbuild 2308 -1998* **Smit Amandla Marine Pty Ltd** - *Durban* *South Africa* Official number: 20102	**1,731** 821 -	Class: (BV)	**1997-01 Pacific Ocean Engineering & Trading Pte Ltd (POET) — Singapore** Yd No: 1103 Converted From: Products Tank Barge, Non-propelled-2008 Loa 70.00 Br ex - Dght 3.370 Lbp 67.30 Br md 18.28 Dpth 4.26 Welded, 1 dk	**(B35E2TF) Bunkering Tanker**	**2 oil engines** geared to sc. shafts driving 2 Azimuth electric drive units
9345491 *PHFS* -	**SMIT BRONCO** **Smit Vessel Management Services BV** Boskalis Offshore Marine Services BV *Rotterdam* *Netherlands* MMSI: 246526000	**230** 69 120	Class: BV	**2006-06 IHC DeltaShipyard BV — Sliedrecht** Yd No: 11016 Loa 25.80 Br ex - Dght 2.720 Lbp 22.15 Br md 10.00 Dpth 3.45 Welded, 1 dk	**(B32A2ST) Tug** Cranes: 1x26t Ice Capable	**2 oil engines** reduction geared to sc. shafts driving 2 FP propellers Total Power: 1,492kW (2,028hp) Caterpillar 3508B 2 x Vee 4 Stroke 8 Cy. 170 x 190 each-746kW (1014bhp) Caterpillar Inc-USA AuxGen: 2 x 84kW 400/220V 50Hz a.c Thrusters: 1 Tunnel thruster (f)
9528304 *PBME* -	**SMIT BUFFALO** **Smit Shipping Singapore Pte Ltd** Smit Vessel Management Services BV *Rotterdam* *Netherlands* MMSI: 245038000 Official number: 52506	**230** 59 -	Class: BV	**2009-12 B.V. Scheepswerf Damen Hardinxveld — Hardinxveld-Giessendam** Yd No: 571612 Loa 25.80 Br ex 10.05 Dght - Lbp 23.60 Br md 10.00 Dpth - Welded, 1 dk	**(B32A2ST) Tug** Cranes: 1x26t Ice Capable	**2 oil engines** reduction geared to sc. shafts driving 2 FP propellers Total Power: 1,492kW (2,028hp) Caterpillar 3508B 2 x Vee 4 Stroke 8 Cy. 170 x 190 each-746kW (1014bhp) Caterpillar Inc-USA AuxGen: 2 x 78kW a.c Thrusters: 1 Tunnel thruster (f)
9528299 *PBWD* -	**SMIT BULLDOG** **Smit Shipping Singapore Pte Ltd** Smit Vessel Management Services BV *Rotterdam* *Netherlands* MMSI: 246643000 Official number: 52505	**230** 69 -	Class: BV	**2009-09 B.V. Scheepswerf Damen Hardinxveld — Hardinxveld-Giessendam** (Hull) Yd No: 571611 **2009-09 B.V. Scheepswerf Damen — Gorinchem** Yd No: 571611 Loa 25.80 Br ex 10.05 Dght - Lbp 23.66 Br md 10.00 Dpth - Welded, 1 dk	**(B32A2ST) Tug** Cranes: 1x26t Ice Capable	**2 oil engines** reduction geared to sc. shafts driving 2 FP propellers Total Power: 1,492kW (2,028hp) Caterpillar 3508B 2 x Vee 4 Stroke 8 Cy. 170 x 190 each-746kW (1014bhp) Caterpillar Inc-USA AuxGen: 2 x 78kW 50Hz a.c Thrusters: 1 Tunnel thruster (f)
9457426 *PP7203* -	**SMIT CAIAPO** **SMIT Rebocadores do Brasil SA** - *Rio de Janeiro* *Brazil* MMSI: 710011790 Official number: 3813871827	**397** 119 273	Class: AB	**2009-04 Detroit Brasil Ltda — Itajai** Yd No: 322 Loa 30.25 Br ex - Dght 3.750 Lbp 28.63 Br md 11.00 Dpth 5.28 Welded, 1 dk	**(B32A2ST) Tug**	**2 oil engines** Reduction geared to sc. shafts driving 2 Directional propellers Total Power: 3,372kW (4,584hp) Caterpillar 3516B-HD 2 x Vee 4 Stroke 16 Cy. 170 x 215 each-1686kW (2292bhp) Caterpillar Inc-USA AuxGen: 2 x 92kW a.c
9457414 *PP7390* -	**SMIT CANINDE** **SMIT Rebocadores do Brasil SA** - *Rio de Janeiro* *Brazil* MMSI: 710012010 Official number: 3813871070	*397* 119 273	Class: AB	**2009-02 Detroit Brasil Ltda — Itajai** Yd No: 321 Loa 30.25 Br ex - Dght 3.750 Lbp 24.75 Br md 11.00 Dpth 5.28 Welded, 1 dk	**(B32A2ST) Tug**	**2 oil engines** Reduction geared to sc. shafts driving 2 Directional propellers Total Power: 3,372kW (4,584hp) Caterpillar 3516B-HD 2 x Vee 4 Stroke 16 Cy. 170 x 215 each-1686kW (2292bhp) Caterpillar Inc-USA AuxGen: 2 x 92kW a.c
9457488 *PP7397* -	**SMIT CARAJA** **SMIT Rebocadores do Brasil SA** - SatCom: Inmarsat C 471011198 *Rio de Janeiro* *Brazil* MMSI: 710002030 Official number: 3813872980	*397* 119 270	Class: AB	**2009-10 Detroit Brasil Ltda — Itajai** Yd No: 326 Loa 30.25 Br ex - Dght 4.200 Lbp - Br md 11.00 Dpth 5.25 Welded, 1 dk	**(B32A2ST) Tug**	**2 oil engines** gearing integral to driving 2 Directional propellers Total Power: 3,372kW (4,584hp) Caterpillar 3516B-HD 2 x Vee 4 Stroke 16 Cy. 170 x 215 each-1686kW (2292bhp) Caterpillar Inc-USA

IMO / Call sign	Name / Owner	Tonnage	Classification	Build / Dimensions	Type	Machinery
9457476 *PP7392* -	**SMIT CARIPUNA** **SMIT Rebocadores do Brasil SA** - SatCom: Inmarsat C 471011132 *Rio de Janeiro* *Brazil* MMSI: 710020200 Official number: 3813872556	*397* 119 270	Class: AB	**2009-08 Detroit Brasil Ltda — Itajai** Yd No: 325 Loa 30.30 Br ex - Dght 3.750 Lbp 30.00 Br md 11.00 Dpth 5.25 Welded, 1 dk	**(B32A2ST) Tug**	**2 oil engines** reduction geared to sc. shafts driving 2 Propellers Total Power: 4,000kW (5,438hp) Caterpillar 3516B-HD 2 x Vee 4 Stroke 16 Cy. 170 x 215 each-2000kW (2719bhp) Caterpillar Inc-USA AuxGen: 2 x 92kW a.c
9516284 *5BPS3* -	**SMIT CAYMAN** **Smit Lamnalco Ltd** - *Limassol* *Cyprus*	**285** 85 150	Class: BV	**2008-12 Song Cam Shipyard — Haiphong** (Hull) Yd No: (511551) **2008-12 B.V. Scheepswerf Damen — Gorinchem** Yd No: 511551 Loa 28.67 Br ex 10.43 Dght 3.610 Lbp 25.78 Br md 9.80 Dpth 4.60 Welded, 1 dk	**(B32A2ST) Tug**	**2 oil engines** reduction geared to sc. shafts driving 2 Z propellers Total Power: 3,282kW (4,462hp) Caterpillar 3516B-TA 2 x Vee 4 Stroke 16 Cy. 170 x 190 each-1641kW (2231bhp) Caterpillar Inc-USA AuxGen: 2 x 86kW 50Hz a.c
9457440 *PP7202* -	**SMIT CHARRUA** **SMIT Rebocadores do Brasil SA** - SatCom: Inmarsat C 471011197 *Rio de Janeiro* *Brazil* MMSI: 710001780 Official number: 3813871908	*397* 119 270	Class: AB	**2009-06 Detroit Brasil Ltda — Itajai** Yd No: 324 Loa 30.25 Br ex - Dght 4.200 Lbp 28.63 Br md 11.00 Dpth 5.28 Welded, 1 dk	**(B32A2ST) Tug**	**2 oil engines** Reduction geared to sc. shafts driving 2 Propellers Total Power: 4,000kW (5,438hp) Caterpillar 3516B-HD 2 x Vee 4 Stroke 16 Cy. 170 x 215 each-2000kW (2719bhp) Caterpillar Inc-USA AuxGen: 2 x 92kW a.c
9454876 *C6YB7* -	**SMIT CHEETAH** **Smit Harbour Towage Rotterdam BV** - SatCom: Inmarsat C 43110283 *Nassau* *Bahamas* MMSI: 311028700 Official number: 8001694	**484** 145 -	Class: LR ✠**100A1** SS 09/2009 escort tug, fire fighting Ship 1 (2400m3/h) with water spray **LMC** **UMS** Eq.Ltr: I; Cable: 330.0/24.0 U2 (a)	**2009-09 Song Cam Shipyard — Haiphong** (Hull) Yd No: (513003) **2009-09 B.V. Scheepswerf Damen — Gorinchem** Yd No: 513003 Loa 32.14 Br ex 13.29 Dght 6.000 Lbp 31.64 Br md 12.50 Dpth 5.40 Welded, 1 dk	**(B32A2ST) Tug**	**2 oil engines** integral geared to sc. shafts driving 2 Directional propellers Total Power: 5,420kW (7,370hp) Caterpillar C280-8 2 x 4 Stroke 8 Cy. 280 x 300 each-2710kW (3685bhp) Caterpillar Inc-USA AuxGen: 2 x 162kW 400V 50Hz a.c
9190391 *CFG7577* -	**SMIT CLYDE** **Smit Marine Canada Inc** - *Vancouver, BC* *Canada* MMSI: 316011473 Official number: 831934	**353** 105 175	Class: LR ✠**100A1** SS 03/2010 tug ✠**LMC** **UMS** Eq.Ltr: O†; Cable: 302.5/24.0 U2 (a)	**2000-03 B.V. Scheepswerf Damen — Gorinchem** Yd No: 7937 **2000-03 Stocznia Polnocna (Northern Shipyard) — Gdansk** (Hull) Yd No: 7937 Loa 30.60 Br ex 11.20 Dght 4.050 Lbp 27.44 Br md 10.60 Dpth 5.00 Welded, 1 dk	**(B32A2ST) Tug**	**2 oil engines** reduction geared to sc. shafts driving 2 Directional propellers Total Power: 3,660kW (4,976hp) 13.2kn Wartsila 6L26 2 x 4 Stroke 6 Cy. 260 x 320 each-1830kW (2488bhp) Wartsila NSD Nederland BV-Netherlands AuxGen: 2 x 85kW 400V 50Hz a.c
7917991 *GBVP* -	**SMIT COLLINGWOOD** *ex Collingwood -2007* **Smit Harbour Towage (UK) Ltd (Smit Harbour Towage Liverpool)** - *Liverpool* *United Kingdom* MMSI: 232002704 Official number: 389168	**281** 84 111	Class: LR ✠**100A1** SS 06/2013 tug U.K. coastal service and between River Elbe & Brest ✠**LMC** Eq.Ltr: (F) D; Cable: 247.5/17.5 U2	**1981-01 R. Dunston (Hessle) Ltd. — Hessle** Yd No: H928 Loa 30.64 Br ex 9.33 Dght 2.663 Lbp 28.50 Br md 9.01 Dpth 3.79 Welded, 1 dk	**(B32A2ST) Tug**	**2 oil engines** dr geared to sc. shafts driving 2 Directional propellers Total Power: 1,206kW (1,640hp) 12.5kn Ruston 6RKCM 2 x 4 Stroke 6 Cy. 254 x 305 each-603kW (820bhp) Ruston Diesels Ltd.-Newton-le-Willows AuxGen: 2 x 78kW 440V 50Hz a.c Fuel: 54.0 (d.f.)
9457438 *PP7201* -	**SMIT CRAO** **SMIT Rebocadores do Brasil SA** - SatCom: Inmarsat C 471011121 *Rio de Janeiro* *Brazil* MMSI: 710001770 Official number: 3813871916	**397** 119 273	Class: AB	**2009-05 Detroit Brasil Ltda — Itajai** Yd No: 323 Loa 30.25 Br ex - Dght 3.750 Lbp 28.63 Br md 11.00 Dpth 5.28 Welded, 1 dk	**(B32A2ST) Tug**	**2 oil engines** Reduction geared to sc. shafts driving 2 Directional propellers Total Power: 3,000kW (4,078hp) Caterpillar 3512B-HD 2 x Vee 4 Stroke 12 Cy. 170 x 215 each-1500kW (2039bhp) Caterpillar Inc-USA AuxGen: 2 x 92kW a.c
9309801 *H03975* -	**SMIT CRISTOBAL** **Smit International (Curacao) NV** Smit Harbour Towage Panama Inc *Panama* *Panama* Official number: 33338PEXTF5	**294** 88 166	Class: LR ✠**100A1** SS 12/2009 tug **LMC** **UMS** Eq.Ltr: F; Cable: 275.0/19.0 U2 (a)	**2004-12 PO SevMash Predpriyatiye — Severodvinsk** (Hull) Yd No: (511510) **2004-12 B.V. Scheepswerf Damen — Gorinchem** Yd No: 511510 Loa 28.75 Br ex 10.43 Dght 3.708 Lbp 25.79 Br md 9.80 Dpth 4.60 Welded, 1 dk	**(B32A2ST) Tug**	**2 oil engines** gearing integral to driving 2 Directional propellers Total Power: 3,542kW (4,816hp) Caterpillar 3516B-HD 2 x Vee 4 Stroke 16 Cy. 170 x 215 each-1771kW (2408bhp) Caterpillar Inc-USA AuxGen: 2 x 85kW 400/230V 50Hz a.c Thrusters: 1 Thwart. FP thruster (f) Fuel: 101.0 (d.f.)
9309813 *H04246* -	**SMIT CURACAO** **Rotterdam Tug BV** Smit Harbour Towage Panama Inc *Panama* *Panama* Official number: 34519PEXTF3	**294** 88 -	Class: LR ✠**100A1** SS 04/2010 tug **LMC** **UMS** Eq.Ltr: F; Cable: 275.0/19.0 U2 (a)	**2005-04 PO SevMash Predpriyatiye — Severodvinsk** (Hull) Yd No: (511511) **2005-04 B.V. Scheepswerf Damen — Gorinchem** Yd No: 511511 Loa 28.75 Br ex 10.43 Dght 3.708 Lbp 25.79 Br md 9.80 Dpth 4.60 Welded, 1 dk	**(B32A2ST) Tug**	**2 oil engines** gearing integral to driving 2 Z propellers Total Power: 3,542kW (4,816hp) Caterpillar 3516B-HD 2 x Vee 4 Stroke 16 Cy. 170 x 215 each-1771kW (2408bhp) Caterpillar Inc-USA AuxGen: 2 x 85kW 400V 50Hz a.c Thrusters: 1 Thwart. FP thruster (f)
7603588 *S6F08* -	**SMIT CYCLONE** *ex R. B. Brunel -1978 ex Magnus XI -1975* **Smit Singapore Pte Ltd** - SatCom: Inmarsat M 650397226 *Singapore* *Singapore* MMSI: 563346000 Official number: 389046	**2,700** 810 3,743	Class: GL	**1969-07 Howaldtswerke-Deutsche Werft AG (HDW) — Kiel** Yd No: 530119 Loa 75.98 Br ex 24.03 Dght 3.358 Lbp - Br md 24.02 Dpth 4.68 Welded, 1 dk	**(Y11B4WL) Sheerlegs Pontoon** Derricks: 1x1000t	**2 oil engines** sr geared to sc. shafts driving 2 Directional propellers Total Power: 882kW (1,200hp) G.M. (Detroit Diesel) 16V-92 2 x Vee 2 Stroke 16 Cy. 123 x 127 each-441kW (600bhp) Detroit Diesel-Detroit, Mi AuxGen: 1 x 355kW 380V 50Hz a.c, 2 x 175kW 380V 50Hz a.c Thrusters: 1 Thwart. FP thruster (f)
9359521 *C6VA4* -	**SMIT DAMIETTA** *launched as Ege-7 -2005* **Rotterdam Tug BV** Smit Terminals Division Rotterdam BV *Nassau* *Bahamas* MMSI: 308954000 Official number: 8001105	**409** 122 -	Class: BV	**2005-11 Anadolu Deniz Insaat Kizaklari San. ve Tic. Ltd. Sti. — Tuzla** Yd No: 195 Loa 30.25 Br ex - Dght 3.750 Lbp - Br md 11.00 Dpth 5.28 Welded, 1 dk	**(B32A2ST) Tug**	**2 oil engines** reduction geared to sc. shafts driving 2 Directional propellers Total Power: 3,600kW (4,894hp) 12.5kn Caterpillar 3516B 2 x Vee 4 Stroke 16 Cy. 170 x 190 each-1800kW (2447bhp) Caterpillar Inc-USA AuxGen: 2 x 80kW 380V 50Hz a.c
9396426 *C6ZN7* -	**SMIT DANE** *ex Smit Trinidad -2009* **Smit Singapore Pte Ltd** SMIT Rebocadores do Brasil SA *Nassau* *Bahamas* MMSI: 311060700 Official number: 8001957	**294** 88 142	Class: GL (LR) ✠ Classed LR until 23/7/10	**2008-05 Santierul Naval Damen Galati S.A. — Galati** (Hull) Yd No: 1125 **2008-05 B.V. Scheepswerf Damen — Gorinchem** Yd No: 511532 Loa 28.75 Br ex 10.43 Dght 3.610 Lbp 25.78 Br md 9.80 Dpth 4.60	**(B32A2ST) Tug**	**2 oil engines** gearing integral to driving 2 Z propellers Total Power: 3,728kW (5,068hp) Caterpillar 3516B-HD 2 x Vee 4 Stroke 16 Cy. 170 x 215 each-1864kW (2534bhp) Caterpillar Inc-USA AuxGen: 2 x 84kW 400V 50Hz a.c
9351256 *C6VG6* -	**SMIT DIARE** **Smit Lamnalco Netherlands BV** - *Nassau* *Bahamas* MMSI: 309131000 Official number: 8001149	**313** 93 120	Class: LR ✠**100A1** SS 02/2011 tug **LMC** **UMS** Eq.Ltr: F; Cable: 275.0/19.0 U2 (a)	**2006-02 Stal-Rem SA — Gdansk** (Hull) Yd No: (511727) **2006-02 B.V. Scheepswerf Damen — Gorinchem** Yd No: 511727 Loa 29.80 Br ex 10.20 Dght 3.788 Lbp 28.03 Br md 9.40 Dpth 4.80 Welded, 1 dk	**(B32A2ST) Tug** Ice Capable	**2 oil engines** gearing integral to driving 2 Directional propellers Total Power: 3,728kW (5,068hp) 12.3kn Caterpillar 3516B-HD 2 x Vee 4 Stroke 16 Cy. 170 x 215 each-1864kW (2534bhp) Caterpillar Inc-USA AuxGen: 2 x 85kW 400V 50Hz a.c
9389473 *MRSV3* -	**SMIT DONAU** **Smit Harbour Towage (UK) Ltd (Smit Harbour Towage Liverpool)** - *Liverpool* *United Kingdom* MMSI: 235054738 Official number: 913015	**289** 86 -	Class: LR (BV) **100A1** SS 05/2012 tug **LMC** **UMS**	**2007-05 Damen Shipyards Gdynia SA — Gdynia** (Hull) Yd No: (511533) **2007-05 B.V. Scheepswerf Damen — Gorinchem** Yd No: 511533 Loa 28.75 Br ex 10.43 Dght 4.740 Lbp 25.78 Br md 9.80 Dpth 4.60 Welded, 1 dk	**(B32A2ST) Tug**	**2 oil engines** reduction geared to sc. shafts driving 2 Z propellers Total Power: 3,730kW (5,072hp) Caterpillar 3516B-HD 2 x Vee 4 Stroke 16 Cy. 170 x 215 each-1865kW (2536bhp) Caterpillar Inc-USA AuxGen: 2 x 85kW 400V 50Hz a.c

IMO / Call sign	Name / Owner	Tonnage	Class	Builder / Dimensions	Type	Machinery
9476408 *C6XZ2* -	**SMIT EBRO** **Smit Shipping Singapore Pte Ltd** Smit Harbour Towage Rotterdam BV *Nassau* Bahamas MMSI: 311026500 Official number: 8001681	285 85 160	Class: BV	2009-08 **Santierul Naval Damen Galati S.A. — Galati** (Hull) Yd No: 1158 2009-08 **B.V. Scheepswerf Damen — Gorinchem** Yd No: 511546 Loa 28.67 Br ex 10.43 Dght 4.800 Lbp 25.78 Br md 9.80 Dpth 4.60 Welded, 1 dk	**(B32A2ST) Tug**	**2 oil engines** reduction geared to sc. shafts driving 2 Propellers Total Power: 3,678kW (5,000hp) Caterpillar 3516B-HD 2 x Vee 4 Stroke 16 Cy. 170 x 215 each-1839kW (2500bhp) Caterpillar Inc-USA
9389485 *C6XN2* -	**SMIT ELBE** **Smit Shipping Singapore Pte Ltd** Smit Vessel Management Services BV *Nassau* Bahamas MMSI: 311014600 Official number: 8001602	289 86 -	Class: BV	2007-07 **Damen Shipyards Gdynia SA — Gdynia** (Hull) Yd No: (511534) 2007-07 **B.V. Scheepswerf Damen — Gorinchem** Yd No: 511534 Loa 28.67 Br ex 10.43 Dght 3.610 Lbp 25.79 Br md 9.80 Dpth 4.60 Welded, 1 dk	**(B32A2ST) Tug**	**2 oil engines** reduction geared to sc. shafts driving 2 Z propellers Total Power: 3,730kW (5,072hp) Caterpillar 3516B 2 x Vee 4 Stroke 16 Cy. 170 x 190 each-1865kW (2536bhp) Caterpillar Inc-USA
9483748 *ORQG* -	**SMIT EMOE** *ex* Rt Tango *-2011* *ex* Midlum II *-2011* **Smit Shipping Singapore Pte Ltd** Smit International (Smit Internationale Nederland BV) *Zeebrugge* Belgium MMSI: 205618000 Official number: 02 00041 2012	377 113 139	Class: BV (GL)	2011-06 **PT ASL Shipyard Indonesia — Batam** Yd No: 896 Loa 28.30 Br ex 12.00 Dght 3.300 Lbp 26.10 Br md 11.50 Dpth 5.24 Welded, 1 dk	**(B32A2ST) Tug**	**3 oil engines** gearing integral to driving 3 Z propellers Total Power: 5,280kW (7,179hp) A.B.C. 8DZC 3 x 4 Stroke 8 Cy. 256 x 310 each-1760kW (2393bhp) Anglo Belgian Corp NV (ABC)-Belgium AuxGen: 2 x 130kW 400V a.c
9144172 *ZR3448* -	**SMIT ENERGY** *ex* Pentow Energy *-2008* **Smit Amandla Marine Pty Ltd** - *Durban* South Africa Official number: 29605	1,777 985 3,678	Class: (BV)	1996-11 **Dorbyl Marine Pty. Ltd. — Cape Town** Yd No: SC9407 Conv to DH-2008 Loa 64.80 Br ex - Dght 4.845 Lbp 63.60 Br md 15.10 Dpth 5.70 Welded, 1 dk	**(B35E2TF) Bunkering Tanker** Double Hull (13F) Liq: 3,634; Liq (Oil): 3,634	**2 oil engines** reduction geared to sc. shafts driving 2 Directional propellers Total Power: 750kW (1,020hp) 5.0kn Caterpillar 3408TA 2 x Vee 4 Stroke 8 Cy. 137 x 152 each-375kW (510bhp) Caterpillar Inc-USA AuxGen: 2 x 145kW 380V 50Hz a.c Thrusters: 1 Water jet (f) Fuel: 12.5 (d.f.) 6.0pd
9396220 *C6WI9* -	**SMIT EUROPE** *launched as* Bogazici 1 *-2007* **Smit Lamnalco Ltd** Smit Terminals Europe Ltd *Nassau* Bahamas MMSI: 308403000 Official number: 8001399	465 139 -	Class: BV	2007-07 **Ge-Ta Corp. — Istanbul** Yd No: 006 Loa 32.50 Br ex - Dght 4.300 Lbp 27.60 Br md 11.70 Dpth 5.60 Welded, 1 dk	**(B32A2ST) Tug**	**2 oil engines** gearing integral to driving 2 Z propellers Total Power: 3,840kW (5,220hp) 13.0kn Caterpillar 3516B 2 x Vee 4 Stroke 16 Cy. 170 x 190 each-1920kW (2610bhp) Caterpillar Inc-USA AuxGen: 3 x 139kW 50Hz a.c Thrusters: 1 Directional thruster (f)
9396414 *HO5072* -	**SMIT GRENADA** **Smit International (Curacao) NV** Smit Harbour Towage Panama Inc *Panama* Panama Official number: 37095PEXTF3	294 88 -	Class: LR ✠ **100A1** SS 02/2013 tug **LMC** **UMS** Eq.Ltr: F; Cable: 275.0/19.0 U2 (a)	2008-02 **Santierul Naval Damen Galati S.A. — Galati** (Hull) Yd No: 1124 2008-02 **B.V. Scheepswerf Damen — Gorinchem** Yd No: 511531 Loa 28.67 Br ex 10.43 Dght 4.700 Lbp 25.79 Br md 9.80 Dpth 4.60 Welded, 1 dk	**(B32A2ST) Tug**	**2 oil engines** gearing integral to driving 2 Z propellers Total Power: 3,728kW (5,068hp) Caterpillar 3516B-HD 2 x Vee 4 Stroke 16 Cy. 170 x 215 each-1864kW (2534bhp) Caterpillar Inc-USA AuxGen: 2 x 84kW 400V 50Hz a.c
9476381 *HP5027* -	**SMIT GUADELOUPE** **Smit Shipping Singapore Pte Ltd** Smit Harbour Towage Panama Inc *Panama* Panama Official number: 39892PEXTF1	285 85 160	Class: BV	2009-05 **Santierul Naval Damen Galati S.A. — Galati** (Hull) Yd No: 1156 2009-05 **B.V. Scheepswerf Damen — Gorinchem** Yd No: 511544 Loa 28.67 Br ex 10.43 Dght 4.700 Lbp 25.78 Br md 9.80 Dpth 4.60 Welded, 1 dk	**(B32A2ST) Tug**	**2 oil engines** reduction geared to sc. shafts driving 2 Directional propellers Total Power: 3,678kW (5,000hp) Caterpillar 3516B-HD 2 x Vee 4 Stroke 16 Cy. 170 x 215 each-1839kW (2500bhp) Caterpillar Inc-USA
9402421 *C6XH8* -	**SMIT HUDSON** **Smit Shipping Singapore Pte Ltd** Smit Vessel Management Services BV *Nassau* Bahamas MMSI: 311010100 Official number: 8001559	285 - 150	Class: BV	2008-07 **Santierul Naval Damen Galati S.A. — Galati** (Hull) Yd No: 1126 2008-07 **B.V. Scheepswerf Damen — Gorinchem** Yd No: 511535 Loa 28.67 Br ex 10.43 Dght 3.610 Lbp - Br md 9.80 Dpth 4.60 Welded, 1 dk	**(B32A2ST) Tug**	**2 oil engines** reduction geared to sc. shafts driving 2 Directional propellers Total Power: 3,626kW (4,930hp) Caterpillar 3516B-TA 2 x Vee 4 Stroke 16 Cy. 170 x 190 each-1813kW (2465bhp) Caterpillar Inc-USA AuxGen: 2 x 94kW 400/230V 50Hz a.c
9190406 *CFN6647* -	**SMIT HUMBER** **Smit Marine Canada Inc** - *Vancouver, BC* Canada MMSI: 316020345 Official number: 835712	354 106 175	Class: LR (BV) ✠ **100A1** SS 10/2009 tug ✠ **LMC** **UMS** Eq.Ltr: G; Cable: 302.5/24.0 U2 (a)	2000-04 **B.V. Scheepswerf Damen — Gorinchem** Yd No: 7938 2000-04 **Stocznia Polnocna SA (Northern Shipyard) — Gdansk** (Hull) Yd No: 7938 Loa 30.60 Br ex 11.20 Dght 4.940 Lbp 27.44 Br md 10.60 Dpth 5.32 Welded, 1 dk	**(B32A2ST) Tug**	**2 oil engines** reduction geared to sc. shafts driving 2 Directional propellers Total Power: 3,660kW (4,976hp) 13.2kn Wartsila 6L26 2 x 4 Stroke 6 Cy. 260 x 320 each-1830kW (2488bhp) Wartsila NSD Nederland BV-Netherlands AuxGen: 2 x 85kW 400V 50Hz a.c
9434826 *C6XV8* -	**SMIT JAGUAR** **Smit Lamnalco Netherlands BV** - SatCom: Inmarsat C 431100285 *Nassau* Bahamas MMSI: 311023400 Official number: 8001655	484 145 260	Class: LR ✠ **100A1** SS 07/2009 escort tug, fire-fighting Ship 1 (2400 m3/h) with water spray **LMC** **UMS** Eq.Ltr: I; Cable: 330.0/24.0 U2 (a)	2009-07 **Song Cam Shipyard — Haiphong** (Hull) Yd No: (513002) 2009-02 **B.V. Scheepswerf Damen — Gorinchem** Yd No: 513002 Loa 32.14 Br ex 13.29 Dght 6.148 Lbp 31.64 Br md 12.50 Dpth 5.40 Welded, 1 dk	**(B32A2ST) Tug**	**2 oil engines** gearing integral to driving 2 Directional propellers Total Power: 5,420kW (7,370hp) Caterpillar C280-8 2 x 4 Stroke 8 Cy. 280 x 300 each-2710kW (3685bhp) Caterpillar Inc-USA AuxGen: 2 x 150kW 400V 50Hz a.c
9322607 *J7BP9* -	**SMIT KAMARA** **Smit Shipping Singapore Pte Ltd** Smit Singapore Pte Ltd *Portsmouth* Dominica MMSI: 325448000 Official number: ZA750	2,588 776 1,700	Class: AB (LR) Classed LR until 12/9/10	2005-10 **Keppel Singmarine Pte Ltd — Singapore** Yd No: 285 Loa 70.90 Br ex 16.24 Dght 5.600 Lbp 63.60 Br md 16.00 Dpth 7.00 Welded, 1 dk	**(B21B20A) Anchor Handling Tug Supply** Cranes: 1x25t	**2 oil engines** with clutches, flexible couplings & sr reverse geared to sc. shafts driving 2 CP propellers Total Power: 4,920kW (6,690hp) 12.5kn Wartsila 6R32LN 2 x 4 Stroke 6 Cy. 320 x 350 each-2460kW (3345bhp) Wartsila Finland Oy-Finland AuxGen: 2 x 570kW 440V 60Hz a.c, 2 x 1200kW 440V 60Hz a.c Thrusters: 2 Thwart. CP thruster (f); 1 Thwart. CP thruster (a) Fuel: 970.0 (r.f.)
9454321 *ORQF* -	**SMIT KIWI** *ex* RT Samba *-2011* *ex* Exact *-2011* **URS Belgie NV** *Zeebrugge* Belgium MMSI: 205619000 Official number: 02 00042 2012	377 134 97	Class: BV (GL)	2011-06 **PT ASL Shipyard Indonesia — Batam** Yd No: 895 Loa 28.30 Br ex 12.00 Dght 3.450 Lbp 26.10 Br md 11.50 Dpth 5.24 Welded, 1 dk	**(B32A2ST) Tug**	**3 oil engines** gearing integral to driving 3 Z propellers Total Power: 5,280kW (7,179hp) A.B.C. 8DZC 3 x 4 Stroke 8 Cy. 256 x 310 each-1760kW (2393bhp) Anglo Belgian Corp NV (ABC)-Belgium AuxGen: 2 x 130kW 400V a.c
9328273 *C6VD5* -	**SMIT KOMODO** **Smit Singapore Pte Ltd** *Nassau* Bahamas MMSI: 308193000 Official number: 8001137	2,593 778 2,126	Class: AB	2006-01 **Keppel Singmarine Pte Ltd — Singapore** Yd No: 286 Loa 70.90 Br ex - Dght 5.600 Lbp 63.60 Br md 16.00 Dpth 7.00 Welded, 1 dk	**(B21B20A) Anchor Handling Tug Supply** Cranes: 1x30t	**2 oil engines** geared to sc. shafts driving 2 CP propellers Total Power: 4,920kW (6,690hp) 12.5kn Wartsila 6R32LN 2 x 4 Stroke 6 Cy. 320 x 350 each-2460kW (3345bhp) Wartsila Finland Oy-Finland AuxGen: 5 x 570kW a.c, 2 x 1200kW a.c Thrusters: 2 Tunnel thruster (f); 1 Tunnel thruster (a) Fuel: 970.0 (r.f.)
9557587 *VHIB* -	**SMIT KOONGO** **Smit Lamnalco Singapore Pte Ltd** Smit Vessel Management Services BV *Gladstone, Qld* Australia MMSI: 503641000 Official number: 859650	455 136 304	Class: BV	2010-08 **Uzmar Gemi Insa Sanayi ve Ticaret AS — Basiskele** Yd No: 34 Loa 30.25 Br ex 12.05 Dght 4.240 Lbp 26.60 Br md 11.75 Dpth 5.28 Welded, 1 dk	**(B32A2ST) Tug**	**2 oil engines** geared to sc. shafts driving 2 Directional propellers Total Power: 3,946kW (5,364hp) Caterpillar 3516B-TA 2 x Vee 4 Stroke 16 Cy. 170 x 190 each-1973kW (2682bhp) Caterpillar Inc-USA AuxGen: 2 x 86kW 50Hz a.c
9578517 *VHIF* -	**SMIT KULLAROO** **Smit Shipping Singapore Pte Ltd** Smit Marine Australia Pty Ltd *Gladstone, Qld* Australia MMSI: 503647000 Official number: 589698	455 136 304	Class: BV	2010-11 **Uzmar Gemi Insa Sanayi ve Ticaret AS — Basiskele** Yd No: 57 Loa 30.25 Br ex 12.05 Dght 4.240 Lbp 26.60 Br md 11.75 Dpth 5.28 Welded, 1 dk	**(B32A2ST) Tug**	**2 oil engines** reduction geared to sc.shafts driving 2 Z propellers Total Power: 3,946kW (5,364hp) Caterpillar 3516B-HD 2 x Vee 4 Stroke 16 Cy. 170 x 215 each-1973kW (2682bhp) Caterpillar Inc-USA

IMO / Call sign	Name / Owner / Flag	Tonnage	Class	Builder / Dimensions	Type	Machinery
9380180 *9VBS6* -	**SMIT LAISA** **Smit Lamnalco Netherlands BV** - *Singapore* *Singapore* MMSI: 565754000 Official number: 393671	**1,751** 525 1,811	Class: LR (AB) **100A1** SS 07/2013 tug, fire-fighting Ship 1 (3000m3/h) with water spray **LMC**	**2008-07 Keppel Nantong Shipyard Co Ltd — Nantong JS** (Hull) Yd No: 004 **2008-07 Keppel Singmarine Pte Ltd — Singapore** Yd No: 322 Loa 60.00 Br ex - Dght 4.850 Lbp - Br md 16.00 Dpth 6.00 Welded, 1 dk	**(B21B20A) Anchor Handling Tug Supply**	**2 oil engines** reduction geared to sc. shafts driving 2 CP propellers Total Power: 4,414kW (6,002hp) Yanmar 8N280M-SV 2 x 4 Stroke 8 Cy. 280 x 380 each-2207kW (3001bhp) Yanmar Diesel Engine Co Ltd-Japan AuxGen: 2 x 400kW a.c, 1 x 600kW a.c
9371452 *9VBU4* -	**SMIT LANGKAWI** **Smit Lamnalco Netherlands BV** - *Singapore* *Singapore* MMSI: 565325000 Official number: 392689	**1,727** 518 1,826	Class: LR (AB) **100A1** SS 01/2012 TOC Contemplated	**2006-12 Keppel Singmarine Pte Ltd — Singapore** Yd No: 303 Loa 60.00 Br ex - Dght 4.200 Lbp 54.00 Br md 15.98 Dpth 5.97 Welded, 1 dk	**(B21B20A) Anchor Handling Tug Supply**	**2 oil engines** reduction geared to sc. shafts driving 2 CP propellers Total Power: 4,414kW (6,002hp) Yanmar 8N280M-SV 2 x 4 Stroke 8 Cy. 280 x 380 each-2207kW (3001bhp) Yanmar Diesel Engine Co Ltd-Japan AuxGen: 2 x 400kW a.c, 1 x 600kW a.c Fuel: 560.0 (r.f.)
9488724 *VHIG* -	**SMIT LEOPARD** **Smit Lamnalco Singapore Pte Ltd** Smit Vessel Management Services BV *Gladstone, Qld* *Australia* MMSI: 503643000 Official number: 859668	**374** 112 238	Class: LR ✠**100A1** SS 10/2010 escort tug, fire fighting Ship 1 (2400 m3/h) ✠**LMC** **UMS** Eq.Ltr: H; Cable: 302.5/22.0 U2 (a)	**2010-10 Penglai Bohai Shipyard Co Ltd — Penglai SD** (Hull) Yd No: (511216) **2010-10 B.V. Scheepswerf Damen — Gorinchem** Yd No: 511216 Loa 32.50 Br ex 11.24 Dght 4.250 Lbp 29.01 Br md 10.60 Dpth 5.00 Welded, 1 dk	**(B32A2ST) Tug**	**2 oil engines** reduction geared to sc. shafts driving 2 Directional propellers Total Power: 4,180kW (5,684hp) 13.0kn Caterpillar 3516B-HD 2 x Vee 4 Stroke 16 Cy. 170 x 215 each-2090kW (2842bhp) Caterpillar Inc-USA AuxGen: 2 x 84kW 400V 50Hz a.c
9371464 *9VCL6* -	**SMIT LINGGA** **Smit Lamnalco Netherlands BV** - *Singapore* *Singapore* MMSI: 565371000 Official number: 392783	**1,727** 518 1,823	Class: BV (AB)	**2007-02 Keppel Singmarine Pte Ltd — Singapore** Yd No: 304 Loa 60.00 Br ex - Dght 4.200 Lbp 54.00 Br md 16.00 Dpth 6.00 Welded, 1 dk	**(B21B20A) Anchor Handling Tug Supply**	**2 oil engines** reduction geared to sc. shafts driving 2 CP propellers Total Power: 4,414kW (6,002hp) Yanmar 8N280M-SV 2 x 4 Stroke 8 Cy. 280 x 380 each-2207kW (3001bhp) Yanmar Diesel Engine Co Ltd-Japan AuxGen: 2 x 400kW a.c, 1 x 600kW a.c Thrusters: 1 Tunnel thruster (f) Fuel: 560.0 (r.f.)
9537408 *ORQS* -	**SMIT LION** *ex Multratug 3 -2012* **Smit International (Smit Internationale Nederland BV)** URS Belgie NV *Zeebrugge* *Belgium* MMSI: 205636000	**484** 145 276	Class: BV (LR) (GL) ✠ Classed LR until 27/12/11	**2010-10 Song Cam Shipyard — Haiphong** (Hull) Yd No: (513015) **2010-10 B.V. Scheepswerf Damen — Gorinchem** Yd No: 513015 Loa 32.14 Br ex 13.29 Dght 4.250 Lbp 29.35 Br md 12.52 Dpth 5.39 Welded, 1 dk	**(B32A2ST) Tug**	**2 oil engines** reduction geared to sc. shafts driving 2 Directional propellers Total Power: 5,420kW (7,370hp) Caterpillar C280-8 2 x 4 Stroke 8 Cy. 280 x 300 each-2710kW (3685bhp) Caterpillar Inc-USA AuxGen: 2 x 162kW 400V 50Hz a.c
8735883 *ZRSL* -	**SMIT LIPUMA** **Smit Amandla Marine Pty Ltd** - *Durban* *South Africa* Official number: 20743	**2,398** 1,621 -		**2008-01 Dormac (Pty) Ltd — Durban** Yd No: 108 Loa 71.40 Br ex - Dght 5.710 Lbp 69.00 Br md 18.00 Dpth 7.20 Welded, 1 dk	**(B35E2TF) Bunkering Tanker** Double Hull Liq: 4,700; Liq (Oil): 4,700	**2 diesel electric oil engines** geared to sc. shafts driving 2 Azimuth electric drive units Total Power: 1,066kW (1,450hp) 6.0kn Caterpillar C18 2 x 4 Stroke 6 Cy. 145 x 183 each-533kW (725bhp) Caterpillar Inc-USA Thrusters: 1 Thwart. FP thruster (f)
8125052 -	**SMIT-LLOYD 27** **Smit Singapore Pte Ltd** SEACOR Marine (Asia) Pte Ltd	**1,089** 326 1,082	Class: (AB) (IR)	**1982-12 Scheepswerf Ferus Smit BV — Westerbroek** Yd No: 231 Loa 57.46 Br ex 12.22 Dght 4.501 Lbp 50.02 Br md 12.21 Dpth 5.82 Welded, 1 dk	**(B21B20A) Anchor Handling Tug Supply** Passengers: berths: 12	**2 oil engines** with flexible couplings & sr gearedto sc. shafts driving 2 CP propellers Total Power: 3,356kW (4,562hp) 11.5kn Kromhout 9FHD240 2 x 4 Stroke 9 Cy. 240 x 260 each-1678kW (2281bhp) Stork Werkspoor Diesel BV-Netherlands AuxGen: 1 x 150kW 440V 60Hz a.c, 2 x 140kW 440V 60Hz a.c Thrusters: 1 Thwart. CP thruster (f) Fuel: 433.5 (d.f.) 7.0pd
8213914 *C6OH6* -	**SMIT-LLOYD 33** **Smit Shipping Singapore Pte Ltd** Smit Amandla Marine Pty Ltd *Nassau* *Bahamas* MMSI: 309707000 Official number: 728137	**1,089** 326 1,104	Class: BV (AB)	**1984-04 Tille Scheepsbouw B.V. — Kootstertille** Yd No: 235 Loa 57.43 Br ex 12.53 Dght 4.811 Lbp 50.02 Br md 12.21 Dpth 5.82 Welded, 1 dk	**(B21B20A) Anchor Handling Tug Supply**	**2 oil engines** with flexible couplings & sr gearedto sc. shafts driving 2 CP propellers Total Power: 3,356kW (4,562hp) 11.5kn Kromhout 9FHD240 2 x 4 Stroke 9 Cy. 240 x 260 each-1678kW (2281bhp) Stork Werkspoor Diesel BV-Netherlands AuxGen: 1 x 150kW 440V 60Hz a.c, 2 x 140kW 440V 60Hz a.c Thrusters: 1 Thwart. CP thruster (f) Fuel: 433.5 (d.f.) 7.0pd
9190494 *C6RC7* -	**SMIT LOIRE** **Smit Lamnalco Ltd** Smit-Lloyd (Antilles) NV *Nassau* *Bahamas* MMSI: 308433000 Official number: 8000097	**353** 105 175	Class: BV (LR) ✠ Classed LR until 30/3/11	**2000-05 Stocznia Polnocna SA (Northern Shipyard) — Gdansk** (Hull) **2000-05 B.V. Scheepswerf Damen — Gorinchem** Yd No: 7948 Loa 30.60 Br ex 11.20 Dght 4.250 Lbp 27.44 Br md 10.60 Dpth 5.00 Welded, 1 dk	**(B32A2ST) Tug**	**2 oil engines** reduction geared to sc. shafts driving 2 Directional propellers Total Power: 3,660kW (4,976hp) 13.2kn Wartsila 6L26 2 x 4 Stroke 6 Cy. 260 x 320 each-1830kW (2488bhp) Wartsila NSD Nederland BV-Netherlands AuxGen: 2 x 85kW 400V 50Hz a.c
9366316 *9VAN8* -	**SMIT LOMBOK** *ex Hadi 20 -2006* **Smit Lamnalco Lombok Pte Ltd** Smit Amandla Marine Pty Ltd *Singapore* *Singapore* MMSI: 565148000 Official number: 392167	**1,727** 518 1,833	Class: AB	**2006-03 Keppel Singmarine Pte Ltd — Singapore** Yd No: 289 Loa 60.00 Br ex 16.08 Dght 4.200 Lbp 54.00 Br md 16.00 Dpth 6.00 Welded, 1 dk	**(B21B20T) Offshore Tug/Supply Ship**	**2 oil engines** reduction geared to sc. shafts driving 2 CP propellers Total Power: 4,354kW (5,920hp) Yanmar 8N280-SN 2 x 4 Stroke 8 Cy. 280 x 380 each-2177kW (2960bhp) Yanmar Diesel Engine Co Ltd-Japan Thrusters: 1 Tunnel thruster (f)
9047025 *C6TA6* -	**SMIT LUCAYA** *ex Azami -2003* **Smit-Lloyd (Antilles) NV** - *Nassau* *Bahamas* MMSI: 311559000 Official number: 8000666	**368** 110 199	Class: BV	**1991-12 Hanasaki Zosensho K.K. — Yokosuka** Yd No: 225 Loa 36.30 Br ex - Dght 3.510 Lbp 30.80 Br md 10.00 Dpth 4.40 Welded, 1 dk	**(B32A2ST) Tug**	**2 oil engines** with clutches, flexible couplings & sr geared to sc. shafts driving 2 FP propellers Total Power: 2,648kW (3,600hp) Niigata 6L28HX 2 x 4 Stroke 6 Cy. 280 x 370 each-1324kW (1800bhp) Niigata Engineering Co Ltd-Japan
9380178 *9VBS5* -	**SMIT LUMBA** **Afrikdelta Shipping Services Pte Ltd** Smit Lamnalco Netherlands BV *Singapore* *Singapore* MMSI: 565753000 Official number: 393670	**1,751** 525 1,835	Class: BV (AB)	**2008-05 Keppel Nantong Shipyard Co Ltd — Nantong JS** (Hull) Yd No: 003 **2008-05 Keppel Singmarine Pte Ltd — Singapore** Yd No: 321 Loa 60.00 Br ex - Dght 5.100 Lbp 56.53 Br md 16.00 Dpth 6.00 Welded, 1 dk	**(B21B20A) Anchor Handling Tug Supply**	**2 oil engines** reduction geared to sc. shafts driving 2 CP propellers Total Power: 4,414kW (6,002hp) 12.5kn Yanmar 8N280M-SV 2 x 4 Stroke 8 Cy. 280 x 380 each-2207kW (3001bhp) Yanmar Diesel Engine Co Ltd-Japan AuxGen: 2 x 400kW a.c, 1 x 600kW a.c Fuel: 560.0
9380166 *9VBS3* -	**SMIT LUMUT** **Smit Lamnalco Netherlands BV** - *Singapore* *Singapore* MMSI: 565751000	**1,751** 525 1,828	Class: LR (AB) **100A1** SS 01/2013 tug, fire-fighting Ship 1 (3000m3/h) with water spray **LMC**	**2008-01 Keppel Nantong Shipyard Co Ltd — Nantong JS** (Hull) Yd No: 002 **2008-01 Keppel Singmarine Pte Ltd — Singapore** Yd No: 320 Loa 60.00 Br ex - Dght 4.850 Lbp 54.00 Br md 16.00 Dpth 6.00 Welded, 1 dk	**(B21B20A) Anchor Handling Tug Supply**	**2 oil engines** reduction geared to sc. shafts driving 2 CP propellers Total Power: 4,414kW (6,002hp) Yanmar 8N280M-SV 2 x 4 Stroke 8 Cy. 280 x 380 each-2207kW (3001bhp) Yanmar Diesel Engine Co Ltd-Japan AuxGen: 2 x 400kW a.c, 1 x 600kW a.c Fuel: 560.0 (r.f.)
9380154 *9VBS4* -	**SMIT LUZON** **Smit Lamnalco Netherlands BV** - *Singapore* *Singapore* MMSI: 565752000 Official number: 393669	**1,751** 525 1,817	Class: LR (AB) **100A1** SS 03/2013 TOC contemplated	**2008-03 Keppel Nantong Shipyard Co Ltd — Nantong JS** (Hull) Yd No: 001 **2008-03 Keppel Singmarine Pte Ltd — Singapore** Yd No: 319 Loa 60.00 Br ex - Dght 4.850 Lbp 58.70 Br md 16.00 Dpth 6.00 Welded, 1 dk	**(B21B20A) Anchor Handling Tug Supply**	**2 oil engines** reduction geared to sc. shafts driving 2 CP propellers Total Power: 4,414kW (6,002hp) Yanmar 8N280M-SV 2 x 4 Stroke 8 Cy. 280 x 380 each-2207kW (3001bhp) Yanmar Diesel Engine Co Ltd-Japan AuxGen: 2 x 400kW a.c, 1 x 600kW a.c Thrusters: 1 Tunnel thruster (f) Fuel: 560.0

9488712 *9V6931* -	**SMIT LYNX** **Smit Shipping Singapore Pte Ltd** Smit Singapore Pte Ltd *Singapore* *Singapore* MMSI: 566547000 Official number: 397915	**374** 112 -	Class: LR **✠100A1** SS 11/2010 escort tug, fire fighting Ship 1 (2400m3/h) **LMC** **UMS** Eq.Ltr: H; Cable: 302.5/22.0 U2 (a)	**2010-11 Penglai Bohai Shipyard Co Ltd — Penglai SD** (Hull) Yd No: (511215) **2010-11 B.V. Scheepswerf Damen — Gorinchem** Yd No: 511215 Loa 32.50 Br ex - Dght 4.250 Lbp 29.01 Br md 10.60 Dpth 5.00 Welded, 1 dk	**(B32A2ST) Tug**	**2 oil engines** reduction geared to sc. shafts driving 2 Directional propellers Total Power: 3,542kW (4,816hp) 13.0kn Caterpillar 3516B-HD 2 x Vee 4 Stroke 16 Cy. 170 x 215 each-1771kW (2408bhp) Caterpillar Inc-USA AuxGen: 2 x 84kW 400V 50Hz a.c
9397925 *C6XO7* -	**SMIT MADAGASCAR** **Smit Lamnalco Ltd** Smit Terminals Europe Ltd *Nassau* *Bahamas* MMSI: 311017600 Official number: 8001614	**329** 98 120	Class: BV (LR) ✠ Classed LR until 03/2/10	**2009-01 PT ASL Shipyard Indonesia — Batam** Yd No: 809 Loa 28.00 Br ex 9.90 Dght 4.000 Lbp 23.94 Br md 9.80 Dpth 4.80 Welded, 1 dk	**(B32A2ST) Tug**	**2 oil engines** gearing integral to driving 2 Z propellers Total Power: 2,646kW (3,598hp) 12.0kn Niigata 6L25HX 2 x 4 Stroke 6 Cy. 250 x 350 each-1323kW (1799bhp) Niigata Engineering Co Ltd-Japan AuxGen: 2 x 99kW 415V 50Hz a.c Fuel: 130.0 (d.f.)
8714891 *ZR8600* -	**SMIT MADURA** *ex Salvatore -2003* **Smit Amandla Marine Pty Ltd** - *Cape Town* *South Africa* MMSI: 601980000 Official number: 11010	**1,070** 321 947	Class: AB (RI)	**1988-12 Cant. Navale "Ferrari" S.p.A. — La Spezia** Yd No: 68 Loa 50.00 Br ex 14.55 Dght 5.713 Lbp 43.50 Br md 14.30 Dpth 6.70 Welded, 1 dk	**(B32A2ST) Tug** A-frames: 1	**2 oil engines** with clutches, flexible couplings & sr geared to sc. shafts driving 2 CP propellers Total Power: 6,620kW (9,000hp) 15.5kn Nohab 16V25 2 x Vee 4 Stroke 16 Cy. 250 x 300 each-3310kW (4500bhp) Wartsila Diesel AB-Sweden AuxGen: 3 x 400kW 380V 50Hz a.c Thrusters: 2 Thwart. FP thruster (f) Fuel: 531.0 (d.f.) 108.0 (r.f.) 31.3pd
9213674 *HO2416* -	**SMIT MANDJI** **Smit International (Gabon) SA** - *Panama* *Panama* MMSI: 357264000 Official number: 3069705A	**322** 96 -	Class: BV	**2004-12 Stal-Rem SA — Gdansk** (Hull) Yd No: (511606) **2004-12 B.V. Scheepswerf Damen — Gorinchem** Yd No: 511606 Loa 35.53 Br ex - Dght 4.070 Lbp - Br md 8.84 Dpth 4.40 Welded, 1 dk	**(B32A2ST) Tug**	**2 oil engines** geared to sc. shafts driving 2 FP propellers Total Power: 2,910kW (3,956hp) 12.9kn Caterpillar 3516TA 2 x Vee 4 Stroke 16 Cy. 170 x 190 each-1455kW (1978bhp) Caterpillar Inc-USA
9179000 *C6QQ9* -	**SMIT MANZANILLO** *ex Smit Ile-Ife -2010* **Smit Shipping Singapore Pte Ltd** SMIT Rebocadores do Brasil SA *Nassau* *Bahamas* MMSI: 308097000 Official number: 732236	**305** 91 223	Class: LR **✠100A1** SS 06/2009 tug **✠LMC** **UMS** Eq.Ltr: F; Cable: 275.0/19.0 U2	**1999-06 PO SevMash Predpriyatiye — Severodvinsk** (Hull) **1999-06 B.V. Scheepswerf Damen — Gorinchem** Yd No: 7926 Loa 30.82 Br ex 10.20 Dght 3.758 Lbp 26.00 Br md 9.40 Dpth 4.80 Welded, 1 dk	**(B32A2ST) Tug**	**2 oil engines** with clutches, flexible couplings & sr geared to sc. shafts driving 2 Directional propellers Total Power: 3,132kW (4,258hp) 10.5kn Caterpillar 3516B-TA 2 x Vee 4 Stroke 16 Cy. 170 x 190 each-1566kW (2129bhp) Caterpillar Inc-USA AuxGen: 2 x 85kW 380V 50Hz a.c Fuel: 115.0 (d.f.) 8.0pd
9402445 *C6XL2* -	**SMIT MARTINIQUE** **Smit Lamnalco Ltd** Smit Lamnalco Netherlands BV *Nassau* *Bahamas* MMSI: 311012900 Official number: 8001584	**294** 88 150	Class: BV (LR) ✠ Classed LR until 3/2/10	**2008-11 Santierul Naval Damen Galati S.A. — Galati** (Hull) Yd No: 1128 **2008-11 B.V. Scheepswerf Damen — Gorinchem** Yd No: 511537 Loa 28.75 Br ex 10.43 Dght 3.690 Lbp 25.78 Br md 9.80 Dpth 4.60 Welded, 1 dk	**(B32A2ST) Tug**	**2 oil engines** reduction geared to sc. shafts driving 2 Directional propellers Total Power: 3,728kW (5,068hp) Caterpillar 3516B-HD 2 x Vee 4 Stroke 16 Cy. 170 x 215 each-1864kW (2534bhp) Caterpillar Inc-USA AuxGen: 2 x 84kW 400V 50Hz a.c
9397937 *C6XQ3* -	**SMIT MAURITIUS** *launched as ASL Mauritius -2009* **Smit Lamnalco Ltd** Smit Lamnalco Netherlands BV *Nassau* *Bahamas* MMSI: 311018900 Official number: 8001633	**329** 98 120	Class: BV (LR) ✠ Classed LR until 3/2/10	**2009-03 PT ASL Shipyard Indonesia — Batam** (Hull) Yd No: 810 **2009-03 ASL Shipyard Pte Ltd — Singapore** Yd No: 810 Loa 28.00 Br ex 9.90 Dght 4.000 Lbp 23.94 Br md 9.80 Dpth 4.80 Welded, 1 dk	**(B32A2ST) Tug**	**2 oil engines** gearing integral to driving 2 Z propellers Total Power: 2,646kW (3,598hp) 12.0kn Niigata 6L25HX 2 x 4 Stroke 6 Cy. 250 x 350 each-1323kW (1799bhp) Niigata Engineering Co Ltd-Japan AuxGen: 2 x 99kW 415V 50Hz a.c Fuel: 130.0 (d.f.)
9187241 *CFN5283* -	**SMIT MISSISSIPPI** **Smit International (Smit Internationale Nederland BV)** Smit Marine Canada Inc *Vancouver, BC* *Canada* MMSI: 316013397 Official number: 832964	**353** 105 240	Class: LR **✠100A1** SS 09/2013 tug **✠LMC** **UMS** Eq.Ltr: G; Cable: 302.5/24.0 U2	**1999-03 B.V. Scheepswerf Damen — Gorinchem** Yd No: 7933 **1999-03 Stocznia Polnocna SA (Northern Shipyard) — Gdansk** (Hull) Yd No: 7933 Loa 30.60 Br ex 11.20 Dght 5.010 Lbp 27.44 Br md 10.60 Dpth 5.00 Welded, 1 dk	**(B32A2ST) Tug**	**2 oil engines** reduction geared to sc. shafts driving 2 Directional propellers Total Power: 3,660kW (4,976hp) 12.7kn Wartsila 6L26 2 x 4 Stroke 6 Cy. 260 x 320 each-1830kW (2488bhp) Wartsila NSD Nederland BV-Netherlands AuxGen: 2 x 105kW 480V 60Hz a.c Fuel: 88.3 (d.f.)
9187277 *C6QN4* -	**SMIT MISSOURI** **Smit Lamnalco Ltd** SMIT Terminals (Bahamas) *Nassau* *Bahamas* Official number: 732207	**353** 105 225	Class: BV (LR) ✠ Classed LR until 6/9/07	**1999-11 Stocznia Polnocna SA (Northern Shipyard) — Gdansk** (Hull) **1999-11 B.V. Scheepswerf Damen — Gorinchem** Yd No: 7936 Loa 30.60 Br ex 11.20 Dght 4.050 Lbp 24.74 Br md 10.60 Dpth 5.00 Welded, 1 dk	**(B32A2ST) Tug**	**2 oil engines** reduction geared to sc. shafts driving 2 Directional propellers Total Power: 3,660kW (4,976hp) 12.7kn Wartsila 6L26 2 x 4 Stroke 6 Cy. 260 x 320 each-1830kW (2488bhp) Wartsila NSD Nederland BV-Netherlands AuxGen: 2 x 105kW 480V 60Hz a.c
9516272 *5BPT3* -	**SMIT MONTSERRAT** **Smit Singapore Pte Ltd** Smit Vessel Management Services BV *Limassol* *Cyprus* MMSI: 210045000	**285** 85 150	Class: BV	**2008-12 Song Cam Shipyard — Haiphong** (Hull) Yd No: (511550) **2008-12 B.V. Scheepswerf Damen — Gorinchem** (Hull) Yd No: 511550 Loa 28.67 Br ex 10.43 Dght 3.610 Lbp 25.78 Br md 9.80 Dpth 4.60 Welded, 1 dk	**(B32A2ST) Tug**	**2 oil engines** reduction geared to sc. shafts driving 2 Z propellers Total Power: 3,282kW (4,462hp) Caterpillar 3516B-TA 2 x Vee 4 Stroke 16 Cy. 170 x 190 each-1641kW (2231bhp) Caterpillar Inc-USA AuxGen: 2 x 86kW 50Hz a.c
7803140 *VD3119* -	**SMIT NASS** *ex S/Vm T.P. 2 -2009 ex T. P. 2 -1985* *ex S/VM T.P. 2 -1984* **Minette Bay Ship Docking Ltd** - *Vancouver, BC* *Canada* MMSI: 316018737 Official number: 391202	*361* 233 168	Class: (LR) ✠ Classed LR until 24/11/95	**1979-03 E S Fox Ltd — Niagara Falls ON** (Hull launched by) Yd No: 4801 **1983-12 Vito Steel Boat & Barge Construction Ltd — Delta BC** (Hull completed by) Yd No: 159 Converted From: Shunter Pontoon-1983 Loa 30.94 Br ex 11.61 Dght 1.991 Lbp 26.67 Br md 10.98 Dpth 3.66 Welded, 1 dk	**(B32A2ST) Tug**	**1 oil engine** with clutches, flexible couplings & epicyclic geared to sc. shafts driving 2 Z propellers Total Power: 2,648kW (3,600hp) Alco 16V251F 1 x Vee 4 Stroke 16 Cy. 229 x 267 2648kW (3600bhp) Bombardier Inc-Canada AuxGen: 1 x 135kW 575V 60Hz a.c
9322592 *J7AY6* -	**SMIT NICOBAR** **Smit Shipping Singapore Pte Ltd** Smit Singapore Pte Ltd *Portsmouth* *Dominica* MMSI: 325228000 Official number: 8001190	**2,606** 781 1,930	Class: AB	**2006-05 Keppel Singmarine Pte Ltd — Singapore** Yd No: 287 Loa 70.90 Br ex - Dght 5.600 Lbp 63.60 Br md 16.00 Dpth 7.00 Welded, 1 dk	**(B22A20R) Offshore Support Vessel**	**2 oil engines** geared to sc. shafts driving 2 CP propellers Total Power: 7,380kW (10,034hp) 13.5kn Wartsila 9R32 2 x 4 Stroke 9 Cy. 320 x 350 each-3690kW (5017bhp) Wartsila Finland Oy-Finland AuxGen: 2 x 700kW 440V 60Hz a.c, 2 x 1200kW 440V 60Hz a.c Thrusters: 2 Tunnel thruster (f); 1 Tunnel thruster (a)
9187253 *A8ZW8* -	**SMIT NIDA** *ex Smit Mersey -2009* **Smit Lamnalco Netherlands BV** - *Monrovia* *Liberia* MMSI: 636092280 Official number: 92280	**353** 105 238	Class: LR **✠100A1** SS 04/2009 tug **✠LMC** **UMS** Eq.Ltr: G; Cable: 302.5/24.0 U2	**1999-04 B.V. Scheepswerf Damen — Gorinchem** Yd No: 7934 **1999-04 Stocznia Polnocna SA (Northern Shipyard) — Gdansk** (Hull) Yd No: 7934 Loa 30.60 Br ex 11.20 Dght 4.050 Lbp 27.74 Br md 10.60 Dpth 5.00 Welded, 1 dk	**(B32A2ST) Tug**	**2 oil engines** reduction geared to sc. shafts driving 2 Directional propellers Total Power: 3,660kW (4,976hp) 12.7kn Wartsila 6L26 2 x 4 Stroke 6 Cy. 260 x 320 each-1830kW (2488bhp) Wartsila NSD Nederland BV-Netherlands AuxGen: 2 x 105kW 480V 60Hz a.c Fuel: 88.3 (d.f.)
8137055 - -	**SMIT NORMAN** *ex Rivtow Norman -2008 ex Rivtow Spirit -1991* **Smit Marine Canada Inc** - *Vancouver, BC* *Canada* Official number: 395742	*136* 57 -		**1980 John Manly Shipyard Ltd — Vancouver BC** Loa 18.60 Br ex 7.32 Dght - Lbp - Br md - Dpth 3.05 Welded, 1 dk	**(B32A2ST) Tug**	**2 oil engines** driving 2 FP propellers Total Power: 706kW (960hp) G.M. (Detroit Diesel) 16V-71-N 2 x Vee 2 Stroke 16 Cy. 108 x 127 each-353kW (480bhp) General Motors Detroit DieselAllison Divn-USA
9344605 *UDIF* -	**SMIT NOVIK** *ex SMIT-FEMCO NOVIK -2011* **High Latitude Shipping Inc** Smit Vessel Management Services BV *Kholmsk* *Russia* MMSI: 273311060	**130** 42 235	Class: RS (LR) ✠ 19/7/06	**2006-07 Santierul Naval Damen Galati S.A. — Galati** (Hull) Yd No: 1069 **2006-07 B.V. Scheepswerf Damen — Gorinchem** Yd No: 509612 Loa 22.57 Br ex 7.88 Dght 3.160 Lbp 20.41 Br md 7.84 Dpth 3.74 Welded, 1 dk	**(B32A2ST) Tug** Ice Capable	**2 oil engines** with clutches, flexible couplings & sr reverse geared to sc. shafts driving 2 FP propellers Total Power: 2,028kW (2,758hp) 11.3kn Caterpillar 3512B-TA 2 x Vee 4 Stroke 12 Cy. 170 x 190 each-1014kW (1379bhp) Caterpillar Inc-USA AuxGen: 2 x 50kW 230/400V 50Hz a.c Fuel: 32.0 (d.f.)

9187265 *C6QN6* -	**SMIT ONEIDA** *ex Smit Marne -2007* **Smit Lamnalco Ltd** SMIT Terminals (Bahamas) *Nassau* *Bahamas* MMSI: 308831000 Official number: 732209	**353** 105 240	Class: BV (LR) ✠ Classed LR until 6/9/07	**1999-07 Stocznia Polnocna SA (Northern Shipyard) — Gdansk** (Hull) **1999-07 B.V. Scheepswerf Damen — Gorinchem** Yd No: 7935 Loa 30.60 Br ex 11.20 Dght 4.050 Lbp 29.74 Br md 10.60 Dpth 5.00 Welded, 1 dk	**(B32A2ST) Tug**	**2 oil engines** reduction geared to sc. shafts driving 2 Directional propellers Total Power: 3,660kW (4,976hp) 12.7kn Wartsila 6L26 2 x 4 Stroke 6 Cy. 260 x 320 each-1830kW (2488bhp) Wartsila NSD Nederland BV-Netherlands AuxGen: 2 x 105kW 480V 60Hz a.c Fuel: 88.3 (d.f.)
8213885 *ORNX* -	**SMIT ORCA** *ex Orca -1986* **Boskalis Offshore Marine Services BV** Unie van Redding - en Sleepdienst NV (Union de Remorquage et de Sauvetage SA) (Towage & Salvage Union Ltd) *Antwerpen* *Belgium* MMSI: 205466000 Official number: 01 00635 2006	**835** 250 835	Class: BV	**1983-12 Barkmeijer Stroobos B.V. — Stroobos** Yd No: 224 Loa 49.87 Br ex 11.79 Dght 4.210 Lbp 43.01 Br md 11.51 Dpth 4.73 Welded, 1 dk	**(B22A2OR) Offshore Support Vessel** Cranes: 1x16t	**2 oil engines** with flexible couplings & sr gearedto sc. shafts driving 2 CP propellers Total Power: 1,288kW (1,752hp) 11.3kn MAN 7L20/27 2 x 4 Stroke 7 Cy. 200 x 270 each-644kW (876bhp) Brons Industrie NV-Netherlands AuxGen: 3 x 250kW 440V 60Hz a.c, 1 x 125kW 440V 60Hz a.c, 1 x 55kW 440V 60Hz a.c Thrusters: 1 Thwart. FP thruster (f)
9424998 *CFN5087* -	**SMIT ORLEANS** *ex T. P. 3 -2008* **Smit Marine Canada Inc** - *Vancouver, BC* *Canada* MMSI: 316012721 Official number: 832019	**402** 120 -		**2008-10 Nichols Bros. Boat Builders, Inc. — Freeland, Wa** Yd No: S-152 Loa 30.50 Br ex - Dght - Lbp - Br md 12.19 Dpth 4.97 Welded, 1 dk	**(B32A2ST) Tug**	**2 oil engines** gearing integral to driving 2 Z propellers Total Power: 5,050kW (6,866hp) Caterpillar 3516C 2 x Vee 4 Stroke 16 Cy. 170 x 215 each-2525kW (3433bhp) Caterpillar Inc-USA AuxGen: 2 x 215kW a.c
9351268 *C6VI9* -	**SMIT OWENA** - **Smit Lamnalco Netherlands BV** - *Nassau* *Bahamas* MMSI: 308022000 Official number: 8001169	**313** 93 -	Class: LR ✠ **100A1** SS 04/2011 tug **LMC** **UMS** Eq.Ltr: F; Cable: 275.0/19.0 U2 (a)	**2006-04 Stal-Rem SA — Gdansk** (Hull) Yd No: (511728) **2006-04 B.V. Scheepswerf Damen — Gorinchem** Yd No: 511728 Loa 29.80 Br ex 10.20 Dght 3.788 Lbp 28.03 Br md 9.40 Dpth 4.80 Welded, 1 dk	**(B32A2ST) Tug**	**2 oil engines** reduction geared to sc. shafts driving 2 Directional propellers Total Power: 3,728kW (5,068hp) 12.3kn Caterpillar 3516B-HD 2 x Vee 4 Stroke 16 Cy. 170 x 215 each-1864kW (2534bhp) Caterpillar Inc-USA AuxGen: 2 x 85kW 400V 50Hz a.c
9366756 *HP2348* -	**SMIT OZOURI** - **Smit International (Gabon) SA** - *Panama* *Panama* MMSI: 370757000 Official number: 4016209	**322** 96 -	Class: BV	**2006-12 Santierul Naval Damen Galati S.A. — Galati** (Hull) Yd No: 1115 **2006-12 B.V. Scheepswerf Damen — Gorinchem** Yd No: 511614 Loa 35.53 Br ex - Dght 4.550 Lbp 32.43 Br md 8.84 Dpth 4.40 Welded, 1 dk	**(B32A2ST) Tug**	**2 oil engines** reduction geared to sc. shafts driving 2 Directional propellers Total Power: 2,948kW (4,008hp) Caterpillar 3516B 2 x Vee 4 Stroke 16 Cy. 170 x 190 each-1474kW (2004bhp) Caterpillar Inc-USA AuxGen: 3 x 84kW 50Hz a.c
9276822 *HO3883* -	**SMIT PANAMA** - **Smit International (Curacao) NV** Smit Harbour Towage Panama Inc *Panama* *Panama* Official number: 33101PEXTF4	**294** 88 148	Class: LR ✠ **100A1** SS 08/2009 tug **LMC** **UMS** Eq.Ltr: F; Cable: 275.0/19.0 U2 (a)	**2004-08 Santierul Naval Damen Galati S.A. — Galati** (Hull) Yd No: 976 **2004-08 B.V. Scheepswerf Damen — Gorinchem** Yd No: 511505 Loa 28.75 Br ex 10.43 Dght 3.708 Lbp 25.79 Br md 9.80 Dpth 4.60 Welded, 1 dk	**(B32A2ST) Tug**	**2 oil engines** reduction geared to sc. shafts driving 2 Z propellers Total Power: 3,450kW (4,690hp) Caterpillar 3516B-HD 1 x Vee 4 Stroke 16 Cy. 170 x 215 1725kW (2345bhp) Caterpillar Inc-USA AuxGen: 2 x 85kW 400/230V 50Hz a.c Thrusters: 1 Thwart. FP thruster (f) Fuel: 117.0 (d.f.)
9434814 *C6XV7* -	**SMIT PANTHER** - **Smit Harbour Towage Rotterdam BV** - SatCom: Inmarsat C 431100286 *Nassau* *Bahamas* MMSI: 311023500 Official number: 8001654	**484** 145 262	Class: LR ✠ **100A1** SS 06/2009 escort tug, fire fighting Ship 1 (2400m/h) with water spray **LMC** **UMS** Eq.Ltr: I; Cable: 330.0/24.0 U2 (a)	**2009-06 Song Cam Shipyard — Haiphong** (Hull) Yd No: (513001) **2009-06 B.V. Scheepswerf Damen — Gorinchem** Yd No: 513001 Loa 32.14 Br ex 13.29 Dght 6.148 Lbp 31.64 Br md 12.50 Dpth 5.40 Welded, 1 dk	**(B32A2ST) Tug**	**2 oil engines** gearing integral to driving 2 Directional propellers Total Power: 5,420kW (7,370hp) Caterpillar C280-8 2 x 4 Stroke 8 Cy. 280 x 300 each-2710kW (3685bhp) Caterpillar Inc-USA AuxGen: 2 x 150kW 400V 50Hz a.c Fuel: 173.0 (d.f.)
9668661 *PPSA* -	**SMIT PARECI** - **SMIT Rebocadores do Brasil SA** - *Rio de Janeiro* *Brazil* MMSI: 710005000	*271* 81 136	Class: AB	**2013-12 TWB SA — Navegantes** Yd No: H1003 Loa 24.40 Br ex 10.28 Dght 3.000 Lbp 22.00 Br md 10.25 Dpth 4.31 Welded, 1 dk	**(B32A2ST) Tug**	**2 oil engines** reduction geared to sc. shafts driving 2 Z propellers Total Power: 2,760kW (3,752hp) Caterpillar 3512C-HD 2 x Vee 4 Stroke 12 Cy. 170 x 215 each-1380kW (1876bhp) Caterpillar Inc-USA Fuel: 75.0 (d.f.)
9668659 *PPYX* -	**SMIT PATAXO** - **SMIT Rebocadores do Brasil SA** - *Rio de Janeiro* *Brazil* MMSI: 710012550	**271** 81 136	Class: AB	**2013-06 TWB SA — Navegantes** Yd No: H1002 Loa 24.40 Br ex 10.28 Dght 3.000 Lbp 22.00 Br md 10.25 Dpth 4.31 Welded, 1 dk	**(B32A2ST) Tug**	**2 oil engines** reduction geared to sc. shafts driving 2 Z propellers Total Power: 2,760kW (3,752hp) Caterpillar 3512C-HD 2 x Vee 4 Stroke 12 Cy. 170 x 215 each-1380kW (1876bhp) Caterpillar Inc-USA AuxGen: 2 x 99kW a.c Fuel: 75.0 (d.f.)
9359533 *C6VA5* -	**SMIT PORT SAID** *completed as Ege-8 -2005* **Smit Internationale Sleepbootmaatschappij - Smit Salvor BV** Smit Terminals Division Rotterdam BV *Nassau* *Bahamas* MMSI: 308013000 Official number: 8001103	**409** 122 -	Class: BV	**2005-11 Anadolu Deniz Insaat Kizaklari San. ve Tic. Ltd. Sti. — Tuzla** Yd No: 196 Loa 30.25 Br ex - Dght 3.750 Lbp - Br md 11.00 Dpth 5.28 Welded, 1 dk	**(B32A2ST) Tug**	**2 oil engines** reduction geared to sc. shafts driving 2 Directional propellers Total Power: 3,600kW (4,894hp) 12.5kn Caterpillar 3516B 2 x Vee 4 Stroke 16 Cy. 170 x 190 each-1800kW (2447bhp) Caterpillar Inc-USA
9190509 *C6RC6* -	**SMIT RHONE** - **Smit Lamnalco Ltd** Smit-Lloyd (Antilles) NV *Nassau* *Bahamas* MMSI: 309691000 Official number: 8000095	**353** 105 175	Class: BV (LR) ✠ Classed LR until 23/8/09	**2000-07 Stocznia Polnocna SA (Northern Shipyard) — Gdansk** (Hull) **2000-07 B.V. Scheepswerf Damen — Gorinchem** Yd No: 7949 Loa 30.60 Br ex 11.20 Dght 4.050 Lbp 27.44 Br md 10.60 Dpth 5.00 Welded, 1 dk	**(B32A2ST) Tug**	**2 oil engines** reduction geared to sc. shafts driving 2 Directional propellers Total Power: 3,660kW (4,976hp) 13.2kn Wartsila 6L26 2 x 4 Stroke 6 Cy. 260 x 320 each-1830kW (2488bhp) Wartsila NSD Nederland BV-Netherlands AuxGen: 2 x 85kW 400V 50Hz a.c
9179012 *C6QR2* -	**SMIT RIMA** - **Smit Lamnalco Netherlands BV** - SatCom: Inmarsat C 430866720 *Nassau* *Bahamas* MMSI: 308667000 Official number: 732237	**305** 91 175	Class: LR ✠ **100A1** SS 07/2009 tug ✠ **LMC** **UMS** Eq.Ltr: F; Cable: 275.0/19.0 U2	**1999-07 Stocznia Tczew Sp z oo — Tczew** (Hull) **1999-07 B.V. Scheepswerf Damen — Gorinchem** Yd No: 7927 Loa 30.82 Br ex 10.20 Dght 3.760 Lbp 26.00 Br md 9.40 Dpth 4.80 Welded, 1 dk	**(B32A2ST) Tug**	**2 oil engines** with clutches, flexible couplings & reduction geared to sc. shafts driving 2 Directional propellers Total Power: 3,124kW (4,248hp) Caterpillar 3516B-TA 2 x Vee 4 Stroke 16 Cy. 170 x 190 each-1562kW (2124bhp) Caterpillar Inc-USA AuxGen: 2 x 85kW 380V 60Hz a.c
9394179 *C6WP7* -	**SMIT RIO MUNI** - **Smit Lamnalco Netherlands BV** - *Nassau* *Bahamas* MMSI: 308811000 Official number: 8001434	**374** 112 307	Class: LR ✠ **100A1** SS 03/2013 escort tug, restricted services Port of Malabo, Equatorial Guinea, fire fighting Ship 1 (2400 m3/h with water spray) **LMC** **UMS** Eq.Ltr: H; Cable: 302.5/22.0 U2 (a)	**2008-03 Damen Shipyards Gdynia SA — Gdynia** (Hull) Yd No: 511214 **2008-03 B.V. Scheepswerf Damen — Gorinchem** Yd No: 511214 Loa 32.50 Br ex 10.64 Dght 4.250 Lbp 29.01 Br md 10.60 Dpth 5.00 Welded, 1 dk	**(B32A2ST) Tug**	**2 oil engines** reduction geared to sc. shafts driving 2 Directional propellers Total Power: 4,180kW (5,684hp) Caterpillar 3516B-HD 2 x Vee 4 Stroke 16 Cy. 170 x 215 each-2090kW (2842bhp) Caterpillar Inc-USA AuxGen: 2 x 84kW 400V 50Hz a.c
9476379 *HP3257* -	**SMIT SABA** - **Smit Shipping Singapore Pte Ltd** Smit Harbour Towage Panama Inc *Panama* *Panama* MMSI: 352744000 Official number: 39884PEXTF1	**285** 85 160	Class: BV	**2009-04 Santierul Naval Damen Galati S.A. — Galati** (Hull) Yd No: 1155 **2009-04 B.V. Scheepswerf Damen — Gorinchem** Yd No: 511543 Loa 28.67 Br ex - Dght 4.800 Lbp 25.78 Br md 10.43 Dpth 4.60 Welded, 1 dk	**(B32A2ST) Tug**	**2 oil engines** reduction geared to sc. shafts driving 2 FP propellers Total Power: 3,728kW (5,068hp) Caterpillar 3516B-TA 2 x Vee 4 Stroke 16 Cy. 170 x 190 each-1864kW (2534bhp) Caterpillar Inc-USA AuxGen: 2 x 92kW 50Hz a.c

IMO / Call sign	Name / Owner / Port	Tonnage	Class	Builder / Dimensions	Type	Machinery
8127830 *UFXQ* -	**SMIT SAKHALIN** *ex Iscaroo -1998 ex Canmar Miscaroo -1998* *ex Miscaroo -1995* **Smit Lamnalco Netherlands BV** - *Kholmsk* *Russia* MMSI: 273438220	**3,143** 942 1,965	Class: RS (LR) ✠ Classed LR until 6/6/13	**1983-07 Vancouver Shipyards Co Ltd — North Vancouver BC** Yd No: 106 Loa 79.25 Br ex 17.58 Dght 8.160 Lbp 69.12 Br md 17.23 Dpth 9.71 Welded, 1 dk	**(B21B20A) Anchor Handling Tug Supply** Cranes: 2x5t Ice Capable	**4 oil engines** with clutches, flexible couplings & sr geared to sc. shafts driving 2 CP propellers Total Power: 10,956kW (14,896hp) 14.7kn Wartsila 8R32 4 x 4 Stroke 8 Cy. 320 x 350 each-2739kW (3724bhp) Oy Wartsila Ab-Finland AuxGen: 2 x 1000kW 460V 60Hz a.c, 2 x 395kW 460V 60Hz a.c, 1 x 250kW 460V 60Hz a.c Thrusters: 1 Thwart. FP thruster (f); 1 Water jet (a) Fuel: 1251.0 (d.f.) 43.5pd
9120152 *2CPS8* -	**SMIT SANDON** *ex Schelde 20 -2009* **Smit Harbour Towage (UK) Ltd (Smit Harbour Towage Liverpool)** - *Liverpool* *United Kingdom* MMSI: 235074754 Official number: 916062	**398** 119 255	Class: LR ✠ **100A1** SS 03/2011 tug ✠ **LMC** **UMS** Eq.Ltr: G; Cable: 302.5/20.5 U2	**1996-03 Astilleros Armon SA — Navia** Yd No: 369 Loa 30.60 Br ex 11.04 Dght 3.400 Lbp 28.50 Br md 11.00 Dpth 4.50 Welded, 1 dk	**(B32A2ST) Tug**	**2 oil engines** gearing integral to driving 2 Voith-Schneider propellers Total Power: 3,000kW (4,078hp) 13.0kn Deutz SBV8M628 2 x 4 Stroke 8 Cy. 240 x 280 each-1500kW (2039bhp) Motoren Werke Mannheim AG (MWM)-Mannheim AuxGen: 2 x 144kW 380V 50Hz a.c, 1 x 72kW 380V 50Hz a.c
9402433 *C6XI5* -	**SMIT SCHELDE** **Smit Shipping Singapore Pte Ltd** Smit Vessel Management Services BV *Nassau* *Bahamas* MMSI: 311010600 Official number: 8001565	**285** 86 150	Class: BV	**2008-09 Santierul Naval Damen Galati S.A. — Galati** (Hull) Yd No: 1127 **2008-09 B.V. Scheepswerf Damen — Gorinchem** Yd No: 511536 Loa 28.67 Br ex 10.43 Dght 4.860 Lbp 27.90 Br md 9.80 Dpth 4.60 Welded, 1 dk	**(B32A2ST) Tug**	**2 oil engines** reduction geared to sc. shafts driving 2 Directional propellers Total Power: 3,626kW (4,930hp) Caterpillar 3516B-TA 2 x Vee 4 Stroke 16 Cy. 170 x 190 each-1813kW (2465bhp) Caterpillar Inc-USA AuxGen: 2 x 84kW 400/230V 50Hz a.c Fuel: 85.0 (d.f.)
9476393 *C6XY2* -	**SMIT SEINE** **Smit Singapore Pte Ltd** Smit Internationale NV *Nassau* *Bahamas* MMSI: 311025600 Official number: 8001673	**285** 85 160	Class: BV	**2009-09 Santierul Naval Damen Galati S.A. — Galati** (Hull) Yd No: 1157 **2009-09 B.V. Scheepswerf Damen — Gorinchem** Yd No: 511545 Loa 28.67 Br ex - Dght 4.800 Lbp 25.78 Br md 10.43 Dpth 4.60 Welded, 1 dk	**(B32A2ST) Tug**	**2 oil engines** reduction geared to sc. shafts driving 2 Propellers Total Power: 3,678kW (5,000hp) Caterpillar 3516B-HD 2 x Vee 4 Stroke 16 Cy. 170 x 215 each-1839kW (2500bhp) Caterpillar Inc-USA
9662356 *9V9846* -	**SMIT SENTOSA** **Smit Singapore Pte Ltd** - *Singapore* *Singapore* MMSI: 566803000 Official number: 397656	**1,463** 439 925	Class: AB	**2013-04 Guangxi Guijiang Shipyard — Wuzhou GX** Yd No: 01-2010-19 Loa 51.80 Br ex - Dght 5.000 Lbp 44.40 Br md 15.00 Dpth 6.50 Welded, 1 dk	**(B21B20A) Anchor Handling Tug Supply**	**2 oil engines** reduction geared to sc. shafts driving 2 Propellers Total Power: 5,440kW (7,396hp) Wartsila 8L26 2 x 4 Stroke 8 Cy. 260 x 320 each-2720kW (3698bhp) Wartsila Finland Oy-Finland AuxGen: 2 x 1000kW a.c, 2 x 425kW a.c, 1 x 340kW a.c Thrusters: 2 Tunnel thruster (f)
9662368 *9V9845* -	**SMIT SERAYA** **Smit Singapore Pte Ltd** - *Singapore* *Singapore* MMSI: 566804000 Official number: 397655	**1,463** 439 933	Class: AB	**2013-07 Guangxi Guijiang Shipyard — Wuzhou GX** Yd No: 01-2010-20 Loa 51.80 Br ex - Dght 5.000 Lbp 44.40 Br md 15.00 Dpth 6.50 Welded, 1 dk	**(B21B20A) Anchor Handling Tug Supply** Cranes: 1x32t	**2 oil engines** reduction geared to sc. shafts driving 2 Propellers Total Power: 5,440kW (7,396hp) Wartsila 8L26 2 x 4 Stroke 8 Cy. 260 x 320 each-2720kW (3698bhp) Wartsila Finland Oy-Finland AuxGen: 2 x 1000kW a.c, 2 x 425kW a.c Thrusters: 2 Tunnel thruster (f) Fuel: 550.0 (d.f.)
9191058 - -	**SMIT SHOALRUNNER I** *launched as Shoalrunner -1999* **Smit International (Gabon) SA** - *Port-Gentil* *Gabon* MMSI: 626004000	**134** 40 -	Class: BV	**1999-03 Damen Shipyards Changde Co Ltd — Changde HN** (Hull) Yd No: 6911 **1999-03 B.V. Scheepswerf Damen — Gorinchem** Yd No: 6911 Loa 24.80 Br ex 9.00 Dght 2.200 Lbp 21.66 Br md 8.50 Dpth 3.20 Welded, 1 dk	**(B32A2ST) Tug**	**2 oil engines** geared to sc. shafts driving 2 FP propellers Total Power: 1,000kW (1,360hp) 9.0kn Caterpillar 3412TA 2 x Vee 4 Stroke 12 Cy. 137 x 152 each-500kW (680bhp) Caterpillar Inc-USA
9479709 *C6YN5* -	**SMIT SIYANDA** **Smit Shipping Singapore Pte Ltd** Smit Amandla Marine Pty Ltd *Nassau* *Bahamas* MMSI: 311039200 Official number: 8001766	**1,438** 431 1,037	Class: BV	**2010-09 Keppel Nantong Shipyard Co Ltd — Nantong JS** Yd No: 027 Loa 49.50 Br ex 15.02 Dght 6.200 Lbp 47.00 Br md 15.00 Dpth 6.75 Welded, 1 dk	**(B32A2ST) Tug** Cranes: 1	**2 oil engines** reduction geared to sc. shafts driving 2 Z propellers Total Power: 5,200kW (7,070hp) Wartsila 8L26 2 x 4 Stroke 8 Cy. 260 x 320 each-2600kW (3535bhp) Wartsila Italia SpA-Italy AuxGen: 2 x 700kW 440V 60Hz a.c, 2 x 260kW 440V 60Hz a.c Thrusters: 1 Tunnel thruster (f) Fuel: 497.0
7803138 *VD3118* -	**SMIT SKEENA** *ex S/Vm T.P. 1 -1999 ex T. P. 1 -1985* *ex S/VM T.P. 1 -1984* **Minette Bay Ship Docking Ltd** - *Vancouver, BC* *Canada* MMSI: 316018947 Official number: 391201	*361* 233 168	Class: (LR) ✠ Classed LR until 24/11/95	**1979-03 E S Fox Ltd — Niagara Falls ON** (Hull launched by) Yd No: 4800 **1983-12 Vito Steel Boat & Barge Construction Ltd — Delta BC** (Hull completed by) Yd No: 158 Converted From: Shunter Pontoon-1983 Loa 30.94 Br ex 11.61 Dght 1.991 Lbp 26.67 Br md 10.98 Dpth 3.66 Welded, 1 dk	**(B32A2ST) Tug**	**1 oil engine** with clutches, flexible couplings & epicyclic geared to sc. shafts driving 2 Z propellers Total Power: 2,648kW (3,600hp) Alco 16V251F 1 x Vee 4 Stroke 16 Cy. 229 x 267 2648kW (3600bhp) Bombardier Inc-Canada AuxGen: 1 x 135kW 575V 60Hz a.c
9266645 *VQGC7* -	**SMIT SPEY** **Smit International (Scotland) Ltd** *United Kingdom* MMSI: 235008177	**140** - 12		**2003-03 FBMA-Babcock Marine Inc — Balamban** Yd No: 2219 Loa 27.84 Br ex - Dght 1.700 Lbp 24.00 Br md 6.70 Dpth 3.35 Welded, 1 dk	**(B34K2QT) Training Ship** Hull Material: Aluminium Alloy	**3 oil engines** geared to sc. shafts driving 2 FP propellers , 1 Water jet Total Power: 1,305kW (1,775hp) 20.0kn Cummins 6CTA8.3-M1 1 x 4 Stroke 6 Cy. 114 x 135 261kW (355bhp) Cummins Engine Co Ltd-United Kingdom Cummins KTA-19-M4 2 x 4 Stroke 6 Cy. 159 x 159 each-522kW (710bhp) Cummins Engine Co Ltd-United Kingdom
9179024 *C6QR9* -	**SMIT TABOGUILLA** *ex Smit Yerwa -2010* **Smit Shipping Singapore Pte Ltd** SMIT Rebocadores do Brasil SA *Nassau* *Bahamas* MMSI: 309244000 Official number: 732244	**305** 91 224	Class: LR ✠ **100A1** SS 09/2009 tug ✠ **LMC** **UMS** Eq.Ltr: F; Cable: 275.0/19.0 U2 (a)	**1999-09 Stocznia Tczew Sp z oo — Tczew** (Hull) **1999-09 B.V. Scheepswerf Damen — Gorinchem** Yd No: 7928 Loa 30.82 Br ex 10.20 Dght 3.758 Lbp 26.00 Br md 9.40 Dpth 4.80 Welded, 1 dk	**(B32A2ST) Tug**	**2 oil engines** with clutches, flexible couplings & sr geared to sc. shafts driving 2 Directional propellers Total Power: 3,132kW (4,258hp) 12.8kn Caterpillar 3516B-TA 2 x Vee 4 Stroke 16 Cy. 170 x 190 each-1566kW (2129bhp) Caterpillar Inc-USA AuxGen: 2 x 85kW 380V 60Hz a.c Fuel: 114.0 (d.f.) 5.0pd
8844531 *C6QH5* -	**SMIT TAHITI** *ex Kurobe Maru -1998* **Smit-Lloyd (Antilles) NV** Smit International (Antilles) NV *Nassau* *Bahamas* MMSI: 308063000 Official number: 731100	**263** 79 -	Class: BV	**1990-07 Keihin Dock Co Ltd — Yokohama** Yd No: 218 Loa 30.80 Br ex - Dght 2.800 Lbp 27.00 Br md 8.80 Dpth 3.58 Welded, 1 dk	**(B32A2ST) Tug**	**2 oil engines** driving 2 FP propellers Total Power: 2,206kW (3,000hp) Niigata 6L25CXE 2 x 4 Stroke 6 Cy. 250 x 320 each-1103kW (1500bhp) Niigata Engineering Co Ltd-Japan
9457335 *PP6260* -	**SMIT TAMOIO** **SMIT Rebocadores do Brasil SA** - *Rio de Janeiro* *Brazil* MMSI: 710003530 Official number: 3813869318	**293** 88 107	Class: AB	**2008-08 Detroit Brasil Ltda — Itajai** Yd No: 316 Loa 24.40 Br ex - Dght 2.750 Lbp 22.00 Br md 10.25 Dpth 4.31 Welded, 1 dk	**(B32A2ST) Tug**	**2 oil engines** driving 2 Propellers Total Power: 3,000kW (4,078hp) Caterpillar 3512B-HD 2 x Vee 4 Stroke 12 Cy. 170 x 215 each-1500kW (2039bhp) Caterpillar Inc-USA AuxGen: 2 x 92kW a.c
9457323 *PS9784* -	**SMIT TAPAJO** **SMIT Rebocadores do Brasil SA** - *Rio de Janeiro* *Brazil* MMSI: 710003920 Official number: 3810522392	**293** 88 103	Class: AB	**2008-05 Detroit Brasil Ltda — Itajai** Yd No: 315 Loa 24.40 Br ex - Dght 2.750 Lbp 22.92 Br md 10.25 Dpth 5.05 Welded, 1 dk	**(B32A2ST) Tug**	**2 oil engines** Reduction geared to sc. shafts driving 2 Propellers Total Power: 2,758kW (3,750hp) Caterpillar 3512B-HD 2 x Vee 4 Stroke 12 Cy. 170 x 215 each-1379kW (1875bhp) Caterpillar Inc-USA AuxGen: 2 x 92kW a.c

9457361 *PP6258* -	**SMIT TAPEBA** *ex* Detroit Brasil 319 *-2008* **SMIT Rebocadores do Brasil SA** - *Rio de Janeiro* *Brazil* MMSI: 710003560 Official number: 3813869270	**293** 88 104	Class: AB	**2008**-07 **Detroit Brasil Ltda — Itajai** Yd No: 319 Loa 24.40 Br ex - Dght 2.750 Lbp 22.92 Br md 10.25 Dpth 5.05 Welded, 1 dk	**(B32A2ST) Tug**	**2 oil engines** reduction geared to sc. shafts driving 2 Propellers Total Power: 2,758kW (3,750hp) Caterpillar 3512B-HD 2 x Vee 4 Stroke 12 Cy. 170 x 215 each-1379kW (1875bhp) Caterpillar Inc-USA AuxGen: 2 x 92kW a.c
9457347 *PP6256* -	**SMIT TARIANA** **SMIT Rebocadores do Brasil SA** - *Rio de Janeiro* *Brazil* MMSI: 710003540 Official number: 3813868681	**293** 88 97	Class: AB	**2008**-06 **Detroit Brasil Ltda — Itajai** Yd No: 317 Loa 24.40 Br ex - Dght 2.750 Lbp 22.00 Br md 10.25 Dpth 4.31 Welded, 1 dk	**(B32A2ST) Tug**	**2 oil engines** Reduction geared to sc. shafts driving 2 Propellers Total Power: 2,758kW (3,750hp) Caterpillar 3512B-HD 2 x Vee 4 Stroke 12 Cy. 170 x 215 each-1379kW (1875bhp) Caterpillar Inc-USA AuxGen: 2 x 92kW a.c
9449144 *PS9785* -	**SMIT TERENA** **SMIT Rebocadores do Brasil SA** - *Rio de Janeiro* *Brazil* MMSI: 710003450 Official number: 3810522384	**293** 88 109	Class: AB	**2008**-03 **Detroit Brasil Ltda — Itajai** Yd No: 313 Loa 24.40 Br ex - Dght 2.750 Lbp 22.00 Br md 10.25 Dpth 5.05 Welded, 1 dk	**(B32A2ST) Tug**	**2 oil engines** reduction geared to sc. shafts driving 2 Z propellers Total Power: 2,760kW (3,752hp) 11.0kn Caterpillar 3512B-HD 2 x Vee 4 Stroke 12 Cy. 170 x 215 each-1380kW (1876bhp) Caterpillar Inc-USA AuxGen: 2 x 92kW a.c Fuel: 68.8 (d.f.)
9449132 *PS9412* -	**SMIT TICUNA** *ex* Detroit Brasil 312 *-2008* **SMIT Rebocadores do Brasil SA** - *Rio de Janeiro* *Brazil* MMSI: 710003720 Official number: 3810522406	**293** 88 82	Class: AB	**2008**-02 **Detroit Brasil Ltda — Itajai** Yd No: 312 Loa 24.40 Br ex - Dght 2.750 Lbp 22.92 Br md 10.25 Dpth 5.05 Welded, 1 dk	**(B32A2ST) Tug**	**2 oil engines** reduction geared to sc. shafts driving 2 Z propellers Total Power: 2,758kW (3,750hp) Caterpillar 3512B-HD 2 x Vee 4 Stroke 12 Cy. 170 x 215 each-1379kW (1875bhp) Caterpillar Inc-USA AuxGen: 2 x 92kW a.c
9454888 *ORPO* -	**SMIT TIGER** **Smit Shipping Singapore Pte Ltd** Unie van Redding - en Sleepdienst NV (Union de Remorquage et de Sauvetage SA) (Towage & Salvage Union Ltd) *Zeebrugge* *Belgium* MMSI: 205565000 Official number: 02 00022 2010	**484** 145 -	Class: LR ✠ **100A1** SS 10/2009 escort tug, fire fighting Ship 1 (2400m3/h) with water spray **LMC** **UMS** Eq.Ltr: I; Cable: 330.0/24.0 U2 (a)	**2009**-10 **Song Cam Shipyard — Haiphong** (Hull) Yd No: (513004) **2009**-10 **B.V. Scheepswerf Damen — Gorinchem** Yd No: 513004 Loa 32.14 Br ex 13.29 Dght 6.000 Lbp 31.64 Br md 12.50 Dpth 5.40 Welded, 1 dk	**(B32A2ST) Tug**	**2 oil engines** integral geared to sc. shafts driving 2 Directional propellers Total Power: 5,420kW (7,370hp) Caterpillar C280-8 2 x 4 Stroke 8 Cy. 280 x 300 each-2710kW (3685bhp) Caterpillar Inc-USA AuxGen: 2 x 162kW 400V 50Hz a.c
8953540 - -	**SMIT TIGER SUN** *ex* Smit Tiger *-2011* *ex* Tiger Sun *-2011* **Smit Harbour Towage Vancouver Inc** Smit Marine Canada Inc *Vancouver, BC* *Canada* MMSI: 316005623 Official number: 820966	*147* 110 -		**1999 Sylte Shipyard Ltd — Maple Ridge BC** Yd No: 79 L reg 21.69 Br ex - Dght - Lbp - Br md 10.68 Dpth 3.87 Welded, 1 dk	**(B32A2ST) Tug**	**2 oil engines** gearing integral to driving 2 Z propellers Total Power: 3,972kW (5,400hp) 13.0kn M.T.U. 16V4000M70 2 x Vee 4 Stroke 16 Cy. 165 x 190 each-1986kW (2700bhp) MTU Friedrichshafen GmbH-Friedrichshafen AuxGen: 1 x 13kW a.c
8209987 *HP9414* -	**SMIT TOBAGO** *ex* Take Maru No. 38 *-1998* *ex* Sumida Maru *-1990* **Smit International (Curacao) NV** Smit Harbour Towage Panama Inc *Panama* *Panama* Official number: 27534PEXTF7	**246** 73 67	Class: LR (BV) **100A1** SS 04/2013 tug coastal service **LMC** Eq.Ltr: I; Cable: 330.0/24.0 U2 (a)	**1982**-07 **Hanasaki Zosensho K.K. — Yokosuka** Yd No: 186 Loa 30.31 Br ex 9.05 Dght 3.070 Lbp 29.01 Br md 8.81 Dpth 3.61 Welded, 1 dk	**(B32A2ST) Tug**	**2 oil engines** driving 2 Directional propellers Total Power: 3,000kW (4,078hp) 12.5kn Niigata 6L25CX 2 x 4 Stroke 6 Cy. 250 x 320 each-1500kW (2039bhp) Niigata Engineering Co Ltd-Japan AuxGen: 2 x 60kW 380V 60Hz a.c
9578505 *VHIE* -	**SMIT TONDOON** **Smit Shipping Singapore Pte Ltd** Smit Marine Australia Pty Ltd *Gladstone, Qld* *Australia* MMSI: 503648000 Official number: 859701	**455** 136 304	Class: BV	**2010**-10 **Uzmar Gemi Insa Sanayi ve Ticaret AS — Basiskele** Yd No: 56 Loa 30.25 Br ex 12.05 Dght 4.240 Lbp 26.60 Br md 11.75 Dpth 5.28 Welded, 1 dk	**(B32A2ST) Tug**	**2 oil engines** geared to sc. shafts driving 2 Directional propellers Total Power: 3,946kW (5,364hp) Caterpillar 3516B-HD 2 x Vee 4 Stroke 16 Cy. 170 x 215 each-1973kW (2682bhp) Caterpillar Inc-USA AuxGen: 2 x 86kW 50Hz a.c
9449091 *PS9431* -	**SMIT TORA** **SMIT Rebocadores do Brasil SA** - *Rio de Janeiro* *Brazil* MMSI: 710003710 Official number: 3810522325	**293** 88 107	Class: AB	**2008**-01 **Detroit Brasil Ltda — Itajai** Yd No: 311 Loa 24.40 Br ex - Dght 2.750 Lbp 22.92 Br md 10.25 Dpth 5.05 Welded, 1 dk	**(B32A2ST) Tug**	**2 oil engines** reduction geared to sc. shafts driving 2 Z propellers Total Power: 2,758kW (3,750hp) Caterpillar 3512B-HD 2 x Vee 4 Stroke 12 Cy. 170 x 215 each-1379kW (1875bhp) Caterpillar Inc-USA AuxGen: 2 x 92kW a.c
9266633 *VQGC9* -	**SMIT TOWY** **Smit International (Scotland) Ltd** - *United Kingdom* MMSI: 235008179	**140** - 12		**2003**-03 **FBMA-Babcock Marine Inc — Balamban** Yd No: 2218 Loa 27.84 Br ex - Dght 1.700 Lbp 24.00 Br md 6.70 Dpth 3.35 Welded, 1 dk	**(B34K2QT) Training Ship** Hull Material: Aluminium Alloy	**3 oil engines** geared to sc. shafts driving 2 FP propellers , 1 Water jet Total Power: 1,305kW (1,775hp) 20.0kn Cummins 6CTA8.3-M1 1 x 4 Stroke 6 Cy. 114 x 135 261kW (355bhp) Cummins Engine Co Ltd-United Kingdom Cummins KTA-19-M4 2 x 4 Stroke 6 Cy. 159 x 159 each-522kW (710bhp) Cummins Engine Co Ltd-United Kingdom
9449156 *PS9786* -	**SMIT TUCANO** **SMIT Rebocadores do Brasil SA** - *Rio de Janeiro* *Brazil* MMSI: 710000266 Official number: 3810522414	*293* 88 116	Class: AB	**2008**-04 **Detroit Brasil Ltda — Itajai** Yd No: 314 Loa 24.40 Br ex - Dght 2.750 Lbp 22.00 Br md 10.25 Dpth 4.31 Welded, 1 dk	**(B32A2ST) Tug**	**2 oil engines** reduction geared to sc. shafts driving 2 Z propellers Total Power: 2,760kW (3,752hp) Caterpillar 3512B-HD 2 x Vee 4 Stroke 12 Cy. 170 x 215 each-1380kW (1876bhp) Caterpillar Inc-USA AuxGen: 2 x 92kW a.c
9457359 *PP6262* -	**SMIT TUPARI** **SMIT Rebocadores do Brasil SA** - *Rio de Janeiro* *Brazil* MMSI: 710003550 Official number: 3813869296	**293** 88 107	Class: AB	**2008**-10 **Detroit Brasil Ltda — Itajai** Yd No: 318 Loa 24.40 Br ex — Dght 2.750 Lbp 22.92 Br md 10.25 Dpth 4.31 Welded, 1 dk	**(B32A2ST) Tug**	**2 oil engines** Reduction geared to sc. shafts driving 2 Propellers Total Power: 3,000kW (4,078hp) Caterpillar 3512B-HD 2 x Vee 4 Stroke 12 Cy. 170 x 215 each-1500kW (2039bhp) Caterpillar Inc-USA AuxGen: 2 x 92kW a.c
9449077 *PS9354* -	**SMIT TUPI** **SMIT Rebocadores do Brasil SA** - *Rio de Janeiro* *Brazil* MMSI: 710003640 Official number: 3810522317	**293** 88 107	Class: AB	**2007**-12 **Detroit Brasil Ltda — Itajai** Yd No: 309 Loa 24.40 Br ex - Dght 2.750 Lbp 22.00 Br md 10.25 Dpth 5.05 Welded, 1 dk	**(B32A2ST) Tug**	**2 oil engines** reduction geared to sc. shafts driving 2 Z propellers Total Power: 2,720kW (3,698hp) Caterpillar 3512B-HD 2 x Vee 4 Stroke 12 Cy. 170 x 215 each-1360kW (1849bhp) Caterpillar Inc-USA
9457373 *PP6263* -	**SMIT TUPINAMBA** *ex* Detroit Brasil 320 *-2008* **SMIT Rebocadores do Brasil SA** - *Rio de Janeiro* *Brazil* MMSI: 710003830 Official number: 3813869300	**293** 88 107	Class: AB	**2008**-10 **Detroit Brasil Ltda — Itajai** Yd No: 320 Loa 24.40 Br ex - Dght 2.750 Lbp 22.92 Br md 10.25 Dpth 5.05 Welded, 1 dk	**(B32A2ST) Tug**	**2 oil engines** Reduction geared to sc. shafts driving 2 Propellers Total Power: 3,000kW (4,078hp) Caterpillar 3512B-HD 2 x Vee 4 Stroke 12 Cy. 170 x 215 each-1500kW (2039bhp) Caterpillar Inc-USA AuxGen: 2 x 92kW a.c
9449089 *PS9430* -	**SMIT TUXA** **SMIT Rebocadores do Brasil SA** - *Rio de Janeiro* *Brazil* MMSI: 710000259 Official number: 3810522295	**293** 88 107	Class: AB	**2008**-01 **Detroit Brasil Ltda — Itajai** Yd No: 310 Loa 24.40 Br ex — Dght 2.750 Lbp 22.92 Br md 10.25 Dpth 5.05 Welded, 1 dk	**(B32A2ST) Tug**	**2 oil engines** reduction geared to sc. shafts driving 2 Z propellers Total Power: 2,758kW (3,750hp) Caterpillar 3512B-HD 2 x Vee 4 Stroke 12 Cy. 170 x 215 each-1379kW (1875bhp) Caterpillar Inc-USA AuxGen: 2 x 92kW a.c

9402457 *C6ZO3* -	**SMIT VENTA** *ex* Smit Dominica *-2009* **Smit Shipping Singapore Pte Ltd** SMIT Rebocadores do Brasil SA *Nassau* *Bahamas* MMSI: 311061200 Official number: 8001961	**294** 88 -	Class: LR ✠**100A1** SS 02/2014 tug **LMC** **UMS** Eq.Ltr: F; Cable: 275.0/19.0 U2 (a)	**2009-02 Santierul Naval Damen Galati S.A. — Galati** (Hull) Yd No: 1129 **2009-02 B.V. Scheepswerf Damen — Gorinchem** Yd No: 511538 Loa 28.75 Br ex 10.43 Dght 3.690 Lbp 25.79 Br md 9.80 Dpth 4.60 Welded, 1 dk	**(B32A2ST) Tug**	**2 oil engines** reduction geared to sc. shafts driving 2 Directional propellers Total Power: 3,728kW (5,068hp) Caterpillar 3516B-HD 1 x Vee 4 Stroke 16 Cy. 170 x 215 1864kW (2534bhp) Caterpillar Inc-USA Caterpillar 3516TA 1 x Vee 4 Stroke 16 Cy. 170 x 190 1864kW (2534bhp) Caterpillar Inc-USA AuxGen: 2 x 84kW 400V 50Hz a.c
8610289 *GJJB* -	**SMIT WATERLOO** *ex* Adsteam Waterloo *-2007* *ex* Waterloo *-2005* **Smit Harbour Towage (UK) Ltd (Smit Harbour Towage Liverpool)** - *Liverpool* *United Kingdom* MMSI: 232101000 Official number: 704492	**298** 89 96	Class: LR ✠**100A1** SS 06/2012 tug for near Continental trading area service ✠**LMC** Eq.Ltr: (G) ; Cable: 302.5/17.0 U2 (a)	**1987-06 McTay Marine Ltd. — Bromborough** Yd No: 77 Loa 31.15 Br ex 9.76 Dght 4.582 Lbp 28.91 Br md 9.31 Dpth 3.81 Welded, 1 dk	**(B32A2ST) Tug**	**2 oil engines** with flexible couplings & dr gearedto sc. shafts driving 2 Directional propellers Total Power: 1,282kW (1,744hp) 12.0kn Ruston 6RK270M 2 x 4 Stroke 6 Cy. 270 x 305 each-641kW (872bhp) Ruston Diesels Ltd.-Newton-le-Willows AuxGen: 2 x 80kW 440V 50Hz a.c
9557599 *VHIC* -	**SMIT YALLARM** **Smit Lamnalco Singapore Pte Ltd** Smit Internationale NV *Gladstone, Qld* *Australia* MMSI: 503642000 Official number: 859657	**455** 136 304	Class: BV	**2010-09 Uzmar Gemi Insa Sanayi ve Ticaret AS — Basiskele** Yd No: 35 Loa 30.25 Br ex 12.05 Dght 4.240 Lbp 26.60 Br md 11.75 Dpth 5.28 Welded, 1 dk	**(B32A2ST) Tug**	**2 oil engines** geared to sc. shafts driving 2 Directional propellers Total Power: 3,946kW (5,364hp) Caterpillar 3516B-HD 2 x Vee 4 Stroke 16 Cy. 170 x 215 each-1973kW (2682bhp) Caterpillar Inc-USA
9266621 *VQGD2* -	**SMIT YARE** **Smit International (Scotland) Ltd** *Aberdeen* *United Kingdom* MMSI: 235008181	**140** - 12		**2003-03 FBMA-Babcock Marine Inc — Balamban** Yd No: 2217 Loa 27.84 Br ex - Dght 1.700 Lbp 24.00 Br md 6.70 Dpth 3.35 Welded, 1 dk	**(B34K2QT) Training Ship** Hull Material: Aluminium Alloy	**3 oil engines** geared to sc. shafts driving 2 FP propellers , 1 Water jet Total Power: 1,305kW (1,775hp) 20.0kn Cummins 6CTA8.3-M1 1 x 4 Stroke 6 Cy. 114 x 135 261kW (355bhp) Cummins Engine Co Ltd-United Kingdom Cummins KTA-19-M4 2 x 4 Stroke 6 Cy. 159 x 159 each-522kW (710bhp) Cummins Engine Co Ltd-United Kingdom
9427328 *WDD5428* -	**SMITH INVADER** **Smith Towing LLC** KJS Towing Inc *Morgan City, LA* *United States of America* MMSI: 367158250 Official number: 1193486	**238** 71 -	Class: AB	**2006-12 Mariner LLC — Houma LA** Yd No: 141 Loa 25.30 Br ex - Dght - Lbp - Br md 9.75 Dpth 3.66 Welded, 1 dk	**(B32A2ST) Tug**	**2 oil engines** reduction geared to sc. shafts driving 2 FP propellers Total Power: 1,472kW (2,002hp) Caterpillar 3508B 2 x Vee 4 Stroke 8 Cy. 170 x 190 each-736kW (1001bhp) Caterpillar Inc-USA
7534672 *WYR2927* -	**SMITH ISLAND** *ex* FS 216 (Col. William J. McKiernan) *-2005* **Omega Protein Inc** - *Reedville, VA* *United States of America* MMSI: 367088140 Official number: 563942	*541* 367 -	Class: (AB)	**1944 Higgins Industries, Inc. — New Orleans, La** Yd No: 82 Converted From: Replenishment Dry Cargo Vessel L reg 51.46 Br ex 9.78 Dght - Lbp - Br md - Dpth 3.56 Welded, 1 dk	**(B11B2FV) Fishing Vessel**	**1 oil engine** driving 1 FP propeller Total Power: 1,324kW (1,800hp)
9518775 *WDE4416* -	**SMITH PREDATOR** **KJS Towing Inc** - *Morgan City, LA* *United States of America* MMSI: 367352890 Official number: 1211313	**238** 71 145	Class: AB	**2008-04 Mariner LLC — Houma LA** Yd No: 145 Loa 26.82 Br ex - Dght 3.110 Lbp - Br md 9.75 Dpth 3.86 Welded, 1 dk	**(B32A2ST) Tug**	**2 oil engines** reduction geared to sc. shafts driving 2 FP propellers Total Power: 1,940kW (2,638hp) Caterpillar 3512B 2 x Vee 4 Stroke 12 Cy. 170 x 190 each-970kW (1319bhp) Caterpillar Inc-USA AuxGen: 2 x 55kW a.c
9376232 - -	**SMITH TIDE** **Tidewater Properties Ltd** Tidewater Marine International Inc	**1,868** 588 2,018	Class: AB	**2007-11 PT Pan-United Shipyard Indonesia — Batam** Yd No: 156 Loa 64.80 Br ex - Dght 4.200 Lbp 58.70 Br md 16.00 Dpth 5.80 Welded, 1 dk	**(B21B20A) Anchor Handling Tug Supply**	**2 oil engines** reduction geared to sc. shafts driving 2 CP propellers Total Power: 5,280kW (7,178hp) Caterpillar 3608 2 x 4 Stroke 8 Cy. 280 x 300 each-2640kW (3589bhp) Caterpillar Inc-USA AuxGen: 2 x 320kW a.c Fuel: 510.0 (d.f.)
7417173 *WDE4096* -	**SMITHBRIDGE SUN** *ex* Gulf Sun *-2011* *ex* Sun New York *-2008* *ex* Seabulk New York *-2006* *ex* Alaskan Empire *-2000* *ex* Lavaca Seahorse *-1991* *ex* L'Olonnois *-1980* **Guam Marine Services Inc** - *Piti, GU* *United States of America* MMSI: 368563000 Official number: 569386	**1,022** 306 990	Class: (AB)	**1975-07 Halter Marine, Inc. — Moss Point, Ms** Yd No: 458 Converted From: Fishing Vessel-1997 Converted From: Offshore Tug/Supply Ship-1991 Lengthened-1997 Lengthened-1991 Loa 71.63 Br ex 12.20 Dght 4.496 Lbp 65.07 Br md 12.19 Dpth 5.18 Welded, 1 dk	**(B21A20S) Platform Supply Ship** Ice Capable	**2 oil engines** reverse reduction geared to sc. shafts driving 2 FP propellers Total Power: 3,530kW (4,800hp) 12.0kn MWM TBD441V16 2 x Vee 4 Stroke 16 Cy. 230 x 270 each-1765kW (2400bhp) Motoren Werke Mannheim AG (MWM)-West Germany AuxGen: 2 x 150kW Thrusters: 1 Thwart. FP thruster (f) Fuel: 483.5 (d.f.)
9281683 *AUMN* -	**SMITI** *ex* Formosapetro Forever *-2006* **Essar Shipping Ltd** - SatCom: Inmarsat Mini-M 763615429 *Mumbai* *India* MMSI: 419592000 Official number: 3222	**149,274** 90,656 281,396 T/cm 170.0	Class: AB IR	**2005-07 IHI Marine United Inc — Kure HS** Yd No: 3178 Loa 330.00 (BB) Br ex - Dght 20.430 Lbp 316.60 Br md 60.00 Dpth 28.90 Welded, 1 Dk.	**(A13A2TV) Crude Oil Tanker** Double Hull (13F) Liq: 313,335; Liq (Oil): 313,335 Compartments: 5 Ta, 10 Wing Ta, ER, 2 Wing Slop Ta 10 Cargo Pump (s): 6x5000m³/hr, 4x2400m³/hr Manifold: Bow/CM: 154m	**1 oil engine** driving 1 FP propeller Total Power: 22,680kW (30,836hp) 14.0kn Sulzer 7RTA84T 1 x 2 Stroke 7 Cy. 840 x 3150 22680kW (30836bhp) Diesel United Ltd.-Aioi AuxGen: 3 x 930kW 450V 60Hz a.c Fuel: 402.0 (d.f.) 6485.0 (r.f.)
8715247 *9A6582* -	**SMJELI** *ex* Vega *-1998* *ex* Smjeli *-1993* **'Brodospas' dd Split** - SatCom: Inmarsat C 423816310 *Split* *Croatia* MMSI: 238163000	**353** 106 180	Class: CS (JR)	**1990-10 Brodogradiliste 'Jozo Lozovina-Mosor' (Brodomosor) — Trogir** Yd No: 198 Loa 29.92 Br ex 10.72 Dght 4.150 Lbp 25.40 Br md 10.70 Dpth 5.28 Welded, 1 dk	**(B32A2ST) Tug**	**2 oil engines** with hydraulic couplings & sr geared to sc. shafts driving 2 Directional propellers Total Power: 2,900kW (3,942hp) Pielstick 6PA6L280 2 x 4 Stroke 6 Cy. 280 x 290 each-1450kW (1971bhp) Tvornica Dizel Motora 'Jugoturbina'-Yugoslavia Fuel: 165.0
8986418 *MKEY3* -	**SMOKE DRAGON OF LONDON** **First Anglo American Marine Ltd** - *London* *United Kingdom* MMSI: 235018752 Official number: 714445	*124* - -		**1986 Versilcraft — Viareggio** Loa 26.00 Br ex - Dght 2.000 Lbp - Br md 5.85 Dpth - Bonded, 1 dk	**(X11A2YP) Yacht** Hull Material: Reinforced Plastic	**3 oil engines** geared to sc. shafts driving 3 Propellers Total Power: 2,382kW (3,240hp) 13.0kn G.M. (Detroit Diesel) 12V-92-TA 3 x Vee 2 Stroke 12 Cy. 123 x 127 each-794kW (1080bhp) General Motors Detroit DieselAllison Divn-USA Thrusters: 1 Thwart. FP thruster (f); 1 Thwart. FP thruster (a)
9466893 *V7VC8* -	**SMOLENSK** *ex* Fesco Smolensk *-2013* **Novik Maritime Ltd** Far-Eastern Shipping Co (FESCO) (Dalnevostochnoye Morskoye Parokhodstvo) *Majuro* *Marshall Islands* MMSI: 538004089 Official number: 4089	**33,044** 19,231 57,000 T/cm 58.8	Class: BV	**2012-01 Qingshan Shipyard — Wuhan HB** Yd No: 20060373 Loa 189.99 (BB) Br ex - Dght 12.800 Lbp 185.00 Br md 32.26 Dpth 18.00 Welded, 1 dk	**(A21A2BC) Bulk Carrier** Grain: 71,634; Bale: 68,200 Compartments: 5 Ho, ER 5 Ha: 4 (21.3 x 18.3)ER (18.9 x 18.3) Cranes: 4x30t	**1 oil engine** driving 1 FP propeller Total Power: 9,480kW (12,889hp) 14.5kn MAN-B&W 6S50MC-C 1 x 2 Stroke 6 Cy. 500 x 2000 9480kW (12889bhp) Doosan Engine Co Ltd-South Korea AuxGen: 3 x 600kW 60Hz a.c
8847131 *UBVW* -	**SMOLNINSKIY** **Vladkristall Co Ltd (OOO 'Vladkristall')** - *Nakhodka* *Russia* MMSI: 273257000 Official number: 890127	**2,483** 1,006 1,557	Class: RS	**1990-05 Sudostroitelnyy Zavod "Baltiya" — Klaypeda** Yd No: 532 Converted From: Stern Trawler-2007 Loa 85.10 Br ex 13.04 Dght 4.650 Lbp 76.80 Br md 13.00 Dpth 6.50 Welded, 1 dk	**(A34A2GR) Refrigerated Cargo Ship** Ins: 2,500 Compartments: 2 Ho, ER 2 Ha: ER 2 (2.2 x 3.4) Cranes: 1x3.2t Ice Capable	**1 oil engine** driving 1 FP propeller Total Power: 852kW (1,158hp) 11.3kn S.K.L. 8NVD48A-2U 1 x 4 Stroke 8 Cy. 320 x 480 852kW (1158bhp) VEB Schwermaschinenbau "KarlLiebknecht" (SKL)-Magdeburg AuxGen: 2 x 320kW a.c, 1 x 150kW a.c

IMO / Call sign / Flag	Name / Owner / Port	Tonnage	Class	Builder / Dimensions	Type / Cargo	Machinery
8860834 - -	**SMOLNYY** - **Uvas-Trans Ltd** - *Kerch* *Ukraine* MMSI: 272635000	**4,510** 1,353 4,056	Class: (RS)	**1992**-10 **Sudostroitelnyy Zavod "Krasnoye Sormovo" — Nizhniy Novgorod** Yd No: 81 Loa 113.20 Br ex 16.60 Dght 4.800 Lbp 105.83 Br md - Dpth 7.40 Welded, 1 dk	**(B34G2SE) Pollution Control Vessel** Cranes: 1x12.5t Ice Capable	**2 oil engines** sr geared to sc. shafts driving 2 FP propellers Total Power: 2,530kW (3,440hp) 10.0kn Dvigatel Revolyutsii 6CHRNP36/45 2 x 4 Stroke 6 Cy. 360 x 450 each-1265kW (1720bhp) Zavod "Dvigatel Revolyutsii"-Nizhniy Novgorod AuxGen: 3 x 320kW 400V 50Hz a.c Thrusters: 1 Thwart. FP thruster (f); 2 Directional thruster (a) Fuel: 152.4 (d.f.) (Part Heating Coils) 358.7 (r.f.) 15.0pd
9569657 *5IXY09* -	**SMOOTH** - **NITC** - *Zanzibar* *Tanzania* MMSI: 677010800	**164,796** 108,706 317,536 T/cm 181.2	Class: (LR) ✠ Classed LR until 12/7/13	**2013**-07 **Shanghai Waigaoqiao Shipbuilding Co Ltd — Shanghai** Yd No: 1225 Loa 333.00 (BB) Br ex 60.05 Dght 22.640 Lbp 320.00 Br md 60.00 Dpth 30.50 Welded, 1 dk	**(A13A2TV) Crude Oil Tanker** Double Hull (13F) Liq: 334,900; Liq (Oil): 334,900 Cargo Heating Coils Compartments: 5 Ta, 10 Wing Ta, ER, 2 Wing Slop Ta 3 Cargo Pump (s): 3x5500m³/hr Manifold: Bow/CM: 165.2m	**1 oil engine** driving 1 FP propeller Total Power: 31,640kW (43,018hp) 16.1kn Wartsila 7RT-flex82T 1 x 2 Stroke 7 Cy. 820 x 3375 31640kW (43018bhp) Wartsila Finland Oy-Finland AuxGen: 3 x 1600kW 450V 60Hz a.c Boilers: e (ex.g.) 26.5kgf/cm² (26.0bar), WTAuxB (o.f.) 23.0kgf/cm² (22.6bar) Fuel: 480.0 (d.f.) 8440.0 (r.f.)
8601630 *HSB2921* -	**SMOOTH SEA** *ex* Tsurufuji Maru No. 8 *-2002* *ex* Kakumei Maru *-1996* **Smooth Sea Co Ltd** - SatCom: Inmarsat C 456700279 *Bangkok* *Thailand* MMSI: 567038700 Official number: 451001011	**2,983** 1,494 4,974	Class: (NK)	**1986**-06 **Taihei Kogyo K.K. — Hashihama, Imabari** Yd No: 1895 Loa 104.20 (BB) Br ex 15.50 Dght 6.401 Lbp 96.02 Br md - Dpth 7.93 Welded, 1 dk	**(A13B2TP) Products Tanker** Double Bottom Entire Compartment Length Liq: 5,440; Liq (Oil): 5,440 Compartments: 8 Ta, ER	**1 oil engine** driving 1 CP propeller Total Power: 2,427kW (3,300hp) Hanshin 6EL40 1 x 4 Stroke 6 Cy. 400 x 800 2427kW (3300bhp) The Hanshin Diesel Works Ltd-Japan Thrusters: 1 Thwart. CP thruster (f)
8223660 *HSB3059* -	**SMOOTH SEA 2** *ex* Oriental Joaquim *-2003* *ex* Golden Joaquim *-1999* *ex* Naniwa Maru No. 58 *-1999* **Smooth Sea Co Ltd** - SatCom: Inmarsat C 456700368 *Bangkok* *Thailand* MMSI: 567000550 Official number: 460003012	**1,989** 914 3,044 T/cm 9.5	Class: (NK)	**1983**-08 **Mitsubishi Heavy Industries Ltd. — Shimonoseki** Yd No: 857 Loa 75.49 (BB) Br ex 14.84 Dght 5.160 Lbp 71.76 Br md 14.81 Dpth 6.33 Welded, 1 dk	**(A13B2TP) Products Tanker** Double Bottom Entire Compartment Length Liq: 3,378; Liq (Oil): 3,378 Compartments: 10 Ta, ER 2 Cargo Pump (s): 2x750m³/hr Manifold: Bow/CM: 34m	**1 oil engine** driving 1 CP propeller Total Power: 1,765kW (2,400hp) 11.5kn Hanshin 6EL35 1 x 4 Stroke 6 Cy. 350 x 700 1765kW (2400bhp) The Hanshin Diesel Works Ltd-Japan AuxGen: 2 x 300kW 450V 60Hz a.c, 1 x 180kW 450V 60Hz a.c Thrusters: 1 Thwart. CP thruster (f) Fuel: 30.0 (d.f.) 160.0 (r.f.) 7.0pd
8303616 *HSB3190* -	**SMOOTH SEA 3** *ex* Andhika Aryandhi *-2004* **Smooth Sea Co Ltd** - SatCom: Inmarsat C 456761352 *Bangkok* *Thailand* MMSI: 567287000 Official number: 470003399	**4,301** 1,916 6,801 T/cm 15.7	Class: (NK)	**1983**-12 **Fukuoka Shipbuilding Co Ltd — Fukuoka FO** Yd No: 1109 Conv to DH-2009 Loa 107.02 (BB) Br ex 18.24 Dght 6.600 Lbp 99.01 Br md 18.20 Dpth 8.11 Welded, 1 dk	**(A12B2TR) Chemical/Products Tanker** Double Hull (13F) Liq: 6,603; Liq (Oil): 7,643 Cargo Heating Coils Compartments: 10 Wing Ta, ER 2 Cargo Pump (s): 2x600m³/hr Manifold: Bow/CM: 44m	**1 oil engine** driving 1 FP propeller Total Power: 2,868kW (3,899hp) 10.5kn Mitsubishi 6UEC37L 1 x 2 Stroke 6 Cy. 370 x 880 2868kW (3899bhp) Kobe Hatsudoki KK-Japan AuxGen: 2 x 260kW
8301486 *HSB2886* -	**SMOOTH SEA 4** *ex* Tasco 3 *-2005* *ex* Tatsumi Maru No. 58 *-2002* **Smooth Sea Co Ltd** - *Bangkok* *Thailand* MMSI: 567208000 Official number: 451000594	**1,997** 817 3,521 T/cm 9.6	Class: (NK)	**1983**-06 **Murakami Hide Zosen K.K. — Imabari** Yd No: 210 Conv to DH-2009 Loa 91.44 Br ex - Dght 5.960 Lbp 85.02 Br md 13.00 Dpth 6.61 Welded, 1 dk	**(A12B2TR) Chemical/Products Tanker** Double Hull (13F) Liq: 2,475; Liq (Oil): 2,475 Compartments: 5 Ta, ER 2 Cargo Pump (s): 2x350m³/hr Manifold: Bow/CM: 45.5m	**1 oil engine** driving 1 CP propeller Total Power: 1,765kW (2,400hp) 10.8kn Hanshin 6EL35 1 x 4 Stroke 6 Cy. 350 x 700 1765kW (2400bhp) The Hanshin Diesel Works Ltd-Japan AuxGen: 2 x 240kW 450V 60Hz a.c, 1 x 120kW 450V 60Hz a.c, 1 x 40kW 450V 60Hz a.c Thrusters: 1 Thwart. CP thruster (f) Fuel: 17.0 (d.f.) 70.0 (r.f.) 3.5pd
9033402 *HSB3850* -	**SMOOTH SEA 5** *ex* Shiragiku Maru *-2008* **Smooth Sea Co Ltd** - SatCom: Inmarsat C 456761352 *Bangkok* *Thailand* MMSI: 567053900 Official number: 510082643	**981** 335 1,283	Class: (IR) (NK)	**1992**-02 **K.K. Mukai Zosensho — Nagasaki** Yd No: 636 Loa 68.20 Br ex - Dght 4.100 Lbp 63.00 Br md 10.80 Dpth 4.50 Welded, 1 dk	**(A13C2LA) Asphalt/Bitumen Tanker** Double Bottom Entire Compartment Length Liq: 1,280; Liq (Oil): 1,280; Asphalt: 1,280 Cargo Heating Coils 2 Cargo Pump (s): 2x400m³/hr	**1 oil engine** reverse geared to sc. shaft driving 1 FP propeller Total Power: 1,324kW (1,800hp) 11.3kn Akasaka A31R 1 x 4 Stroke 6 Cy. 310 x 600 1324kW (1800bhp) Akasaka Tekkosho KK (Akasaka DieselLtd)-Japan
8514045 *HSB4352* -	**SMOOTH SEA 28** *ex* Hung Kuk No. 15 *-2009* *ex* Shoun Polestar *-1991* **Smooth Sea Co Ltd** - *Bangkok* *Thailand* MMSI: 567058900 Official number: 520085431	**4,481** 2,171 6,756	Class: (KR) (NK)	**1986**-01 **Kochi Jyuko K.K. — Kochi** Yd No: 2441 Loa 113.32 (BB) Br ex - Dght 6.318 Lbp 104.02 Br md 18.01 Dpth 8.01 Welded, 1 dk	**(A12B2TR) Chemical/Products Tanker** Liq: 7,403; Liq (Oil): 7,403 Compartments: 15 Ta, ER	**1 oil engine** driving 1 FP propeller Total Power: 2,992kW (4,068hp) 13.2kn B&W 6L35MC 1 x 2 Stroke 6 Cy. 350 x 1050 2992kW (4068bhp) Hitachi Zosen Corp-Japan AuxGen: 2 x 240kW 450V a.c
9420899 *HSB4341* -	**SMOOTH SEA 102** *ex* Zhen Xing You 16 *-2009* **Smooth Sea Co Ltd** - *Bangkok* *Thailand* MMSI: 567054500 Official number: 540000223	**1,993** 887 3,325		**2006**-08 **Zhejiang Hongguan Ship Industry Co Ltd — Linhai ZJ** Loa 88.02 Br ex - Dght - Lbp 79.98 Br md 13.50 Dpth 6.00 Welded, 1 dk	**(A13B2TP) Products Tanker** Double Hull (13F)	**1 oil engine** reduction geared to sc. shaft driving 1 FP propeller Total Power: 735kW (999hp) 8.0kn Chinese Std. Type G6300ZCA 1 x 4 Stroke 6 Cy. 300 x 380 735kW (999bhp) Ningbo CSI Power & Machinery GroupCo Ltd-China
9615640 *9WLF8* -	**SMOOTH WATER 1** - **Smooth Water Sdn Bhd** - *Kuching* *Malaysia* MMSI: 533002990 Official number: 333352	**326** 98 285	Class: BV	**2011**-08 **Sarawak Land Shipyard Sdn Bhd — Miri** Yd No: 16 Loa 31.00 Br ex - Dght 3.500 Lbp 28.26 Br md 9.15 Dpth 4.30 Welded, 1 dk	**(B32A2ST) Tug**	**2 oil engines** reduction geared to sc. shaft driving 2 FP propellers Total Power: 1,776kW (2,414hp) Chinese Std. Type 12V190 2 x Vee 4 Stroke 12 Cy. 190 x 210 each-888kW (1207bhp) Jinan Diesel Engine Co Ltd-China AuxGen: 2 x 80kW 50Hz a.c Fuel: 240.0 (d.f.)
9066590 *XCMR* -	**SMR MANZANILLO** - **Grupo TMM SA de CV** - *Manzanillo* *Mexico*	**212** 63 168	Class: GL (LR) ✠ Classed LR until 17/5/01	**1998**-03 **Stocznia Tczew Sp z oo — Tczew** (Hull) **1998**-03 **B.V. Scheepswerf Damen — Gorinchem** Yd No: 3187 Loa 30.50 Br ex 8.42 Dght 4.000 Lbp 27.05 Br md 7.80 Dpth 4.05 Welded, 1 dk	**(B32A2ST) Tug**	**2 oil engines** with clutches, flexible couplings & sr reverse geared to sc. shafts driving 2 FP propellers Total Power: 3,134kW (4,260hp) Caterpillar 3516B-TA 2 x Vee 4 Stroke 16 Cy. 170 x 190 each-1567kW (2130bhp) Caterpillar Inc-USA AuxGen: 2 x 65kW 440V 60Hz a.c Fuel: 102.0 (d.f.)
9510204 *YDA4488* -	**SMS ABEL** - **PT Wintermar** - *Jakarta* *Indonesia* MMSI: 525019489 Official number: 5834	**270** 81 96	Class: AB	**2008**-10 **Sam Aluminium Engineering Pte Ltd — Singapore** Yd No: H76 Loa 40.25 Br ex - Dght 1.300 Lbp 38.07 Br md 7.79 Dpth 3.40 Welded, 1 dk	**(B34J2SD) Crew Boat** Hull Material: Aluminium Alloy Passengers: unberthed: 82	**3 oil engines** reduction geared to sc. shafts driving 3 Propellers Total Power: 3,696kW (5,025hp) 28.0kn Caterpillar C32 3 x Vee 4 Stroke 12 Cy. 145 x 162 each-1232kW (1675bhp) Caterpillar Inc-USA AuxGen: 2 x 90kW a.c
9510216 *HP9948* -	**SMS ABLE** - **PT Wintermar** - *Panama* *Panama* MMSI: 370988000 Official number: 4008409	**270** 81 95	Class: AB	**2008**-12 **Sam Aluminium Engineering Pte Ltd — Singapore** Yd No: H79 Loa 40.25 Br ex - Dght 1.300 Lbp 38.07 Br md 7.79 Dpth 3.40 Welded, 1 dk	**(B34J2SD) Crew Boat** Hull Material: Aluminium Alloy	**3 oil engines** reduction geared to sc. shafts driving 3 Propellers Total Power: 3,090kW (4,200hp) 25.0kn Caterpillar C32 3 x Vee 4 Stroke 12 Cy. 145 x 162 each-1030kW (1400bhp) Caterpillar Inc-USA AuxGen: 2 x 90kW a.c
8962450 *YB4334* -	**SMS ARIAL** - **PT Pann (Persero)** PT Arial Niaga Nusantara *Palembang* *Indonesia*	**119** 71 -	Class: KI	**2000**-02 **P.T. Mariana Bahagia — Palembang** Loa 25.25 Br ex - Dght - Lbp - Br md 8.22 Dpth 2.59 Welded, 1 dk	**(B34L2QU) Utility Vessel**	**2 oil engines** reduction geared to sc. shafts driving 2 FP propellers Total Power: 514kW (698hp) 8.0kn Yanmar 6HAL-HTE 2 x 4 Stroke 6 Cy. 130 x 150 each-257kW (349bhp) (made 1998) Yanmar Diesel Engine Co Ltd-Japan

IMO / Call sign / Flag	Name / Owner	Tonnage	Class	Builder	Type	Machinery
9587324 *PNSD* -	**SMS ASSURANCE** *ex AHT Pacific -2010* **PT Sentosa Segara Mulia Shipping** PT Wintermar *Jakarta* *Indonesia* MMSI: 525018000 Official number: 2705/PPM	**573** 172 328	Class: AB	**2010-07 Jiangsu Wuxi Shipyard Co Ltd — Wuxi JS** (Hull) Yd No: (1351) **2010-07 Pacific Ocean Engineering & Trading Pte Ltd (POET) — Singapore** Yd No: 1351 Loa 41.80 Br ex 10.05 Dght 3.200 Lbp 37.40 Br md 10.00 Dpth 4.60 Welded, 1 dk	**(B21B20A) Anchor Handling Tug Supply**	**2 oil engines** reduction geared to sc. shafts driving 2 Propellers Total Power: 2,648kW (3,600hp) 11.0kn Yanmar 8N21A-EN 2 x 4 Stroke 8 Cy. 210 x 290 each-1324kW (1800bhp) Yanmar Diesel Engine Co Ltd-Japan AuxGen: 3 x 226kW a.c Fuel: 260.0 (d.f.)
9598141 *PNQC* -	**SMS DISCOVERY** **PT Sentosa Segara Mulia Shipping** PT Wintermar *Jakarta* *Indonesia* MMSI: 525003051	**541** 163 -	Class: BV KI	**2010-06 PT Bumi Laut Perkasa — Batam** Yd No: 192 Loa 48.00 Br ex 11.02 Dght 2.500 Lbp 44.87 Br md 11.00 Dpth 3.50 Welded, 1 dk	**(B22A20R) Offshore Support Vessel**	**2 oil engines** reduction geared to sc. shafts driving 2 FP propellers Total Power: 2,420kW (3,290hp) Mitsubishi S12R-MPTK 2 x Vee 4 Stroke 12 Cy. 170 x 180 each-1210kW (1645bhp) Mitsubishi Heavy Industries Ltd-Japan
9554339 *XCVJ9* -	**SMS DOS BOCAS** *ex Svitzer Kestrel -2013* **Consignataria San Miguel SA de CV** - *Dos Bocas* *Mexico* MMSI: 345050042 Official number: 2701351532 2	**442** 132 286	Class: LR ✠ **100A1** SS 12/2011 tug, fire-fighting Ship 1 (2400m3/h) with water spray *IWS WDL (5t/m2 from aft to frame 15) ✠ **LMC** **UMS** Eq.Ltr: H; Cable: 302.5/24.0 U2 (a)	**2011-12 Jiangsu Zhenjiang Shipyard Co Ltd — Zhenjiang JS** Yd No: VZJ6173-0805 Loa 30.80 Br ex 11.32 Dght 5.100 Lbp 26.80 Br md 11.00 Dpth 6.10 Welded, 1 dk	**(B32A2ST) Tug**	**2 oil engines** gearing integral to driving 2 Z propellers Total Power: 3,676kW (4,998hp) Niigata 6L28HX 2 x 4 Stroke 6 Cy. 280 x 370 each-1838kW (2499bhp) Niigata Engineering Co Ltd-Japan AuxGen: 2 x 120kW 400V 50Hz a.c
9656606 *JZAL* -	**SMS ENDEAVOUR** **PT Wintermar** - *Jakarta* *Indonesia* MMSI: 525003109 Official number: 3382	**1,461** 438 1,322	Class: AB	**2013-03 Guangdong Yuexin Ocean Engineering Co Ltd — Guangzhou GD** Yd No: 3159 Loa 58.70 Br ex 14.62 Dght 4.750 Lbp 53.20 Br md 14.60 Dpth 5.50 Welded, 1 dk	**(B21B20A) Anchor Handling Tug Supply** Cranes: 1x3t	**2 oil engines** reduction geared to sc. shaft (s) driving 2 CP propellers Total Power: 3,788kW (5,150hp) 13.5kn Caterpillar 3516C 2 x Vee 4 Stroke 16 Cy. 170 x 190 each-1894kW (2575bhp) Caterpillar Inc-USA AuxGen: 2 x 800kW a.c, 2 x 350kW a.c Thrusters: 2 Thwart. CP thruster (f) Fuel: 470.0 (d.f.)
9576698 *PORI* -	**SMS EXPLORER** *ex Aht Explorer -2012* **PT Sentosa Segara Mulia Shipping** PT Wintermar *Jakarta* *Indonesia* MMSI: 525003161	**573** 172 325	Class: AB	**2011-08 Wuxue Janda Shipbuilding Co Ltd — Wuxue HB** (Hull) Yd No: (1325) **2011-08 Pacific Ocean Engineering & Trading Pte Ltd (POET) — Singapore** Yd No: 1325 Loa 41.80 Br ex 10.05 Dght 3.200 Lbp 37.40 Br md 10.00 Dpth 4.20 Welded, 1 dk	**(B21B20A) Anchor Handling Tug Supply**	**2 oil engines** reduction geared to sc. shafts driving 2 CP propellers Total Power: 2,942kW (4,000hp) Mitsubishi S8U-MPTK 2 x 4 Stroke 8 Cy. 240 x 260 each-1471kW (2000bhp) Mitsubishi Heavy Industries Ltd-Japan AuxGen: 3 x 280kW a.c
8508981 *YB4633* -	**SMS EXPRESS** *ex Ruby Express -2008 ex Angelica -2004* **PT Wintermar Offshore Marine** *Jakarta* *Indonesia* MMSI: 525019390	**190** 70 21	Class: BV	**1986-03 Soc. Francaise de Cons. Nav. — Villeneuve-la-Garenne** Yd No: 842/1 Loa 34.90 Br ex 6.46 Dght 1.201 Lbp 28.00 Br md 6.30 Dpth 2.80 Welded	**(B34J2SD) Crew Boat** Passengers: unberthed: 60	**2 oil engines** geared to sc. shafts driving 2 Water jets Total Power: 2,780kW (3,780hp) 27.0kn G.M. (Detroit Diesel) 16V-149-TI 2 x Vee 2 Stroke 16 Cy. 146 x 146 each-1390kW (1890bhp) General Motors Detroit DieselAllison Divn-USA AuxGen: 2 x 64kW 380V 50Hz a.c
9456381 *YDA4279* -	**SMS FRONTIER** **PT Sentosa Segara Mulia Shipping** PT Wintermar *Jakarta* *Indonesia*	**159** 48 -	Class: KI (BV)	**2007-06 P.T. Mariana Bahagia — Palembang** Yd No: 047 Loa 25.00 Br ex - Dght 2.700 Lbp 22.00 Br md 7.60 Dpth 3.50 Welded, 1 dk	**(B34L2QU) Utility Vessel**	**2 oil engines** reduction geared to sc. shafts driving 2 FP propellers Total Power: 1,220kW (1,658hp) Yanmar 6AYM-ETE 2 x 4 Stroke 6 Cy. 155 x 180 each-610kW (829bhp) Yanmar Diesel Engine Co Ltd-Japan AuxGen: 2 x 35kW 400V a.c
9409601 *H07401* -	**SMS JOL** **PT Wintermar** - *Panama* *Panama* MMSI: 355360000 Official number: 44519PEXT1	**264** 80 96	Class: AB	**2006-09 Sam Aluminium Engineering Pte Ltd — Singapore** Yd No: H71 Loa 40.25 Br ex - Dght 1.300 Lbp 37.40 Br md 7.80 Dpth 3.40 Welded, 1 dk	**(B34J2SD) Crew Boat** Hull Material: Aluminium Alloy Passengers: unberthed: 80	**3 oil engines** reduction geared to sc. shafts driving 3 FP propellers Total Power: 3,132kW (4,257hp) 22.0kn Caterpillar C32 3 x Vee 4 Stroke 12 Cy. 145 x 162 each-1044kW (1419bhp) Caterpillar Inc-USA
6524773 *YHGW* -	**SMS KARTA NEGARA** *ex Gonj-Zhu 5 -2002 ex Princess -2002* *ex Prinses Margriet -1996* **PT Sekawan Maju Sejahtera** *Surabaya* *Indonesia* MMSI: 525493596	**4,457** 1,860 673		**1964-07 van der Giessen-de Noord NV — Krimpen a/d IJssel** Yd No: 815 Loa 101.99 Br ex 18.06 Dght 4.830 Lbp 97.29 Br md 18.01 Dpth 5.29 Welded, 1 dk	**(A36A2PR) Passenger/Ro-Ro Ship (Vehicles)** Passengers: unberthed: 1000 Bow door Len: 7.00 Wid: 4.20 Swl: - Stern door Len: 7.00 Wid: 4.20 Swl: - Lane-Len: 402 Lane-Wid: 6.00 Lane-clr ht: 4.00 Cars: 85	**4 diesel electric oil engines** driving 4 gen. each 750kW 300V d.c Connecting to 4 elec. motors driving 2 Propellers aft, 1 fwd Total Power: 3,428kW (4,660hp) 16.0kn MAN G8V30/45ATL 4 x 4 Stroke 8 Cy. 300 x 450 each-857kW (1165bhp) J & K Smit's Machinehandel NV-Netherlands AuxGen: 3 x 150kW 390V 50Hz a.c Fuel: 208.5 (d.f.)
9059262 *MHIU8* -	**SMS LEAH** *ex Willpower -2013 ex Karin S -2005* *ex Diamante -1998* **Sinbad Marine Services Ltd** *Southampton* *United Kingdom* MMSI: 235024568 Official number: 909950	**120** - -	Class: BV	**1995-06 Stocznia 'Odra' — Szczecin** (Hull) **1995-06 B.V. Scheepswerf Damen — Gorinchem** Yd No: 6105 Loa 19.50 Br ex 6.04 Dght 2.000 Lbp 19.01 Br md 6.00 Dpth 2.70 Welded, 1 dk	**(B32A2ST) Tug**	**2 oil engines** geared to sc. shafts driving 2 FP propellers Total Power: 810kW (1,102hp) 10.0kn Caterpillar 3408TA 2 x Vee 4 Stroke 8 Cy. 137 x 152 each-405kW (551bhp) Caterpillar Inc-USA
8748335 *V3NX5* -	**SMS MARINE 128** *ex Yue Dong Guan Chui 0138 -2011* **Winton Enterprises Ltd** *Belize City* *Belize* Official number: 441120033	**2,523** 757 -		**2006-01 Dongguan Dongsheng Shipyard Co Ltd — Dongguan GD** Loa 58.00 Br ex 19.80 Dght - Lbp - Br md 19.80 Dpth 5.50 Welded, 1 dk	**(B33A2DU) Dredger (unspecified)**	**4 oil engines** driving 4 Propellers 9.0kn Cummins 4 x 4 Stroke
9581617 *XCAB8* -	**SMS MEXICO** *ex Svitzer Nereid -2013* **Svitzer (Americas) Ltd** Freepoint Tug & Towing Services *Dos Bocas* *Mexico* MMSI: 345050044 Official number: 11291	**630** 189 471	Class: LR ✠ **100A1** SS 02/2012 escort tug, fire-fighting Ship 1 (2400m3/h) with water spray *IWS WDL (5t/m2 from fr 0 to fr 15) ✠ **LMC** **UMS** Eq.Ltr: I; Cable: 330.0/24.0 U2 (a)	**2012-02 Qingdao Qianjin Shipyard — Qingdao SD** Yd No: 8Z2031 Loa 33.30 Br ex 13.84 Dght 4.500 Lbp 28.60 Br md 13.00 Dpth 6.10 Welded, 1 dk	**(B32A2ST) Tug**	**2 oil engines** gearing integral to driving 2 Z propellers Total Power: 4,412kW (5,998hp) Niigata 8L28HX 2 x 4 Stroke 8 Cy. 280 x 370 each-2206kW (2999bhp) Niigata Engineering Co Ltd-Japan AuxGen: 3 x 224kW 400V 50Hz a.c
8718562 *JZFW* -	**SMS MULAWARMAN** *ex Vayu -2013* **PT Sekawan Maju Sejahtera** *Indonesia* MMSI: 525023144	*1,529* - 803		**1988-06 Naikai Shipbuilding & Engineering Co Ltd — Onomichi HS (Setoda Shipyard)** Yd No: 529 Loa 83.44 (BB) Br ex 14.52 Dght 3.814 Lbp 76.00 Br md 14.50 Dpth 5.40 Welded, 2 dks	**(A36A2PR) Passenger/Ro-Ro Ship (Vehicles)** Passengers: unberthed: 470 Bow door & ramp Len: 8.30 Wid: 4.50 Swl: - Stern door/ramp Len: 8.70 Wid: 5.40 Swl: - Trailers: 23	**2 oil engines** with clutches, flexible couplings & sr reverse geared to sc. shafts driving 2 FP propellers Total Power: 3,384kW (4,600hp) 16.3kn Daihatsu 6DLM-32 2 x 4 Stroke 6 Cy. 320 x 400 each-1692kW (2300bhp) Daihatsu Diesel Manufacturing Co Lt-Japan AuxGen: 2 x 480kW 450V 60Hz a.c Thrusters: 1 Thwart. CP thruster (f)
9556325 *PMSU* -	**SMS MULIA** **PT Wintermar Offshore Marine** PT Wintermar *Jakarta* *Indonesia* MMSI: 525019421	**690** 207 -	Class: KI	**2009-02 PT Bumi Laut Perkasa — Batam** Yd No: 191 Loa 53.00 Br ex - Dght 2.760 Lbp 48.35 Br md 13.72 Dpth 3.66 Welded, 1 dk	**(A35D2RL) Landing Craft** Bow ramp (centre)	**2 oil engines** reduction geared to sc. shafts driving 2 FP propellers Total Power: 894kW (1,216hp) Cummins KTA-19-M3 2 x 4 Stroke 6 Cy. 159 x 159 each-447kW (608bhp) Cummins Engine Co Inc-USA

Ship / Owner	Tonnage	Class	Builder / Dimensions	Type	Machinery
9675389 **SMS PARGO** *JZJP* *ex* AHT Pargo *-2013* - **PT Sentosa Segara Mulia Shipping** PT Wintermar Offshore Marine *Jakarta* *Indonesia* MMSI: 525024138	**573** 172 313	Class: AB	**2013-07 Wuxue Janda Shipbuilding Co Ltd — Wuxue HB** (Hull) Yd No: (1381) **2013-06 Pacific Ocean Engineering & Trading Pte Ltd (POET) — Singapore** Yd No: 1381 Loa 41.80 Br ex - Dght 3.200 Lbp 37.40 Br md 10.00 Dpth 4.60 Welded, 1 dk	**(B21B20A) Anchor Handling Tug Supply**	**2 oil engines** reduction geared to sc. shafts driving 2 FP propellers Total Power: 2,984kW (4,058hp) Mitsubishi S8U-MPTK 2 x 4 Stroke 8 Cy. 240 x 260 each-1492kW (2029bhp) Mitsubishi Heavy Industries Ltd-Japan AuxGen: 3 x 225kW a.c Fuel: 270.0
9637521 **SMS PINANG** *POFP* *launched as* ASD Everglades *-2011* - **PT Sentosa Segara Mulia Shipping** - *Jakarta* *Indonesia*	**372** 111 180	Class: AB	**2011-11 Bengbu Shenzhou Machinery Co Ltd — Bengbu AH** Yd No: 1358 Loa 29.36 Br ex - Dght 4.100 Lbp 24.19 Br md 9.80 Dpth 5.00 Welded, 1 dk	**(B32A2ST) Tug**	**2 oil engines** reduction geared to sc. shafts driving 2 Z propellers Total Power: 2,648kW (3,600hp) Yanmar 8N21A-EN 2 x 4 Stroke 8 Cy. 210 x 290 each-1324kW (1800bhp) Yanmar Diesel Engine Co Ltd-Japan AuxGen: 2 x 99kW a.c Fuel: 180.0 (d.f.)
9232010 **SMS POWER** *YDA4088* - **PT Lautan Lestari** - *Jakarta* *Indonesia* MMSI: 525019426	**134** 41 126	Class: KI (NK)	**2000-05 Yii Brothers Shipbuilding Contractor Co — Sibu** Yd No: 87 Loa 23.50 Br ex - Dght 2.712 Lbp 21.07 Br md 7.32 Dpth 3.20 Welded, 1 dk	**(B32A2ST) Tug**	**2 oil engines** reduction geared to sc. shafts driving 2 FP propellers Total Power: 894kW (1,216hp) 10.0kn Cummins KTA-19-M3 2 x 4 Stroke 6 Cy. 159 x 159 each-447kW (608bhp) Cummins Engine Co Inc-USA AuxGen: 2 x 21kW 380/220V a.c Fuel: 97.0 (d.f.)
9642318 **SMS PRESTIGE** *JZAN* - **PT Wintermar** Seacoral Maritime Pte Ltd *Jakarta* *Indonesia* MMSI: 525019639 Official number: 3429	**190** 57 73	Class: AB	**2013-05 Sam Aluminium Engineering Pte Ltd — Singapore** Yd No: H103 Loa 35.50 Br ex - Dght 1.250 Lbp 32.48 Br md 7.00 Dpth 3.40 Welded, 1 dk	**(B34J2SD) Crew Boat** Hull Material: Aluminium Alloy	**3 oil engines** reduction geared to sc. shafts driving 3 Propellers Total Power: 2,238kW (3,042hp) Caterpillar C32 ACERT 3 x Vee 4 Stroke 12 Cy. 145 x 162 each-746kW (1014bhp) Caterpillar Motoren (Guangdong) CoLtd-China
8508993 **SMS PRIMA** *YB4632* *ex* Opal *-2008* *ex* Delima Express *-2005* - *ex* Aida *-2004* **PT Wintermar Offshore Marine** - *Jakarta* *Indonesia* MMSI: 525019392	**190** 70 -	Class: BV	**1986-03 Soc. Francaise de Cons. Nav. — Villeneuve-la-Garenne** Yd No: 842/2 Loa 34.90 Br ex 6.46 Dght 1.201 Lbp 28.00 Br md 6.30 Dpth 2.80 Welded	**(B34J2SD) Crew Boat** Passengers: unberthed: 90	**2 oil engines** geared to sc. shafts driving 2 Directional propellers Total Power: 2,780kW (3,780hp) 27.0kn G.M. (Detroit Diesel) 16V-149-TI 2 x Vee 2 Stroke 16 Cy. 146 x 146 each-1390kW (1890bhp) General Motors Detroit DieselAllison Divn-USA
9531399 **SMS RAINBOW** *YDA4692* - **PT Wintermar** Seacoral Maritime Pte Ltd *Jakarta* *Indonesia* MMSI: 525003043 Official number: 6451	**282** 84 88	Class: AB	**2010-08 Sam Aluminium Engineering Pte Ltd — Singapore** Yd No: H86 Loa 40.38 Br ex - Dght 1.300 Lbp 38.93 Br md 7.80 Dpth 3.40 Welded, 1 dk	**(B34L2QU) Utility Vessel** Hull Material: Aluminium Alloy Passengers: unberthed: 100	**3 oil engines** reduction geared to sc. shafts driving 3 Propellers Total Power: 2,460kW (3,345hp) Caterpillar C32 3 x Vee 4 Stroke 12 Cy. 145 x 162 each-820kW (1115bhp) Caterpillar Inc-USA AuxGen: 2 x 56kW a.c
7923316 **SMS RIVER** *PNYB* *ex* Rush River *-2011* *ex* Mr. Buster *-1997* - *ex* Theresa Bruce *-1989* **PT Wintermar** - *Jakarta* *Indonesia* Official number: 3193/PPM	**656** 196 1,200	Class: AB KI	**1980-09 Halter Marine, Inc. — Lockport, La** Yd No: 885 Loa 54.86 Br ex - Dght 3.658 Lbp 50.66 Br md 12.50 Dpth 4.27 Welded, 1 dk	**(B21A20S) Platform Supply Ship** Grain: 127; Liq: 937; Liq (Oil): 937	**2 oil engines** reverse reduction geared to sc. shafts driving 2 FP propellers Total Power: 1,854kW (2,520hp) 12.0kn EMD (Electro-Motive) 12-645-E2 2 x Vee 2 Stroke 12 Cy. 230 x 254 each-927kW (1260bhp) (Re-engined , Reconditioned & fitted 1980) General Motors Detroit DieselAllison Divn-USA AuxGen: 2 x 99kW Thrusters: 1 Thwart. FP thruster (f)
9263796 **SMS SAKTI** *YDA4119* - **PT Lautan Lestari** - *Jakarta* *Indonesia*	**181** 55 87	Class: KI (NK)	**2002-01 Lingco Shipbuilding Pte Ltd — Singapore** Yd No: 2601 Loa 25.05 Br ex - Dght 2.712 Lbp 23.08 Br md 8.00 Dpth 3.50 Welded, 1 dk	**(B32B2SP) Pusher Tug**	**2 oil engines** driving 2 FP propellers Total Power: 1,204kW (1,636hp) 11.0kn Mitsubishi S6R2-MPTK 2 x 4 Stroke 6 Cy. 170 x 220 each-602kW (818bhp) (made 2002) Mitsubishi Heavy Industries Ltd-Japan AuxGen: 2 x 45kW a.c
9637519 **SMS SANGATTA** *POFO* *ex* ASD Eversole *-2011* - **PT Sentosa Segara Mulia Shipping** PT Wintermar *Jakarta* *Indonesia* Official number: 397332	**372** 111 183	Class: AB	**2011-11 Bengbu Shenzhou Machinery Co Ltd — Bengbu AH** Yd No: (1357) **2011* Pacific Ocean Engineering & Trading Pte Ltd (POET) — Singapore** Yd No: 1357 Loa 29.36 Br ex - Dght 4.100 Lbp 24.19 Br md 9.80 Dpth 5.00 Welded, 1 dk	**(B32A2ST) Tug**	**2 oil engines** reduction geared to sc. shafts driving 2 Directional propellers Total Power: 2,648kW (3,600hp) Yanmar 8N21A-EN 2 x 4 Stroke 8 Cy. 210 x 290 each-1324kW (1800bhp) Yanmar Diesel Engine Co Ltd-Japan AuxGen: 2 x 99kW a.c
9557604 **SMS SHOALBUSTER** *2BYF6* - **Gareloch Support Services (Plant) Ltd** - SatCom: Inmarsat C 423506093 *Southampton* *United Kingdom* MMSI: 235070418 Official number: 916038	**212** 63 200	Class: BV	**2009-06 Damen Shipyards Kozle Sp z oo — Kedzierzyn-Kozle** (Hull) Yd No: 1139 **2009-06 B.V. Scheepswerf Damen Hardinxveld — Hardinxveld-Giessendam** Yd No: 571619 Loa 26.02 Br ex 9.32 Dght 2.650 Lbp 23.90 Br md 9.10 Dpth 3.60 Welded, 1 dk	**(B32A2ST) Tug**	**2 oil engines** reduction geared to sc. shafts driving 2 FP propellers Total Power: 1,640kW (2,230hp) 10.0kn Caterpillar 3508B-TA 2 x Vee 4 Stroke 8 Cy. 170 x 190 each-820kW (1115bhp) Caterpillar Inc-USA AuxGen: 2 x 69kW 50Hz a.c Thrusters: 1 Retract. directional thruster (f)
9336555 **SMS SUPPORTER** *PNYA* *ex* Neptune Trident *-2011* *ex* Nor Sea *-2008* - **PT Wintermar** - *Jakarta* *Indonesia* MMSI: 525019583	**1,951** 585 1,790	Class: AB	**2005-04 P.T. Jaya Asiatic Shipyard — Batam** Yd No: 845 Loa 70.05 Br ex - Dght 4.950 Lbp 63.00 Br md 14.95 Dpth 6.10 Welded, 1 dk	**(B21B20A) Anchor Handling Tug Supply**	**2 oil engines** reduction geared to sc. shafts driving 2 CP propellers Total Power: 4,050kW (5,506hp) 12.0kn Wartsila 6L26A 2 x 4 Stroke 6 Cy. 260 x 320 each-2025kW (2753bhp) Wartsila Finland Oy-Finland AuxGen: 2 x 1228kW 440V 60Hz a.c, 2 x 370kW 440V 60Hz a.c Thrusters: 2 Thwart. CP thruster (f); 1 Thwart. CP thruster (a)
8981573 **SMS SWAKARYA** *YFTB* - **PT Wintermar Offshore Marine** - *Jakarta* *Indonesia* MMSI: 525019060	**757** 228 -	Class: KI	**1997-08 P.T. Sentosa Mulia Shipyard — Batam** Loa 53.58 Br ex - Dght 2.530 Lbp 47.33 Br md 13.72 Dpth 3.43 Welded, 1 dk	**(A35D2RL) Landing Craft** Bow ramp (centre)	**2 oil engines** geared to sc. shafts driving 2 Propellers Total Power: 736kW (1,000hp) Cummins 2 x 4 Stroke each-368kW (500bhp) Cummins Engine Co Inc-USA
9426520 **SMS TANGGUH** *YCEH* - **PT Wintermar Offshore Marine** PT Wintermar *Jakarta* *Indonesia* MMSI: 525019351 Official number: 4435/L	**785** 236 1,392	Class: KI RI	**2007-02 PT Bumi Laut Perkasa — Batam** Yd No: 184 Loa 56.42 Br ex - Dght 3.180 Lbp 49.63 Br md 12.00 Dpth 4.10 Welded, 1 dk	**(A35D2RL) Landing Craft** Bow ramp (centre)	**2 oil engines** reduction geared to sc. shafts driving 2 FP propellers Total Power: 942kW (1,280hp) Cummins KTA-19-M3 2 x 4 Stroke 6 Cy. 159 x 159 each-471kW (640bhp) Cummins Engine Co Inc-USA AuxGen: 2 x 90kW 415V a.c
9204037 **SMS TRANSPORTER** *YHFE* - **PT Wintermar** - *Jakarta* *Indonesia* MMSI: 525023093	**1,845** 554 1,785	Class: BV (GL) (KI)	**1998-09 Forward Shipbuilding Enterprise Sdn Bhd — Sibu** Yd No: 1057 Converted From: Products Tanker-2012 Loa 69.82 Br ex 17.07 Dght 3.003 Lbp 64.63 Br md 17.07 Dpth 3.96 Welded, 1 dk	**(B22A20R) Offshore Support Vessel** Double Hull Passengers: berths: 92 Liq: 1,787; Liq (Oil): 1,787 Cranes: 1x3t	**2 oil engines** reduction geared to sc. shafts driving 2 FP propellers Total Power: 1,390kW (1,890hp) 9.1kn Dorman SEAKING-8 2 x 4 Stroke 8 Cy. 160 x 190 each-695kW (945bhp) Dorman Diesels Ltd.-Stafford AuxGen: 2 x 150kW 220/380V a.c Thrusters: 1 Tunnel thruster (f)

IMO / Call sign / Flag	Name / Owner	Tonnage	Class	Builder / Dimensions	Type	Machinery
9581394 *YDA4811* -	**SMS VALIANT** **PT Wintermar** - *Jakarta* *Indonesia* MMSI: 525019582	**244** 83 76	Class: AB	**2011-04 Sam Aluminium Engineering Pte Ltd — Singapore** Yd No: H92 Loa 36.63 Br ex - Dght 1.800 Lbp 35.19 Br md 7.80 Dpth 3.40 Welded, 1 dk	**(B34L2QU) Utility Vessel** Hull Material: Aluminium Alloy	**3 oil engines** reduction geared to sc. shafts driving 3 FP propellers Total Power: 2,460kW (3,345hp) Caterpillar C32 3 x Vee 4 Stroke 12 Cy. 145 x 162 each-820kW (1115bhp) Caterpillar Inc-USA AuxGen: 2 x 56kW a.c Fuel: 100.0 (d.f.)
9642306 *YB4887* -	**SMS VALUE** **PT Wintermar** Seacoral Maritime Pte Ltd *Jakarta* *Indonesia* MMSI: 525019635 Official number: NO.3550/BA	*270* 81 72	Class: AB	**2013-04 Sam Aluminium Engineering Pte Ltd — Singapore** (Hull) Yd No: (H107) **2013-04 P.T. Adiguna Shipbuilding & Engineering — Jakarta** Yd No: H107 Loa 36.63 Br ex - Dght 1.300 Lbp 33.65 Br md 7.80 Dpth 3.64 Welded, 1 dk	**(B34J2SD) Crew Boat** Hull Material: Aluminium Alloy	**3 oil engines** reduction geared to sc. shafts driving 3 Water jets Total Power: 3,243kW (4,410hp) Caterpillar C32 ACERT 3 x Vee 4 Stroke 12 Cy. 145 x 162 each-1081kW (1470bhp) Caterpillar Motoren (Guangdong) CoLtd-China AuxGen: 2 x 56kW a.c Fuel: 99.0 (d.f.)
9572941 *YDA4705* -	**SMS VANDA** *ex* TW Vanda *-2010* **PT Sentosa Segara Mulia Shipping** PT Wintermar *Jakarta* *Indonesia*	**249** 74 150	Class: AB	**2010-06 Bengbu Shenzhou Machinery Co Ltd — Bengbu AH** (Hull) Yd No: (1321) **2010-06 Pacific Ocean Engineering & Trading Pte Ltd (POET) — Singapore** Yd No: 1321 Loa 29.50 Br ex - Dght 3.500 Lbp 27.00 Br md 9.00 Dpth 4.16 Welded, 1 dk	**(B32A2ST) Tug**	**2 oil engines** reduction geared to sc. shafts driving 2 FP propellers Total Power: 2,984kW (4,058hp) Cummins KTA-50-M2 2 x Vee 4 Stroke 16 Cy. 159 x 159 each-1492kW (2029bhp) Cummins Engine Co Inc-USA AuxGen: 2 x 37kW a.c
9581409 *YDA4834* -	**SMS VENTURE** **PT Wintermar** - *Jakarta* *Indonesia* MMSI: 525019585	**244** 83 77	Class: AB	**2011-07 Sam Aluminium Engineering Pte Ltd — Singapore** Yd No: H93 Loa 36.63 Br ex - Dght 1.800 Lbp 35.19 Br md 7.80 Dpth 3.40 Welded, 1 dk	**(B34L2QU) Utility Vessel** Hull Material: Aluminium Alloy	**3 oil engines** reduction geared to sc. shafts driving 3 FP propellers Total Power: 3,243kW (4,410hp) Caterpillar C32 3 x Vee 4 Stroke 12 Cy. 145 x 162 each-1081kW (1470bhp) Caterpillar Inc-USA AuxGen: 2 x 56kW a.c Fuel: 100.0 (d.f.)
9642291 *YB4886* -	**SMS VIKING** **PT Wintermar** Seacoral Maritime Pte Ltd *Jakarta* *Indonesia* MMSI: 525019636 Official number: NO.3549/BA	*270* 81 70	Class: AB	**2013-04 Sam Aluminium Engineering Pte Ltd — Singapore** (Hull) Yd No: (H102) **2013-04 P.T. Adiguna Shipbuilding & Engineering — Jakarta** Yd No: H102 Loa 36.63 Br ex - Dght 1.300 Lbp 33.65 Br md 7.80 Dpth 3.64 Welded, 1 dk	**(B34J2SD) Crew Boat** Hull Material: Aluminium Alloy	**3 oil engines** reduction geared to sc. shafts driving 3 Water jets Total Power: 3,243kW (4,410hp) Caterpillar C32 ACERT 3 x Vee 4 Stroke 12 Cy. 145 x 162 each-1081kW (1470bhp) Caterpillar Motoren (Guangdong) CoLtd-China AuxGen: 2 x 56kW a.c Fuel: 99.0 (d.f.)
9459228 *YB4656* -	**SMS VINCENT** **PT Wintermar** - *Jakarta* *Indonesia* MMSI: 525019391 Official number: PK673/1/16/DK-08	**268** 81 96	Class: AB KI	**2007-10 Sam Aluminium Engineering Pte Ltd — Singapore** Yd No: H75 Loa 40.25 Br ex - Dght 1.300 Lbp 38.07 Br md 7.80 Dpth 3.40 Welded, 1 dk	**(B34J2SD) Crew Boat** Hull Material: Aluminium Alloy Passengers: unberthed: 82	**3 oil engines** reduction geared to sc. shafts driving 3 FP propellers Total Power: 3,696kW (5,025hp) Caterpillar C32 3 x Vee 4 Stroke 12 Cy. 145 x 162 each-1232kW (1675bhp) Caterpillar Inc-USA AuxGen: 2 x 90kW a.c Thrusters: 1 Tunnel thruster (f) Fuel: 97.2 (d.f.)
9581382 *YDA4743* -	**SMS VISION** **PT Sentosa Segara Mulia Shipping** PT Wintermar *Jakarta* *Indonesia* MMSI: 525019575 Official number: 6583	**244** 83 79	Class: AB	**2010-12 Sam Aluminium Engineering Pte Ltd — Singapore** Yd No: H91 Loa 36.63 Br ex - Dght 1.300 Lbp 35.19 Br md 7.80 Dpth 3.40 Welded, 1 dk	**(B34L2QU) Utility Vessel** Hull Material: Aluminium Alloy	**3 oil engines** reduction geared to sc. shafts driving 3 FP propellers Total Power: 2,460kW (3,345hp) Caterpillar C32 3 x Vee 4 Stroke 12 Cy. 145 x 162 each-820kW (1115bhp) Caterpillar Inc-USA AuxGen: 2 x 56kW a.c
9642289 *YB4884* -	**SMS VOSPER** **PT Wintermar** Seacoral Maritime Pte Ltd *Jakarta* *Indonesia* MMSI: 525019632 Official number: 7715	**244** - 71	Class: AB	**2013-02 Sam Aluminium Engineering Pte Ltd — Singapore** (Hull) Yd No: (H101) **2013-02 P.T. Adiguna Shipbuilding & Engineering — Jakarta** Yd No: 101 Loa 36.63 Br ex - Dght 1.300 Lbp 33.65 Br md 7.80 Dpth 3.64 Welded, 1 dk	**(B34J2SD) Crew Boat** Hull Material: Aluminium Alloy	**3 oil engines** reduction geared to sc. shafts driving 3 Propellers Total Power: 3,243kW (4,410hp) Caterpillar C32 ACERT 3 x Vee 4 Stroke 12 Cy. 145 x 162 each-1081kW (1470bhp) Caterpillar Motoren (Guangdong) CoLtd-China AuxGen: 2 x 56kW a.c Fuel: 99.0 (d.f.)
9569891 *PNAP* -	**SMS VOYAGER** **PT Wintermar** - SatCom: Inmarsat C 452501377 *Jakarta* *Indonesia* MMSI: 525019511 Official number: 5835	**498** 150 -	Class: BV	**2009-08 Forward Marine Enterprise Sdn Bhd — Sibu** Yd No: FM-48 Loa 48.00 Br ex - Dght 2.500 Lbp 45.00 Br md 11.00 Dpth 3.50 Welded, 1 dk	**(B21B20T) Offshore Tug/Supply Ship**	**2 oil engines** reduction geared to sc. shafts driving 2 FP propellers Total Power: 2,080kW (2,828hp) Mitsubishi S12R-MPTK 2 x Vee 4 Stroke 12 Cy. 170 x 180 each-1040kW (1414bhp) Mitsubishi Heavy Industries Ltd-Japan AuxGen: 3 x 130kW 50Hz a.c Thrusters: 1 Tunnel thruster (f) Fuel: 176.0
9097800 - -	**SMU EXODUS** *ex* Fortuna I *-2010* **PT SMU Transliner** - *Samarinda* *Indonesia*	**114** 35 -	Class: KI	**2006-12 in Indonesia** Loa 23.50 Br ex - Dght - Lbp 21.80 Br md 6.50 Dpth 2.50 Welded, 1 dk	**(B32A2ST) Tug**	**2 oil engines** reduction geared to sc. shafts driving 2 Propellers Total Power: 810kW (1,102hp) Mitsubishi 10DC11 2 x Vee 4 Stroke 10 Cy. 141 x 152 each-405kW (551bhp) Mitsubishi Heavy Industries Ltd-Japan
8942759 *WDD5770* -	**SMUGGLER'S POINT** *ex* Croyance *-2006* *ex* Mon Repos *-1999* *ex* Rest Express *-1998* *ex* Monrepos Express *-1998* *ex* Earl Bull Shepard *-1995* **Big King Transportation S de RL** *United States of America* MMSI: 367163370	*470* 376 -		**1943-01 Sturgeon Bay Shipbuilding & Dry Dock Corp — Sturgeon Bay WI** Yd No: 103746 L reg 53.80 Br ex - Dght - Lbp - Br md 9.75 Dpth 3.81 Welded, 1 dk	**(A31A2GX) General Cargo Ship**	**2 oil engines** driving 2 FP propellers Total Power: 736kW (1,000hp) 10.0kn General Motors 2 x each-368kW (500bhp) General Motors Corp-USA
9275218 *XPWG* -	**SMYRIL** **Foroyar Landsstyri** Strandfaraskip Landsins SatCom: Inmarsat C 423130010 *Torshavn* *Faeroe Islands (Danish)* MMSI: 231300000	**12,670** 3,801 2,652	Class: NV (LR) ✠ Classed LR until 18/12/07	**2005-09 Navantia SA — San Fernando (Sp)** Yd No: 399 Loa 138.00 (BB) Br ex 23.00 Dght 5.813 Lbp 123.00 Br md 22.70 Dpth 13.70 Welded, 3 dks	**(A36A2PR) Passenger/Ro-Ro Ship (Vehicles)** Passengers: unberthed: 976; cabins: 34; berths: 100 Stern door/ramp (p. a.) Len: 10.60 Wid: 6.50 Swl: - Stern door/ramp (s. a.) Len: 10.60 Wid: 6.50 Swl: - Lane-Len: 970 Cars: 200	**4 oil engines** with clutches, flexible couplings & sr geared to sc. shafts driving 2 CP propellers Total Power: 13,440kW (18,272hp) 21.0kn MAN 7L32/40 3 x 4 Stroke 7 Cy. 320 x 400 each-3360kW (4568bhp) Manises Diesel Engine Co. S.A.-Valencia MAN-B&W 7L32/40 1 x 4 Stroke 7 Cy. 320 x 400 3360kW (4568bhp) Manises Diesel Engine Co. S.A.-Valencia AuxGen: 2 x 1235kW 400V 50Hz a.c, 4 x 515kW 400V 50Hz a.c Boilers: TOH (o.f.) 10.2kgf/cm² (10.0bar) Thrusters: 2 Thwart. CP thruster (f)
9416941 *J8B3818* -	**SMYRNA** **Smyrna Shipping Ltd** ABC Maritime AG *Kingstown* *St Vincent & The Grenadines* MMSI: 376456000 Official number: 10291	**1,025** 308 703	Class: BV	**2008-05 Gelibolu Gemi Insa Sanayi ve Ticaret AS — Gelibolu** Yd No: 35 Loa 48.00 Br ex - Dght 4.100 Lbp 44.22 Br md 12.60 Dpth 5.20 Welded, 1 dk	**(B21A20S) Platform Supply Ship** Cranes: 1x10t	**2 oil engines** reduction geared to sc. shafts driving 2 CP propellers Total Power: 2,354kW (3,200hp) 11.5kn Cummins KTA-50-M2 2 x Vee 4 Stroke 16 Cy. 159 x 159 each-1177kW (1600bhp) Cummins Engine Co Inc-USA AuxGen: 3 x 225kW 380V 50Hz a.c Thrusters: 1 Tunnel thruster (f) Fuel: 240.0 (d.f.)

9149952 *YJTQ2* -	**SMYRNA** *ex* Avatar *-2014* *ex* Messenger K *-2010* *ex* F. Camellia *-2008* *ex* Tong Xing *-2004* **Alcor Maritime Ltd** Troy Denizcilik Turizm Ltd Sti (Troy Shipping & Tourism Co Ltd) *Port Vila* *Vanuatu* MMSI: 577212000 Official number: 2274	**3,796** 1,480 4,509	Class: (BV) (NK) (CC)	**1996**-07 **Jiangsu Yangzijiang Shipbuilding Co Ltd — Jiangyin JS** Yd No: 327-1 Loa 93.00 Br ex - Dght 5.812 Lbp 84.80 Br md 17.60 Dpth 7.80 Welded, 1 dk	**(A31A2GX) General Cargo Ship** Bale: 5,426 3 Ha: (18.9 x 12.6) (25.4 x 12.6)ER (6.5 x 7.8)	**1 oil engine** driving 1 FP propeller Total Power: 2,206kW (2,999hp) Hudong 6E34/82SDZC 1 x 2 Stroke 6 Cy. 340 x 820 2206kW (2999bhp) Hudong Shipyard-China Fuel: 330.0 (r.f.)
9493779 *A8YB6* -	**SMYRNI** **Pisces Finance Ltd** Dynacom Tankers Management Ltd *Monrovia* *Liberia* MMSI: 636015015 Official number: 15015	**83,562** 49,022 149,998 T/cm 119.8	Class: AB	**2011**-08 **Jiangsu Rongsheng Shipbuilding Co Ltd — Rugao JS** Yd No: 1073 Loa 274.50 (BB) Br ex 48.04 Dght 16.483 Lbp 264.00 Br md 48.00 Dpth 23.70 Welded, 1 dk	**(A13A2TV) Crude Oil Tanker** Double Hull (13F) Liq: 167,550; Liq (Oil): 167,500 Cargo Heating Coils Compartments: 12 Wing Ta, 2 Wing Slop Ta, ER 3 Cargo Pump (s): 3x3500m³/hr Manifold: Bow/CM: 138.8m	**1 oil engine** driving 1 FP propeller Total Power: 18,660kW (25,370hp) 15.1kn MAN-B&W 6S70MC-C 1 x 2 Stroke 6 Cy. 700 x 2800 18660kW (25370bhp) Doosan Engine Co Ltd-South Korea AuxGen: 3 x 940kW a.c Fuel: 240.0 (d.f.) 4500.0 (r.f.)
9225469 *PQ3923* -	**SN ABROLHOS** **Sulnorte Servicos Maritimos Ltda** H Dantas Comercio Navegacao e Industrias Ltda *Rio de Janeiro* *Brazil* Official number: 3810485187	**298** 89 870	Class: (BV)	**1998**-08 **H. Dantas Construcoes e Reparos Navais Ltda. — Aracaju** Yd No: 578 Loa 31.34 Br ex - Dght 4.000 Lbp 29.45 Br md 9.80 Dpth 4.50 Welded, 1 dk	**(B32A2ST) Tug**	**2 oil engines** reduction geared to sc. shafts driving 2 Directional propellers Total Power: 2,984kW (4,058hp) 14.6kn Caterpillar 3516B 2 x Vee 4 Stroke 16 Cy. 170 x 190 each-1492kW (2029bhp) Caterpillar Inc-USA
8732623 *PS7401* -	**SN ARAGIPE** **Sulnorte Servicos Maritimos Ltda** H Dantas Comercio Navegacao e Industrias Ltda *Rio de Janeiro* *Brazil* MMSI: 710001120 Official number: 3810514446	**227** 68 -		**2005**-01 **H. Dantas Construcoes e Reparos Navais Ltda. — Aracaju** Loa 24.39 Br ex - Dght 3.250 Lbp - Br md 9.15 Dpth 4.35 Welded, 1 dk	**(B32A2ST) Tug**	**2 oil engines** reduction geared to sc. shafts driving 2 Directional propellers Total Power: 3,000kW (4,078hp) Caterpillar 3512B-HD 2 x Vee 4 Stroke 12 Cy. 170 x 215 each-1500kW (2039bhp) Caterpillar Inc-USA
9256236 *IBFE* -	**SN AZZURRA** *ex* Blue Dolphin *-2011* *ex* Stena Commander *-2006* *ex* Blue Dolphin *-2003* **Scerni di Navigazione Srl** - *Genoa* *Italy* MMSI: 247077200	**40,763** 20,395 72,344 T/cm 67.0	Class: RI (AB)	**2003**-03 **Hudong-Zhonghua Shipbuilding (Group) Co Ltd — Shanghai** Yd No: H1302A Loa 228.64 (BB) Br ex - Dght 14.020 Lbp 218.60 Br md 32.26 Dpth 20.20 Welded, 1 dk	**(A13B2TP) Products Tanker** Double Hull (13F) Liq: 75,273; Liq (Oil): 75,273 Compartments: 12 Wing Ta, ER 3 Cargo Pump (s): 3x2000m³/hr Manifold: Bow/CM: 113.8m	**1 oil engine** driving 1 FP propeller Total Power: 11,290kW (15,350hp) 14.0kn MAN-B&W 5S60MC-C 1 x 2 Stroke 5 Cy. 600 x 2400 11290kW (15350bhp) Hudong Heavy Machinery Co Ltd-China AuxGen: 3 x 600kW a.c Fuel: 102.0 (d.f.) 2218.0 (r.f.)
8732611 *PS7334* -	**SN CAETE** **Sulnorte Servicos Maritimos Ltda** H Dantas Comercio Navegacao e Industrias Ltda *Rio de Janeiro* *Brazil* MMSI: 710000960 Official number: 3810513075	**227** 68 -		**2004**-01 **H. Dantas Construcoes e Reparos Navais Ltda. — Aracaju** Loa 24.39 Br ex - Dght 3.250 Lbp - Br md 9.15 Dpth 4.04 Welded, 1 dk	**(B32A2ST) Tug**	**2 oil engines** reduction geared to sc. shafts driving 2 Directional propellers Total Power: 2,080kW (2,828hp) Volvo Penta D49 2 x Vee 4 Stroke 12 Cy. 170 x 180 each-1040kW (1414bhp) AB Volvo Penta-Sweden
8732635 - -	**SN CHUI** **Sulnorte Servicos Maritimos Ltda** H Dantas Comercio Navegacao e Industrias Ltda *Rio de Janeiro* *Brazil* Official number: 3810517224	**227** 68 -		**2006**-01 **H. Dantas Construcoes e Reparos Navais Ltda. — Aracaju** Yd No: 593 Loa 24.39 Br ex - Dght 3.250 Lbp - Br md 9.15 Dpth 4.35 Welded, 1 dk	**(B32A2ST) Tug**	**2 oil engines** reduction geared to sc. shafts driving 2 Directional propellers Total Power: 3,000kW (4,078hp) Caterpillar 3512B-HD 2 x Vee 4 Stroke 12 Cy. 170 x 215 each-1500kW (2039bhp) Caterpillar Inc-USA
9429182 *IBKF* -	**SN CLAUDIA** *ex* D. T. Mariano *-2011* **Scerni di Navigazione Srl** - *Genoa* *Italy* MMSI: 247274100	**60,185** 33,762 109,010 T/cm 91.3	Class: RI (AB)	**2009**-11 **Hudong-Zhonghua Shipbuilding (Group) Co Ltd — Shanghai** Yd No: H1544A Loa 243.00 (BB) Br ex 42.03 Dght 15.350 Lbp 233.00 Br md 42.00 Dpth 22.00 Welded, 1 dk	**(A13A2TV) Crude Oil Tanker** Double Hull (13F) Liq: 123,030; Liq (Oil): 103,056 Cargo Heating Coils Compartments: 12 Wing Ta, 2 Wing Slop Ta, ER 3 Cargo Pump (s): 3x2500m³/hr Manifold: Bow/CM: 118.5m	**1 oil engine** driving 1 FP propeller Total Power: 13,570kW (18,450hp) 14.7kn MAN-B&W 7S60MC 1 x 2 Stroke 7 Cy. 600 x 2292 13570kW (18450bhp) Hudong Heavy Machinery Co Ltd-China AuxGen: 3 x 680kW 450V 60Hz a.c Fuel: 125.0 (d.f.) 2700.0 (r.f.)
9225471 *PQ3924* -	**SN DAVID** **Sulnorte Servicos Maritimos Ltda** H Dantas Comercio Navegacao e Industrias Ltda *Rio de Janeiro* *Brazil* Official number: 3810485179	**302** 90 135	Class: (AB) (BV)	**1998**-01 **H. Dantas Construcoes e Reparos Navais Ltda. — Aracaju** Yd No: 579 Loa 31.34 Br ex - Dght 3.600 Lbp 29.45 Br md 9.80 Dpth 4.50 Welded, 1 dk	**(B32A2ST) Tug**	**2 oil engines** reduction geared to sc. shafts driving 1 Directional propeller , 1 FP propeller Total Power: 2,982kW (4,054hp) Caterpillar 3516B 1 x Vee 4 Stroke 16 Cy. 170 x 190 1491kW (2027bhp) Caterpillar Inc-USA
9256248 *IBZJ* -	**SN FEDERICA** *ex* White Dolphin *-2011* *ex* Stena Comanche *-2007* *ex* White Dolphin *-2004* **Scerni di Navigazione Srl** - *Genoa* *Italy* MMSI: 247077300	**40,763** 20,395 72,344 T/cm 65.0	Class: RI (AB)	**2003**-05 **Hudong-Zhonghua Shipbuilding (Group) Co Ltd — Shanghai** Yd No: H1303A Loa 228.64 (BB) Br ex 32.29 Dght 14.015 Lbp 218.60 Br md 32.26 Dpth 20.20 Welded, 1 dk	**(A13B2TP) Products Tanker** Double Hull (13F) Liq: 75,273; Liq (Oil): 80,000 Cargo Heating Coils Compartments: 12 Wing Ta, 1 Slop Ta, ER 3 Cargo Pump (s): 3x2000m³/hr Manifold: Bow/CM: 113.8m	**1 oil engine** driving 1 FP propeller Total Power: 11,290kW (15,350hp) 14.0kn MAN-B&W 5S60MC-C 1 x 2 Stroke 5 Cy. 600 x 2400 11290kW (15350bhp) Hudong Heavy Machinery Co Ltd-China AuxGen: 3 x 600kW a.c
9225457 *PQ3922* -	**SN GUARAPARI** **Sulnorte Servicos Maritimos Ltda** H Dantas Comercio Navegacao e Industrias Ltda *Rio de Janeiro* *Brazil* Official number: 3810485152	**302** 90 870	Class: (BV)	**1998**-05 **H. Dantas Construcoes e Reparos Navais Ltda. — Aracaju** Yd No: 577 Loa 31.34 Br ex - Dght 4.000 Lbp 29.28 Br md 9.80 Dpth 4.50 Welded, 1 dk	**(B32A2ST) Tug**	**2 oil engines** geared to sc. shafts driving 2 Propellers Total Power: 4,054kW (5,512hp) 14.6kn Caterpillar 3516B 2 x Vee 4 Stroke 16 Cy. 170 x 190 each-2027kW (2756bhp) Caterpillar Inc-USA
9020003 *DSFK6* -	**SN HARMONY** *ex* Hoam *-2011* *ex* Harvest Ace *-2000* *ex* Asian Harmony *-1993* **Seanet Shipping Co Ltd** - SatCom: Inmarsat A 1341357 *Jeju* *South Korea* MMSI: 440991000 Official number: JJR-000981	**8,255** 3,495 10,030	Class: KR (NK)	**1991**-04 **Higaki Zosen K.K. — Imabari** Yd No: 395 Loa 116.84 (BB) Br ex 19.62 Dght 8.064 Lbp 108.00 Br md 19.60 Dpth 14.50 Welded, 1 dk	**(A31A2GX) General Cargo Ship** Grain: 19,673; Bale: 18,259 Compartments: 2 Ho, ER 2 Ha: 2 (29.4 x 12.6)ER Derricks: 4x20t	**1 oil engine** driving 1 FP propeller Total Power: 3,089kW (4,200hp) 12.3kn Mitsubishi 6UEC37LA 1 x 2 Stroke 6 Cy. 370 x 880 3089kW (4200bhp) Mitsubishi Heavy Industries Ltd-Japan AuxGen: 3 x 168kW a.c
8732659 - -	**SN JATOBA** **Sulnorte Servicos Maritimos Ltda** H Dantas Comercio Navegacao e Industrias Ltda *Rio de Janeiro* *Brazil* Official number: 3813868320	**227** 68 -		**2008**-01 **H. Dantas Construcoes e Reparos Navais Ltda. — Aracaju** Loa 24.39 Br ex - Dght 3.250 Lbp - Br md 9.15 Dpth 4.35 Welded, 1 dk	**(B32A2ST) Tug**	**2 oil engines** reduction geared to sc. shafts driving 2 Directional propellers Total Power: 3,000kW (4,078hp) Caterpillar 3512B-HD 2 x Vee 4 Stroke 12 Cy. 170 x 215 each-1500kW (2039bhp) Caterpillar Inc-USA
8732532 *PS6772* -	**SN JAUA** **Sulnorte Servicos Maritimos Ltda** H Dantas Comercio Navegacao e Industrias Ltda *Rio de Janeiro* *Brazil* Official number: 3810512877	**227** 68 -		**2004**-01 **Detroit Brasil Ltda — Itajai** Loa 24.39 Br ex - Dght 3.250 Lbp - Br md 9.15 Dpth 4.04 Welded, 1 dk	**(B32A2ST) Tug**	**2 oil engines** reduction geared to sc. shafts driving 2 Directional propellers Total Power: 2,080kW (2,828hp) Volvo Penta D49 2 x Vee 4 Stroke 12 Cy. 170 x 180 each-1040kW (1414bhp) AB Volvo Penta-Sweden
8732647 - -	**SN OIAPOQUE** **Sulnorte Servicos Maritimos Ltda** H Dantas Comercio Navegacao e Industrias Ltda *Rio de Janeiro* *Brazil* Official number: 3810517992	**227** 68 -		**2006**-01 **H. Dantas Construcoes e Reparos Navais Ltda. — Aracaju** Yd No: 594 Loa 24.39 Br ex - Dght 3.250 Lbp - Br md 9.15 Dpth 4.35 Welded, 1 dk	**(B32A2ST) Tug**	**2 oil engines** reduction geared to sc. shafts driving 2 Directional propellers Total Power: 3,000kW (4,078hp) Caterpillar 3512B-HD 2 x Vee 4 Stroke 12 Cy. 170 x 215 each-1500kW (2039bhp) Caterpillar Inc-USA

9437983 *IBKC* -	**SN OLIVIA** *ex* D. T. Vincenzo P. *-2011* **Scerni di Navigazione Srl** - SatCom: Inmarsat C 424702879 *Genoa* *Italy* MMSI: 247283800	**60,193** 33,762 109,005 T/cm 91.3	Class: RI (AB)	**2010**-01 **Hudong-Zhonghua Shipbuilding (Group) Co Ltd — Shanghai** Yd No: H1545A Loa 243.00 (BB) Br ex 42.03 Dght 15.350 Lbp 233.00 Br md 42.00 Dpth 22.00 Welded, 1 dk	**(A13A2TV) Crude Oil Tanker** Double Hull (13F) Liq: 123,030; Liq (Oil): 103,056 Cargo Heating Coils Compartments: 12 Wing Ta, 2 Wing Slop Ta, ER 3 Cargo Pump (s): 3x2500m³/hr Manifold: Bow/CM: 118.5m	**1 oil engine** driving 1 FP propeller Total Power: 13,570kW (18,450hp) 14.7kn MAN-B&W 7S60MC 1 x 2 Stroke 7 Cy. 600 x 2292 13570kW (18450bhp) Hudong Heavy Machinery Co Ltd-China AuxGen: 3 x 720kW a.c Fuel: 125.0 (d.f.) 2700.0 (r.f.)
8732594 *PR2255* -	**SN PALMARES** *ex* Palmares *-2010* **Sulnorte Servicos Maritimos Ltda** H Dantas Comercio Navegacao e Industrias Ltda *Rio de Janeiro* *Brazil* MMSI: 710002550 Official number: 2810244901	**349** 104 -		**1992**-12 Loa 29.95 Br ex - Dght 3.300 Lbp - Br md 11.58 Dpth 4.57 Welded, 1 dk	**(B32A2ST) Tug**	**2 oil engines** geared to sc. shafts driving 2 Propellers Total Power: 1,824kW (2,480hp) Caterpillar D399 2 x Vee 4 Stroke 16 Cy. 159 x 203 each-912kW (1240bhp) Caterpillar Inc-USA
9197179 *3FPI9* -	**SN QUEEN** *ex* Bright 1 *-2009* *ex* Bright Star *-2009* *ex* Colima Star *-2008* *ex* Sun Breeze *-2007* **MK Maritime SA** Seanet Shipping Co Ltd *Panama* *Panama* MMSI: 371157000 Official number: 4020009A	**7,816** 3,670 11,478	Class: KR (NK)	**1999**-02 **K.K. Miura Zosensho — Saiki** Yd No: 1216 Loa 109.30 (BB) Br ex - Dght 9.264 Lbp 99.80 Br md 19.80 Dpth 13.80 Welded, 1 dk	**(A31A2GX) General Cargo Ship** Grain: 15,655; Bale: 14,812 Compartments: 2 Ho, ER 2 Ha: 2 (26.3 x 15.4)ER Cranes: 2x30.7t; Derricks: 2x30t	**1 oil engine** driving 1 FP propeller Total Power: 3,965kW (5,391hp) 13.5kn Mitsubishi 7UEC33LSII 1 x 2 Stroke 7 Cy. 330 x 1050 3965kW (5391bhp) Akasaka Tekkosho KK (Akasaka DieselLtd)-Japan
8816821 *CUEN* -	**SNABMAR** **Sociedade Nacional dos Armadores de Pesca SA (SNAB)** Sociedade de Pesca do Miradouro Lda SatCom: Inmarsat C 426351510 *Lisbon* *Portugal* MMSI: 263515000	*184* 72 110	Class: (LR) ✠ Classed LR until 23/1/96	**1989**-07 **Polyships S.A. — Vigo** Yd No: 90017 Loa 28.50 Br ex 8.25 Dght 3.100 Lbp 23.60 Br md 8.00 Dpth 4.20 Bonded, 1 dk	**(B11A2FT) Trawler** Hull Material: Reinforced Plastic	**1 oil engine** with clutches, flexible couplings & sr geared to sc. shaft driving 1 CP propeller Total Power: 570kW (775hp) 10.0kn Caterpillar 3508TA 1 x Vee 4 Stroke 8 Cy. 170 x 190 570kW (775bhp) Caterpillar Inc-USA AuxGen: 1 x 128kW 380V 50Hz a.c, 1 x 128kW 380V 50Hz a.c
9021643 *CUEU* LX-87-N	**SNABPESCA** **Sociedade Nacional dos Armadores de Pesca SA (SNAB)** Sociedade de Pesca do Miradouro Lda SatCom: Inmarsat C 426351910 *Lisbon* *Portugal* MMSI: 263519000	**217** 65 116	Class: (LR) ✠ Classed LR until 31/10/95	**1991**-07 **Polyships S.A. — Vigo** Yd No: 90018 Loa 28.90 Br ex 8.25 Dght 3.100 Lbp 23.60 Br md 8.00 Dpth 4.20 Bonded, 1 dk	**(B11A2FT) Trawler** Hull Material: Reinforced Plastic Ins: 138	**1 oil engine** with clutches, flexible couplings & sr geared to sc. shaft driving 1 CP propeller Total Power: 519kW (706hp) 10.0kn Caterpillar 3508TA 1 x Vee 4 Stroke 8 Cy. 170 x 190 519kW (706bhp) Caterpillar Inc-USA AuxGen: 1 x 128kW 380V 50Hz a.c, 1 x 128kW 380V 50Hz a.c
8704913 *UBCI6* -	**SNABZHENETS** *ex* Kilstraum *-2011* **'Supplier' Co Ltd (OOO Snabzhenets)** *Nakhodka* *Russia* MMSI: 273357840	**2,894** 1,397 4,618 T/cm 11.2	Class: RS (GL) (NV)	**1988**-03 **Aukra Industrier AS — Aukra** Yd No: 80 Conv to DH-2009 Loa 85.70 (BB) Br ex 15.30 Dght 6.690 Lbp 80.40 Br md 15.20 Dpth 8.80 Welded, 1 dk	**(A12B2TR) Chemical/Products Tanker** Double Hull (13F) Liq: 4,994; Liq (Oil): 5,096 Cargo Heating Coils Compartments: 18 Wing Ta (s.stl), ER 18 Cargo Pump (s): 18x175m³/hr Manifold: Bow/CM: 42.5m Ice Capable	**1 oil engine** with flexible couplings & sr gearedto sc. shaft driving 1 CP propeller Total Power: 2,205kW (2,998hp) 12.5kn Wartsila 6R32 1 x 4 Stroke 6 Cy. 320 x 350 2205kW (2998bhp) Wartsila Diesel Oy-Finland AuxGen: 1 x 671kW 440V 60Hz a.c, 3 x 230kW 440V 60Hz a.c Thrusters: 1 Tunnel thruster (f) Fuel: 50.0 (d.f.) 237.0 (r.f.) 10.0pd
8930782 - -	**SNABZHENETS** **MASCO JSC (ZAO 'Malaya Sudokhodnaya Kompaniya')** - *Murmansk* *Russia* Official number: 740269	**212** 74 145	Class: RS (Class contemplated)	**1975**-05 **Kanonerskiy Sudoremontnyy Zavod — Leningrad** Yd No: 3 Loa 36.12 Br ex 7.40 Dght 2.000 Lbp 32.50 Br md 7.30 Dpth 3.10 Welded, 1 dk	**(A34A2GR) Refrigerated Cargo Ship** Ins: 199 Compartments: 2 Ho 2 Ha: (3.0 x 2.5) (3.0 x 2.0) Cranes: 1x3t Ice Capable	**1 oil engine** geared to sc. shaft driving 1 FP propeller Total Power: 165kW (224hp) 9.0kn Daldizel 6CHNSP18/22 1 x 4 Stroke 6 Cy. 180 x 220 165kW (224bhp) Daldizel-Khabarovsk AuxGen: 3 x 30kW a.c Fuel: 7.0 (d.f.)
8930794 *UHFY* -	**SNABZHENETS-1** **Vostok Trans Ltd** - *Petropavlovsk-Kamchatskiy* *Russia* Official number: 792193	**208** 63 144	Class: RS	**1979**-10 **Kanonerskiy Sudoremontnyy Zavod — Leningrad** Yd No: 12 Loa 36.12 Br ex 7.40 Dght 2.000 Lbp 32.50 Br md 7.30 Dpth 3.10 Welded, 1 dk	**(A34A2GR) Refrigerated Cargo Ship** Ins: 201 Compartments: 2 Ho Cranes: 1x3t Ice Capable	**1 oil engine** geared to sc. shaft driving 1 FP propeller Total Power: 165kW (224hp) 9.0kn Daldizel 6CHNSP18/22 1 x 4 Stroke 6 Cy. 180 x 220 165kW (224bhp) Daldizel-Khabarovsk AuxGen: 3 x 30kW a.c Fuel: 6.0 (d.f.)
8930811 *UCFA* -	**SNABZHENETS-8** **OOO 'Vit Co Ltd'** - *Nakhodka* *Russia*	**258** 100 116	Class: RS	**1977**-07 **Kanonerskiy Sudoremontnyy Zavod — Leningrad** Yd No: 8 Loa 36.12 Br ex 7.40 Dght 2.000 Lbp 32.50 Br md 7.38 Dpth 3.10 Welded, 1 dk	**(A34A2GR) Refrigerated Cargo Ship** Ins: 199 Compartments: 2 Ho 2 Ha: (3.0 x 2.5) (3.0 x 2.0) Cranes: 1x3.2t Ice Capable	**1 oil engine** driving 1 FP propeller Total Power: 157kW (213hp) 9.0kn Daldizel 6CHNSP18/22 1 x 4 Stroke 6 Cy. 180 x 220 157kW (213bhp) (new engine 1994) Daldizel-Khabarovsk AuxGen: 2 x 30kW a.c Fuel: 7.0 (d.f.)
8220515 - -	**SNAEFARI** *ex* Bjarnarey *-1995* *ex* Gideon *-1992* **Agropesca SA** - *Paita* *Peru* Official number: PT-12295-PT	*221* 76 155	Class: (LR) ✠ Classed LR until 6/9/00	**1984**-03 **Stocznia Polnocna im Bohaterow Westerplatte — Gdansk** Yd No: B277/01 Loa 32.95 (BB) Br ex 8.41 Dght 3.831 Lbp 29.09 Br md 8.03 Dpth 6.33 Welded, 2 dks	**(B11A2FS) Stern Trawler** Ins: 209 Compartments: 1 Ho, ER 1 Ha: ER Ice Capable	**1 oil engine** with clutches, flexible couplings & sr geared to sc. shaft driving 1 CP propeller Total Power: 618kW (840hp) Sulzer 6AL20/24 1 x 4 Stroke 6 Cy. 200 x 240 618kW (840bhp) Zaklady Przemyslu Metalowego 'HCegielski' SA-Poznan AuxGen: 1 x 100kW 440V 50Hz a.c, 1 x 80kW 440V 50Hz a.c Fuel: 42.5 (d.f.)
6828923 *TFBY* EA 110	**SNAEFELL** *ex* Akureyrin *-2009* *ex* Slettbakur *-2002* *ex* Stella Kristina *-1973* **Samherji hf** - SatCom: Inmarsat C 425107910 *Akureyri* *Iceland* MMSI: 251079000 Official number: 1351	**1,319** 393 712	Class: NV	**1968**-10 **Soviknes Verft AS — Sovik** Yd No: 70 Converted From: Stern Trawler-1987 Loa 69.75 (BB) Br ex 10.24 Dght 4.973 Lbp 62.34 Br md 10.20 Dpth 7.01 Welded, 2 dks	**(B11A2FG) Factory Stern Trawler** Ins: 956 Compartments: 2 Ho, ER 2 Ha: (2.9 x 1.9) (3.5 x 2.9)ER Derricks: 2x1t Ice Capable	**1 oil engine** reduction geared to sc. shaft driving 1 CP propeller Total Power: 2,207kW (3,001hp) 14.0kn Normo BRM-6 1 x 4 Stroke 6 Cy. 320 x 360 2207kW (3001bhp) (new engine 1987) AS Bergens Mek Verksteder-Norway AuxGen: 1 x 380V 50Hz a.c, 1 x 380V 50Hz a.c Fuel: 20.0 (d.f.) 280.0 (r.f.) 6.0pd
7739064 - -	**SNAIL** *ex* Camaron 4 *-1984* *ex* Rama Cay *-1979* - -	*117* 87 -		**1977 Pacsa — El Bluff** L reg 22.56 Br ex - Dght - Lbp - Br md 6.71 Dpth 2.29 Bonded, 1 dk	**(B11A2FS) Stern Trawler** Hull Material: Reinforced Plastic	**1 oil engine** driving 1 FP propeller Total Power: 268kW (364hp) 10.0kn Caterpillar 3408TA 1 x Vee 4 Stroke 8 Cy. 137 x 152 268kW (364bhp) Caterpillar Tractor Co-USA
7533771 *XUAK4* -	**SNAKE** *ex* Albacore *-2009* *ex* Barkhatovo *-2004* **Furin LLC** - *Phnom Penh* *Cambodia* MMSI: 514345000 Official number: 0975392	**165** 49 88	Class: (RS)	**1975 Zavod 'Nikolayevsk-na-Amure' — Nikolayevsk-na-Amure** Yd No: 124 Loa 33.96 Br ex 7.09 Dght 2.899 Lbp 30.13 Br md 7.00 Dpth 3.69 Welded, 1 dk	**(B11B2FV) Fishing Vessel** Bale: 115 Compartments: 1 Ho, ER 1 Ha: (1.6 x 1.3) Derricks: 2x2t; Winches: 2 Ice Capable	**1 oil engine** driving 1 FP propeller Total Power: 224kW (305hp) 9.5kn S.K.L. 8NVD36-1U 1 x 4 Stroke 8 Cy. 240 x 360 224kW (305bhp) VEB Schwermaschinenbau "KarlLiebknecht" (SKL)-Magdeburg
9026150 *XCCL1* -	**SNAKE RIVER** *ex* C/Plunderer *-2004* **Corporativo de Arrendamiento y Fondeo SAPI de CV SOFOM ENR (CAF)** Consultoria y Servicios Petroleros SA de CV (CSP) *Ciudad del Carmen* *Mexico* MMSI: 345070140	**164** 49 164	Class: RI	**1980**-01 **Swiftships Inc — Morgan City LA** Yd No: 229 Loa 36.02 Br ex - Dght 1.820 Lbp 33.30 Br md 7.32 Dpth 2.96 Welded, 1 dk	**(B34J2SD) Crew Boat** Hull Material: Aluminium Alloy	**4 oil engines** reduction geared to sc. shafts driving 4 FP propellers Total Power: 1,640kW (2,228hp) 18.0kn G.M. (Detroit Diesel) 12V-71-TI 4 x Vee 2 Stroke 12 Cy. 108 x 127 each-410kW (557bhp) General Motors Detroit DieselAllison Divn-USA AuxGen: 2 x 30kW a.c
8853556 *DUA2559* -	**SNAPPER** **Malayan Towage & Salvage Corp (SALVTUG)** - *Manila* *Philippines* Official number: MNLD007631	*145* 99 -		**1945 Platzer Boat Works — Houston, Tx** Loa - Br ex - Dght - Lbp 28.65 Br md 7.59 Dpth 3.38 Welded, 1 dk	**(B32A2ST) Tug**	**1 oil engine** driving 1 FP propeller

IMO / Call sign	Name / Owner / Port / Flag	Tonnage	Class	Builder / Dimensions	Type	Machinery
8008151 *9YCAJ* -	**SNAPPER** **Bristol Marine Consultants Inc** - *Port of Spain* *Trinidad & Tobago*	**269** 80 -	Class: (LR) ✠ Classed LR until 29/9/12	**1981**-03 **B.V. Scheepswerven v/h H.H. Bodewes — Millingen a/d Rijn** Yd No: 757 Loa 31.12 Br ex 9.61 Dght 3.218 Lbp 28.00 Br md 9.50 Dpth 4.60 Welded, 1 dk	**(B32A2ST) Tug**	**2 oil engines** reverse reduction geared to sc. shafts driving 2 FP propellers Total Power: 2,400kW (3,264hp) MaK 6M332AK 2 x 4 Stroke 6 Cy. 240 x 330 each-1200kW (1632bhp) Krupp MaK Maschinenbau GmbH-Kiel AuxGen: 2 x 90kW 240/415V 60Hz a.c, 1 x 10kW 240/415V 60Hz a.c
8500862 *YJSV4* -	**SNAPPER** *ex* Geco Snapper *-2010* *ex* Arctic Ivik *-1997* **Offshore Service Vessels LLC** Edison Chouest Offshore International Ltd *Port Vila* *Vanuatu* MMSI: 576842000 Official number: 1478	**2,526** 757 1,475	Class: LR ✠ **100A1** SS 07/2011 seismic survey vessel Ice Class 1 CASPPR - Ice Class 2 ✠ **LMC** Eq.Ltr: P; Cable: 440.0/38.0 U3	**1985**-07 **Allied Shipbuilders Ltd — North Vancouver BC** Yd No: 243 Converted From: Offshore Tug/Supply Ship-1997 Loa 68.41 Br ex 14.46 Dght 4.879 Lbp 62.13 Br md 14.00 Dpth 5.80 Welded, 1 dk	**(B31A2SR) Research Survey Vessel** Ice Capable	**2 oil engines** with clutches, flexible couplings & sr geared to sc. shafts driving 2 CP propellers Total Power: 5,040kW (6,852hp) 15.0kn Alpha 12U28L-VO 2 x Vee 4 Stroke 12 Cy. 280 x 320 each-2520kW (3426bhp) MAN B&W Diesel A/S-Denmark AuxGen: 1 x 430kW 460V 60Hz a.c, 1 x 300kW 460V 60Hz a.c Thrusters: 1 Thwart. CP thruster (f); 1 Tunnel thruster (a) Fuel: 748.5 (d.f.) 24.0pd
6605345 *HO4012* -	**SNARSUND** *ex* Naseer I *-2009* *ex* Nour Al Abdallah *-2007* *ex* Ebla I *-2003* *ex* Voline *-1995* *ex* Mirna *-1992* *ex* Karterados II *-1992* *ex* Alexfay II *-1987* *ex* Nordhafen *-1983* *ex* Snarsund *-1975* *ex* Kai *-1974* **Emad Abdul Zahra El Ghadban** - *Panama* *Panama* MMSI: 352660000 Official number: 03629PEXT2	*1,199* 837 2,300	Class: (GL)	**1965**-07 **Gebr. Schuerenstedt KG Schiffs- u. Bootswerft — Berne** Yd No: 1307 Loa 73.61 Br ex 11.61 Dght 5.279 Lbp 67.11 Br md 11.51 Dpth 6.30 Welded, 2 dks	**(A31A2GX) General Cargo Ship** Grain: 3,024; Bale: 2,723 Compartments: 1 Ho, ER 2 Ha: 2 (16.7 x 7.0)ER Derricks: 2x5t,2x3t; Winches: 4 Ice Capable	**1 oil engine** driving 1 FP propeller Total Power: 1,030kW (1,400hp) 12.0kn MaK 8M451AK 1 x 4 Stroke 8 Cy. 320 x 450 1030kW (1400bhp) Maschinenbau Kiel AG (MaK)-Kiel AuxGen: 3 x 42kW 380V Fuel: 84.5 (d.f.) 5.0pd
9358747 *LNQE* -	**SNARVEIEN** **Bergen-Nordhordaland Rutelag AS** - *Bergen* *Norway* MMSI: 259280000	**232** 81 22		**2005**-07 **Oma Baatbyggeri AS — Stord** Yd No: 521 Loa 25.96 Br ex - Dght - Lbp 25.55 Br md 9.00 Dpth 3.39 Welded, 1 dk	**(A37B2PS) Passenger Ship** Hull Material: Aluminium Alloy Passengers: unberthed: 181	**2 oil engines** reduction geared to sc. shafts driving 2 CP propellers Total Power: 1,100kW (1,496hp) Scania DI16 M 2 x Vee 4 Stroke 8 Cy. 127 x 154 each-550kW (748bhp) Scania AB-Sweden
8416308 *IBEA* -	**SNAV ADRIATICO** *ex* Stena Baltica *-2013* *ex* Koningin Beatrix *-2002* **Snav SpA** - *Naples* *Italy* MMSI: 247334600	**31,910** 13,080 4,456	Class: GL (Class contemplated) (LR) (NV) Classed LR until 6/12/13	**1986**-04 **van der Giessen-de Noord BV — Krimpen a/d IJssel** Yd No: 935 Lengthened-2005 Loa 164.41 (BB) Br ex - Dght 6.300 Lbp 146.77 Br md 27.61 Dpth 18.52 Welded	**(A36A2PR) Passenger/Ro-Ro Ship (Vehicles)** Passengers: 1200; unberthed: 145; cabins: 379; berths: 949 Bow door & ramp (centre) Len: 14.00 Wid: 6.00 Swl: - Stern door/ramp (p) Len: 11.50 Wid: 4.85 Swl: - Stern door/ramp (s) Len: 11.50 Wid: 4.85 Swl: - Lane-Len: 1850 Lane-clr ht: 4.35 Cars: 466	**4 oil engines** with clutches, flexible couplings & reduction geared to sc. shafts driving 2 CP propellers Total Power: 19,360kW (26,320hp) 19.5kn MAN 8L40/45 4 x 4 Stroke 8 Cy. 400 x 450 each-4840kW (6580bhp) MAN B&W Diesel GmbH-Augsburg AuxGen: 4 x 900kW 450V 60Hz a.c Boilers: WTAuxB (o.f.) Thrusters: 2 Thwart. CP thruster (f)
9038957 *IRXA* -	**SNAV ALCIONE** *ex* Alcione Primo *-1997* *ex* Alcione *-1991* **Snav SpA** - *Naples* *Italy* MMSI: 247058700 Official number: 1811	**570** 189 100	Class: RI (NV)	**1991**-05 **Kvaerner Fjellstrand AS — Omastrand** Yd No: 1605 Loa 40.20 Br ex - Dght 1.690 Lbp - Br md 10.10 Dpth 3.92 Welded, 1 dk	**(A37B2PS) Passenger Ship** Hull Material: Aluminium Alloy Passengers: unberthed: 352	**2 oil engines** geared to sc. shafts driving 2 Water jets Total Power: 3,758kW (5,110hp) M.T.U. 16V396TE74 2 x Vee 4 Stroke 16 Cy. 165 x 185 each-1879kW (2555bhp) MTU Friedrichshafen GmbH-Friedrichshafen
9048718 *IKVW* -	**SNAV ALDEBARAN** *ex* Viking Express II *-1996* *ex* Orca Spirit *-1995* **Ustica Lines SpA** - *Naples* *Italy* MMSI: 247036700 Official number: 1975	**522** 171 100	Class: RI (BV) (NV)	**1992**-01 **Kvaerner Fjellstrand AS — Omastrand** Yd No: 1610 Loa 40.20 Br ex - Dght 1.609 Lbp 36.00 Br md 10.10 Dpth 3.97 Welded	**(A37B2PS) Passenger Ship** Passengers: unberthed: 296	**2 oil engines** geared to sc. shafts driving 2 Water jets Total Power: 3,998kW (5,436hp) M.T.U. 16V396TE74L 2 x Vee 4 Stroke 16 Cy. 165 x 185 each-1999kW (2718bhp) MTU Friedrichshafen GmbH-Friedrichshafen AuxGen: 2 x 68kW 380V 50Hz a.c
8911865 *IINS* -	**SNAV ALTAIR** *ex* Sirius *-1996* **Snav SpA** - *Naples* *Italy* MMSI: 247058800 Official number: 1957	**494** 170 31	Class: RI (RS)	**1990**-08 **AB Nya Oskarshamns Varv — Oskarshamn (Hull)** Yd No: 525 **1990**-08 **Westamarin AS — Mandal** Yd No: 106 Loa 41.00 Br ex - Dght 1.590 Lbp - Br md 10.00 Dpth 4.07 Welded, 1 dk	**(A37B2PS) Passenger Ship** Hull Material: Aluminium Alloy Passengers: unberthed: 292	**2 oil engines** geared to sc. shafts driving 2 FP propellers Total Power: 4,080kW (5,548hp) 33.0kn M.T.U. 16V396TB84 2 x Vee 4 Stroke 16 Cy. 165 x 185 each-2040kW (2774bhp) MTU Friedrichshafen GmbH-Friedrichshafen AuxGen: 2 x 64kW a.c
8708402 *IZAU* -	**SNAV ANDROMEDA** *ex* Pilen 3 *-2001* *ex* Vindile *-1990* **Snav SpA** - *Naples* *Italy* MMSI: 247037900 Official number: 2060	**332** 121 50	Class: RI (NV)	**1988**-05 **AB Nya Oskarshamns Varv — Oskarshamn** Yd No: 510 Loa 37.01 Br ex 9.81 Dght 1.701 Lbp 31.09 Br md 9.50 Dpth 3.67 Welded, 1 dk	**(A37B2PS) Passenger Ship** Hull Material: Aluminium Alloy Passengers: unberthed: 332	**2 oil engines** with flexible couplings & sr gearedto sc. shaft driving 2 Water jets Total Power: 4,080kW (5,548hp) 40.5kn M.T.U. 16V396TB84 2 x Vee 4 Stroke 16 Cy. 165 x 185 each-2040kW (2774bhp) MTU Friedrichshafen GmbH-Friedrichshafen AuxGen: 2 x 56kW 220V 50Hz a.c
8911853 *IINQ* -	**SNAV ANTARES** *ex* Irbis *-1996* **Snav SpA** - *Naples* *Italy* MMSI: 247058900 Official number: 1958	**493** 170 31	Class: RI (RS)	**1990**-08 **AB Nya Oskarshamns Varv — Oskarshamn (Hull)** Yd No: 524 **1990**-08 **Westamarin AS — Mandal** Yd No: 105 Loa 41.00 Br ex - Dght 1.590 Lbp 37.20 Br md 10.00 Dpth 4.07 Welded, 1 dk	**(A37B2PS) Passenger Ship** Hull Material: Aluminium Alloy Passengers: unberthed: 292	**2 oil engines** geared to sc. shafts driving 2 FP propellers Total Power: 4,080kW (5,548hp) 33.0kn M.T.U. 16V396TB84 2 x Vee 4 Stroke 16 Cy. 165 x 185 each-2040kW (2774bhp) MTU Friedrichshafen GmbH-Friedrichshafen AuxGen: 2 x 64kW a.c
9008809 *ITYJ* -	**SNAV AQUARIUS** *ex* Springaren *-2001* **Ustica Lines SpA** - *Naples* *Italy* MMSI: 247029300	**442** 156 50	Class: RI (BV) (NV)	**1991**-06 **Kvaerner Fjellstrand AS — Omastrand** Yd No: 1608 Loa 38.80 Br ex - Dght 1.590 Lbp 36.50 Br md 9.44 Dpth 3.96 Welded, 1 dk	**(A37B2PS) Passenger Ship** Passengers: unberthed: 255	**2 oil engines** sr geared to sc. shafts driving 2 Water jets Total Power: 3,998kW (5,436hp) 33.0kn M.T.U. 16V396TE74 2 x Vee 4 Stroke 16 Cy. 165 x 185 each-1999kW (2718bhp) MTU Friedrichshafen GmbH-Friedrichshafen AuxGen: 2 x 64kW 380V 50Hz a.c
9059171 *IJCM2* -	**SNAV AQUILA** *ex* Benchi Express *-2012* *ex* SNAV Aquila *-2009* *ex* Saelen *-2002* **Marinvest Srl** Fred Olsen SA *Naples* *Italy* MMSI: 247318800	**490** 158 100	Class: RI (NV)	**1993**-05 **Kvaerner Fjellstrand AS — Omastrand** Yd No: 1613 Loa 40.20 Br ex - Dght 1.870 Lbp 36.00 Br md 10.10 Dpth 3.92 Welded	**(A37B2PS) Passenger Ship** Hull Material: Aluminium Alloy Passengers: unberthed: 288	**2 oil engines** reduction geared to sc. shafts driving 2 Water jets Total Power: 3,998kW (5,436hp) 34.0kn M.T.U. 16V396TE74L 2 x Vee 4 Stroke 16 Cy. 165 x 185 each-1999kW (2718bhp) MTU Friedrichshafen GmbH-Friedrichshafen AuxGen: 2 x 68kW 380V 50Hz a.c Fuel: 10.4 (d.f.)
8807492 *IFEB* -	**SNAV ARIES** *ex* Waterways 1 *-2000* *ex* Condor 8 *-1997* **Snav SpA** - *Naples* *Italy* MMSI: 247058600 Official number: 2048	**324** 119 31	Class: RI (NV)	**1988**-04 **Fairey Marinteknik Shipbuilders (S) Pte Ltd — Singapore** Yd No: 115 Loa 36.33 Br ex 9.43 Dght 1.405 Lbp 30.76 Br md 9.40 Dpth 3.46 Welded, 1 dk	**(A37B2PS) Passenger Ship** Hull Material: Aluminium Alloy Passengers: unberthed: 300	**2 oil engines** with clutches & sr geared to sc. shafts driving 2 Water jets Total Power: 3,880kW (5,276hp) 35.0kn M.T.U. 16V396TB84 2 x Vee 4 Stroke 16 Cy. 165 x 185 each-1940kW (2638bhp) MTU Friedrichshafen GmbH-Friedrichshafen AuxGen: 2 x 39kW 380V 50Hz a.c Fuel: 6.1 (d.f.)
8911360 *IZJS* -	**SNAV AURORA** *ex* Svalan *-2002* *ex* Merkuriy *-1995* **Snav SpA** - *Naples* *Italy* MMSI: 247066100 Official number: 2076	**424** 142 29	Class: (RI) (NV) (RS)	**1990**-04 **Kvaerner Fjellstrand AS — Omastrand** Yd No: 1598 Loa 38.80 Br ex - Dght 1.590 Lbp 36.00 Br md 9.44 Dpth 3.92 Welded, 1 dk	**(A37B2PS) Passenger Ship** Passengers: unberthed: 286	**2 oil engines** sr geared to sc. shafts driving 2 Water jets Total Power: 4,080kW (5,548hp) 28.0kn M.T.U. 16V396TB84 2 x Vee 4 Stroke 16 Cy. 165 x 185 each-2040kW (2774bhp) MTU Friedrichshafen GmbH-Friedrichshafen AuxGen: 2 x 64kW 380V 50Hz a.c

IMO / Call sign	Name / Owner	Tonnage	Class	Builder / Dimensions	Type / Capacity	Machinery
8712520 *IBUH* -	**SNAV LAZIO** *ex* Pride of Portsmouth *-2005* *ex* Olau Britannia *-1994* **Snav SpA** - *Naples* *Italy* MMSI: 247163100 Official number: 517/SEZ. I	**33,336** 17,001 4,100	Class: RI (LR) (GL) **CCS** Classed LR until 26/4/06	**1990**-05 **Schichau Seebeckwerft AG — Bremerhaven** Yd No: 1068 Loa 161.00 (BB) Br ex 33.46 Dght 6.526 Lbp 144.00 Br md 29.00 Dpth 18.90 Welded, 4 dks	**(A36A2PR) Passenger/Ro-Ro Ship (Vehicles)** Passengers: unberthed: 391; cabins: 423; berths: 1414 Bow door & ramp (f) Len: 12.00 Wid: 6.00 Swl: - Stern door/ramp (p) Len: 6.30 Wid: 8.00 Swl: - Stern door/ramp (s) Len: 6.30 Wid: 8.00 Swl: - Lane-Len: 1440 Lane-Wid: 3.00 Lane-clr ht: 4.40 Cars: 538 Cargo Heating Coils Ice Capable	**4 oil engines** with clutches, flexible couplings & dr geared to sc. shafts driving 2 CP propellers Total Power: 19,600kW (26,648hp) 19.0kn Sulzer 8ZAL40S 4 x 4 Stroke 8 Cy. 400 x 560 each-4900kW (6662bhp) Zaklady Urzadzen Technicznych'Zgoda' SA-Poland AuxGen: 4 x 1890kW 660V 60Hz a.c, 1 x 532kW 660V 60Hz a.c Boilers: AuxB (o.f.) Thrusters: 2 Thwart. CP thruster (f) Fuel: 77.7 (d.f.) (Heating Coils) 897.6 (r.f.) 72.0pd
9305922 *IRBQ* -	**SNAV ORION** - **Marinvest Srl** Snav SpA *Naples* *Italy* MMSI: 247128500	**590** 233 50	Class: RI	**2005**-04 **Marinteknik Shipbuilders (S) Pte Ltd — Singapore** Yd No: 188 Loa 49.86 Br ex - Dght 1.340 Lbp 44.86 Br md 9.00 Dpth 3.37 Welded, 1 dk	**(A37B2PS) Passenger Ship** Hull Material: Aluminium Alloy Passengers: unberthed: 688	**4 oil engines** reduction geared to sc. shafts driving 4 Propellers Total Power: 7,884kW (10,720hp) M.T.U. 16V396TE74L 4 x Vee 4 Stroke 16 Cy. 165 x 185 each-1971kW (2680bhp) MTU Friedrichshafen GmbH-Friedrichshafen Thrusters: 2 Tunnel thruster (f)
8712518 *IBUB* -	**SNAV SARDEGNA** *ex* Pride of Le Havre *-2005* *ex* Olau Hollandia *-1994* **Snav SpA** - *Naples* *Italy* MMSI: 247163900 Official number: 516/1 SEZ	**33,336** 17,001 4,100	Class: RI (LR) (GL) Classed LR until 20/5/06	**1989**-09 **Schichau Seebeckwerft AG — Bremerhaven** Yd No: 1067 Loa 161.00 (BB) Br ex 33.40 Dght 6.526 Lbp 144.00 Br md 29.00 Dpth 18.93 Welded, 4 dks	**(A36A2PR) Passenger/Ro-Ro Ship (Vehicles)** Passengers: unberthed: 391; cabins: 411; berths: 1354 Bow door & ramp (f) Len: 12.00 Wid: 6.00 Swl: - Stern door/ramp (p) Len: 6.30 Wid: 8.00 Swl: - Stern door/ramp (s) Len: 6.30 Wid: 8.00 Swl: - Lane-Len: 1440 Lane-Wid: 3.00 Lane-clr ht: 4.40 Cars: 538 Cargo Heating Coils Ice Capable	**4 oil engines** with clutches, flexible couplings & dr geared to sc. shafts driving 2 CP propellers Total Power: 19,600kW (26,648hp) 19.0kn Sulzer 8ZAL40S 4 x 4 Stroke 8 Cy. 400 x 560 each-4900kW (6662bhp) (made 1988) Zaklady Urzadzen Technicznych'Zgoda' SA-Poland AuxGen: 4 x 1890kW 660V 60Hz a.c, 1 x 532kW 660V 60Hz a.c Boilers: AuxB (o.f.) Thrusters: 2 Thwart. CP thruster (f) Fuel: 77.7 (d.f.) (Heating Coils) 897.6 (r.f.) 72.0pd
7826790 *ICKK* -	**SNAV TOSCANA** *ex* Peter Wessel *-2008* *ex* Wasa Star *-1984* **Snav SpA** - *Naples* *Italy* MMSI: 247237700	**30,318** 16,956 3,630	Class: RI (NV)	**1981**-06 **Oresundsvarvet AB — Landskrona** Yd No: 279 Lengthened-1988 Loa 168.48 (BB) Br ex 24.52 Dght 5.711 Lbp 155.07 Br md 24.01 Dpth 16.57 Welded, 5 dks	**(A36A2PR) Passenger/Ro-Ro Ship (Vehicles)** Passengers: unberthed: 350; cabins: 530; berths: 1850 Bow door & ramp Len: 18.30 Wid: 8.00 Swl: - Stern door/ramp (p) Len: 14.40 Wid: 3.50 Swl: - Stern door/ramp (s) Len: 14.40 Wid: 3.50 Swl: - Stern door/ramp (centre) Len: 15.80 Wid: 10.50 Swl: - Lane-Len: 650 Lane-Wid: 2.50 Lane-clr ht: 4.60 Cars: 650, Trailers: 42 Ice Capable	**4 oil engines** sr geared to sc. shafts driving 2 CP propellers Total Power: 21,480kW (29,204hp) 19.0kn B&W 8K45GF 4 x 2 Stroke 8 Cy. 450 x 900 each-5370kW (7301bhp) AB Gotaverken-Sweden AuxGen: 2 x 1700kW 380V 50Hz a.c, 3 x 1660kW 380V 50Hz a.c Thrusters: 2 Thwart. FP thruster (f) Fuel: 89.0 (d.f.) 789.0 (r.f.) 77.0pd
9194098 *PHJN* -	**SNEEKERDIEP** *ex* Suono *-2012* *ex* Sneekerdiep *-2011* *ex* Callisto *-2002* **Beheermaatschappij ms Sneekerdiep II BV** Feederlines BV *Groningen* *Netherlands* MMSI: 244456000 Official number: 36288	**3,170** 1,876 4,537	Class: GL (BV)	**2000**-12 **Rousse Shipyard JSC — Rousse** Yd No: 407 Loa 98.94 Br ex - Dght 5.740 Lbp 92.75 Br md 13.80 Dpth 7.40 Welded, 1 dk	**(A31A2GX) General Cargo Ship** Grain: 6,255 TEU 282 C.Ho 162/20' (40') C.Dk 120/20' (40') Compartments: 2 Ho, ER 2 Ha: ER Ice Capable	**1 oil engine** with flexible couplings & reductiongeared to sc. shaft driving 1 CP propeller Total Power: 2,880kW (3,916hp) 13.5kn MaK 6M32 1 x 4 Stroke 6 Cy. 320 x 480 2880kW (3916bhp) MaK Motoren GmbH & Co. KG-Kiel AuxGen: 1 x 325kW 380V 50Hz a.c, 2 x 160kW 380V 50Hz a.c Thrusters: 1 Thwart. CP thruster (f) Fuel: 55.0 (d.f.) (Heating Coils) 250.0 (r.f.) 12.5pd
7644049 *UFLU* -	**SNEGIRYOVO** *ex* RS-300 No. 92 *-2002* **OOO Rybnaya Kompaniya 'Nord-Ost'** - *Petropavlovsk-Kamchatskiy* *Russia* Official number: 761246	**172** 51 88	Class: (RS)	**1977 Astrakhanskaya Sudoverf im. "Kirova" — Astrakhan** Yd No: 92 Loa 34.02 Br ex 7.12 Dght 2.874 Lbp 29.98 Br md 7.00 Dpth 3.71 Welded, 1 dk	**(B11B2FV) Fishing Vessel** Bale: 95 Compartments: 1 Ho, ER 1 Ha: (1.3 x 1.6) Derricks: 2x2t; Winches: 2 Ice Capable	**1 oil engine** driving 1 CP propeller Total Power: 224kW (305hp) 9.5kn S.K.L. 8NVD36-1U 1 x 4 Stroke 8 Cy. 240 x 360 224kW (305bhp) VEB Schwermaschinenbau "KarlLiebknecht" (SKL)-Magdeburg Fuel: 22.0 (d.f.)
5332628 - -	**SNEKKAR** - **Argenpez SA** - -	*413* 133 340	Class: (LR) (BV) ✠ Classed LR until 7/69	**1961**-08 **Stocznia Polnocna (Northern Shipyard) — Gdansk** Yd No: B21/10 Loa 47.76 Br ex 8.41 Dght 3.798 Lbp 43.77 Br md 8.31 Dpth 4.70 Riveted\Welded	**(B11A2FT) Trawler** Ins: 334	**1 oil engine** driving 1 CP propeller Total Power: 1,015kW (1,380hp) 14.0kn MAN G7V40/60 1 x 4 Stroke 7 Cy. 400 x 600 1015kW (1380bhp) Maschinenbau Augsburg Nuernberg (MAN)-Augsburg AuxGen: 2 x 40kW 110V Fuel: 112.0 (d.f.)
8732788 - -	**SNELLIUS** - **HHC Malta Ltd** -	**1,500** - -	Class: (RI)	**1952**-02 **Machinefabriek en Scheepswerf van P. Smit Jr. N.V. — Rotterdam** Yd No: 595 Converted From: Research Vessel-2008 Loa 71.40 Br ex 10.82 Dght 2.130 Lbp 65.00 Br md 10.80 Dpth 6.35 Welded, 1 dk	**(A37A2PC) Passenger/Cruise**	**2 oil engines** driving 2 FP propellers Total Power: 1,472kW (2,002hp) 0.2kn Stork 2 x each-736kW (1001bhp) Koninklijke Machinefabriek GebrStork & Co NV-Netherlands
7029641 *UEEP* -	**SNEZHKA** *ex* Sniezka *-2007* - - *Russia* MMSI: 273442390	**545** 172 616	Class: (PR)	**1970 Stocznia 'Wisla' — Gdansk** Yd No: ZW1/01 Converted From: Water Tanker-1997 Loa 57.61 Br ex 9.45 Dght 3.020 Lbp 54.02 Br md 9.02 Dpth 3.76 Welded, 1 dk	**(B34E2SW) Waste Disposal Vessel** Compartments: 4 Ta, ER 2 Cargo Pump (s): 2x150m³/hr Manifold: Bow/CM: 32m Ice Capable	**1 oil engine** reverse reduction geared to sc. shaft driving 1 CP propeller Total Power: 294kW (400hp) 8.5kn Sulzer 8BAH22 1 x 2 Stroke 8 Cy. 220 x 320 294kW (400bhp) Zaklady Przemyslu Metalowego 'HCegielski' SA-Poznan AuxGen: 3 x 80kW 400V a.c Fuel: 18.5 (d.f.) 2.5pd
8111740 *IIPO2* -	**SNIPE** *ex* Seabulk Snipe *-2008* *ex* Red Snipe *-2001* **Micoperi Srl** Leadership Management & Services SatCom: Inmarsat C 424702488 *Ravenna* *Italy* MMSI: 247256900 Official number: 34	**958** 287 1,148	Class: RI (BV) (GL)	**1982**-08 **JG Hitzler Schiffswerft und Masch GmbH & Co KG — Lauenburg** Yd No: 772 Loa 60.00 Br ex 13.34 Dght 4.250 Lbp 54.36 Br md 13.01 Dpth 4.91 Welded, 1 dk	**(B21B20A) Anchor Handling Tug Supply** Grain: 170; Bale: 145	**2 oil engines** sr geared to sc. shafts driving 2 CP propellers Total Power: 3,236kW (4,400hp) MaK 6M453AK 2 x 4 Stroke 6 Cy. 320 x 420 each-1618kW (2200bhp) Krupp MaK Maschinenbau GmbH-Kiel AuxGen: 2 x 200kW 230/400V 50Hz a.c, 1 x 100kW 230/400V 50Hz a.c Thrusters: 1 Thwart. CP thruster (f) Fuel: 563.5 (d.f.)
9466166 *DSQB7* -	**SNK LADY** - **DaeHo Shipping Co Ltd** Kumjin Shipping Co Ltd *Jeju* *South Korea* MMSI: 441520000 Official number: JJR-088666	**2,091** 901 3,606	Class: KR (NK)	**2008**-03 **Nantong Yahua Shipbuilding Co Ltd — Nantong JS** Yd No: LC-716 Loa 84.90 Br ex - Dght 5.900 Lbp 79.02 Br md 13.00 Dpth 7.50 Welded, 1 dk	**(A31A2GX) General Cargo Ship** Bale: 3,118 Compartments: 1 Ho, ER 1 Ha: ER (45.0 x 10.0)	**1 oil engine** driving 1 FP propeller Total Power: 1,618kW (2,200hp) 12.9kn Niigata 6M34BT 1 x 4 Stroke 6 Cy. 340 x 620 1618kW (2200bhp) Niigata Engineering Co Ltd-Japan AuxGen: 3 x 144kW 445V a.c

9466178 *3ERE6* -	**SNK LUCKY** **Phoenix Line Corp SA** Kumjin Shipping Co Ltd SatCom: Inmarsat C 437002210 *Panama* *Panama* MMSI: 370022000 Official number: 3393008A	**2,086** 895 3,609	Class: KR (NK)	**2008-05 Nantong Yahua Shipbuilding Co Ltd — Nantong JS** Yd No: LC-717 Loa 84.90 Br ex - Dght 5.901 Lbp 79.02 Br md 13.00 Dpth 7.50 Welded, 1 dk	**(A31A2GX) General Cargo Ship** Bale: 3,118 Compartments: 1 Ho, ER 1 Ha: ER (45.0 x 10.0)	**1 oil engine** driving 1 FP propeller Total Power: 1,618kW (2,200hp) 12.5kn Niigata 6M34BFT 1 x 4 Stroke 6 Cy. 340 x 620 1618kW (2200bhp) Niigata Engineering Co Ltd-Japan
9256212 *A8DZ2* -	**SNL COLOMBO** *ex* YM Colombo *-2012* *ex* Norasia Integra *-2007* *completed as* E. R. Auckland *-2004* **Auckland Marine Inc** Danaos Shipping Co Ltd *Monrovia* *Liberia* MMSI: 636013289 Official number: 13289	**41,855** 25,310 53,610 T/cm 71.6	Class: GL	**2004-03 Hyundai Samho Heavy Industries Co Ltd — Samho** Yd No: S178 Loa 264.20 (BB) Br ex - Dght 12.750 Lbp 249.00 Br md 32.20 Dpth 19.50 Welded, 1 dk	**(A33A2CC) Container Ship (Fully Cellular)** TEU 4300 C Ho 1610 TEU C Dk 2690 TEU incl 520 ref C. Compartments: ER, 7 Cell Ho	**1 oil engine** driving 1 FP propeller Total Power: 36,560kW (49,707hp) 24.1kn MAN-B&W 8K90MC-C 1 x 2 Stroke 8 Cy. 900 x 2300 36560kW (49707bhp) Hyundai Heavy Industries Co Ltd-South Korea AuxGen: 2 x 2280kW 450/230V 60Hz a.c, 2 x 1700kW 450/230V 60Hz a.c Thrusters: 1 Thwart. CP thruster (f)
9202546 *PCHF* -	**SNOEKGRACHT** **Rederij Snoekgracht** Spliethoff's Bevrachtingskantoor BV *Amsterdam* *Netherlands* MMSI: 245816000 Official number: 36734	**16,641** 6,700 21,402 T/cm 35.1	Class: LR ✠ **100A1** SS 03/2009 strengthened for heavy cargoes, container cargoes in holds, on upper deck and upper deck hatch covers timber deck cargoes tank top suitable for regular discharge by grabs LA LI *IWS Ice Class 1A (Finnish-Swedish Ice Class Rules 1985) Max draught midship 10.943m Max/min draught aft 11.47/6.6m Max/min draught forward 11.47/4.2m ✠ **LMC** **UMS** Eq.Ltr: 0†; Cable: 605.0/70.0 U2	**2000-03 Mitsubishi Heavy Industries Ltd. — Shimonoseki** Yd No: 1062 Loa 168.15 (BB) Br ex 25.42 Dght 10.740 Lbp 159.14 Br md 25.20 Dpth 14.60 Welded, 1 dk	**(A31A2GX) General Cargo Ship** Grain: 23,786; Bale: 23,786 TEU 1127 C Ho 478 TEU C Dk 649 TEU incl 120 ref C. Compartments: 3 Ho, ER 3 Ha: (26.6 x 15.2)Tappered (38.4 x 17.8) (31.9 x 20.4)ER Cranes: 3x120t Ice Capable	**1 oil engine** with flexible couplings & sr reverse geared to sc. shaft driving 1 CP propeller Total Power: 12,060kW (16,397hp) 19.5kn Wartsila 6L64 1 x 4 Stroke 6 Cy. 640 x 900 12060kW (16397bhp) Wartsila Italia SpA-Italy AuxGen: 1 x 1000kW 445V 60Hz a.c, 3 x 450kW 445V 60Hz a.c Boilers: TOH (o.f.) 10.2kgf/cm² (10.0bar), TOH (ex.g.) 10.2kgf/cm² (10.0bar) Thrusters: 1 Thwart. CP thruster (f) Fuel: 275.0 (d.f.) (Heating Coils) 1750.0 (r.f.) 45.0pd
7227384 *WDB9022* -	**SNOHOMISH** *ex* Neptune *-1994* *ex* Mister David *-1986* **Dunlap Towing Co** - *La Conner, WA* *United States of America* MMSI: 303465000 Official number: 540290	**347** 104 -	Class: (AB)	**1972 Halter Marine Services, Inc. — New Orleans, La** Yd No: 311 Loa 31.81 Br ex - Dght 4.242 Lbp 31.78 Br md 9.48 Dpth 4.98 Welded, 1 dk	**(B32A2ST) Tug**	**2 oil engines** reverse reduction geared to sc. shafts driving 2 FP propellers Total Power: 2,484kW (3,378hp) Caterpillar 3516 2 x Vee 4 Stroke 16 Cy. 170 x 190 each-1242kW (1689bhp) (new engine 1994) Caterpillar Inc-USA AuxGen: 2 x 60kW Fuel: 366.0 (d.f.)
8971384 *WDC9943* -	**SNOHOMISH** *ex* Dami Dew *-2004* *ex* Sarah Rose *-2002* *ex* Snohomish (WYT-98) *-1998* **Viking I LLC** - *Chesapeake City, MD* *United States of America* Official number: 920435	*195* 116 -		**1944-05 Ira S. Bushey & Son, Inc. — New York, NY** Loa 33.50 Br ex - Dght 3.750 Lbp 31.77 Br md 8.18 Dpth 4.61 Welded, 1 dk	**(B32A2ST) Tug** Ice Capable	**2 diesel electric oil engines** driving 2 gen. Connecting to 1 elec. Motor of (736kW) driving 1 FP propeller Total Power: 882kW (1,200hp)
8302090 *GDHX* -	**SNOLDA** *ex* Filla *-2003* **Government of The United Kingdom (Shetland Islands Council Ferry Services)** - *Lerwick* *United Kingdom* MMSI: 232003608 Official number: 399394	*130* 49 151	Class: (LR) ✠ Classed LR until 16/11/84	**1983-10 Th Hellesoy Skipsbyggeri AS — Lofallstrand** Yd No: 49 Loa 24.41 Br ex 7.07 Dght 3.501 Lbp 20.40 Br md 7.01 Dpth 3.81 Welded, 1 dk	**(A36A2PR) Passenger/Ro-Ro Ship (Vehicles)** Passengers: unberthed: 12 Stern door/ramp Len: 1.40 Wid: 4.20 Swl: - Lane-Len: 26 Lane-Wid: 5.48 Cars: 6 Compartments: 1 Ho, ER 1 Ha: (7.2 x 3.4) Cranes: 1	**1 oil engine** sr geared to sc. shaft driving 1 CP propeller Total Power: 346kW (470hp) 10.0kn Kelvin TASC8 1 x 4 Stroke 8 Cy. 165 x 184 346kW (470bhp) Kelvin Diesels Ltd., GECDiesels-Glasgow AuxGen: 3 x 20kW 230V 50Hz a.c Thrusters: 1 Thwart. FP thruster (f) Fuel: 15.0 (d.f.)
7911193 *DUH2143* -	**SNOOPY** **Mabuhay Vinyl** *Cebu* *Philippines* Official number: CDO7000558	*399* 243 539		**1980-07 Philippine Iron Construction & Marine Works Inc. — Jasaan** Yd No: 44 Loa - Br ex - Dght 0.931 Lbp 42.45 Br md 10.00 Dpth 2.57 Welded, 1 dk	**(A12A2TC) Chemical Tanker**	**2 oil engines** geared to sc. shafts driving 2 FP propellers Total Power: 536kW (728hp) Caterpillar 2 x 4 Stroke each-268kW (364bhp) Caterpillar Tractor Co-USA
7823023 *VG6223* -	**SNOW DRIFT** **Taginello Ventures Ltd** - *Vancouver, BC* *Canada* Official number: 391861	*115* 32 -		**1979-03 Allied Shipbuilders Ltd — North Vancouver BC** Yd No: 215 Loa 24.31 Br ex 7.01 Dght - Lbp 22.03 Br md 7.00 Dpth 3.66 Welded	**(B11B2FV) Fishing Vessel**	**1 oil engine** reverse reduction geared to sc. shaft driving 1 FP propeller Total Power: 382kW (519hp) Caterpillar 3412PCTA 1 x Vee 4 Stroke 12 Cy. 137 x 152 382kW (519bhp) Caterpillar Tractor Co-USA
9142629 *PHQP* -	**SNOW STAR** **Erik Thun AB (Thunship Management Holland)** Marin Ship Management BV SatCom: Inmarsat C 424571710 *Delfzijl* *Netherlands* MMSI: 245717000 Official number: 32028	**2,904** 1,656 5,398	Class: BV	**1996-12 Scheepswerf Ferus Smit BV — Westerbroek** Yd No: 307 Loa 89.00 (BB) Br ex 13.40 Dght 7.000 Lbp 84.99 Br md 13.35 Dpth 8.80 Welded, 1 dk	**(A31A2GX) General Cargo Ship** Grain: 5,990 Compartments: 1 Ho, ER 3 Ha: 3 (18.9 x 10.4)ER Ice Capable	**1 oil engine** geared to sc. shaft driving 1 CP propeller Total Power: 2,400kW (3,263hp) 12.5kn Wartsila 6R32E 1 x 4 Stroke 6 Cy. 320 x 350 2400kW (3263bhp) Wartsila Diesel Oy-Finland AuxGen: 1 x 360kW 440V a.c Thrusters: 1 Thwart. FP thruster (f) Fuel: 21.0 (d.f.) 247.0 (r.f.) 10.0pd
7422180 *9LD2138* -	**SNOW WHITE** *ex* Abnett Snow *-2007* *ex* Ouirgane *-2002* **Eldora Shipping Co** BIA Shipping Co *Freetown* *Sierra Leone* MMSI: 667639000 Official number: SL100639	**2,791** 1,362 3,357	Class: DR (IS) (BV)	**1975-12 J.J. Sietas Schiffswerft — Hamburg** Yd No: 766 Loa 93.45 (BB) Br ex 14.74 Dght 5.560 Lbp 83.55 Br md 14.50 Dpth 7.95 Welded, 2 dks	**(A31A2GX) General Cargo Ship** Grain: 5,740; Bale: 5,439; Ins: 5,739 TEU 195 C Ho 94 TEU C Dk 101 TEU incl 20 ref C. Compartments: 1 Ho, ER 1 Ha: (51.3 x 10.3)ER Ice Capable	**1 oil engine** reduction geared to sc. shaft driving 1 CP propeller Total Power: 2,502kW (3,402hp) 14.5kn MaK 6M551AK 1 x 4 Stroke 6 Cy. 450 x 550 2502kW (3402bhp) MaK Maschinenbau GmbH-Kiel AuxGen: 3 x 220kW 380V 50Hz a.c Thrusters: 1 Thwart. FP thruster (f)
1010404 *ZGBD* -	**SNOWBIRD** *launched as* Pretty Woman *-2010* **Snowbird Charter Ltd** Edmiston Yacht Management Ltd *George Town* *Cayman Islands (British)* Official number: 742967	**368** 110 -	Class: LR ✠ **100A1** SS 07/2010 SSC Yacht, mono, G6 **LMC** **UMS** Cable: 275.0/17.0 U2 (a)	**2010-07 Scheepswerf Made B.V. — Made** (Hull) Yd No: (245) **2010-07 Scheepsbouw en Machinefabriek Hakvoort B.V. — Monnickendam** Yd No: 245 Loa 39.00 (BB) Br ex 8.20 Dght 2.550 Lbp 31.86 Br md 8.00 Dpth 4.30 Welded, 1 dk	**(X11A2YP) Yacht**	**2 oil engines** with clutches, flexible couplings & sr reverse geared to sc. shafts driving 2 FP propellers Total Power: 894kW (1,216hp) Caterpillar C18 2 x 4 Stroke 6 Cy. 145 x 183 each-447kW (608bhp) Caterpillar Inc-USA AuxGen: 2 x 105kW 400V 50Hz a.c
9112313 *ZCBV6* -	**SNOWDON** *launched as* SG Creation *-1998* **Topeka Navigation Ltd** Zodiac Maritime Agencies Ltd SatCom: Inmarsat C 431026311 *Hamilton* *Bermuda (British)* MMSI: 310263000 Official number: 731261	**85,848** 55,402 170,079 T/cm 122.6	Class: LR (AB) **100A1** SS 08/2013 bulk carrier strengthened for heavy cargoes, Nos. 2, 4, 6 & 8 holds may be empty *IWS ESP LI ESN-Hold 1 **LMC** **UMS** Eq.Ltr: Y†; Cable: 742.5/97.0 U3 (a)	**1998-08 Samsung Heavy Industries Co Ltd — Geoje** Yd No: 1168 Loa 292.00 (BB) Br ex - Dght 17.300 Lbp 281.00 Br md 46.00 Dpth 23.20 Welded, 1 dk	**(A21A2BC) Bulk Carrier** Grain: 185,460 Compartments: 9 Ho, ER 9 Ha: (13.7 x 14.5)7 (13.7 x 21.1) (13.7 x 14.5)ER	**1 oil engine** driving 1 FP propeller Total Power: 16,192kW (22,015hp) 14.6kn B&W 6S70MC 1 x 2 Stroke 6 Cy. 700 x 2674 16192kW (22015bhp) Samsung Heavy Industries Co Ltd-South Korea AuxGen: 3 x 650kW a.c

8412417 *J8B3277* -	**SNOWLARK** *ex* RMS Snowlark *-2008* *ex* RMS Walsum *-2005* *ex* Mosa *-1998* **Snow Maritime Inc** AS Vista Shipping Agency *Kingstown* *St Vincent & The Grenadines* MMSI: 375203000 Official number: 9749	**1,289** 386 1,555	Class: GL	**1984-10 Hermann Suerken GmbH & Co. KG — Papenburg** Yd No: 331 Loa 74.91 (BB) Br ex 10.60 Dght 3.391 Lbp 70.52 Br md 10.51 Dpth 5.69 Welded, 2 dks	**(A31A2GX) General Cargo Ship** Grain: 2,351; Bale: 2,310 Compartments: 1 Ho, ER 1 Ha: (46.8 x 8.2)ER	**1 oil engine** reverse reduction geared to sc. shaft driving 1 FP propeller Total Power: 441kW (600hp) 10.0kn Deutz SBA6M528 1 x 4 Stroke 6 Cy. 220 x 280 441kW (600bhp) Kloeckner Humboldt Deutz AG-West Germany AuxGen: 2 x 94kW 380V 50Hz a.c Thrusters: 1 Thwart. FP thruster (f)
9193537 - -	**SNP-2** **Instituto Del Mar Del Peru (IMARPE)** *Callao* *Peru*	**150** 118	Class: (LR) ✠ Classed LR until 16/9/09	**1999-02 SIMA Serv. Ind. de la Marina Callao (SIMAC) — Callao** Yd No: 064 Loa 21.50 Br ex 5.44 Dght 2.088 Lbp 18.70 Br md 5.30 Dpth 2.50 Welded, 1 dk	**(B11A2FS) Stern Trawler**	**1 oil engine** with clutches & sr reverse geared to sc. shaft driving 1 FP propeller Total Power: 272kW (370hp) 10.0kn Caterpillar 3406B 1 x 4 Stroke 6 Cy. 137 x 165 272kW (370bhp) (new engine 2006) Caterpillar Inc-USA AuxGen: 2 x 27kW 220V 60Hz a.c
8510166 - -	**SNS LEO** *ex* Shinko Maru No. 13 *-2009* **Sutan Nazaar Services Pte Ltd** -	**263** - 378		**1985-10 Maeno Zosen KK — Sanyoonoda YC** Yd No: 115 Loa 40.01 Br ex 7.83 Dght 3.001 Lbp 36.02 Br md 7.80 Dpth 3.20 Welded, 1 dk	**(A12A2TC) Chemical Tanker** Liq: 310 Compartments: 6 Ta, ER	**1 oil engine** sr geared to sc. shaft driving 1 FP propeller Total Power: 257kW (349hp) Daihatsu 6PKT-16 1 x 4 Stroke 6 Cy. 160 x 210 257kW (349bhp) Daihatsu Diesel Manufacturing Co Lt-Japan
8625595 *9MLV7* -	**SNS VIRGO** *ex* Uno Maru *-2011* - - *Port Klang* *Malaysia* MMSI: 533063300 Official number: 334367	*318* 95 563		**1986-01 Nakamura Shipbuilding & Engine Works Co. Ltd. — Yanai** Yd No: 156 Loa 46.84 Br ex - Dght 3.201 Lbp 43.01 Br md 7.80 Dpth 3.38 Welded, 1 dk	**(A13B2TP) Products Tanker**	**1 oil engine** driving 1 FP propeller Total Power: 515kW (700hp) 10.0kn Yanmar MF24-DT 1 x 4 Stroke 6 Cy. 240 x 420 515kW (700bhp) Yanmar Diesel Engine Co Ltd-Japan
9603922 - -	**SO BAEK** - **Namsung Yesun Co Ltd** - *Pyeongtaek* *South Korea* MMSI: 440012230 Official number: PTR-104747	**273** - 167	Class: KR	**2010-10 Samkwang Shipbuilding & Engineering Co Ltd — Incheon** Yd No: SKSB-191 Loa 36.50 Br ex 10.02 Dght 3.312 Lbp 32.49 Br md 10.00 Dpth 4.50 Welded, 1 dk	**(B32A2ST) Tug**	**2 oil engines** reduction geared to sc. shafts driving 2 Propellers Total Power: 3,310kW (4,500hp) Niigata 6L28HX 2 x 4 Stroke 6 Cy. 280 x 370 each-1655kW (2250bhp) Niigata Engineering Co Ltd-Japan
8658267 *HMPR* -	**SO BAEK SAN** *ex* Feng Shin 1 *-2012* **Korea Kumbyol Trading Co** - *Nampho* *North Korea* MMSI: 445025000 Official number: 5805157	**2,895** 1,669 4,925	Class: KC (Class contemplated)	**2008-12 Ma'anshan Tianyu Shipbuilding Co Ltd — Dangtu County AH** Loa 98.22 Br ex - Dght 5.550 Lbp 91.00 Br md 16.20 Dpth 6.95 Welded, 1 dk	**(A31A2GX) General Cargo Ship** Grain: 6,165; Bale: 6,050 Compartments: 2 Ho, ER 2 Ha: ER	**1 oil engine** reduction geared to sc. shaft driving 1 FP propeller Total Power: 2,000kW (2,719hp) Chinese Std. Type G8300ZC 1 x 4 Stroke 8 Cy. 300 x 380 2000kW (2719bhp) Ningbo CSI Power & Machinery GroupCo Ltd-China AuxGen: 3 x 90kW a.c
8817289 *HMPX* -	**SO BAEK SU** *ex* Tae Won 188 *-2012* *ex* Ever Spring *-2009* *ex* Sumiyoshi Maru No. 38 *-2002* **Korea Lyeming Shipping Co** - *Nampho* *North Korea* MMSI: 445030000 Official number: 3804644	**1,894** 1,289 1,443	Class: KC	**1988-07 Shin Kurushima Dockyard Co. Ltd. — Akitsu** Yd No: 2576 Loa 66.45 (BB) Br ex - Dght 4.441 Lbp 60.00 Br md 13.20 Dpth 7.25 Welded, 1 dk	**(B33A2DG) Grab Dredger** Grain: 833 Compartments: 1 Ho, ER 1 Ha: ER	**1 oil engine** geared to sc. shaft driving 1 FP propeller Total Power: 736kW (1,001hp) Hanshin 6LU35G 1 x 4 Stroke 6 Cy. 350 x 550 736kW (1001bhp) The Hanshin Diesel Works Ltd-Japan
8743660 *HMYR7* -	**SO GYONG** *ex* Zhe Le Ji 888 *-2007* **Korea Sogyong Trading Corp** - *Nampho* *North Korea* MMSI: 445263000 Official number: 5704874	**498** 278 1,130	Class: KC (Class contemplated)	**2007-06 in the People's Republic of China** Yd No: 712 Loa 52.80 Br ex - Dght 3.430 Lbp 48.25 Br md 8.80 Dpth 4.08 Welded, 1 dk	**(A31A2GX) General Cargo Ship**	**1 oil engine** reduction geared to sc. shaft driving 1 FP propeller Total Power: 215kW (292hp) Chinese Std. Type 1 x 4 Stroke 215kW (292bhp) Jinan Diesel Engine Co Ltd-China
8891883 *HMIR* -	**SO GYONG 2** *ex* Dae Ryong Gang *-2005* *ex* Hae Gum 21 *-2005* *ex* Daikoku Maru *-2005* **Korea Sogyong Trading Corp** - *Wonsan* *North Korea* MMSI: 445226000 Official number: 1700812	*298* 119 358	Class: KC	**1967 in Japan** Loa 43.90 Br ex - Dght 3.330 Lbp - Br md 8.10 Dpth - Welded, 1 dk	**(B12B2FC) Fish Carrier**	**1 oil engine** driving 1 FP propeller Niigata 1 x 4 Stroke Niigata Engineering Co Ltd-Japan
8002274 *HMYJ7* -	**SO HUNG 1** *ex* Verna *-2003* *ex* Tortola *-2000* *ex* Silverfull No. 2 *-1997* *ex* Komatsushima Maru *-1995* **Korea Kangsong Shipping & Trading Co** - *Nampho* *North Korea* MMSI: 445293000 Official number: 3001289	**1,212** 649 1,586	Class: KC	**1980-03 Yamanaka Zosen K.K. — Imabari** Yd No: 222 Loa 68.70 Br ex - Dght 4.352 Lbp 64.01 Br md 11.51 Dpth 6.13 Welded, 1 dk	**(A31A2GX) General Cargo Ship**	**1 oil engine** driving 1 FP propeller Total Power: 1,324kW (1,800hp) Makita GSLH633 1 x 4 Stroke 6 Cy. 330 x 530 1324kW (1800bhp) Makita Diesel Co Ltd-Japan
8832710 *6WDR* DAK 821	**SOACHIP 11** *ex* Soachip XI *-2011* **Zhoushan Marine Fisheries Co** - *Dakar* *Senegal*	*299* 89 -	Class: (CC)	**1987 Dalian Fishing Vessel Co — Dalian LN** Loa 44.38 Br ex - Dght - Lbp 38.00 Br md 7.60 Dpth 3.75 Welded	**(B11B2FV) Fishing Vessel**	**1 oil engine** geared to sc. shaft driving 1 FP propeller Total Power: 736kW (1,001hp) 12.0kn Chinese Std. Type 8300 1 x 4 Stroke 8 Cy. 300 x 380 736kW (1001bhp) Dalian Fishing Vessel Co-China AuxGen: 2 x 120kW 400V a.c
8832734 *6WDM* DAK 822	**SOACHIP 12** *ex* Soachip XII *-2011* **Zhoushan Marine Fisheries Co** - *Dakar* *Senegal*	*299* 89 -	Class: (CC)	**1987 Dalian Fishing Vessel Co — Dalian LN** Loa 44.38 Br ex - Dght - Lbp 38.00 Br md 7.60 Dpth 3.75 Welded	**(B11B2FV) Fishing Vessel**	**1 oil engine** geared to sc. shaft driving 1 FP propeller Total Power: 441kW (600hp) 12.0kn Chinese Std. Type 8300 1 x 4 Stroke 8 Cy. 300 x 380 441kW (600bhp) Dalian Fishing Vessel Co-China AuxGen: 2 x 120kW 400V a.c
8917716 *PBIX* -	**SOAVE** *ex* Smaragden *-2007* **Merwesingel BV** Rederij Chr Kornet & Zonen BV *Werkendam* *Netherlands* MMSI: 244936000 Official number: 51358	**3,828** 2,016 4,452 T/cm 15.0	Class: BV (LR) (GL) Classed LR until 27/9/07	**1991-08 J.J. Sietas KG Schiffswerft GmbH & Co. — Hamburg** Yd No: 1058 Loa 103.50 (BB) Br ex 16.24 Dght 6.070 Lbp 96.90 Br md 16.00 Dpth 8.00 Welded, 1 dk	**(A31A2GX) General Cargo Ship** Grain: 6,820; Bale: 6,603 TEU 372 C.Ho 134/20' (40') C.Dk 238/20' (40') incl. 50 ref C. Compartments: 2 Ho, ER 3 Ha: (12.4 x 10.3)2 (25.1 x 12.8)ER Ice Capable	**1 oil engine** with flexible couplings & sr geared to sc. shaft driving 1 CP propeller Total Power: 3,330kW (4,527hp) 15.3kn Wartsila 9R32D 1 x 4 Stroke 9 Cy. 320 x 350 3330kW (4527bhp) Wartsila Diesel Oy-Finland AuxGen: 1 x 500kW 220/380V 50Hz a.c, 2 x 228kW 220/380V 50Hz a.c Thrusters: 1 Thwart. FP thruster (f)
8709925 *EFJA* -	**SOBAREIRO** **Pesquera Loira SL** *Marin* *Spain* Official number: 3-2358/	**329** 98 169	Class: (LR) ✠ Classed LR until 1/10/05	**1988-09 Factoria Naval de Marin S.A. — Marin** Yd No: 22 Loa 34.00 Br ex 8.37 Dght 3.452 Lbp 28.53 Br md 8.31 Dpth 3.51 Welded, 1 dk	**(B11A2FS) Stern Trawler** Ins: 165	**1 oil engine** with flexible couplings & sr geared to sc. shaft driving 1 CP propeller Total Power: 640kW (870hp) Deutz SBA8M528 1 x 4 Stroke 8 Cy. 220 x 280 640kW (870bhp) Hijos de J Barreras SA-Spain AuxGen: 2 x 120kW 380V 50Hz a.c, 1 x 80kW 380V 50Hz a.c
9036935 - -	**SOBHAN** - **IRISL Marine Services & Engineering Co** - *Bandar Abbas* *Iran* Official number: 3.10132	*453* - 750	Class: AS (LR) (BV) Classed LR until 27/5/04	**1991 B.V. Scheepswerf Damen Bergum — Bergum** (Hull) **1991 B.V. Scheepswerf Damen — Gorinchem** Yd No: 6721 Loa 40.00 Br ex 10.01 Dght 2.601 Lbp 38.80 Br md 9.97 Dpth 3.26 Welded, 1 dk	**(B35E2TF) Bunkering Tanker** Compartments: 6 Ta, ER	**2 oil engines** with clutches & reduction geared to sc. shafts driving 2 FP propellers Total Power: 268kW (364hp) 6.0kn G.M. (Detroit Diesel) 6-71-N 2 x 2 Stroke 6 Cy. 108 x 127 each-134kW (182bhp) (made 1980, fitted 1991) Detroit Diesel Corporation-Detroit, Mi AuxGen: 2 x 62kW 380V 50Hz a.c

IMO / Call sign	Ship / Owner	Tonnage	Class	Builder / Dimensions	Type	Machinery
8922084 *9BTQ* -	**SOBHAN 2** *ex* Daiei Maru *-2009* **Abdol Amir Marhounian Nezhad & Abdol Mohammad Karampour Dashti** - *Iran* MMSI: 422829000	*398* - 450		**1990-08 Imura Zosen K.K. — Komatsushima** Yd No: 250 Loa - (BB) Br ex - Dght 2.700 Lbp 49.00 Br md 9.00 Dpth 4.80 Welded, 1 dk	**(A31A2GX) General Cargo Ship** Bale: 936 Compartments: 1 Ho, ER 1 Ha: (29.2 x 6.8)ER	**1 oil engine** with clutches & reverse geared to sc. shaft driving 1 FP propeller Total Power: 405kW (551hp) 10.5kn Yanmar MF26-HT 1 x 4 Stroke 6 Cy. 260 x 500 405kW (551bhp) Yanmar Diesel Engine Co Ltd-Japan
9126675 *EAMD* -	**SOBIA** *ex* Celache Dos *-2005* **Navinorte SA** G Junquera Maritima SA *Bilbao* *Spain* MMSI: 224362590 Official number: 5-3/1996	**682** 380 1,447	Class: BV	**1996-02 Astilleros Zamakona SA — Santurtzi** Yd No: 316 Loa 40.90 Br ex - Dght 4.881 Lbp 39.26 Br md 11.20 Dpth 5.40 Welded, 1 dk	**(B35E2TF) Bunkering Tanker** Double Bottom Entire Compartment Length Liq: 1,635; Liq (Oil): 1,635 Part Cargo Heating Coils Compartments: 10 Ta, ER 2 Cargo Pump (s): 2x250m³/hr	**2 oil engines** gearing integral to driving 2 Z propellers Total Power: 736kW (1,000hp) 6.0kn GUASCOR E318TA-SP 2 x Vee 4 Stroke 12 Cy. 150 x 150 each-368kW (500bhp) Gutierrez Ascunce Corp (GUASCOR)-Spain AuxGen: 2 x 320kW 380V 50Hz a.c Thrusters: 1 Directional thruster (f) Fuel: 13.0 (d.f.) 3.0pd
8859380 - -	**SOBIRAKI MARU** - -	*172* - 513		**1991-12 Osaki Zosen KK — Awaji HG** Loa 50.00 Br ex - Dght 3.220 Lbp 45.00 Br md 8.40 Dpth 5.00 Welded, 1 dk	**(A31A2GX) General Cargo Ship** Compartments: 1 Ho, ER 1 Ha: (26.0 x 6.2)ER	**1 oil engine** driving 1 FP propeller Total Power: 368kW (500hp) 9.5kn Sumiyoshi S25G 1 x 4 Stroke 6 Cy. 250 x 450 368kW (500bhp) Sumiyoshi Marine Diesel Co Ltd-Japan
8859897 *UEQB* -	**SOBOLEVO** *ex* Sea Fox *-2001* *ex* Kirganik *-1998* **Sea Eagle JSC (ZAO 'Morskoy Orel')** - *Petropavlovsk-Kamchatskiy* *Russia* MMSI: 273429070	**515** 154 188	Class: (RS) (NV)	**1992-05 AO Zavod 'Nikolayevsk-na-Amure' — Nikolayevsk-na-Amure** Yd No: 1285 Loa 44.88 Br ex - Dght 3.770 Lbp 39.37 Br md 9.47 Dpth 5.13 Welded, 1 dk	**(B11A2FS) Stern Trawler** Ice Capable	**1 oil engine** driving 1 FP propeller Total Power: 588kW (799hp) 11.5kn S.K.L. 8NVD48A-2U 1 x 4 Stroke 8 Cy. 320 x 480 588kW (799bhp) SKL Motoren u. Systemtechnik AG-Magdeburg
7204734 *J7CJ2* -	**SOBRE WORLD** *ex* Taisei Maru No. 55 *-1978* **Quadrant Navigation Inc** Ocean Tankers (Pte) Ltd *Dominica* MMSI: 325591000	**1,800** 1,172 3,493 T/cm 9.5	Class: (NK)	**1971-12 Asakawa Zosen K.K. — Imabari** Yd No: 196 Loa 86.37 Br ex 13.85 Dght 5.460 Lbp 81.01 Br md 13.80 Dpth 6.35 Riveted\Welded, 1 dk	**(A13B2TP) Products Tanker** Liq: 4,287; Liq (Oil): 4,287 2 Cargo Pump (s)	**2 oil engines** geared to sc. shaft driving 1 FP propeller Total Power: 1,912kW (2,600hp) 12.0kn Daihatsu 6DSM-26F 2 x 4 Stroke 6 Cy. 260 x 320 each-956kW (1300bhp) Daihatsu Diesel Manufacturing Co Lt-Japan
5332824 - B-42	**SOBROSO** - **Sociedade de Pesca de Mariscos Lda (PESCAMAR)** Pescanova SA *Beira* *Mozambique*	*573* 295 -	Class: (BV)	**1962 Astilleros Construcciones SA — Meira** Yd No: 35 L reg 48.80 Br ex 8.36 Dght 4.230 Lbp 48.80 Br md 8.31 Dpth 4.75 Riveted\Welded, 1 dk	**(B11A2FT) Trawler** 2 Ha: 2 (1.9 x 1.3)	**1 oil engine** driving 1 FP propeller Total Power: 971kW (1,320hp) 12.3kn Deutz RBV8M545 1 x 4 Stroke 8 Cy. 320 x 450 971kW (1320bhp) Kloeckner Humboldt Deutz AG-West Germany Fuel: 172.5 (d.f.)
6611667 - -	**SOBY-FAERGEN** *ex* Ostbornholm *-1980* - -	**850** 255 471	Class: (BV)	**1966-07 Kalmar Varv AB — Kalmar** Yd No: 416 Converted From: General Cargo Ship-1979 Loa 49.20 Br ex 9.53 Dght 3.201 Lbp 44.51 Br md 9.50 Dpth 8.01 Welded, 1 dk & S dk	**(A36A2PR) Passenger/Ro-Ro Ship (Vehicles)** Passengers: unberthed: 200 Grain: 1,800; Bale: 1,630 Compartments: 1 Ho, ER, 1 Tw Dk 1 Ha: (2.9 x 3.9)ER Ice Capable	**1 oil engine** sr geared to sc. shaft driving 1 Directional propeller Total Power: 588kW (799hp) 12.0kn Deutz RBV6M545 1 x 4 Stroke 6 Cy. 320 x 450 588kW (799bhp) Kloeckner Humboldt Deutz AG-West Germany AuxGen: 2 x 37kW 380V a.c Fuel: 61.0 (d.f.)
9583263 *T2NL3* -	**SOC ENDEAVOUR** *ex* Oranda 2 *-2012* **Koi Marine Ltd** Global Workboats Pte Ltd *Funafuti* *Tuvalu* MMSI: 572912000 Official number: 26261111	**3,914** 1,174 2,832	Class: AB	**2012-05 Zhejiang Shenzhou Shipbuilding Co Ltd — Xiangshan County ZJ** Yd No: SZ08006 Loa 75.00 (BB) Br ex 20.42 Dght 5.500 Lbp 68.00 Br md 20.40 Dpth 7.00 Welded, 1 dk	**(B34T2QR) Work/Repair Vessel** Cranes: 1x45t	**2 oil engines** reduction geared to sc. shafts driving 2 CP propellers Total Power: 3,200kW (4,350hp) Wartsila 8L20 2 x 4 Stroke 8 Cy. 200 x 280 each-1600kW (2175bhp) Wartsila Finland Oy-Finland AuxGen: 5 x 590kW a.c Fuel: 1250.0 (d.f.)
7314034 *XVBC* -	**SOC TRANG 01** *ex* Can Tho *-1993* *ex* Kaishin Maru No. 32 *-1993* **Soc Trang Shipping Co (Cong Ty Van Tai Bien Soc Trang)** - *Saigon* *Vietnam*	**265** - 230	Class: (VR)	**1973 Miho Zosensho K.K. — Shimizu** Yd No: 889 Loa 41.70 Br ex 7.55 Dght 2.800 Lbp 36.00 Br md 7.52 Dpth 3.10 Welded, 1 dk	**(B11B2FV) Fishing Vessel** Ins: 270	**1 oil engine** driving 1 FP propeller Total Power: 552kW (750hp) 11.0kn Niigata 6M26KGHS 1 x 4 Stroke 6 Cy. 260 x 400 552kW (750bhp) Niigata Engineering Co Ltd-Japan AuxGen: 2 x 150kW a.c
9107320 *9HCD9* -	**SOCAR** *ex* BOA Master *-2009* *ex* Cinhco *-1997* **Palmali Tugs Co Ltd** Palmali Gemicilik ve Acentelik AS (Palmali Shipping & Agency) *Valletta* *Malta* MMSI: 256774000 Official number: 9107320	**359** 107 287	Class: RS (NV) (BV)	**1994-09 Astilleros Armon SA — Navia** Yd No: 326 Loa 30.00 Br ex 10.00 Dght 4.480 Lbp 26.80 Br md 9.85 Dpth 5.40 Welded, 1 dk	**(B32A2ST) Tug**	**2 oil engines** reduction geared to sc. shafts driving 2 Directional propellers Total Power: 2,942kW (4,000hp) 12.0kn Caterpillar 3516TA 2 x Vee 4 Stroke 16 Cy. 170 x 190 each-1471kW (2000bhp) Caterpillar Inc-USA Fuel: 210.0
9232993 *9HA2805* -	**SOCAR-2** *ex* Citta Di Ancona *-2011* **Palmali Tugs 2 Co Ltd** Palmali Gemicilik ve Acentelik AS (Palmali Shipping & Agency) *Valletta* *Malta* MMSI: 215911000 Official number: 9232993	**304** 91 -	Class: RS (RI)	**2001-03 Cooperativa Ing G Tommasi Cantiere Navale Srl — Ancona** Yd No: 104 Loa 30.00 Br ex - Dght 4.000 Lbp 26.30 Br md 10.00 Dpth 5.00 Welded, 1 dk	**(B32A2ST) Tug**	**2 oil engines** reduction geared to sc. shafts driving 2 Directional propellers Total Power: 2,880kW (3,916hp) 13.2kn Wartsila 8L20 2 x 4 Stroke 8 Cy. 200 x 280 each-1440kW (1958bhp) Wartsila Finland Oy-Finland AuxGen: 2 x 100kW 220/400V 50Hz a.c Fuel: 112.0 (d.f.) 12.0pd
9665839 *9LD2462* -	**SOCHI** *ex* Zatu-S Savari *-2012* **Concord Management & Consulting LLC** - *Freetown* *Sierra Leone* MMSI: 667005162	**350** 150 -		**2012-06 Cizgi Yat Imalat Turizm Sanayi Ticaret Ltd Sti — Istanbul (Tuzla)** Yd No: 04 Loa 39.85 Br ex - Dght - Lbp - Br md 8.50 Dpth - Welded, 1 dk	**(A37B2PS) Passenger Ship**	**2 oil engines** reduction geared to sc. shafts driving 2 Propellers Total Power: 602kW (818hp) Scania DI12 M 2 x 4 Stroke 6 Cy. 127 x 154 each-301kW (409bhp) Scania AB-Sweden
9022154 *D6BZ9* -	**SOCHI** *ex* TB 205 *-2004* *ex* TB 614 *-2004* **Raiko Hristov EAD** - *Moroni* *Union of Comoros* MMSI: 616204000 Official number: 1200247	**398** 119	Class: (BR)	**1976-01 'Ilya Boyadzhiev' Shipyard — Bourgas** Loa 54.46 Br ex - Dght 2.070 Lbp 52.00 Br md 7.70 Dpth 3.50 Welded, 1 dk	**(A31A2GX) General Cargo Ship**	**2 oil engines** reduction geared to sc. shafts driving 2 Propellers Total Power: 442kW (600hp) Barnaultransmash 3D12A 2 x Vee 4 Stroke 12 Cy. 150 x 180 each-221kW (300bhp) Bryanskiy Mashinostroitelnyy Zavod (BMZ)-Bryansk
9144976 *UBIH7* -	**SOCHI-1** *ex* Rapparee *-2011* *ex* Fastcat-Ryde *-2010* *ex* Supercat 17 *-2000* *ex* Water Jet 1 *-1999* **Federal State Unitary Enterprise Rosmorport** - *Sochi* *Russia* MMSI: 273351130	**478** 168 46	Class: RS (NV)	**1996-03 Kvaerner Fjellstrand (S) Pte Ltd — Singapore** Yd No: 018 Loa 40.00 Br ex 10.10 Dght 1.610 Lbp 36.00 Br md - Dpth 3.97 Welded, 1 dk	**(A37B2PS) Passenger Ship** Passengers: 370	**2 oil engines** reduction geared to sc. shafts driving 2 Water jets Total Power: 4,000kW (5,438hp) 34.0kn M.T.U. 16V396TE74L 2 x Vee 4 Stroke 16 Cy. 165 x 185 each-2000kW (2719bhp) MTU Friedrichshafen GmbH-Friedrichshafen AuxGen: 2 x a.c
8888513 *UBIH6* -	**SOCHI-2** *ex* Fastcat-Shanklin *-2011* *ex* Supercat 18 *-2000* *ex* Water Jet 2 *-1999* **Federal State Unitary Enterprise Rosmorport** 'Solen+' Ltd Co *Sochi* *Russia* MMSI: 273350130	**482** 169 50	Class: RS (NV)	**1996-03 Kvaerner Fjellstrand (S) Pte Ltd — Singapore** Yd No: 020 Loa 40.00 Br ex 10.10 Dght 1.621 Lbp - Br md - Dpth 3.97 Welded, 1 dk	**(A37B2PS) Passenger Ship** Passengers: unberthed: 360	**2 oil engines** reduction geared to sc. shaft (s) driving 2 Water jets Total Power: 4,000kW (5,438hp) 34.0kn M.T.U. 16V396TE74L 2 x Vee 4 Stroke 16 Cy. 165 x 185 each-2000kW (2719bhp) MTU Friedrichshafen GmbH-Friedrichshafen AuxGen: 2 x a.c
9666376 *3FRP6* -	**SOCHIMA** - **Tonimas Nigeria Ltd** - *Panama* *Panama* MMSI: 354618000 Official number: 45410PEXT	**4,047** 1,940 6,770	Class: BV	**2014-03 Rui'an Jiangnan Shiprepair & Building Yard — Rui'an ZJ** Yd No: RAJN009 Loa 103.00 Br ex - Dght 7.000 Lbp 96.50 Br md 16.00 Dpth 8.70 Welded, 1 dk	**(A12B2TR) Chemical/Products Tanker** Double Hull (13F) Liq: 7,085; Liq (Oil): 7,085 Cargo Heating Coils Compartments: 10 Wing Ta, 2 Wing Slop Ta, ER 2 Cargo Pump (s): 2x750m³/hr Ice Capable	**1 oil engine** reduction geared to sc. shaft driving 1 Propeller Total Power: 2,574kW (3,500hp) 12.5kn Yanmar 6N330-EN 1 x 4 Stroke 6 Cy. 330 x 440 2574kW (3500bhp) Qingdao Zichai Boyang Diesel EngineCo Ltd-China AuxGen: 3 x 350kW 440V 60Hz a.c Thrusters: 1 Tunnel thruster (f) Fuel: 107.0 (d.f.) 300.0 (r.f.)

9664861 *EABV* -	**SOCIB** - **Government of Spain (Coastal Ocean Observing & Forecast System Balearic Islands ICTS (SOCIB))** - *Palma de Mallorca* Spain MMSI: 225950380 Official number: 393930	149 45 -		2012-07 **Rodman Polyships S.A. — Vigo** Yd No: 82004 Loa 23.62 Br ex 9.19 Dght 1.500 Lbp 23.15 Br md 9.00 Dpth 3.40 Welded, 1 dk	**(B31A2SR) Research Survey Vessel**	**2 oil engines** reduction geared to sc. shafts driving 2 Propellers Total Power: 2,440kW (3,318hp) M.T.U. 12V2000M84 2 x Vee 4 Stroke 12 Cy. 135 x 156 each-1220kW (1659bhp) MTU Friedrichshafen GmbH-Friedrichshafen
9570010 *HIRD659* -	**SOCO** *ex* Ulupinar VIII *-2010* **Caucedo Marine Services Inc** Remolcadores Dominicanos SA SatCom: Inmarsat C 432780410 *Santo Domingo* Dominican Rep. MMSI: 327804000	276 136 -	Class: BV (Class contemplated) RI	2010-01 **Pirlant Shipyard — Tuzla** Yd No: 22 Loa 24.39 Br ex - Dght 4.040 Lbp 23.20 Br md 9.15 Dpth 4.04 Welded, 1 dk	**(B32A2ST) Tug**	**2 oil engines** reduction geared to sc. shafts driving 2 Z propellers Total Power: 2,460kW (3,344hp) 12.0kn Caterpillar 3512B-TA 2 x Vee 4 Stroke 12 Cy. 170 x 190 each-1230kW (1672bhp) Caterpillar Inc-USA AuxGen: 2 x 65kW 380V 50Hz a.c
8427644 *DUH2341* -	**SOCOR 3** *ex* Paco *-1973* **Socor Shipping Lines Inc** - *Cebu* Philippines Official number: CEB1000779	*464* 255 -		1973 **at Lapu-Lapu** Loa - Br ex 10.72 Dght - Lbp 51.49 Br md 10.70 Dpth 2.42 Welded, 1 dk	**(A35D2RL) Landing Craft**	**2 oil engines** driving 2 FP propellers Total Power: 882kW (1,200hp)
8428844 - -	**SOCOTRA** - **Yemen Fishing Corp** - *Aden* Yemen	286 84 -		1976 **Guangzhou Fishing Vessel Shipyard — Guangzhou GD** Loa 44.82 Br ex 7.60 Dght 2.200 Lbp - Br md - Dpth 2.70 Welded, 1 dk	**(B11B2FV) Fishing Vessel**	**1 oil engine** geared to sc. shaft driving 1 FP propeller Total Power: 441kW (600hp) Chinese Std. Type 6300 1 x 4 Stroke 6 Cy. 300 x 380 441kW (600bhp) Guangzhou Diesel Engine Factory CoLtd-China
8881797 - -	**SOCOTRA** *ex* 1604 *-1973* **Government of The Yemeni Republic (Ministry of Fish Wealth)** - *Aden* Yemen	723 216 414	Class: (RS)	1989 **Zavod "Leninskaya Kuznitsa" — Kiyev** Yd No: 1604 Loa 54.82 Br ex 10.15 Dght 4.140 Lbp 50.30 Br md 9.95 Dpth 5.00 Welded, 1 dk	**(B11A2FS) Stern Trawler**	**1 oil engine** driving 1 FP propeller Total Power: 852kW (1,158hp) 12.0kn S.K.L. 8NVD48A-2U 1 x 4 Stroke 8 Cy. 320 x 480 852kW (1158bhp) VEB Schwermaschinenbau "KarlLiebknecht" (SKL)-Magdeburg
9597599 *UBRH6* -	**SOCRAT** - **The Sea Commercial Port of St Petersburg (A/O Morskoy Port Sankt-Peterburg)** - *St Petersburg* Russia MMSI: 273358830	400 - 270	Class: NV RS	2010-12 **OAO Moskovskiy Sudostroitelnyy i Sudoremontnyy Zavod — Moscow** Yd No: 382 Loa 37.50 Br ex 8.60 Dght 2.700 Lbp 32.00 Br md 8.30 Dpth 4.40 Welded, 1 dk	**(X11A2YP) Yacht**	**2 oil engines** reduction geared to sc. shafts driving 2 FP propellers Total Power: 820kW (1,114hp) Caterpillar 3406E-TA 2 x 4 Stroke 6 Cy. 137 x 165 each-410kW (557bhp) Caterpillar Inc-USA AuxGen: 2 x 99kW a.c Thrusters: 1 Tunnel thruster (f)
9390692 *A8OE2* -	**SOCRATES** - **Kerry Trading Co Ltd** Tsakos Columbia Shipmanagement (TCM) SA *Monrovia* Liberia MMSI: 636013615 Official number: 13615	41,676 21,792 74,327 T/cm 67.2	Class: AB	2008-03 **Sungdong Shipbuilding & Marine Engineering Co Ltd — Tongyeong** Yd No: 3004 Loa 228.00 (BB) Br ex - Dght 14.300 Lbp 219.00 Br md 32.24 Dpth 20.60 Welded, 1 dk	**(A13A2TW) Crude/Oil Products Tanker** Double Hull (13F) Liq: 78,928; Liq (Oil): 83,104 Cargo Heating Coils Compartments: 12 Wing Ta, 2 Wing Slop Ta, ER 3 Cargo Pump (s): 3x2000m³/hr Manifold: Bow/CM: 113.1m	**1 oil engine** driving 1 FP propeller Total Power: 12,240kW (16,642hp) 15.3kn MAN-B&W 6S60MC 1 x 2 Stroke 6 Cy. 600 x 2292 12240kW (16642bhp) STX Engine Co Ltd-South Korea AuxGen: 3 x 680kW a.c Fuel: 122.0 (d.f.) 2138.0 (r.f.)
7216555 *WBE2534* -	**SOCRATES** - **Capital Oil & Gas Industries Ltd** - *Charleston, SC* United States of America MMSI: 366856440 Official number: 502838	273 81 -		1966 **Burton Shipyard Co., Inc. — Port Arthur, Tx** Yd No: 369 Loa - Br ex 8.95 Dght 3.556 Lbp 35.13 Br md 8.87 Dpth 4.09 Welded, 1 dk	**(B32A2ST) Tug**	**2 oil engines** driving 2 FP propellers Total Power: 2,354kW (3,200hp) Fairbanks, Morse 8-38D8-1/8 2 x 2 Stroke 8 Cy. 207 x 254 each-1177kW (1600bhp) (made 1954) Fairbanks Morse & Co.-New Orleans, La
8941547 - -	**SOCRATES I** *ex* Ibrahim Buzi *-1998* *ex* Kanina *-1998* - -	*112* 75 -		1978-10 **Kantieri Detar "Durres" — Durres** Yd No: 119.2 Loa 25.00 Br ex - Dght - Lbp - Br md 6.20 Dpth 2.50 Welded, 1 dk	**(A31A2GX) General Cargo Ship**	**1 oil engine** driving 1 FP propeller Total Power: 425kW (578hp) S.K.L. 1 x 4 Stroke 425kW (578bhp) VEB Schwermaschinenbau "KarlLiebknecht" (SKL)-Magdeburg
9452517 *V7ZK2* -	**SOCRATIS** *ex* Thalassini Kyra *-2012* **Myrtos Shipping SA** Navina Maritime SA *Majuro* Marshall Islands MMSI: 538004843 Official number: 4843	34,374 19,565 58,609 T/cm 59.1	Class: AB	2010-06 **SPP Plant & Shipbuilding Co Ltd — Sacheon** Yd No: H1032 Loa 196.00 (BB) Br ex - Dght 13.000 Lbp 189.00 Br md 32.26 Dpth 18.60 Welded, 1 dk	**(A21A2BC) Bulk Carrier** Grain: 75,531; Bale: 70,734 Compartments: 5 Ho, ER 5 Ha: ER Cranes: 4x36t	**1 oil engine** driving 1 FP propeller Total Power: 9,973kW (13,559hp) 14.5kn MAN-B&W 6S50MC-C 1 x 2 Stroke 6 Cy. 500 x 2000 9973kW (13559bhp) Doosan Engine Co Ltd-South Korea AuxGen: 3 x 600kW a.c Fuel: 137.0 (d.f.) 2177.0 (r.f.)
9245524 *A7D6427* -	**SODA NATHEEL** - **Qatar Shipping Co (Q Ship) SPC** - *Doha* Qatar Official number: 172/2001	448 134 293	Class: AB	2001-05 **Bharati Shipyard Ltd — Ratnagiri** Yd No: 280 Loa 33.00 Br ex 10.90 Dght 4.500 Lbp 31.65 Br md 10.70 Dpth 5.50 Welded, 1 dk	**(B32A2ST) Tug**	**2 oil engines** with flexible couplings & reductiongeared to sc. shafts driving 2 FP propellers Total Power: 3,380kW (4,596hp) 12.0kn Wartsila 9L20 2 x 4 Stroke 9 Cy. 200 x 280 each-1690kW (2298bhp) Wartsila Finland Oy-Finland AuxGen: 2 x 145kW a.c Thrusters: 1 Thwart. FP thruster (f) Fuel: 156.0 (d.f.) 5.0pd
9655640 *A7D6716* -	**SODANATHEEL II** - **Qatar Navigation QSC (Milaha)** - *Doha* Qatar MMSI: 466501430	294 88 160	Class: LR ✠ **100A1** SS 11/2013 tug, fire-fighting Ship 1 (2400m3/h) **LMC** **UMS** Eq.Ltr: F; Cable: 275.0/19.0 U2 (a)	2013-11 **Nakilat Damen Shipyards Qatar Ltd — Ras Laffan** (Hull) Yd No: (511589) 2013-11 **B.V. Scheepswerf Damen — Gorinchem** Yd No: 511589 Loa 28.67 Br ex 10.43 Dght 5.000 Lbp 25.78 Br md 9.80 Dpth 4.60 Welded, 1 dk	**(B32A2ST) Tug**	**2 oil engines** gearing integral to driving 2 Directional propellers Total Power: 3,728kW (5,068hp) 12.9kn Caterpillar 3516C 2 x Vee 4 Stroke 16 Cy. 170 x 215 each-1864kW (2534bhp) Caterpillar Inc-USA AuxGen: 2 x 86kW 400V 50Hz a.c
9284312 *SBFW* -	**SODERARM** - **Waxholms Angfartygs AB** - *Vaxholm* Sweden MMSI: 265538450	686 206 70		2004-04 **AS Rigas Kugu Buvetava (Riga Shipyard) — Riga** (Hull) Yd No: 008/3 2004-04 **Moen Slip AS — Kolvereid** Yd No: 56 Loa 39.90 Br ex - Dght 2.850 Lbp 37.20 Br md 10.30 Dpth 4.40 Welded, 1 dk	**(A37B2PS) Passenger Ship** Passengers: unberthed: 350 Ice Capable	**2 oil engines** geared to sc. shafts driving 2 Directional propellers Total Power: 1,060kW (1,442hp) 12.0kn Mitsubishi S6R2-MPTK 2 x 4 Stroke 6 Cy. 170 x 220 each-530kW (721bhp) Mitsubishi Heavy Industries Ltd-Japan AuxGen: 2 x 168kW Thrusters: 1 Tunnel thruster (f)
7204930 *YDLG* -	**SOECHI ANINDYA** *ex* Bobo IV *-2005* *ex* Virgon *-1981* *ex* Hakuryu Maru *-1977* **PT Armada Bumi Pratiwi Lines (ABP Lines)** - *Jakarta* Indonesia MMSI: 525016102	*3,259* 1,794 4,992	Class: KI (NK)	1971-10 **Watanabe Zosen KK — Imabari EH** Yd No: 141 Loa 102.80 Br ex 15.27 Dght 6.000 Lbp 96.02 Br md 15.22 Dpth 7.80 Riveted\Welded, 1 dk	**(A13B2TP) Products Tanker** Liq: 6,185; Liq (Oil): 6,185 Compartments: 5 Ta, ER	**1 oil engine** driving 1 FP propeller Total Power: 3,089kW (4,200hp) 13.5kn Hanshin 6LU54 1 x 4 Stroke 6 Cy. 540 x 860 3089kW (4200bhp) Hanshin Nainenki Kogyo-Japan AuxGen: 2 x 120kW 445V a.c Fuel: 639.0 14.5pd
9110145 *PNWN* -	**SOECHI ASIA XXIX** *ex* Golden Asia *-2011* **PT Inti Energi Line** PT Sukses Osean Khatulistiwa Line *Jakarta* Indonesia MMSI: 525015817 Official number: 2011 PST NO.6824/L	3,868 1,749 6,312 T/cm 13.8	Class: KI NK	1994-08 **Murakami Hide Zosen K.K. — Imabari** Yd No: 362 Loa 104.99 (BB) Br ex - Dght 6.742 Lbp 97.50 Br md 16.60 Dpth 7.80 Welded, 1 dk	**(A12B2TR) Chemical/Products Tanker** Double Hull Liq: 6,190; Liq (Oil): 6,316 Cargo Heating Coils Compartments: 14 Wing Ta 14 Cargo Pump (s): 14x200m³/hr Manifold: Bow/CM: 53.9m	**1 oil engine** driving 1 FP propeller Total Power: 3,089kW (4,200hp) 12.5kn Mitsubishi 6UEC37LA 1 x 2 Stroke 6 Cy. 370 x 880 3089kW (4200bhp) Akasaka Tekkosho KK (Akasaka DieselLtd)-Japan AuxGen: 3 x 163kW a.c Fuel: 70.0 (d.f.) 350.0 (r.f.)
8403296 *YHIB* -	**SOECHI CHEMICAL I** *ex* Kyokuho Maru No. 7 *-2002* **PT Sukses Osean Khatulistiwa Line** - *Jakarta* Indonesia MMSI: 525019185	*674* 222 1,176	Class: KI	1984-06 **Teraoka Shipyard Co Ltd — Minamiawaji HG** Yd No: 235 Loa 63.00 Br ex 9.84 Dght 4.150 Lbp 57.99 Br md 9.81 Dpth 4.60 Welded, 1 dk	**(A12A2TC) Chemical Tanker** Liq: 899	**1 oil engine** driving 1 FP propeller Total Power: 883kW (1,201hp) Hanshin 6LU28 1 x 4 Stroke 6 Cy. 280 x 440 883kW (1201bhp) The Hanshin Diesel Works Ltd-Japan

8513948 *YHKY* -	**SOECHI CHEMICAL III** *ex* Etsuzan Maru No. 3 *-2004* **PT Sukses Osean Khatulistiwa Line** - *Jakarta* *Indonesia* MMSI: 525016099	**936** 326 1,498	Class: KI	**1985**-11 **Imamura Zosen — Kure** Yd No: 310 Loa 68.00 Br ex 11.05 Dght 4.390 Lbp 65.03 Br md 11.02 Dpth 5.16 Welded, 1 dk	**(A12A2TC) Chemical Tanker** Liq: 1,288	**1 oil engine** with clutches, flexible couplings & reverse reduction geared to sc. shaft driving 1 FP propeller Total Power: 956kW (1,300hp) Hanshin LH28G 1 x 4 Stroke 6 Cy. 280 x 460 956kW (1300bhp) The Hanshin Diesel Works Ltd-Japan
8319158 *YHPW* -	**SOECHI CHEMICAL V** *ex* Jeci *-2003* *ex* Hoshin *-1999* *ex* Hoshin Maru *-1990* **PT Sukses Osean Khatulistiwa Line** - *Jakarta* *Indonesia* Official number: 8552	**1,002** 491 1,714	Class: KI (NK)	**1983**-11 **Kochi Jyuko (Kaisei Zosen) K.K. — Kochi** Yd No: 1615 Loa 72.52 (BB) Br ex - Dght 4.417 Lbp 67.01 Br md 11.51 Dpth 5.16 Welded, 1 dk	**(A12B2TR) Chemical/Products Tanker** Liq: 1,398; Liq (Oil): 1,398 Compartments: 16 Ta, ER	**1 oil engine** driving 1 FP propeller Total Power: 1,103kW (1,500hp) 11.0kn Akasaka A28 1 x 4 Stroke 6 Cy. 280 x 550 1103kW (1500bhp) Akasaka Tekkosho KK (Akasaka DieselLtd)-Japan AuxGen: 2 x 104kW
8709585 *YHTH* -	**SOECHI CHEMICAL VII** *ex* Mar Lucia *-2004* **PT Sukses Osean Khatulistiwa Line** - *Jakarta* *Indonesia* MMSI: 525016302	**3,570** 1,441 4,409 T/cm 12.2	Class: KI (LR) ✠ Classed LR until 15/9/09	**1989**-06 **Union Naval de Levante SA (UNL) — Valencia** Yd No: 173 Loa 107.63 (BB) Br ex 15.53 Dght 6.011 Lbp 97.87 Br md 15.50 Dpth 7.40 Welded, 1 dk	**(A12A2TC) Chemical Tanker** Double Bottom Entire Compartment Length Liq: 4,798 Cargo Heating Coils Compartments: 6 Ta, 8 Wing Ta, 2 Wing Slop Ta, ER 16 Cargo Pump (s)	**1 oil engine** driving 1 FP propeller Total Power: 2,280kW (3,100hp) 14.5kn B&W 5L35MC 1 x 2 Stroke 5 Cy. 350 x 1050 2280kW (3100bhp) Astilleros Espanoles SA (AESA)-Spain AuxGen: 2 x 290kW 380V 50Hz a.c, 1 x 250kW 380V 50Hz a.c, 1 x 250kW 380V 50Hz a.c Thrusters: 1 Thwart. FP thruster (f); 1 Thwart. FP thruster (a) Fuel: 24.5 (d.f.) 238.9 (r.f.)
8403624 *PMAT* -	**SOECHI CHEMICAL XIX** *ex* GG Chemist *-2007* *ex* Sunyang Chemi 1 *-2003* *ex* Southern Princess 8 *-1999* *ex* Poemi Symphony *-1996* *ex* Southern Princess *-1991* **PT Sukses Osean Khatulistiwa Line** - *Jakarta* *Indonesia* MMSI: 525019373	**2,904** 1,380 4,901 T/cm 12.0	Class: KI (NK)	**1984**-09 **Fukuoka Shipbuilding Co Ltd — Fukuoka FO** Yd No: 1110 Loa 95.80 (BB) Br ex 15.04 Dght 6.449 Lbp 89.00 Br md 15.00 Dpth 7.73 Welded, 1 dk	**(A12B2TR) Chemical/Products Tanker** Liq: 5,113; Liq (Oil): 5,113 Cargo Heating Coils Compartments: 18 Ta, ER 12 Cargo Pump (s)	**1 oil engine** driving 1 FP propeller Total Power: 2,060kW (2,801hp) 12.1kn Hanshin 6EL38 1 x 4 Stroke 6 Cy. 380 x 760 2060kW (2801bhp) The Hanshin Diesel Works Ltd-Japan AuxGen: 2 x 280kW a.c Fuel: 500.0 (r.f.)
8609838 *PMKJ* -	**SOECHI CHEMICAL XXI** *ex* Siam Suchada *-2008* *ex* Sinar Perak *-2005* *ex* Tabah *-2001* *ex* Dovechem I *-1996* *ex* Suchinda *-1989* **PT Inti Energi Line** - *Jakarta* *Indonesia* MMSI: 525019401	**1,446** 666 2,235 T/cm 7.4	Class: KI (NK)	**1986**-10 **Towa Zosen K.K. — Shimonoseki** Yd No: 577 Loa 75.95 (BB) Br ex - Dght 5.111 Lbp 69.95 Br md 12.01 Dpth 6.30 Welded, 1 dk	**(A12B2TR) Chemical/Products Tanker** Double Bottom Entire Compartment Length Liq: 2,515; Liq (Oil): 2,515 Compartments: 1 Ta, 8 Wing Ta, ER 1 Cargo Pump (s): 1x200m³/hr	**1 oil engine** reverse geared to sc. shaft driving 1 FP propeller Total Power: 956kW (1,300hp) 11.0kn Akasaka A28 1 x 4 Stroke 6 Cy. 280 x 550 956kW (1300bhp) Akasaka Tekkosho KK (Akasaka DieselLtd)-Japan AuxGen: 2 x 120kW a.c Fuel: 140.0 (r.f.)
8013522 *YHYH* -	**SOECHI PRATIWI** *ex* Forgea I *-2006* *ex* Spring Grace *-2002* *ex* Shamrock Tres *-1998* *ex* Naniwa Maru No. 80 *-1991* **PT Sukses Osean Khatulistiwa Line** - *Jakarta* *Indonesia* MMSI: 525019268	**3,362** 1,636 5,280 T/cm 13.4	Class: KI (NK)	**1980**-08 **Higaki Zosen K.K. — Imabari** Yd No: 246 Loa 103.26 (BB) Br ex - Dght 6.031 Lbp 95.81 Br md 15.51 Dpth 7.32 Welded, 1 dk	**(A13B2TP) Products Tanker** Double Bottom Entire Compartment Length Liq: 5,847; Liq (Oil): 5,847 2 Cargo Pump (s)	**1 oil engine** driving 1 FP propeller Total Power: 3,310kW (4,500hp) 13.0kn Hanshin 6LU54 1 x 4 Stroke 6 Cy. 540 x 860 3310kW (4500bhp) The Hanshin Diesel Works Ltd-Japan AuxGen: 2 x 300kW 445V 60Hz a.c Fuel: 48.0 (d.f.) 372.5 (r.f.) 14.0pd
9036739 *YHCO* -	**SOECHI PRESTASI** *ex* Eishin Maru *-2001* **PT Sukses Osean Khatulistiwa Line** - *Jakarta* *Indonesia* MMSI: 525019132	**986** 407 1,728	Class: KI	**1992**-02 **Nakatani Shipyard Co. Ltd. — Etajima** Yd No: 546 Loa 70.94 (BB) Br ex - Dght 4.720 Lbp 65.00 Br md 11.30 Dpth 5.15 Welded, 1 dk	**(A12A2TC) Chemical Tanker**	**1 oil engine** geared to sc. shaft driving 1 FP propeller Total Power: 1,324kW (1,800hp) Hanshin 6EL30G 1 x 4 Stroke 6 Cy. 300 x 600 1324kW (1800bhp) The Hanshin Diesel Works Ltd-Japan Thrusters: 1 Thwart. FP thruster (f)
7518551 *PLVY* -	**SOEMANTRI BRODJONEGORO** **PT Pupuk Sriwidjaja Palembang (PUSRI)** - *Jakarta* *Indonesia* MMSI: 525018003	**7,404** 2,527 11,196	Class: KI (GL)	**1977**-03 **Mitsubishi Heavy Industries Ltd. — Yokohama** Yd No: 968 Loa 114.51 Br ex 20.05 Dght 6.035 Lbp 109.40 Br md 20.01 Dpth 10.01 Welded, 1 dk	**(A24C2BU) Urea Carrier** Grain: 12,751 Compartments: 1 Ho, ER 10 Ha: (4.5 x 3.5)9 (6.3 x 3.5)ER	**2 oil engines** reduction geared to sc. shafts driving 2 FP propellers Total Power: 3,678kW (5,000hp) 12.0kn Daihatsu 8DSM-32 2 x 4 Stroke 8 Cy. 320 x 380 each-1839kW (2500bhp) Daihatsu Diesel Manufacturing Co Lt-Japan AuxGen: 2 x 450kW 400V 50Hz a.c, 1 x 100kW 400V 50Hz a.c Thrusters: 1 Thwart. FP thruster (f) Fuel: 510.0 (d.f.) 20.0pd
8817447 *YE9030* -	**SOERYA 81** **PT Sinar Abadi Cemerlang** - *Ambon* *Indonesia*	*166* 99 -	Class: KI (NV)	**1989**-05 **Ocean Shipyards (WA) Pty Ltd — Fremantle WA** Yd No: 177 Loa 24.97 Br ex - Dght 3.401 Lbp - Br md 7.80 Dpth 7.79 Welded	**(B11A2FT) Trawler**	**1 oil engine** with clutches & reverse reduction geared to sc. shaft driving 1 FP propeller Total Power: 296kW (402hp) 8.7kn Caterpillar 3408TA 1 x Vee 4 Stroke 8 Cy. 137 x 152 296kW (402bhp) Caterpillar Inc-USA AuxGen: 2 x 85kW 415V 50Hz a.c
8817485 *YE9067* -	**SOERYA 82** **PT Sinar Abadi Cemerlang** - *Ambon* *Indonesia*	*166* 99 -	Class: KI (NV)	**1989**-08 **Ocean Shipyards (WA) Pty Ltd — Fremantle WA** Yd No: 181 Loa 24.97 Br ex - Dght 3.401 Lbp - Br md 7.80 Dpth - Welded, 1 dk	**(B11A2FT) Trawler**	**1 oil engine** with clutches & reverse reduction geared to sc. shaft driving 1 FP propeller Total Power: 296kW (402hp) 8.7kn Caterpillar 3408TA 1 x Vee 4 Stroke 8 Cy. 137 x 152 296kW (402bhp) Caterpillar Inc-USA AuxGen: 2 x 85kW 415V 50Hz a.c
8817459 *YE9031* -	**SOERYA 83** **PT Sinar Abadi Cemerlang** - *Ambon* *Indonesia*	*166* 99 -	Class: KI (NV)	**1989**-05 **Ocean Shipyards (WA) Pty Ltd — Fremantle WA** Yd No: 178 Loa 24.97 Br ex - Dght 3.401 Lbp - Br md 7.79 Dpth - Welded	**(B11A2FT) Trawler**	**1 oil engine** with clutches & reverse reduction geared to sc. shaft driving 1 FP propeller Total Power: 296kW (402hp) 8.7kn Caterpillar 3408TA 1 x Vee 4 Stroke 8 Cy. 137 x 152 296kW (402bhp) Caterpillar Inc-USA AuxGen: 2 x 85kW 415V 50Hz a.c
8817497 *YE9068* -	**SOERYA 85** **PT Sinar Abadi Cemerlang** - *Ambon* *Indonesia*	*166* 99 -	Class: KI (NV)	**1989**-08 **Ocean Shipyards (WA) Pty Ltd — Fremantle WA** Yd No: 182 Loa 24.97 Br ex - Dght 3.401 Lbp - Br md 7.80 Dpth - Welded, 1 dk	**(B11A2FT) Trawler**	**1 oil engine** geared to sc. shaft driving 1 FP propeller Total Power: 296kW (402hp) 8.7kn Caterpillar 3408TA 1 x Vee 4 Stroke 8 Cy. 137 x 152 296kW (402bhp) Caterpillar Inc-USA AuxGen: 2 x 85kW 415V 50Hz a.c
8817502 *YE9069* -	**SOERYA 86** **PT Sinar Abadi Cemerlang** - *Ambon* *Indonesia*	*166* 99 -	Class: KI (NV)	**1989**-10 **Ocean Shipyards (WA) Pty Ltd — Fremantle WA** Yd No: 183 Loa 24.97 Br ex - Dght 3.401 Lbp - Br md 7.80 Dpth - Welded, 1 dk	**(B11A2FT) Trawler**	**1 oil engine** with clutches & reverse reduction geared to sc. shaft driving 1 FP propeller Total Power: 296kW (402hp) 8.7kn Caterpillar 3408TA 1 x Vee 4 Stroke 8 Cy. 137 x 152 296kW (402bhp) Caterpillar Inc-USA AuxGen: 2 x 85kW 415V 50Hz a.c
8817514 *YE9070* -	**SOERYA 87** **PT Sinar Abadi Cemerlang** - *Ambon* *Indonesia*	*166* 99 -	Class: KI (NV)	**1989**-10 **Ocean Shipyards (WA) Pty Ltd — Fremantle WA** Yd No: 184 Loa 24.97 Br ex - Dght 3.401 Lbp - Br md 7.80 Dpth - Welded, 1 dk	**(B11A2FT) Trawler**	**1 oil engine** with clutches & reverse reduction geared to sc. shaft driving 1 FP propeller Total Power: 296kW (402hp) 8.7kn Caterpillar 3408TA 1 x Vee 4 Stroke 8 Cy. 137 x 152 296kW (402bhp) Caterpillar Inc-USA AuxGen: 2 x 85kW 415V 50Hz a.c
8817526 *YE9073* -	**SOERYA 88** **PT Sinar Abadi Cemerlang** - *Ambon* *Indonesia*	*166* 99 -	Class: KI (NV)	**1989**-12 **Ocean Shipyards (WA) Pty Ltd — Fremantle WA** Yd No: 185 Loa 24.97 Br ex - Dght 3.401 Lbp - Br md 7.80 Dpth - Welded, 1 dk	**(B11A2FT) Trawler**	**1 oil engine** geared to sc. shaft driving 1 FP propeller Total Power: 296kW (402hp) 8.7kn Caterpillar 3408TA 1 x Vee 4 Stroke 8 Cy. 137 x 152 296kW (402bhp) Caterpillar Inc-USA AuxGen: 2 x 85kW 415V 50Hz a.c

IMO / Call sign	Name / Owner	Tonnage	Class	Build / Dimensions	Type	Machinery
8817899 *YE9074* -	**SOERYA 89** **PT Sinar Abadi Cemerlang** - *Ambon* *Indonesia*	*166* 99 -	Class: KI (NV)	**1989-12 Ocean Shipyards (WA) Pty Ltd — Fremantle WA** Yd No: 186 Loa 24.97 Br ex - Dght 3.401 Lbp - Br md 7.80 Dpth - Welded, 1 dk	**(B11A2FT) Trawler**	**1 oil engine** geared to sc. shaft driving 1 FP propeller Total Power: 296kW (402hp) 8.7kn Caterpillar 3408TA 1 x Vee 4 Stroke 8 Cy. 137 x 152 296kW (402bhp) Caterpillar Inc-USA AuxGen: 2 x 85kW 415V 50Hz a.c
9222065 *OPAR* Z 18	**SOETKIN** **Rederij Versluys-Couwyzer BVBA** - *Zeebrugge* *Belgium* MMSI: 205306000 Official number: 01 00415 1999	**386** 115 -		**2000-09 'Crist' Sp z oo — Gdansk** (Hull) **2000-09 Scheepswerf van der Werff en Visser — Irnsum** Yd No: 318 Loa 37.79 Br ex - Dght 5.400 Lbp 33.01 Br md 8.56 Dpth 4.76 Welded, 1 dk	**(B11A2FT) Trawler** Bale: 200	**1 oil engine** geared to sc. shaft driving 1 FP propeller Total Power: 883kW (1,201hp) A.B.C. 8DZC 1 x 4 Stroke 8 Cy. 256 x 310 883kW (1201bhp) Anglo Belgian Corp NV (ABC)-Belgium
8319615 *J8II2* -	**SOFALA** *ex* Pentow Service *-2012* *ex* Osam Service *-1993* **Smit Amandla Marine Pty Ltd** - SatCom: Inmarsat C 437601314 *Kingstown* *St Vincent & The Grenadines* MMSI: 376617000 Official number: 6016	**736** 221 840	Class: BV (AB)	**1983-09 Tonoura Dock Co. Ltd. — Miyazaki** Yd No: 73 Loa 42.02 Br ex 12.70 Dght 4.480 Lbp 36.00 Br md 12.50 Dpth 5.01 Welded, 1 dk	**(B21B20T) Offshore Tug/Supply Ship**	**2 oil engines** sr geared to sc. shafts driving 2 CP propellers Total Power: 2,236kW (3,040hp) 10.0kn Fuji 8M23C 2 x 4 Stroke 8 Cy. 230 x 260 each-1118kW (1520bhp) Fuji Diesel Co Ltd-Japan AuxGen: 1 x 240kW 415V 50Hz a.c, 1 x 160kW 415V 50Hz a.c Thrusters: 1 Thwart. CP thruster (f) Fuel: 374.0 (d.f.) 7.0pd
8204573 *4RAX* -	**SOFIA** *ex* Sofia 1 *-2008* *ex* Commander *-2007* *ex* Green Saikai *-1999* **Capital City Marine Services (Pvt) Ltd** Ocean Ship Management Pte Ltd *Colombo* *Sri Lanka* MMSI: 417222311 Official number: 1282	**11,315** 6,871 18,433 T/cm 29.2	Class: NK	**1983-03 Sasebo Heavy Industries Co. Ltd. — Sasebo Yard, Sasebo** Yd No: 310 Loa 147.87 (BB) Br ex 23.14 Dght 9.300 Lbp 138.82 Br md 23.11 Dpth 12.63 Welded, 1 dk	**(A21A2BC) Bulk Carrier** Grain: 24,130; Bale: 23,574 Compartments: 4 Ho, ER 4 Ha: (17.6 x 9.6)3 (19.2 x 11.2)ER Derricks: 4x25t	**1 oil engine** driving 1 FP propeller Total Power: 4,413kW (6,000hp) 14.0kn Mitsubishi 6UEC52/125H 1 x 2 Stroke 6 Cy. 520 x 1250 4413kW (6000bhp) Kobe Hatsudoki KK-Japan AuxGen: 2 x 400kW 450V 60Hz a.c Fuel: 139.0 (d.f.) 1191.5 (r.f.) 18.5pd
1011874 *V7ZB6* -	**SOFIA** **Ferrum Investments Ltd** - *Bikini* *Marshall Islands* MMSI: 538070874 Official number: 70874	**469** 140 335	Class: LR ✠ **100A1** SS 03/2013 SSC Yacht, mono, G6 **LMC** Cable: 302.5/19.0 U2 (a)	**2013-03 Moonen Shipyards B.V. — 's-Hertogenbosch** Yd No: 194 Loa 40.80 Br ex 8.40 Dght - Lbp 35.10 Br md 8.20 Dpth 4.25 Welded, 1 dk	**(X11A2YP) Yacht**	**2 oil engines** with clutches, flexible couplings & sr reverse geared to sc. shafts driving 2 FP propellers Total Power: 1,492kW (2,028hp) Caterpillar C32 2 x Vee 4 Stroke 12 Cy. 145 x 162 each-746kW (1014bhp) Caterpillar Inc-USA AuxGen: 1 x 80kW 400V 50Hz a.c, 1 x 50kW 400V 50Hz a.c Thrusters: 1 Thwart. FP thruster (f); 1 Thwart. FP thruster (a)
8816730 *CNA2479* -	**SOFIA** **Asmaroc SA** Grupo Amasua SA *Casablanca* *Morocco*	**395** 118 300	Class: (BV)	**1989-10 Construcciones Navales P Freire SA — Vigo** Yd No: 367 Loa 37.17 Br ex 8.52 Dght 4.050 Lbp 31.53 Br md 8.51 Dpth 6.23 Welded, 1 dk	**(B11A2FS) Stern Trawler** Ins: 315	**1 oil engine** with flexible couplings & sr gearedto sc. shaft driving 1 FP propeller Total Power: 772kW (1,050hp) 11.0kn Wartsila 6R22 1 x 4 Stroke 6 Cy. 220 x 240 772kW (1050bhp) Construcciones Echevarria SA-Spain
9312690 *PJKK* -	**SOFIA** **ms 'Sofia' Schiffahrtsgesellschaft mbH & Co Reederei KG** Intersee Schiffahrtsgesellschaft mbH & Co KG SatCom: Inmarsat C 430674910 *Willemstad* *Curacao* MMSI: 306749000	**3,870** 2,132 5,780 T/cm 13.0	Class: BV	**2005-06 Maritim Shipyard Sp z oo — Gdansk** (Hull) **2005-06 Niestern Sander B.V. — Delfzijl** Yd No: 823 Loa 106.12 (BB) Br ex - Dght 6.140 Lbp 100.05 Br md 14.40 Dpth 8.10 Welded, 1 dk	**(A31A2GX) General Cargo Ship** Grain: 7,645 TEU 240 Ice Capable	**1 oil engine** geared to sc. shaft driving 1 CP propeller Total Power: 2,700kW (3,671hp) 13.0kn MaK 9M25 1 x 4 Stroke 9 Cy. 255 x 400 2700kW (3671bhp) Caterpillar Motoren GmbH & Co. KG-Germany AuxGen: 2 x 288kW 400/220V 50Hz a.c, 1 x 360kW 400/220V 50Hz a.c Thrusters: 1 Tunnel thruster (f) Fuel: 88.0 (d.f.) 245.0 (r.f.)
9460409 *CXCS* -	**SOFIA** *ex* Sea & Sea *-2014* *ex* Sofia I *-2009* *ex* Sea & Sea *-2009* *ex* Ning Hu 28 *-2007* **Sirius Tankers SA** - *Uruguay* MMSI: 770576318	**2,951** 1,556 4,900		**2007-04 Rui'an Jiangnan Shiprepair & Building Yard — Rui'an ZJ** Yd No: 28 Loa 99.86 Br ex - Dght 6.200 Lbp 93.00 Br md 15.20 Dpth 7.60 Welded, 1 dk	**(A13B2TP) Products Tanker** Double Hull (13F)	**1 oil engine** geared to sc. shaft driving 1 Propeller Total Power: 1,765kW (2,400hp) 12.0kn Chinese Std. Type G8300ZC 1 x 4 Stroke 8 Cy. 300 x 380 1765kW (2400bhp) Wuxi Antai Power Machinery Co Ltd-China
9472086 *A8WY7* -	**SOFIA** **Cheyenne Maritime Co** Goldenport Shipmanagement Ltd *Monrovia* *Liberia* MMSI: 636014863 Official number: 14863	**32,983** 19,191 56,899 T/cm 58.8	Class: NK	**2011-07 COSCO (Zhoushan) Shipyard Co Ltd — Zhoushan ZJ** Yd No: ZS07038 Loa 189.99 (BB) Br ex - Dght 12.818 Lbp 185.00 Br md 32.26 Dpth 18.00 Welded, 1 dk	**(A21A2BC) Bulk Carrier** Grain: 71,634; Bale: 68,200 Compartments: 5 Ho, ER 5 Ha: ER Cranes: 4x30t	**1 oil engine** driving 1 FP propeller Total Power: 9,480kW (12,889hp) 14.2kn MAN-B&W 6S50MC-C 1 x 2 Stroke 6 Cy. 500 x 2000 9480kW (12889bhp) Mitsui Engineering & Shipbuilding CLtd-Japan Fuel: 2400.0
9507283 *V7WO2* -	**SOFIA 3** *ex* Le Yana *-2011* *ex* Macalulu *-2009* **Sofia 3 Ltd** - *Bikini* *Marshall Islands* MMSI: 538070791 Official number: 70791	**419** 125 104	Class: AB	**2008-05 Baglietto S.p.A. — Varazze** Yd No: 10196 Loa 42.75 (BB) Br ex 8.90 Dght 2.950 Lbp 37.40 Br md 8.40 Dpth 4.75 Welded, 1 dk	**(X11A2YP) Yacht**	**2 oil engines** reduction geared to sc. shafts driving 2 FP propellers Total Power: 1,940kW (2,638hp) 14.5kn Caterpillar 3512B 2 x Vee 4 Stroke 12 Cy. 170 x 190 each-970kW (1319bhp) Caterpillar Inc-USA AuxGen: 2 x 86kW a.c
9450404 *DGZT2* -	**SOFIA EXPRESS** **Hapag-Lloyd AG** - SatCom: Inmarsat C 421836610 *Hamburg* *Germany* MMSI: 218366000 Official number: 22527	**93,750** 37,699 104,007 T/cm 122.0	Class: GL	**2010-06 Hyundai Heavy Industries Co Ltd — Ulsan** Yd No: 2077 Loa 335.06 (BB) Br ex - Dght 14.610 Lbp 319.00 Br md 42.80 Dpth 24.50 Welded, 1 dk	**(A33A2CC) Container Ship (Fully Cellular)** TEU 8749	**1 oil engine** driving 1 FP propeller Total Power: 57,200kW (77,769hp) 25.2kn MAN-B&W 10K98ME 1 x 2 Stroke 10 Cy. 980 x 2660 57200kW (77769bhp) Hyundai Heavy Industries Co Ltd-South Korea AuxGen: 1 x 4000kW 6600/690V a.c, 2 x 3900kW 6600/690V a.c, 2 x 2700kW 6600/690V a.c Thrusters: 1 Tunnel thruster (f)
1010325 *V7ON6* -	**SOFIA II** **Losa Ltd** - *Bikini* *Marshall Islands* MMSI: 538070577 Official number: 70577	**191** 57 -	Class: LR ✠ **100A1** SS 11/2013 SSC Yacht, mono, G6 **LMC** Cable: 240.0/16.0 SH	**2008-11 Jachtwerf Jongert B.V. — Medemblik** (Hull) Yd No: (190) **2008-11 Moonen Shipyards B.V. — 's-Hertogenbosch** Yd No: 190 Loa 30.38 Br ex 7.30 Dght 2.000 Lbp 26.05 Br md 7.00 Dpth 3.86 Welded, 1 dk	**(X11A2YP) Yacht**	**2 oil engines** with clutches, flexible couplings & reverse reduction geared to sc. shafts driving 2 FP propellers Total Power: 894kW (1,216hp) 15.0kn Caterpillar C18 2 x 4 Stroke 6 Cy. 145 x 183 each-447kW (608bhp) Caterpillar Inc-USA AuxGen: 2 x 40kW 230V 50Hz a.c Thrusters: 1 Thwart. FP thruster (f)
9392511 *C9Y77* -	**SOFIA III** *ex* Shelf Explorer *-2009* **Mozambique Minerals Ltd** Kenmare Resources Plc *Maputo* *Mozambique* MMSI: 650148000 Official number: 9392511	**178** 54 146	Class: LR (NK) **100A1** SS 10/2011 tug **LMC**	**2006-10 Bonafile Shipbuilders & Repairs Sdn Bhd — Sandakan** Yd No: 33/04 Loa 26.20 Br ex - Dght 2.910 Lbp 24.72 Br md 8.00 Dpth 3.83 Welded, 1 dk	**(B32A2ST) Tug**	**2 oil engines** reduction geared to sc. shafts driving 2 Propellers Total Power: 1,220kW (1,658hp) 11.0kn Yanmar 2 x 4 Stroke each-610kW (829bhp) Yanmar Diesel Engine Co Ltd-Japan
8735089 *CULJ7* S-2103-C	**SOFIA ISABEL** - - *Setubal* *Portugal*	**164** - -		**2001 Estaleiros Navais Lda. (ASTINAVA) — Figueira da Foz** Loa 24.00 Br ex - Dght - Lbp 19.87 Br md - Dpth - Welded, 1 dk	**(B11A2FS) Stern Trawler**	**1 oil engine** driving 1 Propeller Total Power: 447kW (608hp)
8328094 *HP2032* -	**SOFIA LYNN** *ex* Genesis I *-2003* *ex* Geminis *-2000* **Agropesquera Industrial Bahia Cupica SA** - *Panama* *Panama* Official number: 3069605A	**736** 509 -	Class: (RI)	**1967 J M Martinac Shipbuilding Corp — Tacoma WA** Loa 47.86 Br ex 10.42 Dght - Lbp - Br md - Dpth 5.80 Riveted\Welded, 1 dk	**(B11B2FV) Fishing Vessel**	**1 oil engine** driving 1 FP propeller Total Power: 2,096kW (2,850hp) 10.0kn EMD (Electro-Motive) 12-645-E5 1 x Vee 2 Stroke 12 Cy. 230 x 254 2096kW (2850bhp) General Motors Corp-USA

IMO / Call sign	Name / Owner	Tonnage	Class	Builder / Dimensions	Type / Cargo	Machinery
9593634 *IIYA2* -	**SOFIA M** - **Ustica Lines SpA** - *Palermo* *Italy* MMSI: 247294200 Official number: 381011	**242** 72 112	Class: RI (BV)	**2010**-06 **Air Naval Srl — Torre Annunziata** Yd No: 1011 Loa 37.50 Br ex 7.00 Dght 1.500 Lbp 31.60 Br md 7.00 Dpth 2.49 Welded, 1 dk	**(A37B2PS) Passenger Ship** Hull Material: Aluminium Alloy Passengers: unberthed: 206	**3 oil engines** reduction geared to sc. shafts driving 3 FP propellers Total Power: 3,243kW (4,410hp) 30.0kn Caterpillar C32 ACERT 3 x Vee 4 Stroke 12 Cy. 145 x 162 each-1081kW (1470bhp) Caterpillar Inc-USA Thrusters: 1 Tunnel thruster (f)
7331434 - - -	**SOFIA No. 7** *ex* Taisho Maru No. 11 *-1990* *ex* Jinpo Maru No. 65 *-1984* *ex* Taisei Maru No. 38 *-1982* **Gold Fish Co Ltd** - *San Lorenzo* *Honduras* Official number: L-1923048	*233* 114 296		**1973 Nishii Dock Co. Ltd. — Ise** Yd No: 252 Loa 44.51 Br ex 7.73 Dght 2.998 Lbp 38.87 Br md 7.70 Dpth 3.31 Riveted\Welded, 1 dk	**(B11B2FV) Fishing Vessel**	**1 oil engine** driving 1 FP propeller Total Power: 625kW (850hp) Niigata 6L28X 1 x 4 Stroke 6 Cy. 280 x 440 625kW (850bhp) Niigata Engineering Co Ltd-Japan
9686194 - -	**SOFIA ONE** *ex* Xiang Chang De Huo 1111 *-2013* **Auraphie Pacific Corp** -	**1,857** 557 4,500	Class: ZC (Class contemplated)	**2012**-10 **Taoyuan Hengsheng Shipyard — Taoyuan County HN** Loa 83.80 Br ex 19.03 Dght 3.400 Lbp 80.00 Br md 19.00 Dpth 4.30 Welded, 1 dk	**(A31C2GD) Deck Cargo Ship**	**2 oil engines** reduction geared to sc. shafts driving 2 Propellers Total Power: 1,150kW (1,564hp) Chinese Std. Type 8170ZLC 2 x 4 Stroke 8 Cy. 170 x 200 each-575kW (782bhp) Zibo Diesel Engine Factory-China
9423308 *LW3427*	**SOFIA R** - **Bunkerbaires SA** Risler SA *Buenos Aires* *Argentina* MMSI: 701006126 Official number: 02560	*219* - 550		**2006**-11 **Riopal SA — Escobar** Yd No: 01 Loa 45.60 Br ex - Dght 2.400 Lbp 43.50 Br md 8.35 Dpth 2.95 Welded, 1 dk	**(B35E2TF) Bunkering Tanker** Double Hull (13F)	**2 oil engines** reduction geared to sc. shafts driving 2 FP propellers Total Power: 560kW (762hp) Cummins NTA-855-M 2 x 4 Stroke 6 Cy. 140 x 152 each-280kW (381bhp) Cummins Engine Co Inc-USA
9530967 *D5AN5* -	**SOFIA R** - **Fairsea Navigation Corp** John J Rigos Marine Enterprises SA SatCom: Inmarsat C 463712458 *Monrovia* *Liberia* MMSI: 636015406 Official number: 15406	**22,733** 12,330 36,093 T/cm 46.1	Class: LR ✠ **100A1** SS 05/2012 bulk carrier CSR BC-A GRAB (20) Nos. 2 and 4 holds may be empty ESP Shipright (ACS (B),CM) *IWS LI ✠ **LMC** **UMS** Eq.Ltr: J†; Cable: 605.0/66.0 U3 (a)	**2012**-05 **Hyundai Mipo Dockyard Co Ltd — Ulsan** Yd No: 6020 Loa 186.40 (BB) Br ex 27.84 Dght 10.918 Lbp 178.00 Br md 27.80 Dpth 15.60 Welded, 1 dk	**(A21A2BC) Bulk Carrier** Grain: 47,922; Bale: 47,692 Compartments: 5 Ho, ER 5 Ha: ER Cranes: 4x30t	**1 oil engine** driving 1 FP propeller Total Power: 7,860kW (10,686hp) 14.8kn MAN-B&W 6S46MC-C 1 x 2 Stroke 6 Cy. 460 x 1932 7860kW (10686bhp) Hyundai Heavy Industries Co Ltd-South Korea AuxGen: 3 x 540kW 450V 60Hz a.c Boilers: AuxB (Comp) 9.2kgf/cm² (9.0bar)
9462873 *2CKX3* -	**SOFICO** - **ING Lease France SA** Waterman Marine Consultancy Sarl *Douglas* *Isle of Man (British)* MMSI: 235073659 Official number: 741893	**499** 272 55	Class: RI	**2009**-07 **C.R.N. Cant. Nav. Ancona S.r.l. — Ancona** Yd No: 43/04 Loa 42.60 Br ex - Dght 2.350 Lbp 36.16 Br md 8.65 Dpth 4.60 Welded, 1 dk	**(X11A2YP) Yacht** Hull Material: Reinforced Plastic	**2 oil engines** reduction geared to sc. shafts driving 2 FP propellers Total Power: 2,088kW (2,838hp) 13.0kn Caterpillar C32 2 x Vee 4 Stroke 12 Cy. 145 x 162 each-1044kW (1419bhp) Caterpillar Inc-USA AuxGen: 2 x 80kW a.c
8962345 *LCSR* N-6-V	**SOFIE** *ex* Birgerson *-2008* *ex* Vestoy *-2006* *ex* Karoliussen *-2006* **Sofie Svolvaer AS** - *Tromso* *Norway* MMSI: 257475500	**134** 53 -		**1957 Kvernenes Skipsbyggeri — Brandasund** Yd No: 35/1 Loa 21.20 Br ex - Dght - Lbp - Br md 6.40 Dpth 3.88 Welded, 1 dk	**(B11B2FV) Fishing Vessel**	**1 oil engine** driving 1 FP propeller Total Power: 294kW (400hp) 10.0kn Caterpillar 1 x 4 Stroke 294kW (400bhp) (new engine 1965) Caterpillar Tractor Co-USA
9310604 *9HSI8* -	**SOFIE BULKER** - **Lauritzen Bulkers A/S** - *Valletta* *Malta* MMSI: 256367000 Official number: 9310604	**17,663** 10,133 28,682	Class: NK	**2007**-03 **Shin Kochi Jyuko K.K. — Kochi** Yd No: 7197 Loa 176.63 (BB) Br ex - Dght 9.633 Lbp 169.40 Br md 26.00 Dpth 13.60 Welded, 1 dk	**(A21A2BC) Bulk Carrier** Grain: 39,052; Bale: 37,976 Compartments: 5 Ho, ER 5 Ha: 4 (19.5 x 17.8)ER (17.9 x 12.8) Cranes: 4x30.5t	**1 oil engine** driving 1 FP propeller Total Power: 5,900kW (8,022hp) 14.1kn Mitsubishi 5UEC52LA 1 x 2 Stroke 5 Cy. 520 x 1600 5900kW (8022bhp) Kobe Hatsudoki KK-Japan Fuel: 93.0 (d.f.) 1024.0 (r.f.)
9146479 *OZUN2* -	**SOFIE MAERSK** - **A P Moller - Maersk A/S** A P Moller SatCom: Inmarsat B 321977620 *Copenhagen* *Denmark (DIS)* MMSI: 219776000 Official number: D3660	**92,198** 53,625 110,381 T/cm 124.0	Class: AB	**1998**-12 **Odense Staalskibsvaerft A/S — Munkebo (Lindo Shipyard)** Yd No: 165 Loa 346.98 (BB) Br ex - Dght 14.940 Lbp 331.54 Br md 42.80 Dpth 24.10 Welded, 1 dk	**(A33A2CC) Container Ship (Fully Cellular)** TEU 9578 incl 817 ref C Compartments: ER, 20 Cell Ho 20 Ha: ER	**1 oil engine** driving 1 FP propeller Total Power: 54,898kW (74,639hp) 25.0kn B&W 12K90MC 1 x 2 Stroke 12 Cy. 900 x 2550 54898kW (74639bhp) Hitachi Zosen Corp-Japan AuxGen: 5 x 3000kW 6600V 60Hz a.c Thrusters: 1 Thwart. FP thruster (f); 2 Thwart. FP thruster (a)
9297151 *OUQV2* -	**SOFIE THERESA** *launched as* Aylin *-2004* **Herning Shipping A/S** - *Struer* *Denmark (DIS)* MMSI: 220264000 Official number: D4062	**2,660** 1,085 3,418 T/cm 10.8	Class: BV (LR) Classed LR until 5/6/13	**2004**-08 **Dearsan Gemi Insaat ve Sanayii Koll. Sti. — Tuzla** Yd No: 27 Loa 92.86 (BB) Br ex - Dght 5.600 Lbp 86.65 Br md 14.10 Dpth 7.20 Welded, 1 dk	**(A12B2TR) Chemical/Products Tanker** Double Hull (13F) Liq: 4,018; Liq (Oil): 4,018 Cargo Heating Coils Compartments: 1 Ta, ER, 12 Wing Ta 3 Cargo Pump (s): 3x257m³/hr Manifold: Bow/CM: 54.1m Ice Capable	**1 oil engine** with clutches, flexible couplings & sr geared to sc. shaft driving 1 CP propeller Total Power: 2,040kW (2,774hp) 13.5kn MAN-B&W 6L27/38 1 x 4 Stroke 6 Cy. 270 x 380 2040kW (2774bhp) (made 2003) MAN B&W Diesel A/S-Denmark AuxGen: 3 x 320kW 50Hz a.c Boilers: WTAuxB (o.f.) 10.2kgf/cm² (10.0bar) Thrusters: 1 Tunnel thruster (f) Fuel: 45.0 (d.f.) 268.0 (d.f.) 7.5pd
6618172 *YYV2347* -	**SOFIGNE** *ex* Zuliano XI *-2003* *ex* Condor VI *-1993* *ex* Condor *-1992* **Servicios Remolcadores del Caribe CA (SERECA)** - *Puerto Sucre* *Venezuela* Official number: APNN-8.515	*222* 184 203	Class: (AB)	**1966 Mitsubishi Heavy Industries Ltd. — Shimonoseki** Yd No: 605 Loa 33.28 Br ex 8.72 Dght 4.687 Lbp 31.40 Br md 8.69 Dpth 5.19 Welded, 1 dk	**(B32A2ST) Tug**	**2 oil engines** reverse reduction geared to sc. shafts driving 2 FP propellers Total Power: 2,206kW (3,000hp) General Motors 16-278-A 2 x Vee 2 Stroke 16 Cy. 222 x 267 each-1103kW (1500bhp) (Re-engined ,made 1943, Reconditioned & fitted 1966) General Motors Corp-USA AuxGen: 2 x 350kW Fuel: 163.5
9383481 *5BEN2* -	**SOFRANA JOINVILLE** *ex* Mcp Salzburg *-2013* *ex* Micronesian Pride *-2013* *ex* MCP Salzburg *-2012* **mv Unterloiben Shipping Co Ltd** Oesterreichischer Lloyd Seereederei (Cyprus) Ltd *Limassol* *Cyprus* MMSI: 212031000 Official number: 9383481	**5,272** 2,309 7,852	Class: CC	**2008**-06 **Huanghai Shipbuilding Co Ltd — Rongcheng SD** Yd No: HCY-62 Loa 117.00 (BB) Br ex 19.74 Dght 6.450 Lbp 110.00 Br md 19.70 Dpth 8.50 Welded, 1 dk	**(A31A2GX) General Cargo Ship** Grain: 9,523; Bale: 9,422 TEU 629 C Ho 199 TEU C Dk 430 TEU incl 60 ref C. Compartments: 3 Ho, ER 3 Ha: (25.4 x 15.0) (31.9 x 15.0)ER (19.5 x 15.0) Ice Capable	**2 oil engines** reverse reduction geared to sc. shafts driving 2 FP propellers Total Power: 5,000kW (6,798hp) 13.8kn Daihatsu 8DKM-28 2 x 4 Stroke 8 Cy. 280 x 390 each-2500kW (3399bhp) Shaanxi Diesel Heavy Industry Co Lt-China AuxGen: 3 x 270kW 450V 60Hz a.c Fuel: 230.0 (d.f.) 380.0 (r.f.)
9295529 *V2CN5* -	**SOFRANA SURVILLE** *ex* Monia *-2007* **ms 'Monia' tom Worden GmbH & Co KG** Schiffahrtskontor tom Worden GmbH & Co KG *Saint John's* *Antigua & Barbuda* MMSI: 305051000 Official number: 4284	**9,935** 5,198 12,343	Class: GL	**2007**-06 **Jiangsu Eastern Heavy Industry Co Ltd — Jingjiang JS** Yd No: 02C-019 Loa 140.67 (BB) Br ex 23.60 Dght 8.700 Lbp - Br md 23.20 Dpth 11.50 Welded, 1 dk	**(A33A2CC) Container Ship (Fully Cellular)** TEU 887 C Ho 322 TEU C Dk 565 TEU incl 200 ref C Cranes: 2x45t Ice Capable	**1 oil engine** reduction geared to sc. shaft driving 1 FP propeller Total Power: 8,400kW (11,421hp) 18.0kn MaK 9M43 1 x 4 Stroke 9 Cy. 430 x 610 8400kW (11421bhp) Caterpillar Motoren GmbH & Co. KG-Germany Thrusters: 1 Tunnel thruster (f); 1 Tunnel thruster (a)

9408372 *A8QY2* -	**SOFRANA TOURVILLE** *ex Avra -2010* **Sea Plantain Corp** Cosmoship Management SA *Monrovia* *Liberia* MMSI: 636014031 Official number: 14031	**9,684** 4,716 12,502	Class: BV (GL)	**2009-10 Dae Sun Shipbuilding & Engineering Co Ltd — Busan** Yd No: 481 Loa 142.70 (BB) Br ex - Dght 8.200 Lbp 133.50 Br md 22.60 Dpth 11.20 Welded, 1 dk	**(A33A2CC) Container Ship (Fully Cellular)** Double Hull TEU 1037 incl 180 ref C Compartments: 5 Cell Ho, ER Cranes: 2x40t,1	**1 oil engine** driving 1 FP propeller Total Power: 7,860kW (10,686hp) 18.0kn MAN-B&W 6S46MC-C 1 x 2 Stroke 6 Cy. 460 x 1932 7860kW (10686bhp) STX Engine Co Ltd-South Korea AuxGen: 3 x 615kW 445V 60Hz a.c Thrusters: 1 Tunnel thruster (f) Fuel: 687.0 (d.f.)
6829264 - -	**SOFRIMA No. 1** *ex Dae Yong No. 1 -1982* *ex Fukujin Maru No. 21 -1977* *ex Hokuetsu Maru No. 21 -1977* **Sofrima** Daerim Fishery Co Ltd *Nouadhibou* *Mauritania*	*123* 40 -	Class: (KR)	**1968 Nichiro Zosen K.K. — Hakodate** Yd No: 266 Loa 35.51 Br ex 6.53 Dght 2.490 Lbp 29.60 Br md 6.51 Dpth 2.80 Welded, 1 dk	**(B11A2FS) Stern Trawler** Ins: 104 1 Ha: (6.7 x 1.9)	**1 oil engine** driving 1 FP propeller Total Power: 662kW (900hp) 10.5kn Fuji 6S27.5CH2F 1 x 4 Stroke 6 Cy. 275 x 410 662kW (900bhp) Fuji Diesel Co Ltd-Japan AuxGen: 2 x 28kW 225V a.c
6509151 - -	**SOFU MARU** - **San-Chuan Marine Pte Ltd**	*145* 43 -	Class: (NK) (NV)	**1964 Shin Yamamoto Shipbuilding & Engineering Co Ltd — Kochi KC** Yd No: 37 Loa 26.42 Br ex 7.57 Dght 2.515 Lbp 24.01 Br md 7.50 Dpth 3.41 Welded, 1 dk	**(B32A2ST) Tug**	**2 oil engines** driving 2 FP propellers Total Power: 1,472kW (2,002hp) 13.0kn Fuji 2 x 4 Stroke 6 Cy. 350 x 480 each-736kW (1001bhp) Fuji Diesel Co Ltd-Japan AuxGen: 1 x 24kW 225V 60Hz a.c
8618516 *JJ3503* -	**SOFU MARU** - **Hayakoma Unyu KK** - *Kobe, Hyogo* *Japan* Official number: 129160	*164* - -		**1987-02 Kanagawa Zosen — Kobe** Yd No: 294 Loa 30.87 Br ex - Dght 2.701 Lbp 26.01 Br md 8.81 Dpth 3.81 Welded, 1 dk	**(B32A2ST) Tug**	**2 oil engines** Geared Integral to driving 2 Z propellers Total Power: 1,912kW (2,600hp) 12.9kn Fuji 6L27.5G 2 x 4 Stroke 6 Cy. 275 x 320 each-956kW (1300bhp) Fuji Diesel Co Ltd-Japan
8860262 - -	**SOFULAR 1** - **Sofuoglu Denizcilik ve Ticaret AS** - *Istanbul* *Turkey* Official number: 3908	*275* 157 500		**1960 Torlaklar Tersanesi — Istanbul** Loa 48.00 Br ex - Dght - Lbp 45.00 Br md 7.27 Dpth 2.95 Welded, 1 dk	**(A31A2GX) General Cargo Ship** Cranes: 3x3t	**1 oil engine** driving 1 FP propeller Total Power: 315kW (428hp) 10.0kn S.K.L. 1 x 4 Stroke 315kW (428bhp) VEB Schwermaschinenbau "KarlLiebknecht" (SKL)-Magdeburg
9151424 *3FDR8* -	**SOGA** - **Taga Line SA** Tagashira Kaiun Co Ltd SatCom: Inmarsat B 335199610 *Panama* *Panama* MMSI: 351996000 Official number: 2538398C	**13,448** 5,857 17,224 T/cm 31.5	Class: NK	**1998-02 Shin Kochi Jyuko K.K. — Kochi** Yd No: 7095 Loa 159.53 (BB) Br ex - Dght 8.718 Lbp 150.00 Br md 25.00 Dpth 12.80 Welded, 1 dk	**(A33A2CC) Container Ship (Fully Cellular)** Bale: 3,093 TEU 1157 C Ho 464 TEU C Dk 673 TEU incl 120 ref C. 15 Ha: (9.8 x 8.5)2 (12.6 x 8.0)6 (12.8 x 10.6)6 (12.6 x 10.6)ER Cranes: 2x40t	**1 oil engine** driving 1 FP propeller Total Power: 9,628kW (13,090hp) 18.0kn Mitsubishi 7UEC50LSII 1 x 2 Stroke 7 Cy. 500 x 1950 9628kW (13090bhp) Kobe Hatsudoki KK-Japan AuxGen: 4 x 438kW 440/100V 60Hz a.c Thrusters: 1 Thwart. CP thruster (f) Fuel: 1680.0
8110980 *LLPV* -	**SOGN** *ex Alversund -1996* **Fjord1 AS** - *Maaloy* *Norway* MMSI: 257205400	**2,528** 997 150	Class: (NV)	**1982-12 Tronderverftet AS — Hommelvik** Yd No: 50 Loa 80.12 Br ex 14.33 Dght 4.000 Lbp 70.80 Br md 14.30 Dpth 7.12 Welded, 2 dks	**(A36A2PR) Passenger/Ro-Ro Ship (Vehicles)** Passengers: unberthed: 650 Bow door & ramp (centre) Stern door & ramp (centre) Lane-Len: 29 Lane-Wid: 8.00 Lane-clr ht: 4.50 Cars: 140, Trailers: 12	**1 oil engine** with clutches, flexible couplings & sr geared to sc. shaft driving 2 CP propellers 1 fwd and 1 aft Total Power: 1,942kW (2,640hp) 14.5kn Normo KVMB-12 1 x Vee 4 Stroke 12 Cy. 250 x 300 1942kW (2640bhp) AS Bergens Mek Verksteder-Norway AuxGen: 2 x 116kW 220V 50Hz a.c
8311302 *LNEG* -	**SOGNEFJORD** - **Fjord1 AS** - *Floro* *Norway* MMSI: 257373400	**1,439** 470 607	Class: (NV)	**1984-05 Tronderverftet AS — Hommelvik** Yd No: 52 Loa 73.51 Br ex 13.90 Dght 3.731 Lbp 65.72 Br md 13.71 Dpth 4.50 Welded, 1 dk	**(A36A2PR) Passenger/Ro-Ro Ship (Vehicles)** Passengers: unberthed: 399 Bow door & ramp Len: - Wid: 7.50 Swl: - Stern door & ramp Len: - Wid: 7.50 Swl: - Lane-Len: 450 Cars: 90, Trailers: 9 Ice Capable	**1 oil engine** driving 2 CP propellers 1 fwd and 1 aft Total Power: 2,207kW (3,001hp) 14.8kn Wichmann 7AXA 1 x 2 Stroke 7 Cy. 300 x 450 2207kW (3001bhp) Wichmann Motorfabrikk AS-Norway AuxGen: 2 x 120kW 220V 50Hz a.c Thrusters: 1 Thwart. CP thruster (f)
9018816 *LEAQ* -	**SOGNEPRINS** *ex Fosningen -2008* **Fjordcharter Norway AS** - *Floro* *Norway* MMSI: 257273500	**141** 56 38	Class: (NV)	**1991-06 Lindstols Skips- & Baatbyggeri AS — Risor** Yd No: 298 Loa 22.50 Br ex 7.62 Dght 1.100 Lbp 19.50 Br md 7.60 Dpth 3.15 Welded, 1 dk	**(A37B2PS) Passenger Ship** Hull Material: Aluminium Alloy Passengers: unberthed: 118	**2 oil engines** geared to sc. shafts driving 2 FP propellers Total Power: 1,098kW (1,492hp) 26.0kn M.T.U. 12V183TE92 2 x Vee 4 Stroke 12 Cy. 128 x 142 each-549kW (746bhp) MTU Friedrichshafen GmbH-Friedrichshafen
8003175 *A6E3038* -	**SOHA FOLK** *ex Columbia Tide -2005 ex Wise Tide -1984* **Folk Shipping LLC** - *Dubai* *United Arab Emirates* MMSI: 470880000 Official number: 5199	**764** 229 1,200	Class: AB (RI)	**1980-05 Halter Marine, Inc. — Moss Point, Ms** Yd No: 881 Loa 54.87 Br ex - Dght 3.683 Lbp 51.82 Br md 12.20 Dpth 4.27 Welded, 1 dk	**(B21B20T) Offshore Tug/Supply Ship**	**2 oil engines** reverse reduction geared to sc. shafts driving 2 FP propellers Total Power: 1,654kW (2,248hp) 10.0kn Caterpillar D399SCAC 2 x Vee 4 Stroke 16 Cy. 159 x 203 each-827kW (1124bhp) Caterpillar Tractor Co-USA AuxGen: 2 x 125kW 450V 60Hz a.c Thrusters: 1 Thwart. FP thruster (f)
9036650 *EPCK8* -	**SOHAIL 10** *ex Arman -2013 ex Sanmanyoshi 4 -2013* *ex Koei Maru No. 3 -2009* **Mohammad Mozaffari Nasab & Abdolali Mozaffari** - - *Iran* MMSI: 422049200	*191* - 550	Class: IZ	**1991-08 Kegoya Dock K.K. — Kure** Yd No: 925 Loa 55.10 (BB) Br ex 9.02 Dght 3.260 Lbp 49.90 Br md 9.00 Dpth 5.40 Welded, 1 dk	**(A31A2GX) General Cargo Ship** Compartments: 1 Ho, ER	**1 oil engine** driving 1 FP propeller Total Power: 625kW (850hp) Niigata 6M26BGT 1 x 4 Stroke 6 Cy. 260 x 460 625kW (850bhp) Niigata Engineering Co Ltd-Japan
9210816 *H9ZZ* -	**SOHAR LNG** *ex Lakshmi -2003 ex Sohar Lng -2002* *ex Lakshmi -2002* **Energy Spring LNG Carrier SA** Oman Ship Management Co SAOC SatCom: Inmarsat C 435718610 *Panama* *Panama* MMSI: 357186000 Official number: 3052005B	**111,203** 33,361 71,997 T/cm 108.8	Class: NK	**2001-11 Mitsubishi Heavy Industries Ltd. — Nagasaki** Yd No: 2162 Loa 297.50 (BB) Br ex 45.84 Dght 11.252 Lbp 283.00 Br md 45.75 Dpth 25.50 Welded, 1 dk	**(A11A2TN) LNG Tanker** Double Hull Liq (Gas): 135,850 6 x Gas Tank (s); 5 independent Kvaerner-Moss (alu) sph , ER 10 Cargo Pump (s): 10x1200m³/hr Manifold: Bow/CM: 119.8m	**1 Steam Turb** reduction geared to sc. shaft driving 1 FP propeller Total Power: 26,800kW (36,437hp) 19.5kn Mitsubishi MS40-2 1 x steam Turb 26800kW (36437shp) Mitsubishi Heavy Industries Ltd-Japan AuxGen: 2 x 2000kW a.c, 1 x 2000kW a.c Thrusters: 1 Thwart. FP thruster (f) Fuel: 5060.0
7738709 *9BPZ* -	**SOHEIL DARYA** *ex Herald Bluff -2000* **Mostafa Farz & Partner** - *Bushehr* *Iran* MMSI: 422565000 Official number: 17534	**116** 35 -	Class: AS	**1976 Ocean Shipyards (WA) Pty Ltd — Fremantle WA** Converted From: Fishing Vessel-2000 Loa 22.53 Br ex - Dght - Lbp - Br md 6.76 Dpth 2.47 Welded, 1 dk	**(A31A2GX) General Cargo Ship**	**1 oil engine** driving 1 FP propeller Total Power: 775kW (1,054hp) 9.5kn Caterpillar 3412 1 x Vee 4 Stroke 12 Cy. 137 x 152 775kW (1054bhp) Caterpillar Tractor Co-USA
6522000 *SUVC* -	**SOHEIR** *ex Suehiro Maru No. 18 -1978* *ex Denei No. 1 -1971* **Mobil Oil Egypt (SAA)** - *Port Said* *Egypt* MMSI: 622111005	*905* 596 1,583	Class: (AB)	**1965 Watanabe Zosen KK — Imabari EH** Yd No: 65 Loa 62.36 Br ex 9.50 Dght 4.476 Lbp 57.00 Br md 9.48 Dpth 4.93 Riveted\Welded, 1 dk	**(A13B2TP) Products Tanker** Liq: 1,931; Liq (Oil): 1,931 Compartments: 8 Ta, ER	**1 oil engine** driving 1 FP propeller Total Power: 956kW (1,300hp) 12.5kn Nippon Hatsudoki HS6NV138 1 x 4 Stroke 6 Cy. 380 x 540 956kW (1300bhp) Nippon Hatsudoki-Japan AuxGen: 2 x 20kW Fuel: 92.5 5.0pd
8985983 *9BEE* -	**SOHEYL 1** *ex Soheyl I -2005 ex Sonbak 9-I -2003* **Soheyl Hourmouzghan Marine Transportation Cooperative Co** - *Bandar Abbas* *Iran* MMSI: 422770000 Official number: 806	**370** 111 502	Class: AS	**2003-03 Wonsan Shipyard — Wonsan** Loa 56.60 Br ex 10.80 Dght 1.800 Lbp 50.00 Br md 10.50 Dpth 2.60 Welded, 1 dk	**(A35D2RL) Landing Craft**	**2 oil engines** driving 2 Propellers Total Power: 486kW (660hp) Yanmar 2 x 4 Stroke each-243kW (330bhp) Yanmar Diesel Engine Co Ltd-Japan

IMO / Call sign	Name / Owner	Tonnage	Class	Builder / Dimensions	Type	Machinery
9328429 *9BEF* -	**SOHEYL 2** *ex* Sonbak 201 *-2004* **Soheyl Hourmouzghan Marine Transportation Cooperative Co** - *Bandar Abbas* *Iran* MMSI: 422431000 Official number: 807	**496** 202 1,000	Class: AS	**2004**-03 **Wonsan Shipyard — Wonsan** Yd No: 201-03 Loa 58.39 Br ex 13.80 Dght 2.400 Lbp 51.79 Br md 13.50 Dpth 3.16 Welded, 1 dk	**(A35D2RL) Landing Craft** Bow door/ramp (f)	**2 oil engines** reduction geared to sc. shafts driving 2 Propellers Total Power: 882kW (1,200hp) Yanmar 6AYM-ETE 2 x 4 Stroke 6 Cy. 155 x 180 each-441kW (600bhp) Yanmar Diesel Engine Co Ltd-Japan
9452282 *9BPQ* -	**SOHEYL 3** **Hormouz Sea Safe Co** *Bandar Abbas* *Iran* MMSI: 422710000 Official number: 11542	**498** 150 800	Class: AS (BV)	**2007**-05 **Arvandan Shipbuilding Co., — Iran** Yd No: 11171 Loa 49.70 Br ex 11.67 Dght 2.500 Lbp 46.90 Br md 11.65 Dpth 3.50 Welded, 1 dk	**(A35D2RL) Landing Craft**	**2 oil engines** driving 2 Propellers Total Power: 1,104kW (1,500hp) Mitsubishi S6R2-MPTK 2 x 4 Stroke 6 Cy. 170 x 220 each-552kW (750bhp) Mitsubishi Heavy Industries Ltd-Japan
9163817 *J8B4790* -	**SOHEYLI** *ex* Basith *-2013* **Cotswold Shipholding SA** EDT Shipmanagement Ltd *Kingstown* *St Vincent & The Grenadines* MMSI: 375805000 Official number: 11263	**443** 132 350	Class: LR ✠ **100A1** SS 11/2012 tug ✠ **LMC** Eq.Ltr: G; Cable: 302.5/22.0 U2	**1997**-11 **Stocznia Tczew Sp z oo — Tczew** (Hull) **1997**-11 **B.V. Scheepswerf Damen — Gorinchem** Yd No: 4719 Loa 40.00 Br ex 9.31 Dght 3.858 Lbp 34.12 Br md 9.00 Dpth 4.75 Welded, 1 dk	**(B32A2ST) Tug**	**2 oil engines** with clutches, flexible couplings & sr reverse geared to sc. shafts driving 2 FP propellers Total Power: 1,200kW (1,632hp) 12.0kn Caterpillar 3508TA 2 x Vee 4 Stroke 8 Cy. 170 x 190 each-600kW (816bhp) Caterpillar Inc-USA AuxGen: 2 x 144kW 380V 50Hz a.c Thrusters: 1 Thwart. FP thruster (f) Fuel: 195.0 (d.f.)
7938892 - -	**SOHO MARU** - -	*111* 35 -		**1971 Kimura Zosen K.K. — Nagasaki** L reg 29.51 Br ex - Dght - Lbp - Br md 6.80 Dpth 2.70 Welded, 1 dk	**(B11B2FV) Fishing Vessel**	**1 oil engine** driving 1 FP propeller
9234537 *JE3176* -	**SOHO MARU No. 16** **KK Fukushima Gyogyo** - *Hachinohe, Aomori* *Japan* Official number: 136272	*310* - -		**2000**-04 **Nagasaki Zosen K.K. — Nagasaki** Yd No: 1170 Loa 61.12 (BB) Br ex - Dght 3.650 Lbp 52.50 Br md 8.76 Dpth 4.15 Welded, 1 dk	**(B11B2FV) Fishing Vessel**	**1 oil engine** driving 1 CP propeller Total Power: 1,221kW (1,660hp) Niigata 6MG34HX 1 x 4 Stroke 6 Cy. 340 x 450 1221kW (1660bhp) Niigata Engineering Co Ltd-Japan AuxGen: 1 x 530kW 225V a.c, 1 x 353kW 225V a.c
9021320 *JE3037* -	**SOHO MARU No. 17** **KK Fukushima Gyogyo** - *Hachinohe, Aomori* *Japan* Official number: 130885	*340* - -		**1991**-04 **Nagasaki Zosen K.K. — Nagasaki** Yd No: 1083 Loa 62.82 (BB) Br ex 9.02 Dght 3.952 Lbp 56.00 Br md 9.00 Dpth 4.43 Welded	**(B11B2FV) Fishing Vessel**	**1 oil engine** with clutches & sr geared to sc. shaft driving 1 CP propeller Total Power: 1,140kW (1,550hp) Daihatsu 6DKM-32 1 x 4 Stroke 6 Cy. 320 x 360 1140kW (1550bhp) Daihatsu Diesel Manufacturing Co Lt-Japan Thrusters: 1 Thwart. FP thruster (f)
8804115 *JE2879* -	**SOHO MARU No. 26** *ex* Nisshin Maru No. 26 *-1994* **KK Fukushima Gyogyo** - *Hachinohe, Aomori* *Japan* Official number: 130527	*273* - 535		**1988**-07 **K.K. Murakami Zosensho — Ishinomaki** Yd No: 1221 Loa 52.60 (BB) Br ex - Dght 3.657 Lbp 45.30 Br md 8.91 Dpth 4.25 Welded, 1 dk	**(B11B2FV) Fishing Vessel**	**1 oil engine** with clutches, flexible couplings & sr geared to sc. shaft driving 1 CP propeller Total Power: 1,155kW (1,570hp) Yanmar 8Z280L-ET 1 x 4 Stroke 8 Cy. 280 x 360 1155kW (1570bhp) Yanmar Diesel Engine Co Ltd-Japan
8610071 - -	**SOHO MARU No. 36** *ex* Shoshin Maru No. 30 *-2002* *ex* Hakuryu Maru No. 72 *-1991* **Jaehwa Corp** - *South Korea*	*245* - -		**1986**-08 **K.K. Murakami Zosensho — Ishinomaki** Yd No: 1193 Loa 51.74 (BB) Br ex - Dght - Lbp 44.61 Br md 8.31 Dpth 4.20 Welded, 1 dk	**(B11B2FV) Fishing Vessel**	**1 oil engine** driving 1 FP propeller Total Power: 861kW (1,171hp) Niigata 6MG28BXF 1 x 4 Stroke 6 Cy. 280 x 350 861kW (1171bhp) Niigata Engineering Co Ltd-Japan
8904630 - -	**SOHO MARU NO. 37** *ex* Shoshin Maru No. 18 *-2002* *ex* Myojin Maru No. 78 *-2001* - -	*332* - 627		**1989**-05 **K.K. Izutsu Zosensho — Nagasaki** Yd No: 966 Loa 60.30 (BB) Br ex - Dght 4.205 Lbp 54.70 Br md 9.00 Dpth 4.40 Welded	**(B11B2FV) Fishing Vessel**	**1 oil engine** driving 1 FP propeller Total Power: 1,250kW (1,700hp) Niigata 6MG32CLX 1 x 4 Stroke 6 Cy. 320 x 420 1250kW (1700bhp) Niigata Engineering Co Ltd-Japan Thrusters: 1 Thwart. FP thruster (f)
8804024 - -	**SOHO MARU No. 58** **Pesquera Arnippo SA** Continental Armadores de Pesca SA (CONARPESA) *Argentina* Official number: 02611	*589* - 1,058		**1988**-04 **Kitanihon Zosen K.K. — Hachinohe** Yd No: 228 Loa 71.30 (BB) Br ex 10.62 Dght 4.187 Lbp 61.02 Br md 10.60 Dpth 7.00 Welded, 2 dks	**(B11B2FV) Fishing Vessel** Ins: 1,482	**1 oil engine** with clutches, flexible couplings & sr geared to sc. shaft driving 1 CP propeller Total Power: 1,324kW (1,800hp) Niigata 6M31AFTE 1 x 4 Stroke 6 Cy. 310 x 530 1324kW (1800bhp) Niigata Engineering Co Ltd-Japan Thrusters: 1 Thwart. CP thruster (f)
8820638 - -	**SOHO MARU No. 63** - -	*135* - -		**1989**-02 **Nagasaki Zosen K.K. — Nagasaki** Yd No: 1053 Loa 45.40 (BB) Br ex - Dght 2.800 Lbp 36.50 Br md 7.82 Dpth 3.20 Welded	**(B11B2FV) Fishing Vessel**	**1 oil engine** driving 1 FP propeller Total Power: 861kW (1,171hp) Niigata 6MG28HX 1 x 4 Stroke 6 Cy. 280 x 370 861kW (1171bhp) Niigata Engineering Co Ltd-Japan
9606235 *7JIR* -	**SOHO MARU NO. 63** **KK Fukushima Gyogyo** - *Hachinohe, Aomori* *Japan* Official number: 141367	*279* 89 418		**2011**-03 **Miho Zosensho K.K. — Shimizu** Yd No: 1544 Loa 60.08 Br ex - Dght 3.740 Lbp 51.20 Br md 11.40 Dpth 6.08 Welded, 1 dk	**(B11B2FV) Fishing Vessel**	**1 oil engine** reduction geared to sc. shaft driving 1 Propeller Total Power: 2,647kW (3,599hp) Niigata 6MG34HX 1 x 4 Stroke 6 Cy. 340 x 450 2647kW (3599bhp) Niigata Engineering Co Ltd-Japan
9195004 *JCBO* -	**SOHO MARU No. 68** **KK Fukushima Gyogyo** - *Hachinohe, Aomori* *Japan* MMSI: 431219000 Official number: 133356	*160* - 191		**1998**-12 **Niigata Engineering Co Ltd — Niigata NI** Yd No: 2362 Loa 37.00 (BB) Br ex - Dght 3.306 Lbp 32.00 Br md 7.60 Dpth 4.60 Welded, 1 dk	**(B11B2FV) Fishing Vessel** Ins: 109	**1 oil engine** with clutches, flexible couplings & sr geared to sc. shaft driving 1 CP propeller Total Power: 1,030kW (1,400hp) Niigata 6MG28HX 1 x 4 Stroke 6 Cy. 280 x 370 1030kW (1400bhp) Niigata Engineering Co Ltd-Japan
9474187 *JD2565* -	**SOHO MARU NO. 83** **KK Fukushima Gyogyo** - *Hachinohe, Aomori* *Japan* MMSI: 432635000 Official number: 140693	*329* - 598		**2008**-02 **Miho Zosensho K.K. — Shimizu** Yd No: 1528 Loa 64.60 Br ex - Dght 4.080 Lbp - Br md 11.60 Dpth 6.69 Welded, 1 dk	**(B11B2FV) Fishing Vessel**	**1 oil engine** reduction geared to sc. shaft driving 1 CP propeller Total Power: 2,942kW (4,000hp) Daihatsu 6DKM-36 1 x 4 Stroke 6 Cy. 360 x 480 2942kW (4000bhp) Daihatsu Diesel Manufacturing Co Lt-Japan Thrusters: 1 Tunnel thruster (f)
8001933 - -	**SOHO MARU No. 83** - - *Chinese Taipei*	*116* 24 -		**1980**-03 **Nagasaki Zosen K.K. — Nagasaki** Yd No: 732 Loa 37.01 Br ex 7.50 Dght 2.371 Lbp 31.07 Br md 7.01 Dpth 2.80 Welded, 1 dk	**(B11B2FV) Fishing Vessel**	**1 oil engine** reduction geared to sc. shaft driving 1 FP propeller Total Power: 861kW (1,171hp) Daihatsu 6DSM-28FSL 1 x 4 Stroke 6 Cy. 280 x 340 861kW (1171bhp) Daihatsu Diesel Manufacturing Co Lt-Japan
9346392 *7JAJ* -	**SOHO MARU NO. 88** **KK Fukushima Gyogyo** - *Hachinohe, Aomori* *Japan* MMSI: 432497000 Official number: 140097	*300* - -		**2005**-03 **Miho Zosensho K.K. — Shimizu** Yd No: 1512 Loa 61.35 Br ex 11.61 Dght 4.030 Lbp 51.00 Br md 11.60 Dpth 6.60 Welded, 1 dk	**(B11B2FV) Fishing Vessel**	**1 oil engine** geared to sc. shaft driving 1 CP propeller Total Power: 2,942kW (4,000hp) Daihatsu 6DKM-36 1 x 4 Stroke 6 Cy. 360 x 480 2942kW (4000bhp) Daihatsu Diesel Manufacturing Co Lt-Japan Thrusters: 1 Tunnel thruster (f)
7123215 - -	**SOHO MARU No. 163** *ex* Soho Maru No. 83 *-1980* - -	*111* 35 132		**1971 Usuki Iron Works Co Ltd — Usuki OT** Yd No: 810 Loa 36.45 Br ex 6.94 Dght 2.426 Lbp 30.82 Br md 6.91 Dpth 2.80 Welded, 1 dk	**(B11A2FT) Trawler**	**1 oil engine** driving 1 FP propeller Total Power: 883kW (1,201hp) Daihatsu 6DSM-26 1 x 4 Stroke 6 Cy. 260 x 320 883kW (1201bhp) Daihatsu Diesel Manufacturing Co Lt-Japan

9209245 *DSQS6* -	**SOHOH** **KDB Capital Corp** Khana Marine Ltd *Jeju* *South Korea* MMSI: 441690000 Official number: JJR-101951	**4,504** 2,220 5,456	Class: KR (NK)	**1999-08 Kyokuyo Shipyard Corp — Shimonoseki YC** Yd No: 427 Loa 120.75 (BB) Br ex - Dght 7.110 Lbp 112.90 Br md 16.60 Dpth 10.00 Welded, 3 dks	**(A34A2GR) Refrigerated Cargo Ship** Ins: 6,655 Compartments: 3 Ho, ER, 6 Tw Dk 3 Ha: 3 (7.1 x 6.4)ER Derricks: 6x5t	**1 oil engine** driving 1 FP propeller Total Power: 4,119kW (5,600hp) 15.8kn Mitsubishi 8UEC37LA 1 x 2 Stroke 8 Cy. 370 x 880 4119kW (5600bhp) Kobe Hatsudoki KK-Japan Thrusters: 1 Tunnel thruster (f) Fuel: 890.0
9413391 *9BJR* -	**SOHRAB** **Government of The Islamic Republic of Iran (Ports & Maritime Organisation)** - *Bandar Abbas* *Iran* MMSI: 422558000	**260** 99 126	Class: (BV)	**2007-07 Penglai Bohai Shipyard Co Ltd — Penglai SD** Yd No: PBZ05-53 Loa 31.54 Br ex - Dght 3.600 Lbp 28.34 Br md 9.60 Dpth 4.50 Welded, 1 dk	**(B32A2ST) Tug**	**2 oil engines** reduction geared to sc. shafts driving 2 Z propellers Total Power: 2,400kW (3,264hp) 12.0kn MaK 6M20 2 x 4 Stroke 6 Cy. 200 x 300 each-1200kW (1632bhp) Caterpillar Motoren GmbH & Co. KG-Germany Fuel: 106.0 (r.f.)
7802782 - -	**SOHRAB** *launched as* Shipyard 2 *-1983* **Karachi Port Trust** - *Karachi* *Pakistan*	*282* 78 111	Class: (LR) ✠ Classed LR until 27/4/94	**1983-03 Karachi Shipyard & Engineering Works Ltd. — Karachi** Yd No: 144 Loa 36.96 Br ex 9.40 Dght 3.355 Lbp 30.66 Br md 9.01 Dpth 4.65 Welded, 1 dk	**(B32A2ST) Tug**	**2 oil engines** with clutches, flexible couplings & sr reverse geared to sc. shafts driving 2 FP propellers Total Power: 1,618kW (2,200hp) 12.0kn Sulzer 6ASL25/30 2 x 4 Stroke 6 Cy. 250 x 300 each-809kW (1100bhp) Zaklady Przemyslu Metalowego 'HCegielski' SA-Poznan AuxGen: 2 x 77kW 380V 50Hz a.c, 1 x 40kW 380V 50Hz a.c Fuel: 47.0 (d.f.) 0.5pd
9524372 - -	**SOIREE** **Sail Lord Ltd** - *Douglas* *Isle of Man (British)* Official number: 742225	**235** 70 30	Class: RI	**2009-04 ISA Produzione Srl — Ancona** Yd No: 120.08 Loa 36.40 Br ex - Dght 1.500 Lbp 30.00 Br md 7.40 Dpth 3.66 Bonded, 1 dk	**(X11A2YP) Yacht** Hull Material: Reinforced Plastic	**3 oil engines** reduction geared to sc. shafts driving 3 Water jets Total Power: 5,370kW (7,302hp) 33.0kn M.T.U. 16V2000M93 3 x Vee 4 Stroke 16 Cy. 135 x 156 each-1790kW (2434bhp) MTU Friedrichshafen GmbH-Friedrichshafen
8745618 *MCSJA* -	**SOJANA** **SOJANA LLP** - *Cowes* *United Kingdom* MMSI: 232852000 Official number: 907716	*115* 35 -		**2003-12 GM Offshore Composites Ltd — Lymington** (Hull) Yd No: 133 **2003-12 Fast Cruising Ltd — Cowes** Yd No: 1 Loa 35.00 Br ex - Dght 4.500 Lbp 31.78 Br md 7.62 Dpth 1.22 Bonded, 1 dk	**(X11A2YP) Yacht** Hull Material: Reinforced Plastic	**1 oil engine** reduction geared to sc. shaft driving 1 Propeller Total Power: 276kW (375hp) Lugger 61.842 1 x 4 Stroke 276kW (375bhp)
8716057 *HLLW* -	**SOJIN NO. 101** *ex* Chung Yong No. 23 *-2004* **Sojin Shipping Co Ltd** - *Busan* *South Korea* MMSI: 440801000 Official number: 9512321-6260002	*378* - 419	Class: KR	**1987-03 ShinA Shipbuilding Co Ltd — Tongyeong** Yd No: 316 Loa 53.32 Br ex - Dght 3.650 Lbp 47.25 Br md 8.72 Dpth 3.76 Welded, 1 dk	**(B11B2FV) Fishing Vessel**	**1 oil engine** with clutches, flexible couplings & reverse reduction geared to sc. shaft driving 1 FP propeller Total Power: 883kW (1,201hp) 12.8kn Niigata 6M28AFTE 1 x 4 Stroke 6 Cy. 280 x 480 883kW (1201bhp) Ssangyong Heavy Industries Co Ltd-South Korea AuxGen: 2 x 560kW 225V a.c
6708953 - -	**SOKHNA ANTA** *ex* Le Malouin *-1991* *ex* Valloire *-1972* **Fari Peche Ltd** -	*156* 52 -	Class: (BV)	**1966 Ateliers & Chantiers de La Rochelle-Pallice — La Rochelle** Yd No: 5150 Loa 27.13 Br ex 6.74 Dght 2.661 Lbp - Br md 6.68 Dpth 3.56 Welded, 1 dk	**(B11A2FT) Trawler** Ins: 100 2 Ha: 2 (0.9 x 1.0)	**1 oil engine** driving 1 FP propeller Total Power: 412kW (560hp) 11.0kn Deutz RBV6M536 1 x 4 Stroke 6 Cy. 270 x 360 412kW (560bhp) Kloeckner Humboldt Deutz AG-West Germany Fuel: 30.0 (d.f.)
7015107 *EFFK* -	**SOKO EDER** *ex* Jaime Lopez Tapia *-1988* **Fondomar SL** - *Bilbao* *Spain* Official number: 5-10/1992	*125* 47 -	Class: (GL)	**1970 SA Juliana Constructora Gijonesa — Bilbao** Yd No: 15 Loa 24.64 Br ex - Dght 2.693 Lbp 22.03 Br md 6.81 Dpth 3.20 Welded, 1 dk	**(B32A2ST) Tug**	**1 oil engine** sr geared to sc. shaft driving 1 FP propeller Total Power: 544kW (740hp) 9.0kn MAN V6V16/18 1 x Vee 4 Stroke 12 Cy. 160 x 180 544kW (740bhp) EN Bazan de Construcciones NavalesMilitares SA-Spain
6520923 *HC4526* -	**SOKOL** **Entreg SA** Industrial Pesquera Junin SA (JUNSA) *Guayaquil* *Ecuador* Official number: P-00-0836	*136* 64 183	Class: (BV)	**1965 AG Weser, Werk Seebeck — Bremerhaven** Yd No: 893 Loa 25.46 Br ex 7.24 Dght - Lbp 21.26 Br md 7.01 Dpth 3.51 Welded	**(B11B2FV) Fishing Vessel**	**1 oil engine** driving 1 FP propeller Total Power: 399kW (542hp) Caterpillar D353SCAC 1 x 4 Stroke 6 Cy. 159 x 203 399kW (542bhp) Caterpillar Tractor Co-USA
8726052 - -	**SOKOL** **Port-Petrovsk Joint-Stock Fish Processing Commercial Co (A/O 'Port-Petrovsk Rybopromyshlennaya Kommercheskaya Kompaniya')** -	**191** 85 314	Class: (RS)	**1987 Svetlovskiy Sudoremontnyy Zavod — Svetlyy** Yd No: 36 Loa 29.45 Br ex 8.15 Dght 3.120 Lbp 28.50 Br md - Dpth 3.60 Welded, 1 dk	**(B34G2SE) Pollution Control Vessel** Liq: 332; Liq (Oil): 332 Compartments: 8 Ta Ice Capable	**1 oil engine** geared to sc. shaft driving 1 FP propeller Total Power: 165kW (224hp) 7.5kn Daldizel 6CHNSP18/22 1 x 4 Stroke 6 Cy. 180 x 220 165kW (224bhp) Daldizel-Khabarovsk AuxGen: 1 x 50kW, 1 x 25kW Fuel: 12.0 (d.f.)
8924721 *UHMV* -	**SOKOLOVKA** **Tayfun Co Ltd** - *Sovetskaya Gavan* *Russia* MMSI: 273419300 Official number: 922027	**117** 35 30	Class: RS	**1993-11 Sretenskiy Sudostroitelnyy Zavod — Sretensk** Yd No: 308 Loa 25.45 Br ex 6.80 Dght 2.390 Lbp 22.00 Br md 6.80 Dpth 3.30 Welded, 1 dk	**(B11A2FS) Stern Trawler** Ins: 64 Ice Capable	**1 oil engine** driving 1 FP propeller Total Power: 220kW (299hp) 10.0kn S.K.L. 6NVD26A-2 1 x 4 Stroke 6 Cy. 180 x 260 220kW (299bhp) SKL Motoren u. Systemtechnik AG-Magdeburg AuxGen: 2 x 16kW a.c Fuel: 12.0 (d.f.)
9232682 *TCCX3* -	**SOKULLU MEHMED PASA** **Istanbul Deniz Otobusleri Sanayi ve Ticaret AS (IDO)** - *Istanbul* *Turkey* MMSI: 271002383 Official number: 7735	**395** 119 39	Class: TL (NV)	**2000-08 Turkiye Gemi Sanayii A.S. — Pendik** (Assembled by) Yd No: 025 **2000-08 Kvaerner Fjellstrand AS — Omastrand** (Parts for assembly by) Loa 35.00 Br ex - Dght 2.501 Lbp 32.22 Br md 10.10 Dpth 3.91 Welded, 2 dks	**(A37B2PS) Passenger Ship** Passengers: unberthed: 450	**4 oil engines** geared to sc shafts driving 2 FP propellers Total Power: 2,424kW (3,296hp) 32.0kn M.T.U. 12V183TE72 4 x Vee 4 Stroke 12 Cy. 128 x 142 each-606kW (824bhp) MTU Friedrichshafen GmbH-Friedrichshafen AuxGen: 2 x 70kW a.c
7533898 *UHIG* -	**SOKUR** **FC Pribrezhnyy Lov Co Ltd** - SatCom: Inmarsat C 427320951 *Petropavlovsk-Kamchatskiy* *Russia*	**172** 51 94	Class: (RS)	**1975 Sretenskiy Sudostroitelnyy Zavod — Sretensk** Yd No: 81 Loa 33.96 Br ex 7.09 Dght 2.899 Lbp 30.00 Br md 7.00 Dpth 3.69 Welded, 1 dk	**(B11B2FV) Fishing Vessel** Bale: 96 Compartments: 1 Ho, ER 1 Ha: (1.3 x 1.6) Derricks: 2x2t; Winches: 2 Ice Capable	**1 oil engine** driving 1 FP propeller Total Power: 224kW (305hp) 9.0kn S.K.L. 8NVD36-1U 1 x 4 Stroke 8 Cy. 240 x 360 224kW (305bhp) VEB Schwermaschinenbau "KarlLiebknecht" (SKL)-Magdeburg Fuel: 20.0 (d.f.)
8663523 *YDA3166* -	**SOL 1001** **PT Pelayaran Nasional Sandico Ocean Line** - *Batam* *Indonesia* MMSI: 525020118 Official number: 2012 PPM NO.228/L	**137** 42 -	Class: KI	**2012-05 PT Karyasindo Samudra Biru Shipyard — Batam** Yd No: 138 Loa 23.50 Br ex - Dght 2.390 Lbp 21.69 Br md 7.32 Dpth 3.20 Welded, 1 dk	**(B32A2ST) Tug**	**2 oil engines** reduction geared to sc. shafts driving 2 FP propellers Total Power: 894kW (1,216hp) Cummins KTA-19-M3 2 x 4 Stroke 6 Cy. 159 x 159 each-447kW (608bhp) Chongqing Cummins Engine Co Ltd-China AuxGen: 2 x 35kW 400V a.c
9657820 *YDA3090* -	**SOL 1002** **PT Pelayaran Nasional Sandico Ocean Line** - *Batam* *Indonesia*	**138** 41 74	Class: KI	**2012-04 Capricorn Central Shipbuilding Sdn Bhd — Sibu** Yd No: 010 Loa 23.16 Br ex - Dght 2.390 Lbp 21.60 Br md 6.70 Dpth 2.89 Welded, 1 dk	**(B32A2ST) Tug**	**2 oil engines** reduction geared to sc. shafts driving 2 FP propellers Total Power: 894kW (1,216hp) Cummins KTA-19-M3 2 x 4 Stroke 6 Cy. 159 x 159 each-447kW (608bhp) Chongqing Cummins Engine Co Ltd-China AuxGen: 2 x 32kW 415V a.c
8663535 *YDA3259* -	**SOL 1003** **PT Pelayaran Nasional Sandico Ocean Line** - *Batam* *Indonesia* MMSI: 525007170 Official number: 2012 PPM.NO.2530/L	**137** 42 -	Class: KI	**2012-09 PT Karyasindo Samudra Biru Shipyard — Batam** Yd No: 145 Loa 23.50 Br ex - Dght 2.390 Lbp 21.69 Br md 7.32 Dpth 3.20 Welded, 1 dk	**(B32A2ST) Tug**	**2 oil engines** reduction geared to sc. shafts driving 2 FP propellers Total Power: 894kW (1,216hp) Cummins KTA-19-M3 2 x 4 Stroke 6 Cy. 159 x 159 each-447kW (608bhp) Chongqing Cummins Engine Co Ltd-China AuxGen: 2 x 35kW 400V a.c

8663547 *YDA3292* -	**SOL 1005** - **PT Pelayaran Nasional Sandico Ocean Line** - *Batam* *Indonesia* MMSI: 525009087 Official number: 2012 PPM NO.2563/L	**152** 46 -	Class: KI	**2012-09 PT Buana Cipta Mandala — Batam** Yd No: 003 Loa 23.50 Br ex - Dght 2.590 Lbp 22.76 Br md 7.32 Dpth 3.20 Welded, 1 dk	**(B32A2ST) Tug**	**2 oil engines** reduction geared to sc. shafts driving 2 FP propellers Total Power: 980kW (1,332hp) Mitsubishi S6A3-MPTK 2 x 4 Stroke 6 Cy. 150 x 175 each-490kW (666bhp) Mitsubishi Heavy Industries Ltd-Japan AuxGen: 2 x 24kW 400V a.c
9018658 *ELQQ4* -	**SOL DO BRASIL** - **Esplanade Shipping Corp** Maritime Services Aleuropa GmbH SatCom: Inmarsat A 1252254 *Monrovia* *Liberia* MMSI: 636010032 Official number: 10032	**15,218** 4,566 19,653	Class: GL	**1994-11 Kvaerner Floro AS — Floro** Yd No: 253 Loa 172.00 (BB) Br ex - Dght 9.510 Lbp 160.60 Br md 26.00 Dpth 14.50 Welded, 1 dk	**(A14E2LJ) Fruit Juice Carrier, Refrigerated** Ins: 12,320; Liq: 12,374 TEU 480 Compartments: 16 Wing Ta, ER 8 Cargo Pump (s): 8x80m³/hr	**1 oil engine** driving 1 CP propeller Total Power: 10,800kW (14,684hp) 18.0kn Sulzer 6RTA62 1 x 2 Stroke 6 Cy. 620 x 2150 10800kW (14684bhp) H Cegielski Poznan SA-Poland AuxGen: 1 x 1264kW 440V 60Hz a.c, 3 x 750kW 220/440V 60Hz a.c Thrusters: 1 Thwart. FP thruster (f) Fuel: 264.0 (d.f.) 1787.0 (r.f.)
8706313 - -	**SOL DO MAIO** - **Interbase EP** - *Sao Vicente* *Cape Verde*	*121* 40 -	Class: (BV)	**1985-11 VSR BV — Made** (Hull) **1985-11 B.V. Scheepswerf Damen — Gorinchem** Yd No: 4123 Loa 22.71 Br ex - Dght - Lbp - Br md 7.01 Dpth 3.51 Welded, 1 dk	**(B11B2FV) Fishing Vessel**	**1 oil engine** geared to sc. shaft driving 1 FP propeller Total Power: 220kW (299hp) Caterpillar 3306PCTA 1 x 4 Stroke 6 Cy. 121 x 152 220kW (299bhp) Caterpillar Tractor Co-USA
8876285 *5NKD* -	**SOL I** *ex* Seamark I *-2008* **Southern Offshore Ltd** - *Lagos* *Nigeria* Official number: SR641	**193** 57		**1977 Halter Marine, Inc. — Pierre Part, La** Yd No: 663 Loa 33.53 Br ex - Dght - Lbp - Br md 7.92 Dpth 3.20 Welded, 1 dk	**(B34R2QY) Supply Tender**	**1 oil engine** driving 1 FP propeller General Motors General Motors Corp-USA
9114282 *5NKD2* -	**SOL II** *ex* Oil Siluko *-2010* **Southern Offshore Ltd** - *Lagos* *Nigeria* Official number: SR1096	**150** 45 93	Class: (AB) (GL)	**1994-09 Aluminum Boats, Inc. — Marrero, La** Yd No: 374 L reg 31.85 Br ex - Dght - Lbp 28.11 Br md 7.16 Dpth 3.35 Welded, 1 dk	**(B21A2OC) Crew/Supply Vessel** Hull Material: Aluminium Alloy	**2 oil engines** with clutches, flexible couplings & sr geared to sc. shafts driving 2 FP propellers Total Power: 838kW (1,140hp) 20.0kn Caterpillar 3412TA 2 x Vee 4 Stroke 12 Cy. 137 x 152 each-419kW (570bhp) Caterpillar Inc-USA AuxGen: 2 x 50kW 380V 50Hz a.c Fuel: 17.3 (d.f.)
8108767 - -	**SOL LUESHING** *ex* Avgerinos *-2007* *ex* Suzac *-2005* *ex* Stor *-2000* **Sol Lueshing Inc** -	**2,510** 1,306 4,040 T/cm 11.3	Class: (BV) (GL)	**1981-12 Schichau-Unterweser AG — Bremerhaven** Yd No: 2277 Loa 89.08 Br ex 15.04 Dght 5.609 Lbp 84.00 Br md 15.02 Dpth 5.80 Welded, 1 dk.	**(A12A2TC) Chemical Tanker** Liq: 4,464 Cargo Heating Coils Compartments: 10 Wing Ta, ER 11 Cargo Pump (s): 10x100m³/hr, 1x40m³/hr Ice Capable	**1 oil engine** with flexible couplings & sr gearedto sc. shaft driving 1 CP propeller Total Power: 1,751kW (2,381hp) 12.0kn MaK 6M453AK 1 x 4 Stroke 6 Cy. 320 x 420 1751kW (2381bhp) Krupp MaK Maschinenbau GmbH-Kiel AuxGen: 2 x 370kW 440V 60Hz a.c Thrusters: 1 Thwart. FP thruster (f) Fuel: 24.0 (d.f.) 92.0 (d.f.)
8822569 *MWRC6* RN 1	**SOLA FIDE** - **Buchan (WN1) Ltd** - SatCom: Inmarsat A 1454401 *Runcorn* *United Kingdom* MMSI: 234402000 Official number: B14900	*527* 158 -		**1989-12 Barkmeijer Stroobos B.V. — Stroobos** Yd No: 245 Loa 43.97 Br ex - Dght 3.830 Lbp 39.27 Br md 9.00 Dpth 5.10 Welded, 1 dk	**(B11A2FT) Trawler**	**1 oil engine** reduction geared to sc. shaft driving 1 FP propeller Total Power: 1,471kW (2,000hp) Stork-Werkspoor 6SW280 1 x 4 Stroke 6 Cy. 280 x 300 1471kW (2000bhp) Stork Werkspoor Diesel BV-Netherlands Thrusters: 1 Tunnel thruster (f)
7367732 - -	**SOLA GRATIA** *ex* Prins Maurits *-1980* **Chandernagor International Inc** Ruisvis BV	**281** 84 -		**1974-03 Scheepswerf- en Reparatiebedrijf "Harlingen" B.V. — Harlingen** Yd No: 42 Lengthened-1986 Loa 38.18 Br ex 7.88 Dght - Lbp 33.86 Br md 7.80 Dpth 4.12 Welded, 1 dk	**(B11B2FV) Fishing Vessel**	**1 oil engine** driving 1 FP propeller Total Power: 1,325kW (1,801hp) Kromhout 9FCHD240 1 x 4 Stroke 9 Cy. 240 x 260 1325kW (1801bhp) (new engine 1986) Stork Werkspoor Diesel BV-Netherlands
6820268 - -	**SOLA No. 6** *ex* Taiyo Maru No. 6 *-1983* *ex* Manryo Maru No. 32 *-1983* - -	*377* 187 -		**1967 Narasaki Zosen KK — Muroran HK** Yd No: 618 Loa 48.82 Br ex 8.41 Dght 3.404 Lbp 42.80 Br md 8.39 Dpth 3.81 Welded, 2 dks	**(B11B2FV) Fishing Vessel**	**1 oil engine** driving 1 FP propeller Total Power: 1,030kW (1,400hp) Niigata 6M37AHS 1 x 4 Stroke 6 Cy. 370 x 540 1030kW (1400bhp) Niigata Engineering Co Ltd-Japan
1006910 *ZCFQ7* -	**SOLAIA** - **Pettittco Ltd** - *George Town* *Cayman Islands (British)* MMSI: 319563000 Official number: 734505	**427** 128 -	Class: LR ✠ **100A1** SS 03/2011 SSC Yacht mono G6 service area ✠ **LMC** Cable: 137.5/19.0 U2 (a)	**2001-03 Scheepsbouw en Machinefabriek Hakvoort B.V. — Monnickendam** Yd No: 230 Loa 40.00 Br ex 8.85 Dght 2.700 Lbp 36.22 Br md 8.60 Dpth 4.80 Welded, 2 dks	**(X11A2YP) Yacht**	**2 oil engines** with clutches, flexible couplings & sr reverse geared to sc. shafts driving 2 FP propellers Total Power: 1,074kW (1,460hp) 12.5kn Caterpillar 3412C-TA 2 x Vee 4 Stroke 12 Cy. 137 x 152 each-537kW (730bhp) Caterpillar Inc-USA AuxGen: 2 x 79kW 400V 50Hz a.c Thrusters: 1 Thwart. FP thruster (f)
9449003 *2DOS2* -	**SOLAN** - **Shetland Islands Council Towage Operations** - SatCom: Inmarsat C 423592458 *Lerwick* *United Kingdom* MMSI: 235080775 Official number: 916763	**852** 255 540	Class: LR ✠ **100A1** SS 11/2010 escort tug ✠ **LMC** **UMS** Eq.Ltr: J; Cable: 357.5/32.0 U2 (a)	**2010-11 Union Naval Valencia SA (UNV) — Valencia** Yd No: 471 Loa 40.00 Br ex 14.05 Dght 4.451 Lbp 37.50 Br md 14.00 Dpth 5.50 Welded, 1 dk	**(B32A2ST) Tug**	**2 oil engines** gearing integral to driving 2 Voith-Schneider propellers Total Power: 6,570kW (8,932hp) 14.0kn MAN-B&W 9L27/38 2 x 4 Stroke 9 Cy. 270 x 380 each-3285kW (4466bhp) MAN B&W Diesel AG-Augsburg AuxGen: 3 x 184kW 415V 50Hz a.c
9395317 *9HA2320* -	**SOLANA** - **Nestor I Maritime Ltd** Heidmar Inc SatCom: Inmarsat C 424833010 *Valletta* *Malta* MMSI: 248330000 Official number: 9395317	**156,651** 98,944 296,790 T/cm 177.4	Class: AB	**2010-05 Shanghai Jiangnan Changxing Shipbuilding Co Ltd — Shanghai** Yd No: H2408 Loa 330.00 (BB) Br ex 60.04 Dght 21.500 Lbp 316.00 Br md 60.00 Dpth 29.70 Welded, 1 dk	**(A13A2TV) Crude Oil Tanker** Double Hull (13F) Liq: 324,815; Liq (Oil): 333,528 Compartments: 5 Ta, 10 Wing Ta, 2 Wing Slop Ta, ER 3 Cargo Pump (s): 3x5500m³/hr Manifold: Bow/CM: 162m	**1 oil engine** driving 1 FP propeller Total Power: 25,480kW (34,643hp) 15.8kn MAN-B&W 7S80MC 1 x 2 Stroke 7 Cy. 800 x 3056 25480kW (34643bhp) CSSC MES Diesel Co Ltd-China AuxGen: 3 x 1050kW a.c Fuel: 430.0 (d.f.) 8000.0 (r.f.)
8023163 *H03894* -	**SOLANA** *ex* Harris *-2005* **La Mar Shipping Services SA** Maroos Shipping Co LLC *Panama* *Panama* MMSI: 351468000 Official number: 1170582G	**302** 91 261	Class: LR ✠ **100A1** SS 10/2010 offshore tug/supply ship ✠ **LMC** Eq.Ltr: (H) ; Cable: 357.5/26.0 U2 (a)	**1981-10 Sing Koon Seng Pte Ltd — Singapore** Yd No: SKS569 Loa 34.24 Br ex 9.25 Dght 3.214 Lbp 30.99 Br md 9.01 Dpth 3.61 Welded, 1 dk	**(B21B20T) Offshore Tug/Supply Ship**	**2 oil engines** dr reverse geared to sc. shafts driving 2 FP propellers Total Power: 992kW (1,348hp) 11.0kn Caterpillar D379SCAC 2 x Vee 4 Stroke 8 Cy. 159 x 203 each-496kW (674bhp) Caterpillar Tractor Co-USA AuxGen: 2 x 110kW 415V 50Hz a.c Thrusters: 1 Thwart. FP thruster (f)
8992637 *WCY5602* -	**SOLANA** *ex* Golden Eagle *-2005* *ex* Mormon Island *-2005* **Taurus Marine Inc** Cross Link Inc (Westar Marine Services) *San Francisco, CA* *United States of America* Official number: 569110	*150* 102 -		**1975-01 Louis G. Ortis Boat Co., Inc. — Krotz Springs, La** Yd No: 12 L reg 19.93 Br ex - Dght - Lbp - Br md 7.35 Dpth 2.74 Welded, 1 dk	**(B32A2ST) Tug**	**1 oil engine** driving 1 Propeller
6904595 *9LB2218* -	**SOLAND** *ex* Steve-B *-2003* *ex* Crest Tide *-1985* *ex* Tide Hal III *-1970* **Corona Corp** - *Freetown* *Sierra Leone* MMSI: 667202200 Official number: SL102022	*679* 335 1,006	Class: (AB)	**1969 Verolme Scheepswerf Alblasserdam N.V. — Alblasserdam** Yd No: 805 Loa 50.50 Br ex 11.87 Dght 3.893 Lbp 46.61 Br md 11.56 Dpth 4.42 Welded, 1 dk	**(B21A20S) Platform Supply Ship**	**2 oil engines** reverse reduction geared to sc. shafts driving 2 FP propellers Total Power: 1,250kW (1,700hp) 11.0kn Caterpillar D398B 2 x Vee 4 Stroke 12 Cy. 153 x 203 each-625kW (850bhp) Caterpillar Tractor Co-USA AuxGen: 2 x 100kW 450V 60Hz a.c Thrusters: 1 Thwart. FP thruster (f) Fuel: 132.0 (d.f.)

IMO / Call sign	Name / Owner	Tonnage	Class	Builder / Dimensions	Type	Machinery
9423463 *VMQ9273* -	**SOLANDER** - **The Australian Institute of Marine Science** - *Townsville, Qld* *Australia* MMSI: 503540000 Official number: 858417	**384** 115 105	Class: AB	**2007-11 Tenix Defence Pty Ltd (Marine Division) — Fremantle WA** Yd No: 359 Loa 35.80 Br ex - Dght 2.800 Lbp 31.70 Br md 8.60 Dpth 4.20 Welded, 1 dk	**(B31A2SR) Research Survey Vessel**	**2 oil engines** reduction geared to sc. shafts driving 2 FP propellers Total Power: 942kW (1,280hp) Cummins KTA-19-M3 2 x 4 Stroke 6 Cy. 159 x 159 each-471kW (640bhp) Cummins Engine Co Inc-USA AuxGen: 2 x 136kW a.c Thrusters: 1 Tunnel thruster (f) Fuel: 61.6 (d.f.)
8975500 *3DYJ* -	**SOLANDER II** *ex* Chidori Maru No. 75 *-1984* **Solander Pacific Ltd** - *Suva* *Fiji* MMSI: 520113000 Official number: 00424	**172** 52 -		**1974 Ofunato Zosen Tekko K.K. — Ofunato** L reg 30.23 (BB) Br ex - Dght - Lbp - Br md 7.02 Dpth 1.63 Welded, 1 dk	**(B11B2FV) Fishing Vessel**	**1 oil engine** driving 1 Propeller Total Power: 372kW (506hp) 8.0kn Cummins 1 x 4 Stroke 372kW (506bhp) (new engine 1999, fitted 1999) Cummins Engine Co Inc-USA
8653152 *3DQH* 1005	**SOLANDER III** *ex* Ika 3 *-1994* *ex* Hatsutori Maru No. 3 *-1979* *ex* Shinei Maru No. 11 *-1979* **Solander Pacific Ltd** - *Suva* *Fiji* MMSI: 520021000 Official number: 373770	**101** 33 -		**1973-01 K.K. Tago Zosensho — Nishi-Izu** Shortened-2004 Loa 30.00 Br ex 5.55 Dght - Lbp - Br md 5.10 Dpth 2.39 Welded, 1 dk	**(B11B2FV) Fishing Vessel**	**1 oil engine** reduction geared to sc. shaft driving 1 Propeller Total Power: 380kW (517hp) Cummins KT-19-M 1 x 4 Stroke 6 Cy. 159 x 159 380kW (517bhp) (new engine 2004) Cummins Engine Co Inc-USA
8653164 *3DVD* 1006	**SOLANDER IV** *ex* Shimpo No. 7 *-1995* *ex* Shinryu Maru No. 1 *-1990* **Solander Pacific Ltd** - SatCom: Inmarsat C 452001710 *Suva* *Fiji* MMSI: 520022000 Official number: 00015	**112** 29 -		**1981-11 Higashi Kyushu Shipbuilding Co Ltd — Usuki OT** Yd No: 518 Loa 33.25 Br ex 5.85 Dght - Lbp - Br md 5.44 Dpth 2.25 Bonded, 1 dk	**(B11B2FV) Fishing Vessel** Hull Material: Reinforced Plastic	**1 oil engine** reduction geared to sc. shaft driving 1 Propeller Total Power: 380kW (517hp) Cummins KT-19-M 1 x 4 Stroke 6 Cy. 159 x 159 380kW (517bhp) (new engine 2004) Cummins Engine Co Inc-USA
8972118 *3DWW* 1009	**SOLANDER IX** *ex* Highlander II *-2002* *ex* Kaiyo Maru *-1999* **Solander Pacific Ltd** - SatCom: Inmarsat C 452008810 *Suva* *Fiji* MMSI: 520088000 Official number: 00339	**113** 34 -		**1979-05 Nishinippon FRP Zosen K.K. — Hohoku** Yd No: 5348 Loa 33.30 (BB) Br ex - Dght - Lbp 26.80 Br md 5.56 Dpth 2.40 Bonded, 1 dk	**(B11B2FV) Fishing Vessel** Hull Material: Reinforced Plastic	**1 oil engine** reduction geared to sc. shaft driving 1 FP propeller Total Power: 380kW (517hp) 14.0kn Cummins KT-19-M 1 x 4 Stroke 6 Cy. 159 x 159 380kW (517bhp) (new engine 2002) Cummins Engine Co Inc-USA
8114481 *3DYK* 1012	**SOLANDER KARIQA** *ex* Kariqa *-2002* *ex* Solomon Kariqa *-1991* **Solander Pacific Ltd** - *Suva* *Fiji* MMSI: 520114100 Official number: 00428	*181* 54 -		**1981-10 K.K. Murakami Zosensho — Ishinomaki** Yd No: 1078 L reg 28.73 (BB) Br ex - Dght - Lbp 27.00 Br md 6.41 Dpth 2.60 Welded, 1 dk	**(B12D2FR) Fishery Research Vessel**	**1 oil engine** geared to sc. shaft driving 1 FP propeller Total Power: 380kW (517hp) 9.0kn Cummins KT-19-M 1 x 4 Stroke 6 Cy. 159 x 159 380kW (517bhp) (new engine 2004) Cummins Engine Co Inc-USA AuxGen: 2 x 225V 60Hz a.c
8875554 *3DVL* 1007	**SOLANDER V** *ex* Pyunghwa 36 *-1997* **Solander Pacific Ltd** - SatCom: Inmarsat C 452001810 *Suva* *Fiji* MMSI: 520023000 Official number: 00117	**143** 42 103	Class: (KR)	**1991-06 Kwangyang Shipbuilding & Engineering Co Ltd — Janghang** Yd No: 75 Loa 34.03 Br ex - Dght 2.509 Lbp 29.51 Br md 5.80 Dpth - Welded, 1 dk	**(B11B2FV) Fishing Vessel**	**1 oil engine** driving 1 FP propeller Yanmar 1 x 4 Stroke Kwangyang Diesel Engine Co Ltd-South Korea
8653176 *3DVS* 1008	**SOLANDER VI** *ex* Santa Lucia *-1999* *ex* Taisei Maru No. 5 *-1995* **Solander Pacific Ltd** - SatCom: Inmarsat C 451200234 *Suva* *Fiji* Official number: 00193	**102** 47 -		**1981-12 YK Kamiryo Zosensho — Hagi YC** Yd No: 278 L reg 25.95 Br ex 4.94 Dght - Lbp - Br md 4.72 Dpth 2.07 Bonded, 1 dk	**(B11B2FV) Fishing Vessel** Hull Material: Reinforced Plastic	**1 oil engine** reduction geared to sc. shaft driving 1 Propeller Total Power: 380kW (517hp) Cummins KT-19-M 1 x 4 Stroke 6 Cy. 159 x 159 380kW (517bhp) (new engine 2004) Cummins Engine Co Inc-USA
9269154 *3DWN* 1010	**SOLANDER X** *ex* Winfull 3 *-2004* **Solander Pacific Ltd** - SatCom: Inmarsat C 452002811 *Suva* *Fiji* MMSI: 520028000 Official number: 000299	**158** 47 84	Class: (BV)	**2001 Zhoushan Zhentai Shipbuilding — Zhoushan ZJ** Yd No: D01 Loa 29.77 Br ex - Dght 3.000 Lbp 26.40 Br md 6.40 Dpth 3.00 Welded, 1 dk	**(B11B2FV) Fishing Vessel**	**1 oil engine** driving 1 FP propeller Total Power: 447kW (608hp) Cummins KTA-19-M3 1 x 4 Stroke 6 Cy. 159 x 159 447kW (608bhp) Chongqing Cummins Engine Co Ltd-China AuxGen: 2 x 200kW
8653188 *3DWK* 1011	**SOLANDER XI** *ex* Waimanu Catcher *-2002* *ex* Masa Maru No. 28 *-2000* *ex* Sanko Maru No. 11 *-1995* *ex* Manju Maru No. 11 *-1985* **Solander Pacific Ltd** - *Suva* *Fiji* MMSI: 520148100 Official number: 000271	**104** 45 -		**1979-03 Yamaha Motor Co. Ltd. — Kitamura** Yd No: 025 Loa 25.53 Br ex 5.45 Dght - Lbp - Br md - Dpth 2.30 Bonded, 1 dk	**(B11B2FV) Fishing Vessel** Hull Material: Reinforced Plastic	**1 oil engine** reduction geared to sc. shaft driving 1 Propeller Total Power: 380kW (517hp) Cummins KT-19-M 1 x 4 Stroke 6 Cy. 159 x 159 380kW (517bhp) (new engine 2004) Cummins Engine Co Inc-USA
8879407 *3DSP* 1039	**SOLANDER XII** *ex* Shinryo Maru No. 8 *-2009* *ex* Shinsen Maru No. 5 *-2009* **Solander Viti Ltd** - SatCom: Inmarsat C 452017010 *Suva* *Fiji* MMSI: 520170100 Official number: 000796	*117* 34 -		**1981-03 Nishii Dock Co. Ltd. — Ise** Yd No: 646 Loa 36.44 Br ex 5.92 Dght 2.250 Lbp 27.50 Br md 5.85 Dpth 2.50 Bonded, 1 dk	**(B11B2FV) Fishing Vessel** Hull Material: Reinforced Plastic	**1 oil engine** driving 1 FP propeller Total Power: 933kW (1,269hp) 11.0kn Yanmar T250-ET2 1 x 4 Stroke 6 Cy. 260 x 330 933kW (1269bhp) Yanmar Diesel Engine Co Ltd-Japan
8950926 *3DNA* -	**SOLANDER XIV** *ex* Junyo Maru No. 11 *-2011* *ex* Ryusho Maru No. 1 *-2006* *ex* Ofusa Maru No. 11 *-2006* **Solander Viti Ltd** - SatCom: Inmarsat C 452019710 *Suva* *Fiji* Official number: 000914	*110* 33 -		**1982-01 Higashi Kyushu Shipbuilding Co Ltd — Usuki OT** Yd No: 512 Loa 35.20 Br ex - Dght 2.200 Lbp 27.50 Br md 5.50 Dpth 2.52 Bonded, 1 dk	**(B11B2FV) Fishing Vessel** Hull Material: Reinforced Plastic	**1 oil engine** driving 1 FP propeller Total Power: 420kW (571hp) 11.1kn Yanmar 6G-TA 1 x 4 Stroke 6 Cy. 240 x 290 420kW (571bhp) Yanmar Diesel Engine Co Ltd-Japan
8931449 *3DVY* -	**SOLANDER XV** *ex* Koryo Maru No. 58 *-2011* *ex* Jintoku Maru No. 12 *-2011* **Solander Pacific Ltd** - SatCom: Inmarsat C 452024010 *Suva* *Fiji* Official number: 001067	*115* 34 -		**1981-12 Nishii Dock Co. Ltd. — Ise** Converted From: Fishing Vessel-2011 L reg 29.00 Br ex - Dght - Lbp - Br md 5.75 Dpth 2.45 Bonded, 1 dk	**(B12B2FC) Fish Carrier** Hull Material: Reinforced Plastic	**1 oil engine** driving 1 FP propeller Total Power: 745kW (1,013hp) 11.0kn Daihatsu 6DLM-26 1 x 4 Stroke 6 Cy. 260 x 340 745kW (1013bhp) (new engine 2000) Daihatsu Diesel Manufacturing Co Lt-Japan

IMO / Call sign / Flag	Name / Owner	Tonnage	Class	Builder / Dimensions	Type	Machinery
1011575 *ZGDC5* -	**SOLANDGE** *ex* Niki *-2013* **Oceanic Explorations Ltd** Master Yachts Consultancy SL *George Town* *Cayman Islands (British)* MMSI: 319418000 Official number: 743875	**2,899** 869 401	Class: LR ✠ **100A1** SS 10/2013 SSC, Yacht (P), mono, G6 ✠ **LMC** **UMS** Cable: 440.0/34.0 U2 (a)	**2013-10 Kroeger Werft GmbH & Co. KG — Schacht-Audorf** Yd No: 13673 Loa 85.00 (BB) Br ex 14.21 Dght 3.900 Lbp 68.40 Br md 13.80 Dpth 7.00 Welded, 1 dk	**(X11A2YP) Yacht**	**2 oil engines** with clutches, flexible couplings & sr reverse geared to sc. shafts driving 2 FP propellers Total Power: 4,000kW (5,438hp) 17.5kn Caterpillar 3516B HD DITA 2 x Vee 4 Stroke 16 Cy. 170 x 215 each-2000kW (2719bhp) Caterpillar Inc-USA AuxGen: 1 x 456kW 400V 50Hz a.c, 2 x 364kW 400V 50Hz a.c Thrusters: 1 Thwart. CP thruster (f); 1 Water jet (a)
9428073 *SDJU* -	**SOLANDO** *ex* Soley-1 *-2013* *ex* Messinia *-2009* **Donso Shipping KB** Rederi AB Donsotank *Donso* *Sweden* MMSI: 266421000	**13,472** 6,361 19,992 T/cm 30.9	Class: NV (BV)	**2009-09 Soli Shipyard — Izmit** Yd No: 06 Loa 149.95 (BB) Br ex 23.40 Dght 9.915 Lbp 142.80 Br md 23.20 Dpth 13.00 Welded, 1 dk	**(A12A2TC) Chemical Tanker** Double Hull (13F) Liq: 20,916 Compartments: 14 Wing Ta, 2 Wing Slop Ta, ER 14 Cargo Pump (s): 14x350m³/hr Manifold: Bow/CM: 71.1m Ice Capable	**1 oil engine** driving 1 CP propeller Total Power: 6,917kW (9,404hp) 14.0kn MAN-B&W 8S35ME-B 1 x 2 Stroke 8 Cy. 350 x 1550 6917kW (9404bhp) MAN Diesel A/S-Denmark AuxGen: 1 x 1200kW 450V 60Hz a.c, 3 x 750kW 450V 60Hz a.c Thrusters: 1 Tunnel thruster (f) Fuel: 158.0 (d.f.) 545.0 (r.f.)
8028486 *HP7723* -	**SOLANJO** *ex* Stako *-2006* **Salina AS** - *Panama* *Panama* MMSI: 355637000 Official number: 4347412	**1,533** 517 1,450	Class: IS (NV)	**1981-12 FEAB-Marstrandverken — Marstrand** (Hull) Yd No: 155 **1981-12 Fosen Mek. Verksteder AS — Rissa** Yd No: 31 Loa 67.77 Br ex 13.82 Dght 3.050 Lbp 61.50 Br md 13.80 Dpth 7.01 Welded, 1 dk	**(A23A2BD) Bulk Carrier, Self-discharging** Grain: 2,407; Bale: 2,265 Compartments: 2 Ho, ER 2 Ha: 2 (14.0 x 8.9)ER Derricks: 1 Ice Capable	**1 oil engine** driving 1 FP propeller Total Power: 1,177kW (1,600hp) 12.6kn Wichmann 6AXAG 1 x 2 Stroke 6 Cy. 300 x 450 1177kW (1600bhp) Wichmann Motorfabrikk AS-Norway AuxGen: 2 x 184kW 380V 50Hz a.c Thrusters: 1 Thwart. FP thruster (f)
8988416 *WDB7930* -	**SOLANO** - **San Francisco Bay Area Water Emergency Transportation Authority (WETA)** - *Vallejo, CA* *United States of America* MMSI: 366950020 Official number: 1155022	**541** 174 38		**2004-07 Dakota Creek Industries Inc — Anacortes WA** Yd No: 44 Loa 41.30 Br ex - Dght 1.500 Lbp - Br md 11.50 Dpth 3.90 Welded, 1 dk	**(A37B2PS) Passenger Ship** Hull Material: Aluminium Alloy Passengers: unberthed: 328	**2 oil engines** geared to sc. shafts driving 2 Water jets Total Power: 4,640kW (6,308hp) M.T.U. 16V4000M70 2 x Vee 4 Stroke 16 Cy. 165 x 190 each-2320kW (3154bhp) Detroit Diesel Corporation-Detroit, Mi
9426128 *A8XH4* -	**SOLAR AFRICA** - **Natural Maritime SA** Sojitz Marine & Engineering Corp (SOMEC) SatCom: Inmarsat C 463709518 *Monrovia* *Liberia* MMSI: 636014894 Official number: 14894	**32,372** 19,458 58,064 T/cm 57.4	Class: NK	**2011-03 Tsuneishi Heavy Industries (Cebu) Inc — Balamban** Yd No: SC-129 Loa 189.99 (BB) Br ex - Dght 12.826 Lbp 185.60 Br md 32.26 Dpth 18.00 Welded, 1 dk	**(A21A2BC) Bulk Carrier** Grain: 72,689; Bale: 70,122 Compartments: 5 Ho, ER 5 Ha: ER Cranes: 4x30t	**1 oil engine** driving 1 FP propeller Total Power: 8,400kW (11,421hp) 14.5kn MAN-B&W 6S50MC-C 1 x 2 Stroke 6 Cy. 500 x 2000 8400kW (11421bhp) Mitsui Engineering & Shipbuilding CLtd-Japan Fuel: 2389.0 (r.f.)
9056533 *3ETX8* -	**SOLAR ARION** *ex* Merilla *-2010* *ex* Tien Shan *-2009* **NHR Shipping SA** Polaris Shipping Co Ltd SatCom: Inmarsat C 435196211 *Panama* *Panama* MMSI: 351962000 Official number: 4221411	**66,600** 42,445 128,826 T/cm 98.2	Class: CR KR (NK)	**1994-02 Hashihama Shipbuilding Co Ltd — Tadotsu KG** (Hull) Yd No: 1020 **1994-02 Tsuneishi Shipbuilding Co Ltd — Fukuyama HS** Yd No: 1020 Loa 265.00 (BB) Br ex - Dght 16.326 Lbp 255.00 Br md 41.00 Dpth 22.30 Welded, 1 dk	**(A21A2BC) Bulk Carrier** Grain: 144,478 Compartments: 9 Ho, ER 9 Ha: (13.2 x 13.6)8 (14.9 x 18.7)ER	**1 oil engine** driving 1 FP propeller Total Power: 11,620kW (15,799hp) 13.5kn B&W 6S70MC 1 x 2 Stroke 6 Cy. 700 x 2674 11620kW (15799bhp) Mitsui Engineering & Shipbuilding CLtd-Japan AuxGen: 1 x 500kW 450V 60Hz a.c, 2 x 560kW 450V 60Hz a.c Fuel: 104.0 (d.f.) 2564.0 (r.f.) 40.6pd
9237266 *V7AJ7* -	**SOLAR BREEZE** *ex* Great Pheasant *-2013* **KSF 23 International SA** Polaris Shipping Co Ltd *Majuro* *Marshall Islands* MMSI: 538005012 Official number: 5012	**90,876** 57,695 178,820	Class: KR (NK)	**2000-09 Hyundai Heavy Industries Co Ltd — Ulsan** Yd No: 1307 Loa 289.97 (BB) Br ex - Dght 17.620 Lbp 280.10 Br md 47.00 Dpth 24.00 Welded, 1 dk	**(A21A2BC) Bulk Carrier** Grain: 194,179 Compartments: 9 Ho, ER 9 Ha: 7 (15.3 x 21.2)2 (15.3 x 16.0)ER	**1 oil engine** driving 1 FP propeller Total Power: 16,860kW (22,923hp) 14.5kn MAN-B&W 6S70MC 1 x 2 Stroke 6 Cy. 700 x 2674 16860kW (22923bhp) Hyundai Heavy Industries Co Ltd-South Korea Fuel: 4750.0
9146596 *3FB06* -	**SOLAR EMBER** *ex* Su-Oh *-2013* **EOS Line Inc** Polaris Shipping Co Ltd *Panama* *Panama* MMSI: 356525000 Official number: 44993PEXT1	**84,318** 56,081 171,081 T/cm 114.9	Class: KR (NK)	**1997-02 Ishikawajima-Harima Heavy Industries Co Ltd (IHI) — Kure** Yd No: 3072 Loa 289.00 (BB) Br ex - Dght 17.625 Lbp 277.00 Br md 45.00 Dpth 23.80 Welded, 1 dk	**(A21A2BC) Bulk Carrier** Grain: 186,674 Compartments: 9 Ho, ER 9 Ha: (18.4 x 17.0)2 (17.8 x 20.4)5 (13.8 x 20.4) (16.8 x 13.8)ER	**1 oil engine** driving 1 FP propeller Total Power: 16,040kW (21,808hp) 14.8kn Sulzer 6RTA72 1 x 2 Stroke 6 Cy. 720 x 2500 16040kW (21808bhp) Diesel United Ltd.-Aioi Fuel: 4620.0 (r.f.)
9303754 *5BYV3* -	**SOLAR N** *ex* Mark Twain *-2013* *ex* Emirates Eminence *-2009* *ex* CMA CGM Respect *-2009* *completed as* Mark Twain *-2006* **Prometheus Shipping Corp** Navios Shipmanagement Inc *Limassol* *Cyprus* MMSI: 210839000 Official number: 9303754	**35,581** 19,407 44,053	Class: GL	**2006-03 Hanjin Heavy Industries & Construction Co Ltd — Busan** Yd No: 149 Loa 222.50 (BB) Br ex - Dght 12.000 Lbp 212.00 Br md 32.20 Dpth 19.30 Welded, 1 dk	**(A33A2CC) Container Ship (Fully Cellular)** TEU 3398 incl 300 ref C.	**1 oil engine** driving 1 FP propeller Total Power: 28,880kW (39,265hp) 22.7kn MAN-B&W 8K80MC-C 1 x 2 Stroke 8 Cy. 800 x 2300 28880kW (39265bhp) Doosan Engine Co Ltd-South Korea AuxGen: 4 x 1200kW 450/230V a.c Thrusters: 1 Thwart. CP thruster (f)
8656312 *UBOH3* G-0919	**SOLAR NO. 101** - **LLC Go-Raizing Sakhalin** - *Nevelsk* *Russia* MMSI: 273351630 Official number: 877353	**890** 427 809	Class: RS (Class contemplated)	**1988-06 Lien Ho Shipbuilding Co, Ltd — Kaohsiung** Loa 64.80 Br ex - Dght 3.850 Lbp 56.65 Br md 10.00 Dpth 4.20 Welded, 1 dk	**(B11B2FV) Fishing Vessel**	**1 oil engine** with clutches & sr reverse geared to sc. shaft driving 1 FP propeller Total Power: 1,343kW (1,826hp) 12.0kn Niigata 6M31AFTE 1 x 4 Stroke 6 Cy. 310 x 530 1343kW (1826bhp) Niigata Engineering Co Ltd-Japan AuxGen: 2 x 540kW a.c, 1 x 360kW a.c Fuel: 320.0 (d.f.)
8911499 *DSOV2* -	**SOLAR ORION** *ex* Chenebourg *-2011* *ex* Lowlands Grace *-2006* *ex* CSK Everest *-1993* **Shinhan Capital Co Ltd** Polaris Shipping Co Ltd SatCom: Inmarsat C 444095959 *Jeju* *South Korea* MMSI: 440395000 Official number: JJR-069680	**77,273** 47,299 149,518 T/cm 106.3	Class: KR (BV)	**1991-01 China Shipbuilding Corp (CSBC) — Kaohsiung** Yd No: 508 Loa 270.08 (BB) Br ex 43.02 Dght 17.325 Lbp 260.03 Br md 42.96 Dpth 23.90 Welded, 1 dk	**(A21A2BC) Bulk Carrier** Grain: 164,597; Bale: 162,730 Compartments: 9 Ho, ER 9 Ha: 9 (14.2 x 18.4)ER	**1 oil engine** driving 1 FP propeller Total Power: 12,431kW (16,901hp) 12.6kn B&W 5L80MCE 1 x 2 Stroke 5 Cy. 800 x 2592 12431kW (16901bhp) Kawasaki Heavy Industries Ltd-Japan AuxGen: 3 x 500kW 450V 60Hz a.c Fuel: 217.0 (d.f.) 2853.0 (r.f.) 38.0pd
5333335 - -	**SOLAR STAR** - **The Star Ferry Co Ltd** - *Hong Kong* *Hong Kong* Official number: 196866	*164* 40 -		**1957 Hong Kong & Whampoa Dock Co Ltd — Hong Kong** Loa 33.78 Br ex 9.22 Dght - Lbp - Br md 8.57 Dpth 2.61 Welded, 1 dk	**(A37B2PS) Passenger Ship** Passengers: unberthed: 555	**1 oil engine** driving 1 FP propeller Total Power: 352kW (479hp) Crossley HGN6 1 x 2 Stroke 6 Cy. 267 x 343 352kW (479bhp) Crossley Bros. Ltd.-Manchester
8899249 - -	**SOLAR TIDE** - **Multiplan Nigeria Ltd**	**204** 61 -	Class: AB	**1980-01 Fred Settoon, Inc. — Pierre Part, La** Yd No: 244 L reg 33.52 Br ex - Dght 2.720 Lbp - Br md 8.53 Dpth 3.20 Welded, 1 dk	**(B34R2QY) Supply Tender**	**2 oil engines** reverse reduction geared to sc. shafts driving 2 FP propellers Total Power: 764kW (1,038hp) 10.0kn Caterpillar 3412TA 2 x Vee 4 Stroke 12 Cy. 137 x 152 each-382kW (519bhp) Caterpillar Tractor Co-USA AuxGen: 2 x 50kW a.c Fuel: 83.0 (d.f.)
9273521 *WDE9879* -	**SOLAR TIDE II** - **Regions Equipment Finance Corp** Tidex Nigeria Ltd *New Orleans, LA* *United States of America* MMSI: 369289000 Official number: 1140537	**1,235** 473 1,675	Class: AB	**2003-07 Quality Shipyards LLC — Houma LA** Yd No: 1236 Loa 79.50 Br ex - Dght 4.200 Lbp 64.31 Br md 14.02 Dpth 5.18 Welded, 1 dk	**(B21A20S) Platform Supply Ship**	**2 oil engines** geared to sc. shafts driving 2 FP propellers Total Power: 3,370kW (4,582hp) Caterpillar 3516B-HD 2 x Vee 4 Stroke 16 Cy. 170 x 215 each-1685kW (2291bhp) Caterpillar Inc-USA

8906236 *IIOP2* -	**SOLARIA** *ex* Annelise Theresa *-2009* *ex* Elka Theresa *-2002* **Morfini SpA** - SatCom: Inmarsat C 424702484 *Bari* *Italy* MMSI: 247256800 Official number: 339	**1,475** 535 2,345 T/cm 8.2	Class: RI (LR) ✠ Classed LR until 2/2/09	**1990-12 J.H. van Eijk & Zonen B.V. — Sliedrecht** Yd No: 370 Loa 79.90 Br ex 10.94 Dght 4.362 Lbp 75.25 Br md 10.90 Dpth 6.55 Welded, 1 dk	**(A13B2TP) Products Tanker** Double Hull Liq: 2,478; Liq (Oil): 2,478 Cargo Heating Coils Compartments: 10 Ta, ER 2 Cargo Pump (s): 2x225m³/hr Manifold: Bow/CM: 39m Ice Capable	**1 oil engine** with clutches, flexible couplings & sr reverse geared to sc. shaft driving 1 FP propeller Total Power: 1,102kW (1,498hp) 10.0kn A.B.C. 6MDZC 1 x 4 Stroke 6 Cy. 256 x 310 1102kW (1498bhp) Anglo Belgian Corp NV (ABC)-Belgium AuxGen: 2 x 90kW 380V 50Hz a.c Boilers: 2 AuxB (o.f.) 12.2kgf/cm² (12.0bar) Thrusters: 1 Thwart. FP thruster (f) Fuel: 80.0 (d.f.)
8990483 *WDB7832* -	**SOLARIS** - **Freeport Shipbuilding Hull 267 Inc** - *Fort Walton Beach, FL* *United States of America* Official number: 1149929	**355** 108 -		**2004 Freeport Shipbuilding & Marine Repair, Inc. — Freeport, Fl** Yd No: 267 Loa 38.10 Br ex - Dght 1.400 Lbp - Br md 7.92 Dpth 2.13 Welded, 1 dk	**(A37B2PS) Passenger Ship** Passengers: unberthed: 125	**2 oil engines** geared to sc. shafts driving 2 Propellers Total Power: 442kW (600hp) Caterpillar 3406 2 x 4 Stroke 6 Cy. 137 x 165 each-221kW (300bhp) Caterpillar Inc-USA AuxGen: 2 x 63kW
9108099 *IBJS* -	**SOLARO** - **Carbonor SpA** Carbofin SpA SatCom: Inmarsat B 324702930 *Genoa* *Italy* MMSI: 247080000 Official number: 007	**25,300** 9,784 38,427 T/cm 46.0	Class: AB RI	**1996-04 Sestri Cant. Nav. SpA — Genova** Yd No: 5962 Loa 180.51 (BB) Br ex 29.00 Dght 12.620 Lbp 169.05 Br md 28.99 Dpth 17.90 Welded, 1 dk	**(A11B2TG) LPG Tanker** Double Hull (13F) Liq (Gas): 37,314 4 x Gas Tank (s); 4 independent pri horizontal 8 Cargo Pump (s): 8x350m³/hr Manifold: Bow/CM: 93m Ice Capable	**1 oil engine** driving 1 FP propeller Total Power: 11,100kW (15,092hp) 15.9kn Sulzer 5RTA62U 1 x 2 Stroke 5 Cy. 620 x 2150 11100kW (15092bhp) Fincantieri Cantieri NavaliItaliani SpA-Italy AuxGen: 1 x 1400kW 450V 60Hz a.c, 3 x 1000kW 450V 60Hz a.c Fuel: 221.0 (d.f.) 2499.0 (r.f.) 41.0pd
8210285 *D6FM9* -	**SOLARTE** *ex* African Trader *-2010* *ex* Tukanas *-2008* *ex* Oriana I *-1997* *ex* Hakko Fontaine *-1995* **Baltic Atlant Shipping SL** - SatCom: Inmarsat C 461688510 *Moroni* *Union of Comoros* MMSI: 616885000	**3,261** 1,590 3,919	Class: IV (NV) (NK)	**1982-12 Kochi Jyuko (Eiho Zosen) K.K. — Kochi** Yd No: 1550 Loa 92.23 (BB) Br ex - Dght 6.568 Lbp 85.02 Br md 16.21 Dpth 6.86 Welded, 3 dks	**(A34A2GR) Refrigerated Cargo Ship** Ins: 4,329 Compartments: 3 Ho, ER 3 Ha: 3 (4.9 x 4.9) Derricks: 6x4t	**1 oil engine** sr geared to sc. shaft driving 1 FP propeller Total Power: 3,310kW (4,500hp) 14.5kn Pielstick 6PC2-6L-400 1 x 4 Stroke 6 Cy. 400 x 460 3310kW (4500bhp) Ishikawajima Harima Heavy IndustrieCo Ltd (IHI)-Japan AuxGen: 1 x 640kW 450V 60Hz a.c, 2 x 600kW 450V 60Hz a.c Fuel: 134.0 (d.f.) 590.0 (r.f.) 12.5pd
8802636 *9WTE* -	**SOLAS** - **Government of Malaysia (Director of Marine - Sabah)** - *Labuan* *Malaysia* Official number: M66	**684** 205 -	Class: (LR) ✠ Classed LR until 5/7/00	**1989-02 Sabah Shipyard Sdn Bhd — Labuan** Yd No: 142 Loa 51.60 Br ex 10.72 Dght 2.601 Lbp 47.60 Br md 10.50 Dpth 4.00 Welded, 1 dk	**(B34Q2QL) Buoy & Lighthouse Tender**	**1 oil engine** with clutches, flexible couplings & sr geared to sc. shaft driving 1 CP propeller Total Power: 691kW (939hp) Blackstone ESL6MK2 1 x 4 Stroke 6 Cy. 222 x 292 691kW (939bhp) Mirrlees Blackstone (Stamford)Ltd.-Stamford AuxGen: 2 x 160kW 240/415V 50Hz a.c Thrusters: 1 Thwart. FP thruster (f)
8604008 *UBCQ* -	**SOLBORG** *ex* Faroe Prawns *-1992* **Aspect Co Ltd (OOO 'Aspect')** - *Petropavlovsk-Kamchatskiy* *Russia* MMSI: 273317030	**2,015** 744 1,060	Class: RS (NV)	**1987-01 Salthammer Baatbyggeri AS — Vestnes** (Hull) **1987-01 Langsten Slip & Baatbyggeri AS — Tomrefjord** Yd No: 121 Loa 63.80 (BB) Br ex - Dght 5.622 Lbp 55.43 Br md 13.00 Dpth 8.12 Welded, 1 dk	**(B11A2FS) Stern Trawler** Ins: 1,749 Ice Capable	**1 oil engine** geared to sc. shaft driving 1 CP propeller Total Power: 2,251kW (3,060hp) 15.0kn Wartsila 6R32D 1 x 4 Stroke 6 Cy. 320 x 350 2251kW (3060bhp) Wartsila Diesel Oy-Finland AuxGen: 1 x 1456kW 440V 60Hz a.c, 2 x 406kW 440V 60Hz a.c
9224245 *TFUS* RE 270	**SOLBORG** *ex* Gardar *-2006* **Brim hf** - *Reykjavik* *Iceland* MMSI: 251603110 Official number: 2464	*116* 35 54	Class: (NV)	**2001-04 Dalian Fishing Vessel Co — Dalian LN** Yd No: 99-200-8 Loa 21.50 Br ex - Dght 2.000 Lbp 19.50 Br md 6.40 Dpth 3.20 Welded, 1 dk	**(B11B2FV) Fishing Vessel** Ice Capable	**1 oil engine** reduction geared to sc. shaft driving 1 CP propeller Total Power: 440kW (598hp) 11.3kn Cummins KTA-19-M3 1 x 4 Stroke 6 Cy. 159 x 159 440kW (598bhp) Cummins Engine Co Inc-USA
8130980 *HQJL6* -	**SOLCHEM** *ex* Showa Maru *-1992* **Asian Chemical Carriers Ltd** - *San Lorenzo* *Honduras* Official number: L-1324205	*699* 494 1,803		**1982-04 Ube Dockyard Co. Ltd. — Ube** Yd No: 171 Loa 70.62 Br ex 11.03 Dght 4.611 Lbp 65.03 Br md 11.00 Dpth 5.01 Welded, 1 dk	**(A13B2TP) Products Tanker** Liq: 2,148; Liq (Oil): 2,148 Compartments: 10 Ta, ER	**1 oil engine** driving 1 CP propeller Total Power: 1,324kW (1,800hp) Hanshin 6EL30 1 x 4 Stroke 6 Cy. 300 x 600 1324kW (1800bhp) Hanshin Nainenki Kogyo-Japan
8942486 - -	**SOLDADO OSPREY** - **Trinmar Ltd** - *Port of Spain* *Trinidad & Tobago*	**114** 34 -		**1960 Halter Marine Services, Inc. — U.S.A.** Loa - Br ex - Dght 2.590 Lbp 26.82 Br md 7.31 Dpth 2.89 Welded, 1 dk	**(B21A2OS) Platform Supply Ship**	**2 oil engines** geared to sc. shafts driving 2 FP propellers Total Power: 514kW (698hp) G.M. (Detroit Diesel) 12V-71 2 x Vee 2 Stroke 12 Cy. 108 x 127 each-257kW (349bhp) General Motors Detroit DieselAllison Divn-USA
9618111 *9V9439* -	**SOLDOY** - **Soldoy Shipping Pte Ltd** Densan Deniz Nakliyat ve Sanayi AS (Densan Shipping Co Inc) *Singapore* *Singapore* MMSI: 566211000 Official number: 397084	**33,042** 19,132 56,830 T/cm 58.8	Class: NV (GL)	**2011-12 Yangfan Group Co Ltd — Zhoushan ZJ** Yd No: 2194 Loa 190.00 (BB) Br ex - Dght 12.800 Lbp 185.00 Br md 32.26 Dpth 18.00 Welded, 1 dk	**(A21A2BC) Bulk Carrier** Grain: 71,634; Bale: 68,200 Compartments: 5 Ho, ER 5 Ha: ER Cranes: 4x36t	**1 oil engine** driving 1 FP propeller Total Power: 9,480kW (12,889hp) 14.5kn MAN-B&W 6S50MC-C 1 x 2 Stroke 6 Cy. 500 x 2000 9480kW (12889bhp) STX Engine Co Ltd-South Korea AuxGen: 3 x a.c
9314583 *DBFH* -	**SOLEA** - **Government of The Federal Republic of Germany (Bundesanstalt fuer Landwirtschaft und Ernahrung BLE) (Federal Office for Agriculture & Food)** - *Cuxhaven* *Germany* MMSI: 211417590	**638** 191 135	Class: GL	**2004-06 Muhlhan Sp z oo — Szczecin** (Hull) **2004-06 Fr Fassmer GmbH & Co KG — Berne** Yd No: 1940 Loa 42.70 Br ex 10.20 Dght 3.400 Lbp 39.40 Br md 9.80 Dpth 4.80 Welded, 1 dk	**(B12D2FR) Fishery Research Vessel** Ice Capable	**2 diesel electric oil engines** driving 2 gen. each 664kW 400V a.c Connecting to 1 elec. Motor of (950kW) driving 1 FP propeller Total Power: 1,424kW (1,936hp) M.T.U. 16V2000M50 2 x Vee 4 Stroke 16 Cy. 130 x 150 each-712kW (968bhp) MTU Friedrichshafen GmbH-Friedrichshafen Thrusters: 1 Tunnel thruster (f)
8818142 - -	**SOLEA** - **Francoise Burdinat** Sud Clearance Sarl	**235** 74 326	Class: (LR) ✠ Classed LR until 1/6/10	**1989-07 Campbeltown Shipyard Ltd. — Campbeltown** Yd No: 085 Converted From: Live-Fish Carrier (Well Boat)-2010 Loa 33.51 Br ex 7.62 Dght 3.413 Lbp 30.20 Br md 7.60 Dpth 3.80 Welded, 1 dk	**(A31A2GX) General Cargo Ship** Grain: 260 Compartments: 2 Ho, ER 2 Ha: ER Cranes: 1x2t	**1 oil engine** with clutches, flexible couplings & sr geared to sc. shaft driving 1 CP propeller Total Power: 530kW (721hp) 8.5kn Caterpillar 3412TA 1 x Vee 4 Stroke 12 Cy. 137 x 152 530kW (721bhp) (new engine 1996) Caterpillar Inc-USA AuxGen: 2 x 60kW 415V 50Hz a.c, 1 x 15kW 415V 50Hz a.c Thrusters: 1 Thwart. CP thruster (f)
7349089 *J8Y4093* -	**SOLEA** - **Esperance Ltd** Philippe Bracht *Kingstown* *St Vincent & The Grenadines* MMSI: 377122000 Official number: 40563	**387** 116 102	Class: GL	**1974-05 Schiffswerft u. Maschinenfabrik Max Sieghold — Bremerhaven** Yd No: 162 Converted From: Trawler-2005 Loa 36.19 Br ex 9.05 Dght 3.300 Lbp 29.19 Br md 9.00 Dpth 4.40 Welded, 1 dk	**(X11A2YP) Yacht** Derricks: 1x3t Ice Capable	**1 oil engine** reverse reduction geared to sc. shaft driving 1 CP propeller Total Power: 640kW (870hp) 12.0kn Deutz SBA6M528 1 x 4 Stroke 6 Cy. 220 x 280 640kW (870bhp) Kloeckner Humboldt Deutz AG-West Germany AuxGen: 2 x 76kW 380/220V a.c
8922620 - - -	**SOLEDA** *ex* Wei Kai No. 16 *-1992* - -	**560** 248 -		**1990 Fong Kuo Shipbuilding Co Ltd — Kaohsiung** Loa - Br ex - Dght - Lbp 47.50 Br md 8.70 Dpth 3.75 Welded, 1 dk	**(B11B2FV) Fishing Vessel**	**1 oil engine** driving 1 FP propeller Total Power: 883kW (1,201hp) 11.0kn Niigata 1 x 4 Stroke 6 Cy. 883kW (1201bhp) Niigata Engineering Co Ltd-Japan
6700755 *EFHE* -	**SOLEDAD** - **Plana y Cia SL** - *Vigo* *Spain* Official number: 3-8643/	*169* 88 314	Class: (BV)	**1966 Construcciones Navales Santodomingo SA — Vigo** Yd No: 347 Loa 28.12 Br ex 6.43 Dght 3.302 Lbp 25.07 Br md 6.41 Dpth 3.56 Welded, 1 dk	**(B11A2FT) Trawler** Ins: 65 Compartments: 1 Ho, ER 3 Ha: (0.5 x 0.4)2 (1.0 x 1.0)ER	**1 oil engine** driving 1 FP propeller Total Power: 294kW (400hp) 10.0kn Deutz RA8M528 1 x 4 Stroke 8 Cy. 220 x 280 294kW (400bhp) Kloeckner Humboldt Deutz AG-West Germany Fuel: 43.0 (d.f.)

8200008 **SOLEDAD RUA**
LW3008
-
RUA Remolcadores Unidos Argentinos SAM y C
-
Argentina
MMSI: 701007048
Official number: 02508

289 / 163 / 195
Class: (AB)

1982-12 **Astilleros Mestrina S.A. — Tigre**
Yd No: 65
Loa - Br ex - Dght 3.201
Lbp 33.00 Br md 9.42 Dpth 4.32
Welded, 1 dk

(B32A2ST) Tug

2 oil engines sr reverse geared to sc. shafts driving 2 CP propellers
Total Power: 1,788kW (2,430hp) 13.0kn
MAN 9L25/30
2 x 4 Stroke 9 Cy. 250 x 300 each-894kW (1215bhp)
Industrias Argentinas MAN SAIC-Argentina
AuxGen: 2 x 80kW a.c
Thrusters: 1 Thwart. FP thruster (f)

8965048 **SOLEFISH**
H03799
ex Leon Grigsby *-2006*
-
Hercules Oilfield Services Ltd
Hercules Liftboat Co LLC
Panama *Panama*
Official number: 1177382I

299 / 73 / -

1978 Sun Contractors, Inc. — Harvey, La
L reg 22.55 Br ex - Dght -
Lbp - Br md 11.58 Dpth 2.13
Welded, 1 dk

(B22A2ZM) Offshore Construction Vessel, jack up

4 oil engines reduction geared to sc. shafts driving 2 FP propellers
Total Power: 1,176kW (1,600hp)
General Motors
4 x each-294kW (400bhp)
General Motors Corp-USA

8896687 **SOLEIL 51**
6WJG
DAK 1178
ex CNFC 9514 *-2011*
China National Fisheries Corp
-
Dakar *Senegal*

327 / 98 / 160
Class: (CC)

1995 Guangzhou Fishing Vessel Shipyard — Guangzhou GD
Loa 44.86 Br ex - Dght 3.000
Lbp 38.00 Br md 8.00 Dpth 4.00
Welded, 1 dk

(B11B2FV) Fishing Vessel
Ins: 464

1 oil engine geared to sc. shaft driving 1 FP propeller
Total Power: 735kW (999hp) 12.0kn
Chinese Std. Type 8300
1 x 4 Stroke 8 Cy. 300 x 380 735kW (999bhp)
Dalian Fishing Vessel Co-China
AuxGen: 2 x 120kW 400V a.c

8896699 **SOLEIL 61**
6WJH
DAK 1179
ex CNFC 9515 *-2011*
China National Fisheries Corp
-
Dakar *Senegal*

327 / 98 / 160
Class: (CC)

1995 Guangzhou Fishing Vessel Shipyard — Guangzhou GD
Loa 44.86 Br ex - Dght 3.000
Lbp 38.00 Br md 8.00 Dpth 4.00
Welded, 1 dk

(B11B2FV) Fishing Vessel
Ins: 464

1 oil engine geared to sc. shaft driving 1 FP propeller
Total Power: 735kW (999hp) 12.0kn
Chinese Std. Type 8300
1 x 4 Stroke 8 Cy. 300 x 380 735kW (999bhp)
Dalian Fishing Vessel Co-China
AuxGen: 2 x 120kW 400V a.c

6807553 **SOLEIL D'ORIENT**
-
ex Seahire II *-1984* *ex* Gulf Queen *-1977*
ex Alibut I *-1969*
-

219 / 140 / -

1967 Scheepswerf Vooruit B.V. — Zaandam
L reg 25.30 Br ex 7.01 Dght -
Lbp - Br md - Dpth -
Welded, 1 dk

(B11B2FV) Fishing Vessel

1 oil engine driving 1 FP propeller
Total Power: 313kW (426hp) 9.5kn
Caterpillar D353SCAC
1 x 4 Stroke 6 Cy. 159 x 203 313kW (426bhp)
Caterpillar Tractor Co-USA

8316170 **SOLEIMAN**
EQOF
-
Bahregan Marine Services Co Ltd
-
Bushehr *Iran*
MMSI: 422149000
Official number: 434

1,019 / 305 / 1,550
Class: AS (LR)
✠ Classed LR until 31/5/00

1984-05 **Kanrei Zosen K.K. — Naruto** (Hull)
Yd No: 302
1984-05 **Mitsui Ocean Development & Eng. Co. Ltd. — Japan** Yd No: 178
Loa 61.12 Br ex 12.76 Dght 3.900
Lbp 55.50 Br md 12.21 Dpth 5.01
Welded, 1 dk

(B21A2OS) Platform Supply Ship

2 oil engines with clutches, flexible couplings & sr reverse geared to sc. shafts driving 2 FP propellers
Total Power: 2,722kW (3,700hp) 13.0kn
Deutz SBV8M628
2 x 4 Stroke 8 Cy. 240 x 280 each-1361kW (1850bhp)
Kloeckner Humboldt Deutz AG-West Germany
AuxGen: 2 x 240kW 385V 50Hz a.c
Thrusters: 1 Thwart. CP thruster (f)
Fuel: 510.5 (d.f.)

1006544 **SOLEMAR**
ZCIR3
-
Dunellen Holdings Ltd
Pacific Yacht Operations
George Town *Cayman Islands (British)*
MMSI: 319868000
Official number: 735677

1,149 / 344 / -
Class: LR
✠ **100A1** SS 06/2013
SSC
Yacht (P), mono, G6
✠ **LMC** **UMS**
Cable: 440.0/26.0 U2 (a)

2003-06 **Damen Shipyards Gdynia SA — Gdynia** (Hull)
2003-06 **Amels Schelde BV — Vlissingen**
Yd No: 435
Loa 61.50 Br ex 11.02 Dght 3.750
Lbp 53.48 Br md 10.60 Dpth 5.70
Welded, 1 dk

(X11A2YP) Yacht

2 oil engines with clutches, flexible couplings & sr reverse geared to sc. shafts driving 2 FP propellers
Total Power: 3,878kW (5,272hp) 17.0kn
Caterpillar 3516B-TA
2 x Vee 4 Stroke 16 Cy. 170 x 190 each-1939kW (2636bhp)
Caterpillar Inc-USA
AuxGen: 2 x 216kW 400V 50Hz a.c
Thrusters: 1 Thwart. FP thruster (f)

1010337 **SOLEMATES**
ZGAS8
-
Solemates Marine Ltd
Dynamic Yacht Management LLC
George Town *Cayman Islands (British)*
MMSI: 319032800
Official number: 742891

1,218 / 365 / 189
Class: LR
✠ **100A1** SS 07/2010
SSC
Yacht, mono, G6
✠ **LMC** **UMS**
Eq.Ltr: J;
Cable: 332.0/24.0 U2 (a)

2010-07 **Luerssen Bardenfleth GmbH & Co KG — Berne** (Hull) Yd No: (13661)
2010-07 **Fr. Luerssen Werft GmbH & Co. — Bremen** Yd No: 13661
Loa 60.00 Br ex 11.41 Dght 3.500
Lbp 48.72 Br md 11.10 Dpth 6.27
Welded, 1 dk

(X11A2YP) Yacht

2 oil engines with clutches, flexible couplings & sr reverse geared to sc. shafts driving 2 FP propellers
Total Power: 2,908kW (3,954hp) 12.0kn
Caterpillar 3512B
2 x Vee 4 Stroke 12 Cy. 170 x 190 each-1454kW (1977bhp)
Caterpillar Inc-USA
AuxGen: 3 x 280kW 400V 50Hz a.c
Thrusters: 1 Thwart. FP thruster (f)

8933198 **SOLENA**
HQUW9
ex Nikita *-1999* *ex* Noble Vickie *-1997*
ex Golden Hull *-1997* *ex* Gonave Family *-1997*
Solena Transportation Inc
-
SatCom: Inmarsat C 433472910
San Lorenzo *Honduras*
MMSI: 334729000
Official number: L-0327338

368 / 116 / 500

1945 Milwaukee Iron & Steel Works — Milwaukee, Wi
Loa 40.54 Br ex - Dght 3.000
Lbp 38.92 Br md 9.14 Dpth 4.26
Welded, 1 dk

(A31A2GX) General Cargo Ship

2 oil engines driving 2 FP propellers
Total Power: 588kW (800hp)
General Motors
2 x each-294kW (400bhp)
General Motors Corp-USA

9226322 **SOLENT**
9HXG6
ex CSAV Livorno *-2006* *ex* Solent *-2003*
ms 'Provence' Schiffahrtsgesellschaft mbH & Co KG
FH Bertling Reederei GmbH
Valletta *Malta*
MMSI: 215205000
Official number: 7185

24,918 / 12,535 / 35,079
Class: NV

2002-03 **Jiangdu Yahai Shipbuilding Co Ltd — Jiangdu JS** Yd No: BC32000-001
Loa 188.00 (BB) Br ex 27.73 Dght 11.300
Lbp 177.00 Br md 27.70 Dpth 15.50
Welded, 1 dk

(A31A2GX) General Cargo Ship
Double Hull
Grain: 45,069
TEU 1874 incl 100 ref C.
Compartments: 5 Ho, ER
9 Ha: (12.8 x 20.0)8 (12.8 x 23.0)ER
Cranes: 4x35t

1 oil engine driving 1 FP propeller
Total Power: 8,730kW (11,869hp) 15.0kn
Sulzer 6RTA48T-B
1 x 2 Stroke 6 Cy. 480 x 2000 8730kW (11869bhp)
Yichang Marine Diesel Engine Co Ltd-China
AuxGen: 3 x 600kW 60Hz a.c

9118173 **SOLENT FISHER**
C6TW6
-
James Fisher Everard Ltd
James Fisher (Shipping Services) Ltd
Nassau *Bahamas*
MMSI: 311799000
Official number: 8000868

3,368 / 1,367 / 4,970 / T/cm / 12.6
Class: LR
✠ **100A1** SS 10/2012
Double Hull oil tanker
ESP
LI
✠ **LMC** **UMS**
Eq.Ltr: S; Cable: 552.5/44.0 U2

1997-10 **Qiuxin Shipyard — Shanghai** Yd No: 1245
Loa 91.00 (BB) Br ex 15.63 Dght 6.200
Lbp 86.00 Br md 15.60 Dpth 7.80
Welded, 1 dk

(A13B2TP) Products Tanker
Double Hull (13F)
Liq: 4,756; Liq (Oil): 4,756
Cargo Heating Coils
Compartments: 12 Wing Ta, ER
12 Cargo Pump (s): 10x300m³/hr, 2x250m³/hr
Manifold: Bow/CM: 44.6m

1 oil engine with clutches, flexible couplings & sr geared to sc. shaft driving 1 CP propeller
Total Power: 2,640kW (3,589hp) 12.1kn
MaK 6M32
1 x 4 Stroke 6 Cy. 320 x 480 2640kW (3589bhp)
MaK Motoren GmbH & Co. KG-Kiel
AuxGen: 1 x 1000kW 415V 50Hz a.c, 1 x 630kW 415V 50Hz a.c, 1 x 505kW 415V 50Hz a.c
Boilers: TOH (o.f.) 5.1kgf/cm² (5.0bar), TOH (ex.g.) 5.1kgf/cm² (5.0bar)
Thrusters: 1 Thwart. FP thruster (f)
Fuel: 49.0 (d.f.) 211.0 (r.f.)

7340344 **SOLENT SCENE**
GUKV
-
Blue Line Cruises Ltd
-
Poole *United Kingdom*
MMSI: 235003665
Official number: 362081

131 / 76 / -

1974 Bideford Shipyard (1973) Ltd. — Bideford
Yd No: Y55
Loa 27.44 Br ex 6.99 Dght 1.448
Lbp 25.91 Br md 6.72 Dpth 2.29
Welded, 2 dks

(A37B2PS) Passenger Ship
Passengers: unberthed: 249

2 oil engines geared to sc. shafts driving 2 FP propellers
Total Power: 226kW (308hp) 10.0kn
Gardner 8LXB
2 x 4 Stroke 8 Cy. 121 x 152 each-113kW (154bhp)
L. Gardner & Sons Ltd.-Manchester

9206061 **SOLENT STAR**
A8OG9
-
Star Reefers Shipowning Inc
Star Reefers Poland Sp z oo
SatCom: Inmarsat C 463701273
Monrovia *Liberia*
MMSI: 636013624
Official number: 13624

10,804 / 5,320 / 9,709 / T/cm / 25.7
Class: NV (NK)

2001-01 **Shikoku Dockyard Co. Ltd. — Takamatsu**
Yd No: 894
Loa 150.00 (BB) Br ex - Dght 9.018
Lbp 140.00 Br md 23.00 Dpth 13.30
Welded, 1 dk

(A34A2GR) Refrigerated Cargo Ship
Ins: 14,335
TEU 306 C Ho 84 TEU C Dk 222 TEU incl 100 ref C
Compartments: 4 Ho, ER, 10 Tw Dk
4 Ha: 4 (12.6 x 7.8)ER
Cranes: 2x40t,2x8t

1 oil engine driving 1 FP propeller
Total Power: 12,640kW (17,185hp) 21.0kn
B&W 8S50MC-C
1 x 2 Stroke 8 Cy. 500 x 2000 12640kW (17185bhp)
Mitsui Engineering & Shipbuilding CLtd-Japan
AuxGen: 4 x 800kW 450V 60Hz a.c
Fuel: 172.6 (d.f.) 1545.0 (r.f.) 45.0pd

9428085 **SOLERO**
SFAP
ex Soley-2 *-2013* *ex* Monfiero *-2009*
Donso Shipping KB
Brostrom AB
Donso *Sweden*
MMSI: 266420000

13,472 / 6,361 / 19,992 / T/cm / 30.9
Class: NV (BV)

2009-09 **Soli Shipyard — Izmit** Yd No: 07
Loa 149.95 (BB) Br ex 23.40 Dght 9.915
Lbp 143.60 Br md 23.20 Dpth 13.05
Welded, 1 dk

(A12A2TC) Chemical Tanker
Double Hull (13F)
Liq: 20,914
Compartments: 14 Wing Ta, 2 Wing Slop Ta, ER
14 Cargo Pump (s): 14x350m³/hr
Manifold: Bow/CM: 71.1m
Ice Capable

1 oil engine driving 1 CP propeller
Total Power: 6,917kW (9,404hp) 14.0kn
MAN-B&W 8S35ME-B
1 x 2 Stroke 8 Cy. 350 x 1550 6917kW (9404bhp)
MAN Diesel A/S-Denmark
AuxGen: 1 x 1200kW 450V 60Hz a.c, 3 x 750kW 450V 60Hz a.c
Thrusters: 1 Tunnel thruster (f)
Fuel: 182.0 (d.f.) 893.0 (r.f.)

8104204 *TUN5022* -	**SOLEVANT** *ex* Santa Maria *-2011* **Armement Solevant Pecheries** Armement CMB et Compagnie *Abidjan* *Cote d'Ivoire* MMSI: 619002000	*760* 349 -	Class: BV	**1982-08 Ateliers et Chantiers de La Manche — St-Malo** Yd No: 1298 Loa 55.43 (BB) Br ex 10.90 Dght 5.310 Lbp 47.50 Br md 10.61 Dpth 7.70 Welded, 2 dks	**(B11B2FV) Fishing Vessel** Ins: 800 Compartments: 10 Ho, ER 10 Ha: ER	**2 oil engines** with clutches, flexible couplings & sr geared to sc. shaft driving 1 CP propeller Total Power: 2,060kW (2,800hp) MaK 8M282AK 2 x 4 Stroke 8 Cy. 240 x 280 each-1030kW (1400bhp) Krupp MaK Maschinenbau GmbH-Kiel
8318441 *TFHA* SH 124	**SOLEY** *ex* Silfurnes *-2011* *ex* Hrisey *-2011* *ex* Harpa *-1992* **Soffanias Cecilsson hf** - *Grundarfjordur* *Iceland* MMSI: 251248110 Official number: 1674	*201* 74 -		**1985-03 Velsmidja Seydisfjardar h/f — Seydisfjordur** Yd No: 18 Loa 26.01 Br ex 7.01 Dght 5.650 Lbp 24.39 Br md 5.21 Dpth 3.46 Welded, 1 dk	**(B11B2FV) Fishing Vessel**	**1 oil engine** geared to sc. shaft driving 1 FP propeller Total Power: 416kW (566hp) Caterpillar 1 x 4 Stroke 416kW (566bhp) Caterpillar Tractor Co-USA
8607270 *V3PU5* -	**SOLEY** *ex* El Nino *-2008* *ex* Sevina-2 *-2004* *ex* Fyodor Korobkov *-2004* **Levert Shipping Co Ltd** - *Belize City* *Belize* MMSI: 312891000 Official number: 350430048	**7,765** 2,329 3,372	Class: RS	**1989-10 VEB Volkswerft Stralsund — Stralsund** Yd No: 818 Loa 120.47 Br ex 19.03 Dght 6.630 Lbp 108.12 Br md 19.00 Dpth 12.22 Welded, 2 dks	**(B11A2FG) Factory Stern Trawler** Ins: 3,900 Ice Capable	**2 oil engines** with clutches, flexible couplings & reduction geared to sc. shaft driving 1 CP propeller Total Power: 5,298kW (7,204hp) 14.9kn S.K.L. 6VDS48/42AL-2 2 x 4 Stroke 6 Cy. 420 x 480 each-2649kW (3602bhp) VEB Schwermaschinenbau "KarlLiebknecht" (SKL)-Magdeburg AuxGen: 2 x 1500kW a.c, 2 x 760kW a.c
7711103 *TFDL* -	**SOLEY** *ex* Norbrit Waal *-1988* *ex* Selbydyke *-1985* **Bjorgun Ehf** - *Reykjavik* *Iceland* MMSI: 251191110 Official number: 1894	**1,705** 512 2,995	Class: GL (LR) ✠ Classed LR until 14/1/88	**1979-02 Cochrane Shipbuilders Ltd. — Selby** Yd No: 106 Converted From: General Cargo Ship-1988 Loa 79.43 Br ex 13.26 Dght 4.920 Lbp 74.02 Br md 13.20 Dpth 6.00 Welded, 1 dk	**(B33B2DS) Suction Hopper Dredger** Grain: 3,245; Bale: 3,222; Hopper: 1,453	**1 oil engine** with flexible couplings & reductiongeared to sc. shaft driving 1 CP propeller Total Power: 2,207kW (3,001hp) 13.0kn Mirrlees KMR-6 1 x 4 Stroke 6 Cy. 381 x 457 2207kW (3001bhp) Mirrlees Blackstone (Stockport)Ltd.-Stockport AuxGen: 2 x 109kW 220/380V 50Hz a.c Thrusters: 1 Thwart. FP thruster (f) Fuel: 323.0 (r.f.)
8616207 *TFSH* GK 200	**SOLEY SIGURJONS** *ex* Solbakur *-2008* *ex* Raudinupur *-2005* *ex* Julius Havsteen *-1997* *ex* Qaasiut II *-1995* **Nesfiskur Ehf** - SatCom: Inmarsat A 1251131 *Gardur* *Iceland* MMSI: 251338110 Official number: 2262	**737** 246 508	Class: LR (NV) **100A1** SS 07/2012 stern trawler **LMC** Eq.Ltr: F; Cable: 334.0/24.0	**1987-08 Danyard Aalborg A/S — Aalborg** (Hull) **1987-08 Johs Kristensen Skibsbyggeri A/S — Hvide Sande** Yd No: 183 Loa 43.26 (BB) Br ex 10.40 Dght 4.580 Lbp 41.98 Br md 10.22 Dpth 4.65 Welded	**(B11A2FS) Stern Trawler** Ins: 300	**1 oil engine** with clutches, flexible couplings & dr geared to sc. shaft driving 1 CP propeller Total Power: 1,240kW (1,686hp) Wartsila 8R22 1 x 4 Stroke 8 Cy. 220 x 240 1240kW (1686bhp) Wartsila Diesel Oy-Finland AuxGen: 1 x 828kW 380V 50Hz a.c, 2 x 384kW 380V 50Hz a.c
7434767 - -	**SOLHEIMFISK** *ex* Bergstral *-2001* *ex* Bergstral Senior *-1999* *ex* Thorunn Havsteen *-1999* *ex* Julius Havsteen *-1999* -	**343** 102 -		**1976-10 Skipasmidastod Thorgeir & Ellert h/f — Akranes** Yd No: 32 Loa 36.76 Br ex - Dght - Lbp 31.32 Br md 8.01 Dpth 5.75 Welded, 1 dk	**(B11A2FS) Stern Trawler**	**1 oil engine** driving 1 FP propeller MaK 8M451AK 1 x 4 Stroke 8 Cy. 320 x 450 MaK Maschinenbau GmbH-Kiel
8701428 *MGFW6* PH 63	**SOLI DEO GLORIA** *ex* Cornelia J *-2004* **Osprey (PD63) Ltd** - *Plymouth* *United Kingdom* MMSI: 235021304 Official number: C18314	**546** 163 -		**1988-02 Stocznia im Komuny Paryskiej — Gdynia** (Hull) Yd No: 432 **1988-02 B.V. Scheepswerf Damen — Gorinchem** Yd No: 4497 Loa 45.70 (BB) Br ex - Dght 3.830 Lbp 40.57 Br md 9.01 Dpth 5.31 Welded, 1 dk	**(B11B2FV) Fishing Vessel**	**1 oil engine** with clutches, flexible couplings & sr reverse geared to sc. shaft driving 1 CP propeller Total Power: 2,821kW (3,835hp) Deutz SBV16M628 1 x Vee 4 Stroke 16 Cy. 240 x 280 2821kW (3835bhp) Kloeckner Humboldt Deutz AG-West Germany
9557525 *9WHP8* -	**SOLID 8** - **Tropical Ray Sdn Bhd** - *Kuching* *Malaysia* MMSI: 533966000 Official number: 332951	**299** 89 -	Class: (BV)	**2009-01 Robin Dockyard & Engineering Sdn Bhd — Kuching** Yd No: 1 Loa 31.20 Br ex - Dght 3.600 Lbp 27.85 Br md 9.00 Dpth 4.20 Welded, 1 dk	**(B32A2ST) Tug**	**2 oil engines** geared to sc. shafts driving 2 FP propellers Total Power: 2,238kW (3,042hp) Cummins KTA-38-M2 2 x Vee 4 Stroke 12 Cy. 159 x 159 each-1119kW (1521bhp) Cummins Engine Co Ltd-United Kingdom
8604565 *DUA2707* -	**SOLID ACE** *ex* Cosmo Angel *-1996* **Solid Shipping Lines Corp** - *Manila* *Philippines* Official number: 00-0000795	**4,717** 2,955 7,371	Class: NK	**1986-09 Dae Sun Shipbuilding & Engineering Co Ltd — Busan** Yd No: 300 Loa 100.25 (BB) Br ex 17.53 Dght 7.610 Lbp 91.25 Br md 17.51 Dpth 10.50 Welded, 2 dks	**(A31A2GX) General Cargo Ship** Grain: 10,807; Bale: 10,063 TEU 176 C. 176/20' Compartments: 2 Ho, ER, 2 Tw Dk 2 Ha: 2 (28.6 x 13.0)ER Derricks: 2x30t,2x20t	**1 oil engine** driving 1 FP propeller Total Power: 2,501kW (3,400hp) 12.3kn Makita LS42L 1 x 4 Stroke 6 Cy. 420 x 840 2501kW (3400bhp) Makita Diesel Co Ltd-Japan Fuel: 485.0 (r.f.)
9643702 *4DFB5*	**SOLID GEM** - **Solid Shipping Lines Corp** - *Manila* *Philippines* MMSI: 548042500	**4,680** 1,783 6,757	Class: NK	**2013-08 Nakatani Shipyard Co. Ltd. — Etajima** Yd No: 630 Loa 104.16 (BB) Br ex - Dght 7.190 Lbp 97.00 Br md 17.50 Dpth 8.90 Welded, 1 dk	**(A31A2GX) General Cargo Ship** Bale: 6,397 TEU 278 Compartments: 2 Ho, ER 2 Ha: ER Cranes: 2x30.7t; Derricks: 1x30t	**1 oil engine** driving 1 FP propeller Total Power: 2,427kW (3,300hp) 12.5kn Akasaka A41 1 x 4 Stroke 6 Cy. 410 x 800 2427kW (3300bhp) Akasaka Tekkosho KK (Akasaka DieselLtd)-Japan AuxGen: 3 x 230kW a.c Fuel: 405.0
8324995 *DUKR* -	**SOLID GOLD** *ex* Dang Melati *-1994* *ex* Eastern Muse *-1988* *ex* Oriente Reina *-1986* **Solid Shipping Lines Corp** - *Manila* *Philippines* Official number: 00-0000787	**3,955** 2,355 6,424	Class: NK	**1984-07 Dae Sun Shipbuilding & Engineering Co Ltd — Busan** Yd No: 279 Loa 109.05 Br ex 16.44 Dght 6.725 Lbp 101.42 Br md 16.41 Dpth 8.26 Welded, 1 dk	**(A31A2GX) General Cargo Ship** Grain: 8,885; Bale: 8,402 TEU 160 C. 160/20' (40') Compartments: 2 Ho, ER 2 Ha: (29.0 x 10.4) (30.0 x 10.4)ER Derricks: 2x30t,2x25t	**1 oil engine** driving 1 FP propeller Total Power: 3,001kW (4,080hp) 12.5kn B&W 6L35MC 1 x 2 Stroke 6 Cy. 350 x 1050 3001kW (4080bhp) Makita Diesel Co Ltd-Japan AuxGen: 2 x 280kW a.c Fuel: 450.0 (r.f.)
7921758 - -	**SOLID HAWK** *ex* Meiyu No. 23 *-2010* *ex* Choyo Maru No. 23 *-2004* *ex* Shinkai Maru No. 23 *-2003* *ex* Choyo Maru No. 23 *-2002* -	*199* 62 -		**1979-09 Sokooshi Zosen K.K. — Osakikamijima** Yd No: 257 Loa 33.91 Br ex - Dght 3.148 Lbp 30.61 Br md 8.40 Dpth 3.61 Welded, 1 dk	**(B32A2ST) Tug**	**1 oil engine** driving 1 FP propeller Total Power: 1,471kW (2,000hp) Hanshin 6LU28G 1 x 4 Stroke 6 Cy. 280 x 440 1471kW (2000bhp) The Hanshin Diesel Works Ltd-Japan
9368132 *9WGI4*	**SOLID I** - **Concrete Teamwork Sdn Bhd** - *Kuching* *Malaysia* Official number: 330665	**200** 60 185	Class: BV (NK)	**2005-10 Jana Seribu Shipbuilding (M) Sdn Bhd — Sibu** Yd No: 2015 Loa 27.50 Br ex - Dght 3.012 Lbp 25.55 Br md 8.30 Dpth 3.81 Welded, 1 dk	**(B32A2ST) Tug**	**2 oil engines** reduction geared to sc. shafts driving 2 Propellers Total Power: 1,516kW (2,062hp) Mitsubishi S6R2-MPTK 2 x 4 Stroke 6 Cy. 170 x 220 each-758kW (1031bhp) Mitsubishi Heavy Industries Ltd-Japan
8325004 *DXBY* -	**SOLID JADE** *ex* Dang Raihana *-1995* *ex* Takaozan Maru *-1985* **Solid Shipping Lines Corp** - *Manila* *Philippines* Official number: 00-0000788	**4,066** 2,577 6,425	Class: NK	**1984-09 Dae Sun Shipbuilding & Engineering Co Ltd — Busan** Yd No: 280 Loa 109.05 Br ex 16.44 Dght 6.741 Lbp 101.42 Br md 16.40 Dpth 8.26 Welded, 1 dk	**(A31A2GX) General Cargo Ship** Grain: 8,885; Bale: 8,402 TEU 160 C.160/20' (40') Compartments: 2 Ho, ER 2 Ha: (29.0 x 10.0) (30.0 x 10.0)ER Derricks: 2x30t,2x25t	**1 oil engine** driving 1 FP propeller Total Power: 3,001kW (4,080hp) 12.5kn B&W 6L35MC 1 x 2 Stroke 6 Cy. 350 x 1050 3001kW (4080bhp) Makita Diesel Co Ltd-Japan AuxGen: 2 x 280kW a.c Fuel: 450.0 (r.f.)
8510635 *DUA2708* -	**SOLID LINK** *ex* Momoshima Maru *-1996* **Solid Shipping Lines Corp** - *Manila* *Philippines* Official number: 00-0000796	**4,769** 2,282 6,507	Class: NK	**1986-05 Dae Sun Shipbuilding & Engineering Co Ltd — Busan** Yd No: 295 Loa 100.25 (BB) Br ex 17.53 Dght 6.651 Lbp 91.25 Br md 17.51 Dpth 10.50 Welded, 2 dks	**(A31A2GX) General Cargo Ship** Grain: 11,138; Bale: 10,290 TEU 188 C. 188/20' (40') Compartments: 2 Ho, ER 2 Ha: ER Derricks: 2x25t,2x22t	**1 oil engine** driving 1 FP propeller Total Power: 2,501kW (3,400hp) 12.3kn Makita LS42L 1 x 4 Stroke 6 Cy. 420 x 840 2501kW (3400bhp) Makita Diesel Co Ltd-Japan Fuel: 510.0 (r.f.)
9643697 *4DEX2* -	**SOLID MARINE** - **Solid Shipping Lines Corp** - *Manila* *Philippines* MMSI: 548025500 Official number: MC-000727	**4,680** 1,783 6,795	Class: NK	**2013-02 Nakatani Shipyard Co. Ltd. — Etajima** Yd No: 628 Loa 104.16 (BB) Br ex - Dght 7.190 Lbp 97.00 Br md 17.50 Dpth 8.90 Welded, 1 dk	**(A31A2GX) General Cargo Ship** Bale: 6,396 TEU 278 Cranes: 2x30.7t; Derricks: 1x30t	**1 oil engine** driving 1 Propeller Total Power: 2,427kW (3,300hp) 14.0kn Akasaka A41 1 x 4 Stroke 6 Cy. 410 x 800 2427kW (3300bhp) Akasaka Tekkosho KK (Akasaka DieselLtd)-Japan AuxGen: 3 x 260kW a.c Fuel: 400.0

9085089 *DUA3108* -	**SOLID OCEAN** *ex* Rio Bella *-2009* *ex* Oriental Ace *-2003* *ex* China First *-2003* **Solid Shipping Lines Corp** - *Manila* *Philippines* Official number: 00-0000023	**4,767** 1,712 5,480	Class: NK	**1994-12 Tsuneishi Shipbuilding Co Ltd — Fukuyama HS** Yd No: 1040 Loa 96.17 (BB) Br ex 17.23 Dght 6.725 Lbp 87.00 Br md 17.20 Dpth 11.50 Welded, 2 dks	**(A31A2GX) General Cargo Ship** Grain: 9,387; Bale: 8,953 TEU 216 C. 216/20' Compartments: 2 Ho, ER 2 Ha: (12.6 x 12.6) (30.8 x 12.6)ER Derricks: 3x30t	**1 oil engine** driving 1 FP propeller Total Power: 2,060kW (2,801hp) 12.0kn Hanshin 6LU40 1 x 4 Stroke 6 Cy. 400 x 640 2060kW (2801bhp) The Hanshin Diesel Works Ltd-Japan AuxGen: 3 x a.c Fuel: 300.0 (r.f.)
8406030 *DUA2697* -	**SOLID PEARL** *ex* Dang Mahligai *-1996* *ex* Oriental Venus *-1985* **Solid Shipping Lines Corp** - *Manila* *Philippines* Official number: 00-0000789	**4,618** 2,109 5,968	Class: (AB) (KR) (NK)	**1984-10 Kegoya Dock K.K. — Kure** Yd No: 846 Loa 98.25 Br ex - Dght 6.574 Lbp 89.95 Br md 17.51 Dpth 10.50 Welded, 2 dks	**(A31A2GX) General Cargo Ship** Grain: 10,625; Bale: 10,018 Compartments: 2 Ho, ER 2 Ha: 2 (24.8 x 10.4)ER Derricks: 2x30t,2x20t	**1 oil engine** driving 1 FP propeller Total Power: 2,427kW (3,300hp) 11.3kn Akasaka A41 1 x 4 Stroke 6 Cy. 410 x 800 2427kW (3300bhp) Akasaka Tekkosho KK (Akasaka DieselLtd)-Japan AuxGen: 2 x 160kW 445V a.c
8513936 *DYCS* -	**SOLID STAR** *ex* Erica *-1999* **Solid Shipping Lines Corp** - *Manila* *Philippines* Official number: 00-0000786	**4,498** 2,223 5,806	Class: NK	**1985-07 Imai Shipbuilding Co Ltd — Kochi KC** Yd No: 539 Loa 96.78 (BB) Br ex - Dght 6.586 Lbp 89.95 Br md 18.01 Dpth 10.52 Welded, 1 dk	**(A31A2GX) General Cargo Ship** Grain: 10,525; Bale: 10,141 TEU 194 C. 194/20' Compartments: 2 Ho, ER 2 Ha: (24.7 x 12.5) (26.0 x 12.5)ER Derricks: 2x30t,2x22t	**1 oil engine** driving 1 FP propeller Total Power: 2,207kW (3,001hp) 12.0kn Mitsubishi 6UEC37L 1 x 2 Stroke 6 Cy. 370 x 880 2207kW (3001bhp) Kobe Hatsudoki KK-Japan AuxGen: 3 x 148kW a.c Fuel: 450.0 (r.f.)
8821539 *DYGL* -	**SOLID SUN** *ex* Southern Rouge *-2001* *ex* Southern Cross *-1998* *ex* Southern Rouge *-1997* *ex* Westwind Glory *-1993* **Solid Shipping Lines Corp** - SatCom: Inmarsat A 1700414 *Manila* *Philippines* Official number: 00-0000794	**4,717** 2,486 5,964	Class: NK	**1989-06 Dae Sun Shipbuilding & Engineering Co Ltd — Busan** Yd No: 350 Loa 100.25 (BB) Br ex - Dght 6.639 Lbp 91.25 Br md 17.50 Dpth 10.50 Welded, 2 dks	**(A31A2GX) General Cargo Ship** Grain: 10,850; Bale: 10,077 TEU 80 C. 80/20' Compartments: 2 Ho, ER, 2 Tw Dk 2 Ha: (25.4 x 12.5) (26.7 x 12.5)ER Derricks: 2x30t,2x20t	**1 oil engine** driving 1 FP propeller Total Power: 2,501kW (3,400hp) 12.3kn Makita LS42L 1 x 4 Stroke 6 Cy. 420 x 840 2501kW (3400bhp) Makita Diesel Co Ltd-Japan AuxGen: 3 x 179kW a.c Fuel: 505.0 (r.f.)
8813934 *YJZC9* -	**SOLIDARNOSC** - **Saturn One Shipping Ltd** Polska Zegluga Morska PP (POLSTEAM) *Port Vila* *Vanuatu* MMSI: 576005000 Official number: 705	**41,252** 25,569 73,470 T/cm 70.0	Class: NV PR	**1991-03 B&W Skibsvaerft A/S — Copenhagen** Yd No: 934 Loa 228.55 Br ex - Dght 14.119 Lbp 224.55 Br md 32.24 Dpth 19.00 Welded, 1 dk	**(A21A2BC) Bulk Carrier** Double Hull Grain: 84,960 Compartments: 9 Ho, ER 9 Ha: (11.2 x 9.0)8 (16.0 x 13.5)ER	**1 oil engine** driving 1 FP propeller Total Power: 7,995kW (10,870hp) 14.2kn B&W 5S60MC 1 x 2 Stroke 5 Cy. 600 x 2292 7995kW (10870bhp) Hyundai Heavy Industries Co Ltd-South Korea AuxGen: 3 x 550kW 440V 60Hz a.c Fuel: 297.7 (d.f.) 1852.0 (r.f.)
7614599 *UBEE* -	**SOLIDAT** *ex* Saymenskiy Kanal *-2006* *ex* Ladoga-10 *-1978* **Ladoga Shipping Co Ltd (OOO Sudokhodnaya Kompaniya 'Ladoga')** - *Astrakhan* *Russia* MMSI: 273327300 Official number: 770283	**1,590** 742 2,155	Class: RS	**1978-05 Rauma-Repola Oy — Uusikaupunki** Yd No: 285 Loa 80.96 Br ex 11.94 Dght 4.360 Lbp 77.68 Br md 11.76 Dpth 5.59 Welded, 1 dk	**(A31A2GX) General Cargo Ship** Grain: 2,635; Bale: 2,623 TEU 62 C. 62/20' Compartments: 2 Ho, ER 2 Ha: (16.9 x 8.2) (24.6 x 8.2)ER Ice Capable	**2 oil engines** reverse reduction geared to sc. shafts driving 2 FP propellers Total Power: 1,280kW (1,740hp) 12.3kn S.K.L. 6NVD48A-2U 2 x 4 Stroke 6 Cy. 320 x 480 each-640kW (870bhp) VEB Schwermaschinenbau "KarlLiebknecht" (SKL)-Magdeburg AuxGen: 3 x 50kW a.c Thrusters: 1 Thwart. FP thruster (f) Fuel: 229.0 (d.f.)
7618246 - -	**SOLIDOR 2** *ex* Solidor II *-1994* *ex* Langeland II *-1989* *ex* Langeland To *-1978* - - -	**3,401** 1,020 622	Class: (LR) (BV) ✠ Classed LR until 7/4/89	**1977-07 Scheepswerf Hoogezand B.V. — Hoogezand** (Hull) Yd No: 184 **1977-07 "Combiship" B.V. — Hoogezand** Yd No: C128 Loa 70.01 (BB) Br ex 16.24 Dght 3.810 Lbp 63.51 Br md 15.87 Dpth 10.14 Welded, 2 dks, intermediate dk portside (2nd & intermediate dks light cargoes only)	**(A36A2PR) Passenger/Ro-Ro Ship (Vehicles)** Passengers: unberthed: 650 Bow door/ramp Stern door/ramp Cars: 90 Ice Capable	**2 oil engines** sr geared to sc. shafts driving 2 CP propellers Total Power: 2,640kW (3,590hp) 15.5kn MaK 6M452AK 2 x 4 Stroke 6 Cy. 320 x 450 each-1320kW (1795bhp) MaK Maschinenbau GmbH-Kiel AuxGen: 2 x 360kW 380V 60Hz a.c, 1 x 350kW 380V 60Hz a.c Thrusters: 1 Thwart. CP thruster (f) Fuel: 30.5 (d.f.) 61.0 (r.f.) 15.0pd
7436416 *UAXX* ME-0314	**SOLIGALICH** - **Expo-Holding Co Ltd** - *Murmansk* *Russia*	**746** 224 343	Class: (RS)	**1974-11 Yaroslavskiy Sudostroitelnyy Zavod — Yaroslavl** Yd No: 314 Loa 53.73 (BB) Br ex 10.72 Dght 4.290 Lbp 47.92 Br md - Dpth 6.02 Welded, 1 dk	**(B11A2FS) Stern Trawler** Ins: 218 Compartments: 1 Ho, ER 2 Ha: 2 (1.6 x 1.6) Derricks: 2x1.5t Ice Capable	**1 oil engine** driving 1 CP propeller Total Power: 971kW (1,320hp) 12.8kn S.K.L. 8NVD48A-2U 1 x 4 Stroke 8 Cy. 320 x 480 971kW (1320bhp) VEB Schwermaschinenbau "KarlLiebknecht" (SKL)-Magdeburg Thrusters: 1 Thwart. FP thruster (f); 1 Tunnel thruster (a)
8986987 *V3RU4* -	**SOLIKAMSK** *ex* Volgo-Don 229 *-2005* **Saluta Shipping Ltd** Kent Shipping & Chartering Ltd SatCom: Inmarsat C 431236210 *Belize City* *Belize* MMSI: 312362000 Official number: 141120195	**3,991** 1,197 5,462	Class: IV RR (RS)	**1979-12 Navashinskiy Sudostroitelnyy Zavod 'Oka' — Navashino** Yd No: 1130 Loa 138.30 Br ex 16.70 Dght 3.420 Lbp 135.00 Br md 16.50 Dpth 5.50 Welded, 1 dk	**(A31A2GX) General Cargo Ship** Grain: 6,270	**2 oil engines** driving 2 FP propellers Total Power: 1,324kW (1,800hp) 10.0kn Dvigatel Revolyutsii 6CHRN36/45 2 x 4 Stroke 6 Cy. 360 x 450 each-662kW (900bhp) Zavod "Dvigatel Revolyutsii"-Gorkiy
9629483 *9AA8522* -	**SOLIN** - **April Marine Inc** Jadroplov International Maritime Transport Ltd (Jadroplov dd) *Split* *Croatia* MMSI: 238303000	**30,092** 17,852 51,545	Class: BV CS	**2012-07 Brodosplit - Brodogradiliste doo — Split** Yd No: 470 Loa 189.90 (BB) Br ex - Dght 12.371 Lbp 182.00 Br md 32.24 Dpth 17.10 Welded, 1 dk	**(A21A2BC) Bulk Carrier** Grain: 64,986 Compartments: 5 Ho, ER 5 Ha: ER Cranes: 4x36t	**1 oil engine** driving 1 FP propeller Total Power: 7,500kW (10,197hp) 14.5kn MAN-B&W 6S50MC-C8 1 x 2 Stroke 6 Cy. 500 x 2000 7500kW (10197bhp) Brodosplit Tvornica Dizel Motoradoo-Croatia AuxGen: 3 x 730kW 60Hz a.c
9496252 *C6ZL4* -	**SOLINA** - **Erato Seven Shipping Ltd** Polska Zegluga Morska PP (POLSTEAM) *Nassau* *Bahamas* MMSI: 311058500 Official number: 8001934	**20,603** 9,299 29,691	Class: NV PR	**2012-01 Nantong Mingde Heavy Industry Co Ltd — Tongzhou JS** Yd No: -30000LBC-07 Loa 190.00 (BB) Br ex - Dght 10.220 Lbp 182.60 Br md 23.60 Dpth 14.60 Welded, 1 dk	**(A21A2BC) Bulk Carrier** Grain: 38,340 Compartments: 6 Ho, ER 6 Ha: ER Cranes: 3 Ice Capable	**1 oil engine** driving 1 FP propeller Total Power: 8,730kW (11,869hp) 14.5kn Wartsila 6RTA48T-B 1 x 2 Stroke 6 Cy. 480 x 2000 8730kW (11869bhp) H Cegielski Poznan SA-Poland Thrusters: 1 Tunnel thruster (f)
9425370 *9VCE2* -	**SOLITAIRE** - **Hong Lam Marine Pte Ltd** - *Singapore* *Singapore* MMSI: 565610000 Official number: 392239	**5,307** 2,779 9,000 T/cm 17.6	Class: BV	**2008-01 Guangzhou Hangtong Shipbuilding & Shipping Co Ltd — Jiangmen GD** Yd No: 062001 Loa 110.00 (BB) Br ex 18.62 Dght 7.900 Lbp 105.05 Br md 18.60 Dpth 10.00 Welded, 1 dk	**(A12B2TR) Chemical/Products Tanker** Double Hull (13F) Liq: 9,721; Liq (Oil): 9,721 Part Cargo Heating Coils Compartments: 12 Wing Ta, 2 Wing Slop Ta, ER 3 Cargo Pump (s): 3x750m³/hr Manifold: Bow/CM: 55.7m	**1 oil engine** reduction geared to sc. shaft driving 1 FP propeller Total Power: 2,645kW (3,596hp) 12.7kn Daihatsu 8DKM-32 1 x 4 Stroke 8 Cy. 320 x 360 2645kW (3596bhp) Daihatsu Diesel Manufacturing Co Lt-Japan
7129049 *3ECI8* -	**SOLITAIRE** *ex* Solitaire I *-1993* *ex* Comship *-1992* *ex* Akdeniz S *-1992* *ex* Trentwood *-1990* *ex* Interbulk Vanguard *-1988* *ex* Trentwood *-1988* **Societe d'Exploitation du Solitaire SA** Allseas Engineering BV SatCom: Inmarsat A 1363452 *Panama* *Panama* MMSI: 351597000 Official number: 1906090D	**94,855** 28,456 - T/cm 92.6	Class: LR (BV) (AB) **100A1** SS 02/2013 LA LI ✠ **LMC** Eq.Ltr: A*; Cable: 742.5/95.0 U3	**1972-03 Mitsubishi Heavy Industries Ltd. — Hiroshima** Yd No: 223 Converted From: Bulk Carrier-1998 Lengthened-1998 Loa 299.90 (BB) Br ex 40.64 Dght 9.300 Lbp 248.65 Br md 40.60 Dpth 24.00 Welded, 1 dk	**(B22C20X) Pipe Layer** Grain: 139,800 Cranes: 1x300t,1x40t,2x35t,1x18t	**8 diesel electric oil engines** driving 8 gen. each 6026kW 10000V a.c Connecting to 8 elec. motors each (4330kW) driving 8 Directional propellers Total Power: 45,200kW (61,456hp) 13.0kn Wartsila 6R46B 8 x 4 Stroke 6 Cy. 460 x 580 each-5650kW (7682bhp) (new engine 1998, fitted 1998) Wartsila NSD Finland Oy-Finland AuxGen: 1 x 900kW 460V 60Hz a.c Boilers: 8 TOH New (ex.g.) (fitted: 1972) 13.3kgf/cm² (13.0bar), 2 TOH New (o.f.) (fitted: 1972) 10.2kgf/cm² (10.0bar) Thrusters: 1 Tunnel thruster (f) Fuel: 5435.0 (r.f.)
9227962 *H3FH* -	**SOLITAIRE 1** *ex* Sea Bell *-2013* *ex* Ocean Velvet *-2004* **Mersin Shipping Co** Karlog Shipping Co Ltd *Panama* *Panama* MMSI: 353047000 Official number: 2704500CH	**15,609** 8,745 24,997	Class: NK	**2000-04 Iwagi Zosen Co Ltd — Kamijima EH** Yd No: 191 Loa 159.92 (BB) Br ex - Dght 9.801 Lbp 149.80 Br md 26.00 Dpth 13.50 Welded, 1 dk	**(A21A2BC) Bulk Carrier** Grain: 31,961; Bale: 30,892 Compartments: 4 Ho, ER 4 Ha: (18.4 x 17.6)3 (24.8 x 22.0) Cranes: 3x30.5t	**1 oil engine** driving 1 FP propeller Total Power: 6,157kW (8,371hp) 14.5kn B&W 6S42MC 1 x 2 Stroke 6 Cy. 420 x 1764 6157kW (8371bhp) Makita Corp-Japan Fuel: 1954.0 (r.f.)

7824118 - -	**SOLITUDE ONE** *ex* Big Blue Explorer *-2012* *ex* Hakuo Maru *-1998* **CKM-Squared Pte Ltd** - *Singapore* *Singapore* MMSI: 563664000 Official number: 09042-L/12	*491* 242 -		**1979-07 Hayashikane Shipbuilding & Engineering Co Ltd — Shimonoseki YC** Yd No: 1227 Converted From: Fishery Patrol Vessel-2003 Lengthened-1982 Loa 51.21 Br ex 8.62 Dght 3.901 Lbp 47.20 Br md 8.60 Dpth 6.20 Welded, 1 dk	**(A37A2PC) Passenger/Cruise** Passengers: cabins: 12; berths: 24	**1 oil engine** driving 1 FP propeller Total Power: 1,986kW (2,700hp) 14.0kn Akasaka AH40 1 x 4 Stroke 6 Cy. 400 x 600 1986kW (2700bhp) Akasaka Tekkosho KK (Akasaka DieselLtd)-Japan
8230120 *ERPJ* -	**SOLKA 2** *ex* Volgo-Balt 126 *-2003* **Solka Shipping Ltd** Private Enterprise 'SVS Management' *Giurgiulesti* *Moldova* MMSI: 214181610	**2,457** 1,006 3,173	Class: UA (IS) (RR) (RS)	**1970 Zavody Tazkeho Strojarstva (ZTS) — Komarno** Yd No: 1326 Loa 114.00 Br ex 13.23 Dght 3.450 Lbp 110.00 Br md 13.01 Dpth 5.50 Welded, 1 dk	**(A31A2GX) General Cargo Ship** Grain: 4,720 Compartments: 4 Ho, ER 4 Ha: (18.6 x 11.2)2 (18.8 x 11.2) (20.3 x 11.2)ER	**2 oil engines** driving 2 FP propellers Total Power: 1,030kW (1,400hp) 10.0kn Skoda 6L275IIIPN 2 x 4 Stroke 6 Cy. 275 x 350 each-515kW (700bhp) Skoda-Praha
7222293 - -	**SOLKATTEN** *ex* Fjordtroll *-1988* - - *United Arab Emirates*	*144* 58 -	Class: (NV)	**1972 Westermoen Hydrofoil AS — Mandal** Yd No: 24 Loa 26.65 Br ex - Dght - Lbp 26.09 Br md 9.00 Dpth 2.60 Welded, 1 dk	**(A37B2PS) Passenger Ship** Hull Material: Aluminium Alloy Passengers: unberthed: 140	**2 oil engines** sr geared to sc. shafts driving 2 FP propellers Total Power: 1,618kW (2,200hp) 28.0kn M.T.U. 12V493TY70 2 x Vee 4 Stroke 12 Cy. 175 x 205 each-809kW (1100bhp) MTU Friedrichshafen GmbH-Friedrichshafen AuxGen: 1 x 12kW 220V 50Hz a.c
9155250 *UHVT* -	**SOLL TAMAN** *ex* KST 41 *-2001* **Smit Lamnalco Singapore Pte Ltd** Soll-R LLC *Novorossiysk* *Russia* MMSI: 273422770	**272** 81 123	Class: RS (LR) (AB) Classed LR until 10/7/10	**1997-06 Keppel Singmarine Dockyard Pte Ltd — Singapore** Yd No: 217 Loa 30.00 Br ex 9.00 Dght 3.750 Lbp 22.50 Br md 9.00 Dpth 4.70 Welded, 1 dk	**(B32A2ST) Tug**	**2 oil engines** driving 2 Z propellers Total Power: 2,942kW (4,000hp) Niigata 6L26HLX 2 x 4 Stroke 6 Cy. 260 x 350 each-1471kW (2000bhp) Niigata Engineering Co Ltd-Japan AuxGen: 2 x 80kW 380V 50Hz a.c
9155262 *UHZD* -	**SOLL TEMRYUK** *ex* KST 42 *-2001* **Smit Lamnalco Singapore Pte Ltd** Soll-R LLC *Novorossiysk* *Russia* MMSI: 273421770	**272** 81 122	Class: RS (LR) (BV) (AB) Classed LR until 29/6/07	**1997-06 Keppel Singmarine Dockyard Pte Ltd — Singapore** Yd No: 218 Loa 30.00 Br ex - Dght 3.750 Lbp 22.50 Br md 9.00 Dpth 4.70 Welded, 1 dk	**(B32A2ST) Tug**	**2 oil engines** driving 2 Z propellers Total Power: 2,942kW (4,000hp) Niigata 6L26HLX 2 x 4 Stroke 6 Cy. 260 x 350 each-1471kW (2000bhp) Niigata Engineering Co Ltd-Japan AuxGen: 2 x 80kW 380V 50Hz a.c
9269300 *LYTJ*	**SOLL TENGIZ** **Smit Internationale Sleepbootmaatschappij - Smit Salvor BV** Soll-R LLC *Klaipeda* *Lithuania* MMSI: 277447000 Official number: 837	**896** 269 791	Class: BV (RS)	**2002-05 Yantai Raffles Shipyard Co Ltd — Yantai SD** Yd No: YRF2000-117 Loa 48.00 Br ex - Dght 4.825 Lbp 43.20 Br md 13.00 Dpth 5.80 Welded, 1 dk	**(B22A2OR) Offshore Support Vessel**	**2 oil engines** geared to sc. shafts driving 2 CP propellers Total Power: 2,880kW (3,916hp) 12.5kn Wartsila 8L20 2 x 4 Stroke 8 Cy. 200 x 280 each-1440kW (1958bhp) Wartsila Finland Oy-Finland Thrusters: 1 Tunnel thruster (f)
9562996 *LNFR* -	**SOLLIFJELL** **Boreal Transport Nord AS** - *Hammerfest* *Norway* MMSI: 257473000	**329** 118 20		**2010-03 Batservice Mandal AS — Mandal** Yd No: 84 Loa 35.00 Br ex - Dght 1.500 Lbp - Br md 10.50 Dpth 3.35 Bonded, 1 dk	**(A37B2PS) Passenger Ship** Hull Material: Carbon Fibre Sandwich Passengers: unberthed: 250	**2 oil engines** reduction geared to sc. shafts driving 2 CP propellers Total Power: 2,160kW (2,936hp) 33.0kn M.T.U. 12V2000M72 2 x Vee 4 Stroke 12 Cy. 135 x 156 each-1080kW (1468bhp) MTU Friedrichshafen GmbH-Friedrichshafen AuxGen: 2 x 28kW 280V 50Hz a.c
7922659 *S9NF* -	**SOLMAR V** *ex* Isla de Arosa III *-1994* **Solmar SA** - *Sao Tome* *Sao Tome & Principe*	*264* 135 215	Class: (RP) (BV)	**1980-03 Factoria Naval de Marin S.A. — Marin** Yd No: 2 Loa 30.00 Br ex - Dght 1.801 Lbp 25.48 Br md 10.49 Dpth 3.00 Welded, 1 dk	**(A36A2PR) Passenger/Ro-Ro Ship (Vehicles)**	**2 oil engines** reduction geared to sc. shafts driving 2 FP propellers Total Power: 632kW (860hp) Baudouin DNP12M 2 x Vee 4 Stroke 12 Cy. 150 x 150 each-316kW (430bhp) Societe des Moteurs Baudouin SA-France
8227408 *UDVZ* -	**SOLNECHNIK** **Taymshit JSC (OOO 'Taymshit Commercial Firm')** - *Murmansk* *Russia* Official number: 831913	*171* 51 88	Class: (RS)	**1984 Astrakhanskaya Sudoverf im. "Kirova" — Astrakhan** Yd No: 169 Loa 34.02 Br ex 7.12 Dght 2.901 Lbp 29.98 Br md - Dpth 3.66 Welded, 1 dk	**(B11B2FV) Fishing Vessel** Ice Capable	**1 oil engine** driving 1 FP propeller Total Power: 224kW (305hp) 9.0kn S.K.L. 8NVD36-1U 1 x 4 Stroke 8 Cy. 240 x 360 224kW (305bhp) VEB Schwermaschinenbau "KarlLiebknecht" (SKL)-Magdeburg AuxGen: 2 x 75kW, 1 x 28kW Fuel: 17.0 (d.f.)
8925309 *UBFF* -	**SOLNECHNOGORSK** **JSC 'Lesosibirsk Port' (OAO Lesosibirskiy Port)** JSC Yenisey River Shipping Co (A/O Yeniseyskoye Parokhodstvo) *Taganrog* *Russia* MMSI: 273389200	**1,843** 633 2,083	Class: (RS) (RR)	**1965-09 Zavody Tazkeho Strojarstva (ZTS) — Komarno** Yd No: 2051 Loa 103.50 Br ex 12.20 Dght 2.840 Lbp 97.30 Br md - Dpth 4.90 Welded, 1 dk	**(A31A2GX) General Cargo Ship** Ice Capable	**2 oil engines** driving 2 FP propellers Total Power: 772kW (1,050hp) Skoda 6L275PN 2 x 4 Stroke 6 Cy. 275 x 360 each-386kW (525bhp) CKD Praha-Praha
7405479 - -	**SOLNECHNYY** *ex* Adonis *-2001* *ex* Hyun II No. 201 *-2000* *ex* Reefer No. 2 *-1997* *ex* Ocean Dynamic *-1985* - -	**5,024** 2,201 5,688	Class: (KR) (RS) (NK)	**1975-03 Kishimoto Zosen — Osakikamijima** Yd No: 445 Loa 124.11 (BB) Br ex 17.45 Dght 6.922 Lbp 114.99 Br md 17.40 Dpth 7.50 Welded, 2 dks	**(A34A2GR) Refrigerated Cargo Ship** Ins: 6,676 4 Ha: (5.3 x 5.9)3 (5.6 x 5.9)ER Derricks: 8x10t	**1 oil engine** sr geared to sc. shaft driving 1 FP propeller Total Power: 6,620kW (9,001hp) 17.5kn B&W 12U50HU 1 x Vee 4 Stroke 12 Cy. 500 x 540 6620kW (9001bhp) Hitachi Zosen Corp-Japan AuxGen: 3 x 360kW 445V 60Hz a.c Fuel: 242.0 (d.f.) 744.5 (r.f.) 27.5pd
7611755 *LEWE* -	**SOLNOR** **Fjord1 AS** - *Aalesund* *Norway* MMSI: 257375400	**765** 247 264	Class: (NV)	**1977-03 A.M. Liaaen Skipsverft & Mek. Verksted — Aalesund** Yd No: 127 Loa 64.40 Br ex 11.45 Dght 3.099 Lbp 54.00 Br md 11.28 Dpth 4.20 Welded, 1 dk	**(A36A2PR) Passenger/Ro-Ro Ship (Vehicles)** Passengers: unberthed: 300 Bow ramp (centre) Stern ramp (centre) Lane-clr ht: 4.50 Cars: 50	**1 oil engine** driving 2 Propellers 1 fwd and 1 aft Total Power: 883kW (1,201hp) 12.0kn MWM TBD484-6 1 x 4 Stroke 6 Cy. 320 x 480 883kW (1201bhp) Motoren Werke Mannheim AG (MWM)-West Germany
8302258 *UBFH7* -	**SOLNTSE VOSTOKA** *ex* Ali S *-2010* *ex* Huong Giang *-2003* *ex* Mira *-1997* *ex* Bydgoszcz *-1993* **North Eastern Shipping Co Ltd (NESCO Ltd) (OOO 'Severo-Vostochnoye Morskoye Parokhodstvo')** - *Nakhodka* *Russia* MMSI: 273355720	**11,583** 6,026 13,593 T/cm 27.1	Class: RS (GL) (PR)	**1989-01 Stocznia im Komuny Paryskiej — Gdynia** Yd No: B354/07 Loa 149.27 (BB) Br ex - Dght 9.140 Lbp 139.91 Br md 21.98 Dpth 12.02 Welded, 2 dks, 3rd dk in No.5 hold	**(A31A2GX) General Cargo Ship** Passengers: berths: 12 Grain: 15,373; Bale: 14,596; Ins: 2,660; Liq: 608 TEU 302 C Ho 170 TEU C Dk 132 TEU incl 20 ref C. Compartments: 1 Cell Ho, 4 Ho, ER, 1 Tw Dk in Fo'c's'l, 6 Tw Dk 9 Ha: (12.6 x 7.8)2 (19.2 x 7.8)4 (12.8 x 7.8)2 (10.2 x 7.6)ER Cranes: 3x25t,3x12.5t; Derricks: 2x5t Ice Capable	**1 oil engine** driving 1 FP propeller Total Power: 7,080kW (9,626hp) 16.0kn Sulzer 6RTA58 1 x 2 Stroke 6 Cy. 580 x 1700 7080kW (9626bhp) Zaklady Przemyslu Metalowego 'HCegielski' SA-Poznan AuxGen: 1 x 1000kW 400V 50Hz a.c, 3 x 800kW 400V 50Hz a.c Thrusters: 1 Thwart. CP thruster (f) Fuel: 261.0 (d.f.) 1459.0 (r.f.) 30.5pd
8820705 *JVTR4* -	**SOLO** *ex* Nan You 11 *-1993* *ex* Seiho Maru No. 5 *-1989* **Nanan City Channel Marine Transport Co Ltd** - *Ulaanbaatar* *Mongolia* MMSI: 457531000 Official number: 30741288	**1,017** 569 1,907	Class: SC	**1989-02 Sasaki Shipbuilding Co Ltd — Osakikamijima HS** Yd No: 528 Loa 74.43 (BB) Br ex - Dght 4.708 Lbp 69.95 Br md 11.50 Dpth 5.20 Welded, 1 dk	**(A13B2TP) Products Tanker** Compartments: 10 Ta, ER	**1 oil engine** driving 1 CP propeller Total Power: 1,324kW (1,800hp) Akasaka A31 1 x 4 Stroke 6 Cy. 310 x 600 1324kW (1800bhp) (made 1988) Akasaka Tekkosho KK (Akasaka DieselLtd)-Japan Thrusters: 1 Thwart. CP thruster (f)
8826058 *9V3417* -	**SOLO** *ex* Bali *-1999* *ex* Solo *-1994* *ex* Kutilang *-1990* *ex* Kirby Smith *-1970* **Ocean Tankers (Pte) Ltd** - *Singapore* *Singapore* MMSI: 564416000 Official number: 384239	**172** 51 -	Class: AB (KI)	**1970-09 Halter Marine Services, Inc. — New Orleans, La** Yd No: 277 Loa 34.40 Br ex - Dght 1.200 Lbp 30.80 Br md 7.30 Dpth 3.48 Welded, 1 dk	**(B21B2OT) Offshore Tug/Supply Ship**	**2 oil engines** reverse reduction geared to sc. shaft driving 1 FP propeller Total Power: 994kW (1,352hp) 14.0kn G.M. (Detroit Diesel) 12V-149-NA 2 x Vee 2 Stroke 12 Cy. 146 x 146 each-497kW (676bhp) General Motors Detroit DieselAllison Divn-USA AuxGen: 2 x 40kW a.c Fuel: 43.0

IMO / Call sign	Name / Owner / Port	Tonnage	Class	Builder / Dimensions	Type	Machinery
8002339 - -	**SOLO 2** **Solo Fishing Co Pty Ltd** K F V Fisheries (Qld) Pty Ltd *Townsville, Qld* *Australia* Official number: 385748	*138* 84 -	Class: (NV)	**1980**-10 **Australian Shipbuilding Industries (WA) Pty Ltd — Fremantle WA** Yd No: 177 Loa 22.59 Br ex 6.89 Dght 2.752 Lbp 21.26 Br md 6.23 Dpth 3.10 Welded	**(B11A2FT) Trawler**	**1 oil engine** driving 1 FP propeller Total Power: 268kW (364hp) Caterpillar 3408PCTA 1 x Vee 4 Stroke 8 Cy. 137 x 152 268kW (364bhp) Caterpillar Tractor Co-USA
8023929 - -	**SOLO 3** **Solo Fishing Co Pty Ltd** K F V Fisheries (Qld) Pty Ltd *Townsville, Qld* *Australia* Official number: 385749	*138* 84 -	Class: (NV)	**1980**-11 **Australian Shipbuilding Industries (WA) Pty Ltd — Fremantle WA** Yd No: 190 Loa 23.02 Br ex 6.89 Dght - Lbp 21.37 Br md 6.27 Dpth 3.10 Welded, 1 dk	**(B11A2FT) Trawler**	**1 oil engine** driving 1 FP propeller Total Power: 268kW (364hp) 9.5kn Caterpillar 3408TA 1 x Vee 4 Stroke 8 Cy. 137 x 152 268kW (364bhp) Caterpillar Tractor Co-USA
7727322 *SFXY*	**SOLOGA** **Waxholms Angfartygs AB** *Vaxholm* *Sweden* MMSI: 265522530	**202** 80 40		**1978**-06 **Gotaverken Finnboda AB — Stockholm** Yd No: 403 Loa 27.51 Br ex 7.19 Dght 2.960 Lbp 26.40 Br md - Dpth 3.51 Welded, 1 dk	**(A37B2PS) Passenger Ship** Passengers: unberthed: 233	**1 oil engine** geared to sc. shaft driving 1 CP propeller Total Power: 405kW (551hp) 11.0kn Hedemora V6A/9 1 x Vee 4 Stroke 6 Cy. 185 x 210 405kW (551bhp) Hedemora Diesel AB-Sweden
7328102 *VTNW* -	**SOLOMON** *ex* Morlang Mette *-1987* *ex* Mette Steen *-1977* **Ellon Hinengo Ltd** *Kolkata* *India* MMSI: 419030400 Official number: 2308	**791** 380 912	Class: IR (NV) (BV)	**1973**-07 **p/f Skala Skipasmidja — Skali** Yd No: 23 Loa 55.28 Br ex 10.52 Dght 3.670 Lbp 49.69 Br md 10.49 Dpth 5.67 Welded, 2 dks	**(A31A2GX) General Cargo Ship** Grain: 1,812; Bale: 1,587 Compartments: 1 Ho, ER 1 Ha: (25.4 x 6.1)ER Derricks: 1x5t,1x3t; Winches: 2 Ice Capable	**1 oil engine** driving 1 CP propeller Total Power: 596kW (810hp) 8.5kn Alpha 408-26VO 1 x 2 Stroke 8 Cy. 260 x 400 596kW (810bhp) Alpha Diesel A/S-Denmark AuxGen: 1 x 32kW 380V 50Hz a.c, 1 x 48kW 380V 50Hz a.c
8717568 *UHNE* -	**SOLOMON** *ex* Sviola *-2010* *ex* Satsuma Seiun Maru *-2002* **Arcovo Co Ltd** - SatCom: Inmarsat C 427304550 *Petropavlovsk-Kamchatskiy* *Russia* MMSI: 273453080	**777** 209 392	Class: RS	**1988**-02 **Goriki Zosensho — Ise** Yd No: 1001 Loa 55.57 Br ex - Dght 3.700 Lbp 47.72 Br md 9.01 Dpth 3.92 Welded, 1 dk	**(B11B2FV) Fishing Vessel**	**1 oil engine** driving 1 FP propeller Total Power: 1,103kW (1,500hp) Niigata 6M31AFTE 1 x 4 Stroke 6 Cy. 310 x 530 1103kW (1500bhp) Niigata Engineering Co Ltd-Japan
9212292 *H4NC* -	**SOLOMON EMERALD** *ex* Mazpesca *-2007* **National Fisheries Developments Ltd** - *Honiara* *Solomon Islands* MMSI: 557000500 Official number: 2503145333-3	*718* 216 478	Class: IS	**2001**-04 **Industria Naval de Mazatlan S.A. de C.V. — Mazatlan** Yd No: 736 Loa 45.72 (BB) Br ex - Dght 4.270 Lbp - Br md 9.75 Dpth 6.60 Welded, 1 dk	**(B11B2FV) Fishing Vessel** Ins: 500	**1 oil engine** reduction geared to sc. shaft driving 1 FP propeller Total Power: 942kW (1,281hp) Caterpillar 3512B 1 x Vee 4 Stroke 12 Cy. 170 x 190 942kW (1281bhp) Caterpillar Inc-USA
8647464 *H4DT* -	**SOLOMON ENDEAVOUR** *ex* Soltai 6 *-2010* **National Fisheries Developments Ltd** - *Honiara* *Solomon Islands* Official number: 595	**103** 41 -		**1980**-01 **Iisaku Zosen K.K. — Nishi-Izu** L reg 28.04 Br ex - Dght - Lbp - Br md 5.65 Dpth 2.65 Welded, 1 dk	**(B11B2FV) Fishing Vessel**	**1 oil engine** driving 1 Propeller Total Power: 441kW (600hp) Akasaka 1 x 4 Stroke 6 Cy. 441kW (600bhp) Akasaka Tekkosho KK (Akasaka DieselLtd)-Japan
9211183 *H4AB* -	**SOLOMON JADE** *ex* Azteca 12 *-2009* **National Fisheries Developments Ltd** - *Honiara* *Solomon Islands* Official number: 968	**718** 215 478		**2001**-03 **Industria Naval del Pacifico S.A. de C.V. — Guaymas** Yd No: 741 Loa 45.72 (BB) Br ex - Dght 4.270 Lbp - Br md 9.75 Dpth 6.60 Welded, 1 dk	**(B11B2FV) Fishing Vessel** Ins: 500	**1 oil engine** reduction geared to sc. shaft driving 1 FP propeller Total Power: 942kW (1,281hp) 11.0kn Caterpillar 3512TA 1 x Vee 4 Stroke 12 Cy. 170 x 190 942kW (1281bhp) Caterpillar Inc-USA
9212319 *H4AL* -	**SOLOMON OPAL** *ex* Camila *-2009* **National Fisheries Developments Ltd** - *Honiara* *Solomon Islands* Official number: 970	*718* 215 478		**2001**-11 **Industria Naval de Mazatlan S.A. de C.V. — Mazatlan** Yd No: 738 Loa 45.72 (BB) Br ex - Dght 4.270 Lbp - Br md 9.75 Dpth 6.60 Welded, 1 dk	**(B11B2FV) Fishing Vessel** Ins: 500	**1 oil engine** reduction geared to sc. shaft driving 1 FP propeller Total Power: 942kW (1,281hp) Caterpillar 3512B 1 x Vee 4 Stroke 12 Cy. 170 x 190 942kW (1281bhp) Caterpillar Inc-USA
9211171 *H4ND* -	**SOLOMON PEARL** *ex* Azteca 11 *-2007* **National Fisheries Developments Ltd** - *Honiara* *Solomon Islands* MMSI: 557000400 Official number: 2503140933-4	**718** 215 478	Class: IS	**2001**-03 **Industria Naval del Pacifico S.A. de C.V. — Guaymas** Yd No: 740 Loa 45.72 (BB) Br ex - Dght 4.400 Lbp - Br md 9.75 Dpth 6.60 Welded, 1 dk	**(B11B2FV) Fishing Vessel** Ins: 500	**1 oil engine** reduction geared to sc. shaft driving 1 FP propeller Total Power: 942kW (1,281hp) 11.0kn Caterpillar 3512TA 1 x Vee 4 Stroke 12 Cy. 170 x 190 942kW (1281bhp) Caterpillar Inc-USA
9212307 *H4AM* -	**SOLOMON RUBY** *ex* Tamara *-2009* **National Fisheries Developments Ltd** - *Honiara* *Solomon Islands* Official number: 969	*718* 215 478		**2001**-03 **Industria Naval de Mazatlan S.A. de C.V. — Mazatlan** Yd No: 737 Loa 45.72 (BB) Br ex - Dght 4.270 Lbp - Br md 9.75 Dpth 6.60 Welded, 1 dk	**(B11B2FV) Fishing Vessel** Ins: 500	**1 oil engine** reduction geared to sc. shaft driving 1 FP propeller Total Power: 942kW (1,281hp) Caterpillar 3512B 1 x Vee 4 Stroke 12 Cy. 170 x 190 942kW (1281bhp) Caterpillar Inc-USA
8734918 *ZDFG2*	**SOLONA** *ex* Caneli *-2009* **Seawind Enterprises Ltd** David Batstone *Gibraltar* *Gibraltar (British)* MMSI: 236121000 Official number: 735333	**149** 44 -	Class: RI	**2002**-03 **Cant. Nav. San Lorenzo SpA — Viareggio** Yd No: 415 Loa 28.90 Br ex - Dght 1.900 Lbp 27.00 Br md 6.61 Dpth 3.25 Bonded, 1 dk	**(X11A2YP) Yacht** Hull Material: Reinforced Plastic	**2 oil engines** geared to sc. shafts driving 2 FP propellers Total Power: 2,880kW (3,916hp) M.T.U. 16V2000M90 2 x Vee 4 Stroke 16 Cy. 130 x 150 each-1440kW (1958bhp) MTU Friedrichshafen GmbH-Friedrichshafen
8600765 - -	**SOLONCY MOURA** **Superintendencia do Desenvolvimento da Pesca Sudepe** - SatCom: Inmarsat M 671002410 *Brazil*	**145** - 100		**1998**-07 **Estaleiro Itajai S.A. (EISA) — Itajai** Yd No: 163 Loa - Br ex - Dght 2.800 Lbp 22.00 Br md 7.90 Dpth 3.60 Welded, 1 dk	**(B11A2FT) Trawler**	**1 oil engine** geared to sc. shaft driving 1 FP propeller Total Power: 268kW (364hp) 9.5kn Cummins NTA-855-M 1 x 4 Stroke 6 Cy. 140 x 152 268kW (364bhp) Cummins Engine Co Inc-USA
8862569 *OXQL2* -	**SOLOVEN** *ex* Lovenorn *-2003* **O Log Shipping ApS** - *Copenhagen* *Denmark (DIS)* MMSI: 219570000 Official number: H255	**390** 117 -		**1960** **Orlogsvaerftet (Naval Dockyard) — Copenhagen** Converted From: Buoy & Lighthouse Tender-2009 Loa 45.99 Br ex - Dght - Lbp - Br md 8.50 Dpth 3.50 Welded, 1 dk	**(B31A2SR) Research Survey Vessel** Derricks: 1x5t	**1 oil engine** driving 1 CP propeller Total Power: 530kW (721hp) 11.5kn Alpha 1 x 4 Stroke 6 Cy. 530kW (721bhp) Alpha Diesel A/S-Denmark AuxGen: 1 x 72kW 380V a.c
5372965 *SDGO* -	**SOLSKAR** *ex* Underas Sandtag III *-1980* **Rederi A/B Skargardsgrus** *Varmdo* *Sweden* MMSI: 265611390	**202** 60 320		**1946** **Hjalmare Docka — Arboga** Lengthened-1959 Loa 37.77 Br ex 6.91 Dght 2.801 Lbp - Br md 6.86 Dpth - Welded	**(A24D2BA) Aggregates Carrier** 1 Ha: (23.8 x 5.4)ER	**2 oil engines** geared to sc. shaft driving 1 FP propeller Total Power: 226kW (308hp) 7.5kn Skandiaverken 2 x 2 Stroke 6 Cy. 380 x 410 each-113kW (154bhp) Skandiaverken AB-Sweden AuxGen: 1 x 40kW 380V Fuel: 3.0 (d.f.)
6506264 *LNYK* M-107-G	**SOLSKJAER** *ex* Breistrand *-1985* *ex* Andenesfisk V *-1978* *ex* Andenesfisk II *-1973* **K/S Solskjaer A/S** Ottar Thu Dodsbo *Aalesund* *Norway* MMSI: 259207000	**499** 149 -	Class: (NV)	**1965** **Kaarbos Mek. Verksted AS — Harstad** Yd No: 46 Loa 41.31 Br ex 8.06 Dght 4.325 Lbp 29.01 Br md 8.01 Dpth 6.35 Welded, 1 dk	**(B11A2FS) Stern Trawler** Compartments: 1 Ho, ER 1 Ha: (3.9 x 2.9) Derricks: 1x2t; Winches: 1	**1 oil engine** driving 1 FP propeller Total Power: 809kW (1,100hp) MaK 6M452AK 1 x 4 Stroke 6 Cy. 320 x 450 809kW (1100bhp) (new engine 1990) Krupp MaK Maschinenbau GmbH-Kiel AuxGen: 1 x 110kW 220V 50Hz a.c, 1 x 97kW 220V 50Hz a.c
8010544 *LJVT* -	**SOLSKJEL** **Fjord1 AS** *Kristiansund* *Norway* MMSI: 257377400	**844** 265 250	Class: (NV)	**1981**-06 **Nordfjord Verft AS — Nordfjordeid** (Hull) **1981**-06 **A.M. Liaaen AS — Aalesund** Yd No: 137 Loa 64.34 Br ex 11.26 Dght 3.100 Lbp 56.01 Br md 11.26 Dpth 4.32 Welded, 1 dk	**(A36A2PR) Passenger/Ro-Ro Ship (Vehicles)** Passengers: unberthed: 399 Bow door & ramp Stern door & ramp Cars: 50	**1 oil engine** driving 1 CP propeller , 1 fwd Total Power: 919kW (1,249hp) MWM TBD484-6 1 x 4 Stroke 6 Cy. 320 x 480 919kW (1249bhp) Motoren Werke Mannheim AG (MWM)-West Germany AuxGen: 2 x 80kW 220V 50Hz a.c

8211605 *5IM033* -	**SOLSKY** *ex* Mamba *-2004* **Alpha Logistics TZ Ltd** - *Dar es Salaam* *Tanzania* MMSI: 674010029 Official number: 10050	**170** 51 154	Class: IS (LR) ✠ Classed LR until 1/10/97	**1982-10 Scheepsbouw Alblas B.V. — Krimpen a/d IJssel** (Hull) **1982-10 B.V. Scheepswerf Damen — Gorinchem** Yd No: 3122 Loa 26.40 Br ex 8.16 Dght 3.261 Lbp 22.92 Br md 7.80 Dpth 4.04 Welded, 1 dk	**(B32A2ST) Tug**	**2 oil engines** with clutches, flexible couplings & sr reverse geared to sc. shafts driving 2 FP propellers Total Power: 2,210kW (3,004hp) Deutz SBV6M628 2 x 4 Stroke 6 Cy. 240 x 280 each-1105kW (1502bhp) Kloeckner Humboldt Deutz AG-West Germany AuxGen: 2 x 48kW 240/416V 50Hz a.c
8222147 *9LYFN9* -	**SOLSTAR** *ex* Nguvu II *-2006* **Corona Corp** - *Freetown* *Sierra Leone* MMSI: 667076000 Official number: SL100076	**362** 109 203	Class: IS (LR) ✠ Classed LR until 19/11/04	**1984-04 Ferguson-Ailsa Ltd — Troon** Yd No: 561 Loa 36.00 Br ex 10.29 Dght 3.514 Lbp 32.21 Br md 9.76 Dpth 4.45 Welded, 1 dk	**(B32A2ST) Tug**	**2 oil engines** with clutches, flexible couplings & sr geared to sc. shafts driving 2 CP propellers Total Power: 3,164kW (4,302hp) 14.5kn Ruston 8RKCM 2 x Vee 4 Stroke 8 Cy. 254 x 305 each-1582kW (2151bhp) Ruston Diesels Ltd.-Newton-le-Willows AuxGen: 2 x 85kW 440V 50Hz a.c, 1 x 20kW 440V 50Hz a.c Fuel: 100.0 (d.f.) 3.5pd
8972728 *ZNYO6* BF56	**SOLSTICE** *ex* Seonaid M *-2005* **Solstice FR492 Ltd** - *Banff* *United Kingdom* MMSI: 235003080 Official number: C17445	**166** 65 -		**2001 Astilleros Armon SA — Navia** Yd No: 527 Lengthened-2009 Loa 24.00 (BB) Br ex - Dght - Lbp - Br md 7.26 Dpth 4.10 Welded, 1 dk	**(B11A2FS) Stern Trawler** Ins: 100	**1 oil engine** reduction geared to sc. shaft driving 1 FP propeller Total Power: 620kW (843hp) 10.5kn Caterpillar 3508B 1 x Vee 4 Stroke 8 Cy. 170 x 190 620kW (843bhp) Caterpillar Inc-USA Fuel: 24.5 (d.f.)
8913708 *LDEB3* -	**SOLSTRAUM** - **Utkilen Shipping AS** Utkilen AS SatCom: Inmarsat C 425713610 *Bergen* *Norway (NIS)* MMSI: 257136000	**3,998** 1,914 6,519 T/cm 14.7	Class: NV	**1990-10 Aukra Industrier AS — Aukra** Yd No: 84 Loa 101.70 (BB) Br ex 18.25 Dght 7.013 Lbp 94.00 Br md 18.20 Dpth 8.90 Welded, 1 dk	**(A12B2TR) Chemical/Products Tanker** Double Hull (13F) Liq: 6,710; Liq (Oil): 6,847 Cargo Heating Coils Compartments: 14 Wing Ta, ER 14 Cargo Pump (s): 14x200m³/hr Manifold: Bow/CM: 52m Ice Capable	**1 oil engine** geared to sc. shaft driving 1 CP propeller Total Power: 3,233kW (4,396hp) 14.0kn Normo BRM-8 1 x 4 Stroke 8 Cy. 320 x 360 3233kW (4396bhp) Bergen Diesel AS-Norway AuxGen: 1 x 990kW 440V 60Hz a.c, 3 x 322kW 440V 60Hz a.c Thrusters: 1 Tunnel thruster (f) Fuel: 174.0 (d.f.) 320.0 (r.f.) 15.0pd
7005346 *SBQN* -	**SOLSUND** *ex* Strilfjord *-1990* *ex* Austra *-1989* *ex* Torghatten *-1987* **Olandsfarjan AB** - *Monsteras* *Sweden* MMSI: 265523070	**526** 278 -	Class: (NV)	**1969 Sandnessjoen Slip & Mek. Verksted — Sandnessjoen** Yd No: 21 Loa 33.86 Br ex 8.95 Dght 2.650 Lbp 30.00 Br md 8.89 Dpth 3.76 Welded, 1 dk	**(A36A2PR) Passenger/Ro-Ro Ship (Vehicles)** Passengers: unberthed: 175 Bow door & ramp Stern door & ramp Cars: 16 Derricks: 1x5t,1x2t Ice Capable	**2 oil engines** with clutches, flexible couplings & sr geared to sc. shafts driving 2 CP propellers Total Power: 400kW (544hp) 9.0kn Scania DSI11 2 x 4 Stroke 6 Cy. 127 x 145 each-200kW (272bhp) (new engine 1980) Scania AB-Sweden AuxGen: 2 x 50kW 220V 50Hz a.c Thrusters: 1 Thwart. FP thruster (f) Fuel: 30.0 (d.f.) 1.2pd
7950565 - -	**SOLTAI 61** *ex* Yakushi Maru No. 11 *-1989* *ex* Meisho Maru No. 53 *-1983* *ex* Dai Maru No. 15 *-1980* **Solomon Taiyo Ltd** - *Honiara* *Solomon Islands*	*297* 149 -		**1970 Kochiken Zosen — Kochi** Yd No: 390 L reg 42.01 Br ex - Dght - Lbp - Br md 8.11 Dpth 3.51 Welded, 1 dk	**(B11B2FV) Fishing Vessel**	**1 oil engine** driving 1 FP propeller Total Power: 721kW (980hp) Daihatsu 1 x 4 Stroke 721kW (980bhp) Daihatsu Diesel Manufacturing Co Lt-Japan
7379462 - -	**SOLTAI 77** *ex* Daijin Maru No. 3 *-1994* *ex* Kosho Maru No. 11 *-1990* *ex* Kyoyo Maru No. 11 *-1987* *ex* Meisho Maru No. 85 *-1981* *ex* Nadayoshi Maru No. 15 *-1978* **Solomon Taiyo Ltd** - *Solomon Islands*	*439* 218 556		**1973 Miho Zosensho K.K. — Shimizu** Yd No: 931 Loa 57.46 Br ex 9.02 Dght 3.506 Lbp 49.00 Br md 9.00 Dpth 4.12 Welded, 1 dk	**(B11B2FV) Fishing Vessel**	**1 oil engine** driving 1 FP propeller Total Power: 1,324kW (1,800hp) Hanshin 6LU35 1 x 4 Stroke 6 Cy. 350 x 550 1324kW (1800bhp) Hanshin Nainenki Kogyo-Japan
9380922 *H4PU* -	**SOLTAI NO. 101** - **Government of The Solomon Islands (National Fisheries Development)** - *Honiara* *Solomon Islands* Official number: 916	*199* 60 -		**2006-02 Miho Zosensho K.K. — Shimizu** Yd No: 1517 Loa 37.65 Br ex - Dght 2.530 Lbp 30.00 Br md 6.40 Dpth 2.80 Welded, 1 dk	**(B11B2FV) Fishing Vessel**	**1 oil engine** reduction geared to sc. shaft driving 1 FP propeller Total Power: 662kW (900hp) 10.5kn Yanmar 6N18A-SV 1 x 4 Stroke 6 Cy. 180 x 280 662kW (900bhp) Yanmar Diesel Engine Co Ltd-Japan
9380934 *H4PT* -	**SOLTAI NO. 105** - **Government of The Solomon Islands (National Fisheries Development)** Soltuna Ltd *Honiara* *Solomon Islands* Official number: 917	*199* 60 -		**2006-02 Miho Zosensho K.K. — Shimizu** Yd No: 1518 Loa 37.65 Br ex - Dght 2.530 Lbp 30.00 Br md 6.40 Dpth 2.80 Welded, 1 dk	**(B11B2FV) Fishing Vessel**	**1 oil engine** reduction geared to sc. shaft driving 1 FP propeller Total Power: 662kW (900hp) 10.5kn Yanmar 6N18A-SV 1 x 4 Stroke 6 Cy. 180 x 280 662kW (900bhp) Yanmar Diesel Engine Co Ltd-Japan
9587922 *EZHB* -	**SOLTAN** *ex* Posh Rapid *-2012* **GAC Marine SA** - *Turkmenbashy* *Turkmenistan* MMSI: 434121800	**2,588** 766 2,446	Class: AB	**2011-11 PaxOcean Engineering (Zhuhai) Co Ltd — Zhuhai GD** Yd No: PY1003 Loa 71.50 (BB) Br ex - Dght 5.900 Lbp 61.20 Br md 16.60 Dpth 7.20 Welded, 1 dk	**(B21B20A) Anchor Handling Tug Supply** TEU 4 incl 4 ref C Cranes: 1x5t	**2 oil engines** reduction geared to sc. shafts driving 2 CP propellers Total Power: 5,840kW (7,940hp) 13.0kn MAN-B&W 8L27/38 2 x 4 Stroke 8 Cy. 270 x 380 each-2920kW (3970bhp) MAN Diesel A/S-Denmark AuxGen: 2 x 1200kW 440V 60Hz a.c, 2 x 425kW 440V 60Hz a.c Thrusters: 2 Tunnel thruster (f); 1 Tunnel thruster (a) Fuel: 763.0
7120251 *9A2173* -	**SOLTANKA** - **Jadrolinija** - *Rijeka* *Croatia* MMSI: 238116140 Official number: 2T-297	*426* 222 181	Class: CS (JR)	**1971 Brodogradiliste 'Titovo' — Kraljevica** Yd No: 405 Loa 48.01 Br ex 10.80 Dght 2.201 Lbp 41.46 Br md 9.02 Dpth 2.49 Welded, 1 dk	**(A36A2PR) Passenger/Ro-Ro Ship (Vehicles)** Bow door & ramp	**2 oil engines** driving 2 FP propellers Total Power: 846kW (1,150hp) 11.5kn Isotta Fraschini ID36SS8V 2 x Vee 4 Stroke 8 Cy. 170 x 170 each-423kW (575bhp) (new engine 1989) Isotta Fraschini SpA-Italy AuxGen: 1 x 80kW 220V 50Hz a.c
9158654 *EI7195* -	**SOLUNDOY** *ex* Oystrand *-2000* **Finbar & Jeremiah Kieran O'Driscoll** The Solundoy Trading Co Ltd *Skibbereen* *Irish Republic* MMSI: 250100900 Official number: 403752	**265** 79 300		**1997-08 Aas Mek. Verksted AS — Vestnes** Yd No: 147 Loa 30.60 (BB) Br ex - Dght - Lbp 27.77 Br md 7.50 Dpth 4.20 Welded, 1 dk	**(B12B2FC) Fish Carrier**	**1 oil engine** with clutches & sr geared to sc. shaft driving 1 CP propeller Total Power: 750kW (1,020hp) 10.7kn Caterpillar 3508TA 1 x Vee 4 Stroke 8 Cy. 170 x 190 750kW (1020bhp) Caterpillar Inc-USA AuxGen: 2 x 165kW 230V 50Hz a.c Thrusters: 1 Thwart. FP thruster (f); 1 Tunnel thruster (a) Fuel: 35.0 (d.f.) 4.0pd
9609809 *WDF6808* -	**SOLUTION** - **Westport Shipyard Inc** - *Westport, MA* *United States of America* MMSI: 368168000 Official number: 1229855	**316** 94 70	Class: AB	**2010-10 Westport Shipyard, Inc. — Westport, Wa** Yd No: GRC-4301 Loa 43.53 Br ex - Dght 2.370 Lbp 37.19 Br md 7.92 Dpth 3.17 Bonded, 1 dk	**(B34H2SQ) Patrol Vessel** Hull Material: Reinforced Plastic	**2 oil engines** reduction geared to sc. shafts driving 2 Propellers Total Power: 5,884kW (8,000hp) M.T.U. 2 x 4 Stroke each-2942kW (4000bhp) MTU Friedrichshafen GmbH-Friedrichshafen
8935251 *5NJD* -	**SOLUWA** *ex* Acemis I *-2013* *ex* Lamnalco 28 *-2004* *ex* Bull Run *-1994* **Omed International Nigeria Ltd** - *Lagos* *Nigeria* MMSI: 657824000	**126** 37 -	Class: BV	**1977 Swiftships Inc — Morgan City LA** Yd No: 126 Loa 30.53 Br ex - Dght - Lbp 28.46 Br md 6.58 Dpth 2.83 Welded, 1 dk	**(B21A20C) Crew/Supply Vessel** Hull Material: Aluminium Alloy	**3 oil engines** reduction geared to sc. shafts driving 3 FP propellers Total Power: 1,170kW (1,590hp) 18.0kn G.M. (Detroit Diesel) 12V-71 3 x Vee 2 Stroke 12 Cy. 108 x 127 each-390kW (530bhp) General Motors Corp-USA AuxGen: 2 x 60kW 110V 60Hz a.c

IMO / Call sign / Fishing no.	Name / Owner / Port	Tonnage	Class	Builder / Dimensions	Type / Cargo	Machinery
8309971 *LMFG* F-42-M	**SOLVAERGUTT** *ex* Gimsoytral *-2013* *ex* Knausen *-1999* *ex* Sulejenta *-1992* **Solvaergutt AS** - *Svolvaer* *Norway* MMSI: 257866500	*140* 56 -		**1983-07 H. & E. Nordtveit Skipsbyggeri AS — Nordtveitgrend** Yd No: 74 Loa 21.49 Br ex 7.12 Dght - Lbp 18.62 Br md - Dpth 3.26 Welded, 1 dk	**(B11B2FV) Fishing Vessel**	**1 oil engine** geared to sc. shaft driving 1 FP propeller Total Power: 346kW (470hp) Yanmar 6LAAL-DT 1 x 4 Stroke 6 Cy. 148 x 165 346kW (470bhp) Yanmar Diesel Engine Co Ltd-Japan
9514133 *LCJG* F-10-H	**SOLVAERSKJAER** **Seiland Kystfiske AS** - *Hammerfest* *Norway* MMSI: 257128000	**494** 148 -		**2009-04 'Crist' Sp z oo — Gdansk** (Hull) Yd No: B34/02 **2009-04 Larsnes Mek. Verksted AS — Larsnes** Yd No: 48 Loa 34.99 (BB) Br ex - Dght 4.900 Lbp 28.70 Br md 9.25 Dpth 6.20 Welded, 1 dk	**(B11B2FV) Fishing Vessel**	**1 oil engine** reduction geared to sc. shaft driving 1 Propeller Total Power: 745kW (1,013hp) Yanmar 8N21L-EV 1 x 4 Stroke 8 Cy. 210 x 290 745kW (1013bhp) Yanmar Diesel Engine Co Ltd-Japan Thrusters: 1 Tunnel thruster (f); 1 Tunnel thruster (a)
7723687 *V2LG* -	**SOLVEIG K** *ex* Minchen D *-2008* *ex* Schulau *-1999* **'Solveig K' GmbH & Co KG** Reederei Konig GmbH *Saint John's* *Antigua & Barbuda* MMSI: 304010360 Official number: 2268	**1,678** 724 1,964	Class: (GL)	**1978-11 J.J. Sietas KG Schiffswerft GmbH & Co. — Hamburg** Yd No: 862 Loa 72.29 (BB) Br ex 12.83 Dght 4.447 Lbp 65.51 Br md 12.81 Dpth 6.80 Welded, 2 dks	**(A31A2GX) General Cargo Ship** Grain: 3,215; Bale: 3,139 TEU 127 C.Ho 53/20' (40') C.Dk 74/20' (40') Compartments: 1 Ho, ER 1 Ha: (43.7 x 10.2)ER Ice Capable	**1 oil engine** driving 1 FP propeller Total Power: 1,103kW (1,500hp) 12.5kn MWM TBD484-8 1 x 4 Stroke 8 Cy. 320 x 480 1103kW (1500bhp) Motoren Werke Mannheim AG (MWM)-West Germany AuxGen: 2 x 76kW 220/380V 50Hz a.c Fuel: 176.0 6.0pd
9589607 *C6ZW5* -	**SOLVIK SUPPLIER** - **Solvik Supplier AS** Norfield Offshore AS *Nassau* *Bahamas* MMSI: 311070200 Official number: 8002017	**4,366** 1,813 4,900	Class: NV	**2011-10 OAO Sudostroitelnyy Zavod "Severnaya Verf" — St.-Peterburg** Yd No: 696 Loa 85.00 (BB) Br ex 20.03 Dght 7.000 Lbp 77.70 Br md 20.00 Dpth 8.60 Welded, 1 dk	**(B21A2OS) Platform Supply Ship** Ice Capable	**4 diesel electric oil engines** driving 4 gen. Connecting to 2 elec. motors driving 2 Azimuth electric drive units Total Power: 6,988kW (9,500hp) 12.5kn Caterpillar 3516B 4 x Vee 4 Stroke 16 Cy. 170 x 190 each-1747kW (2375bhp) Caterpillar Inc-USA Thrusters: 2 Tunnel thruster (f); 1 Retract. directional thruster (f)
9321689 *LAJC6* -	**SOLVIKEN** - **Viken Fleet I AS** Viken Shipping AS SatCom: Inmarsat C 425868210 *Bergen* *Norway (NIS)* MMSI: 258682000	**61,653** 35,445 114,523 T/cm 99.1	Class: NV	**2007-01 Samsung Heavy Industries Co Ltd — Geoje** Yd No: 1572 Loa 246.00 (BB) Br ex 43.89 Dght 14.900 Lbp 239.00 Br md 43.80 Dpth 21.30 Welded, 1 dk	**(A13A2TV) Crude Oil Tanker** Double Hull (13F) Liq: 123,862; Liq (Oil): 123,862 Cargo Heating Coils Compartments: 12 Wing Ta, 2 Wing Slop Ta, ER 3 Cargo Pump (s): 3x3800m³/hr Manifold: Bow/CM: 125.6m Ice Capable	**1 oil engine** driving 1 FP propeller Total Power: 15,820kW (21,509hp) 14.2kn MAN-B&W 7S60MC-C 1 x 2 Stroke 7 Cy. 600 x 2400 15820kW (21509bhp) Doosan Engine Co Ltd-South Korea AuxGen: 3 x a.c Thrusters: 1 Tunnel thruster (f) Fuel: 201.3 (d.f.) 2793.2 (r.f.)
7305203 *UGDF* -	**SOLVYCHEGODSK** - **DV Kurs Co Ltd** - *Nakhodka* *Russia* MMSI: 273878200	**700** 210 305	Class: (RS)	**1972-11 Yaroslavskiy Sudostroitelnyy Zavod — Yaroslavl** Yd No: 303 Loa 49.92 (BB) Br ex 10.72 Dght 4.250 Lbp 46.21 Br md - Dpth 6.02 Welded, 1 dk	**(B11A2FS) Stern Trawler** Ins: 275 Compartments: 1 Ho, ER 2 Ha: 2 (1.6 x 1.6) Derricks: 2x1.5t; Winches: 2 Ice Capable	**1 oil engine** driving 1 CP propeller Total Power: 971kW (1,320hp) 13.0kn S.K.L. 8NVD48A-2U 1 x 4 Stroke 8 Cy. 320 x 480 971kW (1320bhp) VEB Schwermaschinenbau "KarlLiebknecht" (SKL)-Magdeburg AuxGen: 1 x 300kW, 3 x 160kW Thrusters: 1 Thwart. FP thruster (f); 1 Tunnel thruster (a) Fuel: 191.0 (d.f.)
9320491 *C6VB4* -	**SOLWAY FISHER** - **FSL-4 Inc** James Fisher (Shipping Services) Ltd *Nassau* *Bahamas* MMSI: 308665000 Official number: 8001113	**3,501** 1,444 5,422 T/cm 13.3	Class: LR ✠ **100A1** SS 06/2011 Double Hull oil tanker, bottom strengthened for loading and unloading aground ESP LI ✠ **LMC** **UMS** Eq.Ltr: U; Cable: 470.5/40.0 U3 (a)	**2006-06 Santierul Naval Damen Galati S.A. — Galati** (Hull) Yd No: 1067 **2006-06 B.V. Scheepswerf Damen Bergum — Bergum** Yd No: 9379 Loa 85.32 (BB) Br ex 17.20 Dght 6.313 Lbp 81.12 Br md 17.04 Dpth 8.95 Welded, 1 dk	**(A13B2TP) Products Tanker** Double Hull (13F) Liq: 5,734; Liq (Oil): 5,734 Compartments: 10 Wing Ta, 1 Slop Ta, ER 10 Cargo Pump (s): 10x200m³/hr Manifold: Bow/CM: 35.3m	**1 oil engine** with clutches, flexible couplings & sr geared to sc. shaft driving 1 CP propeller Total Power: 2,640kW (3,589hp) 12.2kn MaK 8M25 1 x 4 Stroke 8 Cy. 255 x 400 2640kW (3589bhp) Caterpillar Motoren GmbH & Co. KG-Germany AuxGen: 2 x 450kW 400V 50Hz a.c, 1 x 355kW 400V 50Hz a.c Boilers: TOH (ex.g.) 10.2kgf/cm² (10.0bar), TOH (o.f.) 10.2kgf/cm² (10.0bar) Thrusters: 1 Thwart. FP thruster (f) Fuel: 28.5 (d.f.) 161.6 (r.f.)
5344736 - -	**SOLWAY LASS** *ex* Tui Nasavusavu *-1985* *ex* Lawedua *-1985* *ex* Sundeved *-1976* *ex* Bent *-1976* *ex* Solway Lass *-1938* *ex* Adolf *-1938* *ex* Stina *-1938* **Matilda Cruises Pty Ltd** - *Sydney, NSW* *Australia* Official number: 852167	*128* 87 157		**1902 Gebr. G. & H. Bodewes — Hoogezand** Converted From: General Cargo Ship-1985 Loa 27.61 Br ex 5.90 Dght 2.699 Lbp - Br md 5.87 Dpth - Riveted	**(A37B2PS) Passenger Ship** Hull Material: Iron Passengers: unberthed: 60	**1 oil engine** driving 1 FP propeller Total Power: 81kW (110hp) Alpha 1 x 2 Stroke 2 Cy. 81kW (110bhp) (new engine 1980) Frederikshavn Jernstoberi ogMaskinfabrik-Denmark AuxGen: 1 x 30kW 24V
8703830 *UBLK8* -	**SOLYARIS** *ex* O Yang No. 205 *-2013* **Paroos Co Ltd (Paroos 000)** - *Nevelsk* *Russia* MMSI: 273336280	**606** 262 427	Class: KR RS	**1987-11 Daedong Shipbuilding Co Ltd — Busan** Yd No: 335 Loa 56.07 Br ex 8.81 Dght 3.490 Lbp 49.60 Br md 8.80 Dpth 3.84 Welded, 1 dk	**(B11B2FV) Fishing Vessel** Bale: 577; Ins: 469	**1 oil engine** sr reverse geared to sc. shaft driving 1 FP propeller Total Power: 882kW (1,199hp) 12.5kn Niigata 6M28AFTE 1 x 4 Stroke 6 Cy. 280 x 480 882kW (1199bhp) Ssangyong Heavy Industries Co Ltd-South Korea AuxGen: 2 x 308kW 220V a.c Fuel: 248.0 (d.f.)
9167344 *P3WG9* -	**SOLYMAR** - **Harren & Partner Schiffahrts GmbH & Co KG ms 'Paragon'** Held Bereederungs GmbH & Co KG *Limassol* *Cyprus* MMSI: 209664000 Official number: P448	**2,820** 1,503 4,106	Class: GL (BV)	**1998-06 Bodewes' Scheepswerven B.V. — Hoogezand** Yd No: 583 Loa 89.72 (BB) Br ex - Dght 5.690 Lbp 84.98 Br md 13.60 Dpth 7.20 Welded, 1 dk	**(A31A2GX) General Cargo Ship** Double Hull Grain: 5,628 TEU 246 C.Ho 111/20' C.Dk 135/20' Compartments: 1 Ho, ER 1 Ha: (62.9 x 11.0)ER Ice Capable	**1 oil engine** geared to sc. shaft driving 1 CP propeller Total Power: 2,400kW (3,263hp) 13.0kn MaK 8M25 1 x 4 Stroke 8 Cy. 255 x 400 2400kW (3263bhp) MaK Motoren GmbH & Co. KG-Kiel AuxGen: 1 x 292kW 230/400V 50Hz a.c, 2 x 252kW 230/400V 50Hz a.c Thrusters: 1 Thwart. FP thruster (f) Fuel: 38.8 (d.f.) (Heating Coils) 276.0 (r.f.) 10.5pd
9174880 - -	**SOMA 11** *ex* Sanaga IV *-2004* **SOMASCIR Groupe MAOA Peche** ARPECO SA *Nouadhibou* *Mauritania*	**202** 61 -	Class: (BV)	**1998-09 Construcciones Navales Santodomingo SA — Vigo** Yd No: 629 Loa 27.50 Br ex - Dght 3.750 Lbp 22.50 Br md 7.20 Dpth 5.60 Welded, 1 dk	**(B11A2FS) Stern Trawler** Ins: 110 Compartments: 1 Ho 1 Ha:	**1 oil engine** with flexible couplings & sr gearedto sc. shaft driving 1 FP propeller Total Power: 526kW (715hp) 10.1kn Caterpillar 3508TA 1 x Vee 4 Stroke 8 Cy. 170 x 190 526kW (715bhp) Caterpillar Inc-USA
9169885 *TJPAE* -	**SOMA 12** *ex* Andela V *-2005* **SOMASCIR Groupe MAOA Peche** ARPECO SA *Douala* *Cameroon*	**202** 61 111	Class: (BV)	**1998-03 Construcciones Navales P Freire SA — Vigo** Yd No: 483 Loa 27.50 Br ex - Dght 3.000 Lbp 22.50 Br md 7.20 Dpth 5.60 Welded, 1 dk	**(B11A2FS) Stern Trawler** Compartments: 1 Ho 1 Ha:	**1 oil engine** reduction geared to sc. shaft driving 1 FP propeller Total Power: 519kW (706hp) 9.7kn Caterpillar 3508TA 1 x Vee 4 Stroke 8 Cy. 170 x 190 519kW (706bhp) Caterpillar Inc-USA AuxGen: 2 x 135kW a.c Fuel: 92.0 (d.f.)
9123350 *JBLV* -	**SOMA MARU** - **Mitsui OSK Lines Ltd, MOL Ocean Expert Co Ltd** MOL Ship Management Co Ltd (MOLSHIP) SatCom: Inmarsat C 443179010 *Soma, Fukushima* *Japan* MMSI: 431790000 Official number: 133327	**55,610** 27,029 90,844	Class: NK	**1995-09 Koyo Dockyard Co Ltd — Mihara HS** Yd No: 2062 Loa 239.94 (BB) Br ex 43.04 Dght 12.771 Lbp 230.00 Br md 43.00 Dpth 19.70 Welded, 1 dk	**(A21A2BC) Bulk Carrier** Grain: 118,335 Compartments: 7 Ho, ER 7 Ha: (17.0 x 20.8)4 (17.9 x 20.8) (15.3 x 20.8) (17.0 x 17.6)ER	**1 oil engine** driving 1 FP propeller Total Power: 11,254kW (15,301hp) 14.0kn Sulzer 7RTA62 1 x 2 Stroke 7 Cy. 620 x 2150 11254kW (15301bhp) Mitsubishi Heavy Industries Ltd-Japan Fuel: 2780.0 (r.f.)
6823545 *5TAO* NDB 330	**SOMACOPP IV** *ex* Kashima Maru No. 8 *-1987* *ex* Shoichi Maru No. 52 *-1987* **Somacopp SA** - *Nouadhibou* *Mauritania*	*349* 168 -	Class: (RI)	**1968 Yamanishi Shipbuilding Co Ltd — Ishinomaki MG** Yd No: 583 Loa 50.60 Br ex 8.82 Dght 3.328 Lbp 44.61 Br md 8.79 Dpth 3.79 Welded, 2 dks	**(B11A2FT) Trawler**	**1 oil engine** driving 1 FP propeller Total Power: 1,250kW (1,700hp) Akasaka 6DH38SS 1 x 4 Stroke 6 Cy. 380 x 560 1250kW (1700bhp) Akasaka Tekkosho KK (Akasaka DieselLtd)-Japan

6908228 5TAP -	**SOMACOPP V** ex Shinsei Maru No. 5 -1981 **Somacopp SA** - Nouadhibou Mauritania	371 144 -	Class: (RI)	**1968 Yamanishi Shipbuilding Co Ltd — Ishinomaki MG** Yd No: 595 Loa 53.19 Br ex 8.82 Dght 3.328 Lbp 47.02 Br md 8.79 Dpth 3.79 Welded, 2 dks	**(B11B2FV) Fishing Vessel**	**1 oil engine** driving 1 FP propeller Total Power: 1,250kW (1,700hp) Akasaka 6DH38SS 1 x 4 Stroke 6 Cy. 380 x 560 1250kW (1700bhp) Akasaka Tekkosho KK (Akasaka DieselLtd)-Japan
6723159 - -	**SOMACOPP VII** ex Balboa No. 1 -1986 ex Dae Yang No. 12 -1983 ex Kyoshin Maru No. 57 -1982 **Somacopp SA** - Nouadhibou Mauritania	549 184 1,245	Class: (RI) (KR) (NK)	**1967 Niigata Engineering Co Ltd — Niigata NI** Yd No: 703 Loa 57.36 Br ex 9.73 Dght 3.760 Lbp 51.75 Br md 9.70 Dpth 4.15 Welded, 2 dks	**(B11A2FT) Trawler** Ins: 475 Compartments: 2 Ho, ER 2 Ha: (1.1 x 1.1) (2.2 x 3.2)ER Derricks: 2x1.5t	**1 oil engine** driving 1 FP propeller Total Power: 1,103kW (1,500hp) 12.0kn Niigata 6M37HS 1 x 4 Stroke 6 Cy. 370 x 540 1103kW (1500bhp) Niigata Engineering Co Ltd-Japan AuxGen: 2 x 240kW 445V a.c Fuel: 231.5
7900481 HO4569 -	**SOMANG** ex Elpis -2006 ex Seasafico 01 -2002 ex Seaprodex 05 -1990 ex Eastern Reefer -1989 **Elpis Corp** Taerim Corp Ltd Panama Panama MMSI: 371275000 Official number: 34552LG	1,211 447 1,175	Class: (NK)	**1979-03 Kishigami Zosen K.K. — Akitsu** Yd No: 1300 Loa 65.85 Br ex - Dght 4.370 Lbp 60.49 Br md 12.20 Dpth 7.00 Welded, 2 dks	**(A34A2GR) Refrigerated Cargo Ship** Ins: 1,507	**1 oil engine** reverse geared to sc. shaft driving 1 FP propeller Total Power: 1,324kW (1,800hp) 12.3kn Akasaka AH33 1 x 4 Stroke 6 Cy. 330 x 500 1324kW (1800bhp) Akasaka Tekkosho KK (Akasaka DieselLtd)-Japan AuxGen: 3 x 160kW a.c
7227475 - -	**SOMAPECHE RAJA 1** ex Rosso I -1989 ex Shoyo Maru -1989 - - Nouadhibou Mauritania	349 165 -	Class: (RI)	**1972 Narasaki Zosen KK — Muroran HK** Yd No: 801 Loa 56.98 Br ex 9.02 Dght 3.455 Lbp 51.72 Br md 9.00 Dpth 5.72 Welded, 2 dks	**(B11A2FT) Trawler**	**1 oil engine** driving 1 FP propeller Total Power: 1,692kW (2,300hp) Niigata 8MG31AX 1 x 4 Stroke 8 Cy. 310 x 380 1692kW (2300bhp) Niigata Engineering Co Ltd-Japan
7302457 - -	**SOMAURIPECT 1** ex Shoun Maru No. 18 -1987 ex Eiho Maru No. 132 -1983 **Satema** - Nouadhibou Mauritania	124 41 -	Class: (RI)	**1973 Narasaki Zosen KK — Muroran HK** Yd No: 825 Loa 37.72 Br ex 7.42 Dght 2.280 Lbp 31.12 Br md 7.40 Dpth 5.14 Welded, 2 dks	**(B11A2FT) Trawler**	**1 oil engine** driving 1 CP propeller Total Power: 993kW (1,350hp) Hanshin 6LUN28 1 x 4 Stroke 6 Cy. 280 x 480 993kW (1350bhp) Hanshin Nainenki Kogyo-Japan AuxGen: 1 x 208kW 220V 60Hz a.c
8116960 V3JO3 -	**SOMAYA** ex Castor -2012 ex Arklow Day -2003 ex Diane Green -2000 ex Sarine 2 -1996 ex Fastnes -1993 ex Fjellnes -1986 **Best Leaders International SA** Mallah Ship Management Co Ltd Belize City Belize MMSI: 312444000 Official number: 291330158	8,351 4,305 12,334 T/cm 21.4	Class: RI (LR) (TL) (GL) (NV) Classed LR until 31/8/12	**1982-08 Miho Zosensho K.K. — Shimizu** Yd No: 1209 Loa 129.04 (BB) Br ex 20.02 Dght 8.405 Lbp 122.03 Br md 20.01 Dpth 11.21 Welded, 1 dk	**(A31A2GX) General Cargo Ship** Grain: 15,170; Bale: 15,035 Compartments: 4 Ho, ER 4 Ha: 2 (19.2 x 16.5)2 (12.8 x 12.9)ER Cranes: 2	**1 oil engine** sr reverse geared to sc. shaft driving 1 FP propeller Total Power: 4,306kW (5,854hp) 14.5kn Pielstick 9PC2-5L-400 1 x 4 Stroke 9 Cy. 400 x 460 4306kW (5854bhp) Nippon Kokan KK (NKK Corp)-Japan AuxGen: 2 x 367kW 440V 60Hz a.c Boilers: e (ex.g.) 5.2kgf/cm^2 (5.1bar), AuxB (o.f.) 5.6kgf/cm^2 (5.5bar)
8506012 YEMU -	**SOMBAR** ex Hanjani -2010 **PT Arpeni Pratama Ocean Line Tbk** - SatCom: Inmarsat A 1525273 Jakarta Indonesia MMSI: 525011037	6,302 2,643 7,761	Class: KI (NK)	**1985-11 Nishi Shipbuilding Co Ltd — Imabari EH** Yd No: 339 Loa 104.15 Br ex 18.52 Dght 7.498 Lbp 96.02 Br md 18.51 Dpth 13.00 Welded, 2 dks	**(A31A2GX) General Cargo Ship** Grain: 14,792; Bale: 13,775 Compartments: 2 Ho, ER 2 Ha: 2 (25.3 x 13.3)ER Cranes: 2x25t; Derricks: 2x20t	**1 oil engine** driving 1 FP propeller Total Power: 3,001kW (4,080hp) 12.5kn B&W 6L35MC 1 x 2 Stroke 6 Cy. 350 x 1050 3001kW (4080bhp) Hitachi Zosen Corp-Japan Fuel: 600.0 (r.f.)
9292113 ONHD -	**SOMBEKE** ex BW Sombeke -2011 **Exmar Shipping NV** Exmar Marine NV SatCom: Inmarsat C 420560910 Antwerpen Belgium MMSI: 205609000 Official number: 01 00790 2011	25,994 7,799 29,213 T/cm 44.7	Class: NV	**2006-10 Daewoo Shipbuilding & Marine Engineering Co Ltd — Geoje** Yd No: 2309 Loa 180.00 (BB) Br ex 29.23 Dght 10.422 Lbp 172.00 Br md 29.20 Dpth 18.20 Welded, 1 dk	**(A11B2TG) LPG Tanker** Double Bottom Entire Compartment Length Liq (Gas): 38,436 3 x Gas Tank (s); 3 independent (C.mn.stl) cyl horizontal 6 Cargo Pump (s): 6x465m^3/hr Manifold: Bow/CM: 92.3m	**1 oil engine** driving 1 FP propeller Total Power: 9,988kW (13,580hp) 16.4kn MAN-B&W 6S50MC-C 1 x 2 Stroke 6 Cy. 500 x 2000 9988kW (13580bhp) Doosan Engine Co Ltd-South Korea AuxGen: 3 x 800kW a.c Thrusters: 1 Tunnel thruster (f) Fuel: 257.0 (d.f.) 2603.0 (r.f.)
8726715 UCMQ -	**SOMERI** ex Symeri -1992 **Shipping Co 'River-Sea' LLC (River-Sea Shipping Agency Co Ltd)** - Astrakhan Russia MMSI: 273352060	270 81 89	Class: RS	**1987-01 Brodogradiliste 'Tito' — Belgrade** Yd No: 1112 Loa 35.78 Br ex 9.49 Dght 3.280 Lbp 30.10 Br md 9.00 Dpth 4.50 Welded, 1 dk	**(B32A2ST) Tug** Ice Capable	**2 oil engines** driving 1 CP propeller Total Power: 1,854kW (2,520hp) 13.5kn Sulzer 6ASL25D 2 x 4 Stroke 6 Cy. 250 x 300 each-927kW (1260bhp) in Yugoslavia AuxGen: 2 x 927kW a.c Fuel: 50.0 (d.f.)
9431604 PBHH -	**SOMERS ISLES** ex Ideaal -2013 **Scheepvaart Onderneming Ideaal** Amasus Shipping BV Sneek Netherlands MMSI: 244796000	2,702 810 3,300	Class: BV	**2012-01 Hong Ha Shipbuilding Co Ltd — Haiphong** Yd No: 08 Loa 89.98 (BB) Br ex - Dght 4.850 Lbp 84.98 Br md 13.75 Dpth 6.25 Welded, 1 dk	**(A31A2GX) General Cargo Ship** Grain: 4,870 TEU 300 Compartments: 1 Ho, ER 1 Ha: ER (61.8 x 10.8) Ice Capable	**1 oil engine** reduction geared to sc. shaft driving 1 CP propeller Total Power: 1,980kW (2,692hp) 13.0kn MaK 6M25 1 x 4 Stroke 6 Cy. 255 x 400 1980kW (2692bhp) Caterpillar Motoren GmbH & Co. KG-Germany AuxGen: 1 x 468kW 400V 50Hz a.c, 2 x 232kW 400V 50Hz a.c Thrusters: 1 Tunnel thruster (f) Fuel: 400.0
7609697 V7GI4 -	**SOMERSET** ex Anangel Might -2001 **Labbeholmen Shipping AS** SMT Shipmanagement & Transport Gdynia Ltd Sp z oo SatCom: Inmarsat C 453846157 Majuro Marshall Islands MMSI: 538002101 Official number: 2101	13,491 5,301 23,500 T/cm 31.6	Class: BV (AB)	**1978-09 Ishikawajima-Harima Heavy Industries Co Ltd (IHI) — Aioi HG** Yd No: 2560 Converted From: General Cargo Ship-2006 Loa 164.32 (BB) Br ex - Dght 10.100 Lbp 155.43 Br md 22.86 Dpth 14.15 Welded, 1 dk	**(A24A2BT) Cement Carrier** Grain: 30,425 Compartments: 4 Ho, ER	**1 oil engine** sr geared to sc. shaft driving 1 CP propeller Total Power: 5,737kW (7,800hp) 12.0kn Pielstick 12PC2-5V-400 1 x Vee 4 Stroke 12 Cy. 400 x 460 5737kW (7800bhp) Ishikawajima Harima Heavy IndustrieCo Ltd (IHI)-Japan AuxGen: 1 x 450kW 450V 60Hz a.c, 1 x 160kW 450V 60Hz a.c Fuel: 134.0 (d.f.) (Part Heating Coils) 1115.5 (r.f.) 24.5pd
9661089 AVQQ -	**SOMESHWAR** - **United Shippers Ltd** - Mumbai India MMSI: 419000471 Official number: 3930	1,068 517 1,750	Class: IR	**2012-05 Goa Ore Carriers — Goa** Yd No: 11 Loa 67.10 Br ex 12.02 Dght 3.200 Lbp 64.03 Br md 12.00 Dpth 4.35 Welded, 1 dk	**(A31A2GX) General Cargo Ship** Bale: 2,003 Compartments: 1 Ho, ER 1 Ha: ER	**2 oil engines** reduction geared to sc. shafts driving 2 FP propellers Total Power: 402kW (546hp) 7.6kn Cummins NT-855-M 2 x 4 Stroke 6 Cy. 140 x 152 each-201kW (273bhp) Cummins India Ltd-India
1004041 PEPK -	**SOMETHING COOL** ex Something Cool II -2001 ex Louise III -2001 **Eurotrust BV** - Netherlands	136 79 -	Class: LR **100A1** SS 06/2009 Yacht **LMC**	**1964 N.V. Dok- en Werf-Mij. Wilton-Fijenoord — Schiedam** Loa 29.70 Br ex 5.61 Dght 1.700 Lbp 26.77 Br md - Dpth 2.89 Welded, 1 dk	**(X11A2YP) Yacht**	**2 oil engines** geared to sc. shafts driving 2 FP propellers Total Power: 706kW (960hp) G.M. (Detroit Diesel) 12V-71 2 x Vee 2 Stroke 12 Cy. 108 x 127 each-353kW (480bhp) General Motors Corp-USA
9368015 9BQZ -	**SOMIA** ex Iran Torkaman -2010 **Khazar Sea Shipping Lines** - Bandar Anzali Iran MMSI: 422750000	5,676 3,334 7,004 T/cm 22.0	Class: IN (LR) (RS) Classed LR until 1/9/11	**2008-05 OAO Volgogradskiy Sudostroitelnyy Zavod — Volgograd** Yd No: 244 Loa 139.95 (BB) Br ex 16.72 Dght 4.600 Lbp 135.69 Br md 16.50 Dpth 6.00 Welded, 1 dk	**(A31A2GX) General Cargo Ship** Double Bottom Entire, Double Sides Partial Grain: 10,956 TEU 274 C Ho 204 TEU C Dk 70 TEU Compartments: 4 Ho, ER 4 Ha: ER	**2 oil engines** with flexible couplings & reduction geared to sc. shafts driving 2 FP propellers Total Power: 2,400kW (3,264hp) 10.5kn Wartsila 6L20 2 x 4 Stroke 6 Cy. 200 x 280 each-1200kW (1632bhp) Wartsila Finland Oy-Finland AuxGen: 3 x 240kW a.c Boilers: WTAuxB (o.f.) 7.1kgf/cm^2 (7.0bar), WTAuxB (ex.g.) 7.1kgf/cm^2 (7.0bar) Thrusters: 1 Thwart. FP thruster (f)
9253375 - -	**SOMJAI 1** - - Bangkok Thailand Official number: 431001724	426 290 -		**2000-12 in Thailand** Loa 41.50 Br ex 8.50 Dght - Lbp - Br md - Dpth 5.00 Welded, 1 dk	**(B11B2FV) Fishing Vessel**	**1 oil engine** geared to sc. shaft driving 1 FP propeller Total Power: 1,015kW (1,380hp) Caterpillar 3512TA 1 x Vee 4 Stroke 12 Cy. 170 x 190 1015kW (1380bhp) Caterpillar Inc-USA

Number	Name / Owner	Tonnage	Class	Builder / Dimensions	Type	Machinery
8711150 *JXWA* N-105-VR	**SOMMAROYVAERING** *ex* Heidi Anita *-1996* **Jarle Bergs's Sonner AS** - *Tromso* *Norway* MMSI: 257806500	**192** 57 -		**1988-04 Sletta Baatbyggeri AS — Mjosundet** Yd No: 68 Loa 19.97 (BB) Br ex 6.41 Dght - Lbp - Br md - Dpth 3.41 Welded, 1 dk	**(B11B2FV) Fishing Vessel**	**1 oil engine** geared to sc. shaft driving 1 FP propeller Total Power: 385kW (523hp) Mercedes Benz 0M424A 1 x Vee 4 Stroke 12 Cy. 128 x 142 385kW (523bhp) Daimler Benz AG-West Germany Thrusters: 1 Tunnel thruster (f)
9669811 - -	**SOMMER S** - **Shaver Transportation Co** - *Portland, OR* *United States of America* Official number: 1231637	**267** 213 -		**2012-06 Diversified Marine, Inc. — Portland, Or** Yd No: 24 Loa 23.62 Br ex - Dght - Lbp - Br md 10.97 Dpth 4.35 Welded, 1 dk	**(B32A2ST) Tug**	**2 diesel electric oil engines** reduction geared to sc. shafts driving 2 Azimuth electric drive units Total Power: 4,000kW (5,438hp) M.T.U. 16V4000M61 2 x Vee 4 Stroke 16 Cy. 165 x 190 each-2000kW (2719bhp) Detroit Diesel Corporation-Detroit, Mi
9713090 - -	**SOMMIT** - **Sommit Enterprise Ltd** - *Chittagong* *Bangladesh* Official number: C1870	**998** - 1,659	Class: RI	**2014-01 Narayangonj Engineering & Shipbuilding Ltd (NESL) — Bandar** Yd No: NESL 15 Loa 68.60 Br ex - Dght 3.900 Lbp 63.50 Br md 10.80 Dpth 5.30 Welded, 1 dk	**(A13B2TP) Products Tanker** Double Hull (13F)	**2 oil engines** reduction geared to sc. shafts driving 2 FP propellers Total Power: 1,080kW (1,468hp) 10.0kn AuxGen: 2 x 40kW a.c
9638886 *D5BZ7* -	**SOMNIUM AUSTRALIS** - **Lucretia Shipping SA** Santoku Senpaku Co Ltd SatCom: Inmarsat C 463712452 *Monrovia* *Liberia* MMSI: 636015640 Official number: 15640	**91,349** 58,425 176,491 T/cm 120.6	Class: NK	**2012-06 Shanghai Jiangnan Changxing Shipbuilding Co Ltd — Shanghai** Yd No: 1270 Loa 292.00 (BB) Br ex 45.05 Dght 18.320 Lbp 282.00 Br md 45.00 Dpth 24.80 Welded, 1 dk	**(A21A2BC) Bulk Carrier** Grain: 194,179; Bale: 183,425 Compartments: 9 Ho, ER 9 Ha: ER	**1 oil engine** driving 1 FP propeller Total Power: 16,860kW (22,923hp) 14.0kn MAN-B&W 6S70MC-C8 1 x 2 Stroke 6 Cy. 700 x 2800 16860kW (22923bhp) CSSC MES Diesel Co Ltd-China Fuel: 5120.0
8221222 *HMYD6* -	**SON BONG 1** *ex* Hung Song 8 *-2010* *ex* Pine Tree 8 *-2003* *ex* Sonamu No. 8 *-2003* *ex* Hakuyo Maru No. 8 *-1998* **Korea Sonbong General Trading Co** - SatCom: Inmarsat C 444529210 *Nampho* *North Korea* MMSI: 445292000 Official number: 3200861	**979** 405 1,127		**1982-02 K.K. Murakami Zosensho — Naruto** Yd No: 133 Converted From: General Cargo Ship-2009 Loa 60.10 Br ex - Dght 3.850 Lbp 55.00 Br md 10.50 Dpth 6.00 Welded, 1 dk	**(A31A2GX) General Cargo Ship** Grain: 1,949; Bale: 1,899 Compartments: 1 Ho, ER 1 Ha: (32.2 x 8.0)ER	**1 oil engine** driving 1 FP propeller Total Power: 883kW (1,201hp) Hanshin 6LU28 1 x 4 Stroke 6 Cy. 280 x 440 883kW (1201bhp) The Hanshin Diesel Works Ltd-Japan
7827237 *9HWQ8* -	**SON I** *ex* Samos Island *-2010* *ex* Sea Star *-2007* *ex* Islay Trader *-2005* *ex* Sea Kestrel *-2003* *ex* Pentland *-2000* *ex* Capacity *-1994* *ex* Lizzonia *-1989* **Son Shipping & Trading Ltd** Derin Gemi Acenteligi ve Gemi Isletmeciligi Sanayi ve Ticaret Ltd Sti (Derin Shipping Agency & Shipping Management Trade Ltd Co) *Valletta* *Malta* MMSI: 256532000 Official number: 7827237	**909** 518 1,315	Class: RI (LR) ✠ Classed LR until 26/1/07	**1980-02 Cochrane Shipbuilders Ltd. — Selby** Yd No: 109 Loa 60.30 Br ex 11.28 Dght 3.896 Lbp 56.01 Br md 11.21 Dpth 4.60 Welded, 1 dk	**(A31A2GX) General Cargo Ship** Grain: 1,781; Bale: 1,633 Compartments: 1 Ho, ER 1 Ha: (30.9 x 8.5)ER	**1 oil engine** reverse reduction geared to sc. shaft driving 1 FP propeller Total Power: 728kW (990hp) 12.0kn Blackstone ESL8MK2 1 x 4 Stroke 8 Cy. 222 x 292 728kW (990bhp) Mirrlees Blackstone (Stamford)Ltd.-Stamford AuxGen: 2 x 80kW 415V 50Hz a.c Fuel: 62.0
9578189 *XVXJ* -	**SON LOC 09** - **Son Loc Sea River Transport Services Co Ltd** - *Haiphong* *Vietnam* MMSI: 574000460	**1,599** 1,032 3,126	Class: VR	**2010-07 Nam Ha Shipyard — Nam Ha** Yd No: BTB-819 Loa 78.68 Br ex 12.62 Dght 5.220 Lbp 73.58 Br md 12.60 Dpth 6.48 Welded, 1 dk	**(A21A2BC) Bulk Carrier** Grain: 3,948; Bale: 3,556 Compartments: 2 Ho, ER 2 Ha: ER 2 (19.8 x 8.4)	**1 oil engine** reduction geared to sc. shaft driving 1 FP propeller Total Power: 1,103kW (1,500hp) 10.0kn Chinese Std. Type 8300ZLC 1 x 4 Stroke 8 Cy. 300 x 380 1103kW (1500bhp) Zibo Diesel Engine Factory-China AuxGen: 2 x 80kW 400V a.c Fuel: 80.0 (r.f.)
8748256 *XVMJ* -	**SON LONG 08** *ex* Son Long 18 *-2012* **Son Long Joint Stock Co** Thanh Dat Seagoing Vessel JSC *Haiphong* *Vietnam* MMSI: 574012287 Official number: VN-2610-VT	**1,598** 1,062 3,098	Class: VR	**2008-06 Haiphong Mechanical & Trading Co. — Haiphong** Yd No: THB25-04 Loa 79.80 Br ex 12.82 Dght 5.040 Lbp 74.80 Br md 12.80 Dpth 6.08 Welded, 1 dk	**(A31A2GX) General Cargo Ship** Grain: 3,498 Compartments: 2 Ho, ER 2 Ha: ER 2 (20.4 x 8.4)	**1 oil engine** driving 1 FP propeller Total Power: 734kW (998hp) 10.0kn Chinese Std. Type 8300ZLC 1 x 4 Stroke 8 Cy. 300 x 380 734kW (998bhp) Zibo Diesel Engine Factory-China AuxGen: 2 x 75kW 400V a.c
7306477 - -	**SON MAR 9** *ex* Propemex G-26 *-2012* *launched as* Banfoco 107 *-1973* **Pesquera Selecta de Guaymas SA de CV** - *Guaymas* *Mexico*	*124* 79 -	Class: (LR) ✠ Classed LR until 30/1/76	**1973-01 Astilleros Monarca S.A. — Guaymas** Yd No: 16 Loa 21.95 Br ex 6.18 Dght 2.560 Lbp 19.51 Br md 6.05 Dpth 3.41 Welded, 1 dk	**(B11B2FV) Fishing Vessel** Compartments: 1 Ho, ER 1 Ha: (2.7 x 1.8)	**1 oil engine** reverse reduction geared to sc. shaft driving 1 FP propeller Total Power: 252kW (343hp) Rolls Royce C8TFLM 1 x 4 Stroke 8 Cy. 130 x 152 252kW (343bhp) Rolls Royce Ltd.-Shrewsbury AuxGen: 1 x 5kW 32V d.c, 1 x 1kW 32V d.c
7306489 - -	**SON MAR 10** *ex* Propemex G-27 *-1973* *launched as* Banfoco 108 *-1973* **Pesquera Selecta de Guaymas SA de CV** - *Guaymas* *Mexico*	*124* 79 -	Class: (LR) ✠ Classed LR until 30/1/76	**1973-01 Astilleros Monarca S.A. — Guaymas** Yd No: 17 Loa 21.95 Br ex 6.18 Dght 2.560 Lbp 19.51 Br md 6.05 Dpth 3.41 Welded, 1 dk	**(B11B2FV) Fishing Vessel** Compartments: 1 Ho, ER 1 Ha: (2.7 x 1.8)	**1 oil engine** reverse reduction geared to sc. shaft driving 1 FP propeller Total Power: 252kW (343hp) Rolls Royce C8TFLM 1 x 4 Stroke 8 Cy. 130 x 152 252kW (343bhp) Rolls Royce Ltd.-Shrewsbury AuxGen: 1 x 5kW 32V d.c, 1 x 1kW 32V d.c
7306491 - -	**SON MAR 11** *ex* Propemex G-28 *-1973* *launched as* Banfoco 109 *-1973* **Pesquera Selecta de Guaymas SA de CV** - *Guaymas* *Mexico*	*124* 79 -	Class: (LR) ✠ Classed LR until 30/1/76	**1973-05 Astilleros Monarca S.A. — Guaymas** Loa 21.95 Br ex 6.18 Dght 2.560 Lbp 19.51 Br md 6.05 Dpth 3.41 Welded	**(B11B2FV) Fishing Vessel** Compartments: 1 Ho, ER 1 Ha: (2.7 x 1.8)	**1 oil engine** reverse reduction geared to sc. shaft driving 1 FP propeller Total Power: 252kW (343hp) Rolls Royce C8TFLM 1 x 4 Stroke 8 Cy. 130 x 152 252kW (343bhp) Rolls Royce Ltd.-Shrewsbury AuxGen: 1 x 5kW 32V d.c, 1 x 1kW 32V d.c
7306506 - -	**SON MAR 12** *ex* Propemex G-29 *-1973* *launched as* Banfoco 110 *-1973* **Pesquera Selecta de Guaymas SA de CV** - *Guaymas* *Mexico*	*124* 79 -	Class: (LR) ✠ Classed LR until 30/1/76	**1973-05 Astilleros Monarca S.A. — Guaymas** Loa 21.95 Br ex 6.18 Dght 2.560 Lbp 19.51 Br md 6.05 Dpth 3.41 Welded	**(B11B2FV) Fishing Vessel** Compartments: 1 Ho, ER 1 Ha: (2.7 x 1.8)	**1 oil engine** reverse reduction geared to sc. shaft driving 1 FP propeller Total Power: 252kW (343hp) Rolls Royce C8TFLM 1 x 4 Stroke 8 Cy. 130 x 152 252kW (343bhp) Rolls Royce Ltd.-Shrewsbury AuxGen: 1 x 5kW 32V d.c, 1 x 1kW 32V d.c
7356082 - -	**SON MAR 13** *ex* Propemex G-30 *-1973* *ex* Banfoco 111 *-1975* **Pesquera Selecta de Guaymas SA de CV** - *Guaymas* *Mexico*	*124* 79 -	Class: (LR) ✠ Classed LR until 28/5/76	**1975-04 Astilleros Monarca S.A. — Guaymas** Yd No: 20 Loa 21.95 Br ex 6.18 Dght 2.560 Lbp 19.51 Br md 6.05 Dpth 3.41 Welded, 1 dk	**(B11B2FV) Fishing Vessel**	**1 oil engine** reverse reduction geared to sc. shaft driving 1 FP propeller Total Power: 252kW (343hp) Rolls Royce C8TFLM 1 x 4 Stroke 8 Cy. 130 x 152 252kW (343bhp) Rolls Royce Motors Ltd.-Shrewsbury AuxGen: 1 x 5kW 32V d.c
8663743 *XVZF* -	**SON THINH 19** *ex* Tan Thanh 18 *-2013* **Son Thinh Import Export JSC** - *Haiphong* *Vietnam* MMSI: 574012469	**499** 317 959	Class: VR	**2009-05 Thanh Long Shipbuilding Industry Co Ltd — Haiphong** Loa 56.60 Br ex - Dght 3.500 Lbp 53.00 Br md 9.00 Dpth 4.30 Welded, 1 dk	**(A31A2GX) General Cargo Ship**	**1 oil engine** reduction geared to sc. shaft driving 1 Propeller Total Power: 1,080kW (1,468hp) Chinese Std. Type X6170ZCA 1 x 4 Stroke 6 Cy. 170 x 200 1080kW (1468bhp)
9023316 - -	**SON TRA** - **Da Nang Port (Cang Da Nang)** - *Da Nang* *Vietnam* Official number: VNDN-163-LD	**185** 55 -	Class: VR	**1981-01 Bach Dang Shipyard — Haiphong** Yd No: L-19 Loa 29.70 Br ex 8.32 Dght 3.750 Lbp 28.00 Br md 8.30 Dpth 4.00 Welded, 1 dk	**(B32A2ST) Tug**	**1 oil engine** driving 1 FP propeller Total Power: 588kW (799hp) 10.0kn S.K.L. 8NVD48 1 x 4 Stroke 8 Cy. 320 x 480 588kW (799bhp) (made 1967, added 1981) SKL Motoren u. Systemtechnik AG-Magdeburg

8700060 *UBIG7* -	**SONA** *ex Ladoga-106 -2008* **Caspius 2012 LLC** - SatCom: Inmarsat C 427300030 *Astrakhan* *Russia* MMSI: 273357400	**1,853** 822 2,075	Class: RS	**1989-04 Rauma-Repola Oy — Uusikaupunki** Yd No: 331 Loa 82.50 (BB) Br ex 11.40 Dght 4.001 Lbp 77.75 Br md 11.26 Dpth 5.80 Welded, 1 dk	**(A31A2GX) General Cargo Ship** Bale: 3,040 Ice Capable	**2 oil engines** with clutches, flexible couplings & reverse reduction geared to sc. shafts driving 2 FP propellers Total Power: 882kW (1,200hp) 10.3kn S.K.L. 6VDS26/20AL-1 2 x 4 Stroke 6 Cy. 200 x 260 each-441kW (600bhp) VEB Schwermaschinenbau "KarlLiebknecht" (SKL)-Magdeburg AuxGen: 2 x 80kW 390V 50Hz a.c, 1 x 40kW 390V 50Hz a.c Thrusters: 1 Thwart. FP thruster (f) Fuel: 159.0 (d.f.) 4.9pd
8617433 *6WHY* DAK 1138	**SONA** - - *Dakar* *Senegal*	**138** 42 100	Class: (AB)	**1988-01 S.L. Ardeag — Bilbao** Yd No: 146 Loa 27.72 Br ex 7.22 Dght 2.554 Lbp 24.16 Br md 7.21 Dpth 3.41 Welded, 1 dk	**(B11A2FS) Stern Trawler**	**2 oil engines** sr geared to sc. shafts driving 2 FP propellers Total Power: 540kW (734hp) 12.0kn Volvo Penta TAMD121C 2 x 4 Stroke 6 Cy. 130 x 150 each-270kW (367bhp) AB Volvo Penta-Sweden
9558347 *AUOY* -	**SONA-II** *ex Vignesh Fabricators 7 -2009* **KVR Offshore Pvt Ltd** - *Visakhapatnam* *India* MMSI: 419078300 Official number: 3284	**317** 96 254	Class: IR	**2009-02 in India** Yd No: 7 Loa 35.40 Br ex - Dght 3.000 Lbp - Br md 9.00 Dpth 3.50 Welded, 1 dk	**(B34R2QY) Supply Tender**	**2 oil engines** reduction geared to sc. shafts driving 2 Propellers Total Power: 942kW (1,280hp) 10.0kn Cummins KTA-19-M3 2 x 4 Stroke 6 Cy. 159 x 159 each-471kW (640bhp) Cummins India Ltd-India
9688441 *HP5610* -	**SONAGAS UNO** - **SI Global SA** - *Panama* *Panama* Official number: 019922739PE	**283** 65 250	Class: PD	**2012-12 Metalships & Docks, S.A. — Vigo** Yd No: 102 Loa 39.50 Br ex - Dght 3.650 Lbp 32.50 Br md 8.00 Dpth 3.70 Welded, 1 dk	**(A31A2GX) General Cargo Ship** Grain: 215	**1 oil engine** driving 1 Propeller Total Power: 1,030kW (1,400hp) 12.0kn GUASCOR 1 x 1030kW (1400bhp) Gutierrez Ascunce Corp (GUASCOR)-Spain
8738756 *AUAC* -	**SONALI** - **United Divers Pvt Ltd** Vighnahar Ship Management & Services Pvt Ltd *Visakhapatnam* *India* Official number: 2971	**189** 57 -		**2001-01 Santosh Fabricators — Kakinada** Loa 24.80 Br ex - Dght - Lbp 22.78 Br md 8.00 Dpth - Welded, 1 dk	**(B22A20V) Diving Support Vessel**	**2 oil engines** reduction geared to sc. shafts driving 2 Propellers Total Power: 682kW (928hp) MWM TD2V8 2 x Vee 4 Stroke 8 Cy. 120 x 130 each-341kW (464bhp) Greaves Ltd-India
9482304 *C6YM7* -	**SONANGOL BENGUELA** - **Sonangol Benguela Ltd** Sociedad Nacional de Combustiveis de Angola (SONANGOL) *Nassau* *Bahamas* MMSI: 311038100 Official number: 9000345	**104,537** 31,361 89,806 T/cm 106.7	Class: AB	**2011-12 Daewoo Shipbuilding & Marine Engineering Co Ltd — Geoje** Yd No: 2282 Loa 291.08 (BB) Br ex 43.44 Dght 12.700 Lbp 280.00 Br md 43.40 Dpth 26.50 Welded, 1 dk	**(A11A2TN) LNG Tanker** Double Hull Liq (Gas): 160,500 1 x Gas Tank (s); ER	**1 Steam Turb** reduction geared to sc. shaft driving 1 FP propeller Total Power: 28,300kW (38,477hp) 19.2kn Kawasaki UA-400 1 x steam Turb 28300kW (38477shp) Kawasaki Heavy Industries Ltd-Japan AuxGen: 2 x 3800kW a.c Thrusters: 1 Tunnel thruster (f) Fuel: 519.7 (d.f.) 6195.0 (r.f.)
9575589 *C6ZU3* -	**SONANGOL CABINDA** - **Sonangol Cabinda Ltd** Sociedad Nacional de Combustiveis de Angola (SONANGOL) *Nassau* *Bahamas* MMSI: 311066500 Official number: 7000156	**83,753** 49,262 157,747 T/cm 118.0	Class: AB	**2013-01 Daewoo Shipbuilding & Marine Engineering Co Ltd — Geoje** Yd No: 5353 Loa 274.00 (BB) Br ex 48.04 Dght 17.000 Lbp 264.00 Br md 48.00 Dpth 23.70 Welded, 1 dk	**(A13A2TV) Crude Oil Tanker** Double Hull (13F) Liq: 168,000; Liq (Oil): 168,000 Cargo Heating Coils Compartments: 12 Wing Ta, ER, 2 Wing Slop Ta 3 Cargo Pump (s): 3x3500m³/hr Manifold: Bow/CM: 137.5m	**1 oil engine** driving 1 FP propeller Total Power: 16,850kW (22,909hp) 15.5kn MAN-B&W 6S70MC-C8 1 x 2 Stroke 6 Cy. 700 x 2800 16850kW (22909bhp) Hyundai Heavy Industries Co Ltd-South Korea AuxGen: 3 x 900kW a.c Fuel: 340.0 (d.f.) 3450.0 (r.f.)
9482299 *C6YM5* -	**SONANGOL ETOSHA** - **Sonangol Etosha Ltd** Sociedad Nacional de Combustiveis de Angola (SONANGOL) *Nassau* *Bahamas* MMSI: 311027800 Official number: 9000341	**104,537** 31,361 89,932 T/cm 106.7	Class: AB	**2011-11 Daewoo Shipbuilding & Marine Engineering Co Ltd — Geoje** Yd No: 2281 Loa 291.08 (BB) Br ex - Dght 11.900 Lbp 280.00 Br md 43.40 Dpth 26.50 Welded, 1 dk	**(A11A2TN) LNG Tanker** Double Hull Liq (Gas): 160,500	**1 Steam Turb** reduction geared to sc. shaft driving 1 FP propeller Total Power: 28,300kW (38,477hp) 19.2kn Kawasaki UA-400 1 x steam Turb 28300kW (38477shp) Kawasaki Heavy Industries Ltd-Japan AuxGen: 3 x 3800kW a.c Fuel: 519.7 (d.f.) 6195.3 (r.f.)
9180114 *C6QR8* -	**SONANGOL GIRASSOL** - **Sonangol Shipping Girassol Ltd** Stena Bulk LLC SatCom: Inmarsat C 430928211 *Nassau* *Bahamas* MMSI: 309282000 Official number: 732243	**81,230** 50,687 159,057 T/cm 116.9	Class: AB	**2000-01 Daewoo Heavy Industries Ltd — Geoje** Yd No: 5138 Loa 274.00 (BB) Br ex - Dght 17.020 Lbp 264.00 Br md 48.00 Dpth 23.20 Welded, 1 dk	**(A13A2TV) Crude Oil Tanker** Double Hull (13F) Liq: 166,668; Liq (Oil): 169,865 Cargo Heating Coils Compartments: 12 Wing Ta, 2 Wing Slop Ta, ER 3 Cargo Pump (s): 3x3500m³/hr Manifold: Bow/CM: 134m	**1 oil engine** driving 1 FP propeller Total Power: 16,859kW (22,921hp) 15.2kn B&W 6S70MC 1 x 2 Stroke 6 Cy. 700 x 2674 16859kW (22921bhp) HSD Engine Co Ltd-South Korea AuxGen: 3 x 850kW a.c Fuel: 4347.0 (r.f.)
9575565 *C6ZB9* -	**SONANGOL HUILA** - **Sonangol Huila Ltd** Stena Bulk LLC SatCom: Inmarsat C 431106611 *Nassau* *Bahamas* MMSI: 311066400 Official number: 7000155	**83,753** 49,262 157,871 T/cm 118.0	Class: AB	**2012-06 Daewoo Shipbuilding & Marine Engineering Co Ltd — Geoje** Yd No: 5351 Loa 274.00 (BB) Br ex 48.04 Dght 17.000 Lbp 264.00 Br md 48.00 Dpth 23.70 Welded, 1 dk	**(A13A2TV) Crude Oil Tanker** Double Hull (13F) Liq: 168,551; Liq (Oil): 168,000 Cargo Heating Coils Compartments: 12 Wing Ta, ER, 2 Wing Slop Ta 3 Cargo Pump (s): 3x3500m³/hr Manifold: Bow/CM: 137.5m	**1 oil engine** driving 1 FP propeller Total Power: 16,850kW (22,909hp) 15.5kn MAN-B&W 6S70MC-C8 1 x 2 Stroke 6 Cy. 700 x 2800 16850kW (22909bhp) Hyundai Heavy Industries Co Ltd-South Korea AuxGen: 3 x 900kW a.c Fuel: 349.0 (d.f.) 3454.0 (r.f.)
9575553 *C62B4* -	**SONANGOL KALANDULA** - **Sonangol Kalandula Ltd** International Tanker Management Holding Ltd (ITM Holding) SatCom: Inmarsat C 431101294 *Nassau* *Bahamas* MMSI: 311035500 Official number: 7000151	**83,753** 49,262 157,955 T/cm 118.0	Class: AB	**2011-10 Daewoo Shipbuilding & Marine Engineering Co Ltd — Geoje** Yd No: 5350 Loa 274.00 (BB) Br ex 48.04 Dght 17.010 Lbp 264.00 Br md 48.00 Dpth 23.70 Welded, 1 dk	**(A13A2TV) Crude Oil Tanker** Double Hull (13F) Liq: 168,000; Liq (Oil): 168,000 Cargo Heating Coils Compartments: 12 Wing Ta, 2 Wing Slop Ta, ER 3 Cargo Pump (s): 3x3500m³/hr Manifold: Bow/CM: 137.5m	**1 oil engine** driving 1 FP propeller Total Power: 16,850kW (22,909hp) 15.5kn MAN-B&W 6S70MC-C8 1 x 2 Stroke 6 Cy. 700 x 2800 16850kW (22909bhp) Hyundai Heavy Industries Co Ltd-South Korea AuxGen: 3 x 900kW a.c Fuel: 349.0 (d.f.) 3454.0 (r.f.)
9315654 *C6UO2* -	**SONANGOL KASSANJE** - **Sonangol Shipping Kassanje Ltd** Stena Bulk LLC *Nassau* *Bahamas* MMSI: 311974000 Official number: 8001012	**83,469** 48,922 158,706 T/cm 118.7	Class: AB	**2005-06 Daewoo Shipbuilding & Marine Engineering Co Ltd — Geoje** Yd No: 5276 Loa 274.00 (BB) Br ex - Dght 17.023 Lbp 264.00 Br md 48.00 Dpth 23.70 Welded, 1 dk	**(A13A2TV) Crude Oil Tanker** Double Hull (13F) Liq: 167,811; Liq (Oil): 167,811 Cargo Heating Coils Compartments: 12 Wing Ta, 2 Wing Slop Ta, ER 3 Cargo Pump (s): 3x3500m³/hr Manifold: Bow/CM: 134m	**1 oil engine** driving 1 FP propeller Total Power: 17,092kW (23,238hp) 15.0kn B&W 6S70MC 1 x 2 Stroke 6 Cy. 700 x 2674 17092kW (23238bhp) Doosan Engine Co Ltd-South Korea AuxGen: 3 x 850kW a.c Fuel: 403.1 (d.f.) 4348.1 (r.f.)
9203772 *C6RO5* -	**SONANGOL KIZOMBA** - **Sonangol Shipping Kizomba Ltd** Stena Bulk LLC SatCom: Inmarsat C 431112510 *Nassau* *Bahamas* MMSI: 311125000 Official number: 8000255	**81,230** 50,687 159,165 T/cm 116.9	Class: AB	**2001-01 Daewoo Shipbuilding & Marine Engineering Co Ltd — Geoje** Yd No: 5154 Loa 274.00 (BB) Br ex - Dght 17.020 Lbp 264.00 Br md 48.00 Dpth 23.20 Welded, 1 dk	**(A13A2TV) Crude Oil Tanker** Double Hull (13F) Liq: 166,684; Liq (Oil): 166,684 Cargo Heating Coils Compartments: 12 Wing Ta, 2 Wing Slop Ta, ER 3 Cargo Pump (s): 3x3500m³/hr Manifold: Bow/CM: 134m	**1 oil engine** driving 1 FP propeller Total Power: 16,858kW (22,920hp) 15.2kn MAN-B&W 6S70MC 1 x 2 Stroke 6 Cy. 700 x 2674 16858kW (22920bhp) HSD Engine Co Ltd-South Korea AuxGen: 3 x 850kW 440/220V 60Hz a.c Fuel: 327.0 (d.f.) 4224.0 (r.f.) 71.0pd
9203760 *C6RH7* -	**SONANGOL LUANDA** - **Sonangol Shipping Luanda Ltd** Stena Bulk LLC SatCom: Inmarsat C 431103610 *Nassau* *Bahamas* MMSI: 311036000 Official number: 8000177	**81,230** 50,687 159,178 T/cm 117.0	Class: AB	**2000-09 Daewoo Heavy Industries Ltd — Geoje** Yd No: 5153 Loa 274.00 (BB) Br ex - Dght 17.020 Lbp 264.00 Br md 48.00 Dpth 23.20 Welded, 1 dk	**(A13A2TV) Crude Oil Tanker** Double Hull (13F) Liq: 166,684; Liq (Oil): 166,684 Cargo Heating Coils Compartments: 12 Wing Ta, 2 Wing Slop Ta, ER 3 Cargo Pump (s): 3x3500m³/hr Manifold: Bow/CM: 134m	**1 oil engine** driving 1 FP propeller Total Power: 16,859kW (22,921hp) 15.2kn B&W 6S70MC 1 x 2 Stroke 6 Cy. 700 x 2674 16859kW (22921bhp) HSD Engine Co Ltd-South Korea AuxGen: 3 x 850kW 440/220V 60Hz a.c Fuel: 326.5 (d.f.) 4307.0 (r.f.) 71.0pd

IMO / Call sign	Name / Owner / Flag	Tonnage	Class	Construction	Type / Cargo	Machinery
9325049 *C6VR3* -	**SONANGOL NAMIBE** - **Sonangol Shipping Namibe Ltd** Stena Bulk LLC SatCom: Inmarsat Mini-M 761119165 *Nassau* *Bahamas* MMSI: 309072000 Official number: 9000209	**83,469** 48,922 158,425 T/cm 118.0	Class: AB	**2007-03 Daewoo Shipbuilding & Marine Engineering Co Ltd — Geoje** Yd No: 5277 Loa 274.00 (BB) Br ex 48.04 Dght 17.000 Lbp 264.00 Br md 48.00 Dpth 23.70 Welded, 1 dk	**(A13A2TV) Crude Oil Tanker** Double Hull (13F) Liq: 167,811; Liq (Oil): 167,811 Cargo Heating Coils Compartments: 12 Wing Ta, 2 Wing Slop Ta, ER 3 Cargo Pump (s): 3x3500m^3/hr Manifold: Bow/CM: 134m	**1 oil engine** driving 1 FP propeller Total Power: 16,860kW (22,923hp) 15.0kn MAN-B&W 6S70MC 1 x 2 Stroke 6 Cy. 700 x 2674 16860kW (22923bhp) Doosan Engine Co Ltd-South Korea AuxGen: 3 x 850kW a.c Fuel: 226.0 (d.f.) 4136.0 (r.f.)
9575577 *C6ZBB* -	**SONANGOL PORTO AMBOIM** - **Sonangol Porto Amboim Ltd** Sociedad Nacional de Combustiveis de Angola (SONANGOL) *Nassau* *Bahamas* MMSI: 311066300 Official number: 7000154	**83,753** 49,262 157,639 T/cm 118.0	Class: AB	**2012-07 Daewoo Shipbuilding & Marine Engineering Co Ltd — Geoje** Yd No: 5352 Loa 274.00 (BB) Br ex 48.04 Dght 17.000 Lbp 264.00 Br md 48.00 Dpth 23.70 Welded, 1 dk	**(A13A2TV) Crude Oil Tanker** Double Hull (13F) Liq: 168,550; Liq (Oil): 168,000 Cargo Heating Coils Compartments: 12 Wing Ta, 2 Wing Slop Ta, ER 3 Cargo Pump (s): 3x3500m^3/hr Manifold: Bow/CM: 137.5m	**1 oil engine** driving 1 FP propeller Total Power: 16,850kW (22,909hp) 15.5kn MAN-B&W 6S70MC-C8 1 x 2 Stroke 6 Cy. 700 x 2800 16850kW (22909bhp) Hyundai Heavy Industries Co Ltd-South Korea AuxGen: 3 x 900kW a.c Fuel: 349.0 (d.f.) 3454.0 (r.f.)
9575541 *C6ZF3* -	**SONANGOL RANGEL** - **Sonangol Rangel Ltd** Sociedad Nacional de Combustiveis de Angola (SONANGOL) SatCom: Inmarsat C 431101242 *Nassau* *Bahamas* MMSI: 311069200 Official number: 8001917	**83,753** 49,262 157,755 T/cm 118.0	Class: AB	**2011-07 Daewoo Shipbuilding & Marine Engineering Co Ltd — Geoje** Yd No: 5349 Loa 274.00 (BB) Br ex 48.04 Dght 17.000 Lbp 264.00 Br md 48.00 Dpth 23.70 Welded, 1 dk	**(A13A2TV) Crude Oil Tanker** Double Hull (13F) Liq: 168,550; Liq (Oil): 168,000 Cargo Heating Coils Compartments: 12 Wing Ta, 2 Wing Slop Ta, 1 Slop Ta, ER 3 Cargo Pump (s): 3x3500m^3/hr Manifold: Bow/CM: 137.5m	**1 oil engine** driving 1 FP propeller Total Power: 16,850kW (22,909hp) 15.5kn MAN-B&W 6S70MC-C8 1 x 2 Stroke 6 Cy. 700 x 2800 16850kW (22909bhp) Hyundai Heavy Industries Co Ltd-South Korea AuxGen: 3 x 900kW a.c Fuel: 349.0 (d.f.) 3454.0 (r.f.)
9475600 *C6YM6* -	**SONANGOL SAMBIZANGA** - **Sonangol Sambizanga Ltd** Sociedad Nacional de Combustiveis de Angola (SONANGOL) *Nassau* *Bahamas* MMSI: 311027900 Official number: 9000343	**104,537** 31,361 89,742 T/cm 106.7	Class: AB	**2011-10 Daewoo Shipbuilding & Marine Engineering Co Ltd — Geoje** Yd No: 2280 Loa 291.08 (BB) Br ex - Dght 11.900 Lbp 280.00 Br md 43.40 Dpth 26.50 Welded, 1 dk	**(A11A2TN) LNG Tanker** Double Hull Liq (Gas): 160,500	**1 Steam Turb** reduction geared to sc. shaft driving 1 FP propeller Total Power: 28,300kW (38,477hp) 19.2kn Kawasaki UA-400 1 x steam Turb 28300kW (38477shp) Kawasaki Heavy Industries Ltd-Japan AuxGen: 5 x 3800kW Fuel: 570.5 (d.f.) 6260.9 (r.f.)
7720063 *ES2358* EK-9801	**SONAR** *ex* Kan *-1998* *ex* Kangilineq *-1995* *ex* Eldborgtral *-1987* **Reyktal Ltd (AS Reyktal)** - *Tallinn* *Estonia* MMSI: 276226000 Official number: 198FB03	**718** 246 413	Class: NV	**1978-10 Tomren Verft AS — Tomrefjord** Yd No: 43 Loa 45.39 (BB) Br ex - Dght 4.300 Lbp 40.99 Br md 9.52 Dpth 6.56 Welded, 2 dks	**(B11A2FT) Trawler** Compartments: 1 Ho, ER 1 Ha: (2.2 x 1.9)ER Ice Capable	**1 oil engine** sr geared to sc. shaft driving 1 CP propeller Total Power: 1,140kW (1,550hp) Normo LDMB-8 1 x 4 Stroke 8 Cy. 250 x 300 1140kW (1550bhp) AS Bergens Mek Verksteder-Norway AuxGen: 1 x 540kW 230V 50Hz a.c, 1 x 112kW 230V 50Hz a.c
7019438 *S2KD* -	**SONAR KAMOL** *ex* Saima IV *-1984* *ex* Masayoshi *-1984* *ex* Masayoshi Maru No. 1 *-1981* **Orient Riverine Transportation Ltd** - *Chittagong* *Bangladesh* Official number: C.160	*537* 337 1,100	Class: (NK)	**1969 Nishi Shipbuilding Co Ltd — Imabari EH** Yd No: 118 Loa 54.01 Br ex 9.22 Dght 4.049 Lbp 49.59 Br md 9.20 Dpth 4.50 Welded, 1 dk	**(A12B2TR) Chemical/Products Tanker** Liq: 1,298; Liq (Oil): 1,298 Compartments: 2 Ta, ER	**1 oil engine** driving 1 FP propeller Total Power: 552kW (750hp) 10.0kn Sumiyoshi S6YDTSS 1 x 4 Stroke 6 Cy. 280 x 420 552kW (750bhp) Sumiyoshi Marine Diesel Co Ltd-Japan
7535066 *S2KS* -	**SONAR TARI** *ex* Hoei Maru No. 3 *-1983* **Alpha Shipping Pvt Ltd** - *Chittagong* *Bangladesh* Official number: C.507	*663* 439 1,688		**1971 Shimoda Dockyard Co. Ltd. — Shimoda** Loa 60.00 Br ex 9.53 Dght 4.153 Lbp 57.00 Br md 9.50 Dpth 4.50 Welded, 1 dk	**(A13B2TP) Products Tanker** Liq: 1,728; Liq (Oil): 1,728 Compartments: 4 Ta, ER	**1 oil engine** driving 1 FP propeller Total Power: 515kW (700hp) 9.0kn Matsui 1 x 4 Stroke 515kW (700bhp) Matsui Iron Works Co Ltd-Japan
8725199 - -	**SONATA** *ex* PTR-50 No. 32 *-1993* - -	**187** 56 77	Class: (RS)	**1987-08 Astrakhanskaya Sudoverf im. "Kirova" — Astrakhan** Yd No: 32 Loa 31.85 Br ex 7.08 Dght 2.100 Lbp 27.80 Br md - Dpth 3.15 Welded, 1 dk	**(B12B2FC) Fish Carrier** Ins: 100 Compartments: 2 Ho	**1 oil engine** geared to sc. shaft driving 1 FP propeller Total Power: 221kW (300hp) 10.2kn Daldizel 6CHNSP18/22-300 1 x 4 Stroke 6 Cy. 180 x 220 221kW (300bhp) Daldizel-Khabarovsk AuxGen: 2 x 25kW Fuel: 14.0 (d.f.)
8948181 *ERCV* -	**SONATA-1** *ex* Ariadna *-2007* *ex* Perm *-2004* **ADF Oil Inc** - *Giurgiulesti* *Moldova* MMSI: 214180322	*1,850* 646 3,438	Class: (RS) (RR)	**1966-06 Zavody Tazkeho Strojarstva (ZTS) — Komarno** Yd No: 1162 Loa 103.58 Br ex 12.40 Dght 4.000 Lbp 100.00 Br md 12.20 Dpth 4.90 Welded, 1 dk	**(A31A2GX) General Cargo Ship** Grain: 3,400 Compartments: 4 Ho, ER 4 Ha: 4 (15.5 x 8.0)ER	**2 oil engines** driving 2 FP propellers Total Power: 772kW (1,050hp) Skoda 6L275PN 2 x 4 Stroke 6 Cy. 275 x 360 each-386kW (525bhp) CKD Praha-Praha AuxGen: 2 x 44kW Fuel: 68.0 (d.f.)
9454242 *V2GD6* -	**SONDERBORG STRAIT** - **ms 'Sonderborg Strait' GmbH & Co KG** Carsten Rehder Schiffsmakler und Reederei GmbH & Co KG *Saint John's* *Antigua & Barbuda* MMSI: 305904000	**12,514** 5,339 14,222	Class: GL	**2012-11 Nanjing Wujiazui Shipbuilding Co Ltd — Nanjing JS** Yd No: WJZ034 Loa 158.01 (BB) Br ex - Dght 8.600 Lbp 148.50 Br md 23.50 Dpth 11.90 Welded, 1 dk	**(A33A2CC) Container Ship (Fully Cellular)** TEU 1085 C Ho 372 TEU C Dk 713 incl 250 ref C Ice Capable	**1 oil engine** driving 1 FP propeller Total Power: 9,720kW (13,215hp) 18.5kn Wartsila 6RT-flex50 1 x 2 Stroke 6 Cy. 500 x 2050 9720kW (13215bhp) Hitachi Zosen Corp-Japan Thrusters: 1 Tunnel thruster (f)
7731608 *LKPV* -	**SONDMORINGEN** *ex* Norengen *-2007* **Arfinn John Klungsoyr Karlsen** - *Aalesund* *Norway* MMSI: 257566500	**204** 61 -		**1967-01 Langsten Slip & Baatbyggeri AS — Tomrefjord** Yd No: 33 Loa 28.96 Br ex 6.51 Dght - Lbp - Br md - Dpth - Welded, 1 dk	**(B11B2FV) Fishing Vessel**	**1 oil engine** driving 1 FP propeller Total Power: 338kW (460hp) Callesen 4-427-DOT 1 x 4 Stroke 4 Cy. 270 x 400 338kW (460bhp) (new engine 1971) Aabenraa Motorfabrik, HeinrichCallesen A/S-Denmark
7531735 *TC7825* -	**SONDUREN-2** - **Government of The Republic of Turkey (Kiyi Emniyeti ve Gemicilik Kurtarma Isletmesi Genel Mudurlugu Gemicilik Kur Dairesi Bsk)** Government of The Republic of Turkey (Turkiye Cumhuriyeti Devlet Demir Yollari - Haydarpasa Liman Isletmesi) (Turkish Republic State Railways - Haydarpasa Harbour Management) *Mersin* *Turkey* MMSI: 271010246 Official number: 4987	**295** 167 188	Class: (TL) (AB)	**1981-08 Denizcilik Bankasi T.A.O. — Alaybey, Izmir** Yd No: 37 Loa 36.23 Br ex 9.30 Dght 3.869 Lbp 32.80 Br md 8.91 Dpth 5.11 Welded, 1 dk	**(B32A2ST) Tug**	**1 oil engine** sr geared to sc. shaft driving 1 CP propeller Total Power: 1,824kW (2,480hp) 13.0kn Alpha 16V23L-VO 1 x Vee 4 Stroke 16 Cy. 225 x 300 1824kW (2480bhp) B&W Alpha Diesel A/S-Denmark AuxGen: 2 x 80kW a.c Fuel: 56.0 (d.f.)
7531670 *TC7122* -	**SONDUREN-3** - **Government of The Republic of Turkey (Kiyi Emniyeti ve Gemicilik Kurtarma Isletmesi Genel Mudurlugu Gemicilik Kur Dairesi Bsk)** - *Istanbul* *Turkey* MMSI: 271010112	*295* 166 188	Class: TL (AB)	**1982-03 Denizcilik Bankasi T.A.O. — Alaybey, Izmir** Yd No: 38 Loa 36.23 Br ex 9.30 Dght 3.869 Lbp 32.80 Br md 8.91 Dpth 5.11 Welded, 1 dk	**(B32A2ST) Tug**	**1 oil engine** sr geared to sc. shaft driving 1 CP propeller Total Power: 1,824kW (2,480hp) 13.0kn Alpha 16V23L-VO 1 x Vee 4 Stroke 16 Cy. 225 x 300 1824kW (2480bhp) B&W Alpha Diesel A/S-Denmark AuxGen: 2 x 80kW a.c Fuel: 56.0 (d.f.)
7531711 *TC6204* -	**SONDUREN-4** - **Government of The Republic of Turkey (Kiyi Emniyeti ve Gemicilik Kurtarma Isletmesi Genel Mudurlugu Gemicilik Kur Dairesi Bsk)** - *Istanbul* *Turkey* MMSI: 271010089 Official number: 7674	*295* 166 188	Class: TL (AB)	**1982-04 Denizcilik Bankasi T.A.O. — Alaybey, Izmir** Yd No: 39 Loa 36.23 Br ex 9.30 Dght 3.869 Lbp 32.80 Br md 8.91 Dpth 5.11 Welded, 1 dk	**(B32A2ST) Tug**	**1 oil engine** sr geared to sc. shaft driving 1 CP propeller Total Power: 1,824kW (2,480hp) 13.0kn Alpha 16V23L-VO 1 x Vee 4 Stroke 16 Cy. 225 x 300 1824kW (2480bhp) B&W Alpha Diesel A/S-Denmark AuxGen: 2 x 80kW a.c Fuel: 56.0 (d.f.)

7531723 *TC8920* -	**SONDUREN-5** **Government of The Republic of Turkey (Kiyi Emniyeti ve Gemicilik Kurtarma Isletmesi Genel Mudurlugu Gemicilik Kur Dairesi Bsk)** - *Istanbul* *Turkey* MMSI: 271010091 Official number: 3915	*295* 166 188	Class: TL (AB)	**1982-12 Denizcilik Bankasi T.A.O. — Alaybey, Izmir** Yd No: 40 Loa 36.23 Br ex 9.30 Dght 3.869 Lbp 33.98 Br md 8.91 Dpth 3.90 Welded, 1 dk	**(B32A2ST) Tug**	**1 oil engine** sr geared to sc. shaft driving 1 CP propeller Total Power: 1,824kW (2,480hp) 13.0kn Alpha 16V23L-VO 1 x Vee 4 Stroke 16 Cy. 225 x 300 1824kW (2480bhp) B&W Alpha Diesel A/S-Denmark AuxGen: 2 x 80kW a.c Fuel: 56.0 (d.f.)
7531694 *TC9566* -	**SONDUREN-6** **Government of The Republic of Turkey (Kiyi Emniyeti ve Gemicilik Kurtarma Isletmesi Genel Mudurlugu Gemicilik Kur Dairesi Bsk)** - *Izmir* *Turkey* MMSI: 271035008 Official number: 9301	*295* 166 188	Class: TL (AB)	**1983-03 Denizcilik Bankasi T.A.O. — Alaybey, Izmir** Yd No: 41 Loa 36.23 Br ex 9.30 Dght 3.869 Lbp 32.80 Br md 8.91 Dpth 5.11 Welded, 1 dk	**(B32A2ST) Tug**	**1 oil engine** sr geared to sc. shaft driving 1 CP propeller Total Power: 1,824kW (2,480hp) 13.0kn Alpha 16V23L-VO 1 x Vee 4 Stroke 16 Cy. 225 x 300 1824kW (2480bhp) B&W Alpha Diesel A/S-Denmark AuxGen: 2 x 80kW a.c Fuel: 56.0 (d.f.)
7531656 *TC9392* -	**SONDUREN-7** **Government of The Republic of Turkey (Kiyi Emniyeti ve Gemicilik Kurtarma Isletmesi Genel Mudurlugu Gemicilik Kur Dairesi Bsk)** - *Istanbul* *Turkey* MMSI: 271010014 Official number: 4307	*295* 166 188	Class: TL (AB)	**1984-03 Denizcilik Bankasi T.A.O. — Alaybey, Izmir** Yd No: 42 Loa 36.23 Br ex 9.30 Dght 3.869 Lbp 32.80 Br md 8.91 Dpth 5.11 Welded, 1 dk	**(B32A2ST) Tug**	**1 oil engine** sr geared to sc. shaft driving 1 CP propeller Total Power: 1,824kW (2,480hp) 13.0kn Alpha 16V23L-VO 1 x Vee 4 Stroke 16 Cy. 225 x 300 1824kW (2480bhp) B&W Alpha Diesel A/S-Denmark AuxGen: 2 x 80kW a.c Fuel: 56.0 (d.f.)
7531682 *TC7826* -	**SONDUREN-8** **Government of The Republic of Turkey (Iskenderun Liman Isletmesi)** - *Iskenderun* *Turkey* MMSI: 271010852 Official number: 5502	**290** 152 -	Class: TL (AB)	**1986-06 Turkiye Gemi Sanayii A.S. — Alaybey, Izmir** Yd No: 43 Loa 36.23 Br ex 9.30 Dght 3.500 Lbp 33.61 Br md 8.91 Dpth 3.60 Welded, 1 dk	**(B32A2ST) Tug**	**1 oil engine** sr geared to sc. shaft driving 1 CP propeller Total Power: 1,712kW (2,328hp) 13.0kn Alpha 16V23L-VO 1 x Vee 4 Stroke 16 Cy. 225 x 300 1712kW (2328bhp) MAN B&W Diesel A/S-Denmark AuxGen: 2 x 80kW a.c Fuel: 56.0 (d.f.)
7531709 *TC6576* -	**SONDUREN-9** **Government of The Republic of Turkey (Kiyi Emniyeti ve Gemicilik Kurtarma Isletmesi Genel Mudurlugu Gemicilik Kur Dairesi Bsk)** Government of The Republic of Turkey (Turkiye Cumhuriyeti Devlet Demir Yollari - Haydarpasa Liman Isletmesi) (Turkish Republic State Railways - Haydarpasa Harbour Management) *Istanbul* *Turkey* MMSI: 271010853 Official number: 5081	**299** 126 -	Class: TL (AB)	**1982-08 Denizcilik Bankasi T.A.O. — Haskoy, Istanbul** Yd No: 85 Loa 36.23 Br ex 9.45 Dght 4.220 Lbp 32.80 Br md 8.91 Dpth 5.11 Welded, 1 dk	**(B32A2ST) Tug**	**1 oil engine** sr geared to sc. shaft driving 1 CP propeller Total Power: 1,824kW (2,480hp) 13.0kn Alpha 16V23L-VO 1 x Vee 4 Stroke 16 Cy. 225 x 300 1824kW (2480bhp) B&W Alpha Diesel A/S-Denmark AuxGen: 2 x 80kW a.c Fuel: 51.0 (d.f.)
7531644 *TC6663* -	**SONDUREN-10** **Government of The Republic of Turkey (Kiyi Emniyeti ve Gemicilik Kurtarma Isletmesi Genel Mudurlugu Gemicilik Kur Dairesi Bsk)** - *Istanbul* *Turkey* MMSI: 271002400 Official number: 5523	*394* 82 -	Class: TL (AB)	**1987-01 Turkiye Gemi Sanayii A.S. — Haskoy, Istanbul** Yd No: 88 Loa 36.25 Br ex - Dght 3.652 Lbp 33.00 Br md 8.91 Dpth 5.11 Welded, 1 dk	**(B32A2ST) Tug**	**1 oil engine** sr geared to sc. shaft driving 1 CP propeller Total Power: 1,824kW (2,480hp) 13.0kn Alpha 16V23L-VO 1 x Vee 4 Stroke 16 Cy. 225 x 300 1824kW (2480bhp) MAN B&W Diesel A/S-Denmark AuxGen: 2 x 80kW a.c Fuel: 50.0 (d.f.)
7531747 *TC6583* -	**SONDUREN-12** **TCDD Isletmesi Genel Mudurlugu** - *Istanbul* *Turkey* MMSI: 271010819 Official number: 5186	*394* 82 -	Class: (TL) (AB)	**1982-07 Denizcilik Bankasi T.A.O. — Halic, Istanbul** Yd No: 205 Loa 36.45 Br ex - Dght 4.220 Lbp 32.31 Br md 8.91 Dpth 5.11 Welded, 1 dk	**(B32A2ST) Tug**	**1 oil engine** sr geared to sc. shaft driving 1 CP propeller Total Power: 1,824kW (2,480hp) 13.0kn Alpha 16V23L-VO 1 x Vee 4 Stroke 16 Cy. 225 x 300 1824kW (2480bhp) B&W Alpha Diesel A/S-Denmark AuxGen: 2 x 80kW a.c Fuel: 53.0 (d.f.)
8893439 *3WCZ* -	**SONG BIEN 04** **Water Way Transport Co No 3 (Cong Ty Van Tai Thuy 3)** - *Haiphong* *Vietnam*	**166** 86 200	Class: (VR)	**1989 Kien An Shipbuilding Works — Haiphong** Loa 36.35 Br ex 7.46 Dght 1.950 Lbp 33.50 Br md - Dpth 2.50 Welded, 1 dk	**(A31A2GX) General Cargo Ship**	**1 oil engine** reduction geared to sc. shaft driving 1 FP propeller Total Power: 99kW (135hp) 8.0kn Skoda 6L160 1 x 4 Stroke 6 Cy. 160 x 225 99kW (135bhp) CKD Praha-Praha
8930330 *3WDF* -	**SONG BIEN 08** **Thanh Long Co Ltd (Cong Ty Tnhh Thanh Long)** *Haiphong* *Vietnam*	**129** 61 150	Class: (VR)	**1990 at Quang Ninh** Loa 40.25 Br ex - Dght 1.200 Lbp - Br md 8.20 Dpth 2.00 Welded, 1 dk	**(A31A2GX) General Cargo Ship** Bale: 380 Compartments: 2 Ho 2 Ha: (9.6 x 5.0) (10.8 x 5.0)	**1 oil engine** reduction geared to sc. shaft driving 1 FP propeller Total Power: 99kW (135hp) 8.0kn Skoda 6L160 1 x 4 Stroke 6 Cy. 160 x 225 99kW (135bhp) (made 1984) CKD Praha-Praha AuxGen: 1 x 5kW a.c
8894160 - -	**SONG BIEN 10** **Water Way Transport Co No 3 (Cong Ty Van Tai Thuy 3)** - *Haiphong* *Vietnam*	**130** 61 150	Class: (VR)	**1989 Song Cam Shipyard — Haiphong** Loa 40.25 Br ex - Dght 1.900 Lbp 38.00 Br md 6.20 Dpth 2.80 Welded, 1 dk	**(A31A2GX) General Cargo Ship** Compartments: 2 Ho, ER 2 Ha: 2 (9.0 x 4.0)ER	**1 oil engine** reduction geared to sc. shaft driving 1 FP propeller Total Power: 99kW (135hp) 9.0kn Skoda 6L160 1 x 4 Stroke 6 Cy. 160 x 225 99kW (135bhp) CKD Praha-Praha
8894110 - -	**SONG BIEN 16** **Water Way Transport Co No 3 (Cong Ty Van Tai Thuy 3)** - *Haiphong* *Vietnam*	*129* - 150	Class: (VR)	**1990 at Haiphong** Loa 39.10 Br ex - Dght 1.200 Lbp 38.00 Br md 8.20 Dpth 2.00 Welded, 1 dk	**(A31A2GX) General Cargo Ship**	**1 oil engine** reduction geared to sc. shaft driving 1 FP propeller Total Power: 99kW (135hp) 7.0kn Skoda 6L160 1 x 4 Stroke 6 Cy. 160 x 225 99kW (135bhp) (made 1983) CKD Praha-Praha
8925660 *3WEP* -	**SONG BIEN 20** **Thanh Dat Co Ltd (Cong Ty Tnhh Thanh Dat)** - *Haiphong* *Vietnam*	**160** 63 150	Class: (VR)	**1991 at Haiphong** Loa 39.10 Br ex - Dght 1.200 Lbp 38.00 Br md 8.00 Dpth 2.00 Welded, 1 dk	**(A31A2GX) General Cargo Ship** Bale: 334 Compartments: 2 Ho	**1 oil engine** reduction geared to sc. shaft driving 1 FP propeller Total Power: 99kW (135hp) Skoda 6L160 1 x 4 Stroke 6 Cy. 160 x 225 99kW (135bhp) CKD Praha-Praha
8132421 - -	**SONG CHANG** *ex Kakuho Maru No. 8 -2010* **Song Chong-Yun** *Busan* *South Korea*	*191* - 350		**1981-12 K.K. Tago Zosensho — Nishi-Izu** Yd No: 180 Loa 33.80 Br ex - Dght 3.240 Lbp 30.00 Br md 7.20 Dpth 3.38 Welded, 1 dk	**(A13B2TP) Products Tanker**	**1 oil engine** driving 1 FP propeller Total Power: 228kW (310hp) 9.0kn Sumiyoshi S623TE 1 x 4 Stroke 6 Cy. 230 x 400 228kW (310bhp) Sumiyoshi Tekkosho-Japan
8656465 *XVCI* -	**SONG CHANH 36** **Song Chanh Maritime Transport JSC** - *Haiphong* *Vietnam* MMSI: 574999640	**1,598** 1,062 3,090	Class: VR	**2009-07 Song Chanh Shipbuilding JSC — Yen Hung** Loa 79.80 Br ex 12.82 Dght 5.040 Lbp 74.80 Br md 12.80 Dpth 6.08 Welded, 1 dk	**(A31A2GX) General Cargo Ship** Grain: 3,498 Compartments: 2 Ho, ER 2 Ha: ER 2 (20.4 x 8.4)	**1 oil engine** reduction geared to sc. shaft driving 1 FP propeller Total Power: 720kW (979hp) 10.0kn Chinese Std. Type CW8200ZC 1 x 4 Stroke 8 Cy. 200 x 270 720kW (979bhp) Weichai Power Co Ltd-China AuxGen: 2 x 76kW 380V a.c
9631917 *XVRD* -	**SONG CHANH 66** **Song Chanh Maritime Transport JSC** - *Haiphong* *Vietnam* Official number: VN-3232-VT	**999** 618 1,926	Class: VR	**2011-04 Song Chanh Shipbuilding JSC — Yen Hung** Yd No: TKT-31-06 Loa 67.50 Br ex 11.02 Dght 4.500 Lbp 63.70 Br md 11.00 Dpth 5.30 Welded, 1 dk	**(A31A2GX) General Cargo Ship** Grain: 2,012 Compartments: 2 Ho, ER 2 Ha: (14.6 x 7.3)ER (15.4 x 7.3)	**1 oil engine** reduction geared to sc. shaft driving 1 FP propeller Total Power: 600kW (816hp) 11.0kn Chinese Std. Type Z8170ZL 1 x 4 Stroke 8 Cy. 170 x 200 600kW (816bhp) Zibo Diesel Engine Factory-China AuxGen: 2 x 60kW 390V a.c

IMO / Call sign	Name / Owner	Tonnage	Class	Builder / Dimensions	Type / Capacity	Machinery
9111034 *3WRU8* -	**SONG CHAU 1** *ex* Terban 1 *-2010* **Song Chau Petro JSC** - SatCom: Inmarsat C 457489610 *Saigon* *Vietnam* MMSI: 574896000 Official number: VNSG-1994-TD	**2,934** 1,744 4,920	Class: VR (AB)	**1996-06 Kepphil Shipyard Inc — Bauan** Yd No: 69 Loa 98.50 (BB) Br ex 15.53 Dght 5.624 Lbp 92.00 Br md 15.50 Dpth 7.50 Welded, 1 dk	**(A13B2TP) Products Tanker** Double Hull Liq: 6,000; Liq (Oil): 6,000 Compartments: 10 Ta, ER 2 Cargo Pump (s): 2x500m³/hr	**1 oil engine** with flexible couplings & sr reverse geared to sc. shaft driving 1 FP propeller Total Power: 2,266kW (3,081hp) Caterpillar 3608TA 1 x 4 Stroke 8 Cy. 280 x 300 2266kW (3081bhp) Caterpillar Inc-USA
9218703 *3WDF9* -	**SONG CHAU 3** *ex* Jasa Ketiga *-2011* *ex* Samho Family *-2002* **Song Chau Petro JSC** - *Saigon* *Vietnam* MMSI: 574001050 Official number: VNSG-2074-TD	**3,321** 1,858 4,999	Class: NK VR (BV) (AB) (KR)	**2000-10 Haedong Shipbuilding Co Ltd — Tongyeong** Yd No: 1028 Loa 102.25 (BB) Br ex 15.72 Dght 6.132 Lbp 95.01 Br md 15.60 Dpth 7.80 Welded, 1 dk	**(A13B2TP) Products Tanker** Double Hull (13F)	**1 oil engine** driving 1 FP propeller Total Power: 2,574kW (3,500hp) Hanshin LH41LA 1 x 4 Stroke 6 Cy. 410 x 800 2574kW (3500bhp) The Hanshin Diesel Works Ltd-Japan AuxGen: 2 x 430kW a.c Fuel: 277.0
9024451 - -	**SONG DAO** - **Financial Leasing Company II of Vietnam Bank for Agriculture & Rural Development (Financial Leasing Co II)** - *Saigon* *Vietnam*	**499** 270 840	Class: VR	**2002-09 An Phu Works — Ho Chi Minh City** Yd No: THK-01-03NC Loa 49.18 Br ex 9.70 Dght 2.900 Lbp 46.25 Br md 9.50 Dpth 3.50 Welded, 1 dk	**(A31A2GX) General Cargo Ship** Bale: 855 Compartments: 1 Ho, ER 1 Ha: ER (32.5 x 7.7)	**2 oil engines** reduction geared to sc. shafts driving 2 FP propellers Total Power: 442kW (600hp) 12.0kn Niigata NSF-G 2 x 4 Stroke 6 Cy. 132 x 160 each-221kW (300bhp) (made 1974, fitted 2002) Niigata Engineering Co Ltd-Japan AuxGen: 1 x 13kW 220V a.c
8869086 - -	**SONG DIEM 02** *ex* Tra Ly 02 *-1996* **Song Diem-Thai Binh Maritrans Enterprise (Xi Nghiep Van Tai Song Diem- Thai Binh)** - *Haiphong* *Vietnam* Official number: VN-1073-VT	**204** 105 323	Class: (VR)	**1985 Thai Binh Mechanical Works — Thai Binh** Lengthened & Deepened-2000 Loa 40.85 Br ex 7.32 Dght 2.250 Lbp 37.84 Br md 7.10 Dpth 2.80 Welded, 1 dk	**(A31A2GX) General Cargo Ship** Grain: 311 Compartments: 2 Ho, ER 2 Ha: 2 (7.0 x 4.0)ER	**1 oil engine** reduction geared to sc. shaft driving 1 FP propeller Total Power: 99kW (135hp) 8.5kn Skoda 6L160 1 x 4 Stroke 6 Cy. 160 x 225 99kW (135bhp) CKD Praha-Praha AuxGen: 1 x 6kW a.c
8869036 - -	**SONG DIEM 05** *ex* Tra Ly 08 *-1996* **Song Diem-Thai Binh Maritrans Enterprise (Xi Nghiep Van Tai Song Diem- Thai Binh)** - *Haiphong* *Vietnam* Official number: VN-1079-VT	**154** 88 200	Class: VR	**1989 Thai Binh Mechanical Works — Thai Binh** Loa 36.35 Br ex 7.22 Dght 1.950 Lbp 33.75 Br md 7.00 Dpth 2.50 Welded, 1 dk	**(A31A2GX) General Cargo Ship** Grain: 311 Compartments: 2 Ho, ER 2 Ha: 2 (7.0 x 4.0)ER	**1 oil engine** reduction geared to sc. shaft driving 1 FP propeller Total Power: 99kW (135hp) 8.5kn S.K.L. 4NVD26-2 1 x 4 Stroke 4 Cy. 180 x 260 99kW (135bhp) VEB Schwermaschinenbau "KarlLiebknecht" (SKL)-Magdeburg AuxGen: 1 x 6kW a.c
8894342 - -	**SONG DIEM 09** - **Song Diem-Thai Binh Maritrans Enterprise (Xi Nghiep Van Tai Song Diem- Thai Binh)** - *Haiphong* *Vietnam* Official number: VN-1080-VT	**173** 89 200	Class: (VR)	**1994 Thai Binh Mechanical Works — Thai Binh** Loa 36.35 Br ex 7.18 Dght 1.950 Lbp 33.25 Br md 7.16 Dpth 2.70 Welded, 1 dk	**(A31A2GX) General Cargo Ship**	**1 oil engine** reduction geared to sc. shaft driving 1 FP propeller Total Power: 99kW (135hp) Skoda 6L160 1 x 4 Stroke 6 Cy. 160 x 225 99kW (135bhp) CKD Praha-Praha
8416891 *XVSJ* -	**SONG DINH 01** *ex* Neftegaz-32 *-1987* **Marine Transport & Diving Service Division VIETSOVPETRO Vietnam Soviet Joint Venture Corp** - SatCom: Inmarsat C 457408210 *Saigon* *Vietnam* MMSI: 574082072 Official number: VNSG-1206K-TH	**2,140** 642 1,382	Class: VR (RS)	**1985-10 Stocznia Gdanska im Lenina — Gdansk** Yd No: B92/58 Loa 81.18 Br ex 16.30 Dght 4.940 Lbp 71.46 Br md 15.96 Dpth 7.20 Welded, 2 dks	**(B21B20T) Offshore Tug/Supply Ship**	**2 oil engines** reduction geared to sc. shafts driving 2 CP propellers Total Power: 5,300kW (7,206hp) 13.0kn Sulzer 6ZL40/48 2 x 4 Stroke 6 Cy. 400 x 480 each-2650kW (3603bhp) Zaklady Urzadzen Technicznych'Zgoda' SA-Poland AuxGen: 3 x 384kW 400V 50Hz a.c Thrusters: 1 Thwart. FP thruster (f) Fuel: 359.0
8839031 - -	**SONG DOC 01** - **Hau Giang Fishery & Sea Products Processing Co (HGFS) (Cong Ty Khai Thac Va Che Bien Thuy San Hau Giang)** - *Saigon* *Vietnam*	*145* 80 100	Class: (VR)	**1987 at Ho Chi Minh City** Loa 26.70 Br ex - Dght 2.600 Lbp - Br md 6.80 Dpth 3.40 Welded, 1 dk	**(A34A2GR) Refrigerated Cargo Ship**	**1 oil engine** reduction geared to sc. shaft driving 1 FP propeller Total Power: 382kW (519hp) 7.0kn Caterpillar 3412TA 1 x Vee 4 Stroke 12 Cy. 137 x 152 382kW (519bhp) Caterpillar Inc-USA AuxGen: 1 x 65kW a.c, 1 x 42kW a.c
8801280 *3ERK5* -	**SONG DOC PRIDE MV 19** *ex* Ocean Ride *-2008* *ex* Ocean Pride *-2007* *ex* Cabo Tamar *-2004* *ex* Reliable Energy *-1996* *ex* Cabo de Hornos *-1991* **Song Doc MV 19 BV** Modec Management Services Pte Ltd SatCom: Inmarsat C 437008010 *Panama* *Panama* MMSI: 370080000 Official number: 3428708A	**40,103** 13,532 62,482 T/cm 64.3	Class: AB (LR) ✠ Classed LR until 5/3/08	**1990-12 Hudong Shipyard — Shanghai** Yd No: 1182 Converted From: Crude Oil/Products Tanker-2007 Loa 224.64 (BB) Br ex 32.24 Dght 12.751 Lbp 217.00 Br md 32.20 Dpth 19.60 Welded, 1 dk	**(B22E20F) FPSO, Oil** Double Sides Entire Compartment Length Liq: 59,620; Liq (Oil): 74,176 Cargo Heating Coils	**1 oil engine** driving 1 FP propeller Total Power: 9,195kW (12,502hp) 12.5kn B&W 6L60MC 1 x 2 Stroke 6 Cy. 600 x 1944 9195kW (12502bhp) Hudong Shipyard-China AuxGen: 3 x 600kW 440V 60Hz a.c Boilers: AuxB (Comp) 11.7kgf/cm² (11.5bar), AuxB (o.f.) 18.4kgf/cm² (18.0bar)
9400722 *3WTP* -	**SONG GIANH** - **Vinashin Ocean Shipping Co Ltd** - SatCom: Inmarsat C 457407410 *Haiphong* *Vietnam* MMSI: 574074000	**13,365** 4,144 12,336	Class: VR	**2007-02 Nam Trieu Shipbuilding Industry Co. Ltd. — Haiphong** Yd No: H-165 Loa 180.69 Br ex - Dght 6.000 Lbp 156.00 Br md 25.05 Dpth 12.00 Welded, 1 dk	**(A38B2GB) Barge Carrier**	**2 oil engines** reduction geared to sc. shafts driving 2 FP propellers Total Power: 3,530kW (4,800hp) 13.0kn Guangzhou 8320ZC 2 x 4 Stroke 8 Cy. 320 x 440 each-1765kW (2400bhp) Guangzhou Diesel Engine Factory CoLtd-China
9022582 *XVFO* -	**SONG GIANH 09** *ex* Dai Duong 17 *-2010* *ex* Minh Tuan 18 *-2005* *ex* ND 0694 *-1999* **Thang Loi Construction Co Ltd** - *Haiphong* *Vietnam* MMSI: 574561000 Official number: VN-1330-VT	**252** 164 475	Class: VR	**1996-01 189 Company — Haiphong** Loa 45.50 Br ex 7.48 Dght 2.550 Lbp 42.65 Br md 7.24 Dpth 3.20 Welded, 1 dk	**(A31A2GX) General Cargo Ship** Grain: 640; Bale: 593 Compartments: 2 Ho, ER 2 Ha: (9.5 x 4.3)ER (8.5 x 4.3)	**2 oil engines** driving 2 FP propellers Total Power: 239kW (325hp) 8.0kn Skoda 6L160 1 x 4 Stroke 6 Cy. 160 x 225 99kW (135bhp) (made 1988) CKD Praha-Praha Skoda 6L160PN 1 x 4 Stroke 6 Cy. 160 x 225 140kW (190bhp) (made 1995) CKD Praha-Praha AuxGen: 1 x 12kW 220V a.c
8106800 *HMYL5* -	**SONG GWANG RYON** *ex* Jin Asia *-2003* *ex* Tsurugi *-1999* *ex* Ken Wood *-1990* *ex* Goddess *-1987* **Korea 56 Trading Co** - *Songnim* *North Korea* MMSI: 445196000 Official number: 3001855	**2,393** 1,594 4,661	Class: KC (KR) (NK)	**1980-11 K.K. Imai Seisakusho — Kamijima** Yd No: 210 Loa 88.25 Br ex - Dght 6.429 Lbp 82.00 Br md 15.20 Dpth 7.60 Welded, 1 dk	**(A31A2GX) General Cargo Ship** Grain: 5,518; Bale: 5,018 2 Ha: (15.1 x 8.5) (26.0 x 8.5)ER Derricks: 3x15t	**1 oil engine** driving 1 FP propeller Total Power: 1,692kW (2,300hp) 11.0kn Akasaka DM38AK 1 x 4 Stroke 6 Cy. 380 x 600 1692kW (2300bhp) Akasaka Tekkosho KK (Akasaka DieselLtd)-Japan AuxGen: 2 x 104kW 450V a.c
8520381 *XUGV6* -	**SONG HAE** *ex* Kouros V *-2010* *ex* Green Space *-2007* *ex* Sungreen *-2005* *ex* Vilma VIII *-2002* *ex* Havelland *-1999* **Carbuncle Business Co Ltd** Shenghao Marine (Hong Kong) Ltd *Phnom Penh* *Cambodia* MMSI: 515254000	**13,371** 6,858 17,088 T/cm 30.0	Class: (LR) (GL) (DS) ✠ Classed LR until 25/4/88	**1987-01 VEB Schiffswerft Neptun — Rostock** Yd No: 204/1464 Loa 158.07 (BB) Br ex 23.09 Dght 10.102 Lbp 146.01 Br md 23.06 Dpth 13.42 Welded, 2 dks	**(A31A2GX) General Cargo Ship** Grain: 22,284; Bale: 20,975 TEU 928 C.Ho 373 TEU C Dk 550 TEU incl 66 ref C. Compartments: 4 Ho, ER, 5 Tw Dk 7 Ha: (12.7 x 10.8)Tappered 2 (25.3 x 7.7)2 (25.3 x 10.1) (12.7 x 7.7) (12.7 x 10.1)ER Cranes: 2,1 Ice Capable	**1 oil engine** driving 1 CP propeller Total Power: 7,598kW (10,330hp) 16.8kn MAN K5SZ70/125BL 1 x 2 Stroke 5 Cy. 700 x 1250 7598kW (10330bhp) VEB Dieselmotorenwerk Rostock-Rostock AuxGen: 1 x 1000kW 390V 50Hz a.c, 2 x 684kW 390V 50Hz a.c, 1 x 408kW 390V 50Hz a.c Thrusters: 1 Thwart. CP thruster (f) Fuel: 290.0 (d.f.) 900.0 (r.f.) 35.0pd
9155327 *BOHO* -	**SONG HAI** - **COSCO Bulk Carrier Co Ltd (COSCO BULK)** - SatCom: Inmarsat B 341221210 *Tianjin* *China* MMSI: 412212000	**27,585** 14,848 47,500 T/cm 53.0	Class: CC	**1998-07 Hudong Shipbuilding Group — Shanghai** Yd No: H1247A Loa 189.94 (BB) Br ex - Dght 11.700 Lbp 180.00 Br md 32.20 Dpth 16.60 Welded, 1 dk	**(A21A2BC) Bulk Carrier** Grain: 57,104; Bale: 55,962 Compartments: 5 Ho, ER 5 Ha: (16.0 x 15.0)4 (17.6 x 15.0)ER Cranes: 4x30t	**1 oil engine** driving 1 FP propeller Total Power: 7,330kW (9,966hp) 13.8kn B&W 6L50MC 1 x 2 Stroke 6 Cy. 500 x 1620 7330kW (9966bhp) Hudong Shipyard-China

9224013 - -	**SONG HAN** **Da Nang Port (Cang Da Nang)** - *Da Nang* *Vietnam* Official number: VNDN-175-LD	**180** 54 178	Class: VR (NK)	**2000-03 Forward Shipbuilding Enterprise Sdn Bhd — Sibu** Yd No: 71 Loa 26.00 Br ex 8.20 Dght 3.012 Lbp 23.50 Br md 7.92 Dpth 3.65 Welded, 1 dk	**(B32A2ST) Tug**	**2 oil engines** reduction geared to sc. shafts driving 2 FP propellers Total Power: 1,268kW (1,724hp) 10.0kn Cummins KTA-38-M0 2 x Vee 4 Stroke 12 Cy. 159 x 159 each-634kW (862bhp) Cummins Engine Co Inc-USA Fuel: 150.0 (d.f.)
8868410 *XVOM* -	**SONG HIEU 01** **Song Thu Co of Region 5 of Army Command (Cong Ty Song Tha Quan Khu V)** - *Da Nang* *Vietnam*	**130** 61 180	Class: (VR)	**1988 at Haiphong** Loa 35.40 Br ex - Dght 2.100 Lbp - Br md 6.50 Dpth 2.90 Welded, 1 dk	**(A31A2GX) General Cargo Ship** Compartments: 2 Ho, ER 2 Ha: 2 (7.0 x 4.0)ER	**1 oil engine** reduction geared to sc. shaft driving 1 FP propeller Total Power: 132kW (179hp) 10.0kn Gardner 6LXB 1 x 4 Stroke 6 Cy. 121 x 152 132kW (179bhp) L. Gardner & Sons Ltd.-Manchester
8922412 *HMYB3* -	**SONG HOA 2** *ex* Li Yuan *-2002* *ex* Chang Da *-1999* *ex* Yun Da *-1996* *ex* Stream *-1993* *ex* Sun-Beam *-1992* **Korea Solsong Shipping Co** - *Nampho* *North Korea* MMSI: 445370000 Official number: 3900147	**1,584** 476 2,013	Class: KC (CC) (GL)	**1989-11 VEB Elbewerften Boizenburg/Rosslau — Rosslau** Yd No: 352 Loa 82.86 Br ex - Dght 3.810 Lbp 78.65 Br md 11.60 Dpth 4.00 Welded, 1 dk	**(A31A2GX) General Cargo Ship** Grain: 1,986; Bale: 1,940 TEU 70 C.Ho 34/20' C.Dk 36/20' incl. 10 ref C. Compartments: 2 Ho, ER 2 Ha: 2 (19.6 x 9.2)ER	**2 oil engines** dr reverse geared to sc. shafts driving 2 FP propellers Total Power: 882kW (1,200hp) 11.2kn S.K.L. 8VD36/24A-1 2 x 4 Stroke 8 Cy. 240 x 360 each-441kW (600bhp) VEB Schwermaschinenbau "KarlLiebknecht" (SKL)-Magdeburg AuxGen: 2 x 100kW 380V a.c
9622320 *3WBK9* -	**SONG HONG 04** **Bui Van Nha** - *Saigon* *Vietnam*	**299** 90 348	Class: VR	**2010-10 in Vietnam** Loa 32.35 Br ex 9.20 Dght 3.600 Lbp 29.85 Br md 9.00 Dpth 4.50 Welded, 1 dk	**(B32A2ST) Tug**	**2 oil engines** reduction geared to sc. shafts driving 2 FP propellers Total Power: 2,984kW (4,058hp) Cummins KTA-50-M2 2 x Vee 4 Stroke 16 Cy. 159 x 159 each-1492kW (2029bhp) Cummins Engine Co Inc-USA AuxGen: 2 x 48kW 380V a.c
8839043 *XVNC* -	**SONG LAM** **Vietnam Petroleum Transport JSC (VIPCO) (Cong Ty Van Tai Xang Dau Duong Thuy 1)** - *Haiphong* *Vietnam*	*338* 102 300	Class: (VR)	**1972 in the People's Republic of China** L reg 39.01 Br ex - Dght 2.983 Lbp - Br md 8.19 Dpth 3.49 Welded, 1 dk	**(A13B2TU) Tanker (unspecified)**	**1 oil engine** geared to sc. shaft driving 1 FP propeller Total Power: 294kW (400hp) Chinese Std. Type 6300 1 x 4 Stroke 6 Cy. 300 x 380 294kW (400bhp) in China
8867349 *XVMU* -	**SONG LAM 08** **Quoc Nam Nguyen** *Haiphong* *Vietnam*	**385** 169 400	Class: (VR)	**1985 Ben Kien Mechanical Factory — Haiphong** Loa 48.50 Br ex - Dght 3.200 Lbp - Br md 8.00 Dpth 4.10 Welded, 1 dk	**(A31A2GX) General Cargo Ship** Grain: 660 Compartments: 2 Ho, ER 2 Ha: (12.5 x 4.7) (11.5 x 4.7)ER	**1 oil engine** reduction geared to sc. shaft driving 1 FP propeller Total Power: 294kW (400hp) 8.0kn S.K.L. 8NVD26A-2 1 x 4 Stroke 8 Cy. 180 x 260 294kW (400bhp) VEB Schwermaschinenbau "KarlLiebknecht" (SKL)-Magdeburg AuxGen: 2 x 50kW a.c
9264570 *VRYD9* -	**SONG LIN WAN** **Williden Agents Ltd** China Shipping Tanker Co Ltd *Hong Kong* *Hong Kong* MMSI: 477381000 Official number: HK-0934	**56,358** 32,355 105,965 T/cm 90.0	Class: BV	**2002-11 Namura Shipbuilding Co Ltd — Imari SG** Yd No: 238 Loa 241.03 Br ex - Dght 14.920 Lbp 232.00 Br md 42.00 Dpth 21.20 Welded, 1 dk	**(A13A2TV) Crude Oil Tanker** Double Hull (13F) Liq: 115,636; Liq (Oil): 119,700 Part Cargo Heating Coils Compartments: 12 Wing Ta, 2 Wing Slop Ta, Wing ER 3 Cargo Pump (s): 3x2500m³/hr Manifold: Bow/CM: 118.5m	**1 oil engine** driving 1 FP propeller Total Power: 11,770kW (16,002hp) 14.5kn B&W 6S60MC 1 x 2 Stroke 6 Cy. 600 x 2292 11770kW (16002bhp) Hitachi Zosen Corp-Japan AuxGen: 3 x 1740kW 440/110V 60Hz a.c Fuel: 225.0 (d.f.) 2650.0 (r.f.)
8869191 - -	**SONG LO 04** **Water Mechanical Materials Supply Enterprise (Xi Nghiep Cung Ung Vat Tu Co Khi Thuy)** - *Haiphong* *Vietnam*	*129* - 150	Class: (VR)	**1988 Song Lo Shipyard — Vinh Phu** Loa 40.35 Br ex - Dght 1.500 Lbp - Br md 6.20 Dpth 2.80 Welded, 1 dk	**(A31A2GX) General Cargo Ship**	**1 oil engine** reduction geared to sc. shaft driving 1 FP propeller Total Power: 99kW (135hp) 8.0kn Skoda 6L160 1 x 4 Stroke 6 Cy. 160 x 225 99kW (135bhp) CKD Praha-Praha
8869177 - -	**SONG MA 01** **Thanh Hoa Maritrans Co (Xi Nghiep Van Tai Song Bien Thanh Hoa)** - *Haiphong* *Vietnam* Official number: VN-820-VT	**154** 88 185	Class: (VR)	**1987 Thanh Hoa Shipbuilding JSC — Thanh Hoa** Loa 36.55 Br ex 7.12 Dght 1.950 Lbp 33.75 Br md 7.10 Dpth 2.50 Welded, 1 dk	**(A31A2GX) General Cargo Ship** Grain: 277 Compartments: 2 Ho 2 Ha: 2 (6.5 x 4.0)	**1 oil engine** reduction geared to sc. shaft driving 1 FP propeller Total Power: 103kW (140hp) 8.0kn Yanmar 5KDGGE 1 x 4 Stroke 5 Cy. 145 x 170 103kW (140bhp) (made 1977) Yanmar Diesel Engine Co Ltd-Japan
8869139 - -	**SONG MA 06** **Thanh Hoa Maritrans Co (Xi Nghiep Van Tai Song Bien Thanh Hoa)** *Haiphong* *Vietnam* Official number: VN-876-VT	**166** 86 216	Class: VR	**1987-01 LISEMCO — Haiphong** Loa 36.35 Br ex 7.36 Dght 1.950 Lbp 33.75 Br md 7.16 Dpth 2.50 Welded, 1 dk	**(A31A2GX) General Cargo Ship** Grain: 277 Compartments: 2 Ho, ER 2 Ha: 2 (6.5 x 4.0)ER	**1 oil engine** reduction geared to sc. shaft driving 1 FP propeller Total Power: 103kW (140hp) 8.0kn Yanmar 5KDGGE 1 x 4 Stroke 5 Cy. 145 x 170 103kW (140bhp) (made 1977) Yanmar Diesel Engine Co Ltd-Japan
8893594 - -	**SONG MA 10** **Thanh Hoa Maritrans Co (Xi Nghiep Van Tai Song Bien Thanh Hoa)** *Haiphong* *Vietnam*	**155** - 200	Class: (VR)	**1989 at Haiphong** Loa 35.40 Br ex - Dght 2.100 Lbp 33.50 Br md 6.20 Dpth 2.90 Welded, 1 dk	**(A31A2GX) General Cargo Ship** Compartments: 2 Ho, ER 2 Ha: 2 (6.5 x 4.0)ER	**1 oil engine** reduction geared to sc. shaft driving 1 FP propeller Total Power: 103kW (140hp) 8.5kn Yanmar 5KDGGE 1 x 4 Stroke 5 Cy. 145 x 170 103kW (140bhp) (made 1977) Yanmar Diesel Engine Co Ltd-Japan AuxGen: 1 x 5kW a.c
8893740 - -	**SONG MA 18** **Thanh Hoa Maritrans Co (Xi Nghiep Van Tai Song Bien Thanh Hoa)** *Haiphong* *Vietnam*	**130** 61 170	Class: (VR)	**1991 at Haiphong** Loa 36.03 Br ex - Dght 2.200 Lbp 35.20 Br md 6.20 Dpth 2.80 Welded, 1 dk	**(A31A2GX) General Cargo Ship**	**1 oil engine** reduction geared to sc. shaft driving 1 FP propeller Total Power: 99kW (135hp) 9.0kn Skoda 6L160 1 x 4 Stroke 6 Cy. 160 x 225 99kW (135bhp) CKD Praha-Praha AuxGen: 1 x 6kW a.c
9192026 *XVDS* -	**SONG NGAN** *launched as* Asian Gutty *-1999* **Vietnam Ocean Shipping JSC (VOSCO) (Cong Ty Co Phan Van Tai Bien Viet Nam)** - *Haiphong* *Vietnam* MMSI: 574058048 Official number: VN-1276-VT	**4,726** 2,085 6,205 T/cm 13.4	Class: NK VR	**1999-01 Sanyo Zosen K.K. — Onomichi** Yd No: 1085 Loa 96.70 (BB) Br ex - Dght 7.346 Lbp 84.90 Br md 17.40 Dpth 11.60 Welded, 2 dks	**(A31A2GX) General Cargo Ship** Grain: 10,437; Bale: 9,705 Compartments: 2 Ho, ER, 2 Tw Dk 2 Ha: (14.7 x 12.6) (28.0 x 12.6)ER Derricks: 1x30t,2x25t	**1 oil engine** driving 1 FP propeller Total Power: 2,427kW (3,300hp) 11.8kn Akasaka A41 1 x 4 Stroke 6 Cy. 410 x 800 2427kW (3300bhp) Akasaka Tekkosho KK (Akasaka DieselLtd)-Japan AuxGen: 2 x 240kW 445V 60Hz a.c Fuel: 69.0 (d.f.) (Heating Coils) 439.5 (r.f.) 10.9pd
7828097 *DUL2007* -	**SONG OF DOLLY 3** *ex* Shiokaze *-1999* **Sarangani Transport & Trading Corp** - *General Santos* *Philippines* Official number: 12-0001487	*120* 22 44		**1978 Binan Senpaku Kogyo K.K. — Onomichi** Yd No: 5303 Loa 33.05 Br ex - Dght 1.800 Lbp 27.00 Br md 5.80 Dpth 2.40 Welded, 1 dk	**(A37B2PS) Passenger Ship**	**1 oil engine** driving 1 FP propeller Total Power: 368kW (500hp) Yanmar 1 x 4 Stroke 368kW (500bhp) Yanmar Diesel Engine Co Ltd-Japan
9042960 - -	**SONG RONG** *ex* Shoei Maru *-2010* **Shanghai Shanwei Dredging Engineering Co Ltd**	*499* - 1,600		**1992-06 Yamakawa Zosen Tekko K.K. — Kagoshima** Yd No: 710 L reg 64.10 Br ex - Dght 4.300 Lbp 62.00 Br md 13.30 Dpth 6.80 Welded, 1 dk	**(A24D2BA) Aggregates Carrier**	**1 oil engine** driving 1 FP propeller Total Power: 736kW (1,001hp) Niigata 6M34AGT 1 x 4 Stroke 6 Cy. 340 x 620 736kW (1001bhp) Niigata Engineering Co Ltd-Japan
9135573 *VRMP9* -	**SONG SHAN** *ex* Kun Lun Shan *-2013* *ex* Hai Young *-2012* *ex* Asian Rose *-2008* *ex* Maple Aries *-2003* **Forge Ahead Shipping Ltd** Dalian Changtian Shipping Ltd *Hong Kong* *Hong Kong* MMSI: 477065500 Official number: HK-3489	**7,633** 2,336 11,288	Class: KR (NK)	**1996-03 Shin Kurushima Dockyard Co. Ltd. — Akitsu** Yd No: 2897 Loa 113.22 (BB) Br ex 19.62 Dght 8.519 Lbp 105.40 Br md 19.60 Dpth 13.20 Welded, 2 dks	**(A31A2GX) General Cargo Ship** Grain: 16,580; Bale: 14,923 TEU 40 Compartments: 2 Ho, ER 2 Ha: (20.3 x 12.6) (33.6 x 12.6)ER Cranes: 2x25t; Derricks: 1x25t	**1 oil engine** driving 1 FP propeller Total Power: 3,884kW (5,281hp) 13.3kn B&W 6L35MC 1 x 2 Stroke 6 Cy. 350 x 1050 3884kW (5281bhp) Makita Corp-Japan

IMO / Call sign	Name / Owner	Tonnage	Class	Builder / Dimensions	Type / Capacity	Machinery
9160243 *BORK* -	**SONG SHAN HAI** **COSCO Bulk Carrier Co Ltd (COSCO BULK)** - SatCom: Inmarsat B 341224610 *Tianjin* *China* MMSI: 412246000	**39,361** 25,643 73,605 T/cm 64.0	Class: CC	**1998-01 Jiangnan Shipyard (Group) Co Ltd — Shanghai** Yd No: H2233 Loa 225.00 Br ex - Dght 14.010 Lbp 217.00 Br md 32.26 Dpth 19.20 Welded, 1 dk	**(A21A2BC) Bulk Carrier** Grain: 90,838; Bale: 86,170 Compartments: 7 Ho, ER 7 Ha: (15.5 x 13.2)6 (15.5 x 15.0)ER	**1 oil engine** driving 1 FP propeller Total Power: 8,662kW (11,777hp) 14.4kn Sulzer 5RTA58 1 x 2 Stroke 5 Cy. 580 x 1700 8662kW (11777bhp) Shanghai Shipyard-China
8507341 *BORO* -	**SONG SHI HAI** *ex* Sea Emerald *-2004* *ex* Marif *-1995* **Tianjin Yuanhua Shipping Co Ltd** - *Tianjin* *China* MMSI: 413009000	**15,813** 9,229 26,596 T/cm 37.6	Class: (CC) (NK)	**1985-10 KK Kanasashi Zosen — Toyohashi AI** Yd No: 3068 Loa 167.21 (BB) Br ex - Dght 9.545 Lbp 160.00 Br md 26.01 Dpth 13.31 Welded, 1 dk	**(A21A2BC) Bulk Carrier** Grain: 33,918; Bale: 32,682 Compartments: 5 Ho, ER 5 Ha: (13.8 x 13.1)4 (19.2 x 13.1)ER Cranes: 4x30t	**1 oil engine** driving 1 FP propeller Total Power: 5,075kW (6,900hp) 14.0kn B&W 6L50MCE 1 x 2 Stroke 6 Cy. 500 x 1620 5075kW (6900bhp) Mitsui Engineering & Shipbuilding CLtd-Japan AuxGen: 4 x 286kW a.c Fuel: 127.0 (d.f.) 1254.5 (r.f.) 20.0pd
8317382 *BIOF* -	**SONG TAI SHAN 5** *ex* Zhao Shang Er *-2006* *ex* Kaiho Maru *-2004* **Shanghai Huachen Shipping Co Ltd** - *Shanghai* *China* MMSI: 413370810	*563* 315 774	Class: CC (NK)	**1983-09 Shirahama Zosen K.K. — Honai** Yd No: 116 Loa 61.96 Br ex - Dght 3.947 Lbp 56.22 Br md 10.01 Dpth 4.42 Welded, 1 dk	**(A11B2TG) LPG Tanker** Liq (Gas): 1,156 2 x Gas Tank (s);	**1 oil engine** driving 1 FP propeller Total Power: 1,214kW (1,651hp) 12.0kn Hanshin 6LU32 1 x 4 Stroke 6 Cy. 320 x 510 1214kW (1651bhp) (made 1983) The Hanshin Diesel Works Ltd-Japan
8106422 *BIOG* -	**SONG TAI SHAN 6** *ex* Zhao Shang San *-2006* *ex* Koyo Maru No. 5 *-1999* **Shanghai Huachen Shipping Co Ltd** - *Shanghai* *China* MMSI: 413370820	**824** 461 744	Class: (CC) (NK)	**1981-11 Sanyo Zosen K.K. — Onomichi** Yd No: 823 Loa 61.95 Br ex - Dght 3.756 Lbp 56.20 Br md 10.00 Dpth 4.40 Welded, 1 dk	**(A11B2TG) LPG Tanker** Liq (Gas): 1,186 2 x Gas Tank (s);	**1 oil engine** with clutches, flexible couplings & sr geared to sc. shaft driving 1 CP propeller Total Power: 1,177kW (1,600hp) 12.0kn Daihatsu 6DSM-28S 1 x 4 Stroke 6 Cy. 280 x 340 1177kW (1600bhp) Daihatsu Diesel Manufacturing Co Lt-Japan AuxGen: 3 x 128kW a.c
9015149 *BIQS* -	**SONG TAI SHAN 16** *ex* Chun Xing 138 *-2008* *ex* Golden Crux No. 15 *-2004* **Shanghai Huachen Shipping Co Ltd** - *Shanghai* *China* MMSI: 413374370	**3,306** 992 3,481 T/cm 12.6	Class: CC (NK)	**1991-09 Usuki Shipyard Co Ltd — Usuki OT** Yd No: 1611 Loa 99.98 Br ex - Dght 5.679 Lbp 93.80 Br md 16.00 Dpth 7.00 Welded, 1 dk	**(A11B2TG) LPG Tanker** Liq (Gas): 3,513 2 x Gas Tank (s); 2 Cargo Pump (s): 2x300m³/hr	**1 oil engine** driving 1 CP propeller Total Power: 2,942kW (4,000hp) 14.0kn Akasaka A45 1 x 4 Stroke 6 Cy. 450 x 880 2942kW (4000bhp) Akasaka Tekkosho KK (Akasaka DieselLtd)-Japan AuxGen: 3 x 240kW a.c
8866436 *3WSK* -	**SONG THU 02** *ex* Nam Hai *-2000* *ex* An Bien 01 *-1992* **Song Thu Co of Region 5 of Army Command (Cong Ty Song Tha Quan Khu V)** - *Da Nang* *Vietnam* Official number: VNDN-171-VTNL	**438** 210 600	Class: VR	**1992 Constructional Engineering Works — Ho Chi Minh City** Loa 46.20 Br ex 9.22 Dght 3.250 Lbp 43.80 Br md 9.20 Dpth 3.80 Welded, 1 dk	**(A13B2TP) Products Tanker**	**2 oil engines** reduction geared to sc. shafts driving 2 FP propellers Total Power: 294kW (400hp) 8.0kn S.K.L. 6NVD26-2 2 x 4 Stroke 6 Cy. 180 x 260 each-147kW (200bhp) SKL Motoren u. Systemtechnik AG-Magdeburg AuxGen: 1 x 44kW a.c, 1 x 30kW a.c
8651300 *HMXX* -	**SONG UN** *ex* Chang Jin 25 *-2000* **JPL Ship Management Co Ltd** Korea Samhung Corp *Nampho* *North Korea* MMSI: 445013000 Official number: 5005519	**1,737** 850 2,615		**2000-03 Zhejiang Yueqing Qiligang Ship Industry Co Ltd — Yueqing ZJ** Yd No: ZWZ-00004 Loa 84.10 Br ex - Dght 4.400 Lbp 78.60 Br md 13.20 Dpth 5.40 Welded, 1 dk	**(A31A2GX) General Cargo Ship**	**1 oil engine** driving 1 FP propeller Total Power: 970kW (1,319hp) S.K.L. 8NVD48A-2U 1 x 4 Stroke 8 Cy. 320 x 480 970kW (1319bhp) Zhenjiang Marine Diesel Works-China
8893477 *3WAZ* -	**SONG VAN 01** **Haiphong Transportation & Construction Co (Cong Ty Van Tai Va Xai Dung Haiphong)** - *Haiphong* *Vietnam*	**154** 88 200	Class: (VR)	**1985 Kien An Shipbuilding Works — Haiphong** Loa 36.50 Br ex - Dght 1.950 Lbp 34.20 Br md 7.46 Dpth 2.55 Welded, 1 dk	**(A31A2GX) General Cargo Ship** Grain: 309 Compartments: 2 Ho, ER 2 Ha: 2 (8.0 x 5.0)ER	**1 oil engine** reduction geared to sc. shaft driving 1 FP propeller Total Power: 99kW (135hp) 8.0kn Skoda 6L160 1 x 4 Stroke 6 Cy. 160 x 225 99kW (135bhp) CKD Praha-Praha
8868848 *XVLJ* -	**SONG VAN 10** **Tien Lang-Hai Phong Waterline Transport Co (Cong Ty Van Tai Thuy Tien Lang Hai Phong)** - *Haiphong* *Vietnam*	**322** 224 450	Class: (VR)	**1992 at Haiphong** Yd No: 46 Loa 49.30 Br ex - Dght 2.400 Lbp - Br md 8.60 Dpth 3.00 Welded, 1 dk	**(A31A2GX) General Cargo Ship** Grain: 683 Compartments: 2 Ho, ER	**1 oil engine** reduction geared to sc. shaft driving 1 FP propeller Total Power: 221kW (300hp) 9.0kn Barnaultransmash 3D12A 1 x Vee 4 Stroke 12 Cy. 150 x 180 221kW (300bhp) AO Barnaultransmash-Barnaul AuxGen: 1 x 24kW a.c
8893489 - -	**SONG VAN 12** **Haiphong Transportation & Construction Co (Cong Ty Van Tai Va Xai Dung Haiphong)** - *Haiphong* *Vietnam*	**226** 99 339	Class: (VR)	**1993 Ha Long Shipbuilding Engineering JSC — Haiphong** Loa 42.72 Br ex - Dght 2.400 Lbp 40.00 Br md 6.40 Dpth 3.00 Welded, 1 dk	**(A31A2GX) General Cargo Ship** Compartments: 2 Ho, ER 2 Ha: (8.0 x 5.0) (8.5 x 5.0)ER	**1 oil engine** driving 1 FP propeller Total Power: 160kW (218hp) S.K.L. 6NVD36-1U 1 x 4 Stroke 6 Cy. 240 x 360 160kW (218bhp) (made 1968) VEB Schwermaschinenbau "KarlLiebknecht" (SKL)-Magdeburg AuxGen: 1 x 16kW a.c
8827557 *6MOJ* -	**SONG WON No. 59** *ex* Dae Nam No. 103 *-1992* **Choi In-Duk** - *Busan* *South Korea* Official number: 9506026-6210003	**198** - 317	Class: (KR)	**1989-08 Jinhae Ship Construction Industrial Co Ltd — Changwon** Loa 45.40 Br ex - Dght 3.250 Lbp 38.90 Br md 7.70 Dpth 3.40 Welded, 1 dk	**(B12B2FC) Fish Carrier** Ins: 328	**1 oil engine** driving 1 FP propeller Total Power: 1,030kW (1,400hp) 12.3kn Niigata 6M28AFTE 1 x 4 Stroke 6 Cy. 280 x 480 1030kW (1400bhp) Ssangyong Heavy Industries Co Ltd-South Korea AuxGen: 2 x 192kW 225V a.c
9160700 *3FRF8* -	**SONG YUN HE** **COSCO Line 'New York Inc'** COSCO Container Lines Co Ltd (COSCON) SatCom: Inmarsat B 335215310 *Panama* *Panama* MMSI: 352153000 Official number: 2585398C	**16,737** 9,236 23,831 T/cm 40.9	Class: CC (AB)	**1998-09 Imabari Shipbuilding Co Ltd — Marugame KG (Marugame Shipyard)** Yd No: 1300 Loa 182.80 (BB) Br ex 27.60 Dght 10.000 Lbp 172.00 Br md 27.60 Dpth 14.00 Welded, 1 dk	**(A33A2CC) Container Ship (Fully Cellular)** TEU 1432 C Ho 570 TEU C Dk 862 TEU incl 130 ref C. Compartments: 5 Cell Ho, ER	**1 oil engine** driving 1 FP propeller Total Power: 11,769kW (16,001hp) 19.1kn B&W 6S60MC 1 x 2 Stroke 6 Cy. 600 x 2292 11769kW (16001bhp) Kawasaki Heavy Industries Ltd-Japan AuxGen: 3 x 560kW a.c
9423645 *V7ER9* -	**SONGA BREEZE** *ex* Clipper Makishio *-2014* **Songa Chemical AS** - *Majuro* *Marshall Islands* MMSI: 538005523 Official number: 5523	**11,919** 6,206 19,999 T/cm 30.3	Class: NK	**2009-02 Fukuoka Shipbuilding Co Ltd — Nagasaki NS** Yd No: 2021 Loa 146.57 (BB) Br ex 24.23 Dght 9.542 Lbp 138.10 Br md 24.19 Dpth 12.90 Welded, 1 dk	**(A12B2TR) Chemical/Products Tanker** Double Hull (13F) Liq: 20,562; Liq (Oil): 20,527 Cargo Heating Coils Compartments: 18 Wing Ta (s.stl), 2 Wing Slop Ta (s.stl), ER 18 Cargo Pump (s): 12x330m³/hr, 6x220m³/hr Manifold: Bow/CM: 74.3m	**1 oil engine** driving 1 FP propeller Total Power: 6,480kW (8,810hp) 14.6kn MAN-B&W 6S42MC 1 x 2 Stroke 6 Cy. 420 x 1764 6480kW (8810bhp) Makita Corp-Japan AuxGen: 3 x 540kW a.c Thrusters: 1 Tunnel thruster Fuel: 95.0 (d.f.) 923.0 (r.f.)
9409510 *V7CZ8* -	**SONGA CHALLENGE** *ex* Global Challenge *-2013* **Songa Chemical AS** Navig8 Chemicals Inc *Majuro* *Marshall Islands* MMSI: 538005355 Official number: 5355	**11,623** 6,056 19,993 T/cm 28.8	Class: KR	**2009-08 Usuki Shipyard Co Ltd — Usuki OT** Yd No: 1717 Loa 145.50 (BB) Br ex 23.73 Dght 9.709 Lbp 137.00 Br md 23.70 Dpth 13.35 Welded, 1 dk	**(A12B2TR) Chemical/Products Tanker** Double Hull (13F) Liq: 21,384; Liq (Oil): 22,500 Cargo Heating Coils Compartments: 20 Wing Ta (s.stl), 2 Wing Slop Ta, ER (s.stl) 22 Cargo Pump (s): 8x200m³/hr, 14x300m³/hr Manifold: Bow/CM: 72.4m	**1 oil engine** driving 1 FP propeller Total Power: 6,150kW (8,362hp) 14.7kn MAN-B&W 6S42MC 1 x 2 Stroke 6 Cy. 420 x 1764 6150kW (8362bhp) Hitachi Zosen Corp-Japan AuxGen: 3 x 440kW a.c Thrusters: 1 Tunnel thruster (f) Fuel: 127.0 (d.f.) 886.0 (r.f.)
9378321 *V7LH4* -	**SONGA CRYSTAL** *ex* Samho Crystal *-2006* **Songa Product & Chemical Tankers AS** Navig8 Chemicals Inc *Majuro* *Marshall Islands* MMSI: 538002745 Official number: 2745	**8,485** 4,031 12,927 T/cm 23.0	Class: KR (NV)	**2006-10 Samho Shipbuilding Co Ltd — Tongyeong** Yd No: 1075 Loa 127.20 (BB) Br ex 20.43 Dght 8.714 Lbp 119.00 Br md 20.40 Dpth 11.50 Welded, 1 dk	**(A12B2TR) Chemical/Products Tanker** Double Hull (13F) Liq: 13,387; Liq (Oil): 13,387 Cargo Heating Coils Compartments: 12 Wing Ta, 2 Wing Slop Ta, Wing ER 12 Cargo Pump (s): 12x300m³/hr Manifold: Bow/CM: 59.4m	**1 oil engine** driving 1 FP propeller Total Power: 4,440kW (6,037hp) 13.5kn MAN-B&W 6S35MC 1 x 2 Stroke 6 Cy. 350 x 1400 4440kW (6037bhp) STX Engine Co Ltd-South Korea AuxGen: 3 x 490kW 440/220V 50Hz a.c Thrusters: 1 Tunnel thruster (f) Fuel: 72.0 (d.f.) (Heating Coils) 683.0 (r.f.)

8751095 *V7KB4* -	**SONGA DEE** *ex* Stena Dee *-2006* *ex* Dyvi Stena *-1996* **Songa Offshore SE** Songa Management Ltd *Majuro* *Marshall Islands* MMSI: 538002597 Official number: 2597	**15,757** 4,728 -	Class: NV (AB)	**1984**-09 **Mitsubishi Heavy Industries Ltd. — Hiroshima** Yd No: H326 Loa 112.00 Br ex 72.65 Dght 20.000 Lbp - Br md 68.00 Dpth 34.00 Welded, 1 dk	**(Z11C3ZE) Drilling Rig, semi Submersible** Passengers: berths: 116 Cranes: 2x60t	**4 diesel electric oil engines** driving 4 gen. Connecting to 4 elec. motors driving 4 Azimuth electric drive units Total Power: 10,504kW (14,280hp) 6.0kn Nohab 1 x 2251kW (3060bhp) (new engine 2004) Nohab 3 x each-2251kW (3060bhp) (new engine 2004) Fuel: 1190.0 (r.f.)
8756590 *LFFM* -	**SONGA DELTA** *ex* Deepsea Delta *-2009* *ex* West Delta *-2004* *ex* Dyvi Delta *-2001* **Songa Delta Ltd** Songa Management Ltd *Oslo* *Norway* MMSI: 257097000	**23,535** 7,204 -	Class: NV	**1981**-01 **Rauma-Repola Oy — Pori** Yd No: 12 Loa 122.44 Br ex 86.05 Dght 24.384 Lbp - Br md - Dpth 46.17 Welded, 1 dk	**(Z11C3ZE) Drilling Rig, semi Submersible** Passengers: berths: 100 Cranes: 3x50t	**4 diesel electric oil engines** driving 4 gen. each 3000kW 6000V a.c Connecting to 4 elec. motors driving 2 CP propellers Total Power: 12,600kW (17,132hp) 7.0kn Wartsila 18V200 4 x Vee 4 Stroke 18 Cy. 200 x 240 each-3150kW (4283bhp) Wartsila France SA-France
9460459 *V7PS4* -	**SONGA DIAMOND** **Songa Product & Chemical Tankers AS** Navig8 Chemicals Inc *Majuro* *Marshall Islands* MMSI: 538003277 Official number: 3277	**11,259** 5,265 17,543 T/cm 28.5	Class: KR	**2009**-01 **Samho Shipbuilding Co Ltd — Tongyeong** Yd No: 1204 Loa 144.00 (BB) Br ex - Dght 9.214 Lbp 135.00 Br md 22.60 Dpth 12.50 Welded, 1 dk	**(A12B2TR) Chemical/Products Tanker** Double Hull (13F) Liq: 17,897; Liq (Oil): 19,020 Cargo Heating Coils Compartments: 14 Wing Ta, 2 Wing Slop Ta, ER 14 Cargo Pump (s): 8x300m³/hr, 6x200m³/hr Manifold: Bow/CM: 73m	**1 oil engine** driving 1 FP propeller Total Power: 5,920kW (8,049hp) 14.0kn MAN-B&W 8S35MC 1 x 2 Stroke 8 Cy. 350 x 1400 5920kW (8049bhp) Mitsui Engineering & Shipbuilding CLtd-Japan AuxGen: 3 x 750kW 450V a.c Thrusters: 1 Thwart. FP thruster (f) Fuel: 112.0 (d.f.) 914.0 (r.f.)
9461714 *V7VC3* -	**SONGA EAGLE** **Songa Product & Chemical Tankers II AS** Lorentzens Skibs Management AS *Majuro* *Marshall Islands* MMSI: 538004084 Official number: 4084	**8,505** 4,055 13,250 T/cm 23.1	Class: KR (AB) (NV)	**2008**-12 **Jinse Shipbuilding Co Ltd — Busan** Yd No: 1008 Loa 127.90 (BB) Br ex 20.43 Dght 8.750 Lbp 119.70 Br md 20.40 Dpth 11.50 Welded, 1 dk	**(A12B2TR) Chemical/Products Tanker** Double Hull (13F) Liq: 13,265; Liq (Oil): 13,941 Cargo Heating Coils Compartments: 12 Wing Ta, 2 Wing Slop Ta, ER 12 Cargo Pump (s): 12x300m³/hr Manifold: Bow/CM: 59.6m	**1 oil engine** driving 1 FP propeller Total Power: 4,440kW (6,037hp) 13.6kn MAN-B&W 6S35MC 1 x 2 Stroke 6 Cy. 350 x 1400 4440kW (6037bhp) STX Engine Co Ltd-South Korea AuxGen: 3 x 480kW a.c Thrusters: 1 Tunnel thruster (f) Fuel: 64.0 (d.f.) 616.0 (r.f.)
9473937 *V7RO7* -	**SONGA EMERALD** **Songa Product & Chemical Tankers IV AS** Navig8 Chemicals Inc SatCom: Inmarsat C 453834431 *Majuro* *Marshall Islands* MMSI: 538003552 Official number: 3552	**11,259** 5,265 17,567 T/cm 28.5	Class: KR	**2009**-07 **Samho Shipbuilding Co Ltd — Tongyeong** Yd No: 1208 Loa 144.06 (BB) Br ex - Dght 9.214 Lbp 136.00 Br md 22.60 Dpth 12.50 Welded, 1 dk	**(A12B2TR) Chemical/Products Tanker** Double Hull (13F) Liq: 17,902; Liq (Oil): 17,902 Cargo Heating Coils Compartments: 14 Wing Ta, 2 Wing Slop Ta, ER 14 Cargo Pump (s): 8x300m³/hr, 6x200m³/hr Manifold: Bow/CM: 71m	**1 oil engine** driving 1 FP propeller Total Power: 5,920kW (8,049hp) 14.0kn MAN-B&W 8S35MC 1 x 2 Stroke 8 Cy. 350 x 1400 5920kW (8049bhp) STX Engine Co Ltd-South Korea AuxGen: 3 x 750kW 450V a.c Thrusters: 1 Tunnel thruster (f) Fuel: 112.0 (d.f.) 914.0 (r.f.)
9482653 *V7VC4* -	**SONGA FALCON** **Ross Chemical III AS** Lorentzens Skibs Management AS *Majuro* *Marshall Islands* MMSI: 538004085 Official number: 4085	**8,505** 4,055 13,224 T/cm 23.1	Class: AB	**2009**-03 **Jinse Shipbuilding Co Ltd — Busan** Yd No: 1009 Loa 127.90 (BB) Br ex 20.43 Dght 8.764 Lbp 119.70 Br md 20.40 Dpth 11.50 Welded, 1 dk	**(A12B2TR) Chemical/Products Tanker** Double Hull (13F) Liq: 13,242; Liq (Oil): 13,264 Cargo Heating Coils Compartments: 12 Wing Ta, 2 Wing Slop Ta, ER 12 Cargo Pump (s): 12x300m³/hr Manifold: Bow/CM: 59.6m	**1 oil engine** driving 1 FP propeller Total Power: 4,457kW (6,060hp) 13.4kn MAN-B&W 6S35MC 1 x 2 Stroke 6 Cy. 350 x 1400 4457kW (6060bhp) STX Engine Co Ltd-South Korea AuxGen: 3 x 480kW a.c Thrusters: 1 Tunnel thruster (f) Fuel: 61.0 (d.f.) 678.0 (r.f.)
9482665 *V7RQ8* -	**SONGA HAWK** **Songa Product & Chemical Tankers II AS** Navig8 Chemicals Inc SatCom: Inmarsat C 453834252 *Majuro* *Marshall Islands* MMSI: 538003566 Official number: 3566	**8,505** 4,055 13,265 T/cm 23.3	Class: KR (NV) (AB)	**2009**-05 **Jinse Shipbuilding Co Ltd — Busan** Yd No: 1010 Loa 127.90 (BB) Br ex 20.43 Dght 8.764 Lbp 119.70 Br md 20.40 Dpth 11.50 Welded, 1 dk	**(A12B2TR) Chemical/Products Tanker** Double Hull (13F) Liq: 13,257; Liq (Oil): 13,257 Part Cargo Heating Coils Compartments: 12 Wing Ta, 2 Wing Slop Ta, ER 12 Cargo Pump (s): 12x300m³/hr Manifold: Bow/CM: 59.9m	**1 oil engine** driving 1 FP propeller Total Power: 4,440kW (6,037hp) 13.4kn MAN-B&W 6S35MC 1 x 2 Stroke 6 Cy. 350 x 1400 4440kW (6037bhp) STX Engine Co Ltd-South Korea AuxGen: 3 x 480kW a.c Thrusters: 1 Tunnel thruster (f) Fuel: 74.0 (d.f.) 570.0 (r.f.)
9473925 *V7RO6* -	**SONGA JADE** **Songa Product & Chemical Tankers IV AS** Navig8 Chemicals Inc SatCom: Inmarsat C 453834387 *Majuro* *Marshall Islands* MMSI: 538003551 Official number: 3551	**11,259** 5,265 17,604 T/cm 28.7	Class: KR	**2009**-06 **Samho Shipbuilding Co Ltd — Tongyeong** Yd No: 1207 Loa 144.06 (BB) Br ex - Dght 9.214 Lbp 136.37 Br md 22.60 Dpth 12.50 Welded, 1 dk	**(A12B2TR) Chemical/Products Tanker** Double Hull (13F) Liq: 17,902; Liq (Oil): 17,902 Cargo Heating Coils Compartments: 14 Wing Ta, 2 Wing Slop Ta, ER 14 Cargo Pump (s): 8x300m³/hr, 6x200m³/hr Manifold: Bow/CM: 71m	**1 oil engine** driving 1 FP propeller Total Power: 5,920kW (8,049hp) 15.0kn MAN-B&W 8S35MC 1 x 2 Stroke 8 Cy. 350 x 1400 5920kW (8049bhp) STX Engine Co Ltd-South Korea AuxGen: 3 x 750kW 450V 60Hz a.c Thrusters: 1 Tunnel thruster (f) Fuel: 112.0 (d.f.) 914.0 (r.f.)
9473913 *V7RO5* -	**SONGA OPAL** **Songa Product & Chemical Tankers IV AS** Navig8 Chemicals Inc SatCom: Inmarsat C 453834323 *Majuro* *Marshall Islands* MMSI: 538003550 Official number: 3550	**11,259** 5,265 17,588 T/cm 28.7	Class: KR	**2009**-05 **Samho Shipbuilding Co Ltd — Tongyeong** Yd No: 1206 Loa 144.06 (BB) Br ex - Dght 9.214 Lbp 136.00 Br md 22.60 Dpth 12.50 Welded, 1 dk	**(A12B2TR) Chemical/Products Tanker** Double Hull (13F) Liq: 17,897; Liq (Oil): 17,897 Cargo Heating Coils Compartments: 14 Wing Ta, 2 Wing Slop Ta, ER 14 Cargo Pump (s): 8x300m³/hr, 6x200m³/hr Manifold: Bow/CM: 71m	**1 oil engine** driving 1 FP propeller Total Power: 5,920kW (8,049hp) 14.0kn MAN-B&W 8S35MC 1 x 2 Stroke 8 Cy. 350 x 1400 5920kW (8049bhp) STX Engine Co Ltd-South Korea AuxGen: 3 x 750kW 450V 60Hz a.c Thrusters: 1 Tunnel thruster (f) Fuel: 112.0 (d.f.) 894.0 (r.f.)
9409522 *V7CY5* -	**SONGA PEACE** *ex* Global Peace *-2013* **Songa Chemical AS** Navig8 Chemicals Inc *Majuro* *Marshall Islands* MMSI: 538005348 Official number: 5348	**11,623** 6,056 19,992 T/cm 28.8	Class: KR	**2009**-11 **Usuki Shipyard Co Ltd — Usuki OT** Yd No: 1718 Loa 145.53 (BB) Br ex 23.70 Dght 9.709 Lbp 137.00 Br md 23.70 Dpth 13.35 Welded, 1 dk	**(A12B2TR) Chemical/Products Tanker** Double Hull (13F) Liq: 21,497; Liq (Oil): 22,500 Cargo Heating Coils Compartments: 20 Wing Ta (s.stl), 2 Wing Slop Ta (s.stl), ER 22 Cargo Pump (s): 8x200m³/hr, 14x300m³/hr Manifold: Bow/CM: 72.4m	**1 oil engine** driving 1 FP propeller Total Power: 6,150kW (8,362hp) 14.7kn MAN-B&W 6S42MC 1 x 2 Stroke 6 Cy. 420 x 1764 6150kW (8362bhp) Hitachi Zosen Corp-Japan AuxGen: 3 x a.c Thrusters: 1 Tunnel thruster (f) Fuel: 140.0 (d.f.) 880.0 (r.f.)
9444455 *V7OL4* -	**SONGA PEARL** **Songa Product & Chemical Tankers AS** Navig8 Chemicals Inc *Majuro* *Marshall Islands* MMSI: 538003108 Official number: 3108	**11,259** 5,265 17,539 T/cm 28.5	Class: KR	**2008**-05 **Samho Shipbuilding Co Ltd — Tongyeong** Yd No: 1201 Loa 144.00 (BB) Br ex - Dght 9.214 Lbp 136.00 Br md 22.60 Dpth 12.50 Welded, 1 dk	**(A12B2TR) Chemical/Products Tanker** Double Hull (13F) Liq: 17,893; Liq (Oil): 19,020 Cargo Heating Coils Compartments: 14 Wing Ta, 2 Wing Slop Ta, ER 14 Cargo Pump (s): 8x300m³/hr, 6x200m³/hr Manifold: Bow/CM: 72.2m	**1 oil engine** driving 1 FP propeller Total Power: 5,943kW (8,080hp) 14.0kn MAN-B&W 8S35MC 1 x 2 Stroke 8 Cy. 350 x 1400 5943kW (8080bhp) (made 2008) STX Engine Co Ltd-South Korea AuxGen: 3 x 750kW 450V 60Hz a.c Thrusters: 1 Tunnel thruster (f) Fuel: 112.0 (d.f.) 914.0 (r.f.)
9444479 *V7OL5* -	**SONGA RUBY** **Songa Product & Chemical Tankers AS** Navig8 Chemicals Inc *Majuro* *Marshall Islands* MMSI: 538003109 Official number: 3109	**11,259** 5,265 17,604 T/cm 28.5	Class: KR	**2008**-08 **Samho Shipbuilding Co Ltd — Tongyeong** Yd No: 1203 Loa 144.00 (BB) Br ex - Dght 9.214 Lbp 136.00 Br md 22.60 Dpth 12.50 Welded, 1 dk	**(A12B2TR) Chemical/Products Tanker** Double Hull (13F) Liq: 17,893; Liq (Oil): 19,020 Cargo Heating Coils Compartments: 14 Wing Ta, 2 Wing Slop Ta, ER 14 Cargo Pump (s): 8x300m³/hr, 6x200m³/hr Manifold: Bow/CM: 71m	**1 oil engine** driving 1 FP propeller Total Power: 5,920kW (8,049hp) 14.0kn MAN-B&W 8S35MC 1 x 2 Stroke 8 Cy. 350 x 1400 5920kW (8049bhp) STX Engine Co Ltd-South Korea AuxGen: 3 x 749kW 450V a.c Thrusters: 1 Tunnel thruster (f) Fuel: 112.0 (d.f.) 914.0 (r.f.)
9444467 *V7OL6* -	**SONGA SAPPHIRE** **Songa Product & Chemical Tankers AS** Navig8 Chemicals Inc *Majuro* *Marshall Islands* MMSI: 538003110 Official number: 3110	**11,259** 5,265 17,539 T/cm 28.5	Class: KR	**2008**-06 **Samho Shipbuilding Co Ltd — Tongyeong** Yd No: 1202 Loa 144.00 (BB) Br ex - Dght 9.214 Lbp 136.00 Br md 22.60 Dpth 12.50 Welded, 1 dk	**(A12B2TR) Chemical/Products Tanker** Double Hull (13F) Liq: 17,893; Liq (Oil): 19,020 Cargo Heating Coils Compartments: 14 Wing Ta, 2 Wing Slop Ta, ER 14 Cargo Pump (s): 8x300m³/hr, 6x200m³/hr Manifold: Bow/CM: 71m	**1 oil engine** driving 1 FP propeller Total Power: 5,349kW (7,273hp) 14.0kn MAN-B&W 8S35MC 1 x 2 Stroke 8 Cy. 350 x 1400 5349kW (7273bhp) STX Engine Co Ltd-South Korea AuxGen: 3 x 750kW 450V 60Hz a.c Thrusters: 1 Tunnel thruster (f) Fuel: 112.0 (d.f.) 914.0 (r.f.)

9460461 *V7PS6* -	**SONGA TOPAZ** **Songa Product & Chemical Tankers IV AS** Navig8 Chemicals Inc *Majuro* *Marshall Islands* MMSI: 538003279 Official number: 3279	**11,259** 5,265 17,596 T/cm 28.5	Class: KR	**2009-04 Samho Shipbuilding Co Ltd — Tongyeong** Yd No: 1205 Loa 144.06 (BB) Br ex - Dght 9.214 Lbp 135.00 Br md 22.60 Dpth 12.50 Welded, 1 dk	**(A12B2TR) Chemical/Products Tanker** Double Hull (13F) Liq: 17,897; Liq (Oil): 19,020 Cargo Heating Coils Compartments: 14 Wing Ta, 2 Wing Slop Ta, ER 14 Cargo Pump (s): 8x300m^3/hr, 6x200m^3/hr Manifold: Bow/CM: 71m	**1 oil engine** driving 1 FP propeller Total Power: 5,920kW (8,049hp) 15.0kn MAN-B&W 8S35MC 1 x 2 Stroke 8 Cy. 350 x 1400 5920kW (8049bhp) STX Engine Co Ltd-South Korea AuxGen: 3 x 750kW 450V 60Hz a.c Thrusters: 1 Tunnel thruster (f) Fuel: 112.0 (d.f.) 914.0 (r.f.)
8752271 *LFEX* -	**SONGA TRYM** *ex* Deepsea Trym *-2009* *ex* La Muralla *-1995* *ex* Daysland One *-1988* *ex* Nortrym *-1987* **Songa Offshore SE** Songa Management Ltd *Oslo* *Norway* MMSI: 257091000	**12,143** 3,851 -	Class: NV	**1976-09 Aker Verdal AS — Verdal** (Hull launched by) **1976-09 AS Bergens Mek. Verksteder — Bergen** (Hull completed by) Yd No: 708 Loa 108.20 Br ex 67.36 Dght - Lbp - Br md - Dpth 36.58 Welded, 1 dk	**(Z11C3ZE) Drilling Rig, semi Submersible** Cranes: 2x40t	**4 diesel electric oil engines** driving 4 gen. each 1750kW 720V d.c Connecting to 4 elec. motors driving 2 Propellers Total Power: 6,472kW (8,800hp) 6.0kn Bergens KVGB-12 2 x Vee 4 Stroke 12 Cy. 250 x 300 each-1618kW (2200bhp) (new engine 1976) AS Bergens Mek Verksteder-Norway Bergens KVGB-12 2 x Vee 4 Stroke 12 Cy. 250 x 300 each-1618kW (2200bhp) (new engine 2005) AS Bergens Mek Verksteder-Norway
9416109 *V7ZP4* -	**SONGA WINDS** **Songa Chemical AS** Navig8 Chemicals Inc *Majuro* *Marshall Islands* MMSI: 538004885 Official number: 4885	**11,662** 6,295 19,954 T/cm 29.8	Class: NK	**2009-06 Fukuoka Shipbuilding Co Ltd — Fukuoka FO** Yd No: 1276 Loa 144.09 (BB) Br ex 24.23 Dght 9.632 Lbp 136.00 Br md 24.19 Dpth 12.90 Welded, 1 dk	**(A12B2TR) Chemical/Products Tanker** Double Hull (13F) Liq: 20,523; Liq (Oil): 41,046 Cargo Heating Coils Compartments: 9 Ta, 18 Wing Ta, 2 Wing Slop Ta, ER 20 Cargo Pump (s): 12x300m^3/hr, 8x200m^3/hr Manifold: Bow/CM: 72.2m	**1 oil engine** driving 1 FP propeller Total Power: 6,230kW (8,470hp) 14.5kn Mitsubishi 7UEC45LA 1 x 2 Stroke 7 Cy. 450 x 1350 6230kW (8470bhp) Akasaka Tekkosho KK (Akasaka DieselLtd)-Japan AuxGen: 3 x 420kW a.c Thrusters: 1 Tunnel thruster (f) Fuel: 511.0 (d.f.) 761.0 (r.f.)
9280017 *CUOQ8* LG-1348-C	**SONHO DE INFANCIA** **Sociedade Pesca Sonho de Infancia, Lda** - *Lagos* *Portugal* MMSI: 263413370	*142* - -		**2004-04 Navalfoz - Com. E Desenvolvimento de Proj. Navais Lda. — Figueira da Foz** Yd No: 41 Loa 23.00 Br ex - Dght - Lbp - Br md 6.40 Dpth 3.00 Welded	**(B11B2FV) Fishing Vessel**	**1 oil engine** geared to sc. shaft driving 1 Propeller Total Power: 313kW (426hp) Cummins KT-19-M 1 x 4 Stroke 6 Cy. 159 x 159 313kW (426bhp) Cummins Engine Co Ltd-United Kingdom
9397743 *SVAS6* -	**SONIA** **Sonia Transportation Special Maritime Enterprise (ENE)** Neda Maritime Agency Co Ltd SatCom: Inmarsat C 424092810 *Piraeus* *Greece* MMSI: 240928000 Official number: 11924	**91,373** 58,745 177,974 T/cm 120.6	Class: AB	**2009-09 Shanghai Waigaoqiao Shipbuilding Co Ltd — Shanghai** Yd No: 1094 Loa 292.00 (BB) Br ex - Dght 18.300 Lbp 282.00 Br md 45.00 Dpth 24.80 Welded, 1 dk	**(A21A2BC) Bulk Carrier** Grain: 194,486; Bale: 183,425 Compartments: 9 Ho, ER 9 Ha: 7 (15.5 x 20.0)ER 2 (15.5 x 16.5)	**1 oil engine** driving 1 FP propeller Total Power: 16,860kW (22,923hp) 14.0kn MAN-B&W 6S70MC 1 x 2 Stroke 6 Cy. 700 x 2674 16860kW (22923bhp) Hudong Heavy Machinery Co Ltd-China AuxGen: 3 x 750kW a.c
8109333 *VTDY* -	**SONIA** *launched as* Lakshmi *-1981* **Marshall Seafoods Pvt Ltd** *Mumbai* *India* Official number: 1941	*115* 38 81	Class: IR (LR) ✠ Classed LR until 1/12/93	**1981-11 B.V. Scheepswerf "De Hoop" — Hardinxveld-Giessendam** Yd No: 760 Loa 23.68 Br ex 6.58 Dght 2.909 Lbp 21.24 Br md 6.51 Dpth 3.43 Welded, 1 dk	**(B11A2FT) Trawler** Ins: 70	**1 oil engine** with clutches, flexible couplings & sr reverse geared to sc. shaft driving 1 FP propeller Total Power: 405kW (551hp) Caterpillar 3408TA 1 x Vee 4 Stroke 8 Cy. 137 x 152 405kW (551bhp) Caterpillar Tractor Co-USA AuxGen: 2 x 12kW 380V 50Hz a.c
8522676 - -	**SONIA ESPERANZA** *ex* Lady Rhona *-1977* **Bob McNab** *Roatan* *Honduras* Official number: RH-U25005	*127* 85		**1977 Desco Marine — Saint Augustine, Fl** Loa 28.88 Br ex - Dght - Lbp - Br md 6.71 Dpth 2.75 Bonded, 1 dk	**(B11A2FT) Trawler** Hull Material: Reinforced Plastic	**1 oil engine** driving 1 FP propeller Total Power: 268kW (364hp) Caterpillar 3412PCTA 1 x Vee 4 Stroke 12 Cy. 137 x 152 268kW (364bhp) Caterpillar Tractor Co-USA
5408623 *CXNI* -	**SONIA I** *ex* Hakko Reefer *-1982* *ex* Kinshu Maru *-1977* *ex* Sanwa Maru *-1977* **Tuna Sur SA** - *Uruguay*	*328* 180 482	Class: (NK)	**1963 KK Kanasashi Zosen — Shizuoka SZ** Yd No: 528 Converted From: Fishing Vessel-1977 Loa 50.60 Br ex 7.95 Dght 3.425 Lbp 44.51 Br md 7.90 Dpth 3.76 Welded, 1 dk	**(A34A2GR) Refrigerated Cargo Ship** Ins: 634 3 Ha: 3 (1.6 x 1.6)ER	**1 oil engine** driving 1 FP propeller Total Power: 699kW (950hp) 10.5kn Makita 1 x 4 Stroke 6 Cy. 350 x 500 699kW (950bhp) Makita Tekkosho-Japan
7644465 *OWXN* -	**SONIA KIIL II** *ex* Klondyke *-1993* *ex* Hatlagutt *-1987* *ex* Eidefisk *-1986* *ex* Kormt *-1982* **Greenland Scallops & Seafood ApS** - *Nuuk* *Denmark* Official number: H1140	*141* 65 152	Class: (NV)	**1977-02 Haakonsens Mek. Verksted AS — Skudeneshavn** Yd No: 6 Loa 24.44 Br ex - Dght - Lbp 19.51 Br md 7.62 Dpth 3.81 Welded, 1 dk	**(B11B2FV) Fishing Vessel**	**1 oil engine** driving 1 FP propeller Total Power: 416kW (566hp) Caterpillar D379SCAC 1 x Vee 4 Stroke 8 Cy. 159 x 203 416kW (566bhp) Caterpillar Tractor Co-USA AuxGen: 2 x 36kW 220V 50Hz a.c
7739014 - -	**SONIA MC II** *ex* Shallow Water *-1985* **B & S Fishery Co S de RL** - *Roatan* *Honduras* Official number: RHU-52424	*112* 75 -		**1978 Steiner Shipyard, Inc. — Bayou La Batre, Al** L reg 20.46 Br ex 6.71 Dght - Lbp - Br md - Dpth 3.43 Welded, 1 dk	**(B11A2FT) Trawler**	**1 oil engine** driving 1 FP propeller Total Power: 268kW (364hp) Caterpillar D353TA 1 x 4 Stroke 6 Cy. 159 x 203 268kW (364bhp) Caterpillar Tractor Co-USA
6822228 - -	**SONIA ROSAL** **Peix Cameroon SA** - *Cameroon*	*217* 73 144	Class: (BV)	**1968 Astilleros Zamakona SA — Santurtzi** Yd No: 28 Loa 31.09 Br ex 7.22 Dght 3.680 Lbp 26.50 Br md 7.19 Dpth 3.92 Welded, 1 dk	**(B11A2FT) Trawler** Grain: 160 Compartments: 2 Ho, ER 2 Ha: 2 (1.3 x 1.3)ER	**1 oil engine** reduction geared to sc. shaft driving 1 FP propeller Total Power: 427kW (581hp) 10.5kn Stork RHO218K 1 x 4 Stroke 8 Cy. 210 x 300 427kW (581bhp) Naval Stork Werkspoor SA-Spain AuxGen: 2 x 80kW 220V a.c, 1 x 30kW 220V a.c Fuel: 52.0 (d.f.)
9398204 *YJVW8* -	**SONIA TIDE** **Green Fleet Ltd** Tidewater Marine International Inc *Port Vila* *Vanuatu* MMSI: 576136000 Official number: 1874	**494** 148 681	Class: AB	**2006-09** Yd No: 81 Loa 53.30 Br ex - Dght 2.963 Lbp 46.94 Br md 10.37 Dpth 4.27 Welded, 1 dk	**(B21A20C) Crew/Supply Vessel** Hull Material: Aluminium Alloy Passengers: unberthed: 175	**4 oil engines** reduction geared to sc. shafts driving 4 FP propellers Total Power: 5,368kW (7,300hp) 16.0kn Cummins KTA-50-M2 4 x Vee 4 Stroke 16 Cy. 159 x 159 each-1342kW (1825bhp) Cummins Engine Co Inc-USA AuxGen: 2 x 175kW a.c Fuel: 120.0
7018240 *HQJE7* -	**SONIC RO/RO** *ex* Asagiri Maru No. 2 *-1991* **Philko Marine S de RL** - *San Lorenzo* *Honduras* Official number: L-0123031	*637* 230 306		**1970 Shin Yamamoto Shipbuilding & Engineering Co Ltd — Kochi KC** Yd No: 129 Loa 55.73 Br ex 12.02 Dght 2.585 Lbp 50.02 Br md 11.99 Dpth 3.81 Riveted\Welded, 1 dk	**(A36A2PR) Passenger/Ro-Ro Ship (Vehicles)** Passengers: unberthed: 300 Cars: 12	**2 oil engines** driving 2 FP propellers Total Power: 1,472kW (2,002hp) 13.0kn Daihatsu 8PSHTCM-26D 2 x 4 Stroke 8 Cy. 260 x 320 each-736kW (1001bhp) Daihatsu Kogyo-Japan AuxGen: 2 x 60kW Fuel: 43.5 5.0pd
9373723 *WDD2812* -	**SONIE** **Tug Sonie LLC** Wilmington Tug Inc *New Castle, DE* *United States of America* Official number: 1186151	**263** 78 -		**2006-11 Washburn & Doughty Associates Inc — East Boothbay ME** Yd No: 88 Loa 24.37 Br ex - Dght 3.960 Lbp - Br md 9.14 Dpth 4.32 Welded, 1 dk	**(B32A2ST) Tug**	**2 oil engines** gearing integral to driving 2 Z propellers Total Power: 2,640kW (3,590hp) M.T.U. 12V4000M60 2 x Vee 4 Stroke 12 Cy. 165 x 190 each-1320kW (1795bhp) Detroit Diesel Corporation-Detroit, Mi
9344370 *V2CR8* -	**SONJA** *ex* Susan K *-2012* *ex* Sonja *-2007* **Nimmrich & Prahm Reederei GmbH & Co KG ms 'Sonja'** Nimmrich & Prahm Bereederung GmbH & Co KG *Saint John's* *Antigua & Barbuda* MMSI: 305089000 Official number: 4319	**3,642** 1,790 4,464	Class: GL	**2007-06 Rousse Shipyard JSC — Rousse** Yd No: 873 Loa 100.71 (BB) Br ex 15.44 Dght 5.625 Lbp 95.20 Br md 15.20 Dpth 7.30 Welded, 1 dk	**(A31A2GX) General Cargo Ship** Grain: 6,457 TEU 281 Compartments: 2 Ho, ER 2 Ha: (31.2 x 12.8)ER (28.4 x 12.8) Cranes: 2x60t Ice Capable	**1 oil engine** geared to sc. shaft driving 1 CP propeller Total Power: 2,361kW (3,210hp) 13.0kn MaK 8M25 1 x 4 Stroke 8 Cy. 255 x 400 2361kW (3210bhp) Caterpillar Motoren GmbH & Co. KG-Germany AuxGen: 2 x 216kW a.c, 1 x 440kW a.c

7524627 *OPAS* Z 19
SONJA
Rederij Thysebaerdt BVBA
-
Zeebrugge *Belgium*
MMSI: 205239000
Official number: 01 00310 1996
159 47 -
1973 N.V. Scheepswerven L. de Graeve — Zeebrugge
Loa 30.70 Br ex - Dght -
Lbp 26.76 Br md 7.19 Dpth -
Welded, 1 dk
(B11A2FT) Trawler
1 oil engine driving 1 FP propeller
Total Power: 515kW (700hp) 11.0kn
A.B.C. 8MDX
1 x 4 Stroke 8 Cy. 242 x 320 515kW (700bhp)
Anglo Belgian Co NV (ABC)-Belgium

8648298 *OXEW* FN 338
SONJAN I
Jan Sondergaard & Martin Sondergaard Larsen
-
Strandby *Denmark*
Official number: H838
128 62 -
1981 Strandby Skibsvaerft I/S — Strandby
Yd No: 76
Loa 22.11 Br ex - Dght -
Lbp - Br md 5.80 Dpth 3.91
Welded, 1 dk
(B11B2FV) Fishing Vessel
1 oil engine driving 1 Propeller

6726280 *OF2611* FIN-130-V
SONNE
ex Sunnanland *-1997* *ex* Luna *-1977*
Dan Granfors & Soner
-
Narpes *Finland*
MMSI: 230995870
Official number: 11968
233 69 179
Class: (BV)
1967 VEB Rosslauer Schiffswerft — Rosslau
Yd No: S.750/14
Loa 33.63 Br ex 6.61 Dght 2.699
Lbp 29.55 Br md 6.58 Dpth 3.31
Welded, 1 dk
(B11B2FV) Fishing Vessel
Ins: 146
Compartments: 2 Ho, ER
4 Ha: 4 (1.2 x 1.2)ER
Derricks: 2x0.3t
1 oil engine driving 1 CP propeller
Total Power: 662kW (900hp) 11.0kn
Nohab F26R
1 x 4 Stroke 6 Cy. 250 x 300 662kW (900bhp)
Nydqvist & Holm AB-Sweden
Fuel: 28.5 (d.f.)

6909777 *DFCG* -
SONNE
RF Forschungsschiffahrt GmbH
-
SatCom: Inmarsat B 321843910
Bremen *Germany*
MMSI: 211216200
Official number: 4216
3,557 1,067 4,734
Class: GL
1969-03 Rickmers Rhederei GmbH Rickmers Werft — Bremerhaven Yd No: 350
Converted From: Stern Trawler-1977
Lengthened-1991
Loa 97.61 (BB) Br ex 14.23 Dght 6.000
Lbp 89.90 Br md 14.20 Dpth 9.30
Welded, 3 dks
(B31A2SR) Research Survey Vessel
Cranes: 1x8t; Derricks: 1x5t
3 diesel electric oil engines driving 3 gen. each 1600kW 660V a.c Connecting to 2 elec. motors each (1150kW) driving 1 FP propeller
Total Power: 4,800kW (6,525hp) 13.0kn
MaK 8M282
3 x 4 Stroke 8 Cy. 240 x 280 each-1600kW (2175bhp)
Atlas MaK Maschinenbau GmbH-Kiel
AuxGen: 3 x 1600kW 660V 50Hz a.c
Thrusters: 1 Retract. directional thruster (f)
Fuel: 918.0 (d.f.) 8.0pd

8404771 *OJKN* -
SONNSKAR
ex Vingaskar av Styrso *-2003*
ex Vingaborg *-2001* *ex* Still Waters *-1996*
ex Santos *-1993* *ex* Tirana *-1993*
OY Sonnfish AB
-
Kaskinen *Finland*
Official number: 12255
385 115 324
1985-07 Kalmar Fartygsreparationer AB — Kalmar Yd No: 464
Loa 33.66 Br ex 8.69 Dght 4.280
Lbp 30.03 Br md 8.62 Dpth 6.51
Welded, 1 dk
(B11A2FS) Stern Trawler
Ins: 250
Ice Capable
1 oil engine with flexible couplings & sr gearedto sc. shaft driving 1 CP propeller
Total Power: 1,103kW (1,500hp)
Deutz SBV6M628
1 x 4 Stroke 6 Cy. 240 x 280 1103kW (1500bhp)
Kloeckner Humboldt Deutz AG-West Germany
Thrusters: 1 Thwart. CP thruster (f)

6903395 *5VAO9* -
SONNY
ex Orca I *-2010* *ex* Sonny *-2002*
ex Anne Wonsild *-1994* *ex* Anne Mac *-1978*
Ravenwood Maritime SA
Ocean Marine Management Inc
Lome *Togo*
MMSI: 671125000
Official number: TG-00128
1,141 652 2,110
Class: (BV)
1968-12 A/S Svendborg Skibsvaerft — Svendborg
Yd No: 124
Lengthened-1978
Loa 74.30 Br ex 10.24 Dght 4.841
Lbp 69.47 Br md 10.20 Dpth 5.74
Welded, 1 dk.
(A13B2TP) Products Tanker
Liq: 2,414; Liq (Oil): 2,414
Cargo Heating Coils
Compartments: 14 Wing Ta, ER
4 Cargo Pump (s)
1 oil engine driving 1 CP propeller
Total Power: 809kW (1,100hp) 11.5kn
MaK 6M451AK
1 x 4 Stroke 6 Cy. 320 x 450 809kW (1100bhp)
Atlas MaK Maschinenbau GmbH-Kiel
AuxGen: 2 x 137kW 380V 50Hz a.c, 1 x 39kW 380V 50Hz a.c
Fuel: 59.0 (d.f.) (Heating Coils) 3.5pd

8660569 *2BIY6* -
SONO
ex Mimi La Sardine *-2012*
Sweet Yacht Management LLP
-
United Kingdom
MMSI: 235066502
Official number: 914664
125 - -
2008-01 Princess Yachts International Plc — Plymouth
Loa 28.40 Br ex - Dght 1.830
Lbp 23.98 Br md 7.01 Dpth -
Bonded, 1 dk
(X11A2YP) Yacht
Hull Material: Reinforced Plastic
2 oil engines reduction geared to sc. shafts driving 2 Propellers
Total Power: 3,580kW (4,868hp)
M.T.U. 16V2000M93
2 x Vee 4 Stroke 16 Cy. 135 x 156 each-1790kW (2434bhp)
MTU Friedrichshafen GmbH-Friedrichshafen

9123520 *V7UO2* -
SONOMA
ex Vento Di Nortada *-2012* *ex* Sonoma *-2012*
ex Nordcloud *-2011* *ex* Libra Patagonia *-2009*
ex Nordcloud *-2003* *ex* Niver Austral *-1999*
ex Nordcloud *-1998*
Olive Shipping Investments LLC
Conbulk Shipping SA
Majuro *Marshall Islands*
MMSI: 538004399
Official number: 4399
16,252 8,916 22,384
Class: BV GL
1997-04 Stocznia Szczecinska SA — Szczecin
Yd No: B186/3/10
Loa 179.23 (BB) Br ex - Dght 9.940
Lbp 167.26 Br md 25.30 Dpth 13.50
Welded, 1 dk
(A33A2CC) Container Ship (Fully Cellular)
Grain: 29,676
TEU 1684 C Ho 630 TEU C Dk 1054 TEU incl 120 ref C.
9 Ha:
Cranes: 3x45t
Ice Capable
1 oil engine driving 1 FP propeller
Total Power: 13,328kW (18,121hp) 19.0kn
Sulzer 6RTA62U
1 x 2 Stroke 6 Cy. 620 x 2150 13328kW (18121bhp)
H Cegielski Poznan SA-Poland
AuxGen: 1 x 920kW 440V a.c, 3 x 540kW 440/220V a.c
Thrusters: 1 Tunnel thruster (f)
Fuel: 1647.0

9236195 *9HDS8* -
SONOMA
ex Yong Kang *-2005*
Karmen Shipping Co Ltd
TMS Bulkers Ltd
Valletta *Malta*
MMSI: 215865000
Official number: 9576
40,437 25,855 74,786 T/cm 67.0
Class: BV (CC)
2001-05 Hudong-Zhonghua Shipbuilding (Group) Co Ltd — Shanghai Yd No: H1284A
Loa 225.00 (BB) Br ex - Dght 14.260
Lbp 217.00 Br md 32.26 Dpth 19.60
Welded, 1 dk
(A21A2BC) Bulk Carrier
Grain: 91,718; Bale: 89,882
Compartments: 7 Ho, ER
7 Ha: (14.6 x 13.2)6 (14.6 x 15.0)ER
1 oil engine driving 1 FP propeller
Total Power: 10,224kW (13,901hp) 14.5kn
MAN-B&W 5S60MC
1 x 2 Stroke 5 Cy. 600 x 2292 10224kW (13901bhp)
Hudong Heavy Machinery Co Ltd-China
AuxGen: 3 x 530kW 450V a.c

7355026 - -
SONRISA
ex Hokuo Maru No. 25 *-1986*
ex Choyo Maru No. 55 *-1986*
-
-
351 159 -
Class: (RI)
1974-02 Narasaki Zosen KK — Muroran HK
Yd No: 861
Loa 57.51 Br ex 9.02 Dght 3.455
Lbp 50.50 Br md 9.00 Dpth 5.59
Welded, 2 dks
(B11B2FV) Fishing Vessel
1 oil engine driving 1 FP propeller
Total Power: 1,692kW (2,300hp)
Hanshin 6LUS40
1 x 4 Stroke 6 Cy. 400 x 640 1692kW (2300bhp)
Hanshin Nainenki Kogyo-Japan

7315301 *URCE* -
SONRISA
ex Blangbintang I *-1997* *ex* Polar Viking *-1992*
ex Polarfisk *-1984* *ex* Helgoyfjord *-1981*
Fishing Co Foros Ltd
Chuan-Chuan Yoo International Trade Ltd
Sevastopol *Ukraine*
437 131 -
Class: (NV)
1973-05 AS Tromso Skipsverft & Mek. Verksted — Tromso Yd No: 41
Loa 35.49 Br ex 8.67 Dght 4.018
Lbp 30.99 Br md 8.62 Dpth 6.25
Welded, 2 dks
(B11B2FV) Fishing Vessel
Ice Capable
1 oil engine driving 1 FP propeller
Total Power: 736kW (1,001hp)
Wichmann 4AXA
1 x 2 Stroke 4 Cy. 300 x 450 736kW (1001bhp)
Wichmann Motorfabrikk AS-Norway
AuxGen: 2 x 112kW 220V 50Hz a.c

6923539 - -
SONT
ex Telco Sont *-1999* *ex* Everdina *-1990*
ex Anna Lydia *-1984*
-
-
-
200 60 -
Class: (BV)
1969 Scheepswerf Vooruit B.V. — Zaandam
Yd No: 331
Converted From: Trawler-1990
Lengthened-1976
Loa 35.36 Br ex - Dght -
Lbp - Br md 7.04 Dpth 3.28
Welded, 1 dk
(B22G2OY) Standby Safety Vessel
1 oil engine driving 1 FP propeller
Total Power: 662kW (900hp)
Stork
1 x 662kW (900bhp) (new engine 1975)
Stork Werkspoor Diesel BV-Netherlands

7344364 *ATPR* -
SONU
ex Sumathi *-2006* *ex* Souri *-1978*
Kei-Rsos Maritime Ltd
-
Visakhapatnam *India*
MMSI: 419033700
Official number: 1713
337 130 144
Class: IR (LR)
✠ Classed LR until 5/12/80
1976-08 Hooghly Docking & Engineering Co. Ltd. — Haora Yd No: 418
Loa 36.56 Br ex 8.92 Dght 3.614
Lbp 31.91 Br md 8.50 Dpth 5.01
Welded, 1 dk
(B32A2ST) Tug
2 oil engines reverse reduction geared to sc. shafts driving 2 FP propellers
Total Power: 1,766kW (2,402hp) 11.5kn
MAN G6V30/45ATL
2 x 4 Stroke 6 Cy. 300 x 450 each-883kW (1201bhp)
Garden Reach Workshops Ltd-India
AuxGen: 2 x 128kW 415V 50Hz a.c
Fuel: 65.0 (d.f.)

9506057 *J7BC8* -
SONWA PRINCESS
Mega Trade Links (Singapore) Pte Ltd
Mohan Mutha Exports Pvt Ltd
Portsmouth *Dominica*
MMSI: 325344000
Official number: 50344
270 81 298
Class: KR (NK)
2008-02 Celtug Service Shipyard Sdn Bhd — Sibu
Yd No: 0611
Loa 30.20 Br ex - Dght 3.612
Lbp 27.06 Br md 8.60 Dpth 4.30
Welded, 1 dk
(B32A2ST) Tug
2 oil engines reduction geared to sc. shaft (s) driving 2 Propellers
Total Power: 1,518kW (2,064hp)
Mitsubishi S6R2-MPTK
1 x 4 Stroke 6 Cy. 170 x 220 759kW (1032bhp)
Mitsubishi Heavy Industries Ltd-Japan
AuxGen: 2 x 90kW a.c
Fuel: 220.0

6928187 *D8SS* -
SOO YANG
Ssangyong Shipping Co Ltd
-
Busan *South Korea*
Official number: BSR-695801
3,787 2,391 5,654
Class: (KR) (NK)
1969-06 Nipponkai Heavy Ind. Co. Ltd. — Toyama
Yd No: 144
Loa 110.24 Br ex 15.02 Dght 6.503
Lbp 103.99 Br md 15.00 Dpth 8.41
Welded, 1 dk
(A24A2BT) Cement Carrier
Grain: 4,988
1 oil engine driving 1 FP propeller
Total Power: 2,207kW (3,001hp) 12.0kn
Akasaka 6DM51SS
1 x 4 Stroke 6 Cy. 510 x 840 2207kW (3001bhp)
Akasaka Tekkosho KK (Akasaka DieselLtd)-Japan
AuxGen: 2 x 140kW 445V a.c
Fuel: 317.0 9.5pd

IMO / Call sign	Name / Owner	Tonnage	Class	Builder / Dimensions	Type	Machinery
8327478 *D9IW* -	**SOO YOUNG No. 7** *ex* Chung Gu 7 *-2000* *ex* Anna *-1997* *ex* Dong Kuk No. 88 *-1996* *ex* Sand Carry No. 1 *-1984* **Soo Young Shipping Co Ltd** - *Busan* *South Korea* Official number: BSR-825526	*779* 199 1,518	Class: (KR)	**1982 Sungkwang Shipbuilding Co Ltd — Tongyeong** Loa 59.42 Br ex - Dght 4.697 Lbp 53.01 Br md 10.51 Dpth 5.21 Welded, 1 dk	**(B33A2DU) Dredger (unspecified)** Hopper: 875 1 Ha: (19.8 x 8.4) Cranes: 1x9t	**1 oil engine** driving 1 FP propeller Total Power: 883kW (1,201hp) 11.5kn Hanshin 6LU28 1 x 4 Stroke 6 Cy. 280 x 440 883kW (1201bhp) Ssangyong Heavy Industries Co Ltd-South Korea AuxGen: 1 x 60kW 225V a.c
9614531 *9V9715* -	**SOOCHOW** - **The China Navigation Co Pte Ltd** - *Singapore* *Singapore* MMSI: 564135000 Official number: 397502	**25,483** 11,817 30,721	Class: LR ✠ **100A1** SS 01/2014 container ship, hold Nos. 3 & 4 strengthened for heavy cargo **ShipRight** ACS (B) *IWS LI EP ✠ **LMC** **UMS** Eq.Ltr: M†; Cable: 638.5/73.0 U3 (a)	**2014-01 Zhejiang Ouhua Shipbuilding Co Ltd — Zhoushan ZJ** Yd No: 643 Loa 199.90 (BB) Br ex 28.28 Dght 10.500 Lbp 188.79 Br md 28.20 Dpth 15.50 Welded, 1 dk	**(A33A2CC) Container Ship (Fully Cellular)** TEU 2082 C Ho 916 TEU C Dk 1166 TEU incl 147 ref C Compartments: 2 Ho, 2 Tw Dk, 3 Cell Ho, ER Cranes: 4x60t	**1 oil engine** driving 1 FP propeller Total Power: 13,560kW (18,436hp) 15.5kn Wartsila 6RT-flex58T 1 x 2 Stroke 6 Cy. 580 x 2416 13560kW (18436bhp) Hudong Heavy Machinery Co Ltd-China AuxGen: 3 x 1058kW 450V 60Hz a.c Boilers: AuxB (Comp) 8.4kgf/cm² (8.2bar) Thrusters: 1 Tunnel thruster (f)
8740280 - -	**SOON FONG** - **PT Hutan Hijau Mas** - *Samarinda* *Indonesia*	**213** 64 -	Class: KI	**2009-01 C.V. Karya Lestari Industri — Samarinda** Loa 36.40 Br ex - Dght - Lbp - Br md 8.00 Dpth 2.40 Welded, 1 dk	**(A35D2RL) Landing Craft**	**2 oil engines** driving 2 Propellers Total Power: 514kW (698hp) Yanmar 6HA2M-HTE 2 x 4 Stroke 6 Cy. 130 x 165 each-257kW (349bhp) Yanmar Diesel Engine Co Ltd-Japan
9115872 - -	**SOON LEE NO. 1** *ex* Siang Ping 93 *-2013* **Soon Lee Heavy Machinery Services** - *Muara* *Brunei* Official number: 0059	**498** 150 880	Class: NK	**1994-07 Tai Chung Hua Shipyard Sdn Bhd — Malaysia** Yd No: 04 Loa 48.78 Br ex - Dght 2.336 Lbp 47.40 Br md 12.12 Dpth 3.05 Welded, 1 dk	**(A35D2RL) Landing Craft** Bow ramp (centre)	**2 oil engines** reduction geared to sc. shafts driving 2 FP propellers Total Power: 514kW (698hp) 7.0kn Cummins NTA-855-M 2 x 4 Stroke 6 Cy. 140 x 152 each-257kW (349bhp) Cummins Engine Co Inc-USA AuxGen: 2 x 20kW a.c Fuel: 25.0 (d.f.)
8327935 *D8GK* -	**SOON PUNG** *ex* Tacoma No. 3 *-1990* **Semo Marine Co Ltd** - *Yeosu* *South Korea* Official number: YSR-834071	**104** - 15	Class: (KR)	**1983 Korea Tacoma Marine Industries Ltd — Changwon** Yd No: 10209 Loa 26.01 Br ex - Dght - Lbp 23.09 Br md 10.20 Dpth 2.70 Welded, 1 dk	**(A37B2PS) Passenger Ship**	**2 oil engines** driving 2 FP propellers Total Power: 1,510kW (2,052hp) 30.9kn M.T.U. 8V396TB83 2 x Vee 4 Stroke 8 Cy. 165 x 185 each-755kW (1026bhp) MTU Friedrichshafen GmbH-Friedrichshafen AuxGen: 1 x 30kW 220V a.c
7338547 - -	**SOOND** *ex* Sound of Scarba *-2000* *ex* Olandssund III *-2000* - -	*175* 67 91		**1960 AB Asi-Verken — Amal** Converted From: Ferry (Passenger/Vehicle)-2001 Loa 32.52 Br ex 8.02 Dght 2.680 Lbp - Br md - Dpth - Welded	**(A37B2PS) Passenger Ship** Bow ramp (centre) Len: 1.20 Wid: 3.58 Swl: -	**4 oil engines** with belt drive & sr geared to sc. shafts driving 2 CP propellers 1 fwd and 1 aft Total Power: 440kW (600hp) 7.0kn Scania DSI11 4 x 4 Stroke 6 Cy. 127 x 145 each-110kW (150bhp) AB Scania Vabis-Sweden AuxGen: 1 x 8kW 230V 50Hz a.c Fuel: 9.5 (d.f.) 1.0pd
9681388 - -	**SOOYOUNG NO. 3** *completed as* Zhe Jiao Ji 110 *-2013* **Taizhou Circumsail Import & Export Co Ltd** -	**622** 348 993	Class: IZ	**2013-01 Taizhou Donghai Shiprepair & Building Co Ltd — Wenling ZJ** Yd No: DH201218 Loa 59.05 Br ex - Dght - Lbp - Br md 9.20 Dpth 4.35 Welded, 1 dk	**(A13B2TP) Products Tanker** Double Hull (13F)	**1 oil engine** reduction geared to sc. shaft driving 1 Propeller Total Power: 956kW (1,300hp) Daihatsu 6DKM-20 1 x 4 Stroke 6 Cy. 200 x 300 956kW (1300bhp) Anqing Marine Diesel Engine Works-China
7380148 - -	**SOPECHE III** *ex* Koshin Maru *-2013* *ex* Koshin Maru No. 21 *-1984* *ex* Choyo Maru No. 57 *-1984* **Inter-Arika SA** - *Nouadhibou* *Mauritania*	*347* 153 -	Class: (RI)	**1974-11 Narasaki Zosen KK — Muroran HK** Yd No: 877 Loa 57.49 Br ex 8.23 Dght 3.226 Lbp 50.50 Br md 8.21 Dpth 3.61 Welded, 1 dk	**(B11B2FV) Fishing Vessel**	**1 oil engine** driving 1 FP propeller Total Power: 1,692kW (2,300hp) Akasaka AH40 1 x 4 Stroke 6 Cy. 400 x 600 1692kW (2300bhp) Akasaka Tekkosho KK (Akasaka DieselLtd)-Japan
7643007 - -	**SOPELAGIC** *ex* Themis *-2010* *ex* Nimber *-2009* *ex* Ganthi V *-1987* **Sopelagic Ltd** Jelti Noumairi	**452** 135 -	Class: (NV)	**1976-09 Falkenbergs Varv AB — Falkenberg** Yd No: 172 Loa 39.12 Br ex - Dght 3.150 Lbp 34.04 Br md 8.25 Dpth 4.20 Welded, 1 dk	**(B11A2FS) Stern Trawler** Compartments: 2 Ho, ER 3 Ha: (3.0 x 1.9)2 (2.0 x 1.9)ER Ice Capable	**1 oil engine** sr geared to sc. shaft driving 1 FP propeller Total Power: 1,545kW (2,101hp) 12.0kn Nohab F212V 1 x Vee 4 Stroke 12 Cy. 250 x 300 1545kW (2101bhp) AB Bofors NOHAB-Sweden AuxGen: 1 x 52kW 380V 50Hz a.c, 1 x 26kW 380V 50Hz a.c Thrusters: 1 Thwart. FP thruster (f) Fuel: 72.0 (d.f.)
8614625 *PP2452* -	**SOPESCA II A** *ex* Sopesca Iii *-1995* **Gentil** - *Itajai* *Brazil* Official number: 4430063192	*148* 44 -		**1987-09 Empresa Brasileira de Construcao Naval S.A. (EBRASA) — Itajai** Yd No: 176 Loa - Br ex - Dght - Lbp - Br md - Dpth - Welded, 1 dk	**(B11A2FT) Trawler**	**1 oil engine** driving 1 FP propeller
8317370 *PNCP* -	**SOPHIA** *ex* Sumise Maru No. 21 *-2009* *ex* Sumise Maru No. 38 *-1985* **PT Pelayaran Andalas Bahtera Baruna** - *Jakarta* *Indonesia* MMSI: 525015574	**2,118** 774 2,955	Class: KI	**1984-03 Shinhama Dockyard Co. Ltd. — Anan** Yd No: 752 Loa 90.89 Br ex - Dght 3.966 Lbp 86.90 Br md 15.02 Dpth 5.97 Welded, 1 dk	**(A24A2BT) Cement Carrier** Grain: 2,416 Compartments: 8 Ho, ER	**2 oil engines** driving 2 FP propellers Total Power: 956kW (1,300hp) 9.5kn Niigata 6M24FT 2 x 4 Stroke 6 Cy. 240 x 410 each-478kW (650bhp) Niigata Engineering Co Ltd-Japan AuxGen: 1 x 240kW 225V a.c, 2 x 64kW 225V a.c Fuel: 15.0 (d.f.) 70.0 (r.f.) 4.5pd
6918091 - -	**SOPHIA** *ex* Gevostar *-2007* **Fairwinds Maritime Services Ltd** -	**1,088** 326 1,458	Class: (NV)	**1969 Gerh. Voldnes AS — Fosnavaag** Yd No: 9 Loa 72.70 Br ex 11.54 Dght 3.474 Lbp 67.62 Br md 11.50 Dpth 5.31 Welded, 2 dks	**(B35E2TF) Bunkering Tanker** Liq: 1,550; Liq (Oil): 1,550 Cargo Heating Coils Compartments: 8 Ta, ER 3 Cargo Pump (s) Ice Capable	**1 oil engine** driving 1 CP propeller Total Power: 1,214kW (1,651hp) 12.5kn MaK 8MU452AK 1 x 4 Stroke 8 Cy. 320 x 450 1214kW (1651bhp) Atlas MaK Maschinenbau GmbH-Kiel AuxGen: 2 x 72kW 220V 50Hz a.c Fuel: 60.0 (r.f.) 6.5pd
9141986 *A8JT3* -	**SOPHIA** *ex* Liberty Ace *-2006* *ex* Liberty Arc *-2005* *ex* Liberty Hawk *-2005* **Cambridge Shipping Ltd** White Sea Navigation SA *Monrovia* *Liberia* MMSI: 636012989 Official number: 12989	**26,021** 15,520 45,758 T/cm 50.5	Class: NK	**1996-04 Imabari Shipbuilding Co Ltd — Marugame KG (Marugame Shipyard)** Yd No: 1252 Loa 189.90 (BB) Br ex 31.03 Dght 11.660 Lbp 179.80 Br md 31.00 Dpth 16.50 Welded, 1 dk	**(A21A2BC) Bulk Carrier** Grain: 58,881; Bale: 56,201 Compartments: 5 Ho, ER 5 Ha: (20.0 x 16.0)4 (20.8 x 16.0)ER Cranes: 4x30.5t	**1 oil engine** driving 1 FP propeller Total Power: 8,561kW (11,640hp) 14.0kn B&W 6S50MC 1 x 2 Stroke 6 Cy. 500 x 1910 8561kW (11640bhp) Hitachi Zosen Corp-Japan Fuel: 1870.0 (r.f.)
9433456 *V2DM8* -	**SOPHIA** - **MarTrust Ship No Two GmbH & Co KG** Kapitan Manfred Draxl Schiffahrts GmbH & Co KG *Saint John's* *Antigua & Barbuda* MMSI: 305260000 Official number: 4482	**7,464** 3,165 8,166 T/cm 22.0	Class: GL	**2008-07 Fujian Mawei Shipbuilding Ltd — Fuzhou FJ** Yd No: 437-35 Loa 129.60 (BB) Br ex - Dght 7.400 Lbp 120.34 Br md 20.60 Dpth 10.80 Welded, 1 dk	**(A33A2CC) Container Ship (Fully Cellular)** Double Bottom Entire Compartment Length TEU 698 C Ho 226 TEU C Dk 472 TEU incl 120 ref C. Ice Capable	**1 oil engine** reduction geared to sc. shaft driving 1 CP propeller Total Power: 7,200kW (9,789hp) 17.5kn MaK 8M43C 1 x 4 Stroke 8 Cy. 430 x 610 7200kW (9789bhp) Caterpillar Motoren GmbH & Co. KG-Germany AuxGen: 1 x 1000kW 450/230V a.c, 3 x 450kW 450/230V a.c Thrusters: 1 Tunnel thruster (f)
9448891 *V7LV2* -	**SOPHIA** - **Pearl Sophia Shipping Ltd** N G Livanos Maritime Co Ltd *Majuro* *Marshall Islands* MMSI: 538002812 Official number: 2812	**5,034** 1,686 6,388 T/cm 16.1	Class: AB	**2009-04 Zhenjiang Sopo Shiprepair & Building Co Ltd — Zhenjiang JS** Yd No: SP09 Loa 100.12 (BB) Br ex - Dght 6.000 Lbp 94.00 Br md 18.00 Dpth 9.60 Welded, 1 dk	**(A12B2TR) Chemical/Products Tanker** Double Hull (13F) Liq: 7,253; Liq (Oil): 7,401 Compartments: 12 Wing Ta, 2 Wing Slop Ta, ER	**1 oil engine** reduction geared to sc. shaft driving 1 CP propeller Total Power: 2,970kW (4,038hp) 12.0kn MaK 9M25C 1 x 4 Stroke 9 Cy. 255 x 400 2970kW (4038bhp) Caterpillar Motoren GmbH & Co. KG-Germany AuxGen: 3 x 360kW a.c Fuel: 100.0 (d.f.) 290.0 (r.f.)

9323912 *C4VZ2* -	**SOPHIA** **Soffive Shipping Corp** Safety Management Overseas SA *Limassol* *Cyprus* MMSI: 210970000 Official number: 9323912	**46,982** 26,950 86,949 T/cm 79.7	Class: LR ✠ **100A1** SS 06/2012 bulk carrier BC-A strengthened for heavy cargoes, Nos. 2, 4 & 6 holds may be empty ESP **ShipRight** (SDA, FDA, CM) ESN *IWS LI ✠ **LMC** **UMS** Eq.Ltr: Q†; Cable: 691.6/81.0 U3 (a)	**2007**-06 **IHI Marine United Inc — Yokohama KN** Yd No: 3246 Loa 229.00 (BB) Br ex 36.54 Dght 14.100 Lbp 219.90 Br md 36.50 Dpth 19.90 Welded, 1 dk	**(A21A2BC) Bulk Carrier** Double Hull Grain: 98,800; Bale: 94,844 Compartments: 7 Ho, ER 7 Ha: ER	**1 oil engine** driving 1 FP propeller Total Power: 10,300kW (14,004hp) 14.5kn Sulzer 6RTA58T 1 x 2 Stroke 6 Cy. 580 x 2416 10300kW (14004bhp) Diesel United Ltd.-Aioi AuxGen: 3 x 600kW 450V 60Hz a.c Boilers: AuxB (Comp) 7.1kgf/cm^2 (7.0bar)
8030582 *WBO6548* -	**SOPHIA CHRISTINE** *ex* Saga Service *-1988* *ex* Marsea Eleven *-1988* - - *New Orleans, LA* *United States of America* Official number: 640553	*282* 192 1,200	Class: (AB)	**1981**-09 **Halter Marine, Inc. — Moss Point, Ms** Yd No: 1011 Loa 54.87 Br ex - Dght 3.664 Lbp 50.60 Br md 12.20 Dpth 4.27 Welded, 1 dk	**(B21A2OS) Platform Supply Ship**	**2 oil engines** reverse reduction geared to sc. shafts driving 2 FP propellers Total Power: 1,654kW (2,248hp) 12.0kn Caterpillar D399SCAC 2 x Vee 4 Stroke 16 Cy. 159 x 203 each-827kW (1124bhp) Caterpillar Tractor Co-USA AuxGen: 2 x 135kW 440V 60Hz a.c Thrusters: 1 Thwart. FP thruster (f) Fuel: 241.0 (d.f.) 10.0pd
9330642 *V7QP5* -	**SOPHIA D** *ex* Sophia *-2008* **Sophia Shipping Inc** Densan Deniz Nakliyat ve Sanayi AS (Densan Shipping Co Inc) *Majuro* *Marshall Islands* MMSI: 538003414 Official number: 3414	**32,583** 18,070 53,565 T/cm 57.3	Class: NV	**2008**-04 **Nam Trieu Shipbuilding Industry Co. Ltd. — Haiphong** Yd No: HR-53-NT02 Loa 190.00 (BB) Br ex 32.29 Dght 12.600 Lbp 183.25 Br md 32.26 Dpth 17.50 Welded, 1 dk	**(A21A2BC) Bulk Carrier** Double Hull Grain: 65,900; Bale: 64,000 Compartments: 5 Ho, ER 5 Ha: 4 (21.6 x 22.4)ER (19.2 x 20.8) Cranes: 4x36t	**1 oil engine** driving 1 FP propeller Total Power: 9,481kW (12,890hp) 14.2kn MAN-B&W 6S50MC-C 1 x 2 Stroke 6 Cy. 500 x 2000 9481kW (12890bhp) Dalian Marine Diesel Works-China AuxGen: 3 x 680kW 450V 60Hz a.c Fuel: 215.0 (d.f.) 2000.0 (r.f.) 34.5pd
9546007 *D5FJ4* -	**SOPHIA I** *ex* Aoli 6 *-2013* **Sophia Steamship Ltd** INTRESCO GmbH *Monrovia* *Liberia* MMSI: 636016284 Official number: 16284	**7,988** 4,126 12,232	Class: RI	**2011**-04 **Zhejiang Aoli Shipbuilding Co Ltd — Yueqing ZJ** Yd No: AL0812 Loa 140.30 (BB) Br ex - Dght 7.790 Lbp 131.00 Br md 20.00 Dpth 10.50 Welded, 1 dk	**(A31A2GX) General Cargo Ship** Double Hull (13F) Grain: 14,787; Bale: 13,308 Compartments: 3 Ho, ER 3 Ha: 2 (24.5 x 15.0)ER (23.1 x 15.0) Cranes: 2x25t Ice Capable	**1 diesel electric oil engine** reduction geared to sc. shaft driving 1 FP propeller Total Power: 3,310kW (4,500hp) 12.0kn Yanmar 8N330-EN 1 x 4 Stroke 8 Cy. 330 x 440 3310kW (4500bhp) Qingdao Zichai Boyang Diesel EngineCo Ltd-China AuxGen: 3 x 300kW 400V 50Hz a.c
9374557 *9VLP6* -	**SOPHIA KOSAN** **LKT Gas Carriers Pte Ltd** Lauritzen Kosan A/S *Singapore* *Singapore* MMSI: 565843000 Official number: 394075	**9,175** 2,753 10,348 T/cm 21.3	Class: BV (NV)	**2008**-10 **STX Shipbuilding Co Ltd — Busan** Yd No: 5026 Loa 120.42 (BB) Br ex 19.82 Dght 8.814 Lbp 112.35 Br md 19.80 Dpth 11.21 Welded, 1 dk	**(A11B2TG) LPG Tanker** Double Hull Liq (Gas): 9,000 2 x Gas Tank (s); 2 independent (5% Ni.stl) cyl horizontal 2 Cargo Pump (s): 2x450m^3/hr Manifold: Bow/CM: 56.5m	**1 oil engine** driving 1 FP propeller Total Power: 5,180kW (7,043hp) 16.0kn MAN-B&W 7S35MC 1 x 2 Stroke 7 Cy. 350 x 1400 5180kW (7043bhp) STX Engine Co Ltd-South Korea AuxGen: 3 x 1100kW 60Hz a.c Fuel: 150.0 (d.f.) 1008.0 (r.f.)
9664249 *5NXI2* -	**SOPHIA MARIA** *ex* Pearl Star 60579 *-2013* **SLOK Nigeria Ltd** - *Lagos* *Nigeria* MMSI: 657100000 Official number: SR 2130	**2,908** 872 3,229	Class: AB	**2013**-06 **Fujian Southeast Shipyard — Fuzhou FJ** Yd No: DN75M-12 Loa 75.00 (BB) Br ex - Dght 6.500 Lbp 67.85 Br md 17.25 Dpth 8.00 Welded, 1 dk	**(B21A2OS) Platform Supply Ship**	**2 oil engines** reduction geared to sc. shafts driving 2 Z propellers Total Power: 4,412kW (5,998hp) 10.0kn Niigata 8L28HX 2 x 4 Stroke 8 Cy. 280 x 370 each-2206kW (2999bhp) Niigata Engineering Co Ltd-Japan AuxGen: 3 x 450kW 415V 50Hz a.c, 2 x 1000kW 415V 50Hz a.c Thrusters: 2 Thwart. CP thruster (f)
9445708 *C6XX8* -	**SOPHIA Z** **Calm Ocean Shipping SA** Saint Michael Shipping Co Ltd *Nassau* *Bahamas* MMSI: 311025400 Official number: 8001671	**33,280** 19,342 57,285 T/cm 57.3	Class: NK (LR) ✠ Classed LR until 12/1/12	**2009**-11 **STX (Dalian) Shipbuilding Co Ltd — Wafangdian LN** Yd No: D2003 Loa 190.00 (BB) Br ex 32.62 Dght 13.000 Lbp 183.30 Br md 32.26 Dpth 18.50 Welded, 1 dk	**(A21A2BC) Bulk Carrier** Grain: 71,967 Compartments: 5 Ho, ER 5 Ha: 4 (19.7 x 18.3)ER (18.0 x 18.3) Cranes: 4x36t	**1 oil engine** driving 1 FP propeller Total Power: 9,480kW (12,889hp) 14.5kn MAN-B&W 6S50MC-C 1 x 2 Stroke 6 Cy. 500 x 2000 9480kW (12889bhp) STX Engine Co Ltd-South Korea AuxGen: 3 x 625kW 450V 60Hz a.c Boilers: AuxB (Comp) 9.2kgf/cm^2 (9.0bar) Fuel: 2210.0
9131278 *ELXL6* -	**SOPHIE** *ex* Sophie Rickmers *-2010* *ex* CCNI Aviles *-2008* *ex* CCNI Antofagasta *-2005* *ex* CSAV Barcelona *-2002* *ex* CCNI Antofagasta *-2002* *ex* CSAV Barcelona *-2002* *ex* CCNI Antofagasta *-2001* *ex* Contship Mexico *-2001* *ex* CCNI Antofagasta *-1999* **Sophie Rickmers Schiffahrtsgesellschaft mbH & Cie KG** Rickmers Reederei GmbH & Cie KG *Monrovia* *Liberia* MMSI: 636090564 Official number: 90564	**22,817** 11,005 35,230	Class: GL (LR) ✠ Classed LR until 14/12/99	**1999**-10 **Stocznia Szczecinska Porta Holding SA — Szczecin** Yd No: B577/2/1 Loa 171.20 (BB) Br ex - Dght 11.650 Lbp 161.80 Br md 30.60 Dpth 16.20 Welded, 1 dk	**(A31A2GX) General Cargo Ship** Grain: 38,636 TEU 1644 C Ho 824 TEU C Dk 820 TEU incl 66 ref C. Cargo Heating Coils Compartments: 4 Ho, 4 Cell Ho, ER 8 Ha: (12.6 x 12.8)7 (12.6 x 28.0)ER Cranes: 3x40t	**1 oil engine** driving 1 FP propeller Total Power: 12,000kW (16,315hp) 16.0kn Sulzer 6RTA58T 1 x 2 Stroke 6 Cy. 580 x 2416 12000kW (16315bhp) H Cegielski Poznan SA-Poland AuxGen: 3 x 904kW 450V 60Hz a.c Fuel: 240.9 (d.f.) (Heating Coils) 3019.8 (r.f.) 42.0pd
9553270 *9V9319* -	**SOPHIE 9** *launched as* CF Bron *-2011* **DH Marine Pte Ltd** Hong Lam Marine Pte Ltd *Singapore* *Singapore* MMSI: 566011000 Official number: 396922	**4,568** 1,871 6,141	Class: BV	**2011**-05 **Rongcheng Shenfei Shipbuilding Co Ltd — Rongcheng SD** Yd No: FS1014 Loa 102.70 (BB) Br ex - Dght 6.500 Lbp 95.00 Br md 17.80 Dpth 8.80 Welded, 1 dk	**(A13B2TP) Products Tanker** Double Hull (13F) Liq: 6,746; Liq (Oil): 6,869 Cargo Heating Coils Compartments: 10 Wing Ta, 2 Wing Slop Ta, ER 3 Cargo Pump (s): 2x750m^3/hr, 1x300m^3/hr	**1 oil engine** reduction geared to sc. shaft driving 1 CP propeller Total Power: 2,620kW (3,562hp) 11.7kn Hyundai Himsen 9H25/33P 1 x 4 Stroke 9 Cy. 250 x 330 2620kW (3562bhp) Hyundai Heavy Industries Co Ltd-South Korea AuxGen: 2 x 410kW 440V 60Hz a.c, 1 x 400kW 440V 60Hz a.c Thrusters: 1 Tunnel thruster (f) Fuel: 387.5 (r.f.)
8979893 *CRXK3* -	**SOPHIE BLUE** **Oceanglen Ltd** - *Madeira* *Portugal (MAR)* MMSI: 255901270	**426** 127 -	Class: (RI)	**1998 CBI Navi Srl — Viareggio** Yd No: 32 Loa 41.00 Br ex - Dght - Lbp 32.00 Br md 8.48 Dpth 4.75 Welded, 1 dk	**(X11A2YP) Yacht** Passengers: cabins: 6; berths: 12	**2 oil engines** geared to sc. shafts driving 2 Propellers Total Power: 2,684kW (3,650hp) Caterpillar 3512 2 x Vee 4 Stroke 12 Cy. 170 x 190 each-1342kW (1825bhp) Caterpillar Inc-USA AuxGen: 2 x 80kW 380V 50Hz a.c
8904355 *FGVH* LO 726643	**SOPHIE MARIA** *ex* Freedom *-1998* **Dever Ar Mor Sarl** - *Lorient* *France* MMSI: 227812000 Official number: 686912	*113* - -		**1990**-07 **Forges Caloin — Etaples** (Hull) Yd No: 60 **1990**-07 **Chantier du Ponant — La Rochelle** Loa - (BB) Br ex - Dght 3.761 Lbp 24.95 Br md 7.20 Dpth 4.42 Welded	**(B11A2FS) Stern Trawler** Ins: 100	**1 oil engine** geared to sc. shaft driving 1 FP propeller Total Power: 397kW (540hp) A.B.C. 6MDXS 1 x 4 Stroke 6 Cy. 242 x 320 397kW (540bhp) Anglo Belgian Corp NV (ABC)-Belgium
9138109 *C6LX* -	**SOPHIE OLDENDORFF** **Oldendorff Carriers GmbH & Co KG** - *Madeira* *Portugal (MAR)* MMSI: 255805390 Official number: TEMP163M	**41,428** 19,161 70,037	Class: NK (LR) (NV) Classed LR until 1/10/10	**2000**-09 **Jiangnan Shipyard (Group) Co Ltd — Shanghai** Yd No: H2228 Loa 225.00 (BB) Br ex - Dght 14.420 Lbp 215.00 Br md 32.18 Dpth 19.51 Welded, 1 dk	**(A23A2BD) Bulk Carrier, Self-discharging** Grain: 66,332 Compartments: 7 Ho, ER 8 Ha: 2 (12.0 x 6.0)6 (14.0 x 15.4)ER	**1 oil engine** driving 1 FP propeller Total Power: 10,784kW (14,662hp) 15.0kn MAN-B&W 6S60MC 1 x 2 Stroke 6 Cy. 600 x 2292 10784kW (14662bhp) Dalian Marine Diesel Works-China AuxGen: 2 x 1300kW a.c, 2 x 625kW a.c Thrusters: 1 Thwart. FP thruster (f) Fuel: 345.0 (d.f.) 1564.0 (r.f.) 39.7pd

No. / Call sign	Name / Owner	Tonnage	Class	Builder / Dimensions	Type	Machinery
9265756 *VRJH3* -	**SOPHIE SCHULTE** *ex* Atlantic Galaxy *-2011* *launched as* Yerotsakos *-2005* **Lamma Island Shipping Ltd** Bernhard Schulte Shipmanagement (Isle of Man) Ltd *Hong Kong* *Hong Kong* MMSI: 477328300 Official number: HK3247	**61,991** 34,668 115,583 T/cm 98.1	Class: AB	**2005-06 Sanoyas Hishino Meisho Corp — Kurashiki OY** Yd No: 1224 Loa 249.00 (BB) Br ex 44.04 Dght 14.825 Lbp 238.00 Br md 44.00 Dpth 21.20 Welded, 1 dk	**(A13A2TV) Crude Oil Tanker** Double Hull (13F) Liq: 124,637; Liq (Oil): 124,637 Cargo Heating Coils Compartments: 12 Wing Ta, 2 Wing Slop Ta, Wing ER 3 Cargo Pump (s): 3x2800m³/hr Manifold: Bow/CM: 126.2m	**1 oil engine** driving 1 FP propeller Total Power: 13,549kW (18,421hp) 14.7kn MAN-B&W 6S60MC-C 1 x 2 Stroke 6 Cy. 600 x 2400 13549kW (18421bhp) Kawasaki Heavy Industries Ltd-Japan AuxGen: 2 x 700kW a.c, 1 x 660kW a.c Fuel: 220.0 (d.f.) 3400.0 (r.f.)
9334545 *JWLS3* -	**SOPHIE SIEM** **Siem Offshore Rederi AS** Siem Offshore AS *Aalesund* *Norway (NIS)* MMSI: 257855000	**2,465** 859 3,555	Class: NV	**2006-01 SC Aker Braila SA — Braila** (Hull) Yd No: 1081 **2006-01 Aker Langsten AS — Tomrefjord** Yd No: 205 Loa 73.40 (BB) Br ex 16.63 Dght 6.500 Lbp 64.00 Br md 16.60 Dpth 7.60 Welded, 1 dk	**(B21A20S) Platform Supply Ship**	**2 oil engines** geared to sc. shafts driving 2 CP propellers Total Power: 4,060kW (5,520hp) 14.5kn Caterpillar 3606 2 x 4 Stroke 6 Cy. 280 x 300 each-2030kW (2760bhp) Caterpillar Inc-USA AuxGen: 2 x 345kW 60Hz a.c, 2 x 520kW 60Hz a.c Thrusters: 2 Tunnel thruster (f); 2 Tunnel thruster (a)
1004053 *MXKA3* -	**SOPHISTICATED LADY** *ex* Zulu Charlie *-2005* *ex* Mary Fisher *-2005* **Bridgeport Yachting Ltd** - *London* *United Kingdom* Official number: 305193	*158* 84 -	Class: (LR) ✠ Classed LR until 25/11/96	**1964-05 James A Silver Ltd — Helensburgh** (Hull launched by) **1964-05 Wm. Denny & Bros. Ltd. — Dumbarton** (Hull completed by) Loa 29.46 Br ex - Dght 2.440 Lbp 26.44 Br md 5.73 Dpth 3.35 Welded, 1 dk	**(X11A2YP) Yacht**	**2 oil engines** driving 2 FP propellers Total Power: 530kW (720hp) Baudouin 2 x 4 Stroke 6 Cy. 150 x 150 each-265kW (360bhp) Societe des Moteurs Baudouin SA-France
8916607 *SWBZ* -	**SOPHOCLES V** *ex* Sofoklis Venizelos *-1999* *ex* Hermes *-1999* **Anonymos Naftiliaki Eteria Kritis AE (ANEK Lines SA)** - SatCom: Inmarsat C 423959310 *Chania* *Greece* MMSI: 239593000 Official number: 26	**29,991** 13,844 6,987 T/cm 37.1	Class: RI (HR) (NK)	**1990-07 Mitsubishi Heavy Industries Ltd. — Shimonoseki** Yd No: 937 Loa 192.00 (BB) Br ex 29.00 Dght 6.716 Lbp 175.00 Br md 27.00 Dpth 9.90 Welded, 9 dks	**(A36A2PR) Passenger/Ro-Ro Ship (Vehicles)** Passengers: unberthed: 1413; cabins: 180; berths: 637; driver berths: 76 Stern door/ramp Len: 15.00 Wid: 6.64 Swl: 40 Quarter bow door/ramp (s) Len: 21.20 Wid: 7.20 Swl: 40 Quarter stern door/ramp (s) Len: 18.00 Wid: 6.64 Swl: 40 Lane-Len: 1890 Lane-Wid: 2.86 Lane-clr ht: 4.50 Cars: 473	**2 oil engines** with flexible couplings & sr geared to sc. shafts driving 2 CP propellers Total Power: 26,186kW (35,602hp) 25.0kn Pielstick 12PC4-2V-570 2 x Vee 4 Stroke 12 Cy. 570 x 620 each-13093kW (17801bhp) Nippon Kokan KK (NKK Corp)-Japan AuxGen: 2 x 1250kW 440V a.c, 3 x 1020kW 440V a.c Thrusters: 2 Thwart. CP thruster (f); 1 Thwart. CP thruster (a) Fuel: 164.1 (d.f.) (Heating Coils) 985.6 (r.f.) 122.0pd
8725838 - -	**SOPOCHNOYE** **UTRF-Holding JSC (OAO 'UTRF-Holding')** -	**773** 231 303	Class: (RS)	**1986-09 Volgogradskiy Sudostroitelnyy Zavod — Volgograd** Yd No: 234 Loa 53.74 (BB) Br ex 10.71 Dght 4.360 Lbp 47.92 Br md - Dpth 6.50 Welded, 1 dk	**(B11A2FS) Stern Trawler** Ice Capable	**1 oil engine** driving 1 CP propeller Total Power: 871kW (1,184hp) 12.7kn S.K.L. 8NVD48A-2U 1 x 4 Stroke 8 Cy. 320 x 480 871kW (1184bhp) VEB Schwermaschinenbau "KarlLiebknecht" (SKL)-Magdeburg AuxGen: 1 x 300kW a.c, 3 x 160kW a.c, 2 x 135kW a.c
8972924 - -	**SOPOTI** **Isa Popa** - *Durres* *Albania* Official number: 115-115	**112** 79 120		**1974 Kantieri Detar "Durres" — Durres** Loa 25.00 Br ex 6.20 Dght 2.740 Lbp - Br md 6.00 Dpth 3.20 Welded, 1 dk	**(A31A2GX) General Cargo Ship**	**1 oil engine** driving 1 FP propeller Total Power: 294kW (400hp) S.K.L. 8NVD26A-2 1 x 4 Stroke 8 Cy. 180 x 260 294kW (400bhp) VEB Schwermaschinenbau "KarlLiebknecht" (SKL)-Magdeburg
6872285 *HP7555* -	**SOPRUS** **Transporte y Turismo Bocatoreno SA** - *Panama* *Panama* Official number: 22854PEXT2	**462** 138 191	Class: (RS)	**1956-03 Admiralteyskiy Sudostroitelnyy Zavod — Leningrad** Yd No: 685 Loa 45.60 Br ex 11.03 Dght 2.701 Lbp - Br md 10.62 Dpth 4.02 Welded, 1 dk	**(A36A2PR) Passenger/Ro-Ro Ship (Vehicles)** Ice Capable	**2 oil engines** driving 2 FP propellers Total Power: 442kW (600hp) 10.5kn S.K.L. R8DV136 2 x 4 Stroke 8 Cy. 240 x 360 each-221kW (300bhp) VEB Schwermaschinenbau "KarlLiebknecht" (SKL)-Magdeburg AuxGen: 2 x 64kW Fuel: 30.0 (d.f.)
9084463 *PKOW* -	**SOPUTAN** **Government of The Republic of Indonesia (Markas Besar TNI Angkatan Laut - Indonesian Navy)** - *Indonesia*	**1,279** 383 983	Class: (LR) ✠	**1995-07 Dae Sun Shipbuilding & Engineering Co Ltd — Busan** Yd No: 405 Loa 66.21 Br ex 11.94 Dght 4.513 Lbp 60.20 Br md 11.70 Dpth 5.60 Welded, 1 dk	**(B32A2ST) Tug**	**2 oil engines** geared to sc. shafts driving 2 CP propellers Total Power: 3,530kW (4,800hp) 13.5kn Pielstick 8PA5L 2 x 4 Stroke 8 Cy. 255 x 270 each-1765kW (2400bhp) Ssangyong Heavy Industries Co Ltd-South Korea AuxGen: 2 x 435kW 440V 60Hz a.c, 2 x 105kW 440V 60Hz a.c Thrusters: 1 Thwart. FP thruster (f)
7004562 - -	**SOR BANTADTHAI 29** *ex* Chow Tha H. 4 *-1999* **Government of The Kingdom of Thailand (Marine Department)** - *Bangkok* *Thailand* Official number: 131002905	*823* 322 661	Class: (LR) ✠ Classed LR until 2/71	**1969-09 Hayashikane Shipbuilding & Engineering Co Ltd — Nagasaki NS** Yd No: 713 Loa 58.30 Br ex 10.04 Dght 3.512 Lbp 52.71 Br md 10.01 Dpth 4.53 Welded, 1 dk	**(B33B2DT) Trailing Suction Hopper Dredger** Hopper: 404	**2 oil engines** driving 2 FP propellers Total Power: 750kW (1,020hp) Niigata 6L25BX 2 x 4 Stroke 6 Cy. 250 x 320 each-375kW (510bhp) Niigata Engineering Co Ltd-Japan AuxGen: 2 x 136kW 225V 50Hz a.c, 1 x 80kW 225V 50Hz a.c
9253337 - -	**SOR SAPCHAROENSAMUT 1** **Thavee Sirithaveesap**	**295** 201 -		**2001-01 PSP Marine Co Ltd — Samut Sakhon** Loa 38.10 Br ex 8.00 Dght - Lbp - Br md - Dpth 4.50 Welded, 1 dk	**(B11B2FV) Fishing Vessel**	**1 oil engine** driving 1 FP propeller Total Power: 736kW (1,001hp) Cummins KTA-38-M1 1 x Vee 4 Stroke 12 Cy. 159 x 159 736kW (1001bhp) Cummins Engine Co Inc-USA
8982450 - -	**SOR SOMBOON 19** **Vichai Pattanawittayanont** - *Bangkok* *Thailand* Official number: 460002888	**296** 201 -		**2003-09 Mahachai Dockyard Co., Ltd. — Samut Sakhon** Loa 39.00 Br ex - Dght - Lbp 36.30 Br md 8.00 Dpth 4.00 Welded, 1 dk	**(B12B2FC) Fish Carrier**	**1 oil engine** geared to sc. shaft driving 1 Propeller Total Power: 746kW (1,014hp) Cummins KTA-38-M1 1 x Vee 4 Stroke 12 Cy. 159 x 159 746kW (1014bhp) Cummins Engine Co Inc-USA
8324311 *7LNU* -	**SORACHI** **Government of Japan (Ministry of Land, Infrastructure & Transport) (The Coastguard)** - *Tokyo* *Japan* MMSI: 431800065 Official number: 128063	*330* - -		**1984-08 Tohoku Shipbuilding Co Ltd — Shiogama MG** Yd No: 209 Loa 67.80 Br ex 7.92 Dght 2.800 Lbp 60.00 Br md 7.90 Dpth 4.40 Welded, 1 dk	**(B34H2SQ) Patrol Vessel**	**2 oil engines** driving 2 CP propellers Total Power: 2,206kW (3,000hp) Niigata 6M31EX 2 x 4 Stroke 6 Cy. 310 x 460 each-1103kW (1500bhp) Niigata Engineering Co Ltd-Japan
9281736 - -	**SORAK** **Kum Gang Maritime Co Ltd** - *Pyeongtaek* *South Korea* MMSI: 440001820 Official number: PTR-023105	**215** - -	Class: (KR)	**2002-11 Yeunsoo Shipbuilding Co Ltd — Janghang** Yd No: 11 Loa 34.10 Br ex - Dght 3.100 Lbp 28.60 Br md 9.50 Dpth 4.00 Welded, 1 Dk.	**(B32A2ST) Tug**	**2 oil engines** geared to sc. shafts driving 2 FP propellers Total Power: 3,230kW (4,392hp) M.T.U. 16V4000M60 2 x Vee 4 Stroke 16 Cy. 165 x 190 each-1615kW (2196bhp) MTU Friedrichshafen GmbH-Friedrichshafen
9666314 - -	**SORAK** **Kum Gang Maritime Co Ltd** - *Pyeongtaek* *South Korea* MMSI: 440016320 Official number: PTR-127309	**281** - 173	Class: KR	**2012-07 Samkwang Shipbuilding & Engineering Co Ltd — Incheon** Yd No: SKSB-204 Loa 36.50 Br ex 10.02 Dght 3.300 Lbp 31.15 Br md 10.00 Dpth 4.50 Welded, 1 dk	**(B32A2ST) Tug**	**2 oil engines** reduction geared to sc. shafts driving 2 Propellers Total Power: 3,840kW (5,220hp) Yanmar 6EY26 2 x 4 Stroke 6 Cy. 260 x 385 each-1920kW (2610bhp) Yanmar Diesel Engine Co Ltd-Japan Fuel: 63.0 (d.f.)
8723361 *UAYO* -	**SORAKSAN** *ex* Zolotaya Dolina *-1999* **OOO Zolotaya Dolina** Vostoktransshipping Co Ltd *Vladivostok* *Russia* MMSI: 273449080 Official number: 846478	**6,648** 2,525 4,900	Class: RS (BV) (NV)	**1986-03 GP Sudostroitelnyy Zavod im. "61 Kommunara" — Nikolayev** Yd No: 1122 Loa 126.60 (BB) Br ex 18.00 Dght 7.480 Lbp 115.00 Br md - Dpth 10.70 Welded, 3 dks	**(A34A2GR) Refrigerated Cargo Ship** Ins: 6,650 Compartments: 4 Ho, ER 4 Ha: ER Derricks: 8x3.2t Ice Capable	**1 oil engine** driving 1 FP propeller Total Power: 3,970kW (5,398hp) 15.3kn B&W 6DKRN45/120 1 x 2 Stroke 6 Cy. 450 x 1200 3970kW (5398bhp) Bryanskiy Mashinostroitelnyy Zavod (BMZ)-Bryansk AuxGen: 3 x 500kW a.c

IMO / Call sign	Name / Owner	Tonnage	Class	Builder / Dimensions	Type	Machinery
8502157 *JWQY* F-350-M	**SORBOEN** **Storvik Shipping ANS** *Trondheim* *Norway* MMSI: 257563500	**272** 108 -		**1985**-09 **Herfjord Slip & Verksted AS — Revsnes i Fosna** (Hull) **1985**-09 **Solstrand Slip & Baatbyggeri AS — Tomrefjord** Yd No: 41 Loa 27.44 Br ex - Dght - Lbp - Br md 8.01 Dpth 4.35 Welded, 1 dk	**(B11A2FS) Stern Trawler**	**1 oil engine** geared to sc. shaft driving 1 FP propeller Total Power: 397kW (540hp) Caterpillar 3508TA 1 x Vee 4 Stroke 8 Cy. 170 x 190 397kW (540bhp) Caterpillar Tractor Co-USA Thrusters: 1 Thwart. FP thruster (f); 2 Tunnel thruster (a)
9356787 *V7JK7* -	**SORCHA** *ex* Lia Fail *-2006* **Sorcha Inc** - *Bikini* *Marshall Islands* MMSI: 538070187 Official number: 70187	**498** 149	Class: AB	**2005**-08 **Northern Marine Inc — Anacortes WA** Yd No: 15001 Loa 46.30 Br ex 9.07 Dght 1.980 Lbp 39.70 Br md 8.84 Dpth 4.11 Bonded, 1 dk	**(X11A2YP) Yacht** Hull Material: Reinforced Plastic	**2 oil engines** geared to sc. shafts driving 2 CP propellers Total Power: 2,244kW (3,050hp) 12.0kn Caterpillar 3512B 2 x Vee 4 Stroke 12 Cy. 170 x 190 each-1122kW (1525bhp) Caterpillar Inc-USA Thrusters: 1 Tunnel thruster (f)
8737611 *EA3566* 3-TA-31-98	**SORD** **Sord 97 SL** - *Tarragona* *Spain* Official number: 3-1/1998	**127** - -		**1998**-04 **EN Bazan de Construcciones Navales Militares SA — San Fernando (Sp)** Yd No: 351 Loa 27.00 Br ex - Dght 1.700 Lbp 23.00 Br md 7.80 Dpth 2.85 Bonded, 1 dk	**(B11A2FS) Stern Trawler** Hull Material: Reinforced Plastic	**2 oil engines** driving 2 Propellers
6700652 *LCKA* -	**SORDYROY** *ex* Snaefugl *-2008* *ex* Gudmundur Olafur II *-2003* *ex* Gudmundur Olafur *-2003* *ex* Krossanes *-1983* *ex* Arnarnes *-1981* *ex* Bjarni Olafsson *-1978* *ex* Borkur II *-1973* *ex* Borkur *-1972* **Fisketransport AS** DBS Consultancy AS *Kristiansand* *Norway* MMSI: 257151000	**611** 183 -	Class: (NV)	**1966**-11 **Ankerlokken Verft Floro AS — Floro** Yd No: 74 Lengthened-1996 Lengthened-1975 Loa 50.22 Br ex 7.65 Dght 3.760 Lbp 47.60 Br md 7.60 Dpth 5.82 Welded, 1 dk	**(B11B2FV) Fishing Vessel** Compartments: 2 Ho, ER 2 Ha: 2 (2.5 x 1.6)ER Derricks: 1; Winches: 1 Ice Capable	**1 oil engine** geared to sc. shaft driving 1 CP propeller Total Power: 588kW (799hp) Blackstone ESS8 1 x 4 Stroke 8 Cy. 222 x 292 588kW (799bhp) Lister Blackstone Marine Ltd.-Dursley AuxGen: 2 x 42kW 220V 50Hz a.c
8734451 *YD6456* -	**SOREANG** *ex* Atlantic Star 8 *-2012* **PT Perusahaan Pelayaran Tonasa Lines** - *Samarinda* *Indonesia*	**225** 68 -	Class: KI	**1999 P.T. Karya Mulyo Teknik — Samarinda** Loa 29.75 Br ex - Dght - Lbp 25.50 Br md 8.00 Dpth 3.75 Welded, 1 dk	**(B32A2ST) Tug**	**2 oil engines** driving 2 Propellers Total Power: 1,324kW (1,800hp) Niigata 2 x 4 Stroke 6 Cy. each-662kW (900bhp) Niigata Engineering Co Ltd-Japan
8112079 *EQLG* -	**SOREH** **Government of The Islamic Republic of Iran (Ports & Maritime Organisation)** - *Chabahar* *Iran* MMSI: 422774000 Official number: 588	**206** 62 135	Class: AS (LR) ✠ Classed LR until 17/6/92	**1983**-06 **Scheepsbouw Alblas B.V. — Krimpen a/d IJssel** (Hull) **1983**-06 **B.V. Scheepswerf Damen — Gorinchem** Yd No: 3127 Loa 30.21 Br ex 8.06 Dght 3.310 Lbp 26.95 Br md 7.80 Dpth 4.04 Welded, 1 dk	**(B32A2ST) Tug**	**2 oil engines** with clutches, flexible couplings & sr reverse geared to sc. shafts driving 2 FP propellers Total Power: 2,140kW (2,910hp) Deutz SBV6M628 2 x 4 Stroke 6 Cy. 240 x 280 each-1070kW (1455bhp) Kloeckner Humboldt Deutz AG-West Germany AuxGen: 2 x 64kW 380V 50Hz a.c Fuel: 68.0 (d.f.)
5413082 - -	**SOREL POINT** *ex* Uno *-1984* *ex* Susse W *-1980* *ex* Danasund *-1977* *ex* Volmer *-1974* *ex* Rainer Carstens *-1965* **Francis Shurland Jnr** - *Georgetown* *Guyana* Official number: 0000157	**299** 169 470	Class: (GL)	**1963 Martin Jansen GmbH & Co. KG Schiffsw. u. Masch. — Leer** Yd No: 55 Loa 42.70 Br ex 7.55 Dght 2.780 Lbp 39.15 Br md 7.50 Dpth 3.10 Welded, 1 dk	**(A31A2GX) General Cargo Ship** Grain: 651; Bale: 595 Compartments: 1 Ho, ER 1 Ha: (20.5 x 5.0)ER	**1 oil engine** reverse reduction geared to sc. shaft driving 1 FP propeller Total Power: 272kW (370hp) 9.5kn Cummins KT-1150-M 1 x 4 Stroke 6 Cy. 159 x 159 272kW (370bhp) (new engine 1980) Cummins Engine Co Inc-USA AuxGen: 1 x 10kW 220V d.c, 1 x 5kW 220V d.c
1002316 *MGZJ5* -	**SOREMI** *ex* Lady Anfimar *-2002* **Agentspeedy Ltd** Fairdeal Group Management SA *London* *United Kingdom* Official number: 712872	**236** 75	Class: LR ✠ **100A1** SS 04/2012 Yacht ✠ **LMC**	**1987**-09 **Baglietto S.p.A. — Varazze** Loa 35.53 Br ex 7.60 Dght 1.180 Lbp 28.70 Br md - Dpth 3.47 Welded, 1 dk	**(X11A2YP) Yacht** Hull Material: Aluminium Alloy	**2 oil engines** driving 2 Water jets Total Power: 3,140kW (4,270hp) M.T.U. 12V396 2 x Vee 4 Stroke 12 Cy. 165 x 185 each-1570kW (2135bhp) MTU Friedrichshafen GmbH-Friedrichshafen
9202493 *EPAD8* -	**SOREN** *ex* Fortuna II *-2009* **Golden Sea Shipping Co Ltd** Parsian Golden Sea Shipping Co *Bandar Anzali* *Iran* MMSI: 422869000 Official number: 937	**3,185** 1,358 3,850	Class: AS GL (Class contemplated) (RS)	**1999**-03 **OAO Navashinskiy Sudostroitelnyy Zavod 'Oka' — Navashino** Yd No: 1062 Loa 107.40 Br ex - Dght 3.980 Lbp 103.80 Br md 16.70 Dpth 5.50 Welded, 1 dk	**(A31A2GX) General Cargo Ship** Grain: 4,720 TEU 168 C.Ho 90/20' C.Dk 78/20' Compartments: 3 Ho, ER 3 Ha: 3 (18.6 x 12.6)ER Ice Capable	**2 oil engines** with clutches, flexible couplings & sr reverse geared to sc. shafts driving 2 FP propellers Total Power: 1,740kW (2,366hp) 10.0kn Dvigatel Revolyutsii 6CHRN36/45 2 x 4 Stroke 6 Cy. 360 x 450 each-870kW (1183bhp) Zavod "Dvigatel Revolyutsii"-Nizhniy Novgorod AuxGen: 2 x 150kW 380V 50Hz a.c, 1 x 50kW 380V 50Hz a.c Thrusters: 1 Thwart. FP thruster (f) Fuel: 170.0 (d.f.) 6.0pd
6511647 - -	**SORENGANA** - **North Western Trading Co Ltd** - *Madang* *Papua New Guinea*	*115* 51 132		**1965 Tohoku Shipbuilding Co Ltd — Shiogama MG** Yd No: 63C Loa 26.80 Br ex 6.10 Dght 2.185 Lbp 24.46 Br md 5.90 Dpth 2.80 Welded, 1 dk	**(A31A2GX) General Cargo Ship**	**1 oil engine** driving 1 FP propeller Yanmar 1 x 4 Stroke 5 Cy. 200 x 280 Yanmar Diesel Engine Co Ltd-Japan
8033118 *UGKO* -	**SORGU** - **Udarnik-1 Fishing Collective (Rybolovetskiy Kolkhoz 'Udarnik-1')** - *Petropavlovsk-Kamchatskiy* *Russia*	**358** 107 150	Class: (RS)	**1981**-09 **Sudostroitelnyy Zavod "Avangard" — Petrozavodsk** Yd No: 404 Loa 35.72 Br ex 8.82 Dght 3.429 Lbp 31.00 Br md 8.80 Dpth 5.95 Welded, 1 dk	**(B11A2FS) Stern Trawler** Ins: 110 Compartments: 1 Ho, ER 1 Ha: (1.3 x 1.3) Derricks: 2x1.5t Ice Capable	**1 oil engine** geared to sc. shaft driving 1 FP propeller Total Power: 425kW (578hp) 10.5kn S.K.L. 8VD36/24A-1U 1 x 4 Stroke 8 Cy. 240 x 360 425kW (578bhp) VEB Schwermaschinenbau "KarlLiebknecht" (SKL)-Magdeburg AuxGen: 2 x 160kW Fuel: 81.0 (d.f.)
5334561 *LDTY3* -	**SORLANDET** - **Stiftelsen Fullriggeren 'Sorlandet'** - *Kristiansand* *Norway (NIS)* MMSI: 257165000 Official number: 8583	**499** 149 -	Class: NV	**1927**-05 **Hoivolds Motor- & Mek. Verksted — Kristiansand** Yd No: 1 Loa 56.70 Br ex 8.87 Dght 4.420 Lbp 48.16 Br md 8.84 Dpth 5.19 Riveted, 2 dks	**(X11B2QN) Sail Training Ship**	**1 oil engine** driving 1 CP propeller Total Power: 415kW (564hp) Deutz SBA8M816 1 x 4 Stroke 8 Cy. 142 x 160 415kW (564bhp) (new engine 1980) Kloeckner Humboldt Deutz AG-West Germany AuxGen: 1 x 60kW 220V 50Hz a.c, 1 x 12kW 220V 50Hz a.c
7942946 *UCWS* -	**SORMOVO 1** *ex* Voloma *-2013* *ex* Sormovskiy-3001 *-2011* **LLC 'Sormovo Ship'** CJSC 'Line Invest' *St Petersburg* *Russia* MMSI: 273315200	**2,491** 977 3,100	Class: RS	**1981 Shipbuilding & Shiprepairing Yard 'Ivan Dimitrov' — Rousse** Yd No: 371 Loa 114.06 Br ex 13.26 Dght 3.660 Lbp 110.84 Br md 13.02 Dpth 5.52 Welded, 1 dk	**(A31A2GX) General Cargo Ship** Grain: 4,308; Bale: 4,308 Compartments: 4 Ho, ER 4 Ha: (17.5 x 9.4)2 (17.9 x 9.4) (18.6 x 9.4)ER Ice Capable	**2 oil engines** driving 2 FP propellers Total Power: 970kW (1,318hp) 10.5kn S.K.L. 6NVD48A-2U 2 x 4 Stroke 6 Cy. 320 x 480 each-485kW (659bhp) VEB Schwermaschinenbau "KarlLiebknecht" (SKL)-Magdeburg AuxGen: 3 x 50kW Fuel: 113.0 (d.f.)
7005671 *UBEI* -	**SORMOVSKIY-12** - **Orbita Shipping Co Ltd** Meridian Co Ltd SatCom: Inmarsat C 427310352 *Astrakhan* *Russia* MMSI: 273455820 Official number: 691861	**2,478** 1,080 3,353	Class: RS	**1969 Sudostroitelnyy Zavod "Krasnoye Sormovo" — Gorkiy** Yd No: 014 Loa 114.20 Br ex 13.21 Dght 3.800 Lbp 108.01 Br md 13.00 Dpth 5.52 Welded, 1 dk	**(A31A2GX) General Cargo Ship** Bale: 4,297 Compartments: 4 Ho, ER 4 Ha: (17.6 x 9.3)3 (18.1 x 9.3)ER Ice Capable	**2 oil engines** driving 2 FP propellers Total Power: 970kW (1,318hp) 10.8kn S.K.L. 6NVD48A-U 2 x 4 Stroke 6 Cy. 320 x 480 each-485kW (659bhp) VEB Schwermaschinenbau "KarlLiebknecht" (SKL)-Magdeburg AuxGen: 3 x 50kW Fuel: 114.0 (d.f.)
7324273 *UHMP* -	**SORMOVSKIY-29** - **USA Ltd** JSC Sredne-Volzhskaya Sudokhodnaya Kompaniya (Middle Volga Shipping Co) *Astrakhan* *Russia* MMSI: 273329400	**2,481** 1,081 3,134	Class: RS	**1973**-06 **Sudostroitelnyy Zavod "Krasnoye Sormovo" — Gorkiy** Yd No: 39 Loa 114.03 Br ex 13.21 Dght 3.810 Lbp 107.50 Br md 13.00 Dpth 5.52 Welded, 1 dk	**(A31A2GX) General Cargo Ship** Bale: 4,297 Compartments: 4 Ho, ER 4 Ha: (17.6 x 9.3)3 (18.1 x 9.3)ER Ice Capable	**2 oil engines** driving 2 FP propellers Total Power: 970kW (1,318hp) 10.8kn S.K.L. 6NVD48A-U 2 x 4 Stroke 6 Cy. 320 x 480 each-485kW (659bhp) VEB Schwermaschinenbau "KarlLiebknecht" (SKL)-Magdeburg AuxGen: 4 x 50kW Fuel: 94.0 (d.f.)

IMO / Call sign	Ship / Owner	Tonnage	Class	Build	Type / Capacity	Machinery
7329144 *UAAT* -	**SORMOVSKIY-32** *ex XVII Syezd VLKSM -1992* *ex Sormovskiy-32 -1992* **Parkside International Services Ltd** JSC Sredne-Volzhskaya Sudokhodnaya Kompaniya (Middle Volga Shipping Co) *Astrakhan* *Russia* MMSI: 273459910	**2,478** 999 3,353	Class: RS	**1974**-04 **Sudostroitelnyy Zavod "Krasnoye Sormovo" — Gorkiy** Yd No: 45 Loa 114.03 Br ex 13.21 Dght 3.810 Lbp 110.27 Br md 13.00 Dpth 5.52 Welded, 1 dk	**(A31A2GX) General Cargo Ship** Grain: 4,297; Bale: 4,296 Compartments: 4 Ho, ER 4 Ha: (17.6 x 9.3)3 (18.0 x 9.3) Ice Capable	**2 oil engines** driving 2 FP propellers Total Power: 970kW (1,318hp) 10.8kn S.K.L. 6NVD48A-U 2 x 4 Stroke 6 Cy. 320 x 480 each-485kW (659bhp) VEB Schwermaschinenbau "KarlLiebknecht" (SKL)-Magdeburg AuxGen: 4 x 50kW Fuel: 94.0 (d.f.)
7630103 *V3ID* -	**SORMOVSKIY-36** *ex Fyodor Podtelkov -1994* *ex Sormovskiy-36 -1994* *ex Fyodor Podtelkov -1992* **Yucatan Shipping Co Ltd** Joint Stock Co Navigator Group *Belize City* *Belize* Official number: 360120012	**2,466** 977 3,136	Class: RS	**1976**-08 **Sudostroitelnyy Zavod "Krasnoye Sormovo" — Gorkiy** Yd No: 52 Loa 114.03 Br ex 13.21 Dght 3.642 Lbp 108.01 Br md 12.98 Dpth 5.52 Welded, 1 dk	**(A31A2GX) General Cargo Ship** Grain: 4,297 Compartments: 4 Ho, ER 4 Ha: (17.6 x 9.3)3 (18.0 x 9.3) Ice Capable	**2 oil engines** driving 2 FP propellers Total Power: 970kW (1,318hp) 10.8kn S.K.L. 6NVD48A-U 2 x 4 Stroke 6 Cy. 320 x 480 each-485kW (659bhp) VEB Schwermaschinenbau "KarlLiebknecht" (SKL)-Magdeburg AuxGen: 4 x 50kW Fuel: 94.0 (d.f.)
7732016 *UGQY* -	**SORMOVSKIY-40** - **Amur Shipping Co** - *Nikolayevsk-na-Amure* *Russia* MMSI: 273356000	**2,478** 1,075 3,347	Class: RS	**1978**-04 **Sudostroitelnyy Zavod "Krasnoye Sormovo" — Gorkiy** Yd No: 57 Loa 114.03 Br ex 13.21 Dght 3.810 Lbp 107.50 Br md 13.00 Dpth 5.50 Welded, 1 dk	**(A31A2GX) General Cargo Ship** Bale: 4,297 Compartments: 4 Ho, ER 4 Ha: (17.6 x 9.3)3 (18.1 x 9.3)ER Ice Capable	**2 oil engines** driving 2 FP propellers Total Power: 970kW (1,318hp) 10.5kn S.K.L. 6NVD48A-U 2 x 4 Stroke 6 Cy. 320 x 480 each-485kW (659bhp) VEB Schwermaschinenbau "KarlLiebknecht" (SKL)-Magdeburg AuxGen: 3 x 50kW Fuel: 112.0 (d.f.)
7945857 *V3OE9* -	**SORMOVSKIY-43** *ex Sormovskiy 43 -2012* *ex Sormovskiy-43 -2011* **Volgo-Don 203 Shipping Co Ltd** Rosshipcom Marine Ltd *Belize City* *Belize* MMSI: 312063000 Official number: 371120067	**2,466** 1,065 3,134	Class: RS	**1981**-09 **Sudostroitelnyy Zavod "Krasnoye Sormovo" — Gorkiy** Yd No: 69 Loa 114.03 Br ex 13.21 Dght 3.423 Lbp 108.03 Br md 13.00 Dpth 5.54 Welded, 1 dk	**(A31A2GX) General Cargo Ship** Grain: 4,297; Bale: 4,297 Compartments: 4 Ho, ER 4 Ha: (17.6 x 9.3)3 (17.9 x 9.3)ER Ice Capable	**2 oil engines** driving 2 FP propellers Total Power: 970kW (1,318hp) 10.8kn S.K.L. 6NVD48-2U 2 x 4 Stroke 6 Cy. 320 x 480 each-485kW (659bhp) VEB Schwermaschinenbau "KarlLiebknecht" (SKL)-Magdeburg Fuel: 111.0 (d.f.)
8133566 *V4ER2* -	**SORMOVSKIY-45** - **Sormovskiy 45 Ltd** Is-Bir Denizcilik ve Tankercilik Ticaret Ltd Sti *Basseterre* *St Kitts & Nevis* MMSI: 341393000	**2,478** 999 3,346	Class: RS	**1982**-11 **Sudostroitelnyy Zavod "Krasnoye Sormovo" — Gorkiy** Yd No: 74 Loa 114.03 Br ex 13.21 Dght 3.810 Lbp 108.03 Br md 13.00 Dpth 5.54 Welded, 1 dk	**(A31A2GX) General Cargo Ship** Bale: 4,297 Compartments: 4 Ho, ER 4 Ha: (17.6 x 9.3)3 (18.1 x 9.3)ER Ice Capable	**2 oil engines** driving 2 FP propellers Total Power: 970kW (1,318hp) 10.8kn S.K.L. 6NVD48-2U 2 x 4 Stroke 6 Cy. 320 x 480 each-485kW (659bhp) VEB Schwermaschinenbau "KarlLiebknecht" (SKL)-Magdeburg Fuel: 111.0 (d.f.)
8226428 *V4YT2* -	**SORMOVSKIY-48** - **Sormovskiy 48 Ltd** Is-Bir Denizcilik ve Tankercilik Ticaret Ltd Sti *St Kitts & Nevis* MMSI: 341287000	**2,466** 1,065 3,346	Class: RS	**1983**-11 **Sudostroitelnyy Zavod "Krasnoye Sormovo" — Gorkiy** Yd No: 77 Loa 114.03 Br ex 13.21 Dght 3.810 Lbp 107.79 Br md 13.00 Dpth 5.54 Welded, 1 dk	**(A31A2GX) General Cargo Ship** Bale: 4,297 Compartments: 4 Ho, ER 4 Ha: (17.6 x 9.3)3 (17.9 x 9.3)ER Ice Capable	**2 oil engines** driving 2 FP propellers Total Power: 970kW (1,318hp) 10.8kn S.K.L. 6NVD48A-U 2 x 4 Stroke 6 Cy. 320 x 480 each-485kW (659bhp) VEB Schwermaschinenbau "KarlLiebknecht" (SKL)-Magdeburg AuxGen: 3 x 50kW Fuel: 111.0 (d.f.)
8332784 *UAKQ* -	**SORMOVSKIY-49** - **'SA Shipping' Ltd (LLC SA Shipping)** - *Kaliningrad* *Russia* MMSI: 273325200 Official number: 840113	**2,478** 917 3,135	Class: RS	**1984**-07 **Sudostroitelnyy Zavod "Krasnoye Sormovo" — Gorkiy** Yd No: 81 Loa 114.02 Br ex 13.22 Dght 3.671 Lbp 110.76 Br md 13.00 Dpth 5.52 Welded, 1 dk	**(A31A2GX) General Cargo Ship** Bale: 4,297 Compartments: 4 Ho, ER 4 Ha: (17.6 x 9.3)3 (17.9 x 9.3)ER Ice Capable	**2 oil engines** driving 2 FP propellers Total Power: 970kW (1,318hp) 10.7kn S.K.L. 6NVD48-2U 2 x 4 Stroke 6 Cy. 320 x 480 each-485kW (659bhp) VEB Schwermaschinenbau "KarlLiebknecht" (SKL)-Magdeburg Fuel: 84.0 (d.f.)
8628133 *UAKX* -	**SORMOVSKIY-53** - **Western Shipping Co JSC (OAO Zapadnoye Parokhodstvo - 'ZAPADFLOT')** - *Kaliningrad* *Russia* MMSI: 273326000 Official number: 850308	**2,466** 988 3,353	Class: RS	**1986**-07 **Sudostroitelnyy Zavod "Krasnoye Sormovo" — Gorkiy** Yd No: 87 Loa 114.02 Br ex 13.22 Dght 3.810 Lbp 110.76 Br md 13.00 Dpth 5.50 Welded, 1 dk	**(A31A2GX) General Cargo Ship** Bale: 4,297 Compartments: 4 Ho, ER 4 Ha: (17.6 x 9.3)3 (17.9 x 9.3)ER Ice Capable	**2 oil engines** driving 2 FP propellers Total Power: 970kW (1,318hp) 10.7kn S.K.L. 6NVD48-2U 2 x 4 Stroke 6 Cy. 320 x 480 each-485kW (659bhp) VEB Schwermaschinenbau "KarlLiebknecht" (SKL)-Magdeburg
7740764 *UBUK* -	**SORMOVSKIY-54** *ex 60 Let VLKSM -1992* **Yucatan Shipping Co Ltd** Joint Stock Co Navigator Group *Taganrog* *Russia* MMSI: 273371500	**2,466** 988 3,353	Class: RS	**1978**-11 **Sudostroitelnyy Zavod "Krasnoye Sormovo" — Gorkiy** Yd No: 60 Loa 114.03 Br ex 13.21 Dght 3.810 Lbp 108.01 Br md 12.98 Dpth 5.52 Welded, 1 dk	**(A31A2GX) General Cargo Ship** Bale: 4,297 Compartments: 4 Ho, ER 4 Ha: (17.6 x 9.3)3 (17.9 x 9.3)ER Ice Capable	**2 oil engines** driving 2 FP propellers Total Power: 970kW (1,318hp) 10.8kn S.K.L. 6NVD48-2U 2 x 4 Stroke 6 Cy. 320 x 480 each-485kW (659bhp) VEB Schwermaschinenbau "KarlLiebknecht" (SKL)-Magdeburg Fuel: 111.0 (d.f.)
7733515 *UDPV* -	**SORMOVSKIY-116** *ex Mikhail Krivoshlykov -1992* **Yucatan Shipping Co Ltd** Joint Stock Co Navigator Group *Taganrog* *Russia* MMSI: 273376300 Official number: 781771	**2,466** 988 3,353	Class: RS	**1978**-06 **Sudostroitelnyy Zavod im Volodarskogo — Rybinsk** Yd No: 76 Loa 114.03 Br ex 13.21 Dght 3.671 Lbp 108.01 Br md 13.00 Dpth 5.85 Welded, 1 dk	**(A31A2GX) General Cargo Ship** Bale: 4,297 Compartments: 4 Ho, ER 4 Ha: (17.6 x 9.3)3 (17.9 x 9.3)ER Ice Capable	**2 oil engines** driving 2 FP propellers Total Power: 970kW (1,318hp) 10.8kn S.K.L. 6NVD48-2U 2 x 4 Stroke 6 Cy. 320 x 480 each-485kW (659bhp) VEB Schwermaschinenbau "KarlLiebknecht" (SKL)-Magdeburg Fuel: 94.0 (d.f.)
7741392 *UGQZ* -	**SORMOVSKIY-117** - **Amur Shipping Co** - SatCom: Inmarsat C 427320776 *Nikolayevsk-na-Amure* *Russia* MMSI: 273355000 Official number: 782153	**2,478** 1,075 3,294	Class: RS	**1979 Sudostroitelnyy Zavod im Volodarskogo — Rybinsk** Yd No: 79 Loa 114.03 Br ex 13.21 Dght 3.810 Lbp 108.01 Br md 13.00 Dpth 5.52 Welded, 1 dk	**(A31A2GX) General Cargo Ship** Bale: 4,297 Compartments: 4 Ho, ER 4 Ha: (17.6 x 9.3)3 (18.0 x 9.3)ER Ice Capable	**2 oil engines** driving 2 FP propellers Total Power: 970kW (1,318hp) 10.8kn S.K.L. 6NVD48-2U 2 x 4 Stroke 6 Cy. 320 x 480 each-485kW (659bhp) VEB Schwermaschinenbau "KarlLiebknecht" (SKL)-Magdeburg Fuel: 112.0 (d.f.)
7943287 *V4NX* -	**SORMOVSKIY-118** - **Sormovskiy 118 Ltd** Is-Bir Denizcilik ve Tankercilik Ticaret Ltd Sti *Basseterre* *St Kitts & Nevis* MMSI: 341872000	**2,478** 1,075 3,353	Class: RS	**1981**-06 **Sudostroitelnyy Zavod im Volodarskogo — Rybinsk** Yd No: 84 Loa 114.03 Br ex 13.21 Dght 3.810 Lbp 108.03 Br md 13.00 Dpth 5.52 Welded, 1 dk	**(A31A2GX) General Cargo Ship** Bale: 4,297 Compartments: 4 Ho, ER 4 Ha: (17.6 x 9.3)3 (17.9 x 9.3)ER Ice Capable	**2 oil engines** driving 2 FP propellers Total Power: 970kW (1,318hp) 10.8kn S.K.L. 6NVD48-2U 2 x 4 Stroke 6 Cy. 320 x 480 each-485kW (659bhp) VEB Schwermaschinenbau "KarlLiebknecht" (SKL)-Magdeburg Fuel: 92.0 (d.f.)
8035154 *XUBF8* -	**SORMOVSKIY-119** - **Flagship Maritime Ltd** Red to Red Denizcilik Ticaret Ltd Sti *Phnom Penh* *Cambodia* MMSI: 515314000 Official number: 0782843	**2,466** 1,065 3,346	Class: UA (RS)	**1982**-06 **Sudostroitelnyy Zavod im Volodarskogo — Rybinsk** Yd No: 87 Loa 114.03 Br ex 13.21 Dght 3.810 Lbp 108.03 Br md 13.00 Dpth 5.52 Welded, 1 dk	**(A31A2GX) General Cargo Ship** Grain: 4,297; Bale: 4,297 Compartments: 4 Ho, ER 4 Ha: (17.6 x 9.3)3 (17.9 x 9.3)ER Ice Capable	**2 oil engines** driving 2 FP propellers Total Power: 970kW (1,318hp) 10.8kn S.K.L. 6NVD48-2U 2 x 4 Stroke 6 Cy. 320 x 480 each-485kW (659bhp) VEB Schwermaschinenbau "KarlLiebknecht" (SKL)-Magdeburg
8133578 *V3MZ4* -	**SORMOVSKIY 121** *ex Sormovskiy-121 -2008* **Balkan Shipping & Trade Ltd** Trimorya Shipping & Trade Co *Belize City* *Belize* MMSI: 312366000 Official number: 370920048	**2,466** 1,065 3,353	Class: RS	**1982**-11 **Sudostroitelnyy Zavod im Volodarskogo — Rybinsk** Yd No: 88 Loa 114.03 Br ex 13.21 Dght 3.810 Lbp 110.76 Br md 13.00 Dpth 5.54 Welded, 1 dk	**(A31A2GX) General Cargo Ship** Bale: 4,297 Compartments: 4 Ho, ER 4 Ha: (17.6 x 9.3)3 (18.1 x 9.3)ER Ice Capable	**2 oil engines** driving 2 FP propellers Total Power: 970kW (1,318hp) 10.8kn S.K.L. 6NVD48-2U 2 x 4 Stroke 6 Cy. 320 x 480 each-485kW (659bhp) VEB Schwermaschinenbau "KarlLiebknecht" (SKL)-Magdeburg Fuel: 100.0
8227410 *UDPQ* -	**SORMOVSKIY-122** - **LLC Rosshipcom** - *Taganrog* *Russia*	**2,466** 988 3,134	Class: RS	**1984**-05 **Sudostroitelnyy Zavod im Volodarskogo — Rybinsk** Yd No: 89 Loa 114.23 Br ex 13.21 Dght 3.671 Lbp 108.03 Br md 13.00 Dpth 5.54 Welded, 1 dk	**(A31A2GX) General Cargo Ship** Bale: 4,297 Compartments: 4 Ho, ER 4 Ha: (17.6 x 9.3)3 (18.1 x 9.3)ER Ice Capable	**2 oil engines** driving 2 FP propellers Total Power: 970kW (1,318hp) 10.8kn S.K.L. 6NVD48A-U 2 x 4 Stroke 6 Cy. 320 x 480 each-485kW (659bhp) VEB Schwermaschinenbau "KarlLiebknecht" (SKL)-Magdeburg AuxGen: 4 x 50kW Fuel: 111.0 (d.f.)

8035166 *V3MR4* -	**SORMOVSKIY 3006** *ex* Sormovskiy-3006 *-2009* **Volgo-Don 203 Shipping Co Ltd** LLC Rosshipcom *Belize City* *Belize* MMSI: 312162000 Official number: 370920047	**2,491** Class: RS 977 3,100	**1982-06 Shipbuilding & Shiprepairing Yard 'Ivan Dimitrov' — Rousse** Yd No: 376 Loa 114.08 Br ex 13.52 Dght 3.660 Lbp 110.84 Br md 13.02 Dpth 5.52 Welded, 1 dk	**(A31A2GX) General Cargo Ship** Grain: 4,280; Bale: 4,280 Compartments: 4 Ho, ER 4 Ha: (17.5 x 9.4)2 (17.9 x 9.4) (18.6 x 9.4)ER Ice Capable	**2 oil engines** driving 2 FP propellers Total Power: 970kW (1,318hp) 10.5kn S.K.L. 6NVD48A-U 2 x 4 Stroke 6 Cy. 320 x 480 each-485kW (659bhp) VEB Schwermaschinenbau "KarlLiebknecht" (SKL)-Magdeburg AuxGen: 3 x 50kW Fuel: 113.0 (d.f.)
8222367 *UILG* -	**SORMOVSKIY-3051** **VF International Transportation Ltd Co (OOO 'VF Zagranperevozki')** Volga-Neva Ltd *St Petersburg* *Russia* MMSI: 273416080 Official number: 830535	**3,041** Class: RS 936 3,811	**1984-08 Estaleiros Navais de Viana do Castelo S.A. — Viana do Castelo** Yd No: 130 Loa 119.03 Br ex 13.03 Dght 4.260 Lbp 112.05 Br md 13.02 Dpth 6.00 Welded, 1 dk	**(A31A2GX) General Cargo Ship** Grain: 4,751; Bale: 3,000 TEU 90 C. 90/20' (40') Compartments: 4 Ho, ER 4 Ha: 2 (18.7 x 9.2)2 (12.6 x 9.2)ER	**2 oil engines** driving 2 FP propellers Total Power: 1,280kW (1,740hp) 11.3kn S.K.L. 6NVD48A-2U 2 x 4 Stroke 6 Cy. 320 x 480 each-640kW (870bhp) VEB Schwermaschinenbau "KarlLiebknecht" (SKL)-Magdeburg AuxGen: 3 x 100kW 400V 50Hz a.c Thrusters: 1 Thwart. CP thruster (f) Fuel: 57.0 (r.f.)
8222379 *UISO* -	**SORMOVSKIY-3052** **VF International Transportation Ltd Co (OOO 'VF Zagranperevozki')** Volga-Neva Ltd SatCom: Inmarsat C 427310452 *St Petersburg* *Russia* MMSI: 273328500 Official number: 830546	**3,041** Class: RS 1,205 3,832	**1984-11 Estaleiros Navais de Viana do Castelo S.A. — Viana do Castelo** Yd No: 131 Loa 119.21 Br ex 13.42 Dght 4.240 Lbp 112.05 Br md 13.21 Dpth 6.02 Welded, 1 dk	**(A31A2GX) General Cargo Ship** Grain: 4,751; Bale: 3,000 TEU 90 C. 90/20' (40') Compartments: 4 Ho, ER 4 Ha: 2 (18.7 x 9.2)2 (12.6 x 9.2)ER	**2 oil engines** driving 2 FP propellers Total Power: 1,280kW (1,740hp) 10.5kn S.K.L. 6NVD48A-2U 2 x 4 Stroke 6 Cy. 320 x 480 each-640kW (870bhp) VEB Schwermaschinenbau "KarlLiebknecht" (SKL)-Magdeburg AuxGen: 3 x 100kW 400V 50Hz a.c Thrusters: 1 Thwart. CP thruster (f) Fuel: 73.0 (r.f.)
8222381 *UIRT* -	**SORMOVSKIY-3053** **VF International Transportation Ltd Co (OOO 'VF Zagranperevozki')** Volga-Neva Ltd *St Petersburg* *Russia* MMSI: 273329500 Official number: 842528	**3,041** Class: RS 1,027 3,811	**1985-03 Estaleiros Navais de Viana do Castelo S.A. — Viana do Castelo** Yd No: 132 Loa 119.13 Br ex 13.42 Dght 4.250 Lbp 112.43 Br md 13.21 Dpth 6.05 Welded, 1 dk	**(A31A2GX) General Cargo Ship** Grain: 4,751; Bale: 3,000 TEU 90 C. 90/20' (40') Compartments: 4 Ho, ER 4 Ha: 2 (18.7 x 9.2)2 (12.6 x 9.2)ER	**2 oil engines** driving 2 FP propellers Total Power: 1,280kW (1,740hp) 11.3kn S.K.L. 6NVD48A-2U 2 x 4 Stroke 6 Cy. 320 x 480 each-640kW (870bhp) VEB Schwermaschinenbau "KarlLiebknecht" (SKL)-Magdeburg AuxGen: 3 x 100kW 400V 50Hz a.c Thrusters: 1 Thwart. CP thruster (f) Fuel: 82.0 (r.f.)
8222393 *UIRU* -	**SORMOVSKIY-3054** **VF International Transportation Ltd Co (OOO 'VF Zagranperevozki')** JS North-Western Shipping Co (OAO 'Severo-Zapadnoye Parokhodstvo') *St Petersburg* *Russia* MMSI: 273320600	**3,041** Class: RS 1,038 3,811	**1985-05 Estaleiros Navais de Viana do Castelo S.A. — Viana do Castelo** Yd No: 133 Loa 119.13 Br ex 13.42 Dght 4.250 Lbp 112.43 Br md 13.21 Dpth 6.05 Welded, 1 dk	**(A31A2GX) General Cargo Ship** Grain: 4,751; Bale: 3,000 TEU 90 C. 90/20' (40') Compartments: 4 Ho, ER 4 Ha: 2 (18.7 x 9.2)2 (12.6 x 9.2)ER	**2 oil engines** driving 2 FP propellers Total Power: 1,280kW (1,740hp) 10.5kn S.K.L. 6NVD48A-2U 2 x 4 Stroke 6 Cy. 320 x 480 each-640kW (870bhp) VEB Schwermaschinenbau "KarlLiebknecht" (SKL)-Magdeburg AuxGen: 3 x 100kW 400V 50Hz a.c Thrusters: 1 Thwart. CP thruster (f) Fuel: 73.0 (r.f.)
8419611 *UAAO* -	**SORMOVSKIY-3055** **North-Western Fleet (A/O 'Severo-Zapadnyy Flot')** - *St Petersburg* *Russia* MMSI: 273310400 Official number: 853096	**3,041** Class: RS 1,273 3,804	**1986-07 Estaleiros Navais de Viana do Castelo S.A. — Viana do Castelo** Yd No: 134 Loa 119.21 Br ex 13.42 Dght 4.250 Lbp 112.05 Br md 13.02 Dpth 6.05 Welded, 1 dk	**(A31A2GX) General Cargo Ship** Grain: 4,751; Bale: 3,000 TEU 90 C. 90/20' (40') Compartments: 4 Ho, ER 4 Ha: 2 (18.7 x 9.2)2 (12.6 x 9.2)ER Ice Capable	**2 oil engines** driving 2 FP propellers Total Power: 1,280kW (1,740hp) 10.5kn S.K.L. 6NVD48A-2U 2 x 4 Stroke 6 Cy. 320 x 480 each-640kW (870bhp) VEB Schwermaschinenbau "KarlLiebknecht" (SKL)-Magdeburg AuxGen: 3 x 100kW 400V 50Hz a.c Thrusters: 1 Thwart. CP thruster (f) Fuel: 193.0 (r.f.)
8419623 *UDBT* -	**SORMOVSKIY-3056** **North-Western Fleet (A/O 'Severo-Zapadnyy Flot')** - *St Petersburg* *Russia* MMSI: 273316200 Official number: 862822	**3,041** Class: RS 1,202 3,804	**1986-10 Estaleiros Navais de Viana do Castelo S.A. — Viana do Castelo** Yd No: 135 Loa 119.21 Br ex 13.40 Dght 4.250 Lbp 112.80 Br md 13.21 Dpth 6.02 Welded, 1 dk	**(A31A2GX) General Cargo Ship** Grain: 4,751; Bale: 3,000 TEU 90 C. 90/20' (40') Compartments: 4 Ho, ER 4 Ha: 2 (18.7 x 9.2)2 (12.6 x 9.2)ER Ice Capable	**2 oil engines** driving 2 FP propellers Total Power: 1,280kW (1,740hp) 10.5kn S.K.L. 6NVD48A-2U 2 x 4 Stroke 6 Cy. 320 x 480 each-640kW (870bhp) VEB Schwermaschinenbau "KarlLiebknecht" (SKL)-Magdeburg AuxGen: 3 x 100kW 400V 50Hz a.c Thrusters: 1 Thwart. CP thruster (f) Fuel: 193.0 (r.f.)
8419635 *UCVL* -	**SORMOVSKIY-3057** **North-Western Fleet (A/O 'Severo-Zapadnyy Flot')** - *St Petersburg* *Russia* MMSI: 273325400 Official number: 853325	**3,041** Class: RS 1,204 3,853	**1987-01 Estaleiros Navais de Viana do Castelo S.A. — Viana do Castelo** Yd No: 136 Loa 119.21 Br ex 13.42 Dght 4.250 Lbp 112.53 Br md 13.21 Dpth 6.02 Welded, 1 dk	**(A31A2GX) General Cargo Ship** Grain: 4,751; Bale: 3,000 TEU 90 C. 90/20' (40') Compartments: 4 Ho, ER 4 Ha: 2 (18.7 x 9.2)2 (12.6 x 9.2)ER Ice Capable	**2 oil engines** driving 2 FP propellers Total Power: 1,280kW (1,740hp) 10.5kn S.K.L. 6NVD48A-2U 2 x 4 Stroke 6 Cy. 320 x 480 each-640kW (870bhp) VEB Schwermaschinenbau "KarlLiebknecht" (SKL)-Magdeburg AuxGen: 3 x 100kW 400V 50Hz a.c Thrusters: 1 Thwart. CP thruster (f) Fuel: 193.0 (r.f.)
8419647 *UGYM* -	**SORMOVSKIY-3058** **JS North-Western Shipping Co (OAO 'Severo-Zapadnoye Parokhodstvo')** - *St Petersburg* *Russia* MMSI: 273316400 Official number: 863948	**3,041** Class: RS 1,204 3,853	**1987-05 Estaleiros Navais de Viana do Castelo S.A. — Viana do Castelo** Yd No: 137 Loa 119.21 Br ex 13.42 Dght 4.250 Lbp 112.53 Br md 13.21 Dpth 6.02 Welded, 1 dk	**(A31A2GX) General Cargo Ship** Grain: 4,751; Bale: 3,000 TEU 90 C. 90/20' (40') Compartments: 4 Ho, ER 4 Ha: 2 (18.7 x 9.2)2 (12.6 x 9.2)ER Ice Capable	**2 oil engines** driving 2 FP propellers Total Power: 1,280kW (1,740hp) 10.5kn S.K.L. 6NVD48A-2U 2 x 4 Stroke 6 Cy. 320 x 480 each-640kW (870bhp) VEB Schwermaschinenbau "KarlLiebknecht" (SKL)-Magdeburg AuxGen: 3 x 100kW 400V 50Hz a.c Thrusters: 1 Thwart. CP thruster (f) Fuel: 193.0 (r.f.)
8702214 *UISK* -	**SORMOVSKIY-3060** **Western Shipping Co JSC (OAO Zapadnoye Parokhodstvo - 'ZAPADFLOT')** - SatCom: Inmarsat A 1404515 *Kaliningrad* *Russia* MMSI: 273323000 Official number: 875663	**2,998** Class: RS 1,138 3,630 T/cm 13.2	**1988-09 Estaleiros Navais de Viana do Castelo S.A. — Viana do Castelo** Yd No: 141 Loa 118.70 Br ex 13.40 Dght 4.130 Lbp 112.50 Br md 13.21 Dpth 6.02 Welded, 1 dk	**(A31A2GX) General Cargo Ship** Grain: 4,751; Bale: 3,000 TEU 90 C. 90/20' (40') Compartments: 4 Ho, ER 4 Ha: 2 (18.7 x 9.2)2 (12.6 x 9.2)ER Ice Capable	**2 oil engines** driving 2 FP propellers Total Power: 1,280kW (1,740hp) 10.5kn S.K.L. 6NVD48A-2U 2 x 4 Stroke 6 Cy. 320 x 480 each-640kW (870bhp) VEB Schwermaschinenbau "KarlLiebknecht" (SKL)-Magdeburg AuxGen: 3 x 100kW 400V 50Hz a.c Thrusters: 1 Thwart. CP thruster (f)
8702240 *UCYQ* -	**SORMOVSKIY-3063** **JSC Northern River Shipping Lines** - *Arkhangelsk* *Russia* MMSI: 273363000 Official number: 885881	**3,048** Class: RS 1,163 3,721 T/cm 13.2	**1989-04 Estaleiros Navais de Viana do Castelo S.A. — Viana do Castelo** Yd No: 144 Loa 119.20 Br ex 13.40 Dght 4.150 Lbp 112.50 Br md 13.20 Dpth 6.00 Welded, 1 dk	**(A31A2GX) General Cargo Ship** Grain: 4,751; Bale: 3,000 TEU 108 C. 108/20' (40') Compartments: 4 Ho, ER 4 Ha: 2 (18.7 x 9.2)2 (12.6 x 9.2)ER Ice Capable	**2 oil engines** driving 2 FP propellers Total Power: 1,280kW (1,740hp) 10.5kn S.K.L. 6NVD48A-2U 2 x 4 Stroke 6 Cy. 320 x 480 each-640kW (870bhp) VEB Schwermaschinenbau "KarlLiebknecht" (SKL)-Magdeburg AuxGen: 3 x 100kW 400V 50Hz a.c Thrusters: 1 Thwart. CP thruster (f)
8702252 *UIYD* -	**SORMOVSKIY-3064** **NWS Eighteen Balt Shipping Co Ltd** JS North-Western Shipping Co (OAO 'Severo-Zapadnoye Parokhodstvo') *St Petersburg* *Russia* MMSI: 273454300 Official number: 886102	**3,048** Class: RS 1,142 3,630 T/cm 13.2	**1989-07 Estaleiros Navais de Viana do Castelo S.A. — Viana do Castelo** Yd No: 145 Loa 118.70 Br ex 13.40 Dght 4.130 Lbp 112.50 Br md 13.21 Dpth 6.00 Welded, 1 dk	**(A31A2GX) General Cargo Ship** Grain: 4,751; Bale: 3,000 TEU 90 C. 90/20' (40') Compartments: 4 Ho, ER 4 Ha: 2 (18.7 x 9.2)2 (12.6 x 9.2)ER Ice Capable	**2 oil engines** driving 2 FP propellers Total Power: 1,280kW (1,740hp) 10.5kn S.K.L. 6NVD48A-2U 2 x 4 Stroke 6 Cy. 320 x 480 each-640kW (870bhp) VEB Schwermaschinenbau "KarlLiebknecht" (SKL)-Magdeburg AuxGen: 3 x 100kW 400V 50Hz a.c Thrusters: 1 Thwart. CP thruster (f)
8704547 *UFMU* -	**SORMOVSKIY-3066** **LLC 'Leasing Co' Vega** Maritime Trade Port of Khatanga SatCom: Inmarsat C 427310420 *Arkhangelsk* *Russia* MMSI: 273416020	**3,048** Class: RS 1,163 3,721 T/cm 13.2	**1990-03 Estaleiros Navais de Viana do Castelo S.A. — Viana do Castelo** Yd No: 147 Loa 118.70 Br ex 13.40 Dght 4.170 Lbp 112.50 Br md 13.20 Dpth 6.00 Welded, 1 dk	**(A31A2GX) General Cargo Ship** Grain: 4,751; Bale: 3,000 TEU 90 C. 90/20' (40') Compartments: 4 Ho, ER 4 Ha: 2 (18.7 x 9.2)2 (12.6 x 9.2)ER Ice Capable	**2 oil engines** driving 2 FP propellers Total Power: 1,280kW (1,740hp) 10.5kn S.K.L. 6NVD48A-2U 2 x 4 Stroke 6 Cy. 320 x 480 each-640kW (870bhp) VEB Schwermaschinenbau "KarlLiebknecht" (SKL)-Magdeburg AuxGen: 3 x 100kW 400V 50Hz a.c Thrusters: 1 Thwart. FP thruster (f)

8704559 *UBWC* -	**SORMOVSKIY-3067** **NWS Twenty Balt Shipping Co Ltd** JS North-Western Shipping Co (OAO 'Severo-Zapadnoye Parokhodstvo') *St Petersburg* *Russia* MMSI: 273311900 Official number: 896458	**3,048** 1,112 3,391 T/cm 13.2	Class: RS	**1990-07 Estaleiros Navais de Viana do Castelo S.A. — Viana do Castelo** Yd No: 148 Loa 119.20 Br ex 13.40 Dght 4.760 Lbp 112.50 Br md 13.20 Dpth 6.00 Welded, 1 dk	**(A31A2GX) General Cargo Ship** Grain: 4,751; Bale: 3,000 TEU 90 C. 90/20' (40') Compartments: 4 Ho, ER 4 Ha: 2 (18.7 x 9.2)2 (12.6 x 9.2)ER Ice Capable	**2 oil engines** driving 2 FP propellers Total Power: 1,280kW (1,740hp) 10.5kn S.K.L. 6NVD48A-2U 2 x 4 Stroke 6 Cy. 320 x 480 each-640kW (870bhp) VEB Schwermaschinenbau "KarlLiebknecht" (SKL)-Magdeburg AuxGen: 3 x 100kW 400V 50Hz a.c Thrusters: 1 Thwart. CP thruster (f) Fuel: 193.0 (d.f.)
8704561 *UCYR* -	**SORMOVSKIY-3068** **JSC Northern River Shipping Lines** - SatCom: Inmarsat C 427300159 *Arkhangelsk* *Russia* MMSI: 273362000 Official number: 896068	**3,048** 1,112 3,391 T/cm 13.2	Class: RS	**1990-11 Estaleiros Navais de Viana do Castelo S.A. — Viana do Castelo** Yd No: 149 Loa 118.70 Br ex 13.40 Dght 4.080 Lbp 112.50 Br md 13.20 Dpth 6.00 Welded, 1 dk	**(A31A2GX) General Cargo Ship** Grain: 4,751; Bale: 3,000 TEU 108 C. 108/20' Compartments: 4 Ho, ER 4 Ha: 2 (18.7 x 9.2)2 (12.6 x 9.2)ER Ice Capable	**2 oil engines** driving 2 FP propellers Total Power: 1,280kW (1,740hp) 10.5kn S.K.L. 6NVD48A-2U 2 x 4 Stroke 6 Cy. 320 x 480 each-640kW (870bhp) VEB Schwermaschinenbau "KarlLiebknecht" (SKL)-Magdeburg AuxGen: 3 x 100kW 400V 50Hz a.c Thrusters: 1 Thwart. CP thruster (f)
9166780 *OYKJ2* -	**SOROE MAERSK** **A P Moller - Maersk A/S** A P Moller SatCom: Inmarsat C 421980213 *Munkebo* *Denmark (DIS)* MMSI: 219802000 Official number: D3733	**92,198** 53,625 110,387 T/cm 124.0	Class: AB	**1999-06 Odense Staalskibsvaerft A/S — Munkebo (Lindo Shipyard)** Yd No: 167 Loa 346.98 (BB) Br ex - Dght 14.941 Lbp 331.54 Br md 42.80 Dpth 24.10 Welded, 1 dk	**(A33A2CC) Container Ship (Fully Cellular)** TEU 9578 incl 817 ref C Compartments: ER, 20 Cell Ho 20 Ha: ER	**1 oil engine** driving 1 FP propeller Total Power: 54,840kW (74,560hp) 25.0kn B&W 12K90MC-C 1 x 2 Stroke 12 Cy. 900 x 2300 54840kW (74560bhp) Hitachi Zosen Corp-Japan AuxGen: 5 x 3000kW 6600V a.c Thrusters: 1 Thwart. FP thruster (f); 2 Thwart. FP thruster (a)
9217125 *EBRI* -	**SOROLLA** **Cia Trasmediterranea SA (Acciona Trasmediterranea)** - SatCom: Inmarsat C 422460012 *Santa Cruz de Tenerife* *Spain (CSR)* MMSI: 224600000 Official number: 18/2000	**26,916** 14,308 5,000	Class: BV	**2001-05 Hijos de J. Barreras S.A. — Vigo** Yd No: 1580 Loa 172.00 (BB) Br ex - Dght 6.200 Lbp 157.00 Br md 26.20 Dpth 9.20 Welded, 9 dks	**(A36A2PR) Passenger/Ro-Ro Ship (Vehicles)** Passengers: unberthed: 356; cabins: 202; berths: 744 Stern door/ramp (p) Len: 18.00 Wid: 8.50 Swl: - Stern door/ramp (s) Len: 18.00 Wid: 8.50 Swl: - Lane-Len: 1800 Lane-Wid: 3.00 Lane-clr ht: 4.70 Lorries: 98, Cars: 165	**4 oil engines** with clutches, flexible couplings & sr geared to sc. shafts driving 2 CP propellers Total Power: 28,960kW (39,376hp) 23.0kn Wartsila 8L46A 4 x 4 Stroke 8 Cy. 460 x 580 each-7240kW (9844bhp) Wartsila Diesel S.A.-Bermeo AuxGen: 3 x 1570kW 380V a.c, 2 x 1570kW a.c Thrusters: 2 Thwart. FP thruster (f) Fuel: 144.1 (d.f.) (Heating Coils) 707.5 (r.f.)
8737154 - -	**SOROWAKO STAR** *ex* Equator 16 *-2008* **PT International Nickel Indonesia** - *Makassar* *Indonesia*	**180** 55 -	Class: KI	**2008-06 PT Muji Rahayu Shipyard — Tenggarong** Loa 27.00 Br ex - Dght 2.990 Lbp 25.21 Br md 7.50 Dpth 3.60 Welded, 1 dk	**(B32A2ST) Tug**	**2 oil engines** driving 2 Propellers Total Power: 1,220kW (1,658hp) Yanmar 6AYM-ETE 2 x 4 Stroke 6 Cy. 155 x 180 each-610kW (829bhp) Yanmar Diesel Engine Co Ltd-Japan
6704907 *LKEQ* -	**SOROY** **Boreal Transport Nord AS** - *Hammerfest* *Norway* MMSI: 258548000	**336** 158 -	Class: (NV)	**1967 Loland Motorverkstad AS — Leirvik i Sogn** Yd No: 24 Loa 37.65 Br ex 8.74 Dght 3.550 Lbp 33.51 Br md 8.50 Dpth 3.71 Welded, 1 dk	**(A32A2GF) General Cargo/Passenger Ship** Passengers: 98 Compartments: 1 Ho, ER 1 Ha: (3.7 x 2.5)ER Cranes: 1x3t	**1 oil engine** driving 1 FP propeller Total Power: 393kW (534hp) Caterpillar 3408TA 1 x Vee 4 Stroke 8 Cy. 137 x 152 393kW (534bhp) Caterpillar Tractor Co-USA Fuel: 13.0 (d.f.) 2.0pd
9220873 *LJQQ* M-20-A	**SOROYFISK** *ex* Stromsnes *-2012* *ex* Asbjorn Selsbane *-2008* **Soroyfisk AS** - *Aalesund* *Norway* MMSI: 259641000	**377** 113 -		**1999-10 O. Ulvan Baatbyggeri AS — Sandstad** Yd No: 423 Loa 27.40 Br ex 9.20 Dght 5.500 Lbp - Br md - Dpth - Welded, 1 dk	**(B11A2FS) Stern Trawler**	**1 oil engine** geared to sc. shaft driving 1 FP propeller Total Power: 746kW (1,014hp) Caterpillar 3508TA 1 x Vee 4 Stroke 8 Cy. 170 x 190 746kW (1014bhp) Caterpillar Inc-USA
8976786 *LMKJ*	**SOROYSUND** **Seaworks AS** - *Harstad* *Norway* MMSI: 257137000	**907** 347 -		**1972-10 AS Mjellem & Karlsen — Bergen** Yd No: 107 Converted From: Logistics Vessel (Naval Ro-Ro Cargo)-2003 Lengthened-1995 Loa 60.58 Br ex 10.50 Dght 2.100 Lbp - Br md - Dpth 3.50 Welded, 1 dk	**(A35D2RL) Landing Craft**	**2 oil engines** geared to sc. shafts driving 2 FP propellers Total Power: 900kW (1,224hp) 11.7kn MWM TBD234V12 2 x Vee 4 Stroke 12 Cy. 128 x 140 each-450kW (612bhp) (new engine 1995) Motoren Werke Mannheim AG (MWM)-Mannheim
9357626 *3FUB* -	**SORRELLE** **Sorrelle SA** Akron Trade & Transport *Panama* *Panama* MMSI: 352949000 Official number: 4157910	**8,251** 2,997 11,003	Class: NV (CC)	**2010-02 Haidong Shipyard — Taizhou ZJ** Yd No: DBD-2005-031 Loa 129.60 (BB) Br ex 20.20 Dght 7.600 Lbp 123.00 Br md 20.00 Dpth 11.50 Welded, 1 dk	**(A12B2TR) Chemical/Products Tanker** Double Hull (13F) Liq: 12,976; Liq (Oil): 12,976 Compartments: 12 Wing Ta, 2 Wing Slop Ta, ER	**2 oil engines** reduction geared to sc. shafts driving 2 FP propellers Total Power: 4,000kW (5,438hp) 12.5kn Chinese Std. Type G8300ZC 2 x 4 Stroke 8 Cy. 300 x 380 each-2000kW (2719bhp) Ningbo CSI Power & Machinery GroupCo Ltd-China AuxGen: 3 x 320kW 400V a.c
9310408 *9HOL9* -	**SORRENTO** *ex* Federal Maple *-2008* *ex* Maple Ridge *-2007* **Aegean Traders Inc** TMS Bulkers Ltd SatCom: Inmarsat C 424928010 *Valletta* *Malta* MMSI: 249280000 Official number: 9310408	**39,736** 25,754 76,633 T/cm 66.6	Class: NK	**2004-10 Imabari Shipbuilding Co Ltd — Marugame KG (Marugame Shipyard)** Yd No: 1403 Loa 224.94 (BB) Br ex - Dght 14.139 Lbp 217.00 Br md 32.26 Dpth 19.50 Welded, 1 dk	**(A21A2BC) Bulk Carrier** Grain: 90,740 Compartments: 7 Ho, ER 7 Ha: 6 (17.1 x 15.6)ER (17.1 x 12.8)	**1 oil engine** driving 1 FP propeller Total Power: 10,320kW (14,031hp) 15.3kn B&W 6S60MC 1 x 2 Stroke 6 Cy. 600 x 2292 10320kW (14031bhp) Hitachi Zosen Corp-Japan Fuel: 2970.0
9264312 *IBDD* -	**SORRENTO** *ex* Eurostar Valencia *-2007* **Atlantica SpA di Navigazione** Grimaldi Group SatCom: Inmarsat C 424702536 *Palermo* *Italy* MMSI: 247086300 Official number: 120	**25,984** 8,100 7,150	Class: RI	**2003-06 Cantiere Navale Visentini Srl — Porto Viro** Yd No: 197 Loa 186.35 (BB) Br ex - Dght 6.620 Lbp 169.50 Br md 25.60 Dpth 9.14 Welded, 8 dks	**(A36A2PR) Passenger/Ro-Ro Ship (Vehicles)** Passengers: unberthed: 580; cabins: 93; berths: 370 Stern door/ramp (centre) Len: 16.00 Wid: 16.50 Swl: - Lane-Len: 2200 Cars: 160, Trailers: 172	**2 oil engines** geared to sc. shafts driving 2 CP propellers Total Power: 18,900kW (25,696hp) 23.5kn MAN 9L48/60 2 x 4 Stroke 9 Cy. 480 x 600 each-9450kW (12848bhp) MAN B&W Diesel AG-Augsburg AuxGen: 3 x 1800kW 60Hz a.c, 2 x 1800kW 60Hz a.c Thrusters: 2 Tunnel thruster (f) Fuel: 287.0 (d.f.) (Heating Coils) 1280.0 (r.f.) 78.0pd
9261853 *VKV6549* -	**SORRENTO** **Peninsula Searoad Charters Pty Ltd** Peninsula Searoad Transport Pty Ltd (Queenscliff Car Ferry) (Searoad Ferries) (Ferry Terminal Beach Cafe) *Geelong, Vic* *Australia* MMSI: 503169900	**3,200** 650 300		**2001-07 Southern Marine Shiplift Pty Ltd — Launceston TAS** Loa 61.45 Br ex - Dght 2.300 Lbp 57.00 Br md 17.40 Dpth 4.50 Welded, 1 dk	**(A36A2PR) Passenger/Ro-Ro Ship (Vehicles)** Passengers: unberthed: 700 Cars: 80	**2 oil engines** geared to sc. shafts driving 2 Directional propellers contra-rotating propellers Total Power: 1,912kW (2,600hp) 13.5kn Cummins KTA-38-M2 2 x Vee 4 Stroke 12 Cy. 159 x 159 each-956kW (1300bhp) Cummins Engine Co Ltd-United Kingdom AuxGen: 2 x a.c Thrusters: 2 Thwart. CP thruster (f)
8906729 *IUEG* -	**SORRENTO JET** **Navigazione Libera del Golfo Srl** - *Naples* *Italy* MMSI: 247043400 Official number: 1757	*366* 249 38	Class: RI	**1990-06 FBM Marine Ltd. — Cowes** Yd No: 1264 Loa 41.90 Br ex - Dght 1.100 Lbp - Br md 7.65 Dpth 2.84 Welded	**(A37B2PS) Passenger Ship** Hull Material: Aluminium Alloy Passengers: unberthed: 350	**2 oil engines** geared to sc. shafts driving 2 FP propellers Total Power: 2,090kW (2,842hp) 28.0kn M.T.U. 12V396TB83 2 x Vee 4 Stroke 12 Cy. 165 x 185 each-1045kW (1421bhp) MTU Friedrichshafen GmbH-Friedrichshafen
8721569 *XUBB2* -	**SORTIDA** *ex* Estrella *-2011* *ex* Nikopol *-2010* **Yalania Holdings Ltd** - *Phnom Penh* *Cambodia* MMSI: 514445000 Official number: 1086543	**723** 414 414	Class: IS (RS)	**1986-06 Zavod "Leninskaya Kuznitsa" — Kiyev** Yd No: 1566 Loa 54.82 Br ex 9.95 Dght 4.140 Lbp 50.30 Br md - Dpth 5.00 Welded, 1 dk	**(B11A2FS) Stern Trawler** Ice Capable	**1 oil engine** driving 1 CP propeller Total Power: 852kW (1,158hp) 12.0kn S.K.L. 8NVD48A-2U 1 x 4 Stroke 8 Cy. 320 x 480 852kW (1158bhp) VEB Schwermaschinenbau "KarlLiebknecht" (SKL)-Magdeburg AuxGen: 4 x 160kW a.c

Ship	Tonnage	Class	Builder & dimensions	Type	Machinery
9432646 **SORTLAND** *LASE* - **SEB Njord AS** Remoy Management AS *Fosnavaag* *Norway* MMSI: 257736000	**4,025** 1,207 2,100	Class: NV	**2010-07 Societatea Comerciala Severnav S.A. — Drobeta-Turnu Severin** (Hull) Yd No: (52) **2010-07 Myklebust Mek. Verksted AS — Gursken** Yd No: 52 Loa 93.30 (BB) Br ex - Dght 6.200 Lbp 82.40 Br md 16.60 Dpth 8.60 Welded, 1 dk	**(B34H2SQ) Patrol Vessel** Cranes: 1 Ice Capable	**1 diesel electric oil engine** reduction geared to sc. shaft driving 1 CP propeller Total Power: 4,000kW (5,438hp) 15.5kn Bergens B32: 40L8P 1 x 4 Stroke 8 Cy. 320 x 400 4000kW (5438bhp) Rolls Royce Marine AS-Norway AuxGen: 1 x 676kW 50Hz a.c, 3 x 900kW 50Hz a.c, 1 x 1000kW 690V 50Hz a.c Thrusters: 1 Retract. directional thruster (f); 1 Thwart. FP thruster (f); 1 Thwart. FP thruster (a) Fuel: 96.0 (LNG) 555.0 (d.f.)
9020314 **SORVIK** *LCRI* *ex* Trio *-2012* *ex* Sjodur *-2009* ST-36-F *ex* Stadt Viking *-2008* *ex* Tuesund *-2002* *ex* Angeltveit *-1997* **Espen Nilsen AS** - *Maaloy* *Norway* MMSI: 259102000	**144** 57 -		**1990 Stocznia 'Wisla' — Gdansk** Yd No: SN-201 Loa - Br ex - Dght - Lbp 19.97 Br md 6.99 Dpth 4.02 Welded, 1 dk	**(B11B2FV) Fishing Vessel**	**1 oil engine** driving 1 FP propeller Total Power: 345kW (469hp) 10.5kn Volvo Penta TAMD162A 1 x 4 Stroke 6 Cy. 144 x 165 345kW (469bhp) AB Volvo Penta-Sweden Thrusters: 1 Thwart. FP thruster (f); 1 Tunnel thruster (a)
9517977 **SORYO MARU** *JD2876* - **Sowa Kaiun YK** - *Kasaoka, Okayama* *Japan* MMSI: 431000864 Official number: 140943	*498* - 1,296		**2009-02 Suzuki Shipyard Co. Ltd. — Yokkaichi** Yd No: 721 Loa 64.98 Br ex - Dght 4.600 Lbp - Br md 10.00 Dpth 4.50 Welded, 1 dk	**(A12A2TC) Chemical Tanker** Double Hull (13F) Liq: 1,230	**1 oil engine** driving 1 FP propeller Total Power: 1,030kW (1,400hp) 11.0kn Hanshin LH28G 1 x 4 Stroke 6 Cy. 280 x 460 1030kW (1400bhp) The Hanshin Diesel Works Ltd-Japan
9100592 **SORYU MARU** *JNVT* - **Daiichi Chuo Kisen Kaisha** SatCom: Inmarsat A 1206264 *Saikai, Nagasaki* *Japan* MMSI: 431695000 Official number: 134487	**48,458** 26,476 86,868	Class: NK	**1995-01 Sumitomo Heavy Industries Ltd. — Oppama Shipyard, Yokosuka** Yd No: 1199 Loa 233.04 (BB) Br ex - Dght 13.783 Lbp 223.00 Br md 38.00 Dpth 20.10 Welded, 1 dk	**(A21A2BC) Bulk Carrier** Grain: 104,244 Compartments: 5 Ho, ER 8 Ha: (15.8 x 14.3)6 (13.2 x 17.8) (14.1 x 17.8)ER	**1 oil engine** driving 1 FP propeller Total Power: 11,136kW (15,141hp) 14.4kn Sulzer 6RTA62U 1 x 2 Stroke 6 Cy. 620 x 2150 11136kW (15141bhp) Diesel United Ltd.-Aioi Fuel: 2740.0 (r.f.)
8904680 **SORYU MARU** *JJ3653* - **Hayakoma Unyu KK** - *Kobe, Hyogo* *Japan* Official number: 129235	*226* - -		**1989-06 Kanagawa Zosen — Kobe** Yd No: 327 Loa 35.50 Br ex - Dght 3.100 Lbp 31.25 Br md 9.20 Dpth 4.20 Welded, 1 dk	**(B32A2ST) Tug**	**2 oil engines** Geared Integral to driving 2 Z propellers Total Power: 2,574kW (3,500hp) 12.9kn Fuji 6L27.5X 2 x 4 Stroke 6 Cy. 275 x 320 each-1287kW (1750bhp) Fuji Diesel Co Ltd-Japan
8417807 **SOS** - - - -	**187** 59 166	Class: (BV)	**1984-10 Marstal Team Staal ApS — Marstal** Yd No: 89 Loa 26.22 Br ex - Dght 2.601 Lbp 22.81 Br md 7.03 Dpth 5.80 Welded, 2 dks	**(B11A2FS) Stern Trawler** Ice Capable	**2 oil engines** with clutches, flexible couplings & sr geared to sc. shaft driving 1 CP propeller Total Power: 730kW (992hp) MAN D2542MLE 2 x Vee 4 Stroke 12 Cy. 125 x 142 each-365kW (496bhp) Maschinenbau Augsburg Nuernberg (MAN)-Augsburg
9273002 **SOSHANGANA** *9HXT8* - **NYK LNG (Atlantic) Ltd** NYK Shipmanagement Pte Ltd *Valletta* *Malta* MMSI: 256581000 Official number: 9273002	**5,991** 1,798 7,717 T/cm 17.5	Class: NK	**2003-03 Shin Kochi Jyuko K.K. — Kochi** Yd No: 7158 Loa 109.03 Br ex - Dght 7.269 Lbp 104.00 Br md 19.40 Dpth 11.00 Welded, 1 dk	**(A12B2TR) Chemical/Products Tanker** Double Hull (13F) Liq: 5,532; Liq (Oil): 5,532; Asphalt: 5,532 Cargo Heating Coils Compartments: 3 Ta, ER 2 Cargo Pump (s): 2x300m³/hr	**1 oil engine** driving 1 FP propeller Total Power: 4,160kW (5,656hp) 13.7kn Mitsubishi 8UEC37LA 1 x 2 Stroke 8 Cy. 370 x 880 4160kW (5656bhp) Kobe Hatsudoki KK-Japan AuxGen: 3 x 320kW 440V 60Hz a.c Fuel: 150.0 (d.f.) (Heating Coils) 1126.0 (r.f.) 15.7pd
9005144 **SOSHU NO. 1** *JL5885* *ex* Hokuyo Maru No. 11 *-2002* - **KK Soshu** - *Satsumasendai, Kagoshima* *Japan* Official number: 131454	*199* - 600		**1990-05 Shin Yamamoto Shipbuilding & Engineering Co Ltd — Kochi KC** Yd No: 325 Loa - Br ex - Dght - Lbp 47.20 Br md 11.00 Dpth 5.50 Welded	**(A31A2GX) General Cargo Ship**	**1 oil engine** driving 1 FP propeller Sumiyoshi 1 x 4 Stroke Sumiyoshi Marine Diesel Co Ltd-Japan
9142071 **SOSHUN MARU** *JJ3928* - **Hayakoma Kaiun KK** - *Kobe, Hyogo* *Japan* Official number: 134244	*235* - -		**1996-05 Kanagawa Zosen — Kobe** Yd No: 428 Loa 37.50 Br ex - Dght - Lbp 33.00 Br md 9.00 Dpth 4.09 Welded, 1 dk	**(B32A2ST) Tug**	**2 oil engines** Geared Integral to driving 2 Z propellers Total Power: 2,648kW (3,600hp) 14.8kn Niigata 6L28HX 2 x 4 Stroke 6 Cy. 280 x 370 each-1324kW (1800bhp) Niigata Engineering Co Ltd-Japan
8930823 **SOSNOVETS** *UCSN* - **Ecosoyuz Co Ltd** - *Murmansk* *Russia* MMSI: 273136500 Official number: 780016	**217** 73 145	Class: RS	**1979 Kanonerskiy Sudoremontnyy Zavod — Leningrad** Yd No: 11 Loa 36.12 Br ex 7.40 Dght 2.000 Lbp 32.50 Br md 7.38 Dpth 3.10 Welded, 1 dk	**(A34A2GR) Refrigerated Cargo Ship** Ins: 201 Compartments: 2 Ho 2 Ha: (3.0 x 2.5) (3.0 x 2.0) Cranes: 1x3.2t Ice Capable	**1 oil engine** geared to sc. shaft driving 1 FP propeller Total Power: 165kW (224hp) 9.0kn Daldizel 6CHNSP18/22 1 x 4 Stroke 6 Cy. 180 x 220 165kW (224bhp) Daldizel-Khabarovsk AuxGen: 3 x 30kW a.c Fuel: 7.0 (d.f.)
8930964 **SOSNOVKA** *UFRF* - **JSC Baltic Technical Fleet (A/O 'Baltiyskiy Tekhnicheskiy Flot') (Balttekhflot)** - *St Petersburg* *Russia* MMSI: 273449430 Official number: 662178	*589* 154 870	Class: (RS) (RR)	**1967-06 Rizhskiy Sudoremontnyy Zavod — Riga** Yd No: 360 Loa 55.00 Br ex 10.40 Dght 3.580 Lbp 53.30 Br md - Dpth 4.30 Welded, 1 dk	**(B34A2SH) Hopper, Motor** Hopper: 500 Compartments: 1 Ho, ER 1 Ha: (24.8 x 6.7)ER Ice Capable	**2 oil engines** driving 2 FP propellers Total Power: 442kW (600hp) 8.0kn Pervomaysk 6CH25/34-2 2 x 4 Stroke 6 Cy. 250 x 340 each-221kW (300bhp) Pervomaydizelmash (PDM)-Pervomaysk AuxGen: 2 x 64kW a.c Fuel: 60.0 (d.f.)
9582013 **SOSNOVKA-1** *UBCH4* - **Government of The Russian Federation (Kamchattransflot) (State Unitary Enterprise 'Kamchattransflot')** - *Vladivostok* *Russia* MMSI: 273355320	**376** 112 57	Class: RS	**2011-08 Sosnovskiy Sudostroitelnyy Zavod — Sosnovka** Yd No: 10500 Loa 42.60 Br ex 8.82 Dght 2.000 Lbp 38.40 Br md 8.60 Dpth 2.70 Welded, 1 dk	**(A35D2RL) Landing Craft** TEU 12 Cranes: 1x7.3t Ice Capable	**2 oil engines** reduction geared to sc. shafts driving 2 Directional propellers Total Power: 948kW (1,288hp) 9.0kn Cummins QSM11-M 2 x 4 Stroke 6 Cy. 125 x 147 each-474kW (644bhp) Cummins Engine Co Inc-USA
9582025 **SOSNOVKA-2** *UBCH5* - **Government of The Russian Federation (Kamchattransflot) (State Unitary Enterprise 'Kamchattransflot')** - *Vladivostok* *Russia* MMSI: 273356320	**376** 112 57	Class: RS	**2011-08 Sosnovskiy Sudostroitelnyy Zavod — Sosnovka** Yd No: 10501 Loa 42.60 Br ex 8.82 Dght 2.000 Lbp 38.40 Br md 8.60 Dpth 2.70 Welded, 1 dk	**(A35D2RL) Landing Craft** TEU 12 Cranes: 1x7.3t Ice Capable	**2 oil engines** reduction geared to sc. shafts driving 2 Directional propellers Total Power: 948kW (1,288hp) 9.0kn Cummins QSM11-M 2 x 4 Stroke 6 Cy. 125 x 147 each-474kW (644bhp) Cummins Engine Co Inc-USA
9582037 **SOSNOVKA-3** *UBLI3* - **Government of The Russian Federation (Federal Agency of Maritime & River Transport (Rosmorrechflot))** Government of The Russian Federation (Kamchattransflot) (State Unitary Enterprise 'Kamchattransflot') *Vladivostok* *Russia* MMSI: 273359460	**376** 112 280	Class: RS	**2012-11 Sosnovskiy Sudostroitelnyy Zavod — Sosnovka** Yd No: 10502 Loa 42.60 Br ex 8.82 Dght 2.000 Lbp 38.40 Br md 8.60 Dpth 2.70 Welded, 1 dk	**(A35D2RL) Landing Craft** Bow ramp (centre) TEU 12 Cranes: 1x7.3t Ice Capable	**2 oil engines** reduction geared to sc. shafts driving 2 Directional propellers Total Power: 948kW (1,288hp) 9.0kn Cummins QSM11 2 x 4 Stroke 6 Cy. 125 x 147 each-474kW (644bhp) Cummins Engine Co Inc-USA AuxGen: 2 x 140kW a.c Fuel: 50.0 (d.f.)
9020273 **SOSPAN** *HO8016* - **Westminster Dredging Co Ltd** - *Panama* *Panama* Official number: 019922528PE	**718** 215 1,300	Class: (BV)	**1990-05 Scheepsbouwwerf Slob B.V. — Papendrecht** Yd No: 388 Loa 57.03 Br ex - Dght 3.600 Lbp 54.77 Br md 10.01 Dpth 4.30 Welded, 1 dk	**(B33B2DS) Suction Hopper Dredger** Hopper: 970	**1 oil engine** geared to sc. shaft driving 1 FP propeller Total Power: 402kW (547hp) 9.0kn Caterpillar 3412T 1 x Vee 4 Stroke 12 Cy. 137 x 152 402kW (547bhp) Caterpillar Inc-USA Thrusters: 1 Tunnel thruster (f) Fuel: 45.0 (d.f.)

IMO / Call sign	Name / Owner	Tonnage	Class	Builder / Dimensions	Type / Capacity	Machinery
7711062 *PBAL* -	**SOSPAN DAU** *ex* Badebec *-2001* *ex* Adlergrund *-1992* **Sosban CV** - *Papendrecht* *Netherlands* MMSI: 244990000 Official number: 39165	**1,546** 463 2,134	Class: LR (BV) (DS) **100A1** SS 08/2011 hopper dredger dredging within 15 miles from shore or 20 miles from nearest port or when in ballast maximum 200m from nearest port **LMC** **UMS**	**1978-12 Ateliers et Chantiers de La Manche — Dieppe** Yd No: 1267 Converted From: Hopper-2001 Loa 70.36 (BB) Br ex 14.33 Dght 3.126 Lbp 68.36 Br md 14.30 Dpth 3.81 Welded, 1 dk	**(B33B2DT) Trailing Suction Hopper Dredger** Hopper: 1,400 Compartments: 1 Ho, ER	**2 oil engines** with clutches & sr reverse geared to sc. shafts driving 2 FP propellers Total Power: 1,164kW (1,582hp) 9.0kn Caterpillar 3508B-TA 2 x Vee 4 Stroke 8 Cy. 170 x 190 each-582kW (791bhp) (new engine 2003) Caterpillar Inc-USA AuxGen: 2 x 88kW 380V 50Hz a.c Thrusters: 1 Thwart. FP thruster (f)
9453092 - -	**SOSRCEM** - **Government of The Socialist Republic of Vietnam** - *Da Nang* *Vietnam* MMSI: 574988000	**1,044** 313 590		**2010-04 Song Thu Co. — Da Nang** (Hull) Yd No: (553008) **2010-04 B.V. Scheepswerf Damen — Gorinchem** Yd No: 553008 Loa 52.40 Br ex 12.20 Dght 4.500 Lbp 48.45 Br md 12.00 Dpth 4.00 Welded, 1 dk	**(B34G2SE) Pollution Control Vessel**	**2 oil engines** reduction geared to sc. shafts driving 2 CP propellers Total Power: 2,700kW (3,670hp) 12.8kn Caterpillar 3512B-TA 2 x Vee 4 Stroke 12 Cy. 170 x 190 each-1350kW (1835bhp) Caterpillar Inc-USA AuxGen: 2 x a.c Thrusters: 1 Thwart. FP thruster (f)
9555890 *PP6848* -	**SOSSEGO VALE** *ex* Sossego *-2009* **Vale SA** - *Belem* *Brazil* Official number: 1210132362	**448** 134 227		**2009-09 Detroit Brasil Ltda — Itajai** Yd No: 335 Loa 32.00 Br ex - Dght 4.500 Lbp 29.80 Br md 11.60 Dpth 5.36 Welded, 1 dk	**(B32A2ST) Tug**	**2 oil engines** reduction geared to sc. shafts driving 2 Directional propellers Total Power: 4,302kW (5,848hp) 11.0kn GE Marine 12V228 2 x Vee 4 Stroke 12 Cy. 229 x 267 each-2151kW (2924bhp) General Electric Co.-Lynn, Ma
8701715 *D4CP* -	**SOTAVENTO** - **Companhia Nacional de Navegacao 'Arca Verde'** - *Sao Vicente* *Cape Verde*	*499* 209 300	Class: (GL)	**1987-10 Schiffswerft und Maschinenfabrik Cassens GmbH — Emden** Yd No: 179 Loa 45.01 Br ex - Dght 3.010 Lbp 39.02 Br md 9.61 Dpth 4.32 Welded, 1 dk	**(A36A2PR) Passenger/Ro-Ro Ship (Vehicles)** Grain: 510; Bale: 458	**1 oil engine** reduction geared to sc. shaft driving 1 CP propeller Total Power: 599kW (814hp) 10.5kn MAN 6L20/27 1 x 4 Stroke 6 Cy. 200 x 270 599kW (814bhp) MAN B&W Diesel GmbH-Augsburg
8725254 - -	**SOTIRIA** *ex* Svesa *-2012* *ex* PTR-50 No. 23 *-1999* **Thessalia Compania Naviera SA** -	**193** 57 60	Class: (RS)	**1987-04 Astrakhanskaya Sudoverf im. "Kirova" — Astrakhan** Yd No: 23 Loa 31.85 Br ex 7.08 Dght 2.100 Lbp 27.80 Br md 6.90 Dpth 3.15 Welded, 1 dk	**(B12B2FC) Fish Carrier** Ins: 100 Compartments: 2 Ho	**1 oil engine** geared to sc. shaft driving 1 FP propeller Total Power: 221kW (300hp) 10.2kn Daldizel 6CHNSP18/22-300 1 x 4 Stroke 6 Cy. 180 x 220 221kW (300bhp) Daldizel-Khabarovsk AuxGen: 2 x 25kW Fuel: 14.0 (d.f.)
6704397 *SVA2192* -	**SOTIRIA** *ex* Efstathia M *-2008* *ex* Star Stability *-2004* *ex* Stari Grad *-2004* *ex* Green Star *-1997* *ex* Talete *-1985* *ex* Thales *-1972* **Analipsi Maritime Co** Lidmar Shipping & Trading Co Ltd *Piraeus* *Greece* MMSI: 240822000 Official number: 11798	*1,596* 890 1,900	Class: (HR) (PR) (CS) (RI) (BV)	**1967-06 Ateliers et Chantiers du Havre — Le Havre** Yd No: 188 Converted From: LPG Tanker-1996 Loa 80.98 Br ex 11.99 Dght 5.130 Lbp 74.27 Br md 11.97 Dpth 6.60 Welded, 1 dk	**(B35E2TF) Bunkering Tanker** Liq: 2,000; Liq (Oil): 2,000	**1 oil engine** driving 1 FP propeller Total Power: 1,662kW (2,260hp) 11.0kn MAN G8V40/60 1 x 4 Stroke 8 Cy. 400 x 600 1662kW (2260bhp) Maschinenbau Augsburg Nuernberg (MAN)-Augsburg Fuel: 191.0 (d.f.) (Heating Coils)
8866967 *UFWI* -	**SOTNIK** *ex* Maria I *-2007* *ex* Mariya *-2006* *ex* Maria I *-1997* *ex* Mariya *-1995* *ex* Volgo-Balt 127 *-1995* **Yaroslavskiy Kapital Leasing Russia Co Ltd** Transnerud LLC *Taganrog* *Russia* MMSI: 273328900	**2,457** 1,134 3,562	Class: RS	**1970-08 Zavody Tazkeho Strojarstva (ZTS) — Komarno** Yd No: 1327 Loa 114.00 Br ex 13.19 Dght 3.860 Lbp 107.43 Br md 13.01 Dpth 5.50 Welded, 1 dk	**(A31A2GX) General Cargo Ship** Grain: 4,730 Compartments: 4 Ho, ER 4 Ha: (17.9 x 9.4)2 (18.9 x 9.4) (19.2 x 9.4)ER	**2 oil engines** driving 2 FP propellers Total Power: 1,030kW (1,400hp) 10.0kn Skoda 6L275IIPN 2 x 4 Stroke 6 Cy. 275 x 350 each-515kW (700bhp) (new engine 1982) CKD Praha-Praha AuxGen: 2 x 80kW a.c Fuel: 101.0 (d.f.)
9691230 - -	**SOTOKU MARU** - **Hayakoma Unyu KK** - *Japan*	*227* - -	Class: FA	**2013-10 Kanagawa Zosen — Kobe** Yd No: 656 Loa 37.50 Br ex - Dght 4.100 Lbp - Br md 9.00 Dpth - Welded, 1 dk	**(B32A2ST) Tug**	**2 oil engines** reduction geared to sc. shafts driving 2 Propellers Total Power: 3,676kW (4,998hp) Niigata 6L28HX 2 x 4 Stroke 6 Cy. 280 x 370 each-1838kW (2499bhp) Niigata Engineering Co Ltd-Japan
7600330 *9MOC* -	**SOTONG** *ex* Asiatic Charm *-1980* **Government of Malaysia (Royal Malaysian Navy)** - *Malaysia*	*233* 33 -	Class: (AB)	**1977-02 Sea Services Pte Ltd — Singapore** Yd No: Y129 Loa 29.49 Br ex 8.79 Dght 4.250 Lbp - Br md - Dpth - Welded, 1 dk	**(B32A2ST) Tug**	**2 oil engines** geared to sc. shafts driving 2 FP propellers Total Power: 1,176kW (1,598hp) 11.0kn Yanmar 6UAL-ST 2 x 4 Stroke 6 Cy. 200 x 240 each-588kW (799bhp) Yanmar Diesel Engine Co Ltd-Japan
8827052 *LAYN* -	**SOTRAOIL** *ex* O. V. K. IV *-1990* **Bergen Tankers AS** - *Bergen* *Norway* MMSI: 257237500 Official number: 20597	**479** 157 510 T/cm 2.0	Class: NV	**1968 Seutelvens Verksted — Fredrikstad** Yd No: 96 Converted From: Waste Disposal Vessel Loa 42.55 Br ex 9.50 Dght 2.930 Lbp 40.60 Br md 9.10 Dpth 5.13 Welded, 1 dk	**(B35E2TF) Bunkering Tanker** Double Hull Liq: 670; Liq (Oil): 670 Cargo Heating Coils 2 Cargo Pump (s): 2x200m³/hr	**1 oil engine** geared to sc. shaft driving 1 Directional propeller Total Power: 397kW (540hp) Caterpillar 3412TA 1 x Vee 4 Stroke 12 Cy. 137 x 152 397kW (540bhp) (new engine 1990) Caterpillar Inc-USA AuxGen: 2 x 108kW 220V 50Hz a.c Thrusters: 1 Thwart. FP thruster (f)
6407470 *IUKF* -	**SOTTOMARINA** *ex* Virginia *-1964* **Omnia River Srl** - *Chioggia* *Italy* MMSI: 247537000 Official number: 1	**429** 272 417	Class: (RI)	**1964-02 Cantiere Navale Visentini Mario e Figlio — Porto Viro** Yd No: 10 Lengthened-1976 Loa 55.73 Br ex 7.83 Dght 3.041 Lbp 52.74 Br md 7.80 Dpth 3.71 Riveted\Welded, 1 dk	**(A31A2GX) General Cargo Ship** Compartments: 2 Ho, ER	**1 oil engine** geared to sc. shaft driving 1 FP propeller Total Power: 184kW (250hp) 8.5kn Cummins KTA-19-M 1 x 4 Stroke 6 Cy. 159 x 159 184kW (250bhp) (new engine 1984) Cummins Engine Co Inc-USA
9574602 *JD3190* -	**SOUBAN MARU** - **Hayakoma Unyu KK** - *Kobe, Hyogo* *Japan* Official number: 141437	*229* - -		**2011-04 Kanagawa Zosen — Kobe** Yd No: 624 Loa 37.50 Br ex - Dght 3.100 Lbp 33.00 Br md 9.00 Dpth 4.09 Welded, 1 dk	**(B32A2ST) Tug**	**2 diesel electric oil engines** reduction geared to sc. shafts driving 2 Propellers Total Power: 3,676kW (4,998hp) Niigata 6L28HX 2 x 4 Stroke 6 Cy. 280 x 370 each-1838kW (2499bhp) Niigata Engineering Co Ltd-Japan
9176228 *JG5371* -	**SOUBI MARU** - **Corporation for Advanced Transport & Technology & Uyeno Transtech Co Ltd** Uyeno Transtech Co Ltd *Yokohama, Kanagawa* *Japan* MMSI: 431100372 Official number: 136606	*3,494* - 4,999	Class: NK	**1997-10 Naikai Zosen Corp — Onomichi HS (Setoda Shipyard)** Yd No: 630 Loa 104.96 (BB) Br ex - Dght 6.425 Lbp 97.00 Br md 16.00 Dpth 7.70 Welded, 1 dk	**(A13A2TW) Crude/Oil Products Tanker** Double Bottom Entire Compartment Length Liq: 6,117; Liq (Oil): 6,117 Compartments: 10 Wing Ta, ER 2 Cargo Pump (s): 2x1300m³/hr	**1 oil engine** driving 1 FP propeller Total Power: 3,266kW (4,440hp) 13.7kn B&W 6L35MC 1 x 2 Stroke 6 Cy. 350 x 1050 3266kW (4440bhp) Hitachi Zosen Corp-Japan AuxGen: 2 x 400kW a.c Thrusters: 1 Thwart. FP thruster (f) Fuel: 204.0 (r.f.) 12.8pd
9531430 *SVBH5* -	**SOUDA** - **Souda Shipping Co** Avin International SA SatCom: Inmarsat C 424110910 *Piraeus* *Greece* MMSI: 241109000 Official number: 12051	**2,336** 1,038 3,465 T/cm 9.7	Class: BV	**2010-11 in the People's Republic of China** Yd No: CT103 Loa 88.22 (BB) Br ex 13.02 Dght 5.950 Lbp 82.50 Br md 13.00 Dpth 7.25 Welded, 1 dk	**(A12B2TR) Chemical/Products Tanker** Double Hull (13F) Liq: 3,667; Liq (Oil): 3,667 Cargo Heating Coils Compartments: 5 Wing Ta, 5 Wing Ta, 1 Wing Slop Ta, 1 Wing Slop Ta, ER 3 Cargo Pump (s): 2x500m³/hr, 1x300m³/hr Manifold: Bow/CM: 40.1m	**1 oil engine** reduction geared to sc. shafts driving 1 FP propeller Total Power: 1,471kW (2,000hp) 11.2kn Chinese Std. Type LB8250ZLC 1 x 4 Stroke 8 Cy. 250 x 320 1471kW (2000bhp) Zibo Diesel Engine Factory-China AuxGen: 3 x 259kW 50Hz a.c Thrusters: 1 Tunnel thruster (f) Fuel: 43.0 (d.f.) 157.0 (r.f.)
9246190 *SY2659* -	**SOUDA II** - **Georgios Tzanakos** George Tzanakos Shipping & Trading *Piraeus* *Greece* MMSI: 237574100 Official number: 8103	**111** 52 -		**2002 NAFSI S.A. — Piraeus** Loa - Br ex - Dght - Lbp 23.29 Br md 7.00 Dpth 3.45 Welded, 1 dk	**(B32A2ST) Tug**	**2 oil engines** reduction geared to sc. shafts driving 2 FP propellers Total Power: 986kW (1,340hp) Caterpillar 3412TA 2 x Vee 4 Stroke 12 Cy. 137 x 152 each-493kW (670bhp) Caterpillar Inc-USA

IMO / Call sign	Name / Owner	Tonnage	Class	Builder / Dimensions	Type	Machinery
7528415 - -	**SOUELLABA** **L'Office National des Ports du Cameroon (ONPC)** - *Douala* *Cameroon*	*180* 120 -	Class: (BV)	**1975**-09 **B.V. Scheepswerf Damen — Gorinchem** Yd No: 781 Loa 22.18 Br ex - Dght 3.436 Lbp 19.99 Br md 6.01 Dpth 3.43 Welded, 1 dk	**(B32A2ST) Tug**	**2 oil engines** driving 2 FP propellers Total Power: 1,176kW (1,598hp) 12.3kn G.M. (Detroit Diesel) 12V-149 2 x Vee 2 Stroke 12 Cy. 146 x 146 each-588kW (799bhp) General Motors Detroit DieselAllison Divn-USA
9148647 *3FGX2* -	**SOUL OF LUCK** *ex* Hansa Catalina *-2013* *ex* Cap Lobos *-2006* *ex* Hansa Catalina *-2003* *ex* CMA Xiamen *-2000* *ex* P&O Nedlloyd Abidjan *-1999* *ex* Hansa Catalina *-1997* **Osier Holding SA** Victoria Oceanway Ltd *Panama* *Panama* MMSI: 352495000 Official number: 4493613	**16,915** 7,595 21,519 T/cm 38.4	Class: NK (GL)	**1997**-10 **Hanjin Heavy Industries Co Ltd — Ulsan** Yd No: 634 Loa 168.05 (BB) Br ex - Dght 9.215 Lbp 158.00 Br md 27.20 Dpth 13.80 Welded, 1 dk	**(A33A2CC) Container Ship (Fully Cellular)** TEU 1645 C Ho 606 TEU C Dk 1039 TEU incl 108 ref C. Cranes: 2x40t,1x10t Ice Capable	**1 oil engine** driving 1 FP propeller Total Power: 11,954kW (16,253hp) 19.0kn B&W 6S60MC 1 x 2 Stroke 6 Cy. 600 x 2292 11954kW (16253bhp) Hyundai Heavy Industries Co Ltd-South Korea AuxGen: 3 x 600kW 220/440V a.c Thrusters: 1 Tunnel thruster (f)
7390856 - -	**SOULA** *ex* Sotiria *-1990* *ex* Lamnalco 11 *-1987* *ex* Lamnalco Hawk *-1982* - -	**243** 73 253	Class: (LR) (HR) ✠ Classed LR until 18/1/89	**1974**-09 **Halter Marine Services, Inc. — New Orleans, La** Yd No: 426 Converted From: Crewboat-1989 Loa 30.48 Br ex 7.55 Dght 2.631 Lbp 26.45 Br md 7.32 Dpth 3.20 Welded, 1 dk	**(B11B2FV) Fishing Vessel**	**2 oil engines** with clutches & sr reverse geared to sc. shafts driving 2 FP propellers Total Power: 772kW (1,050hp) 10.0kn G.M. (Detroit Diesel) 12V-71 2 x Vee 2 Stroke 12 Cy. 108 x 127 each-386kW (525bhp) General Motors Corp-USA AuxGen: 2 x 24kW 220/440V 60Hz a.c
8882997 *OZHC* -	**SOULVEN** **Casper Fink** - *Struer* *Denmark* Official number: H1197	**140** 42 -		**1966 Orlogsvaerftet (Naval Dockyard) — Copenhagen** Yd No: 218 Loa 30.33 Br ex - Dght - Lbp - Br md 7.65 Dpth 3.40 Welded, 1 dk	**(B22A2OV) Diving Support Vessel**	**1 oil engine** driving 1 FP propeller
7808592 *EQHJ* -	**SOUMAR** *ex* Esteghlal *-1983* *ex* Abtin *-1980* **Government of The Islamic Republic of Iran (Ports & Maritime Organisation)** - *Khorramshahr* *Iran* MMSI: 422719000	*4,415* 2,101 4,965	Class: (LR) ✠ Classed LR until 9/11/94	**1979**-04 **IHC Smit BV — Kinderdijk** Yd No: C01120 Loa 96.02 Br ex 17.56 Dght 6.370 Lbp 88.04 Br md 17.51 Dpth 7.80 Welded, 1 dk	**(B33B2DT) Trailing Suction Hopper Dredger** Hopper: 3,000 Cranes: 1x15t	**2 oil engines** reverse reduction geared to sc. shafts driving 2 FP propellers Total Power: 3,310kW (4,500hp) MWM TBD501-6 2 x 4 Stroke 6 Cy. 360 x 450 each-1655kW (2250bhp) Motoren Werke Mannheim AG (MWM)-West Germany AuxGen: 4 x 310kW 390V 60Hz a.c Thrusters: 1 Thwart. FP thruster (f)
7118870 *5VAE7* -	**SOUMAYA-J** *ex* Lady Ranim *-2008* *ex* Amer-F *-2006* *ex* Mets *-2004* *ex* Aquila *-1994* *ex* Nautic *-1994* *ex* Elmwood *-1990* *ex* Nautic *-1987* *ex* Pepilo *-1982* *ex* Nautic *-1982* **Mariposa Maritime Co** Hamza Shipping Co *Lome* *Togo* MMSI: 671036000	**2,397** 1,298 3,720	Class: IV (GL)	**1971**-11 **J.J. Sietas Schiffswerft — Hamburg** Yd No: 675 Loa 88.52 Br ex 13.85 Dght 6.500 Lbp 80.30 Br md 13.80 Dpth 8.03 Welded, 2 dks	**(A31A2GX) General Cargo Ship** Grain: 4,647; Bale: 4,545 TEU 275 C. 275/20' Compartments: 1 Ho, ER 1 Ha: (50.9 x 10.2)ER Ice Capable	**1 oil engine** driving 1 FP propeller Total Power: 1,765kW (2,400hp) 12.0kn MaK 6MU551AK 1 x 4 Stroke 6 Cy. 450 x 550 1765kW (2400bhp) Atlas MaK Maschinenbau GmbH-Kiel
7110373 *7TEM* -	**SOUMMAM-2** **Entreprise Portuaire d'Arzew (EPA)** - *Alger* *Algeria*	*235* - -	Class: (BV)	**1971 Towa Zosen K.K. — Shimonoseki** Yd No: 395 Loa 32.31 Br ex 8.44 Dght 3.201 Lbp 29.01 Br md 8.40 Dpth 4.02 Welded, 1 dk	**(B32A2ST) Tug**	**2 oil engines** driving 2 CP propellers Total Power: 1,472kW (2,002hp) 12.0kn Pielstick 8PA4V185 2 x Vee 4 Stroke 8 Cy. 185 x 210 each-736kW (1001bhp) Chantiers de l'Atlantique-France AuxGen: 2 x 70kW 220/380V 50Hz a.c Fuel: 69.0 (d.f.)
7110385 *7TEN* -	**SOUMMAM-3** **Entreprise Portuaire de Bejaia (EPB)** - *Alger* *Algeria*	*235* - -	Class: (BV)	**1971 Towa Zosen K.K. — Shimonoseki** Yd No: 396 Loa 32.31 Br ex 8.44 Dght 3.201 Lbp 29.01 Br md 8.40 Dpth 4.02 Welded, 1 dk	**(B32A2ST) Tug**	**2 oil engines** driving 2 CP propellers Total Power: 1,472kW (2,002hp) 12.0kn Pielstick 8PA4V185 2 x Vee 4 Stroke 8 Cy. 185 x 210 each-736kW (1001bhp) Chantiers de l'Atlantique-France AuxGen: 2 x 70kW 220/380V 50Hz a.c Fuel: 69.0 (d.f.)
9414175 *A6E2646* -	**SOUNA** *ex* AOS Venus *-2008* **Gulf Piping Co WLL (GPC)** - *Abu Dhabi* *United Arab Emirates* MMSI: 470343000	**279** 83 270	Class: BV	**2006**-10 **Rushan Shipbuilding Co Ltd — Rushan SD** Yd No: SRC05-19 Loa 32.00 Br ex 9.21 Dght 3.800 Lbp 31.14 Br md 9.20 Dpth 4.50 Welded, 1 dk	**(B32A2ST) Tug**	**2 oil engines** reduction geared to sc. shafts driving 2 FP propellers Total Power: 2,384kW (3,242hp) 12.0kn Cummins KTA-38-M2 2 x Vee 4 Stroke 12 Cy. 159 x 159 each-1192kW (1621bhp) Cummins Engine Co Ltd-United Kingdom
8209585 *YJTK2* -	**SOUND** *ex* Vos Sound *-2013* *ex* DEA Sound *-2009* *ex* Smit-Lloyd Sound *-2003* *ex* TS 52 Sound *-1993* - - *Port Vila* *Vanuatu*	**1,521** 456 1,828	Class: BV (GL)	**1983**-08 **Elsflether Werft AG — Elsfleth** Yd No: 405 Loa 67.59 Br ex 14.05 Dght 5.971 Lbp 62.04 Br md 14.03 Dpth 6.91 Welded, 1 dk	**(B21B20A) Anchor Handling Tug Supply** Grain: 256 Compartments: 4 Ta, ER Cranes: 1x2t Ice Capable	**2 oil engines** with clutches, flexible couplings & sr geared to sc. shafts driving 2 CP propellers Total Power: 5,884kW (8,000hp) 15.5kn MWM TBD510-8 2 x 4 Stroke 8 Cy. 330 x 360 each-2942kW (4000bhp) Motoren Werke Mannheim AG (MWM)-West Germany AuxGen: 2 x 462kW 230/440V 60Hz a.c, 2 x 275kW 230/440V 60Hz a.c Thrusters: 1 Thwart. CP thruster (f) Fuel: 477.0 (d.f.) 8.0pd
9677820 *SFTC*	**SOUND ENTERPRISE** **Marcon-Gruppen I Sverige AB** Svensk Sjoentreprenad AB *Malmo* *Sweden* MMSI: 265702940	**161** 48 -	Class: BV	**2012**-11 **B.V. Scheepswerf Damen — Gorinchem** Yd No: 532518 Loa 25.12 Br ex 10.40 Dght 1.800 Lbp 23.73 Br md 10.00 Dpth 3.50 Welded, 1 dk	**(B21A20C) Crew/Supply Vessel** Hull Material: Aluminium Alloy	**2 oil engines** reduction geared to sc. shafts driving 2 FP propellers Total Power: 1,640kW (2,230hp) 25.0kn Caterpillar C32 2 x Vee 4 Stroke 12 Cy. 145 x 162 each-820kW (1115bhp) Caterpillar Inc-USA AuxGen: 2 x 23kW 50Hz a.c Thrusters: 2 Tunnel thruster (f)
9086538 *A8VF9* -	**SOUND FUTURE** *ex* Darya Yog *-2010* *ex* Maganda *-2004* *ex* Unimaster *-1999* **Vivant Marine Co** Blue Ocean Maritime Inc *Monrovia* *Liberia* MMSI: 636014602 Official number: 14602	**18,495** 10,215 29,156 T/cm 40.3	Class: LR (NK) ✠ **100A1** SS 07/2011 bulk carrier strengthened for heavy cargoes, Nos. 2 & 4 holds may be empty ESP ESN-Hold 1 Ice Class 1D ✠ **LMC** **UMS** Eq.Ltr: H†; Cable: 605.0/62.0 U3 (a)	**1996**-07 **Tianjin Xingang Shipyard — Tianjin** Yd No: 289 Loa 186.60 (BB) Br ex 25.06 Dght 10.020 Lbp 176.00 Br md 25.00 Dpth 14.40 Welded, 1 dk	**(A21A2BC) Bulk Carrier** Grain: 37,566 Compartments: 5 Ho, ER 5 Ha: 5 (16.4 x 12.9)ER Cranes: 4x25t Ice Capable	**1 oil engine** driving 1 FP propeller Total Power: 5,970kW (8,117hp) 14.0kn B&W 6L42MC 1 x 2 Stroke 6 Cy. 420 x 1360 5970kW (8117bhp) Hudong Shipyard-China AuxGen: 3 x 528kW 450V 60Hz a.c
9651151 *ZDKY7* -	**SOUND HORIZON** **Svensk Sjoentreprenad AB** - *Gibraltar* *Gibraltar (British)* MMSI: 236111849	**164** 49 133	Class: BV	**2012**-07 **Neptune Shipyards BV — Aalst (Nl)** Yd No: 416 Loa 23.95 Br ex - Dght 2.100 Lbp 22.00 Br md 9.54 Dpth 3.10 Welded, 1 dk	**(B34L2QU) Utility Vessel**	**2 oil engines** reduction geared to sc. shafts driving 2 FP propellers Total Power: 1,640kW (2,230hp) 9.0kn Caterpillar C32 2 x Vee 4 Stroke 12 Cy. 145 x 162 each-820kW (1115bhp) Caterpillar Inc-USA AuxGen: 2 x 86kW 50Hz a.c
6810926 *VY4372* -	**SOUND OF ISLAY** **Government of Newfoundland & Labrador (Department of Works, Services & Transportation)** - *St John's, NL* *Canada* MMSI: 316001217 Official number: 335016	*280* 135 -	Class: (LR) ✠ Classed LR until 5/69	**1968**-04 **Ferguson Bros (Port Glasgow) Ltd — Port Glasgow** Yd No: 452 Loa 43.41 Br ex 9.53 Dght 1.582 Lbp 38.13 Br md 9.15 Dpth 2.29 Welded, 1 dk	**(A36A2PR) Passenger/Ro-Ro Ship (Vehicles)** Passengers: 93 Stern door/ramp	**2 oil engines** sr reverse geared to sc. shafts driving 2 FP propellers Total Power: 470kW (640hp) 10.8kn Kelvin TA8 2 x 4 Stroke 8 Cy. 165 x 184 each-235kW (320bhp) Bergius Kelvin Co. Ltd.-Glasgow AuxGen: 2 x 24kW 240V 50Hz a.c Thrusters: 1 Water jet (f)

IMO / Call sign	Ship / Owner	Tonnage	Class	Built / Dimensions	Type	Machinery
8928894 *MWUB5* -	**SOUND OF SANDA** *ex* Gemeente Pont 24 *-1996* **The Underwater Centre (Fort William) Ltd** - *Glasgow* *United Kingdom* MMSI: 235008136 Official number: 729223	*403* 129 211 T/cm 4.7		**1964**-07 **Arnhemsche Scheepsbouw Mij NV — Arnhem** Loa 48.43 Br ex 13.87 Dght 2.700 Lbp 47.00 Br md 10.99 Dpth 3.77 Welded, 1 dk	**(A36A2PR) Passenger/Ro-Ro Ship (Vehicles)** Passengers: 220 Bow door/ramp Len: 1.20 Wid: 4.00 Swl: - Stern door/ramp Len: 1.20 Wid: 4.00 Swl: - Lane-Len: 157 Lane-Wid: 2.70 Lane-clr ht: 5.00 Lorries: 4, Cars: 34 Ice Capable	**2 oil engines** with clutches, flexible couplings & sr geared to sc. shafts driving 2 Directional propellers 1 fwd and 1 aft Total Power: 716kW (974hp) 10.3kn Caterpillar 3408TA 2 x Vee 4 Stroke 8 Cy. 137 x 152 each-358kW (487bhp) Caterpillar Tractor Co-USA AuxGen: 2 x 47kW 110/230V 50Hz a.c Fuel: 23.9 (d.f.) 2.5pd
8928882 *MVFY3* -	**SOUND OF SCALPAY** *ex* Gemeente Pont 23 *-1995* **The Underwater Centre (Fort William) Ltd** - *Glasgow* *United Kingdom* MMSI: 235008146 Official number: 728402	*403* 129 211 T/cm 4.6		**1962**-07 **Arnhemsche Scheepsbouw Mij NV — Arnhem** Loa 48.43 Br ex 13.87 Dght 2.700 Lbp 47.00 Br md 10.99 Dpth 3.77 Welded, 1 dk	**(A36A2PR) Passenger/Ro-Ro Ship (Vehicles)** Passengers: 220 Bow door/ramp Len: 1.20 Wid: 4.00 Swl: - Stern door/ramp Len: 1.20 Wid: 4.00 Swl: - Lane-Len: 157 Lane-Wid: 2.70 Lane-clr ht: 5.00 Lorries: 4, Cars: 34 Ice Capable	**2 oil engines** with clutches, flexible couplings & sr geared to sc. shafts driving 2 Directional propellers 1 fwd and 1 aft Total Power: 716kW (974hp) 10.3kn Caterpillar 3408TA 2 x Vee 4 Stroke 8 Cy. 137 x 152 each-358kW (487bhp) Caterpillar Tractor Co-USA AuxGen: 2 x 47kW 110/230V 50Hz a.c Fuel: 23.9 (d.f.) 2.5pd
9237424 *ZNGH7* -	**SOUND OF SCARBA** **Western Ferries (Clyde) Ltd** - *Glasgow* *United Kingdom* MMSI: 235001902 Official number: 904360	**489** 151 229 T/cm 5.2	Class: (LR) ✠ Classed LR until 30/4/06	**2001**-05 **Ferguson Shipbuilders Ltd — Port Glasgow** Yd No: 710 Loa 49.95 Br ex 15.01 Dght 2.504 Lbp 48.00 Br md 13.50 Dpth 3.99 Welded, 1 dk	**(A36A2PR) Passenger/Ro-Ro Ship (Vehicles)** Passengers: unberthed: 220 Bow ramp (centre) Len: 1.40 Wid: 4.50 Swl: - Stern ramp (centre) Len: 1.40 Wid: 4.50 Swl: - Lane-Len: 194 Lane-Wid: 2.67 Lane-clr ht: 5.60 Lorries: 4, Cars: 40	**2 oil engines** gearing integral to driving 2 Z propellers units have contrarotating propellers Total Power: 942kW (1,280hp) 11.0kn Cummins KTA-19-M3 2 x 4 Stroke 6 Cy. 159 x 159 each-471kW (640bhp) Cummins Engine Co Ltd-United Kingdom AuxGen: 2 x 57kW 220/415V 50Hz a.c Fuel: 17.8 (d.f.) 2.0pd
9012082 *TCA3046* -	**SOUND OF SEA** *ex* Metauro *-2013* *ex* Gianmaria *-1994* **Vakif Finansal Kiralama AS** Kalkan Denizcilik Petrol Lojistik Turizm Sanayi ve Ticaret Ltd Sti *Istanbul* *Turkey* MMSI: 271043738	**2,987** 1,264 4,621 T/cm 14.1	Class: BV (RI)	**1991**-12 **Cant. Nav. M. Morini & C. — Ancona** Loa 108.70 (BB) Br ex - Dght 5.184 Lbp 98.60 Br md 15.00 Dpth 7.00 Welded, 1 dk	**(A12B2TR) Chemical/Products Tanker** Double Hull (13F) Liq: 4,370; Liq (Oil): 4,370 Cargo Heating Coils Compartments: 10 Wing Ta (s.stl), 1 Slop Ta (s.stl), 2 Wing Slop Ta (s.stl), ER 12 Cargo Pump (s): 10x150m³/hr, 2x200m³/hr Manifold: Bow/CM: 50.9m	**1 oil engine** reduction geared to sc. shaft driving 1 CP propeller Total Power: 2,945kW (4,004hp) 12.5kn Wartsila 8R32 1 x 4 Stroke 8 Cy. 320 x 350 2945kW (4004bhp) Wartsila Diesel Oy-Finland AuxGen: 3 x 414kW 440/220V 60Hz a.c, 1 x 400kW 440/220V 60Hz a.c Thrusters: 1 Tunnel thruster (f) Fuel: 214.0 (d.f.) 295.0 (r.f.)
9665217 *2GWI2* -	**SOUND OF SEIL** **Western Ferries (Clyde) Ltd** - *Glasgow* *United Kingdom* MMSI: 235101062	**497** 153 230	Class: LR ✠**A1** SS 10/2013 inland waterways ferry, zone 1 Cable: 82.5/17.5 U2 (a)	**2013**-10 **Cammell Laird Shiprepairers & Shipbuilders Ltd — Birkenhead** Yd No: 1387 Loa 49.95 Br ex 15.01 Dght 2.500 Lbp 48.00 Br md 13.50 Dpth 4.00 Welded, 1 dk	**(A36A2PR) Passenger/Ro-Ro Ship (Vehicles)** Passengers: 260 Lane-clr ht: 5.20 Cars: 40	**2 oil engines** reduction geared to sc. shafts driving 2 Contra-rotating propellers Total Power: 894kW (1,216hp) 11.5kn Cummins QSK19-M 2 x 4 Stroke 6 Cy. 159 x 159 each-447kW (608bhp) Cummins Engine Co Inc-USA AuxGen: 2 x 52kW 415V 50Hz a.c
9289441 *MCGF8* -	**SOUND OF SHUNA** **Western Ferries (Clyde) Ltd** - *Glasgow* *United Kingdom* MMSI: 235013197 Official number: 907871	**489** 151 229	Class: LR ✠**100A1** SS 09/2013 passenger and vehicle ferry for service between Hunters Quay/Dunoon and McIroys Point/Gourock with occasional voyages in reasonable weather within the Firth of Clyde. Also voyages with out passengers to ports in west coast of Scotland for docking/overhaul in reasonable weather **LMC** Eq.Ltr: C; Cable: 110.0/16.0 U2 (a)	**2003**-09 **Ferguson Shipbuilders Ltd — Port Glasgow** Yd No: 715 Loa 49.95 Br ex 15.01 Dght 2.500 Lbp 48.00 Br md 13.50 Dpth 3.99 Welded, 1 dk	**(A36A2PR) Passenger/Ro-Ro Ship (Vehicles)** Passengers: unberthed: 220 Bow ramp (centre) Len: 1.40 Wid: 4.30 Swl: - Stern ramp (centre) Len: 1.40 Wid: 4.30 Swl: - Lane-Len: 194 Lane-Wid: 2.67 Lane-clr ht: 5.00 Cars: 40	**2 oil engines** gearing integral to driving 2 Z propellers units have contrarotating propellers Total Power: 942kW (1,280hp) 11.0kn Cummins KTA-19-M3 2 x 4 Stroke 6 Cy. 159 x 159 each-471kW (640bhp) Cummins Engine Co Inc-USA AuxGen: 2 x 57kW 415/240V 50Hz a.c Fuel: 18.0 (d.f.) 2.5pd
9665229 *2GWI3* -	**SOUND OF SOAY** **Western Ferries (Clyde) Ltd** - *Glasgow* *United Kingdom* MMSI: 235101063	**497** 153 270	Class: LR ✠**A1** SS 10/2013 inland waterways ferry, zone 1 Cable: 82.5/17.5 U2 (a)	**2013**-10 **Cammell Laird Shiprepairers & Shipbuilders Ltd — Birkenhead** Yd No: 1388 Loa 49.95 Br ex 15.01 Dght 2.500 Lbp 48.00 Br md 13.50 Dpth 4.00 Welded, 1 dk	**(A36A2PR) Passenger/Ro-Ro Ship (Vehicles)** Passengers: 260 Lane-clr ht: 5.20 Cars: 40	**2 oil engines** reduction geared to sc. shafts driving 2 Contra-rotating propellers Total Power: 894kW (1,216hp) 11.5kn Cummins QSK19-M 2 x 4 Stroke 6 Cy. 159 x 159 each-447kW (608bhp) Cummins Engine Co Inc-USA AuxGen: 2 x 52kW 415V 50Hz a.c
8852382 *WDC5237* -	**SOUND PACER** **Aphrodite Inc** - *Cordova, AK* *United States of America* MMSI: 367037960 Official number: 948793	*115* 68 -		**1989 United Marine Shipbuilding, Inc. — Seattle, Wa** Loa - Br ex - Dght - Lbp 24.44 Br md 6.71 Dpth 2.96 Welded, 1 dk	**(B11B2FV) Fishing Vessel**	**1 oil engine** driving 1 FP propeller
9364538 *SDLC* -	**SOUND PROVIDER** *ex* MCS Alix *-2011* **Marcon-Gruppen I Sverige AB** Svensk Sjoentreprenad AB *Malmo* *Sweden* MMSI: 265660390	**239** 71 300	Class: BV	**2005**-12 **Stocznia Kozle Serwis Sp z oo — Kedzierzyn-Kozle** (Hull) Yd No: (1565) **2005**-12 **B.V. Scheepswerf Damen Hardinxveld — Hardinxveld-Giessendam** Yd No: 1565 Loa 26.08 Br ex 9.12 Dght 2.630 Lbp 23.36 Br md 9.10 Dpth 3.60 Welded, 1 dk	**(B32A2ST) Tug**	**2 oil engines** reduction geared to sc. shafts driving 2 FP propellers Total Power: 1,644kW (2,236hp) 10.0kn Caterpillar 3508B-TA 2 x Vee 4 Stroke 8 Cy. 170 x 190 each-822kW (1118bhp) Caterpillar Inc-USA Thrusters: 1 Tunnel thruster (f)
9277369 *WXAE* -	**SOUND RELIANCE** **Vessel Management Services Inc** Intrepid Ship Management Inc *San Francisco, CA* *United States of America* MMSI: 369580000 Official number: 1122837	**950** 285 945	Class: AB	**2002**-07 **Moss Point Marine, Inc. — Escatawpa, Ms** Yd No: 1938 Loa - Br ex - Dght 5.800 Lbp 38.71 Br md 12.80 Dpth 6.70 Welded	**(B32B2SA) Articulated Pusher Tug**	**2 oil engines** reduction geared to sc. shafts driving 2 FP propellers Total Power: 6,766kW (9,200hp) Caterpillar 3612TA 2 x Vee 4 Stroke 12 Cy. 280 x 300 each-3383kW (4600bhp) Caterpillar Inc-USA AuxGen: 2 x 190kW a.c
9570876 *ZDNH2* -	**SOUND SOLUTION** **Marcon-Gruppen I Sverige AB** Svensk Sjoentreprenad AB *Gibraltar* *Gibraltar (British)* MMSI: 236111925	**200** 60 172	Class: BV	**2009**-12 **Neptune Shipyards BV — Aalst (Nl)** Yd No: 334 Loa 25.10 Br ex - Dght 2.390 Lbp 23.61 Br md 9.90 Dpth 3.50 Welded, 1 dk	**(B34L2QU) Utility Vessel**	**2 oil engines** reduction geared to sc. shafts driving 2 FP propellers Total Power: 1,640kW (2,230hp) 9.0kn Caterpillar C32 2 x Vee 4 Stroke 12 Cy. 145 x 162 each-820kW (1115bhp) Caterpillar Inc-USA AuxGen: 2 x 226kW 380/220V 50Hz a.c Fuel: 80.0
5112688 - -	**SOUNDA** *ex* Farouche *-1978* **L'Agence Transcongolaise des Communications** - *Pointe Noire* *Congo*	*218* - -	Class: (BV)	**1958 Ziegler Freres — Dunkerque** Yd No: 113 Loa 31.73 Br ex 8.36 Dght 3.607 Lbp 29.49 Br md 7.62 Dpth - Riveted\Welded, 1 dk	**(B32A2ST) Tug** 1 Ha: (1.9 x 1.1)	**1 oil engine** driving 1 FP propeller Total Power: 633kW (861hp) 11.0kn Werkspoor 8TM330 1 x 4 Stroke 8 Cy. 330 x 600 633kW (861bhp) Ziegler Freres-Dunkerque AuxGen: 2 x 50kW 110V d.c Fuel: 93.5 (d.f.)

IMO / Call sign	Name / Owner	Tonnage	Class	Builder / Dimensions	Type	Machinery
9312145 *SWGE* -	**SOUNION** **Sounion Special Maritime Enterprise (ENE)** Delta Tankers Ltd SatCom: Inmarsat C 424054210 *Piraeus* *Greece* MMSI: 240542000 Official number: 11535	**84,844** 53,844 163,759 T/cm 123.0	Class: LR ✠ **100A1** SS 12/2010 Double Hull oil tanker ESP **ShipRight** (SDA, FDA plus, CM) *IWS LI SPM EP Ice Class 1A FS at draught 16.3945m Max/min draught fwd 16.3945/5.6245m Max/min draught aft 16.3945/8.7445m Required power 18.6mw, installed power 18.6mw ✠ **LMC** **UMS IGS** Eq.Ltr: Z†; Cable: 742.5/100.0 U3 (a)	**2006-11 Hyundai Samho Heavy Industries Co Ltd — Samho** Yd No: S268 Loa 274.00 (BB) Br ex 50.06 Dght 17.024 Lbp 265.00 Br md 50.00 Dpth 23.10 Welded, 1 dk	**(A13A2TV) Crude Oil Tanker** Double Hull (13F) Liq: 173,962; Liq (Oil): 173,962 Cargo Heating Coils Compartments: 12 Wing Ta, 2 Wing Slop Ta, ER 3 Cargo Pump (s): 3x4000m³/hr Manifold: Bow/CM: 136m Ice Capable	**1 oil engine** driving 1 FP propeller Total Power: 18,610kW (25,302hp) 15.4kn MAN-B&W 6S70MC-C 1 x 2 Stroke 6 Cy. 700 x 2800 18610kW (25302bhp) Hyundai Heavy Industries Co Ltd-South Korea AuxGen: 3 x 860kW 450V 60Hz a.c Boilers: AuxB (Comp) 8.1kgf/cm² (7.9bar), WTAuxB (o.f.) 18.4kgf/cm² (18.0bar) Fuel: 147.9 (d.f.) 4200.9 (r.f.)
9003902 *JVDR5* -	**SOURAJ** *ex* Daikoku Maru *-2013* **Ali Jaddam Abdollahi** - *Ulaanbaatar* *Mongolia* MMSI: 457900062	*199* - 650		**1990-07 K.K. Miura Zosensho — Saiki** Yd No: 888 Loa 58.90 Br ex - Dght 3.130 Lbp 53.00 Br md 9.60 Dpth 5.33 Welded	**(A31A2GX) General Cargo Ship**	**1 oil engine** driving 1 FP propeller Total Power: 588kW (799hp) Niigata 6M28BGT 1 x 4 Stroke 6 Cy. 280 x 480 588kW (799bhp) Niigata Engineering Co Ltd-Japan
8859158 *EPBT7* -	**SOURAN** *ex* Yamato Maru *-2013* - - *Iran* MMSI: 422033800	*171* - 439		**1990-09 YK Furumoto Tekko Zosensho — Osakikamijima** Loa 50.00 Br ex - Dght 3.200 Lbp 45.00 Br md 8.30 Dpth 5.10 Welded, 1 dk	**(A31A2GX) General Cargo Ship**	**1 oil engine** driving 1 FP propeller Total Power: 405kW (551hp) 10.0kn Matsui ML626GSC-1 1 x 4 Stroke 6 Cy. 260 x 480 405kW (551bhp) Matsui Iron Works Co Ltd-Japan
8836235 - -	**SOURDOUGH** - -	**620** 194 661	Class: (RS)	**1945 Brunswick Marine Construction Co — Brunswick, Ga** Loa 53.03 Br ex 9.75 Dght 3.500 Lbp 50.60 Br md - Dpth 4.57 Welded	**(B11B2FV) Fishing Vessel**	**1 oil engine** geared to sc. shaft driving 1 FP propeller Total Power: 955kW (1,298hp) 11.0kn Caterpillar 3512TA 1 x Vee 4 Stroke 12 Cy. 170 x 190 955kW (1298bhp) Caterpillar Tractor Co-USA AuxGen: 1 x 410kW a.c, 1 x 210kW a.c, 1 x 135kW a.c Fuel: 261.0 (d.f.)
9274331 *YKRK* -	**SOURIA** *ex* BBC California *-2007* *completed as* Ostkap Carrier *-2004* **Syrian General Authority for Maritime Transport** - *Lattakia* *Syria* MMSI: 468392000 Official number: 392	**9,611** 4,260 12,716	Class: GL	**2004-06 Qingshan Shipyard — Wuhan HB** Loa 138.07 (BB) Br ex - Dght 8.000 Lbp 130.00 Br md 21.00 Dpth 11.00 Welded, 1 dk	**(A31A2GX) General Cargo Ship** Grain: 15,952 TEU 665 Compartments: 3 Ho, ER 3 Ha: ER Cranes: 2x120t Ice Capable	**1 oil engine** reduction geared to sc. shaft driving 1 CP propeller Total Power: 5,400kW (7,342hp) 15.0kn MaK 6M43 1 x 4 Stroke 6 Cy. 430 x 610 5400kW (7342bhp) Caterpillar Motoren GmbH & Co. KG-Germany AuxGen: 1 x 700kW 400/220V a.c, 3 x 395kW 400/220V a.c Thrusters: 1 Tunnel thruster (f)
8908662 *VB5536* -	**SOURIS LADY** **Mersey Seafoods Ltd** - *Charlottetown, PE* *Canada* MMSI: 316001940 Official number: 812096	*563* 263 -	Class: (AB)	**1989-09 Georgetown Shipyard Inc — Georgetown PE** Yd No: 50 Loa 41.00 Br ex - Dght - Lbp 35.20 Br md 9.80 Dpth 5.70 Welded, 2 dks	**(B11A2FS) Stern Trawler** Ice Capable	**1 oil engine** with clutches, flexible couplings & sr geared to sc. shaft driving 1 FP propeller Total Power: 1,037kW (1,410hp) 11.5kn Caterpillar 3516TA 1 x Vee 4 Stroke 16 Cy. 170 x 190 1037kW (1410bhp) Caterpillar Inc-USA AuxGen: 2 x 135kW
8643080 - -	**SOURS** - -	*698* 499 -		**1981-01 Estaleiros Sao Joao Nilo Tavares Coutinho S.A. — Manaus** Loa 48.93 Br ex 9.17 Dght 1.700 Lbp - Br md - Dpth 3.51 Welded, 1 dk	**(A37B2PS) Passenger Ship** Passengers: unberthed: 492	**1 oil engine** driving 1 Propeller
8802284 - -	**SOUSAH** **Government of Libya (Socialist Ports Co)** *Tripoli* *Libya*	**208** 62	Class: (LR) ✠ Classed LR until 11/9/96	**1991-09 Tczewska Stocznia Rzeczna — Tczew** (Hull) Yd No: HP2600L3 **1991-09 B.V. Scheepswerf Damen — Gorinchem** Yd No: 3167 Loa 30.20 Br ex 8.07 Dght 3.430 Lbp 27.06 Br md 7.80 Dpth 4.05 Welded, 1 dk	**(B32A2ST) Tug**	**2 oil engines** with clutches, flexible couplings & sr reverse geared to sc. shafts driving 2 FP propellers Total Power: 2,400kW (3,264hp) Deutz SBV6M628 2 x 4 Stroke 6 Cy. 240 x 280 each-1200kW (1632bhp) Kloeckner Humboldt Deutz AG-Germany AuxGen: 2 x 68kW 380V 50Hz a.c, 1 x 38kW 380V 50Hz a.c
9522790 *JD3016* -	**SOUSEI MARU** **Japan Railway Construction, Transport & Technology Agency, Asahi Tanker Co Ltd, Nisshin Unyu Co Ltd & Yoshikuni KK** KK DCAM *Tokyo* *Japan* MMSI: 431001136 Official number: 141178	*3,590* - 5,520	Class: NK	**2010-01 Hakata Zosen K.K. — Imabari** Yd No: 712 Loa 104.94 Br ex - Dght 6.660 Lbp 98.00 Br md 16.00 Dpth 8.20 Welded, 1 dk	**(A13B2TP) Products Tanker** Double Hull (13F) Liq: 5,487; Liq (Oil): 5,487	**1 oil engine** driving 1 FP propeller Total Power: 3,900kW (5,302hp) 14.2kn MAN-B&W 6L35MC 1 x 2 Stroke 6 Cy. 350 x 1050 3900kW (5302bhp) The Hanshin Diesel Works Ltd-Japan Fuel: 350.0
9394234 *CQLA* -	**SOUSELAS** *ex* Ismail K *-2012* Ership SAU *Madeira* *Portugal (MAR)* MMSI: 255804840 Official number: 1420	**14,116** 7,329 21,058	Class: LR (NK) (BV) **100A1** SS 11/2012 bulk carrier strengthened for heavy cargo ESP *IWS LI **LMC** **UMS**	**2007-11 Torgem Gemi Insaat Sanayii ve Ticaret a.s. — Tuzla, Istanbul** Yd No: 88 Loa 157.90 (BB) Br ex - Dght 8.930 Lbp 151.90 Br md 23.20 Dpth 12.50 Welded, 1 dk	**(A21A2BC) Bulk Carrier** Grain: 26,631 Compartments: 4 Ho, ER 4 Ha: ER Cranes: 3x30t	**1 oil engine** driving 1 FP propeller Total Power: 5,950kW (8,090hp) 14.5kn MAN-B&W 8S35MC 1 x 2 Stroke 8 Cy. 350 x 1400 5950kW (8090bhp) MAN Diesel A/S-Denmark AuxGen: 3 x 575kW a.c Fuel: 780.0
9672703 *JD3653* -	**SOUSHIN MARU** **Japan Railway Construction, Transport & Technology Agency, Asahi Tanker Co Ltd & Hoyo Kaiun KK** Hoyo Kaiun KK *Tokyo* *Japan* MMSI: 431005248 Official number: 142128	*3,595* - 5,724	Class: NK	**2014-03 Kumamoto Dock K.K. — Yatsushiro** Yd No: 462 Loa 104.95 (BB) Br ex - Dght 6.813 Lbp 98.80 Br md 16.00 Dpth 8.20 Welded, 1 dk	**(A12B2TR) Chemical/Products Tanker** Double Hull (13F)	**1 oil engine** driving 1 FP propeller Total Power: 3,250kW (4,419hp) MAN-B&W 5L35MC 1 x 2 Stroke 5 Cy. 350 x 1050 3250kW (4419bhp) The Hanshin Diesel Works Ltd-Japan
6518205 *HQBS9* -	**SOUSOU EXPRESS** *ex* Masiques *-1987* **Dejacmar Toussaint** - *San Lorenzo* *Honduras* Official number: L-0321624	*304* 163 478	Class: (LR) ✠ Classed LR until 11/12/81	**1966-02 Ast. de Tarragona — Tarragona** Loa 37.01 Br ex 7.50 Dght 3.918 Lbp 32.31 Br md 7.47 Dpth 4.78 Welded, 2 dks	**(A31A2GX) General Cargo Ship**	**1 oil engine** with hydraulic coupling driving 1 CP propeller Total Power: 313kW (426hp) 10.0kn Alpha 405-24VO 1 x 2 Stroke 5 Cy. 240 x 400 313kW (426bhp) Alpha Diesel A/S-Denmark AuxGen: 2 x 5kW 220V 50Hz a.c
9499474 *IILH2* -	**SOUTH** **Best Shipping Srl** - *Palermo* *Italy* MMSI: 247244600	**610** - -	Class: RI	**2008-06 Fratelli Rossi Cantiere Navale Srl — Viareggio** Yd No: FR 019 Loa 53.30 Br ex 10.02 Dght 3.000 Lbp 44.97 Br md 10.00 Dpth 5.00 Welded, 1 dk	**(X11A2YP) Yacht**	**2 oil engines** reduction geared to sc. shafts driving 2 Propellers Total Power: 3,236kW (4,400hp) Caterpillar 3516B 2 x Vee 4 Stroke 16 Cy. 170 x 190 each-1618kW (2200bhp) Caterpillar Inc-USA
9434864 *UBNG7* -	**SOUTH** *ex* Danga South 9 *-2008* **South Management BV** Neptuneflot Co Ltd *St Petersburg* *Russia* MMSI: 273356030	**259** 77 320	Class: BV (RS)	**2008-03 Kian Juan Dockyard Sdn Bhd — Miri** Yd No: 116 Loa 30.00 Br ex 8.69 Dght 3.500 Lbp 27.73 Br md 8.60 Dpth 4.12 Welded, 1 dk	**(B32A2ST) Tug** A-frames: 1	**2 oil engines** reduction geared to sc. shafts driving 2 FP propellers Total Power: 2,088kW (2,838hp) Cummins KTA-38-M2 2 x Vee 4 Stroke 12 Cy. 159 x 159 each-1044kW (1419bhp) Cummins Engine Co Ltd-United Kingdom AuxGen: 2 x 80kW 415/230V 50Hz a.c Thrusters: 1 Tunnel thruster (f) Fuel: 179.0 (d.f.)

8203050 *A6E2446* -	**SOUTH CAROLINA** *ex* Seabulk South Carolina *-2011* *ex* Seamark South Carolina *-1999* *ex* Seabulk South Carolina *-1997* *ex* Seamark South Carolina *-1996* *ex* Seabulk South Carolina *-1992* *ex* Golden Bear *-1989* *ex* PBR/454 *-1985* **Orient Oil Co LLC** - *Sharjah* *United Arab Emirates* MMSI: 470401000 Official number: 6655	**701** 210 1,200	Class: AB	**1983-07 Champion Shipyards, Inc. — Pass Christian, Ms** Yd No: 14 L reg 51.39 Br ex - Dght 3.595 Lbp 54.87 Br md 12.20 Dpth 4.27 Welded, 1 dk	**(B21A20S) Platform Supply Ship**	**2 oil engines** reverse reduction geared to sc. shafts driving 2 FP propellers Total Power: 2,206kW (3,000hp) 12.0kn EMD (Electro-Motive) 12-645-E6 2 x Vee 2 Stroke 12 Cy. 230 x 254 each-1103kW (1500bhp) (Reconditioned , Reconditioned & fitted 1983) General Motors Corp.Electro-Motive Div.-La Grange AuxGen: 2 x 99kW a.c Thrusters: 1 Thwart. FP thruster (f)
7651133 *HQJK5* -	**SOUTH CHINA** *ex* Super June *-1985* *ex* Nippo Maru No. 1 *-1991* **South China Shipping Ltd** - *San Lorenzo* *Honduras* Official number: L-0324189	*498* 267 1,815	Class: (KR)	**1975-07 Y.K. Tokai Zosensho — Tsukumi** Loa 61.50 Br ex - Dght 4.613 Lbp 57.00 Br md 13.01 Dpth 5.41 Welded, 1 dk	**(A31A2GX) General Cargo Ship** Grain: 1,725; Bale: 1,591 1 Ha: (26.4 x 5.0)ER	**1 oil engine** driving 1 FP propeller Total Power: 1,103kW (1,500hp) 12.0kn Fuji 6S30BH 1 x 4 Stroke 6 Cy. 300 x 450 1103kW (1500bhp) Fuji Diesel Co Ltd-Japan AuxGen: 2 x 49kW 225V a.c
9657739 *P2V5549* -	**SOUTH FORTUNE** *ex* Danum 142 *-2013* **Tzen Plantation Ltd** - *Port Moresby* *Papua New Guinea*	**173** 52 171	Class: (BV)	**2012-09 Piasau Slipways Sdn Bhd — Miri** Yd No: 376 Loa 26.80 Br ex - Dght 3.000 Lbp 24.04 Br md 7.32 Dpth 3.65 Welded, 1 dk	**(B32A2ST) Tug**	**2 oil engines** reduction geared to sc. shafts driving 2 FP propellers Total Power: 894kW (1,216hp) Cummins KTA-19-M3 2 x 4 Stroke 6 Cy. 159 x 159 each-447kW (608bhp) Cummins Engine Co Inc-USA Fuel: 150.0 (d.f.)
7110828 *BVAQ* -	**SOUTH GOOD No. 1** - **South Good Fishery Co Ltd** - *Kaohsiung* *Chinese Taipei*	*264* 184	Class: (CR)	**1971 Fong Kuo Shipbuilding Co Ltd — Kaohsiung** Loa 39.20 Br ex 6.91 Dght 2.750 Lbp 33.99 Br md 6.90 Dpth 3.15 Welded, 1 dk	**(B11B2FV) Fishing Vessel** Ins: 255 Compartments: 3 Ho, ER 4 Ha: 2 (1.0 x 1.0)2 (1.2 x 1.0)ER Derricks: 1x1t	**1 oil engine** driving 1 FP propeller Total Power: 478kW (650hp) 10.5kn Hanshin 6L26AGSH 1 x 4 Stroke 6 Cy. 260 x 400 478kW (650bhp) Hanshin Nainenki Kogyo-Japan AuxGen: 2 x 80kW 230V a.c
8412467 *9LY2539* -	**SOUTH HILL 2** *ex* Ryong Nam 2 *-2012* *ex* Panagia Tinou *-2006* *ex* Long Kim *-2001* *ex* Handy Brave *-1998* *ex* Red Stag *-1994* *ex* Southern Brave *-1992* **CM Chartering Ltd** Hua Heng Shipping Ltd *Freetown* *Sierra Leone* MMSI: 667003342 Official number: SL103342	**14,921** 8,855 25,402 T/cm 34.5	Class: KC (NK)	**1984-08 Imabari Shipbuilding Co Ltd — Imabari EH (Imabari Shipyard)** Yd No: 445 Loa 159.76 (BB) Br ex 25.23 Dght 10.240 Lbp 149.99 Br md 25.21 Dpth 14.03 Welded, 1 dk	**(A21A2BC) Bulk Carrier** Grain: 32,014; Bale: 30,501 Compartments: 4 Ho, ER 4 Ha: (18.4 x 12.8)3 (21.6 x 12.8)ER Cranes: 3x30t; Derricks: 1x25t	**1 oil engine** driving 1 FP propeller Total Power: 5,149kW (7,001hp) 13.5kn B&W 6L50MCE 1 x 2 Stroke 6 Cy. 500 x 1620 5149kW (7001bhp) Hitachi Zosen Corp-Japan AuxGen: 3 x 340kW a.c Fuel: 1522.0
9370379 *3ENY2* -	**SOUTH ISLANDER** - **Vega Marine Ltd SA** Hachiuma Steamship Co Ltd (Hachiuma Kisen KK) *Panama* *Panama* MMSI: 353870000 Official number: 3342408A	**18,174** 11,005 18,091	Class: NK	**2007-12 Shin Kochi Jyuko K.K. — Kochi** Yd No: 7207 Loa 160.70 (BB) Br ex 25.00 Dght 9.380 Lbp 151.20 Br md 25.00 Dpth 12.80 Welded	**(A31A2GA) General Cargo Ship (with Ro-Ro facility)** Angled stern door/ramp (centre) Bale: 15,218 TEU 970 incl 100 ref C. Cranes: 2x40t	**1 oil engine** driving 1 FP propeller Total Power: 9,625kW (13,086hp) 18.0kn Mitsubishi 7UEC50LSII 1 x 2 Stroke 7 Cy. 500 x 1950 9625kW (13086bhp) Kobe Hatsudoki KK-Japan AuxGen: 3 x 790kW a.c Thrusters: 1 Tunnel thruster (f) Fuel: 1640.0
7625495 *HP9326* -	**SOUTH MARINE 28** *ex* Grouper *-2012* **South Marine Offshore** - *Panama* *Panama* MMSI: 353731000 Official number: 2696100C	*162* 49 110	Class: (LR) ✠ Classed LR until 10/5/95	**1980-03 Bodewes Scheepswerf "Volharding" Foxhol B.V. — Foxhol** (Hull) **1980-03 B.V. Scheepswerf Damen — Gorinchem** Yd No: 3102 Loa 26.21 Br ex 8.06 Dght 3.261 Lbp 22.92 Br md 7.92 Dpth 4.03 Welded, 1 dk	**(B32A2ST) Tug**	**2 oil engines** reverse reduction geared to sc. shaft driving 2 FP propellers Total Power: 2,060kW (2,800hp) Caterpillar D399TA 2 x Vee 4 Stroke 16 Cy. 159 x 203 each-1030kW (1400bhp) Caterpillar Tractor Co-USA AuxGen: 2 x 50kW 220V 60Hz a.c
8218483 - -	**SOUTH MOLLE REEF** *ex* Telford Reef *-1986* **Ansett Australia Ltd** - *Bowen, Qld* *Australia*	*173* 40 20		**1982-10 North Queensland Engineers & Agents Pty Ltd — Cairns QLD** Yd No: 107 Loa 22.81 Br ex 9.20 Dght 1.601 Lbp 19.51 Br md 8.72 Dpth 2.75 Welded, 1 dk	**(A37B2PS) Passenger Ship** Hull Material: Aluminium Alloy Passengers: unberthed: 220	**2 oil engines** sr reverse geared to sc. shafts driving 2 CP propellers Total Power: 1,176kW (1,598hp) G.M. (Detroit Diesel) 12V-92-TA 2 x Vee 2 Stroke 12 Cy. 123 x 127 each-588kW (799bhp) General Motors Detroit DieselAllison Divn-USA
8428002 *DUH2040* -	**SOUTH PACIFIC** - **Southern Pacific Transport Corp** - *Cebu* *Philippines* Official number: CEB1000001	*230* 115 300		**1975 at Lapu-Lapu** L reg 38.57 Br ex 7.35 Dght - Lbp 37.98 Br md 7.32 Dpth - Welded, 1 dk	**(A32A2GF) General Cargo/Passenger Ship**	**1 oil engine** driving 1 FP propeller Total Power: 294kW (400hp)
8610930 - -	**SOUTH PASSAGE** - **M & G Hoschke Pty Ltd** - *Cairns, Qld* *Australia* MMSI: 503318000 Official number: 853018	*198* 59 -		**1988-06 EMS Holdings Pty Ltd — Fremantle WA** Yd No: 15 Loa 29.01 Br ex 7.40 Dght 3.101 Lbp 25.02 Br md 7.21 Dpth 3.92 Welded, 1 dk	**(B11A2FT) Trawler** Ins: 110	**1 oil engine** with clutches, flexible couplings & sr geared to sc. shaft driving 1 FP propeller Total Power: 526kW (715hp) Caterpillar 3508TA 1 x Vee 4 Stroke 8 Cy. 170 x 190 526kW (715bhp) Caterpillar Inc-USA
1004601 *9HB2853* -	**SOUTH PAW C** *ex* Zulu Sea *-1995* *ex* Janka *-1995* *ex* Laura *-1995* *ex* Gipsy *-1995* **Astra Bay Ltd** - *Valletta* *Malta* Official number: 1004601	**225** 67 -	Class: LR **✠ 100A1** SS 02/2013 Yacht **✠LMC**	**1977-07 Cant. Nav. Ugo Codecasa S.p.A. — Viareggio** Loa 34.52 Br ex 7.10 Dght 2.980 Lbp 30.01 Br md 7.00 Dpth 3.53 Welded, 1 dk	**(X11A2YP) Yacht**	**2 oil engines** geared to sc. shafts driving 2 FP propellers Total Power: 1,156kW (1,572hp) Caterpillar 3508TA 2 x Vee 4 Stroke 8 Cy. 170 x 190 each-578kW (786bhp) Caterpillar Tractor Co-USA
9164794 *ICJH* -	**SOUTH RIVER** *ex* Clipper Stamford *-2010* **Italian Shipping Co (ISC) Srl** Time 2000 Noleggio e Trasporti Marittimi SAS *Naples* *Italy* MMSI: 247286300	**14,118** 6,124 20,731 T/cm 30.8	Class: BV (AB)	**1998-09 Hitachi Zosen Singapore Pte Ltd — Singapore** Yd No: N-024 Loa 159.90 (BB) Br ex - Dght 9.726 Lbp 149.00 Br md 23.10 Dpth 13.80 Welded, 1 dk	**(A31A2GX) General Cargo Ship** Grain: 23,880; Bale: 23,795 TEU 869 C Ho 390 TEU C Dk 479 TEU incl 54 ref C. Compartments: 4 Ho, ER 4 Ha: (25.6 x 18.2)3 (19.2 x 18.2)ER Cranes: 3x36t	**1 oil engine** driving 1 FP propeller Total Power: 6,150kW (8,362hp) 15.0kn B&W 6S42MC 1 x 2 Stroke 6 Cy. 420 x 1764 6150kW (8362bhp) Hitachi Zosen Corp-Japan AuxGen: 3 x 600kW 450V 60Hz a.c Fuel: 64.9 (d.f.) (Heating Coils) 1137.8 (r.f.) 25.0pd
6524620 *9GHD* AFT 65	**SOUTH SEA** *ex* Sierra *-1998* **Toiman Fishing Co Ltd** - *Takoradi* *Ghana* MMSI: 627933000 Official number: 316933	*524* 232 659	Class: RC (BV)	**1966 Ast. Celaya — Bilbao** Yd No: 79 Loa 52.02 Br ex 9.02 Dght 3.747 Lbp 49.61 Br md 9.01 Dpth 4.25 Riveted\Welded, 2 dks	**(B11B2FV) Fishing Vessel** Ins: 555 Compartments: 3 Ho, ER 3 Ha: 3 (1.6 x 1.6)ER Derricks: 2x1t	**1 oil engine** driving 1 FP propeller Total Power: 956kW (1,300hp) 12.8kn MAN G9V30/45ATL 1 x 4 Stroke 9 Cy. 300 x 450 956kW (1300bhp) Cia Euskalduna de Construccion yReparacion de Buques SA-Spain Fuel: 291.0 (d.f.)
9286657 *A8FZ9* -	**SOUTH SEA** - **Huntley Enterprises SA** Dynacom Tankers Management Ltd SatCom: Inmarsat C 463705495 *Monrovia* *Liberia* MMSI: 636012524 Official number: 12524	**78,845** 46,993 149,993 T/cm 118.0	Class: LR **✠ 100A1** SS 10/2010 Double Hull oil tanker ESP *IWS LI SPM **ShipRight** (SDA, FDA plus, CM) **✠LMC** **UMS IGS** Eq.Ltr: A†; Cable: 742.5/97.0 U3 (a)	**2005-10 Universal Shipbuilding Corp — Tsu ME** Yd No: 008 Loa 274.20 (BB) Br ex 48.04 Dght 15.975 Lbp 263.00 Br md 48.00 Dpth 22.40 Welded, 1 dk	**(A13A2TV) Crude Oil Tanker** Double Hull (13F) Liq: 160,636; Liq (Oil): 160,636 Cargo Heating Coils Compartments: 12 Wing Ta, 2 Wing Slop Ta, ER 3 Cargo Pump (s): 3x3500m³/hr Manifold: Bow/CM: 133.8m	**1 oil engine** driving 1 FP propeller Total Power: 16,440kW (22,352hp) 15.4kn Sulzer 6RTA72U 1 x 2 Stroke 6 Cy. 720 x 2500 16440kW (22352bhp) Diesel United Ltd.-Aioi AuxGen: 3 x 800kW 450V 60Hz a.c Boilers: e (ex.g.) 22.9kgf/cm² (22.5bar), WTAuxB (o.f.) 17.9kgf/cm² (17.6bar) Fuel: 275.0 (d.f.) 3500.0 (r.f.)
7120213 - -	**SOUTH SEAS** *ex* Mary S *-1988* **Alpha Fishing Co Inc** - *Venezuela*	*916* 459 -		**1971 San Diego Mar. Co. — San Diego, Ca** Yd No: 173 L reg 55.94 Br ex - Dght - Lbp 59.26 Br md 10.97 Dpth 4.53 Welded, 1 dk	**(B11B2FV) Fishing Vessel**	**1 oil engine** driving 1 FP propeller Total Power: 2,648kW (3,600hp) General Motors 1 x 2 Stroke 2648kW (3600bhp) General Motors Corp-USA

8855906 - -	**SOUTH SEAS '84** - **Sahlman Seafoods Inc** - *Kingstown* *St Vincent & The Grenadines*	*101* 69 -		**1983-01 Steiner Shipyard, Inc. — Bayou La Batre, Al** Loa - Br ex - Dght - Lbp 20.33 Br md 6.71 Dpth 3.32 Welded, 1 dk	**(B11B2FV) Fishing Vessel**	**1 oil engine** driving 1 FP propeller
7314606 - -	**SOUTH STAR** *ex* Isuzu Maru No. 21 *-1987* **TS Corp** Daewoo Marine Co Ltd *Fiji*	*254* 130 315	Class: (KR)	**1973 Yamanishi Shipbuilding Co Ltd — Ishinomaki MG** Yd No: 740 Loa 47.81 Br ex 8.03 Dght 2.998 Lbp 41.20 Br md 8.01 Dpth 3.41 Welded, 1 dk	**(B11B2FV) Fishing Vessel**	**1 oil engine** driving 1 FP propeller Total Power: 809kW (1,100hp) 11.5kn Akasaka AH27 1 x 4 Stroke 6 Cy. 270 x 420 809kW (1100bhp) Akasaka Tekkosho KK (Akasaka DieselLtd)-Japan AuxGen: 2 x 176kW 225V a.c
8400517 *JVJW5* -	**SOUTH STAR** *ex* Florence *-2014* *ex* Celtic *-2006* *ex* Violet Islands *-1993* *ex* Sanko Hydrangea *-1986* - - *Ulaanbaatar* *Mongolia*	**16,582** 9,524 27,652 T/cm 38.8	Class: BV (NK)	**1985-05 Mitsubishi Heavy Industries Ltd. — Nagasaki** Yd No: 1961 Loa 165.51 (BB) Br ex - Dght 9.599 Lbp 157.99 Br md 27.01 Dpth 13.31 Welded, 1 dk	**(A21A2BC) Bulk Carrier** Grain: 34,810; Bale: 34,182 Compartments: 5 Ho, ER 5 Ha: (8.0 x 13.5)4 (19.2 x 13.5)ER Cranes: 4x25t	**1 oil engine** driving 1 FP propeller Total Power: 4,832kW (6,570hp) 13.0kn Mitsubishi 6UE52LA 1 x 2 Stroke 6 Cy. 520 x 1600 4832kW (6570bhp) Mitsubishi Heavy Industries Ltd-Japan AuxGen: 3 x 450kW 450V 60Hz a.c Fuel: 234.5 (d.f.) (Heating Coils) 1258.5 (r.f.) 21.0pd
8305858 *3CM2143* -	**SOUTH STAR** *ex* Jiin Horng 116 *-2002* *ex* Altar 7 *-1998* *ex* Cheog Yang No. 301 *-1995* **Pesquera Jiin Yeong Fishery SA** - *Malabo* *Equatorial Guinea* Official number: EG-968952	*509* 152 350	Class: (KR)	**1983-11 Dae Sun Shipbuilding & Engineering Co Ltd — Busan** Yd No: 271 Loa 49.97 (BB) Br ex 8.62 Dght 3.547 Lbp 44.00 Br md 8.60 Dpth 3.66 Welded, 1 dk	**(B11B2FV) Fishing Vessel** Compartments: 4 Ho, ER 4 Ha: ER	**1 oil engine** sr reverse geared to sc. shaft driving 1 FP propeller Total Power: 736kW (1,001hp) 12.0kn Niigata 6M28AET 1 x 4 Stroke 6 Cy. 280 x 480 736kW (1001bhp) Niigata Engineering Co Ltd-Japan AuxGen: 2 x 280kW 225V 60Hz a.c Thrusters: 1 Thwart. FP thruster (f) Fuel: 350.0 (d.f.) 3.0pd
8823355 - -	**SOUTH STAR UNO** *ex* Aqua Jet No. 1 *-1999* **South Star Navigation Inc** - *Batangas* *Philippines* Official number: BAT5006327	*220* 149 23		**1989-03 Mitsui Eng. & SB. Co. Ltd. — Tamano** Yd No: TH 1613 Loa 34.20 Br ex - Dght 1.250 Lbp 29.00 Br md 8.00 Dpth 3.20 Welded, 1 dk	**(A37B2PS) Passenger Ship** Hull Material: Aluminium Alloy Passengers: unberthed: 196	**2 oil engines** geared to sc. shafts driving 2 Water jets Total Power: 2,898kW (3,940hp) 30.0kn M.T.U. 16V396TB83 2 x Vee 4 Stroke 16 Cy. 165 x 185 each-1449kW (1970bhp) MTU Friedrichshafen GmbH-Friedrichshafen AuxGen: 1 x 32kW a.c, 1 x 8kW a.c
9206059 *A8OH2*	**SOUTHAMPTON STAR** - **Star Reefers Shipowning Inc** Star Reefers Poland Sp z oo SatCom: Inmarsat C 463701274 *Monrovia* *Liberia* MMSI: 636013625 Official number: 13625	**10,804** 5,320 9,709 T/cm 25.7	Class: NV (NK)	**1999-12 Shikoku Dockyard Co. Ltd. — Takamatsu** Yd No: 893 Loa 150.00 (BB) Br ex - Dght 9.018 Lbp 140.00 Br md 23.00 Dpth 13.30 Welded, 1 dk	**(A34A2GR) Refrigerated Cargo Ship** Ins: 14,335 TEU 306 C Ho 84 TEU C Dk 222 TEU incl 100 ref C 4 Ha: 4 (12.6 x 7.8) Cranes: 2x40t,2x8t	**1 oil engine** driving 1 FP propeller Total Power: 12,641kW (17,187hp) 21.0kn B&W 8S50MC-C 1 x 2 Stroke 8 Cy. 500 x 2000 12641kW (17187bhp) Mitsui Engineering & Shipbuilding CLtd-Japan AuxGen: 4 x 800kW 450V 60Hz a.c
8855994 - -	**SOUTHEAST** - **f/v Southeast LLC** - *Astoria, OR* *United States of America* Official number: 694038	*107* 85 -		**1986 Van Peer Boatworks — Fort Bragg, Ca** Yd No: 14 Loa - Br ex - Dght - Lbp 20.12 Br md 6.71 Dpth 3.35 Welded, 1 dk	**(B11B2FV) Fishing Vessel**	**1 oil engine** driving 1 FP propeller
7340887 *V5SH* L737	**SOUTHERN AQUARIUS** *ex* Faroe Venture *-1992* *ex* Andri I *-1990* *ex* Roman I *-1989* *ex* Roman *-1985* **CMI Trawling (Pty) Ltd** Deep Ocean Processors SatCom: Inmarsat C 465900830 *Walvis Bay* *Namibia* Official number: 95WB011	*1,154* 391 984	Class: (LR) (BV) ✠ Classed LR until 92	**1974-05 Ferguson Bros (Port Glasgow) Ltd — Port Glasgow** Yd No: 467 Converted From: Stern Trawler-1989 Converted From: Stern Trawler-1974 Loa 63.00 (BB) Br ex 12.53 Dght 5.335 Lbp 54.51 Br md 12.50 Dpth 8.00 Welded, 2 dks	**(B12A2FF) Fish Factory Ship** Ins: 850	**1 oil engine** sr geared to sc. shaft driving 1 FP propeller Total Power: 2,430kW (3,304hp) 15.0kn Deutz SBV6M640 1 x 4 Stroke 6 Cy. 370 x 400 2430kW (3304bhp) (new engine 1988) Kloeckner Humboldt Deutz AG-West Germany
9355393 *3EEG9*	**SOUTHERN ATLAS** - **Sansho Line SA** Tatsumi Marine (S) Pte Ltd *Panama* *Panama* MMSI: 371896000 Official number: 3181406A	**5,551** 2,785 8,905 T/cm 18.2	Class: NK	**2006-04 Shitanoe Shipbuilding Co Ltd — Usuki OT** Yd No: 1251 Loa 115.50 (BB) Br ex 18.73 Dght 7.613 Lbp 108.50 Br md 18.70 Dpth 10.00 Welded, 1 dk	**(A12B2TR) Chemical/Products Tanker** Double Hull (13F) Liq: 19,384; Liq (Oil): 9,656 Cargo Heating Coils Compartments: 16 Wing Ta (s.stl), 1 Slop Ta (s.stl), ER 16 Cargo Pump (s): 12x300m³/hr, 4x200m³/hr Manifold: Bow/CM: 59.5m	**1 oil engine** driving 1 FP propeller Total Power: 3,883kW (5,279hp) 13.7kn MAN-B&W 6L35MC 1 x 2 Stroke 6 Cy. 350 x 1050 3883kW (5279bhp) Hitachi Zosen Corp-Japan AuxGen: 3 x 400kW 450V a.c Thrusters: 1 Tunnel thruster (f) Fuel: 55.0 (d.f.) 427.0 (r.f.)
9152181 *A8IO7*	**SOUTHERN BAY** *ex* Southern Express *-2005* **'Southern Bay' Schiffahrtsgesellschaft mbH & Co KG** Triton Schiffahrts GmbH *Monrovia* *Liberia* MMSI: 636091012 Official number: 91012	**8,879** 4,366 9,609	Class: BV (NK)	**1997-11 Kitanihon Zosen K.K. — Hachinohe** Yd No: 310 Loa 143.00 (BB) Br ex 22.02 Dght 8.288 Lbp 133.00 Br md 22.00 Dpth 13.00 Welded, 2 dks	**(A34A2GR) Refrigerated Cargo Ship** Ins: 14,853 TEU 202 C.Ho 42 TEU C.Dk 160 TEU incl 73 ref C. Compartments: 4 Ho, ER, 4 Tw Dk 4 Ha: ER Cranes: 1x40t; Derricks: 8x6t	**1 oil engine** driving 1 FP propeller Total Power: 9,628kW (13,090hp) 19.3kn Mitsubishi 7UEC50LSII 1 x 2 Stroke 7 Cy. 500 x 1950 9628kW (13090bhp) Akasaka Tekkosho KK (Akasaka DieselLtd)-Japan AuxGen: 3 x 800kW a.c Fuel: 120.0 (d.f.) 1210.0 (r.f.) 36.0pd
7742554 *WDD3987* -	**SOUTHERN BELL** *ex* Capt Lee *-2006* *ex* Master Bill *-2001* *ex* Robin Paulette *-2001* **Thu Hong Thi Tran** - *Bayou La Batre, AL* *United States of America* MMSI: 367138950 Official number: 591119	*120* 81 -		**1978 Master Marine, Inc. — Bayou La Batre, Al** Yd No: 199 L reg 22.59 Br ex 6.71 Dght - Lbp - Br md - Dpth 3.41 Welded, 1 dk	**(B11B2FV) Fishing Vessel**	**1 oil engine** driving 1 FP propeller Total Power: 331kW (450hp) Caterpillar 3412T 1 x Vee 4 Stroke 12 Cy. 137 x 152 331kW (450bhp) Caterpillar Tractor Co-USA
6603725 *ZR6033* -	**SOUTHERN BELLE** *ex* Chacabuco 1 *-1996* *ex* Langeveld *-1984* *ex* Helge Skog *-1981* *ex* Leinebjorn *-1978* **Premier Fishing (Pty) Ltd** - *Cape Town* *South Africa* MMSI: 601794000 Official number: 19601	*304* 135 -	Class: (NV)	**1965-11 Skaalurens Skipsbyggeri AS — Rosendal** Yd No: 208/22 Lengthened-1969 Loa 38.54 Br ex 7.19 Dght 4.598 Lbp 34.65 Br md 7.17 Dpth 5.14 Welded, 1 dk	**(B11B2FV) Fishing Vessel** Compartments: 2 Ho, 3 Ta, ER 7 Ha: (2.4 x 1.9)6 (2.4 x 1.5)ER Derricks: 1x3t; Winches: 1 Ice Capable	**1 oil engine** driving 1 FP propeller Total Power: 662kW (900hp) Wichmann 6ACA 1 x 2 Stroke 6 Cy. 280 x 420 662kW (900bhp) Wichmann Motorfabrikk AS-Norway AuxGen: 1 x 96kW 220V 50Hz a.c, 1 x 64kW 220V 50Hz a.c, 1 x 40kW 220V 50Hz a.c Thrusters: 1 Thwart. FP thruster (f); 1 Tunnel thruster (a)
9584841 *WDE7492* -	**SOUTHERN BELLE** - **Southern States Offshore Inc** - *Houston, TX* *United States of America* MMSI: 367393920 Official number: 1217664	**385** 115 300		**2009-04 Island Boats Inc — Jeanerette LA** Yd No: 10115 Loa 51.20 Br ex - Dght 2.100 Lbp 46.99 Br md 9.75 Dpth 3.81 Welded, 1 dk	**(B21A2OC) Crew/Supply Vessel** Hull Material: Aluminium Alloy Passengers: unberthed: 75	**4 oil engines** reduction geared to sc. shafts driving 4 FP propellers Total Power: 5,372kW (7,304hp) 25.0kn Cummins QSK50-M 4 x Vee 4 Stroke 16 Cy. 159 x 159 each-1343kW (1826bhp) Cummins Engine Co Inc-USA Thrusters: 2 Thwart. FP thruster (f)
8993007 *WCD9857* -	**SOUTHERN BELLE II** *ex* Anh Vu *-2012* *ex* Maria N II *-2010* **Thu Hong Thi Tran** - *Bayou La Batre, AL* *United States of America* Official number: 992378	*152* 45 -		**1993-01 La Force Shipyard Inc — Coden AL** Yd No: 101 L reg 26.12 Br ex - Dght - Lbp - Br md 7.62 Dpth 3.96 Welded, 1 dk	**(B11B2FV) Fishing Vessel**	**1 oil engine** driving 1 Propeller
9437763 *9HA2127* -	**SOUTHERN BREEZE** *ex* Alfa Moon *-2009* *ex* Chang An Kinay *-2007* **Southern Breeze Maritime Ltd** Sonata doo *Valletta* *Malta* MMSI: 248018000 Official number: 9437763	**4,109** 2,332 6,064 T/cm 14.3	Class: BV (CC)	**2007-11 Chang An Shipbuilding Co Ltd — Linhai ZJ** Yd No: 602 Loa 99.89 (BB) Br ex - Dght 6.700 Lbp 94.60 Br md 16.60 Dpth 8.40 Welded, 1 dk	**(A31A2GX) General Cargo Ship** Grain: 8,005; Bale: 8,005 Compartments: 2 Ho, ER 2 Ha: ER 2 (25.2 x 12.0) Cranes: 2x30t	**1 oil engine** reverse reduction geared to sc. shaft driving 1 FP propeller Total Power: 2,207kW (3,001hp) 12.5kn Yanmar 6N330-UN 1 x 4 Stroke 6 Cy. 330 x 440 2207kW (3001bhp) Qingdao Zichai Boyang Diesel EngineCo Ltd-China AuxGen: 2 x 250kW 440V 50Hz a.c

IMO / Call sign / Flag	Name / Owner / Port	Tonnage	Class	Builder / Dimensions	Type	Machinery
9378785 *3EJN6* -	**SOUTHERN BULL** **Southern Dragon Chemical SA** Sansho Kaiun Co Ltd *Panama* Panama MMSI: 372571000 Official number: 3255207	**8,295** 4,698 14,577 T/cm 23.4	Class: NK	**2007**-03 **Asakawa Zosen K.K. — Imabari** Yd No: 560 Loa 134.16 (BB) Br ex 20.52 Dght 8.813 Lbp 125.00 Br md 20.50 Dpth 11.60 Welded, 1 dk	**(A12B2TR) Chemical/Products Tanker** Double Hull (13F) Liq: 16,162; Liq (Oil): 16,162 Cargo Heating Coils Compartments: 16 Wing Ta (s.stl), ER 16 Cargo Pump (s): 12x300m³/hr, 4x200m³/hr Manifold: Bow/CM: 69.3m	**1 oil engine** driving 1 FP propeller Total Power: 4,440kW (6,037hp) 13.9kn MAN-B&W 6S35MC 1 x 2 Stroke 6 Cy. 350 x 1400 4440kW (6037bhp) Imex Co Ltd-Japan AuxGen: 3 x 450kW a.c Thrusters: 1 Tunnel thruster (f) Fuel: 47.0 (d.f.) 767.0 (r.f.)
8610966 *VWVQ* -	**SOUTHERN CHALLENGER** **Southern Sea Crafts Ltd** - *India*	*157* - -		**1984**-12 **K Shipyard Construction Co — Fremantle WA** Yd No: 96 Loa - Br ex - Dght - Lbp 22.81 Br md - Dpth - Welded, 1 dk	**(B11A2FT) Trawler**	**1 oil engine** geared to sc. shaft driving 1 FP propeller Total Power: 299kW (407hp) Caterpillar 3408PCTA 1 x Vee 4 Stroke 8 Cy. 137 x 152 299kW (407bhp) Caterpillar Tractor Co-USA
7351147 *VHGI* -	**SOUTHERN CHAMPION** *ex* Giljanes *-1998* *ex* Vestborg *-1988* *ex* Giljanes *-1987* *ex* Jutland III *-1980* **Austral Fisheries Pty Ltd** - SatCom: Inmarsat B 350302610 *Fremantle, WA* Australia MMSI: 503057000 Official number: 856107	**2,203** 660 -	Class: BV	**1974**-05 **Soc. Esercizio Cant. S.p.A. — Viareggio** Yd No: 610 Loa 87.20 Br ex 13.64 Dght 5.208 Lbp 77.15 Br md 13.62 Dpth 7.27 Welded, 2 dks	**(B11A2FS) Stern Trawler** Ice Capable	**2 oil engines** geared to sc. shaft driving 1 CP propeller Total Power: 2,206kW (3,000hp) 16.0kn Nohab F212V 2 x Vee 4 Stroke 12 Cy. 250 x 300 each-1103kW (1500bhp) AB NOHAB-Sweden AuxGen: 1 x 350kW 220/380V 50Hz a.c Fuel: 758.5 (d.f.)
9096894 *WDD5209* -	**SOUTHERN COMET** **Southern States Offshore Inc** - *Houston, TX* United States of America MMSI: 367155130 Official number: 1192754	**387** 116 410	Class: (AB)	**2007**-06 **La Force Shipyard Inc — Coden AL** Yd No: 149 Loa 51.83 Br ex - Dght - Lbp 48.18 Br md 9.75 Dpth 3.75 Welded, 1 dk	**(B34J2SD) Crew Boat** Hull Material: Aluminium Alloy Passengers: unberthed: 75	**4 oil engines** reduction geared to sc. shafts driving 4 FP propellers Total Power: 4,920kW (6,688hp) 25.0kn Caterpillar 3512B-TA 4 x Vee 4 Stroke 12 Cy. 170 x 190 each-1230kW (1672bhp) Caterpillar Inc-USA Thrusters: 2 Thwart. FP thruster (f)
7733137 *WYC4493* -	**SOUTHERN COMFORT** **Alvin O Zar** - *New Orleans, LA* United States of America Official number: 585857	*161* 112 -		**1977 Toche Marine, Inc. — Biloxi, Ms** Yd No: 3 L reg 25.09 Br ex - Dght - Lbp - Br md 7.32 Dpth 3.59 Welded, 1 dk	**(B11B2FV) Fishing Vessel**	**1 oil engine** driving 1 FP propeller Total Power: 331kW (450hp)
9441659 *3ELB6* -	**SOUTHERN CONDOR** **Sansho Line SA** Sansho Kaiun Co Ltd *Panama* Panama MMSI: 372903000 Official number: 35791PEXT1	**8,295** 4,698 14,583 T/cm 23.4	Class: NK	**2007**-07 **Asakawa Zosen K.K. — Imabari** Yd No: 561 Loa 134.16 (BB) Br ex 20.52 Dght 8.813 Lbp 125.00 Br md 20.50 Dpth 11.60 Welded, 1 dk	**(A12B2TR) Chemical/Products Tanker** Double Hull (13F) Liq: 16,495; Liq (Oil): 16,167 Cargo Heating Coils Compartments: 16 Wing Ta, ER 16 Cargo Pump (s): 12x300m³/hr, 4x200m³/hr Manifold: Bow/CM: 69.3m	**1 oil engine** driving 1 FP propeller Total Power: 4,440kW (6,037hp) 13.9kn MAN-B&W 6S35MC 1 x 2 Stroke 6 Cy. 350 x 1400 4440kW (6037bhp) Imex Co Ltd-Japan AuxGen: 3 x 430kW a.c Thrusters: 1 Tunnel thruster (f) Fuel: 47.0 (d.f.) 767.0 (r.f.)
8666991 - -	**SOUTHERN CONDOR II** **Southern Shipping Co Pty Ltd** - *Launceston, Tas* Australia Official number: 857011	**298** 89 270		**2002**-05 **FC Management Pty Ltd — Bridport TAS** Loa 34.95 Br ex - Dght 2.200 Lbp 34.20 Br md 10.80 Dpth - Welded, 1 dk	**(A36A2PR) Passenger/Ro-Ro Ship (Vehicles)**	**2 oil engines** reduction geared to sc. shafts driving 2 Propellers
9515292 *3FYA2* -	**SOUTHERN COUGAR** *ex* Hyacinth *-2013* **Barco de Oro International SA** Selandia Ship Management (Singapore) Pte Ltd *Panama* Panama MMSI: 353712000 Official number: 4483313	**7,411** 3,962 12,585 T/cm 21.4	Class: NK	**2009**-09 **Shitanoe Shipbuilding Co Ltd — Usuki OT** Yd No: 1280 Loa 126.50 (BB) Br ex - Dght 8.859 Lbp 118.00 Br md 20.30 Dpth 11.50 Welded, 1 dk	**(A12B2TR) Chemical/Products Tanker** Double Hull (13F) Liq: 13,765; Liq (Oil): 13,765 Cargo Heating Coils Compartments: 14 Wing Ta (s.stl), ER 14 Cargo Pump (s): 12x300m³/hr, 2x200m³/hr Manifold: Bow/CM: 53.6m	**1 oil engine** driving 1 FP propeller Total Power: 4,440kW (6,037hp) 15.0kn MAN-B&W 6S35MC 1 x 2 Stroke 6 Cy. 350 x 1400 4440kW (6037bhp) Hitachi Zosen Corp-Japan AuxGen: 3 x 420kW a.c Thrusters: 1 Tunnel thruster (f) Fuel: 115.0 (d.f.) 740.0 (r.f.)
9290971 *7JFN* -	**SOUTHERN CROSS** **Nippon Yusen Kabushiki Kaisha (NYK Line)** Hachiuma Steamship Co Ltd (Hachiuma Kisen KK) *Tokyo* Japan MMSI: 432710000 Official number: 141048	**48,042** 26,665 88,125 T/cm 79.7	Class: NK	**2004**-05 **Imabari Shipbuilding Co Ltd — Marugame KG (Marugame Shipyard)** Yd No: 1396 Loa 229.93 (BB) Br ex 38.00 Dght 13.819 Lbp 220.00 Br md 38.00 Dpth 19.90 Welded, 1 dk	**(A21A2BC) Bulk Carrier** Double Bottom Entire Compartment Length Grain: 101,695 Compartments: 5 Ho, ER 5 Ha: ER 5 (23.0 x 17.6)	**1 oil engine** driving 1 FP propeller Total Power: 12,092kW (16,440hp) 14.7kn B&W 6S60MC 1 x 2 Stroke 6 Cy. 600 x 2292 12092kW (16440bhp) Mitsui Engineering & Shipbuilding CLtd-Japan AuxGen: 3 x 550kW 440V 60Hz a.c Fuel: 224.0 (d.f.) 2968.0 (r.f.)
8885793 *WBB2413* -	**SOUTHERN CROSS** **Shrimp Vessel Playboy Inc** - *Brownsville, TX* United States of America MMSI: 367132090 Official number: 910032	*118* 94 -		**1987 Roca Construction Co. — Brownsville, Tx** Yd No: 4 L reg 21.95 Br ex - Dght - Lbp - Br md 6.25 Dpth 3.66 Welded, 1 dk	**(B11B2FV) Fishing Vessel**	**1 oil engine** driving 1 FP propeller
9089463 *WDC2550* -	**SOUTHERN CROSS** *ex* Cochise *-2013* *ex* Spring Creek *-2013* *ex* DS 44 *-2013* *ex* DPC 4 *-1945* **Marine Express Inc** Seaway Towing Co *San Francisco, CA* United States of America Official number: 243954	*139* 94 -	Class: (AB)	**1943**-07 **George Lawley & Son Corp. — Boston, Ma** Yd No: 1292 Loa - Br ex - Dght - Lbp 25.00 Br md 7.32 Dpth 3.20 Welded, 1 dk	**(B32A2ST) Tug**	**1 oil engine** geared to sc. shaft driving 1 Propeller Total Power: 515kW (700hp) EMD (Electro-Motive) 8-567 1 x Vee 2 Stroke 8 Cy. 216 x 254 515kW (700bhp) General Motors Corp-USA
6415271 *ZR3506* CT 140	**SOUTHERN CROSS** *ex* Anton D *-1983* *ex* Foulque *-1980* **South West Trawlers** - *Cape Town* South Africa MMSI: 601433000 Official number: 350865	*224* 89 215	Class: (BV)	**1964 Societe des Forges et Chantiers de La Mediterranee — Le Havre** Yd No: 390/2 Loa 28.85 Br ex 7.21 Dght - Lbp 26.50 Br md 7.14 Dpth 3.39 Welded, 1 dk	**(B11B2FV) Fishing Vessel** Ins: 146 Compartments: 9 Ta, ER 8 Ha: 8 (1.4 x 1.4) Derricks: 2x1t; Winches: 2	**1 oil engine** driving 1 FP propeller Total Power: 405kW (551hp) 9.5kn MGO 12V175ASHR 1 x Vee 4 Stroke 12 Cy. 175 x 180 405kW (551bhp) Societe Alsacienne de ConstructionsMecaniques (SACM)-France
7740219 *DTBP5* -	**SOUTHERN CROSS** *ex* Uransu Star *-2002* *ex* Ocean Gold No. 3 *-2002* *ex* Taizan Maru *-1995* **Tae Kyung Shipping Co ltd** - *Wando* South Korea MMSI: 440603000 Official number: 9607457-6461103	**501** 202 650		**1978**-02 **K.K. Mochizuki Zosensho — Osakikamijima** Yd No: 103 Loa 53.01 Br ex - Dght 3.501 Lbp 47.50 Br md 8.81 Dpth 4.81 Welded, 2 dks	**(A31A2GX) General Cargo Ship** 1 Ha: (25.8 x 7.0)	**1 oil engine** driving 1 FP propeller Total Power: 736kW (1,001hp) 12.0kn Niigata 6L28X 1 x 4 Stroke 6 Cy. 280 x 440 736kW (1001bhp) Niigata Engineering Co Ltd-Japan
7801427 *DUH2604* -	**SOUTHERN CROSS** *ex* Toyoshio Maru *-2007* **Sub-See Philippines Inc** - *Cebu* Philippines MMSI: 548536300 Official number: CEB1006875	**297** 201 344	Class: IS	**1978**-09 **Naikai Shipbuilding & Engineering Co Ltd — Onomichi HS (Taguma Shipyard)** Yd No: 439 Converted From: Fishing Vessel-2007 Loa 44.70 Br ex 8.34 Dght 3.200 Lbp 39.00 Br md 8.31 Dpth 4.02 Riveted\Welded, 1 dk	**(B31A2SR) Research Survey Vessel**	**1 oil engine** driving 1 CP propeller Total Power: 720kW (979hp) 10.0kn Daihatsu 6DKM-26 1 x 4 Stroke 6 Cy. 260 x 380 720kW (979bhp) Daihatsu Diesel Manufacturing Co Lt-Japan Thrusters: 1 Thwart. CP thruster
8038493 - -	**SOUTHERN CROSS** *ex* Nightwalker *-2007* **Marty G Kimmons** - *New Orleans, LA* United States of America Official number: 617715	*119* 81 -		**1980 Viguerie Trawlers, Inc. — Dulac, La** L reg 21.19 Br ex 7.32 Dght - Lbp - Br md - Dpth 2.87 Welded, 1 dk	**(B11B2FV) Fishing Vessel**	**1 oil engine** driving 1 FP propeller Total Power: 441kW (600hp)

9558189 *7JJA* -	**SOUTHERN CROSS DREAM** **Mimosa Maritima Ltd** Mitsui OSK Lines Ltd (MOL) SatCom: Inmarsat C 443279410 *Tokyo* *Japan* MMSI: 432794000 Official number: 141398	**92,152** 59,985 180,694	Class: NK	**2011-03 Tsuneishi Heavy Industries (Cebu) Inc — Balamban** Yd No: SC-160 Loa 291.90 (BB) Br ex - Dght 18.068 Lbp 286.90 Br md 45.00 Dpth 24.50 Welded, 1 dk	**(A21A2BC) Bulk Carrier** Grain: 200,998 Compartments: 9 Ho, ER 9 Ha: ER	**1 oil engine** driving 1 FP propeller Total Power: 17,690kW (24,051hp) 14.5kn MAN-B&W 7S65ME-C 1 x 2 Stroke 7 Cy. 650 x 2730 17690kW (24051bhp) Mitsui Engineering & Shipbuilding CLtd-Japan Fuel: 5693.0 (r.f.)
7050107 *WY5797* -	**SOUTHERN CRUSADER** **R & C Fishing Corp** - *New Bedford, MA* *United States of America* MMSI: 366283380 Official number: 514457	*130* 88 -		**1968 Master Marine, Inc. — Bayou La Batre, Al** L reg 22.19 Br ex 6.76 Dght - Lbp - Br md - Dpth 3.56 Welded	**(B11B2FV) Fishing Vessel**	**1 oil engine** driving 1 FP propeller Total Power: 313kW (426hp)
8939647 *WDD2297* -	**SOUTHERN CRUSADER II** *ex St. Mary -2006* **R & C Fishing Corp** - *New Bedford, MA* *United States of America* MMSI: 367113460 Official number: 1038917	**130** 39 -		**1996 Hung V. Le — Cut Off, La** L reg 25.24 Br ex - Dght - Lbp - Br md 7.16 Dpth 3.66 Welded, 1 dk	**(B11B2FV) Fishing Vessel**	**1 oil engine** driving 1 FP propeller
7412135 *WCY9884* -	**SOUTHERN DANCER** *ex Sword Dancer -1999* *ex H. O. S. Sword Dancer -1998* *ex State Yankee -1994* **Jones Act Shipping Inc** - *Cape Canaveral, FL* *United States of America* MMSI: 366764320 Official number: 561685	**668** 211 1,300	Class: (AB)	**1974-12 Blount Marine Corp. — Warren, RI** Yd No: 183 Loa 54.84 Br ex 11.89 Dght 3.547 Lbp 53.29 Br md 11.87 Dpth 4.25 Welded, 1 dk	**(B21B20A) Anchor Handling Tug Supply**	**2 oil engines** reverse reduction geared to sc. shafts driving 2 FP propellers Total Power: 1,654kW (2,248hp) 12.0kn Caterpillar D399SCAC 2 x Vee 4 Stroke 16 Cy. 159 x 203 each-827kW (1124bhp) Caterpillar Tractor Co-USA AuxGen: 2 x 75kW 460V 60Hz a.c Thrusters: 1 Thwart. FP thruster (f) Fuel: 305.0 (d.f.)
9415002 *3ER09* -	**SOUTHERN DRAGON** **Southern Chemical Carriers SA** Sansho Kaiun Co Ltd SatCom: Inmarsat Mini-M 764854541 *Panama* *Panama* MMSI: 370123000 Official number: 3418408A	**7,411** 3,962 12,648 T/cm 21.3	Class: NK	**2008-07 Shitanoe Shipbuilding Co Ltd — Usuki OT** Yd No: 1272 Loa 126.50 (BB) Br ex 20.33 Dght 8.859 Lbp 118.00 Br md 20.30 Dpth 11.50 Welded, 1 dk	**(A12B2TR) Chemical/Products Tanker** Double Hull (13F) Liq: 13,747; Liq (Oil): 13,950 Cargo Heating Coils Compartments: 14 Wing Ta, ER 14 Cargo Pump (s): 12x300m³/hr, 2x200m³/hr Manifold: Bow/CM: 55.2m	**1 oil engine** driving 1 FP propeller Total Power: 4,440kW (6,037hp) 14.0kn MAN-B&W 6S35MC 1 x 2 Stroke 6 Cy. 350 x 1400 4440kW (6037bhp) Imex Co Ltd-Japan AuxGen: 3 x 380kW a.c Thrusters: 1 Tunnel thruster (f) Fuel: 120.0 (d.f.) 740.0 (r.f.)
8745864 - -	**SOUTHERN ELEGANCE** *ex Sioux City Sue -2001 ex Dewitt Clinton -2000* **Associated Marine Services Ltd** - *Port of Spain* *Trinidad & Tobago*	**806** 255 -		**1986 Offshore Shipbuilding Inc — Palatka FL** Yd No: 39 Loa 45.41 Br ex - Dght - Lbp 43.59 Br md 11.12 Dpth - Welded, 1 dk	**(A37B2PS) Passenger Ship**	**2 oil engines** reduction geared to sc. shafts driving 2 Propellers Total Power: 942kW (1,280hp) G.M. (Detroit Diesel) 12V-71 2 x Vee 2 Stroke 12 Cy. 108 x 127 each-471kW (640bhp) Detroit Diesel Corporation-Detroit, Mi
9042271 *C6WM2* -	**SOUTHERN EXPLORER** *ex Polar Explorer -2007 ex Sophie -2007* *ex NDS Benguela -2005 ex Sophie -2004* *ex Pacific Chile -1998 ex Sophie -1993* **Arrow Seismic ASA** - *Nassau* *Bahamas* MMSI: 309032000 Official number: 8001404	**2,881** 925 3,300	Class: (LR) (BV) ✠ Classed LR until 26/3/93	**1992-12 Orskov Christensens Staalskibsvaerft A/S — Frederikshavn** Yd No: 177 Converted From: General Cargo Ship (with Ro-Ro Facility)-2012 Loa 91.63 (BB) Br ex 16.83 Dght 4.450 Lbp 84.98 Br md 16.20 Dpth 6.90 Welded, 1 dk	**(B31A2SR) Research Survey Vessel** Stern ramp Len: 9.16 Wid: 4.70 Swl: 30 Bale: 3,800 Compartments: 1 Ho, ER 4 Ha: ER Ice Capable	**2 oil engines** with clutches, flexible couplings & sr geared to sc. shafts driving 2 CP propellers Total Power: 2,560kW (3,480hp) 14.0kn Alpha 8L23/30 2 x 4 Stroke 8 Cy. 225 x 300 each-1280kW (1740bhp) MAN B&W Diesel A/S-Denmark AuxGen: 2 x 750kW 380V 50Hz a.c, 1 x 139kW 380V 50Hz a.c Thrusters: 1 Thwart. FP thruster (f)
9248459 *H9YO* -	**SOUTHERN EXPLORER** **Fair Wind Navigation SA** Mizuho Sangyo Co Ltd SatCom: Inmarsat C 435415110 *Panama* *Panama* MMSI: 354151000 Official number: 2854202B	**88,552** 58,972 177,493 T/cm 119.0	Class: NK	**2002-05 Mitsui Eng. & SB. Co. Ltd., Chiba Works — Ichihara** Yd No: 1548 Loa 289.00 (BB) Br ex - Dght 17.950 Lbp 279.00 Br md 45.00 Dpth 24.40 Welded, 1 dk	**(A21A2BC) Bulk Carrier** Grain: 197,089 Compartments: 9 Ho, ER 9 Ha: 2 (15.5 x 15.0)7 (15.5 x 20.6)ER	**1 oil engine** driving 1 FP propeller Total Power: 16,858kW (22,920hp) 15.0kn B&W 6S70MC 1 x 2 Stroke 6 Cy. 700 x 2674 16858kW (22920bhp) Mitsui Engineering & Shipbuilding CLtd-Japan Fuel: 3910.0
8855114 *WCW8201* -	**SOUTHERN FAITH** *ex Capt. Tan -2010 ex Lady Ann -1995* **Southern Faithful LLC** - *Palacios, TX* *United States of America* MMSI: 367135670 Official number: 916943	*114* 91 -		**1987 Thu Quoc Le — Amelia, La** Yd No: 1 Loa - Br ex - Dght - Lbp 23.77 Br md 6.71 Dpth 3.05 Welded, 1 dk	**(B11B2FV) Fishing Vessel**	**1 oil engine** driving 1 FP propeller
9414993 *3EQD6* -	**SOUTHERN FALCON** **Sansho Line SA** Sansho Kaiun Co Ltd *Panama* *Panama* MMSI: 352306000 Official number: 3391408	**5,551** 2,785 9,051 T/cm 18.3	Class: NK	**2008-04 Shitanoe Shipbuilding Co Ltd — Usuki OT** Yd No: 1271 Loa 115.50 (BB) Br ex 18.73 Dght 7.693 Lbp 108.50 Br md 18.70 Dpth 10.00 Welded, 1 dk	**(A12B2TR) Chemical/Products Tanker** Double Hull (13F) Liq: 9,656; Liq (Oil): 9,656 Cargo Heating Coils Compartments: 16 Wing Ta, 2 Wing Slop Ta, ER 16 Cargo Pump (s): 12x300m³/hr, 4x200m³/hr Manifold: Bow/CM: 56.3m	**1 oil engine** driving 1 FP propeller Total Power: 3,900kW (5,302hp) 13.7kn MAN-B&W 6L35MC 1 x 2 Stroke 6 Cy. 350 x 1050 3900kW (5302bhp) Hitachi Zosen Corp-Japan AuxGen: 3 x 350kW 450V 60Hz a.c Thrusters: 1 Tunnel thruster (f) Fuel: 55.0 (d.f.) 571.0 (r.f.)
7016412 - L548	**SOUTHERN FISHER** *ex Fisher -1995 ex Southern Fisher -1988* *ex Entente -1982* **Inter Namibia Enterprises** - *Namibia*	*364* 169 -	Class: (BV)	**1970 Con. Mec. de Normandie — Cherbourg** Loa 46.39 Br ex - Dght - Lbp - Br md 8.92 Dpth 4.60 Welded, 1 dk	**(B11A2FT) Trawler**	**1 oil engine** driving 1 FP propeller Total Power: 736kW (1,001hp) 11.0kn MGO 16V175BSHR 1 x Vee 4 Stroke 16 Cy. 175 x 180 736kW (1001bhp) Societe Alsacienne de ConstructionsMecaniques (SACM)-France
9404613 *A8QX9* -	**SOUTHERN FLEUR** *ex Dora C -2012* **Alcione Development Inc** Cosmoship Management SA *Monrovia* *Liberia* MMSI: 636014030 Official number: 14030	**9,684** 4,716 12,502	Class: BV (GL)	**2009-02 Dae Sun Shipbuilding & Engineering Co Ltd — Busan** Yd No: 480 Loa 142.72 (BB) Br ex - Dght 8.210 Lbp 133.50 Br md 22.60 Dpth 11.20 Welded, 1 dk	**(A33A2CC) Container Ship (Fully Cellular)** TEU 1037 incl 180 ref C Cranes: 3x40t	**1 oil engine** driving 1 FP propeller Total Power: 7,089kW (9,638hp) 18.0kn MAN-B&W 6S46MC-C 1 x 2 Stroke 6 Cy. 460 x 1932 7089kW (9638bhp) STX Engine Co Ltd-South Korea AuxGen: 3 x 615kW 445V 60Hz a.c Thrusters: 1 Tunnel thruster (f) Fuel: 796.0
9415014 *3ESP* -	**SOUTHERN GIRAFFE** **Southern Dragon Chemical SA** Sansho Kaiun Co Ltd *Panama* *Panama* MMSI: 370384000 Official number: 3424508A	**7,411** 3,962 12,647 T/cm 21.3	Class: NK	**2008-08 Shitanoe Shipbuilding Co Ltd — Usuki OT** Yd No: 1273 Loa 126.50 (BB) Br ex - Dght 8.850 Lbp 118.00 Br md 20.30 Dpth 11.50 Welded, 1 dk	**(A12B2TR) Chemical/Products Tanker** Double Hull (13F) Liq: 13,748; Liq (Oil): 13,950 Cargo Heating Coils Compartments: 10 Wing Ta, 1 Ta, ER, 1 Wing Slop Ta 13 Cargo Pump (s): 12x300m³/hr, 1x70m³/hr Manifold: Bow/CM: 55.2m	**1 oil engine** driving 1 FP propeller Total Power: 4,440kW (6,037hp) 14.0kn MAN-B&W 6S35MC 1 x 2 Stroke 6 Cy. 350 x 1400 4440kW (6037bhp) Imex Co Ltd-Japan AuxGen: 3 x 350kW 450V 60Hz a.c Thrusters: 1 Tunnel thruster (f) Fuel: 119.0 (d.f.) 737.0 (r.f.)
9552422 *HOHI* -	**SOUTHERN HARMONY** **Fair Wind Navigation SA** Mizuho Sangyo Co Ltd *Panama* *Panama* MMSI: 373508000 Official number: 4405712	**93,288** 60,451 182,249 T/cm 125.0	Class: NK	**2012-07 Kawasaki Heavy Industries Ltd — Sakaide KG** Yd No: 1676 Loa 292.00 (BB) Br ex - Dght 18.226 Lbp 288.00 Br md 45.00 Dpth 24.70 Welded, 1 dk	**(A21A2BC) Bulk Carrier** Grain: 203,226 Compartments: 9 Ho, ER 9 Ha: ER	**1 oil engine** driving 1 FP propeller Total Power: 17,780kW (24,174hp) 14.3kn MAN-B&W 6S70MC-C 1 x 2 Stroke 6 Cy. 700 x 2800 17780kW (24174bhp) Kawasaki Heavy Industries Ltd-Japan Fuel: 4970.0

9534901 *3FXK2* -	**SOUTHERN HAWK** **Rio Brillante SA** Sansho Kaiun Co Ltd *Panama* *Panama* MMSI: 357794000 Official number: 4018109	**8,295** 4,698 14,545 T/cm 23.4	Class: NK	**2009-02 Asakawa Zosen K.K. — Imabari** Yd No: 567 Loa 134.16 (BB) Br ex 20.52 Dght 8.813 Lbp 125.00 Br md 20.50 Dpth 11.60 Welded, 1 dk	**(A12B2TR) Chemical/Products Tanker** Double Hull (13F) Liq: 16,492; Liq (Oil): 16,492 Cargo Heating Coils Compartments: 14 Wing Ta (s.stl), 2 Wing Slop Ta (s.stl), ER 14 Cargo Pump (s): 12x300m^3/hr, 2x200m^3/hr Manifold: Bow/CM: 69.3m	**1 oil engine** driving 1 FP propeller Total Power: 4,440kW (6,037hp) 13.9kn MAN-B&W 6S35MC 1 x 2 Stroke 6 Cy. 350 x 1400 4440kW (6037bhp) Hitachi Zosen Corp-Japan AuxGen: 3 x 430kW a.c Thrusters: 1 Tunnel thruster (f) Fuel: 82.0 (d.f.) 733.0 (r.f.)
9338632 *3EOJ8* -	**SOUTHERN HIGHWAY** **SKD 5500 Shipping SA** Taiyo Nippon Kisen Co Ltd *Panama* *Panama* MMSI: 356580000 Official number: 3358208A	**39,422** 11,827 12,892	Class: NK	**2008-01 Shin Kurushima Dockyard Co. Ltd. — Onishi** Yd No: 5500 Loa 188.03 (BB) Br ex - Dght 8.524 Lbp 178.00 Br md 28.20 Dpth 20.70 Welded, 11 dks, incl. 8 non-continuous dks	**(A35B2RV) Vehicles Carrier** Side door/ramp1 (p) 1 (s) Len: 16.75 Wid: 4.00 Swl: 17 Quarter stern door/ramp (s. a.) Len: 30.30 Wid: 5.50 Swl: 51 Cars: 3,893	**1 oil engine** driving 1 FP propeller Total Power: 10,999kW (14,954hp) 20.0kn Mitsubishi 8UEC50LSII 1 x 2 Stroke 8 Cy. 500 x 1950 10999kW (14954bhp) Kobe Hatsudoki KK-Japan Thrusters: 1 Tunnel thruster (f) Fuel: 2610.0
8940995 *WDE9588* -	**SOUTHERN HORIZON** *ex* Carolyn J *-2009* **Pac Horizon Inc** - *San Diego, CA* *United States of America* MMSI: 367418960 Official number: 1052597	**188** 76 -		**1997 Johnson Shipbuilding & Repair — Bayou La Batre, Al** Yd No: 140 L reg 27.25 Br ex - Dght - Lbp - Br md 7.32 Dpth 3.93 Welded, 1 dk	**(B11B2FV) Fishing Vessel**	**1 oil engine** driving 1 FP propeller
9423695 *3EWF4* -	**SOUTHERN IBIS** **Southern Dragon Chemical SA** Sansho Kaiun Co Ltd *Panama* *Panama* MMSI: 353608000 Official number: 4057009	**11,780** 6,321 19,905 T/cm 29.8	Class: NK	**2009-07 Fukuoka Shipbuilding Co Ltd — Nagasaki NS** Yd No: 2023 Loa 144.09 (BB) Br ex 24.23 Dght 9.652 Lbp 136.00 Br md 24.19 Dpth 12.90 Welded, 1 dk	**(A12B2TR) Chemical/Products Tanker** Double Hull (13F) Liq: 20,527; Liq (Oil): 20,527 Cargo Heating Coils Compartments: 18 Wing Ta (s.stl), 2 Wing Slop Ta (s.stl), ER 18 Cargo Pump (s): 12x300m^3/hr, 6x200m^3/hr Manifold: Bow/CM: 74.8m	**1 oil engine** driving 1 FP propeller Total Power: 6,150kW (8,362hp) 14.5kn MAN-B&W 6S42MC 1 x 2 Stroke 6 Cy. 420 x 1764 6150kW (8362bhp) Imex Co Ltd-Japan AuxGen: 3 x 540kW a.c Thrusters: 1 Tunnel thruster (f) Fuel: 126.0 (d.f.) 894.0 (r.f.)
9416111 *3FMZ* -	**SOUTHERN JAGUAR** *ex* W-O Vashi *-2009* **Southern Dragon Chemical SA** Sansho Kaiun Co Ltd *Panama* *Panama* MMSI: 352746000 Official number: 4088209	**11,757** 6,346 19,997 T/cm 29.8	Class: NK	**2009-09 Fukuoka Shipbuilding Co Ltd — Fukuoka FO** Yd No: 1277 Loa 144.09 (BB) Br ex 24.23 Dght 9.670 Lbp 136.00 Br md 24.19 Dpth 12.90 Welded, 1 dk	**(A12B2TR) Chemical/Products Tanker** Double Hull (13F) Liq: 20,529; Liq (Oil): 20,529 Cargo Heating Coils Compartments: 18 Wing Ta, 2 Wing Slop Ta, ER 18 Cargo Pump (s): 12x300m^3/hr, 6x200m^3/hr Manifold: Bow/CM: 73.2m	**1 oil engine** driving 1 FP propeller Total Power: 6,150kW (8,362hp) 14.5kn MAN-B&W 6S42MC 1 x 2 Stroke 6 Cy. 420 x 1764 6150kW (8362bhp) Makita Corp-Japan AuxGen: 3 x 480kW a.c Thrusters: 1 Tunnel thruster (f) Fuel: 110.0 (d.f.) 909.0 (r.f.)
9577185 *3EXJ3* -	**SOUTHERN KOALA** **Southern Dragon Chemical SA** Sansho Kaiun Co Ltd *Panama* *Panama* MMSI: 355040000 Official number: 4173810	**12,197** 6,534 21,290 T/cm 30.9	Class: NK	**2010-06 Asakawa Zosen K.K. — Imabari** Yd No: 600 Loa 149.00 (BB) Br ex 24.03 Dght 9.715 Lbp 140.00 Br md 24.00 Dpth 12.80 Welded, 1 dk	**(A12B2TR) Chemical/Products Tanker** Double Hull (13F) Liq: 20,009; Liq (Oil): 22,100 Cargo Heating Coils Compartments: 18 Wing Ta, 2 Wing Slop Ta, ER 18 Cargo Pump (s): 2x200m^3/hr, 16x300m^3/hr Manifold: Bow/CM: 74.7m	**1 oil engine** driving 1 FP propeller Total Power: 6,150kW (8,362hp) 14.5kn MAN-B&W 6S42MC 1 x 2 Stroke 6 Cy. 420 x 1764 6150kW (8362bhp) Hitachi Zosen Corp-Japan AuxGen: 3 x 520kW 450V 60Hz a.c Thrusters: 1 Tunnel thruster (f) Fuel: 134.0 (d.f.) 1069.0 (r.f.)
9567752 *3FBG9* -	**SOUTHERN LION** **Southern Chemical Carriers SA** Sansho Kaiun Co Ltd SatCom: Inmarsat C 437111510 *Panama* *Panama* MMSI: 371115000 Official number: 4308711	**7,424** 3,962 12,651 T/cm 21.4	Class: NK	**2011-08 Shitanoe Shipbuilding Co Ltd — Usuki OT** Yd No: 1292 Loa 126.50 (BB) Br ex 20.33 Dght 8.860 Lbp 118.00 Br md 20.30 Dpth 11.50 Welded, 1 dk	**(A12B2TR) Chemical/Products Tanker** Double Hull (13F) Liq: 12,304; Liq (Oil): 13,651 Cargo Heating Coils Compartments: 6 Wing Ta, 6 Wing Ta, 1 Wing Slop Ta, 1 Wing Slop Ta, ER 12 Cargo Pump (s): 12x300m^3/hr Manifold: Bow/CM: 55.2m	**1 oil engine** driving 1 FP propeller Total Power: 4,440kW (6,037hp) 14.0kn MAN-B&W 6S35MC 1 x 2 Stroke 6 Cy. 350 x 1400 4440kW (6037bhp) Imex Co Ltd-Japan AuxGen: 3 x 350kW Thrusters: 1 Tunnel thruster (f) Fuel: 110.0 (d.f.) 730.0 (r.f.)
8941274 - -	**SOUTHERN LUCILLE** *ex* Lady Gabrielle *-2000* **Kelsey Martin Jones** - *Key West, FL* *United States of America* Official number: 1053985	**139** 41 -		**1997 Rodriguez Boat Builders, Inc. — Coden, Al** Yd No: 161 L reg 24.63 Br ex - Dght - Lbp - Br md 7.32 Dpth 3.75 Welded, 1 dk	**(B11B2FV) Fishing Vessel**	**1 oil engine** driving 1 FP propeller
9282857 *CFG2618* 138052	**SOUTHERN MARINER** **Cape Mariner Enterprises Ltd** - *St John's, NL* *Canada* MMSI: 316004790 Official number: 824301	*149* 111 -		**2002-10 Chantier Naval Forillon Inc — Gaspe QC** L reg 19.10 (BB) Br ex - Dght 4.023 Lbp - Br md 7.90 Dpth 4.50 Welded, 1 dk	**(B11A2FS) Stern Trawler**	**1 oil engine** geared to sc. shaft driving 1 Propeller Total Power: 715kW (972hp) 10.0kn Caterpillar 3508B 1 x Vee 4 Stroke 8 Cy. 170 x 190 715kW (972bhp) Caterpillar Inc-USA Thrusters: 1 Tunnel thruster (f)
9210713 *5WDC* -	**SOUTHERN MOANA** *ex* Opal Harmony *-2014* *ex* Forum Samoa II *-2010* **Pacific Forum Line Ltd & Samoa Shipping Services Ltd** Neptune Pacific Agency Australia Pty Ltd (Neptune Pacific Line) *Apia* *Samoa* MMSI: 561003000	**7,091** 3,492 8,115 T/cm 20.4	Class: GL	**2001-07 Chengxi Shipyard — Jiangyin JS** Yd No: 4324 Loa 126.42 (BB) Br ex - Dght 7.222 Lbp 116.60 Br md 19.40 Dpth 9.50 Welded, 1 dk	**(A31A2GX) General Cargo Ship** Grain: 10,300 TEU 660 C Ho 186 TEU C Dk 474 TEU incl 76 ref C. Compartments: 2 Dp Ta in Hold, 2 Ho, ER 4 Ha: ER Cranes: 2x60t Ice Capable	**1 oil engine** driving 1 CP propeller Total Power: 4,983kW (6,775hp) 16.1kn B&W 5L42MC 1 x 2 Stroke 5 Cy. 420 x 1360 4983kW (6775bhp) Hudong Heavy Machinery Co Ltd-China AuxGen: 2 x 560kW 450V 60Hz a.c Thrusters: 1 Thwart. CP thruster (f) Fuel: 129.0 (d.f.) 578.0 (r.f.) 22.2pd
8127438 *WBE5866* -	**SOUTHERN MOON** **Jackson Marine LLC** Tidewater Marine LLC *New Orleans, LA* *United States of America* Official number: 648914	**674** 202 1,200	Class: AB	**1982-07 Halter Marine, Inc. — Lockport, La** Yd No: 1055 Loa 54.87 Br ex - Dght 3.663 Lbp 51.85 Br md 12.20 Dpth 4.27 Welded, 1 dk	**(B21A20S) Platform Supply Ship**	**2 oil engines** reverse reduction geared to sc. shafts driving 2 FP propellers Total Power: 1,654kW (2,248hp) 12.0kn Caterpillar D399SCAC 2 x Vee 4 Stroke 16 Cy. 159 x 203 each-827kW (1124bhp) Caterpillar Tractor Co-USA AuxGen: 2 x 99kW
7939341 *WYB7134* -	**SOUTHERN NIGHTS** **Southern Nights Trawlers** - *Lafitte, LA* *United States of America* Official number: 600399	*189* 128 -		**1978 Toche Marine, Inc. — Biloxi, Ms** L reg 26.40 Br ex 7.93 Dght - Lbp - Br md - Dpth 3.69 Welded, 1 dk	**(B11B2FV) Fishing Vessel**	**1 oil engine** driving 1 FP propeller Total Power: 493kW (670hp)
9433171 *9HA2366* -	**SOUTHERN OCEAN** *ex* Bourbon Oceanteam 104 *-2011* **Oceanteam Bourbon 4 AS** North Sea Shipping AS *Valletta* *Malta* MMSI: 248437000 Official number: 9433171	**11,014** 3,305 7,000	Class: NV	**2010-05 Metalships & Docks, S.A. — Vigo** Yd No: 288 Loa 133.60 (BB) Br ex - Dght 6.850 Lbp 120.40 Br md 27.00 Dpth 9.70 Welded, 1 dk	**(B22A20R) Offshore Support Vessel** Cranes: 1x250t,1x100t	**4 diesel electric oil engines** driving 4 gen. each 2500kW a.c Connecting to 2 elec. motors each (3500kW) driving 2 Azimuth electric drive units Total Power: 14,760kW (20,068hp) 12.0kn Wartsila 9R32LN 4 x 4 Stroke 9 Cy. 320 x 350 each-3690kW (5017bhp) Wartsila Finland Oy-Finland Thrusters: 2 Tunnel thruster (f); 1 Retract. directional thruster (f) Fuel: 1530.0 (r.f.)
6711742 - -	**SOUTHERN PACIFIC** *ex* Southern Pacific I *-2004* *ex* Norfish Buenaventura *-1989* *ex* Isabella *-1988* *ex* Elektra *-1972* **Aitutaki Fisheries Ltd**	*240* 58 169	Class: (BV)	**1967 VEB Rosslauer Schiffswerft — Rosslau** Loa 33.60 Br ex 6.66 Dght 2.995 Lbp 29.55 Br md 6.60 Dpth 3.30 Welded, 1 dk	**(B11A2FT) Trawler** Ins: 180 Compartments: 2 Ho, ER 2 Ha: 2 (1.6 x 1.2)ER Derricks: 1x3t,1x0.5t; Winches: 2 Ice Capable	**1 oil engine** driving 1 CP propeller Total Power: 625kW (850hp) 12.0kn Caterpillar D398SCAC 1 x Vee 4 Stroke 12 Cy. 159 x 203 625kW (850bhp) (made 1970, fitted 1972) Caterpillar Tractor Co-USA AuxGen: 1 x 16kW 220V d.c, 1 x 12kW 220V d.c Fuel: 19.5 (d.f.)

5092486 *ZR4145* CTA 130	**SOUTHERN PATRIOT** *ex* Harvest Apollo *-1979* *ex* Doncos *-1970* **Premier Fishing (Pty) Ltd** South Atlantic Fishing Co *Cape Town* *South Africa* MMSI: 601707000 Official number: 350629	*519* 220 193	Class: (BV)	**1962 Astilleros Construcciones SA — Meira** Yd No: 33 Converted From: Trawler-1980 L reg 44.96 Br ex 8.23 Dght - Lbp 44.96 Br md 8.21 Dpth 4.50 Riveted\Welded	**(B11B2FV) Fishing Vessel** 2 Ha: 2 (1.9 x 0.9)	**1 oil engine** driving 1 FP propeller Total Power: 699kW (950hp) 11.0kn Krupps 1 x 4 Stroke 6 Cy. 295 x 420 699kW (950bhp) La Maquinista Terrestre y Mar (MTM)-Spain Fuel: 20.5
9074121 *HSB4851* -	**SOUTHERN PEARL** *ex* Eurosea *-2013* *ex* Genmar Revenge *-2011* *ex* Sintra *-2004* *ex* Astro Perseus *-2000* *ex* Yuhsei Maru *-1999* **Top Nautical Star Co Ltd** Khunnathee Co Ltd *Bangkok* *Thailand* MMSI: 567489000 Official number: 570000033	**53,773** 21,938 96,755 T/cm 89.7	Class: AB (Class contemplated) (NV) (NK)	**1994-03 Samsung Heavy Industries Co Ltd — Geoje** Yd No: 1108 Loa 243.50 (BB) Br ex 41.83 Dght 13.618 Lbp 233.00 Br md 41.80 Dpth 20.00 Welded, 1 dk	**(A13A2TV) Crude Oil Tanker** Double Hull (13F) Liq: 104,417; Liq (Oil): 104,417 Cargo Heating Coils Compartments: 7 Ta, 2 Wing Slop Ta, ER 3 Cargo Pump (s): 3x2500m³/hr Manifold: Bow/CM: 124.2m	**1 oil engine** driving 1 FP propeller Total Power: 10,416kW (14,162hp) 14.2kn B&W 6L60MC 1 x 2 Stroke 6 Cy. 600 x 1944 10416kW (14162bhp) Hyundai Heavy Industries Co Ltd-South Korea AuxGen: 3 x 700kW 450V 60Hz a.c Fuel: 138.7 (d.f.) (Part Heating Coils) 2520.3 (r.f.) 39.3pd
9264207 *9VVN8* -	**SOUTHERN PEARL** *ex* Capitaine Wallis *-2011* *launched as* Pac Natuna *-2003* **Neptune Pacific Line Pte Ltd** Neptune Pacific Agency Australia Pty Ltd (Neptune Pacific Line) *Singapore* *Singapore* MMSI: 565760000 Official number: 393622	**5,234** 2,724 6,030	Class: LR (AB) **100A1** SS 04/2013 container ship **LMC** **UMS** Eq.Ltr: Z; Cable: 522.0/48.0 U3 (a)	**2003-04 Jiangsu Yangzijiang Shipbuilding Co Ltd — Jiangyin JS** Yd No: 01YZJ-639C42 Loa 109.39 (BB) Br ex 18.48 Dght 6.700 Lbp 103.20 Br md 18.20 Dpth 8.40 Welded, 1 dk	**(A33A2CC) Container Ship (Fully Cellular)** Grain: 9,300; Bale: 9,300 TEU 513 C Ho 172 TEU C Dk 341 TEU incl 60 ref C. Compartments: 3 Cell Ho, ER 3 Ha: 2 (25.5 x 15.4)ER (19.2 x 12.8) Cranes: 2x45t	**1 oil engine** with clutches, flexible couplings & sr geared to sc. shaft driving 1 CP propeller Total Power: 4,320kW (5,873hp) 16.0kn MaK 9M32C 1 x 4 Stroke 9 Cy. 320 x 480 4320kW (5873bhp) Caterpillar Motoren GmbH & Co. KG-Germany AuxGen: 3 x 370kW 220/440V 60Hz a.c, 1 x 500kW 220/440V 60Hz a.c Boilers: AuxB (Comp) 7.1kgf/cm² (7.0bar) Thrusters: 1 Thwart. CP thruster (f) Fuel: 91.5 (d.f.) 516.2 (r.f.) 15.0pd
8924874 *VVWV* -	**SOUTHERN PIONEER** **R Akoojee Jadwet & Co Pvt Ltd (R A J Lines)** *Visakhapatnam* *India* Official number: 2058	**142** 83 62	Class: (IR)	**1984-10 K Shipyard Construction Co — Fremantle WA** Yd No: 70 Loa 22.80 Br ex 6.52 Dght 3.300 Lbp 21.30 Br md 6.46 Dpth 3.67 Welded, 1 dk	**(B11B2FV) Fishing Vessel**	**1 oil engine** reduction geared to sc. shaft driving 1 FP propeller Total Power: 272kW (370hp) 8.5kn Caterpillar 3408TA 1 x Vee 4 Stroke 8 Cy. 137 x 152 272kW (370bhp) Caterpillar Inc-USA AuxGen: 1 x 80kW 440V 50Hz a.c Fuel: 58.0 (d.f.)
8885846 *WCD4989* -	**SOUTHERN PRIDE** *ex* Virgin Mary *-2013* **David M Stewart** *Biloxi, MS* *United States of America* Official number: 912968	*115* 78 -		**1987 Master Boat Builders, Inc. — Coden, Al** Yd No: 113 L reg 22.84 Br ex - Dght - Lbp - Br md 6.70 Dpth 3.40 Welded, 1 dk	**(B11B2FV) Fishing Vessel**	**1 oil engine** driving 1 FP propeller
8838403 *ZMBA* -	**SOUTHERN PROGRESS** *ex* Yuki Maru No. 7 *-1994* *ex* Kaio Maru No. 28 *-1988* **Okains Bay Vessel Holdings Ltd** *Timaru* *New Zealand* Official number: 876094	**150** 50	Class: (LR) Classed LR until 10/6/11	**1981 Kidoura Shipyard Co Ltd — Kesennuma MG** Yd No: 501 Loa 34.58 (BB) Br ex 6.56 Dght 2.100 Lbp 27.77 Br md 5.65 Dpth 2.60 Welded, 1 dk	**(B11B2FV) Fishing Vessel**	**1 oil engine** with clutches, flexible couplings & reverse geared to sc. shaft driving 1 FP propeller Total Power: 294kW (400hp) Niigata 6M24GTB 1 x 4 Stroke 6 Cy. 240 x 410 294kW (400bhp) Niigata Engineering Co Ltd-Japan AuxGen: 1 x 104kW 220V 60Hz a.c, 1 x 100kW 220V 60Hz a.c
7309003 *HC2304* -	**SOUTHERN QUEEN** *ex* Sanbros I *-1995* *ex* Southern Queen *-1994* **Manacripex Cia Ltda** - *Manta* *Ecuador* Official number: P-04-0408	*148* 103 -		**1947 Tacoma Boatbuilding Co., Inc. — Tacoma, Wa** L reg 27.86 Br ex 8.08 Dght - Lbp - Br md - Dpth 3.15 Welded	**(B11B2FV) Fishing Vessel**	**1 oil engine** driving 1 FP propeller Total Power: 515kW (700hp)
9222637 *WCZ5544* -	**SOUTHERN QUEST** **Southern States Offshore Inc** - *Houston, TX* *United States of America* MMSI: 338644000 Official number: 1089213	**1,124** 337 1,766	Class: AB	**1999-12 Halter Marine, Inc. — Lockport, La** Yd No: 1843 Loa 62.10 Br ex - Dght 4.400 Lbp 57.87 Br md 14.00 Dpth 5.15 Welded, 1 dk	**(B21A2OS) Platform Supply Ship**	**2 oil engines** reverse reduction geared to sc. shafts driving 2 FP propellers Total Power: 2,868kW (3,900hp) 12.0kn EMD (Electro-Motive) 16-645-E2 2 x Vee 2 Stroke 16 Cy. 230 x 254 each-1434kW (1950bhp) General Motors Corp.Electro-Motive Div.-La Grange AuxGen: 2 x 135kW 460V a.c Thrusters: 1 Thwart. FP thruster (f)
5060550 *ZR4291* CTA 139	**SOUTHERN RAIDER** *ex* San Sebastian *-1977* *ex* S. Sebastian *-1973* *ex* Cap d'Ailly *-1968* **Premier Fishing SA (Pty) Ltd & Foodcorp (Pty) Ltd** - *Cape Town* *South Africa* MMSI: 601702000 Official number: 350702	*458* 193 360	Class: (BV) (RI)	**1956 AG Weser, Werk Seebeck — Bremerhaven** Yd No: 812 Converted From: Trawler-1980 Loa 54.31 Br ex 8.97 Dght - Lbp 47.99 Br md 8.92 Dpth 4.65 Riveted	**(B11B2FV) Fishing Vessel** Compartments: 1 Ho, ER 5 Ha: 5 (0.9 x 0.9) Derricks: 3x2t	**2 oil engines** with hydraulic couplings & geared to sc. shaft driving 1 FP propeller Total Power: 1,000kW (1,360hp) 13.0kn Deutz RV6M436 1 x 4 Stroke 6 Cy. 240 x 360 Kloeckner Humboldt Deutz AG-West Germany Deutz SBV8M545 1 x 4 Stroke 8 Cy. 320 x 450 1000kW (1360bhp) Kloeckner Humboldt Deutz AG-West Germany AuxGen: 3 x 40kW 110V d.c Fuel: 157.5 (d.f.)
9043940 *WBO8580* -	**SOUTHERN RESPONDER** *ex* Georgia Responder *-2006* **Marine Spill Response Corp** - *Ingleside, TX* *United States of America* MMSI: 366596000 Official number: 983113	**1,335** 400 1,400	Class: AB	**1993-04 Trinity-Beaumont — Beaumont, Tx** Yd No: 1303 Loa 64.18 Br ex - Dght 4.461 Lbp 60.20 Br md 13.41 Dpth 5.18 Welded	**(B34G2SE) Pollution Control Vessel**	**2 oil engines** reverse reduction geared to sc. shafts driving 2 FP propellers Total Power: 1,884kW (2,562hp) 12.0kn Caterpillar 3512TA 2 x Vee 4 Stroke 12 Cy. 170 x 190 each-942kW (1281bhp) Caterpillar Inc-USA AuxGen: 3 x 250kW a.c Thrusters: 1 Tunnel thruster (f)
9220196 *9V8124* -	**SOUTHERN ROYAL** **Chempioneer Tankers Pte Ltd** Sansho Kaiun Co Ltd *Singapore* *Singapore* MMSI: 564299000 Official number: 395345	**7,098** 4,056 12,675 T/cm 21.0	Class: BV	**1999-12 Asakawa Zosen K.K. — Imabari** Yd No: 415 Loa 124.00 (BB) Br ex 20.22 Dght 8.760 Lbp 116.00 Br md 20.20 Dpth 11.20 Welded, 1 dk	**(A12B2TR) Chemical/Products Tanker** Double Hull (13F) Liq: 13,563; Liq (Oil): 13,563 Cargo Heating Coils Compartments: 22 Wing Ta, 2 Wing Slop Ta, ER 22 Cargo Pump (s): 6x300m³/hr, 16x160m³/hr Manifold: Bow/CM: 56.1m	**1 oil engine** driving 1 FP propeller Total Power: 4,193kW (5,701hp) 13.6kn B&W 6S35MC 1 x 2 Stroke 6 Cy. 350 x 1400 4193kW (5701bhp) Hitachi Zosen Corp-Japan AuxGen: 3 x 400kW 450V 60Hz a.c Thrusters: 1 Thwart. FP thruster (f) Fuel: 55.0 (d.f.) (Part Heating Coils) 625.0 (r.f.) 16.5pd
5306069 *ZR3983* CTA 129	**SOUTHERN SAINT** *ex* St. Jean Baptiste de la Salle *-1977* **Premier Fishing (Pty) Ltd** - *Cape Town* *South Africa* Official number: 350669	*550* 204 -	Class: (BV)	**1958 Handel en Scheepsbouw Mij. Kramer & Booy N.V. — Kootstertille** Yd No: 105 Loa 55.00 Br ex 9.10 Dght - Lbp 47.99 Br md 9.00 Dpth 4.81 Riveted\Welded, 1 dk	**(B11A2FT) Trawler** Derricks: 1x3t	**1 oil engine** driving 1 FP propeller Total Power: 883kW (1,201hp) 14.0kn Deutz RBV6M366 1 x 4 Stroke 6 Cy. 420 x 660 883kW (1201bhp) Kloeckner Humboldt Deutz AG-West Germany Fuel: 149.5 (d.f.)
8203971 *ERTD*	**SOUTHERN SEA** *ex* Lanka Mahapola *-2013* *ex* X-Press Trisuli *-1997* *ex* Lanka Mahapola *-1997* **Ocean Marine Service** Southern Ship Management (Pvt) Ltd *Giurgiulesti* *Moldova* MMSI: 214182004	**8,082** 4,639 11,372	Class: (NK) (IR)	**1983-06 Ishikawajima-Harima Heavy Industries Co Ltd (IHI) — Tokyo** Yd No: 2812 Loa 129.00 Br ex 20.45 Dght 8.621 Lbp 120.00 Br md 20.40 Dpth 11.50 Welded, 1 dk	**(A31A2GX) General Cargo Ship** Grain: 15,511; Bale: 14,832 TEU 410 incl 36 ref C. Compartments: 4 Ho, ER 6 Ha: (6.4 x 6.0) (20.0 x 10.4)4 (20.0 x 8.0)ER Cranes: 1x35t,1x25t	**1 oil engine** driving 1 FP propeller Total Power: 5,649kW (7,680hp) 16.0kn Sulzer 6RLB56 1 x 2 Stroke 6 Cy. 560 x 1150 5649kW (7680bhp) Ishikawajima Harima Heavy IndustrieCo Ltd (IHI)-Japan AuxGen: 3 x 440kW Fuel: 860.0 (r.f.)
8009935 *WCX6191* -	**SOUTHERN SEAHORSE** *ex* Mobile Seahorse *-1998* **Southern States Offshore Inc** - SatCom: Inmarsat C 436628910 *Houston, TX* *United States of America* MMSI: 366990770 Official number: 635750	**540** 162 450	Class: (AB)	**1981-05 Houma Fabricators Inc — Houma LA** Yd No: 69 Loa 48.77 Br ex 11.61 Dght 3.753 Lbp 47.55 Br md 11.59 Dpth 4.35 Welded, 1 dk	**(B21A2OS) Platform Supply Ship**	**2 oil engines** sr reverse geared to sc. shafts driving 2 FP propellers Total Power: 1,250kW (1,700hp) 10.0kn Caterpillar D398SCAC 2 x Vee 4 Stroke 12 Cy. 159 x 203 each-625kW (850bhp) Caterpillar Tractor Co-USA AuxGen: 2 x 75kW 460/225V 60Hz a.c Thrusters: 1 Thwart. FP thruster (f) Fuel: 112.0 (d.f.)

IMO / Call sign	Name / Owner	Tonnage	Class	Builder / Dimensions	Type	Machinery
6708410 *WX6579* -	**SOUTHERN SEAHORSE** *ex* J. H. Levy *-1978* - **Ocean Ventures Inc** - *Morgan City, LA* *United States of America* Official number: 504351	*195* 133 -		**1966 American Marine Corp. — New Orleans, La** Yd No: 953 Loa 47.60 Br ex 11.03 Dght 3.172 Lbp 44.56 Br md 10.98 Dpth 3.81 Welded, 1 dk	**(B21A20S) Platform Supply Ship**	**2 oil engines** driving 2 FP propellers Total Power: 1,250kW (1,700hp) Caterpillar D398SCAC 2 x Vee 4 Stroke 12 Cy. 159 x 203 each-625kW (850bhp) Caterpillar Tractor Co-USA
8945828 *DYSK* -	**SOUTHERN SEAS** - **Southland Express Inc** - *Manila* *Philippines* Official number: MNLD001798	*327* 247 -		**1987 at Manila** L reg 44.61 Br ex - Dght - Lbp - Br md 8.54 Dpth 2.59 Welded, 1 dk	**(A13B2TU) Tanker (unspecified)**	**1 oil engine** driving 1 FP propeller Total Power: 441kW (600hp) Cummins 1 x 4 Stroke 441kW (600bhp) Cummins Engine Co Inc-USA
8990445 *WDC4087* -	**SOUTHERN SPIRIT** - **Southern States Offshore Inc** - *Houston, TX* *United States of America* MMSI: 367018840 Official number: 1164326	**387** 116 -		**2005-05 La Force Shipyard Inc — Coden AL** Yd No: 145 Loa 51.80 Br ex - Dght - Lbp - Br md 9.75 Dpth 3.96 Welded, 1 dk	**(B21A20S) Platform Supply Ship** Hull Material: Aluminium Alloy Passengers: unberthed: 75	**4 oil engines** geared to sc. shafts driving 4 Propellers Total Power: 4,632kW (6,296hp) 25.0kn Caterpillar 3512B 4 x Vee 4 Stroke 12 Cy. 170 x 190 each-1158kW (1574bhp) Caterpillar Inc-USA Thrusters: 2 Thwart. FP thruster (f)
9171125 *3FWV8* -	**SOUTHERN SPIRIT** - **Grand Rich Line Inc** Jacksoon Shipping Safety Management Consultant Co Ltd SatCom: Inmarsat B 335700510 *Panama* *Panama* MMSI: 357005000 Official number: 2603299D	**18,459** 10,119 29,482	Class: NK	**1998-11 Shin Kurushima Dockyard Co. Ltd. — Onishi** Yd No: 2973 Loa 170.03 (BB) Br ex - Dght 9.978 Lbp 162.00 Br md 27.40 Dpth 14.00 Welded, 1 dk	**(A21A2BC) Bulk Carrier** Double Hull Grain: 37,451; Bale: 36,269 Compartments: 5 Ho, ER 5 Ha: (15.2 x 16.9)3 (20.8 x 22.8) (16.0 x 22.8)ER Cranes: 4x30.5t	**1 oil engine** driving 1 FP propeller Total Power: 6,620kW (9,001hp) 14.4kn Mitsubishi 5UEC52LS 1 x 2 Stroke 5 Cy. 520 x 1850 6620kW (9001bhp) Mitsubishi Heavy Industries Ltd-Japan Fuel: 1200.0
9410894 *9HA2148* -	**SOUTHERN SPIRIT** - **The S Spirit Shipping Co Ltd** Interorient Marine Services (Germany) GmbH & Co KG SatCom: Inmarsat C 424805511 *Valletta* *Malta* MMSI: 248055000 Official number: 9410894	**62,775** 34,934 113,043 T/cm 99.7	Class: AB	**2009-10 New Times Shipbuilding Co Ltd — Jingjiang JS** Yd No: 0311515 Loa 250.00 (BB) Br ex 44.04 Dght 14.800 Lbp 240.00 Br md 44.00 Dpth 21.00 Welded, 1 dk	**(A13A2TW) Crude/Oil Products Tanker** Double Hull (13F) Liq: 124,690; Liq (Oil): 124,690 Cargo Heating Coils Compartments: 12 Wing Ta, 2 Wing Slop Ta, ER 3 Cargo Pump (s): 3x3000m³/hr Manifold: Bow/CM: 122.5m	**1 oil engine** driving 1 FP propeller Total Power: 15,820kW (21,509hp) 15.0kn MAN-B&W 7S60MC-C 1 x 2 Stroke 7 Cy. 600 x 2400 15820kW (21509bhp) Hudong Heavy Machinery Co Ltd-China AuxGen: 3 x 900kW a.c Fuel: 220.0 (d.f.) 3100.0 (r.f.)
9344071 *DYQF* -	**SOUTHERN STAR** - **Cygnet Bulk Carriers SA** MMS Co Ltd *Manila* *Philippines* MMSI: 548769000 Official number: MNLA000693	**39,895** 21,193 49,470	Class: NK	**2007-09 Tsuneishi Holdings Corp Tsuneishi Shipbuilding Co — Fukuyama HS** Yd No: 1349 Loa 199.90 Br ex - Dght 11.550 Lbp 191.50 Br md 32.20 Dpth 22.75 Welded, 1 dk	**(A24B2BW) Wood Chips Carrier** Grain: 102,126 Compartments: 6 Ho, ER 6 Ha: ER Cranes: 3x14.7t	**1 oil engine** driving 1 FP propeller Total Power: 8,580kW (11,665hp) 14.6kn MAN-B&W 6S50MC 1 x 2 Stroke 6 Cy. 500 x 1910 8580kW (11665bhp) Mitsui Engineering & Shipbuilding CLtd-Japan Fuel: 2820.0
8987319 *WDG9984* -	**SOUTHERN STAR** *ex* Mr Larry *-2013* *ex* Larry J. Hebert *-2010* *ex* Voyager *-2010* **Southern Star LLC** - *Chesapeake, VA* *United States of America* MMSI: 367593210 Official number: 506327	*145* 98 -		**1966-12 SBA Shipyards Inc — Jennings LA** Yd No: 176 Loa - Br ex - Dght 2.600 Lbp 24.38 Br md 7.30 Dpth 2.90 Welded, 1 dk	**(B32A2ST) Tug**	**2 oil engines** geared to sc. shafts driving 2 Propellers Total Power: 882kW (1,200hp) G.M. (Detroit Diesel) 16V-92 2 x Vee 2 Stroke 16 Cy. 123 x 127 each-441kW (600bhp) General Motors Detroit DieselAllison Divn-USA AuxGen: 2 x 30kW
9068990 *YJS7172* -	**SOUTHERN STAR** - **Government of The Republic of Vanuatu** - *Port Vila* *Vanuatu* Official number: 6153	**277** 83 130	Class: (CC)	**2005-09 Wuhan Nanhua High Speed Ship Engineering Co Ltd — Wuhan HB** Loa 32.60 Br ex - Dght - Lbp 29.60 Br md 7.60 Dpth 3.50 Welded, 1 dk	**(A32A2GF) General Cargo/Passenger Ship** Passengers: unberthed: 60 Bale: 220 Compartments: 2 Ho, ER 2 Ha: ER 2 (3.0 x 3.0) Cranes: 1x1.5t	**2 oil engines** geared to sc. shafts driving 2 Propellers 10.0kn Cummins KTA-19-M4 2 x 4 Stroke 6 Cy. 159 x 159 Chongqing Cummins Engine Co Ltd-China AuxGen: 2 x 50kW 400V a.c
8886591 - -	**SOUTHERN STAR** - **Jenny Trinh** - *Savannah, GA* *United States of America* Official number: 663876	*127* 102 -		**1982 Raffield's Shipbuilding — Port Saint Joe, Fl** Yd No: 103 L reg 18.90 Br ex - Dght - Lbp - Br md 7.47 Dpth 3.65 Bonded, 1 dk	**(B11B2FV) Fishing Vessel** Hull Material: Reinforced Plastic	**1 oil engine** driving 1 FP propeller
8627000 *YJTN2* -	**SOUTHERN STAR** *ex* Lady of the Isles *-1988* *ex* Melbider *-1988* **McKee Shipping Ltd** J McKee & Partners Ltd *Port Vila* *Vanuatu* Official number: 2258	**286** 86 84	Class: GL (NV)	**1973-09 Carrington Slipways Pty Ltd — Newcastle NSW** Yd No: 85 Converted From: Patrol Vessel-1991 Loa 36.85 Br ex 7.95 Dght 2.210 Lbp 33.52 Br md 7.93 Dpth 2.74 Welded, 1 dk	**(B22A20V) Diving Support Vessel** Cranes: 2x3t	**2 oil engines** reduction geared to sc. shafts driving 2 FP propellers Total Power: 716kW (974hp) 9.5kn Kelvin TA8 2 x 4 Stroke 8 Cy. 165 x 184 each-358kW (487bhp) English Electric Diesels Ltd.-Glasgow AuxGen: 3 x 32kW 50Hz a.c
7634305 *WDE6165* -	**SOUTHERN STAR I** *ex* Capt. George *-1992* **New Transport Lines Inc** - *Panama City, FL* *United States of America* MMSI: 367004310 Official number: 593394	*297* 202 1,000	Class: (AB)	**1978-06 Rockport Yacht & Supply Co. (RYSCO) — Rockport, Tx** Yd No: 104 Loa - Br ex - Dght 3.414 Lbp 49.38 Br md 11.59 Dpth 3.97 Welded, 1 dk	**(B21A20S) Platform Supply Ship**	**2 oil engines** reverse reduction geared to sc. shafts driving 2 FP propellers . Total Power: 1,250kW (1,700hp) 12.0kn Caterpillar D398SCAC 2 x Vee 4 Stroke 12 Cy. 159 x 203 each-625kW (850bhp) Caterpillar Tractor Co-USA AuxGen: 2 x 75kW
8971762 - -	**SOUTHERN STAR No. 888** *ex* Hsiang Fa No. 888 *-2002* **Grace Marine Co Ltd** -	**520** 241 -		**2001 Fong Kuo Shipbuilding Co Ltd — Kaohsiung** Yd No: 380 Loa 56.49 Br ex - Dght 3.400 Lbp 48.60 Br md 8.70 Dpth 3.75 Welded, 1 dk	**(B11B2FV) Fishing Vessel**	**1 oil engine** geared to sc. shaft driving 1 FP propeller Total Power: 1,030kW (1,400hp) 13.0kn Hanshin LH28G 1 x 4 Stroke 6 Cy. 280 x 460 1030kW (1400bhp) The Hanshin Diesel Works Ltd-Japan
8427905 *DUAP5* -	**SOUTHERN STAR S** *ex* Roden V *-2002* *ex* Oil Queen V *-2002* **Nautilus Tanker Corp** - *Manila* *Philippines* Official number: MNLD001916	*233* 144 -		**1974 Sandoval Shipyards Inc. — Manila** Loa - Br ex 7.35 Dght - Lbp 35.67 Br md 7.32 Dpth 3.26 Welded, 1 dk	**(A13B2TU) Tanker (unspecified)**	**1 oil engine** driving 1 FP propeller Total Power: 140kW (190hp)
7113002 *VLHJ* -	**SOUTHERN SURVEYOR** *ex* Kurderen *-1982* *ex* Kurd *-1982* *ex* Ranger Callisto *-1973* **RTSS Columbus Shipping Inc** RTSS Maritime Services LLC *Hobart, Tas* *Australia* MMSI: 503049000	**1,594** 479 2,000	Class: LR ✠ **100A1** SS 08/2010 fishing/research ✠ **LMC** **UMS** Eq.Ltr: M; Cable: U2	**1972-05 Brooke Marine Ltd. — Lowestoft** Yd No: 374 Converted From: Diving Support Vessel-1990 Converted From: Stern Trawler-1983 Loa 66.15 Br ex 12.25 Dght 5.300 Lbp 56.85 Br md 12.20 Dpth 7.78 Welded, 2 dks	**(B12D2FR) Fishery Research Vessel** Compartments: 2 Ho, ER 7 Ha: (0.9 x 0.9) (2.2 x 2.2) (0.6 x 0.6) (7.1 x 3.5) (2.1 x 2.1) (0.6 x 0.7) (0.9 x 1.0)	**1 oil engine** with flexible couplings & sr reverse geared to sc. shaft driving 1 CP propeller Total Power: 2,200kW (2,991hp) 14.0kn Wartsila 6R32E 1 x 4 Stroke 6 Cy. 320 x 350 2200kW (2991bhp) (new engine 1994) Wartsila Diesel Oy-Finland AuxGen: 1 x 1500kW 415V 50Hz a.c, 3 x 850kW 415V 60Hz a.c Thrusters: 1 Retract. directional thruster (f); 2 Thwart. CP thruster (f); 2 Thwart. CP thruster (a) Fuel: 255.5 (d.f.)
8719176 *E5U2082* -	**SOUTHERN TIARE** *ex* Manini *-2013* *ex* Southern Tiare *-2013* *ex* Spica *-2004* *ex* Fortuna Coast *-1995* **CIAH (Cook Islands) Ltd** Chatham Islands Shipping Ltd *Rarotonga* *Cook Islands* MMSI: 518132000 Official number: 1159	**1,185** 361 1,210	Class: LR (BV) **100A1** SS 03/2013 **LMC** Eq.Ltr: M; Cable: 385.0/32.0 U2	**1988-03 Svendborg Vaerft A/S — Svendborg** Yd No: 188 Loa 67.35 (BB) Br ex 11.42 Dght 4.350 Lbp 62.55 Br md 11.42 Dpth 5.51 Welded, 1 dk	**(A31A2GX) General Cargo Ship** Grain: 1,630 TEU 61 C Ho 36 TEU C Dk 25 TEU incl 18 ref C Compartments: 1 Ho, ER 1 Ha: (38.7 x 7.8)ER Cranes: 2x20t	**1 oil engine** with flexible couplings & sr geared to sc. shaft driving 1 CP propeller Total Power: 599kW (814hp) 11.0kn MWM TBD440-6 1 x 4 Stroke 6 Cy. 230 x 270 599kW (814bhp) Motoren Werke Mannheim AG (MWM)-West Germany AuxGen: 2 x 230kW 380V 50Hz a.c, 1 x 135kW 380V 50Hz a.c Thrusters: 1 Thwart. FP thruster (f)

IMO / Call sign	Name / Owner	Tonnage	Class	Builder / Dimensions	Type / Cargo	Machinery
9359674 *9VEY2* -	**SOUTHERN TRADER** *ex* Capitaine Tasman *-2013* *ex* Southern Lily *-2011* *ex* Kota Rahmat *-2011* **Pacific International Lines (Pte) Ltd** - *Singapore* *Singapore* MMSI: 565730000 Official number: 393325	**9,725** 4,512 12,985	Class: NK	**2008-01 Shin Kochi Jyuko K.K. — Kochi** Yd No: 7211 Loa 145.93 (BB) Br ex - Dght 8.120 Lbp 135.00 Br md 22.60 Dpth 10.80 Welded, 1 dk	**(A33A2CC) Container Ship (Fully Cellular)** TEU 907 incl 100 ref C. Cranes: 2x40t	**1 oil engine** driving 1 FP propeller Total Power: 6,150kW (8,362hp) 17.1kn MAN-B&W 6S42MC 1 x 2 Stroke 6 Cy. 420 x 1764 6150kW (8362bhp) Mitsui Engineering & Shipbuilding CLtd-Japan AuxGen: 3 x a.c Thrusters: 1 Tunnel thruster (f) Fuel: 1110.0
9269594 *9V8604* -	**SOUTHERN UNICORN** **Chempioneer Tankers Pte Ltd** Sansho Kaiun Co Ltd *Singapore* *Singapore* MMSI: 563188000 Official number: 396005	**6,976** 3,900 11,959 T/cm 20.8	Class: NK	**2002-11 Asakawa Zosen K.K. — Imabari** Yd No: 427 Loa 123.50 (BB) Br ex 20.22 Dght 8.414 Lbp 116.00 Br md 20.20 Dpth 10.85 Welded, 1 dk	**(A12B2TR) Chemical/Products Tanker** Double Hull (13F) Liq: 12,897; Liq (Oil): 12,897 Cargo Heating Coils Compartments: 22 Wing Ta (s.stl), 2 Wing Slop Ta (s.stl), Wing ER 22 Cargo Pump (s): 18x200m³/hr, 4x300m³/hr Manifold: Bow/CM: 66m	**1 oil engine** driving 1 FP propeller Total Power: 4,200kW (5,710hp) 14.1kn MAN-B&W 6S35MC 1 x 2 Stroke 6 Cy. 350 x 1400 4200kW (5710bhp) Imex Co Ltd-Japan AuxGen: 3 x 440kW 60Hz a.c Thrusters: 1 Tunnel thruster (f) Fuel: 73.0 (d.f.) (Heating Coils) 546.0 (r.f.) 18.5pd
9405150 *ZRJZ* -	**SOUTHERN VALOUR** **Unicorn Calulo Bunker Services (Pty) Ltd** Unical Bunker Services (Pty) Ltd *Durban* *South Africa* Official number: 10729	**2,402** 1,179 4,250	Class: NV (BV)	**2008-04 Jiangmen Yinxing Shipbuilding Co Ltd — Jiangmen GD** Yd No: YXI-004 Loa 69.80 Br ex - Dght 5.900 Lbp 67.10 Br md 17.60 Dpth 7.20 Welded, 1 dk	**(B35E2TF) Bunkering Tanker** Double Hull (13F) Compartments: 1 Ta, 10 Wing Ta, ER 4 Cargo Pump (s): 2x500m³/hr, 2x150m³/hr	**2 oil engines** reduction geared to sc. shafts driving 2 FP propellers Total Power: 984kW (1,338hp) 6.0kn Cummins QSK19-M 2 x 4 Stroke 6 Cy. 159 x 159 each-492kW (669bhp) Cummins Engine Co Inc-USA AuxGen: 3 x 410kW a.c Thrusters: 1 Directional thruster (f) Fuel: 103.0 (d.f.)
9405148 *ZRBN* -	**SOUTHERN VENTURE** **Unicorn Calulo Bunker Services (Pty) Ltd** Unical Bunker Services (Pty) Ltd *Durban* *South Africa* Official number: 20741	**2,402** 1,179 4,250	Class: NV (BV)	**2008-04 Jiangmen Yinxing Shipbuilding Co Ltd — Jiangmen GD** Yd No: YXI-003 Loa 69.80 Br ex - Dght 5.900 Lbp 67.10 Br md 17.60 Dpth 7.20 Welded, 1 dk	**(B35E2TF) Bunkering Tanker** Double Hull (13F) Compartments: 1 Ta, 10 Wing Ta, ER	**2 oil engines** gearing integral to driving 2 Directional propellers Total Power: 984kW (1,338hp) 6.0kn Cummins QSK19-M 2 x 4 Stroke 6 Cy. 159 x 159 each-492kW (669bhp) Cummins Engine Co Inc-USA Thrusters: 1 Directional thruster (f)
7644491 *ZR3938* -	**SOUTHERN VICTOR** *ex* Saevaklettur *-1995* *ex* Vagborg *-1992* *ex* Svalbard *-1983* *ex* Signe Helen *-1978* **Premier Fishing (Pty) Ltd** - SatCom: Inmarsat C 460101140 *Cape Town* *South Africa* Official number: 19736	**1,065** 320 -	Class: (NV)	**1978-03 FEAB-Karlstadverken — Karlstad** (Hull launched by) Yd No: 123 **1978-03 p/f Skala Skipasmidja — Skali** (Hull completed by) Yd No: 30 Lengthened-1983 Loa 56.75 Br ex 9.58 Dght 4.311 Lbp 54.28 Br md 9.52 Dpth 9.50 Welded, 2 dks	**(B11A2FT) Trawler** Compartments: 7 Ho, ER 2 Ha: 2 (2.6 x 6.4) Ice Capable	**1 oil engine** driving 1 CP propeller Total Power: 1,545kW (2,101hp) Wichmann 7AX 1 x 2 Stroke 7 Cy. 300 x 450 1545kW (2101bhp) Wichmann Motorfabrikk AS-Norway AuxGen: 2 x 152kW 380V 50Hz a.c Thrusters: 1 Thwart. CP thruster (f)
7928562 - -	**SOUTHERN VOYAGER** *ex* Santa Rosa A *-2012* **Joseph & Marcia Bronwyn Valente Pty Ltd** - *Port Adelaide, SA* *Australia* Official number: 199287	*149* 99 -		**1980-08 Kali Boat Building Pty Ltd — Port Adelaide SA** Yd No: 27 Loa 23.70 Br ex 7.17 Dght - Lbp 21.75 Br md 7.00 Dpth 3.61 Welded, 1 dk	**(B11B2FV) Fishing Vessel**	**1 oil engine** sr geared to sc. shaft driving 1 FP propeller Total Power: 403kW (548hp) Caterpillar D379SCAC 1 x Vee 4 Stroke 8 Cy. 159 x 203 403kW (548bhp) Caterpillar Tractor Co-USA
9264879 *9V9308* -	**SOUTHERN WALLABY** *ex* Bow Wallaby *-2008* **Chempioneer Tankers Pte Ltd** Sansho Kaiun Co Ltd *Singapore* *Singapore* MMSI: 564789000 Official number: 396907	**6,976** 3,900 11,951 T/cm 20.8	Class: NK	**2003-01 Asakawa Zosen K.K. — Imabari** Yd No: 428 Loa 123.50 (BB) Br ex 20.22 Dght 8.414 Lbp 116.00 Br md 20.20 Dpth 10.85 Welded, 1 dk	**(A12B2TR) Chemical/Products Tanker** Double Hull (13F) Liq: 12,893; Liq (Oil): 12,893 Cargo Heating Coils Compartments: 20 Wing Ta (s.stl), 2 Wing Slop Ta (s.stl), ER (s.stl) 20 Cargo Pump (s): 2x300m³/hr, 18x200m³/hr Manifold: Bow/CM: 66.8m	**1 oil engine** driving 1 FP propeller Total Power: 4,200kW (5,710hp) 14.1kn MAN-B&W 6S35MC 1 x 2 Stroke 6 Cy. 350 x 1400 4200kW (5710bhp) Imex Co Ltd-Japan AuxGen: 3 x 380kW a.c Thrusters: 1 Thwart. CP thruster (f) Fuel: 73.0 (d.f.) (Heating Coils) 715.0 (r.f.) 16.9pd
8019801 *WDD3741* -	**SOUTHERN WIND** *ex* Seahawker *-1990* *ex* Sablefish *-1990* **Trident Seafoods Corp** - *Seattle, WA* *United States of America* MMSI: 367892000 Official number: 625927	**493** 147 -		**1980 Mitchel Duane Phares — Los Angeles, La** Yd No: 36 Lengthened-1990 Loa 43.90 Br ex - Dght 3.536 Lbp - Br md 9.76 Dpth 4.17 Welded, 1 dk	**(B11B2FV) Fishing Vessel**	**2 oil engines** geared to sc. shafts driving 2 FP propellers Total Power: 992kW (1,348hp) G.M. (Detroit Diesel) 12V-149 2 x Vee 2 Stroke 12 Cy. 146 x 146 each-496kW (674bhp) General Motors Detroit DieselAllison Divn-USA
9290880 *H8ZG* -	**SOUTHERN WISDOM** **Fair Wind Navigation SA** Mizuho Sangyo Co Ltd SatCom: Inmarsat C 435778010 *Panama* *Panama* MMSI: 357780000 Official number: 3018804B	**88,548** 58,972 177,325 T/cm 119.0	Class: NK	**2004-09 Mitsui Eng. & SB. Co. Ltd., Chiba Works — Ichihara** Yd No: 1593 Loa 289.00 (BB) Br ex - Dght 17.975 Lbp 279.00 Br md 45.00 Dpth 24.40 Welded, 1 dk	**(A21A2BC) Bulk Carrier** Grain: 197,089 Compartments: 9 Ho, ER 9 Ha: 7 (15.5 x 20.6)ER 2 (15.5 x 15.0)	**1 oil engine** driving 1 FP propeller Total Power: 16,858kW (22,920hp) 14.5kn B&W 6S70MC 1 x 2 Stroke 6 Cy. 700 x 2674 16858kW (22920bhp) Mitsui Engineering & Shipbuilding CLtd-Japan Fuel: 3910.0
9312406 *H9DN* -	**SOUTHERN ZEBRA** **Southern Chemical Carriers SA** Sansho Kaiun Co Ltd *Panama* *Panama* MMSI: 352254000 Official number: 3034404B	**5,551** 2,785 8,907 T/cm 18.2	Class: NK	**2004-10 Shitanoe Shipbuilding Co Ltd — Usuki OT** Yd No: 1238 Loa 115.50 (BB) Br ex 18.73 Dght 7.613 Lbp 108.50 Br md 18.70 Dpth 10.00 Welded, 1 dk	**(A12B2TR) Chemical/Products Tanker** Double Hull (13F) Liq: 9,890; Liq (Oil): 9,890 Cargo Heating Coils Compartments: 16 Wing Ta (s.stl), 1 Slop Ta, ER 16 Cargo Pump (s): 12x300m³/hr, 4x200m³/hr Manifold: Bow/CM: 53m	**1 oil engine** driving 1 FP propeller Total Power: 3,900kW (5,302hp) 13.7kn B&W 6L35MC 1 x 2 Stroke 6 Cy. 350 x 1050 3900kW (5302bhp) Hitachi Zosen Corp-Japan AuxGen: 3 x 400kW 450V 60Hz a.c Thrusters: 1 Thwart. CP thruster (f) Fuel: 55.0 (d.f.) 571.0 (r.f.) 16.5pd
9547312 *9WHV7* -	**SOUTHERNLINE 3** **Woodman Southernline Sdn Bhd** - SatCom: Inmarsat C 453300780 *Kuching* *Malaysia* MMSI: 533000795 Official number: 333008	**326** 98 272	Class: NK	**2009-05 Sarawak Land Shipyard Sdn Bhd — Miri** Yd No: 09 Loa 31.00 Br ex - Dght 3.512 Lbp 28.59 Br md 9.15 Dpth 4.30 Welded, 1 dk	**(B32A2ST) Tug**	**2 oil engines** reduction geared to sc. shafts driving 2 Propellers Total Power: 1,518kW (2,064hp) Mitsubishi S6R2-MTK3L 2 x 4 Stroke 6 Cy. 170 x 220 each-759kW (1032bhp) Mitsubishi Heavy Industries Ltd-Japan AuxGen: 2 x 99kW a.c Fuel: 240.0
9550606 *9V8744* -	**SOUTHERNPEC 6** *ex* Hua Hang 106 *-2010* **Southernpec (Singapore) Shipping Pte Ltd** - SatCom: Inmarsat C 456387411 *Singapore* *Singapore* MMSI: 563874000 Official number: 396189	**2,990** 1,321 4,710	Class: BV	**2010-05 Taizhou Yuanhang Shipyard Co Ltd — Wenling ZJ** Yd No: YH0705 Loa 99.86 (BB) Br ex - Dght 6.200 Lbp 93.31 Br md 15.20 Dpth 7.60 Welded, 1 dk	**(A13B2TP) Products Tanker** Double Hull (13F) Liq: 3,620; Liq (Oil): 3,620 Compartments: 8 Wing Ta, ER	**1 oil engine** reduction geared to sc. shaft driving 1 FP propeller Total Power: 1,956kW (2,659hp) 11.5kn MAN-B&W 8L28/32A 1 x 4 Stroke 8 Cy. 280 x 320 1956kW (2659bhp) Zhenjiang Marine Diesel Works-China AuxGen: 3 x 312kW 60Hz a.c
9550591 *9V8316* -	**SOUTHERNPEC 7** *ex* Jnos *-2010* *ex* Hua Hang 105 *-2009* **Southernpec (Singapore) Shipping Pte Ltd** - SatCom: Inmarsat C 456374410 *Singapore* *Singapore* MMSI: 563744000 Official number: 395602	**2,990** 1,321 4,710	Class: BV	**2009-07 Taizhou Yuanhang Shipyard Co Ltd — Wenling ZJ** Yd No: YH0701 Loa 99.86 Br ex - Dght 6.200 Lbp 93.00 Br md 15.20 Dpth 7.60 Welded, 1 dk	**(A13B2TP) Products Tanker** Double Hull (13F) Liq: 4,682; Liq (Oil): 4,682 Compartments: 10 Wing Ta, ER	**1 oil engine** driving 1 FP propeller Total Power: 2,206kW (2,999hp) 11.8kn Yanmar 6N330-EN 1 x 4 Stroke 6 Cy. 330 x 440 2206kW (2999bhp) Qingdao Zichai Boyang Diesel EngineCo Ltd-China AuxGen: 2 x 244kW 60Hz a.c
8906793 *HPXQ* -	**SOUTHERNPEC 8** *ex* Pericles G.C. *-2010* *ex* Taos *-2006* *ex* General Monarch *-1996* *ex* Sea Duke *-1991* **Southernpec (Singapore) Shipping Pte Ltd** Southern Petrochemical Co Ltd *Panama* *Panama* MMSI: 351831000 Official number: 4311511	**144,567** 90,511 275,993 T/cm 167.2	Class: LR (NV) **100A1** SS 09/2010 TOC contemplated	**1990-09 Hitachi Zosen Corp — Nagasu KM** Yd No: 4844 Converted From: Crude Oil Tanker-2014 Loa 326.19 (BB) Br ex - Dght 20.480 Lbp 313.00 Br md 56.60 Dpth 28.60 Welded, 1 dk	**(B22H2OF) FSO, Oil** Single Hull Liq: 306,300; Liq (Oil): 306,300 Compartments: 6 Wing Ta, 6 Ta, 2 Wing Slop Ta, ER 3 Cargo Pump (s): 3x5400m³/hr Manifold: Bow/CM: 158m	**1 oil engine** driving 1 FP propeller Total Power: 16,983kW (23,090hp) 12.0kn B&W 6S80MC 1 x 2 Stroke 6 Cy. 800 x 3056 16983kW (23090bhp) Hitachi Zosen Corp-Japan AuxGen: 3 x 750kW 450V 60Hz a.c Fuel: 396.5 (d.f.) 3680.8 (r.f.) 58.2pd

9613977 *9V9208* -	**SOUTHERNPEC 9** **Southernpec (Singapore) Shipping Pte Ltd** - *Singapore* *Singapore* MMSI: 566068000 Official number: 396772	**3,433** 1,581 5,483	Class: BV (CC)	**2011-08 Taizhou Zhongxing Shipyard — Taizhou ZJ** Yd No: ZX0801 Loa 100.72 Br ex 16.00 Dght 6.200 Lbp 92.70 Br md - Dpth 8.00 Welded, 1 dk	**(A13B2TP) Products Tanker** Double Hull (13F) Liq: 5,518; Liq (Oil): 5,518 Compartments: 6 Wing Ta, 6 Wing Ta, ER Ice Capable	**1 oil engine** reduction geared to sc. shaft driving 1 FP propeller Total Power: 1,914kW (2,602hp) 12.0kn Daihatsu 6DKM-28 1 x 4 Stroke 6 Cy. 280 x 390 1914kW (2602bhp) Shaanxi Diesel Heavy Industry Co Lt-China AuxGen: 3 x 400kW 50Hz a.c Fuel: 290.0
9614115 *9V9209* -	**SOUTHERNPEC 11** **Southernpec (Singapore) Shipping Pte Ltd** - *Singapore* *Singapore* MMSI: 566103000 Official number: 369773	**5,138** 2,272 7,000	Class: BV	**2011-06 Zhejiang Shenzhou Shipbuilding Co Ltd — Xiangshan County ZJ** Yd No: SZ09010 Loa 118.00 Br ex 17.63 Dght 6.600 Lbp 110.00 Br md 17.60 Dpth 9.00 Welded, 1 dk	**(A13B2TP) Products Tanker** Double Hull (13F) Liq: 8,165; Liq (Oil): 8,165 Compartments: 5 Wing Ta, 5 Wing Ta, ER	**1 oil engine** reduction geared to sc. shaft driving 1 FP propeller Total Power: 2,574kW (3,500hp) 12.5kn Yanmar 6N330-EN 1 x 4 Stroke 6 Cy. 330 x 440 2574kW (3500bhp) Qingdao Zichai Boyang Diesel EngineCo Ltd-China AuxGen: 2 x 340kW 60Hz a.c Fuel: 417.8
9620279 *9V9270* -	**SOUTHERNPEC 12** **Southernpec (Singapore) Shipping Pte Ltd** - *Singapore* *Singapore* MMSI: 566094000 Official number: 396858	**5,036** 2,272 7,000	Class: BV	**2011-07 Zhejiang Fanshun Shipbuilding Industry Co Ltd — Yueqing ZJ** Yd No: FS07/06 Converted From: Products Tanker-2013 Loa 118.00 Br ex - Dght 6.600 Lbp 110.00 Br md 17.60 Dpth 9.00 Welded, 1 dk	**(A12B2TR) Chemical/Products Tanker** Double Hull (13F) Liq: 8,050; Liq (Oil): 8,050 Compartments: 5 Wing Ta, 5 Wing Ta, ER	**1 oil engine** reduction geared to sc. shaft driving 1 FP propeller Total Power: 2,665kW (3,623hp) 12.5kn Guangzhou 6G32 1 x 4 Stroke 6 Cy. 320 x 480 2665kW (3623bhp) Guangzhou Diesel Engine Factory CoLtd-China AuxGen: 3 x 312kW 60Hz a.c Fuel: 499.0
9200598 *VRXN7* -	**SOUTHERNPEC 18** *ex* Bow De Jin *-2011* **SPC Oscar Pte Ltd** - *Hong Kong* *Hong Kong* MMSI: 477005000 Official number: HK-0803	**6,294** 3,549 11,752 T/cm 19.7	Class: BV (NK)	**1999-11 Fukuoka Shipbuilding Co Ltd — Fukuoka FO** Yd No: 1209 Loa 117.00 (BB) Br ex - Dght 8.766 Lbp 110.10 Br md 20.00 Dpth 11.20 Welded, 1 dk	**(A12B2TR) Chemical/Products Tanker** Double Hull (13F) Liq: 12,286; Liq (Oil): 12,500 Cargo Heating Coils Compartments: 20 Wing Ta (s.stl), ER 20 Cargo Pump (s): 20x200m³/hr Manifold: Bow/CM: 54m	**1 oil engine** driving 1 FP propeller Total Power: 3,884kW (5,281hp) 13.5kn B&W 6L35MC 1 x 2 Stroke 6 Cy. 350 x 1050 3884kW (5281bhp) Makita Corp-Japan AuxGen: 2 x 450kW a.c Fuel: 81.0 (d.f.) 668.0 (r.f.)
9408530 *V7PO6* -	**SOUTHPORT** **Southport Navigation Ltd** Thome Ship Management Pte Ltd SatCom: Inmarsat C 453832569 *Majuro* *Marshall Islands* MMSI: 538003268 Official number: 3268	**62,856** 35,798 115,462 T/cm 99.7	Class: NV	**2008-09 STX Shipbuilding Co Ltd — Changwon (Jinhae Shipyard)** Yd No: 3002 Loa 249.99 (BB) Br ex 44.03 Dght 14.917 Lbp 239.00 Br md 44.00 Dpth 21.00 Welded, 1 dk	**(A13A2TW) Crude/Oil Products Tanker** Double Hull (13F) Liq: 126,211; Liq (Oil): 126,211 Cargo Heating Coils Compartments: 12 Wing Ta, 2 Wing Slop Ta, ER 3 Cargo Pump (s): 3x3000m³/hr Manifold: Bow/CM: 126.4m	**1 oil engine** driving 1 FP propeller Total Power: 13,560kW (18,436hp) 15.0kn MAN-B&W 6S60MC-C 1 x 2 Stroke 6 Cy. 600 x 2400 13560kW (18436bhp) STX Engine Co Ltd-South Korea AuxGen: 3 x a.c Fuel: 180.0 (d.f.) 2600.0 (r.f.)
7200295 *3DN6001* -	**SOUTHSEA MANA** *ex* F. B. Walker *-1972* **Southsea Island Cruises Ltd** - *Suva* *Fiji* Official number: 333493	*134* 46 -		**1955 F.B. Walker & Sons, Inc. — Pascagoula, Ms** L reg 26.43 Br ex 6.71 Dght - Lbp - Br md - Dpth 2.75 Welded, 1 dk	**(B21A20S) Platform Supply Ship**	**2 oil engines** driving 2 FP propellers Total Power: 442kW (600hp) 10.0kn General Motors 6-110 2 x 2 Stroke 6 Cy. 127 x 142 each-221kW (300bhp) General Motors Corp-USA
9577484 *PJJQ* -	**SOUTHWIND** **Southwind BV** Avra Towage BV *Willemstad* *Curacao* MMSI: 306058000	**298** 89 -	Class: RI (BV)	**2011-03 Vitawani Shipbuilding Sdn Bhd — Sibu** Yd No: VT8 Loa 31.10 Br ex 9.52 Dght 3.500 Lbp 28.72 Br md 9.50 Dpth 4.20 Welded, 1 dk	**(B32A2ST) Tug**	**2 oil engines** reduction geared to sc. shafts driving 2 FP propellers Total Power: 2,354kW (3,200hp) 11.0kn Cummins KTA-50-M2 2 x Vee 4 Stroke 16 Cy. 159 x 159 each-1177kW (1600bhp) Cummins Engine Co Ltd-United Kingdom AuxGen: 2 x 80kW 50Hz a.c
8116609 *FPYC* CH 518388	**SOUVIENS TOI** **CAPAM** - *Cherbourg* *France* MMSI: 228326000 Official number: 518388	*107* 34 45	Class: (BV)	**1982-09 Con. Mec. de Normandie — Cherbourg** Yd No: 23/02 Loa 23.02 Br ex - Dght 3.401 Lbp 19.69 Br md 7.56 Dpth 3.97 Welded, 1 dk	**(B11A2FS) Stern Trawler** Ins: 76 Compartments: 1 Ho, ER 1 Ha:	**1 oil engine** with clutches, flexible couplings & sr geared to sc. shaft driving 1 CP propeller Total Power: 441kW (600hp) 11.0kn Poyaud A12150SRHM 1 x Vee 4 Stroke 12 Cy. 150 x 180 441kW (600bhp) Poyaud S.S.C.M.-Surgeres
8855918 - -	**SOU'WESTER** **Sahlman Seafoods Inc** - *Kingstown* *St Vincent & The Grenadines* Official number: 400265	*101* 69 -		**1984 Steiner Shipyard, Inc. — Bayou La Batre, Al** Loa 22.86 Br ex - Dght - Lbp 20.33 Br md 6.71 Dpth 3.32 Welded, 1 dk	**(B11A2FT) Trawler**	**1 oil engine** geared to sc. shaft driving 1 FP propeller Total Power: 268kW (364hp) Cummins KT-1150-M 1 x 4 Stroke 6 Cy. 159 x 159 268kW (364bhp) Cummins Engine Co Inc-USA
9094444 *JD2183* -	**SOUYOU MARU** *ex* Seiyo Maru *-2006* **Okii Kaiun KK** - *Etajima, Hiroshima* *Japan* MMSI: 431402032 Official number: 140254	*499* - 1,524		**2005-12 K.K. Murakami Zosensho — Naruto** Loa 74.92 Br ex - Dght 3.910 Lbp 70.00 Br md 12.50 Dpth 6.86 Welded, 1 dk	**(A31A2GX) General Cargo Ship** 1 Ha: ER (40.2 x 10.2)	**1 oil engine** driving 1 Propeller Total Power: 1,471kW (2,000hp) 13.0kn Hanshin LH34LA 1 x 4 Stroke 6 Cy. 340 x 640 1471kW (2000bhp) The Hanshin Diesel Works Ltd-Japan
8003149 *WDG5448* -	**SOVEREIGN** *ex* Toby Tide *-2012* **Ocean Marine Services Inc** - *Nikiski, AK* *United States of America* MMSI: 367546770 Official number: 618175	**709** 212 1,200	Class: AB	**1980-03 Halter Marine, Inc. — Moss Point, Ms** Yd No: 878 Loa 54.87 Br ex 12.22 Dght 3.683 Lbp 51.82 Br md 12.20 Dpth 4.27 Welded, 1 dk	**(B21A20S) Platform Supply Ship**	**2 oil engines** reverse reduction geared to sc. shafts driving 2 FP propellers Total Power: 1,654kW (2,248hp) 12.0kn Caterpillar D399SCAC 2 x Vee 4 Stroke 16 Cy. 159 x 203 each-827kW (1124bhp) Caterpillar Tractor Co-USA AuxGen: 2 x 125kW Thrusters: 1 Thwart. FP thruster (f)
8512281 *9HUE9* -	**SOVEREIGN** *ex* Sovereign Of The Seas *-2008* **Pullmantur Cruises Sovereign Ltd** Pullmantur Cruises Ship Management Ltd SatCom: Inmarsat C 424953910 *Valletta* *Malta* MMSI: 249539000 Official number: 8512281	**73,529** 45,194 7,546	Class: GL (NV)	**1987-12 Chantiers de l'Atlantique — St-Nazaire** Yd No: A29 Loa 268.33 (BB) Br ex - Dght 7.800 Lbp 236.02 Br md 32.21 Dpth 15.12 Welded, 6 dks	**(A37A2PC) Passenger/Cruise** Passengers: cabins: 1141; berths: 2524	**4 oil engines** with clutches, flexible couplings & sr geared to sc. shafts driving 2 CP propellers Total Power: 20,476kW (27,840hp) 19.0kn Pielstick 9PC20L400 4 x 4 Stroke 9 Cy. 400 x 550 each-5119kW (6960bhp) Alsthom Atlantique-France AuxGen: 6 x 2110kW 450V a.c Thrusters: 2 Thwart. CP thruster (f) Fuel: 2373.0 (d.f.)
7514000 *XUBC4* -	**SOVEREIGN** *ex* Okhotsk 1 *-2011* *ex* Okhotsk *-2010* *ex* Okhotsk 1 *-2010* *ex* Okhotsk *-2003* *ex* Pere No. 1 *-2003* *ex* Kazu Maru *-1991* *ex* Yusho Maru No. 8 *-1990* *ex* Fukuyo Maru No. 28 *-1984* **Dolmus Ltd** - *Phnom Penh* *Cambodia* MMSI: 514449000 Official number: 1075551	**414** 203 310	Class: IS (RS) (KR)	**1975-10 Niigata Engineering Co Ltd — Niigata NI** Yd No: 1373 Converted From: Fish Carrier-2010 Converted From: Fishing Vessel-2000 Loa 46.02 Br ex 8.03 Dght 3.228 Lbp 40.20 Br md 8.00 Dpth 3.47 Riveted\Welded, 1 dk	**(B11B2FV) Fishing Vessel**	**1 oil engine** driving 1 FP propeller Total Power: 640kW (870hp) Niigata 6M28KGHS 1 x 4 Stroke 6 Cy. 280 x 440 640kW (870bhp) Niigata Engineering Co Ltd-Japan Fuel: 67.0 (d.f.)
9643532 *ZGBZ4* -	**SOVEREIGN** *ex* Harbour Island *-2013* **Northstar Holdings Ltd** Fairport Inc (Fairport Yacht Support) *The Creek* *Cayman Islands (British)* MMSI: 319931000 Official number: 743641	**1,100** 330 -	Class: AB	**2011-10 Newcastle Shipyards LLC — Palm Coast FL** Yd No: 1002 Loa 55.00 Br ex 10.30 Dght 4.130 Lbp 47.31 Br md 10.00 Dpth 5.50 Welded, 1 dk	**(X11A2YP) Yacht**	**2 oil engines** reduction geared to sc. shafts driving 2 FP propellers Total Power: 2,460kW (3,344hp) 12.0kn Caterpillar 3512B 2 x Vee 4 Stroke 12 Cy. 170 x 190 each-1230kW (1672bhp) Caterpillar Inc-USA

9390939 **SOVEREIGN**
A8MJ7
-
Multinvest Inc
Dynacom Tankers Management Ltd
Monrovia *Liberia*
MMSI: 636013353
Official number: 13353

42,331 Class: AB
21,943
74,998
T/cm
69.2

2009-01 Sungdong Shipbuilding & Marine Engineering Co Ltd — Tongyeong
Yd No: 3032
Loa 228.00 (BB) Br ex 32.27 Dght 14.430
Lbp 219.00 Br md 32.24 Dpth 20.90
Welded, 1 dk

(A13A2TW) Crude/Oil Products Tanker
Double Hull (13F)
Liq: 80,609; Liq (Oil): 83,104
Cargo Heating Coils
Compartments: 12 Wing Ta, 2 Wing Slop Ta, ER
3 Cargo Pump (s): 3x2300m³/hr
Manifold: Bow/CM: 113.2m

1 oil engine driving 1 FP propeller
Total Power: 12,240kW (16,642hp) 15.3kn
MAN-B&W 6S60MC
1 x 2 Stroke 6 Cy. 600 x 2292 12240kW (16642bhp)
Doosan Engine Co Ltd-South Korea
AuxGen: 3 x 680kW a.c
Fuel: 127.5 (d.f.) 1995.0 (r.f.)

9120841 **SOVEREIGN MAERSK**
OYGA2
-
A P Moller - Maersk A/S
A P Moller
SatCom: Inmarsat B 321947620
Aarhus *Denmark (DIS)*
MMSI: 219476000
Official number: D3620

92,198 Class: AB (LR)
53,625 ✠ Classed LR until 14/4/09
110,381
T/cm
124.0

1997-09 Odense Staalskibsvaerft A/S — Munkebo (Lindo Shipyard) Yd No: 160
Loa 346.98 (BB) Br ex 42.92 Dght 14.940
Lbp 331.54 Br md 42.80 Dpth 24.10
Welded, 1 dk

(A33A2CC) Container Ship (Fully Cellular)
TEU 9578 incl 817 ref C
Compartments: ER, 20 Cell Ho
20 Ha: ER

1 oil engine driving 1 FP propeller
Total Power: 54,840kW (74,560hp) 24.6kn
B&W 12K90MC
1 x 2 Stroke 12 Cy. 900 x 2550 54840kW (74560bhp)
Mitsui Engineering & Shipbuilding CLtd-Japan
AuxGen: 5 x 3000kW 6600V 60Hz a.c
Boilers: AuxB (o.f.) 10.2kgf/cm² (10.0bar), AuxB (ex.g.) 10.2kgf/cm² (10.0bar)
Thrusters: 1 Thwart. FP thruster (f); 2 Thwart. FP thruster (a)

8213213 **SOVEREIGNTY**
WDB4543 *ex* Dona Liliana *ex* Diamond Express *-1988*
- **Trident Seafoods Corp**

Seattle, WA *United States of America*
MMSI: 366899520
Official number: 651752

585 Class: (NV) (AB)
175
1,200

1982-12 Leevac Shipyards Inc — Jennings LA
Yd No: 287
Converted From: Offshore Supply Ship-1990
Loa 50.30 Br ex - Dght 3.469
Lbp 47.10 Br md 11.60 Dpth 3.97
Welded, 1 dk

(B11A2FS) Stern Trawler

2 oil engines reverse reduction geared to sc. shafts driving 2 FP propellers
Total Power: 1,324kW (1,800hp) 12.0kn
G.M. (Detroit Diesel) 16V-149
2 x Vee 2 Stroke 16 Cy. 146 x 146 each-662kW (900bhp)
General Motors Detroit DieselAllison Divn-USA
AuxGen: 2 x 325kW 440V 60Hz a.c
Thrusters: 1 Thwart. FP thruster (f)

8834249 **SOVETSKAYA GAVAN**
UBIF8 *ex* Daebo Ace *-2008* *ex* Aqua Stoli *-2005*
- *ex* Catherine *-1998* *ex* Nucet *-1993*
Eastern Shipping Co Ltd (Vostochnaya Sudokhodnaya Kompaniya OOO)
-
Nakhodka *Russia*
MMSI: 273335810

7,620 Class: RS (LR) (KR) (RN)
2,883 Classed LR until 5/11/05
9,891
T/cm
19.0

1989-07 Santierul Naval Galati S.A. — Galati
Yd No: 801
Loa 127.72 (BB) Br ex - Dght 7.600
Lbp 117.94 Br md 20.00 Dpth 10.00
Welded, 1 dk

(A13B2TP) Products Tanker
Single Hull
Liq: 9,323; Liq (Oil): 9,323
Compartments: 5 Ta, 6 Wing Ta, ER
3 Cargo Pump (s): 3x63m³/hr
Manifold: Bow/CM: 53m
Ice Capable

1 oil engine driving 1 FP propeller
Total Power: 4,531kW (6,160hp) 11.0kn
MAN K6SZ52/105CL
1 x 2 Stroke 6 Cy. 520 x 1050 4531kW (6160bhp)
U.C.M. Resita S.A.-Resita
AuxGen: 3 x 320kW a.c
Boilers: 2 AuxB (o.f.) 7.1kgf/cm² (7.0bar), e (ex.g.) 7.1kgf/cm² (7.0bar)

8705046 **SOVETSKAYA KONSTITUTSIYA**
UBHR
AB-0034 **JSC Arkhangelsk Trawl Fleet (A/O 'Arkhangelskiy Tralflot')**
-
Murmansk *Russia*
MMSI: 273290700
Official number: 870592

3,816 Class: RS
1,144
1,727

1988-08 Stocznia im Komuny Paryskiej — Gdynia
Yd No: B408/34
Loa 94.00 Br ex 15.92 Dght 5.670
Lbp 85.00 Br md 15.90 Dpth 10.00
Welded, 2 dks

(B11A2FG) Factory Stern Trawler
Grain: 300; Ins: 1,500

1 oil engine geared to sc. shaft driving 1 CP propeller
Total Power: 3,935kW (5,350hp) 15.8kn
Sulzer 6ZL40/48
1 x 4 Stroke 6 Cy. 400 x 480 3935kW (5350bhp)
Zaklady Urzadzen Technicznych'Zgoda' SA-Poland
AuxGen: 1 x 1200kW a.c, 2 x 800kW a.c

7636860 **SOVETSKAYA RODINA**
UFHV
- **Shipping Co 'River-Sea' LLC (River-Sea Shipping Agency Co Ltd)**
River Sea Management Co Ltd
Taganrog *Russia*
MMSI: 273322500

2,827 Class: RS
1,231
3,846

1979-09 Estaleiros Navais de Viana do Castelo S.A. — Viana do Castelo Yd No: 108
Loa 118.80 Br ex 13.21 Dght 4.230
Lbp 112.50 Br md 13.01 Dpth 6.00
Welded, 1 dk

(A31A2GX) General Cargo Ship
Bale: 3,000
Compartments: 4 Ho, ER
4 Ha: 2 (13.1 x 9.2)2 (18.6 x 9.2)ER

2 oil engines driving 2 FP propellers
Total Power: 1,280kW (1,740hp) 11.3kn
S.K.L. 6NVD48A-2U
2 x 4 Stroke 6 Cy. 320 x 480 each-640kW (870bhp)
VEB Schwermaschinenbau "KarlLiebknecht" (SKL)-Magdeburg
AuxGen: 3 x 100kW 400V 50Hz a.c
Thrusters: 1 Thwart. CP thruster (f)
Fuel: 57.0 (r.f.)

8838582 **SOVETSKIY SOYUZ**
UCJJ
- **Government of The Russian Federation**
Federal State Unitary Enterprise 'Atomflot'
SatCom: Inmarsat A 1404104
Murmansk *Russia*
MMSI: 273132300
Official number: 830268

20,646 Class: (RS)
6,194
2,750

1989-12 Baltiyskiy Zavod — Leningrad Yd No: 703
Loa 150.02 Br ex 30.00 Dght 11.000
Lbp 130.59 Br md - Dpth 17.23
Welded, 4 dks

(B34C2SI) Icebreaker
Double Hull
Cranes: 3x16t
Ice Capable

2 turbo electric Steam Turbs driving 6 gen. each 9000kW 780V a.c Connecting to 6 elec. motors each (8800kW) driving 3 FP propellers
Total Power: 55,200kW (75,050hp) 19.5kn
Russkiy TGG-27.50M5
2 x steam Turb each-27600kW (37525shp), made: 1989 in the U.S.S.R.

8826852 **SOVETSKOYE**
UDFM
- **Bosantur DVA Co Ltd**
-
Nakhodka *Russia*
MMSI: 273899500

871 Class: RS
227
332

1989-12 Zavod "Leninskaya Kuznitsa" — Kiyev
Yd No: 273
Loa 53.75 Br ex 10.71 Dght 4.361
Lbp 47.93 Br md 10.50 Dpth 6.02
Welded

(B11A2FS) Stern Trawler
Ins: 218
Ice Capable

1 oil engine driving 1 CP propeller
Total Power: 970kW (1,319hp) 12.6kn
S.K.L. 8NVD48A-2U
1 x 4 Stroke 8 Cy. 320 x 480 970kW (1319bhp)
VEB Schwermaschinenbau "KarlLiebknecht" (SKL)-Magdeburg
AuxGen: 3 x 160kW a.c, 1 x 300kW a.c
Fuel: 164.0 (d.f.)

9211042 **SOVGAVAN**
-
- **Tayfun Co Ltd**
-

117 Class: (RS)
35
37

1999-01 Sretenskiy Sudostroitelnyy Zavod — Sretensk Yd No: 313
Loa 25.45 Br ex 6.80 Dght 2.390
Lbp 22.00 Br md - Dpth 3.30
Welded, 1 dk

(B11A2FS) Stern Trawler
Grain: 64
Ice Capable

1 oil engine driving 1 FP propeller
Total Power: 162kW (220hp)
S.K.L. 6NVD26A-2
1 x 4 Stroke 6 Cy. 180 x 260 162kW (220bhp)
SKL Motoren u. Systemtechnik AG-Magdeburg

8133449 **SOVREMENNIK**
-
- **Ekofim JSC (TOO 'Ekofim')**
-

784 Class: (RS)
235
373

1982-11 Zavod "Leninskaya Kuznitsa" — Kiyev
Yd No: 1515
Loa 54.84 Br ex 9.96 Dght 4.140
Lbp 50.29 Br md 9.80 Dpth 5.06
Welded, 1 dk

(B11A2FG) Factory Stern Trawler
Ins: 414
Ice Capable

1 oil engine driving 1 CP propeller
Total Power: 736kW (1,001hp) 12.0kn
S.K.L. 8NVD48AU
1 x 4 Stroke 8 Cy. 320 x 480 736kW (1001bhp)
VEB Schwermaschinenbau "KarlLiebknecht" (SKL)-Magdeburg
Fuel: 180.0 (d.f.)

8618542 **SOVREMENNIK**
- *ex* Koufuku *-2010* *ex* Polina *-2008*
- *ex* Hiro Maru No. 8 *-2004*
ex Tatsu Maru No. 58 *-2003*
ex Ryoan Maru No. 78 *-1994*
Pacific Fishing JSC
-
Kholmsk *Russia*

494 Class: RS
229
-

1987-02 KK Kanasashi Zosen — Shizuoka SZ
Yd No: 3125
Loa 48.11 (BB) Br ex 8.23 Dght 3.201
Lbp 42.02 Br md 8.21 Dpth 3.51
Welded, 1 dk

(B11B2FV) Fishing Vessel
Ins: 333

1 oil engine with clutches, flexible couplings & sr reverse geared to sc. shaft driving 1 FP propeller
Total Power: 736kW (1,001hp)
Akasaka DM26K
1 x 4 Stroke 6 Cy. 260 x 440 736kW (1001bhp)
Akasaka Tekkosho KK (Akasaka DieselLtd)-Japan

9363209 **SOWA MARU**
JD2194
- **YK Yoshimoto Kisen**
-
Komatsushima, Tokushima *Japan*
Official number: 140264

498
-
1,300

2005-12 KK Ura Kyodo Zosensho — Awaji HG
Yd No: 325
Loa 64.76 Br ex - Dght 4.270
Lbp 60.00 Br md 10.00 Dpth 4.50
Welded, 1 dk

(A12A2TC) Chemical Tanker
Double Hull (13F)
2 Cargo Pump (s): 2x600m³/hr

1 oil engine reduction geared to sc. shaft driving 1 FP propeller
Total Power: 1,029kW (1,399hp) 11.0kn
Niigata 6M28BGT
1 x 4 Stroke 6 Cy. 280 x 480 1029kW (1399bhp)
Niigata Engineering Co Ltd-Japan

9241047 **SOWENA**
UDVL *ex* Swissco Super *-2007*
- **Caspiy Ak Jhelken Ltd**
Ark Shipping Co Ltd
Novorossiysk *Russia*

294 Class: BV
88
-

2000-09 Tuong Aik (Sarawak) Sdn Bhd — Sibu
Yd No: 9902
Loa 36.00 Br ex - Dght -
Lbp - Br md 9.00 Dpth 4.00
Welded, 1 dk

(B32A2ST) Tug

2 oil engines reduction geared to sc. shafts driving 2 FP propellers
Total Power: 1,766kW (2,402hp) 10.5kn
Caterpillar 3512TA
2 x Vee 4 Stroke 12 Cy. 170 x 190 each-883kW (1201bhp)
Caterpillar Inc-USA
AuxGen: 2 x 110kW a.c
Fuel: 200.0 (d.f.)

8651025 **SOWENNA**
EIHB5
S175 **Tadgh O'Callaghan**
-
Skibbereen *Irish Republic*
Official number: 404503

107
44
-

1989 Halmatic Ltd — Havant
Loa 18.04 Br ex - Dght -
Lbp - Br md - Dpth -
Bonded, 1 dk

(B11A2FS) Stern Trawler
Hull Material: Reinforced Plastic

1 oil engine driving 1 Propeller
Total Power: 270kW (367hp)

7718668 *JQUB* -	**SOYA** **Government of Japan (Ministry of Land, Infrastructure & Transport) (The Coastguard)** - *Tokyo* *Japan* MMSI: 431800020 Official number: 121639	*2,973* - -		**1978-11 Nippon Kokan KK (NKK Corp) — Yokohama KN (Tsurumi Shipyard)** Yd No: 961 Loa 98.60 Br ex 15.64 Dght 5.200 Lbp 90.00 Br md 15.60 Dpth 8.00 Welded, 3 dks	**(B34H2SQ) Patrol Vessel** Ice Capable	**2 oil engines** geared to sc. shafts driving 2 FP propellers Total Power: 11,474kW (15,600hp) 20.0kn Pielstick 12PC2-5V-400 2 x Vee 4 Stroke 12 Cy. 400 x 460 each-5737kW (7800bhp) Nippon Kokan KK (NKK Corp)-Japan AuxGen: 1 x 520kW 450V 60Hz a.c, 1 x 120kW 450V 60Hz a.c
8910548 *JH3180* -	**SOYA** *ex* Inuwashi Maru No. 2 *-2012* *ex* Tateiwa Maru No. 2 *-2009* *ex* Akeno Maru *-2008* **Nihon Tug-Boat Co Ltd** - *Ishikari, Hokkaido* *Japan* MMSI: 431301187 Official number: 130073	*196* - -		**1989-09 Kanagawa Zosen — Kobe** Yd No: 331 Loa 33.00 Br ex - Dght 3.100 Lbp 29.50 Br md 9.40 Dpth 4.00 Welded	**(B32A2ST) Tug**	**2 oil engines** Geared Integral to driving 2 Z propellers Total Power: 2,648kW (3,600hp) 13.5kn Niigata 6L28HX 2 x 4 Stroke 6 Cy. 280 x 370 each-1324kW (1800bhp) Niigata Engineering Co Ltd-Japan
9587726 *LFPW* F-100-B	**SOYA** **Arthur AS** Ronny Erlandsen *Vardo* *Norway*	**204** 81 172		**2010-01 Skogsoy Bat AS — Mandal** Yd No: 79 Loa 20.95 Br ex - Dght - Lbp 19.00 Br md 8.00 Dpth 6.00 Welded, 1 dk	**(B11B2FV) Fishing Vessel** Hull Material: Aluminium Alloy	**1 oil engine** reduction geared to sc. shaft driving 1 Propeller Total Power: 478kW (650hp) Volvo Penta D16 1 x 4 Stroke 6 Cy. 144 x 165 478kW (650bhp) AB Volvo Penta-Sweden AuxGen: 1 x 92kW a.c, 1 x 62kW a.c
5302661 *SKYO* -	**SOYA III** *ex* Piltank *-2008* *ex* Rya *-1966* *ex* Shell S 8 *-1958* *ex* Shell 8 *-1947* *ex* Tankman *-1946* *ex* Soya III *-1941* **Walleniusrederierna AB (Wallenius Lines AB)** - *Stockholm* *Sweden* MMSI: 265519920	**131** 39 135		**1936 Lofholmsvarvet — Stockholm** Lengthened-1939 L reg 27.74 Br ex 5.31 Dght 2.198 Lbp - Br md 5.29 Dpth - Riveted, 1 dk	**(A13B2TU) Tanker (unspecified)** Liq: 172; Liq (Oil): 172 Compartments: 8 Ta, ER	**1 oil engine** driving 1 FP propeller Total Power: 74kW (101hp) 7.5kn Jonkopings 1 x 4 Stroke 2 Cy. 270 x 340 74kW (101bhp) AB Jonkopings Motorfabrik-Sweden Fuel: 5.0 (d.f.) 0.5pd
8907462 *V3WE7* -	**SOYA MARU** *ex* Fengshun 19 *-2003* *ex* Komei Maru No. 8 *-2002* **Green Ocean Marine Co Ltd** Dalian Fengshun Shipping Agency Co Ltd *Belize City* *Belize* MMSI: 312064000 Official number: 160210513	**1,924** 1,033 1,409	Class: IT	**1989-05 Hitachi Zosen Mukaishima Marine Co Ltd — Onomichi HS** Yd No: 17 Converted From: Bulk Aggregates Carrier-2003 Loa 65.59 Br ex 13.30 Dght 4.411 Lbp 60.00 Br md 13.20 Dpth 6.20 Welded, 1 dk	**(A31A2GX) General Cargo Ship** Grain: 970 Compartments: 1 Ho, ER 1 Ha: ER	**1 oil engine** geared to sc. shaft driving 1 FP propeller Total Power: 1,471kW (2,000hp) 10.0kn Hanshin 6LU35G 1 x 4 Stroke 6 Cy. 350 x 550 1471kW (2000bhp) The Hanshin Diesel Works Ltd-Japan Thrusters: 1 Thwart. FP thruster (f)
9661211 *D5DA5* -	**SOYA MAY** **Soya May Maritime LLC** Foremost Maritime Corp *Monrovia* *Liberia* MMSI: 636015825 Official number: 15825	**48,090** 27,571 87,146	Class: AB	**2013-03 Hudong-Zhonghua Shipbuilding (Group) Co Ltd — Shanghai** Yd No: H1661A Loa 229.00 (BB) Br ex - Dght 14.200 Lbp 221.00 Br md 36.80 Dpth 19.90 Welded, 1 dk	**(A21A2BC) Bulk Carrier** Grain: 99,636 Compartments: 7 Ho, ER 7 Ha: ER	**1 oil engine** driving 1 FP propeller Total Power: 10,500kW (14,276hp) 14.5kn MAN-B&W 5S60MC-C8 1 x 2 Stroke 5 Cy. 600 x 2400 10500kW (14276bhp) Hudong Heavy Machinery Co Ltd-China AuxGen: 3 x 600kW a.c Fuel: 180.0 (d.f.) 3060.0 (r.f.)
8858207 *UARQ* -	**SOYANA** **Variant Fishing Co (Rybolovetskaya Firma 'Variant')** - *Murmansk* *Russia* MMSI: 273294100	**775** 220 413	Class: RS	**1975-12 Zavod "Leninskaya Kuznitsa" — Kiyev** Yd No: 1416 Loa 54.82 Br ex 9.96 Dght 4.110 Lbp 50.29 Br md 9.80 Dpth 5.00 Welded, 1 dk	**(B11B2FV) Fishing Vessel** Ice Capable	**1 oil engine** driving 1 CP propeller Total Power: 736kW (1,001hp) 11.7kn S.K.L. 8NVD48A-2U 1 x 4 Stroke 8 Cy. 320 x 480 736kW (1001bhp) VEB Schwermaschinenbau "KarlLiebknecht" (SKL)-Magdeburg AuxGen: 2 x 150kW a.c, 2 x 100kW a.c
9552848 *3FDO6* -	**SOYO** **Collie Shipholding SA** Hachiuma Steamship Co Ltd (Hachiuma Kisen KK) *Panama* *Panama* MMSI: 373613000 Official number: 4405212	**50,872** 28,676 91,867	Class: NK	**2012-07 Oshima Shipbuilding Co Ltd — Saikai NS** Yd No: 10700 Loa 235.00 (BB) Br ex - Dght 13.060 Lbp 230.00 Br md 43.00 Dpth 18.55 Welded, 1 dk	**(A21A2BC) Bulk Carrier** Double Hull Grain: 108,633 Compartments: 5 Ho, ER 5 Ha: ER	**1 oil engine** driving 1 FP propeller Total Power: 11,910kW (16,193hp) 14.5kn Mitsubishi 6UEC60LSII 1 x 2 Stroke 6 Cy. 600 x 2300 11910kW (16193bhp) Mitsubishi Heavy Industries Ltd-Japan Fuel: 3810.0
9475208 *C6YN3* -	**SOYO** **Mint LNG I Ltd** Angola LNG Supply Services LLC SatCom: Inmarsat C 431101132 *Nassau* *Bahamas* MMSI: 311038500 Official number: 9000354	**100,723** 32,706 82,858 T/cm 104.4	Class: AB	**2011-08 Samsung Heavy Industries Co Ltd — Geoje** Yd No: 1810 Loa 285.36 (BB) Br ex - Dght 12.150 Lbp 274.00 Br md 43.40 Dpth 26.40 Welded, 1 dk	**(A11A2TN) LNG Tanker** Double Hull Liq (Gas): 154,948 4 x Gas Tank (s); 4 membrane (s.stl) pri horizontal 8 Cargo Pump (s): 8x1850m³/hr Manifold: Bow/CM: 141.7m	**4 diesel electric oil engines** driving 3 gen. each 11000kW 6600V a.c 1 gen. of 5500kW 6600V a.c Connecting to 2 elec. motors each (13600kW) driving 1 FP propeller Total Power: 39,900kW (54,247hp) 19.5kn Wartsila 12V50DF 3 x Vee 4 Stroke 12 Cy. 500 x 580 each-11400kW (15499bhp) (new engine 2011) Wartsila France SA-France Wartsila 6L50DF 1 x 4 Stroke 6 Cy. 500 x 580 5700kW (7750bhp) (new engine 2011) Wartsila France SA-France Thrusters: 1 Tunnel thruster (f) Fuel: 1490.0 (d.f.) 4831.0 (r.f.)
9073452 *JGKL* KN1-777	**SOYO MARU** **Fisheries Research Agency** - SatCom: Inmarsat A 1206232 *Yokohama, Kanagawa* *Japan* MMSI: 431673000 Official number: 134348	*892* - 519		**1994-10 Mitsubishi Heavy Industries Ltd. — Shimonoseki** Yd No: 982 Loa 67.50 (BB) Br ex 11.44 Dght 4.780 Lbp 60.00 Br md 11.40 Dpth 7.10 Welded, 1 dk	**(B31A2SR) Research Survey Vessel**	**2 oil engines** with clutches, flexible couplings & sr geared to sc. shaft driving 1 CP propeller Total Power: 2,354kW (3,200hp) Daihatsu 6DLM-26 2 x 4 Stroke 6 Cy. 260 x 340 each-1177kW (1600bhp) Daihatsu Diesel Manufacturing Co Lt-Japan AuxGen: 1 x 360kW 450V 60Hz a.c, 2 x 300kW 450V 60Hz a.c Thrusters: 1 Thwart. CP thruster (f) Fuel: 16.0 (d.f.) 273.0 (r.f.) 6.5pd
9371634 *YJVA2* -	**SOYO TIDE** **Sonatide Marine Ltd** Tidewater Marine International Inc *Port Vila* *Vanuatu* MMSI: 576044000 Official number: 1710	**549** 164 325	Class: AB	**2007-06 PT Pan-United Shipyard Indonesia — Batam** Yd No: 155 Loa 36.00 Br ex - Dght 4.500 Lbp 31.63 Br md 12.00 Dpth 5.60 Welded, 1 dk	**(B32A2ST) Tug**	**2 oil engines** reduction geared to sc. shafts driving 2 CP propellers Total Power: 4,920kW (6,690hp) Caterpillar 3608 2 x 4 Stroke 8 Cy. 280 x 300 each-2460kW (3345bhp) Caterpillar Inc-USA AuxGen: 2 x 277kW a.c Fuel: 170.0
7213096 *DTAC4* -	**SOYOKAZE** *ex* Soyokaze Maru *-1989* **O Yang Fisheries Co Ltd** - SatCom: Inmarsat C 444074912 *Busan* *South Korea* Official number: 9511004-6260008	**2,984** 1,427 3,580	Class: (KR) (NK)	**1972-06 Taguma Zosen KK — Onomichi HS** Yd No: 106 Loa 97.16 Br ex 14.81 Dght 6.265 Lbp 90.00 Br md 14.79 Dpth 7.60 Riveted\Welded, 1 dk	**(A34A2GR) Refrigerated Cargo Ship** Ins: 3,895 Compartments: 3 Ho, ER 3 Ha: (4.5 x 4.0)2 (4.8 x 4.0)ER Cranes: 6x2t; Derricks: 6x5t	**1 oil engine** driving 1 FP propeller Total Power: 4,119kW (5,600hp) 14.8kn Niigata 12MGV40X 1 x Vee 4 Stroke 12 Cy. 400 x 520 4119kW (5600bhp) Niigata Engineering Co Ltd-Japan AuxGen: 2 x 500kW 450V 60Hz a.c Fuel: 1188.0 22.0pd
7001728 - -	**SOYU MARU** **Dae Han Jung Suru Co Ltd** - *South Korea*	*174* - -		**1969 Osaka Shipbuilding Co Ltd — Osaka OS** Yd No: 310 Loa 24.52 Br ex 8.64 Dght 2.693 Lbp 22.61 Br md 8.62 Dpth 3.79 Riveted\Welded, 1 dk	**(B32A2ST) Tug**	**2 oil engines** driving 2 FP propellers Total Power: 1,544kW (2,100hp) Daihatsu 8PSHTCM-26D 2 x 4 Stroke 8 Cy. 260 x 320 each-772kW (1050bhp) Daihatsu Kogyo-Japan AuxGen: 2 x 48kW 225V a.c Fuel: 41.5 8.0pd
9033115 *JJ3689* -	**SOYU MARU** **Hayakoma Unyu KK** - *Kobe, Hyogo* *Japan* Official number: 129277	*199* - - T/cm 2.6		**1991-02 Kanagawa Zosen — Kobe** Yd No: 355 Loa 33.00 Br ex 11.00 Dght 3.100 Lbp 28.50 Br md 9.20 Dpth 4.20 Welded, 1 dk	**(B32A2ST) Tug**	**2 oil engines** Geared Integral to driving 2 Z propellers Total Power: 2,648kW (3,600hp) 13.7kn Niigata 6L28HX 2 x 4 Stroke 6 Cy. 280 x 370 each-1324kW (1800bhp) Niigata Engineering Co Ltd-Japan AuxGen: 2 x 96kW 225V 60Hz a.c Thrusters: 1 Thwart. FP thruster (f) Fuel: 5.0 (d.f.) 70.0 (r.f.) 7.5pd

8863381 - -	**SOYUZ** *ex* Unions *ex* Popisaare *-1993* - -	**117** 35 36	Class: (RS)	**1978-12 Sosnovskiy Sudostroitelnyy Zavod — Sosnovka** Yd No: 3280 Loa 25.51 Br ex 7.00 Dght 2.390 Lbp 22.00 Br md 6.80 Dpth 3.30 Welded, 1 dk	**(B11A2FS) Stern Trawler**	**1 oil engine** driving 1 FP propeller Total Power: 221kW (300hp) 10.0kn S.K.L. 6NVD26A-2 1 x 4 Stroke 6 Cy. 180 x 260 221kW (300bhp) (made 1977) VEB Schwermaschinenbau "KarlLiebknecht" (SKL)-Magdeburg
8726014 *UEYA* -	**SOYUZ** - **Sea Fishing Port Co Ltd (OOO 'Morskoy Rybnyy Port')** - *St Petersburg* *Russia* Official number: 870744	**270** 81 89	Class: RS	**1988-05 Brodogradiliste 'Tito' — Belgrade** Yd No: 1123 Loa 35.23 Br ex 9.49 Dght 3.270 Lbp 33.10 Br md 9.00 Dpth 4.50 Welded, 1 dk	**(B32A2ST) Tug** Ice Capable	**2 oil engines** driving 1 CP propeller Total Power: 1,854kW (2,520hp) 13.5kn Sulzer 6ASL25D 2 x 4 Stroke 6 Cy. 250 x 300 each-927kW (1260bhp) in Yugoslavia AuxGen: 1 x 150kW a.c
8835982 *UEPD* M-0601	**SOYUZ-1** *ex* Bussi-2 *-1993* **Gela Ltd** - *Murmansk* *Russia* MMSI: 273441350	**190** 57 70	Class: RS	**1990-10 Astrakhanskaya Sudoverf im. "Kirova" — Astrakhan** Yd No: 81 Loa 31.85 Br ex 7.08 Dght 2.101 Lbp 27.80 Br md 6.90 Dpth 3.15 Welded	**(B12B2FC) Fish Carrier** Ins: 100	**1 oil engine** geared to sc. shaft driving 1 FP propeller Total Power: 232kW (315hp) 10.2kn Daldizel 6CHSPN2A18-315 1 x 4 Stroke 6 Cy. 180 x 220 232kW (315bhp) Daldizel-Khabarovsk AuxGen: 2 x 25kW a.c Fuel: 14.0 (d.f.)
8832904 *UERX* -	**SOYUZ-2** *ex* PTR-300 No. 78 *-1993* **OOO Bionord (Bionord Co Ltd)** - *Murmansk* *Russia*	**164** 49 70	Class: (RS)	**1990-06 Astrakhanskaya Sudoverf im. "Kirova" — Astrakhan** Yd No: 78 Loa 31.86 Br ex 7.09 Dght 2.101 Lbp 27.80 Br md 6.90 Dpth 3.18 Welded, 1dk	**(B12B2FC) Fish Carrier** Ins: 100 Compartments: 2 Ho 2 Ha: 2 (2.1 x 2.4) Derricks: 2x1t	**1 oil engine** geared to sc. shaft driving 1 FP propeller Total Power: 232kW (315hp) 10.3kn Daldizel 6CHSPN2A18-315 1 x 4 Stroke 6 Cy. 180 x 220 232kW (315bhp) Daldizel-Khabarovsk AuxGen: 2 x 25kW a.c Fuel: 14.0 (d.f.)
8514734 - -	**SOZAN MARU** - **Rui Xiang HK Marine Co Ltd** -	*226* - -	Class: IZ	**1985-11 Kanagawa Zosen — Kobe** Yd No: 280 Loa 35.51 Br ex - Dght 3.101 Lbp 31.25 Br md 9.21 Dpth 4.22 Welded, 1 dk	**(B32A2ST) Tug**	**2 oil engines** Geared Integral to driving 2 Z propellers Total Power: 2,574kW (3,500hp) 12.9kn Fuji 6L27.5G 2 x 4 Stroke 6 Cy. 275 x 320 each-1287kW (1750bhp) Fuji Diesel Co Ltd-Japan
8306682 *4OAS* -	**SOZINA** - **Luka Bar-Preduzece** - *Bar* *Montenegro* MMSI: 262500080	*169* - -	Class: (JR)	**1983-12 Johann Oelkers KG — Hamburg** Yd No: 587 Loa 25.20 Br ex 8.69 Dght 3.720 Lbp 23.50 Br md 8.50 Dpth 3.61 Welded, 1 dk	**(B32A2ST) Tug**	**2 oil engines** with clutches, flexible couplings & sr geared to sc. shafts driving 2 Directional propellers Total Power: 1,176kW (1,598hp) 11.8kn Deutz RBA6M528 2 x 4 Stroke 6 Cy. 220 x 280 each-588kW (799bhp) Kloeckner Humboldt Deutz AG-West Germany AuxGen: 2 x 33kW 380V 50Hz a.c Fuel: 30.0 (d.f.)
9130717 *YD5066* -	**SOZO GLORY** - **PT Pande Astika Dharma** - *Benoa* *Indonesia*	**117** 35 -	Class: KI (GL)	**1995 Seri Modalwan Sdn Bhd — Sandakan** L reg 21.43 Br ex 6.82 Dght 2.940 Lbp 21.58 Br md 6.80 Dpth 3.50 Welded, 1 dk	**(B32A2ST) Tug**	**2 oil engines** reduction geared to sc. shafts driving 2 FP propellers Total Power: 692kW (940hp) 7.0kn Caterpillar 3408TA 2 x Vee 4 Stroke 8 Cy. 137 x 152 each-346kW (470bhp) Caterpillar Inc-USA AuxGen: 2 x 21kW 220/380V a.c
9401922 *9HA3546* -	**SOZON** *ex* Sanko Marble *-2014* **Sunshine Maritime Ltd** Eastern Mediterranean Maritime Ltd *Valletta* *Malta* MMSI: 229718000 Official number: 9401922	**30,488** 15,289 50,779	Class: NK	**2010-01 Oshima Shipbuilding Co Ltd — Saikai NS** Yd No: 10526 Loa 189.99 (BB) Br ex - Dght 12.260 Lbp 186.00 Br md 32.26 Dpth 17.31 Welded, 1 dk	**(A31A2GO) Open Hatch Cargo Ship** Double Hull Grain: 57,886; Bale: 57,782 TEU 306 Compartments: 8 Ho, ER 8 Ha: ER Cranes: 4x40t	**1 oil engine** driving 1 FP propeller Total Power: 10,187kW (13,850hp) 15.5kn MAN-B&W 5S60MC-C 1 x 2 Stroke 5 Cy. 600 x 2400 10187kW (13850bhp) Kawasaki Heavy Industries Ltd-Japan Fuel: 2350.0
8301840 *LZGB* -	**SOZOPOL-1** *ex* Sozopol *-2008* **Nautilus Metal Trade & Demolition Industry LLC** Valmar Oil Ltd *Bourgas* *Bulgaria* MMSI: 207021000 Official number: 311	**2,453** 990 3,261	Class: BR	**1982-12 Shipbuilding & Shiprepairing Yard 'Ivan Dimitrov' — Rousse** Yd No: 378 Loa 114.61 Br ex 13.26 Dght 3.790 Lbp 111.84 Br md 13.01 Dpth 5.52 Welded, 1 dk	**(A31A2GX) General Cargo Ship** Grain: 4,300; Bale: 4,297 Compartments: 4 Ho, ER 4 Ha: (17.6 x 9.1)3 (18.1 x 9.1)ER Ice Capable	**2 oil engines** driving 2 FP propellers Total Power: 970kW (1,318hp) 10.8kn S.K.L. 6NVD48A-2U 2 x 4 Stroke 6 Cy. 320 x 480 each-485kW (659bhp) VEB Schwermaschinenbau "KarlLiebknecht" (SKL)-Magdeburg
8725840 *UAYD* -	**SOZVEZDIYE** - **Luntos Co Ltd** - SatCom: Inmarsat M 627312210 *Petropavlovsk-Kamchatskiy* *Russia* MMSI: 273849000	**839** 252 338	Class: RS	**1988-07 Volgogradskiy Sudostroitelnyy Zavod — Volgograd** Yd No: 247 Loa 53.74 Br ex 10.71 Dght 4.500 Lbp 47.92 Br md 10.50 Dpth 6.00 Welded, 1 dk	**(B11A2FS) Stern Trawler** Ins: 218 Ice Capable	**1 oil engine** driving 1 CP propeller Total Power: 970kW (1,319hp) 12.7kn S.K.L. 8NVD48A-2U 1 x 4 Stroke 8 Cy. 320 x 480 970kW (1319bhp) VEB Schwermaschinenbau "KarlLiebknecht" (SKL)-Magdeburg AuxGen: 1 x 300kW a.c, 3 x 160kW a.c, 2 x 135kW a.c Fuel: 154.0 (d.f.)
8931164 *UBNG8* -	**SP-01** - **Transit Ltd** - *Petropavlovsk-Kamchatskiy* *Russia* Official number: 790198	**159** 47 164	Class: RS	**1979-07 Petropavlovsk-Kamchatskiy SRZ — Petropavlovsk-Kamchatskiy** Yd No: 1 Loa 35.75 Br ex 7.50 Dght 1.710 Lbp 33.50 Br md 7.20 Dpth 2.40 Welded, 1 dk	**(A31C2GD) Deck Cargo Ship** Ice Capable	**1 oil engine** geared to sc. shaft driving 1 FP propeller Total Power: 165kW (224hp) 8.8kn Daldizel 6CHNSP18/22 1 x 4 Stroke 6 Cy. 180 x 220 165kW (224bhp) Daldizel-Khabarovsk AuxGen: 2 x 14kW Fuel: 5.0 (d.f.)
9704142 *JVGR5* -	**SP 1** - **PT Berjaya Samudera Indonesia** - *Ulaanbaatar* *Mongolia* MMSI: 457900092 Official number: 34211313	**2,438** 905 3,943	Class: RI	**2013-11 Nantong Tongshun Shiprepair & Building Co Ltd — Nantong JS** Yd No: TS20121028 Loa 94.88 Br ex - Dght 4.160 Lbp 89.70 Br md 15.00 Dpth 6.05 Welded, 1 dk	**(B35E2TF) Bunkering Tanker** Double Hull (13F)	**2 oil engines** reduction geared to sc. shafts driving 2 FP propellers Total Power: 912kW (1,240hp) 7.0kn Weifang X6170ZC 2 x 4 Stroke 6 Cy. 170 x 200 each-456kW (620bhp) Weichai Power Co Ltd-China AuxGen: 2 x 60Hz a.c
9704154 *JVJF5* -	**SP 2** - **PT Berjaya Samudera Indonesia** - *Ulaanbaatar* *Mongolia* MMSI: 457900008 Official number: 34591313	**2,438** 905 3,500	Class: RI	**2013-12 Nantong Tongshun Shiprepair & Building Co Ltd — Nantong JS** Yd No: TS20121029 Loa 94.88 Br ex - Dght 4.160 Lbp 89.70 Br md 15.00 Dpth 6.05 Welded, 1 dk	**(B35E2TF) Bunkering Tanker** Double Hull (13F)	**2 oil engines** reduction geared to sc. shafts driving 2 Propellers Total Power: 912kW (1,240hp) 7.0kn Weifang X6170ZC 2 x 4 Stroke 6 Cy. 170 x 200 each-456kW (620bhp) Weichai Power Co Ltd-China
8931152 - -	**SP-02** - **Ust-Khayryuzovskiy Fish Cannery Plant (Ust-Khayryuzovskiy Rybokonservnyy Zavod)** -	**163** 49 161	Class: (RS)	**1980 Petropavlovsk-Kamchatskiy SRZ — Petropavlovsk-Kamchatskiy** Yd No: 2 Loa 35.75 Br ex 7.50 Dght 1.710 Lbp 33.50 Br md - Dpth 2.40 Welded, 1 dk	**(A31C2GD) Deck Cargo Ship** Ice Capable	**1 oil engine** geared to sc. shaft driving 1 FP propeller Total Power: 165kW (224hp) 8.8kn Daldizel 6CHNSP18/22 1 x 4 Stroke 6 Cy. 180 x 220 165kW (224bhp) Daldizel-Khabarovsk AuxGen: 2 x 14kW Fuel: 5.0 (d.f.)
9704166 *JVJG5* -	**SP 3** - **PT Berjaya Samudera Indonesia** - *Ulaanbaatar* *Mongolia* MMSI: 457900009	**2,438** 905 3,500	Class: RI	**2014-03 Nantong Tongshun Shiprepair & Building Co Ltd — Nantong JS** Yd No: TS20121030 Loa 94.88 Br ex - Dght 4.160 Lbp 89.70 Br md 15.00 Dpth 6.05 Welded, 1 dk	**(B35E2TF) Bunkering Tanker** Double Hull (13F)	**2 oil engines** reduction geared to sc. shafts driving 2 Propellers Total Power: 912kW (1,240hp) Weifang X6170ZC 2 x 4 Stroke 6 Cy. 170 x 200 each-456kW (620bhp) Weichai Power Co Ltd-China
8888329 - -	**SP-04** - **Preobrazheniye Trawler Fleet Base (Preobrazhenskaya Baza Tralovogo Flota)** - *Nakhodka* *Russia* Official number: 822187	**145** 58 164	Class: RS	**1982-09 Petropavlovsk-Kamchatskiy SRZ — Petropavlovsk-Kamchatskiy** Yd No: 4 Loa 35.75 Br ex 7.50 Dght 1.710 Lbp 33.48 Br md 7.20 Dpth 2.40 Welded, 1 dk	**(A31C2GD) Deck Cargo Ship**	**1 oil engine** geared to sc. shaft driving 1 FP propeller Total Power: 165kW (224hp) 7.8kn Daldizel 6CHNSP18/22 1 x 4 Stroke 6 Cy. 180 x 220 165kW (224bhp) Daldizel-Khabarovsk AuxGen: 2 x 14kW Fuel: 5.0 (d.f.)

8138736 - -	**SP-05** - **Vostretsovo Fishing Collective (Rybolovetskiy Kolkhoz imeni Vostretsova)** -	*145* 58 148	Class: (RS)	**1983**-08 **Petropavlovsk-Kamchatskiy SRZ — Petropavlovsk-Kamchatskiy** Yd No: 5 Loa 35.75 Br ex 7.50 Dght 1.710 Lbp 33.50 Br md - Dpth 2.42 Welded, 1 dk	**(A31C2GD) Deck Cargo Ship** Ice Capable	**1 oil engine** geared to sc. shaft driving 1 FP propeller Total Power: 165kW (224hp) 8.0kn Daldizel 6CHNSP18/22 1 x 4 Stroke 6 Cy. 180 x 220 165kW (224bhp) Daldizel-Khabarovsk AuxGen: 2 x 14kW Fuel: 7.0 (d.f.)
8228127 - -	**SP-06** - **Kama Co Ltd** - *Vladivostok* *Russia*	**145** 58 156	Class: RS	**1984**-06 **Petropavlovsk-Kamchatskiy SRZ — Petropavlovsk-Kamchatskiy** Yd No: 6 Loa 35.74 Br ex 7.40 Dght 1.710 Lbp 33.50 Br md 7.20 Dpth 2.42 Welded, 1 dk	**(A31C2GD) Deck Cargo Ship** Ice Capable	**1 oil engine** geared to sc. shaft driving 1 FP propeller Total Power: 165kW (224hp) 7.8kn Daldizel 6CHNSP18/22 1 x 4 Stroke 6 Cy. 180 x 220 165kW (224bhp) Daldizel-Khabarovsk AuxGen: 2 x 14kW Fuel: 7.0 (d.f.)
8726258 - -	**SP-08** - **Ustkamchatryba Co Ltd (OOO 'Ustkamchatryba')** -	**159** 47 186	Class: (RS)	**1986**-12 **Petropavlovsk-Kamchatskiy SRZ — Petropavlovsk-Kamchatskiy** Yd No: 8 Loa 35.75 Br ex 7.50 Dght 1.820 Lbp 33.50 Br md - Dpth 2.40 Welded, 1 dk	**(A31C2GD) Deck Cargo Ship** Ice Capable	**1 oil engine** geared to sc. shaft driving 1 FP propeller Total Power: 165kW (224hp) 8.8kn Daldizel 6CHNSP18/22 1 x 4 Stroke 6 Cy. 180 x 220 165kW (224bhp) Daldizel-Khabarovsk AuxGen: 2 x 14kW Fuel: 5.0 (d.f.)
8726272 *UHLX* -	**SP-10** - **MAG-SEA Tranzit Co Ltd** - *Magadan* *Russia*	**159** 47 145	Class: RS	**1988**-07 **Petropavlovsk-Kamchatskiy SRZ — Petropavlovsk-Kamchatskiy** Yd No: 10 Loa 35.75 Br ex 7.50 Dght 1.820 Lbp 33.50 Br md 7.20 Dpth 2.40 Welded, 1 dk	**(A31C2GD) Deck Cargo Ship** Ice Capable	**1 oil engine** geared to sc. shaft driving 1 FP propeller Total Power: 165kW (224hp) 8.8kn Daldizel 6CHNSP18/22 1 x 4 Stroke 6 Cy. 180 x 220 165kW (224bhp) Daldizel-Khabarovsk AuxGen: 2 x 14kW Fuel: 5.0 (d.f.)
8931138 - -	**SP-10** - **Murmansk Sea Construction Trust (A/O 'Murmanskmorstroy Trest)** -	*145* 56 158	Class: (RS)	**1977 Sudoremontnyy Zavod "Krasnaya Kuznitsa" — Arkhangelsk** Yd No: 10 Loa 35.75 Br ex 7.40 Dght 1.710 Lbp 33.50 Br md - Dpth 2.40 Welded, 1 dk	**(A31C2GD) Deck Cargo Ship** Ice Capable	**1 oil engine** geared to sc. shaft driving 1 FP propeller Total Power: 165kW (224hp) 8.5kn Daldizel 6CHNSP18/22 1 x 4 Stroke 6 Cy. 180 x 220 165kW (224bhp) Daldizel-Khabarovsk AuxGen: 1 x 14kW, 1 x 12kW Fuel: 6.0 (d.f.)
8834756 *UGYB* -	**SP-11** - **Velest Co Ltd** - *Petropavlovsk-Kamchatskiy* *Russia*	**159** 47 186	Class: (RS)	**1990**-08 **Petropavlovsk-Kamchatskiy SRZ — Petropavlovsk-Kamchatskiy** Yd No: 11 Loa 35.77 Br ex 7.50 Dght 1.821 Lbp 33.50 Br md 7.20 Dpth 2.42 Welded, 1 dk	**(A31C2GD) Deck Cargo Ship** Ice Capable	**1 oil engine** geared to sc. shaft driving 1 FP propeller Total Power: 165kW (224hp) 8.8kn Daldizel 6CHNSP18/22 1 x 4 Stroke 6 Cy. 180 x 220 165kW (224bhp) Daldizel-Khabarovsk AuxGen: 2 x 14kW Fuel: 5.0 (d.f.)
8931114 *UHQF* -	**SP-103** - **Transit Ltd** - *Petropavlovsk-Kamchatskiy* *Russia*	*161* 48 150	Class: RS	**1970**-07 **Sudoremontnyy Zavod "Yakor" — Sovetskaya Gavan** Yd No: 698/3 Loa 35.75 Br ex 7.50 Dght 1.710 Lbp 33.50 Br md 7.20 Dpth 2.40 Welded, 1 dk	**(A31C2GD) Deck Cargo Ship** Ice Capable	**1 oil engine** geared to sc. shaft driving 1 FP propeller Total Power: 165kW (224hp) 7.8kn Daldizel 6CHNSP18/22 1 x 4 Stroke 6 Cy. 180 x 220 165kW (224bhp) Daldizel-Khabarovsk AuxGen: 1 x 13kW Fuel: 7.8 (d.f.)
8931035 *UGFQ* -	**SP-111** - **Fazil Zabidogly Aliyev** - *Shakhtyorsk* *Russia*	*173* 58 163	Class: RS	**1971**-11 **Sudoremontnyy Zavod "Yakor" — Sovetskaya Gavan** Yd No: 698/11 Loa 35.75 Br ex 7.50 Dght 1.710 Lbp 33.48 Br md 7.22 Dpth 2.42 Welded, 1 dk	**(A31C2GD) Deck Cargo Ship** Ice Capable	**1 oil engine** geared to sc. shaft driving 1 FP propeller Total Power: 165kW (224hp) 7.8kn Daldizel 6CHNSP18/22 1 x 4 Stroke 6 Cy. 180 x 220 165kW (224bhp) (new engine 1976) Daldizel-Khabarovsk AuxGen: 2 x 13kW Fuel: 5.0 (d.f.)
8931009 *UCNG* -	**SP-114** - **Government of The Russian Federation** JSC Ltd 'Magadanskiy Morskoy Torgoviy Port' (JSC Ltd 'Magadan Marine Commerical Port') *Magadan* *Russia*	**161** 48 163	Class: RS	**1972**-08 **Sudoremontnyy Zavod "Yakor" — Sovetskaya Gavan** Yd No: 698/14 Loa 35.75 Br ex 7.50 Dght 1.710 Lbp 33.48 Br md - Dpth 2.42 Welded, 1 dk	**(A31C2GD) Deck Cargo Ship** Ice Capable	**1 oil engine** geared to sc. shaft driving 1 FP propeller Total Power: 165kW (224hp) 7.8kn Daldizel 6CHNSP18/22 1 x 4 Stroke 6 Cy. 180 x 220 165kW (224bhp) Daldizel-Khabarovsk AuxGen: 1 x 13kW a.c Fuel: 5.0 (d.f.)
8930990 *UDTX* -	**SP-115** - **Info-Usluga Co Ltd** - *Nakhodka* *Russia* Official number: 722241	*173* 58 163	Class: RS	**1972**-09 **Sudoremontnyy Zavod "Yakor" — Sovetskaya Gavan** Yd No: 698/15 Loa 35.75 Br ex 7.50 Dght 1.710 Lbp 33.48 Br md 7.20 Dpth 2.42 Welded, 1 dk	**(A31C2GD) Deck Cargo Ship** Ice Capable	**1 oil engine** geared to sc. shaft driving 1 FP propeller Total Power: 165kW (224hp) 7.8kn Daldizel 6CHNSP18/22 1 x 4 Stroke 6 Cy. 180 x 220 165kW (224bhp) Daldizel-Khabarovsk AuxGen: 1 x 12kW a.c Fuel: 12.0 (d.f.)
8966468 *UDJH* -	**SP-118** - **JSC Ltd 'Magadanskiy Morskoy Torgoviy Port' (JSC Ltd 'Magadan Marine Commerical Port')** - *Magadan* *Russia* Official number: 722203	**161** 48 163	Class: RS	**1972**-12 **Sudoremontnyy Zavod "Yakor" — Sovetskaya Gavan** Yd No: 698/18 Loa 35.72 Br ex 7.22 Dght 1.710 Lbp 33.83 Br md 7.20 Dpth 2.40 Welded, 1 dk	**(A31C2GD) Deck Cargo Ship** Ice Capable	**1 oil engine** geared to sc. shaft driving 1 FP propeller Total Power: 165kW (224hp) 7.8kn Daldizel 6CHNSP18/22 1 x 4 Stroke 6 Cy. 180 x 220 165kW (224bhp) Daldizel-Khabarovsk AuxGen: 2 x 12kW Fuel: 12.0 (d.f.)
8930574 - -	**SP-120** - **Boshnyakovskiy Open-Pit Coal Mine JSC (OAO 'Boshnyakovskiy Ugolnyy Razrez')** -	*173* 58 163	Class: (RS)	**1973**-09 **Sudoremontnyy Zavod "Yakor" — Sovetskaya Gavan** Yd No: 698/20 Loa 35.75 Br ex 7.50 Dght 1.710 Lbp 33.48 Br md - Dpth 2.40 Welded, 1 dk	**(A31C2GD) Deck Cargo Ship** Ice Capable	**1 oil engine** geared to sc. shaft driving 1 FP propeller Total Power: 165kW (224hp) 7.8kn Daldizel 6CHNSP18/22 1 x 4 Stroke 6 Cy. 180 x 220 165kW (224bhp) Daldizel-Khabarovsk AuxGen: 1 x 13kW Fuel: 3.0 (d.f.)
8930586 - -	**SP-121** - **Interregional Transportation Corp** - *Okhotsk* *Russia* Official number: 732493	*173* 58 163	Class: RS	**1973**-11 **Sudoremontnyy Zavod "Yakor" — Sovetskaya Gavan** Yd No: 698/21 Loa 35.75 Br ex 7.50 Dght 1.710 Lbp 33.48 Br md - Dpth 2.42 Welded, 1 dk	**(A31C2GD) Deck Cargo Ship** Ice Capable	**1 oil engine** geared to sc. shaft driving 1 FP propeller Total Power: 165kW (224hp) 7.8kn Daldizel 6CHNSP18/22 1 x 4 Stroke 6 Cy. 180 x 220 165kW (224bhp) Daldizel-Khabarovsk AuxGen: 2 x 12kW Fuel: 12.0 (d.f.)
8888331 - -	**SP-123** - **Preobrazhenskiy Fishing Combine JSC (ZAO PRDP 'Preobrazhenskiy Rybokombinat')** - *Nakhodka* *Russia* Official number: 732690	*173* 57 163	Class: RS	**1974**-10 **Sudoremontnyy Zavod "Yakor" — Sovetskaya Gavan** Yd No: 698/123 Loa 35.75 Br ex 7.50 Dght 1.710 Lbp 33.48 Br md 7.50 Dpth 2.42 Welded, 1 dk	**(A31C2GD) Deck Cargo Ship** Ice Capable	**1 oil engine** geared to sc. shaft driving 1 FP propeller Total Power: 165kW (224hp) 7.8kn Daldizel 6CHNSP18/22 1 x 4 Stroke 6 Cy. 180 x 220 165kW (224bhp) Daldizel-Khabarovsk AuxGen: 1 x 14kW a.c, 1 x 13kW a.c Fuel: 5.0 (d.f.)
8930653 - -	**SP-130** - -	**157** 47 163	Class: (RS)	**1976**-12 **Sudoremontnyy Zavod "Yakor" — Sovetskaya Gavan** Yd No: 698/30 Loa 35.75 Br ex 7.50 Dght 1.710 Lbp 33.48 Br md - Dpth 2.40 Welded, 1 dk	**(A31C2GD) Deck Cargo Ship** Ice Capable	**1 oil engine** geared to sc. shaft driving 1 FP propeller Total Power: 165kW (224hp) 7.8kn Daldizel 6CHNSP18/22 1 x 4 Stroke 6 Cy. 180 x 220 165kW (224bhp) Daldizel-Khabarovsk AuxGen: 2 x 13kW Fuel: 6.0 (d.f.)
8930691 - -	**SP-135** - -	*173* 58 163	Class: (RS)	**1978**-05 **Sudoremontnyy Zavod "Yakor" — Sovetskaya Gavan** Yd No: 698/35 Loa 35.75 Br ex 7.50 Dght 1.710 Lbp 33.48 Br md - Dpth 2.40 Welded, 1 dk	**(A31C2GD) Deck Cargo Ship** Ice Capable	**1 oil engine** geared to sc. shaft driving 1 FP propeller Total Power: 165kW (224hp) 8.0kn Daldizel 6CHNSP18/22 1 x 4 Stroke 6 Cy. 180 x 220 165kW (224bhp) Daldizel-Khabarovsk AuxGen: 1 x 13kW a.c Fuel: 3.0 (d.f.)

IMO / Call sign	Name / Owner / Manager / Flag	Tonnage	Class	Build / Dimensions	Type / Cargo	Machinery
9423138 *WDE2808* -	**SP AMBER** **Team Marine LLC** Edison Chouest Offshore LLC *Galliano, LA* *United States of America* MMSI: 368481000 Official number: 1201240	**626** 187 628	Class: AB	**2008-02 Gulf Ship LLC — Gulfport MS** Yd No: 241 Loa 33.52 Br ex - Dght 5.120 Lbp 32.18 Br md 12.80 Dpth 5.71 Welded, 1 dk	**(B32A2ST) Tug**	**2 oil engines** reduction geared to sc. shafts driving 2 Directional propellers Total Power: 4,700kW (6,390hp) Caterpillar 3516C 2 x Vee 4 Stroke 16 Cy. 170 x 215 each-2350kW (3195bhp) Caterpillar Inc-USA AuxGen: 2 x 233kW a.c
9498963 *V7S19* -	**SP AMSTERDAM** *ex* W-O Bondia *-2010* **SP Amsterdam Tanker Corp** Medallion Reederei GmbH *Majuro* *Marshall Islands* MMSI: 538003662 Official number: 3662	**5,256** 2,847 8,828 T/cm 17.6	Class: BV	**2009-12 Yangzhou Kejin Shipyard Co Ltd — Jiangdu JS** Yd No: 06041 Loa 110.00 (BB) Br ex - Dght 7.900 Lbp 105.05 Br md 18.60 Dpth 10.00 Welded, 1 dk	**(A12B2TR) Chemical/Products Tanker** Double Hull (13F) Liq: 9,612; Liq (Oil): 9,612 Cargo Heating Coils Compartments: 10 Wing Ta, ER 3 Cargo Pump (s): 3x750m³/hr Manifold: Bow/CM: 52.7m	**1 oil engine** reduction geared to sc. shaft driving 1 FP propeller Total Power: 2,500kW (3,399hp) 12.0kn Yanmar 6N330-EN 1 x 4 Stroke 6 Cy. 330 x 440 2500kW (3399bhp) Qingdao Zichai Boyang Diesel EngineCo Ltd-China AuxGen: 3 x 360kW 50Hz a.c Thrusters: 1 Tunnel thruster (f) Fuel: 100.0 (d.f.) 250.0 (r.f.)
9498975 *V7SJ2* -	**SP ATHENS** *ex* Buschur *-2010* **SP Athens Tanker Corp** Medallion Reederei GmbH *Majuro* *Marshall Islands* MMSI: 538003663 Official number: 3663	**5,256** 2,847 8,828 T/cm 17.6	Class: BV	**2010-01 Yangzhou Kejin Shipyard Co Ltd — Jiangdu JS** Yd No: 06042 Loa 110.00 (BB) Br ex - Dght 7.900 Lbp 105.05 Br md 18.60 Dpth 10.00 Welded, 1 dk	**(A12B2TR) Chemical/Products Tanker** Double Hull (13F) Liq: 9,623; Liq (Oil): 9,623 Cargo Heating Coils Compartments: 10 Wing Ta, ER 3 Cargo Pump (s): 3x750m³/hr Manifold: Bow/CM: 59.4m	**1 oil engine** reduction geared to sc. shaft driving 1 FP propeller Total Power: 2,500kW (3,399hp) 12.0kn Yanmar 6N330-EN 1 x 4 Stroke 6 Cy. 330 x 440 2500kW (3399bhp) Qingdao Zichai Boyang Diesel EngineCo Ltd-China AuxGen: 3 x 288kW 50Hz a.c Thrusters: 1 Tunnel thruster (f) Fuel: 108.0 (d.f.) 252.0 (r.f.)
9377585 *V7KM2* -	**SP BELGRADE** *ex* W-O Aviva *-2010* *ex* Noronha Sea *-2008* **SP Belgrade Shipping Corp** Medallion Reederei GmbH *Majuro* *Marshall Islands* MMSI: 538003621 Official number: 3621	**4,535** 2,425 7,695 T/cm 16.7	Class: NK (LR) (CC) Classed LR until 6/9/13	**2006-05 Nanjing Shenghua Shipbuilding Co Ltd — Nanjing JS** Yd No: 522 Loa 115.00 (BB) Br ex 17.60 Dght 6.800 Lbp 109.00 Br md 17.60 Dpth 8.70 Welded, 1 dk	**(A13B2TP) Products Tanker** Double Hull (13F) Liq: 8,500; Liq (Oil): 8,317 Compartments: 12 Wing Ta, 2 Wing Slop Ta, ER 2 Cargo Pump (s): 2x750m³/hr Manifold: Bow/CM: 44.1m	**1 oil engine** reverse reduction geared to sc. shaft driving 1 FP propeller Total Power: 2,206kW (2,999hp) 11.0kn Chinese Std. Type G8300ZC 1 x 4 Stroke 8 Cy. 300 x 380 2206kW (2999bhp) Ningbo CSI Power & Machinery GroupCo Ltd-China AuxGen: 3 x 300kW 400V 50Hz a.c Boilers: TOH (o.f.) 10.2kgf/cm² (10.0bar) Thrusters: 1 Thwart. FP thruster (f) Fuel: 275.0
9387152 *V7LT4* -	**SP BERLIN** *ex* W-O Mogba *-2010* *ex* Beckman Sea *-2009* **SP Berlin Shipping Corp** Medallion Reederei GmbH *Majuro* *Marshall Islands* MMSI: 538003623 Official number: 3623	**4,535** 2,425 7,691 T/cm 16.7	Class: NK (LR) (CC) Classed LR until 19/4/13	**2007-02 Nanjing Shenghua Shipbuilding Co Ltd — Nanjing JS** Yd No: 524 Loa 115.00 (BB) Br ex - Dght 6.800 Lbp 109.00 Br md 17.60 Dpth 8.71 Welded, 1 dk	**(A13B2TP) Products Tanker** Double Hull (13F) Liq: 8,317; Liq (Oil): 8,317 Cargo Heating Coils Compartments: 12 Wing Ta, 2 Wing Slop Ta, Wing ER 2 Cargo Pump (s): 2x750m³/hr Manifold: Bow/CM: 44.1m	**1 oil engine** with clutches, flexible couplings & reverse reduction geared to sc. shaft driving 1 FP propeller Total Power: 2,206kW (2,999hp) 11.0kn Chinese Std. Type G8300ZC 1 x 4 Stroke 8 Cy. 300 x 380 2206kW (2999bhp) Ningbo CSI Power & Machinery GroupCo Ltd-China AuxGen: 3 x 300kW 400V 50Hz a.c Boilers: TOH Thrusters: 1 Tunnel thruster (f) Fuel: 156.0 (d.f.) 234.0 (r.f.)
9471173 *V7PP4* -	**SP BOSTON** *ex* W-O Mubarik *-2010* **SP Boston Shipping Corp** Medallion Reederei GmbH *Majuro* *Marshall Islands* MMSI: 538090356 Official number: 3806	**4,599** 2,447 7,695 T/cm 16.7	Class: NK (LR) (CC) Classed LR until 8/8/13	**2008-08 Nanjing Shenghua Shipbuilding Co Ltd — Nanjing JS** Yd No: 538 Loa 115.00 (BB) Br ex 17.60 Dght 6.800 Lbp 109.00 Br md 17.60 Dpth 8.70 Welded, 1 dk	**(A13B2TP) Products Tanker** Double Hull (13F) Liq: 8,317; Liq (Oil): 8,317 Cargo Heating Coils Compartments: 6 Ta, 2 Slop Ta, ER 2 Cargo Pump (s): 2x750m³/hr Manifold: Bow/CM: 56.3m	**1 oil engine** reduction geared to sc. shaft driving 1 FP propeller Total Power: 2,206kW (2,999hp) 11.0kn Chinese Std. Type G8300ZC 1 x 4 Stroke 8 Cy. 300 x 380 2206kW (2999bhp) Ningbo CSI Power & Machinery GroupCo Ltd-China AuxGen: 3 x a.c Thrusters: 1 Tunnel thruster (f) Fuel: 125.0 (d.f.) 210.0 (r.f.)
9387164 *V7MI7* -	**SP BRUSSELS** *ex* W-O Mahalu *-2010* *ex* Tolson Sea *-2009* **SP Brussels Shipping Corp** Medallion Reederei GmbH *Majuro* *Marshall Islands* MMSI: 538003624 Official number: 3624	**4,535** 2,425 7,654 T/cm 16.7	Class: NK (LR) (CC) Classed LR until 3/10/13	**2007-07 Nanjing Shenghua Shipbuilding Co Ltd — Nanjing JS** Yd No: 525 Loa 115.00 (BB) Br ex - Dght 6.800 Lbp 109.00 Br md 17.60 Dpth 8.70 Welded, 1 dk	**(A13B2TP) Products Tanker** Double Hull (13F) Liq: 8,480; Liq (Oil): 8,317 Cargo Heating Coils Compartments: 12 Wing Ta, 2 Wing Slop Ta, ER 2 Cargo Pump (s): 2x750m³/hr Manifold: Bow/CM: 44.1m	**1 oil engine** reverse reduction geared to sc. shaft driving 1 FP propeller Total Power: 2,206kW (2,999hp) 11.0kn Chinese Std. Type G8300ZC 1 x 4 Stroke 8 Cy. 300 x 380 2206kW (2999bhp) Ningbo CSI Power & Machinery GroupCo Ltd-China AuxGen: 3 x 300kW 400V 50Hz a.c Boilers: TOH (o.f.) 10.2kgf/cm² (10.0bar) Thrusters: 1 Thwart. FP thruster (f) Fuel: 275.0
9423140 *WDE2897* -	**SP CORAL** **Team Marine LLC** Edison Chouest Offshore LLC *Galliano, LA* *United States of America* MMSI: 367331070 Official number: 1201242	**626** 187 629	Class: AB	**2008-02 Gulf Ship LLC — Gulfport MS** Yd No: 242 Loa 33.54 Br ex - Dght 5.120 Lbp 32.20 Br md 12.81 Dpth 5.71 Welded, 1 dk	**(B32A2ST) Tug**	**2 oil engines** reduction geared to sc. shafts driving 2 Directional propellers Total Power: 4,700kW (6,390hp) Caterpillar 3516C 2 x Vee 4 Stroke 16 Cy. 170 x 215 each-2350kW (3195bhp) Caterpillar Inc-USA AuxGen: 2 x 234kW a.c Fuel: 333.0 (r.f.)
9418389 *V7QY5* -	**SP DELHI** *ex* W-O Djam *-2010* **SP Delhi Tanker Corp** Medallion Reederei GmbH SatCom: Inmarsat C 453833554 *Majuro* *Marshall Islands* MMSI: 538003474 Official number: 3474	**2,148** 967 3,600 T/cm 10.0	Class: LR ✠ **100A1** SS 01/2014 Double Hull oil tanker carriage of oils with a FP exceeding 60 degree C ESP LI ✠ **LMC** **UMS** Eq.Ltr: R†; Cable: 440.0/34.0 U3 (a)	**2009-01 Hangzhou Dongfeng Shipbuilding Co Ltd — Hangzhou ZJ** (Hull) Yd No: 2006-24 **2009-01 Volharding Shipyards B.V. — Foxhol** Yd No: 629 Loa 83.40 (BB) Br ex 12.94 Dght 5.660 Lbp 79.50 Br md 12.90 Dpth 7.45 Welded, 1 dk	**(A13B2TP) Products Tanker** Double Hull (13F) Liq: 3,478; Liq (Oil): 3,650 Cargo Heating Coils Compartments: 10 Wing Ta, 1 Slop Ta, ER 2 Cargo Pump (s): 2x440m³/hr Manifold: Bow/CM: 39m	**1 oil engine** reduction geared to sc. shaft driving 1 CP propeller Total Power: 1,560kW (2,121hp) Wartsila 8L20 1 x 4 Stroke 8 Cy. 200 x 280 1560kW (2121bhp) Wartsila Finland Oy-Finland AuxGen: 2 x 825kW 440V 60Hz a.c Boilers: TOH (o.f.) 8.2kgf/cm² (8.0bar), TOH (ex.g.) 8.2kgf/cm² (8.0bar) Thrusters: 1 Tunnel thruster (f)
9418391 *V7RL4* -	**SP DUBAI** *ex* W-O Chokdee *-2010* **SP Dubai Tanker Corp** Medallion Reederei GmbH SatCom: Inmarsat C 453834119 *Majuro* *Marshall Islands* MMSI: 538003533 Official number: 3533	**2,148** 967 3,799 T/cm 10.0	Class: LR ✠ **100A1** SS 07/2009 Double Hull oil tanker carriage of oils with a FP exceeding 60 degree C ESP LI ✠ **LMC** **UMS** Eq.Ltr: Q†; Cable: 44.0/34.0 U3 (a)	**2009-07 Hangzhou Dongfeng Shipbuilding Co Ltd — Hangzhou ZJ** (Hull) Yd No: 2006-25 **2009-07 Volharding Shipyards B.V. — Foxhol** Yd No: 654 Loa 83.40 (BB) Br ex 12.94 Dght 5.660 Lbp 79.50 Br md 12.90 Dpth 7.45 Welded, 1 dk	**(A13B2TP) Products Tanker** Double Hull (13F) Liq: 3,476; Liq (Oil): 3,650 Cargo Heating Coils Compartments: 10 Wing Ta, 1 Slop Ta, ER 2 Cargo Pump (s): 2x450m³/hr Manifold: Bow/CM: 39m	**1 oil engine** with clutches, flexible couplings & sr geared to sc. shaft driving 1 CP propeller Total Power: 1,560kW (2,121hp) 11.0kn Wartsila 8L20 1 x 4 Stroke 8 Cy. 200 x 280 1560kW (2121bhp) Wartsila Finland Oy-Finland AuxGen: 2 x 325kW 440V 60Hz a.c Boilers: TOH (o.f.) 10.2kgf/cm² (10.0bar), TOH (ex.g.) 10.2kgf/cm² (10.0bar) Thrusters: 1 Tunnel thruster (f)
9418406 *9HA2661* -	**SP DUBLIN** *ex* W-O Kesak *-2009* **SP Dublin Tanker Corp** Medallion Reederei GmbH *Valletta* *Malta* MMSI: 215164000 Official number: 9418406	**2,143** 967 3,798 T/cm 10.0	Class: LR ✠ **100A1** SS 11/2009 Double Hull oil tanker carriage of oils with a FP exceeding 60 degree C ESP LI ✠ **LMC** **UMS** Eq.Ltr: Q†; Cable: 440.0/34.0 U3 (a)	**2009-11 Hangzhou Dongfeng Shipbuilding Co Ltd — Hangzhou ZJ** (Hull) Yd No: 2006-26 **2009-11 Volharding Shipyards B.V. — Foxhol** Yd No: 655 Loa 83.40 (BB) Br ex 12.94 Dght 5.650 Lbp 79.50 Br md 12.90 Dpth 7.45 Welded, 1 dk	**(A13B2TP) Products Tanker** Double Hull (13F) Liq: 3,476; Liq (Oil): 3,650 Compartments: 10 Wing Ta, 1 Slop Ta, ER 2 Cargo Pump (s): 2x450m³/hr Manifold: Bow/CM: 39m	**1 oil engine** with clutches, flexible couplings & sr geared to sc. shaft driving 1 CP propeller Total Power: 1,560kW (2,121hp) 11.0kn Wartsila 8L20 1 x 4 Stroke 8 Cy. 200 x 280 1560kW (2121bhp) Wartsila Finland Oy-Finland AuxGen: 2 x 325kW 440V 60Hz a.c Boilers: TOH (o.f.) 16.3kgf/cm² (16.0bar), TOH (ex.g.) 16.3kgf/cm² (16.0bar) Thrusters: 1 Tunnel thruster (f)
8915419 *3FRB3* -	**SP GAS 01** *ex* Boral Gas *-2012* **Cong Ty Co Phan Van Tai Dau Khi Sai Gon** - *Panama* *Panama* MMSI: 352172000 Official number: 4501113	**2,602** 780 2,139 T/cm 9.2	Class: AB	**1991-01 Fulton Marine N.V. — Ruisbroek** Yd No: 181 Loa 84.30 (BB) Br ex - Dght 5.010 Lbp 78.30 Br md 13.60 Dpth 7.20 Welded, 1dk	**(A11B2TG) LPG Tanker** Double Bottom Entire Compartment Length Liq (Gas): 2,300 3 x Gas Tank (s); 3 independent (C.mn.stl) cyl horizontal 3 Cargo Pump (s) Manifold: Bow/CM: 44m	**1 oil engine** sr geared to sc. shaft driving 1 FP propeller Total Power: 1,504kW (2,045hp) 13.0kn Wartsila 6R32 1 x 4 Stroke 6 Cy. 320 x 350 1504kW (2045bhp) Wartsila Diesel Oy-Finland AuxGen: 2 x 600kW a.c Thrusters: 1 Tunnel thruster

IMO / Call sign	Name / Owner	Tonnage	Class	Builder / Dimensions	Type	Machinery
8915421 *3FTW2* -	**SP GAS 02** *ex* Pacific Gas *-2013* **Cong Ty Co Phan Van Tai Dau Khi Sai Gon** - *Panama* *Panama* MMSI: 372778000 Official number: 44556PEXT	**2,602** 780 2,139 T/cm 9.4	Class: AB	**1991-04 Fulton Marine N.V. — Ruisbroek** Yd No: 182 Loa 84.30 (BB) Br ex - Dght 5.010 Lbp 78.90 Br md 13.60 Dpth 7.20 Welded, 1 dk	**(A11B2TG) LPG Tanker** Double Bottom Entire Compartment Length Liq (Gas): 2,190 3 x Gas Tank (s); 3 independent (C.mn.stl) cyl horizontal 3 Cargo Pump (s) Manifold: Bow/CM: 44m	**1 oil engine** sr geared to sc. shaft driving 1 CP propeller Total Power: 2,045kW (2,780hp) 13.0kn Wartsila 6R32 1 x 4 Stroke 6 Cy. 320 x 350 2045kW (2780bhp) Wartsila Diesel Oy-Finland AuxGen: 2 x 600kW 415V 50Hz a.c, 1 x 240kW 415V 50Hz a.c Thrusters: 1 Thwart. CP thruster (f) Fuel: 258.9 (d.f.) 9.5pd
9423152 *WDE2900* -	**SP IVORY** - **Team Marine LLC** Edison Chouest Offshore LLC *Galliano, LA* *United States of America* MMSI: 367331110 Official number: 1201238	**626** 187 629	Class: AB	**2008-02 Gulf Ship LLC — Gulfport MS** Yd No: 243 Loa 33.54 Br ex - Dght 5.120 Lbp 32.20 Br md 12.81 Dpth 5.71 Welded, 1 dk	**(B32A2ST) Tug**	**2 oil engines** reduction geared to sc. shafts driving 2 Directional propellers Total Power: 4,700kW (6,390hp) Caterpillar 3516C 2 x Vee 4 Stroke 16 Cy. 170 x 215 each-2350kW (3195bhp) Caterpillar Inc-USA AuxGen: 2 x 233kW a.c Fuel: 333.0 (r.f.)
8865080 - -	**SP MARINE** *ex* Taisho Maru No. 2 *-2008* **SP Marine Engineering Co Ltd** - *Busan* *South Korea* Official number: BSR080221	*198* - 500		**1992-09 Shinosaki Zosen — Kumamoto** Yd No: 105 L reg 44.00 Br ex - Dght 2.900 Lbp - Br md 8.00 Dpth 3.40 Welded, 1 dk	**(A12A2TC) Chemical Tanker**	**1 oil engine** driving 1 FP propeller Total Power: 441kW (600hp) Yanmar MF24-HT 1 x 4 Stroke 6 Cy. 240 x 420 441kW (600bhp) Yanmar Diesel Engine Co Ltd-Japan
9423164 *WDE3266* -	**SP PEARL** - **Team Marine LLC** Edison Chouest Offshore LLC *Galliano, LA* *United States of America* MMSI: 367336580 Official number: 1201239	**626** 187 629	Class: AB	**2008-04 Gulf Ship LLC — Gulfport MS** Yd No: 244 Loa 33.54 Br ex - Dght 5.120 Lbp 32.20 Br md 12.81 Dpth 5.71 Welded, 1 dk	**(B32A2ST) Tug**	**2 oil engines** reduction geared to sc. shafts driving 2 Directional propellers Total Power: 4,700kW (6,390hp) Caterpillar 3516C 2 x Vee 4 Stroke 16 Cy. 170 x 215 each-2350kW (3195bhp) Caterpillar Inc-USA AuxGen: 2 x 234kW a.c Fuel: 333.0 (r.f.)
9547453 *YDA4376* -	**SP POWER I** - **PT Multi Niaga Sukses Jakarta** - *Jakarta* *Indonesia* Official number: 5214	**181** 54 -	Class: KI	**2008-02 Kiong Nguong Shipbuilding Contractor Co — Sibu** Yd No: 2056 Loa 26.00 Br ex - Dght 3.000 Lbp 24.23 Br md 7.93 Dpth 3.65 Welded, 1 dk	**(B32A2ST) Tug**	**2 oil engines** reduction geared to sc. shafts driving 2 Propellers Total Power: 1,618kW (2,200hp) Mitsubishi S12A2-MPTK 2 x Vee 4 Stroke 12 Cy. 150 x 160 each-809kW (1100bhp) Mitsubishi Heavy Industries Ltd-Japan
9547465 *YDA4387* -	**SP POWER II** - **PT Multi Niaga Sukses Jakarta** - *Jakarta* *Indonesia* Official number: 5239	**181** 54 -	Class: KI	**2008-06 Kiong Nguong Shipbuilding Contractor Co — Sibu** Yd No: 2057 Loa 26.00 Br ex - Dght 3.000 Lbp 23.33 Br md 7.93 Dpth 3.65 Welded, 1 dk	**(B32A2ST) Tug**	**2 oil engines** reduction geared to sc. shafts driving 2 Propellers Total Power: 1,716kW (2,334hp) Mitsubishi S12A2-MPTK 2 x Vee 4 Stroke 12 Cy. 150 x 160 each-858kW (1167bhp) Mitsubishi Heavy Industries Ltd-Japan
7612876 *YDA4421* -	**SP POWER IX** *ex* Takasu Maru *-2008* **PT Multi Niaga Sukses Jakarta** - *Jakarta* *Indonesia* Official number: 5428	**252** 76 -	Class: KI	**1976-06 Fukae Zosen K.K. — Etajima** Yd No: 151 Loa 31.55 Br ex - Dght 2.980 Lbp 27.01 Br md 8.81 Dpth 3.81 Welded, 1 dk	**(B32A2ST) Tug**	**2 oil engines** reduction geared to sc. shaft driving 1 FP propeller Total Power: 2,060kW (2,800hp) Yanmar 6ZL-UT 2 x 4 Stroke 6 Cy. 280 x 340 each-1030kW (1400bhp) Yanmar Diesel Engine Co Ltd-Japan
8726296 - -	**SPA-002** - **OOO 'Terminal-Zapad'** - *Petropavlovsk-Kamchatskiy* *Russia* Official number: 863670	**162** 48 167	Class: RS	**1987-06 Sudoremontnyy Zavod "Yakor" — Sovetskaya Gavan** Yd No: 820 Loa 35.82 Br ex 7.20 Dght 1.850 Lbp 33.63 Br md - Dpth 2.40 Welded, 1 dk	**(A31C2GD) Deck Cargo Ship** Ice Capable	**1 oil engine** driving 1 FP propeller Total Power: 220kW (299hp) 8.7kn S.K.L. 6NVD26A-2 1 x 4 Stroke 6 Cy. 180 x 260 220kW (299bhp) VEB Schwermaschinenbau "KarlLiebknecht" (SKL)-Magdeburg AuxGen: 1 x 14kW, 1 x 13kW Fuel: 56.0 (d.f.)
8726313 - -	**SPA-004** - **Sakhalin Basin Emergency-Rescue Department (Sakhalinskoye Basseynovoye Avariyno-Spasatelnoye Upravleniye)** - *Korsakov* *Russia*	**189** 57 118 T/cm 2.0	Class: RS	**1988-07 Sudoremontnyy Zavod "Yakor" — Sovetskaya Gavan** Yd No: 822 Converted From: Deck Cargo Vessel Loa 35.82 Br ex 7.20 Dght 1.850 Lbp 33.63 Br md - Dpth 2.40 Welded, 1 dk	**(B34P2QV) Salvage Ship** Ice Capable	**1 oil engine** geared to sc. shaft driving 1 FP propeller Total Power: 220kW (299hp) 8.7kn Daldizel 6CHNSP18/22-300 1 x 4 Stroke 6 Cy. 180 x 220 220kW (299bhp) Daldizel-Khabarovsk AuxGen: 1 x 14kW, 1 x 13kW Fuel: 16.6 (d.f.) 0.9pd
8726325 - -	**SPA-005** - **Provideniya Port Authority (Providenskiy MTP)** - *Provideniya* *Russia* Official number: 875170	**162** 48 167	Class: RS	**1988-05 Sudoremontnyy Zavod "Yakor" — Sovetskaya Gavan** Yd No: 823 Loa 35.82 Br ex 7.20 Dght 1.850 Lbp 33.63 Br md - Dpth 2.40 Welded, 1 dk	**(A31C2GD) Deck Cargo Ship** Ice Capable	**1 oil engine** geared to sc. shaft driving 1 FP propeller Total Power: 220kW (299hp) 8.7kn Daldizel 6CHNSP18/22-300 1 x 4 Stroke 6 Cy. 180 x 220 220kW (299bhp) Daldizel-Khabarovsk AuxGen: 1 x 14kW, 1 x 13kW Fuel: 56.0 (d.f.)
8726600 *UHPT* -	**SPA-007** - **Aleksandrovsk Sakhalinskiy Marine Port** - *Aleksandrovsk-Sakhalinskiy* *Russia*	**162** 48 167	Class: RS	**1988-09 Sudoremontnyy Zavod "Yakor" — Sovetskaya Gavan** Yd No: 841 Loa 35.82 Br ex 7.20 Dght 1.850 Lbp 33.63 Br md 7.20 Dpth 2.40 Welded, 1 dk	**(A31C2GD) Deck Cargo Ship** Ice Capable	**1 oil engine** geared to sc. shaft driving 1 FP propeller Total Power: 220kW (299hp) 8.7kn Daldizel 6CHNSP18/22-300 1 x 4 Stroke 6 Cy. 180 x 220 220kW (299bhp) Daldizel-Khabarovsk AuxGen: 1 x 14kW, 1 x 13kW Fuel: 56.0 (d.f.)
8729793 *UGFA* -	**SPA-008 KAPITAN MUROMTSEV** *ex* Kapitan Muromtsev *-2011* *ex* SPA-008 *-1992* **MAG-SR Transit Co Ltd** - *Magadan* *Russia* Official number: 883104	**162** 48 167	Class: RS	**1988-12 Sudoremontnyy Zavod "Yakor" — Sovetskaya Gavan** Yd No: 842 Loa 35.84 Br ex - Dght 1.851 Lbp 33.63 Br md 7.21 Dpth 2.42 Welded, 1 dk	**(A31C2GD) Deck Cargo Ship**	**1 oil engine** geared to sc. shaft driving 1 FP propeller Total Power: 230kW (313hp) 8.8kn Daldizel 6CHNSP18/22-300 1 x 4 Stroke 6 Cy. 180 x 220 230kW (313bhp) Daldizel-Khabarovsk AuxGen: 1 x 14kW, 1 x 13kW Fuel: 56.0 (d.f.)
8730388 - -	**SPA-010** - **OOO 'Terminal-Zapad'** - *Petropavlovsk-Kamchatskiy* *Russia*	**162** 48 167	Class: RS	**1989-07 Sudoremontnyy Zavod "Yakor" — Sovetskaya Gavan** Yd No: 851 Loa 35.84 Br ex 7.20 Dght 1.850 Lbp 33.63 Br md - Dpth 2.40 Welded, 1 dk	**(A31C2GD) Deck Cargo Ship** Ice Capable	**1 oil engine** geared to sc. shaft driving 1 FP propeller Total Power: 220kW (299hp) 8.8kn Daldizel 6CHNSP18/22-300 1 x 4 Stroke 6 Cy. 180 x 220 220kW (299bhp) Daldizel-Khabarovsk AuxGen: 1 x 14kW, 1 x 13kW Fuel: 56.0 (d.f.)
8730390 *UDGL* -	**SPA-011** - **Kvant Co Ltd** - *Korsakov* *Russia* MMSI: 273186700 Official number: 886210	**177** 53 167	Class: RS	**1989-09 Sudoremontnyy Zavod "Yakor" — Sovetskaya Gavan** Yd No: 852 Converted From: Deck Cargo Vessel-2005 Loa 33.82 Br ex 7.20 Dght 1.851 Lbp 33.53 Br md 7.00 Dpth 2.42 Welded, 1 dk	**(A31A2GX) General Cargo Ship** Ice Capable	**1 oil engine** geared to sc. shaft driving 1 FP propeller Total Power: 230kW (313hp) 8.7kn Daldizel 6CHNSP18/22-300 1 x 4 Stroke 6 Cy. 180 x 220 230kW (313bhp) Daldizel-Khabarovsk AuxGen: 1 x 14kW, 1 x 13kW Fuel: 56.0 (d.f.)
8826864 *UFGD* -	**SPA-012** - **Aleksandrovsk Sakhalinskiy Marine Port** - *Aleksandrovsk-Sakhalinskiy* *Russia*	**162** 48 167	Class: RS	**1989-12 Sudoremontnyy Zavod "Yakor" — Sovetskaya Gavan** Yd No: 853 Loa 35.84 Br ex 7.21 Dght 1.851 Lbp 33.63 Br md - Dpth 2.42 Welded	**(A31C2GD) Deck Cargo Ship** Ice Capable	**1 oil engine** geared to sc. shaft driving 1 FP propeller Total Power: 230kW (313hp) 8.7kn Daldizel 6CHNSP18/22-300 1 x 4 Stroke 6 Cy. 180 x 220 230kW (313bhp) Daldizel-Khabarovsk AuxGen: 1 x 14kW, 1 x 13kW Fuel: 56.0 (d.f.)
9449869 *PCNR* -	**SPAARNE TRADER** **Stichting ms Spaarne Trader** MCC Transport Singapore Pte Ltd *Winschoten* *Netherlands* MMSI: 246383000	**17,068** 7,036 21,800	Class: GL	**2012-02 Zhejiang Ouhua Shipbuilding Co Ltd — Zhoushan ZJ** Yd No: 525 Loa 180.35 (BB) Br ex - Dght 9.500 Lbp 169.30 Br md 25.00 Dpth 14.20 Welded, 1 dk	**(A33A2CC) Container Ship (Fully Cellular)** TEU 1496 incl 368 ref C	**1 oil engine** reduction geared to sc. shaft driving 1 CP propeller Total Power: 11,120kW (15,119hp) 18.5kn MAN-B&W 8L58/64 1 x 4 Stroke 8 Cy. 580 x 640 11120kW (15119bhp) MAN B&W Diesel AG-Augsburg AuxGen: 3 x 1600kW 450V a.c Thrusters: 1 Tunnel thruster (f)

Vessel	Tonnage	Class	Builder / Dimensions	Type / Cargo	Machinery
9188221 **SPAARNEBORG** *PCGE* - **K/S UL 676** Wagenborg Shipping BV *Delfzijl* *Netherlands* MMSI: 245452000 Official number: 36243	**21,005** 10,601 12,502 T/cm 38.6	Class: BV	**1999-11 Flender Werft AG — Luebeck** Yd No: 676 Loa 183.29 (BB) Br ex Dght 7.500 Lbp 173.00 Br md 25.20 Dpth 15.30 Welded, 2 dks	**(A35A2RR) Ro-Ro Cargo Ship** Passengers: driver berths: 12 Stern door/ramp (centre) Len: 16.00 Wid: 22.70 Swl: 100 Lane-Len: 2475 Lane-clr ht: 5.30 Trailers: 136	**1 oil engine** driving 1 CP propeller Total Power: 10,920kW (14,847hp) 18.0kn Sulzer 7RTA52U 1 x 2 Stroke 7 Cy. 520 x 1800 10920kW (14847bhp) Korea Heavy Industries & ConstrCo Ltd (HANJUNG)-South Korea AuxGen: 2 x 990kW 440/220V 50Hz a.c Thrusters: 2 Thwart. CP thruster (f); 1 Tunnel thruster (a) Fuel: 293.0 (d.f.) 1452.0 (r.f.)
9194062 **SPAARNEDIEP** *PEBZ* *ex Subito -2012 ex Spaarnediep -2011* - **Beheermaatschappij ms Spaarnediep II BV** Feederlines BV *Groningen* *Netherlands* MMSI: 246493000 Official number: 36285	**3,170** 1,876 4,554	Class: GL	**2000-05 Rousse Shipyard JSC — Rousse** Yd No: 404 Loa 98.94 (BB) Br ex - Dght 5.739 Lbp 92.50 Br md 13.80 Dpth 7.40 Welded, 1 dk	**(A31A2GX) General Cargo Ship** Grain: 6,255 TEU 282 C.Ho 120/20' (40') C.Dk 162/20' (40') Compartments: 1 Ho, ER 1 Ha: (70.4 x 11.2)ER Cranes: 1x13t,1x4t Ice Capable	**1 oil engine** reduction geared to sc. shaft driving 1 CP propeller Total Power: 2,640kW (3,589hp) 12.5kn MaK 6M32 1 x 4 Stroke 6 Cy. 320 x 480 2640kW (3589bhp) MaK Motoren GmbH & Co. KG-Kiel AuxGen: 1 x 328kW 380V a.c, 2 x 160kW 380V a.c Thrusters: 1 Thwart. FP thruster (f) Fuel: 254.0 (d.f.)
9202558 **SPAARNEGRACHT** *PDBO* - **Rederij Spaarnegracht** Spliethoff's Bevrachtingskantoor BV *Amsterdam* *Netherlands* MMSI: 246452000 Official number: 36731	**16,641** 6,700 21,402 T/cm 35.1	Class: LR ✠ **100A1** SS 08/2010 strengthened for heavy cargoes, container cargoes in holds, on upper deck and upper deck hatch covers timber deck cargoes tank top suitable for regular discharge by grabs LA *IWS LI Ice Class 1A (Finnish-Swedish Ice Class Rules 1985) Max draught midship 10.943m Max/min draught aft 11.47/6.6m Max/min draught forward 11.47/4.2m ✠ **LMC** **UMS** Eq.Ltr: 0†; Cable: 605.0/70.0 U2	**2000-08 Tsuneishi Shipbuilding Co Ltd — Fukuyama HS** Yd No: 1174 Loa 168.14 (BB) Br ex 25.42 Dght 10.740 Lbp 159.14 Br md 25.20 Dpth 14.60 Welded, 1 dk	**(A31A2GX) General Cargo Ship** Grain: 23,786; Bale: 23,786 TEU 1127 C Ho 478 TEU C Dk 649 TEU incl 120 ref C. Cargo Heating Coils Compartments: 3 Ho, ER 3 Ha: (26.6 x 15.2)Tappered (38.4 x 17.8) (31.9 x 20.4)ER Cranes: 3x120t Ice Capable	**1 oil engine** with flexible couplings & sr reverse geared to sc. shaft driving 1 CP propeller Total Power: 12,060kW (16,397hp) 19.5kn Wartsila 6L64 1 x 4 Stroke 6 Cy. 640 x 900 12060kW (16397bhp) Wartsila Italia SpA-Italy AuxGen: 1 x 1000kW 445V 60Hz a.c, 3 x 450kW 445V 60Hz a.c Boilers: TOH (o.f.) 10.2kgf/cm² (10.0bar), TOH (ex.g.) 10.2kgf/cm² (10.0bar) Thrusters: 1 Thwart. CP thruster (f) Fuel: 275.0 (d.f.) (Heating Coils) 1750.0 (r.f.) 45.0pd
9398955 **SPABUNKER CINCUENTA** *ECLF* - **Boluda Tankers SA** *Santa Cruz de Tenerife* *Spain (CSR)* MMSI: 224220360	**2,893** 1,473 5,200	Class: BV	**2007-05 Union Naval Valencia SA (UNV) — Valencia** Yd No: 399 Loa 84.93 Br ex Dght 5.600 Lbp 79.56 Br md 16.25 Dpth 7.60 Welded, 1 dk	**(B35E2TF) Bunkering Tanker**	**2 oil engines** driving 2 gen. reduction geared to sc. shafts driving 2 Z propellers Total Power: 3,372kW (4,584hp) 12.0kn Caterpillar 3516B-HD 2 x Vee 4 Stroke 16 Cy. 170 x 215 each-1686kW (2292bhp) Caterpillar Inc-USA
9416898 **SPABUNKER CINCUENTAYUNO** *ECNA* - **Boluda Tankers SA** - *Santa Cruz de Tenerife* *Spain (CSR)* MMSI: 224322240	**2,893** 1,427 5,200	Class: BV	**2008-08 Union Naval Valencia SA (UNV) — Valencia** Yd No: 396 Loa 84.93 Br ex - Dght 6.200 Lbp 76.56 Br md 16.26 Dpth 7.60 Welded, 1 dk	**(B35E2TF) Bunkering Tanker** Double Hull (13F) Liq: 5,090; Liq (Oil): 5,090	**2 oil engines** reduction geared to sc. shafts driving 2 Z propellers Total Power: 3,472kW (4,720hp) 10.0kn Caterpillar 3516 2 x Vee 4 Stroke 16 Cy. 170 x 190 each-1736kW (2360bhp) Caterpillar Inc-USA AuxGen: 2 x 400V 50Hz a.c Thrusters: 1 Tunnel thruster (f)
9416886 **SPABUNKER CUARENTA** *EAEN* - **Boluda Tankers SA** - *Santa Cruz de Tenerife* *Spain (CSR)* MMSI: 224473460 Official number: 2-1/2008	**2,551** 1,226 4,200	Class: BV	**2008-03 Union Naval Valencia SA (UNV) — Valencia** Yd No: 394 Loa 73.79 Br ex - Dght 6.200 Lbp 69.78 Br md 16.25 Dpth 7.60 Welded, 1 dk	**(B35E2TF) Bunkering Tanker** Double Hull (13F) Liq: 3,850; Liq (Oil): 3,850	**2 oil engines** reduction geared to sc. shafts driving 2 CP propellers Total Power: 3,000kW (4,078hp) 7.5kn Caterpillar 3516B-HD 2 x Vee 4 Stroke 16 Cy. 170 x 215 each-1500kW (2039bhp) Caterpillar Inc-USA AuxGen: 2 x 936kW 400V 50Hz a.c, 2 x 361kW 451V 50Hz a.c Fuel: 66.0
9127382 **SPABUNKER CUARENTAYUNO** *EALQ* *ex V.B. Veronica -2009* - **Boluda Tankers SA** - *Santa Cruz de Tenerife* *Spain (CSR)* MMSI: 224878000	**1,656** 860 4,000	Class: BV (LR) ✠ Classed LR until 2/5/07	**1996-01 Union Naval de Levante SA (UNL) — Valencia** Yd No: 238 Lengthened-2008 Loa 72.10 Br ex 16.02 Dght 5.300 Lbp 70.43 Br md 16.00 Dpth 6.80 Welded, 1 dk	**(A13B2TP) Products Tanker** Double Bottom Entire Compartment Length Liq: 4,244; Liq (Oil): 3,000 Cargo Heating Coils Compartments: 12 Ta, ER 1 Cargo Pump (s)	**2 oil engines** with flexible couplings & reduction geared to sc. shafts driving 2 Directional propellers Total Power: 1,130kW (1,536hp) 5.0kn Mitsubishi S6R2-MPTA 2 x 4 Stroke 6 Cy. 170 x 220 each-565kW (768bhp) Mitsubishi Heavy Industries Ltd-Japan AuxGen: 2 x 400kW 380V 50Hz a.c, 1 x 135kW 380V 50Hz a.c Boilers: TOH (o.f.) 10.2kgf/cm² (10.0bar) Fuel: 70.0
9014547 **SPABUNKER NUEVE** *EGYW* *ex Campante Dos -2004* - **Boluda Tankers SA** - *Santa Cruz de Tenerife* *Spain (CSR)* MMSI: 224309480	**513** 301 1,100	Class: BV	**1989-09 Union Naval de Levante SA (UNL) — Valencia** Yd No: 188 Loa - Br ex - Dght 4.030 Lbp 38.77 Br md 9.71 Dpth 4.73 Welded, 1 dk	**(B35E2TF) Bunkering Tanker** Liq: 1,216; Liq (Oil): 1,216 Compartments: 8 Wing Ta, ER 4 Cargo Pump (s): 2x200m³/hr, 2x75m³/hr Manifold: Bow/CM: 19m	**2 oil engines** sr geared to sc. shafts driving 2 Directional propellers Total Power: 560kW (762hp) 10.0kn GUASCOR F180T-SP 2 x 4 Stroke 6 Cy. 152 x 165 each-280kW (381bhp) Gutierrez Ascunce Corp (GUASCOR)-Spain AuxGen: 2 x 220kW 380V 50Hz a.c Thrusters: 2 Thwart. FP thruster (a) Fuel: 5.0 (d.f.) 3.0pd
9416874 **SPABUNKER SESENTA** *ECMZ* - **Boluda Tankers SA** - *Las Palmas* *Spain (CSR)* MMSI: 224322230	**2,113** 956 3,517	Class: BV	**2008-03 Union Naval Valencia SA (UNV) — Valencia** Yd No: 395 Loa 63.99 Br ex - Dght 6.200 Lbp 59.28 Br md 16.25 Dpth 7.60 Welded, 1 dk	**(B35E2TF) Bunkering Tanker** Double Hull (13F)	**2 oil engines** reduction geared to sc. shafts driving 2 CP propellers Total Power: 3,840kW (5,220hp) 7.0kn Caterpillar 3516B-HD 2 x Vee 4 Stroke 16 Cy. 170 x 215 each-1920kW (2610bhp) Caterpillar Inc-USA AuxGen: 2 x 400V 50Hz a.c
9120231 **SPABUNKER SESENTAYUNO** *EAHE* *ex Eileen -2009* - **High Light Assets Corp** Boluda Tankers SA *Santa Cruz de Tenerife* *Spain (CSR)* MMSI: 224608620	**1,655** 812 4,148 T/cm 8.2	Class: BV (LR) ✠ Classed LR until 21/3/12	**1995-09 Union Naval de Levante SA (UNL) — Valencia** Yd No: 228 Loa 52.83 Br ex 16.80 Dght 5.300 Lbp 50.83 Br md 16.78 Dpth 6.80 Welded, 1 dk	**(A13B2TP) Products Tanker** Double Hull Liq: 3,031; Liq (Oil): 3,031 Cargo Heating Coils Compartments: 8 Wing Ta, ER 4 Cargo Pump (s): 2x330m³/hr, 2x120m³/hr Manifold: Bow/CM: 22.8m	**2 oil engines** with flexible couplings & reduction geared to sc. shafts driving 2 Directional propellers Total Power: 1,030kW (1,400hp) 6.0kn Mitsubishi S6R2-MPTA 2 x 4 Stroke 6 Cy. 170 x 220 each-515kW (700bhp) Mitsubishi Heavy Industries Ltd-Japan AuxGen: 2 x 400kW 380V 50Hz a.c, 1 x 135kW 380V 50Hz a.c Boilers: TOH (o.f.) 10.2kgf/cm² (10.0bar)
8208555 **SPABUNKER SIETE** - *ex Carol -2001* - **Societe Mauritanienne de Navigation et de Cabotage (SMNC)** - *Mauritania*	**1,209** 716 2,400	Class: (GL) (AB) (BV)	**1984-02 S.A. Balenciaga — Zumaya** Yd No: 307 Loa 72.90 Br ex 11.33 Dght 4.531 Lbp 67.01 Br md 11.31 Dpth 5.36 Welded, 1 dk	**(B35E2TF) Bunkering Tanker** Liq: 2,560; Liq (Oil): 2,560	**1 oil engine** sr reverse geared to sc. shaft driving 1 FP propeller Total Power: 1,103kW (1,500hp) 11.8kn Alpha 12V23HU 1 x Vee 4 Stroke 12 Cy. 225 x 300 1103kW (1500bhp) Construcciones Echevarria SA-Spain AuxGen: 1 x 84kW 220/380V a.c, 2 x 52kW 220/380V a.c
9296638 **SPABUNKER TREINTA** *ECIK* - **Boluda Tankers SA** - *Santa Cruz de Tenerife* *Spain (CSR)* MMSI: 224142890	**2,885** 1,473 5,000	Class: BV	**2006-04 Union Naval Valencia SA (UNV) — Valencia** Yd No: 371 Loa 84.93 Br ex - Dght 6.000 Lbp 79.56 Br md 16.25 Dpth 7.60 Welded, 1 dk	**(B35E2TF) Bunkering Tanker** Double Hull (13F)	**2 oil engines** gearing integral to driving 2 Z propellers Total Power: 3,478kW (4,728hp) 12.0kn Caterpillar 3516 2 x Vee 4 Stroke 16 Cy. 170 x 190 each-1739kW (2364bhp) Caterpillar Inc-USA Thrusters: 1 Tunnel thruster (f)

9237163 *ZDFU5* -	**SPABUNKER TWENTY** *ex* Spabunker Veinte *-2003* **Maritime Gibraltar Ltd** Gibraltar Underwater Contractors Ltd (GIBUNCO) *Gibraltar* *Gibraltar (British)* MMSI: 236053000	**2,896** 1,394 4,999	Class: LR (BV) **100A1** SS 03/2012 oil tanker ESP carriage of oils with a FP exceeding 60 degree C **LMC** **UMS** Eq.Ltr: S; Cable: 467.5/36.0 U3 (a)	**2002-03 Union Naval Valencia SA (UNV) — Valencia** Yd No: 286 Loa 73.40 (BB) Br ex 16.27 Dght 6.000 Lbp 70.70 Br md 16.25 Dpth 7.60 Welded, 1 dk	**(A13B2TP) Products Tanker** Double Hull (13F) Compartments: 10 Wing Ta, 1 Ta, 1 Slop Ta, ER	**2 oil engines** gearing integral to driving 2 Voith-Schneider propellers Total Power: 2,554kW (3,472hp) 8.0kn Deutz TBD620V12 2 x Vee 4 Stroke 12 Cy. 170 x 195 each-1277kW (1736bhp) Deutz AG-Koeln AuxGen: 2 x 932kW 380V 50Hz a.c, 2 x 120kW 380V 50Hz a.c Boilers: TOH (o.f.) 10.2kgf/cm^2 (10.0bar) Thrusters: 1 Thwart. FP thruster (f)
8117794 *3FXE4* -	**SPABUNKER UNO** *ex* Spabunker I *-2005* **ING Lease (Espana) SA EFC** Boluda Tankers SA *Panama* *Panama* MMSI: 370874000 Official number: 41940PEXTF	**2,227** 1,138 4,344	Class: BV	**1983-07 Jose Valina Lavandeira — La Coruna** Yd No: 15 Conv to DH-2011 Loa 76.51 Br ex 16.30 Dght 5.684 Lbp 72.85 Br md 16.00 Dpth 6.81 Welded, 1 dk	**(B35E2TF) Bunkering Tanker** Double Hull (13F) Liq: 5,014; Liq (Oil): 5,014 Part Cargo Heating Coils Compartments: 8 Ta, ER 8 Cargo Pump (s): 8x210m^3/hr	**2 oil engines** with clutches & sr geared to sc. shafts driving 2 FP propellers Total Power: 1,236kW (1,680hp) 7.6kn Deutz SBA12M816 2 x Vee 4 Stroke 12 Cy. 142 x 160 each-618kW (840bhp) Hijos de J Barreras SA-Spain AuxGen: 2 x 480kW 380V 50Hz a.c
9280378 *EABZ* -	**SPABUNKER VEINTIDOS** **Boluda Tankers SA** - *Santa Cruz de Tenerife* *Spain (CSR)* MMSI: 224101930	**2,894** 1,394 4,999	Class: BV	**2003-12 Union Naval Valencia SA (UNV) — Valencia** Yd No: 343 Loa 82.13 Br ex - Dght 5.630 Lbp 77.00 Br md 16.25 Dpth 7.60 Welded	**(B35E2TF) Bunkering Tanker**	**2 oil engines** geared to sc. shafts driving 2 Propellers Total Power: 2,760kW (3,752hp) Deutz TBD620V12 2 x Vee 4 Stroke 12 Cy. 170 x 195 each-1380kW (1876bhp) Deutz AG-Koeln
9259874 *EAFF* -	**SPABUNKER VEINTIUNO** **Boluda Tankers SA** - *Santa Cruz de Tenerife* *Spain (CSR)* MMSI: 224976000	**2,895** 1,394 4,999	Class: BV	**2003-01 Union Naval Valencia SA (UNV) — Valencia** Yd No: 289 Loa 82.07 Br ex - Dght 6.000 Lbp 76.77 Br md 16.25 Dpth 7.60 Welded, 1 dk	**(B35E2TF) Bunkering Tanker**	**2 oil engines** geared to sc. shafts driving 2 FP propellers Total Power: 2,552kW (3,470hp) 8.0kn Deutz TBD620V12 2 x Vee 4 Stroke 12 Cy. 170 x 195 each-1276kW (1735bhp) Deutz AG-Koeln
1009302 *ZCT18* -	**SPACE** **Azur Charters Ltd** Nigel Burgess Ltd (BURGESS) *George Town* *Cayman Islands (British)* MMSI: 319917000 Official number: 740068	**499** 149 -	Class: LR ✠ **100A1** SS 04/2012 SSC Yacht, mono, G6 **LMC** **UMS** Cable: 275.0/19.0 U2 (a)	**2007-07 NMC Alblasserdam BV — Alblasserdam** (Hull) Yd No: (796) **2007-07 Jacht- en Scheepswerf C. van Lent & Zonen B.V. — Kaag** Yd No: 796 Loa 44.65 Br ex - Dght 2.900 Lbp 37.40 Br md 8.80 Dpth 4.55 Welded, 1 dk	**(X11A2YP) Yacht**	**2 oil engines** with clutches, flexible couplings & sr geared to sc. shafts driving 2 FP propellers Total Power: 1,576kW (2,142hp) 14.2kn M.T.U. 12V2000M70 2 x Vee 4 Stroke 12 Cy. 130 x 150 each-788kW (1071bhp) MTU Friedrichshafen GmbH-Friedrichshafen AuxGen: 2 x 150kW 400V 50Hz a.c Thrusters: 1 Thwart. FP thruster (f)
6716625 - -	**SPACE I** *ex* Howard Jones *-1988* *ex* Castle Cove *-1979* **PT Space Jayapura** - *Sorong* *Indonesia*	*192* 58 111	Class: (LR) (KI) (AB) ✠ Classed LR until 20/10/78	**1967-06 Adelaide Ship Construction Pty Ltd — Port Adelaide SA** Yd No: 36 Loa 30.64 Br ex 8.54 Dght 3.887 Lbp 27.67 Br md 8.08 Dpth 4.58 Welded, 1 dk	**(B32A2ST) Tug**	**1 oil engine** reverse reduction geared to sc. shaft driving 1 FP propeller Total Power: 1,192kW (1,621hp) 12.0kn Mirrlees KSSGMR-6 1 x 4 Stroke 6 Cy. 381 x 457 1192kW (1621bhp) Mirrlees National Ltd.-Stockport AuxGen: 2 x 40kW 415V 50Hz a.c Fuel: 32.0
1006271 *ZCRN4* -	**SPADA** **Jarwood Ltd** - *George Town* *Cayman Islands (British)* MMSI: 319342000 Official number: 731933	**271** 81 32	Class: LR ✠ **100A1** SS 11/2013 SSC Yacht mono G6 service area ✠ **LMC** Cable: 603.0/24.0 U2 (a)	**1998-11 Scheepsbouw en Machinefabriek Hakvoort B.V. — Monnickendam** Yd No: 224 Loa 33.50 Br ex - Dght 2.380 Lbp 28.13 Br md 7.82 Dpth 3.90 Welded, 1 dk	**(X11A2YP) Yacht**	**2 oil engines** with flexible couplings & sr reverse geared to sc. shafts driving 2 FP propellers Total Power: 708kW (962hp) 17.0kn Caterpillar 3406TA 2 x 4 Stroke 6 Cy. 137 x 165 each-354kW (481bhp) Caterpillar Inc-USA AuxGen: 2 x 80kW 380V 50Hz a.c, 1 x 50kW 380V 50Hz a.c Thrusters: 1 Thwart. FP thruster (f); 1 Tunnel thruster (a)
9584267 *IJAP2* -	**SPAGNA** **Rimorchiatori Riuniti SpA** - *Genoa* *Italy*	**274** - 145	Class: RI **100A1** 09/2011 Class contemplated	**2011-09 Astilleros Armon Burela SA — Burela** (Hull) **2011-09 Astilleros Armon SA — Navia** Yd No: 699 Loa 24.40 Br ex - Dght 5.150 Lbp - Br md 11.27 Dpth 4.38 Welded, 1 dk	**(B32A2ST) Tug**	**2 oil engines** reduction geared to sc. shafts driving 2 Z propellers Total Power: 3,842kW (5,224hp) Caterpillar 3516C 2 x Vee 4 Stroke 16 Cy. 170 x 190 each-1921kW (2612bhp) Caterpillar Inc-USA Fuel: 84.0 (d.f.)
9086186 *YD4610* -	**SPAJ 023** *ex* Perfect Fortune *-2000* **PT Sumber Penghidupan Abadi Jaya** - *Jakarta* *Indonesia*	**104** 62 111	Class: (KI) (NK)	**1993-08 Super-Light Shipbuilding Contractor — Sibu** Yd No: 6 Loa 23.00 Br ex - Dght 2.388 Lbp 21.76 Br md 7.00 Dpth 2.90 Welded, 1 dk	**(B32A2ST) Tug**	**2 oil engines** reduction geared to sc. shafts driving 2 FP propellers Total Power: 692kW (940hp) 10.5kn Caterpillar 3408TA 2 x Vee 4 Stroke 8 Cy. 137 x 152 each-346kW (470bhp) Caterpillar Inc-USA AuxGen: 2 x 24kW a.c
8891950 *YD8004* -	**SPAJ 024** *ex* E S Pisces *-2000* **PT Sumber Penghidupan Abadi Jaya** - *Bitung* *Indonesia*	**210** 63	Class: (KI) (BV)	**1995 Ningbo Ningxunjie Shipbuilding Co Ltd — Ningbo ZJ** Yd No: 7172 Loa - Br ex - Dght 2.950 Lbp 26.56 Br md 8.00 Dpth 3.48 Welded, 1 dk	**(B32A2ST) Tug**	**2 oil engines** geared to sc. shafts driving 2 FP propellers Total Power: 1,104kW (1,500hp) 12.0kn Chinese Std. Type 6300 2 x 4 Stroke 6 Cy. 300 x 380 each-552kW (750bhp) Ningbo Zhonghua Dongli PowerMachinery Co Ltd -China
8740357 - -	**SPAJ 030** **PT Sumber Penghidupan Abadi Jaya** - *Banjarmasin* *Indonesia*	**215** 65 -	Class: KI	**2006-06 PT Duta Tujuh Bersaudara Sejati — Pleihari** Loa 29.40 Br ex - Dght - Lbp 27.12 Br md 8.46 Dpth 3.70 Welded, 1 dk	**(B32A2ST) Tug**	**2 oil engines** reduction geared to sc. shafts driving 2 FP propellers Total Power: 1,118kW (1,520hp) Cummins QST30-G10 2 x Vee 4 Stroke 12 Cy. 140 x 165 each-559kW (760bhp) Cummins Engine Co Inc-USA AuxGen: 1 x 88kW 400V a.c
8740369 - -	**SPAJ 031** **PT Sumber Penghidupan Abadi Jaya** - *Banjarmasin* *Indonesia*	**231** 70 -	Class: (KI)	**2006-06 PT Duta Tujuh Bersaudara Sejati — Pleihari** Loa 29.40 Br ex - Dght - Lbp 27.45 Br md 8.46 Dpth 3.70	**(B32A2ST) Tug**	**2 oil engines** driving 2 Propellers Total Power: 1,118kW (1,520hp) Cummins QST30-G10 2 x Vee 4 Stroke 12 Cy. 140 x 165 each-559kW (760bhp) Cummins Engine Co Inc-USA
8121032 *DUH3173* -	**SPAN ASIA 1** *ex* Jan D *-2011* *ex* Maersk Canarias *-1999* *ex* Dania *-1994* *ex* Nedlloyd Daisy *-1994* *ex* Dania *-1993* *ex* Alcyone *-1992* *ex* Kastamonu *-1988* *ex* Contship Lugano *-1985* *ex* Kastamonu *-1985* *launched as* Alcyone *-1982* **Philippine Span Asia Carrier Corp (PSACC)** - *Cebu* *Philippines* Official number: CEB1008379	**5,404** 2,718 6,764	Class: GL (NV)	**1982-09 J.J. Sietas KG Schiffswerft GmbH & Co. — Hamburg** Yd No: 846 Loa 113.65 (BB) Br ex 19.05 Dght 6.530 Lbp 103.43 Br md 19.03 Dpth 8.92 Welded, 2 dks	**(A31A2GX) General Cargo Ship** Grain: 8,990; Bale: 8,760 TEU 445 C Ho 172 TEU C Dk 273 TEU incl 56 ref C. Compartments: 2 Ho, ER 2 Ha: ER Cranes: 2x35t Ice Capable	**1 oil engine** sr geared to sc. shaft driving 1 CP propeller Total Power: 2,949kW (4,009hp) 14.5kn MaK 8M551AK 1 x 4 Stroke 8 Cy. 450 x 550 2949kW (4009bhp) Krupp MaK Maschinenbau GmbH-Kiel AuxGen: 1 x 552kW 400V 50Hz a.c, 3 x 240kW 400V 50Hz a.c Thrusters: 1 Thwart. FP thruster (f) Fuel: 138.0 (d.f.) 695.0 (r.f.) 17.5pd
8410378 *DUA3150* -	**SPAN ASIA 2** *ex* Blue Sky *-2011* *ex* Mandeb Bay *-1998* *ex* Blue Sky *-1995* *ex* Saigon Lotus *-1993* *ex* Blue Sky *-1993* *ex* Carme *-1990* *ex* Inka Dede *-1990* *ex* Regency Bay *-1987* *ex* Inka Dede *-1987* **Philippine Span Asia Carrier Corp (PSACC)** - *Cebu* *Philippines* Official number: CEB1008412	**3,120** 1,733 3,676	Class: GL	**1984-07 J.J. Sietas KG Schiffswerft GmbH & Co. — Hamburg** Yd No: 915 Loa 88.63 (BB) Br ex 15.47 Dght 6.454 Lbp 80.52 Br md 15.46 Dpth 8.31 Welded, 2 dks	**(A31A2GX) General Cargo Ship** Grain: 5,553; Bale: 5,471 TEU 256 C.Ho 112/20' C.Dk 144/20' incl. 20 ref C. Compartments: 1 Ho, ER 1 Ha: (51.3 x 12.5)ER Cranes: 2x30t Ice Capable	**1 oil engine** with flexible couplings & sr gearedto sc. shaft driving 1 CP propeller Total Power: 1,070kW (1,455hp) 12.0kn Wartsila 6R32 1 x 4 Stroke 6 Cy. 320 x 350 1070kW (1455bhp) Oy Wartsila Ab-Finland AuxGen: 2 x 300kW 231/400V 50Hz a.c, 1 x 92kW 231/400V 50Hz a.c Thrusters: 1 Thwart. FP thruster (f) Fuel: 64.5 (d.f.) 308.5 (r.f.) 6.0pd
7824613 *DUH3214* -	**SPAN ASIA 3** *ex* Carnation *-2011* *ex* Reykjafoss *-1999* *ex* Regulus *-1984* **Philippine Span Asia Carrier Corp (PSACC)** - *Cebu* *Philippines* Official number: CEB1008538	**4,226** 2,315 5,788	Class: GL	**1979-05 J.J. Sietas KG Schiffswerft GmbH & Co. — Hamburg** Yd No: 825 Converted From: Container Ship (Fully Cellular)-1979 Loa 109.93 (BB) Br ex 16.11 Dght 6.530 Lbp 99.57 Br md 16.01 Dpth 8.46 Welded, 2 dks	**(A31A2GX) General Cargo Ship** Grain: 7,844; Bale: 7,341 TEU 308 C Ho 144 TEU C Dk 164 TEU incl 40 ref C. Compartments: 2 Ho, ER, 2 Tw Dk 2 Ha: (25.3 x 12.7) (38.3 x 12.7)ER Cranes: 2x35t Ice Capable	**1 oil engine** sr geared to sc. shaft driving 1 CP propeller Total Power: 2,207kW (3,001hp) 13.0kn MaK 6M551AK 1 x 4 Stroke 6 Cy. 450 x 550 2207kW (3001bhp) Krupp MaK Maschinenbau GmbH-Kiel AuxGen: 1 x 456kW 220/380V 50Hz a.c, 1 x 228kW 220/380V 50Hz a.c, 2 x 208kW 220/380V 50Hz a.c Thrusters: 1 Thwart. CP thruster (f) Fuel: 87.0 (d.f.) 473.0 (r.f.) 14.0pd

8405000 *DUA3156* -	**SPAN ASIA 5** *ex* Thor Admiral *-2011* *ex* Norasia Odessa *-2007* *ex* Petra *-2005* *ex* BBC Africa *-2005* *ex* Petra *-2004* *ex* Sloman Server *-2003* *ex* Petra *-2003* *ex* CGM Saint Elie *-1997* *ex* Helene *-1997* *ex* Carib Faith *-1996* *ex* Helene *-1992* *ex* Ville du Mistral *-1989* *ex* Helene *-1988* *ex* BCR Dusseldorf *-1987* *ex* Bacol Rio *-1986* *ex* BCR Helene *-1985* *ex* Helene *-1985* **Philippine Span Asia Carrier Corp (PSACC)** - *Cebu* *Philippines* MMSI: 548563200 Official number: CEB1008643	**5,608** 3,088 7,130	Class: GL	**1985-01 Werft Nobiskrug GmbH — Rendsburg** Yd No: 722 Loa 117.02 (BB) Br ex 19.64 Dght 6.133 Lbp 106.86 Br md 19.61 Dpth 8.01 Welded, 2 dks	**(A31A2GA) General Cargo Ship (with Ro-Ro facility)** Stern door/ramp (centre) Len: 13.00 Wid: 6.50 Swl: 100 Lane-Len: 360 Grain: 9,155; Bale: 9,061 TEU 574 C Ho 206 TEU C Dk 368 TEU incl 30 ref C. Compartments: 1 Ho, ER 1 Ha: (76.5 x 15.1)ER Cranes: 2x35t Ice Capable	**1 oil engine** with flexible couplings & sr gearedto sc. shaft driving 1 CP propeller Total Power: 1,898kW (2,581hp) 12.5kn MaK 6M551AK 1 x 4 Stroke 6 Cy. 450 x 550 1898kW (2581bhp) Krupp MaK Maschinenbau GmbH-Kiel Thrusters: 1 Thwart. FP thruster (f) Fuel: 513.0 (r.f.)
8405036 *DUA3176* -	**SPAN ASIA 7** *ex* Astrid *-2012* *ex* Vento di Tramontana *-2003* *ex* Astrid *-2003* *ex* Vento di Tramontana *-2003* *ex* Fas Gemlik *-2002* *ex* BBC Germany *-2001* *ex* Fas Gemlik *-2001* *ex* Cam Ayous Express *-1996* *ex* Nedlloyd Tulip *-1995* *ex* Ville d'Orient *-1992* *ex* Kathe Husmann *-1988* *ex* Bacol Vitoria *-1987* *launched as* Kathe Husmann *-1985* **Philippine Span Asia Carrier Corp (PSACC)** - *Cebu* *Philippines* Official number: CEB1008783	**5,608** 3,088 7,120	Class: GL	**1985-10 Werft Nobiskrug GmbH — Rendsburg** Yd No: 725 Loa 116.96 (BB) Br ex 20.30 Dght 6.130 Lbp 105.85 Br md 19.60 Dpth 8.00 Welded, 2 dks	**(A31A2GA) General Cargo Ship (with Ro-Ro facility)** Stern door/ramp (centre) Lane-Len: 360 Grain: 9,155; Bale: 9,061 TEU 574 C Ho 206 TEU C Dk 368 TEU incl 30 ref C. Compartments: 1 Ho, ER 1 Ha: (76.5 x 15.1)ER Cranes: 2x35t Ice Capable	**1 oil engine** with flexible couplings & sr gearedto sc. shaft driving 1 CP propeller Total Power: 1,899kW (2,582hp) 13.0kn MaK 6M551AK 1 x 4 Stroke 6 Cy. 450 x 550 1899kW (2582bhp) Krupp MaK Maschinenbau GmbH-Kiel AuxGen: 1 x 400kW 440/220V 60Hz a.c, 2 x 240kW 440/220V 60Hz a.c, 1 x 172kW 440/220V 60Hz a.c Thrusters: 1 Thwart. FP thruster (f)
8421224 *DUA3185* -	**SPAN ASIA 9** *ex* Hansewall *-2013* *ex* Mcc Clipper *-2009* *ex* Hansewall *-2005* *ex* Joanna Borchard *-1997* *ex* Levant Lesum *-1996* *ex* Levant Neva *-1996* *ex* Lucy Borchard *-1994* *ex* Miriam Borchard *-1992* *ex* Kalymnos *-1990* *launched as* Hansewall *-1985* **Philippine Span Asia Carrier Corp (PSACC)** - *Cebu* *Philippines* Official number: CEB1008862	**6,659** 2,823 8,331	Class: GL	**1985-02 J.J. Sietas KG Schiffswerft GmbH & Co. — Hamburg** Yd No: 940 Loa 117.51 (BB) Br ex 20.45 Dght 7.484 Lbp 109.40 Br md 20.21 Dpth 10.80 Welded, 2 dks	**(A31A2GX) General Cargo Ship** Grain: 11,000; Bale: 10,870 TEU 541 C Ho 230 TEU C Dk 311 TEU incl 100 ref C. Compartments: 2 Ho, ER, 2 Tw Dk 2 Ha: ER Cranes: 2x35t Ice Capable	**1 oil engine** with flexible couplings & sr gearedto sc. shaft driving 1 CP propeller Total Power: 5,400kW (7,342hp) 16.0kn MaK 8M552C 1 x 4 Stroke 8 Cy. 450 x 520 5400kW (7342bhp) (new engine 1993) Krupp MaK Maschinenbau GmbH-Kiel AuxGen: 1 x 500kW 380/220V a.c, 1 x 280kW 380/220V a.c, 2 x 208kW 380/220V a.c Thrusters: 1 Tunnel thruster (f)
9076351 *DUA3216* -	**SPAN ASIA 10** *ex* CEC Future *-2013* *ex* CMA CGM Tunis *-2004* *ex* CEC Future *-2003* *ex* Arktis Future *-2002* *ex* CEC Future *-2001* *ex* Signet Spirit *-2000* *ex* CEC Future *-2000* *ex* Arktis Future *-1999* *ex* Melbridge Flash *-1996* *ex* Arktis Future *-1994* **Philippine Span Asia Carrier Corp (PSACC)** - *Cebu* *Philippines* Official number: 07-0000130	**4,980** 2,230 7,121 T/cm 16.6	Class: LR (BV) **100A1** SS 12/2009 container cargoes in all holds and on upper deck and on all hatch covers LI **LMC** **UMS** Cable: 534.0/48.0 U3 (a)	**1994-12 Aarhus Flydedok A/S — Aarhus** Yd No: 211 Loa 101.10 (BB) Br ex 19.20 Dght 7.320 Lbp 93.60 Br md 18.80 Dpth 9.30 Welded, 1 dk	**(A31A2GX) General Cargo Ship** Grain: 8,014 TEU 444 C Ho 152 TEU C Dk 292 incl 50 ref C Compartments: 1 Ho, 1 Tw Dk, ER 1 Ha: (58.9 x 15.2)ER Cranes: 2x70t Ice Capable	**1 oil engine** with clutches, flexible couplings & sr geared to sc. shaft driving 1 CP propeller Total Power: 4,500kW (6,118hp) 14.5kn MaK 6M552C 1 x 4 Stroke 6 Cy. 450 x 520 4500kW (6118bhp) Krupp MaK Maschinenbau GmbH-Kiel AuxGen: 1 x 600kW 440V 60Hz a.c, 3 x 320kW 450V 60Hz a.c Boilers: TOH (ex.g.), TOH (o.f.) Thrusters: 1 Thwart. CP thruster (f)
8611946 *DUA3221* -	**SPAN ASIA 11** *ex* Patara *-2013* *ex* BBC Colombia *-2007* *ex* Patara *-2007* *ex* BBC Colombia *-2005* *ex* Hannah *-2001* *ex* Paapsund *-1997* *ex* Paapsand *-1995* *ex* Sun Bay *-1995* *ex* Enno B *-1994* *ex* Myanmar Pioneer *-1992* *ex* Tiger Cliff *-1991* *ex* Enno B *-1990* *ex* Nouakchott *-1990* *ex* Karin B *-1989* *ex* A. I. M. Voyager *-1987* *launched as* Karin B *-1987* **Philippine Span Asia Carrier Corp (PSACC)** - *Cebu* *Philippines* MMSI: 548599200	**3,236** 1,645 4,741	Class: RI (GL)	**1987-01 Schiffswerft u. Masch. Paul Lindenau GmbH & Co. KG — Kiel** Yd No: 224 Loa 101.19 (BB) Br ex 14.05 Dght 5.755 Lbp 94.21 Br md 14.01 Dpth 7.47 Welded, 2 dks	**(A31A2GX) General Cargo Ship** Grain: 5,692; Bale: 5,580 TEU 240 C. 240/20' (40') Compartments: 1 Ho, ER, 1 Tw Dk 1 Ha: (62.3 x 11.1)ER Cranes: 2x25t Ice Capable	**1 oil engine** with flexible couplings & sr gearedto sc. shaft driving 1 CP propeller Total Power: 1,659kW (2,256hp) 12.0kn MWM TBD510-6 1 x 4 Stroke 6 Cy. 330 x 360 1659kW (2256bhp) Motoren Werke Mannheim AG (MWM)-West Germany AuxGen: 3 x 196kW a.c Thrusters: 1 Thwart. FP thruster (f)
8913930 *DUA3222* -	**SPAN ASIA 12** *ex* Sea Bird *-2013* **Philippine Span Asia Carrier Corp (PSACC)** - *Philippines* MMSI: 548603200	**3,273** 1,575 4,100	Class: GL	**1990-06 HDW-Nobiskrug GmbH — Rendsburg** Yd No: 751 Loa 94.40 (BB) Br ex - Dght 6.250 Lbp 86.50 Br md 15.50 Dpth 7.90 Welded, 1 dk, 2nd portable dk in hold	**(A31A2GX) General Cargo Ship** Grain: 5,862 TEU 276 C.Ho 131/20' (40') C.Dk 145/20' (40') incl. 30 ref C. Compartments: 1 Ho, ER 1 Ha: (55.8 x 12.6)ER Cranes: 2x50t Ice Capable	**1 oil engine** with flexible couplings & sr geared to sc. shaft driving 1 CP propeller Total Power: 2,200kW (2,991hp) 13.5kn MaK 6M453C 1 x 4 Stroke 6 Cy. 320 x 420 2200kW (2991bhp) Krupp MaK Maschinenbau GmbH-Kiel AuxGen: 2 x 313kW 220/380V 50Hz a.c, 1 x 260kW 220/380V 50Hz a.c Thrusters: 1 Thwart. FP thruster (f) Fuel: 60.0 (d.f.) 245.0 (r.f.) 10.0pd
8817265 *DYJM* -	**SPAN ASIA 15** *ex* Sulpicio Express Dos *-2013* *ex* Hokuo Maru *-2002* **Philippine Span Asia Carrier Corp (PSACC)** - *Cebu* *Philippines* Official number: 07-0000182	*4,509* 1,387 5,186	Class: NK	**1988-08 Shin Kurushima Dockyard Co. Ltd. — Akitsu** Yd No: 2566 Loa 136.00 (BB) Br ex - Dght 6.166 Lbp 126.00 Br md 20.00 Dpth 14.50 Welded	**(A35A2RR) Ro-Ro Cargo Ship** Lane-Len: 400 Bale: 14,710 TEU 56 C.Dk 56 TEU	**1 oil engine** driving 1 CP propeller Total Power: 7,723kW (10,500hp) 17.0kn B&W 7L50MC 1 x 2 Stroke 7 Cy. 500 x 1620 7723kW (10500bhp) Kobe Hatsudoki KK-Japan AuxGen: 3 x 686kW a.c Thrusters: 1 Thwart. CP thruster (f) Fuel: 400.0 (r.f.)
8817071 *DYJL* -	**SPAN ASIA 16** *ex* Sulpicio Express Tres *-2013* *ex* Honshu Maru *-2002* **Philippine Span Asia Carrier Corp (PSACC)** - *Cebu* *Philippines* Official number: 07-0000183	*6,016* 3,255 4,848	Class: NK	**1989-01 Imabari Shipbuilding Co Ltd — Imabari EH (Imabari Shipyard)** Yd No: 476 Loa 128.53 (BB) Br ex - Dght 6.115 Lbp 120.00 Br md 20.40 Dpth 9.50 Welded	**(A35A2RR) Ro-Ro Cargo Ship** Passengers: cabins: 2; berths: 4 Lane-Len: 500	**1 oil engine** driving 1 CP propeller Total Power: 6,355kW (8,640hp) 17.0kn Mitsubishi 8UEC45LA 1 x 2 Stroke 8 Cy. 450 x 1350 6355kW (8640bhp) Akasaka Tekkosho KK (Akasaka DieselLtd)-Japan AuxGen: 2 x 560kW 450V 60Hz a.c Thrusters: 1 Thwart. FP thruster (f) Fuel: 28.0 (d.f.) 396.0 (r.f.) 23.6pd
7724344 *DUHP5* -	**SPAN ASIA 17** *ex* Sulpicio Express Siete *-2014* *ex* Lily Crown *-2009* *ex* Abeer S *-2004* *ex* Echo Pioneer *-2002* *ex* EAL Saphire *-1990* *ex* Costa Rica *-1989* **Philippine Span Asia Carrier Corp (PSACC)** - *Cebu* *Philippines* Official number: CEB1008035	**9,754** 5,524 11,464	Class: (NV) (GL)	**1981-07 Stocznia Szczecinska im A Warskiego — Szczecin** Yd No: B430/12 Loa 146.23 (BB) Br ex 21.54 Dght 8.402 Lbp 134.40 Br md 21.51 Dpth 11.31 Welded, 2 dks	**(A31A2GX) General Cargo Ship** Grain: 18,562; Bale: 17,164 TEU 454 C Ho 214 TEU C Dk 240 TEU incl 15 ref C. Compartments: 4 Ho, ER, 5 Tw Dk 7 Ha: (12.6 x 7.8)2 (19.2 x 7.8)2 (25.6 x 7.8)2 (12.5 x 7.8)ER Derricks: 6x36t; Winches: 18 Ice Capable	**1 oil engine** driving 1 CP propeller Total Power: 7,282kW (9,901hp) 16.5kn Sulzer 6RND68 1 x 2 Stroke 6 Cy. 680 x 1250 7282kW (9901bhp) Zaklady Przemyslu Metalowego 'HCegielski' SA-Poznan AuxGen: 1 x 664kW 380V 50Hz a.c, 3 x 400kW 380V 50Hz a.c Thrusters: 1 Thwart. FP thruster (f) Fuel: 184.0 (d.f.) (Heating Coils) 993.0 (r.f.) 35.5pd
8027664 *5IM508* -	**SPANIA** *ex* Spruttenberg *-2004* *ex* Montania *-2001* *ex* Thekla *-1996* *ex* Clovis *-1988* *ex* Thekla Wessels *-1986* **mv Spania Shipping GmbH & Co KG** Black Sea Shipping BSS GmbH *Zanzibar* *Tanzania (Zanzibar)* MMSI: 677040800 Official number: 300248	**2,265** 797 3,500	Class: IS MG (GL) (BV)	**1981-06 MAN GHH Dock- u. Schiffbau Rheinwerft Walsum — Duisburg** Yd No: 1143 Loa 98.60 Br ex 11.41 Dght 4.310 Lbp 95.41 Br md 11.34 Dpth 7.15 Welded, 2 dks	**(A31A2GX) General Cargo Ship** Grain: 4,284; Bale: 4,239 TEU 100 C.Ho 60/20' (40') C.Dk 40/20' (40') Compartments: 1 Ho, ER 1 Ha: (66.6 x 9.1)ER Ice Capable	**1 oil engine** sr reverse geared to sc. shaft driving 1 FP propeller Total Power: 971kW (1,320hp) 10.5kn S.K.L. 8NVD48A-2U 1 x 4 Stroke 8 Cy. 320 x 480 971kW (1320bhp) VEB Schwermaschinenbau "KarlLiebknecht" (SKL)-Magdeburg AuxGen: 2 x 104kW 220/380V 50Hz a.c, 1 x 40kW 220/380V 50Hz a.c Thrusters: 1 Thwart. FP thruster (f) Fuel: 238.0 (d.f.) 6.0pd

7925247 *CFD7792* -
SPANISH MIST
ex Ole Rabudal *-1994* *ex* Reus *-1994*
launched as Ebro *-1981*
Les Remorquages IM Inc
-
Halifax, NS *Canada*
MMSI: 316001069
Official number: 817737
366 / 110 / 246
Class: LR (AB)
✠**100A1** SS 05/2009
tug
Ice Class 1D
✠**LMC**
Eq.Ltr: H; Cable: 302.5/22.0 U2
1981-04 **S.L. Ardeag — Bilbao** Yd No: 120
Loa 35.01 Br ex 10.04 Dght 4.401
Lbp 31.53 Br md 9.42 Dpth 5.36
Welded, 1 dk
(B32A2ST) Tug
Ice Capable
1 oil engine sr geared to sc. shaft driving 1 CP propeller
Total Power: 2,088kW (2,839hp) 12.0kn
Caterpillar 3608TA
1 x 4 Stroke 8 Cy. 280 x 300 2088kW (2839bhp) (new engine 2001)
Caterpillar Inc-USA
AuxGen: 2 x 112kW 380V 50Hz a.c, 1 x 28kW 380V 50Hz a.c

7313523 - -
SPANISH QUEEN II
ex Capt. Brett *-1981* *ex* Lori L *-1978*
Spanish Queen Ltd
-
Nassau *Bahamas*
Official number: 384546
140 / 78 / -
1973 Desco Marine — Saint Augustine, Fl Yd No: 121-F
Loa 22.86 Br ex 6.74 Dght 2.744
Lbp - Br md - Dpth 3.81
Bonded, 1 dk
(B11A2FT) Trawler
Hull Material: Reinforced Plastic
1 oil engine geared to sc. shaft driving 1 FP propeller
Total Power: 268kW (364hp) 10.0kn
Caterpillar 3406TA
1 x 4 Stroke 6 Cy. 137 x 165 268kW (364bhp) (Re-engined ,made 1972, Reconditioned & fitted 1980)
Caterpillar Tractor Co-USA

9257838 - -
SPAR
Government of The United States of America (US Coast Guard)
-
Kodiak, AK *United States of America*
1,930 / 579 / 350
Class: (AB)
2001-09 **Marinette Marine Corp — Marinette WI** Yd No: 206
Loa 68.41 Br ex - Dght 4.390
Lbp 62.42 Br md 14.00 Dpth 6.00
Welded, 1 dk
(B34Q2QB) Buoy Tender
2 oil engines reduction geared to sc. shafts driving 2 FP propellers
Total Power: 4,560kW (6,200hp)
Caterpillar 3608
2 x 4 Stroke 8 Cy. 280 x 300 each-2280kW (3100bhp)
Caterpillar Inc-USA

9299290 *LAFQ6* -
SPAR CANIS
Spar Shipping AS
-
Bergen *Norway (NIS)*
MMSI: 257807000
32,474 / 17,790 / 53,565 / T/cm / 57.3
Class: NK NV
2006-03 **Chengxi Shipyard — Jiangyin JS** Yd No: 4208
Loa 189.95 (BB) Br ex 32.27 Dght 12.540
Lbp 182.99 Br md 32.26 Dpth 17.50
Welded, 1 dk
(A21A2BC) Bulk Carrier
Double Hull
Grain: 65,900; Bale: 64,000
Compartments: 5 Ho, ER
5 Ha: 4 (21.6 x 22.4)ER (19.2 x 20.8)
Cranes: 4x36t
1 oil engine driving 1 FP propeller
Total Power: 9,480kW (12,889hp) 14.2kn
MAN-B&W 6S50MC-C
1 x 2 Stroke 6 Cy. 500 x 2000 9480kW (12889bhp)
Hudong Heavy Machinery Co Ltd-China
AuxGen: 3 x 620kW 440/220V 60Hz a.c
Fuel: 215.0 (d.f.) 2000.0 (r.f.) 34.5pd

9490844 *LAKA7* -
SPAR CAPELLA
Spar Shipping AS
Navig8 Bulk Asia Pte Ltd
SatCom: Inmarsat C 425954510
Bergen *Norway (NIS)*
MMSI: 259545000
32,839 / 19,559 / 58,000 / T/cm / 59.2
Class: NV (BV)
2011-01 **Yangzhou Dayang Shipbuilding Co Ltd — Yangzhou JS** Yd No: DY3033
Loa 189.99 (BB) Br ex - Dght 12.950
Lbp 185.00 Br md 32.26 Dpth 18.00
Welded, 1 dk
(A21A2BC) Bulk Carrier
Grain: 71,549; Bale: 69,760
Compartments: 5 Ho, ER
5 Ha: ER
Cranes: 4x35t
1 oil engine driving 1 FP propeller
Total Power: 9,960kW (13,542hp) 14.3kn
MAN-B&W 6S50MC-C
1 x 2 Stroke 6 Cy. 500 x 2000 9960kW (13542bhp)
AuxGen: 3 x a.c

9154608 *LAVC5* -
SPAR CETUS
ex Golden Protea *-2002*
Spar Shipholding AS
Navig8 Bulk Asia Pte Ltd
Bergen *Norway (NIS)*
MMSI: 258604000
25,982 / 15,690 / 45,146 / T/cm / 49.8
Class: NV (LR) (BV)
Classed LR until 10/8/08
1998-09 **Hashihama Shipbuilding Co Ltd — Tadotsu KG** Yd No: 1117
Loa 185.74 (BB) Br ex 30.45 Dght 11.950
Lbp 177.00 Br md 30.40 Dpth 16.50
Welded, 1 dk
(A21A2BC) Bulk Carrier
Grain: 57,208; Bale: 55,564
Compartments: 5 Ho, ER
5 Ha: (20.0 x 15.3)4 (20.8 x 15.3)ER
Cranes: 4x30t
1 oil engine driving 1 FP propeller
Total Power: 7,171kW (9,750hp) 14.5kn
B&W 6S50MC
1 x 2 Stroke 6 Cy. 500 x 1910 7171kW (9750bhp)
Mitsui Engineering & Shipbuilding CLtd-Japan
AuxGen: 3 x 480kW 450V 60Hz a.c, 1 x 80kW 450V 60Hz a.c
Boilers: WTAuxB (Comp) 7.0kgf/cm² (6.9bar)

9497830 *LALU7* -
SPAR CORONA
Spar Shipping AS
Navig8 Bulk Asia Pte Ltd
Bergen *Norway (NIS)*
MMSI: 259965000
32,839 / 19,559 / 58,000 / T/cm / 59.2
Class: NV (BV)
2011-08 **Yangzhou Dayang Shipbuilding Co Ltd — Yangzhou JS** Yd No: DY138
Loa 189.99 (BB) Br ex - Dght 12.950
Lbp 185.00 Br md 32.26 Dpth 18.00
Welded, 1 dk
(A21A2BC) Bulk Carrier
Grain: 71,549; Bale: 69,760
Compartments: 5 Ho, ER
5 Ha: ER
Cranes: 4x35t
1 oil engine driving 1 FP propeller
Total Power: 8,700kW (11,829hp) 14.3kn
MAN-B&W 6S50MC-C
1 x 2 Stroke 6 Cy. 500 x 2000 8700kW (11829bhp)
Doosan Engine Co Ltd-South Korea
AuxGen: 3 x 610kW a.c

9490791 *LAKK7* -
SPAR CORVUS
Spar Shipping AS
-
SatCom: Inmarsat C 425909310
Bergen *Norway (NIS)*
MMSI: 259093000
32,839 / 19,559 / 58,000 / T/cm / 59.2
Class: NV (BV)
2011-01 **Yangzhou Dayang Shipbuilding Co Ltd — Yangzhou JS** Yd No: DY3028
Loa 189.99 (BB) Br ex - Dght 12.950
Lbp 185.00 Br md 32.26 Dpth 18.00
Welded, 1 dk
(A21A2BC) Bulk Carrier
Grain: 71,549; Bale: 69,760
Compartments: 5 Ho, ER
5 Ha: ER
Cranes: 4x35t
1 oil engine driving 1 FP propeller
Total Power: 9,960kW (13,542hp) 14.3kn
MAN-B&W 6S50MC-C
1 x 2 Stroke 6 Cy. 500 x 2000 9960kW (13542bhp)
AuxGen: 3 x 610kW a.c

9299305 *LAFO6* -
SPAR DRACO
Spar Shipholding AS
Navig8 Bulk Asia Pte Ltd
Bergen *Norway (NIS)*
MMSI: 257799000
32,474 / 17,790 / 53,565 / T/cm / 57.3
Class: NK (Class contemplated) NV
2006-07 **Chengxi Shipyard — Jiangyin JS** Yd No: 4209
Loa 189.95 (BB) Br ex 32.29 Dght 12.540
Lbp 183.38 Br md 32.26 Dpth 17.50
Welded, 1 dk
(A21A2BC) Bulk Carrier
Double Hull
Grain: 65,752; Bale: 64,000
Compartments: 5 Ho, ER
5 Ha: 4 (21.6 x 22.4)ER (19.2 x 20.8)
Cranes: 4x36t
1 oil engine driving 1 FP propeller
Total Power: 9,480kW (12,889hp) 14.2kn
MAN-B&W 6S50MC-C
1 x 2 Stroke 6 Cy. 500 x 2000 9480kW (12889bhp)
Hudong Heavy Machinery Co Ltd-China
AuxGen: 3 x 620kW 440V 60Hz a.c
Fuel: 230.0 (d.f.) 2000.0 (r.f.) 34.5pd

9307580 *LAFP6* -
SPAR GEMINI
Spar Shipholding AS
Navig8 Bulk Asia Pte Ltd
Bergen *Norway (NIS)*
MMSI: 257801000
32,474 / 17,790 / 53,565 / T/cm / 57.3
Class: NK (NV)
2007-02 **Chengxi Shipyard Co Ltd — Jiangyin JS** Yd No: CX4211
Loa 189.95 (BB) Br ex 32.24 Dght 12.560
Lbp 183.02 Br md 32.22 Dpth 17.50
Welded, 1 dk
(A21A2BC) Bulk Carrier
Double Hull
Grain: 65,752; Bale: 64,000
Compartments: 5 Ho, ER
5 Ha: 4 (21.6 x 22.4)ER (19.2 x 20.8)
Cranes: 4x36t
1 oil engine driving 1 FP propeller
Total Power: 9,480kW (12,889hp) 14.2kn
MAN-B&W 6S50MC-C
1 x 2 Stroke 6 Cy. 500 x 2000 9480kW (12889bhp)
Hudong Heavy Machinery Co Ltd-China
AuxGen: 3 x 650kW 440V 60Hz a.c
Fuel: 215.0 (d.f.) 2000.0 (r.f.) 34.5pd

9490806 *LAKL7* -
SPAR HYDRA
Spar Shipping AS
-
SatCom: Inmarsat C 425940110
Bergen *Norway (NIS)*
MMSI: 259701000
32,839 / 19,559 / 58,000 / T/cm / 59.2
Class: NV (BV)
2011-01 **Yangzhou Dayang Shipbuilding Co Ltd — Yangzhou JS** Yd No: DY3029
Loa 189.99 (BB) Br ex - Dght 12.950
Lbp 185.00 Br md 32.26 Dpth 18.00
Welded, 1 dk
(A21A2BC) Bulk Carrier
Grain: 71,549; Bale: 69,760
Compartments: 5 Ho, ER
5 Ha: ER
Cranes: 4x35t
1 oil engine driving 1 FP propeller
Total Power: 9,960kW (13,542hp) 14.3kn
MAN-B&W 6S50MC-C
1 x 2 Stroke 6 Cy. 500 x 2000 9960kW (13542bhp)
AuxGen: 3 x 610kW a.c

9328534 *LAMX7* -
SPAR LIBRA
ex Bulk Navigator *-2011* *ex* Arya Payk *-2009*
ex Bulk Navigator *-2006*
Spar Shipping AS
-
Bergen *Norway (NIS)*
MMSI: 259932000
32,474 / 17,790 / 53,565 / T/cm / 57.3
Class: NK NV
2006-04 **Chengxi Shipyard — Jiangyin JS** Yd No: 4213
Loa 189.95 (BB) Br ex 32.28 Dght 12.556
Lbp 183.05 Br md 32.26 Dpth 17.50
Welded, 1 dk
(A21A2BC) Bulk Carrier
Double Hull
Grain: 65,752; Bale: 64,000
Compartments: 5 Ho, ER
5 Ha: 4 (21.6 x 22.4)ER (19.2 x 20.8)
Cranes: 4x36t
1 oil engine driving 1 FP propeller
Total Power: 9,480kW (12,889hp) 14.2kn
MAN-B&W 6S50MC-C
1 x 2 Stroke 6 Cy. 500 x 2000 9480kW (12889bhp)
Hudong Heavy Machinery Co Ltd-China
AuxGen: 3 x 620kW 440V 60Hz a.c
Fuel: 230.0 (d.f.) 2000.0 (r.f.) 34.5pd

9154610 *LAVD5* -
SPAR LUPUS
ex Golden Aloe *-2002*
Spar Shipholding AS
Spar Shipping AS
Bergen *Norway (NIS)*
MMSI: 258605000
25,982 / 15,690 / 47,375 / T/cm / 49.8
Class: NK (LR) (NV) (BV)
Classed LR until 24/8/08
1998-08 **Hashihama Shipbuilding Co Ltd — Tadotsu KG** Yd No: 1127
Loa 185.74 (BB) Br ex - Dght 11.950
Lbp 177.00 Br md 30.40 Dpth 16.50
Welded, 1 dk
(A21A2BC) Bulk Carrier
Grain: 57,208; Bale: 55,564
Compartments: 5 Ho, ER
5 Ha: (20.0 x 15.3)4 (20.8 x 15.3)ER
Cranes: 4x30t
1 oil engine driving 1 FP propeller
Total Power: 7,171kW (9,750hp) 14.5kn
B&W 6S50MC
1 x 2 Stroke 6 Cy. 500 x 1910 7171kW (9750bhp)
Mitsui Engineering & Shipbuilding CLtd-Japan
AuxGen: 3 x 500kW a.c
Fuel: 1790.0 (d.f.)

9289025 *LAZQ5* -
SPAR LYNX
Spar Shipholding AS
Navig8 Bulk Asia Pte Ltd
Bergen *Norway (NIS)*
MMSI: 257321000
32,474 / 17,790 / 53,162 / T/cm / 57.3
Class: NK (NV)
2005-03 **Chengxi Shipyard — Jiangyin JS** Yd No: 4205
Loa 190.00 (BB) Br ex - Dght 12.540
Lbp 183.44 Br md 32.26 Dpth 17.50
Welded, 1 dk
(A21A2BC) Bulk Carrier
Double Hull
Grain: 65,900; Bale: 64,000
Compartments: 5 Ho, ER
5 Ha: 4 (21.6 x 22.4)ER (19.2 x 20.8)
Cranes: 4x36t
1 oil engine driving 1 FP propeller
Total Power: 9,480kW (12,889hp) 14.2kn
MAN-B&W 6S50MC-C
1 x 2 Stroke 6 Cy. 500 x 2000 9480kW (12889bhp)
Hudong Heavy Machinery Co Ltd-China
AuxGen: 3 x 680kW 440/220V 60Hz a.c
Fuel: 199.0 (d.f.) 1927.0 (r.f.) 34.5pd

9289013 *LAZP5* -
SPAR LYRA
Spar Shipholding AS
Navig8 Bulk Asia Pte Ltd
Bergen *Norway (NIS)*
MMSI: 257316000
32,474 / 17,790 / 53,565 / T/cm / 57.3
Class: NK (Class contemplated) NV
2005-01 **Chengxi Shipyard — Jiangyin JS** Yd No: 4204
Loa 190.00 (BB) Br ex - Dght 12.540
Lbp 183.44 Br md 32.26 Dpth 17.50
Welded, 1 dk
(A21A2BC) Bulk Carrier
Double Hull
Grain: 65,752; Bale: 64,000
Compartments: 5 Ho, ER
5 Ha: 4 (21.6 x 22.4)ER (19.2 x 20.8)
Cranes: 4x36t
1 oil engine driving 1 FP propeller
Total Power: 9,480kW (12,889hp) 14.2kn
MAN-B&W 6S50MC-C
1 x 2 Stroke 6 Cy. 500 x 2000 9480kW (12889bhp)
Kawasaki Heavy Industries Ltd-Japan
AuxGen: 3 x 680kW 440/220V 60Hz a.c
Fuel: 230.0 (d.f.) 2000.0 (r.f.) 36.0pd

9490727 *LAJZ7* -
SPAR MIRA
Spar Shipping AS
Navig8 Bulk Asia Pte Ltd
Bergen *Norway (NIS)*
MMSI: 257556000
32,839 / 19,559 / 58,000 / T/cm / 59.2
Class: NV (BV)
2010-09 **Yangzhou Dayang Shipbuilding Co Ltd — Yangzhou JS** Yd No: DY3017
Loa 190.00 (BB) Br ex - Dght 12.950
Lbp 185.00 Br md 32.26 Dpth 18.00
Welded, 1 dk
(A21A2BC) Bulk Carrier
Grain: 71,549; Bale: 69,760
Compartments: 5 Ho, ER
5 Ha: ER
Cranes: 4x35t
1 oil engine driving 1 FP propeller
Total Power: 9,960kW (13,542hp) 14.3kn
MAN-B&W 6S50MC-C
1 x 2 Stroke 6 Cy. 500 x 2000 9960kW (13542bhp)
Doosan Engine Co Ltd-South Korea
AuxGen: 3 x 700kW a.c

9077238 *LACA6* -	**SPAR NEPTUN** *ex* Apollon *-2004* *ex* Gran Trader *-1999* **Spar Shipholding AS** Navig8 Bulk Asia Pte Ltd *Bergen* *Norway (NIS)* MMSI: 257348000	**36,559** 23,279 70,101 T/cm 65.0	Class: NV (NK)	**1994-06 Sumitomo Heavy Industries Ltd. — Oppama Shipyard, Yokosuka** Yd No: 1193 Loa 225.00 (BB) Br ex 32.26 Dght 13.268 Lbp 217.00 Br md 32.00 Dpth 18.30 Welded, 1 dk	**(A21A2BC) Bulk Carrier** Grain: 81,839; Bale: 78,529 Compartments: 7 Ho, ER 7 Ha: (16.7 x 13.4)6 (16.7 x 15.0)ER	**1 oil engine** driving 1 FP propeller Total Power: 7,723kW (10,500hp) 15.6kn Sulzer 6RTA62 1 x 2 Stroke 6 Cy. 620 x 2150 7723kW (10500bhp) Diesel United Ltd.-Aioi AuxGen: 3 x a.c
9114622 *LAWI4* -	**SPAR ORION** *ex* Western Orion *-2001* **Spar Shipholding AS** Spar Shipping AS SatCom: Inmarsat C 425898810 *Bergen* *Norway (NIS)* MMSI: 258988000	**26,449** 16,181 47,639 T/cm 50.9	Class: NV (LR) Classed LR until 18/8/09	**1996-05 Oshima Shipbuilding Co Ltd — Saikai NS** Yd No: 10186 Loa 189.99 (BB) Br ex - Dght 11.820 Lbp 181.60 Br md 30.50 Dpth 16.50 Welded, 1 dk	**(A21A2BC) Bulk Carrier** Grain: 59,923; Bale: 57,372 Compartments: 5 Ho, ER 5 Ha: (16.0 x 15.3)4 (20.8 x 15.3)ER Cranes: 4x25t	**1 oil engine** driving 1 FP propeller Total Power: 7,333kW (9,970hp) 15.9kn B&W 6S50MC 1 x 2 Stroke 6 Cy. 500 x 1910 7333kW (9970bhp) Kawasaki Heavy Industries Ltd-Japan AuxGen: 3 x 440kW 220/440V 60Hz a.c Fuel: 120.0 (d.f.) (Heating Coils) 1780.0 (r.f.) 26.3pd
9557111 *LAIS7* -	**SPAR RIGEL** **Spar Shipholding AS** Navig8 Bulk Asia Pte Ltd SatCom: Inmarsat C 425759310 *Bergen* *Norway (NIS)* MMSI: 257593000 Official number: 16595R	**32,837** 19,559 58,000 T/cm 59.2	Class: NV (BV)	**2010-04 Yangzhou Dayang Shipbuilding Co Ltd — Yangzhou JS** Yd No: DY3064 Loa 189.99 (BB) Br ex - Dght 12.950 Lbp 185.00 Br md 32.26 Dpth 18.00 Welded, 1 dk	**(A21A2BC) Bulk Carrier** Grain: 71,549; Bale: 69,760 Compartments: 5 Ho, ER 5 Ha: ER Cranes: 4x35t	**1 oil engine** driving 1 FP propeller Total Power: 9,960kW (13,542hp) 14.3kn MAN-B&W 6S50MC-C 1 x 2 Stroke 6 Cy. 500 x 2000 9960kW (13542bhp) Doosan Engine Co Ltd-South Korea AuxGen: 3 x 610kW 60Hz a.c
9307578 *LAFN6* -	**SPAR SCORPIO** **Spar Shipholding AS** Navig8 Bulk Asia Pte Ltd *Bergen* *Norway (NIS)* MMSI: 257795000	**32,474** 17,790 53,565 T/cm 57.3	Class: NK NV	**2006-10 Chengxi Shipyard — Jiangyin JS** Yd No: 4210 Loa 190.03 (BB) Br ex 32.29 Dght 12.540 Lbp 183.06 Br md 32.26 Dpth 17.50 Welded, 1 dk	**(A21A2BC) Bulk Carrier** Double Hull Grain: 65,752; Bale: 64,000 Compartments: 5 Ho, ER 5 Ha: 4 (21.6 x 22.4)ER (19.2 x 20.8) Cranes: 4x36t	**1 oil engine** driving 1 FP propeller Total Power: 9,480kW (12,889hp) 14.2kn MAN-B&W 6S50MC-C 1 x 2 Stroke 6 Cy. 500 x 2000 9480kW (12889bhp) Hudong Heavy Machinery Co Ltd-China AuxGen: 3 x 620kW 440V 60Hz a.c Fuel: 230.0 (d.f.) 2000.0 (r.f.) 34.5pd
9104615 *LAWK4* -	**SPAR SIRIUS** *ex* Western Transporter *-2001* **Spar Shipholding AS** Spar Shipping AS SatCom: Inmarsat C 425898510 *Bergen* *Norway (NIS)* MMSI: 258985000	**25,968** 15,778 45,402 T/cm 49.8	Class: NK (Class contemplated) NV (LR) ✠ Classed LR until 11/1/09	**1996-03 Tsuneishi Shipbuilding Co Ltd — Fukuyama HS** Yd No: 1066 Loa 185.74 (BB) Br ex 30.43 Dght 11.620 Lbp 177.00 Br md 30.40 Dpth 16.50 Welded, 1 dk	**(A21A2BC) Bulk Carrier** Grain: 57,208; Bale: 55,565 Compartments: 5 Ho, ER 5 Ha: (20.0 x 15.3)4 (20.8 x 15.3)ER Cranes: 4x25t	**1 oil engine** driving 1 FP propeller Total Power: 7,274kW (9,890hp) 14.6kn B&W 6S50MC 1 x 2 Stroke 6 Cy. 500 x 1910 7274kW (9890bhp) Kawasaki Heavy Industries Ltd-Japan AuxGen: 3 x 400kW 450V 60Hz a.c Boilers: AuxB (Comp) 7.0kgf/cm² (6.9bar) Fuel: 74.0 (d.f.) 1529.0 (r.f.)
9328522 *LAMY7* -	**SPAR SPICA** *ex* Bulk Voyager *-2011* *ex* Arya Payam *-2009* *ex* Bulk Voyager *-2005* *ex* Paracan *-2005* **Spar Shipholding AS** Navig8 Bulk Asia Pte Ltd *Bergen* *Norway (NIS)* MMSI: 259933000	**32,474** 17,790 53,565 T/cm 57.3	Class: NK (Class contemplated) NV	**2005-08 Chengxi Shipyard — Jiangyin JS** Yd No: 4212 Loa 190.00 (BB) Br ex 32.31 Dght 12.600 Lbp 182.95 Br md 32.27 Dpth 17.50 Welded, 1 dk	**(A21A2BC) Bulk Carrier** Double Hull Grain: 65,900; Bale: 64,000 Compartments: 5 Ho, ER 5 Ha: 4 (21.6 x 22.4)ER (19.2 x 20.8) Cranes: 4x36t	**1 oil engine** driving 1 FP propeller Total Power: 9,480kW (12,889hp) 14.2kn MAN-B&W 6S50MC-C 1 x 2 Stroke 6 Cy. 500 x 2000 9480kW (12889bhp) Hudong Heavy Machinery Co Ltd-China AuxGen: 3 x 620kW 440V 60Hz a.c Fuel: 215.0 (d.f.) 2000.0 (r.f.) 33.4pd
9299288 *LAZS5* -	**SPAR TAURUS** **Spar Shipholding AS** Navig8 Bulk Asia Pte Ltd *Bergen* *Norway (NIS)* MMSI: 257325000	**32,474** 17,790 53,565 T/cm 57.3	Class: NK (Class contemplated) NV	**2005-11 Chengxi Shipyard — Jiangyin JS** Yd No: 4207 Loa 189.95 (BB) Br ex 32.29 Dght 12.540 Lbp 183.05 Br md 32.26 Dpth 17.50 Welded, 1 dk	**(A21A2BC) Bulk Carrier** Double Hull Grain: 65,752; Bale: 64,000 Compartments: 5 Ho, ER 5 Ha: 4 (21.6 x 22.4)ER (19.2 x 20.8) Cranes: 4x36t	**1 oil engine** driving 1 FP propeller Total Power: 9,480kW (12,889hp) 14.2kn MAN-B&W 6S50MC-C 1 x 2 Stroke 6 Cy. 500 x 2000 9480kW (12889bhp) Hudong Heavy Machinery Co Ltd-China AuxGen: 3 x 620kW 440/220V 60Hz a.c Fuel: 199.0 (d.f.) 1927.0 (r.f.) 34.5pd
9490856 *LALC7* -	**SPAR URSA** **Spar Shipping AS** - *Bergen* *Norway (NIS)* MMSI: 259794000	**32,839** 19,559 58,000 T/cm 59.2	Class: NV (BV)	**2011-04 Yangzhou Dayang Shipbuilding Co Ltd — Yangzhou JS** Yd No: DY3034 Loa 189.99 (BB) Br ex - Dght 12.950 Lbp 185.00 Br md 32.26 Dpth 18.00 Welded, 1 dk	**(A21A2BC) Bulk Carrier** Grain: 71,549; Bale: 69,760 Compartments: 5 Ho, ER 5 Ha: ER Cranes: 4x35t	**1 oil engine** driving 1 FP propeller Total Power: 9,960kW (13,542hp) 14.3kn MAN-B&W 6S50MC-C 1 x 2 Stroke 6 Cy. 500 x 2000 9960kW (13542bhp) AuxGen: 3 x 610kW a.c
9490870 *LAKB7* -	**SPAR VEGA** **Spar Shipholding AS** Navig8 Bulk Asia Pte Ltd SatCom: Inmarsat C 425909910 *Bergen* *Norway (NIS)* MMSI: 259099000	**32,839** 19,559 57,970 T/cm 59.2	Class: NV (BV)	**2011-01 Yangzhou Dayang Shipbuilding Co Ltd — Yangzhou JS** Yd No: DY3037 Loa 189.99 (BB) Br ex - Dght 12.950 Lbp 185.00 Br md 32.26 Dpth 18.00 Welded, 1 dk	**(A21A2BC) Bulk Carrier** Grain: 71,549; Bale: 69,760 Compartments: 5 Ho, ER 5 Ha: ER Cranes: 4x35t	**1 oil engine** driving 1 FP propeller Total Power: 9,960kW (13,542hp) 14.3kn MAN-B&W 6S50MC-C 1 x 2 Stroke 6 Cy. 500 x 2000 9960kW (13542bhp) AuxGen: 3 x 610kW a.c
9299276 *LAZR5* -	**SPAR VIRGO** **Spar Shipholding AS** Navig8 Bulk Asia Pte Ltd *Bergen* *Norway (NIS)* MMSI: 257323000	**32,474** 17,960 53,000 T/cm 57.3	Class: NK NV	**2005-06 Chengxi Shipyard — Jiangyin JS** Yd No: 4206 Loa 190.00 (BB) Br ex - Dght 12.500 Lbp 183.05 Br md 32.26 Dpth 17.50 Welded, 1 dk	**(A21A2BC) Bulk Carrier** Double Hull Grain: 65,770; Bale: 64,000 Compartments: 5 Ho, ER 5 Ha: 4 (21.6 x 22.4)ER (19.2 x 20.8) Cranes: 4x36t	**1 oil engine** driving 1 FP propeller Total Power: 9,480kW (12,889hp) 14.2kn MAN-B&W 6S50MC-C 1 x 2 Stroke 6 Cy. 500 x 2000 9480kW (12889bhp) Hudong Heavy Machinery Co Ltd-China AuxGen: 3 x 620kW 440/220V 60Hz a.c Fuel: 199.0 (d.f.) 1927.0 (r.f.) 34.5pd
7232975 *INYS* -	**SPARGI** *ex* Curl Curl *-1994* **Alimare Srl** - *Reggio Calabria* *Italy* Official number: 1948	**152** 100 65	Class: (LR) (RI) ✠ Classed LR until 28/5/95	**1972-11 Cantiere Navale L Rodriquez — Messina** Yd No: 155 Loa 28.91 Br ex 10.72 Dght - Lbp 24.36 Br md 5.71 Dpth 3.31 Riveted\Welded, 1 dk	**(A37B2PS) Passenger Ship** Hull Material: Aluminium Alloy Passengers: unberthed: 140	**2 oil engines** reverse reduction geared to sc. shafts driving 2 FP propellers Total Power: 1,618kW (2,200hp) 32.0kn M.T.U. 12V493TY70 2 x Vee 4 Stroke 12 Cy. 175 x 205 each-809kW (1100bhp) MTU Friedrichshafen GmbH-Friedrichshafen AuxGen: 1 x 16kW 415/240V 50Hz a.c, 2 x 1kW 24V 50Hz a.c
7050999 *WY5678* -	**SPARHAWK I** *ex* Mister Lobster Eleni *-1994* *ex* Kon Tiki I *-1994* **Sparhawk Corp** - *New Bedford, MA* *United States of America* Official number: 517542	*189* 95 -		**1968 Atlantic Marine — Jacksonville, Fl** L reg 23.02 Br ex 7.35 Dght - Lbp - Br md - Dpth 2.62 Welded	**(B11B2FV) Fishing Vessel**	**1 oil engine** driving 1 FP propeller Total Power: 313kW (426hp)
9195341 - -	**SPARI** **Government of The Republic of Suriname (Ministry of Defence)** Government of The Republic of Suriname *Paramaribo* *Suriname*	*109* - 12	Class: (LR) ✠ Classed LR until 6/6/01	**1999-04 Rodman Polyships S.A. — Vigo** Yd No: 101.004 Loa 30.00 Br ex 6.51 Dght 1.500 Lbp 24.96 Br md 6.00 Dpth 3.35 Bonded, 1 dk	**(B34H2SQ) Patrol Vessel** Hull Material: Reinforced Plastic	**2 oil engines** with clutches, flexible couplings & sr reverse geared to sc. shafts driving 2 Water jets Total Power: 2,014kW (2,738hp) 30.0kn M.T.U. 12V2000M90 2 x Vee 4 Stroke 12 Cy. 130 x 150 each-1007kW (1369bhp) MTU Friedrichshafen GmbH-Friedrichshafen AuxGen: 2 x 21kW 380V 60Hz a.c
8802698 *MKJX5* N 183	**SPARKLING SEA** **J H McKee Ltd** - *Newry* *United Kingdom* MMSI: 235000743 Official number: A24549	**195** 65 -		**1988-12 Scheepswerf Made B.V. — Made** (Hull) **1988-12 B.V. Scheepswerf Damen — Gorinchem** Yd No: 4173 Loa 23.21 Br ex - Dght 3.201 Lbp - Br md 7.12 Dpth - Welded, 1 dk	**(B11A2FS) Stern Trawler**	**1 oil engine** with clutches, flexible couplings & sr reverse geared to sc. shaft driving 1 FP propeller Total Power: 519kW (706hp) Caterpillar 3508TA 1 x Vee 4 Stroke 8 Cy. 170 x 190 519kW (706bhp) Caterpillar Inc-USA
7392945 *EI6212* D 437	**SPARKLING STAR** **Donal O'Neill** - *Dublin* *Irish Republic* MMSI: 250440000 Official number: 403397	**275** 89 -		**1975-02 Scheepswerf- en Reparatiebedrijf "Harlingen" B.V. — Harlingen** Yd No: 43 Loa 26.60 Br ex - Dght - Lbp - Br md 7.29 Dpth 3.69 Welded	**(B11B2FV) Fishing Vessel**	**1 oil engine** geared to sc. shaft driving 1 FP propeller Total Power: 552kW (750hp) Blackstone EWSL6 1 x 4 Stroke 6 Cy. 222 x 292 552kW (750bhp) Mirrlees Blackstone (Stamford)Ltd.-Stamford
8972558 *ZNZL6* FR 29	**SPARKLING STAR IV** *ex* Ajax *-2012* *ex* Holly B II *-2004* **JJ Corbett** Westward Fishing Co *United Kingdom* MMSI: 235003150 Official number: C17307	**130** 47 -		**2001 JSC Bars — Sankt-Peterburg** (Hull) **2001 Buckie Shipyard Ltd. — Buckie** Loa 17.60 (BB) Br ex - Dght 4.000 Lbp - Br md 6.40 Dpth - Welded, 1 dk	**(B11A2FS) Stern Trawler** Ins: 75	**1 oil engine** reduction geared to sc. shaft driving 1 FP propeller Total Power: 435kW (591hp) 10.1kn Caterpillar 3412TA 1 x Vee 4 Stroke 12 Cy. 137 x 152 435kW (591bhp) Caterpillar Inc-USA Fuel: 15.3 (d.f.)

IMO / Call sign	Name / Owners	Tonnage	Class	Build / Dimensions	Type	Machinery
9317353 *3EDS6* -	**SPARNA** **Lucretia Shipping SA** Santoku Senpaku Co Ltd *Panama* *Panama* MMSI: 371707000 Official number: 3145006A	**31,385** 17,161 54,881 T/cm 55.9	Class: NK	**2006-01 Oshima Shipbuilding Co Ltd — Saikai NS** Yd No: 10401 Loa 189.99 (BB) Br ex - Dght 12.520 Lbp 185.79 Br md 32.26 Dpth 17.62 Welded, 1 dk	**(A21A2BC) Bulk Carrier** Double Hull Grain: 64,824; Bale: 64,391 Compartments: 5 Ho, ER 5 Ha: ER Cranes: 4x30t	**1 oil engine** driving 1 FP propeller Total Power: 8,208kW (11,160hp) 14.5kn B&W 6S50MC-C 1 x 2 Stroke 6 Cy. 500 x 2000 8208kW (11160bhp) Kawasaki Heavy Industries Ltd-Japan Fuel: 1985.0
9171450 *5IQV23* -	**SPARROW** *ex* Clove *-2013* *ex* Semnan *-2012* *ex* Iran Semnan *-2008* **Clove Shipping Co Ltd** NITC *Zanzibar* *Tanzania (Zanzibar)* MMSI: 677002200	**81,479** 50,676 159,681 T/cm 117.5	Class: (LR) (GL) (NV) ✠ Classed LR until 23/5/01	**2000-03 Daewoo Heavy Industries Ltd — Geoje** Yd No: 5134 Loa 274.00 (BB) Br ex 48.04 Dght 17.022 Lbp 264.00 Br md 48.00 Dpth 23.20 Welded, 1 dk	**(A13A2TV) Crude Oil Tanker** Double Hull (13F) Liq: 166,683; Liq (Oil): 166,683 Compartments: 12 Wing Ta, 2 Wing Slop Ta, ER 3 Cargo Pump (s): 3x3500m³/hr Manifold: Bow/CM: 129m	**1 oil engine** driving 1 FP propeller Total Power: 16,846kW (22,904hp) 15.2kn MAN-B&W 6S70MC 1 x 2 Stroke 6 Cy. 700 x 2674 16846kW (22904bhp) HSD Engine Co Ltd-South Korea AuxGen: 3 x 970kW 450V 60Hz a.c Fuel: 282.0 (d.f.) (Heating Coils) 4491.0 (r.f.) 59.4pd
9176278 *V7IB8* -	**SPARROW** *ex* Sea Blue *-2005* *ex* Bay Bulker *-2004* **Sparrow Shipping LLC** Eagle Shipping International (USA) LLC *Majuro* *Marshall Islands* MMSI: 538002354 Official number: 2354	**26,580** 16,450 48,220 T/cm 51.8	Class: LR (BV) (NK) **100A1** SS 02/2010 bulk carrier strengthened for heavy cargoes, Nos. 2 & 4 holds may be empty ESP **LMC** **UMS** Cable: 605.0/66.0 U3 (a)	**2000-02 Oshima Shipbuilding Co Ltd — Saikai NS** Yd No: 10243 Loa 189.33 (BB) Br ex - Dght 11.739 Lbp 178.09 Br md 30.95 Dpth 16.40 Welded, 1 dk	**(A21A2BC) Bulk Carrier** Grain: 60,956; Bale: 59,778 Compartments: 5 Ho, ER 5 Ha: (17.1 x 15.6) (19.8 x 15.6) (19.8 x 15.6)2 (21.6 x 15.6)ER Cranes: 4x30t	**1 oil engine** driving 1 FP propeller Total Power: 8,527kW (11,593hp) 14.5kn Mitsubishi 6UEC50LSII 1 x 2 Stroke 6 Cy. 500 x 1950 8527kW (11593bhp) Mitsubishi Heavy Industries Ltd-Japan AuxGen: 3 x 441kW 450V 60Hz a.c Boilers: WTAuxB (Comp)
7504122 *ERGH* -	**SPARROW** *ex* Sea Pearl *-2006* *ex* Kronborg *-2005* *ex* Christopher Meeder *-2003* **Friends Shipmanagement Inc** El Reedy Shipping Agency *Moldova* MMSI: 214180708	**2,235** 1,136 2,200	Class: MB (GL)	**1976-05 Schiffswerft Hugo Peters — Wewelsfleth** Yd No: 559 Loa 86.92 Br ex 12.98 Dght 4.752 Lbp 78.17 Br md 12.80 Dpth 7.00 Welded, 2 dks	**(A31A2GX) General Cargo Ship** Grain: 4,040; Bale: 3,735 TEU 135 incl 10 ref C. Compartments: 1 Ho, ER 2 Ha: (12.6 x 8.0) (37.1 x 10.2)ER Ice Capable	**1 oil engine** sr geared to sc. shaft driving 1 FP propeller Total Power: 1,434kW (1,950hp) 13.0kn MaK 6M453AK 1 x 4 Stroke 6 Cy. 320 x 420 1434kW (1950bhp) MaK Maschinenbau GmbH-Kiel AuxGen: 2 x 65kW 220/380V 50Hz a.c, 1 x 42kW 220/380V 50Hz a.c Fuel: 129.0 (d.f.) 8.5pd
7945481 - -	**SPARROW** *ex* Kalachevsk *-2007* - -	**497** 149 207	Class: (RS)	**1981-08 Zavod 'Nikolayevsk-na-Amure' — Nikolayevsk-na-Amure** Yd No: 1210 Loa 44.85 Br ex 9.32 Dght 3.750 Lbp 39.37 Br md - Dpth 5.13 Welded, 1 dk	**(B11B2FV) Fishing Vessel** Ins: 210 Compartments: 1 Ho, ER 1 Ha: (1.2 x 1.2) Derricks: 4x3.3t Ice Capable	**1 oil engine** driving 1 FP propeller 11.5kn S.K.L. 6NVD48-2U 1 x 4 Stroke 6 Cy. 320 x 480 VEB Schwermaschinenbau "KarlLiebknecht" (SKL)-Magdeburg
7393779 *9LD2397* -	**SPARROW HAWK** *ex* Keen Express *-2011* *ex* Keen *-2008* *ex* Maersk Feeder *-1989* *ex* Edda Freia *-1979* **Carona Corp** Alpha Logistics Services (EPZ) Ltd *Freetown* *Sierra Leone* MMSI: 667005097 Official number: SL105097	**958** 379 1,095	Class: (RI) (NV)	**1976-04 Bolsones Verft AS — Molde** Yd No: 243 Loa 61.24 Br ex 12.68 Dght 4.936 Lbp 52.00 Br md 12.35 Dpth 5.59 Welded, 1 dk	**(B21B20T) Offshore Tug/Supply Ship** Cranes: 1 Ice Capable	**2 oil engines** geared to sc. shafts driving 2 CP propellers Total Power: 5,178kW (7,040hp) 15.0kn Nohab F216V 2 x Vee 4 Stroke 16 Cy. 250 x 300 each-2589kW (3520bhp) AB Bofors NOHAB-Sweden AuxGen: 2 x 199kW 440/220V 60Hz a.c Thrusters: 1 Thwart. FP thruster (f) Fuel: 350.0 (d.f.) 25.0pd
8809361 *UIBS* -	**SPARTA** *ex* Ocean No. 68 *-2009* *ex* Seisho Maru No. 68 *-2007* **Antey Co Ltd (TOO 'Antey')** - SatCom: Inmarsat C 427303276 *Sovetskaya Gavan* *Russia* MMSI: 273345230	**708** 280 371	Class: RS	**1988-10 Yamanishi Shipbuilding Co Ltd — Ishinomaki MG** Yd No: 968 Loa 55.16 (BB) Br ex 8.82 Dght 3.743 Lbp 48.00 Br md 8.80 Dpth 3.75 Welded, 1 dk	**(B11B2FV) Fishing Vessel** Ins: 430	**1 oil engine** with clutches, flexible couplings & sr geared to sc. shaft driving 1 FP propeller Total Power: 662kW (900hp) 12.0kn Fuji 6S27F 1 x 4 Stroke 6 Cy. 270 x 510 662kW (900bhp) Fuji Diesel Co Ltd-Japan AuxGen: 2 x 280kW 225V a.c Fuel: 200.0 (d.f.)
9372468 *A8HT6* -	**SPARTA** *ex* Jin Chengzhou 29 *-2005* **Sparta Steamship Ltd** INTRESCO GmbH *Monrovia* *Liberia* MMSI: 636012774 Official number: 12774	**7,139** 4,078 10,315	Class: RS (CC)	**2005-09 Linhai Jianghai Shipbuilding Co Ltd — Linhai ZJ** Yd No: 005 Loa 134.00 (BB) Br ex 19.03 Dght 6.790 Lbp 125.80 Br md 19.00 Dpth 9.20 Welded, 1 dk	**(A31A2GX) General Cargo Ship** Grain: 13,924 TEU 486 C Ho 240 TEU C Dk 246 TEU Compartments: 3 Ho, ER 3 Ha: ER 3 (26.0 x 12.0)	**1 oil engine** reduction geared to sc. shaft driving 1 FP propeller Total Power: 2,501kW (3,400hp) 12.5kn Daihatsu 8DKM-28 1 x 4 Stroke 8 Cy. 280 x 390 2501kW (3400bhp) Shaanxi Diesel Heavy Industry Co Lt-China AuxGen: 3 x 120kW a.c
9493860 *V7UG5* -	**SPARTA** *ex* Lotus *-2010* **Sparta LLC** Maritime Equity Management LLC SatCom: Inmarsat C 453835684 *Majuro* *Marshall Islands* MMSI: 538002021 Official number: 2021	**91,373** 58,745 178,005 T/cm 120.6	Class: NV (GL) (AB)	**2010-02 Shanghai Jiangnan Changxing Shipbuilding Co Ltd — Shanghai** Yd No: 1164 Loa 292.00 (BB) Br ex - Dght 18.300 Lbp 282.00 Br md 45.00 Dpth 24.80 Welded, 1 dk	**(A21A2BC) Bulk Carrier** Grain: 194,486; Bale: 183,425 Compartments: 9 Ho, ER 9 Ha: ER	**1 oil engine** driving 1 FP propeller Total Power: 16,860kW (22,923hp) 14.0kn MAN-B&W 6S70MC 1 x 2 Stroke 6 Cy. 700 x 2674 16860kW (22923bhp) Hyundai Heavy Industries Co Ltd-South Korea AuxGen: 3 x 900kW 450V a.c
9403528 *2CPB3* -	**SPARTACUS** **Hayward Corporate Inc** Enterprises Shipping & Trading SA *Douglas* *Isle of Man (British)* MMSI: 235074619 Official number: 741917	**93,196** 59,298 179,156	Class: BV	**2011-08 Sungdong Shipbuilding & Marine Engineering Co Ltd — Tongyeong** Yd No: 1030 Loa 292.00 (BB) Br ex - Dght 18.300 Lbp 283.50 Br md 45.00 Dpth 24.80 Welded, 1 dk	**(A21A2BC) Bulk Carrier** Grain: 198,193; Bale: 182,071 Compartments: 9 Ho, ER 9 Ha: ER	**1 oil engine** driving 1 FP propeller Total Power: 18,660kW (25,370hp) 14.6kn MAN-B&W 6S70MC-C 1 x 2 Stroke 6 Cy. 700 x 2800 18660kW (25370bhp) Hyundai Heavy Industries Co Ltd-South Korea AuxGen: 3 x 730kW 60Hz a.c
9249776 - -	**SPARTACUS** **Molimar** *Naples* *Italy*	**500** - 750		**2000-12 Cantieri Navali Termoli SpA — Termoli** Yd No: 167 Loa 36.00 Br ex - Dght - Lbp - Br md 10.20 Dpth 5.30 Welded, 1 dk	**(B21B20T) Offshore Tug/Supply Ship**	**2 oil engines** reduction geared to sc. shafts driving 2 CP propellers Total Power: 3,240kW (4,406hp) Wartsila 9L20 2 x 4 Stroke 9 Cy. 200 x 280 each-1620kW (2203bhp) Wartsila Finland Oy-Finland
7504158 *5IM611* -	**SPARTACUS** *ex* Joy Star *-2011* *ex* Navigia *-2008* *ex* DFL Hamburg *-1994* *ex* Dana Navigia *-1990* *ex* Navigia *-1990* *ex* Donar *-1979* **El Reedy Shipping Co** - *Zanzibar* *Tanzania (Zanzibar)* MMSI: 677051100 Official number: 300356	**2,240** 1,309 2,560	Class: DR (BR) (GL)	**1975-12 KG Norderwerft GmbH & Co. — Hamburg** (Hull) **1975-12 J.J. Sietas Schiffswerft — Hamburg** Yd No: 783 Loa 81.39 (BB) Br ex 13.42 Dght 5.030 Lbp 74.16 Br md 13.40 Dpth 7.50 Welded, 2 dks	**(A31A2GX) General Cargo Ship** Grain: 4,785; Bale: 4,512 TEU 149 C. 149/20' Compartments: 1 Ho, ER 1 Ha: (50.4 x 10.2)ER Ice Capable	**1 oil engine** reduction geared to sc. shaft driving 1 FP propeller Total Power: 1,470kW (1,999hp) 13.8kn MaK 8M453AK 1 x 4 Stroke 8 Cy. 320 x 420 1470kW (1999bhp) MaK Maschinenbau GmbH-Kiel
7822914 *9LD2507* -	**SPARTAK** *ex* Proje 2 *-2013* *ex* RM 1003 *-2011* **Amonia Enterprises SA** - *Freetown* *Sierra Leone*	*108* 30 -	Class: (TL) (AB)	**1983-07 Denizcilik Bankasi T.A.O. — Istinye, Istanbul** Yd No: 45 Loa 26.17 Br ex 6.71 Dght 3.220 Lbp 24.34 Br md 6.58 Dpth 3.46 Welded, 1 dk	**(B32A2ST) Tug**	**1 oil engine** reverse reduction geared to sc. shaft driving 1 FP propeller Total Power: 754kW (1,025hp) 11.0kn Normo LDM-6 1 x 4 Stroke 6 Cy. 250 x 300 754kW (1025bhp) AS Bergens Mek Verksteder-Norway AuxGen: 2 x 44kW
8332540 *9A6745* -	**SPARTAK** *ex* Iris I *-1999* **Jadran Tuna doo** - *Zadar* *Croatia* MMSI: 238279740 Official number: 3R-116	*119* 39 90	Class: CS	**1983 Brodogradiliste Greben — Vela Luka** Yd No: 815 Loa 23.70 Br ex - Dght 3.271 Lbp 21.01 Br md 6.80 Dpth 3.71 Bonded	**(B11A2FS) Stern Trawler** Hull Material: Reinforced Plastic	**1 oil engine** geared to sc. shaft driving 1 FP propeller Total Power: 820kW (1,115hp) 10.0kn Cummins KTA-38-M1 1 x Vee 4 Stroke 12 Cy. 159 x 159 820kW (1115bhp) Cummins India Ltd-India AuxGen: 1 x 20kW 50Hz a.c
8313996 - -	**SPARTAK** *ex* Sayme *-1994* *ex* Ustritsa *-1994* **Batesko Co (Firma 'Batesko')** -	**255** 76 113	Class: (RS)	**1984-09 Stocznia Ustka SA — Ustka** Yd No: B275/04 Converted From: Trawler Loa 29.80 Br ex 8.00 Dght 3.430 Lbp 26.37 Br md - Dpth 4.02 Welded, 1 dk	**(B31A2SR) Research Survey Vessel**	**1 oil engine** geared to sc. shaft driving 1 CP propeller Total Power: 552kW (750hp) 10.7kn Sulzer 6AL20/24 1 x 4 Stroke 6 Cy. 200 x 240 552kW (750bhp) Zaklady Przemyslu Metalowego 'HCegielski' SA-Poznan AuxGen: 2 x 100kW Fuel: 52.0 (d.f.)

IMO / Call sign	Name, former names, owner, manager, port, flag	Tonnage	Class	Builder, dimensions	Type	Machinery
7725403 *9HCL7* -	**SPARTAN** *ex* Jantar *-2009* *ex* Pacific Salvor *-2001* *ex* Abeille Bretagne *-1996* **Princess Management Ltd** Pella Shipping Co SatCom: Inmarsat M 655300110 *Valletta* *Malta* MMSI: 215102000 Official number: 7478	**668** 200 1,200	Class: BV	**1979**-07 **Ateliers et Chantiers de La Manche — Dieppe** Yd No: 1271 Loa 44.75 Br ex 11.82 Dght 4.800 Lbp 40.01 Br md 11.40 Dpth 5.44 Welded, 1 dk	**(B21B20A) Anchor Handling Tug Supply**	**2 oil engines** geared to sc. shaft driving 2 CP propellers Total Power: 3,530kW (4,800hp) 11.0kn Pielstick 6PA6L280 2 x 4 Stroke 6 Cy. 280 x 290 each-1765kW (2400bhp) Alsthom Atlantique-France AuxGen: 2 x 224kW a.c, 1 x 112kW a.c Thrusters: 1 Thwart. FP thruster (f)
7047461 *WYZ5243* -	**SPARTAN** *ex* Mark Hannah *-2009* *ex* Challenger *-1993* *ex* Gulf Challenger *-1980* *ex* Lead Horse *-1973* **Occidental Chemical Corp** - *Ludington, MI* *United States of America* MMSI: 366891340 Official number: 519204	*190* 129 -		**1969 Burton Shipyard Co., Inc. — Port Arthur, Tx** Yd No: 439 Converted From: Tug-1979 Loa - Br ex - Dght 3.995 Lbp 36.94 Br md 9.73 Dpth 4.37 Welded, 1 dk	**(B32B2SA) Articulated Pusher Tug**	**2 oil engines** reverse reduction geared to sc. shafts driving 2 FP propellers Total Power: 2,500kW (3,400hp) 12.5kn EMD (Electro-Motive) 16-645-C 2 x Vee 2 Stroke 16 Cy. 230 x 254 each-1250kW (1700bhp) General Motors Corp.Electro-Motive Div.-La Grange AuxGen: 2 x 115kW a.c
7105196 - -	**SPARTAN** **Luzon Stevedoring Corp** - *Iloilo* *Philippines* Official number: 213431	*301* 80 -	Class: (AB)	**1971 Iloilo Dock & Engineering Co. — Iloilo** Yd No: 94 Loa 35.06 Br ex 8.54 Dght 3.823 Lbp 31.32 Br md 8.23 Dpth 4.42 Welded, 1 dk	**(B32A2ST) Tug** Derricks: 1x3t; Winches: 1	**2 oil engines** reduction geared to sc. shafts driving 2 FP propellers Total Power: 832kW (1,132hp) 12.0kn MWM 2 x Vee 4 Stroke 12 Cy. 140 x 180 each-416kW (566bhp) Motoren Werke Mannheim AG (MWM)-West Germany AuxGen: 2 x 60kW 220V 60Hz a.c Fuel: 146.5 (d.f.)
8867870 *WBN3018* -	**SPARTAN** **Crowley Marine Services Inc** - *San Francisco, CA* *United States of America* MMSI: 366888760 Official number: 518285	*147* 99 -		**1969 Mangone Shipbuilding Co. — Houston, Tx** Yd No: 88 Loa 30.30 Br ex 9.60 Dght 3.556 Lbp - Br md - Dpth 4.43 Welded, 1 dk	**(B32A2ST) Tug**	**2 oil engines** sr reverse geared to sc. shafts driving 2 FP propellers Total Power: 1,766kW (2,402hp) Caterpillar D399SCAC 2 x Vee 4 Stroke 16 Cy. 159 x 203 each-883kW (1201bhp) Caterpillar Tractor Co-USA
7047526 - -	**SPARTAN II** *ex* Spartan *-1986* *ex* Spartan I *-1986* *ex* Spartan Service *-1986* **Shackle International Ltd** -	**704** 211 508	Class: (AB)	**1969 Burton Shipyard Co., Inc. — Port Arthur, Tx** Yd No: 450 Loa 52.74 Br ex - Dght 3.861 Lbp 51.97 Br md 12.26 Dpth 4.58 Welded, 1 dk	**(B21B20A) Anchor Handling Tug Supply**	**2 oil engines** reverse reduction geared to sc. shafts driving 2 FP propellers Total Power: 1,654kW (2,248hp) 10.0kn Caterpillar D399SCAC 2 x Vee 4 Stroke 16 Cy. 159 x 203 each-827kW (1124bhp) Caterpillar Tractor Co-USA AuxGen: 2 x 100kW Thrusters: 1 Thwart. FP thruster
9030993 *ELLB2* -	**SPARTAN WARRIOR** *ex* Orion Star *-2008* **Soprano SA** Polembros Shipping Ltd SatCom: Inmarsat A 1252260 *Monrovia* *Liberia* MMSI: 636008889 Official number: 8889	**159,766** 98,543 297,237 T/cm 170.0	Class: LR ✠ **100A1** SS 11/2009 Double Hull oil tanker ESP SPM ✠ **LMC** **UMS IGS** Eq.Ltr: D*; Cable: 770.0/114.0 U3	**1994**-11 **Nippon Kokan KK (NKK Corp) — Tsu ME** Yd No: 139 Conv to DH-2010 Loa 331.50 (BB) Br ex 58.04 Dght 22.135 Lbp 317.00 Br md 58.00 Dpth 31.26 Welded, 1 dk	**(A13A2TV) Crude Oil Tanker** Double Hull (13F) Liq: 328,678; Liq (Oil): 328,678 Compartments: 6 Wing Ta, 7 Ta, ER, 2 Wing Slop Ta 3 Cargo Pump (s): 3x5000m³/hr Manifold: Bow/CM: 162.8m	**1 oil engine** driving 1 FP propeller Total Power: 20,230kW (27,505hp) 14.3kn Sulzer 7RTA84M 1 x 2 Stroke 7 Cy. 840 x 2900 20230kW (27505bhp) Diesel United Ltd.-Aioi AuxGen: 3 x 900kW 450V 60Hz a.c Boilers: 2 AuxB (o.f.) 24.5kgf/cm² (24.0bar), e (ex.g.) 28.1kgf/cm² (27.6bar) Fuel: 378.0 (d.f.) 7471.0 (r.f.) 74.0pd
9217644 *SYDH* -	**SPARTIA** **Fowler Transportation Special Maritime Enterprise (ENE)** Neda Maritime Agency Co Ltd *Piraeus* *Greece* MMSI: 239715000 Official number: 10770	**39,783** 25,329 75,115 T/cm 67.3	Class: LR ✠ **100A1** SS 07/2010 bulk carrier strengthened for heavy cargoes, Nos. 2, 4 & 6 holds may be empty ESP ESN *IWS LI **ShipRight** (SDA, FDA, CM) ✠ **LMC** **UMS** Eq.Ltr: P†; Cable: 664.1/78.0 U3 (a)	**2000**-07 **Hitachi Zosen Corp — Maizuru KY** Yd No: 4957 Loa 224.92 (BB) Br ex 32.24 Dght 13.800 Lbp 217.00 Br md 32.20 Dpth 19.15 Welded, 1 dk	**(A21A2BC) Bulk Carrier** Grain: 89,423; Bale: 86,925 Compartments: 7 Ho, ER 7 Ha: (16.3 x 13.0)6 (17.2 x 14.6)ER	**1 oil engine** driving 1 FP propeller Total Power: 10,750kW (14,616hp) 15.0kn B&W 6S60MC 1 x 2 Stroke 6 Cy. 600 x 2292 10750kW (14616bhp) Hitachi Zosen Corp-Japan AuxGen: 3 x 400kW 450V 60Hz a.c Boilers: AuxB (Comp) 7.0kgf/cm² (6.9bar)
9274800 *P3VW9* -	**SPARTO** **Starwave Shipping Co Ltd** Enesel SA SatCom: Inmarsat C 420905510 *Limassol* *Cyprus* MMSI: 209055000 Official number: 9274800	**62,877** 34,548 114,549 T/cm 99.9	Class: NV	**2004**-07 **Samsung Heavy Industries Co Ltd — Geoje** Yd No: 1444 Loa 249.87 (BB) Br ex - Dght 14.900 Lbp 239.00 Br md 43.80 Dpth 21.30 Welded, 1 dk	**(A13A2TW) Crude/Oil Products Tanker** Double Hull (13F) Liq: 124,092; Liq (Oil): 124,092 Cargo Heating Coils Compartments: 12 Wing Ta, 2 Wing Slop Ta, ER 3 Cargo Pump (s): 3x2800m³/hr Manifold: Bow/CM: 125.6m Ice Capable	**1 oil engine** driving 1 FP propeller Total Power: 14,313kW (19,460hp) 15.3kn B&W 7S60MC 1 x 2 Stroke 7 Cy. 600 x 2292 14313kW (19460bhp) Doosan Engine Co Ltd-South Korea AuxGen: 3 x 910kW 450/220V 60Hz a.c Fuel: 146.0 (d.f.) 3615.0 (r.f.) 51.4pd
5422241 *IJAC* -	**SPARVIERO** *ex* Robbenplate *-1986* **Moby SpA** - *Cagliari* *Italy* Official number: 529	*276* 90 142	Class: (RI) (GL)	**1963 AG Weser, Werk Seebeck — Bremerhaven** Yd No: 897 Loa 31.58 Br ex 9.22 Dght 4.241 Lbp 28.00 Br md 8.70 Dpth 4.70 Welded, 1 dk	**(B32A2ST) Tug** Ice Capable	**1 oil engine** reverse reduction geared to sc. shaft driving 1 FP propeller Total Power: 1,177kW (1,600hp) 12.5kn Deutz SBV6M358 1 x 4 Stroke 6 Cy. 400 x 580 1177kW (1600bhp) Kloeckner Humboldt Deutz AG-West Germany AuxGen: 2 x 48kW 380V 50Hz a.c, 1 x 46kW 380V 50Hz a.c
7329405 *ISFA* -	**SPARVIERO** **Cooperativa Pescatori Srl San Pietro Apostolo** - *Cetara* *Italy* Official number: 564	*170* 51	Class: (RI)	**1973 Cant. Nav. Ugo Codecasa S.p.A. — Viareggio** Yd No: 20 Loa 35.49 Br ex 7.14 Dght 2.888 Lbp 28.33 Br md 7.12 Dpth 3.51 Welded, 1 dk	**(B11A2FT) Trawler**	**1 oil engine** driving 1 FP propeller Total Power: 597kW (812hp) Caterpillar 3516TA 1 x Vee 4 Stroke 16 Cy. 170 x 190 597kW (812bhp) (new engine 1998) Caterpillar Inc-USA
9497531 *UBKI6* -	**SPASATEL KAREV** **Government of The Russian Federation** Government of The Russian Federation (Federal Budgetary Enterprise State Marine Emergency Salvage, Rescue & Pollution Prevention Coordination Service of Russian Federation) (SMRPCS) *St Petersburg* *Russia* MMSI: 273357360	**2,530** 760 1,215	Class: RS	**2012**-11 **Nevskiy Sudostroitelnyy i Sudorem. Zavod — Shlisselburg** Yd No: 701 Loa 73.00 Br ex 16.60 Dght 5.100 Lbp 66.30 Br md 15.50 Dpth 6.71 Welded, 1 dk	**(B34P2QV) Salvage Ship** Cranes: 2x20t	**4 diesel electric oil engines** driving 4 gen. Connecting to 2 elec. motors each (2000kW) driving 2 Azimuth electric drive units Total Power: 5,760kW (7,832hp) Wartsila 8L20 4 x 4 Stroke 8 Cy. 200 x 280 each-1440kW (1958bhp) Wartsila Finland Oy-Finland Thrusters: 2 Tunnel thruster (f)
9593933 *UCNA* -	**SPASATEL KAVDEJKIN** **Government of The Russian Federation (Ministry of Transport of the Russian Federation)** - *Murmansk* *Russia* MMSI: 273351190	**2,532** 759 1,180	Class: RS	**2013**-08 **Nevskiy Sudostroitelnyy i Sudorem. Zavod — Shlisselburg** Yd No: 702 Loa 73.00 Br ex 16.60 Dght 5.100 Lbp 66.30 Br md 15.50 Dpth 6.71 Welded, 1 dk	**(B34P2QV) Salvage Ship**	**4 diesel electric oil engines** driving 4 gen. Connecting to 2 elec. motors each (2060kW) driving 2 Azimuth electric drive units Total Power: 5,760kW (7,832hp) Wartsila 8L20 4 x 4 Stroke 8 Cy. 200 x 280 each-1440kW (1958bhp) Wartsila Finland Oy-Finland AuxGen: 4 x 1370kW a.c, 1 x 300kW a.c Thrusters: 2 Tunnel thruster (f) Fuel: 250.0 (d.f.)
9593945 - -	**SPASATEL ZABORSHCHIKOV** **Government of The Russian Federation (Ministry of Transport of the Russian Federation)** - *St Petersburg* *Russia* Official number: MPSV07	**2,634** 760 1,215	Class: RS (Class contemplated)	**2013**-12 **Nevskiy Sudostroitelnyy i Sudorem. Zavod — Shlisselburg** Yd No: 703 Loa 73.00 Br ex 16.60 Dght 5.100 Lbp 64.40 Br md 15.50 Dpth 6.70 Welded, 1 dk	**(B34P2QV) Salvage Ship**	**4 diesel electric oil engines** driving 4 gen. Connecting to 2 elec. motors each (2000kW) driving 2 Azimuth electric drive units Total Power: 5,760kW (7,832hp) Wartsila 8L20 4 x 4 Stroke 8 Cy. 200 x 280 each-1440kW (1958bhp) Wartsila Finland Oy-Finland Thrusters: 2 Tunnel thruster (f)

IMO / Call sign	Name / Owner / Flag	Tonnage	Class	Builder / Dimensions	Type	Machinery
8800975 *PB9476* -	**SPATHOEK** *ex* Schleswig-Holstein *-2011* **NV ms Spathoek** EVT BV *Terschelling* *Netherlands* MMSI: 244730394 Official number: 54500	**1,743** 579 274	Class: GL	**1988**-05 **Husumer Schiffswerft Inh. Gebr. Kroeger GmbH & Co. KG — Husum** Yd No: 1507 Loa 67.85 Br ex 13.42 Dght 1.952 Lbp 64.93 Br md 12.81 Dpth 3.20 Welded, 1 dk	**(A36A2PR) Passenger/Ro-Ro Ship (Vehicles)** Passengers: unberthed: 970 Bow door & ramp Lane-clr ht: 4.20 Cars: 54 Ice Capable	**2 oil engines** with flexible couplings & reverse reduction geared to sc. shafts driving 2 FP propellers Total Power: 1,440kW (1,958hp) 12.0kn MWM TBD440-6 2 x 4 Stroke 6 Cy. 230 x 270 each-720kW (979bhp) Motoren Werke Mannheim AG (MWM)-West Germany AuxGen: 1 x 184kW 220/380V a.c Thrusters: 1 Directional thruster (f) Fuel: 64.8 (d.f.)
9327774 *ICDR* -	**SPAVALDA** **Armamento Setramar SpA** Navimar SA *Ravenna* *Italy* MMSI: 247194900 Official number: 82338	**9,286** 4,398 15,026	Class: RI	**2007**-01 **in Turkey** (Hull) Yd No: 05818 **2007**-01 **Niestern Sander B.V. — Delfzijl** Yd No: 818 Loa 139.95 (BB) Br ex - Dght 7.700 Lbp 134.70 Br md 21.00 Dpth 10.60 Welded, 1 dk	**(A31A2GX) General Cargo Ship** Grain: 16,200 TEU 1200 Compartments: 2 Ho, ER 2 Ha: ER	**1 oil engine** geared to sc. shaft driving 1 FP propeller Total Power: 4,350kW (5,914hp) 14.0kn Wartsila 6L38B 1 x 4 Stroke 6 Cy. 380 x 475 4350kW (5914bhp) Wartsila Finland Oy-Finland AuxGen: 1 x 800kW a.c, 2 x 320kW a.c Thrusters: 1 Tunnel thruster (f) Fuel: 90.0 (d.f.) 600.0 (r.f.)
7430046 - -	**SPEAR I** *ex* Nok Nan Num 7 *-2006* *ex* Shokaku Maru *-2002* *ex* Shinei *-1998* *ex* Harmony III *-1997* *ex* Shokaku Maru *-1990* - -	**672** 418 1,300	Class: IS (GL)	**1975**-04 **Matsuura Tekko Zosen K.K. — Osakikamijima** Yd No: 226 Loa 58.60 Br ex 10.52 Dght 4.192 Lbp 53.98 Br md 10.49 Dpth 4.50 Welded, 1 dk	**(A13B2TP) Products Tanker**	**1 oil engine** driving 1 FP propeller Total Power: 1,073kW (1,459hp) 9.0kn Hanshin 6LU32 1 x 4 Stroke 6 Cy. 320 x 510 1073kW (1459bhp) Hanshin Nainenki Kogyo-Japan
7009615 *H03516* -	**SPEARFISH ANN** *ex* Al Sayang *-2004* *ex* Bhaita Liman *-1998* *ex* Iwashima Maru *-1980* **Linden Shipping International** - *Panama* *Panama* MMSI: 355809000 Official number: 3517113	**250** 75 479	Class: HR IS (KI) (NK)	**1969**-11 **Kanagawa Zosen — Kobe** Yd No: 96 Loa 31.60 Br ex 9.02 Dght 3.306 Lbp 28.50 Br md 9.00 Dpth 4.02 Riveted\Welded, 1 dk	**(B32A2ST) Tug**	**2 oil engines** geared to sc. shafts driving 2 FP propellers Total Power: 2,648kW (3,600hp) 12.0kn Hanshin Z6L38ASH 2 x 4 Stroke 6 Cy. 380 x 570 each-1324kW (1800bhp) Hanshin Nainenki Kogyo-Japan AuxGen: 2 x 40kW 445V a.c Fuel: 67.0 10.0pd
8651180 *J7BY2* -	**SPEARTOOTH** *ex* Jarco *-2011* **GPP Construction Equipment Corp** - *Portsmouth* *Dominica* MMSI: 325513000 Official number: 50513	**160** 48 -		**1980 Offshore Trawlers, Inc. — Bayou La Batre, Al** Yd No: 102 Loa 25.45 Br ex 7.32 Dght - Lbp - Br md - Dpth 2.13 Welded, 1 dk	**(B21A20S) Platform Supply Ship**	**2 oil engines** reduction geared to sc. shafts driving 2 Propellers
7946100 *HCJJ* -	**SPECIAL T** *ex* Pittston T *-2011* *ex* Val-T *-2011* *ex* Merry Queen *-2011* **Acotramar CA** - *Guayaquil* *Ecuador* Official number: TN-00-0143	*484* 434 -	Class: (AB)	**1941 Avondale Marine Ways Inc. — Avondale, La** Yd No: 18 Loa 56.39 Br ex - Dght - Lbp 48.77 Br md 10.06 Dpth 2.54 Welded, 1 dk	**(A13B2TU) Tanker (unspecified)**	**2 oil engines** driving 2 FP propellers Total Power: 354kW (482hp) Fairbanks, Morse 2 x 2 Stroke 6 Cy. 254 x 317 each-177kW (241bhp) Fairbanks Morse & Co.-New Orleans, La
9285184 *2GJY9* -	**SPECIALITY** **FSL-14 Inc** James Fisher (Shipping Services) Ltd *London* *United Kingdom* MMSI: 235098053	**3,859** 1,276 4,426 T/cm 13.6	Class: LR ✠ **100A1** SS 05/2011 Double Hull oil and chemical tanker, Ship Type 2 ESP LI ✠ **LMC** **UMS CCS** Eq.Ltr: U; Cable: 467.5/40.0 U3 (a)	**2006**-05 **Qingshan Shipyard — Wuhan HB** Yd No: 20020401 Converted From: Products Tanker-2011 Loa 95.14 (BB) Br ex 17.12 Dght 5.890 Lbp 87.11 Br md 17.00 Dpth 7.70 Welded, 1 dk	**(A12B2TR) Chemical/Products Tanker** Double Hull (13F) Liq: 4,510; Liq (Oil): 4,510 Compartments: 6 Ta, 1 Slop Ta, ER 6 Cargo Pump (s): 6x375m³/hr Manifold: Bow/CM: 46.2m	**6 diesel electric oil engines** driving 6 gen. each 486kW 690V a.c Connecting to 2 elec. motors each (900kW) driving 2 FP propellers Total Power: 3,090kW (4,200hp) 11.5kn MAN D2840LE 6 x Vee 4 Stroke 10 Cy. 128 x 142 each-515kW (700bhp) MAN Nutzfahrzeuge AG-Nuernberg Boilers: HWH (o.f.) 3.9kgf/cm² (3.8bar) Thrusters: 1 Thwart. FP thruster (f) Fuel: 105.0 (d.f.)
7205104 *WBP2185* -	**SPECIALTY DIVER I** *ex* Cal Diver V *-2005* *ex* Sanah *-2005* *ex* Cal Diver V *-1996* *ex* State Queen *-1991* **Specialty Rentals Inc** - *New Orleans, LA* *United States of America* MMSI: 366967010 Official number: 536440	*194* 132 -	Class: (AB)	**1971 Halter Marine Fabricators, Inc. — Moss Point, Ms** Yd No: 321 Loa - Br ex - Dght 3.380 Lbp 47.25 Br md 11.59 Dpth 3.97 Welded, 1 dk	**(B21B20A) Anchor Handling Tug Supply**	**2 oil engines** reverse reduction geared to sc. shafts driving 2 FP propellers Total Power: 1,176kW (1,598hp) Caterpillar D398B 2 x Vee 4 Stroke 12 Cy. 153 x 203 each-588kW (799bhp) Caterpillar Tractor Co-USA AuxGen: 2 x 75kW Fuel: 154.5 (d.f.)
9535412 *9V7663* -	**SPECTRUM** **Hong Lam Logistics Pte Ltd** Hong Lam Marine Pte Ltd SatCom: Inmarsat C 456310010 *Singapore* *Singapore* MMSI: 563100000 Official number: 394590	**14,355** 5,492 21,999 T/cm 31.4	Class: NK	**2009**-05 **Yangzhou Kejin Shipyard Co Ltd — Jiangdu JS** Yd No: 07050 Loa 138.50 (BB) Br ex 26.02 Dght 9.813 Lbp 130.00 Br md 26.00 Dpth 14.30 Welded, 1 dk	**(A13B2TP) Products Tanker** Double Hull (13F) Liq: 21,315; Liq (Oil): 21,315 Cargo Heating Coils Compartments: 12 Wing Ta, 2 Wing Slop Ta, ER 4 Cargo Pump (s): 4x750m³/hr Manifold: Bow/CM: 74.1m	**2 oil engines** reduction geared to sc. shafts driving 2 FP propellers Total Power: 6,618kW (8,998hp) 12.0kn Daihatsu 6DKM-36 2 x 4 Stroke 6 Cy. 360 x 480 each-3309kW (4499bhp) Daihatsu Diesel Manufacturing Co Lt-Japan AuxGen: 3 x 550kW 450V 60Hz a.c Thrusters: 2 Tunnel thruster (f) Fuel: 100.0 (d.f.) 1200.0 (r.f.)
9145566 *6AFG* -	**SPEED 1** - **Eastmed Marine Transport** Yousef S Khalaf *Alexandria* *Egypt* MMSI: 622176001 Official number: 3301	**436** 202 595	Class: HR	**2007**-01 **General Egyptian Co. — Cairo** Yd No: 1067 Loa 49.00 Br ex - Dght 3.230 Lbp 47.28 Br md 8.00 Dpth 4.30 Welded, 1 dk	**(A12B2TR) Chemical/Products Tanker** Double Hull (13F) Compartments: 8 Ta, 2 Slop Ta, ER	**2 oil engines** geared to sc. shafts driving 2 FP propellers Total Power: 588kW (800hp) Caterpillar 3406TA 2 x 4 Stroke 6 Cy. 137 x 165 each-294kW (400bhp) Caterpillar Inc-USA AuxGen: 2 x 50Hz a.c
8993186 - -	**SPEED 2** *ex* Alter Ego I *-2005* **FAI Rent-a-Yacht SA** Mare-Lux SA *Luxembourg* *Luxembourg*	**145** 43 -		**1996**-01 **Cantiere Navale Arno Srl — Pisa** Yd No: 118/2 Loa 27.00 Br ex 6.05 Dght 1.900 Lbp 22.92 Br md 6.00 Dpth 3.01 Bonded, 1 dk	**(X11A2YP) Yacht** Hull Material: Reinforced Plastic	**2 oil engines** driving 2 Propellers Total Power: 2,646kW (3,598hp) 31.0kn M.T.U. 2 x 4 Stroke each-1323kW (1799bhp) MTU Friedrichshafen GmbH-Friedrichshafen
8816053 *SY2591* -	**SPEED CAT 1** *ex* Panormitis *-2008* *ex* Tallink Express I *-2001* *ex* Sleipner *-1997* **Hellas Speed Cat** - *Piraeus* *Greece* MMSI: 237552900 Official number: 11735	**430** 139 50	Class: (BV) (NV)	**1989**-05 **Fjellstrand AS — Omastrand** Yd No: 1589 Loa 38.84 Br ex 9.44 Dght 1.580 Lbp 36.00 Br md - Dpth 3.91 Riveted	**(A37B2PS) Passenger Ship** Hull Material: Aluminium Alloy Passengers: unberthed: 243	**2 oil engines** geared to sc. shafts driving 2 Water jets Total Power: 4,078kW (5,544hp) 35.0kn M.T.U. 16V396TB84 2 x Vee 4 Stroke 16 Cy. 165 x 185 each-2039kW (2772bhp) MTU Friedrichshafen GmbH-Friedrichshafen AuxGen: 2 x 70kW 230V 50Hz a.c
9125891 *SVAD6* -	**SPEEDRUNNER II** *ex* Tallink Autoexpress 4 *-2007* *ex* St. Matthew *-2004* *ex* Pegasus One *-2002* *ex* Stena Pegasus *-1997* *ex* Pegasus One *-1996* **Jaywick Shipping Co Ltd** Aegean Speed Lines *Piraeus* *Greece* MMSI: 239363100 Official number: 11767	**3,971** 1,191 405	Class: RI (BV) (GL)	**1996**-05 **Fincantieri-Cant. Nav. Italiani S.p.A. — Riva Trigoso** Yd No: 5965 Loa 95.00 Br ex - Dght 2.890 Lbp 82.00 Br md 16.00 Dpth 10.50 Welded, 1 dk	**(A36A2PR) Passenger/Ro-Ro Ship (Vehicles)** Passengers: unberthed: 723 Stern door/ramp Len: 9.00 Wid: 6.00 Swl: - Lane-Len: 730 Cars: 150	**4 oil engines** reduction geared to sc. shafts driving 4 Water jets Total Power: 24,000kW (32,632hp) 32.0kn M.T.U. 20V1163TB73 4 x Vee 4 Stroke 20 Cy. 230 x 280 each-6000kW (8158bhp) MTU Friedrichshafen GmbH-Friedrichshafen AuxGen: 3 x 270kW a.c Thrusters: 1 Thwart. FP thruster (f) Fuel: 87.0 (d.f.) 120.0pd
9141871 *SVAF3* -	**SPEEDRUNNER III** *ex* Superseacat Three *-2009* **Torania Shipping Co Ltd** Aegean Speed Lines SatCom: Inmarsat C 424093210 *Piraeus* *Greece* MMSI: 240932000 Official number: 11886	**4,697** 1,409 340	Class: RI (NV)	**1999**-03 **Fincantieri-Cant. Nav. Italiani S.p.A. — La Spezia** Yd No: 6003 Loa 100.31 Br ex - Dght 2.699 Lbp 88.00 Br md 17.10 Dpth 10.70 Welded, 1 dk	**(A36A2PR) Passenger/Ro-Ro Ship (Vehicles)** Hull Material: Aluminium Alloy Passengers: unberthed: 800 Stern door/ramp (p. a.) Stern door/ramp (s. a.) Cars: 170	**4 oil engines** driving 4 Water jets Total Power: 27,500kW (37,388hp) 34.0kn Ruston 20RK270 4 x Vee 4 Stroke 20 Cy. 270 x 305 each-6875kW (9347bhp) Ruston Paxman Diesels Ltd.-United Kingdom

IMO / Call sign	Name / Owner	Tonnage	Class	Builder / Dimensions	Type	Machinery
9141883 *SVAF2* -	**SPEEDRUNNER IV** *ex* Superseacat Four *-2007* **Kira Navigation Co Ltd** Aegean Speed Lines SatCom: Inmarsat C 424093110 *Piraeus* *Greece* MMSI: 240931000 Official number: 11880	**4,697** 1,409 340	Class: RI	**1998-11 Fincantieri-Cant. Nav. Italiani S.p.A. — Riva Trigoso** Yd No: 6004 Loa 100.31 Br ex - Dght 2.699 Lbp 88.00 Br md 17.10 Dpth 10.70 Welded	**(A36A2PR) Passenger/Ro-Ro Ship (Vehicles)** Hull Material: Aluminium Alloy Passengers: unberthed: 800 Stern door/ramp (p. a.) Stern door/ramp (s. a.) Cars: 170	**4 oil engines** driving 4 Water jets Total Power: 27,500kW (37,388hp) 34.0kn Ruston 20RK270 4 x Vee 4 Stroke 20 Cy. 270 x 305 each-6875kW (9347bhp) Ruston Paxman Diesels Ltd.-United Kingdom
9279367 *HPLJ* -	**SPEEDWELL** **Sealift Maritime SA** Misuga Kaiun Co Ltd SatCom: Inmarsat C 435445010 *Panama* *Panama* MMSI: 354450000 Official number: 2936403B	**27,989** 17,077 50,329 T/cm 53.5	Class: NK	**2003-09 Kawasaki Shipbuilding Corp — Kobe HG** Yd No: 1541 Loa 189.80 (BB) Br ex - Dght 11.925 Lbp 181.00 Br md 32.26 Dpth 16.90 Welded, 1 dk	**(A21A2BC) Bulk Carrier** Grain: 63,198; Bale: 60,713 Compartments: 5 Ho, ER 5 Ha: (20.2 x 18.0)3 (20.2 x 18.0)ER (17.6 x 18.0) Cranes: 4x30.5t	**1 oil engine** driving 1 FP propeller Total Power: 8,091kW (11,001hp) 14.5kn MAN-B&W 6S50MC-C 1 x 2 Stroke 6 Cy. 500 x 2000 8091kW (11001bhp) Kawasaki Heavy Industries Ltd-Japan Fuel: 1770.0
9713870 - -	**SPEEDWELL** **PT Gurita Lintas Samudera** - *Jakarta* *Indonesia*	**256** 77 194	Class: NK	**2013-11 PT Palma Progress Shipyard — Batam** Yd No: 543 Loa 28.05 Br ex - Dght 3.312 Lbp 26.75 Br md 8.60 Dpth 4.30 Welded, 1 dk	**(B32A2ST) Tug**	**2 oil engines** reduction geared to sc. shaft (s) driving 2 FP propellers Total Power: 1,518kW (2,064hp) Mitsubishi S6R2-MTK3L 2 x 4 Stroke 6 Cy. 170 x 220 each-759kW (1032bhp) Mitsubishi Heavy Industries Ltd-Japan Fuel: 220.0
7609154 *DUA2598* -	**SPEEDY VII** *ex* Shinriki Maru No. 18 *-1995* *ex* Taisei Maru No. 18 *-1995* *ex* Soho Maru No. 18 *-1986* *ex* Choei Maru No. 2 *-1986* **Royale Fishing Corp** - *Manila* *Philippines* Official number: MNLD007270	*168* 88 213		**1976-06 KK Kanasashi Zosen — Shizuoka SZ** Yd No: 1217 Loa 37.50 Br ex 6.74 Dght 2.598 Lbp 33.10 Br md 6.71 Dpth 3.00 Welded, 1 dk	**(B11B2FV) Fishing Vessel**	**1 oil engine** driving 1 FP propeller Total Power: 956kW (1,300hp) Yanmar 1 x 4 Stroke 6 Cy. 250 x 390 956kW (1300bhp) Yanmar Diesel Engine Co Ltd-Japan
7506780 *WDC4261* -	**SPENCE** *ex* James Danos *-2004* **TransAtlantic Lines Tugholdings Inc** TransAtlantic Lines LLC *New York, NY* *United States of America* MMSI: 367021860 Official number: 559788	*189* 58 -		**1974 Bollinger Machine Shop & Shipyard, Inc. — Lockport, La** Yd No: 90 Loa - Br ex 7.93 Dght 2.998 Lbp 27.77 Br md - Dpth 3.51 Welded, 1 dk	**(B32A2ST) Tug**	**1 oil engine** driving 1 FP propeller Total Power: 1,618kW (2,200hp)
9404326 - -	**SPENCER F. BAIRD** **Government of The United States of America (Department of The Interior, Fish & Wildlife Service)** - *Cheboygan, MI* *United States of America*	**256** 76 123	Class: (AB)	**2006-06 Conrad Industries, Inc. — Morgan City, La** Yd No: 729 Loa 28.95 Br ex - Dght - Lbp 25.61 Br md 9.14 Dpth 3.93 Welded, 1 dk	**(B12D2FR) Fishery Research Vessel** Ice Capable	**2 oil engines** reduction geared to sc. shafts driving 2 FP propellers Total Power: 1,492kW (2,028hp) Caterpillar 3508B 2 x Vee 4 Stroke 8 Cy. 170 x 190 each-746kW (1014bhp) Caterpillar Inc-USA AuxGen: 2 x 175kW a.c
8741703 *WDE7248* -	**SPENCER PHILIP** **Phil Guilbeau Offshore Inc** - *Golden Meadow, LA* *United States of America* Official number: 1213503	**499** - -		**2009-02 Thoma-Sea Boatbuilders Inc — Houma LA** Yd No: 142 Loa 51.80 Br ex - Dght - Lbp - Br md 10.97 Dpth 3.50 Welded, 1 dk	**(B21A20S) Platform Supply Ship**	**2 oil engines** reduction geared to sc. shafts driving 2 FP propellers Total Power: 1,402kW (1,906hp) 13.0kn Caterpillar 3508TA 2 x Vee 4 Stroke 8 Cy. 170 x 190 each-701kW (953bhp) Caterpillar Inc-USA AuxGen: 2 x 99kW a.c
9121455 *PFDY* BRU 68	**SPERA IN DEO** *ex* Johanna Jacobus *-2000* **Mosselkweekbedrijf W Okkerse BV** - *Bruinisse* *Netherlands* MMSI: 244355000 Official number: 28740	**252** 75 160		**1995-07 Stocznia Tczew Sp z oo — Tczew** (Hull) **1995-07 B.V. Scheepswerf Maaskant — Bruinisse** Yd No: 514 Loa 39.16 Br ex 9.00 Dght 2.060 Lbp 35.91 Br md - Dpth 2.51 Welded, 1 dk	**(B11A2FT) Trawler**	**2 oil engines** reduction geared to sc. shafts driving 2 FP propellers Total Power: 1,060kW (1,442hp) Caterpillar 3412T 2 x Vee 4 Stroke 12 Cy. 137 x 152 each-530kW (721bhp) Caterpillar Inc-USA Thrusters: 1 Water jet (f)
9002609 *HPPO* -	**SPERANZA** *ex* La Esperanza *-2012* *ex* EHM Maersk *-2003* *ex* British Valour *-2002* *ex* Elisabeth Maersk *-1997* **Sino Shipping Holdings Ltd** - SatCom: Inmarsat C 435303510 *Panama* *Panama* MMSI: 353035000 Official number: 2956904C	**158,475** 95,332 299,700 T/cm 172.0	Class: LR (KR) ✠ **100A1** SS 05/2012 oil tanker (Double Hull) SPM ESP LI ✠ **LMC** **UMS IGS** Eq.Ltr: E*; Cable: 770.0/122.0 U3	**1993-05 Odense Staalskibsvaerft A/S — Munkebo (Lindo Shipyard)** Yd No: 142 Converted From: FSO (Floating Storage, Offtake)-2014 Converted From: Crude Oil Tanker-2014 Converted From: Oil Storage Vessel-2013 Converted From: Crude Oil Tanker-2012 Loa 343.71 (BB) Br ex 56.44 Dght 21.575 Lbp 327.54 Br md 56.40 Dpth 30.41 Welded, 1 dk	**(A13A2TV) Crude Oil Tanker** Double Hull (13F) Liq: 321,162; Liq (Oil): 321,162 Compartments: 5 Ta, 10 Wing Ta, 2 Wing Slop Ta, ER 3 Cargo Pump (s): 3x5000m³/hr Manifold: Bow/CM: 172.9m	**1 oil engine** driving 1 FP propeller Total Power: 23,534kW (31,997hp) 14.0kn Mitsubishi 8UEC75LSII 1 x 2 Stroke 8 Cy. 750 x 2800 23534kW (31997bhp) Mitsubishi Heavy Industries Ltd-Japan AuxGen: 3 x 780kW 440V 60Hz a.c Boilers: 2 WTAuxB (o.f.) 18.4kgf/cm² (18.0bar), e (ex.g.) 23.5kgf/cm² (23.0bar) Fuel: 325.0 (d.f.) 7526.1 (r.f.)
9197131 *VRZP6* -	**SPERO** *ex* Seaservice *-2013* **Seaservice Shipping Ltd** - *Hong Kong* *Hong Kong* MMSI: 477623000 Official number: HK-1235	**57,979** 31,829 107,160 T/cm 91.0	Class: LR (NK) **100A1** SS 12/2013 Double Hull oil tanker ESP *IWS LI **LMC** **UMS IGS**	**1998-12 Koyo Dockyard Co Ltd — Mihara HS** Yd No: 2102 Loa 246.80 (BB) Br ex - Dght 14.000 Lbp 235.00 Br md 42.00 Dpth 21.30 Welded, 1 dk	**(A13A2TW) Crude/Oil Products Tanker** Double Hull (13F) Liq: 116,683; Liq (Oil): 116,683 Cargo Heating Coils Compartments: 14 Wing Ta, ER 3 Cargo Pump (s): 3x2500m³/hr Manifold: Bow/CM: 124m	**1 oil engine** driving 1 FP propeller Total Power: 12,799kW (17,402hp) 14.0kn Sulzer 7RTA62 1 x 2 Stroke 7 Cy. 620 x 2150 12799kW (17402bhp) Diesel United Ltd.-Aioi AuxGen: 3 x 680kW 450V 60Hz a.c Fuel: 293.9 (d.f.) (Heating Coils) 3650.2 (r.f.) 45.5pd
9232644 *V7BD7* -	**SPERO** *ex* Nienstedten *-2013* *ex* Wehr Nienstedten *-2012* *ex* African Cheetah *-2011* *ex* Wehr Nienstedten *-2010* *ex* Libra Chile *-2009* *launched as* Wehr Nienstedten *-2001* **Spero AS** Conbulk Shipping SA *Majuro* *Marshall Islands* MMSI: 538005122 Official number: 5122	**16,802** 8,672 22,968 T/cm 37.1	Class: BV GL	**2002-01 Stocznia Szczecinska Porta Holding SA — Szczecin** Yd No: B170/III/16 Loa 184.70 (BB) Br ex - Dght 9.890 Lbp 171.94 Br md 25.30 Dpth 13.50 Welded, 1 dk	**(A33A2CC) Container Ship (Fully Cellular)** Grain: 29,816; Bale: 29,000 TEU 1730 C Ho 634 TEU C Dk 1096 TEU incl 200 ref C. Cranes: 3x45t	**1 oil engine** driving 1 FP propeller Total Power: 13,328kW (18,121hp) 19.0kn Sulzer 6RTA62U 1 x 2 Stroke 6 Cy. 620 x 2150 13328kW (18121bhp) H Cegielski Poznan SA-Poland AuxGen: 3 x 1096kW 440/220V 60Hz a.c Thrusters: 1 Tunnel thruster (f) Fuel: 2405.0 (r.f.)
9030864 *ICSP*	**SPES** **Atlantica SpA di Navigazione** Grimaldi Group SatCom: Inmarsat A 1152116 *Palermo* *Italy* MMSI: 247146000 Official number: 1204	**33,823** 12,558 16,806	Class: RI (AB)	**1993-10 Flender Werft AG — Luebeck** Yd No: 656 Loa 178.09 (BB) Br ex 27.08 Dght 8.764 Lbp 164.00 Br md 26.80 Dpth 16.40 Welded, 8 dks, Nos 1,3,& 5 Hoistable	**(A35B2RV) Vehicles Carrier** Passengers: berths: 12 Side door/ramp (s) Len: 11.80 Wid: 2.80 Swl: - Quarter stern door/ramp (s. a.) Len: 31.00 Wid: 6.20 Swl: - Lane-Len: 1395 Cars: 2,860	**2 oil engines** with clutches, flexible couplings & sr geared to sc. shaft driving 1 CP propeller Total Power: 11,520kW (15,662hp) 19.0kn Sulzer 8ZAL40S 2 x 4 Stroke 8 Cy. 400 x 560 each-5760kW (7831bhp) Zaklady Urzadzen Technicznych'Zgoda' SA-Poland Thrusters: 1 Thwart. FP thruster (f)
8815281 *FHPN* FC 716582	**SPES** **Spes Armement Sarl** - *Fecamp* *France* MMSI: 228976000 Official number: 716582	**173** - -		**1988-11 SOCARENAM — Boulogne** Yd No: 132 Loa 24.60 Br ex 7.38 Dght 3.123 Lbp 21.24 Br md 7.20 Dpth 3.80 Welded, 1 dk	**(B11A2FS) Stern Trawler**	**1 oil engine** with clutches, flexible couplings & sr geared to sc. shaft driving 1 CP propeller Total Power: 441kW (600hp) Baudouin 12F160SR 1 x Vee 4 Stroke 12 Cy. 160 x 190 441kW (600bhp) Societe des Moteurs Baudouin SA-France
5336571 - -	**SPES** **Lamyra Maritime SA** - *Argentina*	*845* 706 1,651	Class: (BV)	**1944 C.R.D. Adriatico — Trieste** Yd No: 1347 Lengthened-1965 L reg 67.21 Br ex 9.94 Dght 4.509 Lbp - Br md 9.91 Dpth 5.74 Welded, 2 dks	**(A31A2GX) General Cargo Ship** Grain: 2,235 Derricks: 4x2t,2x1t	**1 oil engine** driving 1 FP propeller Total Power: 625kW (850hp) MWM 1 x 4 Stroke 6 Cy. 320 x 480 625kW (850bhp) (new engine 1972) Motoren Werke Mannheim AG (MWM)-West Germany

IMO / Call sign	Name / Owner / Port	Tonnage	Class	Builder / Dimensions	Type	Machinery
7720324 - -	**SPES PRIMA** *launched as* Mare Nostrum *-1978* **Cooperativa Mare Nostrum** - *Porto Empedocle* *Italy* Official number: 117	*150* - -		**1978**-09 **G. De Vincenzi — Trapani** Yd No: 11/77 Loa 28.25 Br ex 6.63 Dght - Lbp 22.00 Br md 6.61 Dpth 3.20 Welded, 1 dk	**(B11A2FT) Trawler**	**1 oil engine** reduction geared to sc. shaft driving 1 FP propeller Blackstone ESL8MK2 1 x 4 Stroke 8 Cy. 222 x 292 Mirrlees Blackstone (Stamford)Ltd.-Stamford
8328783 - - -	**SPES UNICA 2** - - -	*127* 55 -	Class: (BV)	**1981 Ateliers du Bastion SA — Les Sables-d'Olonne** Loa 26.09 Br ex 6.91 Dght 3.580 Lbp 22.43 Br md - Dpth 4.09 Welded, 1 dk	**(B11B2FV) Fishing Vessel**	**1 oil engine** sr geared to sc. shaft driving 1 CP propeller Total Power: 423kW (575hp) 11.0kn Duvant 6VJS 1 x 4 Stroke 6 Cy. 255 x 300 423kW (575bhp) Moteurs Duvant-France AuxGen: 2 x 36kW 380V a.c
8701571 *SY2133* -	**SPETSES CAT** *ex* Layar Sinar *-2001* **Spetses Cat Naftiki Eteria** - *Chalkis* *Greece* MMSI: 237485100 Official number: 34	**319** 112 50	Class: (NV)	**1987**-05 **Marinteknik Shipbuilders (S) Pte Ltd — Singapore** Yd No: 103 Loa 34.02 Br ex 9.40 Dght 3.501 Lbp 27.01 Br md - Dpth 3.61 Welded, 1 dk	**(A37B2PS) Passenger Ship** Hull Material: Aluminium Alloy Passengers: unberthed: 70	**2 oil engines** with clutches, flexible couplings & sr geared to sc. shafts driving 2 Water jets Total Power: 2,360kW (3,208hp) M.T.U. 12V396 2 x Vee 4 Stroke 12 Cy. 165 x 185 each-1180kW (1604bhp) MTU Friedrichshafen GmbH-Friedrichshafen AuxGen: 2 x 30kW 380V 50Hz a.c
7628930 - -	**SPETSSTROY-1** *ex* Videle *-2006* **Dunayspetsbut** -	**639** 192 888	Class: (RS) (RN)	**1976**-01 **Santierul Naval Drobeta-Turnu Severin S.A. — Drobeta-Turnu S.** Yd No: 3991 Loa 55.55 Br ex 10.02 Dght 3.600 Lbp 52.48 Br md 10.00 Dpth 4.30 Welded, 1 dk	**(A31A2GX) General Cargo Ship** Grain: 500 Compartments: 1 Ho, ER Ice Capable	**2 oil engines** geared to sc. shafts driving 2 FP propellers Total Power: 442kW (600hp) 8.0kn Pervomaysk 6CH25/34 2 x 4 Stroke 6 Cy. 250 x 340 each-221kW (300bhp) Pervomaydizelmash (PDM)-Pervomaysk AuxGen: 2 x 64kW 220V 50Hz a.c Fuel: 56.0 (d.f.)
9668178 *YDA 3237* -	**SPGM 05** **PT Megah Mandiri Sukses Sejati** - *Batam* *Indonesia* MMSI: 525021139	**145** 44 160	Class: NK	**2012**-12 **Rajang Maju Shipbuilding Sdn Bhd — Sibu** Yd No: RMM0032 Loa 23.90 Br ex - Dght 2.910 Lbp 22.43 Br md 7.30 Dpth 3.50 Welded, 1 dk	**(B32A2ST) Tug**	**2 oil engines** reduction geared to sc. shafts driving 2 FP propellers Total Power: 970kW (1,318hp) Yanmar 6AYM-WST 2 x 4 Stroke 6 Cy. 155 x 180 each-485kW (659bhp) Yanmar Diesel Engine Co Ltd-Japan Fuel: 100.0
8659663 - -	**SPGM 1288** **PT Megah Mandiri Sukses Sejati** - *Batam* *Indonesia*	**137** 42 -	Class: KI	**2011**-11 **PT Karyasindo Samudra Biru Shipyard — Batam** Loa 23.50 Br ex - Dght - Lbp 21.69 Br md 7.32 Dpth 3.20 Welded, 1 dk	**(B32A2ST) Tug**	**2 oil engines** reduction geared to sc. shafts driving 2 FP propellers Total Power: 894kW (1,216hp) Cummins KTA-19-M3 2 x 4 Stroke 6 Cy. 159 x 159 each-447kW (608bhp) Chongqing Cummins Engine Co Ltd-China
9689421 *YDA3393* -	**SPGM 1306** **PT Megah Mandiri Sukses Sejati** - *Batam* *Indonesia*	**151** 46 108	Class: NK	**2013**-10 **SL Shipbuilding Contractor Sdn Bhd — Sibu** Yd No: 159 Loa 23.50 Br ex 7.32 Dght 2.712 Lbp 21.32 Br md 7.32 Dpth 3.20 Welded, 1 dk	**(B32A2ST) Tug**	**2 oil engines** reduction geared to sc. shafts driving 2 FP propellers Total Power: 970kW (1,318hp) Yanmar 6AYM-WST 2 x 4 Stroke 6 Cy. 155 x 180 each-485kW (659bhp) Yanmar Diesel Engine Co Ltd-Japan Fuel: 85.0
9689433 *YDA3421* -	**SPGM 1307** **PT Megah Mandiri Sukses Sejati** - *Batam* *Indonesia*	**143** 43 108	Class: NK	**2014**-03 **SL Shipbuilding Contractor Sdn Bhd — Sibu** Yd No: 160 Loa 23.50 Br ex 7.33 Dght 2.712 Lbp 21.99 Br md 7.32 Dpth 3.20 Welded, 1 dk	**(B32A2ST) Tug**	**2 oil engines** reduction geared to sc. shafts driving 2 Propellers Total Power: 970kW (1,318hp) Yanmar 6AYM-WST 2 x 4 Stroke 6 Cy. 155 x 180 each-485kW (659bhp) Yanmar Diesel Engine Co Ltd-Japan
9297668 *VQNY8* FH 713	**SPICA** **Pesquera Seanmar SL** - *Falmouth* *United Kingdom* MMSI: 235005820 Official number: C17870	**320** 96 -	Class: BV	**2003**-06 **Astilleros Armon Vigo SA — Vigo** Yd No: 33 Loa 34.60 (BB) Br ex - Dght 3.500 Lbp 29.00 Br md 8.30 Dpth 5.65 Welded, 1 dk	**(B11A2FS) Stern Trawler**	**1 oil engine** geared to sc. shaft driving 1 CP propeller Total Power: 530kW (721hp) 12.5kn Caterpillar 3512TA 1 x Vee 4 Stroke 12 Cy. 170 x 190 530kW (721bhp) Caterpillar Inc-USA
9449699 *A8QJ5* -	**SPICA** **ms 'Spica' Schifffahrtsgesellschaft GmbH & Co KG** Reederei Wolfram Sabban GmbH & Co KG SatCom: Inmarsat C 463702741 *Monrovia* *Liberia* MMSI: 636091617 Official number: 91617	**9,996** 4,900 11,807	Class: BV (GL)	**2008**-09 **Yangfan Group Co Ltd — Zhoushan ZJ** Yd No: 2062 Loa 139.17 (BB) Br ex - Dght 8.800 Lbp 130.49 Br md 22.60 Dpth 11.80 Welded, 1 dk	**(A33A2CC) Container Ship (Fully Cellular)** TEU 957 incl 220 ref C. Compartments: 4 Cell Ho, ER 4 Ha: 3 (12.6 x 18.2)ER (12.6 x 15.6)Tappered Cranes: 2x45t Ice Capable	**1 oil engine** reduction geared to sc. shaft (s) driving 1 CP propeller Total Power: 9,600kW (13,052hp) 18.1kn MAN-B&W 8L48/60B 1 x 4 Stroke 8 Cy. 480 x 600 9600kW (13052bhp) MAN B&W Diesel AG-Augsburg AuxGen: 2 x 910kW 450V a.c, 1 x 2000kW 450V a.c Thrusters: 1 Tunnel thruster (f); 1 Tunnel thruster (f)
9438951 *IIYF2* -	**SPICA** *ex* Fairplay-29 *-2011* *ex* Spica *-2008* **Tripnavi SpA** - *Trieste* *Italy* MMSI: 247333900 Official number: 799	**498** - 249	Class: RI (BV)	**2007**-04 **Astilleros Armon SA — Navia** Yd No: 641 Loa 35.00 Br ex - Dght 4.560 Lbp 30.80 Br md 11.20 Dpth 5.40 Welded, 1 dk	**(B32A2ST) Tug**	**2 oil engines** reduction geared to sc. shafts driving 2 Directional propellers Total Power: 3,946kW (5,364hp) 13.0kn Caterpillar 3516B 2 x Vee 4 Stroke 16 Cy. 170 x 190 each-1973kW (2682bhp) Caterpillar Inc-USA AuxGen: 2 x 154kW a.c
8746882 *9MFD9* -	**SPICA** **Government of Malaysia (Director of Marine & Ministry of Transport)** - *Port Klang* *Malaysia* Official number: 332370	**140** 42 25		**2007**-12 **Kay Marine Sdn Bhd — Kuala Terengganu** (Assembled by) Yd No: J104-2 **0000* Inform Marine Technology — Fremantle WA** (Parts for assembly by) Loa 26.00 Br ex - Dght 1.200 Lbp - Br md 9.20 Dpth 2.55 Welded, 1 dk	**(A37B2PS) Passenger Ship** Hull Material: Aluminium Alloy	**2 oil engines** reduction geared to sc. shafts driving 2 Propellers Total Power: 2,206kW (3,000hp) M.T.U. 12V2000M91 2 x Vee 4 Stroke 12 Cy. 130 x 150 each-1103kW (1500bhp) MTU Friedrichshafen GmbH-Friedrichshafen
8836716 - -	**SPICA** **Government of The Republic of Italy (Ministero dei Trasporti e della Navigazione)-ISP TEC-Nucleo Operativo di Venezia** - SatCom: Inmarsat M 624700217 *Italy*	*1,751* 1,070 -	Class: (RI)	**1990 Fincantieri-Cant. Nav. Italiani S.p.A. — La Spezia** Yd No: 5848 Loa 80.70 Br ex 11.82 Dght 4.300 Lbp 71.51 Br md 11.80 Dpth 5.60 Welded, 2 dks	**(B34G2SE) Pollution Control Vessel**	**2 oil engines** driving 2 FP propellers Total Power: 5,840kW (7,940hp) GMT BL230.16V 2 x Vee 4 Stroke 16 Cy. 230 x 310 each-2920kW (3970bhp) Fincantieri Cantieri NavaliItaliani SpA-Italy
9083043 *DIPS* -	**SPICA** *ex* Melfi Italia *-2004* *ex* Containerships IV *-2003* **ms 'Spica' Hans-Peter Wegener KG** Wegener Bereederungsgesellschaft mbH & Co KG (Reederei H - P Wegener) SatCom: Inmarsat C 421121736 *Hamburg* *Germany* MMSI: 211217360 Official number: 17355	**7,550** 3,957 8,932	Class: GL	**1994**-03 **J.J. Sietas KG Schiffswerft GmbH & Co. — Hamburg** Yd No: 1072 Loa 151.14 (BB) Br ex 19.66 Dght 7.420 Lbp 141.40 Br md 19.40 Dpth 9.30 Welded, 1 dk	**(A33A2CC) Container Ship (Fully Cellular)** Grain: 13,221; Bale: 12,568 TEU 749 C Ho 248 TEU C Dk 501 TEU incl 102 ref C. Compartments: 4 Ho, ER 4 Ha: (12.4 x 12.8)3 (25.1 x 15.8)ER Ice Capable	**1 oil engine** with flexible couplings & sr geared to sc. shaft driving 1 CP propeller Total Power: 9,999kW (13,595hp) 21.6kn MaK 8M601C 1 x 4 Stroke 8 Cy. 580 x 600 9999kW (13595bhp) Krupp MaK Maschinenbau GmbH-Kiel AuxGen: 1 x 1276kW 220/380V 50Hz a.c, 2 x 320kW 220/380V 50Hz a.c Thrusters: 1 Thwart. CP thruster (f)
9183594 *HOIP* -	**SPICA** *ex* Admiral 8 *-2011* *ex* Dauntless *-2010* *ex* Hellas Fos *-2005* **Centrus Shipping SA** Artemiz Marine Services JLT *Panama* *Panama* MMSI: 353727000 Official number: 41318PEXT2	**27,645** 12,616 46,168 T/cm 50.7	Class: BV (NV)	**1999**-03 **Hyundai Heavy Industries Co Ltd — Ulsan** Yd No: 1140 Loa 183.20 (BB) Br ex - Dght 12.220 Lbp 174.00 Br md 32.20 Dpth 18.20 Welded, 1 dk	**(A13A2TW) Crude/Oil Products Tanker** Double Hull (13F) Liq: 50,715; Liq (Oil): 52,120 Part Cargo Heating Coils Compartments: 12 Wing Ta, 2 Wing Slop Ta, ER 12 Cargo Pump (s): 12x600m³/hr Manifold: Bow/CM: 92m	**1 oil engine** driving 1 FP propeller Total Power: 7,679kW (10,440hp) 14.2kn MAN-B&W 6S50MC 1 x 2 Stroke 6 Cy. 500 x 1910 7679kW (10440bhp) Hyundai Heavy Industries Co Ltd-South Korea AuxGen: 3 x 830kW 440V 60Hz a.c Fuel: 219.0 (d.f.) (Heating Coils) 1388.0 (r.f.) 34.6pd

7330959 *DUPA5* -	**SPICA** *ex* Inaba Maru *-2000* *ex* Kanda Maru *-1991* *ex* Amagi Maru *-1989* **Harbor Star Shipping Services Inc** - *Manila* *Philippines* Official number: 00-0000348	*213* 104 -		**1973-09 Kanagawa Zosen — Kobe** Yd No: 131 Loa 33.50 Br ex 8.23 Dght 2.293 Lbp 29.49 Br md 8.21 Dpth 3.43 Riveted\Welded, 1 dk	**(B32A2ST) Tug**	**2 oil engines** driving 2 FP propellers Total Power: 1,912kW (2,600hp) Niigata 6L25BX 2 x 4 Stroke 6 Cy. 250 x 320 each-956kW (1300bhp) Niigata Engineering Co Ltd-Japan
9355460 *V2CV3* -	**SPICA J** *ex* C2C Spica *-2009* *completed as* Spica J *-2007* **ms 'Spica J' Schiffahrtsgesellschaft UG (haftungsbeschrankt) & Co KG** Jungerhans Maritime Services GmbH & Co KG *Saint John's* *Antigua & Barbuda* MMSI: 305115000 Official number: 4347	**8,246** 4,002 11,186	Class: GL	**2007-07 Detlef Hegemann Rolandwerft GmbH & Co. KG — Berne** Yd No: 237 Loa 139.60 (BB) Br ex - Dght 7.364 Lbp 133.25 Br md 22.20 Dpth 9.50 Welded, 1 dk	**(A33A2CC) Container Ship (Fully Cellular)** TEU 962 C Ho 218 TEU C Dk 744 TEU incl 170 ref C Compartments: 3 Cell Ho, ER 3 Ha: ER	**1 oil engine** reduction geared to sc. shafts driving 1 CP propeller Total Power: 8,402kW (11,423hp) 17.9kn MaK 9M43 1 x 4 Stroke 9 Cy. 430 x 610 8402kW (11423bhp) Caterpillar Motoren GmbH & Co. KG-Germany AuxGen: 2 x 437kW 440/230V 60Hz a.c, 1 x 1200kW 440/230V 60Hz a.c Thrusters: 1 Thwart. CP thruster (f) Fuel: 160.0 (d.f.) 800.0 (r.f.)
9536909 *9V9599* -	**SPICA LEADER** - **Spica Shipholding Pte Ltd** Nippon Yusen Kabushiki Kaisha (NYK Line) SatCom: Inmarsat C 456646610 *Singapore* *Singapore* MMSI: 566466000 Official number: 397336	**41,886** 12,566 14,378	Class: NK	**2012-05 Shin Kurushima Dockyard Co. Ltd. — Onishi** Yd No: 5673 Loa 190.03 (BB) Br ex - Dght 9.326 Lbp 182.00 Br md 28.20 Dpth 29.43 Welded	**(A35B2RV) Vehicles Carrier** Side door/ramp (s) Len: - Wid: - Swl: 35 Quarter stern door/ramp (s. a.) Len: - Wid: - Swl: 150 Cars: 3,921	**1 oil engine** driving 1 FP propeller Total Power: 11,335kW (15,411hp) 20.0kn Mitsubishi 7UEC52LSE 1 x 2 Stroke 7 Cy. 520 x 2000 11335kW (15411bhp) Kobe Hatsudoki KK-Japan Thrusters: 1 Tunnel thruster (f) Fuel: 2470.0
9089334 *MNDD7* -	**SPICY** - **ING Lease (Italia) SpA** Navilux SA *London* *United Kingdom* MMSI: 232810000 Official number: 911855	**181** 54 -	Class: BV	**2006-03 Overmarine SpA — Viareggio** Yd No: 108/20 Loa 31.51 Br ex - Dght 1.290 Lbp 28.26 Br md 7.09 Dpth 4.87 Bonded, 1 dk	**(X11A2YP) Yacht** Hull Material: Reinforced Plastic	**2 oil engines** reduction geared to sc. shafts driving 2 FP propellers Total Power: 4,080kW (5,548hp) 37.0kn M.T.U. 12V4000M90 2 x Vee 4 Stroke 12 Cy. 165 x 190 each-2040kW (2774bhp) MTU Friedrichshafen GmbH-Friedrichshafen AuxGen: 2 x 33kW a.c
8221258 *9LB2324* -	**SPIDER** *ex* Kazym *-1983* **Multi Group International FZE** - *Freetown* *Sierra Leone* MMSI: 667002163 Official number: SL102163	**118** 36 43	Class: IS	**1983-02 Fukushima Zosen Ltd. — Matsue** Yd No: 309 Loa 21.32 Br ex - Dght 1.501 Lbp 19.61 Br md 9.91 Dpth 1.81 Welded, 1 dk	**(B34X2QA) Anchor Handling Vessel**	**2 oil engines** reduction geared to sc. shafts driving 2 FP propellers G.M. (Detroit Diesel) 12V-92 2 x Vee 2 Stroke 12 Cy. 123 x 127 Detroit Diesel Corporation-Detroit, Mi
9197911 *PCEO* -	**SPIEGELGRACHT** - **Rederij Spiegelgracht** Spliethoff's Bevrachtingskantoor BV *Amsterdam* *Netherlands* MMSI: 245789000 Official number: 36728	**16,641** 6,700 21,402 T/cm 35.1	Class: LR ✠ **100A1** SS 04/2010 strengthened for heavy cargoes, container cargoes in holds, on upper deck and upper deck hatch covers, timber deck cargoes LA LI *IWS Ice Class 1A (Finnish-Swedish Ice Class Rules 1985) at a draught of 10.943m Max/min draught fwd 11.47/4.2m Max/min draught aft 11.47/6.6m ✠ **LMC** **UMS** Eq.Ltr: 0†; Cable: 605.0/70.0 U2	**2000-04 Tsuneishi Shipbuilding Co Ltd — Fukuyama HS** Yd No: 1172 Loa 168.14 (BB) Br ex 25.42 Dght 10.710 Lbp 162.10 Br md 25.20 Dpth 14.60 Welded, 1 dk	**(A31A2GX) General Cargo Ship** Grain: 23,786; Bale: 23,786 TEU 1127 C Ho 478 TEU C Dk 649 TEU incl 120 ref C. Compartments: 3 Ho, ER 3 Ha: (26.6 x 15.2)Tappered (38.4 x 17.8) (31.9 x 20.4)ER Cranes: 3x120t Ice Capable	**1 oil engine** with flexible couplings & sr reverse geared to sc. shaft driving 1 CP propeller Total Power: 12,060kW (16,397hp) 19.5kn Wartsila 6L64 1 x 4 Stroke 6 Cy. 640 x 900 12060kW (16397bhp) Wartsila Italia SpA-Italy AuxGen: 1 x 1000kW 445V 60Hz a.c, 3 x 450kW 445V 60Hz a.c Boilers: TOH (ex.g.) 10.2kgf/cm² (10.0bar), TOH (o.f.) 10.2kgf/cm² (10.0bar) Thrusters: 1 Thwart. CP thruster (f) Fuel: 275.0 (d.f.) (Heating Coils) 1750.0 (r.f.) 45.0pd
9506148 *V2GM5* -	**SPIEKEROOG** - **Reederei M Lauterjung GmbH & Co KG ms 'Spiekeroog'** Reederei M Lauterjung GmbH *Saint John's* *Antigua & Barbuda* MMSI: 305997000	**4,591** - 5,488	Class: GL	**2013-12 Qidong Daoda Marine Heavy Industry — Qidong JS** Yd No: DD016 Loa 108.17 (BB) Br ex - Dght 6.500 Lbp 102.58 Br md 16.60 Dpth 8.80 Welded, 1 dk	**(A31A2GX) General Cargo Ship** Grain: 7,500; Bale: 7,500 TEU 385 C Ho 138 TEU C Dk 247 TEU incl 10 ref C Compartments: 1 Ho, 1 Tw Dk, ER 2 Ha: ER Cranes: 2x60t Ice Capable	**1 oil engine** reduction geared to sc. shaft driving 1 CP propeller Total Power: 3,500kW (4,759hp) 14.5kn MAN-B&W 7L32/40 1 x 4 Stroke 7 Cy. 320 x 400 3500kW (4759bhp) Shaanxi Diesel Heavy Industry Co Lt-China AuxGen: 1 x 500kW a.c, 2 x 350kW a.c Thrusters: 1 Tunnel thruster (f) Fuel: 90.0 (d.f.) 390.0 (r.f.)
8016897 *DCFX* -	**SPIEKEROOG I** - **Nordseebad Spiekeroog GmbH Kurverwaltung & Schiff-Fahrt** - *Spiekeroog* *Germany* MMSI: 211283830 Official number: 3944	**553** 237 130	Class: GL	**1981-05 Julius Diedrich Schiffswerft GmbH & Co KG — Moormerland** Yd No: 141 Loa 46.77 Br ex 9.56 Dght 1.310 Lbp 42.42 Br md 9.52 Dpth 2.98 Welded, 1 dk	**(A37B2PS) Passenger Ship** Passengers: unberthed: 775	**2 oil engines** reverse reduction geared to sc. shafts driving 2 FP propellers Total Power: 540kW (734hp) 11.0kn MWM TBD604-6 2 x 4 Stroke 6 Cy. 160 x 185 each-270kW (367bhp) Motoren Werke Mannheim AG (MWM)-West Germany AuxGen: 1 x 184kW a.c, 1 x 105kW a.c
8024143 *DDCB* -	**SPIEKEROOG II** *ex* Hannover *-1991* *ex* Stadt Neustadt *-1982* *ex* Hannover *-1981* **Nordseebad Spiekeroog GmbH Kurverwaltung & Schiff-Fahrt** - *Spiekeroog* *Germany* MMSI: 211217990 Official number: 4339	**495** 188 116	Class: GL	**1981-04 Martin Jansen GmbH & Co. KG Schiffsw. u. Masch. — Leer** Yd No: 166 Loa 47.91 Br ex 8.51 Dght 1.440 Lbp 43.01 Br md 8.50 Dpth 2.01 Welded, 1 dk	**(A37B2PS) Passenger Ship** Passengers: unberthed: 680 Ice Capable	**2 oil engines** reduction geared to sc. shafts driving 2 FP propellers Total Power: 920kW (1,250hp) 12.0kn Mitsubishi S6R2-MPTA 2 x 4 Stroke 6 Cy. 170 x 220 each-460kW (625bhp) (new engine 2005) Mitsubishi Heavy Industries Ltd-Japan Thrusters: 1 Tunnel thruster (f)
6715102 *DCUH* -	**SPIEKEROOG III** - **Michael Elges** Nordseebad Spiekeroog GmbH Kurverwaltung & Schiff-Fahrt *Spiekeroog* *Germany* MMSI: 211218770 Official number: 3608	**153** 57 54	Class: GL	**1967 Husumer Schiffswerft — Husum** Yd No: 1244 Loa 33.56 Br ex 6.99 Dght 1.450 Lbp 29.52 Br md 6.81 Dpth 2.27 Welded, 1 dk	**(A37B2PS) Passenger Ship** Passengers: unberthed: 300 Ice Capable	**1 oil engine** reverse reduction geared to sc. shaft driving 1 FP propeller Total Power: 309kW (420hp) 11.5kn Deutz SBA8M816 1 x 4 Stroke 8 Cy. 142 x 160 309kW (420bhp) (new engine 1982) Kloeckner Humboldt Deutz AG-West Germany AuxGen: 1 x 8kW 231/400V 50Hz a.c
7824871 *DJFV* -	**SPIEKEROOG IV** *ex* Adler Pomerania *-2010* *ex* Pellworm I *-1997* **Nordseebad Spiekeroog GmbH Kurverwaltung & Schiff-Fahrt** - *Spiekeroog* *Germany* MMSI: 211472890 Official number: 5899	**299** 104 98	Class: GL	**1979-05 Husumer Schiffswerft — Husum** Yd No: 1452 Loa 38.31 Br ex 10.39 Dght 1.501 Lbp 35.21 Br md 10.01 Dpth 3.10 Welded, 1 dk	**(A36A2PR) Passenger/Ro-Ro Ship (Vehicles)** Passengers: unberthed: 296 Bow ramp (centre) Stern ramp (centre) Cars: 20 Ice Capable	**2 oil engines** reduction geared to sc. shaft driving 2 FP propellers Total Power: 570kW (774hp) 10.0kn MWM TBD601-6K 2 x 4 Stroke 6 Cy. 160 x 165 each-285kW (387bhp) MWM AG Lieferwerk MuenchenSueddeutsche Bremsen-Muenchen Thrusters: 1 Water jet (f)
9437672 *9HA2419* -	**SPIKE** - **Spike Shipping Ltd** Genel Denizcilik Nakliyati AS (GEDEN LINES) *Valletta* *Malta* MMSI: 248571000 Official number: 9437672	**61,341** 35,396 115,897 T/cm 99.1	Class: NV	**2010-07 Samsung Heavy Industries Co Ltd — Geoje** Yd No: 1757 Loa 249.97 (BB) Br ex 43.84 Dght 14.900 Lbp 239.00 Br md 43.80 Dpth 21.00 Welded, 1 dk	**(A13A2TV) Crude Oil Tanker** Double Hull (13F) Liq: 123,650; Liq (Oil): 123,650 Cargo Heating Coils Compartments: 12 Wing Ta, 2 Wing Slop Ta, ER 3 Cargo Pump (s): 3x2800m³/hr Manifold: Bow/CM: 123.7m	**1 oil engine** driving 1 FP propeller Total Power: 13,560kW (18,436hp) 15.3kn MAN-B&W 6S60MC-C 1 x 2 Stroke 6 Cy. 600 x 2400 13560kW (18436bhp) Doosan Engine Co Ltd-South Korea AuxGen: 3 x 800kW a.c Fuel: 220.0 (d.f.) 2900.0 (r.f.)
8650899 - -	**SPIKE ISLAND** *ex* Tana *-1997* *ex* L3508 *-1994* **Marine Transport Services Ltd** - *Cork* *Irish Republic* Official number: 403205	**123** 80 -		**1963 John I Thornycroft & Co Ltd — Southampton** Converted From: Infantry Landing Craft-1963 Loa 25.90 Br ex - Dght 1.670 Lbp - Br md 7.89 Dpth - Welded, 1 dk	**(A35D2RL) Landing Craft**	**2 oil engines** reduction geared to sc. shafts driving 2 Directional propellers Total Power: 808kW (1,098hp) Paxman 2 x each-404kW (549bhp) Paxman Diesels Ltd.-Colchester

7016888 *J7AX2* -	**SPINDELERO** *ex* Vastsjo *-2006* *ex* Doverian *-1996* *ex* Whitdale *-1994* *ex* Danae *-1988* *ex* Pass of Chisholm *-1984* *ex* Cordene *-1975* - - *Portsmouth* *Dominica* MMSI: 325214000	**903** 469 1,435	Class: (LR) (BV) (HR) ✠ Classed LR until 15/11/85	**1970-05 Appledore Shipbuilders Ltd — Bideford** Yd No: A.S. 72 Lengthened-1972 Loa 69.83 Br ex 9.96 Dght 4.192 Lbp 65.33 Br md 9.76 Dpth 4.96 Welded, 1 dk	**(A12B2TR) Chemical/Products Tanker** Double Hull Liq: 1,567; Liq (Oil): 1,567 Cargo Heating Coils Compartments: 8 Wing Ta, ER	**2 oil engines** sr geared to sc. shaft driving 1 CP propeller Total Power: 930kW (1,264hp) 11.5kn Paxman 12RPHCM 2 x Vee 4 Stroke 12 Cy. 178 x 197 each-465kW (632bhp) English Electric Diesels Ltd.Paxman Eng. Div.-Colchester AuxGen: 2 x 200kW 415V 50Hz a.c, 1 x 75kW 415V 50Hz a.c Fuel: 61.0 (d.f.) 4.0pd
8992285 *DZIK* -	**SPINE** *ex* Showa Maru No. 8 *-1995* **Irma Fishing & Trading Inc** - *Manila* *Philippines* Official number: MNLD001572	*152* 96 290		**1974-05 Nagato Zosen K.K. — Shimonoseki** Converted From: Oil Tanker-1995 L reg 29.58 Br ex - Dght 2.900 Lbp - Br md 6.20 Dpth 3.10 Welded, 1 dk	**(A14A2LO) Water Tanker** Liq: 318; Liq (Oil): 318	**1 oil engine** geared to sc. shaft driving 1 Propeller Total Power: 221kW (300hp) 8.5kn Yanmar 6M-T 1 x 4 Stroke 6 Cy. 200 x 240 221kW (300bhp) Yanmar Diesel Engine Co Ltd-Japan
6618378 *VM3404* -	**SPINIFEX** **Pelagic Marine Services Pty Ltd** Svitzer Australia Pty Ltd (Svitzer Australasia) *Fremantle, WA* *Australia* MMSI: 503177700 Official number: 196955	*185* 121 91		**1966 John Franetovich & Co — Fremantle WA** Loa 27.34 Br ex 7.68 Dght 1.321 Lbp 27.03 Br md 7.62 Dpth 1.96 Welded, 2 dks	**(A35D2RL) Landing Craft** Bow door/ramp	**4 oil engines** driving 4 FP propellers Total Power: 184kW (250hp) 8.0kn Perkins 6.305 (M) 2 x 2 Stroke 6 Cy. 92 x 127 each-92kW (125bhp) Perkins Engines Ltd.-Peterborough Rolls Royce C6NFLM 2 x 4 Stroke 6 Cy. 130 x 152 Rolls Royce Ltd.-Shrewsbury Fuel: 14.0 (d.f.) 2.0pd
9580003 *3EVV6* -	**SPINNAKER SW** *launched as* Sanko Vega *-2012* **Spinnaker Pescadores SA** Shih Wei Navigation Co Ltd *Panama* *Panama* MMSI: 372014000 Official number: 4440012	**19,836** 10,404 31,657 T/cm 45.1	Class: NK	**2012-11 The Hakodate Dock Co Ltd — Hakodate HK** Yd No: 853 Loa 175.53 (BB) Br ex - Dght 9.641 Lbp 167.00 Br md 29.40 Dpth 13.70 Welded, 1 dk	**(A21A2BC) Bulk Carrier** Double Hull Grain: 38,306; Bale: 39,270 Compartments: 5 Ho, ER 5 Ha: ER Cranes: 4x30t	**1 oil engine** driving 1 FP propeller Total Power: 6,840kW (9,300hp) 14.4kn Mitsubishi 6UEC45LSE 1 x 2 Stroke 6 Cy. 450 x 1840 6840kW (9300bhp) Kobe Hatsudoki KK-Japan Fuel: 1450.0
9218961 *JL6575* -	**SPINNER** **Homasu Kaiso KK** *Anan, Tokushima* *Japan* Official number: 135596	*134* - -		**1999-01 K.K. Watanabe Zosensho — Nagasaki** Yd No: 070 Loa 25.61 Br ex - Dght - Lbp - Br md 9.20 Dpth 6.50 Welded, 1 dk	**(B32A2ST) Tug**	**1 oil engine** driving 1 FP propeller Total Power: 2,942kW (4,000hp) 12.0kn Hanshin LH46LG 1 x 4 Stroke 6 Cy. 460 x 880 2942kW (4000bhp) The Hanshin Diesel Works Ltd-Japan
9083457 *T2RY3* -	**SPINNER DOLPHIN** *ex* ASL Eagle *-2009* *ex* Island Tamara 3 *-2001* **Kim Hock Bee Trading Pte Ltd** ASL Offshore & Marine Pte Ltd *Funafuti* *Tuvalu* Official number: 23309310	*109* 33 98	Class: (GL)	**1993-06 Shanghai Hangjian Shipyard — Shanghai** Yd No: SHJ 37 L reg 20.64 Br ex - Dght 2.833 Lbp - Br md 6.80 Dpth 3.43 Welded, 1 dk	**(B32A2ST) Tug**	**2 oil engines** reduction geared to sc. shafts driving 2 FP propellers Total Power: 514kW (698hp) 10.0kn Cummins NTA-855-M 2 x 4 Stroke 6 Cy. 140 x 152 each-257kW (349bhp) Cummins Engine Co Ltd-United Kingdom AuxGen: 2 x 16kW 220/380V a.c
8967278 *JK5580* -	**SPINNER II** **Tokuyama Genseki Yuso KK** *Shunan, Yamaguchi* *Japan* Official number: 136120	*134* - -		**2001-05 K.K. Watanabe Zosensho — Nagasaki** Yd No: 089 Loa 25.60 Br ex - Dght - Lbp - Br md 9.20 Dpth 6.50 Welded, 1 dk	**(B32A2ST) Tug**	**1 oil engine** driving 1 FP propeller Total Power: 2,795kW (3,800hp) 9.8kn Niigata 6M42GT 1 x 4 Stroke 6 Cy. 420 x 820 2795kW (3800bhp) Niigata Engineering Co Ltd-Japan
9245213 *JM6599* -	**SPINNER NO. 3** **Fuji Kaiun KK** *Sanyoonoda, Yamaguchi* *Japan* MMSI: 431401883 Official number: 136818	*146* - 383		**2001-05 Nakatani Shipyard Co. Ltd. — Etajima** Yd No: 591 Loa 27.00 Br ex - Dght - Lbp 24.00 Br md 17.70 Dpth 6.91 Welded, 1 dk	**(B32B2SA) Articulated Pusher Tug**	**1 oil engine** reduction geared to sc. shaft driving 1 FP propeller Total Power: 1,324kW (1,800hp) 12.5kn Yanmar 6N260-SN 1 x 4 Stroke 6 Cy. 260 x 360 1324kW (1800bhp) Yanmar Diesel Engine Co Ltd-Japan AuxGen: 2 x 180kW a.c Fuel: 104.0 (d.f.)
9495258 *9HZY9* -	**SPINOLA** **Tug Malta Ltd** SatCom: Inmarsat C 424976611 *Valletta* *Malta* MMSI: 249766000 Official number: 9495258	**701** 210 300	Class: RI	**2009-06 Astilleros Armon SA — Navia** Yd No: 677 Loa 36.65 Br ex - Dght 3.830 Lbp 33.75 Br md 13.60 Dpth 4.80 Welded, 1 dk	**(B32A2ST) Tug**	**2 oil engines** reduction geared to sc. shafts driving 2 Voith-Schneider propellers Total Power: 5,280kW (7,178hp) MaK 8M25C 2 x 4 Stroke 8 Cy. 255 x 400 each-2640kW (3589bhp) Caterpillar Motoren GmbH & Co. KG-Germany AuxGen: 3 x 150kW a.c Fuel: 180.0
8873752 *5IM361* -	**SPIRIDON** *ex* Gozde *-2013* *ex* Wella *-2008* *ex* Gredis *-2002* *ex* Mekhanik Cherkasov *-1994* *ex* Volgo-Don 5066 *-1994* **Bosmar Maritime SA** Umar Denizcilik ve Orman Urunleri Dis Ticaret Ltd Sti (Umar Shipping) *Zanzibar* *Tanzania (Zanzibar)* MMSI: 677026100 Official number: 300116	**3,994** 1,435 5,313	Class: IS (RS) (RR)	**1977 Santierul Naval Oltenita S.A. — Oltenita** Yd No: 5066 Loa 138.30 Br ex - Dght 3.520 Lbp 135.00 Br md 16.50 Dpth 5.50 Welded, 1 dk	**(A31A2GX) General Cargo Ship** Grain: 6,270 Compartments: 2 Ho, ER 2 Ha: ER	**2 oil engines** driving 2 FP propellers Total Power: 1,324kW (1,800hp) 11.0kn Dvigatel Revolyutsii 6CHRNP36/45 2 x 4 Stroke 6 Cy. 360 x 450 each-662kW (900bhp) Zavod "Dvigatel Revolyutsii"-Gorkiy AuxGen: 2 x 100kW a.c
7311329 *ODVR* -	**SPIRIDON II** *ex* Mikhail Cheremnykh *-2009* **Rima Tanios El Murr, Joe Joseph Azouri & Mohiba Mekhayel Herro** Murr Shipping SA *Beirut* *Lebanon* MMSI: 450547000 Official number: B-4346	**3,527** 1,622 4,054	Class: PX (RS)	**1973-08 Hollming Oy — Rauma** Yd No: 204 Loa 97.31 Br ex 16.24 Dght 6.360 Lbp 89.95 Br md 16.21 Dpth 7.70 Welded, 1 dk	**(A31A2GX) General Cargo Ship** Grain: 5,966; Bale: 5,892 Compartments: 3 Ho, ER 3 Ha: (10.5 x 10.5)2 (18.5 x 12.9)ER Derricks: 1x35t,1x20t,1x12.5t Ice Capable	**1 oil engine** driving 1 FP propeller Total Power: 2,574kW (3,500hp) 14.0kn B&W 5-50VT2BF-110 1 x 2 Stroke 5 Cy. 500 x 1100 2574kW (3500bhp) Valmet Oy-Finland Fuel: 456.0 (r.f.)
5269003 *KVUB* -	**SPIRIT** *ex* Sea Harvester *-1985* *ex* Palisana *-1978* **Park West Childrens Fund Inc (Friend Ships)** Friend Ships Unlimited *Galveston, TX* *United States of America* MMSI: 367375000 Official number: 249824	*3,809* 2,151 5,310	Class: (AB)	**1945-04 Pennsylvania Shipyards Inc. — Beaumont, Tx** Yd No: 326 Converted From: Fishing Vessel-1989 Converted From: General Cargo Ship-1945 Loa 103.23 Br ex 15.27 Dght 7.138 Lbp 97.95 Br md 15.24 Dpth 8.84 Welded, 2 dks	**(B35A2QZ) Mission Ship** Ins: 3,245 Compartments: 3 Ho, ER 3 Ha: (6.1 x 6.1)2 (12.3 x 6.1)ER Derricks: 2x10t,8x5t; Winches: 10	**1 oil engine** driving 1 FP propeller Total Power: 1,250kW (1,700hp) 10.0kn Nordberg TSM-216 1 x 4 Stroke 6 Cy. 546 x 737 1250kW (1700bhp) Nordberg Manufacturing Co-USA AuxGen: 2 x 250kW 220V d.c Fuel: 990.5
1010820 *ZGBI9* -	**SPIRIT** **Five Rivers Group Ltd** YCO SAM *The Creek* *Cayman Islands (British)* MMSI: 319738000	**656** 196 -	Class: LR ✠ **100A1** SS 05/2011 SSC Yacht, mono, G6 ✠ **LMC** **UMS** Cable: 330.0/20.5 U3 (a)	**2011-05 Damen Shipyards Gdynia SA — Gdynia** (Hull) **2011-05 Amels BV — Vlissingen** Yd No: 459 Loa 52.30 Br ex 9.47 Dght 3.150 Lbp 45.00 Br md 9.00 Dpth 4.90 Welded, 1 dk	**(X11A2YP) Yacht**	**2 oil engines** with clutches, flexible couplings & sr reverse geared to sc. shafts driving 2 FP propellers Total Power: 2,100kW (2,856hp) M.T.U. 16V2000M72 2 x Vee 4 Stroke 16 Cy. 135 x 156 each-1050kW (1428bhp) MTU Friedrichshafen GmbH-Friedrichshafen AuxGen: 2 x 155kW 400V 50Hz a.c Thrusters: 1 Thwart. FP thruster (f)
9360049 *E5U2484* -	**SPIRIT** **Tumi Pasha Spirit Ltd** - *Cook Islands Yacht Squadron* *Cook Islands* Official number: 1573	**304** 91 173	Class: (AB)	**2005-01 New Zealand Yachts Ltd — Whangarei** Yd No: NZY01 Loa 34.09 Br ex - Dght 2.200 Lbp 28.90 Br md 10.84 Dpth 4.05 Welded, 1 dk	**(X11A2YP) Yacht**	**2 oil engines** reduction geared to sc. shafts driving 2 Propellers Total Power: 2,060kW (2,800hp) Caterpillar 3412E 2 x Vee 4 Stroke 12 Cy. 137 x 152 each-1030kW (1400bhp) Caterpillar Inc-USA
8824347 - -	**SPIRIT 42** *ex* Sachi Maru No. 22 *-2008* **PT Pelayaran Taruna Kusan Explosive (TAREXSHIP)** -	**472** 314 1,136		**1989-01 Fuji Kaiji Kogyo — Japan** Yd No: 220 Loa 47.50 Br ex - Dght 2.990 Lbp 45.00 Br md 18.00 Dpth 4.15 Welded, 1 dk	**(B34B2SC) Crane Vessel**	**2 oil engines** driving 2 FP propellers Total Power: 1,030kW (1,400hp) 7.0kn Niigata 2 x 4 Stroke each-515kW (700bhp) Niigata Engineering Co Ltd-Japan

9364423 **SPIRIT OF AMERICA**
WDB8298
-
New York City (Department of Transportation)
New York, NY *United States of America*
MMSI: 366952890
Official number: 1170221

5,901
1,770
1,000

Class: AB

2005-09 Marinette Marine Corp — Marinette WI
Yd No: 513
Loa 94.50 Br ex - Dght 4.170
Lbp 91.59 Br md 21.33 Dpth 6.33
Welded, 1 dk

(A36A2PR) Passenger/Ro-Ro Ship (Vehicles)
Passengers: unberthed: 4400
Cars: 30

3 diesel electric oil engines driving 2 Propellers
Total Power: 8,595kW (11,685hp)
EMD (Electro-Motive) 16-710-G7B
3 x Vee 2 Stroke 16 Cy. 230 x 279 each-2865kW (3895bhp)
General Motors Corp.Electro-Motive Div.-La Grange

8984068 **SPIRIT OF ASHANTI**
CQTN
-
Windcraft Transportes Maritimos Lda
Maritime World Yachting Spanish SLU
Madeira *Portugal (MAR)*
MMSI: 255990000
Official number: 1236

156
46
-

1998 Tecnomarine SpA — La Spezia
Loa 30.60 Br ex - Dght -
Lbp 27.40 Br md 6.36 Dpth 3.06
Bonded, 1 dk

(X11A2YP) Yacht
Hull Material: Reinforced Plastic

2 oil engines reduction geared to sc. shafts driving 2 Propellers
Total Power: 4,480kW (6,092hp)
M.T.U. 16V396TE94
2 x Vee 4 Stroke 16 Cy. 165 x 185 each-2240kW (3046bhp)
MTU Friedrichshafen GmbH-Friedrichshafen

8647696 **SPIRIT OF ATHOS**
SW8861
-
Asteras Naftiki Eteria
Thessaloniki *Greece*
MMSI: 237087900
Official number: 222

499
217
167

Class: HR RS

1996-12 D. Homatas & Sons Ltd. — Thessaloniki/Salonica Yd No: 222
Loa 53.00 Br ex - Dght 2.260
Lbp 46.50 Br md 9.50 Dpth 3.75
Welded, 1 dk

(A37B2PS) Passenger Ship
Passengers: unberthed: 640

2 oil engines driving 2 FP propellers
Total Power: 1,492kW (2,028hp) 12.0kn
MAN
2 x 4 Stroke each-746kW (1014bhp)
MAN Nutzfahrzeuge AG-Nuernberg

9360752 **SPIRIT OF AUCKLAND**
9V2496
ex Bahia *-2013*
-
AR First Navigation Pte Ltd
Rickmers Shipmanagement (Singapore) Pte Ltd
Singapore *Singapore*
MMSI: 564078000
Official number: 399096

41,483
23,894
53,124

Class: GL

2007-02 Daewoo Shipbuilding & Marine Engineering Co Ltd — Geoje Yd No: 4129
Loa 254.06 (BB) Br ex - Dght 12.400
Lbp 242.00 Br md 32.20 Dpth 19.30
Welded, 1 dk

(A33A2CC) Container Ship (Fully Cellular)
Double Bottom Entire Compartment Length
TEU 3752 C Ho 1480 TEU C Dk 2272 TEU incl 844 ref C

1 oil engine driving 1 FP propeller
Total Power: 26,160kW (35,567hp) 22.4kn
MAN-B&W 8S70MC-C
1 x 2 Stroke 8 Cy. 700 x 2800 26160kW (35567bhp)
Doosan Engine Co Ltd-South Korea
AuxGen: 4 x 2500kW 450V a.c
Thrusters: 1 Tunnel thruster (f)
Fuel: 169.4 (d.f.) 5175.2 (r.f.)

9197349 **SPIRIT OF BANGKOK**
V7FY7
ex Sean Rickmers *-2013*
-
ex Delmas Zambia *-2009*
ex Sean Rickmers *-2008* *ex* Kindia *-2004*
ex Indamex Kindia *-2003* *ex* Kindia *-2002*
Spirit of Bangkok Co Ltd
Rickmers Shipmanagement (Singapore) Pte Ltd
Majuro *Marshall Islands*
MMSI: 538090122
Official number: 4738

16,986
7,538
21,184
T/cm
38.4

Class: GL (LR)
Classed LR until 15/5/04

1999-07 Hanjin Heavy Industries & Construction Co Ltd — Ulsan Yd No: 640
Loa 168.00 (BB) Br ex - Dght 9.200
Lbp 158.00 Br md 27.20 Dpth 13.80
Welded, 1 dk

(A33A2CC) Container Ship (Fully Cellular)
TEU 1620 C Ho 610 TEU C Dk 1010 TEU incl 200 ref C
Compartments: 7 Cell Ho, ER
8 Ha: (12.6 x 18.3)Tappered 7 (12.6 x 23.4)ER
Cranes: 3x40t,1x20t

1 oil engine driving 1 FP propeller
Total Power: 15,800kW (21,482hp) 20.0kn
B&W 7S60MC-C
1 x 2 Stroke 7 Cy. 600 x 2400 15800kW (21482bhp)
Hyundai Heavy Industries Co Ltd-South Korea
AuxGen: 3 x 900kW 440/220V 60Hz a.c
Boilers: TOH (o.f.), TOH (ex.g.)
Thrusters: 1 Thwart. CP thruster (f)
Fuel: 112.2 (d.f.) (Heating Coils) 1584.0 (r.f.) 63.0pd

8515740 **SPIRIT OF BRAZIL**
V7OG5
ex Yarrow *-2008* *ex* Alexandraki *-2002*
-
ex Irrawaddy *-2000* *ex* Raijin Maru *-1996*
Rioja Finance Inc
Kristen Marine SA
Majuro *Marshall Islands*
MMSI: 538003084
Official number: 3084

36,591
22,908
70,653

Class: NK

1986-08 Kurushima Dockyard Co. Ltd. — Onishi
Yd No: 2458
Loa 225.00 (BB) Br ex - Dght 13.282
Lbp 216.01 Br md 32.21 Dpth 18.22
Welded, 1 dk

(A21A2BC) Bulk Carrier
Grain: 80,355; Bale: 77,935
Compartments: 7 Ho, ER
7 Ha: 2 (14.0 x 14.0)5 (17.9 x 14.0)ER

1 oil engine driving 1 FP propeller
Total Power: 7,355kW (10,000hp) 13.5kn
B&W 6S60MCE
1 x 2 Stroke 6 Cy. 600 x 2292 7355kW (10000bhp)
Hitachi Zosen Corp-Japan
Fuel: 1935.0 (r.f.)

7305629 **SPIRIT OF BRAZIL VII**
HO2326
ex Adler Clipper *-2007* *ex* Harle Express *-1997*
-
ex Stadt Kiel I *-1983*
ex Stadt Heiligenhafen *-1981* *ex* Elbe *-1976*
Centennial Asset Ltd
EBX SA
Panama *Panama*
MMSI: 372428000
Official number: 3362908A

882
317
186

Class: (RI) (GL)

1973-03 Muetzelfeldtwerft GmbH — Cuxhaven
Yd No: 185
Loa 54.72 (BB) Br ex 10.04 Dght 2.690
Lbp 47.02 Br md 10.01 Dpth 4.09
Welded, 1 dk

(A37B2PS) Passenger Ship
Passengers: unberthed: 710
Ice Capable

2 oil engines reverse reduction geared to sc. shafts driving 2 CP propellers
Total Power: 1,588kW (2,160hp) 15.3kn
MWM TBD440-8
2 x 4 Stroke 8 Cy. 230 x 270 each-794kW (1080bhp)
Motoren Werke Mannheim AG (MWM)-West Germany
AuxGen: 2 x 252kW 220V 50Hz a.c
Thrusters: 1 Thwart. FP thruster (f)

9524231 **SPIRIT OF BRITAIN**
2DXD4
-
SNC Gris-Nez Bail
P&O Ferries France SAS
SatCom: Inmarsat C 423592632
Dover *United Kingdom*
MMSI: 235082716
Official number: 917019

47,592
14,277
9,500

Class: LR
✠ **100A1** SS 01/2011
passenger and vehicle ferry
ShipRight (SDA, CM, ACS (B))
*IWS
EP
✠ **LMC** **UMS**
Eq.Ltr: 0†;
Cable: 660.0/78.0 U3 (a)

2011-01 STX Finland Oy — Rauma Yd No: 1367
Loa 212.00 (BB) Br ex 31.40 Dght 6.540
Lbp 197.90 Br md 30.80 Dpth 21.10
Welded, 9 dks including 3 vehicle decks

(A36A2PR) Passenger/Ro-Ro Ship (Vehicles)
Passengers: unberthed: 1750
Bow door/ramp (centre)
Len: 5.20 Wid: 22.36 Swl: 115
Stern door/ramp (centre)
Lane-Len: 3746
Lorries: 180, Cars: 1,059

4 oil engines with clutches, flexible couplings & sr geared to sc. shafts driving 2 CP propellers
Total Power: 30,400kW (41,332hp) 22.0kn
MAN-B&W 7L48/60
4 x 4 Stroke 7 Cy. 480 x 600 each-7600kW (10333bhp)
MAN B&W Diesel AG-Augsburg
AuxGen: 4 x 1463kW 415V 50Hz a.c, 4 x 3120kW 6600V 50Hz a.c
Boilers: e (ex.g.) 10.4kgf/cm² (10.2bar), AuxB (o.f.) 9.4kgf/cm² (9.2bar)
Thrusters: 3 Thwart. CP thruster (f)

9015668 **SPIRIT OF BRITISH COLUMBIA**
VOSM
-
British Columbia Ferry Services Inc
Victoria, BC *Canada*
MMSI: 316001268
Official number: 815277

18,747
13,893
2,925

Class: AB

1993-02 Integrated Ferry Constructors Ltd — Victoria BC (Aft section) Yd No: 20
1993-02 Allied Shipbuilders Ltd — North Vancouver BC (Fwd section) Yd No: 254
Loa 167.50 (BB) Br ex 32.90 Dght 5.000
Lbp 156.00 Br md 26.60 Dpth 8.00
Welded, 3 dks

(A36A2PR) Passenger/Ro-Ro Ship (Vehicles)
Passengers: unberthed: 2000
Bow door
Stern door
Lane-Len: 2354
Lane-clr ht: 4.60
Vehicles: 470

4 oil engines with clutches, flexible couplings & sr geared to sc. shafts driving 2 CP propellers
Total Power: 15,960kW (21,700hp) 19.0kn
MAN 6L40/54
4 x 4 Stroke 6 Cy. 400 x 540 each-3990kW (5425bhp)
MAN B&W Diesel AG-Augsburg
AuxGen: 2 x 1700kW 600V 60Hz a.c, 1 x 1700kW 600V 60Hz a.c
Thrusters: 2 Thwart. CP thruster (f)
Fuel: 475.0 (d.f.) 33.0pd

9178290 **SPIRIT OF CAPE TOWN**
9V2504
ex Alva Rickmers *-2014* *ex* As Asturia *-2013*
-
ex CSAV Rio Rapel *-2009* *ex* Asturia *-2004*
ex Comanche *-2003* *ex* Ocelot Max *-2002*
AR Alva Navigation Pte Ltd
Rickmers Shipmanagement (Singapore) Pte Ltd
Singapore *Singapore*
MMSI: 564105000
Official number: 399104

26,047
10,209
30,703
T/cm
49.4

Class: GL (BV)

2000-02 China Shipbuilding Corp (CSBC) — Kaohsiung Yd No: 735
Loa 195.60 (BB) Br ex - Dght 11.010
Lbp 185.50 Br md 30.20 Dpth 16.60
Welded, 1 dk

(A33A2CC) Container Ship (Fully Cellular)
TEU 2210 C Ho 868 TEU C Dk 1342 TEU incl 300 ref C.
Compartments: 5 Cell Ho, ER
Cranes: 3x45t

1 oil engine driving 1 FP propeller
Total Power: 20,874kW (28,380hp) 21.0kn
B&W 7S70MC
1 x 2 Stroke 7 Cy. 700 x 2674 20874kW (28380bhp)
Hyundai Heavy Industries Co Ltd-South Korea
AuxGen: 4 x 1200kW 450V 60Hz a.c
Thrusters: 1 Thwart. CP thruster (f)

9178288 **SPIRIT OF COLOMBO**
9V2507
ex Alina Rickmers *-2014* *ex* Aquitania *-2013*
-
ex Corrado *-2003* *ex* Lionmax *-2002*
AR Alina Navigation Pte Ltd
Rickmers Shipmanagement (Singapore) Pte Ltd
Singapore *Singapore*
MMSI: 564094000
Official number: 399109

26,047
10,209
30,703
T/cm
49.4

Class: GL (BV)

2000-04 China Shipbuilding Corp (CSBC) — Kaohsiung Yd No: 734
Loa 195.60 (BB) Br ex - Dght 11.010
Lbp 185.50 Br md 30.20 Dpth 16.60
Welded, 1 dk

(A33A2CC) Container Ship (Fully Cellular)
TEU 2202 C Ho 870 TEU C Dk 1332 TEU incl 300 ref C.
Compartments: 5 Cell Ho, ER
Cranes: 3x45t

1 oil engine driving 1 FP propeller
Total Power: 20,874kW (28,380hp) 21.0kn
B&W 7S70MC
1 x 2 Stroke 7 Cy. 700 x 2674 20874kW (28380bhp)
Hyundai Heavy Industries Co Ltd-South Korea
AuxGen: 4 x 1200kW 450/110V 60Hz a.c
Thrusters: 1 Thwart. CP thruster (f)
Fuel: 3008.0 (r.f.) 86.0pd

8972508 **SPIRIT OF DENARAU**
-
ex FH 31 *-2000*
-
Skeggs Group Ltd
Fiji

176
53
-

2000-08 in New Zealand (Hull launched by)
2000-08 in New Zealand (Hull completed by)
Loa 29.70 Br ex - Dght -
Lbp - Br md 8.52 Dpth 2.42
Welded

(A35D2RL) Landing Craft

1 oil engine driving 1 FP propeller
Total Power: 170kW (231hp) 6.0kn
General Motors
1 x 2 Stroke 170kW (231bhp)
General Motors Detroit DieselAllison Divn-USA

9387607 **SPIRIT OF ENDURANCE**
ZMEN
ex CCL Moji *-2008* *launched as* Panjang *-2008*
-
PIT Pacific Investment & Trading GmbH & Co KG
Pacifica Shipping (1985) Ltd
Lyttelton *New Zealand*
MMSI: 512042000
Official number: 876374

7,464
3,085
8,165
T/cm
22.0

Class: GL

2008-05 Fujian Mawei Shipbuilding Ltd — Fuzhou FJ Yd No: 437-30
Loa 129.62 (BB) Br ex - Dght 7.400
Lbp 120.34 Br md 20.60 Dpth 10.80
Welded, 1 dk

(A33A2CC) Container Ship (Fully Cellular)
Double Bottom Entire Compartment Length
TEU 698 C Ho 226 TEU C Dk 472 TEU incl 120 ref C.

1 oil engine reduction geared to sc. shaft driving 1 CP propeller
Total Power: 7,200kW (9,789hp) 17.5kn
MaK 8M43
1 x 4 Stroke 8 Cy. 430 x 610 7200kW (9789bhp) (new engine 2008)
Caterpillar Motoren GmbH & Co. KG-Germany
AuxGen: 3 x 450kW 450/230V a.c, 1 x 1000kW 450/230V a.c
Thrusters: 1 Tunnel thruster (f)

9533816 *2DXD5* -	**SPIRIT OF FRANCE** **SNC White Cliffs Bail** P&O Ferries France SAS *Dover* *United Kingdom* MMSI: 235082717 Official number: 917512	**47,592** 14,277 9,884	Class: LR ✠**100A1** SS 01/2012 passenger and vehicle ferry **ShipRight** (SDA,CM,ACS (B)) *IWS EP ✠**LMC** **UMS** Eq.Ltr: 0†; Cable: 660.0/78.0 U3 (a)	**2012-01 STX Finland Oy — Rauma** Yd No: 1368 Loa 212.00 (BB) Br ex 31.40 Dght 6.700 Lbp 197.90 Br md 30.80 Dpth 9.70 Welded, 3 dks	**(A36A2PR) Passenger/Ro-Ro Ship (Vehicles)** Passengers: 2000 Bow door/ramp (centre) Len: 5.20 Wid: 27.36 Swl: 115 Stern door/ramp (centre) Lane-Len: 3746 Cars: 195, Trailers: 180	**4 oil engines** with clutches, flexible couplings & sr geared to sc. shafts driving 2 CP propellers Total Power: 30,400kW (41,332hp) 22.0kn MAN-B&W 7L48/60 4 x 4 Stroke 7 Cy. 480 x 600 each-7600kW (10333bhp) MAN B&W Diesel AG-Augsburg AuxGen: 4 x 1463kW 415V 50Hz a.c, 4 x 3120kW 6600V 50Hz a.c Boilers: e (ex.g.) 10.4kgf/cm^2 (10.2bar), AuxB (o.f.) 9.4kgf/cm^2 (9.2bar) Thrusters: 2 Thwart. CP thruster (f); 1 Thwart. CP thruster (a)
8883563 *WDD4938* -	**SPIRIT OF GLACIER BAY** *ex* Spirit of Nantucket *ex* Nantucket Clipper *-2006* **General Electric Capital Corp** - SatCom: Inmarsat C 436712910 *Sitka, AK* *United States of America* MMSI: 367129000 Official number: 677685	**1,471** 511 -	Class: (AB)	**1984 Jeffboat, Inc. — Jeffersonville, In** Yd No: 82-2543 Loa 63.09 Br ex - Dght 2.560 Lbp 52.57 Br md 11.27 Dpth 3.50 Welded, 1 dk	**(A37A2PC) Passenger/Cruise** Passengers: cabins: 51; berths: 107	**2 oil engines** sr geared to sc. shafts driving 2 FP propellers Total Power: 784kW (1,066hp) G.M. (Detroit Diesel) 12V-92 2 x Vee 2 Stroke 12 Cy. 123 x 127 each-392kW (533bhp) General Motors Detroit DieselAllison Divn-USA AuxGen: 3 x 200kW a.c Thrusters: 1 Thwart. FP thruster (f)
9391660 *9V2497* -	**SPIRIT OF HAMBURG** *ex* Bahia Laura *-2013* **AR Fifth Navigation Pte Ltd** Rickmers Shipmanagement (Singapore) Pte Ltd *Singapore* *Singapore* MMSI: 564061000	**41,483** 23,894 53,139	Class: GL	**2007-07 Daewoo Shipbuilding & Marine Engineering Co Ltd — Geoje** Yd No: 4133 Loa 254.06 (BB) Br ex - Dght 12.400 Lbp 242.00 Br md 32.20 Dpth 19.30 Welded, 1 dk	**(A33A2CC) Container Ship (Fully Cellular)** Double Bottom Entire Compartment Length TEU 3752 C Ho 1480 TEU C Dk 2272 TEU incl 844 ref C	**1 oil engine** driving 1 FP propeller Total Power: 24,880kW (33,827hp) 22.4kn MAN-B&W 8S70MC-C 1 x 2 Stroke 8 Cy. 700 x 2800 24880kW (33827bhp) Doosan Engine Co Ltd-South Korea AuxGen: 4 x 2500kW 450V a.c Thrusters: 1 Tunnel thruster (f) Fuel: 169.4 (d.f.) 5175.2 (r.f.)
9007556 *3DZC* -	**SPIRIT OF HARMONY** *ex* Ferry Sazan *-2007* **Patterson Brothers Shipping** - *Suva* *Fiji*	*1,505* - 558		**1991-03 Shinhama Dockyard Co. Ltd. — Anan** Yd No: 807 Loa - Br ex - Dght 3.501 Lbp 65.03 Br md 14.51 Dpth 5.31 Welded	**(A36A2PR) Passenger/Ro-Ro Ship (Vehicles)**	**2 oil engines** driving 2 FP propellers Total Power: 3,384kW (4,600hp) Daihatsu 6DLM-32 2 x 4 Stroke 6 Cy. 320 x 400 each-1692kW (2300bhp) Daihatsu Diesel Manufacturing Co Lt-Japan
9433638 *HPGK* -	**SPIRIT OF HO-PING** **Satsuki Maritime SA** Kitaura Kaiun KK SatCom: Inmarsat C 437226410 *Panama* *Panama* MMSI: 372264000 Official number: 4251811	**43,012** 27,239 82,152 T/cm 70.2	Class: NK	**2011-03 Tsuneishi Shipbuilding Co Ltd — Fukuyama HS** Yd No: 1452 Loa 228.99 Br ex - Dght 14.430 Lbp 222.00 Br md 32.26 Dpth 20.05 Welded, 1 dk	**(A21A2BC) Bulk Carrier** Grain: 97,381 Compartments: 7 Ho, ER 7 Ha: ER	**1 oil engine** driving 1 FP propeller Total Power: 9,710kW (13,202hp) 14.5kn MAN-B&W 6S60MC-C 1 x 2 Stroke 6 Cy. 600 x 2400 9710kW (13202bhp) Mitsui Engineering & Shipbuilding CLtd-Japan Fuel: 3184.0 (r.f.)
9319583 *ZMG2777* -	**SPIRIT OF INDEPENDENCE** *ex* Tini *-2013* **Northeastern Star Shipping Co Ltd** Pacifica Shipping (1985) Ltd *Auckland* *New Zealand* MMSI: 512409000	**6,701** 3,557 8,200 T/cm 20.7	Class: BV (GL)	**2005-01 Zhejiang Yangfan Ship Group Co Ltd — Zhoushan ZJ** Yd No: 2029 Loa 132.60 (BB) Br ex - Dght 7.200 Lbp 123.40 Br md 19.20 Dpth 9.20 Welded, 1 dk	**(A33A2CC) Container Ship (Fully Cellular)** TEU 672 C Ho 228 TEU C Dk 444 TEU incl 75 ref C Ice Capable	**1 oil engine** reduction geared to sc. shaft driving 1 CP propeller Total Power: 6,300kW (8,565hp) 17.0kn MaK 7M43 1 x 4 Stroke 7 Cy. 430 x 610 6300kW (8565bhp) Caterpillar Motoren GmbH & Co. KG-Germany AuxGen: 3 x 352kW 440/220V 60Hz a.c, 1 x 1200kW 440/220V 60Hz a.c Thrusters: 1 Thwart. CP thruster (f)
9289893 *VHS6181* -	**SPIRIT OF KANGAROO ISLAND** **Australia Inbound Pty Ltd** Kangaroo Island Sealink Pty Ltd (SeaLink Travel Group) *Port Adelaide, SA* *Australia* MMSI: 503466000 Official number: 857409	**1,329** 399 350	Class: NV	**2003-12 Austal Ships Pty Ltd — Fremantle WA** Yd No: 117 Loa 50.37 (BB) Br ex 18.00 Dght 2.500 Lbp 49.50 Br md 17.80 Dpth 5.50 Welded, 1 dk	**(A36A2PR) Passenger/Ro-Ro Ship (Vehicles)** Hull Material: Aluminium Alloy Passengers: unberthed: 244 Cars: 55	**2 oil engines** geared to sc. shafts driving 2 FP propellers Total Power: 2,236kW (3,040hp) 15.0kn Caterpillar 3512B 2 x Vee 4 Stroke 12 Cy. 170 x 190 each-1118kW (1520bhp) Caterpillar Inc-USA AuxGen: 2 x 50Hz a.c
9179816 *H3TC* -	**SPIRIT OF LUCK** *ex* Estebroker *-2013* *ex* CSAV Trinidad *-2008* *ex* Hanjin Dubai *-2007* *ex* Trade Bravery *-2005* *ex* TPL Merchant *-2002* *ex* Lykes Crusader *-2001* *ex* TMM Quetzal *-1999* *ex* Widukind *-1999* **Feliz Shipping Co Ltd** Victoria Oceanway Ltd *Panama* *Panama* MMSI: 373022000 Official number: 4519613	**25,705** 12,028 33,843 T/cm 52.0	Class: NK (GL)	**1999-03 Kvaerner Warnow Werft GmbH — Rostock** Yd No: 17 Loa 208.36 (BB) Br ex 30.04 Dght 11.400 Lbp 195.00 Br md 29.80 Dpth 16.40 Welded, 1 dk	**(A33A2CC) Container Ship (Fully Cellular)** Grain: 44,903 TEU 2526 C Ho 960 TEU C Dk 1566 TEU incl 394 ref C. Compartments: 5 Cell Ho 10 Ha: (12.6 x 15.7) (12.6 x 20.8)8 (12.6 x 26.0) Cranes: 3x45t Ice Capable	**1 oil engine** driving 1 FP propeller Total Power: 19,810kW (26,934hp) 21.0kn B&W 7L70MC 1 x 2 Stroke 7 Cy. 700 x 2268 19810kW (26934bhp) Dieselmotorenwerk Rostock GmbH-Rostock AuxGen: 3 x 1360kW a.c, 1 x 1020kW a.c Thrusters: 1 Thwart. CP thruster (f) Fuel: 247.0 (d.f.) (Heating Coils) 2332.0 (r.f.) 98.2pd
9204972 *9V2508* -	**SPIRIT OF MANILA** *ex* Angie Rickmers *-2014* *ex* AS Alicantia *-2013* *ex* Safmarine Illovo *-2010* *ex* Alicantia *-2005* *ex* Commander *-2003* *ex* Jaguar Max *-2002* **AR Angie Navigation Pte Ltd** Rickmers Shipmanagement (Singapore) Pte Ltd *Singapore* *Singapore* MMSI: 564095000 Official number: 399110	**26,047** 10,209 30,554 T/cm 49.4	Class: GL (BV)	**2000-07 China Shipbuilding Corp — Keelung** Yd No: 736 Loa 195.60 (BB) Br ex - Dght 11.010 Lbp 185.50 Br md 30.20 Dpth 16.60 Welded, 1 dk	**(A33A2CC) Container Ship (Fully Cellular)** TEU 2262 C Ho 870 TEU C Dk 1392 TEU incl 435 ref C. Compartments: 3 Cell Ho, ER 9 Ha: (12.6 x 21.0) (12.6 x 25.6)7 (12.6 x 26.1)ER Cranes: 3x45t	**1 oil engine** driving 1 FP propeller Total Power: 24,830kW (33,759hp) 20.0kn B&W 8S70MC 1 x 2 Stroke 8 Cy. 700 x 2674 24830kW (33759bhp) Hyundai Heavy Industries Co Ltd-South Korea AuxGen: 4 x 1470kW 440V 60Hz a.c Thrusters: 1 Thwart. CP thruster (f)
9362413 *9V2500* -	**SPIRIT OF MELBOURNE** *ex* Bahia Grande *-2014* **AR Fourth Navigation Pte Ltd** Rickmers Shipmanagement (Singapore) Pte Ltd *Singapore* *Singapore* MMSI: 564086000 Official number: 399100	**41,483** 23,894 53,176	Class: GL	**2007-05 Daewoo Shipbuilding & Marine Engineering Co Ltd — Geoje** Yd No: 4132 Loa 254.07 (BB) Br ex - Dght 12.400 Lbp 242.00 Br md 32.20 Dpth 19.30 Welded, 1 dk	**(A33A2CC) Container Ship (Fully Cellular)** Double Bottom Entire Compartment Length TEU 3752 C Ho 1480 TEU C Dk 2272 TEU incl 844 ref C	**1 oil engine** driving 1 FP propeller Total Power: 26,160kW (35,567hp) 22.4kn MAN-B&W 8S70MC-C8 1 x 2 Stroke 8 Cy. 700 x 2800 26160kW (35567bhp) Doosan Engine Co Ltd-South Korea AuxGen: 4 x 2470kW 450V a.c Thrusters: 1 Tunnel thruster (f) Fuel: 169.4 (d.f.) 5175.2 (r.f.)
8992998 *WDC4321* -	**SPIRIT OF MOUNT VERNON** *ex* Spirit Of Washington Ii *-2011* **Spirit Marine Co** - *Washington, DC* *United States of America* MMSI: 367022930 Official number: 959325	**867** - -		**1990-01 Service Marine Industries Inc — Amelia LA** Yd No: 158 L reg 48.07 Br ex - Dght - Lbp - Br md 10.06 Dpth 3.35 Welded, 1 dk	**(A37B2PS) Passenger Ship**	**1 oil engine** driving 1 Propeller
9178276 *9V2506* -	**SPIRIT OF MUMBAI** *ex* Amiko Rickmers *-2014* *ex* Anglia *-2013* *ex* Columbus Australia *-2004* *ex* Cherokee *-2003* *ex* Panthermax *-2002* *ex* Canmar Supreme *-2002* *ex* Panther Max *-2001* **AR Amiko Navigation Pte Ltd** Rickmers Shipmanagement (Singapore) Pte Ltd *Singapore* *Singapore* MMSI: 564103000 Official number: 399106	**26,047** 10,209 30,703 T/cm 49.4	Class: GL (BV)	**1999-11 China Shipbuilding Corp (CSBC) — Kaohsiung** Yd No: 733 Loa 195.60 (BB) Br ex - Dght 11.000 Lbp 185.50 Br md 30.20 Dpth 16.60 Welded, 1 dk	**(A33A2CC) Container Ship (Fully Cellular)** TEU 2202 incl 350 ref C. Compartments: 5 Cell Ho, ER 9 Ha: (12.6 x 15.8)8 (12.6 x 21.0)ER Cranes: 3x45t	**1 oil engine** driving 1 FP propeller Total Power: 20,874kW (28,380hp) 18.0kn B&W 7S70MC 1 x 2 Stroke 7 Cy. 700 x 2674 20874kW (28380bhp) Hyundai Heavy Industries Co Ltd-South Korea AuxGen: 4 x 1200kW 450V 60Hz a.c Thrusters: 1 Thwart. CP thruster (f) Fuel: 2330.1 (d.f.) 86.0pd
8975603 *ZMSV* -	**SPIRIT OF NEW ZEALAND** *ex* Spirit of Adventure *-2003* **Spirit of Adventure Trust Board Inc** *Auckland* *New Zealand* Official number: 875169	*184* 55 -		**1986 Thackwray Yachts Ltd. — New Zealand** Loa 45.20 Br ex - Dght 4.000 Lbp 33.25 Br md 9.11 Dpth - Welded, 1 dk	**(X11B2QN) Sail Training Ship** Passengers: 40	**1 oil engine** with clutches & sr reverse geared to sc. shaft driving 1 CP propeller Total Power: 184kW (250hp) 9.0kn Gardner 8L3B 1 x 4 Stroke 8 Cy. 140 x 197 184kW (250bhp) L. Gardner & Sons Ltd.-Manchester AuxGen: 2 x 32kW a.c Thrusters: 1 Thwart. FP thruster (f) Fuel: 21.3 (d.f.) 1.5pd

8984551 - - -	**SPIRIT OF NIUGINI** *ex* Aqua One *-2007* - -	*200* 136 -		**1999 in Thailand** Loa 35.00 Br ex - Dght 1.800 Lbp - Br md 6.10 Dpth 4.00 Welded, 1 dk	**(X11A2YP) Yacht** Passengers: berths: 16	**2 oil engines** geared to sc. shafts driving 2 Propellers Total Power: 2,066kW (2,808hp) Cummins KTA-38-M2 2 x Vee 4 Stroke 12 Cy. 159 x 159 each-1033kW (1404bhp) Cummins Engine Co Inc-USA
8861618 *WDD4552* -	**SPIRIT OF NORFOLK** **Spirit Cruises LLC** - *Norfolk, VA* *United States of America* MMSI: 367146190 Official number: 982944	*1,151* 371 -		**1992 Service Marine Industries Inc — Amelia LA** Yd No: 163 Loa - Br ex - Dght - Lbp 51.57 Br md 11.58 Dpth 3.65 Welded, 1 dk	**(A37B2PS) Passenger Ship**	**1 oil engine** driving 1 FP propeller
9204984 *9V2503*	**SPIRIT OF PIRAEUS** *ex* Akki Rickmers *-2014* *ex* As Andalusia *-2013* *ex* Marfret Provence *-2010* *ex* AS Andalusia *-2008* *ex* Safmarine Mono *-2008* *ex* Andalusia *-2004* *ex* Centurion *-2003* *ex* Puma Max *-2002* **AR Akki Navigation Pte Ltd** Rickmers Shipmanagement (Singapore) Pte Ltd *Singapore* *Singapore* MMSI: 564099000 Official number: 399103	**26,047** 10,209 30,554 T/cm 49.4	Class: GL (BV)	**2001-02 China Shipbuilding Corp — Keelung** Yd No: 760 Loa 195.60 (BB) Br ex - Dght 11.010 Lbp 185.50 Br md 30.20 Dpth 16.60 Welded, 1 dk	**(A33A2CC) Container Ship (Fully Cellular)** TEU 2262 C Ho 870 TEU C Dk 1392 TEU incl 435 ref C. Cranes: 3x45t	**1 oil engine** driving 1 FP propeller Total Power: 24,830kW (33,759hp) 18.0kn B&W 8S70MC 1 x 2 Stroke 8 Cy. 700 x 2674 24830kW (33759bhp) Hyundai Heavy Industries Co Ltd-South Korea AuxGen: 4 x 1200kW 440/110V 60Hz a.c Thrusters: 1 Thwart. CP thruster (f)
9040259 - -	**SPIRIT OF PORT LOUIS** *ex* Ahinora *-2001* *ex* Royal Victoria *-1995* **G & G Marine Services Ltd** Nordic Shipping & Trading SA	**478** 159 100	Class: (NV)	**1991-11 Kvaerner Fjellstrand AS — Omastrand** Yd No: 1609 Loa 40.00 Br ex - Dght 1.612 Lbp 39.92 Br md 10.10 Dpth 3.93 Welded	**(A37B2PS) Passenger Ship** Hull Material: Aluminium Alloy Passengers: unberthed: 302	**2 oil engines** geared to sc. shafts driving 2 Water jets Total Power: 3,998kW (5,436hp) 35.0kn M.T.U. 16V396TE74L 2 x Vee 4 Stroke 16 Cy. 165 x 185 each-1999kW (2718bhp) MTU Friedrichshafen GmbH-Friedrichshafen AuxGen: 2 x 68kW 380V 50Hz a.c
9319894 *MHBV5* -	**SPIRIT OF PORTSMOUTH** **Portsmouth Harbour Ferry Co Plc** - *Portsmouth* *United Kingdom* MMSI: 235024149 Official number: 909851	**377** 126 30		**2005-05 Stocznia 'Wisla' Sp z oo — Gdansk** (Hull) Yd No: 345 **2005-05 VT Halmatic Ltd — Portsmouth** Loa 32.60 Br ex - Dght 1.900 Lbp 30.15 Br md 10.20 Dpth - Welded, 1 dk	**(A37B2PS) Passenger Ship** Passengers: unberthed: 300	**2 oil engines** geared to sc. shafts driving 2 Directional propellers Total Power: 536kW (728hp) 10.0kn Scania DSI12 2 x 4 Stroke 6 Cy. 127 x 145 each-268kW (364bhp) Scania AB-Sweden
9037020 *3FLY2*	**SPIRIT OF SEA** *ex* Quseir *-2012* *ex* Shadwan Island 1 *-2009* *ex* Al Esraa *-2009* *ex* Luta *-1999* *launched as* Turnu Maprele *-1996* **Fairplay Shipping Co SA** Sea Gate Management Co SA *Panama* *Panama* MMSI: 356823000 Official number: 4297111A	**12,233** 7,042 16,113	Class: PR (GL) (RN)	**1996-01 Santierul Naval Galati S.A. — Galati** Yd No: 811 Loa 158.70 (BB) Br ex - Dght 9.920 Lbp 147.00 Br md 22.80 Dpth 13.20 Welded, 2 dks	**(A31A2GX) General Cargo Ship** Grain: 23,272; Bale: 22,189 TEU 526 incl 32 ref C. Compartments: 4 Ho, ER, 3 Tw Dk 4 Ha: ER Cranes: 6x12.5t	**1 oil engine** driving 1 FP propeller Total Power: 6,030kW (8,198hp) 15.0kn MAN K8SZ52/105CL 1 x 2 Stroke 8 Cy. 520 x 1050 6030kW (8198bhp) U.C.M. Resita S.A.-Resita AuxGen: 3 x 500kW 380V 50Hz a.c Fuel: 356.7 (d.f.) 1398.3 (r.f.) 27.5pd
9362401 *9V2499* -	**SPIRIT OF SHANGHAI** *ex* Bahia Castillo *-2013* **AR Third Navigation Pte Ltd** Rickmers Shipmanagement (Singapore) Pte Ltd *Singapore* *Singapore* MMSI: 564067000 Official number: 399099	**41,483** 23,894 53,160	Class: GL	**2007-04 Daewoo Shipbuilding & Marine Engineering Co Ltd — Geoje** Yd No: 4131 Loa 254.07 (BB) Br ex - Dght 12.400 Lbp 241.99 Br md 32.20 Dpth 19.30 Welded, 1 dk	**(A33A2CC) Container Ship (Fully Cellular)** Double Bottom Entire Compartment Length TEU 3752 C Ho 1480 TEU C Dk 2272 TEU incl 844 ref C	**1 oil engine** driving 1 FP propeller Total Power: 26,160kW (35,567hp) 22.4kn MAN-B&W 8S70MC-C8 1 x 2 Stroke 8 Cy. 700 x 2800 26160kW (35567bhp) Doosan Engine Co Ltd-South Korea AuxGen: 4 x 2500kW 450/230V a.c Thrusters: 1 Tunnel thruster (f) Fuel: 169.4 (d.f.) 5175.2 (r.f.)
9362396 *9V2498* -	**SPIRIT OF SINGAPORE** *ex* Bahia Blanca *-2014* **AR Second Navigation Pte Ltd** Rickmers Shipmanagement (Singapore) Pte Ltd *Singapore* *Singapore* MMSI: 564077000 Official number: 399098	**41,483** 23,894 53,093	Class: GL	**2007-02 Daewoo Shipbuilding & Marine Engineering Co Ltd — Geoje** Yd No: 4130 Loa 254.06 (BB) Br ex - Dght 12.400 Lbp 241.99 Br md 32.20 Dpth 19.30 Welded, 1 dk	**(A33A2CC) Container Ship (Fully Cellular)** Double Bottom Entire Compartment Length TEU 3752 C Ho 1480 TEU C Dk 2272 TEU incl 844 ref C	**1 oil engine** driving 1 FP propeller Total Power: 26,160kW (35,567hp) 22.4kn MAN-B&W 8S70MC-C8 1 x 2 Stroke 8 Cy. 700 x 2800 26160kW (35567bhp) Doosan Engine Co Ltd-South Korea AuxGen: 4 x 2500kW 450V a.c Thrusters: 1 Tunnel thruster (f) Fuel: 169.4 (d.f.) 5175.2 (r.f.)
9112210 - -	**SPIRIT OF ST. AGNES** - **St Agnes Boating** - *United Kingdom*	*100* - 20	Class: (LR) ✠	**1994-12 Souter Shipyard Ltd. — Cowes** Yd No: 130 Loa 13.41 Br ex 5.79 Dght - Lbp - Br md - Dpth 1.71 Welded, 1 dk	**(A37B2PS) Passenger Ship** Passengers: unberthed: 80	**2 oil engines** driving 2 FP propellers Total Power: 106kW (144hp) Volvo Penta 2 x 4 Stroke each-53kW (72bhp) AB Volvo Penta-Sweden
9044528 *JPDL* -	**SPIRIT OF ST WORLD** *ex* Akogare *-2013* - - SatCom: Inmarsat C 443135210 *Osaka, Osaka* *Japan* MMSI: 431005001 Official number: 133434	**362** 108 108		**1993-03 Sumitomo Heavy Industries Ltd. — Uraga Shipyard, Yokosuka** Yd No: 1188 Loa 52.16 Br ex - Dght 3.900 Lbp 36.00 Br md 8.60 Dpth 5.90 Welded, 3 dks	**(X11B2QN) Sail Training Ship**	**1 oil engine** with clutches, flexible couplings & reduction geared to sc. shaft driving 1 CP propeller Total Power: 235kW (320hp) 8.5kn Yanmar 6GH-ST 1 x 4 Stroke 6 Cy. 117 x 140 235kW (320bhp) Yanmar Diesel Engine Co Ltd-Japan Thrusters: 1 Thwart. CP thruster (f)
9391672 *9V2501* -	**SPIRIT OF SYDNEY** *ex* Bahia Negra *-2013* *ex* CCNI Shenzhen *-2010* *ex* Bahia Negra *-2008* **AR Sixth Navigation Pte Ltd** Rickmers Shipmanagement (Singapore) Pte Ltd *Singapore* *Singapore* MMSI: 564053000 Official number: 399101	**41,483** 23,894 53,142	Class: GL	**2007-08 Daewoo Shipbuilding & Marine Engineering Co Ltd — Geoje** Yd No: 4134 Loa 254.00 (BB) Br ex 32.20 Dght 12.400 Lbp 242.00 Br md 32.19 Dpth 19.30 Welded, 1 dk	**(A33A2CC) Container Ship (Fully Cellular)** Double Bottom Entire Compartment Length TEU 3752 C Ho 1480 TEU C Dk 2272 TEU incl 844 ref C	**1 oil engine** driving 1 FP propeller Total Power: 26,160kW (35,567hp) 22.4kn MAN-B&W 8S70MC-C 1 x 2 Stroke 8 Cy. 700 x 2800 26160kW (35567bhp) AuxGen: 4 x 2470kW 450V a.c Thrusters: 1 Tunnel thruster (f) Fuel: 169.4 (d.f.) 5175.2 (r.f.)
9158446 *VNGY* -	**SPIRIT OF TASMANIA I** *ex* Superfast IV *-2002* **TT Line Co Pty Ltd** - *Devonport, Tas* *Australia* MMSI: 503432000 Official number: 857101	**29,338** 11,404 5,651	Class: AB HR	**1998-03 Kvaerner Masa-Yards Inc — Turku** Yd No: 1341 Loa 194.33 (BB) Br ex - Dght 6.550 Lbp 176.00 Br md 25.00 Dpth 9.10 Welded, 9 dks,incl 2 hoistable	**(A36A2PR) Passenger/Ro-Ro Ship (Vehicles)** Passengers: unberthed: 886; cabins: 222; berths: 750 Bow door/ramp Len: 20.30 Wid: 4.50 Swl: - Stern door/ramp (p) Len: 11.75 Wid: 5.00 Swl: - Stern door/ramp (s) Len: 11.75 Wid: 8.00 Swl: - Lane-Len: 2507 Lorries: 110, Cars: 140	**4 oil engines** with clutches, flexible couplings & sr geared to sc. shafts driving 2 CP propellers Total Power: 42,240kW (57,428hp) 28.5kn Sulzer 16ZAV40S 4 x Vee 4 Stroke 16 Cy. 400 x 560 each-10560kW (14357bhp) Wartsila NSD France SA-France AuxGen: 3 x 1384kW 440V 60Hz a.c, 2 x 1384kW 440V 60Hz a.c Thrusters: 2 Thwart. CP thruster (f); 1 Tunnel thruster (a) Fuel: 143.0 (d.f.) (Heating Coils) 1222.0 (r.f.) 168.0pd
9158434 *VNSZ* -	**SPIRIT OF TASMANIA II** *ex* Superfast III *-2002* **TT Line Co Pty Ltd** - *Devonport, Tas* *Australia* MMSI: 503433000 Official number: 857102	**29,338** 11,404 5,651	Class: AB HR	**1998-02 Kvaerner Masa-Yards Inc — Turku** Yd No: 1340 Loa 194.30 (BB) Br ex - Dght 6.440 Lbp 176.00 Br md 25.00 Dpth 9.10 Welded, 9 dks,incl 2 hoistable	**(A36A2PR) Passenger/Ro-Ro Ship (Vehicles)** Passengers: unberthed: 886; cabins: 222; berths: 750 Bow door/ramp Len: 20.30 Wid: 4.50 Swl: - Stern door/ramp (p) Len: 11.75 Wid: 5.00 Swl: - Stern door/ramp (s) Len: 11.75 Wid: 8.00 Swl: - Lane-Len: 2507 Lorries: 110, Cars: 140	**4 oil engines** with clutches, flexible couplings & sr geared to sc. shafts driving 2 CP propellers Total Power: 42,240kW (57,428hp) 27.5kn Sulzer 16ZAV40S 4 x Vee 4 Stroke 16 Cy. 400 x 560 each-10560kW (14357bhp) Wartsila NSD France SA-France AuxGen: 3 x 1384kW 440V 60Hz a.c, 2 x 1384kW 440V 60Hz a.c Thrusters: 2 Thwart. CP thruster (f); 1 Tunnel thruster (a) Fuel: 143.0 (d.f.) (Heating Coils) 1222.0 (r.f.) 168.0pd
8846474 - -	**SPIRIT OF THE BAY** *ex* Island Explorer *-2000* *ex* Queenstown Explorer *-1997* *ex* Tamahine Moorea *-1994* *ex* Starship Genesis *-1992* **Spirit of the Bay Pty Ltd** Romano del Bianco & Frank Aquillino *Australia*	**136** - 26	Class: (BV)	**1987 International Catamarans Pty Ltd — Hobart TAS** Loa - Br ex - Dght 0.680 Lbp 19.25 Br md 8.20 Dpth 2.00 Welded, 1 dk	**(A37B2PS) Passenger Ship** Hull Material: Aluminium Alloy Passengers: unberthed: 200	**2 oil engines** reduction geared to sc. shafts driving 2 FP propellers Total Power: 1,912kW (2,600hp) 25.0kn General Motors 2 x 4 Stroke 16 Cy. each-956kW (1300bhp) General Motors Detroit DieselAllison Divn-USA

8748086 - -	**SPIRIT OF THE SEA** *ex* Stenia (P776) *-2011* **John Francois de Sousa** -	**101** 70 49	Class: IS	**1992 D.C.A.N. Direction des Constr. et Armes Navales — Lorient** Loa 24.65 Br ex 5.90 Dght 1.400 Lbp 23.00 Br md 5.75 Dpth 2.51 Bonded, 1 dk	**(B34H2SQ) Patrol Vessel** Hull Material: Reinforced Plastic	**2 oil engines** reduction geared to sc. shafts driving 2 FP propellers Total Power: 1,236kW (1,680hp) Baudouin V12BTI 840 2 x Vee 4 Stroke 12 Cy. 120 x 110 each-618kW (840bhp) Societe des Moteurs Baudouin SA-France
9030682 *CFL2070* -	**SPIRIT OF VANCOUVER ISLAND** **British Columbia Ferry Services Inc** - *Victoria, BC* *Canada* MMSI: 316001269 Official number: 816503	**18,747** 13,894 2,925	Class: AB	**1994-02 Integrated Ferry Constructors Ltd — Victoria BC** (Aft section) Yd No: 21 **1994-02 Allied Shipbuilders Ltd — North Vancouver BC** (Fwd section) Yd No: 255 Loa 167.50 (BB) Br ex 32.90 Dght 5.000 Lbp 156.00 Br md 26.60 Dpth 8.00 Welded, 3 dks	**(A36A2PR) Passenger/Ro-Ro Ship (Vehicles)** Passengers: unberthed: 2000 Bow door Stern door Lane-Len: 2354 Lane-clr ht: 4.60 Vehicles: 470	**4 oil engines** with clutches, flexible couplings & sr geared to sc. shafts driving 2 CP propellers Total Power: 15,960kW (21,700hp) 19.0kn MAN 6L40/54 4 x 4 Stroke 6 Cy. 400 x 540 each-3990kW (5425bhp) MAN B&W Diesel AG-Augsburg AuxGen: 2 x 1700kW 600V 60Hz a.c, 1 x 1700kW 600V 60Hz a.c Thrusters: 2 Thwart. CP thruster (f) Fuel: 475.0 (d.f.) 33.0pd
8967852 *WDD4776* -	**SPIRIT OF WASHINGTON** *ex* Horizon *-2005* **Pegasus Yachts Inc** - *New York, NY* *United States of America* MMSI: 367148880 Official number: 1088208	**1,005** 333 -		**2000 Blount Industries — Warren, RI** Yd No: 303 L reg 39.75 Br ex - Dght - Lbp - Br md 11.80 Dpth 3.20 Welded, 3 dks	**(A37B2PS) Passenger Ship** Passengers: unberthed: 600	**2 oil engines** driving 2 FP propellers Total Power: 956kW (1,300hp) G.M. (Detroit Diesel) 16V-92 2 x Vee 2 Stroke 16 Cy. 123 x 127 each-478kW (650bhp) Detroit Diesel Corporation-Detroit, Mi Thrusters: 1 Thwart. FP thruster (f)
6820842 *9H5822* -	**SPIRO F** *ex* Reedness *-1997* *ex* Kyndill II *-1986* *ex* Kyndill *-1985* *ex* Gerda Brodsgaard *-1973* **SL Spiro Shipping Ltd** SL Ship Management Co Ltd *Valletta* *Malta* MMSI: 248047000 Official number: 5659	**902** 374 1,221	Class: BV	**1968 Frederikshavn Vaerft og Tordok A/S — Frederikshavn** Yd No: 281 Loa 60.64 Br ex 10.29 Dght 4.217 Lbp 56.35 Br md 10.19 Dpth 5.74 Welded, 2 dks	**(B34E2SW) Waste Disposal Vessel** Liq: 1,446; Liq (Oil): 1,446 Cargo Heating Coils Compartments: 12 Ta, ER 4 Cargo Pump (s): 4x165m³/hr Manifold: Bow/CM: 25m Ice Capable	**1 oil engine** driving 1 CP propeller Total Power: 809kW (1,100hp) 11.5kn MaK 1 x 4 Stroke 6 Cy. 320 x 450 809kW (1100bhp) Atlas MaK Maschinenbau GmbH-Kiel AuxGen: 2 x 137kW 380V 50Hz a.c, 1 x 39kW 380V 50Hz a.c Fuel: 59.0 (d.f.) 3.5pd
5204053 *SW3484* -	**SPIROS LEKKAS** *ex* Laurent Chambon *-1987* **Portolos Salvage SA** Portolos Salvage & Towage *Piraeus* *Greece* MMSI: 237116600 Official number: 9245	*248* 62 -	Class: (BV)	**1960 Scheepsw. en Ghbw. v/h Jonker & Stans N.V. — Hendrik-Ido-Ambacht** Yd No: 285 Loa 33.30 Br ex 8.41 Dght 3.703 Lbp - Br md - Dpth 4.50 Welded, 1 dk	**(B32A2ST) Tug**	**1 oil engine** driving 1 FP propeller Total Power: 971kW (1,320hp) 12.5kn Baldwin 1 x 4 Stroke 8 Cy. 310 x 460 971kW (1320bhp) Swiss Locomotive & Machine Works-Switzerland AuxGen: 2 x 50kW 220V d.c
8729391 *UGZX* -	**SPITAK** **OOO 'Polluks' (Polluks Co Ltd)** - *Petropavlovsk-Kamchatskiy* *Russia* MMSI: 273851100 Official number: 882046	**448** 134 207	Class: RS	**1989-05 Zavod 'Nikolayevsk-na-Amure' — Nikolayevsk-na-Amure** Yd No: 1263 Loa 44.89 Br ex 9.47 Dght 3.771 Lbp 39.37 Br md 9.30 Dpth 5.14 Welded, 1 dk	**(B11A2FS) Stern Trawler** Ins: 210 Ice Capable	**1 oil engine** driving 1 FP propeller Total Power: 588kW (799hp) 11.5kn S.K.L. 6NVD48A-2U 1 x 4 Stroke 6 Cy. 320 x 480 588kW (799bhp) VEB Schwermaschinenbau "KarlLiebknecht" (SKL)-Magdeburg AuxGen: 3 x 150kW a.c
9451135 *CFH8987* -	**SPITFIRE III** **Atlantic Reyser Ltd** Atlantic Towing Ltd *Saint John, NB* *Canada* MMSI: 316013045 Official number: 832806	**395** 118 190	Class: LR ✠ **100A1** SS 10/2013 tug, fire fighting Ship 1 (2400m3/h) with water spray *IWS EP Canadian coastal service, 20 miles offshore, east coast of Canada and south to New York, USA ✠ **LMC** **UMS** Eq.Ltr: G; Cable: 305.0/20.5 U2 (a)	**2008-10 East Isle Shipyard Ltd — Georgetown PE** Yd No: 91 Loa 30.80 Br ex 11.16 Dght 5.480 Lbp 29.00 Br md 11.14 Dpth 5.21 Welded, 1 dk	**(B32A2ST) Tug**	**2 oil engines** gearing integral to driving 2 Z propellers Total Power: 3,998kW (5,436hp) Caterpillar 3516B-HD 2 x Vee 4 Stroke 16 Cy. 170 x 190 each-1999kW (2718bhp) (made 2008) Caterpillar Inc-USA AuxGen: 2 x 189kW 440V 60Hz a.c
9290153 *C4BV2* -	**SPITHA** **Lamerdo Shipping Co Ltd** Efnav Co Ltd *Limassol* *Cyprus* MMSI: 209514000 Official number: 9290153	**41,059** 25,433 75,411 T/cm 66.9	Class: GL (LR) ✠ Classed LR until 7/2/12	**2005-04 STX Shipbuilding Co Ltd — Changwon (Jinhae Shipyard)** Yd No: 1138 Loa 225.00 (BB) Br ex 32.28 Dght 14.500 Lbp 216.20 Br md 32.24 Dpth 19.70 Welded, 1 dk	**(A21A2BC) Bulk Carrier** Grain: 90,155 Compartments: 7 Ho, ER 7 Ha: ER	**1 oil engine** driving 1 FP propeller Total Power: 11,060kW (15,037hp) 14.5kn B&W 7S50MC-C 1 x 2 Stroke 7 Cy. 500 x 2000 11060kW (15037bhp) STX Engine Co Ltd-South Korea AuxGen: 3 x 600kW 450V 60Hz a.c Boilers: AuxB (Comp) 6.9kgf/cm² (6.8bar)
8932015 - -	**SPK-165 BLEYKHERT** *ex* SPK-165 *-1998* **OOO 'Novomortekhflot'** - *Novorossiysk* *Russia* MMSI: 273316820	*596* 124 338	Class: RS	**1963-07 VEB Mathias-Thesen-Werft — Wismar** Yd No: 165 Loa 38.28 Br ex 13.98 Dght 1.850 Lbp 38.00 Br md - Dpth 3.48 Welded, 1 dk	**(B34B2SC) Crane Vessel** Ice Capable	**2 oil engines** driving 2 FP propellers Total Power: 588kW (800hp) 8.5kn S.K.L. 8NVD36 2 x 4 Stroke 8 Cy. 240 x 360 each-294kW (400bhp) VEB Schwermaschinenbau "KarlLiebknecht" (SKL)-Magdeburg AuxGen: 2 x 270kW a.c, 1 x 64kW a.c Fuel: 48.0 (d.f.)
9580156 *CBAV* -	**SPL ATACAMA** *ex* Kerkini *-2012* **Empresa Maritima (EMPREMAR) SA** - *Valparaiso* *Chile* MMSI: 725001045	**23,587** 11,598 34,400	Class: AB (NV)	**2012-11 SPP Shipbuilding Co Ltd — Tongyeong** Yd No: H4066 Loa 180.00 Br ex 30.05 Dght 9.900 Lbp 172.00 Br md 30.00 Dpth 14.70 Welded, 1 dk	**(A21A2BC) Bulk Carrier** Grain: 48,766; Bale: 46,815 Compartments: 5 Ho, ER 5 Ha: ER Cranes: 4x35t	**1 oil engine** driving 1 FP propeller Total Power: 7,900kW (10,741hp) 14.0kn MAN-B&W 5S50MC-C 1 x 2 Stroke 5 Cy. 500 x 2000 7900kW (10741bhp) Doosan Engine Co Ltd-South Korea AuxGen: 3 x 600kW a.c
8414582 *9HA2705* -	**SPL PRINCESS ANASTASIA** *ex* Bilbao *-2011* *ex* Pride of Bilbao *-2010* *ex* Olympia *-1993* **Zatarga Ltd** LLC 'St Peter Line Rus' SatCom: Inmarsat C 421535710 *Valletta* *Malta* MMSI: 215357000 Official number: 8414582	**37,583** 23,730 4,000	Class: LR (BV) (NV) **100A1** CS 10/2010 roll on - roll off cargo ship/passenger ship Ice Class 1AS in association with a summer moulded draught of 6.718m **LMC** **UMS CCS**	**1986-04 Oy Wartsila Ab — Turku** Yd No: 1290 Loa 176.82 (BB) Br ex 32.86 Dght 6.719 Lbp 159.59 Br md 28.40 Dpth 14.66 Welded, 8 dks incl. 1 hoistable	**(A36A2PR) Passenger/Ro-Ro Ship (Vehicles)** Passengers: unberthed: 53; cabins: 841; berths: 2500 Bow door & ramp (centre) Len: - Wid: 6.00 Swl: - Stern door/ramp (p) Len: - Wid: 7.10 Swl: - Stern door/ramp (s) Len: - Wid: 7.10 Swl: - Lane-Len: 1120 Lane-clr ht: 4.60 Cars: 600, Trailers: 62 Ice Capable	**4 oil engines** with clutches, flexible couplings & sr geared to sc. shafts driving 2 CP propellers Total Power: 22,988kW (31,256hp) 22.0kn Pielstick 12PC2-6V-400 4 x Vee 4 Stroke 12 Cy. 400 x 460 each-5747kW (7814bhp) Oy Wartsila Ab-Finland AuxGen: 3 x 1050kW 380V 50Hz a.c, 2 x 700kW 380V 50Hz a.c Boilers: AuxB (ex.g.), AuxB (o.f.) Thrusters: 2 Thwart. CP thruster (f) Fuel: 194.6 (d.f.) (Heating Coils) 1148.6 (r.f.) 86.0pd
9580132 *CBTQ* -	**SPL TARAPACA** *ex* St George *-2011* **Empresa Maritima (EMPREMAR) SA** - *Valparaiso* *Chile* MMSI: 725019110 Official number: 3282	**23,440** 11,526 34,431	Class: AB	**2011-08 SPP Shipbuilding Co Ltd — Tongyeong** Yd No: H4064 Loa 180.00 (BB) Br ex - Dght 9.900 Lbp 172.00 Br md 30.00 Dpth 14.70 Welded, 1 dk	**(A21A2BC) Bulk Carrier** Grain: 48,766; Bale: 46,815 Compartments: 5 Ho, ER 5 Ha: ER Cranes: 4x35t	**1 oil engine** driving 1 FP propeller Total Power: 7,900kW (10,741hp) 14.0kn MAN-B&W 5S50MC-C 1 x 2 Stroke 5 Cy. 500 x 2000 7900kW (10741bhp) Doosan Engine Co Ltd-South Korea AuxGen: 3 x 600kW a.c Fuel: 185.0 (d.f.) 1560.0 (r.f.)
9370367 *3EPT4* -	**SPLENDEUR** **Leyte Navigation SA** Toko Kaiun Kaisha Ltd *Panama* *Panama* MMSI: 354988000 Official number: 3363908A	**21,192** 11,444 33,440	Class: NK	**2008-03 Shin Kochi Jyuko K.K. — Kochi** Yd No: 7212 Loa 179.99 (BB) Br ex 28.20 Dght 10.031 Lbp 172.00 Br md 28.20 Dpth 14.30 Welded, 1 dk	**(A31A2GO) Open Hatch Cargo Ship** Double Hull Grain: 44,642; Bale: 43,765 Compartments: 5 Ho, ER 5 Ha: ER Cranes: 4x30.5t	**1 oil engine** driving 1 FP propeller Total Power: 6,250kW (8,498hp) 14.3kn Mitsubishi 6UEC52LA 1 x 2 Stroke 6 Cy. 520 x 1600 6250kW (8498bhp) Kobe Hatsudoki KK-Japan AuxGen: 3 x 317kW a.c Fuel: 1450.0

9015747 *IBAS* -	**SPLENDID** **Grandi Navi Veloci (GRANNAVI) SpA** - SatCom: Inmarsat A 1152201 *Palermo* *Italy* MMSI: 247136000 Official number: 1210	**39,139** 20,073 6,875 T/cm 39.0	Class: RI (AB)	**1994-05 Nuovi Cantieri Apuania SpA — Carrara** Yd No: 1160 Lengthened-1996 Loa 214.21 (BB) Br ex 27.60 Dght 6.550 Lbp 188.97 Br md 26.80 Dpth 8.30 Welded, 2 dks	**(A36A2PR) Passenger/Ro-Ro Ship (Vehicles)** Passengers: unberthed: 305; cabins: 444; berths: 1639; driver berths: 56 Stern door/ramp (p) Len: 13.00 Wid: 7.50 Swl: - Stern door/ramp (s) Len: 13.00 Wid: 7.50 Swl: - Stern door/ramp (centre) Len: 13.00 Wid: 8.90 Swl: - Lane-Len: 2259 Lane-clr ht: 4.30 Cars: 760 Grain: 7,590 Compartments: 1 Ho 2 Ha:	**4 oil engines** with clutches, flexible couplings & dr geared to sc. shafts driving 2 CP propellers Total Power: 23,040kW (31,324hp) 23.0kn Sulzer 8ZAL40S 4 x 4 Stroke 8 Cy. 400 x 560 each-5760kW (7831bhp) Fincantieri Cantieri Navaliltaliani SpA-Italy AuxGen: 3 x 2150kW Thrusters: 1 Thwart. CP thruster (f)
9252228 *HPMT* -	**SPLENDID ACE** **Aurora Car Maritime Transport SA** MOL Ship Management Singapore Pte Ltd *Panama* *Panama* MMSI: 355294000 Official number: 2944403B	**56,439** 17,959 19,893	Class: NK (AB)	**2003-09 Minamininippon Shipbuilding Co Ltd — Usuki OT** Yd No: 676 Loa 198.00 (BB) Br ex 32.23 Dght 9.916 Lbp 188.00 Br md 32.20 Dpth 14.60 Welded, 13 dks incl. 2 liftable dks	**(A35B2RV) Vehicles Carrier** Side door/ramp (s) Len: 17.10 Wid: 4.50 Swl: 22 Quarter stern door/ramp (s. a.) Len: 32.20 Wid: 7.00 Swl: 100 Cars: 6,182	**1 oil engine** driving 1 FP propeller Total Power: 14,160kW (19,252hp) 20.0kn Mitsubishi 8UEC60LS 1 x 2 Stroke 8 Cy. 600 x 2200 14160kW (19252bhp) Kobe Hatsudoki KK-Japan AuxGen: 3 x 950kW 60Hz a.c Thrusters: 1 Tunnel thruster (f); 1 Tunnel thruster (a) Fuel: 180.0 (d.f.) 2800.0 (r.f.) 54.0pd
9004700 *3EDS7* -	**SPLENDOR** *ex Trump Pescadores -2006* *ex Chun Kuan -1998* **Splendor Enterprises SA** Harmony Transportation Co Ltd *Panama* *Panama* MMSI: 371708000 Official number: 3135906A	**5,552** 2,351 7,067	Class: NK (CR)	**1990-07 Shin Kurushima Dockyard Co. Ltd. — Akitsu** Yd No: 2690 Loa 98.17 (BB) Br ex - Dght 7.429 Lbp 89.95 Br md 18.80 Dpth 12.90 Welded, 2 dks	**(A31A2GX) General Cargo Ship** Grain: 13,790; Bale: 12,612 Compartments: 2 Ho, ER 2 Ha: 2 (20.3 x 12.7)ER Derricks: 2x30t,2x25t	**1 oil engine** driving 1 FP propeller Total Power: 2,425kW (3,297hp) 12.4kn Hanshin 6EL40 1 x 4 Stroke 6 Cy. 400 x 800 2425kW (3297bhp) The Hanshin Diesel Works Ltd-Japan AuxGen: 3 x 165kW a.c Fuel: 525.0 (r.f.)
8953631 *9V9999* -	**SPLENDOR** *ex Splendour -2012* **PSA Marine Pte Ltd** - *Singapore* *Singapore* Official number: 397840	**296** 88 450	Class: BV	**1999-12 ASL Shipyard Pte Ltd — Singapore** Yd No: 168 Loa 30.00 Br ex - Dght 5.300 Lbp 28.03 Br md 9.50 Dpth 3.80 Welded, 1 dk	**(B32A2ST) Tug** Passengers: berths: 8	**2 oil engines** reduction geared to sc. shafts driving 2 Z propellers Total Power: 2,464kW (3,350hp) 12.0kn Deutz SBV6M628 2 x 4 Stroke 6 Cy. 240 x 280 each-1232kW (1675bhp) Deutz AG-Koeln AuxGen: 2 x 91kW a.c
8408014 *3FWU2* -	**SPLENDOUR** *ex Natcha Naree -2010* *ex Twilight Success -1996* *ex Natcha Naree -1996* *ex Twilight Success -1996* *ex Harbor Breeze -1994 ex Orange Bridge -1988* **Saanguine Shipping Pvt Ltd** Nepa Projects & Investments Ltd *Panama* *Panama* MMSI: 371685000 Official number: 4146510	**13,720** 8,026 23,593	Class: NK	**1984-07 K.K. Uwajima Zosensho — Uwajima** Yd No: 2351 Loa 155.82 (BB) Br ex - Dght 9.987 Lbp 148.00 Br md 24.60 Dpth 13.60 Welded, 1 dk	**(A21A2BC) Bulk Carrier** Grain: 29,006; Bale: 28,284 Compartments: 4 Ho, ER 4 Ha: (15.2 x 11.2)3 (19.2 x 12.8)ER Cranes: 4x25.4t	**1 oil engine** driving 1 FP propeller Total Power: 5,112kW (6,950hp) 14.2kn Mitsubishi 6UE52LA 1 x 2 Stroke 6 Cy. 520 x 1600 5112kW (6950bhp) Akasaka Tekkosho KK (Akasaka DieselLtd)-Japan AuxGen: 2 x 400kW a.c Fuel: 1025.0 (r.f.)
9357377 *5IS044* -	**SPLENDOUR** *ex Blackstone -2013 ex Rosemary -2012* *ex Sarv -2012* **NITC** - *Zanzibar* *Tanzania (Zanzibar)* MMSI: 677004300	**85,462** 53,441 164,154	Class: (BV) (NV)	**2009-01 Hyundai Samho Heavy Industries Co Ltd — Samho** Yd No: S319 Loa 274.20 (BB) Br ex 50.04 Dght 17.000 Lbp 264.00 Br md 50.00 Dpth 23.10 Welded, 1 dk	**(A13A2TV) Crude Oil Tanker** Double Hull (13F) Liq: 169,000; Liq (Oil): 169,000 Cargo Heating Coils Compartments: 12 Wing Ta, 2 Wing Slop Ta, ER 3 Cargo Pump (s): 3x4000m³/hr	**1 oil engine** driving 1 FP propeller Total Power: 18,660kW (25,370hp) 15.4kn MAN-B&W 6S70MC-C 1 x 2 Stroke 6 Cy. 700 x 2800 18660kW (25370bhp) Hyundai Heavy Industries Co Ltd-South Korea AuxGen: 3 x 1050kW 60Hz a.c Fuel: 4661.0
9535448 *9V7664* -	**SPLENDOUR** **Hong Lam Integration Pte Ltd** Hong Lam Marine Pte Ltd SatCom: Inmarsat C 456440110 *Singapore* *Singapore* MMSI: 564401000 Official number: 394591	**14,355** 5,492 21,946 T/cm 31.4	Class: NK	**2009-11 Yangzhou Kejin Shipyard Co Ltd — Jiangdu JS** Yd No: 07051 Loa 138.50 (BB) Br ex 26.02 Dght 9.817 Lbp 130.00 Br md 26.00 Dpth 14.30 Welded, 1 dk	**(A13B2TP) Products Tanker** Double Hull (13F) Liq: 21,315; Liq (Oil): 21,315 Cargo Heating Coils Compartments: 12 Wing Ta, 2 Wing Slop Ta, ER 4 Cargo Pump (s): 4x750m³/hr Manifold: Bow/CM: 74.1m	**2 oil engines** reduction geared to sc. shafts driving 2 FP propellers Total Power: 6,618kW (8,998hp) 12.0kn Daihatsu 6DKM-36 2 x 4 Stroke 6 Cy. 360 x 480 each-3309kW (4499bhp) Daihatsu Diesel Manufacturing Co Lt-Japan AuxGen: 3 x 550kW a.c Thrusters: 2 Tunnel thruster (f) Fuel: 100.0 (d.f.) 1200.0 (r.f.)
9070632 *C6TZ9* -	**SPLENDOUR OF THE SEAS** **Splendour of the Seas Inc** Royal Caribbean Cruises Ltd (RCCL) *Nassau* *Bahamas* MMSI: 311804000 Official number: 9000121	**69,472** 37,971 5,200	Class: NV	**1996-03 Chantiers de l'Atlantique — St-Nazaire** Yd No: B31 Loa 264.26 (BB) Br ex 36.30 Dght 7.700 Lbp 221.50 Br md 32.00 Dpth 10.45 Welded	**(A37A2PC) Passenger/Cruise** Passengers: cabins: 904; berths: 2074	**5 diesel electric oil engines** driving 5 gen. each 11700kW 6600V a.c Connecting to 2 elec. motors each (21500kW) driving 2 FP propellers Total Power: 57,500kW (78,175hp) 24.0kn Wartsila 12V46 5 x Vee 4 Stroke 12 Cy. 460 x 580 each-11500kW (15635bhp) Wartsila Diesel Oy-Finland Thrusters: 2 Thwart. FP thruster (f); 1 Tunnel thruster (a) Fuel: 235.0 (d.f.) 2071.0 (r.f.) 264.0pd
9154505 *9AIQ* -	**SPLIT** **Split Maritime Inc** Jadroplov International Maritime Transport Ltd (Jadroplov dd) SatCom: Inmarsat B 323814524 *Split* *Croatia* MMSI: 238145000 Official number: 5T-609	**24,533** 13,824 42,584 T/cm 51.4	Class: CS LR ✠ **100A1** SS 05/2008 bulk carrier strengthened for heavy cargoes, Nos. 2 & 4 holds may be empty ESP LI ESN-Hold 1 ✠ **LMC** **UMS** Eq.Ltr: K†; Cable: 646.0/68.0 U3	**1998-05 Brodosplit - Brodogradiliste doo — Split** Yd No: 402 Loa 187.63 (BB) Br ex 30.85 Dght 10.987 Lbp 179.37 Br md 30.80 Dpth 15.45 Welded, 1 dk	**(A21A2BC) Bulk Carrier** Double Bottom Entire Compartment Length Grain: 51,126; Bale: 49,034 Compartments: 5 Ho, ER 5 Ha: (12.8 x 16.0)4 (19.2 x 16.0)ER Cranes: 4x30t	**1 oil engine** driving 1 FP propeller Total Power: 7,150kW (9,721hp) 14.0kn B&W 5S50MC 1 x 2 Stroke 5 Cy. 500 x 1910 7150kW (9721bhp) Brodosplit Tvornica Dizel Motoradoo-Croatia AuxGen: 3 x 592kW 440V 60Hz a.c Boilers: e (ex.g.) 7.1kgf/cm² (7.0bar), AuxB (o.f.) 7.1kgf/cm² (7.0bar) Fuel: 152.2 (d.f.) 1622.0 (r.f.) 30.0pd
8857100 - -	**SPLIT 3** *ex Volna 1 -1999* **NV Besix SA** -	**499** 149 866	Class: (RS)	**1985-07 Deggendorfer Werft u. Eisenbau GmbH — Deggendorf** Yd No: 769 Loa 51.15 Br ex 9.29 Dght 3.000 Lbp 49.80 Br md 9.00 Dpth 4.00 Welded, 1 dk	**(B34A2SH) Hopper, Motor** Hopper: 415 1 Ha: (20.0 x 6.2)ER Ice Capable	**2 oil engines** driving 2 Directional propellers Total Power: 348kW (474hp) 7.5kn Deutz F12L413F 2 x Vee 4 Stroke 12 Cy. 125 x 130 each-174kW (237bhp) Kloeckner Humboldt Deutz AG-West Germany
9237917 *J8B2096* -	**SPLIT 4** **NV Besix SA** - *Kingstown* *St Vincent & The Grenadines* MMSI: 375585000 Official number: 8568	**865** 259 1,200	Class: BV	**2000-09 ASL Shipyard Pte Ltd — Singapore** Yd No: 183 Loa 65.95 Br ex - Dght 3.500 Lbp 62.95 Br md 11.00 Dpth 4.00 Welded, 1 dk	**(B34A2SH) Hopper, Motor** Hopper: 750	**2 oil engines** gearing integral to driving 2 Voith-Schneider propellers Total Power: 820kW (1,114hp) 8.0kn Caterpillar 3408TA 2 x Vee 4 Stroke 8 Cy. 137 x 152 each-410kW (557bhp) Caterpillar Inc-USA
8857112 *J8B2143* -	**SPLIT 5** *ex Volna 2 -2000* **NV Besix SA** - *Kingstown* *St Vincent & The Grenadines* MMSI: 375594000 Official number: 8615	**563** 168 845	Class: BV (RS)	**1985-07 Deggendorfer Werft u. Eisenbau GmbH — Deggendorf** Yd No: 770 Converted From: Hopper-1992 Loa 51.15 Br ex 9.29 Dght 3.000 Lbp 49.80 Br md 9.00 Dpth 4.00 Welded, 1 dk	**(A31C2GD) Deck Cargo Ship** 1 Ha: (20.0 x 6.2)ER Ice Capable	**2 oil engines** driving 2 Directional propellers Total Power: 348kW (474hp) 7.5kn Deutz F12L413F 2 x Vee 4 Stroke 12 Cy. 125 x 130 each-174kW (237bhp) Kloeckner Humboldt Deutz AG-West Germany
8222836 - -	**SPLIT BARGE 46** - **Suez Canal Authority** - *Port Said* *Egypt*	*730* - 1,500	Class: (GL)	**1985-05 Port Said Engineering Works — Port Said** Yd No: 641 Loa 65.89 Br ex 11.03 Dght 3.126 Lbp 62.84 Br md 11.00 Dpth 4.02 Welded, 1 dk	**(B34A2SH) Hopper, Motor** Hopper: 750	**2 oil engines** with clutches, flexible couplings & dr geared to sc. shafts driving 2 Directional propellers Total Power: 814kW (1,106hp) 8.0kn Cummins VTA-1710-M1 2 x Vee 4 Stroke 12 Cy. 140 x 152 each-407kW (553bhp) Cummins Engine Co Inc-USA

IMO / Call sign	Name / Owner / Port	Tonnage	Class	Builder / Dimensions	Type	Machinery
8222848 - -	**SPLIT BARGE 47** **Suez Canal Authority** *Port Said* *Egypt*	*730* - 1,500	Class: (GL)	**1985-10 Port Said Engineering Works — Port Said** Yd No: 642 Loa 65.89 Br ex 11.03 Dght 3.147 Lbp 62.84 Br md 11.00 Dpth 4.02 Welded, 1 dk	**(B34A2SH) Hopper, Motor** Hopper: 750	**2 oil engines** with clutches, flexible couplings & dr geared to sc. shafts driving 2 Directional propellers Total Power: 814kW (1,106hp) Cummins VTA-1710-M1 2 x Vee 4 Stroke 12 Cy. 140 x 152 each-407kW (553bhp) Cummins Engine Co Inc-USA
8222850 - -	**SPLIT BARGE 48** **Suez Canal Authority** - *Port Said* *Egypt*	*780* - 1,500	Class: (GL)	**1986-11 Port Said Engineering Works — Port Said** Yd No: 643 Loa 62.95 Br ex 11.05 Dght 3.417 Lbp 62.84 Br md 11.02 Dpth 4.02 Welded, 1 dk	**(B34A2SH) Hopper, Motor** Hopper: 750	**2 oil engines** reduction geared to sc. shafts driving 2 Directional propellers Total Power: 814kW (1,106hp) 8.0kn Cummins VTA-1710-M 2 x Vee 4 Stroke 12 Cy. 140 x 152 each-407kW (553bhp) Cummins Engine Co Inc-USA AuxGen: 2 x 104kW 220/380V a.c
8222862 - -	**SPLIT BARGE 49** **Suez Canal Authority** - *Port Said* *Egypt*	*780* - 1,500	Class: (GL)	**1987-03 Port Said Engineering Works — Port Said** Yd No: 644 Loa 62.95 Br ex 11.03 Dght 3.126 Lbp 62.84 Br md 11.02 Dpth 4.02 Welded, 1 dk	**(B34A2SH) Hopper, Motor** Hopper: 750	**2 oil engines** with clutches, flexible couplings & dr geared to sc. shafts driving 2 Directional propellers Total Power: 814kW (1,106hp) 8.0kn Cummins VTA-1710-M 2 x Vee 4 Stroke 12 Cy. 140 x 152 each-407kW (553bhp) Cummins Engine Co Inc-USA
9087441 - -	**SPLIT BARGE 57** **Suez Canal Authority** - *Port Said* *Egypt*	*780* - 1,500	Class: (GL)	**1995-01 Port Said Engineering Works — Port Said** Yd No: 501 Loa 65.90 Br ex - Dght 3.700 Lbp 62.95 Br md 11.00 Dpth 4.00 Welded, 1 dk	**(B34A2SH) Hopper, Motor**	**2 oil engines** with clutches, flexible couplings & sr geared to sc. shafts driving 2 FP propellers Total Power: 930kW (1,264hp) Caterpillar 3412TA 2 x Vee 4 Stroke 12 Cy. 137 x 152 each-465kW (632bhp) Caterpillar Inc-USA
9087453 - -	**SPLIT BARGE 58** **Suez Canal Authority** - *Port Said* *Egypt*	*780* - -	Class: (GL)	**1996-03 Port Said Engineering Works — Port Said** Yd No: 502 Loa 65.90 Br ex 11.32 Dght - Lbp 62.95 Br md 11.00 Dpth 3.70 Welded, 1 dk	**(B34A2SH) Hopper, Motor**	**2 oil engines** reduction geared to sc. shafts driving 2 Directional propellers Total Power: 930kW (1,264hp) 8.0kn Caterpillar 3412T 2 x Vee 4 Stroke 12 Cy. 137 x 152 each-465kW (632bhp) Caterpillar Inc-USA
8331388 - -	**SPLIT ONE** - -	*248* 235 -		**1975 Schiffsw. Hans Boost Masch.- u. Stahlbau GmbH & Co. KG — Trier** L reg 41.00 Br ex 8.41 Dght - Lbp - Br md - Dpth 3.08 Welded, 1 dk	**(B34A2SH) Hopper, Motor**	**2 oil engines** driving 2 FP propellers Total Power: 500kW (680hp) 7.5kn Deutz BF12L714 2 x Vee 4 Stroke 12 Cy. 120 x 140 each-250kW (340bhp) Kloeckner Humboldt Deutz AG-West Germany
7012313 *MPVD9* -	**SPLIT THREE** *ex SCG 27 -1992* **ML (UK) Ltd** - *Poole* *United Kingdom* MMSI: 232004152 Official number: 721300	**475** 142 886	Class: (NV)	**1969 Hollming Oy — Rauma** Yd No: 191 Loa 50.62 Br ex 9.25 Dght 2.896 Lbp - Br md 9.20 Dpth 3.15 Welded, 1 dk	**(B34A2SH) Hopper, Motor** Grain: 460; Hopper: 460 Compartments: 1 Ho, ER	**2 oil engines** geared to sc. shaft driving 1 Directional propeller Total Power: 308kW (418hp) 6.0kn Scania DS11 2 x 4 Stroke 6 Cy. 127 x 145 each-154kW (209bhp) AB Scania Vabis-Sweden AuxGen: 1 x 13kW 380V 50Hz a.c Fuel: 153.5 (d.f.)
8633176 *MKES5* -	**SPLIT TWO** *ex SL 75 -1992* **ML (UK) Ltd** - *Poole* *United Kingdom* MMSI: 232004153 Official number: 712265	**325** 97 535		**1975 Deggendorfer Werft u. Eisenbau GmbH — Deggendorf** Loa 37.64 Br ex 8.40 Dght - Lbp - Br md - Dpth 3.10 Welded, 1 dk	**(B34A2SH) Hopper, Motor**	**2 oil engines** with clutches, flexible couplings & geared to sc. shafts driving 2 Directional propellers Total Power: 368kW (500hp) Fiat 821M 2 x 4 Stroke 6 Cy. 137 x 156 each-184kW (250bhp) AIFO, Appl. Ind. FIAT OM S.p.A-Pregnana Milanese
9101730 *V2EA7* -	**SPLITTNES** *ex Kari Arnhild -2002* **Partenreederei ms 'Kari Arnhild'** HJH Shipmanagement GmbH & Co KG SatCom: Inmarsat C 435642310 *Saint John's* *Antigua & Barbuda* MMSI: 304219000 Official number: 3631	**11,538** 5,388 18,886	Class: GL (BV) (NV)	**1994-10 Kvaerner Kleven Leirvik AS — Leirvik i Sogn** Yd No: 261 Lengthened-2006 Loa 166.20 (BB) Br ex - Dght 9.531 Lbp 156.80 Br md 20.50 Dpth 12.80 Welded, 1 dk	**(A23A2BD) Bulk Carrier, Self-discharging** Grain: 14,120 Compartments: 7 Ho, ER 7 Ha: (10.0 x 11.9)5 (10.0 x 14.7) (10.0 x 14.7)ER	**2 oil engines** reduction geared to sc. shafts driving 1 CP propeller Total Power: 4,440kW (6,036hp) 14.5kn Wartsila 6R32 2 x 4 Stroke 6 Cy. 320 x 350 each-2220kW (3018bhp) Wartsila Diesel Oy-Finland AuxGen: 2 x 1500kW 440V 60Hz a.c, 2 x 450kW 440/220V 60Hz a.c Thrusters: 1 Thwart. FP thruster (f); 1 Tunnel thruster (a) Fuel: 219.0 (d.f.) 480.0 (r.f.)
8749614 - -	**SPOB AGUNG JAYA I** - **PT Agung Lisna Sakti Mandiri** - *Tanjung Priok* *Indonesia*	**157** 87 -	Class: KI	**2010-03 P.T. Dok & Perkapalan Kodja Bahari (Unit IV) — Jakarta** Loa 34.00 Br ex - Dght 1.800 Lbp 32.64 Br md 7.30 Dpth 2.40 Welded, 1 dk	**(B35E2TF) Bunkering Tanker**	**2 oil engines** reduction geared to sc. shafts driving 2 Propellers Total Power: 250kW (340hp) Yanmar 6CH-HTE3 2 x 4 Stroke 6 Cy. 105 x 125 each-125kW (170bhp) (made 2008, fitted 2010) Yanmar Diesel Engine Co Ltd-Japan
8737788 - -	**SPOB ARSADE 2** *ex Bawi III -1994* **PT Andoyo Tofan Nugraha** - *Pontianak* *Indonesia*	**347** 226 -	Class: KI	**1985 P.T. Tunas Samudera — Ketapang** Loa 37.20 Br ex - Dght 2.000 Lbp 34.30 Br md 12.20 Dpth 2.74 Welded, 1 dk	**(A13B2TU) Tanker (unspecified)**	**2 oil engines** driving 2 Propellers Total Power: 530kW (720hp) Nissan RE10 2 x Vee 4 Stroke 10 Cy. 135 x 132 each-265kW (360bhp) Nissan Diesel Motor Co. Ltd.-Ageo
8740254 - -	**SPOB BOJONEGORO 1** - **PT Ardila Insan Sejahtera** - *Cirebon* *Indonesia*	**258** 154 -	Class: KI	**2007-06 P.T. Dok & Perkapalan Kodja Bahari (Unit IV) — Jakarta** Loa 35.80 Br ex - Dght 1.890 Lbp 34.50 Br md 10.00 Dpth 2.60 Welded, 1 dk	**(A13B2TU) Tanker (unspecified)**	**2 oil engines** driving 2 Propellers Total Power: 688kW (936hp) MAN D2840LE 2 x Vee 4 Stroke 10 Cy. 128 x 142 each-344kW (468bhp) MAN Nutzfahrzeuge AG-Nuernberg
8651934 - -	**SPOB BOJONEGORO VII** - **PT Ardila Insan Sejahtera** - *Tanjung Priok* *Indonesia*	**285** 129 500	Class: KI	**2010-06 P.T. Dok & Perkapalan Kodja Bahari (Unit IV) — Jakarta** Loa 42.80 Br ex - Dght 2.000 Lbp 41.00 Br md 8.50 Dpth 2.60 Welded, 1 dk	**(A13B2TP) Products Tanker** Double Hull (13F)	**2 oil engines** reduction geared to sc. shafts driving 2 Propellers 9.0kn AuxGen: 1 x 118kW 380/220V a.c
9703564 - -	**SPOB BORNEO PERKASA** - **PT Barokah Gemilang Perkasa** - *Indonesia*	**2,180** 1,091 5,791	Class: KI (Class contemplated)	**2008-11 PT Karya Teknik Utama — Batam** Yd No: KTU-195 Converted From: Products Tank Barge, Non-propelled-2013 Loa 74.68 Br ex - Dght - Lbp - Br md 19.50 Dpth 5.50 Welded, 1 dk	**(A13B2TP) Products Tanker** Double Hull (13F)	**2 oil engines** reduction geared to sc. shafts driving 2 Propellers Total Power: 1,472kW (2,002hp) 13.5kn Mitsubishi 2 x each-736kW (1001bhp) (, added 2013) Mitsubishi Heavy Industries Ltd-Japan
8737726 - -	**SPOB DS 7** - **PT Cakrawala Nusantara Perkasa** - *Jakarta* *Indonesia*	**157** 97 -	Class: KI	**2006-06 P.T. Dok & Perkapalan Kodja Bahari (Unit IV) — Jakarta** Loa - Br ex - Dght - Lbp 32.64 Br md 7.30 Dpth 2.40 Welded, 1 dk	**(A13B2TU) Tanker (unspecified)**	**2 oil engines** driving 2 Propellers Total Power: 338kW (460hp) Chinese Std. Type D683ZLC 2 x 4 Stroke 6 Cy. 114 x 135 each-169kW (230bhp) Shanghai Diesel Engine Co Ltd-China AuxGen: 2 x 30kW 400V a.c
8658877 *YB4786* -	**SPOB LAUTAN INDAH JAYA I** - **PT Komelino Putra Kusuma** - *Palembang* *Indonesia*	**271** 159 -	Class: KI	**2011-07 CV Buana Raya Utama — Palembang** Loa 37.07 Br ex - Dght 2.300 Lbp 35.32 Br md 11.00 Dpth 2.75 Welded, 1 dk	**(A13B2TP) Products Tanker**	**2 oil engines** reduction geared to sc. shafts driving 2 FP propellers AuxGen: 2 x 13kW 380V a.c
9685516 *JZAB* -	**SPOB LUCINDA** *launched as Lucinda -2013* **PT Mitsi Citra Mandiri** - *Batam* *Indonesia* MMSI: 525021162 Official number: GT2384No4660/PPm	**2,384** 1,335 3,000	Class: KI (Class contemplated)	**2013-03 PT Usda Seroja Jaya — Rengat** Yd No: 015 Loa 88.16 Br ex - Dght - Lbp 84.29 Br md 15.00 Dpth 4.80 Welded, 1 dk	**(A13B2TP) Products Tanker** Double Hull (13F)	**2 oil engines** reduction geared to sc. shafts driving 2 Propellers Total Power: 1,938kW (2,634hp) Yanmar 2 x 4 Stroke each-969kW (1317bhp) Yanmar Diesel Engine Co Ltd-Japan

9549724 *PMRA* -	**SPOB MELISSA I** *ex* Melissa I *-2013* **PT Agniputra Jayakusuma** - *Samarinda* *Indonesia* MMSI: 525011085 Official number: 3785	**1,312** 695 2,000	Class: KI	**2008-11 PT Anugerah Wijaya Bersaudara — Samarinda** Yd No: 2800/08 Loa 75.52 Br ex 15.00 Dght 3.150 Lbp 75.50 Br md 15.00 Dpth 4.20 Welded, 1 dk	**(A13B2TP) Products Tanker** Double Hull (13F)	**2 oil engines** reduction geared to sc. shafts driving 2 Propellers Total Power: 1,220kW (1,658hp) Yanmar 6AYM-ETE 2 x 4 Stroke 6 Cy. 155 x 180 each-610kW (829bhp) Yanmar Diesel Engine Co Ltd-Japan AuxGen: 2 x 206kW 400V a.c
8737776 - -	**SPOB MULYA SATU** *ex* Kencana Jaya I *-1991* **PT Ekalima Graha & Co** - *Jakarta* *Indonesia*	**279** 190 518	Class: KI	**1984 Dynamic Marine Pte Ltd — Singapore** Loa 36.45 Br ex - Dght - Lbp - Br md 12.17 Dpth 2.45 Welded, 1 dk	**(B35E2TF) Bunkering Tanker** Compartments: 6 Wing Ta, ER	**2 oil engines** reduction geared to sc. shafts driving 2 Propellers Total Power: 376kW (512hp) Yanmar 6CH-UTE 2 x 4 Stroke 6 Cy. 105 x 125 each-188kW (256bhp) Yanmar Diesel Engine Co Ltd-Japan
9663908 *PONX* -	**SPOB MUSI** **PT PERTAMINA Trans Kontinental** - *Batam* *Indonesia* MMSI: 525010168 Official number: GT2277 no.4114/ppm	**2,370** 1,366 3,540	Class: KI (Class contemplated) RI (Class contemplated)	**2012-05 PT BH Marine & Offshore Engineering — Batam** Yd No: H020 Loa 85.00 Br ex - Dght - Lbp - Br md 20.00 Dpth 5.00 Welded, 1 dk	**(A13B2TP) Products Tanker** Double Hull (13F)	**2 oil engines** reduction geared to sc. shafts driving 2 FP propellers Total Power: 1,472kW (2,002hp) 13.5kn Yanmar 6RY17P-GV 2 x 4 Stroke 6 Cy. 165 x 219 each-736kW (1001bhp) Yanmar Diesel Engine Co Ltd-Japan
8737738 - -	**SPOB NIAGARA V** **PT Cakrawala Nusantara Perkasa** - *Jakarta* *Indonesia*	**157** 97 -	Class: KI	**2006 P.T. Dok & Perkapalan Kodja Bahari (Unit IV) — Jakarta** Loa 34.00 Br ex - Dght 1.790 Lbp 32.30 Br md 7.30 Dpth 2.40 Welded, 1 dk	**(A13B2TU) Tanker (unspecified)**	**2 oil engines** driving 2 Propellers Total Power: 340kW (462hp) Chinese Std. Type D683ZLC 2 x 4 Stroke 6 Cy. 114 x 135 each-170kW (231bhp) Shanghai Diesel Engine Co Ltd-China
7214325 *WYX2004* -	**SPOKANE** **State of Washington (Department of Transportation)** Washington State Department of Transportation (Washington State Ferries) *Seattle, WA* *United States of America* MMSI: 366709780 Official number: 544785	*3,246* 1,198 1,213	Class: (AB)	**1973-02 Todd Pacific Shipyards Corp. — Seattle, Wa** Yd No: 53 Loa 134.12 Br ex 26.52 Dght 5.182 Lbp 127.41 Br md 26.47 Dpth 7.55 Welded, 1 dk	**(A36A2PR) Passenger/Ro-Ro Ship (Vehicles)** Passengers: unberthed: 2000	**4 diesel electric oil engines** driving 4 gen. each 1900kW 325V a.c Connecting to 2 elec. motors driving 2 Propellers aft, 1 fwd Total Power: 8,460kW (11,504hp) 20.0kn EMD (Electro-Motive) 16-645-E7B 4 x Vee 2 Stroke 16 Cy. 230 x 254 each-2115kW (2876bhp) General Motors Corp.Electro-Motive Div.-La Grange AuxGen: 2 x 550kW 450V 60Hz a.c
8730106 *UDNG* -	**SPOKOYNYY** *ex* Irlava *-2004* **Grinda Ltd** - *Korsakov* *Russia* MMSI: 273436860	**190** 57 70	Class: RS	**1989-09 Astrakhanskaya Sudoverf im. "Kirova" — Astrakhan** Yd No: 67 Loa 31.86 Br ex 7.09 Dght 2.320 Lbp 27.82 Br md 6.90 Dpth 3.18 Welded, 1 dk	**(B12B2FC) Fish Carrier** Ins: 100	**1 oil engine** geared to sc. shaft driving 1 FP propeller Total Power: 232kW (315hp) 10.2kn Daldizel 6CHSPN2A18-315 1 x 4 Stroke 6 Cy. 180 x 220 232kW (315bhp) Daldizel-Khabarovsk AuxGen: 2 x 25kW Fuel: 14.0 (d.f.)
9625188 *YJQM2* -	**SPOONER TIDE** **Orange Fleet Ltd** Tidewater Marine International Inc *Port Vila* *Vanuatu* MMSI: 577037000 Official number: 2102	**1,678** 503 1,308	Class: AB	**2012-01 Fujian Southeast Shipyard — Fuzhou FJ** Yd No: DN59M-71 Loa 59.25 Br ex - Dght 4.950 Lbp 52.20 Br md 14.95 Dpth 6.10 Welded, 1 dk	**(B21B20A) Anchor Handling Tug Supply**	**2 oil engines** reduction geared to sc. shafts driving 2 CP propellers Total Power: 3,840kW (5,220hp) 11.0kn Caterpillar 3516C-HD 2 x Vee 4 Stroke 16 Cy. 170 x 215 each-1920kW (2610bhp) Caterpillar Inc-USA AuxGen: 2 x 800kW a.c, 2 x 350kW a.c Thrusters: 2 Tunnel thruster (f) Fuel: 520.0
9035137 *SXLS* -	**SPORADES** **Sporades Special Maritime Enterprise (ENE)** Eletson Corp SatCom: Inmarsat C 423906910 *Piraeus* *Greece* MMSI: 239069000 Official number: 10063	**39,265** 17,954 66,895 T/cm 67.4	Class: LR (NV) **100A1** SS 07/2013 Double Hull oil tanker ESP LI **LMC** **UMS IGS** Eq.Ltr: 0†; Cable: 660.0/78.0 U3	**1993-07 Hyundai Heavy Industries Co Ltd — Ulsan** Yd No: 773 Loa 228.00 (BB) Br ex 32.40 Dght 13.218 Lbp 216.49 Br md 32.20 Dpth 19.70 Welded, 1 dk	**(A13A2TW) Crude/Oil Products Tanker** Double Hull Liq: 71,532; Liq (Oil): 71,532 Cargo Heating Coils Compartments: 14 Wing Ta, 2 Wing Slop Ta, ER 3 Cargo Pump (s): 3x2000m³/hr Manifold: Bow/CM: 115m	**1 oil engine** driving 1 FP propeller Total Power: 7,963kW (10,826hp) 14.7kn B&W 6L60MC 1 x 2 Stroke 6 Cy. 600 x 1944 7963kW (10826bhp) Hyundai Heavy Industries Co Ltd-South Korea AuxGen: 1 x 750kW 450V 60Hz a.c, 2 x 600kW 450V 60Hz a.c Boilers: 2 AuxB (o.f.) 18.4kgf/cm² (18.0bar) Fuel: 134.2 (d.f.) (Heating Coils) 1894.7 (r.f.) 36.2pd
8133671 - -	**SPOSOBNYY** - -	**918** 275 322	Class: (RS)	**1982 Yaroslavskiy Sudostroitelnyy Zavod — Yaroslavl** Yd No: 350 Loa 53.75 (BB) Br ex 10.49 Dght 4.290 Lbp 47.92 Br md - Dpth 6.00 Welded, 1 dk	**(B11A2FS) Stern Trawler** Ins: 218 Compartments: 1 Ho, ER 1 Ha: (1.6 x 1.6) Derricks: 2x1.5t Ice Capable	**1 oil engine** driving 1 FP propeller Total Power: 971kW (1,320hp) 12.8kn S.K.L. 8NVD48A-2U 1 x 4 Stroke 8 Cy. 320 x 480 971kW (1320bhp) VEB Schwermaschinenbau "KarlLiebknecht" (SKL)-Magdeburg Fuel: 195.0 (d.f.)
7945754 *UBOF* -	**SPOSOBNYY** **Trouler Co Ltd** Poseydon Co Ltd *Vladivostok* *Russia* MMSI: 273811610	**172** 51 87	Class: (RS)	**1981-10 Sretenskiy Sudostroitelnyy Zavod — Sretensk** Yd No: 119 Loa 33.96 Br ex 7.09 Dght 2.899 Lbp 30.00 Br md - Dpth 3.69 Welded, 1 dk	**(B11B2FV) Fishing Vessel** Bale: 115 Compartments: 1 Ho, ER 1 Ha: (1.6 x 1.3) Derricks: 2x2t; Winches: 2 Ice Capable	**1 oil engine** driving 1 CP propeller Total Power: 224kW (305hp) 9.5kn S.K.L. 8VD36/24-1 1 x 4 Stroke 8 Cy. 240 x 360 224kW (305bhp) VEB Schwermaschinenbau "KarlLiebknecht" (SKL)-Magdeburg
9487225 *9HSP9* -	**SPOT** **Spot Shipping Ltd** Genel Denizcilik Nakliyati AS (GEDEN LINES) SatCom: Inmarsat C 424941811 *Valletta* *Malta* MMSI: 249418000 Official number: 9487225	**31,117** 18,159 53,100	Class: NV (BV)	**2008-12 Zhejiang Shipbuilding Co Ltd — Ningbo ZJ** Yd No: 07-172 Loa 190.00 (BB) Br ex - Dght 10.700 Lbp 182.00 Br md 32.26 Dpth 17.20 Welded, 1 dk	**(A21A2BC) Bulk Carrier** Grain: 65,049 Compartments: 5 Ho, ER 5 Ha: ER Cranes: 4x35t	**1 oil engine** driving 1 FP propeller Total Power: 9,480kW (12,889hp) 14.7kn MAN-B&W 6S50MC-C 1 x 2 Stroke 6 Cy. 500 x 2000 9480kW (12889bhp) Doosan Engine Co Ltd-South Korea AuxGen: 3 x a.c
9172040 *5IQR19* -	**SPOTLESS** *ex* Lantana *-2013* *ex* Sanandaj *-2012* *ex* Iran Sanandaj *-2008* **Lantana Shipping Co Ltd** NITC *Zanzibar* *Tanzania (Zanzibar)* MMSI: 677001800	**81,479** 50,676 159,681 T/cm 117.5	Class: (GL) (NV)	**1999-11 Daewoo Heavy Industries Ltd — Geoje** Yd No: 5132 Loa 274.00 (BB) Br ex 48.04 Dght 17.022 Lbp 264.00 Br md 48.00 Dpth 23.20 Welded, 1 dk	**(A13A2TV) Crude Oil Tanker** Double Hull (13F) Liq: 166,683; Liq (Oil): 169,880 Compartments: 12 Wing Ta, ER, 2 Wing Slop Ta 3 Cargo Pump (s): 3x3500m³/hr Manifold: Bow/CM: 129m	**1 oil engine** driving 1 FP propeller Total Power: 16,859kW (22,921hp) 14.9kn B&W 6S70MC 1 x 2 Stroke 6 Cy. 700 x 2674 16859kW (22921bhp) Korea Heavy Industries & ConstrCo Ltd (HANJUNG)-South Korea AuxGen: 3 x 970kW 440V 60Hz a.c Fuel: 282.0 (d.f.) (Heating Coils) 4491.0 (r.f.) 73.5pd
8978370 *OJIR* -	**SPOVEN** *ex* Ellosfarjan *-1998* *ex* Ornostrom *-1998* *ex* Farja 61/233 *-1985* **Ansgar Ab** - *Kumlinge* *Finland* MMSI: 230111970	**170** 55 -	Class: FA	**1959 Broderna Larsson Varv & Mekaniska Verkstads — Kristinehamn** Yd No: 394 Loa 36.80 Br ex - Dght 3.100 Lbp 34.64 Br md 8.00 Dpth 4.15 Welded, 1 dk	**(A36A2PR) Passenger/Ro-Ro Ship (Vehicles)** Bow ramp (f) Stern ramp (a)	**4 oil engines** geared to sc. shaft driving 2 CP propellers Total Power: 676kW (920hp) Volvo Penta TMD100C 4 x 4 Stroke 6 Cy. 121 x 140 each-169kW (230bhp) Volvo Pentaverken-Sweden
8931229 *UAQU* -	**SPP-01** **Kamtramp Co Ltd (OOO 'Kamtramp')** - *Petropavlovsk-Kamchatskiy* *Russia*	**193** 58 125	Class: RS	**1978-01 Sudoremontnyy Zavod "Yakor" — Sovetskaya Gavan** Yd No: 4004/1 Loa 35.75 Br ex 7.50 Dght 1.710 Lbp 33.50 Br md 7.20 Dpth 2.40 Welded, 1 dk	**(A31C2GD) Deck Cargo Ship** Ice Capable	**1 oil engine** geared to sc. shaft driving 1 FP propeller Total Power: 165kW (224hp) 8.3kn Daldizel 6CHNSP18/22 1 x 4 Stroke 6 Cy. 180 x 220 165kW (224bhp) Daldizel-Khabarovsk AuxGen: 2 x 12kW a.c Fuel: 5.0 (d.f.)
8931334 - -	**SPP-005** **Beringovskiy Commercial Port (Beringovskiy MTP)** -	**166** 49 164	Class: (RS)	**1980-12 Sudoremontnyy Zavod "Yakor" — Sovetskaya Gavan** Yd No: 10251/5 Loa 35.72 Br ex 7.50 Dght 1.850 Lbp 33.63 Br md - Dpth 2.40 Welded, 1 dk	**(A31C2GD) Deck Cargo Ship** Ice Capable	**1 oil engine** geared to sc. shaft driving 1 FP propeller Total Power: 221kW (300hp) 8.7kn Daldizel 6CHNSP18/22-300 1 x 4 Stroke 6 Cy. 180 x 220 221kW (300bhp) Daldizel-Khabarovsk AuxGen: 2 x 14kW Fuel: 5.0 (d.f.)

IMO / Call sign	Name / Owner / Port	Tonnage	Class	Build / Dimensions	Type	Machinery
8931360 - -	**SPP-011** - **OOO 'Morskiye Ekologicheskiye Tekhnologii'** *Vladivostok* *Russia*	**170** 51 164	Class: RS	**1982-07 Sudoremontnyy Zavod "Yakor" — Sovetskaya Gavan** Yd No: 10251/11 Converted From: Waste Disposal Vessel-2006 Converted From: Deck Cargo Vessel-2005 Loa 35.72 Br ex 7.20 Dght 1.850 Lbp 33.50 Br md 7.20 Dpth 2.40 Welded, 1 dk	**(A13B2TU) Tanker (unspecified)** Ice Capable	**1 oil engine** geared to sc. shaft driving 1 FP propeller Total Power: 221kW (300hp) 8.3kn Daldizel 6CHNSP18/22-300 1 x 4 Stroke 6 Cy. 180 x 220 221kW (300bhp) Daldizel-Khabarovsk AuxGen: 1 x 14kW, 1 x 13kW Fuel: 7.0 (d.f.)
8726428 *UHCQ* -	**SPP-14** - **Uglegorsk Commercial Seaport (Uglegorsk MTP)** - *Korsakov* *Russia*	**193** 58 125	Class: RS	**1985-12 Sudoremontnyy Zavod "Yakor" — Sovetskaya Gavan** Yd No: 4004/14 Loa 35.75 Br ex 7.50 Dght 1.710 Lbp 33.50 Br md 7.20 Dpth 2.40 Welded, 1 dk	**(A31C2GD) Deck Cargo Ship** Ice Capable	**1 oil engine** geared to sc. shaft driving 1 FP propeller Total Power: 165kW (224hp) 8.3kn Daldizel 6CHNSP18/22 1 x 4 Stroke 6 Cy. 180 x 220 165kW (224bhp) Daldizel-Khabarovsk AuxGen: 1 x 14kW, 1 x 13kW Fuel: 4.0 (d.f.)
8139053 - -	**SPP-014** - **Uglegorsk Commercial Seaport (Uglegorsk MTP)** - *Uglegorsk* *Russia* Official number: 822064	**153** 59 164	Class: (RS)	**1983-05 Sudoremontnyy Zavod "Yakor" — Sovetskaya Gavan** Yd No: 10251/14 Loa 35.72 Br ex 7.19 Dght 1.850 Lbp 33.63 Br md - Dpth 2.42 Welded, 1 dk	**(A31C2GD) Deck Cargo Ship** Ice Capable	**1 oil engine** geared to sc. shaft driving 1 FP propeller Total Power: 221kW (300hp) 8.7kn Daldizel 6CHNSP18/22-300 1 x 4 Stroke 6 Cy. 180 x 220 221kW (300bhp) Daldizel-Khabarovsk AuxGen: 1 x 14kW, 1 x 13kW Fuel: 7.0 (d.f.)
8139065 *UBVR* -	**SPP-015** - **Morskie Linii Co Ltd** - *Petropavlovsk-Kamchatskiy* *Russia*	**175** 52 164	Class: RS	**1983-08 Sudoremontnyy Zavod "Yakor" — Sovetskaya Gavan** Yd No: 10251/15 Loa 35.72 Br ex 7.22 Dght 1.850 Lbp 33.63 Br md 7.20 Dpth 2.42 Welded, 1 dk	**(A31C2GD) Deck Cargo Ship** Ice Capable	**1 oil engine** geared to sc. shaft driving 1 FP propeller Total Power: 221kW (300hp) 8.7kn Daldizel 6CHNSP18/22-300 1 x 4 Stroke 6 Cy. 180 x 220 221kW (300bhp) Daldizel-Khabarovsk AuxGen: 1 x 14kW, 1 x 13kW Fuel: 7.0 (d.f.)
8726454 *UAGP* -	**SPP-17** - **Kupez Co Ltd** - *Okhotsk* *Russia*	**193** 58 125	Class: RS	**1986-09 Sudoremontnyy Zavod "Yakor" — Sovetskaya Gavan** Yd No: 4004/17 Loa 35.75 Br ex 7.50 Dght 1.710 Lbp 33.50 Br md 7.20 Dpth 2.40 Welded, 1 dk	**(A31C2GD) Deck Cargo Ship** Ice Capable	**1 oil engine** geared to sc. shaft driving 1 FP propeller Total Power: 165kW (224hp) 8.3kn Daldizel 6CHNSP18/22 1 x 4 Stroke 6 Cy. 180 x 220 165kW (224bhp) Daldizel-Khabarovsk AuxGen: 1 x 14kW, 1 x 13kW Fuel: 4.0 (d.f.)
8228153 - -	**SPP-018** - **Beringovskiy Commercial Port (Beringovskiy MTP)** - *Beringovskiy* *Russia* Official number: 832456	**166** 49 164	Class: (RS)	**1984-06 Sudoremontnyy Zavod "Yakor" — Sovetskaya Gavan** Yd No: 10251/18 Loa 35.74 Br ex 7.22 Dght 1.850 Lbp 33.63 Br md - Dpth 2.42 Welded, 1 dk	**(A31C2GD) Deck Cargo Ship** Ice Capable	**1 oil engine** geared to sc. shaft driving 1 FP propeller Total Power: 221kW (300hp) 8.7kn Daldizel 6CHNSP18/22-300 1 x 4 Stroke 6 Cy. 180 x 220 221kW (300bhp) Daldizel-Khabarovsk AuxGen: 2 x 14kW Fuel: 5.0 (d.f.)
8726662 *UAQE* -	**SPP-19** - **Alexandr N Yablokov** - *Magadan* *Russia*	**193** 58 125	Class: RS	**1987-06 Sudoremontnyy Zavod "Yakor" — Sovetskaya Gavan** Yd No: 4004/19 Loa 35.75 Br ex 7.50 Dght 1.710 Lbp 33.50 Br md 7.20 Dpth 2.40 Welded, 1 dk	**(A31C2GD) Deck Cargo Ship** Ice Capable	**1 oil engine** geared to sc. shaft driving 1 FP propeller Total Power: 165kW (224hp) 8.3kn Daldizel 6CHNSP18/22 1 x 4 Stroke 6 Cy. 180 x 220 165kW (224bhp) Daldizel-Khabarovsk AuxGen: 1 x 14kW, 1 x 13kW Fuel: 4.0 (d.f.)
8726674 - -	**SPP-20** - **Ustkamchatryba Co Ltd (OOO 'Ustkamchatryba')** - *Petropavlovsk-Kamchatskiy* *Russia* Official number: 874336	**193** 58 114	Class: RS	**1987-12 Sudoremontnyy Zavod "Yakor" — Sovetskaya Gavan** Yd No: 4004/20 Loa 35.75 Br ex 7.50 Dght 1.710 Lbp 33.50 Br md 7.20 Dpth 2.40 Welded, 1 dk	**(A31C2GD) Deck Cargo Ship** Ice Capable	**1 oil engine** geared to sc. shaft driving 1 FP propeller Total Power: 165kW (224hp) 8.3kn Daldizel 6CHNSP18/22 1 x 4 Stroke 6 Cy. 180 x 220 165kW (224bhp) Daldizel-Khabarovsk AuxGen: 1 x 14kW, 1 x 13kW Fuel: 4.0 (d.f.)
8228751 *UALS* -	**SPP-020** - **MAG-SEA Tranzit Co Ltd** - *Magadan* *Russia* MMSI: 273434250 Official number: 843272	**170** 51 164	Class: RS	**1984-09 Sudoremontnyy Zavod "Yakor" — Sovetskaya Gavan** Yd No: 10251/20 Loa 35.74 Br ex 7.22 Dght 1.850 Lbp 33.63 Br md 7.20 Dpth 2.42 Welded, 1 dk	**(A31C2GD) Deck Cargo Ship** Ice Capable	**1 oil engine** driving 1 FP propeller Total Power: 221kW (300hp) 8.7kn S.K.L. 6NVD26A-2 1 x 4 Stroke 6 Cy. 180 x 260 221kW (300bhp) VEB Schwermaschinenbau "KarlLiebknecht" (SKL)-Magdeburg AuxGen: 1 x 14kW, 1 x 13kW Fuel: 7.0 (d.f.)
8331651 *UBDL* -	**SPP-021** - **Terneyles JSC (OAO 'Terneyles')** - *Vladivostok* *Russia* Official number: 841493	**169** 50 164	Class: (RS)	**1984-11 Sudoremontnyy Zavod "Yakor" — Sovetskaya Gavan** Yd No: 10251/21 Loa 35.72 Br ex 7.20 Dght 1.850 Lbp 33.63 Br md - Dpth 2.40 Welded, 1 dk	**(A31C2GD) Deck Cargo Ship** Ice Capable	**1 oil engine** driving 1 FP propeller Total Power: 220kW (299hp) 8.7kn S.K.L. 6NVD26A-2 1 x 4 Stroke 6 Cy. 180 x 260 220kW (299bhp) VEB Schwermaschinenbau "KarlLiebknecht" (SKL)-Magdeburg AuxGen: 1 x 14kW, 1 x 13kW Fuel: 7.0 (d.f.)
8726686 - -	**SPP-21** - **Ok Gym Li** -	**193** 58 125	Class: (RS)	**1988-06 Sudoremontnyy Zavod "Yakor" — Sovetskaya Gavan** Yd No: 4004/21 Loa 35.75 Br ex 7.50 Dght 1.710 Lbp 33.50 Br md 7.20 Dpth 2.40 Welded, 1 dk	**(A31C2GD) Deck Cargo Ship** Ice Capable	**1 oil engine** geared to sc. shaft driving 1 FP propeller Total Power: 165kW (224hp) 8.3kn Daldizel 6CHNSP18/22 1 x 4 Stroke 6 Cy. 180 x 220 165kW (224bhp) Daldizel-Khabarovsk AuxGen: 1 x 14kW, 1 x 13kW Fuel: 4.0 (d.f.)
8726698 *UBQV* -	**SPP-022** - **District State Unitary Enterprise 'Chukotsnab' (Gosudarstvennoe Unitarnoe Predpriyatie - Chukotskiy Avtonomnyy Okrug 'Chukotsnab')** - *Anadyr* *Russia*	**166** 49 164	Class: RS	**1985-05 Sudoremontnyy Zavod "Yakor" — Sovetskaya Gavan** Yd No: 10251/22 Loa 35.72 Br ex 7.20 Dght 1.850 Lbp 33.63 Br md - Dpth 2.40 Welded, 1 dk	**(A31C2GD) Deck Cargo Ship** Ice Capable	**1 oil engine** driving 1 FP propeller Total Power: 220kW (299hp) 8.7kn S.K.L. 6NVD26A-2 1 x 4 Stroke 6 Cy. 180 x 260 220kW (299bhp) VEB Schwermaschinenbau "KarlLiebknecht" (SKL)-Magdeburg AuxGen: 1 x 14kW, 1 x 13kW Fuel: 7.0 (d.f.)
8726636 *UDGI* -	**SPP-027** - **RPF 'Kontinent' Co Ltd** - *Korsakov* *Russia* MMSI: 273183700 Official number: 852233	**169** 50 164	Class: (RS)	**1986-07 Sudoremontnyy Zavod "Yakor" — Sovetskaya Gavan** Yd No: 10251/27 Loa 35.72 Br ex 7.20 Dght 1.850 Lbp 33.63 Br md 7.20 Dpth 2.40 Welded, 1 dk	**(A31C2GD) Deck Cargo Ship** Ice Capable	**1 oil engine** driving 1 FP propeller Total Power: 220kW (299hp) 8.7kn S.K.L. 6NVD26A-2 1 x 4 Stroke 6 Cy. 180 x 260 220kW (299bhp) VEB Schwermaschinenbau "KarlLiebknecht" (SKL)-Magdeburg AuxGen: 1 x 14kW, 1 x 13kW Fuel: 7.0 (d.f.)
8726648 *UDYQ* -	**SPP-028** - **Azimut-A Co Ltd** - *Uglegorsk* *Russia*	**166** 49 164	Class: RS	**1986-09 Sudoremontnyy Zavod "Yakor" — Sovetskaya Gavan** Yd No: 10251/28 Loa 35.72 Br ex 7.20 Dght 1.850 Lbp 33.63 Br md - Dpth 2.40 Welded, 1 dk	**(A31C2GD) Deck Cargo Ship** Ice Capable	**1 oil engine** driving 1 FP propeller Total Power: 220kW (299hp) 8.7kn S.K.L. 6NVD26A-2 1 x 4 Stroke 6 Cy. 180 x 260 220kW (299bhp) VEB Schwermaschinenbau "KarlLiebknecht" (SKL)-Magdeburg AuxGen: 1 x 14kW, 1 x 13kW Fuel: 7.0 (d.f.)
8616350 - -	**SPP 52** *ex Settsu Maru -2007* **SPP Shipping Co Ltd** - *Tongyeong* *South Korea* Official number: CMR077970	*135* - -		**1987-03 Osaka Shipbuilding Co Ltd — Osaka OS** Yd No: 444 Loa 30.20 Br ex 9.20 Dght 2.601 Lbp 25.50 Br md 8.30 Dpth 3.58 Welded, 1 dk	**(B32A2ST) Tug**	**2 oil engines** Geared Integral to driving 2 Z propellers Total Power: 1,104kW (1,500hp) 11.0kn Yanmar M200-ST 2 x 4 Stroke 6 Cy. 200 x 260 each-552kW (750bhp) Yanmar Diesel Engine Co Ltd-Japan AuxGen: 2 x 60kW 220V 60Hz a.c Fuel: 22.5 (d.f.) 4.0 (r.f.) 5.5pd

IMO / Call sign	Name / Owner / Registry	Tonnage	Class	Builder / Dimensions	Type	Machinery
7823504 - -	**SPP 53** *ex* Hakuyo Maru *-2007* *ex* Iyo Maru *-1993* **SPP Shipping Co Ltd** - *Tongyeong* South Korea Official number: CMR087814	*200* - -		**1979-03 Hakata Zosen K.K. — Imabari** Yd No: 211 Loa 31.72 Br ex - Dght - Lbp 26.50 Br md 8.60 Dpth 3.51 Welded, 1 dk	**(B32A2ST) Tug**	**2 oil engines** geared integral to driving 2 Z propellers Total Power: 1,912kW (2,600hp) Yanmar G250-ET 2 x 4 Stroke 6 Cy. 250 x 290 each-956kW (1300bhp) Yanmar Diesel Engine Co Ltd-Japan
7929437 - -	**SPP 54** *ex* Hita Maru *-2008* **SPP Shipping Co Ltd** - *Tongyeong* South Korea Official number: CMR087861	*321* - -		**1980-08 Kanbara Zosen K.K. — Onomichi** Yd No: 250 Loa 40.70 Br ex - Dght 3.300 Lbp 32.00 Br md 9.00 Dpth 4.20 Welded, 1 dk	**(B32A2ST) Tug**	**2 oil engines** geared integral to driving 2 Z propellers Total Power: 2,500kW (3,400hp) Niigata 6L28BX 2 x 4 Stroke 6 Cy. 280 x 320 each-1250kW (1700bhp) Niigata Engineering Co Ltd-Japan
9254587 - -	**SPP 55** *ex* Kinjo Maru *-2008* **SPP Shipping Co Ltd** - *Tongyeong* South Korea Official number: CMR-088015	*195* - -	Class: KR	**2002-02 Kanagawa Zosen — Kobe** Yd No: 497 Loa 33.90 Br ex - Dght - Lbp 29.50 Br md 9.40 Dpth 4.00 Welded, 1 dk	**(B32A2ST) Tug**	**2 oil engines** Geared Integral to driving 2 Z propellers Total Power: 2,648kW (3,600hp) 14.0kn Yanmar 6N280-UN 2 x 4 Stroke 6 Cy. 280 x 380 each-1324kW (1800bhp) Yanmar Diesel Engine Co Ltd-Japan AuxGen: 2 x 270kW 220V 60Hz a.c Fuel: 55.0 (d.f.)
8519306 - -	**SPP 56** *ex* Misaki Maru *-2008* **SPP Shipping Co Ltd** - *Tongyeong* South Korea Official number: CMR-088192	*152* - -	Class: KR	**1986-02 Kanagawa Zosen — Kobe** Yd No: 284 Loa 30.20 Br ex - Dght 2.701 Lbp 25.51 Br md 8.60 Dpth 3.81 Welded, 1 dk	**(B32A2ST) Tug**	**2 oil engines** geared integral to driving 2 Z propellers Total Power: 1,912kW (2,600hp) Niigata 6L25CXE 2 x 4 Stroke 6 Cy. 250 x 320 each-956kW (1300bhp) Niigata Engineering Co Ltd-Japan
9063445 - -	**SPP 57** *ex* Tsukama *-2008* *ex* Sapporo Maru *-2008* **SPP Shipping Co Ltd** - *Tongyeong* South Korea Official number: CMR-084431	**149** - 61	Class: KR	**1993-05 Kambara Marine Development & Shipbuilding Co Ltd — Fukuyama HS** Yd No: OE-180 Loa 29.52 Br ex 8.23 Dght 3.010 Lbp 25.50 Br md 8.00 Dpth 3.60 Welded, 1 dk	**(B32A2ST) Tug**	**2 oil engines** Geared Integral to driving 2 Z propellers Total Power: 1,472kW (2,002hp) 12.0kn Niigata 6L22HX 2 x 4 Stroke 6 Cy. 220 x 280 each-736kW (1001bhp) Niigata Engineering Co Ltd-Japan AuxGen: 2 x 80kW 225V 50Hz a.c Fuel: 31.0 (d.f.) 7.0pd
8926195 - -	**SPP 58** *ex* Daiei Maru *-2011* - - South Korea MMSI: 440148610 Official number: CMR-114432	*119* - -		**1996-10 Kanbara Zosen K.K. — Onomichi** Yd No: 488 Loa 28.00 Br ex - Dght - Lbp 25.00 Br md 8.20 Dpth 3.18 Welded, 1 dk	**(B32A2ST) Tug**	**2 oil engines** geared to sc. shafts driving 2 FP propellers Total Power: 1,472kW (2,002hp) 11.0kn Yanmar M220-EN 2 x 4 Stroke 6 Cy. 220 x 300 each-736kW (1001bhp) Yanmar Diesel Engine Co Ltd-Japan
7808279 *UDDD* -	**SPRAVEDLIVYY** - **Federal State Financed Institution 'Far-Eastern Expeditionary Division of Emergency & Rescue Operations'** - *Vladivostok* Russia MMSI: 273813200 Official number: 790465	**3,121** 936 1,474	Class: RS	**1980-01 Oy Wartsila Ab — Helsinki** Yd No: 424 Lengthened Loa 74.41 Br ex 18.32 Dght 6.700 Lbp 65.00 Br md 17.62 Dpth 9.02 Welded, 2 dks	**(B32A2ST) Tug** Cranes: 2x5t,2x3t Ice Capable	**2 oil engines** driving 2 CP propellers Total Power: 5,590kW (7,600hp) 15.0kn Pielstick 6PC2-5L-400 2 x 4 Stroke 6 Cy. 400 x 460 each-2795kW (3800bhp) Oy Wartsila Ab-Finland AuxGen: 3 x 508kW Thrusters: 1 Thwart. FP thruster (f) Fuel: 1400.0 (r.f.)
7934157 *WQZ3918* -	**SPRAY II** - **f/v Spray Inc** - *Gloucester, MA* United States of America Official number: 603749	*150* 102 -		**1979-04 Canaveral Shipbuilding Corp. — Cape Canaveral, Fl** L reg 23.08 Br ex 6.76 Dght - Lbp - Br md - Dpth 3.76 Welded, 1 dk	**(B11A2FS) Stern Trawler**	**1 oil engine** driving 1 FP propeller Total Power: 412kW (560hp) Caterpillar D379SCAC 1 x Vee 4 Stroke 8 Cy. 159 x 203 412kW (560bhp) Caterpillar Tractor Co-USA
5337082 - -	**SPREE** - - -	*132* 46 -	Class: (DS)	**1956 Schiffbau u. Reparaturwerft Stralsund — Stralsund** Yd No: 2011 Loa 26.45 Br ex 6.71 Dght 3.531 Lbp 23.40 Br md - Dpth 3.66 Welded, 1 dk	**(B11B2FV) Fishing Vessel** Compartments: 1 Ho, ER 1 Ha: ER Ice Capable	**1 oil engine** driving 1 FP propeller Total Power: 221kW (300hp) 9.0kn S.K.L. 8NVD36-1U 1 x 4 Stroke 8 Cy. 240 x 360 221kW (300bhp) VEB Schwermaschinenbau "KarlLiebknecht" (SKL)-Magdeburg AuxGen: 2 x 21kW 110V d.c
8748402 *WDA7434* -	**SPREE** - **Spree Expeditions Inc** - *Key West, FL* United States of America MMSI: 366843270 Official number: 572368	**141** 45 50		**1976-06 Swiftships Inc — Morgan City LA** Yd No: 118 Loa 30.48 Br ex 6.83 Dght 2.190 Lbp - Br md 6.83 Dpth 3.14 Welded, 1 dk	**(A37A2PC) Passenger/Cruise** Hull Material: Aluminium Alloy Passengers: unberthed: 24	**3 oil engines** reduction geared to sc. shafts driving 3 FP propellers Total Power: 1,104kW (1,500hp) 13.0kn G.M. (Detroit Diesel) 12V-71-TI 3 x Vee 2 Stroke 12 Cy. 108 x 127 each-368kW (500bhp) General Motors Detroit DieselAllison Divn-USA AuxGen: 2 x 30kW a.c
1001166 *E5U2551* -	**SPREZZATURA** *ex* Foie Gras *-2012* *ex* Caroline Sea *-1995* *ex* Anymore *-1995* *ex* Aliska *-1995* *ex* Bluemar *-1995* **Xanthus Shipping Ltd** - *Rarotonga* Cook Islands MMSI: 518604000 Official number: 1640	**146** 43 -	Class: RI (LR) ✠ Classed LR until 11/10/95	**1971-12 N.V. Scheepswerven "Nicolaas Witsen en Vis" — Alkmaar** Yd No: 984 Loa 30.28 Br ex 6.13 Dght 1.730 Lbp 26.44 Br md 6.10 Dpth 3.38 Welded, 1 dk	**(X11A2YP) Yacht**	**2 oil engines** reduction geared to sc. shafts driving 2 FP propellers Total Power: 1,986kW (2,700hp) 12.0kn M.T.U. 2 x each-993kW (1350bhp) (new engine 2012) MTU Friedrichshafen GmbH-Friedrichshafen
9698604 *V7BG5* -	**SPREZZATURA** *ex* San Lorezo CL33/14 *-2013* **Sprezzatura Ltd** Vessel Safety Management LLC *Bikini* Marshall Islands MMSI: 538070933 Official number: 70933	**184** 55 -		**2013-07 Cant. Nav. San Lorenzo SpA — Viareggio** Yd No: CL33/14 Loa 32.60 Br ex - Dght - Lbp - Br md 7.00 Dpth - Welded, 1 dk	**(X11A2YP) Yacht** Hull Material: Carbon Fibre Sandwich	**2 oil engines** reduction geared to sc. shafts driving 2 Propellers
9654139 *VNJ4295* -	**SPRIGHTLY** - **DMS Maritime Pty Ltd** - *Darwin, NT* Australia MMSI: 503778700 Official number: 860677	**146** 43 59	Class: LR ✠ **100A1** SS 07/2013 tug *IWS Australian coastal service **LMC** **UMS** Eq.Ltr: C; Cable: 274.5/17.5 U2 (a)	**2013-07 Damen Shipyards Changde Co Ltd — Changde HN** (Hull) Yd No: (512407) **2013-07 B.V. Scheepswerf Damen — Gorinchem** Yd No: 512407 Loa 21.19 Br ex 9.48 Dght 3.020 Lbp 18.79 Br md 8.90 Dpth 4.00 Welded, 1 dk	**(B32A2ST) Tug**	**2 oil engines** gearing integral to driving 2 Directional propellers Total Power: 1,940kW (2,638hp) Caterpillar C32 ACERT 2 x Vee 4 Stroke 12 Cy. 145 x 162 each-970kW (1319bhp) Caterpillar Inc-USA AuxGen: 2 x 42kW 400V 50Hz a.c Thrusters: 1 Tunnel thruster (f)
7392000 *P2V5057* -	**SPRIGHTLY** *ex* Thomas Webb *-1994* *ex* Corsair *-1975* **Pacific Towing (PNG) Pty Ltd** - *Port Moresby* Papua New Guinea MMSI: 553111257 Official number: 355779	*166* 24 129	Class: (LR) ✠ Classed LR until 25/4/10	**1975-03 Carrington Slipways Pty Ltd — Newcastle NSW** Yd No: 101 Loa 26.34 Br ex 8.11 Dght 3.429 Lbp 22.79 Br md 7.78 Dpth 4.17 Welded, 1 dk	**(B32A2ST) Tug**	**2 oil engines** reverse reduction geared to sc. shafts driving 2 FP propellers Total Power: 1,472kW (2,002hp) 11.5kn Blackstone ESL6MK2 2 x 4 Stroke 6 Cy. 222 x 292 each-736kW (1001bhp) Mirrlees Blackstone (Stamford)Ltd.-Stamford AuxGen: 2 x 50kW 415V 50Hz a.c
9368027 *9VJC4* -	**SPRING** - **Spring Navigation Pte Ltd** Equatorial Marine Fuel Management Services Pte Ltd *Singapore* Singapore MMSI: 565124000 Official number: 391514	**4,048** 2,083 7,496	Class: NK	**2006-07 Zhenjiang Sopo Shiprepair & Building Co Ltd — Zhenjiang JS** Yd No: SP0403 Loa 90.00 (BB) Br ex - Dght - Lbp 84.46 Br md 17.50 Dpth 9.00 Welded, 1 dk	**(A13B2TP) Products Tanker** Double Hull (13F) Liq: 7,413; Liq (Oil): 7,413 2 Cargo Pump (s): 2x1020m³/hr	**2 oil engines** reduction geared to sc shaft (s) driving 1 FP propeller Total Power: 2,648kW (3,600hp) 13.5kn Yanmar 6N260-SN 2 x 4 Stroke 6 Cy. 260 x 360 each-1324kW (1800bhp) Yanmar Diesel Engine Co Ltd-Japan Fuel: 320.0

9416812 *V7QA8* -	**SPRING** **Montenegro Marine Corp** NGM Energy SA *Majuro* *Marshall Islands* MMSI: 538003325 Official number: 3325	**8,539** 4,117 13,022 T/cm 23.2	Class: AB	**2009-04 21st Century Shipbuilding Co Ltd — Tongyeong** Yd No: 248 Loa 128.60 (BB) Br ex - Dght 8.714 Lbp 120.40 Br md 20.40 Dpth 11.50 Welded, 1 dk	**(A12B2TR) Chemical/Products Tanker** Double Hull (13F) Liq: 13,395; Liq (Oil): 14,094 Cargo Heating Coils Compartments: 12 Wing Ta, 2 Wing Slop Ta, ER 12 Cargo Pump (s): 12x300m^3/hr Manifold: Bow/CM: 60.7m	**1 oil engine** driving 1 FP propeller Total Power: 4,440kW (6,037hp) 13.4kn MAN-B&W 6S35MC 1 x 2 Stroke 6 Cy. 350 x 1400 4440kW (6037bhp) STX Engine Co Ltd-South Korea AuxGen: 3 x 480kW a.c Thrusters: 1 Tunnel thruster (f) Fuel: 75.0 (d.f.) 640.0 (r.f.)
9580209 *3FCI2* -	**SPRING AEOLIAN** **Primavera Montana SA** Shunzan Kaiun KK (Shunzan Kaiun Co Ltd) *Panama* *Panama* MMSI: 354807000 Official number: 4337512	**44,366** 27,201 83,478 T/cm 71.0	Class: NK	**2012-01 Sanoyas Shipbuilding Corp — Kurashiki OY** Yd No: 1321 Loa 229.00 (BB) Br ex - Dght 14.598 Lbp 224.00 Br md 32.24 Dpth 20.20 Welded, 1 dk	**(A21A2BC) Bulk Carrier** Grain: 96,078 Compartments: 7 Ho, ER 7 Ha: ER	**1 oil engine** driving 1 FP propeller Total Power: 10,740kW (14,602hp) 14.0kn MAN-B&W 6S60MC-C 1 x 2 Stroke 6 Cy. 600 x 2400 10740kW (14602bhp) Mitsui Engineering & Shipbuilding CLtd-Japan Fuel: 3200.0
5084180 *DVQM* -	**SPRING BEAUTY** *ex* Benevolent *ex* Kaiki Maru No. 18 *-1971* *ex* Dai Maru No. 15 *-1971* **Frabelle Fishing Corp** - *Manila* *Philippines* Official number: MNLD000390	*366* 186 -		**1961-08 KK Kanasashi Zosen — Shizuoka SZ** Yd No: 418 Loa 48.90 Br ex 7.78 Dght - Lbp 43.16 Br md 7.75 Dpth 3.81 Welded, 1 dk	**(B11B2FV) Fishing Vessel** Compartments: 1 Ho, ER	**1 oil engine** driving 1 FP propeller Total Power: 588kW (799hp) 11.0kn Hanshin Z6WS 1 x 4 Stroke 6 Cy. 350 x 500 588kW (799bhp) Hanshin Nainenki Kogyo-Japan
9406506 *3ENV4* -	**SPRING BRAVE** **Primavera Montana SA** Shunzan Kaiun KK (Shunzan Kaiun Co Ltd) SatCom: Inmarsat C 435300311 *Panama* *Panama* MMSI: 353003000 Official number: 3345108A	**104,730** 66,443 206,306 T/cm 140.2	Class: NK	**2007-12 Imabari Shipbuilding Co Ltd — Saijo EH (Saijo Shipyard)** Yd No: 8050 Loa 299.99 (BB) Br ex 50.00 Dght 18.105 Lbp 291.40 Br md 50.00 Dpth 24.50 Welded, 1 dk	**(A21A2BC) Bulk Carrier** Grain: 220,022 Compartments: 9 Ho, ER 9 Ha: 8 (16.2 x 23.8)ER (16.2 x 20.4)	**1 oil engine** driving 1 FP propeller Total Power: 18,630kW (25,329hp) 14.5kn MAN-B&W 6S70MC-C 1 x 2 Stroke 6 Cy. 700 x 2800 18630kW (25329bhp) Mitsui Engineering & Shipbuilding CLtd-Japan AuxGen: 3 x a.c Fuel: 5500.0
9612351 *VRLH2* -	**SPRING BREEZE** **Spring Breeze Shipping Ltd** Jiangsu Steamship Co Ltd *Hong Kong* *Hong Kong* MMSI: 477305600 Official number: HK-3664	**22,648** 11,229 33,600 T/cm 48.5	Class: NV	**2013-01 Jiangsu Yangzijiang Shipbuilding Co Ltd — Jiangyin JS** Yd No: YZJ2010-964 Loa 181.00 (BB) Br ex 30.05 Dght 9.800 Lbp 172.00 Br md 30.02 Dpth 14.60 Welded, 1 dk	**(A21A2BC) Bulk Carrier** Grain: 47,000 Compartments: 5 Ho, ER 5 Ha: ER Cranes: 4x30t	**1 oil engine** driving 1 FP propeller Total Power: 6,480kW (8,810hp) 13.9kn MAN-B&W 6S42MC 1 x 2 Stroke 6 Cy. 420 x 1764 6480kW (8810bhp) Hudong Heavy Machinery Co Ltd-China AuxGen: 3 x a.c
9610200 *3FIJ9* -	**SPRING BREEZE** **Murakami Sekiyu Co Ltd & Tradewind Navigation SA** Murakami Sekiyu Co Ltd (Murakami Sekiyu KK) SatCom: Inmarsat C 437323010 *Panama* *Panama* MMSI: 373230000 Official number: 4374512	**21,699** 12,253 36,365	Class: NK	**2012-04 Shikoku Dockyard Co. Ltd. — Takamatsu** Yd No: 1071 Loa 176.50 (BB) Br ex - Dght 10.718 Lbp 168.50 Br md 28.80 Dpth 15.20 Welded, 1 dk	**(A21A2BC) Bulk Carrier** Grain: 47,089; Bale: 45,414 Compartments: 5 Ho, ER 5 Ha: ER Cranes: 4x30.5t	**1 oil engine** driving 1 FP propeller Total Power: 7,300kW (9,925hp) 14.5kn MAN-B&W 6S46MC-C 1 x 2 Stroke 6 Cy. 460 x 1932 7300kW (9925bhp) Mitsui Engineering & Shipbuilding CLtd-Japan Fuel: 1950.0
9557862 *3FLF5* -	**SPRING BRIGHT** **Primavera Montana SA** Shunzan Kaiun KK (Shunzan Kaiun Co Ltd) SatCom: Inmarsat C 435767310 *Panama* *Panama* MMSI: 357673000 Official number: 4110110	**91,508** 57,746 174,757 T/cm 122.0	Class: NK	**2010-01 Namura Shipbuilding Co Ltd — Imari SG** Yd No: 333 Loa 289.98 (BB) Br ex - Dght 18.029 Lbp 280.00 Br md 45.00 Dpth 24.70 Welded, 1 dk	**(A21A2BC) Bulk Carrier** Grain: 199,507 Compartments: 9 Ho, ER 9 Ha: 7 (16.2 x 20.2) (16.2 x 15.1)ER (15.3 x 16.8)	**1 oil engine** driving 1 FP propeller Total Power: 16,860kW (22,923hp) 14.8kn MAN-B&W 6S70MC-C 1 x 2 Stroke 6 Cy. 700 x 2800 16860kW (22923bhp) Hitachi Zosen Corp-Japan Fuel: 4830.0
9114660 *VRFF2* -	**SPRING CANARY** *ex* Orient Iris *-2009* **Well Trend Shipping Ltd** Chun An Shipping Ltd *Hong Kong* *Hong Kong* MMSI: 477225600 Official number: HK-2398	**7,416** 2,889 8,125	Class: NK	**1995-04 Usuki Shipyard Co Ltd — Usuki OT** Yd No: 1632 Loa 108.50 (BB) Br ex - Dght 7.436 Lbp 100.00 Br md 20.00 Dpth 13.50 Welded	**(A35A2RR) Ro-Ro Cargo Ship** Quarter stern door/ramp (s) Cars: 222 Cranes: 2x40t; Derricks: 2x25t	**1 oil engine** driving 1 FP propeller Total Power: 3,604kW (4,900hp) 13.7kn Mitsubishi 7UEC37LA 1 x 2 Stroke 7 Cy. 370 x 880 3604kW (4900bhp) Akasaka Tekkosho KK (Akasaka DieselLtd)-Japan AuxGen: 2 x 360kW a.c Fuel: 453.0 (r.f.) 14.2pd
6822230 *VJML* -	**SPRING COVE** **Australian Barge Charter** Qport Marine Services Pty Ltd *Brisbane, Qld* *Australia* MMSI: 503468000 Official number: 332700	*222* - 110	Class: LR ✠ **100A1** SS 09/2008 tug ✠ **LMC** Eq.Ltr: (c) ; Cable: U1	**1968-08 Adelaide Ship Construction Pty Ltd — Port Adelaide SA** Yd No: 44 Loa 30.64 Br ex 8.54 Dght 3.912 Lbp 27.67 Br md 8.08 Dpth 4.58 Welded, 1 dk	**(B32A2ST) Tug**	**1 oil engine** reverse reduction geared to sc. shaft driving 1 FP propeller Total Power: 1,311kW (1,782hp) 12.0kn Mirrlees KMR-6 1 x 4 Stroke 6 Cy. 381 x 457 1311kW (1782bhp) Mirrlees National Ltd.-Stockport AuxGen: 2 x 40kW 415V 50Hz a.c
8967187 - -	**SPRING DELINI 1** *ex* Ocean Bridge No. I *-2008* *ex* Sumiei Maru No. 1 *-2004* **World Shipping Co Ltd** - *Pohang* *South Korea* MMSI: 440412220 Official number: PHB-126826	**618** 185 208	Class: KR (BV)	**2001-03 YK Nakanoshima Zosensho — Kochi KC** Yd No: 215 Loa 29.00 Br ex - Dght 4.868 Lbp 24.50 Br md 10.00 Dpth 7.53 Welded, 1 dk	**(B32B2SP) Pusher Tug**	**2 oil engines** driving 2 FP propellers Total Power: 2,942kW (4,000hp) 10.3kn Niigata 6M38GT 2 x 4 Stroke 6 Cy. 380 x 720 each-1471kW (2000bhp) Niigata Engineering Co Ltd-Japan
9425801 *3FHX3* -	**SPRING EAGLE** **Kyowa Kisen Co Ltd & Green Spanker Shipping SA** Kyowa Kisen Co Ltd *Panama* *Panama* MMSI: 372333000 Official number: 4175010	**32,287** 19,458 58,096 T/cm 57.4	Class: NK	**2010-06 Tsuneishi Heavy Industries (Cebu) Inc — Balamban** Yd No: SC-114 Loa 189.99 (BB) Br ex - Dght 12.826 Lbp 185.60 Br md 32.26 Dpth 18.00 Welded, 1 dk	**(A21A2BC) Bulk Carrier** Grain: 72,689; Bale: 70,122 Compartments: 5 Ho, ER 5 Ha: ER Cranes: 4x30t	**1 oil engine** driving 1 FP propeller Total Power: 8,450kW (11,489hp) 14.5kn MAN-B&W 6S50MC-C 1 x 2 Stroke 6 Cy. 500 x 2000 8450kW (11489bhp) Mitsui Engineering & Shipbuilding CLtd-Japan Fuel: 2388.0 (r.f.)
9392896 *3EKP7* -	**SPRING EURO** **Shokuyu Navigation Co SA** ST Marine Co Ltd *Panama* *Panama* MMSI: 372786000 Official number: 3280407A	**2,579** 1,133 3,947 T/cm 10.8	Class: NK	**2007-06 Shitanoe Shipbuilding Co Ltd — Usuki OT** Yd No: 1277 Loa 88.60 (BB) Br ex 14.62 Dght 6.008 Lbp 83.00 Br md 14.60 Dpth 7.20 Welded, 1 dk	**(A12B2TR) Chemical/Products Tanker** Double Hull (13F) Liq: 4,067; Liq (Oil): 4,068 Cargo Heating Coils Compartments: 8 Wing Ta, 1 Ta, ER 9 Cargo Pump (s): 9x200m^3/hr Manifold: Bow/CM: 44.7m	**1 oil engine** driving 1 FP propeller Total Power: 2,647kW (3,599hp) 13.5kn Akasaka A41S 1 x 4 Stroke 6 Cy. 410 x 800 2647kW (3599bhp) Akasaka Tekkosho KK (Akasaka DieselLtd)-Japan AuxGen: 2 x 330kW a.c Thrusters: 1 Tunnel thruster (f) Fuel: 65.0 (d.f.) 230.0 (r.f.)
9603491 *VRJA2* -	**SPRING GLORY** **Spring Glory Shipping Ltd** Jiangsu Steamship Co Ltd *Hong Kong* *Hong Kong* MMSI: 477397200 Official number: HK-3188	**51,265** 31,203 93,379 T/cm 80.9	Class: CC (AB)	**2011-09 Jiangsu Newyangzi Shipbuilding Co Ltd — Jingjiang JS** Yd No: YZJ2006-927 Loa 229.20 (BB) Br ex 38.04 Dght 14.900 Lbp 222.00 Br md 38.00 Dpth 20.70 Welded, 1 dk	**(A21A2BC) Bulk Carrier** Grain: 110,300 Compartments: 7 Ho, ER 7 Ha: ER	**1 oil engine** driving 1 FP propeller Total Power: 11,800kW (16,043hp) 14.1kn MAN-B&W 6S60MC-C 1 x 2 Stroke 6 Cy. 600 x 2400 11800kW (16043bhp) STX Engine Co Ltd-South Korea AuxGen: 3 x 730kW a.c
9478872 *3FCY5* -	**SPRING HAWK** **Seiun Shipping SA & Tsurumi Kisen Co Ltd** Tsurumi Kisen Co Ltd *Panama* *Panama* MMSI: 354127000 Official number: 4175910	**31,232** 18,516 55,688 T/cm 55.8	Class: NK	**2010-05 Mitsui Eng. & SB. Co. Ltd. — Tamano** Yd No: 1720 Loa 189.99 (BB) Br ex - Dght 12.570 Lbp 182.00 Br md 32.26 Dpth 17.90 Welded, 1 dk	**(A21A2BC) Bulk Carrier** Grain: 70,800; Bale: 68,000 Compartments: 5 Ho, ER 5 Ha: ER Cranes: 4x30t	**1 oil engine** driving 1 FP propeller Total Power: 9,480kW (12,889hp) 14.5kn MAN-B&W 6S50MC-C 1 x 2 Stroke 6 Cy. 500 x 2000 9480kW (12889bhp) Mitsui Engineering & Shipbuilding CLtd-Japan Fuel: 2380.0 (r.f.)
9649524 *VRKG9* -	**SPRING HONOR** **Spring Honor Shipping Ltd** Dalian Chun An Ship Management Co Ltd *Hong Kong* *Hong Kong* MMSI: 477325800 Official number: HK-3451	**7,100** 2,928 8,460	Class: CC	**2012-06 Weihai Donghai Shipyard Co Ltd — Weihai SD** Yd No: DHZ-11-02 Loa 112.21 Br ex - Dght 7.600 Lbp 103.88 Br md 19.00 Dpth 11.50 Welded, 1 dk	**(A31A2GX) General Cargo Ship** Grain: 12,741 Compartments: 2 Ho, ER 2 Ha: (25.9 x 14.4)ER (25.2 x 14.4) Cranes: 2x50t Ice Capable	**1 oil engine** driving 1 FP propeller Total Power: 2,648kW (3,600hp) 12.0kn Hanshin LH41LA 1 x 4 Stroke 6 Cy. 410 x 800 2648kW (3600bhp) The Hanshin Diesel Works Ltd-Japan AuxGen: 3 x 350kW 400V a.c

IMO / Call sign	Name / Owner	Tonnage	Class	Build / Dimensions	Type / Capacity	Machinery
8421315 *XUGV5* -	**SPRING HOPE** *ex* Susango *-2011* *ex* Sun Host *-2007* *ex* Hansung 33 *-2003* *ex* Katalina *-2000* *ex* Happiness *-1993* **Hong Kong Joint Success Ltd** Shenghao Marine (Hong Kong) Ltd *Phnom Penh* *Cambodia* MMSI: 515161000	**9,665** 3,968 13,537	Class: PD (KR) (NK)	**1985-03 Imai Shipbuilding Co Ltd — Kochi KC** Yd No: 531 Loa 117.02 (BB) Br ex - Dght 8.778 Lbp 108.01 Br md 23.00 Dpth 15.02 Welded, 1 dk	**(A31A2GX) General Cargo Ship** Grain: 22,033; Bale: 20,707 Compartments: 2 Ho, ER 2 Ha: 2 (31.5 x 12.8)ER Derricks: 4x15t	**1 oil engine** driving 1 FP propeller Total Power: 3,012kW (4,095hp) 11.5kn B&W 7L35MCE 1 x 2 Stroke 7 Cy. 350 x 1050 3012kW (4095bhp) Hitachi Zosen Corp-Japan AuxGen: 3 x 240kW a.c
6522177 *HSBA* -	**SPRING HORSE** *ex* Kii *-1980* *ex* Kii Maru *-1980* **Sirichai Laobooncharoen** - *Bangkok* *Thailand* Official number: 239001394	*1,049* 542 1,698	Class: (NK)	**1965-06 Usuki Iron Works Co Ltd — Saiki OT** Yd No: 1058 Loa 68.26 Br ex 10.44 Dght 4.776 Lbp 63.02 Br md 10.42 Dpth 5.41 Welded, 1 dk	**(A31A2GX) General Cargo Ship** Grain: 2,102; Bale: 2,007 Compartments: 2 Ho, ER 2 Ha: (16.9 x 7.0) (16.1 x 7.0)ER	**1 oil engine** driving 1 FP propeller Total Power: 1,214kW (1,651hp) 11.0kn Hanshin Z6ZSH 1 x 4 Stroke 6 Cy. 430 x 620 1214kW (1651bhp) Hanshin Nainenki Kogyo-Japan AuxGen: 1 x 48kW Fuel: 68.0
9114529 *VRAJ7* -	**SPRING HUMMER** *ex* Chris-T *-2004* **Spring Hummer Shipping Ltd** Dalian Chun An Ship Management Co Ltd *Hong Kong* *Hong Kong* MMSI: 477640400 Official number: HK-1395	**8,015** 3,172 8,634	Class: NK	**1995-02 KK Kanasashi — Shizuoka SZ** Yd No: 3356 Loa 109.98 (BB) Br ex - Dght 7.815 Lbp 99.95 Br md 20.20 Dpth 13.20 Welded, 1 dk	**(A35A2RR) Ro-Ro Cargo Ship** Angled stern door/ramp (s. a.) Lane-Len: 820 Bale: 15,014 Compartments: 2 Ho, ER 2 Ha: 2 (30.0 x 16.2)ER Cranes: 2x30t	**1 oil engine** driving 1 FP propeller Total Power: 3,089kW (4,200hp) 13.0kn Mitsubishi 6UEC37LA 1 x 2 Stroke 6 Cy. 370 x 880 3089kW (4200bhp) Akasaka Tekkosho KK (Akasaka DieselLtd)-Japan Fuel: 610.0 (r.f.)
9330290 *3EGC3* -	**SPRING HYDRANGEA** **Primavera Montana SA** Shunzan Kaiun KK (Shunzan Kaiun Co Ltd) SatCom: Inmarsat C 435684510 *Panama* *Panama* MMSI: 356845000 Official number: 3197606B	**89,726** 58,801 176,955 T/cm 121.7	Class: NK	**2006-07 Namura Shipbuilding Co Ltd — Imari SG** Yd No: 255 Loa 288.97 (BB) Br ex - Dght 17.955 Lbp 279.00 Br md 45.00 Dpth 24.40 Welded, 1 dk	**(A21A2BC) Bulk Carrier** Grain: 198,809; Bale: 195,968 Compartments: 9 Ho, ER 9 Ha: 7 (16.3 x 20.2) (16.3 x 15.2)ER (16.3 x 16.8)	**1 oil engine** driving 1 FP propeller Total Power: 16,860kW (22,923hp) 14.6kn MAN-B&W 6S70MC 1 x 2 Stroke 6 Cy. 700 x 2674 16860kW (22923bhp) Hitachi Zosen Corp-Japan Fuel: 5080.0
9619567 *VRIT3* -	**SPRING NELSON** **Spring Nelson Shipping Ltd** Dalian Chun An Ship Management Co Ltd *Hong Kong* *Hong Kong* MMSI: 477950800	**7,100** 2,928 8,499	Class: CC	**2011-08 Weihai Donghai Shipyard Co Ltd — Weihai SD** Yd No: HZ-07-07-CCS Loa 112.21 Br ex - Dght 7.600 Lbp 103.00 Br md 19.00 Dpth 11.50 Welded, 1 dk	**(A31A2GX) General Cargo Ship** Grain: 12,741 Compartments: 2 Ho, ER 2 Ha: (25.9 x 14.4)ER (25.2 x 14.4) Cranes: 2x50t Ice Capable	**1 oil engine** driving 1 FP propeller Total Power: 2,648kW (3,600hp) 11.5kn Hanshin LH41LA 1 x 4 Stroke 6 Cy. 410 x 800 2648kW (3600bhp) The Hanshin Diesel Works Ltd-Japan AuxGen: 3 x 350kW 400V a.c
9595400 *3FHP6* -	**SPRING NEXUS** **Primavera Montana SA** Shunzan Kaiun KK (Shunzan Kaiun Co Ltd) *Panama* *Panama* MMSI: 355354000 Official number: 4443312	**106,368** 64,032 206,562	Class: NK	**2012-12 Universal Shipbuilding Corp — Tsu ME** Yd No: 170 Loa 299.70 (BB) Br ex - Dght 18.230 Lbp 291.75 Br md 50.00 Dpth 25.00 Welded, 1 dk	**(A21A2BC) Bulk Carrier** Double Hull Grain: 218,684 Compartments: 9 Ho, ER 9 Ha: ER	**1 oil engine** driving 1 FP propeller Total Power: 16,810kW (22,855hp) 14.0kn MAN-B&W 7S65ME-C 1 x 2 Stroke 7 Cy. 650 x 2730 16810kW (22855bhp) Mitsui Engineering & Shipbuilding CLtd-Japan AuxGen: 3 x 627kW a.c Fuel: 5330.0
9324590 *HOXG* -	**SPRING NOTE** **Shokuyu Navigation Co SA** ST Marine Co Ltd *Panama* *Panama* MMSI: 354718000 Official number: 3052405B	**2,579** 1,133 3,948 T/cm 10.8	Class: NK	**2004-12 Shitanoe Shipbuilding Co Ltd — Usuki OT** Yd No: 1243 Loa 88.60 (BB) Br ex 14.62 Dght 6.009 Lbp 83.00 Br md 14.60 Dpth 7.20 Welded, 1 dk	**(A12B2TR) Chemical/Products Tanker** Double Hull (13F) Liq: 4,071; Liq (Oil): 4,154 Cargo Heating Coils Compartments: 1 Ta, 16 Wing Ta, ER 9 Cargo Pump (s): 9x200m³/hr Manifold: Bow/CM: 44.7m	**1 oil engine** driving 1 FP propeller Total Power: 2,648kW (3,600hp) 13.5kn Akasaka A41S 1 x 4 Stroke 6 Cy. 410 x 800 2648kW (3600bhp) Akasaka Tekkosho KK (Akasaka DieselLtd)-Japan AuxGen: 2 x 350kW 450V 60Hz a.c Thrusters: 1 Tunnel thruster (f) Fuel: 65.0 (d.f.) 229.0 (r.f.)
9304150 *3EJZ5* -	**SPRING PRIDE** **Primavera Montana SA** Shunzan Kaiun KK (Shunzan Kaiun Co Ltd) *Panama* *Panama* MMSI: 372655000 Official number: 3282207A	**58,107** 33,880 106,552 T/cm 97.3	Class: NK	**2007-06 Oshima Shipbuilding Co Ltd — Saikai NS** Yd No: 10431 Loa 255.22 (BB) Br ex - Dght 13.465 Lbp 245.62 Br md 43.00 Dpth 19.39 Welded, 1 dk	**(A21A2BC) Bulk Carrier** Double Hull Grain: 130,679; Bale: 127,298 Compartments: 7 Ho, ER 7 Ha: ER	**1 oil engine** driving 1 FP propeller Total Power: 12,268kW (16,680hp) 14.5kn MAN-B&W 6S60MC 1 x 2 Stroke 6 Cy. 600 x 2292 12268kW (16680bhp) Mitsui Engineering & Shipbuilding CLtd-Japan Fuel: 3610.0
9321897 *C4VG2* -	**SPRING R** *ex* MOL Spring *-2013* *ex* Spring R *-2012* *ex* Nordspring *-2011* **Schifffahrtsgesellschaft ms 'Spring R' mbH & Co KG** Reederei Nord Ltd *Limassol* *Cyprus* MMSI: 210161000	**38,332** 21,924 46,269	Class: GL	**2007-07 STX Shipbuilding Co Ltd — Changwon (Jinhae Shipyard)** Yd No: 1209 Loa 246.86 (BB) Br ex - Dght 12.300 Lbp 232.30 Br md 32.20 Dpth 19.30 Welded, 1 dk	**(A33A2CC) Container Ship (Fully Cellular)** TEU 3586 C Ho 1433 TEU C Dk 2153 TEU incl 500 ref C	**1 oil engine** driving 1 FP propeller Total Power: 32,435kW (44,099hp) 23.4kn MAN-B&W 9K80MC-C 1 x 2 Stroke 9 Cy. 800 x 2300 32435kW (44099bhp) STX Engine Co Ltd-South Korea AuxGen: 4 x 1800kW 450V a.c Thrusters: 1 Tunnel thruster (f)
9217814 *VRCZ6* -	**SPRING RETRIEVER** *ex* Millennium Oak *-2007* **Concept Shipping Ltd** Dalian Chun An Ship Management Co Ltd *Hong Kong* *Hong Kong* MMSI: 477897800 Official number: HK-1940	**4,724** 2,812 7,734	Class: NK	**2000-06 Shin Kochi Jyuko K.K. — Kochi** Yd No: 7128 Loa 99.92 Br ex - Dght 7.241 Lbp 93.00 Br md 19.20 Dpth 8.90 Welded, 1 dk	**(A31A2GX) General Cargo Ship** Grain: 9,806; Bale: 9,200 2 Ha: 2 (25.2 x 10.2) Derricks: 4x25t	**1 oil engine** driving 1 FP propeller Total Power: 3,236kW (4,400hp) 13.3kn B&W 5L35MC 1 x 2 Stroke 5 Cy. 350 x 1050 3236kW (4400bhp) Makita Corp-Japan AuxGen: 2 x 230kW a.c Fuel: 580.0
7216103 *WY5388* -	**SPRING RIVER** *ex* Soring River *-2001* *ex* Nicki Marie Candies *-1997* **Trico Marine Assets Inc** Trico Marine Operators Inc *New Orleans, LA* *United States of America* Official number: 517536	*195* 132 -	Class: (AB)	**1968-11 American Marine Corp. — New Orleans, La** Yd No: 1016 Loa - Br ex - Dght 3.150 Lbp 47.78 Br md 11.59 Dpth 3.81 Welded, 1 dk	**(B21A20S) Platform Supply Ship**	**2 oil engines** reverse reduction geared to sc. shafts driving 2 FP propellers Total Power: 920kW (1,250hp) G.M. (Detroit Diesel) 16V-92 2 x Vee 2 Stroke 16 Cy. 123 x 127 each-460kW (625bhp) (new engine 1982) General Motors Detroit DieselAllison Divn-USA AuxGen: 2 x 75kW Fuel: 107.5 (d.f.)
9156802 *VRGX7* -	**SPRING ROSETTA** *ex* Great Kali *-2010* *ex* Thai Rose *-2009* *ex* Cagayan *-2005* *ex* Celebes *-2001* **Spring Rosetta Shipping Ltd** Dalian Chun An Ship Management Co Ltd *Hong Kong* *Hong Kong* MMSI: 477779900 Official number: HK-2758	**6,264** 3,891 8,668	Class: CC (NK) (IR)	**1997-03 Shin Kurushima Dockyard Co. Ltd. — Hashihama, Imabari** Yd No: 2943 Loa 100.59 (BB) Br ex 18.82 Dght 8.219 Lbp 93.50 Br md 18.80 Dpth 13.00 Welded, 1 dk	**(A31A2GX) General Cargo Ship** Grain: 13,940; Bale: 13,096 Compartments: 4 Ho, ER 4 Ha: 2 (23.9 x 13.0)2 (23.9 x 12.6)ER Cranes: 2x30t; Derricks: 2x25t	**1 oil engine** driving 1 FP propeller Total Power: 3,236kW (4,400hp) 12.4kn B&W 5L35MC 1 x 2 Stroke 5 Cy. 350 x 1050 3236kW (4400bhp) Akasaka Tekkosho KK (Akasaka DieselLtd)-Japan AuxGen: 3 x 840kW a.c Fuel: 650.0
9424235 *3FNG4* -	**SPRING SAMCHEONPO** **Primavera Montana SA** Shunzan Kaiun KK (Shunzan Kaiun Co Ltd) SatCom: Inmarsat C 435373810 *Panama* *Panama* MMSI: 353738000 Official number: 4068509	**64,618** 37,585 119,597	Class: NK	**2009-07 Sanoyas Hishino Meisho Corp — Kurashiki OY** Yd No: 1285 Loa 245.00 (BB) Br ex - Dght 15.404 Lbp 238.00 Br md 43.00 Dpth 21.65 Welded, 1 dk	**(A21A2BC) Bulk Carrier** Grain: 135,683 Compartments: 7 Ho, ER 7 Ha: ER	**1 oil engine** driving 1 FP propeller Total Power: 13,560kW (18,436hp) 14.5kn MAN-B&W 6S60MC-C 1 x 2 Stroke 6 Cy. 600 x 2400 13560kW (18436bhp) Mitsui Engineering & Shipbuilding CLtd-Japan AuxGen: 3 x 480kW 60Hz a.c Fuel: 3484.0
9178094 *VRFV7* -	**SPRING SAPO** *ex* Nozomi *-2009* *ex* Alondra Rainbow *-2000* **Elite Sky Transportation Ltd** Chun An Shipping Ltd *Hong Kong* *Hong Kong* MMSI: 477621600 Official number: HK-2530	**7,762** 2,646 8,913	Class: NK	**1998-05 Shin Kurushima Dockyard Co. Ltd. — Hashihama, Imabari** Yd No: 2968 Loa 113.22 (BB) Br ex - Dght 7.309 Lbp 105.40 Br md 19.60 Dpth 13.20 Welded, 2 dks	**(A31A2GX) General Cargo Ship** Grain: 16,822; Bale: 15,176 Compartments: 2 Ho, ER 2 Ha: (20.3 x 14.8) (33.6 x 14.8)ER Cranes: 2x30t; Derricks: 1x25t	**1 oil engine** driving 1 FP propeller Total Power: 3,884kW (5,281hp) 13.3kn B&W 6L35MC 1 x 2 Stroke 6 Cy. 350 x 1050 3884kW (5281bhp) Makita Corp-Japan Fuel: 780.0
9612375 *VRLV2* -	**SPRING SCENERY** **Spring Scenery Shipping Ltd** China Yantai Shipping Co Ltd *Hong Kong* *Hong Kong* MMSI: 477427700 Official number: HK-3776	**22,648** 11,224 33,847 T/cm 48.5	Class: NV	**2013-04 Jiangsu Yangzijiang Shipbuilding Co Ltd — Jiangyin JS** Yd No: YZJ2010-965 Loa 181.00 (BB) Br ex 30.04 Dght 9.820 Lbp 172.00 Br md 30.00 Dpth 14.60 Welded, 1 dk	**(A21A2BC) Bulk Carrier** Grain: 47,042; Bale: 44,435 Compartments: 5 Ho, ER 5 Ha: 4 (19.2 x 19.2)ER (16.8 x 15.0) Cranes: 4x30t	**1 oil engine** driving 1 FP propeller Total Power: 6,480kW (8,810hp) 13.9kn MAN-B&W 6S42MC 1 x 2 Stroke 6 Cy. 420 x 1764 6480kW (8810bhp) Hudong Heavy Machinery Co Ltd-China AuxGen: 3 x 600kW a.c Fuel: 178.0 (d.f.) 1515.0 (r.f.)

Ship	Tonnage	Class	Builder & dimensions	Type & capacity	Machinery
9619579 **SPRING SHINE** *VRIT2* - **Spring Shine Shipping Ltd** Dalian Chun An Ship Management Co Ltd *Hong Kong* *Hong Kong* MMSI: 477950700 Official number: HK-3141	**7,100** 2,928 8,473	Class: CC	**2011-09 Weihai Donghai Shipyard Co Ltd — Weihai SD** Yd No: DHZ-07-19 Loa 112.21 Br ex - Dght 7.600 Lbp 103.00 Br md 19.00 Dpth 11.50 Welded, 1 dk	**(A31A2GX) General Cargo Ship** Grain: 12,741 Compartments: 2 Ho, ER 2 Ha: (25.9 x 14.4)ER (25.2 x 14.4) Cranes: 2x50t Ice Capable	**1 oil engine** driving 1 FP propeller Total Power: 2,648kW (3,600hp) 11.5kn Hanshin LH41LA 1 x 4 Stroke 6 Cy. 410 x 800 2648kW (3600bhp) The Hanshin Diesel Works Ltd-Japan
9427550 **SPRING SKY** *VRHC7* - **Dynamic Hitter Shipping SA** Cido Shipping (Korea) Co Ltd *Hong Kong* *Hong Kong* MMSI: 477815800 Official number: HK-2798	**25,745** 8,075 9,301	Class: NK	**2010-07 Yamanishi Corp — Ishinomaki MG** Yd No: 1061 Loa 165.00 (BB) Br ex - Dght 7.716 Lbp 154.00 Br md 26.00 Dpth 17.75 Welded	**(A35B2RV) Vehicles Carrier** Side door/ramp (s) Quarter stern door/ramp (s. a.) Cars: 2,520	**1 oil engine** driving 1 FP propeller Total Power: 8,640kW (11,747hp) 17.6kn MAN-B&W 8S42MC 1 x 2 Stroke 8 Cy. 420 x 1764 8640kW (11747bhp) Makita Corp-Japan AuxGen: 3 x 580kW a.c Thrusters: 1 Tunnel thruster (f) Fuel: 1646.0 (r.f.)
9675755 **SPRING SKY** *3EUP6* - **Diamond Camellia SA** - *Panama* MMSI: 370103000 Official number: 45440TJ	**34,764** 20,200 61,413 T/cm 61.4	Class: LR (Class contemplated) **100A1** 01/2014 Class contemplated	**2014-01 Shin Kasado Dockyard Co Ltd — Kudamatsu YC** Yd No: K-053 Loa 199.90 (BB) Br ex - Dght 13.000 Lbp - Br md 32.24 Dpth 18.60 Welded, 1 dk	**(A21A2BC) Bulk Carrier** Grain: 77,674; Bale: 73,552 Compartments: 5 Ho, ER 5 Ha: 4 (23.5 x 19.0)ER (18.7 x 19.0) Cranes: 4x30.7t	**1 oil engine** driving 1 FP propeller Total Power: 9,960kW (13,542hp) 14.5kn MAN-B&W 6S50MC-C8 1 x 2 Stroke 6 Cy. 500 x 2000 9960kW (13542bhp) Hitachi Zosen Corp-Japan AuxGen: 3 x 490kW a.c Fuel: 2565.0
9394507 **SPRING SPLENDOR** *VRHS8* - **Spring Splendor Co Ltd** Big Horizon Shipping Agencies Ltd SatCom: Inmarsat C 447703070 *Hong Kong* *Hong Kong* MMSI: 477986700 Official number: HK-2928	**156,651** 98,944 296,908 T/cm 177.4	Class: AB	**2011-01 Shanghai Jiangnan Changxing Shipbuilding Co Ltd — Shanghai** Yd No: H2421 Loa 330.00 (BB) Br ex 60.04 Dght 21.500 Lbp 316.00 Br md 60.00 Dpth 29.70 Welded, 1 dk	**(A13A2TV) Crude Oil Tanker** Double Hull (13F) Liq: 324,800; Liq (Oil): 324,800 Compartments: 5 Ta, 10 Wing Ta, ER, 2 Wing Slop Ta 3 Cargo Pump (s): 3x5500m³/hr Manifold: Bow/CM: 162m	**1 oil engine** driving 1 FP propeller Total Power: 25,480kW (34,643hp) 15.8kn MAN-B&W 7S80MC 1 x 2 Stroke 7 Cy. 800 x 3056 25480kW (34643bhp) CSSC MES Diesel Co Ltd-China AuxGen: 3 x 1050kW a.c Fuel: 430.0 (d.f.) 7200.0 (r.f.)
9628037 **SPRING SUNRISE** *VRLD4* - **Spring Sunrise Shipping Ltd** Jiangsu Steamship Co Ltd *Hong Kong* *Hong Kong* MMSI: 477464700 Official number: HK-3634	**29,304** 15,757 46,947	Class: LR ✠ **100A1** SS 01/2013 bulk carrier CSR BC-A GRAB (20) Nos. 2 & 4 holds may be empty ESP **ShipRight** ACS (B) *IWS LI ✠ **LMC** **UMS** Eq.Ltr: M†; Cable: 632.5/73.0 U3 (a)	**2013-01 Jiangsu Yangzi Changbo Shipbuilding Co Ltd — Jingjiang JS** Yd No: YZJ2010-962 Loa 189.99 (BB) Br ex 32.30 Dght 10.500 Lbp 185.00 Br md 32.26 Dpth 15.50 Welded, 1 dk	**(A21A2BC) Bulk Carrier** Grain: 59,000 Compartments: 5 Ho, ER 5 Ha: ER Cranes: 4x30t	**1 oil engine** driving 1 FP propeller Total Power: 8,280kW (11,257hp) 14.3kn MAN-B&W 6S46MC-C8 1 x 2 Stroke 6 Cy. 460 x 1932 8280kW (11257bhp) Dalian Marine Diesel Co Ltd-China AuxGen: 3 x 675kW 400V 50Hz a.c Boilers: e (ex.g.) 9.2kgf/cm² (9.0bar), AuxB (Comp) 9.2kgf/cm² (9.0bar)
9628049 **SPRING SUNSHINE** *VRLR6* - **Hua Yang International Marine Transportation Co Ltd** Jiangsu Huaxi Ship Management Co Ltd *Hong Kong* *Hong Kong* MMSI: 477250800 Official number: HK-3748	**29,304** 15,755 46,947	Class: LR ✠ **100A1** SS 03/2013 bulk carrier CSR BC-A GRAB (20) Nos. 2 & 4 holds may be empty ESP **ShipRight** ACS (B) *IWS LI ✠ **LMC** **UMS** Eq.Ltr: M†; Cable: 632.5/73.0 U3 (a)	**2013-03 Jiangsu Yangzi Changbo Shipbuilding Co Ltd — Jingjiang JS** Yd No: YZJ2010-963 Loa 189.99 (BB) Br ex 32.30 Dght 10.900 Lbp 185.00 Br md 32.26 Dpth 15.50 Welded, 1 dk	**(A21A2BC) Bulk Carrier** Grain: 59,000 Compartments: 5 Ho, ER 5 Ha: 4 (21.3 x 18.3)ER (18.7 x 18.3) Cranes: 4x30t	**1 oil engine** driving 1 FP propeller Total Power: 8,280kW (11,257hp) 14.3kn MAN-B&W 6S46MC-C8 1 x 2 Stroke 6 Cy. 460 x 1932 8280kW (11257bhp) Dalian Marine Diesel Co Ltd-China AuxGen: 2 x 780kW 400V 50Hz a.c, 1 x 640kW 400V 50Hz a.c Boilers: e (ex.g.) 7.3kgf/cm² (7.2bar), AuxB (Comp) 7.7kgf/cm² (7.6bar)
9374143 **SPRING SWEETBRIER** *3EXR4* - **Primavera Montana SA** Shunzan Kaiun KK (Shunzan Kaiun Co Ltd) SatCom: Inmarsat C 435448411 *Panama* *Panama* MMSI: 354484000 Official number: 38995KJ	**113,932** 43,997 228,531	Class: NK	**2009-06 Namura Shipbuilding Co Ltd — Imari SG** Yd No: 281 Loa 319.58 (BB) Br ex - Dght 18.127 Lbp 308.00 Br md 54.00 Dpth 24.30 Welded, 1 dk	**(A21B2BO) Ore Carrier** Grain: 146,938 Compartments: 9 Ho, ER 9 Ha: ER	**1 oil engine** driving 1 FP propeller Total Power: 22,432kW (30,499hp) 15.1kn Mitsubishi 6UEC85LSII 1 x 2 Stroke 6 Cy. 850 x 3150 22432kW (30499bhp) Mitsubishi Heavy Industries Ltd-Japan AuxGen: 3 x 640kW 60Hz a.c Fuel: 7050.0
9490117 **SPRING WARBLER** *3EYE8* - **Majuro Ship Finance Co** Daiichi Chuo Marine Co Ltd (DC Marine) *Panama* *Panama* MMSI: 373066000 Official number: 4373012	**41,799** 25,953 78,400	Class: NK	**2012-03 Sanoyas Shipbuilding Corp — Kurashiki OY** Yd No: 1303 Loa 225.00 (BB) Br ex - Dght 14.435 Lbp 220.00 Br md 32.24 Dpth 19.90 Welded, 1 dk	**(A21A2BC) Bulk Carrier** Grain: 91,144 Compartments: 7 Ho, ER 7 Ha: ER	**1 oil engine** driving 1 FP propeller Total Power: 9,560kW (12,998hp) 14.5kn MAN-B&W 7S50MC-C 1 x 2 Stroke 7 Cy. 500 x 2000 9560kW (12998bhp) Mitsui Engineering & Shipbuilding CLtd-Japan Fuel: 2770.0
9603518 **SPRING WEALTH** *VRJE9* - **Spring Wealth Shipping Ltd** Jiangsu Steamship Co Ltd SatCom: Inmarsat C 447798864 *Hong Kong* *Hong Kong* MMSI: 477346200 Official number: HK-3229	**51,265** 31,203 93,347 T/cm 80.9	Class: AB	**2011-10 Jiangsu Newyangzi Shipbuilding Co Ltd — Jingjiang JS** Yd No: YZJ2006-930 Loa 229.20 (BB) Br ex 38.04 Dght 14.900 Lbp 222.00 Br md 38.00 Dpth 20.70 Welded, 1 dk	**(A21A2BC) Bulk Carrier** Grain: 110,330 Compartments: 7 Ho, ER 7 Ha: ER	**1 oil engine** driving 1 FP propeller Total Power: 11,800kW (16,043hp) 14.1kn MAN-B&W 6S60MC-C 1 x 2 Stroke 6 Cy. 600 x 2400 11800kW (16043bhp) STX Engine Co Ltd-South Korea AuxGen: 3 x 730kW a.c Fuel: 233.0 (d.f.) 3598.0 (r.f.)
9427562 **SPRING WIND** *VRHO3* - **Dynamic Boxer Shipping SA** Cido Shipping (Korea) Co Ltd *Hong Kong* *Hong Kong* MMSI: 477961300 Official number: HK-2891	**25,745** 8,075 9,274	Class: NK	**2010-10 Yamanishi Corp — Ishinomaki MG** Yd No: 1062 Loa 165.03 (BB) Br ex - Dght 7.720 Lbp 154.00 Br md 26.00 Dpth 11.65 Welded	**(A35B2RV) Vehicles Carrier** Side door/ramp (s) Quarter stern door/ramp (s. a.) Cars: 2,520	**1 oil engine** driving 1 FP propeller Total Power: 8,640kW (11,747hp) 17.6kn MAN-B&W 8S42MC 1 x 2 Stroke 8 Cy. 420 x 1764 8640kW (11747bhp) Makita Corp-Japan AuxGen: 3 x 580kW a.c Thrusters: 1 Tunnel thruster (f) Fuel: 1646.0 (r.f.)
9446453 **SPRING ZEPHYR** *3FLH2* - **Primavera Montana SA** Shunzan Kaiun KK (Shunzan Kaiun Co Ltd) SatCom: Inmarsat C 437100110 *Panama* *Panama* MMSI: 371001000 Official number: 4199210	**92,756** 60,504 181,725 T/cm 125.0	Class: NK	**2010-09 Imabari Shipbuilding Co Ltd — Saijo EH (Saijo Shipyard)** Yd No: 8090 Loa 291.98 (BB) Br ex - Dght 18.235 Lbp 283.80 Br md 45.00 Dpth 24.70 Welded, 1 dk	**(A21A2BC) Bulk Carrier** Grain: 201,243 Compartments: 9 Ho, ER 9 Ha: ER	**1 oil engine** driving 1 FP propeller Total Power: 18,660kW (25,370hp) 14.0kn MAN-B&W 6S70MC-C 1 x 2 Stroke 6 Cy. 700 x 2800 18660kW (25370bhp) Mitsui Engineering & Shipbuilding CLtd-Japan Fuel: 5839.0 (r.f.)
8219009 **SPRINGTIDE** - - - -	*105* 72 -		**1982 Steiner Shipyard, Inc. — Bayou La Batre, Al** Yd No: 138 Loa 22.81 Br ex - Dght 2.401 Lbp 20.12 Br md 6.71 Dpth 3.36 Welded, 1 dk	**(B11A2FT) Trawler**	**1 oil engine** geared to sc. shaft driving 1 FP propeller Total Power: 268kW (364hp) Cummins KT-1150-M 1 x 4 Stroke 6 Cy. 159 x 159 268kW (364bhp) Cummins Engine Co Inc-USA
5429081 **SPRINT** *ERAH* - *ex* Spring 3 *-2007* *ex* Chelsea Jean *-2004* *ex* Jason Cape *-1997* *ex* Calypso I *-1988* *ex* Calypso *-1984* *ex* Swazi *-1982* *ex* Swazi Coast *-1967* **New Horizon Trade Ltd** - *Chisinau* *Moldova* MMSI: 214180108	**922** 277 1,239	Class: (LR) ✠ Classed LR until 16/10/96	**1963-12 Clelands Shipbuilding Co. Ltd. — Wallsend** Yd No: 269 Converted From: General Cargo/Tanker-1984 Lengthened-1971 Loa 60.84 Br ex 11.23 Dght 4.236 Lbp 56.90 Br md 11.13 Dpth 4.73 Welded, 1 dk	**(B33A2DS) Suction Dredger** Hopper: 800	**2 oil engines** driving 2 FP propellers Total Power: 706kW (960hp) 10.0kn Polar M46I 2 x 2 Stroke 6 Cy. 250 x 420 each-353kW (480bhp) British Polar Engines Ltd.-Glasgow Thrusters: 1 Water jet (f) Fuel: 43.5

IMO / Call sign	Name / Owner / Manager / Registry	Tonnage	Classification	Builder / Dimensions	Type / Cargo	Machinery
9423657 *PHOL* -	**SPRINTER** - **Sprinter Shipping CV** - *Werkendam* *Netherlands* MMSI: 245176000 Official number: 51678	**2,528** 1,053 3,610	Class: NV (LR) ✠ Classed LR until 20/10/11	**2008-04 Leda doo — Korcula** (Hull) **2008-04 Scheepswerf Peters B.V. — Kampen** Yd No: 1209 Loa 89.99 (BB) Br ex 12.58 Dght 5.250 Lbp 84.95 Br md 12.50 Dpth 8.00 Welded, 1 dk	**(A31A2GX) General Cargo Ship** Grain: 4,927 TEU 157 C Ho 105 TEU C Dk 52 TEU Compartments: 1 Ho, ER 1 Ha: ER Ice Capable	**1 oil engine** with clutches, flexible couplings & sr geared to sc. shaft driving 1 CP propeller Total Power: 1,800kW (2,447hp) 13.0kn Wartsila 9L20 1 x 4 Stroke 9 Cy. 200 x 280 1800kW (2447bhp) Wartsila Finland Oy-Finland AuxGen: 1 x 250kW 400V 50Hz a.c, 1 x a.c Thrusters: 1 Thwart. FP thruster (f)
9417763 *A8QJ4* -	**SPRUCE 2** *ex Louise -2012* **Flame Enterprises SA** Cyprus Sea Lines Co Ltd *Monrovia* *Liberia* MMSI: 636013940 Official number: 13940	**42,010** 22,359 73,747 T/cm 67.1	Class: RI (AB)	**2008-11 New Times Shipbuilding Co Ltd — Jingjiang JS** Yd No: 0307356 Loa 228.60 (BB) Br ex - Dght 14.498 Lbp 219.70 Br md 32.26 Dpth 20.80 Welded, 1 dk	**(A13B2TP) Products Tanker** Double Hull (13F) Liq: 81,278; Liq (Oil): 81,278 Cargo Heating Coils Compartments: 12 Wing Ta, 2 Wing Slop Ta, ER 3 Cargo Pump (s): 3x2300m³/hr Manifold: Bow/CM: 112.3m	**1 oil engine** driving 1 FP propeller Total Power: 11,300kW (15,363hp) 14.5kn MAN-B&W 5S60MC-C 1 x 2 Stroke 5 Cy. 600 x 2400 11300kW (15363bhp) Hudong Heavy Machinery Co Ltd-China AuxGen: 3 x 900kW a.c Fuel: 210.0 (d.f.) 1928.0 (r.f.)
9232814 *C6SD9* -	**SPRUCE ARROW** - **Gearbulk Shipowning Ltd** Gearbulk Ltd *Nassau* *Bahamas* MMSI: 311288000 Official number: 8000398	**32,458** 15,387 47,792 T/cm 52.8	Class: NV	**2002-01 Stocznia Gdanska - Grupa Stoczni Gdynia SA — Gdansk** Yd No: 6684/22 Loa 189.79 (BB) Br ex 31.03 Dght 12.800 Lbp 181.83 Br md 30.99 Dpth 18.50 Welded, 1 dk	**(A31A2GO) Open Hatch Cargo Ship** Grain: 62,400 TEU 1550 Compartments: 7 Ho, ER 7 Ha: (13.0 x 23.0)6 (18.0 x 26.0)ER Cranes: 4x36t	**1 oil engine** driving 1 FP propeller Total Power: 9,023kW (12,268hp) 14.2kn B&W 5S60MC 1 x 2 Stroke 5 Cy. 600 x 2292 9023kW (12268bhp) H Cegielski Poznan SA-Poland
9308235 *9V2155* -	**SPRUCE GALAXY** - **Abo Singapore Pte Ltd** Unix Line Pte Ltd *Singapore* *Singapore* MMSI: 563626000 Official number: 398681	**12,105** 6,405 19,995 T/cm 30.3	Class: NK	**2006-12 Shin Kurushima Dockyard Co. Ltd. — Akitsu** Yd No: 5338 Loa 147.83 (BB) Br ex 24.23 Dght 9.446 Lbp 141.00 Br md 24.20 Dpth 12.85 Welded, 1 dk	**(A12B2TR) Chemical/Products Tanker** Double Hull (13F) Liq: 20,878; Liq (Oil): 20,877 Cargo Heating Coils Compartments: 20 Wing Ta (s.stl), 2 Wing Slop Ta (s.stl), ER 20 Cargo Pump (s): 6x200m³/hr, 14x300m³/hr Manifold: Bow/CM: 76.6m	**1 oil engine** driving 1 FP propeller Total Power: 6,230kW (8,470hp) 15.0kn Mitsubishi 7UEC45LA 1 x 2 Stroke 7 Cy. 450 x 1350 6230kW (8470bhp) Kobe Hatsudoki KK-Japan AuxGen: 3 x 460kW 450V 60Hz a.c Thrusters: 1 Tunnel thruster (f) Fuel: 78.0 (d.f.) 1016.0 (r.f.)
8119261 *VOSL* -	**SPRUCEGLEN** *ex Fraser -2002 ex Federal Fraser -2001* *ex Federal St. Louis -1991* *ex Selkirk Settler -1991* **The CSL Group Inc (Canada Steamship Lines)** CSL Americas *Montreal, QC* *Canada* MMSI: 316001844 Official number: 802345	**22,388** 11,648 36,251 T/cm 47.2	Class: LR (AB) ✠ **100A1** Lake SS 01/2012 Great Lakes and River St. Lawrence, also Strait of Belle Isle south of 52N latitude and coastal service south from St. John's Newfoundland to the eastern seaboard of Canada ✠ **LMC** Eq.Ltr: I†; Cable: U3 (a)	**1983-04 Govan Shipbuilders Ltd — Glasgow** Yd No: 256 Loa 222.54 (BB) Br ex 23.17 Dght 9.941 Lbp 216.92 Br md 23.08 Dpth 14.64 Welded, 1 dk	**(A21A2BC) Bulk Carrier** Grain: 47,013; Bale: 46,366 Compartments: 7 Ho, ER 7 Ha: (19.4 x 13.2) (12.7 x 13.2)3 (25.5 x 13.2)2 (12.6 x 13.2)ER Ice Capable	**1 oil engine** driving 1 CP propeller Total Power: 8,002kW (10,880hp) 12.0kn Sulzer 4RLB76 1 x 2 Stroke 4 Cy. 760 x 1600 8002kW (10880bhp) Clark Hawthorn Ltd.-Newcastle AuxGen: 3 x 525kW 440V 60Hz a.c Boilers: AuxB (o.f.) 6.9kgf/cm² (6.8bar), AuxB (ex.g.) 6.9kgf/cm² (6.8bar) Thrusters: 1 Thwart. CP thruster (f) Fuel: 124.0 (d.f.) 1315.5 (r.f.) 27.0pd
9353034 - -	**SPRUT** - **Coast Guard RF** - *Russia*	**1,300** - 134		**2009-05 AO Pribaltiyskiy Sudostroitelnyy Zavod "Yantar" — Kaliningrad** Yd No: 511 Loa 65.90 Br ex - Dght 3.480 Lbp 60.20 Br md 10.60 Dpth 5.50 Welded, 1 dk	**(B34H2SQ) Patrol Vessel**	**1 oil engine** driving 1 Propeller M.T.U. 1 x 4 Stroke
7814400 *5NRQ8* -	**SPSL CLARA** *ex Clara -2002 ex Oil Maintainer -1992* **Adamac Marine Services Ltd (Adamac Group)** - *Lagos* *Nigeria*	**869** 260 823	Class: IS (BV) (AB)	**1979-04 Singapore Slipway & Engineering Co. Pte Ltd — Singapore** Yd No: 138 Loa 55.22 Br ex - Dght 3.350 Lbp 49.87 Br md 12.21 Dpth 4.35 Welded, 1 dk	**(B22A2OR) Offshore Support Vessel** Cranes: 1x15t	**2 oil engines** reverse reduction geared to sc. shafts driving 2 FP propellers Total Power: 1,604kW (2,180hp) 10.5kn Caterpillar D399TA 2 x Vee 4 Stroke 16 Cy. 159 x 203 each-802kW (1090bhp) Caterpillar Tractor Co-USA AuxGen: 3 x 250kW 440V a.c, 1 x 75kW a.c Thrusters: 1 Thwart. FP thruster (f)
8828147 *5NUH4* -	**SPSL DARNELL SERVICE** *ex Darnell Tide -2011* **Adamac Industries Ltd** Adamac Marine Services Ltd (Adamac Group) *Lagos* *Nigeria*	**106** 31 -	Class: IS (AB) (BV)	**1989 B.V. Scheepswerf Damen — Gorinchem** Yd No: 2647 Loa 26.65 Br ex - Dght 2.000 Lbp 25.40 Br md 5.90 Dpth 3.35 Welded, 1 dk	**(B34L2QU) Utility Vessel**	**2 oil engines** geared to sc. shafts driving 2 FP propellers Total Power: 2,156kW (2,932hp) 15.9kn Caterpillar 3512TA 2 x Vee 4 Stroke 12 Cy. 170 x 190 each-1078kW (1466bhp) Caterpillar Inc-USA AuxGen: 2 x 64kW 220V 60Hz a.c Fuel: 14.7 (d.f.)
7435589 *HQWY4* -	**SPSL EARL** *ex Anglian Earl -2002 ex Union Three -1994* **SPSL Earl Nevis Inc** Adamac Marine Services Ltd (Adamac Group) *San Lorenzo* *Honduras* MMSI: 334559000 Official number: L-1528220	**763** 228 498	Class: (LR) (BV) Classed LR until 27/10/04	**1977-03 Beliard-Murdoch S.A. — Oostende** Yd No: 228 Loa 45.62 Br ex - Dght 4.701 Lbp 41.69 Br md 11.51 Dpth 6.13 Welded, 1 dk	**(B21B20A) Anchor Handling Tug Supply**	**2 oil engines** reverse reduction geared to sc. shafts driving 2 FP propellers Total Power: 4,118kW (5,598hp) 13.5kn EMD (Electro-Motive) 16-645-E5 2 x Vee 2 Stroke 16 Cy. 230 x 254 each-2059kW (2799bhp) General Motors Corp-USA AuxGen: 2 x 216kW 220/440V 60Hz a.c Thrusters: 1 Thwart. FP thruster (f) Fuel: 559.0 (d.f.)
8868575 - -	**SPSL GAZELLE** *ex Lamnalco Gazelle -2013* **Adamac Marine Services Ltd (Adamac Group)** - *Lagos* *Nigeria*	**135** 40 -	Class: BV	**1992-01 Gulf Craft Inc — Patterson LA** Yd No: 373 Loa 30.48 Br ex - Dght 1.830 Lbp 27.99 Br md 7.01 Dpth 2.92 Welded, 1 dk	**(B21A20S) Platform Supply Ship**	**2 oil engines** reduction geared to sc. shafts driving 2 FP propellers Total Power: 1,124kW (1,528hp) 20.0kn Caterpillar 3412TA 2 x Vee 4 Stroke 12 Cy. 137 x 152 each-562kW (764bhp) Caterpillar Inc-USA AuxGen: 2 x 40kW 220V 50Hz a.c Fuel: 17.0 (d.f.)
8868563 - -	**SPSL IMPALA** *ex Lamnalco Impala -2013* **Adamac Marine Services Ltd (Adamac Group)** - *Lagos* *Nigeria*	**135** 40 -	Class: BV (AB)	**1992 Gulf Craft Inc — Patterson LA** Yd No: 374 Loa 30.48 Br ex - Dght 1.830 Lbp 27.99 Br md 7.01 Dpth 2.92 Welded, 1 dk	**(B21A20S) Platform Supply Ship**	**2 oil engines** reduction geared to sc. shafts driving 2 FP propellers Total Power: 1,124kW (1,528hp) 20.0kn Caterpillar 3412TA 2 x Vee 4 Stroke 12 Cy. 137 x 152 each-562kW (764bhp) Caterpillar Inc-USA AuxGen: 2 x 40kW 220V 50Hz a.c Fuel: 17.0 (d.f.)
7827263 *ELXO8* -	**SPSL KRANTOR** *ex Krantor -2000* **SPSL Krantor Liberia Inc** Adamac Marine Services Ltd (Adamac Group) SatCom: Inmarsat C 463674280 *Monrovia* *Liberia* MMSI: 636011214 Official number: 11214	**847** 255 700	Class: (GL) (AB)	**1979-08 Sing Koon Seng Pte Ltd — Singapore** Yd No: SKS489 Loa 51.01 Br ex 13.62 Dght 3.544 Lbp 44.96 Br md 13.50 Dpth 4.02 Welded, 1 dk	**(B34P2QV) Salvage Ship** Cranes: 1x100t	**2 oil engines** reverse reduction geared to sc. shafts driving 2 Directional propellers Total Power: 892kW (1,212hp) 10.5kn M.T.U. 8V396TC62 2 x Vee 4 Stroke 8 Cy. 165 x 185 each-446kW (606bhp) MTU Friedrichshafen GmbH-Friedrichshafen AuxGen: 3 x 400kW a.c, 1 x 92kW a.c Thrusters: 1 Thwart. FP thruster (f)
7209332 *HP9518* -	**SPSL MASTER** *ex Dea Master -2000 ex Independent I -1999* *ex Yelcho -1999 ex Smit-Kaylen J -1996* *ex Smit-Lloyd 5 -1995* *ex Smit-Lloyd Matsas 5 -1995* *ex Smit-Lloyd 43 -1986* **SPSL Master Liberia Inc** Adamac Marine Services Ltd (Adamac Group) *Panama* *Panama* MMSI: 357724000 Official number: 27911PEXT5	**836** 250 865	Class: (AB) (HR)	**1972 N.V. Scheepswerven v/h H.H. Bodewes — Millingen a/d Rijn** Yd No: 697 Loa 53.14 Br ex 12.30 Dght 4.439 Lbp 49.31 Br md 12.03 Dpth 4.96 Welded, 1 dk	**(B21B20A) Anchor Handling Tug Supply** Passengers: berths: 12	**2 oil engines** driving 2 CP propellers Total Power: 2,060kW (2,800hp) 13.0kn De Industrie 8D7HD 2 x 4 Stroke 8 Cy. 305 x 460 each-1030kW (1400bhp) NV Motorenfabriek 'De Industrie'-Netherlands AuxGen: 2 x 135kW 220V d.c Thrusters: 1 Thwart. FP thruster (f) Fuel: 274.5 (d.f.)

IMO / Call sign	Name / Owner	Tonnage	Class	Builder / Dimensions	Type	Machinery
7230460 *5NSW3* -	**SPSL SARAH SERVICE** *ex* Shetland Service *-2006* *ex* Shetland Shore *-1980* **Adamac Marine Services Ltd (Adamac Group)** - *Lagos* *Nigeria* MMSI: 657545000	**965** 289 831	Class: IS (LR) ✠ Classed LR until 7/2/07	**1973-01 Richards (Shipbuilders) Ltd — Lowestoft** Yd No: 508 Converted From: Offshore Tug/Supply Ship-1978 Lengthened-1978 Loa 60.05 Br ex 11.92 Dght 4.449 Lbp 54.26 Br md 11.43 Dpth 4.96 Welded, 1 dk	**(B22G20Y) Standby Safety Vessel** Ice Capable	**2 oil engines** reverse reduction geared to sc. shafts driving 2 FP propellers Total Power: 2,942kW (4,000hp) 14.0kn Blackstone ESL16MK2 2 x Vee 4 Stroke 16 Cy. 222 x 292 each-1471kW (2000bhp) Mirrlees Blackstone (Stamford)Ltd.-Stamford AuxGen: 2 x 320kW 440V 60Hz a.c, 1 x 110kW 440V 60Hz a.c Thrusters: 1 Thwart. CP thruster (f); 1 Water jet (f); 1 Tunnel thruster (a)
8200931 *5NUH3* -	**SPSL TIGER SERVICE** *ex* Oil Tiger *-2011* **Adamac Industries Ltd** Adamac Marine Services Ltd (Adamac Group) *Lagos* *Nigeria*	**1,063** 319 1,259	Class: IS (LR) (GL) ✠ Classed LR until 15/12/93	**1983-02 Singapore Slipway & Engineering Co. Pte Ltd — Singapore** Yd No: 158 Loa 58.98 Br ex 13.44 Dght 4.252 Lbp 53.01 Br md 13.20 Dpth 5.01 Welded, 1 dk	**(B21B20A) Anchor Handling Tug Supply**	**2 oil engines** with clutches, flexible couplings & sr reverse geared to sc. shafts driving 2 FP propellers Total Power: 3,538kW (4,810hp) 12.0kn Wartsila 12V22 2 x Vee 4 Stroke 12 Cy. 220 x 240 each-1769kW (2405bhp) Oy Wartsila Ab-Finland AuxGen: 3 x 155kW 440V 60Hz a.c Thrusters: 1 Thwart. FP thruster (f)
8017449 *5NSW2* -	**SPSL VICTORIA SERVICE** *ex* Atlas Service *-2011* *ex* Gulf Fleet No. 42 *-1986* **Adamac Marine Services Ltd (Adamac Group)** - *Lagos* *Nigeria*	**711** 213 1,200	Class: IS (AB) (RI)	**1980-09 Quality Equipment Inc — Houma LA** Yd No: 162 Loa 57.91 Br ex - Dght 3.664 Lbp 51.44 Br md 12.20 Dpth 4.27 Welded, 1 dk	**(B21B20A) Anchor Handling Tug Supply**	**2 oil engines** reverse reduction geared to sc. shafts driving 2 FP propellers Total Power: 2,868kW (3,900hp) 13.0kn EMD (Electro-Motive) 16-567-BC 2 x Vee 2 Stroke 16 Cy. 216 x 254 each-1434kW (1950bhp) (Reconditioned , Reconditioned & fitted 1980) General Motors Corp.Electro-Motive Div.-La Grange AuxGen: 1 x 198kW 220/440V 60Hz a.c, 1 x 110kW 220/440V 60Hz a.c Thrusters: 1 Thwart. FP thruster (f) Fuel: 310.0 (d.f.) 14.0pd
8032712 *YB4564* -	**SPT** *ex* San No. 1 *-2009* *ex* Toei Maru No. 3 *-2006* **PT Bahana Line** - *Tanjung Priok* *Indonesia*	**160** 48 220	Class: KI	**1980-09 Tokuoka Zosen K.K. — Naruto** Yd No: 65 Loa 33.65 Br ex - Dght 2.300 Lbp 29.90 Br md 6.50 Dpth 2.80 Welded, 1 dk	**(A13B2TU) Tanker (unspecified)**	**1 oil engine** driving 1 FP propeller Total Power: 221kW (300hp) Matsui 1 x 4 Stroke 6 Cy. 200 x 240 221kW (300bhp) Matsui Iron Works Co Ltd-Japan
9336402 *C6WG9* -	**SPT CHALLENGER** **Grimstad Shipping Co Ltd** Bergshav Management AS *Nassau* *Bahamas* MMSI: 309518000 Official number: 8001384	**57,657** 32,116 105,786 T/cm 91.5	Class: NV	**2007-06 Tsuneishi Holdings Corp Tsuneishi Shipbuilding Co — Tadotsu KG** Yd No: 1325 Loa 240.50 (BB) Br ex 42.00 Dght 14.887 Lbp 230.01 Br md 41.99 Dpth 21.20 Welded, 1 dk	**(A13A2TV) Crude Oil Tanker** Double Hull (13F) Liq: 114,413; Liq (Oil): 114,413 Cargo Heating Coils Compartments: 12 Wing Ta, 2 Wing Slop Ta, ER 3 Cargo Pump (s): 3x2500m^3/hr Manifold: Bow/CM: 123.2m	**1 oil engine** driving 1 FP propeller Total Power: 10,599kW (14,410hp) 15.0kn MAN-B&W 6S60ME-C 1 x 2 Stroke 6 Cy. 600 x 2400 10599kW (14410bhp) Mitsui Engineering & Shipbuilding CLtd-Japan AuxGen: 3 x a.c Thrusters: 1 Tunnel thruster (f) Fuel: 195.2 (d.f.) 2437.6 (r.f.)
9336397 *C6WD3* -	**SPT CHAMPION** **Lillesand Shipping Co Ltd** Bergshav Management AS *Nassau* *Bahamas* MMSI: 309987000 Official number: 8001356	**57,657** 32,116 105,786 T/cm 91.5	Class: NV	**2007-05 Tsuneishi Holdings Corp Tsuneishi Shipbuilding Co — Tadotsu KG** Yd No: 1324 Loa 240.50 (BB) Br ex 42.00 Dght 14.878 Lbp 230.02 Br md 41.99 Dpth 21.20 Welded, 1 dk	**(A13A2TV) Crude Oil Tanker** Double Hull (13F) Liq: 114,413; Liq (Oil): 114,413 Cargo Heating Coils Compartments: 12 Wing Ta, 2 Wing Slop Ta, ER 3 Cargo Pump (s): 3x2500m^3/hr Manifold: Bow/CM: 123.2m	**1 oil engine** driving 1 FP propeller Total Power: 10,599kW (14,410hp) 15.0kn MAN-B&W 6S60ME-C 1 x 2 Stroke 6 Cy. 600 x 2400 10599kW (14410bhp) Mitsui Engineering & Shipbuilding CLtd-Japan AuxGen: 3 x a.c Thrusters: 1 Tunnel thruster (f) Fuel: 195.2 (d.f.) 2437.6 (r.f.)
7707279 *WDC6636* -	**SPT DEFENDER** *ex* Gulf Defender *-2004* *ex* Biscay Seahorse *-1991* **SPT Offshore LLC** SPT Inc (Skaugen PetroTrans) *Houston, TX* *United States of America* MMSI: 367058843 Official number: 580255	**660** 198 658	Class: AB	**1977-03 Halter Marine, Inc. — Moss Point, Ms** Yd No: 571 Loa 56.39 Br ex - Dght 3.664 Lbp 49.92 Br md 12.20 Dpth 4.27 Welded, 1 dk	**(B21A20S) Platform Supply Ship**	**2 oil engines** reverse reduction geared to sc. shafts driving 2 FP propellers Total Power: 1,654kW (2,248hp) 12.0kn Caterpillar D399SCAC 2 x Vee 4 Stroke 16 Cy. 159 x 203 each-827kW (1124bhp) Caterpillar Tractor Co-USA AuxGen: 2 x 98kW Thrusters: 1 Thwart. FP thruster (f)
9313486 *C6WL3* -	**SPT EXPLORER** **SPT Explorer LLC** Teekay Marine (Glasgow) Ltd *Nassau* *Bahamas* MMSI: 308109000 Official number: 9000243	**57,657** 32,116 105,804 T/cm 91.6	Class: NV	**2008-01 Tsuneishi Holdings Corp Tsuneishi Shipbuilding Co — Tadotsu KG** Yd No: 1328 Loa 240.50 (BB) Br ex 42.03 Dght 14.878 Lbp 230.00 Br md 42.00 Dpth 21.20 Welded, 1 dk	**(A13A2TV) Crude Oil Tanker** Double Hull (13F) Liq: 114,412; Liq (Oil): 118,580 Cargo Heating Coils Compartments: 12 Wing Ta, 2 Wing Slop Ta, ER 3 Cargo Pump (s): 3x2500m^3/hr Manifold: Bow/CM: 123m	**1 oil engine** driving 1 FP propeller Total Power: 13,369kW (18,176hp) 15.0kn MAN-B&W 6S60ME-C 1 x 2 Stroke 6 Cy. 600 x 2400 13369kW (18176bhp) Mitsui Engineering & Shipbuilding CLtd-Japan AuxGen: 3 x a.c Thrusters: 1 Tunnel thruster (f) Fuel: 169.2 (d.f.) 2333.2 (r.f.)
8016419 *V7UJ7* -	**SPT GUARDIAN** *ex* Gulf Guardian *-2004* *ex* H. O. S. Fighting Fox *-1991* *ex* Tom Martin Pugh *-1982* **SPT Guardian Inc** SPT Inc (Skaugen PetroTrans) *Majuro* *Marshall Islands* MMSI: 538003963 Official number: 3963	**626** 188 1,000	Class: AB	**1980-09 RYSCO Shipyard Inc. — Blountstown, Fl** Yd No: 47 Loa - Br ex - Dght 3.682 Lbp 53.35 Br md 11.59 Dpth 4.27 Welded, 1 dk	**(B21A20S) Platform Supply Ship**	**2 oil engines** reverse reduction geared to sc. shafts driving 2 FP propellers Total Power: 1,654kW (2,248hp) 12.0kn Caterpillar D399SCAC 2 x Vee 4 Stroke 16 Cy. 159 x 203 each-827kW (1124bhp) Caterpillar Tractor Co-USA AuxGen: 2 x 99kW Thrusters: 1 Thwart. FP thruster (f)
8603652 *YB4595* -	**SPT II** *ex* Man No. 1 *-2008* *ex* Kiku Maru No. 3 *-2007* **PT Indoline Incomekita** - *Tanjung Priok* *Indonesia*	**288** 97 441	Class: KI	**1986-03 Iisaku Zosen K.K. — Nishi-Izu** Yd No: 85126 Loa 40.72 Br ex 7.83 Dght 2.982 Lbp 36.02 Br md 7.80 Dpth 3.41 Welded, 1 dk	**(A13B2TP) Products Tanker**	**1 oil engine** with clutches & reverse reduction geared to sc. shaft driving 1 FP propeller Total Power: 368kW (500hp) Yanmar MF24-HT 1 x 4 Stroke 6 Cy. 240 x 420 368kW (500bhp) Yanmar Diesel Engine Co Ltd-Japan
8123494 *WDD3217* -	**SPT PEARL** *ex* Gulf Pearl *-2006* *ex* Pearl Graham *-2004* **SPT Offshore LLC** SPT Inc (Skaugen PetroTrans) *Los Angeles, CA* *United States of America* MMSI: 367127440 Official number: 647181	**624** 187 1,200	Class: AB	**1982-04 Offshore Trawlers, Inc. — Bayou La Batre, Al** Yd No: 160 Loa - Br ex - Dght 3.753 Lbp 51.82 Br md 12.20 Dpth 4.35 Welded, 1 dk	**(B21A20S) Platform Supply Ship**	**2 oil engines** reverse reduction geared to sc. shafts driving 2 FP propellers Total Power: 1,368kW (1,860hp) 12.0kn G.M. (Detroit Diesel) 16V-149 2 x Vee 2 Stroke 16 Cy. 146 x 146 each-684kW (930bhp) General Motors Detroit DieselAllison Divn-USA AuxGen: 2 x 99kW Thrusters: 1 Thwart. FP thruster (f)
7643679 *WDC6637* -	**SPT PROTECTOR** *ex* Gulf Protector *-2003* *ex* Labrador *-1991* *ex* Labrador Seahorse *-1989* **SPT Offshore LLC** SPT Inc (Skaugen PetroTrans) *Houston, TX* *United States of America* MMSI: 367058853 Official number: 579571	**659** 197 725	Class: (AB)	**1977-01 Halter Marine, Inc. — Moss Point, Ms** Yd No: 570 Loa 54.87 Br ex - Dght 3.660 Lbp 49.92 Br md 12.20 Dpth 4.27 Welded, 1 dk	**(B21A20S) Platform Supply Ship**	**2 oil engines** reverse reduction geared to sc. shafts driving 2 FP propellers Total Power: 1,654kW (2,248hp) 12.0kn Caterpillar D399SCAC 2 x Vee 4 Stroke 16 Cy. 159 x 203 each-827kW (1124bhp) Caterpillar Tractor Co-USA AuxGen: 2 x 95kW 440V 60Hz a.c Thrusters: 1 Thwart. FP thruster (f) Fuel: 258.0 (d.f.) 15.0pd
8030635 *WDE2255* -	**SPT VICTORY** *ex* Epic Service *-2007* *ex* Marsea Seventeen *-1989* **SPT Offshore LLC** SPT Inc (Skaugen PetroTrans) SatCom: Inmarsat C 436629410 *Houston, TX* *United States of America* MMSI: 367322450 Official number: 643112	**693** 207 1,200	Class: AB	**1981-12 Halter Marine, Inc. — Moss Point, Ms** Yd No: 1016 Loa 54.87 Br ex - Dght 3.664 Lbp 50.60 Br md 12.20 Dpth 4.27 Welded, 1 dk	**(B21A20S) Platform Supply Ship**	**2 oil engines** reverse reduction geared to sc. shafts driving 2 FP propellers Total Power: 1,654kW (2,248hp) 12.0kn Caterpillar D399SCAC 2 x Vee 4 Stroke 16 Cy. 159 x 203 each-827kW (1124bhp) Caterpillar Tractor Co-USA AuxGen: 2 x 135kW 440V 60Hz a.c Thrusters: 1 Thwart. FP thruster (f) Fuel: 241.0 (d.f.) 10.0pd
8030714 *WDD8357* -	**SPT VIGILANCE** *ex* Hilton Tide *-2007* **SPT Offshore LLC** SPT Inc (Skaugen PetroTrans) *Houston, TX* *United States of America* MMSI: 367198110 Official number: 653836	**693** 207 1,200	Class: AB	**1982-12 Halter Marine, Inc. — Moss Point, Ms** Yd No: 1024 Loa - Br ex - Dght 3.664 Lbp 54.87 Br md 12.20 Dpth 4.27 Welded, 1 dk	**(B21A20S) Platform Supply Ship**	**2 oil engines** reverse reduction geared to sc. shafts driving 2 FP propellers Total Power: 1,654kW (2,248hp) 12.0kn Caterpillar D399SCAC 2 x Vee 4 Stroke 16 Cy. 159 x 203 each-827kW (1124bhp) Caterpillar Tractor Co-USA AuxGen: 2 x 135kW Thrusters: 1 Thwart. FP thruster (f)

Number / Name / Owner	Tonnage	Class	Build / Dimensions	Type	Machinery
8987228 **SPUD** *UQK* - **Geo Energi Group LLP** - *Aqtau* *Kazakhstan* Official number: 941314	**303** 91 154	Class: RS	**1995-01 Robishaw Engineering Inc. — Houston, Tx** Yd No: 1213 Loa 35.60 Br ex 12.60 Dght 1.200 Lbp - Br md - Dpth 2.13 Welded, 1 dk	**(B31A2SR) Research Survey Vessel**	**2 oil engines** geared to sc. shafts driving 2 Directional propellers Total Power: 588kW (800hp) 6.0kn G.M. (Detroit Diesel) 8V-71 2 x Vee 2 Stroke 8 Cy. 108 x 127 each-294kW (400bhp) Detroit Diesel Eng. Co.-Detroit, Mi Fuel: 30.0
8974025 **SPUDNIK** *WTL4965* - *ex* Arctic Transport *-2008* **Island Tug & Barge Co** - *Seattle, WA* *United States of America* MMSI: 366207000 Official number: 696457	*487* 445 -		**1945 United States Navy Yard, Charleston — Charleston, SC** L reg 59.64 Br ex - Dght - Lbp - Br md 10.36 Dpth 2.43 Welded, 1 dk	**(B11B2FV) Fishing Vessel**	**1 oil engine** driving 1 FP propeller
9202534 **SPUIGRACHT** *PBBB* - **Rederij Spuigracht** Spliethoff's Bevrachtingskantoor BV *Amsterdam* *Netherlands* MMSI: 245261000 Official number: 38773	**16,639** 6,730 21,349 T/cm 35.1	Class: LR ✠ **100A1** SS 07/2010 strengthened for heavy cargoes, container cargoes in holds on upper deck and upper deck hatch covers, timber deck cargoes, tank top suitable for regular discharge by grabs LI *IWS Ice Class 1A (Finnish-Swedish Ice Class Rules 1985) Max draught midship 10.959m Max/min draught aft 11.47/6.6m Max/min draught fwd 11.47/4.2m ✠ **LMC** **UMS** Eq.Ltr: I†; Cable: 618.3/64.0 U3 (a)	**2001-03 Stocznia Szczecinska Porta Holding SA — Szczecin** Yd No: B587/IV/4 Loa 172.00 (BB) Br ex 25.49 Dght 10.600 Lbp 160.70 Br md 25.30 Dpth 14.60 Welded, 1 dk	**(A31A2GX) General Cargo Ship** Grain: 22,200 TEU 1127 C Ho 478 TEU C Dk 649 TEU incl 120 ref C. Cargo Heating Coils Compartments: 3 Ho, ER 4 Ha: (6.4 x 7.5) (25.6 x 15.2)Tappered (38.4 x 17.8) (32.0 x 20.4)ER Cranes: 3x120t Ice Capable	**1 oil engine** with flexible couplings & sr gearedto sc. shaft driving 1 CP propeller Total Power: 12,060kW (16,397hp) 17.0kn Wartsila 6L64 1 x 4 Stroke 6 Cy. 640 x 900 12060kW (16397bhp) Wartsila Italia SpA-Italy AuxGen: 1 x 1000kW 440V 60Hz a.c, 4 x 450kW 440V 60Hz a.c Boilers: TOH (o.f.) 10.2kgf/cm² (10.0bar), TOH (ex.g.) 10.2kgf/cm² (10.0bar) Thrusters: 1 Thwart. CP thruster (f) Fuel: 275.0 (d.f.) (Heating Coils) 1750.0 (r.f.) 45.0pd
7914494 **SPURN HAVEN II** *MSGL2* - *ex* Ventura *-1993* **Phillips 66 Ltd** Svitzer Marine Ltd *Grimsby* *United Kingdom* MMSI: 232003547 Official number: 723649	**654** 196 750	Class: AB	**1979-11 Bollinger Machine Shop & Shipyard, Inc. — Lockport, La** Yd No: 123 L reg 49.80 Br ex 11.61 Dght 3.396 Lbp - Br md 11.58 Dpth 3.96 Welded, 1 dk	**(B21A20S) Platform Supply Ship**	**2 oil engines** reverse reduction geared to sc. shafts driving 2 FP propellers Total Power: 1,250kW (1,700hp) 12.0kn Caterpillar D398SCAC 2 x Vee 4 Stroke 12 Cy. 159 x 203 each-625kW (850bhp) Caterpillar Tractor Co-USA AuxGen: 2 x 99kW a.c Thrusters: 1 Thwart. FP thruster (f)
9327920 **SPUTNIK** *ZCTV6* - *ex* Penumbra *-2007* *ex* Raven Explorer *-2007* *ex* Borcos Tasneem 2 *-2007* **Belmer Systems Inc** Yacht Management Consultants Sarl (Hill Robinson Yacht Management Consultants) *George Town* *Cayman Islands (British)* MMSI: 319760000 Official number: 740277	**2,307** 692 1,597	Class: AB (LR) ✠ Classed LR until 31/1/08	**2006-10 Boustead Naval Shipyard Sdn Bhd — Lumut** Yd No: 022 Converted From: Maintenance Vessel, Offshore-2007 Loa 60.00 Br ex 16.84 Dght 4.850 Lbp 53.90 Br md 16.00 Dpth 5.50 Welded, 1 dk	**(B34R2QY) Supply Tender**	**2 oil engines** with clutches, flexible couplings & reverse geared to sc. shafts driving 2 CP propellers Total Power: 4,060kW (5,520hp) 12.0kn Caterpillar 3606 2 x 4 Stroke 6 Cy. 280 x 300 each-2030kW (2760bhp) Caterpillar Inc-USA AuxGen: 2 x 280kW 415V 50Hz a.c, 2 x 1000kW 415V 50Hz a.c Thrusters: 1 Thwart. CP thruster (f)
1006570 **SPYK** *ZCSC3* - **Kamal Marine Ltd** - *George Town* *Cayman Islands (British)* MMSI: 319171000 Official number: 732442	**214** 64 -	Class: LR ✠ **100A1** SS 05/2009 SSC Yacht mono HSC LDC G4 **LMC** Eq.Ltr: L; Cable: 110.0/14.0 U1	**1999-05 Cantieri di Pisa — Pisa** Yd No: 659 Loa 32.32 Br ex 7.45 Dght 2.780 Lbp 26.85 Br md 7.40 Dpth 3.70 Bonded, 1 dk	**(X11A2YP) Yacht** Hull Material: Reinforced Plastic	**2 oil engines** with clutches, flexible couplings & sr reverse geared to sc. shafts driving 2 FP propellers Total Power: 3,362kW (4,570hp) M.T.U. 12V396TE94 2 x Vee 4 Stroke 12 Cy. 165 x 185 each-1681kW (2285bhp) MTU Friedrichshafen GmbH-Friedrichshafen AuxGen: 2 x 50kW 380V 50Hz a.c Thrusters: 1 Thwart. FP thruster (f)
7218278 **SPYROS** - - - -	*536* 420 244	Class: (BV)	**1972 "Naus" Shipyard Philippou Bros. S.A. — Piraeus** Loa 55.96 Br ex 9.00 Dght 2.131 Lbp 54.36 Br md - Dpth 3.00 Welded, 1 dk	**(A36A2PR) Passenger/Ro-Ro Ship (Vehicles)**	**2 oil engines** sr geared to sc. shafts driving 2 FP propellers Total Power: 530kW (720hp) 14.0kn Caterpillar D343TA 2 x 4 Stroke 6 Cy. 137 x 165 each-265kW (360bhp) Caterpillar Tractor Co-USA
9315367 **SPYROS** *SWXJ* - **Eleni Efta Special Maritime Enterprise (ENE)** Enesel SA SatCom: Inmarsat C 424059310 *Piraeus* *Greece* MMSI: 240593000 Official number: 11628	**161,175** 110,520 319,247 T/cm 180.0	Class: NV	**2007-07 Hyundai Samho Heavy Industries Co Ltd — Samho** Yd No: S278 Loa 333.00 (BB) Br ex 60.05 Dght 22.522 Lbp 319.00 Br md 60.00 Dpth 30.40 Welded, 1 dk	**(A13A2TV) Crude Oil Tanker** Double Hull (13F) Liq: 339,053; Liq (Oil): 339,053 Compartments: 5 Ta, 10 Wing Ta, 2 Wing Slop Ta, ER 3 Cargo Pump (s): 3x5000m³/hr Manifold: Bow/CM: 165.2m	**1 oil engine** driving 1 FP propeller Total Power: 26,412kW (35,910hp) 15.5kn MAN-B&W 6S90MC-C 1 x 2 Stroke 6 Cy. 900 x 3188 26412kW (35910bhp) Hyundai Heavy Industries Co Ltd-South Korea AuxGen: 3 x a.c Fuel: 311.0 (d.f.) 9077.0 (r.f.)
9308584 **SPYROS** *V7ZZ9* - *ex* Iller Trader *-2012* *ex* Maersk Fuji *-2010* *ex* Iller Trader *-2005* **Spyros Marine LLC** Technomar Shipping Inc *Majuro* *Marshall Islands* MMSI: 538004951 Official number: 4951	**9,981** 4,900 11,798	Class: GL RI	**2005-07 Zhejiang Yangfan Ship Group Co Ltd — Zhoushan ZJ** Yd No: 2017 Loa 139.10 (BB) Br ex - Dght 8.800 Lbp 129.00 Br md 22.60 Dpth 11.80 Welded, 1 dk	**(A33A2CC) Container Ship (Fully Cellular)** Double Bottom Entire Compartment Length TEU 957 incl 240 ref C. Cranes: 2x45t	**1 oil engine** geared to sc. shaft driving 1 CP propeller Total Power: 9,600kW (13,052hp) 18.5kn MAN-B&W 8L48/60B 1 x 4 Stroke 8 Cy. 480 x 600 9600kW (13052bhp) AuxGen: 2 x 910kW 440/220V 60Hz a.c, 1 x 2000kW 440/220V 60Hz a.c Thrusters: 1 Tunnel thruster (f); 1 Tunnel thruster (f)
9565948 **SPYROS K** *A8YS2* - **Marine Velvet SA** Tsakos Columbia Shipmanagement (TCM) SA *Monrovia* *Liberia* MMSI: 636015119 Official number: 15119	**81,314** 51,990 157,648 T/cm 120.0	Class: AB	**2011-05 Sungdong Shipbuilding & Marine Engineering Co Ltd — Tongyeong** Yd No: 2034 Loa 274.27 (BB) Br ex 48.04 Dght 17.150 Lbp 264.00 Br md 48.00 Dpth 23.10 Welded, 1 dk	**(A13A2TW) Crude/Oil Products Tanker** Double Hull (13F) Liq: 165,700; Liq (Oil): 169,693 Compartments: 12 Wing Ta, 2 Wing Slop Ta, ER 3 Cargo Pump (s)	**1 oil engine** driving 1 FP propeller Total Power: 18,660kW (25,370hp) 15.5kn MAN-B&W 6S70MC-C 1 x 2 Stroke 6 Cy. 700 x 2800 18660kW (25370bhp) Hyundai Heavy Industries Co Ltd-South Korea AuxGen: 3 x 987kW a.c Fuel: 230.7 (d.f.) 4511.8 (r.f.)
9480514 **SQUALL** *ZCIF2* - **Debary Ltd** Globaljet SA *George Town* *Cayman Islands (British)* MMSI: 319811000 Official number: 735583	**360** 108 221	Class: AB	**2002-12 Perini Navi SpA (Divisione Picchiotti) — Viareggio** Yd No: 2036 Loa 52.30 Br ex - Dght 4.900 Lbp 47.25 Br md 10.35 Dpth 4.35 Welded, 1 dk	**(X11A2YP) Yacht**	**1 oil engine** geared to sc. shaft driving 1 CP propeller Total Power: 1,044kW (1,419hp) Caterpillar 3412E-TA 1 x Vee 4 Stroke 12 Cy. 137 x 152 1044kW (1419bhp) Caterpillar Inc-USA
7437862 **SQUALO BIANCO** *INSB* - **Navalgiglio di Rum G & C Snc** - *Naples* *Italy* Official number: 1212	*115* 71 14	Class: (RI)	**1973 Cant. Nav. Seaflight — Messina** Yd No: 23 Loa 27.13 Br ex 10.01 Dght 3.501 Lbp 22.66 Br md 6.04 Dpth 2.75 Riveted, 1 dk	**(A37B2PS) Passenger Ship** Hull Material: Aluminium Alloy Passengers: unberthed: 120	**2 oil engines** driving 2 FP propellers Total Power: 1,618kW (2,200hp) 33.0kn M.T.U. 12V493TY60 2 x Vee 4 Stroke 12 Cy. 175 x 205 each-809kW (1100bhp) MTU Friedrichshafen GmbH-Friedrichshafen
6718219 **SQUALUS** *LDST* - **Kvernhusvik Skipsverft AS** - *Trondheim* *Norway* MMSI: 257084600	**253** 75 -	Class: (RI)	**1967 N.V. Scheepswerven v/h H.H. Bodewes — Millingen a/d Rijn** Yd No: 662 Loa 32.97 Br ex 8.62 Dght 2.501 Lbp 30.99 Br md 8.60 Dpth 3.66 Welded, 1 dk	**(B32A2ST) Tug**	**2 oil engines** driving 2 Voith-Schneider propellers Total Power: 1,324kW (1,800hp) Deutz SBV8M536 2 x 4 Stroke 8 Cy. 270 x 360 each-662kW (900bhp) Kloeckner Humboldt Deutz AG-West Germany Fuel: 60.0
8877150 **SQUALUS** *IMRU* - **Rimorchiatori Riuniti Panfido e Compagnia Srl** - *Venice* *Italy* Official number: 8608	**144** 48 100	Class: RI	**1994 Cant. Nav. Rosetti — Ravenna** Yd No: 23 Loa 23.50 Br ex - Dght 3.800 Lbp 21.00 Br md 8.00 Dpth 3.80 Welded, 1 dk	**(B32A2ST) Tug**	**2 oil engines** driving 2 FP propellers Total Power: 1,680kW (2,284hp) 12.6kn MWM TBD604BV8 2 x Vee 4 Stroke 8 Cy. 170 x 195 each-840kW (1142bhp) Motoren Werke Mannheim AG (MWM)-Mannheim

IMO / Call sign / Flag	Name / Former names / Owners / Port	Tonnage (GT/NT/DWT)	Class	Builder / Dimensions	Type / Cargo	Machinery
7636690 - -	**SQUARE I** *ex* Bahati *-1986* **Square General Contracting Co**	*483* 398 640	Class: (HR) (GL)	**1977 JG Hitzler Schiffswerft und Masch GmbH & Co KG — Lauenburg** Yd No: 759 Loa 37.50 Br ex 11.16 Dght 2.702 Lbp 36.00 Br md 11.02 Dpth 4.78 Welded, 1 dk	**(A24A2BT) Cement Carrier**	**2 oil engines** geared to sc. shafts driving 2 FP propellers Total Power: 338kW (460hp) 5.0kn Deutz BF12L714 2 x Vee 4 Stroke 12 Cy. 120 x 140 each-169kW (230bhp) Kloeckner Humboldt Deutz AG-West Germany
7501417 *DUA2270* -	**SQUIRREL** *ex* Tairyo Maru *-1989* **Loadstar Shipping Co Inc** - *Manila* *Philippines* Official number: 00-0000455	*494* 289 1,599	Class: (GL)	**1975-07 Kochi Jyuko K.K. — Kochi** Yd No: 887 Loa - Br ex 11.03 Dght 4.141 Lbp 60.94 Br md 11.00 Dpth 5.85 Riveted\Welded, 1 dk	**(A31A2GX) General Cargo Ship**	**1 oil engine** driving 1 FP propeller Total Power: 1,030kW (1,400hp) 13.4kn Hanshin 6LUD32G 1 x 4 Stroke 6 Cy. 320 x 510 1030kW (1400bhp) Hanshin Nainenki Kogyo-Japan
9099925 - -	**SR STAR 01** - **Rudi Harto Wijaya Suliansyah** - *Samarinda* *Indonesia*	**298** 90 -	Class: KI	**2007-09 C.V. Dok & Galangan Kapal Perlun — Samarinda** Loa 32.76 Br ex - Dght 3.360 Lbp 29.60 Br md 8.50 Dpth 4.00 Welded, 1 dk	**(B32A2ST) Tug**	**2 oil engines** reduction geared to sc. shafts driving 2 Propellers Total Power: 1,766kW (2,402hp) Caterpillar D399 2 x Vee 4 Stroke 16 Cy. 159 x 203 each-883kW (1201bhp) (Re-engined ,made 2000, refitted 2007) Caterpillar Inc-USA
8743593 *YDA6428* -	**SR STAR 02** - **Rudi Harto Wijaya Suliansyah** - *Samarinda* *Indonesia*	**256** 77 -	Class: KI	**2009-12 P.T. Rejeki Abadi Sakti — Samarinda** Loa 30.25 Br ex - Dght 3.090 Lbp 28.46 Br md 8.60 Dpth 3.75 Welded, 1 dk	**(B32A2ST) Tug**	**2 oil engines** reduction geared to sc. shafts driving 2 Propellers Total Power: 1,654kW (2,248hp) Caterpillar D399 2 x Vee 4 Stroke 16 Cy. 159 x 203 each-827kW (1124bhp) (Re-engined ,made 2000, refitted 2009) Caterpillar Inc-USA AuxGen: 2 x 79kW 400V a.c
8653982 - -	**SR STAR 08** - **Rudi Harto Wijaya Suliansyah** - *Samarinda* *Indonesia*	**250** 75 -	Class: KI	**2010-12 PT Mangkupalas Mitra Makmur — Samarinda** Loa 30.25 Br ex - Dght 2.790 Lbp 28.51 Br md 8.60 Dpth 3.75 Welded, 1 dk	**(B32A2ST) Tug**	**2 oil engines** reduction geared to sc. shafts driving 2 FP propellers AuxGen: 2 x 60kW 400V a.c
7414688 *5NKP* -	**SR TRADER** *ex* Zambezi *-2008* *ex* Oranjemund *-2006* **SR Fuel Trading Ltd** Anchor Ocean Ltd *Nigeria* MMSI: 657221000 Official number: 377659	**1,251** 730 2,018 T/cm 6.3	Class: (GL)	**1976-02 Dorman Long (Africa) Ltd. — Durban** Yd No: 2700 Loa 61.02 Br ex 12.02 Dght 4.401 Lbp 56.34 Br md 12.01 Dpth 6.15 Welded, 1 dk	**(A13B2TP) Products Tanker** Single Hull Grain: 352; Bale: 302; Liq: 1,559; Liq (Oil): 1,559 Part Cargo Heating Coils Compartments: 1 Ho, 6 Wing Ta, ER 1 Ha: (27.7 x 9.1)ER 2 Cargo Pump (s): 2x275m³/hr Manifold: Bow/CM: 43m	**2 oil engines** reduction geared to sc. shafts driving 2 CP propellers Total Power: 1,268kW (1,724hp) 11.5kn Caterpillar D398SCAC 2 x Vee 4 Stroke 12 Cy. 159 x 203 each-634kW (862bhp) Caterpillar Tractor Co-USA AuxGen: 3 x 80kW 220/380V 50Hz a.c Thrusters: 1 Thwart. FP thruster (f) Fuel: 109.0 (d.f.) 4.5pd
9062623 *VTLT* -	**SRAVANTHI** - **Bay Liners Ltd** - *Chennai* *India* Official number: F-MDR-009	**354** 123 214	Class: (IR) (NK)	**1993-01 Niigata Engineering Co Ltd — Niigata NI** Yd No: 2170 Loa 42.00 Br ex - Dght 2.800 Lbp 36.67 Br md 7.40 Dpth 3.15 Welded, 1 dk	**(B11B2FV) Fishing Vessel** Ins: 221	**1 oil engine** with clutches, flexible couplings & sr reverse geared to sc. shaft driving 1 FP propeller Total Power: 625kW (850hp) 10.0kn Niigata 6NSC-M 1 x 4 Stroke 6 Cy. 190 x 260 625kW (850bhp) Niigata Engineering Co Ltd-Japan
8657445 *9A9299* -	**SRDELA** *ex* Sefik Reis *-2003* **Ugor doo** - *Rijeka* *Croatia* MMSI: 238988810	**143** 43 -	Class: CS	**2002 in Turkey** Loa 28.20 Br ex - Dght 2.530 Lbp 24.00 Br md 9.40 Dpth 3.10 Welded, 1 dk	**(B11B2FV) Fishing Vessel**	**1 oil engine** reduction geared to sc. shafts driving 1 FP propeller Total Power: 625kW (850hp) 10.0kn Iveco Aifo 8291 SRM85 1 x Vee 4 Stroke 12 Cy. 145 x 130 625kW (850bhp) IVECO AIFO S.p.A.-Pregnana Milanese
7740659 - -	**SREDNEKOLYMSKIY** - - -	**739** 232 350	Class: (RS)	**1978-09 Volgogradskiy Sudostroitelnyy Zavod — Volgograd** Yd No: 879 Loa 53.73 (BB) Br ex 10.72 Dght 4.290 Lbp 47.92 Br md 10.50 Dpth 6.02 Welded, 1 dk	**(B11A2FS) Stern Trawler** Ins: 218 Compartments: 1 Ho, ER 2 Ha: 2 (1.6 x 1.6) Derricks: 2x1.5t Ice Capable	**1 oil engine** driving 1 CP propeller Total Power: 971kW (1,320hp) 12.8kn S.K.L. 8NVD48A-2U 1 x 4 Stroke 8 Cy. 320 x 480 971kW (1320bhp) VEB Schwermaschinenbau "KarlLiebknecht" (SKL)-Magdeburg Thrusters: 1 Thwart. FP thruster (f); 1 Tunnel thruster (a) Fuel: 185.0 (d.f.)
8037190 *ATSM* -	**SREE LAKSHMI** - **Pron Magnate Pvt Ltd** - *Visakhapatnam* *India* Official number: 1768	*116* 79 57	Class: (IR) (AB)	**1978 Ingenieria y Maq. Especializada S.A. (IMESA) — Salina Cruz** Loa 23.17 Br ex 7.35 Dght 2.240 Lbp 21.39 Br md 7.33 Dpth 3.28 Welded, 1 dk	**(B11B2FV) Fishing Vessel**	**1 oil engine** sr geared to sc. shaft driving 1 FP propeller Total Power: 206kW (280hp) 8.5kn Caterpillar D353C 1 x 4 Stroke 6 Cy. 159 x 203 206kW (280bhp) Caterpillar Tractor Co-USA AuxGen: 2 x 10kW 120V 50Hz a.c Fuel: 39.5 (d.f.)
5344877 *9WAC* -	**SRI ASAHAN** *ex* Sungei Asahan *-1973* **Tang & Sim Shipping Sdn Bhd** - *Kuching* *Malaysia* Official number: 324794	*194* 97 231		**1950 N.V. Scheepsw. "De Vooruitgang" v/h D. Boot — Alphen a/d Rijn** Yd No: 1199 Loa 38.89 Br ex 7.32 Dght 2.198 Lbp - Br md 7.27 Dpth - Welded, 1 dk	**(A31A2GX) General Cargo Ship** Bale: 422 Compartments: 1 Ho, ER Winches: 2	**1 oil engine** driving 1 FP propeller 7.0kn De Industrie 1 x 4 Stroke 3 Cy. 280 x 400 NV Motorenfabriek 'De Industrie'-Netherlands Fuel: 8.0
7109568 *YHES* -	**SRI BAHARI** *ex* Langsa *-2003* *ex* Sun Jaya *-2001* *ex* Abadi Jaya *-1996* *ex* Hashima Maru *-1996* *ex* Seiun Maru No. 20 *-1988* **PT Pelayaran Fajar Sribahari Sakti** - SatCom: Inmarsat C 452500394 *Jakarta* *Indonesia* MMSI: 525002044	**1,413** 917 2,203	Class: KI	**1970-12 Kishimoto Zosen — Osakikamijima** Yd No: 396 Loa 72.40 (BB) Br ex 11.80 Dght 5.106 Lbp 67.95 Br md 11.50 Dpth 6.90 Welded, 1 dk	**(A31A2GX) General Cargo Ship** Grain: 3,995; Bale: 3,794 Compartments: 1 Ho, ER 1 Ha: (38.4 x 8.0)ER	**1 oil engine** driving 1 FP propeller Total Power: 1,177kW (1,600hp) 11.0kn Hanshin 6LU35 1 x 4 Stroke 6 Cy. 350 x 550 1177kW (1600bhp) Hanshin Nainenki Kogyo-Japan AuxGen: 2 x 180kW 225V a.c Fuel: 90.5
9643843 *HSB4713* -	**SRI BANDON** - **NTL Marine Co Ltd** Nathalin Co Ltd *Bangkok* *Thailand* MMSI: 567061900 Official number: 550002900	**2,409** 809 3,000	Class: BV	**2012-08 Nanjing East Star Shipbuilding Co Ltd — Nanjing JS** Yd No: ESS100201 Loa 77.00 Br ex 15.03 Dght 4.500 Lbp 72.80 Br md 15.00 Dpth 7.00 Welded, 1 dk	**(A13B2TP) Products Tanker** Double Hull (13F) Liq: 3,380; Liq (Oil): 3,448 Compartments: 8 Wing Ta, ER	**1 oil engine** reduction geared to sc. shaft driving 1 FP propeller Total Power: 1,914kW (2,602hp) 11.5kn Daihatsu 6DKM-28 1 x 4 Stroke 6 Cy. 280 x 390 1914kW (2602bhp) Anqing Marine Diesel Engine Works-China AuxGen: 1 x 190kW 60Hz a.c, 2 x 206kW 60Hz a.c Fuel: 245.0
7627120 *HP6965* -	**SRI BEGA** *ex* Eifuku Maru No. 1 *-1992* *ex* Fukuho Maru No. 11 *-1985* **Mazuda International Inc** Ehara Industries Ltd *Panama* *Panama* Official number: 21998KJ	*447* 274 995		**1977-03 Nippon Zosen Tekko K.K. — Kitakyushu** Yd No: 248 Loa 62.62 Br ex 10.04 Dght 3.614 Lbp 57.00 Br md 10.01 Dpth 6.10 Welded, 2 dks	**(A31A2GX) General Cargo Ship**	**1 oil engine** driving 1 FP propeller Total Power: 883kW (1,201hp) Hanshin 6LU28G 1 x 4 Stroke 6 Cy. 280 x 440 883kW (1201bhp) Hanshin Nainenki Kogyo-Japan
9161223 *YB4733* -	**SRI GEMILANG** - **Government of The Republic of Indonesia (Direktorat Jenderal Perhubungan Darat - Ministry of Land Communications)** - *Jakarta* *Indonesia*	**158** 48 -	Class: (KI)	**1996-01 P.T. Dok & Perkapalan Kodja Bahari — Palembang** Loa 30.00 Br ex - Dght 1.960 Lbp 28.60 Br md 9.15 Dpth 2.50 Welded, 1 dk	**(A36A2PR) Passenger/Ro-Ro Ship (Vehicles)** Bow ramp (centre) Stern ramp (centre) Side ramp (p) Side ramp (s)	**4 oil engines** reduction geared to sc. shafts driving 4 FP propellers Total Power: 308kW (420hp) 7.6kn Yanmar 6CHE 4 x 4 Stroke 6 Cy. 105 x 125 each-77kW (105bhp) Yanmar Diesel Engine Co Ltd-Japan AuxGen: 1 x 70kW 220/380V a.c
7205300 *YCVS* -	**SRI INDRA** *ex* Kitahime Maru *-1981* *ex* Shinyu Maru No. 18 *-1981* **PT Pelayaran Tahta Bahtera** - *Jakarta* *Indonesia*	**1,241** 752 2,841	Class: (KI)	**1972-01 Yoshiura Zosen — Kure** Yd No: 219 Loa 72.83 Br ex 12.07 Dght 5.150 Lbp 72.52 Br md 12.02 Dpth 5.49 Welded, 1 dk	**(A13B2TP) Products Tanker** Liq: 2,788; Liq (Oil): 2,788 Compartments: 10 Ta, ER	**1 oil engine** driving 1 FP propeller Total Power: 1,545kW (2,101hp) 13.5kn Akasaka AH38 1 x 4 Stroke 6 Cy. 380 x 560 1545kW (2101bhp) Akasaka Tekkosho KK (Akasaka DieselLtd)-Japan AuxGen: 2 x 48kW 225V a.c Fuel: 60.0

5337446 *9MTH* -	**SRI KEMASIK** *ex* Sri Rompin *-1966* **Pantai Timor Angkutan Sdn Bhd** - *Penang* *Malaysia* Official number: 324011	*187* 1 -	Class: (LR) ✠ Classed LR until 31/8/81	**1961-03 The Taikoo Dockyard & Engineering Co — Hong Kong** Yd No: 472 Loa 29.42 Br ex 7.55 Dght 3.271 Lbp 26.22 Br md 7.47 Dpth 3.81 Welded, 1 dk	**(B32A2ST) Tug**	**1 oil engine** with flexible couplings & sr reverse geared to sc. shaft driving 1 FP propeller Total Power: 588kW (799hp) Crossley HGN6 1 x 2 Stroke 6 Cy. 267 x 343 588kW (799bhp) Crossley Bros. Ltd.-Manchester AuxGen: 1 x 40kW 220V d.c, 1 x 19kW 220V d.c, 1 x 10kW 220V d.c
8614807 *HSB2969* -	**SRI KRABI** *ex* Hakuyo Maru *-2002* **Nathalin Co Ltd** Nathalin Management Co Ltd *Bangkok* *Thailand* MMSI: 567039100 Official number: 451001639	*985* 587 2,016	Class: (NK)	**1987-01 Hakata Zosen K.K. — Imabari** Yd No: 351 Loa 69.90 Br ex - Dght 4.879 Lbp 66.10 Br md 12.01 Dpth 5.36 Welded, 1 dk	**(A13B2TP) Products Tanker** Liq: 2,199; Liq (Oil): 2,199	**1 oil engine** driving 1 FP propeller Total Power: 1,324kW (1,800hp) 11.5kn Akasaka A31 1 x 4 Stroke 6 Cy. 310 x 600 1324kW (1800bhp) Akasaka Tekkosho KK (Akasaka DieselLtd)-Japan AuxGen: 3 x 88kW a.c
8993899 *9WEQ9* -	**SRI LABUAN LIMA** - **Trans-Link Sdn Bhd** Sin Matu Sdn Bhd *Kota Kinabalu* *Malaysia* MMSI: 533000233 Official number: 329936	**137** 61 -		**2004-07 Yong Choo Kui Shipyard Sdn Bhd — Sibu** Yd No: 2381 Loa 36.76 Br ex 4.28 Dght 1.350 Lbp 33.50 Br md 4.27 Dpth 1.50 Welded, 1 dk	**(A37B2PS) Passenger Ship**	**2 oil engines** reduction geared to sc. shafts driving 2 Propellers Total Power: 1,220kW (1,658hp) Yanmar 6AYM-ETE 2 x 4 Stroke 6 Cy. 155 x 180 each-610kW (829bhp) Yanmar Diesel Engine Co Ltd-Japan
9051882 *9WAK9* -	**SRI LABUAN TIGA** - **Trans-Link Sdn Bhd** - *Kota Kinabalu* *Malaysia* MMSI: 533560000 Official number: 325671	**121** 46 50	Class: NK	**1991-03 Yong Choo Kui Shipyard Sdn Bhd — Sibu** Yd No: 0190 Loa 37.50 Br ex - Dght 1.104 Lbp 33.64 Br md 4.40 Dpth 2.15 Welded	**(A37B2PS) Passenger Ship**	**2 oil engines** geared to sc. shafts driving 2 FP propellers Total Power: 934kW (1,270hp) 28.0kn General Motors 2 x Vee 2 Stroke 16 Cy. 114 x 127 each-467kW (635bhp) General Motors Detroit DieselAllison Divn-USA AuxGen: 1 x 36kW a.c Fuel: 8.0 (d.f.)
7629867 *YCUH* -	**SRI LAMBANG** *ex* Kim In VII *-2002* *ex* Sogetsu Maru *-1976* **PT Kunangan Citra Bahari** - *Jakarta* *Indonesia*	*102* 31 233	Class: (KI) (NK)	**1964-04 Shin Yamamoto Shipbuilding & Engineering Co Ltd — Kochi KC** Yd No: 44 Loa 24.67 Br ex 6.51 Dght 2.579 Lbp 22.89 Br md 6.48 Dpth 2.90 Welded, 1 dk	**(B32A2ST) Tug**	**2 oil engines** driving 2 FP propellers Total Power: 810kW (1,102hp) 12.5kn Fuji 6SD27BH 2 x 4 Stroke 6 Cy. 270 x 400 each-405kW (551bhp) Fuji Diesel Co Ltd-Japan AuxGen: 2 x 17kW
5337472 *9WYX* -	**SRI LANJUT** *ex* Kilkenny *-1976* *ex* Sri Lanjut *-1973* *ex* Sri Trengganu *-1966* **Tang & Sim Shipping Sdn Bhd** - *Kuching* *Malaysia* Official number: 325048	*241* 99 209	Class: (LR) Classed LR until 26/3/76	**1956-05 The Taikoo Dockyard & Engineering Co — Hong Kong** Yd No: 417 Loa 39.17 Br ex 7.68 Dght 1.848 Lbp 36.58 Br md 7.62 Dpth 2.60 Welded, 1 dk	**(A31A2GX) General Cargo Ship** Grain: 360; Bale: 310 Compartments: 1 Ho, ER 1 Ha: (17.6 x 4.8)ER Derricks: 2x2t; Winches: 2	**2 oil engines** sr geared to sc. shafts driving 2 FP propellers Total Power: 194kW (264hp) 8.5kn Kelvin KR6 2 x 4 Stroke 6 Cy. 152 x 229 each-97kW (132bhp) Bergius Co. Ltd.-Glasgow AuxGen: 1 x 30kW 415V d.c Fuel: 7.5 (d.f.)
8708579 - -	**SRI LATA** - **Sharmila Fisheries Pvt Ltd** - *Visakhapatnam* *India* Official number: F-VSM73	**121** 36 47	Class: (IR)	**1991-10 Hooghly Dock & Port Engineers Ltd. — Haora** Yd No: 453 Loa 23.46 Br ex 6.51 Dght 2.650 Lbp 20.97 Br md 6.50 Dpth 3.44 Welded, 1 dk	**(B11A2FS) Stern Trawler**	**1 oil engine** dr geared to sc. shaft driving 1 FP propeller Total Power: 300kW (408hp) 9.0kn Caterpillar 3408PCTA 1 x Vee 4 Stroke 8 Cy. 137 x 152 300kW (408bhp) Caterpillar Inc-USA AuxGen: 2 x 40kW 415V 50Hz a.c Fuel: 30.0 (d.f.)
8623561 - -	**SRI MEWAH III** - **Syarikat Samling Timber Sdn Bhd** - *Miri* *Malaysia* Official number: M-2549	**152** 60 184	Class: (NK)	**1979 Sin Chin Seng Shipyard — Singapore** Loa 34.90 Br ex - Dght 1.659 Lbp 32.69 Br md 6.80 Dpth 2.32 Welded, 1 dk	**(A13B2TU) Tanker (unspecified)**	**1 oil engine** geared to sc. shaft driving 1 FP propeller Total Power: 312kW (424hp) 10.0kn Deutz SBA8M816 1 x 4 Stroke 8 Cy. 142 x 160 312kW (424bhp) Kloeckner Humboldt Deutz AG-West Germany
8623573 - -	**SRI MEWAH IV** - **Syarikat Samling Timber Sdn Bhd** - *Miri* *Malaysia* Official number: M-2550	**152** 60 184	Class: (NK)	**1979 Sin Chin Seng Shipyard — Singapore** Loa 34.90 Br ex - Dght 1.659 Lbp 32.69 Br md 6.80 Dpth 2.32 Welded, 1 dk	**(A13B2TU) Tanker (unspecified)**	**1 oil engine** geared to sc. shaft driving 1 FP propeller Total Power: 312kW (424hp) 10.0kn Deutz SBA8M816 1 x 4 Stroke 8 Cy. 142 x 160 312kW (424bhp) Kloeckner Humboldt Deutz AG-West Germany
8623585 - -	**SRI MEWAH V** - **Syarikat Samling Timber Sdn Bhd** - *Miri* *Malaysia* Official number: M-2563	**152** 60 184	Class: (NK)	**1979 Sin Chin Seng Shipyard — Singapore** Loa 34.90 Br ex - Dght 1.659 Lbp 32.69 Br md 6.80 Dpth 2.32 Welded, 1 dk	**(A13B2TU) Tanker (unspecified)**	**1 oil engine** geared to sc. shaft driving 1 FP propeller Total Power: 312kW (424hp) 10.0kn Deutz SBA8M816 1 x 4 Stroke 8 Cy. 142 x 160 312kW (424bhp) Kloeckner Humboldt Deutz AG-West Germany
7419901 *HSB2241* -	**SRI NAKORN** *ex* Koyo Maru *-1983* **B P P Supply Co Ltd** - *Bangkok* *Thailand* Official number: 361000456	*491* 303 1,165		**1975-03 Towa Zosen K.K. — Shimonoseki** Yd No: 472 Loa 49.46 Br ex 11.00 Dght 3.950 Lbp 46.00 Br md 10.98 Dpth 3.99 Welded, 1 dk	**(A13B2TU) Tanker (unspecified)** Single Hull	**1 oil engine** driving 1 FP propeller Total Power: 809kW (1,100hp) Hanshin 6LU28G 1 x 4 Stroke 6 Cy. 280 x 440 809kW (1100bhp) The Hanshin Diesel Works Ltd-Japan
9286334 - -	**SRI NAKORN 23** *ex* Chonlasab *-2005* **Pramote Cholwisit** - *Bangkok* *Thailand* Official number: 459200033	*297* 202 -		**2002-07 Mits Decisions Co., Ltd. — Samut Sakhon** Loa 33.00 Br ex 7.50 Dght - Lbp - Br md - Dpth 4.30 Welded, 1 dk	**(B12B2FC) Fish Carrier**	**1 oil engine** geared to sc. shaft driving 1 FP propeller Total Power: 351kW (477hp) Cummins KTA-19-M3 1 x 4 Stroke 6 Cy. 159 x 159 351kW (477bhp) Cummins Engine Co Inc-USA
7642962 *9WBN* -	**SRI NAM HUA No. 3** - **Sri Nang Hwa Shipping Sdn Bhd** - *Kuching* *Malaysia* Official number: 324828	*473* 372 -		**1976 Ocean Shipyard Co Sdn Bhd — Sibu** L reg 49.69 Br ex 9.83 Dght - Lbp - Br md - Dpth - Welded, 1 dk	**(A31A2GX) General Cargo Ship**	**2 oil engines** geared to sc. shafts driving 2 FP propellers Total Power: 354kW (482hp) 8.0kn Chinese Std. Type 12V135C 2 x Vee 4 Stroke 12 Cy. 135 x 140 each-177kW (241bhp) Shanghai Diesel Engine Co Ltd-China
9062271 *HSB4844* -	**SRI NARA** *ex* Daiei Maru No. 1 *-2013* **NTL Marine Co Ltd** Nathalin Co Ltd *Bangkok* *Thailand* MMSI: 567001580 Official number: 560003437	*2,920* 1,260 4,999	Class: NK	**1993-03 Higaki Zosen K.K. — Imabari** Yd No: 416 Loa 103.20 (BB) Br ex 15.02 Dght 6.415 Lbp 95.80 Br md 15.00 Dpth 7.50 Welded, 1 dk	**(A13B2TP) Products Tanker** Liq: 5,350; Liq (Oil): 5,350 Compartments: 10 Ta, ER	**1 oil engine** driving 1 CP propeller Total Power: 2,994kW (4,071hp) 13.3kn Hanshin 6EL44 1 x 4 Stroke 6 Cy. 440 x 880 2994kW (4071bhp) Kobe Hatsudoki KK-Japan AuxGen: 3 x 250kW a.c Thrusters: 1 Thwart. CP thruster (f) Fuel: 250.0 (r.f.)
7815129 *HSB2859* -	**SRI PAKNAKHON** *ex* Henda *-2002* *ex* Kahenda III *-1992* *ex* Asano 8 *-1990* *ex* Asano Maru No. 8 *-1990* **B P P Supply Co Ltd** - *Thailand* Official number: 457400077	**770** 321 1,326		**1978-11 Kochi Jyuko K.K. — Kochi** Yd No: 1281 L reg 63.99 Br ex - Dght 4.500 Lbp 59.01 Br md 10.01 Dpth 4.53 Riveted\Welded, 1 dk	**(A13B2TP) Products Tanker**	**1 oil engine** driving 1 FP propeller Total Power: 883kW (1,201hp) Hanshin 6LU28G 1 x 4 Stroke 6 Cy. 280 x 440 883kW (1201bhp) Hanshin Nainenki Kogyo-Japan
6812596 - -	**SRI PERMAISURI** *ex* Weipa *-1980* **Bogor Jaya Sdn Bhd** -	*321* 86 224	Class: (LR) ✠ Classed LR until 8/6/84	**1968-05 North Queensland Engineers & Agents Pty Ltd — Cairns QLD** Yd No: 16 Lengthened-1969 Loa 42.30 Br ex 9.58 Dght 1.817 Lbp 37.95 Br md 9.25 Dpth 2.04 Welded, 1 dk	**(A35D2RL) Landing Craft** Bow door/ramp (centre)	**2 oil engines** sr reverse geared to sc. shafts driving 2 FP propellers Total Power: 346kW (470hp) 9.0kn Cummins NT-335-M 2 x 4 Stroke 6 Cy. 140 x 152 each-173kW (235bhp) Cummins Engine Co Ltd-United Kingdom AuxGen: 1 x 56kW 415V 50Hz a.c, 1 x 25kW 415V 50Hz a.c

8712257 *HSB2979* -	**SRI PHANG-NGA** *ex* Ryoyo Maru *-2003* **NTL Marine Co Ltd** Nathalin Management Co Ltd *Bangkok* *Thailand* MMSI: 567040100 Official number: 460000682	*929* 593 1,998	Class: (NK)	**1987**-11 **Hakata Zosen K.K. — Imabari** Yd No: 362 Loa 69.82 Br ex - Dght 4.400 Lbp 66.00 Br md 12.00 Dpth 5.40 Welded, 1 dk	**(A13B2TP) Products Tanker** Liq: 2,231; Liq (Oil): 2,231	**1 oil engine** driving 1 FP propeller Total Power: 1,324kW (1,800hp) 11.0kn Akasaka A31 1 x 4 Stroke 6 Cy. 310 x 600 1324kW (1800bhp) Akasaka Tekkosho KK (Akasaka DieselLtd)-Japan AuxGen: 3 x 101kW a.c Fuel: 80.0 (d.f.)
8122892 *HSB2616* -	**SRI PHUKET** *ex* Senryo Maru *-1999* **Nathalin Co Ltd** Nathalin Management Co Ltd SatCom: Inmarsat C 456754010 *Bangkok* *Thailand* MMSI: 567012400 Official number: 421000360	**2,894** 1,486 4,997	Class: (NK)	**1982**-07 **Sanuki Shipbuilding & Iron Works Co Ltd — Mitoyo KG** Yd No: 1102 Loa 103.31 (BB) Br ex - Dght 6.457 Lbp 95.00 Br md 15.00 Dpth 7.29 Welded, 1 dk	**(A13A2TW) Crude/Oil Products Tanker** Double Bottom Entire Compartment Length Liq: 5,242; Liq (Oil): 5,349 Compartments: 5 Ta, ER 2 Cargo Pump (s): 2x1000m³/hr	**1 oil engine** driving 1 CP propeller Total Power: 2,427kW (3,300hp) 12.5kn Hanshin 6EL40 1 x 4 Stroke 6 Cy. 400 x 800 2427kW (3300bhp) The Hanshin Diesel Works Ltd-Japan AuxGen: 2 x 240kW 445V 60Hz a.c Thrusters: 1 Tunnel thruster (f) Fuel: 144.0 (d.f.) 228.0 (r.f.)
9239991 *9VMH7* -	**SRI PREM APARNA** *ex* Prem Aparna *-2012* *ex* Spring Seletar *-2006* *ex* Maersk Seletar *-2002* **Mercator Lines (Singapore) Ltd** - SatCom: Inmarsat C 456527210 *Singapore* *Singapore* MMSI: 565272000 Official number: 392522	**38,678** 25,112 73,461 T/cm 66.1	Class: NV (NK)	**2001**-01 **Tsuneishi Shipbuilding Co Ltd — Fukuyama HS** Yd No: 1176 Loa 225.00 Br ex - Dght 13.870 Lbp 216.00 Br md 32.26 Dpth 19.10 Welded, 1 dk	**(A21A2BC) Bulk Carrier** Grain: 88,344 Compartments: 7 Ho, ER 7 Ha: 6 (17.0 x 15.4)ER (15.3 x 12.8) Cranes: 4x30t	**1 oil engine** driving 1 FP propeller Total Power: 9,930kW (13,501hp) 15.0kn B&W 6S60MC 1 x 2 Stroke 6 Cy. 600 x 2292 9930kW (13501bhp) Mitsui Engineering & Shipbuilding CLtd-Japan Fuel: 2445.0 (r.f.)
9074470 *AUKK* -	**SRI PREM POORVA** *ex* Prem Poorva *-2013* *ex* Marvel Timonel *-2005* *ex* Maersk Timonel *-2002* **Mercator Ltd** - *Mumbai* *India* MMSI: 419572000 Official number: 3174	**36,708** 22,997 69,286	Class: IR (LR) (NK) Classed LR until 17/2/14	**1994**-07 **Hashihama Shipbuilding Co Ltd — Tadotsu KG** (Hull) Yd No: 1035 **1994**-07 **Tsuneishi Shipbuilding Co Ltd — Fukuyama HS** Yd No: 1035 Loa 225.00 (BB) Br ex - Dght 13.257 Lbp 215.00 Br md 32.20 Dpth 18.30 Welded, 1 dk	**(A21A2BC) Bulk Carrier** Grain: 81,769; Bale: 78,529 Compartments: 7 Ho, ER 7 Ha: (14.3 x 12.8)6 (16.8 x 14.4)ER Cranes: 4x25t	**1 oil engine** driving 1 FP propeller Total Power: 11,254kW (15,301hp) 14.0kn B&W 6S60MC 1 x 2 Stroke 6 Cy. 600 x 2292 11254kW (15301bhp) Mitsui Engineering & Shipbuilding CLtd-Japan AuxGen: 2 x 560kW 450V 60Hz a.c Boilers: AuxB (Comp) 6.5kgf/cm² (6.4bar) Fuel: 187.0 (d.f.) 2397.0 (r.f.)
9311165 *3FDD4* -	**SRI PREM VARSHA** *ex* Prem Varsha *-2012* *ex* Doric Challenge *-2007* **Varsha Vidya Inc** Mercator Lines (Singapore) Ltd *Panama* *Panama* MMSI: 357544000 Official number: 4333412A	**43,288** 27,638 82,379 T/cm 70.2	Class: LR ✠ **100A1** SS 01/2011 bulk carrier BC-A strengthened for heavy cargoes, Nos. 2, 4 & 6 holds may be empty ESP ESN LI *IWS **ShipRight** (SDA, FDA, CM) ✠ **LMC** **UMS** Eq.Ltr: O†; Cable: 660.0/78.0 U3 (a)	**2006**-01 **Tsuneishi Corp — Tadotsu KG** Yd No: 1309 Loa 228.99 Br ex 32.30 Dght 14.430 Lbp 222.00 Br md 32.26 Dpth 20.03 Welded, 1 dk	**(A21A2BC) Bulk Carrier** Grain: 97,000 Compartments: 7 Ho, ER 7 Ha: 6 (17.8 x 15.4)ER (14.2 x 13.8) Cranes: 4x30t	**1 oil engine** driving 1 FP propeller Total Power: 10,530kW (14,317hp) 14.5kn MAN-B&W 7S50MC-C 1 x 2 Stroke 7 Cy. 500 x 2000 10530kW (14317bhp) Mitsui Engineering & Shipbuilding CLtd-Japan AuxGen: 3 x 560kW 450V 60Hz a.c Boilers: WTAuxB (Comp) 7.1kgf/cm² (7.0bar) Fuel: 173.0 (d.f.) 2379.0 (r.f.)
9336373 *3FSF2* -	**SRI PREM VEENA** *ex* Prem Veena *-2012* *ex* Songa Anmaj *-2007* *ex* Achilles *-2007* **Mercator Lines (Singapore) Ltd** - *Panama* *Panama* MMSI: 355647000 Official number: 4332712A	**43,158** 27,286 82,792 T/cm 70.2	Class: NV (NK)	**2007**-01 **Tsuneishi Holdings Corp Tsuneishi Shipbuilding Co — Fukuyama HS** Yd No: 1341 Loa 228.99 Br ex 32.29 Dght 14.430 Lbp 222.00 Br md 32.26 Dpth 20.03 Welded, 1 dk	**(A21A2BC) Bulk Carrier** Grain: 97,186 Compartments: 7 Ho, ER 7 Ha: ER	**1 oil engine** driving 1 FP propeller Total Power: 9,800kW (13,324hp) 14.5kn MAN-B&W 7S50MC-C 1 x 2 Stroke 7 Cy. 500 x 2000 9800kW (13324bhp) Mitsui Engineering & Shipbuilding CLtd-Japan
9326275 *3FLF4* -	**SRI PREM VIDYA** *ex* Prem Vidya *-2012* *ex* Doric Freedom *-2007* **Varsha Vidya Inc** Mercator Lines (Singapore) Ltd *Panama* *Panama* MMSI: 370357000 Official number: 4333512A	**43,288** 27,565 82,273 T/cm 70.2	Class: LR ✠ **100A1** SS 11/2011 bulk carrier BC-A strengthened for heavy cargoes, Nos. 2, 4 & 6 holds may be empty ESP **ShipRight** (SDA, FDA, CM) ESN LI *IWS ✠ **LMC** **UMS** Eq.Ltr: O†; Cable: 660.0/78.0 U3 (a)	**2006**-11 **Tsuneishi Corp — Tadotsu KG** Yd No: 1344 Loa 228.99 Br ex 32.30 Dght 14.430 Lbp 222.00 Br md 32.26 Dpth 20.03 Welded, 1 dk	**(A21A2BC) Bulk Carrier** Grain: 97,000 Compartments: 7 Ho, ER 7 Ha: ER Cranes: 4x30t	**1 oil engine** driving 1 FP propeller Total Power: 10,530kW (14,317hp) 14.5kn MAN-B&W 7S50MC-C 1 x 2 Stroke 7 Cy. 500 x 2000 10530kW (14317bhp) Mitsui Engineering & Shipbuilding CLtd-Japan AuxGen: 3 x 560kW 450V 60Hz a.c Boilers: WTAuxB (Comp) 7.1kgf/cm² (7.0bar)
7634733 *HP5758* -	**SRI RAMA** *ex* Sam Hong I *-1988* *ex* Kay Chuan VII *-1976* *ex* Harumi Maru *-1976* **Dharma Agung SA** - *Panama* *Panama* Official number: 19984PEXT5	*115* 35 231	Class: (KI) (NK)	**1963**-02 **Setoda Zosensho KK — Onomichi HS** Yd No: 135 Loa 26.29 Br ex 6.99 Dght 2.439 Lbp 24.01 Br md 6.52 Dpth 3.19 Welded, 1 dk	**(B32A2ST) Tug**	**2 oil engines** geared to sc. shafts driving 2 FP propellers Total Power: 824kW (1,120hp) 10.5kn Yanmar 6UA-UT 2 x 4 Stroke 6 Cy. 200 x 240 each-412kW (560bhp) Kobe Hatsudoki KK-Japan AuxGen: 2 x 28kW
9643831 *HSB4684* -	**SRI TAH CHANA** - **NTL Marine Co Ltd** Nathalin Management Co Ltd *Bangkok* *Thailand* MMSI: 567457000 Official number: 550002366	**2,420** 800 3,000	Class: BV	**2012**-07 **Nanjing Yonghua Ship Co Ltd — Nanjing JS** Yd No: YHSC1007-01Y Loa 77.40 Br ex 15.03 Dght 4.800 Lbp 72.00 Br md 15.00 Dpth 7.00 Welded, 1 dk	**(A13B2TU) Tanker (unspecified)** Double Hull (13F) Liq: 3,330; Liq (Oil): 3,330 Compartments: 5 Wing Ta, 5 Wing Ta, ER	**1 oil engine** reduction geared to sc. shaft driving 1 FP propeller Total Power: 1,914kW (2,602hp) 11.5kn Daihatsu 6DKM-28 1 x 4 Stroke 6 Cy. 280 x 390 1914kW (2602bhp) Anqing Marine Diesel Engine Works-China AuxGen: 1 x 200kW a.c, 1 x 200kW a.c Fuel: 188.8
9047283 *HSB4440* -	**SRI TAHTHONG** *ex* Meisho Maru No. 28 *-2010* **NTL Marine Co Ltd** Nathalin Management Co Ltd SatCom: Inmarsat C 456700450 *Bangkok* *Thailand* MMSI: 567001120 Official number: 530000899	**1,005** 588 1,868	Class: NK	**1992**-10 **Shin Kochi Jyuko K.K. — Kochi** Yd No: 7027 Loa 75.02 Br ex - Dght 4.662 Lbp 70.00 Br md 11.20 Dpth 5.10 Welded, 1 dk	**(A13B2TP) Products Tanker** Liq: 2,203; Liq (Oil): 2,203 Compartments: 10 Ta, ER	**1 oil engine** reverse geared to sc. shaft driving 1 FP propeller Total Power: 1,324kW (1,800hp) 11.6kn Hanshin 6EL30G 1 x 4 Stroke 6 Cy. 300 x 600 1324kW (1800bhp) The Hanshin Diesel Works Ltd-Japan AuxGen: 3 x 90kW a.c Fuel: 60.0 (d.f.)
8609151 *HSB3910* -	**SRICHAIYA** *ex* Jasa 98 *-2008* *ex* Teruwa Maru *-1998* **BSL Leasing Co Ltd** - *Thailand* MMSI: 567055200 Official number: 510084491	**1,888** 907 2,898 T/cm 8.5	Class: (NK)	**1986**-06 **Taihei Kogyo K.K. — Hashihama, Imabari** Yd No: 1907 Loa 81.52 (BB) Br ex - Dght 5.568 Lbp 75.01 Br md 13.61 Dpth 6.61 Welded, 1 dk	**(A13B2TP) Products Tanker** Double Bottom Entire Compartment Length Liq: 3,250; Liq (Oil): 3,250 Compartments: 10 Ta, ER	**1 oil engine** with clutches & reduction geared to sc. shaft driving 1 CP propeller Total Power: 1,434kW (1,950hp) 12.3kn Akasaka A37 1 x 4 Stroke 6 Cy. 370 x 720 1434kW (1950bhp) Akasaka Tekkosho KK (Akasaka DieselLtd)-Japan AuxGen: 2 x 128kW 450V 60Hz a.c Fuel: 27.5 (d.f.) 85.5 (r.f.) 6.5pd
8129694 - -	**SRIJANI** - **Government of The People's Republic of Bangladesh (Ministry of Forests)** - *Bangladesh*	*100* - 150	Class: (KR)	**1982**-10 **Chungmu Shipbuilding Co Inc — Tongyeong** Yd No: 113 Loa - Br ex - Dght - Lbp - Br md - Dpth - Welded, 1 dk	**(A37B2PS) Passenger Ship**	**2 oil engines** driving 2 FP propellers Yanmar 2 x 4 Stroke Yanmar Diesel Engine Co Ltd-Japan
8805858 *PLSZ* -	**SRIJAYA 8** *ex* Unity *-2005* *ex* Wakasa *-2002* **PT Pelayaran Fajar Sribahari Sakti** - *Jakarta* *Indonesia* MMSI: 525015085	**680** 215 635	Class: KI	**1988**-05 **Murakami Hide Zosen K.K. — Imabari** Yd No: 283 Loa 56.60 Br ex - Dght 2.901 Lbp 52.02 Br md 9.80 Dpth 5.06 Welded	**(A31A2GX) General Cargo Ship** Grain: 1,450; Bale: 1,403 Compartments: 1 Ho, ER 1 Ha: ER	**1 oil engine** driving 1 FP propeller Total Power: 588kW (799hp) Yanmar MF26-HT 1 x 4 Stroke 6 Cy. 260 x 500 588kW (799bhp) Yanmar Diesel Engine Co Ltd-Japan AuxGen: 1 x 74kW 225V a.c

IMO / Call sign	Name / Owner / Port	Tonnage	Class	Builder / Dimensions	Type	Machinery
8996994 *YB4389* -	**SRIKANDI** **PT Srikandi Bahtera Nusantara** - *Jakarta* *Indonesia*	**107** 33 -	Class: (KI)	**2002-12 P.T. Anggun Segara — Tanjungpinang** Loa 26.88 Br ex - Dght 0.800 Lbp 26.00 Br md 5.20 Dpth 2.30 Bonded, 1 dk	**(A37B2PS) Passenger Ship** Hull Material: Reinforced Plastic	**2 oil engines** reduction geared to sc. shafts driving 2 Propellers Total Power: 1,618kW (2,200hp) MAN D2842LE 2 x Vee 4 Stroke 12 Cy. 128 x 142 each-809kW (1100bhp) (made 2000) MAN Nutzfahrzeuge AG-Nuernberg
9163063 *PMHR* -	**SRIKANDI** **PT Apol Cemerlang** PT Arpeni Pratama Ocean Line Tbk *Jakarta* *Indonesia* MMSI: 525011120	**2,670** 1,210 3,582	Class: NK	**1997-11 Chungmu Shipbuilding Co Inc — Tongyeong** Yd No: 248 Loa 90.00 (BB) Br ex - Dght 5.000 Lbp 85.00 Br md 15.00 Dpth 7.00 Welded, 1 dk	**(A13B2TP) Products Tanker** Double Bottom Partial Compartment Length Liq: 4,530; Liq (Oil): 4,530	**1 oil engine** driving 1 FP propeller Total Power: 1,618kW (2,200hp) 11.5kn Hanshin LH34LA 1 x 4 Stroke 6 Cy. 340 x 640 1618kW (2200bhp) The Hanshin Diesel Works Ltd-Japan Fuel: 230.0
5413836 *HPPI* -	**SRIKANDI** *ex* Taisei Maru No. 12 *-1968* **Yuni Navigation Co Ltd** - *Panama* *Panama* Official number: 47269	*483* 218 716	Class: (BV)	**1957-11 Koyo Dockyard Co Ltd — Mihara HS** Yd No: 50 L reg 47.58 Br ex 8.41 Dght 3.734 Lbp - Br md 8.36 Dpth 4.02 Riveted\Welded, 1 dk	**(A13B2TU) Tanker (unspecified)** Liq: 833; Liq (Oil): 833 Compartments: 8 Ta, ER	**1 oil engine** driving 1 FP propeller Total Power: 478kW (650hp) 12.0kn Niigata M6F31S 1 x 4 Stroke 6 Cy. 310 x 440 478kW (650bhp) Niigata Engineering Co Ltd-Japan AuxGen: 1 x 7kW 110V d.c, 1 x 5kW 110V d.c
8999506 *YB3390* -	**SRIKANDI 99** **PT Srikandi Bahtera Nusantara** - *Batam* *Indonesia*	**154** 47 -	Class: KI	**2002-07 PT Marinatama Gemanusa — Batam** Loa 31.75 Br ex 5.40 Dght 1.000 Lbp 27.20 Br md 5.00 Dpth 2.50 Bonded, 1 dk	**(A37B2PS) Passenger Ship** Hull Material: Reinforced Plastic	**2 oil engines** reduction geared to sc. shafts driving 2 Propellers Total Power: 1,618kW (2,200hp) 30.0kn MAN D2842LE 2 x Vee 4 Stroke 12 Cy. 128 x 142 each-809kW (1100bhp) (made 2001) MAN Nutzfahrzeuge AG-Nuernberg
9705811 *JZOS* -	**SRIKANDI 511** **PT Lima Srikandi Jaya** - *Indonesia* MMSI: 525018192	**2,221** 1,088 2,688	Class: RI	**2013-09 Jiangsu Huatai Shipbuilding Co Ltd — Taixing JS** Yd No: HT-61 Loa 88.28 (BB) Br ex - Dght 3.250 Lbp 83.54 Br md 15.00 Dpth 4.80 Welded, 1 dk	**(A13B2TP) Products Tanker** Double Hull (13F)	**2 oil engines** reduction geared to sc. shafts driving 2 FP propellers Total Power: 1,220kW (1,658hp) Mitsubishi S6R2-MPTK 2 x 4 Stroke 6 Cy. 170 x 220 each-610kW (829bhp) Mitsubishi Heavy Industries Ltd-Japan AuxGen: 2 x 48kW 400V 50Hz a.c
9706188 - -	**SRIKANDI 512** **PT Lima Srikandi Jaya** -	**2,221** 1,088 3,200	Class: RI	**2013-09 Jiangsu Huatai Shipbuilding Co Ltd — Taixing JS** Yd No: HT-62 Loa 88.28 Br ex - Dght 3.250 Lbp 83.54 Br md 15.00 Dpth 4.80 Welded, 1 dk	**(A13B2TP) Products Tanker**	**2 oil engines** reduction geared to sc. shafts driving 2 FP propellers Total Power: 1,220kW (1,658hp) Mitsubishi S6R2-MPTR 2 x 4 Stroke 6 Cy. 170 x 220 each-610kW (829bhp) Mitsubishi Heavy Industries Ltd-Japan AuxGen: 2 x 48kW 400V 50Hz a.c
9710816 *JZOU* -	**SRIKANDI 514** **PT Lima Srikandi Jaya** - *Indonesia*	**1,975** 1,088 3,200	Class: RI (Class contemplated)	**2013-11 Jiangsu Huatai Shipbuilding Co Ltd — Taixing JS** Yd No: HT-63 Loa 88.28 Br ex - Dght - Lbp - Br md 15.00 Dpth 4.80 Welded, 1 dk	**(A12B2TR) Chemical/Products Tanker** Double Hull (13F)	**2 oil engines** reduction geared to sc. shafts driving 2 Propellers Mitsubishi Mitsubishi Heavy Industries Ltd-Japan
9710828 - -	**SRIKANDI 515** **PT Lima Srikandi Jaya** - *Indonesia*	**1,975** 1,088 3,200	Class: RI (Class contemplated)	**2013-11 Jiangsu Huatai Shipbuilding Co Ltd — Taixing JS** Yd No: HT-64 Loa 88.28 Br ex - Dght - Lbp - Br md 15.00 Dpth 4.80 Welded, 1 dk	**(A12B2TR) Chemical/Products Tanker** Double Hull (13F)	**2 oil engines** reduction geared to sc. shafts driving 2 Propellers Mitsubishi Mitsubishi Heavy Industries Ltd-Japan
9726097 *JZOW* -	**SRIKANDI 516** **PT Lima Srikandi Jaya** Union Venture Marine *Indonesia* MMSI: 525018196	**1,975** 1,088 3,200	Class: IZ	**2014-01 Jiangsu Huatai Shipbuilding Co Ltd — Taixing JS** Yd No: HT-65 Loa 88.28 (BB) Br ex - Dght - Lbp - Br md 15.00 Dpth 4.80 Welded, 1 dk	**(A13B2TP) Products Tanker** Double Hull (13F)	**2 oil engines** reduction geared to sc. shaft (s) driving 2 Propellers Total Power: 1,220kW (1,658hp) Mitsubishi S6R2-MPTK 2 x 4 Stroke 6 Cy. 170 x 220 each-610kW (829bhp) Mitsubishi Heavy Industries Ltd-Japan
9697571 *JZOX* -	**SRIKANDI 517** **PT Lima Srikandi Jaya** Union Venture Marine *Indonesia* MMSI: 525018197	**1,975** 1,088 3,200	Class: IZ KI	**2013-12 Jiangsu Hongqiang Marine Heavy Industry Co Ltd — Qidong JS** Yd No: HQ073 Loa 88.28 Br ex - Dght 4.000 Lbp 83.54 Br md 15.00 Dpth 4.80 Welded, 1 dk	**(A12B2TR) Chemical/Products Tanker**	**2 oil engines** reverse reduction geared to sc. shafts driving 2 Propellers Total Power: 1,060kW (1,442hp) Mitsubishi S6R2-MPTK 2 x 4 Stroke 6 Cy. 170 x 220 each-530kW (721bhp) Mitsubishi Co.-Japan
9697583 *JZOY* -	**SRIKANDI 518** **PT Lima Srikandi Jaya** Union Venture Marine *Indonesia* MMSI: 525018198	**2,231** 1,249 3,200	Class: IZ KI (Class contemplated)	**2013-12 Jiangsu Hongqiang Marine Heavy Industry Co Ltd — Qidong JS** Yd No: HQ074 Loa 88.28 Br ex - Dght 4.000 Lbp 83.54 Br md 15.00 Dpth 4.80 Welded, 1 dk	**(A12B2TR) Chemical/Products Tanker**	**2 oil engines** reverse reduction geared to sc. shafts driving 2 Propellers Total Power: 1,060kW (1,442hp) Mitsubishi 1 x 530kW (721bhp) Mitsubishi Co.-Japan Mitsubishi S6R2-MPTK 1 x 4 Stroke 6 Cy. 170 x 220 530kW (721bhp) Mitsubishi Co.-Japan
8216825 *YHLP* -	**SRIKANDI LINE** *ex* Hidezuru Maru *-2004* **PT Bukit Merapin Nusantara Lines** - *Jakarta* *Indonesia* MMSI: 525015268 Official number: 8532	**1,914** 575 767	Class: KI	**1983-09 Hayashikane Shipbuilding & Engineering Co Ltd — Nagasaki NS** Yd No: 913 Loa 65.99 Br ex 13.72 Dght 3.701 Lbp 64.85 Br md 13.70 Dpth 5.00 Welded, 2 dks	**(A36A2PR) Passenger/Ro-Ro Ship (Vehicles)** Passengers: unberthed: 600 Bow door/ramp Stern door/ramp Lane-Len: 100 Cars: 37, Trailers: 21	**2 oil engines** with clutches & sr geared to sc. shafts driving 2 FP propellers Total Power: 2,648kW (3,600hp) 14.9kn Daihatsu 6DSM-28 2 x 4 Stroke 6 Cy. 280 x 340 each-1324kW (1800bhp) Daihatsu Diesel Manufacturing Co Lt-Japan AuxGen: 2 x 240kW 450V 60Hz a.c Thrusters: 1 Thwart. CP thruster (f) Fuel: 24.5 (d.f.) 69.0 (r.f.)
7506247 *YB5167* -	**SRIKANDI NUSANTARA** *ex* Under Grace I *-1997* *ex* Nippo No. 2 *-1996* *ex* Kamagari No. 2 *-1988* **PT Jembatan Nusantara** - *Semarang* *Indonesia*	*476* 143 116	Class: KI	**1975-07 Imamura Zosen — Kure** Yd No: 205 Loa 38.71 Br ex 10.01 Dght 2.007 Lbp 32.49 Br md 8.18 Dpth 2.90 Welded	**(A36A2PR) Passenger/Ro-Ro Ship (Vehicles)** Passengers: unberthed: 364	**1 oil engine** driving 1 FP propeller Total Power: 441kW (600hp) Niigata 6L25BXB 1 x 4 Stroke 6 Cy. 250 x 320 441kW (600bhp) Niigata Engineering Co Ltd-Japan
7712171 - -	**SRIMUKHA** **Kakinada Port Authority** - *Kakinada* *India*	*240* - 250	Class: IR	**1975-11 Bharati Shipyard Ltd — Kakinada** Loa 35.11 Br ex 8.69 Dght 1.531 Lbp 33.02 Br md 8.41 Dpth 2.42 Welded, 1 dk	**(A13B2TP) Products Tanker**	**2 oil engines** geared to sc. shafts driving 2 FP propellers Total Power: 200kW (272hp) Torpedo-Rijeka T534A 2 x 4 Stroke 4 Cy. 112 x 140 each-100kW (136bhp) Tvornica Motora 'Torpedo'-Yugoslavia
9002790 - -	**SRINAKARIN** **Government of The Kingdom of Thailand (Marine Police Division)** - *Bangkok* *Thailand*	*675* - -	Class: (LR) ✠	**1992-02 Italthai Marine Co., Ltd. — Samut Prakan** Yd No: 82 Loa 62.00 Br ex 8.21 Dght 2.400 Lbp 54.98 Br md 8.20 Dpth 4.77 Welded, 1 dk	**(B34H2SQ) Patrol Vessel**	**2 oil engines** with clutches, flexible couplings & sr reverse geared to sc. shafts driving 2 FP propellers Total Power: 7,040kW (9,572hp) 25.0kn Deutz SBV16M628 2 x Vee 4 Stroke 16 Cy. 240 x 280 each-3520kW (4786bhp) Motoren Werke Mannheim AG (MWM)-Mannheim AuxGen: 2 x 215kW 440V 60Hz a.c
6829422 *HSAR* -	**SRINAKORN 15** *ex* Hartford *-2012* *ex* Junta Maru *-1983* *ex* Seisho Maru No. 8 *-1983* **Vichai Pongsasalikul** - *Bangkok* *Thailand* Official number: 260845014	*478* 263 -		**1968 KK Kanasashi Zosen — Shizuoka SZ** Yd No: 841 Lengthened-1979 L reg 53.80 Br ex 8.64 Dght 3.607 Lbp 47.99 Br md 8.62 Dpth 4.09 Welded, 1 dk	**(B11B2FV) Fishing Vessel**	**1 oil engine** driving 1 FP propeller Total Power: 956kW (1,300hp) Ito M356HS 1 x 4 Stroke 6 Cy. 350 x 500 956kW (1300bhp) Ito Tekkosho-Japan
7124130 *HSB2077* -	**SRINAPA** *ex* Kaiko Maru No. 85 *-1983* **Duang Jutha Co Ltd** Nathalin Co Ltd *Bangkok* *Thailand* Official number: 261031862	*499* 322 1,200		**1971 Sanuki Shipbuilding & Iron Works Co Ltd — Mitoyo KG** Yd No: 606 Loa 52.20 Br ex 9.66 Dght 4.242 Lbp 52.02 Br md 9.61 Dpth 4.50 Riveted\Welded, 1 dk	**(A13B2TP) Products Tanker** Single Hull Liq: 1,446; Liq (Oil): 1,446 Compartments: 4 Ta, ER 2 Cargo Pump (s): 2x400m³/hr	**1 oil engine** driving 1 FP propeller Total Power: 1,030kW (1,400hp) 11.5kn Makita FSHC633 1 x 4 Stroke 6 Cy. 330 x 500 1030kW (1400bhp) Makita Tekkosho-Japan Fuel: 406.5 (d.f.)

IMO / Call sign	Name / Owner	Tonnage	Build / Dimensions	Type	Machinery
8954805 - -	**SRINOPPARAT 15** - **Somkiet Kasemteerasomboon** - *Bangkok* *Thailand* Official number: 430900129	**215** 146 447	**1999 in Thailand** Loa 33.00 Br ex 7.00 Dght - Lbp - Br md - Dpth 4.20 Welded, 1 dk	**(A34A2GR) Refrigerated Cargo Ship**	**1 oil engine** driving 1 FP propeller Total Power: 448kW (609hp) Cummins 1 x 4 Stroke 448kW (609bhp) Cummins Engine Co Inc-USA
5323172 *HSKD* -	**SRIPINYO** *ex Shinei Maru No. 8 -1973* **Madam Poonsri Sutharom** - *Bangkok* *Thailand* Official number: 161012760	*1,827* 980 3,053	Class: (NK) **1960-12 Kawasaki Dockyard Co Ltd — Kobe HG** Yd No: 995 Loa 84.97 Br ex 12.76 Dght 5.665 Lbp 78.01 Br md 12.70 Dpth 6.56 Welded, 1 dk	**(A31A2GX) General Cargo Ship** Grain: 3,745; Bale: 3,507 Compartments: 2 Ho, ER 2 Ha: (9.2 x 5.5) (26.6 x 5.5)ER Derricks: 1x40t,6x10t	**1 oil engine** driving 1 FP propeller Total Power: 1,177kW (1,600hp) 10.5kn Kinoshita 6UKNHS 1 x 4 Stroke 6 Cy. 470 x 680 1177kW (1600bhp) Kinoshita Tekkosho-Japan AuxGen: 2 x 50kW 225V d.c Fuel: 187.0 (d.f.)
7205013 - -	**SRIRACHA 3** *ex Tomozuru Maru -1995* **Sriracha Tugboat Co Ltd** - *Thailand* Official number: 382000039	*200* 60 -	**1971 Towa Zosen K.K. — Shimonoseki** Yd No: 416 Loa 29.01 Br ex 8.23 Dght 2.801 Lbp - Br md 8.21 Dpth 3.81 Welded, 1 dk	**(B32A2ST) Tug**	**2 oil engines** driving 2 Voith-Schneider propellers Total Power: 1,618kW (2,200hp) Hanshin 6L32 2 x 4 Stroke 6 Cy. 320 x 390 each-809kW (1100bhp) Hanshin Nainenki Kogyo-Japan AuxGen: 2 x 35kW Fuel: 48.0 4.0pd
6920575 - -	**SRIRACHA 4** *ex Kakusho Maru -1995* **Sriracha Tugboat Co Ltd** - *Thailand* Official number: 382000110	*221* 66 -	**1969 Towa Zosen K.K. — Shimonoseki** Yd No: 373 Loa 29.99 Br ex 8.23 Dght 2.794 Lbp 29.01 Br md 8.21 Dpth 3.79 Welded, 1 dk	**(B32A2ST) Tug**	**2 oil engines** driving 2 Voith-Schneider propellers Total Power: 1,618kW (2,200hp) Hanshin 6L32 2 x 4 Stroke 6 Cy. 320 x 390 each-809kW (1100bhp) Hanshin Nainenki Kogyo-Japan AuxGen: 2 x 28kW Fuel: 48.0 4.0pd
7001649 - -	**SRIRACHA 5** *ex Shinsei Maru -2005* **Sriracha Tugboat Co Ltd** - *Bangkok* *Thailand* Official number: 392000065	*199* 50 -	**1969 Shin Yamamoto Shipbuilding & Engineering Co Ltd — Kochi KC** Yd No: 123 Loa 29.77 Br ex 8.23 Dght 2.794 Lbp 26.98 Br md 8.21 Dpth 3.79 Riveted\Welded, 1 dk	**(B32A2ST) Tug**	**2 oil engines** driving 2 Voith-Schneider propellers Total Power: 1,618kW (2,200hp) Hanshin 6L32 2 x 4 Stroke 6 Cy. 320 x 390 each-809kW (1100bhp) Hanshin Nainenki Kogyo-Japan AuxGen: 2 x 35kW a.c
7353389 *HSB2376* -	**SRIRACHA 6** *ex Shonan Maru -1995* *ex Kyokko Maru No. 5 -1986* **Sriracha Tugboat Co Ltd** - *Thailand* Official number: 381000905	*227* 68 71	**1973 Sanyo Zosen K.K. — Onomichi** Yd No: 672 Loa 32.10 Br ex 8.84 Dght 3.010 Lbp 26.01 Br md 8.82 Dpth 3.85 Riveted\Welded, 1 dk	**(B32A2ST) Tug**	**2 oil engines** reduction geared to sc. shafts driving 2 Z propellers Total Power: 2,428kW (3,302hp) Fuji 6S32FH 2 x 4 Stroke 6 Cy. 320 x 500 each-1214kW (1651bhp) Fuji Diesel Co Ltd-Japan AuxGen: 2 x 35kW 60Hz a.c
6729311 - -	**SRIRACHA 7** *ex Sakai Maru -1996 ex Kyoho Maru -1995* *ex Take Maru No. 32 -1984* *ex Higashi Maru -1984* **Sriracha Tugboat Co Ltd** - *Thailand* Official number: 391000355	*209* 62 -	**1967 Osaka Shipbuilding Co Ltd — Osaka OS** Yd No: 272 L reg 31.95 Br ex 8.22 Dght 2.718 Lbp 30.84 Br md 8.20 Dpth 3.80 Welded, 1 dk	**(B32A2ST) Tug**	**2 oil engines** driving 2 Voith-Schneider propellers Total Power: 1,618kW (2,200hp) Niigata 6L31AX 2 x 4 Stroke 6 Cy. 310 x 380 each-809kW (1100bhp) Niigata Engineering Co Ltd-Japan AuxGen: 2 x 35kW 220V 60Hz a.c
6800701 - -	**SRIRACHA 8** *ex Haruta Maru -1998* **Sriracha Tugboat Co Ltd** - *Bangkok* *Thailand* Official number: 402000026	*197* 53 -	**1967 Towa Zosen K.K. — Shimonoseki** Yd No: 355 Loa 29.61 Br ex 8.22 Dght 2.871 Lbp 28.99 Br md 8.20 Dpth 3.79 Welded, 1 dk	**(B32A2ST) Tug**	**2 oil engines** driving 2 Voith-Schneider propellers Total Power: 1,618kW (2,200hp) Hanshin 6L32 2 x 4 Stroke 6 Cy. 320 x 390 each-809kW (1100bhp) Hanshin Nainenki Kogyo-Japan AuxGen: 2 x 28kW 225V 60Hz a.c
6622159 - -	**SRIRACHA 12** *ex Amagi Maru -1989* *ex V. S. P. Matsushima Maru -1989* **Sriracha Tugboat Co Ltd** - *Thailand* Official number: 321002557	*193* 70 -	**1966 Osaka Shipbuilding Co Ltd — Osaka OS** Yd No: 262 Loa 31.96 Br ex 8.26 Dght 2.718 Lbp 30.87 Br md 8.21 Dpth 3.79 Riveted\Welded, 1 dk	**(B32A2ST) Tug**	**2 oil engines** driving 2 Voith-Schneider propellers Total Power: 1,618kW (2,200hp) Niigata 6L31AX 2 x 4 Stroke 6 Cy. 310 x 380 each-809kW (1100bhp) Niigata Engineering Co Ltd-Japan AuxGen: 2 x 20kW 220V a.c Fuel: 24.0 3.0pd
8402981 *HSB3150* -	**SRIRACHA 16** *ex Atsumi Maru -2004* **Sriracha Tugboat Co Ltd** - *Thailand* MMSI: 567053700 Official number: 470001834	*332* 100 -	**1984-04 Kanagawa Zosen — Kobe** Yd No: 262 Loa 35.00 Br ex - Dght 3.101 Lbp 30.51 Br md 9.61 Dpth 4.22 Welded, 1 dk	**(B32A2ST) Tug**	**2 oil engines** sr geared to sc. shafts driving 2 Z propellers Total Power: 2,574kW (3,500hp) Niigata 6L28BXE 2 x 4 Stroke 6 Cy. 280 x 320 each-1287kW (1750bhp) Niigata Engineering Co Ltd-Japan AuxGen: 2 x 96kW 220V 60Hz a.c
7913763 *HSB3135* -	**SRIRACHA 17** *ex Sekio Maru -2004 ex Horyu Maru -1996* **Sriracha Tugboat Co Ltd** - *Bangkok* *Thailand* MMSI: 567000259 Official number: 470001842	**311** 94 -	**1979-10 Sagami Zosen Tekko K.K. — Yokosuka** Yd No: 200 Loa 33.00 Br ex - Dght 3.100 Lbp 29.72 Br md 9.60 Dpth 4.20 Welded, 1 dk	**(B32A2ST) Tug**	**2 oil engines** driving 2 Z propellers Total Power: 2,354kW (3,200hp) Niigata 8L25BX 2 x 4 Stroke 8 Cy. 250 x 320 each-1177kW (1600bhp) Niigata Engineering Co Ltd-Japan AuxGen: 2 x 80kW 380V 60Hz a.c
8118279 *HSB3193* -	**SRIRACHA 18** *ex Tenryu Maru -2005* **Sriracha Tugboat Co Ltd** - *Bangkok* *Thailand* Official number: 470003242	**296** 89 -	**1981-10 Kanagawa Zosen — Kobe** Yd No: 230 Loa 35.01 Br ex - Dght 3.101 Lbp 30.51 Br md 9.61 Dpth 4.22 Welded, 1 dk	**(B32A2ST) Tug**	**2 oil engines** driving 2 Z propellers Total Power: 2,354kW (3,200hp) Niigata 6MG28BX 2 x 4 Stroke 6 Cy. 280 x 320 each-1177kW (1600bhp) Niigata Engineering Co Ltd-Japan AuxGen: 2 x 80kW 440V 60Hz a.c Fuel: 41.5 (d.f.) 8.5pd
8122270 *HSB3383* -	**SRIRACHA 19** *ex Nunobiki Maru -2006* **Sriracha Tugboat Co Ltd** - *Bangkok* *Thailand* Official number: 490000638	**169** 51 -	**1982-04 Kanagawa Zosen — Kobe** Yd No: 236 Loa 27.01 Br ex 8.16 Dght 2.601 Lbp 24.96 Br md 8.00 Dpth 3.60 Welded, 1 dk	**(B32A2ST) Tug**	**2 oil engines** driving 2 Z propellers Total Power: 1,398kW (1,900hp) Niigata 6MG22LX 2 x 4 Stroke 6 Cy. 220 x 290 each-699kW (950bhp) Niigata Engineering Co Ltd-Japan AuxGen: 2 x 48kW 220V 60Hz a.c Fuel: 20.5 (d.f.) 7.0pd
8020240 *HSB3384* -	**SRIRACHA 20** *ex Hario Maru -2005 ex Kasuga Maru -2005* **Sriracha Tugboat Co Ltd** - *Bangkok* *Thailand* Official number: 490000620	**243** 73 -	**1980-12 Kanagawa Zosen — Kobe** Yd No: 216 Loa 31.60 Br ex 8.62 Dght - Lbp 27.00 Br md 8.60 Dpth 3.80 Welded, 1 dk	**(B32A2ST) Tug**	**2 oil engines** gearing integral to driving 2 Z propellers Total Power: 1,912kW (2,600hp) Niigata 6L25BX 2 x 4 Stroke 6 Cy. 250 x 320 each-956kW (1300bhp) Niigata Engineering Co Ltd-Japan AuxGen: 2 x 48kW 440V a.c
8821151 *HSB3423* -	**SRIRACHA 21** *ex Ube Maru -2006 ex Tamano Maru -2002* **Sriracha Tugboat Co Ltd** - *Bangkok* *Thailand* MMSI: 567000880 Official number: 490001579	**258** 78 -	**1989-01 Kanagawa Zosen — Kobe** Yd No: 321 Loa 36.20 Br ex - Dght 2.800 Lbp 32.00 Br md 8.80 Dpth 3.80 Welded, 1 dk	**(B32A2ST) Tug**	**2 oil engines** reduction geared to sc. shafts driving 2 Z propellers Total Power: 2,574kW (3,500hp) Niigata 6L28BXE 2 x 4 Stroke 6 Cy. 280 x 320 each-1287kW (1750bhp) Niigata Engineering Co Ltd-Japan AuxGen: 2 x 96kW 250V 60Hz a.c
8514992 *HSB4238* -	**SRIRACHA 22** *ex Taiho Maru -2009* **Sriracha Tugboat Co Ltd** - *Bangkok* *Thailand* MMSI: 567001060 Official number: 520081110	**225** 68 80	**1985-12 Osaka Shipbuilding Co Ltd — Osaka OS** Yd No: 438 Loa 31.09 Br ex - Dght 2.901 Lbp 26.52 Br md 8.72 Dpth 3.92 Welded, 1 dk	**(B32A2ST) Tug**	**2 oil engines** sr geared to sc. shaft driving 2 Z propellers Total Power: 2,500kW (3,400hp) Daihatsu 6DLM-28 2 x 4 Stroke 6 Cy. 280 x 360 each-1250kW (1700bhp) Daihatsu Diesel Manufacturing Co Lt-Japan AuxGen: 2 x 72kW 220V 60Hz a.c

ID / Call sign	Name, former names, owner, registry	Tonnage	Class	Builder, dimensions	Type, cargo details	Machinery
8904678 *HSB4422* -	**SRIRACHA 24** *ex* Soya Maru *-2010* *ex* Asagiri *-2001* **Sriracha Tugboat Co Ltd** - *Thailand* MMSI: 567000275 Official number: 5300011004	**216** 89 -		**1989-04 Kanagawa Zosen — Kobe** Yd No: 326 Loa 35.20 Br ex - Dght 3.100 Lbp 30.50 Br md 9.60 Dpth 4.20 Welded	**(B32A2ST) Tug**	**2 oil engines** Geared Integral to driving 2 Z propellers Total Power: 2,574kW (3,500hp) Niigata 6L28BXE 2 x 4 Stroke 6 Cy. 280 x 320 each-1287kW (1750bhp) Niigata Engineering Co Ltd-Japan AuxGen: 2 x 90kW a.c
9128788 *HSB4669* -	**SRIRACHA 25** *ex* Akashia Maru *-2012* **Sriracha Tugboat Co Ltd** - *Thailand* MMSI: 567061700 Official number: 550002390	**272** 82 71		**1995-06 Niigata Engineering Co Ltd — Niigata NI** Yd No: 2281 Loa 31.00 Br ex - Dght 2.680 Lbp 27.00 Br md 8.00 Dpth 3.00 Welded, 1 dk	**(B32A2ST) Tug**	**2 oil engines** with clutches, flexible couplings & dr geared to sc. shafts driving 2 FP propellers Total Power: 2,354kW (3,200hp) Niigata 6L25HX 2 x 4 Stroke 6 Cy. 250 x 350 each-1177kW (1600bhp) Niigata Engineering Co Ltd-Japan
9135377 *HSB4700* -	**SRIRACHA 26** *ex* Mitsu Maru *-2012* **Sriracha Tugboat Co Ltd** - *Thailand* MMSI: 567000349 Official number: 550002405	**272** 82 -		**1995-11 Niigata Engineering Co Ltd — Niigata NI** Yd No: 2282 Loa 31.02 Br ex - Dght 2.670 Lbp 27.00 Br md 8.80 Dpth 3.50 Welded, 1 dk	**(B32A2ST) Tug**	**2 oil engines** geared integral to driving 2 Z propellers Total Power: 2,354kW (3,200hp) 12.5kn Niigata 6L25HX 2 x 4 Stroke 6 Cy. 250 x 350 each-1177kW (1600bhp) Niigata Engineering Co Ltd-Japan
9108142 *HSB4685* -	**SRIRACHA EAGLE** *ex* Dalmacija *-2012* *ex* Banda Sea *-2000* **Khunnathee Co Ltd** - *Bangkok* *Thailand* MMSI: 567458000 Official number: 550001344	**53,639** 27,821 96,168 T/cm 89.8	Class: (BV) (AB) (CS)	**1996-05 Samsung Heavy Industries Co Ltd — Geoje** Yd No: 1137 Loa 243.28 (BB) Br ex 41.84 Dght 13.710 Lbp 233.00 Br md 41.80 Dpth 20.03 Welded, 1 dk	**(A13A2TV) Crude Oil Tanker** Double Hull (13F) Liq: 104,397; Liq (Oil): 104,397 Cargo Heating Coils Compartments: 12 Wing Ta, 2 Wing Slop Ta, ER 3 Cargo Pump (s): 3x2500m³/hr Manifold: Bow/CM: 121.9m	**1 oil engine** driving 1 FP propeller Total Power: 10,416kW (14,162hp) 14.2kn B&W 6L60MC 1 x 2 Stroke 6 Cy. 600 x 1944 10416kW (14162bhp) Hyundai Heavy Industries Co Ltd-South Korea Fuel: 120.4 (d.f.) 2411.7 (r.f.)
8814433 *HSB4656* -	**SRIRACHA LEADER** *ex* Zygi *-2012* *ex* Torm Olga *-2005* *ex* Olga *-2004* *ex* Gunta *-1995* *ex* Argo Europa *-1992* **Khunnathee Co Ltd** - *Bangkok* *Thailand* MMSI: 567456000 Official number: 550000958	**24,731** 12,652 44,484 T/cm 48.4	Class: (LR) ✠ Classed LR until 7/3/12	**1992-03 Dalian Shipyard Co Ltd — Dalian LN** Yd No: PC380/2 Loa 182.06 (BB) Br ex 30.03 Dght 10.870 Lbp 174.55 Br md 30.00 Dpth 17.00 Welded, 1 dk	**(A13A2TW) Crude/Oil Products Tanker** Double Hull (13F) Liq: 46,494; Liq (Oil): 46,495 Cargo Heating Coils Compartments: 7 Ta, 2 Wing Slop Ta, ER 4 Cargo Pump (s): 4x900m³/hr Manifold: Bow/CM: 92.5m	**1 oil engine** driving 1 FP propeller Total Power: 7,060kW (9,599hp) 14.0kn B&W 5L60MC 1 x 2 Stroke 5 Cy. 600 x 1944 7060kW (9599bhp) Dalian Marine Diesel Works-China AuxGen: 3 x 560kW 450V 60Hz a.c Boilers: e (ex.g.) 18.4kgf/cm² (18.0bar), AuxB (o.f.) 18.4kgf/cm² (18.0bar) Fuel: 210.0 (d.f.) 1561.0 (r.f.)
8920086 *HSB4479* -	**SRIRACHA MASTER** *ex* Taiyoh I *-2010* **Khunnathee Co Ltd** - *Bangkok* *Thailand* MMSI: 567056300 Official number: 530001691	**54,931** 27,471 89,960 T/cm 89.0	Class: (NK)	**1991-06 Namura Shipbuilding Co Ltd — Imari SG** Yd No: 912 Loa 241.78 (BB) Br ex 42.03 Dght 12.931 Lbp 232.00 Br md 42.00 Dpth 20.40 Welded, 1 dk	**(A13A2TV) Crude Oil Tanker** Double Sides Entire Compartment Length Liq: 108,355; Liq (Oil): 112,579 Cargo Heating Coils Compartments: 5 Ta, 4 Wing Ta, ER 3 Cargo Pump (s): 3x2500m³/hr Manifold: Bow/CM: 119.6m	**1 oil engine** driving 1 FP propeller Total Power: 9,400kW (12,780hp) 14.0kn Sulzer 7RTA62 1 x 2 Stroke 7 Cy. 620 x 2150 9400kW (12780bhp) Mitsubishi Heavy Industries Ltd-Japan AuxGen: 3 x 600kW 450V 60Hz a.c Fuel: 162.0 (d.f.) 2401.0 (r.f.) 31.7pd
9108647 *HSB3934* -	**SRIRACHA TRADER** *ex* Torm Gotland *-2008* **Khunnathee Co Ltd** Nathalin Co Ltd *Bangkok* *Thailand* MMSI: 567356000 Official number: 520080287	**28,628** 12,678 47,629 T/cm 50.4	Class: (LR) ✠ Classed LR until 30/7/12	**1995-08 Onomichi Dockyard Co Ltd — Onomichi HS** Yd No: 389 Converted From: Chemical/Products Tanker-2009 Loa 182.84 (BB) Br ex 32.23 Dght 12.820 Lbp 172.00 Br md 32.20 Dpth 19.10 Welded, 1 dk	**(A13A2TW) Crude/Oil Products Tanker** Double Hull (13F) Liq: 50,386; Liq (Oil): 50,386 Compartments: 2 Ta, 12 Wing Ta, ER, 2 Wing Slop Ta, 1 Slop Ta 14 Cargo Pump (s): 14x500m³/hr Manifold: Bow/CM: 94.1m	**1 oil engine** driving 1 FP propeller Total Power: 8,580kW (11,665hp) 14.8kn B&W 6S50MC 1 x 2 Stroke 6 Cy. 500 x 1910 8580kW (11665bhp) Mitsui Engineering & Shipbuilding CLtd-Japan AuxGen: 4 x 680kW 450V 60Hz a.c Boilers: 2 AuxB (o.f.) 11.4kgf/cm² (11.2bar), e (ex.g.) 15.0kgf/cm² (14.7bar) Fuel: 245.6 (d.f.) (Heating Coils) 1660.1 (r.f.)
8973796 *HSB2595* -	**SRIVICHAI NAVEE 1** *ex* Darachai 1 *-2012* **Srivichai Navee Co Ltd** - *Bangkok* *Thailand* Official number: 411000651	**834** 250 -		**1998-11 in Thailand** Loa 49.90 Br ex 12.45 Dght - Lbp 47.70 Br md - Dpth 4.75 Welded, 1 dk	**(A31A2GX) General Cargo Ship**	**2 oil engines** geared to sc. shafts driving 2 CP propellers Total Power: 700kW (952hp) Cummins 2 x 4 Stroke each-350kW (476bhp) Cummins Engine Co Inc-USA
9370068 - -	**SRIVICHAI NAVEE 2** - **KTB Leasing Co Ltd** - *Bangkok* *Thailand* Official number: 480001470	**788** 425 1,100		**2005-12 Pronpiya Development & Service Co Ltd — Bang Sai** Loa 49.60 Br ex - Dght - Lbp 48.50 Br md 13.00 Dpth 4.20 Welded, 1 dk	**(A31A2GX) General Cargo Ship**	**2 oil engines** reduction geared to sc. shafts driving 2 Propellers Total Power: 760kW (1,034hp) Cummins 2 x 4 Stroke each-380kW (517bhp) Cummins Engine Co Inc-USA
8001725 *YCSD* -	**SRIWIJAYA BAHARI** *ex* S & B No. 1 *-2012* *ex* Joong-A No. 1 *-2003* *ex* Jadis No. 1 *-2003* *ex* Nichinan Maru *-1996* *ex* Kami Maru No. 7 *-1988* **PT Isna Agung Permata** - *Pontianak* *Indonesia* MMSI: 525371600	**1,434** 1,021 1,496	Class: KI (KR) (NK)	**1980-04 Mategata Zosen K.K. — Namikata** Yd No: 188 Loa 71.13 Br ex - Dght 4.042 Lbp 66.35 Br md 12.00 Dpth 6.45 Welded, 2 dks	**(A31A2GX) General Cargo Ship** Grain: 3,145; Bale: 2,925 1 Ha: (40.6 x 9.3)ER	**1 oil engine** driving 1 FP propeller Total Power: 1,324kW (1,800hp) 11.8kn Akasaka DM36 1 x 4 Stroke 6 Cy. 360 x 540 1324kW (1800bhp) Akasaka Tekkosho KK (Akasaka DieselLtd)-Japan AuxGen: 2 x 72kW 225V a.c
9131553 *YDA4205* -	**SRO 7** - **PT Trans Tirtajasa Gemilang** - *Jakarta* *Indonesia*	**129** 39 137	Class: KI (NK)	**1995-06 Far East Shipyard Co Sdn Bhd — Sibu** Yd No: 02/95 Loa 23.15 Br ex - Dght 2.512 Lbp 21.05 Br md 7.30 Dpth 3.00 Welded, 1 dk	**(B32A2ST) Tug**	**2 oil engines** reduction geared to sc. shafts driving 2 FP propellers Total Power: 692kW (940hp) 9.5kn Caterpillar 3408TA 2 x Vee 4 Stroke 8 Cy. 137 x 152 each-346kW (470bhp) Caterpillar Inc-USA
9131577 - -	**SRO III** - **Samudra Raya Offshore Pte Ltd** -	**153** 46 110	Class: (NK)	**1995-06 Super-Light Shipbuilding Contractor — Sibu** Yd No: 12 Loa 23.50 Br ex - Dght 2.512 Lbp 21.43 Br md 7.50 Dpth 3.10 Welded, 1 dk	**(B32A2ST) Tug**	**2 oil engines** reduction geared to sc. shafts driving 2 FP propellers Total Power: 736kW (1,000hp) 10.5kn Cummins KTA-19-M 2 x 4 Stroke 6 Cy. 159 x 159 each-368kW (500bhp) Cummins Engine Co Inc-USA Fuel: 80.0 (d.f.)
8931372 - -	**SRP-6** - **State Enterprise Kerch Sea Fishing Port** -	*104* 25 155	Class: (RS)	**1970 Sudoremontnyy Zavod "Krasnaya Kuznitsa" — Arkhangelsk** Yd No: 6 Loa 35.72 Br ex 7.50 Dght 1.720 Lbp 33.50 Br md - Dpth 2.40 Welded, 1 dk	**(A31C2GD) Deck Cargo Ship** Ice Capable	**1 oil engine** geared to sc. shaft driving 1 FP propeller Total Power: 165kW (224hp) 7.8kn Daldizel 6CHNSP18/22 1 x 4 Stroke 6 Cy. 180 x 220 165kW (224bhp) (new engine 1980) Daldizel-Khabarovsk Fuel: 3.0 (d.f.)
8931384 - -	**SRP-10** - **Marine Trading Port of Skadovsk** -	*152* 58 163	Class: (RS)	**1972 Sudoremontnyy Zavod "Krasnaya Kuznitsa" — Arkhangelsk** Yd No: 10 Loa 35.75 Br ex 7.50 Dght 1.720 Lbp 33.55 Br md - Dpth 2.40 Welded, 1 dk	**(A31C2GD) Deck Cargo Ship** Ice Capable	**1 oil engine** geared to sc. shaft driving 1 FP propeller Total Power: 165kW (224hp) 7.8kn Daldizel 6CHNSP18/22 1 x 4 Stroke 6 Cy. 180 x 220 165kW (224bhp) (new engine 1986) Daldizel-Khabarovsk AuxGen: 1 x 13kW Fuel: 5.0 (d.f.)
8931396 - -	**SRP-19** - **State Enterprise Berdyansk Commercial Sea Port** - *Berdyansk* *Ukraine* Official number: 743286	*152* 58 163	Class: (RS)	**1974 Sudoremontnyy Zavod "Krasnaya Kuznitsa" — Arkhangelsk** Yd No: 19 Loa 35.75 Br ex 7.50 Dght 1.720 Lbp 33.55 Br md - Dpth 2.40 Welded, 1 dk	**(A31C2GD) Deck Cargo Ship** Ice Capable	**1 oil engine** geared to sc. shaft driving 1 FP propeller Total Power: 165kW (224hp) 7.8kn Daldizel 6CHNSP18/22 1 x 4 Stroke 6 Cy. 180 x 220 165kW (224bhp) (new engine 1987) Daldizel-Khabarovsk AuxGen: 1 x 12kW Fuel: 7.0 (d.f.)

IMO / Call sign / Flag	Name / Owner / Port	GT / NT / DWT	Class	Builder / Dimensions	Type	Machinery
8931401 *UIJR* -	**SRP-21** **Murmansk Region Administration of Salvage & Special Operation (Murmanskoye Basseynovoye Avariyno-Spasatelnoye Upravleniye)** - *Murmansk* *Russia*	**160** 48 163	Class: RS	**1974 Sudoremontnyy Zavod "Krasnaya Kuznitsa" — Arkhangelsk** Yd No: 21 Loa 35.75 Br ex 7.50 Dght 1.720 Lbp 33.55 Br md 7.20 Dpth 2.40 Welded, 1 dk	**(A31C2GD) Deck Cargo Ship** Ice Capable	**1 oil engine** geared to sc. shaft driving 1 FP propeller Total Power: 165kW (224hp) 7.8kn Daldizel 6CHNSP18/22 1 x 4 Stroke 6 Cy. 180 x 220 165kW (224bhp) Daldizel-Khabarovsk AuxGen: 1 x 16kW, 1 x 12kW Fuel: 5.0 (d.f.)
8932730 - -	**SRP-150-15** **Fishing Artel Khayryuzovo** - *Petropavlovsk-Kamchatskiy* *Russia*	**163** 49 163	Class: RS	**1976-09 Sudoremontnyy Zavod "Yakor" — Sovetskaya Gavan** Yd No: 698/15 Loa 35.75 Br ex 7.50 Dght 1.710 Lbp 33.48 Br md 7.20 Dpth 2.42 Welded, 1 dk	**(A31C2GD) Deck Cargo Ship** Ice Capable	**1 oil engine** geared to sc. shaft driving 1 FP propeller Total Power: 165kW (224hp) 7.8kn Daldizel 6CHNSP18/22 1 x 4 Stroke 6 Cy. 180 x 220 165kW (224bhp) Daldizel-Khabarovsk AuxGen: 1 x 12kW a.c Fuel: 5.0 (d.f.)
8932778 - -	**SRP-150-19** **Yu I Koslov & D V Korneyev** - *Nakhodka* *Russia*	*173* 58 163	Class: RS	**1973 Nakhodkinskiy Sudoremontnyy Zavod — Nakhodka** Yd No: 19 Loa 35.75 Br ex 7.50 Dght 1.710 Lbp 33.48 Br md 7.20 Dpth 2.40 Welded, 1 dk	**(A31C2GD) Deck Cargo Ship** Ice Capable	**1 oil engine** geared to sc. shaft driving 1 FP propeller Total Power: 165kW (224hp) 7.8kn Daldizel 6CHNSP18/22 1 x 4 Stroke 6 Cy. 180 x 220 165kW (224bhp) Daldizel-Khabarovsk AuxGen: 1 x 13kW a.c Fuel: 5.0 (d.f.)
8932792 *UCVX* -	**SRP-150-21** **Vostok Construction Cooperative (Staratelnaya Artel 'Vostok')** - *Nikolayevsk-na-Amure* *Russia*	**166** 49 133	Class: RS	**1977-09 Sudoremontnyy Zavod "Yakor" — Sovetskaya Gavan** Yd No: 698/21 Loa 35.75 Br ex 7.50 Dght 1.710 Lbp 33.48 Br md 7.20 Dpth 2.42 Welded, 1 dk	**(A31C2GD) Deck Cargo Ship** Ice Capable	**1 oil engine** geared to sc. shaft driving 1 FP propeller Total Power: 165kW (224hp) 7.8kn Daldizel 6CHNSP18/22 1 x 4 Stroke 6 Cy. 180 x 220 165kW (224bhp) (new engine 1989) Daldizel-Khabarovsk AuxGen: 1 x 12kW Fuel: 12.0 (d.f.)
8932833 - -	**SRP-150-25** -	*173* 58 163	Class: (RS)	**1978-05 Sudoremontnyy Zavod "Yakor" — Sovetskaya Gavan** Yd No: 698/25 Loa 35.75 Br ex 7.50 Dght 1.710 Lbp 33.48 Br md - Dpth 2.40 Welded, 1 dk	**(A31C2GD) Deck Cargo Ship** Ice Capable	**1 oil engine** geared to sc. shaft driving 1 FP propeller Total Power: 165kW (224hp) 7.8kn Daldizel 6CHNSP18/22 1 x 4 Stroke 6 Cy. 180 x 220 165kW (224bhp) Daldizel-Khabarovsk AuxGen: 1 x 13kW a.c Fuel: 5.0 (d.f.)
8932845 - -	**SRP-150-28** **Federal State Unitary Enterprise Rosmorport** Poronaysk Commercial Port (Poronayskiy MTP)	**157** 47 163	Class: (RS)	**1978-06 Sudoremontnyy Zavod "Yakor" — Sovetskaya Gavan** Yd No: 698/28 Loa 35.75 Br ex 7.50 Dght 1.710 Lbp 33.48 Br md - Dpth 2.40 Welded, 1 dk	**(A31C2GD) Deck Cargo Ship** Ice Capable	**1 oil engine** geared to sc. shaft driving 1 FP propeller Total Power: 165kW (224hp) 7.8kn Daldizel 6CHNSP18/22 1 x 4 Stroke 6 Cy. 180 x 220 165kW (224bhp) Daldizel-Khabarovsk AuxGen: 2 x 13kW Fuel: 6.0 (d.f.)
8932869 - -	**SRP-150-31** **Fenu-Invest Co Ltd**	*173* 58 163	Class: (RS)	**1978-09 Sudoremontnyy Zavod "Yakor" — Sovetskaya Gavan** Yd No: 698/31 Loa 35.75 Br ex 7.50 Dght 1.710 Lbp 33.48 Br md - Dpth 2.40 Welded, 1 dk	**(A31C2GD) Deck Cargo Ship** Ice Capable	**1 oil engine** geared to sc. shaft driving 1 FP propeller Total Power: 165kW (224hp) 7.8kn Daldizel 6CHNSP18/22 1 x 4 Stroke 6 Cy. 180 x 220 165kW (224bhp) Daldizel-Khabarovsk AuxGen: 1 x 12kW Fuel: 5.0 (d.f.)
8932871 - -	**SRP-150-32** **Rostorg JSC** - *Nakhodka* *Russia*	*161* 58 163	Class: (RS)	**1978-10 Sudoremontnyy Zavod "Yakor" — Sovetskaya Gavan** Yd No: 698/32 Loa 35.75 Br ex 7.50 Dght 1.710 Lbp 33.48 Br md 7.00 Dpth 2.40 Welded, 1 dk	**(A31C2GD) Deck Cargo Ship** Ice Capable	**1 oil engine** geared to sc. shaft driving 1 FP propeller Total Power: 165kW (224hp) 7.8kn Daldizel 6CHNSP18/22 1 x 4 Stroke 6 Cy. 180 x 220 165kW (224bhp) Daldizel-Khabarovsk AuxGen: 1 x 12kW a.c Fuel: 5.0 (d.f.)
8932883 - -	**SRP-150-35** **Koryakryba JSC (A/O 'Koryakryba')** - *Beringovskiy* *Russia* Official number: 781945	*173* 58 163	Class: (RS)	**1979-05 Sudoremontnyy Zavod "Yakor" — Sovetskaya Gavan** Yd No: 698/35 Loa 35.75 Br ex 7.50 Dght 1.710 Lbp 33.48 Br md - Dpth 2.40 Welded, 1 dk	**(A31C2GD) Deck Cargo Ship** Ice Capable	**1 oil engine** geared to sc. shaft driving 1 FP propeller Total Power: 165kW (224hp) 7.8kn Daldizel 6CHNSP18/22 1 x 4 Stroke 6 Cy. 180 x 220 165kW (224bhp) Daldizel-Khabarovsk AuxGen: 1 x 13kW Fuel: 5.0 (d.f.)
8932895 - -	**SRP-150-37** **Koryakryba JSC (A/O 'Koryakryba')** -	*173* 58 163	Class: (RS)	**1979-06 Sudoremontnyy Zavod "Yakor" — Sovetskaya Gavan** Yd No: 698/37 Loa 35.75 Br ex 7.50 Dght 1.710 Lbp 33.48 Br md - Dpth 2.40 Welded, 1 dk	**(A31C2GD) Deck Cargo Ship** Ice Capable	**1 oil engine** geared to sc. shaft driving 1 FP propeller Total Power: 165kW (224hp) 7.8kn Daldizel 6CHNSP18/22 1 x 4 Stroke 6 Cy. 180 x 220 165kW (224bhp) Daldizel-Khabarovsk AuxGen: 1 x 13kW Fuel: 5.0 (d.f.)
8932924 - -	**SRP-150-42** **JSC Iyanin Kutkh i Losos (ZAO 'Iyanin Kutkh i Losos')** - *Vladivostok* *Russia* Official number: 792231	*173* 58 163	Class: (RS)	**1979-11 Sudoremontnyy Zavod "Yakor" — Sovetskaya Gavan** Yd No: 698/42 Loa 35.75 Br ex 7.50 Dght 1.710 Lbp 33.48 Br md - Dpth 2.40 Welded, 1 dk	**(A31C2GD) Deck Cargo Ship** Ice Capable	**1 oil engine** geared to sc. shaft driving 1 FP propeller Total Power: 166kW (226hp) 7.8kn Daldizel 6CHNSP18/22 1 x 4 Stroke 6 Cy. 180 x 220 166kW (226bhp) Daldizel-Khabarovsk AuxGen: 1 x 12kW Fuel: 3.0 (d.f.)
8933069 - -	**SRP-150K-2** **ZAO 'Stividor'** -	**159** 47 165	Class: (RS)	**1975-11 Krasnogorskiy Sudostroitelnyy Zavod — Krasnogorsk** Yd No: 2 Loa 35.75 Br ex 7.50 Dght 1.720 Lbp 33.50 Br md - Dpth 2.40 Welded, 1 dk	**(A31C2GD) Deck Cargo Ship** Ice Capable	**1 oil engine** geared to sc. shaft driving 1 FP propeller Total Power: 165kW (224hp) 7.8kn Daldizel 6CHNSP18/22 1 x 4 Stroke 6 Cy. 180 x 220 165kW (224bhp) Daldizel-Khabarovsk AuxGen: 2 x 13kW Fuel: 6.0 (d.f.)
8932950 - -	**SRP-150K-5** - -	*167* 56 164	Class: (RS)	**1977 Krasnogorskiy Sudostroitelnyy Zavod — Krasnogorsk** Yd No: 5 Loa 35.75 Br ex 7.50 Dght 1.710 Lbp 33.50 Br md - Dpth 2.40 Welded, 1 dk	**(A31C2GD) Deck Cargo Ship** Ice Capable	**1 oil engine** geared to sc. shaft driving 1 FP propeller Total Power: 165kW (224hp) 9.5kn Daldizel 6CHNSP18/22 1 x 4 Stroke 6 Cy. 180 x 220 165kW (224bhp) Daldizel-Khabarovsk AuxGen: 1 x 13kW Fuel: 6.0 (d.f.)
8228397 *UBCL* -	**SRP-150K-10** **Veteran Mortrans Co Ltd** - *Petropavlovsk-Kamchatskiy* *Russia* Official number: 822577	**159** 47 164	Class: RS	**1984-08 Krasnogorskiy Sudostroitelnyy Zavod — Krasnogorsk** Yd No: 10 Loa 35.74 Br ex 7.40 Dght 1.710 Lbp 33.63 Br md 7.20 Dpth 2.42 Welded, 1 dk	**(A31C2GD) Deck Cargo Ship** Ice Capable	**1 oil engine** geared to sc. shaft driving 1 FP propeller Total Power: 165kW (224hp) 9.5kn Daldizel 6CHNSP18/22 1 x 4 Stroke 6 Cy. 180 x 220 165kW (224bhp) Daldizel-Khabarovsk AuxGen: 2 x 13kW Fuel: 6.0 (d.f.)
8933007 - -	**SRP-154** **OOO 'Morskiye Ekologicheskiye Tekhnologii'** - *Nakhodka* *Russia*	*161* 59 163	Class: RS	**1969 Nakhodkinskiy Sudoremontnyy Zavod — Nakhodka** Yd No: 4 Loa 35.75 Br ex 7.50 Dght 1.710 Lbp 33.48 Br md - Dpth 2.40 Welded, 1 dk	**(A31C2GD) Deck Cargo Ship** Ice Capable	**1 oil engine** geared to sc. shaft driving 1 FP propeller Total Power: 165kW (224hp) 8.5kn Daldizel 6CHNSP18/22 1 x 4 Stroke 6 Cy. 180 x 220 165kW (224bhp) Daldizel-Khabarovsk AuxGen: 1 x 12kW Fuel: 5.0 (d.f.)

6900989 **SRTM-8435** *680* Class: (RS)
\- 252
\- **Bangladesh Fisheries Development Corp** 330
\-
Bangladesh

1966 Khabarovskiy Sudostroitelnyy Zavod im Kirova — Khabarovsk Yd No: 125
Loa 54.21 Br ex 9.30 Dght 3.683
Lbp 49.99 Br md 9.22 Dpth 4.70
Welded, 1 dk

(B11A2FT) Trawler
Ins: 352
Compartments: 2 Ho, ER
2 Ha: 2 (1.5 x 1.6)
Derricks: 1x2t,3x1.5t; Winches: 4
Ice Capable

1 oil engine driving 1 CP propeller
Total Power: 588kW (799hp) 12.0kn
S.K.L. 8NVD48AU
1 x 4 Stroke 8 Cy. 320 x 480 588kW (799bhp)
VEB Schwermaschinenbau "KarlLiebknecht" (SKL)-Magdeburg
AuxGen: 3 x 88kW

6901036 **SRTM-8451** *699* Class: (RS)
\- 262
\- **Bangladesh Fisheries Development Corp** 283
\-
Bangladesh

1966 Khabarovskiy Sudostroitelnyy Zavod im Kirova — Khabarovsk Yd No: 129
Loa 54.21 Br ex 9.30 Dght 3.683
Lbp 49.99 Br md 9.22 Dpth 4.70
Welded, 1 dk

(B11A2FT) Trawler
Ins: 352
Compartments: 2 Ho, ER
2 Ha: 2 (1.5 x 1.6)
Derricks: 1x2t,3x1.5t; Winches: 4
Ice Capable

1 oil engine driving 1 CP propeller
Total Power: 588kW (799hp) 12.0kn
S.K.L. 8NVD48AU
1 x 4 Stroke 8 Cy. 320 x 480 588kW (799bhp)
VEB Schwermaschinenbau "KarlLiebknecht" (SKL)-Magdeburg
AuxGen: 3 x 88kW

9520405 **SS 3201** **262** Class: NK
V7XS7 79
\- **Blueocean Marine Pte Ltd** 301
Seahorse Heavy Transport Pte Ltd
Majuro *Marshall Islands*
MMSI: 538004562
Official number: 4562

2008-11 Forward Marine Enterprise Sdn Bhd — Sibu Yd No: FM-18
Loa 30.00 Br ex - Dght 3.512
Lbp 27.73 Br md 8.60 Dpth 4.12
Welded, 1 dk

(B32A2ST) Tug

2 oil engines reduction geared to sc. shafts driving 2 FP propellers
Total Power: 1,518kW (2,064hp)
Mitsubishi S6R2-MTK3L
2 x 4 Stroke 6 Cy. 170 x 220 each-759kW (1032bhp)
Mitsubishi Heavy Industries Ltd-Japan
AuxGen: 2 x 98kW a.c
Fuel: 200.0

8770912 **SS AMAZONIA** **24,268** Class: BV (AB)
H04389 7,280
\- **Baerfield Drilling LLC** 15,777
Schahin Engenharia SA
Panama *Panama*
MMSI: 355890000
Official number: 36410PEXT1

2011-04 Yantai Raffles Shipyard Co Ltd — Yantai SD Yd No: YRO2006-193
Loa 105.00 Br ex 73.06 Dght 16.760
Lbp - Br md 67.10 Dpth 33.99
Welded, 1 dk

(Z11C3ZE) Drilling Rig, semi Submersible
Cranes: 3x50t

7 diesel electric oil engines driving 7 gen. each 4580kW a.c Connecting to 7 elec. motors driving 7 Directional propellers
Total Power: 32,060kW (43,589hp)
Caterpillar 3616
7 x Vee 4 Stroke 16 Cy. 280 x 300 each-4580kW (6227bhp)
Caterpillar Inc-USA
Fuel: 2900.0

8122115 **SS BARAKUDA** **363** Class: NV (AB) (BV)
PNTI *ex* Mermaid Supporter *-2010* 109
\- *ex* Pacific Pearl *-2003* 272
PT Seascape Surveys Indonesia
\-
Batam *Indonesia*
MMSI: 525006060

1982-04 Imamura Zosen — Kure Yd No: 282
Loa 38.99 Br ex 8.51 Dght 2.809
Lbp 35.01 Br md 8.50 Dpth 3.51
Welded, 1 dk

(B31A2SR) Research Survey Vessel

2 oil engines with clutches & sr reverse geared to sc. shafts driving 2 FP propellers
Total Power: 1,618kW (2,200hp) 12.0kn
Yanmar T220-ET
2 x 4 Stroke 6 Cy. 220 x 280 each-809kW (1100bhp)
Yanmar Diesel Engine Co Ltd-Japan
AuxGen: 3 x 128kW 440V 50Hz a.c
Thrusters: 1 Water jet (f)
Fuel: 88.9 (d.f.) 6.4pd

8971815 **SS DELPHINE** **1,342** Class: (LR)
CQTJ *ex* Delphine *-2003* *ex* Dauntless *-1987* 697 ✠ Classed LR until 62
\- *ex* Delphine *-1968* *ex* Dauntless *-1946* 1,950
ex Delphine *-1942*
Vintage Cruises Lda
\-
SatCom: Inmarsat C 425598610
Madeira *Portugal (MAR)*
MMSI: 255986000
Official number: 1164

1921-05 Great Lakes Engineering Works — Ecorse, Mi Yd No: 239
Converted From: Training Vessel-2002
Converted From: Yacht-1968
Loa 78.50 Br ex 11.15 Dght 4.500
Lbp - Br md 10.82 Dpth 6.72
Riveted\Welded, 2 dks

(A37B2PS) Passenger Ship
Passengers: berths: 28

2 Steam Recips driving 2 FP propellers
Total Power: 1,472kW (2,002hp) 15.0kn
2 x Steam Recip. each-736kW (1001ihp)
Great Lakes Engineering Works-USA

8313518 **SS FAVOUR** **135** Class: (AB)
\- *ex* Fraih 20 *-2007* 40
\- **Sea-Swamp Supplies & Services Ltd** 53
\-
Nigeria
Official number: SR915

1983-11 Yokohama Yacht Co Ltd — Yokohama KN Yd No: 819
Loa 33.61 Br ex Dght 1.601
Lbp 30.36 Br md 6.11 Dpth 3.26
Welded, 1 dk

(B21A2OC) Crew/Supply Vessel

2 oil engines with clutches & sr reverse geared to sc. shafts driving 2 FP propellers
Total Power: 2,354kW (3,200hp) 22.0kn
G.M. (Detroit Diesel) 16V-149-TI
2 x Vee 2 Stroke 16 Cy. 146 x 146 each-1177kW (1600bhp)
General Motors Detroit DieselAllison Divn-USA
AuxGen: 2 x 50kW

6815184 **SS-I** *320* Class: (LR) (GL)
\- *ex* Gol *-2007* *ex* Hassan *-1991* *ex* Hazim *-1975* 125 ✠ Classed LR until 9/11/84
\- - 198
\-

1968-10 Charles D. Holmes & Co. Ltd. — Beverley Yd No: 1011
Loa 40.67 Br ex 10.09 Dght 3.436
Lbp 36.58 Br md 9.61 Dpth 4.37
Welded, 1 dk

(B32A2ST) Tug

1 oil engine reverse reduction geared to sc. shaft driving 1 FP propeller
Total Power: 1,662kW (2,260hp) 11.0kn
Ruston 9ATCM
1 x 4 Stroke 9 Cy. 318 x 368 1662kW (2260bhp)
Ruston & Hornsby Ltd.-Lincoln
AuxGen: 2 x 98kW 220/380V 50Hz a.c
Fuel: 110.5 (d.f.)

8127141 **SS MARINER** **348** Class: AB
9V3314 *ex* Bunker Gulf *-2002* *ex* Bunker SPC IX *-1987* 211
\- *ex* Bee Lan *-1984* 750
Impex Navigation Pte Ltd
\-
Singapore *Singapore*
MMSI: 564732000
Official number: 382835

1982-12 Pan-United Shipping Pte Ltd — Singapore Yd No: P-31
Loa - Br ex - Dght 2.318
Lbp 45.12 Br md 9.77 Dpth 3.05
Welded, 1 dk

(B35E2TF) Bunkering Tanker
Liq: 1,000; Liq (Oil): 1,000
2 Cargo Pump (s)

2 oil engines reverse reduction geared to sc. shafts driving 2 FP propellers
Total Power: 500kW (680hp) 8.0kn
G.M. (Detroit Diesel) 12V-71-N
2 x Vee 2 Stroke 12 Cy. 108 x 127 each-250kW (340bhp)
General Motors Detroit DieselAllison Divn-USA
AuxGen: 2 x 20kW

8770924 **SS PANTANAL** **24,268** Class: BV (AB)
H04400 7,280
\- **Soratu Drilling LLC** 16,036
Schahin Engenharia SA
SatCom: Inmarsat C 435567710
Panama *Panama*
MMSI: 355677000
Official number: 36406PEXT2

2010-11 Yantai Raffles Shipyard Co Ltd — Yantai SD Yd No: YRO2006-200
Loa 105.00 Br ex 73.00 Dght 16.760
Lbp - Br md 67.10 Dpth 33.99
Welded, 1 dk

(Z11C3ZE) Drilling Rig, semi Submersible
Cranes: 1x60t,2x50t

7 diesel electric oil engines driving 7 gen. Connecting to 8 elec. motors driving 8 Directional propellers
Total Power: 32,060kW (43,589hp)
Caterpillar 3616
7 x Vee 4 Stroke 16 Cy. 280 x 300 each-4580kW (6227bhp)
Caterpillar Inc-USA
Fuel: 2900.0

8521309 **SS PROSPERITY** **933** Class: KR (LR) (NV)
9V3236 *ex* Swift Prosperity *-2000* 604 Classed LR until 18/1/11
\- **Chemtank Marine Pte Ltd** 1,674
JR Orion Services Pte Ltd T/cm
Singapore *Singapore* 6.7
MMSI: 563004340
Official number: 383340

1985-08 Asia-Pacific Shipyard Pte Ltd — Singapore Yd No: 842
Loa 55.61 Br ex - Dght 3.571
Lbp 53.32 Br md 13.01 Dpth 4.32
Welded, 1 dk

(A13B2TP) Products Tanker
Single Hull
Ins: 223; Liq: 1,500; Liq (Oil): 1,500
Compartments: 10 Wing Ta, ER
4 Cargo Pump (s): 2x95m³/hr, 2x36m³/hr

2 oil engines gearing integral to driving 2 Z propellers
Total Power: 810kW (1,102hp) 8.0kn
Caterpillar 3408TA
2 x Vee 4 Stroke 8 Cy. 137 x 152 each-405kW (551bhp)
Caterpillar Tractor Co-USA
AuxGen: 2 x 90kW 415V 50Hz a.c
Thrusters: 2 Thwart. FP thruster (f)
Fuel: 73.5 (d.f.)

8018132 **SS ROVER 11** **51,035** Class: (LR)
VJRB *ex* River Boyne *-2013* 16,346 ✠ Classed LR until 17/10/12
\- **River Boyne Pty Ltd** 76,308
Queensland Alumina Ltd (QLD Alumina Ltd) (QAL Contractors) T/cm
SatCom: Inmarsat C 450300064 82.0
Sydney, NSW *Australia*
MMSI: 503000005
Official number: 850245

1982-09 Mitsubishi Heavy Industries Ltd. — Nagasaki Yd No: 1882
Loa 255.02 (BB) Br ex 35.41 Dght 12.820
Lbp 248.01 Br md 35.35 Dpth 18.29
Welded, 1 dk

(A21B2BO) Ore Carrier
Grain: 63,765; Ore: 66,159
Compartments: 3 Ho, ER
8 Ha: (19.2 x 15.5)7 (16.8 x 15.5)ER

1 Steam Turb dr geared to sc. shaft driving 1 FP propeller
Total Power: 13,975kW (19,000hp) 15.8kn
Mitsubishi
1 x steam Turb 13975kW (19000shp)
Mitsubishi Heavy Industries Ltd-Japan
AuxGen: 2 x 1850kW 450V 60Hz a.c, 1 x 700kW 450V 60Hz a.c
Boilers: 2 WTB 75.9kgf/cm² (74.4bar)480°C 64.5kgf/cm² (63.3bar)
Fuel: 3500.0 (c) 20.0 (d.f.) 220.0pd

9032408 **SS ULSAN** **1,535** Class: (KR)
DSOH2 *ex* Uranus *-2005* *ex* Shin Kobe *-2001* 444
\- - 1,125
\-
Jeju *South Korea*
MMSI: 440651000
Official number: JJR-059576

1991-03 Yamanaka Zosen K.K. — Imabari Yd No: 510
Loa 81.60 (BB) Br ex - Dght 3.863
Lbp 74.50 Br md 12.80 Dpth 6.80
Welded, 1 dk

(A31A2GX) General Cargo Ship
Compartments: 1 Ho, ER

1 oil engine sr geared to sc. shaft driving 1 FP propeller
Total Power: 2,574kW (3,500hp) 18.1kn
Pielstick 16PA5V
1 x Vee 4 Stroke 16 Cy. 255 x 270 2574kW (3500bhp)
Niigata Engineering Co Ltd-Japan
Thrusters: 1 Thwart. CP thruster (f)

Identity	Name / Owner	Tonnage	Class	Build / Dimensions	Type / Cargo	Machinery
7721392 - -	**SS VELES** *ex* Abu Zenima *-2011* **Nerei Shipping Ltd** Seaservice Shipping Ltd	**10,022** 6,081 12,402	Class: IS (LR) ✠ Classed LR until 18/3/11	**1983**-06 **Alexandria Shipyard — Alexandria** Yd No: 10025 Loa 132.90 (BB) Br ex 20.55 Dght 9.462 Lbp 121.96 Br md 20.50 Dpth 12.20 Welded, 2 dks	**(A31A2GA) General Cargo Ship (with Ro-Ro facility)** Quarter stern door/ramp (s) Len: 17.00 Wid: 4.00 Swl: - Lane-Len: 760 Grain: 22,180; Bale: 20,345 TEU 380 C Ho 212 TEU C Dk 168 TEU Compartments: 4 Ho, ER, 1 RoRo Tw Dk 4 Ha: (6.7 x 7.3) (14.1 x 10.2)2 (26.9 x 10.5)ER Cranes: 2x25t,3x12.5t Ice Capable	**1 oil engine** driving 1 FP propeller Total Power: 4,928kW (6,700hp) 16.5kn B&W 5L55GFCA 1 x 2 Stroke 5 Cy. 550 x 1380 4928kW (6700bhp) B&W Diesel A/S-Denmark AuxGen: 2 x 504kW 440V 60Hz a.c, 1 x 312kW 440V 60Hz a.c Fuel: 182.0 (d.f.) 734.0 (r.f.)
9358357 *DSO08* -	**SS WIN** *ex* Soon Yang *-2012* **Sean Shipping Co Ltd** Sung Kyung Maritime Co Ltd (SK Maritime) SatCom: Inmarsat C 444095827 *Jeju* *South Korea* MMSI: 441008000 Official number: JJR-068821	**1,928** 896 3,460	Class: KR (NK)	**2005**-07 **Koike Zosen Kaiun KK — Osakikamijima** Yd No: 302 Loa 81.75 Br ex 13.24 Dght 5.939 Lbp 75.00 Br md 13.00 Dpth 7.50 Welded, 1 dk	**(A31A2GX) General Cargo Ship** Bale: 3,150 1 Ha: ER (45.0 x 10.0)	**1 oil engine** driving 1 FP propeller Total Power: 1,618kW (2,200hp) 10.0kn Niigata 6M34BT 1 x 4 Stroke 6 Cy. 340 x 620 1618kW (2200bhp) Niigata Engineering Co Ltd-Japan
8031627 - -	**SSANG YONG** - **Ssangyong Shipping Co Ltd** - *Tongyeong* *South Korea* Official number: CMR-804468	*497* 255 769	Class: (KR)	**1980 Chungmu Shipbuilding Co Inc — Tongyeong** Loa 53.80 Br ex - Dght 3.301 Lbp 48.01 Br md 9.20 Dpth 3.81 Welded, 1 dk	**(A31A2GX) General Cargo Ship** Grain: 1,053; Bale: 1,010 1 Ha: (24.1 x 6.1) Derricks: 1x5t,1x3t	**1 oil engine** driving 1 FP propeller Total Power: 552kW (750hp) 12.3kn Hanshin 6L26BGSH 1 x 4 Stroke 6 Cy. 260 x 400 552kW (750bhp) Ssangyong Heavy Industries Co Ltd-South Korea AuxGen: 2 x 42kW 220V a.c
8804218 - -	**SSANG YONG NO. 5** *ex* Kannon Maru No. 18 *-2002* - -	*446* - 700	Class: KR	**1988**-06 **K.K. Saidaiji Zosensho — Okayama** Yd No: 152 L reg 55.40 Br ex - Dght 5.000 Lbp - Br md 9.40 Dpth 5.50 Welded	**(A31A2GX) General Cargo Ship**	**1 oil engine** reduction geared to sc. shaft driving 1 FP propeller Total Power: 625kW (850hp) 12.1kn Hanshin 6LB26RG 1 x 4 Stroke 6 Cy. 260 x 440 625kW (850bhp) The Hanshin Diesel Works Ltd-Japan
8206026 *V3PJ7* -	**SSE CHARLOTTE** *ex* TTB Singapore *-2010* *ex* Hans Tide *-2009* *ex* Black Lion *-1997* **Singapore Salvage Engineers Pte Ltd** - *Belize City* *Belize* MMSI: 312463000 Official number: 131010838	**315** 94 397	Class: AB	**1982**-11 **Southern Ocean Shipbuilding Co Pte Ltd — Singapore** Yd No: 135 Loa 38.00 Br ex - Dght 3.304 Lbp 36.50 Br md 9.52 Dpth 3.71 Welded, 1 dk	**(B34L2QU) Utility Vessel** Cranes: 1x5t	**2 oil engines** sr reverse geared to sc. shafts driving 2 FP propellers Total Power: 1,472kW (2,002hp) 12.0kn Yanmar T220-ET 2 x 4 Stroke 6 Cy. 220 x 280 each-736kW (1001bhp) Yanmar Diesel Engine Co Ltd-Japan AuxGen: 2 x 80kW a.c Thrusters: 1 Thwart. FP thruster (f) Fuel: 170.0
9674086 *9V2109* -	**SSE OLGA** - **Singapore Salvage Engineers Pte Ltd** - *Singapore* *Singapore* MMSI: 563024970 Official number: 398627	**195** 59 192	Class: NK	**2013**-05 **SL Shipbuilding Contractor Sdn Bhd — Sibu** Yd No: 156 Loa 27.10 Br ex 8.02 Dght 3.012 Lbp 25.34 Br md 8.00 Dpth 3.65 Welded, 1 dk	**(B32A2ST) Tug**	**2 oil engines** reduction geared to sc. shaft (s) driving 2 FP propellers Total Power: 1,220kW (1,658hp) Yanmar 6AYM-WET 2 x 4 Stroke 6 Cy. 155 x 180 each-610kW (829bhp) Yanmar Diesel Engine Co Ltd-Japan AuxGen: 2 x 40kW a.c Fuel: 144.0
6717708 *DUL6703* -	**SSFVPI** *ex* Orion Maru *-1967* **South Sea Fishing Ventures Inc (RD Export Division) RDEX** - *General Santos* *Philippines* Official number: 12-0000114	*157* 44 -		**1967 Towa Zosen K.K. — Shimonoseki** Yd No: 349 Loa 29.42 Br ex 8.26 Dght 2.591 Lbp 26.50 Br md 8.23 Dpth 3.59 Welded, 1 dk	**(B32A2ST) Tug**	**2 oil engines** geared to sc. shaft driving 1 Directional propeller Total Power: 1,618kW (2,200hp) 11.0kn Makita 2 x 4 Stroke 6 Cy. 300 x 380 each-809kW (1100bhp) Makita Tekkosho-Japan AuxGen: 1 x 50kW Fuel: 43.5 7.5pd
8212673 *WDDU* -	**SSG EDWARD A. CARTER JR.** *ex* Sealand Oregon *-2001* *ex* OOCL Innovation *-2000* *ex* Nedlloyd Hudson *-1993* *ex* Nebraska *-1988* *ex* Susan C *-1988* *ex* American Nebraska *-1987* **Maersk Line Ltd** - SatCom: Inmarsat A 1503652 *Norfolk, VA* *United States of America* MMSI: 367015000 Official number: 665785	**57,075** 18,995 58,943	Class: AB (KR)	**1985**-04 **Daewoo Shipbuilding & Heavy Machinery Ltd — Geoje** Yd No: 4007 Loa 289.52 (BB) Br ex 32.31 Dght 12.675 Lbp 279.00 Br md 32.22 Dpth 21.49 Welded, 1 dk	**(A33A2CC) Container Ship (Fully Cellular)** TEU 4614 incl 146 ref C. Compartments: ER, 11 Cell Ho 18 Ha: (13.2 x 10.7)ER 17 (12.7 x 10.7) 36 Wing Ha: 4 (12.7 x 5.9)2 (13.2 x 7.9)30 (12.7 x 8.3) Cranes: 4x36t	**1 oil engine** driving 1 FP propeller Total Power: 20,888kW (28,399hp) 19.1kn Sulzer 7RLB90 1 x 2 Stroke 7 Cy. 900 x 1900 20888kW (28399bhp) Hyundai Engine & Machinery Co Ltd-South Korea AuxGen: 3 x 1000kW 480V 60Hz a.c Fuel: 950.0 (d.f.) 6370.5 (r.f.) 73.5pd
9022245 - -	**SSH 31** - **Civil Engineering & Technical Fleet JSC (Stroitelen i Technicheski Flot)** - *Varna* *Bulgaria* Official number: 262	**418** 77 782	Class: BR	**1978**-01 **'Ilya Boyadzhiev' Shipyard — Bourgas** Loa 56.20 Br ex 9.12 Dght 3.640 Lbp - Br md - Dpth 4.44 Welded, 1 dk	**(A31A2GX) General Cargo Ship**	**2 oil engines** driving 2 Propellers Total Power: 470kW (640hp) S.K.L. 6NVD36A-1U 2 x 4 Stroke 6 Cy. 240 x 360 each-235kW (320bhp) VEB Schwermaschinenbau "KarlLiebknecht" (SKL)-Magdeburg
9022257 - -	**SSH 33** - **Civil Engineering & Technical Fleet JSC (Stroitelen i Technicheski Flot)** - *Varna* *Bulgaria* Official number: 263	**418** 77 782	Class: (BR)	**1979**-01 **'Ilya Boyadzhiev' Shipyard — Bourgas** Loa 56.20 Br ex 9.10 Dght 3.640 Lbp - Br md - Dpth 4.44 Welded, 1 dk	**(A31A2GX) General Cargo Ship**	**2 oil engines** driving 2 Propellers Total Power: 470kW (640hp) S.K.L. 6NVD36A-1U 2 x 4 Stroke 6 Cy. 240 x 360 each-235kW (320bhp) VEB Schwermaschinenbau "KarlLiebknecht" (SKL)-Magdeburg
9022269 - -	**SSH 35** - **Civil Engineering & Technical Fleet JSC (Stroitelen i Technicheski Flot)** - *Varna* *Bulgaria* Official number: 267	**418** 77 782	Class: BR	**1979**-01 **'Ilya Boyadzhiev' Shipyard — Bourgas** Loa 56.20 Br ex 9.10 Dght 3.640 Lbp - Br md - Dpth 4.44 Welded, 1 dk	**(A31A2GX) General Cargo Ship**	**2 oil engines** driving 2 Propellers Total Power: 470kW (640hp) S.K.L. 6NVD36A-1U 2 x 4 Stroke 6 Cy. 240 x 360 each-235kW (320bhp) VEB Schwermaschinenbau "KarlLiebknecht" (SKL)-Magdeburg
9022271 - -	**SSH 37** - **Civil Engineering & Technical Fleet JSC (Stroitelen i Technicheski Flot)** - *Varna* *Bulgaria* Official number: 270	**418** 77 782	Class: BR	**1979**-01 **'Ilya Boyadzhiev' Shipyard — Bourgas** Loa 56.20 Br ex 9.10 Dght 3.640 Lbp - Br md - Dpth 4.44 Welded, 1 dk	**(A31A2GX) General Cargo Ship**	**2 oil engines** driving 2 Propellers Total Power: 470kW (640hp) S.K.L. 6NVD36A-1U 2 x 4 Stroke 6 Cy. 240 x 360 each-235kW (320bhp) VEB Schwermaschinenbau "KarlLiebknecht" (SKL)-Magdeburg
9022283 - -	**SSH 39** - **Civil Engineering & Technical Fleet JSC (Stroitelen i Technicheski Flot)** - *Varna* *Bulgaria* Official number: 274	**418** 77 782	Class: (BR)	**1979**-01 **'Ilya Boyadzhiev' Shipyard — Bourgas** Loa 56.20 Br ex 9.10 Dght 3.640 Lbp - Br md - Dpth 4.44 Welded, 1 dk	**(A31A2GX) General Cargo Ship**	**2 oil engines** driving 2 Propellers Total Power: 470kW (640hp) S.K.L. 6NVD36A-1U 2 x 4 Stroke 6 Cy. 240 x 360 each-235kW (320bhp) VEB Schwermaschinenbau "KarlLiebknecht" (SKL)-Magdeburg
9022295 - -	**SSH 45** - **Civil Engineering & Technical Fleet JSC (Stroitelen i Technicheski Flot)** - *Varna* *Bulgaria* Official number: 281	**418** 77 782	Class: (BR)	**1980**-01 **'Ilya Boyadzhiev' Shipyard — Bourgas** Loa 56.20 Br ex 9.10 Dght 3.620 Lbp - Br md - Dpth 4.42 Welded, 1 dk	**(A31A2GX) General Cargo Ship**	**2 oil engines** driving 2 Propellers Total Power: 470kW (640hp) S.K.L. 6NVD36A-1U 2 x 4 Stroke 6 Cy. 240 x 360 each-235kW (320bhp) VEB Schwermaschinenbau "KarlLiebknecht" (SKL)-Magdeburg

9665360 *V7DC3* -	**SSI DIGNITY** **Felicitas Shipping Inc** Densay Shipping & Trading JLT *Majuro* *Marshall Islands* MMSI: 538005363 Official number: 5363	**44,003** 27,326 81,600 T/cm 71.9	Class: LR (Class contemplated) **100A1** 03/2014 Class contemplated	**2014**-03 **Jinling Shipyard — Nanjing JS** Yd No: JLZ9120404 Loa 229.00 (BB) Br ex Dght 14.450 Lbp 225.50 Br md 32.26 Dpth 20.05 Welded, 1 dk	**(A21A2BC) Bulk Carrier** Grain: 97,000; Bale: 90,784 Compartments: 7 Ho, ER 7 Ha: ER	**1 oil engine** driving 1 FP propeller Total Power: 13,560kW (18,436hp) 14.5kn MAN-B&W 6S60MC-C 1 x 2 Stroke 6 Cy. 600 x 2400 13560kW (18436bhp) AuxGen: 3 x 600kW a.c
9595955 *V7XC5* -	**SSI GLORIOUS** **Blue Adventure Seatrade Inc** Densay Gemi Kiralama ve Acentacilik Denizcilik ve Turizm ve Ticaret AS *Majuro* *Marshall Islands* MMSI: 538004446 Official number: 4446	**32,987** 19,223 56,733 T/cm 58.8	Class: LR ✠ **100A1** SS 07/2012 bulk carrier CSR BC-A Nos. 2 & 4 holds may be empty GRAB (20) ESP LI **ShipRight** (CM,ACS (B)) *IWS EP ✠ **LMC** **UMS** Cable: 632.5/73.0 U3 (a)	**2012**-07 **Jinling Shipyard — Nanjing JS** Yd No: JLZ9100416 Loa 189.99 (BB) Br ex 32.28 Dght 12.800 Lbp 185.00 Br md 32.26 Dpth 18.00 Welded, 1 dk	**(A21A2BC) Bulk Carrier** Grain: 71,634; Bale: 68,200 Compartments: 5 Ho, ER 5 Ha: ER Cranes: 4x30t	**1 oil engine** driving 1 FP propeller Total Power: 9,480kW (12,889hp) 14.2kn MAN-B&W 6S50MC-C 1 x 2 Stroke 6 Cy. 500 x 2000 9480kW (12889bhp) STX (Dalian) Engine Co Ltd-China AuxGen: 3 x 600kW 450V 60Hz a.c Boilers: WTAuxB (Comp) 9.0kgf/cm² (8.8bar)
9250579 *V7SW8* -	**SSI PRIDE** *ex* Ocean Predator *-2009* *ex* Brilliant Star *-2007* **Ocean Crystal Ship & Seatrade Inc** Densay Shipping & Trading JLT *Majuro* *Marshall Islands* MMSI: 538003738 Official number: 3738	**27,656** 16,095 48,635 T/cm 54.0	Class: LR (NK) **100A1** SS 01/2012 bulk carrier, strengthened for heavy cargoes, Nos. 2 & 4 holds may be empty ESP LI ESN *IWS **LMC** Eq.Ltr: L†; Cable: 632.0/70.0 U3 (a)	**2002**-01 **The Hakodate Dock Co Ltd — Hakodate HK** Yd No: 787 Loa 189.95 (BB) Br ex - Dght 11.651 Lbp 182.40 Br md 32.00 Dpth 16.55 Welded, 1 dk	**(A21A2BC) Bulk Carrier** Double Bottom Entire Compartment Length Grain: 61,836; Bale: 59,655 Cargo Heating Coils Compartments: 5 Ho, ER 5 Ha: (16.8 x 17.6)4 (20.8 x 17.6)ER Cranes: 4x30t	**1 oil engine** driving 1 FP propeller Total Power: 7,981kW (10,851hp) 14.2kn Mitsubishi 6UEC52LS 1 x 2 Stroke 6 Cy. 520 x 1850 7981kW (10851bhp) Kobe Hatsudoki KK-Japan AuxGen: 2 x 440kW 450V 60Hz a.c Boilers: AuxB (Comp) 7.1kgf/cm² (7.0bar) Fuel: 172.0 (d.f.) (Heating Coils) 1726.0 (r.f.)
9595943 *V7WO4* -	**SSI VICTORY** **Northshield Shipping Co Ltd** Densay Shipping & Trading JLT SatCom: Inmarsat C 453835994 *Majuro* *Marshall Islands* MMSI: 538004352 Official number: 4352	**32,987** 19,242 56,781 T/cm 58.8	Class: LR ✠ **100A1** SS 01/2012 bulk carrier CSR BC-A Nos. 2 & 4 holds may be empty GRAB (20) ESP LI **ShipRight** (CM,ACS (B)) *IWS EP ✠ **LMC** **UMS** Cable: 632.5/73.0 U3 (a)	**2012**-01 **Jinling Shipyard — Nanjing JS** Yd No: JLZ9100415 Loa 189.99 (BB) Br ex 32.28 Dght 12.800 Lbp 185.00 Br md 32.26 Dpth 18.00 Welded, 1 dk	**(A21A2BC) Bulk Carrier** Grain: 71,634; Bale: 68,768 Compartments: 5 Ho, ER 5 Ha: ER Cranes: 4x30t	**1 oil engine** driving 1 FP propeller Total Power: 9,480kW (12,889hp) 14.2kn MAN-B&W 6S50MC-C 1 x 2 Stroke 6 Cy. 500 x 2000 9480kW (12889bhp) STX (Dalian) Engine Co Ltd-China AuxGen: 3 x 600kW 450V 60Hz a.c Boilers: WTAuxB (Comp) 9.2kgf/cm² (9.0bar)
8747965 *UBXF9* G-0857	**SSK-1** *ex* Maan Shian No. 12 *-2008* **Korifena Co Ltd** - *Nevelsk* *Russia* MMSI: 273331630 Official number: 857	**1,088** 540 881	Class: RS	**1987** **Sen Koh Shipbuilding Corp — Kaohsiung** Yd No: 010310 Loa 64.06 Br ex 10.00 Dght 4.200 Lbp 57.00 Br md 10.00 Dpth 4.50 Welded, 1 dk	**(B11B2FV) Fishing Vessel** Ins: 1,281	**1 oil engine** driving 1 Propeller 11.0kn
8747977 *UBFX7* G-0865	**SSK-2** *ex* Jui Ying *-2009* **Korifena Co Ltd** - *Nevelsk* *Russia* MMSI: 273335230 Official number: 865	**1,177** 462 970	Class: RS	**1996** **Fong Kuo Shipbuilding Co Ltd — Kaohsiung** Yd No: 012939 Loa 59.08 Br ex - Dght 4.000 Lbp 52.20 Br md 10.30 Dpth 4.50 Welded, 1 dk	**(B11B2FV) Fishing Vessel**	**1 oil engine** driving 1 Propeller Daihatsu 1 x 4 Stroke Daihatsu Diesel Manufacturing Co Lt-Japan
8747989 *UBXF8* G-0858	**SSK-3** *ex* Te Wen No. 1 *-2008* **Sayra Co Ltd** - *Nevelsk* *Russia* MMSI: 273330630 Official number: 858	**1,007** 490 789	Class: RS	**1987** **Sen Koh Shipbuilding Corp — Kaohsiung** Yd No: 010430 Loa 64.10 Br ex - Dght 4.100 Lbp 55.30 Br md 9.70 Dpth 4.30 Welded, 1 dk	**(B11B2FV) Fishing Vessel**	**1 oil engine** driving 1 Propeller
8747991 *UBFX6* G-0870	**SSK-5** *ex* Shian Maan No. 12 *-2009* **Sargan LLC** - *Nevelsk* *Russia* MMSI: 273339530 Official number: 867	**959** 421 756	Class: RS	**1984** **San Yang Shipbuilding Co., Ltd. — Kaohsiung** Yd No: 009178 Loa 60.12 Br ex - Dght 4.100 Lbp 52.72 Br md 9.36 Dpth 4.50 Welded, 1 dk	**(B11B2FV) Fishing Vessel**	**1 oil engine** driving 1 Propeller 11.0kn
8748000 *UHRY* G-0866	**SSK-6** *ex* Pei Sheng No. 6 *-2009* **Sayra Co Ltd** - *Nevelsk* *Russia* MMSI: 273338530 Official number: 866	**1,195** 625 988	Class: RS	**2000** **San Yang Shipbuilding Co., Ltd. — Kaohsiung** Yd No: 806 Loa 68.70 Br ex - Dght 4.100 Lbp 60.20 Br md 10.00 Dpth 4.50 Welded, 1 dk	**(B11B2FV) Fishing Vessel**	**1 oil engine** driving 1 Propeller Total Power: 1,119kW (1,521hp)
7200611 *HQJE8* -	**SSP 188** *ex* Murai *-1991* *ex* Independence *-1985* *ex* Fairmount *-1985* *ex* Osage *-1985* **Hacienda Shipping Co Pte Ltd** - *San Lorenzo* *Honduras* Official number: L-1524138	*484* 216 -	Class: (KI)	**1968**-05 **Burton Shipyard Co., Inc. — Port Arthur, Tx** Yd No: 429 Loa 50.29 Br ex 11.59 Dght 3.429 Lbp 47.24 Br md - Dpth 3.97 Welded, 1 dk	**(B21B20A) Anchor Handling Tug Supply**	**2 oil engines** geared to sc. shaft driving 1 FP propeller Total Power: 1,126kW (1,530hp) Caterpillar D398TA 2 x Vee 4 Stroke 12 Cy. 159 x 203 each-563kW (765bhp) Caterpillar Tractor Co-USA
9054341 *YD6582* -	**SSP 788** **PT Perusahaan Pelayaran Rusianto Bersaudara** - *Samarinda* *Indonesia*	**215** 65 -	Class: KI (AB)	**1991**-01 **President Marine Pte Ltd — Singapore** Yd No: 060 Loa 29.00 Br ex - Dght 3.670 Lbp 27.08 Br md 8.59 Dpth 4.11 Welded, 1 dk	**(B32A2ST) Tug**	**2 oil engines** with clutches & reverse reduction geared to sc. shafts driving 2 FP propellers Total Power: 1,766kW (2,402hp) 11.0kn Yanmar M220-EN 2 x 4 Stroke 6 Cy. 220 x 300 each-883kW (1201bhp) Yanmar Diesel Engine Co Ltd-Japan AuxGen: 2 x 98kW 415/388V a.c
8822985 - -	**SSP 878** **PT Perusahaan Pelayaran Rusianto Bersaudara** - *Samarinda* *Indonesia*	**177** 53 128	Class: KI (AB)	**1989** **President Marine Pte Ltd — Singapore** Yd No: 032 Loa - Br ex - Dght 2.410 Lbp 24.40 Br md 8.00 Dpth 3.00 Welded, 1 dk	**(B32A2ST) Tug**	**2 oil engines** reverse reduction geared to sc. shaft driving 2 FP propellers Total Power: 1,176kW (1,598hp) 10.0kn Caterpillar 3412TA 2 x Vee 4 Stroke 12 Cy. 137 x 152 each-588kW (799bhp) Caterpillar Inc-USA AuxGen: 2 x 80kW a.c
8220498 *YD4023* -	**SSP 1999** *ex* Aqua 108 *-2003* **Hacienda Shipping Co Pte Ltd** - *Jakarta* *Indonesia* Official number: 8148+BA	**116** 69 105	Class: (KI) (AB)	**1985**-03 **Keppel Philippines Shipyard Inc — Bauan** Yd No: 55 Loa 23.02 Br ex 7.01 Dght 3.201 Lbp 22.00 Br md 7.00 Dpth 3.55 Welded, 1 dk	**(B32A2ST) Tug**	**2 oil engines** sr reverse geared to sc. shafts driving 2 FP propellers Total Power: 810kW (1,102hp) 10.5kn Niigata 6MG16XA 2 x 4 Stroke 6 Cy. 160 x 200 each-405kW (551bhp) Niigata Engineering Co Ltd-Japan AuxGen: 2 x 24kW 440V 60Hz a.c Thrusters: 1 Thwart. FP thruster (f) Fuel: 66.0 (d.f.) 4.5pd

9280536 *YDA4290* -	**SSS MAHAKAM** *ex* Sds 32 *-2013* **PT Sahabat Samudra Sejahtera** PT Wintermar Offshore Marine *Jakarta* *Indonesia* Official number: 2007PST NO 4651L	**185** 56 178	Class: NK	**2002**-11 **Forward Shipbuilding Enterprise Sdn Bhd — Sibu** Yd No: 85 Loa 26.00 Br ex - Dght 2.962 Lbp 24.12 Br md 8.00 Dpth 3.65 Welded, 1 dk	**(B32A2ST) Tug**	**2 oil engines** geared to sc. shafts driving 2 FP propellers Total Power: 1,204kW (1,636hp) 10.0kn Mitsubishi S6R2-MTK 2 x 4 Stroke 6 Cy. 170 x 220 each-602kW (818bhp) Mitsubishi Heavy Industries Ltd-Japan AuxGen: 2 x 56kW a.c Fuel: 125.0 (d.f.)
9612727 *A8PN2* -	**SSV CATARINA** **Catarina Marine Inc** Ventura Petroleo Ltda *Monrovia* *Liberia* MMSI: 636013800 Official number: 13800	**41,148** 12,345 25,500	Class: NV	**2012**-11 **Daewoo Shipbuilding & Marine Engineering Co Ltd — Geoje** Yd No: 3028 Loa 117.90 Br ex 96.70 Dght 25.000 Lbp 117.90 Br md 78.08 Dpth 45.00 Welded, 1 dk	**(Z11C3ZE) Drilling Rig, semi Submersible**	**8 diesel electric oil engines** driving 8 gen. each 5220kW a.c Connecting to 8 elec. motors driving 8 Azimuth electric drive units Total Power: 43,520kW (59,168hp) 6.9kn Wartsila 16V26 8 x Vee 4 Stroke 16 Cy. 260 x 320 each-5440kW (7396bhp) Wartsila Italia SpA-Italy
8769547 *A8JW4*	**SSV VICTORIA** **Victoria Marine Inc** Ventura Petroleo Ltda SatCom: Inmarsat C 463705375 *Monrovia* *Liberia* MMSI: 636012995 Official number: 12995	**41,160** 12,348 -	Class: NV	**2009**-09 **Daewoo Shipbuilding & Marine Engineering Co Ltd — Geoje** Yd No: 3024 Loa 116.60 Br ex 78.00 Dght 25.000 Lbp - Br md - Dpth 45.00 Welded, 1 dk	**(Z11C3ZE) Drilling Rig, semi Submersible**	**8 diesel electric oil engines** driving 8 gen. Connecting to 8 elec. motors each (3500kW) driving 8 Azimuth electric drive units Total Power: 41,600kW (56,560hp) Wartsila 16V26 8 x Vee 4 Stroke 16 Cy. 260 x 320 each-5200kW (7070bhp) Wartsila Finland Oy-Finland
8963806 - -	**ST-5** **Megaflot Ltd** -	*378* 113 500		**1984 Velikiy Ustyugskiy Sudostroitel. i SR Zavod — Velikiy Ustyug** Loa 61.50 Br ex - Dght - Lbp - Br md 9.00 Dpth 2.20 Welded, 1 dk	**(A31A2GX) General Cargo Ship**	**2 oil engines** geared to sc. shafts driving 2 FP propellers Total Power: 332kW (452hp) 12.0kn Daldizel 6CHNSP18/22 2 x 4 Stroke 6 Cy. 180 x 220 each-166kW (226bhp) Daldizel-Khabarovsk
8963909 *HP9619* -	**ST-7** **Meilans Shipping Corp** - *Panama* *Panama* Official number: 2694100	**490** 231 545		**1985 Velikiy Ustyugskiy Sudostroitel. i SR Zavod — Velikiy Ustyug** Loa 61.50 Br ex - Dght - Lbp - Br md 9.00 Dpth 2.20 Welded, 1 dk	**(A31A2GX) General Cargo Ship**	**2 oil engines** geared to sc. shafts driving 2 FP propellers Total Power: 332kW (452hp) 12.0kn Daldizel 6CHNSP18/22 2 x 4 Stroke 6 Cy. 180 x 220 each-166kW (226bhp) Daldizel-Khabarovsk
8963911 *HP9620* -	**ST-22** **Meilans Shipping Corp** - *Panama* *Panama* Official number: 2692000	**490** 231 545		**1987 Velikiy Ustyugskiy Sudostroitel. i SR Zavod — Velikiy Ustyug** Loa 61.50 Br ex - Dght - Lbp - Br md 9.00 Dpth 2.20 Welded, 1 dk	**(A31A2GX) General Cargo Ship**	**2 oil engines** geared to sc. shafts driving 2 FP propellers Total Power: 332kW (452hp) 12.0kn Daldizel 6CHNSP18/22 2 x 4 Stroke 6 Cy. 180 x 220 each-166kW (226bhp) Daldizel-Khabarovsk
7000114 *D7LZ* -	**ST 101** *ex* Yong Ma No. 1 *-2010* *ex* Sachi Maru *-1979* **Kim Jong-Myoung** - *Masan* *South Korea* MMSI: 440117920 Official number: MSR-694037	*198* 55 60	Class: (KR)	**1969 Hayashikane Shipbuilding & Engineering Co Ltd — Yokosuka KN** Yd No: 677 Loa 32.11 Br ex 8.82 Dght 2.830 Lbp 30.79 Br md 8.79 Dpth 3.89 Welded, 1 dk	**(B32A2ST) Tug**	**2 oil engines** driving 2 FP propellers Total Power: 1,472kW (2,002hp) 12.0kn Niigata 6L25BX 2 x 4 Stroke 6 Cy. 250 x 320 each-736kW (1001bhp) Niigata Engineering Co Ltd-Japan AuxGen: 2 x 48kW 225V a.c Fuel: 29.5
7323126 - -	**ST. AGNES** *ex* Shinko Maru No. 35 *-1996* *ex* Kaiko Maru No. 35 *-1989* **Sal Fishing Corp** - *Iloilo* *Philippines* Official number: ILO3003017	*248* 112 407		**1973 Tokushima Zosen K.K. — Fukuoka** Yd No: 1107 Loa 47.17 Br ex 7.62 Dght 3.201 Lbp 42.02 Br md 7.60 Dpth 3.61 Welded, 1 dk	**(B11B2FV) Fishing Vessel**	**1 oil engine** driving 1 FP propeller Total Power: 1,177kW (1,600hp) Makita KNLH630 1 x 4 Stroke 6 Cy. 300 x 480 1177kW (1600bhp) Makita Tekkosho-Japan
9414761 *C6YQ2* -	**ST. ANDREW** *ex* Nord Manila *-2010* *launched as* Nord London *-2010* **Mergalia Shipping Co Ltd** Tri Bulk Shipping Ltd *Nassau* *Bahamas* MMSI: 311041600 Official number: 8001786	**20,809** 11,689 32,688 T/cm 46.0	Class: BV	**2010**-07 **Jiangmen Nanyang Ship Engineering Co Ltd — Jiangmen GD** Yd No: 108 Loa 179.90 (BB) Br ex - Dght 10.150 Lbp 171.50 Br md 28.40 Dpth 14.10 Welded, 1 dk	**(A21A2BC) Bulk Carrier** Grain: 42,565; Bale: 40,558 Compartments: 5 Ho, ER 5 Ha: 3 (20.0 x 19.2) (18.4 x 19.2)ER (14.4 x 17.6) Cranes: 4x30.5t	**1 oil engine** driving 1 FP propeller Total Power: 6,480kW (8,810hp) 13.7kn MAN-B&W 6S42MC 1 x 2 Stroke 6 Cy. 420 x 1764 6480kW (8810bhp) Yichang Marine Diesel Engine Co Ltd-China AuxGen: 3 x 500kW 60Hz a.c
9401934 *9HA3552* -	**ST ANDREW** *ex* Sanko Mercury *-2014* **Super Sailors Co Ltd** Eastern Mediterranean Maritime Ltd *Valletta* *Malta* MMSI: 229725000 Official number: 9401934	**30,488** 15,289 50,792	Class: NK	**2010**-03 **Oshima Shipbuilding Co Ltd — Saikai NS** Yd No: 10527 Loa 189.99 (BB) Br ex - Dght 12.260 Lbp 186.00 Br md 32.26 Dpth 17.31 Welded, 1 dk	**(A31A2GO) Open Hatch Cargo Ship** Double Hull Grain: 57,886; Bale: 57,782 TEU 306 Compartments: 8 Ho, ER 8 Ha: ER Cranes: 4x40t	**1 oil engine** driving 1 FP propeller Total Power: 10,187kW (13,850hp) 15.5kn MAN-B&W 5S60MC-C 1 x 2 Stroke 5 Cy. 600 x 2400 10187kW (13850bhp) Kawasaki Heavy Industries Ltd-Japan AuxGen: 3 x 520kW 60Hz a.c Fuel: 2350.0
8915471 *ORKG* -	**ST. ANNASTRAND** **URS Belgie NV** Unie van Redding - en Sleepdienst NV (Union de Remorquage et de Sauvetage SA) (Towage & Salvage Union Ltd) *Antwerpen* *Belgium* MMSI: 205057000 Official number: 01 00301 1996	**249** 74 134	Class: BV	**1991**-12 **N.V. Scheepswerf van Rupelmonde — Rupelmonde** Yd No: 465 Loa 30.99 Br ex 8.90 Dght 3.589 Lbp 25.00 Br md 8.70 Dpth 4.64 Welded, 1 dk	**(B32A2ST) Tug**	**2 oil engines** with clutches, flexible couplings & reduction geared to sc. shafts driving 2 FP propellers Total Power: 2,130kW (2,896hp) 13.0kn A.B.C. 6MDZC 2 x 4 Stroke 6 Cy. 256 x 310 each-1065kW (1448bhp) Anglo Belgian Corp NV (ABC)-Belgium AuxGen: 2 x 108kW 400V 50Hz a.c Thrusters: 2 Directional thruster (a)
5171658 - -	**ST. ANNE** *ex* St. Anne of Alderney *-1986* *ex* Baltzborg *-1979* *ex* Juto *-1977* *ex* Jens Rand *-1974* **Francis L Earl** -	*300* 187 550	Class: (BV)	**1963 Orskovs Staalskibsvaerft A/S — Frederikshavn** Yd No: 22 Loa 45.34 Br ex 8.67 Dght 3.099 Lbp 43.21 Br md 8.64 Dpth 3.46 Welded, 1 dk	**(A31A2GX) General Cargo Ship** Grain: 707; Bale: 623 Compartments: 2 Ho, ER 2 Ha: 2 (10.8 x 5.0)ER Derricks: 2x2t; Winches: 2 Ice Capable	**1 oil engine** driving 1 CP propeller Total Power: 313kW (426hp) 10.0kn Alpha 405-24VO 1 x 2 Stroke 5 Cy. 240 x 400 313kW (426bhp) Alpha Diesel A/S-Denmark Fuel: 30.5 (d.f.)
8984161 *WDA9218* -	**ST. ANTHONY** **Le Family Inc** - *New Orleans, LA* *United States of America* MMSI: 366862770 Official number: 1123321	**158** 47 -		**2002 Rodriguez Boat Builders, Inc. — Coden, Al** Yd No: 224 L reg 26.15 Br ex - Dght - Lbp - Br md 7.62 Dpth 3.65 Welded, 1 dk	**(B11B2FV) Fishing Vessel**	**1 oil engine** driving 1 Propeller
8983569 *WDA7819* -	**ST. ANTHONY** **Chuc Tan Nguyen** - *Biloxi, MS* *United States of America* MMSI: 366847530 Official number: 1124639	**187** 56 -		**2002 T.M. Jemison Construction Co., Inc. — Bayou La Batre, Al** Yd No: 172 L reg 26.30 Br ex - Dght - Lbp - Br md 7.92 Dpth 3.96 Welded, 1 dk	**(B11B2FV) Fishing Vessel**	**1 oil engine** driving 1 Propeller
9190585 *OXQB* L 510	**ST. ANTHONY** **Rederi Jane Gierlevsen** - *Thyboron* *Denmark* MMSI: 220507000 Official number: D4276	**498** 149 365	Class: (LR) ✠ Classed LR until 16/3/12	**1999**-03 **Stocznia Polnocna SA (Northern Shipyard) — Gdansk** (Hull) Yd No: B685/04 **1999**-03 **B.V. Scheepswerf Maaskant — Stellendam** Yd No: 542 Loa 42.35 Br ex 8.50 Dght 3.860 Lbp 37.95 Br md 8.50 Dpth 5.15 Welded, 1 dk	**(B11A2FT) Trawler**	**1 oil engine** with flexible couplings & sr geared to sc. shaft driving 1 FP propeller Total Power: 1,470kW (1,999hp) 13.0kn Deutz SBV9M628 1 x 4 Stroke 9 Cy. 240 x 280 1470kW (1999bhp) Deutz AG-Koeln AuxGen: 2 x 100kW 400V 50Hz a.c Thrusters: 1 Thwart. FP thruster (f)
8515128 *DUH2666* -	**ST. ANTHONY DE PADUA** *ex* Cebu Ferry 2 *-2012* *ex* Asakaze *-2009* **2GO Group Inc** - *Cebu* *Philippines* MMSI: 548315100 Official number: CEB1008170	**1,792** 1,254 964		**1986**-03 **Yamanishi Shipbuilding Co Ltd — Ishinomaki MG** Yd No: 918 Loa 88.68 Br ex 15.04 Dght 3.801 Lbp 80.00 Br md 15.00 Dpth 4.80 Welded, 2 dks	**(A36A2PR) Passenger/Ro-Ro Ship (Vehicles)**	**2 oil engines** with clutches, flexible couplings & sr reverse geared to sc. shafts driving 2 FP propellers Total Power: 4,414kW (6,002hp) Daihatsu 8DLM-32 2 x 4 Stroke 8 Cy. 320 x 400 each-2207kW (3001bhp) Daihatsu Diesel Manufacturing Co Lt-Japan

8428014 - -
ST. ANTHONY IV
Lucrecio Dellariarte
-
Zamboanga *Philippines*
Official number: ZAM200056
133 72 -
1982 L. Dellariarte — Zamboanga
Loa - Br ex 6.74 Dght -
Lbp 26.22 Br md 6.71 Dpth 2.90
Welded, 1 dk
(B11B2FV) Fishing Vessel
1 oil engine driving 1 FP propeller
Total Power: 221kW (300hp)

9145607 *FQAV* PV 863687
ST. ANTOINE MARIE
Serge Perez
-
Port-Vendres *France*
MMSI: 228233000
Official number: 863687
150 - 135
1996-06 Chantiers Piriou — Concarneau
Yd No: 182
Loa 24.90 (BB) Br ex 8.40 Dght 2.900
Lbp 23.00 Br md 7.50 Dpth 3.89
Welded, 1 dk
(B11B2FV) Fishing Vessel
1 oil engine reverse reduction geared to sc. shaft driving 1 FP propeller
Total Power: 316kW (430hp) 12.0kn
Mitsubishi S12N-MPTK
1 x Vee 4 Stroke 12 Cy. 160 x 180 316kW (430bhp)
Mitsubishi Heavy Industries Ltd-Japan
Thrusters: 1 Thwart. FP thruster (f); 1 Tunnel thruster (a)

8992065 *WDD2490* -
ST. AQUILINA
Allen Marine Tours Inc
-
Sitka, AK *United States of America*
MMSI: 367115930
Official number: 1156351
244 - -
2004-07 Allen Marine Inc. — Sitka Yd No: 44
Loa 26.80 Br ex - Dght -
Lbp - Br md 8.83 Dpth 2.74
Welded, 1 dk
(A37B2PS) Passenger Ship
Hull Material: Aluminium Alloy
Passengers: unberthed: 150
4 oil engines driving 4 Water jets 29.0kn

8815530 *DUTQ6* -
ST. AUGUSTINE OF HIPPO
ex Cebu Ferry 1 *-2012* *ex* Ferry Kumano *-2007*
2GO Group Inc
-
Cebu *Philippines*
MMSI: 548545300
Official number: MNLD011114
2,778 1,618 1,200
1989-03 Shinhama Dockyard Co. Ltd. — Anan
Yd No: 783
L reg 87.80 Br ex - Dght 5.000
Lbp - Br md 16.00 Dpth 10.20
Welded
(A36A2PR) Passenger/Ro-Ro Ship (Vehicles)
Passengers: unberthed: 520
Bow door/ramp
Stern door/ramp
Lane-Len: 330
Trailers: 37
2 oil engines driving 2 FP propellers
Total Power: 3,310kW (4,500hp) 16.8kn
Daihatsu 6DLM-40
2 x 4 Stroke 6 Cy. 400 x 480 each-1655kW (2250bhp)
Daihatsu Diesel Manufacturing Co Lt-Japan

7406021 *J8B2227* -
ST. BARBARA
ex Zealous *-2001* *ex* OSV Zealous *-1996*
ex Gray Seal *-1994* *ex* Seaforth Clansman *-1988*
St Barbara Navigation Co Ltd
Miliana Shipmanagement Ltd
SatCom: Inmarsat C 460100953
Kingstown *St Vincent & The Grenadines*
MMSI: 375666000
Official number: 8699
2,324 697 1,180
Class: LR
✠ **100A1** SS 06/2011
Ice Class 3
✠ **LMC**
Eq.Ltr: P; Cable: U2
1977-08 Cochrane & Sons Ltd. — Selby
Yd No: 1574
Converted From: Buoy & Lighthouse Tender-2001
Converted From: Diving Support Vessel-1988
Loa 80.02 Br ex 14.08 Dght 5.012
Lbp 68.71 Br md 13.71 Dpth 6.76
Welded, 1 dk, 2nd dk in way of hold
(B31A2SR) Research Survey Vessel
Cranes: 1x30t
Ice Capable
4 oil engines with clutches, flexible couplings & dr geared to sc. shafts driving 2 CP propellers
Total Power: 5,384kW (7,320hp) 13.0kn
Blackstone ESL12
4 x Vee 4 Stroke 12 Cy. 222 x 292 each-1346kW (1830bhp)
Mirrlees Blackstone (Stamford)Ltd.-Stamford
AuxGen: 2 x 441kW 440V 60Hz a.c, 2 x 300kW 440V 60Hz a.c
Thrusters: 1 Thwart. CP thruster (f); 1 Tunnel thruster (a)
Fuel: 413.0 (d.f.)

9373113 *DSBJ7* -
ST BLISS
ex Sea Star *-2013* *ex* JL Brave *-2011*
ex Green Willow *-2007*
Seatras Marine Co Ltd
-
Jeju *South Korea*
MMSI: 440010000
Official number: JJR-071861
1,972 1,395 3,429
Class: KR (CC)
2005-12 Rongcheng Xixiakou Shipyard Co Ltd — Rongcheng SD Yd No: 008
Loa 81.00 (BB) Br ex - Dght 5.500
Lbp 76.00 Br md 13.60 Dpth 6.80
Welded, 1 dk
(A31A2GX) General Cargo Ship
Grain: 4,468
Compartments: 2 Ho, ER
2 Ha: ER 2 (18.6 x 9.0)
Ice Capable
1 oil engine reduction geared to sc. shaft driving 1 FP propeller
Total Power: 1,618kW (2,200hp) 12.3kn
Daihatsu 6DKM-26
1 x 4 Stroke 6 Cy. 260 x 380 1618kW (2200bhp)
Anqing Marine Diesel Engine Works-China
AuxGen: 2 x 150kW 400V a.c

9135705 *DUH2638* -
ST. BRAQUIEL
ex Supercat 32 *-2007*
ex Parque Das Nacoes *-2009*
ex Hansepfeil *-2001*
Supercat Fast Ferry Corp
-
Cebu *Philippines*
Official number: CEB1008004
224 81 18
Class: (GL)
1996-07 Lindstols Skips- & Baatbyggeri AS — Risor (Hull launched by) Yd No: 306
1996-07 Schiffs- u. Yachtwerft Abeking & Rasmussen GmbH & Co. — Lemwerder
(Hull completed by) Yd No: 6443
Loa 27.94 Br ex 9.24 Dght 1.650
Lbp 27.50 Br md 9.00 Dpth 3.23
Welded, 1 dk
(A37B2PS) Passenger Ship
Hull Material: Aluminium Alloy
Passengers: unberthed: 202
2 oil engines with flexible couplings & sr gearedto sc. shafts driving 2 CP propellers
Total Power: 2,000kW (2,720hp) 35.0kn
M.T.U. 8V396TE74
2 x Vee 4 Stroke 8 Cy. 165 x 185 each-1000kW (1360bhp)
MTU Friedrichshafen GmbH-Friedrichshafen

7645548 *EI5890* -
ST BRIDGET
ex Galway Bay *-2013* *ex* Brittania *-1989*
Eugene Garrihy
-
Galway *Irish Republic*
MMSI: 250216000
Official number: 403293
109 45 40
Class: (BV)
1976 Ch. Pierre Glehen — Audierne Yd No: 103
Loa 38.99 Br ex - Dght 1.910
Lbp 34.02 Br md 7.51 Dpth 3.46
Welded, 1 dk
(A37B2PS) Passenger Ship
2 oil engines driving 2 FP propellers
Total Power: 1,618kW (2,200hp) 16.5kn
MGO UD30V16
2 x Vee 4 Stroke 16 Cy. 175 x 180 each-809kW (1100bhp)
Societe Alsacienne de ConstructionsMecaniques (SACM)-France

7025566 - -
ST. CATHERINE I
ex Maria Josefa 29 *-2006*
ex Choun Maru No. 18 *-1986*
ex Yamada Maru No. 27 *-1979*
G D Fishing Corp
-
Iloilo *Philippines*
Official number: ILO3001100
169 94 -
1970-04 Nagasaki Zosen K.K. — Nagasaki
Yd No: 251
Loa 35.74 Br ex 6.13 Dght 2.286
Lbp 31.02 Br md 6.10 Dpth 2.85
Welded, 1 dk
(B11B2FV) Fishing Vessel
1 oil engine driving 1 FP propeller
Total Power: 515kW (700hp)
Niigata 6L25BX
1 x 4 Stroke 6 Cy. 250 x 320 515kW (700bhp)
Niigata Engineering Co Ltd-Japan

8518546 *MFJT9* -
ST. CECILIA
WIGHTlink Ltd (Isle of Wight Ferries)
-
London *United Kingdom*
MMSI: 235031617
Official number: 712850
2,968 904 594 T/cm 10.0
1987-03 Cochrane Shipbuilders Ltd. — Selby
Yd No: 135
Loa 76.94 Br ex 17.02 Dght 2.486
Lbp 75.00 Br md 16.81 Dpth 4.53
Welded, 1 dk
(A36A2PR) Passenger/Ro-Ro Ship (Vehicles)
Passengers: unberthed: 784
Bow door/ramp
Len: 5.90 Wid: 3.70 Swl: 18
Stern door/ramp
Len: 5.90 Wid: 3.70 Swl: 18
Cars: 142
3 oil engines gearing integral to driving 3 Voith-Schneider propellers 1 fwd and 2 aft
Total Power: 2,403kW (3,267hp) 12.0kn
MAN 6L25/30
3 x 4 Stroke 6 Cy. 250 x 300 each-801kW (1089bhp)
MAN B&W Diesel GmbH-Augsburg
AuxGen: 3 x 156kW 415V 50Hz a.c
Fuel: 125.0 (r.f.) 6.5pd

9003938 *DSP05* -
ST CHAMPION
ex JI Champion *-2011* *ex* JFE-2 *-2007*
ex Taisei Maru *-2004*
Jang-Ho Shipping Co Ltd
-
Jeju *South Korea*
MMSI: 441335000
Official number: JJR-071886
1,867 953 2,100
Class: KR (BV) (NK)
1990-05 Hitachi Zosen Mukaishima Marine Co Ltd — Onomichi HS Yd No: 30
Loa 79.19 (BB) Br ex - Dght 4.822
Lbp 73.00 Br md 13.00 Dpth 7.90
Welded, 1 dk
(A31A2GX) General Cargo Ship
Grain: 2,850; Bale: 2,848
Compartments: 1 Ho, ER
1 Ha: ER
1 oil engine driving 1 CP propeller
Total Power: 1,471kW (2,000hp) 14.2kn
B&W 6S26MC
1 x 2 Stroke 6 Cy. 260 x 980 1471kW (2000bhp)
The Hanshin Diesel Works Ltd-Japan

9327504 *FWBM* -
ST CHARLOTTE
ex FS Charlotte *-2009*
SEA-tankers Shipping SAS
ST Management (SAAM)
SatCom: Inmarsat C 463501051
Marseille *France (FIS)*
MMSI: 228331700
Official number: 924615S
9,416 2,824 12,497 T/cm 25.6
Class: BV
2006-03 Turkter Tersane ve Deniz Isl. A.S. — Tuzla (Hull) Yd No: (40)
2006-03 Yardimci Tersanesi A.S. — Tuzla
Yd No: 40
Loa 129.00 (BB) Br ex 22.02 Dght 8.200
Lbp 123.90 Br md 22.00 Dpth 12.50
Welded, 1 dk
(A12B2TR) Chemical/Products Tanker
Double Hull (13F)
Liq: 10,457; Liq (Oil): 10,457; Asphalt: 10,457
Cargo Heating Coils
Compartments: 1 Ta, 10 Wing Ta, ER
6 Cargo Pump (s): 2x100m³/hr, 2x337m³/hr, 2x400m³/hr
Manifold: Bow/CM: 64.5m
1 oil engine reduction geared to sc. shaft driving 1 CP propeller
Total Power: 5,400kW (7,342hp) 14.0kn
MaK 6M43
1 x 4 Stroke 6 Cy. 430 x 610 5400kW (7342bhp)
Caterpillar Motoren GmbH & Co. KG-Germany
AuxGen: 1 x 1490kW a.c, 3 x 750kW a.c
Thrusters: 1 Tunnel thruster (f)
Fuel: 70.0 (d.f.) 736.0 (r.f.) 20.0pd

9027269 - -
ST. CHRISTOPHER
ex Liao Chang Yu 6420 *-2006*
-
-
178 77 -
2003-01 Rongcheng Haida Shipbuilding Co Ltd — Rongcheng SD
L reg 35.73 Br ex - Dght -
Lbp - Br md 6.60 Dpth 3.20
Welded, 1 dk
(B11A2FT) Trawler
1 oil engine driving 1 Propeller
Total Power: 441kW (600hp) 11.0kn
Chinese Std. Type Z8E160C
1 x 4 Stroke 8 Cy. 160 x 225 441kW (600bhp)
Jinan Diesel Engine Co Ltd-China

8856003 *WDG7423* -
ST. CHRISTOPHER
Mary Dang Nguyen
-
Orange, TX *United States of America*
MMSI: 367567130
Official number: 929099
158 107 -
1988 Sneed Shipbuilding Inc — Orange TX
Yd No: 291
Loa - Br ex - Dght -
Lbp 24.41 Br md 7.32 Dpth 3.51
Welded, 1 dk
(B11B2FV) Fishing Vessel
1 oil engine driving 1 FP propeller

7043271 *WBK5750* -
ST CHRISTOPHER
W L & O Inc
-
Brownsville, TX *United States of America*
MMSI: 367198510
Official number: 519019
133 90 -
1969 Master Marine, Inc. — Bayou La Batre, Al
Yd No: 102
L reg 22.19 Br ex 6.76 Dght -
Lbp - Br md - Dpth 3.56
Welded
(B11B2FV) Fishing Vessel
1 oil engine driving 1 FP propeller
Total Power: 257kW (349hp)

Identification	Tonnage	Classification	Builder / Dimensions	Type	Machinery
5145984 - - - **ST. CHRISTOPHER** *ex* Heinz-Heino *-1980* *ex* Aeolus *-1956* *ex* Heinz Brey *-1954* **St Christopher Services LLC** -	*158* 112 -	Class: (BV) (GL)	**1932 Gebr. Niestern N.V. Scheepswerven en Mfbk — Delfzijl** Converted From: General Cargo Ship-1980 Lengthened-1957 L reg 34.14 Br ex 5.77 Dght - Lbp 32.21 Br md 5.74 Dpth 2.39 Riveted, 1 dk	**(A37B2PS) Passenger Ship** 2 Ha: (7.2 x 3.3) (9.8 x 3.5) Derricks: 2x0.5t; Winches: 1	**1 oil engine** driving 1 FP propeller Total Power: 74kW (101hp) 6.0kn Deutsche Werke 1 x 4 Stroke 2 Cy. 270 x 420 74kW (101bhp) Deutsche Werke Kiel AG (DWK)-Kiel Fuel: 4.0 (d.f.)
8891443 *MFBZ4* - **ST. CICALA** *ex* Cicala *-2004* **Karen McAvoy** White Water Recovery Ltd *Manchester* *United Kingdom* MMSI: 235018152 Official number: 909034	**272** 81 -		**1970-11 Charles D. Holmes & Co. Ltd. — Beverley** Yd No: 1021 Loa 31.02 Br ex 9.02 Dght - Lbp - Br md 8.53 Dpth 4.11 Welded, 1 dk	**(B34R2QY) Supply Tender**	**1 oil engine** geared to sc. shaft driving 1 FP propeller Total Power: 485kW (659hp) 12.0kn Blackstone ERS8M 1 x 4 Stroke 8 Cy. 222 x 292 485kW (659bhp) Lister Blackstone Marine Ltd.-Dursley
7403990 *WZA4027* - **ST. CLAIR** **Bell Steamship Co** American Steamship Co *Philadelphia, PA* *United States of America* MMSI: 366938750 Official number: 571875	*27,482* 22,681 45,648 T/cm 63.6	Class: AB	**1976-03 Bay Shipbuilding Co — Sturgeon Bay WI** Yd No: 714 Loa 234.73 Br ex 28.05 Dght 9.170 Lbp 231.66 Br md 27.97 Dpth 15.85 Welded, 1 dk	**(A23A2BK) Bulk Carrier, Self-discharging, Laker** Compartments: 5 Ho, ER 26 Ha: ER	**3 oil engines** sr geared to sc. shaft driving 1 CP propeller Total Power: 7,944kW (10,800hp) 14.5kn EMD (Electro-Motive) 20-645-E7 3 x Vee 2 Stroke 20 Cy. 230 x 254 each-2648kW (3600bhp) General Motors Corp.Electro-Motive Div.-La Grange AuxGen: 2 x 600kW Thrusters: 1 Thwart. FP thruster (f); 1 Tunnel thruster (a) Fuel: 678.5 (d.f.)
9236949 *ZNNR5* - **ST CLARE** **ING Lease UK Ltd** WIGHTlink Ltd (Isle of Wight Ferries) *London* *United Kingdom* MMSI: 235002514 Official number: 904282	**5,359** 1,607 769	Class: LR ✠ **100A1** CS 07/2011 passenger/vehicle ferry Portsmouth to Isle of Wight service ✠ **LMC** Eq.Ltr: V; Cable: 495.0/42.0 U3 (a)	**2001-07 Gdanska Stocznia 'Remontowa' SA — Gdansk** Yd No: 653 Loa 86.97 Br ex 18.40 Dght 2.600 Lbp 84.50 Br md 18.00 Dpth 4.60 Welded, 1 dk	**(A36A2PR) Passenger/Ro-Ro Ship (Vehicles)** Passengers: unberthed: 878 Bow ramp (centre) Len: - Wid: 5.20 Swl: - Stern ramp (centre) Len: - Wid: 5.20 Swl: - Cars: 204	**4 oil engines** gearing integral to driving 4 Voith-Schneider propellers 2 fwd and 2 aft Total Power: 3,300kW (4,488hp) 13.0kn Wartsila 5L20 4 x 4 Stroke 5 Cy. 200 x 280 each-825kW (1122bhp) Wartsila Finland Oy-Finland AuxGen: 3 x 252kW 415V 50Hz a.c Fuel: 25.0 (d.f.) 46.0 (r.f.) 14.0pd
5425334 *HQVH6* - **ST. COLMAN** *ex* Velda *-1999* *ex* Concierge *-1993* *ex* Orpena *-1991* *ex* Claudia P *-1983* *ex* Saint Colman *-1981* **Roseda Shipping Inc** - *San Lorenzo* *Honduras* MMSI: 334850000 Official number: L-0327472	**858** 451 1,250	Class: (LR) (BV) ✠ Classed LR until 17/2/88	**1963-06 Scheepswerf "De Gideon" v/h J. Koster Hzn. — Groningen** Yd No: 251 Loa 62.46 Br ex 10.04 Dght - Lbp 58.55 Br md 9.91 Dpth 4.42 Riveted\Welded, 1 dk	**(A31A2GX) General Cargo Ship** Grain: 1,777; Bale: 1,668 Compartments: 2 Ho, ER 2 Ha: (8.7 x 5.4) (17.5 x 7.1)ER Derricks: 3x3t; Winches: 3	**1 oil engine** sr reverse geared to sc. shaft driving 1 FP propeller Total Power: 714kW (971hp) 12.0kn English Electric 1 x 4 Stroke 8 Cy. 203 x 254 714kW (971bhp) English Electric Co. Ltd.-Newton-le-Willows AuxGen: 2 x 30kW 220V d.c, 1 x 15kW 220V d.c Fuel: 71.0 (d.f.)
8912869 *UESZ* - **ST CONFIDENCE** *ex* St Konfidens *-2008* *ex* ST Confidence *-2008* *ex* Thyra *-2004* *ex* Gastello *-2000* **Sovfracht JSC (A/O 'Sovfrakht')** - *Vostochnyy* *Russia* MMSI: 273443870	**3,972** 1,617 4,705	Class: RS (BV) (NV)	**1993-03 Sedef Gemi Endustrisi A.S. — Gebze** Yd No: 91 Loa 97.80 Br ex 17.34 Dght 6.010 Lbp 90.22 Br md 17.30 Dpth 7.00 Welded, 1 dk	**(A31A2GX) General Cargo Ship** Grain: 5,242; Bale: 5,227 TEU 221 C.Ho 111/20' C.Dk 110/20' incl. 12 ref C. Compartments: 2 Ho, ER 2 Ha: 2 (25.7 x 12.5)ER Cranes: 2x25t Ice Capable	**1 oil engine** driving 1 CP propeller Total Power: 3,354kW (4,560hp) 12.5kn B&W 6L35MC 1 x 2 Stroke 6 Cy. 350 x 1050 3354kW (4560bhp) H Cegielski Poznan SA-Poland AuxGen: 1 x 300kW 220/380V 50Hz a.c, 2 x 264kW 220/380V 50Hz a.c Fuel: 90.0 (d.f.) 275.0 (r.f.) 12.7pd
9203710 *9HA2873* - **ST. CONSTANTINE** *ex* Boris Shcherbina *-2007* **Kogos Shipping Co Ltd** BSBS Ltd *Valletta* *Malta* MMSI: 256510000 Official number: 9203710	**3,467** 1,595 4,520	Class: RS	**2002-06 AT Kyyivskyi Sudnobudivnyi-Sudnoremontnyi Zavod — Kyyiv** Yd No: 001 Loa 103.23 Br ex - Dght 4.580 Lbp 97.54 Br md 16.42 Dpth 6.21 Welded, 1 dk	**(A31A2GX) General Cargo Ship** Grain: 5,440 TEU 209 C.Ho 98/20' C.Dk 111/20' Compartments: 2 Ho, ER 2 Ha: ER 2 (31.5 x 13.4)	**1 oil engine** driving 1 FP propeller Total Power: 1,800kW (2,447hp) 11.0kn S.K.L. 8VDS29/24AL-2 1 x 4 Stroke 8 Cy. 240 x 290 1800kW (2447bhp) SKL Motoren u. Systemtechnik AG-Magdeburg AuxGen: 3 x 174kW a.c Thrusters: 1 Tunnel thruster (f)
8600272 *ZR3398* - **ST. CROIX** *ex* HEL-151 *-1995* **Dyer Eiland Visserye (Pty) Ltd** - *Cape Town* *South Africa* MMSI: 601628000 Official number: 19507	*178* 53 126	Class: (PR)	**1988-10 Stocznia Ustka SA — Ustka** Yd No: B280/02 Loa 26.73 Br ex - Dght 3.200 Lbp - Br md 7.41 Dpth 3.66 Welded, 1 dk	**(B11A2FS) Stern Trawler**	**1 oil engine** geared to sc. shaft driving 1 FP propeller Total Power: 419kW (570hp) 10.0kn Sulzer 6AL20/24 1 x 4 Stroke 6 Cy. 200 x 240 419kW (570bhp) Zaklady Przemyslu Metalowego 'HCegielski' SA-Poznan
8941420 *WCX6748* - **ST. DANIEL PHILLIP III** **Daniel Phillip III Inc** - *Port Lavaca, TX* *United States of America* Official number: 1055674	**140** 42 -		**1997 T.M. Jemison Construction Co., Inc. — Bayou La Batre, Al** Yd No: 110 L reg 24.14 Br ex - Dght - Lbp - Br md 7.32 Dpth 3.63 Welded, 1 dk	**(B11B2FV) Fishing Vessel**	**1 oil engine** driving 1 FP propeller
1009508 *2BHL9* - **ST. DAVID** *ex* St Ekaterina *-2012* *ex* Xanadu *-2010* **Endless Leisure Ltd** Camper & Nicholsons France SARL *Douglas* *Isle of Man (British)* MMSI: 235066164 Official number: 739334	**969** 290 171	Class: LR ✠ **100A1** SS 11/2008 SSC Yacht, mono, G6 **LMC** Cable: 330.0/22.0 U3 (a)	**2008-11 Azimut-Benetti SpA — Livorno** Yd No: FB239 Loa 59.40 (BB) Br ex 10.63 Dght 3.200 Lbp 49.70 Br md 10.40 Dpth 5.45 Welded, 1 dk	**(X11A2YP) Yacht**	**2 oil engines** with clutches, flexible couplings & dr reverse geared to sc. shafts driving 2 FP propellers Total Power: 2,760kW (3,752hp) Caterpillar 3512B 2 x Vee 4 Stroke 12 Cy. 170 x 215 each-1380kW (1876bhp) Caterpillar Inc-USA AuxGen: 2 x 200kW 380V 50Hz a.c Thrusters: 1 Thwart. FP thruster (f)
8958071 *WDB8235* - **ST. DOMINIC II** *ex* Tiffany Anna *-2005* *ex* Black Eagle II *-2000* *ex* B & B *-1999* **Thuc & Hang LLC** - *Allen, TX* *United States of America* MMSI: 366955160 Official number: 1079273	**144** 43 -		**1999 J & J Marine, Inc. — Bayou La Batre, Al** Yd No: 161 L reg 24.71 Br ex - Dght - Lbp - Br md 7.31 Dpth 3.84 Welded, 1 dk	**(B11B2FV) Fishing Vessel**	**1 oil engine** driving 1 FP propeller
7617125 *3ENT2* - **ST EFREM** *ex* Efrem *-2007* *ex* Evanthia *-1997* *ex* Sila *-1991* *ex* Sinoex *-1986* *ex* Sincere Trader *-1982* **San Evans Maritime Co Ltd** Livanbros Marine SA *Panama* *Panama* MMSI: 352226000 Official number: 3438408	**9,144** 5,489 15,134	Class: (BV) (PR) (CR) (AB)	**1977-11 Taiwan Shipbuilding Corp — Keelung** Yd No: N-068 Loa 143.41 (BB) Br ex 19.84 Dght 9.050 Lbp 134.12 Br md 19.80 Dpth 12.35 Welded, 2 dks	**(A31A2GX) General Cargo Ship** Grain: 20,161; Bale: 19,001 Compartments: 4 Ho, ER 5 Ha: (19.8 x 9.9)4 (9.1 x 9.9)ER Derricks: 12x10t; Winches: 12	**1 oil engine** sr geared to sc. shaft driving 1 FP propeller Total Power: 3,339kW (4,540hp) 11.0kn Pielstick 12PC2-2V-400 1 x Vee 4 Stroke 12 Cy. 400 x 460 3339kW (4540bhp) Ishikawajima Harima Heavy IndustrieCo Ltd (IHI)-Japan AuxGen: 2 x 310kW 450V 60Hz a.c, 1 x 200kW 450V 60Hz a.c
9594999 *9HA2890* - **ST ELMO** **Tug Malta Ltd** - *Valletta* *Malta* MMSI: 256606000 Official number: 9594999	**455** 136 228	Class: RI	**2011-11 Astilleros Zamakona Pasaia SL — Pasaia** Yd No: 700 Loa 30.25 Br ex - Dght 3.750 Lbp - Br md 11.75 Dpth 5.33 Welded, 1 dk	**(B32A2ST) Tug** Cranes: 1	**2 oil engines** reduction geared to sc. shafts driving 2 Directional propellers Total Power: 3,372kW (4,584hp) 12.9kn Caterpillar 3516B-HD 2 x Vee 4 Stroke 16 Cy. 170 x 215 each-1686kW (2292bhp) Caterpillar Inc-USA AuxGen: 2 x 130kW a.c
5422540 *SGFI* - **ST. ERIK** *ex* Kung Erik *-1996* *ex* St. Erik *-1976* *ex* Solo *-1966* *ex* St. Erik *-1963* **Stromma Turism & Sjofart AB** - *Gothenburg* *Sweden* MMSI: 265625300	**246** 99 -		**1880 Motala Co. — Goteborg** L reg 37.28 Br ex 6.13 Dght 2.701 Lbp - Br md 6.08 Dpth - Riveted, 1 dk	**(A37B2PS) Passenger Ship** Passengers: unberthed: 298	**1 oil engine** driving 1 FP propeller Total Power: 287kW (390hp) 12.0kn Polar M46I 1 x 2 Stroke 6 Cy. 250 x 420 287kW (390bhp) (new engine 1951) Nydqvist & Holm AB-Sweden
8706325 - - **ST. EUGENE 5** *ex* Saint Eugene V *-1963* -	*251* 141 50	Class: (BV)	**1988-04 Soc. Francaise de Cons. Nav. — Villeneuve-la-Garenne** Yd No: 855 Loa 35.01 Br ex 6.46 Dght 1.251 Lbp 28.00 Br md 6.32 Dpth 2.80 Welded, 1 dk	**(A37B2PS) Passenger Ship** Hull Material: Aluminium Alloy Passengers: unberthed: 200	**2 oil engines** with clutches, flexible couplings & sr geared to sc. shafts driving 2 FP propellers , 2 Water jets Total Power: 2,500kW (3,400hp) 27.0kn MWM TBD604BV12 2 x Vee 4 Stroke 12 Cy. 170 x 195 each-1250kW (1700bhp) Kloeckner Humboldt Deutz AG-West Germany

IMO / Call sign	Name / Owner	Tonnage	Class	Build / Dimensions	Type / Details	Machinery
5070127 *GTSF* -	**ST. EVAL** *ex Chieftain -1967* **Blueridge Investments Ltd** Washington Yachting Group *Falmouth* *United Kingdom* MMSI: 233217000 Official number: 161905	*209* 9 -	Class: (LR) ✠ Classed LR until 6/94	**1930-04 Scott & Sons — Bowling** Yd No: 317 Converted From: Tug-1987 Loa 34.45 Br ex 7.35 Dght 3.664 Lbp 32.52 Br md 7.32 Dpth 3.81 Riveted	**(X11A2YP) Yacht**	**1 oil engine** driving 1 FP propeller Total Power: 1,030kW (1,400hp) 10.5kn General Motors 16-278-A 1 x Vee 2 Stroke 16 Cy. 222 x 267 1030kW (1400bhp) (Re-engined ,made 1944, Reconditioned & refitted 1990) General Motors Corp-USA AuxGen: 1 x 30kW 220V d.c, 1 x 15kW 220V d.c Thrusters: 1 Thwart. FP thruster (f)
8224004 - -	**ST EXPLORER** *ex Asian Winner 1 -2001 ex Jin Song -2008* *ex Shozui -2002 ex Shozui Maru -2002* **Sea-Tech Transport Inc** - *Zamboanga* *Philippines* Official number: ZAM2D01786	**2,960** 2,013 5,514	Class: (NK)	**1983-05 Ube Dockyard Co. Ltd. — Ube** Yd No: 178 Loa 99.50 Br ex 15.55 Dght 6.517 Lbp 92.03 Br md 15.51 Dpth 7.73 Welded, 1 dk	**(A31A2GX) General Cargo Ship** Grain: 6,046; Bale: 5,826 Compartments: 2 Ho, ER 2 Ha: (24.7 x 7.5) (25.2 x 7.5)ER	**1 oil engine** driving 1 FP propeller Total Power: 2,574kW (3,500hp) 12.5kn Hanshin 6LU46A 1 x 4 Stroke 6 Cy. 460 x 740 2574kW (3500bhp) The Hanshin Diesel Works Ltd-Japan AuxGen: 2 x 130kW 440V 60Hz a.c Fuel: 29.0 (d.f.) 97.0 (r.f.) 10.5pd
8907228 *MMDA5* -	**ST. FAITH** **WIGHTlink Ltd (Isle of Wight Ferries)** - *London* *United Kingdom* MMSI: 235031618 Official number: 718794	**3,009** 914 574 T/cm 10.0		**1990-07 Cochrane Shipbuilders Ltd. — Selby** Yd No: 169 Loa 76.09 Br ex 24.40 Dght 2.486 Lbp 72.38 Br md 17.22 Dpth 4.52 Welded, 1 dk	**(A36A2PR) Passenger/Ro-Ro Ship (Vehicles)** Passengers: unberthed: 784 Bow door/ramp Len: 5.05 Wid: 5.20 Swl: 18 Stern door/ramp Len: 5.05 Wid: 5.20 Swl: 18 Lane-Wid: 5.20 Lane-clr ht: 4.65 Cars: 142	**3 oil engines** gearing integral to driving 3 Voith-Schneider propellers 1 fwd and 2 aft Total Power: 2,406kW (3,270hp) 12.0kn Sulzer 6ASL25/30 3 x 4 Stroke 6 Cy. 250 x 300 each-802kW (1090bhp) MAN B&W Diesel AG-West Germany AuxGen: 3 x 300kW 415V 50Hz a.c, 3 x 156kW 415V 50Hz a.c Fuel: 125.0 (r.f.) 6.5pd
7928794 *D6GD3* -	**ST FILIP** *ex Fast Filip -2010 ex Smaragd -1992* **Voyager International Trade & Ship Management LLC** Sudoservice Shipping Consultancy & Trading Ltd *Moroni* *Union of Comoros* MMSI: 616999020 Official number: 1201167	**1,740** 734 1,990	Class: BR (PR) (GL)	**1980-04 J.J. Sietas KG Schiffswerft GmbH & Co. — Hamburg** Yd No: 919 Loa 85.86 (BB) Br ex 11.38 Dght 3.480 Lbp 84.04 Br md 11.31 Dpth 6.00 Welded, 2 dks	**(A31A2GX) General Cargo Ship** Grain: 3,260; Bale: 3,247 TEU 90 C.Ho 54/20' (40') C.Dk 36/20' (40') Compartments: 1 Ho, ER 1 Ha: (55.3 x 8.9) Ice Capable	**1 oil engine** reduction geared to sc. shaft driving 1 FP propeller Total Power: 441kW (600hp) 10.8kn Deutz SBA8M528 1 x 4 Stroke 8 Cy. 220 x 280 441kW (600bhp) Kloeckner Humboldt Deutz AG-West Germany AuxGen: 3 x 61kW 220/380V 50Hz a.c Thrusters: 1 Thwart. FP thruster (f)
8899201 *5NQJ1* -	**ST GABRIEL** *ex Gulf Shark -2013* **Multiplan International Ltd** *Nigeria*	**213** 63 -	Class: AB	**1981-01 Hudson Shipbuilders, Inc. (HUDSHIP) — Pascagoula, Ms** Yd No: 87 Loa 34.14 Br ex - Dght 3.030 Lbp - Br md 7.92 Dpth 3.35 Welded, 1 dk	**(B34L2QU) Utility Vessel**	**2 oil engines** reverse reduction geared to sc. shafts driving 2 FP propellers Total Power: 1,104kW (1,500hp) 10.0kn G.M. (Detroit Diesel) 16V-92 2 x Vee 2 Stroke 16 Cy. 123 x 127 each-552kW (750bhp) General Motors Detroit DieselAllison Divn-USA AuxGen: 2 x 50kW a.c Fuel: 68.0 (d.f.)
9304590 *9V2426* -	**ST. GABRIEL** **OCM Singapore Njord Holdings St Gabriel Pte Ltd** Parakou Shipmanagement Pte Ltd *Singapore* *Singapore* MMSI: 564875000 Official number: 399003	**30,068** 13,602 51,266 T/cm 52.0	Class: NV	**2006-01 STX Shipbuilding Co Ltd — Changwon (Jinhae Shipyard)** Yd No: 1183 Loa 183.00 (BB) Br ex 32.23 Dght 13.130 Lbp 173.90 Br md 32.20 Dpth 19.10 Welded, 1 dk	**(A12B2TR) Chemical/Products Tanker** Double Hull (13F) Liq: 54,100; Liq (Oil): 54,100 Cargo Heating Coils Compartments: 12 Wing Ta, 2 Wing Slop Ta, ER 12 Cargo Pump (s): 12x600m³/hr Manifold: Bow/CM: 92m	**1 oil engine** driving 1 FP propeller Total Power: 9,488kW (12,900hp) 14.2kn MAN-B&W 6S50MC-C 1 x 2 Stroke 6 Cy. 500 x 2000 9488kW (12900bhp) STX Engine Co Ltd-South Korea AuxGen: 3 x 900kW 440/220V 60Hz a.c Fuel: 114.0 (d.f.) 1570.0 (r.f.) 36.5pd
9437517 *C6YR2* -	**ST. GEORGE** *ex Nord Shanghai -2010* **Koronia Shipping Co Ltd** Tri Bulk Shipping Ltd *Nassau* *Bahamas* MMSI: 311042500 Official number: 8001796	**20,748** 11,689 32,688 T/cm 45.9	Class: BV	**2009-08 Jiangmen Nanyang Ship Engineering Co Ltd — Jiangmen GD** Yd No: 111 Loa 179.90 Br ex - Dght 10.150 Lbp 171.50 Br md 28.40 Dpth 14.10 Welded, 1 dk	**(A21A2BC) Bulk Carrier** Grain: 42,565; Bale: 40,558 Compartments: 5 Ho, ER 5 Ha: 3 (20.0 x 19.2) (18.4 x 19.2)ER (14.4 x 17.6) Cranes: 4x30.5t	**1 oil engine** driving 1 FP propeller Total Power: 6,480kW (8,810hp) 13.7kn MAN-B&W 6S42MC 1 x 2 Stroke 6 Cy. 420 x 1764 6480kW (8810bhp) STX Engine Co Ltd-South Korea
8328886 - -	**ST. GEORGE** **Earthmovers Solomons Ltd** - *Honiara* *Solomon Islands*	*124* - -		**1970 New Guinea SB. Co. Pty. Ltd. — Rabaul** L reg 24.05 Br ex 6.41 Dght - Lbp - Br md - Dpth - Welded, 1 dk	**(A31A2GX) General Cargo Ship**	**2 oil engines** driving 2 FP propellers Total Power: 98kW (134hp) Cummins 2 x 4 Stroke each-49kW (67bhp) Cummins Engine Co Inc-USA
7333872 *GDNT* PZ 1053	**ST. GEORGES** *ex Jacob -1984 ex Soli Deo Gloria -1980* **W Stevenson & Sons** - *Penzance* *United Kingdom* MMSI: 232005630 Official number: A18835	*237* 71 -		**1974-03 Holland Launch N.V. — Zaandam** Yd No: 521 Loa 34.96 Br ex 7.57 Dght - Lbp 30.87 Br md 7.50 Dpth 4.02 Welded, 1 dk	**(B11A2FT) Trawler**	**1 oil engine** driving 1 FP propeller Total Power: 809kW (1,100hp) Deutz 1 x 4 Stroke 6 Cy. 809kW (1100bhp) Kloeckner Humboldt Deutz AG-West Germany
9254068 *FGA5123* -	**ST. GERMAIN** **Gie Pirmil Bail** Societe de Transports Fluviaux Maritimes de l'Ouest (STFMO) *St-Nazaire* *France* MMSI: 227009430 Official number: 916032	**1,155** - 1,900	Class: BV	**2001-09 Shipyard Nista — Amsterdam** (Hull) **2001-09 B.V. Scheepswerf Damen — Gorinchem** Yd No: 563350 Loa 75.09 Br ex 12.00 Dght 4.000 Lbp 72.00 Br md 11.90 Dpth 4.50 Welded, 1 dk	**(B33B2DT) Trailing Suction Hopper Dredger** Hopper: 1,150	**2 oil engines** reduction geared to sc. shafts driving 2 FP propellers Total Power: 1,500kW (2,040hp) 11.5kn Caterpillar 3508B-TA 2 x Vee 4 Stroke 8 Cy. 170 x 190 each-750kW (1020bhp) Caterpillar Inc-USA AuxGen: 2 x 145kW 380/220V 50Hz a.c Thrusters: 1 Water jet (f)
9257204 *DSPR3* -	**ST GLORY** *ex Core Ami -2012 ex Kai Yuan -2008* *ex Chang An Ace -2005* **Moriah Merchant Marine Co Ltd** Union Marine Co Ltd *Jeju* *South Korea* MMSI: 441426000 Official number: JJR-088864	**1,998** 1,294 3,275	Class: KR (CC)	**2001-09 Taizhou Zhongyuan Shipyard — Taizhou ZJ** Yd No: 001 Loa 81.20 Br ex - Dght 5.500 Lbp 76.00 Br md 13.00 Dpth 6.80 Welded, 1 dk	**(A31A2GX) General Cargo Ship** Grain: 4,541; Bale: 4,541 Compartments: 2 Ho, ER 2 Ha: ER 2 (18.6 x 9.0) Ice Capable	**1 oil engine** reduction geared to sc. shaft driving 1 FP propeller Total Power: 1,103kW (1,500hp) 8.0kn Chinese Std. Type G6300ZC 1 x 4 Stroke 6 Cy. 300 x 380 1103kW (1500bhp) Ningbo CSI Power & Machinery GroupCo Ltd-China AuxGen: 2 x 150kW 400V a.c
9414759 *C6YO5* -	**ST. GREGORY** *ex Nord Copenhagen -2010* **Haryana Shipping Co Ltd** Tri Bulk Shipping Ltd *Nassau* *Bahamas* MMSI: 311040200 Official number: 8001774	**20,809** 11,689 32,688 T/cm 46.0	Class: BV	**2010-06 Jiangmen Nanyang Ship Engineering Co Ltd — Jiangmen GD** Yd No: 107 Loa 179.90 (BB) Br ex - Dght 10.150 Lbp 171.50 Br md 28.40 Dpth 14.10 Welded, 1 dk	**(A21A2BC) Bulk Carrier** Grain: 42,565; Bale: 40,558 Compartments: 5 Ho, ER 5 Ha: 3 (20.0 x 19.2) (18.4 x 19.2)ER (14.4 x 17.6) Cranes: 4x30.5t	**1 oil engine** driving 1 FP propeller Total Power: 6,480kW (8,810hp) 13.7kn MAN-B&W 6S42MC 1 x 2 Stroke 6 Cy. 420 x 1764 6480kW (8810bhp) STX Engine Co Ltd-South Korea AuxGen: 3 x 440kW 60Hz a.c Fuel: 1635.0 (r.f.)
9042726 *4DEJ5* -	**ST. GREGORY THE GREAT** *ex Superferry 20 -2012* *ex Sun Flower Kogane -2010* **2GO Group Inc** Negros Navigation Co Inc *Manila* *Philippines* MMSI: 548394100 Official number: 00-0000305	**19,468** 5,840 3,516	Class: BV (NK)	**1992-07 KK Kanasashi — Toyohashi AI** Yd No: 3280 Loa 150.88 (BB) Br ex - Dght 5.471 Lbp 140.00 Br md 25.00 Dpth 13.30 Welded, 2 dks	**(A36A2PR) Passenger/Ro-Ro Ship (Vehicles)** Passengers: 942 Bow door & ramp Quarter stern door/ramp (p) Quarter stern door/ramp (s) Lane-Len: 1000 Lane-clr ht: 5.20 Lorries: 100, Cars: 60	**2 oil engines** with flexible couplings & sr geared to sc. shafts driving 2 CP propellers Total Power: 18,536kW (25,202hp) 22.1kn Sulzer 14ZAV40S 2 x Vee 4 Stroke 14 Cy. 400 x 560 each-9268kW (12601bhp) Hitachi Zosen Corp-Japan AuxGen: 2 x 1000kW a.c, 2 x 880kW a.c, 1 x 360kW a.c Thrusters: 1 Thwart. CP thruster (f); 1 Tunnel thruster (a) Fuel: 361.0 (r.f.) 70.8pd
8120569 *GDBB* -	**ST. HELEN** **WIGHTlink Ltd (Isle of Wight Ferries)** - *London* *United Kingdom* MMSI: 235031619 Official number: 705464	**2,983** 908 538 T/cm 10.0		**1983-11 Henry Robb Ltd. — Leith** Yd No: 535 Loa 76.97 Br ex 17.23 Dght 2.486 Lbp 75.01 Br md 16.81 Dpth 4.53 Welded, 1 dk	**(A36A2PR) Passenger/Ro-Ro Ship (Vehicles)** Passengers: unberthed: 784 Bow door/ramp Len: 5.90 Wid: 3.70 Swl: 18 Stern door/ramp Len: 5.90 Wid: 3.70 Swl: 18 Lane-clr ht: 4.32 Cars: 142	**3 oil engines** gearing integral to driving 3 Voith-Schneider propellers 1 fwd and 2 aft Total Power: 1,986kW (2,700hp) 12.0kn MAN 6L25/30 3 x 4 Stroke 6 Cy. 250 x 300 each-662kW (900bhp) Harland and Wolff Ltd.-Belfast AuxGen: 3 x 156kW 415V 50Hz a.c Fuel: 125.0 (r.f.) 6.5pd

IMO / Call sign	Name / Owner / Manager / Flag	Tonnage	Class	Builder / Dimensions	Type / Cargo	Machinery
9229350 *9HFW7* -	**ST. HELEN** **Brave Shipping Ltd** Thenamaris (Ships Management) Inc *Valletta* *Malta* MMSI: 215203000 Official number: 7651	**57,301** 32,526 105,661 T/cm 92.0	Class: LR **✠100A1** SS 04/2012 Double Hull oil tanker ESP *IWS SPM **ShipRight** (SDA, FDA, CM) **✠LMC** **UMS IGS** Eq.Ltr: T†; Cable: 715.0/87.0 U3 (a)	**2002-04 Samho Heavy Industries Co Ltd — Samho** Yd No: 133 Loa 244.00 (BB) Br ex 42.03 Dght 14.919 Lbp 234.00 Br md 42.00 Dpth 21.00 Welded, 1 dk	**(A13A2TV) Crude Oil Tanker** Double Hull (13F) Liq: 117,963; Liq (Oil): 118,084 Cargo Heating Coils Compartments: 12 Wing Ta, 2 Wing Slop Ta, ER 3 Cargo Pump (s): 3x3000m^3/hr Manifold: Bow/CM: 122.8m	**1 oil engine** driving 1 FP propeller Total Power: 11,327kW (15,400hp) 14.5kn B&W 6S60MC 1 x 2 Stroke 6 Cy. 600 x 2292 11327kW (15400bhp) Hyundai Heavy Industries Co Ltd-South Korea AuxGen: 3 x 730kW 450/220V 60Hz a.c Boilers: WTAuxB (Comp) 8.1kgf/cm^2 (7.9bar), WTAuxB (o.f.) 18.3kgf/cm^2 (17.9bar) Fuel: 195.0 (d.f.) (Heating Coils) 2417.0 (r.f.)
8716306 *MMHE5* -	**ST. HELENA** **St Helena Line Ltd** Andrew Weir Shipping Ltd SatCom: Inmarsat B 323266910 *London* *United Kingdom* MMSI: 232669000 Official number: 718836	**6,767** 2,030 3,130 T/cm 15.3	Class: LR **✠100A1** CS 10/2010 passenger ship cargo oil (FP 60~C and above) in DTm CG **✠LMC** **UMS** Eq.Ltr: (X) ; Cable: 498.0/56.0 U2	**1990-10 A. & P. Appledore Aberdeen — Aberdeen** Yd No: 1000 Loa 105.00 Br ex 19.23 Dght 6.016 Lbp 95.00 Br md 19.20 Dpth 10.00 Welded, 2 dks, 3rd dk (f & a of DTm)	**(A32A2GF) General Cargo/Passenger Ship** Passengers: cabins: 49; berths: 128 Bale: 3,750 TEU 52 C Ho 36 TEU C Dk 16 TEU incl 12 ref C. Compartments: 2 Ho, 2 Ta, ER 2 Ha: (6.5 x 6.0) (13.3 x 11.0) Cranes: 2x12.5t; Derricks: 2x10t	**2 oil engines** with clutches & reduction geared to sc. shafts driving 2 CP propellers Total Power: 6,532kW (8,880hp) 14.5kn Mirrlees KMR6MK3 2 x 4 Stroke 6 Cy. 400 x 457 each-3266kW (4440bhp) Mirrlees Blackstone (Stockport)Ltd.-Stockport AuxGen: 2 x 1000kW 415V 50Hz a.c, 2 x 1000kW 415V 50Hz a.c Boilers: 2 AuxB (o.f.) 9.2kgf/cm^2 (9.0bar), AuxB (ex.g.) 9.2kgf/cm^2 (9.0bar) Fuel: 54.0 (d.f.) 760.0 (r.f.) 21.0pd
9103582 *DUF2063* -	**ST I** *ex* Shin Sumiho Maru *-2010* **Vicente T Poraque** - *Legaspi* *Philippines* Official number: 05-0000029	**245** 129 650		**1993-07 KK Ouchi Zosensho — Matsuyama EH** Yd No: 503 Loa 57.57 Br ex - Dght - Lbp 53.00 Br md 9.50 Dpth 5.34 Welded, 1 dk	**(A31A2GX) General Cargo Ship** Grain: 1,314; Bale: 1,280 Compartments: 1 Ho 1 Ha: (31.4 x 7.5)	**1 oil engine** driving 1 FP propeller Total Power: 662kW (900hp) 11.0kn Hanshin LH26G 1 x 4 Stroke 6 Cy. 260 x 440 662kW (900bhp) The Hanshin Diesel Works Ltd-Japan
9097135 *WDD7860* -	**ST. IGNATIUS LOYOLA** - Harvey Gulf International Marine LLC *New Orleans, LA* *United States of America* MMSI: 367192310 Official number: 1200624	**447** 134 -		**2007-07 Master Boat Builders, Inc. — Coden, Al** Yd No: 393 Loa 45.72 Br ex - Dght - Lbp - Br md 10.97 Dpth 3.65 Welded, 1 dk	**(B21A20S) Platform Supply Ship**	**2 oil engines** reduction geared to sc. shaft driving 2 Propellers Total Power: 1,492kW (2,028hp) 12.0kn Caterpillar 3508B 1 x Vee 4 Stroke 8 Cy. 170 x 190 746kW (1014bhp) Caterpillar Inc-USA AuxGen: 2 x 99kW 480V 50Hz a.c Thrusters: 1 Thwart. FP thruster (f)
8805157 *DUH3109* -	**ST. IGNATIUS OF LOYOLA** *ex* Cebu Ferry 3 *-2012* *ex* Esan *-2010* **2GO Group Inc** - *Cebu* *Philippines* MMSI: 548422100 Official number: CEB1008337	*2,825* 1,977 1,836		**1988-09 Naikai Shipbuilding & Engineering Co Ltd — Onomichi HS (Setoda Shipyard)** Yd No: 532 Loa 104.65 (BB) Br ex 16.20 Dght 4.713 Lbp 95.00 Br md 16.00 Dpth 11.46 Welded	**(A35A2RR) Ro-Ro Cargo Ship** Lane-Len: 255 Vehicles: 42	**2 oil engines** with clutches, flexible couplings & sr reverse geared to sc. shaft driving 2 FP propellers Total Power: 5,884kW (8,000hp) 17.5kn Daihatsu 6DLM-40 2 x 4 Stroke 6 Cy. 400 x 480 each-2942kW (4000bhp) Daihatsu Diesel Manufacturing Co Lt-Japan AuxGen: 3 x 400kW 450V 60Hz a.c Thrusters: 1 Thwart. CP thruster (f)
8864359 *DUF2069* -	**ST-III** *ex* Kinju Maru No. 10 *-2010* **Vicente T Poraque** - *Legaspi* *Philippines* Official number: 05-0000178	**245** 149 699		**1992-02 K.K. Kamishima Zosensho — Osakikamijima** Yd No: 527 Loa 56.87 (BB) Br ex - Dght 3.130 Lbp 51.00 Br md 9.50 Dpth 5.30 Welded, 1 dk	**(A31A2GX) General Cargo Ship** Compartments: 1 Ho, ER	**1 oil engine** reverse geared to sc. shaft driving 1 FP propeller Total Power: 956kW (1,300hp) 12.0kn Hanshin LH26G 1 x 4 Stroke 6 Cy. 260 x 440 956kW (1300bhp) The Hanshin Diesel Works Ltd-Japan Thrusters: 1 Thwart. FP thruster (f)
8729157 *4LMZ2* -	**ST. ILIA** *ex* Grot *-2010* *ex* PTR-50 No. 65 *-1994* **Iepl Ilia State University** - *Georgia* MMSI: 213973000 Official number: C-00472	**190** 57 70	Class: (RS)	**1989-07 Astrakhanskaya Sudoverf im. "Kirova" — Astrakhan** Yd No: 65 Loa 31.85 Br ex 7.08 Dght 2.100 Lbp 27.80 Br md - Dpth 3.15 Welded, 1 dk	**(B12B2FC) Fish Carrier** Ins: 100	**1 oil engine** geared to sc. shaft driving 1 FP propeller Total Power: 232kW (315hp) 10.3kn Daldizel 6CHSPN2A18-315 1 x 4 Stroke 6 Cy. 180 x 220 232kW (315bhp) Daldizel-Khabarovsk AuxGen: 2 x 25kW Fuel: 14.0 (d.f.)
9689160 *9V7494* -	**ST. JACOBI** **Shenlong Maritime Pte Ltd** Maruta Industries Co Ltd (Maruta Sangyo KK) *Singapore* *Singapore* MMSI: 563673000 Official number: 398490	**29,656** 13,843 50,529	Class: NK	**2014-01 SPP Shipbuilding Co Ltd — Sacheon** Yd No: H4101 Loa 183.00 (BB) Br ex - Dght 13.315 Lbp 174.00 Br md 32.20 Dpth 19.10 Welded, 1 dk	**(A12B2TR) Chemical/Products Tanker** Double Hull (13F) Liq: 52,800; Liq (Oil): 52,800	**1 oil engine** driving 1 FP propeller
7045994 *WDC3084* -	**ST. JAMES** *ex* Bay Prince *-2004* *ex* Larkin Hale *-2004* *ex* Quita *-2004* *ex* Tester *-1986* **Moran Towing Corp** - *New Orleans, LA* *United States of America* MMSI: 367002410 Official number: 517050	*189* 129 -	Class: (AB)	**1968 Main Iron Works, Inc. — Houma, La** Yd No: 209 Loa - Br ex 8.39 Dght 3.791 Lbp 29.34 Br md 8.26 Dpth 4.22 Welded, 1 dk	**(B32A2ST) Tug**	**2 oil engines** reverse reduction geared to sc. shaft driving 1 FP propeller Total Power: 1,704kW (2,316hp) G.M. (Detroit Diesel) 16V-149 2 x Vee 2 Stroke 16 Cy. 146 x 146 each-852kW (1158bhp) General Motors Corp-USA AuxGen: 2 x 60kW Fuel: 150.5
8712556 *FHPF* BL 734689	**ST. JEAN BAPTISTE** *ex* Yann Marie *-2003* *ex* Natalys *-2001* **Michel Jules Francois Caloin** - *Boulogne* *France* MMSI: 227105100 Official number: 734689	**164** - -		**1988-06 Forges Caloin — Etaples** Yd No: 53 Loa 24.00 Br ex - Dght - Lbp 20.50 Br md 6.80 Dpth 3.80 Welded, 1 dk	**(B11A2FS) Stern Trawler**	**1 oil engine** reduction geared to sc. shaft driving 1 FP propeller Total Power: 441kW (600hp) MGO UD30V12 1 x Vee 4 Stroke 12 Cy. 175 x 180 441kW (600bhp) Societe Alsacienne de ConstructionsMecaniques (SACM)-France
9135717 *DUH2635* -	**ST. JHUDIEL** *ex* Supercat 30 *-2001* *ex* Bairro Alto *-2001* *ex* Hanseblitz *-2001* **Supercat Fast Ferry Corp** - *Cebu* *Philippines* Official number: CEB1008003	**224** 81 18	Class: (GL)	**1996-07 Lindstols Skips- & Baatbyggeri AS — Risor** Yd No: 305 Loa 27.70 Br ex 9.24 Dght 1.650 Lbp - Br md 9.04 Dpth 3.25 Welded, 1 dk	**(A37B2PS) Passenger Ship** Hull Material: Aluminium Alloy Passengers: unberthed: 202	**2 oil engines** geared to sc. shafts driving 2 CP propellers Total Power: 2,000kW (2,720hp) 35.0kn M.T.U. 8V396TE74 2 x Vee 4 Stroke 8 Cy. 165 x 185 each-1000kW (1360bhp) MTU Friedrichshafen GmbH-Friedrichshafen
7314371 *DZPL* -	**ST. JOAN OF ARC** *ex* Superferry 5 *-2012* *ex* Aboitiz Superferry V *-1996* *ex* Ferry Cosmo *-1994* *ex* Ferry Hakozaki *-1992* **2GO Group Inc** - *Manila* *Philippines* MMSI: 548082100 Official number: 00-0000441	**11,638** 6,466 2,919	Class: (AB)	**1973-05 Onomichi Dockyard Co Ltd — Onomichi HS** Yd No: 240 Loa 138.61 (BB) Br ex 22.15 Dght 5.890 Lbp 128.00 Br md 22.10 Dpth 8.20 Riveted\Welded, 2 dks	**(A36A2PR) Passenger/Ro-Ro Ship (Vehicles)** Passengers: 2476 Bow ramp Stern ramp Lane-Len: 780 Cars: 370	**2 oil engines** driving 2 FP propellers Total Power: 11,180kW (15,200hp) 19.0kn MAN V7V-40/54 2 x Vee 4 Stroke 14 Cy. 400 x 540 each-5590kW (7600bhp) Mitsubishi Heavy Industries Ltd-Japan AuxGen: 3 x 570kW 445V 60Hz a.c Fuel: 51.0 (d.f.) 231.0 (r.f.) 23.0pd
9313462 *VRCG6* -	**ST. JOHANNIS** **Pretty Harmony Shipping SA** Parakou Shipmanagement Pte Ltd *Hong Kong* *Hong Kong* MMSI: 477607100 Official number: HK-1787	**30,068** 13,602 51,218 T/cm 52.0	Class: NV	**2007-02 STX Shipbuilding Co Ltd — Changwon (Jinhae Shipyard)** Yd No: 1203 Loa 183.06 (BB) Br ex 32.23 Dght 13.147 Lbp 173.90 Br md 32.20 Dpth 19.10 Welded, 1 dk	**(A12B2TR) Chemical/Products Tanker** Double Hull (13F) Liq: 52,047; Liq (Oil): 54,100 Cargo Heating Coils Compartments: 12 Wing Ta, 2 Wing Slop Ta, Wing ER 12 Cargo Pump (s): 12x600m^3/hr Manifold: Bow/CM: 92.1m	**1 oil engine** driving 1 FP propeller Total Power: 9,488kW (12,900hp) 14.2kn MAN-B&W 6S50MC-C 1 x 2 Stroke 6 Cy. 500 x 2000 9488kW (12900bhp) STX Engine Co Ltd-South Korea AuxGen: 3 x 900kW 440/220V 60Hz a.c Fuel: 114.0 (d.f.) 1570.0 (r.f.) 36.5pd
7527992 *WDD2991* -	**ST. JOHN** **State of Louisiana (Department of Transportation & Development)** - *New Orleans, LA* *United States of America* MMSI: 367122430 Official number: 582890	*656* 446 200	Class: (AB)	**1978 Equitable Shipyards, Inc. — New Orleans, La** Yd No: 1688 Loa - Br ex - Dght 1.524 Lbp 45.73 Br md 20.01 Dpth 3.03 Welded	**(A36A2PR) Passenger/Ro-Ro Ship (Vehicles)**	**2 oil engines** driving 2 FP propellers Total Power: 1,412kW (1,920hp) Caterpillar D346TA 2 x Vee 4 Stroke 8 Cy. 137 x 165 each-706kW (960bhp) Caterpillar Tractor Co-USA

IMO / Call sign	Name / Owner	Tonnage	Class	Builder / Dimensions	Type	Machinery
7043192 *WY6134* -	**ST. JOHN** *ex* Miss Mona Marie *-2001* **Pho Van Pham** - *Rockport, TX* *United States of America* Official number: 519139	*103* 70 -		**1969 Toche Enterprises, Inc. — Ocean Springs, Ms** Yd No: 1027 L reg 20.88 Br ex 6.74 Dght - Lbp - Br md - Dpth 3.41 Welded	**(B11B2FV) Fishing Vessel**	**1 oil engine** driving 1 FP propeller Total Power: 257kW (349hp)
7121700 - -	**ST. JOHN** *ex* Bonaparte *-1988* *ex* Snekkar *-1986* *ex* Dogger Bank *-1982* **Blumar Seafoods** -	*691* 236 418	Class: (BV)	**1972 Stocznia im Komuny Paryskiej — Gdynia** Yd No: B423/02 Loa 54.21 Br ex - Dght 4.601 Lbp 48.37 Br md 11.04 Dpth 4.70 Welded, 2 dks	**(B11A2FS) Stern Trawler** Ins: 510	**1 oil engine** geared to sc. shaft driving 1 CP propeller Total Power: 1,471kW (2,000hp) 14.5kn Crepelle 12PSN 1 x Vee 4 Stroke 12 Cy. 260 x 280 1471kW (2000bhp) Crepelle et Cie-France AuxGen: 2 x 197kW 380V 50Hz a.c, 1 x 144kW 380V 50Hz a.c Fuel: 205.5 (d.f.)
8521713 *YJQT9* -	**ST. JOHN** - **St John Shipping Ltd** Pacific Blue Ltd *Port Vila* *Vanuatu* MMSI: 576206000 Official number: 1999	312 94 -	Class: IS (LR) ✠ Classed LR until 31/1/05	**1987-03 Amels BV — Makkum** Yd No: 410 Converted From: Trawler Loa 36.50 Br ex 8.11 Dght - Lbp 32.47 Br md 8.01 Dpth 4.37 Welded, 1 dk	**(B22G2OY) Standby Safety Vessel** Ins: 175	**1 oil engine** with clutches, flexible couplings & dr reverse geared to sc. shaft driving 1 FP propeller Total Power: 1,103kW (1,500hp) 12.8kn Deutz SBV8M628 1 x 4 Stroke 8 Cy. 240 x 280 1103kW (1500bhp) Kloeckner Humboldt Deutz AG-West Germany AuxGen: 2 x 100kW 220/380V 50Hz a.c, 1 x 80kW 220/380V 50Hz a.c Thrusters: 1 Thwart. FP thruster (f)
8654388 *WDC3083* -	**ST. JOHN** *ex* Harbor Queen *-1982* **Moran Towing Corp** - *New Orleans, LA* *United States of America* Official number: 272543	**128** 42 -		**1956 Parker Bros. & Co., Inc. — Houston, Tx** Yd No: 24 Loa 25.60 Br ex - Dght - Lbp - Br md 7.92 Dpth 2.80 Welded, 1 dk	**(B32A2ST) Tug**	**1 oil engine** driving 1 Propeller
8941030 *WCX8040* -	**ST. JOHN BOSCO** - **Khan Van Tran** - *Larose, LA* *United States of America* MMSI: 366739880 Official number: 1056070	*153* 123 -		**1997 Khan V. Tran — Larose, La** L reg 22.86 Br ex - Dght - Lbp - Br md 7.47 Dpth 3.81 Welded, 1 dk	**(B11B2FV) Fishing Vessel**	**1 oil engine** driving 1 FP propeller
9238870 *S6NO9*	**ST. JOHN MERCY** *ex* Macau Trader *-2014* *ex* PAC Antlia *-2014* *launched as* H. H. Ruth *-2001* **Antlia Shipping Ltd** PACCship (UK) Ltd *Singapore* *Singapore* MMSI: 564682000 Official number: 389907	**13,764** 5,157 16,794	Class: AB	**2001-10 Jurong Shipyard Pte Ltd — Singapore** Yd No: 1060 Loa 154.00 (BB) Br ex 25.04 Dght 9.500 Lbp 145.00 Br md 25.00 Dpth 13.60 Welded, 1 dk	**(A33A2CC) Container Ship (Fully Cellular)** TEU 1078 incl 150 ref C. Cranes: 2x40t	**1 oil engine** driving 1 FP propeller Total Power: 13,387kW (18,201hp) 19.5kn B&W 7L60MC 1 x 2 Stroke 7 Cy. 600 x 1944 13387kW (18201bhp) Hudong Heavy Machinery Co Ltd-China AuxGen: 3 x 830kW a.c Thrusters: 1 Tunnel thruster (f)
9188180 *WCY2315* -	**ST. JOHNS** - **Seabulk Towing Inc** - *Port Everglades, FL* *United States of America* MMSI: 367343230 Official number: 1063615	**317** 95 -	Class: (AB)	**1998-04 Halter Marine, Inc. — Lockport, La** Yd No: 1706 Loa - Br ex 15.15 Dght 1.620 Lbp 27.53 Br md - Dpth 3.27 Welded, 1 dk	**(B32A2ST) Tug**	**2 oil engines** gearing integral to driving 2 Z propellers Total Power: 2,942kW (4,000hp) 12.0kn Caterpillar 3516TA 2 x Vee 4 Stroke 16 Cy. 170 x 190 each-1471kW (2000bhp) Caterpillar Inc-USA AuxGen: 2 x 73kW a.c
8984159 *WDC3859* -	**ST. JOSEPH** - **Cao Family Inc** - *New Orleans, LA* *United States of America* MMSI: 367015370 Official number: 1123025	**158** 47 -		**2002 Rodriguez Boat Builders, Inc. — Coden, Al** Yd No: 222 L reg 26.15 Br ex - Dght - Lbp - Br md 7.62 Dpth 3.65 Welded, 1 dk	**(B11B2FV) Fishing Vessel**	**1 oil engine** driving 1 Propeller
8940098 *WDE2220* -	**ST. JOSEPH** - **L-T Inc** - *Palacios, TX* *United States of America* Official number: 1039485	**148** 44 -		**1996 Master Boat Builders, Inc. — Coden, Al** Yd No: 217 L reg 24.87 Br ex - Dght - Lbp - Br md 7.32 Dpth 3.81 Welded, 1 dk	**(B11B2FV) Fishing Vessel**	**1 oil engine** driving 1 FP propeller
8855889 - -	**ST. JOSEPH** - **Hue Stacey Nguyen** - *Port Arthur, TX* *United States of America* Official number: 683310	*134* 91 -		**1985 Quality Marine, Inc. — Bayou La Batre, Al** Yd No: 179 Loa 25.30 Br ex - Dght - Lbp 22.89 Br md 6.77 Dpth 3.54 Welded, 1 dk	**(B11B2FV) Fishing Vessel**	**1 oil engine** driving 1 FP propeller Total Power: 530kW (721hp) Caterpillar 3412TA 1 x Vee 4 Stroke 12 Cy. 137 x 152 530kW (721bhp) Caterpillar Tractor Co-USA
8944898 *DUA2038* -	**ST. JOSEPH 1** *ex* YFU-54 *-1988* **Tanjuan Shipping Inc** - *Cebu* *Philippines* Official number: CEB1000461	*234* 138 -		**1988 at Cebu** Loa - Br ex - Dght - Lbp 44.66 Br md 9.75 Dpth 1.65 Welded, 1 dk	**(A35D2RL) Landing Craft**	**1 oil engine** driving 1 FP propeller Total Power: 368kW (500hp) Cummins 1 x 4 Stroke 368kW (500bhp) Cummins Engine Co Inc-USA
9622655 *WDF8656*	**ST. JOSEPH THE WORKER** - **Harvey Cougar LLC** Harvey Gulf International Marine LLC *New Orleans, LA* *United States of America* MMSI: 367497160 Official number: 1232182	**878** 263 1,230	Class: AB	**2011-08 Master Boat Builders, Inc. — Coden, Al** Yd No: 417 Loa 56.40 Br ex - Dght 3.820 Lbp 53.66 Br md 14.03 Dpth 4.57 Welded, 1 dk	**(B21A2OS) Platform Supply Ship**	**2 oil engines** reduction geared to sc. shafts driving 2 Propellers Total Power: 2,238kW (3,042hp) Caterpillar 3512C 2 x Vee 4 Stroke 12 Cy. 170 x 190 each-1119kW (1521bhp) Caterpillar Inc-USA AuxGen: 2 x 910kW 60Hz a.c
8986767 *WDE4802* -	**ST. JOSEPH VII** *ex* St. Paul *-2004* **My Julie LLC** - *New Orleans, LA* *United States of America* MMSI: 367357950 Official number: 1139728	**182** 54 -		**2003** Yd No: 249 Loa - Br ex - Dght - Lbp - Br md - Dpth - Welded, 1 dk	**(B11B2FV) Fishing Vessel**	**1 oil engine** driving 1 Propeller
8855877 *WDE4456* -	**ST. JUDE** *ex* Capt. D & A *-2004* **Joseph E Malley** - *Pago Pago, AS* *United States of America* Official number: 917554	*174* 118 -		**1987 Universal Shipbuilding, Inc. — New Iberia, La** Yd No: 7 Loa - Br ex - Dght - Lbp 26.06 Br md 7.32 Dpth 3.60 Welded, 1 dk	**(B11B2FV) Fishing Vessel**	**1 oil engine** driving 1 FP propeller
8870346 *WAV8495* -	**ST. JUDE** *ex* Clipper *-2004* **Daniel G Curry** - *Ketchikan, AK* *United States of America* MMSI: 366164050 Official number: 518545	*136* 40 -		**1969 Universal Iron Works — Houma, La** Loa 28.65 Br ex - Dght - Lbp - Br md 7.32 Dpth 3.14 Welded, 1 dk	**(B34R2QY) Supply Tender**	**1 oil engine** driving 1 FP propeller
8969783 *WDA9381* -	**ST. JUDE I** - **Hung V Tran** - *New Orleans, LA* *United States of America* MMSI: 366864540 Official number: 1118281	**186** 55 -		**2001 T.M. Jemison Construction Co., Inc. — Bayou La Batre, Al** Yd No: 161 L reg 26.30 Br ex - Dght - Lbp - Br md 7.62 Dpth 3.96 Welded, 1 dk	**(B11B2FV) Fishing Vessel**	**1 oil engine** driving 1 FP propeller

9689158 *9V7493* -	**ST. KATHARINEN** **Shenlong Maritime Pte Ltd** Maruta Industries Co Ltd (Maruta Sangyo KK) *Singapore* *Singapore* MMSI: 563648000 Official number: 398488	**29,656** 13,843 50,259	Class: NK	**2013-10 SPP Shipbuilding Co Ltd — Sacheon** Yd No: H4100 Loa 183.00 (BB) Br ex - Dght 13.315 Lbp 174.00 Br md 32.20 Dpth 19.10 Welded, 1 dk	**(A12B2TR) Chemical/Products Tanker** Double Hull (13F) Liq: 52,800; Liq (Oil): 54,170	**1 oil engine** driving 1 FP propeller Total Power: 7,240kW (9,844hp) 14.5kn Fuel: 1540.0
7036292 *DUE2032* -	**ST. KRISTOPHER** *ex Muroran -1990 ex Muroran Maru -1987* **Viva Shipping Lines Co Inc** - *Batangas* *Philippines* Official number: BAT5000380	*716* 397 956		**1970-03 Narasaki Zosen KK — Muroran HK** Yd No: 739 Loa 74.71 (BB) Br ex 12.83 Dght 3.861 Lbp 69.02 Br md 12.81 Dpth 4.70 Welded, 1 dk	**(A36A2PR) Passenger/Ro-Ro Ship (Vehicles)** Passengers: 1652	**4 oil engines** geared to sc. shafts driving 2 FP propellers Total Power: 4,708kW (6,400hp) 17.0kn Daihatsu 8DSM-26 4 x 4 Stroke 8 Cy. 260 x 320 each-1177kW (1600bhp) Daihatsu Diesel Manufacturing Co Lt-Japan AuxGen: 2 x 100kW 225V a.c Fuel: 80.0 (d.f.) 15.0pd
7405273 *DUE2088* -	**ST. LAWRENCE** *ex Ferry Ikitsuki No. 8 -1996* *ex Ferry Takashima -1987* **Sto Domingo Shipping Lines** - *Batangas* *Philippines* Official number: BAT5003374	*256* 115 71		**1974-06 Fukumoto Zosensho — Onomichi** Yd No: 143 Loa 33.63 Br ex 8.44 Dght 2.150 Lbp 28.99 Br md 8.41 Dpth 2.90 Riveted\Welded, 1 dk	**(A37B2PS) Passenger Ship**	**1 oil engine** driving 1 FP propeller Total Power: 515kW (700hp) Kubota 1 x 4 Stroke 6 Cy. 260 x 410 515kW (700bhp) Kubota Tekkosho-Japan
9042764 *4DEJ8* -	**ST. LEO THE GREAT** *ex Superferry 21 -2012* *ex Sun Flower Nishiki -2010* **2GO Group Inc** Negros Navigation Co Inc *Manila* *Philippines* MMSI: 548398100 Official number: 00-0000333	**19,468** 5,840 3,520	Class: BV (NK)	**1992-12 KK Kanasashi — Toyohashi AI** Yd No: 3285 Loa 150.87 (BB) Br ex - Dght 5.471 Lbp 140.00 Br md 25.00 Dpth 13.30 Welded, 2 dks	**(A36A2PR) Passenger/Ro-Ro Ship (Vehicles)** Passengers: 942 Angled stern door/ramp (p. a.) Angled stern door/ramp (s. a.) Lane-Len: 1000 Lorries: 100, Cars: 60	**2 oil engines** with flexible couplings & sr geared to sc. shafts driving 2 CP propellers Total Power: 18,536kW (25,202hp) 22.1kn Sulzer 14ZAV40S 2 x Vee 4 Stroke 14 Cy. 400 x 560 each-9268kW (12601bhp) Hitachi Zosen Corp-Japan AuxGen: 2 x 1000kW a.c Thrusters: 1 Thwart. CP thruster (f); 1 Tunnel thruster (a)
9285304 *WDD3646* -	**ST. LOUIS** **GulfMark Americas Inc** - *New Orleans, LA* *United States of America* MMSI: 367021240 Official number: 1167668	**2,045** 797 3,463	Class: AB	**2005-04 Bender Shipbuilding & Repair Co Inc — Mobile AL** Yd No: 7428 Lengthened-2013 Loa 76.81 Br ex - Dght 4.900 Lbp 74.42 Br md 16.50 Dpth 5.80 Welded, 1 dk	**(B21A20S) Platform Supply Ship**	**3 diesel electric oil engines** driving 2 gen. each 1825kW 480V a.c 1 gen. of 910kW 480V a.c Connecting to 2 elec. motors each (1566kW) driving 2 Z propellers Total Power: 4,560kW (6,199hp) 12.5kn Cummins KTA-38-M 1 x Vee 4 Stroke 12 Cy. 159 x 159 910kW (1237bhp) Cummins Engine Co Inc-USA Cummins QSK60-M 2 x Vee 4 Stroke 16 Cy. 159 x 190 each-1825kW (2481bhp) Cummins Engine Co Inc-USA Thrusters: 2 Thwart. CP thruster (f) Fuel: 641.0 (d.f.)
9243186 *WDD3825* -	**ST LOUIS EXPRESS** *ex CP Yellowstone -2006* *ex TMM Guanajuato -2005* **Wilmington Trust Co, as Trustee** Hapag-Lloyd AG *St Louis, MO* *United States of America* MMSI: 367136680 Official number: 1191641	**40,146** 18,097 40,478 T/cm 64.6	Class: AB	**2002-11 China Shipbuilding Corp (CSBC) — Kaohsiung** Yd No: 792 Loa 243.35 (BB) Br ex - Dght 11.000 Lbp 232.40 Br md 32.20 Dpth 19.50 Welded, 1 dk	**(A33A2CC) Container Ship (Fully Cellular)** TEU 3237 C Ho 1420 TEU C Dk 1817 TEU incl 400 ref C. Cranes: 4x45t	**1 oil engine** driving 1 FP propeller Total Power: 29,243kW (39,759hp) 22.5kn B&W 8K80MC-C 1 x 2 Stroke 8 Cy. 800 x 2300 29243kW (39759bhp) Doosan Engine Co Ltd-South Korea AuxGen: 3 x 2280kW Thrusters: 1 Thwart. CP thruster (f) Fuel: 222.0 (d.f.) 4305.0 (r.f.) 110.0pd
8939271 *WDF4173* -	**ST. LUCAS** **Dinh Nguyen** - *New Orleans, LA* *United States of America* MMSI: 367448830 Official number: 1036744	**149** 44 -		**1995 Master Boat Builders, Inc. — Coden, Al** Yd No: 205 L reg 24.87 Br ex - Dght - Lbp - Br md 7.32 Dpth 3.81 Welded, 1 dk	**(B11B2FV) Fishing Vessel**	**1 oil engine** driving 1 FP propeller
9353993 *S6BB3* -	**ST. LUCIA** **St Lucia Shipping Pte Ltd** Epic Ship Management Pte Ltd *Singapore* *Singapore* MMSI: 565841000 Official number: 392918	**4,253** 1,374 5,035 T/cm 14.7	Class: NK (BV)	**2008-04 Sasaki Shipbuilding Co Ltd — Osakikamijima HS** Yd No: 663 Loa 99.98 (BB) Br ex 17.22 Dght 6.110 Lbp 93.50 Br md 17.20 Dpth 7.80 Welded, 1 dk	**(A11B2TG) LPG Tanker** Liq (Gas): 4,900 2 x Gas Tank (s); 2 independent (stl) cyl horizontal 2 Cargo Pump (s): 2x350m³/hr Manifold: Bow/CM: 45.5m	**1 oil engine** driving 1 FP propeller Total Power: 3,120kW (4,242hp) 13.8kn Mitsubishi 6UEC37LA 1 x 2 Stroke 6 Cy. 370 x 880 3120kW (4242bhp) Akasaka Tekkosho KK (Akasaka DieselLtd)-Japan AuxGen: 2 x 380kW 450V 60Hz a.c Thrusters: 1 Tunnel thruster (f) Fuel: 105.0 (d.f.) 503.0 (r.f.)
9313474 *VRCG4* -	**ST. MARIEN** **Pretty Unity Shipping SA** Parakou Shipmanagement Pte Ltd *Hong Kong* *Hong Kong* MMSI: 477593800 Official number: HK-1785	**30,068** 13,602 51,218 T/cm 52.0	Class: NV	**2007-03 STX Shipbuilding Co Ltd — Changwon (Jinhae Shipyard)** Yd No: 1204 Loa 183.06 (BB) Br ex 32.23 Dght 13.147 Lbp 173.90 Br md 32.20 Dpth 19.10 Welded, 1 dk	**(A12B2TR) Chemical/Products Tanker** Double Hull (13F) Liq: 52,048; Liq (Oil): 52,048 Cargo Heating Coils Compartments: 12 Wing Ta, 2 Wing Slop Ta, ER 12 Cargo Pump (s): 12x600m³/hr Manifold: Bow/CM: 92.1m	**1 oil engine** driving 1 FP propeller Total Power: 8,580kW (11,665hp) 14.2kn MAN-B&W 6S50MC-C 1 x 2 Stroke 6 Cy. 500 x 2000 8580kW (11665bhp) STX Engine Co Ltd-South Korea AuxGen: 3 x 900kW 440/220V 60Hz a.c Fuel: 235.0 (d.f.) 1568.0 (r.f.) 36.5pd
9500508 *VRER2* -	**ST. MARK** **Cotaijet 351 Ltd** Chu Kong High-Speed Ferry Co Ltd *Hong Kong* *Hong Kong* MMSI: 477197300 Official number: HK-2288	**700** 230 84	Class: NV	**2009-03 Austal Ships Pty Ltd — Fremantle WA** Yd No: 351 Loa 47.50 Br ex 12.10 Dght 1.640 Lbp 44.10 Br md 11.80 Dpth 3.80 Welded, 1 dk	**(A37B2PS) Passenger Ship** Hull Material: Aluminium Alloy Passengers: unberthed: 417	**4 oil engines** reduction geared to sc. shafts driving 4 Water jets Total Power: 9,280kW (12,616hp) M.T.U. 16V4000M70 4 x Vee 4 Stroke 16 Cy. 165 x 190 each-2320kW (3154bhp) MTU Friedrichshafen GmbH-Friedrichshafen AuxGen: 2 x a.c
9367358 *LXOX* -	**ST MARSEILLE** **SEA-tankers Shipping SAS** ST Management (SAAM) SatCom: Inmarsat C 425322910 *Luxembourg* *Luxembourg* MMSI: 253229000	**5,218** 2,398 8,015 T/cm 17.0	Class: BV	**2008-03 Anadolu Deniz Insaat Kizaklari San. ve Tic. Ltd. Sti. — Tuzla** Yd No: 205 Loa 121.68 (BB) Br ex 17.20 Dght 6.858 Lbp 115.31 Br md 17.20 Dpth 8.80 Welded, 1 dk	**(A12B2TR) Chemical/Products Tanker** Double Hull (13F) Liq: 8,182; Liq (Oil): 8,182 Cargo Heating Coils Compartments: 1 Slop Ta, 12 Wing Ta, ER 12 Cargo Pump (s): 12x330m³/hr Manifold: Bow/CM: 66m Ice Capable	**1 oil engine** reduction geared to sc. shaft driving 1 CP propeller Total Power: 3,787kW (5,149hp) 14.0kn MaK 8M32C 1 x 4 Stroke 8 Cy. 320 x 480 3787kW (5149bhp) Caterpillar Motoren GmbH & Co. KG-Germany AuxGen: 3 x 580kW 440V 60Hz a.c, 1 x 1200kW 440/230V 60Hz a.c Thrusters: 1 Tunnel thruster (f) Fuel: 64.6 (d.f.) 384.8 (r.f.)
1003619 *MNQZ8* -	**ST. MARTEEN F** **Moracee Ltd** Combet Yacht Consultant *London* *United Kingdom* Official number: 721980	**213** 63 -	Class: (LR) ✠ Classed LR until 16/8/12	**1992-03 Cant. Nav. Ugo Codecasa S.p.A. — Viareggio** Loa 34.70 Br ex 7.00 Dght 2.300 Lbp 30.02 Br md - Dpth 4.14 Welded, 1 dk	**(X11A2YP) Yacht**	**2 oil engines** geared to sc. shafts driving 2 FP propellers Total Power: 1,022kW (1,390hp) Deutz SBA8M816 2 x 4 Stroke 8 Cy. 142 x 160 each-511kW (695bhp) Motoren Werke Mannheim AG (MWM)-Mannheim
8856015 - -	**ST. MARTIN** **Viet Giang Corp** - *New Orleans, LA* *United States of America* Official number: 912915	*112* 89 -		**1987 Binh Van Mai — Morgan City, La** Yd No: 1 Loa - Br ex - Dght - Lbp 22.86 Br md 6.71 Dpth 2.93 Welded, 1 dk	**(B11B2FV) Fishing Vessel**	**1 oil engine** driving 1 FP propeller
8887026 *WTU3573* -	**ST MARTIN** *ex St Martin Ii -2012 ex Nancy III -2007* *ex Capt. Steve -2001* **Men Truong** - *Houston, TX* *United States of America* Official number: 612624	*119* 81 -		**1979 St Augustine Trawlers, Inc. — Saint Augustine, Fl** Yd No: S-41 L reg 19.75 Br ex - Dght - Lbp - Br md 6.70 Dpth 3.10 Welded, 1 dk	**(B11B2FV) Fishing Vessel**	**1 oil engine** driving 1 FP propeller

IMO / Call sign	Name / Owner / Port	Tonnage	Class	Builder / Dimensions	Type / Cargo	Machinery
9364198 *S6BB5* -	**ST. MARTIN** **St Martin Shipping Pte Ltd** Epic Ship Management Pte Ltd *Singapore* *Singapore* MMSI: 565870000 Official number: 392920	**4,303** 1,373 5,024 T/cm 14.7	Class: NK	**2008-04 Kanrei Zosen K.K. — Naruto** Yd No: 407 Loa 99.90 (BB) Br ex 17.63 Dght 6.165 Lbp 93.50 Br md 17.60 Dpth 8.00 Welded, 1 dk	**(A11B2TG) LPG Tanker** Double Bottom Entire Compartment Length Liq (Gas): 5,018 3 x Gas Tank (s); 2 independent cyl horizontal, 1 (stl) 2 Cargo Pump (s): 2x350m³/hr Manifold: Bow/CM: 45.7m	**1 oil engine** driving 1 FP propeller Total Power: 3,250kW (4,419hp) 15.0kn MAN-B&W 5L35MC 1 x 2 Stroke 5 Cy. 350 x 1050 3250kW (4419bhp) Makita Corp-Japan AuxGen: 2 x 380kW 450V 60Hz a.c Thrusters: 1 Tunnel thruster (f) Fuel: 116.0 (d.f.) 467.0 (r.f.)
9097123 *WDD6206* -	**ST. MARTIN DE PORRES** Harvey Gulf International Marine LLC *New Orleans, LA* *United States of America* MMSI: 367169650 Official number: 1191732	**447** 134 -		**2007-02 Master Boat Builders, Inc. — Coden, Al** Yd No: 392 Loa 45.72 Br ex - Dght - Lbp 41.46 Br md 10.97 Dpth 3.65 Welded, 1 dk	**(B21A20S) Platform Supply Ship**	**2 oil engines** reduction geared to sc. shafts driving 2 FP propellers Total Power: 1,250kW (1,700hp) 12.0kn Caterpillar 3508B 2 x Vee 4 Stroke 8 Cy. 170 x 190 each-625kW (850bhp) Caterpillar Inc-USA AuxGen: 2 x 150kW 480V 50Hz a.c Thrusters: 1 Thwart. FP thruster (f)
8969537 *WDE6444* -	**ST. MARTIN IV** *ex* Anna Priscilla *-2005* **Lien Nguyen** *Biloxi, MS* *United States of America* Official number: 1115726	**169** 50 -		**2001** Yd No: 202 L reg 26.18 Br ex - Dght - Lbp - Br md 7.62 Dpth 3.81 Welded, 1 dk	**(B11B2FV) Fishing Vessel**	**1 oil engine** driving 1 FP propeller
8938875 - -	**ST. MARTIN IV** **Lien Bich Nguyen** *Venice, LA* *United States of America* Official number: 1037921	**142** 114 -		**1995 Duyen Van Tran — Gautier, Ms** L reg 23.77 Br ex - Dght - Lbp - Br md 7.32 Dpth 3.47 Welded, 1 dk	**(B11B2FV) Fishing Vessel**	**1 oil engine** driving 1 FP propeller
8969678 *WDA9488* -	**ST. MARTIN V** **Lien Bich Nguyen** *Venice, LA* *United States of America* MMSI: 366865740 Official number: 1116463	**130** 104 -		**2001 Duyen Van Tran — Gautier, Ms** Yd No: 004 L reg 23.77 Br ex - Dght - Lbp - Br md 7.62 Dpth 3.04 Welded, 1 dk	**(B11B2FV) Fishing Vessel**	**1 oil engine** driving 1 FP propeller
8941482 - -	**ST. MARTIN VI** **Tuong Tran** *Larose, LA* *United States of America* Official number: 1050300	*160* 128 -		**1997 Tuong Tran — Larose, La** Yd No: 10 L reg 23.77 Br ex - Dght - Lbp - Br md 7.47 Dpth 3.81 Welded, 1 dk	**(B11B2FV) Fishing Vessel**	**1 oil engine** driving 1 FP propeller
8886113 - -	**ST. MARTYRS V N** **St Martyrs V N Inc** *New Orleans, LA* *United States of America* Official number: 917504	*124* 99 -		**1987 National Shipbuilders Co. — Slidell, La** L reg 23.47 Br ex - Dght - Lbp - Br md 7.01 Dpth 3.21 Welded, 1 dk	**(B11B2FV) Fishing Vessel**	**1 oil engine** driving 1 FP propeller
7100469 *WX9059* -	**ST. MARY** *ex* Miss Jenny II *-2001* *ex* St. Dominic *-1995* *ex* Miss Dianne *-1989* *ex* Neva J *-1989* *ex* Captain Hibo *-1976* *ex* Chief Paul Pitts *-1976* **Bruce Bui** *Houston, TX* *United States of America* Official number: 508927	*101* 69 -		**1967 Rockport Yacht & Supply Co. (RYSCO) — Rockport, Tx** L reg 21.37 Br ex 6.56 Dght - Lbp - Br md - Dpth 2.37 Welded, 1 dk	**(B11B2FV) Fishing Vessel**	**1 oil engine** driving 1 FP propeller Total Power: 279kW (379hp)
9219252 *C4LP2* -	**ST. MARY** *ex* OOCL Manila *-2010* *ex* Venice Express *-2008* *ex* CP Success *-2006* *ex* Canmar Success *-2005* *ex* Brazilian Express *-2005* **Mariona Shipping Co Ltd** TS Lines Ltd *Limassol* *Cyprus* MMSI: 209370000 Official number: 9219252	**16,850** 7,364 21,579 T/cm 38.5	Class: LR (BV) **100A1** SS 01/2011 container ship **LMC** **UMS** Eq.Ltr: J†;	**2001-01 Hanjin Heavy Industries & Construction Co Ltd — Busan** Yd No: 082 Loa 168.80 (BB) Br ex 27.22 Dght 8.750 Lbp 158.00 Br md 27.20 Dpth 13.80 Welded, 1 dk	**(A33A2CC) Container Ship (Fully Cellular)** TEU 1679 C Ho 610 TEU C Dk 1069 TEU incl 194 ref C. Compartments: 7 Cell Ho, ER 7 Ha: ER	**1 oil engine** driving 1 FP propeller Total Power: 15,785kW (21,461hp) 20.0kn MAN-B&W 7S60MC-C 1 x 2 Stroke 7 Cy. 600 x 2400 15785kW (21461bhp) HSD Engine Co Ltd-South Korea AuxGen: 3 x 900kW 440V 60Hz a.c Boilers: TOH (o.f.), TOH (ex.g.) Thrusters: 1 Thwart. CP thruster (f)
8953186 *YYV2599* -	**ST. MARYS EXPRESS** *ex* Lance *-1994* **Lago Boats CA** *Maracaibo* *Venezuela* Official number: AJZL-22798	**148** 103 -		**1981 Universal Iron Works — Houma, La** Converted From: General Cargo Ship Converted From: Offshore Supply Ship L reg 31.85 Br ex - Dght - Lbp - Br md 7.62 Dpth 2.07 Welded, 1 dk	**(B32A2ST) Tug**	**2 oil engines** driving 2 FP propellers Total Power: 1,324kW (1,800hp) 10.0kn G.M. (Detroit Diesel) 16V-71 2 x Vee 2 Stroke 16 Cy. 108 x 127 each-662kW (900bhp) General Motors Detroit DieselAllison Divn-USA
6725949 *DUHF5* -	**ST. MATHEW** *ex* Mintrade 3 *-2001* *ex* Don Ramon *-1990* *ex* Yamakawa Maru *-1978* **Mintrade Shipping Lines Inc** *Davao* *Philippines* Official number: CEB1001137	*497* 308 2,009	Class: (NK)	**1967-05 Kochiken Zosen — Kochi** Yd No: 325 Loa 71.28 Br ex 10.83 Dght 5.004 Lbp 65.00 Br md 10.80 Dpth 5.59 Riveted\Welded, 1 dk	**(A31A2GX) General Cargo Ship** Grain: 2,238; Bale: 2,030 Compartments: 1 Ho, ER 1 Ha: (35.2 x 5.4)ER Derricks: 2x10t	**1 oil engine** driving 1 FP propeller Total Power: 956kW (1,300hp) 11.0kn Nippon Hatsudoki HS6NV138 1 x 4 Stroke 6 Cy. 380 x 540 956kW (1300bhp) Nippon Hatsudoki-Japan AuxGen: 2 x 48kW 230V d.c Fuel: 90.5
9221803 *ONGM* -	**ST MAUD** *ex* FS Maud *-2009* *launched as* Clipper Leader *-2001* **SEA-tankers Shipping SAS** ST Management (SAAM) *Antwerpen* *Belgium* MMSI: 205572000 Official number: 01 00757 2010	**6,519** 3,125 10,018 T/cm 20.0	Class: BV (NV) (AB)	**2001-06 Yardimci Tersanesi A.S. — Tuzla** Yd No: 19 Loa 118.37 (BB) Br ex - Dght 8.220 Lbp 112.00 Br md 19.00 Dpth 10.10 Welded, 1 dk	**(A12B2TR) Chemical/Products Tanker** Double Hull (13F) Liq: 10,956; Liq (Oil): 11,143 Compartments: 2 Ta, 10 Wing Ta, ER, 2 Wing Slop Ta 12 Cargo Pump (s): 12x200m³/hr Manifold: Bow/CM: 57m Ice Capable	**1 oil engine** driving 1 CP propeller Total Power: 4,440kW (6,037hp) 14.0kn B&W 6S35MC 1 x 2 Stroke 6 Cy. 350 x 1400 4440kW (6037bhp) AuxGen: 1 x 500kW 50Hz a.c, 3 x 500kW 50Hz a.c Thrusters: 1 Thwart. CP thruster (f) Fuel: 158.0 (d.f.) (Heating Coils) 545.0 (r.f.) 20.5pd
9344887 *DSPP5* -	**ST MERMAID** *ex* Mao Xing *-2008* **Seatras Co Ltd** *Jeju* *South Korea* MMSI: 441366000 Official number: JJR-071978	**1,999** - 3,347	Class: KR (CC)	**2005-03 Zhejiang Hongxin Shipbuilding Co Ltd — Taizhou ZJ** Yd No: 0401 Loa 81.00 Br ex - Dght 5.500 Lbp 76.00 Br md 13.60 Dpth 6.80 Welded, 1 dk	**(A31A2GX) General Cargo Ship** Grain: 4,450 Ice Capable	**1 oil engine** reduction geared to sc. shaft driving 1 FP propeller Total Power: 1,324kW (1,800hp) 12.0kn Chinese Std. Type G6300ZC 1 x 4 Stroke 6 Cy. 300 x 380 1324kW (1800bhp) Wuxi Antai Power Machinery Co Ltd-China AuxGen: 2 x 120kW 400V a.c
9237723 *WCZ9003* -	**ST. MICHAEL** **Elizabeth Minh Nguyen** *Bayou La Batre, AL* *United States of America* Official number: 1097968	**194** 58 -		**2000 Ocean Marine, Inc. — Bayou La Batre, Al** Yd No: 377 Loa 25.20 Br ex - Dght - Lbp - Br md 7.50 Dpth 4.00 Welded, 1 dk	**(B11B2FV) Fishing Vessel**	**1 oil engine** driving 1 FP propeller
8019734 - -	**ST. MICHAEL** *ex* Capt. B *-1990* *ex* Dr. Henry *-1990* **Cook Islands Seafood Ltd** -	*173* 118 -		**1979 Master Boat Builders, Inc. — Coden, Al** Yd No: 8 L reg 26.89 Br ex 7.47 Dght - Lbp - Br md 7.32 Dpth 3.51 Welded, 1 dk	**(B11B2FV) Fishing Vessel**	**1 oil engine** driving 1 FP propeller Total Power: 441kW (600hp) Caterpillar D399SCAC 1 x Vee 4 Stroke 16 Cy. 159 x 203 441kW (600bhp) Caterpillar Tractor Co-USA
8976970 *WDD2544* -	**ST. MICHAEL II** **Elizabeth Nguyen** *Biloxi, MS* *United States of America* MMSI: 367116620 Official number: 1131967	**194** 58 -		**2002-01 Ocean Marine, Inc. — Bayou La Batre, Al** L reg 27.95 Br ex - Dght - Lbp - Br md 8.22 Dpth 3.96 Welded, 1 dk	**(B11B2FV) Fishing Vessel**	**1 oil engine** driving 1 FP propeller

IMO / Call sign	Name / Owner / Flag	Tonnage	Class	Builder / Dimensions	Type / Capacities	Machinery
5306485 *5ZTO* -	**ST. MICHAEL LIKONI** - **Kenya Bus Services (Mombasa) Ltd** - *Mombasa* *Kenya* Official number: 10055	*105* 88 61	Class: (LR) ✠ Classed LR until 16/10/81	**1960-02 African Marine & General Eng. Co. Ltd. — Mombasa** Yd No: 340 Loa 33.53 Br ex 10.55 Dght 1.016 Lbp 27.44 Br md 10.52 Dpth 1.73 Welded, 1 dk	**(A37B2PS) Passenger Ship** Passengers: unberthed: 300	**2 oil engines** through fluid couplings driving 2 Directional propellers Total Power: 214kW (290hp) 7.0kn Gardner 6L3B 2 x 4 Stroke 6 Cy. 140 x 197 each-107kW (145bhp) L. Gardner & Sons Ltd.-Manchester Fuel: 3.5 (d.f.)
9000455 *DUH3152* -	**ST MICHAEL THE ARCHANGEL** *ex* St Michael Archangel *-2011* *ex* Queen *-2011* *ex* Queen Mary *-2011* *ex* Blue Diamond *-2008* **Caprotec Corp** Negros Navigation Co Inc *Cebu* *Philippines* MMSI: 548572300 Official number: CEB1008357	**17,781** 5,334 3,665	Class: KR	**1990-07 Shin Kurushima Dockyard Co. Ltd. — Onishi** Yd No: 2671 Loa 150.87 Br ex - Dght 5.471 Lbp 140.00 Br md 25.00 Dpth 13.00 Welded	**(A36A2PR) Passenger/Ro-Ro Ship (Vehicles)** Passengers: unberthed: 844; cabins: 24; berths: 98 Bow door & ramp Stern door/ramp Lane-Len: 900 Lorries: 105, Cars: 50	**2 oil engines** geared to sc. shafts driving 2 CP propellers Total Power: 18,536kW (25,202hp) 22.2kn Sulzer 14ZAV40S 2 x Vee 4 Stroke 14 Cy. 400 x 560 each-9268kW (12601bhp) Hitachi Zosen Corp-Japan AuxGen: 2 x 880kW a.c
9482926 *9HXI9* -	**ST. NICOLAS** - **Kogos Shipping Co Ltd** BSBS Ltd *Valletta* *Malta* MMSI: 249674000 Official number: 9482926	**5,897** 3,451 6,716	Class: RS	**2009-09 OAO Khersonskiy Sudostroitelnyy Zavod — Kherson** Yd No: 18019 Loa 139.22 Br ex 16.50 Dght 4.800 Lbp 133.20 Br md 16.20 Dpth 6.20 Welded, 1 dk	**(A31A2GX) General Cargo Ship** Grain: 11,401 TEU 262 C Ho 192 TEU C Dk 70 TEU Compartments: 3 Ho, ER 3 Ha: ER Ice Capable	**1 oil engine** reduction geared to sc. shaft driving 1 FP propeller Total Power: 1,800kW (2,447hp) 9.8kn Wartsila 9L20 1 x 4 Stroke 9 Cy. 200 x 280 1800kW (2447bhp) Wartsila Finland Oy-Finland AuxGen: 3 x 180kW a.c Thrusters: 1 Tunnel thruster (f) Fuel: 331.0 (d.f.)
9313254 *S6AG2* -	**ST. NIKOLAI** - **Shenlong Maritime Pte Ltd** Maruta Industries Co Ltd (Maruta Sangyo KK) *Singapore* *Singapore* MMSI: 564674000 Official number: 390576	**26,909** 13,695 47,297 T/cm 50.3	Class: NK	**2005-04 Onomichi Dockyard Co Ltd — Onomichi HS** Yd No: 508 Loa 182.50 (BB) Br ex 32.23 Dght 12.617 Lbp 172.00 Br md 32.20 Dpth 18.10 Welded, 1 dk	**(A13B2TP) Products Tanker** Double Hull (13F) Liq: 52,628; Liq (Oil): 50,560 Cargo Heating Coils Compartments: 12 Wing Ta, 2 Wing Slop Ta, 1 Slop Ta, ER 4 Cargo Pump (s): 4x1000m³/hr Manifold: Bow/CM: 91.8m	**1 oil engine** driving 1 FP propeller Total Power: 8,580kW (11,665hp) 15.3kn B&W 6S50MC 1 x 2 Stroke 6 Cy. 500 x 1910 8580kW (11665bhp) Mitsui Engineering & Shipbuilding CLtd-Japan AuxGen: 3 x a.c Fuel: 101.9 (d.f.) 1561.1 (r.f.)
9170274 *A8ZL2* -	**ST. NIKON** *ex* Augusta A *-2012* *ex* Lowlands Sumida *-2011* *ex* Federal Sumida *-2006* **Nikon Maritime Inc** Unimor Shipping Agency *Monrovia* *Liberia* MMSI: 636015236 Official number: 15236	**37,689** 24,199 72,493 T/cm 66.6	Class: NK	**1998-06 Imabari Shipbuilding Co Ltd — Marugame KG (Marugame Shipyard)** Yd No: 1306 Loa 224.94 (BB) Br ex - Dght 13.553 Lbp 217.00 Br md 32.20 Dpth 18.70 Welded, 1 dk	**(A21A2BC) Bulk Carrier** Grain: 85,596 Compartments: 7 Ho, ER 7 Ha: (13.0 x 12.8)5 (17.9 x 14.4) (16.3 x 14.4)ER	**1 oil engine** driving 1 FP propeller Total Power: 10,224kW (13,901hp) 14.5kn Sulzer 6RTA62 1 x 2 Stroke 6 Cy. 620 x 2150 10224kW (13901bhp) Diesel United Ltd.-Aioi Fuel: 3080.0
9227089 *DUH2444* -	**ST. NURIEL** *ex* Supercat 22 *-2012* *ex* Mt. Samat Ferry 3 *-2006* **Supercat Fast Ferry Corp** - *Cebu* *Philippines* Official number: CEB1004789	**242** 169 20	Class: (NV)	**2000-09 FBMA-Babcock Marine Inc — Balamban** Yd No: 1005 Loa 28.00 Br ex - Dght 1.600 Lbp 25.20 Br md 8.50 Dpth 3.10 Welded, 1 dk	**(A37B2PS) Passenger Ship** Hull Material: Aluminium Alloy Passengers: unberthed: 180	**2 oil engines** geared to sc. shafts driving 2 FP propellers Total Power: 1,618kW (2,200hp) 28.0kn Caterpillar 3412T 2 x Vee 4 Stroke 12 Cy. 137 x 152 each-809kW (1100bhp) Caterpillar Inc-USA AuxGen: 1 x 65kW a.c
7109609 *ESUD* -	**ST. OLA** *ex* Eck *-1992* *ex* Eckero *-1991* *ex* Svea Scarlett *-1982* **OU Elwell Capital** Saaremaa Shipping Co Ltd (AS Saaremaa Laevakompanii) *Roomassaare* *Estonia* MMSI: 276509000 Official number: 3P02J01	**4,833** 1,449 711	Class: LR ✠ **100A1** CS 02/2009 Baltic Sea service Ice Class 1 ✠ **LMC** Eq.Ltr: S; Cable: U2	**1971-07 Jos L Meyer — Papenburg** Yd No: 564 Loa 85.95 (BB) Br ex 16.77 Dght 4.000 Lbp 79.46 Br md 16.31 Dpth 10.20 Welded, 1 dk, 2nd dk clear of mchy. space	**(A36A2PR) Passenger/Ro-Ro Ship (Vehicles)** Passengers: unberthed: 600 Bow door & ramp Len: 5.30 Wid: 4.60 Swl: 13 Stern door/ramp Len: 6.30 Wid: 6.00 Swl: 13 Lane-Len: 820 Lane-Wid: 4.60 Lane-clr ht: 4.20 Lorries: 25, Cars: 180, Trailers: 14 Ice Capable	**4 oil engines** with flexible couplings & sr geared to sc. shafts driving 2 FP propellers Total Power: 4,032kW (5,480hp) 16.5kn Wartsila 824TS 4 x 4 Stroke 8 Cy. 240 x 310 each-1008kW (1370bhp) (new engine 1987) Wartsila Diesel Oy-Finland AuxGen: 2 x 480kW 400V 50Hz a.c, 5 x 140kW 400V 50Hz a.c
9113020 *V4YA2* -	**ST.OLGA** *ex* Asta *-2014* *ex* Torm Asta *-2002* *ex* Asta *-2002* **Breeze Corp** Erma Shipping Co Ltd *Basseterre* *St Kitts & Nevis* MMSI: 341187000 Official number: SKN 1002658	**3,891** 2,533 5,820 T/cm 14.1	Class: NK (LR) (AB) ✠ Classed LR until 11/10/09	**1996-11 AB "Baltijos" Laivu Statykla — Klaipeda** (Hull launched by) Yd No: 301 **1996-11 Ast. de Huelva S.A. — Huelva** (Hull completed by) Yd No: 565 Loa 102.83 (BB) Br ex 15.94 Dght 6.554 Lbp 97.20 Br md 15.85 Dpth 8.10 Welded, 1 dk	**(A31A2GX) General Cargo Ship** Grain: 6,881 TEU 353 C incl 50 ref C Compartments: 2 Ho, ER 2 Ha: 2 (32.7 x 13.3)ER Cranes: 2x36t Ice Capable	**1 oil engine** with flexible couplings & sr gearedto sc. shaft driving 1 CP propeller Total Power: 3,520kW (4,786hp) 13.5kn MAN 8L32/40 1 x 4 Stroke 8 Cy. 320 x 400 3520kW (4786bhp) MAN B&W Diesel AG-Augsburg AuxGen: 1 x 560kW 380V 50Hz a.c, 2 x 348kW 380V 50Hz a.c Boilers: AuxB (Comp) 9.2kgf/cm² (9.0bar) Thrusters: 1 Thwart. FP thruster (f) Fuel: 220.0 48.0
6804393 *V5KW* L176	**ST. PADARN** *ex* Stormy *-1979* *ex* Nordsjobas *-1978* **Namibian Fishing Industries Ltd (Namfish)** - *Luderitz* *Namibia* MMSI: 659071000 Official number: 91LB072	*341* 209 -	Class: (LR) (NV) ✠ Classed LR until 10/83	**1967-07 Smedvik Mek. Verksted AS — Tjorvaag** Yd No: 13 Lengthened-1970 Loa 47.12 Br ex 8.31 Dght 4.876 Lbp 42.02 Br md 8.26 Dpth 6.46 Welded, 2 dks	**(B11B2FV) Fishing Vessel** Compartments: 2 Ho, 3 Ta, ER 5 Ha: 3 (1.8 x 2.5) (2.5 x 3.2) (2.9 x 3.2)ER Derricks: 1x3t; Winches: 1	**1 oil engine** driving 1 CP propeller Total Power: 736kW (1,001hp) 12.0kn Deutz RBV8M545 1 x 4 Stroke 8 Cy. 320 x 450 736kW (1001bhp) Kloeckner Humboldt Deutz AG-West Germany AuxGen: 2 x 136kW 440V 60Hz a.c, 1 x 60kW 440V 60Hz a.c Thrusters: 1 Thwart. FP thruster (f); 1 Tunnel thruster (a) Fuel: 122.0 (d.f.) 4.0pd
8731318 *DUH2504* -	**ST PADRE PIO** *ex* San Padre Pio - 2 *-2011* **Medallion Transport** - *Cebu* *Philippines* Official number: CEB1006115	*248* 127 -		**2000-01 on Negros** L reg 45.00 Br ex - Dght - Lbp - Br md 8.00 Dpth 3.20 Welded, 1 dk	**(A31A2GX) General Cargo Ship**	**1 oil engine** driving 1 Propeller
8969379 *WDA6927* -	**ST. PAUL** - **Dang Nguyen** - *Palacios, TX* *United States of America* MMSI: 366837630 Official number: 1121129	**161** 48 -		**2001 Master Boat Builders, Inc. — Coden, Al** Yd No: 324 L reg 25.96 Br ex - Dght - Lbp - Br md 7.62 Dpth 3.80 Welded, 1 dk	**(B11B2FV) Fishing Vessel**	**1 oil engine** driving 1 Propeller
8941638 *WDD3780* -	**ST PAUL PETER** *ex* St. Benedict *-2006* **Peter Paul of Houma Inc** - *New Orleans, LA* *United States of America* MMSI: 367136110 Official number: 929437	*138* 111 -		**1990 Saigon Shipyard — Dulac, La** L reg 25.91 Br ex - Dght - Lbp - Br md 7.01 Dpth 3.23 Welded, 1 dk	**(B11B2FV) Fishing Vessel**	**1 oil engine** driving 1 FP propeller
8214358 *ZDFJ3* -	**ST. PAULI** *ex* Euphony *-2010* *ex* Smaland *-2002* *ex* Anita Maria *-1997* *ex* Gerd Schepers *-1994* **Lunar Sea Shipping Co Ltd** GBS-Shipmanagement GmbH & Co KG *Gibraltar* *Gibraltar (British)* MMSI: 236002000 Official number: 736282	**3,075** 1,143 3,219	Class: GL	**1983-06 Detlef Hegemann Rolandwerft GmbH & Co. KG — Berne** Yd No: 123 Loa 92.41 Br ex 15.24 Dght 4.384 Lbp 87.00 Br md 15.21 Dpth 7.01 Welded, 2 dks	**(A31A2GX) General Cargo Ship** Grain: 5,747; Bale: 5,715; Liq: 420 TEU 207 C.Ho 135/20' (40') C.Dk 72/20' (40') Compartments: 1 Ho, ER 1 Ha: (51.3 x 9.3)ER Cranes: 2x12t Ice Capable	**1 oil engine** sr geared to sc. shaft driving 1 FP propeller Total Power: 1,471kW (2,000hp) 12.0kn MWM TBD510-6 1 x 4 Stroke 6 Cy. 330 x 360 1471kW (2000bhp) Motoren Werke Mannheim AG (MWM)-West Germany AuxGen: 2 x 148kW 380V 50Hz a.c
9310393 *LXSV* -	**ST PAULINE** *ex* FS Pauline *-2009* **SEA-tankers Shipping SAS** ST Management (SAAM) *Luxembourg* *Luxembourg* MMSI: 253381000	**4,077** 1,812 5,717 T/cm 15.0	Class: BV	**2005-06 Torlak Gemi Insaat Sanayi ve Ticaret A.S. — Tuzla** (Hull) Yd No: 41 **2005-06 Yardimci Tersanesi A.S. — Tuzla** Yd No: 35 Loa 105.50 (BB) Br ex - Dght 6.290 Lbp 99.35 Br md 16.80 Dpth 7.40 Welded, 1 dk	**(A12B2TR) Chemical/Products Tanker** Double Hull (13F) Liq: 6,252; Liq (Oil): 6,252 Cargo Heating Coils Compartments: 10 Wing Ta, ER 10 Cargo Pump (s): 10x200m³/hr Manifold: Bow/CM: 48m Ice Capable	**1 oil engine** geared to sc. shaft driving 1 CP propeller Total Power: 2,720kW (3,698hp) 12.0kn MAN-B&W 8L27/38 1 x 4 Stroke 8 Cy. 270 x 380 2720kW (3698bhp) MAN B&W Diesel AG-Augsburg AuxGen: 3 x 400kW 380/220V 50Hz a.c, 1 x 800kW 380/220V 50Hz a.c Thrusters: 1 Thwart. CP thruster (f) Fuel: 85.9 (d.f.) 274.0 (r.f.) 15.0pd

IMO / Call sign	Name / Owner / Port	Tonnage	Class	Builder / Dimensions	Type	Machinery
5343598 - -	**ST. PAULUS** *ex* St. Pauli *-1999* *ex* Sulldorf *-1978* **Transtejo-Transportes Tejo EP** - *Lisbon* *Portugal*	*274* 126 134		**1959**-05 **Schiffswerft Scheel & Joehnk GmbH — Hamburg** Yd No: 413 Loa 30.10 Br ex 7.50 Dght 3.175 Lbp - Br md - Dpth 3.66 Riveted\Welded, 2 dks	**(A37B2PS) Passenger Ship** Passengers: 607	**1 diesel electric oil engine** driving 1 gen. of 240kW 380V d.c Connecting to 1 elec. Motor driving 1 FP propeller Total Power: 279kW (379hp) Deutz RBV6M536 1 x 4 Stroke 6 Cy. 270 x 360 279kW (379bhp) Kloeckner Humboldt Deutz AG-West Germany AuxGen: 2 x 30kW 110V d.c
7832555 *6MID* -	**ST. PEDRO No. 51** *ex* Hiyoshi Maru No. 18 *-1972* *ex* Fukuyo Maru *-1972* **Hai Chung Industries Co Ltd** - *Busan* *South Korea* Official number: BS-A-526	*183* 96 -	Class: (KR)	**1963 Yamanishi Shipbuilding Co Ltd — Ishinomaki MG** Loa 38.51 Br ex - Dght - Lbp 33.71 Br md 6.90 Dpth 3.15 Welded, 1 dk	**(B11B2FV) Fishing Vessel** Ins: 249 3 Ha: 3 (1.1 x 1.3)	**1 oil engine** driving 1 FP propeller Total Power: 478kW (650hp) 9.5kn Fuji 6SD30 1 x 4 Stroke 6 Cy. 300 x 430 478kW (650bhp) Fuji Diesel Co Ltd-Japan AuxGen: 2 x 51kW 220V a.c
6423084 *6MAR* -	**ST. PEDRO No. 61** *ex* Kaisei No. 113 *-1979* *ex* Shinei Maru No. 1 *-1973* **Hae Woi Industrial Co Ltd** - *Busan* *South Korea* Official number: BS-A-1596	*189* 89 -	Class: (KR) (NK)	**1964 KK Kanasashi Zosen — Shizuoka SZ** Yd No: 591 Loa 39.07 Br ex 6.96 Dght 2.794 Lbp 34.02 Br md 6.91 Dpth 3.10 Welded, 1 dk	**(B11B2FV) Fishing Vessel** Ins: 206	**1 oil engine** driving 1 FP propeller Total Power: 515kW (700hp) 11.0kn Niigata 1 x 4 Stroke 6 Cy. 280 x 440 515kW (700bhp) Niigata Engineering Co Ltd-Japan AuxGen: 2 x 62kW 230V a.c
6400898 *HLBB* -	**ST. PEDRO No. 62** *ex* Choko Maru No. 17 *-1973* **Hae Woi Industrial Co Ltd** - *Busan* *South Korea* Official number: BS-A-1581	*196* 87 -	Class: (KR)	**1963 Miho Zosensho K.K. — Shimizu** Yd No: 382 Loa 38.64 Br ex 6.96 Dght - Lbp 33.89 Br md 6.91 Dpth 3.15 Welded, 1 dk	**(B11B2FV) Fishing Vessel**	**1 oil engine** driving 1 FP propeller Total Power: 456kW (620hp) Akasaka MA6SS 1 x 4 Stroke 6 Cy. 270 x 400 456kW (620bhp) Akasaka Tekkosho KK (Akasaka DieselLtd)-Japan
7646449 *HQAZ9* -	**ST. PEDRO No. 63** *ex* King Star No. 81 *-1979* **Atlas de Honduras Fisheries** - *Honduras*	*449* 155 -	Class: (KR)	**1967 KK Kanasashi Zosen — Shizuoka SZ** Loa 46.33 Br ex - Dght - Lbp 40.98 Br md 7.70 Dpth 3.46 Welded, 1 dk	**(B11B2FV) Fishing Vessel** Ins: 306 4 Ha: 2 (1.0 x 0.8)2 (1.6 x 1.4)	**1 oil engine** driving 1 FP propeller Total Power: 736kW (1,001hp) 10.5kn Akasaka YM6 1 x 4 Stroke 6 Cy. 370 x 520 736kW (1001bhp) Akasaka Tekkosho KK (Akasaka DieselLtd)-Japan AuxGen: 2 x 116kW 230V a.c
8034370 - -	**ST. PETER** *ex* Makandra No. 10 *-1992* **Binh Van Nguyen** - *Bayou La Batre, AL* *United States of America* Official number: 991508	*124* 87 -	Class: (KR)	**1981 Master Marine, Inc. — Bayou La Batre, Al** Yd No: 241 Loa 25.30 Br ex - Dght - Lbp 21.67 Br md 6.72 Dpth 3.81 Welded, 1 dk	**(B11A2FT) Trawler** Ins: 91	**1 oil engine** with clutches & sr geared to sc. shaft driving 1 FP propeller Total Power: 331kW (450hp) Caterpillar 3412T 1 x Vee 4 Stroke 12 Cy. 137 x 152 331kW (450bhp) Caterpillar Tractor Co-USA
8939142 *WDE3617* -	**ST. PETER** *ex* Miss Vivian *-2005* **Thomas K Nguyen** - *Abbeville, LA* *United States of America* MMSI: 367341670 Official number: 1031347	*148* 44 -		**1995 Master Boat Builders, Inc. — Coden, Al** Yd No: 199 L reg 24.87 Br ex - Dght - Lbp - Br md 7.32 Dpth 3.81 Welded, 1 dk	**(B11B2FV) Fishing Vessel**	**1 oil engine** driving 1 FP propeller
8940206 *WCY8932* -	**ST. PETER** - **Tam Minh Nguyen** - *Palacios, TX* *United States of America* Official number: 1045565	**148** 44 -		**1996 Master Boat Builders, Inc. — Coden, Al** Yd No: 230 L reg 24.87 Br ex - Dght - Lbp - Br md 7.32 Dpth 3.81 Welded, 1 dk	**(B11B2FV) Fishing Vessel**	**1 oil engine** driving 1 FP propeller
9437529 *C6YR4* -	**ST. PETER** *ex* Nord Mumbai *-2010* **Orissa Shipping Co Ltd** Tri Bulk Shipping Ltd *Nassau* *Bahamas* MMSI: 311042700 Official number: 8001798	**20,748** 11,689 32,688 T/cm 46.0	Class: BV (LR) Classed LR until 22/8/10	**2009-09 Jiangmen Nanyang Ship Engineering Co Ltd — Jiangmen GD** Yd No: 112 Loa 179.90 (BB) Br ex 28.44 Dght 10.200 Lbp 171.50 Br md 28.40 Dpth 14.10 Welded, 1 dk	**(A21A2BC) Bulk Carrier** Grain: 42,565; Bale: 40,558 Compartments: 5 Ho, ER 5 Ha: 3 (20.0 x 19.2) (18.4 x 19.2)ER (14.4 x 17.6) Cranes: 4x30.5t	**1 oil engine** driving 1 FP propeller Total Power: 6,480kW (8,810hp) 13.7kn MAN-B&W 6S42MC 1 x 2 Stroke 6 Cy. 420 x 1764 6480kW (8810bhp) STX Engine Co Ltd-South Korea AuxGen: 3 x 440kW 450V 60Hz a.c Boilers: AuxB (Comp) 7.9kgf/cm² (7.7bar)
7518408 *DUG2205* -	**ST. PETER THE APOSTLE** *ex* Hankyu No. 32 *-1996* **Negros Navigation Co Inc** - *Manila* *Philippines* Official number: 00-0001420	**6,090** 4,133 2,700	Class: (AB)	**1976-05 Kanda Zosensho K.K. — Kure** Yd No: 202 Loa 151.49 Br ex 22.84 Dght 10.820 Lbp 141.03 Br md 22.81 Dpth 12.50 Welded, 2 dks	**(A36A2PR) Passenger/Ro-Ro Ship (Vehicles)** Passengers: 2060 Bow door & ramp Stern door/ramp Lane-Len: 730	**2 oil engines** reverse reduction geared to sc. shafts driving 2 FP propellers Total Power: 14,710kW (20,000hp) 21.0kn MAN 18V40/54 2 x Vee 4 Stroke 18 Cy. 400 x 540 each-7355kW (10000bhp) Mitsubishi Heavy Industries Ltd-Japan AuxGen: 3 x 572kW 450V 60Hz a.c Fuel: 14.5 (d.f.) 317.5 (r.f.) 66.0pd
9354272 *VRCG5* -	**ST PETRI** *ex* Pretty Time *-2012* **Pretty Time Shipping SA** Parakou Shipmanagement Pte Ltd *Hong Kong* *Hong Kong* MMSI: 477593900 Official number: HK-1786	**30,068** 13,602 51,288 T/cm 52.0	Class: BV	**2007-02 STX Shipbuilding Co Ltd — Changwon (Jinhae Shipyard)** Yd No: 1224 Loa 183.00 (BB) Br ex - Dght 13.200 Lbp 172.57 Br md 32.20 Dpth 19.10 Welded, 1 dk	**(A12B2TR) Chemical/Products Tanker** Double Hull (13F) Liq: 54,100; Liq (Oil): 54,100 Cargo Heating Coils Compartments: 12 Wing Ta, 2 Wing Slop Ta, ER 12 Cargo Pump (s): 12x600m³/hr Manifold: Bow/CM: 92m	**1 oil engine** driving 1 FP propeller Total Power: 9,488kW (12,900hp) 14.2kn MAN-B&W 6S50MC-C 1 x 2 Stroke 6 Cy. 500 x 2000 9488kW (12900bhp) STX Engine Co Ltd-South Korea AuxGen: 3 x 900kW 440/220V 60Hz a.c Fuel: 121.0 (d.f.) (Heating Coils) 1567.0 (r.f.) 36.5pd
8940787 - -	**ST. PHANXICO** *ex* Lucky Daddy *-2004* **Ha T Nguyen** - *New Orleans, LA* *United States of America* Official number: 1040384	**138** 41 -		**1996 Venture Boats, Inc. — Chauvin, La** Yd No: 103 L reg 23.84 Br ex - Dght - Lbp - Br md 7.32 Dpth 3.66 Welded, 1 dk	**(B11B2FV) Fishing Vessel**	**1 oil engine** driving 1 FP propeller
8958382 *WDC6835* -	**ST. PHILLIP** - **St Phillip Inc** - *Palacios, TX* *United States of America* MMSI: 367061950 Official number: 1082130	**148** 44 -		**1999 Master Boat Builders, Inc. — Coden, Al** Yd No: 265 L reg 24.87 Br ex - Dght - Lbp - Br md 7.31 Dpth 3.81 Welded, 1 dk	**(B11B2FV) Fishing Vessel**	**1 oil engine** driving 1 FP propeller
9598751 *FIDX* -	**ST PIERRE** - **Societe de Transports Fluviaux Maritimes de l'Ouest (STFMO)** - *St-Nazaire* *France* MMSI: 228024800 Official number: 929934Y	**2,627** 827 4,325	Class: BV	**2012-09 STX France Lorient SAS — Lanester** Yd No: 839 Loa 84.15 (BB) Br ex - Dght 6.150 Lbp 79.85 Br md 15.60 Dpth 7.00 Welded, 1 dk	**(B33B2DT) Trailing Suction Hopper Dredger** Hopper: 2,462 Compartments: 1 Ho, ER 1 Ha: ER	**2 oil engines** reduction geared to sc. shafts driving 2 CP propellers Total Power: 3,870kW (5,262hp) 13.0kn MAN-B&W 9L21/31 2 x 4 Stroke 9 Cy. 210 x 310 each-1935kW (2631bhp) STX Engine Co Ltd-South Korea Thrusters: 1 Tunnel thruster (f) Fuel: 190.0
7800057 *GYHT* -	**ST PIRAN** *ex* Hallgarth *-2008* **Falmouth Docks & Engineering Co** A & P Group Ltd *Falmouth* *United Kingdom* MMSI: 232004548 Official number: 365819	**223** 66 103	Class: (LR) ✠ Classed LR until 29/9/08	**1979-06 Scott & Sons (Bowling) Ltd. — Bowling** Yd No: 457 Loa 29.47 Br ex 8.94 Dght 2.910 Lbp 27.77 Br md 8.50 Dpth 3.50 Welded, 1 dk	**(B32A2ST) Tug**	**2 oil engines** gearing integral to driving 2 Voith-Schneider propellers Total Power: 1,570kW (2,134hp) 12.0kn Ruston 6RK3CM 2 x 4 Stroke 6 Cy. 254 x 305 each-785kW (1067bhp) Ruston Diesels Ltd.-Newton-le-Willows AuxGen: 3 x 60kW 440V 50Hz a.c

8217051 *DYRY* -	**ST. POPE JOHN PAUL II** *ex* Superferry 12 *-2012* *ex* New Miyako *-1996* **2GO Group Inc** - *Manila* *Philippines* MMSI: 548281100 Official number: 00-0000442	**15,223** 10,192 5,022	Class: KR (LR) (BV) Classed LR until 28/2/10	**1984-01 Kanda Zosensho K.K. — Kawajiri** Yd No: 278 Loa 173.00 (BB) Br ex - Dght 6.181 Lbp 160.00 Br md 26.80 Dpth 14.30 Welded, 2 dks	**(A36A2PR) Passenger/Ro-Ro Ship (Vehicles)** Passengers: unberthed: 2090; berths: 116 Bow door & ramp Stern door/ramp Lane-Len: 1250 Lane-Wid: 2.00 Lane-clr ht: 4.20 Lorries: 136, Cars: 133	**2 oil engines** with flexible couplings & sr reverse geared to sc. shafts driving 2 FP propellers Total Power: 17,654kW (24,002hp) 21.0kn MAN 12V52/55 2 x Vee 4 Stroke 12 Cy. 520 x 550 each-8827kW (12001bhp) Mitsubishi Heavy Industries Ltd-Japan AuxGen: 2 x 1300kW 440V 60Hz a.c, 2 x 440kW 440V 60Hz a.c Boilers: TOH (o.f.) (fitted: 1984) 15.3kgf/cm^2 (15.0bar) Thrusters: 1 Thwart. CP thruster (f); 2 Thwart. CP thruster (a) Fuel: 58.0 (d.f.) 360.0 (r.f.) 33.0pd
8853829 - - -	**ST. PORTO No. 1** *ex* Chien Yuan No. 1 *-1989* - -	**297** 89 -		**1974 Taiwan Machinery Manufacturing Corp. — Kaohsiung** L reg 34.60 Br ex - Dght - Lbp - Br md 6.25 Dpth 2.64 Welded, 1 dk	**(B11B2FV) Fishing Vessel**	**1 oil engine** driving 1 FP propeller Total Power: 405kW (551hp) 8.0kn Niigata 1 x 4 Stroke 405kW (551bhp) Niigata Engineering Co Ltd-Japan
1011757 *ZGCS2* -	**ST. PRINCESS OLGA** - **Serlio Shipping Ltd** Imperial Yachts SARL *George Town* *Cayman Islands (British)* MMSI: 319321000 Official number: 743788	**2,684** 805 -	Class: LR **✠100A1** SS 02/2013 SSC Yacht (P), mono *IWS EP G6 **✠LMC** **UMS** Cable: 440.0/34.0 U3 (a)	**2013-02 Zwijnenburg BV — Krimpen a/d IJssel** (Hull) Yd No: (708) **2013-02 Oceanco Shipyards (Alblasserdam) B.V. — Alblasserdam** Yd No: 708 Loa 88.39 (BB) Br ex 14.20 Dght 4.500 Lbp 71.94 Br md 13.80 Dpth 7.10 Welded, 2 dks	**(X11A2YP) Yacht**	**2 oil engines** with clutches, flexible couplings & sr reverse geared to sc. shafts driving 2 FP propellers Total Power: 7,200kW (9,790hp) M.T.U. 20V4000M73L 2 x Vee 4 Stroke 20 Cy. 170 x 190 each-3600kW (4895bhp) MTU Friedrichshafen GmbH-Friedrichshafen AuxGen: 2 x 308kW 400V 50Hz a.c, 1 x 495kW 400V 50Hz a.c Thrusters: 1 Thwart. FP thruster (f); 1 Thwart. FP thruster (a)
9227871 *3EOD3* -	**ST. ROSSA** *ex* Santa Rossa *-2007* *ex* Century Hope *-2006* *ex* Century Cypress *-2004* **Bergen Shipping Ltd** Ahilleos Ship Management Ltd *Panama* *Panama* MMSI: 355061000 Official number: 3364708B	**9,978** 5,489 16,239	Class: GL (LR) (NK) Classed LR until 24/1/11	**2001-01 Shin Kochi Jyuko K.K. — Kochi** Yd No: 7135 Loa 137.03 (BB) Br ex - Dght 8.316 Lbp 130.00 Br md 23.00 Dpth 11.40 Welded, 1 dk	**(A21A2BC) Bulk Carrier** Grain: 20,322; Bale: 19,850 Compartments: 4 Ho, ER 4 Ha: (13.6 x 11.0)2 (17.6 x 18.2) (17.6 x 13.7)ER Cranes: 4x30t	**1 oil engine** driving 1 FP propeller Total Power: 4,634kW (6,300hp) 13.8kn Mitsubishi 6UEC37LSII 1 x 2 Stroke 6 Cy. 370 x 1290 4634kW (6300bhp) Akasaka Tekkosho KK (Akasaka DieselLtd)-Japan
9356646 *FMLH* -	**ST SARA** *ex* FS Sara *-2009* **SEA-tankers Shipping SAS** ST Management (SAAM) *Marseille* *France (FIS)* MMSI: 228320900 Official number: 926344W	**5,271** 2,398 8,019 T/cm 17.0	Class: BV	**2007-01 Anadolu Deniz Insaat Kizaklari San. ve Tic. Ltd. Sti. — Tuzla** Yd No: 188 Loa 121.68 (BB) Br ex - Dght 6.858 Lbp 113.63 Br md 17.20 Dpth 8.80 Welded, 1 dk	**(A12B2TR) Chemical/Products Tanker** Double Hull (13F) Liq: 8,352; Liq (Oil): 8,352 Cargo Heating Coils Compartments: 1 Slop Ta, 12 Wing Ta, ER 12 Cargo Pump (s): 12x330m^3/hr Ice Capable	**1 oil engine** geared to sc. shaft driving 1 CP propeller Total Power: 3,841kW (5,222hp) 13.5kn MaK 8M32C 1 x 4 Stroke 8 Cy. 320 x 480 3841kW (5222bhp) Caterpillar Motoren GmbH & Co. KG-Germany AuxGen: 3 x 580kW 440V 60Hz a.c, 1 x 1200kW 440V 60Hz a.c Thrusters: 1 Tunnel thruster (f); 2 Water jet (a)
9227091 *DUH2450* -	**ST. SEALTHIEL** *ex* Supercat 25 *-2012* *ex* Mt. Samat Ferry 5 *-2007* **Supercat Fast Ferry Corp** - *Manila* *Philippines* MMSI: 548540300	**180** 118 20	Class: (NV)	**2000-12 FBMA-Babcock Marine Inc — Balamban** Yd No: 1006 Loa 28.00 Br ex - Dght 1.600 Lbp 25.20 Br md 8.50 Dpth 3.10 Welded, 1 dk	**(A37B2PS) Passenger Ship** Hull Material: Aluminium Alloy Passengers: unberthed: 180	**2 oil engines** geared to sc. shafts driving 2 FP propellers Total Power: 1,618kW (2,200hp) 28.0kn Caterpillar 3412T 2 x Vee 4 Stroke 12 Cy. 137 x 152 each-809kW (1100bhp) Caterpillar Inc-USA AuxGen: 1 x 65kW a.c
9282675 *FVDG* -	**ST SOLENE** *ex* FS Solene *-2009* **SEA-tankers Shipping SAS** ST Management (SAAM) SatCom: Inmarsat C 422630210 *Marseille* *France (FIS)* MMSI: 226302000 Official number: 924392Z	**3,997** 1,823 5,820 T/cm 14.7	Class: BV	**2003-10 Torlak Gemi Insaat Sanayi ve Ticaret A.S. — Tuzla** (Hull) Yd No: 34 **2003-10 Yardimci Tersanesi A.S. — Tuzla** Yd No: 27 Loa 105.50 (BB) Br ex - Dght 6.290 Lbp 99.35 Br md 16.80 Dpth 7.40 Welded, 1 dk	**(A12B2TR) Chemical/Products Tanker** Double Hull (13F) Liq: 6,298; Liq (Oil): 6,298 Cargo Heating Coils Compartments: 10 Wing Ta, ER 10 Cargo Pump (s): 10x200m^3/hr Manifold: Bow/CM: 48m Ice Capable	**1 oil engine** geared to sc. shaft driving 1 CP propeller Total Power: 2,720kW (3,698hp) 13.0kn MAN-B&W 8L27/38 1 x 4 Stroke 8 Cy. 270 x 380 2720kW (3698bhp) MAN B&W Diesel A/S-Denmark AuxGen: 3 x 400kW 380/220V 50Hz a.c, 1 x 800kW 380/220V 50Hz a.c Thrusters: 1 Thwart. CP thruster (f) Fuel: 105.0 280.0 (r.f.) 15.0pd
8939635 *WCX2129* -	**ST. TADEO II** - **Mien Thi Tran** - *Pass Christian, MS* *United States of America* MMSI: 366728530 Official number: 1040496	**137** 41 -		**1996 Duong Van Nguyen — Dulac, La** L reg 24.02 Br ex - Dght - Lbp - Br md 7.32 Dpth 3.84 Welded, 1 dk	**(B11B2FV) Fishing Vessel**	**1 oil engine** driving 1 FP propeller
9262259 *ONGV* -	**ST THAIS** *ex* FS Thais *-2010* **SEA-tankers Shipping SAS** ST Management (SAAM) *Antwerpen* *Belgium* MMSI: 205587000 Official number: 01 00770 2010	**11,118** 5,573 19,117 T/cm 29.0	Class: BV	**2003-01 Estaleiros Navais de Viana do Castelo S.A. — Viana do Castelo** Yd No: 212 Loa 140.00 (BB) Br ex - Dght 9.503 Lbp 134.00 Br md 23.00 Dpth 12.40 Welded, 1 dk	**(A12B2TR) Chemical/Products Tanker** Double Hull (13F) Liq: 18,733; Liq (Oil): 19,118 Compartments: 10 Wing Ta, ER, 2 Wing Slop Ta 10 Cargo Pump (s): 10x300m^3/hr Manifold: Bow/CM: 78m Ice Capable	**1 oil engine** with flexible couplings & reduction geared to sc. shaft driving 1 CP propeller Total Power: 6,300kW (8,565hp) 14.0kn MaK 7M43 1 x 4 Stroke 7 Cy. 430 x 610 6300kW (8565bhp) Caterpillar Motoren GmbH & Co. KG-Germany AuxGen: 3 x 750kW 380V 50Hz a.c, 1 x 1500kW a.c Thrusters: 1 Thwart. CP thruster (f) Fuel: 90.0 (d.f.) 901.0 (r.f.)
8864610 *3FDC5* -	**ST UNION** *ex* Chiyo Maru No. 18 *-2010* **Koho Shipping SA** Sung Kyung Maritime Co Ltd (SK Maritime) *Panama* *Panama* MMSI: 353303000 Official number: 4154410	**1,500** 760 1,553	Class: KR	**1992-05 Yamanaka Zosen K.K. — Imabari** Yd No: 525 Loa 74.60 (BB) Br ex - Dght 4.030 Lbp 69.70 Br md 11.50 Dpth 7.20 Welded, 1 dk	**(A31A2GX) General Cargo Ship** Grain: 2,861; Bale: 2,786 Compartments: 1 Ho, ER	**1 oil engine** reverse geared to sc. shaft driving 1 FP propeller Total Power: 736kW (1,001hp) Hanshin LH31G 1 x 4 Stroke 6 Cy. 310 x 530 736kW (1001bhp) The Hanshin Diesel Works Ltd-Japan
9056210 *DUH2581* -	**ST. URIEL** *ex* Supercat 23 *-2010* *ex* Penguin Success *-2010* **Supercat Fast Ferry Corp** - *Cebu* *Philippines* Official number: CEB1006788	**229** 89 50		**1992-12 Aluminium Craft (88) Pte Ltd — Singapore** Yd No: 19 Loa 32.00 Br ex 7.80 Dght - Lbp - Br md 7.40 Dpth 2.75 Welded, 1 dk	**(A37B2PS) Passenger Ship** Hull Material: Aluminium Alloy Passengers: unberthed: 363	**3 oil engines** sr geared to sc. shafts driving 3 FP propellers Total Power: 1,920kW (2,610hp) 26.0kn M.T.U. 12V183TE72 3 x Vee 4 Stroke 12 Cy. 128 x 142 each-640kW (870bhp) MTU Friedrichshafen GmbH-Friedrichshafen AuxGen: 2 x 39kW 240V 50Hz a.c
8839299 *DUF2070* -	**ST-V** *ex* Kosei Maru *-2010* **Santa Clara Shipping Corp** - *Legaspi* *Philippines* Official number: 05-0000236	**248** 152 699		**1989-12 Osaki Zosen KK — Awaji HG** Loa 59.00 Br ex - Dght 3.320 Lbp 53.42 Br md 9.50 Dpth 5.59 Welded, 1 dk	**(A31A2GX) General Cargo Ship**	**1 oil engine** driving 1 FP propeller Total Power: 662kW (900hp) 12.0kn Niigata 6M26AGTE 1 x 4 Stroke 6 Cy. 260 x 460 662kW (900bhp) Niigata Engineering Co Ltd-Japan
9071600 *A8UP7* -	**ST. VASILIOS** *ex* Athena A *-2012* *ex* Delray *-2010* *ex* Lanikai *-2008* *ex* Lacerta *-2008* *ex* Kiyoh *-2000* **Vasilios Maritime Ltd** Unimor Shipping Agency *Monrovia* *Liberia* MMSI: 636014536 Official number: 14536	**37,629** 23,436 71,862 T/cm 65.5	Class: BV (NK)	**1994-02 Shin Kurushima Dockyard Co. Ltd. — Onishi** Yd No: 2786 Loa 225.03 (BB) Br ex - Dght 13.477 Lbp 215.50 Br md 32.26 Dpth 18.60 Welded, 1 dk	**(A21A2BC) Bulk Carrier** Double Hull Grain: 82,893 Compartments: 7 Ho, ER 7 Ha: (14.1 x 13.6)6 (18.1 x 14.0)ER	**1 oil engine** driving 1 FP propeller Total Power: 7,635kW (10,381hp) 14.0kn Mitsubishi 6UEC60LA 1 x 2 Stroke 6 Cy. 600 x 1900 7635kW (10381bhp) Kobe Hatsudoki KK-Japan
9353981 *S6BB2* -	**ST. VINCENT** - **St Vincent Shipping Pte Ltd** Epic Ship Management Pte Ltd *Singapore* *Singapore* MMSI: 565687000 Official number: 393917	**4,253** 1,374 5,023 T/cm 17.7	Class: NK (BV)	**2008-01 Sasaki Shipbuilding Co Ltd — Osakikamijima HS** Yd No: 662 Loa 99.98 (BB) Br ex 17.22 Dght 6.114 Lbp 93.50 Br md 17.20 Dpth 7.80 Welded, 1 dk	**(A11B2TG) LPG Tanker** Double Sides Entire Compartment Length Liq (Gas): 4,925 3 x Gas Tank (s); 2 independent (stl) cyl horizontal, ER 2 Cargo Pump (s): 2x350m^3/hr Manifold: Bow/CM: 46.6m	**1 oil engine** driving 1 FP propeller Total Power: 3,120kW (4,242hp) 13.8kn Mitsubishi 6UEC37LA 1 x 2 Stroke 6 Cy. 370 x 880 3120kW (4242bhp) Akasaka Tekkosho KK (Akasaka DieselLtd)-Japan AuxGen: 2 x 350kW a.c Thrusters: 1 Tunnel thruster (f) Fuel: 105.0 (d.f.) 503.0 (r.f.)

IMO / Call sign	Name / Owner / Port	Tonnage	Class	Builder / Dimensions	Type	Machinery
8886163 - -	**ST. VINCENT 1 B.** - **St Vincent B Inc** - *New Orleans, LA* *United States of America* Official number: 908383	*106* 72 -		**1986 Master Boat Builders, Inc. — Coden, Al** Yd No: 105 L reg 21.33 Br ex - Dght - Lbp - Br md 6.17 Dpth 3.25 Welded, 1 dk	**(B11B2FV) Fishing Vessel**	**1 oil engine** driving 1 FP propeller
9242962 *WDD2459* -	**ST. VINCENT III** *ex* Capt. L C *-2005* **St Peter Joseph Inc** - *Cut Off, LA* *United States of America* MMSI: 367115570 Official number: 1103134	**143** 42 -		**2000** Yd No: 179 Loa 23.95 Br ex - Dght - Lbp - Br md 7.31 Dpth 3.84 Welded, 1 dk	**(B11B2FV) Fishing Vessel**	**1 oil engine** driving 1 FP propeller
8940270 - -	**ST. VINCENT IX T** - **Master Martin Inc** - *Cut Off, LA* *United States of America* Official number: 1039899	*144* 115 -		**1996 Master Martin, Inc. — Cut Off, La** L reg 23.77 Br ex - Dght - Lbp - Br md 7.01 Dpth 3.66 Welded, 1 dk	**(B11B2FV) Fishing Vessel**	**1 oil engine** driving 1 FP propeller
9241580 *WDD2452* -	**ST. VINCENT V** *ex* Miss Theresa II *-2006* **St Theresa Anna Inc** - *Larose, LA* *United States of America* MMSI: 367115490 Official number: 1100249	**163** 48 -		**2000 Master Boat Builders, Inc. — Coden, Al** Yd No: 288 Loa - Br ex - Dght - Lbp 25.83 Br md 7.57 Dpth 3.78 Welded, 1 dk	**(B11A2FT) Trawler**	**2 oil engines** geared to sc. shafts driving 2 Propellers Total Power: 794kW (1,080hp) Caterpillar 3412 2 x Vee 4 Stroke 12 Cy. 137 x 152 each-397kW (540bhp) Caterpillar Inc-USA
8900983 *UBYT* -	**ST WIND** *ex* Noble Spirit *-2004* *ex* Novikovo *-2003* *ex* Zim Saigon *-1999* *ex* Novikovo *-1998* **Avangard-4 Shipping Co SA** Shipping-Trans Group *Vostochnyy* *Russia* MMSI: 273435370	**3,988** 1,618 4,706	Class: RS (NV)	**1991-12 Sedef Gemi Endustrisi A.S. — Gebze** Yd No: 79 Loa 97.80 Br ex - Dght 6.010 Lbp 90.22 Br md 17.30 Dpth 7.00 Welded, 1 dk	**(A31A2GX) General Cargo Ship** Grain: 5,242; Bale: 5,227 TEU 221 C.Ho 111/20' (40') C.Dk 110/20' (40') incl. 6 ref C. Compartments: 2 Ho, ER 2 Ha: 2 (25.7 x 12.5)ER Cranes: 2x25t Ice Capable	**1 oil engine** driving 1 CP propeller Total Power: 3,354kW (4,560hp) 12.5kn B&W 6L35MC 1 x 2 Stroke 6 Cy. 350 x 1050 3354kW (4560bhp) Zaklady Przemyslu Metalowego 'HCegielski' SA-Poznan AuxGen: 1 x 300kW 220/380V 50Hz a.c, 2 x 264kW 220/380V 50Hz a.c Fuel: 90.0 (d.f.) 275.0 (r.f.) 12.7pd
7638507 *FNUG* -	**ST. XAVIER MARIS STELLA III** *ex* Hornelen *-2001* *ex* Bremer Norden *-1990* *ex* Coaster Emmy *-1982* **Societe de Navigation des Tuamotu Sarl** - *Papeete* *France* MMSI: 226223000 Official number: 862769	**1,264** 407 1,150	Class: BV (NV)	**1978-06 Johan Drage AS — Rognan** Yd No: 377 Lengthened-1979 Loa 63.28 Br ex 11.03 Dght 3.798 Lbp 58.30 Br md 11.00 Dpth 8.03 Welded, 1 dk & S dk	**(A31B2GP) Palletised Cargo Ship** Grain: 2,980; Bale: 2,790 TEU 32 C. 32/20' Compartments: 1 Ho, ER 1 Ha: (21.0 x 6.3)ER Derricks: 1x28t; Winches: 1 Ice Capable	**1 oil engine** reduction geared to sc. shaft driving 1 CP propeller Total Power: 827kW (1,124hp) 11.5kn Caterpillar D399SCAC 1 x Vee 4 Stroke 16 Cy. 159 x 203 827kW (1124bhp) Caterpillar Tractor Co-USA AuxGen: 2 x 82kW 220V 50Hz a.c Thrusters: 1 Thwart. FP thruster (f)
8210821 - -	**ST707** *ex* Towada Maru *-2011* *ex* Hakuo Maru *-1992* **Booyeong Development Co Ltd** - *South Korea*	*191* - -		**1982-09 Sagami Zosen Tekko K.K. — Yokosuka** Yd No: 219 Loa 30.50 Br ex - Dght 2.601 Lbp 27.01 Br md 8.81 Dpth 3.40 Welded, 1 dk	**(B32A2ST) Tug**	**2 oil engines** geared integral to driving 2 Z propellers Total Power: 1,912kW (2,600hp) 13.5kn Niigata 6L25BX 2 x 4 Stroke 6 Cy. 250 x 320 each-956kW (1300bhp) Niigata Engineering Co Ltd-Japan AuxGen: 2 x 64kW 225V 60Hz a.c, 1 x 12kW 225V 60Hz a.c Fuel: 25.0 (d.f.)
9649158 *POTE* -	**STA-1** - **PT Steeltech Asia (STA)** - *Batam* *Indonesia* MMSI: 525007280	**305** 92 -	Class: KI (BV)	**2012-02 Taishan Winde Shipbuilding Co Ltd — Taishan GD** Yd No: WD1005 Loa 30.80 Br ex - Dght 3.400 Lbp 28.30 Br md 9.40 Dpth 4.95 Welded, 1 dk	**(B32A2ST) Tug**	**2 oil engines** reduction geared to sc. shafts driving 2 FP propellers Total Power: 2,200kW (2,992hp) Chinese Std. Type LB6250ZLC 2 x 4 Stroke 6 Cy. 250 x 320 each-1100kW (1496bhp) Qingdao Zichai Boyang Diesel EngineCo Ltd-China AuxGen: 2 x 90kW 60Hz a.c
6711699 *DUG2028* -	**STA ANA FFC** *ex* Gawler *-2001* **F F Cruz Shipping Corp** - *Iloilo* *Philippines* Official number: 06-0000586	**175** 52 -	Class: (LR) ✠ Classed LR until 11/72	**1967-06 Adelaide Ship Construction Pty Ltd — Port Adelaide SA** Yd No: 34 Loa 30.10 Br ex 8.49 Dght 4.230 Lbp 27.21 Br md 8.08 Dpth 4.55 Welded, 1 dk	**(B32A2ST) Tug** 1 Ha: (1.3 x 0.9)	**1 oil engine** dr reverse geared to sc. shaft driving 1 FP propeller Total Power: 831kW (1,130hp) 10.0kn English Electric 8RKCM 1 x Vee 4 Stroke 8 Cy. 254 x 305 831kW (1130bhp) English Electric Co. Ltd.-Stafford AuxGen: 2 x 30kW 220V d.c Fuel: 27.0 (d.f.)
7016797 *DUA2241* -	**STA. MARIA** *ex* Ryuyu Maru *-1981* *ex* Nikko Maru No. 2 *-1978* **Phil Asia Interport Services Corp** - *Manila* *Philippines* Official number: 00-0000578	*207* 107 -		**1970-06 Ishikawajima Ship & Chemical Plant Co Ltd — Tokyo** Yd No: 399 Loa 28.40 Br ex 8.67 Dght 2.591 Lbp 25.00 Br md 8.62 Dpth 3.48 Welded, 1 dk	**(B32A2ST) Tug**	**2 oil engines** geared to sc. shafts driving 2 FP propellers Total Power: 1,398kW (1,900hp) Fuji 6MD27.5CH 2 x 4 Stroke 6 Cy. 275 x 320 each-699kW (950bhp) Fuji Diesel Co Ltd-Japan AuxGen: 2 x 36kW 445V a.c
7375856 *DVEW* -	**STA. RITA DE CASIA** *ex* Superferry 1 *-2012* *ex* Aboitiz Superferry I *-1996* *ex* Venus *-1989* **2GO Group Inc** WG & A Jebsens Shipmanagement Inc *Manila* *Philippines* MMSI: 548138100 Official number: 00-0000439	**9,184** 2,987 3,908	Class: (LR) (KR) (NK) Classed LR until 30/6/10	**1975-12 Shikoku Dockyard Co. Ltd. — Takamatsu** Yd No: 780 Loa 132.40 (BB) Br ex 20.63 Dght 6.530 Lbp 120.00 Br md 20.00 Dpth 20.00 Riveted\Welded, 2 dks	**(A36A2PR) Passenger/Ro-Ro Ship (Vehicles)** Passengers: 2042; cabins: 2; berths: 4 Bow ramp Stern door & ramp Lane-Len: 1150 2 Ha: (32.6 x 3.8) (33.5 x 3.8)	**2 oil engines** with flexible couplings & sr geared to sc. shafts driving 2 FP propellers Total Power: 15,600kW (21,210hp) 19.5kn Wartsila 8R46 2 x 4 Stroke 8 Cy. 460 x 580 each-7800kW (10605bhp) (new engine 1994) Wartsila Diesel Oy-Finland AuxGen: 2 x 710kW 440V 60Hz a.c Boilers: AuxB (o.f.) 7.0kgf/cm² (6.9bar) Thrusters: 1 Thwart. FP thruster (f) Fuel: 100.0 (d.f.) 793.0 (r.f.) 57.0pd
8611300 *CSFF4*	**STA. RITA DE CASSIA** - **Camara Municipal de Caminha** - *Caminha* *Portugal* Official number: C-36-TL	**184** 55 90	Class: RP	**1995-02 Estaleiros Sao Jacinto S.A. — Aveiro** Yd No: 162 Loa 36.20 Br ex - Dght 1.400 Lbp 35.00 Br md 11.00 Dpth 2.10 Welded, 1 dk	**(A36A2PR) Passenger/Ro-Ro Ship (Vehicles)** Passengers: unberthed: 138 Bow ramp (centre) Stern ramp (centre)	**2 oil engines** reduction geared to sc. shafts driving 2 FP propellers Total Power: 250kW (340hp) MAN D2866TE 2 x 4 Stroke 6 Cy. 128 x 155 each-125kW (170bhp) MAN Nutzfahrzeuge AG-Nuernberg
8949070 *DUA6387* -	**STA. THERESA** *ex* Santa Theresa *-2012* *ex* Tamashio *-1999* **Phil Asia Interport Services Corp** - *Manila* *Philippines* Official number: 00-0000579	*195* 95 -		**1972-05 K.K. Miura Zosensho — Saiki** Loa 27.80 Br ex - Dght 2.700 Lbp 26.00 Br md 8.80 Dpth 3.58 Welded, 1 dk	**(B32A2ST) Tug**	**2 oil engines** driving 2 Propellers Total Power: 920kW (1,250hp) 12.5kn Fuji 2 x 4 Stroke each-460kW (625bhp) (, fitted 2002) Fuji Diesel Co Ltd-Japan
9588988 *3YKA* H-95-AV	**STAALOY** - **Torbas AS** - *Bergen* *Norway* MMSI: 259855000	**886** 265 -		**2011-05 AS Rigas Kugu Buvetava (Riga Shipyard) — Riga** (Hull) Yd No: 024 **2011-05 Lyng AS — Deknepollen** Yd No: 2 Loa 43.80 (BB) Br ex - Dght - Lbp - Br md 11.00 Dpth 5.50 Welded, 1 dk	**(B11B2FV) Fishing Vessel** Hull Material: Aluminium Alloy	**1 oil engine** reduction geared to sc. shaft driving 1 Propeller Total Power: 1,980kW (2,692hp) MaK 6M25 1 x 4 Stroke 6 Cy. 255 x 400 1980kW (2692bhp) Caterpillar Motoren GmbH & Co. KG-Germany Thrusters: 1 Tunnel thruster (f); 1 Tunnel thruster (a)
9627514 - -	**STAATEN RIVER** *ex* Kim Heng 1233 *-2013* **Sea Swift Pty Ltd** - *Cairns, Qld* *Australia* Official number: 31320QC	**143** 43 112	Class: NK	**2011-07 Kaibuok Shipyard (M) Sdn Bhd — Sibu** Yd No: 0731 Loa 23.50 Br ex - Dght 2.710 Lbp 21.32 Br md 7.32 Dpth 3.20 Welded, 1 dk	**(B32A2ST) Tug**	**2 oil engines** reduction geared to sc. shafts driving 2 FP propellers Total Power: 894kW (1,216hp) Cummins KTA-19-M3 2 x 4 Stroke 6 Cy. 159 x 159 each-447kW (608bhp) Cummins Engine Co Inc-USA Fuel: 89.0 (d.f.)
8816182 - -	**STAATSOLIE 4** - **Staatsolie Maatschappij Surinamen NV** - *Paramaribo* *Suriname*	**831** - 1,500	Class: (BV)	**1989-09 Surinaamse Dok en Scheepsbouw Mij — Paramaribo** Yd No: 8674 Loa 62.01 Br ex 12.50 Dght 2.901 Lbp 59.17 Br md 12.20 Dpth 3.31 Welded, 1 dk	**(A13A2TV) Crude Oil Tanker** Liq: 1,670; Liq (Oil): 1,670 Compartments: 8 Ta, ER	**2 oil engines** sr geared to sc. shafts driving 2 FP propellers Total Power: 1,264kW (1,718hp) G.M. (Detroit Diesel) 12V-71-TA 2 x Vee 2 Stroke 12 Cy. 108 x 127 each-632kW (859bhp) General Motors Detroit DieselAllison Divn-USA

Vessel	Tonnage	Class	Builder / Dimensions	Type	Machinery
8802741 **STAATSOLIE 5** - - **Staatsolie Maatschappij Surinamen NV** - *Paramaribo* *Suriname*	*992* 646 1,535	Class: (BV)	**1988**-11 **Surinaamse Dok en Scheepsbouw Mij — Paramaribo** Yd No: 8616 Loa 62.00 Br ex 12.50 Dght 3.200 Lbp 59.17 Br md 12.21 Dpth 4.00 Welded, 1 dk	**(A13A2TV) Crude Oil Tanker** Liq: 1,670; Liq (Oil): 1,670 Compartments: 8 Ta, ER	**2 oil engines** sr geared to sc. shafts driving 2 FP propellers Total Power: 1,264kW (1,718hp) G.M. (Detroit Diesel) 12V-71-TI 2 x Vee 2 Stroke 12 Cy. 108 x 127 each-632kW (859bhp) General Motors Detroit DieselAllison Divn-USA
9452086 **STABERHUK** *DD5730* - **Government of The Federal Republic of Germany (Wasserschuetzpolizei Schleswig-Holstein)** - *Kiel* *Germany* MMSI: 211462260	**111** 33 15	Class: (GL)	**2009**-07 **Fr Fassmer GmbH & Co KG — Berne** Yd No: 06/1/3011 Loa 27.20 Br ex - Dght 1.600 Lbp 23.03 Br md 6.20 Dpth 3.10 Welded, 1 dk	**(B34H2SQ) Patrol Vessel** Hull Material: Aluminium Alloy	**2 oil engines** reduction geared to sc. shafts driving 2 FP propellers Total Power: 1,800kW (2,448hp) 24.0kn M.T.U. 10V2000M72 2 x Vee 4 Stroke 10 Cy. 135 x 156 each-900kW (1224bhp) MTU Friedrichshafen GmbH-Friedrichshafen Thrusters: 1 Tunnel thruster (f)
7502564 **STACEY FOSS** *WYL4909* - **Foss Maritime Co** - *Seattle, WA* *United States of America* MMSI: 366932970 Official number: 571855	**364** 109 -	Class: (AB)	**1976**-09 **Fairhaven Shipyard, Inc. — Bellingham, Wa** Yd No: 47 Loa 33.53 Br ex 10.39 Dght 4.125 Lbp 32.36 Br md 10.37 Dpth 4.83 Welded, 1 dk	**(B32A2ST) Tug**	**2 oil engines** reverse reduction geared to sc. shafts driving 2 FP propellers Total Power: 2,132kW (2,898hp) 13.0kn EMD (Electro-Motive) 8-645-E2 2 x Vee 2 Stroke 8 Cy. 230 x 254 each-1066kW (1449bhp) General Motors Corp.Electro-Motive Div.-La Grange AuxGen: 2 x 115kW
7742607 **STACEY RAY** - - **John Zar Jr** - *New Orleans, LA* *United States of America* Official number: 591833	*142* 97 -		**1978 Marine Builders, Inc. — Mobile, Al** L reg 23.47 Br ex 6.81 Dght - Lbp - Br md - Dpth 3.41 Welded, 1 dk	**(B11B2FV) Fishing Vessel**	**1 oil engine** reverse reduction geared to sc. shaft driving 1 FP propeller Total Power: 386kW (525hp) G.M. (Detroit Diesel) 12V-71-TI 1 x Vee 2 Stroke 12 Cy. 108 x 127 386kW (525bhp) General Motors Detroit DieselAllison Divn-USA Fuel: 59.0
8517047 **STACIA** - *ex* Azov Wind *-2010* *ex* Nino *-2005* - *ex* G. Ordzhonikidze *-2000* *ex* Grigoriy Ordzhonikidze *-1994* **Stacia Corp SA** White Pearl Naval Services SA	**10,985** 5,140 17,127 T/cm 27.8	Class: (NV) (RS)	**1988**-11 **Brodogradiliste Split (Brodosplit) — Split** Yd No: 355 Converted From: Products Tanker-2006 Loa 151.30 (BB) Br ex - Dght 9.470 Lbp 142.60 Br md 22.40 Dpth 12.15 Welded, 1 dk	**(A12B2TR) Chemical/Products Tanker** Double Hull (13F) Liq: 16,290; Liq (Oil): 16,290 Compartments: 10 Wing Ta, 6 Ta, 2 Wing Slop Ta, ER 16 Cargo Pump (s): 16x250m³/hr Manifold: Bow/CM: 73.6m Ice Capable	**1 oil engine** driving 1 CP propeller Total Power: 5,701kW (7,751hp) 15.0kn B&W 5L50MC 1 x 2 Stroke 5 Cy. 500 x 1620 5701kW (7751bhp) Brodogradiliste Split (Brodosplit)-Yugoslavia AuxGen: 1 x 720kW a.c, 2 x 560kW a.c Thrusters: 1 Thwart. FP thruster (f) Fuel: 68.0 (d.f.) 890.0 (r.f.)
5098935 **STACKE** *SETU* *ex* Einar *-1973* - **M Fries** - *Stockholm* *Sweden*	*155* 52 -	Class: (LR) ✠ Classed LR until 25/7/75	**1948**-04 **Lodose Varv AB — Lodose** Yd No: 90 Loa 26.01 Br ex 7.88 Dght 3.960 Lbp 24.21 Br md 7.80 Dpth 4.20 Riveted\Welded	**(B32A2ST) Tug** Ice Capable	**1 oil engine** driving 1 CP propeller Total Power: 1,214kW (1,651hp) 12.0kn Crossley CRL8 1 x 2 Stroke 8 Cy. 368 x 483 1214kW (1651bhp) (new engine 1960) Crossley Bros. Ltd.-Manchester AuxGen: 1 x 85kW 220V d.c, 1 x 25kW 220V d.c Fuel: 66.0 (d.f.)
8977780 **STACY JO** *WDB7802* *ex* Phyllis Mccall Ii *-2010* - **Offshore Oil Services Inc** - *Freeport, TX* *United States of America* MMSI: 338084000 Official number: 1034178	**237** 71 210		**1995**-09 **Gulf Craft Inc — Patterson LA** Yd No: 404 Loa 41.00 Br ex - Dght 2.000 Lbp 38.00 Br md 8.00 Dpth 3.00 Welded, 1 dk	**(B21A20C) Crew/Supply Vessel** Hull Material: Aluminium Alloy Passengers: 74; cabins: 4	**4 oil engines** reduction geared to sc. shafts driving 4 FP propellers Total Power: 2,060kW (2,800hp) 20.0kn Cummins KTA-19-M 4 x 4 Stroke 6 Cy. 159 x 159 each-515kW (700bhp) Cummins Engine Co Inc-USA AuxGen: 2 x 50kW a.c Fuel: 45.0 (d.f.) 13.0pd
7940417 **STACY LEE** *WDC8003* *ex* Miss Sammie *-2005* - **Stacy Lee Inc** - *Cape May, NJ* *United States of America* Official number: 601984	*132* 89 -		**1979 Eastern Marine, Inc. — Panama City, Fl** Yd No: 10 L reg 21.55 Br ex 6.53 Dght - Lbp - Br md - Dpth 3.69 Welded, 1 dk	**(B11B2FV) Fishing Vessel**	**1 oil engine** driving 1 FP propeller Total Power: 496kW (674hp)
7947790 **STACY M** *WBV7290* *ex* Kay Lynn *-2005* - **Huntress Inc** - *Davisville, RI* *United States of America* MMSI: 366460140 Official number: 611418	*119* 81 -		**1979 Rockport Yacht & Supply Co. (RYSCO) — Rockport, Tx** L reg 22.47 Br ex 6.76 Dght - Lbp - Br md - Dpth 3.05 Welded, 1 dk	**(B11B2FV) Fishing Vessel**	**1 oil engine** driving 1 FP propeller Total Power: 382kW (519hp) Caterpillar 3412PCTA 1 x Vee 4 Stroke 12 Cy. 137 x 152 382kW (519bhp) Caterpillar Tractor Co-USA
8990457 **STACY MCALLISTER** *WDB7607* *ex* Houma (YTB-811) *-2003* - **McAllister Steamship LLC** McAllister Towing of Virginia Inc *New York, NY* *United States of America* MMSI: 366945050 Official number: 1143301	**243** 72 -		**1971**-09 **Peterson Builders, Inc. — Sturgeon Bay, Wi** Loa 33.22 Br ex - Dght 3.657 Lbp 31.24 Br md 8.84 Dpth 4.88 Welded, 1 dk	**(B32A2ST) Tug**	**2 oil engines** geared to sc. shafts driving 2 Z propellers Total Power: 2,942kW (4,000hp) Caterpillar 3516B 2 x Vee 4 Stroke 16 Cy. 170 x 190 each-1471kW (2000bhp) (new engine 2005) Caterpillar Inc-USA
8611207 **STAD** *YJTS3* *ex* Stadum *-2014* *ex* Westerhusen *-2002* - *ex* Alpha *-1999* *ex* Barbel *-1993* **Stad Shipping Ltd** Wakes & Co Ltd *Port Vila* *Vanuatu* MMSI: 577229000 Official number: 2291	**1,984** 1,056 3,233	Class: GL	**1989**-06 **IHC Holland NV Dredgers — Kinderdijk** (Hull) Yd No: 10295 **1989**-06 **B.V. Scheepswerf Damen — Gorinchem** Yd No: 8208 Loa 89.31 Br ex - Dght 4.700 Lbp 86.04 Br md 12.51 Dpth 6.35 Welded, 2 dks	**(A31A2GX) General Cargo Ship** Double Bottom Entire Compartment Length Grain: 3,983 TEU 158 C.Ho 78/20' C.Dk 80/20' Compartments: 1 Ho, ER 1 Ha: (63.4 x 10.1)ER Ice Capable	**1 oil engine** sr reverse geared to sc. shaft driving 1 FP propeller Total Power: 600kW (816hp) 11.0kn MaK 6M332AK 1 x 4 Stroke 6 Cy. 240 x 330 600kW (816bhp) Krupp MaK Maschinenbau GmbH-Kiel AuxGen: 2 x 84kW 220/380V a.c, 1 x 38kW 220/380V a.c
9185554 **STAD AMSTERDAM** *PECA* - **Randstad Clipper Beheer BV & Amsterdam Clipper Beheer BV** Rederij Clipper Stad Amsterdam BV *Amsterdam* *Netherlands* MMSI: 246494000 Official number: 34264	**723** 277 110	Class: LR ✠ **100A1** SS 03/2009 sailing passenger ship *IWS ✠ **LMC** **UMS** Eq.Ltr: H; Cable: 357.5/26.0 U2 (a)	**2000**-06 **Damen Oranjewerf Amsterdam — Amsterdam** Yd No: 6900 Loa 66.56 Br ex 10.59 Dght 4.200 Lbp 53.93 Br md 10.50 Dpth 6.45 Welded, 2 dks	**(A37B2PS) Passenger Ship**	**1 oil engine** with clutches, flexible couplings & sr reverse geared to sc. shaft driving 1 CP propeller Total Power: 746kW (1,014hp) 11.0kn Caterpillar 3508B 1 x Vee 4 Stroke 8 Cy. 170 x 190 746kW (1014bhp) Caterpillar Inc-USA AuxGen: 2 x 160kW 230/400V 60Hz a.c Thrusters: 1 Thwart. FP thruster (f)
8010934 **STADACONA** *C6FS9* *ex* CSL Yarra *-2002* *ex* River Yarra *-2000* - *ex* Audax *-1991* *ex* Star Kanda *-1987* **CSL Pacific Shipping Ltd** CSL Australia Pty Ltd SatCom: Inmarsat C 431130111 *Nassau* *Bahamas* MMSI: 311301000 Official number: 9000032	**22,931** 11,367 32,452	Class: LR ✠ **100A1** SS 12/2009 strengthened for heavy cargoes LI *IWS ✠ **LMC** **UMS** Eq.Ltr: J†; Cable: 605.0/66.0 U3 (a)	**1984**-10 **Kanda Zosensho K.K. — Kawajiri** Yd No: 264 Converted From: Bulk Carrier-1991 Loa 182.86 (BB) Br ex 27.69 Dght 10.851 Lbp 170.01 Br md 27.60 Dpth 15.12 Welded, 1 dk	**(A31A2GE) General Cargo Ship, Self-discharging** Double Sides Entire Compartment Length Grain: 33,525; Bale: 31,000 Compartments: 4 Ho, ER 4 Ha: (32.0 x 20.4) (17.6 x 20.4) (21.6 x 20.4) (20.7 x 20.4)ER	**1 oil engine** driving 1 FP propeller Total Power: 8,238kW (11,200hp) 14.7kn B&W 6L67GFC 1 x 2 Stroke 6 Cy. 670 x 1700 8238kW (11200bhp) Hitachi Zosen Corp-Japan AuxGen: 3 x 544kW 450V 60Hz a.c Boilers: AuxB (Comp) 8.5kgf/cm² (8.3bar) Fuel: 273.0 (d.f.) 868.0 (r.f.)
9535620 **STADE** *V2QH3* - **mv 'Stade' BV** Reederei Heinz Corleis KG *Saint John's* *Antigua & Barbuda* MMSI: 305772000	**8,059** 3,909 10,872	Class: LR ✠ **100A1** SS 07/2011 strengthened for heavy cargoes, container cargoes in holds and on upper deck hatch covers LI Ice Class 1A FS at a draught of 7.574m Max/min draught fwd 7.574/3.60m Max/min draught aft 7.574/4.80m Required power 3558kw, installed power 4320kw ✠ **LMC** **UMS** Eq.Ltr: A†; Cable: 522.5/50.0 U3 (a)	**2011**-07 **Damen Shipyards Yichang Co Ltd — Yichang HB** (Hull) Yd No: 567312 **2011**-07 **B.V. Scheepswerf Damen — Gorinchem** Yd No: 567312 Loa 145.63 (BB) Br ex 18.36 Dght 7.400 Lbp 136.80 Br md 18.25 Dpth 10.30 Welded, 1 dk	**(A31A2GX) General Cargo Ship** Grain: 14,878 TEU 663 incl 60 ref C Compartments: 2 Ho, ER 2 Ha: ER Cranes: 2x80t Ice Capable	**1 oil engine** with flexible couplings & sr reverse geared to sc. shaft driving 1 CP propeller Total Power: 4,320kW (5,873hp) 14.2kn MaK 9M32C 1 x 4 Stroke 9 Cy. 320 x 480 4320kW (5873bhp) Caterpillar Motoren GmbH & Co. KG-Germany AuxGen: 3 x 350kW 400V 50Hz a.c, 1 x 760kW 400V 50Hz a.c Boilers: TOH (ex.g.) 10.2kgf/cm² (10.0bar), TOH (o.f.) 13.3kgf/cm² (13.0bar) Thrusters: 1 Thwart. FP thruster (f)

IMO / Call sign	Name / Owner / Flag	Tonnage	Class	Builder / Dimensions	Type / Capacity	Machinery
9414462 *9HA3070* -	**STADION II** **Stadion Shipping Co SA** Equinox Maritime Ltd *Valletta* *Malta* MMSI: 229101000 Official number: 9414462	**19,999** 10,419 30,200 T/cm 43.5	Class: AB	**2012-08 Tsuji Heavy Industries (Jiangsu) Co Ltd — Zhangjiagang JS** Yd No: NB0023 Loa 178.70 (BB) Br ex - Dght 9.790 Lbp 170.00 Br md 28.00 Dpth 14.00 Welded, 1 dk	**(A21A2BC) Bulk Carrier** Grain: 40,633; Bale: 38,602 Compartments: 5 Ho, ER 5 Ha: 4 (20.8 x 21.0)ER (16.6 x 15.0) Cranes: 4x30t	**1 oil engine** driving 1 FP propeller Total Power: 6,232kW (8,473hp) 14.0kn MAN-B&W 6S42MC 1 x 2 Stroke 6 Cy. 420 x 1764 6232kW (8473bhp) STX Engine Co Ltd-South Korea AuxGen: 3 x 550kW a.c Fuel: 82.0 (d.f.) 1320.0 (r.f.)
9202508 *PDBY* -	**STADIONGRACHT** **Rederij Stadiongracht** Spliethoff's Bevrachtingskantoor BV *Amsterdam* *Netherlands* MMSI: 246466000 Official number: 36727	**16,639** 6,730 21,250 T/cm 35.9	Class: LR ✠ **100A1** SS 06/2010 strengthened for heavy cargoes, container cargoes in holds, on upper deck and upper deck hatch covers timber deck cargoes tank top suitable for regular discharge by grabs *IWS LI Ice Class 1A (Finnish-Swedish Ice Class Rules 1985) Max draught midship 10.959m Max/min draught aft 11.47/6.6m Max/min draught fwd 11.47/4.2m ✠ **LMC** **UMS** Eq.Ltr: I†; Cable: 618.4/64.0 U3 (a)	**2000-09 Stocznia Szczecinska Porta Holding SA — Szczecin** Yd No: B587/IV/1 Loa 172.00 (BB) Br ex 25.50 Dght 10.600 Lbp 160.29 Br md 25.30 Dpth 14.60 Welded, 1 dk	**(A31A2GX) General Cargo Ship** Grain: 22,200 TEU 1127 C Ho 478 TEU C Dk 649 TEU incl 120 ref C. Compartments: 3 Ho, ER 4 Ha: (6.4 x 7.5) (25.6 x 15.2)Tappered (38.4 x 17.8) (32.0 x 20.4)ER Cranes: 3x120t Ice Capable	**1 oil engine** with flexible couplings & sr reverse geared to sc. shaft driving 1 CP propeller Total Power: 12,060kW (16,397hp) 19.1kn Wartsila 6L64 1 x 4 Stroke 6 Cy. 640 x 900 12060kW (16397bhp) Wartsila Italia SpA-Italy AuxGen: 1 x 1000kW 445V 60Hz a.c, 3 x 450kW 445V 60Hz a.c Boilers: TOH (o.f.) 10.2kgf/cm² (10.0bar), TOH (ex.g.) 10.2kgf/cm² (10.0bar) Thrusters: 1 Thwart. CP thruster (f) Fuel: 275.0 (d.f.) (Heating Coils) 1750.0 (r.f.) 45.0pd
8879940 *LCNT* -	**STADT** *ex* Hinnavag *-2011* *ex* Hessa *-1991* *ex* Bjorgvin *-1991* **Britt Janne AS** *Floro* *Norway*	**398** 119 -		**1962-06 Loland Motorverkstad AS — Leirvik i Sogn** Yd No: 16 Loa 40.69 Br ex - Dght - Lbp - Br md 9.50 Dpth - Welded, 1 dk	**(A36A2PR) Passenger/Ro-Ro Ship (Vehicles)** Passengers: unberthed: 380	**1 oil engine** driving 2 FP propellers 1 fwd and 1 aft Total Power: 441kW (600hp) 11.0kn Wichmann 1 x 441kW (600bhp) Wichmann Motorfabrikk AS-Norway
9333060 *V2CX6* -	**STADT AACHEN** **ms 'Stadt Aachen' T & H Schiffahrts GmbH & Co KG** Thien & Heyenga Bereederungs- und Befrachtungsgesellschaft mbH *Saint John's* *Antigua & Barbuda* MMSI: 305905000 Official number: 4367	**35,573** 19,496 44,145	Class: GL	**2007-09 Hanjin Heavy Industries & Construction Co Ltd — Busan** Yd No: 160 Loa 222.51 (BB) Br ex - Dght 12.000 Lbp 212.00 Br md 32.20 Dpth 19.30 Welded, 1 dk	**(A33A2CC) Container Ship (Fully Cellular)** TEU 3398 C Ho 1399 TEU C Dk 1999 TEU incl 300 ref C Compartments: 6 Cell Ho, ER 12 Ha: ER	**1 oil engine** driving 1 FP propeller Total Power: 28,880kW (39,265hp) 22.4kn MAN-B&W 8K80MC-C 1 x 2 Stroke 8 Cy. 800 x 2300 28880kW (39265bhp) Hyundai Heavy Industries Co Ltd-South Korea AuxGen: 4 x 1200kW 450/230V 60Hz a.c Thrusters: 1 Tunnel thruster (f)
8414829 *JWPM* -	**STADT AARDAL** *ex* Pax *-2013* **Stadt Sjotransport AS** - *Haugesund* *Norway* MMSI: 258188000 Official number: 20129	**315** 94 300	Class: NV	**1985-09 Skaalurens Skipsbyggeri AS — Rosendal** Yd No: 239 Loa 29.70 Br ex 9.50 Dght 5.980 Lbp 28.00 Br md 9.01 Dpth 4.65 Welded, 1 dk	**(B32A2ST) Tug** Passengers: cabins: 4	**2 oil engines** with clutches, flexible couplings & sr geared to sc. shafts driving 2 Directional propellers Total Power: 2,200kW (2,992hp) 11.5kn Normo KRMB-6 2 x 4 Stroke 6 Cy. 250 x 300 each-1100kW (1496bhp) AS Bergens Mek Verksteder-Norway AuxGen: 2 x 128kW 380V 50Hz a.c Fuel: 130.0 (d.f.)
9235608 *V2EO5* -	**STADT BREMEN** *ex* EWL Rotterdam *-2008* *ex* Tharos *-2003* *launched as* Stadt Bremen *-2003* **ms 'Stadt Bremen' T & H Schiffharts GmbH & Co KG** Thien & Heyenga Bereederungs- und Befrachtungsgesellschaft mbH *Saint John's* *Antigua & Barbuda* MMSI: 305495000 Official number: 4684	**9,528** 4,703 12,895 T/cm 27.0	Class: GL	**2003-02 Santierul Naval Constanta S.A. — Constanta** (Hull) Yd No: 556 **2003-02 Muetzelfeldtwerft GmbH — Cuxhaven** Yd No: 241 Loa 146.45 (BB) Br ex - Dght 8.312 Lbp 139.00 Br md 22.70 Dpth 11.20 Welded, 1 dk	**(A33A2CC) Container Ship (Fully Cellular)** TEU 1102 C Ho 334 TEU C Dk 768 TEU incl 200 ref C. Cranes: 2x40t	**1 oil engine** reduction geared to sc. shaft driving 1 CP propeller Total Power: 8,997kW (12,232hp) 20.0kn MAN 7L58/64 1 x 4 Stroke 7 Cy. 580 x 640 8997kW (12232bhp) MAN B&W Diesel AG-Augsburg AuxGen: 1 x 1200kW 440V a.c, 3 x 570kW 440/220V a.c Thrusters: 1 Tunnel thruster (f)
9338278 *V7NL4* -	**STADT BREMERHAVEN** *ex* Appen Paula *-2011* *ex* CSAV Atlas *-2009* *ex* Fa Mei Shan *-2008* *launched as* Maersk Recife *-2005* **ms Stadt Bremerhaven T + H Schiffahrts GmbH & Co KG** Thien & Heyenga Bereederungs- und Befrachtungsgesellschaft mbH *Majuro* *Marshall Islands* MMSI: 538090335 Official number: 90335	**9,954** 5,117 13,710 T/cm 28.0	Class: GL	**2006-12 Jiangsu Eastern Heavy Industry Co Ltd — Jingjiang JS** Yd No: 02C-15 Loa 147.87 (BB) Br ex - Dght 8.510 Lbp 140.30 Br md 23.25 Dpth 11.50 Welded, 1 dk	**(A33A2CC) Container Ship (Fully Cellular)** Grain: 16,000; Bale: 16,000 TEU 1118 C Ho 334 TEU C Dk 784 TEU incl 233 ref C Compartments: 5 Cell Ho, ER 7 Ha: ER Cranes: 2x45t	**1 oil engine** driving 1 FP propeller Total Power: 9,488kW (12,900hp) 19.6kn MAN-B&W 6S50MC-C 1 x 2 Stroke 6 Cy. 500 x 2000 9488kW (12900bhp) Yichang Marine Diesel Engine Co Ltd-China AuxGen: 3 x 911kW 450/220V 60Hz a.c Thrusters: 1 Tunnel thruster (f)
9445904 *V2FG7* -	**STADT CADIZ** *ex* Calidris *-2010* **ms Stadt Cadiz T + H Schiffahrts GmbH + Co KG** Thien & Heyenga Bereederungs- und Befrachtungsgesellschaft mbH SatCom: Inmarsat C 430567010 *Saint John's* *Antigua & Barbuda* MMSI: 305670000	**35,878** 14,700 41,234	Class: GL	**2010-11 Guangzhou Wenchong Shipyard Co Ltd — Guangzhou GD** Yd No: 382 Loa 212.48 (BB) Br ex - Dght 12.500 Lbp 195.30 Br md 32.20 Dpth 20.30 Welded, 1 dk	**(A33A2CC) Container Ship (Fully Cellular)** TEU 2758 C Ho 1356 TEU C Dk 1402 TEU incl 499 ref C. Compartments: 5 Cell Ho, ER Cranes: 3x45t,1x35t	**1 oil engine** driving 1 FP propeller Total Power: 25,040kW (34,044hp) 22.3kn Wartsila 8RT-flex68 1 x 2 Stroke 8 Cy. 680 x 2720 25040kW (34044bhp) Hudong Heavy Machinery Co Ltd-China AuxGen: 4 x 1600kW 450V a.c Thrusters: 1 Tunnel thruster (f)
5067053 *LMIT* -	**STADT CHIEF** *ex* Bergslep *-2007* *ex* Big *-1986* *ex* Cement 8 *-1968* **Stadt Sjotransport AS** *Floro* *Norway* MMSI: 257380800 Official number: 12595	**108** 32 -	Class: (NV)	**1947 Glommens Mek Verksted — Fredrikstad** Yd No: 109 Loa 27.89 Br ex 6.35 Dght 2.623 Lbp 25.48 Br md 6.33 Dpth 3.10 Welded, 1 dk	**(B32A2ST) Tug**	**1 oil engine** driving 1 FP propeller Total Power: 883kW (1,201hp) 10.0kn Wichmann 8ACA 1 x 2 Stroke 8 Cy. 280 x 420 883kW (1201bhp) (made 1964, fitted 1971) Wichmann Motorfabrikk AS-Norway AuxGen: 2 x 60kW a.c Thrusters: 1 Thwart. FP thruster (f) Fuel: 10.0 (d.f.)
9450923 *V2QA6* -	**STADT COBURG** *ex* Bunga Raya Lima *-2011* **ms Stadt Coburg T+H Shipping Co Ltd** Thien & Heyenga Bereederungs- und Befrachtungsgesellschaft mbH SatCom: Inmarsat C 430548710 *Saint John's* *Antigua & Barbuda* MMSI: 305487000 Official number: 3040	**42,112** 25,378 54,327	Class: GL	**2009-08 Daewoo Shipbuilding & Marine Engineering Co Ltd — Geoje** Yd No: 4145 Loa 260.31 (BB) Br ex - Dght 12.600 Lbp 247.00 Br md 32.20 Dpth 19.20 Welded, 1 dk	**(A33A2CC) Container Ship (Fully Cellular)** TEU 4380 C Ho 1622 TEU C Dk 2758 TEU incl 360 ref C Compartments: 7 Cell Ho, ER	**1 oil engine** driving 1 FP propeller Total Power: 36,560kW (49,707hp) 24.4kn MAN-B&W 8K90MC-C 1 x 2 Stroke 8 Cy. 900 x 2300 36560kW (49707bhp) Doosan Engine Co Ltd-South Korea AuxGen: 3 x 2430kW 450V a.c Thrusters: 1 Tunnel thruster (f)
9320049 *V2CF4* -	**STADT DRESDEN** *ex* Sci Kiran *-2009* *launched as* Stadt Dresden *-2006* **ms 'Stadt Dresden' T & H Schiffahrts GmbH & Co KG** Thien & Heyenga Bereederungs- und Befrachtungsgesellschaft mbH SatCom: Inmarsat C 430411910 *Saint John's* *Antigua & Barbuda* MMSI: 304119000	**27,971** 13,574 37,937 T/cm 56.8	Class: GL	**2006-12 Aker MTW Werft GmbH — Wismar** (Aft section) Yd No: 126 **2006-12 Aker Warnemuende Operations GmbH — Rostock** (Fwd section) Loa 221.72 (BB) Br ex - Dght 11.430 Lbp 209.62 Br md 29.86 Dpth 16.40 Welded, 1 dk	**(A33A2CC) Container Ship (Fully Cellular)** Double Bottom Entire Compartment Length TEU 2742 C Ho 1112 TEU C Dk 1630 TEU incl 400 ref C. Compartments: 5 Cell Ho, ER 11 Ha: ER	**1 oil engine** driving 1 FP propeller Total Power: 21,769kW (29,597hp) 21.9kn MAN-B&W 7L70MC-C 1 x 2 Stroke 7 Cy. 700 x 2360 21769kW (29597bhp) H Cegielski Poznan SA-Poland AuxGen: 3 x 1330kW 450/230V a.c, 1 x 895kW 450/230V a.c Thrusters: 1 Thwart. CP thruster (f)

IMO / Call sign	Name / Owner / Manager / Flag	Tonnage	Class	Built / Dimensions	Type / Cargo	Machinery
9234379 *V2BD7* -	**STADT EMDEN** *ex* EWL Hispania *-2008* *ex* Stadt Emden *-2006* *ex* P&O Nedlloyd Araucania *-2005* *ex* MOL Rainbow *-2003* *launched as* Lania *-2002* **ms 'Stadt Emden' T & H Schiffahrts GmbH & Co KG** Thien & Heyenga Bereederungs- und Befrachtungsgesellschaft mbH *Saint John's* *Antigua & Barbuda* MMSI: 304422000 Official number: 3974	**9,528** 4,703 12,895 T/cm 27.0	Class: GL	**2002**-06 **Santierul Naval Constanta S.A. — Constanta** (Hull) Yd No: 555 **2002**-06 **Muetzelfeldtwerft GmbH — Cuxhaven** Yd No: 240 Loa 146.45 (BB) Br ex 23.25 Dght 8.312 Lbp 139.00 Br md 22.70 Dpth 11.20 Welded, 1 dk	**(A33A2CC) Container Ship (Fully Cellular)** Double Bottom Entire Compartment Length TEU 1102 C Ho 334 TEU C Dk 768 TEU incl 200 ref C. Cranes: 2x45t	**1 oil engine** reduction geared to sc. shaft driving 1 CP propeller Total Power: 9,730kW (13,229hp) 20.0kn MAN 7L58/64 1 x 4 Stroke 7 Cy. 580 x 640 9730kW (13229bhp) MAN B&W Diesel AG-Augsburg AuxGen: 3 x 565kW 440/220V a.c, 1 x 1200kW 440/220V a.c Thrusters: 1 Thwart. FP thruster (f)
7022485 *DEPL* -	**STADT EMDEN** *ex* Ostsee I *-1991* *ex* Elizabeth *-1977* *ex* Pietertje Elizabeth *-1975* **Fischereibetrieb Viribus Unitis GmbH** - *Emden* *Germany* Official number: 4346	**151** 45 -	Class: (GL)	**1970**-10 **Holland Launch N.V. — Zaandam** Yd No: 467 Lengthened-1976 Loa 31.78 Br ex 7.04 Dght 2.550 Lbp 28.53 Br md 7.00 Dpth 3.40 Welded, 1 dk	**(B11A2FT) Trawler**	**1 oil engine** reverse reduction geared to sc. shaft driving 1 FP propeller Total Power: 1,250kW (1,700hp) Mitsubishi S12R-MPTA 1 x Vee 4 Stroke 12 Cy. 170 x 180 1250kW (1700bhp) (new engine 1993) Mitsubishi Heavy Industries Ltd-Japan
9235610 *V2BD8* -	**STADT FLENSBURG** *ex* EWL Canada *-2008* *launched as* Alassa *-2006* *ex* Melfi Havana *-2003* **ms 'Stadt Flensburg' T & H Schiffahrts GmbH & Co KG** Thien & Heyenga Bereederungs- und Befrachtungsgesellschaft mbH *Saint John's* *Antigua & Barbuda* MMSI: 304517000 Official number: 3975	**9,528** 4,703 12,895 T/cm 27.4	Class: GL	**2003**-10 **OAO Damen Shipyards Okean — Nikolayev** (Hull) **2003**-10 **Muetzelfeldtwerft GmbH — Cuxhaven** Yd No: 242 Loa 146.47 (BB) Br ex - Dght 8.310 Lbp 138.55 Br md 22.70 Dpth 11.29 Welded, 1 dk	**(A33A2CC) Container Ship (Fully Cellular)** TEU 1102 C Ho 334 TEU C Dk 768 TEU incl 200 ref C. Compartments: 5 Cell Ho, ER Cranes: 2x45t	**1 oil engine** geared to sc. shaft driving 1 CP propeller Total Power: 9,730kW (13,229hp) 20.0kn MAN 7L58/64 1 x 4 Stroke 7 Cy. 580 x 640 9730kW (13229bhp) MAN B&W Diesel AG-Augsburg AuxGen: 3 x 600kW 450/230V 60Hz a.c, 1 x 1200kW 450/230V 60Hz a.c Thrusters: 1 Thwart. CP thruster (f) Fuel: 245.0 (d.f.) 1380.0 (r.f.) 44.5pd
9459278 *V2EX3* -	**STADT FREIBURG** **ms Stadt Freiburg T+H Schiffahrts GmbH + Co KG** Thien & Heyenga Bereederungs- und Befrachtungsgesellschaft mbH SatCom: Inmarsat C 430558710 *Saint John's* *Antigua & Barbuda* MMSI: 305587000 Official number: 4754	**42,112** 25,378 54,325	Class: GL	**2010**-05 **Daewoo Shipbuilding & Marine Engineering Co Ltd — Geoje** Yd No: 4170 Loa 259.98 (BB) Br ex - Dght 12.600 Lbp 247.00 Br md 32.20 Dpth 19.20 Welded, 1 dk	**(A33A2CC) Container Ship (Fully Cellular)** TEU 4380 C Ho 1622 TEU C Dk 2758 TEU incl 360 ref C Compartments: ER, 7 Cell Ho	**1 oil engine** driving 1 FP propeller Total Power: 36,560kW (49,707hp) 24.3kn MAN-B&W 8K90MC-C 1 x 2 Stroke 8 Cy. 900 x 2300 36560kW (49707bhp) Doosan Engine Co Ltd-South Korea AuxGen: 3 x 2432kW 450V a.c Thrusters: 1 Tunnel thruster (f) Fuel: 5150.0 (r.f.)
9395094 *C4XY2* -	**STADT GERA** *ex* Maersk Rades *-2009* **ms 'Stadt Gera' T & H Schiffahrts GmbH & Co KG** Thien & Heyenga Bereederungs- und Befrachtungsgesellschaft mbH *Limassol* *Cyprus* MMSI: 210235000	**15,375** 5,938 18,236	Class: GL	**2007**-09 **Zhejiang Ouhua Shipbuilding Co Ltd — Zhoushan ZJ** Yd No: 2042 Loa 166.15 (BB) Br ex - Dght 9.500 Lbp 155.08 Br md 25.00 Dpth 14.20 Welded, 1 dk	**(A33A2CC) Container Ship (Fully Cellular)** TEU 1284 C Ho 472 TEU C Dk 812 TEU incl 390 ref C Cranes: 2x45t	**1 oil engine** reduction geared to sc. shaft driving 1 CP propeller Total Power: 11,200kW (15,228hp) 19.0kn MAN-B&W 8L58/64 1 x 4 Stroke 8 Cy. 580 x 640 11200kW (15228bhp) MAN B&W Diesel AG-Augsburg AuxGen: 4 x 1600kW 450/220V a.c Thrusters: 1 Tunnel thruster (f)
9395135 *V2DG6* -	**STADT GOTHA** *ex* Mell Senang *-2012* *ex* Stadt Gotha *-2011* **ms 'Stadt Gotha' T & H Schiffahrts GmbH & Co KG** Thien & Heyenga Bereederungs- und Befrachtungsgesellschaft mbH SatCom: Inmarsat C 430520710 *Saint John's* *Antigua & Barbuda* MMSI: 305207000 Official number: 4432	**15,375** 5,983 18,298	Class: GL	**2008**-02 **Zhejiang Ouhua Shipbuilding Co Ltd — Zhoushan ZJ** Yd No: 2046 Loa 166.15 (BB) Br ex - Dght 9.500 Lbp 155.08 Br md 25.00 Dpth 14.20 Welded, 1 dk	**(A33A2CC) Container Ship (Fully Cellular)** TEU 1284 C Ho 472 TEU C Dk 812 TEU incl 390 ref C Compartments: 4 Cell Ho, ER Cranes: 2x45t	**1 oil engine** reduction geared to sc. shaft driving 1 CP propeller Total Power: 11,200kW (15,228hp) 19.0kn MAN-B&W 8L58/64 1 x 4 Stroke 8 Cy. 580 x 640 11200kW (15228bhp) MAN Diesel A/S-Denmark AuxGen: 4 x 1600kW 450V a.c Thrusters: 1 Tunnel thruster (f)
9330276 *V2CH3* -	**STADT HAMELN** *ex* APL Galapagos *-2007* *ex* Stadt Hameln *-2007* **ms 'Stadt Hameln' T & H Schiffahrts GmbH & Co KG** Thien & Heyenga Bereederungs- und Befrachtungsgesellschaft mbH *Saint John's* *Antigua & Barbuda* MMSI: 304220000 Official number: 4234	**9,957** 5,020 13,749 T/cm 28.0	Class: GL	**2007**-01 **Kouan Shipbuilding Industry Co — Taizhou JS** Yd No: KA402 Loa 147.87 (BB) Br ex 23.43 Dght 8.510 Lbp 140.30 Br md 23.25 Dpth 11.50 Welded, 1 dk	**(A33A2CC) Container Ship (Fully Cellular)** Double Bottom Partial Compartment Length Grain: 16,000; Bale: 16,000 TEU 1118 C Ho 334 TEU C Dk 784 incl 220 ref C Compartments: 5 Ho, ER 7 Ha: ER Cranes: 2x45t	**1 oil engine** reduction geared to sc. shaft driving 1 CP propeller Total Power: 9,730kW (13,229hp) 19.0kn MAN-B&W 7L58/64 1 x 4 Stroke 7 Cy. 580 x 640 9730kW (13229bhp) MAN B&W Diesel AG-Augsburg AuxGen: 1 x 1400kW 450/230V a.c, 3 x 570kW 450/230V a.c Thrusters: 1 Tunnel thruster (f)
9007001 *P3ZW5* -	**STADT HANNOVER** *ex* Arcadian Faith *-2001* *ex* FLS Colombia *-1997* *ex* Arcadian Faith *-1994* **ms Troll GmbH & Co KG** Thien & Heyenga Bereederungs- und Befrachtungsgesellschaft mbH SatCom: Inmarsat C 420900685 *Limassol* *Cyprus* MMSI: 210836000 Official number: P404	**3,978** 2,267 5,250	Class: GL	**1994**-07 **Astilleros Unidos de Veracruz S.A. de C.V. (AUVER) — Veracruz** (Hull) Yd No: 124 **1994**-07 **Muetzelfeldtwerft GmbH — Cuxhaven** Yd No: 215 Loa 104.75 (BB) Br ex 16.57 Dght 6.550 Lbp 96.70 Br md 16.40 Dpth 8.30 Welded, 2 dks	**(A31A2GX) General Cargo Ship** Grain: 6,744; Bale: 6,744 TEU 373 C Ho 130 TEU C Dk 243 TEU incl 40 ref C. Compartments: 3 Ho, ER 3 Ha: (12.5 x 10.6)2 (26.0 x 13.3)ER Cranes: 2x36t Ice Capable	**1 oil engine** with flexible couplings & sr geared to sc. shaft driving 1 CP propeller Total Power: 3,520kW (4,786hp) 16.0kn MAN 8L32/40 1 x 4 Stroke 8 Cy. 320 x 400 3520kW (4786bhp) MAN B&W Diesel AG-Augsburg AuxGen: 1 x 576kW 220/440V 60Hz a.c, 2 x 252kW 220/440V 60Hz a.c, 1 x 200kW 220/440V 60Hz a.c Thrusters: 1 Thwart. FP thruster (f)
9395056 *V2CM9* -	**STADT JENA** *ex* TS Xiamen *-2008* *launched as* Stadt Jena *-2007* **ms 'Stadt Jena' T & H Schiffahrts GmbH & Co KG** Thien & Heyenga Bereederungs- und Befrachtungsgesellschaft mbH *Saint John's* *Antigua & Barbuda* MMSI: 305047000 Official number: 4280	**15,375** 5,983 18,278	Class: GL	**2007**-05 **Zhejiang Ouhua Shipbuilding Co Ltd — Zhoushan ZJ** Yd No: 2038 Loa 166.15 (BB) Br ex - Dght 9.500 Lbp 155.08 Br md 25.00 Dpth 14.20 Welded, 1 dk	**(A33A2CC) Container Ship (Fully Cellular)** TEU 1284 C Ho 472 TEU C Dk 812 TEU incl 390 ref C Cranes: 2x45t	**1 oil engine** reduction geared to sc. shaft driving 1 CP propeller Total Power: 11,200kW (15,228hp) 19.0kn MAN-B&W 8L58/64 1 x 4 Stroke 8 Cy. 580 x 640 11200kW (15228bhp) MAN B&W Diesel AG-Augsburg AuxGen: 4 x 1600kW 450/220V a.c Thrusters: 1 Tunnel thruster (f)
5337771 *DJUY* -	**STADT KIEL** **Forderverein ms 'Stadt Kiel' eV** - *Kiel* *Germany* MMSI: 211240870	*253* 144 -	Class: GL	**1934 Fried. Krupp Germaniawerft AG — Kiel** Yd No: 532 Lengthened-1943 Loa 28.10 Br ex 7.32 Dght 2.693 Lbp - Br md 7.27 Dpth 3.00 Riveted, 1 dk	**(A37B2PS) Passenger Ship** Passengers: unberthed: 335	**1 oil engine** driving 1 FP propeller Total Power: 382kW (519hp) 11.0kn MaK MAU423 1 x 4 Stroke 8 Cy. 290 x 420 382kW (519bhp) (new engine 1954) Maschinenbau Kiel AG (MaK)-Kiel Fuel: 13.0 (d.f.)
9333058 *V2CP8* -	**STADT KOLN** *ex* Emirates Indus *-2011* *ex* Stadt Koln *-2011* **ms 'Stadt Koln' T & H Schiffahrts GmbH & Co KG** Thien & Heyenga Bereederungs- und Befrachtungsgesellschaft mbH *Saint John's* *Antigua & Barbuda* MMSI: 305075000 Official number: 4303	**35,573** 19,496 44,234	Class: GL	**2007**-07 **Hanjin Heavy Industries & Construction Co Ltd — Busan** Yd No: 159 Loa 222.50 (BB) Br ex - Dght 12.020 Lbp 212.01 Br md 32.21 Dpth 19.30 Welded, 1 dk	**(A33A2CC) Container Ship (Fully Cellular)** TEU 3398 C Ho 1399 TEU C Dk 1999 TEU incl 300 ref C Compartments: 6 Cell Ho, ER 12 Ha: ER	**1 oil engine** driving 1 FP propeller Total Power: 28,880kW (39,265hp) 22.4kn MAN-B&W 8K80MC-C 1 x 2 Stroke 8 Cy. 800 x 2300 28880kW (39265bhp) Doosan Engine Co Ltd-South Korea AuxGen: 4 x 1200kW 450/230V 60Hz a.c Thrusters: 1 Tunnel thruster (f)
9216092 *D5CT3* -	**STADT LUEBECK** *ex* New Confidence *-2010* **Percy Shipping Co** Costamare Shipping Co SA *Monrovia* *Liberia* MMSI: 636015775 Official number: 15775	**13,764** 5,157 16,794	Class: GL (AB)	**2001**-03 **Jurong Shipyard Pte Ltd — Singapore** Yd No: 1058 Loa 154.00 (BB) Br ex 25.04 Dght 9.500 Lbp 145.00 Br md 25.00 Dpth 13.60 Welded, 1 dk	**(A33A2CC) Container Ship (Fully Cellular)** TEU 1078 incl 150 ref C. Compartments: 4 Cell Ho, ER 7 Ha: ER Cranes: 2x40t	**1 oil engine** driving 1 FP propeller Total Power: 13,440kW (18,273hp) 19.5kn B&W 7L60MC 1 x 2 Stroke 7 Cy. 600 x 1944 13440kW (18273bhp) Hudong Heavy Machinery Co Ltd-China AuxGen: 3 x 830kW a.c Thrusters: 1 Tunnel thruster (f)

IMO / Call sign / Fishing no.	Name / Former names / Owner / Manager / Port / Flag	Tonnage	Class	Builder / Dimensions	Type / Cargo	Machinery
9450911 *V2EM8* -	**STADT MARBURG** *ex* Amsterdam Bridge *-2014* *completed as* Stadt Marburg *-2009* **ms Stadt Marburg T+H Schiffahrts GmbH & Co KG** Thien & Heyenga Bereederungs- und Befrachtungsgesellschaft mbH SatCom: Inmarsat C 430548110 *Saint John's* *Antigua & Barbuda* MMSI: 305481000 Official number: 4671	**42,112** 25,378 54,405	Class: GL	**2009**-07 **Daewoo Shipbuilding & Marine Engineering Co Ltd — Geoje** Yd No: 4144 Loa 260.32 (BB) Br ex - Dght 12.600 Lbp 247.00 Br md 32.20 Dpth 19.20 Welded, 1 dk	**(A33A2CC) Container Ship (Fully Cellular)** TEU 4380 C Ho 1622 TEU C Dk 2758 TEU incl 360 ref C Compartments: 7 Cell Ho, ER	**1 oil engine** driving 1 FP propeller Total Power: 36,560kW (49,707hp) 24.4kn MAN-B&W 8K90MC-C 1 x 2 Stroke 8 Cy. 900 x 2300 36560kW (49707bhp) Doosan Engine Co Ltd-South Korea AuxGen: 3 x 2430kW 450V a.c Thrusters: 1 Tunnel thruster (f)
9339064 *C4NS2* -	**STADT RAVENSBURG** *ex* RBD Alexa *-2010* **Dritte Ravensburg Blind Pool GmbH & Co KG** Thien & Heyenga Bereederungs- und Befrachtungsgesellschaft mbH *Limassol* *Cyprus* MMSI: 210160000 Official number: P548	**7,545** 3,165 8,184 T/cm 22.0	Class: GL	**2006**-09 **Fujian Mawei Shipbuilding Ltd — Fuzhou FJ** Yd No: 437-13 Loa 129.57 (BB) Br ex - Dght 7.400 Lbp 120.34 Br md 20.60 Dpth 10.80 Welded, 1 dk	**(A33A2CC) Container Ship (Fully Cellular)** Double Bottom Entire Compartment Length TEU 698 C Ho 226 TEU C Dk 472 TEU incl 120 ref C. 3 Ha: ER Ice Capable	**1 oil engine** reduction geared to sc. shaft driving 1 CP propeller Total Power: 7,200kW (9,789hp) 16.5kn MaK 8M43C 1 x 4 Stroke 8 Cy. 430 x 610 7200kW (9789bhp) Caterpillar Motoren GmbH & Co. KG-Germany AuxGen: 1 x 1000kW 450/230V a.c, 3 x 450kW 450/230V a.c Thrusters: 1 Tunnel thruster (f)
9320037 *V2CE8* -	**STADT ROSTOCK** *ex* Sci Jyoti *-2009* *completed as* Stadt Rostock *-2006* **ms 'Stadt Rostock' Zweite T & H Schiffahrts GmbH & Co KG** Thien & Heyenga Bereederungs- und Befrachtungsgesellschaft mbH *Saint John's* *Antigua & Barbuda* MMSI: 304538000 Official number: 4213	**27,971** 13,574 37,929 T/cm 56.8	Class: GL	**2006**-10 **Aker MTW Werft GmbH — Wismar** (Aft section) Yd No: 125 **2006**-10 **Aker Warnemuende Operations GmbH — Rostock** (Fwd section) Loa 221.73 (BB) Br ex - Dght 11.430 Lbp 209.62 Br md 29.80 Dpth 16.40 Welded, 1 dk	**(A33A2CC) Container Ship (Fully Cellular)** Double Bottom Entire Compartment Length TEU 2742 C Ho 1112 TEU C Dk 1630 TEU incl 400 ref C Compartments: 5 Cell Ho, ER 11 Ha: ER	**1 oil engine** driving 1 FP propeller Total Power: 21,769kW (29,597hp) 21.9kn MAN-B&W 7L70MC-C 1 x 2 Stroke 7 Cy. 700 x 2360 21769kW (29597bhp) H Cegielski Poznan SA-Poland AuxGen: 3 x 1330kW 450/220V a.c, 1 x 1050kW 450/220V a.c Thrusters: 1 Tunnel thruster (f)
9235622 *V2BD9* -	**STADT ROTENBURG** *ex* EWL Central America *-2008* *completed as* Pirsos *-2007* *ex* Melfi Italia II *-2003* **ms 'Stadt Rotenburg' T & H Schiffarts GmbH & Co KG** Thien & Heyenga Bereederungs- und Befrachtungsgesellschaft mbH *Saint John's* *Antigua & Barbuda* MMSI: 304561000 Official number: 3976	**9,528** 4,703 12,864 T/cm 27.4	Class: GL	**2003**-12 **OAO Damen Shipyards Okean — Nikolayev** (Hull) **2003**-12 **Muetzelfeldtwerft GmbH — Cuxhaven** Yd No: 243 Loa 146.47 (BB) Br ex - Dght 8.310 Lbp 138.55 Br md 22.70 Dpth 11.20 Welded, 1 dk	**(A33A2CC) Container Ship (Fully Cellular)** Double Hull TEU 1102 C Ho 334 TEU C Dk 768 TEU incl 200 ref C. Compartments: 5 Cell Ho, ER Cranes: 2x45t	**1 oil engine** geared to sc. shaft driving 1 CP propeller Total Power: 9,730kW (13,229hp) 20.0kn MAN 7L58/64 1 x 4 Stroke 7 Cy. 580 x 640 9730kW (13229bhp) MAN B&W Diesel AG-Augsburg AuxGen: 3 x 600kW 450/230V 60Hz a.c, 1 x 1200kW 450V 60Hz a.c Thrusters: 1 Thwart. CP thruster (f) Fuel: 245.0 (d.f.) (Heating Coils) 1380.0 (r.f.)
9211157 *V2OK* -	**STADT SCHWERIN** *ex* Melfi Halifax *-2008* *ex* MSC Ireland *-2004* *ex* Jork Venture *-2002* *launched as* Armin *-1999* **ms 'Stadt Schwerin' T & H Schiffahrts Gmb & Co KG** Thien & Heyenga Bereederungs- und Befrachtungsgesellschaft mbH *Saint John's* *Antigua & Barbuda* MMSI: 304010999 Official number: 2350	**14,241** 6,256 18,425 T/cm 32.4	Class: GL	**1999**-12 **Stocznia Gdanska - Grupa Stoczni Gdynia SA — Gdansk** Yd No: 125/1 Loa 158.75 (BB) Br ex - Dght 10.212 Lbp 145.00 Br md 24.00 Dpth 13.90 Welded, 1 dk	**(A33A2CC) Container Ship (Fully Cellular)** Grain: 23,216 TEU 1129 C Ho 436 TEU C Dk 693 TEU incl 200 ref C. Compartments: 4 Cell Ho, ER 7 Ha: 2 (12.8 x 15.6)5 (12.8 x 20.6)ER Cranes: 2x43t	**1 oil engine** driving 1 FP propeller Total Power: 10,010kW (13,610hp) 18.0kn B&W 7S50MC 1 x 2 Stroke 7 Cy. 500 x 1910 10010kW (13610bhp) H Cegielski Poznan SA-Poland AuxGen: 3 x 880kW 440/220V 60Hz a.c Thrusters: 1 Tunnel thruster (f)
9440306 *V2EY8* -	**STADT SEVILLA** *launched as* Calandra *-2010* **ms 'Stadt Sevilla' T & H Schiffahrts GmbH & Co KG** Thien & Heyenga Bereederungs- und Befrachtungsgesellschaft mbH *Saint John's* *Antigua & Barbuda* MMSI: 305603000	**35,878** 20,470 41,253	Class: GL	**2010**-09 **Guangzhou Wenchong Shipyard Co Ltd — Guangzhou GD** Yd No: 381 Loa 212.59 (BB) Br ex - Dght 12.500 Lbp 195.30 Br md 32.20 Dpth 20.30 Welded, 1 dk	**(A33A2CC) Container Ship (Fully Cellular)** TEU 2796 C Ho 1356 TEU C Dk 1440 TEU incl 506 ref C Cranes: 3x45t,1x35t	**1 oil engine** driving 1 FP propeller Total Power: 25,040kW (34,044hp) 22.3kn Wartsila 8RT-flex68 1 x 2 Stroke 8 Cy. 680 x 2720 25040kW (34044bhp) Hudong Heavy Machinery Co Ltd-China AuxGen: 4 x 1600kW 450V a.c Thrusters: 1 Tunnel thruster (f)
8414817 *JWPO* -	**STADT SLOVAG** *ex* Dux *-2013* **Stadt Sjotransport AS** - *Haugesund* *Norway* MMSI: 258189000 Official number: 20128	**315** 94 300	Class: NV	**1985**-09 **Skaalurens Skipsbyggeri AS — Rosendal** Yd No: 238 Loa 29.01 Br ex 9.50 Dght 6.000 Lbp 28.00 Br md 9.01 Dpth 4.65 Welded, 1 dk	**(B32A2ST) Tug** Passengers: cabins: 4	**2 oil engines** with clutches, flexible couplings & sr geared to sc. shafts driving 2 Directional propellers Total Power: 2,200kW (2,992hp) 11.5kn Normo KRMB-6 2 x 4 Stroke 6 Cy. 250 x 300 each-1100kW (1496bhp) AS Bergens Mek Verksteder-Norway AuxGen: 2 x 128kW 380V 50Hz a.c Fuel: 109.0 (d.f.)
9336828 *V2BR5* -	**STADT SOLINGEN** *ex* Larch Arrow *-2011* *launched as* Stadt Solingen *-2006* **Reederei M Lauterjung GmbH & Co KG Independent ms 'Stadt Solingen'** Sunship Schiffahrtskontor KG *Saint John's* *Antigua & Barbuda* MMSI: 304904000 Official number: 4098	**30,570** 16,966 50,223 T/cm 52.2	Class: GL (NK)	**2006**-07 **P.T. PAL Indonesia — Surabaya** Yd No: 236 Loa 189.99 (BB) Br ex 30.56 Dght 12.820 Lbp 182.00 Br md 30.50 Dpth 17.50 Welded, 1 dk	**(A21A2BC) Bulk Carrier** Double Hull Grain: 60,000; Bale: 60,000 Compartments: 5 Ho, ER 5 Ha: 4 (20.0 x 25.5)ER (8.8 x 16.0) Cranes: 4x35t	**1 oil engine** driving 1 FP propeller Total Power: 9,480kW (12,889hp) 14.5kn MAN-B&W 6S50MC-C 1 x 2 Stroke 6 Cy. 500 x 2000 9480kW (12889bhp) STX Engine Co Ltd-South Korea AuxGen: 3 x 720kW a.c Fuel: 115.6 (d.f.) 1874.4 (r.f.)
6422377 *TFGF* VE 108	**STAFNES** *ex* Narfi *-2008* *ex* Gissur Hviti *-2008* *ex* Bara *-1978* **Helga Ehf** - *Vestmannaeyjar* *Iceland* MMSI: 251360110 Official number: 0964	**257** 77 -	Class: (NV)	**1964** **Orens Mek. Verksted — Trondheim** Yd No: 32 Loa 33.23 Br ex 6.91 Dght 3.353 Lbp 29.16 Br md 6.86 Dpth 3.54 Welded, 1 dk	**(B11B2FV) Fishing Vessel** Compartments: 2 Ho, ER 2 Ha: (1.6 x 1.4) (2.3 x 1.4)ER Derricks: 1x3t; Winches: 1	**1 oil engine** driving 1 FP propeller Total Power: 331kW (450hp) Stork 1 x 4 Stroke 6 Cy. 210 x 300 331kW (450bhp) Koninklijke Machinefabriek GebrStork & Co NV-Netherlands
9592018 *5BSS3* -	**STAHLA** *launched as* Houheng 1 *-2012* **Corsat Shipping Co Ltd** Katsikis & Sigalas Ltd *Limassol* *Cyprus* MMSI: 209755000 Official number: 9592018	**41,254** 25,658 76,059 T/cm 68.6	Class: CC (Class contemplated) NV (AB)	**2012**-09 **Hudong-Zhonghua Shipbuilding (Group) Co Ltd — Shanghai** Yd No: H1643A Loa 225.00 (BB) Br ex - Dght 14.250 Lbp 217.00 Br md 32.26 Dpth 19.70 Welded, 1 dk	**(A21A2BC) Bulk Carrier** Grain: 91,717; Bale: 89,882 Compartments: 7 Ho, ER 7 Ha: ER	**1 oil engine** driving 1 FP propeller Total Power: 11,300kW (15,363hp) 14.5kn MAN-B&W 5S60MC-C8 1 x 2 Stroke 5 Cy. 600 x 2400 11300kW (15363bhp) Hudong Heavy Machinery Co Ltd-China AuxGen: 3 x a.c
8112677 *UCCG* TH-360	**STAKFELL** **Saami Co Ltd (OOO Firma 'Saami')** - *Murmansk* *Russia* MMSI: 273450930 Official number: 814532	**753** 226 242	Class: RS (NV)	**1982**-06 **AS Storviks Mek. Verksted — Kristiansund** (Hull launched by) Yd No: 95 **1982**-06 **Sterkoder Mek. Verksted AS — Kristiansund** (Hull completed by) Yd No: 95A Loa 50.75 Br ex 10.50 Dght 4.500 Lbp 44.00 Br md 10.33 Dpth 6.76 Welded, 2 dks	**(B11A2FS) Stern Trawler** Ice Capable	**1 oil engine** with clutches, flexible couplings & sr geared to sc. shaft driving 1 FP propeller Total Power: 1,617kW (2,198hp) 13.3kn Wichmann 6AXAG 1 x 2 Stroke 6 Cy. 300 x 450 1617kW (2198bhp) Wichmann Motorfabrikk AS-Norway AuxGen: 1 x 800kW 380V 50Hz a.c, 1 x 226kW 380V 50Hz a.c
7808281 *UASQ* MCH-0425	**STAKHANOVETS** **Murmansk Basin Administration for Fishery Protection & Conservation (Upravleniye 'Murmanrybvod')** - SatCom: Inmarsat C 427321578 *Murmansk* *Russia* MMSI: 273218800 Official number: 790164	**3,120** 936 1,628	Class: (RS)	**1980**-02 **Oy Wartsila Ab — Helsinki** Yd No: 425 Loa 72.07 Br ex 18.32 Dght 6.700 Lbp 65.00 Br md 17.62 Dpth 9.02 Welded, 2 dks	**(B32A2ST) Tug** Cranes: 2x5t,2x3t Ice Capable	**2 oil engines** driving 2 CP propellers Total Power: 5,590kW (7,600hp) 15.0kn Pielstick 6PC2-5L-400 2 x 4 Stroke 6 Cy. 400 x 460 each-2795kW (3800bhp) Oy Wartsila Ab-Finland Thrusters: 1 Thwart. FP thruster (f) Fuel: 1471.0 (r.f.)

Ship	Tonnage	Class	Build / Dimensions	Type	Machinery
5077682 **STALBAS** *LNXH* *ex* Tralbas *-1974* - *ex* Commandant Charcot *-1968* *ex* Jean Charcot *-1955* **Barens Offshore AS** - SatCom: Inmarsat C 425728110 *Aalesund* *Norway* MMSI: 257281000 Official number: 16993	**854** 256 472	Class: NV (BV)	**1955 Beliard, Crichton & Cie. S.A. — Oostende** Yd No: 156 Converted From: Trawler-1974 Loa 58.76 Br ex 9.43 Dght 4.642 Lbp 52.43 Br md 9.40 Dpth 5.34 Riveted\Welded, 2 dks	**(B11B2FV) Fishing Vessel** 2 Ha: 2 (2.8 x 1.0)	**1 oil engine** sr geared to sc. shaft driving 1 CP propeller Total Power: 1,603kW (2,179hp) 12.0kn Wartsila 12V22 1 x Vee 4 Stroke 12 Cy. 220 x 240 1603kW (2179bhp) (new engine ,made 1978, fitted 1987) Oy Wartsila Ab-Finland AuxGen: 2 x 272kW 380V 50Hz a.c, 1 x a.c Thrusters: 1 Directional thruster (f); 1 Tunnel thruster (a)
8906949 **STALEGG** *LKUA* *ex* Unity *-2013* *ex* Torbas *-2001* - *ex* Ocean Way *-1997* **Beitveit Havfiske AS** - *Aalesund* *Norway* MMSI: 257388000	**814** 346 -	Class: LR ✠ **100A1** SS 06/2012 fishing vessel ✠ **LMC** Cable: 357.5/28.0 U2	**1989**-11 **Simek, Sigbjorn Iversen AS — Flekkefjord** Yd No: 68 Loa 44.90 (BB) Br ex 11.08 Dght 4.070 Lbp 37.88 Br md 11.00 Dpth 7.83 Welded, 2 dks	**(B11A2FS) Stern Trawler** Ins: 170	**1 oil engine** with clutches, flexible couplings & sr geared to sc. shaft driving 1 CP propeller Total Power: 2,400kW (3,263hp) Wichmann 8V28B 1 x Vee 4 Stroke 8 Cy. 280 x 360 2400kW (3263bhp) Wartsila Wichmann Diesel AS-Norway
6812912 **STALHOLM** - *ex* Bergholm *-1997* *ex* Lyngholm *-1996* - *ex* Grotle *-1994* - -	**286** 86 -		**1968 Eidsvik Skipsbyggeri AS — Uskedalen** Yd No: 23 Lengthened-1980 Loa 34.75 Br ex 6.84 Dght - Lbp 27.44 Br md 6.80 Dpth 3.48 Welded, 1 dk	**(B11B2FV) Fishing Vessel**	**1 oil engine** driving 1 FP propeller Total Power: 368kW (500hp) Alpha 405-26VO 1 x 2 Stroke 5 Cy. 260 x 400 368kW (500bhp) Alpha Diesel A/S-Denmark
7712755 **STALHOLM** *LAHQ* *ex* Sildey *-2006* *ex* Sildoy *-2001* T-2-LK *ex* Bommelfisk *-1996* **Reisafisk AS** Ervik Havfiske AS *Tromso* *Norway* MMSI: 259114000	**339** 102 -		**1978**-02 **Th Hellesoy Skipsbyggeri AS — Lofallstrand** Yd No: 97 Loa 33.53 Br ex 7.62 Dght - Lbp 29.01 Br md - Dpth 6.51 Welded, 2 dks	**(B11B2FV) Fishing Vessel**	**1 oil engine** driving 1 FP propeller Total Power: 508kW (691hp) Callesen 6-427-FOT 1 x 4 Stroke 6 Cy. 270 x 400 508kW (691bhp) Aabenraa Motorfabrik, HeinrichCallesen A/S-Denmark
9690212 **STALINGRAD** - *ex* Transflot-02 *-2014* - **Transchart Ltd** JSC Trans-Flot *Belize City* *Belize* Official number: 361420136	**4,810** 1,503 6,360	Class: RI	**2014**-03 **Yangzhou Haichuan Shipyard — Yangzhou JS** Yd No: HCR17 Loa 139.90 (BB) Br ex 16.94 Dght 4.000 Lbp 136.60 Br md 16.70 Dpth 6.40 Welded, 1 dk	**(A12B2TR) Chemical/Products Tanker** Double Hull (13F)	**2 oil engines** reduction geared to sc. shaft (s) driving 2 Propellers Total Power: 2,400kW (3,264hp) 10.0kn Wartsila 6L20 2 x 4 Stroke 6 Cy. 200 x 280 each-1200kW (1632bhp) Wartsila Finland Oy-Finland
7640615 **STALKER** *CXZV* *ex* Nemunelis *-2000* *ex* Ivan Polozkov *-1992* - **Apsey SA** - *Montevideo* *Uruguay* MMSI: 770576141 Official number: 8043	**873** 262 350	Class: (RS)	**1976 Yaroslavskiy Sudostroitelnyy Zavod — Yaroslavl** Yd No: 328 Loa 53.73 (BB) Br ex 10.70 Dght 4.290 Lbp 47.92 Br md - Dpth 6.02 Welded, 1 dk	**(B11A2FS) Stern Trawler** Ins: 218 Compartments: 1 Ho, ER 2 Ha: 2 (1.6 x 1.6) Derricks: 2x1.5t; Winches: 2 Ice Capable	**1 oil engine** driving 1 CP propeller Total Power: 971kW (1,320hp) 12.8kn S.K.L. 8NVD48A-2U 1 x 4 Stroke 8 Cy. 320 x 480 971kW (1320bhp) VEB Schwermaschinenbau "KarlLiebknecht" (SKL)-Magdeburg AuxGen: 1 x 300kW, 3 x 160kW Thrusters: 1 Thwart. FP thruster (f); 1 Tunnel thruster (a) Fuel: 201.0 (d.f.)
7430163 **STALKER** - *ex* Toho Maru *-1992* *ex* Hokuho Maru *-1989* - - -	*466* 174 -		**1975**-03 **Narasaki Zosen KK — Muroran HK** Yd No: 829 Loa 49.54 Br ex 8.31 Dght 3.429 Lbp 42.60 Br md 8.28 Dpth 3.79 Welded, 1 dk	**(B11B2FV) Fishing Vessel**	**1 oil engine** driving 1 FP propeller Total Power: 956kW (1,300hp) Niigata 6MG25BX 1 x 4 Stroke 6 Cy. 250 x 320 956kW (1300bhp) Niigata Engineering Co Ltd-Japan AuxGen: 2 x 200kW 225V a.c
8859847 **STALKER** - *ex* Kapitan Zubkov *-2005* - **OOO 'Rino Fish Ko'** -	**404** 121 174	Class: (RS)	**1991**-10 **Khabarovskiy Sudostroitelnyy Zavod im Kirova — Khabarovsk** Yd No: 101 Loa 41.87 Br ex - Dght 3.180 Lbp 37.27 Br md 8.90 Dpth 4.60 Welded, 1 dk	**(B11A2FS) Stern Trawler** Ins: 95 Ice Capable	**1 oil engine** geared to sc. shaft driving 1 CP propeller Total Power: 441kW (600hp) 9.5kn Daldizel 6CHNSP18/22 1 x 4 Stroke 6 Cy. 180 x 220 441kW (600bhp) Daldizel-Khabarovsk AuxGen: 3 x 75kW Fuel: 63.0 (d.f.)
6714172 **STALLION** *DZFA* *ex* Cagayan Express *-1989* *ex* Kiribati II *-1981* - *ex* Choei Maru *-1980* **Satellite Navigation Inc** - *Manila* *Philippines* Official number: S0853	*2,290* 1,423 4,196	Class: (NK)	**1967**-03 **Kurushima Dockyard Co. Ltd. — Imabari** Yd No: 397 Loa 89.62 Br ex 14.46 Dght 6.028 Lbp 83.01 Br md 14.41 Dpth 7.09 Riveted\Welded, 1 dk	**(A31A2GX) General Cargo Ship** Grain: 5,331; Bale: 4,989 Compartments: 2 Ho, ER 2 Ha: (17.6 x 7.0) (27.2 x 7.0)ER Derricks: 3x10t	**1 oil engine** driving 1 FP propeller Total Power: 1,618kW (2,200hp) 11.5kn Hanshin 6L46 1 x 4 Stroke 6 Cy. 460 x 680 1618kW (2200bhp) Hanshin Nainenki Kogyo-Japan AuxGen: 1 x 300kW 445V 60Hz a.c, 2 x 88kW 445V 60Hz a.c Fuel: 127.0 7.0pd
7727413 **STALLOVARRE** *LHBG* *ex* Solbakk *-2001* - **Bjorklids Ferjerederi AS** - *Tromso* *Norway* MMSI: 257374400	**944** 283 258	Class: (NV)	**1978**-07 **Moss Rosenberg Verft AS (Rosenberg Verft) — Stavanger** Yd No: 208 Loa 64.32 Br ex 11.46 Dght 3.101 Lbp 54.01 Br md 11.26 Dpth 4.22 Welded, 1 dk	**(A36A2PR) Passenger/Ro-Ro Ship (Vehicles)** Passengers: unberthed: 399 Bow door & ramp Stern door & ramp Cars: 50	**1 oil engine** geared to sc. shaft driving 1 CP propeller , 1 fwd Total Power: 956kW (1,300hp) 13.5kn Normo LDM-8 1 x 4 Stroke 8 Cy. 250 x 300 956kW (1300bhp) AS Bergens Mek Verksteder-Norway
9309485 **STALO** *C4GF2* - **Staloudi Shipping Corp** Safety Management Overseas SA *Limassol* *Cyprus* MMSI: 209317000 Official number: 9309485	**46,982** 26,950 87,036 T/cm 79.7	Class: LR ✠ **100A1** SS 01/2011 bulk carrier BC-A strengthened for heavy cargoes, Nos. 2, 4 & 6 holds may be empty ESP EP (B) **ShipRight** (SDA, FDA, CM) ESN *IWS LI ✠ **LMC** **UMS** Eq.Ltr: A†; Cable: 687.5/81.0 U3 (a)	**2006**-01 **IHI Marine United Inc — Yokohama KN** Yd No: 3208 Loa 229.00 (BB) Br ex 36.54 Dght 14.100 Lbp 219.90 Br md 36.50 Dpth 19.90 Welded, 1 dk	**(A21A2BC) Bulk Carrier** Double Hull Grain: 98,900 Compartments: 7 Ho, ER 7 Ha: ER	**1 oil engine** driving 1 FP propeller Total Power: 10,300kW (14,004hp) 14.5kn Sulzer 6RTA58T 1 x 2 Stroke 6 Cy. 580 x 2416 10300kW (14004bhp) Diesel United Ltd.-Aioi AuxGen: 3 x 600kW 450V 60Hz a.c Boilers: AuxB (Comp) 7.1kgf/cm² (7.0bar)
7507382 **STALWART** *WBN6512* - **Crowley Marine Services Inc** - *San Francisco, CA* *United States of America* MMSI: 366888850 Official number: 575052	**538** 161 -	Class: AB	**1976**-07 **McDermott Shipyards Inc — Morgan City LA** Yd No: 219 Loa 41.46 Br ex 11.13 Dght 5.182 Lbp 39.22 Br md 11.08 Dpth 5.85 Welded, 1 dk	**(B32A2ST) Tug**	**2 oil engines** reverse reduction geared to sc. shafts driving 2 FP propellers Total Power: 5,148kW (7,000hp) 14.0kn EMD (Electro-Motive) 20-645-E5 2 x Vee 2 Stroke 20 Cy. 230 x 254 each-2574kW (3500bhp) General Motors Corp.Electro-Motive Div.-La Grange AuxGen: 2 x 90kW
5337915 **STALWART** *VVBP* - **Kolkata Port Trust** - *Kolkata* *India*	*456* - -	Class: IR (LR) ✠ Classed LR until 12/63	**1949**-02 **John I Thornycroft & Co Ltd — Southampton** Yd No: 4117 Loa 38.87 Br ex 9.78 Dght 3.842 Lbp 35.84 Br md 9.76 Dpth 4.25 Riveted\Welded	**(B32A2ST) Tug** Winches: 1	**2 Steam Recips** driving 2 FP propellers 11.0kn John I Thornycroft & Co Ltd-United Kingdom AuxGen: 1 x 15kW 220V d.c Fuel: 123.0 (r.f.)
9287273 **STAMATIS** *C6TQ9* - **Riva Marine Investments SA** Samos Steamship Co SatCom: Inmarsat C 431174910 *Nassau* *Bahamas* MMSI: 311749000 Official number: 8000817	**102,112** 66,756 203,266 T/cm 138.0	Class: LR ✠ **100A1** SS 09/2004 bulk carrier strengthened for heavy cargoes, Nos. 2, 4, 6 & 8 holds may be empty ESP ESN LI **ShipRight** (SDA, FDA, CM) ✠ **LMC** **UMS** Eq.Ltr: Y†; Cable: 742.5/97.0 U3 (a)	**2004**-09 **Universal Shipbuilding Corp — Nagasu KM (Ariake Shipyard)** Yd No: 5009 Loa 299.95 (BB) Br ex 50.06 Dght 17.880 Lbp 291.17 Br md 50.00 Dpth 24.10 Welded, 1 dk	**(A21A2BC) Bulk Carrier** Grain: 217,968 Compartments: 9 Ho, ER 9 Ha: ER 7 (15.7 x 23.4)	**1 oil engine** driving 1 FP propeller Total Power: 16,860kW (22,923hp) 14.7kn B&W 6S70MC 1 x 2 Stroke 6 Cy. 700 x 2674 16860kW (22923bhp) Hitachi Zosen Corp-Japan AuxGen: 3 x 560kW 450V 60Hz a.c Boilers: AuxB (Comp) 7.0kgf/cm² (6.9bar) Fuel: 428.0 (d.f.) 5423.0 (r.f.)

5146249 *SV4488* -	**STAMATOULA KALLIOPI** *ex* Vasilios D *-1996* *ex* Petrola 38 *-1996* *ex* Alexis *-1977* *ex* Modus *-1974* *ex* Helen *-1970* **Metaxas D Naftiki Eteria** - *Piraeus* *Greece* MMSI: 237182600 Official number: 6514	*486* 213 880	Class: (NV)	**1962 Seutelvens Verksted — Fredrikstad** Yd No: 78 Loa 59.01 Br ex 8.64 Dght 3.683 Lbp 54.01 Br md 8.60 Dpth 3.92 Welded, 1 dk	**(A13B2TU) Tanker (unspecified)** Liq: 1,147; Liq (Oil): 1,147 Cargo Heating Coils Compartments: 8 Ta, ER Ice Capable	**1 oil engine** driving 1 CP propeller Total Power: 588kW (799hp) 10.5kn MWM 1 x 4 Stroke 6 Cy. 320 x 480 588kW (799bhp) Motoren Werke Mannheim AG (MWM)-West Germany AuxGen: 1 x 104kW 220V 50Hz a.c, 1 x 36kW 220V 50Hz a.c Fuel: 73.0 (d.f.) 5.0pd
8036055 *WDC5575* -	**STAMFORD** *ex* Thomas Tracy *-1971* **McAllister Towing & Transportation Co Inc (MT & T)** - *Dover, DE* *United States of America* MMSI: 367043190 Official number: 261833	*256* 7 -	Class: (GL) (AB)	**1951-05 Levingston SB. Co. — Orange, Tx** Yd No: 464 Loa - Br ex - Dght 3.747 Lbp 30.46 Br md 8.23 Dpth 4.27 Welded, 1 dk	**(B32A2ST) Tug**	**1 oil engine** sr reverse geared to sc. shaft driving 1 FP propeller Total Power: 2,115kW (2,876hp) EMD (Electro-Motive) 16-645-E5 1 x Vee 2 Stroke 16 Cy. 230 x 254 2115kW (2876bhp) General Motors Detroit DieselAllison Divn-USA AuxGen: 2 x 30kW d.c
9636943 *VRJD7* -	**STAMFORD PIONEER** **K/S Danskib 83** Atlas Shipping Ltd 773231838 *Hong Kong* *Hong Kong* MMSI: 477462800 Official number: HK-3219	**20,954** 11,781 32,211 T/cm 46.1	Class: NK (GL) (BV)	**2012-01 Taizhou Maple Leaf Shipbuilding Co Ltd — Linhai ZJ** Yd No: LBC31800-030 Loa 179.91 (BB) Br ex - Dght 10.150 Lbp 171.50 Br md 28.40 Dpth 14.10 Welded, 1 dk	**(A21A2BC) Bulk Carrier** Grain: 43,460; Bale: 41,420 Compartments: 5 Ho, ER 5 Ha: ER Cranes: 4x30t	**1 oil engine** driving 1 FP propeller Total Power: 6,480kW (8,810hp) 13.7kn MAN-B&W 6S42MC 1 x 2 Stroke 6 Cy. 420 x 1764 6480kW (8810bhp) STX Engine Co Ltd-South Korea AuxGen: 3 x a.c Fuel: 1570.0
9603958 *H9JI* -	**STAMINA SW** **Stamina Pescadores SA** Shih Wei Navigation Co Ltd *Panama* *Panama* MMSI: 373766000 Official number: 4416012	**17,902** 10,199 28,000	Class: BV CR (Class contemplated)	**2012-08 Kitanihon Zosen K.K. — Hachinohe** Yd No: 552 Loa 170.00 (BB) Br ex - Dght 9.850 Lbp 162.00 Br md 26.60 Dpth 14.00 Welded, 1 dk	**(A21A2BC) Bulk Carrier** Grain: 39,668 Compartments: 5 Ho, ER 5 Ha: ER Cranes: 4x30t	**1 oil engine** driving 1 FP propeller Total Power: 6,480kW (8,810hp) 14.5kn MAN-B&W 6S42MC 1 x 2 Stroke 6 Cy. 420 x 1764 6480kW (8810bhp) Makita Corp-Japan AuxGen: 3 x 450kW 60Hz a.c Fuel: 1870.0
9167095 *LJCC* N-11-VV	**STAMSUND** *ex* Nordtind *-2000* **Nordland Havfiske AS** Havfisk ASA SatCom: Inmarsat C 425948510 *Svolvaer* *Norway* MMSI: 259485000	**698** 236 532	Class: NV	**1998-06 Astilleros Gondan SA — Castropol** Yd No: 400 Loa 44.95 Br ex - Dght 5.447 Lbp 40.32 Br md 10.20 Dpth 6.65 Welded, 1 dk	**(B11A2FS) Stern Trawler** Bale: 432 Ice Capable	**1 oil engine** reduction geared to sc. shaft driving 1 CP propeller Total Power: 1,800kW (2,447hp) MaK 6M25 1 x 4 Stroke 6 Cy. 255 x 400 1800kW (2447bhp) MaK Motoren GmbH & Co. KG-Kiel AuxGen: 2 x 436kW 220/440V 60Hz a.c Fuel: 170.0 (d.f.)
7819187 *HP9465* -	**STAND KING** *ex* Stanford King *-2011* *ex* Al-Mojil XXVI *-1998* *ex* Gulf Commander *-1993* *ex* Jagrande *-1991* *ex* Hatteras Seahorse *-1987* **Green Ocean Shipping Co Ltd** Global Marine Ship Management & Operations LLC *Panama* *Panama* MMSI: 357115000 Official number: 2673200E	**808** 242 500	Class: BV (AB)	**1979 Halter Marine, Inc. — Moss Point, Ms** Yd No: 731 Loa 56.39 Br ex - Dght 3.658 Lbp 49.92 Br md 12.20 Dpth 4.27 Welded, 1 dk	**(B21A20S) Platform Supply Ship**	**2 oil engines** reverse reduction geared to sc. shafts driving 2 FP propellers Total Power: 3,162kW (4,300hp) 12.0kn EMD (Electro-Motive) 12-645-E7 2 x Vee 2 Stroke 12 Cy. 230 x 254 each-1581kW (2150bhp) General Motors Corp.Electro-Motive Div.-La Grange AuxGen: 2 x 99kW Thrusters: 1 Thwart. FP thruster (f) Fuel: 255.0
7726316 *HO2648* -	**STAND SUPPLIER** *ex* Stanford Supplier *-2011* *ex* Argos *-2001* *ex* Ted Martin *-1981* **Green Ocean Supplier Ltd** Global Marine Ship Management & Operations LLC *Panama* *Panama* MMSI: 352523000 Official number: 2872202B	**664** 199 974	Class: BV (AB)	**1977-04 Halter Marine, Inc. — Moss Point, Ms** Yd No: 585 Loa 54.87 Br ex - Dght 3.620 Lbp 50.45 Br md 11.59 Dpth 4.30 Welded, 1 dk	**(B21A20S) Platform Supply Ship**	**2 oil engines** geared to sc. shafts driving 2 FP propellers Total Power: 1,434kW (1,950hp) 12.0kn EMD (Electro-Motive) 8-645-E6 2 x Vee 2 Stroke 8 Cy. 230 x 254 each-717kW (975bhp) General Motors Corp.Electro-Motive Div.-La Grange AuxGen: 2 x 99kW 440/208V 60Hz a.c Thrusters: 1 Thwart. FP thruster (f)
7636896 *J8B4497* -	**STANE** *ex* Stanechakker *-2010* **Wavernie Ltd** Ship & Shore Services Ltd *Kingstown* *St Vincent & The Grenadines* MMSI: 375318000 Official number: 10970	**423** 126 185	Class: LR ✠ **100A1** CS 05/2008 tug ✠ **LMC** Eq.Ltr: J; Cable: 357.5/30.0 U2	**1978-06 Hall, Russell & Co. Ltd. — Aberdeen** Yd No: 976 Loa 37.98 Br ex 10.55 Dght 4.388 Lbp 32.95 Br md 10.01 Dpth 5.24 Welded, 1 dk	**(B32A2ST) Tug**	**2 oil engines** sr geared to sc. shafts driving 2 CP propellers Total Power: 2,794kW (3,798hp) 14.0kn Ruston 12RKCM 2 x Vee 4 Stroke 12 Cy. 254 x 305 each-1397kW (1899bhp) Ruston Diesels Ltd.-Newton-le-Willows AuxGen: 2 x 80kW 440V 50Hz a.c, 1 x 78kW 440V 50Hz a.c Thrusters: 1 Thwart. FP thruster (f)
7302158 *DUA2906* -	**STANFORD** *ex* Kachina *-2002* *ex* Take Maru No. 33 *-2001* *ex* Hayashio Maru *-1998* **Malayan Towage & Salvage Corp (SALVTUG)** - *Manila* *Philippines* Official number: 00-0001381	*197* 74 -	Class: (AB)	**1973-02 Kanagawa Zosen — Kobe** Yd No: 123 Loa 29.65 Br ex 8.64 Dght 2.598 Lbp 24.52 Br md 8.62 Dpth 3.81 Riveted\Welded, 1 dk	**(B32A2ST) Tug**	**2 oil engines** gearing integral to driving 2 Z propellers Total Power: 1,766kW (2,402hp) Niigata 6L25BX 2 x 4 Stroke 6 Cy. 250 x 320 each-883kW (1201bhp) Niigata Engineering Co Ltd-Japan
9489455 *9V7707* -	**STANFORD ALPHA** *ex* Jaya Alpha *-2010* *launched as* Saag Lyra *-2008* **Stanford Alpha Pte Ltd** Stanford Marine Asia Pte Ltd SatCom: Inmarsat C 456362010 *Singapore* *Singapore* MMSI: 563620000 Official number: 394658	**1,678** 503 1,338	Class: AB	**2008-09 Fujian Southeast Shipyard — Fuzhou FJ** (Hull) Yd No: H885 **2008-09 Jaya Shipbuilding & Engineering Pte Ltd — Singapore** Yd No: 885 Loa 59.25 Br ex - Dght 4.950 Lbp 52.20 Br md 14.95 Dpth 6.10 Welded, 1 dk	**(B21B20A) Anchor Handling Tug Supply**	**2 oil engines** reduction geared to sc. shafts driving 2 CP propellers Total Power: 3,840kW (5,220hp) 11.0kn Caterpillar 3516B-HD 2 x Vee 4 Stroke 16 Cy. 170 x 215 each-1920kW (2610bhp) Caterpillar Inc-USA AuxGen: 3 x 344kW 415V 50Hz a.c Thrusters: 1 Tunnel thruster (f) Fuel: 540.0 (d.f.)
9654177 *J8B4809* -	**STANFORD BATELEUR** **Stanford Bateleur Ltd** Stanford Marine Asia Pte Ltd *Kingstown* *St Vincent & The Grenadines* MMSI: 375822000 Official number: 11282	**3,601** 1,429 5,188	Class: AB	**2013-02 Fujian Mawei Shipbuilding Ltd — Fuzhou FJ** Yd No: 619-36 Loa 87.20 (BB) Br ex - Dght 5.900 Lbp 84.00 Br md 18.40 Dpth 8.00 Welded, 1 dk	**(B21A20S) Platform Supply Ship**	**4 diesel electric oil engines** driving 4 gen. Connecting to 2 elec. motors each (2000kW) driving 2 Azimuth electric drive units Total Power: 7,492kW (10,188hp) 12.0kn Cummins QSK60-M 4 x Vee 4 Stroke 16 Cy. 159 x 190 each-1873kW (2547bhp) Cummins Engine Co Inc-USA Thrusters: 1 Tunnel thruster (f); 1 Retract. directional thruster (f) Fuel: 970.0 (d.f.)
9480746 *J8B4156* -	**STANFORD BREAM** *ex* Waha I *-2013* *ex* Jason Pertama *-2009* **Waha 1 Ltd** Waha Marine Agency LLC SatCom: Inmarsat C 437700116 *Kingstown* *St Vincent & The Grenadines* MMSI: 376267000 Official number: 10629	**1,039** 311 679	Class: AB	**2009-07 Sealink Shipyard Sdn Bhd — Miri** Yd No: 133 Loa 48.00 Br ex - Dght 4.200 Lbp 42.40 Br md 13.20 Dpth 5.20 Welded, 1 dk	**(B21B20A) Anchor Handling Tug Supply**	**2 oil engines** reduction geared to sc. shafts driving 2 CP propellers Total Power: 3,788kW (5,150hp) Caterpillar 3516B-HD 2 x Vee 4 Stroke 16 Cy. 170 x 215 each-1894kW (2575bhp) Caterpillar Inc-USA AuxGen: 3 x 380kW a.c Thrusters: 1 Tunnel thruster (f)
9533634 *J8B4512* -	**STANFORD BUZZARD** **Stanford Buzzard Ltd** Stanford Marine Asia Pte Ltd *Kingstown* *St Vincent & The Grenadines* MMSI: 375587000 Official number: 10985	**3,601** 1,429 5,115	Class: AB	**2011-10 Fujian Mawei Shipbuilding Ltd — Fuzhou FJ** Yd No: 619-9 Loa 87.08 (BB) Br ex - Dght 6.040 Lbp 82.96 Br md 18.80 Dpth 7.40 Welded, 1 dk	**(B21A20S) Platform Supply Ship**	**4 diesel electric oil engines** driving 4 gen. each 1825kW Connecting to 2 elec. motors each (2000kW) driving 2 Azimuth electric drive units Total Power: 7,300kW (9,924hp) 12.0kn Cummins QSK60-M 4 x Vee 4 Stroke 16 Cy. 159 x 190 each-1825kW (2481bhp) Caterpillar Inc-USA Thrusters: 1 Tunnel thruster (f); 1 Retract. directional thruster (f) Fuel: 975.0 (d.f.)

IMO / Call sign / Flag	Name / Owner / Manager	Tonnage	Class	Built / Dimensions	Type	Machinery
9589865 *J8B4475* -	**STANFORD CARACARA** **Stanford Caracara Ltd** Stanford Marine Asia Pte Ltd *Kingstown* *St Vincent & The Grenadines* MMSI: 375762000 Official number: 10948	**1,393** 418 1,314	Class: AB	**2011**-05 **Fujian Mawei Shipbuilding Ltd — Fuzhou FJ** Yd No: 613-7 Loa 57.50 Br ex - Dght 4.500 Lbp 52.00 Br md 13.80 Dpth 5.50 Welded, 1 dk	**(B21A20S) Platform Supply Ship**	**2 oil engines** reduction geared to sc. shafts driving 2 Directional propellers Total Power: 2,940kW (3,998hp) 12.0kn Cummins QSK60-M 2 x Vee 4 Stroke 16 Cy. 159 x 190 each-1470kW (1999bhp) Cummins Engine Co Inc-USA AuxGen: 3 x 350kW a.c Thrusters: 1 Tunnel thruster (f)
9324241 *J8B4140* -	**STANFORD CHALLENGER** *ex* Jaya Supplier 1 *-2009* **Stanford Charter Inc** Stanford Marine LLC *Kingstown* *St Vincent & The Grenadines* MMSI: 377246000 Official number: 10613	**1,470** 441 1,475	Class: BV	**2004**-12 **Guangzhou Hangtong Shipbuilding & Shipping Co Ltd — Jiangmen GD** Yd No: 032002 Loa 58.70 Br ex - Dght 4.750 Lbp 53.20 Br md 14.60 Dpth 5.50 Welded, 1 dk	**(B21B20A) Anchor Handling Tug Supply**	**2 oil engines** geared to sc. shafts driving 2 CP propellers Total Power: 3,494kW (4,750hp) 13.5kn Caterpillar 3516B-HD 2 x Vee 4 Stroke 16 Cy. 170 x 215 each-1747kW (2375bhp) Caterpillar Inc-USA AuxGen: 3 x 320kW 415/220V 50Hz a.c Thrusters: 1 Tunnel thruster (f) Fuel: 470.0 (d.f.)
9589841 *J8B4375* -	**STANFORD CONDOR** **Stanford Condor Ltd** Stanford Marine LLC SatCom: Inmarsat C 437700164 *Kingstown* *St Vincent & The Grenadines* MMSI: 377042000 Official number: 10848	**1,393** 418 1,302	Class: AB	**2010**-12 **Fujian Mawei Shipbuilding Ltd — Fuzhou FJ** Yd No: 613-5 Loa 57.49 Br ex - Dght 5.100 Lbp 51.98 Br md 13.80 Dpth 5.50 Welded, 1 dk	**(B21A20S) Platform Supply Ship**	**2 oil engines** reduction geared to sc. shafts driving 2 Directional propellers Total Power: 2,984kW (4,058hp) 12.0kn Cummins QSK60-M 2 x Vee 4 Stroke 16 Cy. 159 x 190 each-1492kW (2029bhp) Cummins Engine Co Inc-USA AuxGen: 3 x 350kW 415V 50Hz a.c Thrusters: 1 Tunnel thruster (f) Fuel: 450.0 (d.f.)
9537654 *J8B3987* -	**STANFORD DOVE** **Stanford Charter Inc** Stanford Marine LLC *Kingstown* *St Vincent & The Grenadines* MMSI: 377541000 Official number: 10460	**246** 73 140	Class: AB	**2009**-03 **Grandweld — Dubai** Yd No: H042/07 Loa 41.00 Br ex 7.40 Dght 1.750 Lbp 37.30 Br md 7.30 Dpth 3.50 Welded, 1 dk	**(B21A20C) Crew/Supply Vessel** Hull Material: Aluminium Alloy Passengers: unberthed: 60	**3 oil engines** reduction geared to sc. shafts driving 3 FP propellers Total Power: 3,135kW (4,263hp) 20.0kn Caterpillar C32 3 x Vee 4 Stroke 12 Cy. 145 x 162 each-1045kW (1421bhp) Caterpillar Inc-USA AuxGen: 2 x 84kW 380V 50Hz a.c Thrusters: 1 Tunnel thruster (f)
9225304 *J8B4102* -	**STANFORD ENERGY** *ex* Britoil 44 *-2009* **Stanford Charter Inc** Stanford Marine LLC *Kingstown* *St Vincent & The Grenadines* MMSI: 377511000 Official number: 10575	**466** 140 362	Class: AB	**2000**-04 **Jiangsu Wuxi Shipyard Co Ltd — Wuxi JS** Yd No: H8030 Loa 37.00 Br ex - Dght 4.292 Lbp 34.69 Br md 11.40 Dpth 4.95 Welded, 1 dk	**(B21B20A) Anchor Handling Tug Supply**	**2 oil engines** with clutches, flexible couplings & sr reverse geared to sc. shafts driving 2 FP propellers Total Power: 2,318kW (3,152hp) 10.0kn Caterpillar 3512B-TA 2 x Vee 4 Stroke 12 Cy. 170 x 190 each-1159kW (1576bhp) Caterpillar Inc-USA AuxGen: 3 x 300kW 380V 50Hz a.c Thrusters: 1 Thwart. FP thruster (f) Fuel: 200.0 (d.f.) 8.0pd
9065209 *H03485* -	**STANFORD FALCON** *ex* Atco Reem *-2001* **Stanford Marine Inc** Stanford Marine LLC *Panama* *Panama* MMSI: 353821000 Official number: 2990704B	**253** 75 350	Class: AB	**1992**-07 **Neuville Boat Works, Inc. — New Iberia, La** Yd No: 135-2 Loa 41.15 Br ex - Dght 1.980 Lbp 37.58 Br md 7.92 Dpth 3.96 Welded	**(B21A20C) Crew/Supply Vessel** Hull Material: Aluminium Alloy Passengers: unberthed: 25	**3 oil engines** reduction geared to sc. shafts driving 3 FP propellers Total Power: 3,086kW (4,196hp) 12.0kn G.M. (Detroit Diesel) 12V-71 1 x Vee 2 Stroke 12 Cy. 108 x 127 438kW (596bhp) General Motors Detroit DieselAllison Divn-USA G.M. (Detroit Diesel) 16V-92 2 x Vee 2 Stroke 16 Cy. 123 x 127 each-1324kW (1800bhp) General Motors Detroit DieselAllison Divn-USA AuxGen: 2 x 40kW a.c Thrusters: 1 Tunnel thruster (f)
9205445 *J8B4260* -	**STANFORD GOLD** *ex* Jaya Gold *-2009* **Stanford Gold Ltd** Stanford Marine LLC SatCom: Inmarsat C 437717510 *Kingstown* *St Vincent & The Grenadines* MMSI: 377175000 Official number: 10733	**1,094** 328 1,450	Class: AB	**2000**-08 **Myanma Shipyards — Yangon** Yd No: Y-391 Loa 56.80 Br ex - Dght 4.513 Lbp 50.60 Br md 13.60 Dpth 5.20 Welded, 1 dk	**(B21A20S) Platform Supply Ship**	**2 oil engines** reduction geared to sc. shafts driving 2 FP propellers Total Power: 2,236kW (3,040hp) 12.0kn Caterpillar 3512B 2 x Vee 4 Stroke 12 Cy. 170 x 190 each-1118kW (1520bhp) Caterpillar Inc-USA AuxGen: 3 x 300kW 415V 50Hz a.c Thrusters: 1 Tunnel thruster (f)
9589877 *J8B4476* -	**STANFORD GOSHAWK** **Stanford Goshawk Ltd** Stanford Marine LLC *Kingstown* *St Vincent & The Grenadines* MMSI: 377282000 Official number: 10949	**1,399** 419 1,289	Class: AB	**2011**-08 **Fujian Mawei Shipbuilding Ltd — Fuzhou FJ** Yd No: 613-8 Loa 57.50 Br ex - Dght 5.100 Lbp 52.00 Br md 13.80 Dpth 5.50 Welded, 1 dk	**(B21A20S) Platform Supply Ship** Cranes: 1	**2 oil engines** reduction geared to sc. shafts driving 2 Directional propellers Total Power: 2,940kW (3,998hp) 12.0kn Cummins QSK60-M 2 x Vee 4 Stroke 16 Cy. 159 x 190 each-1470kW (1999bhp) Cummins Engine Co Inc-USA AuxGen: 3 x 350kW 415V 50Hz a.c Thrusters: 1 Tunnel thruster (f) Fuel: 450.0 (d.f.)
8972156 *H03125* -	**STANFORD HARRIER** *ex* Miss Mary-Ann *-2003* **Stanford Marine Inc** Stanford Marine LLC *Panama* *Panama* MMSI: 351239000 Official number: 2985004B	**211** 63 105	Class: AB	**1991**-04 **Breaux Brothers Enterprises, Inc. — Loreauville, La** Yd No: 175 Loa 38.10 Br ex - Dght 2.220 Lbp 35.72 Br md 7.92 Dpth 3.59 Welded, 1 dk	**(B21A20C) Crew/Supply Vessel** Hull Material: Aluminium Alloy Passengers: unberthed: 60	**4 oil engines** reverse reduction geared to sc. shafts driving 4 FP propellers Total Power: 2,024kW (2,752hp) 18.0kn G.M. (Detroit Diesel) 12V-92-TA 4 x Vee 2 Stroke 12 Cy. 123 x 127 each-506kW (688bhp) General Motors Detroit DieselAllison Divn-USA AuxGen: 2 x 40kW 208V 60Hz a.c
9658159 *J8B4933* -	**STANFORD HAWK** **Stanford Hawk Ltd** Stanford Marine LLC *Kingstown* *St Vincent & The Grenadines* MMSI: 376955000 Official number: 11406	**3,120** 936 3,693	Class: AB	**2013**-11 **Fujian Mawei Shipbuilding Ltd — Fuzhou FJ** Yd No: 629-2 Loa 75.00 (BB) Br ex - Dght 6.400 Lbp 66.87 Br md 17.20 Dpth 7.80 Welded, 1 dk	**(B21A20S) Platform Supply Ship** Cranes: 1x5t	**4 diesel electric oil engines** driving 4 gen. each 1800kW a.c Connecting to 2 elec. motors each (2000kW) driving 2 Azimuth electric drive units Total Power: 7,200kW (9,788hp) 14.0kn Cummins 2 x each-1800kW (2447bhp) Cummins Engine Co Inc-USA Cummins 2 x 4 Stroke each-1800kW (2447bhp) Cummins Engine Co Inc-USA Thrusters: 2 Tunnel thruster (f) Fuel: 1260.0
9589889 *J8B4477* -	**STANFORD HUDHUD** **Stanford Hudhud Ltd** Stanford Marine Asia Pte Ltd SatCom: Inmarsat C 437565610 *Kingstown* *St Vincent & The Grenadines* MMSI: 375656000 Official number: 10950	**1,399** 419 1,309	Class: AB	**2011**-08 **Fujian Mawei Shipbuilding Ltd — Fuzhou FJ** Yd No: 613-9 Loa 57.50 Br ex - Dght 5.100 Lbp 52.00 Br md 13.80 Dpth 5.50 Welded, 1 dk	**(B21A20S) Platform Supply Ship**	**2 oil engines** reduction geared to sc. shafts driving 2 Z propellers Total Power: 2,940kW (3,998hp) Cummins QSK60-M 2 x Vee 4 Stroke 16 Cy. 159 x 190 each-1470kW (1999bhp) Cummins Engine Co Inc-USA AuxGen: 3 x 350kW 415V 50Hz a.c Thrusters: 1 Tunnel thruster (f) Fuel: 450.0 (d.f.)
9631515 *J8B4826* -	**STANFORD HUNTER** **Stanford Hunter Ltd** Stanford Marine LLC *Kingstown* *St Vincent & The Grenadines* MMSI: 375857000 Official number: 11299	**1,404** 421 1,122	Class: BV	**2013**-05 **Grandweld — Dubai** Yd No: H087/11 Loa 57.00 Br ex 14.20 Dght 4.500 Lbp 55.00 Br md 13.60 Dpth 6.00 Welded, 1 dk	**(B34T2QR) Work/Repair Vessel** Cranes: 1x18t	**2 oil engines** reduction geared to sc. shafts driving 2 FP propellers Total Power: 2,794kW (3,798hp) 12.5kn Caterpillar 3512C 2 x Vee 4 Stroke 12 Cy. 170 x 215 each-1397kW (1899bhp) Caterpillar Inc-USA AuxGen: 2 x 242kW 440V 60Hz a.c Thrusters: 1 Tunnel thruster (f)

9590151 *J8B4316* -	**STANFORD KITE** **Stanford Kite Ltd** Stanford Marine LLC SatCom: Inmarsat C 437755810 *Kingstown* *St Vincent & The Grenadines* MMSI: 375588000 Official number: 10789	**1,393** 418 1,292	Class: AB	**2010-11 Fujian Mawei Shipbuilding Ltd — Fuzhou FJ** Yd No: 613-4 Loa 57.49 Br ex - Dght 5.100 Lbp 51.99 Br md 13.80 Dpth 5.50 Welded, 1 dk	**(B21A2OS) Platform Supply Ship**	**2 oil engines** reduction geared to sc. shafts driving 2 Directional propellers Total Power: 2,984kW (4,058hp) 12.0kn Cummins QSK60-M 2 x Vee 4 Stroke 16 Cy. 159 x 190 each-1492kW (2029bhp) Cummins Engine Co Inc-USA AuxGen: 3 x 350kW 415V 50Hz a.c Thrusters: 1 Tunnel thruster (f) Fuel: 450.0 (d.f.)
9263473 *9V6146* -	**STANFORD MARINER 2** *ex* Jaya Mariner 2 *-2011* **Stanford Mariner 2 Pte Ltd** Stanford Marine Asia Pte Ltd *Singapore* *Singapore* MMSI: 564463000 Official number: 389576	**1,491** 447 1,353	Class: AB	**2002-03 Jaya Shipbuilding & Engineering Pte Ltd — Singapore** Yd No: 827 Loa 56.00 Br ex - Dght 4.800 Lbp 52.60 Br md 14.95 Dpth 5.80 Welded, 1 dk	**(B21B20A) Anchor Handling Tug Supply** Cranes: 1x5.9t	**2 oil engines** reduction geared to sc. shafts driving 2 CP propellers Total Power: 2,750kW (3,738hp) 11.0kn Wartsila 8L20 2 x 4 Stroke 8 Cy. 200 x 280 each-1375kW (1869bhp) Wartsila Nederland BV-Netherlands AuxGen: 3 x 315kW 415V 50Hz a.c Thrusters: 1 Thwart. CP thruster (f) Fuel: 680.0 (d.f.)
9613733 *J8B4598* -	**STANFORD MAYA** *ex* Global Queen *-2012* **Stanford Shipmanagement Inc** Stanford Marine LLC *Kingstown* *St Vincent & The Grenadines* MMSI: 377693000 Official number: 11071	**243** 72 137	Class: AB (LR) ✠ Classed LR until 29/2/12	**2011-11 Grandweld — Dubai** Yd No: H076/10 Loa 41.00 Br ex 7.40 Dght 1.750 Lbp 38.51 Br md 7.30 Dpth 3.48 Welded, 1 dk	**(B34J2SD) Crew Boat** Hull Material: Aluminium Alloy Passengers: unberthed: 85	**3 oil engines** with clutches, flexible couplings & sr reverse geared to sc. shafts driving 3 FP propellers Total Power: 3,246kW (4,413hp) 20.5kn Caterpillar C32 3 x Vee 4 Stroke 12 Cy. 145 x 162 each-1082kW (1471bhp) Caterpillar Inc-USA AuxGen: 2 x 86kW 380V 50Hz a.c Thrusters: 1 Thwart. FP thruster (f) Fuel: 60.0
9425033 *J8B4259* -	**STANFORD MERMAID** *ex* Jaya Mermaid 5 *-2009* *ex* Shanghai Huali 022 *-2008* **Stanford Mermaid Ltd** Stanford Marine Asia Pte Ltd *Kingstown* *St Vincent & The Grenadines* MMSI: 377012000 Official number: 10732	**1,106** 332 860	Class: BV	**2008-01 Shanghai Huali Marine Engineering Co Ltd — Shanghai** Yd No: 022 Loa 49.00 Br ex - Dght 4.500 Lbp 47.50 Br md 13.20 Dpth 5.30 Welded, 1 dk	**(B21B20A) Anchor Handling Tug Supply**	**2 oil engines** reduction geared to sc. shafts driving 2 CP propellers Total Power: 3,788kW (5,150hp) 10.0kn Caterpillar 3516B-TA 2 x Vee 4 Stroke 16 Cy. 170 x 190 each-1894kW (2575bhp) Caterpillar Inc-USA AuxGen: 3 x 340kW 415V 50Hz a.c Thrusters: 1 Tunnel thruster (f)
9537678 *J8B4073* -	**STANFORD NILE** **Stanford Shipmanagement Inc** Stanford Marine LLC *Kingstown* *St Vincent & The Grenadines* MMSI: 376512000 Official number: 10546	**246** 73 140	Class: AB	**2009-04 Grandweld — Dubai** Yd No: H044/07 Loa 41.00 Br ex 7.40 Dght 1.750 Lbp 37.30 Br md 7.30 Dpth 3.50 Welded, 1 dk	**(B21A2OC) Crew/Supply Vessel** Hull Material: Aluminium Alloy Passengers: unberthed: 60	**3 oil engines** reduction geared to sc. shafts driving 3 FP propellers Total Power: 2,460kW (3,345hp) 20.0kn Caterpillar C32 3 x Vee 4 Stroke 12 Cy. 145 x 162 each-820kW (1115bhp) Caterpillar Inc-USA AuxGen: 2 x 86kW 380V 50Hz a.c Thrusters: 1 Tunnel thruster (f) Fuel: 60.0 (d.f.)
9589853 *J8B4373* -	**STANFORD OSPREY** **Stanford Osprey Ltd** Stanford Marine LLC SatCom: Inmarsat C 437762810 *Kingstown* *St Vincent & The Grenadines* MMSI: 377628000 Official number: 10846	**1,393** 418 1,291	Class: AB	**2010-12 Fujian Mawei Shipbuilding Ltd — Fuzhou FJ** Yd No: 613-6 Loa 57.50 Br ex - Dght 5.100 Lbp 52.00 Br md 13.80 Dpth 5.50 Welded, 1 dk	**(B21A2OS) Platform Supply Ship**	**2 oil engines** reduction geared to sc. shafts driving 2 Directional propellers Total Power: 2,984kW (4,058hp) 12.0kn Cummins QSK60-M 2 x Vee 4 Stroke 16 Cy. 159 x 190 each-1492kW (2029bhp) Cummins Engine Co Inc-USA AuxGen: 3 x 350kW 415V 50Hz a.c Thrusters: 1 Tunnel thruster (f)
8964202 *H03372* -	**STANFORD PELICAN** *ex* Miss Janice *-2003* **Stanford Marine Inc** Stanford Marine LLC *Panama* *Panama* MMSI: 352973000 Official number: 3016804B	**211** 63 105	Class: AB	**1991-02 Breaux Brothers Enterprises, Inc. — Loreauville, La** Yd No: 170 Loa 38.10 Br ex - Dght 2.220 Lbp 35.72 Br md 7.92 Dpth 3.59 Welded, 1 dk	**(B21A2OC) Crew/Supply Vessel** Hull Material: Aluminium Alloy Passengers: unberthed: 60	**4 oil engines** reduction geared to sc. shafts driving 4 FP propellers Total Power: 1,492kW (2,028hp) 18.0kn G.M. (Detroit Diesel) 12V-71 4 x Vee 2 Stroke 12 Cy. 108 x 127 each-373kW (507bhp) Detroit Diesel Corporation-Detroit, Mi AuxGen: 2 x 40kW 208V 60Hz a.c
8519605 *J8B3697* -	**STANFORD PRIDE** *ex* Vikingbank *-2004* **Stanford Marine Inc** Stanford Marine LLC *Kingstown* *St Vincent & The Grenadines* MMSI: 376575000 Official number: 10170	**600** 180 150	Class: AB	**1987-07 Scheepswerf "De Waal" B.V. — Zaltbommel** Yd No: 723 Loa 37.44 Br ex - Dght 4.763 Lbp 30.61 Br md 11.02 Dpth 5.52 Welded, 1 dk	**(B32A2ST) Tug**	**2 oil engines** sr geared to sc. shafts driving 2 Directional propellers Total Power: 3,846kW (5,230hp) 10.0kn Wartsila 12V22 2 x Vee 4 Stroke 12 Cy. 220 x 240 each-1923kW (2615bhp) Wartsila Diesel Oy-Finland AuxGen: 1 x 500kW a.c, 2 x 125kW a.c Thrusters: 1 Tunnel thruster (f) Fuel: 375.0 (d.f.)
9517989 *J8B4135* -	**STANFORD PROVIDER** *ex* A-One *-2010* **Stanford Charter Inc** Stanford Marine LLC *Kingstown* *St Vincent & The Grenadines* MMSI: 377439000 Official number: 10608	**497** 149 575	Class: AB (IR)	**2008-03 Aquarius Yard Pvt Ltd — Goa** Yd No: AQM106 Loa 48.00 Br ex - Dght 2.800 Lbp 46.20 Br md 11.00 Dpth 3.50 Welded, 1 dk	**(B34L2QU) Utility Vessel**	**2 oil engines** with clutches & sr reverse geared to sc. shafts driving 2 FP propellers Total Power: 2,238kW (3,042hp) 12.0kn Cummins KTA-38-M2 2 x Vee 4 Stroke 12 Cy. 159 x 159 each-1119kW (1521bhp) Cummins India Ltd-India AuxGen: 2 x 144kW 450V 50Hz a.c Thrusters: 1 Thwart. FP thruster (f)
9537666 *J8B3986* -	**STANFORD PUMA** **Stanford Shipmanagement Inc** Stanford Marine LLC *Kingstown* *St Vincent & The Grenadines* MMSI: 376668000 Official number: 10459	**246** 73 140	Class: AB	**2009-01 Grandweld — Dubai** Yd No: H043/07 Loa 41.00 Br ex 7.40 Dght 1.750 Lbp 37.30 Br md 7.30 Dpth 3.50 Welded, 1 dk	**(B21A2OC) Crew/Supply Vessel** Hull Material: Aluminium Alloy Passengers: unberthed: 60	**3 oil engines** reduction geared to sc. shafts driving 3 FP propellers Total Power: 2,979kW (4,050hp) 20.0kn Caterpillar C32 3 x Vee 4 Stroke 12 Cy. 145 x 162 each-993kW (1350bhp) Caterpillar Inc-USA AuxGen: 2 x 84kW 380V 50Hz a.c Thrusters: 1 Tunnel thruster (f)
9549683 *J8B4075* -	**STANFORD RHINE** **Stanford Shipmanagement Inc** Stanford Marine LLC *Kingstown* *St Vincent & The Grenadines* MMSI: 377126000 Official number: 10548	**240** 72 121	Class: AB	**2009-09 Grandweld — Dubai** Yd No: H046/07 Loa 41.00 Br ex 7.40 Dght 1.750 Lbp 38.52 Br md 7.30 Dpth 3.50 Welded, 1 dk	**(B21A2OC) Crew/Supply Vessel** Hull Material: Aluminium Alloy Passengers: unberthed: 60	**3 oil engines** reduction geared to sc. shafts driving 3 FP propellers Total Power: 2,460kW (3,345hp) 20.0kn Caterpillar C32 3 x Vee 4 Stroke 12 Cy. 145 x 162 each-820kW (1115bhp) Caterpillar Inc-USA AuxGen: 2 x 86kW 380V 50Hz a.c Thrusters: 1 Tunnel thruster (f)
9492983 *J8B4157* -	**STANFORD SEAL** *ex* Waha II *-2013* *ex* Highline Brenda *-2009* **Waha II Ltd** Stanford Marine LLC SatCom: Inmarsat C 437748410 *Kingstown* *St Vincent & The Grenadines* MMSI: 377484000 Official number: 10630	**497** 149 100	Class: BV	**2009-07 Rajang Maju Shipbuilding Sdn Bhd — Sibu** Yd No: 67 Loa 38.00 Br ex - Dght 3.800 Lbp 34.40 Br md 11.80 Dpth 4.80 Welded, 1 dk	**(B32A2ST) Tug**	**2 oil engines** reduction geared to sc. shafts driving 2 FP propellers Total Power: 3,676kW (4,998hp) Niigata 6MG28HX 2 x 4 Stroke 6 Cy. 280 x 370 each-1838kW (2499bhp) Niigata Engineering Co Ltd-Japan AuxGen: 3 x 113kW 50Hz a.c Thrusters: 1 Tunnel thruster (f)
8121850 *J8B4879* -	**STANFORD SERVICE** *ex* Atco Donya *-2005* **Stanford Marine LLC** - *Kingstown* *St Vincent & The Grenadines* MMSI: 376945000	**186** 55 250	Class: AB	**1991-10 Swiftships Inc — Morgan City LA** Yd No: 289 Loa - Br ex - Dght 2.950 Lbp 29.95 Br md 7.92 Dpth 3.35 Welded, 1 dk	**(B21A2OS) Platform Supply Ship**	**2 oil engines** reduction geared to sc. shafts driving 2 FP propellers Total Power: 992kW (1,348hp) G.M. (Detroit Diesel) 16V-92 2 x Vee 2 Stroke 16 Cy. 123 x 127 each-496kW (674bhp) General Motors Detroit DieselAllison Divn-USA Thrusters: 1 Tunnel thruster (f)

9480318 *J8B3829* -	**STANFORD SWAN** **Stanford Charter Inc** Stanford Marine LLC *Kingstown* *St Vincent & The Grenadines* MMSI: 376754000 Official number: 10302	**244** 73 100	Class: AB	**2008-02 Grandweld — Dubai** Yd No: H026/06 Loa 41.00 Br ex - Dght 1.750 Lbp 37.30 Br md 7.30 Dpth 3.50 Welded, 1 dk	**(B21A20C) Crew/Supply Vessel** Hull Material: Aluminium Alloy Passengers: unberthed: 60	**3 oil engines** reduction geared to sc. shafts driving 3 FP propellers Total Power: 3,021kW (4,107hp) 20.0kn Cummins KTA-38-M2 3 x Vee 4 Stroke 12 Cy. 159 x 159 each-1007kW (1369bhp) Cummins Engine Co Inc-USA AuxGen: 2 x 86kW a.c Thrusters: 1 Tunnel thruster (f) Fuel: 53.0 (d.f.)
9331787 *J8B3698* -	**STANFORD SWIFT** **Stanford Marine Inc** Stanford Marine LLC *Kingstown* *St Vincent & The Grenadines* MMSI: 376698000 Official number: 10171	**161** 48 77	Class: AB (BV)	**2004-12 Grandweld — Dubai** Yd No: H005/03 Loa 34.43 Br ex - Dght 1.450 Lbp 30.50 Br md 7.42 Dpth 3.00 Welded, 1 dk	**(B34J2SD) Crew Boat** Hull Material: Aluminium Alloy Passengers: unberthed: 60	**3 oil engines** reverse reduction geared to sc. shafts driving 3 FP propellers Total Power: 1,545kW (2,100hp) 16.0kn Cummins KTA-19-M4 3 x 4 Stroke 6 Cy. 159 x 159 each-515kW (700bhp) Cummins Engine Co Inc-USA AuxGen: 2 x 84kW 380V 50Hz a.c
9549695 *J8B4076* -	**STANFORD TIGRIS** **Stanford Charter Inc** Stanford Marine LLC *Kingstown* *St Vincent & The Grenadines* MMSI: 377378000 Official number: 10549	**240** 72 136	Class: AB	**2009-07 Grandweld — Dubai** Yd No: H047/07 Loa 41.00 Br ex 7.40 Dght 1.750 Lbp 37.30 Br md 7.30 Dpth 3.50 Welded, 1 dk	**(B21A20C) Crew/Supply Vessel** Hull Material: Aluminium Alloy Passengers: unberthed: 60	**3 oil engines** reduction geared to sc. shafts driving 3 FP propellers Total Power: 2,460kW (3,345hp) 20.0kn Caterpillar C32 3 x Vee 4 Stroke 12 Cy. 145 x 162 each-820kW (1115bhp) Caterpillar Inc-USA AuxGen: 2 x 86kW a.c Thrusters: 1 Tunnel thruster (f) Fuel: 50.0
9549671 *J8B4074* -	**STANFORD TYNE** **Stanford Charter Inc** Stanford Marine LLC *Kingstown* *St Vincent & The Grenadines* MMSI: 377206000 Official number: 10547	**240** 72 135	Class: AB	**2009-06 Grandweld — Dubai** Yd No: H045/07 Loa 41.00 Br ex 7.40 Dght 1.750 Lbp 37.30 Br md 7.30 Dpth 3.50 Welded, 1 dk	**(B21A20C) Crew/Supply Vessel** Hull Material: Aluminium Alloy Passengers: unberthed: 52	**3 oil engines** reduction geared to sc. shafts driving 3 FP propellers Total Power: 2,460kW (3,345hp) Caterpillar C32 3 x Vee 4 Stroke 12 Cy. 145 x 162 each-820kW (1115bhp) Caterpillar Inc-USA AuxGen: 2 x 84kW 380V 50Hz a.c Thrusters: 1 Tunnel thruster (f)
8219463 *5BYM2* -	**STANISLAV YUDIN** **SHL Stanislav Yudin Ltd** Seaway Heavy Lifting Contracting Ltd *Limassol* *Cyprus* MMSI: 210334000	**24,822** 7,447 5,600	Class: NV RS	**1985-08 Oy Wartsila Ab — Turku** Yd No: 1284 Loa 183.20 Br ex 40.00 Dght 8.910 Lbp 174.60 Br md 36.40 Dpth 13.40 Welded, 2 dks	**(B34B2SC) Crane Vessel** Cranes: 1x2500t	**3 diesel electric oil engines** driving 3 gen. each 3888kW 660V a.c Connecting to 3 elec. motors each (1400kW) driving 2 Directional propellers Total Power: 12,285kW (16,704hp) 11.5kn Wartsila 12V32 3 x Vee 4 Stroke 12 Cy. 320 x 350 each-4095kW (5568bhp) Oy Wartsila Ab-Finland AuxGen: 2 x 552kW 380V a.c Thrusters: 2 Tunnel thruster (f) Fuel: 1100.0 (r.f.)
8970122 *WDA4819* -	**STANLEY BOY** *ex* Miss Cathy *-2009* *ex* Miss Jade *-2007* **Gina Dung Mai** - *Abbeville, LA* *United States of America* Official number: 1109262	**162** 48 -		**2001 Master Boat Builders, Inc. — Coden, Al** L reg 25.96 Br ex - Dght - Lbp - Br md 7.62 Dpth 3.81 Welded, 1 dk	**(B11B2FV) Fishing Vessel**	**1 oil engine** driving 1 FP propeller
9363845 *2AOT5* -	**STANLEY PARK** **Bayzon Shipping Inc** Zodiac Maritime Agencies Ltd *London* *United Kingdom* MMSI: 235061675 Official number: 914212	**11,590** 6,119 19,994 T/cm 28.8	Class: NK	**2008-03 Usuki Shipyard Co Ltd — Usuki OT** Yd No: 1710 Loa 145.50 (BB) Br ex 23.73 Dght 9.715 Lbp 137.00 Br md 23.70 Dpth 13.35 Welded, 1 dk	**(A12B2TR) Chemical/Products Tanker** Double Hull (13F) Grain: 22,631; Liq: 22,175; Liq (Oil): 22,175 Cargo Heating Coils Compartments: 22 Wing Ta, ER 22 Cargo Pump (s): 16x310m³/hr, 6x200m³/hr Manifold: Bow/CM: 74.3m	**1 oil engine** driving 1 FP propeller Total Power: 6,150kW (8,362hp) 14.6kn MAN-B&W 6S42MC 1 x 2 Stroke 6 Cy. 420 x 1764 6150kW (8362bhp) Kawasaki Heavy Industries Ltd-Japan AuxGen: 3 x 400kW 450V 60Hz a.c Thrusters: 1 Tunnel thruster (f) Fuel: 95.0 (d.f.) 975.0 (r.f.)
7827201 *WDB7882* -	**STANNARD TIDE** *ex* Whirlaway *-2003* *ex* H. O. S. Whirlaway *-1996* *ex* Luke Victor *-1994* **Point Marine LLC** Tidewater Marine International Inc *Wilmington, DE* *United States of America* MMSI: 369242000 Official number: 613673	**997** 299 1,200	Class: (AB)	**1979-10 Halter Marine, Inc. — Lockport, La** Yd No: 814 Loa 56.11 Br ex - Dght 4.179 Lbp 56.09 Br md 12.20 Dpth 4.70 Welded, 1 dk	**(B21A20S) Platform Supply Ship**	**2 oil engines** reverse reduction geared to sc. shafts driving 2 FP propellers Total Power: 2,868kW (3,900hp) 12.0kn EMD (Electro-Motive) 16-645-E6 2 x Vee 2 Stroke 16 Cy. 230 x 254 each-1434kW (1950bhp) (Re-engined ,made 1972, Reconditioned & fitted 1979) General Motors Corp.Electro-Motive Div.-La Grange AuxGen: 2 x 99kW Thrusters: 1 Thwart. FP thruster (f)
7393743 *TFBF* SU 120	**STAPAEY** *ex* Haraldur Bodvarsson *-2006* *ex* Batsfjord *-1976* **HB Grandi hf** - *Djupivogur* *Iceland* MMSI: 251051110 Official number: 1435	**562** 169 319	Class: (NV)	**1975-04 AS Storviks Mek. Verksted — Kristiansund** Yd No: 67 Loa 46.49 Br ex 9.02 Dght 4.534 Lbp 39.86 Br md 9.00 Dpth 4.97 Welded, 2 dks	**(B11A2FS) Stern Trawler** Ins: 1,200 Compartments: 1 Ho, ER 1 Ha: (2.5 x 1.9)ER Derricks: 1x1.5t; Winches: 1 Ice Capable	**1 oil engine** driving 1 CP propeller Total Power: 1,103kW (1,500hp) 13.0kn MaK 8M452AK 1 x 4 Stroke 8 Cy. 320 x 450 1103kW (1500bhp) MaK Maschinenbau GmbH-Kiel AuxGen: 2 x 83kW 220V 50Hz a.c Fuel: 122.0 (d.f.) 6.0pd
9375783 *V2BU8* -	**STAPELMOOR** **ms 'Stapelmoor' Reederei Bojen GmbH & Co KG** Kapitan Siegfried Bojen- Schiffahrtsbetrieb eK *Saint John's* *Antigua & Barbuda* MMSI: 304932000 Official number: 4130	**2,164** 839 2,930	Class: GL	**2006-06 Slovenske Lodenice a.s. — Komarno** Yd No: 2103 Loa 88.53 Br ex - Dght 4.350 Lbp 84.60 Br md 12.40 Dpth 5.70 Welded, 1 dk	**(A31A2GX) General Cargo Ship** Double Bottom Entire Compartment Length Grain: 4,170 TEU 108 C Ho 72 TEU C Dk 36 TEU. Ice Capable	**1 oil engine** reverse reduction geared to sc. shaft driving 1 FP propeller Total Power: 1,125kW (1,530hp) 10.5kn Wartsila 6L20 1 x 4 Stroke 6 Cy. 200 x 280 1125kW (1530bhp) Wartsila Finland Oy-Finland AuxGen: 1 x 170kW 400V a.c, 1 x 96kW 400V a.c, 1 x 92kW 400V a.c Thrusters: 1 Tunnel thruster (f)
7504201 *XPYI* FD 750	**STAPIN** *ex* Eystnes *-2010* *ex* Husoy *-2004* *ex* Knausen *-1989* **P/F Regn** - *Strendur* *Faeroe Islands (Danish)* MMSI: 231343000 Official number: DF4008	**436** 130 -	Class: NV	**1975-12 Th Hellesoy Skipsbyggeri AS — Lofallstrand** Yd No: 93 Lengthened-1982 Loa 37.09 (BB) Br ex 7.33 Dght - Lbp 28.50 Br md 7.29 Dpth 3.87 Welded, 1 dk	**(B11B2FV) Fishing Vessel**	**1 oil engine** driving 1 CP propeller Total Power: 397kW (540hp) 9.5kn Normo LDM-6 1 x 4 Stroke 6 Cy. 250 x 300 397kW (540bhp) AS Bergens Mek Verksteder-Norway
5272804 *A3CR8* -	**STAR** *ex* Alfa *-2001* *ex* Captain Monachos *-1976* *ex* Peene *-1976* **Star International Tug** - *Nuku'alofa* *Tonga* Official number: 1013	*154* 47 -	Class: (AB) (DS)	**1952 VEB Schiffswerft "Edgar Andre" — Magdeburg** Loa 28.30 Br ex 6.35 Dght 3.607 Lbp - Br md - Dpth 3.81 Welded, 1 dk	**(B32A2ST) Tug** Ice Capable	**1 oil engine** driving 1 FP propeller Total Power: 405kW (551hp) Goerlitzer 1 x 4 Stroke 6 Cy. 325 x 440 405kW (551bhp) VEB Goerlitzer Maschinenbau-Goerlitz AuxGen: 1 x 28kW 230V d.c
1011044 *VRLZ8* -	**STAR** *ex* Main C *-2013* **Kingship Marine Ltd** - *Hong Kong* *Hong Kong* MMSI: 477991315 Official number: HK3814	**426** 127 418	Class: LR ✠ **100A1** SS 03/2012 SSC Yacht, mono, G6 Cable: 275.0/19.0 U2 (a)	**2012-03 Kingship Marine Ltd — Zhongshan GD** Yd No: KS006 Loa 41.90 Br ex 8.40 Dght 2.650 Lbp 34.33 Br md 7.99 Dpth 4.47 Welded, 1 dk	**(X11A2YP) Yacht**	**2 oil engines** with clutches, flexible couplings & dr reverse geared to sc. shafts driving 2 FP propellers Total Power: 1,118kW (1,520hp) 14.0kn Caterpillar C32 2 x Vee 4 Stroke 12 Cy. 145 x 162 each-559kW (760bhp) Caterpillar Inc-USA AuxGen: 2 x 90kW 400V 50Hz a.c Thrusters: 1 Thwart. FP thruster (f)
7911131 *V4WQ2* -	**STAR** *ex* Tecne *-2014* - - *St Kitts & Nevis* MMSI: 341044000	*993* 925 2,566 T/cm 9.9	Class: (RI)	**1979-07 Cantiere Navale Ferronavale — La Spezia** Yd No: 500 Loa 72.90 Br ex 14.38 Dght 3.752 Lbp 72.52 Br md 14.37 Dpth 4.55 Welded, 1 dk	**(A13B2TP) Products Tanker** Liq: 3,729; Liq (Oil): 3,729 Compartments: 12 Ta, ER 13 Cargo Pump (s)	**2 oil engines** geared to sc. shafts driving 2 FP propellers Total Power: 1,040kW (1,414hp) Deutz SBA12M816 2 x Vee 4 Stroke 12 Cy. 142 x 160 each-520kW (707bhp) Kloeckner Humboldt Deutz AG-West Germany

Number	Name / Owner	Tonnage	Class	Built	Type	Machinery
9364722 *ESCJ* -	**STAR** **Tallink Group Ltd (AS Tallink Grupp)** - *Tallinn* *Estonia* MMSI: 276672000 Official number: 5P07D01	**36,249** 13,316 4,700	Class: BV	**2007-04 Aker Yards Oy — Helsinki** Yd No: 1356 Loa 186.00 (BB) Br ex - Dght 6.700 Lbp 170.00 Br md 27.70 Dpth 16.00 Welded	**(A36A2PR) Passenger/Ro-Ro Ship (Vehicles)** Passengers: unberthed: 1380; cabins: 131; berths: 520 Bow door/ramp (centre) Len: 18.00 Wid: 4.70 Swl: - Stern door/ramp (centre) Len: 11.00 Wid: 18.00 Swl: - Lane-Len: 1085 Lane-clr ht: 4.90 Cars: 300 Ice Capable	**4 oil engines** reduction geared to sc. shafts driving 2 CP propellers Total Power: 48,000kW (65,260hp) 27.0kn MaK 12M43C 4 x Vee 4 Stroke 12 Cy. 430 x 610 each-12000kW (16315bhp) Caterpillar Motoren GmbH & Co. KG-Germany AuxGen: 2 x 1440kW 50Hz a.c, 3 x 1350kW 50Hz a.c Thrusters: 2 Tunnel thruster (f); 1 Tunnel thruster (a) Fuel: 975.0 (r.f.) 195.0pd
9221786 *9HDX8* -	**STAR 1** *ex* Star *-2005* *ex* Star-1 *-2003* **Chemstar Shipping Ltd** Chemmariner Shipping Ltd SatCom: Inmarsat C 421587210 *Valletta* *Malta* MMSI: 215872000 Official number: 9583	**4,430** 2,101 6,664 T/cm 15.7	Class: (BV)	**2003-09 Dearsan Gemi Insaat ve Sanayii Koll. Sti. — Tuzla** Yd No: 19 Loa 113.50 (BB) Br ex 16.92 Dght 6.785 Lbp 106.20 Br md 16.90 Dpth 8.40 Welded, 1 dk	**(A12B2TR) Chemical/Products Tanker** Double Hull (13F) Liq: 7,101; Liq (Oil): 7,101 Cargo Heating Coils Compartments: 12 Wing Ta, 1 Slop Ta, ER 13 Cargo Pump (s): 10x200m³/hr, 3x120m³/hr Manifold: Bow/CM: 58.7m	**1 oil engine** driving 1 CP propeller Total Power: 3,500kW (4,759hp) 13.5kn MAN-B&W 5S35MC 1 x 2 Stroke 5 Cy. 350 x 1400 3500kW (4759bhp) MAN B&W Diesel A/S-Denmark AuxGen: 3 x 400kW 380/220V 50Hz a.c, 1 x 473kW 400V 50Hz a.c Thrusters: 1 Tunnel thruster (f) Fuel: 62.9 (d.f.) 346.8 (r.f.) 13.5pd
9654452 *3WFF9* -	**STAR 01** **Ngoc Anh Shipping JSC** - *Haiphong* *Vietnam*	**1,599** 1,014 3,233	Class: VR	**2011-12 Cat Tuong Shipyard — Truc Ninh** Yd No: S07-008.08 Loa 78.63 Br ex 12.62 Dght 5.350 Lbp 73.60 Br md 12.60 Dpth 6.48 Welded, 1 dk	**(A31A2GX) General Cargo Ship** Grain: 3,678; Bale: 3,313 Compartments: 2 Ho, ER 2 Ha: (19.2 x 8.4)ER (19.8 x 8.4)	**1 oil engine** reduction geared to sc. shaft driving 1 FP propeller Total Power: 735kW (999hp) 10.0kn Chinese Std. Type G6300ZC 1 x 4 Stroke 6 Cy. 300 x 380 735kW (999bhp) Ningbo CSI Power & Machinery GroupCo Ltd-China AuxGen: 2 x 80kW 380V a.c Fuel: 88.0
8405012 *5IM566*	**STAR-1** *ex* Recco Star *-2012* *ex* Louise *-2007* *ex* Delmas Luanda *-2006* *ex* Gemini J *-2004* *ex* X-Press Renown *-2003* *ex* Harun *-2000* *ex* Bangkok Star *-1999* *ex* Harun *-1999* *ex* Cam Iroko Express *-1996* *ex* Carib Navigator *-1995* *ex* Navigare *-1994* *ex* Ville de Byblos *-1993* *ex* Navigare *-1992* *ex* Seacrest Achiever *-1991* *ex* Navigare *-1989* *ex* Bacol Santos *-1987* *ex* BCR Jane *-1985* *ex* Navigare *-1985* **Al Manar Establishment for Construction Materials Establishment** Tek Management Corp *Zanzibar* *Tanzania (Zanzibar)* MMSI: 677046600 Official number: 300308	**5,608** 3,088 7,120	Class: IU (RI) (GL)	**1985-05 Werft Nobiskrug GmbH — Rendsburg** Yd No: 723 Loa 117.02 (BB) Br ex 19.61 Dght 6.133 Lbp 106.86 Br md 19.41 Dpth 8.01 Welded, 2 dks	**(A31A2GA) General Cargo Ship (with Ro-Ro facility)** Stern door/ramp (centre) Len: 13.00 Wid: 6.50 Swl: 100 Lane-Len: 400 Lane-Wid: 6.50 Lane-clr ht: 5.50 Grain: 9,155; Bale: 9,061 TEU 574 C Ho 206 TEU C Dk 368 TEU incl 30 ref C. Compartments: 1 Ho, ER 1 Ha: (76.5 x 15.1)ER Cranes: 2x35t Ice Capable	**1 oil engine** with flexible couplings & sr gearedto sc. shaft driving 1 CP propeller Total Power: 1,899kW (2,582hp) 13.0kn MaK 6M551AK 1 x 4 Stroke 6 Cy. 450 x 550 1899kW (2582bhp) Krupp MaK Maschinenbau GmbH-Kiel AuxGen: 1 x 400kW 220/440V 60Hz a.c, 2 x 238kW 220/440V 60Hz a.c Thrusters: 1 Thwart. FP thruster (f) Fuel: 80.0 (d.f.) 400.0 (r.f.)
8317318 *UDXQ* -	**STAR-1** *ex* Taiyo Maru No. 11 *-2003* **JSC 'Kurilskiy Rybak'** - *Nevelsk* *Russia* MMSI: 273445520	**197** 59 98	Class: RS	**1984-02 Sanuki Shipbuilding & Iron Works Co Ltd — Mitoyo KG** Yd No: 1122 Loa 37.70 Br ex - Dght 2.360 Lbp 29.90 Br md 6.41 Dpth 2.54 Welded, 1 dk	**(B11B2FV) Fishing Vessel** Ins: 89 Compartments: 9 Ho, ER 9 Ha: ER	**1 oil engine** driving 1 FP propeller Total Power: 592kW (805hp) Pielstick 5PA5 1 x 4 Stroke 5 Cy. 225 x 270 592kW (805bhp) Niigata Engineering Co Ltd-Japan Fuel: 73.0 (d.f.)
6707052 *ERLX* -	**STAR 1** *ex* Sea Mate III *-2011* *ex* Joshua *-2009* *ex* Suparat *-2001* *ex* Priscilla *-1992* *ex* Meridian *-1992* *ex* General Marshall *-1987* *ex* Crescent Seahorse *-1983* *ex* E. R. Levy *-1977* **Sama Marine & Arabian Coast** - *Moldova* MMSI: 214181224	**497** 149 -		**1966 American Marine Corp. — New Orleans, La** Yd No: 923 Loa 47.25 Br ex 11.03 Dght 3.172 Lbp 44.56 Br md 10.98 Dpth 3.81 Welded	**(B21A2OS) Platform Supply Ship**	**2 oil engines** geared to sc. shaft driving 1 FP propeller Total Power: 1,126kW (1,530hp) Caterpillar D398TA 2 x Vee 4 Stroke 12 Cy. 159 x 203 each-563kW (765bhp) Caterpillar Tractor Co-USA
9076820 - -	**STAR-1** - - *Asuncion* *Paraguay*	**741** 222 332	Class: (RS)	**1992-09 ATVT Zavod "Leninska Kuznya" — Kyyiv** Yd No: 280 Loa 53.74 Br ex 10.71 Dght 4.400 Lbp 47.92 Br md - Dpth 6.00 Welded	**(B11A2FS) Stern Trawler** Ice Capable	**1 oil engine** driving 1 FP propeller Total Power: 971kW (1,320hp) 12.5kn S.K.L. 8NVD48A-2U 1 x 4 Stroke 8 Cy. 320 x 480 971kW (1320bhp) SKL Motoren u. Systemtechnik AG-Magdeburg
9693006 *3WFL9* -	**STAR 02-BLC** **BIDV Financial Leasing Co Ltd** Anh Tuan Shipping JSC *Haiphong* *Vietnam*	**1,599** 1,014 3,233	Class: VR	**2013-01 Cat Tuong Shipyard — Truc Ninh** Yd No: S07-008.10 Loa 78.63 Br ex 12.62 Dght 5.350 Lbp 73.60 Br md 12.60 Dpth 6.48 Welded, 1 dk	**(A31A2GX) General Cargo Ship** Grain: 3,677; Bale: 3,312 Compartments: 2 Ho, ER 2 Ha: (19.2 x 8.4)ER (19.8 x 8.4)	**1 oil engine** reduction geared to sc. shaft driving 1 FP propeller Total Power: 441kW (600hp) 9.0kn Chinese Std. Type G6300ZC 1 x 4 Stroke 6 Cy. 300 x 380 441kW (600bhp) Ningbo CSI Power & Machinery GroupCo Ltd-China AuxGen: 1 x 84kW 380V a.c
9608568 *3WJN9* -	**STAR 62** *ex* Star 18 *-2013* **Hung Hung Trade & Transport Co Ltd** - *Haiphong* *Vietnam* MMSI: 574001800	**1,599** - 3,093	Class: VR	**2013-11 Hoang Phong Shipbuilding JSC — Xuan Truong** Yd No: S07.002.59 Loa 78.63 Br ex - Dght 5.220 Lbp 73.60 Br md 12.60 Dpth 6.48 Welded, 1 dk	**(A31A2GX) General Cargo Ship** Grain: 3,869; Bale: 3,486 Compartments: 2 Ho, ER 2 Ha: ER 2 (19.8 x 8.4)	**1 oil engine** reduction geared to sc. shaft driving 1 FP propeller Total Power: 720kW (979hp) 10.3kn Chinese Std. Type CW8200ZC 1 x 4 Stroke 8 Cy. 200 x 270 720kW (979bhp) Weichai Power Co Ltd-China AuxGen: 2 x 90kW 400V a.c Fuel: 89.0
9558139 *3WDS8* -	**STAR 89** *ex* Star 27-Alci *-2011* **Ngoc Phat Transport Service JSC** - SatCom: Inmarsat C 457497110 *Haiphong* *Vietnam* MMSI: 574971000	**1,598** 1,073 2,996	Class: VR	**2009-12 Hoang Phong Shipbuilding JSC — Xuan Truong** Yd No: THB-25-06 Loa 79.80 Br ex 12.82 Dght 4.900 Lbp 74.84 Br md 12.80 Dpth 6.08 Welded, 1 dk	**(A21A2BC) Bulk Carrier** Grain: 3,946; Bale: 3,556 Compartments: 2 Ho, ER 2 Ha: ER 2 (20.4 x 8.4)	**1 oil engine** reduction geared to sc. shaft driving 1 FP propeller Total Power: 736kW (1,001hp) 11.0kn Chinese Std. Type 8300ZLC 1 x 4 Stroke 8 Cy. 300 x 380 736kW (1001bhp) Zibo Diesel Engine Factory-China AuxGen: 2 x 90kW 400V a.c Fuel: 40.0
8428301 - -	**STAR 101** *ex* Seisho *-2011* *ex* Seisho Maru No. 11 *-1985* *ex* Konpira No. 32 *-1985* - -	*194* 86 258	Class: (KR)	**1970 K.K. Honma Zosensho — Niigata** Loa 43.24 Br ex 7.24 Dght - Lbp 37.80 Br md 7.21 Dpth 3.15 Welded, 1 dk	**(B11B2FV) Fishing Vessel** Ins: 240	**1 oil engine** driving 1 FP propeller Total Power: 588kW (799hp) 10.5kn Hanshin 6LUS24 1 x 4 Stroke 6 Cy. 240 x 405 588kW (799bhp) Hanshin Nainenki Kogyo-Japan AuxGen: 2 x 116kW 225V a.c
9511870 *9V7087* -	**STAR ADMIRAL** **PSA Marine Pte Ltd** - SatCom: Inmarsat C 456420110 *Singapore* *Singapore* MMSI: 564201000 Official number: 392808	**394** 118 189	Class: LR ✠ **100A1** SS 05/2009 tug ✠ **LMC** **UMS** Eq.Ltr: G; Cable: 32.0/20.5 U2 (a)	**2009-05 Hin Lee (Zhuhai) Shipyard Co Ltd — Zhuhai GD** (Hull) Yd No: 183 **2009-05 Cheoy Lee Shipyards Ltd — Hong Kong** Yd No: 4956 Loa 30.00 Br ex 12.33 Dght 5.330 Lbp 28.00 Br md 12.00 Dpth 5.00 Welded, 1 dk	**(B32A2ST) Tug**	**2 oil engines** gearing integral to driving 2 Z propellers Total Power: 3,998kW (5,436hp) Caterpillar 3516B-HD 2 x Vee 4 Stroke 16 Cy. 170 x 215 each-1999kW (2718bhp) Caterpillar Inc-USA AuxGen: 3 x 112kW 415V 50Hz a.c

IMO / Call sign / Flag	Name / Former names / Owner / Manager / Port	Tonnage	Classification	Builder / Dimensions	Type / Cargo	Machinery
8007080 *3FWF5* -	**STAR ALPHA** *ex* Star Force *-2011* *ex* Aegean Force *-2010* *ex* Northica *-2006* *ex* Suula *-2000* *ex* Carupano *-1990* *ex* Emden *-1986* *ex* Bomin Emden *-1983* **North Shore Tankers SA** Star Ship Management SA *Panama* *Panama* MMSI: 356524000 Official number: 4321311	**4,462** 1,870 6,679 T/cm 15.1	Class: LR (NV) (GL) **100A1** SS 07/2012 Double Hull oil tanker SG 1.6, MARPOL 13 (G) (1) (c) ESP Ice Class 1A at a draught not exceeding 7.00m Max/min draughts fwd 7.00/3.90m Max/min draughts aft 7.00/3.90m Power required 3320kw, installed 3529kw **LMC** **UMS** Eq.Ltr: X; Cable: 495.0/46.0 U3 (a)	**1980**-12 **Husumer Schiffswerft — Husum** Yd No: 1469 Converted From: Chemical/Products Tanker-2008 Loa 112.40 (BB) Br ex 17.00 Dght 7.001 Lbp 104.40 Br md 16.60 Dpth 8.90 Welded, 1 dk	**(A13B2TP) Products Tanker** Double Hull Liq: 6,322; Liq (Oil): 6,322 Compartments: 12 Wing Ta, ER, 2 Wing Slop Ta 10 Cargo Pump (s): 10x200m³/hr Manifold: Bow/CM: 50m Ice Capable	**1 oil engine** reduction geared to sc. shaft driving 1 CP propeller Total Power: 3,529kW (4,798hp) 13.5kn Deutz SBV8M540 1 x 4 Stroke 8 Cy. 370 x 400 3529kW (4798bhp) Kloeckner Humboldt Deutz AG-West Germany AuxGen: 1 x 400kW 440V 60Hz a.c, 3 x 392kW 440V 60Hz a.c Boilers: AuxB (Comp) Thrusters: 1 Thwart. FP thruster (f)
9041813 - -	**STAR ANN** *ex* Toyofuku Maru *-2009* - -	**546** 305 780	Class: IS	**1991**-11 **Sasaki Shipbuilding Co Ltd — Osakikamijima HS** Yd No: 563 Loa 53.00 Br ex 9.02 Dght 3.700 Lbp 49.80 Br md 9.00 Dpth 4.00 Welded, 1 dk	**(A12A2TC) Chemical Tanker** Double Bottom Entire Compartment Length Compartments: 6 Ta, ER	**1 oil engine** geared to sc. shaft driving 1 FP propeller Total Power: 736kW (1,001hp) Hanshin LH28G 1 x 4 Stroke 6 Cy. 280 x 460 736kW (1001bhp) The Hanshin Diesel Works Ltd-Japan
9365154 *DSOW9* -	**STAR APEX** **Nam Sung Shipping Co Ltd** - *Jeju* *South Korea* MMSI: 440561000 Official number: JJR-069740	**9,522** 4,960 13,002	Class: KR	**2006**-12 **Dae Sun Shipbuilding & Engineering Co Ltd — Busan** Yd No: 466 Loa 142.71 (BB) Br ex 22.60 Dght 8.214 Lbp 133.50 Br md 22.60 Dpth 11.20 Welded, 1 dk	**(A33A2CC) Container Ship (Fully Cellular)** Double Hull TEU 962 incl 120 ref C.	**1 oil engine** driving 1 FP propeller Total Power: 7,877kW (10,710hp) 18.0kn MAN-B&W 6S46MC-C 1 x 2 Stroke 6 Cy. 460 x 1932 7877kW (10710bhp) STX Engine Co Ltd-South Korea AuxGen: 3 x 615kW 445V 60Hz a.c Thrusters: 1 Tunnel thruster (f) Fuel: 85.8 (d.f.) 710.0 (r.f.)
9644897 *T2QF4* -	**STAR APOLLO** **Sino Ling Tao Resources Pte Ltd** Singapore Star Shipping Pte Ltd *Funafuti* *Tuvalu* MMSI: 572695210 Official number: 30221214	**1,537** 461 1,350	Class: BV	**2012**-09 **Guangzhou Hangtong Shipbuilding & Shipping Co Ltd — Jiangmen GD** Yd No: HT082007 Loa 58.70 Br ex - Dght 4.750 Lbp 53.20 Br md 14.60 Dpth 5.50 Welded, 1 dk	**(B21B20A) Anchor Handling Tug Supply**	**2 oil engines** reduction geared to sc. shafts driving 2 CP propellers Total Power: 3,600kW (4,894hp) 13.5kn Wartsila 9L20 2 x 4 Stroke 9 Cy. 200 x 280 each-1800kW (2447bhp) Wartsila Finland Oy-Finland AuxGen: 3 x 450kW 50Hz a.c Fuel: 470.0
9382554 *9V7081* -	**STAR ARIES** *ex* Star Emerald *-2009* **PSA Marine Pte Ltd** - *Singapore* *Singapore* MMSI: 565636000 Official number: 392799	**327** 98 107	Class: LR ✠ **100A1** SS 08/2012 tug ✠ **LMC** **UMS** Eq.Ltr: G; Cable: 312.5/20.5 U2 (a)	**2007**-11 **Hin Lee (Zhuhai) Shipyard Co Ltd — Zhuhai GD** (Hull) Yd No: 132 **2007**-11 **Cheoy Lee Shipyards Ltd — Hong Kong** Yd No: 4907 Loa 27.40 Br ex 11.52 Dght 5.200 Lbp 25.20 Br md 11.50 Dpth 5.00 Welded, 1 dk	**(B32A2ST) Tug**	**2 oil engines** gearing integral to driving 2 Z propellers Total Power: 3,730kW (5,072hp) 12.0kn Caterpillar 3516B 2 x Vee 4 Stroke 16 Cy. 170 x 215 each-1865kW (2536bhp) Caterpillar Inc-USA AuxGen: 2 x 84kW 415V 50Hz a.c
9627863 *T2QG4* -	**STAR ARTEMIS** **Sino Ling Tao Resources Pte Ltd** Singapore Star Shipping Pte Ltd *Funafuti* *Tuvalu* MMSI: 572696210 Official number: 30231114	**1,537** 461 1,350	Class: BV	**2012**-03 **Guangzhou Hangtong Shipbuilding & Shipping Co Ltd — Jiangmen GD** Yd No: HT082006 Loa 58.70 Br ex - Dght 4.500 Lbp 54.11 Br md 14.60 Dpth 5.50 Welded, 1 dk	**(B21B20A) Anchor Handling Tug Supply**	**2 oil engines** reduction geared to sc. shafts driving 2 CP propellers Total Power: 3,600kW (4,894hp) 13.5kn Wartsila 9L20 2 x 4 Stroke 9 Cy. 200 x 280 each-1800kW (2447bhp) Wartsila Finland Oy-Finland AuxGen: 3 x 450kW 50Hz a.c
7221275 *PHUO* -	**STAR ARUBA** *ex* Kropelin *-1992* **Star Bonaire BV** Koole Tanktransport BV *Zaandam* *Netherlands* MMSI: 246392000 Official number: 32786	**1,161** 419 1,515	Class: GL (DS)	**1972**-03 **VEB Elbewerften Boizenburg/Rosslau — Boizenburg** Yd No: 216 Converted From: General Cargo Ship-1993 Loa 70.97 (BB) Br ex 10.37 Dght 4.502 Lbp 65.16 Br md 10.11 Dpth 5.80 Welded, 1 dk	**(A12E2LE) Edible Oil Tanker** Grain: 2,207; Bale: 1,993; Liq: 1,527 Compartments: 10 Ta, ER Ice Capable	**1 oil engine** driving 1 CP propeller Total Power: 870kW (1,183hp) 12.3kn S.K.L. 8NVD48A-2U 1 x 4 Stroke 8 Cy. 320 x 480 870kW (1183bhp) VEB Schwermaschinenbau "KarlLiebknecht" (SKL)-Magdeburg AuxGen: 1 x 128kW 220/380V 50Hz a.c, 1 x 116kW 220/380V 50Hz a.c, 1 x 76kW 220/380V 50Hz a.c, 1 x 14kW 220/380V 50Hz a.c
8419829 *HSB4447* -	**STAR ASIA** *ex* Hung Kuk No. 19 *-2010* *ex* We Carrier *-1995* **Star Tanker Co Ltd** Smooth Sea Co Ltd SatCom: Inmarsat C 456700355 *Thailand* MMSI: 567060900	**4,084** 1,838 6,777 T/cm 14.4	Class: (KR) (NK)	**1985**-05 **Kurinoura Dockyard Co Ltd — Yawatahama EH** Yd No: 211 Loa 108.39 (BB) Br ex 16.54 Dght 7.166 Lbp 99.27 Br md 16.51 Dpth 8.21 Welded, 1 dk	**(A12B2TR) Chemical/Products Tanker** Liq: 7,707; Liq (Oil): 7,707 Cargo Heating Coils Compartments: 12 Ta, ER 6 Cargo Pump (s): 6x400m³/hr Manifold: Bow/CM: 52m	**1 oil engine** driving 1 FP propeller Total Power: 2,648kW (3,600hp) 13.3kn Hanshin 6EL44 1 x 4 Stroke 6 Cy. 440 x 880 2648kW (3600bhp) The Hanshin Diesel Works Ltd-Japan AuxGen: 2 x 200kW 445V 60Hz a.c Fuel: 111.0 (d.f.) 604.5 (r.f.) 11.0pd
9566734 - -	**STAR ASIA** **Salgaocar Mining Industries Pvt Ltd** Singapore Star Shipping Pte Ltd	**163** 49 146	Class: (BV)	**2009**-07 **Sapor Shipbuilding Industries Sdn Bhd — Sibu** Yd No: SAPOR 39 Loa 23.90 Br ex - Dght 2.900 Lbp 22.94 Br md 7.30 Dpth 3.50 Welded, 1 dk	**(B32A2ST) Tug**	**2 oil engines** reduction geared to sc. shafts driving 2 FP propellers Total Power: 970kW (1,318hp) Yanmar 6AYM-STE 2 x 4 Stroke 6 Cy. 155 x 180 each-485kW (659bhp) Yanmar Diesel Engine Co Ltd-Japan AuxGen: 2 x 28kW 50Hz a.c
9497880 *LAOZ7* -	**STAR ATHENA** *completed as* Chun He 123 *-2012* **Grieg Star Bulk AS** Grieg Star AS SatCom: Inmarsat C 425784910 *Bergen* *Norway (NIS)* MMSI: 257849000	**32,839** 19,559 57,809 T/cm 59.2	Class: NV (BV)	**2012**-07 **Yangzhou Dayang Shipbuilding Co Ltd — Yangzhou JS** Yd No: DY145 Loa 189.99 (BB) Br ex - Dght 12.950 Lbp 185.00 Br md 32.26 Dpth 18.00 Welded, 1 dk	**(A21A2BC) Bulk Carrier** Grain: 71,549; Bale: 69,760 Compartments: 5 Ho, ER 5 Ha: ER Cranes: 4x35t	**1 oil engine** driving 1 FP propeller Total Power: 8,700kW (11,829hp) 14.3kn MAN-B&W 6S50MC-C 1 x 2 Stroke 6 Cy. 500 x 2000 8700kW (11829bhp) Doosan Engine Co Ltd-South Korea AuxGen: 3 x 610kW 60Hz a.c
8502834 *LAYG5* -	**STAR ATLANTIC** *ex* Hoegh Mistral *-2004* *ex* Star Texas *-1990* *ex* Texas Rainbow *-1989* **Grieg International II AS** Grieg Star AS *Bergen* *Norway (NIS)* MMSI: 258867000	**20,125** 9,823 30,402 T/cm 37.6	Class: NV (NK)	**1986**-04 **Kurushima Dockyard Co. Ltd. — Onishi** Yd No: 2417 Loa 168.50 (BB) Br ex - Dght 10.970 Lbp 160.40 Br md 26.00 Dpth 16.00 Welded, 1 dk	**(A31A2GO) Open Hatch Cargo Ship** Grain: 39,052; Bale: 37,992 TEU 1198 incl 96 ref C. Compartments: 7 Ho, ER 7 Ha: ER Gantry cranes: 2x40t	**1 oil engine** driving 1 FP propeller Total Power: 7,208kW (9,800hp) 15.0kn Sulzer 6RTA58 1 x 2 Stroke 6 Cy. 580 x 1700 7208kW (9800bhp) Mitsubishi Heavy Industries Ltd-Japan AuxGen: 3 x 550kW 440V 60Hz a.c
9227522 *V7UW7* -	**STAR AURORA** *ex* Nord-Kraft *-2010* **Star Aurora LLC** Starbulk SA SatCom: Inmarsat C 453835966 *Majuro* *Marshall Islands* MMSI: 538004048 Official number: 4048	**85,379** 56,701 171,199 T/cm 124.5	Class: RI (NV) (BV) (NK)	**2000**-06 **Koyo Dockyard Co Ltd — Mihara HS** Yd No: 2118 Loa 288.93 (BB) Br ex - Dght 17.622 Lbp 280.00 Br md 45.00 Dpth 23.80 Welded, 1 dk	**(A21A2BC) Bulk Carrier** Grain: 188,204 Compartments: 9 Ho, ER 9 Ha: (15.7 x 17.6)8 (15.7 x 20.8)ER	**1 oil engine** driving 1 FP propeller Total Power: 16,109kW (21,902hp) 14.3kn B&W 6S70MC 1 x 2 Stroke 6 Cy. 700 x 2674 16109kW (21902bhp) Mitsui Engineering & Shipbuilding CLtd-Japan
8303850 *DUH2434* -	**STAR BACOLOD** *ex* Seto *-2000* **Roble Shipping Lines Inc** - *Manila* *Philippines* Official number: MNLD010297	*238* 157 300		**1983**-06 **Koa Sangyo KK — Takamatsu KG** Yd No: 513 Loa 47.00 Br ex - Dght 2.901 Lbp 43.52 Br md 8.21 Dpth 4.63 Welded, 1 dk	**(A31A2GX) General Cargo Ship** Grain: 978; Bale: 648 Compartments: 1 Ho, ER 1 Ha: ER	**1 oil engine** driving 1 FP propeller Total Power: 405kW (551hp) Hanshin 6LU24G 1 x 4 Stroke 6 Cy. 240 x 410 405kW (551bhp) The Hanshin Diesel Works Ltd-Japan
9186730 *3FTS3* -	**STAR BALBOA** *ex* Libelle *-2013* **Taurus Maritime Tankers SA** Star Tankers Bunkering SA *Panama* *Panama* MMSI: 357689000 Official number: 44868PEXT	**8,116** 4,244 13,050 T/cm 24.2	Class: GL	**1999**-11 **Lindenau GmbH Schiffswerft u. Maschinenfabrik — Kiel** Yd No: 250 Loa 145.61 (BB) Br ex 19.77 Dght 8.360 Lbp 138.51 Br md 19.73 Dpth 10.65 Welded, 1 dk	**(A12B2TR) Chemical/Products Tanker** Double Hull (13F) Liq: 14,498; Liq (Oil): 14,681 Compartments: 10 Wing Ta, 2 Wing Slop Ta, ER 10 Cargo Pump (s): 10x250m³/hr Manifold: Bow/CM: 72.6m Ice Capable	**1 oil engine** with clutches, flexible couplings & sr geared to sc. shaft driving 1 CP propeller Total Power: 4,200kW (5,710hp) 14.0kn MaK 9M32 1 x 4 Stroke 9 Cy. 320 x 480 4200kW (5710bhp) MaK Motoren GmbH & Co. KG-Kiel AuxGen: 1 x 640kW 380V 50Hz a.c, 2 x 920kW 380V 50Hz a.c Thrusters: 1 Thwart. FP thruster (f) Fuel: 129.9 (d.f.) 414.3 (r.f.) 17.0pd

IMO / Call sign	Name / Owner / Manager	Tonnage	Class	Build / Dimensions	Type / Cargo	Machinery
9562609 *T2GB3* -	**STAR BALIKPAPAN** **Sino Ling Tao Resources Pte Ltd** Singapore Star Shipping Pte Ltd *Funafuti* *Tuvalu* MMSI: 572760000 Official number: 21570909	**481** 144 350	Class: AB	**2010-01 in the People's Republic of China** Yd No: HX010 Loa 37.00 Br ex - Dght - Lbp 29.60 Br md 11.40 Dpth 4.95 Welded, 1 dk	**(B32A2ST) Tug**	**2 oil engines** reverse reduction geared to sc. shafts driving 2 FP propellers Total Power: 2,984kW (4,058hp) Cummins KTA-50-M2 2 x Vee 4 Stroke 16 Cy. 159 x 159 each-1492kW (2029bhp) Cummins Engine Co Inc-USA AuxGen: 2 x 120kW a.c
9088108 *HOFX* -	**STAR BALTIC** *ex* Blue Crystal *-2012* *ex* Sea Crystal *-2011* *ex* Vemaoil XV *-2009* *ex* Tsurutama Maru *-2002* **Baltic Tankers SA** Star Ship Management SA *Panama* *Panama* MMSI: 373378000 Official number: 43295PEXT1	**2,283** 920 3,255 T/cm 10.2	Class: BV (NK)	**1994-05 Nishi Shipbuilding Co Ltd — Imabari EH** Yd No: 382 Conv to DH-2005 Loa 91.30 (BB) Br ex 15.02 Dght 5.380 Lbp 85.00 Br md 13.00 Dpth 6.35 Welded, 1 dk	**(A13B2TP) Products Tanker** Double Hull (13F) Liq: 3,332; Liq (Oil): 3,332 Compartments: 10 Ta, ER 2 Cargo Pump (s): 2x1000m³/hr Manifold: Bow/CM: 45.6m	**1 oil engine** driving 1 CP propeller Total Power: 2,427kW (3,300hp) 11.0kn Hanshin LH41LA 1 x 4 Stroke 6 Cy. 410 x 800 2427kW (3300bhp) The Hanshin Diesel Works Ltd-Japan AuxGen: 2 x 280kW a.c Thrusters: 1 Thwart. FP thruster (f) Fuel: 49.5 (d.f.) 169.5 (r.f.)
9350989 *9V9357* -	**STAR BEST** **Grace Ocean Pte Ltd** Cleanseas Shipmanagement Inc *Singapore* *Singapore* MMSI: 566006000 Official number: 396963	**14,030** 6,724 13,191	Class: NK	**2007-03 Shikoku Dockyard Co. Ltd. — Takamatsu** Yd No: 1032 Loa 162.50 (BB) Br ex - Dght 9.720 Lbp 150.00 Br md 26.00 Dpth 14.10 Welded, 1 dk	**(A34A2GR) Refrigerated Cargo Ship** Ins: 17,463 TEU 436 C Ho 112 TEU C Dk 324 TEU incl 200 ref C Compartments: 4 Ho, ER 4 Ha: ER 4 (12.6 x 10.3) Cranes: 2x40t,2x8t	**1 oil engine** driving 1 FP propeller Total Power: 15,820kW (21,509hp) 22.0kn MAN-B&W 7S60MC-C 1 x 2 Stroke 7 Cy. 600 x 2400 15820kW (21509bhp) Mitsui Engineering & Shipbuilding CLtd-Japan AuxGen: 4 x 1150kW a.c Thrusters: 1 Tunnel thruster (f) Fuel: 2370.0 (r.f.) 55.0pd
9116395 *V7V08* -	**STAR BIG** *ex* Bigfish *-2011* *ex* KWK Genesis *-2011* **Star Big LLC** Starbulk SA *Majuro* *Marshall Islands* MMSI: 538004175 Official number: 4175	**85,034** 55,899 168,404 T/cm 114.2	Class: AB	**1996-07 Halla Engineering & Heavy Industries, Ltd. — Samho** Yd No: 1001 Loa 283.00 (BB) Br ex - Dght 18.169 Lbp 271.00 Br md 45.00 Dpth 24.60 Welded, 1 dk	**(A21A2BC) Bulk Carrier** Grain: 185,314; Bale: 176,070 Compartments: 9 Ho, ER 9 Ha: (15.3 x 16.5)8 (15.3 x 20.0)ER	**1 oil engine** driving 1 FP propeller Total Power: 16,860kW (22,923hp) 14.6kn B&W 6S70MC 1 x 2 Stroke 6 Cy. 700 x 2674 16860kW (22923bhp) Hyundai Heavy Industries Co Ltd-South Korea
9041423 *ZDJW5* -	**STAR BIRD** *ex* Felston *-1994* **Star Bird Shipping K/S** J Poulsen Shipping A/S *Gibraltar* *Gibraltar (British)* MMSI: 236574000	**3,351** 1,835 5,215	Class: GL	**1993-07 Marmara Tersanesi — Yarimca** Yd No: 50A Loa 94.38 (BB) Br ex - Dght 6.250 Lbp 87.10 Br md 15.82 Dpth 7.90 Welded, 1 dk	**(A31A2GX) General Cargo Ship** Grain: 6,076; Bale: 5,380 TEU 343 C.Ho 133/20' (40',45') C.Dk 210/20' (40',45') incl. 60 ref C. Compartments: 1 Ho, ER 1 Ha: (55.8 x 12.9)ER Cranes: 2x30t Ice Capable	**1 oil engine** reduction geared to sc. shaft driving 1 CP propeller Total Power: 2,200kW (2,991hp) 15.0kn MaK 8M453C 1 x 4 Stroke 8 Cy. 320 x 420 2200kW (2991bhp) Krupp MaK Maschinenbau GmbH-Kiel AuxGen: 1 x 702kW 220/380V 50Hz a.c, 2 x 313kW 220/380V 50Hz a.c Thrusters: 1 Directional thruster (f)
9148453 *PHHU* -	**STAR BONAIRE** **Star Bonaire BV** Koole Tanktransport BV *Zaandam* *Netherlands* MMSI: 246359000 Official number: 30330	**2,257** 796 3,400	Class: BV	**1997-01 Scheepswerf- en Reparatiebedrijf "Harlingen" B.V. — Harlingen** Yd No: 202 Loa 90.12 (BB) Br ex 11.95 Dght 5.140 Lbp 84.98 Br md 11.90 Dpth 6.55 Welded, 1 dk	**(A12E2LE) Edible Oil Tanker** Double Sides Entire Compartment Length Liq: 2,960 Cargo Heating Coils Compartments: 14 Ta, ER 1 Cargo Pump (s): 1x450m³/hr	**1 oil engine** with flexible couplings & sr gearedto sc. shaft driving 1 CP propeller Total Power: 1,620kW (2,203hp) 12.5kn Wartsila 9L20 1 x 4 Stroke 9 Cy. 200 x 280 1620kW (2203bhp) Stork Wartsila Diesel BV-Netherlands AuxGen: 1 x 168kW 220/380V 50Hz a.c, 1 x 324kW 220/380V 50Hz a.c Thrusters: 1 Thwart. FP thruster (f) Fuel: 137.0 (d.f.)
9587386 *V7WY7* -	**STAR BOREALIS** **Star Borealis LLC** Starbulk SA *Majuro* *Marshall Islands* MMSI: 538004425 Official number: 4425	**93,733** 58,829 179,678 T/cm 123.2	Class: AB	**2011-09 HHIC-Phil Inc — Subic** Yd No: 063 Loa 292.00 (BB) Br ex - Dght 18.200 Lbp 283.00 Br md 45.00 Dpth 24.75 Welded, 1 dk	**(A21A2BC) Bulk Carrier** Grain: 199,393 Compartments: 9 Ho, ER 9 Ha: ER	**1 oil engine** driving 1 FP propeller Total Power: 18,660kW (25,370hp) 14.5kn MAN-B&W 6S70MC-C8 1 x 2 Stroke 6 Cy. 700 x 2800 18660kW (25370bhp) STX Engine Co Ltd-South Korea AuxGen: 3 x 740kW a.c Fuel: 435.0 (d.f.) 6685.0 (r.f.)
9477414 *2DKT5* -	**STAR BREEZE** **Blenheim Shipping UK Ltd** SatCom: Inmarsat C 423591745 *Douglas* *Isle of Man (British)* MMSI: 235079827 Official number: 741974	**51,130** 30,678 91,827	Class: LR ✠ **100A1** SS 11/2010 bulk carrier CSR BC-A GRAB (20) Nos. 2, 4 & 6 holds may be empty ESP **ShipRight** (CM) *IWS LI ✠ **LMC** **UMS** Eq.Ltr: S†; Cable: 687.5/87.0 U3 (a)	**2010-11 Sungdong Shipbuilding & Marine Engineering Co Ltd — Tongyeong** Yd No: 1070 Loa 229.50 (BB) Br ex 37.12 Dght 14.700 Lbp 221.60 Br md 36.92 Dpth 20.50 Welded, 1 dk	**(A21A2BC) Bulk Carrier** Grain: 109,085; Bale: 103,631 Compartments: 7 Ho, ER 7 Ha: ER	**1 oil engine** driving 1 FP propeller Total Power: 11,060kW (15,037hp) 13.8kn MAN-B&W 7S50MC-C 1 x 2 Stroke 7 Cy. 500 x 2000 11060kW (15037bhp) Hyundai Heavy Industries Co Ltd-South Korea AuxGen: 3 x 600kW 450V 60Hz a.c Boilers: AuxB (Comp) 7.0kgf/cm² (6.9bar)
9002594 *V7AB9* -	**STAR BRIGHT** *ex* La Prudencia *-2012* *ex* Maersk Eleo *-2004* *ex* Eleo Maersk *-1998* **Star Bright Pte Ltd** Southernpec (Singapore) Shipping Pte Ltd *Majuro* *Marshall Islands* MMSI: 538004960 Official number: 4960	**158,475** 94,891 298,900 T/cm 171.5	Class: LR ✠ **100A1** SS 01/2013 Double Hull oil tanker ESP SPM **ShipRight** (SDA, FDA, CM) LI ✠ **LMC** **UMS IGS** Eq.Ltr: E*; Cable: 770.0/122.0 U3	**1993-01 Odense Staalskibsvaerft A/S — Munkebo (Lindo Shipyard)** Yd No: 141 Loa 343.71 (BB) Br ex 56.44 Dght 21.530 Lbp 327.54 Br md 56.40 Dpth 30.41 Welded, 1 dk	**(A13A2TV) Crude Oil Tanker** Double Hull (13F) Liq: 321,162; Liq (Oil): 340,813 Compartments: 5 Ta, 10 Wing Ta, 2 Wing Slop Ta, ER 3 Cargo Pump (s): 3x5000m³/hr Manifold: Bow/CM: 172.9m	**1 oil engine** driving 1 FP propeller Total Power: 23,534kW (31,997hp) 14.5kn Mitsubishi 8UEC75LSII 1 x 2 Stroke 8 Cy. 750 x 2800 23534kW (31997bhp) Mitsubishi Heavy Industries Ltd-Japan AuxGen: 3 x 780kW 440V 60Hz a.c Boilers: 2 WTAuxB (o.f.) 18.4kgf/cm² (18.0bar), e (ex.g.) 23.5kgf/cm² (23.0bar) Fuel: 383.0 (d.f.) 7921.0 (r.f.)
9228124 *SVOT* -	**STAR CANOPUS** *ex* Star Mizuho *-2007* **Star Canopus Special Maritime Enterprise (ENE)** Pegasus Maritime Enterprises Inc *Piraeus* *Greece* MMSI: 240665000 Official number: 11627	**25,388** 15,284 45,635	Class: NV (NK)	**2002-01 Oshima Shipbuilding Co Ltd — Saikai NS** Yd No: 10300 Loa 179.99 (BB) Br ex - Dght 11.576 Lbp 172.00 Br md 31.00 Dpth 16.24 Welded, 1 dk	**(A21A2BC) Bulk Carrier** Grain: 57,256; Bale: 56,560 Compartments: 5 Ho, ER 5 Ha: (17.1 x 15.6)2 (21.6 x 15.6) (18.0 x 15.6) (19.8 x 15.6)ER Cranes: 4x30t	**1 oil engine** driving 1 FP propeller Total Power: 7,245kW (9,850hp) 14.3kn B&W 6S46MC-C 1 x 2 Stroke 6 Cy. 460 x 1932 7245kW (9850bhp) Kawasaki Heavy Industries Ltd-Japan
9228071 *SXYH* -	**STAR CAPELLA** *ex* Star Capella 1 *-2007* *ex* Star Capella *-2007* **Star Capella Special Maritime Enterprise (ENE)** Pegasus Maritime Enterprises Inc *Piraeus* *Greece* MMSI: 240638000 Official number: 11608	**25,388** 15,284 45,601	Class: LR (NK) **100A1** SS 09/2011 bulk carrier strengthened for heavy cargoes, Nos. 2 7 4 holds may be empty ESP ESN LI **LMC** **UMS**	**2001-09 Oshima Shipbuilding Co Ltd — Saikai NS** Yd No: 10295 Loa 179.99 (BB) Br ex - Dght 11.576 Lbp 172.00 Br md 31.00 Dpth 16.24 Welded, 1 dk	**(A21A2BC) Bulk Carrier** Grain: 57,256; Bale: 56,560 Compartments: 5 Ho, ER 5 Ha: (19.8 x 15.6) (18.0 x 15.6) (17.1 x 15.6)2 (21.6 x 15.6)ER Cranes: 4x30t	**1 oil engine** driving 1 FP propeller Total Power: 7,240kW (9,844hp) 14.3kn B&W 6S46MC-C 1 x 2 Stroke 6 Cy. 460 x 1932 7240kW (9844bhp) Kawasaki Heavy Industries Ltd-Japan Boilers: AuxB 7.0kgf/cm² (6.9bar)
6721242 *IXQG* -	**STAR CAPRICORN** *ex* Springeren *-1985* **Speedy Lines Srl** - *Trapani* *Italy* MMSI: 247150800 Official number: 732	*133* 73 14	Class: (RI) (NV)	**1967 Cantiere Navale L Rodriquez — Messina** Yd No: 122 Loa 29.01 Br ex 10.22 Dght 1.440 Lbp 24.41 Br md 6.10 Dpth - Riveted, 1 dk	**(A37B2PS) Passenger Ship** Hull Material: Aluminium Alloy Passengers: unberthed: 125	**2 oil engines** driving 2 FP propellers Total Power: 1,986kW (2,700hp) 34.0kn Maybach MB820DB 2 x Vee 4 Stroke 12 Cy. 175 x 205 each-993kW (1350bhp) (new engine 1975) MTU Friedrichshafen GmbH-Friedrichshafen AuxGen: 1 x 10kW 220V 50Hz a.c, 2 x 0kW 220V 50Hz a.c Fuel: 3.0 (d.f.)
9517903 *9V9352* -	**STAR CARE** **Grace Ocean Pte Ltd** Philsynergy Maritime Inc *Singapore* *Singapore* MMSI: 566341000 Official number: 396958	**14,022** 6,724 13,300	Class: NK	**2009-10 Shikoku Dockyard Co. Ltd. — Takamatsu** Yd No: 1050 Loa 162.50 (BB) Br ex - Dght 9.720 Lbp 150.00 Br md 26.00 Dpth 14.10 Welded, 1 dk	**(A34A2GR) Refrigerated Cargo Ship** Bale: 17,504; Ins: 17,504 TEU 436 C Ho 112 TEU C Dk 324 TEU incl 200 ref C Cranes: 2x40t,2x8t	**1 oil engine** driving 1 FP propeller Total Power: 15,820kW (21,509hp) 22.0kn MAN-B&W 7S60MC-C 1 x 2 Stroke 7 Cy. 600 x 2400 15820kW (21509bhp) Mitsui Engineering & Shipbuilding CLtd-Japan AuxGen: 4 x a.c Thrusters: 1 Tunnel thruster (f) Fuel: 2370.0

IMO / Call sign	Name, former names, owner, manager, port, flag	Tonnage	Class	Builder & dimensions	Type & capacity	Machinery
9301304 *DSOA6* -	**STAR CARRIER** - **Nam Sung Shipping Co Ltd** - *Jeju* *South Korea* MMSI: 440484000 Official number: JJR-058870	**9,522** 4,960 13,007	Class: KR	**2005-02 Dae Sun Shipbuilding & Engineering Co Ltd — Busan** Yd No: 449 Loa 142.71 (BB) Br ex - Dght 8.214 Lbp 133.50 Br md 22.60 Dpth 11.20 Welded, 1 dk	**(A33A2CC) Container Ship (Fully Cellular)** Double Hull TEU 962 incl 120 ref C. 5 Ha: 4 (12.6 x 18.2)ER (12.6 x 12.8)	**1 oil engine** driving 1 FP propeller Total Power: 7,860kW (10,686hp) 17.5kn MAN-B&W 6S46MC-C 1 x 2 Stroke 6 Cy. 460 x 1932 7860kW (10686bhp) STX Engine Co Ltd-South Korea AuxGen: 3 x 615kW 440/220V 60Hz a.c Thrusters: 1 Tunnel thruster (f)
8837552 *DUH2484* -	**STAR CEBU** *ex* Maria Angeline *-2005* *ex* Palau Luna *-1997* *ex* Katsu Maru No. 30 *-1990* **Star Philippines Shipping Lines Inc** - *Iloilo* *Philippines* Official number: ILO3002736	*500* 206 1,178		**1973 Taisei Zosen K.K. — Osakikamijima** Loa 55.30 Br ex - Dght 2.800 Lbp 51.00 Br md 11.00 Dpth 5.50 Welded, 1 dk	**(A24D2BA) Aggregates Carrier** Compartments: 1 Ho, ER 1 Ha: (20.0 x 5.7)ER	**1 oil engine** driving 1 FP propeller Total Power: 588kW (799hp) Hanshin 1 x 4 Stroke 588kW (799bhp) The Hanshin Diesel Works Ltd-Japan
9632997 *V7DA8* -	**STAR CHALLENGER** *ex* Supra Challenger I *-2013* **Star Challenger I LLC** Starbulk SA *Majuro* *Marshall Islands* MMSI: 538005359 Official number: 5359	**34,777** 20,209 61,462 T/cm 61.4	Class: RI (NK)	**2012-11 Iwagi Zosen Co Ltd — Kamijima EH** Yd No: 305 Loa 199.99 (BB) Br ex - Dght 13.010 Lbp 195.00 Br md 32.24 Dpth 18.60 Welded, 1 dk	**(A21A2BC) Bulk Carrier** Grain: 77,674; Bale: 73,552 Compartments: 5 Ho, ER 5 Ha: 4 (23.5 x 19.0)ER (18.7 x 19.0) Cranes: 4x30.5t	**1 oil engine** driving 1 FP propeller Total Power: 8,450kW (11,489hp) 14.5kn MAN-B&W 6S50MC-C8 1 x 2 Stroke 6 Cy. 500 x 2000 8450kW (11489bhp) Fuel: 2560.0
9448437 *DSQQ2* -	**STAR CLIPPER** - **Nam Sung Shipping Co Ltd** - *Jeju* *South Korea* MMSI: 441664000 Official number: JJR-101884	**9,520** 4,938 12,980	Class: KR	**2010-03 Dae Sun Shipbuilding & Engineering Co Ltd — Busan** Yd No: 504 Loa 142.71 (BB) Br ex - Dght 8.214 Lbp 132.77 Br md 22.60 Dpth 11.20 Welded, 1 dk	**(A33A2CC) Container Ship (Fully Cellular)** TEU 962 incl 120 ref C	**1 oil engine** driving 1 FP propeller Total Power: 7,860kW (10,686hp) 18.0kn MAN-B&W 6S46MC-C 1 x 2 Stroke 6 Cy. 460 x 1932 7860kW (10686bhp) STX Engine Co Ltd-South Korea AuxGen: 3 x 615kW 445V a.c Thrusters: 1 Tunnel thruster (f)
8915445 *9HA2513* -	**STAR CLIPPER** - **Star Clipper NV** Star Clippers Monaco SAM *Valletta* *Malta* MMSI: 248786000 Official number: 8915445	**2,298** 838 300	Class: NV (LR) ✠ Classed LR until 15/2/01	**1992-03 Scheepswerf van Langerbrugge — Gent** Yd No: 2184 Loa 111.57 Br ex 15.14 Dght 4.700 Lbp 70.30 Br md 15.00 Dpth 9.10 Welded, 3 dks	**(A37A2PC) Passenger/Cruise** Passengers: cabins: 85; berths: 180	**1 oil engine** sr geared to sc. shaft driving 1 CP propeller Total Power: 1,015kW (1,380hp) 12.0kn Caterpillar 3512TA 1 x Vee 4 Stroke 12 Cy. 170 x 190 1015kW (1380bhp) Caterpillar Inc-USA AuxGen: 2 x 560kW 450V 60Hz a.c Thrusters: 1 Thwart. FP thruster (f) Fuel: 180.0 (d.f.)
9242596 *V2OF2* -	**STAR COMET** *ex* Magellan Comet *-2012* *ex* Susan Borchard *-2010* *ex* Gracechurch Comet *-2009* *launched as* Pioneer Eagle *-2002* **Reederei ms 'Magellan Comet' Schiffahrts GmbH & Co KG** Unifeeder A/S *Saint John's* *Antigua & Barbuda* MMSI: 304416000 Official number: 3761	**6,277** 3,249 7,970	Class: NK (GL)	**2002-06 J.J. Sietas KG Schiffswerft GmbH & Co. — Hamburg** (Aft & pt cargo sections) Yd No: 1197 **2002-06 Daewoo-Mangalia Heavy Industries S.A. — Mangalia** (Fwd & pt cargo sections) Yd No: 4022 Loa 133.39 (BB) Br ex 18.95 Dght 7.240 Lbp 125.30 Br md 18.70 Dpth 9.30 Welded, 1 dk	**(A33A2CC) Container Ship (Fully Cellular)** Grain: 10,845; Bale: 9,607 TEU 735 incl 104 ref C. Compartments: 4 Cell Ho (s.stl), ER 4 Ha: ER	**1 oil engine** with flexible couplings & sr geared to sc. shaft driving 1 CP propeller Total Power: 6,600kW (8,973hp) 18.3kn MaK 8M43 1 x 4 Stroke 8 Cy. 430 x 610 6600kW (8973bhp) Caterpillar Motoren GmbH & Co. KG-Germany AuxGen: 1 x 1220kW 380/220V a.c, 1 x 500kW 380/220V a.c, 1 x 320kW 380/220V a.c Thrusters: 1 Thwart. CP thruster (f) Fuel: 900.0
9511882 *9V7357* -	**STAR COMMODORE** - **PSA Marine Pte Ltd** - SatCom: Inmarsat C 456483910 *Singapore* *Singapore* MMSI: 564839000 Official number: 393901	**394** 118 184	Class: LR ✠ **100A** SS 08/2009 tug ✠ **LMC** **UMS** Eq.Ltr: G†; Cable: 32.0/20.0 U2 (a)	**2009-08 Hin Lee (Zhuhai) Shipyard Co Ltd — Zhuhai GD** (Hull) Yd No: 184 **2009-08 Cheoy Lee Shipyards Ltd — Hong Kong** Yd No: 4957 Loa 30.00 Br ex 12.33 Dght 5.330 Lbp 28.00 Br md 12.00 Dpth 5.00 Welded, 1 dk	**(B32A2ST) Tug**	**2 oil engines** gearing integral to driving 2 Z propellers Total Power: 3,998kW (5,436hp) Caterpillar 3516B-HD 2 x Vee 4 Stroke 16 Cy. 170 x 215 each-1999kW (2718bhp) Caterpillar Inc-USA AuxGen: 2 x 112kW 415V 50Hz a.c
9262637 *V7NZ3* -	**STAR COSMO** *ex* Victoria *-2008* *ex* Port Victoria *-2007* *ex* Catharina Oldendorff *-2005* *ex* Atlantic Sun *-2005* **Star Cosmo LLC** Starbulk SA *Majuro* *Marshall Islands* MMSI: 538003041 Official number: 3041	**30,169** 18,159 52,246	Class: RI (NV)	**2005-01 Yangzhou Dayang Shipbuilding Co Ltd — Yangzhou JS** Yd No: JY99142 Loa 189.90 (BB) Br ex - Dght 12.694 Lbp 179.90 Br md 32.20 Dpth 17.50 Welded, 1 dk	**(A21A2BC) Bulk Carrier** Grain: 64,518; Bale: 63,004 Compartments: 5 Ho, ER 5 Ha: 4 (20.8 x 17.7)ER (20.0 x 16.0) Cranes: 4x30t	**1 oil engine** driving 1 FP propeller Total Power: 8,580kW (11,665hp) 13.5kn MAN-B&W 6S50MC 1 x 2 Stroke 6 Cy. 500 x 1910 8580kW (11665bhp) Dalian Marine Diesel Works-China Fuel: 220.0 (d.f.) (Heating Coils) 1500.0 (r.f.)
7218503 *ZR5486* SH 1364	**STAR CREST** *ex* Quo Vadis D. M. *-1978* **Oceana Brands Ltd** - *Cape Town* *South Africa* MMSI: 601541000 Official number: 19404	*381* 127 396	Class: (NV)	**1972 Vaagland Baatbyggeri AS — Vaagland** Yd No: 83 L reg 36.18 Br ex 7.95 Dght - Lbp 33.86 Br md 7.93 Dpth 4.25 Welded, 1 dk	**(B11A2FT) Trawler** Compartments: 6 Ho, ER 6 Ha: 6 (2.4 x 1.4)ER	**1 oil engine** geared to sc. shaft driving 1 FP propeller Total Power: 588kW (799hp) 11.5kn Blackstone ESS8 1 x 4 Stroke 8 Cy. 222 x 292 588kW (799bhp) Mirrlees Blackstone (Stamford)Ltd.-Stamford AuxGen: 1 x 40kW 220V 50Hz a.c, 2 x 32kW 220V 50Hz a.c, 1 x 12kW 220V 50Hz a.c Thrusters: 1 Thwart. FP thruster (f); 1 Tunnel thruster (a)
9402653 *PHPF* -	**STAR CURACAO** - **Star Bonaire BV** Koole Tanktransport BV *Zaandam* *Netherlands* MMSI: 245405000 Official number: 50607	**3,578** 1,073 4,400	Class: BV	**2008-12 in the Netherlands** (Aft & pt cargo sections) Yd No: 220 **2008-12 in the Netherlands** (Fwd & pt cargo sections) Yd No: (220) Loa 109.62 (BB) Br ex 13.62 Dght 5.450 Lbp 106.20 Br md 13.50 Dpth 8.50 Welded, 1 dk	**(A12E2LE) Edible Oil Tanker** Double Hull (13F) Liq: 4,050 Ice Capable	**1 oil engine** reduction geared to sc. shaft driving 1 CP propeller Total Power: 1,800kW (2,447hp) 12.5kn Wartsila 9L20 1 x 4 Stroke 9 Cy. 200 x 280 1800kW (2447bhp) Wartsila France SA-France Thrusters: 1 Tunnel thruster (f)
9216808 *V7NZ9* -	**STAR DELTA** *ex* F Duckling *-2008* *ex* Yasa Aysen *-2006* **Star Delta LLC** Starbulk SA *Majuro* *Marshall Islands* MMSI: 538003045 Official number: 3045	**30,303** 17,734 52,434 T/cm 55.5	Class: RI (NK)	**2000-10 Tsuneishi Shipbuilding Co Ltd — Fukuyama HS** Yd No: 1192 Loa 189.99 (BB) Br ex - Dght 12.026 Lbp 182.00 Br md 32.26 Dpth 17.00 Welded, 1 dk	**(A21A2BC) Bulk Carrier** Grain: 67,756; Bale: 65,601 Compartments: 5 Ho, ER 5 Ha: (20.4 x 18.4)4 (21.3 x 18.4)ER Cranes: 4x30t	**1 oil engine** driving 1 FP propeller Total Power: 7,797kW (10,601hp) 14.5kn B&W 6S50MC 1 x 2 Stroke 6 Cy. 500 x 1910 7797kW (10601bhp) Mitsui Engineering & Shipbuilding CLtd-Japan AuxGen: 3 x 420kW a.c Fuel: 2196.0 (r.f.)
9382542 *9V7080* -	**STAR DIAMOND** - **PSA Marine Pte Ltd** - *Singapore* *Singapore* MMSI: 565635000 Official number: 392798	**327** 98 99	Class: LR ✠ **100A1** SS 10/2012 tug ✠ **LMC** **UMS** Eq.Ltr: G; Cable: 312.5/20.5 U2 (a)	**2007-10 Hin Lee (Zhuhai) Shipyard Co Ltd — Zhuhai GD** (Hull) Yd No: 131 **2007-10 Cheoy Lee Shipyards Ltd — Hong Kong** Yd No: 4906 Loa 27.40 Br ex 12.10 Dght 5.200 Lbp 25.20 Br md 11.50 Dpth 5.00 Welded, 1 dk	**(B32A2ST) Tug**	**2 oil engines** gearing integral to driving 2 Z propellers Total Power: 3,730kW (5,072hp) 12.0kn Caterpillar 3516B 2 x Vee 4 Stroke 16 Cy. 170 x 215 each-1865kW (2536bhp) Caterpillar Inc-USA AuxGen: 2 x 84kW 415V 50Hz a.c
7507265 *LEQZ3* -	**STAR DIEPPE** *ex* Star Shiraz *-1979* *ex* Star Dieppe *-1977* **Grieg Shipping II AS** Grieg Star AS SatCom: Inmarsat C 425743910 *Bergen* *Norway (NIS)* MMSI: 257439000 Official number: N00025	**27,911** 13,492 43,082 T/cm 49.7	Class: NV	**1977-05 Mitsui Eng. & SB. Co. Ltd. — Tamano** Yd No: 1077 Loa 182.88 (BB) Br ex 31.17 Dght 12.031 Lbp 174.52 Br md 31.09 Dpth 16.31 Welded, 1 dk	**(A31A2GO) Open Hatch Cargo Ship** Grain: 47,232 TEU 1272 incl 40 ref C. Compartments: 9 Ho, ER 9 Ha: 9 (12.8 x 26.2)ER Gantry cranes: 2x30t	**1 oil engine** driving 1 FP propeller Total Power: 9,635kW (13,100hp) 15.0kn B&W 7K67GF 1 x 2 Stroke 7 Cy. 670 x 1400 9635kW (13100bhp) Mitsui Engineering & Shipbuilding CLtd-Japan AuxGen: 3 x 670kW 440V 60Hz a.c Fuel: 2830.5 (r.f.) 45.5pd
9382530 *9V7025* -	**STAR DISCOVERY** - **PSA Marine Pte Ltd** - *Singapore* *Singapore* MMSI: 565438000 Official number: 392550	**327** 98 518	Class: LR ✠ **100A1** SS 05/2012 tug ✠ **LMC** **UMS** Eq.Ltr: G; Cable: 302.5/20.5 U2 (a)	**2007-05 Hin Lee (Zhuhai) Shipyard Co Ltd — Zhuhai GD** (Hull) Yd No: 126 **2007-05 Cheoy Lee Shipyards Ltd — Hong Kong** Yd No: 4889 Loa 27.40 Br ex 11.52 Dght 5.200 Lbp 25.20 Br md 11.50 Dpth 5.00 Welded, 1 dk	**(B32A2ST) Tug**	**2 oil engines** gearing integral to driving 2 Z propellers Total Power: 3,730kW (5,072hp) 12.0kn Caterpillar 3516B 2 x Vee 4 Stroke 16 Cy. 170 x 215 each-1865kW (2536bhp) Caterpillar Inc-USA AuxGen: 2 x 112kW 415V 50Hz a.c

9565728 *YD6318* -	**STAR DOLPHIN** **PT Berkat Samudera** Jan Silunadi *Banjarmasin* *Indonesia* MMSI: 525016498 Official number: 3103/IIA	**201** 61 386	Class: KI	**2009**-07 **CV Sumber Jaya — Banjarmasin** Yd No: H-036 Loa 27.50 Br ex - Dght 2.800 Lbp 25.44 Br md 8.00 Dpth 3.30 Welded, 1 dk	**(B32A2ST) Tug**	**2 oil engines** geared to sc. shafts driving 2 Propellers Total Power: 1,500kW (2,040hp) Mitsubishi S12A2-MPTK 2 x Vee 4 Stroke 12 Cy. 150 x 160 each-750kW (1020bhp) Mitsubishi Heavy Industries Ltd-Japan AuxGen: 2 x 56kW a.c
7309106 *WY2455* -	**STAR DUST** **William R Wilson** - *Juneau, AK* *United States of America* Official number: 508438	*125* 85 -		**1967 Master Marine, Inc. — Bayou La Batre, Al** L reg 22.13 Br ex - Dght - Lbp - Br md 6.76 Dpth 3.20 Welded	**(B11B2FV) Fishing Vessel**	**1 oil engine** driving 1 FP propeller Total Power: 279kW (379hp)
8005109 *LAW02* -	**STAR EAGLE** **Grieg Shipping II AS** Grieg Star AS SatCom: Inmarsat C 425770510 *Bergen* *Norway (NIS)* MMSI: 257705000 Official number: N00756	**24,479** 11,773 39,749	Class: NV	**1981**-12 **Mitsui Eng. & SB. Co. Ltd. — Tamano** Yd No: 1234 Loa 179.61 (BB) Br ex 29.44 Dght 11.990 Lbp 170.01 Br md 29.41 Dpth 16.26 Welded, 1 dk	**(A31A2GO) Open Hatch Cargo Ship** Grain: 41,993; Bale: 41,993 TEU 1448 C Ho 648 TEU C Dk 800 TEU Compartments: 9 Ho, ER 9 Ha: 9 (12.3 x 24.6)ER Gantry cranes: 2x40t	**1 oil engine** driving 1 FP propeller Total Power: 9,635kW (13,100hp) 15.0kn B&W 6L67GFCA 1 x 2 Stroke 6 Cy. 670 x 1700 9635kW (13100bhp) Mitsui Engineering & Shipbuilding CLtd-Japan AuxGen: 3 x 800kW 450V 60Hz a.c Thrusters: 1 Thwart. CP thruster (f) Fuel: 372.0 (d.f.) 2384.0 (r.f.) 41.5pd
9321938 *3FOP5* -	**STAR EAGLE** *ex* Nord Strait *-2012* *ex* Gan-Spirit *-2010* **APSF Owning Co 2 Ltd** Norient Product Pool ApS *Panama* *Panama* MMSI: 353265000 Official number: 4456313	**30,068** 13,648 51,213 T/cm 52.0	Class: NV	**2007**-10 **STX Shipbuilding Co Ltd — Changwon (Jinhae Shipyard)** Yd No: 1215 Loa 183.00 (BB) Br ex 32.24 Dght 13.167 Lbp 173.90 Br md 32.21 Dpth 19.10 Welded, 1 dk	**(A12B2TR) Chemical/Products Tanker** Double Hull (13F) Liq: 52,148; Liq (Oil): 521,450 Compartments: 12 Wing Ta, 2 Wing Slop Ta, ER 12 Cargo Pump (s): 12x600m³/hr Manifold: Bow/CM: 92.6m	**1 oil engine** driving 1 FP propeller Total Power: 9,480kW (12,889hp) 14.2kn MAN-B&W 6S50MC-C 1 x 2 Stroke 6 Cy. 500 x 2000 9480kW (12889bhp) STX Engine Co Ltd-South Korea AuxGen: 3 x 900kW a.c Fuel: 202.0 (d.f.) 1209.0 (r.f.)
8303941 *9MLQ5* -	**STAR EMERALD** *ex* Fortress *-2011* *ex* Sea Defender *-2010* *ex* Kyosei Maru *-2009* *ex* Grandeur Pioneer *-2002* *ex* New Horizon *-2001* *ex* Allwell Prelude *-1999* *ex* Kyosei Maru *-1997* **Zone Arctic Sdn Bhd** - *Port Klang* *Malaysia* MMSI: 533059700 Official number: 334320	**1,352** 669 2,517	Class: (GL)	**1983**-07 **Kurinoura Dockyard Co Ltd — Yawatahama EH** Yd No: 184 Loa 82.91 Br ex - Dght 5.152 Lbp 77.02 Br md 12.01 Dpth 5.72 Welded, 1 dk	**(A13B2TP) Products Tanker** Double Bottom Entire Compartment Length Liq: 2,500; Liq (Oil): 2,500 Compartments: 10 Ta, ER 2 Cargo Pump (s): 2x750m³/hr	**1 oil engine** driving 1 Directional propeller Total Power: 1,397kW (1,899hp) 12.0kn Akasaka A34 1 x 4 Stroke 6 Cy. 340 x 660 1397kW (1899bhp) Akasaka Tekkosho KK (Akasaka DieselLtd)-Japan Fuel: 235.0 (d.f.)
9382528 *9V7024* -	**STAR ENDEAVOUR** **PSA Marine Pte Ltd** - *Singapore* *Singapore* MMSI: 565418000 Official number: 392549	**327** 98 98	Class: LR ✠ **100A1** SS 03/2012 tug ✠ **LMC** **UMS** Eq.Ltr: G; Cable: 312.5/20.5 U2 (a)	**2007**-03 **Hin Lee (Zhuhai) Shipyard Co Ltd — Zhuhai GD** (Hull) Yd No: 125 **2007**-03 **Cheoy Lee Shipyards Ltd — Hong Kong** Yd No: 4888 Loa 27.40 Br ex 11.52 Dght 5.200 Lbp 25.20 Br md 11.50 Dpth 5.00 Welded, 1 dk	**(B32A2ST) Tug**	**2 oil engines** gearing integral to driving 2 Z propellers Total Power: 3,730kW (5,072hp) 12.0kn Caterpillar 3516B 2 x Vee 4 Stroke 16 Cy. 170 x 215 each-1865kW (2536bhp) Caterpillar Inc-USA AuxGen: 2 x 112kW 415V 50Hz a.c Fuel: 88.0 (d.f.)
9517927 *9V9397* -	**STAR ENDEAVOUR I** *ex* Star Endeavour *-2011* **Grace Ocean Pte Ltd** Philsynergy Maritime Inc *Singapore* *Singapore* MMSI: 566060000 Official number: 397019	**14,022** 6,724 12,967	Class: NK	**2010**-02 **Shikoku Dockyard Co. Ltd. — Takamatsu** Yd No: 1052 Loa 162.50 (BB) Br ex - Dght 9.720 Lbp 150.00 Br md 26.00 Dpth 14.10 Welded, 1 dk	**(A34A2GR) Refrigerated Cargo Ship** Bale: 17,427; Ins: 17,427 TEU 552 C Ho 112 TEU C Dk 440 TEU incl 200 ref C Cranes: 2x40t	**1 oil engine** driving 1 FP propeller Total Power: 15,820kW (21,509hp) 22.0kn MAN-B&W 7S60MC-C 1 x 2 Stroke 7 Cy. 600 x 2400 15820kW (21509bhp) Mitsui Engineering & Shipbuilding CLtd-Japan Fuel: 2350.0
9216822 *V7NZ7* -	**STAR EPSILON** *ex* G Duckling *-2007* *ex* Yasa Emirhan *-2006* **Star Epsilon LLC** Starbulk SA *Majuro* *Marshall Islands* MMSI: 538003043 Official number: 3043	**30,303** 17,734 52,402 T/cm 55.5	Class: RI (NK)	**2001**-07 **Tsuneishi Shipbuilding Co Ltd — Fukuyama HS** Yd No: 1201 Loa 189.99 (BB) Br ex - Dght 12.024 Lbp 182.00 Br md 32.26 Dpth 17.00 Welded, 1 dk	**(A21A2BC) Bulk Carrier** Grain: 67,756; Bale: 65,601 Compartments: 5 Ho, ER 5 Ha: (20.4 x 18.4)4 (21.3 x 18.4)ER Cranes: 4x30t	**1 oil engine** driving 1 FP propeller Total Power: 7,801kW (10,606hp) 14.5kn B&W 6S50MC 1 x 2 Stroke 6 Cy. 500 x 1910 7801kW (10606bhp) Mitsui Engineering & Shipbuilding CLtd-Japan
9499450 *LAPA7* -	**STAR ERACLE** **Grieg Star Bulk AS** Grieg Star AS *Bergen* *Norway (NIS)* MMSI: 257916000	**32,839** 19,559 58,018 T/cm 59.2	Class: NV (BV)	**2012**-09 **Yangzhou Dayang Shipbuilding Co Ltd — Yangzhou JS** Yd No: DY146 Loa 189.99 (BB) Br ex - Dght 12.970 Lbp 185.00 Br md 32.26 Dpth 18.00 Welded, 1 dk	**(A21A2BC) Bulk Carrier** Grain: 71,549; Bale: 69,760 Compartments: 5 Ho, ER 5 Ha: ER Cranes: 4x35t	**1 oil engine** driving 1 FP propeller Total Power: 8,700kW (11,829hp) 14.3kn MAN-B&W 6S50MC-C 1 x 2 Stroke 6 Cy. 500 x 2000 8700kW (11829bhp) Doosan Engine Co Ltd-South Korea AuxGen: 3 x 610kW 60Hz a.c Fuel: 2376.0
8011330 *LAHE2* -	**STAR EVVIVA** **Grieg Shipping II AS** Grieg Star AS SatCom: Inmarsat A 1310745 *Bergen* *Norway (NIS)* MMSI: 257627000 Official number: N00250	**24,479** 11,773 39,718	Class: NV	**1982**-04 **Mitsui Eng. & SB. Co. Ltd. — Tamano** Yd No: 1235 Loa 179.61 (BB) Br ex 29.44 Dght 11.990 Lbp 170.01 Br md 29.41 Dpth 16.26 Welded, 1 dk	**(A31A2GO) Open Hatch Cargo Ship** Grain: 41,993; Bale: 41,993 TEU 1448 C Ho 648 TEU C Dk 800 TEU Compartments: 9 Ho, ER 9 Ha: 9 (12.3 x 24.6)ER Gantry cranes: 2x40t	**1 oil engine** driving 1 FP propeller Total Power: 9,635kW (13,100hp) 15.0kn B&W 6L67GFCA 1 x 2 Stroke 6 Cy. 670 x 1700 9635kW (13100bhp) Mitsui Engineering & Shipbuilding CLtd-Japan AuxGen: 3 x 800kW 440V 60Hz a.c Thrusters: 1 Thwart. CP thruster (f) Fuel: 431.0 (d.f.) (Heating Coils) 2642.0 (r.f.) 44.0pd
9343285 *9V6727* -	**STAR EXPLORER** **PSA Marine Pte Ltd** *Singapore* *Singapore* MMSI: 563918000 Official number: 391407	**327** 98 107	Class: LR ✠ **100A1** SS 10/2010 tug ✠ **LMC** **UMS** Eq.Ltr: G; Cable: 304.0/24.0 U2 (a)	**2005**-10 **Hin Lee (Zhuhai) Shipyard Co Ltd — Zhuhai GD** (Hull) Yd No: 088 **2005**-10 **Cheoy Lee Shipyards Ltd — Hong Kong** Yd No: 4853 Loa 27.40 Br ex 11.52 Dght 5.200 Lbp 25.20 Br md 11.50 Dpth 5.00 Welded, 1 dk	**(B32A2ST) Tug**	**2 oil engines** gearing integral to driving 2 Z propellers Total Power: 3,730kW (5,072hp) 12.0kn Caterpillar 3516B 2 x Vee 4 Stroke 16 Cy. 170 x 215 each-1865kW (2536bhp) Caterpillar Inc-USA AuxGen: 2 x 84kW 415V 50Hz a.c
9311000 *3EDK9* -	**STAR EXPRESS** **Royal Tankship SA** Synergy Marine Pte Ltd *Panama* *Panama* MMSI: 371604000 Official number: 33831PEXT1	**28,059** 11,645 45,838 T/cm 50.6	Class: NK	**2005**-11 **Shin Kurushima Dockyard Co. Ltd. — Onishi** Yd No: 5303 Loa 179.88 (BB) Br ex 32.23 Dght 12.022 Lbp 172.00 Br md 32.20 Dpth 18.70 Welded, 1 dk	**(A13B2TP) Products Tanker** Double Hull (13F) Liq: 52,050; Liq (Oil): 53,796 Compartments: 10 Wing Ta, 2 Wing Slop Ta, ER 4 Cargo Pump (s): 4x1000m³/hr Manifold: Bow/CM: 88m	**1 oil engine** driving 1 FP propeller Total Power: 9,267kW (12,599hp) 14.6kn Mitsubishi 6UEC60LA 1 x 2 Stroke 6 Cy. 600 x 1900 9267kW (12599bhp) Kobe Hatsudoki KK-Japan Fuel: 156.0 (d.f.) 1740.0 (r.f.)
9545015 *V7UP9* -	**STAR EXPRESS** **H L International SA Corp** Nam Sung Shipping Co Ltd *Majuro* *Marshall Islands* MMSI: 538003999 Official number: 3999	**9,520** 4,938 12,839	Class: KR	**2010**-10 **Dae Sun Shipbuilding & Engineering Co Ltd — Busan** Yd No: 520 Loa 142.70 (BB) Br ex - Dght 8.214 Lbp 133.50 Br md 22.60 Dpth 11.20 Welded, 1 dk	**(A33A2CC) Container Ship (Fully Cellular)** Double Hull TEU 953 incl 120 ref	**1 oil engine** driving 1 FP propeller Total Power: 7,860kW (10,686hp) 18.1kn MAN-B&W 6S46MC-C 1 x 2 Stroke 6 Cy. 460 x 1932 7860kW (10686bhp) STX Engine Co Ltd-South Korea AuxGen: 3 x 615kW 445V a.c Thrusters: 1 Tunnel thruster (f) Fuel: 85.0 (d.f.) 720.0 (r.f.)
9325611 *3EJS5* -	**STAR FALCON** *ex* Freja Selandia *-2012* **APSF Owning Co 1 Ltd** Norient Product Pool ApS *Panama* *Panama* MMSI: 372608000 Official number: 3253207B	**31,433** 14,001 53,815 T/cm 54.3	Class: NK	**2007**-03 **Shin Kurushima Dockyard Co. Ltd. — Onishi** Yd No: 5371 Loa 185.93 (BB) Br ex 32.23 Dght 13.025 Lbp 179.95 Br md 32.20 Dpth 19.67 Welded, 1 dk	**(A13B2TP) Products Tanker** Double Hull (13F) Liq: 56,765; Liq (Oil): 56,765 Cargo Heating Coils Compartments: 12 Wing Ta, 2 Wing Slop Ta, 1 Slop Ta, ER 4 Cargo Pump (s): 4x1000m³/hr Manifold: Bow/CM: 91.7m	**1 oil engine** driving 1 FP propeller Total Power: 10,620kW (14,439hp) 15.8kn Mitsubishi 6UEC60LS 1 x 2 Stroke 6 Cy. 600 x 2200 10620kW (14439bhp) Kobe Hatsudoki KK-Japan AuxGen: 3 x 700kW a.c Fuel: 180.0 (d.f.) 1886.0 (r.f.)

8021866 *DUH2351* -	**STAR FERRY 1** *ex* Nikkai Maru No. 1 *-1997* **168 Shipping Inc** - *Legaspi* *Philippines* Official number: CEB1002382	*324* 273 307	Class: (NK)	**1981-01 Kanda Zosensho K.K. — Japan** Yd No: 265 Loa 46.46 Br ex 10.22 Dght 2.752 Lbp 41.61 Br md 10.20 Dpth 7.42 Welded, 1 dk	**(A36A2PR) Passenger/Ro-Ro Ship (Vehicles)** Passengers: 550 Angled stern door/ramp (s) Len: 5.60 Wid: 5.00 Swl: 25 Angled side door/ramp (s. a.) Len: 3.80 Wid: 5.00 Swl: - Lane-Len: 74 Lane-Wid: 4.50 Lane-clr ht: 4.00 Lorries: 12	**1 oil engine** geared to sc. shaft driving 1 FP propeller Total Power: 1,177kW (1,600hp) 12.8kn Daihatsu 8DSM-26 1 x 4 Stroke 8 Cy. 260 x 320 1177kW (1600bhp) Daihatsu Diesel Manufacturing Co Lt-Japan AuxGen: 2 x 160kW
8712922 - -	**STAR FERRY III** *ex* Horie Maru *-2007* **168 Shipping Inc** - *Legaspi* *Philippines* Official number: LEG6013135	*808* 364 237		**1987-10 Wakamatsu Zosen K.K. — Kitakyushu** Yd No: 366 Loa 46.41 Br ex - Dght 2.801 Lbp 42.63 Br md 11.50 Dpth 3.71 Welded, 1 dk	**(A36A2PR) Passenger/Ro-Ro Ship (Vehicles)** Passengers: unberthed: 320 Cars: 55, Trailers: 14	**2 oil engines** with clutches, flexible couplings & dr reverse geared to sc. shafts driving 2 FP propellers Total Power: 1,472kW (2,002hp) 13.5kn Daihatsu 6DLM-22 2 x 4 Stroke 6 Cy. 220 x 300 each-736kW (1001bhp) Daihatsu Diesel Manufacturing Co Lt-Japan
9642198 *V7DB4* -	**STAR FIGHTER** *ex* Supra Challenger 2 *-2013* **Star Challenger II LLC** Starbulk SA *Majuro* *Marshall Islands* Official number: 5362	**34,777** 20,209 61,455 T/cm 61.4	Class: RI (NK)	**2013-09 Iwagi Zosen Co Ltd — Kamijima EH** Yd No: 306 Loa 199.98 (BB) Br ex - Dght 13.010 Lbp 195.00 Br md 32.24 Dpth 18.60 Welded, 1 dk	**(A21A2BC) Bulk Carrier** Grain: 77,674; Bale: 73,552 Compartments: 5 Ho, ER 5 Ha: 4 (23.5 x 19.0)ER (18.7 x 19.0) Cranes: 4x30t	**1 oil engine** driving 1 FP propeller Total Power: 8,450kW (11,489hp) 14.5kn MAN-B&W 6S50MC-C8 1 x 2 Stroke 6 Cy. 500 x 2000 8450kW (11489bhp) Mitsui Engineering & Shipbuilding CLtd-Japan AuxGen: 3 x 524kW a.c Fuel: 2565.0
9330056 *9V9359*	**STAR FIRST** **Grace Ocean Pte Ltd** Bright Star Shipmanagement Inc *Singapore* *Singapore* MMSI: 566058000 Official number: 396965	**14,030** 6,724 13,202	Class: NK	**2006-03 Shikoku Dockyard Co. Ltd. — Takamatsu** Yd No: 1030 Loa 162.50 (BB) Br ex - Dght 9.700 Lbp 150.00 Br md 26.00 Dpth 14.10 Welded	**(A34A2GR) Refrigerated Cargo Ship** Ins: 17,463 TEU 436 C Ho 112 TEU C Dk 324 TEU incl 200 ref C Compartments: 4 Ho, 4 Tw Dk, ER 4 Ha: ER 4 (12.6 x 10.3) Cranes: 2x40t,2x8t	**1 oil engine** driving 1 FP propeller Total Power: 15,820kW (21,509hp) 22.0kn MAN-B&W 7S60MC-C 1 x 2 Stroke 7 Cy. 600 x 2400 15820kW (21509bhp) Mitsui Engineering & Shipbuilding CLtd-Japan AuxGen: 1 x 1200kW a.c Thrusters: 1 Tunnel thruster (f) Fuel: 2360.0 55.0pd
7702619 *YCGF* -	**STAR FISH** *ex* Selat Gelasa *-2010* **PT Karyasantosa Tatajaya** - *Panjang* *Indonesia*	*157* 48 -	Class: (KI) (NV)	**1977-09 Sterkoder Mek. Verksted AS — Kristiansund** Yd No: 76 Loa 26.04 Br ex - Dght 3.001 Lbp 24.01 Br md 8.01 Dpth 3.80 Welded, 1 dk	**(B32A2ST) Tug**	**1 oil engine** geared to sc. shaft driving 1 FP propeller Total Power: 853kW (1,160hp) Deutz SBA8M528 1 x 4 Stroke 8 Cy. 220 x 280 853kW (1160bhp) Kloeckner Humboldt Deutz AG-West Germany
8218263 - - -	**STAR FISH 178** *ex* Orient Tide *-2012* *ex* Orient Puma *-1997* - -	**729** 218 953	Class: (AB)	**1983-04 Southern Ocean Shipbuilding Co Pte Ltd — Singapore** Yd No: 142 Loa 49.36 Br ex - Dght 4.395 Lbp 44.40 Br md 12.01 Dpth 5.01 Welded, 1 dk	**(B21A2OS) Platform Supply Ship**	**2 oil engines** sr reverse geared to sc. shafts driving 2 FP propellers Total Power: 2,924kW (3,976hp) 14.0kn Yanmar 6Z280L-ET 2 x 4 Stroke 6 Cy. 280 x 360 each-1462kW (1988bhp) Yanmar Diesel Engine Co Ltd-Japan AuxGen: 2 x 128kW Thrusters: 1 Thwart. FP thruster (f)
8309828 *LAVW4* -	**STAR FLORIDA** **Grieg International II AS** Grieg Star AS SatCom: Inmarsat C 425897410 *Bergen* *Norway (NIS)* MMSI: 258974000	**25,345** 11,625 40,790	Class: NV	**1985-02 Hyundai Heavy Industries Co Ltd — Ulsan** Yd No: 319 Loa 187.20 (BB) Br ex 29.47 Dght 11.820 Lbp 178.01 Br md 29.41 Dpth 16.26 Welded, 1 dk	**(A31A2GO) Open Hatch Cargo Ship** Grain: 42,198 TEU 1112 Compartments: 9 Ho, ER 9 Ha: 9 (12.3 x 24.6)ER Gantry cranes: 2x37t	**1 oil engine** driving 1 FP propeller Total Power: 7,377kW (10,030hp) 15.0kn B&W 7L60MCE 1 x 2 Stroke 7 Cy. 600 x 1944 7377kW (10030bhp) Hyundai Engine & Machinery Co Ltd-South Korea AuxGen: 3 x 750kW 450V 60Hz a.c Thrusters: 1 Thwart. FP thruster (f) Fuel: 100.5 (d.f.) 2586.0 (r.f.) 31.0pd
8915433 *9HA2512* -	**STAR FLYER** *launched as* Star Clipper *-1991* **Star Flyer NV** Star Clippers Monaco SAM *Valletta* *Malta* MMSI: 248785000 Official number: 8915433	**2,298** 838 300	Class: NV (LR) ✠ Classed LR until 14/2/01	**1991-05 Scheepswerf van Langerbrugge — Gent** Yd No: 2183 Loa 111.57 Br ex 15.14 Dght 5.501 Lbp 70.30 Br md 15.10 Dpth 9.10 Welded, 3 dks	**(A37A2PC) Passenger/Cruise** Passengers: cabins: 85; berths: 180	**1 oil engine** driving 1 CP propeller Total Power: 1,014kW (1,379hp) 12.0kn Caterpillar 3512TA 1 x Vee 4 Stroke 12 Cy. 170 x 190 1014kW (1379bhp) Caterpillar Inc-USA AuxGen: 2 x 540kW 450V 60Hz a.c Thrusters: 1 Thwart. FP thruster (f) Fuel: 180.0 (d.f.)
8633592 - -	**STAR FLYTE 41** - **Bailey Group Holdings Pty Ltd** - *Fremantle, WA* *Australia* Official number: 851368	*336* 151 60		**1988-10 WaveMaster International Pty Ltd — Fremantle WA** Loa 41.00 Br ex - Dght 1.100 Lbp - Br md 8.50 Dpth 3.10 Welded, 2 dks	**(A37B2PS) Passenger Ship** Hull Material: Aluminium Alloy Passengers: unberthed: 504	**2 oil engines** with clutches, flexible couplings & sr reverse geared to sc. shafts driving 2 FP propellers Total Power: 2,280kW (3,100hp) 26.0kn M.T.U. 12V396TB83 2 x Vee 4 Stroke 12 Cy. 165 x 185 each-1140kW (1550bhp) MTU Friedrichshafen GmbH-Friedrichshafen AuxGen: 2 x 75kW 240/415V a.c Fuel: 13.5 (d.f.)
8663781 *HQXO7* -	**STAR FORTUNE** *ex* Wah Hing *-2014* *ex* Sheng Ze 5 *-2013* *ex* Jun Jie 5 *-2013* *ex* Xin Ming Fa 17 *-2011* **Star Fortune Enterprises Ltd** Sea Rhythm Enterprise Pte Ltd *San Lorenzo* *Honduras* MMSI: 334943000	**2,989** 1,673 6,467	Class: ZC	**2004-09 Zhejiang Yueqing Qiligang Ship Industry Co Ltd — Yueqing ZJ** Loa 97.00 Br ex - Dght 5.800 Lbp 91.60 Br md 14.50 Dpth 7.20 Welded, 1 dk	**(A31A2GX) General Cargo Ship**	**1 oil engine** driving 1 FP propeller Total Power: 1,471kW (2,000hp) Chinese Std. Type G8300ZC6B 1 x 4 Stroke 8 Cy. 300 x 380 1471kW (2000bhp) Ningbo CSI Power & Machinery GroupCo Ltd-China
8309842 *LAVY4* -	**STAR FRASER** **Grieg International II AS** Grieg Star AS SatCom: Inmarsat C 425897310 *Bergen* *Norway (NIS)* MMSI: 258973000	**25,345** 11,625 40,850	Class: NV	**1985-04 Hyundai Heavy Industries Co Ltd — Ulsan** Yd No: 321 Loa 187.31 (BB) Br ex 29.47 Dght 11.820 Lbp 178.01 Br md 29.41 Dpth 16.26 Welded, 1 dk	**(A31A2GO) Open Hatch Cargo Ship** Grain: 42,198 TEU 1112 Compartments: 9 Ho, ER 9 Ha: 9 (12.3 x 24.6)ER Gantry cranes: 2x37t	**1 oil engine** driving 1 FP propeller Total Power: 7,377kW (10,030hp) 15.0kn B&W 7L60MCE 1 x 2 Stroke 7 Cy. 600 x 1944 7377kW (10030bhp) Hyundai Engine & Machinery Co Ltd-South Korea AuxGen: 3 x 750kW 450V 60Hz a.c Thrusters: 1 Thwart. FP thruster (f) Fuel: 100.5 (d.f.) 2586.0 (r.f.) 31.0pd
8309830 *LAVX4* -	**STAR FUJI** **Grieg International II AS** Grieg Star AS SatCom: Inmarsat C 425897210 *Bergen* *Norway (NIS)* MMSI: 258972000	**25,345** 11,625 40,850	Class: NV	**1985-03 Hyundai Heavy Industries Co Ltd — Ulsan** Yd No: 320 Loa 187.20 (BB) Br ex 29.47 Dght 11.821 Lbp 178.01 Br md 29.41 Dpth 16.26 Welded, 1 dk	**(A31A2GO) Open Hatch Cargo Ship** Grain: 42,198 TEU 1064 Compartments: 9 Ho, ER 9 Ha: 9 (12.3 x 24.6)ER Gantry cranes: 2x37t	**1 oil engine** driving 1 FP propeller Total Power: 7,377kW (10,030hp) 15.0kn B&W 7L60MCE 1 x 2 Stroke 7 Cy. 600 x 1944 7377kW (10030bhp) Hyundai Engine & Machinery Co Ltd-South Korea AuxGen: 3 x 750kW 450V 60Hz a.c Thrusters: 1 Thwart. FP thruster (f) Fuel: 100.5 (d.f.) 2586.0 (r.f.) 31.0pd
9249300 *V7OA4* -	**STAR GAMMA** *ex* C Duckling *-2008* *ex* Sun Bulker *-2006* **Star Gamma LLC** Starbulk SA *Majuro* *Marshall Islands* MMSI: 538003047 Official number: 3047	**29,295** 17,592 53,098	Class: RI (BV)	**2002-10 Oshima Shipbuilding Co Ltd — Saikai NS** Yd No: 10338 Loa 188.50 (BB) Br ex - Dght 12.160 Lbp 179.00 Br md 32.26 Dpth 17.15 Welded, 1 dk	**(A21A2BC) Bulk Carrier** Grain: 66,416; Bale: 65,295 Compartments: 5 Ho, ER 5 Ha: 2 (21.3 x 18.6) (18.6 x 18.6) (22.3 x 18.6)ER (16.7 x 18.6) Cranes: 4x30t	**1 oil engine** driving 1 FP propeller Total Power: 9,488kW (12,900hp) 14.5kn B&W 6S50MC-C 1 x 2 Stroke 6 Cy. 500 x 2000 9488kW (12900bhp) Kawasaki Heavy Industries Ltd-Japan
9033373 *H03888* -	**STAR GATE** *ex* Hachiei Maru *-2005* **TC Union Shipping SA** The Century Shipping Co Ltd *Panama* *Panama* MMSI: 353653000 Official number: 3072105A	**2,664** 999 3,488	Class: KR (NK)	**1991-08 K.K. Miura Zosensho — Saiki** Yd No: 1015 Loa 91.00 Br ex - Dght 5.737 Lbp 84.00 Br md 14.00 Dpth 8.33 Welded, 1 dk	**(A24E2BL) Limestone Carrier** Grain: 3,853 1 Ha: (45.5 x 10.5)ER	**1 oil engine** driving 1 FP propeller Total Power: 1,912kW (2,600hp) 12.3kn Akasaka A37 1 x 4 Stroke 6 Cy. 370 x 720 1912kW (2600bhp) Akasaka Tekkosho KK (Akasaka DieselLtd)-Japan AuxGen: 3 x 116kW a.c

7319242 *T8WN* -	**STAR GLOBAL** *ex* Mop 50 *-2013* *ex* Zakher Moon *-2006* *ex* Uto *-2003* *ex* Smit Manila *-1989* *ex* Seaford *-1981* *ex* Seaforth Challenger *-1977* **Star Global Energy FZE** - *Malakal Harbour* *Palau* MMSI: 511011012	*1,203* 360 1,040	Class: (LR) (BV) ✠ Classed LR until 6/88	**1973-10 Drypool Group Ltd. (Cochrane Shipyard) — Selby** Yd No: 1548 Converted From: Minesweeper-2006 Converted From: Offshore Tug/Supply Ship-1989 Loa 55.91 Br ex 12.27 Dght 4.440 Lbp 49.00 Br md 11.80 Dpth 5.21 Welded, 1 dk	**(B21A20S) Platform Supply Ship** Derricks: 1x30t	**2 oil engines** dr geared to sc. shafts driving 2 CP propellers Total Power: 2,238kW (3,042hp) 12.0kn Hedemora V12A/12 2 x Vee 4 Stroke 12 Cy. 185 x 210 each-1119kW (1521bhp) Hedemora Diesel AB-Sweden AuxGen: 3 x 200kW 440V 60Hz a.c
9463750 *V7UH4* -	**STAR GLOBE** *ex* Theresa Guangdong *-2010* *ex* Glory Talent *-2010* **Dulac Maritime SA** Globus Shipmanagement Corp *Majuro* *Marshall Islands* MMSI: 538003950 Official number: 3950	**32,929** 19,132 56,867 T/cm 58.8	Class: GL	**2010-05 Taizhou Kouan Shipbuilding Co Ltd — Taizhou JS** Yd No: TK0110 Loa 190.02 (BB) Br ex - Dght 12.800 Lbp 185.00 Br md 32.26 Dpth 18.00 Welded, 1 dk	**(A21A2BC) Bulk Carrier** Grain: 71,634; Bale: 68,200 Compartments: 5 Ho, ER 5 Ha: ER Cranes: 4x36t	**1 oil engine** driving 1 FP propeller Total Power: 9,480kW (12,889hp) 14.2kn MAN-B&W 6S50MC-C 1 x 2 Stroke 6 Cy. 500 x 2000 9480kW (12889bhp) STX Engine Co Ltd-South Korea AuxGen: 3 x 600kW 450V a.c
9134749 *H9AG* -	**STAR GOETHALS** *ex* Asperity *-2014* **Northport Maritime Tankers SA** Star Tankers Bunkering SA *Panama* *Panama* MMSI: 355171000 Official number: 45493PEXT	**2,965** 1,136 3,778 T/cm 11.0	Class: LR ✠ **100A1** SS 02/2012 Double Hull oil tanker ESP ✠ **LMC** **UMS** Eq.Ltr: S; Cable: 467.5/36.0 U3	**1997-02 Singmarine Dockyard & Engineering Pte Ltd — Singapore** Yd No: 214 Loa 88.76 (BB) Br ex 16.52 Dght 5.600 Lbp 82.20 Br md 16.50 Dpth 7.65 Welded, 1 dk plus trunk dk	**(A13B2TP) Products Tanker** Double Hull (13F) Liq: 4,179; Liq (Oil): 4,180 Compartments: 5 Ta, ER, 1 Slop Ta 5 Cargo Pump (s): 5x550m³/hr Manifold: Bow/CM: 42.3m	**1 oil engine** with clutches, flexible couplings & sr geared to sc. shaft driving 1 CP propeller Total Power: 2,001kW (2,721hp) 11.5kn Normo KRMB-9 1 x 4 Stroke 9 Cy. 250 x 300 2001kW (2721bhp) Ulstein Bergen AS-Norway AuxGen: 1 x 800kW 440V 60Hz a.c, 3 x 435kW 440V 60Hz a.c Boilers: HWH 6.1kgf/cm² (6.0bar) Thrusters: 1 Thwart. FP thruster (f) Fuel: 200.0 (d.f.)
8420799 *LADR4* -	**STAR GRAN** *launched as* Triton *-1986* **Grieg International II AS** Grieg Star AS SatCom: Inmarsat C 425731410 *Bergen* *Norway (NIS)* MMSI: 257314000	**27,192** 12,918 43,759	Class: NV	**1986-05 Mitsui Eng. & SB. Co. Ltd., Chiba Works — Ichihara** Yd No: 1329 Loa 197.80 (BB) Br ex - Dght 11.720 Lbp 188.50 Br md 29.41 Dpth 16.26 Welded, 1 dk	**(A31A2GO) Open Hatch Cargo Ship** Grain: 47,645; Bale: 47,335 TEU 1532 Compartments: 10 Ho, ER 10 Ha: ER Gantry cranes: 2x40t	**1 oil engine** driving 1 FP propeller Total Power: 7,445kW (10,122hp) 16.3kn B&W 6L60MCE 1 x 2 Stroke 6 Cy. 600 x 1944 7445kW (10122bhp) Mitsui Engineering & Shipbuilding CLtd-Japan AuxGen: 3 x 800kW 450V 60Hz a.c Thrusters: 1 Thwart. CP thruster (f)
8420787 *LADQ4* -	**STAR GRIP** **Grieg Shipping II AS** Grieg Star AS SatCom: Inmarsat A 1312164 *Bergen* *Norway (NIS)* MMSI: 257313000	**27,192** 12,918 43,712	Class: NV	**1986-03 Mitsui Eng. & SB. Co. Ltd., Chiba Works — Ichihara** Yd No: 1328 Loa 197.80 (BB) Br ex 29.44 Dght 11.720 Lbp 188.50 Br md 29.41 Dpth 16.26 Welded, 1 dk	**(A31A2GO) Open Hatch Cargo Ship** Grain: 47,645; Bale: 47,335 TEU 1532 Compartments: 10 Ho, ER 10 Ha: ER Gantry cranes: 2x40t	**1 oil engine** driving 1 FP propeller Total Power: 7,443kW (10,120hp) 15.0kn B&W 6L60MCE 1 x 2 Stroke 6 Cy. 600 x 1944 7443kW (10120bhp) Mitsui Engineering & Shipbuilding CLtd-Japan AuxGen: 3 x 800kW 450V 60Hz a.c Thrusters: 1 Thwart. CP thruster (f)
8940775 - -	**STAR GULF** **Van T Tran** - *Chauvin, LA* *United States of America* Official number: 1041578	*138* 111 -		**1996 Van T. Tran — Chauvin, La** L reg 23.93 Br ex - Dght - Lbp - Br md 7.32 Dpth 3.35 Welded, 1 dk	**(B11B2FV) Fishing Vessel**	**1 oil engine** driving 1 FP propeller
9103128 *LAXP4* -	**STAR HANSA** **Grieg Shipping II AS** Grieg Star AS SatCom: Inmarsat C 425972510 *Bergen* *Norway (NIS)* MMSI: 259725000	**32,749** 13,647 46,580 T/cm 53.0	Class: NV	**1995-12 Mitsui Eng. & SB. Co. Ltd. — Tamano** Yd No: 1418 Loa 198.00 (BB) Br ex - Dght 12.319 Lbp 187.04 Br md 31.00 Dpth 15.60 Welded, 1 dk	**(A31A2GO) Open Hatch Cargo Ship** Grain: 61,491; Bale: 58,726 TEU 1950 C Ho 1350 TEU C Dk 600 TEU incl 20 ref C. Compartments: 11 Ho, ER 11 Ha: ER Gantry cranes: 2x40t	**1 oil engine** driving 1 FP propeller Total Power: 10,519kW (14,302hp) 16.0kn B&W 6S60MC 1 x 2 Stroke 6 Cy. 600 x 2292 10519kW (14302bhp) Mitsui Engineering & Shipbuilding CLtd-Japan AuxGen: 2 x 1300kW 220/440V 60Hz a.c, 1 x 720kW 220/440V 60Hz a.c Thrusters: 1 Tunnel thruster (f); 1 Tunnel thruster (a) Fuel: 117.0 (d.f.) 2259.0 (r.f.) 44.7pd
9103130 *LAGB5* -	**STAR HARMONIA** **Grieg International II AS** Grieg Star AS SatCom: Inmarsat A 1316376 *Bergen* *Norway (NIS)* MMSI: 259885000	**32,749** 13,647 46,604 T/cm 53.0	Class: NV	**1998-01 Mitsui Eng. & SB. Co. Ltd. — Tamano** Yd No: 1419 Loa 198.00 (BB) Br ex - Dght 12.019 Lbp 187.00 Br md 31.00 Dpth 19.00 Welded, 1 dk	**(A31A2GO) Open Hatch Cargo Ship** Grain: 61,498; Bale: 58,726 TEU 1950 C Ho 1350 TEU C Dk 600 TEU incl 20 ref C. Compartments: 11 Ho, ER 11 Ha: 11 (12.3 x 26.2)ER Gantry cranes: 2x40t	**1 oil engine** driving 1 FP propeller Total Power: 10,519kW (14,302hp) 16.0kn B&W 6S60MC 1 x 2 Stroke 6 Cy. 600 x 2292 10519kW (14302bhp) Mitsui Engineering & Shipbuilding CLtd-Japan AuxGen: 2 x 1300kW 220/440V 60Hz a.c, 1 x 720kW 220/440V 60Hz a.c Thrusters: 1 Tunnel thruster (f); 1 Tunnel thruster (a) Fuel: 99.3 (d.f.) 2112.0 (r.f.) 44.0pd
9284520 *3FZX9* -	**STAR HARMONY** *ex* Sanko Glory *-2011* **Star Harmony Compania Naviera SA** Dekoil Inc *Panama* *Panama* MMSI: 353071000 Official number: 4323611	**29,372** 17,601 52,980	Class: GL (NK)	**2005-04 Oshima Shipbuilding Co Ltd — Saikai NS** Yd No: 10380 Loa 188.50 (BB) Br ex - Dght 12.163 Lbp 179.00 Br md 32.26 Dpth 17.15 Welded, 1 dk	**(A21A2BC) Bulk Carrier** Double Hull Grain: 66,416; Bale: 65,295 Compartments: 5 Ho, ER 5 Ha: 2 (21.4 x 18.6) (18.6 x 18.6) (22.3 x 18.6)ER (16.7 x 18.6) Cranes: 4x30t	**1 oil engine** driving 1 FP propeller Total Power: 7,686kW (10,450hp) 14.1kn MAN-B&W 6S50MC-C 1 x 2 Stroke 6 Cy. 500 x 2000 7686kW (10450bhp) Kawasaki Heavy Industries Ltd-Japan AuxGen: 3 x 653kW 440/110V 60Hz a.c Fuel: 1620.0
9071557 *LAVD4* -	**STAR HERDLA** **Grieg Shipping II AS** Grieg Star AS SatCom: Inmarsat A 1315631 *Bergen* *Norway (NIS)* MMSI: 258954000	**32,744** 13,647 46,580 T/cm 53.0	Class: NV	**1994-10 Mitsui Eng. & SB. Co. Ltd. — Tamano** Yd No: 1401 Loa 198.00 (BB) Br ex - Dght 12.316 Lbp 187.00 Br md 31.00 Dpth 15.60 Welded, 1 dk	**(A31A2GO) Open Hatch Cargo Ship** Grain: 61,490; Bale: 61,491 TEU 1950 C Ho 1350 TEU C Dk 600 TEU incl 20 ref C. Compartments: 11 Ho, ER 11 Ha: ER Gantry cranes: 2x40t	**1 oil engine** driving 1 FP propeller Total Power: 10,519kW (14,302hp) 16.3kn B&W 6S60MC 1 x 2 Stroke 6 Cy. 600 x 2292 10519kW (14302bhp) Mitsui Engineering & Shipbuilding CLtd-Japan AuxGen: 2 x 1300kW 440V 60Hz a.c, 1 x 720kW 440V 60Hz a.c Thrusters: 1 Tunnel thruster (f); 1 Tunnel thruster (a) Fuel: 2000.0 (r.f.) 42.0pd
9071569 *LAVN4* -	**STAR HIDRA** **Grieg Shipping II AS** Grieg Star AS SatCom: Inmarsat A 1315653 *Bergen* *Norway (NIS)* MMSI: 258964000	**32,744** 13,647 46,547 T/cm 53.0	Class: NV	**1994-12 Mitsui Eng. & SB. Co. Ltd. — Tamano** Yd No: 1402 Loa 198.00 (BB) Br ex - Dght 12.316 Lbp 187.00 Br md 31.00 Dpth 15.60 Welded, 1 dk	**(A31A2GO) Open Hatch Cargo Ship** Grain: 61,490; Bale: 58,726 TEU 1950 C Ho 1350 TEU C Dk 600 TEU incl 20 ref C. Compartments: 11 Ho, ER 11 Ha: ER Gantry cranes: 2x40t	**1 oil engine** driving 1 FP propeller Total Power: 10,519kW (14,302hp) 16.3kn B&W 6S60MC 1 x 2 Stroke 6 Cy. 600 x 2292 10519kW (14302bhp) Mitsui Engineering & Shipbuilding CLtd-Japan AuxGen: 2 x 1300kW 440V 60Hz a.c, 1 x 720kW 440V 60Hz a.c Thrusters: 1 Tunnel thruster (f); 1 Tunnel thruster (a) Fuel: 2000.0 (r.f.) 42.0pd
7373042 *HP9237* -	**STAR HOPE** *ex* Navis Hope *-2012* *ex* Permina Supply No. 15 *-1998* **Star Petroleum Co FZC** - SatCom: Inmarsat C 435354310 *Panama* *Panama* MMSI: 353543000 Official number: 2681600C	*704* 212 921	Class: BV (KI) (AB)	**1974-08 Kanrei Zosen K.K. — Tokushima** Yd No: 187 Loa 50.00 Br ex 11.66 Dght 4.201 Lbp 45.50 Br md 11.59 Dpth 4.88 Welded, 1 dk	**(B21B20A) Anchor Handling Tug Supply**	**2 oil engines** reverse reduction geared to sc. shafts driving 2 FP propellers Total Power: 2,206kW (3,000hp) 13.0kn Niigata 8MG25BX 2 x 4 Stroke 8 Cy. 250 x 320 each-1103kW (1500bhp) Niigata Engineering Co Ltd-Japan AuxGen: 2 x 160kW Thrusters: 1 Thwart. FP thruster (f) Fuel: 341.5 (d.f.)
9145956 *3FDK6* -	**STAR HYPERION** *ex* Ondina *-2009* *ex* Western Ondina *-2004* **Star Hyperion Compania Naviera SA** Dekoil Inc SatCom: Inmarsat A 1360236 *Panama* *Panama* MMSI: 356370000 Official number: 2312396E	**26,449** 16,181 47,639 T/cm 50.9	Class: NV	**1996-07 Oshima Shipbuilding Co Ltd — Saikai NS** Yd No: 10188 Loa 189.99 (BB) Br ex - Dght 11.820 Lbp 181.60 Br md 30.50 Dpth 16.50 Welded, 1 dk	**(A21A2BC) Bulk Carrier** Grain: 59,923; Bale: 57,372 Compartments: 5 Ho, ER 5 Ha: (16.0 x 15.3)4 (20.8 x 15.3)ER Cranes: 4x25t	**1 oil engine** driving 1 FP propeller Total Power: 7,334kW (9,971hp) 14.0kn B&W 6S50MC 1 x 2 Stroke 6 Cy. 500 x 1910 7334kW (9971bhp) Kawasaki Heavy Industries Ltd-Japan AuxGen: 3 x 440kW 220/440V 60Hz a.c

Identity / Owner	Tonnage	Class	Builder / Dimensions	Type / Cargo	Machinery
7709095 **STAR I** *D4GI* *ex* Bright Star I *-2008* *ex* Agios Arsenios *-2006* - *ex* MSC Bosphorus *-2003* *ex* Peltrader *-1999* *ex* Lady Aalke *-1988* *ex* Midsland *-1987* **Moura Co SA** - SatCom: Inmarsat C 461706310 *Sao Vicente* *Cape Verde* MMSI: 617076000	**2,315** 1,367 3,614	Class: (HR) (BV)	**1978-09 Scheepswerf 'Friesland' BV — Lemmer** Yd No: 363 Loa 82.00 Br ex 13.70 Dght 5.649 Lbp 74.43 Br md 13.62 Dpth 7.83 Welded, 2 dks	**(A31A2GX) General Cargo Ship** Grain: 4,716; Bale: 4,575 TEU 166 C.Ho 128/20' incl. 10 ref C. C.Dk 38/20' Compartments: 1 Ho, ER 1 Ha: (50.4 x 10.2)ER	**1 oil engine** reduction geared to sc. shaft driving 1 CP propeller Total Power: 1,765kW (2,400hp) 12.8kn Bolnes 16VDNL150/600 1 x Vee 2 Stroke 16 Cy. 190 x 350 1765kW (2400bhp) 'Bolnes' Motorenfabriek BV-Netherlands AuxGen: 1 x 200kW 380V 50Hz a.c, 2 x 80kW 380V 50Hz a.c Thrusters: 1 Thwart. FP thruster (f) Fuel: 263.0 (d.f.) 9.5pd
8602385 **STAR I** *E5U2550* *ex* Boe Ocean *-2012* *ex* Zuara *-2004* - *ex* Multimax Bremer *-2003* *ex* Multimax Leader *-1999* *ex* Superflex Bond *-1999* *ex* Berounka *-1995* **Melmar Maritime Ltd** ADCO SAL *Avatiu* *Cook Islands* MMSI: 518603000 Official number: 1639	**6,425** 3,320 7,398 T/cm 17.7	Class: BV (LR) ✠ Classed LR until 26/3/04	**1989-06 Tianjin Xingang Shipyard — Tianjin** Yd No: 262 Loa 119.01 Br ex 18.73 Dght 7.400 Lbp 110.01 Br md 18.61 Dpth 10.42 Welded, 2 dks	**(A31A2GX) General Cargo Ship** Grain: 11,651; Bale: 10,751 TEU 126 C. 126/20' Compartments: 3 Ho, ER, 3 Tw Dk 3 Ha: (12.5 x 8.4) (20.0 x 10.4) (12.9 x 10.4)ER Cranes: 4x15t Ice Capable	**1 oil engine** driving 1 FP propeller Total Power: 3,420kW (4,650hp) 13.5kn Sulzer 5RTA38 1 x 2 Stroke 5 Cy. 380 x 1100 3420kW (4650bhp) Shanghai Diesel Engine Co Ltd-China AuxGen: 3 x 320kW 400V 50Hz a.c Boilers: AuxB New (Comp) 7.9kgf/cm² (7.7bar) Fuel: 104.2 (d.f.) 648.7 (r.f.) 14.6pd
9376945 **STAR I** *9HVF8* *ex* Acor *-2013* - **Star Transportation LLC** Norient Product Pool ApS *Valletta* *Malta* MMSI: 256472000 Official number: 9376945	**23,248** 9,915 37,900 T/cm 45.2	Class: NV (AB)	**2007-06 Hyundai Mipo Dockyard Co Ltd — Ulsan** Yd No: 2022 Loa 184.32 (BB) Br ex 27.45 Dght 11.515 Lbp 176.00 Br md 27.40 Dpth 17.20 Welded, 1 dk	**(A12B2TR) Chemical/Products Tanker** Double Hull (13F) Liq: 40,781; Liq (Oil): 40,801 Compartments: 12 Wing Ta, 2 Wing Slop Ta, ER 12 Cargo Pump (s): 10x500m³/hr, 2x300m³/hr Manifold: Bow/CM: 92.6m Ice Capable	**1 oil engine** driving 1 FP propeller Total Power: 9,480kW (12,889hp) 15.0kn MAN-B&W 6S50MC-C 1 x 2 Stroke 6 Cy. 500 x 2000 9480kW (12889bhp) Hyundai Heavy Industries Co Ltd-South Korea AuxGen: 3 x 900kW a.c Thrusters: 1 Tunnel thruster (f) Fuel: 182.7 (d.f.) 1162.9 (r.f.)
9692521 **STAR I** *9V7573* - **Star Ship Marine Pte Ltd** Hai Yin Marine Pte Ltd *Singapore* *Singapore* MMSI: 563022710 Official number: 398254	**496** 207 803	Class: RI	**2013-11 Lianyungang Wuzhou Shipbuilding Co Co Ltd — Guanyun County JS** Yd No: WZ-35 Loa 44.80 (BB) Br ex - Dght 3.250 Lbp 42.00 Br md 10.20 Dpth 4.22 Welded, 1 dk	**(B35E2TF) Bunkering Tanker** Double Hull (13F)	**2 oil engines** geared to sc. shafts driving 2 FP propellers Total Power: 596kW (810hp) 9.5kn Cummins NTA-855-M 2 x 4 Stroke 6 Cy. 140 x 152 each-298kW (405bhp) Chongqing Cummins Engine Co Ltd-China AuxGen: 3 x 265kW 220V 50Hz a.c
9182978 **STAR ISFJORD** *LAOX5* - **Grieg Shipping II AS** Grieg Star AS *Bergen* *Norway (NIS)* MMSI: 257615000	**32,628** 13,538 46,428 T/cm 48.4	Class: NV	**2000-05 Mitsui Eng. & SB. Co. Ltd. — Tamano** Yd No: 1489 Lengthened-2005 Loa 198.00 (BB) Br ex 31.12 Dght 12.320 Lbp 189.02 Br md 31.00 Dpth 19.00 Welded, 1 dk	**(A31A2GO) Open Hatch Cargo Ship** Double Hull Grain: 55,284 TEU 2096 C Ho 1396 TEU C Dk 700 TEU Compartments: 10 Ho, ER 10 Ha: 10 (12.3 x 26.2)ER Gantry cranes: 2x70t Ice Capable	**1 oil engine** driving 1 FP propeller Total Power: 11,047kW (15,020hp) 16.4kn B&W 6S60MC 1 x 2 Stroke 6 Cy. 600 x 2292 11047kW (15020bhp) Mitsui Engineering & Shipbuilding CLtd-Japan AuxGen: 3 x 1196kW 450V 60Hz a.c Thrusters: 1 Thwart. FP thruster (f); 1 Thwart. CP thruster (a) Fuel: 114.9 (d.f.) (Heating Coils) 1950.8 (r.f.) 42.0pd
9182966 **STAR ISMENE** *LANT5* - **Grieg International II AS** Grieg Star AS *Bergen* *Norway (NIS)* MMSI: 257532000	**32,628** 13,538 46,428 T/cm 48.4	Class: NV	**2000-01 Mitsui Eng. & SB. Co. Ltd. — Tamano** Yd No: 1488 Lengthened-2005 Loa 198.00 (BB) Br ex - Dght 12.319 Lbp 189.02 Br md 31.00 Dpth 19.00 Welded, 1 dk	**(A31A2GO) Open Hatch Cargo Ship** Double Hull Grain: 55,284 TEU 2096 C Ho 1396 TEU C Dk 700 TEU Cargo Heating Coils Compartments: 10 Ho, ER 10 Ha: 10 (12.3 x 26.2)ER Gantry cranes: 2x70t	**1 oil engine** driving 1 FP propeller Total Power: 10,518kW (14,300hp) 16.2kn B&W 6S60MC 1 x 2 Stroke 6 Cy. 600 x 2292 10518kW (14300bhp) Mitsui Engineering & Shipbuilding CLtd-Japan AuxGen: 2 x 1300kW 440V 60Hz a.c Thrusters: 1 Thwart. CP thruster (f); 1 Thwart. CP thruster (a) Fuel: 86.3 (d.f.) (Heating Coils) 1639.7 (r.f.) 44.0pd
9182954 **STAR ISTIND** *LAMP5* - **Grieg Shipping II AS** Grieg Star AS SatCom: Inmarsat C 425742410 *Bergen* *Norway (NIS)* MMSI: 257424000	**32,628** 13,538 46,428 T/cm 48.4	Class: NV	**1999-09 Mitsui Eng. & SB. Co. Ltd. — Tamano** Yd No: 1487 Lengthened-2005 Loa 198.00 (BB) Br ex - Dght 12.300 Lbp 187.00 Br md 31.00 Dpth 19.00 Welded, 1 dk	**(A31A2GO) Open Hatch Cargo Ship** Double Hull Grain: 55,284 TEU 2096 C Ho 1396 TEU C Dk 700 TEU Compartments: 10 Ho, ER 10 Ha: 10 (12.3 x 26.2)ER Gantry cranes: 2x70t	**1 oil engine** driving 1 FP propeller Total Power: 10,519kW (14,302hp) 16.2kn B&W 6S60MC 1 x 2 Stroke 6 Cy. 600 x 2292 10519kW (14302bhp) Mitsui Engineering & Shipbuilding CLtd-Japan AuxGen: 2 x 1300kW 450V a.c, 1 x 720kW 450V a.c Thrusters: 1 Thwart. FP thruster (f); 1 Thwart. CP thruster (a) Fuel: 86.3 (d.f.) 1639.7 (r.f.) 40.0pd
8835035 **STAR IV** - *ex* Shoho Maru *-1990* - **Mekar Serunding Sdn Bhd** -	**299** 162 449	Class: IS (NK)	**1975-05 YK Furumoto Tekko Zosensho — Osakikamijima** Yd No: 362 Converted From: Oil Tanker-2007 Loa 43.10 Br ex - Dght 2.997 Lbp 39.00 Br md 7.00 Dpth 3.30 Welded, 1 dk	**(A13B2TP) Products Tanker** Liq: 630; Liq (Oil): 630	**1 oil engine** driving 1 FP propeller Total Power: 441kW (600hp) 9.0kn Hanshin 6L24GSH 1 x 4 Stroke 6 Cy. 240 x 400 441kW (600bhp) The Hanshin Diesel Works Ltd-Japan AuxGen: 2 x 16kW a.c
9528287 **STAR JAKARTA** *T2FD3* - **Sino Ling Tao Resources Pte Ltd** Singapore Star Shipping Pte Ltd *Funafuti* *Tuvalu* MMSI: 572738000	**472** 141 -	Class: BV	**2009-07 Anhui Chaohu Shipbuilding Yard — Chaohu AH** Yd No: AHJT07-21 Loa 36.10 Br ex - Dght 4.000 Lbp 32.25 Br md 10.60 Dpth 4.90 Welded, 1 dk	**(B32A2ST) Tug**	**2 oil engines** reduction geared to sc. shafts driving 2 FP propellers Total Power: 2,984kW (4,058hp) Cummins KTA-50-M2 2 x Vee 4 Stroke 16 Cy. 159 x 159 each-1492kW (2029bhp) Cummins Engine Co Ltd-United Kingdom AuxGen: 2 x 100kW 60Hz a.c Fuel: 360.0
9254654 **STAR JAPAN** *LAZV5* - **Grieg Shipping II AS** Grieg Star AS *Bergen* *Norway (NIS)* MMSI: 257329000	**32,844** 13,085 44,807	Class: NV	**2004-06 Mitsui Eng. & SB. Co. Ltd. — Tamano** Yd No: 1532 Loa 198.00 (BB) Br ex 31.06 Dght 12.000 Lbp 187.00 Br md 31.00 Dpth 19.00 Welded, 1 dk	**(A31A2GO) Open Hatch Cargo Ship** Double Hull Grain: 61,400 TEU 2070 C Ho 1350 TEU C Dk 720 TEU Gantry cranes: 2x68t	**1 oil engine** driving 1 FP propeller Total Power: 10,519kW (14,302hp) 16.6kn B&W 6S60MC 1 x 2 Stroke 6 Cy. 600 x 2292 10519kW (14302bhp) Mitsui Engineering & Shipbuilding CLtd-Japan AuxGen: 2 x 1370kW 440/220V 60Hz a.c, 1 x 760kW 440/220V 60Hz a.c Thrusters: 1 Tunnel thruster (f); 1 Tunnel thruster (a)
9310513 **STAR JAVA** *LAJS6* - **Grieg Shipping II AS** Grieg Star AS *Bergen* *Norway (NIS)* MMSI: 258734000	**32,679** 13,085 44,692	Class: NV	**2006-11 Mitsui Eng. & SB. Co. Ltd. — Tamano** Yd No: 1533 Loa 198.00 (BB) Br ex 31.06 Dght 12.000 Lbp 187.00 Br md 31.00 Dpth 19.00 Welded, 1 dk	**(A31A2GO) Open Hatch Cargo Ship** Double Hull Grain: 61,400 TEU 2070 C Ho 1350 TEU C Dk 720 TEU Compartments: 11 Ho, ER 11 Ha: ER 11 (12.3 x 26.2) Gantry cranes: 2x40t	**1 oil engine** driving 1 FP propeller Total Power: 12,240kW (16,642hp) 16.0kn MAN-B&W 6S60MC 1 x 2 Stroke 6 Cy. 600 x 2292 12240kW (16642bhp) Mitsui Engineering & Shipbuilding CLtd-Japan AuxGen: 2 x 1300kW 440/220V 60Hz a.c, 1 x 700kW 440/220V 60Hz a.c Thrusters: 1 Tunnel thruster (f); 1 Tunnel thruster (a)
9562594 **STAR JAVA** *T2GC3* - **Sino Ling Tao Resources Pte Ltd** Singapore Star Shipping Pte Ltd *Funafuti* *Tuvalu* MMSI: 572761000 Official number: 20340909	**481** 144 350	Class: AB	**2009-10 in the People's Republic of China** Yd No: HX009 Loa 37.00 Br ex - Dght - Lbp 32.60 Br md 11.40 Dpth 4.95 Welded, 1 dk	**(B32A2ST) Tug**	**2 oil engines** reverse reduction geared to sc. shafts driving 2 FP propellers Total Power: 2,386kW (3,244hp) Cummins KTA-50-M2 2 x Vee 4 Stroke 16 Cy. 159 x 159 each-1193kW (1622bhp) Cummins Engine Co Inc-USA AuxGen: 2 x 120kW a.c
9644823 **STAR JING** *9V2205* - **Norr Systems Pte Ltd** - *Singapore* *Singapore* MMSI: 563156000 Official number: 398739	**36,295** 21,607 63,562	Class: AB	**2013-07 Taizhou Kouan Shipbuilding Co Ltd — Taizhou JS** Yd No: TK0801 Loa 199.90 (BB) Br ex - Dght 13.300 Lbp 194.50 Br md 32.26 Dpth 18.50 Welded, 1 dk	**(A21A2BC) Bulk Carrier** Grain: 78,500; Bale: 73,680 Compartments: 5 Ho, ER 5 Ha: ER Cranes: 4x30t	**1 oil engine** driving 1 FP propeller Total Power: 8,050kW (10,945hp) 14.0kn MAN-B&W 5S60MC-C8 1 x 2 Stroke 5 Cy. 600 x 2400 8050kW (10945bhp) Hudong Heavy Machinery Co Ltd-China AuxGen: 3 x 600kW a.c Fuel: 240.0 (d.f.) 2050.0 (r.f.)
9242601 **STAR JUPITER** *V2OE8* *ex* Magellan Jupiter *-2012* - *ex* Miriam Borchard *-2010* *ex* Gracechurch Jupiter *-2008* *completed as* Pioneer Falcon *-2002* **Reederei ms 'Magellan Jupiter' Schiffahrts GmbH & Co KG** Quadrant Bereederungs GmbH & Co KG *Saint John's* *Antigua & Barbuda* MMSI: 304428000 Official number: 3758	**6,277** 3,249 7,977	Class: NK (GL)	**2002-09 J.J. Sietas KG Schiffswerft GmbH & Co. — Hamburg** Yd No: 1198 Loa 133.43 (BB) Br ex 18.95 Dght 7.240 Lbp 125.30 Br md 18.70 Dpth 9.30 Welded, 1 dk	**(A33A2CC) Container Ship (Fully Cellular)** Double Bottom Entire Compartment Length Grain: 10,845; Bale: 9,607 TEU 735 incl 104 ref C. Compartments: 4 Cell Ho, ER 4 Ha: ER	**1 oil engine** with flexible couplings & sr geared to sc. shaft driving 1 CP propeller Total Power: 6,600kW (8,973hp) 18.3kn MaK 8M43 1 x 4 Stroke 8 Cy. 430 x 610 6600kW (8973bhp) Caterpillar Motoren GmbH & Co. KG-Germany AuxGen: 1 x 1220kW 380/220V a.c, 2 x 510kW 380/220V a.c, 1 x 320kW 380/220V a.c Thrusters: 1 Thwart. CP thruster (f) Fuel: 900.0

Ship	Tonnage	Class	Builder / Dimensions	Type / Capacity	Machinery
9254642 **STAR JUVENTAS** *LAZU5* - **Grieg International II AS** Grieg Star AS *Bergen* *Norway (NIS)* MMSI: 257328000	32,679 13,085 44,837	Class: NV	2004-05 **Mitsui Eng. & SB. Co. Ltd. — Tamano** Yd No: 1531 Loa 198.00 (BB) Br ex 31.06 Dght 12.000 Lbp 187.00 Br md 31.00 Dpth 19.00 Welded, 1 dk	**(A31A2GO) Open Hatch Cargo Ship** Double Hull Grain: 61,400 TEU 2070 C Ho 1350 TEU C Dk 720 TEU Gantry cranes: 2x68t	**1 oil engine** driving 1 FP propeller Total Power: 10,520kW (14,303hp) 16.6kn B&W 6S60MC 1 x 2 Stroke 6 Cy. 600 x 2292 10520kW (14303bhp) Mitsui Engineering & Shipbuilding CLtd-Japan AuxGen: 2 x 1370kW 440/220V 60Hz a.c, 1 x 760kW 440/220V 60Hz a.c Thrusters: 1 Tunnel thruster (f); 1 Tunnel thruster (a)
9221126 **STAR KAPPA** *V7OB5* - *ex* E Duckling *-2007* *ex* Artemis II *-2006* *ex* Artemis *-2003* **Star Kappa LLC** Starbulk SA *Majuro* *Marshall Islands* MMSI: 538003052 Official number: 3052	29,499 17,889 52,055 T/cm 55.0	Class: RI (LR) ✠ Classed LR until 18/8/09	2001-10 **Sanoyas Hishino Meisho Corp — Kurashiki OY** Yd No: 1187 Loa 189.90 (BB) Br ex 32.29 Dght 12.020 Lbp 182.00 Br md 32.26 Dpth 17.10 Welded, 1 dk	**(A21A2BC) Bulk Carrier** Double Bottom Entire Compartment Length Grain: 66,597; Bale: 64,545 Cargo Heating Coils Compartments: 5 Ho, ER 5 Ha: (20.3 x 16.6)4 (20.5 x 18.3)ER Cranes: 5x30t	**1 oil engine** driving 1 FP propeller Total Power: 8,730kW (11,869hp) 14.5kn Sulzer 6RTA48T 1 x 2 Stroke 6 Cy. 480 x 2000 8730kW (11869bhp) Diesel United Ltd.-Aioi AuxGen: 3 x 650kW 450V 60Hz a.c Boilers: AuxB (Comp) 6.9kgf/cm² (6.8bar) Fuel: 276.0 (d.f.) (Heating Coils) 2176.0 (r.f.) 32.0pd
9321940 **STAR KESTREL** *3EVC2* - *ex* Nord Sound *-2013* *ex* Gan-Sabre *-2010* **APSF Owning Co 4 Ltd** Interorient Marine Services (Germany) GmbH & Co KG *Panama* *Panama* MMSI: 354190000 Official number: 4459813	30,068 13,648 51,228 T/cm 52.0	Class: NV	2008-01 **STX Shipbuilding Co Ltd — Changwon (Jinhae Shipyard)** Yd No: 1216 Loa 183.00 (BB) Br ex 32.28 Dght 13.167 Lbp 173.90 Br md 32.20 Dpth 19.10 Welded, 1 dk	**(A12B2TR) Chemical/Products Tanker** Double Hull (13F) Liq: 52,133; Liq (Oil): 53,500 Compartments: 12 Wing Ta, 2 Wing Slop Ta, Wing ER 12 Cargo Pump (s): 12x600m³/hr Manifold: Bow/CM: 92.6m	**1 oil engine** driving 1 FP propeller Total Power: 9,480kW (12,889hp) 14.2kn MAN-B&W 6S50MC-C 1 x 2 Stroke 6 Cy. 500 x 2000 9480kW (12889bhp) STX Engine Co Ltd-South Korea AuxGen: 3 x 900kW 440/220V 60Hz a.c Fuel: 201.0 (d.f.) 1460.0 (r.f.)
9396139 **STAR KILIMANJARO** *LAIG7* - **Grieg Shipping II AS** Grieg Star AS SatCom: Inmarsat C 425735010 *Bergen* *Norway (NIS)* MMSI: 257350000	37,158 13,824 49,862	Class: NV	2009-09 **Hyundai Mipo Dockyard Co Ltd — Ulsan** Yd No: 8002 Loa 208.78 (BB) Br ex 32.25 Dght 12.340 Lbp 197.40 Br md 32.20 Dpth 19.50 Welded, 1 dk	**(A31A2GO) Open Hatch Cargo Ship** Grain: 65,357 TEU 1453 C Ho 618 TEU C Dk 835 TEU Compartments: 3 Tw Dk, 9 Ho, ER 10 Ha: ER Gantry cranes: 2x70t	**1 oil engine** driving 1 FP propeller Total Power: 11,300kW (15,363hp) 16.0kn MAN-B&W 5S60MC-C 1 x 2 Stroke 5 Cy. 600 x 2400 11300kW (15363bhp) Hyundai Heavy Industries Co Ltd-South Korea AuxGen: 2 x 800kW a.c, 1 x 750kW a.c Thrusters: 1 Tunnel thruster (f); 1 Tunnel thruster (a)
9396141 **STAR KINN** *LAJF7* - **Grieg International II AS** Grieg Star AS *Bergen* *Norway (NIS)* MMSI: 257457000 Official number: 28164	37,158 13,824 49,850	Class: NV	2010-02 **Hyundai Mipo Dockyard Co Ltd — Ulsan** Yd No: 8003 Loa 208.78 (BB) Br ex 32.25 Dght 12.340 Lbp 197.40 Br md 32.20 Dpth 19.50 Welded, 1 dk	**(A31A2GO) Open Hatch Cargo Ship** Grain: 65,000 TEU 1453 C Ho 618 TEU C Dk 835 TEU Compartments: 10 Ho, ER 10 Ha: ER Gantry cranes: 2x70t	**1 oil engine** driving 1 FP propeller Total Power: 11,300kW (15,363hp) 16.0kn MAN-B&W 5S60MC-C 1 x 2 Stroke 5 Cy. 600 x 2400 11300kW (15363bhp) Hyundai Heavy Industries Co Ltd-South Korea AuxGen: 2 x 1400kW a.c, 1 x a.c Thrusters: 1 Tunnel thruster (f); 1 Tunnel thruster (a)
9396127 **STAR KIRKENES** *LAHR7* - **Grieg International II AS** Grieg Star AS SatCom: Inmarsat C 425731010 *Bergen* *Norway (NIS)* MMSI: 257310000	37,158 13,824 49,924	Class: NV	2009-06 **Hyundai Mipo Dockyard Co Ltd — Ulsan** Yd No: 8001 Loa 208.78 (BB) Br ex 32.25 Dght 12.340 Lbp 197.40 Br md 32.20 Dpth 19.50 Welded, 1 dk	**(A31A2GO) Open Hatch Cargo Ship** Grain: 65,357 TEU 1453 C Ho 618 TEU C Dk 835 TEU Compartments: 10 Ho, ER 10 Ha: ER Gantry cranes: 2x70t	**1 oil engine** driving 1 FP propeller Total Power: 11,300kW (15,363hp) 16.0kn MAN-B&W 5S60MC-C 1 x 2 Stroke 5 Cy. 600 x 2400 11300kW (15363bhp) Hyundai Heavy Industries Co Ltd-South Korea AuxGen: 2 x 1350kW a.c, 1 x 750kW a.c Thrusters: 1 Tunnel thruster (f); 1 Tunnel thruster (a) Fuel: 323.0 (d.f.) 2850.0 (r.f.) 48.0pd
9396153 **STAR KVARVEN** *LAJK7* - **Grieg Shipping II AS** Grieg Star AS *Bergen* *Norway (NIS)* MMSI: 257661000	37,158 13,824 49,856	Class: NV	2010-04 **Hyundai Mipo Dockyard Co Ltd — Ulsan** Yd No: 8004 Loa 208.78 (BB) Br ex 32.25 Dght 12.340 Lbp 197.40 Br md 32.20 Dpth 19.50 Welded, 1 dk	**(A31A2GO) Open Hatch Cargo Ship** Grain: 65,000 TEU 1453 C Ho 618 TEU C Dk 835 TEU Compartments: 10 Ho, ER 10 Ha: ER Gantry cranes: 2x70t	**1 oil engine** driving 1 FP propeller Total Power: 11,300kW (15,363hp) 16.0kn MAN-B&W 5S60MC-C 1 x 2 Stroke 5 Cy. 600 x 2400 11300kW (15363bhp) Hyundai Heavy Industries Co Ltd-South Korea AuxGen: 2 x a.c, 1 x a.c Thrusters: 1 Tunnel thruster (f); 1 Tunnel thruster (a)
9311531 **STAR LADY** *MHLG3* - **Blenheim Shipping UK Ltd** - *Douglas* *Isle of Man (British)* MMSI: 232443000 Official number: 737502	56,204 32,082 105,522 T/cm 89.2	Class: LR ✠ **100A1** SS 06/2010 Double Hull oil tanker ESP LI **ShipRight** (SDA, FDA, CM) *IWS ✠ **LMC** **UMS IGS** Eq.Ltr: R†; Cable: 691.6/84.0 U3 (a)	2005-06 **Sumitomo Heavy Industries Marine & Engineering Co., Ltd. — Yokosuka** Yd No: 1318 Loa 239.00 (BB) Br ex 42.03 Dght 14.880 Lbp 229.00 Br md 42.00 Dpth 21.30 Welded, 1 dk	**(A13A2TV) Crude Oil Tanker** Double Hull (13F) Liq: 115,572; Liq (Oil): 115,571 Cargo Heating Coils Compartments: 12 Wing Ta, 2 Wing Slop Ta, ER 3 Cargo Pump (s): 3x2500m³/hr Manifold: Bow/CM: 117.9m	**1 oil engine** driving 1 FP propeller Total Power: 12,000kW (16,315hp) 14.0kn Wartsila 6RT-flex58T 1 x 2 Stroke 6 Cy. 580 x 2416 12000kW (16315bhp) Diesel United Ltd.-Aioi AuxGen: 3 x 720kW 450V 60Hz a.c Boilers: e (ex.g.) 22.0kgf/cm² (21.6bar), WTAuxB (o.f.) 18.0kgf/cm² (17.7bar) Fuel: 309.0 (d.f.) 3030.0 (r.f.)
9593854 **STAR LAGUNA** *LAPD7* - **Grieg Shipping II AS** Grieg Star AS *Bergen* *Norway (NIS)* MMSI: 257842000	37,447 15,619 50,827	Class: NV	2012-09 **Hyundai Mipo Dockyard Co Ltd — Ulsan** Yd No: 8075 Loa 204.37 (BB) Br ex 32.30 Dght 12.640 Lbp 194.00 Br md 32.26 Dpth 19.00 Welded, 1 dk	**(A31A2GX) General Cargo Ship** Grain: 66,773; Bale: 66,773 TEU 1411 Compartments: 9 Ho, ER 9 Ha: ER Cranes: 4x75t	**1 oil engine** driving 1 FP propeller Total Power: 10,780kW (14,656hp) 15.5kn MAN-B&W 5S60ME-C8 1 x 2 Stroke 5 Cy. 600 x 2400 10780kW (14656bhp) AuxGen: 3 x 750kW a.c Thrusters: 1 Tunnel thruster (f)
9110602 **STAR LAUREL** *C6AS6* - *ex* Rubin Laurel *-2013* **Canis Shipping Corp** Charterwell Maritime SA *Nassau* *Bahamas* MMSI: 311000139 Official number: 7000569	87,281 54,521 167,573 T/cm 121.0	Class: NK	1995-11 **Namura Shipbuilding Co Ltd — Imari SG** Yd No: 943 Loa 289.94 (BB) Br ex - Dght 17.042 Lbp 279.00 Br md 46.00 Dpth 23.50 Welded, 1 dk	**(A21A2BC) Bulk Carrier** Grain: 189,952 Compartments: 9 Ho, ER 9 Ha: (17.6 x 16.3)8 (21.1 x 16.3)ER	**1 oil engine** driving 1 FP propeller Total Power: 19,669kW (26,742hp) 15.0kn B&W 7S70MC 1 x 2 Stroke 7 Cy. 700 x 2674 19669kW (26742bhp) Hitachi Zosen Corp-Japan Fuel: 149.7 (d.f.) 3694.6 (r.f.)
9517939 **STAR LEADER** *9V9350* - **Grace Ocean Pte Ltd** - *Singapore* *Singapore* MMSI: 566042000 Official number: 396956	14,022 6,724 12,944	Class: NK	2010-04 **Shikoku Dockyard Co. Ltd. — Takamatsu** Yd No: 1053 Loa 162.50 Br ex - Dght 9.720 Lbp 150.00 Br md 26.00 Dpth 14.10 Welded, 1 dk	**(A34A2GR) Refrigerated Cargo Ship** Bale: 17,429; Ins: 17,429 TEU 552 C Ho 112 TEU C Dk 440 TEU incl 200 ref C Cranes: 2x40t,2x8t	**1 oil engine** driving 1 FP propeller Total Power: 15,820kW (21,509hp) 22.0kn MAN-B&W 7S60MC-C 1 x 2 Stroke 7 Cy. 600 x 2400 15820kW (21509bhp) Mitsui Engineering & Shipbuilding CLtd-Japan Fuel: 2345.0 (r.f.)
9573828 **STAR LIFE** *5BEH3* - **LifeThree Shipping Corp** Alassia Newships Management Inc SatCom: Inmarsat C 420925710 *Limassol* *Cyprus* MMSI: 209257000 Official number: 9573828	17,033 10,108 28,210 T/cm 39.6	Class: NK	2011-03 **Shimanami Shipyard Co Ltd — Imabari EH** Yd No: 587 Loa 169.37 (BB) Br ex - Dght 9.820 Lbp 160.40 Br md 27.20 Dpth 13.60 Welded, 1 dk	**(A21A2BC) Bulk Carrier** Grain: 37,320; Bale: 35,742 Compartments: 5 Ho, ER 5 Ha: ER Cranes: 4x30.7t	**1 oil engine** driving 1 FP propeller Total Power: 5,850kW (7,954hp) 14.0kn MAN-B&W 6S42MC 1 x 2 Stroke 6 Cy. 420 x 1764 5850kW (7954bhp) Makita Corp-Japan Fuel: 1538.0 (r.f.)
8745395 **STAR LIGHT** - - *ex* Ming Hui 18 *-2010* **Kuiyang United Shipping Co** Ocean Grow International Shipmanagement Consultant Corp *Jieyang, Guangdong* *China* MMSI: 412466350	970 502 -		1994-02 **Zhejiang Dongtou Damen Shipyard — Dongtou County ZJ** Loa 66.70 Br ex - Dght - Lbp - Br md 10.30 Dpth 6.00 Welded, 1 dk	**(A31A2GX) General Cargo Ship**	**1 oil engine** driving 1 Propeller
8421846 **STAR LIGHT** - - **Starlight Shipping Co** -	969 394 1,150	Class: (CC) (BV)	1984-12 **Guangzhou Shipyard — Guangzhou GD** Yd No: B4108 Loa 51.21 Br ex - Dght 3.571 Lbp 48.24 Br md 12.81 Dpth 5.49 Welded, 1 dk	**(A31A2GX) General Cargo Ship** Bale: 1,718 TEU 24 C. 24/20' Compartments: 2 Ho, ER 2 Ha: 2 (12.5 x 9.9)ER Derricks: 1x35t	**2 oil engines** driving 2 FP propellers Total Power: 592kW (804hp) 10.0kn Caterpillar 3408TA 2 x Vee 4 Stroke 8 Cy. 137 x 152 each-296kW (402bhp) Caterpillar Tractor Co-USA
9332391 **STAR LIGHT NO. 1** *VRZT4* - **Macau-Hong Kong Terminal Ltd** - *Hong Kong* *Hong Kong* Official number: HK-1264	897 303 1,032	Class: CC	2004-10 **Guangdong Jiangmen Shipyard Co Ltd — Jiangmen GD** Yd No: 34A Loa 49.96 Br ex - Dght 2.790 Lbp 48.60 Br md 13.00 Dpth 4.75 Welded, 1 dk	**(A31A2GX) General Cargo Ship** Bale: 1,456 TEU 70 C Ho 46 TEC C Dk 24 TEU. Compartments: 1 Ho, ER 1 Ha: ER (37.1 x 10.2)	**2 oil engines** reduction geared to sc. shafts driving 2 Propellers Total Power: 678kW (922hp) 9.2kn Cummins KTA-19-M 2 x 4 Stroke 6 Cy. 159 x 159 each-339kW (461bhp) Chongqing Cummins Engine Co Ltd-China AuxGen: 2 x 50kW 400V a.c

IMO / Call sign	Name / Owner	Tonnage	Class	Construction	Type	Machinery
9370422 *3FRM5* -	**STAR LILY** **Four Land (Panama) SA** Kansai Steamship Co Ltd *Panama* *Panama* MMSI: 370883000 Official number: 4003209A	**21,192** 11,444 33,248	Class: NK	**2008-10 Shin Kochi Jyuko K.K. — Kochi** Yd No: 7220 Loa 179.99 (BB) Br ex - Dght 10.031 Lbp 172.00 Br md 28.20 Dpth 14.30 Welded, 1 dk	**(A21A2BC) Bulk Carrier** Double Bottom Entire Compartment Length Grain: 44,642; Bale: 43,765 Compartments: 5 Ho, ER 5 Ha: ER Cranes: 4x30t	**1 oil engine** driving 1 FP propeller Total Power: 6,250kW (8,498hp) 14.3kn Mitsubishi 6UEC52LA 1 x 2 Stroke 6 Cy. 520 x 1600 6250kW (8498bhp) Kobe Hatsudoki KK-Japan AuxGen: 3 x 317kW a.c Fuel: 1450.0
9593866 *LAPE7* -	**STAR LIMA** **Grieg Shipping II AS** Grieg Star AS *Bergen* *Norway (NIS)* MMSI: 257844000	**37,447** 15,619 50,761	Class: NV	**2012-09 Hyundai Mipo Dockyard Co Ltd — Ulsan** Yd No: 8076 Loa 204.35 (BB) Br ex 32.30 Dght 12.640 Lbp 194.00 Br md 32.26 Dpth 19.00 Welded, 1 dk	**(A31A2GX) General Cargo Ship** Grain: 66,773; Bale: 66,773 TEU 1411 Compartments: 9 Ho, ER 9 Ha: ER Cranes: 4x75t	**1 oil engine** driving 1 FP propeller Total Power: 10,780kW (14,656hp) 15.5kn MAN-B&W 5S60ME-C8 1 x 2 Stroke 5 Cy. 600 x 2400 10780kW (14656bhp) AuxGen: 3 x 750kW a.c Thrusters: 1 Tunnel thruster (f)
9593878 *LAQJ7* -	**STAR LINDESNES** **Grieg International II AS** Grieg Star AS *Bergen* *Norway (NIS)* MMSI: 258014000	**37,447** 15,619 50,748	Class: NV	**2013-01 Hyundai Mipo Dockyard Co Ltd — Ulsan** Yd No: 8077 Loa 204.36 (BB) Br ex 32.30 Dght 12.640 Lbp 194.01 Br md 32.25 Dpth 19.00 Welded, 1 dk	**(A31A2GX) General Cargo Ship** Grain: 66,773; Bale: 66,773 TEU 1411 Compartments: 9 Ho, ER 9 Ha: ER Cranes: 4x75t	**1 oil engine** driving 1 FP propeller Total Power: 10,780kW (14,656hp) 15.5kn MAN-B&W 5S60ME-C8 1 x 2 Stroke 5 Cy. 600 x 2400 10780kW (14656bhp) AuxGen: 3 x a.c Thrusters: 1 Tunnel thruster (f)
9593907 *LAQM7* -	**STAR LIVORNO** **Grieg Shipping II AS** Grieg Star AS *Bergen* *Norway (NIS)* MMSI: 258009000	**37,447** 15,619 50,700	Class: NV	**2013-07 Hyundai Mipo Dockyard Co Ltd — Ulsan** Yd No: 8080 Loa 204.36 (BB) Br ex 32.32 Dght 12.640 Lbp 194.00 Br md 32.26 Dpth 19.00 Welded, 1 dk	**(A31A2GX) General Cargo Ship** Grain: 66,773; Bale: 66,773 TEU 1411 Compartments: 9 Ho, ER 9 Ha: ER Cranes: 4x75t	**1 oil engine** driving 1 FP propeller Total Power: 10,780kW (14,656hp) 15.5kn MAN-B&W 5S60ME-C8 1 x 2 Stroke 5 Cy. 600 x 2400 10780kW (14656bhp) AuxGen: 3 x a.c Thrusters: 1 Tunnel thruster (f)
9603790 *LAQN7* -	**STAR LOEN** **Grieg Shipping II AS** Grieg Star AS *Bergen* *Norway (NIS)* MMSI: 258008000	**37,447** 15,619 50,792	Class: NV	**2013-09 Hyundai Mipo Dockyard Co Ltd — Ulsan** Yd No: 8081 Loa 204.38 (BB) Br ex 32.31 Dght 12.660 Lbp 194.04 Br md 32.26 Dpth 19.00 Welded, 1 dk	**(A31A2GX) General Cargo Ship** Grain: 66,773; Bale: 66,773 TEU 1411 Compartments: 9 Ho, ER 9 Ha: ER Cranes: 4x75t	**1 oil engine** driving 1 FP propeller Total Power: 10,780kW (14,656hp) 15.5kn MAN-B&W 5S60ME-C8 1 x 2 Stroke 5 Cy. 600 x 2400 10780kW (14656bhp) AuxGen: 3 x a.c Thrusters: 1 Tunnel thruster
9593892 *LAQL7* -	**STAR LOFOTEN** **Grieg International II AS** Grieg Star AS *Bergen* *Norway (NIS)* MMSI: 258011000	**37,447** 15,619 50,728	Class: NV	**2013-05 Hyundai Mipo Dockyard Co Ltd — Ulsan** Yd No: 8079 Loa 204.36 (BB) Br ex 32.31 Dght 12.640 Lbp 194.02 Br md 32.26 Dpth 19.00 Welded, 1 dk	**(A31A2GX) General Cargo Ship** Grain: 66,773; Bale: 66,773 TEU 1411 Compartments: 9 Ho, ER 9 Ha: ER Cranes: 4x75t	**1 oil engine** driving 1 FP propeller Total Power: 10,780kW (14,656hp) 15.5kn MAN-B&W 5S60ME-C8 1 x 2 Stroke 5 Cy. 600 x 2400 10780kW (14656bhp) AuxGen: 3 x a.c Thrusters: 1 Tunnel thruster (f)
9593880 *LAQK7* -	**STAR LOUISIANA** **Grieg Shipping II AS** Grieg Star AS *Bergen* *Norway (NIS)* MMSI: 258013000	**37,447** 15,619 50,720	Class: NV	**2013-03 Hyundai Mipo Dockyard Co Ltd — Ulsan** Yd No: 8078 Loa 204.35 (BB) Br ex 32.31 Dght 12.640 Lbp 193.99 Br md 32.26 Dpth 19.00 Welded, 1 dk	**(A31A2GX) General Cargo Ship** Grain: 66,773; Bale: 66,773 TEU 1411 Compartments: 9 Ho, ER 9 Ha: ER Cranes: 4x75t	**1 oil engine** driving 1 FP propeller Total Power: 10,780kW (14,656hp) 15.5kn MAN-B&W 5S60ME-C8 1 x 2 Stroke 5 Cy. 600 x 2400 10780kW (14656bhp) AuxGen: 3 x a.c
8226014 - -	**STAR LUBANG 1** *ex Kwan Kwang Ferry -2002* **B & Y Shipping Inc** - *Manila* *Philippines* Official number: MN000007	*197* 58 59	Class: (KR)	**1983-08 Sun-Il Shipbuilding Co Ltd — Geoje** Yd No: 88 Loa 42.68 Br ex 6.02 Dght 2.010 Lbp 38.00 Br md 6.00 Dpth 3.00 Welded, 1 dk	**(A37B2PS) Passenger Ship** Bale: 24 Compartments: 1 Ho, ER 1 Ha: (1.0 x 2.3)	**1 oil engine** with clutches & sr reverse geared to sc. shaft driving 1 FP propeller Total Power: 1,177kW (1,600hp) 17.0kn Niigata 8MG25BX 1 x 4 Stroke 8 Cy. 250 x 320 1177kW (1600bhp) Ssangyong Heavy Industries Co Ltd-South Korea AuxGen: 1 x 75kW 225V a.c
9603805 *LAQO7* -	**STAR LUSTER** **Grieg Shipping II AS** Grieg Star AS *Bergen* *Norway (NIS)* MMSI: 258007000	**37,447** 15,619 50,740	Class: NV	**2013-10 Hyundai Mipo Dockyard Co Ltd — Ulsan** Yd No: 8082 Loa 204.36 (BB) Br ex 32.32 Dght 12.640 Lbp 194.00 Br md 32.27 Dpth 19.00 Welded, 1 dk	**(A31A2GX) General Cargo Ship** Grain: 66,773; Bale: 66,773 TEU 1411 Compartments: 9 Ho, ER 9 Ha: ER Cranes: 4x75t	**1 oil engine** driving 1 FP propeller Total Power: 10,780kW (14,656hp) 15.5kn MAN-B&W 5S60ME-C8 1 x 2 Stroke 5 Cy. 600 x 2400 10780kW (14656bhp) AuxGen: 3 x a.c Thrusters: 1 Tunnel thruster (f)
9616838 *V7FA7* -	**STAR LYGRA** **MF Lygra Lease Trust** Grieg Star AS *Majuro* *Marshall Islands* MMSI: 538005562 Official number: 5562	**37,447** 15,619 50,741	Class: NV	**2013-12 Hyundai Mipo Dockyard Co Ltd — Ulsan** Yd No: 8083 Loa 204.36 (BB) Br ex 32.31 Dght 12.640 Lbp 194.03 Br md 32.26 Dpth 19.00 Welded, 1 dk	**(A31A2GX) General Cargo Ship** Grain: 66,773; Bale: 66,773 TEU 1411 Compartments: 9 Ho, ER 9 Ha: ER Cranes: 4x75t	**1 oil engine** driving 1 FP propeller Total Power: 10,780kW (14,656hp) 15.5kn MAN-B&W 5S60ME-C8 1 x 2 Stroke 5 Cy. 600 x 2400 10780kW (14656bhp) AuxGen: 3 x a.c Thrusters: 1 Tunnel thruster (f)
9496135 *2CRK8* -	**STAR MANX** **Star Marine Ltd** Grieg Star Shipping AS SatCom: Inmarsat C 423272812 *Douglas* *Isle of Man (British)* MMSI: 235075135 Official number: 741926	**32,354** 19,458 58,133 T/cm 57.4	Class: NK	**2009-11 Tsuneishi Group (Zhoushan) Shipbuilding Inc — Daishan County ZJ** Yd No: SS-067 Loa 189.99 (BB) Br ex - Dght 12.826 Lbp 185.60 Br md 32.26 Dpth 18.00 Welded, 1 dk	**(A21A2BC) Bulk Carrier** Grain: 72,689; Bale: 70,122 Compartments: 5 Ho, ER 5 Ha: ER Cranes: 4x30t	**1 oil engine** driving 1 FP propeller Total Power: 8,400kW (11,421hp) 14.5kn MAN-B&W 6S50MC-C 1 x 2 Stroke 6 Cy. 500 x 2000 8400kW (11421bhp) Mitsui Engineering & Shipbuilding CLtd-Japan AuxGen: 3 x 480kW a.c Fuel: 2150.0
9218959 - -	**STAR MARINE 3** *ex Captain No. 1 -2005* - -	*149* - 20		**1999-01 Sumidagawa Zosen K.K. — Tokyo** Yd No: N10-28 Loa 37.60 Br ex - Dght - Lbp 33.10 Br md 7.44 Dpth 3.00 Welded	**(A37B2PS) Passenger Ship**	**2 oil engines** driving 2 FP propellers Total Power: 4,046kW (5,500hp) 25.6kn Niigata 16V16FX 2 x Vee 4 Stroke 16 Cy. 165 x 185 each-2023kW (2750bhp) Niigata Engineering Co Ltd-Japan
9377901 *YHPC* -	**STAR MARINE I** *ex Muara Sele 03 -2005* **PT Segara Nusantara Marine** - *Balikpapan* *Indonesia*	**605** 182 -	Class: KI	**2005-03 PT Benua Baru Kariangau — Balikpapan** Loa 61.12 Br ex - Dght 2.700 Lbp 55.39 Br md 11.98 Dpth 3.60 Welded, 1 dk	**(A35D2RL) Landing Craft** Bow ramp (f)	**2 oil engines** reduction geared to sc. shafts driving 2 FP propellers Total Power: 588kW (800hp) Mitsubishi 8DC90A 2 x Vee 4 Stroke 8 Cy. 135 x 140 each-294kW (400bhp) Mitsubishi Heavy Industries Ltd-Japan AuxGen: 2 x 110kW 380V a.c
9301316 *DSOE5* -	**STAR MARINER** **Nam Sung Shipping Co Ltd** - *Jeju* *South Korea* MMSI: 440562000 Official number: JJR-059208	**9,522** 4,960 13,007	Class: KR	**2005-04 Dae Sun Shipbuilding & Engineering Co Ltd — Busan** Yd No: 450 Loa 142.71 (BB) Br ex - Dght 8.214 Lbp 133.50 Br md 22.60 Dpth 11.20 Welded, 1 dk	**(A33A2CC) Container Ship (Fully Cellular)** Double Hull TEU 962 incl 120 ref C.	**1 oil engine** driving 1 FP propeller Total Power: 7,860kW (10,686hp) 18.0kn MAN-B&W 6S46MC-C 1 x 2 Stroke 6 Cy. 460 x 1932 7860kW (10686bhp) STX Engine Co Ltd-South Korea AuxGen: 4 x 615kW 445/220V 60Hz a.c Thrusters: 1 Tunnel thruster (f) Fuel: 85.0 (d.f.) 710.0 (r.f.)
7929542 - -	**STAR MARY** *ex Star Enterprise -2007* *ex Confident Exploit -1998* *ex Himesaka Maru -1994* - -	**257** 85 400	Class: IZ (BV)	**1980-01 Maeno Zosen KK — Sanyoonoda YC** Yd No: 57 Loa 40.39 Br ex 7.01 Dght 3.101 Lbp 36.12 Br md 7.00 Dpth 3.20 Welded, 1 dk	**(A13B2TU) Tanker (unspecified)**	**1 oil engine** driving 1 FP propeller Total Power: 368kW (500hp) Hanshin 6L24GS 1 x 4 Stroke 6 Cy. 240 x 400 368kW (500bhp) The Hanshin Diesel Works Ltd-Japan
9166663 *V7OJ6* -	**STAR MASAYA** *ex Masaya -2006 ex Star Masaya -2004* **Mecano Marine Co** Sitinas Shipping Co *Majuro* *Marshall Islands* MMSI: 538003102 Official number: 3102	**24,953** 13,547 42,717 T/cm 48.8	Class: LR (NV) (BV) **100A1** SS 02/2013 bulk carrier strengthened for heavy caroes, Nos. 2 & 4 holds may be empty ESP ESN-Hold LI **LMC** **UMS**	**1998-02 Ishikawajima-Harima Heavy Industries Co Ltd (IHI) — Tokyo** Yd No: 3099 Loa 181.50 (BB) Br ex 30.53 Dght 11.373 Lbp 172.00 Br md 30.50 Dpth 16.40 Welded, 1 dk	**(A21A2BC) Bulk Carrier** Grain: 52,680; Bale: 52,379 Compartments: 5 Ho, ER 5 Ha: (15.2 x 12.8)4 (19.2 x 15.2)ER Cranes: 4	**1 oil engine** driving 1 FP propeller Total Power: 8,165kW (11,101hp) 14.5kn Sulzer 6RTA48T 1 x 2 Stroke 6 Cy. 480 x 2000 8165kW (11101bhp) Diesel United Ltd.-Aioi AuxGen: 3 x 680kW 110/440V 60Hz a.c

IMO / Call sign	Name / Owner / Flag	Tonnage	Class	Builder / Dimensions	Type / Cargo	Machinery
9081033 *V7VB8* -	**STAR MEGA** *ex* Megalodon *-2011* *ex* Cape Ocean *-2010* *ex* Cape Violet *-2001* **Star Mega LLC** Starbulk SA SatCom: Inmarsat C 453835880 *Majuro* *Marshall Islands* MMSI: 538004081 Official number: 4081	**86,026** 56,199 170,631 T/cm 119.0	Class: NK	**1994-10 Mitsubishi Heavy Industries Ltd. — Nagasaki** Yd No: 2085 Loa 288.00 (BB) Br ex 45.15 Dght 17.687 Lbp 279.00 Br md 45.00 Dpth 24.00 Welded, 1 dk	**(A21A2BC) Bulk Carrier** Grain: 187,737 Compartments: 9 Ho, ER 9 Ha: 7 (16.0 x 20.4)2 (16.0 x 17.0)ER	**1 oil engine** driving 1 FP propeller Total Power: 15,888kW (21,601hp) 14.5kn Mitsubishi 6UEC75LSII 1 x 2 Stroke 6 Cy. 750 x 2800 15888kW (21601bhp) Mitsubishi Heavy Industries Ltd-Japan AuxGen: 4 x 680kW 450V 60Hz a.c Fuel: 119.0 (d.f.) 3858.0 (r.f.) 56.0pd
9325609 *3EVX3* -	**STAR MERLIN** *ex* Freja Dania *-2013* **APSF Owning Co 5 Ltd** Norient Product Pool ApS *Panama* *Panama* MMSI: 357324000 Official number: 4467713	**31,500** 14,001 53,755 T/cm 54.3	Class: NK	**2007-02 Shin Kurushima Dockyard Co. Ltd. — Onishi** Yd No: 5370 Loa 185.93 (BB) Br ex 32.23 Dght 13.025 Lbp 179.95 Br md 32.20 Dpth 19.67 Welded, 1 dk	**(A13B2TP) Products Tanker** Double Hull (13F) Liq: 56,760; Liq (Oil): 56,760 Cargo Heating Coils Compartments: 12 Wing Ta, 2 Wing Slop Ta, ER 4 Cargo Pump (s): 4x1000m³/hr Manifold: Bow/CM: 91.7m	**1 oil engine** driving 1 FP propeller Total Power: 10,620kW (14,439hp) 14.9kn Mitsubishi 6UEC60LS 1 x 2 Stroke 6 Cy. 600 x 2200 10620kW (14439bhp) Kobe Hatsudoki KK-Japan AuxGen: 3 x 700kW a.c Fuel: 180.0 (d.f.) 1886.0 (r.f.)
9684225 *D5FJ8* -	**STAR MISTRAL** **Misty Sea Navigation Corp** Primerose Shipping Co Ltd *Monrovia* *Liberia* MMSI: 636016288 Official number: 16288	**35,812** 21,224 63,301 T/cm 62.1	Class: BV	**2014-01 Yangzhou Dayang Shipbuilding Co Ltd — Yangzhou JS** Yd No: DY4028 Loa 199.99 (BB) Br ex - Dght 13.300 Lbp 193.74 Br md 32.26 Dpth 18.50 Welded, 1 dk	**(A21A2BC) Bulk Carrier** Grain: 77,493; Bale: 75,555 Compartments: 5 Ho, ER 5 Ha: 4 (22.1 x 18.6)ER (14.8 x 17.0) Cranes: 4x35t	**1 oil engine** driving 1 FP propeller Total Power: 11,900kW (16,179hp) 14.5kn MAN-B&W 5S60ME-C8 1 x 2 Stroke 5 Cy. 600 x 2400 11900kW (16179bhp) STX (Dalian) Engine Co Ltd-China
9411135 *H0GP* -	**STAR N** *ex* Mekong Star *-2013* **Alkmene Shipping Corp** Navios Tankers Management Inc *Panama* *Panama* MMSI: 371982000 Official number: 45394PEXT	**23,312** 9,972 37,836 T/cm 45.2	Class: LR ✠ **100A1** SS 01/2009 Double Hull oil and chemical tanker, Ship Type 3 CSR ESP *IWS LI ✠ **LMC** **UMS IGS** Eq.Ltr: J†; Cable: 605.0/66.0 U3 (a)	**2009-01 Hyundai Mipo Dockyard Co Ltd — Ulsan** Yd No: 2094 Loa 184.32 (BB) Br ex 27.43 Dght 11.515 Lbp 176.00 Br md 27.40 Dpth 17.20 Welded, 1 dk	**(A12B2TR) Chemical/Products Tanker** Double Hull (13F) Liq: 40,758; Liq (Oil): 42,630 Compartments: 12 Wing Ta, 2 Wing Slop Ta, ER 12 Cargo Pump (s): 10x500m³/hr, 2x300m³/hr Manifold: Bow/CM: 92.6m	**1 oil engine** driving 1 FP propeller Total Power: 7,860kW (10,686hp) 14.5kn MAN-B&W 6S46MC-C 1 x 2 Stroke 6 Cy. 460 x 1932 7860kW (10686bhp) Hyundai Heavy Industries Co Ltd-South Korea AuxGen: 3 x 730kW 450V 60Hz a.c Boilers: e (ex.g.) 9.2kgf/cm² (9.0bar), WTAuxB (o.f.) 9.2kgf/cm² (9.0bar) Fuel: 155.0 (d.f.) 950.0 (r.f.)
9583134 *LAPJ7* -	**STAR NORITA** **Ugland Shipping AS** Ugland Marine Services AS *Grimstad* *Norway (NIS)* MMSI: 257854000	**32,371** 19,458 58,097 T/cm 57.4	Class: NK	**2012-09 Tsuneishi Group (Zhoushan) Shipbuilding Inc — Daishan County ZJ** Yd No: SS-097 Loa 190.00 (BB) Br ex 32.29 Dght 12.830 Lbp 185.60 Br md 32.26 Dpth 18.00 Welded, 1 dk	**(A21A2BC) Bulk Carrier** Grain: 72,689; Bale: 70,122 Compartments: 5 Ho, ER 5 Ha: ER Cranes: 4x30t	**1 oil engine** driving 1 FP propeller Total Power: 8,400kW (11,421hp) 14.5kn MAN-B&W 6S50MC-C 1 x 2 Stroke 6 Cy. 500 x 2000 8400kW (11421bhp) Mitsui Engineering & Shipbuilding CLtd-Japan Fuel: 2380.0
9375927 *3FFM2* -	**STAR OF ABU DHABI** **Abu Dhabi Shipping International SA** MC Shipping Ltd SatCom: Inmarsat C 435167410 *Panama* *Panama* MMSI: 351674000 Official number: 4117010A	**42,751** 26,554 81,426 T/cm 69.7	Class: NK (NV)	**2009-12 Universal Shipbuilding Corp — Maizuru KY** Yd No: 103 Loa 224.90 (BB) Br ex 32.27 Dght 14.380 Lbp 222.00 Br md 32.26 Dpth 20.00 Welded, 1 dk	**(A21A2BC) Bulk Carrier** Grain: 96,030 Compartments: 7 Ho, ER 7 Ha: ER	**1 oil engine** driving 1 FP propeller Total Power: 11,060kW (15,037hp) 14.6kn MAN-B&W 7S50MC-C 1 x 2 Stroke 7 Cy. 500 x 2000 11060kW (15037bhp) Hitachi Zosen Corp-Japan AuxGen: 3 x a.c Fuel: 20155.0
7521091 S 89	**STAR OF HOPE** *ex* Sea Spray Junior *-2011* *ex* Sea Spray *-2004* **Margaret Downey** - *Galway* *Irish Republic* Official number: 401567	**211** 63 -		**1977-02 Campbeltown Shipyard Ltd. — Campbeltown** Yd No: 034 Loa 25.91 Br ex 7.20 Dght 2.740 Lbp 23.90 Br md 6.71 Dpth 3.65 Welded, 1 dk	**(B11A2FT) Trawler**	**1 oil engine** geared to sc. shaft driving 1 FP propeller Total Power: 515kW (700hp) Alpha 407-26VO 1 x 2 Stroke 7 Cy. 260 x 400 515kW (700bhp) Alpha Diesel A/S-Denmark
9095503 *MPSP9* OB 278	**STAR OF JURA** **The Star Fishing Co Ltd** - *Oban* *United Kingdom* MMSI: 235040345 Official number: C18804	**125** 74 -		**2006-10 Parkol Marine Engineering Ltd — Whitby** Yd No: 018 Loa 19.00 (BB) Br ex - Dght - Lbp - Br md 7.00 Dpth 4.05 Welded, 1 dk	**(B11A2FT) Trawler**	**1 oil engine** reduction geared to sc. shaft driving 1 Propeller Total Power: 448kW (609hp) 10.0kn Caterpillar 3412C 1 x Vee 4 Stroke 12 Cy. 137 x 152 448kW (609bhp) Caterpillar Inc-USA
9148659 *3FAH3* -	**STAR OF LUCK** *ex* Hansa Centaur *-2013* *ex* Pacific Merchant *-2001* *ex* CMA Qingdao *-2000* *ex* P&O Nedlloyd Luanda *-1999* *launched as* Hansa Centaur *-1997* **Cole International Holdings SA** Victoria Oceanway Ltd *Panama* *Panama* MMSI: 355399000 Official number: 4509413	**16,915** 7,595 19,260 T/cm 38.4	Class: NK (GL)	**1997-12 Hanjin Heavy Industries Co Ltd — Ulsan** Yd No: 635 Loa 168.00 (BB) Br ex - Dght 9.220 Lbp 158.00 Br md 27.00 Dpth 13.80 Welded, 1 dk	**(A33A2CC) Container Ship (Fully Cellular)** TEU 1645 C Ho 606 TEU C Dk 1039 TEU incl 128 ref C. Cranes: 2x40t,1x10t Ice Capable	**1 oil engine** driving 1 FP propeller Total Power: 12,240kW (16,642hp) 19.0kn B&W 6S60MC 1 x 2 Stroke 6 Cy. 600 x 2292 12240kW (16642bhp) Hyundai Heavy Industries Co Ltd-South Korea AuxGen: 3 x 600kW a.c Thrusters: 1 Thwart. CP thruster (f) Fuel: 1790.0
9279484 *P3TM9* -	**STAR OF NIPPON** *ex* Wismar Winner *-2004* **Scorpio Ocean Ltd** Emirates Trading Agency LLC SatCom: Inmarsat C 421087210 *Limassol* *Cyprus* MMSI: 210872000 Official number: 9279484	**38,851** 25,325 75,611 T/cm 66.6	Class: NK (AB)	**2004-03 Sanoyas Hishino Meisho Corp — Kurashiki OY** Yd No: 1211 Loa 225.00 (BB) Br ex - Dght 13.970 Lbp 217.00 Br md 32.26 Dpth 19.30 Welded, 1 dk	**(A21A2BC) Bulk Carrier** Double Bottom Entire Compartment Length Grain: 89,232 Compartments: 7 Ho, ER 7 Ha: 6 (17.1 x 15.0)ER (16.2 x 13.3)	**1 oil engine** driving 1 FP propeller Total Power: 8,973kW (12,200hp) 14.5kn B&W 7S50MC-C 1 x 2 Stroke 7 Cy. 500 x 2000 8973kW (12200bhp) Kawasaki Heavy Industries Ltd-Japan AuxGen: 3 x 400kW 440/110V 60Hz a.c Fuel: 160.0 (d.f.) 2800.0 (r.f.) 34.5pd
9384930 *3FZT2* -	**STAR OF SAWARA** **Kashima Naviera SA** World Marine Co Ltd *Panama* *Panama* MMSI: 370990000 Official number: 4000408A	**39,737** 25,728 76,553 T/cm 66.6	Class: NK	**2008-11 Shin Kasado Dockyard Co Ltd — Kudamatsu YC** Yd No: K-001 Loa 224.94 (BB) Br ex - Dght 14.140 Lbp 217.00 Br md 32.26 Dpth 19.50 Welded, 1 dk	**(A21A2BC) Bulk Carrier** Grain: 90,643 Compartments: 7 Ho, ER 7 Ha: 6 (17.1 x 15.6)ER (17.1 x 12.8)	**1 oil engine** driving 1 FP propeller Total Power: 10,320kW (14,031hp) 15.3kn MAN-B&W 6S60MC 1 x 2 Stroke 6 Cy. 600 x 2292 10320kW (14031bhp) Kawasaki Heavy Industries Ltd-Japan AuxGen: 4 x 318kW a.c Fuel: 2970.0 (r.f.)
8886503 *WDD7681* -	**STAR OF THE SEA** *ex* Lady Launa *-1995* **f/v Star of the Sea Inc** - *Juneau, AK* *United States of America* MMSI: 367189720 Official number: 633592	*102* 69 -		**1981 Van Peer Boatworks — Fort Bragg, Ca** Yd No: 9 L reg 17.31 Br ex - Dght - Lbp - Br md 6.70 Dpth 3.20 Welded, 1 dk	**(B11B2FV) Fishing Vessel**	**1 oil engine** driving 1 FP propeller
8654625 *J8PU3* -	**STAR OF THE SEA** *ex* Helena Of The Orient *-1995* *ex* Darnice II *-1995* **Blue Star Yachting Ltd** - *Kingstown* *St Vincent & The Grenadines* Official number: 400634	**218** 65 -		**1982 Cantiere Navale M & B Benetti — Viareggio** Yd No: 152 Loa 27.43 Br ex 7.00 Dght - Lbp - Br md - Dpth 4.10 Welded, 1 dk	**(X11A2YP) Yacht**	**2 oil engines** driving 2 Propellers Caterpillar Caterpillar Inc-USA
9313022 *V7OY3* -	**STAR OMICRON** *ex* Nord Wave *-2008* *launched as* Sibulk Dedication *-2005* **Star Omicron LLC** Starbulk SA *Majuro* *Marshall Islands* MMSI: 538003185 Official number: 3185	**30,002** 18,486 53,489	Class: RI (LR) (NK) Cable: 632.5/0.0 Classed LR until 29/11/09	**2005-01 Iwagi Zosen Co Ltd — Kamijima EH** Yd No: 226 Loa 189.94 (BB) Br ex - Dght 12.303 Lbp 182.00 Br md 32.26 Dpth 17.30 Welded, 1 dk	**(A21A2BC) Bulk Carrier** Grain: 68,927; Bale: 65,526 Compartments: 5 Ho, ER 5 Ha: ER 5 (21.1 x 17.6) Cranes: 4x30.5t	**1 oil engine** driving 1 FP propeller Total Power: 9,480kW (12,889hp) 14.5kn B&W 6S50MC-C 1 x 2 Stroke 6 Cy. 500 x 2000 9480kW (12889bhp) Mitsui Engineering & Shipbuilding CLtd-Japan AuxGen: 3 x 400kW 450/110V 60Hz a.c Boilers: WTAuxB (Comp) 8.2kgf/cm² (8.0bar) Fuel: 147.5 (d.f.) 2041.9 (r.f.) 32.0pd

IMO / Call sign	Name / Owner	Tonnage	Class	Builder / Dimensions	Type / Capacity	Machinery
9382592 *9V7090* -	**STAR OPAL** **PSA Marine Pte Ltd** - *Singapore* *Singapore* MMSI: 565766000 Official number: 392811	**327** 98 -	Class: LR ✠**100A1** SS 03/2013 tug ✠**LMC** **UMS** Eq.Ltr: G; Cable: 312.5/20.5 U2 (a)	**2008-03 Hin Lee (Zhuhai) Shipyard Co Ltd — Zhuhai GD** (Hull) Yd No: 134 **2008-03 Cheoy Lee Shipyards Ltd — Hong Kong** Yd No: 4912 Loa 27.40 Br ex 11.52 Dght 5.200 Lbp 25.20 Br md 11.50 Dpth 5.03 Welded, 1 dk	**(B32A2ST) Tug**	**2 oil engines** gearing integral to driving 2 Z propellers Total Power: 3,730kW (5,072hp) 12.0kn Caterpillar 3516B 2 x Vee 4 Stroke 16 Cy. 170 x 215 each-1865kW (2536bhp) Caterpillar Inc-USA AuxGen: 2 x 86kW 415V 50Hz a.c
9682124 *T3ER2* -	**STAR OPTIMUS** *ex* Zhong Sheng Hai 86 *-2014* *launched as* Xiang Han Sou Gong 0078 *-2010* **Starhigh Asia Pacific Pte Ltd** - *Tarawa* *Kiribati* Official number: K-17101491	**2,909** 872 1,140	Class: IZ	**2010-01 Taoyuan Dewei Shipbuilding Co Ltd — Taoyuan County HN** Yd No: TY1001 Loa 85.00 Br ex - Dght 2.400 Lbp 80.54 Br md 17.20 Dpth 5.50 Welded, 1 dk	**(B33B2DT) Trailing Suction Hopper Dredger**	**2 oil engines** reduction geared to sc. shafts driving 2 Propellers Total Power: 1,496kW (2,034hp) Chinese Std. Type 6210ZLC 2 x 4 Stroke 6 Cy. 210 x 290 each-748kW (1017bhp) Zibo Diesel Engine Factory-China
9315068 *3FXX8* -	**STAR OSPREY** *ex* Nord Sea *-2013* *ex* Gan-Shield *-2010* **APSF Owning Co 3 Ltd** Norient Product Pool ApS *Panama* *Panama* MMSI: 352797000 Official number: 44334PEXT	**30,068** 13,648 51,213 T/cm 52.0	Class: NV	**2007-01 STX Shipbuilding Co Ltd — Changwon (Jinhae Shipyard)** Yd No: 1189 Loa 183.00 (BB) Br ex - Dght 13.167 Lbp 173.90 Br md 32.20 Dpth 19.10 Welded, 1 dk	**(A12B2TR) Chemical/Products Tanker** Double Hull (13F) Liq: 52,123; Liq (Oil): 52,123 Compartments: 12 Wing Ta, 2 Wing Slop Ta, ER 12 Cargo Pump (s): 12x600m³/hr Manifold: Bow/CM: 92.6m	**1 oil engine** driving 1 FP propeller Total Power: 9,480kW (12,889hp) 14.2kn MAN-B&W 6S50MC-C 1 x 2 Stroke 6 Cy. 500 x 2000 9480kW (12889bhp) STX Engine Co Ltd-South Korea AuxGen: 3 x 900kW 60Hz a.c Fuel: 204.0 (d.f.) 1209.0 (r.f.)
9122253 *JG5422* -	**STAR PHENIX** **Toyo Marine Co Ltd, Daiichi Marine Co Ltd & Daiichi Tanker Co Ltd** Daiichi Tanker Co Ltd *Tokyo* *Japan* MMSI: 431100206 Official number: 135206	*2,927* 961 2,430	Class: NK	**1995-11 Ishikawajima Ship & Chemical Plant Co Ltd — Tokyo** Yd No: 604 Loa 96.00 (BB) Br ex 15.03 Dght 5.200 Lbp 88.00 Br md 15.00 Dpth 7.50 Welded, 1 dk	**(A11B2TG) LPG Tanker** Liq (Gas): 3,019 2 x Gas Tank (s);	**1 oil engine** reverse geared to sc. shaft driving 1 FP propeller Total Power: 2,942kW (4,000hp) 14.0kn Hanshin 6LF46 1 x 4 Stroke 6 Cy. 460 x 740 2942kW (4000bhp) The Hanshin Diesel Works Ltd-Japan Fuel: 320.0 (r.f.)
9545003 *V7UP8* -	**STAR PIONEER** **B D International SA Corp** Nam Sung Shipping Co Ltd *Majuro* *Marshall Islands* MMSI: 538003998 Official number: 3998	**9,520** 4,820 12,839	Class: KR	**2010-08 Dae Sun Shipbuilding & Engineering Co Ltd — Busan** Yd No: 519 Loa 142.70 (BB) Br ex - Dght 8.200 Lbp 132.77 Br md 22.60 Dpth 11.20 Welded, 1 dk	**(A33A2CC) Container Ship (Fully Cellular)** Double Hull TEU 953 incl 120 ref	**1 oil engine** driving 1 FP propeller Total Power: 7,860kW (10,686hp) 18.1kn MAN-B&W 6S46MC-C 1 x 2 Stroke 6 Cy. 460 x 1932 7860kW (10686bhp) STX Engine Co Ltd-South Korea AuxGen: 3 x 615kW 445V a.c Thrusters: 1 Tunnel thruster (f)
8710857 *C6AV5* -	**STAR PISCES** *ex* Kalypso *-1993* **Star Pisces Ltd** Star Cruises Administrative Services Sdn Bhd (Star Cruises) *Nassau* *Bahamas* MMSI: 311000164	**40,053** 23,777 2,800	Class: NV	**1990-05 Masa-Yards Inc — Turku** Yd No: 1298 Loa 176.75 (BB) Br ex - Dght 6.220 Lbp - Br md 29.61 Dpth 16.85 Welded	**(A36A2PR) Passenger/Ro-Ro Ship (Vehicles)** Passengers: cabins: 829; berths: 2165 Bow door & ramp Stern door/ramp Lane-Len: 1400 Lane-clr ht: 4.60 Cars: 490 Ice Capable	**4 oil engines** geared to sc. shafts driving 2 FP propellers Total Power: 23,748kW (32,288hp) 22.0kn Sulzer 9ZAL40S 4 x 4 Stroke 9 Cy. 400 x 560 each-5937kW (8072bhp) Wartsila Diesel Oy-Finland AuxGen: 4 x 1987kW 380V 50Hz a.c, 1 x 520kW 380V 50Hz a.c Thrusters: 2 Thwart. FP thruster (f)
9316036 *C6AN8* -	**STAR PLANET** *ex* Ocean Planet *-2013* **Planet Shipping Corp** Chartworld Shipping Corp *Nassau* *Bahamas* MMSI: 311000099 Official number: 7000539	**40,042** 25,318 76,812 T/cm 67.3	Class: NK	**2005-09 Sasebo Heavy Industries Co. Ltd. — Sasebo Yard, Sasebo** Yd No: 726 Loa 225.00 Br ex 32.23 Dght 14.221 Lbp 218.00 Br md 32.20 Dpth 19.80 Welded, 1 dk	**(A21A2BC) Bulk Carrier** Grain: 90,911; Bale: 88,950 Compartments: 7 Ho, ER 7 Ha: 6 (17.0 x 14.4)ER (15.3 x 12.8)	**1 oil engine** driving 1 FP propeller Total Power: 9,230kW (12,549hp) 14.5kn B&W 7S50MC-C 1 x 2 Stroke 7 Cy. 500 x 2000 9230kW (12549bhp) Mitsui Engineering & Shipbuilding CLtd-Japan Fuel: 2780.0
9242613 *V2OE9* -	**STAR PLANET** *ex* Magellan Planet *-2012* *ex* Charlotte Borchard *-2009* *ex* Gracechurch Planet *-2007* *completed as* Pioneer Hawk *-2002* **Reederei ms 'Magellan Planet' Schiffahrts GmbH & Co KG** Quadrant Bereederungs GmbH & Co KG *Saint John's* *Antigua & Barbuda* MMSI: 304427000 Official number: 3759	**6,277** 3,249 7,960	Class: GL NK	**2002-09 J.J. Sietas KG Schiffswerft GmbH & Co. — Hamburg** Yd No: 1199 Loa 133.00 (BB) Br ex 18.95 Dght 7.240 Lbp 125.30 Br md 18.70 Dpth 9.30 Welded, 1 dk	**(A33A2CC) Container Ship (Fully Cellular)** Grain: 10,845; Bale: 9,607 TEU 735 incl 114 ref C. Compartments: 4 Cell Ho, ER 4 Ha: ER	**1 oil engine** with flexible couplings & sr geared to sc. shafts driving 1 CP propeller Total Power: 6,600kW (8,973hp) 18.3kn MaK 8M43 1 x 4 Stroke 8 Cy. 430 x 610 6600kW (8973bhp) Caterpillar Motoren GmbH & Co. KG-Germany AuxGen: 1 x 1220kW 440V a.c, 1 x 500kW 440V a.c, 1 x 320kW 440V a.c Thrusters: 1 Thwart. FP thruster (f) Fuel: 930.0
9588457 *V7XE7* -	**STAR POLARIS** **Star Polaris LLC** Starbulk SA SatCom: Inmarsat C 453836965 *Majuro* *Marshall Islands* MMSI: 538004460 Official number: 4460	**93,733** 58,829 179,546 T/cm 123.2	Class: BV (AB)	**2011-11 HHIC-Phil Inc — Subic** Yd No: 064 Loa 292.00 (BB) Br ex - Dght 18.220 Lbp 283.00 Br md 45.00 Dpth 24.75 Welded, 1 dk	**(A21A2BC) Bulk Carrier** Grain: 199,393 Compartments: 9 Ho, ER 9 Ha: ER	**1 oil engine** driving 1 FP propeller Total Power: 18,660kW (25,370hp) 14.5kn MAN-B&W 6S70MC-C8 1 x 2 Stroke 6 Cy. 700 x 2800 18660kW (25370bhp) STX Engine Co Ltd-South Korea AuxGen: 3 x 740kW a.c Fuel: 430.0 (d.f.) 6680.0 (r.f.)
9517915 *9V9351* -	**STAR PRIDE** **Grace Ocean Pte Ltd** Philsynergy Maritime Inc *Singapore* *Singapore* MMSI: 566090000 Official number: 396957	**14,022** 6,724 12,955	Class: NK	**2009-12 Shikoku Dockyard Co. Ltd. — Takamatsu** Yd No: 1051 Loa 162.50 (BB) Br ex - Dght 9.720 Lbp 150.00 Br md 26.00 Dpth 14.10 Welded, 1 dk	**(A34A2GR) Refrigerated Cargo Ship** Bale: 17,425; Ins: 17,425 TEU 436 C Ho 112 TEU C Dk 324 TEU incl 200 ref C Cranes: 2x40t,2x8t	**1 oil engine** driving 1 FP propeller Total Power: 15,820kW (21,509hp) 22.0kn MAN-B&W 7S60MC-C 1 x 2 Stroke 7 Cy. 600 x 2400 15820kW (21509bhp) Mitsui Engineering & Shipbuilding CLtd-Japan AuxGen: 4 x a.c Fuel: 2370.0
9338747 *9V9358* -	**STAR PRIMA** **Grace Ocean Pte Ltd** Cleanseas Shipmanagement Inc *Singapore* *Singapore* MMSI: 566091000 Official number: 396964	**14,030** 6,724 13,189	Class: NK	**2006-12 Shikoku Dockyard Co. Ltd. — Takamatsu** Yd No: 1031 Loa 162.50 (BB) Br ex 26.00 Dght 9.720 Lbp 150.00 Br md 26.00 Dpth 14.10 Welded	**(A34A2GR) Refrigerated Cargo Ship** Ins: 17,463 TEU 436 C Ho 112 TEU C Dk 324 TEU incl 200 ref C Compartments: 4 Ho, 4 Tw Dk, ER 4 Ha: ER 4 (12.6 x 10.3) Cranes: 2x40t,2x8t	**1 oil engine** driving 1 FP propeller Total Power: 15,820kW (21,509hp) 22.0kn MAN-B&W 7S60MC-C 1 x 2 Stroke 7 Cy. 600 x 2400 15820kW (21509bhp) Mitsui Engineering & Shipbuilding CLtd-Japan AuxGen: 4 x 1150kW a.c Thrusters: 1 Tunnel thruster (f) Fuel: 2370.0 (r.f.) 55.0pd
9192363 *ZCDD6* -	**STAR PRINCESS** **GP3 Ltd** Princess Cruise Lines Ltd *Hamilton* *Bermuda (British)* MMSI: 310361000 Official number: 733709	**108,977** 73,347 10,852 T/cm 80.0	Class: LR (RI) ✠**100A1** CS 01/2012 passenger ship *IWS ✠**LMC** **CCS** Eq.Ltr: Y†; Cable: 742.5/97.0 U3 (a)	**2002-01 Fincantieri-Cant. Nav. Italiani S.p.A. — Monfalcone** (Aft section) Yd No: 6051 **2002-01 Fincantieri-Cant. Nav. Italiani S.p.A. — Castellammare di Stabia** (Fwd section) Loa 289.51 (BB) Br ex 36.03 Dght 8.450 Lbp 242.38 Br md 36.00 Dpth 11.40 Welded, 16 dks plus 2 non continuous decks	**(A37A2PC) Passenger/Cruise** Passengers: cabins: 1297; berths: 3300	**6 diesel electric oil engines** driving 4 gen. each 11200kW 6600V a.c 2 gen. each 8400kW 6600V a.c Connecting to 2 elec. motors each (19000kW) driving 2 FP propellers Total Power: 63,360kW (86,146hp) 22.0kn Sulzer 12ZAV40S 2 x Vee 4 Stroke 12 Cy. 400 x 560 each-8640kW (11747bhp) Wartsila Italia SpA-Italy Sulzer 16ZAV40S 4 x Vee 4 Stroke 16 Cy. 400 x 560 each-11520kW (15663bhp) Wartsila Italia SpA-Italy Boilers: 4 e (ex.g.) 11.2kgf/cm² (11.0bar), 2 AuxB (o.f.) 10.3kgf/cm² (10.1bar), 2 e (ex.g.) 11.2kgf/cm² (11.0bar) Thrusters: 3 Thwart. CP thruster (f); 3 Thwart. CP thruster (a) Fuel: 231.1 (d.f.) 3400.1 (r.f.) 270.0pd
9296200 *C6AT9* -	**STAR PRINCESS** *ex* Atlantic Princess *-2013* **Lycabettus Shipping Corp** Chartworld Shipping Corp *Nassau* *Bahamas* MMSI: 311000151 Official number: 7000580	**90,091** 59,287 180,202 T/cm 121.0	Class: NK	**2003-09 Imabari Shipbuilding Co Ltd — Saijo EH (Saijo Shipyard)** Yd No: 8015 Loa 288.93 (BB) Br ex - Dght 18.170 Lbp 280.80 Br md 45.00 Dpth 24.70 Welded, 1 dk	**(A21A2BC) Bulk Carrier** Double Bottom Entire Compartment Length Grain: 199,725 Compartments: 9 Ho, ER 9 Ha: 8 (15.7 x 20.8)ER (15.7 x 17.6)	**1 oil engine** driving 1 FP propeller Total Power: 18,629kW (25,328hp) 14.5kn MAN-B&W 6S70MC-C 1 x 2 Stroke 6 Cy. 700 x 2800 18629kW (25328bhp) Mitsui Engineering & Shipbuilding CLtd-Japan AuxGen: 3 x 660kW 450/110V 60Hz a.c Fuel: 280.0 (d.f.) 5500.0 (r.f.) 61.5pd

Ship	Tonnage	Class	Builder / Dimensions	Type / Capacity	Machinery
9438494 **STAR QUALITY** *9V355* - **Grace Ocean Pte Ltd** Cleanseas Shipmanagement Inc *Singapore* *Singapore* MMSI: 566059000 Official number: 396961	**14,030** 6,724 13,193	Class: NK	**2008-03 Shikoku Dockyard Co. Ltd. — Takamatsu** Yd No: 1041 Loa 162.50 (BB) Br ex - Dght 9.720 Lbp 150.00 Br md 26.00 Dpth 14.10 Welded, 1 dk	**(A34A2GR) Refrigerated Cargo Ship** Bale: 17,498; Ins: 17,497 TEU 552 C Ho 112 TEU C Dk 440 TEU incl 200 ref C Compartments: 4 Ho, ER 4 Ha: ER 4 (12.6 x 10.3) Cranes: 2x40t,2x8t	**1 oil engine** driving 1 Propeller Total Power: 15,820kW (21,509hp) 22.0kn MAN-B&W 7S60MC-C 1 x 2 Stroke 7 Cy. 600 x 2400 15820kW (21509bhp) Mitsui Engineering & Shipbuilding CLtd-Japan Thrusters: 1 Tunnel thruster (f) Fuel: 2370.0
9529358 **STAR QUEST** *9V7519* - **Sino Quest Tankers Pte Ltd** United Maritime Pte Ltd SatCom: Inmarsat C 456360310 *Singapore* *Singapore* MMSI: 563603000 Official number: 394389	**4,010** 1,584 5,618	Class: CC	**2009-06 Weihai Donghai Shipyard Co Ltd — Weihai SD** Yd No: DHZ-07-01 Loa 94.80 (BB) Br ex - Dght 6.500 Lbp 89.00 Br md 16.50 Dpth 9.20 Welded, 1 dk	**(A13B2TP) Products Tanker** Double Hull (13F) Liq: 6,128; Liq (Oil): 6,128 Compartments: 10 Wing Ta, 2 Wing Slop Ta, ER	**1 oil engine** reduction geared to sc. shaft driving 1 FP propeller Total Power: 1,618kW (2,200hp) 10.0kn Daihatsu 6DKM-26 1 x 4 Stroke 6 Cy. 260 x 380 1618kW (2200bhp) Anqing Marine Diesel Engine Works-China AuxGen: 2 x 250kW 400V a.c Thrusters: 1 Tunnel thruster (f)
9074808 **STAR RELIANCE** *ELRP8* - *ex* Sanko Reliance *-2009* *ex* Sanko Robust *-2006* **Naviport SA** Fairport Shipping Ltd SatCom: Inmarsat C 463692310 *Monrovia* *Liberia* MMSI: 636010205 Official number: 10205	**25,676** 13,991 42,529 T/cm 49.1	Class: NK	**1995-04 Namura Shipbuilding Co Ltd — Imari SG** Yd No: 936 Loa 184.93 (BB) Br ex 30.55 Dght 11.535 Lbp 177.00 Br md 30.50 Dpth 16.20 Welded, 1 dk	**(A21A2BC) Bulk Carrier** Grain: 47,753; Bale: 46,536 Compartments: 8 Ho, ER 8 Ha: (8.8 x 13.0) (13.6 x 25.9)2 (12.8 x 25.9)3 (14.4 x 25.9) (8.8 x 16.2)ER Cranes: 4x30t	**1 oil engine** driving 1 FP propeller Total Power: 8,091kW (11,001hp) 14.5kn B&W 6S50MC 1 x 2 Stroke 6 Cy. 500 x 1910 8091kW (11001bhp) Hitachi Zosen Corp-Japan Fuel: 82.0 (d.f.) 1611.0 (r.f.)
9376177 **STAR REX** *DSPA2* - *ex* Han Feng *-2007* **The Century Shipping Co Ltd** *Busan* *South Korea* MMSI: 440674000 Official number: BSR-070196	**1,996** 1,106 2,846	Class: KR (CC)	**2006-03 Qingdao Hyundai Shipbuilding Co Ltd — Jiaonan SD** Yd No: 121 Loa 79.99 Br ex - Dght 5.211 Lbp 74.29 Br md 13.60 Dpth 7.00 Welded, 1 dk	**(A21A2BC) Bulk Carrier** Grain: 4,127; Bale: 3,893	**1 oil engine** reduction geared to sc. shaft driving 1 FP propeller Total Power: 1,080kW (1,468hp) 11.5kn MAN-B&W 8L23/30 1 x 4 Stroke 8 Cy. 225 x 300 1080kW (1468bhp) (made 2005) Zhenjiang Marine Diesel Works-China
9382580 **STAR RUBY** *9V7089* - **PSA Marine Pte Ltd** - *Singapore* *Singapore* MMSI: 565767000 Official number: 392810	**327** 98 119	Class: LR ✠ **100A1** SS 01/2013 tug ✠ **LMC** **UMS** Eq.Ltr: G; Cable: 312.5/20.5 U2 (a)	**2008-01 Hin Lee (Zhuhai) Shipyard Co Ltd — Zhuhai GD** (Hull) Yd No: 133 **2008-01 Cheoy Lee Shipyards Ltd — Hong Kong** Yd No: 4911 Loa 27.40 Br ex 11.52 Dght 5.200 Lbp 25.20 Br md 11.50 Dpth 5.00 Welded, 1 dk	**(B32A2ST) Tug**	**2 oil engines** gearing integral to driving 2 Z propellers Total Power: 3,730kW (5,072hp) 12.0kn Caterpillar 3516B-HD 2 x Vee 4 Stroke 16 Cy. 170 x 215 each-1865kW (2536bhp) Caterpillar Inc-USA AuxGen: 2 x 112kW 415V 50Hz a.c Fuel: 89.3 (d.f.)
8202264 **STAR S** *3FJM4* - *ex* Star Savannah *-2011* *ex* Calliope *-1997* *ex* Calliope Maru *-1994* **Luvia Shipping** Gamma Denizcilik Nakliyat ve Dis Ticaret Ltd Sti (Gamma Shipping Transport & Foreign Trading Ltd) *Panama* *Panama* MMSI: 352201000 Official number: 2160994F	**11,896** 5,457 18,764	Class: NK	**1983-03 K.K. Uwajima Zosensho — Uwajima** Yd No: 2241 Loa 150.50 (BB) Br ex - Dght 9.274 Lbp 142.02 Br md 21.81 Dpth 12.81 Welded, 1 dk	**(A31A2GO) Open Hatch Cargo Ship** Grain: 19,499; Bale: 19,186 TEU 48 Compartments: 5 Ho, ER 5 Ha: (12.7 x 16.8)4 (21.0 x 16.8)ER Cranes: 2x22.3t	**1 oil engine** driving 1 FP propeller Total Power: 3,825kW (5,200hp) 13.5kn Mitsubishi 8UEC37/88H 1 x 2 Stroke 8 Cy. 370 x 880 3825kW (5200bhp) Kobe Hatsudoki KK-Japan AuxGen: 2 x 500kW 450V 60Hz a.c Fuel: 169.0 (d.f.) 860.0 (r.f.) 16.0pd
9168128 **STAR SAN CARLOS** *4DEL6* - *ex* Sinhan Ferry *-2010* **DBP Leasing Corp** All-Star Shipping Group Inc *Manila* *Philippines* Official number: 00-0000306	*389* 117 94	Class: (KR)	**1997-05 Samwon Shipbuilding Co Ltd — Gunsan** Yd No: 96-01 Loa 43.50 Br ex 8.60 Dght 1.069 Lbp - Br md 8.60 Dpth 2.30 Welded, 1 dk	**(A37B2PS) Passenger Ship**	**2 oil engines** geared to sc. shafts driving 2 FP propellers Total Power: 1,400kW (1,904hp) Cummins KTA-38-M 2 x Vee 4 Stroke 12 Cy. 159 x 159 each-700kW (952bhp) Cummins Engine Co Inc-USA
8904927 **STAR SAPPHIRE** *9MLP7* - *ex* Sea Protector *-2010* *ex* Heisei Maru *-2009* **Zone Arctic Sdn Bhd** *Port Klang* *Malaysia* MMSI: 533046600 Official number: 334314	**327** 181 504	Class: (NK)	**1989-08 Sanuki Shipbuilding & Iron Works Co Ltd — Mitoyo KG** Yd No: 1205 Converted From: Chemical Tanker-2009 Loa 49.50 (BB) Br ex - Dght 2.969 Lbp 45.00 Br md 8.20 Dpth 3.05 Welded, 1 dk	**(A13B2TP) Products Tanker** Liq: 430; Liq (Oil): 430	**1 oil engine** driving 1 FP propeller Total Power: 625kW (850hp) 10.5kn Hanshin 6LU26G 1 x 4 Stroke 6 Cy. 260 x 440 625kW (850bhp) The Hanshin Diesel Works Ltd-Japan
8518778 **STAR SEJATI** *PMGA* - *ex* Oriental Profit *-2007* *ex* Heisei 1 *-1999* *ex* Silver Oak *-1989* **PT Pelayaran Putra Sejati** - *Jakarta* *Indonesia* MMSI: 525016212	**2,848** 1,617 4,748	Class: CR KI (NK)	**1986-04 Kochi Jyuko K.K. — Kochi** Yd No: 1881 Loa 97.37 (BB) Br ex 18.51 Dght 4.868 Lbp 89.95 Br md 18.50 Dpth 6.15 Welded, 1 dk	**(A31A2GX) General Cargo Ship** Grain: 5,434; Bale: 5,059 Compartments: 2 Ho, ER 2 Ha: (18.2 x 9.8) (31.5 x 9.8)ER Derricks: 1x30t,2x15t	**1 oil engine** driving 1 FP propeller Total Power: 2,060kW (2,801hp) Akasaka A38 1 x 4 Stroke 6 Cy. 380 x 740 2060kW (2801bhp) Akasaka Tekkosho KK (Akasaka DieselLtd)-Japan AuxGen: 3 x 108kW a.c
9060405 **STAR SERVICE** *9V3726* - *ex* Ultraline *-1994* **GMT Alpha Pte Ltd** Stellar Shipmanagement Services Pte Ltd *Singapore* *Singapore* MMSI: 564068000 Official number: 385256	**1,291** 815 2,217	Class: GL	**1992-06 Greenbay Marine Pte Ltd — Singapore** Yd No: 82 Loa 62.65 Br ex - Dght 4.400 Lbp - Br md 14.00 Dpth 5.65 Welded, 1 dk	**(A13B2TP) Products Tanker** Liq: 2,932; Liq (Oil): 2,932	**2 oil engines** reverse reduction geared to sc. shafts driving 2 FP propellers Total Power: 1,060kW (1,442hp) 10.0kn Mitsubishi S6R2-MPTK 2 x 4 Stroke 6 Cy. 170 x 220 each-530kW (721bhp) Mitsubishi Heavy Industries Ltd-Japan AuxGen: 2 x 48kW 220/380V a.c Fuel: 78.0 (d.f.)
9438482 **STAR SERVICE I** *9V9398* - *ex* Star Service *-2011* **Grace Ocean Pte Ltd** Bright Star Shipmanagement Inc *Singapore* *Singapore* MMSI: 566028000 Official number: 397020	**14,030** 6,724 13,207	Class: NK	**2008-01 Shikoku Dockyard Co. Ltd. — Takamatsu** Yd No: 1040 Loa 162.50 (BB) Br ex - Dght 9.720 Lbp 150.00 Br md 26.00 Dpth 14.10 Welded, 1 dk	**(A34A2GR) Refrigerated Cargo Ship** Ins: 17,463 TEU 436 C Ho 112 TEU C Dk 324 TEU incl 200 ref C 4 Ha: ER 4 (12.6 x 10.3) Cranes: 2x40t	**1 oil engine** driving 1 Propeller Total Power: 15,820kW (21,509hp) 22.0kn MAN-B&W 7S60MC-C 1 x 2 Stroke 7 Cy. 600 x 2400 15820kW (21509bhp) Mitsui Engineering & Shipbuilding CLtd-Japan AuxGen: 4 x 1150kW a.c Thrusters: 1 Tunnel thruster (f) Fuel: 2370.0
8841060 **STAR SHIP** *PMXD* - *ex* Is No. 3 *-2011* *ex* Shinko Maru No. 25 *-2011* **PT Internusa Jaya Lines** - *Tanjung Priok* *Indonesia*	**1,464** 878 1,592	Class: KI	**1990-04 Mategata Zosen K.K. — Namikata** Yd No: 1026 Loa 74.00 Br ex - Dght 4.000 Lbp 69.50 Br md 12.00 Dpth 6.90 Welded, 1 dk	**(A31A2GX) General Cargo Ship** Grain: 2,850; Bale: 2,573 Compartments: 1 Ho, ER 1 Ha: (40.2 x 9.5)ER	**1 oil engine** driving 1 FP propeller Total Power: 1,177kW (1,600hp) 11.0kn Niigata 6M31AFTE 1 x 4 Stroke 6 Cy. 310 x 530 1177kW (1600bhp) Niigata Engineering Co Ltd-Japan AuxGen: 1 x 100kW 225V a.c Fuel: 70.0 (d.f.)
9520883 **STAR SIRIUS** *V7EH3* - *ex* GL Daishan *-2014* **Star Sirius LLC** Starbulk SA *Majuro* *Marshall Islands* MMSI: 538005469 Official number: 5469	**52,186** 32,423 98,681 T/cm 14.4	Class: RI (NK)	**2011-08 Tsuneishi Group (Zhoushan) Shipbuilding Inc — Daishan County ZJ** Yd No: SS-092 Loa 239.99 (BB) Br ex - Dght 14.450 Lbp 236.00 Br md 38.00 Dpth 19.95 Welded, 1 dk	**(A21A2BC) Bulk Carrier** Grain: 113,237 Compartments: 7 Ho, ER 7 Ha: ER	**1 oil engine** driving 1 FP propeller Total Power: 12,700kW (17,267hp) 14.5kn MAN-B&W 6S60MC-C 1 x 2 Stroke 6 Cy. 600 x 2400 12700kW (17267bhp) Mitsui Engineering & Shipbuilding CLtd-Japan Fuel: 4000.0
9488190 **STAR SIRIUS** *4DED5* - **Batangas Bay Carriers Inc** *Manila* *Philippines* MMSI: 548326100 Official number: 00-0000009	**1,306** 675 1,600	Class: AB	**2009-07 Keppel Batangas Shipyard Inc — Bauan** Yd No: H90 Loa 72.50 Br ex - Dght 2.600 Lbp 69.95 Br md 14.80 Dpth 4.00 Welded, 1 dk	**(A13B2TP) Products Tanker** Double Hull (13F)	**2 oil engines** reduction geared to sc. shafts driving 2 FP propellers Total Power: 1,268kW (1,724hp) 9.5kn Cummins KTA-38-M0 2 x Vee 4 Stroke 12 Cy. 159 x 159 each-634kW (862bhp) Cummins Engine Co Inc-USA
9448839 **STAR SKIPPER** *DSQU8* - *ex* Dae Sun 505 *-2010* **Nam Sung Shipping Co Ltd** *Jeju* *South Korea* MMSI: 441709000 Official number: JJR-102138	**9,520** 4,938 12,980	Class: KR	**2010-06 Dae Sun Shipbuilding & Engineering Co Ltd — Busan** Yd No: 505 Loa 142.71 (BB) Br ex - Dght 8.214 Lbp 132.77 Br md 22.60 Dpth 11.20 Welded, 1 dk	**(A33A2CC) Container Ship (Fully Cellular)** TEU 962 incl 120 ref C. Compartments: 5 Cell Ho, ER 5 Ha: 2 (25.2 x 18.2)2 (12.6 x 18.2)ER (12.6 x 7.9)	**1 oil engine** driving 1 FP propeller Total Power: 7,860kW (10,686hp) 18.0kn MAN-B&W 6S46MC-C 1 x 2 Stroke 6 Cy. 460 x 1932 7860kW (10686bhp) STX Engine Co Ltd-South Korea AuxGen: 3 x 615kW 440/220V 60Hz a.c Thrusters: 1 Tunnel thruster (f) Fuel: 75.0 (d.f.) 640.0 (r.f.)

IMO / Call sign	Name / Owner / Manager / Port	Tonnage	Class	Builder / Dimensions	Type / Capacity	Machinery
8708995 - -	**STAR SOGOD** *ex* Weihai *-2013* *ex* Alciona *-2003* *ex* Kazu Maru No. 8 *-2001* - - *Philippines*	**496** 191 517	Class: IS	**1987-05 Shitanoe Shipbuilding Co Ltd — Usuki OT** Yd No: 1067 Loa 50.02 (BB) Br ex 8.34 Dght 3.171 Lbp 45.50 Br md 8.30 Dpth 5.00 Welded, 1 dk	**(A31A2GX) General Cargo Ship** Grain: 920 Compartments: 1 Ho, ER 1 Ha: (25.5 x 6.3)ER	**1 oil engine** geared to sc. shaft driving 1 FP propeller Total Power: 510kW (693hp) 9.0kn Akasaka MH23R 1 x 4 Stroke 6 Cy. 230 x 390 510kW (693bhp) Akasaka Tekkosho KK (Akasaka DieselLtd)-Japan
9438509 *9V9354* -	**STAR STANDARD** **Grace Ocean Pte Ltd** Philsynergy Maritime Inc *Singapore* *Singapore* MMSI: 566041000 Official number: 396960	**14,030** 6,724 13,201	Class: NK	**2009-02 Shikoku Dockyard Co. Ltd. — Takamatsu** Yd No: 1042 Loa 162.50 (BB) Br ex - Dght 9.700 Lbp 150.00 Br md 26.00 Dpth 14.10 Welded, 1 dk	**(A34A2GR) Refrigerated Cargo Ship** Bale: 17,506; Ins: 17,505 TEU 552 C Ho 112 TEU C Dk 440 TEU incl 200 ref C Cranes: 2x40t	**1 oil engine** driving 1 FP propeller Total Power: 15,820kW (21,509hp) 22.0kn MAN-B&W 7S60MC-C 1 x 2 Stroke 7 Cy. 600 x 2400 15820kW (21509bhp) Mitsui Engineering & Shipbuilding CLtd-Japan Thrusters: 1 Tunnel thruster (f) Fuel: 2370.0
9350991 *9V9356* -	**STAR STRATOS** **Grace Ocean Pte Ltd** Cleanseas Shipmanagement Inc *Singapore* *Singapore* MMSI: 566029000 Official number: 396962	**14,030** 6,724 13,186	Class: NK	**2007-05 Shikoku Dockyard Co. Ltd. — Takamatsu** Yd No: 1033 Loa 162.50 (BB) Br ex - Dght 9.720 Lbp 150.00 Br md 26.00 Dpth 14.10 Welded, 1 dk	**(A34A2GR) Refrigerated Cargo Ship** Ins: 17,477 TEU 552 C Ho 112 TEU C Dk 440 TEU incl 200 ref C Compartments: 4 Ho, 4 Tw Dk, ER 4 Ha: ER 4 (12.6 x 10.3) Cranes: 2x40t,2x8t	**1 oil engine** driving 1 FP propeller Total Power: 15,820kW (21,509hp) 22.0kn MAN-B&W 7S60MC-C 1 x 2 Stroke 7 Cy. 600 x 2400 15820kW (21509bhp) Mitsui Engineering & Shipbuilding CLtd-Japan AuxGen: 4 x 1150kW a.c Thrusters: 1 Tunnel thruster (f) Fuel: 2370.0 (r.f.) 69.0pd
9077783 - -	**STAR SUCCESS** *ex* Ben *-2008* *ex* Ysde-Fkppl 3 *-1998* *ex* Ben *-1997* *ex* Brooklyn 2 *-1995* **Sea Glory Shipping Pte Ltd** -	**220** 66 188	Class: (NV) (AB)	**1993-04 President Marine Pte Ltd — Singapore** Yd No: 127 Loa 29.00 Br ex - Dght 3.700 Lbp 28.00 Br md 8.60 Dpth 4.11 Welded, 1 dk	**(B32A2ST) Tug**	**2 oil engines** with flexible couplings & reverse reduction geared to sc. shafts driving 2 FP propellers Total Power: 1,790kW (2,434hp) 11.0kn Yanmar M220-EN 2 x 4 Stroke 6 Cy. 220 x 300 each-895kW (1217bhp) Yanmar Diesel Engine Co Ltd-Japan
9528275 *T2FE3* -	**STAR SUMATRA** **Sino Ling Tao Resources Pte Ltd** Singapore Star Shipping Pte Ltd *Funafuti* *Tuvalu* MMSI: 572739000	**472** 141 -	Class: BV	**2009-05 Anhui Chaohu Shipbuilding Yard — Chaohu AH** Yd No: AHJT07-20 Loa 36.10 Br ex - Dght 4.000 Lbp 32.25 Br md 10.60 Dpth 4.90 Welded, 1 dk	**(B32A2ST) Tug**	**2 oil engines** geared to sc. shafts driving 2 FP propellers Total Power: 2,356kW (3,204hp) Cummins KTA-50-M2 2 x Vee 4 Stroke 16 Cy. 159 x 159 each-1178kW (1602bhp) Cummins Engine Co Ltd-United Kingdom AuxGen: 2 x 50kW 60Hz a.c
9665944 *3EZA4* -	**STAR SUZHOU** *ex* Jin Cheng Zhou 59 *-2013* **Xie Xiaolanhu** Seacon Ships Management Co Ltd *Panama* *Panama* MMSI: 373752000 Official number: 44761PEXTF1	**7,481** 3,789 10,701	Class: CC	**2012-06 Zhejiang Haifeng Shipbuilding Co Ltd — Linhai ZJ** Yd No: HF0701 Loa 134.20 (BB) Br ex - Dght 7.400 Lbp 126.00 Br md 18.60 Dpth 10.10 Welded, 1 dk	**(A21A2BC) Bulk Carrier** Grain: 13,466 Compartments: 4 Ho, ER 4 Ha: ER 4 (14.7 x 11.0) Cranes: 2x20t Ice Capable	**1 oil engine** reduction geared to sc. shaft driving 1 FP propeller Total Power: 2,970kW (4,038hp) 12.5kn MaK 9M25C 1 x 4 Stroke 9 Cy. 255 x 400 2970kW (4038bhp) Caterpillar Motoren GmbH & Co. KG-Germany AuxGen: 3 x 256kW 400V a.c
8914829 *3FAR5* -	**STAR TAURUS** *ex* Fure Star *-2013* *ex* Kollevik *-2001* *ex* Flying Star *-1996* **Cepheus Maritime Tankers SA** Star Tankers Bunkering SA *Panama* *Panama* MMSI: 357139000 Official number: 45267PEXT	**9,382** 4,788 14,972 T/cm 26.5	Class: NV	**1994-07 Siong Huat Shipyard Pte Ltd — Singapore** Yd No: 8632 Converted From: Chemical/Products Tanker-2000 Loa 145.00 (BB) Br ex 22.66 Dght 8.320 Lbp 135.80 Br md 22.50 Dpth 10.80 Welded, 1 dk	**(A13B2TP) Products Tanker** Double Hull (13F) Liq: 16,066; Liq (Oil): 16,066 Cargo Heating Coils Compartments: 12 Wing Ta, 2 Wing Slop Ta, ER 12 Cargo Pump (s): 12x335m³/hr Manifold: Bow/CM: 79m Ice Capable	**1 oil engine** with clutches & sr geared to sc. shaft driving 1 CP propeller Total Power: 4,860kW (6,608hp) 12.5kn Wartsila 12V32E 1 x Vee 4 Stroke 12 Cy. 320 x 350 4860kW (6608bhp) Wartsila Diesel Oy-Finland AuxGen: 1 x 700kW 440V 60Hz a.c, 3 x 635kW 440V 60Hz a.c Thrusters: 1 Thwart. CP thruster (f) Fuel: 100.0 (d.f.) (Part Heating Coils) 480.0 (r.f.) 18.6pd
9266449 *V7OB2*	**STAR THETA** *ex* J Duckling *-2007* *ex* Medi Sydney *-2006* **Star Theta LLC** Starbulk SA *Majuro* *Marshall Islands* MMSI: 538003050 Official number: 3050	**30,054** 18,207 52,425 T/cm 55.5	Class: RI (BV) (NK)	**2003-06 Tsuneishi Heavy Industries (Cebu) Inc — Balamban** Yd No: SC-038 Loa 190.00 (BB) Br ex - Dght 12.024 Lbp 182.00 Br md 32.26 Dpth 17.00 Welded, 1 dk	**(A21A2BC) Bulk Carrier** Grain: 67,500; Bale: 65,601 Compartments: 5 Ho, ER 5 Ha: 4 (21.3 x 18.4)ER (20.4 x 18.4) Cranes: 4x30t	**1 oil engine** driving 1 FP propeller Total Power: 7,796kW (10,599hp) 14.5kn B&W 6S50MC 1 x 2 Stroke 6 Cy. 500 x 1910 7796kW (10599bhp) (made 2003) Mitsui Engineering & Shipbuilding CLtd-Japan
8127749 *YJZY7* -	**STAR TIDE I** *ex* Star 11 *-2012* *ex* Star Tide 1 *-2010* *ex* Star Tide II *-2000* *ex* Star Tide *-1998* *ex* Torrens Tide *-1995* **Gold Fleet Ltd** Tidewater Marine International Inc *Port Vila* *Vanuatu* Official number: 2126	*1,135* 340 1,503	Class: AB	**1983-09 Torrens Shipbuilders Pty Ltd — Port Adelaide SA** Yd No: 42 Loa 53.78 Br ex 13.59 Dght 5.330 Lbp 47.12 Br md 13.30 Dpth 6.00 Welded, 1 dk	**(B21B20A) Anchor Handling Tug Supply**	**2 oil engines** with clutches, flexible couplings & sr geared to sc. shafts driving 2 CP propellers Total Power: 3,042kW (4,136hp) 12.0kn Nohab F38V 2 x Vee 4 Stroke 8 Cy. 250 x 300 each-1521kW (2068bhp) Nohab Diesel AB-Sweden AuxGen: 1 x 405kW 415V 50Hz a.c, 2 x 150kW 415V 50Hz a.c Thrusters: 1 Thwart. CP thruster (f) Fuel: 387.0 (d.f.) 8.5pd
9511909 *9VHY6* -	**STAR TITAN** **PSA Marine Pte Ltd** - *Singapore* *Singapore* MMSI: 566657000 Official number: 398112	**394** 118 227	Class: LR ✠ **100A1** SS 07/2012 tug, fire-fighting Ship 1 (2400m3/h) with water spray *IWS ✠ **LMC** **UMS** Eq.Ltr: G; Cable: 32.0/20.0 U2 (a)	**2012-07 Hin Lee (Zhuhai) Shipyard Co Ltd — Zhuhai GD** (Hull) Yd No: 212 **2012-07 Cheoy Lee Shipyards Ltd — Hong Kong** Yd No: 4966 Loa 30.00 Br ex 12.33 Dght 3.700 Lbp 28.00 Br md 12.00 Dpth 5.00 Welded, 1 dk	**(B32A2ST) Tug**	**2 oil engines** gearing integral to driving 2 Directional propellers Total Power: 3,998kW (5,436hp) Caterpillar 3516B-TA 2 x Vee 4 Stroke 16 Cy. 170 x 190 each-1999kW (2718bhp) Caterpillar Inc-USA AuxGen: 2 x 112kW 415V 50Hz a.c
7907879 - -	**STAR TRADER** *ex* Listraum *-1990* *ex* Alk *-1987* **Marlin Shipping Ltd** -	**1,815** 650 2,710 T/cm 8.9	Class: (BV) (NV)	**1980-04 Mandals Slip & Mekaniske Verksted AS — Mandal** (Hull) **1980-04 Batservice Verft AS — Mandal** Yd No: 658 Loa 79.15 Br ex 14.05 Dght 5.022 Lbp 74.02 Br md 14.01 Dpth 6.91 Welded, 1 dk.	**(A12A2TC) Chemical Tanker** Liq: 2,620 Cargo Heating Coils Compartments: 12 Ta, ER 12 Cargo Pump (s): 12x80m³/hr Ice Capable	**1 oil engine** driving 1 CP propeller Total Power: 1,469kW (1,997hp) 12.5kn Normo KVM-12 1 x Vee 4 Stroke 12 Cy. 250 x 300 1469kW (1997bhp) AS Bergens Mek Verksteder-Norway AuxGen: 3 x 198kW 440V 60Hz a.c Thrusters: 1 Thwart. FP thruster (f) Fuel: 140.0 7.5pd
9438511 *9V9353* -	**STAR TRUST** **Grace Ocean Pte Ltd** Philsynergy Maritime Inc *Singapore* *Singapore* MMSI: 566049000 Official number: 396959	**14,030** 6,724 13,189	Class: NK	**2009-04 Shikoku Dockyard Co. Ltd. — Takamatsu** Yd No: 1043 Loa 162.50 (BB) Br ex - Dght 9.700 Lbp 150.00 Br md 26.00 Dpth 14.10 Welded, 1 dk	**(A34A2GR) Refrigerated Cargo Ship** Bale: 17,509; Ins: 17,463 TEU 436 C Ho 112 TEU C Dk 324 TEU incl 200 ref C Cranes: 2x40t	**1 oil engine** driving 1 Propeller Total Power: 15,820kW (21,509hp) 22.0kn MAN-B&W 7S60MC-C 1 x 2 Stroke 7 Cy. 600 x 2400 15820kW (21509bhp) Mitsui Engineering & Shipbuilding CLtd-Japan Thrusters: 1 Tunnel thruster (f) Fuel: 2370.0
8223921 - -	**STAR TUNA** *ex* Sunny Diamond *-1999* *ex* Kyokuyo Maru *-1986* - -	**4,341** 1,929 6,225 T/cm 14.6	Class: KR (NK)	**1983-03 Shinhama Dockyard Co. Ltd. — Anan** Yd No: 743 Loa 113.32 Br ex 16.82 Dght 6.815 Lbp 105.01 Br md 16.81 Dpth 8.31 Welded, 1 dk	**(A13B2TP) Products Tanker** Double Bottom Entire Compartment Length Liq: 6,896; Liq (Oil): 6,896 Cargo Heating Coils Compartments: 10 Wing Ta, ER 4 Cargo Pump (s): 2x1300m³/hr, 2x400m³/hr Manifold: Bow/CM: 54m	**1 oil engine** driving 1 CP propeller Total Power: 2,427kW (3,300hp) 12.8kn Hanshin 6EL40 1 x 4 Stroke 6 Cy. 400 x 800 2427kW (3300bhp) The Hanshin Diesel Works Ltd-Japan AuxGen: 3 x 256kW 450V 60Hz a.c Fuel: 85.0 (d.f.) 451.0 (r.f.) 10.0pd
8313166 *JVCB5* -	**STAR TWO** *ex* Prosper Two *-2013* *ex* Cheong Bo *-2004* *ex* Nikko Maru No. 10 *-2000* - *Ulaanbaatar* *Mongolia* MMSI: 457786000	**724** 352 1,141	Class: (GL) (KR)	**1983-05 Sasaki Shipbuilding Co Ltd — Osakikamijima HS** Yd No: 370 Converted From: Chemical Tanker-2005 Loa 63.20 Br ex 9.84 Dght 3.840 Lbp 59.11 Br md 9.81 Dpth 4.45 Welded, 1 dk	**(A13B2TP) Products Tanker** Double Bottom Partial Compartment Length Liq: 1,363; Liq (Oil): 1,363 Compartments: 8 Ta, ER 2 Cargo Pump (s): 2x400m³/hr	**1 oil engine** reverse reduction geared to sc. shaft driving 1 FP propeller Total Power: 956kW (1,300hp) 10.0kn Niigata 6M28AGTE 1 x 4 Stroke 6 Cy. 280 x 480 956kW (1300bhp) Niigata Engineering Co Ltd-Japan AuxGen: 1 x 96kW 440V a.c
9365166 *DSPI3* -	**STAR UNIX** **Nam Sung Shipping Co Ltd** - *Jeju* *South Korea* MMSI: 441030000 Official number: JJR-079648	**9,522** 4,960 13,002	Class: KR	**2007-07 Dae Sun Shipbuilding & Engineering Co Ltd — Busan** Yd No: 467 Loa 142.71 (BB) Br ex 22.60 Dght 8.214 Lbp 133.50 Br md 22.60 Dpth 11.20 Welded, 1 dk	**(A33A2CC) Container Ship (Fully Cellular)** Double Hull TEU 962 incl 120 ref C.	**1 oil engine** driving 1 FP propeller Total Power: 7,877kW (10,710hp) 18.0kn MAN-B&W 6S46MC-C 1 x 2 Stroke 6 Cy. 460 x 1932 7877kW (10710bhp) STX Engine Co Ltd-South Korea AuxGen: 3 x 615kW 440/220V 60Hz a.c Thrusters: 1 Tunnel thruster (f) Fuel: 85.8 (d.f.) 710.0 (r.f.)

9520895 *V7EH8* -	**STAR VEGA** *ex GL Qushan -2014* **Star Vega LLC** Starbulk SA *Majuro* *Marshall Islands* MMSI: 538005472 Official number: 5472	**52,186** 32,423 98,681 T/cm 14.4	Class: BV (NK)	**2011-10 Tsuneishi Group (Zhoushan) Shipbuilding Inc — Daishan County ZJ** Yd No: SS-093 Loa 240.00 (BB) Br ex - Dght 14.480 Lbp 236.00 Br md 38.00 Dpth 19.95 Welded, 1 dk	**(A21A2BC) Bulk Carrier** Grain: 113,237 Compartments: 7 Ho, ER 7 Ha: ER	**1 oil engine** driving 1 FP propeller Total Power: 12,700kW (17,267hp) 14.5kn MAN-B&W 6S60MC-C 1 x 2 Stroke 6 Cy. 600 x 2400 12700kW (17267bhp) Mitsui Engineering & Shipbuilding CLtd-Japan Fuel: 4000.0
8307416 *3EVB3* -	**STAR VEGA** *ex Sigana -2003 ex Spring Gannet -1998* *ex Sanko Gannet -1986* **GM Star Vega Compania Naviera SA** Dekoil Inc SatCom: Inmarsat A 1331476 *Panama* *Panama* MMSI: 354143000 Official number: 1493985I	**24,943** 14,148 42,842 T/cm 36.0	Class: NV (NK)	**1985-05 Mitsubishi Heavy Industries Ltd. — Nagasaki** Yd No: 1938 Loa 189.52 (BB) Br ex 30.03 Dght 10.994 Lbp 181.01 Br md 30.01 Dpth 15.73 Welded, 1 dk	**(A21A2BC) Bulk Carrier** Grain: 54,070; Bale: 53,164 Compartments: 5 Ho, ER 5 Ha: 5 (19.2 x 15.0)ER Cranes: 4x25t	**1 oil engine** driving 1 FP propeller Total Power: 5,859kW (7,966hp) 14.3kn Sulzer 6RTA58 1 x 2 Stroke 6 Cy. 580 x 1700 5859kW (7966bhp) Mitsubishi Heavy Industries Ltd-Japan AuxGen: 3 x 450kW 450V 60Hz a.c Fuel: 183.0 (d.f.) (Heating Coils) 1370.0 (r.f.) 27.0pd
8944680 - -	**STAR VISAYAS** *ex Dona Beatriz -1986* **Star Philippines Shipping Lines Inc** - *Cebu* *Philippines* Official number: CEB1000504	*492* 292 -		**1987 at Cebu** L reg 50.00 Br ex - Dght - Lbp - Br md 9.40 Dpth 3.22 Welded, 1 dk	**(A31A2GX) General Cargo Ship**	**1 oil engine** driving 1 FP propeller Total Power: 338kW (460hp)
9644835 *9V2206* -	**STAR VIVIAN** **Norr Systems Pte Ltd** - *Singapore* *Singapore* MMSI: 563192000 Official number: 398740	**36,295** 21,607 63,548	Class: AB	**2013-09 Taizhou Kouan Shipbuilding Co Ltd — Taizhou JS** Yd No: TK0802 Loa 199.90 (BB) Br ex - Dght 13.300 Lbp 194.50 Br md 32.26 Dpth 18.50 Welded, 1 dk	**(A21A2BC) Bulk Carrier** Grain: 78,772; Bale: 73,680 Compartments: 5 Ho, ER 5 Ha: ER Cranes: 4x30t	**1 oil engine** driving 1 FP propeller Total Power: 8,050kW (10,945hp) 14.2kn MAN-B&W 5S60MC-C8 1 x 2 Stroke 5 Cy. 600 x 2400 8050kW (10945bhp) Hudong Heavy Machinery Co Ltd-China AuxGen: 3 x 600kW a.c Fuel: 240.0 (d.f.) 2090.0 (r.f.)
9343297 *9V6728* -	**STAR VOYAGER** **PSA Marine Pte Ltd** - *Singapore* *Singapore* MMSI: 563920000 Official number: 391408	**327** 98 107	Class: LR ✠ **100A1** SS 10/2010 tug ✠ **LMC** **UMS** Eq.Ltr: G; Cable: 304.0/24.0 U2 (a)	**2005-10 Hin Lee (Zhuhai) Shipyard Co Ltd — Zhuhai GD** (Hull) Yd No: 089 **2005-10 Cheoy Lee Shipyards Ltd — Hong Kong** Yd No: 4854 Loa 27.40 Br ex 11.52 Dght 5.200 Lbp 25.20 Br md 11.50 Dpth 5.00 Welded, 1 dk	**(B32A2ST) Tug**	**2 oil engines** gearing integral to driving 2 Z propellers Total Power: 3,730kW (5,072hp) 12.0kn Caterpillar 3516B 2 x Vee 4 Stroke 16 Cy. 170 x 215 each-1865kW (2536bhp) Caterpillar Inc-USA AuxGen: 2 x 84kW 415V 50Hz a.c
9662485 *H3JK* -	**STAR WENZHOU** *ex Jin Cheng Zhou 138 -2013* **Wang Lifu** Seacon Ships Management Co Ltd *Panama* *Panama* MMSI: 373361000 Official number: 44647PEXTF1	**7,450** 3,736 10,814	Class: CC	**2012-06 Zhejiang Haifeng Shipbuilding Co Ltd — Linhai ZJ** Yd No: HF0801 Loa 134.20 (BB) Br ex 18.64 Dght 7.400 Lbp 126.00 Br md 18.60 Dpth 10.10 Welded, 1 dk	**(A21A2BC) Bulk Carrier** Double Sides Entire Compartment Length Grain: 13,413 Compartments: 3 Ho, ER 3 Ha: 2 (19.6 x 11.0)ER (18.2 x 11.0) Cranes: 2x20t Ice Capable	**1 oil engine** reduction geared to sc. shaft driving 1 FP propeller Total Power: 2,970kW (4,038hp) 12.5kn MaK 9M25C 1 x 4 Stroke 9 Cy. 255 x 400 2970kW (4038bhp) Caterpillar Motoren (Guangdong) CoLtd-China AuxGen: 3 x 259kW 400V a.c
8938162 - - -	**STAR WIN 1** *ex Intan Samudera -2000 ex Xiang Feng I -1998* - - *China*	*1,348* 566 -		**1988 Donghai Shipyard — Shanghai** Loa 79.75 Br ex - Dght - Lbp - Br md 11.40 Dpth 5.40 Welded, 1 dk	**(A31A2GX) General Cargo Ship**	**1 oil engine** driving 1 FP propeller Total Power: 882kW (1,199hp) 12.0kn Chinese Std. Type 1 x 4 Stroke 882kW (1199bhp) Ningbo Engine Factory-China
9122904 *C6ZY9* -	**STAR YANDI** *ex Iron Yandi -2012* **Lliedi Maritime Services Corp** Charterwell Maritime SA *Nassau* *Bahamas* MMSI: 311072500 Official number: 8002037	**82,306** 54,327 169,963 T/cm 118.2	Class: NV	**1996-12 Daewoo Heavy Industries Ltd — Geoje** Yd No: 1105 Loa 289.00 (BB) Br ex 45.03 Dght 17.610 Lbp 278.00 Br md 45.00 Dpth 23.90 Welded, 1 dk	**(A21A2BC) Bulk Carrier** Double Bottom Entire Compartment Length Grain: 184,968 Compartments: 9 Ho, ER 9 Ha: 7 (14.6 x 20.4)2 (14.6 x 15.3)ER	**1 oil engine** driving 1 FP propeller Total Power: 15,175kW (20,632hp) 14.0kn B&W 6S70MC 1 x 2 Stroke 6 Cy. 700 x 2674 15175kW (20632bhp) Korea Heavy Industries & ConstrCo Ltd (HANJUNG)-South Korea AuxGen: 3 x 750kW 240/440V 60Hz a.c Fuel: 210.0 (d.f.) (Heating Coils) 3605.0 (r.f.) 53.9pd
9284477 *V7OA5* -	**STAR ZETA** *ex I Duckling -2007 ex Nord Bulker -2006* **Star Zeta LLC** Starbulk SA *Majuro* *Marshall Islands* MMSI: 538003048 Official number: 3048	**29,357** 17,595 52,994 T/cm 54.7	Class: RI (BV) (NK)	**2003-11 Oshima Shipbuilding Co Ltd — Saikai NS** Yd No: 10353 Loa 189.99 (BB) Br ex - Dght 12.163 Lbp 179.00 Br md 32.26 Dpth 17.15 Welded, 1 dk	**(A21A2BC) Bulk Carrier** Grain: 66,416; Bale: 65,295 Compartments: 5 Ho, ER 5 Ha: (21.4 x 18.6) (21.4 x 18.6) (18.6 x 18.6) (22.3 x 18.6)ER (16.7 x 18.6) Cranes: 4x30t	**1 oil engine** driving 1 FP propeller Total Power: 7,686kW (10,450hp) 14.0kn B&W 6S50MC-C 1 x 2 Stroke 6 Cy. 500 x 2000 7686kW (10450bhp) Kawasaki Heavy Industries Ltd-Japan
9381873 *9HTY8* -	**STARA PLANINA** **Varna Maritime Ltd** Navigation Maritime Bulgare *Valletta* *Malta* MMSI: 256416000 Official number: 9381873	**25,327** 14,598 42,704 T/cm 48.3	Class: GL (BV)	**2007-06 Bulyard Shipbuilding Industry AD — Varna** Yd No: 516 Loa 186.45 (BB) Br ex 30.04 Dght 11.810 Lbp 177.00 Br md 30.00 Dpth 16.25 Welded, 1 dk	**(A21A2BC) Bulk Carrier** Grain: 52,656; Bale: 51,674 Compartments: 5 Ho, ER 5 Ha: ER Cranes: 4x30t Ice Capable	**1 oil engine** driving 1 FP propeller Total Power: 8,340kW (11,339hp) 14.3kn MAN-B&W 6S50MC-C 1 x 2 Stroke 6 Cy. 500 x 2000 8340kW (11339bhp) H Cegielski Poznan SA-Poland
9067996 - -	**STARATEL** *ex Koei Maru No. 5 -2013* **ZAO 'Artel Staratelei' 'Kamchatka'**	*199* - 650	Class: IZ RS (Class contemplated)	**1993-12 Y.K. Kaneko Zosensho — Hojo** L reg 47.50 Br ex - Dght - Lbp - Br md 8.80 Dpth 5.00 Welded, 1 dk	**(A31A2GX) General Cargo Ship**	**1 oil engine** driving 1 FP propeller Total Power: 736kW (1,001hp) 10.0kn Yanmar MF26-HT 1 x 4 Stroke 6 Cy. 260 x 500 736kW (1001bhp) Yanmar Diesel Engine Co Ltd-Japan
8807284 *WUR5426* -	**STARBOUND** **Starbound LLC** Aleutian Spray Fisheries Inc SatCom: Inmarsat A 1501354 *Seattle, WA* *United States of America* MMSI: 367161000 Official number: 944658	*1,533* 1,042 1,388	Class: NV	**1989-03 Dakota Creek Industries Inc — Anacortes WA** Yd No: 22 Loa 73.15 Br ex 14.63 Dght 6.116 Lbp 62.72 Br md 14.03 Dpth 6.71 Welded	**(B11A2FG) Factory Stern Trawler** Ins: 1,755 Ice Capable	**1 oil engine** with clutches, flexible couplings & sr geared to sc. shaft driving 1 CP propeller Total Power: 3,520kW (4,786hp) 15.0kn Normo BRM-9 1 x 4 Stroke 9 Cy. 320 x 360 3520kW (4786bhp) Bergen Diesel AS-Norway AuxGen: 3 x 800kW 480V 60Hz a.c, 1 x 300kW 480V 60Hz a.c Thrusters: 1 Thwart. CP thruster (f)
7629104 *WDE6690* -	**STARBRITE** **Instigator Too Inc** - *Cape May, NJ* *United States of America* Official number: 561989	*134* 91 -		**1974 Marine Builders, Inc. — Mobile, Al** L reg 23.47 Br ex 6.84 Dght - Lbp - Br md - Dpth 3.38 Welded, 1 dk	**(B11A2FT) Trawler**	**1 oil engine** driving 1 FP propeller Total Power: 533kW (725hp) Caterpillar D348SCAC 1 x Vee 4 Stroke 12 Cy. 137 x 165 533kW (725bhp) Caterpillar Tractor Co-USA
9672442 *9WPT6*	**STARCITY EXPRESS NO. 3** **Sunrise Entity Sdn Bhd** - *Kuching* *Malaysia* Official number: 334768	**397** 164 -		**2012-08 PT Marinatama Gemanusa — Batam** Yd No: 01SCEMG12 Loa 43.00 Br ex 8.00 Dght 1.550 Lbp 36.50 Br md 7.63 Dpth 2.00 Bonded, 1 dk	**(A37B2PS) Passenger Ship** Hull Material: Reinforced Plastic	**2 oil engines** driving 2 Propellers
9732096 - -	**STARCITY EXPRESS NO. 5** **Sunrise Entity Sdn Bhd** - *Kuching* *Malaysia* Official number: 333471	**460** 180 -	Class: MY (Class contemplated)	**2014-01 PT Marinatama Gemanusa — Batam** Yd No: 02SCEMG13 Loa 47.50 Br ex - Dght 1.512 Lbp 40.13 Br md 8.50 Dpth 2.00 Bonded, 1 dk	**(A37B2PS) Passenger Ship** Hull Material: Reinforced Plastic	**3 oil engines** reduction geared to sc. shafts driving 3 Propellers Mitsubishi Mitsubishi Heavy Industries Ltd-Japan
7827536 *WCZ7080* -	**STARDUST** *ex Heritage -2000 ex Taormina -1995* *ex Janileen III -1995 ex Adler I -1979* **SJ Fisheries Inc** - *New Bedford, MA* *United States of America* Official number: 608514	*180* 122 -		**1979 Steiner Shipyard, Inc. — Bayou La Batre, Al** L reg 23.26 Br ex 7.29 Dght - Lbp - Br md - Dpth 3.64 Welded, 1 dk	**(B11A2FT) Trawler**	**1 oil engine** geared to sc. shaft driving 1 FP propeller Total Power: 530kW (721hp) Cummins KTA-1150-M 1 x 4 Stroke 6 Cy. 159 x 159 530kW (721bhp) Cummins Engine Co Inc-USA

8826462 - -
STARDUST
-
PT Sindumas Katulistiwa
Samarinda *Indonesia*
199 - -
Class: (KI)
1981 Dok Aneka Teknik — Samarinda
Loa 30.35 Br ex 6.10 Dght 1.400
Lbp 28.70 Br md - Dpth 1.83
Welded, 1 dk
(A35D2RL) Landing Craft
Bow door/ramp
2 oil engines geared to sc. shafts driving 2 FP propellers
Total Power: 442kW (600hp)
Cummins 6BTA-5.9
2 x 4 Stroke 6 Cy. 102 x 120 each-221kW (300bhp) (made 1991, fitted 1991)
Cummins Diesel International Ltd-USA

1005734 *J8Y3462* -
STARFIRE
ex Ambrosia *-2004*
BJAV Marine Ltd
Megayacht Technical Services International Inc
Kingstown *St Vincent & The Grenadines*
MMSI: 377618000
Official number: 5931
747 224 -
Class: LR
✠ **100A1** SS 02/2008
Yacht
LMC Cable: 330.0/24.0 U2 (a)
1998-02 Azimut-Benetti SpA — Viareggio
Yd No: FB219
Loa 53.30 Br ex 9.80 Dght 2.480
Lbp 50.00 Br md 9.29 Dpth 5.56
Welded, 1 dk
(X11A2YP) Yacht
2 oil engines with clutches, flexible couplings & sr reverse geared to sc. shafts driving 2 FP propellers
Total Power: 2,314kW (3,146hp) 17.0kn
Deutz SBV6M628
2 x 4 Stroke 6 Cy. 240 x 280 each-1157kW (1573bhp)
Deutz AG-Koeln
AuxGen: 2 x 160kW 380V 50Hz a.c, 1 x 85kW 380V 50Hz a.c
Thrusters: 1 Thwart. FP thruster (f)

8856039 *WDC5892* -
STARFISH
-
f/v Starfish LLC
-
SatCom: Inmarsat C 436753010
Seattle, WA *United States of America*
Official number: 561651
319 95 -
1974 Marine Construction & Design Co. (MARCO) — Seattle, Wa
Loa - Br ex - Dght -
Lbp 27.98 Br md 8.38 Dpth 2.83
Welded, 1 dk
(B11B2FV) Fishing Vessel
1 oil engine driving 1 FP propeller
Total Power: 828kW (1,126hp)

8843044 *J8TM3* -
STARFISH II
ex Sokolniki *-1997*
Namsov Fishing Enterprises Pty Ltd
-
SatCom: Inmarsat C 437601213
Kingstown *St Vincent & The Grenadines*
MMSI: 376602000
Official number: 7505
4,407 1,322 1,810
Class: RS
1991-04 GP Chernomorskiy Sudostroitelnyy Zavod — Nikolayev Yd No: 592
Loa 104.50 Br ex 16.03 Dght 5.900
Lbp 96.40 Br md 16.00 Dpth 10.20
Welded, 2 dks
(B11A2FG) Factory Stern Trawler
Grain: 870; Bale: 420; Ins: 2,219; Liq: 35
2 oil engines reduction geared to sc. shaft driving 1 CP propeller
Total Power: 5,148kW (7,000hp) 16.1kn
Russkiy 6CHN40/46
2 x 4 Stroke 6 Cy. 400 x 460 each-2574kW (3500bhp)
Mashinostroitelnyy Zavod"Russkiy-Dizel"-Leningrad
AuxGen: 2 x 1600kW 220/380V 50Hz a.c, 3 x 200kW 220/380V 50Hz a.c
Fuel: 1226.0 (d.f.) 23.0pd

8023565 - -
STARFISH VIII
ex Singleton Fleets 62 *-1980*
-
-
127 87 -
1980 Desco Marine — Saint Augustine, Fl
Yd No: 251-F
Loa 22.00 Br ex - Dght -
Lbp 21.34 Br md 6.72 Dpth 2.75
Bonded, 1 dk
(B11A2FT) Trawler
Hull Material: Reinforced Plastic
1 oil engine geared to sc. shaft driving 1 FP propeller
Total Power: 268kW (364hp) 10.0kn
Caterpillar 3408TA
1 x Vee 4 Stroke 8 Cy. 137 x 152 268kW (364bhp)
Caterpillar Tractor Co-USA
Fuel: 316.0

8734657 *WDA7014* -
STARFLEET PATRIOT
-
Starfleet Marine Transportation Inc
-
Charleston, SC *United States of America*
MMSI: 366838630
Official number: 1123380
261 78 -
2002-03 Freeport Shipbuilding & Marine Repair, Inc. — Freeport, Fl Yd No: 261
Loa 42.67 Br ex - Dght -
Lbp - Br md 8.22 Dpth 3.53
Welded, 1 dk
(B21A20C) Crew/Supply Vessel
Hull Material: Aluminium Alloy
Passengers: 57
5 oil engines reduction geared to sc. shafts driving 4 FP propellers , 1 Water jet
Total Power: 2,795kW (3,800hp)
Cummins QSK19-M
5 x 4 Stroke 6 Cy. 159 x 159 each-559kW (760bhp) (new engine 2002)
Cummins Engine Co Inc-USA
AuxGen: 2 x 60kW a.c
Thrusters: 1 Tunnel thruster (f)
Fuel: 40.0

9585431 *WDE8934* -
STARFLEET VIKING
-
Starfleet Marine Transportation Inc
-
Charleston, SC *United States of America*
MMSI: 367411370
Official number: 1219235
327 98 -
2009-07 Freeport Shipbuilding & Marine Repair, Inc. — Freeport, Fl Yd No: 274
Loa 48.78 Br ex - Dght 2.900
Lbp 42.68 Br md 8.84 Dpth 3.65
Welded, 1 dk
(B21A20C) Crew/Supply Vessel
Hull Material: Aluminium Alloy
Passengers: unberthed: 57
4 oil engines reduction geared to sc. shafts driving 4 Propellers
Total Power: 4,476kW (6,084hp) 26.0kn
Cummins KTA-38-M2
4 x Vee 4 Stroke 12 Cy. 159 x 159 each-1119kW (1521bhp)
Cummins Engine Co Inc-USA
Thrusters: 1 Tunnel thruster (f)

9200902 *ZMR4078* -
STARFLYTE
-
Fullers Group Ltd
-
Auckland *New Zealand*
MMSI: 512200555
Official number: 876319
172 51 20
1999-10 WaveMaster International Pty Ltd — Fremantle WA Yd No: 179
Loa 32.00 Br ex - Dght -
Lbp - Br md 8.81 Dpth 2.66
Welded
(A37B2PS) Passenger Ship
Hull Material: Aluminium Alloy
Passengers: unberthed: 220
2 oil engines geared to sc. shafts driving 2 Water jets
Total Power: 1,764kW (2,398hp) 27.0kn
Deutz TBD620V8
2 x Vee 4 Stroke 8 Cy. 170 x 195 each-882kW (1199bhp)
Deutz AG-Koeln

8217257 *3FQR8* -
STARFORD
ex Ramita Naree *-2009* *ex* Nancy *-1995*
ex Shuei Queen *-1994* *ex* Koshu Maru *-1989*
Portwood Trading Ltd
Jieheng Shipping Co Ltd
Panama *Panama*
MMSI: 351113000
Official number: 4056209A
13,888 8,044 23,360
Class: NK
1983-08 K.K. Uwajima Zosensho — Uwajima
Yd No: 2281
Loa 158.00 (BB) Br ex - Dght 9.972
Lbp 148.01 Br md 24.60 Dpth 13.62
Welded, 1 dk
(A21A2BC) Bulk Carrier
Grain: 29,224; Bale: 28,308
Compartments: 4 Ho, ER
4 Ha: (19.2 x 11.2)2 (24.8 x 12.8) (24.0 x 12.8)ER
Cranes: 2x26t,2x24.5t
1 oil engine driving 1 FP propeller
Total Power: 4,413kW (6,000hp) 13.8kn
Mitsubishi 6UEC52HA
1 x 2 Stroke 6 Cy. 520 x 1250 4413kW (6000bhp)
Kobe Hatsudoki KK-Japan
AuxGen: 2 x 400kW 450V 60Hz a.c
Fuel: 268.0 (d.f.) 1059.0 (r.f.) 17.0pd

8221478 *3FNL2* -
STARFORD 6
ex Waily *-2011* *ex* Vanguard *-2010*
ex Jin Pacific *-2005* *ex* Kouros V *-2003*
ex Balder Queen *-1998*
Star Strength Ltd
Guangzhou Seaway International Ship Management Co Ltd
Panama *Panama*
MMSI: 371785000
Official number: 41881PEXT
15,272 9,023 25,449 T/cm 34.3
Class: NK
1983-06 Imabari Shipbuilding Co Ltd — Imabari EH (Imabari Shipyard) Yd No: 420
Loa 160.80 (BB) Br ex - Dght 10.229
Lbp 150.02 Br md 25.20 Dpth 14.00
Welded, 1 dk
(A21A2BC) Bulk Carrier
Grain: 32,730; Bale: 31,087
Compartments: 4 Ho, ER
4 Ha: (18.4 x 12.8)3 (21.6 x 12.8)ER
Cranes: 3x25t; Derricks: 1x25t
1 oil engine driving 1 FP propeller
Total Power: 6,707kW (9,119hp) 13.8kn
Mitsubishi 6UEC52HA
1 x 2 Stroke 6 Cy. 520 x 1250 6707kW (9119bhp)
Kobe Hatsudoki KK-Japan
AuxGen: 2 x 400kW 450V 60Hz a.c
Fuel: 108.0 (d.f.) 1180.0 (r.f.) 28.0pd

8301321 *3ELI9* -
STARFORD 8
ex Araucaria N *-2011* *ex* Araucaria *-2007*
ex Asturias *-1999* *ex* Atlantic Trader I *-1994*
ex Atlantic Trader *-1987*
Huge Fortune International Ltd
Guangzhou Seaway International Ship Management Co Ltd
Panama *Panama*
MMSI: 372957000
Official number: 3320307C
14,965 8,853 25,357 T/cm 34.5
Class: NK (AB)
1984-05 Imabari Shipbuilding Co Ltd — Imabari EH (Imabari Shipyard) Yd No: 427
Loa 159.77 (BB) Br ex - Dght 10.240
Lbp 150.02 Br md 25.21 Dpth 14.00
Welded, 1 dk
(A21A2BC) Bulk Carrier
Grain: 32,014; Bale: 30,501
Compartments: 4 Ho, ER
4 Ha: (18.4 x 12.8)3 (21.6 x 12.8)ER
Cranes: 3x25t; Derricks: 1x25t; Winches: 1
1 oil engine driving 1 FP propeller
Total Power: 5,237kW (7,120hp) 13.5kn
Sulzer 6RTA48
1 x 2 Stroke 6 Cy. 480 x 1400 5237kW (7120bhp)
Mitsubishi Heavy Industries Ltd-Japan
AuxGen: 2 x 360kW 450V 60Hz a.c
Fuel: 128.0 (d.f.) 1306.0 (r.f.)

8507755 *3FGJ3* -
STARFORD 9
ex Dd Leader *-2012* *ex* Pacdream *-2004*
ex Bright Ocean *-1994*
Auspicious Day Holdings Ltd
Guangzhou Seaway International Ship Management Co Ltd
Panama *Panama*
MMSI: 355913000
Official number: 4457313
14,868 8,920 25,759 T/cm 36.4
Class: NK
1985-09 Imabari Shipbuilding Co Ltd — Imabari EH (Imabari Shipyard) Yd No: 454
Loa 159.43 (BB) Br ex 26.04 Dght 9.908
Lbp 149.82 Br md 26.01 Dpth 13.62
Welded, 1 dk
(A21A2BC) Bulk Carrier
Grain: 32,461; Bale: 31,095
Compartments: 4 Ho, ER
4 Ha: (18.5 x 12.8)3 (21.6 x 12.8)ER
Cranes: 3x30t; Derricks: 1x25t
1 oil engine driving 1 FP propeller
Total Power: 4,708kW (6,401hp) 13.4kn
Mitsubishi 5UEC52LA
1 x 2 Stroke 5 Cy. 520 x 1600 4708kW (6401bhp)
Akasaka Tekkosho KK (Akasaka DieselLtd)-Japan
AuxGen: 2 x 256kW a.c
Fuel: 1085.0 (r.f.)

5009673 *LKPP* -
STARFRAKT
ex Startrans *-1997* *ex* Aldor Ingebrigtsen *-1988*
Starskip AS
-
Tromso *Norway*
MMSI: 258301000
191 57 -
Class: (NV)
1955 Lindstols Skips- & Baatbyggeri AS — Risor
Yd No: 250
Converted From: General Cargo Ship-1989
Lengthened-1975
Loa 32.67 Br ex 6.71 Dght 3.315
Lbp 29.01 Br md 6.68 Dpth 3.36
Welded, 1 dk
(B12C2FL) Live Fish Carrier (Well Boat)
Ins: 297
Compartments: 1 Ho, ER
1 Ha: (5.4 x 3.5)ER
Derricks: 1x1.5t
1 oil engine geared to sc. shaft driving 1 FP propeller
Total Power: 446kW (606hp)
Cummins KT-19-M
1 x 4 Stroke 6 Cy. 159 x 159 446kW (606bhp) (new engine 1995)
Cummins Engine Co Inc-USA
AuxGen: 1 x 48kW 220V 50Hz a.c, 1 x 40kW 220V 50Hz a.c

1005904 *C6SC9* -
STARGATE
-
Stargate II Ltd
-
Nassau *Bahamas*
MMSI: 311281000
Official number: 8000387
1,723 516 1,260
Class: LR
✠ **100A1** SS 11/2011
Yacht
✠ **LMC** **UMS**
Cable: 445.7/34.0 U2 (a)
2001-11 Southern African Shipyards (Pty.) Ltd. — Durban (Hull) Yd No: (802)
2001-11 Oceanco Shipyards (Alblasserdam) B.V. — Alblasserdam Yd No: 802
Loa 80.40 (BB) Br ex - Dght 4.000
Lbp 71.50 Br md 13.00 Dpth 6.85
Welded, 1 dk
(X11A2YP) Yacht
2 oil engines with clutches, flexible couplings & sr reverse geared to sc. shafts driving 2 FP propellers
Total Power: 13,000kW (17,674hp) 23.5kn
M.T.U. 20V1163TB73
2 x Vee 4 Stroke 20 Cy. 230 x 280 each-6500kW (8837bhp)
MTU Friedrichshafen GmbH-Friedrichshafen
AuxGen: 3 x 296kW 380V 50Hz a.c
Thrusters: 1 Thwart. FP thruster (f); 2 Water jet (a)

9493212 *D5CJ7* -	**STARGATE** *ex* Assodiver VII *-2011* *ex* Star Gate *-2010* **Larchep Shipping Inc** Eastern Pacific Shipping Pte Ltd *Monrovia* *Liberia* MMSI: 636015713 Official number: 15713	**17,025** 10,108 28,221 T/cm 39.6	Class: NK	**2011-01 Shimanami Shipyard Co Ltd — Imabari EH** Yd No: 545 Loa 169.37 (BB) Br ex - Dght 9.820 Lbp 160.40 Br md 27.20 Dpth 13.60 Welded, 1 dk	**(A21A2BC) Bulk Carrier** Grain: 37,320; Bale: 35,742 Compartments: 5 Ho, ER 5 Ha: 4 (19.2 x 17.6)ER (13.6 x 16.0) Cranes: 4x30.5t	**1 oil engine** driving 1 FP propeller Total Power: 5,850kW (7,954hp) 14.0kn MAN-B&W 6S42MC 1 x 2 Stroke 6 Cy. 420 x 1764 5850kW (7954bhp) Makita Corp-Japan AuxGen: 3 x 440kW 60Hz a.c Fuel: 1538.0 (r.f.)
9103178 *3FMB4* -	**STARGOLD TRADER** *ex* Ashiya Star *-2002* **Stargold Shipping Corp** Golden Management Co Ltd SatCom: Inmarsat A 1346634 *Panama* *Panama* MMSI: 353911000 Official number: 2164394CH	**26,081** 14,868 45,228 T/cm 51.0	Class: NK	**1994-08 Shin Kurushima Dockyard Co. Ltd. — Onishi** Yd No: 2803 Loa 188.33 (BB) Br ex - Dght 11.373 Lbp 179.50 Br md 31.00 Dpth 16.30 Welded, 1 dk	**(A21A2BC) Bulk Carrier** Grain: 58,148; Bale: 56,250 Compartments: 5 Ho, ER 5 Ha: (16.8 x 16.0)4 (20.0 x 16.0)ER Cranes: 4x25t	**1 oil engine** driving 1 FP propeller Total Power: 7,943kW (10,799hp) 14.3kn Mitsubishi 6UEC52LS 1 x 2 Stroke 6 Cy. 520 x 1850 7943kW (10799bhp) Kobe Hatsudoki KK-Japan AuxGen: 3 x 400kW 450V 60Hz a.c Fuel: 209.6 (d.f.) 1591.0 (r.f.) 29.5pd
8221442 *3FFP2* -	**STARK** *ex* East Sunrise 28 *-2010* *ex* Armonikos *-2009* *ex* Ocean Jade *-1997* *ex* Ocean Trader *-1993* **Govinda Navigation Ltd** Ark Shipping SA SatCom: Inmarsat B 335346210 *Panama* *Panama* MMSI: 353462000 Official number: 1393084I	**35,744** 19,794 61,748	Class: BV OM (AB)	**1984-01 Hitachi Zosen Corp — Nagasu KM** Yd No: 4750 Loa 225.00 (BB) Br ex 32.24 Dght 12.434 Lbp 215.02 Br md 32.21 Dpth 17.81 Welded, 1 dk	**(A21A2BC) Bulk Carrier** Grain: 75,026; Bale: 73,780 Compartments: 7 Ho, ER 7 Ha: 5 (18.0 x 14.0)2 (15.4 x 14.0)ER	**1 oil engine** driving 1 FP propeller Total Power: 7,811kW (10,620hp) 14.5kn B&W 6L67GB 1 x 2 Stroke 6 Cy. 670 x 1700 7811kW (10620bhp) Hitachi Zosen Corp-Japan AuxGen: 3 x 500kW 450V 60Hz a.c Fuel: 203.0 (d.f.) (Part Heating Coils) 2387.0 (r.f.) 35.5pd
5338971 *SGDC* -	**STARKODDER** - **Noas Industri AB** - *Norrsundet* *Sweden* MMSI: 265563790	**197** 59 -	Class: (LR) ✠ Classed LR until 30/3/79	**1953-06 AB Finnboda Varf — Stockholm** Yd No: 352 Loa 29.72 Br ex 8.13 Dght 4.293 Lbp 26.98 Br md 7.80 Dpth 4.53 Welded	**(B32A2ST) Tug** Derricks: 3; Winches: 1 Ice Capable	**1 oil engine** driving 1 CP propeller Total Power: 750kW (1,020hp) 12.0kn Nohab ML6 1 x 2 Stroke 6 Cy. 345 x 580 750kW (1020bhp) (new engine ,made 1948, fitted 1953) Nydqvist & Holm AB-Sweden AuxGen: 2 x 70kW 220/250V d.c Fuel: 30.5 (d.f.) 3.5pd
5099848 *SV2910* -	**STARLET** *ex* Ekole Creek *-1971* **Maril Naftiki Eteria** - *Piraeus* *Greece* MMSI: 237356700 Official number: 1942	*145* 25 -	Class: (LR) ✠ Classed LR until 1/1/87	**1959-09 P K Harris & Sons Ltd — Bideford** Yd No: 121 Loa 31.09 Br ex 8.77 Dght 2.979 Lbp 28.05 Br md 8.23 Dpth 3.36 Welded, 1 dk	**(B32A2ST) Tug**	**1 oil engine** sr geared to sc. shaft driving 1 FP propeller Total Power: 706kW (960hp) Deutz RBA8M528 1 x 4 Stroke 8 Cy. 220 x 280 706kW (960bhp) (new engine ,made 1962, fitted 1974) Kloeckner Humboldt Deutz AG-West Germany
8401559 *J8B5055* -	**STARLET** *ex* Prosperity *-2014* *ex* Melanie Z *-2005* *ex* RMS Francia *-1998* *ex* Oranje Rotterdam *-1992* *ex* Sea Tamar *-1991* **Ofnav Shipping & Trading Co Ltd** Efe Gemi Isletmeciligi Sanayi ve Ticaret Ltd Sti *Kingstown* *St Vincent & The Grenadines* MMSI: 375166000 Official number: 11528	**1,289** 386 1,555	Class: GL	**1984-08 Hermann Suerken GmbH & Co. KG — Papenburg** Yd No: 325 Loa 74.91 Br ex 10.60 Dght 3.391 Lbp 70.52 Br md 10.51 Dpth 5.72 Welded, 2 dks	**(A31A2GX) General Cargo Ship** Grain: 2,351; Bale: 2,310 Compartments: 1 Ho, ER 1 Ha: (46.8 x 8.2)ER	**1 oil engine** with clutches, flexible couplings & sr reverse geared to sc. shaft driving 1 FP propeller Total Power: 746kW (1,014hp) 10.0kn Caterpillar 3508B 1 x Vee 4 Stroke 8 Cy. 170 x 190 746kW (1014bhp) (new engine 1984) Caterpillar Inc-USA AuxGen: 2 x 67kW 380/220V 50Hz a.c Thrusters: 1 Thwart. FP thruster (f) Fuel: 105.0 (d.f.) 3.0pd
9282687 *9HF09* -	**STARLET** *ex* Panam Serena *-2009* *ex* Clipper Leander *-2003* **Renzlor Shipping Ltd** Oceanwide Shipping Ltd *Valletta* *Malta* MMSI: 256917000 Official number: 9282687	**6,499** 3,220 10,048 T/cm 19.5	Class: RS (AB)	**2003-07 Yardimci Tersanesi A.S. — Tuzla** Yd No: 30 Loa 118.37 (BB) Br ex 19.30 Dght 8.220 Lbp 112.00 Br md 19.00 Dpth 10.10 Welded, 1 dk	**(A12A2TC) Chemical Tanker** Double Hull (13F) Liq: 10,957 Cargo Heating Coils Compartments: 2 Ta, 10 Wing Ta, ER Manifold: Bow/CM: 56m Ice Capable	**1 oil engine** driving 1 CP propeller Total Power: 4,442kW (6,039hp) 14.0kn B&W 6S35MC 1 x 2 Stroke 6 Cy. 350 x 1400 4442kW (6039bhp) MAN B&W Diesel A/S-Denmark AuxGen: 3 x 500kW 380/220V 50Hz a.c, 1 x 500kW 380/220V 50Hz a.c Thrusters: 1 Thwart. CP thruster (f) Fuel: 165.0 (d.f.) (Heating Coils) 637.0 (r.f.) 20.0pd
9606936 - -	**STARLIGHT** *ex* Horizon 7 *-2013* **Global Quest LLC** - *Palm Beach, FL* *United States of America* Official number: 1242375	**317** 82 47	Class: NV	**2010-09 Premier Yacht Co Ltd — Kaohsiung** Yd No: C105502 Loa 32.20 Br ex - Dght 2.670 Lbp 27.18 Br md 7.94 Dpth 3.62 Welded, 1 dk	**(X11A2YP) Yacht**	**2 oil engines** reduction geared to sc. shafts driving 2 FP propellers Total Power: 1,766kW (2,402hp) 12.8kn Caterpillar C18 2 x 4 Stroke 6 Cy. 145 x 183 each-883kW (1201bhp) Caterpillar Inc-USA AuxGen: 2 x a.c Thrusters: 1 Tunnel thruster (f)
7731256 *WYK9909* -	**STARLIGHT** *ex* Mary D *-2005* **Starlight Inc** - *Vinalhaven, ME* *United States of America* Official number: 582665	*176* 143 -		**1977 Eastern Marine, Inc. — Panama City, Fl** Yd No: 1 L reg 23.84 Br ex 7.17 Dght - Lbp - Br md - Dpth 3.71 Welded, 1 dk	**(B11B2FV) Fishing Vessel** Ins: 142	**1 oil engine** driving 1 FP propeller Total Power: 515kW (700hp) G.M. (Detroit Diesel) 16V-71 1 x Vee 2 Stroke 16 Cy. 108 x 127 515kW (700bhp) General Motors Detroit DieselAllison Divn-USA AuxGen: 2 x 50kW
9112791 *MVHK7* PD 786	**STARLIGHT** *ex* Paragon V *-2002* **mv Starlight LLP** - SatCom: Inmarsat C 423380510 *Peterhead* *United Kingdom* MMSI: 233805000 Official number: B14432	**270** 175 -		**1995-10 Jones Buckie Shipyard Ltd. — Buckie** Yd No: 507 Loa 24.30 Br ex - Dght 5.900 Lbp 23.00 Br md 7.89 Dpth - Welded, 1 dk	**(B11A2FS) Stern Trawler**	**1 oil engine** geared to sc. shaft driving 1 CP propeller Total Power: 1,119kW (1,521hp) 11.5kn Caterpillar 3508TA 1 x Vee 4 Stroke 8 Cy. 170 x 190 1119kW (1521bhp) Caterpillar Inc-USA
8988961 *WDC3595* -	**STARLIGHT** - **TMT Vessels LLC** - *Atlantic City, NJ* *United States of America* MMSI: 367010830 Official number: 1157803	**298** 89 -		**2004-07 Eastern Shipbuilding Group — Panama City, Fl** Yd No: 832 Loa 37.20 Br ex - Dght - Lbp - Br md 9.14 Dpth 3.96 Welded, 1 dk	**(B11A2FS) Stern Trawler**	**1 oil engine** driving 1 Propeller Total Power: 809kW (1,100hp)
8416920 - -	**STARLIGHT EHCO** *ex* Zakher Star *-2009* *ex* Sea Titan *-2003* *ex* Atlet-3 *-1993* **Consolidated Discounts Ltd** Ehco Ventures Ltd *Lagos* *Nigeria*	**1,408** 422 397	Class: IS (BV) (RS)	**1985-06 Stocznia Gdanska im Lenina — Gdansk** Yd No: B99/03 Loa 64.20 Br ex 15.26 Dght 2.331 Lbp 60.33 Br md 15.00 Dpth 4.00 Welded, 1 dk	**(B34B2SC) Crane Vessel**	**2 oil engines** geared to sc. shafts driving 2 CP propellers Total Power: 1,118kW (1,520hp) 11.5kn Sulzer 8AL20/24 2 x 4 Stroke 8 Cy. 200 x 240 each-559kW (760bhp) Zaklady Przemyslu Metalowego 'HCegielski' SA-Poznan AuxGen: 2 x 320kW a.c
8965440 *MZRP6* PD 230	**STARLIGHT RAYS** *ex* Sharon Rose *-2003* **J S Thores** Caley Fisheries Ltd *Peterhead* *United Kingdom* MMSI: 232006430 Official number: C17103	**320** 138 -		**2000-10 Richards Dry Dock & Engineering Ltd — Great Yarmouth** (Hull launched by) **2000-10 Coastal Marine (Boatbuilders) Ltd. — Eyemouth** (Hull completed by) Loa 26.40 Br ex - Dght - Lbp 22.50 Br md 8.32 Dpth 4.40 Welded, 1 dk	**(B11A2FS) Stern Trawler**	**1 oil engine** driving 1 CP propeller Total Power: 730kW (993hp) 10.2kn Caterpillar 3508B 1 x Vee 4 Stroke 8 Cy. 170 x 190 730kW (993bhp) Caterpillar Inc-USA Thrusters: 1 Thwart. FP thruster (f)
9297539 *VRAL2* -	**STARLIGHT VENTURE** - **Overseas Shipping Pte Ltd** U-Ming Marine Transport (Singapore) Pte Ltd SatCom: Inmarsat C 447700092 *Hong Kong* *Hong Kong* MMSI: 477680100 Official number: HK-1406	**161,045** 109,921 317,970 T/cm 179.7	Class: BV	**2004-11 Hyundai Heavy Industries Co Ltd — Ulsan** Yd No: 1610 Loa 333.00 Br ex - Dght 21.600 Lbp 319.00 Br md 60.00 Dpth 30.40 Welded, 1 dk	**(A13A2TV) Crude Oil Tanker** Double Hull (13F) Liq: 352,000; Liq (Oil): 352,000 3 Cargo Pump (s) Manifold: Bow/CM: 165m	**1 oil engine** driving 1 FP propeller Total Power: 29,346kW (39,899hp) 16.0kn B&W 6S90MC-C 1 x 2 Stroke 6 Cy. 900 x 3188 29346kW (39899bhp) Hyundai Heavy Industries Co Ltd-South Korea AuxGen: 3 x 1100kW 440/220V 60Hz a.c

IMO / Call sign	Name / Owner	Tonnage	Class	Build	Type	Machinery
9671010 *ZJL8841* -	**STARLING** **Hammersmith Ventures SA** Luxembourg Marine Services SA (LMS) *Road Harbour* *British Virgin Islands* MMSI: 378373000	**499** 149 70	Class: AB	**2013-07 Cant. Nav. San Lorenzo SpA — Viareggio** Yd No: 114/46 Loa 46.00 (BB) Br ex 9.30 Dght 2.650 Lbp 38.02 Br md 8.90 Dpth 4.80 Welded, 1 dk	**(X11A2YP) Yacht**	**2 oil engines** reduction geared to sc. shafts driving 2 FP propellers Total Power: 3,000kW (4,078hp) Caterpillar 3512C-HD 2 x Vee 4 Stroke 12 Cy. 170 x 215 each-1500kW (2039bhp) Caterpillar Inc-USA AuxGen: 2 x 100kW a.c Fuel: 58.0 (d.f.)
9159074 *DSRG7* -	**STARLINK ONE** *ex* Genkai *-2012* *ex* Hokuren Maru No. 2 *-2006* **Panstar Co Ltd** Star Link Co Ltd *Jeju* *South Korea* MMSI: 441828000 Official number: JJR-120017	*12,968* 3,890 10,414	Class: KR (NK)	**1997-06 Imabari Shipbuilding Co Ltd — Imabari EH (Imabari Shipyard)** Yd No: 533 Loa 153.62 (BB) Br ex - Dght 6.740 Lbp 142.80 Br md 21.40 Dpth 13.13 Welded, 2 dks	**(A35A2RR) Ro-Ro Cargo Ship** Angled side door/ramp (s. f.) Quarter stern door/ramp (s) Trailers: 100 Grain: 955 TEU 202	**1 oil engine** reduction geared to sc. shaft driving 1 CP propeller Total Power: 19,417kW (26,399hp) 23.5kn Pielstick 16PC4-2V-570 1 x Vee 4 Stroke 16 Cy. 570 x 620 19417kW (26399bhp) Diesel United Ltd.-Aioi AuxGen: 1 x 960kW 450V 60Hz a.c Thrusters: 1 Thwart. FP thruster (f); 1 Tunnel thruster (a) Fuel: 878.0 (r.f.)
7819228 *WDC4866* -	**STARLITE** **Starlite Fisheries LLC** SatCom: Inmarsat C 436752810 *Seattle, WA* *United States of America* MMSI: 367528000 Official number: 597065	*192* 134 -		**1978-08 Marine Construction & Design Co. (MARCO) — Seattle, Wa** Yd No: 348 Loa 37.34 Br ex 9.71 Dght 3.050 Lbp 33.69 Br md 9.44 Dpth 4.40 Welded, 1 dk	**(B11A2FS) Stern Trawler** Ins: 270 Cranes: 1x11t	**1 oil engine** reverse reduction geared to sc. shaft driving 1 FP propeller Total Power: 827kW (1,124hp) 12.0kn Caterpillar D399SCAC 1 x Vee 4 Stroke 16 Cy. 159 x 203 827kW (1124bhp) Caterpillar Tractor Co-USA AuxGen: 2 x 155kW, 1 x 53kW Thrusters: 1 Thwart. FP thruster (f)
8125624 *DUE2125* -	**STARLITE ANNAPOLIS** *ex* Princess Colleen *-2006* *ex* Tadotsu Maru *-1999* *ex* Yoshinogawa *-1988* **Dockside Port Terminals & Marine Service** - *Batangas* *Philippines* Official number: 04-0002090	*1,176* 753 354		**1982-03 Kanda Zosensho K.K. — Kawajiri** Yd No: 270 Loa 63.25 Br ex 14.23 Dght 3.099 Lbp 60.00 Br md 14.20 Dpth 4.09 Welded, 1 dk	**(A36A2PR) Passenger/Ro-Ro Ship (Vehicles)** Passengers: unberthed: 280	**2 oil engines** with clutches, flexible couplings & dr reverse geared to sc. shafts driving 1 FP propeller Total Power: 2,354kW (3,200hp) 15.0kn Daihatsu 6DSM-28 2 x 4 Stroke 6 Cy. 280 x 340 each-1177kW (1600bhp) Daihatsu Diesel Manufacturing Co Lt-Japan Thrusters: 1 Thwart. CP thruster (f)
7501534 *DUE2184* -	**STARLITE ATLANTIC** *ex* Zhou Du 11 *-2008* *ex* Wakatsuru Maru *-1991* **Starlite Ferries Inc** - *Batangas* *Philippines* Official number: 04-0001852	*1,497* 928 634		**1975-06 Wakamatsu Zosen K.K. — Kitakyushu** Yd No: 260 Loa 71.58 Br ex 13.62 Dght 3.607 Lbp 65.00 Br md 13.59 Dpth 4.81 Welded, 2 dks	**(A36A2PR) Passenger/Ro-Ro Ship (Vehicles)** Passengers: unberthed: 455 Cars: 37, Trailers: 21	**2 oil engines** geared to sc. shafts driving 2 FP propellers Total Power: 2,354kW (3,200hp) 15.0kn Daihatsu 8DSM-26 2 x 4 Stroke 8 Cy. 260 x 320 each-1177kW (1600bhp) Daihatsu Diesel Manufacturing Co Lt-Japan AuxGen: 2 x 240kW 450V 60Hz a.c Thrusters: 1 Thwart. FP thruster (f) Fuel: 24.0 (d.f.) 89.5 (r.f.) 6.0pd
7401473 *DVOC* -	**STARLITE CLIPPER** *ex* Starlite Ferry 3 *-1999* *ex* Princess Mermaid *-1994* *ex* Itsukushima Maru No. 3 *-1993* *ex* Itsukushima *-1992* **Starlite Ferries Inc** - *Manila* *Philippines* Official number: MNLD003472	*229* 63 132		**1973-12 Kanbara Zosen K.K. — Onomichi** Yd No: 198 Loa 29.49 Br ex 7.55 Dght 1.601 Lbp 27.55 Br md 7.52 Dpth 1.95 Riveted\Welded, 1 dk	**(A37B2PS) Passenger Ship** Passengers: 89	**1 oil engine** driving 1 FP propeller Total Power: 279kW (379hp) Mitsubishi 1 x 4 Stroke 6 Cy. 260 x 400 279kW (379bhp) Mitsubishi Heavy Industries Ltd-Japan
8000240 - -	**STARLITE EXPLORER** *ex* Suzuka Maru No. 3 *-2000* **Starlite Ferries Inc** - *Batangas* *Philippines* Official number: BAT5006695	*151* 90 -	Class: (NK)	**1979 Edogawa Shipbuilding Co. Ltd. — Tokyo** Yd No: 148 Loa 26.50 Br ex - Dght 2.301 Lbp 24.50 Br md 8.00 Dpth 2.80 Welded, 1 dk	**(B34G2SE) Pollution Control Vessel**	**2 oil engines** reduction geared to sc. shafts driving 2 FP propellers Total Power: 810kW (1,102hp) 8.7kn Yanmar S185L-ST 2 x 4 Stroke 6 Cy. 185 x 230 each-405kW (551bhp) Yanmar Diesel Engine Co Ltd-Japan AuxGen: 2 x 26kW a.c
7235422 *DUA2062* -	**STARLITE FERRY** *ex* Asagumo *-1994* **Starlite Ferries Inc** - *Batangas* *Philippines* Official number: 04-0001736	**574** 390 178		**1971 Nippon Kokan KK (NKK Corp) — Yokohama KN (Asano Dockyard)** Yd No: 153 Loa 41.41 Br ex 15.91 Dght 2.667 Lbp 39.83 Br md 15.85 Dpth 4.50 Welded, 1 dk	**(A36A2PR) Passenger/Ro-Ro Ship (Vehicles)** Passengers: 572 Cars: 50	**2 oil engines** driving 2 FP propellers Total Power: 956kW (1,300hp) 12.5kn Daihatsu 6PSTBM-26D 2 x 4 Stroke 6 Cy. 260 x 320 each-478kW (650bhp) Daihatsu Diesel Manufacturing Co Lt-Japan AuxGen: 2 x 34kW 205V a.c Fuel: 26.5 4.0pd
6829484 *DUHC4* -	**STARLITE FERRY 5** *ex* Don Calvino *-1997* *ex* Shunan Maru *-1980* **Starlite Ferries Inc** - *Cebu* *Philippines* Official number: CEB1000071	*881* 208 233		**1968 Taguma Zosen KK — Onomichi HS** Yd No: 68 Loa 62.06 Br ex 13.42 Dght 2.998 Lbp 57.00 Br md 13.39 Dpth 4.60 Riveted\Welded, 1 dk	**(A36B2PL) Passenger/Landing Craft** Passengers: unberthed: 404 Bow door/ramp TEU 40	**2 oil engines** driving 2 FP propellers Total Power: 1,956kW (2,660hp) 11.5kn Daihatsu 8PSTM-30 2 x 4 Stroke 8 Cy. 300 x 380 each-978kW (1330bhp) Daihatsu Kogyo-Japan Fuel: 36.5 6.0pd
8505317 *DUE2124* -	**STARLITE NAUTICA** *ex* Omishima No. 7 *-1999* **Starlite Ferries Inc** - *Batangas* *Philippines* Official number: 04-0001850	*284* 179 138		**1985-04 Naikai Shipbuilding & Engineering Co Ltd — Onomichi HS (Taguma Shipyard)** Yd No: 505 Loa 39.78 Br ex 10.04 Dght 2.301 Lbp 35.01 Br md 10.00 Dpth 3.13 Welded, 1 dk	**(A36A2PR) Passenger/Ro-Ro Ship (Vehicles)**	**1 oil engine** with clutches, flexible couplings & sr reverse geared to sc. shaft driving 1 FP propeller Total Power: 699kW (950hp) Daihatsu 6PSHTDM-26H 1 x 4 Stroke 6 Cy. 260 x 320 699kW (950bhp) Daihatsu Diesel Manufacturing Co Lt-Japan
7118727 - -	**STARLITE NAVIGATOR** *ex* Zhou Du No. 6 *-2003* *ex* Hamagiku *-1985* **Starlite Ferries Inc** - *Batangas* *Philippines* Official number: 04-0001851	*1,101* 491 319		**1971-11 Taguma Zosen KK — Onomichi HS** Yd No: 98 Loa 57.33 Br ex 13.52 Dght 2.896 Lbp 52.99 Br md 13.49 Dpth 4.02 Riveted\Welded, 2 dks	**(A36A2PR) Passenger/Ro-Ro Ship (Vehicles)** Passengers: 600 Bow door/ramp Len: - Wid: 3.60 Swl: -	**2 oil engines** driving 2 FP propellers Total Power: 1,766kW (2,402hp) Niigata 8MG25BX 2 x 4 Stroke 8 Cy. 250 x 320 each-883kW (1201bhp) Niigata Engineering Co Ltd-Japan AuxGen: 2 x 80kW 445V a.c Fuel: 55.0 9.5pd
7044225 *DUHE7* -	**STARLITE NEPTUNE** *ex* Calbayog *-2013* *ex* Don Martin Sr 9 *-2005* *ex* Asia Singapore *-2001* *ex* Miyuki Maru *-1993* **Future Stargate Ventures Inc** Starlite Ferries Inc *Batangas* *Philippines* Official number: CEB1000589	**830** 251 411	Class: (BV)	**1970 Kanda Zosensho K.K. — Kure** Yd No: 151 Loa 62.18 Br ex 13.39 Dght 3.099 Lbp 55.00 Br md 11.41 Dpth 4.02 Welded, 2 dks	**(A36A2PR) Passenger/Ro-Ro Ship (Vehicles)** Passengers: 580	**2 oil engines** reduction geared to sc. shafts driving 2 FP propellers Total Power: 1,324kW (1,800hp) 14.0kn Niigata 6MG25BX 2 x 4 Stroke 6 Cy. 250 x 320 each-662kW (900bhp) Niigata Engineering Co Ltd-Japan AuxGen: 2 x 80kW 440V a.c Fuel: 30.5 3.0pd
8301395 *DUE2127* -	**STARLITE PACIFIC** *ex* Seiyo Maru *-1999* **Starlite Ferries Inc** - *Batangas* *Philippines* Official number: 04-0001849	*498* 268 237		**1983-09 Kanda Zosensho K.K. — Kawajiri** Yd No: 279 Loa 48.32 Br ex 11.64 Dght 2.901 Lbp 44.00 Br md 11.60 Dpth 3.81 Welded, 1 dk	**(A36A2PR) Passenger/Ro-Ro Ship (Vehicles)** Passengers: unberthed: 370 Cars: 6, Trailers: 12	**2 oil engines** sr geared to sc. shafts driving 2 FP propellers Total Power: 1,472kW (2,002hp) 14.0kn Daihatsu 6DSM-26A 2 x 4 Stroke 6 Cy. 260 x 300 each-736kW (1001bhp) Daihatsu Diesel Manufacturing Co Lt-Japan
8895700 *DUE2162* -	**STARLITE POLARIS** *ex* Kushima No. 38 *-1999* *ex* Ehime No. 18 *-1999* **Dockside Port Terminals & Marine Service** - *Batangas* *Philippines* Official number: 04-0002089	*240* 153 90		**1975-07 Binan Senpaku Kogyo K.K. — Onomichi** Loa 35.00 Br ex - Dght 2.000 Lbp 31.00 Br md 8.30 Dpth 2.90 Welded, 1 dk	**(A36A2PR) Passenger/Ro-Ro Ship (Vehicles)**	**1 oil engine** driving 1 FP propeller Total Power: 625kW (850hp) 11.3kn Daihatsu 1 x 4 Stroke 625kW (850bhp) Daihatsu Kogyo-Japan
7405338 *DUE2160* -	**STARLITE VOYAGER** *ex* Ferry Tsubaki *-2003* **Starlite Ferries Inc** - *Batangas* *Philippines* Official number: BAT5006980	*1,200* 653 343		**1974-07 Naikai Shipbuilding & Engineering Co Ltd — Onomichi HS (Taguma Shipyard)** Yd No: 386 Loa 68.64 Br ex 13.01 Dght 3.683 Lbp 61.98 Br md 12.98 Dpth 4.60 Riveted\Welded, 1 dk	**(A37B2PS) Passenger Ship** Passengers: unberthed: 500	**2 oil engines** driving 2 FP propellers Total Power: 3,090kW (4,202hp) 15.5kn Hanshin 6LU38 2 x 4 Stroke 6 Cy. 380 x 580 each-1545kW (2101bhp) Hanshin Nainenki Kogyo-Japan AuxGen: 2 x 200kW 445V 60Hz a.c Fuel: 11.5 (d.f.) 46.5 (r.f.) 15.0pd

9671709 - -	**STARNAV ALDEBARAN** - **Starnav Servicos Maritimos Ltda** - *Rio de Janeiro* *Brazil*	**488** 146 391	Class: RB (Class contemplated)	**2013-03 Detroit Brasil Ltda — Itajai** Yd No: 397 Loa 32.00 Br ex - Dght 4.400 Lbp 29.70 Br md 11.60 Dpth 5.43 Welded, 1 dk	**(B32A2ST) Tug**	**2 oil engines** reduction geared to sc. shafts driving 2 Propellers Total Power: 4,000kW (5,438hp) M.T.U. 16V4000M61 2 x Vee 4 Stroke 16 Cy. 165 x 190 each-2000kW (2719bhp) MTU Friedrichshafen GmbH-Friedrichshafen
9555876 - -	**STARNAV ANTARES** - **Starnav Servicos Maritimos Ltda** - *Rio de Janeiro* *Brazil*	**488** 146 387		**2009-11 Detroit Brasil Ltda — Itajai** Yd No: 332 Loa 32.00 Br ex - Dght 4.120 Lbp 30.59 Br md 11.60 Dpth 5.36 Welded, 1 dk	**(B32A2ST) Tug**	**2 oil engines** reduction geared to sc. shafts driving 2 Propellers Total Power: 3,372kW (4,584hp) Caterpillar 3516B-HD 2 x Vee 4 Stroke 16 Cy. 170 x 215 each-1686kW (2292bhp) Caterpillar Inc-USA Thrusters: 1 Tunnel thruster (f)
9696802 *3FZV5* -	**STARNAV AQUARIUS** - **Starnav Servicos Maritimos Ltda** - *Panama* *Panama* MMSI: 353353000 Official number: 45241PEXT	**4,425** 1,700 4,762	Class: AB (Class contemplated)	**2014-03 Guangzhou Huangpu Shipbuilding Co Ltd — Guangzhou GD** Yd No: H2337 Loa 90.00 Br ex 19.05 Dght 6.250 Lbp 84.67 Br md 19.00 Dpth 7.75 Welded, 1 dk	**(B21A2OS) Platform Supply Ship**	**4 oil engines** reduction geared to sc. shafts driving 2 Propellers Total Power: 8,320kW (11,312hp) 13.0kn M.T.U. 16V4000M33S 4 x Vee 4 Stroke 16 Cy. 170 x 210 each-2080kW (2828bhp) MTU Friedrichshafen GmbH-Friedrichshafen
9668738 *PPNK* -	**STARNAV CENTAURUS** - **Starnav Servicos Maritimos Ltda** - *Itajai* *Brazil* MMSI: 710238000	**4,427** 1,696 4,690	Class: AB	**2013-07 Detroit Brasil Ltda — Itajai** Yd No: 369 Loa 90.00 (BB) Br ex 19.05 Dght 5.840 Lbp 84.67 Br md 19.00 Dpth 7.75 Welded, 1 dk	**(B21A2OS) Platform Supply Ship** Cranes: 2	**4 diesel electric oil engines** driving 4 gen. each 1845kW a.c Connecting to 2 elec. motors each (2750kW) driving 2 Azimuth electric drive units Total Power: 8,320kW (11,312hp) 13.0kn M.T.U. 16V4000M33S 4 x Vee 4 Stroke 16 Cy. 170 x 210 each-2080kW (2828bhp) MTU Friedrichshafen GmbH-Friedrichshafen Thrusters: 2 Tunnel thruster (f) Fuel: 390.0
9603441 *PPZQ* -	**STARNAV ORION** - **Starnav Servicos Maritimos Ltda** - *Rio de Janeiro* *Brazil* MMSI: 710005870 Official number: 3813879976	**488** 144 393		**2011-05 Detroit Brasil Ltda — Itajai** Yd No: 339 Loa 32.00 Br ex - Dght 4.360 Lbp - Br md 11.60 Dpth 5.36 Welded, 1 dk	**(B32A2ST) Tug**	**2 oil engines** reduction geared to sc. shafts driving 2 Propellers M.T.U. 2 x 4 Stroke MTU Friedrichshafen GmbH-Friedrichshafen
9603673 *PPZP* -	**STARNAV PEGASUS** - **Starnav Servicos Maritimos Ltda** - *Rio de Janeiro* *Brazil* MMSI: 710005860 Official number: 3813880257	**488** 144 393		**2011-06 Detroit Brasil Ltda — Itajai** Yd No: 340 Loa 32.00 Br ex - Dght 4.360 Lbp - Br md 11.60 Dpth 5.36 Welded, 1 dk	**(B32A2ST) Tug**	**2 oil engines** reduction geared to sc. shafts driving 2 Propellers M.T.U. 2 x 4 Stroke MTU Friedrichshafen GmbH-Friedrichshafen
9668726 *PPYU* -	**STARNAV PERSEUS** - **Starnav Servicos Maritimos Ltda** - *Itajai* *Brazil* MMSI: 710004880	**4,427** 1,696 5,100	Class: AB	**2013-07 Detroit Brasil Ltda — Itajai** Yd No: 368 Loa 90.00 (BB) Br ex 19.05 Dght 5.840 Lbp 84.67 Br md 19.00 Dpth 7.75 Welded, 1 dk	**(B21A2OS) Platform Supply Ship** Cranes: 2	**4 diesel electric oil engines** driving 4 gen. each 1845kW a.c Connecting to 2 elec. motors each (2750kW) driving 2 Azimuth electric drive units Total Power: 8,320kW (11,312hp) 13.0kn M.T.U. 16V4000M33S 4 x Vee 4 Stroke 16 Cy. 170 x 210 each-2080kW (2828bhp) MTU Friedrichshafen GmbH-Friedrichshafen Thrusters: 2 Tunnel thruster (f) Fuel: 390.0
9668752 *PPSQ* -	**STARNAV REGULUS** - **Starnav Servicos Maritimos Ltda** - *Itajai* *Brazil* MMSI: 710335000	**4,427** 1,696 5,100	Class: AB	**2013-12 Detroit Brasil Ltda — Itajai** Yd No: 371 Loa 90.00 (BB) Br ex 19.05 Dght 6.250 Lbp 84.67 Br md 19.00 Dpth 7.75 Welded, 1 dk	**(B21A2OS) Platform Supply Ship** Cranes: 2	**4 diesel electric oil engines** driving 4 gen. each 1845kW Connecting to 2 elec. motors each (2500kW) driving 2 Azimuth electric drive units Total Power: 8,320kW (11,312hp) 13.0kn M.T.U. 16V4000M33S 4 x Vee 4 Stroke 16 Cy. 170 x 210 each-2080kW (2828bhp) MTU Friedrichshafen GmbH-Friedrichshafen Thrusters: 2 Tunnel thruster (f)
9671694 - -	**STARNAV SAGITARIUS** - **Starnav Servicos Maritimos Ltda** - *Rio de Janeiro* *Brazil*	**488** 146 391	Class: RB (Class contemplated)	**2013-02 Detroit Brasil Ltda — Itajai** Yd No: 396 Loa 32.00 Br ex - Dght 4.400 Lbp 29.70 Br md 11.60 Dpth 5.43 Welded, 1 dk	**(B32A2ST) Tug**	**2 oil engines** reduction geared to sc. shafts driving 2 Propellers Total Power: 4,000kW (5,438hp) M.T.U. 16V4000M61 2 x Vee 4 Stroke 16 Cy. 165 x 190 each-2000kW (2719bhp) MTU Friedrichshafen GmbH-Friedrichshafen
9592159 *PY2039* -	**STARNAV SIRIUS** - **Starnav Servicos Maritimos Ltda** - SatCom: Inmarsat C 471011287 *Rio de Janeiro* *Brazil* MMSI: 710005640 Official number: 3813880028	**488** 144 393		**2011-05 Detroit Brasil Ltda — Itajai** Yd No: 338 Loa 32.00 Br ex - Dght 4.360 Lbp 30.59 Br md 11.60 Dpth 5.36 Welded, 1 dk	**(B32A2ST) Tug**	**2 oil engines** reduction geared to sc. shafts driving 2 Propellers Total Power: 3,942kW (5,360hp) M.T.U. 2 x 4 Stroke each-1971kW (2680bhp) MTU Friedrichshafen GmbH-Friedrichshafen
9668740 *PPRC* -	**STARNAV URSUS** - **Starnav Servicos Maritimos Ltda** - *Itajai* *Brazil* MMSI: 710245000	**4,427** 1,696 4,500	Class: AB	**2013-10 Detroit Brasil Ltda — Itajai** Yd No: 370 Loa 90.00 (BB) Br ex 19.05 Dght 5.840 Lbp 84.67 Br md 19.00 Dpth 7.75 Welded, 1 dk	**(B21A2OS) Platform Supply Ship** Cranes: 2	**4 diesel electric oil engines** driving 4 gen. each 1845kW Connecting to 2 elec. motors each (2750kW) driving 2 Azimuth electric drive units Total Power: 8,320kW (11,312hp) 13.0kn M.T.U. 16V4000M33S 4 x Vee 4 Stroke 16 Cy. 170 x 210 each-2080kW (2828bhp) MTU Friedrichshafen GmbH-Friedrichshafen Thrusters: 2 Tunnel thruster (f) Fuel: 390.0
7438050 *UAZL* ME-0213	**STAROBELSK** - **Sevrybkomflot JSC (A/O 'Sevrybkomflot')** - *Murmansk* *Russia* MMSI: 273512600 Official number: 740822	**739** 221 345	Class: RS	**1974 Zavod "Leninskaya Kuznitsa" — Kiyev** Yd No: 213 Loa 53.73 (BB) Br ex 10.72 Dght 4.290 Lbp 47.92 Br md - Dpth 6.02 Welded, 1 dk	**(B11A2FS) Stern Trawler** Ins: 295 Compartments: 1 Ho, ER 2 Ha: 2 (1.6 x 1.6) Derricks: 2x1.5t Ice Capable	**1 oil engine** driving 1 CP propeller Total Power: 971kW (1,320hp) 12.5kn S.K.L. 8NVD48A-2U 1 x 4 Stroke 8 Cy. 320 x 480 971kW (1320bhp) VEB Schwermaschinenbau "KarlLiebknecht" (SKL)-Magdeburg Thrusters: 1 Thwart. FP thruster (f); 1 Tunnel thruster (a) Fuel: 163.0 (d.f.)
8728062 *UDPI* -	**STAROCHERKASSK** *ex Volgo-Balt 222 -1998* **Kadry JSC (A/O 'Kadry')** - *Taganrog* *Russia* MMSI: 273379100 Official number: 792099	**2,516** 1,022 3,174	Class: RS (RR)	**1980-01 Zavody Tazkeho Strojarstva (ZTS) — Komarno** Yd No: 1953 Loa 113.84 Br ex 13.20 Dght 3.640 Lbp 110.40 Br md 13.00 Dpth 5.50 Welded, 1 dk	**(A31A2GX) General Cargo Ship** Grain: 4,720 Compartments: 4 Ho, ER 4 Ha: (18.2 x 9.5)3 (19.5 x 9.5)ER Ice Capable	**2 oil engines** driving 2 FP propellers Total Power: 1,030kW (1,400hp) 9.6kn Skoda 6L275A2 2 x 4 Stroke 6 Cy. 275 x 350 each-515kW (700bhp) CKD Praha-Praha
7336082 *UGPG* -	**STARODUB** - **Gorod 415 Ltd** - *Petropavlovsk-Kamchatskiy* *Russia* Official number: 731490	**174** 52 89	Class: RS	**1973-09 Sretenskiy Sudostroitelnyy Zavod — Sretensk** Yd No: 55 Loa 33.96 Br ex 7.09 Dght 2.900 Lbp 30.00 Br md 7.00 Dpth 3.69 Welded, 1 dk	**(B11B2FV) Fishing Vessel** Bale: 96 Compartments: 1 Ho, ER 1 Ha: (1.3 x 1.6) Derricks: 2x2t Ice Capable	**1 oil engine** driving 1 FP propeller Total Power: 224kW (305hp) 9.0kn S.K.L. 8NVD36-1U 1 x 4 Stroke 8 Cy. 240 x 360 224kW (305bhp) VEB Schwermaschinenbau "KarlLiebknecht" (SKL)-Magdeburg Fuel: 22.0 (d.f.)
8230522 *UIDA* -	**STAROPOLYE** *ex Volgo-Balt 238 -2011* **Transoptimal SPb Co Ltd** Transoptimal Shipping & Trading Co Ltd *St Petersburg* *Russia* MMSI: 273314900	**2,892** 1,660 4,263	Class: RS (RR)	**1982-06 Zavody Tazkeho Strojarstva (ZTS) — Komarno** Yd No: 1969 Loa 114.00 Br ex 13.23 Dght 4.490 Lbp 110.52 Br md 13.01 Dpth 5.50 Welded, 1 dk	**(A31A2GX) General Cargo Ship** Grain: 4,720 Compartments: 4 Ho, ER 4 Ha: (18.6 x 11.2)2 (18.8 x 11.2) (20.3 x 11.2)ER	**2 oil engines** driving 2 FP propellers Total Power: 1,030kW (1,400hp) 11.0kn Skoda 6L275A2 2 x 4 Stroke 6 Cy. 275 x 350 each-515kW (700bhp) Skoda-Praha AuxGen: 2 x 80kW a.c Fuel: 110.0 (d.f.)

8025381 *V3VW4* -	**STARRY-M** *ex* African Gardenia *-2013* **Rezk Shipping SA** Unimar Shipping Management *Belize City* *Belize* MMSI: 312357000 Official number: 141330291	**6,498** 3,338 9,101 T/cm 21.2	Class: NK (AB)	**1981-10 Shimoda Dockyard Co. Ltd. — Shimoda** Yd No: 317 Loa 135.52 (BB) Br ex 19.05 Dght 6.316 Lbp 128.02 Br md 19.00 Dpth 8.51 Welded, 1 dk	**(A21A2BC) Bulk Carrier** Grain: 11,326; Bale: 11,071 Compartments: 4 Ho, ER 4 Ha: (13.3 x 8.9)3 (12.5 x 8.9)ER Cranes: 3x5t	**1 oil engine** driving 1 FP propeller Total Power: 3,825kW (5,200hp) 15.0kn Mitsubishi 8UEC37/88H 1 x 2 Stroke 8 Cy. 370 x 880 3825kW (5200bhp) Akasaka Tekkosho KK (Akasaka DieselLtd)-Japan AuxGen: 2 x 320kW a.c Fuel: 1038.0 (Heating Coils)
7359498 *6YRN6* -	**STARRY METROPOLIS** *ex* Neptune *-2011* *ex* CT Neptune *-2006* *ex* Olvia *-2004* *ex* Kareliya *-1998* *ex* Leonid Brezhnev *-1989* *ex* Kareliya *-1982* **Income China International Group Ltd** Hopewin Ship Management Co Ltd *Montego Bay* *Jamaica* MMSI: 339300680	**15,791** 5,315 2,402	Class: RS	**1976-12 Oy Wartsila Ab — Turku** Yd No: 1223 Converted From: Ferry (Passenger/Vehicle)-1976 Loa 156.27 (BB) Br ex 22.05 Dght 5.920 Lbp 133.99 Br md 21.80 Dpth 16.29 Welded, 3 dks	**(A37A2PC) Passenger/Cruise** Passengers: berths: 775 Stern door/ramp Len: 7.00 Wid: 5.00 Swl: - Ice Capable	**2 oil engines** geared to sc. shafts driving 2 CP propellers Total Power: 13,240kW (18,002hp) 21.0kn Pielstick 18PC2-2V-400 2 x Vee 4 Stroke 18 Cy. 400 x 460 each-6620kW (9001bhp) Oy Wartsila Ab-Finland AuxGen: 4 x 912kW 400V 50Hz a.c, 1 x 168kW 400V 50Hz a.c Thrusters: 1 Thwart. FP thruster (f) Fuel: 680.0 (r.f.)
9520651 *3FEG8* -	**STARRY SKY** **Diamond Camellia SA** MC Shipping Ltd *Panama* *Panama* MMSI: 373157000 Official number: 4464213	**32,319** 19,458 58,109 T/cm 57.4	Class: NK	**2013-02 Tsuneishi Heavy Industries (Cebu) Inc — Balamban** Yd No: SC-171 Loa 189.99 (BB) Br ex - Dght 12.826 Lbp 185.60 Br md 32.26 Dpth 18.00 Welded, 1 dk	**(A21A2BC) Bulk Carrier** Grain: 72,689; Bale: 70,122 Compartments: 5 Ho, ER 5 Ha: ER Cranes: 4x30t	**1 oil engine** driving 1 FP propeller Total Power: 8,400kW (11,421hp) 14.5kn MAN-B&W 6S50MC-C 1 x 2 Stroke 6 Cy. 500 x 2000 8400kW (11421bhp) Mitsui Engineering & Shipbuilding CLtd-Japan Fuel: 2380.0
8887088 *WCW9025* -	**STARS OF THE SEA** *ex* Amazona *-1996* **P & R Fishing Corp** - *New Bedford, MA* *United States of America* MMSI: 367137450 Official number: 671011	*114* 91 -		**1985** L reg 21.23 Br ex - Dght - Lbp - Br md 6.70 Dpth 3.20 Welded, 1 dk	**(B11B2FV) Fishing Vessel**	**1 oil engine** driving 1 FP propeller
9198472 *WCZ3442* -	**STARSHIP EXPRESS** **D & G Marine Inc** - *Avalon, CA* *United States of America* MMSI: 366768030 Official number: 1081393	**403** 140 50		**1999-06 Pequot River Shipworks Inc — New London CT** Yd No: PRS4 Loa 41.00 Br ex - Dght 1.370 Lbp 37.00 Br md 10.48 Dpth 3.90 Welded, 1 dk	**(A37B2PS) Passenger Ship** Hull Material: Aluminium Alloy Passengers: unberthed: 300	**2 oil engines** geared to sc. shafts driving 2 Water jets Total Power: 4,576kW (6,222hp) M.T.U. 16V4000M70 2 x Vee 4 Stroke 16 Cy. 165 x 190 each-2288kW (3111bhp) MTU Friedrichshafen GmbH-Friedrichshafen
9650066 *V7ZQ9* -	**STARSHIP LEO** **HK International Ltd** Nam Sung Shipping Co Ltd *Majuro* *Marshall Islands* MMSI: 538004893 Official number: 4893	**20,920** 6,587 23,927	Class: KR	**2013-02 Hyundai Mipo Dockyard Co Ltd — Ulsan** Yd No: 4072 Loa 172.10 Br ex - Dght 8.500 Lbp 161.58 Br md 27.50 Dpth 16.50 Welded, 1 dk	**(A33A2CC) Container Ship (Fully Cellular)** TEU 1850	**1 oil engine** driving 1 FP propeller Total Power: 6,000kW (8,158hp) 19.2kn MAN-B&W 8S35MC 1 x 2 Stroke 8 Cy. 350 x 1400 6000kW (8158bhp) Hyundai Heavy Industries Co Ltd-South Korea Thrusters: 1 Tunnel thruster (f)
9656759 *V7ZR3* -	**STARSHIP PEGASUS** **SL International Ltd** Nam Sung Shipping Co Ltd *Majuro* *Marshall Islands* MMSI: 538004895 Official number: 4895	**20,920** 6,587 23,927	Class: KR	**2013-03 Hyundai Mipo Dockyard Co Ltd — Ulsan** Yd No: 4074 Loa 172.10 (BB) Br ex - Dght 8.500 Lbp 161.58 Br md 27.50 Dpth 16.50 Welded, 1 dk	**(A33A2CC) Container Ship (Fully Cellular)** TEU 1850	**1 oil engine** driving 1 FP propeller Total Power: 6,000kW (8,158hp) 19.3kn MAN-B&W 8S35MC 1 x 2 Stroke 8 Cy. 350 x 1400 6000kW (8158bhp) Hyundai Heavy Industries Co Ltd-South Korea Thrusters: 1 Tunnel thruster (f)
9650078 *V7ZR2* -	**STARSHIP URSA** **BS International Ltd** Nam Sung Shipping Co Ltd *Majuro* *Marshall Islands* MMSI: 538004894 Official number: 4894	**20,920** 6,587 23,927	Class: KR	**2013-02 Hyundai Mipo Dockyard Co Ltd — Ulsan** Yd No: 4073 Loa 172.10 Br ex - Dght 8.500 Lbp 161.58 Br md 27.50 Dpth 16.50 Welded, 1 dk	**(A33A2CC) Container Ship (Fully Cellular)** TEU 1850	**1 oil engine** driving 1 FP propeller Total Power: 6,000kW (8,158hp) 19.2kn MAN-B&W 8S35MC 1 x 2 Stroke 8 Cy. 350 x 1400 6000kW (8158bhp) Hyundai Heavy Industries Co Ltd-South Korea Thrusters: 1 Tunnel thruster (f)
7200609 *A6E2769* -	**STARSS-1** *ex* Inca Tide *-1986* *ex* Inca *-1977* **Ahmed Ali Khalifa Shipping Agencies Co LLC** - *Dubai* *United Arab Emirates* Official number: 4127	*142* 43 -	Class: (HR)	**1961 Burton Shipyard Co., Inc. — Port Arthur, Tx** Yd No: 308 Loa 28.96 Br ex 6.91 Dght - Lbp - Br md 6.86 Dpth 3.13 Welded, 1 dk	**(B21A20C) Crew/Supply Vessel**	**2 oil engines** driving 2 FP propellers Total Power: 1,618kW (2,200hp) G.M. (Detroit Diesel) 8V-71-N 2 x Vee 2 Stroke 8 Cy. 108 x 127 each-809kW (1100bhp) General Motors Corp-USA
8815126 *UBMI3* -	**START** *ex* Anphu *-2012* *ex* Fukuyoshi Maru No. 75 *-2006* **Paroos Co Ltd (Paroos OOO)** - *Nevelsk* *Russia* MMSI: 273357560	**688** 346 -	Class: RS	**1988-12 Niigata Engineering Co Ltd — Niigata NI** Yd No: 2108 Loa 55.79 (BB) Br ex - Dght 3.486 Lbp 49.15 Br md 8.90 Dpth 3.85 Welded, 1 dk	**(B11B2FV) Fishing Vessel** Ins: 550	**1 oil engine** with clutches, flexible couplings & sr geared to sc. shaft driving 1 CP propeller Total Power: 699kW (950hp) 11.0kn Niigata 6M28BFT 1 x 4 Stroke 6 Cy. 280 x 480 699kW (950bhp) Niigata Engineering Co Ltd-Japan
9231274 *D5FJ9* -	**STARTRADER** *ex* Botafogo *-2013* **Elain Navigation Co** Omicron Ship Management Inc *Monrovia* *Liberia* MMSI: 636016289 Official number: 16289	**39,727** 25,754 76,623 T/cm 66.6	Class: BV (NK)	**2001-07 Imabari Shipbuilding Co Ltd — Marugame KG (Marugame Shipyard)** Yd No: 1337 Loa 224.94 (BB) Br ex - Dght 14.139 Lbp 217.00 Br md 32.26 Dpth 19.50 Welded, 1 dk	**(A21A2BC) Bulk Carrier** Grain: 90,740 Compartments: 7 Ho, ER 7 Ha: (17.1 x 12.8)6 (17.1 x 15.6)ER	**1 oil engine** driving 1 FP propeller Total Power: 10,320kW (14,031hp) 14.0kn MAN-B&W 6S60MC 1 x 2 Stroke 6 Cy. 600 x 2292 10320kW (14031bhp) Mitsui Engineering & Shipbuilding CLtd-Japan AuxGen: 3 x 400kW 60Hz a.c Fuel: 2970.0
9326495 *V7SM3* -	**STARTRAMP** **Startramp Shipping Ltd** Korkyra Shipping Ltd *Majuro* *Marshall Islands* MMSI: 538003680 Official number: 3680	**12,899** 6,023 18,615	Class: BV (LR) (CS) **100A1** 02/2007 Class contemplated	**2007-02 P.T. PAL Indonesia — Surabaya** Yd No: 225 Loa 147.35 (BB) Br ex - Dght 9.400 Lbp 140.30 Br md 22.50 Dpth 12.85 Welded, 1 dk	**(A31A2GX) General Cargo Ship** Grain: 21,500 Compartments: 4 Ho, ER 4 Ha: ER Cranes: 3x40t	**1 oil engine** reduction geared to sc. shaft driving 1 FP propeller Total Power: 5,600kW (7,614hp) 14.0kn MaK 6M43C 1 x 4 Stroke 6 Cy. 430 x 610 5600kW (7614bhp) Caterpillar Motoren GmbH & Co. KG-Germany Thrusters: 1 Tunnel thruster (f)
8016536 *WDC8284* -	**STARWARD** **Starward Fisheries LLC** - *Seattle, WA* *United States of America* MMSI: 367084590 Official number: 617807	*197* 140 -		**1980-02 Marine Construction & Design Co. (MARCO) — Seattle, Wa** Yd No: 383 Loa 37.37 Br ex - Dght 4.877 Lbp 33.69 Br md 9.44 Dpth 4.40 Welded, 1 dk	**(B11A2FS) Stern Trawler** Cranes: 1x11t	**1 oil engine** geared to sc. shaft driving 1 FP propeller Total Power: 827kW (1,124hp) Caterpillar D399SCAC 1 x Vee 4 Stroke 16 Cy. 159 x 203 827kW (1124bhp) Caterpillar Tractor Co-USA
9235957 *A8CG5* -	**STARWAY** *ex* Hibernia *-2013* *ex* Sag Bulk Australia *-2011* *ex* Selinda *-2009* **Bella Luna Ltd** Omicron Ship Management Inc *Monrovia* *Liberia* MMSI: 636016236 Official number: 16236	**17,784** 9,924 28,107 T/cm 39.5	Class: BV (LR) (AB) Classed LR until 1/11/13	**2001-04 Bohai Shipyard — Huludao LN** Yd No: 407-5 Loa 169.00 (BB) Br ex - Dght 9.710 Lbp 160.30 Br md 27.20 Dpth 13.60 Welded, 1 dk	**(A21A2BC) Bulk Carrier** Double Bottom Entire Compartment Length Grain: 37,505; Bale: 35,836 Cargo Heating Coils Compartments: 5 Ho, ER 5 Ha: (13.6 x 16.0)4 (20.0 x 17.6)ER Cranes: 4x30t	**1 oil engine** driving 1 FP propeller Total Power: 7,100kW (9,653hp) 14.3kn Sulzer 5RTA52 1 x 2 Stroke 5 Cy. 520 x 1800 7100kW (9653bhp) Yichang Marine Diesel Engine Co Ltd-China AuxGen: 3 x 520kW 220/440V 60Hz a.c Fuel: 115.9 (d.f.) (Heating Coils) 1439.4 (r.f.)
8721064 *UDHL* -	**STARYY ARBAT** *ex* XVIII Syezd Profsoyuzov *-1996* **Westrybflot JSC (ZAO 'Westrybflot')** Sovrybflot JSC (A/O 'Sovrybflot') *Kaliningrad* *Russia* MMSI: 273258100 Official number: 862112	**4,407** 1,322 1,810	Class: RS	**1987-08 GP Chernomorskiy Sudostroitelnyy Zavod — Nikolayev** Yd No: 562 Loa 104.50 Br ex 16.03 Dght 5.900 Lbp 96.40 Br md 16.00 Dpth 10.20 Welded, 2 dks	**(B11A2FG) Factory Stern Trawler** Ice Capable	**2 oil engines** geared to sc. shaft driving 1 CP propeller Total Power: 5,148kW (7,000hp) 16.1kn Russkiy 6CHN40/46 2 x 4 Stroke 6 Cy. 400 x 460 each-2574kW (3500bhp) Mashinostroitelnyy Zavod"Russkiy-Dizel"-Leningrad AuxGen: 2 x 1600kW 220/380V 50Hz a.c, 3 x 200kW 220/380V 50Hz a.c Fuel: 1226.0 (d.f.)

IMO / Call sign	Name / Owner	Tonnage	Class	Builder / Dimensions	Type	Machinery
9042116 *HPOI* -	**STAS** **Norfolk International Holding Inc** Russochart GmbH *Panama* *Panama* MMSI: 351156000 Official number: 3518213	2,765 1,153 3,069	Class: RS	**2008-12 AO Pribaltiyskiy Sudostroitelnyy Zavod "Yantar" — Kaliningrad** (Hull) Yd No: 201 **2008-12 in Turkey** Yd No: (201) Loa 102.64 Br ex - Dght 4.980 Lbp 96.24 Br md 12.80 Dpth 6.00 Welded	**(A31A2GX) General Cargo Ship** Grain: 4,021 TEU 164 incl 8 ref C. Compartments: 3 Ho, ER 3 Ha: ER 3 (18.5 x 9.2)	**1 oil engine** REDUCTION: reduction geared to sc. shaft (s) driving 1 CP propeller Total Power: 2,074kW (2,820hp) 13.8kn MAN-B&W 6S26MC 1 x 2 Stroke 6 Cy. 260 x 980 2074kW (2820bhp) AO Bryanskiy MashinostroitelnyyZavod (BMZ)-Bryansk AuxGen: 2 x 320kW a.c Fuel: 260.0 (r.f.)
9623207 *2GED7* -	**STATE OF GRACE** **ALT Charters Ltd** Dohle Private Clients Ltd *Douglas* *Isle of Man (British)* MMSI: 235096604 Official number: 742832	256 76 25	Class: AB	**2013-09 Perini Navi SpA (Divisione Picchiotti) — Viareggio** Yd No: 2180 Loa 39.47 Br ex - Dght 1.620 Lbp 34.26 Br md 9.40 Dpth 3.52 Welded, 1 dk	**(X11A2YS) Yacht (Sailing)** Hull Material: Aluminium Alloy	**1 oil engine** reduction geared to sc. shaft driving 1 CP propeller Total Power: 500kW (680hp) Caterpillar C18 1 x 4 Stroke 6 Cy. 145 x 183 500kW (680bhp) Caterpillar Inc-USA AuxGen: 2 x 69kW a.c Fuel: 15.0 (d.f.)
8835217 *WCAH* -	**STATE OF MAINE** *ex* Tanner (T-AGS-40) *-2000* **Government of The United States of America (Department of Transportation - Maritime Administration) (MarAd)** Maine Maritime Academy *Castine, ME* *United States of America* MMSI: 368946000 Official number: 029703	12,517 3,755 -	Class: AB	**1990-09 Bethlehem Steel Corp. SB. Dept. — Sparrows Point, Md** Yd No: 4668 Converted From: Research Vessel-1997 Loa 152.35 Br ex - Dght 9.330 Lbp 142.04 Br md 21.95 Dpth 12.80 Welded, 1 dk	**(B34K2QT) Training Ship**	**1 oil engine** sr geared to sc. shaft driving 1 CP propeller Total Power: 6,001kW (8,159hp) 20.0kn MaK 6M601AK 1 x 4 Stroke 6 Cy. 580 x 600 6001kW (8159bhp) (new engine 1997) Krupp MaK Maschinenbau GmbH-Kiel AuxGen: 3 x 900kW a.c Fuel: 3993.0 (r.f.)
8835451 *WMAP* -	**STATE OF MICHIGAN** *ex* Persistent *-2004* **Government of The United States of America (Department of Transportation - Maritime Administration) (MarAd)** Great Lakes Maritime Academy *United States of America* MMSI: 338940000 Official number: 8835451	1,894 568 2,250	Class: AB	**1985-08 Tacoma Boatbuilding Co., Inc. — Tacoma, Wa** Yd No: 408 Converted From: Research Vessel-2004 Loa 68.28 Br ex - Dght 5.699 Lbp 68.28 Br md 13.11 Dpth 6.10 Welded, 1 dk	**(B34K2QT) Training Ship**	**4 oil engines** geared to sc. shafts driving 2 FP propellers Total Power: 2,532kW (3,444hp) 11.0kn Caterpillar D398TA 4 x Vee 4 Stroke 12 Cy. 159 x 203 each-633kW (861bhp) Caterpillar Tractor Co-USA AuxGen: 4 x 600kW a.c, 1 x 250kW a.c
8919245 *PHSG* -	**STATENDAM** **HAL Nederland NV** Holland America Line NV SatCom: Inmarsat A 1302515 *Rotterdam* *Netherlands* MMSI: 244078000 Official number: 32041	55,819 26,279 7,637	Class: LR ✠ **100A1** CS 01/2013 passenger ship *IWS ✠ **LMC** Eq.Ltr: P†; Cable: 682.0/78.0 U3	**1993-01 Fincantieri-Cant. Nav. Italiani S.p.A. — Monfalcone** Yd No: 5881 Loa 219.21 (BB) Br ex 30.83 Dght 7.716 Lbp 185.00 Br md 30.80 Dpth 19.13 Welded, 5 dks	**(A37A2PC) Passenger/Cruise** Passengers: cabins: 633; berths: 1613	**5 diesel electric oil engines** driving 2 gen. each 9540kW 6600V a.c 3 gen. each 6340kW 6600V a.c Connecting to 2 elec. motors each (12000kW) driving 2 CP propellers Total Power: 34,560kW (46,987hp) 20.0kn Sulzer 12ZAV40S 2 x Vee 4 Stroke 12 Cy. 400 x 560 each-8640kW (11747bhp) Fincantieri Cantieri NavaliItaliani SpA-Italy Sulzer 8ZAL40S 3 x 4 Stroke 8 Cy. 400 x 560 each-5760kW (7831bhp) Fincantieri Cantieri NavaliItaliani SpA-Italy Boilers: 3 e (ex.g.) 11.2kgf/cm² (11.0bar)190°C , 2 e (ex.g.) 11.2kgf/cm² (11.0bar)190°C , 2 AuxB (o.f.) 9.8kgf/cm² (9.6bar) Thrusters: 2 Thwart. CP thruster (f); 1 Tunnel thruster (a) Fuel: 129.5 (d.f.) 1812.3 (r.f.)
9288045 *PHAQ* -	**STATENGRACHT** **Rederij Statengracht** Spliethoff's Bevrachtingskantoor BV *Amsterdam* *Netherlands* MMSI: 244584000 Official number: 42214	16,676 6,730 21,250 T/cm 35.1	Class: LR ✠ **100A1** SS 07/2009 strengthened for heavy cargoes, container cargoes in holds and on upper deck and upper deck hatch covers, timber deck cargoes *IWS LI Finnish-Swedish Ice Class 1A at a draught of 10.959m Max/min draught fwd 11.47/4.20m Max/min draught aft 11.47/6.60m ✠ **LMC** **UMS** Eq.Ltr: L†; Cable: 605.0/64.0 U3 (a)	**2004-07 Stocznia Szczecinska Nowa Sp z oo — Szczecin** Yd No: B587/IV/5 Loa 172.60 (BB) Br ex 25.65 Dght 10.725 Lbp 160.70 Br md 25.30 Dpth 14.60 Welded, 1 dk	**(A31A2GX) General Cargo Ship** Grain: 23,790; Bale: 23,790 TEU 1134 C Ho 478 TEU C Dk 656 TEU incl 120 ref C. Compartments: 3 Ho, ER 3 Ha: (38.4 x 17.8) (32.0 x 20.4)ER (25.6 x 17.8) Cranes: 3x120t Ice Capable	**1 oil engine** with flexible couplings & sr geared to sc. shaft driving 1 CP propeller Total Power: 12,060kW (16,397hp) 17.0kn Wartsila 6L64 1 x 4 Stroke 6 Cy. 640 x 900 12060kW (16397bhp) Wartsila Italia SpA-Italy AuxGen: 1 x 1000kW 445V 60Hz a.c, 3 x 450kW 445V 60Hz a.c Boilers: TOH (o.f.) 10.2kgf/cm² (10.0bar), TOH (ex.g.) 10.2kgf/cm² (10.0bar) Thrusters: 1 Thwart. CP thruster (f)
9655896 *2GFQ5* -	**STATESMAN** *ex* Ulupinar XIV *-2013* **SMS Towage Ltd** *Hull* *United Kingdom* MMSI: 235092996 Official number: 918896	248 136 97	Class: LR (RI) **100A1** SS 06/2012 tug **LMC**	**2012-06 Sanmar Denizcilik Makina ve Ticaret — Istanbul** Yd No: 06 Loa 24.39 Br ex - Dght 3.000 Lbp 23.20 Br md 9.15 Dpth 4.04 Welded, 1 dk	**(B32A2ST) Tug**	**2 oil engines** reduction geared to sc. shafts driving 2 Directional propellers Total Power: 2,428kW (3,302hp) Caterpillar 3512B 2 x Vee 4 Stroke 12 Cy. 170 x 190 each-1214kW (1651bhp) Caterpillar Inc-USA
8975536 *VNTK* -	**STATESMAN** **L D Shipping Pty Ltd** *Launceston, Tas* *Australia* MMSI: 503344000 Official number: 856371	876 - 870		**1999-12 LD Marine & Ship Repairs Pty Ltd — Launceston TAS** L reg 55.00 Br ex - Dght - Lbp - Br md 10.20 Dpth 3.60 Welded, 1 dk	**(A35D2RL) Landing Craft** Bow door/ramp (f) Grain: 918; Bale: 860	**2 oil engines** geared to sc. shafts driving 2 Propellers Total Power: 1,250kW (1,700hp) M.T.U. 12V2000M 2 x Vee 4 Stroke 12 Cy. 130 x 150 each-625kW (850bhp) MTU Friedrichshafen GmbH-Friedrichshafen
9096399 *OWGA2* -	**STATHAV 22** *ex* Esja *-2006* *ex* Skeljungur II *-2000* *ex* BP 22 *-1994* **Statoil A/S** - *Skagen* *Denmark (DIS)* MMSI: 219010252 Official number: H1525	131 72 -		**1971-09 Bolsones Verft AS — Molde** Yd No: 224 Loa 27.35 Br ex - Dght - Lbp - Br md 6.60 Dpth 3.10 Welded, 1 dk	**(A13B2TP) Products Tanker**	**1 oil engine** driving 1 Propeller Total Power: 220kW (299hp) Volvo Penta 1 x 4 Stroke 220kW (299bhp) AB Volvo Penta-Sweden
9417971 *V7TT3* -	**STATIA EXPRESS** **Seabulk Island Transport Inc** Seabulk Towing Inc *Majuro* *Marshall Islands* MMSI: 538003879 Official number: 3879	284 85 182	Class: AB (LR) ✠ Classed LR until 31/12/12	**2007-12 Astilleros Zamakona Pasaia SL — Pasaia** Yd No: 657 Loa 28.00 Br ex 9.60 Dght 4.100 Lbp 25.40 Br md 9.00 Dpth 4.50 Welded, 1 dk	**(B32A2ST) Tug**	**2 oil engines** with clutches, flexible couplings & sr reverse geared to sc. shafts driving 2 FP propellers Total Power: 2,984kW (4,058hp) Caterpillar 3516B-TA 2 x Vee 4 Stroke 16 Cy. 170 x 190 each-1492kW (2029bhp) Caterpillar Inc-USA AuxGen: 2 x 175kW 440V 60Hz a.c
9417995 *V7UF4* -	**STATIA GLORY** **Seabulk Island Transport Inc** Seabulk Towing Inc *Majuro* *Marshall Islands* MMSI: 538003938 Official number: 3938	284 85 -	Class: AB (LR) ✠ Classed LR until 20/4/12	**2008-05 Astilleros Zamakona Pasaia SL — Pasaia** Yd No: 659 Loa 28.00 Br ex 9.60 Dght 3.300 Lbp 25.40 Br md 9.00 Dpth 4.50 Welded, 1 dk	**(B32A2ST) Tug**	**2 oil engines** with clutches, flexible couplings & sr reverse geared to sc. shafts driving 2 FP propellers Total Power: 2,984kW (4,058hp) Caterpillar 3516B 2 x Vee 4 Stroke 16 Cy. 170 x 215 each-1492kW (2029bhp) Caterpillar Inc-USA AuxGen: 2 x 175kW 440V 60Hz a.c
9417983 *V7UC9* -	**STATIA RELIANT** **Seabulk Island Transport Inc** Seabulk Towing Inc *Majuro* *Marshall Islands* MMSI: 538003903 Official number: 3903	284 85 -	Class: AB (LR) ✠ Classed LR until 30/11/11	**2008-04 Astilleros Zamakona Pasaia SL — Pasaia** Yd No: 658 Loa 28.00 Br ex 9.60 Dght 3.300 Lbp 25.40 Br md 9.00 Dpth 4.50 Welded, 1 dk	**(B32A2ST) Tug**	**2 oil engines** with clutches, flexible couplings & sr reverse geared to sc. shafts driving 2 FP propellers Total Power: 2,984kW (4,058hp) Caterpillar 3516B-HD 2 x Vee 4 Stroke 16 Cy. 170 x 215 each-1492kW (2029bhp) Caterpillar Inc-USA AuxGen: 2 x 175kW 440V 60Hz a.c

7417238 *YJW02* -	**STATIA RESPONDER** *ex* Megan D. Gambarella *-1998* *ex* Croyle Tide *-1994* **NuStar Terminals NV** - SatCom: Inmarsat C 457631810 *Port Vila* Vanuatu MMSI: 576318000 Official number: 211	**996** 298 -	Class: NV (AB)	1976-01 **Halter Marine, Inc. — Moss Point, Ms** Yd No: 486 Loa 59.14 Br ex 12.20 Dght 4.471 Lbp 54.77 Br md 12.15 Dpth 5.19 Welded, 1 dk	**(B21B20A) Anchor Handling Tug Supply**	**2 oil engines** reverse reduction geared to sc. shafts driving 2 FP propellers Total Power: 4,230kW (5,752hp) 14.0kn EMD (Electro-Motive) 16-645-E7 2 x Vee 2 Stroke 16 Cy. 230 x 254 each-2115kW (2876bhp) General Motors Corp.Electro-Motive Div.-La Grange AuxGen: 2 x 150kW Thrusters: 2 Thwart. FP thruster (f) Fuel: 602.5 (d.f.)
9513098 *IIXA2* -	**STATIA STAR** *ex* Giuco *-2011* **MPS Leasing & Factoring SpA** Societe Maritime de Remorquage et d'Assistance SARL (Somara) *Naples* Italy MMSI: 247288500	**483** 147 -	Class: GL RI (BV)	2009-10 **Eregli Gemi Insa Sanayi ve Ticaret AS — Karadeniz Eregli** Yd No: 23 Loa 32.00 Br ex - Dght 5.360 Lbp 32.00 Br md 11.60 Dpth 5.36 Welded, 1 dk	**(B32A2ST) Tug**	**2 oil engines** reduction geared to sc. shafts driving 2 Directional propellers Total Power: 3,600kW (4,894hp) Wartsila 9L20 2 x 4 Stroke 9 Cy. 200 x 280 each-1800kW (2447bhp) Wartsila Finland Oy-Finland AuxGen: 2 x 175kW 400V 50Hz a.c Fuel: 139.0 (r.f.)
9418004 *V7UN9* -	**STATIA SUNRISE** - **Seabulk Island Transport Inc** Seabulk Towing Inc *Majuro* Marshall Islands MMSI: 538003984 Official number: 3984	**284** 85 182	Class: AB (LR) ✠ Classed LR until 19/3/12	2008-07 **Astilleros Zamakona Pasaia SL — Pasaia** Yd No: 660 Loa 28.00 Br ex 9.60 Dght 3.800 Lbp 25.40 Br md 9.00 Dpth 4.50 Welded, 1 dk	**(B32A2ST) Tug**	**2 oil engines** with clutches, flexible couplings & sr reverse geared to sc. shafts driving 2 FP propellers Total Power: 2,984kW (4,058hp) Caterpillar 3516B 2 x Vee 4 Stroke 16 Cy. 170 x 215 each-1492kW (2029bhp) Caterpillar Inc-USA AuxGen: 2 x 175kW 440V 60Hz a.c
5339248 *LDRG* -	**STATSRAAD LEHMKUHL** *ex* Grossherzog Friedrich August *-1923* **Stiftelsen Seilskipet Statsraad Lehmkuhl** - SatCom: Inmarsat B 325811310 *Bergen* Norway MMSI: 258113000 Official number: 7860	**1,516** 454 -	Class: NV	1914-03 **Schiffswerft und Maschinenfabrik Joh C Tecklenborg AG — Bremerhaven** Yd No: 263 Loa 84.60 Br ex 12.65 Dght 5.182 Lbp 73.00 Br md 12.60 Dpth 7.32 Riveted, 3 dks	**(X11B2QN) Sail Training Ship** Cranes: 1x2.5t; Derricks: 1	**1 oil engine** driving 1 FP propeller Total Power: 331kW (450hp) Normo 1 x 4 Stroke 8 Cy. 220 x 320 331kW (450bhp) (new engine 1955) AS Bergens Mek Verksteder-Norway AuxGen: 3 x a.c
8422137 *JWNF* SF-5-S	**STATTEGG** *ex* Veststeinen *-2004* *ex* Leinebris *-1997* **Froyanes AS** - *Maaloy* Norway MMSI: 259247000	**492** 219 -		1985-06 **Aas Skipsbyggeri AS — Vestnes** Yd No: 123 Loa 39.48 Br ex - Dght - Lbp - Br md 8.01 Dpth 6.15 Welded, 1 dk	**(B11B2FV) Fishing Vessel**	**1 oil engine** geared to sc. shaft driving 1 FP propeller Total Power: 577kW (784hp) 10.0kn Caterpillar 3508TA 1 x Vee 4 Stroke 8 Cy. 170 x 190 577kW (784bhp) Caterpillar Tractor Co-USA
9669847 *ZGDF5* -	**STATUS QUO** *ex* Richmond Lady *-2013* **Status Quo Inc** - *George Town* Cayman Islands (British) MMSI: 319053800 Official number: 745111	**437** 131 61	Class: AB	2013-06 **Richmond Yachts — Richmond BC** Yd No: SQF Loa 45.72 Br ex 8.45 Dght 2.130 Lbp 36.12 Br md 8.23 Dpth 3.66 Bonded, 1 dk	**(X11A2YP) Yacht** Hull Material: Reinforced Plastic	**2 oil engines** reduction geared to sc. shafts driving 2 Propellers Total Power: 2,832kW (3,850hp) 15.0kn Caterpillar 2 x 4 Stroke each-1416kW (1925bhp) Caterpillar Inc-USA
9401556 *LAGZ7* -	**STAV VIKING** - **O H Meling Tankers KS** Brostrom AB SatCom: Inmarsat C 425993610 *Stavanger* Norway (NIS) MMSI: 259936000	**11,935** 5,133 16,628 T/cm 28.0	Class: NV	2009-04 **Jiangnan Shipyard (Group) Co Ltd — Shanghai** Yd No: H2414 Loa 144.15 (BB) Br ex - Dght 8.900 Lbp 133.80 Br md 23.00 Dpth 12.40 Welded, 1 dk	**(A12B2TR) Chemical/Products Tanker** Double Hull (13F) Liq: 18,800; Liq (Oil): 19,500 Ice Capable	**1 oil engine** reduction geared to sc. shaft driving 1 CP propeller Total Power: 7,200kW (9,789hp) 14.0kn MAN-B&W 6L48/60B 1 x 4 Stroke 6 Cy. 480 x 600 7200kW (9789bhp) MAN B&W Diesel AG-Augsburg AuxGen: 2 x 680kW a.c, 1 x 1500kW a.c, 1 x 700kW a.c Thrusters: 1 Tunnel thruster (f) Fuel: 570.0 (r.f.)
9263758 *LMAR* -	**STAVANGER** - **Norled AS** - *Stavanger* Norway MMSI: 259419000	**2,434** 730 680	Class: (NV)	2003-05 **Fjellstrand AS — Omastrand** Yd No: 1664 Loa 79.40 Br ex 20.80 Dght - Lbp 76.00 Br md 20.00 Dpth 5.98 Welded, 1 dk	**(A36A2PR) Passenger/Ro-Ro Ship (Vehicles)** Hull Material: Aluminium Alloy Passengers: unberthed: 400 Cars: 112	**4 oil engines** geared to sc. shafts driving 2 Directional propellers 2 propellers fwd, 2 aft Total Power: 5,368kW (7,300hp) 22.0kn M.T.U. 12V4000M60 4 x Vee 4 Stroke 12 Cy. 165 x 190 each-1342kW (1825bhp) MTU Friedrichshafen GmbH-Friedrichshafen
9364239 *LAGE7* -	**STAVANGER BLISS** - **DSD Ships 1 AS** Det Stavangerske Dampskibsselskab Shipping AS (DSD Shipping AS) *Stavanger* Norway (NIS) MMSI: 259791000	**55,898** 29,810 105,400 T/cm 88.9	Class: LR ✠ **100A1** SS 09/2013 Double Hull oil tanker ESP **ShipRight** (SDA, FDA, CM) *IWS LI ✠ **LMC** **UMS IGS** Eq.Ltr: R†; Cable: 691.3/84.0 U3 (a)	2008-09 **Sumitomo Heavy Industries Marine & Engineering Co., Ltd. — Yokosuka** Yd No: 1339 Loa 228.60 (BB) Br ex 42.03 Dght 14.808 Lbp 217.80 Br md 42.00 Dpth 21.50 Welded, 1 dk	**(A13A2TV) Crude Oil Tanker** Double Hull (13F) Liq: 101,479; Liq (Oil): 122,000 Cargo Heating Coils Compartments: 10 Wing Ta, 2 Wing Slop Ta, ER 3 Cargo Pump (s): 3x2500m³/hr Manifold: Bow/CM: 116.6m	**1 oil engine** driving 1 FP propeller Total Power: 12,350kW (16,791hp) 14.8kn MAN-B&W 6S60MC-C 1 x 2 Stroke 6 Cy. 600 x 2400 12350kW (16791bhp) Mitsui Engineering & Shipbuilding CLtd-Japan AuxGen: 3 x 800kW 450V 60Hz a.c Boilers: e (ex.g.) 22.4kgf/cm² (22.0bar), WTAuxB (o.f.) 18.4kgf/cm² (18.0bar) Fuel: 223.3 (d.f.) 1156.3 (r.f.)
9337389 *LAEA7* -	**STAVANGER BLOSSOM** - **KS Stavanger Blossom** Det Stavangerske Dampskibsselskab Shipping AS (DSD Shipping AS) *Stavanger* Norway (NIS) MMSI: 259720000	**56,172** 32,082 105,641 T/cm 89.2	Class: LR ✠ **100A1** SS 02/2012 Double Hull oil tanker ESP **ShipRight** (SDA, FDA, CM) LI *IWS ✠ **LMC** **UMS IGS** Eq.Ltr: R†; Cable: 692.7/84.0 U3 (a)	2007-02 **Sumitomo Heavy Industries Marine & Engineering Co., Ltd. — Yokosuka** Yd No: 1329 Loa 239.10 (BB) Br ex 42.03 Dght 14.850 Lbp 229.00 Br md 42.00 Dpth 21.30 Welded, 1 dk	**(A13A2TV) Crude Oil Tanker** Double Hull (13F) Liq: 115,570; Liq (Oil): 115,570 Cargo Heating Coils Compartments: 12 Wing Ta, 2 Wing Slop Ta, ER 3 Cargo Pump (s): 3x2500m³/hr Manifold: Bow/CM: 117m	**1 oil engine** driving 1 FP propeller Total Power: 12,000kW (16,315hp) 14.9kn Sulzer 6RTA58T 1 x 2 Stroke 6 Cy. 580 x 2416 12000kW (16315bhp) Diesel United Ltd.-Aioi AuxGen: 3 x 650kW 450V 60Hz a.c Boilers: e (ex.g.) 22.0kgf/cm² (21.6bar), WTAuxB (o.f.) 18.0kgf/cm² (17.7bar) Fuel: 250.8 (d.f.) 2744.6 (r.f.)
9278507 *LAOQ7* -	**STAVANGER BREEZE** *ex* Nizon *-2012* **Herfo AS** Det Stavangerske Dampskibsselskab Shipping AS (DSD Shipping AS) *Stavanger* Norway (NIS) MMSI: 257772000	**30,093** 11,699 45,780 T/cm 51.8	Class: NV (BV)	2004-08 **STX Shipbuilding Co Ltd — Changwon (Jinhae Shipyard)** Yd No: 1131 Loa 183.00 (BB) Br ex 32.20 Dght 12.216 Lbp 173.90 Br md 32.20 Dpth 19.10 Welded	**(A12B2TR) Chemical/Products Tanker** Double Hull (13F) Liq: 51,931; Liq (Oil): 51,931 Cargo Heating Coils Compartments: 14 Wing Ta, 2 Wing Slop Ta, ER 14 Cargo Pump (s): 10x600m³/hr, 4x300m³/hr Manifold: Bow/CM: 88.6m	**1 oil engine** driving 1 FP propeller Total Power: 9,488kW (12,900hp) 14.5kn B&W 6S50MC-C 1 x 2 Stroke 6 Cy. 500 x 2000 9488kW (12900bhp) STX Engine Co Ltd-South Korea AuxGen: 3 x 900kW 445/220V 60Hz a.c Thrusters: 1 Tunnel thruster (f) Fuel: 172.0 (d.f.) (Heating Coils) 1416.2 (r.f.) 37.3pd
9284726 *H9EL* -	**STAVANGER EAGLE** - **K/S Stavanger Navion** Det Stavangerske Dampskibsselskab Shipping AS (DSD Shipping AS) *Panama* Panama MMSI: 352382000 Official number: 32552PEXT2	**28,059** 11,645 45,898 T/cm 50.6	Class: NK	2004-10 **Shin Kurushima Dockyard Co. Ltd. — Onishi** Yd No: 5245 Loa 179.88 (BB) Br ex 32.23 Dght 12.022 Lbp 172.00 Br md 32.20 Dpth 18.70 Welded, 1 dk	**(A13B2TP) Products Tanker** Double Hull (13F) Liq: 50,753; Liq (Oil): 53,796 Cargo Heating Coils Compartments: 14 Wing Ta, 2 Wing Slop Ta, ER 4 Cargo Pump (s): 4x1000m³/hr Manifold: Bow/CM: 90.8m	**1 oil engine** driving 1 FP propeller Total Power: 9,267kW (12,599hp) 14.6kn Mitsubishi 6UEC60LA 1 x 2 Stroke 6 Cy. 600 x 1900 9267kW (12599bhp) Kobe Hatsudoki KK-Japan Fuel: 170.0 (d.f.) 1800.0 (r.f.)
9231468 *LAVM5* -	**STAVANGER PRINCE** *ex* Stavanger Navion *-2004* **DSD Ships 2 AS** Taurus Tankers Ltd SatCom: Inmarsat C 425862310 *Stavanger* Norway (NIS) MMSI: 258623000	**61,764** 32,515 109,390 T/cm 91.9	Class: NV (LR) ✠ Classed LR until 9/4/05	2002-06 **Dalian New Shipbuilding Heavy Industries Co Ltd — Dalian LN** Yd No: PC1100-11 Loa 244.60 (BB) Br ex 42.03 Dght 15.450 Lbp 235.00 Br md 42.00 Dpth 22.20 Welded, 1 dk	**(A13B2TP) Products Tanker** Double Hull (13F) Liq: 117,921; Liq (Oil): 117,921 Cargo Heating Coils Compartments: 12 Wing Ta, 2 Wing Slop Ta, ER 6 Cargo Pump (s): 6x3000m³/hr Manifold: Bow/CM: 121.8m	**1 oil engine** driving 1 FP propeller Total Power: 15,540kW (21,128hp) 15.3kn Sulzer 7RTA62U 1 x 2 Stroke 7 Cy. 620 x 2150 15540kW (21128bhp) Dalian Marine Diesel Works-China AuxGen: 3 x 780kW 450V 60Hz a.c Boilers: AuxB (ex.g.) 8.2kgf/cm² (8.0bar), WTAuxB (o.f.) 18.4kgf/cm² (18.0bar) Fuel: 190.0 (d.f.) 3450.0 (r.f.)

9344746 **STAVANGERFJORD** **6,994** Class: NV
LICY 2,098
\- **Fjord1 AS** 1,025
Floro *Norway*
MMSI: 259386000

2007-01 SC Aker Tulcea SA — Tulcea (Hull)
Yd No: 345
2007-01 Aker Yards AS Sovikness — Sovik
Yd No: 150
Loa 129.50 (BB) Br ex 19.10 Dght 4.500
Lbp 122.40 Br md 19.10 Dpth 9.20
Welded, 1 dk

(A36A2PR) Passenger/Ro-Ro Ship (Vehicles)
Passengers: unberthed: 587
Bow door (centre)
Stern door (centre)
Cars: 212

5 diesel electric oil engines driving 3 gen. each 409kW a.c 2 gen. each 2650kW a.c Connecting to 4 elec. motors each (2750kW) driving 4 Z propellers
Total Power: 6,623kW (9,006hp) 17.0kn
Bergens KVGS-12G4
2 x Vee 4 Stroke 12 Cy. 250 x 300 each-2650kW (3603bhp)
Rolls Royce Marine AS-Norway
Scania DI16 M
3 x Vee 4 Stroke 8 Cy. 127 x 154 each-441kW (600bhp)
Scania AB-Sweden

9586605 **STAVANGERFJORD** **31,678** Class: NV
OYOW2 14,270
\- **Fjord Skibsholding III A/S** 3,900
Fjord Line Danmark A/S
Hirtshals *Denmark (DIS)*
MMSI: 219347000
Official number: A-539

2013-07 Stocznia Gdansk SA — Gdansk (Hull)
Yd No: 87
2013-07 Fosen Mek. Verksteder AS — Rissa
Yd No: 87
Loa 170.00 (BB) Br ex 32.90 Dght 6.500
Lbp 148.00 Br md 27.50 Dpth 9.30
Welded, 10 dks

(A36A2PR) Passenger/Ro-Ro Ship (Vehicles)
Passengers: 1500; cabins: 306; berths: 1180
Stern door/ramp (p. a.)
Stern door/ramp (s. a.)
Lane-Len: 1350
Cars: 600
Ice Capable

4 oil engines reduction geared to sc. shafts driving 2 CP propellers
Total Power: 21,600kW (29,368hp) 21.5kn
Bergens B35: 40V12PG
4 x Vee 4 Stroke 12 Cy. 350 x 400 each-5400kW (7342bhp)
Rolls Royce Marine AS-Norway
AuxGen: 1 x 1463kW 690V 60Hz a.c, 2 x 1850kW 690V 60Hz a.c, 2 x 1254kW 690V 60Hz a.c, 1 x 1250kW 690V 60Hz a.c
Thrusters: 2 Tunnel thruster (f)
Fuel: 293.0 (LNG) 94.0 (d.f.)

9321380 **STAVFJORD** **4,206** Class: BV
PBIZ *ex Hunzeborg -2013* 2,282
\- **Scheepvaartonderneming Stavfjord BV** 6,100
Fonnes Shipping AS
Delfzijl *Netherlands*
MMSI: 244140000
Official number: 43039

2005-12 Niestern Sander B.V. — Delfzijl
Yd No: 825
Loa 113.76 (BB) Br ex - Dght 6.010
Lbp 107.64 Br md 14.40 Dpth 8.10
Welded, 1 dk

(A31A2GX) General Cargo Ship
Grain: 8,375
TEU 256 C Ho 144 TEU C Dk 112 TEU
Compartments: 2 Ho, ER
2 Ha: (44.5 x 11.7)ER (38.2 x 11.7)
Ice Capable

1 oil engine reduction geared to sc. shaft driving 1 CP propeller
Total Power: 2,999kW (4,077hp) 13.0kn
Wartsila 6L32
1 x 4 Stroke 6 Cy. 320 x 400 2999kW (4077bhp)
Wartsila Finland Oy-Finland
AuxGen: 2 x 185kW a.c
Thrusters: 1 Thwart. FP thruster (f)
Fuel: 89.0 (d.f.) 305.0 (r.f.)

9401544 **STAVFJORD** **11,935** Class: NV
LAHA7 5,129
\- **O H Meling Tankers KS** 16,635
Brostrom AB T/cm
Stavanger *Norway (NIS)* 28.5
MMSI: 259888000

2009-03 Jiangnan Shipyard (Group) Co Ltd — Shanghai Yd No: H2413
Loa 144.21 (BB) Br ex 23.18 Dght 8.900
Lbp 133.82 Br md 23.00 Dpth 12.40
Welded, 1 dk

(A12B2TR) Chemical/Products Tanker
Double Hull (13F)
Liq: 18,481; Liq (Oil): 19,500
Compartments: 12 Wing Ta, 2 Wing Slop Ta, ER
12 Cargo Pump (s): 12x300m³/hr
Manifold: Bow/CM: 73.4m
Ice Capable

1 oil engine reduction geared to sc. shaft driving 1 CP propeller
Total Power: 7,200kW (9,789hp) 14.0kn
MAN-B&W 6L48/60B
1 x 4 Stroke 6 Cy. 480 x 600 7200kW (9789bhp)
MAN B&W Diesel AG-Augsburg
AuxGen: 2 x 680kW a.c, 1 x 1500kW a.c, 1 x 700kW a.c
Thrusters: 1 Thwart. FP thruster (f)
Fuel: 60.0 (d.f.) 450.0 (r.f.)

8947759 **STAVINSKY** *299*
HQMJ2 *ex Sumiei Maru No. 8 -1993* 250
\- **Stavinsky Maritime Inc** 886
\-
San Lorenzo *Honduras*
Official number: L-0324938

1976-12 K.K. Murakami Zosensho — Naruto
L reg 55.28 Br ex - Dght 3.700
Lbp - Br md 9.50 Dpth 6.00
Welded, 1 dk

(A31A2GX) General Cargo Ship
Compartments: 1 Ho, ER
1 Ha: (31.5 x 7.0)ER

1 oil engine driving 1 FP propeller
Total Power: 883kW (1,201hp) 10.0kn
Makita GSLH6275
1 x 4 Stroke 6 Cy. 275 x 450 883kW (1201bhp)
Makita Diesel Co Ltd-Japan

9521241 **STAVR** **294** Class: RS (LR)
UBZF6 88 ✠ Classed LR until 6/8/09
\- **Future Link Shipping Co** 131
JSC Rosnefteflot
St Petersburg *Russia*
MMSI: 273330930

2009-07 Damen Shipyards Changde Co Ltd — Changde HN (Hull) Yd No: (511563)
2009-07 B.V. Scheepswerf Damen — Gorinchem
Yd No: 511563
Loa 28.67 Br ex 10.43 Dght 4.712
Lbp 25.78 Br md 9.80 Dpth 4.60
Welded, 1 dk

(B32A2ST) Tug
Ice Capable

2 oil engines gearing integral to driving 2 Directional propellers
Total Power: 3,132kW (4,258hp) 12.0kn
Caterpillar 3516B-TA
2 x Vee 4 Stroke 16 Cy. 170 x 190 each-1566kW (2129bhp)
Caterpillar Inc-USA
AuxGen: 2 x 85kW 400V 50Hz a.c

9074585 **STAVRONISI** **38,667** Class: LR (NV) (RS)
SXFT 21,281 **100A1** SS 07/2011
\- **Stavronisi Special Maritime Enterprise (ENE)** 68,232 Double Hull oil tanker MARPOL 20.1.3.
Eletson Corp T/cm ESP
Piraeus *Greece* 65.1 LI
MMSI: 239274000 (Ice Class 1C)
Official number: 10416 **LMC** **UMS IGS**
Eq.Ltr: Q†; Cable: 687.5/81.0 U3

1996-07 ATVT Sudnobudivnyi Zavod "Zaliv" — Kerch Yd No: 916
Loa 242.80 (BB) Br ex 32.24 Dght 13.639
Lbp 228.00 Br md 32.20 Dpth 18.00
Welded, 1 dk

(A13A2TW) Crude/Oil Products Tanker
Double Hull (13F)
Liq: 68,152; Liq (Oil): 68,152
Cargo Heating Coils
Compartments: 14 Wing Ta, 2 Wing Slop Ta, ER
4 Cargo Pump (s): 4x1500m³/hr
Manifold: Bow/CM: 124m
Ice Capable

1 oil engine driving 1 FP propeller
Total Power: 13,180kW (17,920hp) 14.0kn
B&W 8DKRN60/195
1 x 2 Stroke 8 Cy. 600 x 1950 13180kW (17920bhp)
AO Bryanskiy MashinostroitelnyyZavod (BMZ)-Bryansk
AuxGen: 1 x 800kW 220/380V 50Hz a.c, 3 x 650kW 220/380V 50Hz a.c
Boilers: 2 WTAuxB (o.f.) 18.6kgf/cm² (18.2bar), AuxB (ex.g.) 6.9kgf/cm² (6.8bar)
Fuel: 420.0 (d.f.) (Heating Coils) 3534.0 (r.f.) 44.5pd

9466908 **STAVROPOL** **33,044** Class: BV
V7VC9 *ex Fesco Stavropol -2013* 19,231
\- **Parys Maritime Ltd** 56,831
Far-Eastern Shipping Co (FESCO) T/cm
(Dalnevostochnoye Morskoye Parokhodstvo) 58.8
SatCom: Inmarsat C 453837550
Majuro *Marshall Islands*
MMSI: 538004090
Official number: 4090

2012-04 Qingshan Shipyard — Wuhan HB
Yd No: 20060374
Loa 189.99 (BB) Br ex - Dght 12.800
Lbp 185.00 Br md 32.26 Dpth 18.00
Welded, 1 dk

(A21A2BC) Bulk Carrier
Grain: 71,634; Bale: 68,200
Compartments: 5 Ho, ER
5 Ha: 4 (21.3 x 18.3)ER (18.9 x 18.3)
Cranes: 4x30t

1 oil engine driving 1 FP propeller
Total Power: 9,480kW (12,889hp) 14.5kn
MAN-B&W 6S50MC-C
1 x 2 Stroke 6 Cy. 500 x 2000 9480kW (12889bhp)
Doosan Engine Co Ltd-South Korea
AuxGen: 3 x 600kW 60Hz a.c
Fuel: 2400.0

9100396 **STAVROS P.** **25,943** Class: NK
V7002 *ex Matira -2008 ex Minoan Pride -2005* 15,480
\- *ex New Generation -2004* 45,863
Gortynia Shipping SA
Lydia Mar Shipping Co SA
Majuro *Marshall Islands*
MMSI: 538003123
Official number: 3123

1994-07 Koyo Dockyard Co Ltd — Mihara HS
Yd No: 2053
Loa 189.83 (BB) Br ex 31.03 Dght 11.660
Lbp 179.80 Br md 31.00 Dpth 16.50
Welded, 1 dk

(A21A2BC) Bulk Carrier
Grain: 58,918; Bale: 56,955
Compartments: 5 Ho, ER
5 Ha: (20.8 x 16.0)4 (20.0 x 17.6)ER
Cranes: 4x25t

1 oil engine driving 1 FP propeller
Total Power: 7,944kW (10,801hp) 14.2kn
Mitsubishi 6UEC52LS
1 x 2 Stroke 6 Cy. 520 x 1850 7944kW (10801bhp)
Akasaka Tekkosho KK (Akasaka DieselLtd)-Japan
AuxGen: 3 x 400kW a.c
Fuel: 1645.0 (r.f.) 21.2pd

9222314 **STAVROS S. NIARCHOS** **493** Class: LR (GL)
MZIU7 *launched as Neptun Princess -2000* 148 **100A1** SS 02/2010
\- **Tall Ships Youth Trust** 60 sailing ship
Tall Ships Ltd **LMC** **UMS**
London *United Kingdom* Cable: 358.1/26.0 U2 (a)
MMSI: 232007330
Official number: 902815

2000-02 Schiffs- u. Yachtwerft Abeking & Rasmussen GmbH & Co. — Lemwerder (Hull launched by) Yd No: 6442
2000-02 Appledore Shipbuilders Ltd — Bideford (Hull completed by) Yd No: A.S.178
Loa 59.35 Br ex 9.98 Dght 3.500
Lbp 40.60 Br md 9.91 Dpth 5.80
Welded

(X11B2QN) Sail Training Ship

2 oil engines with clutches, flexible couplings & sr reverse geared to sc. shafts driving 2 CP propellers
Total Power: 660kW (898hp) 10.0kn
M.T.U. 8V183TE62
2 x Vee 4 Stroke 8 Cy. 128 x 142 each-330kW (449bhp)
MTU Friedrichshafen GmbH-Friedrichshafen
AuxGen: 3 x 80kW 415V 50Hz a.c
Thrusters: 1 Thwart. CP thruster (f)

8879562 **STB-02** *295*
\- *ex Eikichi Maru No. 108 -2013* -
\- **PT Armada Contener Nusantara** 833
\-
Indonesia

1994-11 Kimura Zosen K.K. — Kure Yd No: 128
Loa 63.08 Br ex - Dght 4.100
Lbp 58.60 Br md 10.50 Dpth 6.10
Welded, 1 dk

(A31A2GX) General Cargo Ship

1 oil engine driving 1 FP propeller
Total Power: 736kW (1,001hp) 11.5kn
Matsui MA29GSC-31
1 x 4 Stroke 6 Cy. 290 x 540 736kW (1001bhp)
Matsui Iron Works Co Ltd-Japan

8514772 **STD 2** **577** Class: (KR)
DTBV5 *ex Sun Tai No. 2 -2008* 228
\- *ex Shinsei Maru No. 2 -2002* -
STD Fisheries Co Ltd
\-
Bigeum *South Korea*
MMSI: 441536000
Official number: 0808001-6261108

1985-10 KK Kanasashi Zosen — Shizuoka SZ
Yd No: 3088
Loa 53.52 (BB) Br ex 8.74 Dght 3.401
Lbp 46.89 Br md 8.70 Dpth 3.76
Welded, 1 dk

(B11B2FV) Fishing Vessel

1 oil engine with clutches, flexible couplings & sr reverse geared to sc. shaft driving 1 FP propeller
Total Power: 736kW (1,001hp)
Hanshin 6LUN28AG
1 x 4 Stroke 6 Cy. 280 x 480 736kW (1001bhp)
The Hanshin Diesel Works Ltd-Japan

8508266 **STD NO. 1** **595** Class: KR
DTDV4 *ex Sun Tai No. 1 -2008* 234
\- *ex Showa Maru No. 1 -2002* 461
Dongwon Industries Co Ltd
\-
Busan *South Korea*
MMSI: 441535000
Official number: 0808001-6261402

1985-05 KK Kanasashi Zosen — Shizuoka SZ
Yd No: 3058
Loa 55.48 (BB) Br ex 8.84 Dght 3.452
Lbp 49.00 Br md 8.79 Dpth 3.81
Welded, 1 dk

(B11B2FV) Fishing Vessel

1 oil engine with clutches, flexible couplings & sr reverse geared to sc. shaft driving 1 FP propeller
Total Power: 1,103kW (1,500hp) 11.5kn
Akasaka DM30FD
1 x 4 Stroke 6 Cy. 300 x 480 1103kW (1500bhp)
Akasaka Tekkosho KK (Akasaka DieselLtd)-Japan

9149249 *T2LU4* -	**STEADFAST** *ex* Moscow Sea *-2013* **Sofia Shipping Co Pte Ltd** Raffles Shipmanagement Services Pte Ltd *Funafuti* *Tuvalu* MMSI: 572612210 Official number: 29139813	**27,526** 14,026 47,363 T/cm 52.4	Class: BV (LR) ✠ Classed LR until 14/8/13	**1998-10 Brodotrogir dd - Shipyard Trogir — Trogir** Yd No: 230 Loa 182.43 (BB) Br ex 32.22 Dght 12.197 Lbp 174.80 Br md 32.20 Dpth 17.50 Welded, 1 dk	**(A13B2TP) Products Tanker** Double Hull (13F) Liq: 51,977; Liq (Oil): 51,977 Compartments: 10 Wing Ta, ER 10 Cargo Pump (s): 10x350m^3/hr Manifold: Bow/CM: 91m	**1 oil engine** driving 1 FP propeller Total Power: 8,310kW (11,298hp) 15.0kn B&W 6S50MC 1 x 2 Stroke 6 Cy. 500 x 1910 8310kW (11298bhp) 'Uljanik' Strojogradnja dd-Croatia AuxGen: 2 x 1280kW 450V 60Hz a.c, 1 x 680kW 450V 60Hz a.c Boilers: e (ex.g.) 10.2kgf/cm^2 (10.0bar), AuxB (o.f.) 10.2kgf/cm^2 (10.0bar) Fuel: 158.0 (d.f.) (Heating Coils) 1633.0 (r.f.) 38.0pd
9149160 *9V5418* -	**STEADY** **PSA Marine Pte Ltd** - *Singapore* *Singapore* MMSI: 563000710 Official number: 387660	**291** 87 80	Class: LR ✠ **100A1** SS 03/2012 tug Singapore coastal & 30 miles seaward service ✠ **LMC** Eq.Ltr: F; Cable: 275.0/19.0 U2	**1997-03 Zhenjiang Shipyard — Zhenjiang JS** (Hull) Yd No: KR-96-110801 **1997-03 Kea Resources Pte Ltd — Singapore** Loa 31.00 Br ex 10.10 Dght 2.610 Lbp 28.40 Br md 9.50 Dpth 3.80 Welded, 1 dk	**(B32A2ST) Tug**	**2 oil engines** with clutches, flexible couplings & sr geared to sc. shafts driving 2 Directional propellers Total Power: 2,500kW (3,400hp) 12.0kn Deutz SBV6M628 2 x 4 Stroke 6 Cy. 240 x 280 each-1250kW (1700bhp) Motoren Werke Mannheim AG (MWM)-Mannheim AuxGen: 2 x 85kW 415V 50Hz a.c
5083289 - -	**STEADY MARINER** *ex* Alice D *-1980* *ex* Steady Mariner *-1980* *ex* Alice D *-1977* *ex* Pollux *-1969* *ex* Cycloop *-1963* - -	*226* 10 -	Class: (BV)	**1953 N.V. Scheepsbouwbedrijf v/h Th.J. Fikkers — Foxhol** Yd No: 82 Loa 29.82 Br ex 8.26 Dght 3.452 Lbp 29.60 Br md 8.21 Dpth 4.12 Riveted, 1 dk	**(B32A2ST) Tug** Derricks: 1x2t	**1 oil engine** geared to sc. shaft driving 1 FP propeller Total Power: 706kW (960hp) 11.5kn G.M. (Detroit Diesel) 16V-149 1 x Vee 2 Stroke 16 Cy. 146 x 146 706kW (960bhp) (new engine 1980) General Motors Detroit DieselAllison Divn-USA AuxGen: 1 x 35kW 110V d.c, 1 x 11kW 110V d.c
9430260 *V7RK9* -	**STEALTH BAHLA** *ex* Alpine Endurance *-2012* *completed as* Stealth SV *-2009* **King of Hearts Inc** Oman Ship Management Co SAOC *Majuro* *Marshall Islands* MMSI: 538003530 Official number: 3530	**29,130** 12,052 46,121 T/cm 52.0	Class: LR ✠ **100A1** SS 04/2009 Double Hull oil and chemical tanker, Ship Type 3 CSR ESP *IWS LI ✠ **LMC** **UMS IGS** Eq.Ltr: M†; Cable: 633.0/73.0 U3 (a)	**2009-04 Hyundai Mipo Dockyard Co Ltd — Ulsan** Yd No: 2139 Loa 183.17 (BB) Br ex 32.24 Dght 12.215 Lbp 174.02 Br md 32.20 Dpth 18.80 Welded, 1 dk	**(A12B2TR) Chemical/Products Tanker** Double Hull (13F) Liq: 52,133; Liq (Oil): 93,788 Cargo Heating Coils Compartments: 12 Wing Ta, 2 Wing Slop Ta, ER 12 Cargo Pump (s): 12x600m^3/hr Manifold: Bow/CM: 91.7m	**1 oil engine** driving 1 FP propeller Total Power: 8,598kW (11,690hp) 14.5kn MAN-B&W 6S50MC-C 1 x 2 Stroke 6 Cy. 500 x 2000 8598kW (11690bhp) Hyundai Heavy Industries Co Ltd-South Korea AuxGen: 3 x 730kW 450V 60Hz a.c Boilers: e (ex.g.) 12.2kgf/cm^2 (12.0bar), WTAuxB (o.f.) 9.2kgf/cm^2 (9.0bar) Fuel: 187.0 (d.f.) 1408.0 (r.f.)
9436006 *SVAR3* -	**STEALTH CHIOS** *completed as* Ghibli *-2009* *launched as* Cape Anglia *-2009* **Petrol Duke Inc** Heidmar Inc SatCom: Inmarsat C 424089910 *Piraeus* *Greece* MMSI: 240899000 Official number: 11882	**62,775** 34,934 112,984 T/cm 99.7	Class: AB	**2009-05 New Times Shipbuilding Co Ltd — Jingjiang JS** Yd No: 0311513 Loa 250.00 (BB) Br ex 44.04 Dght 14.800 Lbp 240.00 Br md 44.00 Dpth 21.00 Welded, 1 dk	**(A13A2TV) Crude Oil Tanker** Double Hull (13F) Liq: 124,680; Liq (Oil): 127,452 Cargo Heating Coils Compartments: 12 Wing Ta, 2 Wing Slop Ta, ER 3 Cargo Pump (s): 3x3000m^3/hr Manifold: Bow/CM: 122.5m	**1 oil engine** driving 1 FP propeller Total Power: 15,820kW (21,509hp) 15.0kn MAN-B&W 7S60MC-C 1 x 2 Stroke 7 Cy. 600 x 2400 15820kW (21509bhp) Doosan Engine Co Ltd-South Korea AuxGen: 3 x 900kW a.c Fuel: 210.0 (d.f.) 3100.0 (r.f.)
9396713 *V7OK6* -	**STEALTH II** *ex* Navig8 Stealth Ii *-2013* *completed as* Enterprise *-2008* **Razorblade Inc** Navig8 Shipmanagement Pte Ltd *Majuro* *Marshall Islands* MMSI: 538003103 Official number: 3103	**30,040** 13,312 50,695 T/cm 52.0	Class: NV	**2008-01 SPP Plant & Shipbuilding Co Ltd — Sacheon** Yd No: S1010 Loa 183.00 (BB) Br ex 32.24 Dght 13.017 Lbp 174.00 Br md 32.20 Dpth 19.10 Welded, 1 dk	**(A12B2TR) Chemical/Products Tanker** Double Hull (13F) Liq: 52,150; Liq (Oil): 52,150 Cargo Heating Coils Compartments: 12 Wing Ta, 2 Wing Slop Ta, ER 12 Cargo Pump (s): 12x600m^3/hr Manifold: Bow/CM: 92m	**1 oil engine** driving 1 FP propeller Total Power: 9,480kW (12,889hp) 14.9kn MAN-B&W 6S50MC-C 1 x 2 Stroke 6 Cy. 500 x 2000 9480kW (12889bhp) STX Engine Co Ltd-South Korea AuxGen: 3 x 900kW 60Hz a.c Fuel: 300.0 (d.f.) 1531.0 (r.f.)
9412036 *V7XH2* -	**STEALTH SKYROS** *launched as* Brave Catherine *-2011* **Haven Trading Inc** Stealth Maritime Corp SA SatCom: Inmarsat C 453836728 *Majuro* *Marshall Islands* MMSI: 538004479 Official number: 4479	**62,884** 35,565 115,000 T/cm 99.2	Class: BV	**2011-10 Daewoo Shipbuilding & Marine Engineering Co Ltd — Geoje** Yd No: 5348 Loa 249.90 (BB) Br ex 44.03 Dght 14.810 Lbp 239.00 Br md 44.00 Dpth 21.20 Welded, 1 dk	**(A13A2TW) Crude/Oil Products Tanker** Double Hull (13F) Liq: 124,270; Liq (Oil): 124,270 Cargo Heating Coils Compartments: 12 Wing Ta, 2 Wing Slop Ta, ER 3 Cargo Pump (s): 3x3000m^3/hr Manifold: Bow/CM: 125.6m	**1 oil engine** driving 1 FP propeller Total Power: 14,280kW (19,415hp) 15.1kn MAN-B&W 6S60MC-C8 1 x 2 Stroke 6 Cy. 600 x 2400 14280kW (19415bhp) Doosan Engine Co Ltd-South Korea AuxGen: 3 x 800kW 60Hz a.c Fuel: 190.0 (d.f.) 2570.0 (r.f.)
7431686 *5VAO7* -	**STEAMER** *ex* Lady Amneh *-2010* *ex* Karina K *-2007* *ex* Karina Kokoeva *-2005* *ex* Heinrich Behrmann *-2004* *ex* Bourgogne *-1989* *ex* Komet I *-1978* *ex* Saracen Prince *-1976* *launched as* Komet *-1975* **Hope Shipping Inc** El Reedy Shipping Agency *Lome* *Togo* MMSI: 671117000	**2,240** 1,165 2,560	Class: DR UA (RS) (GL)	**1975-09 KG Norderwerft GmbH & Co. — Hamburg** (Hull) **1975-09 J.J. Sietas Schiffswerft — Hamburg** Yd No: 745 Loa 81.41 Br ex 13.64 Dght 5.042 Lbp 74.17 Br md 13.39 Dpth 5.19 Welded, 2 dks	**(A31A2GX) General Cargo Ship** Grain: 4,730; Bale: 4,417 TEU 149 C.Ho 86/20' C.Dk 63/20' incl. 20ref C. Compartments: 1 Ho, ER 1 Ha: (50.3 x 10.2)ER Ice Capable	**1 oil engine** driving 1 FP propeller Total Power: 1,949kW (2,650hp) 13.5kn MaK 8M453AK 1 x 4 Stroke 8 Cy. 320 x 420 1949kW (2650bhp) MaK Maschinenbau GmbH-Kiel
8008709 *YQLD* -	**STEAUA DE MARE 1** *ex* Delfin *-1975* *ex* TC-02 *-1975* **IRCM** - *Sulina* *Romania* Official number: 57	**134** 44 62	Class: (RN) (PR)	**1981-09 Stocznia Ustka SA — Ustka** Yd No: B410/63 Loa 25.67 Br ex 7.22 Dght 2.910 Lbp 24.37 Br md 7.21 Dpth 3.49 Welded, 1 dk	**(B11A2FS) Stern Trawler** Ins: 125 Compartments: 1 Ho, ER	**1 oil engine** geared to sc. shaft driving 1 CP propeller Total Power: 419kW (570hp) 10.8kn Sulzer 6AL20/24 1 x 4 Stroke 6 Cy. 200 x 240 419kW (570bhp) Puckie Zaklady Mechaniczne Ltd-Puck AuxGen: 1 x 32kW 400V a.c, 1 x 29kW 400V a.c
8030922 - -	**STEAUA DE MARE 3** *ex* TC-03 *-1975* - -	**132** 44 63	Class: (RN) (PR)	**1981-10 Stocznia Ustka SA — Ustka** Yd No: B410/64 Loa 25.67 Br ex - Dght 2.910 Lbp 24.36 Br md 7.22 Dpth 3.49 Welded, 1 dk	**(B11A2FS) Stern Trawler** Ins: 90	**1 oil engine** geared to sc. shaft driving 1 FP propeller Total Power: 419kW (570hp) 11.3kn Sulzer 6AL20/24 1 x 4 Stroke 6 Cy. 200 x 240 419kW (570bhp) Zaklady Przemyslu Metalowego 'HCegielski' SA-Poznan AuxGen: 2 x 45kW 400V a.c
8503503 *OIVR* -	**STEEL** *ex* Finn *-1991* **ESL Shipping Oy** - SatCom: Inmarsat C 423000039 *Helsinki* *Finland* MMSI: 230202000 Official number: 10594	**1,562** 469 431	Class: NV	**1987-04 Hollming Oy — Rauma** Yd No: 263 Loa 41.70 Br ex 15.50 Dght 6.850 Lbp 40.20 Br md 14.37 Dpth 10.01 Welded, 3 dks	**(B32B2SP) Pusher Tug** Ice Capable	**2 oil engines** sr geared to sc. shafts driving 2 CP propellers Total Power: 7,650kW (10,400hp) Sulzer 6ZAL40 2 x 4 Stroke 6 Cy. 400 x 480 each-3825kW (5200bhp) Wartsila Diesel Oy-Finland AuxGen: 1 x 720kW 380V 50Hz a.c, 2 x 523kW 380V 50Hz a.c, 1 x 133kW 380V 50Hz a.c
1009156 *ZCXZ6* -	**STEEL** **International Restoration Cars Ltd** - *George Town* *Cayman Islands (British)* MMSI: 319520000 Official number: 741335	**769** 230 78	Class: LR ✠ **100A1** SS 02/2009 SSC Yacht (P), mono, G6 Ice Class 1A FS at draught of 3.20m Max/min draught fwd 3.20/2.70m Max/min draught aft 3.20/2.70m Required power 1200kw, installed power 1640kw ✠ **LMC** Cable: 385.0/30.0 U2 (a)	**2009-02 Pendennis Shipyard Ltd. — Falmouth** Yd No: 57 Loa 54.85 (BB) Br ex 9.50 Dght 2.850 Lbp 51.15 Br md 9.50 Dpth 4.50 Welded, 3 dks	**(X11A2YP) Yacht** Ice Capable	**2 oil engines** with clutches, flexible couplings & sr reverse geared to sc. shafts driving 2 FP propellers Total Power: 1,640kW (2,230hp) 12.0kn Caterpillar 3512B 2 x Vee 4 Stroke 12 Cy. 170 x 190 each-820kW (1115bhp) Caterpillar Inc-USA AuxGen: 2 x 150kW 400V 50Hz a.c Thrusters: 1 Thwart. FP thruster (f); 1 Thwart. FP thruster (f)
9380594 *9HHN9* -	**STEEL** *ex* Rocket *-2013* **Steel Shipping LLC** Norient Product Pool ApS *Valletta* *Malta* MMSI: 256995000 Official number: 9380594	**23,248** 9,915 37,889 T/cm 46.1	Class: NV (AB)	**2008-07 Hyundai Mipo Dockyard Co Ltd — Ulsan** Yd No: 2032 Loa 184.32 Br ex 27.45 Dght 11.515 Lbp 176.00 Br md 27.40 Dpth 17.20 Welded, 1 dk	**(A12B2TR) Chemical/Products Tanker** Double Hull (13F) Liq: 40,781; Liq (Oil): 40,781 Compartments: 12 Wing Ta, 2 Wing Slop Ta, ER 12 Cargo Pump (s): 10x500m^3/hr, 2x300m^3/hr Manifold: Bow/CM: 92.6m Ice Capable	**1 oil engine** driving 1 FP propeller Total Power: 9,480kW (12,889hp) 15.0kn MAN-B&W 6S50MC-C 1 x 2 Stroke 6 Cy. 500 x 2000 9480kW (12889bhp) Hyundai Heavy Industries Co Ltd-South Korea AuxGen: 3 x a.c

Ship	Tonnage	Class	Builder / Dimensions	Type / Cargo	Machinery
9146003 **STEEL INTEGRITY** *A8FY8* *ex* Juergen Schulte *-2014* - *ex* Frederike Oldendorff *-2009* *ex* Mercury Trader *-2003* **Steelships Three LLC** Dianik Bross Shipping Corp SA *Monrovia* *Liberia* MMSI: 636016326 Official number: 16326	**26,586** 16,450 48,224 T/cm 51.8	Class: NV (NK)	**1997-07 Oshima Shipbuilding Co Ltd — Saikai NS** Yd No: 10207 Loa 189.33 (BB) Br ex - Dght 11.739 Lbp 180.60 Br md 30.95 Dpth 16.40 Welded, 1 dk	**(A21A2BC) Bulk Carrier** Grain: 60,956; Bale: 59,778 Compartments: 5 Ho, ER 5 Ha: (17.1 x 15.6)2 (21.6 x 15.6)2 (19.8 x 15.6)ER Cranes: 4x25t	**1 oil engine** driving 1 FP propeller Total Power: 7,282kW (9,901hp) 14.5kn Mitsubishi 6UEC50LSII 1 x 2 Stroke 6 Cy. 500 x 1950 7282kW (9901bhp) Mitsubishi Heavy Industries Ltd-Japan AuxGen: 3 x 400kW a.c
8905828 **STEEL TITAN** *D5CV4* *ex* Hellenic Sea *-2012* *ex* Nordbulk *-2002* - **Agios Stefanos Maritime SA** Dianik Bross Shipping Corp SA *Monrovia* *Liberia* MMSI: 636015785 Official number: 15785	**36,448** 22,519 65,434 T/cm 64.7	Class: BV (GL) (AB)	**1991-06 Jiangnan Shipyard — Shanghai** Yd No: 2186 Loa 225.00 Br ex - Dght 13.110 Lbp 215.02 Br md 32.21 Dpth 18.00 Welded, 1 dk	**(A21A2BC) Bulk Carrier** Grain: 78,017; Bale: 74,224 Compartments: 7 Ho, ER 7 Ha: (14.6 x 13.2)6 (14.6 x 15.0)ER	**1 oil engine** driving 1 FP propeller Total Power: 9,451kW (12,850hp) 14.4kn B&W 5L70MCE 1 x 2 Stroke 5 Cy. 700 x 2268 9451kW (12850bhp) Dalian Marine Diesel Works-China AuxGen: 2 x 560kW a.c, 1 x 500kW a.c, 1 x 100kW a.c
9234226 **STEEL VISION** *D5ES6* *ex* Kristin Picer *-2013* - **Steelships Two LLC** Dianik Bross Shipping Corp SA *Monrovia* *Liberia* MMSI: 636016153 Official number: 16153	**28,085** 16,065 48,913 T/cm 54.4	Class: BV (NK)	**2001-07 Ishikawajima-Harima Heavy Industries Co Ltd (IHI) — Tokyo** Yd No: 3147 Loa 189.96 Br ex - Dght 11.623 Lbp 181.71 Br md 32.20 Dpth 16.50 Welded, 1 dk	**(A21A2BC) Bulk Carrier** Grain: 61,553; Bale: 59,844 Compartments: 5 Ho, ER 5 Ha: (17.6 x 17.0)4 (20.0 x 17.0)ER Cranes: 4x30t	**1 oil engine** driving 1 FP propeller Total Power: 7,700kW (10,469hp) 14.5kn Sulzer 6RTA48T 1 x 2 Stroke 6 Cy. 480 x 2000 7700kW (10469bhp) Diesel United Ltd.-Aioi Fuel: 2000.0
9071571 **STEEL WISDOM** *D5DR3* *ex* Yoma 6 *-2013* *ex* Progress II *-2009* - *ex* Kavo Portland *-2006* *ex* Star Phoenix *-2003* **Steelships One LLC** Dianik Bross Shipping Corp SA *Monrovia* *Liberia* MMSI: 636015951 Official number: 15951	**27,011** 16,011 46,641	Class: BV (NK) (NV)	**1995-02 Mitsui Eng. & SB. Co. Ltd. — Tamano** Yd No: 1407 Loa 189.80 (BB) Br ex - Dght 11.600 Lbp 181.99 Br md 31.00 Dpth 16.50 Welded, 1 dk	**(A31A2GO) Open Hatch Cargo Ship** Grain: 59,820; Bale: 57,237 Compartments: 5 Ho, ER 5 Ha: (17.6 x 17.2)4 (20.8 x 17.2)ER Cranes: 4x25t	**1 oil engine** driving 1 FP propeller Total Power: 7,429kW (10,100hp) 14.8kn B&W 6S50MC 1 x 2 Stroke 6 Cy. 500 x 1910 7429kW (10100bhp) Mitsui Engineering & Shipbuilding CLtd-Japan AuxGen: 3 x 480kW a.c Fuel: 1621.0 (r.f.) 25.6pd
7940211 **STEELHEAD** *WDG6826* *ex* Obsession *-2013* - **Decomack Marine Inc** - *Bellingham, WA* *United States of America* MMSI: 367561070 Official number: 603285	**182** 54 -		**1978 Sundial Marine Construction & Repair, Inc. — Troutdale, Or** Yd No: 6 L reg 24.21 Br ex 7.93 Dght - Lbp - Br md - Dpth 2.62 Welded, 1 dk	**(B11B2FV) Fishing Vessel**	**1 oil engine** driving 1 FP propeller Total Power: 552kW (750hp)
9313876 **STEENBANK** *PHDG* - **Bankship IV BV** Pot Scheepvaart BV *Delfzijl* *Netherlands* MMSI: 246125000 Official number: 42935	**2,999** 1,643 4,500	Class: BV	**2005-06 Ferus Smit Leer GmbH — Leer** Yd No: 355 Loa 89.78 (BB) Br ex - Dght 5.950 Lbp 84.99 Br md 14.00 Dpth 7.50 Welded, 1 dk	**(A31A2GX) General Cargo Ship** Grain: 6,088 TEU 144 C Ho 102 TEU C Dk 42 Ice Capable	**1 oil engine** geared to sc. shaft driving 1 CP propeller Total Power: 2,640kW (3,589hp) 13.0kn MaK 8M25 1 x 4 Stroke 8 Cy. 255 x 400 2640kW (3589bhp) Caterpillar Motoren GmbH & Co. KG-Germany AuxGen: 2 x 125kW 440/250V 60Hz a.c Thrusters: 1 Tunnel thruster (f)
6719885 **STEENBORG** - *ex* Berta Morgenroth *-1981* - - -	**718** 441 781	Class: (GL)	**1967 Ruhrorter Schiffswerft u. Maschinenfabrik GmbH — Duisburg** Yd No: 408 Loa 54.97 Br ex 9.63 Dght 4.154 Lbp 50.02 Br md 9.61 Dpth 5.39 Welded, 2 dks	**(A31A2GX) General Cargo Ship** Grain: 1,598; Bale: 1,427 Compartments: 1 Ho, ER 2 Ha: (15.6 x 5.4) (8.3 x 5.4)ER Ice Capable	**1 oil engine** driving 1 FP propeller Total Power: 221kW (300hp) 8.8kn MaK 6MU451 1 x 4 Stroke 6 Cy. 320 x 450 221kW (300bhp) Atlas MaK Maschinenbau GmbH-Kiel
7939896 **STEFAMAR** *SV6057* - **Ioannis Laoumtzis & Evdoxia Laoumtzi** - *Kos* *Greece* MMSI: 237001900 Official number: 6	*149* 47 -	Class: (HR)	**1979 Homatas Brothers Shipyard — Thessaloniki** Yd No: 1407 Loa 31.58 Br ex 6.51 Dght 3.001 Lbp 27.61 Br md - Dpth - Welded, 1 dk	**(A37B2PS) Passenger Ship**	**1 oil engine** driving 1 FP propeller Total Power: 324kW (441hp) 11.0kn Kelvin TASC8 1 x 4 Stroke 8 Cy. 165 x 184 324kW (441bhp) Kelvin Diesels Ltd.-Glasgow
7917898 **STEFAN** *5NSS* *ex* Ekulo Explorer *-2013* *ex* Sea Explorer *-2011* - *ex* Australia Eagle *-1996* *ex* Australian Eagle *-1991* *ex* Lady Diana *-1990* *launched as* Longbow *-1981* *Lagos* *Nigeria* MMSI: 657975000 Official number: SR 2083	**1,247** 374 1,389	Class: AB	**1981-03 New South Wales Govt Engineering & Shbldg Undertaking — Newcastle NSW** Yd No: 102 Loa 59.52 Br ex 13.87 Dght 5.120 Lbp 55.02 Br md 13.50 Dpth 5.82 Welded, 1 dk	**(B21B20A) Anchor Handling Tug Supply** Passengers: berths: 9	**2 oil engines** sr geared to sc. shafts driving 2 CP propellers Total Power: 4,230kW (5,752hp) 13.5kn EMD (Electro-Motive) 16-645-E7 2 x Vee 2 Stroke 16 Cy. 230 x 254 each-2115kW (2876bhp) (made 1979) General Motors Corp.Electro-Motive Div.-La Grange AuxGen: 2 x 300kW 415V 50Hz a.c, 1 x 140kW 415V 50Hz a.c Thrusters: 1 Thwart. CP thruster (f) Fuel: 570.0 (d.f.) 15.0pd
6506020 **STEFAN** *SPG2285* - **Przedsiebiorstwo Robot Czerpalnych I Podwodnych Sp z oo (Dredging & Underwater Works Co Ltd)** - *Gdansk* *Poland* Official number: ROG/S/435	**323** 144 -	Class: PR	**1964 VEB Schiffswerft "Edgar Andre" — Magdeburg** Loa 28.76 Br ex 6.53 Dght 2.601 Lbp 26.67 Br md 6.48 Dpth 3.00 Welded, 1 dk	**(B32A2ST) Tug** Ice Capable	**1 oil engine** driving 1 FP propeller Total Power: 294kW (400hp) 10.5kn S.K.L. 6NVD48 1 x 4 Stroke 6 Cy. 320 x 480 294kW (400bhp) VEB Schwermaschinenbau "KarlLiebknecht" (SKL)-Magdeburg AuxGen: 2 x 27kW 230V d.c, 1 x 7kW 230V d.c
9572197 **STEFAN CEL MARE** *YQNK* - **General Inspectorate of Romanian Border Police (Politia de Frontiera Romana)** - *Constanta* *Romania* MMSI: 264900206	**1,028** 308 -	Class: (BV)	**2010-09 Santierul Naval Damen Galati S.A. — Galati** (Hull) Yd No: 1192 **2010-09 B.V. Scheepswerf Damen — Gorinchem** Yd No: 555056 Loa 66.00 Br ex 10.36 Dght 2.900 Lbp 66.00 Br md 10.25 Dpth 4.70 Welded, 1 dk	**(B34H2SQ) Patrol Vessel**	**2 oil engines** reduction geared to sc. shafts driving 2 CP propellers Total Power: 5,046kW (6,860hp) 21.0kn M.T.U. 16V4000M73L 2 x Vee 4 Stroke 16 Cy. 170 x 190 each-2523kW (3430bhp) MTU Friedrichshafen GmbH-Friedrichshafen AuxGen: 3 x 176kW 50Hz a.c Thrusters: 1 Tunnel thruster (f)
9006394 **STEFAN K.** *PBER* - **Rufinia Beheer BV** Bereederungsgesellschaft Alstership GmbH & Co KG *Delfzijl* *Netherlands* MMSI: 246062000 Official number: 40512	**2,449** 1,380 3,710	Class: GL	**1995-04 Peene-Werft GmbH — Wolgast** Yd No: 414 Loa 87.90 (BB) Br ex - Dght 5.460 Lbp 81.84 Br md 12.80 Dpth 7.10 Welded, 1 dk	**(A31A2GX) General Cargo Ship** Grain: 4,666; Bale: 4,635 TEU 252 C Ho 180 TEU C Dk 72 TEU in 6 ref C. Compartments: 1 Ho, ER 1 Ha: (56.6 x 10.2)ER Ice Capable	**1 oil engine** reduction geared to sc. shaft driving 1 FP propeller Total Power: 1,500kW (2,039hp) 10.0kn Deutz SBV8M628 1 x 4 Stroke 8 Cy. 240 x 280 1500kW (2039bhp) Motoren Werke Mannheim AG (MWM)-Mannheim AuxGen: 2 x 168kW 380/220V a.c Thrusters: 1 Tunnel thruster (f) Fuel: 122.0 (d.f.)
9461594 **STEFAN SIBUM** *5BQX3* - **Sibum GmbH & Co KG ms 'Stefan Sibum'** Reederei Bernd Sibum GmbH & Co KG *Limassol* *Cyprus* MMSI: 209792000	**10,585** 5,400 13,172	Class: BV	**2008-12 SSW Schichau Seebeck Shipyard GmbH — Bremerhaven** Yd No: 2034 Loa 151.74 (BB) Br ex - Dght 8.000 Lbp 142.40 Br md 23.40 Dpth 11.75 Welded, 1 dk	**(A33A2CC) Container Ship (Fully Cellular)** TEU 1036 C Ho 322 TEU C Dk 714 TEU incl 250 ref C Compartments: 3 Cell Ho, ER Ice Capable	**1 oil engine** reduction geared to sc. shaft driving 1 CP propeller Total Power: 9,000kW (12,236hp) 18.5kn MaK 9M43C 1 x 4 Stroke 9 Cy. 430 x 610 9000kW (12236bhp) Caterpillar Motoren GmbH & Co. KG-Germany AuxGen: 1 x 1700kW 450V 60Hz a.c, 3 x 550kW 450V 60Hz a.c Thrusters: 1 Tunnel thruster (f) Fuel: 117.0 (d.f.) 1012.0 (r.f.) 36.0pd
8406951 **STEFANI MAE I** - *ex* Wajima Maru No. 28 *-2002* - **Zamboanga Universal Fishing Co** - *Zamboanga* *Philippines* Official number: ZAM2D00803	*146* 74 -		**1983 K.K. Watanabe Zosensho — Nagasaki** Yd No: 1022 Loa 38.31 Br ex - Dght - Lbp 30.51 Br md 7.12 Dpth 2.82 Welded, 1 dk	**(B12B2FC) Fish Carrier**	**1 oil engine** driving 1 FP propeller Total Power: 713kW (969hp) Pielstick 6PA5 1 x 4 Stroke 6 Cy. 255 x 270 713kW (969bhp) Niigata Engineering Co Ltd-Japan

IMO / Call sign / Fishing No.	Name / Former names / Owner / Port / Flag	Tonnage	Class	Builder / Dimensions	Type / Capacity	Machinery
8603999 *MHAP2* N 265	**STEFANIE M** *ex* Daystar *-2002* *ex* Lunar Bow *-1996* **Stefanie M Fishing Co Ltd** - *Newry* *United Kingdom* MMSI: 235004750 Official number: A13280	**631** 234 513	Class: (LR) ✠ Classed LR until 8/1/91	**1987**-07 **Simek, Sigbjorn Iversen AS — Flekkefjord** Yd No: 67 Loa 49.28 (BB) Br ex 8.92 Dght 5.001 Lbp 36.20 Br md 8.91 Dpth 6.61 Welded, 2 dks	**(B11A2FT) Trawler** Ins: 593	**1 oil engine** with clutches, flexible couplings & sr geared to sc. shaft driving 1 CP propeller Total Power: 1,545kW (2,101hp) 10.0kn Caterpillar 3606TA 1 x 4 Stroke 6 Cy. 280 x 300 1545kW (2101bhp) Caterpillar Inc-USA AuxGen: 1 x 1000kW 440V 60Hz a.c, 2 x 135kW 440V 60Hz a.c Thrusters: 1 Thwart. CP thruster (f); 1 Thwart. FP thruster (a) Fuel: 40.0 (d.f.)
9362968 - -	**STEFANO** - **Pesquera Diamante SA** - *Peru*	**500** - -		**2005**-12 **SIMA Serv. Ind. de la Marina Callao (SIMAC) — Callao** Yd No: 91 Loa 46.50 Br ex - Dght - Lbp 40.20 Br md 10.10 Dpth 4.80 Welded, 1 dk	**(B11B2FV) Fishing Vessel**	**1 oil engine** reduction geared to sc. shaft driving 1 FP propeller Total Power: 1,324kW (1,800hp) 13.5kn General Electric 7FDM12 1 x Vee 4 Stroke 12 Cy. 229 x 267 1324kW (1800bhp) General Electric Co.-Lynn, Ma
7343413 *SY2913* -	**STEFANOS F** *ex* Marcantonio Bragadino *-2002* *ex* Xifias *-1978* *ex* T. B. 2 *-1976* **Elktiki Naftiki Eteria** - *Chalkis* *Greece* MMSI: 237570400 Official number: 410	**121** 38	Class: (LR) ✠ Classed LR until 30/9/87	**1973**-08 **Th. Zervas & Sons — Ambelaki** Loa 26.73 Br ex 7.57 Dght 3.029 Lbp 24.08 Br md 7.31 Dpth 3.51 Welded, 1 dk	**(B32A2ST) Tug**	**1 oil engine** reverse reduction geared to sc. shaft driving 1 FP propeller Total Power: 552kW (750hp) Blackstone ETS8 1 x 4 Stroke 8 Cy. 222 x 292 552kW (750bhp) Mirrlees Blackstone (Stamford)Ltd.-Stamford AuxGen: 2 x 30kW 380V 50Hz a.c
9583744 *9HA2700* -	**STEFANOS T** - **Fantasy Shipping Ltd** Modion Maritime Management SA *Valletta* *Malta* MMSI: 215305000 Official number: 9583744	**43,975** 23,017 80,499	Class: LR ✠ **100A1** SS 07/2011 bulk carrier CSR BC-A (holds 2, 4 & 6 may be empty) GRAB (20) ESP **ShipRight** (CM,ACS (B)) *IWS LI ✠ **LMC** **UMS** Eq.Ltr: Q†; Cable: 687.5/81.0 U3 (a)	**2011**-07 **SPP Shipbuilding Co Ltd — Sacheon** Yd No: H1059 Loa 229.00 (BB) Br ex 32.28 Dght 14.460 Lbp 222.00 Br md 32.24 Dpth 20.10 Welded, 1 dk	**(A21A2BC) Bulk Carrier** Grain: 95,414; Bale: 91,164 Compartments: 7 Ho, ER 7 Ha: 3 (15.7 x 15.2)3 (15.7 x 15.2)ER (14.8 x 15.2)	**1 oil engine** driving 1 FP propeller Total Power: 11,060kW (15,037hp) 14.5kn MAN-B&W 7S50MC-C 1 x 2 Stroke 7 Cy. 500 x 2000 11060kW (15037bhp) Doosan Engine Co Ltd-South Korea AuxGen: 3 x 600kW 450V 60Hz a.c Boilers: AuxB (Comp) 9.2kgf/cm² (9.0bar)
6711467 *LLFZ* -	**STEFFEN ANDREAS** *ex* Buavag *-2005* *ex* Freco *-1996* *ex* Tone *-1983* *ex* Freco *-1973* **Angel Frakt AS** - *Sandnessjoen* *Norway* MMSI: 258582000	**468** 140 564	Class: (BV)	**1967**-05 **Orskovs Staalskibsvaerft A/S — Frederikshavn** Yd No: 44 Loa 48.14 Br ex 8.67 Dght 3.118 Lbp 43.26 Br md 8.64 Dpth 3.46 Welded, 1 dk	**(A31A2GX) General Cargo Ship** Grain: 708; Bale: 616 Compartments: 1 Ho, ER 1 Ha: (21.7 x 5.0)ER Winches: 1	**1 oil engine** driving 1 CP propeller Total Power: 313kW (426hp) 10.0kn Alpha 405-VO 1 x 2 Stroke 5 Cy. 230 x 400 313kW (426bhp) Alpha Diesel A/S-Denmark AuxGen: 1 x 8kW 220V d.c, 2 x 6kW 220V d.c Fuel: 32.5 (d.f.) 1.7pd
9180346 *OVOC* GR 6 22	**STEFFEN C** *ex* Petur Jonsson *-2006* **Sikuaq Trawl AS** - *Nuuk* *Denmark* MMSI: 331224000 Official number: D4238	**2,139** 642 -	Class: NV	**1997**-10 **Aukra Industrier AS — Aukra** Yd No: 98 Loa 63.40 Br ex - Dght 5.800 Lbp 56.40 Br md 13.00 Dpth 8.50 Welded, 1 dk	**(B11A2FS) Stern Trawler** Ice Capable	**1 oil engine** reduction geared to sc. shaft driving 1 CP propeller Total Power: 3,690kW (5,017hp) Wartsila 9R32 1 x 4 Stroke 9 Cy. 320 x 350 3690kW (5017bhp) Wartsila Diesel Oy-Finland AuxGen: 1 x 2000kW a.c, 1 x 863kW a.c Thrusters: 1 Thwart. FP thruster (f) Fuel: 473.0 (r.f.)
9523926 *2CTX2* -	**STEFFI C** - **Vectis 8000 Ltd** Carisbrooke Shipping Ltd *Cowes* *United Kingdom* MMSI: 235075723 Official number: 916355	**5,629** 2,877 8,063 T/cm 17.8	Class: LR (GL) **100A1** SS 02/2010 TOC contemplated	**2010**-02 **Jiangsu Yangzijiang Shipbuilding Co Ltd — Jiangyin JS** Yd No: 2008-825 Loa 108.22 (BB) Br ex 18.48 Dght 7.057 Lbp 103.90 Br md 18.20 Dpth 9.00 Welded, 1 dk	**(A31A2GX) General Cargo Ship** Grain: 10,210; Bale: 10,210 Compartments: 3 Ho, ER 3 Ha: 2 (25.9 x 15.2)ER (17.5 x 15.2) Cranes: 2x25t Ice Capable	**1 oil engine** reduction geared to sc. shaft driving 1 CP propeller Total Power: 3,000kW (4,079hp) 12.4kn MaK 6M32C 1 x 4 Stroke 6 Cy. 320 x 480 3000kW (4079bhp) Caterpillar Motoren GmbH & Co. KG-Germany AuxGen: 1 x 360kW 450V a.c, 2 x 365kW 450V a.c Thrusters: 1 Tunnel thruster (f)
7424683 *TFGM* IS 028	**STEFNIR** *ex* Steffen *-2002* *ex* Stefnir *-1999* *ex* Gyllir *-1993* **Hradfrystihusid-Gunnvor hf** - *Isafjordur* *Iceland* MMSI: 251035000 Official number: 1451	**686** 200 -	Class: NV	**1976**-03 **Flekkefjord Slipp & Maskinfabrikk AS AS — Flekkefjord** Yd No: 121 Loa 49.87 Br ex 9.50 Dght 4.431 Lbp 44.01 Br md 9.45 Dpth 5.15 Welded, 2 dks	**(B11A2FS) Stern Trawler** Compartments: 1 Ho, ER 1 Ha: (2.7 x 2.4)ER Ice Capable	**1 oil engine** driving 1 FP propeller Total Power: 1,309kW (1,780hp) MaK 8M452AK 1 x 4 Stroke 8 Cy. 320 x 450 1309kW (1780bhp) MaK Maschinenbau GmbH-Kiel AuxGen: 1 x 220V 50Hz a.c, 1 x a.c
9255048 *LLQC* -	**STEIGEN** - **Polarfjord AS** - *Bodo* *Norway* MMSI: 258599000	**670** 241 650		**2002**-03 **AS Rigas Kugu Buvetava (Riga Shipyard) — Riga** (Hull) **2002**-03 **Sletta Baatbyggeri AS — Mjosundet** Yd No: 97 Loa 41.60 Br ex - Dght - Lbp 37.50 Br md 9.70 Dpth 4.85 Welded, 1 dk	**(B12C2FL) Live Fish Carrier (Well Boat)** Liq: 670	**1 oil engine** reduction geared to sc. shaft driving 1 FP propeller Total Power: 1,350kW (1,835hp) Deutz SBV6M628 1 x 4 Stroke 6 Cy. 240 x 280 1350kW (1835bhp) Deutz AG-Koeln
9281073 *LMFJ* -	**STEIGTIND** - **Torghatten Nord AS** - *Narvik* *Norway* MMSI: 259310000	**539** 162 46	Class: (NV)	**2003**-04 **Image Marine Pty Ltd — Fremantle WA** Yd No: 243 Loa 41.30 Br ex 11.90 Dght 1.450 Lbp 36.20 Br md 11.60 Dpth 4.30 Welded	**(A37B2PS) Passenger Ship** Hull Material: Aluminium Alloy Passengers: unberthed: 216	**2 oil engines** geared to sc. shafts driving 2 Water jets Total Power: 4,596kW (6,248hp) 34.0kn M.T.U. 16V4000M70 2 x Vee 4 Stroke 16 Cy. 165 x 190 each-2298kW (3124bhp) MTU Friedrichshafen GmbH-Friedrichshafen
9241243 *DKYR* -	**STEIN** *ex* Montoriol *-2013* **Schlepp- und Fahrgesellschaft Kiel mbH-SFK** - *Kiel* *Germany* MMSI: 211611070 Official number: 73121	**269** 81 143	Class: GL	**2001**-12 **Astilleros Zamakona SA — Santurtzi** Yd No: 507 Loa 27.00 Br ex - Dght 2.820 Lbp 25.85 Br md 9.70 Dpth 3.90 Welded, 1 dk	**(B32A2ST) Tug**	**2 oil engines** reduction geared to sc. shafts driving 2 Directional propellers Total Power: 2,650kW (3,602hp) 11.0kn Normo KRMB-6 2 x 4 Stroke 6 Cy. 250 x 300 each-1325kW (1801bhp) Rolls Royce Marine AS-Norway
9280691 *V2BT9* -	**STEINAU** - **Reeder Erwin Strahlmann** Reederei Erwin Strahlmann eK *Saint John's* *Antigua & Barbuda* MMSI: 304926000 Official number: 4122	**2,461** 1,369 3,712	Class: GL	**2006**-12 **Slovenske Lodenice a.s. — Komarno** Yd No: 2962 Loa 87.83 (BB) Br ex - Dght 5.498 Lbp 81.00 Br md 12.80 Dpth 7.10 Welded, 1 Dk.	**(A31A2GX) General Cargo Ship** Grain: 4,677; Bale: 4,620 TEU 167 C. Compartments: 1 Ho, ER 1 Ha: ER (56.6 x 10.2) Ice Capable	**1 oil engine** reverse reduction geared to sc. shaft driving 1 FP propeller Total Power: 1,500kW (2,039hp) 11.7kn MaK 8M20 1 x 4 Stroke 8 Cy. 200 x 300 1500kW (2039bhp) Caterpillar Motoren GmbH & Co. KG-Germany AuxGen: 3 x 119kW 380/220V 50Hz a.c Thrusters: 1 Tunnel thruster (f) Fuel: 147.0 (d.f.) 7.5pd
7612644 *DEEH* -	**STEINBOCK** - **Bugsier-, Reederei- und Bergungs-Gesellschaft mbH & Co KG** - *Bremen* *Germany* MMSI: 211215380 Official number: 4233	**213** 64 60	Class: GL	**1977**-09 **Jadewerft Wilhelmshaven GmbH — Wilhelmshaven** Yd No: 140 Loa 28.53 Br ex 8.44 Dght 2.893 Lbp 26.52 Br md 8.40 Dpth 3.43 Welded, 1 dk	**(B32A2ST) Tug** Ice Capable	**2 oil engines** reduction geared to sc. shafts driving 2 Voith-Schneider propellers Total Power: 1,560kW (2,120hp) Deutz SBA8M528 2 x 4 Stroke 8 Cy. 220 x 280 each-780kW (1060bhp) Kloeckner Humboldt Deutz AG-West Germany

8516794 *OW2380* TG 304	**STEINTOR** **P/F Steintor** Jacob P Hammer SatCom: Inmarsat M 623103720 *Hvalba* *Faeroe Islands (Danish)* MMSI: 231037000 Official number: D3044	**828** 248 -	Class: NV	**1985-12 Salthammer Baatbyggeri AS — Vestnes** (Hull) **1985-12 Langsten Slip & Baatbyggeri AS — Tomrefjord** Yd No: 115 Loa 49.20 Br ex - Dght - Lbp 42.40 Br md 10.10 Dpth 4.75 Welded, 2 dks	**(B11A2FT) Trawler** Ice Capable	**1 oil engine** geared to sc. shaft driving 1 FP propeller Total Power: 1,765kW (2,400hp) Wartsila 12V22 1 x Vee 4 Stroke 12 Cy. 220 x 240 1765kW (2400bhp) Oy Wartsila Ab-Finland AuxGen: 1 x 800kW 380V 50Hz a.c, 2 x 331kW 380V 50Hz a.c Thrusters: 1 Thwart. CP thruster (f)
9216731 *V7CI8* -	**STEINTOR** *ex* TS Laemchabang *-2013* *ex* Belgian Express *-2007* **ms 'Steintor' Schiffahrts GmbH & Co KG** Reederei Elbe Shipping GmbH & Co KG SatCom: Inmarsat C 453821710 *Majuro* *Marshall Islands* MMSI: 538090095 Official number: 90095	**16,850** 7,364 21,373 T/cm 38.4	Class: GL (BV)	**2000-09 Hanjin Heavy Industries & Construction Co Ltd — Busan** Yd No: 080 Loa 168.80 (BB) Br ex 27.22 Dght 9.220 Lbp 159.62 Br md 27.20 Dpth 13.80 Welded, 1 dk	**(A33A2CC) Container Ship (Fully Cellular)** TEU 1679 C Ho 610 TEU C Dk 1069 TEU incl 194 ref C. Compartments: 7 Cell Ho, ER 8 Ha: (12.6 x 18.2)7 (12.6 x 23.4)ER	**1 oil engine** driving 1 FP propeller Total Power: 15,807kW (21,491hp) 20.0kn MAN-B&W 7S60MC-C 1 x 2 Stroke 7 Cy. 600 x 2400 15807kW (21491bhp) HSD Engine Co Ltd-South Korea AuxGen: 3 x 900kW 440/220V a.c Thrusters: 1 Thwart. FP thruster (f)
9226475 *TFVA* SF 10	**STEINUNN** *ex* Helga *-2006* **Fjardarey ehf** Skinney-Thinganes hf *Hornafjordur* *Iceland* MMSI: 251453000 Official number: 2449	**327** 133 -	Class: NV	**2001-11 Guangzhou Huangpu Shipyard — Guangzhou GD** Yd No: FV-7 Loa 28.95 Br ex - Dght 3.800 Lbp 26.04 Br md 9.17 Dpth 6.05 Welded, 1 dk	**(B11B2FV) Fishing Vessel** Ice Capable	**1 oil engine** reduction geared to sc. shafts driving 1 FP propeller Total Power: 940kW (1,278hp) Caterpillar 3512B-HD 1 x Vee 4 Stroke 12 Cy. 170 x 215 940kW (1278bhp) Caterpillar Inc-USA AuxGen: 1 x a.c, 1 x a.c
7224485 *TFAG* GK 37	**STEINUNN** *ex* Gudbjorg Steinunn *-2010* *ex* Olafur Magnusson *-2008* *ex* Thorir II *-2008* *ex* Thorir *-2008* **Aquaculture Development Ehf** - *Akranes* *Iceland* MMSI: 251322110 Official number: 1236	**190** 57 -		**1972-06 Stalvik h/f — Gardabaer** Yd No: 20 Lengthened-1973 Loa 30.03 Br ex 6.76 Dght 4.000 Lbp 28.00 Br md 6.74 Dpth 5.65 Welded, 1 dk	**(B11B2FV) Fishing Vessel**	**1 oil engine** reduction geared to sc. shaft driving 1 CP propeller Total Power: 560kW (761hp) Caterpillar D379SCAC 1 x Vee 4 Stroke 8 Cy. 159 x 203 560kW (761bhp) Caterpillar Tractor Co-USA
7041493 *TFNT* SH 167	**STEINUNN** *ex* Ingibjorg *-1973* *ex* Arnfirdingur II *-1972* **Steinunn hf** - *Olafsvik* *Iceland* MMSI: 251233110 Official number: 1134	**236** 71 -		**1971-01 Stalvik h/f — Gardabaer** Yd No: 14 Lengthened-1995 Lengthened-1982 Loa 33.30 Br ex 6.71 Dght - Lbp - Br md 6.68 Dpth 3.36 Welded, 1 dk	**(B11B2FV) Fishing Vessel**	**1 oil engine** driving 1 CP propeller Total Power: 482kW (655hp) Caterpillar D379SCAC 1 x Vee 4 Stroke 8 Cy. 159 x 203 482kW (655bhp) Caterpillar Tractor Co-USA
8845298 *5NLK5* -	**STELAMARIS EHCO** *ex* Zakher View *-2008* *ex* Zakher Blue *-2006* *ex* Vega *-2006* **Consolidated Discounts Ltd** Ehco Ventures Ltd *Lagos* *Nigeria*	**1,360** 457 1,100	Class: (BV) (RN)	**1985-12 Santierul Naval Braila — Braila** Yd No: 1289 Loa 61.15 (BB) Br ex - Dght 4.250 Lbp 56.22 Br md 13.60 Dpth 5.45 Welded, 1 dk	**(B21A2OS) Platform Supply Ship**	**2 oil engines** driving 2 FP propellers Total Power: 3,604kW (4,900hp) 13.4kn Alco 12V251F 2 x Vee 4 Stroke 12 Cy. 229 x 267 each-1802kW (2450bhp) U.C.M. Resita S.A.-Resita
8960933 - -	**STELIE** **Pecheries MV Stelie Ltee** - *Caraquet, NB* *Canada* MMSI: 316003211 Official number: 821565	**149** 112 -		**2000 L'Industrie Marine de Caraquet Ltee — Caraquet NB** L reg 21.20 Br ex - Dght - Lbp - Br md 7.00 Dpth 3.50 Welded, 1 dk	**(B11B2FV) Fishing Vessel**	**1 oil engine** driving 1 FP propeller Total Power: 625kW (850hp) 12.0kn
9452490 *9HA2318* -	**STELIOS B** *ex* Thalassini Axia *-2013* **Stelios B Maritime Ltd** AB Maritime Inc *Valletta* *Malta* MMSI: 248326000 Official number: 9452490	**34,374** 19,565 58,608 T/cm 59.1	Class: AB	**2010-03 SPP Plant & Shipbuilding Co Ltd — Sacheon** Yd No: H1030 Loa 196.00 (BB) Br ex - Dght 13.000 Lbp 189.00 Br md 32.26 Dpth 18.60 Welded, 1 dk	**(A21A2BC) Bulk Carrier** Grain: 75,531; Bale: 70,734 Compartments: 5 Ho, ER 5 Ha: ER Cranes: 4x36t	**1 oil engine** driving 1 FP propeller Total Power: 9,973kW (13,559hp) 14.5kn MAN-B&W 6S50MC-C 1 x 2 Stroke 6 Cy. 500 x 2000 9973kW (13559bhp) Doosan Engine Co Ltd-South Korea AuxGen: 3 x 600kW a.c Fuel: 137.0 (d.f.) 2177.0 (r.f.)
8745840 *SVA3636* -	**STELIOS FILIAGKOS** **Osios David Maritime Co** Agios Nikolaos - Salamina Shipping Co *Piraeus* *Greece* MMSI: 239630600 Official number: 11892	**1,436** 971 -		**2009-11 in Greece** Yd No: 145 Loa 104.90 Br ex - Dght 2.600 Lbp 84.25 Br md 17.50 Dpth - Welded, 1 dk	**(A36A2PR) Passenger/Ro-Ro Ship (Vehicles)**	**4 oil engines** reduction geared to sc. shafts driving 4 Propellers
9258818 *OW2218* FD 1202	**STELKUR** **P/F Faroe Origin** *Runavik* *Faeroe Islands (Danish)* MMSI: 231010000	**464** 140 -	Class: NV (LR) ✠ Classed LR until 14/1/08	**2002-11 Montajes Cies S.L. — Vigo** Yd No: 111 Loa 37.96 (BB) Br ex - Dght 4.750 Lbp 33.32 Br md 9.50 Dpth 7.70 Welded, 1 dk	**(B11A2FS) Stern Trawler**	**1 oil engine** with clutches, flexible couplings & sr geared to sc. shaft driving 1 CP propeller Total Power: 1,118kW (1,520hp) 12.0kn Caterpillar 3512TA 1 x Vee 4 Stroke 12 Cy. 170 x 190 1118kW (1520bhp) Caterpillar Inc-USA AuxGen: 2 x 136kW a.c
9389655 *YLCV* -	**STELLA** **Freeport of Riga Fleet (Rigas Brivostas Flote)** Freeport of Riga Authority (Rigas Brivostas Parvalde) *Riga* *Latvia* MMSI: 275353000	**445** 133 176	Class: (BV)	**2008-06 AS Rigas Kugu Buvetava (Riga Shipyard) — Riga** Yd No: 1502 Loa 34.20 Br ex - Dght 3.900 Lbp 30.39 Br md 12.10 Dpth 5.63 Welded, 1 dk	**(B32A2ST) Tug** Ice Capable	**2 oil engines** reduction geared to sc. shafts driving 2 Directional propellers Total Power: 3,310kW (4,500hp) 13.2kn Caterpillar 3516B 2 x Vee 4 Stroke 16 Cy. 170 x 190 each-1655kW (2250bhp) Caterpillar Inc-USA
9452268 *V7MS5* -	**STELLA** **Pearl Dawn Shipping Ltd** Antares Shipmanagement SA SatCom: Inmarsat C 453836666 *Majuro* *Marshall Islands* MMSI: 538002894 Official number: 2894	**5,031** 1,681 6,448 T/cm 16.1	Class: AB	**2010-11 Zhenjiang Sopo Shiprepair & Building Co Ltd — Zhenjiang JS** Yd No: SP0508 Loa 100.12 Br ex - Dght 6.500 Lbp 94.00 Br md 18.00 Dpth 9.60 Welded, 1 dk	**(A12B2TR) Chemical/Products Tanker** Double Hull (13F) Liq: 7,254; Liq (Oil): 7,254 Compartments: 6 Wing Ta, 6 Wing Ta, 1 Wing Slop Ta, 1 Wing Slop Ta, ER	**1 oil engine** reduction geared to sc. shaft driving 1 CP propeller Total Power: 2,970kW (4,038hp) 12.0kn MaK 9M25 1 x 4 Stroke 9 Cy. 255 x 400 2970kW (4038bhp) Caterpillar Motoren (Guangdong) CoLtd-China AuxGen: 3 x 500kW a.c Fuel: 110.0 (d.f.) 290.0 (r.f.)
9434785 *D5BK6* -	**STELLA** *launched as* Freeway Pioneer *-2009* **Freeway Pioneer SA** Tsakos Columbia Shipmanagement (TCM) SA *Monrovia* *Liberia* MMSI: 636015544 Official number: 15544	**93,916** 59,550 179,700	Class: BV	**2009-08 Daewoo-Mangalia Heavy Industries S.A. — Mangalia** Yd No: 1046 Loa 292.00 (BB) Br ex - Dght 18.200 Lbp 283.00 Br md 45.00 Dpth 24.70 Welded, 1 dk	**(A21A2BC) Bulk Carrier** Grain: 199,293 Compartments: 9 Ho, ER 9 Ha: ER	**1 oil engine** driving 1 FP propeller Total Power: 18,660kW (25,370hp) 14.5kn MAN-B&W 6S70MC-C 1 x 2 Stroke 6 Cy. 700 x 2800 18660kW (25370bhp) Doosan Engine Co Ltd-South Korea AuxGen: 3 x 800kW 60Hz a.c Fuel: 4231.0
9624691 *OJPW* -	**STELLA** **Suomen Lauttaliikenne Oy (Finferries)** - *Turku* *Finland* MMSI: 230634000	**812** - 390	Class: BV	**2012-10 STX Finland Oy — Rauma** Yd No: 1380 Loa 64.40 Br ex - Dght 4.000 Lbp 61.60 Br md 12.70 Dpth - Welded, 1 dk	**(A36A2PR) Passenger/Ro-Ro Ship (Vehicles)** Passengers: unberthed: 250 Bow ramp (centre) Stern ramp (centre) Lorries: 3, Cars: 39 Ice Capable	**2 diesel electric oil engines** driving 2 gen. each 1300kW Connecting to 2 elec. motors each (1300kW) driving 2 Azimuth electric drive units Total Power: 2,600kW (3,534hp) 13.0kn Fuel: 120.0
9646754 *ZJL8464* -	**STELLA** **Aviemore Assets Ltd** Sarnia Yachts Ltd *Road Harbour* *British Virgin Islands* MMSI: 378340000 Official number: 743283	**236** 70 -		**2011-06 Sunseeker International Ltd — Poole** Yd No: 115/01 Loa 34.10 Br ex 7.39 Dght 2.480 Lbp - Br md 7.28 Dpth 3.79 Bonded, 1 dk	**(X11A2YP) Yacht** Hull Material: Reinforced Plastic	**2 oil engines** reduction geared to sc. shafts driving 2 Propellers Total Power: 3,878kW (5,272hp) M.T.U. 16V2000M94 2 x Vee 4 Stroke 16 Cy. 135 x 156 each-1939kW (2636bhp) MTU Friedrichshafen GmbH-Friedrichshafen

8958643 *WDE2039* -	**STELLA** **Loughbeg Fisheries Inc** - *Kodiak, AK* *United States of America* MMSI: 367319530 Official number: 1070580	**116** 93 -		**1998-01 Van Peer Boatworks — Fort Bragg, Ca** Yd No: 25 L reg 17.67 Br ex - Dght - Lbp - Br md 7.31 Dpth 3.81 Welded, 1 dk	**(B11B2FV) Fishing Vessel**	**1 oil engine** driving 1 FP propeller
8957144 *XCXS* -	**STELLA** *ex* Assault *-2002* *ex* H. O. S. Assault *-2002* **Cotemar SA de CV** - *Ciudad del Carmen* *Mexico* MMSI: 345070066	**120** 36 -	Class: GL	**1979 Camcraft, Inc. — Crown Point, La** Yd No: 193 L reg 30.14 Br ex - Dght - Lbp - Br md 6.64 Dpth 2.66 Welded, 1 dk	**(B21A20C) Crew/Supply Vessel** Hull Material: Aluminium Alloy	**3 oil engines** reduction geared to sc. shafts driving 3 FP propellers Total Power: 399kW (543hp) 13.5kn G.M. (Detroit Diesel) 12V-71-TI 3 x Vee 2 Stroke 12 Cy. 108 x 127 each-133kW (181bhp) General Motors Detroit DieselAllison Divn-USA
8883288 - - -	**STELLA** *ex* Natalya Kudryavtseva *-2006* *ex* Kapitan Bogdanov *-2005* - -	**1,857** 557 2,758	Class: RS	**1990-01 Volgogradskiy Sudostroitelnyy Zavod — Volgograd** Yd No: 144 Loa 86.70 Br ex 12.20 Dght 4.100 Lbp 83.80 Br md 12.00 Dpth 5.94 Welded, 1 dk	**(A31A2GX) General Cargo Ship** Grain: 1,856 Compartments: 1 Ho, ER 2 Ha: 2 (19.8 x 9.0)ER	**2 oil engines** driving 2 FP propellers Total Power: 1,030kW (1,400hp) 10.0kn S.K.L. 6NVDS48A-2U 2 x 4 Stroke 6 Cy. 320 x 480 each-515kW (700bhp) VEB Schwermaschinenbau "KarlLiebknecht" (SKL)-Magdeburg AuxGen: 3 x 100kW a.c Fuel: 66.0 (d.f.)
8860157 *YL2759* -	**STELLA** *ex* Mrtk-0813 *-2011* **Vergi Ltd** - *Riga* *Latvia* MMSI: 275416000 Official number: 0841	**112** 33 30	Class: (RS)	**1991-12 Sosnovskiy Sudostroitelnyy Zavod — Sosnovka** Yd No: 813 Loa 25.50 Br ex 7.00 Dght 2.390 Lbp 22.00 Br md - Dpth 3.30 Welded, 1 dk	**(B11A2FS) Stern Trawler** Ice Capable	**1 oil engine** driving 1 FP propeller Total Power: 220kW (299hp) 9.5kn S.K.L. 6NVD26A-2 1 x 4 Stroke 6 Cy. 180 x 260 220kW (299bhp) SKL Motoren u. Systemtechnik AG-Magdeburg
9183398 *DDEH* -	**STELLA** **Bugsier-, Reederei- und Bergungs-Gesellschaft mbH & Co KG** - *Wilhelmshaven* *Germany* MMSI: 211278240 Official number: 435	**359** 107 150	Class: GL	**1998-06 JG Hitzler Schiffswerft u Masch GmbH & Co KG — Lauenburg** Yd No: 812 Loa 30.60 Br ex - Dght 3.000 Lbp 28.85 Br md 11.00 Dpth 4.00 Welded, 1 dk	**(B32A2ST) Tug** Ice Capable	**2 oil engines** gearing integral to driving 2 Voith-Schneider propellers Total Power: 3,690kW (5,016hp) 15.0kn Deutz SBV9M628 2 x 4 Stroke 9 Cy. 240 x 280 each-1845kW (2508bhp) Motoren Werke Mannheim AG (MWM)-Mannheim AuxGen: 2 x 90kW 220/380V a.c
7364900 - - -	**STELLA** *ex* Vernikou Elli II *-1984* - -	*184* 105 269	Class: (AB)	**1975-05 Vernicos Shipyard — Piraeus** Yd No: 1010 Loa 31.50 Br ex 6.20 Dght 2.807 Lbp 28.28 Br md 6.18 Dpth 3.20 Welded, 1 dk	**(A13B2TU) Tanker (unspecified)**	**1 oil engine** driving 1 FP propeller Total Power: 268kW (364hp) Caterpillar D343SCAC 1 x 4 Stroke 6 Cy. 137 x 165 268kW (364bhp) Caterpillar Tractor Co-USA
7724227 *OJPU* -	**STELLA** *ex* Vengsoy 2 *-2012* *ex* Vengsoy *-2011* **Kuljetus-Savolainen Oy** - *Turku* *Finland* MMSI: 230051080	**293** 88 10	Class: (BV)	**1978-08 Skjervoy Skipsverft AS — Skjervoy** Yd No: 5 Loa 33.01 Br ex 9.40 Dght 2.400 Lbp 31.22 Br md 9.20 Dpth 3.81 Welded, 1 dk	**(A36A2PR) Passenger/Ro-Ro Ship (Vehicles)** Passengers: unberthed: 150 Stern ramp Cars: 16	**1 oil engine** driving 1 FP propeller Total Power: 416kW (566hp) Caterpillar D379B 1 x Vee 4 Stroke 8 Cy. 159 x 203 416kW (566bhp) Caterpillar Tractor Co-USA AuxGen: 2 x 110kW a.c
8623731 *D8MB* -	**STELLA** *ex* Dong Kuk No. 99 *-1994* **Dong Kuk Shipping Co Ltd** - *Busan* *South Korea* Official number: BSR-866055	*740* - 1,838	Class: (KR)	**1986-12 Kyungnam Shipbuilding Co Ltd — Busan** Loa 66.50 Br ex - Dght - Lbp 62.29 Br md 12.50 Dpth 4.40 Welded, 1 dk	**(A24D2BA) Aggregates Carrier** Grain: 1,740 Compartments: 1 Ho, ER 1 Ha: (24.5 x 10.0)ER Cranes: 1x5t	**1 oil engine** driving 1 FP propeller Total Power: 736kW (1,001hp) 8.0kn Nippon Hatsudoki S6NV37 1 x 4 Stroke 6 Cy. 370 x 520 736kW (1001bhp) Nippon Hatsudoki-Japan AuxGen: 2 x 64kW 220V a.c
8034150 *IMFJ* -	**STELLA** *ex* BA 815 *-1989* **CEM SpA** Nuova Naviservice Srl *Genoa* *Italy* MMSI: 247246700 Official number: 8706	*1,192* 1,164 -	Class: RI	**1968 N.V. Scheepswerf en Mfbk. "De Liesbosch" — Nieuwegein** Loa 63.43 Br ex 13.77 Dght 3.418 Lbp 59.75 Br md 13.71 Dpth 4.30 Welded, 1 dk	**(B34A2SH) Hopper, Motor**	**2 oil engines** driving 2 FP propellers Total Power: 536kW (728hp) Caterpillar D343 2 x 4 Stroke 6 Cy. 137 x 165 each-268kW (364bhp) Caterpillar Tractor Co-USA
9522714 *9V9082* -	**STELLA ADA** **Stella Ada Shipping Pte Ltd** Stella Ship Management Pte Ltd *Singapore* *Singapore* MMSI: 566089000 Official number: 396604	**94,710** 59,527 180,223 T/cm 124.3	Class: CC	**2011-06 Dalian Shipbuilding Industry Co Ltd — Dalian LN (No 2 Yard)** Yd No: BC1800-37 Loa 295.00 (BB) Br ex - Dght 18.100 Lbp 285.00 Br md 46.00 Dpth 24.80 Welded, 1 dk	**(A21A2BC) Bulk Carrier** Grain: 201,953 Compartments: 9 Ho, ER 9 Ha: 7 (15.5 x 20.0)ER 2 (15.5 x 16.5)	**1 oil engine** driving 1 FP propeller Total Power: 18,660kW (25,370hp) 14.5kn MAN-B&W 6S70MC-C 1 x 2 Stroke 6 Cy. 700 x 2800 18660kW (25370bhp) Doosan Engine Co Ltd-South Korea AuxGen: 3 x 900kW 450V a.c
9522697 *9V9079* -	**STELLA ALICE** *ex* RZS Milestone *-2010* **Stella Alice Shipping Pte Ltd** Stella Ship Management Pte Ltd SatCom: Inmarsat C 456549110 *Singapore* *Singapore* MMSI: 565491000 Official number: 396601	**94,710** 59,527 180,157 T/cm 124.3	Class: CC	**2010-12 Dalian Shipbuilding Industry Co Ltd — Dalian LN (No 2 Yard)** Yd No: BC1800-34 Loa 295.00 (BB) Br ex - Dght 18.100 Lbp 285.00 Br md 46.00 Dpth 24.80 Welded, 1 dk	**(A21A2BC) Bulk Carrier** Grain: 201,953 Compartments: 9 Ho, ER 9 Ha: 7 (15.5 x 20.0)ER 2 (15.5 x 16.5)	**1 oil engine** driving 1 FP propeller Total Power: 18,660kW (25,370hp) 14.5kn MAN-B&W 6S70MC-C 1 x 2 Stroke 6 Cy. 700 x 2800 18660kW (25370bhp) Doosan Engine Co Ltd-South Korea AuxGen: 3 x 900kW 450V a.c
9637791 *9V9080* -	**STELLA ANITA** **Stella Anita Shipping Pte Ltd** Stella Ship Management Pte Ltd *Singapore* *Singapore* MMSI: 566398000 Official number: 396602	**94,710** 59,527 180,355 T/cm 124.3	Class: CC	**2012-01 Dalian Shipbuilding Industry Co Ltd — Dalian LN (No 2 Yard)** Yd No: BC1800-35 Loa 295.00 (BB) Br ex 46.05 Dght 18.100 Lbp 285.00 Br md 46.00 Dpth 24.80 Welded, 1 dk	**(A21A2BC) Bulk Carrier** Grain: 201,953 Compartments: 9 Ho, ER 9 Ha: 7 (15.5 x 20.0)ER 2 (15.5 x 16.5)	**1 oil engine** driving 1 FP propeller Total Power: 18,660kW (25,370hp) 14.5kn MAN-B&W 6S70MC-C 1 x 2 Stroke 6 Cy. 700 x 2800 18660kW (25370bhp) Doosan Engine Co Ltd-South Korea AuxGen: 3 x 900kW 450V a.c
9604196 *9V9081* -	**STELLA ANNABEL** **Stella Annabel Shipping Pte Ltd** Stella Ship Management Pte Ltd SatCom: Inmarsat C 456394010 *Singapore* *Singapore* MMSI: 563940000 Official number: 396603	**94,710** 59,527 180,337 T/cm 124.3	Class: CC	**2011-03 Dalian Shipbuilding Industry Co Ltd — Dalian LN (No 2 Yard)** Yd No: BC1800-36 Loa 295.00 (BB) Br ex - Dght 18.100 Lbp 285.00 Br md 46.00 Dpth 24.80 Welded, 1 dk	**(A21A2BC) Bulk Carrier** Grain: 201,953 Compartments: 9 Ho, ER 9 Ha: 7 (15.5 x 20.0)ER 2 (15.5 x 16.5)	**1 oil engine** driving 1 FP propeller Total Power: 18,660kW (25,370hp) 14.5kn MAN-B&W 6S70MC-C 1 x 2 Stroke 6 Cy. 700 x 2800 18660kW (25370bhp) Doosan Engine Co Ltd-South Korea AuxGen: 3 x 900kW 450V a.c
9469948 *3EVX6* -	**STELLA ATLANTIC** **Acrux Star Ltd** SiSu-Shipping BV *Panama* *Panama* MMSI: 356305000 Official number: 44361PEXT	**3,079** 1,526 3,818	Class: GL	**2013-03 Western Marine Shipyard Ltd — Chittagong** Yd No: 055 Loa 88.60 Br ex 15.20 Dght 6.000 Lbp 80.95 Br md 15.06 Dpth 7.50 Welded, 1 dk	**(A31A2GX) General Cargo Ship** TEU 247 Cranes: 2x60t Ice Capable	**1 oil engine** reduction geared to sc. shaft driving 1 FP propeller Total Power: 3,060kW (4,160hp) 13.5kn Wartsila 9L26 1 x 4 Stroke 9 Cy. 260 x 320 3060kW (4160bhp) Wartsila Finland Oy-Finland Thrusters: 1 Tunnel thruster (f)
9534676 *CBST* -	**STELLA AUSTRALIS** **Transportes Maritimos Geo Australis SA** Navarino Administradora de Naves SA *Valparaiso* *Chile* MMSI: 725017800 Official number: 3259	**4,508** 1,508 485	Class: AB	**2010-12 Astilleros y Servicios Navales S.A. (ASENAV) — Valdivia** Yd No: 159 Loa 89.00 (BB) Br ex 14.90 Dght 3.450 Lbp 82.70 Br md 14.60 Dpth 4.70 Welded, 1 dk	**(A37A2PC) Passenger/Cruise** Passengers: cabins: 100; berths: 210	**2 oil engines** reduction geared to sc. shafts driving 2 Propellers Total Power: 2,088kW (2,838hp) 12.0kn Cummins KTA-50-M2 2 x Vee 4 Stroke 16 Cy. 159 x 159 each-1044kW (1419bhp) Cummins Engine Co Inc-USA AuxGen: 2 x 450kW a.c Fuel: 212.0 (d.f.)
9124225 *3FDB5* -	**STELLA BEAUTY** **Mar Cot SA** Asiana Lines Inc SatCom: Inmarsat C 435504910 *Panama* *Panama* MMSI: 355049000 Official number: 2208295D	**4,735** 2,239 6,298 T/cm 13.4	Class: NK	**1995-05 Sanyo Zosen K.K. — Onomichi** Yd No: 1066 Loa 96.70 (BB) Br ex - Dght 7.348 Lbp 85.78 Br md 17.40 Dpth 11.68 Welded, 1 dk	**(A31A2GX) General Cargo Ship** Grain: 10,590; Bale: 10,100 Derricks: 3x25t	**1 oil engine** driving 1 FP propeller Total Power: 2,427kW (3,300hp) 11.8kn Akasaka A41 1 x 4 Stroke 6 Cy. 410 x 800 2427kW (3300bhp) Akasaka Tekkosho KK (Akasaka DieselLtd)-Japan Fuel: 430.0 (r.f.)

IMO / Call sign	Name / Owner / Manager / Flag	Tonnage	Class	Builder / Dimensions	Type / Cargo	Machinery
9649299 *S6NY5* -	**STELLA BELINDA** **Stella Belinda Shipping Pte Ltd** Cara Shipping Pte Ltd *Singapore* *Singapore* MMSI: 563505000 Official number: 397873	**44,136** 26,760 81,700	Class: NV	**2013-09 Shanghai Jiangnan Changxing Shipbuilding Co Ltd — Shanghai** Yd No: H1280 Loa 228.97 (BB) Br ex - Dght 14.450 Lbp 225.50 Br md 32.27 Dpth 20.04 Welded, 1 dk	**(A21A2BC) Bulk Carrier** Grain: 97,000 Compartments: 7 Ho, ER 7 Ha: ER	**1 oil engine** driving 1 FP propeller Total Power: 14,280kW (19,415hp) 14.5kn MAN-B&W 6S60ME-C 1 x 2 Stroke 6 Cy. 600 x 2400 14280kW (19415bhp) CSSC MES Diesel Co Ltd-China AuxGen: 3 x a.c
9522661 *9V9084* -	**STELLA CHARLENE** **Stella Charlene Shipping Pte Ltd** Stella Ship Management Pte Ltd *Singapore* *Singapore* MMSI: 566516000 Official number: 396606	**91,374** 58,745 176,357 T/cm 120.6	Class: AB NV	**2012-07 Shanghai Waigaoqiao Shipbuilding Co Ltd — Shanghai** Yd No: 1205 Loa 291.95 (BB) Br ex 45.05 Dght 18.320 Lbp 282.00 Br md 45.00 Dpth 24.80 Welded, 1 dk	**(A21A2BC) Bulk Carrier** Grain: 194,179; Bale: 183,425 Compartments: 9 Ho, ER 9 Ha: ER	**1 oil engine** driving 1 FP propeller Total Power: 18,660kW (25,370hp) 14.0kn MAN-B&W 6S70MC-C 1 x 2 Stroke 6 Cy. 700 x 2800 18660kW (25370bhp) CSSC MES Diesel Co Ltd-China AuxGen: 3 x 900kW a.c Fuel: 380.0 (d.f.) 4780.0 (r.f.)
9522659 *9V9083* -	**STELLA CHERISE** *launched as* Rzs Glory *-2010* **Stella Cherise Shipping Pte Ltd** Stella Ship Management Pte Ltd SatCom: Inmarsat C 456566510 *Singapore* *Singapore* MMSI: 565665000 Official number: 396605	**91,407** 57,770 177,832 T/cm 120.6	Class: CC (BV) (HR)	**2010-11 Shanghai Waigaoqiao Shipbuilding Co Ltd — Shanghai** Yd No: 1181 Loa 291.95 (BB) Br ex - Dght 18.300 Lbp 282.00 Br md 45.00 Dpth 24.80 Welded, 1 dk	**(A21A2BC) Bulk Carrier** Grain: 194,486; Bale: 183,425 Compartments: 9 Ho, ER 9 Ha: ER	**1 oil engine** driving 1 FP propeller Total Power: 16,860kW (22,923hp) 14.0kn MAN-B&W 6S70MC 1 x 2 Stroke 6 Cy. 700 x 2674 16860kW (22923bhp) CSSC MES Diesel Co Ltd-China AuxGen: 3 x 900kW 60Hz a.c
9301249 *HOPL* -	**STELLA COSMOS** **Pana Star Line SA** Noma Shipping Co Ltd (Noma Kaiun KK) *Panama* *Panama* MMSI: 354424000 Official number: 3043505B	**6,255** 3,314 9,320	Class: NK	**2004-12 Bach Dang Shipyard — Haiphong** Yd No: 134 Loa 101.20 (BB) Br ex - Dght 9.214 Lbp 91.34 Br md 18.80 Dpth 13.00 Welded, 1 dk	**(A31A2GX) General Cargo Ship** Grain: 13,149; Bale: 12,371 2 Ha: (25.2 x 12.6) (23.1 x 12.6) Cranes: 2x30.7t; Derricks: 1x30t	**1 oil engine** driving 1 FP propeller Total Power: 2,890kW (3,929hp) 13.3kn Mitsubishi 6UEC33LSII 1 x 2 Stroke 6 Cy. 330 x 1050 2890kW (3929bhp) Akasaka Tekkosho KK (Akasaka DieselLtd)-Japan Thrusters: 1 Thwart. FP thruster (f) Fuel: 650.0
9649304 *9V9085* -	**STELLA DAWN** **Stella Dawn Shipping Pte Ltd** Cara Shipping Pte Ltd *Singapore* *Singapore* MMSI: 564150000 Official number: 396607	**44,138** 26,749 81,700	Class: NV	**2014-03 Shanghai Jiangnan Changxing Shipbuilding Co Ltd — Shanghai** Yd No: H1281 Loa 229.00 (BB) Br ex - Dght 14.470 Lbp 225.50 Br md 32.26 Dpth 20.05 Welded, 1 dk	**(A21A2BC) Bulk Carrier** Grain: 97,000	**1 oil engine** driving 1 FP propeller Total Power: 14,280kW (19,415hp) 14.5kn MAN-B&W 6S60ME-C 1 x 2 Stroke 6 Cy. 600 x 2400 14280kW (19415bhp) CSSC MES Diesel Co Ltd-China AuxGen: 3 x a.c
7128899 *IPNP* -	**STELLA DI LIPARI** *ex* Leone B. *-2004* *ex* Le Cellier *-1979* **Marnavi SpA** *Naples* *Italy* MMSI: 247450000 Official number: 705	**1,520** 543 2,137 T/cm 5.8	Class: RI (BV)	**1972-09 Cantiere Navale di Pietra Ligure — Pietra Ligure** Yd No: 14 Converted From: Water Tanker-2004 Loa 80.52 (BB) Br ex 12.30 Dght 5.240 Lbp 71.51 Br md 12.10 Dpth 5.62 Welded, 1 dk	**(A14A2LO) Water Tanker** Liq: 2,107 Compartments: 8 Wing Ta, ER 2 Cargo Pump (s): 2x300m³/hr	**1 oil engine** reduction geared to sc. shaft driving 1 FP propeller Total Power: 2,207kW (3,001hp) 13.5kn MaK 6M551AK 1 x 4 Stroke 6 Cy. 450 x 550 2207kW (3001bhp) MaK Maschinenbau GmbH-Kiel AuxGen: 2 x 270kW 380V 50Hz a.c, 1 x 115kW 380V 50Hz a.c
8744705 *J8Y3482* -	**STELLA FIERA** **Victory Energy Intl Inc** Ozgul Salim Cesur *Kingstown* *St Vincent & The Grenadines* MMSI: 375059000 Official number: 5951	**247** 74 -	Class: (AB)	**1998-12 Azimut-Benetti SpA — Viareggio** Yd No: BC001 Loa 34.95 Br ex - Dght 1.920 Lbp 28.80 Br md 7.20 Dpth 3.85 Bonded, 1 dk	**(X11A2YP) Yacht** Hull Material: Reinforced Plastic	**2 oil engines** reduction geared to sc. shafts driving 2 Propellers Caterpillar 3412TA 2 x Vee 4 Stroke 12 Cy. 137 x 152 Caterpillar Inc-USA
9522673 *S6NY4* -	**STELLA FLORA** **Stella Flora Shipping Pte Ltd** Stella Ship Management Pte Ltd *Singapore* *Singapore* MMSI: 566721000 Official number: 397872	**91,374** 58,745 176,292 T/cm 120.6	Class: CC (AB)	**2012-10 Shanghai Jiangnan Changxing Shipbuilding Co Ltd — Shanghai** Yd No: H1263 Loa 292.00 (BB) Br ex 45.05 Dght 18.300 Lbp 282.00 Br md 45.00 Dpth 24.80 Welded, 1 dk	**(A21A2BC) Bulk Carrier** Grain: 194,179; Bale: 183,425 Compartments: 9 Ho, ER 9 Ha: 7 (15.5 x 20.0)ER 2 (15.5 x 16.5)	**1 oil engine** driving 1 FP propeller Total Power: 16,860kW (22,923hp) 14.0kn MAN-B&W 6S70MC-C 1 x 2 Stroke 6 Cy. 700 x 2800 16860kW (22923bhp) CSSC MES Diesel Co Ltd-China AuxGen: 3 x 900kW 450V a.c
9474967 *9V7105* -	**STELLA GRACE** *ex* C Frontier *-2013* *completed as* DS Challenge *-2012* **Stella Grace Shipping Pte Ltd** Stella Ship Management Pte Ltd *Singapore* *Singapore* MMSI: 566884000 Official number: 398475	**92,050** 58,616 176,000 T/cm 120.8	Class: NV	**2012-06 Jiangsu Rongsheng Shipbuilding Co Ltd — Rugao JS** Yd No: 1084 Loa 291.80 Br ex 45.05 Dght 18.250 Lbp 282.20 Br md 45.00 Dpth 24.75 Welded, 1 dk	**(A21A2BC) Bulk Carrier** Grain: 198,000 Compartments: 9 Ho, ER 9 Ha: ER	**1 oil engine** driving 1 FP propeller Total Power: 16,860kW (22,923hp) 14.5kn MAN-B&W 6S70MC 1 x 2 Stroke 6 Cy. 700 x 2674 16860kW (22923bhp) AuxGen: 3 x a.c
9604029 *V7YX5* -	**STELLA JADE** *ex* Spice *-2012* **Stella Jade Shipping Co Ltd** Stella Ship Management Pte Ltd SatCom: Inmarsat C 453837852 *Majuro* *Marshall Islands* MMSI: 538004758 Official number: 4758	**91,971** 59,546 175,932 T/cm 120.8	Class: AB CC	**2012-11 Jinhai Heavy Industry Co Ltd — Daishan County ZJ** Yd No: J0040 Loa 291.80 (BB) Br ex - Dght 18.250 Lbp 282.20 Br md 45.00 Dpth 24.75 Welded, 1 dk	**(A21A2BC) Bulk Carrier** Grain: 198,243 Compartments: 9 Ho, ER 9 Ha: 7 (15.6 x 20.0)ER 2 (15.6 x 16.5)	**1 oil engine** driving 1 FP propeller Total Power: 16,860kW (22,923hp) 14.9kn MAN-B&W 6S70MC 1 x 2 Stroke 6 Cy. 700 x 2674 16860kW (22923bhp) Hitachi Zosen Corp-Japan AuxGen: 3 x 900kW 450V a.c Fuel: 390.0 (d.f.) 4830.0 (r.f.)
6910570 *UEIF* -	**STELLA KARINA** *ex* Svalbardi *-2001* *ex* Svalbakur *-1996* *ex* Stella Karina *-1973* **Magadanryba Co Ltd (OOO 'Magadanryba')** *Magadan* *Russia* MMSI: 273424560	**1,155** 347 493	Class: RS (NV)	**1969-07 Soviknes Verft AS — Sovik** Yd No: 71 Loa 61.75 Br ex 10.33 Dght 4.730 Lbp 54.36 Br md 10.20 Dpth 7.01 Welded, 2 dks	**(B11A2FS) Stern Trawler** Ins: 958 Compartments: 2 Ho, ER 2 Ha: (2.9 x 1.9) (3.5 x 2.9)ER Derricks: 2x1t Ice Capable	**1 oil engine** driving 1 CP propeller Total Power: 1,620kW (2,203hp) 10.0kn MWM TBRHS345AU 1 x 4 Stroke 8 Cy. 360 x 450 1620kW (2203bhp) Motoren Werke Mannheim AG (MWM)-West Germany AuxGen: 3 x 104kW 380V 50Hz a.c
9373591 *9VHP3* -	**STELLA KOSAN** **LKT Gas Carriers Pte Ltd** Lauritzen Kosan A/S *Singapore* *Singapore* MMSI: 565829000 Official number: 394015	**9,175** 2,753 10,316 T/cm 20.4	Class: BV (NV)	**2008-03 STX Shipbuilding Co Ltd — Busan** Yd No: 5021 Loa 120.36 (BB) Br ex 19.82 Dght 8.900 Lbp 112.44 Br md 19.80 Dpth 11.21 Welded, 1 dk	**(A11B2TG) LPG Tanker** Double Sides Entire Compartment Length Liq (Gas): 9,000 2 x Gas Tank (s); 2 independent (5% Ni.stl) cyl horizontal 3 Cargo Pump (s): 3x450m³/hr Manifold: Bow/CM: 56.5m	**1 oil engine** driving 1 FP propeller Total Power: 4,678kW (6,360hp) 16.0kn MAN-B&W 7S35MC 1 x 2 Stroke 7 Cy. 350 x 1400 4678kW (6360bhp) STX Engine Co Ltd-South Korea AuxGen: 3 x 1100kW 60Hz a.c Fuel: 150.0 (d.f.) 1008.0 (r.f.)
8801084 *PHUJ* -	**STELLA LYRA** **Carnisse BV** Tarbit Tankers BV SatCom: Inmarsat A 1300503 *Rotterdam* *Netherlands* MMSI: 244503000 Official number: 2632	**2,874** 884 3,848 T/cm 5.7	Class: BV	**1989-03 Tille Scheepsbouw B.V. — Kootstertille** Yd No: 266 Loa 95.75 Br ex - Dght 5.712 Lbp 89.95 Br md 14.50 Dpth 8.30 Welded, 1 dk	**(A12B2TR) Chemical/Products Tanker** Double Hull (13F) Liq: 3,803; Liq (Oil): 3,803; Asphalt: 3,803 Cargo Heating Coils Compartments: 6 Wing Ta, ER 3 Cargo Pump (s): 3x270m³/hr Manifold: Bow/CM: 42m	**1 oil engine** with flexible couplings & sr reverse geared to sc. shaft driving 1 FP propeller Total Power: 1,480kW (2,012hp) 12.5kn Wartsila 4R32D 1 x 4 Stroke 4 Cy. 320 x 350 1480kW (2012bhp) Wartsila Diesel Oy-Finland AuxGen: 4 x 130kW 380V 50Hz a.c Thrusters: 1 Thwart. FP thruster (f) Fuel: 151.0 (d.f.) 8.0pd
5113137 *HQBW7* -	**STELLA MARINA** *ex* Mazin *-1986* *ex* Mila *-1980* *ex* Silverfruit *-1976* *ex* Fedala *-1971* **Stella Marina Shipping & Transport Co** - *San Lorenzo* *Honduras* Official number: L-0321790	*486* 251 866	Class: (BV)	**1952-02 NV Werf Gusto v/h Fa A F Smulders — Schiedam** Yd No: 995 Loa 68.51 Br ex 9.78 Dght 3.455 Lbp 61.04 Br md 9.73 Dpth 5.80 Welded, 1 dk & S dk	**(A34A2GR) Refrigerated Cargo Ship** Ins: 1,235 2 Ha: 2 (7.7 x 4.5)ER Derricks: 4x2t; Winches: 4	**1 oil engine** driving 1 FP propeller Total Power: 883kW (1,201hp) 13.0kn Deutz SBV8M545 1 x 4 Stroke 8 Cy. 320 x 450 883kW (1201bhp) (new engine 1968) Kloeckner Humboldt Deutz AG-West Germany Fuel: 110.5 (d.f.)
8880602 *CUGS7* -	**STELLA MARIS** **Sociedade de Pesca da Atalaia Lda** - *Peniche* *Portugal* MMSI: 204218000 Official number: PE-2090-C	**240** 72 -	Class: RP	**1992 Estaleiros Navais do Seixal Lda. — Seixal** Loa 29.50 Br ex - Dght - Lbp - Br md 7.40 Dpth 3.50 Welded, 1 dk	**(B11B2FV) Fishing Vessel**	**1 oil engine** driving 1 FP propeller Total Power: 368kW (500hp) Caterpillar 3412TA 1 x Vee 4 Stroke 12 Cy. 137 x 152 368kW (500bhp) Caterpillar Inc-USA AuxGen: 2 x 102kW 380V 50Hz a.c

9317157 *3ELD7* -	**STELLA MARIS** **Turtle Marine Shipping Second SA** NEOM Maritime (Singapore) Pte Ltd SatCom: Inmarsat C 437292310 *Panama* *Panama* MMSI: 372923000 Official number: 3281807A	**30,046** 18,207 52,454 T/cm 55.5	Class: NK	**2007-06 Tsuneishi Holdings Corp Tsuneishi Shipbuilding Co — Fukuyama HS** Yd No: 1339 Loa 189.99 (BB) Br ex - Dght 12.022 Lbp 182.00 Br md 32.26 Dpth 17.00 Welded, 1 dk	**(A21A2BC) Bulk Carrier** Grain: 67,756; Bale: 65,601 Compartments: 5 Ho, ER 5 Ha: 4 (21.3 x 18.4)ER (20.4 x 18.4) Cranes: 4x30t	**1 oil engine** driving 1 FP propeller Total Power: 7,800kW (10,605hp) 14.5kn MAN-B&W 6S50MC 1 x 2 Stroke 6 Cy. 500 x 1910 7800kW (10605bhp) Mitsui Engineering & Shipbuilding CLtd-Japan Fuel: 2315.0
9297101 *PHCV* -	**STELLA MARIS** *ex* Scipion *-2005* **Baloeran BV** Tarbit Tankers BV *Dordrecht* *Netherlands* MMSI: 246315000 Official number: 44119	**4,064** 1,219 4,531 T/cm 13.3	Class: BV	**2004-04 Zhejiang Shipbuilding Co Ltd — Ningbo ZJ** Yd No: 02-105 Loa 106.00 Br ex 15.80 Dght 6.300 Lbp 98.50 Br md 15.80 Dpth 9.75 Welded, 1 dk	**(A12B2TR) Chemical/Products Tanker** Double Hull (13F) Liq: 4,220; Liq (Oil): 4,220; Asphalt: 4,220 Compartments: 8 Wing Ta, ER 2 Cargo Pump (s): 2x450m³/hr Manifold: Bow/CM: 52m Ice Capable	**1 oil engine** geared to sc. shaft driving 1 CP propeller Total Power: 2,880kW (3,916hp) 14.0kn MaK 6M32C 1 x 4 Stroke 6 Cy. 320 x 480 2880kW (3916bhp) Caterpillar Motoren GmbH & Co. KG-Germany AuxGen: 3 x 370kW 440V 60Hz a.c Fuel: 60.3 (d.f.) 330.6 (r.f.)
8913368 *YDA4397* -	**STELLA MARIS 101** *ex* Super Power *-2008* **PT Yala Kharisma Shipping** *Jakarta* *Indonesia*	*160* - 126	Class: KI (LR) ✠ Classed LR until 20/6/95	**1990-05 Fujian Fishing Vessel Shipyard — Fuzhou FJ** Yd No: 603-1 Loa 25.20 Br ex 8.22 Dght 2.400 Lbp 23.42 Br md 8.00 Dpth 3.00 Welded, 1 dk	**(B32A2ST) Tug**	**2 oil engines** with clutches & sr reverse geared to sc. shafts driving 2 FP propellers Total Power: 1,176kW (1,598hp) 10.0kn MWM TBD234V16 2 x Vee 4 Stroke 16 Cy. 128 x 140 each-588kW (799bhp) Motoren Werke Mannheim AG (MWM)-West Germany AuxGen: 2 x 40kW 380V 50Hz a.c
9649433 *YDA3066* -	**STELLA MARIS 103** **PT Yala Kharisma Shipping** - *Tanjungpinang* *Indonesia*	**189** 58 177	Class: GL	**2012-03 Forward Marine Enterprise Sdn Bhd — Sibu** Yd No: FM-83 Loa 25.97 Br ex - Dght 3.000 Lbp 23.89 Br md 8.02 Dpth 3.65 Welded, 1 dk	**(B32A2ST) Tug**	**2 oil engines** reduction geared to sc. shafts driving 2 FP propellers Total Power: 970kW (1,318hp) Yanmar 6AYM-WST 2 x 4 Stroke 6 Cy. 155 x 180 each-485kW (659bhp) Yanmar Diesel Engine Co Ltd-Japan
9248851 *EBXC* 3-SS-33-01	**STELLA MARIS BERRIA** **Bonifacio Aizpuru Isasti y otros CB** - *Getaria* *Spain* Official number: 3-3/2001	**160** 48 173		**2002-03 Astilleros de Pasaia SA — Pasaia** Yd No: 311 Loa 32.00 Br ex - Dght 3.300 Lbp 27.00 Br md 7.10 Dpth 3.80 Welded, 1 dk	**(B11B2FV) Fishing Vessel**	**1 oil engine** geared to sc. shaft driving 1 FP propeller Total Power: 368kW (500hp) GUASCOR 1 x 4 Stroke 368kW (500bhp) Gutierrez Ascunce Corp (GUASCOR)-Spain
7101372 *DUE2178* -	**STELLA MARIS EXPLORER** *ex* Stella I *-2003* *ex* Caddo *-1986* *ex* Cherokee *-1979* *ex* Chickasaw *-1979* **Stella Maris Explorer SA** Cruise Island Adventure Inc *Batangas* *Philippines* Official number: 040000127	**275** 157 -		**1966-01 Breaux Bay Craft, Inc. — Loreauville, La** Converted From: Crewboat-1986 Loa 37.01 Br ex 7.57 Dght 1.631 Lbp 32.80 Br md 7.28 Dpth 3.46 Welded, 1 dk	**(A37A2PC) Passenger/Cruise** Hull Material: Aluminium Alloy Passengers: cabins: 10; berths: 22	**2 oil engines** with clutches & sr geared to sc. shafts driving 2 FP propellers Total Power: 1,494kW (2,032hp) 14.5kn M.T.U. 8V396TB83 2 x Vee 4 Stroke 8 Cy. 165 x 185 each-747kW (1016bhp) (new engine 1986) MTU Friedrichshafen GmbH-Friedrichshafen
8709494 *LW9847* -	**STELLA MARIS I** *ex* Pegago Quinto *-1996* **Alimenpez SA** - SatCom: Inmarsat C 470106610 *Mar del Plata* *Argentina* MMSI: 701006043 Official number: 0926	*1,195* 458 1,271	Class: (GL)	**1988-10 Ast. de Huelva S.A. — Huelva** Yd No: 353 Loa 69.40 (BB) Br ex - Dght 4.801 Lbp 60.00 Br md 12.00 Dpth 7.30 Welded	**(B11A2FG) Factory Stern Trawler** Ins: 1,660 Ice Capable	**1 oil engine** with flexible couplings & sr gearedto sc. shaft driving 1 CP propeller Total Power: 1,450kW (1,971hp) 11.5kn Stork-Werkspoor 6SW280 1 x 4 Stroke 6 Cy. 280 x 300 1450kW (1971bhp) Stork Werkspoor Diesel BV-Netherlands AuxGen: 1 x 600kW 220/380V a.c, 2 x 400kW 220/380V a.c, 1 x 200kW 220/380V a.c
7413907 *E5U2232* -	**STELLA MARIS II** *ex* Blue Bill *-2013* *ex* Rosaedith *-2009* *ex* Atlantic Sun *-1995* *ex* Okko Bosma *-1978* **Transportes Maritimos Lamol Inc** Interforce Inc *Avatiu* *Cook Islands* MMSI: 518282000 Official number: 1316	**1,939** 1,087 3,022	Class: (LR) (AB) ✠ Classed LR until 6/9/01	**1976-06 Scheepswerf Gebr. Suurmeijer B.V. — Foxhol** Yd No: 236 Loa 83.44 Br ex 14.30 Dght 5.090 Lbp 74.90 Br md 14.00 Dpth 6.20 Welded, 1 dk	**(A31A2GX) General Cargo Ship** Grain: 3,823; Bale: 3,540 Compartments: 1 Ho, ER 2 Ha: (25.8 x 10.5) (10.2 x 10.5)ER Cranes: 2x10t,1x5t; Derricks: 3x5t Ice Capable	**1 oil engine** sr geared to sc. shaft driving 1 FP propeller Total Power: 1,760kW (2,393hp) 12.5kn MaK 8M452AK 1 x 4 Stroke 8 Cy. 320 x 450 1760kW (2393bhp) MaK Maschinenbau GmbH-Kiel AuxGen: 4 x 80kW 380/220V 50Hz a.c Thrusters: 1 Thwart. FP thruster (f) Fuel: 331.0 (d.f.)
9069918 *EI8772* DA.57	**STELLA NOVA** **Supreme Fishing Co Ltd** - *Drogheda* *Irish Republic* MMSI: 250000626 Official number: 403983	**190** - -	Class: (BV)	**2006-08 Vestvaerftet ApS — Hvide Sande** Yd No: 259 Loa 23.50 Br ex - Dght 4.200 Lbp 19.80 Br md 7.20 Dpth 6.20 Welded, 1 dk	**(B11A2FS) Stern Trawler** Ins: 118	**1 oil engine** geared to sc. shaft driving 1 Propeller Total Power: 441kW (600hp) Caterpillar 3508 1 x Vee 4 Stroke 8 Cy. 170 x 190 441kW (600bhp) Caterpillar Inc-USA
8516225 *OXHK* AS 464	**STELLA NOVA VIII** *ex* Stella Nova Av Fotoe *-2010* *ex* Ganthi *-2008* **Fiskeriselskabet Stella Nova ApS** - *Grenaa* *Denmark* MMSI: 219168000 Official number: H1701	**535** 160 -		**1987-08 Johs Kristensen Skibsbyggeri A/S — Hvide Sande** Yd No: 186 Lengthened-2010 Lengthened Loa 47.00 (BB) Br ex 9.68 Dght - Lbp 34.67 Br md 9.61 Dpth 4.40 Welded, 2 dks	**(B11A2FS) Stern Trawler** Ins: 420	**1 oil engine** with clutches, flexible couplings & sr geared to sc. shaft driving 1 CP propeller Total Power: 1,471kW (2,000hp) Nohab F38V 1 x Vee 4 Stroke 8 Cy. 250 x 300 1471kW (2000bhp) Wartsila Diesel AB-Sweden Thrusters: 1 Thwart. FP thruster (f); 1 Tunnel thruster (a)
9265251 *PHGX* -	**STELLA ORION** *ex* Etoile Lava *-2006* **Boerenzij BV** Tarbit Tankers BV *Dordrecht* *Netherlands* MMSI: 246553000 Official number: 49580	**4,074** 1,223 4,999 T/cm 14.2	Class: GL	**2004-02 Rousse Shipyard JSC — Rousse** Yd No: 702 Loa 104.60 (BB) Br ex - Dght 6.250 Lbp 96.60 Br md 15.20 Dpth 9.30 Welded, 1 dk	**(A12B2TR) Chemical/Products Tanker** Double Hull (13F) Liq: 4,200; Liq (Oil): 4,200; Asphalt: 4,200 Cargo Heating Coils Compartments: 8 Wing Ta, ER 2 Cargo Pump (s): 2x370m³/hr Ice Capable	**1 oil engine** geared to sc. shaft driving 1 CP propeller Total Power: 2,880kW (3,916hp) 13.0kn MaK 6M32C 1 x 4 Stroke 6 Cy. 320 x 480 2880kW (3916bhp) Caterpillar Motoren GmbH & Co. KG-Germany AuxGen: 3 x 400kW a.c, 1 x 440kW a.c Thrusters: 1 Tunnel thruster (f)
8117419 *PI4943* -	**STELLA POLARIS** **F Bult** - *Delfzijl* *Netherlands* MMSI: 244153421 Official number: 1862	**107** 32 -		**1981-04 Jachtbouw en Constructiebedrijf Marcon — Hoogezand** Yd No: 3/98 Converted From: Fishing Vessel Lengthened-1987 Loa 24.95 Br ex - Dght 2.290 Lbp 22.46 Br md 5.81 Dpth 3.05 Welded, 1 dk	**(X11A2YP) Yacht**	**1 oil engine** geared to sc. shaft driving 1 FP propeller Total Power: 441kW (600hp) Caterpillar 3412B 1 x Vee 4 Stroke 12 Cy. 137 x 152 441kW (600bhp) (new engine 1998) Caterpillar Inc-USA
9107605 *DMJZ* SH 3	**STELLA POLARIS** **John Much** - *Heiligenhafen* *Germany* MMSI: 218367000 Official number: 52512	**149** 44 196	Class: (GL)	**1995-05 R. Dunston (Hessle) Ltd. — Hessle** (Hull) Yd No: H1008 **1995-05 Scheepswerf Visser B.V. — Den Helder** Yd No: 141 Loa 24.00 Br ex - Dght - Lbp - Br md 6.70 Dpth 4.20 Welded, 1 dk	**(B11A2FT) Trawler**	**1 oil engine** reverse reduction geared to sc. shaft driving 1 FP propeller Total Power: 564kW (767hp) 9.0kn MWM TBD604BL6 1 x 4 Stroke 6 Cy. 170 x 195 564kW (767bhp) Motoren Werke Mannheim AG (MWM)-Mannheim AuxGen: 2 x 116kW a.c
9187057 *PEBD* -	**STELLA POLARIS** **Azollo BV** Tarbit Tankers BV SatCom: Inmarsat C 424591110 *Rotterdam* *Netherlands* MMSI: 245911000 Official number: 35350	**5,396** 1,668 8,297 T/cm 17.8	Class: BV	**1999-04 Schelde Scheepsnieuwbouw B.V. — Vlissingen** Yd No: 389 Loa 117.18 (BB) Br ex 17.12 Dght 7.550 Lbp 111.73 Br md 17.00 Dpth 10.50 Welded, 1 dk	**(A12B2TR) Chemical/Products Tanker** Double Hull (13F) Liq: 6,390; Liq (Oil): 6,390; Asphalt: 6,390 Cargo Heating Coils Compartments: 4 Ta, 4 Wing Ta, ER 8 Cargo Pump (s): 8x600m³/hr Manifold: Bow/CM: 53m Ice Capable	**1 oil engine** with flexible couplings & sr gearedto sc. shaft driving 1 CP propeller Total Power: 3,840kW (5,221hp) 14.0kn MaK 8M32 1 x 4 Stroke 8 Cy. 320 x 480 3840kW (5221bhp) MaK Motoren GmbH & Co. KG-Kiel AuxGen: 2 x 490kW 400V 50Hz a.c, 1 x 360kW 400V 50Hz a.c Thrusters: 1 Thwart. FP thruster (f) Fuel: 70.0 (d.f.) (Heating Coils) 420.0 (r.f.) 17.0pd
8700802 *PHSU* UK 22	**STELLA POLARIS** *ex* Innis Kerragh *-2005* *ex* Marliona *-2004* *ex* Du Bellay *-1995* *ex* Garlodic *-1993* **Adriaantje Holding BV** - SatCom: Inmarsat C 424530810 *Urk* *Netherlands* MMSI: 245308000 Official number: 47625	**224** 68 -	Class: (BV)	**1986-06 Chantiers Piriou — Concarneau** Yd No: 2980 Loa 29.80 Br ex - Dght 3.631 Lbp 25.68 Br md 7.90 Dpth 4.15 Welded, 1 dk	**(B11A2FS) Stern Trawler** Ins: 140	**1 oil engine** geared to sc. shaft driving 1 CP propeller Total Power: 736kW (1,001hp) 11.5kn Deutz SBV6M628 1 x 4 Stroke 6 Cy. 240 x 280 736kW (1001bhp) Kloeckner Humboldt Deutz AG-West Germany AuxGen: 1 x 51kW 220/380V 50Hz a.c, 1 x 20kW 220/380V 50Hz a.c Fuel: 45.7

9265249 *PHKQ* -	**STELLA VIRGO** *ex Horizon Lava -2007* **Cortusa BV** Tarbit Tankers BV SatCom: Inmarsat Mini-M 761133723 *Dordrecht* *Netherlands* MMSI: 244267000 Official number: 50710	**4,074** 1,223 4,999 T/cm 14.2	Class: GL	**2003-11 Rousse Shipyard JSC — Rousse** Yd No: 701 Loa 104.60 (BB) Br ex - Dght 6.250 Lbp 97.00 Br md 15.20 Dpth 9.30 Welded, 1 dk	**(A12B2TR) Chemical/Products Tanker** Double Hull (13F) Liq: 4,173; Liq (Oil): 4,173; Asphalt: 4,173 Cargo Heating Coils Compartments: 8 Wing Ta, ER 2 Cargo Pump (s): 2x370m³/hr Manifold: Bow/CM: 54.6m Ice Capable	**1 oil engine** geared to sc. shaft driving 1 CP propeller Total Power: 2,841kW (3,863hp) 13.0kn MaK 6M32C 1 x 4 Stroke 6 Cy. 320 x 480 2841kW (3863bhp) Caterpillar Motoren GmbH & Co. KG-Germany AuxGen: 3 x 400kW 380/220V 50Hz a.c, 1 x 400kW 380/220V 50Hz a.c Thrusters: 1 Thwart. CP thruster (f) Fuel: 42.0 (d.f.) 314.0 (r.f.)
9136113 *PHHQ* -	**STELLA WEGA** **Ciconia BV** Tarbit Tankers BV SatCom: Inmarsat B 324528410 *Rotterdam* *Netherlands* MMSI: 245284000 Official number: 30295	**3,983** 1,194 4,250 T/cm 13.3	Class: BV	**1996-09 Scheepsw. en Mfbk."De Biesbosch-Dordrecht" B.V. — Dordrecht** Yd No: 869 Loa 105.60 Br ex 15.92 Dght 6.000 Lbp 98.50 Br md 15.80 Dpth 9.40 Welded, 1 dk	**(A12B2TR) Chemical/Products Tanker** Double Hull (13F) Liq: 4,300; Liq (Oil): 4,300; Asphalt: 4,300 Cargo Heating Coils Compartments: 8 Wing Ta, ER 2 Cargo Pump (s): 2x450m³/hr Manifold: Bow/CM: 51m Ice Capable	**1 oil engine** with clutches, flexible couplings & sr geared to sc. shaft driving 1 CP propeller Total Power: 3,520kW (4,786hp) 15.0kn MaK 8M32 1 x 4 Stroke 8 Cy. 320 x 480 3520kW (4786bhp) Krupp MaK Maschinenbau GmbH-Kiel AuxGen: 1 x 350kW 440V 60Hz a.c, 3 x 300kW 440V 60Hz a.c Thrusters: 1 Thwart. FP thruster (f) Fuel: 60.0 (d.f.) (Heating Coils) 300.0 (r.f.) 14.0pd
8332904 *IUKX* -	**STELLA ZENNARO** **Bruno, Felice, Mauro & Renzo Zennaro SDF** - *Chioggia* *Italy* Official number: 3015	**150** 50 -	Class: (RI)	**1981 Cooperativa Metallurgica Ing G Tommasi Srl — Ancona** Yd No: 41 Loa 30.18 Br ex 6.74 Dght 2.920 Lbp 24.01 Br md 6.71 Dpth 3.41 Welded, 1 dk	**(B11B2FV) Fishing Vessel**	**1 oil engine** geared to sc. shaft driving 1 FP propeller Total Power: 588kW (799hp) Deutz SBA6M528 1 x 4 Stroke 6 Cy. 220 x 280 588kW (799bhp) Kloeckner Humboldt Deutz AG-West Germany
9375941 *H9QL* -	**STELLAE MARE** *ex Star Of Rbd -2012* **Sun Cordia Marine SA** MK Shipmanagement (HK) Co Ltd *Panama* *Panama* MMSI: 370736000 Official number: 4013509A	**44,251** 27,095 83,617 T/cm 71.0	Class: NK (AB)	**2008-11 Sanoyas Hishino Meisho Corp — Kurashiki OY** Yd No: 1273 Loa 229.00 (BB) Br ex - Dght 14.551 Lbp 223.00 Br md 32.24 Dpth 20.20 Welded, 1 dk	**(A21A2BC) Bulk Carrier** Grain: 96,110 Compartments: 7 Ho, ER 7 Ha: ER	**1 oil engine** driving 1 FP propeller Total Power: 11,640kW (15,826hp) 14.0kn MAN-B&W 6S60MC-C 1 x 2 Stroke 6 Cy. 600 x 2400 11640kW (15826bhp) Kawasaki Heavy Industries Ltd-Japan AuxGen: 3 x 400kW a.c Fuel: 221.0 (d.f.) 2513.0 (r.f.)
9614751 *FIFV* -	**STELLAMARIS** **Dragages Transports & Travaux Maritimes SAS (DTM)** *La Rochelle* *France* MMSI: 228032800	**3,664** 1,099 4,720	Class: BV	**2012-12 Astilleros de Murueta S.A. — Gernika-Lumo** Yd No: 292 Loa 102.73 Br ex - Dght 6.070 Lbp 95.90 Br md 15.50 Dpth 7.70 Welded, 1 dk	**(A24D2BA) Aggregates Carrier**	**1 oil engine** driving 1 Propeller Total Power: 4,000kW (5,438hp) Wartsila 8L32 1 x 4 Stroke 8 Cy. 320 x 400 4000kW (5438bhp) Wartsila Finland Oy-Finland
9085730 *PHQW* -	**STELLANOVA** **Scheepvaartmaatschappij Stella Vof** Jumbo Shipping Co SA SatCom: Inmarsat C 424578120 *Rotterdam* *Netherlands* MMSI: 245781000 Official number: 28863	**4,962** 1,488 5,204 T/cm 14.8	Class: LR ✠ **100A1** SS 01/2011 strengthened for heavy cargoes CG ✠ **LMC** **UMS** Eq.Ltr: W†; Cable: 497.5/50.0 U2	**1996-01 YVC Ysselwerf B.V. — Capelle a/d IJssel** Yd No: 266 Loa 95.60 (BB) Br ex 18.37 Dght 6.810 Lbp 87.55 Br md 17.75 Dpth 11.32 Welded, 1 dk	**(A38C2GH) Heavy Load Carrier** Compartments: 1 Ho, ER, 1 Tw Dk 1 Ha: (66.1 x 14.0)ER Cranes: 1x250t; Derricks: 1x250t	**1 oil engine** reduction geared to sc. shaft driving 1 CP propeller Total Power: 2,701kW (3,672hp) 14.0kn MaK 6M32 1 x 4 Stroke 6 Cy. 320 x 480 2701kW (3672bhp) Krupp MaK Maschinenbau GmbH-Kiel AuxGen: 1 x 470kW 440V 60Hz a.c, 2 x 650kW 440V 60Hz a.c Boilers: TOH (o.f.) 10.2kgf/cm² (10.0bar), TOH (ex.g.) 10.2kgf/cm² (10.0bar) Thrusters: 1 Thwart. FP thruster (f)
8912326 *PHEA*	**STELLAPRIMA** **Stella Navigation NV** Kahn Scheepvaart BV (Kahn Shipping Ltd) *Willemstad* *Netherlands* MMSI: 246460000 Official number: 18704	**6,902** 2,070 7,572 T/cm 18.1	Class: LR ✠ **100A1** SS 09/2011 strengthened for heavy cargoes, CG ✠ **LMC** **UMS** Eq.Ltr: X; Cable: 495.0/50.0 U2	**1991-09 YVC Ysselwerf B.V. — Capelle a/d IJssel** Yd No: 252 Loa 100.32 (BB) Br ex 20.98 Dght 7.420 Lbp 93.34 Br md 20.50 Dpth 13.32 Welded, 1 dk & removable "tween dk	**(A38C2GH) Heavy Load Carrier** Bale: 11,000 TEU 370 C.Ho 204/20' C.Dk 166/20' Compartments: 1 Ho, ER, 1 Tw Dk 1 Ha: (71.5 x 15.2)ER Cranes: 1x400t,1x250t	**1 oil engine** with flexible couplings & sr geared to sc. shaft driving 1 CP propeller Total Power: 3,300kW (4,487hp) 13.5kn MaK 9M453C 1 x 4 Stroke 9 Cy. 320 x 420 3300kW (4487bhp) Krupp MaK Maschinenbau GmbH-Kiel AuxGen: 1 x 436kW 440V 60Hz a.c, 2 x 436kW 440V 60Hz a.c Boilers: TOH (o.f.) 10.2kgf/cm² (10.0bar), TOH (ex.g.) 10.2kgf/cm² (10.0bar) Fuel: 110.0 (d.f.) 614.0 (r.f.) 14.0pd
7904138 *XUGS5* -	**STELLAR** *ex Swan -2009 ex Mir -2005 ex Daiyu -1997* *ex Daiyu Maru No. 28 -1994* **Marineiro Co Ltd** - *Phnom Penh* *Cambodia* Official number: 1379088	**394** 148 302	Class: IS (RS)	**1979-06 Sanuki Shipbuilding & Iron Works Co Ltd — Mitoyo KG** Yd No: 1027 Loa 46.80 Br ex - Dght 2.850 Lbp 40.01 Br md 7.80 Dpth 3.18 Welded, 1 dk	**(B11B2FV) Fishing Vessel**	**1 oil engine** driving 1 FP propeller Total Power: 662kW (900hp) 10.0kn Hanshin 6LU26G 1 x 4 Stroke 6 Cy. 260 x 440 662kW (900bhp) Hanshin Nainenki Kogyo-Japan AuxGen: 1 x 320kW a.c, 1 x 160kW a.c Fuel: 200.0
9007805 *DSPH9*	**STELLAR COSMO** *ex Suzuka -2007* **KDB Capital Corp** Polaris Shipping Co Ltd SatCom: Inmarsat C 444001110 *Jeju* *South Korea* MMSI: 441011000 Official number: JJR-079556	**148,740** 79,952 261,310	Class: KR (NK)	**1992-10 Kawasaki Heavy Industries Ltd — Sakaide KG** Yd No: 1426 Converted From: Crude Oil Tanker-2008 Loa 338.00 (BB) Br ex 58.36 Dght 19.721 Lbp 322.00 Br md 58.00 Dpth 28.90 Welded, 1 dk	**(A21B2BO) Ore Carrier** Grain: 134,579 Compartments: 10 Ho, ER 10 Ha: 2 (20.4 x 15.4)4 (12.2 x 15.4)2 (23.2 x 15.4)ER 2 (18.3 x 12.0)	**1 oil engine** driving 1 FP propeller Total Power: 25,480kW (34,643hp) 16.3kn MAN-B&W 7S80MC 1 x 2 Stroke 7 Cy. 800 x 3056 25480kW (34643bhp) Kawasaki Heavy Industries Ltd-Japan AuxGen: 1 x 1040kW 450V 60Hz a.c, 2 x 890kW 450V 60Hz a.c Fuel: 200.0 (d.f.) (Part Heating Coils) 5760.0 (r.f.)
9145671 *3FIQ6* -	**STELLAR CUPID** *ex Crimson Galaxy -2005* **Catalina Shipping SA** Shoei Kisen Kaisha Ltd *Panama* *Panama* MMSI: 356570000 Official number: 2306396D	**30,146** 11,850 34,021	Class: NK	**1996-07 Imabari Shipbuilding Co Ltd — Marugame KG (Marugame Shipyard)** Yd No: 1246 Loa 175.17 (BB) Br ex 31.03 Dght 10.115 Lbp 164.00 Br md 31.00 Dpth 18.40 Welded, 1 dk	**(A24B2BW) Wood Chips Carrier** Grain: 74,152 Compartments: 4 Ho, ER 4 Ha: 3 (17.6 x 17.6) (14.4 x 17.6)ER Cranes: 2x14.5t	**1 oil engine** driving 1 FP propeller Total Power: 6,032kW (8,201hp) 14.0kn Mitsubishi 6UEC52LA 1 x 2 Stroke 6 Cy. 520 x 1600 6032kW (8201bhp) Akasaka Tekkosho KK (Akasaka DieselLtd)-Japan Fuel: 1340.0 (r.f.)
9038725 *V7RD9*	**STELLAR DAISY** *ex Sunrise -2008 ex Sunrise III -2006* **Daisy Maritime Ltd** Polaris Shipping Co Ltd SatCom: Inmarsat C 453800660 *Majuro* *Marshall Islands* MMSI: 538003486 Official number: 3486	**148,431** 44,530 266,141 T/cm 164.8	Class: KR (NK)	**1993-07 Mitsubishi Heavy Industries Ltd. — Nagasaki** Yd No: 2072 Converted From: Crude Oil Tanker-2008 Loa 321.95 (BB) Br ex - Dght 20.326 Lbp 310.00 Br md 58.00 Dpth 29.50 Welded, 1 dk	**(A21B2BO) Ore Carrier** Grain: 142,418 Compartments: 5 Ho, ER 10 Ha: 2 (17.9 x 15.0)7 (14.9 x 15.0)ER (14.9 x 13.0)	**1 oil engine** driving 1 FP propeller Total Power: 21,928kW (29,813hp) 16.0kn Mitsubishi 9UEC75LSII 1 x 2 Stroke 9 Cy. 750 x 2800 21928kW (29813bhp) Mitsubishi Heavy Industries Ltd-Japan AuxGen: 2 x 1100kW 450V 60Hz a.c, 1 x 300kW 440V 60Hz a.c, 1 x 260kW 450V 60Hz a.c Fuel: 366.5 (d.f.) (Heating Coils) 4805.8 (r.f.) 81.4pd
9044229 *DSPS2* -	**STELLAR EAGLE** *ex Sylt -2008* **KDB Capital Corp** Polaris Shipping Co Ltd SatCom: Inmarsat C 444000268 *Jeju* *South Korea* MMSI: 441433000 Official number: JJR-088818	**154,759** 46,427 278,258	Class: KR (LR) ✠ Classed LR until 5/12/07	**1993-09 Daewoo Shipbuilding & Heavy Machinery Ltd — Geoje** Yd No: 5075 Converted From: Crude Oil Tanker-2009 Loa 327.50 (BB) Br ex 57.24 Dght 20.774 Lbp 315.00 Br md 57.20 Dpth 30.40 Welded, 1 dk	**(A21B2BO) Ore Carrier** Grain: 155,000 Compartments: 6 Ho, ER 9 Ha: 3 (19.4 x 15.3)5 (14.0 x 15.3)ER (16.7 x 11.9)	**1 oil engine** driving 1 FP propeller Total Power: 23,461kW (31,898hp) 15.5kn B&W 7S80MC 1 x 2 Stroke 7 Cy. 800 x 3056 23461kW (31898bhp) Korea Heavy Industries & ConstrCo Ltd (HANJUNG)-South Korea AuxGen: 3 x 940kW 440V 60Hz a.c Boilers: 2 e (ex.g.) 24.0kgf/cm² (23.5bar), 2 AuxB (o.f.) 18.4kgf/cm² (18.0bar) Fuel: 437.3 (d.f.) 5316.0 (r.f.)
9514004 *V7RJ6* -	**STELLAR EAGLE** **Stellar Eagle Shipping LLC** Eagle Shipping International (USA) LLC *Majuro* *Marshall Islands* MMSI: 538003521 Official number: 3521	**31,532** 18,765 55,989 T/cm 56.9	Class: NK	**2009-03 IHI Marine United Inc — Yokohama KN** Yd No: 3283 Loa 189.96 (BB) Br ex - Dght 12.735 Lbp 185.00 Br md 32.26 Dpth 18.10 Welded, 1 dk	**(A21A2BC) Bulk Carrier** Grain: 72,062; Bale: 67,062 Compartments: 5 Ho, ER 5 Ha: 4 (20.9 x 18.6)ER (14.6 x 18.6) Cranes: 4x30t	**1 oil engine** driving 1 FP propeller Total Power: 8,890kW (12,087hp) 14.5kn Wartsila 6RT-flex50 1 x 2 Stroke 6 Cy. 500 x 2050 8890kW (12087bhp) Diesel United Ltd.-Aioi AuxGen: 3 x a.c Fuel: 2400.0
8915249 *3EGZ8* -	**STELLAR EXPRESS** *ex Stellar Mermaid -2010* *ex Regno Marinus -2008* **Stellar Express SA** MSI Ship Management Pte Ltd SatCom: Inmarsat C 435378711 *Panama* *Panama* MMSI: 353787000 Official number: 1916990E	**40,169** 13,245 48,821	Class: NK	**1990-08 Oshima Shipbuilding Co Ltd — Saikai NS** Yd No: 10128 Loa 209.01 (BB) Br ex - Dght 10.825 Lbp 200.00 Br md 32.20 Dpth 22.10 Welded, 1 dk	**(A24B2BW) Wood Chips Carrier** Grain: 102,155; Bale: 100,325 Compartments: 6 Ho, ER 6 Ha: (12.8 x 18.7)4 (16.0 x 18.7) (16.0 x 14.0)ER Cranes: 3x14.5t	**1 oil engine** driving 1 FP propeller Total Power: 6,326kW (8,601hp) 14.5kn Sulzer 6RTA52 1 x 2 Stroke 6 Cy. 520 x 1800 6326kW (8601bhp) Diesel United Ltd.-Aioi AuxGen: 4 x 598kW a.c Fuel: 1900.0 (r.f.)

IMO / Call sign	Name / Owner / Manager / Flag	Tonnage	Class	Builder / Dimensions	Type / Cargo	Machinery
8908284 *3EWP9* -	**STELLAR FAIR** *ex* Titan Pisces *-2008* *ex* Vasant J Sheth *-2005* *ex* Tsukubasan *-2003* *ex* Tsukubasan Maru *-2000* **SFA Maritime Inc** Polaris Shipping Co Ltd SatCom: Inmarsat C 435436112 *Panama* *Panama* MMSI: 354361000 Official number: 4167610	**147,817** 44,345 266,629	Class: KR (LR) (NK) (IR) Classed LR until 10/9/08	**1990-05 Sasebo Heavy Industries Co. Ltd. — Sasebo Yard, Sasebo** Yd No: 375 Converted From: Crude Oil Tanker-2009 Loa 324.00 (BB) Br ex - Dght 20.233 Lbp 315.00 Br md 56.00 Dpth 29.40 Welded, 1 dk	**(A21B2BO) Ore Carrier** Grain: 138,384 Compartments: 6 Ho, ER 10 Ha: ER	**1 oil engine** driving 1 FP propeller Total Power: 21,770kW (29,598hp) 15.0kn B&W 7L90MC 1 x 2 Stroke 7 Cy. 900 x 2916 21770kW (29598bhp) Mitsui Engineering & Shipbuilding CLtd-Japan AuxGen: 4 x 740kW 450V 60Hz a.c, 1 x 400kW 450V 60Hz a.c Boilers: AuxB (ex.g.) 24.0kgf/cm² (23.5bar), AuxB (o.f.) 18.0kgf/cm² (17.7bar)
9038438 *E5U2727* -	**STELLAR GALAXY** *ex* Pacific Amber *-2010* *ex* Able Dolphin *-2005* *ex* Cosmo Delphinus *-2001* **LTSF PR 2 Inc** Polaris Shipping Co Ltd *Avatiu* *Cook Islands* MMSI: 518780000 Official number: 1816	**147,697** 44,309 263,130 T/cm 164.8	Class: KR (NK)	**1993-03 Mitsubishi Heavy Industries Ltd. — Nagasaki** Yd No: 2071 Converted From: Crude Oil Tanker-2010 Loa 321.95 (BB) Br ex 58.05 Dght 20.230 Lbp 311.00 Br md 58.00 Dpth 29.50 Welded, 1 dk	**(A21B2BO) Ore Carrier** Grain: 142,418 Compartments: 6 Ho, ER 10 Ha: ER 10 (14.9 x 14.2)	**1 oil engine** driving 1 Contra-rotating propeller Total Power: 20,596kW (28,002hp) 15.3kn Mitsubishi 7UEC75LSII 1 x 2 Stroke 7 Cy. 750 x 2800 20596kW (28002bhp) Mitsubishi Heavy Industries Ltd-Japan AuxGen: 2 x 1000kW 450V 60Hz a.c, 1 x 900kW 450V 60Hz a.c, 1 x 220kW 450V 60Hz a.c Fuel: 334.0 (d.f.) (Part Heating Coils) 4795.0 (r.f.) 68.3pd
9060326 *E5U2718* -	**STELLAR HERMES** *ex* Hama Star *-2010* *ex* Hamal Star *-2010* **LTSF PR 3 Inc** Polaris Shipping Co Ltd *Avatiu* *Cook Islands* MMSI: 518771000 Official number: 1807	**160,890** 55,386 295,520 T/cm 167.5	Class: KR (LR) ✠ Classed LR until 30/11/10	**1994-03 Hyundai Heavy Industries Co Ltd — Ulsan** Yd No: 842 Converted From: Crude Oil Tanker-2011 Loa 332.09 (BB) Br ex 58.05 Dght 22.200 Lbp 318.00 Br md 58.00 Dpth 31.50 Welded, 1 dk	**(A21B2BO) Ore Carrier** Grain: 163,250 Compartments: 5 Ho, ER 10 Ha: ER	**1 oil engine** driving 1 FP propeller Total Power: 23,477kW (31,919hp) 14.6kn B&W 7S80MC 1 x 2 Stroke 7 Cy. 800 x 3056 23477kW (31919bhp) Hyundai Heavy Industries Co Ltd-South Korea AuxGen: 3 x 950kW 450V 60Hz a.c Boilers: 2 AuxB (o.f.) 18.1kgf/cm² (17.8bar), e (ex.g.) 22.0kgf/cm² (21.6bar) Fuel: 453.5 (d.f.) (Heating Coils) 7500.0 (r.f.) 85.7pd
9130602 *3FZN5* -	**STELLAR HOPE** **Erica Navigation SA** Toyo Sangyo Co Ltd (Toyo Sangyo KK) *Panama* *Panama* MMSI: 356125000 Official number: 2295796CH	**77,240** 48,830 151,244 T/cm 106.0	Class: NK	**1996-03 Nippon Kokan KK (NKK Corp) — Tsu ME** Yd No: 155 Loa 273.00 (BB) Br ex - Dght 17.419 Lbp 260.00 Br md 43.00 Dpth 23.90 Welded, 1 dk	**(A21A2BC) Bulk Carrier** Grain: 167,769 Compartments: 9 Ho, ER 9 Ha: (14.2 x 18.4)7 (14.2 x 19.8) (14.2 x 14.0)ER	**1 oil engine** driving 1 FP propeller Total Power: 15,403kW (20,942hp) 14.9kn B&W 6S70MC 1 x 2 Stroke 6 Cy. 700 x 2674 15403kW (20942bhp) Mitsui Engineering & Shipbuilding CLtd-Japan AuxGen: 2 x 560kW a.c, 1 x 480kW a.c Fuel: 3682.0 (r.f.) 52.2pd
9083093 *3FSH5* -	**STELLAR IRIS** *ex* Hyundai Star *-2011* **LTSF PR 4 Inc** Polaris Shipping Co Ltd SatCom: Inmarsat C 437190512 *Panama* *Panama* MMSI: 371905000 Official number: 4313711	**154,786** 52,332 288,272	Class: KR (LR) (AB) ✠ Classed LR until 29/10/02	**1995-12 Hyundai Heavy Industries Co Ltd — Ulsan** Yd No: 907 Converted From: Crude Oil Tanker-2011 Loa 330.27 (BB) Br ex 58.05 Dght 21.425 Lbp 314.28 Br md 58.00 Dpth 30.30 Welded, 1 dk	**(A21B2BO) Ore Carrier** Compartments: 6 Ho, 1 Ta 10 Ha: 6 (15.9 x 15.2) (18.6 x 15.2)ER 3 (13.3 x 15.2)	**1 oil engine** driving 1 FP propeller Total Power: 28,729kW (39,060hp) 14.8kn Sulzer 7RTA84T 1 x 2 Stroke 7 Cy. 840 x 3150 28729kW (39060bhp) Hyundai Heavy Industries Co Ltd-South Korea AuxGen: 3 x 940kW 450V 60Hz a.c
9050230 *V7WF6* -	**STELLAR JOURNEY** *ex* Grand *-2011* *ex* Grand Pacific *-2009* *ex* Crane Princess *-2000* *ex* Takao *-1995* **LTSF PR 5 Inc** Polaris Shipping Co Ltd SatCom: Inmarsat C 453835835 *Majuro* *Marshall Islands* MMSI: 538004287 Official number: 4287	**148,847** 44,654 267,006 T/cm 170.5	Class: KR (NK)	**1994-03 Ishikawajima-Harima Heavy Industries Co Ltd (IHI) — Kure** Yd No: 3030 Converted From: Crude Oil Tanker-2011 Loa 333.00 (BB) Br ex 60.04 Dght 19.777 Lbp 319.00 Br md 60.00 Dpth 28.65 Welded, 1 dk	**(A21B2BO) Ore Carrier** Grain: 156,260 Compartments: 5 Ho, ER 10 Ha: (15.8 x 13.0)ER 9 (14.1 x 13.0)	**1 oil engine** driving 1 FP propeller Total Power: 20,059kW (27,272hp) 15.0kn Sulzer 7RTA84T 1 x 2 Stroke 7 Cy. 840 x 3150 20059kW (27272bhp) Diesel United Ltd.-Aioi Fuel: 5015.0 (r.f.)
9048134 *V7ZK4* -	**STELLAR KNIGHT** *ex* Ore Corumba *-2012* *ex* Pherkad Star *-2010* **VP-1 Shipping Inc** Polaris Shipping Co Ltd *Majuro* *Marshall Islands* MMSI: 538004845 Official number: 4845	**160,666** 48,504 301,389 T/cm 167.5	Class: KR (LR) ✠ Classed LR until 13/10/12	**1995-01 Hyundai Heavy Industries Co Ltd — Ulsan** Yd No: 825 Converted From: Crude Oil Tanker-2011 Loa 332.09 (BB) Br ex 58.05 Dght 22.200 Lbp 319.23 Br md 58.00 Dpth 28.90 Welded, 1 dk	**(A21B2BO) Ore Carrier** Grain: 161,413 Compartments: 7 Ho, ER 9 Ha: ER	**1 oil engine** driving 1 FP propeller Total Power: 23,477kW (31,919hp) 14.6kn B&W 7S80MC 1 x 2 Stroke 7 Cy. 800 x 3056 23477kW (31919bhp) Hyundai Heavy Industries Co Ltd-South Korea AuxGen: 3 x 950kW 450V 60Hz a.c Boilers: 2 AuxB (o.f.) 18.1kgf/cm² (17.8bar), e (ex.g.) 22.0kgf/cm² (21.6bar) Fuel: 425.0 (d.f.) 7500.0 (r.f.) 98.8pd
9030955 *V7ZK5* -	**STELLAR LIBERTY** *ex* Ore Salobo *-2012* *ex* Phoenix Star *-2010* **VP-2 Shipping Inc** Polaris Shipping Co Ltd *Majuro* *Marshall Islands* MMSI: 538004846 Official number: 4846	**164,325** 49,297 291,435 T/cm 171.6	Class: KR (LR) ✠ Classed LR until 19/10/12	**1993-11 Mitsubishi Heavy Industries Ltd. — Nagasaki** Yd No: 2065 Converted From: Crude Oil Tanker-2010 Loa 332.50 (BB) Br ex 58.05 Dght 21.625 Lbp 321.74 Br md 58.00 Dpth 31.50 Welded, 1 dk	**(A21B2BO) Ore Carrier** Grain: 161,519 Compartments: 7 Ho, ER 7 Ha: ER	**1 oil engine** driving 1 FP propeller Total Power: 20,594kW (28,000hp) 15.4kn Mitsubishi 7UEC85LSII 1 x 2 Stroke 7 Cy. 850 x 3150 20594kW (28000bhp) Mitsubishi Heavy Industries Ltd-Japan AuxGen: 3 x 1050kW 450V 60Hz a.c Boilers: e (ex.g.) 22.4kgf/cm² (22.0bar), WTAuxB (o.f.) 16.8kgf/cm² (16.5bar), WTAuxB (o.f.) 17.8kgf/cm² (17.5bar) Fuel: 284.0 (d.f.) (Heating Coils) 6483.0 (r.f.) 75.5pd
9499943 *3FNP4* -	**STELLAR LILAC** **Cypress Navigation Co SA** Setsuyo Kisen Co Ltd *Panama* *Panama* MMSI: 370731000 Official number: 4001909A	**7,522** 4,118 12,601 T/cm 21.5	Class: AB	**2008-11 Higaki Zosen K.K. — Imabari** Yd No: 621 Loa 127.70 (BB) Br ex 19.63 Dght 8.700 Lbp 120.24 Br md 19.60 Dpth 11.55 Welded, 1 dk	**(A12B2TR) Chemical/Products Tanker** Double Hull (13F) Liq: 14,129; Liq (Oil): 14,129 Cargo Heating Coils Compartments: 2 Wing Slop Ta, ER, 16 Wing Ta 16 Cargo Pump (s): 16x300m³/hr Manifold: Bow/CM: 58.3m	**1 oil engine** driving 1 FP propeller Total Power: 4,200kW (5,710hp) 13.5kn MAN-B&W 6S35MC 1 x 2 Stroke 6 Cy. 350 x 1400 4200kW (5710bhp) The Hanshin Diesel Works Ltd-Japan AuxGen: 3 x 480kW a.c Thrusters: 1 Tunnel thruster (f) Fuel: 134.0 (d.f.) 668.0 (r.f.)
9549566 *V2QK8* -	**STELLAR MAESTRO** **Stellar Maestro CV** Stellar Navigation BV *Saint John's* *Antigua & Barbuda* MMSI: 305869000 Official number: 3121	**9,963** 4,937 13,524 T/cm 27.0	Class: LR ✠ **100A1** SS 06/2012 strengthened for heavy cargoes, container cargoes in holds and on upperdeck hatchcovers LI Ice Class 1A FS at a draught of 8.450m Max/min draught fwd 8.450/3.82m Max/min draught aft 8.490/5.12m Required power 4488kw, installed power 6000kw ✠ **LMC** **UMS** Eq.Ltr: D†; Cable: 550.0/54.0 U3 (a)	**2012-06 Damen Shipyards Yichang Co Ltd — Yichang HB** (Hull) Yd No: 567501 **2012-06 B.V. Scheepswerf Damen — Gorinchem** Yd No: 567501 Loa 142.00 (BB) Br ex - Dght 8.250 Lbp 137.00 Br md 20.10 Dpth 11.45 Welded, 1 dk	**(A31A2GX) General Cargo Ship** Grain: 17,242; Bale: 17,242 TEU 712 C Ho 312 TEU C Dk 400 TEU Compartments: 2 Ho, ER 2 Ha: (70.0 x 15.8)ER (26.0 x 15.8) Cranes: 2x80t Ice Capable	**1 oil engine** with flexible couplings & sr geared to sc. shaft driving 1 CP propeller Total Power: 6,000kW (8,158hp) 15.5kn MaK 6M43C 1 x 4 Stroke 6 Cy. 430 x 610 6000kW (8158bhp) Caterpillar Motoren GmbH & Co. KG-Germany AuxGen: 3 x 460kW 400V 50Hz a.c, 1 x 1148kW 400V 50Hz a.c Boilers: e (ex.g.) 10.2kgf/cm² (10.0bar), TOH (o.f.) 10.2kgf/cm² (10.0bar) Thrusters: 1 Thwart. FP thruster (f) Fuel: 98.0 (d.f.) 737.0 (r.f.)
9060314 *V7ZK6* -	**STELLAR MAGIC** *ex* Ore Parati *-2012* *ex* Mirfak Star *-2010* **VP-3 Shipping Inc** Polaris Shipping Co Ltd *Majuro* *Marshall Islands* MMSI: 538004847 Official number: 4847	**160,666** 48,504 298,338 T/cm 167.5	Class: KR (LR) ✠ Classed LR until 16/10/12	**1994-05 Hyundai Heavy Industries Co Ltd — Ulsan** Yd No: 841 Converted From: Crude Oil Tanker-2011 Loa 332.09 (BB) Br ex 58.05 Dght 22.200 Lbp 318.00 Br md 58.00 Dpth 28.90 Welded, 1 dk	**(A21B2BO) Ore Carrier** Grain: 163,250 Compartments: 7 Ho, ER 7 Ha: ER	**1 oil engine** driving 1 FP propeller Total Power: 23,477kW (31,919hp) 14.6kn B&W 7S80MC 1 x 2 Stroke 7 Cy. 800 x 3056 23477kW (31919bhp) Hyundai Heavy Industries Co Ltd-South Korea AuxGen: 3 x 950kW 440V 60Hz a.c Boilers: 2 AuxB (o.f.) 18.1kgf/cm² (17.8bar), e (ex.g.) 22.0kgf/cm² (21.6bar) Fuel: 425.0 (d.f.) (Heating Coils) 7500.0 (r.f.) 98.8pd
9172430 *3FCK9* -	**STELLAR NAVIGATOR** **Santorini Maritima SA** Hachiuma Steamship Co Ltd (Hachiuma Kisen KK) SatCom: Inmarsat C 435719410 *Panama* *Panama* MMSI: 357194000 Official number: 2614999D	**87,417** 57,629 172,940 T/cm 119.0	Class: NK	**1999-01 Nippon Kokan KK (NKK Corp) — Tsu ME** Yd No: 176 Loa 289.00 (BB) Br ex - Dght 17.810 Lbp 279.00 Br md 45.00 Dpth 24.10 Welded, 1 dk	**(A21A2BC) Bulk Carrier** Grain: 191,582 Compartments: 9 Ho, ER 9 Ha: (15.2 x 18.8)7 (15.2 x 20.6) (15.2 x 17.5)ER	**1 oil engine** driving 1 FP propeller Total Power: 15,403kW (20,942hp) 15.0kn B&W 6S70MC 1 x 2 Stroke 6 Cy. 700 x 2674 15403kW (20942bhp) Mitsui Engineering & Shipbuilding CLtd-Japan Fuel: 3760.0

9030943 **STELLAR NEPTUNE**
V7ZK7 *ex* Ore Urucum *-2012* *ex* Libra Star *-2010*
\- **VP-4 Shipping Inc**
Polaris Shipping Co Ltd
Majuro *Marshall Islands*
MMSI: 538004848
Official number: 4848

164,325 / 49,297 / 291,435 / T/cm / 171.6

Class: KR (LR)
✠ Classed LR until 29/10/12

1993-09 Mitsubishi Heavy Industries Ltd. — Nagasaki Yd No: 2064
Converted From: Crude Oil Tanker-2011
Loa 332.50 (BB) Br ex 58.05 Dght 21.625
Lbp 319.00 Br md 58.00 Dpth 31.50
Welded, 1 dk

(A21B2BO) Ore Carrier
Grain: 161,519
Compartments: 7 Ho, ER
7 Ha: ER

1 oil engine driving 1 FP propeller
Total Power: 20,594kW (28,000hp) 14.0kn
Mitsubishi 7UEC85LSII
1 x 2 Stroke 7 Cy. 850 x 3150 20594kW (28000bhp)
Mitsubishi Heavy Industries Ltd-Japan
AuxGen: 3 x 1050kW 450V 60Hz a.c
Boilers: 2 AuxB (o.f.) 18.1kgf/cm² (17.8bar), e (ex.g.) 23.1kgf/cm² (22.7bar)
Fuel: 284.0 (d.f.) (Heating Coils) 6483.0 (r.f.) 75.5pd

9030979 **STELLAR OCEAN**
V7ZK8 *ex* Ore Caue *-2012* *ex* Carina Star *-2009*
\- **VP-5 Shipping Inc**
Polaris Shipping Co Ltd
Majuro *Marshall Islands*
MMSI: 538004849
Official number: 4849

162,393 / 48,717 / 305,668

Class: KR (LR)
✠ Classed LR until 7/11/12

1994-02 Nippon Kokan KK (NKK Corp) — Tsu ME Yd No: 137
Converted From: Crude Oil Tanker-2010
Loa 331.50 (BB) Br ex 58.04 Dght 22.100
Lbp 317.00 Br md 58.00 Dpth 31.25
Welded, 1 dk

(A21B2BO) Ore Carrier
Grain: 180,000
Compartments: 7 Ho, ER
7 Ha: ER

1 oil engine driving 1 FP propeller
Total Power: 20,230kW (27,505hp) 14.3kn
Sulzer 7RTA84M
1 x 2 Stroke 7 Cy. 840 x 2900 20230kW (27505bhp)
Diesel United Ltd.-Aioi
AuxGen: 3 x 900kW 450V 60Hz a.c
Boilers: 2 AuxB (o.f.) 24.5kgf/cm² (24.0bar), e (ex.g.) 28.1kgf/cm² (27.6bar)
Fuel: 378.0 (d.f.) (Heating Coils) 7471.0 (r.f.) 74.0pd

9594157 **STELLAR ORCHID**
V7WR3
\- **Blue Forest Shipping Co Ltd**
Unix Line Pte Ltd
Majuro *Marshall Islands*
MMSI: 538004372
Official number: 4372

7,912 / 4,164 / 12,571 / T/cm / 21.7

Class: NK

2011-07 Kitanihon Zosen K.K. — Hachinohe Yd No: 397
Loa 126.00 (BB) Br ex - Dght 8.663
Lbp 118.00 Br md 20.50 Dpth 11.50
Welded, 1 dk

(A12B2TR) Chemical/Products Tanker
Double Hull (13F)
Liq: 13,093; Liq (Oil): 13,093
Cargo Heating Coils
Compartments: 8 Wing Ta, 8 Wing Ta, 1 Wing Slop Ta, 1 Wing Slop Ta, ER
16 Cargo Pump (s): 6x300m³/hr, 8x200m³/hr, 2x100m³/hr
Manifold: Bow/CM: 63.5m

1 oil engine driving 1 FP propeller
Total Power: 4,440kW (6,037hp) 14.5kn
MAN-B&W 6S35MC
1 x 2 Stroke 6 Cy. 350 x 1400 4440kW (6037bhp)
Hitachi Zosen Corp-Japan
AuxGen: 2 x 500kW a.c
Thrusters: 1 Tunnel thruster (f)
Fuel: 62.0 (d.f.) 698.0 (r.f.)

9231585 **STELLAR PEACE**
YJRU2 *ex* Crimson Neptune *-2011*
\- **Stevens Line Co Ltd**
Sato Steamship Co Ltd (Sato Kisen KK)
Port Vila *Vanuatu*
MMSI: 576642000
Official number: 1292

40,360 / 21,658 / 49,923

Class: NK

2001-07 Shin Kurushima Dockyard Co. Ltd. — Onishi Yd No: 5095
Loa 199.99 Br ex - Dght 11.527
Lbp 193.50 Br md 32.20 Dpth 22.75
Welded, 1 dk

(A24B2BW) Wood Chips Carrier
Grain: 102,276
Compartments: 6 Ho, ER
6 Ha: 5 (14.4 x 20.1) (12.8 x 20.1)ER
Cranes: 3x14.5t

1 oil engine driving 1 FP propeller
Total Power: 7,545kW (10,258hp) 14.0kn
Mitsubishi 6UEC52LS
1 x 2 Stroke 6 Cy. 520 x 1850 7545kW (10258bhp)
Kobe Hatsudoki KK-Japan
Fuel: 2775.0

9048110 **STELLAR PIONEER**
V7ZS6 *ex* Ore Paqueta *-2012* *ex* Polaris Star *-2010*
\- **VP-6 Shipping Inc**
Polaris Shipping Co Ltd
Majuro *Marshall Islands*
MMSI: 538004904
Official number: 4904

160,666 / 48,504 / 298,624 / T/cm / 167.5

Class: KR (LR)
✠ Classed LR until 16/11/12

1994-06 Hyundai Heavy Industries Co Ltd — Ulsan Yd No: 823
Converted From: Crude Oil Tanker-2011
Loa 332.09 (BB) Br ex 58.44 Dght 22.200
Lbp 318.00 Br md 58.00 Dpth 28.90
Welded, 1 dk

(A21B2BO) Ore Carrier
Grain: 161,413
Compartments: 7 Ho, ER
7 Ha: ER

1 oil engine driving 1 FP propeller
Total Power: 23,477kW (31,919hp) 14.6kn
B&W 7S80MC
1 x 2 Stroke 7 Cy. 800 x 3056 23477kW (31919bhp)
Hyundai Heavy Industries Co Ltd-South Korea
AuxGen: 3 x 950kW 450V 60Hz a.c
Boilers: 2 AuxB (o.f.) 18.1kgf/cm² (17.8bar), e (ex.g.) 22.0kgf/cm² (21.6bar)
Fuel: 524.0 (d.f.) 8375.0 (r.f.) 98.8pd

9030981 **STELLAR QUEEN**
V7AD3 *ex* Ore Yantai *-2012* *ex* Ore Goro *-2012*
\- *ex* Hydra Star *-2009*
VP-7 Shipping Inc
Polaris Shipping Co Ltd
Majuro *Marshall Islands*
MMSI: 538004969
Official number: 4969

162,393 / 48,717 / 305,846

Class: KR (LR)
✠ Classed LR until 28/12/12

1994-06 Nippon Kokan KK (NKK Corp) — Tsu ME Yd No: 138
Converted From: Crude Oil Tanker-2010
Loa 331.50 (BB) Br ex 58.04 Dght 22.100
Lbp 317.00 Br md 58.00 Dpth 31.25
Welded, 1 dk

(A21B2BO) Ore Carrier
Grain: 180,000
Compartments: 7 Ho, ER
7 Ha: ER

1 oil engine driving 1 FP propeller
Total Power: 20,230kW (27,505hp) 14.3kn
Sulzer 7RTA84M
1 x 2 Stroke 7 Cy. 840 x 2900 20230kW (27505bhp)
Diesel United Ltd.-Aioi
AuxGen: 3 x 900kW 450V 60Hz a.c
Boilers: 2 AuxB (o.f.) 24.5kgf/cm² (24.0bar), e (ex.g.) 28.1kgf/cm² (27.6bar)
Fuel: 378.0 (d.f.) 7471.0 (r.f.) 74.0pd

9244697 **STELLAR RHAPSODY**
9VAL2 *ex* Crimson Mars *-2012*
\- **Lily Virgo Pte Ltd**
Sandigan Ship Services Inc
Singapore *Singapore*
MMSI: 563584000
Official number: 390989

40,360 / 21,658 / 49,917

Class: NK

2002-07 Shin Kurushima Dockyard Co. Ltd. — Onishi Yd No: 5135
Loa 199.99 (BB) Br ex - Dght 11.527
Lbp 193.50 Br md 32.20 Dpth 22.75
Welded, 1 dk

(A24B2BW) Wood Chips Carrier
Grain: 102,276
Compartments: 6 Ho, ER
6 Ha: (12.8 x 20.1)5 (14.4 x 20.1)ER
Cranes: 3x14.5t

1 oil engine driving 1 FP propeller
Total Power: 7,545kW (10,258hp) 14.1kn
Mitsubishi 6UEC52LS
1 x 2 Stroke 6 Cy. 520 x 1850 7545kW (10258bhp)
Kobe Hatsudoki KK-Japan
Fuel: 2780.0

9060338 **STELLAR RIO**
V7AD4 *ex* Ore Santos *-2013* *ex* Shaula Star *-2010*
\- **VP-8 Shipping Inc**
Polaris Shipping Co Ltd
Majuro *Marshall Islands*
MMSI: 538004970
Official number: 4970

160,666 / 48,504 / 298,450 / T/cm / 167.5

Class: KR (LR)
✠ Classed LR until 7/1/13

1994-05 Hyundai Heavy Industries Co Ltd — Ulsan Yd No: 843
Converted From: Crude Oil Tanker-2011
Loa 332.09 (BB) Br ex 58.05 Dght 22.200
Lbp 318.00 Br md 58.00 Dpth 28.90
Welded, 1 dk

(A21B2BO) Ore Carrier
Single Hull
Grain: 161,413
Compartments: 7 Ho, ER
7 Ha: ER

1 oil engine driving 1 FP propeller
Total Power: 23,477kW (31,919hp) 14.6kn
B&W 7S80MC
1 x 2 Stroke 7 Cy. 800 x 3056 23477kW (31919bhp)
Hyundai Heavy Industries Co Ltd-South Korea
AuxGen: 3 x 950kW 440V 60Hz a.c
Boilers: 2 AuxB (o.f.) 18.1kgf/cm² (17.8bar), e (ex.g.) 22.0kgf/cm² (21.6bar)
Fuel: 425.0 (d.f.) (Heating Coils) 7500.0 (r.f.) 98.8pd

9030967 **STELLAR SAMBA**
V7AD5 *ex* Ore Fazendao *-2013* *ex* Al Bali Star *-2010*
\- **VP-9 Shipping Inc**
Polaris Shipping Co Ltd
Majuro *Marshall Islands*
MMSI: 538004971
Official number: 4971

164,325 / 49,297 / 291,435 / T/cm / 171.6

Class: KR (LR)
✠ Classed LR until 3/1/13

1994-01 Mitsubishi Heavy Industries Ltd. — Nagasaki Yd No: 2066
Converted From: Crude Oil Tanker-2010
Loa 332.50 (BB) Br ex 58.05 Dght 21.624
Lbp 319.00 Br md 58.00 Dpth 31.50
Welded, 1 dk

(A21B2BO) Ore Carrier
Grain: 161,519
Compartments: 7 Ho, ER
7 Ha: ER

1 oil engine driving 1 FP propeller
Total Power: 20,602kW (28,010hp) 14.5kn
Mitsubishi 7UEC85LSII
1 x 2 Stroke 7 Cy. 850 x 3150 20602kW (28010bhp)
Mitsubishi Heavy Industries Ltd-Japan
AuxGen: 3 x 1050kW 450V 60Hz a.c
Boilers: 2 AuxB (o.f.) 18.1kgf/cm² (17.8bar), e (ex.g.) 23.1kgf/cm² (22.7bar)
Fuel: 284.0 (d.f.) 6483.0 (r.f.)

9296602 **STELLAR STREAM II**
3EDN2
\- **Pegasus Shipholding SA**
Pegasus Maritime Co Ltd
Panama *Panama*
MMSI: 371627000
Official number: 3141306A

40,253 / 21,658 / 50,471

Class: NK

2005-12 Shin Kurushima Dockyard Co. Ltd. — Onishi Yd No: 5305
Loa 199.99 Br ex - Dght 11.527
Lbp 193.50 Br md 32.20 Dpth 22.75
Welded, 1 dk

(A24B2BW) Wood Chips Carrier
Grain: 102,276
Compartments: 6 Ho, ER
6 Ha: (12.8 x 20.1)ER 5 (14.4 x 20.1)

1 oil engine driving 1 FP propeller
Total Power: 7,545kW (10,258hp) 14.1kn
Mitsubishi 6UEC52LS
1 x 2 Stroke 6 Cy. 520 x 1850 7545kW (10258bhp)
Kobe Hatsudoki KK-Japan
Fuel: 2710.0

9566631 **STELLAR SUNRISE**
3FUB5
\- **Apricot Ship Holding SA**
Nippon Yusen Kabushiki Kaisha (NYK Line)
Panama *Panama*
MMSI: 353153000
Official number: 4474213

43,855 / 19,191 / 53,979

Class: NK

2013-04 Oshima Shipbuilding Co Ltd — Saikai NS Yd No: 10634
Loa 210.00 (BB) Br ex - Dght 11.526
Lbp 203.58 Br md 32.26 Dpth 22.98
Welded, 1 dk

(A24B2BW) Wood Chips Carrier
Grain: 109,093
Compartments: 6 Ho, ER
6 Ha: ER
Cranes: 3x14.7t

1 oil engine driving 1 FP propeller
Total Power: 9,195kW (12,502hp) 14.5kn
Mitsubishi 7UEC50LSII
1 x 2 Stroke 7 Cy. 500 x 1950 9195kW (12502bhp)
Mitsubishi Heavy Industries Ltd-Japan
Fuel: 2830.0

9048122 **STELLAR TOPAZ**
V7AD6 *ex* Ore Itaguai *-2013* *ex* Markab Star *-2010*
\- **VP-10 Shipping Inc**
Polaris Shipping Co Ltd
Majuro *Marshall Islands*
MMSI: 538004972
Official number: 4972

160,454 / 48,504 / 298,468 / T/cm / 167.5

Class: KR (LR)
✠ Classed LR until 31/12/12

1994-11 Hyundai Heavy Industries Co Ltd — Ulsan Yd No: 824
Converted From: Crude Oil Tanker-2011
Loa 332.09 (BB) Br ex 58.05 Dght 22.523
Lbp 318.00 Br md 58.00 Dpth 28.90
Welded, 1 dk

(A21B2BO) Ore Carrier
Grain: 163,250
Compartments: 7 Ho, ER
9 Ha: 4 (18.2 x 18.4) (31.9 x 18.4)ER 3 (13.7 x 18.4) (31.9 x 14.7)

1 oil engine driving 1 FP propeller
Total Power: 23,477kW (31,919hp) 14.6kn
B&W 7S80MC
1 x 2 Stroke 7 Cy. 800 x 3056 23477kW (31919bhp)
Hyundai Heavy Industries Co Ltd-South Korea
AuxGen: 3 x 950kW 450V 60Hz a.c
Boilers: 2 AuxB (o.f.) 18.1kgf/cm² (17.8bar), e (ex.g.) 22.0kgf/cm² (21.6bar)
Fuel: 425.0 (d.f.) 7500.0 (r.f.) 98.8pd

9006734 **STELLAR UNICORN**
V7AQ6 *ex* Sri Prem Putli *-2013* *ex* Prem Putli *-2012*
\- *ex* Musashi Spirit *-2004*
KSF 24 International SA
Polaris Shipping Co Ltd
Majuro *Marshall Islands*
MMSI: 538005049
Official number: 5049

156,352 / 46,906 / 279,022

Class: KR (LR) (IR) (NK) (NV)
Classed LR until 22/3/13

1993-01 Sasebo Heavy Industries Co. Ltd. — Sasebo Yard, Sasebo Yd No: 385
Converted From: Crude Oil Tanker-2009
Loa 330.26 (BB) Br ex 56.04 Dght 20.898
Lbp 319.00 Br md 56.00 Dpth 30.65
Welded, 1 dk

(A21B2BO) Ore Carrier
Compartments: 7 Ho, ER
10 Ha: ER

1 oil engine driving 1 FP propeller
Total Power: 22,918kW (31,159hp) 15.5kn
B&W 7L90MCE
1 x 2 Stroke 7 Cy. 900 x 2916 22918kW (31159bhp)
Mitsui Engineering & Shipbuilding CLtd-Japan
AuxGen: 1 x 740kW 450V 60Hz a.c, 3 x 740kW 450V 60Hz a.c
Boilers: AuxB (ex.g.) 26.0kgf/cm² (25.5bar), AuxB (o.f.) 20.1kgf/cm² (19.7bar)
Fuel: 200.4 (d.f.) (Heating Coils) 7547.0 (r.f.) 109.0pd

IMO / Call sign	Name / Owner	Tonnage	Class	Builder / Dimensions	Type	Machinery
9249180 *C6FV4* -	**STELLAR VOYAGER** **CM Pacific Maritime Corp** Chevron Tankers Ltd *Nassau* *Bahamas* MMSI: 311487000 Official number: 9000062	**58,088** 30,727 104,801 T/cm 91.2	Class: AB	**2003-07 Samsung Heavy Industries Co Ltd — Geoje** Yd No: 1411 Loa 243.54 (BB) Br ex - Dght 14.772 Lbp 234.88 Br md 42.00 Dpth 21.30 Welded, 1 dk	**(A13A2TV) Crude Oil Tanker** Double Hull (13F) Liq: 113,314; Liq (Oil): 120,000 Cargo Heating Coils Compartments: 12 Wing Ta, 2 Wing Slop Ta, ER 3 Cargo Pump (s): 3x2800m^3/hr Manifold: Bow/CM: 120m	**1 oil engine** driving 1 FP propeller Total Power: 13,549kW (18,421hp) 14.5kn MAN-B&W 6S60MC-C 1 x 2 Stroke 6 Cy. 600 x 2400 13549kW (18421bhp) Doosan Engine Co Ltd-South Korea AuxGen: 3 x 740kW a.c Fuel: 163.0 (d.f.) 3512.2 (r.f.)
9096911 *WBS2983* -	**STELLAR WIND** **Cook Inlet Tug & Barge Co** *Anchorage, AK* *United States of America* MMSI: 367186610 Official number: 991625	**147** 100 -		**1993-01 Tri-Star Marine, Inc. — Seattle, Wa** Yd No: F-0105 Loa - Br ex - Dght - Lbp - Br md - Dpth - Welded, 1 dk	**(B32A2ST) Tug**	**2 oil engines** geared to sc. shafts driving 2 Z propellers Total Power: 2,206kW (3,000hp) Caterpillar 3512TA 2 x Vee 4 Stroke 12 Cy. 170 x 190 each-1103kW (1500bhp) Caterpillar Inc-USA
9594145 *V7VY2* -	**STELLAR WISTERIA** **August Vill Shipping Co Ltd** Tokyo Marine Asia Pte Ltd SatCom: Inmarsat C 453836427 *Majuro* *Marshall Islands* MMSI: 538004239 Official number: 4239	**7,912** 4,164 12,601 T/cm 21.7	Class: NK	**2011-06 Kitanihon Zosen K.K. — Hachinohe** Yd No: 396 Loa 126.00 (BB) Br ex 20.53 Dght 8.663 Lbp 118.00 Br md 20.50 Dpth 11.50 Welded, 1 dk	**(A12B2TR) Chemical/Products Tanker** Double Hull (13F) Liq: 12,344; Liq (Oil): 12,344 Cargo Heating Coils Compartments: 8 Wing Ta, 8 Wing Ta, 1 Wing Slop Ta, 1 Wing Slop Ta, ER 16 Cargo Pump (s): 6x300m^3/hr, 8x200m^3/hr, 2x100m^3/hr Manifold: Bow/CM: 63.5m	**1 oil engine** driving 1 FP propeller Total Power: 4,440kW (6,037hp) 14.5kn MAN-B&W 6S35MC 1 x 2 Stroke 6 Cy. 350 x 1400 4440kW (6037bhp) Hitachi Zosen Corp-Japan AuxGen: 3 x 350kW 450V 60Hz a.c Thrusters: 1 Tunnel thruster (f) Fuel: 62.2 (d.f.) 698.6 (r.f.)
8886955 *WCV4623* -	**STELLER** **Dan Foley** *Glacier Bay, AK* *United States of America* MMSI: 366703120 Official number: 991467	*113* 90 -		**1978 Nichols Bros. Boat Builders, Inc. — Freeland, Wa** Yd No: S-37 L reg 21.33 Br ex - Dght - Lbp - Br md 5.86 Dpth 3.50 Welded, 1 dk	**(B11B2FV) Fishing Vessel**	**1 oil engine** driving 1 FP propeller
8504519 *XUGX4* -	**STELS** *ex* Sapsan *-2012* *ex* Dionis *-2011* *ex* Solomon *-2010* *ex* Costa Verde *-2008* *ex* MYS Pensepel *-2007* *ex* Sumiyoshi Maru No. 68 *-2007* **Duvani International Ltd** - *Phnom Penh* *Cambodia* MMSI: 515021000 Official number: 1385139	**498** 248 478	Class: IS (RS)	**1985-07 Miho Zosensho K.K. — Shimizu** Yd No: 1262 Loa 55.61 (BB) Br ex 8.72 Dght 3.491 Lbp 49.03 Br md 8.70 Dpth 3.87 Welded, 1 dk	**(B11B2FV) Fishing Vessel** Ins: 681	**1 oil engine** with clutches, flexible couplings & sr reverse geared to sc. shaft driving 1 FP propeller Total Power: 1,103kW (1,500hp) 13.5kn Niigata 6M31AFTE 1 x 4 Stroke 6 Cy. 310 x 530 1103kW (1500bhp) Niigata Engineering Co Ltd-Japan Fuel: 265.0 (d.f.)
9496458 *PBSO* -	**STEMAT SPIRIT** **Stemat BV** - *Rotterdam* *Netherlands* MMSI: 246543000 Official number: 51712	**5,551** 1,665 6,209	Class: BV	**2010-03 Taizhou Xinggang Shipbuilding Co Ltd — Taizhou JS** (Hull) **2010-03 Stemat BV — Rotterdam** Yd No: NP331 Loa 90.00 (BB) Br ex - Dght 4.920 Lbp 86.88 Br md 28.00 Dpth 6.50 Welded, 1 dk	**(B34D2SL) Cable Layer** Cranes: 1x18t	**2 oil engines** reduction geared to sc. shafts driving 2 Directional propellers Total Power: 2,280kW (3,100hp) 10.0kn Caterpillar 3512B-HD 2 x Vee 4 Stroke 12 Cy. 170 x 215 each-1140kW (1550bhp) Caterpillar Inc-USA AuxGen: 3 x 850kW a.c Thrusters: 2 Retract. directional thruster (f); 1 Tunnel thruster (f) Fuel: 1208.0 (d.f.)
9371610 *ZDIB2* -	**STEN ARNOLD** **K/S Stenship** Rederiet Stenersen AS *Gibraltar* *Gibraltar (British)* MMSI: 236407000 Official number: 9371610	**11,935** 5,131 16,578 T/cm 28.5	Class: NV	**2008-01 Qiuxin Shipyard — Shanghai** (Hull launched by) Yd No: (H2364) **2008-01 Jiangnan Shipyard (Group) Co Ltd — Shanghai** (Hull completed by) Yd No: H2364 Loa 144.10 (BB) Br ex 23.03 Dght 8.900 Lbp 133.80 Br md 23.00 Dpth 12.41 Welded, 1 dk	**(A12B2TR) Chemical/Products Tanker** Double Hull (13F) Liq: 18,490; Liq (Oil): 18,490 Compartments: 12 Wing Ta, 2 Wing Slop Ta, ER 15 Cargo Pump (s): 12x300m^3/hr, 3x150m^3/hr Manifold: Bow/CM: 72.2m	**1 oil engine** reduction geared to sc. shaft driving 1 CP propeller Total Power: 6,300kW (8,565hp) 14.0kn Wartsila 6L46C 1 x 4 Stroke 6 Cy. 460 x 580 6300kW (8565bhp) Wartsila Finland Oy-Finland AuxGen: 2 x a.c, 1 x a.c, 1 x a.c Thrusters: 1 Tunnel thruster (f) Fuel: 70.0 (d.f.) 530.0 (r.f.)
9318565 *LAKI6* -	**STEN AURORA** **Stentank AS** Rederiet Stenersen AS SatCom: Inmarsat C 425895310 *Bergen* *Norway (NIS)* MMSI: 258953000	**11,935** 5,141 16,596 T/cm 28.5	Class: NV	**2007-09 Qiuxin Shipyard — Shanghai** Yd No: H2363 Loa 144.10 (BB) Br ex 23.03 Dght 8.900 Lbp 133.80 Br md 23.00 Dpth 12.40 Welded, 1 dk	**(A12B2TR) Chemical/Products Tanker** Double Hull (13F) Liq: 18,492; Liq (Oil): 19,500 Compartments: 12 Wing Ta, 2 Wing Slop Ta, ER 12 Cargo Pump (s): 12x300m^3/hr Manifold: Bow/CM: 72.2m Ice Capable	**1 oil engine** geared to sc. shaft driving 1 CP propeller Total Power: 6,300kW (8,565hp) 14.0kn Wartsila 6L46 1 x 4 Stroke 6 Cy. 460 x 580 6300kW (8565bhp) Wartsila Finland Oy-Finland AuxGen: 1 x 960kW a.c, 2 x 640kW a.c, 1 x 1500kW a.c Thrusters: 1 Tunnel thruster (f) Fuel: 70.0 (d.f.) 527.0 (r.f.)
9307671 *LADY6* -	**STEN BALTIC** **Stenoil K/S** Rederiet Stenersen AS *Bergen* *Norway (NIS)* MMSI: 257519000	**11,935** 5,137 16,613 T/cm 28.0	Class: NV	**2005-09 Qiuxin Shipyard — Shanghai** Yd No: H2323 Loa 144.05 (BB) Br ex - Dght 8.900 Lbp 133.80 Br md 23.00 Dpth 12.40 Welded, 1 dk	**(A12B2TR) Chemical/Products Tanker** Double Hull (13F) Liq: 18,491; Liq (Oil): 18,491 Compartments: 12 Wing Ta, ER 12 Cargo Pump (s): 12x300m^3/hr Manifold: Bow/CM: 71.8m Ice Capable	**1 oil engine** geared to sc. shaft driving 1 CP propeller Total Power: 6,300kW (8,565hp) 14.0kn Wartsila 6L46C 1 x 4 Stroke 6 Cy. 460 x 580 6300kW (8565bhp) Wartsila Finland Oy-Finland AuxGen: 1 x 1080kW 60Hz a.c, 2 x 720kW 60Hz a.c, 1 x 1500kW 60Hz a.c Thrusters: 1 Tunnel thruster (f)
9407988 *ZDIY8* -	**STEN BERGEN** **Stentank AS** Brostrom AB SatCom: Inmarsat Mini-M 764893367 *Gibraltar* *Gibraltar (British)* MMSI: 236501000	**11,935** 5,141 16,655 T/cm 28.5	Class: NV	**2009-04 Jiangnan Shipyard (Group) Co Ltd — Shanghai** Yd No: H2401 Loa 144.16 (BB) Br ex 23.18 Dght 8.899 Lbp 134.55 Br md 23.00 Dpth 12.40 Welded, 1 dk	**(A12B2TR) Chemical/Products Tanker** Double Hull (13F) Liq: 18,614; Liq (Oil): 18,614 Compartments: 12 Wing Ta, 2 Wing Slop Ta, ER 12 Cargo Pump (s): 12x300m^3/hr Manifold: Bow/CM: 72.2m Ice Capable	**1 oil engine** reduction geared to sc. shaft driving 1 CP propeller Total Power: 6,300kW (8,565hp) 14.0kn Wartsila 6L46C 1 x 4 Stroke 6 Cy. 460 x 580 6300kW (8565bhp) Wartsila Finland Oy-Finland AuxGen: 2 x 720kW a.c, 1 x 1080kW a.c, 1 x a.c Thrusters: 1 Thwart. FP thruster (f) Fuel: 70.0 (d.f.) 525.0 (r.f.)
9378735 *LAEF7* -	**STEN BOTHNIA** **K/S Stenship** Rederiet Stenersen AS *Bergen* *Norway (NIS)* MMSI: 259769000 Official number: 26924	**11,935** 5,133 16,611 T/cm 28.5	Class: NV	**2008-11 Jiangnan Shipyard (Group) Co Ltd — Shanghai** Yd No: H2384 Loa 144.10 (BB) Br ex 23.20 Dght 8.900 Lbp 133.88 Br md 23.02 Dpth 12.40 Welded, 1 dk	**(A12B2TR) Chemical/Products Tanker** Double Hull (13F) Liq: 18,491; Liq (Oil): 18,491 Compartments: 12 Wing Ta, 2 Wing Slop Ta, ER 12 Cargo Pump (s): 12x300m^3/hr Manifold: Bow/CM: 72.2m Ice Capable	**1 oil engine** reduction geared to sc. shaft driving 1 CP propeller Total Power: 6,300kW (8,565hp) 14.0kn Wartsila 6L46C 1 x 4 Stroke 6 Cy. 460 x 580 6300kW (8565bhp) Wartsila Finland Oy-Finland AuxGen: 2 x a.c, 1 x 1500kW a.c, 1 x a.c Thrusters: 1 Tunnel thruster (f) Fuel: 50.0 (d.f.) 410.0 (r.f.)
9460241 *ZDJF5* -	**STEN FJELL** **Stentank AS** Brostrom AB *Gibraltar* *Gibraltar (British)* MMSI: 236522000	**13,283** 5,845 18,561 T/cm 30.4	Class: NV	**2010-01 Jiangnan Shipyard (Group) Co Ltd — Shanghai** Yd No: H2438 Loa 148.80 (BB) Br ex 23.94 Dght 9.270 Lbp 138.22 Br md 23.76 Dpth 12.80 Welded, 1 dk	**(A12B2TR) Chemical/Products Tanker** Double Hull (13F) Liq: 20,752; Liq (Oil): 20,752 Part Cargo Heating Coils Compartments: 12 Wing Ta, 2 Wing Slop Ta, ER 12 Cargo Pump (s): 12x375m^3/hr Manifold: Bow/CM: 74.2m Ice Capable	**1 oil engine** reduction geared to sc. shaft driving 1 CP propeller Total Power: 7,200kW (9,789hp) 14.0kn MAN-B&W 6L48/60B 1 x 4 Stroke 6 Cy. 480 x 600 7200kW (9789bhp) MAN B&W Diesel AG-Augsburg AuxGen: 2 x 680kW a.c, 1 x 1020kW a.c, 1 x 1875kW a.c Thrusters: 1 Tunnel thruster (f) Fuel: 85.0 (d.f.) 630.0 (r.f.)
9187409 *ZDGF3* -	**STEN FJORD** *ex* Falcon *-2009* **Utsten KS** Rederiet Stenersen AS 723676948 *Gibraltar* *Gibraltar (British)* MMSI: 236243000	**8,882** 4,617 13,670 T/cm 25.2	Class: GL	**2004-08 Yangzhou Dayang Shipbuilding Co Ltd — Yangzhou JS** Yd No: JY97126 Loa 145.34 (BB) Br ex - Dght 8.450 Lbp 136.60 Br md 20.80 Dpth 11.20 Welded, 1 dk	**(A12B2TR) Chemical/Products Tanker** Double Hull (13F) Liq: 15,789; Liq (Oil): 16,300 Cargo Heating Coils Compartments: 14 Wing Ta, 1 Slop Ta, 2 Wing Slop Ta, ER 14 Cargo Pump (s): 14x330m^3/hr Manifold: Bow/CM: 78.4m Ice Capable	**1 oil engine** driving 1 CP propeller Total Power: 6,480kW (8,810hp) 14.5kn B&W 6S42MC 1 x 2 Stroke 6 Cy. 420 x 1764 6480kW (8810bhp) Hudong Heavy Machinery Co Ltd-China AuxGen: 3 x 500kW 450V a.c, 1 x 1400kW 450V a.c Thrusters: 1 Tunnel thruster (f) Fuel: 116.0 (d.f.) 509.0 (r.f.)

9407976 **STEN FRIGG**
ZDIY4
\- **Stentank AS**
Rederiet Stenersen AS
Gibraltar *Gibraltar (British)*
MMSI: 236500000

11,935 5,133 16,587 T/cm 28.5
Class: NV

2009-01 Jiangnan Shipyard (Group) Co Ltd — Shanghai Yd No: H2400
Loa 144.13 (BB) Br ex 23.18 Dght 8.900
Lbp 133.75 Br md 23.00 Dpth 12.41
Welded, 1 dk

(A12B2TR) Chemical/Products Tanker
Double Hull (13F)
Liq: 18,612; Liq (Oil): 18,500
Compartments: 12 Wing Ta, 2 Wing Slop Ta, ER
12 Cargo Pump (s): 12x300m³/hr
Manifold: Bow/CM: 72.2m
Ice Capable

1 oil engine reductiion geared to sc. shaft driving 1 CP propeller
Total Power: 6,300kW (8,565hp) 14.0kn
Wartsila 6L46
1 x 4 Stroke 6 Cy. 460 x 580 6300kW (8565bhp)
Wartsila Finland Oy-Finland
AuxGen: 2 x 640kW a.c, 1 x 960kW a.c, 1 x 1500kW a.c
Thrusters: 1 Thwart. FP thruster (f)
Fuel: 50.0 (d.f.) 400.0 (r.f.)

9358931 **STEN HIDRA**
LAJX6
\- **Stenoil K/S**
Rederiet Stenersen AS
Bergen *Norway (NIS)*
MMSI: 258751000

11,935 5,141 16,670 T/cm 28.5
Class: NV

2007-05 Qiuxin Shipyard — Shanghai
Yd No: H2361
Loa 144.12 (BB) Br ex 23.18 Dght 8.900
Lbp 133.80 Br md 23.00 Dpth 12.40
Welded, 1 dk

(A12B2TR) Chemical/Products Tanker
Double Hull (13F)
Liq: 19,172; Liq (Oil): 19,172
Compartments: 12 Wing Ta, 2 Wing Slop Ta, ER
12 Cargo Pump (s): 12x300m³/hr
Manifold: Bow/CM: 72.2m
Ice Capable

1 oil engine geared to sc. shaft driving 1 CP propeller
Total Power: 6,300kW (8,565hp) 14.0kn
Wartsila 6L46C
1 x 4 Stroke 6 Cy. 460 x 580 6300kW (8565bhp)
Wartsila Finland Oy-Finland
AuxGen: 2 x 1020kW a.c, 1 x a.c, 1 x a.c
Thrusters: 1 Tunnel thruster (f)
Fuel: 70.0 (d.f.) 527.0 (r.f.)

9261102 **STEN IDUN**
ZDFM5
\- **Stenoil K/S**
Brostrom AB
Gibraltar *Gibraltar (British)*
MMSI: 236184000
Official number: 736312

11,935 5,137 16,613 T/cm 28.5
Class: NV

2002-12 Jiangnan Shipyard (Group) Co Ltd — Shanghai Yd No: H2285
Loa 144.05 (BB) Br ex 23.03 Dght 8.900
Lbp 133.80 Br md 23.00 Dpth 12.40
Welded, 1 dk

(A12B2TR) Chemical/Products Tanker
Double Hull (13F)
Liq: 18,492; Liq (Oil): 18,492
Compartments: 12 Wing Ta, 2 Wing Slop Ta, ER
12 Cargo Pump (s): 12x300m³/hr
Manifold: Bow/CM: 71.8m
Ice Capable

1 oil engine reduction geared to sc. shaft driving 1 CP propeller
Total Power: 6,300kW (8,565hp) 14.0kn
Wartsila 6L46C
1 x 4 Stroke 6 Cy. 460 x 580 6300kW (8565bhp) (made 2002)
Wartsila Finland Oy-Finland
AuxGen: 1 x 960kW a.c, 2 x 640kW a.c, 1 x 1500kW a.c
Thrusters: 1 Tunnel thruster (f)
Fuel: 570.0 (r.f.)

9341184 **STEN MOSTER**
ZDHG3
\- **Stentank AS**
Rederiet Stenersen AS
Gibraltar *Gibraltar (British)*
MMSI: 236313000

11,935 5,141 16,613 T/cm 28.0
Class: NV

2006-04 Qiuxin Shipyard — Shanghai
Yd No: H2351
Loa 144.10 (BB) Br ex - Dght 8.900
Lbp 133.80 Br md 23.00 Dpth 12.40
Welded, 1 dk

(A12B2TR) Chemical/Products Tanker
Double Hull (13F)
Liq: 18,491; Liq (Oil): 19,172
Compartments: 12 Wing Ta, 2 Wing Slop Ta, ER
12 Cargo Pump (s): 12x300m³/hr
Manifold: Bow/CM: 71.8m
Ice Capable

1 oil engine geared to sc. shaft driving 1 CP propeller
Total Power: 6,300kW (8,565hp) 14.0kn
Wartsila 6L46C
1 x 4 Stroke 6 Cy. 460 x 580 6300kW (8565bhp)
Wartsila Finland Oy-Finland
AuxGen: 1 x a.c, 2 x a.c, 1 x a.c
Thrusters: 1 Tunnel thruster (f)

9351567 **STEN NORDIC**
LAEY6
\- **Utsten II KS**
Rederiet Stenersen AS
Bergen *Norway (NIS)*
MMSI: 257667000

11,935 5,137 16,657 T/cm 28.5
Class: NV

2005-11 Qiuxin Shipyard — Shanghai
Yd No: H2336
Loa 144.05 (BB) Br ex 23.19 Dght 8.889
Lbp 133.80 Br md 23.00 Dpth 12.40
Welded, 1 dk

(A12B2TR) Chemical/Products Tanker
Double Hull (13F)
Liq: 18,491; Liq (Oil): 18,491
Compartments: 12 Wing Ta, 2 Wing Slop Ta, ER
12 Cargo Pump (s): 12x300m³/hr
Manifold: Bow/CM: 71.8m
Ice Capable

1 oil engine reduction geared to sc. shaft driving 1 CP propeller
Total Power: 6,300kW (8,565hp) 14.0kn
Wartsila 6L46C
1 x 4 Stroke 6 Cy. 460 x 580 6300kW (8565bhp)
Wartsila Finland Oy-Finland
AuxGen: 1 x 1080kW 60Hz a.c, 2 x 720kW 60Hz a.c, 1 x 60Hz a.c
Thrusters: 1 Tunnel thruster (f)
Fuel: 70.0 (d.f.) 528.0 (r.f.)

9460239 **STEN SKAGEN**
ZDJD9
\- **Stentank AS**
Brostrom AB
Gibraltar *Gibraltar (British)*
MMSI: 236514000

13,283 5,850 18,531 T/cm 30.5
Class: NV

2009-10 Jiangnan Shipyard (Group) Co Ltd — Shanghai Yd No: H2437
Loa 148.71 (BB) Br ex 23.94 Dght 9.270
Lbp 138.21 Br md 23.76 Dpth 12.80
Welded, 1 dk

(A12B2TR) Chemical/Products Tanker
Double Hull (13F)
Liq: 20,799; Liq (Oil): 20,799
Part Cargo Heating Coils
Compartments: 12 Wing Ta, 2 Wing Slop Ta, ER
12 Cargo Pump (s): 12x375m³/hr
Manifold: Bow/CM: 74.9m
Ice Capable

1 oil engine geared to sc. shaft driving 1 CP propeller
Total Power: 7,200kW (9,789hp) 14.0kn
MAN-B&W 6L48/60B
1 x 4 Stroke 6 Cy. 480 x 600 7200kW (9789bhp)
MAN B&W Diesel AG-Augsburg
AuxGen: 2 x 640kW a.c, 1 x 960kW a.c, 1 x 1875kW a.c
Thrusters: 1 Thwart. FP thruster (f)
Fuel: 70.0 (d.f.) 505.0 (r.f.)

9378723 **STEN SUOMI**
LADP7
\- **K/S Stenship**
Rederiet Stenersen AS
Bergen *Norway (NIS)*
MMSI: 259768000
Official number: 26923

11,935 5,141 16,670 T/cm 28.5
Class: NV

2008-12 Jiangnan Shipyard (Group) Co Ltd — Shanghai Yd No: H2383
Loa 144.05 (BB) Br ex 23.19 Dght 8.900
Lbp 133.80 Br md 23.00 Dpth 12.40
Welded, 1 dk

(A12B2TR) Chemical/Products Tanker
Double Hull (13F)
Liq: 18,491; Liq (Oil): 18,491
Compartments: 12 Wing Ta, 2 Wing Slop Ta, ER
12 Cargo Pump (s): 12x300m³/hr
Manifold: Bow/CM: 71.8m
Ice Capable

1 oil engine reduction geared to sc. shaft driving 1 CP propeller
Total Power: 6,300kW (8,565hp) 14.0kn
Wartsila 6L46C
1 x 4 Stroke 6 Cy. 460 x 580 6300kW (8565bhp)
Wartsila Finland Oy-Finland
AuxGen: 2 x a.c, 1 x a.c, 1 x a.c
Thrusters: 1 Tunnel thruster (f)
Fuel: 71.0 (d.f.) 527.0 (r.f.)

9235529 **STENA ADVENTURER**
VQLZ4
\- **Stena Ropax Ltd**
Stena Line Ltd
London *United Kingdom*
MMSI: 235667000
Official number: 906976

43,532 17,935 9,487 T/cm 51.1
Class: LR
✠ **100A1** CS 05/2013
roll on - roll off cargo and passenger ship
*IWS
Finnish-Swedish Ice Class 1A at draught of 6.80m
Max/min draught forward 4.80/6.80m
Max/min draught aft 4.98/6.80m
✠ **LMC** **UMS**
Eq.Ltr: N†;
Cable: 660.0/76.0 U3 (a)

2003-05 Hyundai Heavy Industries Co Ltd — Ulsan Yd No: 1393
Loa 210.80 (BB) Br ex 29.88 Dght 6.300
Lbp 197.20 Br md 29.30 Dpth 9.50
Welded, 3 dks

(A36A2PR) Passenger/Ro-Ro Ship (Vehicles)
Passengers: 1500; cabins: 148
Bow door/ramp (centre)
Stern door/ramp (centre)
Lane-Len: 3400
Lane-Wid: 6.00
Lane-clr ht: 5.10
Cars: 500
Ice Capable

4 oil engines with clutches, flexible couplings & sr geared to sc. shafts driving 2 CP propellers
Total Power: 25,920kW (35,240hp) 22.0kn
MAN-B&W 9L40/54
4 x 4 Stroke 9 Cy. 400 x 540 each-6480kW (8810bhp)
MAN B&W Diesel AG-Augsburg
AuxGen: 2 x 2400kW 450V 60Hz a.c, 4 x 1200kW 450V 60Hz a.c
Boilers: e (ex.g.) 12.2kgf/cm² (12.0bar), AuxB (o.f.) 9.2kgf/cm² (9.0bar)
Thrusters: 2 Thwart. FP thruster (f)
Fuel: 333.0 (d.f.) 1362.0 (r.f.)

9147291 **STENA ALEGRA**
MYIL6
\- *ex* Norman Trader *-2013* *ex* T Rex *-2010*
ex Ave Luebeck *-2009* *ex* Pau Casals *-2008*
ex Europax Appia *-2006*
ex Dawn Merchant *-2005*
Stena North Sea Ltd
Stena Line BV
London *United Kingdom*
MMSI: 232197000
Official number: 731839

22,152 6,645 7,360
Class: RI (LR)
✠ Classed LR until 26/5/13

1998-09 Astilleros de Sevilla SRL — Seville
Yd No: 287
Loa 179.93 (BB) Br ex 25.24 Dght 6.500
Lbp 168.70 Br md 24.30 Dpth 14.90
Welded, 2 dks plus 4 superstructure dks

(A36A2PR) Passenger/Ro-Ro Ship (Vehicles)
Passengers: unberthed: 138; cabins: 57; berths: 114
Bow door/ramp (centre)
Len: 15.00 Wid: 4.50 Swl: 45
Stern door/ramp (centre)
Len: 13.00 Wid: 17.00 Swl: 90
Lane-Len: 2000
Lane-Wid: 3.00
Lane-clr ht: 5.20
Trailers: 142

4 oil engines with clutches, flexible couplings & sr geared to sc. shafts driving 2 CP propellers
Total Power: 23,760kW (32,304hp) 22.5kn
Wartsila 9R38
4 x 4 Stroke 9 Cy. 380 x 475 each-5940kW (8076bhp)
Wartsila NSD Nederland BV-Netherlands
AuxGen: 2 x 1400kW 450V 60Hz a.c, 2 x 640kW 450V 60Hz a.c, 2 x 880kW 450V 60Hz a.c
Boilers: 2 AuxB (ex.g.) 6.8kgf/cm² (6.7bar), AuxB (o.f.) 6.8kgf/cm² (6.7bar)
Thrusters: 2 Thwart. CP thruster (f)
Fuel: 13.0 (d.f.) 938.0 (r.f.)

9152507 **STENA ALEXITA**
C6AH5
\- **P/R Stena Ugland Shuttle Tanker I DA**
Standard Marine Tonsberg AS
Bahamas
MMSI: 311000046

77,440 34,050 126,955 T/cm 106.5
Class: NV

1998-08 Hashihama Shipbuilding Co Ltd — Tadotsu KG Yd No: 1129
Loa 262.60 (BB) Br ex 46.04 Dght 15.728
Lbp 247.00 Br md 46.00 Dpth 23.70
Welded, 1 dk

(A13A2TS) Shuttle Tanker
Double Hull (13F)
Liq: 134,014; Liq (Oil): 134,001
Cargo Heating Coils
Compartments: 12 Wing Ta, Wing ER, 2 Wing Slop Ta
3 Cargo Pump (s): 3x4000m³/hr
Manifold: Bow/CM: 130m

2 oil engines driving 2 CP propellers
Total Power: 19,272kW (26,202hp) 15.0kn
B&W 7S50MC
2 x 2 Stroke 7 Cy. 500 x 1910 each-9636kW (13101bhp)
Mitsui Engineering & Shipbuilding CLtd-Japan
AuxGen: 2 x 2420kW 220/440V 60Hz a.c, 2 x 1640kW 220/440V 60Hz a.c
Thrusters: 2 Thwart. FP thruster (f); 2 Thwart. FP thruster (a)
Fuel: 254.0 (d.f.) (Heating Coils) 3710.0 (r.f.) 65.0pd

9322827 **STENA ANTARCTICA**
ZCPE
\- *completed as* Four Antarctica *-2006*
Premuda International Sah
Northern Marine Management Ltd
SatCom: Inmarsat C 431956210
George Town *Cayman Islands (British)*
MMSI: 319562000
Official number: 739108

61,371 35,420 114,849 T/cm 99.0
Class: NV

2006-05 Samsung Heavy Industries Co Ltd — Geoje Yd No: 1575
Loa 250.00 (BB) Br ex 43.84 Dght 14.940
Lbp 239.00 Br md 43.80 Dpth 21.00
Welded, 1 dk

(A13A2TV) Crude Oil Tanker
Double Hull (13F)
Liq: 123,860; Liq (Oil): 127,500
Cargo Heating Coils
Compartments: 12 Wing Ta, 2 Wing Slop Ta, ER
3 Cargo Pump (s): 3x2800m³/hr
Manifold: Bow/CM: 125.7m
Ice Capable

1 oil engine driving 1 FP propeller
Total Power: 15,820kW (21,509hp) 15.3kn
MAN-B&W 7S60MC-C
1 x 2 Stroke 7 Cy. 600 x 2400 15820kW (21509bhp)
Doosan Engine Co Ltd-South Korea
AuxGen: 3 x 680kW a.c
Fuel: 210.0 (d.f.) 2700.0 (r.f.)

9305556 **STENA ARCTICA**
2GXH5
\- **Glacia Ltd**
Neste Shipping Oy
London *United Kingdom*
MMSI: 235101274
Official number: 919419

65,293 35,715 117,099 T/cm 98.2
Class: NV

2005-11 Hyundai Heavy Industries Co Ltd — Ulsan Yd No: 1621
Loa 249.79 (BB) Br ex 44.07 Dght 15.422
Lbp 239.00 Br md 44.00 Dpth 22.04
Welded, 1 dk

(A13A2TV) Crude Oil Tanker
Double Hull (13F)
Liq: 130,213; Liq (Oil): 130,213
Compartments: 12 Wing Ta, 1 Slop Ta, ER
3 Cargo Pump (s): 3x3000m³/hr
Manifold: Bow/CM: 125.1m
Ice Capable

1 oil engine driving 1 FP propeller
Total Power: 15,806kW (21,490hp) 14.0kn
MAN-B&W 7S60ME-C
1 x 2 Stroke 7 Cy. 600 x 2400 15806kW (21490bhp)
Hyundai Heavy Industries Co Ltd-South Korea
AuxGen: 3 x 950kW 440/220V 60Hz a.c
Fuel: 189.1 (d.f.) 2842.4 (r.f.)

IMO / Call sign	Name / Owner / Manager / Flag	Tonnage	Class	Builder / Dimensions	Type / Cargo	Machinery
9322839 *ZCPR7* -	**STENA ATLANTICA** *completed as* Four Atlantica *-2006* **Premuda International Sah** Northern Marine Management Ltd SatCom: Inmarsat C 431916110 *George Town* *Cayman Islands (British)* MMSI: 319161000 Official number: 739722	**61,371** 35,420 114,896 T/cm 99.0	Class: NV	**2006-11 Samsung Heavy Industries Co Ltd — Geoje** Yd No: 1576 Loa 250.00 (BB) Br ex 43.80 Dght 14.940 Lbp 239.00 Br md 43.80 Dpth 21.30 Welded, 1 dk	**(A13A2TV) Crude Oil Tanker** Double Hull (13F) Liq: 123,860; Liq (Oil): 123,860 Cargo Heating Coils Compartments: 12 Wing Ta, 2 Wing Slop Ta, ER 3 Cargo Pump (s): 3x2800m^3/hr Manifold: Bow/CM: 125.7m Ice Capable	**1 oil engine** driving 1 FP propeller Total Power: 12,879kW (17,510hp) 15.3kn MAN-B&W 7S60MC-C 1 x 2 Stroke 7 Cy. 600 x 2400 12879kW (17510bhp) Doosan Engine Co Ltd-South Korea AuxGen: 3 x 680kW a.c Fuel: 205.1 (d.f.) 2838.1 (r.f.)
9364978 *2HAL4* -	**STENA BALTICA** *ex* Cotentin *-2013* **SNC Cotentin** Stena Line BV *London* *United Kingdom* MMSI: 235102029	**22,308** 6,692 6,200	Class: BV	**2007-11 Aker Yards Oy — Helsinki** Yd No: 1357 Loa 165.00 (BB) Br ex - Dght 6.500 Lbp 157.50 Br md 26.80 Dpth - Welded	**(A36A2PR) Passenger/Ro-Ro Ship (Vehicles)** Passengers: cabins: 120; berths: 160 Bow door/ramp (f) Len: 17.50 Wid: 6.00 Swl: - Stern door/ramp (a) Len: 7.50 Wid: 12.00 Swl: - Lane-Len: 2200 Lane-clr ht: 5.20 Lorries: 120 Ice Capable	**2 oil engines** reduction geared to sc. shafts driving 2 CP propellers Total Power: 24,000kW (32,630hp) 23.0kn MaK 12M43C 2 x Vee 4 Stroke 12 Cy. 430 x 610 each-12000kW (16315bhp) Caterpillar Motoren GmbH & Co. KG-Germany AuxGen: 2 x 1440kW a.c Thrusters: 2 Tunnel thruster (f)
9315393 *3EFN3* -	**STENA BLUE SKY** *ex* Bluesky *-2011* **Blue Sky LNG Ltd** Stena Bulk AB SatCom: Inmarsat C 435243810 *Panama* *Panama* MMSI: 352438000 Official number: 3199206CH	**97,754** 29,327 84,363 T/cm 104.3	Class: BV (NV)	**2006-06 Daewoo Shipbuilding & Marine Engineering Co Ltd — Geoje** Yd No: 2233 Loa 285.40 (BB) Br ex 43.44 Dght 12.300 Lbp 274.40 Br md 43.40 Dpth 26.00 Welded, 1 dk	**(A11A2TN) LNG Tanker** Double Bottom Entire Compartment Length Liq (Gas): 142,988 4 x Gas Tank (s); 4 membrane (36% Ni.stl) pri horizontal 8 Cargo Pump (s): 8x1700m^3/hr Manifold: Bow/CM: 141.6m Ice Capable	**1 Steam Turb** reduction geared to sc. shaft driving 1 FP propeller Total Power: 21,461kW (29,178hp) 20.4kn Kawasaki UA-360 1 x steam Turb 21461kW (29178shp) Kawasaki Heavy Industries Ltd-Japan AuxGen: 2 x 3200kW 6600V 60Hz a.c, 2 x 1750kW 6600V 60Hz a.c Thrusters: 1 Thwart. CP thruster (f) Fuel: 505.0 (d.f.) 6915.0 (r.f.)
9419175 *2DMO6* -	**STENA BRITANNICA** *launched as* Stena Britannica III *-2010* **Stena Ropax Ltd** Stena Line BV SatCom: Inmarsat C 423506910 *Harwich* *United Kingdom* MMSI: 235080274 Official number: 917031	**64,039** 36,870 11,600	Class: LR ✠ **100A1** SS 09/2010 roll on-roll off cargo and passenger ship *IWS LI EP (P) Ice Class 1B FS at a draught of 6.650m Max/min draughts fwd 6.650/5.316m Max/min draughts aft 6.650/5.016m Power required 4933kw, power instaled 33600kw ✠ **LMC** **UMS** Eq.Ltr: Q†; Cable: 687.5/81.0 U3 (a)	**2010-09 Nordic Yards Wismar GmbH — Wismar** (Aft section) Yd No: 164 **2010-09 Nordic Yards Warnemuende GmbH — Rostock** (Fwd section) Yd No: 164 Loa 240.00 (BB) Br ex 32.02 Dght 6.400 Lbp 224.00 Br md 32.00 Dpth 21.30 Welded, 7 dks	**(A36A2PR) Passenger/Ro-Ro Ship (Vehicles)** Passengers: cabins: 538; berths: 1376 Bow ramp (centre) Len: 5.20 Wid: 22.36 Swl: 115 Bow door/ramp (centre) Stern ramp (centre) Stern door/ramp (centre) Len: 5.08 Wid: 20.13 Swl: 203 Lane-Len: 5566 Lane-clr ht: 4.80 Lorries: 320, Cars: 230 Ice Capable	**4 oil engines** with clutches, flexible couplings & dr geared to sc. shafts driving 2 CP propellers Total Power: 33,600kW (45,682hp) 22.0kn MAN-B&W 6L48/60CR 2 x 4 Stroke 6 Cy. 480 x 600 each-7200kW (9789bhp) MAN B&W Diesel AG-Augsburg MAN-B&W 8L48/60CR 2 x 4 Stroke 8 Cy. 480 x 600 each-9600kW (13052bhp) MAN B&W Diesel AG-Augsburg AuxGen: 2 x 3176kW 440V 60Hz a.c, 3 x 1254kW 440V 60Hz a.c, 1 x 1463kW 440V 60Hz a.c Boilers: e (ex.g.) 10.2kgf/cm^2 (10.0bar), AuxB (o.f.) 10.2kgf/cm^2 (10.0bar) Thrusters: 2 Thwart. CP thruster (f) Fuel: 185.0 (d.f.) 985.0 (r.f.)
9283629 *C6TM9* -	**STENA CALLAS** *ex* Aspropyrgos *-2009* **Aspropyrgos Maritime Ltd** Stena Bulk AB *Nassau* *Bahamas* MMSI: 311702000 Official number: 8000786	**40,690** 21,232 72,854 T/cm 67.2	Class: NK (LR) ✠ Classed LR until 7/10/08	**2004-08 Hudong-Zhonghua Shipbuilding (Group) Co Ltd — Shanghai** Yd No: H1300A Loa 228.60 (BB) Br ex 32.29 Dght 14.015 Lbp 218.60 Br md 32.26 Dpth 20.20 Welded, 1 dk	**(A13A2TW) Crude/Oil Products Tanker** Double Hull (13F) Liq: 78,636; Liq (Oil): 81,000 Cargo Heating Coils Compartments: 12 Wing Ta, 2 Wing Slop Ta, ER 3 Cargo Pump (s): 3x2000m^3/hr Manifold: Bow/CM: 116m	**1 oil engine** driving 1 FP propeller Total Power: 11,500kW (15,635hp) 15.0kn MAN-B&W 6S60MC 1 x 2 Stroke 6 Cy. 600 x 2292 11500kW (15635bhp) Hudong Heavy Machinery Co Ltd-China AuxGen: 3 x 600kW 450V 60Hz a.c Boilers: WTAuxB (Comp) 8.0kgf/cm^2 (7.8bar), WTAuxB (o.f.) 18.4kgf/cm^2 (18.0bar) Fuel: 176.1 (d.f.) 2907.0 (r.f.)
9228887 *ZINH9* -	**STENA CALYPSO** **Stena Florida Line Ltd** Stena Bulk AB SatCom: Inmarsat C 423548410 *London* *United Kingdom* MMSI: 235484000 Official number: 906239	**8,613** 3,288 9,996 T/cm 25.6	Class: AB	**2002-10 Stocznia Gdynia SA — Gdynia** Yd No: 8226/2 Loa 120.65 (BB) Br ex - Dght 6.500 Lbp 117.10 Br md 23.80 Dpth 9.50 Welded, 1 dk	**(A13B2TP) Products Tanker** Double Hull (13F) Ins: 1,280; Liq: 13,272; Liq (Gas): 1,280; Liq (Oil): 12,650 Cargo Heating Coils Compartments: ER, 2 Wing Slop Ta, 16 Wing Ta 16 Cargo Pump (s): 16x300m^3/hr Manifold: Bow/CM: 56.3m	**4 diesel electric oil engines** driving 2 gen. each 2000kW 690V a.c 2 gen. each 600kW 690V a.c Connecting to 2 elec. motors each (2200kW) driving 2 Directional propellers Total Power: 5,740kW (7,804hp) 13.5kn Wartsila 4L20 2 x 4 Stroke 4 Cy. 200 x 280 each-650kW (884bhp) Wartsila France SA-France Wartsila 6R32LND 2 x 4 Stroke 6 Cy. 320 x 350 each-2220kW (3018bhp) Wartsila France SA-France Thrusters: 1 Thwart. FP thruster (f) Fuel: 40.0 (d.f.) 580.0 (r.f.)
9127760 *SGFV* -	**STENA CARISMA** **Stena Line Scandinavia AB** - *Gothenburg* *Sweden* MMSI: 265430000	**8,631** 2,589 480	Class: NV	**1997-06 Westamarin West AS — Mandal** Yd No: 238 Loa 89.75 (BB) Br ex 30.47 Dght 3.900 Lbp 77.50 Br md 30.00 Dpth 9.60 Welded, 1 dk	**(A36A2PR) Passenger/Ro-Ro Ship (Vehicles)** Hull Material: Aluminium Alloy Passengers: unberthed: 900 Stern door (p) Len: 4.80 Wid: 3.80 Swl: - Stern door (s) Len: 4.80 Wid: 3.80 Swl: - Cars: 208	**2 Gas Turbs** reduction geared to sc. shafts driving 2 Water jets Total Power: 35,460kW (48,212hp) 38.0kn Stal-Laval GT35 2 x Gas Turb each-17730kW (24106shp) ABB Stal AB-Sweden AuxGen: 4 x 520kW 230/440V 60Hz a.c Thrusters: 2 Thwart. CP thruster (f) Fuel: 93.0 (d.f.) 243.0pd
9138800 *2DVE7* -	**STENA CARRIER** *ex* Stena Carrier II *-2004* **Stena Carrier AB** Northern Marine Ferries Ltd SatCom: Inmarsat C 423597627 *Harwich* *United Kingdom* MMSI: 235082307 Official number: 916980	**21,171** 6,351 12,350	Class: NV	**2004-03 Soc. Esercizio Cant. S.p.A. — Viareggio** (Hull launched by) Yd No: 1548 **2004-03 Nuovi Cantieri Apuania SpA — Carrara** (Hull completed by) Yd No: 1231 Loa 182.77 (BB) Br ex 25.52 Dght 6.600 Lbp 166.41 Br md 25.50 Dpth 16.62 Welded, 3 dks	**(A35A2RR) Ro-Ro Cargo Ship** Passengers: driver berths: 12 Stern door/ramp (centre) Len: 19.50 Wid: 18.60 Swl: 86 Lane-Len: 2715 Lane-Wid: 17.20 Lane-clr ht: 6.80 Trailers: 189 TEU 800 incl 75 ref C. Ice Capable	**4 oil engines** reduction geared to sc. shafts driving 2 CP propellers Total Power: 18,776kW (25,528hp) 20.5kn Sulzer 8ZA40S 4 x 4 Stroke 8 Cy. 400 x 560 each-4694kW (6382bhp) New Sulzer Diesel France-France AuxGen: 2 x 1700kW a.c, 2 x 1500kW 60Hz a.c Thrusters: 2 Thwart. FP thruster (f)
9364954 *2BKQ8* -	**STENA CARRON** **Stena Carron Lux 3 Sarl** Stena Drilling Ltd SatCom: Inmarsat C 423591072 *Aberdeen* *United Kingdom* MMSI: 235066948 Official number: 737929	**58,294** 17,489 97,000	Class: NV	**2008-08 Samsung Heavy Industries Co Ltd — Geoje** Yd No: 1669 Loa 227.80 Br ex - Dght 12.000 Lbp 219.40 Br md 42.00 Dpth 19.00 Welded, 1 dk	**(B22B20D) Drilling Ship** Liq: 10,000	**6 diesel electric oil engines** driving 6 gen. each 7290kW 690V a.c Connecting to 2 elec. motors each (5500kW) driving 2 Azimuth electric drive units Total Power: 43,740kW (59,466hp) 12.0kn Wartsila 16V32 6 x Vee 4 Stroke 16 Cy. 320 x 400 each-7290kW (9911bhp) Wartsila Finland Oy-Finland Thrusters: 4 Directional thruster
9282625 *C6TN7* -	**STENA CHIRON** *ex* Daedalos *-2008* **Daedalos Maritime Ltd** Stena Bulk AB *Nassau* *Bahamas* MMSI: 311708000 Official number: 8000792	**40,690** 21,247 72,825 T/cm 66.8	Class: NK (LR) ✠ Classed LR until 29/3/09	**2005-03 Hudong-Zhonghua Shipbuilding (Group) Co Ltd — Shanghai** Yd No: H1332A Loa 228.60 (BB) Br ex 32.29 Dght 14.000 Lbp 218.60 Br md 32.26 Dpth 20.20 Welded, 1 dk	**(A13A2TV) Crude Oil Tanker** Double Hull (13F) Liq: 81,300; Liq (Oil): 81,300 Compartments: 12 Wing Ta, 2 Wing Slop Ta, ER 3 Cargo Pump (s) Manifold: Bow/CM: 116m	**1 oil engine** driving 1 FP propeller Total Power: 11,500kW (15,635hp) 15.2kn B&W 6S60MC 1 x 2 Stroke 6 Cy. 600 x 2292 11500kW (15635bhp) Hudong Heavy Machinery Co Ltd-China AuxGen: 3 x 600kW 450V 60Hz a.c Boilers: AuxB (Comp) 8.0kgf/cm^2 (7.8bar), WTAuxB (o.f.) 18.4kgf/cm^2 (18.0bar) Fuel: 2590.0
9283617 *C6TN6* -	**STENA CHRONOS** *ex* Ikaros *-2009* **Ikaros Maritime Ltd** Stena Bulk AB *Nassau* *Bahamas* MMSI: 311707000 Official number: 8000791	**40,690** 21,245 72,829 T/cm 67.2	Class: NK (LR) ✠ Classed LR until 14/12/08	**2004-11 Hudong-Zhonghua Shipbuilding (Group) Co Ltd — Shanghai** Yd No: H1301A Loa 228.60 (BB) Br ex 32.29 Dght 14.015 Lbp 218.60 Br md 32.26 Dpth 20.20 Welded, 1 dk	**(A13A2TW) Crude/Oil Products Tanker** Double Hull (13F) Liq: 78,363; Liq (Oil): 81,000 Cargo Heating Coils Compartments: 12 Wing Ta, 2 Wing Slop Ta, ER 3 Cargo Pump (s): 3x2000m^3/hr Manifold: Bow/CM: 116m	**1 oil engine** driving 1 FP propeller Total Power: 11,500kW (15,635hp) 15.0kn MAN-B&W 6S60MC 1 x 2 Stroke 6 Cy. 600 x 2292 11500kW (15635bhp) Hudong Heavy Machinery Co Ltd-China AuxGen: 3 x 600kW 450V 60Hz a.c Boilers: AuxB (Comp) 8.0kgf/cm^2 (7.8bar), WTAuxB (o.f.) 18.4kgf/cm^2 (18.0bar) Fuel: 2907.0

Identity / Name / Owner	Tonnage / Class	Build / Dimensions	Type / Cargo	Machinery
9413327 **STENA CLEAR SKY** *2GRY8* *launched as* Clearsky *-2011* - **Clear Sky LNG Shipping Ltd** Stena Bulk AB *Stranraer* *United Kingdom* MMSI: 235100007 Official number: 740536	**109,949** Class: BV 34,378 96,811	**2011**-05 **Daewoo Shipbuilding & Marine Engineering Co Ltd — Geoje** Yd No: 2278 Loa 298.00 (BB) Br ex - Dght 12.900 Lbp 279.00 Br md 45.80 Dpth 26.50 Welded, 1 dk	**(A11A2TN) LNG Tanker** Liq (Gas): 173,593 4 x Gas Tank (s); 4 membrane (36% Ni.stl) pri horizontal 8 Cargo Pump (s) Ice Capable	**4 diesel electric oil engines** driving 3 gen. each 9778kW 6600V a.c 1 gen. of 8889kW 6600V a.c Connecting to 2 elec. motors each (13600kW) driving 2 FP propellers Total Power: 44,550kW (60,569hp) 19.5kn Wartsila 12V50DF 3 x Vee 4 Stroke 12 Cy. 500 x 580 each-11700kW (15907bhp) Wartsila Finland Oy-Finland Wartsila 9L46 1 x 4 Stroke 9 Cy. 460 x 580 9450kW (12848bhp) Wartsila Finland Oy-Finland Fuel: 6118.0 (r.f.)
8752996 **STENA CLYDE** *GVEV* *ex* Benloyal *-1996* *ex* Ocean Benloyal *-1992* - *ex* Sea Conquest *-1982* **Stena Holland BV** Stena Drilling Ltd *Leith* *United Kingdom* MMSI: 234418000 Official number: 376547	**11,326** Class: NV 3,398 10,129	**1976**-11 **Rauma-Repola Oy — Pori** Yd No: 5 Loa 108.20 Br ex 56.40 Dght 6.400 Lbp - Br md - Dpth 36.58 Welded, 1 dk	**(Z11C3ZE) Drilling Rig, semi Submersible** Passengers: berths: 100 Cranes: 2x46t	**4 diesel electric oil engines** driving 4 gen. each 1840kW a.c Connecting to 2 elec. motors driving 2 Propellers Total Power: 7,768kW (10,560hp) Ruston 12RK3CM 4 x Vee 4 Stroke 12 Cy. 254 x 305 each-1942kW (2640bhp) Ruston Paxman Diesels Ltd.-United Kingdom
9258595 **STENA CONCERT** *ZCDX9* *ex* Stena Italica *-2008* - **Stena Gentian Ltd** Northern Marine Management USA LLC *Hamilton* *Bermuda (British)* MMSI: 310560000 Official number: 737958	**27,512** Class: NV (LR) (BV) (RI) 13,797 ✠ Classed LR until 7/6/06 47,288 T/cm 52.2	**2004**-07 **'Uljanik' Brodogradiliste dd — Pula** Yd No: 447 Loa 182.50 (BB) Br ex 32.22 Dght 12.197 Lbp 174.80 Br md 32.20 Dpth 17.50 Welded, 1 dk	**(A12B2TR) Chemical/Products Tanker** Double Hull (13F) Liq: 51,976; Liq (Oil): 51,976 Cargo Heating Coils Compartments: 10 Wing Ta, 2 Wing Slop Ta, ER 10 Cargo Pump (s): 10x550m³/hr Manifold: Bow/CM: 90.9m	**1 oil engine** driving 1 FP propeller Total Power: 8,580kW (11,665hp) 14.8kn B&W 6S50MC 1 x 2 Stroke 6 Cy. 500 x 1910 8580kW (11665bhp) 'Uljanik' Strojogradnja dd-Croatia AuxGen: 1 x 1192kW 450V 60Hz a.c, 2 x 725kW 450V 60Hz a.c Boilers: e (ex.g.) 12.5kgf/cm² (12.3bar), AuxB (o.f.) 12.2kgf/cm² (12.0bar) Thrusters: 1 Thwart. FP thruster (f) Fuel: 151.5 (d.f.) 1523.0 (r.f.)
9252448 **STENA CONQUEROR** *ZCDX8* *launched as* Hellenica *-2003* - **Stena Gentian Ltd** Northern Marine Management Ltd SatCom: Inmarsat B 331055910 *Hamilton* *Bermuda (British)* MMSI: 310559000	**27,512** Class: NV (LR) (BV) (RI) 13,797 ✠ Classed LR until 16/10/03 47,323 T/cm 52.4	**2003**-10 **'Uljanik' Brodogradiliste dd — Pula** Yd No: 444 Loa 182.50 (BB) Br ex 32.22 Dght 12.177 Lbp 174.80 Br md 32.20 Dpth 17.50 Welded, 1 dk	**(A12B2TR) Chemical/Products Tanker** Double Hull (13F) Liq: 51,976; Liq (Oil): 51,555 Cargo Heating Coils Compartments: 10 Wing Ta, 2 Wing Slop Ta, ER 10 Cargo Pump (s): 10x550m³/hr Manifold: Bow/CM: 91.1m	**1 oil engine** driving 1 FP propeller Total Power: 8,580kW (11,665hp) 14.5kn B&W 6S50MC 1 x 2 Stroke 6 Cy. 500 x 1910 8580kW (11665bhp) 'Uljanik' Strojogradnja dd-Croatia AuxGen: 2 x 1192kW 450V 60Hz a.c, 1 x 725kW 450V 60Hz a.c Boilers: e (ex.g.) 12.7kgf/cm² (12.5bar), AuxB (o.f.) 12.2kgf/cm² (12.0bar) Thrusters: 1 Thwart. FP thruster (f) Fuel: 112.0 (d.f.) 1508.0 (r.f.) 34.0pd
9252436 **STENA CONQUEST** *ZCDX7* *completed as* Hispanica *-2003* - **Stena Gentian Ltd** Northern Marine Management USA LLC *Hamilton* *Bermuda (British)* MMSI: 310558000	**27,512** Class: NV (LR) (BV) (RI) 13,797 ✠ Classed LR until 24/9/04 47,136 T/cm 51.8	**2003**-06 **'Uljanik' Brodogradiliste dd — Pula** Yd No: 443 Loa 182.43 (BB) Br ex 32.22 Dght 12.197 Lbp 174.80 Br md 32.20 Dpth 17.50 Welded, 1 dk	**(A12B2TR) Chemical/Products Tanker** Double Hull (13F) Liq: 51,976; Liq (Oil): 51,976 Cargo Heating Coils Compartments: 10 Wing Ta, 2 Wing Slop Ta, ER 10 Cargo Pump (s): 10x550m³/hr Manifold: Bow/CM: 90.9m	**1 oil engine** driving 1 FP propeller Total Power: 8,580kW (11,665hp) 14.5kn B&W 6S50MC 1 x 2 Stroke 6 Cy. 500 x 1910 8580kW (11665bhp) 'Uljanik' Strojogradnja dd-Croatia AuxGen: 2 x 1192kW 450V 60Hz a.c, 1 x a.c Boilers: e (ex.g.) 12.7kgf/cm² (12.5bar), AuxB (o.f.) 12.2kgf/cm² (12.0bar) Thrusters: 1 Thwart. FP thruster (f) Fuel: 151.5 (d.f.) 1523.4 (r.f.)
9383900 **STENA CRYSTAL SKY** *2GRR6* *launched as* Crystalsky *-2011* - **Crystal Sky LNG Shipping Ltd** Stena Bulk AB *Stranraer* *United Kingdom* MMSI: 235099946 Official number: 740535	**109,949** Class: BV 34,378 96,889	**2011**-05 **Daewoo Shipbuilding & Marine Engineering Co Ltd — Geoje** Yd No: 2268 Loa 298.00 (BB) Br ex - Dght 12.900 Lbp 279.00 Br md 45.80 Dpth 26.50 Welded, 1 dk	**(A11A2TN) LNG Tanker** Double Hull Liq (Gas): 173,611 4 x Gas Tank (s); 4 membrane (36% Ni.stl) pri horizontal 8 Cargo Pump (s) Ice Capable	**4 diesel electric oil engines** driving 3 gen. each 9778kW 6600V a.c 1 gen. of 8889kW 6600V a.c Connecting to 2 elec. motors each (13600kW) driving 2 FP propellers Total Power: 43,650kW (59,345hp) 19.5kn Wartsila 12V50DF 3 x Vee 4 Stroke 12 Cy. 500 x 580 each-11400kW (15499bhp) Wartsila France SA-France Wartsila 9L46 1 x 4 Stroke 9 Cy. 460 x 580 9450kW (12848bhp) Wartsila France SA-France Fuel: 6118.0 (r.f.)
7907245 **STENA DANICA** *SKFH* - **Stena Line Scandinavia AB** - *Gothenburg* *Sweden* MMSI: 265177000	**28,727** Class: NV (BV) 8,700 2,950	**1983**-02 **Chantiers du Nord et de La Mediterranee (NORMED) — Dunkirk** Yd No: 309 Loa 154.90 (BB) Br ex 28.48 Dght 6.320 Lbp 133.51 Br md 28.01 Dpth 13.62 Welded, 3 dks	**(A36A2PR) Passenger/Ro-Ro Ship (Vehicles)** Passengers: 2274; cabins: 48; berths: 96 Bow door & ramp Len: 11.60 Wid: 7.00 Swl: - Stern door/ramp (p) Len: 10.03 Wid: 9.63 Swl: - Stern door/ramp (s) Len: 10.03 Wid: 9.63 Swl: - Side ramp (p. f.) Side ramp (p. a.) Lane-Len: 1806 Lane-Wid: 6.00 Lane-clr ht: 4.45 Cars: 550, Trailers: 82 Ice Capable	**4 oil engines** with clutches, flexible couplings & sr geared to sc. shafts driving 2 CP propellers Total Power: 25,596kW (34,800hp) 21.0kn Sulzer 12ZV40/48 4 x Vee 2 Stroke 12 Cy. 400 x 480 each-6399kW (8700bhp) Cie de Constructions Mecaniques (CCM), procede Sulzer-France AuxGen: 5 x 910kW 380V 50Hz a.c Thrusters: 2 Thwart. CP thruster (f)
8764418 **STENA DON** *V7GX3* - **Stena Don Cyprus Ltd** Stena Drilling Ltd *Majuro* *Marshall Islands* MMSI: 538002189 Official number: 2189	**20,064** Class: NV 6,019 3,700	**2001**-12 **Kvaerner Warnow Werft GmbH — Rostock** Yd No: NB400 Loa 95.50 Br ex 71.00 Dght 21.500 Lbp - Br md 69.00 Dpth 33.50 Welded, 1 dk	**(Z11C3ZE) Drilling Rig, semi Submersible**	**9 diesel electric oil engines** driving 9 gen. each 3000kW 11000V a.c Connecting to 6 elec. motors each (3300kW) driving 6 Azimuth electric drive units Total Power: 31,500kW (42,831hp) 8.0kn Nohab 16V25 9 x Vee 4 Stroke 16 Cy. 250 x 300 each-3500kW (4759bhp) Wartsila Sweden AB-Sweden
9364942 **STENA DRILLMAX** *2ALV2* - **Stena Drillmax Lux 3 Sarl** Stena Drilling Ltd *Aberdeen* *United Kingdom* MMSI: 235060864 Official number: 737908	**58,294** Class: NV 17,489 97,000	**2007**-12 **Samsung Heavy Industries Co Ltd — Geoje** Yd No: 1650 Loa 227.80 Br ex - Dght 13.000 Lbp 219.40 Br md 42.00 Dpth 19.00 Welded, 1 dk	**(B22B2OD) Drilling Ship** Liq: 10,000	**6 diesel electric oil engines** driving 6 gen. each 7290kW 690V a.c Connecting to 2 elec. motors each (5500kW) driving 2 Azimuth electric drive units Total Power: 43,740kW (59,466hp) 12.0kn Wartsila 16V32 6 x Vee 4 Stroke 16 Cy. 320 x 400 each-7290kW (9911bhp) Wartsila Finland Oy-Finland Thrusters: 4 Directional thruster
7901760 **STENA EUROPE** *VSTA3* *ex* Lion Europe *-1998* *ex* Stena Europe *-1997* - *ex* Stena Saga *-1994* *ex* Kronprinsessan Victoria *-1988* **Stena Ropax Ltd** Stena Line Ltd *Fishguard* *United Kingdom* MMSI: 235004539 Official number: 905449	**24,828** Class: NV 8,338 2,692	**1981**-04 **Gotaverken Arendal AB — Goteborg** Yd No: 908 Loa 149.02 (BB) Br ex 26.55 Dght 6.140 Lbp 131.21 Br md 26.01 Dpth 16.11 Welded, 6 dks	**(A36A2PR) Passenger/Ro-Ro Ship (Vehicles)** Passengers: unberthed: 804; cabins: 572; berths: 1272 Bow door & ramp Len: 16.50 Wid: 7.82 Swl: - Stern door/ramp (p) Len: 16.50 Wid: 3.72 Swl: - Stern door/ramp (s) Len: 16.50 Wid: 6.52 Swl: - Stern door/ramp (centre) Len: 16.50 Wid: 6.52 Swl: - Lane-Len: 900 Lane-Wid: 6.20 Lane-clr ht: 4.40 Trailers: 60 Ice Capable	**4 oil engines** geared to sc. shafts driving 2 CP propellers Total Power: 15,152kW (20,600hp) 20.5kn Wartsila 12V32 4 x Vee 4 Stroke 12 Cy. 320 x 350 each-3788kW (5150bhp) Oy Wartsila Ab-Finland AuxGen: 3 x 1120kW 380V 50Hz a.c, 2 x 1100kW 380V 50Hz a.c, 1 x 440kW 380V 50Hz a.c Thrusters: 2 Thwart. FP thruster (f) Fuel: 101.5 (d.f.) 368.0 (r.f.) 86.5pd

IMO / Call sign	Name / Owner / Manager	Tonnage	Class	Builder / Dimensions	Type / Details	Machinery
9080194 *MVBD8* -	**STENA EXPLORER** **HSS I Ltd** Stena Line Ltd *London* United Kingdom MMSI: 232002562 Official number: 728692	**19,638** 5,892 1,500	Class: NV	**1996**-02 **Finnyards Oy — Rauma** Yd No: 404 Loa 125.00 (BB) Br ex - Dght 4.500 Lbp 107.50 Br md 40.00 Dpth 12.50 Welded, 1 dk	**(A36A2PR) Passenger/Ro-Ro Ship (Vehicles)** Hull Material: Aluminium Alloy Passengers: unberthed: 1520 Stern door (p. inner) Stern door (p. outer) Stern door (s. inner) Stern door (s. outer) Lane-Len: 885 Cars: 375	**4 Gas Turbs** geared to sc. shafts driving 4 Water jets Total Power: 80,000kW (108,768hp) 40.0kn GE Marine LM1600 2 x Gas Turb each-15000kW (20394shp) Kvaerner Brug AS-Norway GE Marine LM2500 2 x Gas Turb each-25000kW (33990shp) Kvaerner Brug AS-Norway AuxGen: 4 x 861kW 230/440V 60Hz a.c Thrusters: 2 Thwart. FP thruster (f) Fuel: 250.0 (d.f.) 200.0pd
9136022 *5BXF3* -	**STENA FERONIA** *ex* Dublin Seaways *-2011* *ex* Dublin Viking *-2010* *ex* Mersey Viking *-2005* **Stena North Sea Ltd** Northern Marine Management Ltd *Limassol* Cyprus MMSI: 209894000	**21,856** 6,580 7,910 T/cm 35.1	Class: NV RI	**1997**-07 **Cantiere Navale Visentini Srl — Porto Viro** Yd No: 180 Loa 186.45 (BB) Br ex 26.00 Dght 5.550 Lbp 169.50 Br md 25.60 Dpth 9.15 Welded, 2 dks	**(A36A2PR) Passenger/Ro-Ro Ship (Vehicles)** Passengers: cabins: 72; berths: 340 Stern door/ramp (p) Len: 14.00 Wid: 6.00 Swl: - Stern door/ramp (s) Len: 14.00 Wid: 16.00 Swl: - Lane-Len: 2460 Cars: 100, Trailers: 164 Ice Capable	**2 oil engines** reduction geared to sc. shafts driving 2 FP propellers Total Power: 15,600kW (21,210hp) 24.0kn Wartsila 8R46 2 x 4 Stroke 8 Cy. 460 x 580 each-7800kW (10605bhp) Wartsila Diesel AB-Sweden AuxGen: 2 x 850kW 220/440V 60Hz a.c, 3 x 1070kW 220/440V 60Hz a.c Thrusters: 2 Thwart. FP thruster (f); 1 Thwart. FP thruster (f) Fuel: 231.5 (d.f.) 981.7 (r.f.) 22.0pd
9417919 *2ASI7* -	**STENA FLAVIA** *ex* Watling Street *-2013* *ex* Pilar Del Mar *-2010* *ex* Watling Street *-2008* **Stena RoRo Navigation Ltd** Stena Ro Ro AB *London* United Kingdom MMSI: 235064391 Official number: 914496	**26,904** 8,912 7,000	Class: RI	**2008**-04 **Cantiere Navale Visentini Srl — Porto Viro** Yd No: 219 Loa 186.42 (BB) Br ex - Dght 6.850 Lbp 177.12 Br md 25.60 Dpth 15.00 Welded, 1 dk	**(A36A2PR) Passenger/Ro-Ro Ship (Vehicles)** Passengers: 852 Stern door/ramp (centre) Lane-Len: 2255 Cars: 195 Ice Capable	**2 oil engines** reduction geared to sc. shafts driving 2 CP propellers Total Power: 21,600kW (29,368hp) 18.0kn MAN-B&W 9L48/60B 2 x 4 Stroke 9 Cy. 480 x 600 each-10800kW (14684bhp) MAN B&W Diesel AG-Augsburg AuxGen: 3 x 1800kW 450/220V a.c, 2 x 1800kW 450/220V a.c
9214678 *SCKZ* -	**STENA FORECASTER** **Stena Ro Ro AB** Northern Marine Ferries Ltd *Gothenburg* Sweden MMSI: 266040000	**24,688** 7,407 12,300	Class: NV	**2003**-04 **Dalian Shipyard Co Ltd — Dalian LN** Yd No: RO123-2 Loa 195.30 (BB) Br ex - Dght 7.300 Lbp 179.20 Br md 25.50 Dpth 16.62 Welded, 3 dks	**(A35A2RR) Ro-Ro Cargo Ship** Stern door/ramp (centre) Len: 19.50 Wid: 18.60 Swl: 86 Lane-Len: 3000 Trailers: 205 TEU 849 incl 75 ref C. Ice Capable	**4 oil engines** geared to sc. shafts driving 2 CP propellers Total Power: 24,000kW (32,632hp) 22.0kn Sulzer 8ZA40S 4 x 4 Stroke 8 Cy. 400 x 560 each-6000kW (8158bhp) AuxGen: 2 x 1700kW 60Hz a.c, 2 x 1500kW 60Hz a.c Thrusters: 2 Thwart. FP thruster (f)
9227259 *SBJP* -	**STENA FORERUNNER** **Stena Ro Ro AB** Northern Marine Ferries Ltd *Gothenburg* Sweden MMSI: 266041000	**24,688** 7,407 12,300	Class: NV	**2003**-08 **Dalian Shipyard Co Ltd — Dalian LN** Yd No: RO123-3 Loa 195.30 (BB) Br ex - Dght 7.300 Lbp - Br md 25.60 Dpth 16.62 Welded, 3 dks	**(A35A2RR) Ro-Ro Cargo Ship** Stern door/ramp (a) Len: 19.50 Wid: 18.60 Swl: 86 Lane-Len: 3000 Trailers: 205 TEU 849 incl 75 ref C. Ice Capable	**4 oil engines** geared to sc. shafts driving 2 CP propellers Total Power: 24,000kW (32,632hp) 22.0kn Sulzer 8ZA40S 4 x 4 Stroke 8 Cy. 400 x 560 each-6000kW (8158bhp) Wartsila Italia SpA-Italy AuxGen: 2 x 1700kW 60Hz a.c, 2 x 1500kW 60Hz a.c Thrusters: 2 Thwart. CP thruster (f)
9214666 *SHXQ* -	**STENA FORETELLER** *ex* Cetam Massilia *-2003* *ex* Stena Foreteller *-2002* **Stena Ro Ro AB** Northern Marine Ferries Ltd *Gothenburg* Sweden MMSI: 265883000	**24,688** 7,407 12,300	Class: NV	**2001**-12 **Dalian Shipyard Co Ltd — Dalian LN** Yd No: RO123-1 Loa 195.30 (BB) Br ex 26.80 Dght 7.300 Lbp 179.20 Br md 25.60 Dpth 16.62 Welded, 3 dks	**(A35A2RR) Ro-Ro Cargo Ship** Stern door/ramp (centre) Len: 19.51 Wid: 18.61 Swl: 86 Lane-Len: 3000 Lane-clr ht: 6.80 Trailers: 205 TEU 849 incl 75 ref C. Ice Capable	**4 oil engines** geared to sc. shafts driving 2 CP propellers Total Power: 24,000kW (32,632hp) 22.0kn Sulzer 8ZA40S 4 x 4 Stroke 8 Cy. 400 x 560 each-6000kW (8158bhp) AuxGen: 2 x 1700kW a.c, 2 x 1500kW a.c Thrusters: 2 Thwart. FP thruster (f) Fuel: 301.0 (d.f.) 1636.0 (r.f.) 79.0pd
9428932 *2COV5* -	**STENA FORTH** **Stena Forth Lux 3 Sarl** Stena Drilling Ltd SatCom: Inmarsat C 423591884 *Aberdeen* United Kingdom MMSI: 235074573 Official number: 737973	**58,294** 17,489 58,307	Class: NV	**2009**-08 **Samsung Heavy Industries Co Ltd — Geoje** Yd No: 1747 Loa 228.34 Br ex - Dght 12.000 Lbp 219.40 Br md 42.00 Dpth 19.00 Welded, 1 dk	**(B22B20D) Drilling Ship** Cranes: 4x85t	**6 diesel electric oil engines** driving 6 gen. each 7000kW 11000V a.c Connecting to 3 elec. motors each (5500kW) driving 3 Azimuth electric drive units Total Power: 48,000kW (65,262hp) 12.0kn Wartsila 16V32 6 x Vee 4 Stroke 16 Cy. 320 x 400 each-8000kW (10877bhp) Wartsila Finland Oy-Finland Thrusters: 3 Thwart. FP thruster
9138795 *2EJP6* -	**STENA FREIGHTER** *launched as* Sea Chieftain *-2004* **Stena Freighter AB** Northern Marine Ferries Ltd SatCom: Inmarsat C 423597654 *Harwich* United Kingdom MMSI: 235085681 Official number: 917435	**21,104** 6,331 10,048	Class: NV	**2004**-03 **Soc. Esercizio Cant. S.p.A. — Viareggio** (Hull launched by) Yd No: 1547 **2004**-03 **Elektromehanika doo — Rijeka** (Hull completed by) Loa 182.76 (BB) Br ex - Dght 7.400 Lbp 166.21 Br md 25.52 Dpth 16.62 Welded, 3 dks	**(A35A2RR) Ro-Ro Cargo Ship** Passengers: driver berths: 12 Stern door/ramp (centre) Len: 19.50 Wid: 18.60 Swl: 86 Lane-Len: 2715 Lane-Wid: 17.20 Lane-clr ht: 6.80 Trailers: 189 TEU 800 incl 75 ref C. Ice Capable	**4 oil engines** reduction geared to sc. shafts driving 2 CP propellers Total Power: 23,040kW (31,324hp) 22.0kn Sulzer 8ZA40S 4 x 4 Stroke 8 Cy. 400 x 560 each-5760kW (7831bhp) New Sulzer Diesel France-France AuxGen: 2 x 1700kW a.c, 2 x 1500kW 60Hz a.c Thrusters: 2 Thwart. FP thruster (f)
9145176 *SLDW* -	**STENA GERMANICA** *ex* Stena Germanica III *-2010* *ex* Stena Hollandica *-2010* **Stena Line Scandinavia AB** - *Gothenburg* Sweden MMSI: 266331000	**51,837** 23,007 10,670 T/cm 42.0	Class: LR (NV) ✠ **100A1** CS 02/2011 roll on-roll off, passenger ferry *IWS LI Ice Class 1A (Finnish-Swedish Ice Class Rules 1985) Max/min draughts fwd 6.15/5.00m Max/min draughts aft 6.15/5.00m Power required 5850kw, power installed 24000kw Service area between the ports of Sweden (Gothenburg and Karlskona), Poland (Gdynia) and Germany (Kiel) - the Baltic Sea, the UK (Harwich) and the Netherlands (Hoek van Holland) - southern part of the North Sea ✠ **LMC** **UMS** Eq.Ltr: L†; Cable: 632.5/70.0 U3 (a)	**2001**-02 **IZAR Construcciones Navales SA — Puerto Real** Yd No: 81 Lengthened-2007 Loa 241.26 (BB) Br ex 29.32 Dght 6.300 Lbp 223.11 Br md 28.70 Dpth 9.00 Welded, 3 dks plus 4 hoistable car decks	**(A36A2PR) Passenger/Ro-Ro Ship (Vehicles)** Passengers: cabins: 500; berths: 1300 Bow ramp (centre) Len: 18.50 Wid: 15.00 Swl: - Stern door (centre) Len: 12.00 Wid: 15.00 Swl: - Lane-Len: 3980 Lane-Wid: 4.80 Lane-clr ht: 5.00 Cars: 1,290 Ice Capable	**4 oil engines** with clutches, flexible couplings & sr geared to sc. shafts driving 2 CP propellers Total Power: 24,000kW (32,632hp) 22.0kn Sulzer 8ZAL40S 4 x 4 Stroke 8 Cy. 400 x 560 each-6000kW (8158bhp) Wartsila Italia SpA-Italy AuxGen: 2 x 1650kW 240/440V 60Hz a.c, 3 x 1088kW 240/440V 60Hz a.c, 1 x 1616kW a.c, 1 x 2402kW a.c Boilers: AuxB (o.f.) 7.1kgf/cm² (7.0bar), WTAuxB (ex.g.) 7.1kgf/cm² (7.0bar) Thrusters: 2 Thwart. FP thruster (f); 1 Thwart. CP thruster (f) Fuel: 355.0 (d.f.) (Heating Coils) 1300.0 (r.f.) 100.0pd
9121637 *2HBG6* -	**STENA HIBERNIA** *ex* Hibernia Seaways *-2011* *ex* Maersk Importer *-2010* **Stena Ropax Ltd** Northern Marine Ferries Ltd *London* United Kingdom MMSI: 235102224 Official number: 919532	**13,017** 3,905 5,700	Class: LR ✠ **100A1** SS 01/2011 roll on - roll off cargo ship *IWS ✠ **LMC** **UMS** Eq.Ltr: E†; Cable: 621.5/56.0 U3	**1996**-10 **Miho Zosensho K.K. — Shimizu** Yd No: 1460 Loa 142.50 (BB) Br ex 23.47 Dght 5.400 Lbp 134.00 Br md 23.20 Dpth 13.15 Welded, 2 dks	**(A35A2RR) Ro-Ro Cargo Ship** Passengers: 12 Stern door/ramp (a) Len: 11.80 Wid: 16.20 Swl: 90 Lane-Len: 1562 Lane-Wid: 3.00 Lane-clr ht: 4.75	**2 oil engines** with flexible couplings & sr gearedto sc. shafts driving 2 CP propellers Total Power: 10,740kW (14,602hp) 18.6kn Sulzer 8ZAL40S 2 x 4 Stroke 8 Cy. 400 x 560 each-5370kW (7301bhp) Hitachi Zosen Corp-Japan AuxGen: 2 x 1000kW 445V 60Hz a.c, 2 x 560kW 445V 60Hz a.c Boilers: AuxB (o.f.) 6.9kgf/cm² (6.8bar), AuxB (ex.g.) 6.9kgf/cm² (6.8bar) Thrusters: 2 Thwart. CP thruster (f) Fuel: 143.8 (d.f.) 1130.4 (r.f.)

9419163 *PBMM* -	**STENA HOLLANDICA** *ex* Stena Hollandica III *-2010* *launched as* Stena Britannica *-2010* **Stena North Sea Ltd** Stena Line BV SatCom: Inmarsat C 424475811 *Hoek van Holland* *Netherlands* MMSI: 244758000 Official number: 53679	**64,039** 36,919 11,600	Class: LR ✠ **100A1** SS 05/2010 roll on-roll off cargo and passenger ship *IWS LI EP (P) Ice Class 1B FS at a draught of 6.650m Max/min draughts fwd 6.650/5.316m Max/min draughts aft 6.650/5.016m Power required 4933kw, installed 33600kw ✠ **LMC** **UMS** Eq.Ltr: Q†; Cable: 687.5/81.0 U3 (a)	**2010-05 Nordic Yards Wismar GmbH — Wismar** (Aft section) Yd No: 159 **2010-05 Nordic Yards Warnemuende GmbH — Rostock** (Fwd section) Yd No: 159 Loa 240.87 (BB) Br ex 33.02 Dght 6.500 Lbp 224.00 Br md 32.00 Dpth 21.30 Welded, 7 dks	**(A36A2PR) Passenger/Ro-Ro Ship (Vehicles)** Passengers: cabins: 538; berths: 1376 Bow ramp (centre) Len: 5.20 Wid: 22.36 Swl: 115 Bow door/ramp (centre) Stern ramp (centre) Stern door/ramp (centre) Len: 5.08 Wid: 20.13 Swl: 203 Lane-Len: 5566 Lane-clr ht: 4.80 Lorries: 300, Cars: 230 Ice Capable	**4 oil engines** with clutches, flexible couplings & dr geared to sc. shafts driving 2 CP propellers Total Power: 33,600kW (45,682hp) 22.5kn MAN-B&W 6L48/60CR 2 x 4 Stroke 6 Cy. 480 x 600 each-7200kW (9789bhp) MAN B&W Diesel AG-Augsburg MAN-B&W 8L48/60CR 2 x 4 Stroke 8 Cy. 480 x 600 each-9600kW (13052bhp) MAN B&W Diesel AG-Augsburg AuxGen: 2 x 3176kW 440V 60Hz a.c, 3 x 1254kW 440V 60Hz a.c, 1 x 1463kW 440V 60Hz a.c Boilers: e (ex.g.) 10.2kgf/cm^2 (10.0bar), AuxB (o.f.) 10.2kgf/cm^2 (10.0bar) Thrusters: 2 Thwart. CP thruster (f) Fuel: 185.0 (d.f.) 985.0 (r.f.)
9517575 *2FMJ5* -	**STENA ICEMAX** **Stena Icemax Ltd** Stena Drilling Ltd *Aberdeen* *United Kingdom* MMSI: 235092459 Official number: 740532	**58,295** 17,489 55,000	Class: NV	**2012-04 Samsung Heavy Industries Co Ltd — Geoje** Yd No: 1755 Loa 227.80 Br ex - Dght 12.000 Lbp 219.40 Br md 42.00 Dpth 19.00 Welded, 1 dk	**(B22B20D) Drilling Ship**	**6 diesel electric oil engines** driving 6 gen. each 7400kW 690V a.c driving 3 Azimuth electric drive units Total Power: 43,740kW (59,466hp) 12.0kn Wartsila 16V32 6 x Vee 4 Stroke 16 Cy. 320 x 400 each-7290kW (9911bhp) Thrusters: 3 Directional thruster (f)
9125944 *SEAN* -	**STENA JUTLANDICA** *ex* Stena Jutlandica III *-1996* **Stena Sessan Rederi AB** Stena Line Scandinavia AB *Gothenburg* *Sweden* MMSI: 265410000	**29,691** 9,046 6,559 T/cm 39.3	Class: LR ✠ **100A1** CS 06/2011 ro-ro cargo, train and passenger ship *IWS Ice Class 1A ✠ **LMC** **UMS** Eq.Ltr: L†; Cable: 648.0/70.0 U3	**1996-06 van der Giessen-de Noord BV — Krimpen a/d IJssel** Yd No: 967 Loa 182.35 (BB) Br ex 28.43 Dght 6.000 Lbp 169.05 Br md 27.80 Dpth 15.20 Welded, 2 dks	**(A36A2PT) Passenger/Ro-Ro Ship (Vehicles/Rail)** Passengers: unberthed: 1500; cabins: 64; berths: 200; driver berths: 200 Bow door & ramp (centre) Len: 16.00 Wid: 5.80 Swl: - Stern door/ramp (centre) Len: 14.00 Wid: 16.00 Swl: - Side door/ramp (p. f.) Len: 6.60 Wid: 6.50 Swl: - Side door/ramp (p. a.) Len: 6.60 Wid: 6.50 Swl: - Lane-Len: 2100 Lane-Wid: 6.20 Lane-clr ht: 4.90 Trailers: 122 Ice Capable	**4 oil engines** with flexible couplings & sr geared to sc. shafts driving 2 CP propellers Total Power: 25,920kW (35,240hp) 22.0kn MAN 9L40/54 4 x 4 Stroke 9 Cy. 400 x 540 each-6480kW (8810bhp) MAN B&W Diesel AG-Augsburg AuxGen: 4 x 1669kW 220/440V 60Hz a.c Boilers: 2 TOH (ex.g.) 10.2kgf/cm^2 (10.0bar), TOH (o.f.) 10.2kgf/cm^2 (10.0bar) Thrusters: 2 Thwart. FP thruster (f); 2 Tunnel thruster (a) Fuel: 87.0 (d.f.) 775.0 (r.f.)
9329849 *2BGR6* -	**STENA LAGAN** *ex* Lagan Seaways *-2011* *ex* Lagan Viking *-2010* **Stena Ropax Ltd** Northern Marine Ferries Ltd SatCom: Inmarsat C 424714114 *Belfast* *United Kingdom* MMSI: 235065969 Official number: 918282	**27,510** 9,367 7,000	Class: LR (RI) **100A1** SS 07/2010 roll on-roll off cargo/passenger ship Ice Class 1D at a maximum draught of 6.760m Max/min draughts fwd 6.760/4.500m Max/min draughts aft 6.760/4.500m Power required 21600kw, power installed 21600kw **LMC** **UMS** Eq.Ltr: I†; Cable: 605.0/64.0 U3 (a)	**2005-06 Cantiere Navale Visentini Srl — Porto Viro** Yd No: 212 Loa 186.46 (BB) Br ex - Dght 6.800 Lbp 177.40 Br md 25.60 Dpth 14.90 Welded, 6 dks	**(A36A2PR) Passenger/Ro-Ro Ship (Vehicles)** Passengers: unberthed: 488; berths: 482 Stern door/ramp (centre) Len: 17.00 Wid: 14.00 Swl: - Lane-Len: 2100 Trailers: 160 Ice Capable	**2 oil engines** with flexible couplings & sr geared to sc. shafts driving 2 CP propellers Total Power: 21,600kW (29,368hp) 23.5kn MAN-B&W 9L48/60 2 x 4 Stroke 9 Cy. 480 x 600 each-10800kW (14684bhp) MAN B&W Diesel AG-Augsburg AuxGen: 2 x 1800kW 440V 60Hz a.c, 3 x 1800kW 440V 60Hz a.c Boilers: e (ex.g.), AuxB (o.f.) Thrusters: 2 Thwart. CP thruster (f) Fuel: 1470.0 (r.f.)
9329851 *2BPR6* -	**STENA MERSEY** *ex* Mersey Seaways *-2011* *ex* Mersey Viking *-2010* **Stena Ropax Ltd** Northern Marine Ferries Ltd *Belfast* *United Kingdom* MMSI: 235068243 Official number: 915280	**27,510** 9,367 7,000	Class: LR (RI) **100A1** SS 11/2010 roll on-roll off cargo/passenger ship LI Ice Class 1D at maximum draught of 6.760m Max/min draughts fwd 6.760/4.5m Max/min draughts aft 6.760/4.5m Power required 21600kw, power installed 21600kw **LMC** **UMS**	**2005-11 Cantiere Navale Visentini Srl — Porto Viro** Yd No: 213 Loa 186.58 (BB) Br ex - Dght 6.800 Lbp 177.40 Br md 25.60 Dpth 15.00 Welded	**(A36A2PR) Passenger/Ro-Ro Ship (Vehicles)** Passengers: unberthed: 488; berths: 482 Stern door/ramp (centre) Len: 17.00 Wid: 14.00 Swl: - Lane-Len: 2100 Trailers: 160 Ice Capable	**2 oil engines** with flexible couplings & sr geared to sc. shafts driving 2 CP propellers Total Power: 21,600kW (29,368hp) 23.5kn MAN-B&W 9L48/60B 2 x 4 Stroke 9 Cy. 480 x 600 each-10800kW (14684bhp) MAN B&W Diesel AG-Augsburg AuxGen: 3 x 1800kW 440V 60Hz a.c Boilers: e (ex.g.), AuxB (o.f.) Thrusters: 2 Thwart. CP thruster (f) Fuel: 1470.0 (r.f.)
9206671 *C6UK4* -	**STENA NATALITA** **P/R Stena Ugland Shuttle Tanker III DA** Standard Marine Tonsberg AS SatCom: Inmarsat C 431181410 *Nassau* *Bahamas* MMSI: 311814000 Official number: 9000134	**63,051** 30,304 108,073 T/cm 93.6	Class: NV	**2001-05 Tsuneishi Shipbuilding Co Ltd — Fukuyama HS** Yd No: 1166 Loa 246.30 (BB) Br ex - Dght 15.019 Lbp 234.00 Br md 43.00 Dpth 21.80 Welded, 1 dk	**(A13A2TS) Shuttle Tanker** Double Hull (13F) Liq: 111,971; Liq (Oil): 111,971 Cargo Heating Coils Compartments: 12 Wing Ta, ER, 2 Wing Slop Ta 3 Cargo Pump (s): 3x2500m^3/hr Manifold: Bow/CM: 123m	**2 oil engines** driving 2 CP propellers Total Power: 15,754kW (21,420hp) 14.0kn B&W 6S46MC-C 2 x 2 Stroke 6 Cy. 460 x 1932 each-7877kW (10710bhp) MAN B&W Diesel A/S-Denmark AuxGen: 4 x 470kW 440V 60Hz a.c Thrusters: 2 Thwart. FP thruster (f); 2 Thwart. CP thruster (a) Fuel: 343.7 (d.f.) (Heating Coils) 3130.0 (r.f.)
8317954 *SGQU* -	**STENA NAUTICA** *ex* Lion King *-1996* *ex* Isle of Innisfree *-1995* *ex* Stena Nautica *-1992* *ex* Niels Klim *-1991* **Stena Rederi AB** Stena Line Scandinavia AB *Gothenburg* *Sweden* MMSI: 265859000	**19,504** 5,851 3,676	Class: LR (BV) **100A1** CS 04/2011 passenger ship/roll on-roll off cargo/ferry Ice Class 1B **LMC** **UMS** Eq.Ltr: G†; Cable: 577.5/60.0 U3 (a)	**1986-04 A/S Nakskov Skibsvaerft — Nakskov** Yd No: 234 Loa 135.46 (BB) Br ex 24.62 Dght 5.840 Lbp 126.00 Br md 24.00 Dpth 8.00 Welded, 9 dks	**(A36A2PR) Passenger/Ro-Ro Ship (Vehicles)** Passengers: 956; cabins: 74; berths: 148 Bow door & ramp Len: 13.30 Wid: 6.60 Swl: - Stern door/ramp (p) Len: 11.10 Wid: 7.90 Swl: - Stern door/ramp (s) Len: 11.10 Wid: 7.90 Swl: - Lane-Len: 1235 Lane-Wid: 5.70 Lane-clr ht: 4.50 Cars: 152, Trailers: 30 Ice Capable	**2 oil engines** driving 2 CP propellers Total Power: 12,480kW (16,968hp) 18.5kn B&W 8L45GB 2 x 2 Stroke 8 Cy. 450 x 1200 each-6240kW (8484bhp) MAN B&W Diesel A/S-Denmark AuxGen: 4 x 1050kW 380V 50Hz a.c, 2 x 1300kW 380V 50Hz a.c Boilers: AuxB (Comp) 10.2kgf/cm^2 (10.0bar) Thrusters: 2 Thwart. CP thruster (f); 1 Tunnel thruster (a) Fuel: 139.0 (d.f.) 329.5 (r.f.) 48.0pd
9215505 *2BX02* -	**STENA NORDICA** *ex* European Ambassador *-2004* **Stena Nordica AB** Stena Line Ltd *London* *United Kingdom* MMSI: 235070241 Official number: 915548	**24,206** 12,201 4,884 T/cm 33.4	Class: LR ✠ **100A1** CS 12/2010 roro passenger ferry ✠ **LMC** **UMS** Eq.Ltr: I†; Cable: 605.0/66.0 U3 (a)	**2000-12 Mitsubishi Heavy Industries Ltd. — Shimonoseki** Yd No: 1068 Loa 169.80 (BB) Br ex 25.82 Dght 6.020 Lbp 161.60 Br md 24.00 Dpth 9.50 Welded, 3 dks	**(A36A2PR) Passenger/Ro-Ro Ship (Vehicles)** Passengers: unberthed: 181; cabins: 81; berths: 224 Bow door/ramp (centre) Len: 7.20 Wid: 6.75 Swl: 44 Stern door/ramp (centre) Len: 18.50 Wid: 8.00 Swl: 150 Lane-Len: 1948 Lane-Wid: 3.00 Lane-clr ht: 5.20 Cars: 375	**4 oil engines** with clutches, flexible couplings & reduction geared to sc. shafts driving 2 CP propellers Total Power: 39,600kW (53,840hp) 25.7kn Wartsila 12V38 2 x Vee 4 Stroke 12 Cy. 380 x 475 each-7920kW (10768bhp) Wartsila Nederland BV-Netherlands Wartsila 18V38 2 x Vee 4 Stroke 18 Cy. 380 x 475 each-11880kW (16152bhp) Wartsila Nederland BV-Netherlands AuxGen: 2 x 1900kW 420V 50Hz a.c, 2 x 1800kW 420V 50Hz a.c Boilers: 2 e (ex.g.) 13.0kgf/cm^2 (12.7bar), AuxB (o.f.) 7.0kgf/cm^2 (6.9bar) Thrusters: 2 Thwart. CP thruster (f) Fuel: 107.0 (d.f.) (Heating Coils) 1018.0 (r.f.) 60.0pd

IMO / Call sign	Name / Owner / Manager	Tonnage	Class	Builder / Dimensions	Type / Cargo	Machinery
9299123 *ZCDP9* -	**STENA PARIS** **CM P-Max I Ltd** Northern Marine Management Ltd SatCom: Inmarsat C 431048610 *Hamilton* *Bermuda (British)* MMSI: 310486000	**36,064** 19,671 65,125 T/cm 66.1	Class: NV	**2005**-12 **Brodosplit - Brodogradiliste doo — Split** Yd No: 441 Loa 182.90 (BB) Br ex 40.00 Dght 13.000 Lbp 175.50 Br md 40.00 Dpth 17.90 Welded, 1 dk	**(A13B2TP) Products Tanker** Double Hull (13F) Liq: 67,315; Liq (Oil): 67,315 Compartments: 10 Wing Ta, Wing ER, 2 Wing Slop Ta 5 Cargo Pump (s): 5x800m^3/hr Manifold: Bow/CM: 89.6m Ice Capable	**2 oil engines** driving 2 CP propellers Total Power: 15,720kW (21,372hp) 14.5kn MAN-B&W 6S46MC-C 2 x 2 Stroke 6 Cy. 460 x 1932 each-7860kW (10686bhp) Brodosplit Tvornica Dizel Motoradoo-Croatia AuxGen: 4 x 865kW a.c Fuel: 204.7 (d.f.) 2217.6 (r.f.)
9391476 *ZCEC9* -	**STENA PENGUIN** **CM P-Max IX Ltd** Northern Marine Management Ltd *Hamilton* *Bermuda (British)* MMSI: 310602000 Official number: 740519	**36,168** 19,475 64,834 T/cm 66.1	Class: NV	**2010**-10 **Brodosplit - Brodogradiliste doo — Split** Yd No: 464 Loa 182.99 (BB) Br ex - Dght 13.015 Lbp 175.50 Br md 40.00 Dpth 17.90 Welded, 1 dk	**(A13B2TP) Products Tanker** Double Hull (13F) Liq: 66,642; Liq (Oil): 66,642 Cargo Heating Coils Compartments: 10 Wing Ta, 2 Wing Slop Ta, ER 10 Cargo Pump (s): 10x800m^3/hr Manifold: Bow/CM: 92.9m Ice Capable	**2 oil engines** driving 2 CP propellers Total Power: 15,720kW (21,372hp) 14.5kn MAN-B&W 6S46MC-C 2 x 2 Stroke 6 Cy. 460 x 1932 each-7860kW (10686bhp) AuxGen: 4 x 865kW 450V 60Hz a.c Fuel: 200.0 (d.f.) 2000.0 (r.f.)
9299159 *ZCDR5* -	**STENA PERFORMANCE** **CM P-Max IV Ltd** Northern Marine Management Ltd *Hamilton* *Bermuda (British)* MMSI: 310515000	**36,168** 19,687 65,065	Class: NV	**2006**-06 **Brodosplit - Brodogradiliste doo — Split** Yd No: 444 Converted From: Products Tanker-2011 Loa 182.90 (BB) Br ex 40.04 Dght 13.000 Lbp 175.50 Br md 40.00 Dpth 17.90 Welded, 1 dk	**(A12B2TR) Chemical/Products Tanker** Double Hull (13F) Liq: 68,012; Liq (Oil): 68,012 Compartments: 10 Wing Ta, Wing ER, 2 Wing Slop Ta 5 Cargo Pump (s): 5x800m^3/hr Manifold: Bow/CM: 89.6m Ice Capable	**2 oil engines** driving 2 CP propellers Total Power: 15,720kW (21,372hp) 14.5kn MAN-B&W 6S46MC-C 2 x 2 Stroke 6 Cy. 460 x 1932 each-7860kW (10686bhp) Brodosplit Tvornica Dizel Motoradoo-Croatia AuxGen: 4 x a.c Fuel: 204.7 (d.f.) 2217.6 (r.f.)
9506227 *2FGR4* -	**STENA PERFORMER** *ex* Seatruck Performance *-2012* **Seatruck Ferries Three Ltd** Seatruck Ferries Ltd *Douglas* *Isle of Man (British)* MMSI: 235091111 Official number: 742869	**19,722** 5,917 5,600	Class: NV	**2012**-04 **Flensburger Schiffbau-Ges. mbH & Co. KG — Flensburg** Yd No: 751 Loa 142.00 (BB) Br ex 25.80 Dght 5.700 Lbp 133.46 Br md 25.00 Dpth 21.35 Welded, 4 dks	**(A35A2RR) Ro-Ro Cargo Ship** Passengers: driver berths: 12 Stern door/ramp (centre) Len: 19.00 Wid: 17.60 Swl: - Lane-Len: 2166 Trailers: 155	**2 oil engines** reduction geared to sc. shafts driving 2 CP propellers Total Power: 16,000kW (21,754hp) 21.0kn MAN-B&W 7L48/60CR 2 x 4 Stroke 7 Cy. 480 x 600 each-8000kW (10877bhp) MAN B&W Diesel AG-Augsburg AuxGen: 2 x 1200kW a.c, 2 x 800kW a.c Thrusters: 2 Tunnel thruster (f)
9312456 *ZCDU7* -	**STENA PERROS** **CM P-Max VI Ltd** Northern Marine Management Ltd *Hamilton* *Bermuda (British)* MMSI: 310554000	**36,168** 19,685 65,086 T/cm 66.1	Class: NV	**2007**-12 **Brodosplit - Brodogradiliste doo — Split** Yd No: 446 Loa 182.99 (BB) Br ex - Dght 13.000 Lbp 175.50 Br md 40.00 Dpth 17.90 Welded, 1 dk	**(A13B2TP) Products Tanker** Double Hull (13F) Liq: 68,012; Liq (Oil): 68,012 Compartments: 10 Wing Ta, Wing ER, 2 Wing Slop Ta 10 Cargo Pump (s): 10x800m^3/hr Manifold: Bow/CM: 89.6m Ice Capable	**2 oil engines** driving 2 CP propellers Total Power: 15,720kW (21,372hp) 14.5kn MAN-B&W 6S46MC-C 2 x 2 Stroke 6 Cy. 460 x 1932 each-7860kW (10686bhp) Brodosplit Tvornica Dizel Motoradoo-Croatia AuxGen: 4 x 865kW a.c Fuel: 1900.0 (r.f.)
9390032 *ZCEB4* -	**STENA POLARIS** **CM P-Max VIII Ltd** Northern Marine Management Ltd *Hamilton* *Bermuda (British)* MMSI: 310587000 Official number: 740498	**36,168** 19,654 64,917 T/cm 66.1	Class: NV	**2010**-02 **Brodosplit - Brodogradiliste doo — Split** Yd No: 463 Loa 182.99 (BB) Br ex - Dght 13.015 Lbp 175.50 Br md 40.00 Dpth 17.90 Welded, 1 dk	**(A13B2TP) Products Tanker** Double Hull (13F) Liq: 67,315; Liq (Oil): 67,315 Cargo Heating Coils Compartments: 10 Wing Ta, 2 Wing Slop Ta, ER 10 Cargo Pump (s): 10x800m^3/hr Manifold: Bow/CM: 92.9m Ice Capable	**2 oil engines** driving 2 CP propellers Total Power: 15,720kW (21,372hp) 14.5kn MAN-B&W 6S46MC-C 2 x 2 Stroke 6 Cy. 460 x 1932 each-7860kW (10686bhp) Brodosplit Tvornica Dizel Motoradoo-Croatia AuxGen: 4 x 865kW a.c Fuel: 220.0 (d.f.) 2000.0 (r.f.)
9334698 *2GXH4* -	**STENA POSEIDON** **Terra Ltd** Northern Marine Management Ltd *London* *United Kingdom* MMSI: 235101273 Official number: 919420	**42,810** 21,999 74,927 T/cm 69.6	Class: NV	**2006**-12 **Brodosplit - Brodogradiliste doo — Split** Yd No: 454 Loa 228.60 (BB) Br ex 32.27 Dght 14.300 Lbp 220.00 Br md 32.24 Dpth 20.45 Welded, 1 dk	**(A13B2TP) Products Tanker** Double Hull (13F) Liq: 81,709; Liq (Oil): 81,720 Compartments: 12 Wing Ta, 2 Wing Slop Ta, 1 Slop Ta, ER 12 Cargo Pump (s): 12x1000m^3/hr Manifold: Bow/CM: 115.9m Ice Capable	**1 oil engine** driving 1 CP propeller Total Power: 12,240kW (16,642hp) 16.0kn MAN-B&W 6S60MC 1 x 2 Stroke 6 Cy. 600 x 2292 12240kW (16642bhp) Brodosplit Tvornica Dizel Motoradoo-Croatia AuxGen: 3 x 910kW a.c Fuel: 191.4 (d.f.) 2381.0 (r.f.)
9506239 *2FMI8* -	**STENA PRECISION** *ex* Seatruck Precision *-2012* **Seatruck Ferries Four Ltd** Seatruck Ferries Ltd *Douglas* *Isle of Man (British)* MMSI: 235092453 Official number: 742870	**19,722** 5,917 5,600	Class: NV	**2012**-06 **Flensburger Schiffbau-Ges. mbH & Co. KG — Flensburg** Yd No: 752 Loa 142.00 (BB) Br ex - Dght 5.700 Lbp 133.46 Br md 25.00 Dpth 21.35 Welded, 4 dks	**(A35A2RR) Ro-Ro Cargo Ship** Passengers: driver berths: 12 Stern door/ramp (centre) Len: 19.00 Wid: 17.60 Swl: - Lane-Len: 2166 Trailers: 151	**2 oil engines** reduction geared to sc. shafts driving 2 CP propellers Total Power: 16,000kW (21,754hp) 21.0kn MAN-B&W 7L48/60CR 2 x 4 Stroke 7 Cy. 480 x 600 each-8000kW (10877bhp) MAN B&W Diesel AG-Augsburg AuxGen: 2 x 1200kW a.c, 2 x 800kW a.c Thrusters: 2 Tunnel thruster (f)
9413523 *ZCEE6* -	**STENA PREMIUM** **CM P-Max X Ltd** Concordia Maritime AB SatCom: Inmarsat C 431061210 *Hamilton* *Bermuda (British)* MMSI: 310612000 Official number: 740534	**36,168** 19,466 65,055	Class: NV	**2011**-06 **Brodosplit - Brodogradiliste doo — Split** Yd No: 465 Converted From: Products Tanker-2011 Loa 182.90 (BB) Br ex 40.04 Dght 13.000 Lbp 175.50 Br md 40.00 Dpth 17.90 Welded, 1 dk	**(A12B2TR) Chemical/Products Tanker** Double Hull (13F) Liq: 68,012; Liq (Oil): 68,012 Compartments: 10 Wing Ta, 2 Wing Slop Ta, ER 10 Cargo Pump (s): 10x800m^3/hr Manifold: Bow/CM: 89.6m Ice Capable	**2 oil engines** driving 2 CP propellers Total Power: 15,720kW (21,372hp) 14.5kn MAN-B&W 6S46MC-C 2 x 2 Stroke 6 Cy. 460 x 1932 each-7860kW (10686bhp) AuxGen: 4 x 900kW a.c Fuel: 205.0 (d.f.) 2220.0 (r.f.)
9312444 *ZCDR6* -	**STENA PRESIDENT** *ex* Brodosplit 445 *-2007* **CM P-Max V Ltd** Northern Marine Management Ltd *Hamilton* *Bermuda (British)* MMSI: 310549000 Official number: 737893	**36,168** 19,665 65,112 T/cm 66.1	Class: NV	**2007**-09 **Brodosplit - Brodogradiliste doo — Split** Yd No: 445 Loa 182.90 (BB) Br ex - Dght 13.000 Lbp 176.00 Br md 40.00 Dpth 17.90 Welded, 1 dk	**(A13B2TP) Products Tanker** Double Hull (13F) Liq: 67,315; Liq (Oil): 67,315 Compartments: 10 Wing Ta, Wing ER, 2 Wing Slop Ta 10 Cargo Pump (s): 10x800m^3/hr Manifold: Bow/CM: 89.6m Ice Capable	**2 oil engines** driving 2 CP propellers Total Power: 15,720kW (21,372hp) 14.5kn MAN-B&W 6S46MC-C 2 x 2 Stroke 6 Cy. 460 x 1932 each-7860kW (10686bhp) Brodosplit Tvornica Dizel Motoradoo-Croatia AuxGen: 4 x 865kW a.c Fuel: 2000.0 (r.f.)
9299147 *2CKO8* -	**STENA PRIMORSK** **CM P-Max III Ltd** Northern Marine Management Ltd SatCom: Inmarsat C 423591823 *Liverpool* *United Kingdom* MMSI: 235073588 Official number: 737891	**36,168** 19,660 65,125 T/cm 66.1	Class: NV	**2006**-05 **Brodosplit - Brodogradiliste doo — Split** Yd No: 443 Loa 182.90 (BB) Br ex 40.04 Dght 13.000 Lbp 175.00 Br md 40.00 Dpth 17.90 Welded, 1 dk	**(A13B2TP) Products Tanker** Double Hull (13F) Liq: 68,012; Liq (Oil): 68,012 Compartments: 10 Wing Ta, Wing ER, 2 Wing Slop Ta 5 Cargo Pump (s): 5x800m^3/hr Manifold: Bow/CM: 89.6m Ice Capable	**2 oil engines** driving 2 CP propellers Total Power: 15,720kW (21,372hp) 14.5kn MAN-B&W 6S46MC-C 2 x 2 Stroke 6 Cy. 460 x 1932 each-7860kW (10686bhp) Brodosplit Tvornica Dizel Motoradoo-Croatia AuxGen: 4 x 865kW a.c Fuel: 204.7 (d.f.) 2217.6 (r.f.)
9390020 *ZCEA9* -	**STENA PROGRESS** **CM P-Max VII Ltd** Northern Marine Management Ltd SatCom: Inmarsat C 437057910 *Hamilton* *Bermuda (British)* MMSI: 310579000 Official number: 740492	**36,168** 19,654 65,125 T/cm 66.1	Class: NV	**2009**-09 **Brodosplit - Brodogradiliste doo — Split** Yd No: 462 Loa 182.90 (BB) Br ex 40.02 Dght 13.000 Lbp 175.50 Br md 40.00 Dpth 17.90 Welded, 1 dk	**(A13B2TP) Products Tanker** Double Hull (13F) Liq: 67,315; Liq (Oil): 67,315 Cargo Heating Coils Compartments: 10 Wing Ta, 2 Wing Slop Ta, ER 10 Cargo Pump (s): 10x800m^3/hr Manifold: Bow/CM: 89.6m Ice Capable	**2 oil engines** driving 2 CP propellers Total Power: 15,720kW (21,372hp) 14.5kn MAN-B&W 6S46MC-C 2 x 2 Stroke 6 Cy. 460 x 1932 each-7860kW (10686bhp) MAN B&W Diesel A/S-Denmark AuxGen: 4 x 865kW a.c Fuel: 250.0 (d.f.) 2125.0 (r.f.)
9299135 *ZCDR3* -	**STENA PROVENCE** **CM P-Max II Ltd** Northern Marine Management Ltd *Hamilton* *Bermuda (British)* MMSI: 310497000	**36,168** 19,682 65,125	Class: NV	**2006**-03 **Brodosplit - Brodogradiliste doo — Split** Yd No: 442 Converted From: Products Tanker-2012 Loa 182.90 (BB) Br ex 40.04 Dght 13.000 Lbp 175.50 Br md 40.00 Dpth 17.90 Welded, 1 dk	**(A12B2TR) Chemical/Products Tanker** Double Hull (13F) Liq: 67,315; Liq (Oil): 67,315 Compartments: 10 Wing Ta, Wing ER, 2 Wing Slop Ta 5 Cargo Pump (s): 5x800m^3/hr Manifold: Bow/CM: 89.6m Ice Capable	**2 oil engines** driving 2 CP propellers Total Power: 15,720kW (21,372hp) 14.5kn MAN-B&W 6S46MC-C 1 x 2 Stroke 6 Cy. 460 x 1932 7860kW (10686bhp) Brodosplit Tvornica Dizel Motoradoo-Croatia AuxGen: 4 x Fuel: 204.7 (d.f.) 2217.6 (r.f.)

IMO / Call sign	Name / Owner	Tonnage	Classification	Builder / Dimensions	Type / Details	Machinery
7911545 *SLVH* -	**STENA SAGA** *ex* Stena Britannica *-1994* *ex* Silvia Regina *-1991* **Stena Rederi AB** Stena Line Scandinavia AB *Stockholm* *Sweden* MMSI: 265001000	**33,967** 19,246 3,898	Class: LR ✠ **100A1** SS 06/2010 ferry Ice Class 1AS at a draught of 6.718m Max/min draughts fwd 7.00/5.550m Max/min draughts aft 7.50/5.700m Power required 9714kw, installed 22948kw ✠ **LMC** **UMS** Eq.Ltr: L; Cable: 632.5/70.0 U3	**1981-06 Oy Wartsila Ab — Turku** Yd No: 1252 Lengthened-2012 Loa 166.70 (BB) Br ex 29.04 Dght 6.719 Lbp 152.71 Br md 28.41 Dpth 9.12 Welded, 3 dks, 1 movable dk (hoistable) in No. 3 (vehicle) tween dk	**(A36A2PR) Passenger/Ro-Ro Ship (Vehicles)** Passengers: unberthed: 334; cabins: 647; berths: 1666 Bow door & ramp Len: 11.70 Wid: 6.40 Swl: 45 Stern door/ramp (p) Len: 9.20 Wid: 7.10 Swl: 45 Stern door/ramp (s) Len: 9.20 Wid: 7.10 Swl: 45 Lane-Len: 1032 Lane-Wid: 6.00 Lane-clr ht: 4.50 Cars: 450 Ice Capable	**4 oil engines** with clutches, flexible couplings & sr geared to sc. shafts driving 2 CP propellers Total Power: 22,948kW (31,200hp) 22.0kn Pielstick 12PC2-5V-400 4 x Vee 4 Stroke 12 Cy. 400 x 460 each-5737kW (7800bhp) Oy Wartsila Ab-Finland AuxGen: 2 x 1300kW 400V 50Hz a.c, 3 x 1776kW 400V 50Hz a.c Boilers: e (ex.g.) (fitted: 1981) 9.2kgf/cm² (9.0bar), AuxB (o.f.) 7.1kgf/cm² (7.0bar), AuxB (o.f.) (fitted: 1981) 8.0kgf/cm² (7.8bar) Thrusters: 2 Thwart. CP thruster (f) Fuel: 194.2 (d.f.) 1264.3 (r.f.) 90.0pd
9235517 *SJLB* -	**STENA SCANDINAVICA** *ex* Stena Scandinavica Iv *-2011* *ex* Britannica *-2011* *ex* Stena Britannica *-2010* *ex* Stena Britannica II *-2003* **Stena North Sea Ltd** Stena Line Scandinavia AB *Gothenburg* *Sweden* MMSI: 266343000 Official number: 906573	**57,958** 30,282 12,200 T/cm 51.1	Class: LR (NV) ✠ **100A1** CS 01/2013 roll on-roll off passenger ferry *IWS LI Service area between the Ports of Sweden (Gothenburg and Karlskrona), Poland (Gdynia) and Germany (Kiel) - the Baltic Sea, the UK (Harwich) and the Netherlands (Hoek van Holland) - southern part of the North Sea Ice Class 1A FS at a draught of 6.8m Max/min draughts fwd 6.8/4.8m Max/min draughts aft 6.8/4.98m Power required 6120kw, power installed 25920kw ✠ **LMC** **UMS** Eq.Ltr: 0†; Cable: 660.0/78.0 U3 (a)	**2003-01 Hyundai Heavy Industries Co Ltd — Ulsan** Yd No: 1392 Lengthened-2007 Loa 240.09 (BB) Br ex 29.88 Dght 6.314 Lbp 226.45 Br md 29.30 Dpth 9.50 Welded, 12 dks	**(A36A2PR) Passenger/Ro-Ro Ship (Vehicles)** Passengers: cabins: 498; berths: 1000 Bow ramp (centre) Len: 17.50 Wid: 6.50 Swl: 45 Stern door/ramp (centre) Len: 12.00 Wid: 15.00 Swl: 45 Side door (p) Side door (s) Lane-Len: 4100 Lane-Wid: 3.20 Lane-clr ht: 5.00 Cars: 1,311 Ice Capable	**4 oil engines** with clutches, flexible couplings & sr geared to sc. shafts driving 2 CP propellers Total Power: 25,920kW (35,240hp) 22.0kn MAN-B&W 9L40/54 4 x 4 Stroke 9 Cy. 400 x 540 each-6480kW (8810bhp) MAN B&W Diesel AG-Augsburg AuxGen: 4 x 1200kW 450V 60Hz a.c, 2 x 2400kW 450V 60Hz a.c Boilers: e (ex.g.) 12.2kgf/cm² (12.0bar), WTAuxB (o.f.) 9.2kgf/cm² (9.0bar) Thrusters: 2 Thwart. CP thruster (f); 1 Tunnel thruster (f) Fuel: 406.0 (d.f.) 1661.0 (r.f.) 110.0pd
7305772 *SLBM* -	**STENA SCANRAIL** *ex* Stena Searider *-1987* *ex* Trucker *-1985* *ex* Stena Searider *-1984* *ex* Searider *-1984* *ex* Stena Searider *-1983* *ex* Bahjah *-1981* *ex* Seatrader *-1976* *launched as* Stena Seatrader *-1973* **Stena Line Scandinavia AB** - *Gothenburg* *Sweden* MMSI: 265285000	**7,504** 2,251 6,726	Class: LR (BV) **100A1** SS 12/2012 passenger/roll on - roll off cargo ship Ice Class 3 **LMC** Eq.Ltr: S; Cable: 495.0/42.0 U2 (a)	**1973-08 A. Vuijk & Zonen's Scheepswerven B.V. — Capelle a/d IJssel** Yd No: 863 Converted From: Ferry (Passenger/Vehicle)-1987 Lengthened-1976 Loa 142.25 (BB) Br ex 16.34 Dght 4.541 Lbp 127.00 Br md 16.00 Dpth 6.00 Welded, 5 dks	**(A36A2PT) Passenger/Ro-Ro Ship (Vehicles/Rail)** Passengers: 65; berths: 32; driver berths: 36 Bow door/ramp (centre) Stern door & ramp (centre) Len: 12.00 Wid: 3.50 Swl: - Lane-Len: 900 Lane-Wid: 9.35 Lane-clr ht: 5.20 Ice Capable	**2 oil engines** with flexible couplings & sr geared to sc. shafts driving 2 CP propellers Total Power: 5,300kW (7,206hp) 16.0kn Werkspoor 6TM410 2 x 4 Stroke 6 Cy. 410 x 470 each-2650kW (3603bhp) Stork Werkspoor Diesel BV-Netherlands AuxGen: 2 x 520kW 400V 50Hz a.c, 1 x 631kW 380V 50Hz a.c Thrusters: 2 Thwart. FP thruster (f) Fuel: 80.5 (d.f.) 571.5 (r.f.)
9121625 *PFSN* -	**STENA SCOTIA** *ex* Scotia Seaways *-2011* *ex* Maersk Exporter *-2010* **Stena Line Ltd** Northern Marine Ferries Ltd SatCom: Inmarsat C 424589610 *Vlaardingen* *Netherlands* MMSI: 245896000 Official number: 29554	**13,017** 3,905 5,928	Class: LR ✠ **100A1** SS 01/2011 roll on - roll off cargo ship LI *IWS ✠ **LMC** **UMS** Eq.Ltr: E†; Cable: 613.5/56.0 U3	**1996-06 Miho Zosensho K.K. — Shimizu** Yd No: 1459 Loa 142.50 (BB) Br ex 23.47 Dght 5.400 Lbp 134.00 Br md 23.20 Dpth 13.15 Welded, 2 dks	**(A35A2RR) Ro-Ro Cargo Ship** Passengers: 12 Stern door/ramp (a) Len: 11.80 Wid: 16.20 Swl: 90 Lane-Len: 1562 Lane-Wid: 3.00 Lane-clr ht: 4.75 Trailers: 120	**2 oil engines** with flexible couplings & sr gearedto sc. shafts driving 2 CP propellers Total Power: 10,736kW (14,596hp) 18.6kn Sulzer 8ZAL40S 2 x 4 Stroke 8 Cy. 400 x 560 each-5368kW (7298bhp) Hitachi Zosen Corp-Japan AuxGen: 2 x 1000kW 445V 60Hz a.c, 2 x 560kW 445V 60Hz a.c Boilers: AuxB (o.f.) 6.9kgf/cm² (6.8bar), AuxB (ex.g.) 6.9kgf/cm² (6.8bar) Thrusters: 2 Thwart. CP thruster (f) Fuel: 143.8 (d.f.) 1130.4 (r.f.)
9188099 *C6AG7*	**STENA SIRITA** **P/R Stena Ugland Shuttle Tanker II DA** Standard Marine Tonsberg AS *Nassau* *Bahamas* MMSI: 311000038	**77,410** 34,036 126,873 T/cm 106.5	Class: NV	**1999-08 Tsuneishi Shipbuilding Co Ltd — Fukuyama HS** Yd No: 1157 Loa 262.61 (BB) Br ex 46.04 Dght 15.728 Lbp 249.12 Br md 46.00 Dpth 23.70 Welded, 1 dk	**(A13A2TS) Shuttle Tanker** Double Hull (13F) Liq: 134,001; Liq (Oil): 134,001 Cargo Heating Coils Compartments: 12 Wing Ta, 2 Wing Slop Ta, ER 3 Cargo Pump (s): 3x4000m³/hr Manifold: Bow/CM: 129.6m	**2 oil engines** driving 2 CP propellers Total Power: 19,272kW (26,202hp) 14.8kn B&W 7S50MC 2 x 2 Stroke 7 Cy. 500 x 1910 each-9636kW (13101bhp) MAN B&W Diesel A/S-Denmark AuxGen: 2 x 2420kW 220/440V 60Hz a.c, 2 x 1640kW 220/440V 60Hz a.c Thrusters: 2 Tunnel thruster (f); 1 Tunnel thruster (a) Fuel: 302.0 (d.f.) 4131.0 (r.f.)
8751681 *GCWP* -	**STENA SPEY** *ex* High Seas Driller *-1983* **Stena Spey Drilling Ltd** Stena Drilling Ltd *London* *United Kingdom* MMSI: 232662000 Official number: 703396	**16,581** 4,818 13,587	Class: NV	**1983-02 Daewoo Shipbuilding & Heavy Machinery Ltd — Geoje** Yd No: 3007 Loa 79.30 Br ex 62.00 Dght - Lbp - Br md - Dpth 35.40 Welded, 1 dk	**(Z11C3ZE) Drilling Rig, semi Submersible**	**4 diesel electric oil engines** driving 4 gen. each 2200kW a.c Connecting to 2 elec. motors driving 2 FP propellers Total Power: 6,472kW (8,800hp) Bergens KVGB-12 4 x Vee 4 Stroke 12 Cy. 250 x 300 each-1618kW (2200bhp) AS Bergens Mek Verksteder-Norway
7907661 *C6ZK8* -	**STENA SPIRIT** *ex* Stena Scandinavica *-2011* *launched as* Stena Germanica *-1988* **Stena (Bermuda) Line Ltd** Stena Line Scandinavia AB *Nassau* *Bahamas* MMSI: 311058100 Official number: 8001927	**39,193** 17,792 4,500	Class: LR ✠ **100A1** CS 02/2013 car ferry Ice Class 2 ✠ **LMC** **UMS** Eq.Ltr: (K†) ; Cable: 632.5/70.0 U3	**1988-01 Stocznia Gdanska im Lenina — Gdansk** Yd No: B494/02 Loa 175.39 (BB) Br ex 30.82 Dght 6.701 Lbp 154.18 Br md 30.46 Dpth 8.62 Welded	**(A36A2PR) Passenger/Ro-Ro Ship (Vehicles)** Passengers: 1700; cabins: 661 Bow door & ramp Len: 13.00 Wid: 7.00 Swl: - Stern door/ramp (p) Len: 12.00 Wid: 9.00 Swl: - Stern door/ramp (s) Len: 12.00 Wid: 9.00 Swl: - Side door (p) Side door (s) Lane-Len: 1628 Lane-Wid: 7.00 Lane-clr ht: 4.50 Cars: 590, Trailers: 26 Ice Capable	**4 oil engines** with clutches, flexible couplings & sr geared to sc. shafts driving 2 FP propellers Total Power: 20,760kW (28,224hp) 18.5kn Sulzer 16ZV40/48 4 x Vee 2 Stroke 16 Cy. 400 x 480 each-5190kW (7056bhp) Zaklady Urzadzen Technicznych'Zgoda' SA-Poland AuxGen: 5 x 1200kW 400V 50Hz a.c Boilers: e (ex.g.) 12.1kgf/cm² (11.9bar), (e (ex.g.)) (7.5kgf/cm² (7.4bar)), e (ex.g.) 12.1kgf/cm² (11.9bar), e (ex.g.) 12.1kgf/cm² (11.9bar), AuxB (o.f.) 7.0kgf/cm² (6.9bar) Thrusters: 1 Thwart. CP thruster (f); 1 Tunnel thruster (a) Fuel: 280.0 (d.f.) 1400.0 (r.f.) 75.0pd
9208033 *C6ST9* -	**STENA SPIRIT** *ex* Erviken *-2002* **Stena Spirit LLC** Petroleo Brasileiro SA (PETROBRAS) SatCom: Inmarsat C 431147110 *Nassau* *Bahamas* MMSI: 311471000 Official number: 8000581	**83,120** 46,633 151,294 T/cm 118.0	Class: NV (AB)	**2001-01 Samsung Heavy Industries Co Ltd — Geoje** Yd No: 1305 Converted From: Crude Oil Tanker-2003 Loa 277.30 (BB) Br ex 48.04 Dght 16.421 Lbp 265.40 Br md 48.00 Dpth 23.60 Welded, 1 dk	**(A13A2TS) Shuttle Tanker** Double Hull (13F) Liq: 168,810; Liq (Oil): 168,810 Cargo Heating Coils Compartments: 12 Wing Ta, ER, 2 Wing Slop Ta 3 Cargo Pump (s): 3x3800m³/hr Manifold: Bow/CM: 137.8m	**1 oil engine** driving 1 CP propeller Total Power: 18,624kW (25,321hp) 15.2kn B&W 6S70MC-C 1 x 2 Stroke 6 Cy. 700 x 2800 18624kW (25321bhp) HSD Engine Co Ltd-South Korea AuxGen: 1 x 900kW a.c, 3 x 900kW a.c Thrusters: 1 Thwart. FP thruster (f) Fuel: 170.0 (d.f.) (Heating Coils) 3680.0 (r.f.) 68.0pd
9579042 *ZCEF5* -	**STENA SUEDE** **Stena Ocean Ltd** Stena Bulk AB SatCom: Inmarsat C 431062210 *Hamilton* *Bermuda (British)* MMSI: 310622000	**81,187** 51,148 159,158 T/cm 119.6	Class: BV	**2011-11 Samsung Heavy Industries Co Ltd — Geoje** Yd No: 1910 Loa 274.00 (BB) Br ex 48.04 Dght 17.000 Lbp 264.00 Br md 48.00 Dpth 23.20 Welded, 1 dk	**(A13A2TV) Crude Oil Tanker** Double Hull (13F) Liq: 167,400; Liq (Oil): 167,400 Cargo Heating Coils Compartments: 12 Wing Ta, 2 Wing Slop Ta, ER 3 Cargo Pump (s): 3x4000m³/hr Manifold: Bow/CM: 137m	**1 oil engine** driving 1 FP propeller Total Power: 15,720kW (21,373hp) 15.5kn MAN-B&W 6S70ME-C8 1 x 2 Stroke 6 Cy. 700 x 2800 15720kW (21373bhp) Doosan Engine Co Ltd-South Korea AuxGen: 3 x 950kW 60Hz a.c Fuel: 4140.0

IMO / Call sign	Name / Owner	Tonnage	Class	Build / Dimensions	Type	Machinery
9592214 *ZCEJ6* -	**STENA SUNRISE** **Stena Ocean Ltd** Stena Bulk AB *Hamilton* *Bermuda (British)* MMSI: 310654000	**81,187** 51,148 159,034 T/cm 119.6	Class: BV	**2013**-01 **Samsung Heavy Industries Co Ltd — Geoje** Yd No: 1936 Loa 274.00 (BB) Br ex 48.04 Dght 17.000 Lbp 264.00 Br md 48.00 Dpth 23.20 Welded, 1 dk	**(A13A2TV) Crude Oil Tanker** Double Hull (13F) Liq: 167,400; Liq (Oil): 167,400 Cargo Heating Coils Compartments: 12 Wing Ta, 2 Wing Slop Ta, ER 3 Cargo Pump (s): 3x4000m³/hr Manifold: Bow/CM: 137m	**1 oil engine** driving 1 FP propeller Total Power: 15,720kW (21,373hp) 14.5kn MAN-B&W 6S70ME-C8 1 x 2 Stroke 6 Cy. 700 x 2800 15720kW (21373bhp) Doosan Engine Co Ltd-South Korea AuxGen: 3 x 950kW 60Hz a.c Fuel: 130.0 (d.f.) 3400.0 (r.f.)
9198941 *2EZR3* -	**STENA SUPERFAST VII** *ex* Superfast VII *-2011* **Baltic SF VII Ltd** Tallink Group Ltd (AS Tallink Grupp) SatCom: Inmarsat C 423592952 *Belfast* *United Kingdom* MMSI: 235089435 Official number: 5226875	**30,285** 10,769 5,915	Class: AB	**2001**-05 **Howaldtswerke-Deutsche Werft AG (HDW) — Kiel** Yd No: 357 Loa 203.30 (BB) Br ex - Dght 6.600 Lbp 185.60 Br md 25.00 Dpth 9.10 Welded, 9 dks.	**(A36A2PR) Passenger/Ro-Ro Ship (Vehicles)** Passengers: 1200; cabins: 51; berths: 194 Bow door/ramp (centre) Len: 21.30 Wid: 4.00 Swl: - Stern door/ramp (p) Len: 12.00 Wid: 8.00 Swl: - Stern door/ramp (s) Len: 12.00 Wid: 5.00 Swl: - Cars: 661 Ice Capable	**4 oil engines** with clutches, flexible couplings & sr geared to sc. shafts driving 2 CP propellers Total Power: 48,000kW (65,260hp) 25.0kn Sulzer 16ZAV40S 4 x Vee 4 Stroke 16 Cy. 400 x 560 each-12000kW (16315bhp) Wartsila Italia SpA-Italy AuxGen: 2 x 1680kW 440V 60Hz a.c, 3 x 1600kW 440V 60Hz a.c Thrusters: 3 Thwart. FP thruster (f); 1 Thwart. FP thruster (a) Fuel: 135.0 (d.f.) 1269.6 (r.f.) 142.0pd
9198953 *2EZR4* -	**STENA SUPERFAST VIII** *ex* Superfast VIII *-2011* **Baltic SF VIII Ltd** Tallink Group Ltd (AS Tallink Grupp) SatCom: Inmarsat C 4235592953 *Belfast* *United Kingdom* MMSI: 235089436 Official number: 5226889	**30,285** 10,769 5,990	Class: AB	**2001**-07 **Howaldtswerke-Deutsche Werft AG (HDW) — Kiel** Yd No: 358 Loa 203.30 (BB) Br ex 25.43 Dght 6.600 Lbp 185.60 Br md 25.00 Dpth 9.10 Welded	**(A36A2PR) Passenger/Ro-Ro Ship (Vehicles)** Passengers: unberthed: 800; cabins: 179; berths: 622 Bow door/ramp (centre) Len: 21.30 Wid: 4.80 Swl: - Stern door/ramp (p) Len: 12.00 Wid: 8.80 Swl: - Stern door/ramp (s) Len: 12.00 Wid: 6.10 Swl: - Lane-Len: 1918 Cars: 482 Ice Capable	**4 oil engines** with clutches, flexible couplings & sr geared to sc. shafts driving 2 CP propellers Total Power: 48,000kW (65,260hp) 26.6kn Sulzer 16ZAV40S 4 x Vee 4 Stroke 16 Cy. 400 x 560 each-12000kW (16315bhp) Wartsila Italia SpA-Italy AuxGen: 2 x 1680kW 440V 60Hz a.c, 3 x 1600kW 440V 60Hz a.c Thrusters: 2 Thwart. FP thruster (f); 1 Thwart. FP thruster (a) Fuel: 135.0 (d.f.) 1269.6 (r.f.) 142.0pd
9579030 *ZCEF1* -	**STENA SUPERIOR** **Stena Ocean Ltd** Stena Bulk AB *Hamilton* *Bermuda (British)* MMSI: 310620000	**81,187** 51,148 159,236 T/cm 119.6	Class: BV	**2011**-09 **Samsung Heavy Industries Co Ltd — Geoje** Yd No: 1909 Loa 274.00 (BB) Br ex 48.04 Dght 17.000 Lbp 264.00 Br md 48.00 Dpth 23.20 Welded, 1 dk	**(A13A2TV) Crude Oil Tanker** Double Hull (13F) Liq: 167,440; Liq (Oil): 167,400 Cargo Heating Coils Compartments: 12 Wing Ta, 2 Wing Slop Ta, ER 3 Cargo Pump (s): 3x3800m³/hr Manifold: Bow/CM: 137m	**1 oil engine** driving 1 FP propeller Total Power: 18,660kW (25,370hp) 15.5kn MAN-B&W 6S70ME-C8 1 x 2 Stroke 6 Cy. 700 x 2800 18660kW (25370bhp) Doosan Engine Co Ltd-South Korea AuxGen: 3 x 950kW 60Hz a.c Fuel: 260.0 (d.f.) 3850.0 (r.f.)
9585895 *ZCEG9* -	**STENA SUPREME** **CM Suez I Ltd** Stena Bulk AB SatCom: Inmarsat C 431064310 *Hamilton* *Bermuda (British)* MMSI: 310643000	**81,187** 51,148 159,031 T/cm 119.6	Class: BV	**2012**-06 **Samsung Heavy Industries Co Ltd — Geoje** Yd No: 1925 Loa 274.00 (BB) Br ex 48.04 Dght 17.000 Lbp 264.00 Br md 48.00 Dpth 23.22 Welded, 1 dk	**(A13A2TV) Crude Oil Tanker** Double Hull (13F) Liq: 168,360; Liq (Oil): 167,400 Cargo Heating Coils Compartments: 12 Wing Ta, 2 Wing Slop Ta, ER 3 Cargo Pump (s): 3x4000m³/hr Manifold: Bow/CM: 137m	**1 oil engine** driving 1 FP propeller Total Power: 15,720kW (21,373hp) 15.5kn MAN-B&W 6S70ME-C8 1 x 2 Stroke 6 Cy. 700 x 2800 15720kW (21373bhp) Doosan Engine Co Ltd-South Korea AuxGen: 3 x 950kW 60Hz a.c Fuel: 4140.0
9469388 *PHJU* -	**STENA TRANSIT** **Stena North Sea Ltd** Stena Line BV SatCom: Inmarsat C 424451314 *Hoek van Holland* *Netherlands* MMSI: 244513000 Official number: 54460	**33,690** 17,330 8,423	Class: LR ✠ **100A1** SS 09/2011 roll on-roll off cargo ship passenger ship *IWS LI EP Ice Class 1A FS at a draught of 6.38m Max/min draught fwd 6.30/4.66m Max/min draught aft 6.57/4.93m Power required 3676kw, power installed 21600kw ✠ **LMC** **UMS** Eq.Ltr: K†; Cable: 632.8/68.0 U3 (a)	**2011**-09 **Samsung Heavy Industries Co Ltd — Geoje** Yd No: 1808 Loa 212.00 (BB) Br ex 31.62 Dght 6.300 Lbp 194.80 Br md 26.70 Dpth 21.50 Welded, 3 dks	**(A36A2PR) Passenger/Ro-Ro Ship (Vehicles)** Passengers: 330 Stern door/ramp (centre) Len: 6.10 Wid: 14.60 Swl: 101 Lane-Len: 4057 Trailers: 280 Ice Capable	**2 oil engines** with clutches & sr geared to sc. shafts driving 2 CP propellers Total Power: 21,600kW (29,368hp) 22.2kn MAN-B&W 9L48/60B 2 x 4 Stroke 9 Cy. 480 x 600 each-10800kW (14684bhp) STX Engine Co Ltd-South Korea AuxGen: 2 x 2050kW 450V 60Hz a.c, 2 x 1450kW 450V 60Hz a.c Boilers: AuxB (o.f.) 9.2kgf/cm² (9.0bar), AuxB (ex.g.) 9.2kgf/cm² (9.0bar) Thrusters: 2 Thwart. CP thruster (f)
9469376 *PCIY* -	**STENA TRANSPORTER** **Stena North Sea Ltd** Stena Line BV SatCom: Inmarsat C 424676210 *Hoek van Holland* *Netherlands* MMSI: 246762000 Official number: 54185	**33,690** 17,330 8,423	Class: LR (NV) ✠ **100A1** SS 01/2011 roll on-roll off cargo ship, passeneger ship *IWS LI EP Ice Class 1A FS at a draught of 6.38m Max/min draughts fwd 6.30/4.66m Max/min draughts aft 6.57/4.93m Power required 3676kw, power installed 21600kw ✠ **LMC** **UMS** Eq.Ltr: K†; Cable: 632.5/68.0 U3 (a)	**2011**-01 **Samsung Heavy Industries Co Ltd — Geoje** Yd No: 1807 Loa 212.00 (BB) Br ex 31.62 Dght 6.300 Lbp 194.80 Br md 26.70 Dpth 9.30 Welded, 3 dks	**(A36A2PR) Passenger/Ro-Ro Ship (Vehicles)** Passengers: 330; cabins: 130; berths: 264 Stern door/ramp (centre) Len: 6.10 Wid: 14.60 Swl: 101 Lane-Len: 4057 Trailers: 280 Ice Capable	**2 oil engines** with clutches & sr geared to sc. shafts driving 2 CP propellers Total Power: 21,600kW (29,368hp) 23.6kn MAN-B&W 9L48/60B 2 x 4 Stroke 9 Cy. 480 x 600 each-10800kW (14684bhp) STX Engine Co Ltd-South Korea AuxGen: 2 x 2050kW 450V 60Hz a.c, 2 x 1450kW 450V 60Hz a.c Boilers: AuxB (o.f.) 9.2kgf/cm² (9.0bar), AuxB (ex.g.) 9.2kgf/cm² (9.0bar) Thrusters: 2 Thwart. FP thruster (f)
7907659 *SKPZ* -	**STENA VISION** *ex* Stena Germanica *-2010* *launched as* Stena Scandinavica *-1987* **Stena Line Scandinavia AB** - SatCom: Inmarsat B 326529210 *Karlskrona* *Sweden* MMSI: 265292000	**39,191** 17,791 4,500	Class: LR ✠ **100A1** SS 04/2012 car ferry Ice Class 2 ✠ **LMC** **UMS** Eq.Ltr: (K†) ; Cable: 632.5/70.0 U3	**1987**-04 **Stocznia im Komuny Paryskiej — Gdynia** Yd No: B494/01 Loa 175.37 (BB) Br ex 30.82 Dght 6.701 Lbp 154.18 Br md 30.46 Dpth 8.62 Welded, 9 dks, incl. movable no. 4 dk (for cars) and movable No.6 dk (for cars) inboard and fixed at sides	**(A36A2PR) Passenger/Ro-Ro Ship (Vehicles)** Passengers: 1700 Bow door & ramp (centre) Len: 13.00 Wid: 7.00 Swl: - Stern door/ramp (p) Len: 12.00 Wid: 9.00 Swl: - Stern door/ramp (s) Len: 12.00 Wid: 9.00 Swl: - Side door (p) Side doors (s) Lane-Len: 1628 Lane-Wid: 5.00 Lane-clr ht: 4.50 Cars: 590, Trailers: 26 Ice Capable	**4 oil engines** with clutches, flexible couplings & sr geared to sc. shafts driving 2 CP propellers Total Power: 20,760kW (28,224hp) 20.0kn Sulzer 16ZV40/48 4 x Vee 2 Stroke 16 Cy. 400 x 480 each-5190kW (7056bhp) Zaklady Urzadzen Technicznych'Zgoda' SA-Poland AuxGen: 5 x 1200kW 400V 50Hz a.c Boilers: 3 AuxB (ex.g.) (New boiler: 1987) 12.2kgf/cm² (12.0bar), 2 e (ex.g.) 7.7kgf/cm² (7.6bar), 2 AuxB (o.f.) 7.0kgf/cm² (6.9bar) Thrusters: 2 Thwart. CP thruster (f) Fuel: 280.0 (d.f.) 1400.0 (r.f.) 75.0pd
9664720 *V7AG9* -	**STENAWECO GLADYS W** **Sterling Ocean Shipping III LLC** Fleet Management Ltd SatCom: Inmarsat C 453838681 *Majuro* *Marshall Islands* MMSI: 538004994 Official number: 4994	**29,940** 13,491 49,995 T/cm 52.0	Class: AB	**2013**-07 **STX Offshore & Shipbuilding Co Ltd — Changwon (Jinhae Shipyard)** Yd No: 1575 Loa 183.00 (BB) Br ex 32.23 Dght 13.100 Lbp 173.90 Br md 32.20 Dpth 19.10 Welded, 1 dk	**(A12B2TR) Chemical/Products Tanker** Double Hull (13F) Liq: 52,170; Liq (Oil): 52,170 Cargo Heating Coils Compartments: 6 Wing Ta, 6 Wing Ta, 1 Wing Slop Ta, 1 Wing Slop Ta, ER 12 Cargo Pump (s): 12x600m³/hr Manifold: Bow/CM: 90.5m	**1 oil engine** driving 1 FP propeller Total Power: 7,570kW (10,292hp) 14.5kn MAN-B&W 6S50ME-C 1 x 2 Stroke 6 Cy. 500 x 2000 7570kW (10292bhp) STX Engine Co Ltd-South Korea AuxGen: 3 x 910kW a.c Fuel: 245.0 (d.f.) 1167.0 (r.f.)
9661247 *V7AG8* -	**STENAWECO JULIA L** **Sterling Ocean Shipping II LLC** Fleet Management Ltd *Majuro* *Marshall Islands* MMSI: 538004993 Official number: 4993	**29,940** 13,467 49,995 T/cm 52.0	Class: AB	**2013**-06 **STX Offshore & Shipbuilding Co Ltd — Changwon (Jinhae Shipyard)** Yd No: 1574 Loa 183.00 (BB) Br ex 32.23 Dght 13.100 Lbp 173.90 Br md 32.20 Dpth 19.10 Welded, 1 dk	**(A12B2TR) Chemical/Products Tanker** Double Hull (13F) Liq: 52,170; Liq (Oil): 52,170 Cargo Heating Coils Compartments: 6 Wing Ta, 6 Wing Ta, 2 Wing Slop Ta, ER 12 Cargo Pump (s): 12x600m³/hr Manifold: Bow/CM: 90.5m	**1 oil engine** driving 1 FP propeller Total Power: 7,570kW (10,292hp) 14.5kn MAN-B&W 6S50ME-C 1 x 2 Stroke 6 Cy. 500 x 2000 7570kW (10292bhp) STX Engine Co Ltd-South Korea AuxGen: 3 x 910kW a.c Fuel: 245.0 (d.f.) 1167.0 (r.f.)

IMO / Call sign	Name / Owners	Tonnage	Class	Builder / Dimensions	Type / Capacity	Machinery
9661235 *V7AG7* -	**STENAWECO MARJORIE K** *ex* Marjorie K *-2013* **Sterling Ocean Shipping I LLC** Elegant Ship Management & Consultancy Services Pvt Ltd *Majuro* *Marshall Islands* MMSI: 538004992 Official number: 4992	**29,940** 13,486 49,995 T/cm 52.0	Class: AB	**2013**-04 **STX Offshore & Shipbuilding Co Ltd — Changwon (Jinhae Shipyard)** Yd No: 1573 Loa 183.00 (BB) Br ex 32.23 Dght 13.100 Lbp 173.90 Br md 32.20 Dpth 19.10 Welded, 1 dk	**(A12B2TR) Chemical/Products Tanker** Double Hull (13F) Liq: 52,170; Liq (Oil): 52,170 Cargo Heating Coils Compartments: 6 Wing Ta, 6 Wing Ta, 1 Wing Slop Ta, 1 Wing Slop Ta, ER 12 Cargo Pump (s): 12x600m³/hr Manifold: Bow/CM: 90.5m	**1 oil engine** driving 1 FP propeller Total Power: 7,570kW (10,292hp) 14.5kn MAN-B&W 6S50ME-C 1 x 2 Stroke 6 Cy. 500 x 2000 7570kW (10292bhp) STX Engine Co Ltd-South Korea AuxGen: 3 x 910kW a.c Fuel: 245.0 (d.f.) 1167.0 (r.f.)
9642019 *D5BM3* -	**STENAWECO SPIRIT** **Edina Marine Ltd** OceanGold Tankers Inc *Monrovia* *Liberia* MMSI: 636015556 Official number: 15556	**30,017** 13,336 49,995 T/cm 52.0	Class: LR ✠ **100A1** SS 10/2012 Double Hull oil and chemical tanker, Ship Type 2 and Ship Type 3 CSR ESP **ShipRight** (CM,ACS (B)) *IWS LI SPM4 ✠ **LMC** **UMS IGS** Cable: 621.0/73.0 U3 (a)	**2012**-10 **SPP Shipbuilding Co Ltd — Tongyeong** Yd No: H4091 Loa 183.00 (BB) Br ex 32.23 Dght 13.028 Lbp 174.00 Br md 32.20 Dpth 19.10 Welded, 1 dk	**(A12B2TR) Chemical/Products Tanker** Double Hull (13F) Liq: 52,080; Liq (Oil): 52,080 Cargo Heating Coils Compartments: 12 Wing Ta, 2 Wing Slop Ta, ER 12 Cargo Pump (s): 12x600m³/hr Manifold: Bow/CM: 90.5m	**1 oil engine** driving 1 FP propeller Total Power: 8,950kW (12,168hp) 14.5kn MAN-B&W 6S50ME-C8 1 x 2 Stroke 6 Cy. 500 x 2000 8950kW (12168bhp) Doosan Engine Co Ltd-South Korea AuxGen: 3 x 900kW 450V 60Hz a.c Boilers: e (ex.g.) 12.2kgf/cm² (12.0bar), WTAuxB (Comp) 9.4kgf/cm² (9.2bar) Fuel: 223.0 (d.f.) 1282.0 (r.f.)
9660657 *D5EA2* -	**STENAWECO VENTURE** **Berdine Shipholding Ltd** OceanGold Tankers Inc *Monrovia* *Liberia* MMSI: 636016018 Official number: 16018	**29,623** 13,711 49,995	Class: LR ✠ **100A1** SS 01/2014 Double Hull oil and chemical tanker, Ship Type 2 and Ship Type 3 CSR ESP **ShipRight** (ACS (B), CM) *IWS LI SPM4 ECO (CRM,EEDI-3,IHM,OW,P) ✠ **LMC** **UMS IGS** Eq.Ltr: M†; Cable: 632.5/73.0 SL	**2014**-01 **SPP Shipbuilding Co Ltd — Tongyeong** Yd No: H1071 Loa 183.00 (BB) Br ex 32.23 Dght 13.300 Lbp 174.00 Br md 32.20 Dpth 19.10 Welded, 1 dk	**(A12B2TR) Chemical/Products Tanker** Double Hull (13F) Compartments: 12 Wing Ta, 2 Wing Slop Ta, ER	**1 oil engine** driving 1 FP propeller Total Power: 10,680kW (14,521hp) MAN-B&W 6S50ME-B9 1 x 2 Stroke 6 Cy. 500 x 2214 10680kW (14521bhp) Doosan Engine Co Ltd-South Korea AuxGen: 3 x 900kW 450V 60Hz a.c Boilers: AuxB (o.f.) 9.2kgf/cm² (9.0bar), WTAuxB (Comp) 9.2kgf/cm² (9.0bar)
9283978 *ZDGA3* -	**STENBERG** **Stentank AS** Rederiet Stenersen AS SatCom: Inmarsat C 423622210 *Gibraltar* *Gibraltar (British)* MMSI: 236222000	**11,935** 5,133 16,600 T/cm 28.5	Class: NV	**2003**-11 **Qiuxin Shipyard — Shanghai** Yd No: H2296 Loa 144.05 (BB) Br ex 23.15 Dght 8.900 Lbp 133.80 Br md 23.00 Dpth 12.40 Welded, 1 dk	**(A12B2TR) Chemical/Products Tanker** Double Hull (13F) Liq: 18,492; Liq (Oil): 19,500 16 Cargo Pump (s) Manifold: Bow/CM: 72m Ice Capable	**1 oil engine** geared to sc. shaft driving 1 CP propeller Total Power: 6,300kW (8,565hp) 14.0kn Wartsila 6L46C 1 x 4 Stroke 6 Cy. 460 x 580 6300kW (8565bhp) Wartsila Finland Oy-Finland AuxGen: 1 x a.c, 2 x a.c, 1 x 1500kW a.c Thrusters: 1 Tunnel thruster (f)
8730429 *YLFD* LZ-6132	**STENDE** **JSC Baltic Marine Fishing Co (AS 'Baltic Marine Fishing Co)** - SatCom: Inmarsat C 427512410 *Riga* *Latvia* MMSI: 275124000 Official number: 0621	**4,407** 1,322 1,810	Class: RS	**1989**-11 **GP Chernomorskiy Sudostroitelnyy Zavod — Nikolayev** Yd No: 581 Loa 104.50 Br ex 16.03 Dght 5.900 Lbp 96.40 Br md - Dpth 10.20 Welded, 2 dks	**(B11A2FG) Factory Stern Trawler** Grain: 870; Ins: 2,219; Liq: 35 Ice Capable	**2 oil engines** reduction geared to sc. shaft driving 1 CP propeller Total Power: 5,148kW (7,000hp) 16.1kn Russkiy 6CHN40/46 2 x 4 Stroke 6 Cy. 400 x 460 each-2574kW (3500bhp) Mashinostroitelnyy Zavod"Russkiy-Dizel"-Leningrad AuxGen: 2 x 1600kW 220/380V 50Hz a.c, 3 x 200kW 220/380V 50Hz a.c Fuel: 1226.0 (d.f.) 23.0pd
9261114 *ZDFR8* -	**STENHEIM** **Stenoil K/S** Brostrom AB *Gibraltar* *Gibraltar (British)* MMSI: 236202000 Official number: 736357	**11,935** 5,138 16,614 T/cm 28.5	Class: NV	**2003**-05 **Jiangnan Shipyard (Group) Co Ltd — Shanghai** Yd No: H2286 Loa 144.05 (BB) Br ex 23.34 Dght 8.900 Lbp 133.80 Br md 23.00 Dpth 12.40 Welded, 1 dk	**(A12B2TR) Chemical/Products Tanker** Double Hull (13F) Liq: 18,491; Liq (Oil): 18,491 Compartments: 12 Wing Ta, 2 Wing Slop Ta, ER 12 Cargo Pump (s): 12x300m³/hr Manifold: Bow/CM: 71.8m	**1 oil engine** geared to sc. shaft driving 1 CP propeller Total Power: 6,300kW (8,565hp) 14.0kn Wartsila 6L46C 1 x 4 Stroke 6 Cy. 460 x 580 6300kW (8565bhp) Wartsila Finland Oy-Finland AuxGen: 1 x 960kW a.c, 2 x 640kW a.c, 1 x 1500kW 60Hz a.c Thrusters: 1 Tunnel thruster (f)
6922846 - -	**STENI** *ex* Sten *-1994* *ex* Alsten *-1991* - - *Zanzibar* *Tanzania*	*172* 60 129	Class: (NV)	**1969 Ejnar S. Nielsen Mek. Verksted AS — Harstad** Yd No: 14 Loa 29.80 Br ex 8.41 Dght 2.972 Lbp 26.12 Br md 8.11 Dpth 3.76 Welded, 1 dk	**(A36A2PR) Passenger/Ro-Ro Ship (Vehicles)** Passengers: unberthed: 175	**1 oil engine** driving 1 FP propeller Total Power: 478kW (650hp) Normo LSMC-5 1 x 4 Stroke 5 Cy. 250 x 300 478kW (650bhp) AS Bergens Mek Verksteder-Norway AuxGen: 2 x 56kW 220V 50Hz a.c Thrusters: 1 Thwart. FP thruster (f)
9552379 *9V8742* -	**STENIA COLOSSUS** **'K' Line Pte Ltd (KLPL)** Kawasaki Kisen Kaisha Ltd (Kawasaki Kisen KK) ('K' Line) SatCom: Inmarsat C 456415710 *Singapore* *Singapore* MMSI: 564157000 Official number: 396181	**33,096** 19,142 58,731 T/cm 59.5	Class: NK	**2011**-03 **Kawasaki Heavy Industries Ltd — Sakaide KG** Yd No: 1677 Loa 197.00 (BB) Br ex - Dght 12.676 Lbp 194.00 Br md 32.26 Dpth 18.10 Welded, 1 dk	**(A21A2BC) Bulk Carrier** Grain: 73,614; Bale: 70,963 Compartments: 5 Ho, ER 5 Ha: ER Cranes: 4x30.5t	**1 oil engine** driving 1 FP propeller Total Power: 8,630kW (11,733hp) 14.5kn MAN-B&W 6S50MC-C 1 x 2 Stroke 6 Cy. 500 x 2000 8630kW (11733bhp) Kawasaki Heavy Industries Ltd-Japan Fuel: 2265.0 (r.f.)
9187394 *ZDEN8* -	**STENSTRAUM** *ex* Milan *-2001* **Utsten KS** Rederiet Stenersen AS *Gibraltar* *Gibraltar (British)* MMSI: 236006000 Official number: 734606	**8,882** 4,593 13,677 T/cm 25.2	Class: NV (GL)	**2001**-09 **Jiangsu Jiangyang Shipyard Group Co Ltd — Yangzhou JS** Yd No: JY97125 Loa 145.20 (BB) Br ex 20.90 Dght 8.450 Lbp 133.60 Br md 20.80 Dpth 11.20 Welded, 1 dk	**(A12B2TR) Chemical/Products Tanker** Double Hull (13F) Liq: 15,305; Liq (Oil): 15,308 Cargo Heating Coils Compartments: 14 Wing Ta, 1 Slop Ta, 2 Wing Slop Ta, ER 14 Cargo Pump (s): 14x330m³/hr Manifold: Bow/CM: 78.4m Ice Capable	**1 oil engine** driving 1 CP propeller Total Power: 5,490kW (7,464hp) 15.5kn MAN-B&W 6S42MC 1 x 2 Stroke 6 Cy. 420 x 1764 5490kW (7464bhp) AuxGen: 1 x 1400kW a.c, 3 x a.c Thrusters: 1 Thwart. FP thruster (f) Fuel: 110.0 (d.f.) 500.0 (r.f.)
1010832 *ZGCG* -	**STEP ONE** **Yane Consultants Ltd** Moran Yacht Management Inc *George Town* *Cayman Islands (British)* MMSI: 319975000 Official number: 743694	**672** 201 176	Class: LR ✠ **100A1** SS 04/2012 SSC Yacht, mono, G6 **LMC** **UMS** Cable: 330.0/20.5 U2 (a)	**2012**-04 **Damen Shipyards Gdynia SA — Gdynia** (Hull) Yd No: (460) **2012**-04 **Amels BV — Vlissingen** Yd No: 460 Loa 52.30 Br ex 9.00 Dght 3.300 Lbp 45.00 Br md 9.00 Dpth 4.90 Welded, 1 dk	**(X11A2YP) Yacht**	**2 oil engines** with clutches & sr reverse geared to sc. shafts driving 2 FP propellers Total Power: 2,100kW (2,856hp) 13.0kn M.T.U. 16V2000M70 2 x Vee 4 Stroke 16 Cy. 130 x 150 each-1050kW (1428bhp) MTU Friedrichshafen GmbH-Friedrichshafen AuxGen: 2 x 155kW 400V 50Hz a.c Thrusters: 1 Thwart. FP thruster (f)
8822533 *UEKC* -	**STEPAN DEMESHEV** **The Northern Dredging Co Ltd (Severnaya Dnouglubitelnaya Kompaniya Ltd)** - *Nakhodka* *Russia* MMSI: 273817910	**2,081** 624 583	Class: RS	**1988**-04 **VEB Schiffswerft Neptun — Rostock** Yd No: 112/1462 Loa 79.97 Br ex 14.80 Dght 3.750 Lbp 70.88 Br md 14.40 Dpth 5.20 Welded, 1 dk	**(B33A2DB) Bucket Ladder Dredger** Cranes: 1x8t; Derricks: 1x5t Ice Capable	**2 diesel electric oil engines** driving 2 gen. each 440kW 1 gen. of 200kW Connecting to 2 elec. motors each (570kW) driving 2 FP propellers Total Power: 1,940kW (2,638hp) 8.7kn S.K.L. 8NVD48A-2 2 x 4 Stroke 8 Cy. 320 x 480 each-970kW (1319bhp) VEB Schwermaschinenbau "KarlLiebknecht" (SKL)-Magdeburg
8308939 *UIUM* -	**STEPAN GEYTS** *ex* Western Lucky *-1996* **JSC Lesprom-Nakhodka (A/O 'Lesprom-Nakhodka')** Primorsklesprom JSC (A/O 'Primorsklesprom') *Nakhodka* *Russia* MMSI: 273415040	**2,875** 1,638 4,833	Class: RS (NK)	**1983**-02 **K.K. Imai Seisakusho — Kamijima** Yd No: 227 Loa 90.51 Br ex 15.24 Dght 6.405 Lbp 83.32 Br md 15.21 Dpth 7.60 Welded, 1 dk	**(A31A2GX) General Cargo Ship** Grain: 5,720; Bale: 5,075 Compartments: 2 Ho, ER 2 Ha: (15.1 x 8.5) (25.9 x 8.5)ER Derricks: 1x20t,2x15t	**1 oil engine** reverse reduction geared to sc. shaft driving 1 FP propeller Total Power: 1,692kW (2,300hp) 11.0kn Akasaka DM38AK 1 x 4 Stroke 6 Cy. 380 x 600 1692kW (2300bhp) Akasaka Tekkosho KK (Akasaka DieselLtd)-Japan AuxGen: 2 x 120kW Fuel: 331.0 (d.f.) 6.5pd

IMO / Call sign / Fishing no.	Name / Owner / Port / Flag	Tonnage	Class	Builder / Dimensions	Type / Cargo	Machinery
8226454 *UDCS* -	**STEPAN VOSTRETSOV** **Nord Strait Co Ltd** - *Okhotsk* *Russia* MMSI: 273860100	**781** 209 332	Class: (RS)	**1983**-10 **Volgogradskiy Sudostroitelnyy Zavod — Volgograd** Yd No: 213 Loa 53.75 Br ex 10.72 Dght 4.290 Lbp 47.92 Br md - Dpth 6.74 Welded, 1 dk	**(B11A2FS) Stern Trawler** Ins: 218 Compartments: 1 Ho, ER 1 Ha: (1.6 x 1.6) Derricks: 2x1.5t Ice Capable	**1 oil engine** driving 1 CP propeller Total Power: 971kW (1,320hp) 12.8kn S.K.L. 8NVD48A-2U 1 x 4 Stroke 8 Cy. 320 x 480 971kW (1320bhp) VEB Schwermaschinenbau "KarlLiebknecht" (SKL)-Magdeburg AuxGen: 1 x 300kW, 3 x 160kW, 2 x 135kW Fuel: 182.0 (d.f.)
9141534 *OPBS* Z 45	**STEPHANIE** **NV Rederij Stephanie** - *Zeebrugge* *Belgium* MMSI: 205227000 Official number: 01 00042 1996	**388** 116 -		**1996**-07 **N.V. Scheepswerven L. de Graeve — Zeebrugge** Loa 37.78 Br ex 8.50 Dght - Lbp - Br md - Dpth 4.80 Welded, 1 dk	**(B11A2FT) Trawler**	**1 oil engine** driving 1 FP propeller Total Power: 300kW (408hp) Stork 1 x 300kW (408bhp) Stork Wartsila Diesel BV-Netherlands
9427433 *9HA3338* -	**STEPHANIE** *ex* Global Sea *-2013* **Stephanie Shipping Ltd** Bunkers Gibraltar Ltd *Valletta* *Malta* MMSI: 229450000 Official number: 9427433	**5,424** 2,444 7,519 T/cm 17.6	Class: BV	**2010**-02 **Taixing Ganghua Ship Industry Co Ltd — Taixing JS** Yd No: GHCY 1001 Loa 112.70 (BB) Br ex 17.63 Dght 7.200 Lbp 106.47 Br md 17.60 Dpth 9.40 Welded, 1 dk	**(A12B2TR) Chemical/Products Tanker** Double Hull (13F) Liq: 8,341; Liq (Oil): 8,500 Cargo Heating Coils Compartments: 18 Wing Ta, 2 Wing Slop Ta, ER 18 Cargo Pump (s): 2x100m³/hr, 16x150m³/hr Manifold: Bow/CM: 51.4m	**2 oil engines** reduction geared to sc. shafts driving 2 CP propellers Total Power: 3,440kW (4,678hp) 14.0kn MAN-B&W 8L21/31 2 x 4 Stroke 8 Cy. 210 x 310 each-1720kW (2339bhp) Shanghai Xinzhong Power MachinePlant-China AuxGen: 2 x 500kW 450V a.c, 3 x 400kW 450V 60Hz a.c Thrusters: 1 Tunnel thruster (f) Fuel: 89.0 (d.f.) 264.0 (r.f.)
8950287 - -	**STEPHANIE '96** **BEV Processors Inc** - *Georgetown* *Guyana* Official number: 0000294	*111* 75 -		**1996 Steiner Shipyard, Inc. — Bayou La Batre, Al** Loa 22.86 Br ex - Dght - Lbp 19.72 Br md 6.70 Dpth 3.35 Welded, 1 dk	**(B11A2FT) Trawler**	**1 oil engine** driving 1 FP propeller Total Power: 313kW (426hp) Cummins 1 x 4 Stroke 313kW (426bhp) Cummins Engine Co Inc-USA
8957704 - -	**STEPHANIE COLLEEN** **C & E Fisheries Ltd** - *St John's, NL* *Canada* MMSI: 316001977 Official number: 820776	*136* 102 -		**1999 TWL Enterprises Ltd — Trinity TB NL** L reg 18.50 Br ex - Dght - Lbp - Br md 7.10 Dpth 3.70 Bonded, 1 dk	**(B11B2FV) Fishing Vessel** Hull Material: Reinforced Plastic	**1 oil engine** driving 1 FP propeller Total Power: 441kW (600hp) 11.0kn
8968600 *WCD9870* -	**STEPHANIE DANN** *ex* Mary de Felice *-1992* **Tug Stephanie Dann Inc** Dann Ocean Towing Inc *Tampa, FL* *United States of America* MMSI: 338871000 Official number: 600517	**240** 72 -		**1978**-12 **Quality Equipment Inc — Houma LA** Yd No: 150 Loa - Br ex - Dght 3.790 Lbp 28.95 Br md 8.53 Dpth 4.26 Welded, 1 dk	**(B32A2ST) Tug**	**2 oil engines** reverse reduction geared to sc. shafts driving 2 FP propellers Total Power: 1,250kW (1,700hp) 11.0kn Caterpillar D398TA 2 x Vee 4 Stroke 12 Cy. 159 x 203 each-625kW (850bhp) Caterpillar Tractor Co-USA AuxGen: 2 x 75kW a.c Fuel: 211.0 (d.f.)
8705149 *FHDB* GV 642093	**STEPHANIE JEROME** **Lapart** - SatCom: Inmarsat C 422748311 *Guilvinec* *France* MMSI: 227483000 Official number: 642093	*131* - -		**1986 Ch. Pierre Glehen — Guilvinec** Loa 22.03 Br ex - Dght - Lbp - Br md 6.81 Dpth - Welded, 1 dk	**(B11A2FS) Stern Trawler**	**1 oil engine** driving 1 FP propeller Total Power: 382kW (519hp) MWM 1 x 4 Stroke 382kW (519bhp) Motoren Werke Mannheim AG (MWM)-West Germany
7743508 *WCY5699* -	**STEPHANIE LEN** **Lively Lobster LLC** - *Bridgeport, CT* *United States of America* Official number: 594110	*129* 88 -		**1978 Desco Marine — Saint Augustine, Fl** Yd No: 243-F Loa 20.83 Br ex 6.74 Dght - Lbp - Br md - Dpth 3.74 Bonded, 1 dk	**(B11A2FT) Trawler** Hull Material: Reinforced Plastic	**1 oil engine** driving 1 FP propeller Cummins 1 x 4 Stroke Cummins Engine Co Inc-USA
7948354 *WDC5147* -	**STEPHANIE LYNN** **Lanh Van Nguyen** - *Pearland, TX* *United States of America* MMSI: 367036650 Official number: 614058	*147* 100 -		**1979 T & J Marine, Inc. — Coden, Al** Yd No: 5 L reg 23.54 Br ex 6.94 Dght - Lbp - Br md - Dpth 3.71 Welded, 1 dk	**(B11B2FV) Fishing Vessel**	**1 oil engine** driving 1 FP propeller Total Power: 382kW (519hp)
8983935 *WDG2103* -	**STEPHANIE M** *ex* Jessica M *-2013* *ex* Orchid Lady *-2011* *ex* Francis X Seelos II *-2005* **Charca Fish III LLC** - *San Diego, CA* *United States of America* MMSI: 367056702 Official number: 1132795	**171** 51 -		**2002** Yd No: 243A L reg 26.94 Br ex - Dght - Lbp - Br md 7.62 Dpth 3.96 Welded, 1 dk	**(B11B2FV) Fishing Vessel**	**1 oil engine** driving 1 Propeller
8427278 *DUJ2188* -	**STEPHANIE MARIE** *ex* Marima III *-1998* **Aleson Shipping Lines Inc** - *Zamboanga* *Philippines* Official number: ZAM2D000672	*770* 316 -		**1973 at Manila** Loa - Br ex 6.74 Dght - Lbp 46.89 Br md 6.71 Dpth 5.62 Welded, 1 dk	**(A31A2GX) General Cargo Ship** Stern ramp (a)	**1 oil engine** driving 1 FP propeller Total Power: 1,324kW (1,800hp)
7717066 *WDB5472* -	**STEPHANIE MORRISON** *ex* Roxane T *-2003* *ex* Janie C *-1989* **Chet Morrison Offshore LLC** - *Houma, LA* *United States of America* MMSI: 366910010 Official number: 585261	**705** 211 450	Class: (AB)	**1977**-08 **Quality Shipbuilders Inc. — Moss Point, Ms** Yd No: 107 Loa - Br ex 11.61 Dght 3.702 Lbp 53.65 Br md 11.59 Dpth 4.27 Welded, 1 dk	**(B21A20S) Platform Supply Ship**	**2 oil engines** reverse reduction geared to sc. shafts driving 2 FP propellers Total Power: 1,986kW (2,700hp) 12.0kn Caterpillar 3516TA 2 x Vee 4 Stroke 16 Cy. 170 x 190 each-993kW (1350bhp) (new engine 1996) Caterpillar Inc-USA AuxGen: 1 x 99kW a.c, 1 x 75kW a.c Thrusters: 1 Thwart. FP thruster (f)
8852318 *WDE7888* -	**STEPHANIE S** **Petchem Inc** - *Cape Canaveral, FL* *United States of America* Official number: 907272	*126* 101 -		**1986 M.F. Martin, Jr. — Brunswick, Ga** Loa - Br ex - Dght 2.720 Lbp 21.06 Br md 7.92 Dpth 3.20 Welded, 1 dk	**(B32A2ST) Tug**	**2 oil engines** reduction geared to sc. shafts driving 2 FP propellers Total Power: 1,426kW (1,938hp) Caterpillar D398 2 x Vee 4 Stroke 12 Cy. 159 x 203 each-713kW (969bhp) Caterpillar Tractor Co-USA
7743510 *WDB5700* -	**STEPHANIE VAUGHN** **C & I Fishing Corp** - *New Bedford, MA* *United States of America* MMSI: 366912540 Official number: 595941	*170* 116 -		**1978 Quality Marine, Inc. — Bayou La Batre, Al** Yd No: 72 Loa 24.85 Br ex 7.32 Dght - Lbp - Br md - Dpth 3.84 Welded, 1 dk	**(B11B2FV) Fishing Vessel**	**1 oil engine** driving 1 FP propeller Total Power: 372kW (506hp) 12.0kn Caterpillar D379TA 1 x Vee 4 Stroke 8 Cy. 159 x 203 372kW (506bhp) Caterpillar Tractor Co-USA
9051777 *YFDQ* -	**STEPHANIE XVIII** **PT Armada Bumi Pratiwi Lines (ABP Lines)** - *Jakarta* *Indonesia* MMSI: 525016041	**1,377** 501 1,500 T/cm 8.3	Class: KI (LR) ✠ Classed LR until 27/11/96	**1995**-02 **P.T. Dok & Perkapalan Kodja Bahari (Unit I) — Jakarta** Yd No: 1156 Loa 65.00 Br ex 15.02 Dght 3.200 Lbp 61.20 Br md 15.00 Dpth 4.50 Welded, 1 dk	**(A13B2TP) Products Tanker** Liq: 2,088; Liq (Oil): 2,088 Compartments: 8 Ta, ER	**2 oil engines** with clutches, flexible couplings & dr reverse geared to sc. shafts driving 2 FP propellers Total Power: 1,176kW (1,598hp) 10.0kn Yanmar M200-EN 2 x 4 Stroke 6 Cy. 200 x 260 each-588kW (799bhp) Yanmar Diesel Engine Co Ltd-Japan AuxGen: 3 x 120kW 440V 60Hz a.c

IMO / Call sign	Name / Owner	Tonnage	Class	Build / Dimensions	Type	Machinery
9013153 *HP7961* -	**STEPHEN B** **The First Motions Corp SA** *Panama* *Panama* Official number: 2219695	**206** 61 -		**1990 La Force Shipyard Inc — Coden AL** Loa - Br ex - Dght - Lbp 25.00 Br md 7.62 Dpth 6.10 Welded	**(B11B2FV) Fishing Vessel**	**1 oil engine** driving 1 FP propeller Total Power: 368kW (500hp) 10.0kn
6514900 *VDJL* -	**STEPHEN B. ROMAN** *ex* Fort William *-1983* **Essroc Canada Inc** Algoma Central Corp (ACC) *Toronto, ON* *Canada* MMSI: 316001717 Official number: 323001	*6,792* 4,339 8,377	Class: LR ✠ **100A1** Lake SS 05/2009 Great Lakes and River St. Lawrence service ✠ **LMC** Eq.Ltr: (b†) ; Cable: SQ	**1965-05 Davie Shipbuilding Ltd — Levis QC** Yd No: 652 Converted From: Palletised Cargo Ship-1982 Loa 148.93 Br ex 17.20 Dght 7.800 Lbp 142.04 Br md 17.07 Dpth 10.83 Welded, 2 dks	**(A24A2BT) Cement Carrier** Grain: 3,984 Compartments: 3 Wing Ho, ER	**4 oil engines** sr geared to sc. shaft driving 1 CP propeller Total Power: 4,410kW (5,996hp) 16.0kn Fairbanks, Morse 10-38D8-1/8 2 x 2 Stroke 10 Cy. 207 x 254 each-1225kW (1666bhp) Canadian Locomotive Co Ltd-Canada Fairbanks, Morse 8-38D8-1/8 2 x 2 Stroke 8 Cy. 207 x 254 each-980kW (1332bhp) Canadian Locomotive Co Ltd-Canada AuxGen: 1 x 200kW 550V 60Hz a.c, 2 x 260kW 600V 60Hz a.c Thrusters: 1 Thwart. FP thruster (f)
8016380 *WDB2111* -	**STEPHEN DANN** *ex* El Rhino Grande *-2003* *ex* Mr. Bill G *-1990* *ex* Perseverance *-1983* **Dann Ocean Towing Inc** - *Tampa, FL* *United States of America* MMSI: 369560000 Official number: 636165	**305** 91 -	Class: AB	**1981-05 Modern Marine Power, Inc. — Houma, La** Yd No: 38 Loa - Br ex - Dght 3.731 Lbp 32.16 Br md 9.76 Dpth 4.37 Welded, 1 dk	**(B32A2ST) Tug**	**2 oil engines** reverse reduction geared to sc. shafts driving 2 FP propellers Total Power: 1,766kW (2,402hp) 11.0kn Caterpillar 3512TA 2 x Vee 4 Stroke 12 Cy. 170 x 190 each-883kW (1201bhp) (new engine 1983) Caterpillar Tractor Co-USA AuxGen: 2 x 75kW
7046170 *WCA3763* -	**STEPHEN REINAUER** *ex* Exxon Bay State *-1993* *ex* Esso Bay State *-1973* **Reinauer Transportation Companies LLC** - *New York, NY* *United States of America* MMSI: 366516370 Official number: 527691	*382* 114 -	Class: (AB)	**1970 Halter Marine Services, Inc. — New Orleans, La** Yd No: 258 Loa 33.23 Br ex 9.61 Dght 4.211 Lbp 31.81 Br md 9.45 Dpth 4.88 Welded, 1 dk	**(B32A2ST) Tug**	**2 oil engines** reverse reduction geared to sc. shafts driving 2 FP propellers Total Power: 2,132kW (2,898hp) 12.5kn EMD (Electro-Motive) 8-645-E5 2 x Vee 2 Stroke 8 Cy. 230 x 254 each-1066kW (1449bhp) General Motors Corp-USA AuxGen: 2 x 75kW 440V 60Hz a.c Fuel: 228.5
7003817 *WCW8842* -	**STEPHEN-SCOTT** *ex* Gulf Duke *-1978* **Reinauer Transportation Companies LLC** - *New York, NY* *United States of America* MMSI: 366245490 Official number: 507413	*188* 127 -	Class: (AB)	**1967 Main Iron Works, Inc. — Houma, La** Yd No: 174 Loa 30.64 Br ex 8.54 Dght 3.791 Lbp 29.34 Br md 8.26 Dpth 4.22 Welded, 1 dk	**(B32A2ST) Tug**	**2 oil engines** reverse reduction geared to sc. shafts driving 2 FP propellers Total Power: 1,250kW (1,700hp) Caterpillar D398TA 2 x Vee 4 Stroke 12 Cy. 159 x 203 each-625kW (850bhp) Caterpillar Tractor Co-USA AuxGen: 2 x 40kW 120V 60Hz a.c Fuel: 123.0
9533658 *YJRS5* -	**STEPHEN WALLACE DICK** **Platinum Fleet Ltd** Tidewater Marine International Inc *Port Vila* *Vanuatu* MMSI: 577010000 Official number: 2078	**3,601** 1,429 5,144	Class: AB	**2011-09 Fujian Mawei Shipbuilding Ltd — Fuzhou FJ** Yd No: 619-11 Loa 87.10 (BB) Br ex - Dght 6.200 Lbp 82.96 Br md 18.80 Dpth 7.40 Welded, 1 dk	**(B21A2OS) Platform Supply Ship**	**4 diesel electric oil engines** driving 4 gen. each 1825kW Connecting to 2 elec. motors each (2000kW) driving 2 Azimuth electric drive units Total Power: 7,300kW (9,924hp) 12.0kn Cummins QSK60-M 4 x Vee 4 Stroke 16 Cy. 159 x 190 each-1825kW (2481bhp) Cummins Engine Co Inc-USA Thrusters: 1 Tunnel thruster (f); 1 Retract. directional thruster (f)
9225548 *FIYL* CC 911313	**STERENN** **Compagnie Francaise Du Thon Oceanique** - *Concarneau* *France* MMSI: 226180000 Official number: 911313	**1,606** 481 1,180	Class: BV	**2000-12 Chantiers Piriou — Concarneau** Yd No: 216 Loa 67.30 Br ex - Dght 6.100 Lbp 61.90 Br md 12.40 Dpth 8.55 Welded, 1 dk	**(B11B2FV) Fishing Vessel**	**1 oil engine** reduction geared to sc. shaft driving 1 CP propeller Total Power: 3,000kW (4,079hp) 15.5kn Wartsila 8R32 1 x 4 Stroke 8 Cy. 320 x 350 3000kW (4079bhp) Wartsila Finland Oy-Finland AuxGen: 2 x 604kW 380/220V 50Hz a.c
9329136 *VJN4336* -	**STERLING** **PSA Marine Pte Ltd** PB Towage (Australia) Pty Ltd *Sydney, NSW* *Australia* MMSI: 503785000 Official number: 860824	**328** 98 -	Class: LR ✠ **100A1** SS 03/2010 tug ✠ **LMC** **UMS** Eq.Ltr: G; Cable: 304.0/20.5 U2 (a)	**2005-03 Hin Lee (Zhuhai) Shipyard Co Ltd — Zhuhai GD** (Hull) Yd No: 078 **2005-03 Cheoy Lee Shipyards Ltd — Hong Kong** Yd No: 4851 Loa 27.40 Br ex 11.52 Dght 5.200 Lbp 25.20 Br md 11.50 Dpth 5.00 Welded, 1 dk	**(B32A2ST) Tug**	**2 oil engines** gearing integral to driving 2 Z propellers Total Power: 3,730kW (5,072hp) 12.0kn Caterpillar 3516B 2 x Vee 4 Stroke 16 Cy. 170 x 215 each-1865kW (2536bhp) Caterpillar Inc-USA AuxGen: 2 x 84kW 415V 50Hz a.c
8657835 *ZIL6396* -	**STERLING** **Smiths Ferry Service Ltd (Tortola Fast Ferry)** - *Road Harbour* *British Virgin Islands* MMSI: 378111236 Official number: 734211	**142** 64 -		**1986 Camcraft, Inc. — Crown Point, La** Yd No: 186 Loa 29.20 Br ex - Dght - Lbp - Br md 6.55 Dpth 2.04 Welded, 1 dk	**(A37B2PS) Passenger Ship** Hull Material: Aluminium Alloy	**1 oil engine** driving 1 Propeller
9040924 *TC5776* -	**STERLING** *ex* Bunker VII *-2004* **Anadolu Uluslararasi Ticaret ve Tasimacilik AS (Anadolu International Trade & Shipping Co Ltd)** - *Istanbul* *Turkey* MMSI: 271010111 Official number: 6198	**287** 170 600		**1991-07 Ceksan Tersanesi — Turkey** Loa 47.75 Br ex - Dght 2.950 Lbp 44.00 Br md 7.70 Dpth 3.35 Welded, 1 dk	**(B35E2TF) Bunkering Tanker**	**1 oil engine** geared to sc. shaft driving 1 FP propeller Total Power: 405kW (551hp) Volvo Penta TAMD162A 1 x 4 Stroke 6 Cy. 144 x 165 405kW (551bhp) AB Volvo Penta-Sweden
9277058 - -	**STERLING ENERGY** *ex* Melisa D *-2013* *ex* Melisa-D *-2012* *ex* Aslan 6 *-2002* **Sterling Fuels (Hamilton) Ltd** - *Hamilton, ON* *Canada* MMSI: 316024041 Official number: 837033	**749** 332 1,231	Class: LR (BV) **100A1** SS 07/2012 Double Hull oil tanker ESP restricted service within the Great Lakes and River St. Lawrence **LMC**	**2002-05 Selahattin Aslan Tersanesi — Tuzla** Yd No: 6 Loa 64.08 Br ex - Dght 3.960 Lbp 58.15 Br md 10.00 Dpth 4.50 Welded	**(A12B2TR) Chemical/Products Tanker** Double Hull (13F) Liq: 1,240; Liq (Oil): 1,459 Part Cargo Heating Coils Compartments: 10 Wing Ta, 1 Slop Ta, ER 2 Cargo Pump (s): 2x215m³/hr	**1 oil engine** reduction geared to sc. shaft driving 1 FP propeller Total Power: 662kW (900hp) GUASCOR F360TA-SP 1 x Vee 4 Stroke 12 Cy. 152 x 165 662kW (900bhp) Gutierrez Ascunce Corp (GUASCOR)-Spain AuxGen: 2 x 160kW 380V 50Hz a.c
6703422 *ZR3481* DNA 47	**STERLING STAR** *ex* Ferina Star *-1993* *ex* Saksaberg *-1991* *ex* Vesturrodin *-1982* *ex* Neptun *-1977* *ex* Smaragd *-1971* **Owen Elroy Geland** - SatCom: Inmarsat C 460101488 *Cape Town* *South Africa* MMSI: 601608000 Official number: 79301	*192* 57 162	Class: (BV)	**1966 VEB Rosslauer Schiffswerft — Rosslau** Loa 29.79 Br ex 7.42 Dght 2.661 Lbp 28.00 Br md 7.40 Dpth 3.41 Welded, 1 dk	**(B11A2FT) Trawler** Ins: 176 Compartments: 2 Ho, ER 2 Ha: 2 (1.2 x 0.9)ER Derricks: 1x0.5t	**1 oil engine** driving 1 CP propeller Total Power: 441kW (600hp) 12.0kn Alpha 406-26VO 1 x 2 Stroke 6 Cy. 260 x 400 441kW (600bhp) (new engine 1970) Alpha Diesel A/S-Denmark Fuel: 26.5 (d.f.)
8522341 *YDA4548* -	**STERLINK RELIANCE** *ex* Abeer Two *-2005* **PT CFS Indonesia** - *Jakarta* *Indonesia* MMSI: 525012055	**126** 37 -	Class: AB KI	**1985-04 Aluminum Boats, Inc. — Marrero, La** Yd No: 298 Loa - Br ex - Dght - Lbp 28.96 Br md 7.01 Dpth 2.85 Welded, 1 dk	**(B21A2OC) Crew/Supply Vessel** Hull Material: Aluminium Alloy	**3 oil engines** reverse reduction geared to sc. shafts driving 3 FP propellers Total Power: 1,125kW (1,530hp) G.M. (Detroit Diesel) 12V-71 3 x Vee 2 Stroke 12 Cy. 108 x 127 each-375kW (510bhp) General Motors Detroit DieselAllison Divn-USA AuxGen: 2 x 40kW a.c
8035178 *UGWK* -	**STERLYAD** **JSC Yuzhmorrybflot** *Nakhodka* *Russia* MMSI: 273841220	**739** 221 332	Class: RS	**1982 Volgogradskiy Sudostroitelnyy Zavod — Volgograd** Yd No: 203 Loa 53.75 (BB) Br ex 10.72 Dght 4.290 Lbp 47.92 Br md 10.50 Dpth 6.00 Welded, 1 dk	**(B11A2FS) Stern Trawler** Ins: 218 Compartments: 1 Ho, ER 1 Ha: (1.6 x 1.6) Derricks: 2x1.5t Ice Capable	**1 oil engine** driving 1 FP propeller Total Power: 971kW (1,320hp) 12.8kn S.K.L. 8NVD48A-2U 1 x 4 Stroke 8 Cy. 320 x 480 971kW (1320bhp) VEB Schwermaschinenbau "KarlLiebknecht" (SKL)-Magdeburg Fuel: 182.0 (d.f.)

Identity	Name / Owner	Tonnage	Class	Built / Dimensions	Type	Machinery
9573244 *PPOR* -	**STERNA** **Wilson Sons Offshore SA** - *Rio de Janeiro* *Brazil* MMSI: 710008840	**4,106** 1,433 4,547	Class: LR ✠ **100A1** SS 03/2012 offshore supply ship *IWS EP ✠ **LMC** **UMS** Eq.Ltr: U; Cable: 495.0/44.0 U3 (a)	**2012**-03 **Wilson, Sons SA — Guaruja** (Hull) Yd No: 129 **2012**-03 **B.V. Scheepswerf Damen — Gorinchem** Yd No: 552016 Loa 87.40 (BB) Br ex 16.19 Dght 6.000 Lbp 81.57 Br md 16.00 Dpth 7.80 Welded, 1 dk	**(B21A2OS) Platform Supply Ship**	**4 diesel electric oil engines** driving 4 gen. each 1600kW 690V a.c Connecting to 2 elec. motors each (2500kW) driving 2 Directional propellers Total Power: 6,520kW (8,864hp) 12.2kn Caterpillar 3512B-TA 4 x Vee 4 Stroke 12 Cy. 170 x 190 each-1630kW (2216bhp) Caterpillar Inc-USA Thrusters: 2 Thwart. FP thruster (f)
7824431 *FGE9973* -	**STERNE** **Compagnie Du Golfe SAS** - *Vannes* *France* MMSI: 227697060 Official number: 911768	*380* - 100		**1980**-06 **Chantiers et Ateliers de La Perriere — Lorient** Yd No: 317 Converted From: Research Vessel-2007 Loa 49.03 Br ex 7.50 Dght 4.701 Lbp 45.01 Br md - Dpth - Welded, 1 dk	**(A37B2PS) Passenger Ship** Passengers: 156	**2 oil engines** geared to sc. shafts driving 2 FP propellers Total Power: 3,090kW (4,202hp) 17.0kn AGO 195V12CSHR 2 x Vee 4 Stroke 12 Cy. 195 x 180 each-1545kW (2101bhp) Societe Alsacienne de ConstructionsMecaniques (SACM)-France
5340871 *Y4EO* SAS 320	**STERNHAI** **Gert und Sebastian Erler** - *Sassnitz* *Germany* MMSI: 211307720 Official number: 1882	**121** 36 -	Class: (DS)	**1958**-01 **VEB Elbewerft — Boizenburg** Loa 26.45 Br ex 6.71 Dght 3.550 Lbp 23.40 Br md - Dpth 3.66 Welded, 1 dk	**(B11B2FV) Fishing Vessel** Compartments: 1 Ho, ER 1 Ha: ER Ice Capable	**1 oil engine** driving 1 FP propeller Total Power: 221kW (300hp) 9.0kn Halberstadt 6NVD36 1 x 4 Stroke 6 Cy. 240 x 360 221kW (300bhp) VEB Maschinenbau Halberstadt-Halberstadt AuxGen: 2 x 29kW 110V d.c
7035420 *SLCU* -	**STERNO** *ex* Seto *-1984* *ex* Ostestrom *-1983* *ex* Mariona *-1972* *launched as* Ostestrom *-1970* **Fiducia Rederi AB** Rederi AB Uman *Kalmar* *Sweden* MMSI: 265276000	**1,300** 395 1,350	Class: GL	**1970**-07 **N.V. Scheepswerf "Appingedam" v/h A. Apol C.V. — Appingedam** (Aft section) Yd No: 209 **1970**-07 **Gebr. Niestern N.V. Scheepswerven en Mfbk — Delfzijl** (Fwd & cargo sections) Yd No: 275 Converted From: General Cargo Ship-1984 Loa 75.69 Br ex 11.08 Dght 3.563 Lbp 70.06 Br md 11.00 Dpth 6.02 Welded, 2 dks	**(A23A2BD) Bulk Carrier, Self-discharging** Grain: 2,885; Bale: 2,620 Compartments: 1 Ho, ER 1 Ha: (43.7 x 8.0)ER Ice Capable	**1 oil engine** driving 1 FP propeller Total Power: 971kW (1,320hp) 12.0kn Deutz RBV8M545 1 x 4 Stroke 8 Cy. 320 x 450 971kW (1320bhp) Kloeckner Humboldt Deutz AG-West Germany AuxGen: 2 x 60kW 220/380V 50Hz a.c, 1 x 30kW 220/380V 50Hz a.c
9581411 *9V8484* -	**STET POLARIS** **Eng Hup Shipping Pte Ltd** - *Singapore* *Singapore* MMSI: 563015950 Official number: 395853	**166** 50 27	Class: BV	**2010**-06 **Sam Aluminium Engineering Pte Ltd — Singapore** Yd No: H95 Loa 25.00 Br ex - Dght 1.300 Lbp 24.00 Br md 6.60 Dpth 6.25 Welded, 1 dk	**(B34K2QT) Training Ship** Hull Material: Aluminium Alloy	**2 oil engines** reduction geared to sc. shafts driving 2 FP propellers Total Power: 2,088kW (2,838hp) 23.0kn Caterpillar C32 2 x Vee 4 Stroke 12 Cy. 145 x 162 each-1044kW (1419bhp) Caterpillar Inc-USA AuxGen: 2 x 50kW 50Hz a.c
7633662 *LFLR*	**STETIND** *ex* Vardenes *-1988* **Torghatten Nord AS** - *Narvik* *Norway* MMSI: 257215500	**2,018** 958 840	Class: (NV)	**1977**-06 **Batservice Verft AS — Mandal** Yd No: 646 Lengthened-1984 Loa 80.02 Br ex - Dght 3.309 Lbp - Br md 11.51 Dpth 4.53 Welded, 2 dks	**(A36A2PR) Passenger/Ro-Ro Ship (Vehicles)** Passengers: 399 Cars: 67	**2 oil engines** with hydraulic couplings & sr geared to sc. shafts driving 2 FP propellers Total Power: 2,022kW (2,750hp) Normo LDM-8 2 x 4 Stroke 8 Cy. 250 x 300 each-1011kW (1375bhp) AS Bergens Mek Verksteder-Norway Thrusters: 1 Thwart. FP thruster (f)
7307031 *WDC2014* -	**STEVE C.** *ex* Mary Lucille J *-1977* *ex* Mi Judy *-1975* *ex* Miss K *-1975* **Dennis J Rankin** - *Warrenton, OR* *United States of America* MMSI: 366986470 Official number: 511697	*134* 91 -		**1967 Bishop Shipbuilding Corp. — Aransas Pass, Tx** L reg 22.35 Br ex - Dght - Lbp - Br md 6.75 Dpth 3.69 Welded, 1 dk	**(B11B2FV) Fishing Vessel**	**1 oil engine** driving 1 FP propeller Total Power: 357kW (485hp)
7340370 *PC9093* -	**STEVE IRWIN** *ex* Robert Hunter *-2007* *ex* Westra *-2006* **Sea Shepherd UK** Sea Shepherd Conservation Society *Rotterdam* *Netherlands* MMSI: 244943000 Official number: 50466	**1,017** 305 517	Class: (LR) ✠ Classed LR until 25/7/07	**1975**-02 **Hall, Russell & Co. Ltd. — Aberdeen** Yd No: 962 Loa 59.52 Br ex 11.08 Dght 4.388 Lbp 52.00 Br md 10.98 Dpth 6.81 Welded, 2 dks	**(B12D2FP) Fishery Patrol Vessel**	**2 oil engines** sr geared to sc. shaft driving 1 CP propeller Total Power: 3,090kW (4,202hp) 12.0kn Polar SF112VS-F 2 x Vee 4 Stroke 12 Cy. 250 x 300 each-1545kW (2101bhp) British Polar Engines Ltd.-Glasgow AuxGen: 3 x 200kW 415V 50Hz a.c Thrusters: 1 Thwart. FP thruster (f)
8211708 - -	**STEVE N** **Government of The Republic of Guyana (Transport & Harbours Department)** - *Georgetown* *Guyana* Official number: 0000014	*1,500* 660 2,160		**1983**-12 **Guyana National Eng. Corp. Ltd. — Georgetown, Demerara** Yd No: 122 Loa 55.53 Br ex 11.51 Dght 4.201 Lbp 51.52 Br md 11.02 Dpth 5.52 Welded, 1 dk	**(B33B2DS) Suction Hopper Dredger** Hopper: 800 Compartments: 1 Ho, ER	**2 oil engines** with clutches, flexible couplings & sr reverse geared to sc. shafts driving 2 FP propellers Total Power: 764kW (1,038hp) Caterpillar 3412PCTA 2 x Vee 4 Stroke 12 Cy. 137 x 152 each-382kW (519bhp) Caterpillar Tractor Co-USA Thrusters: 2 Water jet (f)
8992613 *WDC2820* -	**STEVE RICHOUX** *ex* Warrior Star *-2005* *ex* Christopher D *-2005* **Marquette Transportation Co Gulf-Inland LLC** - *New Orleans, LA* *United States of America* MMSI: 366998110 Official number: 568988	*262* 178 -		**1975**-01 **in the United States of America** Yd No: 01 L reg 25.91 Br ex - Dght - Lbp - Br md 9.14 Dpth 3.05 Welded, 1 dk	**(B32A2ST) Tug**	**1 oil engine** driving 1 Propeller
8875592 *DUA2942* -	**STEVEN** *ex* Joonsul T-2 *-2005* *ex* Hanyang T-2 *-2005* **Asian Shipping Corp** - *Manila* *Philippines* Official number: 00-0001160	*142* 92 -	Class: (KR)	**1972 Sasebo Heavy Industries Co. Ltd. — Sasebo** Loa 27.00 Br ex - Dght 3.300 Lbp 24.00 Br md 6.50 Dpth - Welded, 1 dk	**(B32A2ST) Tug**	**1 oil engine** driving 1 FP propeller Total Power: 736kW (1,001hp) 11.0kn Niigata 6L28X 1 x 4 Stroke 6 Cy. 280 x 440 736kW (1001bhp) Niigata Engineering Co Ltd-Japan AuxGen: 2 x 24kW 225V a.c
5135472 *IOLM* -	**STEVEN** *ex* Grecia *-1992* **COMARIT SpA Costruzioni Marittime Italiane** - *Naples* *Italy* Official number: 1604	*125* 28 -	Class: (RI)	**1958**-12 **Cant. Nav. Solimano — Savona** Yd No: 25 Loa 24.01 Br ex 6.63 Dght 3.499 Lbp 21.01 Br md 6.61 Dpth 3.81 Riveted\Welded, 1 dk	**(B32A2ST) Tug**	**1 oil engine** driving 1 FP propeller Total Power: 590kW (802hp) Deutz RBV6M545 1 x 4 Stroke 6 Cy. 320 x 450 590kW (802bhp) Kloeckner Humboldt Deutz AG-West Germany AuxGen: 2 x 14kW 110V d.c
9450791 *V7SN5* -	**STEVEN C** **One Navigation Co LLC** Apex Bulk Carriers LLC SatCom: Inmarsat C 453834632 *Majuro* *Marshall Islands* MMSI: 538003686 Official number: 3686	**23,456** 11,522 34,340	Class: NK (AB)	**2009**-11 **SPP Shipbuilding Co Ltd — Tongyeong** Yd No: H4003 Loa 180.00 (BB) Br ex - Dght 9.900 Lbp 172.00 Br md 30.00 Dpth 14.70 Welded, 1 dk	**(A21A2BC) Bulk Carrier** Single Hull Grain: 48,765; Bale: 46,815 Compartments: 5 Ho, ER 5 Ha: ER Cranes: 4x35t	**1 oil engine** driving 1 FP propeller Total Power: 7,900kW (10,741hp) 14.0kn MAN-B&W 5S50MC-C 1 x 2 Stroke 5 Cy. 500 x 2000 7900kW (10741bhp) Doosan Engine Co Ltd-South Korea AuxGen: 3 x 750kW a.c Fuel: 1570.0
7336965 *WYZ8558* -	**STEVEN KIM** *ex* Tien Thanh II *-1992* *ex* John Kemp *-1992* **Binh Tran** - *Houston, TX* *United States of America* Official number: 544448	*112* 76 -		**1972 A.W. Covacevich Shipyard, Inc. — Biloxi, Ms** Yd No: 20 L reg 21.25 Br ex 6.10 Dght - Lbp - Br md - Dpth 3.51 Welded	**(B11B2FV) Fishing Vessel**	**1 oil engine** driving 1 FP propeller Total Power: 268kW (364hp)
8940517 - -	**STEVEN MAI II** *ex* Capt. M. K. *-2005* *ex* Linc Mai *-1999* **Trach Xuan Mai** - *Port Arthur, TX* *United States of America* Official number: 1039707	**172** 51 -		**1996 Rodriguez Boat Builders, Inc. — Coden, Al** Yd No: 142 L reg 26.00 Br ex - Dght - Lbp - Br md 7.92 Dpth 3.72 Welded, 1 dk	**(B11B2FV) Fishing Vessel**	**1 oil engine** driving 1 FP propeller

Identity / Owner	Tonnage	Class	Build / Dimensions	Type / Capacity	Machinery
8741777 **STEVEN MCALLISTER** *WDD9664* *ex Okmulgee (YTB-765) -2007* - **Fifth Third Equipment Finance Co** McAllister Towing & Transportation Co Inc (MT & T) *New Orleans, LA* *United States of America* Official number: 1194780	247 74 66		**1963-07 Southern SB. Corp. — Slidell, La** Yd No: 44 Loa 33.22 Br ex - Dght 4.110 Lbp 31.08 Br md 8.83 Dpth 4.96 Welded, 1 dk	**(B32A2ST) Tug**	**2 oil engines** reduction geared to sc. shafts driving 2 Z propellers Total Power: 3,282kW (4,462hp) Caterpillar 3516B-TA 2 x Vee 4 Stroke 16 Cy. 170 x 190 each-1641kW (2231bhp) (new engine 2007) Caterpillar Inc-USA
9377406 **STEVEN N** *A8TC8* - **General Ore Carrier Corp XXI Ltd** Neu Seeschiffahrt GmbH SatCom: Inmarsat C 463706856 *Monrovia* *Liberia* MMSI: 636014328 Official number: 14328	151,448 53,841 297,462	Class: NV	**2010-02 Universal Shipbuilding Corp — Tsu ME** Yd No: 089 Loa 327.00 (BB) Br ex 55.05 Dght 21.400 Lbp 318.00 Br md 55.00 Dpth 29.25 Welded, 1 dk	**(A21B2BO) Ore Carrier** Grain: 180,474 Compartments: 6 Ho, ER 6 Ha: ER	**1 oil engine** driving 1 FP propeller Total Power: 23,280kW (31,651hp) 14.5kn MAN-B&W 6S80MC-C 1 x 2 Stroke 6 Cy. 800 x 3200 23280kW (31651bhp) Hitachi Zosen Corp-Japan AuxGen: 3 x 745kW a.c Fuel: 7444.0 (r.f.)
7233773 **STEVIA** *ZR2998* CTA 66 **Irvin & Johnson Ltd** SatCom: Inmarsat C 460101023 *Cape Town* *South Africa* MMSI: 601221000 Official number: 350693	*801* 270 563	Class: (LR) (BV) ✠ Classed LR until 2/74	**1973-02 Hall, Russell & Co. Ltd. — Aberdeen** Yd No: 959 Loa 60.97 Br ex 11.76 Dght 4.096 Lbp 52.58 Br md 11.74 Dpth 7.40 Welded, 2 dks	**(B11A2FS) Stern Trawler**	**1 oil engine** sr geared to sc. shaft driving 1 CP propeller Total Power: 1,324kW (1,800hp) 13.0kn Ruston 8ATCM 1 x 4 Stroke 8 Cy. 318 x 368 1324kW (1800bhp) Ruston Paxman Diesels Ltd.-United Kingdom AuxGen: 3 x 245kW 380V 50Hz a.c
7533367 **STEVNS** *OXUH2* *ex Goliath Fur -2001* *ex Mimer -1996* - *ex Weswear -1994* *ex Brage -1989* **Stevns Charter & Towage A/S** Nordane Shipping A/S *Svendborg* *Denmark (DIS)* MMSI: 219937000 Official number: D3593	163 48 -	Class: BV	**1975-11 Scheepswerf Haak B.V. — Zaandam** Yd No: 926 Loa 27.49 Br ex 7.52 Dght 3.100 Lbp 25.48 Br md 7.51 Dpth 3.51 Welded, 1 dk	**(B32A2ST) Tug** Ice Capable	**1 oil engine** reduction geared to sc. shaft driving 1 CP propeller Total Power: 1,067kW (1,451hp) Alpha 10V23L-VO 1 x Vee 4 Stroke 10 Cy. 225 x 300 1067kW (1451bhp) Alpha Diesel A/S-Denmark AuxGen: 2 x 104kW 380V a.c Fuel: 69.0
7418335 **STEVNS GUARD** *OWLE2* *ex Grane -2002* *ex Grane III -1992* - *ex Brage -1991* **Stevns Shipping A/S** Nordane Shipping A/S *Copenhagen* *Denmark (DIS)* MMSI: 219000599	*124* - -	Class: LR ✠ **100A1** SS 06/2009 tug Gavle Harbour service Ice Class 1 ✠ **LMC** Eq.Ltr: C; Cable: U2	**1977-03 AB Asi-Verken — Amal** Yd No: 117 Loa 24.39 Br ex 8.18 Dght 4.101 Lbp 21.32 Br md 7.75 Dpth 4.30 Welded, 1 dk	**(B32A2ST) Tug** Ice Capable	**1 oil engine** with hydraulic couplings & sr geared to sc. shaft driving 1 CP propeller Total Power: 1,368kW (1,860hp) 13.0kn Alpha 12V23L-VO 1 x Vee 4 Stroke 12 Cy. 225 x 300 1368kW (1860bhp) Alpha Diesel A/S-Denmark AuxGen: 2 x 88kW 390V 50Hz a.c
7116858 **STEVNS MASTER** *OZTP2* *ex Lankenau -1998* - **Stevns Charter & Towage A/S** Nordane Shipping A/S *Svendborg* *Denmark (DIS)* MMSI: 219942000 Official number: D3797	*282* 84 138	Class: GL	**1971 N.V. Scheepswerven v/h H.H. Bodewes — Millingen a/d Rijn** Yd No: 692 Loa 31.09 Br ex 8.79 Dght 3.871 Lbp 28.71 Br md - Dpth 4.81 Welded, 1 dk	**(B32A2ST) Tug** Ice Capable	**1 oil engine** geared to sc. shaft driving 1 FP propeller Total Power: 1,471kW (2,000hp) Deutz SBV6M358 1 x 4 Stroke 6 Cy. 400 x 580 1471kW (2000bhp) Kloeckner Humboldt Deutz AG-West Germany AuxGen: 1 x 112kW 380V 50Hz a.c, 1 x 61kW 380V 50Hz a.c Thrusters: 1 Thwart. FP thruster (f)
7105495 **STEWART J. CORT** *WDC6055* - **Massmutual Asset Finance LLC** The Interlake Steamship Co *Wilmington, DE* *United States of America* MMSI: 367050550 Official number: 532272	*32,930* 29,918 60,079	Class: AB	**1971-11 Ingalls SB. Div. of Litton Systems Inc. — Pascagoula, Ms** (Fwd & aft sections) Yd No: 1173 **1971-11 Erie Marine, Inc. — Erie, Pa** (Cargo section) Yd No: 101 Loa 304.81 Br ex 32.01 Dght 8.516 Lbp 301.30 Br md 31.88 Dpth 14.94 Welded, 1 dk	**(A23A2BK) Bulk Carrier, Self-discharging, Laker** Grain: 64,500 Compartments: 4 Ho, ER 18 Ha: 18 (3.5 x 6.5)ER	**4 oil engines** geared to sc. shafts driving 2 CP propellers Total Power: 10,592kW (14,400hp) 16.0kn EMD (Electro-Motive) 20-645-E7 4 x Vee 2 Stroke 20 Cy. 230 x 254 each-2648kW (3600bhp) General Motors Corp-USA AuxGen: 4 x 1250kW 450V 60Hz a.c, 1 x 850kW 450V 60Hz a.c Thrusters: 1 Thwart. FP thruster (f); 1 Tunnel thruster (a) Fuel: 415.5
9266504 **STG 168** *YDA4416* *ex Sms Pusaka -2007* - **PT Wintermar Offshore Marine** *Jakarta* *Indonesia* Official number: 2009 PST NO. 5405/L	131 40 103	Class: NK	**2002-04 Lingco Marine Sdn Bhd — Sibu** Yd No: 2901 Loa 23.50 Br ex - Dght 2.712 Lbp 21.76 Br md 7.32 Dpth 3.20 Welded, 1 dk	**(B32B2SP) Pusher Tug**	**2 oil engines** reduction geared to sc. shafts driving 2 FP propellers Total Power: 1,204kW (1,636hp) Mitsubishi S6R2-MPTK 2 x 4 Stroke 6 Cy. 170 x 220 each-602kW (818bhp) Mitsubishi Heavy Industries Ltd-Japan AuxGen: 1 x 15kW a.c Fuel: 90.0 (d.f.)
8652794 **STH 02** - - **Glory Ocean Lines PT** *Batam* *Indonesia*	201 60 -	Class: KI	**2010-09 C.V. Mercusuar Mandiri — Batam** Loa 29.00 Br ex - Dght - Lbp 27.02 Br md 8.00 Dpth 3.70 Welded, 1 dk	**(B32A2ST) Tug**	**2 oil engines** reduction geared to sc. shafts driving 2 Propellers AuxGen: 2 x 44kW 415V a.c
8002781 **STHENO** *SWBA* *ex Mariella -2007* *ex Claudia M -1999* - *ex Claudia I -1997* *ex Claudia Smits -1988* **Stheno Shipping Co** *Piraeus* *Greece* MMSI: 240617000 Official number: 11580	3,720 2,161 6,238	Class: RI (LR) ✠ Classed LR until 10/12/99	**1981-04 Scheepswerf en Machinefabriek de Groot & van Vliet B.V. — Bolnes** Yd No: 404 Converted From: General Cargo Ship-2010 Loa 84.21 (BB) Br ex 17.10 Dght 8.383 Lbp 74.81 Br md 17.00 Dpth 10.15 Welded, 2 dks	**(A23A2BD) Bulk Carrier, Self-discharging** Grain: 6,934; Bale: 6,726 Compartments: 1 Ho, ER 1 Ha: (45.5 x 12.8)ER	**1 oil engine** with flexible couplings & sr gearedto sc. shaft driving 1 FP propeller Total Power: 2,501kW (3,400hp) 11.0kn Werkspoor 6TM410 1 x 4 Stroke 6 Cy. 410 x 470 2501kW (3400bhp) Stork Werkspoor Diesel BV-Netherlands AuxGen: 1 x 240kW 380V 50Hz a.c, 2 x 224kW 380V 50Hz a.c, 1 x 148kW 380V 50Hz a.c Fuel: 71.5 (d.f.) 481.0 (r.f.) 12.5pd
9629926 **STI AMBER** *V7X09* - **STI Amber Shipping Co Ltd** Scorpio Commercial Management SAM *Majuro* *Marshall Islands* MMSI: 538004532 Official number: 4532	29,708 14,103 49,990 T/cm 52.4	Class: AB	**2012-07 Hyundai Mipo Dockyard Co Ltd — Ulsan** Yd No: 2332 Loa 183.31 Br ex 32.23 Dght 13.005 Lbp 174.29 Br md 32.20 Dpth 19.10 Welded, 1 dk	**(A12B2TR) Chemical/Products Tanker** Double Hull (13F) Liq: 53,032; Liq (Oil): 53,032 Compartments: 6 Wing Ta, 6 Wing Ta, 1 Wing Slop Ta, 1 Slop Ta, 1 Wing Slop Ta, ER 12 Cargo Pump (s): 12x600m³/hr Manifold: Bow/CM: 91.7m	**1 oil engine** driving 1 FP propeller Total Power: 8,890kW (12,087hp) 14.5kn MAN-B&W 6S50ME-B9 1 x 2 Stroke 6 Cy. 500 x 2214 8890kW (12087bhp) Hyundai Heavy Industries Co Ltd-South Korea AuxGen: 3 x 800kW a.c Thrusters: 1 Tunnel thruster (f) Fuel: 190.0 (d.f.) 1450.0 (r.f.)
9658379 **STI BERYL** *V7YN4* - **STI Beryl Shipping Co Ltd** Scorpio Commercial Management SAM *Majuro* *Marshall Islands* MMSI: 538004693 Official number: 4693	29,708 14,103 49,990 T/cm 52.0	Class: AB	**2013-04 Hyundai Mipo Dockyard Co Ltd — Ulsan** Yd No: 2369 Loa 183.31 (BB) Br ex 32.24 Dght 11.000 Lbp 174.29 Br md 32.20 Dpth 19.10 Welded, 1 dk	**(A12B2TR) Chemical/Products Tanker** Double Hull (13F) Liq: 53,030; Liq (Oil): 53,030 Compartments: 6 Wing Ta, 6 Wing Ta, 1 Wing Slop Ta, 1 Slop Ta, 1 Wing Slop Ta, ER 12 Cargo Pump (s): 12x600m³/hr Manifold: Bow/CM: 92.3m	**1 oil engine** driving 1 FP propeller Total Power: 8,200kW (11,149hp) 14.5kn MAN-B&W 6S50ME-B9 1 x 2 Stroke 6 Cy. 500 x 2214 8200kW (11149bhp) Hyundai Heavy Industries Co Ltd-South Korea AuxGen: 3 x 800kW a.c Fuel: 195.0 (d.f.) 1457.0 (r.f.)
9669938 **STI DUCHESSA** *V7CA3* - **STI Duchessa Shipping Co Ltd** Scorpio Commercial Management SAM *Majuro* *Marshall Islands* MMSI: 538005225 Official number: 5225	29,785 13,224 51,840 T/cm 52.0	Class: AB	**2014-01 Hyundai Mipo Dockyard Co Ltd — Ulsan** Yd No: 2389 Loa 183.12 (BB) Br ex 32.24 Dght 13.300 Lbp 174.00 Br md 32.20 Dpth 19.40 Welded, 1 dk	**(A12B2TR) Chemical/Products Tanker** Double Hull (13F) Liq: 53,030; Liq (Oil): 53,030 Compartments: 6 Wing Ta, 6 Wing Ta, 1 Wing Slop Ta, 1 Slop Ta, 1 Wing Slop Ta, ER 12 Cargo Pump (s): 12x600m³/hr Manifold: Bow/CM: 92.3m	**1 oil engine** driving 1 FP propeller 14.5kn MAN-B&W 6G50ME-B9 1 x 2 Stroke Hyundai Heavy Industries Co Ltd-South Korea Fuel: 195.0 (d.f.) 1457.0 (r.f.)
9655913 **STI EMERALD** *V7YN5* *ex Hyundai Mipo 2362 -2013* - **STI Emerald Shipping Co Ltd** Scorpio Commercial Management SAM *Majuro* *Marshall Islands* MMSI: 538004694 Official number: 4694	29,708 14,103 49,990 T/cm 52.0	Class: AB	**2013-03 Hyundai Mipo Dockyard Co Ltd — Ulsan** Yd No: 2362 Loa 183.31 (BB) Br ex 32.24 Dght 13.300 Lbp 174.30 Br md 32.20 Dpth 19.10 Welded, 1 dk	**(A12B2TR) Chemical/Products Tanker** Double Hull (13F) Liq: 53,030; Liq (Oil): 53,030 Compartments: 6 Wing Ta, 6 Wing Ta, 1 Wing Slop Ta, 1 Slop Ta, 1 Wing Slop Ta, ER 12 Cargo Pump (s): 12x600m³/hr Manifold: Bow/CM: 92.3m	**1 oil engine** driving 1 FP propeller Total Power: 8,200kW (11,149hp) 14.5kn MAN-B&W 6S50ME-B9 1 x 2 Stroke 6 Cy. 500 x 2214 8200kW (11149bhp) Hyundai Heavy Industries Co Ltd-South Korea AuxGen: 3 x 800kW a.c Fuel: 195.0 (d.f.) 1457.0 (r.f.)

IMO / Call sign	Ship / Owner / Manager / Port / Flag	Tonnage	Class	Build / Dimensions	Type / Cargo	Machinery
9645786 *V7BD2* -	**STI FONTVIEILLE** **STI Fontvieille Shipping Co Ltd** Scorpio Commercial Management SAM *Majuro* *Marshall Islands* MMSI: 538005118 Official number: 5118	**29,715** 13,483 49,990	Class: AB	**2013**-07 **Hyundai Mipo Dockyard Co Ltd — Ulsan** Yd No: 2349 Loa 183.31 (BB) Br ex - Dght 12.900 Lbp 174.00 Br md 32.20 Dpth 19.10 Welded, 1 dk	**(A12B2TR) Chemical/Products Tanker** Double Hull (13F) Liq: 54,099; Liq (Oil): 54,100 Compartments: 6 Wing Ta, 6 Wing Ta, 1 Wing Slop Ta, 1 Wing Slop Ta, ER	**1 oil engine** driving 1 FP propeller Total Power: 8,890kW (12,087hp) 15.2kn MAN-B&W 6S50ME-B9 1 x 2 Stroke 6 Cy. 500 x 2214 8890kW (12087bhp) Hyundai Heavy Industries Co Ltd-South Korea AuxGen: 3 x 900kW a.c Fuel: 294.0 (d.f.) 1440.0 (r.f.)
9629952 *V7XP2* -	**STI GARNET** **STI Garnet Shipping Co Ltd** Scorpio Commercial Management SAM *Majuro* *Marshall Islands* MMSI: 538004533 Official number: 4533	**29,708** 14,103 49,990 T/cm 52.0	Class: AB	**2012**-09 **Hyundai Mipo Dockyard Co Ltd — Ulsan** Yd No: 2335 Loa 183.31 (BB) Br ex 32.24 Dght 13.300 Lbp 174.29 Br md 32.20 Dpth 19.10 Welded, 1 dk	**(A12B2TR) Chemical/Products Tanker** Double Hull (13F) Liq: 53,033; Liq (Oil): 53,033 Compartments: 6 Wing Ta, 6 Wing Ta, 1 Wing Slop Ta, 1 Slop Ta, 1 Wing Slop Ta, ER 12 Cargo Pump (s): 12x600m³/hr Manifold: Bow/CM: 92.3m	**1 oil engine** driving 1 FP propeller Total Power: 8,890kW (12,087hp) 14.5kn MAN-B&W 6S50ME-B9 1 x 2 Stroke 6 Cy. 500 x 2214 8890kW (12087bhp) Hyundai Heavy Industries Co Ltd-South Korea AuxGen: 3 x 800kW a.c Fuel: 195.0 (d.f.) 1457.8 (r.f.)
9334557 *V7VU4* -	**STI HARMONY** *ex* Sanko Harmony *-2010* **STI Harmony Shipping Co Ltd** Scorpio Commercial Management SAM *Majuro* *Marshall Islands* MMSI: 538004214 Official number: 4214	**40,865** 22,274 73,919 T/cm 67.0	Class: AB	**2007**-10 **Onomichi Dockyard Co Ltd — Onomichi HS** Yd No: 526 Loa 228.50 (BB) Br ex 32.23 Dght 14.365 Lbp 218.00 Br md 32.20 Dpth 20.65 Welded, 1 dk	**(A13B2TP) Products Tanker** Double Hull (13F) Liq: 82,135; Liq (Oil): 82,135 Cargo Heating Coils Compartments: 12 Wing Ta, ER, 2 Wing Slop Ta 3 Cargo Pump (s): 3x2000m³/hr Manifold: Bow/CM: 115.5m Ice Capable	**1 oil engine** driving 1 FP propeller Total Power: 13,560kW (18,436hp) 15.6kn MAN-B&W 6S60MC-C 1 x 2 Stroke 6 Cy. 600 x 2400 13560kW (18436bhp) Mitsui Engineering & Shipbuilding CLtd-Japan Fuel: 159.9 (d.f.) 2569.9 (r.f.)
9334569 *V7VU5* -	**STI HERITAGE** *ex* Sanko Heritage *-2010* **STI Heritage Shipping Co Ltd** Scorpio Commercial Management SAM *Majuro* *Marshall Islands* MMSI: 538004215 Official number: 4215	**40,865** 22,274 73,956 T/cm 67.0	Class: AB	**2008**-01 **Onomichi Dockyard Co Ltd — Onomichi HS** Yd No: 527 Loa 228.50 (BB) Br ex 32.23 Dght 14.365 Lbp 218.00 Br md 32.20 Dpth 20.65 Welded, 1 dk	**(A13B2TP) Products Tanker** Double Hull (13F) Liq: 82,135; Liq (Oil): 84,746 Cargo Heating Coils Compartments: 12 Wing Ta, 2 Wing Slop Ta, ER 3 Cargo Pump (s): 3x2000m³/hr Manifold: Bow/CM: 115.5m Ice Capable	**1 oil engine** driving 1 FP propeller Total Power: 13,560kW (18,436hp) 15.6kn MAN-B&W 6S60MC-C 1 x 2 Stroke 6 Cy. 600 x 2400 13560kW (18436bhp) Mitsui Engineering & Shipbuilding CLtd-Japan AuxGen: 3 x 680kW a.c Fuel: 159.9 (d.f.) 2569.9 (r.f.)
9334789 *V7UG4* -	**STI HIGHLANDER** *ex* Panna *-2010* *ex* Jag Panna *-2009* **STI Highlander Shipping Co Ltd** Scorpio Commercial Management SAM *Majuro* *Marshall Islands* MMSI: 538003945 Official number: 3945	**23,304** 10,232 37,145 T/cm 46.1	Class: NV (IR)	**2007**-01 **Hyundai Mipo Dockyard Co Ltd — Ulsan** Yd No: 0471 Loa 182.55 Br ex 27.39 Dght 11.217 Lbp 175.00 Br md 27.34 Dpth 16.70 Welded, 1 dk	**(A12B2TR) Chemical/Products Tanker** Double Hull (13F) Liq: 41,123; Liq (Oil): 41,123 Cargo Heating Coils Compartments: 12 Wing Ta, 2 Wing Slop Ta, ER 12 Cargo Pump (s): 10x500m³/hr, 2x320m³/hr Manifold: Bow/CM: 92.6m Ice Capable	**1 oil engine** driving 1 FP propeller Total Power: 11,400kW (15,499hp) 14.5kn MAN-B&W 7S50MC-C 1 x 2 Stroke 7 Cy. 500 x 2000 11400kW (15499bhp) AO Bryanskiy MashinostroitelnyyZavod (BMZ)-Bryansk AuxGen: 3 x 970kW 440V 60Hz a.c Thrusters: 1 Tunnel thruster (f) Fuel: 176.0 (d.f.) 1229.0 (r.f.)
9131280 *V7XB5* -	**STI JUPITER** *ex* Greenville 16 *-2013* **STI Marshall Inc** Seahorse Heavy Transport Pte Ltd *Majuro* *Marshall Islands* MMSI: 538004440 Official number: 4440	**223** 66 167	Class: KR (Class contemplated) (AB)	**1995**-12 **ASL Shipyard Pte Ltd — Singapore** Yd No: 085 Loa 29.00 Br ex - Dght 3.719 Lbp 26.50 Br md 8.60 Dpth 4.11 Welded, 1 dk	**(B32A2ST) Tug**	**2 oil engines** driving 2 FP propellers Total Power: 1,766kW (2,402hp) 13.0kn Caterpillar 3516TA 2 x Vee 4 Stroke 16 Cy. 170 x 190 each-883kW (1201bhp) Caterpillar Inc-USA
9645774 *V7BD3* -	**STI LARVOTTO** **STI Larvotto Shipping Co Ltd** Scorpio Commercial Management SAM *Majuro* *Marshall Islands* MMSI: 538005119 Official number: 5119	**29,715** 13,483 49,990	Class: AB	**2013**-07 **Hyundai Mipo Dockyard Co Ltd — Ulsan** Yd No: 2348 Loa 183.31 (BB) Br ex - Dght 12.900 Lbp 174.00 Br md 32.26 Dpth 19.10 Welded, 1 dk	**(A12B2TR) Chemical/Products Tanker** Double Hull (13F) Liq: 54,099; Liq (Oil): 54,099 Compartments: 12 Wing Ta, 2 Wing Slop Ta, ER	**1 oil engine** driving 1 FP propeller Total Power: 9,480kW (12,889hp) 15.2kn MAN-B&W 6S50MC-C 1 x 2 Stroke 6 Cy. 500 x 2000 9480kW (12889bhp) Hyundai Heavy Industries Co Ltd-South Korea Fuel: 294.0 (d.f.) 1440.0 (r.f.)
9645762 *V7BC9* -	**STI LE ROCHER** **STI Le Rocher Shipping Co Ltd** Scorpio Commercial Management SAM *Majuro* *Marshall Islands* MMSI: 538005117 Official number: 5117	**29,715** 13,483 49,990	Class: AB	**2013**-06 **Hyundai Mipo Dockyard Co Ltd — Ulsan** Yd No: 2347 Loa 183.31 (BB) Br ex - Dght 12.900 Lbp 174.00 Br md 32.26 Dpth 19.10 Welded, 1 dk	**(A12B2TR) Chemical/Products Tanker** Double Hull (13F) Liq: 54,099; Liq (Oil): 54,099 Compartments: 6 Wing Ta, 6 Wing Ta, 2 Wing Slop Ta, ER	**1 oil engine** driving 1 FP propeller Total Power: 8,890kW (12,087hp) 15.2kn MAN-B&W 6S50ME-B9 1 x 2 Stroke 6 Cy. 500 x 2214 8890kW (12087bhp) Hyundai Heavy Industries Co Ltd-South Korea AuxGen: 3 x 900kW a.c Fuel: 294.0 (d.f.) 1440.0 (r.f.)
9575656 *HP2994* -	**STI MARS** *ex* Dragonet XV *-2011* **TK Global SA** Sea Horse Middle East Marine Services LLC *Panama* *Panama* Official number: 4253411	**281** 85 295	Class: KR (NK)	**2011**-01 **Kaibuok Shipyard (M) Sdn Bhd — Sibu** Yd No: 0713 Loa 30.20 Br ex - Dght 3.812 Lbp 28.45 Br md 9.00 Dpth 4.60 Welded, 1 dk	**(B32A2ST) Tug**	**2 oil engines** reduction geared to sc. shafts driving 2 Propellers Total Power: 1,780kW (2,420hp) Cummins KTA-38-M2 2 x Vee 4 Stroke 12 Cy. 159 x 159 each-890kW (1210bhp) Cummins Engine Co Ltd-United Kingdom Fuel: 245.0
9560596 *A6E2795* -	**STI NEPTUNE** *ex* TCL3203 *-2014* **Sea Horse Middle East Marine Services LLC** - *Abu Dhabi* *United Arab Emirates* MMSI: 470541000	**276** 82	Class: BV	**2010**-08 **Wuhu Dajiang Shipbuilding Co Ltd — Wuhu AH** Yd No: DJ2008112 Loa 32.00 Br ex 9.45 Dght 3.800 Lbp 29.50 Br md 9.20 Dpth 4.50 Welded, 1 dk	**(B32A2ST) Tug**	**2 oil engines** reduction geared to sc. shafts driving 2 FP propellers Total Power: 2,984kW (4,058hp) Cummins KTA-50-M2 2 x Vee 4 Stroke 16 Cy. 159 x 159 each-1492kW (2029bhp) Cummins Engine Co Ltd-United Kingdom AuxGen: 2 x 100kW a.c
9629964 *V7XP5* -	**STI ONYX** **STI Onyx Shipping Co Ltd** Scorpio Commercial Management SAM *Majuro* *Marshall Islands* MMSI: 538004536 Official number: 4536	**29,708** 14,103 51,840 T/cm 52.0	Class: AB	**2012**-09 **Hyundai Mipo Dockyard Co Ltd — Ulsan** Yd No: 2336 Loa 183.31 (BB) Br ex 32.24 Dght 13.300 Lbp 174.29 Br md 32.20 Dpth 19.10 Welded, 1 dk	**(A12B2TR) Chemical/Products Tanker** Double Hull (13F) Liq: 53,030; Liq (Oil): 53,030 Compartments: 6 Wing Ta, 6 Wing Ta, 1 Wing Slop Ta, 1 Slop Ta, 1 Wing Slop Ta, ER Manifold: Bow/CM: 92.3m	**1 oil engine** driving 1 FP propeller Total Power: 8,890kW (12,087hp) 14.5kn MAN-B&W 6S50ME-B9 1 x 2 Stroke 6 Cy. 500 x 2214 8890kW (12087bhp) Hyundai Heavy Industries Co Ltd-South Korea AuxGen: 3 x 800kW a.c Fuel: 195.0 (d.f.) 1457.0 (r.f.)
9669940 *V7CJ3* -	**STI OPERA** **STI Opera Shipping Co Ltd** Hellespont Ship Management GmbH & Co KG *Majuro* *Marshall Islands* MMSI: 538005269 Official number: 5269	**29,785** 13,224 51,840 T/cm 52.0	Class: AB	**2014**-01 **Hyundai Mipo Dockyard Co Ltd — Ulsan** Yd No: 2390 Loa 183.00 (BB) Br ex 32.24 Dght 13.300 Lbp 174.00 Br md 32.20 Dpth 19.40 Welded, 1 dk	**(A12B2TR) Chemical/Products Tanker** Double Hull (13F) Liq: 53,030; Liq (Oil): 53,030 Compartments: 6 Wing Ta, 6 Wing Ta, 1 Wing Slop Ta, 1 Slop Ta, 1 Wing Slop Ta, ER 12 Cargo Pump (s): 12x600m³/hr Manifold: Bow/CM: 92.3m	**1 oil engine** driving 1 FP propeller Total Power: 10,680kW (14,521hp) 14.5kn MAN-B&W 6S50ME-B9 1 x 2 Stroke 6 Cy. 500 x 2214 10680kW (14521bhp) Fuel: 195.0 (d.f.) 1457.0 (r.f.)
9629940 *V7XP4* -	**STI RUBY** **STI Ruby Shipping Co Ltd** Scorpio Commercial Management SAM SatCom: Inmarsat C 453836023 *Majuro* *Marshall Islands* MMSI: 538004535 Official number: 4535	**29,708** 14,103 49,990 T/cm 52.4	Class: AB	**2012**-09 **Hyundai Mipo Dockyard Co Ltd — Ulsan** Yd No: 2334 Loa 183.31 (BB) Br ex 32.23 Dght 13.005 Lbp 174.29 Br md 32.20 Dpth 19.10 Welded, 1 dk	**(A12B2TR) Chemical/Products Tanker** Double Hull (13F) Liq: 53,032; Liq (Oil): 53,032 Compartments: 12 Wing Ta, 1 Slop Ta, 2 Wing Slop Ta, ER 12 Cargo Pump (s): 12x600m³/hr Manifold: Bow/CM: 92.3m	**1 oil engine** driving 1 FP propeller Total Power: 8,890kW (12,087hp) 14.5kn MAN-B&W 6S50ME-B9 1 x 2 Stroke 6 Cy. 500 x 2214 8890kW (12087bhp) Hyundai Heavy Industries Co Ltd-South Korea AuxGen: 3 x 800kW a.c Fuel: 195.0 (d.f.) 1457.0 (r.f.)
9650573 *V7YN3* -	**STI SAPPHIRE** **STI Sapphire Shipping Co Ltd** Scorpio Commercial Management SAM *Majuro* *Marshall Islands* MMSI: 538004692 Official number: 4692	**29,708** 14,103 49,990 T/cm 52.0	Class: AB	**2013**-01 **Hyundai Mipo Dockyard Co Ltd — Ulsan** Yd No: 2361 Loa 183.31 (BB) Br ex 32.24 Dght 11.000 Lbp 174.29 Br md 32.20 Dpth 19.10 Welded, 1 dk	**(A12B2TR) Chemical/Products Tanker** Double Hull (13F) Liq: 53,030; Liq (Oil): 53,030 Compartments: 6 Wing Ta, 6 Wing Ta, 1 Wing Slop Ta, 1 Slop Ta, 1 Wing Slop Ta, ER 12 Cargo Pump (s): 12x600m³/hr Manifold: Bow/CM: 92.3m	**1 oil engine** driving 1 FP propeller Total Power: 8,890kW (12,087hp) 14.5kn MAN-B&W 6S50ME-B9 1 x 2 Stroke 6 Cy. 500 x 2214 8890kW (12087bhp) Hyundai Heavy Industries Co Ltd-South Korea AuxGen: 3 x 800kW a.c Fuel: 195.0 (d.f.) 1457.0 (r.f.)

IMO / Call sign	Name / Owner / Manager	Tonnage	Class	Build / Dimensions	Type / Cargo	Machinery
9501928 *A6E3023* -	**STI SATURN** *ex* Hako 16 *-2014* **Sea Horse Middle East Marine Services LLC** - *Abu Dhabi* *United Arab Emirates*	**261** 79 288	Class: GL	**2008-09 Eastern Marine Shipbuilding Sdn Bhd — Sibu** Yd No: 77 Loa 30.00 Br ex - Dght 3.500 Lbp 27.73 Br md 8.60 Dpth 4.12 Welded, 1 dk	**(B32A2ST) Tug**	**2 oil engines** reverse reduction geared to sc. shafts driving 2 FP propellers Total Power: 1,790kW (2,434hp) Cummins KTA-38-M2 2 x Vee 4 Stroke 12 Cy. 159 x 159 each-895kW (1217bhp) Cummins Engine Co Inc-USA AuxGen: 2 x 80kW 415V a.c
9409259 *V7VG7* -	**STI SPIRIT** *ex* Atlantic Spirit *-2010* **STI Spirit Shipping Co Ltd** Scorpio Commercial Management SAM SatCom: Inmarsat C 453835979 *Majuro* *Marshall Islands* MMSI: 538004118 Official number: 4118	**62,775** 34,934 113,091 T/cm 99.7	Class: AB	**2008-11 New Times Shipbuilding Co Ltd — Jingjiang JS** Yd No: 0311510 Loa 250.00 (BB) Br ex - Dght 14.820 Lbp 240.00 Br md 44.00 Dpth 21.00 Welded, 1 dk	**(A13A2TW) Crude/Oil Products Tanker** Double Hull (13F) Liq: 124,590; Liq (Oil): 127,453 Cargo Heating Coils Compartments: 12 Wing Ta, 2 Wing Slop Ta, ER 3 Cargo Pump (s): 3x3000m³/hr Manifold: Bow/CM: 122.5m	**1 oil engine** driving 1 FP propeller Total Power: 15,820kW (21,509hp) 15.0kn MAN-B&W 7S60MC-C 1 x 2 Stroke 7 Cy. 600 x 2400 15820kW (21509bhp) Hyundai Heavy Industries Co Ltd-South Korea AuxGen: 3 x 1125kW a.c Fuel: 230.0 (d.f.) 3000.0 (r.f.)
9335006 *HO7836* -	**STI T1** *ex* Wm Matahari Satu *-2010* **STI Maritime SA** Seahorse Heavy Transport Pte Ltd *Panama* *Panama* MMSI: 356385000 Official number: 4180110	**284** 86 182	Class: NK	**2004-12 Celtug Service Shipyard Sdn Bhd — Sibu** Yd No: 309 Loa 31.00 Br ex - Dght 3.212 Lbp 27.48 Br md 8.54 Dpth 4.00 Welded, 1 dk	**(B32A2ST) Tug**	**2 oil engines** reduction geared to sc. shafts driving 2 CP propellers Total Power: 1,516kW (2,062hp) 10.0kn Mitsubishi S6R2-MPTK2 2 x 4 Stroke 6 Cy. 170 x 220 each-758kW (1031bhp) Mitsubishi Heavy Industries Ltd-Japan AuxGen: 2 x a.c Fuel: 180.0 (d.f.)
9408059 *HO7982* -	**STI T2** *ex* Barlian 3 *-2006* **STI Panama SA** Seahorse Heavy Transport Pte Ltd *Panama* *Panama* MMSI: 356400000 Official number: 4184110	**266** 80 282	Class: NK	**2006-09 SL Shipbuilding Contractor Sdn Bhd — Sibu** Yd No: 14 Loa 30.00 Br ex - Dght 3.512 Lbp 28.08 Br md 8.60 Dpth 4.12 Welded, 1 dk	**(B32A2ST) Tug**	**2 oil engines** reduction geared to sc. shafts driving 2 FP propellers Total Power: 1,518kW (2,064hp) Mitsubishi S6R2-MPTK 2 x 4 Stroke 6 Cy. 170 x 220 each-759kW (1032bhp) Mitsubishi Heavy Industries Ltd-Japan AuxGen: 2 x 62kW a.c Fuel: 220.0 (d.f.)
9681106 *V7DP5* -	**STI TEXAS CITY** **STI Texas City Shipping Co Ltd** Scorpio Commercial Management SAM *Majuro* *Marshall Islands* MMSI: 538005412 Official number: 5412	**29,732** 13,785 50,300 T/cm 51.9	Class: AB	**2014-03 SPP Shipbuilding Co Ltd — Sacheon** Yd No: S5122 Loa 183.00 (BB) Br ex - Dght 13.000 Lbp 174.00 Br md 32.20 Dpth 19.10 Welded, 1 dk	**(A12B2TR) Chemical/Products Tanker** Double Hull (13F)	**1 oil engine** driving 1 FP propeller Total Power: 8,950kW (12,168hp) 14.9kn MAN-B&W 6S50MC-C8 1 x 2 Stroke 6 Cy. 500 x 2000 8950kW (12168bhp)
9629938 *V7XP3* -	**STI TOPAZ** **STI Topaz Shipping Co Ltd** Scorpio Commercial Management SAM SatCom: Inmarsat C 453836022 *Majuro* *Marshall Islands* MMSI: 538004534 Official number: 4534	**29,708** 14,103 51,840 T/cm 52.4	Class: AB	**2012-08 Hyundai Mipo Dockyard Co Ltd — Ulsan** Yd No: 2333 Loa 183.31 (BB) Br ex 32.23 Dght 13.300 Lbp 174.29 Br md 32.20 Dpth 19.10 Welded, 1 dk	**(A12B2TR) Chemical/Products Tanker** Double Hull (13F) Liq: 53,033; Liq (Oil): 53,033 Compartments: 6 Wing Ta, 6 Wing Ta, 1 Wing Slop Ta, 1 Slop Ta, 1 Wing Slop Ta, ER 12 Cargo Pump (s): 12x600m³/hr Manifold: Bow/CM: 92.3m	**1 oil engine** driving 1 FP propeller Total Power: 8,890kW (12,087hp) 14.5kn MAN-B&W 6S50ME-B9 1 x 2 Stroke 6 Cy. 500 x 2214 8890kW (12087bhp) Hyundai Heavy Industries Co Ltd-South Korea AuxGen: 3 x 800kW a.c Fuel: 190.0 (d.f.) 1450.0 (r.f.)
9434852 *3FSW2* -	**STI VENUS** *ex* Hako 22 *-2011* *ex* Fordeco 81 *-2009* **Goodarab Marine Services SA** Seahorse Heavy Transport Pte Ltd *Panama* *Panama* Official number: 4241111	**256** 77 320	Class: KR (GL)	**2008-02 Sapangar Shipyard Sdn Bhd — Lahad Datu** Yd No: 115 Loa 30.00 Br ex - Dght - Lbp 27.73 Br md 8.60 Dpth 4.12 Welded, 1 dk	**(B32A2ST) Tug**	**2 oil engines** reduction geared to sc. shafts driving 2 FP propellers Total Power: 1,790kW (2,434hp) Cummins KTA-38-M2 2 x Vee 4 Stroke 12 Cy. 159 x 159 each-895kW (1217bhp) Cummins Engine Co Inc-USA
9645798 *V7BD4* -	**STI VILLE** **STI Ville Shipping Co Ltd** Scorpio Commercial Management SAM *Majuro* *Marshall Islands* MMSI: 538005120 Official number: 5120	**29,715** 13,483 49,990	Class: AB	**2013-09 Hyundai Mipo Dockyard Co Ltd — Ulsan** Yd No: 2350 Loa 183.30 (BB) Br ex - Dght 13.300 Lbp 174.00 Br md 32.26 Dpth 19.10 Welded, 1 dk	**(A12B2TR) Chemical/Products Tanker** Double Hull (13F) Liq: 54,000; Liq (Oil): 54,000 Compartments: 6 Wing Ta, 6 Wing Ta, 1 Wing Slop Ta, 1 Wing Slop Ta, ER	**1 oil engine** driving 1 FP propeller Total Power: 8,890kW (12,087hp) 15.2kn MAN-B&W 6S50ME-B9 1 x 2 Stroke 6 Cy. 500 x 2214 8890kW (12087bhp) Hyundai Heavy Industries Co Ltd-South Korea Fuel: 294.0 (d.f.) 1440.0 (r.f.)
9677038 *LEHO* T-L 0	**STIAN-ANDRE** **Partrederiet Stian Andre Ans** - *Tromso* *Norway* MMSI: 257549800	**104** 41 -		**2013-11 Skogsoy Bat AS — Mandal** Yd No: 87 Loa 18.00 (BB) Br ex 6.60 Dght - Lbp 17.27 Br md 6.40 Dpth 3.25 Welded, 1 dk	**(B11B2FV) Fishing Vessel**	**1 oil engine** driving 1 Propeller
8912209 *DEIV* -	**STIER** **Bugsier-, Reederei- und Bergungs-Gesellschaft mbH & Co KG** - *Bremen* *Germany* MMSI: 211290730 Official number: 4625	**219** 65 119	Class: GL	**1990-11 Detlef Hegemann Rolandwerft GmbH — Bremen** Yd No: 153 Loa 28.53 Br ex - Dght 2.803 Lbp 26.50 Br md 8.80 Dpth 3.50 Welded, 1 dk	**(B32A2ST) Tug** Ice Capable	**2 oil engines** gearing integral to driving 2 Voith-Schneider propellers Total Power: 1,840kW (2,502hp) Deutz SBV6M628 2 x 4 Stroke 6 Cy. 240 x 280 each-920kW (1251bhp) Motoren Werke Mannheim AG (MWM)-Mannheim AuxGen: 2 x 42kW 220/380V a.c
6710839 *LJEO* -	**STIG HALLE** *ex* Rodfjell *-2000* *ex* Arklow Day *-1980* *ex* Nordic Clover *-1978* *ex* Nordic Proctor *-1975* *ex* Knudsvig *-1970* **Fosenfrakt AS** - *Namsos* *Norway* MMSI: 258458000	**522** 223 800	Class: (BV)	**1967-04 Sonderborg Skibsvaerft A/S — Sonderborg** Yd No: 53 Loa 52.61 Br ex 9.83 Dght 3.401 Lbp 47.33 Br md 9.81 Dpth 3.79 Welded, 1 dk	**(A31A2GX) General Cargo Ship** Grain: 998; Bale: 840 Compartments: 1 Ho, ER 1 Ha: (22.6 x 5.1)ER Cranes: 1	**1 oil engine** driving 1 CP propeller Total Power: 507kW (689hp) 11.0kn Callesen 6-427-FOT 1 x 4 Stroke 6 Cy. 270 x 400 507kW (689bhp) Aabenraa Motorfabrik, HeinrichCallesen A/S-Denmark Fuel: 37.5 (d.f.) 2.0pd
9121766 *OW2222* -	**STIGABRUGV** *ex* Rostein *-2000* **Kryvjing P/F** Jon Purkhus *Klaksvik* *Faeroe Islands (Danish)*	**245** 90 330		**1995-04 Aas Mek. Verksted AS — Vestnes** Yd No: 137 Loa 26.70 Br ex - Dght - Lbp - Br md 8.00 Dpth 4.80 Welded, 1 dk	**(B12C2FL) Live Fish Carrier (Well Boat)**	**1 oil engine** geared to sc. shaft driving 1 FP propeller Total Power: 530kW (721hp) Caterpillar 3412TA 1 x Vee 4 Stroke 12 Cy. 137 x 152 530kW (721bhp) Caterpillar Inc-USA
8800810 *TFUN* VE 77	**STIGANDI** *ex* Dala Rafn *-2007* *ex* Haey *-2007* *ex* Emma *-2007* **Stigandi Ehf** - *Vestmannaeyjar* *Iceland* MMSI: 251013000 Official number: 1664	**237** 89 -		**1988 Tczewska Stocznia Rzeczna — Tczew** Yd No: PR/0327 Lengthened-1998 Loa 33.95 (BB) Br ex - Dght 3.782 Lbp - Br md 8.01 Dpth 5.24 Welded, 1 dk	**(B11B2FV) Fishing Vessel**	**1 oil engine** geared to sc. shaft driving 1 FP propeller Total Power: 578kW (786hp) 10.5kn Caterpillar 3508B-TA 1 x Vee 4 Stroke 8 Cy. 170 x 190 578kW (786bhp) (new engine 1998) Caterpillar Inc-USA
8911504 *V2OK2* -	**STIGFOSS** *ex* Ice Star *-2014* **Stor Line Ltd** The Iceland Steamship Co Ltd (Eimskip Island Ehf) (Eimskip Ehf) SatCom: Inmarsat C 430584410 *Saint John's* *Antigua & Barbuda* MMSI: 305844000 Official number: 8911504	**3,625** 1,952 3,543	Class: NV (LR) ✠ Classed LR until 7/2/14	**1990-07 Aarhus Flydedok A/S — Aarhus** Yd No: 196 Loa 92.90 (BB) Br ex 15.37 Dght 5.600 Lbp 84.37 Br md 15.10 Dpth 10.50 Welded, 2 dks, 3rd dk in holds 1 & 2	**(A34A2GR) Refrigerated Cargo Ship** Side doors (s) Ins: 5,130 TEU 42 C.Dk 34/20' (40') incl. 7 ref C. Compartments: 2 Ho, ER, 4 Tw Dk 2 Ha: 2 (6.2 x 7.5)ER Cranes: 2x4t Ice Capable	**1 oil engine** driving 1 CP propeller Total Power: 2,209kW (3,003hp) 13.0kn B&W 6S26MC 1 x 2 Stroke 6 Cy. 260 x 980 2209kW (3003bhp) MAN B&W Diesel A/S-Denmark AuxGen: 1 x 504kW 380V 50Hz a.c, 3 x 312kW 380V 50Hz a.c Boilers: HWH (o.f.) (New boiler: 1990) 12.2kgf/cm² (12.0bar) Thrusters: 1 Thwart. CP thruster (f)
9388431 *WDC8583* -	**STIKINE** **Inter-Island Ferry Authority** - *Hollis, AK* *United States of America* MMSI: 367089610 Official number: 1179851	**2,334** 918 -		**2006-04 Dakota Creek Industries Inc — Anacortes WA** Yd No: 48 Loa 60.35 (BB) Br ex 16.20 Dght 3.400 Lbp - Br md 15.54 Dpth - Welded, 1 dk	**(A36A2PR) Passenger/Ro-Ro Ship (Vehicles)** Passengers: 160 Cars: 33	**2 oil engines** reduction geared to sc. shafts driving 2 CP propellers Total Power: 2,206kW (3,000hp) 15.0kn Caterpillar 3512B 2 x Vee 4 Stroke 12 Cy. 170 x 190 each-1103kW (1500bhp) Caterpillar Inc-USA AuxGen: 2 x 330kW 60Hz a.c Thrusters: 1 Water jet (f)

5255040 *HQMZ8* -	**STILIS STAR** *ex* Eleftherios *-1994* *ex* E. Salpadimos *-1990* *ex* Andriana *-1987* *ex* Nikiti *-1984* *ex* Nordenfeld *-1972* **Norton Compania Naviera SA** - *San Lorenzo* *Honduras* Official number: L-0325117	**1,078** 323 877	Class: (HR) (BV) (GL)	**1957**-05 **Schiffswerft H. Rancke — Hamburg** Yd No: 180 Loa 59.06 Br ex 9.30 Dght 3.556 Lbp 52.00 Br md 9.25 Dpth 3.97 Riveted\Welded, 1 dk	**(A31A2GX) General Cargo Ship** Grain: 1,126; Bale: 1,071 Compartments: 2 Ho, ER 2 Ha: (17.9 x 5.4) (9.5 x 5.4)ER Derricks: 3x2t	**1 oil engine** driving 1 FP propeller Total Power: 368kW (500hp) 10.0kn Deutz RBV8M545 1 x 4 Stroke 8 Cy. 320 x 450 368kW (500bhp) Kloeckner Humboldt Deutz AG-West Germany AuxGen: 2 x 4kW 24V d.c, 1 x 2kW 24V d.c
8706674 *MSJP2* LR 111	**STILL OSTREA** *ex* Ostrea *-1992* **Morecombe Bay Dredgers Ltd** - *Lancaster* *United Kingdom* MMSI: 235001525 Official number: 712824	**122** 36 -		**1987**-09 **Amels Holland BV — Makkum** (Hull) Yd No: 418 **1987**-09 **B.V. Scheepswerf Maaskant — Bruinisse** Yd No: 459 Loa 28.02 Br ex - Dght - Lbp - Br md 8.01 Dpth 2.11 Welded, 1 dk	**(B11B2FV) Fishing Vessel**	**2 oil engines** with clutches & sr reverse geared to sc. shafts driving 2 FP propellers Total Power: 442kW (600hp) 11.0kn Cummins NT-855-M 2 x 4 Stroke 6 Cy. 140 x 152 each-221kW (300bhp) Cummins Engine Co Inc-USA Thrusters: 1 Thwart. FP thruster (f)
9207833 *YJUH8* -	**STIM STAR** - **Offshore Service Vessels LLC** Edison Chouest Offshore LLC *Port Vila* *Vanuatu* MMSI: 576945000 Official number: 1579	**2,674** 802 3,031	Class: AB	**1999**-02 **North American Shipbuilding LLC — Larose LA** Yd No: 181 Loa 73.15 Br ex - Dght 5.334 Lbp 67.51 Br md 17.07 Dpth 6.40 Welded, 1 dk	**(B22F20W) Well Stimulation Vessel**	**2 oil engines** gearing integral to driving 2 Z propellers Total Power: 2,516kW (3,420hp) 12.0kn Caterpillar 3516TA 2 x Vee 4 Stroke 16 Cy. 170 x 190 each-1258kW (1710bhp) Caterpillar Inc-USA AuxGen: 2 x 500kW a.c Thrusters: 1 Thwart. FP thruster (f); 1 Retract. directional thruster (f)
9303687 *V7RL5* -	**STIM STAR ANGOLA** *ex* Viking Nereus *-2009* **BFCA 2009-A Trust** SEACOR Worldwide Inc *Majuro* *Marshall Islands* MMSI: 538003534 Official number: 3534	**3,861** 1,158 1,798	Class: AB (NV)	**2004**-03 **UAB Vakaru Laivu Remontas (JSC Western Shiprepair) — Klaipeda** (Hull) Yd No: 15 **2004**-03 **West Contractors AS — Olensvaag** Yd No: 21 Converted From: Offshore Supply Ship-2009 Loa 73.40 (BB) Br ex - Dght 6.500 Lbp 64.00 Br md 16.60 Dpth 7.60 Welded, 1 dk	**(B22F20W) Well Stimulation Vessel**	**2 oil engines** geared to sc. shafts driving 2 CP propellers Total Power: 4,800kW (6,526hp) 12.0kn MaK 8M25 2 x 4 Stroke 8 Cy. 255 x 400 each-2400kW (3263bhp) Caterpillar Motoren GmbH & Co. KG-Germany AuxGen: 3 x 320kW 450/230V 60Hz a.c, 2 x 1440kW a.c Thrusters: 2 Tunnel thruster (f); 2 Tunnel thruster (a) Fuel: 970.0 (r.f.)
9559975 *V7BV7* -	**STIM STAR ARABIAN GULF** *ex* Mason Bee *-2012* **Wells Fargo Bank Northwest** Bee Mar LLC *Majuro* *Marshall Islands* MMSI: 538005207 Official number: 5207	**2,212** 692 3,135	Class: AB	**2011**-12 **Bollinger Machine Shop & Shipyard, Inc. — Lockport, La** Yd No: 570 Loa 71.32 Br ex - Dght 4.530 Lbp 68.88 Br md 17.07 Dpth 5.49 Welded, 1 dk	**(B21A20S) Platform Supply Ship**	**2 oil engines** reduction geared to sc. shafts driving 2 FP propellers Total Power: 2,982kW (4,054hp) 10.0kn Cummins QSK60-M 2 x Vee 4 Stroke 16 Cy. 159 x 190 each-1491kW (2027bhp) Cummins Engine Co Inc-USA AuxGen: 3 x 300kW 480V a.c Thrusters: 2 Tunnel thruster (f); 1 Tunnel thruster (a) Fuel: 630.0 (d.f.)
9485643 *PMAK* -	**STIM STAR BORNEO** - **PT Multi Agung Sarana Ananda** - *Balikpapan* *Indonesia* MMSI: 525015280	**2,079** 624 1,408	Class: BV KI	**2007**-11 **PT Karya Teknik Utama — Batam** Yd No: 166 Loa 68.38 Br ex - Dght 3.410 Lbp 58.22 Br md 20.12 Dpth 4.72 Welded, 1 dk	**(B22F20W) Well Stimulation Vessel** Passengers: 42	**3 oil engines** reduction geared to sc. shafts driving 3 Propellers Total Power: 3,090kW (4,200hp) Cummins KTA-38-M2 3 x Vee 4 Stroke 12 Cy. 159 x 159 each-1030kW (1400bhp) Cummins Engine Co Inc-USA AuxGen: 2 x 1200kW 400V a.c
9202003 *WCY2842* -	**STIM STAR II** *ex* C-Emperor *-2000* **Offshore Service Vessels LLC** Edison Chouest Offshore LLC *Galliano, LA* *United States of America* MMSI: 366747170 Official number: 1064441	**2,248** 745 2,883	Class: AB	**1998**-09 **North American Shipbuilding LLC — Larose LA** Yd No: 178 Loa 73.15 Br ex - Dght 5.336 Lbp 67.51 Br md 17.07 Dpth 6.40 Welded, 1 dk	**(B21B20A) Anchor Handling Tug Supply**	**2 oil engines** gearing integral to driving 2 Z propellers Total Power: 2,388kW (3,246hp) 11.0kn Caterpillar 3516TA 2 x Vee 4 Stroke 16 Cy. 170 x 190 each-1194kW (1623bhp) Caterpillar Inc-USA AuxGen: 2 x 500kW 480V 60Hz a.c Thrusters: 1 Thwart. CP thruster (f); 1 Retract. directional thruster (f) Fuel: 650.0 (d.f.) 31.5pd
9274991 *WDA7484* -	**STIM STAR III** - **Nautical Ventures LLC** Edison Chouest Offshore LLC *Galliano, LA* *United States of America* MMSI: 369050000 Official number: 1124235	**3,191** 957 2,717	Class: AB	**2002**-05 **North American Fabricators LLC — Houma LA** Yd No: 215 Loa 79.25 Br ex - Dght 5.720 Lbp 76.20 Br md 17.10 Dpth 6.40 Welded, 1 dk	**(B22F20W) Well Stimulation Vessel**	**2 oil engines** reduction geared to sc. shafts driving 2 FP propellers Total Power: 3,752kW (5,102hp) Caterpillar 3606TA 2 x 4 Stroke 6 Cy. 280 x 300 each-1876kW (2551bhp) Caterpillar Inc-USA AuxGen: 2 x 1500kW 60Hz a.c, 2 x 910kW 60Hz a.c Fuel: 850.0
7946382 - -	**STIMA** *ex* Hutson Tide *-2007* *ex* Sea Hawk *-1988* **Multiplan Nigeria Ltd** - *Nigeria* Official number: SR666	**169** 50 -	Class: AB	**1980**-01 **Swiftships Inc — Morgan City LA** Yd No: 82 Loa - Br ex - Dght 1.840 Lbp 38.10 Br md 7.09 Dpth 3.18 Welded, 1 dk	**(B35X2XX) Vessel (function unknown)** Hull Material: Aluminium Alloy	**4 oil engines** driving 2 FP propellers Total Power: 1,500kW (2,040hp) G.M. (Detroit Diesel) 12V-71-TI 4 x Vee 2 Stroke 12 Cy. 108 x 127 each-375kW (510bhp) (new engine 1986) General Motors Detroit DieselAllison Divn-USA
8846747 - -	**STIMFALIA** - **Government of The Republic of Greece (Hellenic Navy)** - *Greece*	*866* 506 457	Class: (HR)	**1991 Khalkis Shipyard S.A. — Khalkis** (Hull launched by) **1991 Hellenic Shipyards — Skaramanga** (Hull completed by) Loa 67.00 Br ex - Dght 4.200 Lbp 60.35 Br md 10.00 Dpth 4.65 Welded, 1 dk	**(A14A2LO) Water Tanker** Compartments: 4 Ta, ER	**1 oil engine** geared to sc. shaft driving 1 FP propeller Total Power: 1,184kW (1,610hp) 11.5kn MAN 12V20/27 1 x Vee 4 Stroke 12 Cy. 200 x 270 1184kW (1610bhp) MAN B&W Diesel AG-Augsburg AuxGen: 2 x 247kW 220/380V a.c
9040558 *WCY2270* -	**STIMSON** *ex* Pinnacle *-1988* **State of Alaska (Department of Public Safety Fish & Wildlife)** - *Dutch Harbor, AK* *United States of America* MMSI: 338282000 Official number: 978410	**716** 214 -		**1991**-10 **Homeport Marine Services — Moss Point, Ms** Yd No: 1119 Loa 46.55 Br ex 11.58 Dght 4.240 Lbp 41.37 Br md - Dpth 4.87 Welded, 1 dk	**(B11B2FV) Fishing Vessel** Ins: 473	**2 oil engines** reverse reduction geared to sc. shafts driving 2 FP propellers Total Power: 1,350kW (1,836hp) 9.5kn Caterpillar 3508TA 2 x Vee 4 Stroke 8 Cy. 170 x 190 each-675kW (918bhp) Caterpillar Inc-USA AuxGen: 3 x 250kW a.c Thrusters: 1 Thwart. FP thruster (f) Fuel: 23.2 (d.f.)
8221856 *8PTR* -	**STINA** *ex* Atlantic Start *-2003* *ex* Atlantic Star *-2001* **Stina Shipping Ltd** Holy House Shipping AB *Bridgetown* *Barbados* MMSI: 314236000 Official number: 733486	**10,535** 4,212 10,601	Class: AB (NK)	**1983**-12 **Sasebo Heavy Industries Co. Ltd. — Sasebo Yard, Sasebo** Yd No: 324 Loa 151.52 (BB) Br ex - Dght 8.821 Lbp 141.00 Br md 22.81 Dpth 13.10 Welded, 3 dks, 4th dk in Nos. 2 & 3 holds	**(A34A2GR) Refrigerated Cargo Ship** Side doors (p) Side doors (s) Ins: 13,199 TEU 84 incl 4 ref C Compartments: ER, 4 Ho 4 Ha: ER 4 (12.4 x 9.4) Cranes: 5x10t	**1 oil engine** driving 1 FP propeller Total Power: 10,591kW (14,400hp) 20.0kn Mitsubishi 8UEC60HA 1 x 2 Stroke 8 Cy. 600 x 1500 10591kW (14400bhp) Ube Industries Ltd-Japan AuxGen: 4 x 600kW 450V 60Hz a.c Fuel: 407.0 (d.f.) 1851.5 (r.f.) 45.0pd
1008968 *V7GB4* -	**STINA** *ex* Harmony *-2001* **Stina Shipping Co Ltd** Intersee Schiffahrtsgesellschaft mbH & Co KG *Bikini* *Marshall Islands* MMSI: 538080006 Official number: 80006	**234** 70 -	Class: HR	**2000**-06 **Olympic Marine — Lavrio** Yd No: 227 Loa 38.53 Br ex - Dght 6.170 Lbp 33.50 Br md 14.50 Dpth 7.20 Welded, 1 dk	**(X11A2YP) Yacht**	**2 oil engines** geared to sc. shafts driving 2 Propellers Total Power: 1,548kW (2,104hp) 14.0kn Caterpillar 3412 2 x Vee 4 Stroke 12 Cy. 137 x 152 each-774kW (1052bhp) Caterpillar Inc-USA
9246530 *V2BW7* -	**STINA** *ex* Rachel Borchard *-2013* *ex* Stina *-2009* *ex* Charlotte Borchard *-2006* *launched as* Stina *-2004* **Jan Breuer KG ms 'Stina'** Reederei Jan Breuer eK *Saint John's* *Antigua & Barbuda* MMSI: 304623000 Official number: 4147	**9,962** 8,565 11,376	Class: GL	**2004**-03 **Daewoo-Mangalia Heavy Industries S.A. — Mangalia** (Hull) Yd No: 4042 **2004**-03 **J.J. Sietas KG Schiffswerft GmbH & Co. — Hamburg** Yd No: 1140 Loa 134.44 (BB) Br ex - Dght 8.700 Lbp 124.41 Br md 22.50 Dpth 11.30 Welded, 1 dk	**(A33A2CC) Container Ship (Fully Cellular)** TEU 862 C.Ho 261 TEU C.Dk 601 TEU incl. 150 ref C. Compartments: 4 Cell Ho, ER	**1 oil engine** geared to sc. shaft driving 1 CP propeller Total Power: 8,400kW (11,421hp) 18.5kn MaK 9M43 1 x 4 Stroke 9 Cy. 430 x 610 8400kW (11421bhp) Caterpillar Motoren GmbH & Co. KG-Germany AuxGen: 2 x 530kW 400/220V 50Hz a.c, 1 x 1300kW a.c Thrusters: 1 Thwart. CP thruster (f); 1 Thwart. CP thruster (a) Fuel: 100.0 (d.f.) (Heating Coils) 850.0 (r.f.) 34.0pd

9374569 *9VLP5* -	**STINA KOSAN** **LKT Gas Carriers Pte Ltd** Lauritzen Kosan A/S *Singapore* *Singapore* MMSI: 565842000 Official number: 394074	9,175 2,753 10,348 T/cm 21.3	Class: BV (NV)	2008-04 **STX Shipbuilding Co Ltd — Busan** Yd No: 5022 Loa 120.41 (BB) Br ex 19.82 Dght 8.814 Lbp 112.30 Br md 19.80 Dpth 11.20 Welded, 1 dk	**(A11B2TG) LPG Tanker** Double Sides Partial Compartment Length Liq (Gas): 9,108 2 x Gas Tank (s); 2 independent (5% Ni.stl) cyl horizontal 2 Cargo Pump (s): 2x450m^3/hr Manifold: Bow/CM: 56.5m	**1 oil engine** driving 1 FP propeller Total Power: 4,678kW (6,360hp) 16.0kn MAN-B&W 7S35MC 1 x 2 Stroke 7 Cy. 350 x 1400 4678kW (6360bhp) STX Engine Co Ltd-South Korea AuxGen: 3 x a.c Fuel: 125.0 (d.f.) 920.0 (r.f.)
7629817 - -	**STINE A** *ex* Noordzee *-1998* *ex* Huragan *-1995* **Deepsea Oil & Gas Ltd** -	190 57 -	Class: (GL) (PR)	1975-08 **Stocznia 'Wisla' — Gdansk** Yd No: R27/02 Loa 30.10 Br ex 8.06 Dght 2.860 Lbp 28.33 Br md - Dpth 3.89 Welded, 1 dk	**(B32A2ST) Tug**	**2 oil engines** reduction geared to sc. shaft driving 1 CP propeller Total Power: 882kW (1,200hp) 12.0kn Sulzer 5AR25 2 x 4 Stroke 5 Cy. 250 x 300 each-441kW (600bhp) Zaklady Przemyslu Metalowego 'HCegielski' SA-Poznan AuxGen: 2 x 49kW 400V 50Hz a.c
7050523 - -	**STINGRAY** *ex* Alexia A. IV *-2003* *ex* Lady Marie *-1992* *ex* Carol Ann *-1990* *ex* Gulf Coast II *-1990* - -	*158* 86 -		1968-01 **Houma Welders Inc — Houma LA** Converted From: Fishing Vessel-1992 L reg 26.22 Br ex 7.07 Dght - Lbp - Br md - Dpth 3.41 Welded, 1 dk	**(A31A2GX) General Cargo Ship**	**1 oil engine** driving 1 FP propeller Total Power: 397kW (540hp)
9045003 - -	**STINGRAY** *ex* Zhen Feng *-2013* *ex* Zhen Feng 2 *-2008* *ex* Zheng Feng 2 *-1999* *ex* Zheng Huong No. 2 *-1996* - -	1,593 939 2,300		1992-03 **Jiangxi Jiangzhou Shipyard — Ruichang JX** Yd No: A415 Loa 83.10 Br ex - Dght 4.500 Lbp 76.30 Br md 12.80 Dpth 5.90 Welded, 1 dk	**(A31A2GX) General Cargo Ship** Grain: 3,392	**1 oil engine** driving 1 FP propeller Total Power: 662kW (900hp) Chinese Std. Type 6350 1 x 4 Stroke 6 Cy. 350 x 500 662kW (900bhp) Shanghai Diesel Engine Co Ltd-China
8853568 *4DEH-7* -	**STINGRAY** *ex* Kittaton (YTM-406) *-1987* *ex* Kittaton (YTB-406) *-1962* *ex* YT-406 *-1945* **Cabras Marine Corp** Malayan Towage & Salvage Corp (SALVTUG) *Manila* *Philippines* Official number: 00-0000173	179 54 -		1945-01 **Ira S. Bushey & Son, Inc. — New York, NY** Loa 30.48 Br ex - Dght 3.040 Lbp 28.65 Br md 7.59 Dpth 3.38 Welded, 1 dk	**(B32A2ST) Tug**	**1 oil engine** driving 1 FP propeller
6505337 - -	**STINNE PETER** *ex* Sisu *-1970* **Watson Marine** -	*297* 194 550	Class: (BV)	1965 **Orskovs Staalskibsvaerft A/S — Frederikshavn** Yd No: 31 Converted From: General Cargo Ship-1970 Loa 48.14 Br ex 8.67 Dght 3.099 Lbp 43.21 Br md 8.64 Dpth 3.48 Welded, 1 dk	**(B33A2DS) Suction Dredger** Hopper: 350 Compartments: 1 Ho, ER	**1 oil engine** driving 1 CP propeller Total Power: 313kW (426hp) 9.5kn Alpha 405-24VO 1 x 2 Stroke 5 Cy. 240 x 400 313kW (426bhp) Alpha Diesel A/S-Denmark AuxGen: 3 x 8kW 220V d.c Fuel: 32.5 (d.f.)
8884696 *DBGJ* -	**STINT** *ex* LCM 19 Stint *-1970* **Government of The Federal Republic of Germany (Land Schleswig-Holstein)** - *Luebeck* *Germany* MMSI: 211229450	100 30 52	Class: (GL)	1966 **Gutehoffnungshuette Sterkrade AG Rheinwerft Walsum — Duisburg** Yd No: 1027 Loa - Br ex - Dght 1.149 Lbp 22.90 Br md 6.40 Dpth 1.39 Welded, 1 dk	**(B34G2SE) Pollution Control Vessel**	**2 oil engines** reverse reduction geared to sc. shafts driving 2 FP propellers Total Power: 504kW (686hp) 10.0kn MWM TRHS518A 2 x 4 Stroke 8 Cy. 140 x 180 each-252kW (343bhp) MWM AG Lieferwerk MuenchenSueddeutsche Bremsen-Muenchen
9316581 *YJUL7* -	**STIPE TIDE** **Gulf Fleet Middle East Ltd** Tidewater Marine International Inc *Port Vila* *Vanuatu* MMSI: 576969000 Official number: 1602	1,720 516 1,516	Class: AB	2004-05 **Jiangsu Zhenjiang Shipyard Co Ltd — Zhenjiang JS** Yd No: 86-ZJS200201 Loa 64.00 Br ex - Dght 4.800 Lbp 56.90 Br md 14.95 Dpth 5.80 Welded, 1 dk	**(B21B20A) Anchor Handling Tug Supply**	**2 oil engines** reduction geared to sc. shafts driving 2 CP propellers Total Power: 4,920kW (6,690hp) 12.5kn Wartsila 6R32LNE 2 x 4 Stroke 6 Cy. 320 x 350 each-2460kW (3345bhp) Wartsila Finland Oy-Finland AuxGen: 2 x 300kW a.c, 2 x 1040kW a.c Thrusters: 1 Tunnel thruster (f) Fuel: 620.0 (d.f.)
9611606 *SVA3472* -	**STIRA DIAMOND** **Diamond Lines Maritime Co** *Piraeus* *Greece* MMSI: 239588800 Official number: 11835	803 209 628		2010-04 **Savvas Shipyard S.A. — Eleusis** Yd No: P110 Loa 72.50 Br ex - Dght 2.800 Lbp 65.00 Br md 16.50 Dpth 3.90 Welded, 1 dk	**(A36A2PR) Passenger/Ro-Ro Ship (Vehicles)** Passengers: unberthed: 600 Lane-clr ht: 4.80 Cars: 139	**2 oil engines** reduction geared to sc. shaft driving 2 Propellers Total Power: 2,310kW (3,140hp) 15.0kn GUASCOR SF480 2 x Vee 4 Stroke 16 Cy. 152 x 165 each-1155kW (1570bhp) Gutierrez Ascunce Corp (GUASCOR)-Spain AuxGen: 2 x 125kW a.c, 1 x 60kW a.c Thrusters: 1 Tunnel thruster (f)
6827981 *VHW2579* -	**STIRLING SKATE** *ex* Kuranda *-1970* **Svitzer Offshore Pty Ltd** *Fremantle, WA* *Australia* Official number: 332712	*103* 40 146		1968-07 **Stannard Bros Slipway & Engineering Pty Ltd — Sydney NSW** Yd No: 1260 L reg 21.24 Br ex 6.20 Dght 3.000 Lbp - Br md 6.00 Dpth 3.50 Welded, 1 dk	**(B32A2ST) Tug**	**2 oil engines** reduction geared to sc. shafts driving 2 Propellers Total Power: 544kW (740hp) G.M. (Detroit Diesel) 2 x each-272kW (370bhp) Detroit Diesel Corporation-Detroit, Mi
8020226 - -	**STIRRUP CAY** *ex* Masuei Maru No. 22 *-1999* **Freepoint Tug & Towing Services** Svitzer (Caribbean) Ltd	248 74 -		1980-11 **Kanagawa Zosen — Kobe** Yd No: 211 Loa - Br ex - Dght 3.260 Lbp 26.01 Br md 8.81 Dpth 3.71 Welded, 1 dk	**(B32A2ST) Tug**	**2 oil engines** driving 2 FP propellers Total Power: 1,912kW (2,600hp) Niigata 6L25BX 2 x 4 Stroke 6 Cy. 250 x 320 each-956kW (1300bhp) Niigata Engineering Co Ltd-Japan
8037011 *WDD9698* -	**STIRS ONE** *ex* Sand Mari J *-1999* **Stirs One Inc** *Point Lookout, NY* *United States of America* MMSI: 367315050 Official number: 615326	138 111 -		1979 **St Augustine Trawlers, Inc. — Saint Augustine, Fl** Yd No: S-42 L reg 19.76 Br ex 6.71 Dght - Lbp - Br md - Dpth 3.13 Welded, 1 dk	**(B11B2FV) Fishing Vessel**	**1 oil engine** driving 1 FP propeller Total Power: 382kW (519hp) Caterpillar 3412PCTA 1 x Vee 4 Stroke 12 Cy. 137 x 152 382kW (519bhp) Caterpillar Tractor Co-USA
7311264 - -	**STIVIDOR** **Sea Commercial Port of Odessa (Odesskiy Morskiy Port)** - *Odessa* *Ukraine* MMSI: 272018500 Official number: 723098	269 80 84	Class: (RS)	1973 **Brodogradiliste 'Tito' Beograd - Brod 'Tito' — Belgrade** Yd No: 894 Loa 35.44 Br ex 9.30 Dght 3.150 Lbp 30.00 Br md 9.00 Dpth 4.50 Welded, 1 dk	**(B32A2ST) Tug** Ice Capable	**2 oil engines** driving 2 FP propellers Total Power: 1,692kW (2,300hp) B&W 7-26MTBF-40 2 x 4 Stroke 7 Cy. 260 x 400 each-846kW (1150bhp) Titovi Zavodi 'Litostroj'-Yugoslavia
6725004 *SIDC* VG 95	**STJARNVIK** *ex* Kenya *-1985* *ex* Ekefjord *-1979* *ex* Jonna Kongerslev *-1977* *ex* Ekefjord *-1973* **Mats Bertil Ingvar Johansson** *Traslovslage* *Sweden* MMSI: 265759000	307 92 -	Class: (NV)	1967 **AB Nya Marstrandsverken — Marstrand** Yd No: 9 Loa 31.42 Br ex 6.84 Dght 2.642 Lbp 28.10 Br md 6.71 Dpth 3.61 Welded, 1 dk	**(B11B2FV) Fishing Vessel** Compartments: 1 Ho, ER 4 Ha: (0.9 x 0.6) (0.9 x 1.3) (1.5 x 1.5) (1.5 x 1.2)ER Derricks: 1x2t; Winches: 1 Ice Capable	**1 oil engine** driving 1 FP propeller Total Power: 736kW (1,001hp) Deutz RBV6M545 1 x 4 Stroke 6 Cy. 320 x 450 736kW (1001bhp) Kloeckner Humboldt Deutz AG-West Germany AuxGen: 1 x 16kW 110V d.c, 1 x 7kW 110V d.c
8508369 *9V8703* -	**STJERNEBORG** *ex* Medcoa Lome *-2011* *ex* Frederiksborg *-2009* *ex* Global Africa *-2007* **Medusa (Singapore) Pte Ltd** Thome Ship Management (Thailand) Co Ltd SatCom: Inmarsat Mini-M 765054317 *Singapore* *Singapore* MMSI: 563572000 Official number: 396126	20,370 16,789 14,163	Class: RI (BV)	1994-04 **Cia Comercio e Navegacao (CCN) — Niteroi (Estaleiro Maua)** Yd No: 190 Lengthened-2012 Loa 174.30 (BB) Br ex 25.83 Dght 7.210 Lbp 159.56 Br md 25.80 Dpth 8.71 Welded, 2 dks	**(A35A2RR) Ro-Ro Cargo Ship** Stern door/ramp (centre) Len: 16.00 Wid: 8.00 Swl: - Quarter stern door/ramp (s) Len: 16.00 Wid: 7.00 Swl: 120 Lane-Len: 2882 Lane-clr ht: 7.00 Cars: 372 TEU 891 Cranes: 2x36t Ice Capable	**1 oil engine** driving 1 CP propeller Total Power: 6,540kW (8,892hp) 13.0kn Sulzer 6RTA48 1 x 2 Stroke 6 Cy. 480 x 1400 6540kW (8892bhp) Ishikawajima do Brasil Estaleiros S (ISHIBRAS)-Brazil AuxGen: 3 x 850kW 450/220V 60Hz a.c, 1 x 993kW 450/220V 60Hz a.c Thrusters: 1 Thwart. CP thruster (f) Fuel: 322.0 (d.f.) 1899.0 (r.f.)
9034755 *SCEO* -	**STJERNEBORG** **Ventrafiken AB** *Landskrona* *Sweden* MMSI: 265527020	424 139 100		1990-12 **Moen Slip og Mekanisk Verksted AS — Kolvereid** Yd No: 36 Loa 34.34 Br ex 10.02 Dght 3.800 Lbp - Br md 10.00 Dpth 3.90 Welded, 1 dk	**(A36A2PR) Passenger/Ro-Ro Ship (Vehicles)** Passengers: unberthed: 300 Bow door/ramp Stern door/ramp Lane-Wid: 1.85 Cars: 12	**4 oil engines** with clutches & reduction geared to sc. shafts driving 2 Directional propellers Total Power: 1,080kW (1,468hp) 12.0kn Scania DSI1151A 4 x 4 Stroke 6 Cy. 127 x 145 each-270kW (367bhp) Saab Scania AB-Sweden Thrusters: 1 Thwart. CP thruster (f)

IMO / Call sign	Name / Owner	Tonnage	Class	Build / Dimensions	Type	Machinery
9517197 *LCJH* -	**STJERNOY** **Boreal Transport Nord AS** *Hammerfest* *Norway* MMSI: 257217000	**195** 78 20		**2009-06 Oma Baatbyggeri AS — Stord** Yd No: 528 Loa 24.46 (BB) Br ex - Dght 1.400 Lbp 23.95 Br md 9.00 Dpth 3.33 Welded, 1 dk	**(A37B2PS) Passenger Ship** Hull Material: Aluminium Alloy Passengers: unberthed: 126	**2 oil engines** reduction geared to sc. shafts driving 2 Water jets Total Power: 1,800kW (2,448hp) 30.0kn M.T.U. 10V2000M72 2 x Vee 4 Stroke 10 Cy. 135 x 156 each-900kW (1224bhp) MTU Friedrichshafen GmbH-Friedrichshafen
9295799 *XPVT* FD 1195	**STJORNAN** **P/F Klaksvikar Trolarafelag** P/F J F K Trol *Leirvik* *Faeroe Islands (Danish)* MMSI: 231327000	**592** 178 -	Class: NV	**2004-11 'Crist' Sp z oo — Gdansk** (Hull) Yd No: B36/1 **2004-11 Osey hf — Hafnarfjordur** Yd No: B13 Loa 36.50 Br ex 8.59 Dght 4.100 Lbp 32.00 Br md 8.50 Dpth 4.40 Welded, 1 dk	**(B11A2FS) Stern Trawler**	**1 oil engine** reduction geared to sc. shaft driving 1 CP propeller Total Power: 670kW (911hp) Mitsubishi S6U-MPTK 1 x 4 Stroke 6 Cy. 240 x 260 670kW (911bhp) Mitsubishi Heavy Industries Ltd-Japan AuxGen: 2 x a.c Thrusters: 1 Tunnel thruster (f)
8326046 *UFRQ* -	**STK-1002** **JSC Volga Shipping (OAO Sudokhodnaya Kompaniya 'Volzhskoye Parokhodstvo')** - SatCom: Inmarsat C 427301588 *St Petersburg* *Russia* MMSI: 273344010	**1,408** 422 1,669	Class: RR	**1983-08 VEB Elbewerften Boizenburg/Rosslau — Rosslau** Yd No: 304/3451 Loa 82.02 Br ex 11.92 Dght 2.750 Lbp 78.01 Br md 11.61 Dpth 4.02 Welded, 1 dk	**(A31A2GX) General Cargo Ship** Grain: 1,940 TEU 60 C. 60/20' incl. 10 ref C. Compartments: 2 Ho, ER 2 Ha: 2 (20.0 x 9.4)ER	**2 oil engines** driving 2 FP propellers Total Power: 882kW (1,200hp) 11.2kn S.K.L. 8NVDS36/24A-1 2 x 4 Stroke 8 Cy. 240 x 360 each-441kW (600bhp) VEB Schwermaschinenbau "KarlLiebknecht" (SKL)-Magdeburg AuxGen: 2 x 100kW Fuel: 87.0 (r.f.)
8326058 *UBEL* -	**STK-1003** **JS North-Western Shipping Co (OAO 'Severo-Zapadnoye Parokhodstvo')** - SatCom: Inmarsat C 427301376 *St Petersburg* *Russia* MMSI: 273458720	**1,367** 422 1,669	Class: RR	**1983-12 VEB Elbewerften Boizenburg/Rosslau — Rosslau** Yd No: 305/3452 Loa 82.02 Br ex - Dght 2.501 Lbp 78.01 Br md 11.61 Dpth 4.02 Welded, 1 dk	**(A31A2GX) General Cargo Ship** Grain: 1,940 TEU 60 C. 60/20' incl. 10 ref C. Compartments: 2 Ho, ER 2 Ha: 2 (20.0 x 9.4)ER	**2 oil engines** driving 2 FP propellers Total Power: 882kW (1,200hp) 11.2kn S.K.L. 8NVDS36/24A-1 2 x 4 Stroke 8 Cy. 240 x 360 each-441kW (600bhp) VEB Schwermaschinenbau "KarlLiebknecht" (SKL)-Magdeburg AuxGen: 2 x 100kW Fuel: 88.0 (d.f.)
8326060 *UBEM* -	**STK-1004** **North-Western Fleet (A/O 'Severo-Zapadnyy Flot')** Volga-Neva Ltd *St Petersburg* *Russia* MMSI: 273439130 Official number: 824750	**1,573** 585 1,669	Class: (RS)	**1984-07 VEB Elbewerften Boizenburg/Rosslau — Rosslau** Yd No: 306/3453 Loa 82.00 Br ex 11.94 Dght 2.750 Lbp 78.00 Br md 11.60 Dpth 4.00 Welded, 1 dk	**(A31A2GX) General Cargo Ship** Grain: 1,940 TEU 70 C. 70/20' incl. 10 ref C. Compartments: 2 Ho, ER 2 Ha: 2 (17.8 x 9.2)ER	**2 oil engines** driving 2 FP propellers Total Power: 882kW (1,200hp) 11.2kn S.K.L. 8NVDS36/24A-1 2 x 4 Stroke 8 Cy. 240 x 360 each-441kW (600bhp) VEB Schwermaschinenbau "KarlLiebknecht" (SKL)-Magdeburg
8422620 *UCYS* -	**STK-1005** **JSC Northern River Shipping Lines** - *Arkhangelsk* *Russia* MMSI: 273363200 Official number: 835539	**1,573** 585 1,663	Class: RS	**1984-02 VEB Elbewerften Boizenburg/Rosslau — Rosslau** Yd No: 307/3454 Loa 82.02 Br ex 11.92 Dght 2.760 Lbp 78.01 Br md 11.61 Dpth 4.02 Welded	**(A31A2GX) General Cargo Ship** Grain: 1,940 TEU 70 C. 70/20' incl. 10 ref C. Compartments: 2 Ho, ER 2 Ha: 2 (17.8 x 9.2)ER	**2 oil engines** driving 2 FP propellers Total Power: 882kW (1,200hp) 11.5kn S.K.L. 8NVDS36/24A-1 2 x 4 Stroke 8 Cy. 240 x 360 each-441kW (600bhp) VEB Schwermaschinenbau "KarlLiebknecht" (SKL)-Magdeburg AuxGen: 2 x 100kW a.c, 1 x 50kW a.c Fuel: 88.0 (r.f.)
8422644 *UFRL* -	**STK-1007** **Saimaa Trade Wind Ltd** - *St Petersburg* *Russia* MMSI: 273331600 Official number: 835261	**1,572** 585 2,162	Class: RS	**1984-06 VEB Elbewerften Boizenburg/Rosslau — Rosslau** Yd No: 309/3456 Loa 82.02 Br ex 11.94 Dght 3.900 Lbp 78.01 Br md 11.61 Dpth 4.02 Welded, 1 dk	**(A31A2GX) General Cargo Ship** Compartments: 2 Ho, ER 2 Ha: ER	**2 oil engines** driving 2 FP propellers Total Power: 882kW (1,200hp) 11.0kn S.K.L. 8NVDS36/24A-1 2 x 4 Stroke 8 Cy. 240 x 360 each-441kW (600bhp) VEB Schwermaschinenbau "KarlLiebknecht" (SKL)-Magdeburg Fuel: 89.0 (r.f.)
8422656 *UFRZ* -	**STK-1008** **Saimaa Trade Wind Ltd** - SatCom: Inmarsat C 427330367 *St Petersburg* *Russia* MMSI: 273330600 Official number: 835257	**1,572** 585 1,347	Class: RS	**1984-08 VEB Elbewerften Boizenburg/Rosslau — Rosslau** Yd No: 310/3457 Loa 82.02 Br ex - Dght 2.910 Lbp 78.01 Br md 11.61 Dpth 4.02 Welded, 1 dk	**(A31A2GX) General Cargo Ship** Grain: 1,940 Compartments: 2 Ho, ER 2 Ha: 2 (17.8 x 9.2)ER	**2 oil engines** driving 2 FP propellers Total Power: 882kW (1,200hp) 11.0kn S.K.L. 8NVDS36/24A-1 2 x 4 Stroke 8 Cy. 240 x 360 each-441kW (600bhp) VEB Schwermaschinenbau "KarlLiebknecht" (SKL)-Magdeburg Fuel: 89.0 (r.f.)
8422668 *UFSC* -	**STK-1009** **JS North-Western Shipping Co (OAO 'Severo-Zapadnoye Parokhodstvo')** Volga-Neva Ltd SatCom: Inmarsat C 427301377 *St Petersburg* *Russia* MMSI: 273311310	**1,408** 422 1,669	Class: RR	**1984-09 VEB Elbewerften Boizenburg/Rosslau — Rosslau** Yd No: 311/3458 Loa 82.02 Br ex - Dght 2.750 Lbp 78.01 Br md 11.61 Dpth 4.02 Welded, 1 dk	**(A31A2GX) General Cargo Ship** Grain: 1,940 Compartments: 2 Ho, ER 2 Ha: 2 (17.8 x 9.2)ER	**2 oil engines** driving 2 FP propellers Total Power: 882kW (1,200hp) 11.0kn S.K.L. 8NVDS36/24A-1 2 x 4 Stroke 8 Cy. 240 x 360 each-441kW (600bhp) VEB Schwermaschinenbau "KarlLiebknecht" (SKL)-Magdeburg
8521842 *UBOC* -	**STK-1012** **Upper Lena River Shipping Co (ZAO 'Verkhne-Lenskoye Rechnoye Parokhodstvo')** - *St Petersburg* *Russia* MMSI: 273317800 Official number: 846035	**1,573** 585 1,669	Class: RS	**1985-03 VEB Elbewerften Boizenburg/Rosslau — Rosslau** Yd No: 314/3461 Loa 82.02 Br ex 11.92 Dght 2.751 Lbp 78.30 Br md 11.61 Dpth 4.02 Welded, 1 dk	**(A31A2GX) General Cargo Ship** Grain: 1,920 TEU 70/20' incl. 10 ref C. Compartments: 2 Ho, ER 2 Ha: 2 (17.8 x 9.2)ER	**2 oil engines** driving 2 FP propellers Total Power: 882kW (1,200hp) 11.0kn S.K.L. 8NVDS36/24A-1 2 x 4 Stroke 8 Cy. 240 x 360 each-441kW (600bhp) VEB Schwermaschinenbau "KarlLiebknecht" (SKL)-Magdeburg AuxGen: 2 x 100kW a.c, 1 x 50kW a.c Fuel: 87.0 (d.f.)
8620014 *UBEU* -	**STK-1019** **JS North-Western Shipping Co (OAO 'Severo-Zapadnoye Parokhodstvo')** - *St Petersburg* *Russia* MMSI: 273327700	**1,367** 422 1,706	Class: RR (RS)	**1986-01 VEB Elbewerften Boizenburg/Rosslau — Rosslau** Yd No: 321/3472 Loa 82.02 Br ex - Dght 2.501 Lbp 78.01 Br md 11.61 Dpth 4.02 Welded, 1 dk	**(A31A2GX) General Cargo Ship** Grain: 1,940 Compartments: 2 Ho, ER 1 Ha: (22.4 x 9.2)ER	**2 oil engines** driving 2 FP propellers Total Power: 882kW (1,200hp) 11.0kn S.K.L. 8NVDS36/24A-1 2 x 4 Stroke 8 Cy. 240 x 360 each-441kW (600bhp) VEB Schwermaschinenbau "KarlLiebknecht" (SKL)-Magdeburg
8620026 *UCYT* -	**STK-1020** **JSC Northern River Shipping Lines** - SatCom: Inmarsat C 427300765 *Arkhangelsk* *Russia* MMSI: 273362200	**1,573** 585 1,669	Class: RS RR	**1986-03 VEB Elbewerften Boizenburg/Rosslau — Rosslau** Yd No: 322/3473 Loa 82.00 Br ex 11.94 Dght 2.760 Lbp 78.10 Br md 11.60 Dpth 4.00 Welded, 1 dk	**(A31A2GX) General Cargo Ship** Grain: 1,940 TEU 70 C. 70/20' incl. 10 ref C. Compartments: 2 Cell Ho, ER 2 Ha: 2 (19.6 x 9.1)ER	**2 oil engines** driving 2 FP propellers Total Power: 882kW (1,200hp) 11.5kn S.K.L. 8NVDS36/24A-1 2 x 4 Stroke 8 Cy. 240 x 360 each-441kW (600bhp) VEB Schwermaschinenbau "KarlLiebknecht" (SKL)-Magdeburg AuxGen: 2 x 100kW a.c Fuel: 88.0 (d.f.)
8620052 *UBEO* -	**STK-1023** **North-Western Fleet (A/O 'Severo-Zapadnyy Flot')** - *St Petersburg* *Russia* MMSI: 273310300 Official number: 854920	**1,573** 585 1,669	Class: RR (RS)	**1986-09 VEB Elbewerften Boizenburg/Rosslau — Rosslau** Yd No: 325/3476 Loa 82.02 Br ex 11.92 Dght 2.750 Lbp 78.01 Br md 11.61 Dpth 4.02 Welded, 1 dk	**(A31A2GX) General Cargo Ship** Grain: 1,940 Compartments: 2 Ho, ER 2 Ha: 2 (17.8 x 9.2)ER	**2 oil engines** driving 2 FP propellers Total Power: 882kW (1,200hp) 11.0kn S.K.L. 8NVDS36/24A-1 2 x 4 Stroke 8 Cy. 240 x 360 each-441kW (600bhp) VEB Schwermaschinenbau "KarlLiebknecht" (SKL)-Magdeburg
8719372 *UCYW* -	**STK-1026** **JSC Northern River Shipping Lines** JSC Shipping Co 'Marshall' SatCom: Inmarsat C 427300320 *Arkhangelsk* *Russia* MMSI: 273369100 Official number: 865765	**1,573** 585 1,706	Class: RS	**1987-04 VEB Elbewerften Boizenburg/Rosslau — Rosslau** Yd No: 328/3479 Loa 82.02 Br ex 11.94 Dght 2.501 Lbp 78.01 Br md 11.61 Dpth 4.02 Welded, 1 dk	**(A31A2GX) General Cargo Ship** Grain: 1,940 TEU 68 C. 68/20'	**2 oil engines** driving 2 FP propellers Total Power: 882kW (1,200hp) 11.0kn S.K.L. 8NVDS36/24A-1 2 x 4 Stroke 8 Cy. 240 x 360 each-441kW (600bhp) VEB Schwermaschinenbau "KarlLiebknecht" (SKL)-Magdeburg

8719396 *UBEP* -	**STK-1028** **Upper Lena River Shipping Co (ZAO 'Verkhne-Lenskoye Rechnoye Parokhodstvo')** - SatCom: Inmarsat C 427300749 *St Petersburg* *Russia* MMSI: 273312210 Official number: 865708	**1,575** 585 1,669	Class: RS (RR)	**1987-07 VEB Elbewerften Boizenburg/Rosslau — Rosslau** Yd No: 330/3481 Loa 82.00 Br ex 11.93 Dght 3.350 Lbp 78.30 Br md 11.60 Dpth 4.00 Welded, 1 dk	**(A31A2GX) General Cargo Ship**	**2 oil engines** driving 2 FP propellers Total Power: 882kW (1,200hp) 11.0kn S.K.L. 8NVDS36/24A-1 2 x 4 Stroke 8 Cy. 240 x 360 each-441kW (600bhp) VEB Schwermaschinenbau "KarlLiebknecht" (SKL)-Magdeburg
8719401 *UCYX* -	**STK-1029** **JSC Northern River Shipping Lines** - SatCom: Inmarsat C 427300326 *Arkhangelsk* *Russia* MMSI: 273368100	**1,573** 585 1,663	Class: RS	**1987-09 VEB Elbewerften Boizenburg/Rosslau — Rosslau** Yd No: 331/3482 Loa 82.02 Br ex 11.94 Dght 2.501 Lbp 78.01 Br md 11.61 Dpth 4.02 Welded, 1 dk	**(A31A2GX) General Cargo Ship** Grain: 1,940 TEU 68 C. 68/20' Ice Capable	**2 oil engines** driving 2 FP propellers Total Power: 882kW (1,200hp) 11.0kn S.K.L. 8NVDS36/24A-1 2 x 4 Stroke 8 Cy. 240 x 360 each-441kW (600bhp) VEB Schwermaschinenbau "KarlLiebknecht" (SKL)-Magdeburg
8719425 *UBEQ* -	**STK-1031** **JS North-Western Shipping Co (OAO 'Severo-Zapadnoye Parokhodstvo')** - SatCom: Inmarsat C 427301375 *St Petersburg* *Russia* MMSI: 273312310	**1,408** 422 1,669	Class: RR	**1987-12 VEB Elbewerften Boizenburg/Rosslau — Rosslau** Yd No: 333/3484 Loa 82.02 Br ex - Dght 2.750 Lbp 78.01 Br md 11.61 Dpth 4.02 Welded, 1 dk	**(A31A2GX) General Cargo Ship**	**2 oil engines** driving 2 FP propellers Total Power: 882kW (1,200hp) 11.0kn S.K.L. 8NVDS36/24A-1 2 x 4 Stroke 8 Cy. 240 x 360 each-441kW (600bhp) VEB Schwermaschinenbau "KarlLiebknecht" (SKL)-Magdeburg
8857095 *UBET* -	**STK-1036** **JS North-Western Shipping Co (OAO 'Severo-Zapadnoye Parokhodstvo')** - SatCom: Inmarsat C 427301394 *St Petersburg* *Russia* MMSI: 273313310	**1,408** 422 1,669	Class: RR	**1989-07 VEB Elbewerften Boizenburg/Rosslau — Rosslau** Yd No: 349 Loa 82.00 Br ex 11.94 Dght 2.750 Lbp 78.10 Br md - Dpth 4.00 Welded, 1 dk	**(A31A2GX) General Cargo Ship**	**2 oil engines** driving 2 FP propellers Total Power: 882kW (1,200hp) 11.0kn S.K.L. 8NVDS36/24A-1 2 x 4 Stroke 8 Cy. 240 x 360 each-441kW (600bhp) VEB Schwermaschinenbau "KarlLiebknecht" (SKL)-Magdeburg
8742006 *YD3390* -	**STK PRIMA 5** *ex* Otaki Maru *-2006* **PT Restu Prima Lestari** - *Batam* *Indonesia*	**157** 48 -	Class: KI	**1987-06 Hongawara Zosen K.K. — Fukuyama** Loa 24.46 Br ex - Dght 2.500 Lbp 24.00 Br md 7.40 Dpth 3.00 Welded, 1 dk	**(B32B2SP) Pusher Tug**	**2 oil engines** reduction geared to sc. shafts driving 2 Propellers Total Power: 882kW (1,200hp) Yanmar S185-ET 2 x 4 Stroke 6 Cy. 185 x 230 each-441kW (600bhp) Yanmar Diesel Engine Co Ltd-Japan
9576038 *PNPZ* -	**STK PRIMA 6** *ex* Wan Wei 19 *-2009* **PT Sentun Prima** Sentek Marine & Trading Pte Ltd *Tanjungpinang* *Indonesia*	**354** 107 -	Class: KI	**2009-05 Jiangsu Shenghua Shipbuilding Co Ltd — Zhenjiang JS** Yd No: JSH501 Loa 33.00 Br ex - Dght 3.200 Lbp 29.90 Br md 9.60 Dpth 4.30 Welded, 1 dk	**(B32A2ST) Tug**	**2 oil engines** reduction geared to sc. shafts driving 2 Propellers Total Power: 3,972kW (5,400hp) Chinese Std. Type 2 x 4 Stroke each-1986kW (2700bhp) Zibo Diesel Engine Factory-China
8735754 *9V9145* -	**STL I** *ex* Shun Yang 19 *-2009* **STL I Marine Pte Ltd** - *Singapore* *Singapore* MMSI: 563017640 Official number: 396694	**1,108** 659 -	Class: RI	**2006-11 in the People's Republic of China** Loa 59.80 Br ex - Dght 3.940 Lbp - Br md 13.80 Dpth 4.60 Welded, 1 dk	**(A24D2BA) Aggregates Carrier** Compartments: 1 Ho, ER 1 Ha: ER	**2 oil engines** driving 2 FP propellers Total Power: 678kW (922hp) 10.0kn Chinese Std. Type 2 x 4 Stroke each-339kW (461bhp) in China AuxGen: 2 x a.c
8735728 *9V9146* -	**STL II** *ex* Shun Yang 18 *-2009* **STL II Marine Pte Ltd** - *Singapore* *Singapore* MMSI: 563017650	**919** 497 -	Class: RI	**2006-12 Shantang Navigation Shipyard Co Ltd — Qingyuan GD** Loa 55.55 Br ex - Dght 3.840 Lbp - Br md 12.50 Dpth 4.50 Welded, 1 dk	**(A24D2BA) Aggregates Carrier** Compartments: 1 Ho, ER 1 Ha: ER	**2 oil engines** driving 2 FP propellers Total Power: 576kW (784hp) 9.0kn Chinese Std. Type 2 x 4 Stroke each-288kW (392bhp) in China
8738184 *9V9109* -	**STL III** *ex* Shun Yang 17 *-2009* **STL III Marine Pte Ltd** - *Singapore* *Singapore* MMSI: 563017330 Official number: 396618	**919** 304 -	Class: RI	**2006-12 Shantang Navigation Shipyard Co Ltd — Qingyuan GD** Loa 55.55 Br ex - Dght 3.740 Lbp - Br md 12.50 Dpth 4.50 Welded, 1 dk	**(A24D2BA) Aggregates Carrier**	**2 oil engines** reduction geared to sc. shafts driving 2 Propellers Total Power: 416kW (566hp) 8.0kn Cummins 2 x 4 Stroke each-208kW (283bhp) Cummins Engine Co Inc-USA
8739059 *9V9110* -	**STL IV** *ex* Shun Yang 12 *-2009* *ex* Shun Hong Hai 12 *-2004* **STL IV Marine Pte Ltd** - *Singapore* *Singapore* MMSI: 563017340 Official number: 396619	**1,255** 376 -	Class: RI	**2000-06 Nanchang Shipyard — Nanchang JX** Loa 68.15 Br ex - Dght 3.500 Lbp - Br md 12.98 Dpth 4.38 Welded, 1 dk	**(A24D2BA) Aggregates Carrier**	**2 oil engines** reduction geared to sc. shafts driving 2 FP propellers Total Power: 746kW (1,014hp) 10.0kn Cummins 2 x 4 Stroke each-373kW (507bhp) Cummins Engine Co Inc-USA AuxGen: 2 x a.c
9583407 *9V9066* -	**STL V** *ex* Zhendon 828 *-2010* **STL V Marine Pte Ltd** - *Singapore* *Singapore* MMSI: 563016990 Official number: 396447	**1,146** 641 -	Class: RI	**2009-12 Dongguan Dongsheng Shipyard Co Ltd — Dongguan GD** Loa 63.00 Br ex 14.50 Dght 3.190 Lbp - Br md 14.20 Dpth 3.80 Welded, 1 dk	**(A24D2BA) Aggregates Carrier**	**2 oil engines** geared to sc. shafts driving 2 FP propellers Total Power: 678kW (922hp) 10.0kn Cummins KTA-19-M500 2 x 4 Stroke 6 Cy. 159 x 159 each-339kW (461bhp) Cummins Engine Co Inc-USA
7314266 *DUE2008* -	**STO. DOMINGO** *ex* Ferry Ocean Rose *-1988* *ex* Noheji Maru *-1987* **Sto Domingo Shipping Lines** - *Batangas* *Philippines* Official number: BAT5000042	*924* 416 711		**1973 Nichiro Zosen K.K. — Hakodate** Yd No: 313 Loa 82.89 Br ex 15.37 Dght 3.785 Lbp 76.26 Br md 15.32 Dpth 5.11 Welded, 3 dks	**(A36A2PR) Passenger/Ro-Ro Ship (Vehicles)**	**4 oil engines** geared to sc. shafts driving 2 FP propellers Total Power: 4,708kW (6,400hp) 15.8kn Niigata 8MG25BX 4 x 4 Stroke 8 Cy. 250 x 320 each-1177kW (1600bhp) Niigata Engineering Co Ltd-Japan AuxGen: 3 x 130kW 445V 60Hz a.c Fuel: 151.5 (d.f.) 16.0pd
7425211 *LACF* ST-70-F	**STO KURS** *ex* Skagholm *-2010* *ex* Jaro *-2001* *ex* Rindagutt *-1976* **Hordaland Fylkeskommune Opplaeringdavdelinga** - *Bergen* *Norway* MMSI: 257019640	**223** 66 -		**1975-06 Eidsvik Skipsbyggeri AS — Uskedalen** Yd No: 33 Loa 28.05 Br ex 7.04 Dght - Lbp 25.00 Br md 7.01 Dpth 3.71 Welded, 1 dk	**(B11B2FV) Fishing Vessel**	**1 oil engine** driving 1 CP propeller Total Power: 515kW (700hp) Alpha 407-26VO 1 x 2 Stroke 7 Cy. 260 x 400 515kW (700bhp) Alpha Diesel A/S-Denmark
8931712 - -	**STO LET KRASNOVODSKU** **Turkmen Shipping Co (Turkmenistanyn Denyiz Paroxodjylygy)** - *Turkmenbashy* *Turkmenistan* Official number: 693161	*134* 42 81	Class: (RS)	**1969-12 Astrakhan. SSZ im 10-iy God Oktyabrskoy Revolyutsii — Astrakhan** Yd No: 11 Loa 28.20 Br ex 7.30 Dght 2.750 Lbp 26.00 Br md - Dpth 3.50 Welded, 1 dk	**(B21B2OT) Offshore Tug/Supply Ship** Liq: 68 Compartments: 4 Ta Ice Capable	**2 oil engines** driving 2 FP propellers Total Power: 442kW (600hp) 10.2kn Pervomaysk 6CHRP25/34 2 x 4 Stroke 6 Cy. 250 x 340 each-221kW (300bhp) Pervomaydizelmash (PDM)-Pervomaysk AuxGen: 2 x 60kW a.c Fuel: 10.0 (d.f.)
8944848 *DUA2039* -	**STO. NINO** **Mandaue Shipping & Lighterage Corp** - *Cebu* *Philippines* Official number: CEB1000462	*247* 156 -		**1981 at Cebu** L reg 45.00 Br ex - Dght 1.830 Lbp - Br md 9.76 Dpth - Welded, 1 dk	**(A35D2RL) Landing Craft**	**1 oil engine** driving 1 FP propeller Total Power: 280kW (381hp) Cummins 1 x 4 Stroke 280kW (381bhp) Cummins Engine Co Inc-USA

7376173 **STO. NINO DE BAY** *1,419* Class: (NK)
DUA2611 *ex* Castor Gas *-1996* *ex* Green Sea *-1992* 430
\- **Grand Asian Shipping Lines Inc** 1,412
\- T/cm
Manila *Philippines* 6.9
Official number: MNLD007322

1974-03 **Tokushima Zosen Sangyo K.K. — Komatsushima** Yd No: 368
Loa 73.22 Br ex 12.25 Dght 4.613
Lbp 67.00 Br md 12.22 Dpth 5.52
Welded, 1 dk

(A11B2TG) LPG Tanker
Liq (Gas): 1,624
2 x Gas Tank (s); 2 independent (C.mn.stl) cyl horizontal
2 Cargo Pump (s): 2x300m³/hr
Manifold: Bow/CM: 30m

1 oil engine driving 1 FP propeller
Total Power: 1,545kW (2,101hp) 12.2kn
Akasaka AH38
1 x 4 Stroke 6 Cy. 380 x 560 1545kW (2101bhp)
Akasaka Tekkosho KK (Akasaka DieselLtd)-Japan
AuxGen: 2 x 100kW
Fuel: 65.0 (d.f.) 145.0 (r.f.) 7.5pd

8427400 **STO. NINO DE SOLEDAD** *247*
DUH2147 *ex* Mindanao Cement 3 *-1992* 140
\- **BC Sea Transport** 470
\-
Tacloban *Philippines*
Official number: CEB1001035

1969 Sandoval Shipyards Inc. — Consolacion
L reg 39.10 Br ex 7.29 Dght -
Lbp 38.58 Br md 7.27 Dpth 3.05
Welded, 1 dk

(A31A2GX) General Cargo Ship

1 oil engine driving 1 FP propeller
Total Power: 353kW (480hp)

8808006 **STO NO. 1** **741** Class: KR
DSOJ3 *ex* Cosmo Glory *-2013* *ex* Sanshin Maru *-2005* 330
\- **STO Control Knowledge Co Ltd** 1,143
\-
Jeju *South Korea*
MMSI: 440752000
Official number: JJR-059438

1988-06 **Hakata Zosen K.K. — Imabari** Yd No: 375
Converted From: Chemical Tanker
Loa 64.99 Br ex 10.03 Dght 3.943
Lbp 60.91 Br md 10.00 Dpth 4.50
Welded, 1 dk

(A12B2TR) Chemical/Products Tanker
Double Hull (13F)
Liq: 1,209; Liq (Oil): 1,209
Compartments: 4 Ta, ER
2 Cargo Pump (s): 2x300m³/hr
Manifold: Bow/CM: 35m

1 oil engine driving 1 FP propeller
Total Power: 956kW (1,300hp) 12.2kn
Hanshin 6LUN28A
1 x 4 Stroke 6 Cy. 280 x 480 956kW (1300bhp)
The Hanshin Diesel Works Ltd-Japan
Fuel: 62.0

9019676 **STO NO. 3** **1,224** Class: KR
D8TX *ex* Songwon *-2013* *ex* Chemicarry No. 1 *-2012* 557
\- *ex* Chemicarry No. 31 *-2005* 1,788
STO Control Knowledge Co Ltd T/cm
\- 6.8
Busan *South Korea*
MMSI: 440227000
Official number: BSR-900296

1990-04 **Banguhjin Engineering & Shipbuilding Co Ltd — Ulsan** Yd No: 79
Loa 70.01 Br ex - Dght 4.500
Lbp 64.01 Br md 12.01 Dpth 5.26
Welded, 1 dk

(A12A2TC) Chemical Tanker
Liq: 1,958
Cargo Heating Coils
3 Cargo Pump (s)

1 oil engine driving 1 FP propeller
Total Power: 1,177kW (1,600hp) 11.5kn
Hanshin 6LUN28
1 x 4 Stroke 6 Cy. 280 x 480 1177kW (1600bhp)
Ssangyong Heavy Industries Co Ltd-South Korea
AuxGen: 2 x 128kW 445V 60Hz a.c
Fuel: 27.3 (d.f.) 120.1 (r.f.)

9390305 **STOC MARCIA** **3,219** Class: BV
C4XG2 1,384
\- **Stoc Mare Ltd** 4,634
Stoc Tankers AB T/cm
Limassol *Cyprus* 12.5
MMSI: 212123000

2007-06 **Ceksan Tersanesi — Turkey** Yd No: 30
Loa 99.91 (BB) Br ex - Dght 6.000
Lbp 93.90 Br md 15.00 Dpth 7.40
Welded, 1 dk

(A12B2TR) Chemical/Products Tanker
Double Hull (13F)
Liq: 4,591; Liq (Oil): 4,951
Cargo Heating Coils
Compartments: 8 Wing Ta, 2 Wing Slop Ta, ER
8 Cargo Pump (s): 8x160m³/hr
Manifold: Bow/CM: 53.4m
Ice Capable

1 oil engine reduction geared to sc. shaft driving 1 CP propeller
Total Power: 3,000kW (4,079hp) 12.5kn
Wartsila 6L32
1 x 4 Stroke 6 Cy. 320 x 400 3000kW (4079bhp)
Wartsila Finland Oy-Finland
AuxGen: 3 x 370kW a.c
Thrusters: 1 Tunnel thruster (f)
Fuel: 62.0 (d.f.) 247.0 (r.f.)

5193890 **STOCKHOLM** **658**
SGLD *ex* Korsholm af Westeras *-1998* 215
\- *ex* Korsholm *-1997* *ex* Oland *-1986* -
ex Korsholm *-1986* *ex* Korsholm III *-1967*
ex Oland *-1956*
Stromma Turism & Sjofart AB
\-
Stockholm *Sweden*
MMSI: 265514680

1931-01 **Oskarshamns Mekaniske Verkstad AB — Oskarshamn** Yd No: 280
Lengthened-1958
Loa 48.72 Br ex 8.60 Dght 2.770
Lbp 46.55 Br md - Dpth -
Riveted\Welded, 1 dk pt 2nd dk

(A37B2PS) Passenger Ship
Passengers: unberthed: 354

1 oil engine driving 1 CP propeller 12.0kn

8226612 **STOCKHOLM AV GOTEBORG** *361*
SMYP *ex* Stockholm *-2011* 83
\- *ex* Stockholm Av Goteborg *-2008*
ex Stockholm *-1997*
Rederi AB Ishavet
\-
Gothenburg *Sweden*
MMSI: 265472000

1953 Helsingborgs Varfs AB — Helsingborg
Converted From: Research Vessel-1999
Converted From: Lighthouse Tender-1967
Loa 37.80 Br ex 8.84 Dght -
Lbp - Br md - Dpth 4.37
Welded, 2 dks

(A37A2PC) Passenger/Cruise
Passengers: cabins: 6; berths: 12

1 oil engine driving 1 FP propeller
Total Power: 423kW (575hp) 10.0kn
Nohab ML4
1 x 2 Stroke 4 Cy. 345 x 580 423kW (575bhp)
Nydqvist & Holm AB-Sweden

7047227 **STOCKTON CREEK** *199* Class: (AB)
\- 109
\- **National Port Authority of Monrovia, Liberia**
\-

1970 Equitable Equipment Co. — Madisonville, La Yd No: 1587
Loa - Br ex 8.62 Dght 3.431
Lbp 26.52 Br md 8.60 Dpth 4.02
Welded, 1 dk

(B32A2ST) Tug

2 oil engines sr reverse geared to sc. shafts driving 2 FP propellers
Total Power: 1,250kW (1,700hp)
Caterpillar D398TA
2 x Vee 4 Stroke 12 Cy. 159 x 203 each-625kW (850bhp)
Caterpillar Tractor Co-USA
AuxGen: 2 x 50kW

9585558 **STOJA** **30,092** Class: BV CS (Class contemplated)
C6AK9 -
\- **United Shipping Services Thirteen Inc** 51,500
Uljanik Shipmanagement Inc
Nassau *Bahamas*
MMSI: 311000076

2012-02 **'Uljanik' Brodogradiliste dd — Pula** Yd No: 489
Loa 189.99 (BB) Br ex - Dght 12.350
Lbp 182.00 Br md 32.24 Dpth 17.10
Welded, 1 dk

(A21A2BC) Bulk Carrier
Grain: 64,500
Compartments: 5 Ho, ER
5 Ha: ER
Cranes: 4x30t

1 oil engine driving 1 FP propeller
Total Power: 8,600kW (11,693hp) 14.2kn
MAN-B&W 6S50MC-C
1 x 2 Stroke 6 Cy. 500 x 2000 8600kW (11693bhp)
'Uljanik' Strojogradnja dd-Croatia
AuxGen: 3 x 620kW a.c

9576222 **STOKKE SENIOR** **375**
JWQZ 150
M-12-U **Stokke Senior AS** 500
Sande Regnskapskontor AS
Aalesund *Norway*

2009-12 **AO Yaroslavskiy Sudostroitelnyy Zavod — Yaroslavl** Yd No: 402
Loa 27.49 (BB) Br ex - Dght -
Lbp 23.99 Br md 9.50 Dpth 4.80
Welded, 1 dk

(B11B2FV) Fishing Vessel

4 diesel electric oil engines driving 1 gen. of 1100kW a.c 1 gen. of 320kW Connecting to 1 elec. Motor driving 1 Propeller
Total Power: 1,764kW (2,400hp)
Scania DI16 M
1 x Vee 4 Stroke 8 Cy. 127 x 154 441kW (600bhp)
Scania AB-Sweden
Scania DI16 M
3 x Vee 4 Stroke 8 Cy. 127 x 154 each-441kW (600bhp)
Scania AB-Sweden
Thrusters: 1 Tunnel thruster (f); 1 Tunnel thruster (a)

5018349 **STOKKSNES** **164**
HO3564 *ex* Sigurvik *-1997* *ex* Freyr *-1992* 49
\- *ex* Anna *-1990* -
Van Miert Corp
\-
Panama *Panama*
Official number: 32192PEXT1

1960 Scheepswerf "De Beer" N.V. — Zaandam Yd No: 1183
Loa 28.10 Br ex 6.53 Dght -
Lbp 26.85 Br md 6.51 Dpth 3.23
Welded, 1 dk

(B11A2FT) Trawler

1 oil engine driving 1 FP propeller
Total Power: 368kW (500hp) 10.0kn
Kromhout 8FHD240
1 x 4 Stroke 8 Cy. 240 x 260 368kW (500bhp)
Kromhout Motorenfabriek D. GoedkoopJr. N.V.-Amsterdam

6820921 **STOKSUNDFERJA** **171** Class: (NV)
LAHM *ex* Kvalsundferja *-1990* 51
\- **FosenNamsos Sjo AS** -
\-
Trondheim *Norway*
MMSI: 257380400

1968 Bolsones Verft AS — Molde Yd No: 218
Loa 30.00 Br ex 9.53 Dght 2.674
Lbp 29.01 Br md 9.49 Dpth 3.51
Welded, 1 dk

(A36A2PR) Passenger/Ro-Ro Ship (Vehicles)
Passengers: unberthed: 115
Bow door & ramp
Stern ramp

1 oil engine driving 2 Propellers 1 fwd and 1 aft
Total Power: 349kW (475hp) 10.0kn
Caterpillar D379TA
1 x Vee 4 Stroke 8 Cy. 159 x 203 349kW (475bhp)
Caterpillar Tractor Co-USA
AuxGen: 2 x 25kW 220V 50Hz a.c
Fuel: 10.0 (d.f.)

7942984 **STOLMASUND** **138** Class: (NV)
JXHO *ex* Strilfjord *-1982* *ex* Austra *-1981* 43
\- **Kjell Jakobsen** -
\- -
Bergen *Norway*
MMSI: 257073700

1959 Kaarbos Mek. Verksted AS — Harstad Yd No: 28
Loa 29.01 Br ex 8.01 Dght -
Lbp - Br md - Dpth 3.26
Welded, 1 dk

(A36A2PR) Passenger/Ro-Ro Ship (Vehicles)
Passengers: unberthed: 100
Cars: 16

1 oil engine driving 1 FP propeller
Total Power: 276kW (375hp)
Wichmann 3ACA
1 x 2 Stroke 3 Cy. 280 x 420 276kW (375bhp)
Wichmann Motorfabrikk AS-Norway

9572159 **STOLNIY GRAD YAROSLAVL** **367** Class: RS
UBPG7 102
\- **Government of The Russian Federation** 51
Government of The Russian Federation (Federal Budgetary Enterprise State Marine Emergency Salvage, Rescue & Pollution Prevention Coordination Service of Russian Federation) (SMRPCS)
Astrakhan *Russia*
MMSI: 273359050

2010-10 **AO Yaroslavskiy Sudostroitelnyy Zavod — Yaroslavl** Yd No: 201
Loa 38.35 Br ex 7.92 Dght 2.350
Lbp 36.27 Br md 7.70 Dpth 3.20
Welded, 1 dk

(B22A20V) Diving Support Vessel
Cranes: 1x2t
Ice Capable

2 oil engines reduction geared to sc. shafts driving 2 CP propellers
Total Power: 882kW (1,200hp) 8.0kn
Baudouin 8M26SR
1 x 4 Stroke 8 Cy. 150 x 150 441kW (600bhp)
Societe des Moteurs Baudouin SA-France
AuxGen: 2 x 136kW a.c
Thrusters: 1 Tunnel thruster (f)

Ship	Tonnage	Class	Build / Dimensions	Type / Cargo	Machinery
9124469 **STOLT ACHIEVEMENT** *ZCSQ* - **Stolt Achievement BV** Stolt Tankers BV SatCom: Inmarsat C 431944610 *George Town* *Cayman Islands (British)* MMSI: 319446000 Official number: 732886	**25,196** 12,048 37,141 T/cm 48.5	Class: NV	**1999-11 ACH Construction Navale — Le Havre** Yd No: 294 Loa 176.70 (BB) Br ex 31.60 Dght 11.850 Lbp 168.00 Br md 31.20 Dpth 15.60 Welded, 1 dk	**(A12B2TR) Chemical/Products Tanker** Double Hull (13F) Liq: 40,593; Liq (Oil): 40,593 Compartments: 26 Wing Ta, 2 Wing Slop Ta, 22 Ta 52 Cargo Pump (s): 14x300m³/hr, 38x200m³/hr Manifold: Bow/CM: 86.1m	**4 diesel electric oil engines** driving 3 gen. each 3520kW 6600V a.c 1 gen. of 2350kW 6600V a.c Connecting to 1 elec. Motor of (10000kW) driving 1 FP propeller Total Power: 13,500kW (18,355hp) 16.2kn Wartsila 6R32LN 1 x 4 Stroke 6 Cy. 320 x 350 2430kW (3304bhp) Wartsila NSD Finland Oy-Finland Wartsila 9R32LN 3 x 4 Stroke 9 Cy. 320 x 350 each-3690kW (5017bhp) Wartsila NSD Finland Oy-Finland Thrusters: 1 Thwart. FP thruster (f) Fuel: 110.0 (d.f.) 1835.0 (r.f.)
9391983 **STOLT AGUILA** *ZCYX9* - *launched as* Sichem Yangtze *-2009* **Kaiser Ship Holding SA** Stolt Tankers BV SatCom: Inmarsat C 431900239 *George Town* *Cayman Islands (British)* MMSI: 319014200	**7,603** 3,760 12,260 T/cm 21.6	Class: BV	**2009-10 Sasaki Shipbuilding Co Ltd — Osakikamijima HS** Yd No: 666 Loa 123.85 (BB) Br ex 20.02 Dght 8.915 Lbp 116.52 Br md 20.00 Dpth 11.50 Welded, 1 dk	**(A12B2TR) Chemical/Products Tanker** Double Hull (13F) Liq: 13,016; Liq (Oil): 12,399 Cargo Heating Coils Compartments: 20 Wing Ta, ER, 2 Wing Slop Ta 20 Cargo Pump (s): 20x200m³/hr Manifold: Bow/CM: 61.9m	**1 oil engine** driving 1 FP propeller Total Power: 3,996kW (5,433hp) 13.5kn MAN-B&W 6S35MC 1 x 2 Stroke 6 Cy. 350 x 1400 3996kW (5433bhp) Hitachi Zosen Corp-Japan AuxGen: 3 x 750kW 450V 60Hz a.c Thrusters: 1 Tunnel thruster (f) Fuel: 118.0 (d.f.) 582.0 (r.f.)
9477555 **STOLT AJISAI** *ZGA02* - **Stolt Ajisai Inc** Stolt-Nielsen Singapore Pte Ltd *George Town* *Cayman Islands (British)* MMSI: 319028000 Official number: 742453	**7,242** 3,808 12,798 T/cm 21.1	Class: NK	**2011-06 Usuki Shipyard Co Ltd — Usuki OT** Yd No: 1727 Loa 121.52 (BB) Br ex - Dght 8.814 Lbp 115.00 Br md 20.60 Dpth 11.30 Welded, 1 dk	**(A12B2TR) Chemical/Products Tanker** Double Hull (13F) Liq: 13,142; Liq (Oil): 13,500 Cargo Heating Coils Compartments: 18 Wing Ta, ER 18 Cargo Pump (s): 6x200m³/hr, 12x300m³/hr Manifold: Bow/CM: 62m	**1 oil engine** driving 1 FP propeller Total Power: 4,900kW (6,662hp) 14.3kn MAN-B&W 7S35MC 1 x 2 Stroke 7 Cy. 350 x 1400 4900kW (6662bhp) Hitachi Zosen Corp-Japan AuxGen: 3 x 450kW a.c Thrusters: 1 Tunnel thruster (f) Fuel: 81.0 (d.f.) 632.0 (r.f.)
9360934 **STOLT AMI** *3EAZ5* - **Makino Kaiun Co Ltd & Maki Ocean Shipping SA** Stolt-Nielsen Singapore Pte Ltd SatCom: Inmarsat Mini-M 764637711 *Panama* *Panama* MMSI: 371433000 Official number: 3200806B	**11,708** 6,349 19,963 T/cm 29.8	Class: NK	**2006-07 Fukuoka Shipbuilding Co Ltd — Nagasaki NS** Yd No: 2007 Loa 144.09 (BB) Br ex 24.23 Dght 9.672 Lbp 136.00 Br md 24.19 Dpth 12.90 Welded, 1 dk	**(A12B2TR) Chemical/Products Tanker** Double Hull (13F) Liq: 21,714; Liq (Oil): 22,157 Compartments: 22 Wing Ta, ER Manifold: Bow/CM: 74.2m	**1 oil engine** driving 1 FP propeller Total Power: 6,230kW (8,470hp) 14.5kn Mitsubishi 7UEC45LA 1 x 2 Stroke 7 Cy. 450 x 1350 6230kW (8470bhp) Akasaka Tekkosho KK (Akasaka DieselLtd)-Japan AuxGen: 3 x 450kW 440V 60Hz a.c Thrusters: 1 Tunnel thruster (f) Fuel: 126.0 (d.f.) 993.0 (r.f.)
8309529 **STOLT AQUAMARINE** *ZCSQ2* - **Stolt Aquamarine BV** Stolt Nielsen USA Inc SatCom: Inmarsat C 431944910 *George Town* *Cayman Islands (British)* MMSI: 319449000 Official number: 732887	**23,964** 13,720 38,761 T/cm 48.7	Class: NV	**1986-06 Daewoo Shipbuilding & Heavy Machinery Ltd — Geoje** Yd No: 2010 Conv to DH-2011 Loa 176.82 (BB) Br ex 32.25 Dght 11.428 Lbp 169.56 Br md 32.23 Dpth 15.00 Welded, 1 dk	**(A12B2TR) Chemical/Products Tanker** Double Hull (13F) Liq: 45,413; Liq (Oil): 45,408 Cargo Heating Coils Compartments: 32 Ta, 22 Wing Ta, ER 58 Cargo Pump (s): 12x450m³/hr, 46x255m³/hr Manifold: Bow/CM: 80.7m	**1 oil engine** driving 1 FP propeller Total Power: 11,520kW (15,663hp) 15.0kn MAN-B&W 6L60MC 1 x 2 Stroke 6 Cy. 600 x 1944 11520kW (15663bhp) Hyundai Engine & Machinery Co Ltd-South Korea AuxGen: 3 x 900kW 450V 60Hz a.c Thrusters: 1 Thwart. FP thruster (f) Fuel: 358.0 (d.f.) 1878.0 (r.f.) 37.5pd
9238284 **STOLT AVANCE** *ZGAG6* - *ex* Althea Gas *-2010* **Stolt Avance Inc** Exmar Marine NV *George Town* *Cayman Islands (British)* MMSI: 319096000 Official number: 742390	**46,393** 16,040 53,677 T/cm 68.9	Class: AB	**2003-01 Kawasaki Shipbuilding Corp — Sakaide KG** Yd No: 1515 Loa 227.00 (BB) Br ex - Dght 10.980 Lbp 216.62 Br md 36.00 Dpth 21.90 Welded, 1 dk	**(A11B2TG) LPG Tanker** Double Bottom Entire Compartment Length Liq (Gas): 80,906 4 x Gas Tank (s); 4 independent (C.mn.stl) pri horizontal 8 Cargo Pump (s): 8x550m³/hr Manifold: Bow/CM: 113.6m	**1 oil engine** driving 1 FP propeller Total Power: 13,900kW (18,898hp) 17.0kn MAN-B&W 5S70MC 1 x 2 Stroke 5 Cy. 700 x 2674 13900kW (18898bhp) Kawasaki Heavy Industries Ltd-Japan AuxGen: 3 x 960kW a.c Fuel: 267.0 (d.f.) 3100.0 (r.f.)
9004310 **STOLT AVOCET** *ZCMQ5* - **Stolt Avocet BV** Stolt Tankers BV SatCom: Inmarsat B 331918510 *George Town* *Cayman Islands (British)* MMSI: 319185000 Official number: 731119	**3,853** 1,557 5,749 T/cm 13.7	Class: LR (NK) **100A1** SS 07/2012 Double Hull oil and chemical tanker, Ship Type 2, MARPOL 20.1.3, CR (s.stl), SG 1.55 ESP **LMC** **UMS** Eq.Ltr: V; Cable: 495.0/48.0 U2	**1992-07 Fukuoka Shipbuilding Co Ltd — Fukuoka FO** Yd No: 1167 Loa 99.90 (BB) Br ex 16.84 Dght 6.763 Lbp 92.50 Br md 16.80 Dpth 8.60 Welded, 1 dk	**(A12B2TR) Chemical/Products Tanker** Double Hull (13F) Liq: 5,221; Liq (Oil): 5,221 Cargo Heating Coils Compartments: 14 Wing Ta, ER, 2 Wing Slop Ta 14 Cargo Pump (s): 8x200m³/hr, 6x125m³/hr Manifold: Bow/CM: 50m Ice Capable	**1 oil engine** driving 1 CP propeller Total Power: 2,574kW (3,500hp) 12.7kn Mitsubishi 6UEC37LA 1 x 2 Stroke 6 Cy. 370 x 880 2574kW (3500bhp) Akasaka Tekkosho KK (Akasaka DieselLtd)-Japan AuxGen: 2 x 400kW 450V 60Hz a.c Boilers: 2 AuxB (o.f.) 8.0kgf/cm² (7.8bar), e (ex.g.) 11.4kgf/cm² (11.2bar) Thrusters: 1 Thwart. CP thruster (f) Fuel: 56.0 (d.f.) (Heating Coils) 326.0 (r.f.) 9.7pd
9156541 **STOLT AZAMI** *VRA02* - **NYK Stolt Shipholding Inc** Stolt Tankers BV SatCom: Inmarsat Mini-M 764365492 *Hong Kong* *Hong Kong* MMSI: 477760700 Official number: HK-1430	**6,356** 3,549 11,564 T/cm 19.7	Class: NK	**1997-09 Fukuoka Shipbuilding Co Ltd — Fukuoka FO** Yd No: 1198 Loa 117.27 (BB) Br ex 20.04 Dght 8.760 Lbp 110.00 Br md 20.00 Dpth 11.20 Welded, 1 dk	**(A12B2TR) Chemical/Products Tanker** Double Hull (13F) Liq: 12,304; Liq (Oil): 12,555 Cargo Heating Coils Compartments: 20 Wing Ta, ER 20 Cargo Pump (s): 8x300m³/hr, 12x200m³/hr Manifold: Bow/CM: 54.1m	**1 oil engine** driving 1 FP propeller Total Power: 3,880kW (5,275hp) 13.5kn B&W 6L35MC 1 x 2 Stroke 6 Cy. 350 x 1050 3880kW (5275bhp) Makita Corp-Japan AuxGen: 3 x 400kW 440V 60Hz a.c Thrusters: 1 Thwart. CP thruster (f) Fuel: 98.0 (d.f.) (Heating Coils) 719.0 (r.f.) 17.0pd
9351543 **STOLT BASUTO** *D5DU4* - *ex* Basuto *-2013* *ex* Stolt Basuto *-2010* **NST Basuto Inc** Stolt Tankers BV *Monrovia* *Liberia* MMSI: 636015972 Official number: 15972	**16,442** 7,460 25,197 T/cm 35.5	Class: AB	**2006-05 Fukuoka Shipbuilding Co Ltd — Nagasaki NS** Yd No: 2005 Loa 158.50 (BB) Br ex 25.63 Dght 10.369 Lbp 150.10 Br md 25.60 Dpth 15.20 Welded, 1 dk	**(A12B2TR) Chemical/Products Tanker** Double Hull (13F) Liq: 30,386; Liq (Oil): 30,390 Cargo Heating Coils Compartments: 4 Ta, 24 Wing Ta, ER 28 Cargo Pump (s): 12x300m³/hr, 16x200m³/hr Manifold: Bow/CM: 78.1m	**1 oil engine** driving 1 FP propeller Total Power: 7,980kW (10,850hp) 15.1kn Mitsubishi 6UEC52LS 1 x 2 Stroke 6 Cy. 520 x 1850 7980kW (10850bhp) Akasaka Tekkosho KK (Akasaka DieselLtd)-Japan AuxGen: 3 x 600kW a.c Thrusters: 1 Thwart. FP thruster (f) Fuel: 142.0 (d.f.) 1287.0 (r.f.)
9511167 **STOLT BOBCAT** *A8XZ9* - *ex* Golden Legend *-2011* **Stolt Bobcat BV** Stolt Tankers BV SatCom: Inmarsat Mini-M 765075523 *Monrovia* *Liberia* MMSI: 636015004 Official number: 15004	**13,517** 7,143 23,432 T/cm 32.4	Class: NK	**2009-07 Kurinoura Dockyard Co Ltd — Yawatahama EH** Yd No: 396 Loa 155.00 (BB) Br ex - Dght 10.217 Lbp 145.00 Br md 24.80 Dpth 13.35 Welded, 1 dk	**(A12B2TR) Chemical/Products Tanker** Double Hull (13F) Liq: 24,725; Liq (Oil): 24,500 Cargo Heating Coils Compartments: 24 Wing Ta, 2 Wing Slop Ta, ER 24 Cargo Pump (s): 12x200m³/hr, 12x150m³/hr Manifold: Bow/CM: 74.9m	**1 oil engine** driving 1 FP propeller Total Power: 7,980kW (10,850hp) 14.6kn Mitsubishi 6UEC52LS 1 x 2 Stroke 6 Cy. 520 x 1850 7980kW (10850bhp) Akasaka Tekkosho KK (Akasaka DieselLtd)-Japan AuxGen: 3 x 530kW a.c Thrusters: 1 Tunnel thruster (f) Fuel: 245.0 (d.f.) 1830.0 (r.f.)
9156553 **STOLT BOTAN** *ELVD6* - **NYK Stolt Shipholding Inc** Stolt Tankers BV SatCom: Inmarsat Mini-M 764661159 *Monrovia* *Liberia* MMSI: 636010835 Official number: 10835	**6,415** 3,549 11,553 T/cm 19.6	Class: NK	**1998-02 Fukuoka Shipbuilding Co Ltd — Fukuoka FO** Yd No: 1199 Loa 117.27 (BB) Br ex 20.03 Dght 8.760 Lbp 110.00 Br md 20.00 Dpth 11.20 Welded, 1 dk	**(A12B2TR) Chemical/Products Tanker** Double Hull (13F) Liq: 11,463; Liq (Oil): 12,553 Cargo Heating Coils Compartments: 18 Wing Ta, 2 Wing Slop Ta, ER 18 Cargo Pump (s): 8x300m³/hr, 10x200m³/hr Manifold: Bow/CM: 54.1m	**1 oil engine** driving 1 FP propeller Total Power: 3,880kW (5,275hp) 13.5kn B&W 6L35MC 1 x 2 Stroke 6 Cy. 350 x 1050 3880kW (5275bhp) Makita Corp-Japan AuxGen: 3 x 400kW 440V 60Hz a.c Thrusters: 1 Thwart. CP thruster (f) Fuel: 95.0 (d.f.) (Heating Coils) 708.0 (r.f.) 17.0pd
9414084 **STOLT BRELAND** *ZCXH* - **Stolt Breland BV** Stolt Tankers BV SatCom: Inmarsat Mini-M 765041172 *George Town* *Cayman Islands (British)* MMSI: 319017500 Official number: 740670	**25,881** 13,418 43,475 T/cm 48.5	Class: NV	**2010-03 Wadan Yards Okean OJSC — Nikolayev** (Fwd & aft sections) **2010-03 STX Norway Floro AS — Floro** (Main cargo section) Yd No: 154 Loa 182.72 (BB) Br ex 32.24 Dght 11.870 Lbp 175.22 Br md 32.20 Dpth 15.60 Welded, 1 dk	**(A12B2TR) Chemical/Products Tanker** Double Hull (13F) Liq: 44,495; Liq (Oil): 45,350 Cargo Heating Coils Compartments: 13 Ta, 26 Wing Ta, ER 39 Cargo Pump (s): 24x385m³/hr, 15x220m³/hr Manifold: Bow/CM: 96m	**1 oil engine** driving 1 CP propeller Total Power: 11,060kW (15,037hp) 15.0kn MAN-B&W 7S50MC-C 1 x 2 Stroke 7 Cy. 500 x 2000 11060kW (15037bhp) MAN Diesel A/S-Denmark AuxGen: 2 x 1330kW a.c, 1 x 1100kW a.c Thrusters: 1 Tunnel thruster (f) Fuel: 168.0 (d.f.) 1942.0 (r.f.)

IMO / Call sign	Name / Owner / Manager	Tonnage	Class	Build / Dimensions	Type / Cargo	Machinery
9102124 *ELSN9* -	**STOLT CAPABILITY** **NST Capability Inc** Stolt Tankers BV SatCom: Inmarsat Mini-M 764863572 *Monrovia* *Liberia* MMSI: 636010380 Official number: 10380	**24,625** 11,933 37,042 T/cm 48.6	Class: NV	**1998**-07 **Danyard A/S — Frederikshavn** Yd No: 736 Loa 176.75 (BB) Br ex 31.08 Dght 11.906 Lbp 168.50 Br md 31.00 Dpth 15.62 Welded, 1 dk	**(A12B2TR) Chemical/Products Tanker** Double Hull (13F) Liq: 39,804; Liq (Oil): 39,804 Compartments: 16 Ta (s.stl), 1 Wing Ta, 27 Wing Ta (s.stl), ER (s.stl) 48 Cargo Pump (s): 31x200m³/hr, 17x300m³/hr Manifold: Bow/CM: 86.3m	**4 diesel electric oil engines** driving 3 gen. each 3520kW 6600V a.c 1 gen. of 2350kW 6600V a.c Connecting to 1 elec. Motor of (10000kW) driving 1 FP propeller Total Power: 13,365kW (18,172hp) 16.2kn Wartsila 6R32LN 1 x 4 Stroke 6 Cy. 320 x 350 2430kW (3304bhp) Wartsila NSD Finland Oy-Finland Wartsila 9R32LN 3 x 4 Stroke 9 Cy. 320 x 350 each-3645kW (4956bhp) Wartsila NSD Finland Oy-Finland Thrusters: 1 Thwart. CP thruster (f) Fuel: 153.0 (d.f.) (Heating Coils) 2107.0 (r.f.) 56.8pd
9168647 *ZGBH8* -	**STOLT COMMITMENT** *ex* Bow Century *-2011* **Stolt Commitment BV** Stolt Tankers BV SatCom: Inmarsat B 331900028 *George Town* *Cayman Islands (British)* MMSI: 319025300	**23,206** 11,915 37,438 T/cm 50.2	Class: NV	**2000**-01 **Kvaerner Floro AS — Floro** Yd No: 139 Loa 183.10 (BB) Br ex 32.23 Dght 10.720 Lbp 176.90 Br md 32.20 Dpth 14.00 Welded, 1 dk	**(A12B2TR) Chemical/Products Tanker** Double Hull (13F) Liq: 39,820; Liq (Oil): 39,822 Cargo Heating Coils Compartments: ER (s.stl), 24 Wing Ta (s.stl), 19 Ta (s.stl), ER 47 Cargo Pump (s): 5x500m³/hr, 14x300m³/hr, 24x200m³/hr, 4x100m³/hr Manifold: Bow/CM: 95.3m Ice Capable	**1 oil engine** driving 1 CP propeller Total Power: 10,416kW (14,162hp) 15.5kn B&W 6L60MC 1 x 2 Stroke 6 Cy. 600 x 1944 10416kW (14162bhp) Manises Diesel Engine Co. S.A.-Valencia AuxGen: 1 x 1100kW 450V 60Hz a.c, 2 x 1260kW 450V 60Hz a.c Thrusters: 1 Thwart. CP thruster (f) Fuel: 235.0 (d.f.) (Part Heating Coils) 1571.0 (r.f.) 43.0pd
9178197 *ZCSP2* -	**STOLT CONCEPT** **Stolt Concept BV** Stolt Tankers BV SatCom: Inmarsat Mini-M 764859474 *George Town* *Cayman Islands (British)* MMSI: 319479000 Official number: 732878	**24,495** 11,919 37,236 T/cm 48.6	Class: NV	**1999**-05 **Danyard A/S — Frederikshavn** Yd No: 737 Loa 176.75 (BB) Br ex 31.10 Dght 11.869 Lbp 168.50 Br md 31.00 Dpth 15.60 Welded, 1 dk	**(A12B2TR) Chemical/Products Tanker** Double Hull (13F) Liq: 39,806; Liq (Oil): 39,806 Compartments: 12 Ta (s.stl), 32 Wing Ta (s.stl), ER (s.stl) 47 Cargo Pump (s): 17x300m³/hr, 29x200m³/hr, 1x150m³/hr Manifold: Bow/CM: 86.4m	**4 diesel electric oil engines** driving 4 gen. each 3520kW 6600V a.c Connecting to 1 elec. Motor of (10000kW) driving 1 FP propeller Total Power: 14,760kW (20,068hp) 16.2kn Wartsila 9R32 4 x 4 Stroke 9 Cy. 320 x 350 each-3690kW (5017bhp) Wartsila NSD Finland Oy-Finland Thrusters: 1 Thwart. FP thruster (f) Fuel: 153.0 (d.f.) 2026.0 (r.f.)
9102071 *ZCSP3* -	**STOLT CONFIDENCE** **Stolt Confidence BV** Stolt Tankers BV SatCom: Inmarsat Mini-M 764647098 *George Town* *Cayman Islands (British)* MMSI: 319468000 Official number: 732879	**24,839** 12,146 37,090 T/cm 48.6	Class: NV	**1996**-11 **Danyard A/S — Frederikshavn** Yd No: 731 Loa 176.75 (BB) Br ex 31.08 Dght 11.912 Lbp 168.50 Br md 31.00 Dpth 15.62 Welded, 1 dk	**(A12B2TR) Chemical/Products Tanker** Double Hull (13F) Liq: 40,494; Liq (Oil): 38,404 Cargo Heating Coils Compartments: 14 Ta (s.stl), 1 Wing Ta, 29 Wing Ta (s.stl), ER (s.stl) 48 Cargo Pump (s): 31x200m³/hr, 17x300m³/hr Manifold: Bow/CM: 86.4m	**4 diesel electric oil engines** driving 4 gen. each 3500kW 6600V a.c Connecting to 1 elec. Motor of (10000kW) driving 1 FP propeller Total Power: 14,580kW (19,824hp) 16.2kn Wartsila 9R32LN 4 x 4 Stroke 9 Cy. 320 x 350 each-3645kW (4956bhp) Wartsila Diesel Oy-Finland AuxGen: 4 x a.c Thrusters: 1 Tunnel thruster (f) Fuel: 153.0 (d.f.) 2030.0 (r.f.) 53.2pd
9148960 *ZCSE5* -	**STOLT CORMORANT** **DS-Rendite-Fonds Nr 99 CFS GmbH & Co Produktentanker KG** Stolt Tankers BV SatCom: Inmarsat C 431930145 *George Town* *Cayman Islands (British)* MMSI: 319301000 Official number: 732459	**3,818** 1,518 5,509 T/cm 14.4	Class: LR (RI) (NV) **100A1** SS 08/2009 Double Hull oil & chemical tanker, Ship Type 2 CR (s.stl) SG 1.85 and PV+0.25 bar gauge all tanks, SG 0.86 and PV+0.6 bar gauge all tanks, SG 1.025 and PV+0.25 bar gauge all tanks, SG 2.2 (70% full) and PV+0.25 bar gauge all tanks, maximum carriage temperature 95 degrees C ESP *IWS LI Ice Class 1B at a draught of 6.50m Max/min draughts fwd 6.5/4.0m Max/min draughts aft 6.5/4.0m Power required 2320kw, power installed 2800kw **LMC** **UMS** Eq.Ltr: Q; Cable: 467.5/40.0 U2	**1999**-10 **INMA SpA — La Spezia** Yd No: 4261 Loa 96.19 (BB) Br ex 16.33 Dght 6.546 Lbp 91.20 Br md 16.20 Dpth 8.00 Welded, 1 dk	**(A12B2TR) Chemical/Products Tanker** Double Hull (13F) Liq: 5,360; Liq (Oil): 5,360 Compartments: 16 Wing Ta, ER 16 Cargo Pump (s): 16x200m³/hr Manifold: Bow/CM: 48.7m Ice Capable	**4 diesel electric oil engines** driving 4 gen. each 896kW 440V a.c Connecting to 1 elec. Motor of (2800kW) driving 1 FP propeller Total Power: 3,720kW (5,056hp) 12.5kn Wartsila 6L20 4 x 4 Stroke 6 Cy. 200 x 280 each-930kW (1264bhp) Wartsila NSD Finland Oy-Finland Boilers: 2 TOH (o.f.) Thrusters: 1 Thwart. FP thruster (f) Fuel: 131.0 (d.f.) 336.0 (r.f.)
9296731 *D5BG8* -	**STOLT COURAGE** **Stolt Courage BV** Stolt Tankers BV *Monrovia* *Liberia* MMSI: 636015517 Official number: 15517	**20,058** 8,695 32,858 T/cm 41.5	Class: BV	**2004**-06 **Shin Kurushima Dockyard Co. Ltd. — Onishi** Yd No: 5275 Loa 174.38 (BB) Br ex 27.73 Dght 10.730 Lbp 167.00 Br md 27.70 Dpth 16.00 Welded, 1 dk	**(A12B2TR) Chemical/Products Tanker** Double Hull (13F) Liq: 35,452; Liq (Oil): 35,452 Cargo Heating Coils Compartments: 14 Wing Ta (s.stl), 2 Wing Slop Ta (s.stl), ER 14 Cargo Pump (s): 14x300m³/hr Manifold: Bow/CM: 89.3m	**1 oil engine** driving 1 FP propeller Total Power: 7,980kW (10,850hp) 15.0kn B&W 6S50MC 1 x 2 Stroke 6 Cy. 500 x 1910 7980kW (10850bhp) Mitsui Engineering & Shipbuilding CLtd-Japan AuxGen: 3 x 600kW 450/100V 60Hz a.c Fuel: 123.0 (d.f.) 1621.0 (r.f.)
9102095 *ZCSP4* -	**STOLT CREATIVITY** **Stolt Creativity BV** Stolt Tankers BV SatCom: Inmarsat Mini-M 764682413 *George Town* *Cayman Islands (British)* MMSI: 319498000 Official number: 732880	**24,625** 11,934 37,271 T/cm 48.6	Class: NV	**1997**-08 **Danyard A/S — Frederikshavn** Yd No: 733 Loa 176.75 (BB) Br ex 31.08 Dght 11.909 Lbp 168.50 Br md 31.00 Dpth 15.62 Welded, 1 dk	**(A12B2TR) Chemical/Products Tanker** Double Hull (13F) Liq: 39,808; Liq (Oil): 39,808 Cargo Heating Coils Compartments: 18 Ta (s.stl), 24 Wing Ta (s.stl), ER 46 Cargo Pump (s): 29x200m³/hr, 17x300m³/hr Manifold: Bow/CM: 86.4m	**4 diesel electric oil engines** driving 3 gen. each 3500kW 6600V 1 gen. of 2350kW 6600V Connecting to 1 elec. Motor of (10000kW) driving 1 FP propeller Total Power: 13,365kW (18,172hp) 16.2kn Wartsila 6R32LN 1 x 4 Stroke 6 Cy. 320 x 350 2430kW (3304bhp) Wartsila Diesel Oy-Finland Wartsila 9R32LN 3 x 4 Stroke 9 Cy. 320 x 350 each-3645kW (4956bhp) Wartsila Diesel Oy-Finland Thrusters: 1 Thwart. CP thruster (f) Fuel: 153.0 (d.f.) 2096.0 (r.f.) 60.0pd
8920531 *ZCMY3* -	**STOLT DIPPER** *ex* Margit Terkol *-1996* *ex* Stolt Margit Terkol *-1994* **Stolt Dipper BV** Stolt Tankers BV SatCom: Inmarsat C 431902677 *George Town* *Cayman Islands (British)* MMSI: 319036000 Official number: 731158	**3,206** 1,356 4,738 T/cm 12.4	Class: LR ✠ **100A1** SS 04/2012 Double Hull oil and chemical tanker, Ship Type 2* MARPOL 13H (1) (b) SG 1.8 cargo tanks 3, 4, 5 & 6, SG 1.2 cargo tanks 1, 2 & 7, CR (s.stl) ESP Ice Class 1D ✠ **LMC** **UMS** Eq.Ltr: U; Cable: 467.5/46.0 U2	**1992**-04 **Aarhus Flydedok A/S — Aarhus** Yd No: 199 Loa 96.35 (BB) Br ex 15.32 Dght 6.200 Lbp 87.75 Br md 15.10 Dpth 8.05 Welded, 1 dk	**(A12B2TR) Chemical/Products Tanker** Double Hull (13F) Liq: 4,653; Liq (Oil): 4,654 Cargo Heating Coils Compartments: 1 Ta, 12 Wing Ta, ER, 2 Wing Slop Ta 13 Cargo Pump (s): 13x150m³/hr Manifold: Bow/CM: 49.4m Ice Capable	**1 oil engine** with clutches, flexible couplings & sr geared to sc. shaft driving 1 CP propeller Total Power: 2,999kW (4,077hp) 13.2kn MaK 9M453C 1 x 4 Stroke 9 Cy. 320 x 420 2999kW (4077bhp) Krupp MaK Maschinenbau GmbH-Kiel AuxGen: 1 x 633kW 380V 50Hz a.c, 3 x 335kW 380V 50Hz a.c Boilers: 2 TOH (o.f.) 8.2kgf/cm² (8.0bar), TOH (ex.g.) 8.2kgf/cm² (8.0bar) Thrusters: 1 Thwart. CP thruster (f) Fuel: 63.0 (d.f.) (Part Heating Coils) 535.0 (r.f.) 11.0pd
9276145 *VRIC3* -	**STOLT DISTRIBUTOR** **Stolt Distributor Inc** Stolt Tankers BV *Hong Kong* *Hong Kong* MMSI: 477266100	**2,700** 1,096 3,992 T/cm 11.3	Class: BV	**2002**-12 **Nichizo Iron Works & Marine Corp — Onomichi HS** Yd No: 165 Loa 92.50 (BB) Br ex 15.00 Dght 5.800 Lbp 85.00 Br md 14.86 Dpth 7.20 Welded, 1 dk	**(A12B2TR) Chemical/Products Tanker** Double Hull (13F) Liq: 3,944; Liq (Oil): 3,944 Cargo Heating Coils Compartments: 1 Ta (s.stl), 8 Wing Ta (s.stl), ER 9 Cargo Pump (s): 8x150m³/hr, 1x70m³/hr Manifold: Bow/CM: 40.1m	**1 oil engine** driving 1 FP propeller Total Power: 2,574kW (3,500hp) 12.5kn Hanshin LH41LA 1 x 4 Stroke 6 Cy. 410 x 800 2574kW (3500bhp) The Hanshin Diesel Works Ltd-Japan AuxGen: 2 x 360kW 440/100V 60Hz a.c Fuel: 72.0 (d.f.) (Heating Coils) 346.0 (r.f.) 8.5pd

9102112 ZCSP5 -
STOLT EFFICIENCY
Stolt Efficiency BV
Stolt Tankers BV
SatCom: Inmarsat C 431948878
George Town *Cayman Islands (British)*
MMSI: 319488000
Official number: 732881

24,625 11,933 36,902 T/cm 48.6

Class: NV

1998-03 **Danyard A/S — Frederikshavn** Yd No: 735
Loa 176.75 (BB) Br ex 31.08 Dght 11.903
Lbp 168.50 Br md 31.00 Dpth 15.62
Welded, 1 dk

(A12B2TR) Chemical/Products Tanker
Double Hull (13F)
Liq: 39,806; Liq (Oil): 39,806
Compartments: 12 Ta (s.stl), 24 Wing Ta (s.stl), 8 Wing Ta, ER
4 x Gas Tank (s); 4 independent (stl) cyl horizontal
48 Cargo Pump (s): 31x200m^3/hr, 17x300m^3/hr
Manifold: Bow/CM: 86.4m

4 diesel electric oil engines driving 3 gen. each 3520kW 6600V 1 gen. of 2344kW 6600V Connecting to 1 elec. Motor of (10000kW) driving 1 FP propeller
Total Power: 13,365kW (18,172hp) 16.2kn
Wartsila 6R32LNE
1 x 4 Stroke 6 Cy. 320 x 350 2430kW (3304bhp)
Wartsila NSD Finland Oy-Finland
Wartsila 9R32LN
3 x 4 Stroke 9 Cy. 320 x 350 each-3645kW (4956bhp)
Wartsila NSD Finland Oy-Finland
Thrusters: 1 Thwart. FP thruster (f)
Fuel: 140.0 (d.f.) 1925.0 (r.f.) 60.0pd

9178202 ZCSP6 -
STOLT EFFORT
Stolt Effort BV
Stolt Tankers BV
SatCom: Inmarsat C 431944510
George Town *Cayman Islands (British)*
MMSI: 319445000
Official number: 732882

24,495 11,919 37,155 T/cm 48.6

Class: NV

1999-12 **Danyard A/S — Frederikshavn** Yd No: 738
Loa 176.75 (BB) Br ex 31.10 Dght 11.855
Lbp 168.50 Br md 31.00 Dpth 15.63
Welded, 1 dk

(A12B2TR) Chemical/Products Tanker
Double Hull (13F)
Liq: 39,806; Liq (Oil): 39,818
Cargo Heating Coils
Compartments: 12 Ta, 28 Wing Ta, 4 Wing Slop Ta, ER
44 Cargo Pump (s): 17x300m^3/hr, 27x200m^3/hr
Manifold: Bow/CM: 86.4m

4 diesel electric oil engines driving 3 gen. each 3500kW a.c 1 gen. of 2400kW a.c Connecting to 1 elec. Motor of (10000kW) driving 1 FP propeller
Total Power: 13,523kW (18,385hp) 16.2kn
Wartsila 6R32
1 x 4 Stroke 6 Cy. 320 x 350 2450kW (3331bhp)
Wartsila NSD Finland Oy-Finland
Wartsila 9R32
3 x 4 Stroke 9 Cy. 320 x 350 each-3691kW (5018bhp)
Wartsila NSD Finland Oy-Finland
Thrusters: 1 Tunnel thruster (f)
Fuel: 153.0 (d.f.) 2069.0 (r.f.)

9004308 ZCFE4 -
STOLT EGRET
Stolt Egret BV
Stolt Tankers BV
SatCom: Inmarsat B 331963310
George Town *Cayman Islands (British)*
MMSI: 319633000
Official number: 733851

3,853 1,557 5,758 T/cm 13.7

Class: LR (NK)
100A1 SS 04/2012
Double Hull oil and chemical tanker, MARPOL 13G (1) (c), Ship Type 2
CR (s.stl), SG 1.55
ESP
LMC **UMS**
Eq.Ltr: V; Cable: 495.0/48.0 U2

1992-04 **Fukuoka Shipbuilding Co Ltd — Fukuoka FO** Yd No: 1166
Loa 99.90 (BB) Br ex 17.06 Dght 6.763
Lbp 92.50 Br md 16.80 Dpth 8.60
Welded, 1 dk

(A12B2TR) Chemical/Products Tanker
Double Hull (13F)
Liq: 5,221; Liq (Oil): 5,523
Cargo Heating Coils
Compartments: 14 Wing Ta, 2 Wing Slop Ta, ER
14 Cargo Pump (s): 8x200m^3/hr, 6x125m^3/hr
Manifold: Bow/CM: 48.7m

1 oil engine driving 1 CP propeller
Total Power: 2,574kW (3,500hp) 12.7kn
Mitsubishi 6UEC37LA
1 x 2 Stroke 6 Cy. 370 x 880 2574kW (3500bhp)
Akasaka Tekkosho KK (Akasaka DieselLtd)-Japan
AuxGen: 2 x 400kW 450V 60Hz a.c
Boilers: 2 AuxB (o.f.) 8.0kgf/cm^2 (7.8bar), e (ex.g.) 11.5kgf/cm^2 (11.3bar)
Thrusters: 1 Thwart. CP thruster (f)
Fuel: 77.0 (d.f.) 326.0 (r.f.)

8309543 ZCSQ3 -
STOLT EMERALD
Stolt Emerald BV
Stolt Tankers BV
SatCom: Inmarsat B 331942911
George Town *Cayman Islands (British)*
MMSI: 319429000
Official number: 732888

23,964 13,720 38,719 T/cm 48.8

Class: NV

1986-04 **Daewoo Shipbuilding & Heavy Machinery Ltd — Geoje** Yd No: 2008
Loa 176.80 (BB) Br ex 32.25 Dght 11.428
Lbp 169.50 Br md 32.25 Dpth 15.00
Welded, 1 dk

(A12B2TR) Chemical/Products Tanker
Double Hull (13F)
Liq: 44,020; Liq (Oil): 45,430
Compartments: 32 Ta (s.stl), 22 Wing Ta, ER
58 Cargo Pump (s): 46x255m^3/hr, 12x450m^3/hr
Manifold: Bow/CM: 80.7m

1 oil engine driving 1 FP propeller
Total Power: 9,179kW (12,480hp) 15.0kn
B&W 6L60MCE
1 x 2 Stroke 6 Cy. 600 x 1944 9179kW (12480bhp)
Hyundai Engine & Machinery Co Ltd-South Korea
AuxGen: 3 x 900kW 450V 60Hz a.c, 1 x a.c
Thrusters: 1 Thwart. FP thruster (f)
Fuel: 277.0 (d.f.) 1904.0 (r.f.) 35.0pd

9284697 D5BW5 -
STOLT ENDURANCE
Stolt Endurance BV
Stolt Tankers BV
Monrovia *Liberia*
MMSI: 636015619
Official number: 15619

20,058 8,489 32,858 T/cm 41.5

Class: BV

2004-08 **Shin Kurushima Dockyard Co. Ltd. — Onishi** Yd No: 5276
Loa 174.38 (BB) Br ex 27.73 Dght 10.730
Lbp 167.00 Br md 27.70 Dpth 16.00
Welded, 1 dk

(A12B2TR) Chemical/Products Tanker
Double Hull (13F)
Liq: 35,472; Liq (Oil): 35,472
Cargo Heating Coils
Compartments: 14 Wing Ta, ER, 2 Wing Slop Ta
14 Cargo Pump (s): 14x300m^3/hr
Manifold: Bow/CM: 89.3m

1 oil engine driving 1 FP propeller
Total Power: 7,980kW (10,850hp) 15.0kn
B&W 6S50MC
1 x 2 Stroke 6 Cy. 500 x 1910 7980kW (10850bhp)
Mitsui Engineering & Shipbuilding CLtd-Japan
AuxGen: 3 x 600kW 450/100V 60Hz a.c
Fuel: 123.0 (d.f.) 1621.0 (r.f.)

9359363 ZCXZ4 -
STOLT FACTO
Stolt Gulf Parcel Tanker 1 Ltd
Gulf Stolt Ship Management JLT
George Town *Cayman Islands (British)*
MMSI: 319280000
Official number: 740764

26,328 14,416 46,011 T/cm 52.2

Class: NV

2010-03 **SLS Shipbuilding Co Ltd — Tongyeong** Yd No: 473
Loa 182.88 (BB) Br ex 32.23 Dght 12.070
Lbp 175.60 Br md 32.20 Dpth 16.05
Welded, 1 dk

(A12B2TR) Chemical/Products Tanker
Double Hull (13F)
Liq: 47,729; Liq (Oil): 47,729
Cargo Heating Coils
Compartments: 9 Ta, 20 Wing Ta, ER
29 Cargo Pump (s): 15x220m^3/hr, 14x360m^3/hr
Manifold: Bow/CM: 90.7m

1 oil engine driving 1 FP propeller
Total Power: 11,300kW (15,363hp) 14.5kn
MAN-B&W 5S60MC-C
1 x 2 Stroke 5 Cy. 600 x 2400 11300kW (15363bhp)
STX Engine Co Ltd-South Korea
AuxGen: 3 x a.c
Thrusters: 1 Tunnel thruster (f)
Fuel: 122.4 (d.f.) 2048.5 (r.f.)

9391995 ZGAH7
STOLT FLAMENCO
launched as Sichem Nile *-2010*
Lily Ship Holding SA
Stolt Tankers BV
George Town *Cayman Islands (British)*
MMSI: 319017600

7,603 3,760 12,270 T/cm 21.6

Class: BV

2010-03 **Sasaki Shipbuilding Co Ltd — Osakikamijima HS** Yd No: 667
Loa 123.85 (BB) Br ex 20.02 Dght 8.910
Lbp 116.00 Br md 20.00 Dpth 11.50
Welded, 1 dk

(A12B2TR) Chemical/Products Tanker
Double Hull (13F)
Liq: 12,411; Liq (Oil): 12,411
Cargo Heating Coils
Compartments: 18 Wing Ta, 2 Wing Slop Ta, ER
18 Cargo Pump (s): 18x200m^3/hr
Manifold: Bow/CM: 61.6m

1 oil engine driving 1 FP propeller
Total Power: 4,440kW (6,037hp) 13.5kn
MAN-B&W 6S35MC
1 x 2 Stroke 6 Cy. 350 x 1400 4440kW (6037bhp)
Hitachi Zosen Corp-Japan
AuxGen: 3 x 750kW 60Hz a.c
Thrusters: 1 Tunnel thruster (f)
Fuel: 120.0 (d.f.) 581.0 (r.f.)

9214305 ZGBG -
STOLT FOCUS
ex Bow Favour *-2011*
Stolt Focus BV
Stolt Tankers BV
SatCom: Inmarsat B 331960211
George Town *Cayman Islands (British)*
MMSI: 319602000

23,190 11,915 37,467 T/cm 50.2

Class: NV

2001-09 **Kleven Floro AS — Floro** Yd No: 142
Loa 183.10 (BB) Br ex 32.23 Dght 10.718
Lbp 176.00 Br md 32.20 Dpth 14.00
Welded, 1 dk

(A12B2TR) Chemical/Products Tanker
Double Hull (13F)
Liq: 39,822; Liq (Oil): 39,822
Compartments: 19 Ta, 24 Wing Ta, ER
47 Cargo Pump (s): 5x500m^3/hr, 10x300m^3/hr, 28x200m^3/hr, 4x100m^3/hr
Manifold: Bow/CM: 95.8m
Ice Capable

1 oil engine driving 1 CP propeller
Total Power: 10,415kW (14,160hp) 16.0kn
B&W 7S50MC-C
1 x 2 Stroke 7 Cy. 500 x 2000 10415kW (14160bhp)
MAN B&W Diesel A/S-Denmark
AuxGen: 1 x 1100kW 450V 60Hz a.c, 2 x 1200kW 450V 60Hz a.c
Thrusters: 1 Thwart. FP thruster (f)
Fuel: 230.0 (d.f.) 1694.0 (r.f.)

9468528 2EGO8
STOLT FUJI
Stolt Fuji BV
Stolt Tankers BV
773156614
Cardiff *United Kingdom*
MMSI: 235084915
Official number: 917237

5,539 1,661 6,065 T/cm 16.6

Class: LR
✠ **100A1** SS 10/2010
Double Hull oil & asphalt tanker carriage of oil with a FP exceeding 60 degree C, cargo temp. 200 degree C, in independent tanks
SG 1.04t/m3
pv+0.21 bar gauge
LI
*IWS
✠ **LMC** **UMS**
Eq.Ltr: X;
Cable: 495.0/46.0 U3 (a)

2010-10 **Xinshun Shipyard Group Co Ltd — Yueqing ZJ** Yd No: XS-0805
Loa 106.99 (BB) Br ex 17.62 Dght 6.500
Lbp 101.50 Br md 17.59 Dpth 10.08
Welded, 1 dk

(A13C2LA) Asphalt/Bitumen Tanker
Double Hull (13F)
Liq: 5,680; Liq (Oil): 5,680
Cargo Heating Coils
Compartments: 8 Wing Ta, 2 Wing Slop Ta, ER
2 Cargo Pump (s): 2x400m^3/hr
Manifold: Bow/CM: 49.6m

1 oil engine with clutches, flexible couplings & sr reverse geared to sc. shaft driving 1 CP propeller
Total Power: 3,060kW (4,160hp) 13.0kn
Wartsila 9L26
1 x 4 Stroke 9 Cy. 260 x 320 3060kW (4160bhp)
Wartsila Finland Oy-Finland
AuxGen: 3 x 360kW 440V 60Hz a.c
Boilers: TOH (o.f.) 10.2kgf/cm^2 (10.0bar), TOH (ex.g.) 10.2kgf/cm^2 (10.0bar)
Thrusters: 1 Thwart. CP thruster (f)
Fuel: 111.0 (d.f.) 407.0 (r.f.)

9148972 ZCSY9 -
STOLT FULMAR
DS-Rendite-Fonds Nr 99 CFS GmbH & Co Produktentanker KG
Stolt Tankers BV
SatCom: Inmarsat C 431954147
George Town *Cayman Islands (British)*
MMSI: 319541000
Official number: 733358

3,818 1,518 5,498 T/cm 14.4

Class: LR (RI) (NV)
100A1 SS 08/2010
Double Hull oil & chemical tanker, Ship Type 2
CR (s.stl)
SG 1.85 and PV+0.25 bar gauge all tanks,
SG 0.86 and PV+0.6 bar gauge all tanks,
SG 1.025 and PV+0.25 bar gauge all tanks,
SG 2.2 (70% full) and PV+0.25 bar gauge all tanks,
maximum carriage temperature 95 degrees C
ESP
*IWS
LI
Ice Class 1B at a draught of 6.50m
Max/min draughts fwd 6.5/4.0m
Max/min draughts aft 6.5/4.0m
Power required 2320kw, power installed 2800kw
LMC **UMS**
Eq.Ltr: Q; Cable: 467.5/40.0 U2

2000-08 **INMA SpA — La Spezia** Yd No: 4262
Loa 96.19 (BB) Br ex 16.31 Dght 6.521
Lbp 91.22 Br md 16.20 Dpth 8.03
Welded, 1 dk

(A12B2TR) Chemical/Products Tanker
Double Hull (13F)
Liq: 5,370; Liq (Oil): 5,370
Compartments: 16 Wing Ta (s.stl), ER
16 Cargo Pump (s): 16x200m^3/hr
Manifold: Bow/CM: 48.7m
Ice Capable

4 diesel electric oil engines driving 4 gen. each 980kW 450V Connecting to 1 elec. Motor of (2800kW) driving 1 FP propeller
Total Power: 3,720kW (5,056hp) 13.0kn
Wartsila 6L20
4 x 4 Stroke 6 Cy. 200 x 280 each-930kW (1264bhp)
Wartsila Finland Oy-Finland
Boilers: 2 TOH (o.f.)
Thrusters: 1 Thwart. FP thruster (f)
Fuel: 15.0 (d.f.) 336.0 (r.f.)

9311012 *A8XT9* -	**STOLT GLORY** *ex* Glory *-2013* *ex* Stolt Glory *-2010* **Stolt Glory BV** Stolt Tankers BV SatCom: Inmarsat Mini-M 765070864 *Monrovia* *Liberia* MMSI: 636014973 Official number: 14973	**20,059** 9,017 33,302 T/cm 41.7	Class: BV	**2005**-09 **Shin Kurushima Dockyard Co. Ltd. — Onishi** Yd No: 5325 Loa 174.38 (BB) Br ex 27.73 Dght 11.023 Lbp 167.00 Br md 27.70 Dpth 16.00 Welded, 1 dk	**(A12B2TR) Chemical/Products Tanker** Double Hull (13F) Liq: 34,942; Liq (Oil): 37,388 Cargo Heating Coils Compartments: 26 Wing Ta, 2 Wing Slop Ta, ER 26 Cargo Pump (s): 26x300m³/hr Manifold: Bow/CM: 86.4m	**1 oil engine** driving 1 FP propeller Total Power: 7,980kW (10,850hp) 15.0kn B&W 6S50MC 1 x 2 Stroke 6 Cy. 500 x 1910 7980kW (10850bhp) Mitsui Engineering & Shipbuilding CLtd-Japan AuxGen: 3 x 600kW 450/100V 60Hz a.c Thrusters: 1 Tunnel thruster (f) Fuel: 123.0 (d.f.) 1621.0 (r.f.)
9518799 *2GFD9* -	**STOLT GREENSHANK** *ex* Brovig Barat *-2013* **Brovig Stainless AS** Stolt Tankers BV *Cardiff* *United Kingdom* MMSI: 235096859	**3,327** 1,357 4,350 T/cm 12.9	Class: BV	**2011**-02 **Chongqing Chuandong Shipbuilding Industry Co Ltd — Chongqing** Yd No: HT0119 Loa 90.90 (BB) Br ex - Dght 6.000 Lbp 85.00 Br md 15.60 Dpth 7.80 Welded, 1 dk	**(A12B2TR) Chemical/Products Tanker** Double Hull (13F) Liq: 4,305; Liq (Oil): 4,357 Cargo Heating Coils Compartments: 8 Wing Ta, 2 Wing Slop Ta, ER 8 Cargo Pump (s): 8x200m³/hr Manifold: Bow/CM: 47m Ice Capable	**1 oil engine** reduction geared to sc. shaft driving 1 CP propeller Total Power: 2,640kW (3,589hp) 12.8kn MaK 8M25C 1 x 4 Stroke 8 Cy. 255 x 400 2640kW (3589bhp) Caterpillar Motoren GmbH & Co. KG-Germany AuxGen: 3 x 360kW 450V 60Hz a.c, 1 x 400kW 450V 60Hz a.c Thrusters: 1 Tunnel thruster (f) Fuel: 63.0 (d.f.) 319.0 (r.f.)
9414072 *ZCXG9* -	**STOLT GROENLAND** **Stolt Groenland BV** Stolt Tankers BV SatCom: Inmarsat C 431900235 *George Town* *Cayman Islands (British)* MMSI: 319014300 Official number: 740669	**25,881** 13,418 43,478 T/cm 48.5	Class: NV	**2009**-12 **Wadan Yards Okean OJSC — Nikolayev** (Fwd & aft sections) **2009**-12 **STX Norway Floro AS — Floro** (Main cargo section) Yd No: 153 Loa 182.72 (BB) Br ex 32.24 Dght 11.887 Lbp 175.22 Br md 32.20 Dpth 15.60 Welded, 1 dk	**(A12B2TR) Chemical/Products Tanker** Double Hull (13F) Liq: 44,495; Liq (Oil): 45,350 Cargo Heating Coils Compartments: 13 Ta, 26 Wing Ta, ER 39 Cargo Pump (s): 24x385m³/hr, 15x220m³/hr Manifold: Bow/CM: 96m	**1 oil engine** driving 1 CP propeller Total Power: 11,060kW (15,037hp) 15.0kn MAN-B&W 7S50MC-C 1 x 2 Stroke 7 Cy. 500 x 2000 11060kW (15037bhp) MAN Diesel A/S-Denmark AuxGen: 2 x 1330kW a.c, 1 x 1100kW a.c Thrusters: 1 Tunnel thruster (f) Fuel: 170.0 (d.f.) 1945.0 (r.f.)
8920581 *MAIZ* -	**STOLT GUILLEMOT** *ex* Sasi Terkol *-1996* **Stolt Guillemot BV** Stolt Tankers BV SatCom: Inmarsat C 423500017 *Cardiff* *United Kingdom* MMSI: 235050033 Official number: 731142	**3,204** 1,356 4,676 T/cm 12.4	Class: LR ✠ **100A1** SS 10/2013 Double Hull oil and chemical tanker, Ship Type 2* MARPOL 13H (1) (b) SG 1.8 cargo tanks 3, 4, 5 & 6, SG 1.2 cargo tanks 1,2 & 7, CR (s.stl) ESP Ice Class 1B ✠ **LMC** **UMS** Eq.Ltr: U; Cable: 468.0/46.0 U2	**1993**-10 **Aarhus Flydedok A/S — Aarhus** Yd No: 204 Loa 96.35 (BB) Br ex 15.33 Dght 6.200 Lbp 87.75 Br md 15.10 Dpth 8.05 Welded, 1 dk	**(A12B2TR) Chemical/Products Tanker** Double Hull (13F) Liq: 4,655; Liq (Oil): 4,653 Cargo Heating Coils Compartments: 1 Ta, 12 Wing Ta, 1 Wing Slop Ta, 1 Slop Ta, ER 13 Cargo Pump (s): 13x150m³/hr Manifold: Bow/CM: 49.5m Ice Capable	**1 oil engine** with clutches, flexible couplings & sr geared to sc. shaft driving 1 CP propeller Total Power: 3,000kW (4,079hp) 13.0kn MaK 9M453C 1 x 4 Stroke 9 Cy. 320 x 420 3000kW (4079bhp) Krupp MaK Maschinenbau GmbH-Kiel AuxGen: 1 x 633kW 380V 50Hz a.c, 3 x 335kW 380V 50Hz a.c Boilers: 2 TOH (o.f.) 8.2kgf/cm² (8.0bar), TOH (ex.g.) 8.2kgf/cm² (8.0bar) Thrusters: 1 Thwart. CP thruster (f) Fuel: 120.0 (d.f.) (Part Heating Coils) 300.0 (r.f.)
9359399 *ZCYV9* -	**STOLT GULF MIRDIF** **Stolt Gulf Parcel Tanker 4 Ltd** Gulf Stolt Ship Management JLT *George Town* *Cayman Islands (British)* MMSI: 319014500 Official number: 742309	**26,329** 14,416 46,011 T/cm 52.2	Class: NV	**2010**-07 **SLS Shipbuilding Co Ltd — Tongyeong** Yd No: 476 Loa 182.88 (BB) Br ex 32.23 Dght 12.086 Lbp 175.60 Br md 32.20 Dpth 16.05 Welded, 1 dk	**(A12B2TR) Chemical/Products Tanker** Double Hull (13F) Liq: 47,757; Liq (Oil): 47,729 Compartments: 8 Ta, 21 Wing Ta, ER 29 Cargo Pump (s): 14x360m³/hr, 15x220m³/hr Manifold: Bow/CM: 91m	**1 oil engine** driving 1 FP propeller Total Power: 11,300kW (15,363hp) 14.5kn MAN-B&W 5S60MC-C 1 x 2 Stroke 5 Cy. 600 x 2400 11300kW (15363bhp) STX Engine Co Ltd-South Korea AuxGen: 3 x a.c Thrusters: 1 Tunnel thruster (f) Fuel: 105.0 (d.f.) 1865.0 (r.f.)
9359387 *ZGAB2* -	**STOLT GULF MISHREF** *ex* Stolt Pluto *-2010* **Stolt Gulf Parcel Tanker 3 Ltd** Gulf Stolt Ship Management JLT *George Town* *Cayman Islands (British)* MMSI: 319014400 Official number: 740766	**26,329** 14,416 46,089 T/cm 52.2	Class: NV	**2010**-07 **SLS Shipbuilding Co Ltd — Tongyeong** Yd No: 475 Loa 182.88 (BB) Br ex 32.22 Dght 12.070 Lbp 175.60 Br md 32.20 Dpth 16.05 Welded, 1 dk	**(A12B2TR) Chemical/Products Tanker** Double Hull (13F) Liq: 47,729; Liq (Oil): 47,729 Cargo Heating Coils Compartments: 9 Ta, 20 Wing Ta, ER 29 Cargo Pump (s): 14x360m³/hr, 15x220m³/hr Manifold: Bow/CM: 91m	**1 oil engine** driving 1 FP propeller Total Power: 11,300kW (15,363hp) 14.5kn MAN-B&W 5S60MC-C 1 x 2 Stroke 5 Cy. 600 x 2400 11300kW (15363bhp) STX Engine Co Ltd-South Korea AuxGen: 3 x 1300kW a.c Thrusters: 1 Tunnel thruster (f) Fuel: 122.0 (d.f.) 2048.0 (r.f.)
8906925 *D5DQ6* -	**STOLT HELLULAND** **Stolt Helluland 2 BV** Stolt Tankers BV *Monrovia* *Liberia* MMSI: 636015948 Official number: 15948	**18,994** 11,165 31,454 T/cm 43.5	Class: NV	**1991**-01 **Kleven Floro AS — Floro** Yd No: 122 Loa 174.70 (BB) Br ex 29.50 Dght 10.142 Lbp 167.20 Br md 29.46 Dpth 13.25 Welded, 1 dk	**(A12B2TR) Chemical/Products Tanker** Double Bottom Entire Compartment Length Liq: 37,293; Liq (Oil): 37,311 Cargo Heating Coils Compartments: 21 Ta (s.stl), 2 Wing Ta (s.stl), 14 Wing Ta, 2 Slop Ta, ER 39 Cargo Pump (s): 39x300m³/hr Manifold: Bow/CM: 83m	**1 oil engine** driving 1 CP propeller Total Power: 9,173kW (12,472hp) 15.5kn B&W 6L60MC 1 x 2 Stroke 6 Cy. 600 x 1944 9173kW (12472bhp) (made 1990) Bryanskiy Mashinostroitelnyy Zavod (BMZ)-Bryansk AuxGen: 3 x 869kW 450V 60Hz a.c Thrusters: 1 Thwart. CP thruster (f) Fuel: 295.0 (d.f.) 2472.0 (r.f.) 33.0pd
8819093 *ZCOZ7* -	**STOLT HILL** *ex* Montana Star *-2006* *ex* Star Sapphire *-2002* **Stolt Hill BV** Stolt-Nielsen Singapore Pte Ltd SatCom: Inmarsat B 331926210 *George Town* *Cayman Islands (British)* MMSI: 319262000 Official number: 738564	**22,620** 13,088 39,005 T/cm 49.1	Class: NV (LR) ✠	**1992**-07 **'Uljanik' Brodogradiliste dd — Pula** Yd No: 395 Conv to DH-2007 Loa 176.00 (BB) Br ex 32.30 Dght 11.247 Lbp 169.43 Br md 32.01 Dpth 15.09 Welded, 1 dk	**(A12B2TR) Chemical/Products Tanker** Double Hull (13F) Liq: 43,224; Liq (Oil): 43,224 Cargo Heating Coils Compartments: 12 Ta, 12 Wing Ta, 2 Wing Slop Ta, ER 24 Cargo Pump (s): 6x550m³/hr, 18x250m³/hr Manifold: Bow/CM: 89m	**1 oil engine** driving 1 FP propeller Total Power: 7,830kW (10,646hp) 14.3kn B&W 5L60MC 1 x 2 Stroke 5 Cy. 600 x 1944 7830kW (10646bhp) 'Uljanik' Strojogradnja dd-Croatia AuxGen: 1 x 1200kW 450V 60Hz a.c, 1 x 1000kW 450V 60Hz a.c, 1 x 849kW 450V 60Hz a.c Fuel: 250.0 (d.f.) (Heating Coils) 1370.0 (r.f.)
9102069 *ZCSP7* -	**STOLT INNOVATION** **Stolt Innovation BV** Stolt Tankers BV SatCom: Inmarsat Mini-M 761134470 *George Town* *Cayman Islands (British)* MMSI: 319489000 Official number: 732883	**24,846** 12,146 36,876 T/cm 48.6	Class: NV	**1996**-05 **Danyard A/S — Frederikshavn** Yd No: 730 Loa 176.75 (BB) Br ex 31.08 Dght 11.881 Lbp 168.50 Br md 31.00 Dpth 15.61 Welded, 1 dk	**(A12B2TR) Chemical/Products Tanker** Double Hull (13F) Liq: 40,488; Liq (Oil): 40,488 Cargo Heating Coils Compartments: 12 Ta (s.stl), 1 Wing Ta, 29 Wing Ta (s.stl), ER (s.stl) 48 Cargo Pump (s): 17x200m³/hr, 31x300m³/hr Manifold: Bow/CM: 86.4m	**4 diesel electric oil engines** driving 4 gen. each 3500kW 6600V Connecting to 1 elec. Motor of (10000kW) driving 1 FP propeller Total Power: 14,580kW (19,824hp) 16.2kn Wartsila 9R32LN 4 x 4 Stroke 9 Cy. 320 x 350 each-3645kW (4956bhp) Wartsila Diesel Oy-Finland AuxGen: 4 x a.c Thrusters: 1 Thwart. CP thruster (f) Fuel: 155.0 (d.f.) 2100.0 (r.f.) 53.2pd
9102083 *ZCSP8* -	**STOLT INSPIRATION** **Stolt Inspiration BV** Stolt Tankers BV SatCom: Inmarsat B 331949911 *George Town* *Cayman Islands (British)* MMSI: 319499000 Official number: 732884	**24,625** 11,934 37,205 T/cm 48.6	Class: NV	**1997**-04 **Danyard A/S — Frederikshavn** Yd No: 732 Loa 176.75 (BB) Br ex 31.08 Dght 11.884 Lbp 168.50 Br md 31.00 Dpth 15.60 Welded, 1 dk	**(A12B2TR) Chemical/Products Tanker** Double Hull (13F) Liq: 39,806; Liq (Oil): 39,806 Cargo Heating Coils Compartments: 12 Ta (s.stl), 1 Wing Ta, 29 Wing Ta (s.stl), ER (s.stl) 46 Cargo Pump (s): 29x200m³/hr, 17x300m³/hr Manifold: Bow/CM: 86.4m	**4 diesel electric oil engines** driving 3 gen. each 3500kW 6600V a.c 1 gen. of 2350kW 6600V a.c Connecting to 1 elec. Motor of (10000kW) driving 1 FP propeller Total Power: 13,395kW (18,213hp) 16.2kn Wartsila 6R32LN 1 x 4 Stroke 6 Cy. 320 x 350 2460kW (3345bhp) Wartsila Diesel Oy-Finland Wartsila 9R32LN 3 x 4 Stroke 9 Cy. 320 x 350 each-3645kW (4956bhp) Wartsila Diesel Oy-Finland Thrusters: 1 Thwart. CP thruster (f) Fuel: 155.0 (d.f.) 2110.0 (r.f.) 53.2pd
9102100 *ELSN7* -	**STOLT INVENTION** **NST Invention Inc** Stolt Tankers BV SatCom: Inmarsat Mini-M 764810987 *Monrovia* *Liberia* MMSI: 636010378 Official number: 10378	**24,634** 11,934 36,905 T/cm 48.6	Class: NV	**1997**-11 **Danyard A/S — Frederikshavn** Yd No: 734 Loa 176.75 (BB) Br ex 31.08 Dght 11.895 Lbp 168.50 Br md 31.00 Dpth 15.60 Welded, 1 dk	**(A12B2TR) Chemical/Products Tanker** Double Hull (13F) Liq: 39,806; Liq (Oil): 38,600 Cargo Heating Coils Compartments: 18 Ta (s.stl), 24 Wing Ta (s.stl), ER, 2 Ta 48 Cargo Pump (s): 31x200m³/hr, 17x300m³/hr Manifold: Bow/CM: 86.4m	**4 diesel electric oil engines** driving 3 gen. each 3520kW 6600V 1 gen. of 2345kW 6600V Connecting to 1 elec. Motor of (10000kW) driving 1 FP propeller Total Power: 13,365kW (18,172hp) 16.3kn Wartsila 6R32LN 1 x 4 Stroke 6 Cy. 320 x 350 2430kW (3304bhp) Wartsila Diesel Oy-Finland Wartsila 9R32LN 3 x 4 Stroke 9 Cy. 320 x 350 each-3645kW (4956bhp) Wartsila Diesel Oy-Finland Thrusters: 1 Thwart. CP thruster (f) Fuel: 153.0 (d.f.) 2417.0 (r.f.) 53.2pd
9414058 *ZCXG7* -	**STOLT ISLAND** **Stolt Island BV** Stolt Tankers BV SatCom: Inmarsat C 431996310 *George Town* *Cayman Islands (British)* MMSI: 319963000 Official number: 740667	**25,834** 13,427 43,593 T/cm 48.5	Class: NV	**2009**-03 **Wadan Yards Okean OJSC — Nikolayev** (Fwd & aft sections) **2009**-03 **STX Norway Floro AS — Floro** (Main cargo section) Yd No: 151 Loa 182.72 (BB) Br ex - Dght 11.870 Lbp 175.22 Br md 32.20 Dpth 15.60 Welded, 1 dk	**(A12B2TR) Chemical/Products Tanker** Double Hull (13F) Liq: 44,495; Liq (Oil): 45,350 Cargo Heating Coils Compartments: 13 Ta, 26 Wing Ta, ER 39 Cargo Pump (s): 24x385m³/hr, 15x220m³/hr Manifold: Bow/CM: 96m	**1 oil engine** driving 1 CP propeller Total Power: 11,060kW (15,037hp) 15.0kn MAN-B&W 7S50MC-C 1 x 2 Stroke 7 Cy. 500 x 2000 11060kW (15037bhp) MAN Diesel A/S-Denmark AuxGen: 2 x 1330kW a.c, 1 x 1100kW a.c Thrusters: 1 Tunnel thruster (f) Fuel: 168.0 (d.f.) 1942.0 (r.f.)

8320119 **STOLT JADE**
ZCSQ4
-
Stolt Jade BV
Stolt Tankers BV
SatCom: Inmarsat B 331943915
George Town *Cayman Islands (British)*
MMSI: 319439000
Official number: 732889

23,964 13,720 38,720 T/cm 48.8

Class: NV

1986-08 Daewoo Shipbuilding & Heavy Machinery Ltd — Geoje Yd No: 2011
Loa 176.82 (BB) Br ex 32.25 Dght 11.436
Lbp 169.02 Br md 32.23 Dpth 15.00
Welded, 1 dk

(A12B2TR) Chemical/Products Tanker
Double Bottom Entire Compartment Length
Liq: 45,416; Liq (Oil): 45,416
Cargo Heating Coils
Compartments: 2 Ta, 9 Wing Ta, 33 Ta (s.stl), 10 Wing Ta (s.stl), ER (s.stl)
58 Cargo Pump (s): 46x255m³/hr, 12x450m³/hr
Manifold: Bow/CM: 81.2m

1 oil engine driving 1 FP propeller
Total Power: 9,179kW (12,480hp) 15.0kn
B&W 6L60MCE
1 x 2 Stroke 6 Cy. 600 x 1944 9179kW (12480bhp)
Hyundai Engine & Machinery Co Ltd-South Korea
AuxGen: 3 x 900kW 450V 60Hz a.c, 1 x a.c
Thrusters: 1 Thwart. FP thruster (f)
Fuel: 277.0 (d.f.) 1877.3 (r.f.)

9314715 **STOLT JASMINE**
H3EM
-
Zakkine Maritime Co SA
Stolt Tankers BV
Panama *Panama*
MMSI: 356934000
Official number: 3052305B

6,868 3,838 12,430 T/cm 21.0

Class: NK

2005-01 Fukuoka Shipbuilding Co Ltd — Fukuoka FO Yd No: 1238
Loa 123.22 (BB) Br ex 20.02 Dght 8.752
Lbp 115.85 Br md 20.00 Dpth 11.20
Welded, 1 dk

(A12B2TR) Chemical/Products Tanker
Double Hull (13F)
Liq: 13,572; Liq (Oil): 13,572
Cargo Heating Coils
Compartments: 18 Wing Ta, 2 Wing Slop Ta, ER
18 Cargo Pump (s): 8x200m³/hr, 10x300m³/hr
Manifold: Bow/CM: 61.8m

1 oil engine driving 1 FP propeller
Total Power: 3,640kW (4,949hp) 13.0kn
Mitsubishi 7UEC37LA
1 x 2 Stroke 7 Cy. 370 x 880 3640kW (4949bhp)
Akasaka Tekkosho KK (Akasaka DieselLtd)-Japan
AuxGen: 2 x 450kW a.c
Thrusters: 1 Tunnel thruster (f)
Fuel: 102.0 (d.f.) 671.0 (r.f.)

9009528 **STOLT KESTREL**
ZCMR7
-
Stolt Kestrel BV
Stolt Tankers BV
SatCom: Inmarsat C 431925210
George Town *Cayman Islands (British)*
MMSI: 319252000
Official number: 730378

3,853 1,557 5,742 T/cm 13.7

Class: LR (NK)
100A1 SS 11/2012
Double Hull oil and chemical tanker, Ship Type 2
MARPOL 13G (1) (c)
SG 1.55 CR (s.stl)
ESP
LMC **UMS**
Eq.Ltr: V; Cable: 495.0/48.0 U2

1992-12 Fukuoka Shipbuilding Co Ltd — Fukuoka FO Yd No: 1169
Loa 99.90 (BB) Br ex 17.06 Dght 6.763
Lbp 92.70 Br md 16.80 Dpth 8.60
Welded, 1 dk

(A12B2TR) Chemical/Products Tanker
Double Hull (13F)
Liq: 5,221; Liq (Oil): 5,221
Cargo Heating Coils
Compartments: 14 Wing Ta, 2 Wing Slop Ta, ER
14 Cargo Pump (s): 8x200m³/hr, 6x125m³/hr
Manifold: Bow/CM: 48.7m

1 oil engine driving 1 CP propeller
Total Power: 2,574kW (3,500hp) 12.7kn
Mitsubishi 6UEC37LA
1 x 2 Stroke 6 Cy. 370 x 880 2574kW (3500bhp)
Akasaka Tekkosho KK (Akasaka DieselLtd)-Japan
AuxGen: 2 x 440kW 450V 60Hz a.c
Boilers: 2 AuxB (o.f.) 8.0kgf/cm² (7.8bar), e (ex.g.) 11.5kgf/cm² (11.3bar)
Thrusters: 1 Thwart. CP thruster (f)
Fuel: 60.0 (d.f.) (Heating Coils) 340.0 (r.f.) 9.7pd

9156565 **STOLT KIKYO**
ELUI5
-
NYK Stolt Shipholding Inc
Stolt-Nielsen Singapore Pte Ltd
SatCom: Inmarsat B 363681510
Monrovia *Liberia*
MMSI: 636010682
Official number: 10682

6,426 3,549 11,545 T/cm 19.6

Class: NK

1998-07 Fukuoka Shipbuilding Co Ltd — Fukuoka FO Yd No: 1202
Loa 117.27 (BB) Br ex 20.83 Dght 8.760
Lbp 110.00 Br md 20.80 Dpth 11.20
Welded, 1 dk

(A12B2TR) Chemical/Products Tanker
Double Hull (13F)
Liq: 12,313; Liq (Oil): 12,299
Cargo Heating Coils
Compartments: 18 Wing Ta, 2 Wing Slop Ta, ER
18 Cargo Pump (s): 8x300m³/hr, 10x200m³/hr
Manifold: Bow/CM: 54.1m

1 oil engine driving 1 FP propeller
Total Power: 3,884kW (5,281hp) 13.4kn
B&W 6L35MC
1 x 2 Stroke 6 Cy. 350 x 1050 3884kW (5281bhp)
Makita Corp-Japan
AuxGen: 3 x 400kW 450V 60Hz a.c
Thrusters: 1 Thwart. CP thruster (f)
Fuel: 194.0 (d.f.) (Heating Coils) 708.0 (r.f.) 16.5pd

9154323 **STOLT KINGFISHER**
2EQD7
ex Multitank Batavia -2011
-
Stolt Kingfisher BV
Stolt Tankers BV
SatCom: Inmarsat C 43592856
Cardiff *United Kingdom*
MMSI: 235087256
Official number: 917545

3,726 1,681 5,890 T/cm 14.0

Class: LR (GL)
100A1 SS 06/2013
Double Hull oil and chemical tanker, Ship Type 2
ESP
CR (s.stl)
Ice Class 1A at a maximum draught of 6.95m
Max/min draughts fwd 6.95/3.50m
Max/min draughts aft 6.95/4.90m
Power required 2866kw, power installed 4165kw
LMC **UMS IGS**

1998-06 Estaleiros Navais de Viana do Castelo S.A. — Viana do Castelo Yd No: 195
Loa 99.99 (BB) Br ex 16.53 Dght 6.800
Lbp 94.90 Br md 16.50 Dpth 8.30
Welded, 1 dk

(A12B2TR) Chemical/Products Tanker
Double Hull (13F)
Liq: 5,976; Liq (Oil): 5,976
Compartments: 18 Wing Ta (s.stl), 2 Wing Slop Ta (s.stl), ER
20 Cargo Pump (s): 20x100m³/hr
Manifold: Bow/CM: 50.8m
Ice Capable

1 oil engine driving 1 CP propeller
Total Power: 4,165kW (5,663hp) 15.0kn
MAN-B&W 7S35MC
1 x 2 Stroke 7 Cy. 350 x 1400 4165kW (5663bhp)
MAN B&W Diesel A/S-Denmark
AuxGen: 2 x 673kW 380/220V 50Hz a.c, 1 x 640kW 380/220V 50Hz a.c
Thrusters: 1 Thwart. FP thruster (f)
Fuel: 150.0 (d.f.) 355.0 (r.f.)

8920555 **STOLT KITE**
ZCMW9
ex Randi Terkol -1996
-
Stolt Kite BV
Stolt Tankers BV
SatCom: Inmarsat Mini-M 764623976
George Town *Cayman Islands (British)*
MMSI: 319206000
Official number: 731143

3,206 1,356 4,735 T/cm 12.4

Class: LR
✠100A1 SS 10/2012
Double Hull oil and chemical tanker, Ship Type 2*,
MARPOL 13H (1) (b)
SG 1.8 tanks 3, 4, 5 & 6, SG 1.2 tanks 1, 2 & 7,
CR (s.stl)
ESP
Ice Class 1D
✠LMC **UMS**
Eq.Ltr: U; Cable: 467.5/46.0 U2

1992-10 Aarhus Flydedok A/S — Aarhus Yd No: 201
Loa 96.35 (BB) Br ex 15.33 Dght 6.210
Lbp 88.13 Br md 15.10 Dpth 8.05
Welded, 1 dk

(A12B2TR) Chemical/Products Tanker
Double Hull (13F)
Liq: 4,653; Liq (Oil): 4,653
Compartments: 1 Ta, 2 Wing Slop Ta, 12 Wing Ta, ER
13 Cargo Pump (s): 13x150m³/hr
Manifold: Bow/CM: 45m
Ice Capable

1 oil engine with clutches, flexible couplings & sr geared to sc. shaft driving 1 CP propeller
Total Power: 2,999kW (4,077hp) 13.2kn
MaK 9M453C
1 x 4 Stroke 9 Cy. 320 x 420 2999kW (4077bhp)
Krupp MaK Maschinenbau GmbH-Kiel
AuxGen: 1 x 633kW 380V 50Hz a.c, 3 x 335kW 380V 50Hz a.c
Boilers: 2 TOH (o.f.) 8.2kgf/cm² (8.0bar), TOH (ex.g.) 8.2kgf/cm² (8.0bar)
Thrusters: 1 Thwart. CP thruster (f)
Fuel: 136.0 (d.f.) (Part Heating Coils) 324.0 (r.f.) 11.0pd

8920579 **STOLT KITTIWAKE**
MAIT
ex Astrid Terkol -1996
-
Stolt Kittiwake BV
Stolt Tankers BV
SatCom: Inmarsat C 423500015
Cardiff *United Kingdom*
MMSI: 235050032
Official number: 731180

3,204 1,359 4,710 T/cm 12.4

Class: LR
✠100A1 SS 06/2013
Double Hull oil and chemical tanker, Ship Type 2*
MARPOL 13H (1) (b)
SG 1.8 cargo tanks 3, 4, 5 & 6, SG 1.2 cargo tanks 1, 2 & 7 ,
CR (s.stl)
ESP
Ice Class 1B
✠LMC **UMS**
Eq.Ltr: U; Cable: 468.0/46.0 U2

1993-06 Aarhus Flydedok A/S — Aarhus Yd No: 203
Loa 96.35 (BB) Br ex 15.33 Dght 6.200
Lbp 87.75 Br md 15.10 Dpth 8.05
Welded, 1 dk

(A12B2TR) Chemical/Products Tanker
Double Hull (13F)
Liq: 4,662; Liq (Oil): 4,662
Cargo Heating Coils
Compartments: 1 Ta, 2 Wing Slop Ta, 12 Wing Ta, ER
13 Cargo Pump (s): 13x150m³/hr
Manifold: Bow/CM: 49.7m
Ice Capable

1 oil engine with clutches, flexible couplings & sr geared to sc. shaft driving 1 CP propeller
Total Power: 3,000kW (4,079hp) 13.2kn
MaK 9M453C
1 x 4 Stroke 9 Cy. 320 x 420 3000kW (4079bhp)
Krupp MaK Maschinenbau GmbH-Kiel
AuxGen: 1 x 633kW 380V 50Hz a.c, 3 x 335kW 380V 50Hz a.c
Boilers: 2 TOH (o.f.) 8.2kgf/cm² (8.0bar), TOH (ex.g.) 8.2kgf/cm² (8.0bar)
Thrusters: 1 Thwart. CP thruster (f)
Fuel: 63.0 (d.f.) (Part Heating Coils) 405.0 (r.f.)

8906937 **STOLT MARKLAND**
D5DN3
-
Stolt Markland 2 BV
Stolt Tankers BV
Monrovia *Liberia*
MMSI: 636015924
Official number: 15924

18,994 11,165 31,433 T/cm 43.4

Class: NV

1991-09 Kvaerner Kleven Floro AS — Floro (Aft section) Yd No: 123
1991-09 Kvaerner Kleven Floro AS — Forde (Fwd section) Yd No: 123
Loa 174.70 (BB) Br ex 29.53 Dght 10.142
Lbp 167.20 Br md 29.50 Dpth 13.25
Welded, 1 dk

(A12B2TR) Chemical/Products Tanker
Double Bottom Entire Compartment Length
Liq: 36,700; Liq (Oil): 36,709
Cargo Heating Coils
Compartments: 23 Ta (s.stl), 16 Wing Ta, ER
39 Cargo Pump (s): 39x300m³/hr
Manifold: Bow/CM: 78.6m

1 oil engine driving 1 CP propeller
Total Power: 9,173kW (12,472hp) 15.5kn
B&W 6L60MC
1 x 2 Stroke 6 Cy. 600 x 1944 9173kW (12472bhp)
Bryanskiy Mashinostroitelnyy Zavod (BMZ)-Bryansk
AuxGen: 1 x 1160kW 450V 60Hz a.c, 3 x 869kW 450V 60Hz a.c
Thrusters: 1 Thwart. CP thruster (f)
Fuel: 295.0 (d.f.) 2472.0 (r.f.) 33.0pd

9425980 **STOLT MEGAMI**
V7PL3
-
East Powership SA
Thome Ship Management Pte Ltd
SatCom: Inmarsat C 453833379
Majuro *Marshall Islands*
MMSI: 538003254
Official number: 3254

12,099 6,436 19,997 T/cm 30.4

Class: NK

2008-07 Shin Kurushima Dockyard Co. Ltd. — Akitsu Yd No: 5490
Loa 147.83 (BB) Br ex - Dght 9.504
Lbp 141.00 Br md 24.20 Dpth 12.85
Welded, 1 dk

(A12B2TR) Chemical/Products Tanker
Double Hull (13F)
Liq: 20,854; Liq (Oil): 21,947
Cargo Heating Coils
Compartments: 22 Wing Ta, 2 Wing Slop Ta, ER
22 Cargo Pump (s): 12x330m³/hr, 10x200m³/hr
Manifold: Bow/CM: 76.9m

1 oil engine driving 1 FP propeller
Total Power: 6,230kW (8,470hp) 15.0kn
Mitsubishi 7UEC45LA
1 x 2 Stroke 7 Cy. 450 x 1350 6230kW (8470bhp)
Kobe Hatsudoki KK-Japan
AuxGen: 3 x 460kW a.c
Thrusters: 1 Tunnel thruster (f)
Fuel: 95.0 (d.f.) 1135.0 (r.f.)

9470545 **STOLT MOMIJI**
ZGAN9
-
Stolt Momiji Inc
Stolt-Nielsen Singapore Pte Ltd
George Town *Cayman Islands (British)*
MMSI: 319034900
Official number: 742451

7,228 3,836 12,829 T/cm 21.1

Class: NK

2010-07 Usuki Shipyard Co Ltd — Usuki OT Yd No: 1722
Converted From: Chemical Tanker-2010
Loa 121.52 (BB) Br ex - Dght 8.814
Lbp 115.00 Br md 20.60 Dpth 11.30
Welded, 1 dk

(A12B2TR) Chemical/Products Tanker
Double Hull (13F)
Liq: 13,241; Liq (Oil): 13,500
Cargo Heating Coils
Compartments: 18 Wing Ta, ER, 2 Wing Slop Ta
18 Cargo Pump (s): 12x300m³/hr, 6x200m³/hr
Manifold: Bow/CM: 62m

1 oil engine driving 1 FP propeller
Total Power: 4,900kW (6,662hp) 14.2kn
MAN-B&W 7S35MC
1 x 2 Stroke 7 Cy. 350 x 1400 4900kW (6662bhp)
Hitachi Zosen Corp-Japan
AuxGen: 3 x 400kW 450V 60Hz a.c
Fuel: 88.0 (d.f.) 702.7 (r.f.)

9005390 **STOLT MOUNTAIN**
ZCOZ6
ex Montana Sun -2006 ex Sun Sapphire -2002
-
Stolt Mountain BV
Stolt Tankers BV
SatCom: Inmarsat B 331927610
George Town *Cayman Islands (British)*
MMSI: 319276000
Official number: 738563

22,620 13,095 39,005 T/cm 49.1

Class: NV (LR)
✠ Classed LR until 27/5/99

1994-07 'Uljanik' Brodogradiliste dd — Pula Yd No: 399
Conv to DH-2007
Loa 176.00 (BB) Br ex 32.03 Dght 11.247
Lbp 169.00 Br md 32.00 Dpth 15.10
Welded, 1 dk

(A12B2TR) Chemical/Products Tanker
Double Hull (13F)
Liq: 44,072; Liq (Oil): 48,035
Cargo Heating Coils
Compartments: 12 Wing Ta, ER, 12 Ta, 2 Wing Slop Ta
24 Cargo Pump (s): 6x550m³/hr, 18x250m³/hr
Manifold: Bow/CM: 90m

1 oil engine driving 1 FP propeller
Total Power: 7,830kW (10,646hp) 14.0kn
B&W 5L60MC
1 x 2 Stroke 5 Cy. 600 x 1944 7830kW (10646bhp)
'Uljanik' Strojogradnja dd-Croatia
AuxGen: 1 x 1200kW 450V 60Hz a.c, 1 x 1000kW 450V 60Hz a.c, 1 x 850kW 450V 60Hz a.c
Fuel: 214.0 (d.f.) 1311.0 (r.f.) 30.5pd

9414060 *ZCXG8* -	**STOLT NORLAND** **Stolt Norland BV** Stolt Tankers BV SatCom: Inmarsat C 431937710 *George Town Cayman Islands (British)* MMSI: 319377000 Official number: 740668	**25,881** 13,418 43,593 T/cm 48.5	Class: NV	**2009-06 Wadan Yards Okean OJSC — Nikolayev** (Fwd & aft sections) **2009-06 STX Norway Floro AS — Floro** (Main cargo section) Yd No: 152 Loa 182.72 (BB) Br ex 32.24 Dght 11.890 Lbp 175.22 Br md 32.20 Dpth 15.60 Welded, 1 dk	**(A12B2TR) Chemical/Products Tanker** Double Hull (13F) Liq: 44,495; Liq (Oil): 45,350 Cargo Heating Coils Compartments: 13 Ta, 26 Wing Ta, ER 39 Cargo Pump (s): 24x385m^3/hr, 15x220m^3/hr Manifold: Bow/CM: 96m	**1 oil engine** driving 1 CP propeller Total Power: 11,060kW (15,037hp) 15.0kn MAN-B&W 7S50MC-C 1 x 2 Stroke 7 Cy. 500 x 2000 11060kW (15037bhp) MAN Diesel A/S-Denmark AuxGen: 2 x 1330kW a.c, 1 x 1100kW a.c Thrusters: 1 Tunnel thruster (f) Fuel: 170.0 (d.f.) 1945.0 (r.f.) 47.2pd
9459539 *A8YA2* -	**STOLT OCELOT** *ex* Golden Ivy *-2011* **Stolt Ocelot BV** Stolt Tankers BV *Monrovia Liberia* MMSI: 636015005 Official number: 15005	**13,517** 7,143 23,324 T/cm 32.4	Class: NK	**2008-04 Kurinoura Dockyard Co Ltd — Yawatahama EH** Yd No: 395 Loa 155.00 (BB) Br ex - Dght 10.217 Lbp 145.00 Br md 24.80 Dpth 13.35 Welded, 1 dk	**(A12B2TR) Chemical/Products Tanker** Double Hull (13F) Liq: 23,463; Liq (Oil): 23,463 Cargo Heating Coils Compartments: 2 Wing Slop Ta, 28 Wing Ta, ER 28 Cargo Pump (s): 12x300m^3/hr, 16x200m^3/hr Manifold: Bow/CM: 72.6m	**1 oil engine** driving 1 FP propeller Total Power: 7,175kW (9,755hp) 14.6kn MAN-B&W 7S42MC 1 x 2 Stroke 7 Cy. 420 x 1764 7175kW (9755bhp) Makita Corp-Japan Thrusters: 1 Tunnel thruster (f) Fuel: 260.0 (d.f.) 1820.0 (r.f.)
9016882 *2EA09* -	**STOLT PELICAN** *ex* Isebek *-2008* *ex* Multitank Saxonia *-1997* **Stolt Pelican BV** Stolt Tankers BV SatCom: Inmarsat Mini-M 765068471 *Cardiff United Kingdom* MMSI: 235083501 Official number: 741344	**3,711** 1,669 5,797 T/cm 14.7	Class: LR (GL) **100A1** SS 11/2011 Double Hull oil and chemical tanker, Ship Type 2 ESP Ice Class 1A at a maximum draught of 6.78m Max/min draughts fwd 6.78/8.50m Max/min draughts aft 6.78/4.90m Power required 2882kw, power installed 3840kw **LMC UMS IGS** Eq.Ltr: U; Cable: 467.0/40.0 U3 (a)	**1996-10 AO Baltiyskiy Zavod — Sankt-Peterburg** Yd No: 422 Loa 99.90 (BB) Br ex 16.53 Dght 6.783 Lbp 95.33 Br md 16.50 Dpth 8.30 Welded, 1 dk	**(A12B2TR) Chemical/Products Tanker** Double Hull (13F) Liq: 5,938; Liq (Oil): 6,057 Cargo Heating Coils Compartments: 20 Wing Ta, ER 20 Cargo Pump (s): 20x100m^3/hr Manifold: Bow/CM: 46.4m Ice Capable	**1 oil engine** driving 1 CP propeller Total Power: 3,840kW (5,221hp) 15.0kn B&W 6L42MC 1 x 2 Stroke 6 Cy. 420 x 1360 3840kW (5221bhp) AO Bryanskiy MashinostroitelnyyZavod (BMZ)-Bryansk AuxGen: 1 x 550kW 400V 50Hz a.c, 2 x 630kW 400V 50Hz a.c Boilers: TOH (ex.g.) 10.2kgf/cm^2 (10.0bar), TOH (o.f.) 10.2kgf/cm^2 (10.0bar) Thrusters: 1 Thwart. FP thruster (f) Fuel: 53.0 (d.f.) 367.0 (r.f.)
9124471 *ZCGE5* -	**STOLT PERSEVERANCE** **Stolt Perseverance BV** Stolt Tankers BV SatCom: Inmarsat Mini-M 761154925 *George Town Cayman Islands (British)* MMSI: 319645000 Official number: 734915	**25,196** 12,048 37,059 T/cm 48.5	Class: LR ✠ **100A1** SS 12/2011 Double Hull oil & chemical tanker, Ship Type 1 SG 1.025, PV+0.6 bar gauge and max. cargo temp. 95 degrees C, all integral cargo tanks SG 1.25, PV+0.25 bar gauge and max. cargo temp. 55 degrees C, integral centre cargo tanks SG 1.55, PV+0.25 bar gauge and max. cargo temp. 55 degrees C, integral centre cargo tanks 80% full SG 1.85, PV+0.25 bar gauge and max. cargo temp. 55 degrees C, integral wing cargo tanks SG 2.2, PV+0.25 bar gauge and max. cargo temp. 55 degrees C, integral wing cargo tanks 70% full SG 1.85, PV+0.7 bar gauge and max. cargo temp. 95 degrees C, independent cargo deck tanks SG 2.2, PV+0.7 bar gauge and max. cargo temp. 55 degrees C, independent cargo deck tanks 70% full CR (s.stl) TC ESP LI centralised control for liq cargoes, bunker ta seperated from cargo ta by coffer dams ✠ **LMC UMS IGS** Cable: 632.5/76.0 U3 (a)	**2001-12 ACH Construction Navale — Le Havre** (Hull launched by) Yd No: 295 **2001-12 'Uljanik' Brodogradiliste dd — Pula** (Hull completed by) Loa 176.70 (BB) Br ex 31.23 Dght 11.891 Lbp 168.00 Br md 31.20 Dpth 15.60 Welded, 1 dk	**(A12B2TR) Chemical/Products Tanker** Double Hull (13F) Liq: 40,593; Liq (Oil): 40,623 Cargo Heating Coils Compartments: 20 Ta (s.stl), 1 Wing Ta, 25 Wing Ta (s.stl), 2 Wing Slop Ta (s.stl), ER (s.stl) 54 Cargo Pump (s): 14x300m^3/hr, 40x200m^3/hr Manifold: Bow/CM: 86.1m	**4 diesel electric oil engines** driving 3 gen. each 3520kW 6600V a.c 1 gen. of 2344kW 6600V a.c Connecting to 1 elec. Motor of (10000kW) driving 1 FP propeller Total Power: 13,365kW (18,172hp) 16.2kn Wartsila 6R32LN 1 x 4 Stroke 6 Cy. 320 x 350 2430kW (3304bhp) Wartsila Finland Oy-Finland Wartsila 9R32LN 3 x 4 Stroke 9 Cy. 320 x 350 each-3645kW (4956bhp) Wartsila Finland Oy-Finland Boilers: e (ex.g.) 15.8kgf/cm^2 (15.5bar), WTAuxB (o.f.) 15.4kgf/cm^2 (15.1bar) Thrusters: 1 Thwart. CP thruster (f) Fuel: 137.0 (d.f.) (Heating Coils) 1848.0 (r.f.) 58.0pd
8920543 *MVRC3* -	**STOLT PETREL** *ex* Edny Terkol *-1996* **Stolt Petrel BV** Stolt Tankers BV SatCom: Inmarsat Mini-M 764623981 *Cardiff United Kingdom* MMSI: 235050801 Official number: 731173	**3,206** 1,357 4,761 T/cm 12.4	Class: LR ✠ **100A1** SS 08/2012 Double Hull oil and chemical tanker, Ship Type 2* MARPOL 13H (1) (b) SG 1.8 tanks 3, 4, 5 & 6, SG 1.2 tanks 1, 2 & 7, CR (s.stl) ESP Ice Class 1D ✠ **LMC UMS** Eq.Ltr: U; Cable: 467.5/46.0 U2	**1992-08 Aarhus Flydedok A/S — Aarhus** Yd No: 200 Loa 96.35 (BB) Br ex 15.33 Dght 6.200 Lbp 88.65 Br md 15.10 Dpth 8.05 Welded, 1 dk	**(A12B2TR) Chemical/Products Tanker** Double Hull (13F) Liq: 4,657; Liq (Oil): 4,657 Cargo Heating Coils Compartments: 1 Ta, 12 Wing Ta, ER, 2 Wing Slop Ta 13 Cargo Pump (s): 13x80m^3/hr Manifold: Bow/CM: 48.2m Ice Capable	**1 oil engine** with clutches, flexible couplings & sr geared to sc. shaft driving 1 CP propeller Total Power: 2,999kW (4,077hp) 13.0kn MaK 9M453C 1 x 4 Stroke 9 Cy. 320 x 420 2999kW (4077bhp) Krupp MaK Maschinenbau GmbH-Kiel AuxGen: 1 x 633kW 380V 50Hz a.c, 3 x 335kW 380V 50Hz a.c Boilers: 2 TOH (o.f.) 8.2kgf/cm^2 (8.0bar), TOH (ex.g.) 8.2kgf/cm^2 (8.0bar) Thrusters: 1 Thwart. CP thruster (f) Fuel: 133.0 (d.f.) (Part Heating Coils) 329.0 (r.f.) 11.0pd
9374521 *3EMR4* -	**STOLT PONDO** *ex* Pondo *-2012* *ex* Stolt Pondo *-2010* **ST Ocean Shipping SA** Stolt-Nielsen Singapore Pte Ltd *Panama Panama* MMSI: 371101000 Official number: 3327107B	**19,380** 9,740 33,232 T/cm 40.9	Class: NK	**2007-10 Kitanihon Zosen K.K. — Hachinohe** Yd No: 371 Loa 170.00 (BB) Br ex 26.63 Dght 11.316 Lbp 162.00 Br md 26.60 Dpth 16.00 Welded, 1 dk	**(A12B2TR) Chemical/Products Tanker** Double Hull (13F) Liq: 36,919; Liq (Oil): 36,919 Cargo Heating Coils Compartments: 26 Wing Ta, 2 Wing Slop Ta, ER 26 Cargo Pump (s): 14x220m^3/hr, 12x330m^3/hr Manifold: Bow/CM: 83.5m	**1 oil engine** driving 1 FP propeller Total Power: 7,980kW (10,850hp) 14.7kn Mitsubishi 6UEC52LS 1 x 2 Stroke 6 Cy. 520 x 1850 7980kW (10850bhp) Akasaka Tekkosho KK (Akasaka DieselLtd)-Japan AuxGen: 3 x 620kW 450V 60Hz a.c Thrusters: 1 Tunnel thruster Fuel: 487.0 (d.f.) 1734.0 (r.f.) 28.7pd
9009530 *ZCFE5* -	**STOLT PUFFIN** **Stolt Puffin BV** Stolt Tankers BV SatCom: Inmarsat B 331964310 *George Town Cayman Islands (British)* MMSI: 319643000 Official number: 733852	**3,853** 1,557 5,737 T/cm 13.7	Class: LR (NK) **100A1** SS 01/2013 Double Hull oil and chemical tanker, MARPOL 13G (1) (c), Ship Type 2 SG 1.5, CR (s.stl) ESP **LMC UMS** Eq.Ltr: V; Cable: 495.0/48.0 U2	**1993-01 Fukuoka Shipbuilding Co Ltd — Fukuoka FO** Yd No: 1170 Loa 99.90 (BB) Br ex 17.06 Dght 6.763 Lbp 92.70 Br md 16.80 Dpth 8.60 Welded, 1 dk	**(A12B2TR) Chemical/Products Tanker** Double Hull (13F) Liq: 5,221; Liq (Oil): 5,221 Cargo Heating Coils Compartments: 14 Wing Ta, 2 Wing Slop Ta, ER 14 Cargo Pump (s): 8x200m^3/hr, 6x125m^3/hr Manifold: Bow/CM: 48.7m Ice Capable	**1 oil engine** driving 1 CP propeller Total Power: 2,574kW (3,500hp) 12.7kn Mitsubishi 6UEC37LA 1 x 2 Stroke 6 Cy. 370 x 880 2574kW (3500bhp) Akasaka Tekkosho KK (Akasaka DieselLtd)-Japan AuxGen: 2 x 400kW 450V 60Hz a.c Boilers: 2 AuxB (o.f.) 8.0kgf/cm^2 (7.8bar), e (ex.g.) 11.4kgf/cm^2 (11.2bar) Thrusters: 1 Thwart. CP thruster (f) Fuel: 78.0 (d.f.) (Heating Coils) 327.0 (r.f.) 9.7pd
9376660 *ZCYS4* -	**STOLT QUETZAL** *launched as* Sichem Amazon *-2009* **Irene Ship Holding SA** Stolt Tankers BV SatCom: Inmarsat C 431999410 *George Town Cayman Islands (British)* MMSI: 319994000 Official number: 741489	**7,603** 3,760 12,260 T/cm 21.6	Class: BV	**2009-06 Sasaki Shipbuilding Co Ltd — Osakikamijima HS** Yd No: 665 Loa 123.85 (BB) Br ex 20.03 Dght 8.915 Lbp 116.00 Br md 20.00 Dpth 11.51 Welded, 1 dk	**(A12B2TR) Chemical/Products Tanker** Double Hull (13F) Liq: 13,016; Liq (Oil): 12,399 Cargo Heating Coils Compartments: 18 Wing Ta, 2 Wing Slop Ta, ER 18 Cargo Pump (s): 18x200m^3/hr Manifold: Bow/CM: 61.6m	**1 oil engine** driving 1 FP propeller Total Power: 3,510kW (4,772hp) 13.0kn MAN-B&W 6L35MC 1 x 2 Stroke 6 Cy. 350 x 1050 3510kW (4772bhp) The Hanshin Diesel Works Ltd-Japan AuxGen: 3 x 750kW 60Hz a.c Thrusters: 1 Tunnel thruster (f) Fuel: 118.0 (d.f.) 582.0 (r.f.)

IMO / Call sign	Name / Owner / Manager / Flag	Tonnage	Classification	Builder / Dimensions	Ship type / Cargo	Machinery
9016870 *2AD07* -	**STOLT RAZORBILL** *ex* Multitank Iberia *-2007* **Stolt Razorbill BV** Stolt Tankers BV SatCom: Inmarsat Mini-M 764804691 *Cardiff* *United Kingdom* MMSI: 235058838 Official number: 913669	**3,716** 1,671 5,797 T/cm 14.7	Class: LR (GL) **100A1** SS 08/2010 oil & chemical tanker, Ship Type 2 ESP Ice Class 1A at a maximum draught of 6.92m Max/min draught fwd 6.92/3.50m Max/min draught aft 6.92/4.90m Power required 2882kw, installed 3840kw **LMC** **UMS IGS** Eq.Ltr: U; Cable: 467.0/40.0 U3 (a)	**1995-08 AO Baltiyskiy Zavod — Sankt-Peterburg** Yd No: 421 Loa 99.91 (BB) Br ex - Dght 6.800 Lbp 95.33 Br md 16.50 Dpth 8.30 Welded, 1 dk	**(A12B2TR) Chemical/Products Tanker** Double Hull (13F) Liq: 5,943; Liq (Oil): 5,942 Cargo Heating Coils Compartments: 20 Wing Ta (s.stl), ER (s.stl) 20 Cargo Pump (s): 20x100m^3/hr Manifold: Bow/CM: 46.4m Ice Capable	**1 oil engine** driving 1 CP propeller Total Power: 3,840kW (5,221hp) 15.0kn MAN-B&W 6L42MC 1 x 2 Stroke 6 Cy. 420 x 1360 3840kW (5221bhp) AO Bryanskiy MashinostroitelnyyZavod (BMZ)-Bryansk AuxGen: 2 x 630kW 400V 50Hz a.c, 1 x 550kW 400V 50Hz a.c Boilers: TOH (o.f.) 10.2kgf/cm^2 (10.0bar), TOH (ex.g.) 10.2kgf/cm^2 (10.0bar) Thrusters: 1 Thwart. FP thruster (f) Fuel: 53.0 (d.f.) 367.0 (r.f.)
9566746 *2EXV5* -	**STOLT REDSHANK** *ex* Brovig Levanto *-2011* **Brovig Stainless AS** Stolt Tankers BV *Cardiff* *United Kingdom* MMSI: 235089046 Official number: 917842	**3,327** 1,357 4,449 T/cm 12.7	Class: BV	**2011-07 Chongqing Chuandong Shipbuilding Industry Co Ltd — Chongqing** Yd No: HT0121 Loa 90.90 (BB) Br ex - Dght 6.010 Lbp 85.00 Br md 15.60 Dpth 8.00 Welded, 1 dk	**(A12B2TR) Chemical/Products Tanker** Double Hull (13F) Liq: 4,314; Liq (Oil): 4,314 Cargo Heating Coils Compartments: 4 Wing Ta, 4 Wing Ta, 1 Wing Slop Ta, 1 Wing Slop Ta, ER 8 Cargo Pump (s): 8x200m^3/hr Manifold: Bow/CM: 47m Ice Capable	**1 oil engine** reduction geared to sc. shaft driving 1 CP propeller Total Power: 2,640kW (3,589hp) 12.8kn MaK 8M25C 1 x 4 Stroke 8 Cy. 255 x 400 2640kW (3589bhp) Caterpillar Motoren GmbH & Co. KG-Germany AuxGen: 3 x 320kW 450V 60Hz a.c, 1 x 400kW 60Hz a.c Thrusters: 1 Tunnel thruster (f) Fuel: 97.0 (d.f.) 319.0 (r.f.)
9314765 *H3WM* -	**STOLT RINDO** **Fast Shipping SA** Dongkuk Marine Co Ltd *Panama* *Panama* MMSI: 352258000 Official number: 3060305B	**6,944** 3,619 11,519 T/cm 21.0	Class: NK	**2005-01 Sasaki Shipbuilding Co Ltd — Osakikamijima HS** Yd No: 650 Loa 122.00 (BB) Br ex 20.05 Dght 8.414 Lbp 115.00 Br md 20.00 Dpth 10.90 Welded, 1 dk	**(A12B2TR) Chemical/Products Tanker** Double Hull (13F) Liq: 11,694; Liq (Oil): 12,766 Cargo Heating Coils Compartments: 18 Wing Ta, ER, 2 Wing Slop Ta 18 Cargo Pump (s): 18x200m^3/hr Manifold: Bow/CM: 61.7m	**1 oil engine** driving 1 FP propeller Total Power: 3,515kW (4,779hp) 13.5kn B&W 6L35MC 1 x 2 Stroke 6 Cy. 350 x 1050 3515kW (4779bhp) Makita Corp-Japan AuxGen: 2 x 440kW 450V 50Hz a.c Fuel: 106.0 (d.f.) 571.0 (r.f.)
9352200 *ZCTV7* -	**STOLT SAGALAND** **Stolt Sagaland BV** Stolt Tankers BV SatCom: Inmarsat C 431928210 *George Town* *Cayman Islands (British)* MMSI: 319282000 Official number: 740278	**25,884** 13,427 44,044 T/cm 52.3	Class: NV	**2008-02 Aker Yards AS Floro — Floro** (Aft & pt cargo sections) Yd No: 149 **2008-02 OAO Damen Shipyards Okean — Nikolayev** (Fwd & pt cargo sections) Loa 182.72 (BB) Br ex 32.23 Dght 11.870 Lbp 175.22 Br md 32.20 Dpth 15.62 Welded, 1 dk	**(A12B2TR) Chemical/Products Tanker** Double Hull (13F) Liq: 40,587; Liq (Oil): 45,350 Cargo Heating Coils Compartments: 13 Ta, 26 Wing Ta, ER 39 Cargo Pump (s): 15x220m^3/hr, 24x385m^3/hr Manifold: Bow/CM: 86.1m	**1 oil engine** driving 1 CP propeller Total Power: 11,060kW (15,037hp) 15.0kn MAN-B&W 7S50MC-C 1 x 2 Stroke 7 Cy. 500 x 2000 11060kW (15037bhp) Kawasaki Heavy Industries Ltd-Japan AuxGen: 2 x 1265kW a.c, 1 x 1100kW a.c Thrusters: 1 Tunnel thruster (f) Fuel: 239.0 (d.f.) 2320.0 (r.f.)
9432969 *ZGAN8* -	**STOLT SAKURA** **Stolt Sakura Inc** Stolt Tankers BV 773204114 *George Town* *Cayman Islands (British)* MMSI: 319673000 Official number: 742450	**7,228** 3,837 12,817 T/cm 20.1	Class: NK	**2010-05 Usuki Shipyard Co Ltd — Usuki OT** Yd No: 1721 Loa 121.52 (BB) Br ex - Dght 8.814 Lbp 115.00 Br md 20.60 Dpth 11.33 Welded, 1 dk	**(A12B2TR) Chemical/Products Tanker** Double Hull (13F) Liq: 13,236; Liq (Oil): 13,500 Cargo Heating Coils Compartments: 18 Wing Ta (s.stl), ER 18 Cargo Pump (s): 12x300m^3/hr, 6x200m^3/hr Manifold: Bow/CM: 62m	**1 oil engine** driving 1 FP propeller Total Power: 4,900kW (6,662hp) 14.2kn MAN-B&W 7S35MC 1 x 2 Stroke 7 Cy. 350 x 1400 4900kW (6662bhp) Hitachi Zosen Corp-Japan AuxGen: 3 x 450kW a.c Thrusters: 1 Tunnel thruster (f) Fuel: 87.0 (d.f.) 702.0 (r.f.)
9518804 *2GBH7* -	**STOLT SANDERLING** *ex* Brovig Cierzo *-2012* **Brovig Stainless AS** Stolt Tankers BV *Cardiff* *United Kingdom* MMSI: 235095972 Official number: 918737	**3,327** 1,357 4,453 T/cm 12.9	Class: BV	**2011-05 Chongqing Chuandong Shipbuilding Industry Co Ltd — Chongqing** Yd No: HT0120 Loa 90.90 (BB) Br ex - Dght 6.000 Lbp 85.00 Br md 15.60 Dpth 8.00 Welded, 1 dk	**(A12B2TR) Chemical/Products Tanker** Double Hull (13F) Liq: 4,305; Liq (Oil): 4,315 Cargo Heating Coils Compartments: 4 Wing Ta, 4 Wing Ta, ER, 2 Wing Slop Ta 8 Cargo Pump (s): 8x200m^3/hr Manifold: Bow/CM: 47m Ice Capable	**1 oil engine** reduction geared to sc. shaft driving 1 CP propeller Total Power: 2,640kW (3,589hp) 12.8kn MaK 8M25C 1 x 4 Stroke 8 Cy. 255 x 400 2640kW (3589bhp) Caterpillar Motoren GmbH & Co. KG-Germany AuxGen: 3 x 320kW 450V 60Hz a.c, 1 x 400kW 450V 60Hz a.c Thrusters: 1 Thwart. FP thruster (f) Fuel: 60.0 (d.f.) 319.0 (r.f.)
9566758 *2EY08* -	**STOLT SANDPIPER** **Brovig Stainless AS** Stolt Tankers BV *Cardiff* *United Kingdom* MMSI: 235089284 Official number: 917857	**3,327** 1,357 4,449 T/cm 12.7	Class: BV	**2011-10 Chongqing Chuandong Shipbuilding Industry Co Ltd — Chongqing** Yd No: HT0122 Loa 90.90 (BB) Br ex - Dght 6.000 Lbp 85.00 Br md 15.60 Dpth 8.00 Welded, 1 dk	**(A12B2TR) Chemical/Products Tanker** Double Hull (13F) Liq: 4,304; Liq (Oil): 4,385 Cargo Heating Coils Compartments: 4 Wing Ta, 4 Wing Ta, 2 Wing Slop Ta, ER 8 Cargo Pump (s): 8x200m^3/hr Manifold: Bow/CM: 47m Ice Capable	**1 oil engine** reduction geared to sc. shaft driving 1 CP propeller Total Power: 2,640kW (3,589hp) 12.8kn MaK 8M25C 1 x 4 Stroke 8 Cy. 255 x 400 2640kW (3589bhp) Caterpillar Motoren GmbH & Co. KG-Germany AuxGen: 3 x 320kW 450V 60Hz a.c, 1 x 400kW 450V 60Hz a.c Thrusters: 1 Tunnel thruster (f) Fuel: 63.0 (d.f.) 326.0 (r.f.)
8309531 *ELEG2* -	**STOLT SAPPHIRE** **NYK Stolt Tankers SA** Stolt Tankers BV SatCom: Inmarsat C 463659910 *Monrovia* *Liberia* MMSI: 636007679 Official number: 7679	**23,964** 13,720 38,746 T/cm 48.7	Class: NV	**1986-01 Daewoo Shipbuilding & Heavy Machinery Ltd — Geoje** Yd No: 2007 Loa 176.80 (BB) Br ex - Dght 11.430 Lbp 169.50 Br md 32.23 Dpth 15.00 Welded, 1 dk	**(A12B2TR) Chemical/Products Tanker** Double Bottom Entire Compartment Length Liq: 45,441; Liq (Oil): 45,441 Cargo Heating Coils Compartments: 30 Ta (s.stl), 2 Ta, 22 Wing Ta (s.stl), 1 Wing Slop Ta, 1 Wing Slop Ta (s.stl), ER (s.stl) 58 Cargo Pump (s): 12x450m^3/hr, 46x255m^3/hr Manifold: Bow/CM: 80.7m	**1 oil engine** driving 1 FP propeller Total Power: 9,179kW (12,480hp) 15.0kn B&W 6L60MC 1 x 2 Stroke 6 Cy. 600 x 1944 9179kW (12480bhp) Hyundai Engine & Machinery Co Ltd-South Korea AuxGen: 3 x 900kW 450V 60Hz a.c, 1 x 900kW 450V 60Hz a.c Thrusters: 1 Thwart. FP thruster (f) Fuel: 278.0 (d.f.) 1877.0 (r.f.) 35.0pd
9149495 *ZCSQ7* -	**STOLT SEA** **Stolt Sea BV** Stolt Tankers BV SatCom: Inmarsat C 431947810 *George Town* *Cayman Islands (British)* MMSI: 319478000 Official number: 733292	**14,900** 7,228 22,198 T/cm 34.1	Class: LR (NV) **100A1** SS 04/2009 Double Hull oil & chemical tanker Ship Type 1 ESP LI *IWS SG 1.45 and PV+0.25 bar gauge all integral tanks, SG 1.85 and PV+0.25 bar gauge at 78% full, all integral tanks, SG 1.025 and PV+0.6 bar gauge all integral tanks, SG 1.45 and PV+0.6/-0.2 bar gauge deck tanks, SG 1.84 and PV+0.6/-0.2 bar gauge at 77% full, deck tanks. Maximum carriage temperature up to 90 deg C integral tanks, Maximum carriage temperature up to 60 deg C deck tanks. **LMC** **UMS** Eq.Ltr: G†; Cable: 577.5/62.0 U3	**1999-05 Astilleros de Sestao SRL — Sestao** Yd No: 309 Loa 162.60 (BB) Br ex 23.72 Dght 10.110 Lbp 154.10 Br md 23.70 Dpth 13.35 Welded, 1 dk	**(A12B2TR) Chemical/Products Tanker** Double Hull (13F) Liq: 24,713; Liq (Oil): 24,713 Cargo Heating Coils Compartments: 10 Ta, 30 Wing Ta, ER 40 Cargo Pump (s): 40x220m^3/hr Manifold: Bow/CM: 82m	**3 diesel electric oil engines** driving 2 gen. each 3200kW 1100V a.c 1 gen. of 2300kW 1100V a.c Connecting to 1 elec. Motor of (6554kW) driving 1 FP propeller Total Power: 8,800kW (11,964hp) 15.2kn Wartsila 6R32E 1 x 4 Stroke 6 Cy. 320 x 350 2320kW (3154bhp) Wartsila NSD Finland Oy-Finland Wartsila 8R32E 2 x 4 Stroke 8 Cy. 320 x 350 each-3240kW (4405bhp) Wartsila NSD Finland Oy-Finland Boilers: 3 TOH (ex.g.) 10.2kgf/cm^2 (10.0bar), 2 TOH (o.f.) 10.2kgf/cm^2 (10.0bar) Thrusters: 1 Tunnel thruster (f) Fuel: 63.0 (d.f.) 1572.0 (r.f.)

9148958 *ZCRD9* -	**STOLT SHEARWATER** **DS-Rendite-Fonds Nr 99 CFS GmbH & Co Produktentanker KG** Stolt Tankers BV SatCom: Inmarsat C 431940211 *George Town* *Cayman Islands (British)* MMSI: 319402000 Official number: 731201	**3,811** 1,518 5,498 T/cm 14.4	Class: LR (RI) (NV) **100A1** SS 10/2013 Double Hull oil & chemical tanker, Ship Type 2 CR (s.stl), SG 1.85, PV+0.25 bar gauge all tanks, SG 0.86, PV+0.6 bar gauge all tanks, SG 1.025, PV+0.25 bar gauge all tanks, SG 2.2 (70% full), PV+0.25 bar gauge all tanks, Maximum carriage temp. 95 degrees C ESP LI Ice Class 1B at a draught of 6.50m Max/min draughts fwd 6.5/4.0m Max/min draughts aft 6.5/4.0m Power required 2320kw, power installed 2800kw **LMC** **UMS** Eq.Ltr: Q; Cable: 467.5/40.0 U2	**1998**-10 **INMA SpA — La Spezia** Yd No: 4260 Loa 96.19 (BB) Br ex 16.31 Dght 6.532 Lbp 91.20 Br md 16.20 Dpth 8.03 Welded, 1 dk	**(A12B2TR) Chemical/Products Tanker** Double Hull (13F) Liq: 5,359; Liq (Oil): 5,359 Cargo Heating Coils Compartments: 16 Wing Ta (s.stl), ER 16 Cargo Pump (s): 16x200m³/hr Manifold: Bow/CM: 48.7m Ice Capable	**4 diesel electric oil engines** driving 4 gen. each 896kW 440V a.c Connecting to 1 elec. Motor of (2800kW) driving 1 FP propeller Total Power: 3,720kW (5,056hp) 12.5kn Wartsila 6L20 4 x 4 Stroke 6 Cy. 200 x 280 each-930kW (1264bhp) Wartsila NSD Finland Oy-Finland Boilers: 2 TOH (o.f.) Thrusters: 1 Thwart. FP thruster (f) Fuel: 75.0 (d.f.) 336.0 (r.f.)
9359375 *ZCYJ2* -	**STOLT SISTO** **Stolt Gulf Parcel Tanker 2 Ltd** Gulf Stolt Ship Management JLT *George Town* *Cayman Islands (British)* MMSI: 319004100 Official number: 740765	**26,329** 14,416 46,011 T/cm 52.2	Class: NV	**2010**-02 **SLS Shipbuilding Co Ltd — Tongyeong** Yd No: 474 Loa 182.88 (BB) Br ex 32.23 Dght 12.086 Lbp 175.60 Br md 32.20 Dpth 16.05 Welded, 1 dk	**(A12B2TR) Chemical/Products Tanker** Double Hull (13F) Liq: 47,729; Liq (Oil): 47,729 Cargo Heating Coils Compartments: 9 Ta, 20 Wing Ta, ER 29 Cargo Pump (s): 15x220m³/hr, 14x360m³/hr Manifold: Bow/CM: 91m	**1 oil engine** driving 1 FP propeller Total Power: 11,300kW (15,363hp) 14.5kn MAN-B&W 5S60MC-C 1 x 2 Stroke 5 Cy. 600 x 2400 11300kW (15363bhp) STX Engine Co Ltd-South Korea AuxGen: 3 x 1300kW 450V 60Hz a.c Thrusters: 1 Tunnel thruster (f) Fuel: 122.0 (d.f.) 2048.0 (r.f.)
9199311 *ZCPQ2* -	**STOLT SKUA** *ex* Bow Wave *-2006* *ex* Yao Ru *-2000* **Stolt Skua BV** Stolt Tankers BV SatCom: Inmarsat C 431912110 *George Town* *Cayman Islands (British)* MMSI: 319121000 Official number: 739709	**5,342** 2,642 8,594 T/cm 18.2	Class: NV (NK)	**1999**-06 **Usuki Shipyard Co Ltd — Usuki OT** Yd No: 1659 Loa 112.00 (BB) Br ex 19.20 Dght 7.514 Lbp 105.00 Br md 19.00 Dpth 10.00 Welded, 1 dk	**(A12B2TR) Chemical/Products Tanker** Double Hull (13F) Liq: 9,227; Liq (Oil): 9,227 Cargo Heating Coils Compartments: 18 Wing Ta (s.stl), 2 Wing Slop Ta, ER 18 Cargo Pump (s): 18x250m³/hr Manifold: Bow/CM: 56.5m	**1 oil engine** driving 1 FP propeller Total Power: 3,089kW (4,200hp) 13.3kn Mitsubishi 6UEC37LA 1 x 2 Stroke 6 Cy. 370 x 880 3089kW (4200bhp) Akasaka Tekkosho KK (Akasaka DieselLtd)-Japan AuxGen: 2 x 480kW a.c Thrusters: 1 Tunnel thruster (f) Fuel: 83.0 (d.f.) 642.0 (r.f.)
9352212 *ZCTY8* -	**STOLT SNELAND** **Stolt Sneland BV** Stolt Tankers BV SatCom: Inmarsat Mini-M 764869480 *George Town* *Cayman Islands (British)* MMSI: 319627000 Official number: 740603	**25,884** 13,427 44,080 T/cm 48.5	Class: NV	**2008**-09 **Wadan Yards Okean OJSC — Nikolayev** (Fwd & aft sections) **2008**-09 **Aker Yards AS Floro — Floro** (Main cargo section) Yd No: 150 Loa 182.72 (BB) Br ex 32.24 Dght 11.870 Lbp 175.22 Br md 32.20 Dpth 15.60 Welded, 1 dk	**(A12B2TR) Chemical/Products Tanker** Double Hull (13F) Liq: 44,170; Liq (Oil): 45,350 Cargo Heating Coils Compartments: 13 Ta, 26 Wing Ta, 2 Wing Slop Ta, ER 39 Cargo Pump (s): 24x385m³/hr, 15x220m³/hr Manifold: Bow/CM: 96m	**1 oil engine** driving 1 CP propeller Total Power: 11,060kW (15,037hp) 15.0kn MAN-B&W 7S50MC-C 1 x 2 Stroke 7 Cy. 500 x 2000 11060kW (15037bhp) Kawasaki Heavy Industries Ltd-Japan AuxGen: 2 x 1330kW a.c, 1 x 1100kW a.c Thrusters: 1 Tunnel thruster (f) Fuel: 110.0 (d.f.) 1835.0 (r.f.)
9149524 *ELVQ7* -	**STOLT SPAN** **Stolt Span Ltd** Stolt Tankers BV SatCom: Inmarsat C 463678040 *Monrovia* *Liberia* MMSI: 636010915 Official number: 10915	**14,900** 7,228 22,273 T/cm 34.1	Class: LR (NV) **100A1** SS 05/2009 Double Hull oil & chemical tanker Ship Type 1 ESP LI SG 1.45 and PV+0.25 bar gauge all integral tanks, SG 1.85 and PV+0.25 bar gauge at 78% full, all integral tanks, SG 1.025 and PV+0.6 bar gauge all integral tanks, SG 1.45 and PV+0.6/-0.2 bar gauge deck tanks, SG 1.84 and PV+0.6/-0.2 bar gauge at 77% full, deck tanks. Maximum carriage temperature up to 90 deg C integral tanks, Maximum carriage temperature up to 60 deg C deck tanks. **LMC** **UMS** Eq.Ltr: G†; Cable: 577.5/62.0 U3	**1998**-12 **Juliana Constructora Gijonesa SA — Gijon** Yd No: 360 Loa 162.60 (BB) Br ex 23.72 Dght 10.116 Lbp 154.10 Br md 23.72 Dpth 13.35 Welded, 1 dk	**(A12B2TR) Chemical/Products Tanker** Double Hull (13F) Liq: 24,720; Liq (Oil): 24,720 Compartments: 10 Ta, 26 Wing Ta, ER 40 Cargo Pump (s): 40x220m³/hr Manifold: Bow/CM: 82m	**3 diesel electric oil engines** driving 1 gen. of 3200kW 690V a.c 1 gen. of 3200kW 690V a.c 1 gen. of 2300kW 690V a.c Connecting to 1 elec. Motor of (6554kW) driving 1 FP propeller Total Power: 8,940kW (12,155hp) 15.2kn Wartsila 6R32 1 x 4 Stroke 6 Cy. 320 x 350 2460kW (3345bhp) Wartsila Diesel S.A.-Bermeo Wartsila 8R32 2 x 4 Stroke 8 Cy. 320 x 350 each-3240kW (4405bhp) Wartsila Diesel S.A.-Bermeo Boilers: 3 TOH (ex.g.) 10.2kgf/cm² (10.0bar), 2 TOH (o.f.) 10.2kgf/cm² (10.0bar) Thrusters: 1 Thwart. FP thruster (f) Fuel: 52.0 (d.f.) 1478.0 (r.f.)
9168611 *ZCSQ9* -	**STOLT SPRAY** **Stolt Spray BV** Stolt Tankers BV SatCom: Inmarsat B 331959111 *George Town* *Cayman Islands (British)* MMSI: 319591000 Official number: 733294	**14,900** 7,228 22,201 T/cm 32.0	Class: NV	**2000**-07 **Juliana Constructora Gijonesa SA — Gijon** Yd No: 362 Loa 162.60 (BB) Br ex - Dght 10.116 Lbp 154.10 Br md 23.72 Dpth 13.35 Welded, 1 dk	**(A12B2TR) Chemical/Products Tanker** Double Hull (13F) Liq: 23,340; Liq (Oil): 24,372 Cargo Heating Coils Compartments: 10 Ta, 26 Wing Ta, 1 Slop Ta, ER 40 Cargo Pump (s): 40x220m³/hr Manifold: Bow/CM: 82m	**3 diesel electric oil engines** driving 2 gen. each 3130kW 690V a.c 1 gen. of 2000kW 690V a.c Connecting to 1 elec. Motor of (6473kW) driving 1 FP propeller Total Power: 9,020kW (12,263hp) 15.2kn Wartsila 6R32LN 1 x 4 Stroke 6 Cy. 320 x 350 2460kW (3345bhp) Wartsila NSD Finland Oy-Finland Wartsila 8R32LN 2 x 4 Stroke 8 Cy. 320 x 350 each-3280kW (4459bhp) Wartsila NSD Finland Oy-Finland Thrusters: 1 Thwart. FP thruster (f) Fuel: 63.0 (d.f.) (Heating Coils) 1522.0 (r.f.)
9169940 *ZCSR* -	**STOLT STREAM** **Stolt Stream BV** Stolt Tankers BV SatCom: Inmarsat B 331946911 *George Town* *Cayman Islands (British)* MMSI: 319469000 Official number: 733295	**14,900** 7,228 22,199 T/cm 34.0	Class: NV	**2000**-05 **Juliana Constructora Gijonesa SA — Gijon** Yd No: 361 Loa 162.60 (BB) Br ex - Dght 10.100 Lbp 154.04 Br md 23.72 Dpth 13.35 Welded, 1 dk	**(A12B2TR) Chemical/Products Tanker** Double Hull (13F) Liq: 24,720; Liq (Oil): 24,720 Cargo Heating Coils Compartments: ER, 10 Ta, 30 Wing Ta 40 Cargo Pump (s): 40x220m³/hr Manifold: Bow/CM: 82m	**3 diesel electric oil engines** driving 2 gen. each 3130kW 690V a.c 1 gen. of 2300kW 690V a.c Connecting to 1 elec. Motor of (6473kW) driving 1 FP propeller Total Power: 8,899kW (12,100hp) 15.2kn Wartsila 6R32 1 x 4 Stroke 6 Cy. 320 x 350 2427kW (3300bhp) Wartsila Finland Oy-Finland Wartsila 8R32LN 2 x 4 Stroke 8 Cy. 320 x 350 each-3236kW (4400bhp) Wartsila Finland Oy-Finland Thrusters: 1 Thwart. FP thruster (f) Fuel: 63.0 (d.f.) (Heating Coils) 1514.0 (r.f.)
9311024 *A8XU2* -	**STOLT STRENGTH** *ex* Strength *-2014* *ex* Stolt Strength *-2010* **Stolt Strength BV** Stolt Tankers BV SatCom: Inmarsat Mini-M 765070634 *Monrovia* *Liberia* MMSI: 636014974 Official number: 14974	**20,059** 9,017 33,209 T/cm 41.7	Class: BV	**2005**-11 **Shin Kurushima Dockyard Co. Ltd. — Onishi** Yd No: 5326 Loa 174.38 (BB) Br ex 27.73 Dght 11.023 Lbp 167.00 Br md 27.70 Dpth 16.00 Welded, 1 dk	**(A12B2TR) Chemical/Products Tanker** Double Hull (13F) Liq: 34,950; Liq (Oil): 37,388 Cargo Heating Coils Compartments: 26 Wing Ta, 2 Wing Slop Ta, ER 26 Cargo Pump (s): 26x300m³/hr Manifold: Bow/CM: 86.4m	**1 oil engine** driving 1 FP propeller Total Power: 8,580kW (11,665hp) 15.0kn MAN-B&W 6S50MC 1 x 2 Stroke 6 Cy. 500 x 1910 8580kW (11665bhp) Mitsui Engineering & Shipbuilding CLtd-Japan AuxGen: 3 x 600kW 450/100V 60Hz a.c Thrusters: 1 Thwart. FP thruster (f) Fuel: 124.0 (d.f.) 1622.0 (r.f.)
9156577 *VRDL8* -	**STOLT SUISEN** **NYK Stolt Shipholding Inc** Stolt Tankers BV SatCom: Inmarsat Mini-M 764804798 *Hong Kong* *Hong Kong* MMSI: 477985800 Official number: HK-2038	**6,426** 3,549 11,538 T/cm 19.6	Class: NK	**1998**-10 **Fukuoka Shipbuilding Co Ltd — Fukuoka FO** Yd No: 1203 Loa 117.27 (BB) Br ex 20.83 Dght 8.760 Lbp 110.00 Br md 20.80 Dpth 11.20 Welded, 1 dk	**(A12B2TR) Chemical/Products Tanker** Double Hull (13F) Liq: 12,305; Liq (Oil): 12,302 Cargo Heating Coils Compartments: ER, 20 Wing Ta 20 Cargo Pump (s): 8x300m³/hr, 12x200m³/hr Manifold: Bow/CM: 54.1m	**1 oil engine** driving 1 FP propeller Total Power: 3,883kW (5,279hp) 12.5kn B&W 6L35MC 1 x 2 Stroke 6 Cy. 350 x 1050 3883kW (5279bhp) Makita Corp-Japan AuxGen: 3 x 380kW 450V 60Hz a.c Thrusters: 1 Thwart. CP thruster (f) Fuel: 95.7 (d.f.) 708.7 (r.f.)

9149512 *ZCSR2* -	**STOLT SUN** **Stolt Sun BV** Stolt Tankers BV SatCom: Inmarsat B 331945911 *George Town* *Cayman Islands (British)* MMSI: 319459000 Official number: 733296	**14,900** 7,228 22,198 T/cm 34.2	Class: LR (NV) **100A1** SS 02/2010 Double Hull oil & chemical tanker Ship Type 1 ESP LI SG 1.45 and PV+0.25 bar gauge all integral tanks, SG 1.85 and PV+0.25 bar gauge at 78% full, all integral tanks, SG 1.025 and PV+0.6 bar gauge all integral tanks, SG 1.45 and PV+0.6/-0.2 bar gauge deck tanks, SG 1.84 and PV+0.6/-0.2 bar gauge at 77% full, deck tanks. Maximum carriage temperature up to 90 deg C integral tanks, Maximum carriage temperature up to 60 deg C deck tanks. **LMC** **UMS**	**2000**-01 **Astilleros de Sestao SRL — Sestao** Yd No: 311 Loa 162.60 (BB) Br ex 23.73 Dght 10.116 Lbp 154.10 Br md 23.70 Dpth 13.35 Welded, 1 dk	**(A12B2TR) Chemical/Products Tanker** Double Hull (13F) Liq: 24,713; Liq (Oil): 24,713 Compartments: 10 Ta, 26 Wing Ta, ER 40 Cargo Pump (s): 40x220m³/hr Manifold: Bow/CM: 82m	**3 diesel electric oil engines** driving 2 gen. each 3200kW 1 gen. of 2300kW Connecting to 1 elec. Motor of (6554kW) driving 1 FP propeller Total Power: 8,800kW (11,964hp) 15.2kn Wartsila 6R32E 1 x 4 Stroke 6 Cy. 320 x 350 2320kW (3154bhp) Wartsila NSD Finland Oy-Finland Wartsila 8R32E 2 x 4 Stroke 8 Cy. 320 x 350 each-3240kW (4405bhp) Wartsila NSD Finland Oy-Finland Boilers: 3 TOH (ex.g.) 10.2kgf/cm² (10.0bar), 2 TOH (o.f.) 10.2kgf/cm² (10.0bar) Thrusters: 1 Thwart. CP thruster (f) Fuel: 63.0 (d.f.) 1540.0 (r.f.)
9168623 *ZCSR3* -	**STOLT SURF** **Stolt Surf BV** Stolt Tankers BV SatCom: Inmarsat C 431999011 *George Town* *Cayman Islands (British)* MMSI: 319545000 Official number: 733297	**14,900** 7,228 22,198 T/cm 32.0	Class: NV	**2000**-12 **Juliana Constructora Gijonesa SA — Gijon** Yd No: 363 Loa 162.60 (BB) Br ex - Dght 10.116 Lbp 154.10 Br md 23.72 Dpth 13.35 Welded, 1 dk	**(A12B2TR) Chemical/Products Tanker** Double Hull (13F) Liq: 24,726; Liq (Oil): 24,726 Compartments: ER, 12 Ta (s.stl), 30 Wing Ta (s.stl) 40 Cargo Pump (s): 40x220m³/hr Manifold: Bow/CM: 82m	**3 diesel electric oil engines** driving 2 gen. each 3100kW 690V a.c 1 gen. of 2000kW 690V a.c Connecting to 1 elec. Motor of (6473kW) driving 1 FP propeller Total Power: 9,020kW (12,263hp) 15.2kn Wartsila 6R32LN 1 x 4 Stroke 6 Cy. 320 x 350 2460kW (3345bhp) Wartsila Finland Oy-Finland Wartsila 8R32LN 2 x 4 Stroke 8 Cy. 320 x 350 each-3280kW (4459bhp) Wartsila Finland Oy-Finland Thrusters: 1 Tunnel thruster (f) Fuel: 63.0 (d.f.) 1540.0 (r.f.)
9199323 *ZCPT8* -	**STOLT TEAL** *ex Bow Wind -2006 ex Gui Zhen -2000* **Stolt Teal BV** Stolt Tankers BV SatCom: Inmarsat C 431919410 *George Town* *Cayman Islands (British)* MMSI: 319194000 Official number: 739741	**5,342** 2,642 8,587 T/cm 17.7	Class: NV (NK)	**1999**-08 **Usuki Shipyard Co Ltd — Usuki OT** Yd No: 1660 Loa 112.00 (BB) Br ex 19.03 Dght 7.514 Lbp 105.00 Br md 19.00 Dpth 10.00 Welded, 1 dk	**(A12B2TR) Chemical/Products Tanker** Double Hull (13F) Liq: 9,230; Liq (Oil): 9,420 Cargo Heating Coils Compartments: 18 Wing Ta (s.stl), 2 Slop Ta (s.stl), ER 18 Cargo Pump (s): 18x250m³/hr Manifold: Bow/CM: 56.5m	**1 oil engine** driving 1 FP propeller Total Power: 3,089kW (4,200hp) 13.3kn Mitsubishi 6UEC37LA 1 x 2 Stroke 6 Cy. 370 x 880 3089kW (4200bhp) Akasaka Tekkosho KK (Akasaka DieselLtd)-Japan AuxGen: 2 x 450kW 440V 60Hz a.c Thrusters: 1 Tunnel thruster (f) Fuel: 86.0 (d.f.) (Heating Coils) 652.0 (r.f.) 11.8pd
8920529 *MVRB8* -	**STOLT TERN** *ex Jytte Terkol -1996 ex Stolt Jytte Terkol -1992* **Stolt Tern BV** Stolt Tankers BV SatCom: Inmarsat Mini-M 764623986 *Cardiff* *United Kingdom* MMSI: 235050795 Official number: 731116	**3,206** 1,358 4,759 T/cm 12.4	Class: LR ✠**100A1** SS 12/2011 Double Hull oil and chemical tanker, Ship Type 2*, MARPOL 13H (1) (b) SG 1.8 tanks 3, 4, 5 & 6, SG 1.2 tanks 1, 2 & 7, CR (s.stl) ESP Ice Class 1D ✠**LMC** **UMS** Eq.Ltr: U; Cable: 467.5/46.0 U2	**1991**-12 **Aarhus Flydedok A/S — Aarhus** Yd No: 198 Loa 96.35 (BB) Br ex 15.33 Dght 6.211 Lbp 87.75 Br md 15.10 Dpth 8.05 Welded, 1 dk	**(A12B2TR) Chemical/Products Tanker** Double Hull (13F) Liq: 4,659; Liq (Oil): 4,659 Cargo Heating Coils Compartments: 1 Ta, 12 Wing Ta, 2 Slop Ta, ER 13 Cargo Pump (s): 13x150m³/hr Manifold: Bow/CM: 49.5m Ice Capable	**1 oil engine** with clutches, flexible couplings & sr geared to sc. shaft driving 1 CP propeller Total Power: 2,999kW (4,077hp) 13.2kn MaK 9M453C 1 x 4 Stroke 9 Cy. 320 x 420 2999kW (4077bhp) Krupp MaK Maschinenbau GmbH-Kiel AuxGen: 1 x 633kW 380V 50Hz a.c, 3 x 335kW 380V 50Hz a.c Boilers: 2 TOH (o.f.) 8.2kgf/cm² (8.0bar), TOH (ex.g.) 8.2kgf/cm² (8.0bar), sg 6.1kgf/cm² (6.0bar) Thrusters: 1 Thwart. CP thruster (f) Fuel: 133.0 (d.f.) (Part Heating Coils) 330.0 (r.f.) 11.0pd
8309555 *ZCSQ6* -	**STOLT TOPAZ** **Stolt Topaz BV** Stolt Tankers BV SatCom: Inmarsat B 331941911 *George Town* *Cayman Islands (British)* MMSI: 319419000 Official number: 733291	**23,964** 13,720 38,818 T/cm 48.8	Class: NV	**1986**-05 **Daewoo Shipbuilding & Heavy Machinery Ltd — Geoje** Yd No: 2009 Loa 176.80 (BB) Br ex - Dght 11.428 Lbp 169.00 Br md 32.25 Dpth 15.00 Welded, 1 dk	**(A12B2TR) Chemical/Products Tanker** Double Bottom Entire Compartment Length Liq: 45,444; Liq (Oil): 45,444 Compartments: 26 Ta (s.stl), 7 Wing Ta (s.stl), 21 Wing Ta, ER 58 Cargo Pump (s): 12x450m³/hr, 46x255m³/hr Manifold: Bow/CM: 81.2m	**1 oil engine** driving 1 FP propeller Total Power: 9,179kW (12,480hp) 15.0kn B&W 6L60MCE 1 x 2 Stroke 6 Cy. 600 x 1944 9179kW (12480bhp) Hyundai Engine & Machinery Co Ltd-South Korea AuxGen: 3 x 900kW 450V 60Hz a.c, 1 x a.c Thrusters: 1 Thwart. FP thruster (f) Fuel: 277.0 (d.f.) 1877.0 (r.f.) 37.5pd
9191280 *VRDB7* -	**STOLT TRANSPORTER** *ex Akane -2007 ex Ao Xing -2007* *ex Akane -2005* **Akane Tankers Ltd** Stolt Tankers BV SatCom: Inmarsat Mini-M 764859487 *Hong Kong* *Hong Kong* MMSI: 477898600 Official number: HK-1957	**2,676** 1,093 3,989 T/cm 11.3	Class: NK (CC) (BV)	**1998**-11 **Hitachi Zosen Mukaishima Marine Co Ltd — Onomichi HS** Yd No: 131 Loa 92.50 (BB) Br ex - Dght 5.762 Lbp 85.00 Br md 15.00 Dpth 7.20 Welded, 1 dk	**(A12B2TR) Chemical/Products Tanker** Double Hull (13F) Liq: 4,020; Liq (Oil): 4,020 Cargo Heating Coils Compartments: 1 Ta, ER, 8 Wing Ta 9 Cargo Pump (s): 8x150m³/hr, 1x70m³/hr Manifold: Bow/CM: 42.8m	**1 oil engine** driving 1 FP propeller Total Power: 2,574kW (3,500hp) 12.1kn Hanshin LH41LA 1 x 4 Stroke 6 Cy. 410 x 800 2574kW (3500bhp) The Hanshin Diesel Works Ltd-Japan AuxGen: 2 x 360kW 445V 60Hz a.c Fuel: 72.0 (d.f.) (Heating Coils) 346.0 (r.f.) 7.5pd
9477543 *ZGAO* -	**STOLT TSUBAKI** **Stolt Tsubaki Inc** Stolt Tankers BV SatCom: Inmarsat C 431918912 *George Town* *Cayman Islands (British)* MMSI: 319027200 Official number: 742452	**7,242** 3,808 12,812 T/cm 21.1	Class: NK	**2011**-04 **Usuki Shipyard Co Ltd — Usuki OT** Yd No: 1726 Loa 121.52 (BB) Br ex 20.63 Dght 8.814 Lbp 115.00 Br md 20.60 Dpth 11.33 Welded, 1 dk	**(A12B2TR) Chemical/Products Tanker** Double Hull (13F) Liq: 13,142; Liq (Oil): 13,500 Cargo Heating Coils Compartments: 9 Wing Ta, 9 Wing Ta, ER 18 Cargo Pump (s): 6x200m³/hr, 12x300m³/hr Manifold: Bow/CM: 62m	**1 oil engine** driving 1 FP propeller Total Power: 4,900kW (6,662hp) 14.3kn MAN-B&W 7S35MC 1 x 2 Stroke 7 Cy. 350 x 1400 4900kW (6662bhp) Hitachi Zosen Corp-Japan AuxGen: 3 x 450kW 60Hz a.c Thrusters: 1 Tunnel thruster (f) Fuel: 81.0 (d.f.) 632.0 (r.f.)
9274305 *D5AF5* -	**STOLT VANGUARD** **Stolt Vanguard BV** Stolt Tankers BV *Monrovia* *Liberia* MMSI: 636015366 Official number: 15366	**15,711** 7,830 25,261 T/cm 34.7	Class: NK	**2004**-08 **Watanabe Zosen KK — Imabari EH** Yd No: 339 Loa 158.83 (BB) Br ex 25.52 Dght 10.515 Lbp 150.00 Br md 25.50 Dpth 15.00 Welded, 1 dk	**(A12B2TR) Chemical/Products Tanker** Double Hull (13F) Liq: 30,300; Liq (Oil): 30,299 Cargo Heating Coils Compartments: 4 Ta, 24 Wing Ta, ER 28 Cargo Pump (s): 10x330m³/hr, 18x220m³/hr Manifold: Bow/CM: 80.9m	**1 oil engine** driving 1 FP propeller Total Power: 7,979kW (10,848hp) 14.5kn Mitsubishi 6UEC52LS 1 x 2 Stroke 6 Cy. 520 x 1850 7979kW (10848bhp) Akasaka Tekkosho KK (Akasaka DieselLtd)-Japan AuxGen: 3 x 520kW a.c Thrusters: 1 Thwart. FP thruster (f) Fuel: 127.0 (d.f.) 1240.0 (r.f.)
8911669 *D5DB2* -	**STOLT VESTLAND** **Stolt Vestland BV** Stolt Tankers BV *Monrovia* *Liberia* MMSI: 636015829 Official number: 15829	**19,034** 11,165 31,434 T/cm 43.6	Class: NV	**1992**-11 **Kvaerner Kleven Floro AS — Floro** (Aft section) Yd No: 125 **1992**-11 **Kvaerner Kleven Floro AS — Forde** (Fwd section) Yd No: 125 Loa 174.70 (BB) Br ex 29.54 Dght 10.122 Lbp 167.20 Br md 29.50 Dpth 13.25 Welded, 1 dk	**(A12B2TR) Chemical/Products Tanker** Double Bottom Entire Compartment Length Liq: 36,706; Liq (Oil): 3,670 Cargo Heating Coils Compartments: 23 Ta (s.stl), 16 Wing Ta, ER, 2 Wing Slop Ta 39 Cargo Pump (s): 39x300m³/hr Manifold: Bow/CM: 83.6m	**1 oil engine** driving 1 CP propeller Total Power: 9,173kW (12,472hp) 15.5kn B&W 6L60MC 1 x 2 Stroke 6 Cy. 600 x 1944 9173kW (12472bhp) AO Bryanskiy MashinostroitelnyyZavod (BMZ)-Bryansk AuxGen: 1 x 1160kW 450V 60Hz a.c, 3 x 869kW 450V 60Hz a.c Thrusters: 1 Thwart. CP thruster (f) Fuel: 295.0 (d.f.) 2463.0 (r.f.) 33.0pd
9196711 *ZCON9* -	**STOLT VIKING** *ex Isola Blu -2005* **Stolt Viking BV** Stolt Tankers BV SatCom: Inmarsat Mini-M 76114711 *George Town* *Cayman Islands (British)* MMSI: 319515000 Official number: 738212	**16,967** 8,322 26,707 T/cm 39.3	Class: NV (BV) (RI)	**2001**-03 **Fincantieri-Cant. Nav. Italiani S.p.A. — Ancona** Yd No: 6054 Loa 166.62 (BB) Br ex 26.93 Dght 10.332 Lbp 155.60 Br md 26.90 Dpth 13.60 Welded, 1 dk	**(A12B2TR) Chemical/Products Tanker** Double Hull (13F) Liq: 27,043; Liq (Oil): 27,043 Compartments: 10 Ta (s.stl), 18 Wing Ta (s.stl), 1 Wing Slop Ta, 1 Slop Ta (s.stl), 1 Wing Slop Ta (s.stl), ER (s.stl) 32 Cargo Pump (s): 2x750m³/hr, 18x300m³/hr, 9x200m³/hr, 3x70m³/hr Manifold: Bow/CM: 83.8m	**3 diesel electric oil engines** driving 3 gen. Connecting to 2 elec. motors each (3300kW) driving 1 FP propeller Total Power: 11,000kW (14,955hp) 15.2kn Wartsila 6L32 1 x 4 Stroke 6 Cy. 320 x 400 3000kW (4079bhp) Wartsila Finland Oy-Finland Wartsila 8L32 2 x 4 Stroke 8 Cy. 320 x 400 each-4000kW (5438bhp) Wartsila Finland Oy-Finland Thrusters: 1 Thwart. FP thruster (f) Fuel: 186.0 (d.f.) 1527.0 (r.f.) 35.0pd

IMO / Call sign / Name / Owner	Tonnage	Class	Builder & Dimensions	Type & Cargo	Machinery
8911657 **STOLT VINLAND** *D5DM9* - **Stolt Vinland BV** Stolt Tankers BV *Monrovia* *Liberia* MMSI: 636015920 Official number: 15920	**19,034** 11,165 31,434 T/cm 43.4	Class: NV	**1992-03 Kvaerner Kleven Floro AS — Floro** (Aft section) Yd No: 124 **1992-03 Kvaerner Kleven Floro AS — Forde** (Fwd section) Yd No: 124 Loa 174.70 (BB) Br ex 29.54 Dght 10.140 Lbp 167.20 Br md 29.50 Dpth 13.25 Welded, 1 dk	**(A12B2TR) Chemical/Products Tanker** Double Bottom Entire Compartment Length Liq: 38,575; Liq (Oil): 36,534 Cargo Heating Coils Compartments: 23 Ta (s.stl), 16 Wing Ta, ER 41 Cargo Pump (s): 39x300m^3/hr, 2x80m^3/hr Manifold: Bow/CM: 83.6m	**1 oil engine** driving 1 CP propeller Total Power: 9,173kW (12,472hp) 15.5kn B&W 6L60MC 1 x 2 Stroke 6 Cy. 600 x 1944 9173kW (12472bhp) AO Bryanskiy MashinostroitelnyyZavod (BMZ)-Bryansk AuxGen: 1 x 1160kW 440V 60Hz a.c, 3 x 869kW 450V 60Hz a.c Thrusters: 1 Thwart. CP thruster (f) Fuel: 286.0 (d.f.) 2423.0 (r.f.) 33.0pd
9279707 **STOLT VIOLET** *H9BK* - **Fast Shipping SA** Stolt-Nielsen Singapore Pte Ltd *Panama* *Panama* MMSI: 351481000 Official number: 3027704B	**5,376** 2,621 8,792 T/cm 17.9	Class: NK	**2004-09 Shin Kurushima Dockyard Co. Ltd. — Hashihama, Imabari** Yd No: 5228 Loa 113.98 (BB) Br ex 18.20 Dght 7.450 Lbp 108.50 Br md 18.20 Dpth 9.65 Welded, 1 dk	**(A12B2TR) Chemical/Products Tanker** Double Hull (13F) Liq: 9,363; Liq (Oil): 9,363 Cargo Heating Coils Compartments: 16 Wing Ta (s.stl), ER, 2 Wing Slop Ta 16 Cargo Pump (s): 16x200m^3/hr Manifold: Bow/CM: 56.7m	**1 oil engine** driving 1 FP propeller Total Power: 3,900kW (5,302hp) 13.8kn B&W 6L35MC 1 x 2 Stroke 6 Cy. 350 x 1050 3900kW (5302bhp) Makita Corp-Japan AuxGen: 2 x 400kW a.c Fuel: 43.0 (d.f.) 395.0 (r.f.)
9274317 **STOLT VIRTUE** *9VGK6* - **United Sky Shipping Pte Ltd** Stolt Tankers BV *Singapore* *Singapore* MMSI: 564738000 Official number: 391330	**15,715** 7,830 25,230 T/cm 34.7	Class: NK	**2004-12 Watanabe Zosen KK — Imabari EH** Yd No: 340 Loa 158.83 (BB) Br ex 25.53 Dght 10.514 Lbp 150.00 Br md 25.50 Dpth 15.00 Welded, 1 dk	**(A12B2TR) Chemical/Products Tanker** Double Hull (13F) Liq: 30,281; Liq (Oil): 30,281 Cargo Heating Coils Compartments: 2 Ta (s.stl), 24 Wing Ta (s.stl), 2 Wing Slop Ta (s.stl), ER 26 Cargo Pump (s): 10x330m^3/hr, 16x220m^3/hr Manifold: Bow/CM: 82.2m	**1 oil engine** driving 1 FP propeller Total Power: 7,980kW (10,850hp) 14.5kn Mitsubishi 6UEC52LS 1 x 2 Stroke 6 Cy. 520 x 1850 7980kW (10850bhp) Akasaka Tekkosho KK (Akasaka DieselLtd)-Japan AuxGen: 3 x 610kW 440/220V 60Hz a.c Thrusters: 1 Thwart. CP thruster (f) Fuel: 105.0 (d.f.) 1165.0 (r.f.)
9274329 **STOLT VISION** *D5CM9* - **Stolt Vision BV** Stolt Tankers BV SatCom: Inmarsat C 463712773 *Monrovia* *Liberia* MMSI: 636015738 Official number: 15738	**15,976** 7,838 25,147 T/cm 34.7	Class: AB	**2005-03 Watanabe Zosen KK — Imabari EH** Yd No: 341 Loa 158.83 (BB) Br ex 25.53 Dght 10.515 Lbp 150.00 Br md 25.50 Dpth 15.00 Welded, 1 dk	**(A12B2TR) Chemical/Products Tanker** Double Hull (13F) Liq: 30,287; Liq (Oil): 30,287 Cargo Heating Coils Compartments: 2 Ta (s.stl), 1 Wing Ta, 23 Wing Ta (s.stl), 2 Wing Slop Ta (s.stl), ER (s.stl) 26 Cargo Pump (s): 10x330m^3/hr, 16x220m^3/hr Manifold: Bow/CM: 82.2m	**1 oil engine** driving 1 FP propeller Total Power: 7,980kW (10,850hp) 14.5kn Mitsubishi 6UEC52LS 1 x 2 Stroke 6 Cy. 520 x 1850 7980kW (10850bhp) Kobe Hatsudoki KK-Japan AuxGen: 3 x 560kW a.c Thrusters: 1 Tunnel thruster (f) Fuel: 169.0 (d.f.) 1240.0 (r.f.)
9297292 **STOLT VOYAGER** *VRGG4* *ex* Samho Prince *-2009* - **Stolt Voyager Ltd** Stolt Tankers BV *Hong Kong* *Hong Kong* MMSI: 477682400 Official number: HK-2617	**2,761** 1,172 3,560 T/cm 10.1	Class: KR	**2003-12 Samho Shipbuilding Co Ltd — Tongyeong** Yd No: 1042 Loa 91.50 (BB) Br ex - Dght 5.713 Lbp 84.00 Br md 14.40 Dpth 7.50 Welded, 1 dk	**(A12B2TR) Chemical/Products Tanker** Double Hull (13F) Liq: 3,998; Liq (Oil): 3,998 Cargo Heating Coils Compartments: 8 Wing Ta (s.stl), ER, 5 Ta (s.stl), 1 Slop Ta 10 Cargo Pump (s): 10x200m^3/hr Manifold: Bow/CM: 48.5m	**1 oil engine** driving 1 FP propeller Total Power: 2,405kW (3,270hp) 13.0kn MAN-B&W 6S26MC 1 x 2 Stroke 6 Cy. 260 x 980 2405kW (3270bhp) STX Corp-South Korea AuxGen: 3 x 320kW 445V a.c Thrusters: 1 Tunnel thruster (f) Fuel: 74.0 (d.f.) 168.0 (r.f.)
9351531 **STOLT ZULU** *D5DU3* - **NST Zulu Inc** Stolt Tankers BV *Monrovia* *Liberia* MMSI: 636015971 Official number: 15971	**16,442** 7,460 25,197 T/cm 35.5	Class: AB	**2006-02 Fukuoka Shipbuilding Co Ltd — Nagasaki NS** Yd No: 2003 Loa 158.50 (BB) Br ex 25.63 Dght 10.369 Lbp 149.00 Br md 25.60 Dpth 15.20 Welded, 1 dk	**(A12B2TR) Chemical/Products Tanker** Double Hull (13F) Liq: 30,386; Liq (Oil): 30,386 Cargo Heating Coils Compartments: 24 Wing Ta, 4 Ta, ER 28 Cargo Pump (s): 12x330m^3/hr, 16x220m^3/hr Manifold: Bow/CM: 78.1m	**1 oil engine** driving 1 FP propeller Total Power: 7,980kW (10,850hp) 15.1kn Mitsubishi 6UEC52LS 1 x 2 Stroke 6 Cy. 520 x 1850 7980kW (10850bhp) Mitsubishi Heavy Industries Ltd-Japan AuxGen: 3 x 600kW a.c Thrusters: 1 Thwart. FP thruster (f) Fuel: 142.0 (d.f.) 1114.0 (r.f.)
8971736 **STON** *9A4929* - **Jadrolinija** - *Rijeka* *Croatia* MMSI: 238107840	**478** 144 180	Class: CS	**1997-01 Brodosplit - Brodogradiliste Specijalnih Objekata doo — Split** Yd No: 585 Loa 41.20 Br ex - Dght - Lbp 32.40 Br md 16.00 Dpth 3.60 Welded, 1 dk	**(A36A2PR) Passenger/Ro-Ro Ship (Vehicles)** Bow ramp (f) Stern ramp (a)	**2 diesel electric oil engines** driving 2 gen. Connecting to 2 elec. motors each (290kW) driving 2 FP propellers Total Power: 1,766kW (2,402hp) 9.5kn Cummins KTA-19-M4 2 x 4 Stroke 6 Cy. 159 x 159 each-883kW (1201bhp) Cummins Engine Co Inc-USA AuxGen: 3 x 824kW 380V 50Hz a.c
8841539 **STONE** *V3QO9* *ex* Slavutich-14 *-2008* - **Merout Corp** Nova Mar Srl *Belize City* *Belize* MMSI: 312852000 Official number: 141220242	**2,193** 658 3,221	Class: RS (RR)	**1990-12 Kiyevskiy Sudostroitelnyy Sudoremontnyy Zavod — Kiyev** Yd No: 14 Loa 109.00 Br ex 16.22 Dght 3.200 Lbp 105.20 Br md 16.00 Dpth 4.00 Welded, 1 dk	**(A31A2GX) General Cargo Ship**	**2 oil engines** driving 2 FP propellers Total Power: 1,294kW (1,760hp) S.K.L. 8NVD48-2U 2 x 4 Stroke 8 Cy. 320 x 480 each-647kW (880bhp) VEB Schwermaschinenbau "KarlLiebknecht" (SKL)-Magdeburg
6917516 **STONE** *LAUT* *ex* Henric *-2007* *ex* Njord *-2003* *ex* Henric *-1998* *ex* Brackengarth *-1995* **Miljostein Shipping AS** - *Holmestrand* *Norway* MMSI: 259531000	**347** 105 -	Class: LR ✠ **100A1** SS 07/2009 tug ✠ **LMC** Eq.Ltr: (e) ; Cable: U1	**1969-08 Appledore Shipbuilders Ltd — Bideford** Yd No: A.S. 67 Loa 36.56 Br ex 10.01 Dght 3.963 Lbp 31.70 Br md 9.45 Dpth 4.65 Welded, 1 dk	**(B32A2ST) Tug**	**2 oil engines** dr geared to sc. shaft driving 1 CP propeller Total Power: 2,486kW (3,380hp) 14.0kn Ruston 6ATCM 2 x 4 Stroke 6 Cy. 318 x 368 each-1243kW (1690bhp) English Electric Diesels Ltd.-Glasgow AuxGen: 1 x 100kW 440V 60Hz a.c, 1 x 98kW 440V 60Hz a.c Fuel: 87.5 (d.f.)
8414518 **STONE BUCCANEER** *WCX8802* *ex* Eastern Sun *-1998* - **John W Stone Oil Distributor LLC** - *New Orleans, LA* *United States of America* MMSI: 368670000 Official number: 679193	*1,576* 1,068 3,549 T/cm 10.5	Class: AB	**1985-05 Jeffboat, Inc. — Jeffersonville, In** Yd No: 83-2635 Loa 85.43 Br ex 13.97 Dght 5.017 Lbp 82.61 Br md 13.72 Dpth 6.10 Welded, 1 dk	**(A13B2TP) Products Tanker** Liq: 4,173; Liq (Oil): 4,173 Cargo Heating Coils Compartments: 12 Ta, ER 4 Cargo Pump (s): 3x477m^3/hr, 1x397m^3/hr Manifold: Bow/CM: 25m	**2 oil engines** with clutches, flexible couplings & sr reverse geared to sc. shafts driving 2 FP propellers Total Power: 2,178kW (2,962hp) 12.5kn EMD (Electro-Motive) 8-645-E7 2 x Vee 2 Stroke 8 Cy. 230 x 254 each-1089kW (1481bhp) General Motors Corp.Electro-Motive Div.-La Grange AuxGen: 2 x 120kW 480V 60Hz a.c Thrusters: 1 Thwart. FP thruster (f); 1 Tunnel thruster (a) Fuel: 77.0 (d.f.) 9.0pd
9380582 **STONE I** *9HHM9* *ex* Rock *-2013* - **Stone Shipping LLC** Norient Product Pool ApS SatCom: Inmarsat Mini-M 761129014 *Valletta* *Malta* MMSI: 256994000 Official number: 9380582	**23,248** 9,915 37,889 T/cm 45.2	Class: NV (AB)	**2008-05 Hyundai Mipo Dockyard Co Ltd — Ulsan** Yd No: 2031 Loa 184.32 (BB) Br ex 27.45 Dght 11.515 Lbp 176.00 Br md 27.40 Dpth 17.20 Welded, 1 dk	**(A12B2TR) Chemical/Products Tanker** Double Hull (13F) Liq: 40,781; Liq (Oil): 40,801 Compartments: 12 Wing Ta, 2 Wing Slop Ta, ER 12 Cargo Pump (s): 10x500m^3/hr, 2x300m^3/hr Manifold: Bow/CM: 92.6m Ice Capable	**1 oil engine** driving 1 FP propeller Total Power: 9,480kW (12,889hp) 14.5kn MAN-B&W 6S50MC-C 1 x 2 Stroke 6 Cy. 500 x 2000 9480kW (12889bhp) Hyundai Heavy Industries Co Ltd-South Korea AuxGen: 3 x 900kW a.c Thrusters: 1 Tunnel thruster (f)
8033596 **STONE MOUNTAIN** - - - -	*121* 82 -		**1979 at Amelia, La** L reg 21.07 Br ex 7.35 Dght - Lbp - Br md - Dpth 2.98 Welded, 1 dk	**(B32A2ST) Tug**	**1 oil engine** driving 1 FP propeller Total Power: 1,383kW (1,880hp)
8992584 **STONE POWER** *WBF2379* - **John W Stone Oil Distributor LLC** - *New Orleans, LA* *United States of America* MMSI: 366954130 Official number: 557119	*169* 115 -		**1974-01 Houma Shipbuilding Co Inc — Houma LA** Yd No: 53 L reg 21.34 Br ex - Dght - Lbp - Br md 7.32 Dpth 3.05 Welded, 1 dk	**(B32A2ST) Tug**	**1 oil engine** driving 1 Propeller
9226396 **STONES** *V2OG9* - **Partenreederei H-J Hartmann ms 'Stones'** HJH Shipmanagement GmbH & Co KG *Saint John's* *Antigua & Barbuda* MMSI: 304267000 Official number: 3777	**17,357** 5,748 28,115	Class: GL	**2001-05 J.J. Sietas KG Schiffswerft GmbH & Co. — Hamburg** Yd No: 1176 Loa 166.72 (BB) Br ex 24.75 Dght 10.490 Lbp 160.58 Br md 24.50 Dpth 14.00 Welded, 1 dk	**(A23A2BD) Bulk Carrier, Self-discharging** Double Bottom Entire Compartment Length Grain: 20,046 Compartments: 7 Ho, ER 7 Ha: (12.6 x 14.0) (13.3 x 14.0)5 (14.7 x 14.0)ER	**1 oil engine** with flexible couplings & sr gearedto sc. shaft driving 1 CP propeller Total Power: 7,300kW (9,925hp) 14.1kn MaK 8M43 1 x 4 Stroke 8 Cy. 430 x 610 7300kW (9925bhp) Caterpillar Motoren GmbH & Co. KG-Germany AuxGen: 1 x 1800kW 460/230V 60Hz a.c, 4 x 682kW 460/230V 60Hz a.c Thrusters: 1 Thwart. CP thruster (f); 1 Tunnel thruster (a) Fuel: 233.5 (d.f.) 1022.3 (r.f.)

8853180 **STONINGTON JO** 193
WDA3427 *ex* Carolina Girl II *-2001* 138
\- **Stonington Fish & Lobster Inc** -
\-
Stonington, CT *United States of America*
MMSI: 366798340
Official number: 941588

1988 Duckworth Steel Boats, Inc. — Tarpon Springs, Fl Yd No: 301
Loa - Br ex - Dght -
Lbp 25.51 Br md 7.62 Dpth 3.90
Welded, 1 dk

(B11B2FV) Fishing Vessel

1 oil engine driving 1 FP propeller

5341526 **STOR ERIK** *113*
SGOU -
\- **Joel Malmstrom** -
\-
Stockholm *Sweden*

1893 Jonkopings Mekaniska Verkstad AB — Jonkoping
Loa 26.62 Br ex 6.00 Dght 3.501
Lbp - Br md 5.95 Dpth -
Riveted, 1 dk

(B32A2ST) Tug

1 Steam Recip driving 1 FP propeller 9.0kn
AB Jonkopings Motorfabrik-Sweden
Fuel: 40.5 (r.f.)

8513601 **STORD** **2,871** Class: (NV)
JXLL 861
\- **Norled AS** 817
Tide ASA
Bergen *Norway*
MMSI: 257026800

1987-02 Ankerlokken Verft Forde AS — Forde Yd No: 24
Loa 87.00 Br ex - Dght -
Lbp 76.82 Br md 14.80 Dpth 7.40
Welded, 2 dks

(A36A2PR) Passenger/Ro-Ro Ship (Vehicles)
Passengers: unberthed: 500
Bow door & ramp
Stern door & ramp
Lane-Wid: 7.00
Lane-clr ht: 4.50
Lorries: 12, Cars: 49

1 oil engine geared to sc. shaft driving 2 FP propellers
Total Power: 1,984kW (2,697hp) 15.0kn
Wichmann WX28V8
1 x Vee 4 Stroke 8 Cy. 280 x 360 1984kW (2697bhp)
Wichmann Motorfabrikk AS-Norway
AuxGen: 2 x 175kW 230V 50Hz a.c, 2 x 64kW 230V 50Hz a.c

5341564 **STORD I** *469*
LEYT *ex* O. T. Moe *-1987* *ex* Stord *-1969* 256
\- **Stiftelsen D/S Stord I** 267
\-
Bergen *Norway*
MMSI: 257786980

1913-04 Laxevaags Maskin- og Jernskipsbyggeri — Bergen Yd No: 110
Converted From: Accommodation Vessel, Stationary-1987
Converted From: General Cargo/Passenger Ship-1969
Lengthened-1931
L reg 47.49 Br ex 7.30 Dght 2.700
Lbp - Br md - Dpth 3.77
Riveted, 2 dks

(A32A2GF) General Cargo/Passenger Ship
Passengers: unberthed: 386
Compartments: 2 Ho
2 Ha:

1 Steam Recip driving 1 Propeller
1 x Steam Recip.
?United Kingdom

7725893 **STORDAL** **1,094** Class: (NV)
LICB *ex* Seimstrand *-1993* 341
\- **Fjord1 AS** 300
\-
Aalesund *Norway*
MMSI: 257381400

1979-03 Hasund Mek. Verksted AS — Ulsteinvik (Hull) Yd No: 23
1979-03 A.M. Liaaen AS — Aalesund Yd No: 132
Loa 69.50 Br ex - Dght 3.401
Lbp 62.41 Br md 13.71 Dpth 4.50
Welded, 1 dk

(A36A2PR) Passenger/Ro-Ro Ship (Vehicles)
Passengers: unberthed: 399
Bow door/ramp (centre)
Stern door/ramp (centre)
Lane-Len: 68
Lane-Wid: 7.40
Lane-clr ht: 4.50
Cars: 70, Trailers: 6

1 oil engine geared to sc. shaft driving 1 CP propeller , 1 fwd
Total Power: 1,214kW (1,651hp) 13.5kn
Normo LDMB-9
1 x 4 Stroke 9 Cy. 250 x 300 1214kW (1651bhp)
AS Bergens Mek Verksteder-Norway

7931167 **STORDOY** **597** Class: NV
LJGP *ex* Fagerfjord *-1988* 214
\- **Erling Boen & Sonner AS** 512
\-
Stavanger *Norway*
MMSI: 258374000
Official number: 19483

1980-08 Johan Drage AS — Rognan Yd No: 380
Loa 39.98 Br ex 9.83 Dght 3.649
Lbp 35.41 Br md 9.81 Dpth 7.57
Welded, 2 dks

(A31B2GP) Palletised Cargo Ship
Stern door/ramp (centre)
Len: 6.00 Wid: 4.00 Swl: -
Bale: 1,000
Compartments: 1 Ho, ER
1 Ha: (21.4 x 6.0)ER
Derricks: 1x20t; Winches: 3
Ice Capable

2 oil engines sr geared to sc. shaft driving 2 FP propellers
Total Power: 598kW (814hp) 10.0kn
Caterpillar 3408B
2 x Vee 4 Stroke 8 Cy. 137 x 152 each-299kW (407bhp)
(new engine 1992)
Caterpillar Inc-USA
AuxGen: 1 x 80kW 220V 50Hz a.c, 1 x 56kW 220V 50Hz a.c
Thrusters: 1 Tunnel thruster (f)
Fuel: 58.0 (d.f.) 2.5pd

6706802 **STOREBAELT** **187** Class: (BV)
S9TD *ex* Birkholn *-1997* *ex* Carl Dammann *-1987* 56
\- *ex* Carl Frigast *-1971* 400
\-
Sao Tome *Sao Tome & Principe*
MMSI: 668115810

1965 Scheepsbouw- en Constructiebedr. K. Hakvoort N.V. — Monnickendam Yd No: 108
Loa 36.25 Br ex 7.29 Dght 2.502
Lbp 33.91 Br md 7.24 Dpth 3.00
Welded, 1 dk

(B33B2DU) Hopper/Dredger (unspecified)
Grain: 200; Hopper: 200
Compartments: 1 Ho, ER
Derricks: 1x3.5t; Winches: 1

1 oil engine driving 1 CP propeller
Total Power: 250kW (340hp)
Alpha 404-24VO
1 x 2 Stroke 4 Cy. 240 x 400 250kW (340bhp)
Alpha Diesel A/S-Denmark

9244752 **STOREGG** **320**
LLLP *ex* Brattskjaer *-2012* 122
M-345-V **Storegg AS** 130
\-
Aalesund *Norway*
MMSI: 257564600

2001-05 Moen Slip AS — Kolvereid Yd No: 46
Lengthened-2007
Loa 27.99 (BB) Br ex - Dght -
Lbp - Br md 8.00 Dpth 4.00
Welded, 1 dk

(B11B2FV) Fishing Vessel

1 oil engine reduction geared to sc. shaft driving 1 FP propeller
Total Power: 736kW (1,001hp)
Mitsubishi S12R-MPTA
1 x Vee 4 Stroke 12 Cy. 170 x 180 736kW (1001bhp)
Mitsubishi Heavy Industries Ltd-Japan

9143570 **STOREKNUT** **2,138** Class: NV
LMDO *ex* Kings Cross *-2003* 641
\- **Dronen Havfiske AS** 2,500
\-
Bergen *Norway*
MMSI: 259242000

1996-12 Th Hellesoy Skipsbyggeri AS — Lofallstrand Yd No: 131
Loa 70.60 Br ex - Dght 7.000
Lbp 61.80 Br md 13.60 Dpth 8.60
Welded, 1 dk

(B11A2FS) Stern Trawler
Ice Capable

1 oil engine geared to sc. shaft driving 1 CP propeller
Total Power: 4,920kW (6,689hp) 16.0kn
Wartsila 12V32E
1 x Vee 4 Stroke 12 Cy. 320 x 350 4920kW (6689bhp)
Wartsila Diesel Oy-Finland
AuxGen: 1 x 1600kW a.c, 1 x 715kW a.c, 1 x 500kW a.c
Thrusters: 1 Thwart. FP thruster (f); 1 Tunnel thruster (a)

6930477 **STORESUND** **122** Class: GL
OZRZ2 *ex* Stein *-1998* 36
\- **Svendborg Bugser A/S (Svendborg Towing Co Ltd)** 54
\-
Svendborg *Denmark (DIS)*
MMSI: 219000548
Official number: D3775

1969 D.W. Kremer Sohn — Elmshorn Yd No: 1141
Loa 25.00 Br ex 7.62 Dght 3.128
Lbp 22.00 Br md 7.22 Dpth 3.79
Welded, 1 dk

(B32A2ST) Tug
Ice Capable

1 oil engine driving 1 FP propeller
Total Power: 809kW (1,100hp)
MWM TBD484-6
1 x 4 Stroke 6 Cy. 320 x 480 809kW (1100bhp)
Motoren Werke Mannheim AG (MWM)-West Germany

9528469 **STORFJORD** **2,967** Class: (NV)
LDKO 891
\- **Fjord1 AS** 970
\-
Molde *Norway*
MMSI: 259098000

2011-01 Stocznia Polnocna SA (Northern Shipyard) — Gdansk (Hull) Yd No: B609/1
2011-01 Gdanska Stocznia 'Remontowa' SA — Gdansk Yd No: 1894/I/1
Loa 109.54 Br ex 17.40 Dght 3.425
Lbp 99.49 Br md 16.99 Dpth 5.35
Welded, 1 dk

(A36A2PR) Passenger/Ro-Ro Ship (Vehicles)
Passengers: unberthed: 292
Bow ramp (centre)
Stern ramp (centre)

2 oil engines reduction geared to sc. shafts driving 2 Z propellers
Total Power: 2,420kW (3,290hp)
Mitsubishi S16R-MPTK
2 x Vee 4 Stroke 16 Cy. 170 x 180 each-1210kW (1645bhp)
Mitsubishi Heavy Industries Ltd-Japan
AuxGen: 2 x 250kW 230V a.c

9004762 **STORK** **497** Class: IS
XUFV4 *ex* Falcon 101 *-2013* *ex* Divine *-2013* 185
\- *ex* Lucky *-2010* *ex* Skif *-2009* 348
ex Kaihatsu Maru No. 2 *-2006*
ex Sano Maru No. 38 *-2003*
Khan Shipping SA
\-
Phnom Penh *Cambodia*
\-
MMSI: 514060000
Official number: 1390053

1990-10 Yamanishi Shipbuilding Co Ltd — Ishinomaki MG Yd No: 982
Converted From: Fishing Vessel
Loa 55.16 (BB) Br ex - Dght 3.700
Lbp 48.00 Br md 8.80 Dpth 3.74
Welded

(A34A2GR) Refrigerated Cargo Ship
Ins: 432

1 oil engine with clutches, flexible couplings & sr geared to sc. shaft driving 1 FP propeller
Total Power: 736kW (1,001hp)
Niigata 6M28HFT
1 x 4 Stroke 6 Cy. 280 x 480 736kW (1001bhp)
Niigata Engineering Co Ltd-Japan

8961937 **STORM** **696** Class: BR (BV)
9LD2515 *ex* Ina *-2013* *ex* Ralitza *-2004* 344
\- **Storm Maritime Co Ltd** 1,005
\-
Freetown *Sierra Leone*
MMSI: 667005215

1981 'Ilya Boyadzhiev' Shipyard — Bourgas Yd No: 554-57
Converted From: Hopper-1995
Loa 56.21 Br ex - Dght 3.543
Lbp 55.08 Br md 9.10 Dpth 4.42
Welded, 1 dk

(A31A2GX) General Cargo Ship

2 oil engines driving 2 FP propellers
Total Power: 470kW (640hp)
S.K.L. 6NVD36
2 x 4 Stroke 6 Cy. 240 x 360 each-235kW (320bhp)
VEB Schwermaschinenbau "KarlLiebknecht" (SKL)-Magdeburg

7607649 **STORM** **2,934** Class: RI (LR)
IBFA *ex* Starman Africa *-1986* 880 ✠ Classed LR until 9/87
\- **S Marco Shipping Srl** 2,015
\-
SatCom: Inmarsat C 424738520
Crotone *Italy*
MMSI: 247004400
Official number: 45

1977-06 Martin Jansen GmbH & Co. KG Schiffsw. u. Masch. — Leer Yd No: 146
Loa 93.85 Br ex 16.13 Dght 4.649
Lbp 83.50 Br md 16.01 Dpth 7.32
Welded, 1 dk

(A38C2GH) Heavy Load Carrier
Stern door/ramp
Len: 7.00 Wid: 11.00 Swl: -
Side ramp (p)
Len: 6.00 Wid: 9.00 Swl: -
Side ramp (s)
Len: 6.00 Wid: 9.00 Swl: -
Lane-Len: 240
Lane-Wid: 11.00
Grain: 1,520; Bale: 1,515
Compartments: 1 Ho, ER
1 Ha: (31.2 x 9.0)ER
Derricks: 1x300t
Ice Capable

2 oil engines sr geared to sc. shafts driving 2 FP propellers
Total Power: 2,590kW (3,522hp) 12.0kn
Deutz RBV8M545
2 x 4 Stroke 8 Cy. 320 x 450 each-1295kW (1761bhp)
Kloeckner Humboldt Deutz AG-West Germany
AuxGen: 2 x 420kW 440V 60Hz a.c, 1 x 280kW 440V 60Hz a.c
Thrusters: 1 Thwart. CP thruster (f)

IMO / Call sign	Ship / Owners	GT / NT / DWT	Class	Builder / Dimensions	Type	Machinery
7903885 - -	**STORM** *ex* Hercules *-2008* *ex* Ryosei Maru No. 1 *-2004* *ex* Shoyo Maru No. 38 *-2004* - -	275 82 126		**1979-07 Narasaki Senpaku Kogyo K.K. — Muroran** Yd No: 150 Loa 37.90 (BB) Br ex - Dght 2.801 Lbp 30.97 Br md 7.38 Dpth 4.63 Welded, 2 dks	**(B11B2FV) Fishing Vessel**	**1 oil engine** reduction geared to sc. shaft driving 1 FP propeller Total Power: 552kW (750hp) Akasaka 6U28 1 x 4 Stroke 6 Cy. 280 x 340 552kW (750bhp) Akasaka Tekkosho KK (Akasaka DieselLtd)-Japan
9477658 *WDF8260* -	**STORM** *ex* Gulf Storm *-2011* **Jackson Offshore Holdings LLC** Jackson Offshore Operators LLC *Houston, TX* *United States of America* MMSI: 367493060 Official number: 1216981	**368** 110 105	Class: AB	**2009-06 Swiftships Shipbuilders LLC — Morgan City LA** Yd No: 585 Loa 51.80 Br ex - Dght 2.740 Lbp 46.56 Br md 9.14 Dpth 3.89 Welded, 1 dk	**(B21A20C) Crew/Supply Vessel** Passengers: unberthed: 70	**4 oil engines** reduction geared to sc. shafts driving 4 Water jets Total Power: 5,668kW (7,708hp) 31.0kn Cummins KTA-50-M2 4 x Vee 4 Stroke 16 Cy. 159 x 159 each-1417kW (1927bhp) Cummins Engine Co Inc-USA AuxGen: 2 x 180kW a.c Thrusters: 1 Retract. directional thruster (f) Fuel: 88.0 (d.f.)
9403358 *J8B3609* -	**STORM** *ex* LM Oceanic *-2006* **Borinken Towing & Salvage LLC** *Kingstown* *St Vincent & The Grenadines* MMSI: 376736000 Official number: 10082	**264** 80 270	Class: GL (NK)	**2006-08 Lingco Shipbuilding Pte Ltd — Singapore** Yd No: 4705 Loa 30.10 Br ex - Dght 3.508 Lbp 28.15 Br md 8.60 Dpth 4.35 Welded, 1 dk	**(B32A2ST) Tug**	**2 oil engines** reverse reduction geared to sc. shafts. driving 2 FP propellers Total Power: 1,790kW (2,434hp) Cummins KTA-38-M2 2 x Vee 4 Stroke 12 Cy. 159 x 159 each-895kW (1217bhp) Cummins Engine Co Inc-USA AuxGen: 1 x 80kW 40V a.c, 2 x 40kW 400V a.c Fuel: 225.0 (r.f.)
5285174 *LMJG* -	**STORM AINE** *ex* Birgitta *-1977* *ex* Prins Georg *-1967* *ex* Birgitta *-1938* *ex* Baldur *-1938* **Nils Olai Kalve** - *Oslo* *Norway*	*130* 82 163	Class: (BV)	**1920 Fried. Krupp Germaniawerft AG — Kiel** Yd No: 257 Loa 31.12 Br ex 6.30 Dght 2.896 Lbp 27.13 Br md 6.25 Dpth 3.10 Riveted, 1 dk	**(A31A2GX) General Cargo Ship** Compartments: 1 Ho, ER 1 Ha: (10.5 x 3.5)ER Derricks: 1x1t; Winches: 1	**1 oil engine** driving 1 FP propeller Total Power: 99kW (135hp) 8.5kn Alpha 343V 1 x 2 Stroke 3 Cy. 200 x 340 99kW (135bhp) (new engine 1957) Alpha Diesel A/S-Denmark
8006309 *CZ7289* -	**STORM BANDIT** *ex* Bandera *-2012* **Ledcor Resources & Transportation Inc** - *Vancouver, BC* *Canada* MMSI: 316005616 Official number: 394166	*144* - -		**1980-09 Allied Shipbuilders Ltd — North Vancouver BC** Yd No: 226 Loa 21.95 Br ex 7.75 Dght 3.556 Lbp - Br md 7.32 Dpth - Welded, 1 dk	**(B32A2ST) Tug**	**2 oil engines** geared to sc. shafts driving 2 FP propellers Total Power: 992kW (1,348hp) G.M. (Detroit Diesel) 12V-149 2 x Vee 2 Stroke 12 Cy. 146 x 146 each-496kW (674bhp) General Motors Corp-USA
9193161 *VHA2365* -	**STORM BAY** **Government of The Commonwealth of Australia (Australian Customs Service, National Maritime Unit)** - *Australia* MMSI: 503371000	**240** 72 30	Class: NV	**2000-08 Austal Ships Pty Ltd — Fremantle WA** Yd No: 138 Loa 34.95 Br ex - Dght 1.857 Lbp 32.00 Br md 7.20 Dpth 3.63 Welded, 1 dk	**(B34H2SQ) Patrol Vessel** Hull Material: Aluminium Alloy	**2 oil engines** reduction geared to sc. shafts driving 2 FP propellers Total Power: 2,100kW (2,856hp) 20.5kn M.T.U. 16V2000M70 2 x Vee 4 Stroke 16 Cy. 130 x 150 each-1050kW (1428bhp) MTU Friedrichshafen GmbH-Friedrichshafen AuxGen: 2 x 135kW a.c Thrusters: 1 Thwart. FP thruster (f)
8501311 - -	**STORM BIRD** - - *Nigeria*	*139* 89 -		**1984-12 Quality Shipyards Inc — Houma LA** Yd No: 175 Loa 27.16 Br ex - Dght - Lbp - Br md - Dpth - Welded, 1 dk	**(B11A2FT) Trawler**	**1 oil engine** driving 1 FP propeller Total Power: 460kW (625hp) Caterpillar 3412PCTA 1 x Vee 4 Stroke 12 Cy. 137 x 152 460kW (625bhp) Caterpillar Tractor Co-USA
7041259 - -	**STORM COVE** *ex* Shell Cove *-1986* **Tasmanian Ports Corporation Pty Ltd (TasPorts)** - *Hobart, Tas* *Australia* Official number: 343940	*223* - -	Class: (LR) ✠ Classed LR until 27/1/84	**1971-02 Carrington Slipways Pty Ltd — Newcastle NSW** Yd No: 60 Loa 29.88 Br ex 9.73 Dght 3.442 Lbp 24.90 Br md 9.40 Dpth 3.89 Welded	**(B32A2ST) Tug**	**2 oil engines** driving 2 Directional propellers Total Power: 1,398kW (1,900hp) 11.5kn Daihatsu 8PSHTB-26D 2 x 4 Stroke 8 Cy. 260 x 320 each-699kW (950bhp) Daihatsu Diesel Manufacturing Co Lt-Japan AuxGen: 2 x 60kW 415V 50Hz a.c Fuel: 32.5 (d.f.)
8012308 *WCZ6533* -	**STORM PETREL** **Evening Star Inc** Icicle Seafoods Inc *Seattle, WA* *United States of America* MMSI: 338671000 Official number: 620769	*276* 187 -		**1980-07 Marine Construction & Design Co. (MARCO) — Seattle, Wa** Yd No: 384 Loa 37.32 Br ex 9.73 Dght - Lbp 33.66 Br md 9.43 Dpth 4.02 Welded, 1 dk	**(B11A2FS) Stern Trawler** Ins: 269 Compartments: 3 Ho, ER Cranes: 1x12t,1x8t	**1 oil engine** geared to sc. shaft driving 1 FP propeller Total Power: 827kW (1,124hp) Caterpillar D399SCAC 1 x Vee 4 Stroke 16 Cy. 159 x 203 827kW (1124bhp) Caterpillar Tractor Co-USA AuxGen: 1 x 155kW, 1 x 55kW
9082738 *C6TE6* -	**STORM RANGER** *ex* Lorenzina *-2003* *ex* Brilliance *-2000* **Astir Navigation** Enterprises Shipping & Trading SA *Nassau* *Bahamas* MMSI: 311606000 Official number: 8000706	**26,071** 15,556 45,744	Class: BV (RI) (NK)	**1995-04 Imabari Shipbuilding Co Ltd — Marugame KG (Marugame Shipyard)** Yd No: 1238 Loa 189.83 (BB) Br ex 31.03 Dght 11.600 Lbp 179.80 Br md 31.00 Dpth 16.50 Welded, 1 dk	**(A21A2BC) Bulk Carrier** Grain: 58,890; Bale: 56,210 Compartments: 5 Ho, ER 5 Ha: (20.0 x 16.0)4 (20.8 x 17.6)ER Cranes: 4x30t	**1 oil engine** driving 1 FP propeller Total Power: 8,562kW (11,641hp) 14.0kn B&W 6S50MC 1 x 2 Stroke 6 Cy. 500 x 1910 8562kW (11641bhp) Hitachi Zosen Corp-Japan
9595357 *5BKG3* -	**STORM RIDER** **Ivory Shipmanagement Inc** Grecomar Shipping Agency Ltd *Limassol* *Cyprus* MMSI: 212712000 Official number: 9595357	**22,413** 11,653 34,154	Class: NK (AB)	**2011-11 Dae Sun Shipbuilding & Engineering Co Ltd — Busan** Yd No: 531 Loa 180.40 (BB) Br ex - Dght 9.920 Lbp 171.40 Br md 30.00 Dpth 14.40 Welded, 1 dk	**(A21A2BC) Bulk Carrier** Double Hull Grain: 46,663; Bale: 44,525 Compartments: 5 Ho, ER 5 Ha: ER Cranes: 4x30t	**1 oil engine** driving 1 FP propeller Total Power: 6,480kW (8,810hp) 13.9kn MAN-B&W 6S42MC7 1 x 2 Stroke 6 Cy. 420 x 1764 6480kW (8810bhp) STX Engine Co Ltd-South Korea AuxGen: 3 x 570kW a.c Fuel: 270.0 (d.f.) 1565.0 (r.f.)
8400062 *LCHX3* -	**STORM WEST** *ex* Kamito *-2008* **Storm Offshore AS** - *Bergen* *Norway (NIS)* MMSI: 257146000	**416** 124 221	Class: NV (BV) (GL)	**1984-12 Orskov Christensens Staalskibsvaerft A/S — Frederikshavn** Yd No: 137 Converted From: Stern Trawler-2008 Loa 32.24 Br ex 8.03 Dght 3.950 Lbp 30.00 Br md 8.00 Dpth 6.40 Welded, 2 dks	**(B31A2SR) Research Survey Vessel** Ice Capable	**1 oil engine** with clutches, flexible couplings & sr geared to sc. shaft driving 1 CP propeller Total Power: 809kW (1,100hp) 11.5kn Alpha 6L23/30 1 x 4 Stroke 6 Cy. 225 x 300 809kW (1100bhp) MAN B&W Diesel A/S-Denmark AuxGen: 2 x 80kW 220/380V 50Hz a.c Thrusters: 1 Thwart. FP thruster (f) Fuel: 64.0 (d.f.)
8600014 *H04190* -	**STORMBAS** *ex* Lis Kemi *-2007* *ex* Lunafjord *-1992* **Storm Offshore AS** - *Panama* *Panama* MMSI: 355243000 Official number: 3410708A	**241** 86 -	Class: PC	**1985-01 Knol's Maskinfabrik A/S, Vesterborg — Nakskov** Yd No: 9 Converted From: Stern Trawler-2009 Lengthened-1989 Loa 30.70 Br ex - Dght 3.552 Lbp 27.44 Br md 7.23 Dpth 5.80 Welded, 1 dk	**(B22A20R) Offshore Support Vessel**	**1 oil engine** geared to sc. shaft driving 1 CP propeller Total Power: 606kW (824hp) Cummins 1 x 4 Stroke 606kW (824bhp) (new engine 1985) Cummins Engine Co Inc-USA Thrusters: 1 Tunnel thruster (f)
9099054 *V4EM2* -	**STORMBAS II** *ex* La Couronnee III *-2011* **Storm Offshore AS** - *Basseterre* *St Kitts & Nevis* MMSI: 341365000 Official number: SKN 1002110	**299** 92 75	Class: BV	**1986-11 Chantier J Chauvet — Paimboeuf** Loa 34.95 Br ex - Dght 2.830 Lbp 30.48 Br md 7.80 Dpth 3.70 Welded, 1 dk	**(B34N2QP) Pilot Vessel**	**2 oil engines** reduction geared to sc. shafts driving 2 CP propellers Total Power: 368kW (500hp) 12.0kn MWM TBD604L6 2 x 4 Stroke 6 Cy. 160 x 185 each-184kW (250bhp) in Germany
9569695 *5IXR03* -	**STORMBERG** *ex* Dew Drop *-2013* **NITC** - *Zanzibar* *Tanzania (Zanzibar)* MMSI: 677010200	**165,359** 107,827 318,000		**2013-05 Dalian Shipbuilding Industry Co Ltd — Dalian LN (No 2 Yard)** Yd No: T3000-49 Loa 332.95 Br ex - Dght 22.600 Lbp 320.00 Br md 60.00 Dpth 30.50 Welded, 1 dk	**(A13A2TV) Crude Oil Tanker** Double Hull (13F) Liq: 330,000; Liq (Oil): 330,000 Compartments: 5 Wing Ta, 5 Ta, 5 Wing Ta, 1 Wing Slop Ta, 1 Wing Slop Ta, ER 3 Cargo Pump (s): 3x5000m³/hr	**1 oil engine** driving 1 FP propeller Total Power: 31,640kW (43,018hp) 15.0kn Wartsila 7RT-flex82T 1 x 2 Stroke 7 Cy. 820 x 3375 31640kW (43018bhp) Qingdao Zichai Boyang Diesel EngineCo Ltd-China AuxGen: 3 x 1120kW a.c
8856053 - -	**STORMBIRD** **Stormbird Inc** - *Kodiak, AK* *United States of America* Official number: 656842	*164* 141 -		**1983 Weldit Corp. — Bellingham, Wa** Loa - Br ex - Dght - Lbp 24.26 Br md 7.92 Dpth 2.44 Welded, 1 dk	**(B11B2FV) Fishing Vessel**	**1 oil engine** driving 1 FP propeller

8861149 *LGFC* M-30-A	**STORMEN SENIOR** *ex* Julsund Senior *-2013* *ex* Harto *-2008* *ex* Borgeson *-2000* *ex* Saro *-1993* **Hauge Kystfiske AS** - *Aalesund* *Norway* MMSI: 257574500	**156** 62 -		**1988 Karlstadsverken AB — Karlstad** Loa 20.30 Br ex 6.47 Dght - Lbp - Br md - Dpth - Welded, 1 dk	**(B11B2FV) Fishing Vessel**	**1 oil engine** geared to sc. shaft driving 1 FP propeller Total Power: 716kW (973hp) Caterpillar 3508TA 1 x Vee 4 Stroke 8 Cy. 170 x 190 716kW (973bhp) Caterpillar Inc-USA
7629233 *CZ7003* -	**STORMFORCE** - **Pacific Cachalot Ltd** - *Vancouver, BC* *Canada* MMSI: 316013539 Official number: 370331	*136* 1 -		**1975 Benson Bros Shipbuilding Co (1960) Ltd — Vancouver BC** L reg 19.57 Br ex 7.70 Dght - Lbp - Br md - Dpth 4.09 Welded, 1 dk	**(B32A2ST) Tug**	**2 oil engines** driving 1 FP propeller Total Power: 1,066kW (1,450hp) 11.0kn Caterpillar D348SCAC 2 x Vee 4 Stroke 12 Cy. 137 x 165 each-533kW (725bhp) Caterpillar Tractor Co-USA
6620814 *LIWS* M-38-AV	**STORMFUGLEN** - **Partrederiet Stormfuglens Rederi DA** Eva Torill Strand *Kristiansund* *Norway*	**395** 118 -		**1966-10 Vaagland Baatbyggeri AS — Vaagland** Yd No: 72 Lengthened-1972 Loa 39.02 Br ex 7.65 Dght - Lbp 35.16 Br md 7.62 Dpth 3.81 Welded, 1 dk	**(B11A2FT) Trawler**	**1 oil engine** driving 1 FP propeller Total Power: 507kW (689hp) Callesen 6-427-FOT 1 x 4 Stroke 6 Cy. 270 x 400 507kW (689bhp) Aabenraa Motorfabrik, HeinrichCallesen A/S-Denmark
9213870 *V4VD2* -	**STORMHAV** *ex* Catherine R *-2013* **Storm Offshore AS** - *Basseterre* *St Kitts & Nevis* MMSI: 341575000	**293** - 140	Class: NV (LR) ✠ Classed LR until 10/9/13	**2001-04 Astilleros Armon SA — Navia** Yd No: 522 Loa 30.62 (BB) Br ex - Dght 3.150 Lbp 25.90 Br md 8.50 Dpth 3.70 Welded, 1 dk	**(B11A2FS) Stern Trawler** Ins: 182	**1 oil engine** reduction geared to sc. shaft driving 1 CP propeller Total Power: 1,066kW (1,449hp) 12.0kn A.B.C. 6MDZC 1 x 4 Stroke 6 Cy. 256 x 310 1066kW (1449bhp) Anglo Belgian Corp NV (ABC)-Belgium AuxGen: 2 x 67kW a.c Thrusters: 1 Thwart. FP thruster (f) Fuel: 96.3 (d.f.)
8851742 *WAA2812* -	**STORMIE C** - **Stormie C LLC** - *Coos Bay, OR* *United States of America* MMSI: 366925980 Official number: 936611	*120* 96 -		**1988 Giddings Boat Works, Inc. — Charleston, Or** Yd No: 12 Converted From: Ferry (Passenger only)-1988 Loa - Br ex - Dght - Lbp 20.73 Br md 7.32 Dpth 3.35 Welded, 1 dk	**(B11B2FV) Fishing Vessel**	**1 oil engine** driving 1 FP propeller Total Power: 496kW (674hp)
9257292 *PBHO* -	**STORMMEEUW** - **Government of The Kingdom of The Netherlands (Rijkswaterstaat Directie Noordzee)** - *Rijswijk, Zuid Holland* *Netherlands* MMSI: 244306000 Official number: 40314	**197** 59 -	Class: LR ✠ **100A1** SS 03/2013 SSC patrol mono HSC G2 **LMC** **UMS** Cable: 60.0/18.0 U2 (a)	**2003-03 Scheepswerf Made B.V. — Made** (Hull) **2003-03 B.V. Scheepswerf Damen — Gorinchem** Yd No: 549956 Loa 34.30 Br ex 7.20 Dght 1.500 Lbp 31.14 Br md 7.05 Dpth 3.10 Welded, 1 dk	**(B34H2SQ) Patrol Vessel** Ice Capable	**2 oil engines** with clutches, flexible couplings & sr reverse geared to sc. shafts driving 2 FP propellers Total Power: 1,634kW (2,222hp) 16.5kn Caterpillar 3412E-TA 2 x Vee 4 Stroke 12 Cy. 137 x 152 each-817kW (1111bhp) Caterpillar Inc-USA AuxGen: 2 x 71kW 400V 50Hz a.c Thrusters: 1 Thwart. FP thruster (f)
6927248 *TFGZ* BA 326	**STORMUR** *ex* Bjarmi *-2012* *ex* Johannes Ivar *-2012* *ex* Julius *-1993* *ex* Reynir *-1992* *ex* Bye Senior *-1973* **Fiskeldistaekni Ehf** - SatCom: Inmarsat C 425140510 *Hafnarfjordur* *Iceland* MMSI: 251405110 Official number: 1321	**242** 67 -	Class: (NV)	**1969 Brastad Skipsbyggeri AS — Vestnes** Yd No: 314 Lengthened-1998 Loa 33.86 Br ex 6.43 Dght - Lbp - Br md 6.41 Dpth 3.51 Welded, 1 dk	**(B11B2FV) Fishing Vessel** Compartments: 1 Ho, ER 1 Ha: Derricks: 1x2.5t; Winches: 1	**1 oil engine** driving 1 FP propeller Total Power: 419kW (570hp) 11.8kn Caterpillar D379SCAC 1 x Vee 4 Stroke 8 Cy. 159 x 203 419kW (570bhp) Caterpillar Tractor Co-USA AuxGen: 1 x 8kW 220V 50Hz a.c Fuel: 25.5 (d.f.) 2.0pd
8308642 *OPBY* O 51	**STORMVOGEL** - **Rederij Versluys-Decuypere PVBA** - *Ostend* *Belgium* MMSI: 205277000 Official number: 01 00309 1996	**217** 65 -		**1983-03 Scheepswerven Seghers N.V. — Oostende** Yd No: 15 Loa 30.59 Br ex - Dght - Lbp 27.18 Br md 7.92 Dpth 3.61 Welded, 1 dk	**(B11A2FT) Trawler** Ins: 140 Compartments: 1 Ho, ER 2 Ha:	**1 oil engine** geared to sc. shaft driving 1 FP propeller Total Power: 662kW (900hp) A.B.C. 6MDXC 1 x 4 Stroke 6 Cy. 242 x 320 662kW (900bhp) Anglo Belgian Corp NV (ABC)-Belgium
8985127 *MRBW9* -	**STORMVOGEL** - **Woodstown Bay Shellfish Swansea Ltd** - *Belfast* *United Kingdom* Official number: C18875	**131** 39 -		**1986-10 Gebr. Kooiman B.V. Scheepswerf en Machinefabriek — Zwijndrecht** Yd No: 134 Loa 35.98 Br ex - Dght - Lbp 33.70 Br md 7.00 Dpth 2.47 Welded, 1 dk	**(B11B2FV) Fishing Vessel**	**1 oil engine** driving 1 Propeller Caterpillar 3412 1 x Vee 4 Stroke 12 Cy. 137 x 152 Caterpillar Tractor Co-USA
8898221 *OWUL* L 415	**STORMY** *ex* Soraya *-2009* **Stormy ApS** - SatCom: Inmarsat C 422013810 *Thyboron* *Denmark* MMSI: 220138000 Official number: H976	**124** 58 -		**1987 Strandby Skibsvaerft I/S — Strandby** Yd No: 86 Loa 23.35 Br ex 5.80 Dght - Lbp - Br md - Dpth 2.90 Welded, 1 dk	**(B11B2FV) Fishing Vessel**	**1 oil engine** driving 1 FP propeller
8510958 *OVUR* HM 220	**STORMY** *ex* Susan Vendelbo *-2012* *ex* Betty Borsmose *-2005* **Mindbo ApS** - SatCom: Inmarsat C 421914010 *Hanstholm* *Denmark* MMSI: 219140000 Official number: D3008	**654** 287 495	Class: BV	**1986-06 A/S Nakskov Skibsvaerft — Nakskov** (Hull launched by) **1986-06 Marstal Team Staal ApS — Marstal** (Hull completed by) Yd No: 102 **1986-06 Poul Ree A/S — Stokkemarke** Yd No: 5251 Loa 44.23 (BB) Br ex - Dght - Lbp 38.99 Br md 9.01 Dpth 7.01 Welded, 1 dk	**(B11A2FS) Stern Trawler**	**1 oil engine** geared to sc. shaft driving 1 CP propeller Total Power: 1,177kW (1,600hp) 11.0kn MaK 6M332AK 1 x 4 Stroke 6 Cy. 240 x 330 1177kW (1600bhp) Krupp MaK Maschinenbau GmbH-Kiel
7938505 *WAO7524* -	**STORMY ELIZABETH** *ex* Papa's Girls *-2005* **William J Mulvey** - *Boston, MA* *United States of America* MMSI: 367151950 Official number: 598951	*111* 75 -		**1978 at Bayou La Batre, Al** Yd No: 3 L reg 21.10 Br ex 6.71 Dght - Lbp - Br md - Dpth 3.41 Welded, 1 dk	**(B11B2FV) Fishing Vessel**	**1 oil engine** driving 1 FP propeller Total Power: 257kW (349hp)
7224057 *WDD4589* -	**STORMY NIGHT** *ex* Vatican *-2010* **K C Trawlers Inc** - *Port Isabel, TX* *United States of America* MMSI: 367146680 Official number: 535091	*103* 70 -		**1971 Marine Mart, Inc. — Port Isabel, Tx** L reg 19.69 Br ex 6.13 Dght - Lbp - Br md - Dpth 3.46 Welded	**(B11B2FV) Fishing Vessel**	**1 oil engine** driving 1 FP propeller Total Power: 268kW (364hp)
7733307 *WSB7864* -	**STORMY SEA** *ex* YO-170 *-1944* **Frederick S Magill** - SatCom: Inmarsat A 1511564 *Sitka, AK* *United States of America* MMSI: 367089140 Official number: 586415	*469* 390 -		**1944 Ira S. Bushey & Son, Inc. — New York, NY** Yd No: 556 L reg 45.94 Br ex - Dght - Lbp - Br md 9.25 Dpth 4.07 Welded, 1 dk	**(B11B2FV) Fishing Vessel**	**1 oil engine** driving 1 FP propeller Total Power: 662kW (900hp)
8719956 - -	**STORMY WEATHER '86** - **Sahlman Seafoods Inc** -	*101* 69 -		**1987-01 Steiner Shipyard, Inc. — Bayou La Batre, Al** Loa 22.86 Br ex - Dght - Lbp 20.33 Br md 6.70 Dpth 3.32 Welded	**(B11B2FV) Fishing Vessel**	**1 oil engine** geared to sc. shaft driving 1 FP propeller Total Power: 268kW (364hp) Cummins KT-1150-M 1 x 4 Stroke 6 Cy. 159 x 159 268kW (364bhp) Cummins Engine Co Inc-USA

IMO / Call sign	Name / Owner	Tonnage	Class	Builder / Dimensions	Type	Machinery
8615306 *JXOK* T-2-I	**STORNES** *ex* Brodd *-2008* *ex* Arctic Eagle *-2006* *ex* Arctic Swan 1 *-2004* *ex* Arctic Swan *-2002* *ex* Remoytral *-1999* *ex* Ringvassoy *-1993* **Engenes Fiskeriselskap AS** AS Roaldnes SatCom: Inmarsat C 425839710 *Aalesund* *Norway* MMSI: 258397000 Official number: 20372	**999** 299 -	Class: NV	**1987-09 Sterkoder Mek. Verksted AS — Kristiansund** Yd No: 105 Loa 47.70 Br ex 11.23 Dght 5.535 Lbp 40.20 Br md 11.20 Dpth 7.50 Welded, 2 dks	**(B11A2FS) Stern Trawler** Ins: 450 Ice Capable	**1 oil engine** geared to sc. shaft driving 1 FP propeller Total Power: 1,839kW (2,500hp) 14.3kn Wichmann 8V28B 1 x Vee 4 Stroke 8 Cy. 280 x 360 1839kW (2500bhp) Wartsila Wichmann Diesel AS-Norway AuxGen: 1 x 1250kW 440V 60Hz a.c, 1 x 344kW 440V 60Hz a.c
9549035 *PCKX* -	**STORNES** - **Van Oord Marine Services BV** CSL Norway AS *Rotterdam* *Netherlands* MMSI: 246695000 Official number: 53526	**19,950** 8,209 27,323	Class: AB	**2011-06 Yantai Raffles Shipyard Co Ltd — Yantai SD** Yd No: YR2007-215 Loa 175.00 (BB) Br ex - Dght 10.568 Lbp 169.40 Br md 26.00 Dpth 14.50 Welded, 1 dk	**(B22K20B) Pipe Burying Vessel** Grain: 24,200 Compartments: 6 Ho, ER 6 Ha: ER	**2 oil engines** reduction geared to sc. shafts driving 2 CP propellers Total Power: 8,000kW (10,876hp) 14.7kn Bergens B32: 40L8P 2 x 4 Stroke 8 Cy. 320 x 400 each-4000kW (5438bhp) Rolls Royce Marine AS-Norway AuxGen: 2 x 2200kW a.c, 4 x 1800kW a.c Thrusters: 1 Tunnel thruster (f); 1 Retract. directional thruster (a); 1 Tunnel thruster (a); 2 Retract. directional thruster (f)
5341813 *SGPD* -	**STORSKAR** *ex* Strengnas Express *-1940* **Waxholms Angfartygs AB** - *Vaxholm* *Sweden* MMSI: 265522420	**256** 102 -		**1908 Lindholmens Verkstads AB — Goteborg** Yd No: 399 Loa 38.97 Br ex 7.01 Dght 3.000 Lbp - Br md 6.99 Dpth - Riveted, 1 dk	**(A37B2PS) Passenger Ship** Passengers: unberthed: 418	**1 Steam Recip** driving 1 FP propeller Total Power: 485kW (659hp) 13.0kn 1 x Steam Recip. 485kW (659ihp) Lindholmens Varv AB-Sweden AuxGen: 2 x 10kW 220V d.c Fuel: 7.0 (d.f.)
7636951 - -	**STORTEBEKER** *ex* Adler X *-2011* *ex* Stella Polaris *-1993* *ex* Poseidon *-1989* *ex* Palucca *-1988* **Adler-Schiffe GmbH & Co KG** - *Altwarp* *Germany*	*214* 143 40	Class: (GL)	**1977-05 Husumer Schiffswerft — Husum** Yd No: 1420 Loa 31.78 Br ex 6.56 Dght 1.661 Lbp 27.46 Br md 6.51 Dpth 2.82 Welded, 1 dk	**(A37B2PS) Passenger Ship** Passengers: berths: 275 Ice Capable	**1 oil engine** reverse reduction geared to sc. shaft driving 1 FP propeller Total Power: 400kW (544hp) 10.5kn Deutz SBA12M816 1 x Vee 4 Stroke 12 Cy. 142 x 160 400kW (544bhp) Kloeckner Humboldt Deutz AG-West Germany AuxGen: 2 x 26kW 220/380V a.c Thrusters: 1 Thwart. FP thruster (f)
7935319 *PB4549* -	**STORTEBEKER** - **Wyker Dampfschiffs-Reederei Foehr-Amrum GmbH** - *Netherlands* MMSI: 244630119 Official number: 34150	**114** 53 -	Class: (GL)	**1969 Husumer Schiffswerft — Husum** Yd No: 1284 Lengthened-1972 Loa 30.51 Br ex 6.30 Dght 1.101 Lbp 24.16 Br md - Dpth 2.01 Welded, 1 dk	**(A37B2PS) Passenger Ship** Passengers: unberthed: 202	**2 oil engines** driving 2 FP propellers Total Power: 346kW (470hp) 13.0kn Deutz SBF6M716 2 x 4 Stroke 6 Cy. 135 x 160 each-173kW (235bhp) Kloeckner Humboldt Deutz AG-West Germany
9040417 *DMYA* -	**STORTEBEKER** - **Entsorgungsreederei GmbH & Co KG** AG Reederei Norden-Frisia *Norden* *Germany* MMSI: 211232500 Official number: 4347	*286* 86 350	Class: GL	**1991-07 Deutsche Binnenwerften GmbH — Genthin** Yd No: 124 Loa 45.00 Br ex 10.85 Dght 1.702 Lbp 41.20 Br md 10.50 Dpth 2.45 Welded	**(A35A2RR) Ro-Ro Cargo Ship** Stern door/ramp (centre) Len: 6.50 Wid: 6.50 Swl: -	**2 oil engines** reverse reduction geared to sc. shafts driving 2 FP propellers Total Power: 692kW (940hp) 10.0kn Volvo Penta TAMD162A 2 x 4 Stroke 6 Cy. 144 x 165 each-346kW (470bhp) AB Volvo Penta-Sweden
9195377 *ZDEG7* -	**STORTEBEKER** - **Briese Schiffahrts GmbH & Co KG ms 'Stortebeker'** Briese Schiffahrts GmbH & Co KG *Gibraltar* *Gibraltar (British)* MMSI: 236119000	**2,301** 1,289 3,159	Class: GL	**2000-10 Daewoo-Mangalia Heavy Industries S.A. — Mangalia** (Hull) Yd No: 1018 **2000-10 Scheepswerf Pattje B.V. — Waterhuizen** Yd No: 418 Loa 82.50 Br ex - Dght 5.250 Lbp 78.20 Br md 12.40 Dpth 6.70 Welded, 1 dk	**(A31A2GX) General Cargo Ship** Double Hull Grain: 4,782; Bale: 4,782 TEU 132 C Ho 96 TEU C Dk 36 TEU incl 12 ref C. Compartments: 1 Ho, ER 1 Ha: (56.3 x 10.2)ER Ice Capable	**1 oil engine** reduction geared to sc. shaft driving 1 CP propeller Total Power: 1,800kW (2,447hp) 12.5kn MaK 6M25 1 x 4 Stroke 6 Cy. 255 x 400 1800kW (2447bhp) Caterpillar Motoren GmbH & Co. KG-Germany AuxGen: 1 x 240kW 220/380V a.c, 2 x 90kW 220/380V a.c Thrusters: 1 Thwart. FP thruster (f) Fuel: 184.0 (d.f.)
5018612 *PHTK* -	**STORTEMELK** *ex* Joke *-1992* *ex* Klaasje *-1985* *ex* Anna Lydia *-1968* **M J de Jonge** - SatCom: Inmarsat C 424449010 *Middelburg* *Netherlands* MMSI: 244602000 Official number: 1734	**109** 55 -		**1961 Scheepswerf Fa. Hijlkema & Zonen — Hoogezand** Yd No: 2/75 Converted From: Fishing Vessel-1992 Loa 29.40 Br ex 6.61 Dght 2.550 Lbp 25.03 Br md 6.49 Dpth 3.40 Welded	**(A37B2PS) Passenger Ship**	**1 oil engine** driving 1 FP propeller Total Power: 588kW (799hp) Kromhout 6FEHD240 1 x 4 Stroke 6 Cy. 240 x 260 588kW (799bhp) (new engine 1980) Stork Werkspoor Diesel BV-Netherlands
6505349 - -	**STORTEMELK** *ex* Ostsee *-2003* *ex* Sund Clipper *-1990* *ex* Baltic Clipper *-1984* *ex* Ems Clipper *-1979* *ex* Sundbuss Henrik II *-1976* - -	**298** 110 39	Class: (GL) (NV)	**1964-12 Lindstols Skips- & Baatbyggeri AS — Risor** Yd No: 260 Lengthened-1986 Loa 37.62 Br ex 7.52 Dght 2.013 Lbp 32.57 Br md 7.31 Dpth 2.62 Welded, 1 dk	**(A37B2PS) Passenger Ship** Passengers: unberthed: 240 Ice Capable	**2 oil engines** driving 2 CP propellers Total Power: 294kW (400hp) 12.0kn Volvo Penta TMD100A 2 x 4 Stroke 6 Cy. 121 x 140 each-147kW (200bhp) Volvo Pentaverken-Sweden AuxGen: 2 x 49kW 220V 50Hz a.c Fuel: 12.0 (d.f.) 1.0pd
9308065 *C6ZT8* -	**STORVIKEN** - **Viken Fleet I AS** Viken Shipping AS *Nassau* *Bahamas* MMSI: 311066100	**82,647** 46,578 152,013 T/cm 118.4	Class: NV (AB)	**2006-02 Samsung Heavy Industries Co Ltd — Geoje** Yd No: 1556 Loa 274.55 (BB) Br ex 48.03 Dght 16.380 Lbp 264.00 Br md 48.00 Dpth 23.60 Welded, 1 dk	**(A13A2TV) Crude Oil Tanker** Double Hull (13F) Liq: 168,852; Liq (Oil): 175,000 Cargo Heating Coils Compartments: 12 Wing Ta, 2 Wing Slop Ta, ER 3 Cargo Pump (s): 3x3800m³/hr Manifold: Bow/CM: 138m	**1 oil engine** driving 1 CP propeller Total Power: 18,623kW (25,320hp) 15.2kn MAN-B&W 6S70ME-C 1 x 2 Stroke 6 Cy. 700 x 2800 18623kW (25320bhp) Doosan Engine Co Ltd-South Korea AuxGen: 3 x a.c, 1 x a.c Thrusters: 1 Tunnel thruster (f) Fuel: 241.0 (d.f.) 4275.0 (r.f.)
9286700 *LMCE* N-0001-ME	**STOTTFJORD** - **Brodrene Bakken AS** - *Bodo* *Norway* MMSI: 257580600	**361** 144 -		**2003-08 AS Rigas Kugu Buvetava (Riga Shipyard) — Riga** (Hull) **2003-08 Sletta Baatbyggeri AS — Mjosundet** Yd No: 100 Loa 27.43 Br ex - Dght - Lbp - Br md 9.40 Dpth 4.15 Welded, 1 dk	**(B11B2FV) Fishing Vessel**	**1 oil engine** geared to sc. shaft driving 1 CP propeller
8868587 *LHAJ* N-39-BO	**STOTTVAERINGEN** - **Havbor AS** - *Bodo* *Norway* MMSI: 257436500	**173** 69 -		**1978 Saltdal Patentslip & Skipsbyggeri — Rognan** Yd No: 136 Lengthened-1992 Loa 27.47 Br ex 6.70 Dght 3.890 Lbp - Br md - Dpth - Welded, 1 dk	**(B11B2FV) Fishing Vessel**	**1 oil engine** reduction geared to sc. shaft driving 1 FP propeller Total Power: 382kW (519hp) 10.5kn Caterpillar 3412TA 1 x Vee 4 Stroke 12 Cy. 137 x 152 382kW (519bhp) Caterpillar Tractor Co-USA
9182485 *LAHF5* -	**STOVE CAMPBELL** *ex* Western Onyx *-2001* **Stove Rederi AS** Wilhelmsen Ship Management Singapore Pte Ltd SatCom: Inmarsat B 325735910 *Oslo* *Norway (NIS)* MMSI: 257359000	**26,966** 15,344 46,223 T/cm 50.7	Class: NK (NV)	**1999-02 Oshima Shipbuilding Co Ltd — Saikai NS** Yd No: 10233 Loa 185.73 Br ex 30.95 Dght 11.785 Lbp 177.00 Br md 30.50 Dpth 16.40 Welded, 1 dk	**(A21A2BC) Bulk Carrier** Double Hull Grain: 56,703; Bale: 54,673 TEU 1036 C Ho 690 TEU C Dk 346 TEU Compartments: 5 Ho, ER 5 Ha: (17.0 x 16.0)Tappered 3 (20.3 x 25.4) (20.3 x 22.0)ER Cranes: 4x30t	**1 oil engine** driving 1 FP propeller Total Power: 7,451kW (10,130hp) 14.5kn B&W 6S50MC-C 1 x 2 Stroke 6 Cy. 500 x 2000 7451kW (10130bhp) Kawasaki Heavy Industries Ltd-Japan AuxGen: 3 x 680kW 220/440V 60Hz a.c Fuel: 125.6 (d.f.) (Heating Coils) 1621.1 (r.f.) 26.6pd
9552953 *3FXU* -	**STOVE OCEAN** - **Stove Rederi AS** The Sanko Steamship Co Ltd (Sanko Kisen KK) *Panama* *Panama* MMSI: 371055000 Official number: 4508513	**31,864** 16,746 55,861 T/cm 55.8	Class: NK	**2013-05 Oshima Shipbuilding Co Ltd — Saikai NS** Yd No: 10641 Loa 189.99 (BB) Br ex - Dght 12.568 Lbp 185.79 Br md 32.26 Dpth 17.87 Welded, 1 dk	**(A21A2BC) Bulk Carrier** Double Hull Grain: 64,634; Bale: 64,064 TEU 306 Compartments: 5 Ho, ER 5 Ha: 4 (21.1 x 18.9)ER (17.6 x 18.9) Cranes: 4x30t	**1 oil engine** driving 1 FP propeller Total Power: 7,615kW (10,353hp) 14.5kn MAN-B&W 6S50MC-C 1 x 2 Stroke 6 Cy. 500 x 2000 7615kW (10353bhp) Kawasaki Heavy Industries Ltd-Japan AuxGen: 3 x a.c Fuel: 2160.0

IMO / Call sign	Name / Owner / Manager / Flag	Tonnage	Class	Construction	Type / Cargo	Machinery
9182497 *LAHG5* -	**STOVE TRADER** *ex Western Obelisk -2001* **Stove Rederi AS** Wilhelmsen Ship Management Singapore Pte Ltd SatCom: Inmarsat C 425740210 *Oslo* *Norway (NIS)* MMSI: 257402000 Official number: 999252	**26,966** 15,344 46,223 T/cm 50.7	Class: NK (NV)	**1999-05 Oshima Shipbuilding Co Ltd — Saikai NS** Yd No: 10234 Loa 185.73 (BB) Br ex - Dght 11.785 Lbp 177.00 Br md 30.50 Dpth 16.40 Welded, 1 dk	**(A21A2BC) Bulk Carrier** Double Hull Grain: 56,703; Bale: 54,673 TEU 1036 C Ho 690 TEU C Dk 346 TEU Compartments: 5 Ho, ER 5 Ha: (17.0 x 16.0)Tappered 3 (20.3 x 25.4) (20.3 x 22.0)ER Cranes: 4x30t	**1 oil engine** driving 1 FP propeller Total Power: 7,451kW (10,130hp) 14.5kn B&W 6S50MC-C 1 x 2 Stroke 6 Cy. 500 x 2000 7451kW (10130bhp) Kawasaki Heavy Industries Ltd-Japan AuxGen: 3 x 680kW 220/440V 60Hz a.c Fuel: 126.1 (d.f.) (Heating Coils) 1652.7 (r.f.) 25.0pd
9182461 *LAHD5* -	**STOVE TRADITION** *ex Western Opal -2001* **Stove Rederi AS** Wilhelmsen Ship Management Singapore Pte Ltd SatCom: Inmarsat B 325996210 *Oslo* *Norway (NIS)* MMSI: 259962000	**26,966** 15,344 46,223 T/cm 50.7	Class: NK (NV)	**1998-06 Oshima Shipbuilding Co Ltd — Saikai NS** Yd No: 10231 Loa 185.73 (BB) Br ex 30.95 Dght 11.785 Lbp 177.00 Br md 30.95 Dpth 16.40 Welded, 1 dk	**(A21A2BC) Bulk Carrier** Double Hull Grain: 56,703; Bale: 54,673 TEU 1036 C Ho 690 TEU C Dk 346 TEU Compartments: 5 Ho, ER 5 Ha: (17.0 x 16.0)Tappered 3 (20.3 x 25.4) (20.3 x 22.0)ER Cranes: 4x30t	**1 oil engine** driving 1 FP propeller Total Power: 7,451kW (10,130hp) 16.0kn B&W 6S50MC-C 1 x 2 Stroke 6 Cy. 500 x 2000 7451kW (10130bhp) Kawasaki Heavy Industries Ltd-Japan AuxGen: 3 x 680kW 220/440V 60Hz a.c Fuel: 111.0 (d.f.) 1588.0 (r.f.) 23.0pd
9182473 *LAHE5* -	**STOVE TRANSPORT** *ex Western Olivin -2001* **Stove Rederi AS** Wilhelmsen Ship Management Singapore Pte Ltd SatCom: Inmarsat C 425996710 *Oslo* *Norway (NIS)* MMSI: 259967000	**26,966** 15,344 46,223 T/cm 50.7	Class: NK NV	**1998-08 Oshima Shipbuilding Co Ltd — Saikai NS** Yd No: 10232 Loa 185.73 Br ex - Dght 11.785 Lbp 177.00 Br md 30.95 Dpth 16.40 Welded, 1 dk	**(A21A2BC) Bulk Carrier** Double Hull Grain: 56,703; Bale: 54,673 TEU 1036 C Ho 690 TEU C Dk 346 TEU Compartments: 5 Ho, ER 5 Ha: (17.0 x 16.0)Tappered 3 (20.3 x 25.4) (20.3 x 22.0)ER Cranes: 4x30t	**1 oil engine** driving 1 FP propeller Total Power: 7,451kW (10,130hp) 16.0kn B&W 6S50MC-C 1 x 2 Stroke 6 Cy. 500 x 2000 7451kW (10130bhp) Diesel United Ltd.-Aioi AuxGen: 3 x 680kW 220/440V 60Hz a.c Fuel: 1870.0 (d.f.)
7037698 *UERT* -	**STOZHARY** **Wella Ltd** - *Petropavlovsk-Kamchatskiy* *Russia* MMSI: 273437670	*172* 43 94	Class: RS	**1968-08 Zavod 'Nikolayevsk-na-Amure' — Nikolayevsk-na-Amure** Yd No: 8 Converted From: Fishing Vessel-1988 Loa 33.96 Br ex 7.09 Dght 2.880 Lbp 30.69 Br md - Dpth 3.69	**(A37B2PS) Passenger Ship** Passengers: unberthed: 29 Ice Capable	**1 oil engine** driving 1 FP propeller 9.5kn S.K.L. 1 x 4 Stroke 8 Cy. 240 x 360 VEB Schwermaschinenbau "KarlLiebknecht" (SKL)-Magdeburg
5097606 *WM5464* -	**STR EDWARD L RYERSON** *ex Edward L. Ryerson -2009* **Indiana Harbor Steamship Co** Central Marine Logistics Inc *Indiana Harbor, IN* *United States of America* MMSI: 367126970 Official number: 282106	*12,170* 7,637 30,442	Class: AB	**1960-08 Manitowoc Shipbuilding Inc — Manitowoc WI** Yd No: 425 Loa 222.51 Br ex 22.92 Dght 8.435 Lbp 217.02 Br md 22.86 Dpth 11.89 Riveted\Welded, 1 dk	**(A21A2BG) Bulk Carrier, Laker Only** Compartments: 4 Ho, ER 18 Ha: 18 (6.1 x 14.6)ER	**1 Steam Turb** dr geared to sc. shaft driving 1 FP propeller Total Power: 7,282kW (9,901hp) 12.0kn General Electric 1 x steam Turb 7282kW (9901shp) General Electric Co.-Lynn, Ma AuxGen: 2 x 600kW Fuel: 782.5 (r.f.)
6875732 - -	**STR NO. 6123** - -	*132* - 52	Class: (RS)	**1965 VEB Schiffswerft "Edgar Andre" — Magdeburg** Yd No: 6123 Loa 28.81 Br ex 6.51 Dght 2.401 Lbp 25.63 Br md - Dpth 3.00 Welded	**(B32A2ST) Tug**	**1 oil engine** driving 1 FP propeller Total Power: 294kW (400hp)
5389554 *WDA2769* -	**STR WILFRED SYKES** *ex Wilfred Sykes -2006* **Indiana Harbor Steamship Co** Central Marine Logistics Inc *Indiana Harbor, IN* *United States of America* MMSI: 366790980 Official number: 259193	*12,729* 7,875 21,845	Class: AB	**1950 American Shipbuilding Co — Lorain OH** Yd No: 866 Loa 202.70 Br ex 21.39 Dght 7.843 Lbp 201.17 Br md 21.34 Dpth 11.28 Riveted\Welded, 1 dk	**(A23A2BK) Bulk Carrier, Self-discharging, Laker** Grain: 21,500 Compartments: 6 Ho, ER 18 Ha: ER	**1 Steam Turb** dr geared to sc. shaft driving 1 FP propeller Total Power: 5,663kW (7,699hp) 13.5kn Westinghouse 1 x steam Turb 5663kW (7699shp) Westinghouse Elec. Corp.-Chester, Pa AuxGen: 2 x 500kW Thrusters: 1 Thwart. FP thruster (f) Fuel: 569.0 (r.f.)
9070175 *D6HV8* -	**STRADER** *ex Athens Trader -2014 ex Belem 2 -2011* *ex MSC Belem -2010 ex Trade Harvest -2002* **Ancient Shipping Industries Ltd** - *Moroni* *Union of Comoros* Official number: 1201555	**29,195** 17,589 35,534 T/cm 51.7	Class: LR ✠**100A1** SS 06/2010 container ship LI ✠**LMC** **UMS** Eq.Ltr: N†; Cable: 660.0/76.0 U3	**1995-06 Hyundai Heavy Industries Co Ltd — Ulsan** Yd No: 871 Loa 196.36 (BB) Br ex 32.30 Dght 11.500 Lbp 184.00 Br md 32.25 Dpth 18.80 Welded, 1 dk	**(A33A2CC) Container Ship (Fully Cellular)** TEU 2227 C Ho 1164 TEU C Dk 1063 TEU incl 99 ref C. Compartments: ER, 6 Cell Ho 10 Ha: ER	**1 oil engine** driving 1 FP propeller Total Power: 19,257kW (26,182hp) 20.0kn B&W 7S70MC 1 x 2 Stroke 7 Cy. 700 x 2674 19257kW (26182bhp) Hyundai Heavy Industries Co Ltd-South Korea AuxGen: 3 x 800kW 440V 60Hz a.c Boilers: AuxB (Comp) 6.9kgf/cm² (6.8bar) Thrusters: 1 Thwart. CP thruster (f) Fuel: 210.0 (d.f.) 2573.0 (r.f.)
8023096 *VOFG* -	**STRAIT EXPLORER** *ex Pennysmart -2009* **Superport Marine Services Ltd** - *St John's, NL* *Canada* MMSI: 316254000 Official number: 801268	*753* 225 393	Class: (LR) ✠Classed LR until 15/6/85	**1982-04 Dorbyl Marine Pty. Ltd. — Durban** Yd No: 6800 Converted From: Stern Trawler-2007 Loa 45.70 (BB) Br ex 11.43 Dght 4.650 Lbp 39.02 Br md 11.20 Dpth 4.77 Welded, 2 dks	**(B31A2SR) Research Survey Vessel** Ins: 376 Compartments: 1 Ho, ER 1 Ha: ER Ice Capable	**1 oil engine** with flexible couplings & sr gearedto sc. shaft driving 1 CP propeller Total Power: 2,200kW (2,991hp) MaK 6M453AK 1 x 4 Stroke 6 Cy. 320 x 420 2200kW (2991bhp) Krupp MaK Maschinenbau GmbH-Kiel AuxGen: 1 x 712kW 450V 60Hz a.c, 1 x 150kW 450V 60Hz a.c Fuel: 133.0 (d.f.)
7208455 *XJAW* -	**STRAIT HUNTER** *ex Geosounder -2011 ex Geograph -2006* *ex Sea Beam -1987 ex Anne Bravo -1985* **Superport Marine Services Ltd** - *Halifax, NS* *Canada* MMSI: 316020186 Official number: 835613	**1,035** 311 1,008	Class: NV	**1972-05 Martin Jansen GmbH & Co. KG Schiffsw. u. Masch. — Leer** Yd No: 102 Loa 57.92 Br ex 10.24 Dght 3.988 Lbp 53.78 Br md 10.19 Dpth 6.35 Welded, 2 dks	**(B31A2SR) Research Survey Vessel** Passengers: cabins: 23; berths: 36 Grain: 1,770; Bale: 1,657 Compartments: 1 Ho, ER, 1 Tw Dk 2 Ha: (19.2 x 8.0) (6.0 x 5.0)ER A-frames: 1x15t,1x8t; Winches: 1 Ice Capable	**1 oil engine** reduction geared to sc. shaft driving 1 CP propeller Total Power: 920kW (1,251hp) 10.0kn Alpha 10V23L-VO 1 x Vee 4 Stroke 10 Cy. 225 x 300 920kW (1251bhp) Alpha Diesel A/S-Denmark AuxGen: 1 x 150kW 440V 60Hz a.c, 3 x 96kW 440V 60Hz a.c Thrusters: 1 Tunnel thruster (a); 1 Tunnel thruster (f) Fuel: 119.0 (d.f.) 5.0pd
9219214 *VTQW* -	**STRAIT ISLAND** - **Government of The Republic of India (Andaman & Nicobar Administration)** ABS Marine Services Pvt Ltd *Mumbai* *India* MMSI: 419052500 Official number: 2910	**449** 135 135	Class: IR	**2005-05 Hindustan Shipyard Ltd — Visakhapatnam** Yd No: 11110 Loa 40.40 Br ex 8.62 Dght 2.660 Lbp 36.50 Br md 8.40 Dpth 4.00 Welded, 1 dk	**(A37B2PS) Passenger Ship** Passengers: unberthed: 100	**2 oil engines** geared to sc. shafts driving 2 FP propellers Total Power: 1,324kW (1,800hp) 12.0kn Yanmar M200-EN 2 x 4 Stroke 6 Cy. 200 x 260 each-662kW (900bhp) Yanmar Diesel Engine Co Ltd-Japan AuxGen: 2 x 80kW 415V 50Hz a.c Fuel: 43.0 (d.f.)
9104134 *POQT* -	**STRAIT MAS** *ex Acx Cherry -2012* **PT Tirtamas Express** PT Pelayaran Tempuran Emas Tbk (TEMAS Line) *Jakarta* *Indonesia* MMSI: 525005120	**13,941** 7,039 18,103	Class: NK	**1994-11 Imabari Shipbuilding Co Ltd — Imabari EH (Imabari Shipyard)** Yd No: 509 Loa 163.66 (BB) Br ex - Dght 8.915 Lbp 152.00 Br md 26.00 Dpth 13.40 Welded, 1 dk	**(A33A2CC) Container Ship (Fully Cellular)** TEU 1241 incl 197 ref C. Compartments: 4 Cell Ho, ER 8 Ha: ER	**1 oil engine** driving 1 FP propeller Total Power: 8,664kW (11,780hp) 18.0kn Mitsubishi 7UEC50LSII 1 x 2 Stroke 7 Cy. 500 x 1950 8664kW (11780bhp) Kobe Hatsudoki KK-Japan AuxGen: 3 x 825kW 440V 60Hz a.c Thrusters: 1 Thwart. CP thruster (f) Fuel: 128.0 (d.f.) 1414.0 (r.f.) 36.0pd
9457191 *2CWS2* -	**STRAIT OF MESSINA** - **Prospect Number 60 Ltd** Pacific Basin Shipping Ltd SatCom: Inmarsat C 423592676 *London* *United Kingdom* MMSI: 235076416 Official number: 917176	**29,429** 8,829 11,415	Class: NV	**2011-03 Odense Staalskibsvaerft A/S — Munkebo (Lindo Shipyard)** Yd No: 220 Loa 193.00 (BB) Br ex - Dght 7.000 Lbp 182.39 Br md 26.00 Dpth 16.70 Welded, 4 dks	**(A35A2RR) Ro-Ro Cargo Ship** Stern door/ramp (centre) Len: 15.00 Wid: 17.00 Swl: 120 Lane-Len: 3663 Lane-clr ht: 6.80 Trailers: 254	**2 oil engines** reduction geared to sc. shafts driving 2 CP propellers Total Power: 18,000kW (24,472hp) 21.5kn MaK 9M43C 2 x 4 Stroke 9 Cy. 430 x 610 each-9000kW (12236bhp) Caterpillar Motoren GmbH & Co. KG-Germany AuxGen: 2 x 900kW a.c, 2 x a.c Thrusters: 1 Tunnel thruster (f); 1 Tunnel thruster (a)
9625360 - -	**STRAIT SHOOTER** - **Weipa Tug Services** - *Australia*	**192** 57 60		**2011-01 Richardson Devine Marine Constructions Pty Ltd — Hobart TAS** Yd No: 052 Loa 28.00 Br ex - Dght 1.400 Lbp 27.10 Br md 8.50 Dpth 3.40 Welded, 1 dk	**(B21A2OC) Crew/Supply Vessel** Hull Material: Aluminium Alloy Passengers: unberthed: 36 Cranes: 1x6.5t	**2 oil engines** reduction geared to sc. shafts driving 2 Propellers Total Power: 2,162kW (2,940hp) 22.0kn Caterpillar C32 ACERT 2 x Vee 4 Stroke 12 Cy. 145 x 162 each-1081kW (1470bhp) Caterpillar Inc-USA

IMO / Call sign	Name / Owner / Port	Tonnage	Class	Builder / Dimensions	Type / Cargo	Machinery
6719407 *VOTR* -	**STRAIT SIGNET** *ex* Sub Sig II *-2003* *ex* Scotia Port *-1975* **Superport Marine Services Ltd** *Halifax, NS* *Canada* MMSI: 316004990 Official number: 328504	*322* 96 -	Class: (LR) ✠ Classed LR until 4/8/72	**1967-08 Saint John Shipbuilding & Dry Dock Co Ltd — Saint John NB** Yd No: 1089 Converted From: Stern Trawler-1975 Loa 35.97 Br ex 8.64 Dght 3.353 Lbp 29.57 Br md 8.54 Dpth 4.12 Welded, 1 dk	**(B12D2FR) Fishery Research Vessel**	**1 oil engine** sr reverse geared to sc. shaft driving 1 FP propeller Total Power: 750kW (1,020hp) 11.0kn Caterpillar D398TA 1 x Vee 4 Stroke 12 Cy. 159 x 203 750kW (1020bhp) Caterpillar Tractor Co-USA AuxGen: 2 x 55kW 220V 60Hz a.c Thrusters: 1 Thwart. FP thruster (f); 1 Tunnel thruster (a) Fuel: 352.5 (d.f.)
9003744 *9MPM4* -	**STRAITS 1** *ex* Suo *-2011* - - *Port Klang* *Malaysia* MMSI: 533065400 Official number: 334399	*299* - 770		**1990-10 Koa Sangyo KK — Takamatsu KG** Yd No: 556 Loa 52.37 Br ex - Dght 3.660 Lbp 48.00 Br md 8.60 Dpth 3.80 Welded, 1 dk	**(A13B2TP) Products Tanker** Liq: 521; Liq (Oil): 521 Compartments: 6 Ta, ER	**1 oil engine** reverse geared to sc. shaft driving 1 FP propeller Total Power: 883kW (1,201hp) Hanshin LH26G 1 x 4 Stroke 6 Cy. 260 x 440 883kW (1201bhp) The Hanshin Diesel Works Ltd-Japan
9115573 *9MPN8* -	**STRAITS 3** *ex* Taishin Maru *-2012* **Primus Maritime Sdn Bhd** - *Port Klang* *Malaysia* MMSI: 533001350 Official number: 334417	*749* - 1,887	Class: (NK)	**1994-10 K.K. Watanabe Zosensho — Nagasaki** Yd No: 023 Loa 74.85 Br ex - Dght 4.743 Lbp 69.95 Br md 11.50 Dpth 5.20 Welded, 1 dk	**(A12B2TR) Chemical/Products Tanker** Liq: 4,400; Liq (Oil): 4,400	**1 oil engine** driving 1 FP propeller Total Power: 1,471kW (2,000hp) 11.8kn Hanshin LH34LG 1 x 4 Stroke 6 Cy. 340 x 640 1471kW (2000bhp) The Hanshin Diesel Works Ltd-Japan AuxGen: 3 x a.c Fuel: 76.0
9419709 *YDA4375* -	**STRAITS BALIKPAPAN** *ex* Topniche 8 *-2008* **PT Indo Straits Tbk** - *Jakarta* *Indonesia*	**274** 83 -	Class: KI (BV)	**2007-01 Bonafile Shipbuilders & Repairs Sdn Bhd — Sandakan** Yd No: 57/04 Loa 29.20 Br ex - Dght 3.840 Lbp 27.00 Br md 9.00 Dpth 4.84 Welded, 1 dk	**(B32A2ST) Tug**	**2 oil engines** reduction geared to sc. shafts driving 2 FP propellers Total Power: 1,766kW (2,402hp) 10.0kn Cummins KTA-38-M2 2 x Vee 4 Stroke 12 Cy. 159 x 159 each-883kW (1201bhp) Cummins Engine Co Ltd-United Kingdom AuxGen: 2 x 90kW 415V a.c
8737946 *YB6348* -	**STRAITS BARITO** **PT Indo Straits Tbk** - *Samarinda* *Indonesia*	**128** 39 -	Class: (KI)	**2007-03 C.V. Karya Lestari Industri — Samarinda** Loa 32.20 Br ex - Dght - Lbp 29.20 Br md 6.50 Dpth 2.10 Welded, 1 dk	**(B32A2ST) Tug**	**2 oil engines** driving 2 Propellers Total Power: 514kW (698hp) Yanmar 6HA2M-HTE 2 x 4 Stroke 6 Cy. 130 x 165 each-257kW (349bhp) Yanmar Diesel Engine Co Ltd-Japan
9186950 *9MQN4* -	**STRAITS CHALLENGER** *ex* Kassel *-2013* **Souffle Shipholding SA** Wilhelmsen Ship Management Sdn Bhd *Port Klang* *Malaysia* MMSI: 533130128 Official number: 334593	**51,204** 15,362 17,297	Class: NK NV	**1999-03 Tsuneishi Shipbuilding Co Ltd — Fukuyama HS** Yd No: 1147 Loa 179.90 (BB) Br ex - Dght 9.620 Lbp 170.00 Br md 32.20 Dpth 15.07 Welded, 12 dks incl. 3 hoistable dks	**(A35B2RV) Vehicles Carrier** Side door/ramp (p) Len: 20.00 Wid: 4.20 Swl: 30 Side door/ramp (s) Len: 20.00 Wid: 4.20 Swl: 30 Quarter stern door/ramp (s) Len: 35.00 Wid: 8.00 Swl: 100 Cars: 4,368	**1 oil engine** driving 1 FP propeller Total Power: 14,121kW (19,199hp) 19.0kn Mitsubishi 8UEC60LS 1 x 2 Stroke 8 Cy. 600 x 2200 14121kW (19199bhp) Mitsubishi Heavy Industries Ltd-Japan AuxGen: 3 x 1304kW 450V 60Hz a.c Thrusters: 1 Thwart. FP thruster (f); 1 Thwart. FP thruster (a) Fuel: 87.1 (d.f.) (Heating Coils) 3547.8 (r.f.) 53.2pd
9426635 *9V7682* -	**STRAITS SKY** *launched as* MK Sky *-2009* **Straits Shipping 4 Pte Ltd** National Shipping SA *Singapore* *Singapore* MMSI: 564400000 Official number: 394626	**4,445** 1,963 6,863	Class: AB	**2009-04 Jiangmen Yinxing Shipbuilding Co Ltd — Jiangmen GD** Yd No: GMG0620 Loa 100.50 (BB) Br ex 18.02 Dght 6.800 Lbp 95.10 Br md 18.00 Dpth 9.50 Welded, 1 dk	**(B35E2TF) Bunkering Tanker** Double Hull (13F) Liq: 7,209; Liq (Oil): 7,209 Compartments: 10 Wing Ta, 2 Wing Slop Ta, ER 3 Cargo Pump (s)	**2 oil engines** reduction geared to sc. shafts driving 2 FP propellers Total Power: 3,236kW (4,400hp) 12.0kn Daihatsu 6DKM-26 2 x 4 Stroke 6 Cy. 260 x 380 each-1618kW (2200bhp) Anqing Marine Diesel Engine Works-China AuxGen: 3 x 320kW a.c Fuel: 160.0 (d.f.) 300.0 (r.f.)
8218055 *YDZX* -	**STRAITS TEAMWORK** **PT Indo Straits Tbk** - *Jakarta* *Indonesia*	*209* 8 191	Class: (KI) (AB)	**1983-11 ASD Marine Pte Ltd — Singapore** Yd No: 102 Loa 28.02 Br ex - Dght 3.509 Lbp 25.51 Br md 8.11 Dpth 4.02 Welded, 1 dk	**(B32A2ST) Tug**	**2 oil engines** sr geared to sc. shafts driving 2 FP propellers Total Power: 2,612kW (3,552hp) 12.0kn Waukesha L5792DSIM 2 x Vee 4 Stroke 12 Cy. 216 x 216 each-1306kW (1776bhp) Waukesha Engine Div. DresserIndustries Inc.-Waukesha, Wi AuxGen: 2 x 52kW 200/400V a.c
8613188 *9MLI6* -	**STRAITS VOYAGER** *ex* Columbia Leader *-2010* *ex* Green Bay *-2001* **Straits Auto Logistics Sdn Bhd** Wilhelmsen Ship Management Sdn Bhd *Port Klang* *Malaysia* MMSI: 533052100 Official number: 334221	**38,659** 11,597 13,491	Class: NK (AB)	**1987-10 Mitsui Eng. & SB. Co. Ltd. — Tamano** Yd No: 1344 Loa 182.00 (BB) Br ex - Dght 9.021 Lbp 170.01 Br md 30.01 Dpth 20.78 Welded, 1 dk	**(A35B2RV) Vehicles Carrier** Side door/ramp (p) Side door/ramp (s) Quarter stern door/ramp (s) Len: - Wid: - Swl: 30 Cars: 3,830	**1 oil engine** driving 1 FP propeller Total Power: 8,606kW (11,701hp) 18.4kn B&W 6S60MCE 1 x 2 Stroke 6 Cy. 600 x 2292 8606kW (11701bhp) Mitsui Engineering & Shipbuilding CLtd-Japan AuxGen: 3 x 720kW 450V a.c
9323704 *ZMSM* -	**STRAITSMAN** *ex* Dueodde *-2010* **Straitsman Ltd** Strait Shipping Ltd *Wellington* *New Zealand* MMSI: 512002959	**13,906** 5,142 4,168	Class: BV (LR) ✠ Classed LR until 7/12/05	**2005-04 Volharding Shipyards B.V. — Foxhol** (Hull) Yd No: 579 **2005-04 Merwede Shipyard BV — Hardinxveld** Yd No: 703 Loa 124.90 (BB) Br ex - Dght 5.600 Lbp 114.95 Br md 23.40 Dpth 14.30 Welded, 3 dks	**(A36A2PR) Passenger/Ro-Ro Ship (Vehicles)** Passengers: unberthed: 340; berths: 60 Stern door/ramp (centre) Lane-Len: 1235 Lane-Wid: 3.10 Lane-clr ht: 4.50 Cars: 280, Trailers: 92 Ice Capable	**2 oil engines** with clutches, flexible couplings & sr geared to sc. shafts driving 2 CP propellers Total Power: 8,640kW (11,746hp) 18.8kn MaK 9M32 2 x 4 Stroke 9 Cy. 320 x 480 each-4320kW (5873bhp) Caterpillar Motoren GmbH & Co. KG-Germany AuxGen: 2 x 1160kW 400V 50Hz a.c, 3 x 515kW 400V 50Hz a.c Boilers: TOH (ex.g.) 10.2kgf/cm² (10.0bar), TOH (o.f.) 10.2kgf/cm² (10.0bar) Thrusters: 2 Thwart. CP thruster (f)
9391127 *9HBX9* -	**STRAITVIEW** *launched as* Sureyya Vardal *-2007* **Dudman Investment & Finance SA** Nordic Tankers A/S SatCom: Inmarsat C 425676510 *Valletta* *Malta* MMSI: 256765000 Official number: 9391127	**2,222** 1,064 3,550 T/cm 10.4	Class: AB	**2007-08 Dentas Gemi Insaat ve Onarim Sanayii A.S. — Istanbul** Yd No: 79 Loa 88.31 (BB) Br ex 13.54 Dght 5.600 Lbp 82.25 Br md 13.50 Dpth 6.50 Welded, 1 dk	**(A12B2TR) Chemical/Products Tanker** Double Hull (13F) Liq: 3,751; Liq (Oil): 3,836 Cargo Heating Coils Compartments: 2 Wing Slop Ta, ER, 12 Wing Ta 12 Cargo Pump (s): 12x100m³/hr Manifold: Bow/CM: 44.5m	**1 oil engine** reduction geared to sc. shaft driving 1 CP propeller Total Power: 1,499kW (2,038hp) 13.5kn MaK 6M25 1 x 4 Stroke 6 Cy. 255 x 400 1499kW (2038bhp) Caterpillar Motoren GmbH & Co. KG-Germany AuxGen: 2 x 345kW a.c, 1 x 535kW a.c Thrusters: 1 Tunnel thruster (f) Fuel: 37.0 (d.f.) 159.0 (r.f.)
8922254 *C6UN9* -	**STRAMI** *ex* Arklow Fame *-2005* *ex* MB Avon *-1997* **Misje Bulk AS** Misje Rederi AS *Nassau* *Bahamas* MMSI: 311973000 Official number: 8001010	**2,373** 1,434 4,245 T/cm 10.6	Class: GL	**1992-07 Scheepswerf Ferus Smit BV — Westerbroek** Yd No: 285 Loa 88.25 (BB) Br ex 13.21 Dght 5.463 Lbp 84.90 Br md 13.17 Dpth 7.00 Welded, 1 dk	**(A31A2GX) General Cargo Ship** Grain: 5,222 TEU 96 C.96/20' Compartments: 1 Ho, ER 2 Ha: 2 (26.0 x 10.2)ER Ice Capable	**1 oil engine** with flexible couplings & sr geared to sc. shaft driving 1 CP propeller Total Power: 1,600kW (2,175hp) 12.0kn Caterpillar 3606TA 1 x 4 Stroke 6 Cy. 280 x 300 1600kW (2175bhp) Caterpillar Inc-USA AuxGen: 1 x 110kW 220/380V a.c Thrusters: 1 Thwart. FP thruster (f)
8112639 *LKVZ* -	**STRAND** **Norled AS** - *Stavanger* *Norway* MMSI: 257074700	**1,479** 534 446	Class: (NV)	**1982-04 Sterkoder Mek. Verksted AS — Kristiansund** Yd No: 94 Loa 74.66 Br ex 13.90 Dght 3.590 Lbp 61.22 Br md 13.71 Dpth 4.53 Welded, 1 dk	**(A36A2PR) Passenger/Ro-Ro Ship (Vehicles)** Passengers: unberthed: 500 Cars: 90	**1 oil engine** driving 1 CP propeller , 1 fwd Total Power: 1,497kW (2,035hp) 13.0kn Wichmann 7AXA 1 x 2 Stroke 7 Cy. 300 x 450 1497kW (2035bhp) Wichmann Motorfabrikk AS-Norway AuxGen: 2 x 110kW 220V 50Hz a.c Fuel: 46.5 (d.f.) 8.5pd
9195779 *LJRS* -	**STRAND SENIOR** **Strand Senior AS** - *Aalesund* *Norway* MMSI: 259574000	**1,969** 590 -	Class: NV	**1999-02 SC Santierul Naval SA Braila — Braila** (Hull) Yd No: 1393 **1999-02 Slipen Mek. Verksted AS — Sandnessjoen** Yd No: 61 Loa 67.40 Br ex 13.03 Dght 6.966 Lbp 60.00 Br md 13.00 Dpth 5.80 Welded, 1 dk	**(B11A2FS) Stern Trawler** Ins: 1,200 Ice Capable	**1 oil engine** geared to sc. shaft driving 1 FP propeller Total Power: 5,517kW (7,501hp) 17.5kn Wartsila 12V32 1 x Vee 4 Stroke 12 Cy. 320 x 400 5517kW (7501bhp) Wartsila NSD Norway AS-Norway AuxGen: 1 x 2300kW 230/440V 60Hz a.c, 3 x 482kW 230/440V 60Hz a.c Thrusters: 1 Thwart. FP thruster (f); 1 Tunnel thruster (a)

Ship	Tonnage	Class	Build / Dimensions	Type	Machinery
8400074 **STRANDE** *DFRQ* - **Schlepp- und Fahrgesellschaft Kiel mbH-SFK** - *Kiel* *Germany* MMSI: 211896000 Official number: 2405	**266** 105 50	Class: (GL)	**1984-06 Schiffswerft u. Masch. Paul Lindenau GmbH & Co. KG — Kiel** Yd No: 214 Loa 32.90 (BB) Br ex 7.90 Dght 2.253 Lbp 29.49 Br md 7.60 Dpth 3.31 Welded, 1 dk	**(A37B2PS) Passenger Ship** Passengers: unberthed: 300	**1 oil engine** with flexible couplings & sr reverse geared to sc. shaft driving 1 FP propeller Total Power: 250kW (340hp) 11.5kn MWM D440-6 1 x 4 Stroke 6 Cy. 230 x 270 250kW (340bhp) Motoren Werke Mannheim AG (MWM)-West Germany Thrusters: 1 Thwart. FP thruster (f)
7112204 **STRANDEBARM** *LARA* - **Norled AS** Tide ASA *Bergen* *Norway* MMSI: 257383400	**743** 304 -	Class: (NV)	**1971-05 Hasund Smie & Sveiseverk AS — Ulsteinvik** (Hull) Yd No: 12 **1971-05 Hatlo Verksted AS — Ulsteinvik** Yd No: 42 Loa 44.35 Br ex 10.60 Dght - Lbp 40.52 Br md 10.55 Dpth 4.22 Welded, 1 dk	**(A36A2PR) Passenger/Ro-Ro Ship (Vehicles)** Cars: 35	**1 oil engine** driving 1 FP propeller Total Power: 662kW (900hp) Wichmann 6ACA 1 x 2 Stroke 6 Cy. 280 x 420 662kW (900bhp) Wichmann Motorfabrikk AS-Norway AuxGen: 2 x 50kW 220V 50Hz a.c Thrusters: 1 Thwart. FP thruster (f)
9564140 **STRANDJA** *9HA2483* - *ex* Federal Yangtze *-2010* *launched as* Eastwind York *-2010* **Balkan Navigation Ltd** Navigation Maritime Bulgare *Valletta* *Malta* MMSI: 248724000 Official number: 9564140	**19,865** 10,279 29,800	Class: LR (AB) **100A1** SS 08/2010 bulk carrier CSR BC-A GRAB (20) Nos. 2, 4 & 6 holds may be empty ESP LI *IWS Ice Class 1C FS at a draught of 10.639m Max/min draught fwd 10.750/3.800m Max/min draught aft 11.321/6.000m Power required 6480kw, power installed 7200kw **LMC** **UMS**	**2010-08 Shanhaiguan Shipbuilding Industry Co Ltd — Qinhuangdao HE** Yd No: 026 Loa 186.00 (BB) Br ex 23.76 Dght 10.400 Lbp 178.80 Br md 23.70 Dpth 14.60 Welded, 1 dk	**(A21A2BC) Bulk Carrier** Grain: 39,091 Compartments: 6 Ho, ER 6 Ha: ER Cranes: 3x30t Ice Capable	**1 oil engine** driving 1 FP propeller Total Power: 7,860kW (10,686hp) 14.0kn MAN-B&W 6S46MC-C 1 x 2 Stroke 6 Cy. 460 x 1932 7860kW (10686bhp) Yichang Marine Diesel Engine Co Ltd-China
9303065 **STRANGE ATTRACTOR** *V7CE5* - *ex* Tokiwa Glory *-2013* **Glory Supra Shipping LLC** Starbulk SA *Majuro* *Marshall Islands* MMSI: 538005251 Official number: 5251	**31,279** 17,709 55,742 T/cm 55.8	Class: BV (NK)	**2006-02 Mitsui Eng. & SB. Co. Ltd. — Tamano** Yd No: 1609 Loa 189.99 (BB) Br ex - Dght 12.550 Lbp 182.00 Br md 32.26 Dpth 17.90 Welded, 1 dk	**(A21A2BC) Bulk Carrier** Grain: 70,811; Bale: 66,122 Compartments: 5 Ho, ER 5 Ha: 4 (21.1 x 18.9)ER (17.6 x 18.9) Cranes: 4x30t	**1 oil engine** driving 1 FP propeller Total Power: 9,480kW (12,889hp) 14.5kn MAN-B&W 6S50MC-C 1 x 2 Stroke 6 Cy. 500 x 2000 9480kW (12889bhp) Mitsui Engineering & Shipbuilding CLtd-Japan Fuel: 2260.0
1003217 **STRANGELOVE** *ZCNR5* - *ex* Paris *-2004* *ex* Paminusch *-2004* **David Hoey** *George Town* *Cayman Islands (British)* MMSI: 319095000 Official number: 398975	**426** 127 -	Class: LR ✠**100A1** SS 07/2009 Yacht ✠**LMC**	**1982-02 de Vries Scheepsbouw B.V. — Aalsmeer** Yd No: 624 Loa 45.99 Br ex 8.32 Dght 2.680 Lbp 41.78 Br md - Dpth - Welded, 1 dk	**(X11A2YP) Yacht**	**2 oil engines** reverse reduction geared to sc. shafts driving 2 FP propellers Total Power: 1,250kW (1,700hp) Caterpillar D398TA 2 x Vee 4 Stroke 12 Cy. 159 x 203 each-625kW (850bhp) Caterpillar Tractor Co-USA
6926311 **STRANGFORD FERRY** *MFWZ7* - **Down County Council (Department for Regional Development Roads Service)** *Belfast* *United Kingdom* MMSI: 235004601 Official number: 334439	*186* 83 65		**1969 Verolme Cork Dockyard Ltd — Cobh** Yd No: 811 Loa 50.14 Br ex 11.08 Dght 1.651 Lbp - Br md - Dpth - Welded, 1 dk	**(A36A2PR) Passenger/Ro-Ro Ship (Vehicles)** Bow ramp (f) Len: 1.22 Wid: 4.57 Swl: 60 Stern ramp (a) Len: 1.22 Wid: 4.57 Swl: 60	**2 oil engines** driving 2 FP propellers Total Power: 224kW (304hp) 10.0kn Kelvin T8 2 x 4 Stroke 8 Cy. 165 x 184 each-112kW (152bhp) GEC Diesels Ltd.Kelvin Marine Div.-Glasgow
8667323 **STRANNEFJORD** *SLCQ* VG-392 **Jonas Nilsson** - *Traslovslage* *Sweden* MMSI: 266147000	**162** 48 -		**2000 O-varvet AB — Ockero** Yd No: 111 Loa 22.98 Br ex - Dght - Lbp - Br md 6.67 Dpth - Welded, 1 dk	**(B11B2FV) Fishing Vessel**	**1 oil engine** driving 1 FP propeller
5342192 **STRANTON** - - - - -	*145* - -	Class: (LR) ✠ Classed LR until 1/63	**1959-11 P K Harris & Sons Ltd — Bideford** Yd No: 124 Loa 31.40 Br ex 8.21 Dght 2.902 Lbp 28.35 Br md 7.88 Dpth 3.59 Welded, 1 dk	**(B32A2ST) Tug** 1 Ha: (1.9 x 1.0)	**2 oil engines** geared to sc. shafts driving 2 FP propellers Total Power: 882kW (1,200hp) Blackstone ERS8 2 x 4 Stroke 8 Cy. 222 x 292 each-441kW (600bhp) Lister Blackstone Marine Ltd.-Dursley AuxGen: 2 x 46kW 110V d.c
9648075 **STRATEGIC ALLIANCE** *9V7193* **SBC Alliance Pte Ltd** *Singapore* *Singapore* MMSI: 563642000 Official number: 398140	**24,641** 13,203 39,848	Class: AB	**2014-01 Tianjin Xingang Shipbuilding Industry Co Ltd — Tianjin** Yd No: NB008-1 Loa 179.99 (BB) Br ex 30.04 Dght 10.500 Lbp 176.60 Br md 30.00 Dpth 15.04 Welded, 1 dk	**(A21A2BC) Bulk Carrier** Double Hull Grain: 48,500 Compartments: 5 Ho, ER 5 Ha: ER Cranes: 4x30t	**1 oil engine** driving 1 FP propeller Total Power: 6,050kW (8,226hp) 14.0kn MAN-B&W 5S50ME-B9 1 x 2 Stroke 5 Cy. 500 x 2214 6050kW (8226bhp) Yichang Marine Diesel Engine Co Ltd-China AuxGen: 3 x 650kW a.c Fuel: 158.0 (d.f.) 1564.0 (r.f.)
9475739 **STRATEGIC ENCOUNTER** *9V2495* - *ex* Peace Lucky *-2014* **SBC Encounter Pte Ltd** MTM Ship Management Pte Ltd *Singapore* *Singapore* MMSI: 564171000 Official number: 399095	**19,992** 11,369 33,000	Class: NK (Class contemplated) (LR) (CC) ✠ Classed LR until 23/4/12	**2010-08 Zhejiang Zhenghe Shipbuilding Co Ltd — Zhoushan ZJ** Yd No: 3024 Loa 177.40 (BB) Br ex 28.66 Dght 10.218 Lbp 168.00 Br md 28.20 Dpth 14.20 Welded, 1 dk	**(A21A2BC) Bulk Carrier** Grain: 42,700 Compartments: 5 Ho, ER 5 Ha: 4 (19.2 x 16.8)ER (14.4 x 15.2) Cranes: 4x30t	**1 oil engine** driving 1 FP propeller Total Power: 7,900kW (10,741hp) 13.9kn MAN-B&W 5S50MC-C 1 x 2 Stroke 5 Cy. 500 x 2000 7900kW (10741bhp) AO Bryanskiy MashinostroitelnyyZavod (BMZ)-Bryansk AuxGen: 3 x 520kW 450V 60Hz a.c Boilers: WTAuxB (Comp) 9.0kgf/cm² (8.8bar)
9475727 **STRATEGIC ENDEAVOR** *9V2493* - *ex* Peace Fortune *-2014* **SBC Endeavor Pte Ltd** MTM Ship Management Pte Ltd *Singapore* *Singapore* MMSI: 564180000 Official number: 399094	**19,992** 11,905 33,078	Class: CC NK (LR) ✠ Classed LR until 5/1/12	**2010-05 Zhejiang Zhenghe Shipbuilding Co Ltd — Zhoushan ZJ** Yd No: 3023 Loa 177.40 (BB) Br ex 28.24 Dght 10.218 Lbp 168.00 Br md 28.20 Dpth 14.20 Welded, 1 dk	**(A21A2BC) Bulk Carrier** Grain: 42,700 Compartments: 5 Ho, ER 5 Ha: 4 (19.2 x 16.8)ER (14.4 x 15.2) Cranes: 4x30t	**1 oil engine** driving 1 FP propeller Total Power: 7,900kW (10,741hp) 13.9kn MAN-B&W 5S50MC-C 1 x 2 Stroke 5 Cy. 500 x 2000 7900kW (10741bhp) AO Bryanskiy MashinostroitelnyyZavod (BMZ)-Bryansk AuxGen: 3 x 520kW 450V 60Hz a.c Boilers: WTAuxB (Comp) 9.0kgf/cm² (8.8bar)
8964109 **STRATEGIC HORIZON** *WCX9870* - *ex* Gulf Miracle *-2006* *ex* Brother *-2005* **Foss Maritime Co** *Long Beach, CA* *United States of America* Official number: 1060958	**309** 92 -		**1999-01** Yd No: 32 Loa 42.70 Br ex - Dght 2.100 Lbp 38.40 Br md 8.83 Dpth 3.81 Welded, 1 dk	**(B21A2OC) Crew/Supply Vessel** Hull Material: Aluminium Alloy	**4 oil engines** reduction geared to sc. shafts driving 4 FP propellers Total Power: 3,580kW (4,868hp) 20.0kn Caterpillar 3508B 4 x Vee 4 Stroke 8 Cy. 170 x 190 each-895kW (1217bhp) (new engine 2000) Caterpillar Inc-USA Fuel: 68.0 (d.f.)
8729107 **STRATIS Z** - - *ex* Akhtiar *-2008* **Kazakh Agency of Applied Ecology JSC** - *Aqtau* *Kazakhstan*	**1,178** 353 391	Class: BV (Class contemplated) (LR) (RS) Classed LR until 24/4/13	**1989-07 Yaroslavskiy Sudostroitelnyy Zavod — Yaroslavl** Yd No: 233 Loa 58.55 Br ex 12.67 Dght 4.760 Lbp 51.60 Br md 12.64 Dpth 5.90 Welded	**(B32A2ST) Tug**	**2 diesel electric oil engines** driving 2 gen. each 1300kW a.c Connecting to 1 elec. Motor of (1900kW) driving 1 FP propeller Total Power: 2,600kW (3,534hp) 13.5kn Kolomna 6CHN1A30/38 2 x 4 Stroke 6 Cy. 300 x 380 each-1300kW (1767bhp) Kolomenskiy Zavod-Kolomna AuxGen: 2 x 300kW, 2 x 160kW Thrusters: 1 Tunnel thruster (f) Fuel: 331.0 (d.f.)
6705987 **STRATOS S** *HQCC8* - *ex* Achaios *-2008* *ex* Coriolanus *-1981* **Atlantida Compania Naviera SA** Lagousses Shipping Co SA *San Lorenzo* *Honduras* Official number: L-1931887	*1,498* 663 -	Class: (LR) ✠ Classed LR until 3/6/87	**1967-05 Yarrow & Co Ltd — Glasgow** Yd No: 2270 L reg 63.37 Br ex 11.92 Dght 4.573 Lbp 59.14 Br md 11.89 Dpth 7.62 Welded, 2 dks	**(B11A2FS) Stern Trawler** Ins: 481 Ice Capable	**1 oil engine** driving 1 CP propeller Total Power: 1,728kW (2,349hp) 15.5kn Mirrlees KLSSDM-8 1 x 4 Stroke 8 Cy. 381 x 508 1728kW (2349bhp) Mirrlees National Ltd.-Stockport AuxGen: 2 x 330kW 220V d.c, 2 x 57kW 220V d.c

9406726 *LACE7* -	**STRAUM** **Utkilen Shipping AS** Utkilen AS *Bergen* *Norway (NIS)* MMSI: 259894000	**12,862** 6,639 19,537 T/cm 32.0	Class: GL	2010-01 **Qingshan Shipyard — Wuhan HB** Yd No: 20060409 Loa 164.36 (BB) Br ex 23.25 Dght 9.550 Lbp 155.40 Br md 23.20 Dpth 12.80 Welded, 1 dk	**(A12B2TR) Chemical/Products Tanker** Double Hull (13F) Liq: 22,384; Liq (Oil): 23,200 Cargo Heating Coils Compartments: 14 Wing Ta, 2 Wing Slop Ta, ER 14 Cargo Pump (s): 2x150m³/hr, 10x300m³/hr, 2x500m³/hr Manifold: Bow/CM: 79.4m Ice Capable	**1 oil engine** driving 1 CP propeller Total Power: 7,860kW (10,686hp) 15.5kn MAN-B&W 6S46MC-C 1 x 2 Stroke 6 Cy. 460 x 1932 7860kW (10686bhp) STX Engine Co Ltd-South Korea AuxGen: 3 x 910kW 440V a.c Thrusters: 1 Tunnel thruster (f)
9656395 *LDEF* -	**STRAUMBERG** **Straumberg AS** - *Mosjoen* *Norway* MMSI: 257177000	**932** 279 650	Class: NV	**2014-01 'Crist' SA — Gdansk** (Hull) Yd No: (51) **2014-01 Larsnes Mek. Verksted AS — Larsnes** Yd No: 51 Loa 46.55 Br ex - Dght 4.500 Lbp 39.60 Br md 12.00 Dpth 5.20 Welded, 1 dk	**(B11B2FV) Fishing Vessel**	**1 oil engine** driving 1 Propeller
7925156 *LIOD* N-2-LF	**STRAUMBERG 1** *ex* Straumberg *-2013* **Straumberg AS** - *Mosjoen* *Norway* MMSI: 258035000	**423** 132 -		1979-07 **Rabben Mek. Verksted AS — Bekkjarvik** Yd No: 110 Loa 30.33 Br ex 8.26 Dght 5.052 Lbp 25.81 Br md - Dpth 6.71 Welded, 2 dks	**(B11B2FV) Fishing Vessel**	**1 oil engine** geared to sc. shaft driving 1 CP propeller Total Power: 625kW (850hp) Caterpillar D353SCAC 1 x 4 Stroke 6 Cy. 159 x 203 625kW (850bhp) Caterpillar Tractor Co-USA
7042291 *LEYJ* -	**STRAUMVIK** *ex* Harvest Caroline *-2008* *ex* Fjordbulk 2 *-2006* *ex* Fjord Trader *-2006* *ex* Irene *-1982* *ex* Lundoy *-1979* *ex* Briland *-1973* **Roslagen AS** Mostraum Management AS *Bergen* *Norway* MMSI: 258260000	**712** 375 593	Class: (NV)	**1971-01 VEB Elbewerften Boizenburg/Rosslau — Rosslau** Yd No: 416/3329 Loa 49.59 Br ex 10.11 Dght 3.118 Lbp 45.22 Br md 10.06 Dpth 5.62 Welded, 1 dk	**(A31A2GX) General Cargo Ship** Grain: 1,487; Bale: 1,345 Compartments: 1 Ho, ER 1 Ha: (22.5 x 6.1)ER Derricks: 1x15t,1x5t; Winches: 2 Ice Capable	**1 oil engine** driving 1 CP propeller Total Power: 827kW (1,124hp) 11.8kn Caterpillar D399TA 1 x Vee 4 Stroke 16 Cy. 159 x 203 827kW (1124bhp) (new engine 1979) Caterpillar Tractor Co-USA AuxGen: 1 x 32kW 220V 50Hz a.c, 2 x 30kW 220V 50Hz a.c
8897758 *YL2297* -	**STRAUPE** *ex* MRTK-2101 *-1996* **Vetra S Ltd (SIA 'Vetra S')** - *Riga* *Latvia* MMSI: 275220000 Official number: 0799	**109** 32 32	Class: (RS)	**1994 Admiralteyskiy Sudostroitelnyy Zavod — Sankt-Peterburg** Yd No: 201 Loa 25.33 Br ex 6.80 Dght 2.500 Lbp 22.00 Br md - Dpth 3.30 Welded, 1 dk	**(B11A2FS) Stern Trawler** Ins: 61 Ice Capable	**1 oil engine** driving 1 FP propeller Total Power: 220kW (299hp) 10.0kn S.K.L. 6NVD26A-2 1 x 4 Stroke 6 Cy. 180 x 260 220kW (299bhp) SKL Motoren u. Systemtechnik AG-Magdeburg AuxGen: 2 x 16kW a.c Fuel: 12.0 (d.f.)
9306471 *C4AD2* -	**STRAUSS** *ex* Antonia Schulte *-2014* *ex* Maersk Navia *-2009* *completed as* P&O Nedlloyd Mariana *-2005* *ex* Antonia Schulte *-2005* **ms 'Strauss' Schiffahrtsgesellschaft mbH & Co KG** Ocean Shipmanagement GmbH *Limassol* *Cyprus* MMSI: 212187000	**25,406** 12,540 33,900	Class: NV (GL)	**2005-03 Aker MTW Werft GmbH — Wismar** (Aft section) Yd No: 107 **2005-03 Aker Warnemuende Operations GmbH — Rostock** (Fwd section) Loa 207.40 (BB) Br ex - Dght 11.400 Lbp 195.40 Br md 29.80 Dpth 16.40 Welded, 1 dk	**(A33A2CC) Container Ship (Fully Cellular)** TEU 2478 C Ho 992 TEU C Dk 1486 TEU incl 400 ref C. Cranes: 3x45t	**1 oil engine** driving 1 FP propeller Total Power: 21,770kW (29,598hp) 22.2kn B&W 7L70MC-C 1 x 2 Stroke 7 Cy. 700 x 2360 21770kW (29598bhp) Hitachi Zosen Corp-Japan AuxGen: 3 x 1400kW 440/220V 60Hz a.c, 1 x 950kW 440/220V 60Hz a.c Thrusters: 1 Thwart. CP thruster (f)
8834330 - -	**STRAVON** **Government of The Republic of Greece (Hellenic Navy)** - *Piraeus* *Greece* Official number: 4467	**117** 53 -	Class: (HR)	**1988 "Naus" Shipyard Philippou Bros. S.A. — Piraeus** Loa 32.72 Br ex - Dght 2.000 Lbp 29.20 Br md 6.10 Dpth 3.50 Welded, 1 dk	**(B31A2SR) Research Survey Vessel**	**2 oil engines** driving 1 FP propeller Total Power: 2,648kW (3,600hp) 13.0kn MAN D2542MTE 2 x Vee 4 Stroke 12 Cy. 125 x 142 each-1324kW (1800bhp) MAN Nutzfahrzeuge AG-Nuernberg AuxGen: 2 x 220kW 380V a.c
7643784 *SPG2263* -	**STRAZAK-5** **Zarzad Portu Gdansk SA (Port of Gdansk Authority)** - *Gdansk* *Poland* Official number: ROG1959	*276* 72 41	Class: PR	**1976-12 Stocznia Remontowa 'Nauta' SA — Gdynia** Yd No: SP2700/357 Loa 37.32 Br ex 9.78 Dght 2.620 Lbp 36.12 Br md 9.24 Dpth 3.61 Welded, 1 dk	**(B34F2SF) Fire Fighting Vessel** Ice Capable	**1 oil engine** reduction geared to sc. shaft driving 1 CP propeller Total Power: 1,986kW (2,700hp) 14.0kn Fiat B300.12SS 1 x Vee 4 Stroke 12 Cy. 300 x 450 1986kW (2700bhp) Zaklady Przemyslu Metalowego 'HCegielski' SA-Poznan AuxGen: 2 x 120kW 380V 50Hz a.c, 1 x 48kW 400V 50Hz a.c Thrusters: 1 Thwart. FP thruster (f)
7724320 *SPG2205* -	**STRAZAK-14** **Port Gdynia Holding SA** - *Gdynia* *Poland* MMSI: 261003510 Official number: ROG10	*276* 72 42	Class: PR	**1977-06 Stocznia Remontowa 'Nauta' SA — Gdynia** Yd No: SP2700/368 Loa 37.34 Br ex 10.01 Dght 3.099 Lbp 36.12 Br md 9.22 Dpth 3.61 Welded, 1 dk	**(B34F2SF) Fire Fighting Vessel** Ice Capable	**1 oil engine** reduction geared to sc. shaft driving 1 CP propeller Total Power: 1,986kW (2,700hp) 14.0kn Fiat B300.12SS 1 x Vee 4 Stroke 12 Cy. 300 x 450 1986kW (2700bhp) Zaklady Przemyslu Metalowego 'HCegielski' SA-Poznan AuxGen: 2 x 120kW 380V 50Hz a.c, 1 x 48kW 400V 50Hz a.c Thrusters: 1 Thwart. FP thruster (f)
7909918 *SPS2028* -	**STRAZAK-25** **Fairplay Polska Sp z oo & Co Sp k** - *Szczecin* *Poland* MMSI: 261001100 Official number: ROS/S/419	*276* 72 -	Class: PR	**1978-12 Stocznia Remontowa 'Nauta' SA — Gdynia** Yd No: 2700/372 Loa 37.34 Br ex - Dght 3.600 Lbp 36.17 Br md 9.22 Dpth 3.61 Welded, 1 dk	**(B34F2SF) Fire Fighting Vessel** Ice Capable	**1 oil engine** reduction geared to sc. shaft driving 1 CP propeller Total Power: 1,986kW (2,700hp) 14.0kn Fiat B300.12SS 1 x Vee 4 Stroke 12 Cy. 300 x 450 1986kW (2700bhp) Zaklady Przemyslu Metalowego 'HCegielski' SA-Poznan AuxGen: 2 x 120kW 380V, 1 x 48kW 400V a.c Thrusters: 1 Thwart. FP thruster (f)
8133528 - -	**STRAZH** *ex* RS-300 No. 156 *-2005* **Government of The Republic of Ukraine Management of Renewal & Conservation of Fishing Resources & Fishery Regulation in the Southern Basin ('Yuzhrybvod')** - *Skadovsk* *Ukraine* Official number: 821146	*163* 39 88	Class: (RS)	**1982 Astrakhanskaya Sudoverf im. "Kirova" — Astrakhan** Yd No: 156 Converted From: Fishing Vessel Loa 34.01 Br ex 7.10 Dght 2.900 Lbp 29.98 Br md - Dpth 3.66 Welded, 1 dk	**(B12D2FP) Fishery Patrol Vessel** Ice Capable	**1 oil engine** driving 1 CP propeller Total Power: 224kW (305hp) 9.5kn S.K.L. 8VD36/24-1 1 x 4 Stroke 8 Cy. 240 x 360 224kW (305bhp) VEB Schwermaschinenbau "KarlLiebknecht" (SKL)-Magdeburg
9479979 *V7XD3* -	**STREAM LUNA** *ex* Pacific Luna *-2011* **Stream Luna KS** Utkilen AS *Majuro* *Marshall Islands* MMSI: 538004451 Official number: 4451	**11,757** 6,346 19,998 T/cm 29.8	Class: NK	**2010-04 Shitanoe Shipbuilding Co Ltd — Usuki OT** Yd No: 7057 Loa 144.09 (BB) Br ex 24.23 Dght 9.668 Lbp 136.00 Br md 24.20 Dpth 12.90 Welded, 1 dk	**(A12B2TR) Chemical/Products Tanker** Double Hull (13F) Liq: 20,530; Liq (Oil): 21,717 Cargo Heating Coils Compartments: 20 Wing Ta, 2 Wing Slop Ta, ER 20 Cargo Pump (s): 8x200m³/hr, 12x300m³/hr Manifold: Bow/CM: 73.2m	**1 oil engine** driving 1 FP propeller Total Power: 6,480kW (8,810hp) 14.5kn MAN-B&W 6S42MC 1 x 2 Stroke 6 Cy. 420 x 1764 6480kW (8810bhp) Makita Corp-Japan AuxGen: 3 x 460kW 400V 60Hz a.c Thrusters: 1 Tunnel thruster (f) Fuel: 110.0 (d.f.) 909.0 (r.f.)
9407093 *V7WN9* -	**STREAM MIA** *ex* Golden Mia *-2011* **Stream Mia KS** Utkilen AS *Majuro* *Marshall Islands* MMSI: 538004400 Official number: 4400	**11,645** 6,326 19,702 T/cm 29.8	Class: NK	**2008-09 Fukuoka Shipbuilding Co Ltd — Nagasaki NS** Yd No: 2019 Loa 144.03 (BB) Br ex 24.23 Dght 9.591 Lbp 136.00 Br md 24.19 Dpth 12.80 Welded, 1 dk	**(A12B2TR) Chemical/Products Tanker** Double Hull (13F) Liq: 21,003; Liq (Oil): 21,654 Cargo Heating Coils Compartments: 26 Wing Ta, 2 Wing Slop Ta, ER 26 Cargo Pump (s): 14x200m³/hr, 12x300m³/hr Manifold: Bow/CM: 73.4m	**1 oil engine** driving 1 FP propeller Total Power: 6,230kW (8,470hp) 14.5kn Mitsubishi 7UEC45LA 1 x 2 Stroke 7 Cy. 450 x 1350 6230kW (8470bhp) Akasaka Tekkosho KK (Akasaka DieselLtd)-Japan AuxGen: 3 x 450kW a.c Thrusters: 1 Tunnel thruster (f) Fuel: 126.0 (d.f.) 1153.0 (r.f.)
8866711 *D6FV5* -	**STREAMLINE** *ex* Omskiy-98 *-2009* **Seamann Investitionen Ltd** Vals Marine Ltd SatCom: Inmarsat C 461696310 *Moroni* *Union of Comoros* MMSI: 616963000	**2,447** 966 3,152	Class: IV (RS) (RR)	**1978 Santierul Naval Oltenita S.A. — Oltenita** Yd No: 110 Loa 108.40 Br ex 14.80 Dght 3.260 Lbp 102.23 Br md - Dpth 5.00 Welded, 1 dk	**(A31A2GX) General Cargo Ship** Compartments: 4 Ho, ER 4 Ha: ER 4 (11.1 x 15.8) Ice Capable	**2 oil engines** driving 2 FP propellers Total Power: 1,320kW (1,794hp) S.K.L. 6NVD48A-2U 2 x 4 Stroke 6 Cy. 320 x 480 each-660kW (897bhp) VEB Schwermaschinenbau "KarlLiebknecht" (SKL)-Magdeburg

8741791 *V7AF7* -	**STREGA** *ex* Anna J *-2012* *ex* Mostro *-2010* **Strega Marine Ltd** - *Bikini* *Marshall Islands* MMSI: 538070905 Official number: 70905	**199** 60 130		**2000 Palmer Johnson Yachts LLC — Sturgeon Bay WI** Yd No: 225 Loa 35.66 Br ex - Dght - Lbp - Br md 7.32 Dpth - Welded, 1 dk	**(X11A2YP) Yacht**	**2 oil engines** with clutches, flexible couplings & sr reverse geared to sc. shafts driving 2 FP propellers Total Power: 4,080kW (5,548hp) 27.0kn M.T.U. 12V4000M90 2 x Vee 4 Stroke 12 Cy. 165 x 190 each-2040kW (2774bhp) MTU Friedrichshafen GmbH-Friedrichshafen
8889414 *UHXQ* -	**STRELA** *ex* Tiksi *-2003* **Cotris Ltd** Ardis Co Ltd *Vladivostok* *Russia* MMSI: 273315640	**2,360** 870 3,183	Class: RS	**1980-09 Santierul Naval Oltenita S.A. — Oltenita** Yd No: 18 Loa 108.40 Br ex 15.00 Dght 3.190 Lbp 105.00 Br md 14.80 Dpth 5.00 Welded, 1 dk	**(A31A2GX) General Cargo Ship** Compartments: 4 Ho, ER 4 Ha: ER 4 (15.5 x 10.9)	**2 oil engines** driving 2 FP propellers Total Power: 1,030kW (1,400hp) 9.0kn S.K.L. 6NVD48A-2U 2 x 4 Stroke 6 Cy. 320 x 480 each-515kW (700bhp) VEB Schwermaschinenbau "KarlLiebknecht" (SKL)-Magdeburg AuxGen: 3 x 50kW a.c Fuel: 84.0 (d.f.)
9246956 *DBVE* -	**STRELASUND** **Government of The Federal Republic of Germany (Umweltministerium Mecklenburg-Vorpommern, Abt 5, Immissionsschutz, Abfall)** Government of The Federal Republic of Germany (Staatlichen Amt fuer Umwelt u Natur) *Stralsund* *Germany* MMSI: 211378550 Official number: 3636	**302** 90 285	Class: GL	**2002-10 Neue Germersheimer Schiffswerft GmbH — Germersheim** Yd No: 870 Loa 32.50 Br ex - Dght 2.600 Lbp 30.00 Br md 8.40 Dpth 3.80 Welded, 1 dk	**(B34G2SE) Pollution Control Vessel** Ice Capable	**2 oil engines** geared to sc. shafts driving 2 Directional propellers Total Power: 750kW (1,020hp) 11.0kn MAN D2842LE 2 x Vee 4 Stroke 12 Cy. 128 x 142 each-375kW (510bhp) MAN Nutzfahrzeuge AG-Nuernberg Thrusters: 1 Water jet (f)
9158197 *UDHM* -	**STRELETS** *ex* Newfoundland Marten *-2007* *launched as* Sevryba IV *-2003* **Strelets Co Ltd (OOO 'Strelets')** Murmansk Trawl Fleet Co (OAO 'Murmanskiy Tralovyy Flot') *Murmansk* *Russia* MMSI: 273312270	**2,015** 605 1,021	Class: NV RS	**2003-06 Orskov Christensens Staalskibsvaerft A/S — Frederikshavn** Yd No: 197 Loa 57.80 Br ex 13.80 Dght 5.700 Lbp 51.50 Br md 13.50 Dpth 8.10 Welded, 1 dk	**(B11A2FS) Stern Trawler** Liq: 970 Ice Capable	**1 oil engine** driving 1 CP propeller Total Power: 2,942kW (4,000hp) Alpha 12V28/32 1 x Vee 4 Stroke 12 Cy. 280 x 320 2942kW (4000bhp) MAN B&W Diesel A/S-Denmark Thrusters: 1 Thwart. CP thruster (f)
8331596 *UFVX* -	**STRELETS** *ex* Lao *-2013* *ex* MRTK-0661 *-1985* **Karelfish Co Ltd (Kommercheskaya Firma 'Karelryba')** - *Murmansk* *Russia* Official number: 842941	**122** 36 30	Class: RS	**1984-11 Sosnovskiy Sudostroitelnyy Zavod — Sosnovka** Yd No: 661 Loa 25.50 Br ex 7.00 Dght 2.390 Lbp 22.00 Br md 6.80 Dpth 3.30 Welded, 1 dk	**(B11B2FV) Fishing Vessel** Ins: 64 Compartments: 1 Ho, ER 1 Ha: (1.3 x 1.5)ER Ice Capable	**1 oil engine** driving 1 FP propeller Total Power: 221kW (300hp) 9.5kn S.K.L. 6NVD26A-2 1 x 4 Stroke 6 Cy. 180 x 260 221kW (300bhp) VEB Schwermaschinenbau "KarlLiebknecht" (SKL)-Magdeburg AuxGen: 2 x 12kW Fuel: 15.0 (d.f.)
9363120 *3FHZ8* -	**STRELITZIA** **Olamar Navegacion SA** Usui Kaiun KK (Usui Kaiun Co Ltd) *Panama* *Panama* MMSI: 351800000 Official number: 4162810	**49,720** 18,358 64,484	Class: NK	**2010-05 Sanoyas Hishino Meisho Corp — Kurashiki OY** Yd No: 1263 Loa 209.99 (BB) Br ex - Dght 12.029 Lbp 204.00 Br md 37.00 Dpth 22.85 Welded, 1 dk	**(A24B2BW) Wood Chips Carrier** Grain: 123,617 Compartments: 6 Ho, ER 6 Ha: ER Cranes: 3x15.5t	**1 oil engine** driving 1 FP propeller Total Power: 9,480kW (12,889hp) 14.6kn MAN-B&W 6S50MC-C 1 x 2 Stroke 6 Cy. 500 x 2000 9480kW (12889bhp) Mitsui Engineering & Shipbuilding CLtd-Japan Fuel: 3050.0 (r.f.)
7336094 - -	**STRELKA** **Novomirovets JSC (A/O 'Novomirovets')** -	**172** 51 89	Class: (RS)	**1973-09 Sretenskiy Sudostroitelnyy Zavod — Sretensk** Yd No: 56 Loa 33.96 Br ex 7.09 Dght 2.899 Lbp 30.00 Br md - Dpth 3.69 Welded, 1 dk	**(B11B2FV) Fishing Vessel** Bale: 96 Compartments: 1 Ho, ER 1 Ha: (1.3 x 1.6) Derricks: 2x2t Ice Capable	**1 oil engine** driving 1 FP propeller Total Power: 224kW (305hp) 9.0kn S.K.L. 8NVD36-1U 1 x 4 Stroke 8 Cy. 240 x 360 224kW (305bhp) VEB Schwermaschinenbau "KarlLiebknecht" (SKL)-Magdeburg
8521983 - -	**STRELNA** *ex* Luda *-2007* *ex* Ursula Sea *-2002* *ex* Osinovka *-1995* - -	**1,907** 572 690	Class: (RS)	**1985-01 VEB Volkswerft Stralsund — Stralsund** Yd No: 664 Loa 62.26 Br ex 13.82 Dght 5.220 Lbp 55.02 Br md 13.81 Dpth 9.22 Welded, 2 dks	**(B11A2FS) Stern Trawler** Ins: 580 Ice Capable	**2 oil engines** sr geared to sc. shaft driving 1 CP propeller Total Power: 1,766kW (2,402hp) 12.9kn S.K.L. 8VD26/20AL-2 2 x 4 Stroke 8 Cy. 200 x 260 each-883kW (1201bhp) VEB Schwermaschinenbau "KarlLiebknecht" (SKL)-Magdeburg AuxGen: 1 x 640kW a.c, 3 x 568kW a.c, 1 x 260kW d.c Fuel: 364.0 (d.f.)
8726959 *UHMK* KI-8108	**STRELNYA** **JSC Atlantrybflot Scientific-Industrial Association (OAO Nauchno-Promyshlennoye Obyedineniye 'Atlantrybflot')** - *Kaliningrad* *Russia* MMSI: 273245200 Official number: 861694	**802** 240 391	Class: (RS)	**1987-04 Zavod "Leninskaya Kuznitsa" — Kiyev** Yd No: 316 Loa 54.82 Br ex 9.95 Dght 4.140 Lbp 50.30 Br md 9.80 Dpth 5.00 Welded, 1 dk	**(B11A2FS) Stern Trawler** Ice Capable	**1 oil engine** driving 1 CP propeller Total Power: 852kW (1,158hp) 12.0kn S.K.L. 8NVD48A-2U 1 x 4 Stroke 8 Cy. 320 x 480 852kW (1158bhp) VEB Schwermaschinenbau "KarlLiebknecht" (SKL)-Magdeburg AuxGen: 4 x 160kW a.c
7630490 - -	**STRELSK** **Magadanrybprom JSC (A/O 'Magadanrybprom')** -	**172** 51 89	Class: (RS)	**1976 Sretenskiy Sudostroitelnyy Zavod — Sretensk** Yd No: 84 Loa 33.96 Br ex 7.09 Dght 2.899 Lbp 30.00 Br md - Dpth 3.69 Welded, 1 dk	**(B11B2FV) Fishing Vessel** Bale: 96 Compartments: 1 Ho, ER 1 Ha: (1.3 x 1.6) Derricks: 2x2t; Winches: 2 Ice Capable	**1 oil engine** driving 1 FP propeller Total Power: 224kW (305hp) 9.0kn S.K.L. 8NVD36-1U 1 x 4 Stroke 8 Cy. 240 x 360 224kW (305bhp) VEB Schwermaschinenbau "KarlLiebknecht" (SKL)-Magdeburg AuxGen: 1 x 86kW, 1 x 60kW Fuel: 20.0 (d.f.)
5342427 *IUOD* -	**STRENUUS** **Calabria di Navigazione Srl** - *Palermo* *Italy* Official number: 1249	**250** 75 -	Class: RI	**1959 Cant. Nav. Breda S.p.A. — Venezia** Yd No: 211 Loa 35.04 Br ex 8.31 Dght 3.760 Lbp 31.02 Br md 8.28 Dpth 4.50 Riveted\Welded, 1 dk	**(B32A2ST) Tug** Derricks: 1x3t	**1 oil engine** driving 1 FP propeller Total Power: 1,103kW (1,500hp) 13.0kn Deutz RBV6M366 1 x 4 Stroke 6 Cy. 420 x 660 1103kW (1500bhp) Kloeckner Humboldt Deutz AG-West Germany AuxGen: 2 x 50kW 115V d.c, 1 x 12kW 115V d.c
9239927 *SWXT* -	**STRESA** **Stresa Transportation Special Maritime Enterprise (ENE)** Neda Maritime Agency Co Ltd *Piraeus* *Greece* MMSI: 239903000 Official number: 11019	**56,899** 31,164 105,357 T/cm 95.1	Class: LR ✠ **100A1** SS 06/2012 Double Hull oil tanker ESP *IWS LI SPM ShipRight (SDA, FDA, CM) ✠ **LMC** **UMS IGS** Eq.Ltr: U†; Cable: 715.0/90.0 U3 (a)	**2002-06 Daewoo Shipbuilding & Marine Engineering Co Ltd — Geoje** Yd No: 5215 Loa 248.00 (BB) Br ex 43.04 Dght 14.320 Lbp 238.00 Br md 43.00 Dpth 21.00 Welded, 1 dk	**(A13A2TV) Crude Oil Tanker** Double Hull (13F) Liq: 123,000; Liq (Oil): 123,000 Compartments: 12 Wing Ta, 2 Wing Slop Ta, ER 3 Cargo Pump (s)	**1 oil engine** driving 1 FP propeller Total Power: 14,039kW (19,087hp) 15.2kn MAN-B&W 5S70MC-C 1 x 2 Stroke 5 Cy. 700 x 2800 14039kW (19087bhp) Doosan Engine Co Ltd-South Korea AuxGen: 3 x 700kW 450V 60Hz a.c Boilers: e (ex.g.) 23.5kgf/cm² (23.0bar), WTAuxB (o.f.) 18.9kgf/cm² (18.5bar)
8618126 *IXXJ* -	**STRETTO MESSINA** *launched as* Stretto di Messina *-1988* **Caronte & Tourist SpA** - *Reggio Calabria* *Italy* MMSI: 247054300 Official number: 255	**1,459** 402 1,327	Class: RI	**1988-05 Cantiere Navale Visentini di Visentini F e C SAS — Porto Viro** Yd No: 155 Loa 94.11 Br ex 17.02 Dght 3.239 Lbp 85.95 Br md 17.00 Dpth 4.95 Welded, 1 dk	**(A36A2PR) Passenger/Ro-Ro Ship (Vehicles)** Passengers: unberthed: 600 Bow door/ramp (f) Stern door/ramp (a)	**2 oil engines** gearing integral to driving 2 Voith-Schneider propellers 1 fwd and 1 aft Total Power: 3,678kW (5,000hp) Nohab F212V 2 x Vee 4 Stroke 12 Cy. 250 x 300 each-1839kW (2500bhp) Wartsila Diesel AB-Sweden
9422926 *YJVM7* -	**STRICKLIN TIDE** **Tidewater Boats Ltd** Tidewater Marine LLC *Port Vila* *Vanuatu* MMSI: 576472000 Official number: 1801	**1,713** 514 1,816	Class: AB	**2009-04 PT ASL Shipyard Indonesia — Batam** Yd No: 874 Loa 60.00 Br ex - Dght 4.800 Lbp 53.90 Br md 16.00 Dpth 6.00 Welded, 1 dk	**(B21B20A) Anchor Handling Tug Supply**	**2 oil engines** reduction geared to sc. shafts driving 2 CP propellers Total Power: 3,678kW (5,000hp) Niigata 6MG28HX 2 x 4 Stroke 6 Cy. 280 x 370 each-1839kW (2500bhp) Niigata Engineering Co Ltd-Japan AuxGen: 2 x 320kW a.c Thrusters: 1 Tunnel thruster (f)

IMO / Call sign	Name / Owner / Manager	Tonnage	Class	Builder / Dimensions	Type	Machinery
9418482 *9V2096* -	**STRIDE** *ex* Zaliv Anadyr *-2013* **Minerva Tankers Pte Ltd** Transpetrol Maritime Services Ltd *Singapore* *Singapore* MMSI: 566907000 Official number: 398613	**60,325** 31,496 103,023 T/cm 92.0	Class: NV	**2009-05 Hyundai Heavy Industries Co Ltd — Ulsan** Yd No: 2025 Loa 245.38 (BB) Br ex 42.04 Dght 14.920 Lbp 234.00 Br md 42.00 Dpth 22.00 Welded, 1 dk	**(A13A2TV) Crude Oil Tanker** Double Hull (13F) Liq: 121,797; Liq (Oil): 103,000 Cargo Heating Coils Compartments: 12 Wing Ta, 2 Wing Slop Ta, ER 3 Cargo Pump (s): 3x2750m³/hr Manifold: Bow/CM: 123.1m Ice Capable	**1 oil engine** driving 1 FP propeller Total Power: 15,820kW (21,509hp) 14.8kn MAN-B&W 7S60MC-C 1 x 2 Stroke 7 Cy. 600 x 2400 15820kW (21509bhp) Hyundai Heavy Industries Co Ltd-South Korea AuxGen: 3 x 1130kW a.c Fuel: 222.0 (d.f.) 2503.0 (r.f.) 56.5pd
9514494 *V7QI5* -	**STRIDER** *ex* Bluegreen Tigre *-2014* **Bluegreen A Ltd** Pentagon Shipping & Logistics Pte Ltd *Majuro* *Marshall Islands* MMSI: 538003371 Official number: 3371	**5,083** 2,411 7,682 T/cm 17.6	Class: RI (BV)	**2009-02 Ningbo Xinle Shipbuilding Co Ltd — Ningbo ZJ** Yd No: 8800-03 Loa 118.00 Br ex 17.73 Dght 6.800 Lbp 110.00 Br md 17.60 Dpth 9.00 Welded, 1 dk	**(A12B2TR) Chemical/Products Tanker** Double Hull (13F) Liq: 8,124; Liq (Oil): 8,124 Cargo Heating Coils Compartments: 12 Wing Ta, 2 Wing Slop Ta, ER 12 Cargo Pump (s): 8x150m³/hr, 4x120m³/hr Manifold: Bow/CM: 52m	**1 oil engine** reduction geared to sc. shaft driving 1 FP propeller Total Power: 2,970kW (4,038hp) 13.0kn MaK 9M25C 1 x 4 Stroke 9 Cy. 255 x 400 2970kW (4038bhp) Caterpillar Motoren GmbH & Co. KG-Germany AuxGen: 3 x 280kW 400V 50Hz a.c, 1 x 320kW 400V 50Hz a.c Thrusters: 1 Tunnel thruster (f) Fuel: 48.0 (d.f.) 373.0 (r.f.)
9465710 *9HWB9* -	**STRIGGLA** - **Metis Owning Co Ltd** TMS Dry Ltd *Valletta* *Malta* MMSI: 249620000 Official number: 9465710	**40,170** 25,603 75,196	Class: AB	**2009-01 Hudong-Zhonghua Shipbuilding (Group) Co Ltd — Shanghai** Yd No: H1569A Loa 225.00 (BB) Br ex 32.30 Dght 14.250 Lbp 217.00 Br md 32.26 Dpth 19.60 Welded, 1 dk	**(A21A2BC) Bulk Carrier** Grain: 91,717; Bale: 89,882 Compartments: 7 Ho, ER 7 Ha: 6 (14.6 x 15.0)ER (14.6 x 13.2)	**1 oil engine** driving 1 FP propeller Total Power: 8,990kW (12,223hp) 14.0kn MAN-B&W 5S60MC-C 1 x 2 Stroke 5 Cy. 600 x 2400 8990kW (12223bhp) Hudong Heavy Machinery Co Ltd-China AuxGen: 3 x 570kW a.c
8703921 *UESR* -	**STRIGUN** *ex* Utyos *-2010* *ex* Angara *-2009* *ex* Chung Yong No. 27 *-2006* **JSC Pacific Marine (JSC 'Pasifik Marin')** - *Vladivostok* *Russia* MMSI: 273310630	**651** 314 321	Class: RS (KR)	**1987-06 ShinA Shipbuilding Co Ltd — Tongyeong** Yd No: 319 Loa 53.50 (BB) Br ex - Dght 3.400 Lbp 48.00 Br md 8.91 Dpth 3.76 Welded, 1 dk	**(B11B2FV) Fishing Vessel** Ins: 598	**1 oil engine** with clutches, flexible couplings & reverse reduction geared to sc. shaft driving 1 FP propeller Total Power: 883kW (1,201hp) 12.5kn Niigata 6M28AFTE 1 x 4 Stroke 6 Cy. 280 x 480 883kW (1201bhp) Ssangyong Heavy Industries Co Ltd-South Korea AuxGen: 2 x 280kW 225V a.c
8938904 - -	**STRIKE THREE** - **Strike Three Inc** - *Bayou La Batre, AL* *United States of America* Official number: 1030554	**135** 47 -		**1995 J & J Marine, Inc. — Bayou La Batre, Al** Yd No: 103 L reg 23.35 Br ex - Dght - Lbp - Br md 7.32 Dpth 3.84 Welded, 1 dk	**(B11B2FV) Fishing Vessel**	**1 oil engine** driving 1 FP propeller
8938899 - -	**STRIKE TWO** - **J & V Marine Inc** - *Bayou La Batre, AL* *United States of America* Official number: 1029658	**134** 47 -		**1995 J & J Marine, Inc. — Bayou La Batre, Al** Yd No: 102 L reg 23.35 Br ex - Dght - Lbp - Br md 7.32 Dpth 3.84 Welded, 1 dk	**(B11B2FV) Fishing Vessel**	**1 oil engine** driving 1 FP propeller
8964159 *WDE7237* -	**STRIKER** *ex* Hilda Mccall *-2008* **Striker Marine Offshore LLC** Comar Marine LLC *Morgan City, LA* *United States of America* MMSI: 367390760 Official number: 1050529	**346** 103 -		**1997-02 Gulf Craft Inc — Patterson LA** Yd No: 413 Loa 45.96 Br ex - Dght - Lbp - Br md 9.14 Dpth 3.65 Welded, 1 dk	**(B21A20C) Crew/Supply Vessel** Hull Material: Aluminium Alloy	**4 oil engines** geared to sc. shafts driving 4 FP propellers Total Power: 3,824kW (5,200hp) 26.0kn Cummins KTA-38-M2 4 x Vee 4 Stroke 12 Cy. 159 x 159 each-956kW (1300bhp) Cummins Engine Co Inc-USA Thrusters: 1 Tunnel thruster (f)
8615954 *VM5303* -	**STRIKER** - **Seafresh Holdings Pty Ltd & Fabron Holdings Pty Ltd** - *Fremantle, WA* *Australia* Official number: 852352	*131* 39 -		**1986-12 Ocean Shipyards (WA) Pty Ltd — Fremantle WA** Yd No: 158 Loa 24.87 Br ex 6.74 Dght - Lbp - Br md 6.71 Dpth 3.79 Welded	**(B11A2FS) Stern Trawler** Ins: 75	**1 oil engine** with clutches & sr geared to sc. shaft driving 1 FP propeller Total Power: 300kW (408hp) Caterpillar 3408TA 1 x Vee 4 Stroke 8 Cy. 137 x 152 300kW (408bhp) Caterpillar Tractor Co-USA
7922764 - -	**STRIKER** *ex* Montado *-2012* *ex* Montnegre *-2008* **Eleanor Corp** Prometheus Maritime Ltd	*129* - 60	Class: (BV)	**1982-02 Union Naval de Levante SA (UNL) — Valencia** Yd No: 500 Loa 26.34 Br ex - Dght 2.650 Lbp 23.02 Br md 7.51 Dpth 3.10 Welded, 1 dk	**(B32A2ST) Tug**	**2 oil engines** reduction geared to sc. shaft driving 1 CP propeller Total Power: 882kW (1,200hp) Baudouin DNP12M 2 x Vee 4 Stroke 12 Cy. 150 x 150 each-441kW (600bhp) Internacional Diesel S.A.-Zumaya
6507397 *ZR5298* -	**STRIKER** *ex* Ocean Striker *-2008* *ex* Southern Striker *-1989* *ex* Ursinus *-1980* **Viking Fishing Co (Deep Sea) Pty Ltd (Viking Fishing Group)** - *Durban* *South Africa* MMSI: 601481000 Official number: 350858	*324* 146		**1964 N.V. Sleephelling Mij. "Scheveningen" — Scheveningen** Yd No: 188 Loa 43.31 Br ex 7.29 Dght 3.296 Lbp 38.71 Br md 7.19 Dpth 3.97 Welded	**(B11A2FT) Trawler**	**1 oil engine** driving 1 FP propeller Deutz RBV8M545 1 x 4 Stroke 8 Cy. 320 x 450 Kloeckner Humboldt Deutz AG-West Germany
9420174 *LAQI* -	**STRIL CHALLENGER** - **Stril Offshore AS** Simon Mokster Shipping AS SatCom: Inmarsat C 425828610 *Stavanger* *Norway* MMSI: 258286000	**2,807** 850 2,798	Class: NV (LR) ✠ Classed LR until 7/9/10	**2009-06 Cemre Muhendislik Gemi Insaat Sanayi ve Ticaret Ltd Sti-Pendik** (Hull) Yd No: (098) **2009-06 Havyard Leirvik AS — Leirvik i Sogn** Yd No: 098 Loa 74.50 (BB) Br ex 17.60 Dght 6.900 Lbp 64.80 Br md 17.20 Dpth 8.00 Welded, 1 dk	**(B21B20A) Anchor Handling Tug Supply** Cranes: 2x5t	**2 oil engines** with clutches, flexible couplings & sr reverse geared to sc. shafts driving 2 CP propellers Total Power: 12,000kW (16,316hp) 15.0kn MaK 12M32C 2 x Vee 4 Stroke 12 Cy. 320 x 420 each-6000kW (8158bhp) Caterpillar Motoren GmbH & Co. KG-Germany AuxGen: 2 x 2400kW 440V 60Hz a.c, 2 x 548kW 440V 60Hz a.c Boilers: AuxB 9.2kgf/cm² (9.0bar) Thrusters: 1 Tunnel thruster (f); 1 Tunnel thruster (a); 1 Retract. directional thruster (f)
9420150 *LAQG* -	**STRIL COMMANDER** - **Stril Offshore AS** Simon Mokster Shipping AS SatCom: Inmarsat C 425855510 *Stavanger* *Norway* MMSI: 258555000	**2,807** 850 3,000	Class: NV (LR) ✠ Classed LR until 6/10/10	**2009-01 Cemre Muhendislik Gemi Insaat Sanayi ve Ticaret Ltd Sti — Altinova** (Hull) Yd No: (093) **2009-01 Havyard Leirvik AS — Leirvik i Sogn** Yd No: 093 Loa 74.50 (BB) Br ex 17.60 Dght 5.500 Lbp 64.80 Br md 17.20 Dpth 8.00 Welded, 1 dk	**(B21B20A) Anchor Handling Tug Supply** Cranes: 2x5t Ice Capable	**2 oil engines** with clutches, flexible couplings & sr reverse geared to sc. shafts driving 2 CP propellers Total Power: 12,000kW (16,316hp) 15.0kn MaK 12M32C 2 x Vee 4 Stroke 12 Cy. 320 x 420 each-6000kW (8158bhp) Caterpillar Motoren GmbH & Co. KG-Germany AuxGen: 2 x 548kW 440V 60Hz a.c, 2 x 1920kW 440V 60Hz a.c Boilers: AuxB 9.2kgf/cm² (9.0bar) Thrusters: 2 Thwart. CP thruster (f); 1 Thwart. CP thruster (a)
9484845 *2EBI9* -	**STRIL EXPLORER** *launched as* Abyss Dweller *-2010* **Mokster Polar AS** Simon Mokster Shipping AS *Douglas* *Isle of Man (British)* MMSI: 235083693 Official number: 742814	**3,650** 1,090 1,400	Class: NV	**2010-09 CHT Denizcilik Gemi Insaa Sanayi Ticaret Ltd Sti — Istanbul (Tuzla)** (Hull) Yd No: 06 **2010-09 West Contractors AS — Olensvaag** Yd No: 33 Loa 76.40 (BB) Br ex - Dght 4.750 Lbp 69.86 Br md 16.20 Dpth 5.45 Welded, 1 dk	**(B22A20R) Offshore Support Vessel** Side door (p) Cranes: 1x60t	**4 diesel electric oil engines** driving 4 gen. each 2231kW Connecting to 2 elec. motors driving 2 Azimuth electric drive units Total Power: 6,564kW (8,924hp) 12.0kn Caterpillar 3516B 1 x Vee 4 Stroke 16 Cy. 170 x 190 1641kW (2231bhp) Caterpillar Inc-USA Caterpillar 3516B 3 x Vee 4 Stroke 16 Cy. 170 x 190 each-1641kW (2231bhp) Caterpillar Inc-USA Thrusters: 1 Tunnel thruster (f); 2 Retract. directional thruster (f) Fuel: 600.0

IMO / Call sign / Flag	Name / Owner / Manager	GT / NT / DWT	Class	Builder / Dimensions	Type	Machinery
9404259 *LAJD* -	**STRIL HERKULES** **Mokster Safety A/S** Simon Mokster Shipping AS SatCom: Inmarsat C 425969010 *Stavanger* *Norway* MMSI: 259690000	**6,251** 1,875 2,100	Class: NV	**2008-12 'Crist' Sp z oo — Gdansk** (Hull launched by) Yd No: 482 **2008-12 West Contractors AS — Olensvaag** (Hull completed by) **2008-12 Palmer Johnson Norway AS — Feda** Yd No: 189 Loa 97.55 (BB) Br ex 19.24 Dght 6.500 Lbp 84.85 Br md 19.20 Dpth 8.00 Welded, 1 dk	**(B21B20T) Offshore Tug/Supply Ship**	**2 oil engines** reduction geared to sc. shafts driving 2 CP propellers Total Power: 9,000kW (12,236hp) 21.5kn MaK 9M32C 2 x 4 Stroke 9 Cy. 320 x 480 each-4500kW (6118bhp) Caterpillar Motoren GmbH & Co. KG-Germany AuxGen: 2 x 970kW a.c, 2 x 1700kW a.c, 1 x 2350kW a.c Thrusters: 1 Retract. directional thruster (f); 1 Tunnel thruster (f); 2 Tunnel thruster (a)
9489493 *OZ2083* -	**STRIL MARINER** **Stril Power AS** Simon Mokster Shipping AS SatCom: Inmarsat C 423129510 *Torshavn* *Faeroe Islands (Danish)* MMSI: 231295000 Official number: 311079399	**3,117** 1,342 3,755	Class: NV	**2009-10 SIMEK AS — Flekkefjord** Yd No: 121 Loa 78.60 (BB) Br ex 17.60 Dght 6.600 Lbp 69.00 Br md 17.38 Dpth 7.70 Welded, 1 dk	**(B21A20S) Platform Supply Ship**	**4 diesel electric oil engines** driving 4 gen. each 1291kW a.c Connecting to 2 elec. motors each (1600kW) driving 2 Azimuth electric drive units Total Power: 5,968kW (8,116hp) 11.0kn Cummins KTA-50-M1 4 x Vee 4 Stroke 16 Cy. 159 x 159 each-1492kW (2029bhp) Cummins Engine Co Ltd-United Kingdom AuxGen: 1 x 115kW a.c Thrusters: 2 Tunnel thruster (f) Fuel: 828.0
9407897 *9HA2720* -	**STRIL MERKUR** **Mokster Safety A/S** Simon Mokster Shipping AS *Valletta* *Malta* MMSI: 215393000 Official number: 9407897	**6,272** 1,882 2,100	Class: NV	**2011-07 Astilleros Gondan SA — Castropol** Yd No: 450 Loa 97.55 (BB) Br ex 19.21 Dght 6.500 Lbp 84.85 Br md 19.20 Dpth 8.00 Welded, 1 dk	**(B21B20T) Offshore Tug/Supply Ship**	**2 oil engines** Connecting to 2 elec. motors each (2000kW) reduction geared to sc. shafts driving 2 CP propellers Total Power: 9,000kW (12,236hp) 20.0kn MaK 9M32C 2 x 4 Stroke 9 Cy. 320 x 480 each-4500kW (6118bhp) Caterpillar Motoren GmbH & Co. KG-Germany AuxGen: 2 x 1700kW a.c, 2 x a.c, 1 x a.c Thrusters: 1 Retract. directional thruster (f); 2 Tunnel thruster (a); 1 Tunnel thruster (f)
9538529 *LGVY* -	**STRIL MERMAID** **KS North Sea Safety** Simon Mokster Shipping AS *Bronnoysund* *Norway* MMSI: 257475000	**3,129** 1,275 3,755	Class: NV	**2010-03 SIMEK AS — Flekkefjord** Yd No: 122 Loa 78.60 (BB) Br ex - Dght 6.550 Lbp 68.40 Br md 17.60 Dpth 7.70 Welded, 1 dk	**(B21A20S) Platform Supply Ship**	**4 diesel electric oil engines** driving 4 gen. Connecting to 2 elec. motors driving 2 Azimuth electric drive units Total Power: 6,416kW (8,724hp) 11.0kn Cummins KTA-50-M2 2 x Vee 4 Stroke 16 Cy. 159 x 159 each-1492kW (2029bhp) Cummins Engine Co Ltd-United Kingdom Cummins QSK60-M 2 x Vee 4 Stroke 16 Cy. 159 x 190 each-1716kW (2333bhp) Cummins Engine Co Ltd-United Kingdom Thrusters: 1 Tunnel thruster (f); 1 Retract. directional thruster (f)
9243370 *LLTU* -	**STRIL MYSTER** **Stril Myster AS** Simon Mokster Shipping AS *Stavanger* *Norway* MMSI: 259698000	**3,557** 1,067 4,500	Class: NV	**2003-01 SC Aker Tulcea SA — Tulcea** (Hull) Yd No: 288 **2003-01 Aker Aukra AS — Aukra** Yd No: 105 Loa 90.20 (BB) Br ex 19.03 Dght 6.900 Lbp 77.20 Br md 19.00 Dpth 7.45 Welded, 1 dk	**(B21A20S) Platform Supply Ship**	**5 diesel electric oil engines** driving 5 gen. each 1825kW Connecting to 2 elec. motors driving 2 Directional propellers azimuth thrusters contra rotating propellers Total Power: 9,505kW (12,925hp) Caterpillar 3516B 5 x Vee 4 Stroke 16 Cy. 170 x 190 each-1901kW (2585bhp) Caterpillar Inc-USA Thrusters: 2 Thwart. FP thruster (f); 1 Retract. directional thruster (f)
9201786 *OZ2151* -	**STRIL NEPTUN** **Sp/F Mariner** Simon Mokster Shipping AS *Torshavn* *Faeroe Islands (Danish)* MMSI: 231067000	**2,423** 800 3,010	Class: NV	**1999-12 YVC Ysselwerf B.V. — Capelle a/d IJssel** Yd No: 275 Loa 70.40 (BB) Br ex - Dght 7.000 Lbp 60.80 Br md 16.00 Dpth 8.00 Welded, 1 dk	**(B21B20T) Offshore Tug/Supply Ship**	**2 oil engines** reduction geared to sc. shafts driving 2 CP propellers Total Power: 5,422kW (7,372hp) 13.0kn Caterpillar 3608 2 x 4 Stroke 8 Cy. 280 x 300 each-2711kW (3686bhp) Caterpillar Inc-USA AuxGen: 2 x 260kW 450V 60Hz a.c, 2 x 1372kW 440V 60Hz a.c Thrusters: 1 Thwart. CP thruster (f); 1 Retract. directional thruster (f); 1 Thwart. CP thruster (a)
9351969 *LNLZ* -	**STRIL ODIN** **Stril Power AS** Simon Mokster Shipping AS *Stavanger* *Norway* MMSI: 258427000	**3,357** 1,198 4,500	Class: NV	**2006-05 SC Aker Tulcea SA — Tulcea** (Hull) Yd No: 341 **2006-05 Aker Yards AS Langsten — Tomrefjord** Yd No: 208 Loa 85.65 (BB) Br ex 19.72 Dght 6.180 Lbp 77.80 Br md 19.70 Dpth 7.45 Welded, 1 dk	**(B21A20P) Pipe Carrier**	**4 diesel electric oil engines** driving 4 gen. each 1901kW 690V a.c Connecting to 2 elec. motors each (2500kW) driving 2 Directional propellers Total Power: 7,604kW (10,340hp) 15.3kn Caterpillar 3516B-TA 4 x Vee 4 Stroke 16 Cy. 170 x 190 each-1901kW (2585bhp) Caterpillar Inc-USA Thrusters: 1 Retract. directional thruster (f); 2 Tunnel thruster (f)
9584554 *3YUU* -	**STRIL ORION** **Simon Mokster Rederi AS** Simon Mokster Shipping AS *Stavanger* *Norway* MMSI: 259977000	**4,323** 1,882 4,900	Class: NV	**2011-10 STX OSV Tulcea SA — Tulcea** (Hull) **2011-10 STX OSV Sovikness — Sovik** Yd No: 729 Loa 93.50 (BB) Br ex - Dght 6.600 Lbp 84.54 Br md 19.00 Dpth 8.00 Welded, 1 dk	**(B21A20S) Platform Supply Ship** Ice Capable	**4 diesel electric oil engines** driving 4 gen. each 1825kW a.c Connecting to 2 elec. motors driving 2 Azimuth electric drive units Total Power: 7,060kW (9,600hp) 12.5kn Caterpillar 3516C-HD 4 x Vee 4 Stroke 16 Cy. 170 x 215 each-1765kW (2400bhp) Caterpillar Inc-USA Thrusters: 2 Tunnel thruster (f); 1 Retract. directional thruster (f)
9258430 *LLVM* -	**STRIL PIONER** *ex Viking Energy -2003* **Simon Mokster Rederi AS** Simon Mokster Shipping AS *Stavanger* *Norway* MMSI: 258169000	**5,073** 1,521 6,013	Class: NV	**2003-04 Santierul Naval Constanta S.A. — Constanta** (Hull) Yd No: 566 **2003-04 Kleven Verft AS — Ulsteinvik** Yd No: 301 Loa 94.90 (BB) Br ex 20.62 Dght 7.899 Lbp 81.60 Br md 20.40 Dpth 9.60 Welded, 1 dk	**(B21A20S) Platform Supply Ship** Cranes: 2x10t	**4 diesel electric oil engines** driving 4 gen. each 1920kW 690V a.c Connecting to 2 elec. motors each (3000kW) & gearing integral to driving 2 Azimuth electric drive units contra rotating azimuth thruster Total Power: 8,040kW (10,932hp) 15.5kn Wartsila 6R32DF 4 x 4 Stroke 6 Cy. 320 x 350 each-2010kW (2733bhp) Wartsila Finland Oy-Finland Thrusters: 2 Thwart. FP thruster (f); 1 Retract. directional thruster (f) Fuel: 80.0 (LNG) 17.0pd
9590565 *3YUW* -	**STRIL POLAR** **Mokster Supply KS** Simon Mokster Shipping AS *Stavanger* *Norway* MMSI: 257013000	**4,283** 1,882 4,900	Class: NV	**2012-02 STX OSV Tulcea SA — Tulcea** (Hull) **2012-02 STX OSV Soviknes — Sovik** Yd No: 748 Loa 93.50 (BB) Br ex 20.80 Dght 6.500 Lbp 84.54 Br md 19.00 Dpth 8.00 Welded, 1 dk	**(B21A20S) Platform Supply Ship** Ice Capable	**4 diesel electric oil engines** driving 4 gen. Connecting to 2 elec. motors each (3000kW) driving 2 Azimuth electric drive units Total Power: 7,300kW (9,924hp) 12.5kn Caterpillar 3516C-HD 4 x Vee 4 Stroke 16 Cy. 170 x 215 each-1825kW (2481bhp) Caterpillar Inc-USA Thrusters: 1 Retract. directional thruster (f); 2 Tunnel thruster (f)
9269099 *LMDC* -	**STRIL POSEIDON** **Mokster Safety A/S** Simon Mokster Shipping AS *Stavanger* *Norway* MMSI: 258117000	**4,785** 1,435 2,000	Class: NV	**2003-07 Tangen Verft AS — Kragero** (Hull) Yd No: 190 **2003-07 Aker Langsten AS — Tomrefjord** Yd No: 190 Loa 91.40 (BB) Br ex - Dght 5.100 Lbp 78.25 Br md 18.20 Dpth 7.50 Welded, 1 dk	**(B22G20Y) Standby Safety Vessel**	**2 oil engines** with clutches, flexible couplings & sr geared to sc. shafts driving 2 CP propellers Total Power: 8,500kW (11,556hp) 20.0kn Caterpillar 3612TA 2 x Vee 4 Stroke 12 Cy. 280 x 300 each-4250kW (5778bhp) Caterpillar Inc-USA AuxGen: 2 x 1700kW 690/230V 60Hz a.c, 3 x 968kW 690/230V 60Hz a.c Thrusters: 1 Tunnel thruster (f); 2 Retract. directional thruster (f); 2 Tunnel thruster (a) Fuel: 1180.0 (d.f.) 50.0pd

9150224 **STRIL POWER**
LINO
-
Stril Power AS
Simon Mokster Shipping AS
SatCom: Inmarsat B 325939810
Stavanger *Norway*
MMSI: 259398000

2,926 Class: NV
1,045
3,044

1997-04 Aukra Industrier AS — Aukra Yd No: 92
Loa 74.90 Br ex - Dght 6.600
Lbp 64.40 Br md 18.00 Dpth 8.00
Welded, 1 dk

(B21B20A) Anchor Handling Tug Supply
Cranes: 1x10t,1x3t
Ice Capable

2 oil engines with clutches, flexible couplings & sr geared to sc. shafts driving 2 CP propellers
Total Power: 10,840kW (14,738hp) 13.0kn
Caterpillar 3616TA
2 x Vee 4 Stroke 16 Cy. 280 x 300 each-5420kW (7369bhp)
Caterpillar Inc-USA
AuxGen: 2 x 1920kW 230/440V 60Hz a.c, 2 x 250kW 230/440V 60Hz a.c
Thrusters: 1 Retract. directional thruster (f); 1 Thwart. FP thruster (f); 1 Tunnel thruster (a)
Fuel: 881.5 (d.f.) 56.6pd

9158666 **STRILBORG**
LIZB
-
Simon Mokster Rederi AS
Simon Mokster Shipping AS
SatCom: Inmarsat B 325946910
Stavanger *Norway*
MMSI: 259469000

2,957 Class: NV
1,082
3,037

1998-02 Aukra Industrier AS — Aukra Yd No: 93
Loa 74.90 Br ex - Dght 6.610
Lbp 64.40 Br md 18.00 Dpth 8.00
Welded, 1 dk

(B21B20A) Anchor Handling Tug Supply
Ice Capable

2 oil engines reduction geared to sc. shafts driving 2 CP propellers
Total Power: 11,034kW (15,002hp) 14.5kn
Caterpillar 3616TA
2 x Vee 4 Stroke 16 Cy. 280 x 300 each-5517kW (7501bhp)
Caterpillar Inc-USA
AuxGen: 2 x 1920kW 440V 60Hz a.c, 2 x 254kW 440V 60Hz a.c
Thrusters: 1 Retract. directional thruster (f); 1 Thwart. FP thruster (f); 1 Tunnel thruster (a)
Fuel: 963.0 (r.f.)

9391139 **STRILEN**
3ERL2
-
KP 2 International SA
Nordic Womar Pte Ltd
Panama *Panama*
MMSI: 370088000
Official number: 3411608

12,560 Class: KR
6,106
19,996
T/cm
31.1

2008-05 Sekwang Heavy Industries Co Ltd — Ulsan Yd No: 1161
Loa 149.61 (BB) Br ex 24.23 Dght 9.400
Lbp 142.60 Br md 24.20 Dpth 12.80
Welded, 1 dk

(A12B2TR) Chemical/Products Tanker
Double Hull (13F)
Liq: 20,866; Liq (Oil): 20,866
Compartments: 16 Wing Ta, 2 Wing Slop Ta, ER
16 Cargo Pump (s): 14x300m³/hr, 2x200m³/hr
Manifold: Bow/CM: 71.5m

1 oil engine driving 1 FP propeller
Total Power: 6,480kW (8,810hp) 14.7kn
MAN-B&W 6S42MC
1 x 2 Stroke 6 Cy. 420 x 1764 6480kW (8810bhp)
STX Engine Co Ltd-South Korea
AuxGen: 3 x 500kW 450V 60Hz a.c
Thrusters: 1 Tunnel thruster (f)
Fuel: 260.0 (d.f.) 1073.0 (r.f.)

9328546 **STRILMOY**
LMYV
-
Simon Mokster Rederi AS
Simon Mokster Shipping AS
Stavanger *Norway*
MMSI: 258366000

3,331 Class: NV
1,212
4,248

2005-08 SC Aker Braila SA — Braila (Hull) Yd No: 1075
2005-08 Aker Langsten AS — Tomrefjord Yd No: 200
Loa 85.65 (BB) Br ex 19.72 Dght 6.180
Lbp 77.80 Br md 19.70 Dpth 7.45
Welded, 1 dk

(B21A20S) Platform Supply Ship

4 diesel electric oil engines driving 4 gen. each 1901kW 690V a.c Connecting to 2 elec. motors each (2500kW) driving 2 Azimuth electric drive units
Total Power: 7,604kW (10,340hp) 12.0kn
Caterpillar 3516B-TA
4 x Vee 4 Stroke 16 Cy. 170 x 190 each-1901kW (2585bhp)
Caterpillar Inc-USA
Thrusters: 1 Retract. directional thruster (f); 2 Tunnel thruster (f)
Fuel: 1190.0 (d.f.) 12.3pd

6808753 **STRILSTAD**
LLYK *ex Skjerstad -1991*
- **Marine Harvest Norway AS**
-
Stavanger *Norway*
MMSI: 257386400

228 Class: (NV)
82
-

1967 Sterkoder Mek. Verksted AS — Kristiansund Yd No: 5
Loa 32.47 Br ex 8.95 Dght 2.794
Lbp 30.00 Br md 8.92 Dpth 3.76
Welded, 1 dk

(A36A2PR) Passenger/Ro-Ro Ship (Vehicles)
Passengers: unberthed: 195

1 oil engine driving 1 FP propeller
Total Power: 441kW (600hp) 11.5kn
Wichmann 4ACA
1 x 2 Stroke 4 Cy. 280 x 420 441kW (600bhp)
Wichmann Motorfabrikk AS-Norway
Fuel: 19.5 (d.f.) 1.0pd

9667942 **STRIMON**
SVBR4
-
Rosse Maritime SA
Pleiades Shipping Agents SA
Piraeus *Greece*
MMSI: 241252000
Official number: 12176

29,940 Class: AB
13,496
49,997
T/cm
52.0

2013-07 STX Offshore & Shipbuilding Co Ltd — Changwon (Jinhae Shipyard) Yd No: 1581
Loa 183.00 (BB) Br ex 32.23 Dght 13.100
Lbp 173.90 Br md 32.20 Dpth 19.10
Welded, 1 dk

(A12B2TR) Chemical/Products Tanker
Double Hull (13F)
Liq: 52,229; Liq (Oil): 52,170
Cargo Heating Coils
Compartments: 6 Wing Ta, 6 Wing Ta, 1 Wing Slop Ta, 1 Slop Ta, 1 Wing Slop Ta, ER
12 Cargo Pump (s): 12x600m³/hr
Manifold: Bow/CM: 92m

1 oil engine driving 1 FP propeller
Total Power: 7,570kW (10,292hp) 14.5kn
MAN-B&W 6S50ME-C
1 x 2 Stroke 6 Cy. 500 x 2000 7570kW (10292bhp)
STX Engine Co Ltd-South Korea
AuxGen: 3 x 910kW a.c
Fuel: 200.0 (d.f.) 1520.0 (r.f.)

9319545 **STROFADES**
SVET *ex LMZ Nafsika -2007*
- **Strofades Special Maritime Enterprise (ENE)**
Eletson Corp
Piraeus *Greece*
MMSI: 240678000
Official number: 11656

40,038 Class: LR (AB)
20,190 **100A1** SS 03/2011
69,431 Double Hull oil tanker
T/cm ESP
67.5 *IWS
LI
SPM
EP (bar above)
LMC **UMS IGS**
Cable: 660.0/78.0 U3 (a)

2006-03 Daewoo-Mangalia Heavy Industries S.A. — Mangalia Yd No: 5005
Loa 228.00 (BB) Br ex 32.22 Dght 13.600
Lbp 219.00 Br md 32.20 Dpth 19.80
Welded, 1 dk

(A13A2TV) Crude Oil Tanker
Double Hull (13F)
Liq: 76,492; Liq (Oil): 76,492
Compartments: 12 Wing Ta, 2 Wing Slop Ta, ER
12 Cargo Pump (s): 12x900m³/hr
Manifold: Bow/CM: 111.5m

1 oil engine driving 1 FP propeller
Total Power: 10,365kW (14,092hp) 14.6kn
MAN-B&W 5S60MC
1 x 2 Stroke 5 Cy. 600 x 2292 10365kW (14092bhp)
Doosan Engine Co Ltd-South Korea
AuxGen: 3 x 900kW 440V 60Hz a.c
Boilers: AuxB (Comp) 7.7kgf/cm² (7.6bar), AuxB (o.f.) 11.0kgf/cm² (10.8bar)
Fuel: 247.0 (d.f.) 2033.0 (r.f.)

8883848 **STROGIY**
UBWV
-
JSC Amur Shipbuilding Plant (OAO Amurskiy Sudostroitelnyy Zavod')
-
Vladivostok *Russia*

470 Class: (RS)
141
215

1959-03 in the People's Republic of China Yd No: 7
Loa 45.79 Br ex 9.82 Dght 3.900
Lbp 42.00 Br md 9.40 Dpth 5.03
Welded, 1 dk

(B32A2ST) Tug
Ice Capable

2 oil engines driving 2 FP propellers
Total Power: 880kW (1,196hp) 11.0kn
Russkiy 6DR30/50-6-2
2 x 2 Stroke 6 Cy. 300 x 500 each-440kW (598bhp)
Mashinostroitelnyy Zavod"Russkiy-Dizel"-Leningrad
AuxGen: 2 x 63kW a.c
Fuel: 170.0 (d.f.)

8827026 **STROITELNYY NO. 19**
-
-
-
-

205 Class: (RS)
62
34

1989-11 Ilyichyovskiy Sudoremontnyy Zavod im. "50-letiya SSSR" — Ilyichyovsk Yd No: 19
Loa 37.62 Br ex 7.21 Dght 1.691
Lbp 34.02 Br md - Dpth 2.93
Welded

(A37B2PS) Passenger Ship

3 oil engines reduction geared to sc. shafts driving 3 FP propellers
Total Power: 960kW (1,306hp) 16.5kn
Barnaultransmash 3D6C
2 x 4 Stroke 6 Cy. 150 x 180 each-110kW (150bhp)
Barnaultransmash-Barnaul
Zvezda M401A-1
1 x Vee 4 Stroke 12 Cy. 180 x 200 740kW (1006bhp)
"Zvezda"-Leningrad
AuxGen: 2 x 16kW a.c

8881890 **STROMBOLI**
- *ex Markarna -1995*
-
-
-

145
109
-

1990 Bridport Marine — Bridport TAS
Loa 23.95 Br ex - Dght -
Lbp - Br md 7.20 Dpth 2.38
Welded, 1 dk

(B11B2FV) Fishing Vessel
Ice Capable

1 oil engine driving 1 FP propeller
Cummins
1 x 4 Stroke
Cummins Engine Co Inc-USA

8331663 **STROMBUS**
-
-
JSC Atlanttralflot
Rustuna Co Ltd

944 Class: (RS)
283
533

1985-07 Pribaltiyskiy Sudostroitelnyy Zavod "Yantar" — Kaliningrad Yd No: 018
Loa 55.53 Br ex 11.09 Dght 5.010
Lbp 49.82 Br md - Dpth 7.50
Welded, 1 dk

(B11B2FV) Fishing Vessel

1 oil engine driving 1 CP propeller
Total Power: 1,673kW (2,275hp) 14.4kn
Kolomna 8CHNRP30/38
1 x 4 Stroke 8 Cy. 300 x 380 1673kW (2275bhp)
Kolomenskiy Zavod-Kolomna
AuxGen: 3 x 280kW a.c

9698068 **STROMCRONA**
SKDZ
-
KaringoTrafiken AB
-
Karingon *Sweden*
MMSI: 265704540

166
50
-

2013-06 AS Rigas Kugu Buvetava (Riga Shipyard) — Riga (Hull) Yd No: 141
2013-06 Swede Ship Marine AB — Fagerfjall Yd No: 475
Loa 24.38 Br ex 6.59 Dght 1.700
Lbp 21.38 Br md 6.50 Dpth 3.34
Welded, 1 dk

(A37B2PS) Passenger Ship
Passengers: unberthed: 150
Ice Capable

2 oil engines reduction geared to sc. shafts driving 2 FP propellers
Total Power: 662kW (900hp) 12.0kn
Scania DI13 M
2 x 4 Stroke 6 Cy. 130 x 160 each-331kW (450bhp)
Scania AB-Sweden

7414157 **STROMNES II**
- *ex Stromnes -2004*
- **Fishing Company Briz Ltd**
-
Ukraine

865 Class: (NV)
259
630

1975-06 Mandals Slip & Mekaniske Verksted AS — Mandal (Hull) Yd No: 52
1975-06 Batservice Verft AS — Mandal Yd No: 613
Lengthened-1980
Loa 54.21 Br ex 9.50 Dght -
Lbp 40.62 Br md 9.48 Dpth 7.52
Welded, 2 dks

(B11B2FV) Fishing Vessel
Compartments: 1 Ho, 6 Ta, ER
7 Ha: (1.9 x 3.9)2 (1.9 x 2.4)4 (1.9 x 1.6)ER
Ice Capable

1 oil engine geared to sc. shaft driving 1 CP propeller
Total Power: 1,596kW (2,170hp)
Alpha 14V23L-VO
1 x Vee 4 Stroke 14 Cy. 225 x 300 1596kW (2170bhp)
Alpha Diesel A/S-Denmark
AuxGen: 2 x 200kW 380V 50Hz a.c
Thrusters: 1 Thwart. FP thruster (f); 1 Tunnel thruster (a)

9428695 **STROMSTIERNA**
SMVD
-
KaringoTrafiken AB
-
Karingon *Sweden*
MMSI: 265587220

180
70
-

2007-01 Swede Ship Marine AB — Fagerfjall Yd No: 424
Loa 28.13 Br ex 6.60 Dght 1.830
Lbp - Br md 6.53 Dpth 3.06
Welded, 1 dk

(A37B2PS) Passenger Ship
Passengers: 200

2 oil engines reduction geared to sc. shafts driving 2 FP propellers
Total Power: 662kW (900hp)
Scania DI12 M
2 x 4 Stroke 6 Cy. 127 x 154 each-331kW (450bhp)
Scania AB-Sweden

8017487 - -	**STROMSUND** *ex* Beinta *-1990* *ex* Seringa *-1984* - -	**470** 141 270	Class: (LR) (NV) ✠ Classed LR until 6/88	**1981-09 Brodrene Lothe AS, Flytedokken — Haugesund** (Hull) Yd No: 42 **1981-09 Haakonsens Mek. Verksted AS — Skudeneshavn** Yd No: 9 Loa 42.72 Br ex 8.02 Dght 4.552 Lbp 26.83 Br md 8.01 Dpth 6.33 Welded, 2 dks	**(B11B2FV) Fishing Vessel**	**1 oil engine** with clutches, flexible couplings & sr geared to sc. shaft driving 1 CP propeller Total Power: 853kW (1,160hp) Alpha 8V23HU 1 x Vee 4 Stroke 8 Cy. 225 x 300 853kW (1160bhp) B&W Alpha Diesel A/S-Denmark AuxGen: 1 x 125kW 230V 50Hz a.c, 2 x 87kW 230V 50Hz a.c Thrusters: 1 Thwart. FP thruster (f); 1 Thwart. FP thruster (a)
7634331 *WDD9335* -	**STRONG** *ex* Caroline *-1991* *ex* J. J. Oberdorf *-1985* **Foss International Inc** *Seattle, WA* *United States of America* MMSI: 368533000 Official number: 598665	**1,094** 328 -	Class: (AB)	**1978-11 Marinette Marine Corp — Marinette WI** Yd No: 1 Loa 45.75 Br ex - Dght 6.770 Lbp 41.00 Br md 12.20 Dpth 7.50 Welded, 1 dk	**(B32B2SA) Articulated Pusher Tug**	**2 oil engines** reverse reduction geared to sc. shafts driving 2 FP propellers Total Power: 5,030kW (6,838hp) 15.5kn EMD (Electro-Motive) 20-645-E7B 2 x Vee 2 Stroke 20 Cy. 230 x 254 each-2515kW (3419bhp) General Motors Corp.Electro-Motive Div.-La Grange AuxGen: 2 x 300kW a.c
9692208 - -	**STRONG** **Asian Shipping Corp** *Manila* *Philippines* Official number: M: TG000074	**423** 126 -	Class: ZC (Class contemplated)	**2013-03 Yizheng Xinyang Shipbuilding Co Ltd — Yizheng JS** Yd No: VHX623-2 Loa 36.10 Br ex - Dght - Lbp - Br md 10.20 Dpth 4.66 Welded, 1 dk	**(B32A2ST) Tug**	**2 oil engines** reduction geared to sc. shafts driving 2 Propellers Total Power: 2,942kW (4,000hp) Chinese Std. Type LB8250ZLC 2 x 4 Stroke 8 Cy. 250 x 320 each-1471kW (2000bhp)
8987979 *DUH2540*	**STRONG FAITH** *ex* Glacy Jammar *-2003* **Key west Shipping Line Corp** Jensen Shipping Corp *Cebu* *Philippines* Official number: TAC8000017	*267* 168 480		**1992 DMC Shipbuilders Inc — Zamboanga** Loa - Br ex - Dght - Lbp 36.00 Br md 6.60 Dpth 5.15 Welded, 1 dk	**(A31A2GX) General Cargo Ship**	**1 oil engine** driving 1 Propeller Total Power: 294kW (400hp) Matsui 1 x 4 Stroke 294kW (400bhp) Matsui Iron Works Co Ltd-Japan
8427266 *DUH2162* -	**STRONG HEART** *ex* St. Gabriel *-2004* *ex* Marielle *-2004* **Key west Shipping Line Corp** Jensen Shipping Corp *Cebu* *Philippines* Official number: CEB1000519	*216* 116 276	Class: (NK)	**1979 Filipino Shipyard & Iron Works Inc. — Manila** Loa 36.89 Br ex 6.76 Dght 2.501 Lbp 34.14 Br md 6.71 Dpth 3.36 Welded, 1 dk	**(A31A2GX) General Cargo Ship** Grain: 468; Bale: 400 Compartments: 1 Ho, ER 2 Ha: (6.4 x 4.2) (7.0 x 4.2)ER	**1 oil engine** driving 1 FP propeller Total Power: 132kW (179hp) 6.8kn AuxGen: 2 x 22kW a.c
7326582 *DUH2129* -	**STRONG HEART 1** *ex* Asia Japan *-2004* *ex* Atsumi Maru *-1988* **Key west Shipping Line Corp** *Cebu* *Philippines* Official number: CEB1000291	*1,302* 359 403	Class: (BV)	**1973-07 Naikai Shipbuilding & Engineering Co Ltd — Onomichi HS (Taguma Shipyard)** Yd No: 374 Loa 64.45 Br ex 13.06 Dght 3.010 Lbp 60.00 Br md 13.01 Dpth 4.20 Riveted\Welded, 2 dks	**(A36A2PR) Passenger/Ro-Ro Ship (Vehicles)** Passengers: 504	**2 oil engines** driving 2 FP propellers Total Power: 2,942kW (4,000hp) 16.2kn Niigata 6L31EZ 2 x 4 Stroke 6 Cy. 310 x 380 each-1471kW (2000bhp) Niigata Engineering Co Ltd-Japan
8425440 *DXNW* -	**STRONG HOPE** *ex* Adam *-2004* *ex* Ana Cristina *-2002* **Key west Shipping Line Corp** *Cebu* *Philippines* Official number: CDO7000023	*249* 170 500		**1972 Philippine Iron Construction & Marine Works Inc. — Jasaan** Loa - Br ex 8.54 Dght 2.741 Lbp 42.68 Br md 8.50 Dpth - Welded, 1 dk	**(B32A2ST) Tug**	**1 oil engine** driving 1 FP propeller 8.0kn
5342518 *LGCV* -	**STRONSTAD** **P/R Vesteraalen Stotteforening** Peter Conradsen *Stokmarknes* *Norway* MMSI: 257318500	**165** 65 -	Class: (NV)	**1955 P. Hoivolds Mek. Verksted AS — Kristiansand** Yd No: 6 Loa 28.91 Br ex 6.81 Dght 2.439 Lbp - Br md 6.79 Dpth 3.23 Riveted\Welded, 1 dk	**(A32A2GF) General Cargo/Passenger Ship** Passengers: unberthed: 140 Compartments: 1 Ho, ER 1 Ha: (1.5 x 1.5)ER Derricks: 1x2.5t	**1 oil engine** driving 1 FP propeller Total Power: 184kW (250hp) 9.5kn Normo 1 x 4 Stroke 5 Cy. 220 x 320 184kW (250bhp) AS Bergens Mek Verksteder-Norway
9356543 *PBSE* -	**STROOMBANK** **Bankship IV BV** Pot Scheepvaart BV SatCom: Inmarsat C 424461710 *Delfzijl* *Netherlands* MMSI: 244617000 Official number: 43771	**2,999** 1,662 4,550	Class: BV	**2009-06 Bijlsma Shipyard BV — Lemmer** Yd No: 707 Loa 89.95 (BB) Br ex - Dght 5.830 Lbp 84.98 Br md 14.40 Dpth 7.35 Welded, 1 dk	**(A31A2GX) General Cargo Ship** Grain: 6,059 TEU 106 Compartments: 1 Ho, ER 1 Ha:	**1 oil engine** geared to sc. shaft driving 1 CP propeller Total Power: 1,860kW (2,529hp) 12.5kn Wartsila 6L26 1 x 4 Stroke 6 Cy. 260 x 320 1860kW (2529bhp) Wartsila Finland Oy-Finland AuxGen: 1 x 312kW a.c Thrusters: 1 Tunnel thruster (f)
9178056 *C6UU8*	**STROVOLOS** *ex* Ioannis *-2005* **Strovolos Shipping Co Ltd** World Tankers Management Pte Ltd *Nassau* *Bahamas* MMSI: 309562000 Official number: 8001060	**28,546** 12,369 47,106 T/cm 50.3	Class: LR (NK) **100A1** SS 06/2009 Double Hull oil tanker ESP *IWS LI **LMC** **UMS IGS** Eq.Ltr: M†; Cable: 632.5/73.0 U3 (a)	**1999-06 Onomichi Dockyard Co Ltd — Onomichi HS** Yd No: 438 Loa 182.50 (BB) Br ex 32.20 Dght 12.666 Lbp 172.00 Br md 32.20 Dpth 19.10 Welded, 1 dk	**(A13B2TP) Products Tanker** Double Hull (13F) Liq: 50,326; Liq (Oil): 50,335 Cargo Heating Coils Compartments: 2 Ta, 14 Wing Ta, 2 Wing Slop Ta, ER 4 Cargo Pump (s): 4x1000m³/hr	**1 oil engine** driving 1 FP propeller Total Power: 8,561kW (11,640hp) 14.8kn B&W 6S50MC 1 x 2 Stroke 6 Cy. 500 x 1910 8561kW (11640bhp) Mitsui Engineering & Shipbuilding CLtd-Japan AuxGen: 3 x 420kW 450V 60Hz a.c Boilers: e (ex.g.) 21.9kgf/cm² (21.5bar), WTAuxB (o.f.) 18.0kgf/cm² (17.7bar) Fuel: 107.0 (d.f.) 1229.0 (r.f.)
7641944 *UGGS* -	**STROYNYY** **Gold Fish Co Ltd (OOO 'Gold Fish')** *Petropavlovsk-Kamchatskiy* *Russia* MMSI: 273567500	**737** 221 333	Class: (RS)	**1972-11 Zavod "Leninskaya Kuznitsa" — Kiyev** Yd No: 204 Loa 49.23 (BB) Br ex 10.70 Dght 4.250 Lbp 44.41 Br md 10.50 Dpth 6.02 Welded, 1 dk	**(B11A2FS) Stern Trawler** Ins: 275 Compartments: 1 Ho, ER 2 Ha: 2 (1.6 x 1.6) Derricks: 2x1.5t; Winches: 2 Ice Capable	**1 oil engine** driving 1 CP propeller Total Power: 971kW (1,320hp) 13.0kn S.K.L. 8NVD48A-2U 1 x 4 Stroke 8 Cy. 320 x 480 971kW (1320bhp) VEB Schwermaschinenbau "KarlLiebknecht" (SKL)-Magdeburg AuxGen: 1 x 300kW, 3 x 160kW, 2 x 135kW Thrusters: 1 Thwart. FP thruster (f); 1 Tunnel thruster (a) Fuel: 191.0 (d.f.)
9290919 *SVNT* -	**STRYMON** **Empire Navigation Ltd** Sun Enterprises Ltd *Chios* *Greece* MMSI: 240278000 Official number: 416	**30,020** 12,196 47,120 T/cm 51.0	Class: LR ✠ **100A1** SS 01/2010 Double Hull oil & chemical tanker, Ship Type 2 & Ship Type 3 ESP LI *IWS SPM **ShipRight** (SDA, FDA plus, CM) ✠ **LMC** **UMS IGS** Eq.Ltr: M†; Cable: 625.5/73.0 U3 (a)	**2005-01 STX Shipbuilding Co Ltd — Changwon (Jinhae Shipyard)** Yd No: 1159 Loa 183.00 (BB) Br ex 32.23 Dght 12.430 Lbp 173.90 Br md 32.20 Dpth 19.10 Welded, 1 dk	**(A12B2TR) Chemical/Products Tanker** Double Hull (13F) Liq: 52,200; Liq (Oil): 52,200 Compartments: 12 Wing Ta, 2 Wing Slop Ta, ER 12 Cargo Pump (s): 12x600m³/hr Manifold: Bow/CM: 91m	**1 oil engine** driving 1 FP propeller Total Power: 9,620kW (13,079hp) 14.5kn B&W 6S50MC-C 1 x 2 Stroke 6 Cy. 500 x 2000 9620kW (13079bhp) STX Engine Co Ltd-South Korea AuxGen: 3 x 740kW 450/220V 60Hz a.c Boilers: AuxB (Comp) 9.2kgf/cm² (9.0bar), WTAuxB (o.f.) 9.2kgf/cm² (9.0bar) Thrusters: 1 Thwart. FP thruster (f) Fuel: 116.3 (d.f.) (Heating Coils) 1433.0 (r.f.) 40.5pd
7804998 *LIID* -	**STRYN** *ex* Bjorgvin *-1994* *ex* Gloppen *-1991* **Fjord1 AS** *Floro* *Norway* MMSI: 257387400	**996** 298 530	Class: (NV)	**1979-06 Eid Verft AS — Nordfjordeid** (Hull) Yd No: 14 **1979-06 Smedvik Mek. Verksted AS — Tjorvaag** Yd No: 70 Lengthened & Rebuilt-1991 Loa 83.30 Br ex 15.20 Dght 2.940 Lbp 74.83 Br md 11.27 Dpth 4.20 Welded, 1 dk	**(A36A2PR) Passenger/Ro-Ro Ship (Vehicles)** Passengers: unberthed: 360 Lane-Len: 216 Cars: 50, Trailers: 4 Ice Capable	**2 oil engines** driving 2 Propellers Total Power: 956kW (1,300hp) Wichmann 4AXA 2 x 2 Stroke 4 Cy. 300 x 450 each-478kW (650bhp) Wichmann Motorfabrikk AS-Norway AuxGen: 2 x 80kW 220V 50Hz a.c
8875176 *OUVM* -	**STRYNBOEN** **A/S Stryno-Rudkobing Faergefart** *Stryno* *Denmark* MMSI: 219000779 Official number: B252	**119** 38 -		**1966-01 Blaalid Slip & Mek Verksted AS — Raudeberg** Yd No: 17 Lengthened-1995 Loa 25.69 Br ex - Dght - Lbp - Br md 7.56 Dpth 2.58 Welded, 1 dk	**(A37B2PS) Passenger Ship**	**1 oil engine** driving 1 FP propeller
9664524 *OUWR* -	**STRYNOE FAERGE** **Langelands Kommune** *Rudkobing* *Denmark* MMSI: 219017917 Official number: A556	**310** 93 160	Class: BV	**2013-07 A/S Hvide Sande Skibs- og Baadebyggeri — Hvide Sande** Yd No: 129 Loa 38.20 Br ex 11.10 Dght 2.200 Lbp 35.13 Br md 10.80 Dpth 3.50 Welded, 1 dk	**(A36A2PR) Passenger/Ro-Ro Ship (Vehicles)**	**2 oil engines** reduction geared to sc. shafts driving 2 CP propellers Total Power: 736kW (1,000hp) 10.0kn Volvo Penta D13MH 2 x 4 Stroke 6 Cy. 131 x 158 each-368kW (500bhp) AB Volvo Penta-Sweden AuxGen: 2 x 174kW 50Hz a.c Fuel: 18.0 (d.f.)

IMO / Call sign	Name / Owner	Tonnage	Class	Build	Type / Capacity	Machinery
8993162 - -	**STS-19** **Marine Ecology Co Ltd (OOO 'Ekologiya Morya')** - *Petropavlovsk-Kamchatskiy* *Russia* Official number: 833552	*122* - 72	Class: RS	**1984**-07 **in the U.S.S.R.** Yd No: 19 Loa 31.40 Br ex 6.18 Dght 1.000 Lbp 30.00 Br md - Dpth 1.60 Welded, 1 dk	**(A14A2LO) Water Tanker** Liq: 30	**1 oil engine** driving 1 FP propeller Total Power: 110kW (150hp) 8.5kn Russkiy 6CHSP15/18 1 x 4 Stroke 6 Cy. 150 x 180 110kW (150bhp) in the U.S.S.R. Fuel: 3.0 (d.f.)
9162069 *3WHP9* -	**STS PIONEER** *ex Nipayia -2012 ex Golden Diane -2002* **STS Petroleum & Logistics Service JSC** - SatCom: Inmarsat C 457400183 *Saigon* *Vietnam* MMSI: 574001590 Official number: VNSG-2099-TD	**5,357** 2,589 8,742 T/cm 17.6	Class: NK	**1997**-10 **Usuki Shipyard Co Ltd — Usuki OT** Yd No: 1650 Loa 112.00 (BB) Br ex 19.20 Dght 7.514 Lbp 105.00 Br md 19.00 Dpth 10.00 Welded, 1 dk	**(A12B2TR) Chemical/Products Tanker** Double Hull (13F) Liq: 8,711; Liq (Oil): 8,711 Cargo Heating Coils Compartments: 10 Wing Ta, 2 Wing Slop Ta, ER 9 Cargo Pump (s): 7x300m³/hr, 2x150m³/hr Manifold: Bow/CM: 59.6m	**1 oil engine** driving 1 FP propeller Total Power: 3,089kW (4,200hp) 13.0kn Mitsubishi 6UEC37LA 1 x 2 Stroke 6 Cy. 370 x 880 3089kW (4200bhp) Akasaka Tekkosho KK (Akasaka DieselLtd)-Japan AuxGen: 2 x a.c Thrusters: 1 Thwart. FP thruster (f) Fuel: 80.0 (d.f.) 586.0 (r.f.)
8902266 *V3OV6* -	**STS STAR** *ex Ht Blade -2011 ex Adsteam Deben -2007* *ex Deben -2005* **Brightwell Investments Ltd SA** Ultramarine Ltd *Belize City* *Belize* MMSI: 312735000 Official number: 37110064	**371** 111 -	Class: RS (LR) ✠ Classed LR until 30/7/11	**1990**-03 **Richards (Shipbuilders) Ltd — Great Yarmouth** Yd No: 583 Loa 30.64 Br ex 10.24 Dght 4.116 Lbp 25.00 Br md 9.60 Dpth 4.80 Welded, 1 dk	**(B32A2ST) Tug**	**2 oil engines** with clutches, flexible couplings & sr geared to sc. shafts driving 2 Directional propellers Total Power: 2,584kW (3,514hp) 12.0kn Ruston 6RK270M 2 x 4 Stroke 6 Cy. 270 x 305 each-1292kW (1757bhp) Ruston Diesels Ltd.-Newton-le-Willows AuxGen: 2 x 325kW 440V 50Hz a.c Thrusters: 1 Thwart. FP thruster (f)
8510087 *HSB4428* -	**STT1** *ex Sun Spring -2010 ex Kotoku -1990* *ex Kotoku Maru -1990* **Ayudhya Development Leasing Co Ltd (ADLC)** Chemstar Shipping Co Ltd SatCom: Inmarsat C 456700330 *Bangkok* *Thailand* MMSI: 567393000 Official number: 530001007	**961** 493 1,775	Class: BV (NK)	**1985**-11 **Kishimoto Zosen K.K. — Kinoe** Yd No: 552 Loa 65.50 Br ex - Dght 4.760 Lbp 61.50 Br md 11.40 Dpth 5.50 Welded, 1 dk	**(A12B2TR) Chemical/Products Tanker** Liq: 1,856; Liq (Oil): 1,856 Compartments: 4 Ta, ER	**1 oil engine** driving 1 FP propeller Total Power: 1,103kW (1,500hp) 11.0kn Akasaka A28 1 x 4 Stroke 6 Cy. 280 x 550 1103kW (1500bhp) Akasaka Tekkosho KK (Akasaka DieselLtd)-Japan AuxGen: 2 x 104kW a.c Fuel: 125.0 (r.f.)
6513774 *Y4HK* -	**STUBNITZ** **Tragerverein Rostocker Kulturschiff Stubnitz eV** Motorschiff Stubnitz eV *Rostock* *Germany* MMSI: 211218820	**2,541** 762 1,350	Class: GL (DS)	**1964 VEB Volkswerft Stralsund — Stralsund** Yd No: 351 Converted From: Fish Carrier-2000 Loa 79.81 Br ex - Dght 4.480 Lbp 71.00 Br md 13.20 Dpth 9.50 Welded, 2 dks	**(B35A2QE) Exhibition Vessel** Grain: 1,850; Ins: 1,310 Compartments: 3 Ho, ER, 1 Tw Dk 3 Ha: Derricks: 2x1.5t; Winches: 2 Ice Capable	**2 oil engines** geared to sc. shaft driving 1 CP propeller Total Power: 986kW (1,340hp) 11.8kn S.K.L. 8NVD48 2 x 4 Stroke 8 Cy. 320 x 480 each-493kW (670bhp) VEB Schwermaschinenbau "KarlLiebknecht" (SKL)-Magdeburg AuxGen: 4 x 216kW 230V d.c, 1 x 80kW 230V d.c Fuel: 458.0 (d.f.)
9190432 *LYLW* -	**STUMBRAS** **Authority of Klaipeda State Seaport (Klaipedos Valstybinio Juru Uosto Direkcija)** - *Klaipeda* *Lithuania* MMSI: 277150000 Official number: 570	**313** 93 270	Class: LR ✠ **100A1** SS 01/2010 tug coastal service between Kiel and St. Petersburg **LMC** Cable: 137.5/19.0 U2 (a)	**2000**-01 **PO SevMash Predpriyatiye — Severodvinsk** (Hull) **2000**-01 **B.V. Scheepswerf Damen — Gorinchem** Yd No: 7941 Loa 30.82 Br ex - Dght 3.760 Lbp 28.03 Br md 9.40 Dpth 4.80 Welded, 1 dk	**(B32A2ST) Tug**	**2 oil engines** with clutches & sr geared to sc. shafts driving 2 Directional propellers Total Power: 3,132kW (4,258hp) 12.0kn Caterpillar 3516B-TA 2 x Vee 4 Stroke 16 Cy. 170 x 190 each-1566kW (2129bhp) Caterpillar Inc-USA AuxGen: 2 x 85kW 380V 60Hz a.c Fuel: 116.8 (d.f.) 16.3pd
7623186 - -	**STUPINA** -	**606** 137 888	Class: (RN)	**1974 Santierul Naval Drobeta-Turnu Severin S.A. — Drobeta-Turnu S.** Yd No: 3984 Loa 55.14 Br ex - Dght 3.599 Lbp 52.41 Br md 10.42 Dpth 4.30 Welded, 1 dk	**(A31A2GX) General Cargo Ship** Grain: 500 Compartments: 1 Ho, ER 1 Ha: ER Ice Capable	**2 oil engines** geared to sc. shafts driving 2 FP propellers Total Power: 442kW (600hp) 8.0kn Pervomaysk 6CH25/34 2 x 4 Stroke 6 Cy. 250 x 340 each-221kW (300bhp) Pervomaydizelmash (PDM)-Pervomaysk AuxGen: 2 x 64kW 220V 50Hz a.c Fuel: 59.0 (d.f.)
7611298 *UGGW* -	**STUPINO** **Sakhalin Asia Shipping JSC (A/O 'Sakhalin Aziya Shipping')** - *Nevelsk* *Russia* MMSI: 273561600 Official number: 751808	**759** 227 358	Class: (RS)	**1975 Volgogradskiy Sudostroitelnyy Zavod — Volgograd** Yd No: 865 Loa 53.73 (BB) Br ex 10.70 Dght 4.287 Lbp 47.92 Br md - Dpth 6.02 Welded, 1 dk	**(B11A2FS) Stern Trawler** Ins: 218 Compartments: 1 Ho, ER 2 Ha: 2 (1.6 x 1.6) Derricks: 2x1.5t; Winches: 2 Ice Capable	**1 oil engine** driving 1 CP propeller Total Power: 971kW (1,320hp) 12.5kn S.K.L. 8NVD48A-2U 1 x 4 Stroke 8 Cy. 320 x 480 971kW (1320bhp) VEB Schwermaschinenbau "KarlLiebknecht" (SKL)-Magdeburg Thrusters: 1 Thwart. FP thruster (f); 1 Tunnel thruster (a)
8657457 *9AA5282* -	**STURAGO** **Maistra dd za hotelijerstovo i turizam** - *Pula* *Croatia* Official number: 1T-200	**130** 39 -	Class: CS	**2008**-01 **Shipyard Izola plc — Izola** Yd No: 701 Loa 25.65 Br ex - Dght 1.560 Lbp 22.00 Br md 6.60 Dpth 2.50 Welded, 1 dk	**(A35A2RR) Ro-Ro Cargo Ship**	**2 oil engines** reduction geared to sc. shaft driving 1 FP propeller Total Power: 760kW (1,034hp) 8.0kn Cummins 6CTA8.3-M 2 x 4 Stroke 6 Cy. 114 x 135 each-380kW (517bhp) Cummins Engine Co Ltd-United Kingdom
7647869 - -	**STURGEON** *ex R. V. Marsys Resolute -2004 ex D K -1991* **US Geological Survey** - *Cheboygan, MI* *United States of America*	*300* - 180	Class: (AB)	**1976 J.R. Long — Sausalito, Ca** Converted From: Fishing Vessel-2004 Rebuilt-2004 Loa 30.79 Br ex - Dght 3.048 Lbp - Br md 7.32 Dpth 4.57 Welded, 1dk	**(B12D2FR) Fishery Research Vessel**	**2 oil engines** reduction geared to sc. shafts driving 2 FP propellers Total Power: 1,104kW (1,500hp) 10.0kn G.M. (Detroit Diesel) SERIES 60 2 x 4 Stroke 6 Cy. 106 x 168 each-552kW (750bhp) (new engine 2004) Detroit Diesel Corporation-Detroit, Mi AuxGen: 2 x 99kW a.c Thrusters: 1 Thwart. FP thruster (f)
5342582 *WJ6383* -	**STURGEON** *ex Signet Magic -2006 ex Sturgeon -2004* **Signet Maritime Corp** - *Brownsville, TX* *United States of America* Official number: 275580	*196* 133 -	Class: (AB)	**1957 Gulfport Shipbuilding Corp. — Port Arthur, Tx** Yd No: 509 Loa 32.47 Br ex 8.51 Dght 3.871 Lbp 30.56 Br md 8.26 Dpth 4.27 Welded, 1 dk	**(B32A2ST) Tug**	**1 oil engine** sr reverse geared to sc. shaft driving 1 FP propeller Total Power: 1,177kW (1,600hp) General Motors 16-278-A 1 x Vee 2 Stroke 16 Cy. 222 x 267 1177kW (1600bhp) (Re-engined ,made 1943, refitted 1957) General Motors Corp-USA AuxGen: 2 x 60kW 230V d.c, 1 x 20kW 230V d.c Fuel: 84.5 (d.f.)
9058933 *9MQJ7* -	**STURGEON** *ex Fujikawa Maru -2013* **Sturgeon Asia Ltd** Skips Marine Services Pte Ltd *Malaysia* MMSI: 533130995	*199* - 530		**1993**-03 **Taiyo Shipbuilding Co Ltd — Sanyoonoda YC** Yd No: 235 Loa 48.03 Br ex 8.05 Dght 3.200 Lbp 44.15 Br md 8.00 Dpth 3.45 Welded, 1 dk	**(A13B2TP) Products Tanker** Liq: 570; Liq (Oil): 570 Compartments: 6 Wing Ta, ER	**1 oil engine** with clutches & reverse geared to sc. shaft driving 1 FP propeller Total Power: 735kW (999hp) Hanshin LH26G 1 x 4 Stroke 6 Cy. 260 x 440 735kW (999bhp) The Hanshin Diesel Works Ltd-Japan
8700577 *PHVW* -	**STURGEON** - - SatCom: Inmarsat C 424424220 *Rotterdam* *Netherlands* MMSI: 244242000 Official number: 2296	**1,605** 481 1,259 T/cm 9.4	Class: BV	**1988**-02 **Tille Scheepsbouw B.V. — Kootstertille** Yd No: 261 Loa 92.76 Br ex 11.40 Dght 3.000 Lbp 88.68 Br md 11.34 Dpth 6.00 Welded, 1 dk	**(A11B2TG) LPG Tanker** Single Hull Liq (Gas): 1,958 6 x Gas Tank (s); 6 independent (C.mn.stl) cyl horizontal 2 Cargo Pump (s): 2x100m³/hr Manifold: Bow/CM: 46.3m	**1 oil engine** with clutches & sr greaed to sc. shaft driving 1 FP propeller Total Power: 795kW (1,081hp) 11.0kn Kromhout 6FEHD240 1 x 4 Stroke 6 Cy. 240 x 260 795kW (1081bhp) Stork Werkspoor Diesel BV-Netherlands AuxGen: 2 x 220kW 220/380V 50Hz a.c Thrusters: 1 Thwart. FP thruster (f) Fuel: 69.0 (d.f.)
8635198 *NSXB* -	**STURGEON BAY** **Government of The United States of America (US Coast Guard)** - *United States of America* MMSI: 366999984	*500* - -		**1988**-08 **Bay City Marine, Inc. — San Diego, Ca** Loa 42.67 Br ex - Dght 3.658 Lbp 39.62 Br md 11.28 Dpth - Welded, 1 dk	**(B32A2ST) Tug** Ice Capable	**2 diesel electric oil engines** driving 2 gen. each 1200kW Connecting to 1 elec. Motor of (1839kW) driving 1 FP propeller Total Power: 1,838kW (2,498hp) 12.0kn Fairbanks, Morse 10-38D8-1/8 2 x 2 Stroke 10 Cy. 207 x 254 each-919kW (1249bhp) Colt Industries Fairbanks MorseEngine Div.-U.S.A. AuxGen: 1 x 125kW a.c Fuel: 71.0

6721216 *TFBO* GK 012	**STURLA** *ex* Gudmundur *-2004* *ex* Tunu *-1999* *ex* Gudmundur *-1998* *ex* Senior *-1973* **Thorbjorn Fiskanes hf** - *Grindavik* *Iceland* MMSI: 251164000 Official number: 1272	**672** 202 610	Class: NV	**1967-05 Karmsund Verft & Mek. Verksted — Avaldsnes** Yd No: 6 Lengthened-1970 Loa 52.91 (BB) Br ex 8.56 Dght 4.630 Lbp 48.06 Br md 8.54 Dpth 6.33 Welded, 1 dk	**(B11B2FV) Fishing Vessel** Compartments: 3 Ho, ER 3 Ha: 3 (2.9 x 3.5)ER Derricks: 1x5t; Winches: 1 Ice Capable	**1 oil engine** driving 1 CP propeller Total Power: 809kW (1,100hp) 13.0kn MaK 6M451AK 1 x 4 Stroke 6 Cy. 320 x 450 809kW (1100bhp) Atlas MaK Maschinenbau GmbH-Kiel AuxGen: 1 x 350kW 380V 50Hz a.c, 2 x 116kW 380V 50Hz a.c Thrusters: 1 Thwart. FP thruster (f); 1 Tunnel thruster (a) Fuel: 43.5 (d.f.) 4.5pd
8003993 *TFGH* AK 010	**STURLAUGUR H BODVARSSON** *ex* Sigurfari II *-1986* **HB Grandi hf** - SatCom: Inmarsat C 425105010 *Akranes* *Iceland* MMSI: 251050110 Official number: 1585	**712** 213 -	Class: (BV)	**1981-07 Skipasmidastod Thorgeir & Ellert h/f — Akranes** Yd No: 35 Loa 50.86 Br ex - Dght 4.152 Lbp 44.02 Br md 9.01 Dpth 4.22 Welded, 1 dk	**(B11A2FS) Stern Trawler**	**1 oil engine** reverse reduction geared to sc. shaft driving 1 FP propeller Total Power: 1,640kW (2,230hp) Alco 12V251E 1 x Vee 4 Stroke 12 Cy. 229 x 267 1640kW (2230bhp) Alco Power Inc-USA
9038907 *DGBE* -	**STUTTGART EXPRESS** - **Hapag-Lloyd AG** - SatCom: Inmarsat A 1123251 *Hamburg* *Germany* MMSI: 211208940 Official number: 17310	**53,815** 23,499 67,640 T/cm 82.3	Class: GL	**1993-12 Samsung Heavy Industries Co Ltd — Geoje** Yd No: 1096 Loa 294.09 (BB) Br ex - Dght 13.500 Lbp 281.60 Br md 32.25 Dpth 21.40 Welded, 1 dk	**(A33A2CC) Container Ship (Fully Cellular)** TEU 4639 C Ho 2342 TEU C Dk 2297 TEU incl 452 ref C. Compartments: ER, 7 Cell Ho 18 Ha: (12.9 x 13.0)Tappered (12.9 x 18.1) (12.9 x 23.2)Tappered (12.9 x 28.4)Tappered 3 (6.4 x 28.4)ER 11 (12.9 x 28.4)	**1 oil engine** driving 1 FP propeller Total Power: 36,510kW (49,639hp) 23.0kn B&W 9K90MC 1 x 2 Stroke 9 Cy. 900 x 2550 36510kW (49639bhp) Hyundai Heavy Industries Co Ltd-South Korea AuxGen: 2 x 2200kW 220/440V 60Hz a.c, 2 x 1650kW 220/440V 60Hz a.c Thrusters: 1 Thwart. CP thruster (f) Fuel: 7362.0
7915838 *WNFX* -	**STUYVESANT** - **The Dutra Group Inc** - *Mobile, AL* *United States of America* MMSI: 368098000 Official number: 648540	**8,432** 2,771 9,950	Class: AB	**1982-06 Avondale Shipyards Inc. — Avondale, La** Yd No: 2332 Loa 124.01 Br ex - Dght 8.411 Lbp 103.03 Br md 21.95 Dpth 10.37 Welded, 1 dk	**(B33B2DT) Trailing Suction Hopper Dredger** Hopper: 8,460	**2 oil engines** reverse reduction geared to sc. shafts driving 2 FP propellers Total Power: 10,150kW (13,800hp) 15.0kn Werkspoor 9TM410 2 x 4 Stroke 9 Cy. 410 x 470 each-5075kW (6900bhp) Stork Werkspoor Diesel BV-Netherlands AuxGen: 3 x 800kW Thrusters: 1 Thwart. FP thruster (f)
8133683 - -	**STVOR** *ex* SPP-013 *-1995* **Krasnogorsk Port Authority (Krasnogorskiy MTP)** - *Korsakov* *Russia* Official number: 822098	**175** 52 162	Class: (RS)	**1982-11 Sudoremontnyy Zavod "Yakor" — Sovetskaya Gavan** Yd No: 10251/13 Loa 35.72 Br ex 7.50 Dght 1.850 Lbp 33.58 Br md - Dpth 2.40 Welded, 1 dk	**(A31C2GD) Deck Cargo Ship** Ice Capable	**1 oil engine** geared to sc. shaft driving 1 FP propeller Total Power: 221kW (300hp) 8.7kn Daldizel 6CHNSP18/22-300 1 x 4 Stroke 6 Cy. 180 x 220 221kW (300bhp) Daldizel-Khabarovsk AuxGen: 2 x a.c Fuel: 7.0 (d.f.)
9510515 *3FUG9* -	**STX ACACIA** - **POS Maritime QY SA** STX Marine Service Co Ltd SatCom: Inmarsat C 435220010 *Panama* *Panama* MMSI: 352200000 Official number: 4223011A	**92,080** 58,719 175,292 T/cm 120.8	Class: KR (NV)	**2010-11 New Times Shipbuilding Co Ltd — Jingjiang JS** Yd No: 0117625 Loa 291.80 (BB) Br ex - Dght 18.250 Lbp 282.20 Br md 45.00 Dpth 24.75 Welded, 1 dk	**(A21A2BC) Bulk Carrier** Grain: 197,132 Compartments: 9 Ho, ER 9 Ha: 4 (26.6 x 32.7)2 (24.8 x 32.7)ER 3 (25.7 x 32.7)	**1 oil engine** driving 1 FP propeller Total Power: 16,860kW (22,923hp) 14.5kn MAN-B&W 6S70MC 1 x 2 Stroke 6 Cy. 700 x 2674 16860kW (22923bhp) STX Engine Co Ltd-South Korea
9346067 *3EEH2* -	**STX ACE 1** - **POS Maritime FX SA** Pan Ocean Co Ltd *Panama* *Panama* MMSI: 371898000 Official number: 3144606A	**30,027** 11,735 46,176 T/cm 51.7	Class: KR	**2006-02 STX Shipbuilding Co Ltd — Changwon (Jinhae Shipyard)** Yd No: 1221 Loa 183.00 (BB) Br ex 32.30 Dght 12.220 Lbp 173.90 Br md 32.20 Dpth 19.10 Welded, 1 dk	**(A12B2TR) Chemical/Products Tanker** Double Hull (13F) Liq: 52,199; Liq (Oil): 52,199 Cargo Heating Coils Compartments: 12 Wing Ta, 2 Wing Slop Ta, ER 12 Cargo Pump (s): 12x600m³/hr Manifold: Bow/CM: 92.3m	**1 oil engine** driving 1 FP propeller Total Power: 8,165kW (11,101hp) 14.7kn MAN-B&W 6S50MC-C 1 x 2 Stroke 6 Cy. 500 x 2000 8165kW (11101bhp) STX Engine Co Ltd-South Korea AuxGen: 3 x 740kW 450V a.c Fuel: 193.2 (d.f.) 1484.0 (r.f.)
9346079 *3EEK8* -	**STX ACE 2** - **POS Maritime GX SA** Pan Ocean Co Ltd *Panama* *Panama* MMSI: 371929000 Official number: 3156806A	**30,027** 11,735 46,185 T/cm 51.8	Class: KR	**2006-03 STX Shipbuilding Co Ltd — Changwon (Jinhae Shipyard)** Yd No: 1222 Loa 183.00 (BB) Br ex 32.23 Dght 12.220 Lbp 173.90 Br md 32.20 Dpth 19.10 Welded, 1 dk	**(A12B2TR) Chemical/Products Tanker** Double Hull (13F) Liq: 52,196; Liq (Oil): 52,196 Compartments: 12 Wing Ta, 2 Wing Slop Ta, ER 12 Cargo Pump (s): 12x600m³/hr Manifold: Bow/CM: 92.3m	**1 oil engine** driving 1 FP propeller Total Power: 8,165kW (11,101hp) 14.7kn MAN-B&W 6S50MC-C 1 x 2 Stroke 6 Cy. 500 x 2000 8165kW (11101bhp) STX Engine Co Ltd-South Korea AuxGen: 3 x 740kW 450V a.c Fuel: 137.4 (d.f.) 1452.9 (r.f.)
9375317 *3EIG9* -	**STX ACE 5** - **POS Maritime IX SA** Pan Ocean Co Ltd *Panama* *Panama* MMSI: 372172000 Official number: 3241307A	**30,027** 11,735 46,176 T/cm 51.8	Class: KR	**2006-11 STX Shipbuilding Co Ltd — Changwon (Jinhae Shipyard)** Yd No: 1227 Loa 183.00 (BB) Br ex 32.30 Dght 12.210 Lbp 173.90 Br md 32.20 Dpth 19.10 Welded, 1 dk	**(A12B2TR) Chemical/Products Tanker** Double Hull (13F) Liq: 52,196; Liq (Oil): 52,196 Compartments: 12 Wing Ta, 2 Wing Slop Ta, ER 14 Cargo Pump (s): 12x600m³/hr, 1x150m³/hr, 1x100m³/hr Manifold: Bow/CM: 92.3m	**1 oil engine** driving 1 FP propeller Total Power: 8,170kW (11,108hp) 14.5kn MAN-B&W 6S50MC-C 1 x 2 Stroke 6 Cy. 500 x 2000 8170kW (11108bhp) STX Engine Co Ltd-South Korea AuxGen: 3 x 740kW 450V a.c Fuel: 137.4 (d.f.) 1452.9 (r.f.)
9375329 *3EIW4* -	**STX ACE 6** - **POS Maritime JX SA** Pan Ocean Co Ltd *Panama* *Panama* MMSI: 372419000 Official number: 3263007A	**30,027** 11,735 46,177 T/cm 51.8	Class: KR	**2007-02 STX Shipbuilding Co Ltd — Changwon (Jinhae Shipyard)** Yd No: 1229 Loa 183.00 (BB) Br ex 32.30 Dght 12.200 Lbp 173.90 Br md 32.20 Dpth 19.10 Welded, 1 dk	**(A12B2TR) Chemical/Products Tanker** Double Hull (13F) Liq: 52,220; Liq (Oil): 52,220 Compartments: 12 Wing Ta, 2 Wing Slop Ta, ER 12 Cargo Pump (s): 12x600m³/hr Manifold: Bow/CM: 92.3m	**1 oil engine** driving 1 FP propeller Total Power: 9,480kW (12,889hp) 14.5kn MAN-B&W 6S50MC-C 1 x 2 Stroke 6 Cy. 500 x 2000 9480kW (12889bhp) STX Engine Co Ltd-South Korea AuxGen: 3 x a.c Fuel: 130.0 (d.f.) 1400.0 (r.f.)
9425265 *3ENU2* -	**STX ACE 7** - **POS Maritime SX SA** Pan Ocean Co Ltd *Panama* *Panama* MMSI: 352618000 Official number: 3370508	**30,027** 11,735 46,149 T/cm 51.8	Class: KR	**2007-12 STX Shipbuilding Co Ltd — Changwon (Jinhae Shipyard)** Yd No: 3007 Loa 183.00 (BB) Br ex 32.23 Dght 12.216 Lbp 173.90 Br md 32.20 Dpth 19.10 Welded, 1 dk	**(A12B2TR) Chemical/Products Tanker** Double Hull (13F) Liq: 52,197; Liq (Oil): 52,197 Cargo Heating Coils Compartments: 12 Wing Ta, 2 Wing Slop Ta, ER 12 Cargo Pump (s): 12x600m³/hr Manifold: Bow/CM: 92.3m	**1 oil engine** driving 1 FP propeller Total Power: 9,480kW (12,889hp) 14.2kn MAN-B&W 6S50MC-C 1 x 2 Stroke 6 Cy. 500 x 2000 9480kW (12889bhp) STX Engine Co Ltd-South Korea AuxGen: 3 x 740kW 450V a.c Fuel: 325.0 (d.f.) 1530.0 (r.f.)
9443877 *3EPV8* -	**STX ACE 10** - **POS Maritime RX SA** Pan Ocean Co Ltd *Panama* *Panama* MMSI: 354252000 Official number: 3407508A	**30,027** 11,735 46,159 T/cm 51.7	Class: KR	**2008-03 STX Shipbuilding Co Ltd — Changwon (Jinhae Shipyard)** Yd No: 1301 Loa 183.00 (BB) Br ex 32.23 Dght 12.216 Lbp 173.90 Br md 32.20 Dpth 19.10 Welded, 1 dk	**(A12B2TR) Chemical/Products Tanker** Double Hull (13F) Liq: 52,211; Liq (Oil): 52,211 Compartments: 12 Wing Ta, 2 Wing Slop Ta, ER 6 Cargo Pump (s): 6x600m³/hr Manifold: Bow/CM: 89.4m	**1 oil engine** driving 1 FP propeller Total Power: 9,480kW (12,889hp) 14.5kn MAN-B&W 6S50MC-C 1 x 2 Stroke 6 Cy. 500 x 2000 9480kW (12889bhp) STX Engine Co Ltd-South Korea AuxGen: 2 x 740kW 450V a.c Fuel: 166.0 (d.f.) 1373.0 (r.f.)
9384007 *3ETG3* -	**STX ACE 12** - **POS Maritime NX SA** Pan Ocean Co Ltd *Panama* *Panama* MMSI: 370549000 Official number: 3448508	**30,027** 11,735 46,188 T/cm 51.8	Class: KR	**2008-09 STX Shipbuilding Co Ltd — Changwon (Jinhae Shipyard)** Yd No: 1249 Loa 183.00 (BB) Br ex - Dght 12.216 Lbp 173.90 Br md 32.20 Dpth 19.10 Welded, 1 dk	**(A12B2TR) Chemical/Products Tanker** Double Hull (13F) Liq: 53,500; Liq (Oil): 53,500 Compartments: 12 Wing Ta, 2 Wing Slop Ta, ER 12 Cargo Pump (s): 12x600m³/hr Manifold: Bow/CM: 92m	**1 oil engine** driving 1 FP propeller Total Power: 9,960kW (13,542hp) 14.5kn MAN-B&W 6S50MC-C 1 x 2 Stroke 6 Cy. 500 x 2000 9960kW (13542bhp) STX Engine Co Ltd-South Korea AuxGen: 4 x 450V a.c Fuel: 197.0 (d.f.) 1529.0 (r.f.)
9613288 *V7YS2* -	**STX ARBORELLA** - **POS Maritime CA SA** Pan Ocean Co Ltd *Majuro* *Marshall Islands* MMSI: 538004720 Official number: 4720	**39,009** 16,720 57,540	Class: KR NV	**2012-09 STX Offshore & Shipbuilding Co Ltd — Changwon (Jinhae Shipyard)** Yd No: 1539 Loa 199.92 (BB) Br ex 32.31 Dght 12.723 Lbp 191.80 Br md 32.26 Dpth 19.30 Welded, 1 dk	**(A31A2GO) Open Hatch Cargo Ship** Grain: 62,500; Bale: 62,430 Compartments: 8 Ho, ER 8 Ha: 6 (18.4 x 28.2) (12.8 x 28.2)ER (12.0 x 18.0) Cranes: 4x45t	**1 oil engine** driving 1 FP propeller Total Power: 9,960kW (13,542hp) 14.5kn MAN-B&W 6S50ME-C8 1 x 2 Stroke 6 Cy. 500 x 2000 9960kW (13542bhp) STX Engine Co Ltd-South Korea AuxGen: 3 x 910kW 450V a.c Fuel: 3040.0

9441879 *3FSM3* -	**STX BEGONIA** **POS Maritime TX SA** STX Marine Service Co Ltd *Panama* *Panama* MMSI: 370900000 Official number: 4034009	**33,115** 19,036 57,307 T/cm 57.3	Class: KR	**2009-04 STX (Dalian) Shipbuilding Co Ltd — Wafangdian LN** Yd No: D2001 Loa 190.00 (BB) Br ex - Dght 13.020 Lbp 183.30 Br md 32.26 Dpth 18.50 Welded, 1 dk	**(A21A2BC) Bulk Carrier** Grain: 71,850 Compartments: 5 Ho, ER 5 Ha: 4 (19.7 x 18.3)ER (18.0 x 18.3) Cranes: 4x30t	**1 oil engine** driving 1 FP propeller Total Power: 9,480kW (12,889hp) 14.5kn MAN-B&W 6S50MC-C 1 x 2 Stroke 6 Cy. 500 x 2000 9480kW (12889bhp) STX Engine Co Ltd-South Korea
9626015 *V7YM2* -	**STX BONITA** **POS Maritime GZ SA** Pan Ocean Co Ltd SatCom: Inmarsat C 45387729 *Majuro* *Marshall Islands* MMSI: 538004689 Official number: 4689	**24,504** 12,325 38,140	Class: KR	**2012-06 STX (Dalian) Shipbuilding Co Ltd — Wafangdian LN** Yd No: D1082 Loa 189.00 (BB) Br ex - Dght 10.350 Lbp 178.13 Br md 30.00 Dpth 15.00 Welded, 1 dk	**(A21A2BC) Bulk Carrier** Double Hull Grain: 46,000 Compartments: 5 Ho, ER 5 Ha: 4 (19.4 x 21.0)ER (16.2 x 14.7) Cranes: 4x30t	**1 oil engine** driving 1 FP propeller Total Power: 7,150kW (9,721hp) 14.0kn MAN-B&W 5S50MC 1 x 2 Stroke 5 Cy. 500 x 1910 7150kW (9721bhp) STX (Dalian) Engine Co Ltd-China
9509499 *3EXW2* -	**STX CHAMPION** **POS Maritime ZY SA** STX Marine Service Co Ltd SatCom: Inmarsat C 437284411 *Panama* *Panama* MMSI: 372844000 Official number: 4239511	**92,053** 60,938 175,293 T/cm 120.8	Class: KR (GL)	**2010-08 New Times Shipbuilding Co Ltd — Jingjiang JS** Yd No: 0117634 Loa 291.80 (BB) Br ex - Dght 18.250 Lbp 282.20 Br md 45.00 Dpth 24.75 Welded, 1 dk	**(A21A2BC) Bulk Carrier** Grain: 197,132 Compartments: 9 Ho, ER 9 Ha: 4 (26.7 x 32.7)2 (24.8 x 32.7)ER 3 (25.8 x 32.7)	**1 oil engine** driving 1 FP propeller Total Power: 16,860kW (22,923hp) 14.5kn MAN-B&W 6S70MC 1 x 2 Stroke 6 Cy. 700 x 2674 16860kW (22923bhp) Hyundai Heavy Industries Co Ltd-South Korea
9621417 *V7YI7* -	**STX CLOVER** **POS Maritime AA SA** Pan Ocean Co Ltd SatCom: Inmarsat C 453837733 *Majuro* *Marshall Islands* MMSI: 538004668 Official number: 4668	**44,098** 27,714 81,177 T/cm 71.9	Class: KR	**2012-05 New Century Shipbuilding Co Ltd — Jingjiang JS** Yd No: 0108203 Loa 229.00 (BB) Br ex 32.30 Dght 14.450 Lbp 225.50 Br md 32.26 Dpth 20.05 Welded, 1 dk	**(A21A2BC) Bulk Carrier** Grain: 97,000; Bale: 90,784 Compartments: 7 Ho, ER 7 Ha: 6 (17.3 x 15.0)ER (14.7 x 12.8) Cranes: 4x35t	**1 oil engine** driving 1 FP propeller Total Power: 9,800kW (13,324hp) 14.1kn MAN-B&W 5S60MC-C8 1 x 2 Stroke 5 Cy. 600 x 2400 9800kW (13324bhp) STX (Dalian) Engine Co Ltd-China
9441881 *3FBW6* -	**STX CROCUS** **POS Maritime UX SA** STX Marine Service Co Ltd SatCom: Inmarsat C 435219612 *Panama* *Panama* MMSI: 352196000 Official number: 4056309	**33,115** 19,036 57,269 T/cm 57.3	Class: KR	**2009-05 STX (Dalian) Shipbuilding Co Ltd — Wafangdian LN** Yd No: D2002 Loa 190.00 (BB) Br ex - Dght 13.020 Lbp 183.30 Br md 32.26 Dpth 18.50 Welded, 1 dk	**(A21A2BC) Bulk Carrier** Grain: 71,850 Compartments: 5 Ho, ER 5 Ha: 4 (19.7 x 18.3)ER (18.0 x 18.3) Cranes: 4x30t	**1 oil engine** driving 1 FP propeller Total Power: 9,480kW (12,889hp) 14.5kn MAN-B&W 6S50MC-C 1 x 2 Stroke 6 Cy. 500 x 2000 9480kW (12889bhp) STX Engine Co Ltd-South Korea
9613317 *V7AQ5* -	**STX DELICATA** **POS Maritime FA SA** STX Marine Service Co Ltd *Majuro* *Marshall Islands* MMSI: 538005048 Official number: 5048	**39,009** 16,720 56,473	Class: KR (NV)	**2013-05 STX Offshore & Shipbuilding Co Ltd — Changwon (Jinhae Shipyard)** Yd No: 1542 Loa 199.90 (BB) Br ex 32.32 Dght 12.700 Lbp 191.80 Br md 32.26 Dpth 19.30 Welded, 1 dk	**(A31A2GO) Open Hatch Cargo Ship** Grain: 62,500; Bale: 62,430 Compartments: 8 Ho, ER 8 Ha: 6 (18.4 x 28.2) (12.8 x 28.2)ER (12.0 x 18.0) Cranes: 4x45t	**1 oil engine** driving 1 FP propeller Total Power: 9,480kW (12,889hp) 14.5kn MAN-B&W 6S50MC-C 1 x 2 Stroke 6 Cy. 500 x 2000 9480kW (12889bhp) STX Engine Co Ltd-South Korea
9452828 *3FFJ8* -	**STX EASTERN** **POS Maritime TY SA** STX Marine Service Co Ltd *Panama* *Panama* MMSI: 371321000 Official number: 4135610	**8,231** 3,723 12,825 T/cm 21.8	Class: KR	**2009-09 STX Offshore & Shipbuilding Co Ltd — Busan** Yd No: 5036 Loa 120.00 (BB) Br ex - Dght 8.664 Lbp 113.29 Br md 20.40 Dpth 11.90 Welded, 1 dk	**(A12B2TR) Chemical/Products Tanker** Double Hull (13F) Liq: 12,982; Liq (Oil): 12,982 Cargo Heating Coils Compartments: 10 Wing Ta, 2 Wing Slop Ta, ER 10 Cargo Pump (s): 10x300m³/hr Manifold: Bow/CM: 45.4m	**1 oil engine** driving 1 FP propeller Total Power: 4,440kW (6,037hp) 13.6kn MAN-B&W 6S35MC 1 x 2 Stroke 6 Cy. 350 x 1400 4440kW (6037bhp) STX Engine Co Ltd-South Korea Thrusters: 1 Tunnel thruster (f) Fuel: 70.0 (d.f.) 545.0 (r.f.)
9468358 *3FGP4* -	**STX EMERALD** **POS Maritime MZ SA** Pan Ocean Co Ltd SatCom: Inmarsat C 437311710 *Panama* *Panama* MMSI: 373117000 Official number: 4375712	**92,071** 59,451 174,964 T/cm 120.8	Class: KR	**2012-04 New Times Shipbuilding Co Ltd — Jingjiang JS** Yd No: 0117619 Loa 291.80 (BB) Br ex 45.10 Dght 18.250 Lbp 282.20 Br md 45.00 Dpth 24.75 Welded, 1 dk	**(A21A2BC) Bulk Carrier** Grain: 198,000 Compartments: 9 Ho, ER 9 Ha: 4 (26.6 x 32.7)2 (24.8 x 32.7)ER 3 (25.7 x 32.7)	**1 oil engine** driving 1 FP propeller Total Power: 16,860kW (22,923hp) 14.5kn MAN-B&W 6S70MC 1 x 2 Stroke 6 Cy. 700 x 2674 16860kW (22923bhp) STX Engine Co Ltd-South Korea Fuel: 4700.0
9621405 *V7XV3* -	**STX ENERGEN** **POS Maritime ZZ SA** Pan Ocean Co Ltd *Majuro* *Marshall Islands* MMSI: 538004579 Official number: 4579	**44,098** 27,714 81,170 T/cm 71.9	Class: KR	**2012-03 New Times Shipbuilding Co Ltd — Jingjiang JS** Yd No: 0108202 Loa 229.00 (BB) Br ex 32.30 Dght 14.472 Lbp 225.50 Br md 32.26 Dpth 20.05 Welded, 1 dk	**(A21A2BC) Bulk Carrier** Grain: 97,000; Bale: 90,784 Compartments: 7 Ho, ER 7 Ha: 6 (17.3 x 15.0)ER (14.7 x 12.8) Cranes: 4x35t	**1 oil engine** driving 1 FP propeller Total Power: 9,800kW (13,324hp) 14.1kn MAN-B&W 5S60MC-C8 1 x 2 Stroke 5 Cy. 600 x 2400 9800kW (13324bhp) STX (Dalian) Engine Co Ltd-China Fuel: 2520.0
9452830 *3EWW5* -	**STX FORTE** **POS Maritime TY SA** STX Marine Service Co Ltd *Panama* *Panama* MMSI: 370265000 Official number: 4135810	**8,231** 3,723 12,814 T/cm 21.8	Class: KR	**2010-01 STX Offshore & Shipbuilding Co Ltd — Busan** Yd No: 5039 Loa 120.00 (BB) Br ex - Dght 8.650 Lbp 113.29 Br md 20.40 Dpth 11.90 Welded, 1 dk	**(A12B2TR) Chemical/Products Tanker** Double Hull (13F) Liq: 12,982; Liq (Oil): 12,982 Cargo Heating Coils Compartments: 10 Wing Ta, 2 Wing Slop Ta, ER 10 Cargo Pump (s): 10x300m³/hr Manifold: Bow/CM: 69.8m	**1 oil engine** driving 1 FP propeller Total Power: 4,008kW (5,449hp) 13.6kn MAN-B&W 6S35MC 1 x 2 Stroke 6 Cy. 350 x 1400 4008kW (5449bhp) STX Engine Co Ltd-South Korea AuxGen: 3 x 450V Thrusters: 1 Tunnel thruster (f) Fuel: 70.0 (d.f.) 540.0 (r.f.)
9444247 *V7SB5* -	**STX FREESIA** **POS Maritime OY SA** Pan Ocean Co Ltd SatCom: Inmarsat C 453834423 *Majuro* *Marshall Islands* MMSI: 538003616 Official number: 3616	**95,047** 60,025 180,736 T/cm 124.0	Class: KR	**2009-07 STX Offshore & Shipbuilding Co Ltd — Changwon (Jinhae Shipyard)** Yd No: 1302 Loa 292.00 (BB) Br ex - Dght 18.220 Lbp 283.00 Br md 45.00 Dpth 24.80 Welded, 1 dk	**(A21A2BC) Bulk Carrier** Double Bottom Entire Compartment Length Grain: 199,366 Compartments: 9 Ho, ER 9 Ha: 7 (15.8 x 20.4)ER 2 (15.8 x 15.3)	**1 oil engine** driving 1 FP propeller Total Power: 18,660kW (25,370hp) 14.3kn MAN-B&W 6S70MC-C 1 x 2 Stroke 6 Cy. 700 x 2800 18660kW (25370bhp) STX Engine Co Ltd-South Korea AuxGen: 3 x 850kW a.c Fuel: 230.0 (d.f.) 4105.0 (r.f.)
9449510 *V7TH8* -	**STX GLORIS** **POS Maritime PY SA** Pan Ocean Co Ltd *Majuro* *Marshall Islands* MMSI: 538003809 Official number: 3809	**20,763** 11,627 32,975 T/cm 46.1	Class: KR (CC)	**2010-02 Taizhou Maple Leaf Shipbuilding Co Ltd — Linhai ZJ** Yd No: 32500-018 Loa 179.90 (BB) Br ex - Dght 10.167 Lbp 171.50 Br md 28.40 Dpth 14.10 Welded, 1 dk	**(A31A2GO) Open Hatch Cargo Ship** Grain: 42,779; Bale: 42,565 Compartments: 5 Ho, ER 5 Ha: 3 (20.0 x 19.2) (18.4 x 19.2)ER (14.4 x 17.6) Cranes: 4x30.5t	**1 oil engine** driving 1 FP propeller Total Power: 6,480kW (8,810hp) 13.7kn MAN-B&W 6S42MC 1 x 2 Stroke 6 Cy. 420 x 1764 6480kW (8810bhp) STX Engine Co Ltd-South Korea
9468712 *3FQI* -	**STX GOLD** **POS Maritime OZ SA** Pan Ocean Co Ltd SatCom: Inmarsat B 356723000 *Panama* *Panama* MMSI: 356723000 Official number: 4316611A	**92,080** 59,495 175,089 T/cm 120.8	Class: KR (NV)	**2011-09 New Times Shipbuilding Co Ltd — Jingjiang JS** Yd No: 0117621 Loa 291.80 (BB) Br ex 45.03 Dght 18.286 Lbp 282.02 Br md 45.00 Dpth 24.75 Welded, 1 dk	**(A21A2BC) Bulk Carrier** Grain: 197,350 Compartments: 9 Ho, ER 9 Ha: 4 (26.6 x 32.7)2 (24.8 x 32.7)ER 3 (25.7 x 32.7)	**1 oil engine** driving 1 FP propeller Total Power: 16,860kW (22,923hp) 14.9kn MAN-B&W 6S70MC 1 x 2 Stroke 6 Cy. 700 x 2674 16860kW (22923bhp) STX Engine Co Ltd-South Korea Fuel: 4710.0
9341330 *H3TY* -	**STX HERO** *completed as* Marida Aiolos *-2009* **POS Maritime HY SA** STX Marine Service Co Ltd SatCom: Inmarsat C 435547713 *Panama* *Panama* MMSI: 355477000 Official number: 4075109	**10,549** 4,082 15,212 T/cm 26.9	Class: KR (NV)	**2009-07 STX RO Offshore Braila SA — Braila** (Hull) Yd No: 1092 **2009-07 STX Norway Offshore AS Brevik — Brevik** Yd No: 52 Loa 149.60 (BB) Br ex 22.03 Dght 8.500 Lbp 139.25 Br md 22.00 Dpth 12.95 Welded, 1 dk	**(A12B2TR) Chemical/Products Tanker** Double Hull (13F) Liq: 17,905; Liq (Oil): 17,905 Compartments: 14 Wing Ta, 2 Wing Slop Ta, ER 14 Cargo Pump (s): 14x350m³/hr Manifold: Bow/CM: 67.9m Ice Capable	**1 oil engine** reduction geared to sc. shaft driving 1 CP propeller Total Power: 5,760kW (7,831hp) 15.0kn MAN-B&W 8L40/54 1 x 4 Stroke 8 Cy. 400 x 540 5760kW (7831bhp) MAN B&W Diesel AG-Augsburg AuxGen: 3 x a.c Thrusters: 1 Tunnel thruster (f) Fuel: 52.0 (d.f.) 647.0 (r.f.)

9468724 **STX HOPE**
3EZL9
\- **POS Maritime HZ SA**
Pan Ocean Co Ltd
SatCom: Inmarsat C 437013710
Panama *Panama*
MMSI: 370137000
Official number: 4329811A

92,080 Class: KR (NV)
59,495
175,021
T/cm
120.8

2011-12 New Times Shipbuilding Co Ltd — Jingjiang JS Yd No: 0117622
Loa 291.80 (BB) Br ex 45.05 Dght 18.250
Lbp 282.22 Br md 45.00 Dpth 24.75
Welded, 1 dk

(A21A2BC) Bulk Carrier
Grain: 197,132; Bale: 191,218
Compartments: 9 Ho, ER
9 Ha: 4 (26.6 x 32.7)2 (24.8 x 32.7)ER 3 (25.7 x 32.7)

1 oil engine driving 1 FP propeller
Total Power: 16,860kW (22,923hp) 14.9kn
MAN-B&W 6S70MC
1 x 2 Stroke 6 Cy. 700 x 2674 16860kW (22923bhp)
STX Engine Co Ltd-South Korea
AuxGen: 3 x 900kW 450V a.c
Fuel: 4700.0

9341342 **STX INFINITY**
3FSV8
completed as Marida Okeanos *-2009*
\- **POS Maritime IY SA**
Pan Ocean Co Ltd
SatCom: Inmarsat C 435519510
Panama *Panama*
MMSI: 355195000
Official number: 4087109

10,549 Class: KR (NV)
4,082
15,212
T/cm
26.9

2009-07 STX RO Offshore Braila SA — Braila (Hull) Yd No: 1093
2009-07 STX Norway Offshore AS Brevik — Brevik Yd No: 53
Loa 149.60 (BB) Br ex 22.03 Dght 8.514
Lbp 139.25 Br md 22.00 Dpth 12.95
Welded, 1 dk

(A12B2TR) Chemical/Products Tanker
Double Hull (13F)
Liq: 17,905; Liq (Oil): 17,905
Compartments: 14 Wing Ta, 2 Wing Slop Ta, ER
14 Cargo Pump (s): 14x350m³/hr
Manifold: Bow/CM: 67.9m
Ice Capable

1 oil engine reduction geared to sc. shaft driving 1 CP propeller
Total Power: 5,760kW (7,831hp) 15.0kn
MAN-B&W 8L40/54
1 x 4 Stroke 8 Cy. 400 x 540 5760kW (7831bhp)
MAN B&W Diesel AG-Augsburg
AuxGen: 3 x 500kW 440V a.c
Thrusters: 1 Tunnel thruster (f)
Fuel: 59.0 (d.f.) 738.0 (r.f.)

9372963 **STX KOLT**
3FNM7
\- **KLT 5 International SA**
STX Marine Service Co Ltd
SatCom: Inmarsat C 437079910
Panama *Panama*
MMSI: 370799000
Official number: 4018609

100,189 Class: KR NV
30,065
86,778

2008-12 Hanjin Heavy Industries & Construction Co Ltd — Busan Yd No: 192
Loa 288.60 (BB) Br ex 44.04 Dght 12.500
Lbp 276.00 Br md 44.00 Dpth 26.20
Welded, 1 dk

(A11A2TN) LNG Tanker
Double Hull
Liq (Gas): 145,700
4 x Gas Tank (s); 4 membrane (s.stl) pri horizontal
8 Cargo Pump (s): 8x2800m³/hr

1 Steam Turb reduction geared to sc. shaft driving 1 FP propeller
Total Power: 29,273kW (39,800hp) 20.3kn
Kawasaki UA-400
1 x steam Turb 29273kW (39800shp)
Kawasaki Heavy Industries Ltd-Japan
AuxGen: 1 x 3500kW 6600V a.c, 2 x 3500kW 6600V a.c
Thrusters: 1 Tunnel thruster (f)
Fuel: 360.0 (d.f.) 6524.0 (r.f.) 239.0pd

9545297 **STX MARGARET**
3FFH3
\- **POS Maritime GB SA**
Pan Ocean Co Ltd
Panama *Panama*
MMSI: 353267000
Official number: 44202SC

95,047 Class: KR
60,025
180,705
T/cm
124.0

2013-02 STX Offshore & Shipbuilding Co Ltd — Changwon (Jinhae Shipyard) Yd No: 3025
Loa 292.00 (BB) Br ex - Dght 18.200
Lbp 283.00 Br md 45.00 Dpth 24.80
Welded, 1 dk

(A21A2BC) Bulk Carrier
Grain: 199,364
Compartments: 9 Ho, ER
9 Ha: 7 (15.8 x 20.4)ER 2 (15.8 x 15.3)

1 oil engine driving 1 FP propeller
Total Power: 18,623kW (25,320hp) 14.3kn
MAN-B&W 6S70MC-C
1 x 2 Stroke 6 Cy. 700 x 2800 18623kW (25320bhp)
STX Engine Co Ltd-South Korea

9621390 **STX MUTIARA**
V7XJ9
\- **POS Maritime YZ SA**
Pan Ocean Co Ltd
Majuro *Marshall Islands*
MMSI: 538004499
Official number: 4499

44,098 Class: KR
27,714
81,177
T/cm
71.9

2011-12 New Times Shipbuilding Co Ltd — Jingjiang JS Yd No: 0108201
Loa 229.00 (BB) Br ex 32.30 Dght 14.472
Lbp 224.79 Br md 32.26 Dpth 20.05
Welded, 1 dk

(A21A2BC) Bulk Carrier
Grain: 97,000; Bale: 90,784
Compartments: 7 Ho, ER
7 Ha: 6 (17.3 x 15.0)ER (14.7 x 12.8)
Cranes: 4x35t

1 oil engine driving 1 FP propeller
Total Power: 9,800kW (13,324hp) 14.0kn
MAN-B&W 5S60MC-C8
1 x 2 Stroke 5 Cy. 600 x 2400 9800kW (13324bhp)
STX (Dalian) Engine Co Ltd-China
Fuel: 2580.0

9487407 **STX PRIDE**
3FXC5
\- **POS Maritime BZ SA**
Pan Ocean Co Ltd
Panama *Panama*
MMSI: 371572000
Official number: 4271811

33,001 Class: KR
19,332
56,907
T/cm
58.8

2011-05 COSCO (Zhoushan) Shipyard Co Ltd — Zhoushan ZJ Yd No: N187
Loa 189.99 (BB) Br ex - Dght 12.818
Lbp 185.60 Br md 32.26 Dpth 18.00
Welded, 1 dk

(A21A2BC) Bulk Carrier
Grain: 71,634; Bale: 68,200
Compartments: 5 Ho, ER
5 Ha: 4 (21.3 x 18.3)ER (18.9 x 18.3)
Cranes: 4x30t

1 oil engine driving 1 FP propeller
Total Power: 9,480kW (12,889hp) 14.2kn
MAN-B&W 6S50MC-C
1 x 2 Stroke 6 Cy. 500 x 2000 9480kW (12889bhp)
STX Engine Co Ltd-South Korea

9487419 **STX QUEEN**
3FUP4
\- **POS Maritime CZ SA**
Pan Ocean Co Ltd
Panama *Panama*
MMSI: 354968000
Official number: 4272911

33,001 Class: KR
19,332
56,907
T/cm
58.8

2011-05 COSCO (Zhoushan) Shipyard Co Ltd — Zhoushan ZJ Yd No: N188
Loa 189.99 (BB) Br ex - Dght 12.818
Lbp 185.60 Br md 32.26 Dpth 18.00
Welded, 1 dk

(A21A2BC) Bulk Carrier
Grain: 71,634; Bale: 68,200
Compartments: 5 Ho, ER
5 Ha: 4 (21.3 x 18.3)ER (18.9 x 18.3)
Cranes: 4x30t

1 oil engine driving 1 FP propeller
Total Power: 9,480kW (12,889hp) 14.2kn
MAN-B&W 6S50MC-C
1 x 2 Stroke 6 Cy. 500 x 2000 9480kW (12889bhp)
STX (Dalian) Engine Co Ltd-China
AuxGen: 3 x 600kW 450V a.c

9487421 **STX RAPIDO**
3FQI8
\- **POS Maritime DZ SA**
Pan Ocean Co Ltd
Panama *Panama*
MMSI: 351878000
Official number: 41945SC

33,001 Class: KR
19,332
56,915
T/cm
58.8

2011-07 COSCO (Zhoushan) Shipyard Co Ltd — Zhoushan ZJ Yd No: N189
Loa 189.99 (BB) Br ex 32.30 Dght 12.818
Lbp 185.64 Br md 32.26 Dpth 18.00
Welded, 1 dk

(A21A2BC) Bulk Carrier
Grain: 71,634; Bale: 68,200
Compartments: 5 Ho, ER
5 Ha: 4 (21.3 x 18.3)ER (18.9 x 18.3)
Cranes: 4x30t

1 oil engine driving 1 FP propeller
Total Power: 9,480kW (12,889hp) 14.2kn
MAN-B&W 6S50MC-C
1 x 2 Stroke 6 Cy. 500 x 2000 9480kW (12889bhp)
STX Engine Co Ltd-South Korea
Fuel: 2280.0

9487433 **STX SPIRIT**
H3OR
\- **POS Maritime EZ SA**
Pan Ocean Co Ltd
Panama *Panama*
MMSI: 371334000
Official number: 4322311

33,001 Class: KR
19,332
56,891
T/cm
58.8

2011-10 COSCO (Zhoushan) Shipyard Co Ltd — Zhoushan ZJ Yd No: N190
Loa 189.99 (BB) Br ex 32.30 Dght 12.818
Lbp 185.60 Br md 32.26 Dpth 18.00
Welded, 1 dk

(A21A2BC) Bulk Carrier
Grain: 71,634; Bale: 68,200
Compartments: 5 Ho, ER
5 Ha: 4 (21.3 x 18.3)ER (18.9 x 18.3)
Cranes: 4x30t

1 oil engine driving 1 FP propeller
Total Power: 9,480kW (12,889hp) 14.2kn
MAN-B&W 6S50MC-C
1 x 2 Stroke 6 Cy. 500 x 2000 9480kW (12889bhp)
STX (Dalian) Engine Co Ltd-China
AuxGen: 3 x 600kW 450V a.c
Fuel: 2280.0

9625827 **STX TOPAZ**
3FMZ5
\- **POS Maritime WA SA**
STX Marine Service Co Ltd
SatCom: Inmarsat C 437307910
Panama *Panama*
MMSI: 373079000
Official number: 4373212

45,055 Class: KR
26,973
82,787
T/cm
71.9

2012-03 STX (Dalian) Shipbuilding Co Ltd — Wafangdian LN Yd No: D2051
Loa 229.00 (BB) Br ex - Dght 14.519
Lbp 225.50 Br md 32.24 Dpth 20.20
Welded, 1 dk

(A21A2BC) Bulk Carrier
Grain: 95,172
Compartments: 7 Ho, ER
7 Ha: 6 (17.2 x 15.0)ER (16.3 x 12.1)

1 oil engine driving 1 FP propeller
Total Power: 9,859kW (13,404hp) 14.5kn
MAN-B&W 6S60MC-C
1 x 2 Stroke 6 Cy. 600 x 2400 9859kW (13404bhp)
STX (Dalian) Engine Co Ltd-China
AuxGen: 3 x 615kW 450V 60Hz a.c
Fuel: 2160.0

9625839 **STX UNITY**
3EXM5
\- **POS Maritime XA SA**
Pan Ocean Co Ltd
Panama *Panama*
MMSI: 373572000
Official number: 4418512

45,055 Class: KR
26,973
82,709
T/cm
71.9

2012-08 STX (Dalian) Shipbuilding Co Ltd — Wafangdian LN Yd No: D2052
Loa 229.00 (BB) Br ex - Dght 14.519
Lbp 225.60 Br md 32.24 Dpth 20.20
Welded, 1 dk

(A21A2BC) Bulk Carrier
Grain: 95,172
Compartments: 7 Ho, ER
7 Ha: 6 (17.2 x 15.0)ER (16.3 x 12.1)

1 oil engine driving 1 FP propeller
Total Power: 9,659kW (13,132hp) 14.1kn
MAN-B&W 6S60MC-C
1 x 2 Stroke 6 Cy. 600 x 2400 9659kW (13132bhp)
STX (Dalian) Engine Co Ltd-China
AuxGen: 3 x 615kW 450V 60Hz a.c
Fuel: 2160.0

9453494 **STX VIVA**
3FDN3
ex Jing Lu 17 *-2010* *ex* Naruto *-2010*
\- **POS Maritime KZ SA**
STX Marine Service Co Ltd
SatCom: Inmarsat C 435784110
Panama *Panama*
MMSI: 357841000
Official number: 4232411

41,101 Class: KR (BV)
25,643
75,209
T/cm
68.3

2010-10 Penglai Zhongbai Jinglu Ship Industry Co Ltd — Penglai SD Yd No: JL0017 (B)
Loa 225.00 (BB) Br ex - Dght 14.219
Lbp 217.00 Br md 32.26 Dpth 19.60
Welded, 1 dk

(A21A2BC) Bulk Carrier
Grain: 89,728
Compartments: 7 Ho, ER
7 Ha: 6 (15.5 x 14.4)ER (14.6 x 13.2)

1 oil engine driving 1 FP propeller
Total Power: 11,300kW (15,363hp) 14.5kn
MAN-B&W 5S60MC-C
1 x 2 Stroke 5 Cy. 600 x 2400 11300kW (15363bhp)
Hyundai Heavy Industries Co Ltd-South Korea

9331476 **STYBARROW VENTURE MV16**
3EIX5
\- **Stybarrow MV 16 BV**
Modec Inc
SatCom: Inmarsat C 437229210
Panama *Panama*
MMSI: 372292000
Official number: 3333207A

83,245 Class: AB
47,688
155,273

2007-01 Samsung Heavy Industries Co Ltd — Geoje Yd No: 1579
Loa 274.60 (BB) Br ex - Dght 16.000
Lbp 264.50 Br md 49.00 Dpth 24.00
Welded, 1 dk

(B22E2OF) FPSO, Oil
Liq: 155,614; Liq (Oil): 155,614
Compartments: 12 Wing Ta, 2 Wing Slop Ta, ER

1 oil engine driving 1 FP propeller
Total Power: 17,091kW (23,237hp) 15.0kn
MAN-B&W 6S70MC-C
1 x 2 Stroke 6 Cy. 700 x 2800 17091kW (23237bhp)
Doosan Engine Co Ltd-South Korea
AuxGen: 3 x 840kW a.c
Fuel: 3121.0 (d.f.)

9380570 **STYLE**
9HBE9
ex Cargo *-2013*
\- **Style Shipping LLC**
Norient Product Pool ApS
Valletta *Malta*
MMSI: 256715000
Official number: 9380570

23,248 Class: NV (AB)
9,915
37,923
T/cm
45.2

2008-01 Hyundai Mipo Dockyard Co Ltd — Ulsan Yd No: 2030
Loa 184.32 (BB) Br ex 27.45 Dght 11.515
Lbp 176.00 Br md 27.40 Dpth 17.20
Welded, 1 dk

(A12B2TR) Chemical/Products Tanker
Double Hull (13F)
Liq: 40,781; Liq (Oil): 40,781
Compartments: 12 Wing Ta, 2 Wing Slop Ta, ER
12 Cargo Pump (s): 10x500m³/hr, 2x300m³/hr
Manifold: Bow/CM: 92.6m
Ice Capable

1 oil engine driving 1 FP propeller
Total Power: 9,480kW (12,889hp) 15.0kn
MAN-B&W 6S50MC-C
1 x 2 Stroke 6 Cy. 500 x 2000 9480kW (12889bhp)
Hyundai Heavy Industries Co Ltd-South Korea
AuxGen: 3 x 900kW a.c
Thrusters: 1 Tunnel thruster (f)

9600607 *9HA2535* -	**STYLIANI Z** **Ionia Shipping Overseas SA** Q-Shipping BV SatCom: Inmarsat C 424883110 *Valletta* *Malta* MMSI: 248831000 Official number: 9600607	**15,545** 8,149 25,000	Class: BV	**2011-01 Ningbo Xinle Shipbuilding Co Ltd — Ningbo ZJ** Yd No: XL-132 Loa 157.00 (BB) Br ex 24.83 Dght 9.800 Lbp 149.80 Br md 24.80 Dpth 13.70 Welded, 1 dk	**(A21A2BC) Bulk Carrier** Grain: 30,915; Bale: 30,297 Compartments: 4 Ho, ER 4 Ha: ER Cranes: 3x30t	**1 oil engine** driving 1 FP propeller Total Power: 4,900kW (6,662hp) 13.0kn MAN-B&W 7S35MC 1 x 2 Stroke 7 Cy. 350 x 1400 4900kW (6662bhp) STX Engine Co Ltd-South Korea AuxGen: 3 x 540kW 50Hz a.c
6403084 *LHBW* -	**STYRBJORN** *ex* Atlet *-1980* *ex* Styrbjorn *-1963* **Norsk Veteranskibsklub** - *Oslo* *Norway* MMSI: 258042500	**162** 48 -		**1910 AB Goteborgs Varv — Goteborg** Yd No: 318 L reg 28.56 Br ex 6.96 Dght - Lbp - Br md 6.91 Dpth - Riveted, 1 dk	**(B32A2ST) Tug**	**1 Steam Recip** driving 1 FP propeller Total Power: 198kW (269hp) 1 x Steam Recip. 198kW (269ihp) AB Goteborgs Varv-Sweden
9116084 *TCRW* -	**SU** *ex* Resit Atasoy *-2010* **HK Denizcilik Gemicilik ve Insaat Sanayi Ticaret AS** - SatCom: Inmarsat M 627110911 *Istanbul* *Turkey* MMSI: 271000423 Official number: 6889	**5,447** 3,336 8,258 T/cm 16.5	Class: BV	**1996-04 Gisa — Tuzla** Yd No: 16 Loa 116.00 (BB) Br ex - Dght 7.550 Lbp 107.32 Br md 17.20 Dpth 9.80 Welded, 1 dk	**(A31A2GX) General Cargo Ship** Grain: 11,404; Bale: 10,311 Compartments: 3 Ho, ER 3 Ha: (12.3 x 7.8) (25.4 x 12.8) (18.4 x 12.8)ER Cranes: 2x20t	**1 oil engine** with flexible couplings & sr gearedto sc. shaft driving 1 CP propeller Total Power: 3,643kW (4,953hp) 13.0kn Wartsila 9R32E 1 x 4 Stroke 9 Cy. 320 x 350 3643kW (4953bhp) Wartsila Diesel Oy-Finland AuxGen: 3 x 300kW 380V 50Hz a.c Fuel: 131.0 (d.f.) 320.0 (r.f.) 13.0pd
9129225 - -	**SU** *ex* Rubis Express *-2006* **National Infrastructure Development Co Ltd (NIDCO)** - *Port of Spain* *Trinidad & Tobago*	**630** 217 50	Class: (TL) (NV) (BV)	**1996-11 Marinteknik Shipbuilders (S) Pte Ltd — Singapore** Yd No: 136 Loa 45.00 Br ex - Dght - Lbp 38.60 Br md 11.00 Dpth - Welded, 1dk	**(A37B2PS) Passenger Ship** Hull Material: Aluminium Alloy Passengers: unberthed: 445	**4 oil engines** reduction geared to sc. shafts driving 4 Water jets 42.0kn M.T.U. 16V396TE74L 4 x Vee 4 Stroke 16 Cy. 165 x 185 MTU Friedrichshafen GmbH-Friedrichshafen
9472957 *TCTO3* -	**SU-B** **Viya Denizcilik Sanayi ve Ticaret Ltd Sti** - *Istanbul* *Turkey* MMSI: 271002706	**1,324** 567 1,845 T/cm 6.1	Class: (BV)	**2009-02 Cide Gemi ve Yat Sanayi Ticaret AS — Cide** Yd No: 01 Loa 77.86 (BB) Br ex - Dght 4.274 Lbp 71.81 Br md 10.60 Dpth 5.10 Welded, 1 dk	**(A12B2TR) Chemical/Products Tanker** Double Hull (13F) Liq: 2,085; Liq (Oil): 2,085 Cargo Heating Coils Compartments: 10 Wing Ta, 1 Slop Ta, ER 4 Cargo Pump (s): 2x291m³/hr, 2x411m³/hr Manifold: Bow/CM: 41m	**1 oil engine** reduction geared to sc. shaft driving 1 CP propeller Total Power: 960kW (1,305hp) 11.0kn MAN-B&W 6L23/30A 1 x 4 Stroke 6 Cy. 225 x 300 960kW (1305bhp) MAN Diesel A/S-Denmark AuxGen: 2 x 312kW 50Hz a.c Thrusters: 1 Tunnel thruster (f) Fuel: 83.0 (d.f.)
8850011 *P5JN* -	**SU CHAE BONG 1** *ex* Kinsho Maru No. 21 *-2002* **Rajin Export Fishery Co** - *Rajin* *North Korea* Official number: 2707217	**209** 77 117		**1977 KK Toyo Zosen Tekkosho — Kamaishi IW** Loa 36.60 Br ex - Dght - Lbp - Br md 6.36 Dpth 2.50 Welded, 1 dk	**(B11B2FV) Fishing Vessel**	**1 oil engine** driving 1 FP propeller Total Power: 346kW (470hp) Matsui 1 x 4 Stroke 346kW (470bhp) Matsui Iron Works Co Ltd-Japan
8106642 *D7KW* -	**SU HAE No. 1** *ex* Seo Hae No. 1 *-1990* *ex* Yawata Maru No. 1 *-1987* **Il Woo Maritime Corp** - *Yeosu* *South Korea* MMSI: 440317130 Official number: YSR-873151	*302* 175 -	Class: KR	**1981-05 Towa Zosen K.K. — Shimonoseki** Yd No: 534 Loa 34.02 Br ex 9.63 Dght 3.150 Lbp 29.01 Br md 9.61 Dpth 4.30 Welded, 1 dk	**(B32A2ST) Tug**	**2 oil engines** geared to sc. shafts driving 2 Directional propellers Total Power: 2,500kW (3,400hp) 13.7kn Fuji 6L27.5G 2 x 4 Stroke 6 Cy. 275 x 320 each-1250kW (1700bhp) Fuji Diesel Co Ltd-Japan AuxGen: 2 x 44kW 225V a.c
8865547 - -	**SU HAE NO. 7** *ex* Iseshio *-2000* **Il Woo Maritime Corp** - *Yeosu* *South Korea* Official number: YSR-995717	*208* - -	Class: KR	**1989-12 Kanbara Zosen K.K. — Onomichi** Yd No: 395 Loa 33.52 Br ex - Dght 3.100 Lbp 28.00 Br md 9.60 Dpth 4.09 Welded, 1 dk	**(B32A2ST) Tug**	**2 oil engines** with clutches, flexible couplings & dr reverse geared to sc. shafts driving 2 FP propellers Total Power: 2,648kW (3,600hp) 13.5kn Niigata 6L28HX 2 x 4 Stroke 6 Cy. 280 x 370 each-1324kW (1800bhp) Niigata Engineering Co Ltd-Japan AuxGen: 2 x 160kW a.c
8875994 *DSDA250* -	**SU HYUP HO No. 1** **National Federation of Fisheries Cooperatives** - *Ulsan* *South Korea* Official number: USR-947725	**131** - 289	Class: (KR)	**1994 Kyungnam Shipbuilding Co Ltd — Busan** Yd No: 93-5 Loa 36.17 Br ex - Dght - Lbp 32.00 Br md 6.20 Dpth 3.20 Welded, 1 dk	**(A13B2TU) Tanker (unspecified)**	**1 oil engine** driving 1 FP propeller Total Power: 419kW (570hp) 10.2kn Yanmar 6LAH-STE3 1 x 4 Stroke 6 Cy. 150 x 165 419kW (570bhp) Kwangyang Diesel Engine Co Ltd-South Korea AuxGen: 3 x 54kW 445V a.c Fuel: 8.0 (d.f.)
7221110 *D9AD* -	**SU HYUP No. 1** **National Federation of Fisheries Cooperatives** - *Incheon* *South Korea* Official number: ICR-670350	*306* 189 413	Class: (KR)	**1968 Dae Sun Shipbuilding & Engineering Co Ltd — Busan** Loa 43.79 Br ex 7.24 Dght - Lbp 39.02 Br md 7.22 Dpth 3.41 Welded, 1 dk	**(A13B2TU) Tanker (unspecified)** Liq: 583; Liq (Oil): 583	**1 oil engine** driving 1 FP propeller Total Power: 405kW (551hp) 10.8kn Niigata 6M26HS 1 x 4 Stroke 6 Cy. 260 x 400 405kW (551bhp) Niigata Engineering Co Ltd-Japan AuxGen: 2 x 32kW 230V a.c
7221134 *D8OZ* -	**SU HYUP No. 3** **Park Jae-Sung** - *Incheon* *South Korea* Official number: ICR-680400	*120* 62 196	Class: (KR)	**1969 Busan Shipbuilding Co Ltd — Busan** Loa 30.51 Br ex 5.44 Dght - Lbp 27.41 Br md 5.41 Dpth 2.49 Welded, 1 dk	**(A13B2TU) Tanker (unspecified)** Liq: 190; Liq (Oil): 190	**1 oil engine** driving 1 FP propeller Total Power: 147kW (200hp) 10.8kn Niigata 6MG16 1 x 4 Stroke 6 Cy. 160 x 200 147kW (200bhp) Niigata Engineering Co Ltd-Japan AuxGen: 2 x 15kW 230V a.c
8832772 *BHUA* -	**SU LIAN YU 601** **Lianyungang Ocean Fisheries Co** - *Lianyungang, Jiangsu* *China*	*274* 86 106	Class: (CC)	**1987 Lianyungang Fishing Vessel Shipyard — Lianyungang JS** Loa 43.50 Br ex - Dght 2.800 Lbp 37.00 Br md 7.60 Dpth 3.80 Welded, 1 dk	**(B11B2FV) Fishing Vessel**	**1 oil engine** geared to sc. shaft driving 1 FP propeller Total Power: 441kW (600hp) 12.0kn Chinese Std. Type 8300 1 x 4 Stroke 8 Cy. 300 x 380 441kW (600bhp) Zibo Diesel Engine Factory-China AuxGen: 2 x 64kW 400V a.c
8832760 - -	**SU LIAN YU 602** **Lianyungang Ocean Fisheries Co** - *Lianyungang, Jiangsu* *China*	*274* 86 106	Class: (CC)	**1987 Lianyungang Fishing Vessel Shipyard — Lianyungang JS** Loa 43.50 Br ex - Dght 2.800 Lbp 37.00 Br md 7.60 Dpth 3.80 Welded, 1 dk	**(B11B2FV) Fishing Vessel**	**1 oil engine** geared to sc. shaft driving 1 FP propeller Total Power: 441kW (600hp) 12.0kn Chinese Std. Type 8300 1 x 4 Stroke 8 Cy. 300 x 380 441kW (600bhp) Zibo Diesel Engine Factory-China AuxGen: 2 x 64kW 400V a.c
9109885 *BAOX* -	**SU RUI 139** *ex* Gas Tabangao *-2006* **Dalian Surui Shipping Co Ltd** - *Dalian, Liaoning* *China* MMSI: 413232000	**3,496** 1,049 3,045 T/cm 12.5	Class: CC (NK)	**1995-05 Fukuoka Shipbuilding Co Ltd — Fukuoka FO** Yd No: 1185 Loa 94.50 (BB) Br ex - Dght 4.514 Lbp 88.50 Br md 16.60 Dpth 7.10 Welded, 1 dk	**(A11B2TG) LPG Tanker** Liq (Gas): 3,514 2 x Gas Tank (s); 2 independent (C.mn.stl) cyl horizontal 2 Cargo Pump (s): 2x300m³/hr Manifold: Bow/CM: 47m	**1 oil engine** driving 1 FP propeller Total Power: 2,405kW (3,270hp) 13.0kn B&W 6S26MC 1 x 2 Stroke 6 Cy. 260 x 980 2405kW (3270bhp) Makita Corp-Japan
9142966 *BAHD* -	**SU RUI 169** *ex* Su Rui *-2007* *ex* Chepstow *-2007* **Dalian Surui Shipping Co Ltd** - *Dalian, Liaoning* *China* MMSI: 413313000	**4,484** 1,346 5,242 T/cm 15.4	Class: CC (NK)	**1996-08 Higaki Zosen K.K. — Imabari** Yd No: 468 Loa 99.95 (BB) Br ex 19.63 Dght 5.650 Lbp 94.90 Br md 19.60 Dpth 7.70 Welded, 1 dk	**(A11B2TG) LPG Tanker** Double Hull Liq (Gas): 5,016 2 x Gas Tank (s); 2 independent (C.mn.stl) horizontal 2 Cargo Pump (s): 2x300m³/hr Manifold: Bow/CM: 46.4m	**1 oil engine** driving 1 FP propeller Total Power: 3,884kW (5,281hp) 13.5kn B&W 6L35MC 1 x 2 Stroke 6 Cy. 350 x 1050 3884kW (5281bhp) The Hanshin Diesel Works Ltd-Japan AuxGen: 2 x a.c Fuel: 115.1 (d.f.) 546.9 (r.f.)
8029985 *HMYU9* -	**SU SAM 1** *ex* Zhu Yuan Hao *-2011* *ex* Houyou Maru *-2006* *ex* Kami Maru No. 11 *-2004* **Korea Kangsong Trading Co** - *Sinuiju* *North Korea* MMSI: 445454000 Official number: 3105580	**1,401** 857 1,000	Class: IC	**1981-04 K.K. Yoshida Zosen Kogyo — Arida** Yd No: 357 Loa - Br ex - Dght - Lbp 66.02 Br md 12.01 Dpth 6.46 Welded, 1 dk	**(A31A2GX) General Cargo Ship**	**1 oil engine** driving 1 FP propeller Total Power: 1,324kW (1,800hp) Makita GSLH633 1 x 4 Stroke 6 Cy. 330 x 530 1324kW (1800bhp) Makita Diesel Co Ltd-Japan

8955366 *BUSI* -	**SU SHUN** **Changjiang LPG Transport & Trade Co Ltd** - *Nanjing, Jiangsu* *China* MMSI: 412077250	**1,918** 1,074 1,221	Class: CC	**1998-10 Qingshan Shipyard — Wuhan HB** Loa 81.30 Br ex - Dght 3.920 Lbp 75.60 Br md 13.60 Dpth 6.00 Welded, 1 dk	**(A11B2TG) LPG Tanker** Liq (Gas): 1,180 2 x Gas Tank (s); 2 independent cyl horizontal	**2 oil engines** geared to sc. shafts driving 2 FP propellers Total Power: 1,624kW (2,208hp) 11.7kn Chinese Std. Type 6300 2 x 4 Stroke 6 Cy. 300 x 380 each-812kW (1104bhp) Guangzhou Diesel Engine Factory CoLtd-China AuxGen: 3 x 156kW 400V a.c
7402178 *HMYM* -	**SU SONG CHON** *ex* Haigum 31 *ex* Fukuichi Maru No. 68 *ex* Kaiho Maru No. 18 **Korea Kumbyol Trading Co** - *Wonsan* *North Korea* Official number: 2402051	**284** 141 736	Class: KC	**1974-05 Miho Zosensho K.K. — Shimizu** Yd No: 926 Converted From: Fishing Vessel-1974 Loa 50.42 Br ex 8.44 Dght 3.050 Lbp 42.98 Br md 8.41 Dpth 3.38 Welded, 1 dk	**(B12B2FC) Fish Carrier**	**1 oil engine** driving 1 FP propeller Total Power: 809kW (1,100hp) Akasaka AH28 1 x 4 Stroke 6 Cy. 280 x 440 809kW (1100bhp) Akasaka Tekkosho KK (Akasaka DieselLtd)-Japan
8600911 *VVJQ* -	**SU WANG** **Four Seasons Fisheries (Pvt) Ltd** - *Visakhapatnam* *India* Official number: 2156	*116* 35 82	Class: (IR) (AB)	**1987-01 Alcock, Ashdown & Co. Ltd. — Bhavnagar** Yd No: 133 Loa 23.50 Br ex 7.45 Dght 2.650 Lbp 20.40 Br md 7.21 Dpth 3.41 Welded, 1 dk	**(B11A2FT) Trawler** Ins: 70	**1 oil engine** with clutches & sr reverse geared to sc. shaft driving 1 FP propeller Total Power: 296kW (402hp) 9.5kn Caterpillar 3408T 1 x Vee 4 Stroke 8 Cy. 137 x 152 296kW (402bhp) Caterpillar Inc-USA AuxGen: 2 x 40kW 440V 50Hz a.c Fuel: 49.0 (d.f.)
8312435 *HMYB* -	**SU YANG SAN 2** *ex* Xin Xin *-2013* *ex* New Lucky III *-2008* *ex* Kitty *-2003* **Korea Suyangsan Shipping Co** - *North Korea*	**2,669** 1,530 3,920	Class: (NK)	**1984-03 Kinoura Zosen K.K. — Imabari** Yd No: 112 Loa 86.34 Br ex - Dght 6.128 Lbp 80.02 Br md 14.00 Dpth 8.72 Welded, 2 dks	**(A31A2GX) General Cargo Ship** Grain: 6,277; Bale: 5,618 Compartments: 2 Ho, ER, 2 Tw Dk 2 Ha: (14.0 x 8.4) (27.3 x 8.4)ER Derricks: 3x25t	**1 oil engine** driving 1 FP propeller Total Power: 1,618kW (2,200hp) 11.0kn Akasaka A34 1 x 4 Stroke 6 Cy. 340 x 660 1618kW (2200bhp) Akasaka Tekkosho KK (Akasaka DieselLtd)-Japan AuxGen: 2 x 120kW Fuel: 50.0 (d.f.) 224.0 (r.f.) 6.0pd
9586851 *BHWJ* -	**SU YOU HAO** **Jiangsu Oil Exploration Corp** - *Yangzhou, Jiangsu* *China* MMSI: 412360970 Official number: 090030	**476** 143 106	Class: CC	**2011-08 Jiangsu Zhenjiang Shipyard Co Ltd — Zhenjiang JS** Yd No: 1-804 Loa 46.80 Br ex 9.75 Dght 1.900 Lbp 38.00 Br md 8.80 Dpth 3.70 Welded, 1 dk	**(B31A2SR) Research Survey Vessel** Ice Capable	**2 oil engines** reduction geared to sc. shafts driving 2 Propellers Total Power: 676kW (920hp) 10.0kn Cummins KTA-19-M500 2 x 4 Stroke 6 Cy. 159 x 159 each-338kW (460bhp) Chongqing Cummins Engine Co Ltd-China AuxGen: 2 x 150kW 400V a.c
8832801 *BHOP* -	**SU YU 601** **Jiangsu Province Marine Fishing Co** - *Shanghai* *China*	*272* 82 -	Class: (CC)	**1985 Ningbo Fishing Vessel Shipyard — Ningbo ZJ** Loa 43.50 Br ex - Dght 2.860 Lbp 37.00 Br md 7.60 Dpth 3.80 Welded, 1 dk	**(B11B2FV) Fishing Vessel**	**1 oil engine** geared to sc. shaft driving 1 FP propeller Total Power: 441kW (600hp) 12.0kn Chinese Std. Type 8300 1 x 4 Stroke 8 Cy. 300 x 380 441kW (600bhp) Zibo Diesel Engine Factory-China AuxGen: 2 x 64kW 400V a.c
8832813 - -	**SU YU 602** **Jiangsu Province Marine Fishing Co** - *Shanghai* *China*	*274* 82 -	Class: (CC)	**1985 Ningbo Fishing Vessel Shipyard — Ningbo ZJ** Loa 43.50 Br ex - Dght 2.760 Lbp 37.00 Br md 7.60 Dpth 3.80 Welded, 1 dk	**(B11B2FV) Fishing Vessel**	**1 oil engine** geared to sc. shaft driving 1 FP propeller Total Power: 441kW (600hp) 12.0kn Chinese Std. Type 8300 1 x 4 Stroke 8 Cy. 300 x 380 441kW (600bhp) Zibo Diesel Engine Factory-China AuxGen: 2 x 64kW 400V a.c
8832825 *BHOQ* -	**SU YU 603** **Jiangsu Province Marine Fishing Co** - *Shanghai* *China*	*274* 82 131	Class: (CC)	**1986 Jiangsu Marine Fishing Co Fishing Vessel Shipyard — Taicang JS** Loa 43.50 Br ex - Dght 2.760 Lbp 37.00 Br md 7.60 Dpth 3.80 Welded, 1 dk	**(B11B2FV) Fishing Vessel**	**1 oil engine** geared to sc. shaft driving 1 FP propeller Total Power: 441kW (600hp) 12.0kn Chinese Std. Type 8300 1 x 4 Stroke 8 Cy. 300 x 380 441kW (600bhp) Wuxi Antai Power Machinery Co Ltd-China AuxGen: 2 x 64kW 400V a.c
8832837 - -	**SU YU 604** **Jiangsu Province Marine Fishing Co** - *Shanghai* *China*	*274* 82 131	Class: (CC)	**1986 Jiangsu Marine Fishing Co Fishing Vessel Shipyard — Taicang JS** Loa 43.50 Br ex - Dght 2.760 Lbp 37.00 Br md 7.60 Dpth 3.80 Welded, 1 dk	**(B11B2FV) Fishing Vessel**	**1 oil engine** geared to sc. shaft driving 1 FP propeller Total Power: 441kW (600hp) 12.0kn Chinese Std. Type 8300 1 x 4 Stroke 8 Cy. 300 x 380 441kW (600bhp) Wuxi Antai Power Machinery Co Ltd-China AuxGen: 2 x 64kW 400V a.c
8832849 *BHPW* -	**SU YU 605** **Jiangsu Province Marine Fishing Co** - *Liuhe, Jiangsu* *China*	*274* 86 129	Class: (CC)	**1987 Lianyungang Fishing Vessel Shipyard — Lianyungang JS** Loa 43.50 Br ex - Dght 2.800 Lbp 37.00 Br md 7.60 Dpth 3.80 Welded, 1 dk	**(B11B2FV) Fishing Vessel**	**1 oil engine** geared to sc. shaft driving 1 FP propeller Total Power: 441kW (600hp) 12.0kn Chinese Std. Type 8300 1 x 4 Stroke 8 Cy. 300 x 380 441kW (600bhp) Wuxi Antai Power Machinery Co Ltd-China AuxGen: 2 x 64kW 400V a.c
8832851 - -	**SU YU 606** **Jiangsu Province Marine Fishing Co** - *Liuhe, Jiangsu* *China*	*274* 86 129	Class: (CC)	**1987 Jiangsu Marine Fishing Co Fishing Vessel Shipyard — Taicang JS** Loa 43.50 Br ex - Dght 2.800 Lbp 37.00 Br md 7.60 Dpth 3.80 Welded, 1 dk	**(B11B2FV) Fishing Vessel**	**1 oil engine** geared to sc. shaft driving 1 FP propeller Total Power: 441kW (600hp) 12.0kn Chinese Std. Type 8300 1 x 4 Stroke 8 Cy. 300 x 380 441kW (600bhp) Wuxi Antai Power Machinery Co Ltd-China AuxGen: 2 x 64kW 400V a.c
9030632 *BOAM* -	**SU ZHOU HAO** *ex* Lu Xun *-1993* **Shanghai International Ferry Co Ltd** - SatCom: Inmarsat A 1571511 *Shanghai* *China* MMSI: 412395000	**14,410** 4,371 2,235	Class: CC (NK)	**1992-04 Shin Kurushima Dockyard Co. Ltd. — Onishi** Yd No: 2721 Loa 154.73 (BB) Br ex - Dght 6.015 Lbp 140.00 Br md 22.00 Dpth 9.85 Welded, 1 dk	**(A36A2PR) Passenger/Ro-Ro Ship (Vehicles)** Passengers: 322 Angled stern door/ramp (s) Len: 20.00 Wid: 8.00 Swl: 55 Lane-Len: 600 TEU 200 Compartments: 1 Cell Ho, ER	**2 oil engines** driving 2 FP propellers Total Power: 12,358kW (16,802hp) 21.0kn Mitsubishi 7UEC45LA 2 x 2 Stroke 7 Cy. 450 x 1350 each-6179kW (8401bhp) Kobe Hatsudoki KK-Japan AuxGen: 3 x 680kW 450V 60Hz a.c Thrusters: 1 Thwart. FP thruster (f)
9000376 *HOZZ* -	**SUAH** *ex* Astra *-2011* *ex* Frio Olympic *-2004* *ex* Reefer Pegasus *-2000* **Nok Co Ltd SA** Khana Marine Ltd *Panama* *Panama* MMSI: 356386000 Official number: 4337912	**4,444** 2,287 5,591	Class: NK (BV) (NV)	**1990-12 Kyokuyo Shipyard Corp — Shimonoseki YC** Yd No: 363 Loa 120.70 (BB) Br ex - Dght 7.110 Lbp 112.90 Br md 16.60 Dpth 10.00 Welded, 1dk, 2nd & 3rd dk in holds only	**(A34A2GR) Refrigerated Cargo Ship** Ins: 6,711 Compartments: 3 Ho, ER, 6 Tw Dk 3 Ha: (7.1 x 5.4)2 (7.1 x 6.4)ER Derricks: 6x5t	**1 oil engine** driving 1 FP propeller Total Power: 4,120kW (5,602hp) 15.8kn Mitsubishi 8UEC37LA 1 x 2 Stroke 8 Cy. 370 x 880 4120kW (5602bhp) Kobe Hatsudoki KK-Japan AuxGen: 4 x 306kW a.c Fuel: 880.0
5342702 - -	**SUAKIN** *ex* El Suakin *-1958* **Government of The Democratic Republic of The Sudan (Railways Department)** - *Sudan*	*162* - -	Class: (LR) ✠	**1951-08 Scott & Sons — Bowling** Yd No: 394 Loa 29.39 Br ex 7.37 Dght 2.960 Lbp - Br md - Dpth - Riveted, 1 dk	**(B32A2ST) Tug**	**1 Steam Recip** driving 1 FP propeller Total Power: 368kW (500hp) 1 x Steam Recip. 368kW (500ihp) Plenty & Son Ltd.-Newbury
6603713 *EEWH* -	**SUANCES** *launched as* J. C. P.-G. 8 *-1966* **Naviera Peninsular SA & Manipulaciones Ferreas del Norte SL** - *Cadiz* *Spain* Official number: 5-1/1998	*998* 511 -	Class: (LR) ✠ Classed LR until 16/1/76	**1966-11 Sociedad Espanola de Construccion Naval SA — Puerto Real** Yd No: 124 Loa 61.02 Br ex 11.74 Dght 4.058 Lbp 57.99 Br md 11.50 Dpth 4.81 Welded, 1 dk	**(B34A2SH) Hopper, Motor**	**1 oil engine** driving 1 FP propeller Total Power: 809kW (1,100hp) 10.0kn Stork 1 x 4 Stroke 8 Cy. 270 x 500 809kW (1100bhp) Naval Stork Werkspoor SA-Spain
9222974 *A8AW2* -	**SUAPE EXPRESS** *ex* E. R. Kobe *-2011* *ex* CSCL Kobe *-2011* *launched as* E. R. Kobe *-2001* **Reederei ms 'ER Kobe' Beteiligungs GmbH & Co KG** ER Schiffahrt GmbH & Cie KG *Monrovia* *Liberia* MMSI: 636090587 Official number: 90587	**66,058** 34,043 68,196	Class: GL	**2001-06 Samsung Heavy Industries Co Ltd — Geoje** Yd No: 1350 Loa 277.22 (BB) Br ex - Dght 14.000 Lbp 263.15 Br md 40.00 Dpth 24.30 Welded, 1 dk	**(A33A2CC) Container Ship (Fully Cellular)** TEU 5762 C Ho 2602 TEU C Dk 3160 TEU incl 500 ref C. Compartments: ER, 8 Cell Ho 15 Ha: (12.7 x 17.7) (12.7 x 25.9) (12.7 x 31.0)ER 10 (12.7 x 36.2)2 (12.7 x 21.2)	**1 oil engine** driving 1 FP propeller Total Power: 54,898kW (74,639hp) 24.9kn B&W 12K90MC 1 x 2 Stroke 12 Cy. 900 x 2550 54898kW (74639bhp) Doosan Engine Co Ltd-South Korea AuxGen: 4 x 2200kW a.c Thrusters: 1 Thwart. CP thruster (f) Fuel: 310.7 (d.f.) (Heating Coils) 5676.4 (r.f.) 228.0pd

Ship	Tonnage	Class	Build / Dimensions	Type	Machinery
9250000 **SUAR VIGO** *ECDY* - **Flota Suardiaz SL** - SatCom: Inmarsat C 422449930 *Santa Cruz de Tenerife* *Spain (CSR)* MMSI: 224499000 Official number: 15/2003	**16,361** 4,908 4,500	Class: LR ✠ **100A1** SS 12/2013 roll on - roll off cargo ship LI *IWS ✠ **LMC** **UMS** Eq.Ltr: C†; Cable: 550.0/54.0 U3 (a)	**2003-12 Hijos de J. Barreras S.A. — Vigo** Yd No: 1593 Loa 149.38 (BB) Br ex 21.44 Dght 6.014 Lbp 139.50 Br md 21.00 Dpth 20.69 Welded, 7 dks	**(A35B2RV) Vehicles Carrier** Stern door/ramp (centre) Len: 5.70 Wid: 15.85 Swl: 76 Lane-Len: 1500 Cars: 1,404	**2 oil engines** with clutches, flexible couplings & sr geared to sc. shafts driving 2 CP propellers Total Power: 12,960kW (17,620hp) 18.5kn MAN 9L40/54 2 x 4 Stroke 9 Cy. 400 x 540 each-6480kW (8810bhp) MAN B&W Diesel AG-Augsburg AuxGen: 2 x 648kW 400V 50Hz a.c, 2 x 648kW 400V 50Hz a.c Boilers: AuxB (Comp) 8.2kgf/cm² (8.0bar) Thrusters: 1 Thwart. CP thruster (f)
7933270 **SUARAN PERMAI** *YGYM* *ex* Miracle I *-2001* *ex* Koryu Maru *-1994* - **PT Samudra Alam Raya** - *Surabaya* *Indonesia*	**1,246** 623 1,599	Class: KI (KR)	**1979-08 Mategata Zosen K.K. — Namikata** Yd No: 163 Loa 65.60 Br ex - Dght 4.290 Lbp - Br md 11.51 Dpth 6.30 Welded, 1 dk	**(A31A2GX) General Cargo Ship**	**1 oil engine** driving 1 FP propeller Total Power: 1,177kW (1,600hp) Hanshin 6LU35 1 x 4 Stroke 6 Cy. 350 x 550 1177kW (1600bhp) The Hanshin Diesel Works Ltd-Japan
9070515 **SUAT BEY** *3FMY4* *ex* Nady *-2009* *ex* Forest-1 *-2008* - *ex* Fergana *-1997* **A&D Ship Management Co SA** Team Gemi Kiralama ve Acenteligi Ltd Sti (Team Chartering & Shipping Services Ltd) *Panama* *Panama* MMSI: 356959000 Official number: 4130610	**2,608** 1,158 3,114	Class: RS (NV) (GL) (RN)	**1993-06 Societatea Comerciala Severnav S.A. — Drobeta-Turnu Severin** Yd No: 008 Loa 86.04 (BB) Br ex - Dght 5.553 Lbp 79.84 Br md 14.50 Dpth 6.70 Welded, 1 dk	**(A31A2GX) General Cargo Ship** Grain: 4,122; Bale: 4,038 TEU 96 C. 96/20' Compartments: 2 Ho, ER 2 Ha: ER	**1 oil engine** driving 1 FP propeller Total Power: 1,802kW (2,450hp) 13.0kn B&W 4L35MCE 1 x 2 Stroke 4 Cy. 350 x 1050 1802kW (2450bhp) Hudong Shipyard-China AuxGen: 2 x 264kW 220/380V a.c
9391452 **SUAT KARABEKIR** *TCTA9* - **Kerem Denizcilik ve Ticaret Ltd** Karma Gemi Isletmeciligi ve Ticaret Ltd Sti *Istanbul* *Turkey* MMSI: 271001038	**4,179** 2,144 6,000	Class: BV	**2008-06 Gisan Gemi Ins. San — Istanbul** Yd No: 41 Loa 100.30 (BB) Br ex - Dght 6.750 Lbp 90.54 Br md 17.00 Dpth 8.64 Welded, 1 dk	**(A31A2GX) General Cargo Ship** Grain: 7,715	**1 oil engine** reduction geared to sc. shaft driving 1 CP propeller Total Power: 2,998kW (4,076hp) 11.0kn MaK 6M32C 1 x 4 Stroke 6 Cy. 320 x 480 2998kW (4076bhp) (new engine 2008) Caterpillar Motoren GmbH & Co. KG-Germany AuxGen: 2 x 244kW a.c
8037748 **SUBA SUBA** - *ex* Shamrock Girls *-2007* *ex* Cajun Girls *-2001* - **Sergio Valenciano Ulloa** - *San Lorenzo* *Honduras* Official number: L-1528236	*161* 114 -		**1980 at Biloxi, Ms** L reg 25.30 Br ex 7.17 Dght 2.820 Lbp - Br md - Dpth 3.26 Welded, 1 dk	**(B11B2FV) Fishing Vessel**	**1 oil engine** driving 1 FP propeller Total Power: 515kW (700hp)
9296561 **SUBAHI** - - **Government of The State of Kuwait (Coast Guard)** - *Kuwait*	**185** 55 15	Class: (LR) ✠ 20/8/03	**2003-09 OCEA SA — St-Nazaire** Yd No: 308 Loa 35.20 Br ex 7.17 Dght 1.230 Lbp 29.85 Br md 6.80 Dpth 3.80 Welded, 1 dk	**(B34H2SQ) Patrol Vessel** Hull Material: Aluminium Alloy	**2 oil engines** with clutches, flexible couplings & sr reverse geared to sc. shafts driving 2 Water jets Total Power: 3,480kW (4,732hp) M.T.U. 12V4000M70 2 x Vee 4 Stroke 12 Cy. 165 x 190 each-1740kW (2366bhp) MTU Friedrichshafen GmbH-Friedrichshafen AuxGen: 2 x 78kW 415V 50Hz a.c
8993734 **SUBALI I** - - **PT Pelabuhan Indonesia III (Persero) (Indonesia Port Corp III) (PELINDO III)** - *Surabaya* *Indonesia*	*191* 57 -	Class: KI	**1990-06 PT Dumas — Surabaya** Loa 27.75 Br ex - Dght 1.400 Lbp 25.25 Br md 8.60 Dpth 2.70 Welded, 1 dk	**(B32A2ST) Tug**	**2 oil engines** geared to sc. shafts driving 2 Propellers Total Power: 840kW (1,142hp) 12.4kn MAN D2842LE 2 x Vee 4 Stroke 12 Cy. 128 x 142 each-420kW (571bhp) (, fitted 1985) MAN Nutzfahrzeuge AG-Nuernberg
8993746 **SUBALI II** *YD5010* - **PT Pelabuhan Indonesia III (Persero) (Indonesia Port Corp III) (PELINDO III)** - *Surabaya* *Indonesia*	*201* 61 -	Class: KI	**1990-01 PT Dumas — Surabaya** Loa 27.50 Br ex - Dght 2.700 Lbp 24.30 Br md 8.60 Dpth 3.50 Welded, 1 dk	**(B32A2ST) Tug**	**2 oil engines** reduction geared to sc. shafts driving 2 Propellers Total Power: 956kW (1,300hp) 10.0kn MWM TBD234V12 2 x Vee 4 Stroke 12 Cy. 128 x 140 each-478kW (650bhp) Motoren Werke Mannheim AG (MWM)-West Germany
6616461 **SUBARNAREKHA** *ATBC* - **Kolkata Port Trust** - *Kolkata* *India* Official number: 1220	*2,514* 1,072 2,484	Class: (LR) (IR) ✠ Classed LR until 3/68	**1966-10 Orenstein-Koppel u. Luebecker Maschinenbau AG — Luebeck** Yd No: 640 Loa 94.04 Br ex 15.32 Dght 4.319 Lbp 89.01 Br md 15.21 Dpth 5.80 Riveted\Welded, 1 dk	**(B33B2DT) Trailing Suction Hopper Dredger** Hopper: 1,274 5 Ha: 2 (1.8 x 1.8)3 (0.6 x 0.6)ER Derricks: 1x8t	**2 oil engines** reverse reduction geared to sc. shafts driving 2 FP propellers Total Power: 1,530kW (2,080hp) 11.0kn MAN G7V30/45 2 x 4 Stroke 7 Cy. 300 x 450 each-765kW (1040bhp) Maschinenbau Augsburg Nuernberg (MAN)-Augsburg AuxGen: 4 x 162kW 420V 50Hz a.c Fuel: 193.0 (d.f.)
9188439 **SUBARU** *JNDG* - **NTT Finance Corp** NTT World Engineering Marine Corp SatCom: Inmarsat B 343136912 *Tokyo* *Japan* MMSI: 431369000 Official number: 136650	**9,557** 2,867 6,843	Class: NK	**1999-02 Mitsubishi Heavy Industries Ltd. — Shimonoseki** Yd No: 1057 Loa 123.33 Br ex - Dght 7.018 Lbp 104.58 Br md 21.00 Dpth 12.20 Welded, 1 dk	**(B34D2SL) Cable Layer** Bale: 2,788 A-frames: 1; Cranes: 2x5t	**4 diesel electric oil engines** driving 4 gen. each 2800kW Connecting to 2 elec. motors each (1986kW) driving 2 Directional propellers Total Power: 11,768kW (16,000hp) 13.2kn Daihatsu 8DKM-32L 4 x 4 Stroke 8 Cy. 320 x 360 each-2942kW (4000bhp) Daihatsu Diesel Manufacturing Co Lt-Japan Thrusters: 1 Thwart. FP thruster (f); 1 Retract. directional thruster (f) Fuel: 1430.0
9181819 **SUBARU** *3FIJ8* *ex* Napili *-2007* - **Stella Phils Inc** Yokohama Marine & Merchant Corp SatCom: Inmarsat B 335473310 *Panama* *Panama* MMSI: 354733000 Official number: 2555198CH	**6,178** 3,057 8,560	Class: NK	**1998-04 Nishi Shipbuilding Co Ltd — Imabari EH** Yd No: 409 Loa 100.64 Br ex - Dght 8.189 Lbp 92.75 Br md 18.80 Dpth 13.00 Welded, 1 dk	**(A31A2GX) General Cargo Ship** Grain: 14,711; Bale: 13,536 Compartments: 2 Ho, ER 2 Ha: 2 (21.7 x 12.8)ER Cranes: 1x30.5t,2x25t	**1 oil engine** driving 1 FP propeller Total Power: 3,236kW (4,400hp) 12.5kn B&W 5L35MC 1 x 2 Stroke 5 Cy. 350 x 1050 3236kW (4400bhp) Makita Corp-Japan Fuel: 550.0
8810310 **SUBARU** *UEKN* *ex* Subaru Reefer *-1992* - **'SubTrop' Co Ltd** Ost-Rossa Co Ltd SatCom: Inmarsat A 140473114 *Vladivostok* *Russia* MMSI: 273819710 Official number: 886422	**1,415** 503 1,354 T/cm 6.6	Class: RS (NK)	**1988-11 KK Kanasashi Zosen — Toyohashi AI** Yd No: 3185 Loa 71.00 (BB) Br ex 12.42 Dght 4.369 Lbp 65.00 Br md 12.40 Dpth 7.10 Welded, 2 dks	**(A34A2GR) Refrigerated Cargo Ship** Ins: 1,792 Compartments: 3 Ho, ER 3 Ha: ER Derricks: 6x5t	**1 oil engine** driving 1 FP propeller Total Power: 1,250kW (1,700hp) 12.8kn Akasaka A34 1 x 4 Stroke 6 Cy. 340 x 660 1250kW (1700bhp) Akasaka Tekkosho KK (Akasaka DieselLtd)-Japan AuxGen: 2 x 360kW 445V 60Hz a.c Fuel: 86.4 (d.f.) 299.2 (r.f.) 5.9pd
8314237 **SUBBA RAO** *VWCS* - **Satyasai Marines Pvt Ltd** - *Visakhapatnam* *India* Official number: 2007	**110** 33 81	Class: (LR) ✠ Classed LR until 6/85	**1984-03 B.V. Scheepswerf "De Hoop" — Hardinxveld-Giessendam** Yd No: 780 Loa 23.68 Br ex 6.58 Dght 2.909 Lbp 21.24 Br md 6.51 Dpth 3.43 Welded, 1 dk	**(B11A2FT) Trawler** Ins: 70	**1 oil engine** with clutches, flexible couplings & sr reverse geared to sc. shaft driving 1 FP propeller Total Power: 405kW (551hp) 9.5kn Caterpillar 3408TA 1 x Vee 4 Stroke 8 Cy. 137 x 152 405kW (551bhp) Caterpillar Tractor Co-USA AuxGen: 2 x 26kW 380V 50Hz a.c Fuel: 38.5 (d.f.)
9683465 **SUBERKO-01** *YD5203* - **PT Orela Bahari** - *Surabaya* *Indonesia* MMSI: 525024193 Official number: 22515A	**193** 58 143	Class: BV (Class contemplated)	**2013-08 Pt Orela Shipyard — Surabaya** Yd No: L-02 Loa 36.40 Br ex - Dght 2.000 Lbp 32.10 Br md 7.60 Dpth 3.35 Welded, 1 dk	**(B34J2SD) Crew Boat** Hull Material: Aluminium Alloy	**3 oil engines** reduction geared to sc. shafts driving 3 Propellers Total Power: 3,090kW (4,200hp) MAN D2862LE 3 x Vee 4 Stroke 12 Cy. 128 x 157 each-1030kW (1400bhp) MAN Nutzfahrzeuge AG-Nuernberg
9090008 **SUBHADRA KUMARI CHAUHAN** *AUKC* - **Government of The Republic of India (Coast Guard)** - *India* Official number: 233	**350** 105 54	Class: (AB) (IR)	**2006-04 Goa Shipyard Ltd. — Goa** Yd No: 1190 Loa 48.14 Br ex 7.51 Dght 2.100 Lbp 44.12 Br md 7.50 Dpth 4.35 Welded, 1 dk	**(B34H2SQ) Patrol Vessel** Hull Material: Aluminium Alloy	**3 oil engines** reduction geared to sc. shafts driving 3 Water jets Total Power: 8,160kW (11,094hp) M.T.U. 16V4000M90 3 x Vee 4 Stroke 16 Cy. 165 x 190 each-2720kW (3698bhp) MTU Friedrichshafen GmbH-Friedrichshafen AuxGen: 2 x 120kW 415V 50Hz a.c Fuel: 35.0 (d.f.)

Identity / Owner	Tonnage / Class	Builder / Dimensions	Type	Machinery
8037231 ATSV - **SUBHASHINI** **Srinivasa Sea Foods Pvt Ltd** *Visakhapatnam* *India* Official number: 1788	*116* 79 57 Class: (IR) (AB)	**1978 Ingenieria y Maq. Especializada S.A. (IMESA) — Coatzacoalcos** Loa 23.17 Br ex 7.47 Dght 2.255 Lbp 21.39 Br md 7.33 Dpth 3.28 Welded, 1 dk	**(B11B2FV) Fishing Vessel**	**1 oil engine** sr geared to sc. shaft driving 1 FP propeller Total Power: 279kW (379hp) 8.5kn Caterpillar D353TA 1 x 4 Stroke 6 Cy. 159 x 203 279kW (379bhp) Caterpillar Tractor Co-USA AuxGen: 2 x 10kW 120V 50Hz a.c Fuel: 39.5 (d.f.)
9208344 *5BQR3* - **SUBHIKSHA** *ex Boa King -2007* **Varun Cyprus Ltd** Varun Shipping Co Ltd *Limassol* *Cyprus* MMSI: 210557000 Official number: 9208344	**2,655** 797 2,271 Class: NV (IR)	**2001-06 Dalian Shipyard Co Ltd — Dalian LN** Yd No: AH23-2 Loa 70.00 (BB) Br ex 18.43 Dght 6.574 Lbp 61.40 Br md 18.40 Dpth 7.60 Welded, 1 dk	**(B21B20A) Anchor Handling Tug Supply**	**2 oil engines** reduction geared to sc. shafts driving 2 CP propellers Total Power: 12,504kW (17,000hp) 16.0kn Caterpillar 3616TA 2 x Vee 4 Stroke 16 Cy. 280 x 300 each-6252kW (8500bhp) Caterpillar Inc-USA AuxGen: 1 x 500kW 440V 60Hz a.c, 1 x 1360kW 440V 60Hz a.c, 2 x 2000kW 440V 60Hz a.c Thrusters: 1 Tunnel thruster (f); 1 Tunnel thruster (a); 1 Retract. directional thruster (f) Fuel: 925.0 (d.f.)
7426033 *DYAU* - **SUBIC BAY 1** *ex Camellia -2004 ex Saroma -1990* **Carlos A Gothong Lines Inc** - *Cebu* *Philippines* MMSI: 548110100 Official number: CEB1006423	*15,439* 4,631 3,878	**1975-11 Naikai Shipbuilding & Engineering Co Ltd — Onomichi HS (Setoda Shipyard)** Yd No: 255 Loa 166.53 Br ex 24.01 Dght 9.710 Lbp 155.00 Br md 23.98 Dpth 14.70 Riveted\Welded, 2 dks	**(A36A2PR) Passenger/Ro-Ro Ship (Vehicles)** Passengers: unberthed: 526; berths: 102 Stern door Quarter bow door/ramp (s) Lane-Len: 920 Lane-clr ht: 4.00 Lorries: 120, Cars: 51	**2 oil engines** sr geared to sc. shafts driving 2 FP propellers Total Power: 14,710kW (20,000hp) 20.8kn MAN 18V40/54 2 x Vee 4 Stroke 18 Cy. 400 x 540 each-7355kW (10000bhp) Mitsubishi Heavy Industries Ltd-Japan AuxGen: 3 x 680kW 450V 60Hz a.c Fuel: 57.5 (d.f.) 586.5 (r.f.) 67.5pd
8923222 *DUA2651* - **SUBIC EAGLE I** - **Eagle Ferry Cruises Inc** - *Philippines*	*133* 43 -	**1996-01 Image Marine Pty Ltd — Fremantle WA** Yd No: 132 Loa 22.00 Br ex - Dght 1.089 Lbp - Br md 7.00 Dpth 2.33 Welded, 1 dk	**(A37B2PS) Passenger Ship** Passengers: unberthed: 154	**1 oil engine** geared to sc. shaft driving 1 FP propeller Total Power: 788kW (1,071hp) 28.5kn MAN D2842LE 1 x Vee 4 Stroke 12 Cy. 128 x 142 788kW (1071bhp) MAN Nutzfahrzeuge AG-Nuernberg
8923210 *DUA2650* - **SUBIC EAGLE II** - **Eagle Ferry Cruises Inc** - *Philippines*	*133* 43 -	**1996-01 Image Marine Pty Ltd — Fremantle WA** Yd No: 133 Loa 22.00 Br ex - Dght 1.089 Lbp - Br md 7.00 Dpth 2.33 Welded, 1 dk	**(A37B2PS) Passenger Ship** Passengers: unberthed: 154	**1 oil engine** geared to sc. shaft driving 1 FP propeller 28.5kn MAN D2842LE 1 x Vee 4 Stroke 12 Cy. 128 x 142 MAN Nutzfahrzeuge AG-Nuernberg
8138138 *EQHF* - **SUBSAHEL 1** **Government of The Islamic Republic of Iran (Coastal Regional Water & Power)** - *Bandar Abbas* *Iran* Official number: 3.8093	*223* 106 - Class: AS (GL)	**1980 Homatas Brothers Shipyard — Thessaloniki** Yd No: 53 Loa 35.62 Br ex 8.84 Dght 1.861 Lbp 32.52 Br md 8.81 Dpth 2.32 Welded, 1 dk	**(A36A2PR) Passenger/Ro-Ro Ship (Vehicles)**	**2 oil engines** reverse geared to sc. shafts driving 2 FP propellers Total Power: 404kW (550hp) 8.5kn Caterpillar 3406PCTA 2 x 4 Stroke 6 Cy. 137 x 165 each-202kW (275bhp) (made 1975, fitted 1980) Caterpillar Tractor Co-USA AuxGen: 1 x 56kW 380/220V a.c
8137158 *EQHT* - **SUBSAHEL 2** **Government of The Islamic Republic of Iran (Coastal Regional Water & Power)** - *Bandar Abbas* *Iran* MMSI: 422804000 Official number: 11495	**196** 59 - Class: AS (GL)	**1980 Homatas Brothers Shipyard — Thessaloniki** Yd No: 54 Loa 35.62 Br ex 8.82 Dght 1.861 Lbp 32.52 Br md 8.03 Dpth 2.32 Welded, 1 dk	**(A36A2PR) Passenger/Ro-Ro Ship (Vehicles)**	**2 oil engines** reverse geared to sc. shafts driving 2 FP propellers Total Power: 404kW (550hp) 8.5kn Caterpillar 3406PCTA 2 x 4 Stroke 6 Cy. 137 x 165 each-202kW (275bhp) Caterpillar Tractor Co-USA AuxGen: 1 x 56kW 220/320V a.c
7504756 *V4MU* - **SUBSEA 5** *ex Fratelli Neri -2007 ex Asso Cinque -1999* *ex Augustea Cinque -1998* *ex OFF Barcelona -1987* **Subsea Petroleum Services** - *Basseterre* *St Kitts & Nevis* MMSI: 341331000 Official number: SKN 1001331	**1,194** 358 1,118 Class: (RI) (GL)	**1977-11 Maritima de Axpe S.A. — Bilbao** Yd No: 97 Loa 60.20 Br ex 13.26 Dght 4.950 Lbp 54.01 Br md 13.01 Dpth 6.00 Welded, 1 dk	**(B21B20A) Anchor Handling Tug Supply**	**2 oil engines** with flexible couplings & sr gearedto sc. shafts driving 2 CP propellers Total Power: 2,250kW (3,060hp) 8.0kn MaK 9M453AK 2 x 4 Stroke 9 Cy. 320 x 420 each-1125kW (1530bhp) MaK Maschinenbau GmbH-Kiel AuxGen: 3 x 360kW 440V 60Hz a.c Thrusters: 1 Thwart. CP thruster (f) Fuel: 700.0 (d.f.) 22.5pd
9585376 *XCAF3* - **SUBSEA 88** - **Transportacion Maritima Mexicana SA de CV** - *Dos Bocas* *Mexico* Official number: 2701353932-4	**1,123** 337 1,102 Class: AB (BV)	**2010-08 Guangzhou Panyu Lingshan Shipyard Ltd — Guangzhou GD** Yd No: 188 Loa 55.00 Br ex 13.84 Dght 4.760 Lbp 48.00 Br md 13.80 Dpth 5.50 Welded, 1 dk	**(B21B20A) Anchor Handling Tug Supply**	**2 oil engines** reduction geared to sc. shafts driving 2 CP propellers Total Power: 3,788kW (5,150hp) 12.5kn Caterpillar 3516B-HD 2 x Vee 4 Stroke 16 Cy. 170 x 215 each-1894kW (2575bhp) Caterpillar Inc-USA AuxGen: 2 x 450kW 415V 50Hz a.c, 2 x 400kW 415V 50Hz a.c Thrusters: 1 Tunnel thruster (f); 1 Tunnel thruster (a)
9585388 *YJQH4* - **SUBSEA 89** - **Subsea Petroleum Services** - SatCom: Inmarsat C 457649310 *Port Vila* *Vanuatu* MMSI: 576493000 Official number: 1947	**1,123** 337 1,102 Class: AB (BV)	**2011-06 Guangzhou Panyu Lingshan Shipyard Ltd — Guangzhou GD** Yd No: 189 Loa 55.00 Br ex 13.84 Dght 4.760 Lbp 48.00 Br md 13.80 Dpth 5.50 Welded, 1 dk	**(B21B20A) Anchor Handling Tug Supply**	**2 oil engines** reduction geared to sc. shafts driving 2 CP propellers Total Power: 3,840kW (5,220hp) 12.5kn Caterpillar 3516B-HD 2 x Vee 4 Stroke 16 Cy. 170 x 215 each-1920kW (2610bhp) Caterpillar Inc-USA AuxGen: 2 x 450kW 415V 50Hz a.c, 2 x 400kW 415V 50Hz a.c Thrusters: 1 Tunnel thruster (f); 1 Tunnel thruster (a) Fuel: 410.0
8218225 - - **SUBSEA 99** *ex Oil Trojan -2006 ex Neel Jalini -1995* *ex Oil Trojan -1990 ex Mirsal Alyem -1987* *ex Black Leopard -1986 ex Mirsal Alyem -1985* **Government of The Arab Republic of Egypt (Naval Forces)** - *Egypt*	**1,085** 325 1,565 Class: (AB) (GL) (BV) (IR)	**1983-09 Sing Koon Seng Pte Ltd — Singapore** Yd No: 603 Loa 61.30 Br ex - Dght 4.520 Lbp 57.28 Br md 13.10 Dpth 5.20 Welded, 1 dk	**(B21B20A) Anchor Handling Tug Supply**	**2 oil engines** sr reverse geared to sc. shafts driving 2 CP propellers Total Power: 3,528kW (4,796hp) 13.1kn Yanmar 8Z280L-ET 2 x 4 Stroke 8 Cy. 280 x 360 each-1764kW (2398bhp) Yanmar Diesel Engine Co Ltd-Japan AuxGen: 2 x 175kW 415V 50Hz a.c, 1 x 65kW a.c Thrusters: 1 Thwart. FP thruster (f) Fuel: 556.0 (d.f.)
9585390 *YJQH7* - **SUBSEA 204** - **Subsea Petroleum Services** - *Port Vila* *Vanuatu* MMSI: 576495000 Official number: 1948	**1,123** 337 1,115 Class: AB (BV)	**2011-09 Guangzhou Panyu Lingshan Shipyard Ltd — Guangzhou GD** Yd No: 204 Loa 55.00 Br ex 13.84 Dght 4.760 Lbp 48.00 Br md 13.80 Dpth 5.50 Welded, 1 dk	**(B21B20A) Anchor Handling Tug Supply**	**2 oil engines** reeduction geared to sc. shafts driving 2 CP propellers Total Power: 3,788kW (5,150hp) 12.5kn Caterpillar 3516B-TA 2 x Vee 4 Stroke 16 Cy. 170 x 190 each-1894kW (2575bhp) Caterpillar Inc-USA AuxGen: 2 x 285kW 415V 50Hz a.c, 2 x 285kW 415V 50Hz a.c Thrusters: 2 Tunnel thruster (f)
9182899 *LJJL* - **SUBSEA VIKING** - **Eidesvik Shipping AS** Eidesvik AS SatCom: Inmarsat B 325957810 *Haugesund* *Norway* MMSI: 259578000	**7,401** 2,220 6,350 Class: NV	**1999-05 Umoe Sterkoder AS — Kristiansund** Yd No: 188 Loa 103.00 (BB) Br ex - Dght 7.840 Lbp 88.80 Br md 22.00 Dpth 9.80 Welded, 1 dk	**(B22A20R) Offshore Support Vessel** Cranes: 1x100t Ice Capable	**4 diesel electric oil engines** driving 4 gen. each 2400kW 690V Connecting to 2 elec. motors each (2750kW) driving 2 Directional propellers Total Power: 10,440kW (14,196hp) 12.0kn MaK 9M25 4 x 4 Stroke 9 Cy. 255 x 400 each-2610kW (3549bhp) MaK Motoren GmbH & Co. KG-Kiel AuxGen: 4 x 690/450V Thrusters: 2 Thwart. FP thruster (f); 1 Directional thruster (f)
7385289 *ZUGG* - **SUBTECH CHALLENGER** *ex S. A. Kuswag V -1999* **Horacio de Nascimento da Silva Gomes** - *Durban* *South Africa* Official number: 350709	*148* 62 173 Class: (AB)	**1974-08 Sandock-Austral Ltd. — Durban** Yd No: 61 Loa 28.91 Br ex 6.43 Dght 2.718 Lbp 26.70 Br md 6.38 Dpth 3.33 Welded, 1 dk	**(B34G2SE) Pollution Control Vessel** Compartments: 2 Ho, ER, 2 Ta 2 Ha: (5.1 x 2.7) (5.4 x 2.7)ER	**1 oil engine** driving 1 CP propeller Total Power: 588kW (799hp) 10.0kn Alpha 408-26VO 1 x 2 Stroke 8 Cy. 260 x 400 588kW (799bhp) Alpha Diesel A/S-Denmark Fuel: 61.0 (d.f.) 3.0pd

IMO / Call sign / Flag	Name / Former names / Owner / Port	Tonnage	Class	Builder / Dimensions	Type	Machinery
7701823 *YFMB* -	**SUBUR** *ex* Tenan Maru *-1985* **PT Berlian Eka Sakti Tangguh** - *Balikpapan* *Indonesia*	**1,270** 649 2,013 T/cm 6.8	Class: (KI) (NK)	**1977**-08 **K.K. Taihei Kogyo — Akitsu** Yd No: 322 Loa 75.04 Br ex - Dght 4.893 Lbp 70.41 Br md 11.21 Dpth 5.62 Welded, 1 dk	**(A12D2LV) Vegetable Oil Tanker** Liq: 2,397 2 Cargo Pump (s)	**1 oil engine** driving 1 FP propeller Total Power: 1,471kW (2,000hp) 12.0kn Hanshin 6LU38 1 x 4 Stroke 6 Cy. 380 x 580 1471kW (2000bhp) Hanshin Nainenki Kogyo-Japan
8340250 *YCLS* -	**SUBUR No. 1** *ex* Wan Tzung No. 1 *-1985* **PT Daya Guna Samudera** - *Ambon* *Indonesia*	*493* 372 -	Class: (KI)	**1972 Kaohsiung Shipbuilding Co. Ltd. — Kaohsiung** Loa 41.51 Br ex - Dght 2.850 Lbp 36.00 Br md 7.00 Dpth 3.31 Welded, 1 dk	**(B11B2FV) Fishing Vessel**	**1 oil engine** driving 1 FP propeller Total Power: 809kW (1,100hp) Makita GNLH6275 1 x 4 Stroke 6 Cy. 275 x 450 809kW (1100bhp) Makita Diesel Co Ltd-Japan
8340262 *YCLT* -	**SUBUR No. 2** *ex* Wan Tzung No. 2 *-1985* **PT Daya Guna Samudera** - *Ambon* *Indonesia*	*493* 372 -	Class: (KI)	**1972 Kaohsiung Shipbuilding Co. Ltd. — Kaohsiung** Loa 41.51 Br ex - Dght 2.850 Lbp 36.00 Br md 7.00 Dpth 3.31 Welded, 1 dk	**(B11B2FV) Fishing Vessel**	**1 oil engine** driving 1 FP propeller Total Power: 809kW (1,100hp) Makita 1 x 4 Stroke 809kW (1100bhp) Makita Diesel Co Ltd-Japan
8743127 - -	**SUBUR REJEKI 1** **Bambang Harianto** - *Samarinda* *Indonesia*	**119** 36 -	Class: KI	**2009**-11 **C.V. Karya Lestari Industri — Samarinda** Loa 23.00 Br ex - Dght 2.000 Lbp 21.40 Br md 6.50 Dpth 2.80 Welded, 1 dk	**(B32A2ST) Tug**	**2 oil engines** reduction geared to sc. shafts driving 2 Propellers Total Power: 882kW (1,200hp) Mitsubishi 10M20 2 x Vee 4 Stroke 10 Cy. 146 x 150 each-441kW (600bhp) Mitsubishi Heavy Industries Ltd-Japan AuxGen: 2 x 74kW 400V a.c
6417451 *EAFR* -	**SUCAR DIEZ** *ex* Sea Nostromo Tercero *-2008* *ex* Schelde III *-2004* **Remolsucar SL** - SatCom: Inmarsat C 422541851 *Las Palmas* *Spain (CSR)* MMSI: 224084630 Official number: 2/2008	**106** 32 -	Class: (BV)	**1964 Arnhemsche Scheepsbouw Mij NV — Arnhem** Yd No: 425 Loa 27.67 Br ex 6.86 Dght 2.902 Lbp 24.62 Br md 6.30 Dpth 3.20 Welded, 1 dk	**(B32A2ST) Tug**	**1 oil engine** geared to sc. shaft driving 1 FP propeller Total Power: 829kW (1,127hp) 12.5kn Deutz SBA16M816 1 x Vee 4 Stroke 16 Cy. 142 x 160 829kW (1127bhp) (new engine 1982) Kloeckner Humboldt Deutz AG-West Germany Fuel: 11.5 (d.f.)
6828909 *ECBB* -	**SUCAR DOCE** *ex* Sea Nostromo Quinto *-2009* *ex* Condor III *-2003* *ex* Smit-Lloyd Cairo *-1991* *ex* Palmer Surveyor *-1989* *ex* Smit-Lloyd Cairo *-1986* *ex* Smit-Lloyd 32 *-1982* **Remolsucar SL** - *Las Palmas* *Spain (CSR)* MMSI: 224081730	*816* 305 406	Class: (BV) (AB) (HR)	**1968 Adelaide Ship Construction Pty Ltd — Port Adelaide SA** Yd No: 54 Loa 59.75 Br ex 11.71 Dght 4.315 Lbp 53.52 Br md 11.31 Dpth 5.16 Welded, 1 dk	**(B21B20A) Anchor Handling Tug Supply** Derricks: 1x10t	**2 oil engines** driving 2 CP propellers Total Power: 1,986kW (2,700hp) 14.0kn De Industrie 6D8HD 2 x 4 Stroke 6 Cy. 400 x 600 each-993kW (1350bhp) NV Motorenfabriek 'De Industrie'-Netherlands AuxGen: 2 x 100kW 220V d.c, 1 x 20kW 220V d.c Thrusters: 1 Water jet (f) Fuel: 253.0 (d.f.)
7049328 *WY7819* -	**SUCCESS** *ex* State Jack *-1976* **Swamp Irish Inc** - *Brownsville, TX* *United States of America* Official number: 522949	*158* 107 -		**1969 Bender Welding & Machine Co Inc — Mobile AL** L reg 24.36 Br ex 7.35 Dght - Lbp - Br md - Dpth 3.46 Welded	**(B11B2FV) Fishing Vessel**	**1 oil engine** driving 1 FP propeller Total Power: 313kW (426hp) Caterpillar D353SCAC 1 x 4 Stroke 6 Cy. 159 x 203 313kW (426bhp) Caterpillar Tractor Co-USA
7621827 *WCW5540* -	**SUCCESS** *ex* H. O. S. Success *-1996* *ex* Point Success *-1991* **Point Marine LLC** Tidewater Marine LLC *Wilmington, DE* *United States of America* Official number: 577810	**695** 208 -	Class: (AB)	**1976**-11 **Halter Marine, Inc. — Moss Point, Ms** Yd No: 567 Loa 56.39 Br ex - Dght 3.671 Lbp 51.49 Br md 12.20 Dpth 4.27 Welded, 1 dk	**(B21B20A) Anchor Handling Tug Supply** Ice Capable	**2 oil engines** reverse reduction geared to sc. shafts driving 2 FP propellers Total Power: 2,206kW (3,000hp) 12.0kn EMD (Electro-Motive) 12-645-E6 2 x Vee 2 Stroke 12 Cy. 230 x 254 each-1103kW (1500bhp) (Re-engined ,made 1954, Reconditioned & fitted 1976) General Motors Corp.Electro-Motive Div.-La Grange AuxGen: 2 x 99kW Thrusters: 1 Thwart. FP thruster (f) Fuel: 302.0 (d.f.)
7905120 *V4VL2* -	**SUCCESS** *ex* Farid *-2013* *ex* Atlantsfarid *-2010* *ex* Courage *-2004* *ex* Azalea *-1998* **Success Enterprises International LLC** Seatraffic Ltd *Charlestown* *St Kitts & Nevis* MMSI: 341659000 Official number: SKN1002584	**906** 359 -	Class: LR ✠ **100A1** SS 05/2009 fishing vessel **LMC** Eq.Ltr: K; Cable: 440.0/24.0 U1 (a)	**1980**-01 **Eid Verft AS — Nordfjordeid** (Hull) Yd No: 15 **1980**-01 **Smedvik Mek. Verksted AS — Tjorvaag** Yd No: 71 **1987 Karstensens Skibsvaerft A/S — Skagen** (Additional cargo section) Lengthened-1987 Loa 62.15 (BB) Br ex 9.10 Dght 5.801 Lbp 53.80 Br md 9.00 Dpth 7.15 Welded, 2 dks	**(B11A2FT) Trawler**	**1 oil engine** with clutches, flexible couplings & sr geared to sc. shaft driving 1 CP propeller Total Power: 1,618kW (2,200hp) 12.5kn MaK 6M453AK 1 x 4 Stroke 6 Cy. 320 x 420 1618kW (2200bhp) Krupp MaK Maschinenbau GmbH-Kiel AuxGen: 1 x 245kW 380V 50Hz a.c, 1 x 160kW 380V 50Hz a.c Thrusters: 1 Thwart. FP thruster (f); 1 Tunnel thruster (a)
7823580 - -	**SUCCESS** *ex* Leader 1 *-1997* *ex* Hai Ying *-1996* *ex* Kissho *-1989* *ex* Kosei Maru No. 31 *-1988* **Hainan Nanyang Shipping Industrial Co Ltd** -	**680** 332 1,200	Class: (CC)	**1979**-05 **Kurinoura Dockyard Co Ltd — Yawatahama EH** Yd No: 134 Loa 58.35 Br ex - Dght 4.060 Lbp 54.00 Br md 10.50 Dpth 4.60 Welded, 1 dk	**(A13B2TP) Products Tanker**	**1 oil engine** driving 1 FP propeller Total Power: 1,030kW (1,400hp) Hanshin 6LUN28AG 1 x 4 Stroke 6 Cy. 280 x 480 1030kW (1400bhp) The Hanshin Diesel Works Ltd-Japan
8877631 - -	**SUCCESS** *ex* Transporter *-2011* *ex* Fog *-2011* *ex* Gendai *-2010* *ex* Sevela *-2005* *ex* Kinsei *-2004* *ex* Kinsei Maru No. 11 *-2003* **Worldwide Cargo Transportation Co Ltd** -	**203** 88 140		**1994 K.K. Yoshida Zosen Tekko — Kesennuma** Yd No: 385 Converted From: Fishing Vessel-2005 Loa 37.75 Br ex - Dght 2.400 Lbp 30.65 Br md 6.60 Dpth 2.60 Welded, 1 dk	**(A31A2GX) General Cargo Ship**	**1 oil engine** with clutches, flexible couplings & sr geared to sc. shaft driving 1 FP propeller Total Power: 592kW (805hp) Sumiyoshi S26G 1 x 4 Stroke 6 Cy. 260 x 470 592kW (805bhp) Sumiyoshi Marine Diesel Co Ltd-Japan
9357353 *5ISK40* -	**SUCCESS** *ex* Baikal *-2013* *ex* Blossom *-2012* *ex* Sima *-2012* **NITC** - *Zanzibar* *Tanzania (Zanzibar)* MMSI: 677003900	**85,462** 53,441 164,154	Class: (BV) (NV)	**2008**-05 **Hyundai Samho Heavy Industries Co Ltd — Samho** Yd No: S317 Loa 274.18 (BB) Br ex 50.04 Dght 17.000 Lbp 265.07 Br md 50.00 Dpth 23.10 Welded, 1 dk	**(A13A2TV) Crude Oil Tanker** Double Hull (13F) Liq: 169,000; Liq (Oil): 169,000 Cargo Heating Coils Compartments: 6 Wing Ta, 6 Wing Ta, 1 Wing Slop Ta, 1 Wing Slop Ta, ER 3 Cargo Pump (s): 3x4000m³/hr	**1 oil engine** driving 1 FP propeller Total Power: 18,660kW (25,370hp) 15.4kn MAN-B&W 6S70MC-C 1 x 2 Stroke 6 Cy. 700 x 2800 18660kW (25370bhp) Hyundai Heavy Industries Co Ltd-South Korea AuxGen: 3 x 1050kW 60Hz a.c
7727566 *PMOA* -	**SUCCESS 2** *ex* Well Success 103 *-2008* *ex* Seatrade *-2003* *ex* Hector *-2001* *ex* Abdallah Bnou Yassine *-2000* *ex* Hirotsuki Maru *-1985* **PT Pelayaran Berkah Setanggi Timur** - *Tanjung Priok* *Indonesia*	**4,709** 1,432 6,000	Class: KI (CR) (BV) (NK)	**1978**-11 **Honda Zosen — Saiki** Yd No: 660 Loa 120.58 Br ex - Dght 7.430 Lbp 113.49 Br md 17.11 Dpth 9.60 Welded, 2 dks	**(A34A2GR) Refrigerated Cargo Ship** Ins: 6,256 Compartments: 3 Ho, ER 3 Ha: 3 (17.1 x 6.1)ER Derricks: 6x5t	**1 oil engine** driving 1 FP propeller Total Power: 5,737kW (7,800hp) 18.0kn Pielstick 12PC2-5V-400 1 x Vee 4 Stroke 12 Cy. 400 x 460 5737kW (7800bhp) Niigata Engineering Co Ltd-Japan AuxGen: 3 x 440kW 445V 60Hz a.c Fuel: 600.0 (d.f.) 916.0 (r.f.) 28.0pd
7740130 - -	**SUCCESS 50** *ex* Uni-Glory 1 *-2003* *ex* Koei Maru No. 8 *-1993* **Success Blossom Ltd** -	**462** 162 670	Class: (GL)	**1978**-02 **Kogushi Zosen K.K. — Okayama** Yd No: 207 Loa 49.20 Br ex - Dght 3.230 Lbp - Br md 8.21 Dpth 3.81 Welded, 1 dk	**(A13B2TU) Tanker (unspecified)** Liq: 633; Liq (Oil): 633	**1 oil engine** reverse geared to sc shaft driving 1 FP propeller Total Power: 552kW (750hp) 10.0kn Hanshin 6L26BGSH 1 x 4 Stroke 6 Cy. 260 x 400 552kW (750bhp) Hanshin Nainenki Kogyo-Japan AuxGen: 1 x 48kW a.c
9147435 *YGXD* -	**SUCCESS CHALLENGER XXXVII** *ex* Maran Altair *-2013* *ex* Astro Altair *-2009* **PT Armada Maritime Offshore** Soechi Group *Jakarta* *Indonesia* MMSI: 525019644	**53,074** 28,469 98,880 T/cm 95.1	Class: AB	**1997**-08 **Daewoo Heavy Industries Ltd — Geoje** Yd No: 5102 Loa 248.00 (BB) Br ex 43.04 Dght 13.500 Lbp 238.00 Br md 43.00 Dpth 19.80 Welded, 1 dk	**(A13A2TW) Crude/Oil Products Tanker** Double Hull (13F) Liq: 112,095; Liq (Oil): 112,095 Cargo Heating Coils Compartments: 12 Wing Ta, ER 3 Cargo Pump (s): 3x2500m³/hr Manifold: Bow/CM: 125m	**1 oil engine** driving 1 FP propeller Total Power: 14,048kW (19,100hp) 15.5kn MAN-B&W 5S70MC 1 x 2 Stroke 5 Cy. 700 x 2674 14048kW (19100bhp) Hyundai Heavy Industries Co Ltd-South Korea AuxGen: 3 x 750kW 440V 60Hz a.c Fuel: 167.7 (d.f.) (Heating Coils) 3026.0 (r.f.) 58.0pd

9136498 *POGC* -	**SUCCESS ENERGY XXXII** *ex* White Cattleya 10 *-2011* *ex* Crane Neptune *-2002* **PT Putra Utama Line** PT Sukses Osean Khatulistiwa Line *Jakarta* *Indonesia* MMSI: 525015923	**4,627** 2,432 7,901 T/cm 17.3	Class: NK	**1996**-03 **Higaki Zosen K.K. — Imabari** Yd No: 467 Loa 112.09 (BB) Br ex 18.62 Dght 6.935 Lbp 104.00 Br md 18.60 Dpth 8.60 Welded, 1 dk	**(A12B2TR) Chemical/Products Tanker** Double Bottom Entire Compartment Length Liq: 7,655; Liq (Oil): 8,647 Cargo Heating Coils Compartments: 6 Ta (s.stl), 10 Wing Ta, 2 Wing Slop Ta, ER 16 Cargo Pump (s): 6x200m^3/hr, 10x150m^3/hr Manifold: Bow/CM: 57.4m	**1 oil engine** driving 1 FP propeller Total Power: 3,089kW (4,200hp) 12.7kn Mitsubishi 6UEC37LA 1 x 2 Stroke 6 Cy. 370 x 880 3089kW (4200bhp) Kobe Hatsudoki KK-Japan AuxGen: 3 x 280kW 450V a.c Fuel: 79.0 (d.f.) 490.0 (r.f.) 12.8pd
9243150 *JZRB* -	**SUCCESS FORTUNE XL** *ex* BW Luna *-2013* *ex* World Luna *-2008* **PT Sukses Osean Khatulistiwa Line** *Jakarta* *Indonesia* MMSI: 525012284	**158,993** 110,268 298,555 T/cm 170.7	Class: NV	**2003**-02 **Daewoo Shipbuilding & Marine Engineering Co Ltd — Geoje** Yd No: 5198 Loa 332.07 (BB) Br ex 58.04 Dght 22.022 Lbp 320.01 Br md 58.01 Dpth 31.20 Welded, 1 dk	**(A13A2TV) Crude Oil Tanker** Double Hull (13F) Liq: 337,418; Liq (Oil): 337,418 Compartments: 5 Ta, 10 Wing Ta, 2 Wing Slop Ta, ER 3 Cargo Pump (s): 3x5000m^3/hr	**1 oil engine** driving 1 FP propeller Total Power: 25,487kW (34,652hp) 15.3kn B&W 7S80MC 1 x 2 Stroke 7 Cy. 800 x 3056 25487kW (34652bhp) Doosan Engine Co Ltd-South Korea AuxGen: 3 x 1180kW 440/220V 60Hz a.c Fuel: 377.0 (d.f.) 7106.0 (r.f.) 100.0pd
9222716 *H3CZ* -	**SUCCESS MARLINA XXXIII** *ex* Golden Jane *-2012* **Success Marlina XXXIII SA** Shintoku Marine Co Ltd *Panama* *Panama* MMSI: 352428000 Official number: 2720100D	**9,599** 5,132 16,476 T/cm 26.5	Class: NK	**2000**-05 **Kurinoura Dockyard Co Ltd — Yawatahama EH** Yd No: 356 Loa 149.00 (BB) Br ex 22.03 Dght 9.100 Lbp 138.00 Br md 22.00 Dpth 11.65 Welded, 1 dk	**(A12B2TR) Chemical/Products Tanker** Double Hull (13F) Liq: 16,960; Liq (Oil): 17,860 Cargo Heating Coils Compartments: 24 Wing Ta (s.stl), 2 Wing Slop Ta (s.stl), ER 24 Cargo Pump (s): 10x300m^3/hr, 8x200m^3/hr, 6x100m^3/hr Manifold: Bow/CM: 70.7m	**1 oil engine** driving 1 FP propeller Total Power: 5,296kW (7,200hp) 13.5kn Mitsubishi 6UEC45LA 1 x 2 Stroke 6 Cy. 450 x 1350 5296kW (7200bhp) Kobe Hatsudoki KK-Japan AuxGen: 3 x 370kW a.c Thrusters: 1 Tunnel thruster (f) Fuel: 117.0 (d.f.) 939.0 (r.f.)
9164536 *JZDI* -	**SUCCESS PEGASUS XXXVI** *ex* AS Oceania *-2013* *ex* St. Katharinen *-2012* **PT Sukses Maritime Line** Soechi Lines Pte Ltd *Jakarta* *Indonesia* MMSI: 525007290 Official number: 4499	**25,202** 11,959 43,760 T/cm 48.8	Class: GL (LR) ✠ Classed LR until 8/6/04	**1999**-06 **Dalian Shipyard Co Ltd — Dalian LN** Yd No: PC440-1 Loa 182.00 (BB) Br ex 30.03 Dght 10.200 Lbp 174.00 Br md 30.00 Dpth 17.25 Welded, 1 dk	**(A13A2TW) Crude/Oil Products Tanker** Double Hull (13F) Liq: 44,771; Liq (Oil): 44,771 Cargo Heating Coils Compartments: 4 Wing Ta, 5 Ta, 2 Wing Slop Ta, ER 4 Cargo Pump (s): 4x500m^3/hr Manifold: Bow/CM: 88.3m	**1 oil engine** driving 1 FP propeller Total Power: 7,859kW (10,685hp) 13.6kn MAN-B&W 6S50MC 1 x 2 Stroke 6 Cy. 500 x 1910 7859kW (10685bhp) Dalian Marine Diesel Works-China AuxGen: 2 x 560kW 440V 60Hz a.c, 1 x 552kW 440V 60Hz a.c Boilers: e (ex.g.) 22.4kgf/cm^2 (22.0bar), AuxB (o.f.) 18.4kgf/cm^2 (18.0bar) Fuel: 129.0 (d.f.) (Heating Coils) 1205.0 (r.f.) 29.0pd
9108702 *POWF* -	**SUCCESS PIONEER XXXV** *ex* Genmar Ajax *-2012* *ex* Julie *-1998* **PT Putra Utama Line** Aquarius Maritime Pte Ltd *Jakarta* *Indonesia* MMSI: 525021055	**53,829** 27,269 96,183 T/cm 89.8	Class: NV	**1996**-07 **Samsung Heavy Industries Co Ltd — Geoje** Yd No: 1138 Loa 243.28 (BB) Br ex 41.83 Dght 13.617 Lbp 233.00 Br md 41.80 Dpth 20.00 Welded, 1 dk	**(A13A2TV) Crude Oil Tanker** Double Hull (13F) Liq: 104,262; Liq (Oil): 104,262 Cargo Heating Coils Compartments: 7 Ta, 2 Wing Slop Ta, ER 6 Cargo Pump (s): 6x2500m^3/hr Manifold: Bow/CM: 121.4m	**1 oil engine** driving 1 FP propeller Total Power: 11,475kW (15,601hp) 14.2kn B&W 6L60MC 1 x 2 Stroke 6 Cy. 600 x 1944 11475kW (15601bhp) Hyundai Heavy Industries Co Ltd-South Korea AuxGen: 3 x 700kW 220/440V 60Hz a.c Fuel: 210.0 (d.f.) 2260.0 (r.f.)
7809431 *9WK02* -	**SUCCESS SATRIA 1** *ex* Tembusu *-2012* *ex* Dolphin III *-2007* *ex* RSG Unity *-1997* *ex* G. S. Supply *-1990* **Success Blossom Sdn Bhd** Success Blossom Trading Pte Ltd *Kota Kinabalu* *Malaysia* MMSI: 533130969	**909** 421 1,604	Class: GL (AB)	**1979**-06 **Shanghai Shipbuilding Pte Ltd — Singapore** Yd No: SH02-T Loa 55.00 Br ex - Dght 2.901 Lbp 53.01 Br md 15.02 Dpth 3.92 Welded, 1 dk	**(B35E2TF) Bunkering Tanker** Liq: 1,426; Liq (Oil): 1,426	**2 oil engines** geared to sc. shafts driving 2 FP propellers Total Power: 792kW (1,076hp) 11.0kn Deutz SBA8M816 2 x 4 Stroke 8 Cy. 142 x 160 each-396kW (538bhp) Kloeckner Humboldt Deutz AG-West Germany AuxGen: 2 x 56kW a.c
8913605 *PNZW* -	**SUCCESS TOTAL XXXI** *ex* Dimitra *-2011* *ex* Vanguard *-2011* *ex* Ostankino *-2004* **PT Putra Utama Mandiri Lines** PT Sukses Osean Khatulistiwa Line *Jakarta* *Indonesia* MMSI: 525015897	**28,223** 13,568 47,059 T/cm 51.2	Class: LR (NV) **100AT** SS 03/2012 moored storage ship *IWS for service at Bawean **LMC** **UMS IGS**	**1992**-03 **Halla Engineering & Heavy Industries Ltd — Incheon** Yd No: 175 Converted From: Chemical/Products Tanker-2012 Loa 183.20 (BB) Br ex 32.36 Dght 12.205 Lbp 174.00 Br md 32.20 Dpth 18.00 Welded, 1 dk	**(B22H2OF) FSO, Oil** Double Hull Liq: 54,080; Liq (Oil): 54,080 Cargo Heating Coils Compartments: 8 Ta, 2 Wing Slop Ta, ER 8 Cargo Pump (s): 8x850m^3/hr Manifold: Bow/CM: 90m Ice Capable	**1 oil engine** driving 1 FP propeller Total Power: 9,135kW (12,420hp) 14.5kn B&W 6S50MC 1 x 2 Stroke 6 Cy. 500 x 1910 9135kW (12420bhp) Hyundai Heavy Industries Co Ltd-South Korea AuxGen: 3 x 600kW 450V 60Hz a.c Fuel: 178.3 (d.f.) (Heating Coils) 1404.8 (r.f.) 37.8pd
9218090 *POWH* -	**SUCCESS VICTORY XXXIV** *ex* Sun Victory *-2012* **PT Armada Maritime Offshore** Soechi Group *Jakarta* *Indonesia* MMSI: 525021054	**3,866** 2,064 6,568 T/cm 14.2	Class: NK	**2000**-02 **Murakami Hide Zosen K.K. — Imabari** Yd No: 508 Loa 105.00 (BB) Br ex - Dght 6.950 Lbp 97.00 Br md 16.80 Dpth 8.40 Welded, 1 dk	**(A12B2TR) Chemical/Products Tanker** Single Hull Liq: 7,272; Liq (Oil): 7,405 Cargo Heating Coils Compartments: 9 Ta (s.stl), 8 Wing Ta, 1 Slop Ta, ER (s.stl) 17 Cargo Pump (s): 9x300m^3/hr, 8x200m^3/hr Manifold: Bow/CM: 52.5m	**1 oil engine** driving 1 FP propeller Total Power: 3,089kW (4,200hp) 12.8kn Mitsubishi 6UEC37LA 1 x 2 Stroke 6 Cy. 370 x 880 3089kW (4200bhp) Akasaka Tekkosho KK (Akasaka DieselLtd)-Japan AuxGen: 2 x 308kW a.c Fuel: 85.0 (d.f.) 455.0 (r.f.)
8746026 *9LY2351* -	**SUCCESS WAY** *ex* Great Age *-2013* *ex* OU XING HUA *-2011* *ex* You Bang 1 *-2010* **Zhoushan Success Way Shipping Co Ltd** Success Way International Shipping Ltd *Freetown* *Sierra Leone* MMSI: 667003154 Official number: SL103154	*2,972* 1,781 5,239	Class: SL	**2009**-09 **Zhejiang Xifeng Shipbuilding Co Ltd — Fenghua ZJ** Yd No: HG0803 Loa 96.90 Br ex - Dght 5.850 Lbp 89.80 Br md 15.80 Dpth 7.40 Welded, 1 dk	**(A31A2GX) General Cargo Ship** Grain: 6,800; Bale: 6,500	**1 oil engine** reduction geared to sc. shaft driving 1 Propeller Total Power: 1,765kW (2,400hp) 11.0kn Chinese Std. Type 1 x 4 Stroke 1765kW (2400bhp) Ningbo CSI Power & Machinery GroupCo Ltd-China
9321158 *C4SZ2* -	**SUCCESSOR** **Cape Victory Navigation Co Ltd** Seascope Shipping Agency Ltd SatCom: Inmarsat C 421208910 *Limassol* *Cyprus* MMSI: 212089000 Official number: 123456	**89,985** 55,963 173,748 T/cm 119.4	Class: NV (NK)	**2007**-03 **Bohai Shipbuilding Heavy Industry Co Ltd — Huludao LN** Yd No: 410-5 Loa 289.70 (BB) Br ex 45.04 Dght 18.200 Lbp 278.20 Br md 45.00 Dpth 24.10 Welded, 1 dk	**(A21A2BC) Bulk Carrier** Double Hull Grain: 186,170 Compartments: 9 Ho, ER 9 Ha: 7 (15.5 x 20.0)ER 2 (15.5 x 16.5)	**1 oil engine** driving 1 FP propeller Total Power: 17,640kW (23,983hp) 14.0kn Wartsila 6RTA68T 1 x 2 Stroke 6 Cy. 680 x 2720 17640kW (23983bhp) Dalian Marine Diesel Works-China AuxGen: 3 x 910kW 450V 60Hz a.c
9559987 - -	**SUCESSO** **EPINOSUL - Empresa de Pilotagem de Norte Sul e Servicos Sarl** - *Angola*	**250** - -		**2010**-05 **Francisco Cardama, SA — Vigo** Yd No: 223 Loa 24.50 Br ex - Dght 3.500 Lbp - Br md 8.00 Dpth 4.00 Welded, 1 dk	**(B32A2ST) Tug**	**2 oil engines** reduction geared to sc. shafts driving 2 Propellers Total Power: 1,940kW (2,638hp) Caterpillar 3512B 2 x Vee 4 Stroke 12 Cy. 170 x 190 each-970kW (1319bhp) Caterpillar Inc-USA
8986573 - -	**SUCEVENI 3** **SC Canal Services Srl** - *Constanta* *Romania* MMSI: 264900186 Official number: 748	**113** - -		**1980 Santierul Naval Drobeta-Turnu Severin S.A. — Drobeta-Turnu S.** Loa 23.80 Br ex 6.96 Dght 2.350 Lbp - Br md - Dpth 3.30 Welded, 1 dk	**(B32A2ST) Tug**	**2 oil engines** geared to sc. shafts driving 2 Propellers Total Power: 442kW (600hp) Maybach MB836B 2 x 4 Stroke 6 Cy. 175 x 205 each-221kW (300bhp) Uzina 23 August Bucuresti-Bucuresti
8648535 - -	**SUCEVENI 4** **SC Port Dredging SA** - *Constanta* *Romania* Official number: 726	*111* 33 -		**1980**-01 **Santierul Naval Drobeta-Turnu Severin S.A. — Drobeta-Turnu S.** Loa - Br ex - Dght - Lbp - Br md - Dpth - Welded, 1 dk	**(B32A2ST) Tug**	**1 oil engine** driving 1 Propeller
8648547 - -	**SUCEVENI 6** **Administration of Constanta Port (Administratia Portului Constantza)** - *Constanta* *Romania* Official number: 59	*112* 33 -		**1980**-01 **Santierul Naval Drobeta-Turnu Severin S.A. — Drobeta-Turnu S.** Loa - Br ex - Dght - Lbp - Br md - Dpth - Welded, 1 dk	**(B32A2ST) Tug**	**1 oil engine** driving 1 Propeller

9104495 HSPA2 - **SUCHADA NAREE**
ex Cynthia Winner *-1997*
Precious Stars Ltd
Great Circle Shipping Agency Ltd
Bangkok *Thailand*
MMSI: 567027000
Official number: 401000552
14,431 8,741 23,732 T/cm 33.6
Class: NK
1994-08 Shin Kurushima Dockyard Co. Ltd. — Onishi Yd No: 2817
Loa 150.52 (BB) Br ex - Dght 9.566
Lbp 143.00 Br md 26.00 Dpth 13.20
Welded, 1 dk
(A21A2BC) Bulk Carrier
Grain: 31,249; Bale: 30,169
Compartments: 4 Ho, ER
4 Ha: (17.9 x 12.8)3 (19.5 x 17.8)ER
Cranes: 4x30t
1 oil engine driving 1 FP propeller
Total Power: 5,296kW (7,200hp) 13.9kn
Mitsubishi 6UEC45LA
1 x 2 Stroke 6 Cy. 450 x 1350 5296kW (7200bhp)
Akasaka Tekkosho KK (Akasaka DieselLtd)-Japan
AuxGen: 3 x 261kW a.c
Fuel: 850.0 (r.f.)

9188685 VWT - **SUCHETA KRIPLANI**
Government of The Republic of India (Coast Guard)
-
India
306 91 50
Class: (AB) (IR)
1998-03 Garden Reach Shipbuilders & Engineers Ltd. — Kolkata Yd No: 2046
Loa 46.00 Br ex - Dght 1.870
Lbp 43.50 Br md 7.50 Dpth 4.30
Welded, 1 dk
(B34H2SQ) Patrol Vessel
2 oil engines reverse reduction geared to sc. shafts driving 2 FP propellers
Total Power: 3,236kW (4,400hp) 23.0kn
M.T.U. 12V538TB82
2 x Vee 4 Stroke 12 Cy. 185 x 200 each-1618kW (2200bhp)
MTU Friedrichshafen GmbH-Friedrichshafen
AuxGen: 3 x 80kW a.c

9098892 LXSD - **SUD**
Optimum Management Sarl
Magellan Management & Consulting SA
Luxembourg *Luxembourg*
MMSI: 253249000
Official number: 8-18
112 33 -
Class: RI
2007-10 Falcon Yacht Service — Viareggio Yd No: FV180
Loa 26.10 Br ex 6.40 Dght -
Lbp 23.45 Br md 6.20 Dpth 3.00
Welded, 1 dk
(X11A2YP) Yacht
2 oil engines reduction geared to sc. shafts driving 2 Propellers
Total Power: 2,206kW (3,000hp)
M.T.U. 12V2000M91
2 x Vee 4 Stroke 12 Cy. 130 x 150 each-1103kW (1500bhp)
MTU Friedrichshafen GmbH-Friedrichshafen

9466207 LXCB - **SUD**
ex Luna Y Sol *-2013*
Optimum Management Sarl
-
Luxembourg *Luxembourg*
149 44 -
Class: RI
2007-07 Cant. Nav. San Lorenzo SpA — Viareggio Yd No: 501
Loa 28.75 Br ex 6.63 Dght 1.900
Lbp 24.78 Br md 6.61 Dpth 3.25
Bonded, 1 dk
(X11A2YP) Yacht
Hull Material: Reinforced Plastic
2 oil engines reduction geared to sc. shafts driving 2 Propellers
Total Power: 3,260kW (4,432hp)
M.T.U.
2 x 4 Stroke each-1630kW (2216bhp)
MTU Friedrichshafen GmbH-Friedrichshafen

9149770 HZEP - **SUDAIR**
ex Al Noof *-2013*
United Arab Shipping Co (UASC)
-
Dammam *Saudi Arabia*
MMSI: 403523001
Official number: SA1171
48,154 26,721 49,993 T/cm 75.2
Class: LR
✠ **100A1** SS 11/2008
container ship
CCSA
*IWS
LI
✠ **LMC** **UMS**
Eq.Ltr: R†; Cable: 688.8/84.0 U3
1998-11 Kawasaki Heavy Industries Ltd — Sakaide KG Yd No: 1477
Loa 276.50 (BB) Br ex 32.30 Dght 12.500
Lbp 259.90 Br md 32.20 Dpth 21.20
Welded, 1 dk
(A33A2CC) Container Ship (Fully Cellular)
TEU 3802 C Ho 2068 TEU C Dk 1734 TEU incl 360 ref C.
Compartments: ER, 8 Cell Ho
16 Ha: (6.4 x 18.4) (13.2 x 18.4)Tappered (12.6 x 23.6)Tappered ER 13 (12.6 x 28.7)
1 oil engine driving 1 FP propeller
Total Power: 34,348kW (46,700hp) 24.1kn
B&W 10L80MC
1 x 2 Stroke 10 Cy. 800 x 2592 34348kW (46700bhp)
Kawasaki Heavy Industries Ltd-Japan
AuxGen: 3 x 2280kW 450V 60Hz a.c
Boilers: e (ex.g.) 12.0kgf/cm² (11.8bar), AuxB (o.f.) 8.1kgf/cm² (7.9bar)
Thrusters: 1 Thwart. CP thruster (f)
Fuel: 440.0 (d.f.) (Heating Coils) 5460.0 (r.f.) 138.0pd

9208332 5BQV3 - **SUDAKSHA**
ex Boa Queen *-2007*
Varun Cyprus Ltd
Varun Shipping Co Ltd
Limassol *Cyprus*
MMSI: 210139000
2,655 797 2,200
Class: NV (IR)
2001-06 Dalian Shipyard Co Ltd — Dalian LN Yd No: AH23-1
Loa 70.00 (BB) Br ex 18.43 Dght 6.570
Lbp 61.40 Br md 18.40 Dpth 7.60
Welded, 1 dk
(B21B20A) Anchor Handling Tug Supply
2 oil engines reduction geared to sc. shafts driving 2 CP propellers
Total Power: 12,504kW (17,000hp) 16.0kn
Caterpillar 3616TA
2 x Vee 4 Stroke 16 Cy. 280 x 300 each-6252kW (8500bhp)
Caterpillar Inc-USA
AuxGen: 1 x 500kW 440V 60Hz a.c, 1 x 1360kW 440V 60Hz a.c, 2 x 2000kW 440V 60Hz a.c
Thrusters: 1 Tunnel thruster (f); 1 Tunnel thruster (a); 1 Retract. directional thruster (f)
Fuel: 925.0 (d.f.)

7634422 - - **SUDARWAN II**
PT Pelayaran Djangkar Sakti
-
Jakarta *Indonesia*
175 83 -
Class: (KI)
1974 P.T. Djantra Dock & Shipbuilding — Jakarta
Loa - Br ex - Dght -
Lbp 32.52 Br md 6.51 Dpth 2.75
Welded, 1 dk
(A31A2GX) General Cargo Ship
1 oil engine driving 1 FP propeller
Total Power: 184kW (250hp) 8.0kn
Chinese Std. Type 6160A
1 x 4 Stroke 6 Cy. 160 x 225 184kW (250bhp) (made 1971, fitted 1974)
Shanghai Diesel Engine Co Ltd-China
AuxGen: 1 x 5kW 110/115V a.c, 1 x 2kW 110/115V a.c

9508378 TCSX6 - **SUDE-S**
Sener Petrol Denizcilik Ticaret AS
Istanbul *Turkey*
MMSI: 271002550
2,802 1,172 3,500
Class: BV
2009-01 Yildirim Gemi Insaat Sanayii A.S. — Tuzla Yd No: 113
Loa 93.10 Br ex - Dght 5.700
Lbp 86.60 Br md 14.50 Dpth 7.20
Welded, 1 dk
(A12B2TR) Chemical/Products Tanker
Double Hull (13F)
Ice Capable
1 oil engine REDUCTION: reduction geared to sc. shaft (s) driving 1 FP propeller
Total Power: 1,960kW (2,665hp) 13.5kn
MAN-B&W 8L28/32A
1 x 4 Stroke 8 Cy. 280 x 320 1960kW (2665bhp)
MAN B&W Diesel A/S-Denmark
AuxGen: 3 x 450kW a.c

9313682 V2BE1 - **SUDERAU**
Roland Ship Administration GmbH & Co KG
Reederei Erwin Strahlmann eK
Saint John's *Antigua & Barbuda*
MMSI: 304797000
Official number: 3977
2,461 1,369 3,707
Class: GL
2005-07 Slovenske Lodenice a.s. — Komarno Yd No: 2957
Loa 87.98 (BB) Br ex - Dght 5.510
Lbp 81.00 Br md 12.80 Dpth 7.10
Welded, 1 dk
(A31A2GX) General Cargo Ship
Grain: 4,612; Bale: 4,585
Compartments: 1 Ho, ER
1 Ha: ER (56.6 x 10.2)
Ice Capable
1 oil engine reverse reduction geared to sc. shaft driving 1 FP propeller
Total Power: 1,500kW (2,039hp) 11.7kn
MaK 8M20
1 x 4 Stroke 8 Cy. 200 x 300 1500kW (2039bhp)
Caterpillar Motoren GmbH & Co. KG-Germany
AuxGen: 3 x 119kW 380/220V 50Hz a.c, 1 x 49kW 380/220V 50Hz a.c
Thrusters: 1 Tunnel thruster (f)
Fuel: 147.0 (d.f.) 7.5pd

8137160 - - **SUDERAUE**
-
-
104 34 55
1980 Husumer Schiffswerft — Husum Yd No: 1465
Lengthened-1981
Loa 25.28 Br ex 8.03 Dght 1.001
Lbp 25.20 Br md 8.02 Dpth 1.60
Welded, 1 dk
(B33A2DU) Dredger (unspecified)
2 oil engines reverse geared to sc. shafts driving 2 FP propellers
6.0kn
Deutz F6L912
2 x 4 Stroke 6 Cy. 100 x 120
Kloeckner Humboldt Deutz AG-West Germany
AuxGen: 1 x 24kW 220/380V a.c

9256327 ZDHC8 - **SUDEROOG**
Briese Schiffahrts GmbH & Co KG ms 'Suderoog'
Briese Schiffahrts GmbH & Co KG
Gibraltar *Gibraltar (British)*
MMSI: 236300000
15,633 6,717 16,939
Class: GL
2005-12 Shandong Weihai Shipyard — Weihai SD Yd No: CZ043
Loa 161.35 (BB) Br ex - Dght 9.900
Lbp 151.00 Br md 25.00 Dpth 13.90
Welded, 1 dk
(A33A2CC) Container Ship (Fully Cellular)
TEU 1402 C Ho 910 TEU C Dk 492 TEU incl 250 ref C.
Compartments: 4 Cell Ho, ER
8 Ha: ER
Cranes: 2x45t
Ice Capable
1 oil engine driving 1 FP propeller
Total Power: 13,560kW (18,436hp) 19.0kn
MAN-B&W 6S60MC-C
1 x 2 Stroke 6 Cy. 600 x 2400 13560kW (18436bhp)
Dalian Marine Diesel Works-China
AuxGen: 3 x 1020kW 450/220V 60Hz a.c
Thrusters: 1 Thwart. FP thruster (f)
Fuel: 120.0 (d.f.) 1600.0 (r.f.)

5232646 LIRP R-14-ES **SUDEROY**
ex Skarholm *-2011* *ex* Omland *-2011*
ex Hallo *-2007* *ex* Kenty *-2003*
ex Merete Lau *-1979*
Skaar AS
-
Egersund *Norway*
MMSI: 259430000
199 134 -
1959-01 Scheepsbouw- en Constructiebedr. K. Hakvoort N.V. — Monnickendam Yd No: 75
Loa 28.00 Br ex 6.23 Dght -
Lbp - Br md - Dpth -
Welded
(B11B2FV) Fishing Vessel
1 oil engine driving 1 FP propeller
Total Power: 375kW (510hp)
Alpha 406-FO
1 x 2 Stroke 6 Cy. 230 x 400 375kW (510bhp)
Alpha Diesel A/S-Denmark

7217858 CXTG - **SUDESTADA**
ex Caiquen II *-1994* *ex* Roebourne *-1992*
Kios SA
-
Montevideo *Uruguay*
Official number: 7843
268 80 -
Class: (LR)
✠ Classed LR until 15/5/09
1972-07 Carrington Slipways Pty Ltd — Newcastle NSW Yd No: 71
Loa 32.01 Br ex 10.09 Dght 4.649
Lbp 28.50 Br md 9.76 Dpth 5.16
Welded, 1 dk
(B32A2ST) Tug
2 oil engines reverse reduction geared to sc. shafts driving 2 FP propellers
Total Power: 2,354kW (3,200hp)
Blackstone ESL16MK2
2 x Vee 4 Stroke 16 Cy. 222 x 292 each-1177kW (1600bhp)
Lister Blackstone MirrleesMarine Ltd.-Dursley
AuxGen: 2 x 40kW 415V 50Hz a.c

9582518 D5CZ4 - **SUDETY**
Galatea Two Navigation Ltd
Polska Zegluga Morska PP (POLSTEAM)
Monrovia *Liberia*
MMSI: 636015816
Official number: 15816
43,025 27,217 82,138 T/cm 70.2
Class: PR (NK)
2013-03 Tsuneishi Shipbuilding Co Ltd — Tadotsu KG Yd No: 1486
Loa 228.99 Br ex - Dght 14.430
Lbp 222.00 Br md 32.26 Dpth 20.05
Welded, 1 dk
(A21A2BC) Bulk Carrier
Grain: 97,000
Compartments: 7 Ho, ER
7 Ha: 6 (17.8 x 15.4)ER (16.2 x 13.8)
1 oil engine driving 1 FP propeller
Total Power: 13,560kW (18,436hp) 14.5kn
MAN-B&W 6S60MC-C
1 x 2 Stroke 6 Cy. 600 x 2400 13560kW (18436bhp)

9146510 **SUDHIRMULJI** **288** Class: IR
VWF0 87
\- **Gol Offshore Ltd** 117
\-
Mumbai *India*
MMSI: 419007300
Official number: 2740

1998-04 Bharati Shipyard Ltd — Ratnagiri Yd No: 264
Loa 31.00 Br ex - Dght 4.790
Lbp 30.00 Br md 9.60 Dpth 3.90
Welded, 1 dk

(B32A2ST) Tug
Passengers: berths: 7

2 oil engines geared to sc. shafts driving 2 Z propellers
Total Power: 2,670kW (3,630hp) 10.0kn
Normo KRMB-6
2 x 4 Stroke 6 Cy. 250 x 300 each-1335kW (1815bhp)
Ulstein Bergen AS-Norway
AuxGen: 2 x 60kW 415V 50Hz a.c
Fuel: 69.0 (d.f.)

9210294 **SUDKAP** **6,170** Class: GL
V2OH9 *ex* Scm Athina *-2009* *ex* BBC Atlantic *-2003* 2,958
\- *ex* Sudkap *-2001* 7,734
Krey Schiffahrts GmbH & Co ms 'Sudkap' KG
Krey Schiffahrts GmbH
Saint John's *Antigua & Barbuda*
MMSI: 304137000
Official number: 3786

2000-11 Stocznia Gdanska - Grupa Stoczni Gdynia SA — Gdansk Yd No: 8203/06
Loa 107.76 Br ex - Dght 7.806
Lbp 102.10 Br md 18.20 Dpth 10.10
Welded, 1 dk

(A31A2GX) General Cargo Ship
Grain: 10,401; Bale: 10,401
TEU 371 C. 371/20' (40')
Compartments: 2 Ho, ER
2 Ha: ER
Cranes: 2x80t
Ice Capable

1 oil engine reduction geared to sc. shaft driving 1 CP propeller
Total Power: 3,456kW (4,699hp) 14.3kn
MAN 8L32/40
1 x 4 Stroke 8 Cy. 320 x 400 3456kW (4699bhp)
MAN B&W Diesel AG-Augsburg
AuxGen: 1 x 424kW 220/380V a.c, 2 x 312kW 220/380V a.c

8726650 **SUDOREMONTNIK** **191** Class: RS
\- 85
\- **Veteran Mortrans Co Ltd** 323
\-
Petropavlovsk-Kamchatskiy *Russia*
Official number: 850670

1985-07 Svetlovskiy Sudoremontnyy Zavod — Svetlyy Yd No: 25
Loa 29.45 Br ex 8.15 Dght 3.120
Lbp 28.50 Br md 7.58 Dpth 3.60
Welded, 1 dk

(B34G2SE) Pollution Control Vessel
Liq: 332; Liq (Oil): 332
Compartments: 8 Ta
Ice Capable

1 oil engine geared to sc. shaft driving 1 FP propeller
Total Power: 165kW (224hp) 7.5kn
Daldizel 6CHNSP18/22
1 x 4 Stroke 6 Cy. 180 x 220 165kW (224bhp)
Daldizel-Khabarovsk
AuxGen: 1 x 50kW, 1 x 25kW
Fuel: 13.0 (d.f.)

8929525 **SUDOREMONTNIK** **182** Class: RS
\- 54
\- **Sudoremont-Zapad (OGUP)** 46
\-
Kaliningrad *Russia*

1973-12 "Petrozavod" — Leningrad Yd No: 835
Loa 29.30 Br ex 8.49 Dght 3.080
Lbp 27.00 Br md 8.30 Dpth 4.34
Welded, 1 dk

(B32A2ST) Tug
Ice Capable

2 oil engines driving 2 CP propellers
Total Power: 882kW (1,200hp) 11.4kn
Russkiy 6D30/50-4-2
2 x 2 Stroke 6 Cy. 300 x 500 each-441kW (600bhp)
Mashinostroitelnyy Zavod"Russkiy-Dizel"-Leningrad
AuxGen: 2 x 25kW a.c
Fuel: 36.0 (d.f.)

7742085 **SUDRINGUR** **671** Class: NV
OW2203 *ex* Suthringur *-1998* *ex* Oyrnafjall *-1995* 201
TG 600 *ex* Suthringur *-1990* -
Sudringur P/F
J C Marner Lisberg
SatCom: Inmarsat M 623102920
Tvoroyri *Faeroe Islands (Danish)*
MMSI: 231029000
Official number: D2619

1977 p/f Skala Skipasmidja — Skali Yd No: 31
Loa 45.62 Br ex 9.33 Dght 4.600
Lbp 39.81 Br md 9.30 Dpth 6.86
Welded, 1 dk & S dk

(B11A2FS) Stern Trawler
Ice Capable

1 oil engine reduction geared to sc. shaft driving 1 FP propeller
Total Power: 1,942kW (2,640hp)
Nohab F212V
1 x Vee 4 Stroke 12 Cy. 250 x 300 1942kW (2640bhp)
AB Bofors NOHAB-Sweden
AuxGen: 2 x 152kW 380V 50Hz a.c

9015058 **SUDUREY** **497**
TFOS *ex* Thorunn Sveinsdottir *-2008* 145
VE 012 **Isfelag Vestmannaeyja hf** 592
\-
Vestmannaeyjar *Iceland*
MMSI: 251019110
Official number: 2020

1991-07 Slippstodin h/f — Akureyri Yd No: 72
Loa 36.86 (BB) Br ex 8.00 Dght 3.000
Lbp 34.18 Br md 8.00 Dpth 7.29
Welded, 1 dk

(B11A2FS) Stern Trawler
Ins: 300

1 oil engine with clutches, flexible couplings & sr geared to sc. shaft driving 1 CP propeller
Total Power: 730kW (993hp) 11.3kn
Kromhout 6FGHD240
1 x 4 Stroke 6 Cy. 240 x 260 730kW (993bhp)
Stork Wartsila Diesel BV-Netherlands
AuxGen: 1 x 208kW 380V 50Hz a.c, 1 x 200kW 380V 50Hz a.c
Thrusters: 1 Thwart. FP thruster (f)

8851118 **SUE KOSSOW** *117*
WDE2544 *ex* Massac *-2005* 79
\- **Ingram Barge Co** -
\-
St Louis, MO *United States of America*
MMSI: 367192680
Official number: 641018

1981 Berry Bros. General Contractors, Inc. — Berwick, La Yd No: 8
Loa - Br ex - Dght -
Lbp 18.14 Br md 7.35 Dpth 2.65
Welded, 1 dk

(B32A2ST) Tug

1 oil engine driving 1 FP propeller

8982101 **SUE LEON LAB** **309**
WDE6715 *ex* Rapid Runner *-2009* 92
\- **Laborde Marine LLC** -
\-
Chalmette, LA *United States of America*
MMSI: 338402000
Official number: 1047287

1997-02 Breaux Bay Craft, Inc. — Loreauville, La Yd No: 1691
Loa 46.33 Br ex - Dght 1.670
Lbp 44.20 Br md 9.15 Dpth 3.81
Welded, 1 dk

(B21A2OC) Crew/Supply Vessel
Hull Material: Aluminium Alloy

4 oil engines Reduction geared to sc. shafts driving 4 FP propellers
Total Power: 4,200kW (5,712hp) 20.0kn
M.T.U. 16V2000M70
4 x Vee 4 Stroke 16 Cy. 130 x 150 each-1050kW (1428bhp)
Detroit Diesel Corporation-Detroit, Mi
AuxGen: 2 x 60Hz a.c

9153020 **SUECIA SEAWAYS** **24,196** Class: NV
OVPB2 *ex* Tor Suecia *-2011* 7,258
\- **DFDS A/S** 11,089
\- T/cm
Copenhagen *Denmark (DIS)* 41.0
MMSI: 220284000
Official number: D4107

1999-10 Fincantieri-Cant. Nav. Italiani S.p.A. — Ancona Yd No: 6021
Loa 197.02 (BB) Br ex 25.96 Dght 7.500
Lbp 180.55 Br md 25.90 Dpth 16.60
Welded, 3 dks incl. 1 hoistable

(A35A2RR) Ro-Ro Cargo Ship
Passengers: 12
Stern door/ramp (a)
Len: 14.00 Wid: 20.80 Swl: 180
Side door/ramp (s)
Lane-Len: 2772
Lane-Wid: 2.95
Lane-clr ht: 6.20
Trailers: 198
Cranes: 1x35t

2 oil engines with clutches, flexible couplings & sr geared to sc. shafts driving 2 CP propellers
Total Power: 21,600kW (29,368hp) 21.0kn
Sulzer 9ZA50S
2 x 4 Stroke 9 Cy. 500 x 660 each-10800kW (14684bhp)
Grandi Motori Trieste-Italy
AuxGen: 2 x 1400kW 380V 50Hz a.c, 3 x 960kW 380V 50Hz a.c
Thrusters: 2 Thwart. CP thruster (f)
Fuel: 54.0 (d.f.) (Heating Coils) 700.0 (r.f.) 80.0pd

9442299 **SUEGNO** **176** Class: RI
IO6899 -
\- **UniCredit Leasing SpA** -
\-
SatCom: Inmarsat Mini-M 761136244
Viareggio *Italy*
MMSI: 247207100

2007-03 Cantieri Navali Ferretti SpA — Fano Yd No: CL97/04
Loa 26.25 Br ex - Dght -
Lbp - Br md 6.97 Dpth 3.50
Bonded, 1 dk

(X11A2YP) Yacht
Hull Material: Reinforced Plastic

2 oil engines geared to sc. shaft driving 1 Propeller
Total Power: 3,580kW (4,868hp)
M.T.U. 16V2000M93
2 x Vee 4 Stroke 16 Cy. 135 x 156 each-1790kW (2434bhp)
MTU Friedrichshafen GmbH-Friedrichshafen

8404355 **SUEHIRO** *452*
\- *ex* Suehiro Maru *-1999* -
\- **-** 1,118
\-

1984-06 Nakatani Shipyard Co. Ltd. — Etajima Yd No: 491
Loa 74.20 (BB) Br ex - Dght 3.501
Lbp 69.02 Br md 11.61 Dpth 3.61
Welded, 2 dks

(A31A2GX) General Cargo Ship
Grain: 2,420; Bale: 2,280

1 oil engine reverse geared to sc. shaft driving 1 FP propeller
Total Power: 956kW (1,300hp)
Akasaka A28
1 x 4 Stroke 6 Cy. 280 x 550 956kW (1300bhp)
Akasaka Tekkosho KK (Akasaka DieselLtd)-Japan

8990249 **SUEHIRO MARU** *168*
JD2009 -
\- **Kushiro Tug Boat KK** -
\-
Kushiro, Hokkaido *Japan*
Official number: 140035

2004-05 Kanto Kogyo K.K. — Hakodate
Loa 32.51 Br ex - Dght 2.800
Lbp 27.00 Br md 9.00 Dpth 3.62
Welded, 1 dk

(B32A2ST) Tug

2 oil engines Geared Integral to driving 2 Z propellers
Total Power: 2,354kW (3,200hp) 13.3kn
Niigata 6L26HLX
2 x 4 Stroke 6 Cy. 260 x 350 each-1177kW (1600bhp)
Niigata Engineering Co Ltd-Japan

8738299 **SUEHIRO MARU** *748*
JD2718 -
\- **Funakoshi Sangyo KK** 2,400
\-
Kure, Hiroshima *Japan*
MMSI: 431000636
Official number: 140786

2008-07 K.K. Watanabe Zosensho — Nagasaki Yd No: 151
Loa 82.52 Br ex - Dght -
Lbp 77.00 Br md 13.60 Dpth 8.15
Welded, 1 dk

(A31A2GX) General Cargo Ship
Bale: 3,100

1 oil engine driving 1 Propeller
Total Power: 2,648kW (3,600hp) 14.5kn
Hanshin LH41LA
1 x 4 Stroke 6 Cy. 410 x 800 2648kW (3600bhp)
The Hanshin Diesel Works Ltd-Japan

9574559 **SUEHIRO MARU** *181*
JD3090 -
\- **Yokkaichi Eisen YK (Yokkaichi Tug Service)** -
\-
Yokkaichi, Mie *Japan*
Official number: 141286

2010-09 Kanagawa Zosen — Kobe Yd No: 616
Loa 33.20 Br ex - Dght 3.100
Lbp 29.00 Br md 9.20 Dpth 3.90
Welded, 1 dk

(B32A2ST) Tug

2 oil engines reduction geared to sc. shafts driving 2 Propellers
Total Power: 2,942kW (4,000hp)
Niigata 6L26HLX
2 x 4 Stroke 6 Cy. 260 x 350 each-1471kW (2000bhp)
Niigata Engineering Co Ltd-Japan

9566124 **SUEHIRO MARU NO. 8** *749*
JD2986 -
\- **Suehiro Kisen KK** 1,900
\-
Fukuyama, Hiroshima *Japan*
MMSI: 431001086
Official number: 141129

2009-11 Suzuki Shipyard Co. Ltd. — Yokkaichi Yd No: 725
Loa 68.00 Br ex - Dght -
Lbp - Br md 11.80 Dpth -
Welded, 1 dk

(A13B2TP) Products Tanker
Double Hull (13F)

1 oil engine driving 1 FP propeller
Total Power: 1,618kW (2,200hp)
Hanshin LA32G
1 x 4 Stroke 6 Cy. 320 x 680 1618kW (2200bhp)
The Hanshin Diesel Works Ltd-Japan

IMO / Call sign / Flag	Name / Owner / Manager / Port	Tonnage	Class	Built / Dimensions	Type / Cargo	Machinery
9203057 *JL6510* -	**SUEHIRO MARU No. 8** **Kigyo Kumiai Osaki Zosen Tekkosho** - *Kanonji, Kagawa* *Japan* Official number: 136473	*199* - -		**1998**-03 **Tokuoka Zosen K.K. — Naruto** Yd No: 250 Loa 58.16 Br ex - Dght - Lbp 52.00 Br md 9.50 Dpth 5.50 Welded, 1 dk	**(A31A2GX) General Cargo Ship** Compartments: 1 Ho, ER 1 Ha: (30.0 x 7.3)ER	**1 oil engine** driving 1 FP propeller Total Power: 736kW (1,001hp) 11.5kn Niigata 6M28BGT 1 x 4 Stroke 6 Cy. 280 x 480 736kW (1001bhp) Niigata Engineering Co Ltd-Japan
9124160 *JK5423* -	**SUEHIRO MARU No. 8** **Funakoshi Sangyo KK** Tokuyama Senpaku KK *Kure, Hiroshima* *Japan* MMSI: 431400446 Official number: 134668	*731* - 1,800		**1995**-06 **Nakatani Shipyard Co. Ltd. — Etajima** Yd No: 566 Loa 87.70 (BB) Br ex - Dght 4.400 Lbp 80.00 Br md 12.70 Dpth 7.70 Welded, 2 dks	**(A31A2GX) General Cargo Ship** Bale: 3,936 Compartments: 1 Ho, ER 1 Ha: ER Cranes: 1	**1 oil engine** driving 1 CP propeller Total Power: 2,648kW (3,600hp) Akasaka A41S 1 x 4 Stroke 6 Cy. 410 x 800 2648kW (3600bhp) Akasaka Tekkosho KK (Akasaka DieselLtd)-Japan Thrusters: 1 Thwart. FP thruster (f)
7728572 *LW2962* -	**SUEMAR DOS** **Sociedad Mixta Olivos SA** - SatCom: Inmarsat C 470138910 - *Puerto Madryn* *Argentina* MMSI: 701000619 Official number: 01508	*221* 107 200	Class: (LR) (GL) Classed LR until 22/12/09	**1979**-05 **Construcciones Navales Santodomingo SA — Vigo** Yd No: 426 Lengthened-1982 Loa 39.50 Br ex 8.31 Dght 3.552 Lbp 34.75 Br md 8.28 Dpth 5.62 Welded, 2 dks	**(B11A2FS) Stern Trawler**	**1 oil engine** reverse reduction geared to sc. shaft driving 1 FP propeller Total Power: 599kW (814hp) 11.8kn Alpha 6T23LU 1 x 4 Stroke 6 Cy. 225 x 300 599kW (814bhp) Construcciones Echevarria SA-Spain AuxGen: 1 x 275kW 220/380V 50Hz a.c
9329033 - -	**SUENOS** **Pescabrava Sociedade Armadora Pesca Lda** - *Tangier* *Morocco*	**115** 34 -		**2004**-05 **Francisco Cardama, SA — Vigo** Yd No: 222 Loa 20.50 Br ex - Dght 2.500 Lbp 18.17 Br md 6.30 Dpth 5.05 Welded, 1 dk	**(B11B2FV) Fishing Vessel**	**1 oil engine** geared to sc. shaft driving 1 FP propeller Total Power: 441kW (600hp) Volvo Penta TAMD165A 1 x 4 Stroke 6 Cy. 144 x 165 441kW (600bhp) AB Volvo Penta-Sweden
9081100 *V7OS4* -	**SUERTE** *ex* Anna *-2008* *ex* Nordmax *-2004* **Bonalma Marine Inc** Alexandria Shipping (Hellas) SA *Majuro* *Marshall Islands* MMSI: 538003146 Official number: 3146	**39,027** 24,110 72,516 T/cm 66.4	Class: AB (GL)	**1995**-01 **Daewoo Heavy Industries Ltd — Geoje** Yd No: 1083 Loa 224.80 (BB) Br ex - Dght 13.820 Lbp 216.00 Br md 32.20 Dpth 19.10 Welded, 1 dk	**(A21A2BC) Bulk Carrier** Grain: 85,704 Compartments: 7 Ho, ER 7 Ha: ER	**1 oil engine** driving 1 FP propeller Total Power: 9,345kW (12,705hp) 14.5kn B&W 6S60MC 1 x 2 Stroke 6 Cy. 600 x 2292 9345kW (12705bhp) Hyundai Heavy Industries Co Ltd-South Korea AuxGen: 3 x 500kW 440/220V a.c Fuel: 171.0 (d.f.) 2379.8 (r.f.)
9036492 - -	**SUEZ 1** **Government of The Arab Republic of Egypt (Ministry of Maritime Transport - Ports & Lighthouses Administration)** - *Alexandria* *Egypt*	**250** - 120	Class: LR ✠**100A1** SS 06/2010 oil tanker Egyptian coastal service ✠**LMC** Eq.Ltr: D; Cable: 247.5/17.5 U2	**1994**-10 **Egyptian Shipbuilding & Repairs Co. — Alexandria** Yd No: 904 Loa 32.90 Br ex 6.90 Dght 2.250 Lbp 30.80 Br md 6.60 Dpth 2.75 Welded, 1 dk	**(A13B2TP) Products Tanker** Compartments: 4 Ta, ER	**2 oil engines** with clutches, flexible couplings & sr reverse geared to sc. shafts driving 2 FP propellers Total Power: 428kW (582hp) M.T.U. 10V183AA61 2 x Vee 4 Stroke 10 Cy. 128 x 142 each-214kW (291bhp) MTU Friedrichshafen GmbH-Friedrichshafen AuxGen: 1 x 48kW 380V 50Hz a.c
9230311 *HODM* -	**SUEZ CANAL BRIDGE** **Virgo Carriers Corp SA** Sea Quest Ship Management Inc SatCom: Inmarsat C 435370410 *Panama* *Panama* MMSI: 353704000 Official number: 2854302C	**68,687** 25,395 71,359	Class: AB (Class contemplated) NK	**2002**-05 **Hyundai Heavy Industries Co Ltd — Ulsan** Yd No: 1370 Loa 284.60 (BB) Br ex - Dght 14.022 Lbp 271.27 Br md 40.00 Dpth 24.40 Welded, 1 dk	**(A33A2CC) Container Ship (Fully Cellular)** TEU 5610 C Ho 2802 TEU C Dk 2808 TEU incl 500 ref C. 16 Ha: 12 (12.6 x 35.8) (12.6 x 33.4) (12.6 x 27.9) (12.6 x 20.5) (6.4 x 15.5)ER	**1 oil engine** driving 1 FP propeller Total Power: 58,840kW (79,999hp) 25.1kn MAN-B&W 11K98MC 1 x 2 Stroke 11 Cy. 980 x 2660 58840kW (79999bhp) Hyundai Heavy Industries Co Ltd-South Korea AuxGen: 4 x 2600kW 440/220V 60Hz a.c Thrusters: 1 Thwart. CP thruster (f) Fuel: 10140.0
7012507 *SUSL* -	**SUEZ FLOWER** *ex* Mas Flower *-1994* *ex* Ibn Jubair *-1992* *ex* Atlan Esmeralda *-1974* **Mohamed Abdel Monim Abdel Samea** - *Alexandria* *Egypt* Official number: 1221	*1,179* 771 1,727	Class: (LR) ✠ Classed LR until 4/3/98	**1970**-04 **Sociedad Metalurgica Duro Felguera — Gijon** Yd No: 58 Loa 72.70 Br ex 11.54 Dght 5.195 Lbp 64.01 Br md 11.51 Dpth 6.10 Welded, 2 dks	**(A31A2GX) General Cargo Ship** Grain: 2,266; Bale: 2,112; Ins: 891 Compartments: 3 Ho, ER, 3 Tw Dk 3 Ha: (14.5 x 5.2)2 (5.5 x 5.2)ER Derricks: 2x20t,4x5t,4x3t	**1 oil engine** driving 1 FP propeller Total Power: 1,103kW (1,500hp) 15.0kn Deutz RBV6M358 1 x 4 Stroke 6 Cy. 400 x 580 1103kW (1500bhp) Hijos de J Barreras SA-Spain AuxGen: 1 x 125kW 400V 50Hz a.c, 2 x 118kW 400V 50Hz a.c
9524449 *V7WJ6* -	**SUEZ FUZEYYA** **Suez Fuzeyya Ltd** Empire Navigation Inc *Majuro* *Marshall Islands* MMSI: 538004316 Official number: 4316	**81,282** 52,295 158,574 T/cm 118.2	Class: AB	**2011**-06 **Hyundai Heavy Industries Co Ltd — Gunsan** Yd No: 2300 Loa 274.33 (BB) Br ex 48.04 Dght 17.170 Lbp 264.00 Br md 48.00 Dpth 23.10 Welded, 1 dk	**(A13A2TV) Crude Oil Tanker** Double Hull (13F) Liq: 170,613; Liq (Oil): 167,500 Cargo Heating Coils Compartments: 12 Wing Ta, 2 Wing Slop Ta, ER 3 Cargo Pump (s): 3x4000m³/hr Manifold: Bow/CM: 137.4m	**1 oil engine** driving 1 FP propeller Total Power: 19,620kW (26,675hp) 16.0kn MAN-B&W 6S70MC-C8 1 x 2 Stroke 6 Cy. 700 x 2800 19620kW (26675bhp) Hyundai Heavy Industries Co Ltd-South Korea AuxGen: 3 x 800kW a.c Fuel: 587.0 (d.f.) 4030.0 (r.f.)
9513139 *V7DU6* -	**SUEZ GEORGE** *ex* Hero *-2014* **Suez George Ltd** Empire Navigation Inc *Majuro* *Marshall Islands* MMSI: 538005435 Official number: 5435	**83,850** 49,031 156,532 T/cm 119.8	Class: AB (NV)	**2011**-03 **Jiangsu Rongsheng Shipbuilding Co Ltd — Rugao JS** Yd No: 1080 Loa 274.50 (BB) Br ex 48.03 Dght 17.000 Lbp 264.00 Br md 48.00 Dpth 23.70 Welded, 1 dk	**(A13A2TV) Crude Oil Tanker** Double Hull (13F) Liq: 167,550; Liq (Oil): 167,500 Cargo Heating Coils Compartments: 12 Wing Ta, 2 Wing Slop Ta, ER 3 Cargo Pump (s): 3x3500m³/hr Manifold: Bow/CM: 138.8m	**1 oil engine** driving 1 FP propeller Total Power: 18,660kW (25,370hp) 15.1kn MAN-B&W 6S70MC-C 1 x 2 Stroke 6 Cy. 700 x 2800 18660kW (25370bhp) AuxGen: 3 x 960kW a.c Fuel: 240.0 (d.f.) 4500.0 (r.f.)
9524463 *V7WJ8* -	**SUEZ HANS** **Suez Hans Ltd** Empire Navigation Inc *Majuro* *Marshall Islands* MMSI: 538004318 Official number: 4318	**81,282** 52,295 158,564 T/cm 118.2	Class: AB	**2011**-07 **Hyundai Heavy Industries Co Ltd — Gunsan** Yd No: 2302 Loa 274.33 (BB) Br ex 48.04 Dght 17.150 Lbp 264.00 Br md 48.00 Dpth 23.10 Welded, 1 dk	**(A13A2TV) Crude Oil Tanker** Double Hull (13F) Liq: 170,613; Liq (Oil): 167,500 Cargo Heating Coils Compartments: 12 Wing Ta, 2 Wing Slop Ta, ER 3 Cargo Pump (s): 3x4000m³/hr Manifold: Bow/CM: 137.4m	**1 oil engine** driving 1 FP propeller Total Power: 19,620kW (26,675hp) 16.0kn MAN-B&W 6S70MC-C8 1 x 2 Stroke 6 Cy. 700 x 2800 19620kW (26675bhp) Hyundai Heavy Industries Co Ltd-South Korea AuxGen: 3 x 800kW a.c Fuel: 587.0 (d.f.) 4030.0 (r.f.)
9524475 *V7WJ9* -	**SUEZ RAJAN** **Suez Rajan Ltd** Empire Navigation Inc *Majuro* *Marshall Islands* MMSI: 538004319 Official number: 4319	**81,282** 52,295 158,564 T/cm 118.2	Class: AB	**2011**-08 **Hyundai Heavy Industries Co Ltd — Gunsan** Yd No: 2303 Loa 274.33 (BB) Br ex 48.04 Dght 17.150 Lbp 264.00 Br md 48.00 Dpth 23.10 Welded, 1 dk	**(A13A2TV) Crude Oil Tanker** Double Hull (13F) Liq: 170,612; Liq (Oil): 167,500 Cargo Heating Coils Compartments: 12 Wing Ta, 2 Wing Slop Ta, ER 3 Cargo Pump (s): 3x4000m³/hr Manifold: Bow/CM: 137.4m	**1 oil engine** driving 1 FP propeller Total Power: 19,620kW (26,675hp) 16.0kn MAN-B&W 6S70MC-C8 1 x 2 Stroke 6 Cy. 700 x 2800 19620kW (26675bhp) Hyundai Heavy Industries Co Ltd-South Korea AuxGen: 3 x 800kW a.c Fuel: 587.1 (d.f.) 4030.0 (r.f.)
9524451 *V7WJ7* -	**SUEZ VASILIS** **Suez Vasilis Ltd** Empire Navigation Inc *Majuro* *Marshall Islands* MMSI: 538004317 Official number: 4317	**81,282** 52,295 158,601 T/cm 118.2	Class: AB	**2011**-06 **Hyundai Heavy Industries Co Ltd — Gunsan** Yd No: 2301 Loa 274.33 (BB) Br ex 48.04 Dght 17.150 Lbp 264.00 Br md 48.00 Dpth 23.10 Welded, 1 dk	**(A13A2TV) Crude Oil Tanker** Double Hull (13F) Liq: 170,613; Liq (Oil): 167,500 Cargo Heating Coils Compartments: 12 Wing Ta, 2 Wing Slop Ta, ER 3 Cargo Pump (s): 3x4000m³/hr Manifold: Bow/CM: 137.4m	**1 oil engine** driving 1 FP propeller Total Power: 19,620kW (26,675hp) 16.0kn MAN-B&W 6S70MC-C8 1 x 2 Stroke 6 Cy. 700 x 2800 19620kW (26675bhp) Hyundai Heavy Industries Co Ltd-South Korea AuxGen: 3 x 800kW a.c Fuel: 587.0 (d.f.) 4030.0 (r.f.)
8802600 *4Z2601* -	**SUFA** **Ashdod Port Co Ltd** - *Ashdod* *Israel* Official number: 001323	**492** 147 780	Class: LR ✠**100A1** SS 07/2009 tug **LMC** **UMS** Eq.Ltr: (H) ; Cable: 335.0/22.0 U2	**1989**-07 **Israel Shipyards Ltd. — Haifa** Yd No: 1064 Loa 35.00 Br ex 11.44 Dght - Lbp 33.51 Br md 11.41 Dpth 4.25 Welded, 1 dk	**(B32A2ST) Tug**	**2 oil engines** gearing integral to driving 2 Voith-Schneider propellers Total Power: 3,200kW (4,350hp) Deutz SBV8M628 2 x 4 Stroke 8 Cy. 240 x 280 each-1600kW (2175bhp) Kloeckner Humboldt Deutz AG-West Germany AuxGen: 2 x 128kW 400V 50Hz a.c
6815304 *MMFK9* LT 372	**SUFFOLK CHIEFTAIN** **Pescacarino SA** - *Lowestoft* *United Kingdom* MMSI: 232006830 Official number: A18989	**400** 120 -	Class: LR ✠**100A1** SS 06/2009 fishing vessel ✠**LMC** Eq.Ltr: (I) ; Cable: 192.5/25.4 U1	**1968**-06 **Appledore Shipbuilders Ltd — Bideford** Yd No: A.S. 56 Converted From: Standby Safety Vessel-1987 Converted From: Trawler-1981 Loa 38.31 Br ex 7.88 Dght - Lbp 33.53 Br md 7.78 Dpth 3.97 Welded, 1 dk	**(B11A2FT) Trawler**	**1 oil engine** with flexible couplings & sr reverse geared to sc. shaft driving 1 FP propeller Total Power: 809kW (1,100hp) 12.3kn Ruston 6ARM 1 x 4 Stroke 6 Cy. 260 x 368 809kW (1100bhp) Ruston & Hornsby Ltd.-Lincoln AuxGen: 1 x 76kW 220V 50Hz a.c, 1 x 56kW 220V 50Hz a.c Fuel: 56.0 (d.f.)

9676917 *2FIG9* -	**SUFFOLK SPIRIT** - **Shire Maritime Ltd** - *Ipswich* *United Kingdom* MMSI: 235091503 Official number: 918210	**146** 146 -		**2012-06 Kocurek Excavators Ltd — Ipswich** Loa 26.00 Br ex - Dght 2.600 Lbp 22.00 Br md 10.40 Dpth 3.35 Welded, 1 dk	**(B34T2QR) Work/Repair Vessel**	**2 oil engines** reduction geared to sc. shafts driving 2 Propellers Total Power: 1,176kW (1,598hp) 10.0kn Thrusters: 1 Thwart. FP thruster (f)
8409604 *FUZK* CN 652468	**SUFFREN** - **Nicolas Cauvin** - SatCom: Inmarsat C 422794510 *Caen* *France* MMSI: 227945000	**171** 121 -		**1985-07 Ch. Normands Reunis — Courseulles-sur-Mer** (Hull) **1985-07 Ateliers et Chantiers de La Manche — Dieppe** Yd No: 1328 Loa - Br ex - Dght - Lbp - Br md - Dpth - Welded, 1 dk	**(B11A2FS) Stern Trawler**	**1 oil engine** driving 1 FP propeller
7612022 *WYT9764* -	**SUGAM No. 21** - **Dole Food Co** - *Astoria, OR* *United States of America* Official number: 556533	*110* 75 -		**1974 Bender Welding & Machine Co Inc — Mobile AL** L reg 20.85 Br ex 6.71 Dght - Lbp - Br md - Dpth 3.38 Welded, 1 dk	**(B11A2FT) Trawler**	**1 oil engine** driving 1 FP propeller Total Power: 313kW (426hp) Caterpillar D353SCAC 1 x 4 Stroke 6 Cy. 159 x 203 313kW (426bhp) Caterpillar Tractor Co-USA
7336020 - -	**SUGAR 6** *ex Sugar -2008 ex Ayanka -2005* **Tianmu Fishing Co** -	**176** 52 88	Class: (RS)	**1973 Zavod 'Nikolayevsk-na-Amure' — Nikolayevsk-na-Amure** Yd No: 81 Loa 33.96 Br ex 7.09 Dght 2.899 Lbp 29.97 Br md - Dpth 3.66 Welded, 1 dk	**(B11B2FV) Fishing Vessel** Bale: 115 Compartments: 1 Ho, ER 1 Ha: (1.3 x 1.6) Derricks: 2x2t; Winches: 2 Ice Capable	**1 oil engine** driving 1 FP propeller Total Power: 224kW (305hp) 9.5kn S.K.L. 8NVD36-1U 1 x 4 Stroke 8 Cy. 240 x 360 224kW (305bhp) VEB Schwermaschinenbau "KarlLiebknecht" (SKL)-Magdeburg
7734454 *WYC4443* -	**SUGAR BEAR** *ex T. P. One -1991 ex Sugar Bear -1991* **Robert L Hunt** - *Juneau, AK* *United States of America* Official number: 587060	*114* 77 -		**1977 Quality Marine, Inc. — Theodore, Al** L reg 21.71 Br ex - Dght - Lbp - Br md 6.71 Dpth 3.20 Welded, 1 dk	**(B11B2FV) Fishing Vessel**	**1 oil engine** driving 1 FP propeller Total Power: 382kW (519hp) G.M. (Detroit Diesel) 12V-149 1 x Vee 2 Stroke 12 Cy. 146 x 146 382kW (519bhp) General Motors Detroit DieselAllison Divn-USA
7309819 *WU5179* -	**SUGAR DADDY** *ex Mis Hijas -2009 ex Miss Davi Nicole -1992* *ex Country Girl -1990 ex Capt. Wayne -1978* *ex Virginia Rose -1976* **Deborah A Koole** - *Galveston, TX* *United States of America* Official number: 297630	*102* 69 -		**1965 Capell Marine, Inc. — Freeport, Tx** Yd No: 6 Converted From: Yacht-1976 L reg 20.67 Br ex 6.20 Dght - Lbp - Br md - Dpth 3.31 Welded, 1 dk	**(B11B2FV) Fishing Vessel**	**1 oil engine** driving 1 FP propeller Total Power: 257kW (349hp)
7938361 *WDD4727* -	**SUGAR FOOT** *ex Miss Ursula -2005 ex Alida Marie -1996* **Debbie Sue LLC** - *Barnegat Light, NJ* *United States of America* Official number: 599042	*127* 86 -		**1978 Gulf Coast Marine Builders, Inc. — Bayou La Batre, Al** Yd No: 17 L reg 23.69 Br ex 6.76 Dght - Lbp - Br md - Dpth 3.54 Welded, 1 dk	**(B11A2FS) Stern Trawler**	**1 oil engine** driving 1 FP propeller Total Power: 257kW (349hp) G.M. (Detroit Diesel) 12V-71-N 1 x Vee 2 Stroke 12 Cy. 108 x 127 257kW (349bhp) General Motors Detroit DieselAllison Divn-USA
7807720 *V7KY3* -	**SUGAR ISLAND** - **Great Lakes Dredge & Dock Co LLC** - *Majuro* *Marshall Islands* MMSI: 538002695 Official number: 2695	**2,820** 846 4,357	Class: AB	**1979-05 Southern SB. Corp. — Slidell, La** Yd No: 119 Loa 85.65 Br ex 15.91 Dght 5.360 Lbp 80.78 Br md 15.87 Dpth 6.56 Welded, 1 dk	**(B33B2DT) Trailing Suction Hopper Dredger** Hopper: 2,754	**2 oil engines** reverse reduction geared to sc. shafts driving 2 FP propellers Total Power: 3,162kW (4,300hp) 12.0kn EMD (Electro-Motive) 12-645-E7B 2 x Vee 2 Stroke 12 Cy. 230 x 254 each-1581kW (2150bhp) General Motors Corp.Electro-Motive Div.-La Grange AuxGen: 2 x 500kW Thrusters: 1 Thwart. FP thruster (f)
7926863 *WDD3817* -	**SUGARFOOT II** *ex Charlotte G -2011* **Timothy Bellanceau** - *Portland, ME* *United States of America* MMSI: 367136560 Official number: 606024	*119* 81 -		**1979 James K. Walker Marine, Inc. — Moss Point, Ms** Yd No: 236 L reg 21.74 Br ex 6.71 Dght - Lbp - Br md - Dpth 3.69 Welded, 1 dk	**(B11A2FT) Trawler**	**1 oil engine** geared to sc. shaft driving 1 FP propeller Total Power: 400kW (544hp) Caterpillar D353TA 1 x 4 Stroke 6 Cy. 159 x 203 400kW (544bhp) Caterpillar Tractor Co-USA
7922972 - - -	**SUGAWARA MARU** - - -	*479* 247 -		**1979-06 Muneta Zosen K.K. — Akashi** Yd No: 823 Loa - Br ex - Dght - Lbp 44.20 Br md 14.00 Dpth 3.00 Welded, 1 dk	**(B34B2SC) Crane Vessel**	**2 oil engines** driving 1 FP propeller Total Power: 882kW (1,200hp) Yanmar 6MAL-DHT 2 x 4 Stroke 6 Cy. 200 x 240 each-441kW (600bhp) Yanmar Diesel Engine Co Ltd-Japan
5343287 - -	**SUGI** *ex Soegi -2011* **PT PERTAMINA (PERSERO)** - *Palembang* *Indonesia*	*214* - -	Class: (LR) (KI) ✠ Classed LR until 18/12/81	**1957-05 N.V. Scheepswerf "Alphen" P. de Vries Lentsch — Alphen a/d Rijn** Yd No: 380 Loa 31.50 Br ex 7.73 Dght 2.700 Lbp 28.20 Br md 7.51 Dpth 3.61 Welded	**(B32A2ST) Tug**	**1 oil engine** with flexible couplings & dr reverse geared to sc. shaft driving 1 FP propeller Total Power: 588kW (799hp) Werkspoor 8TMAF338 1 x 4 Stroke 8 Cy. 330 x 600 588kW (799bhp) NV Werkspoor-Netherlands
7117838 - -	**SUGREEVA** - **Visakhapatnam Port Trust** - *Visakhapatnam* *India*	*1,020* - 1,341	Class: IR (LR) ✠ Classed LR until 23/4/76	**1971-09 Garden Reach Workshops Ltd. — Kolkata** Yd No: 808 Loa 63.81 Br ex 13.90 Dght 2.998 Lbp 58.93 Br md 13.50 Dpth 3.81 Welded, 1 dk	**(B34A2SH) Hopper, Motor**	**2 oil engines** driving 2 Directional propellers Total Power: 640kW (870hp) 8.0kn Caterpillar 3406TA 2 x 4 Stroke 6 Cy. 137 x 165 each-320kW (435bhp) Caterpillar Tractor Co-USA AuxGen: 2 x 56kW 415V 50Hz a.c Fuel: 27.5 (d.f.)
7035901 *D8VS* -	**SUH KANG CHALLENGER** *ex Global Challenger -1993 ex Mini Look -1974* *ex American Main -1973* *launched as Mini Look -1971* **Korea Development Leasing Corp** Suh Kang Co Ltd *Gwangyang* *South Korea* Official number: KYR-715873	*1,569* 997 3,031	Class: (KR) (AB)	**1971-04 K.K. Taihei Kogyo — Akitsu** (Hull) Yd No: 253 **1971-04 The Hakodate Dock Co Ltd — Japan** Yd No: 487 Loa 65.47 Br ex 15.32 Dght 4.955 Lbp 62.80 Br md 15.30 Dpth 6.60 Welded, 1 dk	**(A31A2GX) General Cargo Ship** Grain: 3,671; Bale: 3,564 Compartments: 2 Ho, ER 4 Ha: 4 (19.5 x 5.1)ER Cranes: 2x15t	**2 oil engines** reduction geared to sc. shafts driving 2 FP propellers Total Power: 1,104kW (1,500hp) 10.0kn Daihatsu 6PSHTCM-26D 2 x 4 Stroke 6 Cy. 260 x 320 each-552kW (750bhp) Daihatsu Diesel Manufacturing Co Lt-Japan AuxGen: 2 x 48kW 445V 60Hz a.c Fuel: 106.5 (d.f.)
8619182 - -	**SUHAE No. 15** *ex Koho Maru -1999* *ex Yahata Maru No. 1 -1995* **Suhae Maritime Corp** - *Daesan* *South Korea* MMSI: 440200111 Official number: DSR-999018	*198* - 88	Class: KR	**1987-05 K.K. Odo Zosen Tekko — Shimonoseki** Yd No: 332 Loa 34.00 Br ex 9.45 Dght 3.120 Lbp 29.00 Br md 9.20 Dpth 4.20 Welded, 1 dk	**(B32A2ST) Tug**	**2 oil engines** with flexible couplings & dr gearedto sc. shafts driving 2 FP propellers Total Power: 2,500kW (3,400hp) 14.5kn Fuji 6L27.5G 2 x 4 Stroke 6 Cy. 275 x 320 each-1250kW (1700bhp) Fuji Diesel Co Ltd-Japan AuxGen: 1 x 80kW 225V a.c
8741466 - -	**SUHAE NO. 45** - **Suhae Maritime Corp** - *Daesan* *South Korea* Official number: DSR-082459	*289* - 171	Class: KR	**2008-12 Namyang Shipbuilding Co Ltd — Yeosu** Yd No: 1086 Loa 38.00 Br ex - Dght 3.445 Lbp 34.23 Br md 10.00 Dpth 4.53 Welded, 1 dk	**(B32A2ST) Tug**	**2 oil engines** reduction geared to sc. shafts driving 2 Propellers Total Power: 2,434kW (3,310hp) Niigata 6L28HX 2 x 4 Stroke 6 Cy. 280 x 370 each-1217kW (1655bhp) Niigata Engineering Co Ltd-Japan
9639270 - -	**SUHAE NO. 51** - **Il Woo Maritime Corp** - *Yeosu* *South Korea* Official number: YSR-112805	**296** - 164	Class: KR	**2011-03 Namyang Shipbuilding Co Ltd — Yeosu** Yd No: 1107 Loa 38.00 Br ex - Dght 3.512 Lbp 32.30 Br md 10.00 Dpth 4.60 Welded, 1 dk	**(B32A2ST) Tug**	**2 oil engines** reduction geared to sc. shafts driving 2 Propellers Total Power: 3,840kW (5,220hp) Yanmar 6EY26 2 x 4 Stroke 6 Cy. 260 x 385 each-1920kW (2610bhp) Yanmar Diesel Engine Co Ltd-Japan

9639268 - -	**SUHAE NO. 53** - **Suhae Maritime Corp** - *Daesan* *South Korea* MMSI: 440210040 Official number: DSR-117801	**296** - 164	Class: KR	**2011-02 Namyang Shipbuilding Co Ltd — Yeosu** Yd No: 1106 Loa 38.00 Br ex - Dght 3.512 Lbp 32.30 Br md 10.00 Dpth 4.60 Welded, 1 dk	**(B32A2ST) Tug**	**2 oil engines** reduction geared to sc. shafts driving 2 Propellers Total Power: 3,840kW (5,220hp) Yanmar 6EY26 2 x 4 Stroke 6 Cy. 260 x 385 each-1920kW (2610bhp) Yanmar Diesel Engine Co Ltd-Japan
8746894 *9MHW9* -	**SUHAIL** - **Government of Malaysia (Director of Marine & Ministry of Transport)** - *Port Klang* *Malaysia* Official number: 333808	**140** 42 25		**2007-12 Kay Marine Sdn Bhd — Kuala Terengganu** (Assembled by) Yd No: J104-3 **0000* Inform Marine Technology — Fremantle WA** (Parts for assembly by) Loa 26.00 Br ex - Dght 1.200 Lbp - Br md 9.20 Dpth 2.55 Welded, 1 dk	**(A37B2PS) Passenger Ship** Hull Material: Aluminium Alloy	**2 oil engines** reduction geared to sc. shafts driving 2 Propellers Total Power: 2,206kW (3,000hp) M.T.U. 12V2000M91 2 x Vee 4 Stroke 12 Cy. 130 x 150 each-1103kW (1500bhp) MTU Friedrichshafen GmbH-Friedrichshafen
8037243 *ATSU*	**SUHASINI** - **Srinivasa Sea Foods Pvt Ltd** - *Visakhapatnam* *India* Official number: 1787	*116* 79 57	Class: (IR) (AB)	**1978 Ingenieria y Maq. Especializada S.A. (IMESA) — Coatzacoalcos** Loa 23.17 Br ex 7.47 Dght 2.255 Lbp 21.39 Br md 7.33 Dpth 3.28 Welded, 1 dk	**(B11B2FV) Fishing Vessel**	**1 oil engine** sr geared to sc. shaft driving 1 FP propeller Total Power: 279kW (379hp) 8.5kn Caterpillar D353TA 1 x 4 Stroke 6 Cy. 159 x 203 279kW (379bhp) Caterpillar Tractor Co-USA AuxGen: 2 x 10kW 120V 50Hz a.c Fuel: 39.5 (d.f.)
9029645 *AULA* -	**SUHELI** - **Government of The Republic of India (Administration of Union Territory of Lakshadweep)** Lakshadweep Development Corp Ltd *Mumbai* *India* MMSI: 419324000 Official number: 2253	**164** 49 110	Class: IR	**1987-03 Alcock, Ashdown & Co. Ltd. — Bhavnagar** Yd No: 141 Loa 30.20 Br ex 7.57 Dght 1.710 Lbp 28.25 Br md 7.25 Dpth 2.60 Welded, 1 dk	**(A13B2TU) Tanker (unspecified)**	**2 oil engines** sr geared to sc. shafts driving 2 FP propellers Total Power: 350kW (476hp) 11.0kn Cummins NT-743-M 2 x 4 Stroke 6 Cy. 130 x 152 each-175kW (238bhp) Kirloskar Oil Engines Ltd-India AuxGen: 2 x 6kW 415V 50Hz a.c Fuel: 7.0 (d.f.)
9553347 *YM2181*	**SUHEYLA** - **Karyat Karadeniz Yatcilik ve Turizm AS (Karyacht Karadeniz Yachting & Tourism Inc)** - *Istanbul* *Turkey* Official number: TUGS1282	**146** 44 -		**1990-01 Selah Makina Sanayi ve Ticaret A.S. — Tuzla, Istanbul** Yd No: 19275 Loa 37.96 Br ex - Dght 4.200 Lbp 33.77 Br md 6.20 Dpth 4.89 Welded, 1 dk	**(X11A2YS) Yacht (Sailing)**	**1 oil engine** reduction geared to sc. shaft driving 1 Propeller Total Power: 397kW (540hp) Caterpillar 1 x 4 Stroke 397kW (540bhp) Caterpillar Inc-USA
8125997 *JM5153*	**SUHO MARU** - **Nishi Nippon Kaiun KK** - *Kitakyushu, Fukuoka* *Japan* Official number: 124912	*198* - -		**1982-05 K.K. Odo Zosen Tekko — Shimonoseki** Yd No: 280 Loa 30.61 Br ex 8.84 Dght 2.601 Lbp 27.01 Br md 8.81 Dpth 3.51 Welded, 1 dk	**(B32A2ST) Tug**	**2 oil engines** Geared Integral to driving 2 Z propellers Total Power: 2,206kW (3,000hp) Fuji 6M27.5H 2 x 4 Stroke 6 Cy. 275 x 320 each-1103kW (1500bhp) Fuji Diesel Co Ltd-Japan
9415492 *TCSY7* -	**SUHULET** *ex Ceksan 41 -2007* **Istanbul Deniz Otobusleri Sanayi ve Ticaret AS (IDO)** - *Istanbul* *Turkey* MMSI: 271002544	**1,065** 608 250	Class: TL	**2007-12 Ceksan Tersanesi — Turkey** Yd No: 41 Loa 73.20 Br ex - Dght 2.600 Lbp 71.10 Br md 18.00 Dpth 4.40 Welded, 1 dk	**(A36A2PR) Passenger/Ro-Ro Ship (Vehicles)** Passengers: unberthed: 600 Cars: 80	**4 oil engines** reduction geared to sc. shafts driving 2 Voith-Schneider propellers 2 propellers aft, 2 fwd. Total Power: 2,440kW (3,316hp) 12.5kn Mitsubishi S6R2-MPTA 4 x 4 Stroke 6 Cy. 170 x 220 each-610kW (829bhp) Mitsubishi Heavy Industries Ltd-Japan AuxGen: 2 x 77kW a.c
8426860 *BRON* -	**SUI HAI GONG 109** - **Guangzhou Maritime Transport (Group) Co Ltd** - *Guangzhou, Guangdong* *China* MMSI: 412050670	*789* 335 1,000		**1980 Guangdong New China Shipyard Co Ltd — Dongguan GD** Loa 67.40 Br ex - Dght 4.071 Lbp 60.00 Br md 10.00 Dpth 4.50 Welded, 1 dk	**(A13B2TU) Tanker (unspecified)**	**1 oil engine** driving 1 FP propeller Total Power: 662kW (900hp) 10.5kn Chinese Std. Type 6350ZC 1 x 4 Stroke 6 Cy. 350 x 500 662kW (900bhp) Shanghai Diesel Engine Co Ltd-China AuxGen: 2 x 250kW 400V 50Hz a.c
8847557 - -	**SUI HANG 012** - **Government of The People's Republic of China** - *China*	*131* 68 -		**1988 in the People's Republic of China** Loa - Br ex - Dght - Lbp - Br md - Dpth - Welded, 1 dk	**(A31A2GX) General Cargo Ship**	**1 oil engine** driving 1 FP propeller
8936889 - -	**SUI HANG 315** - - - *China* Official number: 5101V78038	*233* 130 300		**1978-06 Guangzhou Zhujiang Shipyard — Guangzhou GD** Loa 40.56 Br ex - Dght - Lbp - Br md 8.00 Dpth 2.20 Welded, 1 dk	**(A13B2TU) Tanker (unspecified)**	**1 oil engine** driving 1 FP propeller Chinese Std. Type 1 x 4 Stroke Nantong Diesel Engine Co Ltd-China
9090890 *BMQL*	**SUI JIN YANG 6** *ex Gui Jin Yang 1 -2011 ex HAI TONG 118 -2011* *ex Min Yuan Yu Yun 1 -2006* **Guangzhou Coast Logistics Co Ltd** - *Guangzhou, Guangdong* *China* MMSI: 413503260 Official number: 090111000146	**1,587** 889 -	Class: ZC	**1984-06 Duchang County Shipyard — Duchang County JX** Loa 78.87 Br ex - Dght 4.510 Lbp 73.00 Br md 12.60 Dpth 5.80 Welded, 1 dk	**(A31A2GX) General Cargo Ship**	**1 oil engine** driving 1 FP propeller Total Power: 970kW (1,319hp) S.K.L. 8NVD48A-2U 1 x 4 Stroke 8 Cy. 320 x 480 970kW (1319bhp) VEB Schwermaschinenbau "KarlLiebknecht" (SKL)-Magdeburg
8833051 - -	**SUI JIU SHUI 1** - **Guangzhou Salvage Bureau of the Ministry of Communications PRC** - *Guangzhou, Guangdong* *China*	*351* 197 400		**1984-01 Guangdong Jiangmen Shipyard — Jiangmen GD** Loa 40.30 Br ex - Dght 3.500 Lbp 36.90 Br md 8.00 Dpth 4.20 Welded, 2 dks	**(B21A20S) Platform Supply Ship**	**1 oil engine** geared to sc. shaft driving 1 FP propeller Total Power: 294kW (400hp) 9.0kn Chinese Std. Type 6300 1 x 4 Stroke 6 Cy. 300 x 380 294kW (400bhp) Guangzhou Diesel Engine Factory CoLtd-China AuxGen: 2 x 50kW 400V a.c
8832992 - -	**SUI JIU TUO 11** - **Guangzhou Salvage Bureau of the Ministry of Communications PRC** - *Guangzhou, Guangdong* *China*	*102* 30 -		**1984-01 Guangdong Jiangmen Shipyard — Jiangmen GD** Loa 25.40 Br ex - Dght 1.790 Lbp 23.13 Br md 5.60 Dpth 2.70 Welded, 1 dk	**(B32A2ST) Tug**	**2 oil engines** geared to sc. shafts driving 2 FP propellers Total Power: 272kW (370hp) Chinese Std. Type 6160A 2 x 4 Stroke 6 Cy. 160 x 225 each-136kW (185bhp) Weifang Diesel Engine Factory-China AuxGen: 2 x 24kW 400V a.c
8833013 *BSGX* -	**SUI JIU YOU 3** - **Guangzhou Salvage Bureau of the Ministry of Communications PRC** - *Guangzhou, Guangdong* *China*	*485* 271 -		**1985-01 Guangdong Jiangmen Shipyard — Jiangmen GD** Loa 49.52 Br ex - Dght 3.500 Lbp 44.00 Br md 9.19 Dpth 4.20 Welded, 1 dk	**(A13B2TU) Tanker (unspecified)**	**1 oil engine** geared to sc. shaft driving 1 FP propeller Total Power: 294kW (400hp) Chinese Std. Type 6300 1 x 4 Stroke 6 Cy. 300 x 380 294kW (400bhp) Guangzhou Diesel Engine Factory CoLtd-China AuxGen: 2 x 64kW 400V a.c
9186261 *BZWA* -	**SUI YU LENG 8** - **Guangzhou Ocean Fishery Co** - SatCom: Inmarsat C 450301879 *Guangzhou, Guangdong* *China* MMSI: 412462080	**1,413** 424 1,250	Class: CC	**1998-01 Guangzhou Fishing Vessel Shipyard — Guangzhou GD** Yd No: 95-1351 Loa - Br ex - Dght 4.180 Lbp 63.00 Br md 11.40 Dpth 6.40 Welded, 1 dk	**(B11B2FV) Fishing Vessel**	**1 oil engine** driving 1 FP propeller Total Power: 1,334kW (1,814hp)
8664802 *BZWA29* -	**SUI YUAN YU 29** - **Guangzhou Pelagic Fisheries Intergrated (China) Co** - *Guangzhou, Guangdong* *China* MMSI: 412460022 Official number: 4400002011060006	**268** 80 -		**2011-06 Guangzhou Southern Shipbuilding Co Ltd — Guangzhou GD** L reg 34.00 Br ex - Dght - Lbp - Br md 6.90 Dpth 3.80 Welded, 1 dk	**(B11B2FV) Fishing Vessel**	**1 oil engine** reduction geared to sc. shaft driving 1 Propeller Total Power: 426kW (579hp) Chinese Std. Type X6170ZC 1 x 4 Stroke 6 Cy. 170 x 200 426kW (579bhp)

IMO / Call sign	Name / Owner / Port	Tonnage	Class	Builder / Dimensions	Type / Capacity	Machinery
6604810 *WCN3591* -	**SUIATTLE** *ex* Mariner *-1994* **Dunlap Towing Co** - *La Conner, WA* *United States of America* MMSI: 303296000 Official number: 298539	**351** 105 -	Class: (AB)	**1965 Main Iron Works, Inc. — Houma, La** Yd No: 139 Loa 36.58 Br ex 9.20 Dght 4.858 Lbp 35.26 Br md 9.15 Dpth 5.26 Welded, 1 dk	**(B32A2ST) Tug**	**1 oil engine** reverse reduction geared to sc. shaft driving 1 FP propeller Total Power: 2,258kW (3,070hp) 12.5kn EMD (Electro-Motive) 16-645-E7B 1 x Vee 2 Stroke 16 Cy. 230 x 254 2258kW (3070bhp) (new engine 1982) General Motors Corp.Electro-Motive Div.-La Grange AuxGen: 2 x 99kW Fuel: 203.0 (r.f.)
7321192 - -	**SUIDERKUS** *ex* Glen Helen *-1989* *ex* Velia *-1979* - -	*353* 105 183	Class: (LR) ✠ Classed LR until 19/12/89	**1973-09 R. Dunston (Hessle) Ltd. — Hessle** Yd No: S892 L reg 32.92 Br ex 8.36 Dght 3.506 Lbp 32.01 Br md 8.26 Dpth 4.81 Welded, 1 dk	**(B11A2FS) Stern Trawler**	**1 oil engine** sr geared to sc. shaft driving 1 CP propeller Total Power: 919kW (1,249hp) Blackstone ESL8MK2 1 x 4 Stroke 8 Cy. 222 x 292 919kW (1249bhp) Mirrlees Blackstone (Stamford)Ltd.-Stamford AuxGen: 1 x 80kW 440V 50Hz a.c, 1 x 70kW 440V 50Hz a.c Thrusters: 1 Thwart. FP thruster
9536791 *3EWI4* -	**SUIGO** **Picer Marine SA** Biko Kisen Co Ltd *Panama* *Panama* MMSI: 371040000 Official number: 4329911	**91,508** 57,746 174,802 T/cm 122.0	Class: NK	**2011-11 Namura Shipbuilding Co Ltd — Imari SG** Yd No: 318 Loa 289.98 (BB) Br ex - Dght 18.030 Lbp 280.00 Br md 45.00 Dpth 24.70 Welded, 1 dk	**(A21A2BC) Bulk Carrier** Grain: 199,507; Bale: 195,968 Compartments: 9 Ho, ER 9 Ha: ER	**1 oil engine** driving 1 FP propeller Total Power: 16,860kW (22,923hp) 14.8kn MAN-B&W 6S70MC-C 1 x 2 Stroke 6 Cy. 700 x 2800 16860kW (22923bhp) Mitsui Engineering & Shipbuilding CLtd-Japan Fuel: 5180.0
9374179 *3ETD8* -	**SUIKAI** **El Sol Maritime SA** Toyo Sangyo Co Ltd (Toyo Sangyo KK) *Panama* *Panama* MMSI: 370532000 Official number: 3434508A	**50,933** 30,116 93,579	Class: NK	**2008-09 Namura Shipbuilding Co Ltd — Imari SG** Yd No: 290 Loa 234.88 (BB) Br ex - Dght 14.225 Lbp 226.00 Br md 38.00 Dpth 20.00 Welded, 1 dk	**(A21A2BC) Bulk Carrier** Double Hull Grain: 111,527 Compartments: 6 Ho, ER 6 Ha: ER	**1 oil engine** driving 1 FP propeller Total Power: 12,240kW (16,642hp) 14.7kn MAN-B&W 6S60MC 1 x 2 Stroke 6 Cy. 600 x 2292 12240kW (16642bhp) Mitsui Engineering & Shipbuilding CLtd-Japan AuxGen: 4 x 379kW a.c Fuel: 3130.0 (r.f.)
8859445 - -	**SUIKEN MARU NO. 2** *ex* Asaka Maru No. 8 *-2004* **Sambong Corp** - *South Korea* MMSI: 440110110	**445** 133 -		**1991-12 Kanbara Zosen K.K. — Onomichi** Yd No: 421 Loa 31.80 Br ex - Dght 4.200 Lbp 29.05 Br md 9.60 Dpth 5.80 Welded, 1 dk	**(B32B2SP) Pusher Tug**	**2 oil engines** driving 2 FP propellers Total Power: 1,472kW (2,002hp) Matsui M31M28 2 x 4 Stroke 6 Cy. 310 x 550 each-736kW (1001bhp) Matsui Iron Works Co Ltd-Japan
8984575 - - -	**SUIKEN MARU NO. 3** *ex* Hyuga Maru *-2004* - -	**161** 48 -		**1983 Hongawara Zosen K.K. — Fukuyama** Loa 24.85 Br ex - Dght - Lbp - Br md 7.40 Dpth 3.00 Welded, 1 dk	**(B32B2SP) Pusher Tug**	**1 oil engine** driving 1 Propeller Niigata 1 x 4 Stroke Niigata Engineering Co Ltd-Japan
7383487 *3DYS* -	**SUILVEN** **Venu Shipping Ltd** *Suva* *Fiji* MMSI: 520090000	**3,638** 1,091 1,920	Class: (LR) ✠ Classed LR until 11/2/09	**1974-08 Moss Rosenberg Verft AS (Moss Verft) — Moss** Yd No: 180 Converted From: Ferry (Passenger/Vehicle)-1974 Loa 86.52 Br ex 16.03 Dght 4.960 Lbp 78.26 Br md 15.50 Dpth 10.34 Welded, 2 dks	**(A35A2RR) Ro-Ro Cargo Ship** Bow door/ramp Len: 4.11 Wid: 3.68 Swl: 25 Stern door/ramp Len: 4.11 Wid: 3.36 Swl: 25 Lane-Len: 252 Lane-Wid: 3.68 Lane-clr ht: 4.11 Lorries: 20, Cars: 122	**2 oil engines** driving 2 CP propellers Total Power: 2,574kW (3,500hp) 15.8kn Wichmann 7AXA 2 x 2 Stroke 7 Cy. 300 x 450 each-1287kW (1750bhp) Wichmann Motorfabrikk AS-Norway AuxGen: 3 x 152kW 230V 50Hz a.c Thrusters: 2 Thwart. FP thruster (f)
9372080 - -	**SUINLI III** **Superintendencia del Terminal Petrolero de La Libertad (SUINLI)** - *Salinas* *Ecuador* Official number: R-06-0000	**223** 67 209		**2006-04 Varaderos y Talleres Duran SA (VATADUR) — Duran** Yd No: R251 Loa 25.00 Br ex - Dght 3.400 Lbp 21.50 Br md 8.50 Dpth 4.70 Welded, 1 dk	**(B32A2ST) Tug**	**2 oil engines** reduction geared to sc. shafts driving 2 FP propellers Total Power: 1,618kW (2,200hp) Caterpillar 3512 1 x Vee 4 Stroke 12 Cy. 170 x 190 809kW (1100bhp) Caterpillar Inc-USA Caterpillar 3512B 1 x Vee 4 Stroke 12 Cy. 170 x 190 809kW (1100bhp) Caterpillar Inc-USA
9132739 *3EGA2* -	**SUIREI MARU** **Belsally Shipping SA** Taiyo Nippon Kisen Co Ltd *Panama* *Panama* MMSI: 356359000 Official number: 3184206A	**48,937** 28,041 88,736	Class: NK	**1996-05 Kawasaki Heavy Industries Ltd — Sakaide KG** Yd No: 1452 Loa 234.97 (BB) Br ex - Dght 13.850 Lbp 225.00 Br md 38.00 Dpth 19.90 Welded, 1 dk	**(A21A2BC) Bulk Carrier** Grain: 106,299 Compartments: 5 Ho, ER 8 Ha: (16.0 x 14.2)6 (13.6 x 17.8) (14.4 x 17.8)ER	**1 oil engine** driving 1 FP propeller Total Power: 12,269kW (16,681hp) 14.4kn B&W 6S60MC 1 x 2 Stroke 6 Cy. 600 x 2292 12269kW (16681bhp) Kawasaki Heavy Industries Ltd-Japan Fuel: 2275.0 (r.f.)
7725116 *JG3697* -	**SUIRYU** **Government of Japan (Ministry of Land, Infrastructure & Transport) (The Coastguard)** - *Tokyo* *Japan* Official number: 121452	*207* - -		**1978-03 Yokohama Yacht Co Ltd — Yokohama KN** Yd No: 741 Loa 27.50 Br ex 10.41 Dght 2.220 Lbp 25.50 Br md 10.39 Dpth 3.79 Welded, 1 dk	**(B34F2SF) Fire Fighting Vessel**	**2 oil engines** driving 2 FP propellers Total Power: 1,618kW (2,200hp) Maybach MB820DB 2 x Vee 4 Stroke 12 Cy. 175 x 205 each-809kW (1100bhp) Ikegai Tekkosho-Japan
9663831 *JD3388* -	**SUIRYU** **Japan Railway Construction, Transport & Technology Agency & Fuji Kaiun KK** Fuji Kaiun KK *Sanyoonoda, Yamaguchi* *Japan* MMSI: 431003726 Official number: 141719	*999* - 2,289	Class: NK	**2012-07 Kumamoto Dock K.K. — Yatsushiro** Yd No: 461 Loa 78.35 Br ex - Dght 5.150 Lbp 74.35 Br md 12.00 Dpth 5.60 Welded, 1 dk	**(A13B2TP) Products Tanker** Double Hull (13F) Liq: 2,301; Liq (Oil): 2,301	**1 oil engine** reduction geared to sc. shaft driving 1 FP propeller Total Power: 1,765kW (2,400hp) Hanshin LA34G 1 x 4 Stroke 6 Cy. 340 x 720 1765kW (2400bhp) The Hanshin Diesel Works Ltd-Japan Fuel: 120.0
9005039 *JF2145* -	**SUISEI** **Sado Kisen KK** - *Sado, Niigata* *Japan* MMSI: 431700543 Official number: 120094	*169* - 32		**1991-04 Kawasaki Heavy Industries Ltd — Kobe HG** Yd No: F010 Loa 31.24 Br ex - Dght 1.560 Lbp 23.99 Br md 8.53 Dpth 2.59 Welded	**(A37B2PS) Passenger Ship** Hull Material: Aluminium Alloy Passengers: unberthed: 262	**2 Gas Turbs** geared to sc. shafts driving 2 Water jets Total Power: 5,590kW (7,600hp) 43.0kn Allison 501-KF 2 x Gas Turb each-2795kW (3800shp) General Motors Detroit DieselAllison Divn-USA AuxGen: 2 x 50kW 450V 60Hz a.c
9116278 *JD2727* -	**SUISEN** **Shin-Nihonkai Ferry Co Ltd** - SatCom: Inmarsat M 643186010 *Otaru, Hokkaido* *Japan* MMSI: 431860000 Official number: 132873	*17,329* - 5,851 T/cm 33.9		**1996-05 Ishikawajima-Harima Heavy Industries Co Ltd (IHI) — Tokyo** Yd No: 3063 Loa 199.45 (BB) Br ex - Dght 7.080 Lbp 187.00 Br md 25.00 Dpth 9.50 Welded, 2 dks	**(A36A2PR) Passenger/Ro-Ro Ship (Vehicles)** Passengers: cabins: 106; berths: 475; driver berths: 32 Stern door/ramp (centre) Len: 4.30 Wid: 7.50 Swl: 25 Quarter stern door/ramp (s) Len: 4.30 Wid: 7.00 Swl: 40 Lane-Len: 1220 Lorries: 126, Cars: 80	**2 oil engines** with flexible couplings & sr gearedto sc. shafts driving 2 CP propellers Total Power: 47,660kW (64,798hp) 29.4kn Pielstick 18PC4-2BV570 2 x Vee 4 Stroke 18 Cy. 570 x 660 each-23830kW (32399bhp) Diesel United Ltd.-Aioi AuxGen: 1 x 1600kW 450V 60Hz a.c, 1 x 1300kW 450V 60Hz a.c, 3 x 1200kW 450V 60Hz a.c Thrusters: 1 Thwart. CP thruster (f); 1 Thwart. CP thruster (a) Fuel: 33.5 (d.f.) 667.0 (r.f.) 213.0pd
9607057 *7JKP* -	**SUISEN** **Shin-Nihonkai Ferry Co Ltd** - *Otobe, Hokkaido* *Japan* MMSI: 431003671 Official number: 141566	**34,326** - 7,891		**2012-07 Mitsubishi Heavy Industries Ltd. — Nagasaki** Yd No: 2277 Loa 224.50 (BB) Br ex - Dght 7.400 Lbp 207.72 Br md 26.00 Dpth 18.61 Welded, 1 dk	**(A36A2PR) Passenger/Ro-Ro Ship (Vehicles)** Passengers: cabins: 128; berths: 613 Stern door/ramp (s. a.) Len: 7.80 Wid: 6.00 Swl: - Quarter stern door/ramp (s) Len: 16.00 Wid: 6.10 Swl: - Lorries: 158, Cars: 58	**2 diesel electric oil engines** driving 2 gen. each 8700kW a.c Connecting to 2 elec. motors each (6450kW) driving 2 Directional propellers Total Power: 17,400kW (23,658hp) 29.4kn Wartsila 12V38 2 x Vee 4 Stroke 12 Cy. 380 x 475 each-8700kW (11829bhp) Wartsila Finland Oy-Finland Thrusters: 2 Tunnel thruster (f) Fuel: 1050.0 (r.f.)
8028797 - -	**SUITO** - - *Honiara* *Solomon Islands*	*188* - -		**1981-03 Kanagawa Zosen — Kobe** Yd No: 219 Loa - Br ex - Dght 1.751 Lbp 28.02 Br md 7.01 Dpth 2.72 Welded, 1 dk	**(B32A2ST) Tug**	**2 oil engines** driving 2 FP propellers Total Power: 1,176kW (1,598hp) Niigata 6L20CX 2 x 4 Stroke 6 Cy. 200 x 260 each-588kW (799bhp) Niigata Engineering Co Ltd-Japan

IMO / Call sign / Reg.	Name / Former names / Owner / Port	Tonnage (GT/NT/DWT)	Class	Builder / Dimensions	Type	Machinery
6709505 *9GSJ* -	**SUJIN** *ex* Puk Yang No. 6 *-1995* *ex* Merced No. 3 *-1983* *ex* Shoshin Maru No. 8 *-1975* **Danac Fisheries Ltd** - *Takoradi* *Ghana* Official number: 316869	*283* 133 235	Class: (KR)	**1966 Niigata Engineering Co Ltd — Niigata NI** Yd No: 668 Loa 44.79 Br ex 8.34 Dght 3.368 Lbp 39.71 Br md 8.31 Dpth 3.18 Welded, 2 dks	**(B11A2FS) Stern Trawler** Ins: 338 3 Ha: 3 (1.7 x 1.7)ER	**1 oil engine** driving 1 FP propeller Total Power: 919kW (1,249hp) 10.5kn Niigata 6MG31X 1 x 4 Stroke 6 Cy. 310 x 380 919kW (1249bhp) Niigata Engineering Co Ltd-Japan AuxGen: 2 x 80kW 225V a.c
9116307 *HSED2* -	**SUJITRA NAREE** *ex* Tiger Durban *-2004* **Precious Minerals Ltd** Great Circle Shipping Agency Ltd *Bangkok* *Thailand* MMSI: 567290000 Official number: 470003195	**18,302** 9,064 28,290	Class: NK	**1995-12 Nippon Kokan KK (NKK Corp) — Yokohama KN (Tsurumi Shipyard)** Yd No: 1066 Loa 166.00 (BB) Br ex 27.30 Dght 9.717 Lbp 158.68 Br md 27.00 Dpth 14.40 Welded, 1 dk	**(A21A2BC) Bulk Carrier** Grain: 37,510; Bale: 35,728 Compartments: 5 Ho, ER 5 Ha: (19.6 x 12.0)4 (19.2 x 13.5)ER Cranes: 4x30.5t	**1 oil engine** driving 1 FP propeller Total Power: 5,480kW (7,451hp) 14.0kn B&W 5L50MC 1 x 2 Stroke 5 Cy. 500 x 1620 5480kW (7451bhp) Mitsui Engineering & Shipbuilding CLtd-Japan AuxGen: 2 x 440kW a.c Fuel: 1340.0 (r.f.) 20.3pd
8988739 *9MAG3* -	**SUKA EKSPRESS** - **Fast Ferry Ventures Sdn Bhd** - *Penang* *Malaysia* MMSI: 533003100 Official number: 325423	**111** 49 12		**1988 WaveMaster International Pty Ltd — Fremantle WA** Yd No: 017 Loa 26.01 Br ex 6.17 Dght 0.830 Lbp 23.40 Br md 6.10 Dpth 1.50 Welded, 1 dk	**(A37B2PS) Passenger Ship** Hull Material: Aluminium Alloy	**2 oil engines** driving 2 Propellers Total Power: 1,176kW (1,598hp) Mitsubishi 2 x each-588kW (799bhp) Mitsubishi Heavy Industries Ltd-Japan
9106003 *EAAU* 3-ST-41-94	**SUKARI PRIMERO** - **Sukarri SL** - *Santander* *Spain* MMSI: 224052970 Official number: 3-1/1994	**232** 69 100		**1994-05 Astilleros Armon SA — Navia** Yd No: 343 Loa - Br ex - Dght 3.100 Lbp 25.50 Br md 7.50 Dpth 3.50 Welded, 1 dk	**(B11B2FV) Fishing Vessel**	**1 oil engine** geared to sc. shaft driving 1 FP propeller Total Power: 1,119kW (1,521hp) Caterpillar 3508TA 1 x Vee 4 Stroke 8 Cy. 170 x 190 1119kW (1521bhp) Caterpillar Inc-USA
8627816 *YHNE* -	**SUKARIA** *ex* Seifuku Maru *-2002* **Tjhin Jeffriy Soetanto** - *Jakarta* *Indonesia*	*490* 219 510	Class: KI	**1985-08 K.K. Kamishima Zosensho — Osakikamijima** Yd No: 171 Loa 50.77 Br ex - Dght 3.150 Lbp 46.00 Br md 8.31 Dpth 5.31 Welded, 1 dk	**(A31A2GX) General Cargo Ship**	**1 oil engine** driving 1 FP propeller Total Power: 478kW (650hp) 10.0kn Matsui 6M26KGHS 1 x 4 Stroke 6 Cy. 260 x 400 478kW (650bhp) Matsui Iron Works Co Ltd-Japan
7701809 *PMNR* -	**SUKARIA I** *ex* Sang Thai Beryl *-2008* *ex* Hanasakisan Maru *-1991* **PT Pelayaran Sejahtera Bahtera Agung** - *Surabaya* *Indonesia*	**1,215** 656 2,135	Class: KI (NK)	**1977-04 Suzuki Shipyard Co. Ltd. — Yokkaichi** Yd No: 275 Loa 67.85 Br ex 11.54 Dght 4.201 Lbp 64.35 Br md 11.50 Dpth 6.10 Welded, 1 dk	**(A31A2GX) General Cargo Ship** Grain: 2,560; Bale: 2,500 1 Ha: (39.6 x 8.9)ER Derricks: 1x10t,1x5t	**1 oil engine** driving 1 FP propeller Total Power: 1,177kW (1,600hp) 12.0kn Akasaka DM33 1 x 4 Stroke 6 Cy. 330 x 500 1177kW (1600bhp) Akasaka Tekkosho KK (Akasaka DieselLtd)-Japan AuxGen: 3 x 45kW a.c
9640736 *AVOC* -	**SUKHAM** - **Sadhav Shipping Ltd** - *Mumbai* *India* MMSI: 419000371 Official number: 3886	**1,323** 652 2,240	Class: IR	**2011-11 Waterways Shipyard Pvt Ltd — Goa** Yd No: 149 Loa 70.00 Br ex 14.02 Dght 3.200 Lbp 67.12 Br md 14.00 Dpth 4.40 Welded, 1 dk	**(A31A2GX) General Cargo Ship** Bale: 2,584 Compartments: 1 Ho, ER 1 Ha: ER	**2 oil engines** reduction geared to sc. shafts driving 2 FP propellers Total Power: 596kW (810hp) 10.4kn Cummins NTA-855-M 2 x 4 Stroke 6 Cy. 140 x 152 each-298kW (405bhp) Cummins India Ltd-India
7645419 - -	**SUKHANOVO** - - -	**962** 288 313	Class: (RS)	**1977-07 Zavod "Leninskaya Kuznitsa" — Kiyev** Yd No: 229 Loa 53.73 (BB) Br ex 10.72 Dght 4.410 Lbp 47.92 Br md 10.50 Dpth 6.02 Welded, 1 dk	**(B11A2FS) Stern Trawler** Ins: 220 Compartments: 1 Ho, ER 2 Ha: 2 (1.6 x 1.6) Derricks: 2x1.5t Ice Capable	**1 oil engine** driving 1 CP propeller Total Power: 971kW (1,320hp) 12.5kn S.K.L. 8NVD48A-2U 1 x 4 Stroke 8 Cy. 320 x 480 971kW (1320bhp) VEB Schwermaschinenbau "KarlLiebknecht" (SKL)-Magdeburg Thrusters: 1 Thwart. FP thruster (f); 1 Tunnel thruster (a) Fuel: 185.0 (d.f.)
7501508 *SUMD* -	**SUKHNA** *ex* Hokuto Maru *-1977* **Arab Petroleum Pipelines Co (SUMED)** - *Alexandria* *Egypt*	*290* 107 -	Class: AB (BV)	**1975-04 Sagami Zosen Tekko K.K. — Yokosuka** Yd No: 178 Loa 34.88 Br ex 9.61 Dght 3.134 Lbp 30.26 Br md 9.58 Dpth 4.17 Welded, 1 dk	**(B32A2ST) Tug**	**2 oil engines** reverse reduction geared to sc. shafts driving 2 FP propellers Total Power: 2,354kW (3,200hp) 12.0kn Niigata 8L25BX 2 x 4 Stroke 8 Cy. 250 x 320 each-1177kW (1600bhp) Niigata Engineering Co Ltd-Japan AuxGen: 2 x 80kW
8312253 *SSCF* -	**SUKHNA 2** *ex* Willic *-1987* **Arab Petroleum Pipelines Co (SUMED)** - *Alexandria* *Egypt* MMSI: 622122503 Official number: 2938	**1,297** 389 1,857	Class: NV (CC)	**1984-06 Imamura Zosen — Kure** Yd No: 302 Loa 55.63 Br ex 13.29 Dght 5.931 Lbp 51.62 Br md 13.01 Dpth 6.75 Welded, 1 dk	**(B21B20T) Offshore Tug/Supply Ship**	**2 oil engines** with clutches, flexible couplings & sr geared to sc. shafts driving 2 CP propellers Total Power: 4,414kW (6,002hp) 14.5kn Daihatsu 6DVM-26 2 x Vee 4 Stroke 12 Cy. 260 x 300 each-2207kW (3001bhp) Daihatsu Diesel Manufacturing Co Lt-Japan AuxGen: 3 x 200kW 440V 60Hz a.c Thrusters: 1 Thwart. CP thruster (f)
9292797 *6ACE* -	**SUKHNA 4** - **Arab Petroleum Pipelines Co (SUMED)** - *Alexandria* *Egypt* MMSI: 622122445	**354** 32 335	Class: LR ✠ **100A1** SS 12/2008 tug fire fighting Ship 1 (2400 cubic m/hr) ✠ **LMC** Eq.Ltr: H; Cable: 302.5/22.0 U2 (a)	**2003-12 Astilleros Zamakona SA — Santurtzi** Yd No: 601 Loa 31.00 Br ex 10.48 Dght - Lbp 27.00 Br md 9.85 Dpth 5.40 Welded, 1 dk	**(B32A2ST) Tug**	**2 oil engines** geared to sc. shafts driving 2 Directional propellers Total Power: 3,430kW (4,664hp) Deutz SBV8M628 2 x 4 Stroke 8 Cy. 240 x 280 each-1715kW (2332bhp) Deutz AG-Koeln AuxGen: 2 x 120kW 400V 50Hz a.c
6929117 - -	**SUKHONA** - **Bakrybkholodflot** -	*1,115* 426 605	Class: (RS)	**1970-05 VEB Mathias-Thesen-Werft — Wismar** Yd No: 149 Loa 65.69 Br ex 11.13 Dght 3.620 Lbp 59.82 Br md 11.10 Dpth 5.36 Welded, 2 dks	**(B11B2FV) Fishing Vessel** Ins: 1,150 Compartments: 2 Ho, ER 4 Ha: 2 (2.2 x 2.2) Cranes: 2x2t Ice Capable	**1 oil engine** driving 1 FP propeller Total Power: 647kW (880hp) 11.0kn S.K.L. 8NVD48-2U 1 x 4 Stroke 8 Cy. 320 x 480 647kW (880bhp) VEB Schwermaschinenbau "KarlLiebknecht" (SKL)-Magdeburg AuxGen: 2 x 272kW 380V a.c, 1 x 192kW 380V a.c Fuel: 173.0 (d.f.)
8966107 *HP9618* -	**SUKHONA** - **Meilans Shipping Corp** - *Panama* *Panama* Official number: 2704200	**508** 306 765	Class: (RS)	**1961 VEB Schiffswerft "Edgar Andre" — Magdeburg** L reg 61.97 Br ex - Dght - Lbp - Br md 8.16 Dpth 2.60 Welded, 1 dk	**(A31A2GX) General Cargo Ship**	**1 oil engine** driving 1 FP propeller S.K.L. 1 x 4 Stroke VEB Schwermaschinenbau "KarlLiebknecht" (SKL)-Magdeburg
7630505 - -	**SUKHOPOL** - **000 'Kompaniya Sit'** -	**172** 51 89	Class: (RS)	**1976 Sretenskiy Sudostroitelnyy Zavod — Sretensk** Yd No: 86 Loa 33.96 Br ex 7.09 Dght 2.899 Lbp 30.00 Br md - Dpth 3.69 Welded, 1 dk	**(B11B2FV) Fishing Vessel** Bale: 96 Compartments: 1 Ho, ER 1 Ha: (1.6 x 1.3) Derricks: 2x2t; Winches: 2 Ice Capable	**1 oil engine** driving 1 FP propeller Total Power: 224kW (305hp) 9.0kn S.K.L. 8NVD36-1U 1 x 4 Stroke 8 Cy. 240 x 360 224kW (305bhp) VEB Schwermaschinenbau "KarlLiebknecht" (SKL)-Magdeburg AuxGen: 1 x 86kW, 1 x 60kW Fuel: 22.0 (d.f.)
7368786 - -	**SUKI I** *ex* Jacob Nielsen *-1989* *ex* Finnmarkvaering *-1986* *ex* Skjongnes *-1978* - -	*173* 59 -	Class: (NV)	**1974-02 Langsten Slip & Baatbyggeri AS — Tomrefjord** Yd No: 67 Loa 29.77 Br ex 7.12 Dght - Lbp 28.35 Br md 7.09 Dpth 3.81 Welded, 2 dks	**(B11B2FV) Fishing Vessel** Ice Capable	**1 oil engine** geared to sc. shaft driving 1 FP propeller Total Power: 662kW (900hp) Grenaa 6FR24TK 1 x 4 Stroke 6 Cy. 240 x 300 662kW (900bhp) (new engine 1984) A/S Grenaa Motorfabrik-Denmark AuxGen: 2 x 157kW 220V 50Hz a.c

9280196 *TCCS7* -
SUKRAN-C
Selay Uluslararasi Deniz Tasimaciligi Sanayi ve Ticaret Ltd Sti
Selay Denizcilik Sanayi ve Ticaret Ltd Sti
SatCom: Inmarsat C 427122356
Istanbul *Turkey*
MMSI: 271000746
2,798 1,361 3,900 T/cm 11.5
Class: BV (TL)
2004-03 Torlak Gemi Insaat Sanayi ve Ticaret A.S. — Tuzla Yd No: 37
Loa 96.30 (BB) Br ex - Dght 6.100
Lbp 88.61 Br md 14.20 Dpth 8.00
Welded, 1 dk
(A12B2TR) Chemical/Products Tanker
Double Hull (13F)
Liq: 4,822; Liq (Oil): 4,822
Cargo Heating Coils
Compartments: 12 Wing Ta, ER
12 Cargo Pump (s): 12x200m³/hr
Manifold: Bow/CM: 45.2m
1 oil engine sr geared to sc. shaft driving 1 CP propeller
Total Power: 2,040kW (2,774hp) 13.0kn
MAN-B&W 6L27/38
1 x 4 Stroke 6 Cy. 270 x 380 2040kW (2774bhp)
MAN B&W Diesel A/S-Denmark
AuxGen: 1 x 720kW 400/230V 50Hz a.c, 2 x 400kW 400/230V 50Hz a.c
Thrusters: 1 Tunnel thruster (f)
Fuel: 45.0 (d.f.) 135.0 (r.f.)

8218392 *TCBJ8* -
SUKRAN CAMUZ
ex Senkayalar *-2004* *ex* Haci Hakki Deval *-1995*
Nurce Denizcilik ve Tasimacilik Ith Ihrsan ve Ticaret Ltd
Camuzlar Su Urunleri Petrol Tas Turizm Ticaret Ltd Sti
Istanbul *Turkey*
MMSI: 271002052
Official number: 5251
1,384 896 1,740
Class: (TL) (BV) (AB)
1984-02 Marmara Tersanesi — Yarimca Yd No: 26A
Loa 67.01 Br ex - Dght 4.680
Lbp 61.02 Br md 11.00 Dpth 5.52
Welded, 1 dk
(A31A2GX) General Cargo Ship
Grain: 2,009; Bale: 1,834
Compartments: 2 Ho, ER
2 Ha: ER
1 oil engine sr geared to sc. shaft driving 1 Directional propeller
Total Power: 971kW (1,320hp) 10.5kn
S.K.L. 8NVD48A-2U
1 x 4 Stroke 8 Cy. 320 x 480 971kW (1320bhp)
VEB Schwermaschinenbau "KarlLiebknecht" (SKL)-Magdeburg
AuxGen: 2 x 97kW 380V 50Hz a.c
Fuel: 93.5 (d.f.) 6.5pd

8201002 *TCKB* -
SUKRAN S.
ex Sevket Yardimci *-1995*
launched as Karadeniz 6 *-1985*
Simge Denizcilik ve Ticaret AS
Karma Gemi Isletmeciligi ve Ticaret Ltd Sti
Istanbul *Turkey*
MMSI: 271000056
Official number: 5401
3,996 2,575 6,479
Class: BV (AB)
1985-08 Degas Izmir Tersanesi Gemi Insaat ve Demir Imalat — Izmir Yd No: 27
Loa 107.60 (BB) Br ex - Dght 6.908
Lbp 99.37 Br md 16.51 Dpth 8.82
Welded, 1 dk
(A31A2GX) General Cargo Ship
Grain: 8,948; Bale: 8,240
Compartments: 3 Ho, ER
3 Ha: ER
Derricks: 2x22t,2x10t
1 oil engine driving 1 FP propeller
Total Power: 2,942kW (4,000hp) 13.5kn
Hanshin 6EL44
1 x 4 Stroke 6 Cy. 440 x 880 2942kW (4000bhp)
The Hanshin Diesel Works Ltd-Japan
AuxGen: 2 x 180kW a.c, 1 x 80kW a.c

8922395 *9HIU7* -
SUKRIYE
ex Modisk 3 *-2008* *ex* Emerald *-2002*
ex Tavriya-6 *-2001*
Eurasia International Shipping Ltd
Unimarin Denizcilik Sanayi ve Ticaret Ltd Sti
Valletta *Malta*
MMSI: 215283000
Official number: 7880
1,717 705 2,834
Class: RS (RR)
1989-03 VEB Elbewerften Boizenburg/Rosslau — Rosslau Yd No: 350/3492
Deepened-2007
Loa 82.02 Br ex 11.94 Dght 4.720
Lbp 78.49 Br md 11.61 Dpth 6.20
Welded, 1 dk
(A31A2GX) General Cargo Ship
TEU 70 C. 70/20' incl. 10 ref C.
Compartments: 2 Ho, ER
2 Ha: 2 (19.8 x 9.2)ER
2 oil engines driving 2 FP propellers
Total Power: 882kW (1,200hp) 11.2kn
S.K.L. 8VD36/24A-1
2 x 4 Stroke 8 Cy. 240 x 360 each-441kW (600bhp)
VEB Schwermaschinenbau "KarlLiebknecht" (SKL)-Magdeburg
AuxGen: 2 x 100kW a.c

8652029 - -
SUKSES BERSAMA
Sarana Kapuas CV
-
Pontianak *Indonesia*
595 409 -
Class: KI
2010-11 CV Bina Citra — Pontianak
Loa - Br ex - Dght -
Lbp 47.00 Br md 12.60 Dpth 3.60
Welded, 1 dk
(A35D2RL) Landing Craft
Bow ramp (centre)
2 oil engines reduction geared to sc. shafts driving 2 Propellers

---

9099365 *PMOC* -
SUKSES GLOBAL
ex Serena Ii *-2014* *ex* Zhe Xing Hai 202 *-2008*
PT Pelayaran Sherin Kapuas Raya
-
Tanjung Priok *Indonesia*
MMSI: 525016306
2,234 1,198 3,794
Class: KI
2007-01 Wenling Yongli Shiprepair & Building Yard — Wenling ZJ
Loa 91.12 Br ex - Dght 5.450
Lbp 84.80 Br md 13.60 Dpth 6.40
Welded, 1 dk
(A13B2TP) Products Tanker
Double Hull (13F)
1 oil engine reduction geared to sc. shaft driving 1 FP propeller
Total Power: 725kW (986hp)
Chinese Std. Type LB8250ZLC
1 x 4 Stroke 8 Cy. 250 x 320 725kW (986bhp)
Zibo Diesel Engine Factory-China

7925792 *YDZC* -
SUKSES XI
ex Siren *-2005* *ex* Urzhum *-1999*
PT Sukses Osean Khatulistiwa Line
-
Jakarta *Indonesia*
MMSI: 525019295
17,199 11,916 29,990 T/cm 37.7
Class: KI (LR) (NV) (RI)
✠ Classed LR until 21/7/91
1983-01 Hellenic Shipyards — Skaramanga Yd No: 1128
Loa 170.69 (BB) Br ex 26.04 Dght 10.767
Lbp 162.15 Br md 26.00 Dpth 14.46
Welded, 1 dk
(A13B2TP) Products Tanker
Single Hull
Liq: 39,336; Liq (Oil): 39,336
Cargo Heating Coils
Compartments: 7 Ta, ER, 14 Wing Ta, 2 Wing Slop Ta
4 Cargo Pump (s): 4x900m³/hr
Manifold: Bow/CM: 78m
1 oil engine driving 1 FP propeller
Total Power: 8,826kW (12,000hp) 15.5kn
B&W 6L67GFCA
1 x 2 Stroke 6 Cy. 670 x 1700 8826kW (12000bhp)
Zaklady Przemyslu Metalowego 'HCegielski' SA-Poznan
AuxGen: 3 x 528kW 440V 60Hz a.c
Fuel: 211.0 (d.f.) 1592.0 (r.f.)

8614651 - -
SUL ATLANTICO XII
Sul Atlantica
100 - -
1988-01 Empresa Brasileira de Construcao Naval S.A. (EBRASA) — Itajai Yd No: 183
Loa - Br ex - Dght -
Lbp - Br md - Dpth -
Welded, 1 dk
(B11A2FT) Trawler
1 oil engine driving 1 FP propeller

9099133 *LM3739* -
SULA
ex Blink *-2008*
Marin Odysse AS
-
Aalesund *Norway*
MMSI: 257225500
153 46 -
1967-01 Georg Eides Sonner AS — Hoylandsbygd Yd No: 74
Loa 27.66 Br ex - Dght -
Lbp 23.25 Br md 6.20 Dpth 3.20
Welded, 1 dk
(B34Q2QL) Buoy & Lighthouse Tender
1 oil engine driving 1 Propeller
Total Power: 165kW (224hp)
Wichmann 3DCT
1 x 2 Stroke 3 Cy. 200 x 300 165kW (224bhp)
Wichmann Motorfabrikk AS-Norway

9006306 *C6ZR9* -
SULA
ex Baltic Sea *-2012* *ex* RMS Sonsbeck *-2009*
ex Baltic Sea *-2006* *ex* Uranus *-2005*
Berge Rederi AS
Nassau *Bahamas*
MMSI: 311064400
2,449 1,380 3,713
Class: NV (GL)
1992-12 Peene-Werft GmbH — Wolgast Yd No: 405
Loa 87.86 (BB) Br ex 12.81 Dght 5.480
Lbp 81.00 Br md 12.80 Dpth 7.10
Welded, 2 dks
(A31A2GX) General Cargo Ship
Grain: 4,666; Bale: 4,635
TEU 180 C.Ho 108/20' C.Dk 72/20' incl. 6 ref C.
Compartments: 1 Ho, ER
1 Ha: (56.6 x 10.2)ER
Ice Capable
1 oil engine with flexible couplings & sr reverse geared to sc. shaft driving 1 FP propeller
Total Power: 1,500kW (2,039hp) 10.0kn
Deutz SBV8M628
1 x 4 Stroke 8 Cy. 240 x 280 1500kW (2039bhp)
Kloeckner Humboldt Deutz AG-Germany
AuxGen: 2 x 168kW 220/380V a.c
Thrusters: 1 Directional thruster (f)

8933526 *V7IP4* -
SULA
Joyce Marine Co
Jaluit *Marshall Islands*
MMSI: 538070150
Official number: 70150
149 44 -
1968-04 Georg Eides Sonner AS — Hoylandsbygd Yd No: 81
Converted From: Work/Repair Vessel-2007
Lengthened-1987
Loa 27.64 Br ex - Dght -
Lbp 24.90 Br md 6.20 Dpth 2.32
Welded, 1 dk
(X11A2YP) Yacht
Derricks: 1x2t
1 oil engine driving 1 CP propeller
Total Power: 338kW (460hp) 10.5kn
Callesen 4-427-DOT
1 x 4 Stroke 4 Cy. 270 x 400 338kW (460bhp) (new engine 1968)
Aabenraa Motorfabrik, HeinrichCallesen A/S-Denmark
AuxGen: 2 x 17kW 20V d.c
Fuel: 7.0 (d.f.)

8950031 *A9D2916* -
SULAITI-20
ex Aali *-2007* *ex* Interballast 1 *-1999*
ex Anton Mijsing *-1988*
Al Sulaiti Trading & Marine Services Agency
-
Manama *Bahrain*
MMSI: 408375000
602 352 -
Class: BV
1970 NV Scheepswerf G Bijlsma & Zoon — Wartena Yd No: 583
Loa 70.00 Br ex - Dght 2.450
Lbp 68.21 Br md 8.12 Dpth 3.25
Welded, 1 dk
(B33B2DT) Trailing Suction Hopper Dredger
Grain: 555; Hopper: 555
Compartments: 1 Ho, ER
1 oil engine reduction geared to sc. shaft driving 1 FP propeller
Total Power: 500kW (680hp) 16.0kn
Caterpillar 3412TA
1 x Vee 4 Stroke 12 Cy. 137 x 152 500kW (680bhp) (new engine 1986)
Caterpillar Tractor Co-USA
AuxGen: 2 x 78kW 220/380V a.c

8222161 *AVJL* -
SULAWESI
ex Smit Sulawesi *-2010* *ex* Mwokozi *-1990*
Samson Maritime Ltd
Mumbai *India*
MMSI: 419000225
Official number: 3793
747 224 578
Class: IR LR
✠ **100A1** SS 10/2012
tug
✠ **LMC**
Eq.Ltr: J; Cable: 357.5/26.0 U2
1984-08 Ferguson-Ailsa Ltd — Port Glasgow Yd No: 492
Loa 45.65 Br ex 12.02 Dght 4.568
Lbp 41.00 Br md 11.51 Dpth 5.36
Welded, 1 dk
(B32A2ST) Tug
2 oil engines with clutches, flexible couplings & sr geared to sc. shafts driving 2 CP propellers
Total Power: 4,744kW (6,450hp)
Ruston 12RKCM
2 x Vee 4 Stroke 12 Cy. 254 x 305 each-2372kW (3225bhp)
Ruston Diesels Ltd.-Newton-le-Willows
AuxGen: 3 x 84kW 440V 50Hz a.c
Thrusters: 1 Tunnel thruster (f)
Fuel: 311.5 (d.f.)

8106501 *HP6313* -
SULAWESI-1
ex Daishin Maru No. 11 *-1991*
ex Sanko Maru No. 11 *-1989*
Sulawesi Marine Pte Ltd
PT Perikanan Perkan Utama
Panama *Panama*
Official number: 1982791A
220 66 -
1980-10 K.K. Tago Zosensho — Nishi-Izu Yd No: 176
Loa 41.05 Br ex 7.60 Dght 2.601
Lbp 32.52 Br md 6.15 Dpth 2.87
Welded, 1 dk
(B11B2FV) Fishing Vessel
1 oil engine driving 1 FP propeller
Total Power: 353kW (480hp)
Daihatsu 6DS-26D
1 x 4 Stroke 6 Cy. 260 x 320 353kW (480bhp)
Daihatsu Diesel Manufacturing Co Lt-Japan

7381740 *PKCR* -
SULAWESI II
PT (Persero) Pengerukan Indonesia
-
Jakarta *Indonesia*
MMSI: 525019037
3,934 1,181 4,740
Class: (KI) (BV)
1974-12 van der Giessen-de Noord BV — Krimpen a/d IJssel Yd No: 903
Loa 92.00 Br ex 16.06 Dght 6.401
Lbp 85.50 Br md 16.01 Dpth 8.01
Welded, 1 dk
(B33B2DT) Trailing Suction Hopper Dredger
Hopper: 2,654
2 oil engines driving 2 FP propellers
Total Power: 3,178kW (4,320hp) 11.0kn
Smit-Bolnes 309HD
2 x 2 Stroke 9 Cy. 300 x 550 each-1589kW (2160bhp)
Motorenfabriek Smit & Bolnes NV-Netherlands
Thrusters: 1 Thwart. FP thruster (f)

9385049 **SULAWESI PALM**
PNHO
- **Petroline Shipping Pte Ltd**
PACC Ship Managers Pte Ltd
Jakarta *Indonesia*
MMSI: 525019522
Official number: GT.11248 NO.1262/PPA

11,243 Class: AB KI
5,097
16,945
T/cm
28.0

2008-04 Taizhou Sanfu Ship Engineering Co Ltd — Taizhou JS Yd No: SF050205
Loa 144.00 (BB) Br ex - Dght 8.800
Lbp 135.60 Br md 23.00 Dpth 12.50
Welded, 1 dk

(A12B2TR) Chemical/Products Tanker
Double Hull (13F)
Liq: 18,896; Liq (Oil): 19,414
Cargo Heating Coils
Compartments: 12 Wing Ta, 2 Wing Slop Ta, ER

1 oil engine driving 1 FP propeller
Total Power: 4,440kW (6,037hp) 13.0kn
MAN-B&W 6S35MC
1 x 2 Stroke 6 Cy. 350 x 1400 4440kW (6037bhp)
STX Engine Co Ltd-South Korea
AuxGen: 3 x 660kW 440V a.c
Fuel: 78.0 (d.f.) 687.0 (r.f.)

8611958 **SULE VIKING**
J8B4775 *ex* Gudrun II *-2007* *ex* Gudrun *-1990*
- **Nye Sulevaer AS**
-
Kingstown *St Vincent & The Grenadines*
MMSI: 375102000
Official number: 11248

1,599 Class: BV (GL)
858
2,262

1987-02 C. Luehring Schiffswerft GmbH & Co. KG — Brake Yd No: 8602
Lengthened-1994
Loa 80.31 Br ex - Dght 4.374
Lbp 74.95 Br md 11.31 Dpth 5.92
Welded, 2 dks

(A31A2GX) General Cargo Ship
Grain: 2,936; Bale: 2,826
TEU 84 C.Ho 48/20' C.Dk 36/20'
Compartments: 1 Ho, ER, 1 Tw Dk
1 Ha: (51.3 x 9.0)ER
Ice Capable

1 oil engine with clutches, flexible couplings & reverse reduction geared to sc. shaft driving 1 FP propeller
Total Power: 599kW (814hp) 11.0kn
Deutz SBV6M628
1 x 4 Stroke 6 Cy. 240 x 280 599kW (814bhp)
Kloeckner Humboldt Deutz AG-West Germany
Thrusters: 1 Thwart. FP thruster (f)

8318063 **SULEDROTT**
J8B4763 *ex* Ute *-2004*
- **Nye Sulevaer AS**
-
Kingstown *St Vincent & The Grenadines*
MMSI: 376185000
Official number: 11236

1,525 Class: BV (GL)
783
1,837

1984-03 Husumer Schiffswerft Inh. Gebr. Kroeger GmbH & Co. KG — Husum Yd No: 1488
Lengthened-1994
Loa 76.45 (BB) Br ex 11.46 Dght 3.860
Lbp 70.70 Br md 11.30 Dpth 5.72
Welded, 2 dks

(A31A2GX) General Cargo Ship
Grain: 3,032; Bale: 3,005
Compartments: 1 Ho, ER
1 Ha: ER
Ice Capable

1 oil engine reduction geared to sc. shaft driving 1 CP propeller
Total Power: 588kW (799hp) 10.0kn
Callesen 6-427-FOTK
1 x 4 Stroke 6 Cy. 270 x 400 588kW (799bhp)
Aabenraa Motorfabrik, HeinrichCallesen A/S-Denmark
AuxGen: 1 x 96kW 380V 50Hz a.c, 1 x 50kW 380V 50Hz a.c, 1 x 24kW 380V 50Hz a.c
Thrusters: 1 Thwart. FP thruster (f)

9218636 **SULEHAV**
LJJZ
SF-1-SU **Lending Rederi AS**
-
Floro *Norway*
MMSI: 259586000

333
145
-

1999-04 Norrona Verft AS — Hommelvik Yd No: 74
Loa 21.33 Br ex - Dght -
Lbp 18.50 Br md 7.50 Dpth 3.70
Welded, 1 dk

(B11B2FV) Fishing Vessel

1 oil engine reduction geared to sc. shaft driving 1 FP propeller
Total Power: 750kW (1,020hp)
Caterpillar 3508TA
1 x Vee 4 Stroke 8 Cy. 170 x 190 750kW (1020bhp)
Caterpillar Inc-USA
AuxGen: 2 x 178kW a.c
Thrusters: 1 Thwart. FP thruster (f)

8721375 **SULEYMAN STALSKIY**
UITE *ex* Amur-2511 *-2009*
- **SP-Shipping LLC**
Olya-Shipping LLC
Astrakhan *Russia*
MMSI: 273434720

3,086 Class: (RS) (RR)
999
3,337

1986-02 Zavody Tazkeho Strojarstva (ZTS) — Komarno Yd No: 2311
Loa 115.70 Br ex 13.43 Dght 4.130
Lbp 112.40 Br md 13.00 Dpth 6.00
Welded, 1 dk

(A31A2GX) General Cargo Ship
Grain: 4,064
TEU 102 C.Ho 62/20' (40') C.Dk 40/20' (40')
Compartments: 3 Ho, ER
3 Ha: (11.6 x 10.1) (23.0 x 10.1) (24.0 x 10.1)ER

2 oil engines reverse reduction geared to sc. shafts driving 2 FP propellers
Total Power: 1,030kW (1,400hp) 10.0kn
Skoda 6L275A2
2 x 4 Stroke 6 Cy. 275 x 350 each-515kW (700bhp)
CKD Praha-Praha
AuxGen: 3 x 120kW 220/380V a.c, 1 x 50kW 220/380V a.c, 1 x 25kW 220/380V a.c
Thrusters: 1 Thwart. FP thruster (f)
Fuel: 157.0 (d.f.) 7.5pd

8322179 **SULINA**
5VCC2 *ex* Hiba. K *-2013* *ex* Biga *-2007*
- *ex* Uralar Septimo *-1996*
Arwad Full Marine SA
ISM Group Inc
Lome *Togo*
MMSI: 671361000

2,692 Class: GM (BV)
1,489
4,130

1984-10 S.A. Balenciaga — Zumaya Yd No: 313
Loa 91.32 Br ex - Dght 6.436
Lbp 83.01 Br md 14.41 Dpth 8.72
Welded, 1 dk

(A31A2GX) General Cargo Ship
Grain: 5,403; Bale: 5,251
TEU 162 C. 162/20' (40')
Compartments: 2 Ho, ER
2 Ha: ER

1 oil engine sr geared to sc. shaft driving 1 FP propeller
Total Power: 1,471kW (2,000hp) 12.0kn
Deutz RBV6M358
1 x 4 Stroke 6 Cy. 400 x 580 1471kW (2000bhp)
Hijos de J Barreras SA-Spain
AuxGen: 2 x 112kW 220V 50Hz a.c, 1 x 50kW 220V 50Hz a.c
Fuel: 192.0 (d.f.) 5.0pd

9100114 **SULLBERG**
ZDIC3
- **Partenreederei ms 'Sullberg'**
Vega-Reederei Friedrich Dauber GmbH & Co KG
Gibraltar *Gibraltar (British)*
MMSI: 236414000

1,969 Class: GL (BV)
936
3,280

1994-10 Barkmeijer Stroobos B.V. — Stroobos Yd No: 271
Converted From: General Cargo Ship-2007
Rebuilt-2007
Loa 89.50 Br ex - Dght 4.770
Lbp 84.98 Br md 12.50 Dpth 6.00
Welded, 1 dk

(A13B2TP) Products Tanker
Double Bottom Entire Compartment Length
Liq: 3,459; Liq (Oil): 3,459
Compartments: 12 Wing Ta, ER
3 Cargo Pump (s): 3x323m³/hr

1 oil engine reverse reduction geared to sc. shaft driving 1 FP propeller
Total Power: 1,235kW (1,679hp) 10.0kn
Deutz SBV6M628
1 x 4 Stroke 6 Cy. 240 x 280 1235kW (1679bhp)
Motoren Werke Mannheim AG (MWM)-Mannheim
AuxGen: 2 x 82kW a.c, 1 x 400kW a.c
Thrusters: 1 Thwart. FP thruster (f)
Fuel: 152.0 (d.f.)

5343627 **SULOY**
LEZN
- **Arvid Dalen**
-
Vardo *Norway*

150 Class: (NV)
71
183

1920 AS Rosenberg Mek. Verksted — Stavanger Yd No: 48
Lengthened-1932
Loa 36.68 Br ex 5.95 Dght 3.080
Lbp 33.71 Br md 5.90 Dpth 3.28
Riveted, 1 dk

(B11B2FV) Fishing Vessel
Grain: 212
Compartments: 1 Ho, ER
1 Ha: (10.4 x 2.9)
Derricks: 1x3t; Winches: 1

1 oil engine driving 1 CP propeller
Total Power: 206kW (280hp) 10.0kn
AuxGen: 3 x 32kW 220V d.c
Fuel: 20.5 (d.f.) 1.5pd

9077044 **SULPHUR ENTERPRISE**
KAKB
- **BMO Harris Equipment Finance Co**
LMS Shipmanagement Inc
SatCom: Inmarsat A 1534415
Mobile, AL *United States of America*
MMSI: 303520000
Official number: 1024115

16,771 Class: AB
5,031
21,649

1994-10 McDermott Shipyards Inc — Amelia LA Yd No: 294
Loa 159.71 (BB) Br ex - Dght 10.050
Lbp 151.36 Br md 27.43 Dpth 14.47
Welded, 1 dk

(A12A2LP) Molten Sulphur Tanker
Double Bottom Entire Compartment Length
Liq: 27,372
Cargo Heating Coils
Compartments: 4 Ta, ER

1 oil engine sr geared to sc. shaft driving 1 CP propeller
Total Power: 7,238kW (9,841hp) 15.0kn
Wartsila 8R46
1 x 4 Stroke 8 Cy. 460 x 580 7238kW (9841bhp)
Wartsila Diesel Oy-Finland
AuxGen: 3 x 800kW a.c
Thrusters: 1 Thwart. FP thruster (f)
Fuel: 1020.0

9124251 **SULPHUR ESPOIR**
3FXA2
- **Espoir Shipping SA**
Saehan Marine Service Co Ltd
Panama *Panama*
MMSI: 373734000
Official number: 4403312

2,976 Class: NK
893
3,999
T/cm
11.8

1995-09 Shin Kochi Jyuko K.K. — Kochi Yd No: 7066
Loa 99.92 (BB) Br ex - Dght 5.715
Lbp 94.00 Br md 14.50 Dpth 7.80
Welded, 1 dk

(A12A2LP) Molten Sulphur Tanker
Double Bottom Entire Compartment Length
Liq: 2,164
Cargo Heating Coils
Compartments: 8 Wing Ta, ER
4 Cargo Pump (s): 4x90m³/hr
Manifold: Bow/CM: 48m

1 oil engine driving 1 FP propeller
Total Power: 2,427kW (3,300hp) 12.7kn
Hanshin 6EL40
1 x 4 Stroke 6 Cy. 400 x 800 2427kW (3300bhp)
The Hanshin Diesel Works Ltd-Japan
AuxGen: 2 x 240kW a.c
Fuel: 83.0 (d.f.) 254.0 (r.f.) 8.6pd

9209013 **SULPHUR GARLAND**
3FRE9 *ex* Sulphur Spirit *-2011*
- **Palm SA**
Daiichi Tanker Co Ltd
Panama *Panama*
MMSI: 357708000
Official number: 2662099C

3,498 Class: NK
1,050
4,965
T/cm
13.4

1999-09 Hitachi Zosen Mukaishima Marine Co Ltd — Onomichi HS Yd No: 135
Loa 101.05 (BB) Br ex - Dght 6.281
Lbp 93.00 Br md 16.00 Dpth 7.80
Welded, 1 dk

(A12A2LP) Molten Sulphur Tanker
Double Bottom Entire Compartment Length
Liq: 2,758
Cargo Heating Coils
Compartments: 12 Wing Ta, ER
3 Cargo Pump (s): 3x275m³/hr
Manifold: Bow/CM: 46.1m

1 oil engine driving 1 FP propeller
Total Power: 3,236kW (4,400hp) 13.3kn
B&W 5L35MC
1 x 2 Stroke 5 Cy. 350 x 1050 3236kW (4400bhp)
The Hanshin Diesel Works Ltd-Japan
AuxGen: 3 x 387kW a.c
Thrusters: 1 Thwart. FP thruster (f)
Fuel: 139.0 (d.f.) 347.0 (r.f.)

9511789 **SULPHUR GENESIS**
9HA2898
- **DT Chemical SA**
Daiichi Tanker Co Ltd
Valletta *Malta*
MMSI: 256656000
Official number: 9511789

3,235 Class: NK
971
4,451
T/cm
11.5

2008-08 KK Onishigumi Zosensho — Mihara HS Yd No: 360
Loa 94.86 (BB) Br ex 14.52 Dght 6.673
Lbp 89.50 Br md 14.50 Dpth 8.50
Welded, 1 dk

(A12A2LP) Molten Sulphur Tanker
Double Hull
Liq: 2,241
Cargo Heating Coils
Compartments: 8 Ta, ER
Manifold: Bow/CM: 46.6m

1 oil engine driving 1 FP propeller
Total Power: 2,647kW (3,599hp) 13.2kn
Akasaka A41
1 x 4 Stroke 6 Cy. 410 x 800 2647kW (3599bhp)
Akasaka Tekkosho KK (Akasaka DieselLtd)-Japan
AuxGen: 2 x 320kW a.c
Thrusters: 1 Tunnel thruster (f)
Fuel: 300.0

9072862 **SULPHUR GLORY**
H9GE
- **DT Chemical SA**
Daiichi Tanker Co Ltd
SatCom: Inmarsat C 457624310
Panama *Panama*
MMSI: 353294000
Official number: 2797701B

2,283 Class: NK
685
2,999
T/cm
9.8

1993-10 Shin Kurushima Dockyard Co. Ltd. — Hashihama, Imabari Yd No: 2788
Loa 92.52 (BB) Br ex - Dght 5.465
Lbp 86.00 Br md 13.60 Dpth 7.00
Welded, 1 dk

(A12A2LP) Molten Sulphur Tanker
Double Hull
Liq: 1,531
Cargo Heating Coils
Compartments: 8 Ta, ER
4 Cargo Pump (s): 4x90m³/hr
Manifold: Bow/CM: 44.6m

1 oil engine driving 1 FP propeller
Total Power: 2,060kW (2,801hp) 13.0kn
Hanshin 6EL38
1 x 4 Stroke 6 Cy. 380 x 760 2060kW (2801bhp)
The Hanshin Diesel Works Ltd-Japan
AuxGen: 3 x 191kW a.c
Fuel: 54.0 (d.f.) 202.0 (r.f.)

9606986 **SULPHUR GUARDIAN**
3FMC3
- **Palm SA**
Daiichi Tanker Co Ltd
Panama *Panama*
MMSI: 373343000
Official number: 4329711

9,465 Class: NK
2,840
14,785

2011-12 Shitanoe Shipbuilding Co Ltd — Usuki OT Yd No: 1306
Loa 138.00 (BB) Br ex - Dght 8.250
Lbp 129.00 Br md 23.00 Dpth 11.40
Welded, 1 dk

(A12A2LP) Molten Sulphur Tanker
Double Hull (13F)
Liq: 7,207

1 oil engine driving 1 FP propeller
Total Power: 6,150kW (8,362hp) 13.8kn
MAN-B&W 6S42MC
1 x 2 Stroke 6 Cy. 420 x 1764 6150kW (8362bhp)
Hitachi Zosen Corp-Japan
Fuel: 1300.0

IMO / Call sign	Name / Owner	Tonnage	Class	Builder / Dimensions	Type	Machinery
9009839 *JNYN* -	**SULPHUR MERCATOR** - **Kokuka Sangyo Co Ltd** - *Tokyo* *Japan* MMSI: 431574000 Official number: 131679	*696* - 1,225	Class: (NK)	1990-09 **Hitachi Zosen Mukaishima Marine Co Ltd — Onomichi HS** Yd No: 32 Loa 64.50 (BB) Br ex - Dght 3.980 Lbp 60.00 Br md 11.00 Dpth 5.00 Welded, 1 dk	**(A12A2LP) Molten Sulphur Tanker** Liq: 619 Compartments: 3 Ta, ER	**1 oil engine** with clutches & geared to sc. shaft driving 1 CP propeller Total Power: 1,618kW (2,200hp) 11.2kn Akasaka A34 1 x 4 Stroke 6 Cy. 340 x 660 1618kW (2200bhp) Akasaka Tekkosho KK (Akasaka DieselLtd)-Japan AuxGen: 3 x 96kW a.c
9118989 *JGPK* -	**SULPHUR TRIPPER** - **Mitsubishi Chemical Logistics Corp (Mitsubishi Kagaku Butsuryo KK)** Iino Gas Transport Co Ltd *Tokyo* *Japan* MMSI: 431301411 Official number: 134997	*697* - 1,156	Class: NK	1995-02 **Mukaishima Zoki Co. Ltd. — Onomichi** Yd No: 300 Loa 64.50 Br ex 11.02 Dght 3.995 Lbp 60.00 Br md 11.00 Dpth 5.00 Welded, 1 dk	**(A12A2LP) Molten Sulphur Tanker** Liq: 596 Compartments: 6 Ta, ER	**1 oil engine** driving 1 CP propeller Total Power: 1,324kW (1,800hp) 12.6kn Hanshin LH31G 1 x 4 Stroke 6 Cy. 310 x 530 1324kW (1800bhp) The Hanshin Diesel Works Ltd-Japan AuxGen: 2 x 144kW a.c Thrusters: 1 Thwart. CP thruster (f) Fuel: 90.0 (d.f.)
7429360 *DUHI7* -	**SULPICIO CONTAINER 12** *ex* Yukoh Trader *-1986* *ex* First Trader *-1985* *ex* Pros Trader *-1985* *ex* Hoko Maru *-1983* **Philippine Span Asia Carrier Corp (PSACC)** - *Cebu* *Philippines* Official number: CEB1000050	*4,585* 1,227 7,128	Class: (BV) (NK)	1975-10 **Geibi Zosen Kogyo — Kure** Yd No: 263 Loa 107.60 Br ex 17.02 Dght 5.830 Lbp 100.60 Br md 17.00 Dpth 8.50 Welded, 1 dk	**(A31A2GX) General Cargo Ship** Grain: 9,709; Bale: 9,216 TEU 204 C. 204/20'	**1 oil engine** driving 1 FP propeller Total Power: 3,310kW (4,500hp) 12.9kn Hanshin 6LU54 1 x 4 Stroke 6 Cy. 540 x 860 3310kW (4500bhp) Hanshin Nainenki Kogyo-Japan AuxGen: 2 x 144kW 144V a.c Fuel: 65.0 (d.f.) 516.0 (r.f.) 12.5pd
6828155 *DUHG7* -	**SULPICIO CONTAINER IX** *ex* Ethel *-1983* *ex* Hokuryo Maru *-1977* **Philippine Span Asia Carrier Corp (PSACC)** - *Cebu* *Philippines* Official number: CEB1000077	*915* 602 1,787	Class: (BV) (NK)	1968 **Kurushima Dockyard Co. Ltd. — Imabari** Yd No: 460 Loa 68.13 Br ex 10.62 Dght 4.801 Lbp 63.02 Br md 10.60 Dpth 5.41 Riveted\Welded, 1 dk	**(A31A2GX) General Cargo Ship** Grain: 2,031; Bale: 1,769 TEU 60 C. 60/20' Compartments: 1 Ho, ER 2 Ha: (16.5 x 6.5) (16.2 x 6.5)ER Derricks: 2x10t	**1 oil engine** driving 1 FP propeller Total Power: 919kW (1,249hp) 11.0kn Akasaka 6DH35SS 1 x 4 Stroke 6 Cy. 350 x 520 919kW (1249bhp) Akasaka Tekkosho KK (Akasaka DieselLtd)-Japan AuxGen: 2 x 64kW 445V a.c Fuel: 86.5 5.0pd
5308902 *YBCR* -	**SULSEL** *ex* Sampang *-1974* **PT Pelayaran Green Windhu Line** - *Surabaya* *Indonesia*	*387* 65 183	Class: (KI)	1958-03 **Scheepswerf "De Waal" N.V. — Zaltbommel** Yd No: 667 Loa 40.72 Br ex 8.74 Dght 3.302 Lbp 36.99 Br md 8.70 Dpth 3.97 Riveted\Welded, 1 dk	**(B32A2ST) Tug**	**1 oil engine** driving 1 FP propeller Total Power: 603kW (820hp) 11.0kn Werkspoor 1 x 4 Stroke 6 Cy. 390 x 680 603kW (820bhp) NV Werkspoor-Netherlands AuxGen: 1 x 100kW 110V
7223651 *IHNO* -	**SULTAN** *ex* Gian Maria Paolini *-1989* *ex* G. 95 Paolini *-1989* *ex* Marcantonio Colonna *-1978* **ENEA di Cocia Andrea & C** - *Rome* *Italy* Official number: 575	*369* 160 70	Class: (RI)	1966 **Cantiere Navale M & B Benetti — Viareggio** Yd No: 65 Loa 39.25 Br ex 7.73 Dght 2.515 Lbp 33.08 Br md 7.70 Dpth 3.81 Welded, 1 dk	**(A37B2PS) Passenger Ship**	**1 oil engine** driving 1 FP propeller Total Power: 390kW (530hp) Ansaldo Q320/6RS 1 x 4 Stroke 6 Cy. 320 x 420 390kW (530bhp) SA Ansaldo Stabilimento Meccaniche-Italy
7636339 *J2HN* -	**SULTAN** *ex* Prisma *-2012* **Sovereign Global (UK) Ltd** - *Djibouti* *Djibouti* Official number: 30011278	**1,341** 403 600	Class: SC	1978-06 **Rauma-Repola Oy — Savonlinna** Yd No: 411 Loa 60.00 Br ex - Dght 2.630 Lbp 57.09 Br md 13.00 Dpth 3.50 Welded, 1 dk	**(B31A2SR) Research Survey Vessel**	**2 oil engines** reduction geared to sc. shafts driving 2 Directional propellers Total Power: 220kW (300hp) Scania D11 2 x 4 Stroke 6 Cy. 127 x 145 each-110kW (150bhp) Saab Scania AB-Sweden Thrusters: 1 Directional thruster (f)
8218847 *J8B3611* -	**SULTAN** *ex* Seawitch *-2004* *ex* Sea Challenge *-1990* *ex* Pacific Adventure *-1989* *ex* State Power *-1987* **Bellini Marine Services Ltd** Whitesea Shipping & Supply (LLC) *Kingstown* *St Vincent & The Grenadines* MMSI: 376834000 Official number: 10084	**813** 243 1,200	Class: BV (AB)	1983-05 **Bender Shipbuilding & Repair Co Inc — Mobile AL** Yd No: 1005 Loa 58.50 Br ex - Dght 3.682 Lbp 55.60 Br md 12.20 Dpth 4.27 Welded, 1 dk	**(B21B20A) Anchor Handling Tug Supply** Cranes: 1x21t,1x5t	**2 oil engines** reverse reduction geared to sc. shafts driving 2 FP propellers Total Power: 2,868kW (3,900hp) 10.0kn EMD (Electro-Motive) 16-645-E6 2 x Vee 2 Stroke 16 Cy. 230 x 254 each-1434kW (1950bhp) (Re-engined ,made 1975, Reconditioned & fitted 1983) General Motors Corp.Electro-Motive Div.-La Grange AuxGen: 2 x 125kW 208/120V 60Hz a.c Thrusters: 1 Thwart. FP thruster (f)
9101821 - -	**SULTAN** *ex* Sepiyeti *-2012* - -	**189** 57 73	Class: RS (Class contemplated)	1993-09 **OAO Astrakhanskaya Sudoverf — Astrakhan** Yd No: 110 Loa 31.85 Br ex 7.08 Dght 2.100 Lbp 27.80 Br md - Dpth 3.15 Welded, 1 dk	**(B12B2FC) Fish Carrier** Ins: 100 Compartments: 2 Ho 2 Ha: 2 (2.1 x 2.4) Derricks: 2x1t Ice Capable	**1 oil engine** geared to sc. shaft driving 1 FP propeller Total Power: 232kW (315hp) 10.2kn Daldizel 6CHSPN2A18-315 1 x 4 Stroke 6 Cy. 180 x 220 232kW (315bhp) Daldizel-Khabarovsk AuxGen: 2 x 25kW Fuel: 14.0 (d.f.)
8861060 *WAQ3510* -	**SULTAN** - **Highland Light Seafoods LLC** - *Seattle, WA* *United States of America* MMSI: 366485000 Official number: 638851	**289** 86 -		1981 **Eastern Marine, Inc. — Panama City, Fl** Yd No: 35 Loa - Br ex - Dght - Lbp 34.53 Br md 9.14 Dpth 3.51 Welded, 1 dk	**(B11B2FV) Fishing Vessel**	**2 oil engines** driving 2 FP propellers Total Power: 1,016kW (1,382hp) G.M. (Detroit Diesel) 16V-92 2 x Vee 2 Stroke 16 Cy. 123 x 127 each-508kW (691bhp) General Motors Corp-USA
9361081 *HMVN5* -	**SULTAN 1** *launched as* Kamille *-2008* **Brook Motors FZC** Brook General Trading Co LLC *Wonsan* *North Korea* MMSI: 445629000 Official number: 5503110	**497** 298 1,200		2008-03 **Mauban Shipyard — Mauban** Yd No: 10 Loa 67.00 Br ex - Dght - Lbp 61.28 Br md 12.19 Dpth 3.35 Welded, 1 dk	**(A35D2RL) Landing Craft** Bow ramp (f)	**2 oil engines** reduction geared to sc. shafts driving 2 Propellers Total Power: 898kW (1,220hp) Volvo Penta 2 x 4 Stroke 6 Cy. each-449kW (610bhp) AB Volvo Penta-Sweden
9565467 *TCYG9* -	**SULTAN ATASOY** - **Nehir Denizcilik Lojistik Insaat Taah Turizm Yat Sanayi Ltd Sti** Atasoy Group of Shipping Companies (Atasoy Grup Denizcilik Ticaret Ltd Sti) *Istanbul* *Turkey* MMSI: 271040963 Official number: 1331	**4,807** 2,561 6,634	Class: BV	2010-06 **Yasarsan Gemi Insaa Sanayi ve Ticaret Ltd Sti — Altinova** Yd No: 01 Loa 109.00 (BB) Br ex - Dght 6.860 Lbp 99.50 Br md 16.30 Dpth 8.15 Welded, 1 dk	**(A21A2BC) Bulk Carrier** Grain: 8,632 Compartments: 2 Ho, ER 2 Ha: (38.5 x 13.5)ER (29.4 x 13.5)	**1 oil engine** reduction geared to sc. shafts driving 1 CP propeller Total Power: 1,980kW (2,692hp) 12.0kn MaK 6M25 1 x 4 Stroke 6 Cy. 255 x 400 1980kW (2692bhp) Caterpillar Motoren GmbH & Co. KG-Germany AuxGen: 2 x 230kW 60Hz a.c Thrusters: 1 Tunnel thruster (f)
8996970 - -	**SULTAN BABULLAH** - **PT Pann (Persero)** PT Elsafa *Jakarta* *Indonesia*	**155** 131 -	Class: (KI)	1990-12 **P.T. Adiguna Fibrindo Utama — Jakarta** Loa 22.20 Br ex - Dght 0.750 Lbp 19.50 Br md 6.20 Dpth 2.70 Bonded, 1 dk	**(A37B2PS) Passenger Ship** Hull Material: Reinforced Plastic	**2 oil engines** reduction geared to sc. shafts driving 2 Propellers Total Power: 1,082kW (1,472hp) G.M. (Detroit Diesel) 1 x 2 Stroke 541kW (736bhp) Detroit Diesel Eng. Co.-Detroit, Mi G.M. (Detroit Diesel) 1 x 2 Stroke 541kW (736bhp) Detroit Diesel-Detroit, Mi
9366768 *J2HI* -	**SULTAN HABIB A. HOUMED** - **Port Autonome International de Djibouti** - *Djibouti* *Djibouti* MMSI: 621819000	**313** 93 -	Class: (LR) ✠ Classed LR until 13/10/07	2006-07 **PO SevMash Predpriyatiye — Severodvinsk** (Hull) Yd No: (511725) 2006-07 **B.V. Scheepswerf Damen — Gorinchem** Yd No: 511725 Loa 30.82 Br ex 10.20 Dght 4.700 Lbp 28.03 Br md 9.40 Dpth 4.80 Welded, 1 dk	**(B32A2ST) Tug**	**2 oil engines** reduction geared to sc. shafts driving 2 Directional propellers Total Power: 3,730kW (5,072hp) 12.3kn Caterpillar 3516B-TA 2 x Vee 4 Stroke 16 Cy. 170 x 190 each-1865kW (2536bhp) Caterpillar Inc-USA AuxGen: 2 x 84kW 380V 50Hz a.c
9366794 *J2HJ* -	**SULTAN HOUMED L. BOKO** - **Port Autonome International de Djibouti** - *Djibouti* *Djibouti* MMSI: 621819001	**313** 93 224	Class: LR ✠ **100A1** SS 04/2012 tug **LMC** Eq.Ltr: F; Cable: 275.0/19.0 U2 (a)	2007-04 **Stal-Rem SA — Gdansk** (Hull) Yd No: (511732) 2007-04 **B.V. Scheepswerf Damen — Gorinchem** Yd No: 511732 Loa 30.82 Br ex 10.20 Dght 3.758 Lbp 28.03 Br md 9.40 Dpth 4.80 Welded, 1 dk	**(B32A2ST) Tug**	**2 oil engines** gearing integral to driving 2 Directional propellers Total Power: 3,542kW (4,816hp) 12.3kn Caterpillar 3516B-HD 2 x Vee 4 Stroke 16 Cy. 170 x 215 each-1771kW (2408bhp) Caterpillar Inc-USA AuxGen: 2 x 85kW 400V 50Hz a.c

IMO / Call sign	Name / Owner / Port	Tonnage	Class	Builder / Dimensions	Type	Machinery
9645827 - -	**SULTAN I** **PT Karindo Mandiri** PT Karyamas Kaltim Prima *Samarinda* *Indonesia*	**478** 159 1,000	Class: (KI)	**2011-10 PT Karindo Mandiri — Samarinda** Yd No: 2/2011 Loa 62.00 Br ex - Dght 2.000 Lbp 60.20 Br md 12.00 Dpth 3.00 Welded, 1 dk	**(A35D2RL) Landing Craft**	**2 oil engines** reduction geared to sc. shafts driving 2 Propellers Total Power: 824kW (1,120hp) Caterpillar D379 2 x Vee 4 Stroke 8 Cy. 159 x 203 each-412kW (560bhp) Caterpillar Inc-USA
9521174 *A6E2672* -	**SULTAN II** **Liwa Marine Services LLC** *Abu Dhabi* *United Arab Emirates* MMSI: 470523000	**482** 302 700	Class: BV	**2008-04 RRT Marine Services Co — Manila** Yd No: 009 Loa 50.88 Br ex - Dght 2.300 Lbp 47.72 Br md 11.00 Dpth 3.00 Welded, 1 dk	**(A35D2RL) Landing Craft**	**2 oil engines** reduction geared to sc. shafts driving 2 Propellers Total Power: 810kW (1,102hp) Volvo Penta 2 x 4 Stroke 6 Cy. each-405kW (551bhp) AB Volvo Penta-Sweden
8303240 *YDOS* -	**SULTAN MAHMUD BADARUDDIN II** **PT Pupuk Indonesia (Persero)** - *Jakarta* *Indonesia* MMSI: 525018008 Official number: 285+PST	**7,305** 2,580 7,259	Class: KI (LR) (GL) ✠ Classed LR until 4/90	**1984-06 Jos L Meyer GmbH & Co — Papenburg** Yd No: 606 Lengthened-1990 Loa 144.70 Br ex 16.34 Dght 6.780 Lbp 136.20 Br md 16.30 Dpth 10.90 Welded, 1 dk	**(A11B2TG) LPG Tanker** Double Bottom Entire Compartment Length Liq (Gas): 8,700 4 x Gas Tank (s); 1 independent dcc horizontal, 3 independent dcy horizontal	**1 oil engine** with flexible couplings & sr geared to sc. shaft driving 1 FP propeller Total Power: 4,560kW (6,200hp) 15.0kn MaK 8M552AK 1 x 4 Stroke 8 Cy. 450 x 520 4560kW (6200bhp) Krupp MaK Maschinenbau GmbH-Kiel AuxGen: 3 x 550kW 220/440V 50Hz a.c, 1 x 100kW 220/440V 50Hz a.c Thrusters: 1 Thwart. CP thruster (f)
8846553 - -	**SULTANA** **Bay Pacific Carriers Ltd** - *Chittagong* *Bangladesh* Official number: C.874	*384* 239 640	Class: (NK)	**1989-05 Highspeed Shipbuilding & Heavy Engineering Co Ltd — Dhaka** Yd No: 106 Loa - Br ex - Dght 2.364 Lbp 47.25 Br md 10.66 Dpth 2.75 Welded, 1 dk	**(A13B2TU) Tanker (unspecified)**	**2 oil engines** driving 2 FP propellers Total Power: 530kW (720hp) Yanmar 2 x 4 Stroke each-265kW (360bhp) Yanmar Diesel Engine Co Ltd-Japan
9415519 *TCA2893* -	**SULTANAHMET** **Istanbul Deniz Otobusleri Sanayi ve Ticaret AS (IDO)** - *Istanbul* *Turkey* MMSI: 271002578	**1,065** 608 250	Class: TL	**2008-06 Ceksan Tersanesi — Turkey** Yd No: 43 Loa 73.20 Br ex - Dght 2.600 Lbp 70.10 Br md 18.00 Dpth 4.40 Welded, 1 dk	**(A36A2PR) Passenger/Ro-Ro Ship (Vehicles)** Bow ramp (f) Stern ramp (a) Cars: 80	**4 oil engines** reduction geared to sc. shafts driving 2 Voith-Schneider propellers 2 propellers aft, 2 fwd. Total Power: 2,440kW (3,316hp) Mitsubishi S6R2-MPTA 4 x 4 Stroke 6 Cy. 170 x 220 each-610kW (829bhp) Mitsubishi Heavy Industries Ltd-Japan AuxGen: 1 x 71kW a.c, 1 x 62kW a.c
5310785 *YBCQ* -	**SULTENG** *ex* Sandangan *-1974* **PT Pelayaran Surya** - *Surabaya* *Indonesia*	*432* 207 660	Class: (KI)	**1958-02 P.T. Pakin — Jakarta** Yd No: 443 Loa 55.40 Br ex 9.25 Dght 2.998 Lbp 51.74 Br md 9.20 Dpth 3.05 Welded, 1 dk & S dk	**(A31A2GX) General Cargo Ship** 3 Ha: 2 (8.7 x 5.0) (1.3 x 5.0)ER Derricks: 2x6t,2x3t	**1 oil engine** driving 1 FP propeller Total Power: 298kW (405hp) 10.0kn Werkspoor TMAS276 1 x 4 Stroke 6 Cy. 270 x 500 298kW (405bhp) NV Werkspoor-Netherlands AuxGen: 1 x 19kW 110V d.c Fuel: 51.0
8825494 *YDWZ* -	**SULTRA JAYA** *ex* Minatani 01 *-1974* *ex* Lucia No. 6 *-1974* *ex* Pescanip No. 1 *-1974* **PT Putra Sultra S Up Jaman Tedja** - *Jakarta* *Indonesia*	*438* 169 -	Class: (KI)	**1978 KK Kanasashi Zosen — Shizuoka SZ** Loa - Br ex - Dght - Lbp 48.23 Br md 8.20 Dpth 3.60 Welded, 1 dk	**(B11B2FV) Fishing Vessel**	**1 oil engine** geared to sc. shaft driving 1 FP propeller Total Power: 368kW (500hp) Matsui MS24GH 1 x 4 Stroke 6 Cy. 240 x 470 368kW (500bhp) Matsui Iron Works Co Ltd-Japan AuxGen: 1 x 400kW 450V a.c
7433892 *DUA2103* -	**SULU VENTURE** *ex* Legend *-1991* **United Salvage & Towage (Phils) Inc** - *Manila* *Philippines* MMSI: 548403100 Official number: 00-0001581	**679** 203 1,000	Class: AB	**1976-06 Halter Marine, Inc. — Moss Point, Ms** Yd No: 519 Loa 54.87 Br ex 12.20 Dght 3.683 Lbp 49.92 Br md 12.15 Dpth 4.27 Welded, 1 dk	**(B21A20S) Platform Supply Ship**	**2 oil engines** reverse reduction geared to sc. shafts driving 2 FP propellers Total Power: 2,206kW (3,000hp) 12.0kn EMD (Electro-Motive) 12-645-E6 2 x Vee 2 Stroke 12 Cy. 230 x 254 each-1103kW (1500bhp) General Motors Corp.Electro-Motive Div.-La Grange AuxGen: 2 x 150kW a.c Thrusters: 1 Thwart. FP thruster (f) Fuel: 222.5 (d.f.)
9058086 - -	**SUMA MARU No. 8** **KK Amamoto Jyari**	*460* - 1,200		**1993-06 Shinhama Dockyard Co. Ltd. — Tamano** Yd No: 258 Loa 51.00 Br ex - Dght - Lbp 47.00 Br md 12.00 Dpth 3.70 Welded, 1 dk	**(A24D2BA) Aggregates Carrier**	**1 oil engine** driving 1 FP propeller Total Power: 1,177kW (1,600hp) Hanshin 1 x 4 Stroke 1177kW (1600bhp) The Hanshin Diesel Works Ltd-Japan
8026476 *VWLE* -	**SUMAI TANGKAS** *ex* Oil Rider *-1990* **Hind Offshore Pvt Ltd** - *Mumbai* *India* MMSI: 419020500 Official number: 2820	**142** 43 130	Class: BV IR	**1980-04 Cal Marine Pte Ltd — Singapore** Yd No: 153 Loa 30.51 Br ex - Dght 1.601 Lbp 28.12 Br md 6.41 Dpth 3.13 Welded, 1 dk	**(B21A20C) Crew/Supply Vessel** Passengers: unberthed: 42	**2 oil engines** geared to sc. shafts driving 2 FP propellers Total Power: 1,294kW (1,760hp) 13.0kn G.M. (Detroit Diesel) 16V-92-TA 2 x Vee 2 Stroke 16 Cy. 123 x 127 each-647kW (880bhp) General Motors Detroit DieselAllison Divn-USA AuxGen: 2 x 25kW 400V 50Hz a.c Fuel: 25.0 (d.f.)
8972091 *YDZF* -	**SUMANGALO** *ex* P. K. Prosperity *-2010* **Ratna Williem Dan Ronald Sumangalo** - *Surabaya* *Indonesia*	**1,940** 1,046 3,003	Class: KI	**1980 Israel Shipyards Ltd. — Haifa** Loa 84.20 Br ex - Dght 6.200 Lbp 75.30 Br md 12.30 Dpth 7.09 Welded, 1 dk	**(A31A2GX) General Cargo Ship** Grain: 3,759; Bale: 3,627 Compartments: 2 Ho, ER Cranes: 1x5t; Derricks: 2x3t	**1 oil engine** driving 1 FP propeller Total Power: 1,103kW (1,500hp) 10.0kn Werkspoor TMABS396 1 x 4 Stroke 6 Cy. 390 x 680 1103kW (1500bhp) NV Werkspoor-Netherlands AuxGen: 2 x 148kW 440V a.c
7809376 *YHJC* -	**SUMATERA FORTUNE** *ex* Kris Merubi *-2003* *ex* Mulpha Kluang *-1994* *ex* Tunghai Career *-1984* **PT Indonesian Fortune Lloyd (IFL)** - *Jakarta* *Indonesia* MMSI: 525014010	**4,129** 1,941 4,028	Class: KI (NK)	**1979-01 Usuki Iron Works Co Ltd — Usuki OT** Yd No: 995 Loa 96.40 (BB) Br ex 20.05 Dght 5.515 Lbp 88.92 Br md 20.00 Dpth 8.00 Welded, 1 dk	**(A33A2CC) Container Ship (Fully Cellular)** TEU 210 C Ho 118 TEU C Dk 92 TEU incl 18 ref C Compartments: 4 Ho, ER 7 Ha: (12.8 x 10.6)6 (12.8 x 7.9)ER Gantry cranes: 1x30t	**1 oil engine** driving 1 FP propeller Total Power: 2,060kW (2,801hp) 12.0kn Makita GSLH641 1 x 4 Stroke 6 Cy. 410 x 650 2060kW (2801bhp) Makita Diesel Co Ltd-Japan AuxGen: 3 x 200kW a.c Fuel: 215.0 (d.f.) 11.0pd
8822090 *POJW* -	**SUMATERA LEADER** *ex* Straits Success *-2012* *ex* Toyofuku Maru *-2006* **PT NYK Line Indonesia** PT Salam Pacific Indonesia Lines *Jakarta* *Indonesia* MMSI: 525015933	**8,772** 3,296 2,662	Class: KI (NK)	**1989-08 Kanda Zosensho K.K. — Kawajiri** Yd No: 325 Loa 108.00 (BB) Br ex - Dght 5.615 Lbp 99.90 Br md 19.60 Dpth 5.96 Welded, 2 dks	**(A35B2RV) Vehicles Carrier** Quarter stern door/ramp (p. a.) Quarter stern door/ramp (s. a.) Cars: 652	**1 oil engine** driving 1 CP propeller Total Power: 4,119kW (5,600hp) 16.0kn B&W 7L35MC 1 x 2 Stroke 7 Cy. 350 x 1050 4119kW (5600bhp) Hitachi Zosen Corp-Japan AuxGen: 3 x 400kW 450V a.c Thrusters: 1 Thwart. CP thruster (f) Fuel: 335.0 (r.f.)
5343718 *LW4048* -	**SUMATRA** **Armadora Patagonica SA** - *Mar del Plata* *Argentina* Official number: 01105	**173** 106 85	Class: (BV)	**1958-01 Ateliers et Chantiers de La Manche — Dieppe** Yd No: 1149 Loa 34.47 Br ex 6.89 Dght - Lbp 29.52 Br md 6.84 Dpth 3.81 Riveted\Welded, 1 dk	**(B11A2FT) Trawler** 3 Ha: 2 (0.9 x 0.9) (0.8 x 0.8)	**1 oil engine** driving 1 CP propeller Total Power: 552kW (750hp) 12.8kn Deutz RBV6M545 1 x 4 Stroke 6 Cy. 320 x 450 552kW (750bhp) Kloeckner Humboldt Deutz AG-West Germany Fuel: 36.5 (d.f.)
9408047 *PORK* -	**SUMATRA PALM** **PT Jaya Prima Nusantara** PACC Ship Managers Pte Ltd *Batam* *Indonesia* MMSI: 525020109	**11,248** 5,040 16,989 T/cm 28.0	Class: AB	**2008-06 Taizhou Sanfu Ship Engineering Co Ltd — Taizhou JS** Yd No: SF050206 Loa 144.00 (BB) Br ex - Dght 8.800 Lbp 135.60 Br md 23.00 Dpth 12.50 Welded, 1 dk	**(A12B2TR) Chemical/Products Tanker** Double Hull (13F) Liq: 18,896; Liq (Oil): 19,411 Cargo Heating Coils Compartments: 12 Wing Ta, 2 Wing Slop Ta, ER	**1 oil engine** driving 1 FP propeller Total Power: 4,440kW (6,037hp) 13.0kn MAN-B&W 6S35MC 1 x 2 Stroke 6 Cy. 350 x 1400 4440kW (6037bhp) STX Engine Co Ltd-South Korea AuxGen: 3 x 580kW a.c Fuel: 78.0 (d.f.) 687.0 (r.f.)
9256951 *J7AP6* -	**SUMAYA SUCCESS** *ex* Marina Stellar *-2006* **Blue Marine Logistics (S) Pte Ltd** Blue Marine Logistics Pvt Ltd *Portsmouth* *Dominica* Official number: 50287	**205** 62 215	Class: NK	**2001-08 Super-Light Shipbuilding Contractor — Sibu** Yd No: 47 Loa 26.00 Br ex - Dght 3.012 Lbp 23.96 Br md 8.00 Dpth 3.65 Welded, 1 dk	**(B32A2ST) Tug**	**2 oil engines** driving 2 FP propellers Total Power: 1,204kW (1,636hp) Mitsubishi S6R2-MPTK 2 x 4 Stroke 6 Cy. 170 x 220 each-602kW (818bhp) Mitsubishi Heavy Industries Ltd-Japan Fuel: 130.0 (d.f.)

Identity	Name / Owner	Tonnage / Class	Build / Dimensions	Type	Machinery
8216552 *AVNG* -	**SUMAYLA ONE** *ex Dickerson Tide -2011* **Transtar Marine & Offshore Services** Amba Shipping & Logistics Pvt Ltd *Mumbai* *India* MMSI: 419000346 Official number: 3868	**1,078** Class: IR (AB) 323 1,047	**1984-03 McDermott Shipyards Inc — New Iberia LA** Yd No: 162 Converted From: Offshore Supply Ship-1991 Loa 59.14 Br ex 12.45 Dght 3.658 Lbp 54.87 Br md 12.20 Dpth 4.27 Welded, 1 dk	**(B22A2OR) Offshore Support Vessel**	**2 oil engines** sr reverse geared to sc. shafts driving 2 FP propellers Total Power: 1,654kW (2,248hp) 11.0kn Caterpillar D399TA 2 x Vee 4 Stroke 16 Cy. 159 x 203 each-827kW (1124bhp) (Re-engined) Caterpillar Tractor Co-USA AuxGen: 2 x 135kW 480V 60Hz a.c Thrusters: 1 Thwart. FP thruster (f) Fuel: 367.5 (d.f.) 7.5pd
9435387 *EZCV* -	**SUMBAR** *completed as Samur River -2009* **The Turkmen Marine Merchant Fleet Authority** Turkmen Maritime & River Lines (Turkmen Deniz Deryayollary) SatCom: Inmarsat C 443400019 *Turkmenbashy* *Turkmenistan* MMSI: 434113700	**4,681** Class: RS 2,273 7,075	**2009-07 Sudostroitelnyy Zavod "Krasnoye Sormovo" — Nizhniy Novgorod** Yd No: 07006 Loa 139.95 Br ex 16.83 Dght 4.600 Lbp 134.50 Br md 16.60 Dpth 6.00 Welded, 1 dk	**(A13B2TP) Products Tanker** Double Hull (13F) Liq: 7,833; Liq (Oil): 7,833 Cargo Heating Coils Compartments: 6 Ta, ER 6 Cargo Pump (s): 6x150m³/hr	**2 oil engines** reduction geared to sc. shafts driving 2 Directional propellers Total Power: 2,160kW (2,936hp) 10.5kn Wartsila 6L20 2 x 4 Stroke 6 Cy. 200 x 280 each-1080kW (1468bhp) AuxGen: 3 x 292kW a.c Thrusters: 1 Tunnel thruster (f)
7710135 *YCHG* -	**SUMBAWA** **Government of The Republic of Indonesia (Direktorat Jenderal Perhubungan Laut - Ministry of Sea Communications)** - *Jakarta* *Indonesia*	*2,838* Class: (KI) (NK) 1,184 2,247	**1978-08 Ishikawajima Ship & Chemical Plant Co Ltd — Tokyo** Yd No: 496 Loa 85.02 Br ex 16.41 Dght 4.001 Lbp 80.02 Br md 16.40 Dpth 6.02 Welded, 1 dk	**(B33B2DT) Trailing Suction Hopper Dredger** Hopper: 1,200 Cranes: 1x5t	**2 oil engines** with flexible couplings & reductiongeared to sc. shafts driving 2 CP propellers Total Power: 2,354kW (3,200hp) 12.0kn Niigata 8MG25BX 2 x 4 Stroke 8 Cy. 250 x 320 each-1177kW (1600bhp) Niigata Engineering Co Ltd-Japan AuxGen: 3 x 1520kW Thrusters: 1 Thwart. FP thruster (f)
8622256 *YFWK* -	**SUMBER ABADI 178** *ex Sinar Abadi 7 -2007 ex Jasa Prima -2007* *ex Sun Glory I -1998 ex Daisenzan Maru -1997* *ex Shoei Maru No. 35 -1992* **PT Alexindo Yakin Prima** - *Jakarta* *Indonesia* MMSI: 525016487	**1,316** Class: KI 520 1,505	**1983-09 K.K. Yoshida Zosen Kogyo — Arida** Yd No: 387 Loa 75.30 Br ex - Dght 4.250 Lbp 70.00 Br md 11.50 Dpth 6.60 Welded, 1 dk	**(A31A2GX) General Cargo Ship**	**1 oil engine** driving 1 FP propeller Total Power: 883kW (1,201hp) 11.0kn Akasaka DM28AFD 1 x 4 Stroke 6 Cy. 280 x 460 883kW (1201bhp) Akasaka Tekkosho KK (Akasaka DieselLtd)-Japan
9029724 *YHVM* -	**SUMBER ANUGERAH** **PT Pelayaran Sumber Rejeki Bahari Permai** *Ambon* *Indonesia*	**328** Class: KI 99 390	**2003-09 C.V. Jaya Terang — Sorong** Loa 41.50 Br ex - Dght 2.100 Lbp 39.84 Br md 9.00 Dpth 3.30 Welded, 1 dk	**(A35D2RL) Landing Craft** Bow ramp (centre)	**2 oil engines** geared to sc. shafts driving 2 Propellers Total Power: 596kW (810hp) 8.0kn Yanmar 6HA2M-DTE 2 x 4 Stroke 6 Cy. 130 x 165 each-298kW (405bhp) (made 2003) Yanmar Diesel Engine Co Ltd-Japan AuxGen: 2 x 13kW 400V a.c
8837318 *YEHA* -	**SUMBER BAHAGIA SEMESTA I** *ex Kumala Seri -1998* **PT Sarana Bahari Prima** - *Palembang* *Indonesia*	*322* Class: (KI) 179 -	**1987 P.T. Mariana Bahagia — Palembang** Loa 42.50 Br ex - Dght 2.500 Lbp 38.65 Br md 8.00 Dpth 3.00 Welded, 1 dk	**(A31A2GX) General Cargo Ship**	**1 oil engine** geared to sc. shaft driving 1 FP propeller Total Power: 294kW (400hp) 8.0kn Yanmar 6LA-DTE 1 x 4 Stroke 6 Cy. 148 x 165 294kW (400bhp) Yanmar Diesel Engine Co Ltd-Japan AuxGen: 2 x 5kW 115V a.c
8837320 *YEGZ* -	**SUMBER BAHAGIA SEMESTA II** *ex Kumala Karya -1997* **PT Yudi Samudera Pacific** - *Palembang* *Indonesia*	*323* Class: KI 226 -	**1988-03 P.T. Mariana Bahagia — Palembang** Loa 42.50 Br ex - Dght 2.500 Lbp 38.65 Br md 8.00 Dpth 3.00 Welded, 1 dk	**(A31A2GX) General Cargo Ship**	**1 oil engine** geared to sc. shaft driving 1 FP propeller Total Power: 294kW (400hp) 8.0kn Yanmar 6LA-DTE 1 x 4 Stroke 6 Cy. 148 x 165 294kW (400bhp) Yanmar Diesel Engine Co Ltd-Japan AuxGen: 2 x 5kW 115V a.c
9026203 *YB4388* -	**SUMBER BANGKA 6** **PT Sumber Sumatra Raya** - *Palembang* *Indonesia* MMSI: 525016062	**280** Class: KI 84 55	**2001-12 P.T. Sumber Sumatera Raya — Palembang** L reg 36.50 Br ex - Dght 2.480 Lbp 34.00 Br md 7.50 Dpth 2.80 Welded, 1 dk	**(A37B2PS) Passenger Ship** Hull Material: Aluminium Alloy	**3 oil engines** geared to sc. shafts driving 3 Propellers Total Power: 3,150kW (4,284hp) 27.0kn M.T.U. 16V2000M70 3 x Vee 4 Stroke 16 Cy. 130 x 150 each-1050kW (1428bhp) (made 2000) MTU Friedrichshafen GmbH-Friedrichshafen
9026215 *YB4433* -	**SUMBER BANGKA 7** **PT Sumber Sumatra Raya** - *Palembang* *Indonesia*	**292** Class: KI 88 -	**2003-02 P.T. Sumber Sumatera Raya — Palembang** Loa 36.50 Br ex - Dght - Lbp 34.00 Br md 7.50 Dpth 2.80 Welded, 1 dk	**(A37B2PS) Passenger Ship** Hull Material: Aluminium Alloy	**3 oil engines** geared to sc. shafts driving 3 Propellers Total Power: 3,150kW (4,284hp) 30.0kn M.T.U. 16V2000M70 3 x Vee 4 Stroke 16 Cy. 130 x 150 each-1050kW (1428bhp) (made 2001) MTU Friedrichshafen GmbH-Friedrichshafen AuxGen: 2 x 96kW 380V a.c
9028213 *YB4537* -	**SUMBER BANGKA 8** **PT Sumber Sumatra Raya** - *Palembang* *Indonesia*	**201** Class: KI 61 -	**2006-05 P.T. Sumber Sumatera Raya — Palembang** Loa 32.00 Br ex - Dght - Lbp 29.40 Br md 7.00 Dpth 1.80 Welded, 1 dk	**(A37B2PS) Passenger Ship** Hull Material: Aluminium Alloy	**3 oil engines** driving 3 Propellers Total Power: 3,150kW (4,284hp) 36.0kn M.T.U. 16V2000M70 3 x Vee 4 Stroke 16 Cy. 130 x 150 each-1050kW (1428bhp) (made 2005) MTU Friedrichshafen GmbH-Friedrichshafen AuxGen: 2 x 144kW 380V a.c
9026186 - -	**SUMBER BANGKA II** **PT Sumber Sumatra Raya** - *Palembang* *Indonesia*	**140** Class: (KI) 42 -	**1997-05 P.T. Sumber Sumatera Raya — Palembang** L reg 37.00 Br ex - Dght 1.490 Lbp 35.35 Br md 5.00 Dpth 2.00 Welded, 1 dk	**(A37B2PS) Passenger Ship**	**3 oil engines** geared to sc. shafts driving 3 Propellers Total Power: 2,208kW (3,003hp) 25.0kn MAN D2842LE 3 x Vee 4 Stroke 12 Cy. 128 x 142 each-736kW (1001bhp) MAN Nutzfahrzeuge AG-Nuernberg
8847545 *YGQS* -	**SUMBER CAHAYA** *ex Teck Heng -1997 ex Colonial Chief -1992* *ex Keian Maru No. 6 -1991* **PT Transindo Bahari Perkasa** - *Semarang* *Indonesia*	**660** Class: KI 273 718	**1974-05 Ikeda Zosen K.K. — Osakikamijima** Loa 55.10 Br ex - Dght 3.100 Lbp 50.00 Br md 10.00 Dpth 5.00 Welded, 1 dk	**(A31A2GX) General Cargo Ship**	**1 oil engine** driving 1 FP propeller Total Power: 956kW (1,300hp) 10.0kn Hanshin 6LUN28G 1 x 4 Stroke 6 Cy. 280 x 480 956kW (1300bhp) The Hanshin Diesel Works Ltd-Japan
7812361 *PMVX* -	**SUMBER CAHAYA 18** *ex Meitoku Maru No. 28 -2011* - - *Indonesia*	*699* - 1,380	**1979-04 K.K. Miura Zosensho — Saiki** Yd No: 560 Loa - Br ex - Dght 3.601 Lbp 59.01 Br md 10.51 Dpth 5.72 Welded, 1 dk	**(A31A2GX) General Cargo Ship**	**1 oil engine** geared to sc. shaft driving 1 FP propeller Total Power: 1,030kW (1,400hp) Daihatsu 6DS-26 1 x 4 Stroke 6 Cy. 260 x 320 1030kW (1400bhp) Daihatsu Diesel Manufacturing Co Lt-Japan
9083641 *PMWS* -	**SUMBER CAHAYA 68** *ex Wakaba Maru -2009 ex Sahei Maru -2002* **PT Berlian Khatulistiwa Line** PT Tanjung Mas Bahari Perkasa *Dumai* *Indonesia*	**1,018** Class: KI 578 2,053	**1994-02 Miho Zosensho K.K. — Shimizu** Yd No: 1429 Loa 74.08 (BB) Br ex - Dght 4.470 Lbp 70.00 Br md 11.50 Dpth 5.30 Welded, 1 dk	**(A13B2TP) Products Tanker** Liq: 2,250; Liq (Oil): 2,250	**1 oil engine** driving 1 FP propeller Total Power: 1,471kW (2,000hp) Yanmar MF33-ST 1 x 4 Stroke 6 Cy. 330 x 620 1471kW (2000bhp) Yanmar Diesel Engine Co Ltd-Japan Thrusters: 1 Thwart. FP thruster (f)
8202422 *YFRP* -	**SUMBER CAHAYA 88** *ex Big Top -2007* *ex Kyokuyo Maru No. 17 -1997* **PT Tanjung Mas Bahari Perkasa** - *Surabaya* *Indonesia* MMSI: 525690313	*1,075* Class: KI 648 1,620	**1982-10 K.K. Miura Zosensho — Saiki** Yd No: 660 Loa 66.53 (BB) Br ex - Dght 5.100 Lbp 62.01 Br md 10.61 Dpth 6.23 Welded, 2 dks	**(A31A2GX) General Cargo Ship** Grain: 2,211; Bale: 2,170 Compartments: 1 Ho, ER 1 Ha: ER	**1 oil engine** with clutches, flexible couplings & sr reverse geared to sc. shaft driving 1 FP propeller Total Power: 1,030kW (1,400hp) Niigata 6M31AFT 1 x 4 Stroke 6 Cy. 310 x 530 1030kW (1400bhp) Niigata Engineering Co Ltd-Japan
8414362 *YHAL* -	**SUMBER CAHAYA II** *ex Yoko Maru No. 3 -2001* **PT Binaindo Transportasi Bahari Co** - *Dumai* *Indonesia*	**610** Class: KI 340 450	**1984-09 Namikata Shipbuilding Co Ltd — Imabari EH** Yd No: 123 Loa 54.46 Br ex 9.02 Dght 2.801 Lbp 49.51 Br md 9.01 Dpth 5.31 Welded, 2 dks	**(A31A2GX) General Cargo Ship** Grain: 1,218; Bale: 900 Compartments: 1 Ho, ER 1 Ha: ER	**1 oil engine** with clutches & reverse reduction geared to sc. shaft driving 1 FP propeller Total Power: 405kW (551hp) Sumiyoshi S25G 1 x 4 Stroke 6 Cy. 250 x 450 405kW (551bhp) Sumiyoshi Marine Diesel Co Ltd-Japan

Number / Call sign	Name / Owner / Port	Tonnage	Class	Built / Dimensions	Type	Machinery
8626460 *YB3405* -	**SUMBER CAHAYA VIII** *ex* Hiyoshi Maru No. 2 *-2002* **PT Tanjung Mas Bahari Perkasa** *Dumai* Indonesia	**476** 265 750	Class: KI	**1985-04 Y.K. Okajima Zosensho — Matsuyama** Loa 47.60 Br ex - Dght 3.050 Lbp 42.50 Br md 8.21 Dpth 4.91 Welded, 1 dk	**(A31A2GX) General Cargo Ship** Grain: 870; Bale: 800	**1 oil engine** driving 1 FP propeller Total Power: 353kW (480hp) 9.5kn Niigata 6M22GT 1 x 4 Stroke 6 Cy. 220 x 280 353kW (480bhp) (made 1984) Niigata Engineering Co Ltd-Japan
8627103 *YB3417* -	**SUMBER CAHAYA XI** *ex* Sumiho Maru No. 11 *-2002* **PT Harita Prima Abadi Mineral** - *Dumai* Indonesia	*596* 384 699	Class: KI	**1984-07 Yano Zosen K.K. — Imabari** Yd No: 111 Loa 56.14 Br ex - Dght 3.350 Lbp 50.60 Br md 9.00 Dpth 5.30 Welded, 1 dk	**(A31A2GX) General Cargo Ship**	**1 oil engine** reverse geared to sc. shaft driving 1 FP propeller Total Power: 405kW (551hp) 9.5kn Akasaka DM26R 1 x 4 Stroke 6 Cy. 260 x 440 405kW (551bhp) Akasaka Tekkosho KK (Akasaka DieselLtd)-Japan
8730687 *YB3523* -	**SUMBER CARRIER** **PT Tonggak Yakin Mulia** - *Tanjungpinang* Indonesia	**177** 54 -	Class: (KI)	**2005-01 P.T. Sumber Teknik — Indonesia** L reg 36.70 Br ex - Dght 1.790 Lbp 31.90 Br md 8.50 Dpth 2.50 Welded, 1 dk	**(A35D2RL) Landing Craft**	**2 oil engines** reduction geared to sc. shafts driving 2 Propellers Total Power: 794kW (1,080hp) G.M. (Detroit Diesel) 12V-71-TI 2 x Vee 2 Stroke 12 Cy. 108 x 127 each-397kW (540bhp) Detroit Diesel Corporation-Detroit, Mi
8944393 *YBNV* -	**SUMBER CARRIER II** *ex* Merbau Carrier II *-2008* **PT Limin Marine & Offshore** Limin Marine Pte Ltd *Tanjungpinang* Indonesia	**370** 111 583	Class: KI	**1990 Dynamic Marine Pte Ltd — Singapore** Loa 48.60 Br ex - Dght 2.480 Lbp 40.45 Br md 13.00 Dpth 3.30 Welded, 1 dk	**(A35D2RL) Landing Craft**	**2 oil engines** driving 2 FP propellers Total Power: 662kW (900hp) Matsui 3.62DGSC 2 x 4 Stroke 3 Cy. each-331kW (450bhp) Matsui Iron Works Co Ltd-Japan AuxGen: 1 x 24kW 415V a.c, 1 x 38kW 415V a.c
7116212 *YEBG* -	**SUMBER GLORY** *ex* Tropical Rose *-2005* *ex* Eishin No. 8 *-1986* *ex* Zao Maru No. 5 *-1985* **PT Pelayaran Lintas Benua** - *Jakarta* Indonesia	**2,243** 1,307 2,711	Class: KI (NK)	**1971-06 Imamura Zosen — Kure** Yd No: 772 Loa 86.72 Br ex 12.53 Dght 5.080 Lbp 80.02 Br md 12.50 Dpth 7.70 Welded, 2 dks	**(A31A2GX) General Cargo Ship** Grain: 4,465; Bale: 4,216 2 Ha: (13.2 x 8.0) (30.0 x 8.9)ER Derricks: 3x15t	**1 oil engine** driving 1 FP propeller Total Power: 1,912kW (2,600hp) 13.0kn Hanshin 6L46 1 x 4 Stroke 6 Cy. 460 x 680 1912kW (2600bhp) Hanshin Nainenki Kogyo-Japan AuxGen: 2 x 100kW a.c Fuel: 218.5 9.5pd
8826981 - -	**SUMBER IX** **PT Armada Prima Nusantera** - *Palembang* Indonesia	*105* 32 -	Class: (KI)	**1983-02 P.T. Sumber Sumatera Raya — Palembang** Loa 23.16 Br ex 6.52 Dght - Lbp - Br md - Dpth 2.45 Welded, 1 dk	**(B32A2ST) Tug**	**2 oil engines** driving 2 FP propellers Total Power: 1,236kW (1,680hp) 13.0kn Caterpillar 3408TA 2 x Vee 4 Stroke 8 Cy. 137 x 152 each-618kW (840bhp) (made 1982) Caterpillar Tractor Co-USA AuxGen: 1 x 3kW 230V a.c
8937649 - -	**SUMBER JAYA** **PT Sumber Jaya Bahari Abadi** -	**316** 102 -		**1997 Tung Lung Shipbuilding — Sibu** Loa 37.75 Br ex - Dght 2.090 Lbp 35.75 Br md 7.07 Dpth 2.70 Welded, 1 dk	**(A37B2PS) Passenger Ship**	**1 oil engine** driving 1 FP propeller Total Power: 255kW (347hp) M.T.U. 1 x 4 Stroke 255kW (347bhp) MTU Friedrichshafen GmbH-Friedrichshafen
9205146 - -	**SUMBER JAYA II** **PT Sumber Jaya Bahari Abadi** -	**364** 114 247		**1998-01 Tung Lung Shipbuilding — Sibu** Yd No: 260297 Loa 34.35 Br ex - Dght 2.200 Lbp 32.70 Br md 6.95 Dpth 2.70 Welded	**(A37B2PS) Passenger Ship**	**1 oil engine** driving 1 FP propeller Total Power: 255kW (347hp) M.T.U. 1 x 4 Stroke 255kW (347bhp) MTU Friedrichshafen GmbH-Friedrichshafen
8331132 *YETV* -	**SUMBER KARUNIA** *ex* Sumber Hotama II *-2006* *ex* Jinei Maru No. 3 *-1992* *ex* Kaiko Maru No. 2 *-1988* **PT Sarana Bahari Prima** - *Jakarta* Indonesia	**557** 205 500	Class: (KI)	**1976-07 Takeshima Zosen K.K. — Japan** Loa 49.81 Br ex - Dght 3.801 Lbp 46.51 Br md 9.01 Dpth 5.21 Welded, 1 dk	**(A31A2GX) General Cargo Ship** Compartments: 1 Ho, ER 1 Ha: (26.4 x 6.0)ER	**1 oil engine** driving 1 FP propeller Total Power: 74kW (101hp) 10.5kn Niigata 1 x 4 Stroke 74kW (101bhp) Niigata Engineering Co Ltd-Japan
8118451 *YFQC* -	**SUMBER LESTARI** *ex* Gunung Maras *-2004* *ex* Chokyu Maru No. 17 *-1997* **PT Sarana Bahari Prima** - *Jakarta* Indonesia	**1,269** 793 1,599	Class: KI	**1982-01 K.K. Miura Zosensho — Saiki** Yd No: 637 Loa 69.27 Br ex - Dght 4.301 Lbp 65.03 Br md 11.51 Dpth 6.35 Welded, 1 dk	**(A31A2GX) General Cargo Ship**	**1 oil engine** driving 1 FP propeller Total Power: 736kW (1,001hp) Hanshin 6LUN28A 1 x 4 Stroke 6 Cy. 280 x 480 736kW (1001bhp) The Hanshin Diesel Works Ltd-Japan
8884103 *YB7021* -	**SUMBER LESTARI III** *ex* Akebono Maru No. 5 *-1995* **PT Anugrah Makmur Sejahti** - *Makassar* Indonesia	**245** 127 313	Class: KI	**1976-12 Takuma Zosen K.K. — Mitoyo** Loa 36.00 Br ex - Dght 2.900 Lbp 32.00 Br md 7.00 Dpth 4.50 Welded, 1 dk	**(A31A2GX) General Cargo Ship** Compartments: 1 Ho 1 Ha: (18.4 x 5.3)	**1 oil engine** driving 1 FP propeller Total Power: 250kW (340hp) 9.0kn Yanmar 6M-HT 1 x 4 Stroke 6 Cy. 200 x 240 250kW (340bhp) Yanmar Diesel Engine Co Ltd-Japan AuxGen: 1 x 10kW 110/220V a.c
9026227 - -	**SUMBER MAHKOTA 08** **PT Sumber Mahkota Penghidupan** - *Banjarmasin* Indonesia	**113** 67 -	Class: (KI)	**1997-12 CV Sumber Jaya — Banjarmasin** L reg 17.50 Br ex - Dght 2.240 Lbp 16.80 Br md 5.00 Dpth 2.80 Welded, 1 dk	**(B32A2ST) Tug**	**2 oil engines** geared to sc. shafts driving 2 Propellers Total Power: 618kW (840hp) Caterpillar 3408B 2 x Vee 4 Stroke 8 Cy. 137 x 152 each-309kW (420bhp) (made 1995) Caterpillar Inc-USA
8661018 - -	**SUMBER MAKMUR 8** *ex* Citra 08 *-2013* **PT Setiakawan Makmur Bersama** - *Batam* Indonesia Official number: 2013 PPM NO. 2883/L	**152** 46 -	Class: KI (Class contemplated)	**2012-10 PT Citra Shipyard — Batam** Yd No: TB 016 Loa 21.59 Br ex - Dght - Lbp - Br md 7.32 Dpth 3.20 Welded, 1 dk	**(B32A2ST) Tug**	**2 oil engines** reduction geared to sc. shafts driving 2 Propellers Total Power: 894kW (1,216hp) Caterpillar C18 ACERT 2 x 4 Stroke 6 Cy. 145 x 183 each-447kW (608bhp) Caterpillar Inc-USA
9027051 - -	**SUMBER MAS 3** **PT Sumber Mas Timber** - *Samarinda* Indonesia	**215** 102 -	Class: (KI)	**1979-07 P.T. Sumber Mas Timber — Samarinda** L reg 42.60 Br ex - Dght 1.450 Lbp 37.75 Br md 9.20 Dpth 2.00 Welded, 1 dk	**(A35D2RL) Landing Craft** Bow ramp (centre)	**2 oil engines** geared to sc. shafts driving 2 Propellers Total Power: 404kW (550hp) Caterpillar 3406 2 x 4 Stroke 6 Cy. 137 x 165 each-202kW (275bhp) (, fitted 1979) Caterpillar Tractor Co-USA
8837667 - -	**SUMBER MAS No. 5** **PT Sumber Mas Timber** - *Samarinda* Indonesia	*146* 75 -	Class: (KI)	**1981 P.T. Sumber Mas Timber — Samarinda** Loa 27.10 Br ex - Dght 1.450 Lbp 26.75 Br md 7.55 Dpth 1.90 Welded, 1 dk	**(A35D2RL) Landing Craft** Bow door/ramp	**2 oil engines** driving 2 FP propellers Total Power: 272kW (370hp) General Motors 2 x 2 Stroke 6 Cy. each-136kW (185bhp) General Motors Detroit DieselAllison Divn-USA
9026239 - -	**SUMBER MAS XVIII** **PT Mitratirta Lokalestari** - *Jambi* Indonesia	**290** 188 -	Class: KI	**1998-12 PT Mitratirta Lokalestari — Jambi** L reg 37.10 Br ex - Dght 1.970 Lbp 36.25 Br md 10.60 Dpth 2.45 Welded, 1 dk	**(A35D2RL) Landing Craft** Bow ramp (centre)	**2 oil engines** geared to sc. shafts driving 2 Propellers Total Power: 592kW (804hp) Caterpillar 3408 2 x Vee 4 Stroke 8 Cy. 137 x 152 each-296kW (402bhp) Caterpillar Inc-USA
7122156 *YDAP* -	**SUMBER MINA 1** *ex* Indofish No. 7 *-1981* *ex* Fukutoku Maru No. 28 *-1980* **PT Sumber Mina Raya** - *Sabang* Indonesia	*284* 142 -	Class: (NK) (KI)	**1970-12 KK Kanasashi Zosen — Shizuoka SZ** Yd No: 676 Loa 49.20 Br ex 7.83 Dght 3.150 Lbp 44.42 Br md 7.80 Dpth 3.46 Welded, 1 dk	**(B11B2FV) Fishing Vessel**	**1 oil engine** driving 1 FP propeller Total Power: 625kW (850hp) Sumiyoshi S6HAHS 1 x 4 Stroke 6 Cy. 330 x 520 625kW (850bhp) Sumiyoshi Marine Diesel Co Ltd-Japan
7048439 - -	**SUMBER MINA 2** *ex* Indofish No. 5 *-1971* *ex* Marukyoboshi Maru No. 18 *-1971* *ex* Sakura Maru No. 18 *-1971* **PT Sumber Mina Raya** - *Sabang* Indonesia	*254* 129 311	Class: (NK) (KI)	**1971-02 Uchida Zosen — Ise** Yd No: 693 Loa 46.66 Br ex 7.93 Dght - Lbp 40.67 Br md 7.90 Dpth 3.46 Riveted\Welded, 1 dk	**(B11B2FV) Fishing Vessel** Ins: 307 3 Ha: 2 (1.3 x 1.0) (1.6 x 1.6)ER	**1 oil engine** driving 1 FP propeller Total Power: 699kW (950hp) 11.5kn Hanshin 6LU28 1 x 4 Stroke 6 Cy. 280 x 440 699kW (950bhp) Hanshin Nainenki Kogyo-Japan AuxGen: 2 x 176kW

7003374 *YCJD* -	**SUMBER MINA 4** *ex* Fukuseki Maru No. 25 *-1979* *ex* Ino Maru No. 15 *-1979* **PT Sumber Mina Raya** - *Jakarta* *Indonesia* Official number: 4560/L	*224* 112 250	Class: (KI)	**1969-10 KK Kanasashi Zosen — Shizuoka SZ** Yd No: 953 Loa 44.81 Br ex 7.22 Dght 2.731 Lbp 39.30 Br md 7.21 Dpth 3.26 Welded, 1 dk	**(B11B2FV) Fishing Vessel** Ins: 239 Compartments: 3 Ho, ER 5 Ha: 2 (0.9 x 0.9) (1.3 x 0.9)2 (1.6 x 1.5)ER	**1 oil engine** driving 1 FP propeller Total Power: 515kW (700hp) Akasaka 6MH25SS 1 x 4 Stroke 6 Cy. 250 x 400 515kW (700bhp) Akasaka Tekkosho KK (Akasaka DieselLtd)-Japan
6921646 - -	**SUMBER MINA 6** *ex* Kanbay *-1979* *ex* Shoun Maru No. 22 *-1981* *ex* Fukuyo Maru No. 5 *-1981* **PT Sumber Mina Raya** - *Jakarta* *Indonesia*	*224* 103 297	Class: (NK) (KI)	**1969-05 Yamanishi Shipbuilding Co Ltd — Ishinomaki MG** Yd No: 608 Loa 43.24 Br ex 7.73 Dght 2.900 Lbp 37.90 Br md 7.70 Dpth 3.33 Welded, 1 dk	**(B11B2FV) Fishing Vessel** Ins: 229	**1 oil engine** driving 1 FP propeller Total Power: 625kW (850hp) 10.5kn Niigata 6L20AX 1 x 4 Stroke 6 Cy. 200 x 260 625kW (850bhp) Niigata Engineering Co Ltd-Japan AuxGen: 2 x 128kW
9439993 *PNSS*	**SUMBER MITRA KENCANA 1** *ex* Pelangi Gunung Surya *-2012* *ex* ZD Glory *-2007* *ex* Zhong Da You 8 *-2007* **PT Pelayaran Sumber Bahari** PT Sumber Surya Kencana Inhu *Jakarta* *Indonesia* MMSI: 525019573	**1,993** 918 3,116	Class: KI	**2007-02 Yueqing Jiangnan Ship Co Ltd — Yueqing ZJ** Loa 88.20 Br ex - Dght 5.200 Lbp 79.98 Br md 13.50 Dpth 6.00 Welded, 1 dk	**(A13B2TP) Products Tanker** Double Hull (13F)	**1 oil engine** geared to sc. shaft driving 1 Propeller Total Power: 735kW (999hp) 8.0kn Chinese Std. Type G6300ZCA 1 x 4 Stroke 6 Cy. 300 x 380 735kW (999bhp) Ningbo CSI Power & Machinery GroupCo Ltd-China
6711065 *PLZB* -	**SUMBER MUTIARA IV** *ex* Shinpo Maru No. 2 *-1977* *ex* Eishin Maru No. 17 *-1977* - - *Jakarta* *Indonesia*	*571* 331 999	Class: (KI) (NK)	**1967-01 Sasaki Shipbuilding Co Ltd — Osakikamijima HS** Yd No: 102 Converted From: Oil Tanker Loa 54.41 Br ex 9.02 Dght 4.001 Lbp 49.00 Br md 9.01 Dpth 4.40 Welded, 1 dk	**(A12D2LV) Vegetable Oil Tanker** Liq: 1,205; Liq (Oil): 1,205 Compartments: 4 Ta, ER	**1 oil engine** driving 1 FP propeller Total Power: 736kW (1,001hp) 12.5kn Kanegafuchi B6D53EHSB 1 x 4 Stroke 6 Cy. 330 x 460 736kW (1001bhp) Kanegafuchi Diesel-Japan AuxGen: 2 x 20kW 225V a.c Fuel: 35.5 3.0pd
8330061 *PLTL*	**SUMBER MUTIARA IX** *ex* Istana IV *-1977* *ex* Delima 112 *-1977* - - *Jakarta* *Indonesia* MMSI: 525015516	**802** 466 -	Class: KI	**1965 Kurushima Dock Co. Ltd. — Japan** Loa - Br ex - Dght - Lbp 55.50 Br md 9.50 Dpth 4.75 Welded, 1 dk	**(A13B2TU) Tanker (unspecified)**	**1 oil engine** driving 1 FP propeller Total Power: 625kW (850hp) Otsuka SODHS6X26 1 x 4 Stroke 6 Cy. 260 x 410 625kW (850bhp) KK Otsuka Diesel-Japan
8978447 *YCZU* -	**SUMBER POWER** *ex* PN Sukses 3 *-2006* *ex* Poh Hwa No. 5 *-2006* **Maskur** - *Tanjungpinang* *Indonesia*	**431** 130 -	Class: KI	**1999 Tai Chung Hua Shipyard Sdn Bhd — Malaysia** Loa 44.65 Br ex - Dght - Lbp 36.75 Br md 14.58 Dpth 2.88 Welded, 1 dk	**(A31A2GX) General Cargo Ship**	**2 oil engines** reduction geared to sc. shafts driving 2 Propellers Total Power: 536kW (728hp) Cummins 1 x 4 Stroke 268kW (364bhp) Cummins Engine Co Inc-USA Cummins NT-855-M 1 x 4 Stroke 6 Cy. 140 x 152 268kW (364bhp) Cummins Engine Co Inc-USA AuxGen: 2 x 74kW 415V a.c
5396416 - -	**SUMBER POWER IV** *ex* You Yangs *-1997* - -	**166** 50	Class: (LR) ✠ Classed LR until 14/9/84	**1962-12 Adelaide Ship Construction Pty Ltd — Port Adelaide SA** Yd No: 15 Loa 28.96 Br ex 7.57 Dght 3.163 Lbp 26.78 Br md 7.17 Dpth 3.66 Welded, 1 dk	**(B32A2ST) Tug** 1 Ha: (0.9 x 1.2)	**1 oil engine** with hydraulic couplings & sr reverse geared to sc. shaft driving 1 FP propeller Total Power: 874kW (1,188hp) Ruston 6ATCM 1 x 4 Stroke 6 Cy. 318 x 368 874kW (1188bhp) Ruston & Hornsby Ltd.-Lincoln AuxGen: 2 x 35kW 220V d.c
8979336 - -	**SUMBER POWER VI** - **PT Sumber Maritim** - *Indonesia*	*160* 50 -		**1990 P.T. Sumber Teknik — Indonesia** Loa - Br ex - Dght - Lbp 23.70 Br md 7.17 Dpth 3.20 Welded, 1 dk	**(B32A2ST) Tug**	**2 oil engines** driving 2 Propellers Total Power: 882kW (1,200hp)
9055137 *YD4583* -	**SUMBER POWER XVIII** *ex* Sugih *-2005* *ex* MHKL 16 *-2002* *ex* Venkat II *-1999* **PT Sumber Maritim** - *Batam* *Indonesia*	**131** 79 -	Class: KI (AB)	**1992-03 Jiangsu Wuxi Shipyard Co Ltd — Wuxi JS** Yd No: 1008 Loa 22.50 Br ex - Dght 2.400 Lbp 21.30 Br md 7.50 Dpth 3.20 Welded, 1 dk	**(B32A2ST) Tug**	**2 oil engines** reverse reduction geared to sc. shafts driving 2 FP propellers Total Power: 992kW (1,348hp) 10.5kn Cummins VTA-28-M2 2 x Vee 4 Stroke 12 Cy. 140 x 152 each-496kW (674bhp) (made 1990) Cummins Engine Co Inc-USA AuxGen: 2 x 40kW a.c
9084724 *PNES* -	**SUMBER REJEKI 68** *ex* Kakuryu Maru *-2010* *ex* Zuikai Maru *-1997* **PT Berlian Khatulistiwa Line** PT Tanjung Mas Bahari Perkasa *Dumai* *Indonesia*	**1,122** 593 2,100	Class: KI	**1993-11 Hakata Zosen K.K. — Imabari** Yd No: 558 Loa 77.03 Br ex - Dght 4.750 Lbp 73.30 Br md 11.50 Dpth 5.33 Welded, 1 dk	**(A13B2TP) Products Tanker**	**1 oil engine** driving 1 FP propeller Total Power: 1,324kW (1,800hp) Yanmar MF33-ST 1 x 4 Stroke 6 Cy. 330 x 620 1324kW (1800bhp) Yanmar Diesel Engine Co Ltd-Japan
9005089 *PNDS*	**SUMBER REJEKI 88** *ex* Toei Maru No. 2 *-2012* **PT Binaindo Transportasi Bahari Co** - *Indonesia*	*494* - 1,200		**1991-02 K.K. Murakami Zosensho — Naruto** Yd No: 200 Loa 71.82 (BB) Br ex - Dght 4.223 Lbp 66.00 Br md 11.00 Dpth 6.60 Welded	**(A31A2GX) General Cargo Ship** Grain: 2,412; Bale: 2,191 Compartments: 1 Ho, ER 1 Ha: ER	**1 oil engine** reverse geared to sc. shaft driving 1 FP propeller Total Power: 736kW (1,001hp) Akasaka A31R 1 x 4 Stroke 6 Cy. 310 x 600 736kW (1001bhp) Akasaka Tekkosho KK (Akasaka DieselLtd)-Japan
8909795 *YCRF* -	**SUMBER REJEKI VIII** *ex* Genyou *-2008* *ex* Genyo Maru No. 26 *-2007* *ex* Shin Kyokuto Maru *-1994* **PT Tanjung Mas Bahari Perkasa** - *Dumai* *Indonesia* MMSI: 525015708	*1,116* 540 1,900	Class: KI	**1989-12 Mukaishima Zoki Co. Ltd. — Onomichi** Yd No: 258 Converted From: Chemical Tanker-2008 Loa 74.67 Br ex - Dght 4.400 Lbp 69.98 Br md 11.20 Dpth 5.30 Welded, 1 dk	**(A31A2GX) General Cargo Ship**	**1 oil engine** with clutches, flexible couplings & reverse geared to sc. shaft driving 1 FP propeller Total Power: 1,471kW (2,000hp) Hanshin 6EL32G 1 x 4 Stroke 6 Cy. 320 x 640 1471kW (2000bhp) Hanshin Nainenki Kogyo-Japan AuxGen: 2 x 140kW 450V a.c
8737037 *PMPX* -	**SUMBER SEJAHTERA ABADI 2** - **Muhammad Nur** - *Samarinda* *Indonesia*	**348** 105 500	Class: KI	**2008-08 CV Lestari Abadi — Samarinda** Loa 50.30 Br ex - Dght 2.750 Lbp 44.80 Br md 9.00 Dpth 3.00 Welded, 1 dk	**(A35D2RL) Landing Craft** Bow ramp (centre)	**2 oil engines** driving 2 Propellers Total Power: 596kW (810hp) 7.5kn Yanmar 6HA2M-DTE 2 x 4 Stroke 6 Cy. 130 x 165 each-298kW (405bhp) Yanmar Diesel Engine Co Ltd-Japan
7905027 *PNOP* -	**SUMBER SUKSES UTAMA** *ex* Sunshine *-2011* *ex* Progress *-2008* *ex* Reefer Lake *-1996* *ex* Reefer Baroness *-1991* *ex* Pacific Baroness *-1990* **PT Sumber Laut Utama** - *Jakarta* *Indonesia* MMSI: 525010170	**1,884** 953 2,043	Class: KI (LR) ✠ Classed LR until 16/5/01	**1980-01 Frederikshavn Vaerft A/S — Frederikshavn** Yd No: 385 Loa 75.37 (BB) Br ex 13.29 Dght 5.011 Lbp 67.29 Br md 13.21 Dpth 7.27 Welded, 2 dks	**(A34A2GR) Refrigerated Cargo Ship** Ins: 2,960 TEU 8 C.Dk 8/20' Compartments: 3 Ho, ER 3 Ha: (8.6 x 4.7)2 (7.0 x 4.7)ER Derricks: 3x5t; Winches: 3	**1 oil engine** sr geared to sc. shaft driving 1 CP propeller Total Power: 1,368kW (1,860hp) 11.5kn Alpha 12V23L-VO 1 x Vee 4 Stroke 12 Cy. 225 x 300 1368kW (1860bhp) B&W Alpha Diesel A/S-Denmark AuxGen: 3 x 280kW 440V 60Hz a.c, 1 x 44kW 440V 60Hz a.c
8504363 - -	**SUMBER TRUST** *ex* Pacific Trust *-2013* *ex* Tohoku Maru *-2008* - - *Indonesia*	**247** 74 250		**1985-06 Ishikawajima Ship & Chemical Plant Co Ltd — Tokyo** Yd No: 568 Loa 30.99 Br ex - Dght 3.580 Lbp 27.01 Br md 8.62 Dpth 3.61 Welded, 1 dk	**(B32A2ST) Tug**	**2 oil engines** with clutches & dr geared to sc. shafts driving 2 Directional propellers Total Power: 2,206kW (3,000hp) Yanmar T260-ET 2 x 4 Stroke 6 Cy. 260 x 330 each-1103kW (1500bhp) Yanmar Diesel Engine Co Ltd-Japan
8329256 *YCZJ* -	**SUMBER VI** - **PT Pelayaran Nelly Dwi Putri** - *Palembang* *Indonesia*	*100* 60 -	Class: KI	**1981 P.T. Sumber Sumatera Raya — Palembang** L reg 23.17 Br ex - Dght 2.500 Lbp 20.16 Br md 6.52 Dpth 2.85 Welded, 1 dk	**(B32A2ST) Tug**	**2 oil engines** driving 2 FP propellers Total Power: 764kW (1,038hp) Caterpillar 3412TA 2 x Vee 4 Stroke 12 Cy. 137 x 152 each-382kW (519bhp) Caterpillar Tractor Co-USA
8329244 *YD4455* -	**SUMBER VII** - **PT Cahaya Perdana Transalam** - *Palembang* *Indonesia* MMSI: 525015145	*107* 33 -	Class: KI	**1981 P.T. Sumber Sumatera Raya — Palembang** Loa 23.27 Br ex - Dght - Lbp - Br md 6.52 Dpth 2.54 Welded, 1 dk	**(B32A2ST) Tug**	**2 oil engines** driving 2 FP propellers Total Power: 626kW (852hp) Caterpillar D353SCAC 2 x 4 Stroke 6 Cy. 159 x 203 each-313kW (426bhp) Caterpillar Tractor Co-USA

Number / Call sign	Name / Owner	Tonnage	Class	Build / Dimensions	Type	Machinery
8826979 *YDHA* -	**SUMBER VIII** **PT Pelayaran Nelly Dwi Putri** - *Palembang* *Indonesia*	*102* 61 -	Class: KI	**1982 P.T. Sumber Sumatera Raya — Palembang** Loa - Br ex 6.52 Dght - Lbp 22.65 Br md - Dpth 2.45 Welded, 1 dk	**(B32A2ST) Tug**	**2 oil engines** driving 2 FP propellers Total Power: 810kW (1,102hp) Yanmar S165L-ST 2 x 4 Stroke 6 Cy. 165 x 210 each-405kW (551bhp) Yanmar Diesel Engine Co Ltd-Japan AuxGen: 1 x 6kW 220V a.c
8826993 *YD4458* -	**SUMBER X** **PT Sumber Sumatra Raya** - *Palembang* *Indonesia*	*123* 37 -	Class: KI	**1985-05 P.T. Sumber Sumatera Raya — Palembang** Loa 23.00 Br ex 6.50 Dght 2.500 Lbp - Br md - Dpth 2.85 Welded, 1 dk	**(B32A2ST) Tug**	**2 oil engines** driving 2 FP propellers Total Power: 810kW (1,102hp) 10.0kn Yanmar S165L-ST 2 x 4 Stroke 6 Cy. 165 x 210 each-405kW (551bhp) (made 1984) Yanmar Diesel Engine Co Ltd-Japan AuxGen: 1 x 6kW 230V a.c
9027063 *YD4283* -	**SUMBER XI** **PT Spectra Tirta Segara Line** - *Palembang* *Indonesia*	**121** 37 -	Class: KI	**1990-07 P.T. Sumber Sumatera Raya — Palembang** Loa - Br ex - Dght 2.500 Lbp 23.00 Br md 6.50 Dpth 2.85 Welded, 1 dk	**(B32A2ST) Tug**	**2 oil engines** reduction geared to sc. shafts driving 2 Propellers Total Power: 592kW (804hp) Caterpillar 3408B 2 x Vee 4 Stroke 8 Cy. 137 x 152 each-296kW (402bhp) Caterpillar Inc-USA
9027075 - -	**SUMBER XXV** **PT Sumber Sumatra Raya** - *Palembang* *Indonesia*	**139** 42 -	Class: KI	**1998-09 P.T. Sumber Sumatera Raya — Palembang** L reg 25.50 Br ex - Dght 2.490 Lbp 24.67 Br md 7.00 Dpth 3.25 Welded, 1 dk	**(B32A2ST) Tug**	**2 oil engines** geared to sc. shafts driving 2 Propellers Total Power: 1,060kW (1,442hp) 11.0kn MAN 2 x Vee 4 Stroke 12 Cy. each-530kW (721bhp) (made 1998) MAN B&W Diesel AG-Augsburg
7616028 - -	**SUMBER Z PELLER** *ex* Goho Maru *-2003* *ex* Sakura *-1983* **Maskur** -	**238** 71 140		**1976-11 Imamura Zosen — Kure** Yd No: 218 Loa 31.73 Br ex 9.02 Dght 2.701 Lbp 26.52 Br md 8.62 Dpth 3.51 Welded, 1 dk	**(B32A2ST) Tug**	**2 oil engines** driving 2 FP propellers Total Power: 2,124kW (2,888hp) 13.0kn Yanmar G250-E 2 x 4 Stroke 6 Cy. 250 x 290 each-1062kW (1444bhp) Yanmar Diesel Engine Co Ltd-Japan
7909047 *DUL6525* -	**SUMBERMAS SEGARA 7** *ex* Gracia *-1999* *ex* Taiyo Maru No. 18 *-1995* *ex* Daiei Maru No. 18 *-1992* **Damalerio Fishing Enterprise** - *Davao* *Philippines* Official number: DAV4003517	*147* 74 -		**1979-07 Nagasaki Zosen K.K. — Nagasaki** Yd No: 702 L reg 32.00 Br ex - Dght - Lbp 32.52 Br md 6.71 Dpth 2.80 Welded, 1 dk	**(B11B2FV) Fishing Vessel**	**1 oil engine** driving 1 FP propeller Total Power: 883kW (1,201hp) Niigata 6MG25BX 1 x 4 Stroke 6 Cy. 250 x 320 883kW (1201bhp) Niigata Engineering Co Ltd-Japan
7821685 *DUL6266* -	**SUMBERMAS SEGARA 801** *ex* Southern Coast *-2001* *ex* Mondai Maru No. 8 *-1993* **DFC Tuna Venture Corp** - *Davao* *Philippines* Official number: DAV4000113	*343* 168 362		**1979-02 Miho Zosensho K.K. — Shimizu** Yd No: 1116 Loa 54.16 Br ex 8.51 Dght 3.556 Lbp 45.98 Br md 8.50 Dpth 3.92 Welded, 1 dk	**(B11A2FS) Stern Trawler**	**1 oil engine** reverse geared to sc. shaft driving 1 FP propeller Total Power: 1,214kW (1,651hp) Akasaka DM28AR 1 x 4 Stroke 6 Cy. 280 x 460 1214kW (1651bhp) Akasaka Tekkosho KK (Akasaka DieselLtd)-Japan
8021098 *HP2327* -	**SUMERIAN** *ex* Magadir *-1993* *ex* Bardsey *-2005* *ex* Sten *-1986* **Sama Marine Shipping Inc** Meramar Shipping & Trading Co Inc *Panama* *Panama* MMSI: 373326000 Official number: 4497313	**1,144** 613 1,767 T/cm 6.6	Class: (LR) (BV) (NK) Classed LR until 3/4/12	**1981-02 Kitanihon Zosen K.K. — Hachinohe** Yd No: 166 Loa 69.52 Br ex 11.82 Dght 4.313 Lbp 64.01 Br md 11.80 Dpth 5.16 Welded, 1 dk	**(A13B2TP) Products Tanker** Single Hull Liq: 2,075; Liq (Oil): 2,075 Compartments: 8 Wing Ta, ER, 2 Wing Slop Ta 3 Cargo Pump (s): 3x660m³/hr	**1 oil engine** with clutches & dr reverse geared to sc. shaft driving 1 FP propeller Total Power: 1,030kW (1,400hp) 10.5kn Yanmar 6ZL-DT 1 x 4 Stroke 6 Cy. 280 x 340 1030kW (1400bhp) Yanmar Diesel Engine Co Ltd-Japan AuxGen: 2 x 320kW 440V 60Hz a.c, 1 x 96kW 440V 60Hz a.c Boilers: TOH (o.f.) 4.1kgf/cm² (4.0bar), wtdb (o.f.) Fuel: 95.0 (d.f.) 5.0pd
8989587 *JL6646* -	**SUMI MARU NO. 3** **YK Kochi Tugboat** - *Kochi, Kochi* *Japan* MMSI: 431501772 Official number: 136508	*194* - -		**2003-10 Daio Zoki K.K. — Japan** Yd No: 673 Loa 35.60 Br ex - Dght - Lbp 32.00 Br md 9.80 Dpth 5.14 Welded, 1 dk	**(B32B2SP) Pusher Tug**	**2 oil engines** driving 2 Propellers Total Power: 2,942kW (4,000hp) 11.4kn Hanshin LH32LG 2 x 4 Stroke 6 Cy. 320 x 640 each-1471kW (2000bhp) The Hanshin Diesel Works Ltd-Japan
8948569 *T2GV4* -	**SUMI MARU No. 25** **PT Lima Srikandi Jaya** - *Funafuti* *Tuvalu*	*101* - -		**1962-08 Hakata Zosen K.K. — Imabari** Loa 28.00 Br ex - Dght 2.500 Lbp 25.00 Br md 6.50 Dpth 2.90 Welded, 1 dk	**(B32A2ST) Tug**	**1 oil engine** driving 1 FP propeller Total Power: 441kW (600hp) Niigata 6M26HS 1 x 4 Stroke 6 Cy. 260 x 400 441kW (600bhp) Niigata Engineering Co Ltd-Japan
8736710 *JD2511* -	**SUMIEI 5** **Ryoichi Shinohara** JFE Logistics Corp *Anan, Tokushima* *Japan* Official number: 140646	*498* - 1,800		**2007-10 Tokuoka Zosen K.K. — Naruto** Yd No: 307 Loa 73.00 Br ex - Dght 4.450 Lbp 69.00 Br md 11.80 Dpth 7.52 Welded, 1 dk	**(A31A2GX) General Cargo Ship** Grain: 2,546; Bale: 2,546 Compartments: 1 Ho, ER 1 Ha: ER (40.0 x 9.5)	**1 oil engine** driving 1 Propeller Total Power: 1,618kW (2,200hp) 11.0kn Niigata 6M34BGT 1 x 4 Stroke 6 Cy. 340 x 620 1618kW (2200bhp) Niigata Engineering Co Ltd-Japan
8718445 *JJ3578* -	**SUMIEI MARU** **Sanei Kaiun Kensetsu KK** Azumi Kaiun KK *Himeji, Hyogo* *Japan* Official number: 130793	*483* - 1,356		**1988-03 K.K. Matsuura Zosensho — Osakikamijima** Yd No: 353 Loa 57.87 (BB) Br ex 12.53 Dght 4.484 Lbp 52.00 Br md 12.50 Dpth 5.90 Welded, 2 dks	**(A24D2BA) Aggregates Carrier** Grain: 810 Compartments: 1 Ho, ER 1 Ha: ER	**1 oil engine** with clutches & reverse reduction geared to sc. shaft driving 1 FP propeller Total Power: 736kW (1,001hp) Hanshin 6LU32 1 x 4 Stroke 6 Cy. 320 x 510 736kW (1001bhp) The Hanshin Diesel Works Ltd-Japan
8718689 *JJ3564* -	**SUMIEI MARU No. 5** *ex* Sumiei Maru No. 3 *-1996* **YK Sumiei Kogyo** - *Himeji, Hyogo* *Japan* Official number: 129308	*499* - 1,196		**1987-12 Usuki Iron Works Co Ltd — Saiki OT** Yd No: 1341 Loa 65.51 (BB) Br ex - Dght - Lbp 61.73 Br md 13.50 Dpth 6.81 Welded, 2 dks	**(A24D2BA) Aggregates Carrier** Grain: 840 Compartments: 1 Ho, ER 1 Ha: ER	**1 oil engine** with clutches, flexible couplings & reverse reduction geared to sc. shaft driving 1 FP propeller Total Power: 736kW (1,001hp) Akasaka DM36KR 1 x 4 Stroke 6 Cy. 360 x 540 736kW (1001bhp) Akasaka Tekkosho KK (Akasaka DieselLtd)-Japan Thrusters: 1 Thwart. FP thruster (f)
8608793 - -	**SUMIEI MARU No. 8** *ex* Shinei Maru No. 8 *-1988* **Aleson Shipping Lines Inc** *Philippines*	*499* - 1,600		**1986-09 Matsuura Tekko Zosen K.K. — Osakikamijima** Yd No: 323 Loa 67.44 (BB) Br ex 13.26 Dght 4.452 Lbp 61.02 Br md 13.01 Dpth 7.01 Welded, 1 dk	**(B33A2DG) Grab Dredger** Grain: 988; Bale: 951 Compartments: 1 Ho, ER 1 Ha: ER	**1 oil engine** with clutches & reverse reduction geared to sc. shaft driving 1 FP propeller Total Power: 1,324kW (1,800hp) Hanshin 6LU35G 1 x 4 Stroke 6 Cy. 350 x 550 1324kW (1800bhp) The Hanshin Diesel Works Ltd-Japan Thrusters: 1 Thwart. CP thruster (f)
8864490 - -	**SUMIFUKU** *ex* Sumifuku Maru *-2013* **PT Indo Shipping Operator** - *Indonesia*	*199* - 630		**1992-05 Sokooshi Zosen K.K. — Osakikamijima** Yd No: 313 Loa 57.03 Br ex - Dght 3.190 Lbp 52.50 Br md 9.50 Dpth 5.40 Welded, 1 dk	**(A31A2GX) General Cargo Ship**	**1 oil engine** reverse geared to sc. shaft driving 1 FP propeller Total Power: 588kW (799hp) 10.5kn Akasaka T26SR 1 x 4 Stroke 6 Cy. 260 x 440 588kW (799bhp) Akasaka Tekkosho KK (Akasaka DieselLtd)-Japan
8980581 *JL6495* -	**SUMIFUKU MARU** **Mifuku Kaiun YK** - *Uchinomi, Kagawa* *Japan* Official number: 137047	*498* - 1,600		**2003-06 Tokuoka Zosen K.K. — Naruto** Yd No: 275 Loa 74.59 Br ex - Dght 2.500 Lbp 69.00 Br md 12.10 Dpth 7.42 Welded, 1 dk	**(A31A2GX) General Cargo Ship** Grain: 2,636	**1 oil engine** driving 1 Propeller Total Power: 736kW (1,001hp) 11.5kn Niigata 6M34BGT 1 x 4 Stroke 6 Cy. 340 x 620 736kW (1001bhp) Niigata Engineering Co Ltd-Japan
9660475 *JD3367* -	**SUMIFUKU MARU** **Sumifuku Unyu KK** - *Iki, Nagasaki* *Japan* MMSI: 431003685 Official number: 141685	*499* - 1,700		**2012-08 K.K. Matsuura Zosensho — Osakikamijima** Yd No: 580 Loa 76.02 (BB) Br ex - Dght 4.390 Lbp 70.00 Br md 12.00 Dpth 7.35 Welded, 1 dk	**(A31A2GX) General Cargo Ship** Grain: 2,495 Compartments: 1 Ho, ER 1 Ha: ER (40.0 x 9.5)	**1 oil engine** reduction geared to sc. shaft driving 1 FP propeller Total Power: 1,618kW (2,200hp) 12.5kn Niigata 6M34BGT 1 x 4 Stroke 6 Cy. 340 x 620 1618kW (2200bhp) Niigata Engineering Co Ltd-Japan Thrusters: 1 Thwart. FP thruster (f)

9625097 *JD3058* -	**SUMIFUKU MARU NO. 5** - **Mifuku Kaiun YK** - *Shodoshima, Kagawa* *Japan* Official number: 141232	*499* - 1,840	**2010-04 Tokuoka Zosen K.K. — Naruto** Yd No: 322 L reg 71.56 Br ex - Dght 4.450 Lbp 69.00 Br md 11.80 Dpth 7.52 Welded, 1 dk	**(A31A2GX) General Cargo Ship** Grain: 2,546; Bale: 2,546 1 Ha: ER (40.0 x 9.5)	**1 oil engine** reduction geared to sc. shaft driving 1 Propeller Total Power: 1,618kW (2,200hp) 12.0kn Niigata 6M34BGT 1 x 4 Stroke 6 Cy. 340 x 620 1618kW (2200bhp) Niigata Engineering Co Ltd-Japan
8823666 *JL5773* -	**SUMIFUKU MARU No. 5** - **Awa Kaiun YK** - *Naruto, Tokushima* *Japan* Official number: 130592	*498* - 699	**1988-12 Kurinoura Dockyard Co Ltd — Yawatahama EH** Loa 50.99 Br ex - Dght 3.420 Lbp 47.00 Br md 10.50 Dpth 5.63 Welded, 1 dk	**(B33A2DG) Grab Dredger**	**1 oil engine** driving 1 FP propeller Total Power: 736kW (1,001hp) Hanshin 6LU26G 1 x 4 Stroke 6 Cy. 260 x 440 736kW (1001bhp) The Hanshin Diesel Works Ltd-Japan
8806266 *JK4737* -	**SUMIFUKU MARU No. 8** - **YK Eisho Kaiun** - *Himeji, Hyogo* *Japan* Official number: 129575	*499* - 1,390	**1988-01 Shin Kurushima Dockyard Co. Ltd. — Akitsu** Yd No: 2550 Loa 66.20 (BB) Br ex - Dght 4.449 Lbp 61.80 Br md 13.01 Dpth 7.01 Welded, 1 dk	**(B33A2DG) Grab Dredger** Grain: 830 Compartments: 1 Ho, ER 1 Ha: ER	**1 oil engine** with flexible couplings & reverse reduction geared to sc. shaft driving 1 FP propeller Total Power: 736kW (1,001hp) Fuji 6S32G 1 x 4 Stroke 6 Cy. 320 x 610 736kW (1001bhp) Fuji Diesel Co Ltd-Japan
9601613 *JD3168* -	**SUMIHIRO MARU** - **Tahiro Kaiun YK** - *Kainan, Tokushima* *Japan* MMSI: 431002283 Official number: 141404	*298* - 995	**2011-01 Tokuoka Zosen K.K. — Naruto** L reg 59.63 Br ex - Dght 3.720 Lbp 58.00 Br md 10.20 Dpth 6.00 Welded, 1 dk	**(A31A2GX) General Cargo Ship**	**1 oil engine** driving 1 Propeller Total Power: 736kW (1,001hp)
8627062 - -	**SUMIHISA MARU** - - - *Chinese Taipei*	*199* - 699	**1984 Sokooshi Zosen K.K. — Osakikamijima** Yd No: 292 Loa 54.00 Br ex - Dght 3.370 Lbp 49.50 Br md 9.00 Dpth 5.30 Welded, 1 dk	**(A31A2GX) General Cargo Ship** Grain: 1,275; Bale: 1,136	**1 oil engine** driving 1 FP propeller Total Power: 405kW (551hp) 10.8kn Hanshin 6LU26G 1 x 4 Stroke 6 Cy. 260 x 440 405kW (551bhp) The Hanshin Diesel Works Ltd-Japan
8742666 *JD2828* -	**SUMIHO MARU** - **Sumiho Kaiun YK** - *Kure, Hiroshima* *Japan* Official number: 140883	*499* - 1,800	**2008-11 K.K. Murakami Zosensho — Naruto** Loa 74.49 Br ex - Dght 4.340 Lbp 69.60 Br md 12.00 Dpth 7.37 Welded, 1 dk	**(A31A2GX) General Cargo Ship** Grain: 2,852; Bale: 2,430 Compartments: 1 Ho, ER 1 Ha: ER (40.0 x 9.5)	**1 oil engine** reverse reduction geared to sc. shaft driving 1 FP propeller Total Power: 1,323kW (1,799hp) 10.5kn Niigata 6M31BFT 1 x 4 Stroke 6 Cy. 310 x 530 1323kW (1799bhp) Niigata Engineering Co Ltd-Japan
9676694 *JD3378* -	**SUMIHO MARU** - **Sumiho Kisen YK** - *Kure, Hiroshima* *Japan* Official number: 141704	*298* - -	**2012-06 Tokuoka Zosen K.K. — Naruto** L reg 59.63 Br ex - Dght 3.720 Lbp 58.00 Br md 10.20 Dpth 6.00 Welded, 1 dk	**(A31A2GX) General Cargo Ship**	**1 oil engine** reduction geared to sc. shaft driving 1 Propeller Total Power: 735kW (999hp)
7910369 - -	**SUMIHO MARU No. 8** - **Seong Shin Fisheries Co Ltd** - *South Korea*	*199* - -	**1979-03 K.K. Watanabe Zosensho — Nagasaki** Yd No: 778 Loa 45.01 Br ex 6.91 Dght - Lbp 38.00 Br md 6.80 Dpth 3.26 Welded, 1 dk	**(B12C2FL) Live Fish Carrier (Well Boat)**	**1 oil engine** reduction geared to sc. shaft driving 1 FP propeller Total Power: 463kW (629hp) Yanmar G250-E 1 x 4 Stroke 6 Cy. 250 x 290 463kW (629bhp) Yanmar Diesel Engine Co Ltd-Japan
9145724 *JL6474* -	**SUMIHO MARU NO. 15** *ex Satsuki Maru -2002* **Shichiho Kaiun YK** - *Bizen, Okayama* *Japan* Official number: 135509	*199* - 700	**1996-09 Imura Zosen K.K. — Komatsushima** Yd No: 281 Loa 57.40 Br ex - Dght - Lbp 52.00 Br md 9.20 Dpth 5.60 Welded, 1 dk	**(A31A2GX) General Cargo Ship** Compartments: 1 Ho, ER 1 Ha: (30.0 x 7.1)ER	**1 oil engine** driving 1 FP propeller Total Power: 662kW (900hp) 10.5kn Hanshin LH26G 1 x 4 Stroke 6 Cy. 260 x 440 662kW (900bhp) The Hanshin Diesel Works Ltd-Japan
9146223 *JK5506* -	**SUMIHO MARU No. 18** - **YK Inoue Kaiun** - *Kure, Hiroshima* *Japan* Official number: 135254	*199* - 700	**1996-11 KK Ura Kyodo Zosensho — Awaji HG** Yd No: 310 Loa 55.85 Br ex - Dght - Lbp 51.00 Br md 9.50 Dpth 5.60 Welded, 1 dk	**(A31A2GX) General Cargo Ship** Bale: 1,328	**1 oil engine** driving 1 FP propeller Total Power: 736kW (1,001hp) 11.0kn Niigata 6M26AGTE 1 x 4 Stroke 6 Cy. 260 x 460 736kW (1001bhp) Niigata Engineering Co Ltd-Japan
8980476 *JL6677* -	**SUMIHO MARU No. 21** *ex Taikei Maru No. 68 -2011* **Sumiho Maru Katsugyo Unpan KK** - *Uwajima, Ehime* *Japan* Official number: 136573	*296* - -	**2003-01 YK Nakanoshima Zosensho — Kochi KC** L reg 47.00 Br ex - Dght - Lbp - Br md 8.60 Dpth 3.80 Welded, 1 dk	**(B11B2FV) Fishing Vessel**	**1 oil engine** driving 1 Propeller
8889165 - -	**SUMIHO MARU No. 25** *ex Wakamiya Maru No. 63 -2009* - -	*324* - -	**1995-04 YK Nakanoshima Zosensho — Kochi KC** Loa 50.15 Br ex - Dght - Lbp - Br md 8.60 Dpth 3.90 Welded, 1 dk	**(B11B2FV) Fishing Vessel**	**1 oil engine** driving 1 FP propeller Niigata 1 x 4 Stroke Niigata Engineering Co Ltd-Japan
8803408 *JL5520* -	**SUMIHO MARU No. 31** - **Sumiho Maru Katsugyo Unpan KK** - *Uwajima, Ehime* *Japan* MMSI: 431269000 Official number: 129034	*322* - -	**1987-11 Honai Jukogyo K.K. — Honai** Yd No: 55 Loa - Br ex - Dght - Lbp 49.41 Br md 8.50 Dpth 4.02 Welded	**(B11B2FV) Fishing Vessel**	**1 oil engine** driving 1 FP propeller
9235749 *JL6638* -	**SUMIHO MARU No. 32** - **Sumiho Maru Katsugyo Unpan KK** - *Uwajima, Ehime* *Japan* MMSI: 432199000 Official number: 136511	*299* - -	**2000-07 K.K. Izutsu Zosensho — Nagasaki** Yd No: 1090 Loa 55.00 Br ex 8.32 Dght 3.530 Lbp 47.50 Br md 8.30 Dpth 4.00 Welded, 1 dk	**(B11B2FV) Fishing Vessel**	**1 oil engine** driving 1 FP propeller Total Power: 736kW (1,001hp) Akasaka 1 x 4 Stroke 736kW (1001bhp) Akasaka Tekkosho KK (Akasaka DieselLtd)-Japan
9054781 *JL5985* -	**SUMIHO MARU No. 38** - **Sumiho Maru Katsugyo Unpan KK** - *Uwajima, Ehime* *Japan* Official number: 133013	*402* - 753	**1992-11 K.K. Izutsu Zosensho — Nagasaki** Yd No: 1020 L reg 53.40 Br ex - Dght 4.000 Lbp - Br md 8.90 Dpth 4.50 Welded	**(B12B2FC) Fish Carrier**	**1 oil engine** driving 1 FP propeller Total Power: 736kW (1,001hp) Akasaka 1 x 4 Stroke 736kW (1001bhp) Akasaka Tekkosho KK (Akasaka DieselLtd)-Japan Thrusters: 1 Tunnel thruster (f)
8015283 *JL4663* -	**SUMIHO MARU No. 51** - **Sumiho Maru Katsugyo Unpan KK** - *Uwajima, Ehime* *Japan* MMSI: 431250000 Official number: 124079	*298* - 53	**1980-03 K.K. Watanabe Zosensho — Nagasaki** Yd No: 816 Loa 48.01 Br ex 7.80 Dght - Lbp 43.46 Br md 7.60 Dpth 3.61 Welded, 1 dk	**(B12C2FL) Live Fish Carrier (Well Boat)**	**1 oil engine** reduction geared to sc. shaft driving 1 FP propeller Total Power: 566kW (770hp) Yanmar 6Z-ST 1 x 4 Stroke 6 Cy. 280 x 340 566kW (770bhp) Yanmar Diesel Engine Co Ltd-Japan
9140073 *JL6308* -	**SUMIHO MARU No. 58** - **Sumiho Maru Katsugyo Unpan KK** - *Uwajima, Ehime* *Japan* MMSI: 431196000 Official number: 134885	*199* - -	**1996-03 K.K. Izutsu Zosensho — Nagasaki** Yd No: 1055 Loa 48.65 (BB) Br ex - Dght 3.250 Lbp 42.80 Br md 7.80 Dpth 3.70 Welded, 1 dk	**(B11B2FV) Fishing Vessel**	**1 oil engine** with clutches, flexible couplings & sr reverse geared to sc. shaft driving 1 FP propeller Total Power: 736kW (1,001hp) 12.5kn Akasaka K28SFD 1 x 4 Stroke 6 Cy. 280 x 500 736kW (1001bhp) Akasaka Tekkosho KK (Akasaka DieselLtd)-Japan AuxGen: 1 x 120kW a.c, 1 x 104kW a.c Fuel: 55.2 (d.f.)
9015292 *JL5832* -	**SUMIHO MARU No. 68** - **Sumiho Maru Katsugyo Unpan KK** - *Uwajima, Ehime* *Japan* MMSI: 431149000 Official number: 129948	*324* - -	**1989-07 Kurinoura Dockyard Co Ltd — Yawatahama EH** Yd No: 268 Loa 55.64 (BB) Br ex - Dght 3.555 Lbp 49.00 Br md 8.50 Dpth 4.00 Welded	**(B12B2FC) Fish Carrier**	**1 oil engine** reverse geared to sc. shaft driving 1 FP propeller Total Power: 736kW (1,001hp) Akasaka K28SFD 1 x 4 Stroke 6 Cy. 280 x 500 736kW (1001bhp) Akasaka Tekkosho KK (Akasaka DieselLtd)-Japan Thrusters: 1 Thwart. FP thruster (f)

8703799 - -	**SUMIHO MARU No. 75** - -	*349* - 967		1987-05 **Yamanishi Shipbuilding Co Ltd — Ishinomaki MG** Yd No: 933 Loa 68.81 (BB) Br ex 10.62 Dght 4.606 Lbp 60.51 Br md 10.61 Dpth 6.91 Welded, 1 dk	**(B11B2FV) Fishing Vessel** Bale: 989	**1 oil engine** with clutches, flexible couplings & sr reverse geared to sc. shaft driving 1 FP propeller Total Power: 956kW (1,300hp) Niigata 6M31AFTE 1 x 4 Stroke 6 Cy. 310 x 530 956kW (1300bhp) Niigata Engineering Co Ltd-Japan Thrusters: 1 Thwart. CP thruster (f)
9597331 *3FVU6* -	**SUMIHOU** **Mi-Das Line SA** Doun Kisen KK (Doun Kisen Co Ltd) SatCom: Inmarsat C 435299811 *Panama* *Panama* MMSI: 352998000 Official number: 4246911	**40,341** 24,954 74,940 T/cm 67.3	Class: NK	2011-02 **Sasebo Heavy Industries Co. Ltd. — Sasebo Yard, Sasebo** Yd No: 801 Loa 225.00 (BB) Br ex - Dght 14.140 Lbp 218.00 Br md 32.20 Dpth 19.80 Welded, 1 dk	**(A21A2BC) Bulk Carrier** Double Hull Grain: 90,771; Bale: 88,783 Compartments: 7 Ho, ER 7 Ha: ER	**1 oil engine** driving 1 FP propeller Total Power: 9,230kW (12,549hp) 14.5kn MAN-B&W 7S50MC-C 1 x 2 Stroke 7 Cy. 500 x 2000 9230kW (12549bhp) Mitsui Engineering & Shipbuilding CLtd-Japan Fuel: 2746.0 (r.f.)
9243540 *JI3686* -	**SUMINOE MARU** **Osaka-shi Kowan Kyoku (Port & Harbour Bureau)** - *Osaka, Osaka* *Japan* Official number: 137066	*194* - -		2001-03 **Kanagawa Zosen — Kobe** Yd No: 492 Loa 33.80 Br ex - Dght - Lbp 30.42 Br md 9.20 Dpth 4.20 Welded, 1 dk	**(B32A2ST) Tug**	**2 oil engines** Geared Integral to driving 2 Z propellers Total Power: 3,678kW (5,000hp) 13.7kn Niigata 6L28HX 2 x 4 Stroke 6 Cy. 280 x 370 each-1839kW (2500bhp) Niigata Engineering Co Ltd-Japan
9153070 *9V2582* -	**SUMIRE** **Sumire Shipping Pte Ltd** Asiatic Lloyd Shipping Pte Ltd *Singapore* *Singapore* MMSI: 564391000	**14,089** 7,023 17,732	Class: NK	1997-10 **Imabari Shipbuilding Co Ltd — Imabari EH (Imabari Shipyard)** Yd No: 535 Loa 163.66 (BB) Br ex - Dght 8.916 Lbp 152.00 Br md 26.00 Dpth 13.40 Welded, 1 dk	**(A33A2CC) Container Ship (Fully Cellular)** TEU 1177 incl 200 ref C. 16 Ha: Cranes: 2x40t	**1 oil engine** driving 1 FP propeller Total Power: 9,628kW (13,090hp) 18.0kn Mitsubishi 7UEC50LSII 1 x 2 Stroke 7 Cy. 500 x 1950 9628kW (13090bhp) Akasaka Tekkosho KK (Akasaka DieselLtd)-Japan AuxGen: 3 x a.c Thrusters: 1 Tunnel thruster (f) Fuel: 1880.0
8202563 *JL4875* -	**SUMIRIKI MARU No. 2** **Sumiriki Kisen KK** - *Imabari, Ehime* *Japan* Official number: 126195	*474* - 1,168	Class: NK	1982-05 **Shirahama Zosen K.K. — Honai** Yd No: 107 Loa 73.00 Br ex - Dght 3.763 Lbp 68.03 Br md 11.51 Dpth 6.28 Welded, 1 dk	**(A31A2GX) General Cargo Ship** Grain: 2,600; Bale: 2,510 TEU 72 C.72/20' Compartments: 1 Ho, ER 1 Ha: (39.0 x 8.5)ER	**1 oil engine** reverse reduction geared to sc. shaft driving 1 FP propeller Total Power: 956kW (1,300hp) 10.5kn Niigata 6M28AFT 1 x 4 Stroke 6 Cy. 280 x 480 956kW (1300bhp) Niigata Engineering Co Ltd-Japan AuxGen: 3 x 60kW a.c Fuel: 100.0 (r.f.)
8808355 *JK4749* -	**SUMIRIKI MARU No. 7** **Okada Sekizai KK** - *Fukuyama, Hiroshima* *Japan* Official number: 129587	*494* - 1,424		1988-07 **Hitachi Zosen Mukaishima Marine Co Ltd — Onomichi HS** Yd No: 10 Loa 67.50 Br ex 13.28 Dght 4.370 Lbp 62.00 Br md 13.20 Dpth 7.00 Welded, 1 dk	**(B33A2DG) Grab Dredger** Grain: 840 Compartments: 1 Ho 1 Ha:	**1 oil engine** with clutches & reverse reduction geared to sc. shaft driving 1 FP propeller Total Power: 736kW (1,001hp) Niigata 6M34AGT 1 x 4 Stroke 6 Cy. 340 x 620 736kW (1001bhp) Niigata Engineering Co Ltd-Japan
9054121 *JK5109* -	**SUMIRIKI MARU No. 8** **Okada Sekizai KK** - *Fukuyama, Hiroshima* *Japan* Official number: 133069	*490* - 1,496		1993-01 **K.K. Murakami Zosensho — Naruto** Yd No: 207 Loa 67.43 Br ex - Dght 4.200 Lbp 62.00 Br md 13.20 Dpth 7.00 Welded, 1 dk	**(A24D2BA) Aggregates Carrier** Grain: 2,601 Compartments: 1 Ho, ER 1 Ha: ER	**1 oil engine** driving 1 FP propeller Total Power: 736kW (1,001hp) Niigata 6M34AGT 1 x 4 Stroke 6 Cy. 340 x 620 736kW (1001bhp) Niigata Engineering Co Ltd-Japan
8618475 - -	**SUMIRIKI MARU No. 8** **Asnim Poniman** - *Indonesia*	*457* - 443		1987-05 **Hamamoto Zosensho K.K. — Tokushima** Yd No: 681 Loa 50.86 (BB) Br ex - Dght 2.801 Lbp 46.00 Br md 10.51 Dpth 5.36 Welded, 2 dks	**(A31A2GX) General Cargo Ship** Compartments: 1 Ho, ER, 1 Tw Dk 1 Ha: ER	**1 oil engine** driving 1 FP propeller Total Power: 515kW (700hp) Niigata 6M26AGTE 1 x 4 Stroke 6 Cy. 260 x 460 515kW (700bhp) Niigata Engineering Co Ltd-Japan
8703000 *JJ3442* -	**SUMIRIKI MARU No. 15** **Sumiriki Kaiun Kensetsu KK** - *Ieshima, Hyogo* *Japan* Official number: 125385	*459* - 1,000		1987-03 **Sasaki Shipbuilding Co Ltd — Osakikamijima HS** Yd No: 505 Loa 57.36 (BB) Br ex 13.52 Dght 4.342 Lbp 53.01 Br md 13.50 Dpth 6.20 Welded, 2 dks	**(B33A2DG) Grab Dredger** Grain: 565 Compartments: 1 Ho, ER 1 Ha: ER	**1 oil engine** with clutches, flexible couplings & reverse reduction geared to sc. shaft driving 1 FP propeller Total Power: 736kW (1,001hp) Akasaka DM36KR 1 x 4 Stroke 6 Cy. 360 x 540 736kW (1001bhp) Akasaka Tekkosho KK (Akasaka DieselLtd)-Japan
9067946 *JK5225* -	**SUMIRIKI MARU No. 22** **YK Sumiriki Shoji** - *Fukuyama, Hiroshima* *Japan* Official number: 133077	*116* - -		1993-12 **Kanbara Zosen K.K. — Onomichi** Yd No: 450 Loa 23.95 Br ex - Dght 2.600 Lbp 21.95 Br md 7.89 Dpth 3.50 Welded, 1 dk	**(B32B2SP) Pusher Tug**	**1 oil engine** driving 1 FP propeller Total Power: 736kW (1,001hp) 11.0kn Niigata 6M34AGT 1 x 4 Stroke 6 Cy. 340 x 620 736kW (1001bhp) Niigata Engineering Co Ltd-Japan
9266164 *JM6632* -	**SUMISE MARU NO. 2** **Corporation for Advanced Transport & Technology & Narasaki Stax Co Ltd & Kyushu Marine Co Ltd** Kyushu Marine KK *Kitakyushu, Fukuoka* *Japan* MMSI: 431602146 Official number: 136840	*5,468* - 8,881	Class: NK	2002-10 **Kanrei Zosen K.K. — Naruto** Yd No: 393 Loa 117.78 Br ex - Dght 7.279 Lbp 110.00 Br md 18.80 Dpth 9.20 Welded, 1 dk	**(A24A2BT) Cement Carrier** Grain: 6,881	**1 oil engine** driving 1 FP propeller Total Power: 3,884kW (5,281hp) 12.0kn B&W 6L35MC 1 x 2 Stroke 6 Cy. 350 x 1050 3884kW (5281bhp) Makita Corp-Japan Fuel: 230.0
9113903 *JK5237* -	**SUMISE MARU No. 3** **Maruichi Kisen KK** - *Onomichi, Hiroshima* *Japan* MMSI: 431400421 Official number: 134727	*5,375* - 8,579	Class: NK	1995-05 **Kanrei Zosen K.K. — Naruto** Yd No: 367 Loa 117.29 Br ex - Dght 6.815 Lbp 110.00 Br md 18.80 Dpth 9.10 Welded, 1 dk	**(A24A2BT) Cement Carrier** Grain: 6,925; Ore: 6,750	**1 oil engine** driving 1 FP propeller Total Power: 3,884kW (5,281hp) 12.8kn B&W 6L35MC 1 x 2 Stroke 6 Cy. 350 x 1050 3884kW (5281bhp) Makita Corp-Japan Fuel: 220.0 (r.f.)
9189847 *JE3162* -	**SUMISE MARU No. 5** **Hachinohe Senpaku KK & Izumi Kisen KK** Izumi Kisen KK (Izumi Shipping Co Ltd) *Hachinohe, Aomori* *Japan* MMSI: 431700423 Official number: 133357	*3,634* - 6,100	Class: NK	1998-11 **Kanrei Zosen K.K. — Naruto** Yd No: 381 Loa 96.00 Br ex - Dght 6.915 Lbp 90.00 Br md 17.00 Dpth 8.40 Welded, 1 dk	**(A24A2BT) Cement Carrier** Grain: 4,971	**1 oil engine** driving 1 FP propeller Total Power: 3,236kW (4,400hp) 12.7kn B&W 5L35MC 1 x 2 Stroke 5 Cy. 350 x 1050 3236kW (4400bhp) Makita Corp-Japan Fuel: 270.0
9459905 *JD2570* -	**SUMISE MARU NO. 7** *ex Omi Maru -2012* **Yahata Kisen Co Ltd (Yahata Kisen KK)** - *Imabari, Ehime* *Japan* MMSI: 431000548 Official number: 140696	*4,011* - 6,040	Class: NK	2008-03 **Higaki Zosen K.K. — Imabari** Yd No: 611 Loa 106.10 Br ex - Dght 6.613 Lbp 100.20 Br md 16.50 Dpth 8.40 Welded, 1 dk	**(A24A2BT) Cement Carrier** Grain: 5,012	**1 oil engine** driving 1 FP propeller Total Power: 3,309kW (4,499hp) 13.5kn Akasaka A45S 1 x 4 Stroke 6 Cy. 450 x 880 3309kW (4499bhp) Akasaka Tekkosho KK (Akasaka DieselLtd)-Japan AuxGen: 2 x a.c Fuel: 310.0
9209594 *JK5581* -	**SUMISE MARU No. 8** **Corporation for Advanced Transport & Technology & Maruichi Kisen Co Ltd** Maruichi Kisen KK *Onomichi, Hiroshima* *Japan* MMSI: 431401788 Official number: 135286	*3,601* - 6,138	Class: NK	1999-06 **Kanrei Zosen K.K. — Naruto** Yd No: 385 Loa 96.00 Br ex - Dght 6.915 Lbp 90.00 Br md 17.00 Dpth 8.40 Welded, 1 dk	**(A24A2BT) Cement Carrier** Grain: 4,971; Ore: 4,880	**1 oil engine** driving 1 FP propeller Total Power: 3,310kW (4,500hp) 12.6kn Mitsubishi 6UEC33LSII 1 x 2 Stroke 6 Cy. 330 x 1050 3310kW (4500bhp) Akasaka Tekkosho KK (Akasaka DieselLtd)-Japan AuxGen: 3 x 280kW a.c Thrusters: 1 Thwart. FP thruster (f) Fuel: 58.0 (d.f.) 216.0 (r.f.) 12.7pd
9142112 *JG5478* -	**SUMISE MARU No. 20** **Sumise Kaiun KK** - *Tokyo* *Japan* MMSI: 431100268 Official number: 135842	*5,363* - 8,562	Class: NK	1996-09 **Kanrei Zosen K.K. — Naruto** Yd No: 373 Loa 117.80 (BB) Br ex - Dght 7.015 Lbp 110.00 Br md 18.80 Dpth 9.10 Welded, 1 dk	**(A24A2BT) Cement Carrier** Grain: 6,925	**1 oil engine** driving 1 CP propeller Total Power: 3,884kW (5,281hp) 12.8kn B&W 6L35MC 1 x 2 Stroke 6 Cy. 350 x 1050 3884kW (5281bhp) Makita Corp-Japan AuxGen: 1 x 680kW a.c, 2 x 320kW a.c Thrusters: 1 Thwart. FP thruster (f) Fuel: 60.0 (d.f.) 224.0 (r.f.) 15.0pd

Identity	Name / Owner	Tonnage	Class	Builder / Dimensions	Type	Machinery
9511090 *JD2938* -	**SUMISE MARU NO. 21** **Japan Railway Construction, Transport & Technology Agency & Sumise Kaiun Co Ltd** Sumise Kaiun KK *Tokyo* *Japan* MMSI: 431001077 Official number: 141053	*3,914* - 6,300	Class: NK	**2009-10 Shin Kurushima Dockyard Co. Ltd. — Hashihama, Imabari** Yd No: 5570 Loa 95.97 (BB) Br ex - Dght 6.900 Lbp 89.95 Br md 17.00 Dpth 8.60 Welded, 1 dk	**(A24A2BT) Cement Carrier** Grain: 5,259	**1 oil engine** driving 1 FP propeller Total Power: 3,310kW (4,500hp) 12.5kn Mitsubishi 6UEC33LSII 1 x 2 Stroke 6 Cy. 330 x 1050 3310kW (4500bhp) Akasaka Tekkosho KK (Akasaka DieselLtd)-Japan AuxGen: 2 x a.c Fuel: 267.0
9682813 *JD3589* -	**SUMISE MARU NO. 22** **Japan Railway Construction, Transport & Technology Agency & Sumise Kaiun Co Ltd** Sumise Kaiun KK *Tokyo* *Japan* MMSI: 431005246 Official number: 142034	**5,830** - 8,950	Class: NK	**2014-02 Shin Kurushima Dockyard Co. Ltd. — Hashihama, Imabari** Yd No: 5800 Loa 115.53 Br ex - Dght 7.012 Lbp 110.00 Br md 19.00 Dpth 9.10 Welded, 1 dk	**(A24A2BT) Cement Carrier**	**1 oil engine** driving 1 FP propeller Total Power: 3,900kW (5,302hp) MAN-B&W 6L35MC 1 x 2 Stroke 6 Cy. 350 x 1050 3900kW (5302bhp) Makita Corp-Japan
9054169 *JI3505* -	**SUMISE MARU No. 23** **Sumise Kaiun KK** - *Tokyo* *Japan* MMSI: 431301191 Official number: 133419	*2,617* - 3,674		**1992-08 Shinhama Dockyard Co. Ltd. — Anan** Yd No: 816 Loa 93.00 Br ex - Dght 4.163 Lbp 88.50 Br md 17.50 Dpth 6.20 Welded	**(A24A2BT) Cement Carrier** Grain: 3,050 Compartments: 4 Ho, ER	**2 oil engines** sr geared to sc. shafts driving 2 FP propellers Total Power: 1,766kW (2,402hp) Daihatsu 6DLM-28 2 x 4 Stroke 6 Cy. 280 x 360 each-883kW (1201bhp) Daihatsu Diesel Manufacturing Co Lt-Japan
9152375 *JM6420* -	**SUMISE MARU No. 25** **Sumise Kaiun KK** - *Tokyo* *Japan* MMSI: 431400609 Official number: 134610	*749* - 1,708	Class: NK	**1996-11 K.K. Miura Zosensho — Saiki** Yd No: 1175 Loa 70.00 Br ex - Dght 4.547 Lbp 65.00 Br md 11.50 Dpth 5.12 Welded, 1 dk	**(A24A2BT) Cement Carrier** Grain: 1,428	**1 oil engine** driving 1 FP propeller Total Power: 1,324kW (1,800hp) 11.0kn Hanshin LH30L 1 x 4 Stroke 6 Cy. 300 x 600 1324kW (1800bhp) The Hanshin Diesel Works Ltd-Japan Fuel: 70.0 (d.f.)
9145803 *JM6532* -	**SUMISE MARU No. 30** **Shinwa Kaiun KK** - *Kumamoto, Kumamoto* *Japan* Official number: 134636	*360* - 732	Class: NK	**1996-06 Kanmon Zosen K.K. — Shimonoseki** Yd No: 572 Loa 49.99 (BB) Br ex 9.61 Dght 3.770 Lbp 46.50 Br md 9.60 Dpth 4.00 Welded, 1 dk	**(A24A2BT) Cement Carrier** Grain: 555 Compartments: 4 Ho, ER 4 Ha: ER	**1 oil engine** driving 1 FP propeller Total Power: 735kW (999hp) 10.5kn Hanshin LH26G 1 x 4 Stroke 6 Cy. 260 x 440 735kW (999bhp) The Hanshin Diesel Works Ltd-Japan Thrusters: 1 Thwart. CP thruster (f) Fuel: 35.0 (d.f.)
9145815 *JM6543* -	**SUMISE MARU No. 31** **Narasaki Stax Co Ltd & Kyushu Marine Co Ltd** Kyushu Marine KK *Kitakyushu, Fukuoka* *Japan* Official number: 135393	*360* - 732	Class: NK	**1996-11 Kanmon Zosen K.K. — Shimonoseki** Yd No: 573 Loa 49.99 Br ex - Dght 3.770 Lbp 46.50 Br md 9.60 Dpth 4.00 Welded, 1 dk	**(A24A2BT) Cement Carrier** Grain: 555; Bale: 550 Compartments: 6 Ho, ER 6 Ha: ER	**1 oil engine** driving 1 FP propeller Total Power: 883kW (1,201hp) Hanshin LH26G 1 x 4 Stroke 6 Cy. 260 x 440 883kW (1201bhp) The Hanshin Diesel Works Ltd-Japan Thrusters: 1 Thwart. CP thruster (f) Fuel: 35.0 (d.f.)
8021359 - -	**SUMISE No. 36** *ex Sumise Maru No. 36 -1999* - -	*199* - 400		**1981-01 K.K. Miura Zosensho — Saiki** Yd No: 616 Loa - Br ex - Dght 2.812 Lbp 38.51 Br md 8.21 Dpth 3.03 Welded, 1 dk	**(A24A2BT) Cement Carrier**	**1 oil engine** driving 1 FP propeller Total Power: 478kW (650hp) Yanmar 6U-ST 1 x 4 Stroke 6 Cy. 200 x 240 478kW (650bhp) Yanmar Diesel Engine Co Ltd-Japan
9058658 *JK2542* -	**SUMISEI MARU No. 2** **Taizan Kaiun YK** - *Imabari, Ehime* *Japan* Official number: 133705	*498* - 1,600		**1993-02 Kegoya Dock K.K. — Kure** Yd No: 938 Loa 73.85 (BB) Br ex 11.77 Dght 4.470 Lbp 68.00 Br md 11.00 Dpth 7.20 Welded, 2 dks	**(A31A2GX) General Cargo Ship** Compartments: 1 Ho, ER	**1 oil engine** reverse geared to sc. shaft driving 1 FP propeller Total Power: 736kW (1,001hp) Akasaka K31R 1 x 4 Stroke 6 Cy. 310 x 530 736kW (1001bhp) Akasaka Tekkosho KK (Akasaka DieselLtd)-Japan Thrusters: 1 Thwart. FP thruster (f)
8957027 - -	**SUMISEI MARU No. 18** **SK Shipping Co Ltd** - *South Korea*	*104* - -		**1974-06 Abe Koma Zosensho — Nandan** Loa 26.00 Br ex - Dght 2.400 Lbp 23.00 Br md 7.50 Dpth 2.99 Welded, 1 dk	**(B32A2ST) Tug**	**2 oil engines** driving 2 FP propellers Total Power: 2,206kW (3,000hp) 9.0kn Otsuka 2 x 4 Stroke each-1103kW (1500bhp) KK Otsuka Diesel-Japan
8844414 - -	**SUMITOKU MARU** - *Indonesia*	*405* - 970		**1990-08 K.K. Yoshida Zosen Kogyo — Arida** Loa 70.98 Br ex - Dght 3.370 Lbp 65.00 Br md 11.40 Dpth 6.30 Welded, 1 dk	**(A31A2GX) General Cargo Ship** 1 Ha: (37.0 x 9.0)ER	**1 oil engine** driving 1 FP propeller Total Power: 736kW (1,001hp) 10.5kn Niigata 6M28BGT 1 x 4 Stroke 6 Cy. 280 x 480 736kW (1001bhp) Niigata Engineering Co Ltd-Japan
8806292 *JK4738* -	**SUMITOKU MARU No. 11** *ex Myojin Maru No. 51 -1992* *ex Tamayoshi Maru No. 5 -1991* *ex Myojin Maru No. 51 -1990* **Wakamiya Kaiun Kensetsu KK** - *Himeji, Hyogo* *Japan* Official number: 129576	*499* - 1,377		**1988-02 Shin Kurushima Dockyard Co. Ltd. — Akitsu** Yd No: 2556 Loa 65.74 (BB) Br ex - Dght 4.350 Lbp 62.21 Br md 13.21 Dpth 7.24 Welded, 1 dk	**(A24D2BA) Aggregates Carrier** Grain: 1,530 Compartments: 1 Ho, ER 1 Ha: ER	**1 oil engine** reverse reduction geared to sc. shaft driving 1 FP propeller Total Power: 736kW (1,001hp) Hanshin 6LU35G 1 x 4 Stroke 6 Cy. 350 x 550 736kW (1001bhp) The Hanshin Diesel Works Ltd-Japan Thrusters: 1 Thwart. CP thruster (f)
8946482 - -	**SUMIWAKA MARU No. 1** - -	*250* - 481		**1969-06 T. Honda — Tsukumi** Loa 44.50 Br ex - Dght 3.320 Lbp 36.00 Br md 8.00 Dpth 4.60 Welded, 1 dk	**(A24D2BA) Aggregates Carrier** Compartments: 1 Ho, ER 1 Ha: (12.0 x 6.0)ER Cranes: 1	**1 oil engine** driving 1 FP propeller Total Power: 736kW (1,001hp) 11.0kn Yanmar 1 x 4 Stroke 736kW (1001bhp) Yanmar Diesel Engine Co Ltd-Japan
9072642 *JL6169* -	**SUMIWAKA MARU No. 3** **Sumiwaka Kaiun KK** - *Matsushige, Tokushima* *Japan* Official number: 133912	*493* - 1,348		**1993-07 Matsuura Tekko Zosen K.K. — Osakikamijima** Yd No: 376 Loa 67.85 Br ex - Dght 4.460 Lbp 62.00 Br md 13.00 Dpth 7.20 Welded, 2 dks	**(A24D2BA) Aggregates Carrier** Compartments: 1 Ho, ER	**1 oil engine** reverse geared to sc. shaft driving 1 FP propeller Total Power: 1,471kW (2,000hp) Niigata 6M34AGT 1 x 4 Stroke 6 Cy. 340 x 620 1471kW (2000bhp) Niigata Engineering Co Ltd-Japan
8926133 *JJ3840* -	**SUMIWAKA MARU NO. 28** *ex Seiei Maru No. 28 -2003* **Japan Railway Construction, Transport & Technology Agency & Sumiwaka Kaiun KK** Sumiwaka Kaiun KK *Matsushige, Tokushima* *Japan* Official number: 134185	*499* - 1,006		**1996-11 Nagashima Zosen KK — Kihoku ME** Yd No: 502 Loa 70.63 Br ex - Dght 4.150 Lbp 62.60 Br md 13.50 Dpth 6.90 Welded, 1 dk	**(A24D2BA) Aggregates Carrier**	**1 oil engine** driving 1 FP propeller Total Power: 1,471kW (2,000hp) 12.5kn Akasaka A37 1 x 4 Stroke 6 Cy. 370 x 720 1471kW (2000bhp) Akasaka Tekkosho KK (Akasaka DieselLtd)-Japan
8923882 *JL6468* -	**SUMIWAKA MARU No. 30** **Sumiwaka Kaiun KK** - *Matsushige, Tokushima* *Japan* Official number: 135503	*498* - 1,399		**1996-06 Tokuoka Zosen K.K. — Naruto** Yd No: 227 Loa 73.64 Br ex - Dght 4.150 Lbp 65.00 Br md 13.50 Dpth 6.97 Welded, 1 dk	**(A31A2GX) General Cargo Ship**	**1 oil engine** driving 1 FP propeller Total Power: 736kW (1,001hp) 11.7kn Niigata 6M34AGT 1 x 4 Stroke 6 Cy. 340 x 620 736kW (1001bhp) Niigata Engineering Co Ltd-Japan
9140140 *JL6430* -	**SUMIWAKA MARU No. 38** **Sakazaki Kaiun KK** - *Matsushige, Tokushima* *Japan* Official number: 135134	*497* - 1,270		**1995-11 Kurinoura Dockyard Co Ltd — Yawatahama EH** Yd No: 334 Loa 67.50 Br ex 13.22 Dght 4.350 Lbp 62.00 Br md 13.20 Dpth 7.20 Welded, 1 dk	**(A31A2GX) General Cargo Ship** Grain: 1,218 Compartments: 1 Ho, ER 1 Ha: ER	**1 oil engine** driving 1 FP propeller Total Power: 736kW (1,001hp) Niigata 6M34AGT 1 x 4 Stroke 6 Cy. 340 x 620 736kW (1001bhp) Niigata Engineering Co Ltd-Japan
9162552 *JL6562* -	**SUMIWAKA MARU No. 51** **Sumiwaka Kaiun KK** - *Matsushige, Tokushima* *Japan* Official number: 135582	*135* - 158		**1997-03 Matsuura Tekko Zosen K.K. — Osakikamijima** Yd No: 500 Loa - Br ex - Dght 3.570 Lbp 30.15 Br md 9.60 Dpth 5.80 Welded, 1 dk	**(B32B2SP) Pusher Tug**	**2 oil engines** driving 2 FP propellers Total Power: 2,942kW (4,000hp) Niigata 6M34BGT 2 x 4 Stroke 6 Cy. 340 x 620 each-1471kW (2000bhp) Niigata Engineering Co Ltd-Japan

9203045 *JL6509* -	**SUMIWAKA MARU No. 52** **Sumiwaka Kaiun KK** - *Iki, Nagasaki* *Japan* Official number: 136472	*135* - -		**1998**-01 **Tokuoka Zosen K.K. — Naruto** Yd No: 238 Loa 32.66 Br ex - Dght - Lbp 30.15 Br md 9.60 Dpth 5.80 Welded, 1 dk	**(A24D2BA) Aggregates Carrier**	**2 oil engines** driving 2 FP propellers Total Power: 2,942kW (4,000hp) 11.0kn Niigata 6M34BLGT 2 x 4 Stroke 6 Cy. 340 x 680 each-1471kW (2000bhp) Niigata Engineering Co Ltd-Japan
9240598 *JJ4024* -	**SUMIWAKA MARU No. 56** **Sumiwaka Kaiun KK** - *Matsushige, Tokushima* *Japan* Official number: 135967	*414* - -		**2000**-04 **Nagashima Zosen KK — Kihoku ME** Yd No: 533 Loa 29.97 Br ex - Dght - Lbp - Br md 17.65 Dpth 7.53 Welded, 1 dk	**(B32B2SP) Pusher Tug**	**2 oil engines** driving 2 FP propellers Total Power: 2,942kW (4,000hp) 11.0kn Niigata 6M37GT 2 x 4 Stroke 6 Cy. 370 x 720 each-1471kW (2000bhp) Niigata Engineering Co Ltd-Japan
8967216 *JI3684* -	**SUMIWAKA MARU No. 57** **Sumiwaka Kaiun KK** - *Matsushige, Tokushima* *Japan* Official number: 137064	*413* - -		**2001**-01 **Nagashima Zosen KK — Kihoku ME** Yd No: 556 Loa 29.97 Br ex - Dght - Lbp - Br md 17.65 Dpth 7.53 Welded, 1 dk	**(B32B2SP) Pusher Tug**	**2 oil engines** driving 2 FP propellers Total Power: 2,942kW (4,000hp) 11.5kn Niigata 6M37GT 2 x 4 Stroke 6 Cy. 370 x 720 each-1471kW (2000bhp) Niigata Engineering Co Ltd-Japan Fuel: 98.0 (d.f.)
8974635 *JJ4032* -	**SUMIWAKA MARU NO. 58** **KK Sumiwaka** - *Kobe, Hyogo* *Japan* Official number: 135977	**414** - -		**2001**-09 **Hangzhou Dongfeng Shipbuilding Co Ltd — Hangzhou ZJ** Yd No: 616 L reg 24.66 Br ex - Dght 5.500 Lbp 24.50 Br md 17.65 Dpth 7.53 Welded, 1 dk	**(B32B2SP) Pusher Tug**	**2 oil engines** driving 2 Propellers Total Power: 2,942kW (4,000hp) 10.5kn Akasaka A34C 2 x 4 Stroke 6 Cy. 340 x 620 each-1471kW (2000bhp) Akasaka Tekkosho KK (Akasaka DieselLtd)-Japan
8980385 *JL6670* -	**SUMIWAKA MARU NO. 61** **Sumiwaka Kaiun YK** - *Matsushige, Tokushima* *Japan* Official number: 137021	*297* - -		**2002**-07 **Hangzhou Dongfeng Shipbuilding Co Ltd — Hangzhou ZJ** Loa 28.05 Br ex - Dght 5.200 Lbp 24.20 Br md 13.87 Dpth 7.02 Welded, 1 dk	**(B32B2SP) Pusher Tug**	**2 oil engines** geared to sc. shafts driving 2 Propellers Total Power: 2,206kW (3,000hp) Niigata 6MG26HLX 2 x 4 Stroke 6 Cy. 260 x 350 each-1103kW (1500bhp) Niigata Engineering Co Ltd-Japan
9204142 *JI3652* -	**SUMIYO MARU** **Daisen Butsuryu KK** - *Osaka, Osaka* *Japan* MMSI: 431300835 Official number: 135954	*499* - -		**1998**-04 **K.K. Yoshida Zosen Kogyo — Arida** Yd No: 510 Loa 76.32 Br ex - Dght - Lbp 70.00 Br md 12.00 Dpth 7.00 Welded, 1 dk	**(A31A2GX) General Cargo Ship**	**1 oil engine** driving 1 FP propeller Total Power: 1,177kW (1,600hp) 11.5kn Yanmar DY28-EN 1 x 4 Stroke 6 Cy. 280 x 530 1177kW (1600bhp) Yanmar Diesel Engine Co Ltd-Japan
8936516 *JM6665* -	**SUMIYOSHI MARU** **YK Wada Kaiun** - *Kitakyushu, Fukuoka* *Japan* Official number: 136402	*120* - -		**1997**-12 **Amakusa Zosen K.K. — Amakusa** Yd No: 121 Loa 22.10 Br ex - Dght - Lbp 20.00 Br md 9.00 Dpth 3.20 Welded, 1 dk	**(B32A2ST) Tug**	**2 oil engines** driving 2 FP propellers Total Power: 1,472kW (2,002hp) 10.0kn Niigata 6MG22HX 2 x 4 Stroke 6 Cy. 220 x 280 each-736kW (1001bhp) Niigata Engineering Co Ltd-Japan
8869787 *JM6223* -	**SUMIYOSHI MARU** **Yamaichi Kaiun YK** - *Iki, Nagasaki* *Japan* Official number: 133523	*199* - 599		**1993**-02 **K.K. Kamishima Zosensho — Osakikamijima** Yd No: 553 Loa 57.54 Br ex - Dght 3.320 Lbp 47.00 Br md 9.00 Dpth 5.20 Welded, 1 dk	**(A31A2GX) General Cargo Ship** Grain: 1,185; Bale: 1,174	**1 oil engine** driving 1 FP propeller Total Power: 736kW (1,001hp) 10.0kn Matsui ML626GSC-4 1 x 4 Stroke 6 Cy. 260 x 480 736kW (1001bhp) Matsui Iron Works Co Ltd-Japan
8824567 *JJ3648* -	**SUMIYOSHI MARU** *ex Daiei Maru -1997* **Seiichi Takahama** - *Awaji, Hyogo* *Japan* Official number: 129230	*155* - 495		**1989**-05 **K.K. Kamishima Zosensho — Osakikamijima** Yd No: 237 Loa 49.70 Br ex - Dght 3.100 Lbp 44.00 Br md 8.30 Dpth 5.00 Welded, 1 dk	**(A31A2GX) General Cargo Ship**	**1 oil engine** geared to sc. shaft driving 1 FP propeller Total Power: 441kW (600hp) Hanshin 6LB26G 1 x 4 Stroke 6 Cy. 260 x 440 441kW (600bhp) The Hanshin Diesel Works Ltd-Japan
8032487 - -	**SUMIYOSHI MARU** *ex Koun Maru -1985* **Century Product Inc** - *Indonesia*	*152* - 349		**1980**-06 **KK Ouchi Zosensho — Matsuyama EH** Yd No: 159 Loa - Br ex - Dght 2.810 Lbp 38.00 Br md 7.41 Dpth 4.50 Welded, 1 dk	**(A31A2GX) General Cargo Ship**	**1 oil engine** driving 1 FP propeller Total Power: 324kW (441hp) 10.5kn Otsuka 1 x 4 Stroke 324kW (441bhp) KK Otsuka Diesel-Japan
8619209 - -	**SUMIYOSHI MARU** **Keum Dan Industry Co** - *South Korea*	*290* - 300		**1987**-04 **Shirahama Zosen K.K. — Honai** Yd No: 130 Loa 31.09 Br ex 9.83 Dght 3.952 Lbp 28.00 Br md 9.81 Dpth 4.81 Welded, 1 dk	**(B32A2ST) Tug**	**2 oil engines** with clutches, flexible couplings & reverse reduction geared to sc. shafts driving 2 FP propellers Total Power: 2,206kW (3,000hp) Niigata 6M31AGTE 2 x 4 Stroke 6 Cy. 310 x 530 each-1103kW (1500bhp) Niigata Engineering Co Ltd-Japan
8889684 *JM6405* -	**SUMIYOSHI MARU No. 2** **Meiwa Kaiun YK** - *Karatsu, Saga* *Japan* Official number: 134563	*199* - 649		**1995**-05 **Y.K. Okajima Zosensho — Matsuyama** Yd No: 246 Loa 58.03 Br ex - Dght 3.210 Lbp 52.00 Br md 9.50 Dpth 5.42 Welded, 1 dk	**(A31A2GX) General Cargo Ship**	**1 oil engine** driving 1 FP propeller Total Power: 736kW (1,001hp) 11.9kn Niigata 6M26AGTE 1 x 4 Stroke 6 Cy. 260 x 460 736kW (1001bhp) Niigata Engineering Co Ltd-Japan
9711418 *JD3665* -	**SUMIYOSHI MARU NO. 2** **Meiwa Kaiun YK** - *Japan* MMSI: 431005214	*283* - 820	Class: FA	**2014**-02 **Yano Zosen K.K. — Imabari** Yd No: 281 Loa 61.95 Br ex - Dght 3.470 Lbp - Br md 9.80 Dpth - Welded, 1 dk	**(A31A2GX) General Cargo Ship** Double Hull Grain: 1,374; Bale: 1,333	**1 oil engine** reduction geared to sc. shaft driving 1 Propeller Total Power: 1,029kW (1,399hp) Niigata 6M28BGT 1 x 4 Stroke 6 Cy. 280 x 480 1029kW (1399bhp) Niigata Engineering Co Ltd-Japan
8859500 *JK5094* -	**SUMIYOSHI MARU No. 5** **KK Seisei** - *Fukuyama, Hiroshima* *Japan* Official number: 132481	*494* - 1,486		**1991**-10 **Azumi Zosen Kensetsu K.K. — Himeji** Loa 63.00 (BB) Br ex - Dght 4.800 Lbp - Br md 13.20 Dpth 7.80 Welded, 1 dk	**(B33A2DS) Suction Dredger** Compartments: 1 Ho 1 Ha: (22.8 x 9.6) Cranes: 1	**1 oil engine** driving 1 FP propeller Total Power: 736kW (1,001hp) 11.3kn Niigata 1 x 4 Stroke 736kW (1001bhp) Niigata Engineering Co Ltd-Japan
8618580 - -	**SUMIYOSHI MARU No. 5** - -	*469* - 645		**1987**-04 **Miho Zosensho K.K. — Shimizu** Yd No: 1279 Loa 57.76 Br ex 9.12 Dght 3.639 Lbp 50.78 Br md 9.11 Dpth 4.17 Welded, 1 dk	**(B11B2FV) Fishing Vessel** Grain: 845; Bale: 758	**1 oil engine** with clutches, flexible couplings & sr geared to sc. shaft driving 1 FP propeller Total Power: 1,103kW (1,500hp) Niigata 6M31AFTE 1 x 4 Stroke 6 Cy. 310 x 530 1103kW (1500bhp) Niigata Engineering Co Ltd-Japan
8223608 - -	**SUMIYOSHI MARU No. 5** **PT Armada Contener Nusantara**	*199* 100 496		**1983**-03 **Maeno Zosen KK — Sanyoonoda YC** Yd No: 85 Loa 46.72 (BB) Br ex - Dght 3.101 Lbp 42.02 Br md 8.01 Dpth 3.36 Welded, 1 dk	**(A12A2TC) Chemical Tanker** Liq: 345 Compartments: 6 Ta, ER	**1 oil engine** sr geared to sc. shaft driving 1 FP propeller Total Power: 478kW (650hp) Matsui 6M26KGHS 1 x 4 Stroke 6 Cy. 260 x 400 478kW (650bhp) Matsui Iron Works Co Ltd-Japan
8858893 *JK4815* -	**SUMIYOSHI MARU NO. 8** *ex Sakata Maru No. 8 -2007* - - *Onomichi, Hiroshima* *Japan* Official number: 131081	*131* - -		**1991**-08 **Ishida Zosen Kogyo YK — Onomichi HS** Yd No: 110 Loa 30.50 Br ex - Dght 2.700 Lbp 26.50 Br md 7.80 Dpth 3.30 Welded, 1 dk	**(B32A2ST) Tug**	**1 oil engine** driving 1 FP propeller Total Power: 736kW (1,001hp) 12.0kn Yanmar MF29-ST 1 x 4 Stroke 6 Cy. 290 x 520 736kW (1001bhp) Yanmar Diesel Engine Co Ltd-Japan
8806400 - -	**SUMIYOSHI MARU No. 8** - -	*430* - 575		**1988**-06 **Shirahama Zosen K.K. — Honai** Yd No: 135 Loa 47.50 (BB) Br ex - Dght 3.320 Lbp 43.01 Br md 10.51 Dpth 5.01 Welded, 1 dk	**(A24D2BA) Aggregates Carrier** Grain: 680; Bale: 650 Compartments: 1 Ho, ER 1 Ha: (16.8 x 8.0)ER	**1 oil engine** with clutches & reverse reduction geared to sc. shaft driving 1 FP propeller Total Power: 515kW (700hp) Akasaka T26SR 1 x 4 Stroke 6 Cy. 260 x 440 515kW (700bhp) Akasaka Tekkosho KK (Akasaka DieselLtd)-Japan

IMO / Call sign / Fishing no.	Name / Former names / Owner / Port	Tonnage	Class	Built / Builder / Dimensions	Type / Cargo	Machinery
8707886 *JJ3566* -	**SUMIYOSHI MARU No. 10** - **Ogyoku Kaiun YK** - *Ieshima, Hyogo* *Japan* Official number: 129310	*410* - 1,053		**1987-12 Hamamoto Zosensho K.K. — Tokushima** Yd No: 688 Loa - (BB) Br ex - Dght 4.201 Lbp 52.02 Br md 12.01 Dpth 5.90 Welded, 2 dks	**(B33A2DG) Grab Dredger** Compartments: 1 Ho, ER 1 Ha: ER	**1 oil engine** driving 1 FP propeller Total Power: 736kW (1,001hp) Niigata 6M28BGT 1 x 4 Stroke 6 Cy. 280 x 480 736kW (1001bhp) Niigata Engineering Co Ltd-Japan
9152222 *JEYM* KN1-726	**SUMIYOSHI MARU No. 10** - **Sumiyoshi Gyogyo KK** - SatCom: Inmarsat B 343188910 *Miura, Kanagawa* *Japan* MMSI: 431889000 Official number: 134959	*499* - 507		**1996-11 Miho Zosensho K.K. — Shimizu** Yd No: 1478 Loa 58.00 (BB) Br ex - Dght 3.607 Lbp 51.30 Br md 9.10 Dpth 3.96 Welded, 1 dk	**(B11B2FV) Fishing Vessel** Ins: 556	**1 oil engine** with flexible couplings & sr gearedto sc. shaft driving 1 FP propeller Total Power: 736kW (1,001hp) 12.6kn Niigata 6M28HFT 1 x 4 Stroke 6 Cy. 280 x 480 736kW (1001bhp) Niigata Engineering Co Ltd-Japan AuxGen: 2 x 320kW 445V a.c Fuel: 325.0 (d.f.) 3.0pd
9078737 *JJ3809* -	**SUMIYOSHI MARU No. 11** - **KK Shosei** - *Himeji, Hyogo* *Japan* MMSI: 431300097 Official number: 132311	*989* - 2,183		**1993-08 K.K. Mukai Zosensho — Nagasaki** Yd No: 653 Loa 73.45 Br ex - Dght 5.520 Lbp 68.00 Br md 14.80 Dpth 8.95 Welded	**(A31A2GX) General Cargo Ship** 1 Ha: (23.4 x 11.8) Cranes: 1x20t	**1 oil engine** driving 1 FP propeller Total Power: 1,471kW (2,000hp) Niigata 6M34AFT 1 x 4 Stroke 6 Cy. 340 x 620 1471kW (2000bhp) Niigata Engineering Co Ltd-Japan
8915938 - -	**SUMIYOSHI MARU No. 12** - - - *South Korea*	*389* - 907		**1990-06 Hamamoto Zosensho K.K. — Tokushima** Yd No: 733 Loa 59.62 (BB) Br ex - Dght 4.022 Lbp 52.00 Br md 12.00 Dpth 5.90 Welded, 1 dk	**(A24D2BA) Aggregates Carrier** Compartments: 1 Ho, ER 1 Ha: (17.0 x 9.0)ER	**1 oil engine** driving 1 FP propeller Total Power: 736kW (1,001hp) Niigata 6M30GT 1 x 4 Stroke 6 Cy. 300 x 530 736kW (1001bhp) Niigata Engineering Co Ltd-Japan
9004944 *JJ3760* -	**SUMIYOSHI MARU No. 15** - **Shirakawa Kisen KK** - *Ieshima, Hyogo* *Japan* Official number: 131878	*483* - 1,000		**1990-10 Hamamoto Zosensho K.K. — Tokushima** Yd No: 737 Loa 62.78 (BB) Br ex - Dght 4.422 Lbp 55.00 Br md 12.00 Dpth 6.30 Welded, 1 dk	**(B33A2DG) Grab Dredger** Compartments: 1 Ho, ER 1 Ha: ER	**1 oil engine** driving 1 FP propeller Total Power: 736kW (1,001hp) Niigata 6M31AGTE 1 x 4 Stroke 6 Cy. 310 x 530 736kW (1001bhp) Niigata Engineering Co Ltd-Japan
9073543 *JM6350* -	**SUMIYOSHI MARU No. 18** - **Sakamoto Kaiun YK** - *Matsuura, Nagasaki* *Japan* Official number: 132698	*199* - 700		**1994-04 Nippon Zosen Tekko K.K. — Kitakyushu** Yd No: 348 Loa 55.94 (BB) Br ex 9.51 Dght 3.280 Lbp 51.00 Br md 9.50 Dpth 5.50 Welded, 1 dk	**(A31A2GX) General Cargo Ship** Grain: 1,092; Bale: 1,090 Compartments: 1 Ho, ER 1 Ha: ER	**1 oil engine** with clutches & reverse geared to sc. shaft driving 1 FP propeller Total Power: 736kW (1,001hp) Hanshin LH28G 1 x 4 Stroke 6 Cy. 280 x 460 736kW (1001bhp) The Hanshin Diesel Works Ltd-Japan
8905311 *JJ3624* -	**SUMIYOSHI MARU No. 28** - **Goko Kaiun YK** Yashima Senpaku Kyodo Kumiai *Himeji, Hyogo* *Japan* Official number: 130840	*372* - 999		**1989-03 K.K. Matsuura Zosensho — Osakikamijima** Yd No: 362 Loa 58.64 (BB) Br ex 12.02 Dght 4.140 Lbp 52.00 Br md 12.00 Dpth 6.00 Welded, 1 dk	**(B33A2DG) Grab Dredger** Grain: 673 Compartments: 1 Ho, ER 1 Ha: ER	**1 oil engine** driving 1 FP propeller Total Power: 736kW (1,001hp) Makita LN31L 1 x 4 Stroke 6 Cy. 310 x 600 736kW (1001bhp) Makita Diesel Co Ltd-Japan
9087702 *JK5227* -	**SUMIYOSHI MARU NO. 30** *ex Sumiyoshi Maru No. 35 -2002* **Yoshiyama Kisen YK** - *Imabari, Ehime* *Japan* Official number: 133078	*497* - 1,344		**1994-04 Hitachi Zosen Mukaishima Marine Co Ltd — Onomichi HS** Yd No: 82 Loa 67.36 (BB) Br ex - Dght 4.572 Lbp 61.00 Br md 13.00 Dpth 7.53 Welded, 1 dk	**(A24D2BA) Aggregates Carrier** Grain: 1,329 Compartments: 1 Ho, ER 1 Ha: ER	**1 oil engine** with clutches & reverse geared to sc. shaft driving 1 FP propeller Total Power: 735kW (999hp) Hanshin 6LU35G 1 x 4 Stroke 6 Cy. 350 x 550 735kW (999bhp) The Hanshin Diesel Works Ltd-Japan Thrusters: 1 Thwart. FP thruster (f)
9162564 *JJ3936* -	**SUMIYOSHI MARU No. 33** - **Goko Kaiun YK** Yashima Senpaku Kyodo Kumiai *Himeji, Hyogo* *Japan* Official number: 134191	*499* - 1,500		**1997-03 K.K. Matsuura Zosensho — Osakikamijima** Yd No: 522 Loa - Br ex - Dght 4.300 Lbp 63.00 Br md 13.50 Dpth 7.20 Welded, 1 dk	**(A31A2GX) General Cargo Ship**	**1 oil engine** driving 1 FP propeller Total Power: 736kW (1,001hp) Akasaka A34C 1 x 4 Stroke 6 Cy. 340 x 620 736kW (1001bhp) Akasaka Tekkosho KK (Akasaka DieselLtd)-Japan
8717128 *JCMV* KN1-687	**SUMIYOSHI MARU No. 71** - **Nanyo Suisan KK** - *Miura, Kanagawa* *Japan* MMSI: 431424000 Official number: 130293	*498* - 681		**1988-04 Miho Zosensho K.K. — Shimizu** Yd No: 1327 Loa 59.52 (BB) Br ex 9.12 Dght 3.731 Lbp 52.41 Br md 9.10 Dpth 4.10 Welded, 1 dk	**(B11B2FV) Fishing Vessel** Ins: 624	**1 oil engine** with clutches, flexible couplings & sr reverse geared to sc. shaft driving 1 FP propeller Total Power: 1,103kW (1,500hp) Niigata 6M31AFTE 1 x 4 Stroke 6 Cy. 310 x 530 1103kW (1500bhp) Niigata Engineering Co Ltd-Japan
8703593 *JBPI* KN1-680	**SUMIYOSHI MARU No. 73** - **Sumiyoshi Gyogyo KK** - SatCom: Inmarsat B 343185410 *Miura, Kanagawa* *Japan* MMSI: 431854000 Official number: 129736	*469* - 646		**1987-05 Miho Zosensho K.K. — Shimizu** Yd No: 1311 Loa 57.76 (BB) Br ex 9.12 Dght 3.631 Lbp 50.75 Br md 9.11 Dpth 4.02 Welded, 1 dk	**(B11B2FV) Fishing Vessel** Grain: 845; Bale: 758	**1 oil engine** with clutches, flexible couplings & sr geared to sc. shaft driving 1 FP propeller Total Power: 1,103kW (1,500hp) Niigata 6M31AFTE 1 x 4 Stroke 6 Cy. 310 x 530 1103kW (1500bhp) Niigata Engineering Co Ltd-Japan
9234238 *JQZA* KN1-739	**SUMIYOSHI MARU No. 75** - **Koyo Suisan KK** - *Miura, Kanagawa* *Japan* MMSI: 432276000 Official number: 136949	*499* - 508		**2000-10 Miho Zosensho K.K. — Shimizu** Yd No: 1492 Loa 58.00 (BB) Br ex - Dght 3.601 Lbp 51.00 Br md 9.00 Dpth - Welded, 1 dk	**(B11B2FV) Fishing Vessel** Grain: 830; Bale: 766	**1 oil engine** with clutches, flexible couplings & sr geared to sc. shaft driving 1 FP propeller Total Power: 736kW (1,001hp) 12.7kn Niigata 6M28HFT 1 x 4 Stroke 6 Cy. 280 x 480 736kW (1001bhp) Niigata Engineering Co Ltd-Japan AuxGen: 2 x 320kW 445V 60Hz a.c
8839902 - -	**SUMIYOSHI MARU No. 78** - - - *China*	*118* - -		**1989-07 Shunkei Abe — Nandan, Hyogo Pref.** Yd No: 188 Loa 29.95 Br ex - Dght 2.300 Lbp 26.00 Br md 7.30 Dpth 3.48 Welded, 1 dk	**(B32A2ST) Tug**	**1 oil engine** driving 1 FP propeller Yanmar 1 x 4 Stroke Yanmar Diesel Engine Co Ltd-Japan
9189079 *JCFC* KN1-733	**SUMIYOSHI MARU No. 81** - **Sumiyoshi Gyogyo KK** - *Miura, Kanagawa* *Japan* MMSI: 431395000 Official number: 136617	*499* - 511		**1998-08 Miho Zosensho K.K. — Shimizu** Yd No: 1486 Loa 58.00 Br ex - Dght 3.604 Lbp 51.30 Br md 9.10 Dpth 3.96 Welded, 1 dk	**(B11B2FV) Fishing Vessel** Grain: 613; Bale: 555	**1 oil engine** with clutches, flexible couplings & sr reverse geared to sc. shaft driving 1 FP propeller Total Power: 736kW (1,001hp) Niigata 6M28HFT 1 x 4 Stroke 6 Cy. 280 x 480 736kW (1001bhp) Niigata Engineering Co Ltd-Japan
8876766 - -	**SUMIYOSHI No. 18** *ex Sumiyoshi Maru No. 18 -1994* *ex Taiyo Maru No. 7 -1994* - -	*199* 116 658		**1975-05 K.K. Mochizuki Zosensho — Osakikamijima** Loa 50.00 Br ex 8.40 Dght 3.100 Lbp 48.00 Br md - Dpth 5.00 Welded, 1 dk	**(A31A2GX) General Cargo Ship** Compartments: 1 Ho, ER 1 Ha: (27.0 x 6.0)ER	**1 oil engine** driving 1 FP propeller Total Power: 736kW (1,001hp) Otsuka 1 x 4 Stroke 736kW (1001bhp) KK Otsuka Diesel-Japan
9427275 *V7OA9*	**SUMMER** **Carmenta Shipholding SA** NGM Energy SA SatCom: Inmarsat C 453834249 *Majuro* *Marshall Islands* MMSI: 538003326 Official number: 3326	**8,539** 4,117 13,023 T/cm 23.2	Class: AB	**2009-06 21st Century Shipbuilding Co Ltd — Tongyeong** Yd No: 249 Loa 128.60 (BB) Br ex 20.43 Dght 8.714 Lbp 120.40 Br md 20.40 Dpth 11.50 Welded, 1 dk	**(A12B2TR) Chemical/Products Tanker** Double Hull (13F) Liq: 13,398; Liq (Oil): 687 Cargo Heating Coils Compartments: 12 Wing Ta, 2 Wing Slop Ta, ER 12 Cargo Pump (s): 12x600m³/hr Manifold: Bow/CM: 60.7m	**1 oil engine** driving 1 FP propeller Total Power: 4,440kW (6,037hp) 13.4kn MAN-B&W 6S35MC 1 x 2 Stroke 6 Cy. 350 x 1400 4440kW (6037bhp) STX Engine Co Ltd-South Korea AuxGen: 3 x 480kW a.c Thrusters: 1 Tunnel thruster (f) Fuel: 76.0 (d.f.) 674.0 (r.f.)

IMO / Call sign	Name / Owner	Tonnage	Class	Builder / Dimensions	Type	Machinery
8410586 *C6RO3* -	**SUMMER BAY** *ex* Summer Breeze *-2000* *ex* Chiquita Baracoa *-1996* *ex* Ellen D *-1990* **Bay Shipping Corp** Chartworld Shipping Corp SatCom: Inmarsat A 1105643 *Nassau* *Bahamas* MMSI: 311123000 Official number: 8000253	**12,660** 6,755 13,613	Class: NK (Class contemplated) (NV) (AB)	**1985-12 Kurushima Dockyard Co. Ltd. — Onishi** Yd No: 2393 Loa 169.09 (BB) Br ex - Dght 9.529 Lbp 158.53 Br md 24.01 Dpth 13.21 Welded, 4 dks	**(A34A2GR) Refrigerated Cargo Ship** Ins: 15,744 TEU 180 incl 82 ref C Compartments: ER, 4 Ho 4 Ha: ER Cranes: 3x36t,1x10t	**1 oil engine** driving 1 FP propeller Total Power: 19,810kW (26,934hp) 24.3kn B&W 7L70MC 1 x 2 Stroke 7 Cy. 700 x 2268 19810kW (26934bhp) Mitsui Engineering & Shipbuilding CLtd-Japan AuxGen: 4 x 980kW a.c
8036847 - -	**SUMMER BREEZE** *ex* Charlie Brown *-1990* -	*193* 131 -		**1980 at Coden, Al** L reg 28.56 Br ex 8.01 Dght - Lbp - Br md - Dpth 3.69 Welded, 1 dk	**(B11B2FV) Fishing Vessel**	**1 oil engine** driving 1 FP propeller Total Power: 883kW (1,201hp)
9219953 *H3KY* -	**SUMMER CORAL** **Coral Canal SA** Star Management Associates *Panama* *Panama* MMSI: 354836000 Official number: 2723600CH	**3,549** 1,064 4,096 T/cm 13.2	Class: BV	**2000-07 Hitachi Zosen Mukaishima Marine Co Ltd — Onomichi HS** Yd No: 150 Loa 96.70 (BB) Br ex 16.52 Dght 5.300 Lbp 89.70 Br md 16.50 Dpth 7.25 Welded, 1 dk	**(A11B2TG) LPG Tanker** Double Bottom Entire Compartment Length Liq (Gas): 3,589 2 x Gas Tank (s); 2 independent cyl horizontal 2 Cargo Pump (s): 2x250m³/hr Manifold: Bow/CM: 39.4m	**1 oil engine** driving 1 FP propeller Total Power: 2,648kW (3,600hp) 12.5kn Hanshin LH41LA 1 x 4 Stroke 6 Cy. 410 x 800 2648kW (3600bhp) The Hanshin Diesel Works Ltd-Japan AuxGen: 2 x 360kW 440/100V 60Hz a.c Fuel: 140.0 (d.f.) 458.0 (r.f.)
9321902 *C4VF2* -	**SUMMER E** *ex* MOL Summer *-2012* *ex* Nordsummer *-2011* *ex* Orange River Bridge *-2011* *ex* Nordsummer *-2007* **Schifffahrtsgesellschaft ms 'Summer E' GmbH & Co KG** Reederei Nord Ltd SatCom: Inmarsat C 421047310 *Limassol* *Cyprus* MMSI: 210473000 Official number: 9321902	**38,332** 21,924 46,321	Class: GL	**2007-07 STX Shipbuilding Co Ltd — Changwon (Jinhae Shipyard)** Yd No: 1210 Loa 246.83 (BB) Br ex - Dght 12.300 Lbp 232.30 Br md 32.20 Dpth 19.30 Welded, 1 dk	**(A33A2CC) Container Ship (Fully Cellular)** TEU 3586 C Ho 1433 TEU C Dk 2153 TEU incl 500 ref C	**1 oil engine** driving 1 FP propeller Total Power: 32,435kW (44,099hp) 23.4kn MAN-B&W 9K80MC-C 1 x 2 Stroke 9 Cy. 800 x 2300 32435kW (44099bhp) STX Engine Co Ltd-South Korea AuxGen: 4 x 1800kW 450V a.c Thrusters: 1 Tunnel thruster (f)
8413019 *C6RO2* -	**SUMMER FLOWER** *ex* Chiquita Baru *-1996* *ex* Vivian M *-1990* **Flower Shipping Corp** Chartworld Shipping Corp *Nassau* *Bahamas* MMSI: 311122000 Official number: 8000252	**12,659** 6,755 13,584	Class: BV (NV) (AB)	**1984-12 Sasebo Heavy Industries Co. Ltd. — Sasebo Yard, Sasebo** Yd No: 351 Loa 169.09 (BB) Br ex - Dght 9.502 Lbp 157.61 Br md 24.01 Dpth 13.21 Welded, 4 dks	**(A34A2GR) Refrigerated Cargo Ship** Side doors (p) Side doors (s) Ins: 16,367 TEU 180 incl 82 ref C Compartments: ER, 4 Ho 4 Ha: ER Cranes: 3x36t,1x10t	**1 oil engine** driving 1 FP propeller Total Power: 19,810kW (26,934hp) 22.5kn B&W 7L70MC 1 x 2 Stroke 7 Cy. 700 x 2268 19810kW (26934bhp) Mitsui Engineering & Shipbuilding CLtd-Japan AuxGen: 4 x 980kW 440/110V 60Hz a.c
9184938 *9HA3409* -	**SUMMER LADY** *ex* Legato *-2013* **Mirabel Shipholding Corp** Aims Shipping Corp *Valletta* *Malta* MMSI: 229564000 Official number: 9184938	**37,457** 23,766 72,083	Class: RI (NK)	**1999-07 Kanasashi Heavy Industries Co Ltd — Toyohashi AI** Yd No: 3485 Loa 224.99 (BB) Br ex - Dght 13.477 Lbp 215.50 Br md 32.26 Dpth 18.60 Welded, 1 dk	**(A21A2BC) Bulk Carrier** Grain: 84,964; Bale: 82,066 Compartments: 7 Ho, ER 7 Ha: (17.9 x 12.7)6 (18.1 x 14.0)ER	**1 oil engine** driving 1 FP propeller Total Power: 9,268kW (12,601hp) 14.3kn Mitsubishi 6UEC60LA 1 x 2 Stroke 6 Cy. 600 x 1900 9268kW (12601bhp) Kobe Hatsudoki KK-Japan Fuel: 2507.0 (r.f.)
8407814 *C6RN9* -	**SUMMER MEADOW** *ex* Chiquita Bocas *-1996* *ex* Irma M *-1990* **Meadow Shipping Corp** Chartworld Shipping Corp *Nassau* *Bahamas* MMSI: 311121000 Official number: 8000251	**12,659** 6,755 13,584	Class: NK (Class contemplated) (NV) (AB)	**1985-02 Kurushima Dockyard Co. Ltd. — Onishi** Yd No: 2375 Loa 169.09 (BB) Br ex - Dght 9.502 Lbp 157.61 Br md 24.01 Dpth 13.21 Welded, 4 dks	**(A34A2GR) Refrigerated Cargo Ship** Ins: 16,707 TEU 180 incl 82 ref C Compartments: ER, 4 Ho 4 Ha: ER Cranes: 3x36t,1x10t	**1 oil engine** driving 1 FP propeller Total Power: 19,810kW (26,934hp) 20.3kn B&W 7L70MC 1 x 2 Stroke 7 Cy. 700 x 2268 19810kW (26934bhp) Mitsui Engineering & Shipbuilding CLtd-Japan AuxGen: 4 x 980kW a.c
8992792 *WBS8546* -	**SUMMER SPLENDOR** *ex* Splendor *-2013* *ex* P. G.'s Jester *-2013* *ex* Reality *-2005* **Commercial Realty Development LLC** - *Pass Christian, MS* *United States of America* Official number: 959738	*121* 36 -		**1989-01 Broward Marine Inc — Fort Lauderdale FL** Yd No: 244 Loa 28.62 Br ex - Dght - Lbp - Br md 5.88 Dpth 3.05 Welded, 1 dk	**(X11A2YP) Yacht** Hull Material: Aluminium Alloy	**2 oil engines** driving 2 FP propellers 17.0kn
9114139 *A8G03* -	**SUMMER WIND** *ex* Nena M *-2013* *ex* Pacific Mayor *-2002* **Sea Galaxy Marine SA** Cleopatra Shipping Agency Ltd SatCom: Inmarsat C 463714181 *Monrovia* *Liberia* MMSI: 636012617 Official number: 12617	**25,503** 14,222 43,176 T/cm 50.8	Class: GL (KR) (NV)	**1995-06 Hyundai Heavy Industries Co Ltd — Ulsan** Yd No: 898 Loa 185.06 (BB) Br ex 30.03 Dght 11.216 Lbp 177.00 Br md 30.00 Dpth 16.00 Welded, 1 dk	**(A21A2BC) Bulk Carrier** Grain: 54,232; Bale: 52,442 Compartments: 5 Ho, ER 5 Ha: (14.4 x 15.3)4 (19.2 x 15.3)ER Cranes: 4x25t	**1 oil engine** driving 1 FP propeller Total Power: 7,779kW (10,576hp) 14.5kn B&W 6S50MC 1 x 2 Stroke 6 Cy. 500 x 1910 7779kW (10576bhp) Hyundai Heavy Industries Co Ltd-South Korea AuxGen: 3 x 600kW 220/450V 60Hz a.c Fuel: 160.0 (d.f.) 1400.0 (r.f.) 29.0pd
8410574 *C6RN8* -	**SUMMER WIND** *ex* Chiquita Burica *-1996* *ex* Edyth L *-1990* **Wind Shipping Corp** Chartworld Shipping Corp SatCom: Inmarsat A 1105647 *Nassau* *Bahamas* MMSI: 311119000 Official number: 8000250	**12,660** 6,755 13,636	Class: NK (Class contemplated) (NV) (AB)	**1985-11 Kurushima Dockyard Co. Ltd. — Onishi** Yd No: 2392 Loa 169.09 (BB) Br ex - Dght 9.530 Lbp 158.53 Br md 24.01 Dpth 13.21 Welded, 4 dks	**(A34A2GR) Refrigerated Cargo Ship** Ins: 16,707 TEU 180 incl 82 ref C Compartments: ER, 4 Ho 4 Ha: ER Cranes: 3x36t,1x10t	**1 oil engine** driving 1 FP propeller Total Power: 19,810kW (26,934hp) 24.0kn B&W 7L70MC 1 x 2 Stroke 7 Cy. 700 x 2268 19810kW (26934bhp) Mitsui Engineering & Shipbuilding CLtd-Japan AuxGen: 4 x 980kW a.c
8035025 *OG8046* -	**SUMMERSEA** *ex* Agat *-1998* **Marine Lines Oy** - *Hanko* *Finland* MMSI: 230980760 Official number: 11917	**124** 46 20	Class: (RS)	**1982 Ilyichyovskiy Sudoremontnyy Zavod im. "50-letiya SSSR" — Ilyichyovsk** Yd No: 15 Loa 28.70 Br ex 6.35 Dght 1.480 Lbp 27.00 Br md - Dpth 2.50 Welded, 1 dk	**(A37B2PS) Passenger Ship** Passengers: unberthed: 250	**2 oil engines** driving 2 FP propellers Total Power: 220kW (300hp) 10.4kn Barnaultransmash 3D6C 2 x 4 Stroke 6 Cy. 150 x 180 each-110kW (150bhp) Barnaultransmash-Barnaul AuxGen: 2 x 1kW Fuel: 2.0 (d.f.)
9687100 *V7DA2* -	**SUMMERTIME DREAM** **Scorpio Carriers Ltd** Daiichi Chuo Marine Co Ltd (DC Marine) *Majuro* *Marshall Islands* MMSI: 538005357 Official number: 5357	**31,505** 18,683 56,104 T/cm 55.9	Class: NK	**2014-02 Oshima Shipbuilding Co Ltd — Saikai NS** Yd No: 10680 Loa 189.99 (BB) Br ex - Dght 12.569 Lbp 185.79 Br md 32.26 Dpth 17.87 Welded, 1 dk	**(A21A2BC) Bulk Carrier** Grain: 69,872; Bale: 68,798 Compartments: 5 Ho, ER 5 Ha: ER Cranes: 4x30t	**1 oil engine** driving 1 FP propeller Total Power: 5,247kW (7,134hp) 14.5kn AuxGen: 3 x a.c
9492660 *H06357* -	**SUMMIT 1** *ex* Carina 1 *-2013* *ex* Swissco Super *-2011* **Summit Shipping Inc** Bushra Ship Management Pvt Ltd *Panama* *Panama* MMSI: 352224000 Official number: 45012PEXT	**367** 110 350	Class: BV	**2008-06 Guangzhou Panyu Lingshan Shipyard Ltd — Guangzhou GD** Yd No: 159 Loa 36.30 Br ex - Dght 3.580 Lbp 32.28 Br md 9.80 Dpth 4.30 Welded, 1 dk	**(B21B20T) Offshore Tug/Supply Ship**	**2 oil engines** Reduction geared to sc. shafts driving 2 FP propellers Total Power: 2,400kW (3,264hp) 12.0kn Cummins KTA-38-M2 2 x Vee 4 Stroke 12 Cy. 159 x 159 each-1200kW (1632bhp) Cummins Engine Co Inc-USA AuxGen: 2 x 136kW 415V 50Hz a.c Thrusters: 1 Tunnel thruster (f) Fuel: 250.0 (r.f.) 6.5pd
7522473 - -	**SUMMIT 1** *ex* Utoku Maru No. 1 *-1988* *ex* Howa Maru No. 17 *-1982* **Summit Industrial & Mercantile Corp (Pvt) Ltd** - *Chittagong* *Bangladesh* Official number: C.803	*720* 358 1,107		**1975-12 K.K. Ichikawa Zosensho — Ise** Yd No: 1329 Loa - Br ex 9.43 Dght 4.204 Lbp 49.51 Br md 9.40 Dpth 4.40 Riveted\Welded, 1 dk	**(A13B2TU) Tanker (unspecified)**	**1 oil engine** driving 1 FP propeller Total Power: 956kW (1,300hp) Matsui MS28FSC 1 x 4 Stroke 6 Cy. 280 x 420 956kW (1300bhp) Matsui Iron Works Co Ltd-Japan

IMO / Call sign	Name / Owner / Manager	Tonnage	Class	Builder / Dimensions	Type / Cargo	Machinery
9348235 *H05804* -	**SUMMIT 2** *ex* Aquila *-2013* *ex* Swissco Star *-2011* **Faraz Energy Dena Co** - *Panama* *Panama* MMSI: 355986000 Official number: 45011PEXT	**499** 149 -	Class: BV	**2005-11 Guangzhou Panyu Lingshan Shipyard Ltd — Guangzhou GD** Yd No: 123 Loa 45.00 Br ex 11.25 Dght 3.200 Lbp 40.00 Br md 11.00 Dpth 4.00 Welded, 1 dk	**(B21B20A) Anchor Handling Tug Supply**	**2 oil engines** reduction geared to sc. shafts driving 2 FP propellers Total Power: 2,206kW (3,000hp) 12.0kn Caterpillar 3512B 2 x Vee 4 Stroke 12 Cy. 170 x 190 each-1103kW (1500bhp) Caterpillar Inc-USA AuxGen: 2 x 215kW 415/220V 50Hz a.c Thrusters: 1 Tunnel thruster (f) Fuel: 275.0 (d.f.)
9550709 *5BUH2* -	**SUMMIT AFRICA** **Y K Yalu River (Cyprus) Shipping Ltd** Donnelly Tanker Management Ltd SatCom: Inmarsat C 421006310 *Limassol* *Cyprus* MMSI: 210063000 Official number: 9550709	**42,010** 22,361 73,427 T/cm 67.0	Class: AB	**2009-08 New Times Shipbuilding Co Ltd — Jingjiang JS** Yd No: 0307366 Loa 228.60 (BB) Br ex 32.26 Dght 14.498 Lbp 219.70 Br md 32.20 Dpth 20.65 Welded, 1 dk	**(A13B2TP) Products Tanker** Double Hull (13F) Liq: 81,177; Liq (Oil): 81,177 Compartments: 12 Wing Ta, 2 Wing Slop Ta, ER 3 Cargo Pump (s): 3x2300m³/hr Manifold: Bow/CM: 114.1m	**1 oil engine** driving 1 FP propeller Total Power: 11,300kW (15,363hp) 14.7kn MAN-B&W 5S60MC-C 1 x 2 Stroke 5 Cy. 600 x 2400 11300kW (15363bhp) Hudong Heavy Machinery Co Ltd-China AuxGen: 3 x 900kW a.c Fuel: 211.6 (d.f.) 1881.1 (r.f.)
9336505 *C4MR2* -	**SUMMIT AMERICA** **Uniwide Shipping Co Ltd** Donnelly Tanker Management Ltd *Limassol* *Cyprus* MMSI: 210317000 Official number: 9336505	**41,021** 22,158 74,996 T/cm 67.1	Class: GL	**2006-10 Onomichi Dockyard Co Ltd — Onomichi HS** Yd No: 518 Loa 228.49 (BB) Br ex 32.23 Dght 14.332 Lbp 218.00 Br md 32.20 Dpth 20.65 Welded, 1 dk	**(A13B2TP) Products Tanker** Double Hull (13F) Liq: 82,135; Liq (Oil): 82,075 Cargo Heating Coils Compartments: 12 Wing Ta, 2 Wing Slop Ta, ER 3 Cargo Pump (s): 3x2000m³/hr Manifold: Bow/CM: 115.5m	**1 oil engine** driving 1 FP propeller Total Power: 12,268kW (16,680hp) 15.4kn Mitsubishi 6UEC60LSII 1 x 2 Stroke 6 Cy. 600 x 2300 12268kW (16680bhp) Akasaka Tekkosho KK (Akasaka DieselLtd)-Japan AuxGen: 3 x 600kW 450/225V 60Hz a.c Fuel: 159.9 (d.f.) 2569.9 (r.f.)
9336490 *C4LK2* -	**SUMMIT EUROPE** **Navmore Shipping Co Ltd** Donnelly Tanker Management Ltd *Limassol* *Cyprus* MMSI: 209293000 Official number: 9336490	**41,021** 22,158 74,997 T/cm 67.1	Class: GL	**2006-08 Onomichi Dockyard Co Ltd — Onomichi HS** Yd No: 517 Loa 228.49 (BB) Br ex 32.23 Dght 14.330 Lbp 218.00 Br md 32.20 Dpth 20.65 Welded, 1 dk	**(A13B2TP) Products Tanker** Double Hull (13F) Liq: 82,075; Liq (Oil): 82,075 Cargo Heating Coils Compartments: 12 Wing Ta, 2 Wing Slop Ta, ER 3 Cargo Pump (s): 3x2000m³/hr Manifold: Bow/CM: 115.5m	**1 oil engine** driving 1 FP propeller Total Power: 12,268kW (16,680hp) 15.6kn Mitsubishi 6UEC60LSII 1 x 2 Stroke 6 Cy. 600 x 2300 12268kW (16680bhp) Akasaka Tekkosho KK (Akasaka DieselLtd)-Japan AuxGen: 3 x 600kW 450/225V a.c Fuel: 159.9 (d.f.) 2569.9 (r.f.)
9369461 *3ERT4* -	**SUMMIT RIVER** **Whale Line SA** Kawasaki Kisen Kaisha Ltd (Kawasaki Kisen KK) ('K' Line) *Panama* *Panama* MMSI: 370163000 Official number: 3415808A	**46,046** 13,814 52,991 T/cm 72.2	Class: NK	**2008-07 Kawasaki Shipbuilding Corp — Sakaide KG** Yd No: 1595 Loa 226.00 Br ex 37.24 Dght 11.224 Lbp 222.00 Br md 37.20 Dpth 21.00 Welded, 1 dk	**(A11B2TG) LPG Tanker** Double Hull Liq (Gas): 78,566 9 x Gas Tank (s); 8 independent (C.mn.stl) pri horizontal, ER 8 Cargo Pump (s): 8x600m³/hr Manifold: Bow/CM: 113.3m	**1 oil engine** driving 1 FP propeller Total Power: 16,860kW (22,923hp) 17.0kn MAN-B&W 7S60MC-C 1 x 2 Stroke 7 Cy. 600 x 2400 16860kW (22923bhp) Kawasaki Heavy Industries Ltd-Japan Fuel: 200.0 (d.f.) 2700.0 (r.f.)
9404833 *C6WZ6* -	**SUMMIT SPIRIT** **Summit Spirit LLC** Teekay Marine (Singapore) Pte Ltd SatCom: Inmarsat C 430902210 *Nassau* *Bahamas* MMSI: 309022000 Official number: 9000265	**81,732** 51,287 160,451 T/cm 119.7	Class: LR ✠ **100A1** SS 10/2013 Double Hull oil tanker ESP **ShipRight** (SDA, FDA, CM) *IWS LI ✠ **LMC** **UMS IGS** Eq.Ltr: Y†; Cable: 742.5/97.0 U3 (a)	**2008-10 Samsung Heavy Industries Co Ltd — Geoje** Yd No: 1717 Loa 274.39 (BB) Br ex 48.04 Dght 17.020 Lbp 264.00 Br md 48.00 Dpth 23.20 Welded, 1 dk	**(A13A2TV) Crude Oil Tanker** Double Hull (13F) Liq: 167,456; Liq (Oil): 167,456 Cargo Heating Coils Compartments: 12 Wing Ta, 2 Wing Slop Ta, ER 3 Cargo Pump (s): 3x3800m³/hr Manifold: Bow/CM: 137.6m	**1 oil engine** driving 1 FP propeller Total Power: 18,660kW (25,370hp) 15.5kn MAN-B&W 6S70ME-C 1 x 2 Stroke 6 Cy. 700 x 2800 18660kW (25370bhp) Doosan Engine Co Ltd-South Korea AuxGen: 3 x 950kW 450V 60Hz a.c Boilers: e (ex.g.) 22.4kgf/cm² (22.0bar), WTAuxB (o.f.) 18.4kgf/cm² (18.0bar) Fuel: 190.0 (d.f.) 3800.0 (r.f.)
9195494 *FNAO* -	**SUMMIT TERRA** *ex* Anne Laure *-2006* **TH Corp SA** Geogas Trading SA *Marseille* *France (FIS)* MMSI: 228071000 Official number: 924302B	**46,613** 15,473 53,488 T/cm 67.2	Class: BV	**2000-06 Daewoo Heavy Industries Ltd — Geoje** Yd No: 2301 Loa 224.50 (BB) Br ex - Dght 11.720 Lbp 213.00 Br md 36.00 Dpth 22.30 Welded, 1 dk	**(A11B2TG) LPG Tanker** Double Bottom Entire Compartment Length Liq (Gas): 77,105 Cargo Heating Coils 4 x Gas Tank (s); 4 independent (s.stl) pri horizontal 10 Cargo Pump (s): 8x550m³/hr, 2x550m³/hr Manifold: Bow/CM: 113m	**1 oil engine** driving 1 FP propeller Total Power: 16,013kW (21,771hp) 16.5kn Sulzer 7RTA62U 1 x 2 Stroke 7 Cy. 620 x 2150 16013kW (21771bhp) HSD Engine Co Ltd-South Korea AuxGen: 3 x 1150kW 440/220V 60Hz a.c Fuel: 287.3 (d.f.) (Heating Coils) 3740.7 (r.f.) 65.3pd
8816390 - -	**SUMMIT UNITED-1** *ex* Kaiei Maru No. 3 *-1998* **Summit United Shipping Ltd** - *Chittagong* *Bangladesh* Official number: C.1303	**860** 582 1,491	Class: (NK)	**1988-12 K.K. Matsuura Zosensho — Osakikamijima** Yd No: 360 Loa 72.89 (BB) Br ex 12.02 Dght 4.711 Lbp 68.50 Br md 12.00 Dpth 5.30 Welded, 1 dk	**(A13B2TP) Products Tanker** Liq: 2,250; Liq (Oil): 2,250	**1 oil engine** driving 1 FP propeller Total Power: 1,324kW (1,800hp) Hanshin 6LU32G 1 x 4 Stroke 6 Cy. 320 x 510 1324kW (1800bhp) The Hanshin Diesel Works Ltd-Japan Fuel: 62.0 (d.f.)
8911190 - -	**SUMMIT UNITED-2** *ex* Koki Maru No. 7 *-1998* **Summit United Shipping Ltd** - *Chittagong* *Bangladesh* Official number: C.1310	**493** 264 1,185	Class: (NK)	**1989-12 Shitanoe Shipbuilding Co Ltd — Usuki OT** Yd No: 1105 Loa 58.47 Br ex - Dght 4.081 Lbp 55.00 Br md 10.50 Dpth 4.50 Welded, 1 dk	**(A12B2TR) Chemical/Products Tanker** Liq: 1,283; Liq (Oil): 1,283 Compartments: 8 Ta, ER	**1 oil engine** with clutches & reverse geared to sc. shaft driving 1 FP propeller Total Power: 736kW (1,001hp) Niigata 6M28AGTE 1 x 4 Stroke 6 Cy. 280 x 480 736kW (1001bhp) Niigata Engineering Co Ltd-Japan
9075204 *NZAU* -	**SUMNER** **Government of The United States of America (Department of The Navy)** - *Norfolk, VA* *United States of America* MMSI: 303872000 Official number: CG048042	**4,260** 1,278 2,328	Class: AB	**1995-05 Halter Marine, Inc. — Moss Point, Ms** Yd No: 1262 Loa 100.13 Br ex - Dght 5.790 Lbp 94.48 Br md 17.67 Dpth 8.53 Welded	**(B31A2SR) Research Survey Vessel** Ice Capable	**4 diesel electric oil engines** driving 2 gen. each 2435kW 2 gen. each 1825kW Connecting to 2 elec. motors each (2942kW) driving 2 Z propellers Total Power: 9,020kW (12,264hp) 16.0kn EMD (Electro-Motive) 12-645-F7B 2 x Vee 2 Stroke 12 Cy. 230 x 254 each-1900kW (2583bhp) General Motors Corp.Electro-Motive Div.-La Grange EMD (Electro-Motive) 16-645-F7B 2 x Vee 2 Stroke 16 Cy. 230 x 254 each-2610kW (3549bhp) General Motors Corp.Electro-Motive Div.-La Grange Thrusters: 1 Thwart. FP thruster (f) Fuel: 1241.0 (d.f.)
8222238 *V8ST* -	**SUMPIT-SUMPIT** **Government of The State of Brunei** - *Bandar Seri Begawan* *Brunei* Official number: 0090	*236* 65 463	Class: (LR) ✠ Classed LR until 1/5/01	**1983-11 Cheoy Lee Shipyards Ltd — Hong Kong** Yd No: 3980 Loa 30.51 Br ex 8.92 Dght 3.152 Lbp 28.25 Br md 8.51 Dpth 3.69 Welded, 1 dk	**(B32A2ST) Tug**	**2 oil engines** with clutches, flexible couplings & dr reverse geared to sc. shafts driving 2 FP propellers Total Power: 1,214kW (1,650hp) 11.5kn Blackstone ESL6MK2 2 x 4 Stroke 6 Cy. 222 x 292 each-607kW (825bhp) Mirrlees Blackstone (Stamford)Ltd.-Stamford AuxGen: 2 x 72kW 380V 50Hz a.c Fuel: 45.0 (d.f.)
8904616 -	**SUMURATNA** **Sumura Maritime Trades Ltd** *Visakhapatnam* *India*	*343* - 243	Class: (NV) (IR)	**1989-07 Goriki Zosensho — Ise** Yd No: 877 Loa 42.30 Br ex - Dght 3.050 Lbp 37.00 Br md 7.50 Dpth 3.40 Welded, 1 dk	**(B12D2FR) Fishery Research Vessel** Ins: 330	**1 oil engine** driving 1 FP propeller Total Power: 625kW (850hp) Yanmar M200-EN 1 x 4 Stroke 6 Cy. 200 x 260 625kW (850bhp) Yanmar Diesel Engine Co Ltd-Japan AuxGen: 2 x 144kW 220V 50Hz a.c
8740292 *YB2094* -	**SUMUT I** **Government of The Republic of Indonesia (Direktorat Jenderal Perhubungan Darat - Ministry of Land Communications)** - *Belawan* *Indonesia*	**183** 55 -	Class: KI	**2009-06 PT Bayu Bahari Sentosa — Jakarta** Loa 32.00 Br ex - Dght 2.000 Lbp 27.00 Br md 8.00 Dpth 2.50 Welded, 1 dk	**(A35D2RL) Landing Craft**	**2 oil engines** driving 2 Propellers Total Power: 514kW (698hp) Yanmar 6HA2M-HTE 2 x 4 Stroke 6 Cy. 130 x 165 each-257kW (349bhp) Yanmar Diesel Engine Co Ltd-Japan
9612480 - -	**SUMUT II** **Government of The Republic of Indonesia (Direktorat Jenderal Perhubungan Darat - Ministry of Land Communications)** - *Belawan* *Indonesia*	**246** 74 -	Class: (KI)	**2010-02 PT Bayu Bahari Sentosa — Jakarta** Loa 32.00 Br ex - Dght 2.000 Lbp 27.00 Br md 8.00 Dpth 2.50 Welded, 1 dk	**(A35D2RL) Landing Craft** Bow ramp (centre)	**2 oil engines** reduction geared to sc. shafts driving 2 Propellers Total Power: 736kW (1,000hp) Yanmar 6HYM-ETE 2 x 4 Stroke 6 Cy. 133 x 165 each-368kW (500bhp) Yanmar Diesel Engine Co Ltd-Japan AuxGen: 2 x 43kW 380V a.c

9663233 *3FBC3* -	**SUN** *ex* Aeolian Sun *-2013* **Louros Maritime Inc** Araxos Maritime Inc *Panama* *Panama* MMSI: 354265000 Official number: 45060PEXT	**36,353** 21,605 63,672	Class: LR ✠ **100A1** SS 11/2013 bulk carrier CSR BC-A GRAB (20) Nos. 2 & 4 holds may be empty ESP **ShipRight** (ACS (B). CM) *IWS LI ✠ **LMC** **UMS** Cable: 660.0/78.0 U3 (a)	**2013-11 Jinling Shipyard — Nanjing JS** Yd No: JLZ9110415 Loa 199.90 (BB) Br ex 32.32 Dght 13.300 Lbp 194.50 Br md 32.26 Dpth 18.50 Welded, 1 dk	**(A21A2BC) Bulk Carrier** Grain: 78,500; Bale: 73,680 Compartments: 5 Ho, ER 5 Ha: ER Cranes: 4x36t	**1 oil engine** driving 1 FP propeller Total Power: 11,900kW (16,179hp) 14.2kn MAN-B&W 5S60ME-C8 1 x 2 Stroke 5 Cy. 600 x 2400 11900kW (16179bhp) Hudong Heavy Machinery Co Ltd-China AuxGen: 3 x 665kW 450V 60Hz a.c Boilers: AuxB (Comp) 7.4kgf/cm^2 (7.3bar)
8843434 - -	**SUN ACE** *ex* New Princess *-2003* *ex* Kaifuku Maru No. 2 *-1991* - -	**496** 236 695	Class: GM (KR)	**1976 Shin Nippon Jukogyo K.K. — Osakikamijima** Loa 52.50 Br ex - Dght 3.320 Lbp 48.00 Br md 8.40 Dpth 5.00 Welded, 1 dk	**(A31A2GX) General Cargo Ship**	**1 oil engine** driving 1 FP propeller Total Power: 588kW (799hp) Matsui 1 x 4 Stroke 588kW (799bhp) Matsui Iron Works Co Ltd-Japan
8623597 *HQWA9* -	**SUN ANGEL** *ex* Sri Mewah VI *-2001* **Ahmad Pamy Bin Abdul Malik** - *San Lorenzo* *Honduras* Official number: L-1327749	**158** 81 184	Class: (NK)	**1979 Sin Chin Seng Shipyard — Singapore** Loa 34.90 Br ex - Dght 1.659 Lbp 32.69 Br md 6.80 Dpth 2.32 Welded, 1 dk	**(A13B2TU) Tanker (unspecified)**	**1 oil engine** geared to sc. shaft driving 1 FP propeller Total Power: 312kW (424hp) 10.0kn Deutz SBA8M816 1 x 4 Stroke 8 Cy. 142 x 160 312kW (424bhp) Kloeckner Humboldt Deutz AG-West Germany
9349942 *C6WM7* -	**SUN ARROWS** **Maple LNG Transport Inc** Mitsui OSK Lines Ltd (MOL) *Nassau* *Bahamas* MMSI: 309296000 Official number: 8001409	**20,620** 6,186 11,142	Class: NK	**2007-11 Kawasaki Shipbuilding Corp — Sakaide KG** Yd No: 1593 Loa 151.00 (BB) Br ex - Dght 7.629 Lbp 140.00 Br md 28.00 Dpth 16.00 Welded, 1 dk	**(A11A2TN) LNG Tanker** Double Hull Liq (Gas): 19,531 4 x Gas Tank (s); 3 independent Kvaerner-Moss (alu) sph , ER 6 Cargo Pump (s) Ice Capable	**1 Steam Turb** reduction geared to sc. shaft driving 1 CP propeller Total Power: 8,830kW (12,005hp) 18.1kn Kawasaki UA-120 1 x steam Turb 8830kW (12005shp) Kawasaki Heavy Industries Ltd-Japan AuxGen: 3 x 1000kW a.c Fuel: 1923.0
9123348 *D8BY* -	**SUN ASTER** *ex* Ratih *-2013* *ex* Oriental Lily *-2004* **Inficess Shipping Co Ltd** - *Jeju* *South Korea* MMSI: 441972000 Official number: JJR-131035	**5,979** 3,254 10,329 T/cm 19.6	Class: KR (NK)	**1996-04 Asakawa Zosen K.K. — Imabari** Yd No: 391 Loa 125.00 (BB) Br ex 18.82 Dght 7.764 Lbp 117.00 Br md 18.80 Dpth 9.90 Welded, 1 dk	**(A12B2TR) Chemical/Products Tanker** Double Hull (13F) Liq: 11,341; Liq (Oil): 11,341 Cargo Heating Coils Compartments: 4 Ta, 14 Wing Ta, 2 Wing Slop Ta, ER 18 Cargo Pump (s): 4x300m^3/hr, 2x200m^3/hr, 12x150m^3/hr Manifold: Bow/CM: 62.5m	**1 oil engine** driving 1 FP propeller Total Power: 3,884kW (5,281hp) 13.5kn B&W 6L35MC 1 x 2 Stroke 6 Cy. 350 x 1050 3884kW (5281bhp) Hitachi Zosen Corp-Japan AuxGen: 2 x 450kW 450V 60Hz a.c Thrusters: 1 Thwart. CP thruster (f) Fuel: 99.0 (d.f.) (Part Heating Coils) 586.0 (r.f.) 18.0pd
9415636 *V2FS5* -	**SUN BIRD** *launched as* Vechtetal *-2009* **H&P ms 'Combi Dock' Betriebs GmbH & Co KG** Harren & Partner Ship Management GmbH & Co KG SatCom: Inmarsat C 430578110 *Saint John's* *Antigua & Barbuda* MMSI: 305781000 Official number: 4917	**3,199** 1,403 4,409	Class: GL	**2009-05 Shipyard ATG Giurgiu Srl — Giurgiu** (Hull) **2009-05 Bodewes' Scheepswerven B.V. — Hoogezand** Yd No: 690 Loa 89.96 (BB) Br ex - Dght 5.250 Lbp 84.98 Br md 15.20 Dpth 6.90 Welded, 1 dk	**(A31A2GX) General Cargo Ship** Grain: 6,392 TEU 218 Compartments: 1 Ho, ER 1 Ha: ER (61.5 x 12.7) Cranes: 2x36t Ice Capable	**1 oil engine** reduction geared to sc. shaft driving 1 CP propeller Total Power: 1,850kW (2,515hp) 12.0kn MaK 6M25 1 x 4 Stroke 6 Cy. 255 x 400 1850kW (2515bhp) Caterpillar Motoren GmbH & Co. KG-Germany AuxGen: 1 x 424kW 400V a.c, 1 x 348kW 400V a.c Thrusters: 1 Tunnel thruster
9073256 *9MQA7* -	**SUN BIRDIE** *ex* Tenwa Maru *-2002* **Teguh Samudera Sdn Bhd** - *Port Klang* *Malaysia* MMSI: 533130045 Official number: 334475	**742** 325 1,138 T/cm 5.0	Class: BV (NK)	**1993-09 Fujishin Zosen K.K. — Kamo** Yd No: 582 Loa 65.52 (BB) Br ex - Dght 4.030 Lbp 60.30 Br md 10.00 Dpth 4.40 Welded, 1 dk	**(A12A2TC) Chemical Tanker** Double Hull Liq: 1,204 Compartments: 10 Wing Ta, ER 2 Cargo Pump (s): 2x300m^3/hr Manifold: Bow/CM: 31m	**1 oil engine** with clutches & reverse geared to sc. shaft driving 1 FP propeller Total Power: 1,029kW (1,399hp) 10.5kn Akasaka K28R 1 x 4 Stroke 6 Cy. 280 x 480 1029kW (1399bhp) Akasaka Tekkosho KK (Akasaka DieselLtd)-Japan AuxGen: 2 x 120kW 440/100V 60Hz a.c Fuel: 20.0 (d.f.) 55.0 (r.f.)
9601261 *HPMZ* -	**SUN BLUESPIRE** **Duck Marine SA, Marujyu Marine Co Ltd & Yoshichu Transportation Co Ltd** Pacific Ship Management Co Ltd SatCom: Inmarsat C 437118110 *Panama* *Panama* MMSI: 371181000 Official number: 4241411A	**8,718** 3,926 12,318 T/cm 20.0	Class: NK	**2011-01 Higaki Zosen K.K. — Imabari** Yd No: 650 Loa 116.94 (BB) Br ex - Dght 9.120 Lbp 109.01 Br md 19.60 Dpth 14.00 Welded, 1 dk	**(A31A2GX) General Cargo Ship** Grain: 17,256; Bale: 16,023 Compartments: 2 Ho, 2 Tw Dk, ER 2 Ha: (28.5 x 15.0)ER (27.0 x 15.0) Cranes: 2x30.7t	**1 oil engine** driving 1 FP propeller Total Power: 3,900kW (5,302hp) 13.4kn MAN-B&W 6L35MC 1 x 2 Stroke 6 Cy. 350 x 1050 3900kW (5302bhp) The Hanshin Diesel Works Ltd-Japan Fuel: 789.0 (r.f.)
9444211 *3WQR* -	**SUN BRIGHT** **Viethan Shipping & Trading Co Ltd** - SatCom: Inmarsat C 457448710 *Haiphong* *Vietnam* MMSI: 574487000	**4,341** 2,660 7,080	Class: VR	**2007-10 Vinacoal Shipbuilding Co — Ha Long** Yd No: HT-126 Loa 105.67 Br ex - Dght 6.800 Lbp 98.50 Br md 16.80 Dpth 8.80 Welded, 1 dk	**(A31A2GX) General Cargo Ship** Compartments: 2 Ho, ER 2 Ha: ER 2 (28.0 x 10.0) Cranes: 3x9t	**1 oil engine** geared to sc. shaft driving 1 FP propeller Total Power: 2,206kW (2,999hp) 12.5kn Chinese Std. Type G8300ZC 1 x 4 Stroke 8 Cy. 300 x 380 2206kW (2999bhp) Wuxi Antai Power Machinery Co Ltd-China AuxGen: 3 x 152kW 400V a.c
8994453 *WTM3609* -	**SUN COAST** *ex* Dixie Warrior *-2002* **Sun Coast LC** Dann Marine Towing LC *Wilmington, DE* *United States of America* MMSI: 367029870 Official number: 299565	**145** 98 -		**1965-01 Main Iron Works, Inc. — Houma, La** Yd No: 146 Loa 26.00 Br ex - Dght - Lbp - Br md 8.26 Dpth 2.74 Welded, 1 dk	**(B32A2ST) Tug**	**2 oil engines** reduction geared to sc. shafts driving 2 Propellers Total Power: 2,648kW (3,600hp) Caterpillar D398 2 x Vee 4 Stroke 12 Cy. 159 x 203 each-1324kW (1800bhp) Caterpillar Tractor Co-USA
8711021 *3EE06* -	**SUN CROWN** **Oceanic Enterprise Ltd** Ocean Grow International Shipmanagement Consultant Corp *Panama* *Panama* MMSI: 355909000 Official number: 1761288F	**1,292** 525 1,999 T/cm 7.3	Class: (NK)	**1987-12 Murakami Hide Zosen K.K. — Imabari** Yd No: 275 Loa 75.32 Br ex 12.02 Dght 4.734 Lbp 70.01 Br md 12.01 Dpth 5.41 Welded, 1 dk	**(A12A2TC) Chemical Tanker** Liq: 1,969 Manifold: Bow/CM: 39m	**1 oil engine** driving 1 FP propeller Total Power: 1,324kW (1,800hp) 11.5kn Akasaka A31 1 x 4 Stroke 6 Cy. 310 x 600 1324kW (1800bhp) Akasaka Tekkosho KK (Akasaka DieselLtd)-Japan AuxGen: 3 x 106kW Fuel: 160.0 (r.f.)
9116852 *DURA9* -	**SUN CRUISER II** *ex* Flying Emerald *-2002* *ex* White Dolphin II *-1996* **Sole Cruises Inc** Magsaysay Maritime Corp *Manila* *Philippines* Official number: 00-0000863	**200** 20 50	Class: BV	**1995-03 Fast Craft International Pty Ltd — Fremantle WA** Yd No: 003 Loa 26.00 Br ex 9.00 Dght 1.100 Lbp 23.32 Br md 8.70 Dpth 1.95 Welded, 1 dk	**(A37B2PS) Passenger Ship** Hull Material: Aluminium Alloy Passengers: unberthed: 300	**2 oil engines** with flexible couplings & sr geared to sc. shafts driving 2 FP propellers Total Power: 1,940kW (2,638hp) 27.0kn Wartsila UD23V12M5D 2 x Vee 4 Stroke 12 Cy. 142 x 166 each-970kW (1319bhp) Wartsila SACM Diesel SA-France AuxGen: 2 x 37kW a.c Fuel: 6.0 (d.f.) 6.6pd
8401731 *9LY2650* -	**SUN CRYSTAL** *ex* Yong Sheng *-2014* *ex* Sea Walrus *-2013* *ex* Sang Thai Heaven *-2000* *ex* Wymarine *-1994* **YH Marine Co Ltd** - *Freetown* *Sierra Leone* MMSI: 667038000 Official number: SL103350	**4,365** 2,112 5,040	Class: (NK)	**1984-05 Hakata Zosen K.K. — Imabari** Yd No: 302 Loa 97.22 Br ex - Dght 5.810 Lbp 89.50 Br md 18.20 Dpth 9.00 Welded, 2 dks	**(A31A2GX) General Cargo Ship** Grain: 9,622; Bale: 8,950 Compartments: 2 Ho, ER 2 Ha: (16.8 x 11.2) (33.6 x 11.2)ER Derricks: 3x25t	**1 oil engine** driving 1 FP propeller Total Power: 2,059kW (2,799hp) 10.0kn Hanshin 6EL38 1 x 4 Stroke 6 Cy. 380 x 760 2059kW (2799bhp) The Hanshin Diesel Works Ltd-Japan AuxGen: 2 x 132kW Fuel: 460.0 (r.f.)
9477749 *D8CF* -	**SUN DAISY** *ex* Beech 1 *-2013* *ex* Weymouth *-2011* *ex* CF Weymouth *-2010* **Wonwoo Shipping Co Ltd** - *Jeju* *South Korea* MMSI: 441978000 Official number: JJR-131072	**4,570** 1,871 5,500	Class: KR (BV)	**2008-11 Zhejiang Fanshun Shipbuilding Industry Co Ltd — Yueqing ZJ** Yd No: FS1003 Loa 102.70 (BB) Br ex - Dght 6.500 Lbp 95.00 Br md 17.80 Dpth 8.80 Welded, 1 dk	**(A13B2TP) Products Tanker** Double Hull (13F) Liq: 6,860; Liq (Oil): 6,860 Cargo Heating Coils Compartments: 10 Wing Ta, 2 Wing Slop Ta, ER 3 Cargo Pump (s): 2x750m^3/hr, 1x300m^3/hr	**1 oil engine** reduction geared to sc. shaft driving 1 CP propeller Total Power: 2,620kW (3,562hp) 11.7kn Hyundai Himsen 9H25/33P 1 x 4 Stroke 9 Cy. 250 x 330 2620kW (3562bhp) Hyundai Heavy Industries Co Ltd-South Korea AuxGen: 2 x 400kW a.c, 1 x 400kW a.c Thrusters: 1 Tunnel thruster (f) Fuel: 182.0 (r.f.)

8949965 *V3TD5* -	**SUN DANCER II** *ex* Ranger V *-1996* **Sun Dancer (Belize) Ltd** - *Belize City* *Belize* MMSI: 312881000 Official number: 019610642	**371** 118 -		**1974 Robert E Derecktor Inc — Mamaroneck NY** Converted From: Diving Support Vessel-2009 Loa 42.06 Br ex - Dght - Lbp - Br md 7.62 Dpth 3.44 Welded, 1 dk	**(X11A2YP) Yacht** Hull Material: Aluminium Alloy Passengers: driver berths: 20	**1 oil engine** driving 1 FP propeller Total Power: 1,618kW (2,200hp) 12.0kn General Motors 1 x 1618kW (2200bhp) General Motors Detroit DieselAllison Divn-USA
9409508 *3FLE*	**SUN DIANA** **Shokuyu Navigation Co SA** Sun Technomarine Co Ltd SatCom: Inmarsat C 435515413 *Panama* *Panama* MMSI: 355154000 Official number: 38970TJ	**7,215** 3,829 12,906 T/cm 21.1	Class: NK	**2009-06 Usuki Shipyard Co Ltd — Usuki OT** Yd No: 1716 Loa 121.52 (BB) Br ex 20.62 Dght 8.814 Lbp 115.00 Br md 20.60 Dpth 11.30 Welded, 1 dk	**(A12B2TR) Chemical/Products Tanker** Double Hull (13F) Liq: 12,742; Liq (Oil): 12,742 Cargo Heating Coils Compartments: 16 Wing Ta, 1 Slop Ta, ER 16 Cargo Pump (s): 16x200m³/hr Manifold: Bow/CM: 63.8m	**1 oil engine** driving 1 FP propeller Total Power: 4,635kW (6,302hp) 14.2kn Mitsubishi 6UEC37LSII 1 x 2 Stroke 6 Cy. 370 x 1290 4635kW (6302bhp) Akasaka Tekkosho KK (Akasaka DieselLtd)-Japan AuxGen: 2 x 450kW a.c Thrusters: 1 Tunnel thruster (f) Fuel: 93.0 (d.f.) 727.0 (r.f.)
7529067 *V3TC9* -	**SUN ESSEX** *ex* Lucas *-2012* *ex* Susanne A *-2007* *ex* Big *-2002* *ex* Sun Essex *-2000* **Sovlot BV** - *Belize City* *Belize* MMSI: 312540000 Official number: 141310275	**227** 83 175	Class: IV (LR) ✠ Classed LR until 15/1/13	**1977-07 R. Dunston (Hessle) Ltd. — Hessle** Yd No: H910 Loa 32.92 Br ex 9.61 Dght 4.172 Lbp 29.01 Br md 9.15 Dpth 4.91 Welded, 1 dk	**(B32A2ST) Tug**	**1 oil engine** dr geared to sc. shaft driving 1 CP propeller Total Power: 1,522kW (2,069hp) 12.0kn Ruston 12RKCM 1 x Vee 4 Stroke 12 Cy. 254 x 305 1522kW (2069bhp) Ruston Paxman Diesels Ltd.-Colchester AuxGen: 3 x 127kW 440V 50Hz a.c Thrusters: 1 Tunnel thruster (f) Fuel: 92.0 (d.f.)
9242572 *V2OE7* -	**SUN EXPRESS** *ex* Conmar Cape *-2012* *ex* Magellan Star *-2012* *ex* Judith Borchard *-2009* *ex* Gracechurch Star *-2008* *launched as* Pioneer Albatros *-2002* **Schiffahrtsgesellschaft Conmar Cape mbH & Co KG** Conmar Shipping GmbH & Co KG *Saint John's* *Antigua & Barbuda* MMSI: 304408000 Official number: 2626	**6,277** 3,249 7,933	Class: GL	**2002-05 J.J. Sietas KG Schiffswerft GmbH & Co. — Hamburg** (Aft & pt cargo sections) Yd No: 1195 **2002-05 Daewoo-Mangalia Heavy Industries S.A. — Mangalia** (Fwd & pt cargo sections) Yd No: 4021 Loa 133.53 (BB) Br ex 18.95 Dght 7.240 Lbp 125.30 Br md 18.70 Dpth 9.30 Welded, 1 dk	**(A33A2CC) Container Ship (Fully Cellular)** TEU 735 incl 104 ref C. Compartments: 4 Cell Ho, ER 4 Ha: ER	**1 oil engine** with flexible couplings & sr gearedto sc. shaft driving 1 CP propeller Total Power: 7,200kW (9,789hp) 18.3kn MaK 8M43 1 x 4 Stroke 8 Cy. 430 x 610 7200kW (9789bhp) Caterpillar Motoren GmbH & Co. KG-Germany Thrusters: 1 Thwart. CP thruster (f)
7633181 *JVKA4*	**SUN FLORA** *ex* Rich River *-2008* *ex* King Luck *-2003* *ex* Ya Mei *-2003* *ex* Ao Xiang *-2001* *ex* Pyrgos Star *-1994* *ex* Pyrgos *-1993* *ex* Markinch *-1987* **Sun Flora Shipping SA** Chinaland Shipping Pte Ltd *Ulaanbaatar* *Mongolia* MMSI: 457392000 Official number: 28471192	**2,134** 1,200 3,186	Class: UB (LR) (CC) ✠ Classed LR until 18/6/94	**1978-01 Appledore Shipbuilders Ltd — Bideford** Yd No: A.S.119 Loa 91.52 (BB) Br ex 13.31 Dght 5.157 Lbp 84.92 Br md 13.25 Dpth 6.33 Welded, 1 dk	**(A31A2GX) General Cargo Ship** Grain: 4,029; Bale: 3,659 TEU 60 C.Ho 36/20' C.Dk 24/20' Compartments: 1 Ho, ER 2 Ha: 2 (22.8 x 9.3)ER Ice Capable	**1 oil engine** reverse reduction geared to sc. shaft driving 1 FP propeller Total Power: 1,795kW (2,440hp) 13.0kn Blackstone ESL16MK2 1 x Vee 4 Stroke 16 Cy. 222 x 292 1795kW (2440bhp) Mirrlees Blackstone (Stamford)Ltd.-Stamford AuxGen: 3 x 88kW 415V 50Hz a.c Fuel: 34.0 (d.f.) 172.0 (r.f.)
9113264 *D9QT* -	**SUN FLOWER** **Dae A Express Shipping Co Ltd** - *Pohang* *South Korea* MMSI: 440400310 Official number: PHR-956064	**2,394** 640 174	Class: KR (NV)	**1995-07 Incat Tasmania Pty Ltd — Hobart TAS** Yd No: 037 Loa 79.18 Br ex - Dght 2.156 Lbp 71.00 Br md 19.00 Dpth 5.65 Welded, 1 dk	**(A36A2PR) Passenger/Ro-Ro Ship (Vehicles)** Hull Material: Aluminium Alloy Passengers: unberthed: 769 Cars: 32	**4 oil engines** geared to sc. shafts driving 4 Water jets Total Power: 21,680kW (29,476hp) Caterpillar 3616TA 4 x Vee 4 Stroke 16 Cy. 280 x 300 each-5420kW (7369bhp) Caterpillar Inc-USA
9125932 *DSJA2*	**SUN FLOWER 2** *ex* Orange 2 *-2012* *ex* High Speed 1 *-2011* *ex* Captain George *-1997* **Dae A Express Shipping Co Ltd** - *Pohang* *South Korea* MMSI: 440159000 Official number: PHR-111034	**4,480** 1,344 1,500	Class: KR (RI) (NV)	**1996-04 Schelde Scheepsnieuwbouw B.V. — Vlissingen** Yd No: 379 Loa 77.60 Br ex 22.15 Dght 3.159 Lbp 68.80 Br md 21.75 Dpth 7.20 Welded, 1 dk	**(A36A2PR) Passenger/Ro-Ro Ship (Vehicles)** Hull Material: Aluminium Alloy Passengers: unberthed: 726 Stern door/ramp Lane-Len: 160 Cars: 152	**4 oil engines** geared to sc. shafts driving 2 Water jets Total Power: 22,800kW (31,000hp) 33.0kn Caterpillar 3616TA 4 x Vee 4 Stroke 16 Cy. 280 x 300 each-5700kW (7750bhp) Caterpillar Inc-USA AuxGen: 4 x 169kW 220/380V 50Hz a.c Fuel: 78.0 (d.f.)
8513871 *DSPI5*	**SUN FLOWER 7** *ex* Ji Sung *-2006* *ex* Fukushio *-1999* *ex* Fukushio Maru *-1993* **Ji Sung Shipping Co Ltd** - *Jeju* *South Korea* MMSI: 441034000 Official number: JJR-079662	**3,244** 1,593 3,962	Class: KR (NK)	**1986-01 Kochi Jyuko (Eiho Zosen) K.K. — Kochi** Yd No: 1868 Loa 92.23 (BB) Br ex - Dght 6.568 Lbp 85.02 Br md 16.20 Dpth 6.85 Welded, 1 dk, 2nd & 3rd dks in holds	**(A34A2GR) Refrigerated Cargo Ship** Ins: 4,518 Compartments: 3 Ho, ER 3 Ha: 3 (5.0 x 5.0)ER Derricks: 6x5t	**1 oil engine** driving 1 FP propeller Total Power: 2,427kW (3,300hp) 13.6kn Hanshin 6EL40 1 x 4 Stroke 6 Cy. 400 x 800 2427kW (3300bhp) The Hanshin Diesel Works Ltd-Japan AuxGen: 2 x 480kW a.c
9162174 *JI3646* -	**SUN FLOWER COBALT** **Ferry Sunflower Ltd** - *Osaka, Osaka* *Japan* MMSI: 431300775 Official number: 135943	*9,245* - 3,648		**1998-03 Mitsubishi Heavy Industries Ltd. — Shimonoseki** Yd No: 1037 Loa 153.00 (BB) Br ex 26.63 Dght 5.450 Lbp 140.00 Br md 25.00 Dpth 16.47 Welded, 2 dks. 1 hoistable	**(A36A2PR) Passenger/Ro-Ro Ship (Vehicles)** Passengers: unberthed: 325; cabins: 97; berths: 382; driver berths: 70 Bow door & ramp Len: 12.40 Wid: 6.80 Swl: - Quarter stern door/ramp (p) Len: 18.00 Wid: 6.40 Swl: - Quarter stern door/ramp (s) Len: 18.00 Wid: 6.40 Swl: - Lane-Len: 1620 Lane-Wid: 5.00 Lane-clr ht: 4.40 Lorries: 120, Cars: 100	**2 oil engines** with flexible couplings & sr gearedto sc. shafts driving 2 CP propellers Total Power: 19,860kW (27,002hp) 22.5kn Pielstick 18PC2-6V-400 2 x Vee 4 Stroke 18 Cy. 400 x 460 each-9930kW (13501bhp) Nippon Kokan KK (NKK Corp)-Japan AuxGen: 2 x 1200kW 440V 50Hz a.c, 2 x 1200kW 440V 60Hz a.c Thrusters: 1 Thwart. CP thruster (f); 1 Tunnel thruster (a) Fuel: 51.8 (d.f.) 843.6 (r.f.) 74.6pd
9236705 *JM6684* -	**SUN FLOWER DAISETSU** *ex* New Rainbow Love *-2007* **Tsugarukaikyo Ferry Co Ltd** MOL Ferry Co Ltd *Oarai, Ibaraki* *Japan* MMSI: 431602067 Official number: 136432	*11,401* - 6,277	Class: (NK)	**2001-06 Mitsubishi Heavy Industries Ltd. — Shimonoseki** Yd No: 1079 Loa 190.00 (BB) Br ex - Dght 6.872 Lbp 175.00 Br md 26.40 Dpth 20.50 Welded, 4 dks	**(A36A2PR) Passenger/Ro-Ro Ship (Vehicles)** Passengers: unberthed: 600; berths: 70; driver berths: 70 Stern door/ramp Len: 9.00 Wid: 6.00 Swl: - Quarter bow door/ramp (s) Len: 23.00 Wid: 6.50 Swl: - Quarter stern door/ramp (s) Len: 26.00 Wid: 6.50 Swl: - Lane-Len: 2010 Cars: 62, Trailers: 161	**2 oil engines** reduction geared to sc. shafts driving 2 CP propellers Total Power: 29,160kW (39,646hp) 25.0kn Pielstick 12PC4-2V-570 2 x Vee 4 Stroke 12 Cy. 570 x 620 each-14580kW (19823bhp) Nippon Kokan KK (NKK Corp)-Japan AuxGen: 2 x 1020kW a.c Thrusters: 2 Thwart. FP thruster (f); 1 Tunnel thruster (a) Fuel: 700.0 (d.f.) 103.4pd
9061590 *JD2705* -	**SUN FLOWER FURANO** *ex* Hestia *-2007* **MOL Ferry Co Ltd** - *Oarai, Ibaraki* *Japan* MMSI: 431800070 Official number: 128510	*13,539* 6,730 6,805	Class: (NK)	**1993-11 Mitsubishi Heavy Industries Ltd. — Shimonoseki** Yd No: 979 Loa 192.00 (BB) Br ex 27.03 Dght 6.716 Lbp 175.00 Br md 27.00 Dpth 9.95 Welded, 4 dks	**(A36A2PR) Passenger/Ro-Ro Ship (Vehicles)** Passengers: unberthed: 391; cabins: 88; berths: 252; driver berths: 60 Stern door/ramp Side door/ramp (s. f.) Quarter stern door/ramp (s) Lane-Len: 1750 Lorries: 154, Cars: 77	**2 oil engines** with flexible couplings & sr geared to sc. shafts driving 2 CP propellers Total Power: 26,186kW (35,602hp) 24.0kn Pielstick 12PC4-2V-570 2 x Vee 4 Stroke 12 Cy. 570 x 620 each-13093kW (17801bhp) Nippon Kokan KK (NKK Corp)-Japan AuxGen: 2 x 1250kW a.c, 3 x 1020kW a.c Thrusters: 2 Thwart. CP thruster (f); 1 Tunnel thruster (a)
9162162 *JI3634* -	**SUN FLOWER IVORY** **Ferry Sunflower Ltd** - *Osaka, Osaka* *Japan* MMSI: 431300686 Official number: 135933	*9,245* - 3,648 T/cm 28.8		**1997-11 Mitsubishi Heavy Industries Ltd. — Shimonoseki** Yd No: 1036 Loa 153.00 (BB) Br ex 25.03 Dght 5.450 Lbp 140.00 Br md 25.00 Dpth 16.47 Welded, 2 dks	**(A36A2PR) Passenger/Ro-Ro Ship (Vehicles)** Passengers: unberthed: 325; cabins: 97; berths: 382; driver berths: 70 Bow door & ramp Len: 12.40 Wid: 6.80 Swl: - Quarter stern door/ramp (p) Len: 18.00 Wid: 6.40 Swl: - Quarter stern door/ramp (s) Len: 18.00 Wid: 6.40 Swl: - Lane-Len: 1020 Lorries: 120, Cars: 100	**2 oil engines** with flexible couplings & sr gearedto sc. shafts driving 2 CP propellers Total Power: 19,860kW (27,002hp) 22.4kn Pielstick 18PC2-6V-400 2 x Vee 4 Stroke 18 Cy. 400 x 460 each-9930kW (13501bhp) Nippon Kokan KK (NKK Corp)-Japan AuxGen: 2 x 1200kW 450V 50Hz a.c, 2 x 1200kW 450V 60Hz a.c Thrusters: 1 Thwart. CP thruster (f); 1 Tunnel thruster (a) Fuel: 500.0 (d.f.) 72.5pd

LR/IMO No. / Call sign	Name / Owner / Flag	Tonnage	Class	Builder / Dimensions	Type / Capacity	Machinery
9035125 *JG5213* -	**SUN FLOWER KIRISHIMA** - **Ferry Sunflower Ltd** - *Tokyo* *Japan* MMSI: 431586000 Official number: 133868	*12,418* - 5,790		**1993-08 Mitsubishi Heavy Industries Ltd. — Shimonoseki** Yd No: 965 Loa 186.00 (BB) Br ex 27.51 Dght 6.600 Lbp 170.00 Br md 25.50 Dpth 14.90 Welded, 2 dks	**(A36A2PR) Passenger/Ro-Ro Ship (Vehicles)** Passengers: 484 Quarter bow door/ramp (s) Len: 22.50 Wid: 6.00 Swl: - Quarter stern door/ramp (s) Len: 20.50 Wid: 6.00 Swl: - Lane-Len: 1020 Lane-clr ht: 5.25 Lorries: 175, Vehicles: 140	**2 oil engines** with flexible couplings & sr geared to sc. shafts driving 2 CP propellers Total Power: 25,156kW (34,202hp) 23.0kn Pielstick 12PC4-2V-570 2 x Vee 4 Stroke 12 Cy. 570 x 620 each-12578kW (17101bhp) Nippon Kokan KK (NKK Corp)-Japan Thrusters: 1 Thwart. FP thruster (f); 1 Tunnel thruster (a)
9184574 *JD2739* -	**SUN FLOWER SAPPORO** *ex Varuna -2005* **MOL Ferry Co Ltd** - *Oarai, Ibaraki* *Japan* MMSI: 431800850 Official number: 128520	*13,654* - 6,511	Class: (NK)	**1998-10 Mitsubishi Heavy Industries Ltd. — Shimonoseki** Yd No: 1056 Loa 192.00 Br ex - Dght 6.716 Lbp 175.00 Br md 27.00 Dpth 9.90 Welded, 1 dk	**(A36A2PR) Passenger/Ro-Ro Ship (Vehicles)** Passengers: unberthed: 630 Lane-Len: 1600 Lorries: 154, Cars: 77	**2 oil engines** reduction geared to sc. shafts driving 2 FP propellers Total Power: 26,186kW (35,602hp) 24.0kn Pielstick 12PC4-2V-570 2 x Vee 4 Stroke 12 Cy. 570 x 620 each-13093kW (17801bhp) Nippon Kokan KK (NKK Corp)-Japan
9035113 *JG5189* -	**SUN FLOWER SATSUMA** - **Ferry Sunflower Ltd** - *Tokyo* *Japan* MMSI: 431319000 Official number: 133835	*12,415* - 5,814		**1993-03 Mitsubishi Heavy Industries Ltd. — Shimonoseki** Yd No: 964 Loa 186.00 (BB) Br ex - Dght 6.600 Lbp 170.00 Br md 25.50 Dpth 14.90 Welded, 2 dks	**(A36A2PR) Passenger/Ro-Ro Ship (Vehicles)** Passengers: 1051 Quarter bow door/ramp (s) Len: 22.50 Wid: 6.00 Swl: - Quarter stern door/ramp (s) Len: 20.50 Wid: 6.00 Swl: - Lane-Len: 2208 Lane-clr ht: 5.25 Lorries: 175, Vehicles: 140	**2 oil engines** with flexible couplings & sr geared to sc. shafts driving 2 CP propellers Total Power: 25,156kW (34,202hp) 22.9kn Pielstick 12PC4-2V-570 2 x Vee 4 Stroke 12 Cy. 570 x 620 each-12578kW (17101bhp) Nippon Kokan KK (NKK Corp)-Japan AuxGen: 3 x 1230kW 450V 60Hz a.c Thrusters: 1 Thwart. CP thruster (f); 1 Tunnel thruster (a) Fuel: 144.0 (d.f.) 606.0 (r.f.) 87.9pd
9236717 *JM6685* -	**SUN FLOWER SHIRETOKO** *ex New Rainbow Bell -2007* **MOL Ferry Co Ltd** - *Oarai, Ibaraki* *Japan* MMSI: 431602076 Official number: 136852	*11,410* - 6,277	Class: (NK)	**2001-09 Mitsubishi Heavy Industries Ltd. — Shimonoseki** Yd No: 1080 Loa 190.00 (BB) Br ex - Dght 6.872 Lbp 175.00 Br md 26.40 Dpth 20.50 Welded	**(A36A2PR) Passenger/Ro-Ro Ship (Vehicles)** Passengers: unberthed: 600; berths: 70; driver berths: 70 Stern door/ramp Len: 9.00 Wid: 6.00 Swl: - Quarter bow door/ramp (s) Len: 23.00 Wid: 6.50 Swl: - Quarter stern door/ramp (s) Len: 26.00 Wid: 6.50 Swl: - Lane-Len: 2010 Cars: 62, Trailers: 161	**2 oil engines** reduction geared to sc. shafts driving 2 FP propellers Total Power: 29,160kW (39,646hp) 25.0kn Pielstick 12PC4-2V-570 2 x Vee 4 Stroke 12 Cy. 570 x 620 each-14580kW (19823bhp) Nippon Kokan KK (NKK Corp)-Japan AuxGen: 2 x 1020kW a.c Thrusters: 2 Thwart. FP thruster (f); 1 Tunnel thruster (a) Fuel: 700.0 (d.f.) 103.4pd
9356775 *DSMD3* -	**SUN FORTUNE** - **KDB Capital Corp** Seok Chang Maritime Co Ltd *Jeju* *South Korea* MMSI: 441942000 Official number: JJR-111007	**1,997** 1,106 2,846	Class: KR (CC)	**2005-10 Qingdao Hyundai Shipbuilding Co Ltd — Jiaonan SD** Yd No: 119 Loa 79.99 Br ex - Dght 5.200 Lbp 74.00 Br md 13.60 Dpth 7.00 Welded, 1 dk	**(A21A2BC) Bulk Carrier** Grain: 4,127; Bale: 3,893 Compartments: 1 Ho, ER 1 Ha: ER (38.4 x 10.0) Ice Capable	**1 oil engine** geared to sc. shaft driving 1 FP propeller Total Power: 1,080kW (1,468hp) 11.7kn MAN-B&W 8L23/30 1 x 4 Stroke 8 Cy. 225 x 300 1080kW (1468bhp) Zhenjiang Marine Diesel Works-China AuxGen: 3 x 90kW 100V
8036043 - -	**SUN FOX** *ex Lamnalco Fox -2000* **Albwardy Marine Engineering LLC** - *Dubai* *United Arab Emirates* Official number: 4700	*393* 36 140	Class: (BV)	**1978-07 Deltawerf BV — Sliedrecht** Yd No: 198 Loa - Br ex - Dght 1.830 Lbp 24.50 Br md 6.86 Dpth 3.00 Welded, 1 dk	**(A31A2GX) General Cargo Ship**	**2 oil engines** driving 2 FP propellers Total Power: 536kW (728hp) 10.0kn Caterpillar 3408TA 2 x Vee 4 Stroke 8 Cy. 137 x 152 each-268kW (364bhp) Caterpillar Tractor Co-USA
9312353 *H8DH* -	**SUN FUTURE** - **KN Shipping SA** Noma Shipping Co Ltd (Noma Kaiun KK) *Panama* *Panama* MMSI: 356717000 Official number: 3006904B	**6,002** 3,163 9,430	Class: NK	**2004-06 Nishi Shipbuilding Co Ltd — Imabari EH** Yd No: 439 Loa 97.61 Br ex - Dght 9.200 Lbp 89.95 Br md 18.80 Dpth 13.00 Welded, 1 dk	**(A31A2GX) General Cargo Ship** Grain: 12,106; Bale: 11,372 Cranes: 2x30.7t; Derricks: 1x30t	**1 oil engine** driving 1 FP propeller Total Power: 3,398kW (4,620hp) 13.3kn Mitsubishi 6UEC33LSII 1 x 2 Stroke 6 Cy. 330 x 1050 3398kW (4620bhp) Mitsubishi Heavy Industries Ltd-Japan Fuel: 635.0
9172753 *D7LT* -	**SUN GAS** *ex Karin Kosan -2012 ex Jia Long -2011* *ex Karin Kosan -2008 ex Sun Gas -2004* **Myung Shin Shipping Co Ltd** - *Ulsan* *South Korea* MMSI: 441891000 Official number: USR-124811	**3,392** 1,018 3,318 T/cm 12.3	Class: KR (NK) (CC)	**1998-04 Shitanoe Shipbuilding Co Ltd — Usuki OT** Yd No: 1196 Loa 95.97 (BB) Br ex 16.03 Dght 5.113 Lbp 88.10 Br md 16.00 Dpth 7.10 Welded, 1 dk	**(A11B2TG) LPG Tanker** Double Bottom Entire Compartment Length Liq (Gas): 3,514 2 x Gas Tank (s); 2 independent (C.mn.stl) 2 Cargo Pump (s): 2x300m³/hr Manifold: Bow/CM: 43.8m	**1 oil engine** driving 1 FP propeller Total Power: 2,700kW (3,671hp) 13.0kn Mitsubishi 5UEC33LSII 1 x 2 Stroke 5 Cy. 330 x 1050 2700kW (3671bhp) Akasaka Tekkosho KK (Akasaka DieselLtd)-Japan AuxGen: 2 x 400kW 450V a.c Fuel: 88.0 (d.f.) 413.0
9386316 *9H9453* -	**SUN GLIDER II** *ex Isa 120.02 -2006* **Eurocommerce Sun Glider Ltd** - *Valletta* *Malta* Official number: 9386316	**235** 70 -	Class: RI	**2006-07 ISA Produzione Srl — Ancona** Yd No: 120.02 Loa 36.45 Br ex - Dght 1.460 Lbp 30.00 Br md 7.40 Dpth 3.67 Bonded, 1 dk	**(X11A2YP) Yacht** Hull Material: Reinforced Plastic	**3 oil engines** reduction geared to sc. shafts driving 3 FP propellers Total Power: 4,413kW (6,000hp) M.T.U. 16V2000M91 3 x Vee 4 Stroke 16 Cy. 130 x 150 each-1471kW (2000bhp) MTU Friedrichshafen GmbH-Friedrichshafen
9340506 *9HA2857* -	**SUN GLOBE** *ex Lowlands Patrasche -2011* **Longevity Maritime Ltd** Globus Shipmanagement Corp *Valletta* *Malta* MMSI: 256415000 Official number: 9340506	**32,387** 19,450 58,790 T/cm 57.4	Class: BV (AB)	**2007-08 Tsuneishi Heavy Industries (Cebu) Inc — Balamban** Yd No: SC-075 Loa 189.99 (BB) Br ex - Dght 12.800 Lbp 185.75 Br md 32.26 Dpth 18.00 Welded, 1 dk	**(A21A2BC) Bulk Carrier** Grain: 72,358; Bale: 70,120 Compartments: 5 Ho, ER 5 Ha: ER Cranes: 4x30t	**1 oil engine** driving 1 FP propeller Total Power: 8,396kW (11,415hp) 14.5kn MAN-B&W 6S50MC-C 1 x 2 Stroke 6 Cy. 500 x 2000 8396kW (11415bhp) Mitsui Engineering & Shipbuilding CLtd-Japan AuxGen: 3 x 480kW 440/220V 60Hz a.c Fuel: 162.6 (d.f.) 2195.1 (r.f.)
9232307 *DSPC8* -	**SUN GLORY** *ex Southern Odyssey -2007* **Sun Ace Shipping Co Ltd** - *Jeju* *South Korea* MMSI: 440833000 Official number: JJR-079301	**4,438** 2,588 7,362	Class: KR (NK)	**2000-06 Hakata Zosen K.K. — Imabari** Yd No: 621 Loa 100.78 Br ex - Dght 7.164 Lbp 94.00 Br md 18.50 Dpth 9.00 Welded, 1 dk	**(A31A2GX) General Cargo Ship** Grain: 8,676; Bale: 8,132 Compartments: 2 Ho, ER 2 Ha: (20.3 x 10.0) (35.0 x 10.0)ER Cranes: 3x30t	**1 oil engine** driving 1 FP propeller Total Power: 3,089kW (4,200hp) 12.5kn Mitsubishi 6UEC37LA 1 x 2 Stroke 6 Cy. 370 x 880 3089kW (4200bhp) Akasaka Tekkosho KK (Akasaka DieselLtd)-Japan AuxGen: 2 x 240kW 110/440V 60Hz a.c Fuel: 110.5 (d.f.) (Heating Coils) 380.9 (r.f.) 10.0pd
9254276 *HOBT* -	**SUN GRACE** - **Pana Star Line SA** Noma Shipping Co Ltd (Noma Kaiun KK) *Panama* *Panama* MMSI: 353058000 Official number: 2852402B	**6,381** 3,658 10,090	Class: NK	**2002-04 Shin Kurushima Dockyard Co. Ltd. — Hashihama, Imabari** Yd No: 5152 Loa 100.60 Br ex - Dght 9.219 Lbp 93.50 Br md 18.80 Dpth 13.00 Welded, 2 dks	**(A31A2GX) General Cargo Ship** Grain: 13,999; Bale: 12,858 Cranes: 2x30.7t; Derricks: 1x30t	**1 oil engine** driving 1 FP propeller Total Power: 3,250kW (4,419hp) 12.5kn B&W 5L35MC 1 x 2 Stroke 5 Cy. 350 x 1050 3250kW (4419bhp) Makita Corp-Japan Fuel: 700.0
7624348 - -	**SUN H** *ex Sun-S -2013 ex Sun -2007 ex Valiant -2003* **Seven Hill Marine Trade Ltd** ES Deniz Tasimaciligi Ticaret Ltd Sti *Port Vila* *Vanuatu* MMSI: 577144000 Official number: 2207	**1,839** 1,114 3,064	Class: BR (BV)	**1977-09 Scheepsbouw- en Reparatiebedrijf Gebr. Sander B.V. — Delfzijl** Yd No: 275 Loa 80.40 Br ex 13.64 Dght 5.536 Lbp 73.51 Br md 13.42 Dpth 6.74 Welded, 1 dk	**(A31A2GX) General Cargo Ship** Grain: 3,964; Bale: 3,800 Compartments: 2 Ho, ER 2 Ha: (13.7 x 7.3) (25.0 x 9.5)ER	**1 oil engine** driving 1 FP propeller Total Power: 1,103kW (1,500hp) 12.0kn Brons 16GV-A 1 x Vee 2 Stroke 16 Cy. 220 x 380 1103kW (1500bhp) NV Appingedammer Bronsmotorenfabrie-Netherlands AuxGen: 2 x 31kW 220/380V 50Hz a.c Fuel: 120.0 (d.f.)
7373822 *DTBV8* -	**SUN HAE NO. 315** *ex Oryong No. 56 -2009* *ex Haeng Bok No. 501 -1993* **Sun Hae Fisheries Co Ltd** - *Busan* *South Korea* MMSI: 441562000 Official number: 9505010-6210003	*443* 220 510	Class: (KR)	**1974-02 Mie Shipyard Co. Ltd. — Yokkaichi** Yd No: 106 Loa 55.66 Br ex - Dght 3.733 Lbp 49.00 Br md 9.00 Dpth 4.02 Welded, 1 dk	**(B11B2FV) Fishing Vessel** Ins: 568	**1 oil engine** driving 1 FP propeller Total Power: 1,103kW (1,500hp) 12.1kn Akasaka AH30 1 x 4 Stroke 6 Cy. 300 x 480 1103kW (1500bhp) Akasaka Tekkosho KK (Akasaka DieselLtd)-Japan AuxGen: 2 x 180kW 225V a.c

9312365 *H8OL* -	**SUN HAPPINESS** **Pana Star Line SA** Yokohama Marine & Merchant Corp *Panama* *Panama* MMSI: 352962000 Official number: 3016704C	**6,002** 3,163 9,423	Class: NK	**2004-09 Nishi Shipbuilding Co Ltd — Imabari EH** Yd No: 440 Loa 97.61 Br ex - Dght 9.200 Lbp 89.95 Br md 18.80 Dpth 13.00 Welded, 1 dk	**(A31A2GX) General Cargo Ship** Grain: 12,106; Bale: 11,372 Cranes: 2x30.7t; Derricks: 1x30t	**1 oil engine** driving 1 Propeller Total Power: 3,400kW (4,623hp) 13.3kn Mitsubishi 6UEC33LSII 1 x 2 Stroke 6 Cy. 330 x 1050 3400kW (4623bhp) Akasaka Tekkosho KK (Akasaka DieselLtd)-Japan Fuel: 635.0
8884452 - -	**SUN HING NO. 8** **Sun Kong Petroleum Co Ltd** - *Hong Kong* *Hong Kong* Official number: HK-0183	**233** 81 260	Class: CC	**1994 Lingnan Shipyard — Guangzhou GD** Loa 35.00 Br ex - Dght 2.450 Lbp 33.30 Br md 7.40 Dpth 2.96 Welded, 1 dk	**(A13B2TP) Products Tanker**	**2 oil engines** geared to sc. shafts driving 2 FP propellers Total Power: 232kW (316hp) 9.1kn Chinese Std. Type 6160A 2 x 4 Stroke 6 Cy. 160 x 225 each-116kW (158bhp) Weifang Diesel Engine Factory-China AuxGen: 2 x 24kW 400V a.c
9175896 *3FSA7* -	**SUN HOPE** **Shokuyu Navigation Co SA** ST Marine Co Ltd *Panama* *Panama* MMSI: 351575000 Official number: 2503297C	**2,170** 861 3,345 T/cm 13.0	Class: NK	**1997-09 Hitachi Zosen Mukaishima Marine Co Ltd — Onomichi HS** Yd No: 116 Loa 89.50 (BB) Br ex - Dght 5.494 Lbp 83.30 Br md 14.00 Dpth 6.50 Welded, 1 dk	**(A12B2TR) Chemical/Products Tanker** Double Bottom Entire Compartment Length Liq: 2,903; Liq (Oil): 3,150 Compartments: 8 Wing Ta, ER 2 Cargo Pump (s): 2x400m³/hr Manifold: Bow/CM: 43.6m	**1 oil engine** driving 1 FP propeller Total Power: 2,060kW (2,801hp) 12.5kn Akasaka A38 1 x 4 Stroke 6 Cy. 380 x 740 2060kW (2801bhp) Akasaka Tekkosho KK (Akasaka DieselLtd)-Japan Fuel: 52.0 (d.f.) 194.0 (r.f.)
5404835 *D7DR* -	**SUN HWA No. 1** *ex Hanyo Maru -1979* **Kum Dan Mining Industrial Co Ltd** - *Incheon* *South Korea* Official number: ICR-630014	*179* 31 88	Class: (KR)	**1963 Shin Yamamoto Shipbuilding & Engineering Co Ltd — Kochi KC** Yd No: 20 Loa 27.59 Br ex 7.83 Dght 2.591 Lbp 25.00 Br md 7.80 Dpth 3.61 Riveted\Welded, 1 dk	**(B32A2ST) Tug**	**2 oil engines** driving 2 FP propellers Total Power: 1,176kW (1,598hp) 12.0kn Fuji 6MD34E 2 x 4 Stroke 6 Cy. 340 x 470 each-588kW (799bhp) Fuji Diesel Co Ltd-Japan AuxGen: 1 x 20kW 220V a.c Fuel: 40.5 0.5pd
8413667 *6LBL* -	**SUN IL No. 102** **Choi Yang-Jae** - *Busan* *South Korea* Official number: BS-A-2124	*109* 60 -		**1984-02 Sun-Il Shipbuilding Co Ltd — Geoje** Yd No: 102 Loa 35.72 Br ex 5.72 Dght 2.301 Lbp 30.64 Br md 5.71 Dpth 2.72 Welded, 1 dk	**(B11B2FV) Fishing Vessel** Ins: 117	**1 oil engine** with clutches, flexible couplings & reverse reduction geared to sc. shaft driving 1 FP propeller Total Power: 441kW (600hp) Niigata 6M22EGT 1 x 4 Stroke 6 Cy. 220 x 380 441kW (600bhp) Ssangyong Heavy Industries Co Ltd-South Korea
8413679 *6LBK* -	**SUN IL No. 103** **Choi Uk-Sung** - *Busan* *South Korea* Official number: BS-A-2125	*109* 60 -		**1984-02 Sun-Il Shipbuilding Co Ltd — Geoje** Yd No: 103 Loa 35.72 Br ex 5.72 Dght 2.301 Lbp 30.64 Br md 5.71 Dpth 2.72 Welded, 1 dk	**(B11B2FV) Fishing Vessel** Ins: 117	**1 oil engine** with clutches, flexible couplings & reverse reduction geared to sc. shaft driving 1 FP propeller Total Power: 441kW (600hp) Niigata 6M22EGT 1 x 4 Stroke 6 Cy. 220 x 380 441kW (600bhp) Ssangyong Heavy Industries Co Ltd-South Korea
9207857 *DSRE4* -	**SUN IRIS** *ex Chemical Celeste -2011* *ex Panam Celeste -2009* **Inficess Shipping Co Ltd** - *Jeju* *South Korea* MMSI: 441800000 Official number: JJR-111047	**5,994** 3,253 10,226 T/cm 19.6	Class: KR (NK)	**1999-09 Asakawa Zosen K.K. — Imabari** Yd No: 411 Loa 125.00 (BB) Br ex 18.82 Dght 7.764 Lbp 117.00 Br md 18.80 Dpth 9.90 Welded, 1 dk	**(A12B2TR) Chemical/Products Tanker** Double Hull (13F) Liq: 11,322; Liq (Oil): 11,554 Cargo Heating Coils Compartments: 5 Ta (s.stl), 16 Wing Ta (s.stl), ER 21 Cargo Pump (s): 7x300m³/hr, 14x150m³/hr Manifold: Bow/CM: 63.2m	**1 oil engine** driving 1 FP propeller Total Power: 3,884kW (5,281hp) 13.5kn B&W 6L35MC 1 x 2 Stroke 6 Cy. 350 x 1050 3884kW (5281bhp) Hitachi Zosen Corp-Japan AuxGen: 2 x 450kW 450V 60Hz a.c Thrusters: 1 Thwart. FP thruster (f) Fuel: 99.0 (d.f.) 585.0 (r.f.) 16.0pd
9342243 *3EGN3* -	**SUN ISLAND** **Pana Star Line SA** Noma Shipping Co Ltd (Noma Kaiun KK) *Panama* *Panama* MMSI: 356048000 Official number: 3217206	**7,104** 3,878 10,959	Class: NK	**2006-11 Bach Dang Shipyard — Haiphong** Yd No: H-136 Loa 111.75 Br ex 18.83 Dght 9.214 Lbp 99.75 Br md 18.80 Dpth 13.00 Welded, 2 dks	**(A31A2GX) General Cargo Ship** Grain: 14,540; Bale: 13,662 Cranes: 1x60t,2x30.7t; Derricks: 1x30t	**1 oil engine** driving 1 FP propeller Total Power: 3,398kW (4,620hp) 12.0kn Mitsubishi 6UEC33LSII 1 x 2 Stroke 6 Cy. 330 x 1050 3398kW (4620bhp) Akasaka Tekkosho KK (Akasaka DieselLtd)-Japan Fuel: 600.0
9473511 *3EPJ6* -	**SUN JEWELRY** **Ocean VIP SA** Miyamoto Kisen KK *Panama* *Panama* MMSI: 353983000 Official number: 3373808A	**7,727** 2,819 9,045	Class: NK	**2008-03 Kanasashi Heavy Industries Co Ltd — Shizuoka SZ** Yd No: 8205 Loa 104.83 Br ex 20.02 Dght 8.220 Lbp 96.00 Br md 20.00 Dpth 13.80 Welded, 1 dk	**(A31A2GX) General Cargo Ship** Grain: 15,738; Bale: 14,865 Compartments: 2 Ho, ER 2 Ha: ER Cranes: 2x30.7t	**1 oil engine** driving 1 FP propeller Total Power: 3,309kW (4,499hp) 13.5kn Hanshin LH46LA 1 x 4 Stroke 6 Cy. 460 x 880 3309kW (4499bhp) The Hanshin Diesel Works Ltd-Japan AuxGen: 2 x 268kW 440V 50Hz a.c Fuel: 810.0
8912235 - -	**SUN JIANG** *ex Ta Kang No. 6 -2004* **Ta Kang Petroleum Products Co Ltd** - *Hong Kong* *Hong Kong* Official number: 711303	**253** 105 442 T/cm 2.5		**1989-01 Fai Wong Engineering Co. — Hong Kong** Loa 33.52 Br ex - Dght 2.720 Lbp 31.25 Br md 8.25 Dpth 3.36 Welded, 1 dk	**(A13B2TP) Products Tanker** Liq: 454; Liq (Oil): 454 Compartments: 6 Ta, ER	**2 oil engines** sr geared to sc. shaft driving 2 FP propellers Total Power: 448kW (610hp) 10.0kn Cummins NT-855-M 2 x 4 Stroke 6 Cy. 140 x 152 each-224kW (305bhp) Cummins Brasil Ltda-Brazil AuxGen: 1 x 13kW 220V 60Hz a.c
9182394 *DSQB5* -	**SUN JIN** *ex Sea Dream -2008 ex Ocean Dream -2005* **Sun Ace Shipping Co Ltd** - *Jeju* *South Korea* MMSI: 441518000 Official number: JJR-088528	**4,380** 2,709 6,502	Class: KR (NK)	**1998-04 Watanabe Zosen KK — Imabari EH** Yd No: 307 Loa 100.79 Br ex - Dght 6.829 Lbp 92.70 Br md 17.20 Dpth 9.00 Welded, 1 dk	**(A31A2GX) General Cargo Ship** Grain: 9,386; Bale: 8,404 Compartments: 2 Ho, ER 2 Ha: (27.3 x 10.2) (28.0 x 10.2)ER Cranes: 2x25.5t; Derricks: 2x15t	**1 oil engine** driving 1 FP propeller Total Power: 2,795kW (3,800hp) 12.5kn Mitsubishi 6UEC37LA 1 x 2 Stroke 6 Cy. 370 x 880 2795kW (3800bhp) Akasaka Tekkosho KK (Akasaka DieselLtd)-Japan
8629802 *D9RT* -	**SUN JIN No. 1** **Sunjin Consolidated Co Ltd** - *Ulsan* *South Korea* MMSI: 440127990 Official number: USR-878050	**146** - -	Class: KR	**1987-10 Inchon Engineering & Shipbuilding Corp — Incheon** Yd No: 136 Loa 29.08 Br ex - Dght - Lbp 27.56 Br md 8.60 Dpth 3.80 Welded, 1 dk	**(B32A2ST) Tug**	**2 oil engines** geared to sc. shafts driving 2 Z propellers Total Power: 1,912kW (2,600hp) 12.5kn Pielstick 6PA5 2 x 4 Stroke 6 Cy. 255 x 270 each-956kW (1300bhp) Ssangyong Heavy Industries Co Ltd-South Korea AuxGen: 1 x 64kW 225V a.c
9126936 *DSAZ6* -	**SUN JIN No. 2** **Sunjin Consolidated Co Ltd** - *Ulsan* *South Korea* MMSI: 440102098 Official number: USR-957730	**126** - 67	Class: KR	**1995-05 Kyeong-In Engineering & Shipbuilding Co Ltd — Incheon** Yd No: 535 Loa 28.72 Br ex - Dght 2.712 Lbp 24.00 Br md 8.00 Dpth 3.50 Welded, 1 dk	**(B32A2ST) Tug**	**2 oil engines** gearing integral to driving 2 Z propellers Total Power: 2,066kW (2,808hp) 12.0kn Cummins KTA-50-M 2 x Vee 4 Stroke 16 Cy. 159 x 159 each-1033kW (1404bhp) Cummins Engine Co Ltd-United Kingdom AuxGen: 2 x 95kW 220V 60Hz a.c Fuel: 45.0 (d.f.) 2.2pd
9230567 - -	**SUN JIN No. 3** **Sunjin Consolidated Co Ltd** - *Ulsan* *South Korea* MMSI: 440100580 Official number: USR-008293	**124** - 81	Class: KR	**2000-04 Samkwang Shipbuilding & Engineering Co Ltd — Incheon** Yd No: 99-04 Loa 28.00 Br ex 8.15 Dght - Lbp 24.20 Br md 8.00 Dpth 3.60 Welded, 1 dk	**(B32A2ST) Tug**	**2 oil engines** with clutches, flexible couplings & sr geared to sc. shafts driving 2 Z propellers Total Power: 1,764kW (2,398hp) 12.0kn Niigata 6L22HX 2 x 4 Stroke 6 Cy. 220 x 280 each-882kW (1199bhp) Niigata Engineering Co Ltd-Japan AuxGen: 2 x 208kW 225V a.c
9322360 - -	**SUN JIN NO. 7** **Sunjin Consolidated Co Ltd** - *Ulsan* *South Korea* MMSI: 440108240 Official number: USR-048239	**192** - -	Class: KR	**2004-05 Namyang Shipbuilding Co Ltd — Yeosu** Yd No: 1072 Loa 33.50 Br ex - Dght 3.100 Lbp 28.00 Br md 9.20 Dpth 4.00 Welded, 1 dk	**(B32A2ST) Tug**	**2 oil engines** geared to sc. shafts driving 2 Z propellers Total Power: 2,400kW (3,264hp) Hyundai Himsen 6H21/32P 2 x 4 Stroke 6 Cy. 210 x 320 each-1200kW (1632bhp) Hyundai Heavy Industries Co Ltd-South Korea
7354527 *D9HC* -	**SUN JIN No. 7** *ex Mikawa Maru -1981* **Sunjin Consolidated Co Ltd** - *Ulsan* *South Korea* Official number: USR-738044	*272* 93 109	Class: (KR)	**1974-01 Ishikawajima Ship & Chemical Plant Co Ltd — Tokyo** Yd No: 457 Loa 32.85 Br ex 9.53 Dght 3.175 Lbp 26.50 Br md 9.50 Dpth 4.30 Welded, 1 dk	**(B32A2ST) Tug**	**2 oil engines** geared to sc. shafts driving 2 FP propellers Total Power: 2,354kW (3,200hp) 13.3kn Fuji 6L27.5X 2 x 4 Stroke 6 Cy. 275 x 320 each-1177kW (1600bhp) Fuji Diesel Co Ltd-Japan AuxGen: 2 x 60kW 445V a.c

IMO / Call sign	Name / Owner	Tonnage	Class	Construction	Type	Machinery
9181247 - -	**SUN JIN NO. 8** *ex* Hae Kwang No. 5 *-2005* *ex* Fuji *-2001* **Sunjin Consolidated Co Ltd** - *Ulsan* *South Korea* MMSI: 440126810 Official number: USR-018237	*108* - -	Class: KR	**1997-03 Hatayama Zosen KK — Yura WK** Yd No: 225 Loa 28.77 Br ex - Dght - Lbp 24.50 Br md 7.30 Dpth 3.34 Welded, 1 dk	**(B32A2ST) Tug**	**2 oil engines** driving 2 Z propellers Total Power: 956kW (1,300hp) 11.6kn Yanmar M200-SN 2 x 4 Stroke 6 Cy. 200 x 260 each-478kW (650bhp) Yanmar Diesel Engine Co Ltd-Japan
8325963 *D9HL* -	**SUN JIN No. 9** **Sunjin Consolidated Co Ltd** - *Ulsan* *South Korea* MMSI: 440145590 Official number: USR-828212	*162* 44 62	Class: KR	**1983-03 Donghae Shipbuilding Co Ltd — Ulsan** Yd No: 8236 Loa 27.26 Br ex 8.16 Dght 2.601 Lbp 26.01 Br md 8.01 Dpth 3.51 Welded, 1 dk	**(B32A2ST) Tug**	**2 oil engines** with clutches, flexible couplings & dr geared to sc. shafts driving 2 Z propellers Total Power: 1,176kW (1,598hp) 11.6kn Niigata 6L20CX 2 x 4 Stroke 6 Cy. 200 x 260 each-588kW (799bhp) Ssangyong Heavy Industries Co Ltd-South Korea AuxGen: 2 x 40kW 225V a.c
7530377 *D7YB* -	**SUN JIN No. 12** *ex* Masuei Maru No. 35 *-1985* **Sunjin Consolidated Co Ltd** - *Ulsan* *South Korea* MMSI: 440126780 Official number: USR-768085	**149** - 122	Class: KR	**1976-03 Kanagawa Zosen — Kobe** Yd No: 164 Loa - Br ex 8.64 Dght 2.601 Lbp 25.48 Br md 8.62 Dpth 3.81 Welded, 1 dk	**(B32A2ST) Tug**	**2 oil engines** driving 2 Z propellers Total Power: 1,912kW (2,600hp) 12.8kn Niigata 6L25BX 2 x 4 Stroke 6 Cy. 250 x 320 each-956kW (1300bhp) Niigata Engineering Co Ltd-Japan AuxGen: 2 x 112kW 445V a.c
8210168 *D8WG* -	**SUN JIN No. 202** *ex* Masuei Maru No. 27 *-1989* **Sunjin Consolidated Co Ltd** - *Ulsan* *South Korea* MMSI: 440107930 Official number: USR-897786	**153** - 117	Class: KR	**1982-07 Kanagawa Zosen — Kobe** Yd No: 239 Loa 30.31 Br ex - Dght 2.721 Lbp 26.01 Br md 8.81 Dpth 3.71 Welded, 1 dk	**(B32A2ST) Tug**	**2 oil engines** sr geared to sc. shafts driving 2 Z propellers Total Power: 1,912kW (2,600hp) 13.2kn Niigata 6L25BX 2 x 4 Stroke 6 Cy. 250 x 320 each-956kW (1300bhp) Niigata Engineering Co Ltd-Japan
9080314 *DSAI4* -	**SUN JIN No. 303** **Sunjin Consolidated Co Ltd** - *Ulsan* *South Korea* MMSI: 440118970 Official number: USR-937802	**197** - 63	Class: KR	**1993-09 Dae Sun Shipbuilding & Engineering Co Ltd — Busan** Yd No: 401 Loa 28.72 Br ex - Dght - Lbp 25.42 Br md 8.00 Dpth 3.50 Welded, 1 dk	**(B32A2ST) Tug**	**2 oil engines** reduction geared to sc. shafts driving 2 Z propellers Total Power: 956kW (1,300hp) 11.4kn Niigata 6NSD-M 2 x 4 Stroke 6 Cy. 160 x 210 each-478kW (650bhp) Ssangyong Heavy Industries Co Ltd-South Korea AuxGen: 2 x 48kW 225V a.c
9080326 *DSAI3* -	**SUN JIN No. 505** **Sunjin Consolidated Co Ltd** - *Ulsan* *South Korea* MMSI: 440114010 Official number: USR-937810	**322** - 100	Class: KR	**1993-10 Dae Sun Shipbuilding & Engineering Co Ltd — Busan** Yd No: 402 Loa 35.58 Br ex - Dght - Lbp 31.61 Br md 9.40 Dpth 4.20 Welded, 1 dk	**(B32A2ST) Tug**	**2 oil engines** sr geared to sc. shafts driving 2 Z propellers Total Power: 2,648kW (3,600hp) 14.2kn Pielstick 6PA5L255 2 x 4 Stroke 6 Cy. 255 x 270 each-1324kW (1800bhp) Ssangyong Heavy Industries Co Ltd-South Korea AuxGen: 2 x 64kW 225V a.c
9380491 - -	**SUN JIN NO. 606** **Sunjin Consolidated Co Ltd** - *Ulsan* *South Korea* Official number: USR-058311	**275** - -	Class: KR	**2006-01 Namyang Shipbuilding Co Ltd — Yeosu** Yd No: 1075 Loa 37.30 Br ex - Dght 3.300 Lbp 31.15 Br md 10.00 Dpth 4.50 Welded, 1 dk	**(B32A2ST) Tug**	**2 oil engines** reduction geared to sc. shafts driving 2 Z propellers Total Power: 3,308kW (4,498hp) 13.0kn Niigata 6L28HX 2 x 4 Stroke 6 Cy. 280 x 370 each-1654kW (2249bhp) Niigata Engineering Co Ltd-Japan
9149550 - -	**SUN JIN No. 707** **Sunjin Consolidated Co Ltd** - *Ulsan* *South Korea* MMSI: 440117940 Official number: USR-967843	**197** - 119	Class: KR	**1996-05 Kyeong-In Engineering & Shipbuilding Co Ltd — Incheon** Yd No: 546 Loa 33.80 Br ex - Dght - Lbp 28.50 Br md 9.30 Dpth 4.15 Welded, 1 dk	**(B32A2ST) Tug**	**2 oil engines** with clutches, flexible couplings & dr geared to sc. shafts driving 2 Z propellers Total Power: 2,700kW (3,670hp) 13.4kn Caterpillar 3516TA 2 x Vee 4 Stroke 16 Cy. 170 x 190 each-1350kW (1835bhp) Caterpillar Inc-USA
9535474 *DSHP3* -	**SUN JIN NO. 801** **Sunjin Consolidated Co Ltd** - *Ulsan* *South Korea* MMSI: 440313260 Official number: USR-088260	**484** - -	Class: KR	**2008-09 Namyang Shipbuilding Co Ltd — Yeosu** Yd No: 1087 Loa 37.00 Br ex - Dght 3.400 Lbp 31.80 Br md 10.00 Dpth 4.50 Welded, 1 dk	**(B32A2ST) Tug**	**2 oil engines** reduction geared to sc. shafts driving 2 Z propellers Total Power: 3,310kW (4,500hp) Niigata 6L28HX 2 x 4 Stroke 6 Cy. 280 x 370 each-1655kW (2250bhp) Niigata Engineering Co Ltd-Japan
9583483 - -	**SUN JIN NO. 802** **Sunjin Consolidated Co Ltd** - *Ulsan* *South Korea* Official number: USR-098299	**166** - 85	Class: KR	**2009-12 Namyang Shipbuilding Co Ltd — Yeosu** Yd No: 1090 Loa 30.65 Br ex - Dght 2.912 Lbp 28.20 Br md 8.60 Dpth 3.80 Welded, 1 dk	**(B32A2ST) Tug**	**2 oil engines** reduction geared to sc. shafts driving 2 Z propellers Total Power: 1,568kW (2,132hp) 13.0kn Niigata 6L25HX 2 x 4 Stroke 6 Cy. 250 x 350 each-784kW (1066bhp) Niigata Engineering Co Ltd-Japan AuxGen: 2 x 52kW 440V a.c
9166340 *DSOC4* -	**SUN JIN No. 808** **Sunjin Consolidated Co Ltd** - *Ulsan* *South Korea* MMSI: 440513000 Official number: USR-978271	**263** 120 94	Class: KR	**1997-05 Kyeong-In Engineering & Shipbuilding Co Ltd — Incheon** Yd No: 158 Loa 37.30 Br ex - Dght 4.300 Lbp 33.55 Br md 10.60 Dpth 4.54 Welded, 1 dk	**(B32A2ST) Tug**	**2 oil engines** geared to sc. shafts driving 2 Z propellers Total Power: 3,178kW (4,320hp) 13.0kn Pielstick 8PA5L 2 x 4 Stroke 8 Cy. 255 x 270 each-1589kW (2160bhp) Ssangyong Heavy Industries Co Ltd-South Korea
9183960 *DSOJ7* -	**SUN JIN No. 909** **Sunjin Consolidated Co Ltd** - *Ulsan* *South Korea* MMSI: 440763000 Official number: USR-978388	*198* - 139	Class: KR	**1997-12 Kyeong-In Engineering & Shipbuilding Co Ltd — Incheon** Yd No: 161 Loa 33.80 Br ex - Dght - Lbp 28.50 Br md 9.30 Dpth 4.15 Welded, 1 dk	**(B32A2ST) Tug**	**2 oil engines** with clutches, flexible couplings & dr geared to sc. shafts driving 2 Z propellers Total Power: 2,646kW (3,598hp) 13.5kn Pielstick 6PA5 2 x 4 Stroke 6 Cy. 255 x 270 each-1323kW (1799bhp) Ssangyong Heavy Industries Co Ltd-South Korea AuxGen: 2 x 150kW 225V a.c
9044061 *DSBF2* -	**SUN JUNE** *ex* Tiger Hope *-2002* **Sun Ace Shipping Co Ltd** - *Jeju* *South Korea* MMSI: 440009000 Official number: JJR-002641	**4,233** 2,653 6,817	Class: KR	**1992-04 Daedong Shipbuilding Co Ltd — Busan** Yd No: 377 Loa 110.80 (BB) Br ex - Dght 6.891 Lbp 101.66 Br md 16.40 Dpth 8.55 Welded, 1 dk	**(A31A2GX) General Cargo Ship** Grain: 9,387; Bale: 8,518 Compartments: 2 Ho, ER 2 Ha: ER Derricks: 2x22t,2x20t	**1 oil engine** driving 1 FP propeller Total Power: 2,942kW (4,000hp) 15.3kn Akasaka A45 1 x 4 Stroke 6 Cy. 450 x 880 2942kW (4000bhp) Akasaka Tekkosho KK (Akasaka DieselLtd)-Japan AuxGen: 2 x 480kW 450V a.c
9249609 *H9TZ* -	**SUN JUPITER** **Shokuyu Navigation Co SA** Sun Technomarine Co Ltd *Panama* *Panama* MMSI: 353963000 Official number: 2832802CH	**5,359** 2,636 8,833 T/cm 18.3	Class: NK	**2002-01 Usuki Shipyard Co Ltd — Usuki OT** Yd No: 1672 Loa 112.00 (BB) Br ex 19.02 Dght 7.564 Lbp 105.00 Br md 19.00 Dpth 10.00 Welded, 1 dk	**(A12B2TR) Chemical/Products Tanker** Double Hull (13F) Liq: 9,224; Liq (Oil): 9,412 Cargo Heating Coils Compartments: 1 Ta, 14 Wing Ta, ER 15 Cargo Pump (s): 13x200m³/hr, 2x300m³/hr Manifold: Bow/CM: 43.5m	**1 oil engine** driving 1 FP propeller Total Power: 3,640kW (4,949hp) 13.5kn Mitsubishi 7UEC37LA 1 x 2 Stroke 7 Cy. 370 x 880 3640kW (4949bhp) Akasaka Tekkosho KK (Akasaka DieselLtd)-Japan AuxGen: 2 x 400kW a.c Thrusters: 1 Tunnel thruster (f) Fuel: 120.0 (d.f.) 579.0 (r.f.)
8913394 - -	**SUN KONG** - -	**202** 60 208		**1989-03 Guangzhou Zhujiang Shipyard — Guangzhou GD** Yd No: 8815 Loa - Br ex - Dght 2.401 Lbp 30.23 Br md 7.41 Dpth 2.98 Welded, 1 dk	**(A13B2TP) Products Tanker**	**2 oil engines** geared to sc. shafts driving 2 FP propellers Total Power: 328kW (446hp) 10.0kn Chinese Std. Type 6160A 2 x 4 Stroke 6 Cy. 160 x 225 each-164kW (223bhp) (made 1987) Weifang Diesel Engine Factory-China
8327923 *D7YX* -	**SUN KWANG No. 3** *ex* Sun Jin No. 1 *-1985* *ex* Ikuta Maru *-1973* **Sun Kwang Enterprises Co Ltd** - *Incheon* *South Korea* Official number: ICR-638021	*162* 40 92	Class: (KR)	**1963 Kurushima Dockyard Co. Ltd. — Imabari** Yd No: 156 Loa 28.48 Br ex - Dght - Lbp 26.09 Br md 8.01 Dpth 3.81 Welded, 1 dk	**(B32A2ST) Tug**	**2 oil engines** driving 2 FP propellers 12.5kn Hanshin Z6WS 2 x 4 Stroke 6 Cy. 350 x 500 The Hanshin Diesel Works Ltd-Japan AuxGen: 1 x 2kW 110V a.c

9405631 *3ETH2* -	**SUN LAUREL** - **Laurel Shipholding SA** VIKO Offshore & Marine Co Ltd *Panama* *Panama* MMSI: 370559000 Official number: 3463309A	**4,067** 1,821 5,741 T/cm 14.5	Class: KR	**2008-12 Dongbang Co Ltd — Samho** Yd No: 101 Loa 105.60 (BB) Br ex - Dght 6.613 Lbp 98.00 Br md 16.60 Dpth 8.60 Welded, 1 dk	**(A12B2TR) Chemical/Products Tanker** Double Hull (13F) Liq: 6,137; Liq (Oil): 6,137 Cargo Heating Coils Compartments: 10 Wing Ta 10 Cargo Pump (s): 10x200m^3/hr Manifold: Bow/CM: 45.3m	**1 oil engine** reduction geared to sc. shaft driving 1 FP propeller Total Power: 2,880kW (3,916hp) 13.2kn MaK 6M32C 1 x 4 Stroke 6 Cy. 320 x 480 2880kW (3916bhp) Caterpillar Motoren GmbH & Co. KG-Germany AuxGen: 3 x 500kW 450V a.c Thrusters: 1 Tunnel thruster Fuel: 64.0 (d.f.) 257.0 (r.f.)
9376438 *XUHA6* -	**SUN LIGHT** *ex Jinmao -2013 ex Hou Ri 18 -2010* *ex Outsailing 5 -2008* **Sun Marine Co Ltd** - *Phnom Penh* *Cambodia* MMSI: 515468000 Official number: 1305208	**1,972** 1,395 3,300	Class: UB (CC)	**2005-12 Zhejiang Hongxin Shipbuilding Co Ltd — Taizhou ZJ** Yd No: 0407 Loa 81.00 Br ex - Dght 5.500 Lbp 76.00 Br md 13.60 Dpth 6.80 Welded, 1 dk	**(A31A2GX) General Cargo Ship** Grain: 4,479; Bale: 4,390	**1 oil engine** reduction geared to sc. shaft driving 1 FP propeller Total Power: 1,324kW (1,800hp) 12.0kn Chinese Std. Type G6300ZC 1 x 4 Stroke 6 Cy. 300 x 380 1324kW (1800bhp) Wuxi Antai Power Machinery Co Ltd-China
7359125 *9LD2543* -	**SUN LIGHT** *ex Bewa -2013 ex Havso -1993* *ex Karin Bewa -1976* **Dania Marine Ltd** Unimed Navigation SA *Freetown* *Sierra Leone* MMSI: 667005243 Official number: SL105243	**1,920** 1,117 2,753	Class: (BV)	**1975-03 Orskov Christensens Staalskibsvaerft A/S — Frederikshavn** Yd No: 73 Lengthened-1979 Loa 79.91 Br ex 13.01 Dght 5.590 Lbp 74.00 Br md 13.00 Dpth 6.76 Welded, 2 dks	**(A31A2GX) General Cargo Ship** Grain: 4,106; Bale: 3,794 2 Ha: (25.9 x 8.5) (18.5 x 8.5)ER Cranes: 3x3t Ice Capable	**1 oil engine** reduction geared to sc. shaft driving 1 CP propeller Total Power: 1,100kW (1,496hp) 10.0kn MaK 6M332AK 1 x 4 Stroke 6 Cy. 240 x 330 1100kW (1496bhp) (new engine 1986) Krupp MaK Maschinenbau GmbH-Kiel AuxGen: 3 x 120kW 380V 50Hz a.c Fuel: 98.0 (d.f.)
9284714 *DSMA3* -	**SUN LILAC** *ex Sunrise Lilac -2010* **Inficess Shipping Co Ltd** - *Jeju* *South Korea* MMSI: 441939000 Official number: JJR-103461	**5,546** 2,589 8,629 T/cm 13.6	Class: KR (NK)	**2004-02 Shin Kurushima Dockyard Co. Ltd. — Hashihama, Imabari** Yd No: 5280 Loa 113.98 (BB) Br ex - Dght 7.478 Lbp 108.50 Br md 18.20 Dpth 9.75 Welded, 1 dk	**(A12A2TC) Chemical Tanker** Double Hull (13F) Liq: 7,495 Cargo Heating Coils Compartments: 14 Ta, ER, 2 Wing Slop Ta 14 Cargo Pump (s): 12x250m^3/hr, 2x150m^3/hr Manifold: Bow/CM: 58.2m	**1 oil engine** driving 1 FP propeller Total Power: 3,900kW (5,302hp) 14.2kn MAN-B&W 6L35MC 1 x 2 Stroke 6 Cy. 350 x 1050 3900kW (5302bhp) Makita Corp-Japan AuxGen: 3 x 560kW 450V 60Hz a.c Thrusters: 1 Tunnel thruster (f) Fuel: 77.0 (d.f.) 422.0 (r.f.)
9032410 - -	**SUN LINER** - **-** -	*149* - 87		**1991-04 Yokohama Yacht Co Ltd — Yokohama KN** Yd No: 892 Loa 34.05 (BB) Br ex - Dght 1.200 Lbp 30.00 Br md 6.40 Dpth 3.20 Welded, 1 dk	**(A37B2PS) Passenger Ship** Passengers: unberthed: 200	**2 oil engines** with clutches, flexible couplings & sr geared to sc. shafts driving 2 FP propellers Total Power: 2,412kW (3,280hp) G.M. (Detroit Diesel) 16V-149-TI 2 x Vee 2 Stroke 16 Cy. 146 x 146 each-1206kW (1640bhp) General Motors Detroit DieselAllison Divn-USA
9714408 *7JOG* -	**SUN LINER 2** - **Haboro Enika Ferry KK** - *Tomakomai, Hokkaido* *Japan* Official number: 141874	*122* - -		**2013-03 Sumidagawa Zosen K.K. — Tokyo** Loa 35.00 (BB) Br ex - Dght - Lbp - Br md 6.00 Dpth 2.70 Welded, 1 dk	**(A37B2PS) Passenger Ship** Passengers: unberthed: 130	**2 oil engines** reduction geared to sc. shafts driving 2 Propellers Total Power: 2,160kW (2,936hp) 23.0kn M.T.U. 12V2000M70 2 x Vee 4 Stroke 12 Cy. 130 x 150 each-1080kW (1468bhp) MTU Friedrichshafen GmbH-Friedrichshafen
9142033 - -	**SUN LIVE** *ex Hikari Maru No. 2 -2013* **Three Oceans Pte Ltd**	*141* - 373	Class: IO	**1996-03 Imura Zosen K.K. — Komatsushima** Yd No: 278 Loa 37.58 Br ex - Dght 3.100 Lbp 34.00 Br md 7.00 Dpth 3.40 Welded, 1 dk	**(A13B2TP) Products Tanker** Liq: 350; Liq (Oil): 350 Compartments: 6 Ta, ER	**1 oil engine** driving 1 FP propeller Total Power: 441kW (600hp) Sumiyoshi S23G 1 x 4 Stroke 6 Cy. 230 x 400 441kW (600bhp) Sumiyoshi Tekkosho-Japan
9626895 *3FEX4* -	**SUN LUCIA** - **Sun Lucia Maritime SA** STX Marine Service Co Ltd SatCom: Inmarsat C 437326510 *Panama* *Panama* MMSI: 373265000 Official number: 4384312	**33,057** 19,229 56,568 T/cm 58.8	Class: KR	**2012-04 Jiangsu Hantong Ship Heavy Industry Co Ltd — Tongzhou JS** Yd No: HT57-108 Loa 189.99 (BB) Br ex 32.66 Dght 12.818 Lbp 185.00 Br md 32.26 Dpth 18.00 Welded, 1 dk	**(A21A2BC) Bulk Carrier** Grain: 71,634; Bale: 68,200 Compartments: 5 Ho, ER 5 Ha: 4 (21.6 x 18.6)ER (19.2 x 18.6) Cranes: 4x36t	**1 oil engine** driving 1 FP propeller Total Power: 9,480kW (12,889hp) 14.2kn MAN-B&W 6S50MC-C 1 x 2 Stroke 6 Cy. 500 x 2000 9480kW (12889bhp) Hyundai Heavy Industries Co Ltd-South Korea
7629245 *CZ4548* -	**SUN MAIDEN** - **Gale Ventures Ltd** - *Victoria, BC* *Canada* MMSI: 316003459 Official number: 368895	*148* 76 -		**1974 Centre Shipyard Ltd — Victoria BC** L reg 22.74 Br ex 6.71 Dght - Lbp - Br md - Dpth 3.66 Welded, 1 dk	**(B11B2FV) Fishing Vessel**	**1 oil engine** driving 1 FP propeller Total Power: 416kW (566hp) 10.0kn Caterpillar D379SCAC 1 x Vee 4 Stroke 8 Cy. 159 x 203 416kW (566bhp) Caterpillar Tractor Co-USA
7221122 *D8OY* -	**SUN MANG No. 2** *ex Su Hyup No. 2 -1983* **Mackerel Purse-Seine Fishing Corp** - *Busan* *South Korea* Official number: BSR-686104	*177* 90 220	Class: (KR)	**1969 Busan Shipbuilding Co Ltd — Busan** Loa 32.92 Br ex 6.02 Dght 2.836 Lbp 29.49 Br md 6.00 Dpth 3.00 Welded, 1 dk	**(A13B2TU) Tanker (unspecified)** Liq: 278; Liq (Oil): 278	**1 oil engine** driving 1 FP propeller Total Power: 221kW (300hp) 10.5kn Niigata 6MG16HS 1 x 4 Stroke 6 Cy. 160 x 200 221kW (300bhp) Niigata Engineering Co Ltd-Japan AuxGen: 2 x 15kW 230V a.c
8816510 - -	**SUN MANG No. 88** - **Large Purse-Seiner Fish Cooperative** - *Busan* *South Korea* Official number: BSR-880097	**113** - 242	Class: (KR)	**1988-02 Jinhae Ship Construction Industrial Co Ltd — Changwon** Yd No: 8768 Loa 33.89 Br ex - Dght - Lbp 30.03 Br md 6.81 Dpth 3.13 Welded, 1 dk	**(A13B2TU) Tanker (unspecified)** Liq: 280; Liq (Oil): 280	**1 oil engine** driving 1 FP propeller Total Power: 441kW (600hp) 11.1kn Niigata 6L18CX 1 x 4 Stroke 6 Cy. 180 x 240 441kW (600bhp) Ssangyong Heavy Industries Co Ltd-South Korea AuxGen: 1 x 104kW 225V a.c
7513630 *HP6339* -	**SUN MARINE** *ex Hoshin Maru No. 3 -1991* *ex Sankyo Maru -1981* **Both Good Shipping Corp** - *Panama* *Panama* Official number: 20979SC	*199* 121 699		**1975-12 Kimura Zosen K.K. — Kure** Yd No: 60 Loa - Br ex 9.02 Dght 3.379 Lbp 53.98 Br md 9.00 Dpth 5.49 Welded, 1 dk	**(A31A2GX) General Cargo Ship**	**1 oil engine** driving 1 FP propeller Total Power: 809kW (1,100hp) Hanshin 1 x 4 Stroke 809kW (1100bhp) Hanshin Nainenki Kogyo-Japan
9460681 *V7VU6* -	**SUN MASTER** - **Ocean Cross Lines Corp** Kobe Shipmanagement Co Ltd SatCom: Inmarsat C 453836043 *Majuro* *Marshall Islands* MMSI: 538004216 Official number: 4216	**29,179** 15,527 50,714	Class: BV (NK)	**2011-02 Oshima Shipbuilding Co Ltd — Saikai NS** Yd No: 10618 Loa 182.98 (BB) Br ex - Dght 12.150 Lbp 179.30 Br md 32.26 Dpth 17.15 Welded, 1 dk	**(A21A2BC) Bulk Carrier** Double Hull Grain: 59,117; Bale: 58,700 Compartments: 5 Ho, ER 5 Ha: 4 (20.5 x 25.8)ER (14.8 x 19.8) Cranes: 4x30t	**1 oil engine** driving 1 FP propeller Total Power: 7,980kW (10,850hp) 14.5kn Mitsubishi 6UEC50LSII 1 x 2 Stroke 6 Cy. 500 x 1950 7980kW (10850bhp) Mitsubishi Heavy Industries Ltd-Japan AuxGen: 3 x 440kW 60Hz a.c
9291444 *HPWW* -	**SUN MERCURY** - **Shokuyu Navigation Co SA** Sun Technomarine Co Ltd *Panama* *Panama* MMSI: 356789000 Official number: 2971604B	**5,359** 2,637 8,817 T/cm 17.7	Class: NK	**2004-02 Usuki Shipyard Co Ltd — Usuki OT** Yd No: 1684 Loa 112.02 (BB) Br ex 19.02 Dght 7.564 Lbp 105.00 Br md 19.00 Dpth 10.00 Welded, 1 dk	**(A12A2TC) Chemical Tanker** Double Hull (13F) Liq: 9,236 Cargo Heating Coils Compartments: 1 Ta (s.stl), 2 Wing Slop Ta (s.stl), Wing ER, 14 Wing Ta (s.stl) 15 Cargo Pump (s): 2x300m^3/hr, 13x200m^3/hr Manifold: Bow/CM: 53m	**1 oil engine** driving 1 FP propeller Total Power: 3,640kW (4,949hp) 13.5kn Mitsubishi 7UEC37LA 1 x 2 Stroke 7 Cy. 370 x 880 3640kW (4949bhp) Akasaka Tekkosho KK (Akasaka DieselLtd)-Japan AuxGen: 2 x 485kW 440/110V 60Hz a.c Thrusters: 1 Thwart. CP thruster (f) Fuel: 110.4 (d.f.) 600.0 (r.f.) 15.0pd
9566239 *3FCH6* -	**SUN MERMAID** - **Mackerel Marine SA** Blue Marine Management Corp *Panama* *Panama* MMSI: 354817000 Official number: 4135910	**7,167** 3,131 10,463	Class: NK	**2010-02 Higaki Zosen K.K. — Imabari** Yd No: 637 Loa 108.50 Br ex - Dght 8.600 Lbp 99.80 Br md 19.60 Dpth 13.20 Welded, 1 dk	**(A31A2GX) General Cargo Ship** Grain: 15,011; Bale: 13,924 Cranes: 1x60t,2x30.7t	**1 oil engine** driving 1 FP propeller Total Power: 3,900kW (5,302hp) 13.1kn MAN-B&W 6L35MC 1 x 2 Stroke 6 Cy. 350 x 1050 3900kW (5302bhp) The Hanshin Diesel Works Ltd-Japan

9084188 - -	**SUN MOON** *ex* Hoei Maru No. 12 *-2013* *ex* Hosho Maru *-2008* **Three Oceans Pte Ltd** -	*199* - 536	Class: IZ	**1994-04 Koa Sangyo KK — Takamatsu KG** Yd No: 578 Loa 49.61 (BB) Br ex - Dght 3.119 Lbp 45.00 Br md 7.80 Dpth 3.30 Welded, 1 dk	**(A13B2TP) Products Tanker** Liq: 650; Liq (Oil): 650 Compartments: 6 Ta, ER	**1 oil engine** driving 1 FP propeller Total Power: 736kW (1,001hp) Yanmar MF26-ST 1 x 4 Stroke 6 Cy. 260 x 500 736kW (1001bhp) Yanmar Diesel Engine Co Ltd-Japan
9363807 *3EMK7* -	**SUN NEPTUNE** **Shokuyu Navigation Co SA** Sun Technomarine Co Ltd *Panama* *Panama* MMSI: 371097000 Official number: 3315207	**7,215** 3,829 12,909 T/cm 21.1	Class: NK	**2007-09 Usuki Shipyard Co Ltd — Usuki OT** Yd No: 1706 Loa 121.52 (BB) Br ex - Dght 8.814 Lbp 115.00 Br md 20.60 Dpth 11.30 Welded, 1 dk	**(A12A2TC) Chemical Tanker** Double Hull (13F) Liq: 13,500 Cargo Heating Coils Compartments: 16 Wing Ta (s.stl) 16 Cargo Pump (s): 16x200m³/hr Manifold: Bow/CM: 63.8m	**1 oil engine** driving 1 FP propeller Total Power: 4,635kW (6,302hp) 14.2kn Mitsubishi 6UEC37LSII 1 x 2 Stroke 6 Cy. 370 x 1290 4635kW (6302bhp) Akasaka Tekkosho KK (Akasaka DieselLtd)-Japan AuxGen: 3 x 422kW a.c Thrusters: 1 Thwart. FP thruster (f) Fuel: 93.0 (d.f.) 727.0 (r.f.)
7629764 - - - - - -	**SUN No. 11** *ex* Samwon No. 17 *-2002* *ex* Jung Hwa No. 3 *-2002* *ex* Woo Jung No. 3 *-1983* *ex* Daito Maru No. 68 *-1972* - -	*347* 192 515	Class: (KR)	**1966 Narasaki Zosen KK — Muroran HK** Yd No: 568 Loa 51.87 Br ex - Dght 4.000 Lbp 47.68 Br md 8.21 Dpth 5.74 Welded, 1 dk	**(B11A2FS) Stern Trawler** Ins: 470 3 Ha: 2 (1.5 x 1.4) (1.5 x 2.4)	**1 oil engine** driving 1 FP propeller Total Power: 1,324kW (1,800hp) 11.5kn Hanshin 6L38SH 1 x 4 Stroke 6 Cy. 380 x 570 1324kW (1800bhp) Hanshin Nainenki Kogyo-Japan AuxGen: 2 x 92kW 225V a.c
8004260 *DTAC2* -	**SUN No. 31** *ex* Koyo Maru No. 12 *-1994* **Tae Heung Fishery Co Ltd** - *Busan* *South Korea* MMSI: 440812000 Official number: 9807001-6260004	**498** 187 420	Class: KR	**1980-08 Hayashikane Shipbuilding & Engineering Co Ltd — Yokosuka KN** Yd No: 759 Loa 52.91 Br ex 8.92 Dght 3.652 Lbp 46.46 Br md 8.91 Dpth 6.00 Welded, 1 dk	**(B11B2FV) Fishing Vessel**	**1 oil engine** driving 1 FP propeller Total Power: 883kW (1,201hp) 11.0kn Niigata 6L28X 1 x 4 Stroke 6 Cy. 280 x 440 883kW (1201bhp) Niigata Engineering Co Ltd-Japan AuxGen: 2 x 240kW 445V a.c
9459917 *3EQI2* -	**SUN NOBLE** **Seraphic Maritime SA** Setsuyo Kisen Co Ltd SatCom: Inmarsat C 435539110 *Panama* *Panama* MMSI: 355391000 Official number: 3379708A	**8,620** 3,900 12,131	Class: NK	**2008-04 Higaki Zosen K.K. — Imabari** Yd No: 613 Loa 116.99 Br ex - Dght 9.115 Lbp 109.10 Br md 19.60 Dpth 14.00 Welded, 1 dk	**(A31A2GX) General Cargo Ship** Grain: 17,507; Bale: 16,362 Compartments: 2 Ho, 2 Tw Dk, ER 2 Ha: ER Cranes: 3x30.7t; Derricks: 1x30t	**1 oil engine** driving 1 FP propeller Total Power: 4,200kW (5,710hp) 13.8kn MAN-B&W 6S35MC 1 x 2 Stroke 6 Cy. 350 x 1400 4200kW (5710bhp) The Hanshin Diesel Works Ltd-Japan Fuel: 850.0
9408358 *3FMU* -	**SUN OCEAN** *ex* Genius Sun *-2012* *ex* Tjore Olivia *-2010* *ex* UBT Gulf *-2010* **Sun Ocean Shipping Inc** Lissome Marine Services LLC *Panama* *Panama* MMSI: 357171000 Official number: 4461213	**6,149** 2,874 9,250 T/cm 18.9	Class: BV	**2008-10 Dongfang Shipbuilding Group Co Ltd — Yueqing ZJ** Yd No: DF90-3 Loa 117.60 (BB) Br ex - Dght 7.500 Lbp 109.60 Br md 19.00 Dpth 10.00 Welded, 1 dk	**(A12B2TR) Chemical/Products Tanker** Double Hull (13F) Liq: 9,437; Liq (Oil): 10,325 Cargo Heating Coils Compartments: 10 Wing Ta, 2 Wing Slop Ta, ER 10 Cargo Pump (s): 10x300m³/hr Manifold: Bow/CM: 61.6m	**1 oil engine** reduction geared to sc. shaft driving 1 FP propeller Total Power: 2,970kW (4,038hp) 13.5kn MaK 9M25 1 x 4 Stroke 9 Cy. 255 x 400 2970kW (4038bhp) Caterpillar Motoren GmbH & Co. KG-Germany AuxGen: 3 x 417kW a.c Thrusters: 1 Thwart. FP thruster (f) Fuel: 76.0 (d.f.) 376.0 (r.f.)
8861694 *ERVC* -	**SUN OIL I** *ex* Navodari *-2010* **BTZ Valleta Co Ltd & Mediterranean Samac Co Ltd** BTZ Valleta Co Ltd *Giurgiulesti* *Moldova*	**729** 388 1,212	Class: DR (RN)	**1986-02 Santierul Naval Tulcea — Tulcea** Yd No: N45 Loa 54.23 Br ex - Dght 3.650 Lbp 52.20 Br md 10.00 Dpth 4.95 Welded, 1 dk	**(B35E2TF) Bunkering Tanker**	**2 oil engines** geared to sc. shafts driving 1 FP propeller Total Power: 412kW (560hp) Maybach MB836BB 2 x 4 Stroke 8 Cy. 175 x 205 each-206kW (280bhp) (made 1982) Uzina 23 August Bucuresti-Bucuresti
8340066 - -	**SUN ON I** *ex* Hung Yea I *-2010* **PT Daya Guna Samudera** - *Ambon* *Indonesia* Official number: 2282	*157* - -	Class: (KI)	**1971 in Chinese Taipei** Loa 33.71 Br ex - Dght 2.401 Lbp 29.49 Br md 5.81 Dpth 2.80 Welded, 1 dk	**(B11B2FV) Fishing Vessel**	**1 oil engine** driving 1 FP propeller Total Power: 294kW (400hp) Alpha 1 x 4 Stroke 5 Cy. 294kW (400bhp)
8340054 - -	**SUN ON II** *ex* Hung Yea II *-2010* **PT Daya Guna Samudera** - *Ambon* *Indonesia*	*157* - -	Class: (KI)	**1971 in Chinese Taipei** Loa 33.71 Br ex - Dght 2.401 Lbp 29.49 Br md 5.81 Dpth 2.80 Welded, 1 dk	**(B11B2FV) Fishing Vessel**	**1 oil engine** driving 1 FP propeller Total Power: 294kW (400hp) Alpha 1 x 4 Stroke 294kW (400bhp)
9468401 *3EVH6* -	**SUN ORCHID** *ex* STX Orchid *-2013* **LTSF SPO 1 Inc** Pan Ocean Co Ltd *Panama* *Panama* MMSI: 355067000 Official number: 4218611B	**95,047** 60,025 180,717 T/cm 124.0	Class: KR (NV)	**2010-09 STX Offshore & Shipbuilding Co Ltd — Changwon (Jinhae Shipyard)** Yd No: 1311 Loa 292.00 (BB) Br ex - Dght 18.220 Lbp 283.00 Br md 45.00 Dpth 24.80 Welded, 1 dk	**(A21A2BC) Bulk Carrier** Double Bottom Entire Compartment Length Grain: 199,000 Compartments: 9 Ho, ER 9 Ha: 7 (15.8 x 20.4)ER 2 (15.8 x 15.3)	**1 oil engine** driving 1 FP propeller Total Power: 18,660kW (25,370hp) 14.9kn MAN-B&W 6S70MC-C 1 x 2 Stroke 6 Cy. 700 x 2800 18660kW (25370bhp) STX Engine Co Ltd-South Korea AuxGen: 3 x 900kW 450V a.c Fuel: 5560.0
9024889 *T3KP2* -	**SUN ORION** *ex* Chang Da 217 *-2013* *ex* Xing Long Zhou 289 *-2006* **Sun Fleet International Co Ltd** Hunchun Sino Unity Shipping (HongKong) Co Ltd *Tarawa* *Kiribati* MMSI: 529664000 Official number: K17051322	**2,983** 1,932 5,326	Class: IZ IT	**2005-09 Wenling Yongli Shiprepair & Building Yard — Wenling ZJ** Loa 99.80 (BB) Br ex - Dght 5.640 Lbp 92.90 Br md 15.80 Dpth 7.10 Welded, 1 dk	**(A31A2GX) General Cargo Ship** Grain: 6,427 Compartments: 4 Ho, ER	**1 oil engine** geared to sc. shaft driving 1 Propeller Total Power: 1,765kW (2,400hp) 11.0kn Chinese Std. Type G8300ZC 1 x 4 Stroke 8 Cy. 300 x 380 1765kW (2400bhp) Ningbo CSI Power & Machinery GroupCo Ltd-China
8624773 *VLW2296* -	**SUN PARADISE** **The Trust Co (PTAL) Ltd** - *Hayman Island, Qld* *Australia* Official number: 852686	*226* 67 100	Class: (NV)	**1987-07 WaveMaster International Pty Ltd — Fremantle WA** (Hull) **1987-07 Oceanfast International Pty Ltd — Fremantle WA** Loa 37.70 Br ex 7.60 Dght 1.100 Lbp - Br md 7.20 Dpth 3.50 Welded, 1 dk	**(A37B2PS) Passenger Ship** Hull Material: Aluminium Alloy Passengers: unberthed: 96	**2 oil engines** with clutches & dr geared to sc. shafts driving 2 Water jets Total Power: 1,822kW (2,478hp) M.T.U. 12V396TC82 2 x Vee 4 Stroke 12 Cy. 165 x 185 each-911kW (1239bhp) MTU Friedrichshafen GmbH-Friedrichshafen AuxGen: 2 x 60kW 415V 50Hz a.c
7706500 *3EGW6* -	**SUN PEAK** *ex* Fu Xiu *-2008* *ex* Heng Li *-2006* *ex* Helen M *-2001* *ex* Fereniki *-1997* *ex* Mayfair *-1993* *ex* Denmark Maru *-1989* *ex* Aster *-1982* *ex* Scan Eastern *-1982* **Sun Peaks Resources Ltd** Shanghai Shenyue Ship Management Co Ltd *Panama* *Panama* MMSI: 355138000 Official number: 34765PEXT1	**11,070** 6,226 17,587 T/cm 27.4	Class: (NK)	**1977-07 Tsuneishi Shipbuilding Co Ltd — Fukuyama HS** Yd No: 405 Loa 146.00 (BB) Br ex - Dght 9.281 Lbp 138.03 Br md 22.30 Dpth 12.45 Welded, 1 dk	**(A21A2BC) Bulk Carrier** Grain: 21,529; Bale: 20,972 Compartments: 4 Ho, ER 4 Ha: (13.5 x 9.7)3 (19.5 x 11.2)ER Derricks: 3x22.5t,1x15.5t	**1 oil engine** driving 1 FP propeller Total Power: 5,811kW (7,901hp) 14.1kn B&W 9K45GF 1 x 2 Stroke 9 Cy. 450 x 900 5811kW (7901bhp) Mitsui Engineering & Shipbuilding CLtd-Japan AuxGen: 3 x 280kW a.c Fuel: 125.0 (d.f.) 1112.5 (r.f.) 28.5pd
9201700 *DSNX2* -	**SUN PENATES** *ex* Ky Penates *-2008* *ex* Ocean Grace *-2004* **Sun Ace Shipping Co Ltd** - *Jeju* *South Korea* MMSI: 440388000 Official number: JJR-042021	**4,456** 2,722 6,569	Class: KR (NK)	**1999-02 Watanabe Zosen KK — Imabari EH** Yd No: 316 Loa 100.75 Br ex - Dght 6.820 Lbp 92.70 Br md 17.20 Dpth 9.00 Welded, 1 dk	**(A31A2GX) General Cargo Ship** Grain: 9,351; Bale: 8,668 Compartments: 2 Ho, ER 2 Ha: (27.3 x 10.2) (28.0 x 10.2)ER Cranes: 2x25.5t; Derricks: 2x15t	**1 oil engine** driving 1 FP propeller Total Power: 2,795kW (3,800hp) 12.5kn Mitsubishi 6UEC37LA 1 x 2 Stroke 6 Cy. 370 x 880 2795kW (3800bhp) Akasaka Tekkosho KK (Akasaka DieselLtd)-Japan
9191230 *DSRN2* -	**SUN PEONY** *ex* Clipper Trinidad *-2013* *ex* Botany Trust *-2006* **Brise Shipping Co Ltd** Inficess Shipping Co Ltd *Jeju* *South Korea* MMSI: 441920000 Official number: JJR-131019	**5,483** 2,602 8,823 T/cm 17.2	Class: KR (AB) (NK)	**1998-08 Hitachi Zosen Mukaishima Marine Co Ltd — Onomichi HS** Yd No: 128 Loa 112.50 (BB) Br ex 19.00 Dght 7.750 Lbp 105.00 Br md 18.80 Dpth 9.65 Welded, 1 dk	**(A12B2TR) Chemical/Products Tanker** Double Hull (13F) Liq: 9,066; Liq (Oil): 9,067 Cargo Heating Coils Compartments: 16 Wing Ta, Wing ER 16 Cargo Pump (s): 2x300m³/hr, 8x200m³/hr, 6x100m³/hr Manifold: Bow/CM: 48m	**1 oil engine** driving 1 FP propeller Total Power: 3,884kW (5,281hp) 13.8kn B&W 6L35MC 1 x 2 Stroke 6 Cy. 350 x 1050 3884kW (5281bhp) The Hanshin Diesel Works Ltd-Japan AuxGen: 2 x 440kW 450V 60Hz a.c Fuel: 92.0 (d.f.) 540.0 (r.f.)

IMO / Call sign	Name / Owner	Tonnage	Class	Builder / Dimensions	Type / Cargo	Machinery
9369124 *3EHD5* -	**SUN PIONEER** **Doman Shipping SA** Setsuyo Kisen Co Ltd SatCom: Inmarsat C 437202810 *Panama* *Panama* MMSI: 372028000 Official number: 3224706A	**8,621** 3,900 12,192	Class: NK	**2006-10 Higaki Zosen K.K. — Imabari** Yd No: 600 Loa 116.99 Br ex - Dght 9.115 Lbp 109.04 Br md 19.60 Dpth 14.00 Welded, 1 dk	**(A31A2GX) General Cargo Ship** Grain: 17,507; Bale: 16,362 Compartments: 2 Ho, 2 Tw Dk, ER 2 Ha: ER Cranes: 4x30t	**1 oil engine** driving 1 FP propeller Total Power: 4,200kW (5,710hp) 13.6kn MAN-B&W 6S35MC 1 x 2 Stroke 6 Cy. 350 x 1400 4200kW (5710bhp) Makita Corp-Japan Fuel: 850.0
9171113 - -	**SUN PRIME** *ex Southern Fighter -2013* **Sun Ace Shipping Co Ltd** - *Jeju* *South Korea* MMSI: 440112000 Official number: JJR-131065	**18,459** 10,119 29,478	Class: KR (NK)	**1998-09 Shin Kurushima Dockyard Co. Ltd. — Onishi** Yd No: 2972 Loa 170.03 Br ex - Dght 9.978 Lbp 162.00 Br md 27.40 Dpth 14.00 Welded, 1 dk	**(A21A2BC) Bulk Carrier** Double Hull Grain: 37,451; Bale: 36,269 Compartments: 5 Ho, ER 5 Ha: (15.2 x 16.9)3 (20.8 x 22.8) (16.0 x 22.8)ER Cranes: 4x30.5t	**1 oil engine** driving 1 FP propeller Total Power: 6,620kW (9,001hp) 14.5kn Mitsubishi 5UEC52LS 1 x 2 Stroke 5 Cy. 520 x 1850 6620kW (9001bhp) Kobe Hatsudoki KK-Japan Fuel: 1200.0
8738316 *JD2776* -	**SUN PRINCE** **Arita Kaiun KK** - *Osaka, Osaka* *Japan* Official number: 140811	*499* - 1,750		**2008-06 Tokuoka Zosen K.K. — Naruto** Yd No: 311 Loa 74.95 Br ex - Dght 4.400 Lbp 69.00 Br md 11.80 Dpth 7.41 Welded, 1 dk	**(A31A2GX) General Cargo Ship** Bale: 2,596	**1 oil engine** driving 1 Propeller Total Power: 1,618kW (2,200hp) 13.0kn Niigata 6M34BGT 1 x 4 Stroke 6 Cy. 340 x 620 1618kW (2200bhp) Niigata Engineering Co Ltd-Japan
9000259 *ZCBU6* -	**SUN PRINCESS** **COROT Shipping Corp (Sociedada Unipessoal) Ltd** Princess Cruise Lines Ltd SatCom: Inmarsat C 463646810 *Hamilton* *Bermuda (British)* MMSI: 310438000	**77,441** 44,193 8,293	Class: LR (RI) ✠ **100A1** CS 11/2010 passenger ship *IWS ✠ **LMC** **CCS** Eq.Ltr: U†; Cable: 715.0/90.0 U3 (a)	**1995-11 Fincantieri-Cant. Nav. Italiani S.p.A. — Monfalcone** Yd No: 5909 Loa 261.31 (BB) Br ex 32.28 Dght 8.100 Lbp 221.40 Br md 32.25 Dpth 11.30 Welded, 5 dks	**(A37A2PC) Passenger/Cruise** Passengers: cabins: 1011; berths: 2272	**4 diesel electric oil engines** driving 4 gen. each 11128kW 6600V a.c Connecting to 2 elec. motors each (14000kW) driving 2 FP propellers Total Power: 46,080kW (62,652hp) 21.4kn Sulzer 16ZAV40S 4 x Vee 4 Stroke 16 Cy. 400 x 560 each-11520kW (15663bhp) Fincantieri Cantieri Navaliltaliani SpA-Italy AuxGen: 1 x 600kW 440V 60Hz a.c Boilers: e (ex.g.) 11.2kgf/cm² (11.0bar), AuxB (o.f.) 10.0kgf/cm² (9.8bar) Thrusters: 2 Thwart. CP thruster (f); 2 Thwart. CP thruster (a) Fuel: 99.3 (d.f.) 2330.1 (r.f.)
9333113 *3EEJ* -	**SUN PRINCESS** **Shokuyu Navigation Co SA** ST Marine Co Ltd *Panama* *Panama* MMSI: 371916000 Official number: 3152306A	**2,371** 990 3,301 T/cm 10.8	Class: NK	**2006-03 Naikai Zosen Corp — Onomichi HS (Innoshima Shipyard)** Yd No: 711 Loa 89.30 (BB) Br ex 14.02 Dght 5.512 Lbp 83.30 Br md 14.00 Dpth 6.50 Welded, 1 dk	**(A12B2TR) Chemical/Products Tanker** Double Hull (13F) Liq: 3,567; Liq (Oil): 3,567 Cargo Heating Coils Compartments: 8 Wing Ta 8 Cargo Pump (s): 8x150m³/hr Manifold: Bow/CM: 42.5m	**1 oil engine** driving 1 Propeller Total Power: 2,059kW (2,799hp) 12.5kn Akasaka A38 1 x 4 Stroke 6 Cy. 380 x 740 2059kW (2799bhp) Akasaka Tekkosho KK (Akasaka DieselLtd)-Japan Fuel: 282.0 (r.f.)
9190975 *3FMK8* -	**SUN QUEEN** **Shokuyu Navigation Co SA** ST Marine Co Ltd SatCom: Inmarsat B 335115310 *Panama* *Panama* MMSI: 351153000 Official number: 2566898C	**2,487** 909 3,526 T/cm 10.3	Class: NK	**1998-05 Kyoei Zosen KK — Mihara HS** Yd No: 287 Loa 92.00 (BB) Br ex 14.02 Dght 5.612 Lbp 84.90 Br md 14.00 Dpth 6.80 Welded, 1 dk	**(A12B2TR) Chemical/Products Tanker** Double Hull Liq: 3,264; Liq (Oil): 3,330 Cargo Heating Coils Compartments: 8 Wing Ta, 2 Wing Slop Ta, ER 8 Cargo Pump (s): 8x150m³/hr Manifold: Bow/CM: 39.7m	**1 oil engine** with clutches & reverse geared to sc. shaft driving 1 FP propeller Total Power: 2,060kW (2,801hp) 12.0kn Akasaka A38 1 x 4 Stroke 6 Cy. 380 x 740 2060kW (2801bhp) Akasaka Tekkosho KK (Akasaka DieselLtd)-Japan AuxGen: 2 x 360kW 50Hz a.c Fuel: 64.0 (d.f.) (Heating Coils) 277.0 (r.f.) 8.5pd
8742678 *JD2829* -	**SUN QUEEN** **Arita Kaiun KK** - *Osaka, Osaka* *Japan* Official number: 140884	*499* - 1,800		**2008-09 Tokuoka Zosen K.K. — Naruto** Yd No: 312 Loa 76.50 Br ex - Dght 4.370 Lbp 69.00 Br md 11.80 Dpth 7.41 Welded, 1 dk	**(A31A2GX) General Cargo Ship** Compartments: 1 Ho, ER 1 Ha: ER (40.0 x 9.5)	**1 oil engine** driving 1 FP propeller Total Power: 1,471kW (2,000hp)
6911237 *HQIG3* -	**SUN REEFER No. 25** *ex Ebisu Maru No. 25 -1991* **Naviera Copioso S de RL** - *San Lorenzo* *Honduras* Official number: L-0323862	*299* 155 -		**1969 Kochiken Zosen — Kochi** Yd No: 355 Loa - Br ex 7.98 Dght 3.302 Lbp 42.30 Br md 7.95 Dpth 3.61 Welded, 1 dk	**(B11A2FT) Trawler**	**1 oil engine** driving 1 FP propeller Total Power: 699kW (950hp) Daihatsu 1 x 4 Stroke 8 Cy. 260 x - 699kW (950bhp) Daihatsu Kogyo-Japan
8840664 - -	**SUN REEFER No. 31** *ex Fukuyoshi Maru No. 31 -1991* **Naviera Composio S de RL** - *San Lorenzo* *Honduras* Official number: L-0324144	*126* 37 -		**1969 Yamanishi Shipbuilding Co Ltd — Ishinomaki MG** L reg 28.60 Br ex - Dght 2.100 Lbp - Br md 6.20 Dpth 2.60 Welded, 1 dk	**(B11B2FV) Fishing Vessel**	**1 oil engine** driving 1 FP propeller
9002714 *DYMS* -	**SUN RIGHT** *ex Ever Right -2005* **Sirius Carriers Corp SA** Sea Quest Ship Management Inc *Manila* *Philippines* MMSI: 548723000 Official number: MNLA000653	**53,359** 29,561 57,904	Class: NK (AB)	**1993-07 Onomichi Dockyard Co Ltd — Onomichi HS** Yd No: 363 Lengthened-1993 Loa 294.03 (BB) Br ex 32.30 Dght 12.632 Lbp 281.29 Br md 32.22 Dpth 21.25 Welded, 1 dk	**(A33A2CC) Container Ship (Fully Cellular)** Bale: 100,836 TEU 4229 C Ho 2066 TEU C Dk 2163 TEU incl 450 ref C. Compartments: ER, 9 Cell Ho 18 Ha: ER	**1 oil engine** driving 1 FP propeller Total Power: 34,380kW (46,743hp) 23.0kn Sulzer 9RTA84C 1 x 2 Stroke 9 Cy. 840 x 2400 34380kW (46743bhp) Diesel United Ltd.-Aioi AuxGen: 4 x 1700kW 440V 60Hz a.c, 1 x 125kW 440V 60Hz a.c Thrusters: 1 Thwart. CP thruster (f) Fuel: 347.0 (d.f.) 5334.0 (r.f.) 124.5pd
9623219 *V7ZD3* -	**SUN RISE** *ex STX Rose 2 -2013* **POS Maritime BA SA** Pan Ocean Co Ltd *Majuro* *Marshall Islands* MMSI: 538004795 Official number: 4795	**22,499** 6,749 24,173	Class: KR NV	**2012-10 STX (Dalian) Shipbuilding Co Ltd — Wafangdian LN** Yd No: D2101 Loa 168.50 Br ex 44.00 Dght 7.123 Lbp 158.00 Br md 40.00 Dpth 10.30 Welded, 1 dk	**(A38C3GH) Heavy Load Carrier, semi submersible**	**3 oil engines** reduction geared to sc. shafts driving 2 Directional propellers Total Power: 12,000kW (16,314hp) 13.0kn MAN-B&W 8L32/40 3 x 4 Stroke 8 Cy. 320 x 400 each-4000kW (5438bhp) STX Engine Co Ltd-South Korea AuxGen: 2 x 6600V a.c Thrusters: 1 Tunnel thruster (f) Fuel: 2160.0
8312291 - -	**SUN RISE 313** *ex Shinei Maru No. 8 -1998* *ex Wakashio Maru No. 8 -1998* - -	**551** 165 -		**1983-08 KK Kanasashi Zosen — Shizuoka SZ** Yd No: 3005 Loa 53.90 (BB) Br ex 8.74 Dght 3.401 Lbp 47.50 Br md 8.70 Dpth 3.76 Welded, 1 dk	**(B11B2FV) Fishing Vessel** Compartments: 5 Ho, ER 5 Ha: ER	**1 oil engine** with clutches, flexible couplings & sr geared to sc. shaft driving 1 FP propeller Total Power: 883kW (1,201hp) Hanshin 6LUN28AG 1 x 4 Stroke 6 Cy. 280 x 480 883kW (1201bhp) The Hanshin Diesel Works Ltd-Japan
8005616 - -	**SUN-RISE No. 1** *ex Dairin Maru No. 85 -1995* *ex Ryuho Maru No. 85 -1992* **Sun-Rise Fisheries & Co Ltd** -	**658** 245 -		**1980-06 Sanuki Shipbuilding & Iron Works Co Ltd — Mitoyo KG** Yd No: 1065 Loa - Br ex - Dght - Lbp 44.30 Br md 8.50 Dpth 3.51 Welded, 1 dk	**(B11B2FV) Fishing Vessel**	**1 oil engine** driving 1 FP propeller Total Power: 809kW (1,100hp) Akasaka DM28R 1 x 4 Stroke 6 Cy. 280 x 460 809kW (1100bhp) Akasaka Tekkosho KK (Akasaka DieselLtd)-Japan
7819682 *WDE6902* -	**SUN RIVER** *ex Sun Aquarius -2008 ex Sandy River -2008* *ex Blanche Candies -1997* **Legacy Offshore LLC** - *Morgan City, LA* *United States of America* MMSI: 338366000 Official number: 615324	**961** 288 750	Class: AB	**1979-12 Halter Marine, Inc. — Lockport, La** Yd No: 720 Loa 51.82 Br ex - Dght 3.987 Lbp 51.36 Br md 13.41 Dpth 4.27 Welded, 1 dk	**(B21A2OS) Platform Supply Ship**	**2 oil engines** reverse reduction geared to sc. shafts driving 2 FP propellers Total Power: 1,810kW (2,460hp) 12.0kn EMD (Electro-Motive) 12-645-E2 2 x Vee 2 Stroke 12 Cy. 230 x 254 each-905kW (1230bhp) (Re-engined , Reconditioned & fitted 1979) General Motors Corp.Electro-Motive Div.-La Grange AuxGen: 3 x 150kW Thrusters: 1 Thwart. FP thruster (f)

9001332 *DYIN* -	**SUN ROAD** *ex* Ever Royal *-2005* **Aquarius Carriers Corp SA** Sea Quest Ship Management Inc *Manila* *Philippines* MMSI: 548719000 Official number: MNLA000650	**53,359** 29,561 57,904	Class: NK (AB)	**1993**-03 **Onomichi Dockyard Co Ltd — Onomichi HS** Yd No: 362 Lengthened-1993 Loa 294.03 (BB) Br ex 32.30 Dght 12.620 Lbp 281.29 Br md 32.22 Dpth 21.25 Welded, 1 dk	**(A33A2CC) Container Ship (Fully Cellular)** Bale: 100,836 TEU 4229 C Ho 2066 TEU C Dk 2163 TEU incl 450 ref C. Compartments: ER, 9 Cell Ho 18 Ha: ER	**1 oil engine** driving 1 FP propeller Total Power: 34,380kW (46,743hp) 23.0kn Sulzer 9RTA84C 1 x 2 Stroke 9 Cy. 840 x 2400 34380kW (46743bhp) Diesel United Ltd.-Aioi AuxGen: 4 x 1700kW 440V 60Hz a.c, 1 x 125kW 440V 60Hz a.c Thrusters: 1 Thwart. CP thruster (f) Fuel: 342.0 (d.f.) 5250.0 (r.f.) 124.5pd
9002726 *DYMW* -	**SUN ROUND** *ex* Ever Round *-2005* **Taurus Carriers Corp SA** Sea Quest Ship Management Inc *Manila* *Philippines* MMSI: 548726000 Official number: MNLA000657	**53,359** 29,561 57,904	Class: NK (AB)	**1993**-10 **Onomichi Dockyard Co Ltd — Onomichi HS** Yd No: 364 Lengthened-1993 Loa 294.03 (BB) Br ex - Dght 12.632 Lbp 281.29 Br md 32.22 Dpth 21.25 Welded, 1 dk	**(A33A2CC) Container Ship (Fully Cellular)** TEU 4229 C Ho 2066 TEU C Dk 2163 TEU incl 450 ref C. Compartments: ER, 9 Cell Ho 18 Ha: ER	**1 oil engine** driving 1 FP propeller Total Power: 34,380kW (46,743hp) 23.0kn Sulzer 9RTA84C 1 x 2 Stroke 9 Cy. 840 x 2400 34380kW (46743bhp) Diesel United Ltd.-Aioi AuxGen: 4 x 1700kW 440V 60Hz a.c, 1 x 125kW 440V 60Hz a.c Thrusters: 1 Thwart. CP thruster (f) Fuel: 342.0 (d.f.) 5250.0 (r.f.) 124.5pd
9264702 *H9YB* -	**SUN ROYAL** **Taikyo Marine SA** ST Marine Co Ltd *Panama* *Panama* MMSI: 351343000 Official number: 2841702B	**2,282** 906 3,365 T/cm 10.1	Class: NK	**2002**-03 **Hitachi Zosen Mukaishima Marine Co Ltd — Onomichi HS** Yd No: 160 Loa 89.30 (BB) Br ex 14.02 Dght 5.512 Lbp 83.30 Br md 14.00 Dpth 6.50 Welded, 1 dk	**(A12B2TR) Chemical/Products Tanker** Double Hull (13F) Liq: 3,341; Liq (Oil): 3,341 Cargo Heating Coils Compartments: 10 Wing Ta, 1 Slop Ta, ER 10 Cargo Pump (s): 8x200m³/hr, 2x300m³/hr Manifold: Bow/CM: 43.8m	**1 oil engine** reverse reduction geared to sc. shaft driving 1 FP propeller Total Power: 2,059kW (2,799hp) 12.5kn Akasaka A38 1 x 4 Stroke 6 Cy. 380 x 740 2059kW (2799bhp) Akasaka Tekkosho KK (Akasaka DieselLtd)-Japan AuxGen: 2 x 200kW 450V 60Hz a.c Thrusters: 1 Tunnel thruster (f) Fuel: 114.0 (d.f.) 579.0 (r.f.)
9274551 *VRZU4* -	**SUN RUBY** **Pacific Basin Chartering (No 3) Ltd** Pacific Basin Shipping (HK) Ltd *Hong Kong* *Hong Kong* MMSI: 477789000 Official number: HK-1272	**19,887** 11,140 32,754 T/cm 43.8	Class: NK	**2004**-03 **Kanda Zosensho K.K. — Kawajiri** Yd No: 443 Loa 177.00 (BB) Br ex - Dght 10.019 Lbp 168.50 Br md 28.40 Dpth 14.25 Welded, 1 dk	**(A21A2BC) Bulk Carrier** Grain: 42,857; Bale: 40,896 Compartments: 5 Ho, ER 5 Ha: 4 (20.0 x 19.0)ER (15.2 x 15.8) Cranes: 4x30.5t	**1 oil engine** driving 1 FP propeller Total Power: 6,620kW (9,001hp) 13.5kn Mitsubishi 6UEC52LA 1 x 2 Stroke 6 Cy. 520 x 1600 6620kW (9001bhp) Kobe Hatsudoki KK-Japan Fuel: 70.0 (d.f.) 1260.0 (r.f.)
8017748 - -	**SUN SEA** *ex* Harin Panich 19 *-2010* *ex* Eifuku Maru No. 2 *-1995* **Sun & Rshiya Co Ltd** -	*767* 403 1,250		**1980**-11 **K.K. Matsuura Zosensho — Osakikamijima** Yd No: 281 Loa 57.38 Br ex 9.53 Dght 4.850 Lbp - Br md 9.50 Dpth 5.72 Welded, 1 dk	**(A31A2GX) General Cargo Ship**	**1 oil engine** driving 1 FP propeller Total Power: 809kW (1,100hp) Matsui MS245GTSC 1 x 4 Stroke 6 Cy. 245 x 470 809kW (1100bhp) Matsui Iron Works Co Ltd-Japan
7908988 - -	**SUN SHINE** **Ali Shan Navigation Corp** - *Chinese Taipei*	*275* - 24		**1979**-03 **Mitsui Eng. & SB. Co. Ltd., Chiba Works — Ichihara** Yd No: 1600 Loa 32.82 Br ex 9.22 Dght 1.251 Lbp 30.51 Br md 9.20 Dpth 2.82 Welded, 2 dks	**(A37B2PS) Passenger Ship** Hull Material: Aluminium Alloy	**2 oil engines** geared to sc. shafts driving 2 FP propellers Total Power: 3,736kW (5,080hp) Pielstick 16PA4V185VG 2 x Vee 4 Stroke 16 Cy. 185 x 210 each-1868kW (2540bhp) Fuji Diesel Co Ltd-Japan
8653217 *XYTS2* -	**SUN SHINE** **Thuriya Sandar Win Co Ltd** *Yangon* *Myanmar* Official number: 6610 (A)	**1,914** 1,222 -		**2011**-06 **Myanma Port Authority — Yangon (Theinphyu Dockyard)** Yd No: 34MPA Loa 82.92 Br ex - Dght - Lbp - Br md 19.51 Dpth - Welded, 1 dk	**(A35D2RL) Landing Craft**	**3 oil engines** driving 3 Propellers Total Power: 1,314kW (1,788hp)
9471616 *H9JL* -	**SUN SHINE** *ex* STX Rose 1 *-2013* **POS Maritime CY SA** Pan Ocean Co Ltd *Panama* *Panama* MMSI: 370708000 Official number: 38157PEXT1	**17,824** 5,348 16,715	Class: AB KR	**2008**-12 **STX Shipbuilding Co Ltd — Changwon (Jinhae Shipyard)** Yd No: 8001 Loa 174.20 (BB) Br ex 48.00 Dght 5.028 Lbp 165.00 Br md 40.00 Dpth 8.50 Welded, 1 dk	**(A38C3GH) Heavy Load Carrier, semi submersible**	**2 oil engines** reduction geared to sc. shafts driving 2 FP propellers Total Power: 7,680kW (10,442hp) 11.7kn MAN-B&W 8L32/40 2 x 4 Stroke 8 Cy. 320 x 400 each-3840kW (5221bhp) STX Engine Co Ltd-South Korea AuxGen: 3 x 440kW a.c Thrusters: 1 Tunnel thruster (f) Fuel: 145.0 (d.f.) 681.0 (r.f.) 40.0pd
9134385 *DSOV7* -	**SUN STAR** *ex* Formosa Queen *-2006* **Sun Ace Shipping Co Ltd** - *Jeju* *South Korea* MMSI: 440441000 Official number: JJR-069665	**4,137** 1,889 5,779	Class: KR (NK)	**1996**-05 **Shin Kochi Jyuko K.K. — Kochi** Yd No: 7080 Loa 97.94 (BB) Br ex - Dght 6.018 Lbp 89.95 Br md 18.40 Dpth 9.20 Welded, 1 dk	**(A31A2GX) General Cargo Ship** Grain: 8,675; Bale: 8,153 Compartments: 2 Ho, ER 2 Ha: (37.8 x 10.4) (18.9 x 10.4)ER Derricks: 2x30t,1x25t	**1 oil engine** driving 1 FP propeller Total Power: 2,060kW (2,801hp) 12.0kn Akasaka A38 1 x 4 Stroke 6 Cy. 380 x 740 2060kW (2801bhp) Akasaka Tekkosho KK (Akasaka DieselLtd)-Japan
8740345 - -	**SUN STAR** - - *Samarinda* *Indonesia*	**180** 54 -	Class: KI	**2006**-03 **PT Menumbar Kaltim — Samarinda** Loa 27.00 Br ex - Dght 2.800 Lbp 24.72 Br md 7.50 Dpth 3.75 Welded, 1 dk	**(B32A2ST) Tug**	**2 oil engines** driving 2 Propellers Total Power: 1,220kW (1,658hp) Yanmar 6AYM-ETE 2 x 4 Stroke 6 Cy. 155 x 180 each-610kW (829bhp) Yanmar Diesel Engine Co Ltd-Japan
8850839 - -	**SUN STAR** *ex* Take Maru No. 3 *-2000* **Sun Hwa Co Ltd** - *Incheon* *South Korea* MMSI: 440011460 Official number: ICR-002599	*143* - -	Class: KR	**1991**-03 **Kanbara Zosen K.K. — Onomichi** Yd No: 412 Loa 29.50 Br ex - Dght 2.500 Lbp 25.20 Br md 8.40 Dpth 3.57 Welded, 1 dk	**(B32A2ST) Tug**	**2 oil engines** driving 2 Directional propellers Total Power: 1,618kW (2,200hp) 12.2kn Niigata 6L22HX 2 x 4 Stroke 6 Cy. 220 x 280 each-809kW (1100bhp) Niigata Engineering Co Ltd-Japan AuxGen: 2 x 160kW 225V a.c
8988844 - -	**SUN STAR 2** *ex* Jin Hai 2 *-2004* **Dalian Jinguang Fishery Co Ltd** - *Fiji*	**144** 44 -		**2001 Rongcheng Shipbuilding Industry Co Ltd — Rongcheng SD** L reg 34.00 Br ex - Dght - Lbp - Br md 6.60 Dpth 2.80 Welded, 1 dk	**(B11B2FV) Fishing Vessel**	**1 oil engine** geared to sc. shaft driving 1 Propeller Total Power: 330kW (449hp) 10.0kn Chinese Std. Type G6190ZLC 1 x 4 Stroke 6 Cy. 190 x 210 330kW (449bhp) Jinan Diesel Engine Co Ltd-China
8648482 *3DOQ* -	**SUN STAR 3** **Dalian Jinguang Fishery Co Ltd** - *Suva* *Fiji* Official number: 000543	**173** 63 -		**2006**-08 **Huanghai Shipbuilding Co Ltd — Rongcheng SD** Loa 36.00 Br ex 6.40 Dght 2.350 Lbp - Br md - Dpth 3.05 Welded, 1 dk	**(B11B2FV) Fishing Vessel**	**1 oil engine** reduction geared to sc. shaft driving 1 Propeller Total Power: 330kW (449hp) Chinese Std. Type Z6170ZL 1 x 4 Stroke 6 Cy. 170 x 200 330kW (449bhp) Weifang Diesel Engine Factory-China
8647517 *BZTH9* -	**SUN STAR 6** **Dalian Jinguang Fishery Co Ltd** - *Dalian, Liaoning* *China* Official number: 412200115	**242** 73 -		**2010**-03 **Dalian Zhangzidao Hongyuan Dockyard Co Ltd — Changhai County LN** Loa 37.25 Br ex - Dght - Lbp - Br md 7.00 Dpth 3.60 Welded, 1 dk	**(B11B2FV) Fishing Vessel**	**1 oil engine** driving 1 Propeller Total Power: 450kW (612hp) Chinese Std. Type 1 x 4 Stroke 6 Cy. 450kW (612bhp) Henan Diesel Engine Industry Co Ltd-China
8647529 *BZTY2* -	**SUN STAR 7** **Dalian Jinguang Fishery Co Ltd** - *Dalian, Liaoning* *China* Official number: 412200116	**242** 73 -		**2010**-03 **Dalian Zhangzidao Hongyuan Dockyard Co Ltd — Changhai County LN** Loa 37.25 Br ex - Dght - Lbp - Br md 7.00 Dpth 3.60 Welded, 1 dk	**(B11B2FV) Fishing Vessel**	**1 oil engine** driving 1 Propeller Total Power: 450kW (612hp) Chinese Std. Type 1 x 4 Stroke 6 Cy. 450kW (612bhp) Henan Diesel Engine Industry Co Ltd-China
6801729 *GCCW* -	**SUN SWALE** *ex* Clairvoyant *-1981* **TP Towage Co Ltd** - *London* *United Kingdom* Official number: 398886	**195** 58 -	Class: (BV)	**1967**-12 **Ziegler Freres — Dunkerque** Yd No: 161 Loa 29.01 Br ex 8.51 Dght 4.503 Lbp 27.01 Br md 8.01 Dpth 6.30 Welded, 1 dk	**(B32A2ST) Tug**	**1 oil engine** gearing integral to driving 1 Voith-Schneider propeller Total Power: 1,052kW (1,430hp) 12.5kn Crepelle 8SN1 1 x 4 Stroke 8 Cy. 260 x 280 1052kW (1430bhp) (new engine 1970) Crepelle et Cie-France AuxGen: 1 x 48kW 125V d.c, 1 x 20kW 125V d.c Fuel: 34.5 (d.f.)

IMO / Call sign	Name / Owner	Tonnage	Class	Builder / Dimensions	Type	Machinery
8813922 - -	**SUN TAI ON** **Palytone Ltd**	*338* 180 500		**1988-07 Guangzhou Fishing Vessel Shipyard — Guangzhou GD** Loa 35.56 Br ex - Dght 2.801 Lbp 33.66 Br md 8.51 Dpth 3.71 Welded, 1 dk	**(A31A2GX) General Cargo Ship** Bale: 443 Compartments: ER, 2 Ho 2 Ha: ER Derricks: 1	**1 oil engine** geared to sc. shaft driving 1 FP propeller Total Power: 342kW (465hp) 12.0kn Caterpillar 3412TA 1 x Vee 4 Stroke 12 Cy. 137 x 152 342kW (465bhp) Caterpillar Inc-USA AuxGen: 2 x 33kW 400V 50Hz a.c Fuel: 13.5 (d.f.)
7517868 - -	**SUN TIDE** **Seafarer Boat LLC** Tidewater Marine International Inc	**1,165** 349 -	Class: AB	**1976-10 Tacoma Boatbuilding Co., Inc. — Tacoma, Wa** Yd No: 265 Loa 66.45 Br ex 13.42 Dght 5.027 Lbp 60.18 Br md 13.12 Dpth 5.80 Welded, 1 dk	**(B21B20A) Anchor Handling Tug Supply** Ice Capable	**4 oil engines** reverse reduction geared to sc. shafts driving 2 CP propellers Total Power: 5,736kW (7,800hp) 16.0kn EMD (Electro-Motive) 16-645-E6 4 x Vee 2 Stroke 16 Cy. 230 x 254 each-1434kW (1950bhp) General Motors Corp.Electro-Motive Div.-La Grange AuxGen: 2 x 250kW Thrusters: 1 Thwart. FP thruster (f)
9021241 *T3ME2* -	**SUN TREASURE** *ex* Hoei Maru No. 10 *-2014* **Three Oceans Pte Ltd** *Tarawa* *Kiribati* Official number: K-17911474	*199* - 600		**1991-06 Katsuura Dockyard Co. Ltd. — Nachi-Katsuura** Yd No: 311 L reg 44.10 Br ex - Dght - Lbp - Br md 8.00 Dpth 3.50 Welded, 1 dk	**(A13B2TP) Products Tanker**	**1 oil engine** driving 1 FP propeller Total Power: 588kW (799hp) Yanmar M220-UN 1 x 4 Stroke 6 Cy. 220 x 300 588kW (799bhp) Yanmar Diesel Engine Co Ltd-Japan
9178422 *T8XQ* -	**SUN UNICORN** *ex* Stefania Mikhaela *-2014* *ex* Bonnie Rois *-2010* **Stefania Mikhaela Shipping Ltd** Sun Unicorn Navigation AG *Malakal Harbour* *Palau* MMSI: 511011035	**2,990** 1,311 4,791 T/cm 14.0	Class: BV IS (GL)	**1998-12 Kroeger Werft GmbH & Co. KG — Schacht-Audorf** Yd No: 1546 Loa 99.54 (BB) Br ex 17.05 Dght 5.910 Lbp 92.14 Br md 16.90 Dpth 7.55 Welded, 1 dk	**(A31A2GX) General Cargo Ship** Double Hull Grain: 4,450; Bale: 4,165 TEU 366 C Ho 80 TEU C Dk 286 TEU incl 60 ref C. Compartments: 1 Cell Ho, ER 3 Ha: (25.6 x 10.6)Tappered (25.6 x 13.2) (6.2 x 10.6)ER Ice Capable	**1 oil engine** with clutches, flexible couplings & sr geared to sc. shaft driving 1 CP propeller Total Power: 3,920kW (5,330hp) 15.0kn Alpha 16V28/32A 1 x Vee 4 Stroke 16 Cy. 280 x 320 3920kW (5330bhp) MAN B&W Diesel A/S-Denmark AuxGen: 2 x 626kW 450V 60Hz a.c, 2 x 256kW 450V 60Hz a.c Thrusters: 1 Thwart. FP thruster (f) Fuel: 40.8 (d.f.) (Heating Coils) 233.9 (r.f.) 19.5pd
9098517 *T3HG2* -	**SUN UNION** *ex* Hongwin *-2013* *ex* Yue Chao 1 *-2008* **Royal Apex International Corp** Hunchun Sino Unity Shipping (HongKong) Co Ltd *Tarawa* *Kiribati* MMSI: 529609000 Official number: K16951363	**3,802** 2,260 -	Class: IZ IT (MG)	**1995-01 Hubei Shipyard — Wuhan HB** Loa 107.66 Br ex - Dght - Lbp - Br md 16.20 Dpth 7.80 Welded, 1 dk	**(A31A2GX) General Cargo Ship**	**1 oil engine** driving 1 FP propeller Total Power: 1,911kW (2,598hp) 10.0kn Hanshin 6LU40 1 x 4 Stroke 6 Cy. 400 x 640 1911kW (2598bhp) The Hanshin Diesel Works Ltd-Japan
8736382 *9LY2156* -	**SUN UNITY** *ex* Fei Yun 207 *-2009* **Jin & Liu Co Ltd** Royal Armadas International Co Ltd *Freetown* *Sierra Leone* MMSI: 667857000 Official number: SL100857	**2,574** 1,491 -		**2007-10 Nanjing Sanxing Shipyard — Nanjing JS** Loa 85.20 (BB) Br ex - Dght 6.000 Lbp - Br md 14.00 Dpth 7.00 Welded, 1 dk	**(A31A2GX) General Cargo Ship**	**1 oil engine** reduction geared to sc. shaft driving 1 Propeller Total Power: 1,765kW (2,400hp) 11.0kn Chinese Std. Type G8300ZC 1 x 4 Stroke 8 Cy. 300 x 380 1765kW (2400bhp) Ningbo CSI Power & Machinery GroupCo Ltd-China
9528536 *3FOQ4* -	**SUN UNIVERSE** **Suntree Shipping SA** Setsuyo Kisen Co Ltd SatCom: Inmarsat C 437164710 *Panama* *Panama* MMSI: 371647000 Official number: 4066509	**8,620** 3,941 12,146	Class: NK	**2009-08 Higaki Zosen K.K. — Imabari** Yd No: 632 Loa 116.99 (BB) Br ex - Dght 9.115 Lbp 109.10 Br md 19.60 Dpth 14.00 Welded, 1 dk	**(A31A2GX) General Cargo Ship** Grain: 17,507; Bale: 16,361 Compartments: 2 Ho, 2 Tw Dk, ER 2 Ha: ER Cranes: 2x30.7t; Derricks: 1x30t	**1 oil engine** driving 1 FP propeller Total Power: 4,200kW (5,710hp) 13.8kn MAN-B&W 6S35MC 1 x 2 Stroke 6 Cy. 350 x 1400 4200kW (5710bhp) The Hanshin Diesel Works Ltd-Japan AuxGen: 3 x a.c Fuel: 850.0
9217785 *DSQV4* -	**SUN VIEW** *ex* Asian Green *-2010* **Sun Ace Shipping Co Ltd** - *Jeju* *South Korea* MMSI: 441716000 Official number: JJR-102244	**4,205** 2,519 6,397	Class: KR (NK)	**2000-02 Shin Kochi Jyuko K.K. — Kochi** Yd No: 7123 Loa 98.41 Br ex - Dght 6.526 Lbp 89.95 Br md 18.40 Dpth 9.20 Welded, 1 dk	**(A31A2GX) General Cargo Ship** Grain: 9,074; Bale: 8,699 Compartments: 2 Ho, ER 2 Ha: (16.1 x 10.4) (35.8 x 10.4)ER Cranes: 3x30t	**1 oil engine** driving 1 FP propeller Total Power: 2,060kW (2,801hp) 11.8kn Akasaka A38 1 x 4 Stroke 6 Cy. 380 x 740 2060kW (2801bhp) Akasaka Tekkosho KK (Akasaka DieselLtd)-Japan AuxGen: 2 x 180kW 450V 60Hz a.c Fuel: 76.5 (d.f.) (Heating Coils) 423.0 (r.f.) 9.1pd
9643178 *ZGDJ* -	**SUN VIL II** **Sun Vil Shipping SA** Equinox Maritime Ltd *George Town* *Cayman Islands (British)* MMSI: 319054200 Official number: 745141	**31,756** 18,653 56,042 T/cm 55.8	Class: NK	**2013-08 Mitsui Eng. & SB. Co. Ltd., Chiba Works — Ichihara** Yd No: 1851 Loa 189.99 (BB) Br ex - Dght 12.715 Lbp 182.00 Br md 32.25 Dpth 18.10 Welded, 1 dk	**(A21A2BC) Bulk Carrier** Grain: 71,346; Bale: 68,733 Compartments: 5 Ho, ER 5 Ha: 4 (21.1 x 18.9)ER (17.6 x 18.9) Cranes: 4x30t	**1 oil engine** driving 1 FP propeller Total Power: 8,000kW (10,877hp) 14.5kn MAN-B&W 6S50MC-C8 1 x 2 Stroke 6 Cy. 500 x 2000 8000kW (10877bhp) Mitsui Engineering & Shipbuilding CLtd-Japan AuxGen: 3 x 520kW a.c Fuel: 2314.0
9033713 *9HFA8* -	**SUN VITA** *ex* Spirit of Foynes *-2008* *ex* Sun Vita *-2006* *ex* Iduna *-2005* *ex* CMB Iduna *-1995* *ex* Iduna *-1994* **Leo Marine Co Ltd** Alpha Shipping Co SIA *Valletta* *Malta* MMSI: 215913000 Official number: 9654	**3,585** 2,013 4,150	Class: GL	**1991-12 Schiffswerft und Maschinenfabrik Cassens GmbH — Emden** Yd No: 192 Loa 98.80 (BB) Br ex 16.30 Dght 6.100 Lbp 90.70 Br md 16.20 Dpth 7.80 Welded, 1 dk	**(A31A2GX) General Cargo Ship** Grain: 6,000 TEU 361 C incl 40 ref C. Compartments: 1 Ho, ER 2 Ha: 2 (32.5 x 13.4)ER	**1 oil engine** with flexible couplings & sr geared to sc. shaft driving 1 CP propeller Total Power: 1,798kW (2,445hp) 14.6kn MaK 8M453C 1 x 4 Stroke 8 Cy. 320 x 420 1798kW (2445bhp) Krupp MaK Maschinenbau GmbH-Kiel AuxGen: 1 x 500kW 220/380V a.c, 2 x 230kW 220/380V a.c Thrusters: 1 Thwart. FP thruster (f)
8950782 *DUQA4* -	**SUN WARM NO. 1** *ex* Peche No. 131 *-2002* *ex* Jeffe No. 31 *-1994* **Sun Warm Tuna Corp** *Philippines* Official number: MNLD010559	*707* 269 -		**1987 Shin Tien Erh Shipbuilding Co, Ltd — Kaohsiung** Loa 50.50 Br ex - Dght - Lbp 47.60 Br md 8.80 Dpth 3.70 Welded, 1 dk	**(B11B2FV) Fishing Vessel**	**1 oil engine** driving 1 FP propeller 12.0kn Niigata 1 x 4 Stroke 6 Cy. Niigata Engineering Co Ltd-Japan
9163453 *3FJL7* -	**SUN WING** **Shokuyu Navigation Co SA** ST Marine Co Ltd *Panama* *Panama* MMSI: 351221000 Official number: 2400897C	**2,243** 1,009 3,404 T/cm 10.3	Class: NK	**1997-06 Shitanoe Shipbuilding Co Ltd — Usuki OT** Yd No: 1190 Loa 91.60 (BB) Br ex 14.02 Dght 5.512 Lbp 85.00 Br md 14.00 Dpth 6.65 Welded, 1 dk	**(A12B2TR) Chemical/Products Tanker** Double Bottom Entire Compartment Length Liq: 3,596; Liq (Oil): 3,596 Compartments: 4 Ta, 12 Wing Ta, ER 6 Cargo Pump (s): 2x200m³/hr, 4x150m³/hr Manifold: Bow/CM: 51.1m	**1 oil engine** driving 1 FP propeller Total Power: 2,060kW (2,801hp) 12.5kn Akasaka A38 1 x 4 Stroke 6 Cy. 380 x 740 2060kW (2801bhp) Akasaka Tekkosho KK (Akasaka DieselLtd)-Japan AuxGen: 2 x 260kW 450V 60Hz a.c Fuel: 52.0 (d.f.) (Heating Coils) 186.0 (r.f.) 7.0pd
6905898 *D8SF* -	**SUN YANG** **Ssangyong Shipping Co Ltd** - SatCom: Inmarsat C 444044015 *Busan* *South Korea* Official number: BSR-686051	*3,327* 1,976 5,044	Class: (KR) (NK)	**1968-12 Tohoku Shipbuilding Co Ltd — Shiogama MG** Yd No: 114 Loa 104.55 Br ex 15.04 Dght 6.310 Lbp 97.52 Br md 15.00 Dpth 7.60 Welded, 1 dk	**(A24A2BT) Cement Carrier** Grain: 4,427	**1 oil engine** driving 1 FP propeller Total Power: 1,839kW (2,500hp) 12.3kn Hanshin 6L46 1 x 4 Stroke 6 Cy. 460 x 680 1839kW (2500bhp) Hanshin Nainenki Kogyo-Japan AuxGen: 2 x 170kW 445V a.c Fuel: 260.0
6710023 *D7OR* -	**SUN YANG No. 7** *ex* Chemicarry No. 7 *-1986* *ex* Ansei Maru No. 8 *-1974* **Dong Bang Yu Jo Sa** - *Ulsan* *South Korea* Official number: USR-668047	*484* 261 870	Class: (KR)	**1966 K.K. Taihei Kogyo — Akitsu** Yd No: 178 Loa 54.87 Br ex 8.54 Dght 3.804 Lbp 50.02 Br md 8.51 Dpth 4.07 Welded, 1 dk	**(A12A2TC) Chemical Tanker** Liq: 776 Compartments: 6 Ta, ER 2 Cargo Pump (s): 2x120m³/hr	**1 oil engine** driving 1 FP propeller Total Power: 588kW (799hp) 11.3kn Fuji 6SD27.5BH 1 x 4 Stroke 6 Cy. 275 x 410 588kW (799bhp) Fuji Diesel Co Ltd-Japan AuxGen: 2 x 12kW 225V a.c Fuel: 40.5 (Part Heating Coils) 2.5pd
9182411 *DSNY8* -	**SUN YOUNG** *ex* Ocean Venus *-2004* **Sun Ace Shipping Co Ltd** - *Jeju* *South Korea* MMSI: 440434000 Official number: JJR-042205	**4,380** 2,709 6,502	Class: KR (NK)	**1998-07 Watanabe Zosen KK — Imabari EH** Yd No: 309 Loa 100.79 Br ex - Dght 6.929 Lbp 92.70 Br md 17.20 Dpth 9.00 Welded, 1 dk	**(A31A2GX) General Cargo Ship** Grain: 9,386; Bale: 8,404 Compartments: 2 Ho, ER 2 Ha: (28.0 x 10.2) (27.3 x -)ER Cranes: 2x25.5t; Derricks: 2x15t	**1 oil engine** driving 1 FP propeller Total Power: 2,795kW (3,800hp) 12.5kn Mitsubishi 6UEC37LA 1 x 2 Stroke 6 Cy. 370 x 880 2795kW (3800bhp) Akasaka Tekkosho KK (Akasaka DieselLtd)-Japan

9080986 *UHXG* -	**SUNA** **Baltasar Shipping SA** Orion Shipping Co *St Petersburg* *Russia* MMSI: 273331000	**2,889** 1,034 4,143	Class: RS	**1994**-01 **Schiffswerft und Maschinenfabrik Cassens GmbH — Emden** Yd No: 199 Loa 96.00 Br ex 13.40 Dght 5.130 Lbp 93.00 Br md 13.20 Dpth 6.90 Welded, 1 dk	**(A31A2GX) General Cargo Ship** Grain: 5,250 TEU 160 C. 160/20' Compartments: 1 Ho, ER 1 Ha: ER	**1 oil engine** with flexible couplings & sr reverse geared to sc. shaft driving 1 FP propeller Total Power: 1,600kW (2,175hp) 11.0kn MaK 8M332C 1 x 4 Stroke 8 Cy. 240 x 330 1600kW (2175bhp) Krupp MaK Maschinenbau GmbH-Kiel AuxGen: 2 x 200V 50Hz a.c, 1 x 103kW a.c Thrusters: 1 Thwart. FP thruster (f) Fuel: 204.0 (d.f.)
7407348 *C9QC* Q-19	**SUNA** *ex* Ifcor II *-1978* **Sipel** - *Maputo* *Mozambique*	*109* 74 -	Class: (AB)	**1975**-02 **Sandock-Austral Ltd. — Durban** Yd No: 63 Loa 22.89 Br ex 6.48 Dght 2.464 Lbp 20.73 Br md 6.38 Dpth 3.33 Welded, 1 dk	**(B11A2FS) Stern Trawler**	**1 oil engine** reverse reduction geared to sc. shaft driving 1 FP propeller Total Power: 313kW (426hp) 8.5kn Caterpillar D353SCAC 1 x 4 Stroke 6 Cy. 159 x 203 313kW (426bhp) Caterpillar Tractor Co-USA AuxGen: 2 x 20kW a.c Fuel: 26.5 (d.f.)
7946497 *TC5705* -	**SUNA 1** *ex* Dogruyollar III *-1995* *ex* Ertug *-1994* *ex* Turnak-I *-1994* **Yunus Marin Gemicilik Ticaret AS** Su-Ta Denizcilik Ltd *Mersin* *Turkey* Official number: 3824	*335* 195 650		**1944 J. Readhead & Sons Ltd. — South Shields** Loa 49.94 Br ex - Dght 2.601 Lbp 47.88 Br md 7.17 Dpth 3.11 Welded, 1 dk	**(A31A2GX) General Cargo Ship**	**1 oil engine** driving 1 FP propeller Total Power: 368kW (500hp) 7.0kn S.K.L. 1 x 4 Stroke 6 Cy. 240 x 360 368kW (500bhp) VEB Schwermaschinenbau "KarlLiebknecht" (SKL)-Magdeburg
9408281 *3EXN4* -	**SUNBAY** *ex* Sunray *-2010* **Sunbay Maritime SA** Navig8 Bulk Asia Pte Ltd *Panama* *Panama* MMSI: 352760000 Official number: 4237711	**32,957** 19,231 56,842 T/cm 58.8	Class: KR (BV)	**2008**-11 **Jiangsu Hantong Ship Heavy Industry Co Ltd — Tongzhou JS** Yd No: 001 Loa 189.99 (BB) Br ex - Dght 12.800 Lbp 185.00 Br md 32.26 Dpth 18.00 Welded, 1 dk	**(A21A2BC) Bulk Carrier** Grain: 71,634; Bale: 68,200 Compartments: 5 Ho, ER 5 Ha: ER Cranes: 4x35t	**1 oil engine** driving 1 FP propeller Total Power: 9,473kW (12,879hp) 14.2kn MAN-B&W 6S50MC-C 1 x 2 Stroke 6 Cy. 500 x 2000 9473kW (12879bhp) Doosan Engine Co Ltd-South Korea
9184158 *MYTS7* FR 487	**SUNBEAM** **Sunbeam Fishing (Fraserburgh) LLP** - *Fraserburgh* *United Kingdom* MMSI: 232503000 Official number: C16691	**1,349** 404 800	Class: LR ✠ **100A1** SS 07/2009 fishing vessel ✠ **LMC** Cable: 385.0/32.0 U2	**1999**-09 **Astilleros Zamakona SA — Santurtzi** Yd No: 423 Lengthened-2004 Loa 56.17 (BB) Br ex 11.67 Dght 6.300 Lbp 48.82 Br md 11.50 Dpth 8.40 Welded, 1 dk	**(B11B2FV) Fishing Vessel**	**1 oil engine** sr geared to sc. shaft. driving 1 CP propeller Total Power: 2,651kW (3,604hp) 13.0kn MaK 8M32 1 x 4 Stroke 8 Cy. 320 x 480 2651kW (3604bhp) MaK Motoren GmbH & Co. KG-Kiel AuxGen: 1 x 1600kW 440V 60Hz a.c, 2 x 565kW 440V 60Hz a.c Thrusters: 1 Thwart. FP thruster (f); 1 Tunnel thruster (a) Fuel: 320.0 (d.f.)
9233246 *V7DK4* -	**SUNBELT SPIRIT** **Great American Lines Inc** Fairfield-Maxwell Services Ltd SatCom: Inmarsat C 453832024 *Majuro* *Marshall Islands* MMSI: 538001657 Official number: 1657	**60,587** 23,315 17,950	Class: NK	**2002**-03 **Sumitomo Heavy Industries Ltd. — Yokosuka Shipyard, Yokosuka** Yd No: 1284 Loa 212.08 (BB) Br ex - Dght 9.820 Lbp 202.00 Br md 32.26 Dpth 33.95 Welded	**(A35B2RV) Vehicles Carrier** Side door/ramp (s) Quarter stern door/ramp (s. a.) Cars: 6,190	**1 oil engine** driving 1 FP propeller Total Power: 17,760kW (24,146hp) 20.0kn Sulzer 8RTA62 1 x 2 Stroke 8 Cy. 620 x 2150 17760kW (24146bhp) Diesel United Ltd.-Aioi AuxGen: 4 x 5075kW a.c Thrusters: 1 Tunnel thruster (f) Fuel: 3620.0
9323821 *C6UU2* -	**SUNBIRD ARROW** **Glory Ocean Shipping SA** Gearbulk Ltd *Nassau* *Bahamas* MMSI: 309037000 Official number: 8001051	**12,959** 3,888 15,001	Class: NV	**2006**-02 **Kanrei Zosen K.K. — Naruto** Yd No: 398 Loa 144.00 (BB) Br ex 23.53 Dght 8.960 Lbp 134.00 Br md 23.50 Dpth 13.50 Welded, 1 dk	**(A13C2LA) Asphalt/Bitumen Tanker** Double Hull (13F) Liq: 13,720; Liq (Oil): 13,720; Asphalt: 13,720 Compartments: 10 Wing Ta, ER 3 Cargo Pump (s): 3x450m³/hr	**1 oil engine** driving 1 CP propeller Total Power: 7,175kW (9,755hp) 14.5kn MAN-B&W 7S42MC 1 x 2 Stroke 7 Cy. 420 x 1764 7175kW (9755bhp) Makita Corp-Japan AuxGen: 2 x 880kW a.c, 1 x 1000kW a.c Thrusters: 1 Thwart. CP thruster (f)
9475272 *PCQM* -	**SUNBORN BARCELONA** **Sunborn Marine OU** - *Netherlands* MMSI: 246879000	**15,000** - 2,500	**100A1** 05/2013 Class contemplated	**2013**-05 **Boustead Naval Shipyard Sdn Bhd — Lumut** Yd No: 024 Loa 141.20 (BB) Br ex - Dght 3.800 Lbp 127.30 Br md 21.00 Dpth 10.30 Welded, 1 dk	**(A37B2PS) Passenger Ship**	**4 diesel electric oil engines** driving 4 gen. each 800kW 400V a.c Connecting to 2 elec. motors each (920kW) driving 2 Directional propellers Total Power: 3,500kW (4,760hp) 9.0kn Caterpillar C32 4 x Vee 4 Stroke 12 Cy. 145 x 162 each-875kW (1190bhp) Caterpillar Inc-USA Thrusters: 1 Tunnel thruster (f)
9097472 *ZCPK5* -	**SUNCHASER** **SCR Inc** - *George Town* *Cayman Islands (British)* MMSI: 319094000 Official number: 739161	**395** 118 -	Class: AB	**2006**-07 **Richmond Yachts — Richmond BC** Yd No: 3 Loa - Br ex 8.22 Dght 2.280 Lbp 43.28 Br md 8.20 Dpth 3.65 Bonded, 1 dk	**(X11A2YP) Yacht** Hull Material: Reinforced Plastic	**2 oil engines** reduction geared to sc. shafts driving 2 FP propellers Total Power: 2,940kW (3,998hp) 16.0kn M.T.U. 16V2000M91 2 x Vee 4 Stroke 16 Cy. 130 x 150 each-1470kW (1999bhp) MTU Friedrichshafen GmbH-Friedrichshafen AuxGen: 2 x 80kW a.c
5344425 *MECR* -	**SUNCREST** *ex* Sunwind *-1985* *ex* Sun XXIII *-1984* **General Marine** - *London* *United Kingdom*	*144* - -	Class: (LR) ✠ Classed LR until 3/7/02	**1961**-03 **Philip & Son Ltd. — Dartmouth** Yd No: 1320 Loa 28.58 Br ex 7.45 Dght 3.372 Lbp 26.22 Br md 7.32 Dpth 3.74 Riveted\Welded, 1 dk	**(B32A2ST) Tug**	**1 oil engine** reverse geared to sc. shaft driving 1 FP propeller Total Power: 794kW (1,080hp) 11.0kn Mirrlees KLSSDM-6 1 x 4 Stroke 6 Cy. 381 x 508 794kW (1080bhp) Mirrlees, Bickerton & Day-Stockport AuxGen: 2 x 43kW 440V 60Hz a.c
9046007 *D9ZP* -	**SUNCRUISER** *ex* Tezroc *-2004* *ex* Han Ma Eum Ho *-1997* **Daeboo Shipping Co Ltd** - *Incheon* *South Korea* Official number: ICR-927844	**530** 218 83	Class: (KR) (NV)	**1995**-06 **Hyundai Heavy Industries Co Ltd — Ulsan** Yd No: P062 Loa 45.50 Br ex - Dght 1.810 Lbp 43.13 Br md 11.40 Dpth 5.10 Welded, 2 dks	**(A37B2PS) Passenger Ship** Passengers: unberthed: 300	**2 oil engines** with clutches, flexible couplings & sr geared to sc. shafts driving 2 Water jets Total Power: 6,040kW (8,212hp) 35.0kn Paxman 18RP200-2 2 x Vee 4 Stroke 18 Cy. 197 x 216 each-3020kW (4106bhp) Hyundai Heavy Industries Co Ltd-South Korea
8008424 *SBCA* -	**SUND** *ex* Kostersund *-2009* *ex* Biskopsbussen *-1989* **Bjare Shipping HB** - *Torekov* *Sweden* MMSI: 265587850	**189** 56 50	Class: (NV)	**1980**-04 **AS Fjellstrand Aluminium Yachts — Omastrand** Yd No: 1527 Loa 27.07 Br ex 9.34 Dght 1.600 Lbp - Br md - Dpth 3.48 Welded, 1 dk	**(A37B2PS) Passenger Ship** Hull Material: Aluminium Alloy Passengers: unberthed: 194	**2 oil engines** geared to sc. shafts driving 2 FP propellers Total Power: 1,766kW (2,402hp) M.T.U. 12V396TC62 2 x Vee 4 Stroke 12 Cy. 165 x 185 each-883kW (1201bhp) MTU Friedrichshafen GmbH-Friedrichshafen AuxGen: 2 x 24kW 220V 50Hz a.c
9609902 *ICSD* -	**SUNDAISY E** **Ireos E Srl** - *Genoa* *Italy* MMSI: 247299500	**10,154** 5,112 15,332	Class: RI	**2011**-07 **Zhejiang Aoli Shipbuilding Co Ltd — Yueqing ZJ** Yd No: AL0818 Loa 145.60 (BB) Br ex - Dght 8.200 Lbp 136.80 Br md 21.00 Dpth 11.30 Welded, 1 dk	**(A21A2BC) Bulk Carrier** Grain: 19,950 Compartments: 4 Ho, ER 4 Ha: ER Cranes: 2x25t Ice Capable	**1 oil engine** reduction geared to sc. shaft driving 1 FP propeller Total Power: 3,310kW (4,500hp) 13.0kn Yanmar 8N330-EN 1 x 4 Stroke 8 Cy. 330 x 440 3310kW (4500bhp) Qingdao Zichai Boyang Diesel EngineCo Ltd-China AuxGen: 3 x 300kW a.c Thrusters: 1 Tunnel thruster (f)
8633762 *OWCD* -	**SUNDANCE** *ex* Solent Enterprise *-2005* *ex* Gay Enterprise *-1979* **M H Madsen** - *Svendborg* *Denmark* Official number: R104	*273* - -		**1971**-06 **James & Stone (Brightlingsea) Ltd. — Brightlingsea** Yd No: 464 Converted From: Ferry (Passenger only)-2007 Loa 29.99 Br ex - Dght 1.670 Lbp - Br md 9.15 Dpth - Welded, 1 dk	**(X11A2YP) Yacht**	**2 oil engines** driving 2 Propellers 1 fwd and 1 aft Total Power: 541kW (735hp) Dorman 6QTCWM 1 x 4 Stroke 6 Cy. 159 x 165 173kW (235bhp) Dorman Diesels Ltd.-Stafford Dorman 8QTCWM 1 x 4 Stroke 8 Cy. 159 x 165 368kW (500bhp) Dorman Diesels Ltd.-Stafford
8120222 - -	**SUNDANCER** **Ocean Fisheries (Nigeria) Ltd** - *Lagos* *Nigeria* Official number: 375852	*154* 113 -		**1980**-12 **Quality Marine, Inc. — Bayou La Batre, Al** Yd No: 154 Loa 27.16 Br ex - Dght - Lbp 24.69 Br md 7.01 Dpth - Welded, 1 dk	**(B11A2FS) Stern Trawler**	**1 oil engine** driving 1 FP propeller Total Power: 382kW (519hp) Caterpillar 3412TA 1 x Vee 4 Stroke 12 Cy. 137 x 152 382kW (519bhp) Caterpillar Tractor Co-USA

8901975 *VWVI* -	**SUNDARAM** *ex Atco Daina -1999* **Shiv Vani Oil & Gas Exploration Services Ltd** Modest Maritime Services Pvt Ltd *Mumbai India* MMSI: 419072100 Official number: 2859	122 36 30	Class: IR (AB)	**1988 Halter Marine, Inc. — New Orleans, La** Yd No: 1147 Loa 30.99 Br ex 6.48 Dght 1.520 Lbp 29.07 Br md 6.40 Dpth 2.90 Welded	**(B21A2OC) Crew/Supply Vessel** Hull Material: Aluminium Alloy	**3 oil engines** reverse reduction geared to sc. shafts driving 3 FP propellers Total Power: 1,125kW (1,530hp) 15.0kn G.M. (Detroit Diesel) 12V-71-TI 3 x Vee 2 Stroke 12 Cy. 108 x 127 each-375kW (510bhp) General Motors Detroit DieselAllison Divn-USA AuxGen: 2 x 30kW 220V 50Hz a.c Fuel: 14.0 (d.f.)
9266695 *VWSJ* -	**SUNDARANAR** **Chennai Port Trust** - *Chennai India* Official number: 2938	397 119 152	Class: (IR)	**2002-11 Goodwill Engineering Works — Pondicherry** Yd No: 45 Loa 32.60 Br ex 10.72 Dght 4.650 Lbp 31.00 Br md 10.70 Dpth 4.00 Welded, 1 dk	**(B32A2ST) Tug**	**2 oil engines** reduction geared to sc. shafts driving 2 FP propellers Total Power: 2,624kW (3,568hp) 12.0kn Yanmar 8N21A-EN 2 x 4 Stroke 8 Cy. 210 x 290 each-1312kW (1784bhp) Yanmar Diesel Engine Co Ltd-Japan AuxGen: 2 x 80kW 415V 50Hz a.c Fuel: 42.0 (d.f.)
9384291 *SY7841* -	**SUNDAY** **Mediterranean Sun MCPY** - *Piraeus Greece* MMSI: 240559000	748 224 166	Class: LR (HR) (AB) **100A1** SS 08/2011 SSC Yacht, mono, G6 **LMC**	**2006-05 Azimut-Benetti SpA — Livorno** Yd No: FB235 Loa 58.30 Br ex - Dght 3.100 Lbp 50.80 Br md 10.40 Dpth 5.45 Welded, 1 dk	**(X11A2YP) Yacht**	**2 oil engines** reduction geared to sc. shafts driving 2 FP propellers Total Power: 2,722kW (3,700hp) Caterpillar 3512B 2 x Vee 4 Stroke 12 Cy. 170 x 190 each-1361kW (1850bhp) Caterpillar Inc-USA AuxGen: 3 x a.c Thrusters: 1 Tunnel thruster (f)
9294903 *LMJP* N-100-O	**SUNDEROY** **Prestfjord AS** - *Sortland Norway* MMSI: 258052000	1,874 565 1,026	Class: NV	**2004-08 Astilleros Gondan SA — Castropol** Yd No: 423 Loa 56.20 (BB) Br ex - Dght 6.000 Lbp 49.20 Br md 14.00 Dpth 5.50 Welded, 1 dk	**(B11A2FS) Stern Trawler** Ice Capable	**1 oil engine** geared to sc. shaft driving 1 CP propeller Total Power: 4,500kW (6,118hp) 16.0kn Bergens B32: 40L9P 1 x 4 Stroke 9 Cy. 320 x 400 4500kW (6118bhp) Rolls Royce Marine AS-Norway AuxGen: 1 x a.c, 1 x a.c Thrusters: 1 Thwart. CP thruster (f) Fuel: 510.0 (d.f.)
5344724 *HQLD6* -	**SUNDET** **Milford Marine Nigeria Ltd** Eastern Bulkcem Co Ltd *San Lorenzo Honduras* Official number: L-1724625	137 41 -	Class: (LR) ✠ Classed LR until 5/10/01	**1960-08 Solvesborgs Varv AB — Solvesborg** Yd No: 57 Loa 26.00 Br ex 7.40 Dght 2.921 Lbp 23.70 Br md 7.21 Dpth 3.97 Welded, 1 dk	**(B32A2ST) Tug** Ice Capable	**1 oil engine** with flexible couplings & sr reverse geared to sc. shaft driving 1 FP propeller Total Power: 802kW (1,090hp) 11.0kn Ruston 8VEBCM 1 x 4 Stroke 8 Cy. 260 x 368 802kW (1090bhp) Ruston & Hornsby Ltd.-Lincoln AuxGen: 2 x 48kW 220V d.c, 1 x 25kW 220V d.c, 1 x 7kW 220V d.c Fuel: 51.0 (d.f.)
8875504 *LFVQ* -	**SUNDFERJA** *ex Kvaloy -2011* **Bergen-Nordhordaland Rutelag AS** - *Bergen Norway* MMSI: 257295400	180 54 -		**1977-09 Skjervoy Skipsverft AS — Skjervoy** Yd No: 3 Loa 31.59 Br ex - Dght - Lbp 28.50 Br md 9.50 Dpth 3.50 Welded, 1 dk	**(A36A2PR) Passenger/Ro-Ro Ship (Vehicles)** Passengers: unberthed: 88 Lane-Len: 28 Cars: 16	**2 oil engines** driving 2 FP propellers Total Power: 184kW (250hp) 8.5kn Deutz F6M716 2 x 4 Stroke 6 Cy. 135 x 160 each-92kW (125bhp) Kloeckner Humboldt Deutz AG-West Germany
9187655 *5ISG36* -	**SUNDIAL** *ex Crystal -2013 ex Pluto -2012* *ex Abadeh -2012 ex Iran Abadeh -2008* **NITC** - *Zanzibar Tanzania (Zanzibar)* MMSI: 677003500	56,068 29,042 99,030 T/cm 94.5	Class: KR (LR) ✠ Classed LR until 27/3/12	**2000-10 Daewoo Heavy Industries Ltd — Geoje** Yd No: 5148 Loa 248.00 Br ex 43.03 Dght 13.500 Lbp 238.00 Br md 43.00 Dpth 19.80 Welded, 1 dk	**(A13A2TW) Crude/Oil Products Tanker** Double Hull (13F) Liq: 111,556; Liq (Oil): 111,556 Compartments: 12 Wing Ta, 2 Wing Slop Ta, ER 3 Cargo Pump (s): 3x2500m³/hr Manifold: Bow/CM: 84m	**1 oil engine** driving 1 FP propeller Total Power: 14,312kW (19,459hp) 15.4kn Sulzer 7RTA58T 1 x 2 Stroke 7 Cy. 580 x 2416 14312kW (19459bhp) HSD Engine Co Ltd-South Korea AuxGen: 3 x 860kW 450V 60Hz a.c Boilers: 2 AuxB (o.f.) 18.7kgf/cm² (18.3bar), e (ex.g.) 21.9kgf/cm² (21.5bar) Fuel: 210.0 (d.f.) (Heating Coils) 3246.0 (r.f.) 60.0pd
8308587 - -	**SUNDOWNER** *ex Phoenix II -2008 ex Makandra No. 15 -1998* - - -	*134* 91 -		**1983 Master Marine, Inc. — Bayou La Batre, Al** Yd No: 257 Loa 25.30 Br ex - Dght 3.000 Lbp 21.67 Br md 6.72 Dpth 3.81 Welded, 1 dk	**(B11A2FT) Trawler** Ins: 91	**1 oil engine** reduction geared to sc. shaft driving 1 FP propeller Total Power: 331kW (450hp) Caterpillar 3412T 1 x Vee 4 Stroke 12 Cy. 137 x 152 331kW (450bhp) Caterpillar Tractor Co-USA
8855645 - -	**SUNDOWNER '84** **Sahlman Seafoods Inc** - *Kingstown St Vincent & The Grenadines*	*101* 69 -		**1984 Steiner Shipyard, Inc. — Bayou La Batre, Al** Loa 22.86 Br ex - Dght - Lbp 20.33 Br md 6.71 Dpth 3.32 Welded, 1 dk	**(B11A2FT) Trawler**	**1 oil engine** geared to sc. shaft driving 1 FP propeller Total Power: 268kW (364hp) Cummins KT-1150-M 1 x 4 Stroke 6 Cy. 159 x 159 268kW (364bhp) Cummins Engine Co Inc-USA
8920567 *LIFL3* -	**SUNDSTRAUM** *ex Maj-Britt Terkol -1996* **Utkilen Shipping AS** Utkilen AS SatCom: Inmarsat C 425936010 *Bergen Norway (NIS)* MMSI: 259360000	3,206 1,358 4,737 T/cm 12.4	Class: NV (LR) ✠ Classed LR until 6/8/96	**1993-03 Aarhus Flydedok A/S — Aarhus** Yd No: 202 Loa 96.35 (BB) Br ex 15.33 Dght 6.211 Lbp 88.25 Br md 15.30 Dpth 8.05 Welded, 1 dk	**(A12B2TR) Chemical/Products Tanker** Double Hull (13F) Liq: 5,088; Liq (Oil): 4,885 Cargo Heating Coils Compartments: 1 Ta, 2 Wing Slop Ta, 12 Wing Ta, ER 15 Cargo Pump (s): 7x150m³/hr, 8x275m³/hr Manifold: Bow/CM: 49.7m Ice Capable	**1 oil engine** with clutches, flexible couplings & sr geared to sc. shaft driving 1 CP propeller Total Power: 2,970kW (4,038hp) 13.2kn MaK 9M453C 1 x 4 Stroke 9 Cy. 320 x 420 2970kW (4038bhp) Krupp MaK Maschinenbau GmbH-Kiel AuxGen: 1 x 633kW 220/380V 50Hz a.c, 3 x 335kW 220/380V 50Hz a.c Thrusters: 1 Thwart. CP thruster (f) Fuel: 71.0 (d.f.) (Part Heating Coils) 328.0 (r.f.)
5344750 *LJHX* -	**SUNDVAG** *ex Borre -1993 ex Sundvag -1986* *ex Sund 2 -1955 ex VIC 49 -1953* **Bjoroya Fiskeoppdrett AS** - *Oslo Norway*	*183* 108 249	Class: (LR) ✠ Classed LR until 19/6/97	**1944-06 I. Pimblott & Sons Ltd. — Northwich** Yd No: 659 Lengthened-1964 Loa 33.96 Br ex 6.20 Dght 2.540 Lbp 31.73 Br md 6.10 Dpth 2.90 Welded, 1 dk	**(A31A2GX) General Cargo Ship** Grain: 340 Compartments: 1 Ho, ER 1 Ha: (14.6 x 3.6)ER Derricks: 1x2.3t; Winches: 1	**1 oil engine** driving 1 CP propeller Total Power: 154kW (209hp) 8.0kn Normo Z3 1 x 2 Stroke 3 Cy. 300 x 360 154kW (209bhp) (new engine 1963) AS Bergens Mek Verksteder-Norway Fuel: 8.0 (d.f.)
9362580 *PHDF* -	**SUNERGON** **Sunergon Shipping CV** - *Nijkerk Netherlands* MMSI: 246374000 Official number: 44312	2,241 1,077 3,121	Class: LR (RS) **100A1** SS 04/2011 container cargoes in holds and on hatch covers, strengthend for heavy cargoes ✠ **LMC** **UMS** Eq.Ltr: Q; Cable: 440.0/34.0 U3 (a)	**2006-04 Cherepovetskiy Sudostroitelnyy i Sudoremontnyy Zavod — Cherepovets** (Hull) **2006-04 Instalho BV — Werkendam** Yd No: 2004/001 Loa 88.65 Br ex 12.76 Dght 5.000 Lbp 84.64 Br md 12.50 Dpth 6.50 Welded, 1 dk	**(A31A2GX) General Cargo Ship** Grain: 3,999 TEU 164 C Ho 74 TEU C Dk 90 TEU incl 12 ref C Cranes: 1x30t	**1 oil engine** with flexible couplings & sr geared to sc. shaft driving 1 FP propeller Total Power: 1,440kW (1,958hp) Wartsila 8L20 1 x 4 Stroke 8 Cy. 200 x 280 1440kW (1958bhp) Wartsila Finland Oy-Finland AuxGen: 1 x 301kW 440V 50Hz a.c, 1 x 266kW 440V 50Hz a.c Boilers: TOH (Comp) Thrusters: 1 Thwart. FP thruster (f)
8963064 *HQSC8* -	**SUNFAST** *ex Changda 505 -1997* **Loyal India Ocean Shipping Co Ltd** - *San Lorenzo Honduras* Official number: L-0326410	795 445 -		**1996-01 Xiamen Shipyard — Xiamen FJ** Loa - Br ex - Dght - Lbp 54.40 Br md 9.78 Dpth 4.57 Welded, 1 dk	**(A31A2GX) General Cargo Ship**	**1 oil engine** geared to sc. shaft driving 1 FP propeller Total Power: 433kW (589hp) 12.0kn Chinese Std. Type 8300 1 x 4 Stroke 8 Cy. 300 x 380 433kW (589bhp) Zibo Diesel Engine Factory-China
7740087 - -	**SUNFENG** *ex Hua Hang Hai -2007 ex Ever Safety -2005* *ex Xin Tai Yuan -2004 ex Lian Chang 343 -2003* *ex Athena -2003 ex Zenith -1998* *ex Phoenix No. 2 -1996* *ex Koun Maru No. 11 -1982* **Tai Yuan Shipping Co Ltd** -	984 551 1,072	Class: (NK)	**1978 K.K. Yoshida Zosen Kogyo — Arida** Yd No: 278 Loa 60.30 Br ex - Dght 3.723 Lbp 55.00 Br md 10.40 Dpth 5.62 Welded, 1 dk	**(A31A2GX) General Cargo Ship** Grain: 2,048; Bale: 1,612 1 Ha: (30.8 x 8.0)ER	**1 oil engine** driving 1 FP propeller Total Power: 956kW (1,300hp) 12.5kn Makita GNLH630 1 x 4 Stroke 6 Cy. 300 x 480 956kW (1300bhp) Makita Diesel Co Ltd-Japan AuxGen: 2 x 48kW

IMO / Call sign / Flag	Name, Owner, Registry	Tonnage	Class	Built	Type / Capacity	Machinery
9060431 *J8LV6* -	**SUNFISH** *ex* Starfish *-1995* **Namsov Fishing Enterprises Pty Ltd** - SatCom: Inmarsat Mini-M 761689681 *Kingstown St Vincent & The Grenadines* MMSI: 376601000 Official number: 6748	**4,407** 1,322 1,820	Class: RS (NV)	**1993**-04 **DAHK Chernomorskyi Sudnobudivnyi Zavod — Mykolayiv** Yd No: 603 Loa 104.50 Br ex - Dght 5.900 Lbp 96.40 Br md 16.00 Dpth 10.20 Welded, 1 dk	**(B11A2FG) Factory Stern Trawler** Grain: 420; Ins: 2,219 Ice Capable	**2 oil engines** reduction geared to sc. shaft driving 1 CP propeller Total Power: 5,152kW (7,004hp) 16.1kn Russkiy 6CHN40/46 2 x 4 Stroke 6 Cy. 400 x 460 each-2576kW (3502bhp) Mashinostroitelnyy Zavod"Russkiy-Dizel"-Sankt-Peterburg AuxGen: 2 x 1600kW 220/380V 50Hz a.c, 3 x 200kW 220/380V 50Hz a.c Fuel: 1226.0 (d.f.) 23.0pd
7647273 *WYC2233* -	**SUNFLOWER** *ex* Bender *-1995* - - *New Bedford, MA United States of America* Official number: 578559	*146* 102 -		**1976 Bender Welding & Machine Co Inc — Mobile AL** L reg 22.96 Br ex 6.71 Dght - Lbp - Br md - Dpth 3.38 Welded, 1 dk	**(B11B2FV) Fishing Vessel**	**1 oil engine** driving 1 FP propeller Total Power: 416kW (566hp)
6803868 *DVPB* -	**SUNFLOWER 88** *ex* Pelagis 102 *-2010* *ex* Sunflower *-2000* *ex* Hoyo Maru *-1981* *ex* Kaio Maru No. 18 *-1981* **Frabelle Fishing Corp** - *Manila Philippines* Official number: 00-0000220	*995* 528 780		**1967**-09 **KK Kanasashi Zosen — Shizuoka SZ** Yd No: 769 Loa 68.00 Br ex 11.20 Dght 4.573 Lbp 61.17 Br md 11.18 Dpth 5.08 Welded, 1 dk	**(B11B2FV) Fishing Vessel** Compartments: ER	**1 oil engine** reduction geared to sc. shaft driving 1 FP propeller Total Power: 1,330kW (1,808hp) 12.0kn Caterpillar 1 x 4 Stroke 1330kW (1808bhp) (new engine 2010) Caterpillar Inc-USA AuxGen: 2 x 250kW 445V a.c, 1 x 5kW 100V a.c Fuel: 496.0
8810035 *DUA2440* -	**SUNFLOWER 888** *ex* Zora *-1994* **Frabelle Fishing Corp** - SatCom: Inmarsat C 454858510 *Manila Philippines* Official number: MNLD001222	**994** 506 1,105	Class: (NV)	**1990**-02 **K Shipyard Construction & Repairs Pty Ltd — Port Adelaide SA** Yd No: 10 Loa 56.00 (BB) Br ex 11.84 Dght 4.960 Lbp 46.95 Br md 11.60 Dpth 7.63 Welded, 1 dk	**(B11B2FV) Fishing Vessel** Ins: 800	**1 oil engine** with flexible couplings & sr geared to sc. shaft driving 1 FP propeller Total Power: 1,821kW (2,476hp) 12.0kn Caterpillar 3606TA 1 x 4 Stroke 6 Cy. 280 x 300 1821kW (2476bhp) Caterpillar Inc-USA AuxGen: 1 x 350kW 240V 50Hz a.c, 1 x 280kW 240V 50Hz a.c, 1 x 48kW 240V 50Hz a.c Thrusters: 1 Thwart. FP thruster (f); 1 Thwart. FP thruster (a) Fuel: 316.0 (d.f.) 10.0pd
9549669 *IBVW* -	**SUNFLOWER E** **Energy Shipping SpA** Altomar Maritime Inc SatCom: Inmarsat C 424702894 *Genoa Italy* MMSI: 247284600 Official number: R.I. N.141	**8,604** 5,499 13,000	Class: BV	**2009**-03 **Zhejiang Donghong Shipbuilding Co Ltd — Xiangshan County ZJ** Yd No: C4088-3 Loa 120.50 (BB) Br ex - Dght 8.200 Lbp 113.80 Br md 22.00 Dpth 11.00 Welded, 1 dk	**(A31A2GX) General Cargo Ship** Grain: 16,300 Compartments: 4 Ho, ER 4 Ha: ER 4 (16.8 x 15.0) Cranes: 2x20t Ice Capable	**1 oil engine** reduction geared to sc. shaft driving 1 FP propeller Total Power: 3,310kW (4,500hp) 11.0kn Yanmar 8N330-EN 1 x 4 Stroke 8 Cy. 330 x 440 3310kW (4500bhp) Yanmar Diesel Engine Co Ltd-Japan
9376335 *JD2460* -	**SUNFLOWER GOLD** **Ferry Sunflower Ltd** - *Oita, Oita Japan* MMSI: 431000331 Official number: 140584	*11,178* - 4,458		**2007**-11 **Mitsubishi Heavy Industries Ltd. — Shimonoseki** Yd No: 1124 Loa 165.50 (BB) Br ex - Dght 6.000 Lbp 154.70 Br md 27.00 Dpth 14.30 Welded	**(A36A2PR) Passenger/Ro-Ro Ship (Vehicles)** Passengers: 748 Bow door/ramp (centre) Stern door/ramp (centre) Side door/ramp (s. a.) Cars: 222	**2 oil engines** reduction geared to sc. shaft driving 1 CP propeller Total Power: 18,000kW (24,472hp) 23.2kn Pielstick 12PC2.6B 2 x Vee 4 Stroke 12 Cy. 400 x 500 each-9000kW (12236bhp) Nippon Kokan KK (NKK Corp)-Japan Thrusters: 1 Tunnel thruster (f); 3 Tunnel thruster (a) Fuel: 133.0 (d.f.) 468.0 (r.f.)
9284219 *JL6711* -	**SUNFLOWER HAKATA** **Shunzan Kaiun KK (Shunzan Kaiun Co Ltd)** - *Imabari, Ehime Japan* MMSI: 431501764 Official number: 137053	*10,507* - 6,204	Class: NK	**2003**-10 **Mitsubishi Heavy Industries Ltd. — Shimonoseki** Yd No: 1097 Loa 166.90 Br ex - Dght 6.625 Lbp 158.00 Br md 27.00 Dpth 7.38 Welded	**(A35A2RR) Ro-Ro Cargo Ship** Lane-Len: 1920 Cars: 201, Trailers: 160	**1 oil engine** driving 1 FP propeller Total Power: 15,345kW (20,863hp) 25.0kn Mitsubishi 9UEC52LSEII 1 x 2 Stroke 9 Cy. 520 x 2000 15345kW (20863bhp) Mitsubishi Heavy Industries Ltd-Japan AuxGen: 4 x 1050kW a.c Fuel: 610.0
7331290 *DUA2476* -	**SUNFLOWER I** *ex* Izumi Maru No. 10 *-1989* **Delsan Transport Lines Inc** - *Batangas Philippines* Official number: 231431	*698* 409 750	Class: (NK)	**1973**-06 **Miyoshi Shipbuilding Co Ltd — Uwajima EH** Yd No: 215 Loa 60.80 Br ex 10.04 Dght 3.804 Lbp 55.00 Br md 10.00 Dpth 4.60 Riveted\Welded, 1 dk	**(A11B2TG) LPG Tanker** Liq (Gas): 1,014 2 x Gas Tank (s);	**1 oil engine** driving 1 FP propeller Total Power: 1,177kW (1,600hp) 12.5kn Daihatsu 8DSM-26 1 x 4 Stroke 8 Cy. 260 x 320 1177kW (1600bhp) Daihatsu Diesel Manufacturing Co Lt-Japan AuxGen: 2 x 40kW a.c Fuel: 65.0 7.5pd
9376347 *JD2496* -	**SUNFLOWER PEARL** **Ferry Sunflower Ltd** - *Oita, Oita Japan* MMSI: 431000406 Official number: 140627	*11,177* - 4,000		**2008**-01 **Mitsubishi Heavy Industries Ltd. — Shimonoseki** Yd No: 1125 Loa 165.50 (BB) Br ex - Dght 6.000 Lbp 154.00 Br md 27.00 Dpth 14.30 Welded, 6 dks plus 1 moveable dk	**(A36A2PR) Passenger/Ro-Ro Ship (Vehicles)** Double Hull Passengers: 748; cabins: 223 Bow door/ramp (f) Stern door/ramp (a) Quarter stern door/ramps (s. a.) Lorries: 75, Trailers: 9, Vehicles: 36	**2 oil engines** reduction geared to sc. shafts driving 2 CP propellers Total Power: 18,000kW (24,472hp) 23.2kn Pielstick 12PC2.6B 2 x Vee 4 Stroke 12 Cy. 400 x 500 each-9000kW (12236bhp) Nippon Kokan KK (NKK Corp)-Japan AuxGen: 1 x 1350kW a.c, 1 x 1800kW a.c, 2 x 1280kW a.c Thrusters: 1 Tunnel thruster (f); 3 Tunnel thruster (a) Fuel: 130.0 (d.f.) 465.0 (r.f.) 68.0pd
9284221 *JH3422* -	**SUNFLOWER TOKYO** **Japan Railway Construction, Transport & Technology Agency & Hosei Kisen Co Ltd** Hosei Kisen KK *Kamo, Shizuoka Japan* MMSI: 431200647 Official number: 134435	*10,503* - 6,204	Class: NK	**2003**-11 **Mitsubishi Heavy Industries Ltd. — Shimonoseki** Yd No: 1098 Loa 166.90 (BB) Br ex - Dght 6.625 Lbp 158.00 Br md 27.00 Dpth 7.38 Welded	**(A35A2RR) Ro-Ro Cargo Ship** Lane-Len: 1920 Cars: 251, Trailers: 160	**1 oil engine** driving 1 FP propeller Total Power: 11,915kW (16,200hp) 25.0kn Mitsubishi 9UEC52LSEII 1 x 2 Stroke 9 Cy. 520 x 2000 11915kW (16200bhp) Mitsubishi Heavy Industries Ltd-Japan AuxGen: 3 x 1370kW a.c Fuel: 610.0
7380265 - -	**SUNFORD No. 1** *ex* Sachi Maru No. 81 *-1989* - -	*254* 122 307	Class: (KR)	**1974**-03 **Niigata Engineering Co Ltd — Niigata NI** Yd No: 1305 Loa 45.65 Br ex 7.93 Dght 3.250 Lbp 40.19 Br md 7.90 Dpth 3.51 Welded, 1 dk	**(B11B2FV) Fishing Vessel**	**1 oil engine** driving 1 FP propeller Total Power: 625kW (850hp) Niigata 6L28X 1 x 4 Stroke 6 Cy. 280 x 440 625kW (850bhp) Niigata Engineering Co Ltd-Japan
8840597 - -	**SUNG AN** *ex* Sejong *-2012* *ex* Taisei Maru *-2005* **Kings Marine Co Ltd** - *Busan South Korea* MMSI: 440600170 Official number: BSR-013710	*125* - -	Class: KR	**1989**-10 **Kanto Kogyo K.K. — Hakodate** Yd No: 120 Loa 28.00 Br ex - Dght 2.100 Lbp 25.00 Br md 8.20 Dpth 3.47 Welded, 1 dk	**(B32A2ST) Tug**	**2 oil engines** driving 2 Directional propellers Total Power: 1,618kW (2,200hp) Niigata 6L22X 2 x 4 Stroke 6 Cy. 220 x 250 each-809kW (1100bhp) Niigata Engineering Co Ltd-Japan
9111412 - -	**SUNG HAE** **GS-Caltex Corp** Hansun Shipping Co Ltd SatCom: Inmarsat C 444000136 *Yeosu South Korea* MMSI: 440309560 Official number: YSR-075682	**5,914** 2,670 11,816	Class: KR	**1995**-07 **Korea Tacoma Marine Industries Ltd — Changwon** Yd No: 003 Loa 119.82 Br ex - Dght 8.386 Lbp - Br md 19.00 Dpth 10.30 Welded, 1 dk	**(A13B2TP) Products Tanker** Single Hull Liq: 12,790; Liq (Oil): 12,790	**1 oil engine** driving 1 CP propeller Total Power: 2,806kW (3,815hp) 12.0kn B&W 7S26MC 1 x 2 Stroke 7 Cy. 260 x 980 2806kW (3815bhp) Ssangyong Heavy Industries Co Ltd-South Korea
7829431 *6MXU* -	**SUNG HAE No. 21** *ex* Dong Kang No. 111 *-1986* *ex* Dae Heung No. 3 *-1984* **Lee Sung-Man** - *Busan South Korea* Official number: BS-A-1578	*124* 56 139	Class: (KR)	**1979**-01 **ShinA Shipbuilding Co Ltd — Tongyeong** Loa 39.12 Br ex - Dght - Lbp 30.21 Br md 6.30 Dpth 2.80 Welded, 1 dk	**(B11A2FS) Stern Trawler** Ins: 127 4 Ha: (1.1 x 1.1)3 (1.3 x 1.3)	**1 oil engine** driving 1 FP propeller Total Power: 588kW (799hp) 11.0kn Akasaka 6MH25SSR 1 x 4 Stroke 6 Cy. 250 x 400 588kW (799bhp) Akasaka Tekkosho KK (Akasaka DieselLtd)-Japan AuxGen: 2 x 80kW 225V a.c

IMO / Call sign	Name / Owner	Tonnage	Class	Builder / Dimensions	Type	Machinery	Speed / Model
7829443 - -	**SUNG HAE No. 22** *ex* Dong Kang No. 112 *-1986* *ex* Dae Heung No. 5 *-1984* **Lee Sung-Man** - *Busan* *South Korea* Official number: BS-A-1579	*125* 56 140	Class: (KR)	**1979-01 ShinA Shipbuilding Co Ltd — Tongyeong** Loa 39.12 Br ex - Dght - Lbp 30.21 Br md 6.30 Dpth 2.80 Welded, 1 dk	**(B11A2FS) Stern Trawler** Ins: 127 4 Ha: (1.1 x 1.1)3 (1.3 x 1.3)	**1 oil engine** driving 1 FP propeller Total Power: 588kW (799hp) Akasaka 1 x 4 Stroke 6 Cy. 250 x 400 588kW (799bhp) Akasaka Tekkosho KK (Akasaka DieselLtd)-Japan AuxGen: 2 x 80kW 225V a.c	11.0kn 6MH25SSR
7014749 *6KCK* -	**SUNG HAE No. 51** *ex* Kiku Maru No. 12 *-1984* **Jung Seung-Il & Besides One** - *Busan* *South Korea* Official number: BS-A-2612	*115* 43 -	Class: (KR)	**1969 Hayashikane Shipbuilding & Engineering Co Ltd — Nagasaki NS** Yd No: 728 Loa 34.27 Br ex 6.33 Dght 2.388 Lbp 28.78 Br md 6.30 Dpth 2.85 Welded, 1 dk	**(B11B2FV) Fishing Vessel**	**1 oil engine** driving 1 FP propeller Total Power: 515kW (700hp) Niigata 1 x 4 Stroke 6 Cy. 250 x 320 515kW (700bhp) Niigata Engineering Co Ltd-Japan	6L25BX
8947462 *YJSW4* -	**SUNG HUI** **Sung Hui Ocean Co Ltd** Sung Hui Fishery Co Ltd *Port Vila* *Vanuatu* MMSI: 576850000 Official number: 1486	**498** 220 -		**1997 Fong Kuo Shipbuilding Co Ltd — Kaohsiung** L reg 48.60 Br ex - Dght - Lbp - Br md 8.70 Dpth 3.75 Welded, 1 dk	**(B11B2FV) Fishing Vessel**	**1 oil engine** driving 1 FP propeller Total Power: 1,030kW (1,400hp) Akasaka 1 x 4 Stroke 1030kW (1400bhp) Akasaka Tekkosho KK (Akasaka DieselLtd)-Japan	13.0kn
7327419 *HMCO* -	**SUNG JIN 3** *ex* Dae Hung 5 *-2007* *ex* Sea Hawk *-2003* *ex* Kaikata Maru No. 38 *-1992* **Korea Sungjin Shipping Co** - *Wonsan* *North Korea* MMSI: 445183000 Official number: 2306110	**490** 195 424	Class: KC	**1973 Miho Zosensho K.K. — Shimizu** Yd No: 918 Loa 50.40 Br ex 8.23 Dght 3.379 Lbp 44.02 Br md 8.21 Dpth 3.61 Welded, 1 dk	**(B11B2FV) Fishing Vessel**	**1 oil engine** driving 1 FP propeller Total Power: 736kW (1,001hp) Niigata 1 x 4 Stroke 6 Cy. 280 x 440 736kW (1001bhp) Niigata Engineering Co Ltd-Japan	6M28KHS
6706199 *6MNT* -	**SUNG JIN No. 101** *ex* Hwa Sung No. 6 *-1992* *ex* Kwan Ak San No. 3 *-1990* *ex* Kanei Maru No. 12 *-1972* **Tower Shipping Co Ltd** - *Busan* *South Korea* Official number: 9607023-6461303	**380** 114 200	Class: (KR)	**1966 Uchida Zosen — Ise** Yd No: 637 L reg 38.32 Br ex 7.24 Dght 3.099 Lbp 38.00 Br md 7.22 Dpth 3.48 Riveted\Welded, 1 dk	**(B11B2FV) Fishing Vessel** 2 Ha: (1.1 x 1.4) (1.2 x 1.1)ER	**1 oil engine** driving 1 FP propeller Total Power: 662kW (900hp) Hanshin 1 x 4 Stroke 6 Cy. 350 x 500 662kW (900bhp) Hanshin Nainenki Kogyo-Japan AuxGen: 2 x 80kW 230V a.c	10.5kn Z6WS
7853286 - -	**SUNG JIN NO. 333** *ex* Fuji Maru *-2001* - - *Philippines*	**1,287** 687 300	Class: GM	**1976 Toura Zosen — Japan** Loa 65.51 Br ex - Dght 3.150 Lbp 59.59 Br md 11.41 Dpth 8.06 Welded, 1 dk	**(A35B2RV) Vehicles Carrier** Compartments: 2 Ho, ER	**2 oil engines** driving 2 FP propellers Total Power: 1,912kW (2,600hp) Akasaka 2 x 4 Stroke each-956kW (1300bhp) Akasaka Tekkosho KK (Akasaka DieselLtd)-Japan	13.5kn
5099446 - -	**SUNG JIN NO. 777** *ex* Sea Star 77 *-1999* *ex* Pioneer No. 7 *-1999* *ex* Hondu Pioneer *-1992* *ex* Silver Pacific *-1992* *ex* Kyuho Maru No. 58 *-1989* *ex* Eitan Maru *-1984* - -	*449* 214 375		**1962-01 KK Kanasashi Zosen — Shizuoka SZ** Yd No: 435 Converted From: Fishing Vessel-1999 Loa 56.62 Br ex 9.05 Dght - Lbp 50.47 Br md 9.00 Dpth 4.30 Welded, 1 dk	**(A34A2GR) Refrigerated Cargo Ship** Compartments: 3 Ho, ER	**1 oil engine** driving 1 FP propeller Total Power: 883kW (1,201hp) Akasaka 1 x 4 Stroke 6 Cy. 420 x 600 883kW (1201bhp) Akasaka Tekkosho KK (Akasaka DieselLtd)-Japan AuxGen: 2 x 120kW 230V a.c	12.3kn UZ6SS
6401933 *6LWA* -	**SUNG KYUNG No. 2** *ex* Dai Ho No. 2 *-1986* *ex* Katsu Maru No. 16 *-1972* **Sung Kyung Fisheries Co Ltd** - *Busan* *South Korea* Official number: BS-A-148	*250* 126 282	Class: (KR)	**1963 KK Kanasashi Zosen — Shizuoka SZ** Yd No: 540 Loa 43.72 Br ex 7.57 Dght - Lbp 38.54 Br md 7.50 Dpth 3.31 Welded, 1 dk	**(B11B2FV) Fishing Vessel** Grain: 392; Bale: 299 4 Ha: 2 (1.0 x 0.9)2 (1.3 x 1.2)	**1 oil engine** driving 1 FP propeller Total Power: 478kW (650hp) Hanshin 1 x 4 Stroke 6 Cy. 320 x 450 478kW (650bhp) Hanshin Nainenki Kogyo-Japan AuxGen: 2 x 82kW 220V a.c	11.0kn V6
7418165 *6LCT* -	**SUNG KYUNG No. 5** *ex* Saraton No. 2 *-1990* *ex* Chance No. 62 *-1988* *ex* O Dae Yang No. 306 *-1981* **Sung Kyung Fisheries Co Ltd** - *Busan* *South Korea* Official number: 9507082-6260003	**292** - 330	Class: (KR)	**1974 Koo-Il Industries Co Ltd — Busan** Yd No: 202 Loa 44.48 Br ex - Dght 3.092 Lbp 38.51 Br md 8.01 Dpth 3.20 Welded, 1 dk	**(B11B2FV) Fishing Vessel** Ins: 245 4 Ha: 2 (1.2 x 8.4) (1.5 x 1.5) (8.0 x 8.0)ER	**1 oil engine** driving 1 FP propeller Total Power: 552kW (750hp) Makita 1 x 4 Stroke 6 Cy. 230 x 410 552kW (750bhp) Makita Diesel Co Ltd-Japan AuxGen: 2 x 80kW 230V a.c	12.5kn GNLH623
7408299 *6MXF* -	**SUNG KYUNG NO. 505** *ex* Dong Won No. 608 *-2009* *ex* Hae Chang No. 77 *-1984* **Sung Kyung Fisheries Co Ltd** Korea Ship Safety Technology Authority *Busan* *South Korea* MMSI: 440815000 Official number: 9512147-6260004	**718** 254 484	Class: (KR)	**1974-07 Miho Zosensho K.K. — Shimizu** Yd No: 993 Loa 55.50 Br ex 9.02 Dght 3.585 Lbp 49.00 Br md 9.00 Dpth 3.94 Welded, 1 dk	**(B11B2FV) Fishing Vessel** Ins: 545 Compartments: 3 Ho, ER 3 Ha: (1.9 x 1.9)2 (1.3 x 0.9)	**1 oil engine** driving 1 FP propeller Total Power: 1,103kW (1,500hp) Akasaka 1 x 4 Stroke 6 Cy. 300 x 480 1103kW (1500bhp) Akasaka Tekkosho KK (Akasaka DieselLtd)-Japan AuxGen: 2 x 200kW 225V a.c Fuel: 291.5 (d.f.)	11.8kn AH30
8745802 *DSQY5* -	**SUNG SHIN** - **Sung Shin Marine Co Ltd** - *Busan* *South Korea* MMSI: 441755000 Official number: BSR-806373	**469** 140 741	Class: KR	**1980-05 Dadaepo Shipbuilding & Engineering Co — Busan** Yd No: DDP-80-1 Loa 42.15 Br ex - Dght 3.400 Lbp 37.00 Br md 9.50 Dpth 4.03 Welded, 1 dk	**(B32A2ST) Tug**	**2 oil engines** reduction geared to sc. shafts driving 2 Propellers Total Power: 2,942kW (4,000hp) Hanshin 2 x 4 Stroke each-1471kW (2000bhp) The Hanshin Diesel Works Ltd-Japan	
6818423 *HLLL* -	**SUNG SHIN No. 8** *ex* Il Kwang No. 6 *-1989* *ex* Zenrin Maru No. 8 *-1979* **Kim Bun-Sen & Besides One** - *Busan* *South Korea* Official number: BS0201-A1583	*114* 48 -	Class: (KR)	**1968 Tokushima Zosen K.K. — Fukuoka** Yd No: 732 Loa 34.75 Br ex 6.13 Dght 2.617 Lbp 29.01 Br md 6.10 Dpth 2.85 Welded, 1 dk	**(B11B2FV) Fishing Vessel** Ins: 140 5 Ha: 5 (0.9 x 1.2)	**1 oil engine** driving 1 FP propeller Total Power: 478kW (650hp) Hanshin 1 x 4 Stroke 6 Cy. 270 x 400 478kW (650bhp) Hanshin Nainenki Kogyo-Japan AuxGen: 2 x 24kW 230V a.c	11.5kn Z76
7046754 *D9JC* -	**SUNG SHIN T3** *ex* Hyo Dong No. 7 *-2010* *ex* Halla Seung *-1993* *ex* Koyo Maru *-1983* **Lee Dong-Gwon** - *Busan* *South Korea* MMSI: 440301020 Official number: BSR-710101	*106* 28 40	Class: (KR)	**1971 Shin Yamamoto Shipbuilding & Engineering Co Ltd — Kochi KC** Yd No: 144 Loa 24.90 Br ex 6.56 Dght 2.240 Lbp 22.00 Br md 6.51 Dpth 3.00 Riveted\Welded, 1 dk	**(B32A2ST) Tug**	**2 oil engines** driving 2 FP propellers Total Power: 514kW (698hp) Fuji 2 x 4 Stroke 6 Cy. 230 x 370 each-257kW (349bhp) Fuji Diesel Co Ltd-Japan AuxGen: 2 x 25kW 225V a.c Fuel: 30.5 5.0pd	6S23E2F
6606789 *6KDC* -	**SUNG WON No. 17** *ex* Nam Hae No. 257 *-1980* **Sung Won Fisheries Co Ltd** - *Busan* *South Korea* Official number: BS-A-1884	*171* 74 168	Class: (KR)	**1966 Ateliers et Chantiers de La Manche — Dieppe** Yd No: 1195 Loa 30.31 Br ex 6.53 Dght 2.515 Lbp 25.00 Br md 6.51 Dpth 3.10 Welded, 1 dk	**(B11B2FV) Fishing Vessel** Ins: 119 3 Ha: 3 (0.8 x 0.8)ER	**1 oil engine** driving 1 FP propeller Total Power: 338kW (460hp) Fiat 1 x 4 Stroke 8 Cy. 230 x 350 338kW (460bhp) SA Fiat SGM-Torino AuxGen: 2 x 25kW 220V d.c Fuel: 70.0 (d.f.)	9.0kn L230.8S
8325054 *D7GX* -	**SUNG WOON No. 22** - **Sam Han Gang Co Ltd** - *Incheon* *South Korea* Official number: ICR-852106	**719** - 1,526	Class: (KR)	**1985-06 Namyang Shipbuilding & Engineering Co Ltd — Mokpo** Yd No: 3 Loa 66.50 Br ex 11.82 Dght 4.312 Lbp 60.00 Br md 11.80 Dpth 5.01 Welded, 1 dk	**(A24D2BA) Aggregates Carrier** Grain: 1,200 Compartments: 1 Ho, ER 1 Ha: ER	**1 oil engine** sr geared to sc. shaft driving 1 FP propeller Total Power: 883kW (1,201hp) Hanshin 1 x 4 Stroke 6 Cy. 280 x 440 883kW (1201bhp) The Hanshin Diesel Works Ltd-Japan AuxGen: 2 x 64kW 225V a.c	12.5kn 6LU28G
5346071 *6NON* -	**SUNG YOUNG No. 99** *ex* Bo Kyung No. 5 *-1987* *ex* Sea Dragon No. 2 *-1985* *ex* Nike No. 2 *-1976* *ex* Suwa Maru No. 32 *-1971* **Lee Sung-Ho** - *Busan* *South Korea* Official number: BS-A-1809	*332* 175 -	Class: (KR)	**1962 Uchida Zosen — Ise** Yd No: 576 Loa 48.60 Br ex 7.95 Dght 3.175 Lbp 42.96 Br md 7.90 Dpth 3.81 Riveted\Welded, 1 dk	**(B11B2FV) Fishing Vessel** Ins: 453 3 Ha: 2 (1.4 x 1.4) (1.3 x 1.0)ER	**1 oil engine** driving 1 FP propeller Total Power: 736kW (1,001hp) Akasaka 1 x 4 Stroke 6 Cy. 350 x 500 736kW (1001bhp) Akasaka Tekkosho KK (Akasaka DieselLtd)-Japan AuxGen: 2 x 128kW 230V a.c	SR6SS

IMO / Call sign / Flag	Name / Owner	Tonnage	Class	Build / Dimensions	Type / Capacity	Machinery
7203950 *YDAU* -	**SUNGAI BONE** *ex* Melton Clipper *-1983* *ex* Gitta *-1980* **PT Pelayaran Surya** - *Jakarta* *Indonesia*	**1,215** 432 1,130	Class: (GL) (KI)	**1972-06 Handel en Scheepsbouw Mij. Kramer & Booy N.V. — Kootstertille** Yd No: 173 Loa 64.14 Br ex 10.09 Dght 3.911 Lbp 58.60 Br md 9.99 Dpth 6.25 Welded, 2 dks	**(A31A2GX) General Cargo Ship** Grain: 2,362; Bale: 2,213 Compartments: 1 Ho, ER 1 Ha: (31.3 x 7.7)ER Derricks: 1x5t,1x3t; Winches: 2 Ice Capable	**1 oil engine** driving 1 FP propeller Total Power: 662kW (900hp) 11.0kn MWM TBD440-8 1 x 4 Stroke 8 Cy. 230 x 270 662kW (900bhp) Motoren Werke Mannheim AG (MWM)-West Germany AuxGen: 2 x 40kW 220/380V 50Hz a.c, 1 x 25kW 220/380V 50Hz a.c Fuel: 76.0 (d.f.)
7809170 *YGYW* -	**SUNGAI DIGUL** *ex* Marina I *-2001* *ex* Nichido Maru *-1987* **PT Era Globalindo Sentosa SA** - *Palembang* *Indonesia* MMSI: 525023030	*1,778* 720 2,359	Class: KI (BV) (NK)	**1978-07 Usuki Iron Works Co Ltd — Usuki OT** Yd No: 992 Loa 79.66 Br ex 11.54 Dght 5.371 Lbp 72.01 Br md 11.51 Dpth 6.30 Welded, 1 dk	**(A21B2BO) Ore Carrier** Grain: 1,732 1 Ha: (37.8 x 8.0)ER	**1 oil engine** driving 1 CP propeller Total Power: 1,545kW (2,101hp) 11.5kn Akasaka DM38A 1 x 4 Stroke 6 Cy. 380 x 600 1545kW (2101bhp) Akasaka Tekkosho KK (Akasaka DieselLtd)-Japan AuxGen: 1 x 120kW 445V 60Hz a.c, 1 x 90kW 445V 60Hz a.c Fuel: 11.0 (d.f.) 99.5 (r.f.) 7.5pd
6724373 - -	**SUNGAI DJANG II** *ex* Meiyo Maru *-1974* **PT West Irian Fishing Industry Co Ltd** - *Indonesia*	*185* 70 234		**1967-08 Wakamatsu Zosen K.K. — Kitakyushu** Yd No: 168 Loa 37.32 Br ex 6.84 Dght - Lbp 31.91 Br md 6.81 Dpth 3.18 Welded, 1 dk	**(B11B2FV) Fishing Vessel**	**1 oil engine** driving 1 FP propeller Total Power: 625kW (850hp) Niigata 6M28KHS 1 x 4 Stroke 6 Cy. 280 x 440 625kW (850bhp) Niigata Engineering Co Ltd-Japan
9509906 *POJO* -	**SUNGAI GERONG** **PT PERTAMINA (PERSERO)** - *Jakarta* *Indonesia* MMSI: 525008073	**24,167** 7,253 29,756	Class: KI NV	**2011-12 Zhejiang Chenye Shipbuilding Co Ltd — Daishan County ZJ** Yd No: 0803 Loa 180.09 (BB) Br ex 30.53 Dght 9.000 Lbp 173.00 Br md 30.50 Dpth 15.90 Welded, 1 dk	**(A13B2TP) Products Tanker** Double Hull (13F) Liq: 33,000; Liq (Oil): 33,000	**1 oil engine** driving 1 FP propeller Total Power: 6,480kW (8,810hp) 14.0kn MAN-B&W 6S42MC 1 x 2 Stroke 6 Cy. 420 x 1764 6480kW (8810bhp) Hyundai Heavy Industries Co Ltd-South Korea AuxGen: 3 x a.c
8982981 - -	**SUNGAI JULAN 1** **PT Sandi Adi Perkasa** - *Indonesia*	**271** 81 -	Class: (BV)	**2003-03 Piasau Slipways Sdn Bhd — Miri** Yd No: 151 Loa 31.00 Br ex - Dght 3.000 Lbp 27.47 Br md 8.50 Dpth 3.80 Welded, 1 dk	**(B32A2ST) Tug**	**2 oil engines** geared to sc. shafts driving 2 Propellers Total Power: 1,204kW (1,636hp) 10.0kn Mitsubishi S6R2-MPTK 2 x 4 Stroke 6 Cy. 170 x 220 each-602kW (818bhp) Mitsubishi Heavy Industries Ltd-Japan AuxGen: 2 x 97kW a.c
5054393 - -	**SUNGAI KAPUAS** *ex* Slamet XV *-1974* *ex* Slamet Limabelas *-1970* *ex* Bryne *-1967* **PT Cahaya Kalbar Tbk** PT Cahaya Kalbar Tbk *Jakarta* *Indonesia*	*489* 204 660	Class: (KI) (NV)	**1957-01 Glommens Mek Verksted — Fredrikstad** Yd No: 155 Loa 55.07 Br ex 8.67 Dght 3.595 Lbp 49.48 Br md 8.51 Dpth 3.66 Welded, 1 dk	**(A13B2TU) Tanker (unspecified)** Liq: 576; Liq (Oil): 576 Cargo Heating Coils Compartments: 1 Ho, 8 Ta, ER 1 Ha: (1.4 x 0.7) Derricks: 1x2t; Winches: 1 Ice Capable	**1 oil engine** driving 1 FP propeller Total Power: 485kW (659hp) 12.0kn Sulzer 1 x 2 Stroke 6 Cy. 320 x 450 485kW (659bhp) Sulzer Bros Ltd-Switzerland AuxGen: 1 x 27kW 220V 50Hz a.c, 1 x 15kW 220V 50Hz a.c Fuel: 48.0 (d.f.) 2.5pd
9133343 *YD4728* -	**SUNGAI KAPUAS NO. 1** *ex* Abasa No. 3 *-2001* **PT Mercusuar Lintasindo** - *Pontianak* *Indonesia*	**117** 36 112	Class: (KI) (NK)	**1995-03 Yong Choo Kui Shipyard Sdn Bhd — Sibu** Yd No: 1294 Loa 23.17 Br ex - Dght 2.388 Lbp 21.76 Br md 7.00 Dpth 2.90 Welded, 1 dk	**(B32A2ST) Tug**	**2 oil engines** reduction geared to sc. shafts driving 2 FP propellers Total Power: 794kW (1,080hp) 9.5kn Caterpillar 3412TA 2 x Vee 4 Stroke 12 Cy. 137 x 152 each-397kW (540bhp) Caterpillar Inc-USA Fuel: 99.0 (d.f.)
9311945 *9WFM7* -	**SUNGAI LAYUN 1** **Woodman Sdn Bhd** - SatCom: Inmarsat C 453346820 *Kuching* *Malaysia* MMSI: 533468000 Official number: 329567	**261** 79 155	Class: NK	**2004-01 Celtug Service Shipyard Sdn Bhd — Sibu** Yd No: 301 Loa 31.00 Br ex - Dght 3.012 Lbp 28.72 Br md 8.54 Dpth 3.80 Welded, 1 dk	**(B32A2ST) Tug**	**2 oil engines** geared to sc. shafts driving 2 FP propellers Total Power: 1,490kW (2,026hp) Cummins KTA-38-M 2 x Vee 4 Stroke 12 Cy. 159 x 159 each-745kW (1013bhp) Cummins Engine Co Inc-USA AuxGen: 2 x a.c Fuel: 165.0 (d.f.)
7350832 *YB4013* -	**SUNGAI MEMBERAMO** *ex* Sandika I *-2000* *ex* Menara II *-1989* **PT Pelayaran Armada Bandar Bangun Persada** - *Jakarta* *Indonesia*	*151* 61 -	Class: (KI)	**1974-05 P.T. Djantra Dock & Shipbuilding — Jakarta** Yd No: 175B/076 L reg 30.50 Br ex - Dght - Lbp 30.51 Br md 6.00 Dpth 2.29 Welded, 1 dk	**(A31A2GX) General Cargo Ship**	**1 oil engine** driving 1 FP propeller Total Power: 1,000kW (1,360hp) 8.0kn AuxGen: 1 x 3kW 105V
7398690 - -	**SUNGAI PAKNING** **PT PERTAMINA (PERSERO)** - *Jakarta* *Indonesia*	*222* 67 99	Class: KI (NK)	**1973-09 Robin Shipyard Pte Ltd — Singapore** Loa 30.51 Br ex - Dght 3.023 Lbp 27.65 Br md 8.79 Dpth 3.81 Welded, 1 dk	**(B32A2ST) Tug**	**2 oil engines** driving 2 FP propellers Total Power: 2,428kW (3,302hp) 13.0kn Fuji 8S23HZF 2 x 4 Stroke 8 Cy. 320 x 500 each-1214kW (1651bhp) Fuji Diesel Co Ltd-Japan AuxGen: 2 x 44kW 225V
7617096 *YCGU* -	**SUNGAI SEPAKU** **Government of The Republic of Indonesia (Direktorat Jenderal Perhubungan Laut - Ministry of Sea Communications)** PT Pelabuhan Indonesia IV (Persero) Cabang Balikpapan (Indonesia Port Corp IV, Balikpapan) *Balikpapan* *Indonesia*	*160* 48 -	Class: (KI) (NV)	**1977-12 Ulstein Hatlo AS — Ulsteinvik** Yd No: 152 Loa 26.32 Br ex - Dght 3.001 Lbp 24.01 Br md 8.01 Dpth 3.81 Welded, 1 dk	**(B32A2ST) Tug**	**1 oil engine** geared to sc. shaft driving 1 FP propeller Total Power: 640kW (870hp) Deutz SBA8M528 1 x 4 Stroke 8 Cy. 220 x 280 640kW (870bhp) Kloeckner Humboldt Deutz AG-West Germany
8995043 *9WFH6* -	**SUNGAI SILAT 1** **Woodman Sdn Bhd** - *Kuching* *Malaysia* MMSI: 533170000 Official number: 329468	**271** 81 -	Class: BV	**2002-09 Piasau Slipways Sdn Bhd — Miri** Yd No: 132 Loa 31.00 Br ex - Dght 3.000 Lbp 24.79 Br md 8.50 Dpth 3.80 Welded, 1 dk	**(B32A2ST) Tug**	**2 oil engines** geared to sc. shafts driving 2 FP propellers Total Power: 1,204kW (1,636hp) 11.0kn Mitsubishi S6R2-MPTK 2 x 4 Stroke 6 Cy. 170 x 220 each-602kW (818bhp) Mitsubishi Heavy Industries Ltd-Japan AuxGen: 2 x a.c
8329220 - -	**SUNGAI YANG I** **PN Aneka Tambang** - *Tanjungpinang* *Indonesia*	*187* 77 -	Class: (KI)	**1965 in Japan** Loa - Br ex - Dght - Lbp 32.01 Br md 7.51 Dpth 2.80 Welded, 1 dk	**(A31A2GX) General Cargo Ship**	**1 oil engine** driving 1 FP propeller Total Power: 177kW (241hp) Caterpillar D342TA 1 x 4 Stroke 6 Cy. 146 x 203 177kW (241bhp) Caterpillar Tractor Co-USA
8329153 - -	**SUNGAI YANG II** **PN Aneka Tambang** - *Tanjungpinang* *Indonesia*	*192* 77 -	Class: (KI)	**1965 in Japan** Loa - Br ex - Dght - Lbp 32.01 Br md 7.51 Dpth 2.80 Welded, 1 dk	**(A31A2GX) General Cargo Ship**	**1 oil engine** driving 1 FP propeller Total Power: 268kW (364hp) Caterpillar D343 1 x 4 Stroke 6 Cy. 137 x 165 268kW (364bhp) Caterpillar Tractor Co-USA
7928160 *V3NC8* -	**SUNGARI** *ex* Omo Wonz *-2010* *ex* Mercandian Merchant II *-1986* **Inderton Ltd SA** Natie Shipping Co Ltd *Belize City* *Belize* MMSI: 312802000 Official number: 571030003	**5,535** 1,661 3,500	Class: IB (NV)	**1981-09 Frederikshavn Vaerft A/S — Frederikshavn** Yd No: 391 Loa 105.62 (BB) Br ex 19.23 Dght 4.971 Lbp 96.00 Br md 18.81 Dpth 10.57 Welded, 2 dks	**(A35A2RR) Ro-Ro Cargo Ship** Stern door/ramp (centre) Len: 15.40 Wid: 8.60 Swl: - Side door/ramp (s. a.) Len: 13.35 Wid: 4.60 Swl: - Lane-Len: 870 Cars: 450, Trailers: 63 Grain: 10,371; Bale: 10,313 TEU 256 C RoRo Dk 58 TEU C Dk 198 TEU incl 50 ref C. Compartments: 1 Ho, ER	**1 oil engine** sr geared to sc. shaft driving 1 FP propeller Total Power: 3,310kW (4,500hp) 10.0kn MaK 12M453AK 1 x Vee 4 Stroke 12 Cy. 320 x 420 3310kW (4500bhp) Krupp MaK Maschinenbau GmbH-Kiel AuxGen: 3 x 280kW 440V 60Hz a.c Thrusters: 1 Thwart. FP thruster (f) Fuel: 133.0 (d.f.) 482.0 (r.f.)
8916011 - -	**SUNGARI** *ex* Phoenix *-2012* *ex* Shoei Maru No. 52 *-2010* **Farisel Corp Ltd** -	*495* 203 -		**1989-11 KK Kanasashi Zosen — Shizuoka SZ** Yd No: 3211 Converted From: Fishing Vessel-2010 Loa 50.03 (BB) Br ex - Dght 3.250 Lbp 43.50 Br md 8.40 Dpth 3.60 Welded, 1 dk	**(B12B2FC) Fish Carrier** Ins: 419	**1 oil engine** with clutches, flexible couplings & sr reverse geared to sc. shaft driving 1 FP propeller Total Power: 736kW (1,001hp) Akasaka K28FD 1 x 4 Stroke 6 Cy. 280 x 480 736kW (1001bhp) Akasaka Tekkosho KK (Akasaka DieselLtd)-Japan

IMO / Call sign	Name / Owner / Flag	Tonnage	Class	Build / Dimensions	Type / Cargo	Machinery
9357365 *5ISH37* -	**SUNGARY** *ex Suneast -2013 ex Azalea -2012* *ex Sina -2012* **NITC** - *Zanzibar* *Tanzania (Zanzibar)* MMSI: 677003600	**85,462** 53,441 164,154	Class: (BV) (NV)	**2008-07 Hyundai Samho Heavy Industries Co Ltd — Samho** Yd No: S318 Loa 274.18 (BB) Br ex 50.04 Dght 17.000 Lbp 264.00 Br md 50.00 Dpth 23.10 Welded, 1 dk	**(A13A2TV) Crude Oil Tanker** Double Hull (13F) Liq: 169,000; Liq (Oil): 169,000 Cargo Heating Coils Compartments: 6 Wing Ta, 6 Wing Ta, 1 Wing Slop Ta, 1 Wing Slop Ta, ER 3 Cargo Pump (s): 3x4000m^3/hr	**1 oil engine** driving 1 FP propeller Total Power: 18,660kW (25,370hp) 15.4kn MAN-B&W 6S70MC-C 1 x 2 Stroke 6 Cy. 700 x 2800 18660kW (25370bhp) Hyundai Heavy Industries Co Ltd-South Korea AuxGen: 3 x 1050kW 60Hz a.c
5344891 *9WAT* -	**SUNGEI PANNAI** **Chien Say Kup** - *Kuching* *Malaysia* Official number: 324806	*176* 114 242	Class: (BV)	**1950 Spaarndammer Scheepswerf Stapel N.V. — Spaarndam** Yd No: 20 Loa 38.89 Br ex 7.32 Dght 2.198 Lbp - Br md 7.27 Dpth 2.57 Welded, 1 dk	**(A31A2GX) General Cargo Ship** Bale: 422 Compartments: 1 Ho, ER 2 Ha: 2 (5.1 x 2.9)ER Derricks: 2x2t; Winches: 2	**1 oil engine** driving 1 FP propeller Total Power: 99kW (135hp) 7.0kn De Industrie 1 x 4 Stroke 3 Cy. 280 x 400 99kW (135bhp) NV Motorenfabriek 'De Industrie'-Netherlands Fuel: 8.0 (d.f.)
9611395 - -	**SUNJIN NO. 803** **Sunjin Consolidated Co Ltd** - *Ulsan* *South Korea* Official number: USR-108278	**166** - 85	Class: KR	**2010-07 Namyang Shipbuilding Co Ltd — Yeosu** Yd No: 1091 Loa 30.65 Br ex - Dght 2.912 Lbp 28.20 Br md 8.60 Dpth 3.80 Welded, 1 dk	**(B32A2ST) Tug**	**2 oil engines** reduction geared to sc. shafts driving 2 Z propellers Total Power: 2,132kW (2,898hp) 13.0kn Niigata 6L25HX 2 x 4 Stroke 6 Cy. 250 x 350 each-1066kW (1449bhp) Niigata Engineering Co Ltd-Japan
9177222 - -	**SUNKIN No. 1** **Teck Chin Yong** New Temburong Quarry *Muara* *Brunei* Official number: 0018	**355** 107 500	Class: NK	**1997-09 New Island Shipping — Brunei** Yd No: 8096 Loa 36.60 Br ex - Dght 1.959 Lbp 35.52 Br md 12.20 Dpth 2.60 Welded, 1 dk	**(A35D2RL) Landing Craft**	**2 oil engines** reduction geared to sc. shafts driving 2 FP propellers Total Power: 286kW (388hp) 7.5kn Cummins N-855-M 2 x 4 Stroke 6 Cy. 140 x 152 each-143kW (194bhp) Cummins Engine Co Inc-USA Fuel: 10.0 (d.f.)
9460526 *3FPJ9* -	**SUNLEAF GRACE** **Sun Leaf Shipping SA** Toko Kisen Co Ltd (Toko Kisen YK) SatCom: Inmarsat C 435259011 *Panama* *Panama* MMSI: 352590000 Official number: 4310911	**33,900** 20,020 61,683 T/cm 60.0	Class: AB	**2011-09 Oshima Shipbuilding Co Ltd — Saikai NS** Yd No: 10547 Loa 199.98 (BB) Br ex - Dght 12.780 Lbp 196.00 Br md 32.26 Dpth 18.33 Welded, 1 dk	**(A21A2BC) Bulk Carrier** Grain: 76,895; Bale: 75,294 Compartments: 5 Ho, ER 5 Ha: ER Cranes: 4x30t	**1 oil engine** driving 1 FP propeller Total Power: 8,201kW (11,150hp) 14.5kn MAN-B&W 6S50MC-C 1 x 2 Stroke 6 Cy. 500 x 2000 8201kW (11150bhp) Kawasaki Heavy Industries Ltd-Japan AuxGen: 3 x 440kW a.c
8960098 *WDB4636* -	**SUNLIGHT** *ex Lady Elizabeth -2006* **O'Hara Corp** - *Rockland, ME* *United States of America* MMSI: 366900670 Official number: 1098004	**338** 117 -		**2000-01 La Force Shipyard Inc — Coden AL** Yd No: 93 Loa 33.07 Br ex 9.14 Dght - Lbp - Br md - Dpth 4.17 Welded, 1 dk	**(B11B2FV) Fishing Vessel**	**1 oil engine** driving 1 FP propeller
8877174 *HQGW3* -	**SUNLIGHT 2** *ex Max No. 3 -2006 ex Kyoei Maru No. 3 -1990* - - *San Lorenzo* *Honduras* Official number: L-1723502	*108* 34 -		**1973-03 KK Ura Kyodo Zosensho — Awaji HG** Loa 28.30 Br ex - Dght 2.100 Lbp 25.50 Br md 6.70 Dpth 2.99 Welded, 1 dk	**(B32A2ST) Tug**	**1 oil engine** driving 1 FP propeller Total Power: 736kW (1,001hp) 10.0kn Matsui 1 x 4 Stroke 736kW (1001bhp) Matsui Iron Works Co Ltd-Japan
9338864 *C6XP8* -	**SUNLIGHT ACE** **Snowscape Car Carriers SA** MOL Ship Management Singapore Pte Ltd SatCom: Inmarsat C 431100427 *Nassau* *Bahamas* MMSI: 311018600 Official number: 8001630	**58,911** 18,159 18,855	Class: NK	**2009-06 Minaminippon Shipbuilding Co Ltd — Usuki OT** Yd No: 704 Loa 199.95 (BB) Br ex 32.26 Dght 9.816 Lbp 190.00 Br md 32.20 Dpth 14.70 Welded, 12 dks	**(A35B2RV) Vehicles Carrier** Side door/ramp (s) Quarter stern door/ramp (s. a.) Cars: 6,233	**1 oil engine** driving 1 FP propeller Total Power: 15,820kW (21,509hp) 20.0kn MAN-B&W 7S60MC-C 1 x 2 Stroke 7 Cy. 600 x 2400 15820kW (21509bhp) Mitsui Engineering & Shipbuilding CLtd-Japan Thrusters: 1 Tunnel thruster (f) Fuel: 2660.0
7737470 - -	**SUNLIGHT ALICE No. 1** *ex Matsumi Maru No. 3 -1976* - -	*100* 25 -	Class: (NK)	**1974 Makihata Dock K.K. — Onomichi** Loa 26.14 Br ex - Dght 2.750 Lbp 24.01 Br md 7.01 Dpth 3.00 Welded, 1 dk	**(B32A2ST) Tug**	**1 oil engine** driving 1 FP propeller Total Power: 1,103kW (1,500hp) 12.5kn Fuji 6S30B 1 x 4 Stroke 6 Cy. 300 x 450 1103kW (1500bhp) Fuji Diesel Co Ltd-Japan AuxGen: 2 x 24kW
7619525 *ODUX* -	**SUNLIGHT BEY** *ex Warsan -2007 ex Merchant Venture -2003* *ex Merchant Isle -1987 ex Argentea -1987* *ex Med Adriatico -1985 ex Farman -1982* **Sunlight Shipping Co SARL** ADCO SAL SatCom: Inmarsat C 445052710 *Beirut* *Lebanon* MMSI: 450527000 Official number: B-4332	**6,056** 1,816 3,671	Class: IV PX (LR) (RI) ✠ Classed LR until 9/7/03	**1979-08 Estaleiros Navais de Viana do Castelo S.A. — Viana do Castelo** Yd No: 103 Converted From: Ro-Ro Cargo Ship-2008 Deepened-1988 Loa 119.44 (BB) Br ex 19.51 Dght 5.217 Lbp 108.74 Br md 17.51 Dpth 10.72 Welded, 2 dks, 2nd dk light cargoes only	**(A38A2GL) Livestock Carrier**	**2 oil engines** sr geared to sc. shafts driving 2 CP propellers Total Power: 6,400kW (8,702hp) 17.0kn Sulzer 16ASV25/30 2 x Vee 4 Stroke 16 Cy. 250 x 300 each-3200kW (4351bhp) Maschinenbau Augsburg Nuernberg (MAN)-Augsburg AuxGen: 2 x 206kW 380V 50Hz a.c, 2 x 170kW 380V 50Hz a.c Boilers: 2 e 7.0kgf/cm² (6.9bar), AuxB (o.f.) 7.0kgf/cm² (6.9bar) Thrusters: 1 Thwart. FP thruster (f) Fuel: 88.0 (d.f.) 544.5 (r.f.)
7737482 - -	**SUNLIGHT DIANA** *ex Kaiko Maru No. 3 -1976* - -	*100* 25 -	Class: (NK)	**1974 Makihata Dock K.K. — Onomichi** Loa 26.14 Br ex - Dght 2.750 Lbp 24.01 Br md 7.01 Dpth 3.00 Welded, 1 dk	**(B32A2ST) Tug**	**1 oil engine** driving 1 FP propeller Total Power: 1,103kW (1,500hp) 12.5kn Fuji 6S30B 1 x 4 Stroke 6 Cy. 300 x 450 1103kW (1500bhp) Fuji Diesel Co Ltd-Japan AuxGen: 2 x 24kW
9459266 *3FMK7* -	**SUNLIGHT EXPRESS** **Ocean Transit Carrier SA** Yamamaru Kisen KK (Yamamaru Kisen Co Ltd) SatCom: Inmarsat C 435100112 *Panama* *Panama* MMSI: 351001000 Official number: 4243411	**28,725** 12,012 45,931 T/cm 51.3	Class: NK	**2011-02 Shin Kurushima Dockyard Co. Ltd. — Onishi** Yd No: 5606 Loa 181.53 Br ex 32.23 Dght 12.171 Lbp 174.00 Br md 32.20 Dpth 18.70 Welded, 1 dk	**(A13B2TP) Products Tanker** Double Hull (13F) Liq: 51,005; Liq (Oil): 51,005 Compartments: 14 Wing Ta, 2 Wing Slop Ta, ER 4 Cargo Pump (s): 4x1000m^3/hr	**1 oil engine** driving 1 FP propeller Total Power: 9,480kW (12,889hp) 15.2kn MAN-B&W 6S50MC-C 1 x 2 Stroke 6 Cy. 500 x 2000 9480kW (12889bhp) Mitsui Engineering & Shipbuilding CLtd-Japan Fuel: 1967.0 (r.f.)
9539341 *3FHB* -	**SUNLIGHT LILY** **Fair Wind Panama SA** Daido Kaiun Co Ltd SatCom: Inmarsat C 437352210 *Panama* *Panama* MMSI: 373522000 Official number: 4413612	**21,213** 11,615 33,642	Class: NK	**2012-06 Shin Kochi Jyuko K.K. — Kochi** Yd No: 7245 Loa 179.99 Br ex - Dght 10.100 Lbp 172.00 Br md 28.20 Dpth 14.30 Welded, 1 dk	**(A21A2BC) Bulk Carrier** Double Hull Grain: 44,039; Bale: 43,164 Compartments: 5 Ho, ER 5 Ha: 3 (20.8 x 23.8) (19.2 x 23.8)ER (16.8 x 17.2) Cranes: 4x30t	**1 oil engine** driving 1 FP propeller Total Power: 6,250kW (8,498hp) 14.2kn Mitsubishi 6UEC45LSE 1 x 2 Stroke 6 Cy. 450 x 1840 6250kW (8498bhp) Kobe Hatsudoki KK-Japan Fuel: 1620.0
6811803 - -	**SUNLIGHT No. 20** *ex Koryo Maru No. 86 -1974* **Dai Ho Industrial Co Ltd** - *Busan* *South Korea* Official number: BS-A-1251	*367* 193 -	Class: (KR)	**1967 Niigata Engineering Co Ltd — Niigata NI** Yd No: 732 Loa 52.28 Br ex 8.31 Dght 3.201 Lbp 47.81 Br md 8.28 Dpth 3.61 Welded, 1 dk	**(B11A2FS) Stern Trawler** Ins: 399 3 Ha: 2 (1.6 x 8.0) (1.6 x 1.3)ER	**1 oil engine** driving 1 FP propeller Total Power: 1,030kW (1,400hp) 10.0kn Niigata 6L31EZ 1 x 4 Stroke 6 Cy. 310 x 380 1030kW (1400bhp) Niigata Engineering Co Ltd-Japan AuxGen: 2 x 104kW
8879081 - -	**SUNLY SAMUDERA** *ex Kazuryu No. 2 -2012* - - *Indonesia*	*414* - 1,112		**1994-07 K.K. Kamishima Zosensho — Osakikamijima** Yd No: 562 Loa 68.50 Br ex - Dght 4.120 Lbp 61.50 Br md 10.70 Dpth 6.20 Welded, 1 dk	**(A31A2GX) General Cargo Ship**	**1 oil engine** reverse geared to sc. shaft driving 1 FP propeller Total Power: 736kW (1,001hp) 11.0kn Akasaka A28S 1 x 4 Stroke 6 Cy. 280 x 550 736kW (1001bhp) Akasaka Tekkosho KK (Akasaka DieselLtd)-Japan
9073581 *C6WS3* -	**SUNMI** *ex Fehn Sun -2007 ex Apollo Fox -2006* *ex Nesserland -2003 ex Swift -2000* **Misje Bulk AS** Misje Rederi AS *Nassau* *Bahamas* MMSI: 309937000 Official number: 8001448	**2,825** 1,604 4,148	Class: GL (LR) ✠ Classed LR until 8/10/01	**1993-12 Bodewes' Scheepswerven B.V. — Hoogezand** Yd No: 569 Loa 90.46 (BB) Br ex 13.44 Dght 5.600 Lbp 84.60 Br md 13.20 Dpth 7.10 Welded, 1 dk	**(A31A2GX) General Cargo Ship** Compartments: 1 Ta, ER Ice Capable	**1 oil engine** with flexible couplings & sr geared to sc. shaft driving 1 CP propeller Total Power: 1,840kW (2,502hp) 11.5kn Stork-Werkspoor 6SW280 1 x 4 Stroke 6 Cy. 280 x 300 1840kW (2502bhp) Stork Wartsila Diesel BV-Netherlands AuxGen: 1 x 234kW 380/220V 50Hz a.c, 1 x 126kW 380/220V 50Hz a.c Thrusters: 1 Thwart. FP thruster (f)

IMO / Call sign	Name / Owner / Port	Tonnage	Class	Builder / Dimensions	Type / Cargo	Machinery
8719114 *OZ2147* -	**SUNNA** *ex* Sava Ocean *-2013* **Havnarnes Sp/F** Nes hf *Torshavn* *Faeroes (FAS)* MMSI: 231837000	**2,026** 911 3,090 T/cm 8.3	Class: GL (RS) (NV)	**1993**-06 **Brodogradiliste 'Sava' — Macvanska Mitrovica** Yd No: 301 Loa 74.65 (BB) Br ex - Dght 6.100 Lbp 69.10 Br md 12.70 Dpth 8.60 Welded, 1 dk	**(A31A2GX) General Cargo Ship** Double Hull Grain: 3,792 TEU 98 C.Ho 20/20' C.Dk 78/20' Compartments: 1 Ho, ER, 1 Tw Dk 1 Ha: (47.0 x 10.2)ER Ice Capable	**1 oil engine** with flexible couplings & reduction geared to sc. shaft driving 1 CP propeller Total Power: 1,470kW (1,999hp) 11.0kn Normo KRM-8 1 x 4 Stroke 8 Cy. 250 x 300 1470kW (1999bhp) Bergen Diesel AS-Norway AuxGen: 1 x 440kW 380V 50Hz a.c, 2 x 176kW 380V 50Hz a.c Thrusters: 1 Thwart. CP thruster (f) Fuel: 133.0 (d.f.) 5.0pd
5169772 *CB2667* -	**SUNNAN 1** *ex* Singo *-1968* *ex* Jane *-1966* **Sociedad Pesquera Sunnan Ltda** - *Valparaiso* *Chile* Official number: 2140	*120* 49 -	Class: (BV)	**1961 N.V. Sleephelling Mij. "Scheveningen" — Scheveningen** Yd No: 161 Loa 27.79 Br ex 6.43 Dght 2.801 Lbp 24.54 Br md 6.41 Dpth 3.13 Welded, 1 dk	**(B11A2FT) Trawler**	**1 oil engine** driving 1 FP propeller Total Power: 375kW (510hp) 12.0kn Alpha 406-24VO 1 x 2 Stroke 6 Cy. 240 x 400 375kW (510bhp) Alpha Diesel A/S-Denmark Fuel: 31.0 (d.f.)
7030808 *CB2670* -	**SUNNAN IV** *ex* Jean Nicole *-1976* *ex* Cutter XV *-1973* **Viento Sur (Sociedad Pesquera) Ltda** - *Valparaiso* *Chile* Official number: 2143	*410* 171 -	Class: (BV)	**1970 VEB Elbewerften Boizenburg/Rosslau — Rosslau** Loa 37.70 Br ex 8.21 Dght 3.468 Lbp 33.00 Br md 8.18 Dpth 5.49 Welded, 1 dk	**(B11A2FS) Stern Trawler** Ins: 332 Compartments: 1 Ho, ER 1 Ha: ER	**1 oil engine** sr geared to sc. shaft driving 1 FP propeller Total Power: 588kW (799hp) 11.0kn Deutz SBA8M528 1 x 4 Stroke 8 Cy. 220 x 280 588kW (799bhp) (new engine 1974) Kloeckner Humboldt Deutz AG-West Germany AuxGen: 2 x 89kW 380V 50Hz a.c Fuel: 76.5 (d.f.)
7023594 - -	**SUNNAN V** *ex* Jean Eliane *-1976* *ex* Cutter VII *-1974* - - -	*411* 171 -	Class: (BV)	**1970 VEB Elbewerften Boizenburg/Rosslau — Rosslau** Loa 37.70 Br ex 8.21 Dght 3.468 Lbp 33.00 Br md 8.18 Dpth 5.49 Welded, 1 dk	**(B11A2FS) Stern Trawler** Ins: 332 Compartments: 1 Ho, ER 1 Ha: ER	**1 oil engine** sr geared to sc. shaft driving 1 FP propeller Total Power: 588kW (799hp) 10.8kn Deutz SBA8M528 1 x 4 Stroke 8 Cy. 220 x 280 588kW (799bhp) (new engine 1972) Kloeckner Humboldt Deutz AG-West Germany AuxGen: 2 x 89kW 380V 50Hz a.c Fuel: 76.5 (d.f.)
9341160 *OZ2103* -	**SUNNANHAV** - **Erik Thun AB (Thunship Management Holland)** - *Torshavn* *Faeroe Islands (Danish)* MMSI: 231790000	**5,325** 2,572 9,402 T/cm 16.7	Class: BV	**2006**-07 **Ferus Smit Leer GmbH — Leer** Yd No: 373 Loa 110.00 (BB) Br ex 16.00 Dght 7.850 Lbp 106.65 Br md 15.85 Dpth 10.46 Welded, 1 dk	**(A31A2GE) General Cargo Ship, Self-discharging** Grain: 9,551; Bale: 9,220 Compartments: 2 Ho, ER 2 Ha: ER 2 (33.8 x 13.1) Ice Capable	**1 oil engine** geared to sc. shaft driving 1 CP propeller Total Power: 4,000kW (5,438hp) 13.0kn Wartsila 8L32 1 x 4 Stroke 8 Cy. 320 x 400 4000kW (5438bhp) Wartsila Finland Oy-Finland Thrusters: 1 Tunnel thruster (f) Fuel: 62.1 (d.f.) 334.4 (r.f.)
9222041 *SMPD* -	**SUNNANLAND** *ex* Astrid Marie *-2013* **Daniel Axelsson** - *Roro* *Sweden* MMSI: 265824000	**599** 179 -	Class: (NV)	**2000**-07 **Finomar Sp z oo — Szczecin** (Hull) **2000**-07 **Batservice Verft AS — Mandal** Yd No: 690 Loa 37.60 Br ex - Dght 5.700 Lbp 32.50 Br md 10.00 Dpth 7.05 Welded, 1 dk	**(B11A2FT) Trawler** Liq: 430	**1 oil engine** geared to sc. shaft driving 1 CP propeller Wartsila 8L26 1 x 4 Stroke 8 Cy. 260 x 320 Wartsila NSD Nederland BV-Netherlands
5408180 - -	**SUNNANLAND** *ex* Emilia *-1997* *ex* Valo *-1990* *ex* Raymona *-1971* *ex* Gullskar *-1963* - - -	**182** 54 -	Class: (NV)	**1960 Marstrands Mekaniska Verkstad AB — Marstrand** Yd No: 36 Lengthened-1979 Loa 31.15 Br ex 6.79 Dght 3.226 Lbp - Br md 6.68 Dpth 3.61 Welded, 1 dk	**(B11A2FT) Trawler** 4 Ha: 2 (0.8 x 1.1)2 (1.3 x 1.3)ER Derricks: 1x1t; Winches: 1 Ice Capable	**1 oil engine** driving 1 FP propeller Total Power: 618kW (840hp) Jonkopings 1 x 4 Stroke 7 Cy. 260 x 400 618kW (840bhp) (new engine 1967) AB Jonkopings Motorfabrik-Sweden AuxGen: 2 x 4kW 110V d.c
7633375 *SHAF* -	**SUNNANVIK** - **Sunnanvik Shipping Ltd** Eureka Shipping Ltd *Slite* *Sweden* MMSI: 265088000	**7,454** 2,264 9,060	Class: BV (LR) ✠ Classed LR until 26/4/10	**1978**-09 **J.J. Sietas KG Schiffswerft GmbH & Co. — Hamburg** Yd No: 832 Loa 124.01 Br ex 18.04 Dght 7.702 Lbp 120.02 Br md 18.01 Dpth 10.42 Welded, 1 dk	**(A24A2BT) Cement Carrier** Grain: 7,498 Compartments: 2 Ho, ER 2 Ha: ER Ice Capable	**1 oil engine** geared to sc. shaft driving 1 CP propeller Total Power: 4,413kW (6,000hp) 14.0kn Pielstick 12PC2-3V-400 1 x Vee 4 Stroke 12 Cy. 400 x 460 4413kW (6000bhp) Blohm + Voss AG-West Germany AuxGen: 4 x 504kW 400V 50Hz a.c Boilers: HWH (o.f.) 6.1kgf/cm² (6.0bar) Thrusters: 1 Thwart. CP thruster (f); 1 Tunnel thruster (a) Fuel: 112.0 (d.f.) 207.0 (r.f.)
5416917 - -	**SUNNANVIND** *ex* Nordkap II *-1964* *ex* Tylo *-1963* *ex* Theod. Mannheimer *-1947* **Rederi Sjobris K/B** -	*235* 134 350		**1884 Motala Co. — Motala** Loa 32.31 Br ex 6.68 Dght 3.810 Lbp - Br md 6.63 Dpth - Riveted, 1 dk	**(B11B2FV) Fishing Vessel** Derricks: 2; Winches: 2	**1 oil engine** driving 1 FP propeller Total Power: 177kW (241hp) 8.0kn Alpha 1 x 2 Stroke 177kW (241bhp) (new engine 1947) Frederikshavn Jernstoberi ogMaskinfabrik-Denmark
7710501 *LHCR* -	**SUNNFJORD** - **Fjord1 AS** - *Floro* *Norway* MMSI: 257389400	**855** 260 250	Class: (NV)	**1978**-06 **Hasund Mek. Verksted AS — Ulsteinvik** (Hull) Yd No: 22 **1978**-06 **A.M. Liaaen AS — Aalesund** Yd No: 131 Loa 64.50 Br ex - Dght 3.652 Lbp 59.42 Br md 11.46 Dpth 4.20 Welded, 1 dk	**(A36A2PR) Passenger/Ro-Ro Ship (Vehicles)** Passengers: unberthed: 399 Bow door & ramp Len: - Wid: 5.50 Swl: - Stern door & ramp Len: - Wid: 5.50 Swl: - Cars: 65, Trailers: 4 Ice Capable	**1 oil engine** driving 2 Propellers aft, 1 fwd Total Power: 919kW (1,249hp) 13.0kn Normo LDM-8 1 x 4 Stroke 8 Cy. 250 x 300 919kW (1249bhp) AS Bergens Mek Verksteder-Norway
8914855 *UBEG7* -	**SUNNIVA** *ex* Southern Hawk *-1997* **JSC 'Kamchatnefteprodukt'** - *Petropavlovsk-Kamchatskiy* *Russia* MMSI: 273342530	**5,006** 2,645 9,009 T/cm 17.6	Class: RS (NK)	**1990**-06 **Asakawa Zosen K.K. — Imabari** Yd No: 350 Loa 112.00 (BB) Br ex - Dght 7.604 Lbp 104.30 Br md 18.80 Dpth 9.50 Welded, 1 dk	**(A12B2TR) Chemical/Products Tanker** Double Hull Liq: 9,585; Liq (Oil): 9,585 Cargo Heating Coils Compartments: 8 Wing Ta, 7 Ta, ER 16 Cargo Pump (s): 5x150m³/hr, 10x300m³/hr, 1x200m³/hr Manifold: Bow/CM: 56.8m Ice Capable	**1 oil engine** driving 1 FP propeller Total Power: 3,604kW (4,900hp) 13.0kn Mitsubishi 7UEC37LA 1 x 2 Stroke 7 Cy. 370 x 880 3604kW (4900bhp) Akasaka Tekkosho KK (Akasaka DieselLtd)-Japan AuxGen: 2 x 320kW 450V 60Hz a.c Thrusters: 1 Tunnel thruster (f) Fuel: 81.0 (d.f.) 520.0 (r.f.)
8322650 *OZ2095* -	**SUNNMORE** - **Skipafelagid Nor Lines Sp/f** Nor Lines Rederi AS *Torshavn* *Faeroes (FAS)* MMSI: 231763000	**2,706** 1,462 2,000	Class: BV (NV)	**1985**-01 **Fosen Mek. Verksteder AS — Rissa** Yd No: 35 Loa 79.91 (BB) Br ex - Dght 5.012 Lbp 73.21 Br md 15.02 Dpth 10.72 Welded, 3 dks	**(A31B2GP) Palletised Cargo Ship** Side door/ramp (p) Bale: 5,380 TEU 39 C.Ho 27/20' C.DK 12/20' Compartments: 3 Ho, ER 3 Ha: ER Cranes: 1x40t Ice Capable	**1 oil engine** with clutches, flexible couplings & sr geared to sc. shaft driving 1 CP propeller Total Power: 2,023kW (2,750hp) MWM TBD510-6 1 x 4 Stroke 6 Cy. 330 x 360 2023kW (2750bhp) Motoren Werke Mannheim AG (MWM)-West Germany AuxGen: 2 x 250kW 440V 60Hz a.c Thrusters: 1 Thwart. CP thruster (f)
7214260 - -	**SUNNUBERG** *ex* Fiskeskjer *-1999* *ex* Staaloy I *-1995* *ex* Staaloy *-1995* **Jonc Overseas Corp** NCP Zeevisserij BV *Peru*	**1,288** 390 -	Class: (NV)	**1972**-07 **Ulstein Mek. Verksted AS — Ulsteinvik** (Hull launched by) Yd No: 66 **1972**-07 **Fitjar Mek. Verksted AS — Fitjar** (Hull completed by) **1972**-07 **Molde Verft AS — Hjelset** Lengthened Loa 65.13 Br ex 10.02 Dght 6.501 Lbp 55.02 Br md 10.01 Dpth 7.91 Welded, 2 dks	**(B11B2FV) Fishing Vessel** Compartments: 3 Ho, 3 Ta, ER 8 Ha: 6 (2.2 x 1.6) (2.2 x 3.2) (2.5 x 1.6)ER Derricks: 3x5t Ice Capable	**1 oil engine** driving 1 CP propeller Total Power: 2,207kW (3,001hp) 14.0kn Wichmann 9AXAG 1 x 2 Stroke 9 Cy. 300 x 450 2207kW (3001bhp) (new engine 1977) Wichmann Motorfabrikk AS-Norway AuxGen: 2 x 248kW 220V 50Hz a.c, 1 x 76kW 220V 50Hz a.c Thrusters: 1 Thwart. FP thruster (f); 1 Tunnel thruster (a)
7921136 *3CM2153* -	**SUNNY** *ex* Ryh Chun No. 1 *-2000* *ex* Mito Maru No. 35 *-1994* **Sunny Panama SA** Fa Chun Ocean Fishery Co Ltd *Malabo* *Equatorial Guinea* Official number: EGF-968962	**488** 178 360		**1979**-10 **Niigata Engineering Co Ltd — Niigata NI** Yd No: 1651 Loa 48.87 (BB) Br ex - Dght 3.360 Lbp 42.83 Br md 8.51 Dpth 3.64 Welded, 1 dk	**(B11B2FV) Fishing Vessel**	**1 oil engine** reduction geared to sc. shaft driving 1 FP propeller Total Power: 809kW (1,100hp) Niigata 6M28GX 1 x 4 Stroke 6 Cy. 280 x 440 809kW (1100bhp) Niigata Engineering Co Ltd-Japan
7851056 - -	**SUNNY** *ex* Israt *-1986* *ex* Setoji *-1982* **Marine Adventure Inc** - *Ukraine* MMSI: 272409000	*400* 190		**1966 Kochiken Zosen — Kochi** Yd No: 305 Loa 41.00 Br ex - Dght 2.450 Lbp 38.00 Br md 9.01 Dpth 3.46 Welded, 1 dk	**(A36A2PR) Passenger/Ro-Ro Ship (Vehicles)** Passengers: unberthed: 202	**1 oil engine** driving 1 FP propeller Total Power: 736kW (1,001hp) 12.0kn Daihatsu 6PSTCM-30 1 x 4 Stroke 6 Cy. 300 x 380 736kW (1001bhp) Daihatsu Diesel Manufacturing Co Lt-Japan

6929777 - - -	**SUNNY 93** *ex Mirae 89 -2009 ex Queen Marina -2009* *ex SRTM-8483 -2009* **Okean Voctok Co Ltd** -	**613** 194 335	Class: (RS)	**1966 Yaroslavskiy Sudostroitelnyy Zavod — Yaroslavl** Yd No: 23 Loa 54.23 Br ex 9.33 Dght 3.830 Lbp 49.99 Br md 9.22 Dpth 4.73 Welded, 1 dk	**(B11A2FT) Trawler** Ins: 352 Compartments: 2 Ho, ER 2 Ha: 2 (1.5 x 1.6) Derricks: 1x2t; Winches: 1 Ice Capable	**1 oil engine** driving 1 FP propeller Total Power: 588kW (799hp) 12.0kn S.K.L. 8NVD48AU 1 x 4 Stroke 8 Cy. 320 x 480 588kW (799bhp) VEB Schwermaschinenbau "KarlLiebknecht" (SKL)-Magdeburg AuxGen: 3 x 100kW Fuel: 155.0 (d.f.)
9302803 *3EBR7* -	**SUNNY ACE** **CS Sunny SA** Chugoku Sougyo Co Ltd *Panama* *Panama* MMSI: 371207000 Official number: 3090705A	**30,807** 18,103 55,888 T/cm 56.1	Class: NK	**2005-07 Kawasaki Shipbuilding Corp — Kobe HG** Yd No: 1559 Loa 189.90 (BB) Br ex - Dght 12.522 Lbp 185.00 Br md 32.26 Dpth 17.80 Welded, 1 dk	**(A21A2BC) Bulk Carrier** Grain: 69,450; Bale: 66,368 Compartments: 5 Ho, ER 5 Ha: 4 (20.5 x 18.6)ER (17.8 x 18.6) Cranes: 4x30.5t	**1 oil engine** driving 1 FP propeller Total Power: 8,200kW (11,149hp) 14.5kn B&W 6S50MC-C 1 x 2 Stroke 6 Cy. 500 x 2000 8200kW (11149bhp) Kawasaki Heavy Industries Ltd-Japan Fuel: 1790.0
9102148 *H9DI* -	**SUNNY AMAZON** *ex MOL Maas -2010 ex Maas -2001* **Sunny Amazon Maritime SA** Mitsui OSK Lines Ltd (MOL) *Panama* *Panama* MMSI: 352208000 Official number: 3036004B	**60,133** 23,180 62,905	Class: NK	**1995-01 Ishikawajima-Harima Heavy Industries Co Ltd (IHI) — Kure** Yd No: 3046 Loa 299.95 (BB) Br ex - Dght 13.031 Lbp 283.00 Br md 37.10 Dpth 21.80 Welded, 1 dk	**(A33A2CC) Container Ship (Fully Cellular)** TEU 4743 C Ho 2264 TEU C Dk 2479 TEU incl 350 ref C. Compartments: ER, 8 Cell Ho 18 Ha: ER	**1 oil engine** driving 1 FP propeller Total Power: 43,840kW (59,605hp) 24.5kn Sulzer 12RTA84C 1 x 2 Stroke 12 Cy. 840 x 2400 43840kW (59605bhp) Diesel United Ltd.-Aioi AuxGen: 4 x 1600kW 450V a.c, 1 x 1500kW 450V a.c, 1 x 1200kW 450V a.c Thrusters: 1 Thwart. CP thruster (f) Fuel: 6766.0 (r.f.)
9287948 *H8CD* -	**SUNNY BRIGHT** **Ocean Gas Transports SA** JX Ocean Co Ltd *Panama* *Panama* MMSI: 356825000 Official number: 2989904B	**45,965** 13,790 49,999 T/cm 70.3	Class: NK	**2004-05 Mitsubishi Heavy Industries Ltd. — Nagasaki** Yd No: 2188 Loa 230.00 (BB) Br ex 36.63 Dght 10.784 Lbp 219.00 Br md 36.60 Dpth 20.80 Welded, 1 dk	**(A11B2TG) LPG Tanker** Double Bottom Entire Compartment Length Liq (Gas): 77,340 4 x Gas Tank (s); 4 independent (Ni.stl) pri horizontal 8 Cargo Pump (s): 8x550m³/hr Manifold: Bow/CM: 113.9m	**1 oil engine** driving 1 FP propeller Total Power: 12,360kW (16,805hp) 16.7kn Mitsubishi 7UEC60LS 1 x 2 Stroke 7 Cy. 600 x 2200 12360kW (16805bhp) Mitsubishi Heavy Industries Ltd-Japan AuxGen: 3 x 880kW 440/100V 60Hz a.c Fuel: 381.0 (d.f.) 2776.0 (r.f.) 52.0pd
9044140 *D8FY* -	**SUNNY CEDAR** **Korea Marine Transport Co Ltd (KMTC)** SatCom: Inmarsat A 1660745 *Jeju* *South Korea* MMSI: 440023000 Official number: JJR-920573	**3,986** 1,878 5,940	Class: KR	**1992-06 Dae Sun Shipbuilding & Engineering Co Ltd — Busan** Yd No: 387 Loa 107.00 (BB) Br ex 17.22 Dght 6.513 Lbp 97.50 Br md 17.20 Dpth 8.30 Welded, 1 dk	**(A33A2CC) Container Ship (Fully Cellular)** TEU 342 C Ho 132 TEU C Dk 210 TEU incl 25 ref C Compartments: 3 Cell Ho, ER 5 Ha: ER	**1 oil engine** driving 1 FP propeller Total Power: 3,913kW (5,320hp) 14.9kn B&W 7L35MC 1 x 2 Stroke 7 Cy. 350 x 1050 3913kW (5320bhp) Hyundai Heavy Industries Co Ltd-South Korea Thrusters: 1 Tunnel thruster (f)
8885810 - -	**SUNNY DAY** **Land & Marine Contracting Services Ltd** - *Port of Spain* *Trinidad & Tobago* Official number: TT033008	*103* 82 -		**1987 Manuel Dupre — Chauvin, La** L reg 23.77 Br ex - Dght - Lbp - Br md 6.17 Dpth 2.03 Welded, 1 dk	**(B11B2FV) Fishing Vessel**	**1 oil engine** geared to sc. shaft driving 1 FP propeller Caterpillar 1 x 4 Stroke Caterpillar Inc-USA
9511117 *3FPL7* -	**SUNNY DREAM** **Asahi Tanker Co Ltd & Solar Shipping & Trading SA** Asahi Tanker Co Ltd SatCom: Inmarsat C 437158910 *Panama* *Panama* MMSI: 371589000 Official number: 4066809	**7,771** 3,464 12,222 T/cm 21.4	Class: NK	**2009-08 Shin Kurushima Dockyard Co. Ltd. — Hashihama, Imabari** Yd No: 5572 Loa 124.03 (BB) Br ex 19.63 Dght 8.278 Lbp 118.50 Br md 19.60 Dpth 11.50 Welded, 1 dk	**(A12B2TR) Chemical/Products Tanker** Double Hull (13F) Liq: 11,746; Liq (Oil): 11,745 Cargo Heating Coils Compartments: 14 Wing Ta (s.stl), 2 Wing Slop Ta (s.stl), ER 14 Cargo Pump (s): 14x200m³/hr Manifold: Bow/CM: 61.9m	**1 oil engine** driving 1 FP propeller Total Power: 3,900kW (5,302hp) 13.3kn MAN-B&W 6L35MC 1 x 2 Stroke 6 Cy. 350 x 1050 3900kW (5302bhp) Hitachi Zosen Corp-Japan AuxGen: 3 x 420kW 60Hz a.c Thrusters: 1 Tunnel thruster (f) Fuel: 90.0 (d.f.) 695.0 (r.f.)
9008108 *3EMA9* -	**SUNNY GREEN** **Golden Gas Transports SA** Wilhelmsen Ship Management Sdn Bhd SatCom: Inmarsat A 1336250 *Panama* *Panama* MMSI: 354503000 Official number: 2024792D	**44,690** 13,407 50,667 T/cm 69.4	Class: NK	**1992-03 Mitsubishi Heavy Industries Ltd. — Nagasaki** Yd No: 2056 Loa 230.00 (BB) Br ex 36.63 Dght 10.836 Lbp 219.00 Br md 36.60 Dpth 20.40 Welded, 1 dk	**(A11B2TG) LPG Tanker** Double Bottom Entire Compartment Length Liq (Gas): 78,488 Cargo Heating Coils 4 x Gas Tank (s); 4 independent (C.mn.stl) pri 8 Cargo Pump (s): 8x550m³/hr	**1 oil engine** driving 1 FP propeller Total Power: 12,357kW (16,801hp) 16.7kn Mitsubishi 7UEC60LS 1 x 2 Stroke 7 Cy. 600 x 2200 12357kW (16801bhp) Mitsubishi Heavy Industries Ltd-Japan AuxGen: 3 x 880kW a.c Fuel: 126.0 (d.f.) 2043.0 (r.f.) 43.7pd
8703141 *9H5467* - -	**SUNNY HILL** *ex Alyssa- M -2006 ex Candace -1999* *ex Colombaio Sky -1999 ex Colombaio -1992* **Bastia Marine Ltd** SatCom: Inmarsat M 624969510 *Valletta* *Malta* MMSI: 249695000 Official number: 5147	**179** 53 -	Class: (HR) ✠ **100A1** SS 06/2011 ✠ **LMC** Cable: U2 (a)	**1987-06 Scheepswerf "De Amstel" B.V. — Ouderkerk a/d Amstel** Yd No: D160A Loa 36.00 Br ex 8.34 Dght 3.415 Lbp 30.10 Br md 8.00 Dpth 4.86 Welded, 1 dk	**(A37A2PC) Passenger/Cruise** Passengers: cabins: 5; berths: 12	**1 oil engine** with clutches, flexible couplings & sr reverse geared to sc. shaft driving 1 CP propeller Total Power: 279kW (379hp) Isotta Fraschini T11312MH14 1 x Vee 4 Stroke 12 Cy. 130 x 140 279kW (379bhp) Isotta Fraschini SpA-Italy AuxGen: 1 x 44kW 380V 50Hz a.c Thrusters: 1 Tunnel thruster (f)
9482134 *3EVB9* -	**SUNNY HOPE** **CS Sunny SA** Kawasaki Kisen Kaisha Ltd (Kawasaki Kisen KK) ('K' Line) *Panama* *Panama* MMSI: 353096000 Official number: 4292011	**33,138** 19,142 58,787 T/cm 59.5	Class: NK	**2011-08 Kawasaki Heavy Industries Ltd — Kobe HG** Yd No: 1645 Loa 197.00 (BB) Br ex - Dght 12.680 Lbp 194.00 Br md 32.26 Dpth 18.10 Welded, 1 dk	**(A21A2BC) Bulk Carrier** Grain: 73,614; Bale: 70,963 Compartments: 5 Ho, ER 5 Ha: ER Cranes: 4x30.5t	**1 oil engine** driving 1 FP propeller Total Power: 8,630kW (11,733hp) 14.5kn MAN-B&W 6S50MC-C 1 x 2 Stroke 6 Cy. 500 x 2000 8630kW (11733bhp) Kawasaki Heavy Industries Ltd-Japan Fuel: 2260.0
9597379 *VRKQ4* -	**SUNNY HORIZON** **CM Trans Copious Shipping Co Ltd** MSI Ship Management (Qingdao) Co Ltd SatCom: Inmarsat C 447704244 *Hong Kong* *Hong Kong* MMSI: 477978200 Official number: HK-3527	**32,987** 19,225 56,686 T/cm 58.8	Class: RI (LR) ✠ Classed LR until 30/4/13	**2012-06 Xiamen Shipbuilding Industry Co Ltd — Xiamen FJ** Yd No: XSI409J Loa 189.99 (BB) Br ex 32.27 Dght 12.800 Lbp 185.63 Br md 32.26 Dpth 18.00 Welded, 1 dk	**(A21A2BC) Bulk Carrier** Grain: 71,634; Bale: 68,200 Compartments: 5 Ho, ER 5 Ha: ER Cranes: 4x30t	**1 oil engine** driving 1 FP propeller Total Power: 9,480kW (12,889hp) 14.2kn MAN-B&W 6S50MC-C 1 x 2 Stroke 6 Cy. 500 x 2000 9480kW (12889bhp) Hyundai Heavy Industries Co Ltd-South Korea AuxGen: 3 x 600kW 450V 60Hz a.c Boilers: AuxB (Comp) 8.0kgf/cm² (7.8bar)
9213222 *H3AG* -	**SUNNY IRIS** **Solar Shipping & Trading SA** Asahi Tanker Co Ltd *Panama* *Panama* MMSI: 351059000 Official number: 2685400C	**5,160** 2,420 7,849 T/cm 16.8	Class: NK	**2000-02 Fukuoka Shipbuilding Co Ltd — Fukuoka FO** Yd No: 1211 Loa 110.00 (BB) Br ex 18.53 Dght 7.213 Lbp 103.00 Br md 18.50 Dpth 9.60 Welded, 1 dk	**(A12B2TR) Chemical/Products Tanker** Double Hull (13F) Liq: 8,133; Liq (Oil): 8,075 Compartments: 10 Wing Ta, 2 Wing Slop Ta, ER 14 Cargo Pump (s): 12x330m³/hr, 2x100m³/hr Manifold: Bow/CM: 51.9m	**1 oil engine** driving 1 FP propeller Total Power: 3,884kW (5,281hp) 13.7kn B&W 6L35MC 1 x 2 Stroke 6 Cy. 350 x 1050 3884kW (5281bhp) Imex Co Ltd-Japan AuxGen: 3 x 455kW 450V 60Hz a.c Fuel: 86.2 (d.f.) (Heating Coils) 522.5 (r.f.) 14.6pd
9669639 *V7CN8* -	**SUNNY IRIS** **Marina Pissenlet Shipping Ltd** Korea Marine Transport Co Ltd (KMTC) *Majuro* *Marshall Islands* MMSI: 538005291 Official number: 5291	**9,910** 5,118 12,454	Class: KR	**2013-11 Dae Sun Shipbuilding & Engineering Co Ltd — Busan** Yd No: 557 Loa 146.20 (BB) Br ex - Dght 8.214 Lbp 137.00 Br md 22.60 Dpth 11.20 Welded, 1 dk	**(A33A2CC) Container Ship (Fully Cellular)** TEU 1048	**1 oil engine** driving 1 FP propeller Total Power: 6,900kW (9,381hp) 18.0kn MAN-B&W 6S46ME-B8 1 x 2 Stroke 6 Cy. 460 x 1932 6900kW (9381bhp) STX Engine Co Ltd-South Korea AuxGen: 3 x 615kW 445V a.c Fuel: 700.0
9206384 *H3PY* -	**SUNNY JOY** **Grande Shipping Navigation SA** JX Ocean Co Ltd 773190843 *Panama* *Panama* MMSI: 356950000 Official number: 2751401C	**45,965** 13,790 49,999 T/cm 70.3	Class: NK	**2000-10 Mitsubishi Heavy Industries Ltd. — Nagasaki** Yd No: 2150 Loa 230.00 (BB) Br ex 36.63 Dght 10.782 Lbp 219.00 Br md 36.60 Dpth 20.80 Welded, 1 dk	**(A11B2TG) LPG Tanker** Double Bottom Entire Compartment Length Liq (Gas): 77,297 4 x Gas Tank (s); 4 independent (Ni.stl) pri vertical 8 Cargo Pump (s): 8x550m³/hr Manifold: Bow/CM: 113.7m	**1 oil engine** driving 1 FP propeller Total Power: 12,357kW (16,801hp) 16.7kn Mitsubishi 7UEC60LS 1 x 2 Stroke 7 Cy. 600 x 2200 12357kW (16801bhp) Mitsubishi Heavy Industries Ltd-Japan AuxGen: 3 x 880kW a.c Fuel: 379.0 (d.f.) (Heating Coils) 2776.0 (r.f.) 50.0pd

8925218 *JM6575* -	**SUNNY KISSHO** **Jinko Odo** *Kitakyushu, Fukuoka* *Japan* Official number: 135436	*199* - 699		**1996-09 Yano Zosen K.K. — Imabari** Yd No: 167 Loa 58.80 Br ex - Dght 3.200 Lbp 52.80 Br md 9.50 Dpth 5.40 Welded, 1 dk	**(A31A2GX) General Cargo Ship**	**1 oil engine** driving 1 FP propeller Total Power: 736kW (1,001hp) 11.0kn Matsui MA28GSC-33 1 x 4 Stroke 6 Cy. 280 x 540 736kW (1001bhp) Matsui Iron Works Co Ltd-Japan
8921664 *D9TE* -	**SUNNY LAUREL** **Korea Marine Transport Co Ltd (KMTC)** - SatCom: Inmarsat C 444056712 *Jeju* *South Korea* MMSI: 440333000 Official number: JJR-892402	**4,025** 1,103 5,956 T/cm 14.8	Class: KR	**1989-12 Dae Sun Shipbuilding & Engineering Co Ltd — Busan** Yd No: 360 Loa 107.00 (BB) Br ex 17.21 Dght 6.513 Lbp 97.50 Br md 17.20 Dpth 8.30 Welded, 1 dk	**(A33A2CC) Container Ship (Fully Cellular)** TEU 330 C Ho 132 TEU C Dk 198 TEU incl 25 ref C. 5 Ha: (12.5 x 8.0)4 (12.5 x 13.2)ER	**1 oil engine** driving 1 FP propeller Total Power: 3,354kW (4,560hp) 14.4kn B&W 6L35MC 1 x 2 Stroke 6 Cy. 350 x 1050 3354kW (4560bhp) Ssangyong Heavy Industries Co Ltd-South Korea AuxGen: 2 x 250kW 445V 60Hz a.c Fuel: 91.5 (d.f.) 496.4 (r.f.) 13.0pd
9427419 *JD3282* -	**SUNNY LEO** **Asahi Tanker Co Ltd** - *Tokyo* *Japan* MMSI: 431003072 Official number: 141568	**4,552** 2,090 6,821 T/cm 15.8	Class: NK	**2008-03 Niigata Shipbuilding & Repair Inc — Niigata NI** Yd No: 0027 Loa 109.61 (BB) Br ex 17.22 Dght 6.763 Lbp 103.10 Br md 17.20 Dpth 8.90 Welded, 1 dk	**(A12B2TR) Chemical/Products Tanker** Double Hull (13F) Liq: 7,056; Liq (Oil): 7,102 Cargo Heating Coils Compartments: 10 Wing Ta, 2 Wing Slop Ta, ER 3 Cargo Pump (s): 3x800m³/hr Manifold: Bow/CM: 49.1m	**1 oil engine** driving 1 FP propeller Total Power: 3,250kW (4,419hp) 13.4kn MAN-B&W 5L35MC 1 x 2 Stroke 5 Cy. 350 x 1050 3250kW (4419bhp) Imex Co Ltd-Japan AuxGen: 4 x a.c Fuel: 70.0 (d.f.) 386.0 (r.f.)
9691761 *V7ER5* -	**SUNNY LILY** **DAT Atlantic Maritime SA** DAT Maritime Co Ltd *Majuro* *Marshall Islands* MMSI: 538005519 Official number: 5519	**9,988** 4,575 12,248	Class: KR	**2014-04 Hyundai Mipo Dockyard Co Ltd — Ulsan** Yd No: 4079 Loa 146.00 (BB) Br ex 22.90 Dght 8.365 Lbp 139.35 Br md 22.70 Dpth 11.20 Welded, 1 dk	**(A33A2CC) Container Ship (Fully Cellular)** TEU 1000	**1 oil engine** driving 1 FP propeller
7826142 *V4JU2* -	**SUNNY LINA** *ex* Lembeta *-2003* *ex* Vega *-1997* *ex* Terral *-1994* **Sunplan Ltd SA** Shipdeal Corp SatCom: Inmarsat C 434100092 *Charlestown* *St Kitts & Nevis* MMSI: 341091000 Official number: SKN1002259	**2,493** 941 1,927	Class: RS (PR)	**1980-06 Stocznia im Komuny Paryskiej — Gdynia** Yd No: B361/01 Loa 90.99 Br ex 13.42 Dght 5.370 Lbp 86.84 Br md 13.40 Dpth 7.19 Welded, 2 dks	**(A34A2GR) Refrigerated Cargo Ship** Ins: 2,441 Derricks: 6x3t Ice Capable	**1 oil engine** geared to sc. shaft driving 1 FP propeller Total Power: 3,089kW (4,200hp) 15.5kn Sulzer 6ZL40/48 1 x 4 Stroke 6 Cy. 400 x 480 3089kW (4200bhp) Zaklady Urzadzen Technicznych'Zgoda' SA-Poland AuxGen: 3 x 400kW 400V a.c Fuel: 269.0 (d.f.)
9115779 *DSNC9* -	**SUNNY LINDEN** **Korea Marine Transport Co Ltd (KMTC)** - *Jeju* *South Korea* MMSI: 441300000 Official number: JJR-029404	**3,996** 2,023 5,845 T/cm 14.8	Class: KR	**1995-03 ShinA Shipbuilding Co Ltd — Tongyeong** Yd No: 375 Loa 107.55 (BB) Br ex 17.60 Dght 6.513 Lbp 97.60 Br md 17.20 Dpth 8.30 Welded, 1 dk	**(A33A2CC) Container Ship (Fully Cellular)** TEU 342 C Ho 132 TEU C Dk 210 TEU incl 50 ref C Compartments: 5 Cell Ho, ER 5 Ha: ER	**1 oil engine** driving 1 FP propeller Total Power: 3,913kW (5,320hp) 16.5kn B&W 7L35MC 1 x 2 Stroke 7 Cy. 350 x 1050 3913kW (5320bhp) Ssangyong Heavy Industries Co Ltd-South Korea
7359278 *V4JW2* -	**SUNNY LISA** *ex* Igloo Lion *-1995* *ex* Lindo *-1986* **Baltor & Co SA** Shipdeal Corp SatCom: Inmarsat C 434100091 *Charlestown* *St Kitts & Nevis* MMSI: 341095000 Official number: SKN1002261	**1,327** 532 1,666	Class: RS (LR) (BV) ✠ Classed LR until 5/4/92	**1975-03 Uudenkaupungin Telakka Oy (Nystads Varv Ab) — Uusikaupunki** Yd No: 276 Loa 74.12 (BB) Br ex 11.05 Dght 4.712 Lbp 67.32 Br md 11.00 Dpth 6.56 Welded, 2 dks	**(A34A2GR) Refrigerated Cargo Ship** Ins: 2,048 Compartments: 2 Ho, ER, 2 Tw Dk 4 Ha: (4.1 x 3.5)3 (5.3 x 3.5)ER Derricks: 8x2t; Winches: 8	**1 oil engine** sr geared to sc. shaft driving 1 CP propeller Total Power: 1,618kW (2,200hp) 13.5kn Nohab F212V 1 x Vee 4 Stroke 12 Cy. 250 x 300 1618kW (2200bhp) AB NOHAB-Sweden AuxGen: 1 x 225kW 450V 60Hz a.c, 3 x 135kW 450V 60Hz a.c Fuel: 256.0 (d.f.) 6.5pd
9641156 *3FYW7* -	**SUNNY LOTUS** **SB Global SA** Korea Marine Transport Co Ltd (KMTC) *Panama* *Panama* MMSI: 373407000 Official number: 44601PEXT1	**9,910** 5,118 12,750	Class: KR (Class contemplated)	**2013-05 Dae Sun Shipbuilding & Engineering Co Ltd — Busan** Yd No: 512 Loa 143.90 (BB) Br ex - Dght 8.200 Lbp 136.02 Br md 22.60 Dpth 11.20 Welded, 1 dk	**(A33A2CC) Container Ship (Fully Cellular)** TEU 1050	**1 oil engine** driving 1 FP propeller Total Power: 7,860kW (10,686hp) 18.0kn MAN-B&W 6S46MC-C 1 x 2 Stroke 6 Cy. 460 x 1932 7860kW (10686bhp) STX Engine Co Ltd-South Korea AuxGen: 3 x 615kW 445V a.c Thrusters: 1 Tunnel thruster (f)
9133484 *DSFS5* -	**SUNNY MAPLE** **Korea Marine Transport Co Ltd (KMTC)** - SatCom: Inmarsat A 1360513 *Jeju* *South Korea* MMSI: 441158000 Official number: JJR-011231	**3,987** 2,023 5,834 T/cm 14.8	Class: KR	**1996-11 ShinA Shipbuilding Co Ltd — Tongyeong** Yd No: 388 Loa 107.45 (BB) Br ex - Dght 6.513 Lbp 97.60 Br md 17.20 Dpth 8.30 Welded, 1 dk	**(A33A2CC) Container Ship (Fully Cellular)** TEU 342 C Ho 132 TEU C Dk 210 TEU incl 30 ref C.	**1 oil engine** driving 1 FP propeller Total Power: 3,913kW (5,320hp) 16.5kn B&W 7L35MC 1 x 2 Stroke 7 Cy. 350 x 1050 3913kW (5320bhp) Ssangyong Heavy Industries Co Ltd-South Korea AuxGen: 3 x 320kW 445V a.c Thrusters: 1 Tunnel thruster (f)
7734545 *V4JX2* -	**SUNNY MARIA** *ex* Karat Reefer *-2007* *ex* Issli *-2004* *ex* Snowdrop *-2004* **Baltor & Co SA** Shipdeal Corp SatCom: Inmarsat C 434100090 *Charlestown* *St Kitts & Nevis* MMSI: 341096000 Official number: SKN1002262	**1,263** 581 1,423	Class: RS (BV)	**1978 p/f Skala Skipasmidja — Skali** Yd No: 32 Loa 67.29 Br ex 12.02 Dght 4.441 Lbp 61.37 Br md 12.00 Dpth 6.51 Welded, 2 dks	**(A34A2GR) Refrigerated Cargo Ship** Grain: 1,847; Ins: 1,850 Compartments: 3 Ho, ER 3 Ha: 3 (2.9 x 4.5)ER Derricks: 3x5t Ice Capable	**1 oil engine** driving 1 CP propeller Total Power: 1,250kW (1,700hp) 13.7kn MaK 6M452AK 1 x 4 Stroke 6 Cy. 320 x 450 1250kW (1700bhp) MaK Maschinenbau GmbH-Kiel AuxGen: 4 x 123kW 380V a.c Fuel: 239.0 (d.f.)
9474345 *JD3283* -	**SUNNY MARS** **Asahi Tanker Co Ltd** - *Tokyo* *Japan* MMSI: 431003073 Official number: 141569	**4,551** 2,090 6,729 T/cm 15.8	Class: NK	**2008-06 Niigata Shipbuilding & Repair Inc — Niigata NI** Yd No: 0028 Loa 109.61 (BB) Br ex 17.22 Dght 6.763 Lbp 103.00 Br md 17.20 Dpth 8.90 Welded, 1 dk	**(A12B2TR) Chemical/Products Tanker** Double Hull (13F) Liq: 7,102; Liq (Oil): 7,102 Cargo Heating Coils Compartments: 10 Wing Ta, 2 Wing Slop Ta, ER 2 Cargo Pump (s): 2x800m³/hr Manifold: Bow/CM: 54.1m	**1 oil engine** driving 1 FP propeller Total Power: 3,250kW (4,419hp) 13.4kn MAN-B&W 5L35MC 1 x 2 Stroke 5 Cy. 350 x 1050 3250kW (4419bhp) Hitachi Zosen Corp-Japan AuxGen: 2 x a.c Fuel: 60.0 (d.f.) 325.0 (r.f.)
9059119 *3FDK8* -	**SUNNY NAPIER II** **Ocean Woodland Shipping Co Ltd** Universal Marine Corp SatCom: Inmarsat A 1361616 *Panama* *Panama* MMSI: 351990000 Official number: 2554698D	**15,714** 6,784 23,842 T/cm 37.1	Class: NK	**1993-02 Imabari Shipbuilding Co Ltd — Imabari EH (Imabari Shipyard)** Yd No: 498 Loa 168.53 (BB) Br ex 24.64 Dght 9.434 Lbp 160.00 Br md 24.60 Dpth 13.30 Welded, 1 dk	**(A21A2BC) Bulk Carrier** Grain: 26,958 Compartments: 5 Ho, ER 5 Ha: (20.3 x 18.7)4 (22.7 x 18.7)ER Cranes: 2x27.9t	**1 oil engine** driving 1 FP propeller Total Power: 5,149kW (7,001hp) 14.0kn Mitsubishi 6UEC52LA 1 x 2 Stroke 6 Cy. 520 x 1600 5149kW (7001bhp) Akasaka Tekkosho KK (Akasaka DieselLtd)-Japan AuxGen: 4 x 343kW a.c Fuel: 1410.0 (r.f.)
8970043 *WDA5864* -	**SUNNY NGUYEN** **Hung Van Nguyen** - *New Iberia, LA* *United States of America* MMSI: 366825020 Official number: 1111691	**161** 48 -		**2001 Master Boat Builders, Inc. — Coden, Al** Yd No: 309 L reg 25.96 Br ex - Dght - Lbp - Br md 7.62 Dpth 3.10 Welded, 1 dk	**(B11B2FV) Fishing Vessel**	**1 oil engine** driving 1 FP propeller
7227528 *HQCH9* -	**SUNNY No. 77** *ex* Riasu Maru No. 2 *-1987* **Golden Sea Product S de RL** - *San Lorenzo* *Honduras* Official number: L-1921943	*424* 163 -	Class: (KR)	**1972 Narasaki Zosen KK — Muroran HK** Yd No: 784 Loa 49.13 Br ex 8.23 Dght 3.175 Lbp 42.35 Br md 8.21 Dpth 3.79 Welded, 1 dk	**(B11B2FV) Fishing Vessel**	**1 oil engine** driving 1 FP propeller Total Power: 380kW (517hp) 12.0kn Niigata 6MG16S 1 x 4 Stroke 6 Cy. 160 x 200 380kW (517bhp) Niigata Engineering Co Ltd-Japan AuxGen: 1 x 160kW 225V Fuel: 285.5

9474357 *JD3284* -	**SUNNY NOAH** **Asahi Tanker Co Ltd** - *Tokyo* *Japan* MMSI: 431003074 Official number: 141570	**4,551** 2,090 6,690 T/cm 15.8	Class: NK	**2008-09 Niigata Shipbuilding & Repair Inc — Niigata NI** Yd No: 0029 Loa 109.61 (BB) Br ex 17.22 Dght 6.763 Lbp 103.00 Br md 17.20 Dpth 8.90 Welded, 1 dk	**(A12B2TR) Chemical/Products Tanker** Double Hull (13F) Liq: 7,301; Liq (Oil): 7,102 Cargo Heating Coils Compartments: 10 Wing Ta, 2 Wing Slop Ta, ER 2 Cargo Pump (s): 2x800m³/hr Manifold: Bow/CM: 54.1m	**1 oil engine** driving 1 FP propeller Total Power: 3,250kW (4,419hp) 13.4kn MAN-B&W 5L35MC 1 x 2 Stroke 5 Cy. 350 x 1050 3250kW (4419bhp) Imex Co Ltd-Japan AuxGen: 2 x a.c Fuel: 63.0 (d.f.) 369.0 (r.f.)
9102849 *DSEX8* -	**SUNNY OAK** **Korea Marine Transport Co Ltd (KMTC)** - SatCom: Inmarsat C 444067112 *Jeju* *South Korea* MMSI: 440567000 Official number: JJR-990139	**3,996** 2,036 5,800 T/cm 14.8	Class: KR	**1995-10 Kwangyang Shipbuilding & Engineering Co Ltd — Janghang** Yd No: 106 Loa 107.55 (BB) Br ex 17.60 Dght 6.513 Lbp 97.60 Br md 17.20 Dpth 8.30 Welded, 1 dk	**(A33A2CC) Container Ship (Fully Cellular)** TEU 342 C Ho 132 TEU C Dk 210 TEU incl 50 ref C. Compartments: 5 Cell Ho, ER 5 Ha: ER	**1 oil engine** driving 1 FP propeller Total Power: 3,913kW (5,320hp) 14.9kn B&W 7L35MC 1 x 2 Stroke 7 Cy. 350 x 1050 3913kW (5320bhp) Ssangyong Heavy Industries Co Ltd-South Korea AuxGen: 2 x 280kW 445V 60Hz a.c Fuel: 96.0 (d.f.) (Heating Coils) 489.0 (r.f.) 13.0pd
9102150 *3FBU5* -	**SUNNY OASIS** *ex* MOL Rhine *-2010* *ex* Hyundai Dubai *-2009* *ex* APL Dubai *-2008* *ex* MOL Rhine *-2002* *ex* Rhine *-2001* **Sunny Oasis Maritime SA** Mitsui OSK Lines Ltd (MOL) *Panama* *Panama* MMSI: 353987000 Official number: 2211395G	**60,133** 23,180 62,905	Class: NK	**1995-04 Ishikawajima-Harima Heavy Industries Co Ltd (IHI) — Kure** Yd No: 3047 Loa 299.95 (BB) Br ex - Dght 13.031 Lbp 283.00 Br md 37.10 Dpth 21.80 Welded, 1 dk	**(A33A2CC) Container Ship (Fully Cellular)** TEU 4743 C Ho 2264 TEU C Dk 2479 TEU incl 350 ref C. Compartments: ER, 8 Cell Ho 18 Ha: ER	**1 oil engine** driving 1 FP propeller Total Power: 43,844kW (59,610hp) 24.5kn Sulzer 12RTA84C 1 x 2 Stroke 12 Cy. 840 x 2400 43844kW (59610bhp) Diesel United Ltd.-Aioi AuxGen: 4 x 1600kW 450V a.c Thrusters: 1 Thwart. CP thruster (f) Fuel: 196.0 (d.f.) 6964.0 (r.f.) 111.0pd
9072197 *DSQM4* -	**SUNNY OCEAN** *ex* Cupid Arrow *-1999* **NYK Bulkship (Korea) Co Ltd** STX Marine Service Co Ltd *Jeju* *South Korea* MMSI: 441625000 Official number: JJR-094071	**36,074** 23,452 68,621 T/cm 64.7	Class: KR (NK)	**1994-07 Sasebo Heavy Industries Co. Ltd. — Sasebo Yard, Sasebo** Yd No: 392 Loa 224.00 (BB) Br ex - Dght 13.289 Lbp 215.00 Br md 32.20 Dpth 18.20 Welded, 1 dk	**(A21A2BC) Bulk Carrier** Grain: 81,337 Compartments: 7 Ho, ER 7 Ha: (14.4 x 12.8)6 (17.6 x 12.4)ER	**1 oil engine** driving 1 FP propeller Total Power: 9,350kW (12,712hp) 13.9kn B&W 5S60MC 1 x 2 Stroke 5 Cy. 600 x 2292 9350kW (12712bhp) Mitsui Engineering & Shipbuilding CLtd-Japan AuxGen: 3 x 450kW 450V 60Hz a.c Fuel: 78.0 (d.f.) 1785.5 (r.f.) 27.5pd
8906676 *3FGU* -	**SUNNY OCEAN** *ex* Cape Australia *-2012* **Faithful Marine SA** Winning Shipping (HK) Co Ltd SatCom: Inmarsat C 435631810 *Panama* *Panama* MMSI: 356318000 Official number: 4454613	**77,096** 47,175 149,512 T/cm 106.3	Class: CR NK (AB)	**1990-10 China Shipbuilding Corp (CSBC) — Kaohsiung** Yd No: 502 Loa 270.03 (BB) Br ex 43.03 Dght 17.325 Lbp 260.00 Br md 43.00 Dpth 23.90 Welded, 1 dk	**(A21A2BC) Bulk Carrier** Grain: 164,597; Bale: 162,730 Compartments: 9 Ho, ER 9 Ha: 9 (14.2 x 18.4)ER	**1 oil engine** driving 1 FP propeller Total Power: 12,431kW (16,901hp) 13.9kn B&W 5L80MCE 1 x 2 Stroke 5 Cy. 800 x 2592 12431kW (16901bhp) Hitachi Zosen Corp-Japan AuxGen: 3 x 500kW a.c Fuel: 217.0 (d.f.) 2853.0 (r.f.) 38.0pd
9116759 *DSNI6* -	**SUNNY OLIVE** **Korea Marine Transport Co Ltd (KMTC)** - *Jeju* *South Korea* MMSI: 441358000 Official number: JJR-039419	**3,996** 2,023 5,848 T/cm 14.8	Class: KR	**1995-09 ShinA Shipbuilding Co Ltd — Tongyeong** Yd No: 379 Loa 107.55 (BB) Br ex 17.60 Dght 6.509 Lbp 97.60 Br md 17.20 Dpth 8.30 Welded, 1 dk	**(A33A2CC) Container Ship (Fully Cellular)** TEU 342 C Ho 132 TEU C Dk 210 TEU incl 50 ref C. Compartments: 5 Cell Ho, ER 5 Ha: ER	**1 oil engine** driving 1 FP propeller Total Power: 3,913kW (5,320hp) 14.9kn B&W 7L35MC 1 x 2 Stroke 7 Cy. 350 x 1050 3913kW (5320bhp) Ssangyong Heavy Industries Co Ltd-South Korea AuxGen: 2 x 280kW 445V 60Hz a.c Fuel: 96.0 (d.f.) (Heating Coils) 489.0 (r.f.) 13.0pd
9511143 *3EWD7* -	**SUNNY ORION** **Asahi Tanker Co Ltd & Solar Shipping & Trading SA** Asahi Tanker Co Ltd *Panama* *Panama* MMSI: 354663000 Official number: 4161810	**7,771** 3,464 12,203 T/cm 21.5	Class: NK	**2010-04 Shin Kurushima Dockyard Co. Ltd. — Hashihama, Imabari** Yd No: 5576 Loa 124.03 (BB) Br ex 19.63 Dght 8.278 Lbp 118.50 Br md 19.60 Dpth 11.50 Welded, 1 dk	**(A12B2TR) Chemical/Products Tanker** Double Hull (13F) Liq: 13,086; Liq (Oil): 13,086 Cargo Heating Coils Compartments: 14 Wing Ta, 2 Wing Slop Ta, ER 14 Cargo Pump (s): 14x200m³/hr Manifold: Bow/CM: 61.9m	**1 oil engine** driving 1 FP propeller Total Power: 3,900kW (5,302hp) 13.3kn MAN-B&W 6L35MC 1 x 2 Stroke 6 Cy. 350 x 1050 3900kW (5302bhp) Hitachi Zosen Corp-Japan AuxGen: 3 x 380kW 450V 60Hz a.c Thrusters: 1 Tunnel thruster (f) Fuel: 90.0 (d.f.) 695.0 (r.f.)
8890023 *JK5432* -	**SUNNY OSAKI** **Osaki Kisen KK** *Takehara, Hiroshima* *Japan* Official number: 134735	*384* - -		**1995-08 K.K. Kawamoto Zosensho — Osakikamijima** Yd No: 136 L reg 39.00 Br ex - Dght - Lbp - Br md 11.00 Dpth 3.90 Welded, 1 dk	**(A37B2PS) Passenger Ship** Passengers: unberthed: 300	**1 oil engine** driving 1 FP propeller Total Power: 1,324kW (1,800hp) 12.1kn Yanmar 6N260-SN 1 x 4 Stroke 6 Cy. 260 x 360 1324kW (1800bhp) Yanmar Diesel Engine Co Ltd-Japan
9128300 *DSEK8* -	**SUNNY PALM** **Korea Marine Transport Co Ltd (KMTC)** - *Jeju* *South Korea* MMSI: 440119000 Official number: JJR-961131	**3,996** 1,967 5,848 T/cm 14.9	Class: KR	**1996-07 ShinA Shipbuilding Co Ltd — Tongyeong** Yd No: 384 Loa 107.45 (BB) Br ex 17.24 Dght 6.513 Lbp 97.60 Br md 17.20 Dpth 8.30 Welded, 1 dk	**(A33A2CC) Container Ship (Fully Cellular)** TEU 342 C Ho 132 TEU C Dk 210 TEU incl 30 ref C. Compartments: 5 Cell Ho, ER 5 Ha: ER	**1 oil engine** driving 1 FP propeller Total Power: 3,913kW (5,320hp) 16.5kn B&W 7L35MC 1 x 2 Stroke 7 Cy. 350 x 1050 3913kW (5320bhp) Ssangyong Heavy Industries Co Ltd-South Korea AuxGen: 3 x 320kW 445V 60Hz a.c Thrusters: 1 Thwart. CP thruster (f) Fuel: 83.0 (d.f.) 395.0 (r.f.)
9305946 *H8NV* -	**SUNNY PESCADORES** **Sunny Pescadores SA (Panama)** Shih Wei Navigation Co Ltd *Panama* *Panama* MMSI: 352778000 Official number: 3015704B	**7,271** 4,796 12,535	Class: BV	**2004-07 Higaki Zosen K.K. — Imabari** Yd No: 556 Loa 127.81 Br ex - Dght 8.170 Lbp 119.83 Br md 19.60 Dpth 11.00 Welded, 1 dk	**(A31A2GX) General Cargo Ship** Grain: 17,150; Bale: 16,362 Compartments: 3 Ho, ER 3 Ha: ER Cranes: 2x30.5t; Derricks: 1x30t	**1 oil engine** driving 1 FP propeller Total Power: 3,900kW (5,302hp) 13.3kn MAN-B&W 6L35MC 1 x 2 Stroke 6 Cy. 350 x 1050 3900kW (5302bhp) The Hanshin Diesel Works Ltd-Japan AuxGen: 2 x 640kW 450V 60Hz a.c
9044138 *D8FX* -	**SUNNY PINE** **Korea Marine Transport Co Ltd (KMTC)** - SatCom: Inmarsat C 444061612 *Jeju* *South Korea* MMSI: 440024000 Official number: JJR-920442	**3,986** 1,878 5,965	Class: KR	**1992-04 Dae Sun Shipbuilding & Engineering Co Ltd — Busan** Yd No: 386 Loa 107.00 (BB) Br ex 17.22 Dght 6.513 Lbp 97.50 Br md 17.20 Dpth 8.30 Welded, 1 dk	**(A33A2CC) Container Ship (Fully Cellular)** TEU 342 C Ho 132 TEU C Dk 210 TEU incl 25 ref C Compartments: 3 Cell Ho, ER 5 Ha: ER	**1 oil engine** driving 1 FP propeller Total Power: 3,913kW (5,320hp) 14.9kn B&W 7L35MC 1 x 2 Stroke 7 Cy. 350 x 1050 3913kW (5320bhp) Hyundai Heavy Industries Co Ltd-South Korea
9258131 *D7NC* -	**SUNNY POSEIDON** *ex* Eastern Jubilee *-2014* **Hyo Cheon Marine Bunkering Co Ltd** Asahi Tanker Co Ltd *Jeju* *South Korea* MMSI: 440221000 Official number: JJR-141014	**4,374** 1,729 6,135 T/cm 15.6	Class: KR (Class contemplated) (NK)	**2003-01 Shin Kurushima Dockyard Co. Ltd. — Hashihama, Imabari** Yd No: 5202 Loa 107.84 (BB) Br ex 16.83 Dght 6.027 Lbp 102.00 Br md 16.80 Dpth 8.40 Welded, 1 dk	**(A12B2TR) Chemical/Products Tanker** Double Hull (13F) Liq: 6,170; Liq (Oil): 6,170 Cargo Heating Coils Compartments: 2 Wing Slop Ta, ER, 14 Wing Ta 14 Cargo Pump (s): 14x200m³/hr Manifold: Bow/CM: 57.5m	**1 oil engine** driving 1 FP propeller Total Power: 3,236kW (4,400hp) 13.2kn MAN-B&W 5L35MC 1 x 2 Stroke 5 Cy. 350 x 1050 3236kW (4400bhp) (made 2003) Mitsui Engineering & Shipbuilding CLtd-Japan AuxGen: 2 x 300kW 450V 60Hz a.c Thrusters: 1 Tunnel thruster (f) Fuel: 89.0 (d.f.) 473.0 (r.f.)
9651280 *9VFX2* -	**SUNNY PUTNEY** **Sunny Blue Shipping Pte Ltd** Noma Shipping Co Ltd (Noma Kaiun KK) *Singapore* *Singapore* MMSI: 566826000 Official number: 398181	**40,350** 24,954 74,940 T/cm 67.3	Class: NK	**2013-02 Sasebo Heavy Industries Co. Ltd. — Sasebo Yard, Sasebo** Yd No: 809 Loa 225.00 (BB) Br ex 32.25 Dght 14.136 Lbp 218.00 Br md 32.20 Dpth 19.80 Welded, 1 dk	**(A21A2BC) Bulk Carrier** Double Hull Grain: 90,771; Bale: 88,783 Compartments: 7 Ho, ER 7 Ha: ER	**1 oil engine** driving 1 FP propeller Total Power: 8,700kW (11,829hp) 14.5kn MAN-B&W 7S50MC-C8 1 x 2 Stroke 7 Cy. 500 x 2000 8700kW (11829bhp) Mitsui Engineering & Shipbuilding CLtd-Japan Fuel: 2730.0
7720611 - -	**SUNNY ROSE** **PT Salam Pacific Indonesia Lines** *Jakarta* *Indonesia* MMSI: 525017035	**3,677** 1,908 5,470	Class: (KI) (KR)	**1978-08 Dae Sun Shipbuilding & Engineering Co Ltd — Busan** Yd No: 196 Loa 106.03 (BB) Br ex - Dght 6.825 Lbp 97.01 Br md 16.01 Dpth 8.31 Welded, 1 dk	**(A33A2CC) Container Ship (Fully Cellular)** Grain: 6,571; Bale: 5,536 TEU 270 incl 30 ref C. 6 Ha: (12.9 x 8.0)5 (12.3 x 13.2)	**1 oil engine** driving 1 FP propeller Total Power: 3,310kW (4,500hp) 15.8kn Mitsubishi 6UET45/80D 1 x 2 Stroke 6 Cy. 450 x 800 3310kW (4500bhp) Akasaka Tekkosho KK (Akasaka DieselLtd)-Japan AuxGen: 3 x 240kW 445V a.c

9482122 *3FZZ5* -	**SUNNY ROYAL** **CS Sunny SA** Kawasaki Kisen Kaisha Ltd (Kawasaki Kisen KK) ('K' Line) SatCom: Inmarsat C 435721313 *Panama* *Panama* MMSI: 357213000 Official number: 4267411	**33,138** 19,142 58,772 T/cm 59.5	Class: NK	**2011**-05 **Kawasaki Heavy Industries Ltd — Kobe HG** Yd No: 1644 Loa 197.00 (BB) Br ex - Dght 12.680 Lbp 194.00 Br md 32.26 Dpth 18.10 Welded, 1 dk	**(A21A2BC) Bulk Carrier** Grain: 73,614; Bale: 70,963 Compartments: 5 Ho, ER 5 Ha: ER Cranes: 4x30.5t	**1 oil engine** driving 1 FP propeller Total Power: 8,630kW (11,733hp) 14.5kn MAN-B&W 6S50MC-C 1 x 2 Stroke 6 Cy. 500 x 2000 8630kW (11733bhp) Kawasaki Heavy Industries Ltd-Japan Fuel: 2265.0 (r.f.)
9604756 *3FIL6* -	**SUNNY SKY** **Diamond Camellia SA** Daiichi Chuo Marine Co Ltd (DC Marine) *Panama* *Panama* MMSI: 373412000 Official number: 4346912	**17,019** 10,108 28,390 T/cm 39.7	Class: NK	**2011**-12 **Imabari Shipbuilding Co Ltd — Imabari EH (Imabari Shipyard)** Yd No: 709 Loa 169.37 (BB) Br ex - Dght 9.820 Lbp 160.40 Br md 27.20 Dpth 13.60 Welded, 1 dk	**(A21A2BC) Bulk Carrier** Grain: 37,320; Bale: 35,742 Compartments: 5 Ho, ER 5 Ha: ER Cranes: 4x30.5t	**1 oil engine** driving 1 FP propeller Total Power: 5,850kW (7,954hp) 14.5kn MAN-B&W 6S42MC 1 x 2 Stroke 6 Cy. 420 x 1764 5850kW (7954bhp) Makita Corp-Japan Fuel: 1530.0
7808889 *DUD6037* -	**SUNNY SKY 888** *ex* Serrekunda 77 *-1999* *ex* Take Maru No. 31 *-1990* **Sun Warm Tuna Corp** - *Manila* *Philippines* Official number: MNLD010832	**561** 211 -		**1978**-06 **Kochi Jyuko K.K. — Kochi** Yd No: 1268 Loa - Br ex - Dght 3.201 Lbp 43.62 Br md 8.51 Dpth 3.56 Riveted\Welded, 1 dk	**(B11B2FV) Fishing Vessel**	**1 oil engine** driving 1 FP propeller Total Power: 736kW (1,001hp) Hanshin 6LU28 1 x 4 Stroke 6 Cy. 280 x 440 736kW (1001bhp) Hanshin Nainenki Kogyo-Japan
9641857 *D5DG3* -	**SUNNY SMILE** **Citrus Hope Shipping SA** Kawana Kaiun Co Ltd *Monrovia* *Liberia* MMSI: 636015871 Official number: 15871	**50,625** 31,470 95,768	Class: NK	**2013**-01 **Imabari Shipbuilding Co Ltd — Marugame KG (Marugame Shipyard)** Yd No: 1578 Loa 234.98 (BB) Br ex - Dght 14.468 Lbp 227.00 Br md 38.00 Dpth 19.90 Welded, 1 dk	**(A21A2BC) Bulk Carrier** Grain: 109,476 Compartments: 7 Ho, ER 7 Ha: ER	**1 oil engine** driving 1 FP propeller Total Power: 12,950kW (17,607hp) 14.5kn MAN-B&W 6S60MC-C 1 x 2 Stroke 6 Cy. 600 x 2400 12950kW (17607bhp) Mitsui Engineering & Shipbuilding CLtd-Japan AuxGen: 3 x 540kW a.c Fuel: 3900.0
9121041 *DSFP2* -	**SUNNY SPRUCE** **Korea Marine Transport Co Ltd (KMTC)** SatCom: Inmarsat C 435614110 *Jeju* *South Korea* MMSI: 441107000 Official number: JJR-010503	**3,987** 2,023 5,821 T/cm 14.8	Class: KR	**1996**-04 **ShinA Shipbuilding Co Ltd — Tongyeong** Yd No: 382 Loa 107.35 (BB) Br ex 17.24 Dght 6.509 Lbp 97.60 Br md 17.20 Dpth 8.30 Welded, 1 dk	**(A33A2CC) Container Ship (Fully Cellular)** TEU 342 C Ho 132 TEU C Dk 210 TEU incl 25 ref C. Compartments: 5 Cell Ho, ER 5 Ha: (12.9 x 8.4)4 (12.9 x 13.6)ER	**1 oil engine** driving 1 FP propeller Total Power: 3,913kW (5,320hp) 14.8kn B&W 7L35MC 1 x 2 Stroke 7 Cy. 350 x 1050 3913kW (5320bhp) Ssangyong Heavy Industries Co Ltd-South Korea AuxGen: 3 x 353kW 445V 60Hz a.c Thrusters: 1 Thwart. CP thruster (f) Fuel: 95.6 (d.f.) 490.4 (r.f.) 13.0pd
8920517 *3FIX8* -	**SUNNY STAR** *ex* Cape America *-2012* **Sunny Star Shipping SA** Qingdao Winning International Ships Management Co Ltd *Panama* *Panama* MMSI: 373458000 Official number: 4423412	**77,096** 47,175 149,515 T/cm 106.3	Class: CR NK (AB)	**1991**-02 **China Shipbuilding Corp (CSBC) — Kaohsiung** Yd No: 515 Loa 270.00 (BB) Br ex 43.03 Dght 17.325 Lbp 260.00 Br md 43.00 Dpth 23.90 Welded, 1 dk	**(A21A2BC) Bulk Carrier** Grain: 164,597; Bale: 162,730 Compartments: 9 Ho, ER 9 Ha: 9 (14.2 x 18.4)ER	**1 oil engine** driving 1 FP propeller Total Power: 12,607kW (17,140hp) 13.9kn B&W 5L80MCE 1 x 2 Stroke 5 Cy. 800 x 2592 12607kW (17140bhp) Kawasaki Heavy Industries Ltd-Japan AuxGen: 3 x 500kW 220/440V 60Hz a.c Fuel: 217.0 (d.f.) 2853.0 (r.f.) 38.0pd
9607758 *3FWR6* -	**SUNNY VISTA** **Gas Venture SA** JX Ocean Co Ltd *Panama* *Panama* MMSI: 355817000 Official number: 4462413	**47,914** 14,375 55,154 T/cm 71.3	Class: NK	**2013**-03 **Mitsubishi Heavy Industries Ltd. — Nagasaki** Yd No: 2288 Loa 230.00 (BB) Br ex - Dght 11.580 Lbp 219.00 Br md 36.60 Dpth 21.65 Welded, 1 dk	**(A11B2TG) LPG Tanker** Liq (Gas): 83,332	**1 oil engine** driving 1 FP propeller Total Power: 13,000kW (17,675hp) 16.7kn Mitsubishi 7UEC60LSII 1 x 2 Stroke 7 Cy. 600 x 2300 13000kW (17675bhp) Mitsubishi Heavy Industries Ltd-Japan Fuel: 3700.0
9489041 *DSBL4* -	**SUNNY YOUNG** **Joong Ang Shipping Co Ltd** SatCom: Inmarsat C 444000520 *Jeju* *South Korea* MMSI: 440001000 Official number: JJR-111023	**44,290** - 81,967	Class: KR	**2011**-03 **Daewoo Shipbuilding & Marine Engineering Co Ltd — Geoje** Yd No: 1188 Loa 229.00 (BB) Br ex - Dght 14.520 Lbp 218.25 Br md 32.26 Dpth 20.20 Welded, 1 dk	**(A21A2BC) Bulk Carrier** Grain: 96,500 Compartments: 7 Ho, ER 7 Ha: 6 (15.2 x 15.0)ER (15.2 x 13.3)	**1 oil engine** driving 1 FP propeller Total Power: 10,050kW (13,664hp) 14.5kn MAN-B&W 6S60MC-C8 1 x 2 Stroke 6 Cy. 600 x 2400 10050kW (13664bhp) Hyundai Heavy Industries Co Ltd-South Korea
8851455 *WDC6949* -	**SUNNYVALE** **Sunnyvale Ventures LLC** - *Juneau, AK* *United States of America* Official number: 257403	*140* 118 -		**1949 Weldit Tank & Steel Co. — Bellingham, Wa** Loa - Br ex - Dght - Lbp 23.38 Br md 7.35 Dpth 1.98 Welded, 1 dk	**(B12B2FC) Fish Carrier**	**1 oil engine** driving 1 FP propeller Total Power: 199kW (271hp)
8403222 *7KSL* -	**SUNOURA MARU No. 8** *ex* Shumei Maru No. 25 *-1994* *ex* Kashima Maru No. 32 *-1991* **Yasunari Nakajima** - *Uozu, Toyama* *Japan* MMSI: 431082000 Official number: 126644	*192* - -		**1984**-04 **Sanuki Shipbuilding & Iron Works Co Ltd — Mitoyo KG** Yd No: 1131 Loa - (BB) Br ex - Dght 2.710 Lbp 30.99 Br md 6.80 Dpth 3.00 Welded, 1 dk	**(B11B2FV) Fishing Vessel** Ins: 149 Compartments: 11 Ho, ER 12 Ha: ER	**1 oil engine** sr geared to sc. shaft driving 1 FP propeller Total Power: 699kW (950hp) Niigata 6M28AFTE 1 x 4 Stroke 6 Cy. 280 x 480 699kW (950bhp) Niigata Engineering Co Ltd-Japan
1010351 *ZGAF2* -	**SUNRAYS** **Rose Gem Enterprise Ltd** Nigel Burgess Ltd (BURGESS) *George Town* *Cayman Islands (British)* MMSI: 319015100	**2,867** 860 -	Class: LR ✠**100A1** SS 03/2010 SSC Yacht (P), mono, G6 ✠**LMC** **UMS** Cable: 440.0/34.0 U3 (a)	**2010**-03 **Zwijnenburg BV — Krimpen a/d IJssel** (Hull) Yd No: (705) **2010**-03 **Aluship Technology Sp z oo — Gdansk** (Upper part) Yd No: (705) **2010**-03 **Oceanco Shipyards (Alblasserdam) B.V. — Alblasserdam** Yd No: 705 Loa 85.43 (BB) Br ex 14.24 Dght 3.950 Lbp 71.96 Br md 13.80 Dpth 7.10 Welded, 1 dk	**(X11A2YP) Yacht**	**2 oil engines** with clutches, flexible couplings & sr reverse geared to sc. shafts driving 2 FP propellers Total Power: 7,200kW (9,790hp) 19.0kn M.T.U. 16V595TE70 2 x Vee 4 Stroke 16 Cy. 190 x 210 each-3600kW (4895bhp) MTU Friedrichshafen GmbH-Friedrichshafen AuxGen: 3 x 308kW 400V 50Hz a.c Thrusters: 1 Thwart. FP thruster (f); 1 Thwart. FP thruster (a)
1005409 *ZCFY3* -	**SUNRISE** *ex* Amoixa *-2013* *ex* Sunrise *-2013* **Sunrise Ltd** Nigel Burgess Ltd (BURGESS) *George Town* *Cayman Islands (British)* MMSI: 319674000 Official number: 904044	**638** 191 -	Class: LR ✠**100A1** SS 09/2010 Yacht **LMC** Cable: 330.0/24.0 U2	**2000**-09 **Southern African Shipyards (Pty.) Ltd. — Durban** (Hull) Yd No: 232.3 **2000* De Waal Shipyards B.V. — Dreumel** Yd No: 502 Loa 51.80 Br ex 9.87 Dght 3.500 Lbp 47.43 Br md 9.45 Dpth 5.50 Welded, 1 dk	**(X11A2YP) Yacht**	**2 oil engines** with clutches, flexible couplings & sr reverse geared to sc. shafts driving 2 FP propellers Total Power: 2,520kW (3,426hp) 16.0kn M.T.U. 12V396TE74 2 x Vee 4 Stroke 12 Cy. 165 x 185 each-1260kW (1713bhp) MTU Friedrichshafen GmbH-Friedrichshafen AuxGen: 2 x 107kW 380V 50Hz a.c Thrusters: 1 Thwart. FP thruster (f)
7308085 *WX9033* -	**SUNRISE** *ex* Shell Ridge *-2007* **Dung Van Tran** - *Bayou La Batre, AL* *United States of America* MMSI: 366702440 Official number: 506813	*113* 77 -		**1966 Graham Boats, Inc. — Pascagoula, Ms** Yd No: 110 L reg 23.11 Br ex 6.71 Dght - Lbp - Br md - Dpth 3.41 Welded	**(B11B2FV) Fishing Vessel**	**1 oil engine** driving 1 FP propeller Total Power: 268kW (364hp)
7359670 - -	**SUNRISE** *ex* Transgas *-2011* *ex* Edouard L D *-2008* **Amethyst International Ltd** Thome Ship Management Pte Ltd	**79,272** 23,781 67,460 T/cm 94.2	Class: BV (AB)	**1977**-12 **Ateliers et Chantiers de France-Dunkerque — Dunkirk** Yd No: 290 Loa 280.63 (BB) Br ex 41.64 Dght 11.218 Lbp 266.02 Br md 41.61 Dpth 27.51 Welded, 1 dk	**(A11A2TN) LNG Tanker** Double Hull Liq (Gas): 126,813 5 x Gas Tank (s); 5 membrane Gas Transport (36% Ni.stl) pri horizontal 10 Cargo Pump (s): 10x1250m³/hr Manifold: Bow/CM: 133m	**1 Steam Turb** dr geared to sc. shaft driving 1 FP propeller Total Power: 33,100kW (45,003hp) 19.0kn Stal-Laval APG 310/108 1 x steam Turb 33100kW (45003shp), made: 1975, fitted 2000 Alsthom Atlantique-France AuxGen: 2 x 2600kW a.c, 1 x 1400kW a.c Thrusters: 1 Thwart. FP thruster (f) Fuel: 431.0 (d.f.) 4135.0 (r.f.)

IMO / Call sign / Fishing no.	Name / Owner / Registry	Tonnage	Class	Build / Dimensions	Type / Capacity	Machinery
7429449 *DSHL* -	**SUNRISE** *ex* Pana Ace *-2004* *ex* Korea Sunrise *-2000* *ex* Ethylene Sunrise *-1982* **DaeHo Shipping Co Ltd** - *Busan* *South Korea* MMSI: 440301030 Official number: BSR-905231	**2,008** 1,351 2,287	Class: (KR) (NK)	**1975-06 K.K. Ichikawa Zosensho — Ise** Yd No: 1326 Loa 88.02 Br ex 14.03 Dght 4.815 Lbp 82.00 Br md 14.00 Dpth 6.81 Riveted\Welded, 1 dk	**(A11B2TG) LPG Tanker** Liq (Gas): 2,100 2 x Gas Tank (s);	**1 oil engine** driving 1 FP propeller Total Power: 2,059kW (2,799hp) 12.8kn Hanshin 6LUS40 1 x 4 Stroke 6 Cy. 400 x 640 2059kW (2799bhp) Hanshin Nainenki Kogyo-Japan AuxGen: 2 x 176kW 445V a.c
8324555 *GDXH* FR 359	**SUNRISE** **MFV Sunrise LLP** Caley Fisheries Ltd SatCom: Inmarsat C 423363610 *Fraserburgh* *United Kingdom* MMSI: 233636000 Official number: A11608	*225* 143 77		**1984-07 Campbeltown Shipyard Ltd. — Campbeltown** Yd No: 067 Loa 26.01 Br ex 7.22 Dght 3.001 Lbp 23.35 Br md 7.21 Dpth 3.76 Welded, 1 dk	**(B11A2FT) Trawler** Ins: 160	**1 oil engine** with clutches & sr geared to sc. shaft driving 1 CP propeller Total Power: 478kW (650hp) 10.8kn Caterpillar 3508TA 1 x Vee 4 Stroke 8 Cy. 170 x 190 478kW (650bhp) Caterpillar Tractor Co-USA Fuel: 18.0 (d.f.)
8517774 *VVJC* -	**SUNRISE** **Rainbow Seafoods Pvt Ltd** - *Mormugao* *India* Official number: 2133	**104** 31 58	Class: (IR)	**1986-08 Chowgule & Co Pvt Ltd — Goa** Yd No: 90 Loa 23.09 Br ex 7.19 Dght 2.531 Lbp 20.02 Br md 7.01 Dpth 3.20 Welded, 1 dk	**(B11A2FS) Stern Trawler** Ins: 40	**1 oil engine** with clutches & sr reverse geared to sc. shaft driving 1 FP propeller Total Power: 313kW (426hp) 10.0kn Caterpillar 3412TA 1 x Vee 4 Stroke 12 Cy. 137 x 152 313kW (426bhp) Caterpillar Tractor Co-USA AuxGen: 2 x 13kW 240V 50Hz a.c Fuel: 43.5 (d.f.)
8827416 *DTAD3* -	**SUNRISE** **Dongwon Industries Co Ltd** - SatCom: Inmarsat B 344025510 *Busan* *South Korea* MMSI: 440927000 Official number: 9706001-6260008	**647** 251 466	Class: KR	**1989-06 Jinhae Ship Construction Industrial Co Ltd — Changwon** Yd No: 8880 Loa 54.00 Br ex - Dght 3.650 Lbp 48.10 Br md 8.90 Dpth 3.75 Welded, 1 dk	**(B11B2FV) Fishing Vessel** Grain: 662; Bale: 555	**1 oil engine** driving 1 FP propeller Total Power: 883kW (1,201hp) 12.2kn Akasaka K28FD 1 x 4 Stroke 6 Cy. 280 x 480 883kW (1201bhp) Akasaka Tekkosho KK (Akasaka DieselLtd)-Japan AuxGen: 2 x 608kW 225V a.c
9087659 *JM6321* -	**SUNRISE** **Ariakekai Ferryboat KK (Ariakekai Jidosha Kososen Kumiai)** *Nagasu, Kumamoto* *Japan* Official number: 133646	*888* - 150		**1994-02 Hayashikane Dockyard Co Ltd — Nagasaki NS** Yd No: 1008 Loa - Br ex - Dght 2.700 Lbp 55.00 Br md 13.40 Dpth 3.90 Welded	**(A37B2PS) Passenger Ship**	**2 oil engines** reduction geared to sc. shafts driving 2 FP propellers Total Power: 2,648kW (3,600hp) Niigata 6MG26HLX 2 x 4 Stroke 6 Cy. 260 x 350 each-1324kW (1800bhp) Niigata Engineering Co Ltd-Japan
9182655 *D6HO8* -	**SUNRISE** *ex* Sun *-2013* *ex* Chemtrans Sun *-2013* *ex* Emerald Sun *-2003* **Barford Industries Corp** Transtanko Shipping (FZE) *Moroni* *Union of Comoros* MMSI: 616999319	**40,516** 20,305 71,675 T/cm 66.6	Class: (AB)	**1999-08 Hudong Shipbuilding Group — Shanghai** Yd No: H1261A Loa 227.00 (BB) Br ex - Dght 14.018 Lbp 217.00 Br md 32.26 Dpth 20.20 Welded, 1 dk	**(A13A2TW) Crude/Oil Products Tanker** Double Hull (13F) Liq: 74,220; Liq (Oil): 74,220 Cargo Heating Coils Compartments: 1 Ta, 10 Wing Ta, 2 Wing Slop Ta, ER 3 Cargo Pump (s): 3x2000m³/hr Manifold: Bow/CM: 113.6m	**1 oil engine** driving 1 FP propeller Total Power: 10,200kW (13,868hp) 15.0kn B&W 5S60MC 1 x 2 Stroke 5 Cy. 600 x 2292 10200kW (13868bhp) Hudong Heavy Machinery Co Ltd-China AuxGen: 3 x 600kW a.c Fuel: 181.0 (d.f.) 2303.0 (r.f.)
9571741 *XVDJ* -	**SUNRISE** **Agribank Leasing Co II** Loan Cuong Import-Export Investment JSC *Haiphong* *Vietnam* MMSI: 574000070	**2,963** 1,815 5,064	Class: VR	**2010-02 Haiphong Fishery Shipbuilding JSC — Haiphong** Yd No: HT-109.04 Loa 92.25 Br ex 15.33 Dght 6.480 Lbp 84.96 Br md 15.30 Dpth 7.85 Welded, 1 dk	**(A21A2BC) Bulk Carrier** Grain: 6,567 Compartments: 2 Ho, ER 2 Ha: (23.8 x 9.4)ER (15.8 x 9.4)	**1 oil engine** reduction geared to sc. shaft driving 1 FP propeller Total Power: 1,765kW (2,400hp) 10.0kn Chinese Std. Type G8300ZC 1 x 4 Stroke 8 Cy. 300 x 380 1765kW (2400bhp) (made 2009) Ningbo CSI Power & Machinery GroupCo Ltd-China AuxGen: 2 x 280kW 400V a.c
9590060 *V2FL2* -	**SUNRISE** *ex* POS Winner *-2013* *ex* Sunrise *-2011* **Doric Zweite Navigation GmbH & Co KG** Sunship Schiffahrtskontor KG *Saint John's* *Antigua & Barbuda* MMSI: 305710000 Official number: 4857	**93,010** 59,356 179,168	Class: GL (NV)	**2011-04 Sungdong Shipbuilding & Marine Engineering Co Ltd — Tongyeong** Yd No: 1122 Loa 292.00 (BB) Br ex - Dght 18.300 Lbp 283.50 Br md 45.00 Dpth 24.80 Welded, 1 dk	**(A21A2BC) Bulk Carrier** Grain: 199,500; Bale: 187,719 Compartments: 9 Ho, ER 9 Ha: 7 (15.6 x 20.6)ER 2 (15.6 x 17.2)	**1 oil engine** driving 1 FP propeller Total Power: 18,660kW (25,370hp) 14.3kn MAN-B&W 6S70ME-C 1 x 2 Stroke 6 Cy. 700 x 2800 18660kW (25370bhp) MAN Diesel A/S-Denmark AuxGen: 3 x a.c
9393620 *C6XM3* -	**SUNRISE** **Westaway Investments Ltd** Samos Steamship Co *Nassau* *Bahamas* MMSI: 311013800 Official number: 8001595	**22,697** 12,674 37,268	Class: AB	**2009-01 Saiki Heavy Industries Co Ltd — Saiki OT** Yd No: 1173 Loa 177.85 (BB) Br ex - Dght 10.800 Lbp 169.80 Br md 28.60 Dpth 15.00 Welded, 1 dk	**(A21A2BC) Bulk Carrier** Double Hull Grain: 46,030; Bale: 45,707 Compartments: 5 Ho, ER 5 Ha: ER Cranes: 4x30t	**1 oil engine** driving 1 FP propeller Total Power: 7,080kW (9,626hp) 14.5kn Mitsubishi 6UEC52LA 1 x 2 Stroke 6 Cy. 520 x 1600 7080kW (9626bhp) Akasaka Tekkosho KK (Akasaka DieselLtd)-Japan AuxGen: 3 x 440kW a.c
7648124 - -	**SUNRISE 1** *ex* Koryu Maru *-2006* *ex* Otsurugi *-1992* *ex* Nisshin Maru *-1990* **Prima Bridge Island Pte Ltd**	*499* - 566		**1973-10 Fujimi Shipbuilding Co. Ltd. — Kobe** Loa 42.02 Br ex - Dght 2.801 Lbp 37.80 Br md 14.00 Dpth 3.51 Welded, 1dk	**(A31A2GX) General Cargo Ship** Bale: 1,150	**1 oil engine** driving 1 FP propeller Total Power: 552kW (750hp) 8.0kn Yanmar 1 x 4 Stroke 552kW (750bhp) Yanmar Diesel Engine Co Ltd-Japan
8350229 - -	**SUNRISE 2** *ex* Geiyo Maru No. 2 *-1992* **East Sunrise Shipping SA** - *Panama* *Panama* Official number: 2047892	**448** 197 578		**1976 Y.K. Takasago Zosensho — Naruto** Loa 49.31 Br ex - Dght 3.220 Lbp 46.00 Br md 8.01 Dpth 4.91 Welded, 1 dk	**(A31A2GX) General Cargo Ship**	**1 oil engine** driving 1 FP propeller Total Power: 588kW (799hp) 10.0kn Yanmar 1 x 4 Stroke 588kW (799bhp) Yanmar Diesel Engine Co Ltd-Japan
8500977 *3WCR* -	**SUNRISE 6** *ex* Phuong Dong 1 *-2011* *ex* West Islands *-2000* **Mai Mai Trading JSC** Dai Phu Maritime Transport Shipping Co Ltd SatCom: Inmarsat C 457412510 *Haiphong* *Vietnam* MMSI: 574125115 Official number: VN-3287-VT	**8,995** 6,239 15,136 T/cm 24.3	Class: VR (LR) ✠ Classed LR until 20/4/09	**1986-07 Smith's Dock Ltd — South Bank, Middlesbrough** Yd No: 1358 Loa 144.02 Br ex 20.45 Dght 8.872 Lbp 137.52 Br md 20.43 Dpth 11.76 Welded, 1 dk, 2nd dk except in No. 5 hold	**(A31A2GX) General Cargo Ship** Grain: 21,379; Bale: 19,536 TEU 126 C Ho 82 TEU C Dk 44 TEU Compartments: ER, 5 Ho, 3 Tw Dk 5 Ha: (11.6 x 6.7) (13.7 x 8.5)2 (12.9 x 8.5)ER (11.4 x 6.7) Derricks: 6x15t,4x10t; Winches: 10	**1 oil engine** driving 1 FP propeller Total Power: 4,925kW (6,696hp) 14.5kn Sulzer 5RLB56 1 x 2 Stroke 5 Cy. 560 x 1150 4925kW (6696bhp) Clark Kincaid Ltd.-Greenock AuxGen: 3 x 350kW 450V 60Hz a.c Boilers: AuxB (Comp) 7.4kgf/cm² (7.3bar) Fuel: 130.0 (d.f.) 989.5 (r.f.)
9621065 *3WFS9* -	**SUNRISE 69** **Rang Dong Shipping Agency Co Ltd** *Haiphong* *Vietnam* MMSI: 574001340	**4,417** 2,753 7,043	Class: VR	**2011-12 Ben Thuy Shipyard — Nghi Xuan** Yd No: HP718 Loa 105.86 Br ex 17.03 Dght 7.150 Lbp 97.50 Br md 17.00 Dpth 9.10 Welded, 1 dk	**(A31A2GX) General Cargo Ship** Compartments: 2 Ho, ER 2 Ha: (27.3 x 10.0)ER (24.8 x 10.0) Cranes: 3x15t	**1 oil engine** reduction geared to sc. shaft driving 1 FP propeller Total Power: 2,620kW (3,562hp) 13.5kn Hyundai Himsen 9H25/33P 1 x 4 Stroke 9 Cy. 250 x 330 2620kW (3562bhp) Hyundai Heavy Industries Co Ltd-South Korea AuxGen: 2 x 280kW 400V a.c Fuel: 450.0
8950299 - -	**SUNRISE '94** **BEV Processors Inc** *Georgetown* *Guyana* Official number: 0000290	*112* 56 -		**1994 Steiner Shipyard, Inc. — Bayou La Batre, Al** Loa 22.86 Br ex - Dght - Lbp 19.72 Br md 6.70 Dpth 3.35 Welded, 1 dk	**(B11A2FT) Trawler**	**1 oil engine** driving 1 FP propeller Total Power: 313kW (426hp) Cummins 1 x 4 Stroke 313kW (426bhp) Cummins Engine Co Inc-USA
9624196 *3WIP9* -	**SUNRISE 689** **Haiphong Sea Product Shipbuilding JSC** - *Haiphong* *Vietnam* MMSI: 574001690 Official number: VN-3451-TD	**4,080** 1,814 5,929	Class: VR	**2012-06 Haiphong Fishery Shipbuilding JSC — Haiphong** Yd No: HTD-10 Loa 99.91 Br ex 16.33 Dght 6.500 Lbp 94.00 Br md 16.30 Dpth 8.50 Welded, 1 dk	**(A13B2TP) Products Tanker** Double Hull (13F) Liq: 6,381; Liq (Oil): 6,381 Compartments: 1 Ta, 4 Ta, ER	**1 oil engine** reduction geared to sc. shaft driving 1 FP propeller Total Power: 2,500kW (3,399hp) 10.0kn Chinese Std. Type G8320ZC 1 x 4 Stroke 8 Cy. 320 x 440 2500kW (3399bhp) in China Fuel: 422.5

IMO / Call sign	Name / Owner	Tonnage	Class	Builder / Dimensions	Type	Machinery
8400294 3FTB4 -	**SUNRISE 2000** ex Sunrise -1994 **Technip Ships (Netherlands) BV** Technip UK Ltd SatCom: Inmarsat A 1550554 Panama Panama MMSI: 352102000 Official number: 2187195D	**10,781** 3,234 10,045	Class: LR (NK) **100A1** SS 09/2012 **LMC** Eq.Ltr: Z; Cable: 552.5/48.0 U3	**1984-10 KK Kanasashi Zosen — Toyohashi AI** Yd No: 3031 Converted From: Heavy Load Carrier-1995 Loa 123.01 (BB) Br ex 30.03 Dght 4.874 Lbp 117.00 Br md 30.01 Dpth 9.80 Welded, 1 dk	**(B22C20X) Pipe Layer** Passengers: berths: 80 Cranes: 1x75t,1x30t,1x15t	**2 oil engines** with clutches, flexible couplings & sr geared to sc. shafts driving 2 FP propellers Total Power: 3,236kW (4,400hp) 11.8kn Hanshin 6ELS32 2 x 4 Stroke 6 Cy. 320 x 640 each-1618kW (2200bhp) The Hanshin Diesel Works Ltd-Japan AuxGen: 2 x 240kW 450V 60Hz a.c Boilers: 2 AuxB (ex.g.) 5.9kgf/cm^2 (5.8bar), AuxB (o.f.) 6.9kgf/cm^2 (6.8bar) Thrusters: 2 Directional thruster (f); 2 Directional thruster (a)
9338840 C6XL9 -	**SUNRISE ACE** **Snowscape Car Carriers SA** MOL Ship Management Singapore Pte Ltd Nassau Bahamas MMSI: 311013600 Official number: 8001593	**58,685** 18,167 18,864	Class: NK	**2008-12 Minaminippon Shipbuilding Co Ltd — Usuki OT** Yd No: 702 Loa 199.95 (BB) Br ex - Dght 9.800 Lbp 190.00 Br md 32.20 Dpth 14.70 Welded, 12 dks	**(A35B2RV) Vehicles Carrier** Side door/ramp (s) Quarter stern door/ramp (s. a.) Cars: 6,237	**1 oil engine** driving 1 FP propeller Total Power: 15,130kW (20,571hp) 20.0kn MAN-B&W 7S60MC-C 1 x 2 Stroke 7 Cy. 600 x 2400 15130kW (20571bhp) Mitsui Engineering & Shipbuilding CLtd-Japan Thrusters: 1 Tunnel thruster (f) Fuel: 2660.0
9297230 DUEC -	**SUNRISE CAMIA** ex Kemal Telli -2012 **Transnational Uyeno Corp** Transnational Uyeno Maritime Inc Manila Philippines MMSI: 548856000 Official number: 00-0002119	**2,286** 1,040 3,454	Class: BV	**2005-04 Turkter Tersane ve Deniz Isl. A.S. — Tuzla** Yd No: 12 Loa 88.42 Br ex - Dght 5.940 Lbp 82.15 Br md 13.00 Dpth 7.25 Welded, 1 dk	**(A12B2TR) Chemical/Products Tanker** Double Hull (13F) Liq: 3,691; Liq (Oil): 3,691 Compartments: 10 Ta, 2 Slop Ta, ER 10 Cargo Pump (s): 10x150m^3/hr Manifold: Bow/CM: 20m Ice Capable	**1 oil engine** geared to sc. shaft driving 1 CP propeller Total Power: 1,850kW (2,515hp) 12.5kn MaK 6M25 1 x 4 Stroke 6 Cy. 255 x 400 1850kW (2515bhp) Caterpillar Motoren GmbH & Co. KG-Germany AuxGen: 3 x 325kW 440/220V 60Hz a.c, 1 x 600kW 440/220V 60Hz a.c Thrusters: 1 Tunnel thruster (f) Fuel: 45.0 (d.f.) 179.0 (r.f.) 7.5pd
8019655 - -	**SUNRISE COMMAND** ex Seacor Osprey -2006 ex Tasmanian Island -1992 ex Tasmanian Command -1989 **IMI Del Peru SAC** - Talara Peru	**724** 217 1,200	Class: (AB)	**1981-03 Halter Marine, Inc. — New Orleans, La** Yd No: 922 Converted From: Offshore Supply Ship-1992 Loa 56.39 Br ex - Dght 3.663 Lbp 50.70 Br md 12.20 Dpth 4.27 Welded, 1 dk	**(B21A20S) Platform Supply Ship**	**2 oil engines** reverse reduction geared to sc. shafts driving 2 CP propellers Total Power: 1,986kW (2,700hp) 10.0kn Wichmann 4AXA 2 x 2 Stroke 4 Cy. 300 x 450 each-993kW (1350bhp) Wichmann Motorfabrikk AS-Norway AuxGen: 2 x 150kW Thrusters: 1 Thwart. FP thruster (f)
7433971 - -	**SUNRISE CONFIDENCE** ex Capt. Sean -2006 ex Marion C II -2004 ex El Inspector -1994 ex Northern Light -1987 **Petro-Tech Peruana SA** -	**762** 228 971	Class: (AB)	**1976-02 Halter Marine, Inc. — Lockport, La** Yd No: 511 Loa 59.44 Br ex 12.81 Dght 4.115 Lbp 53.40 Br md 12.76 Dpth 4.73 Welded, 1 dk	**(B21B20A) Anchor Handling Tug Supply** Ice Capable	**2 oil engines** reverse reduction geared to sc. shafts driving 2 FP propellers Total Power: 4,230kW (5,752hp) 12.0kn EMD (Electro-Motive) 16-645-E5 2 x Vee 2 Stroke 16 Cy. 230 x 254 each-2115kW (2876bhp) General Motors Corp.Electro-Motive Div.-La Grange AuxGen: 2 x 200kW Thrusters: 1 Thwart. FP thruster (f)
9291315 DSMY2 -	**SUNRISE ECO** ex Sunrise Rosa -2010 **Sunrise Shipping Co Ltd** Dong Jin Shipping Co Ltd Jeju South Korea MMSI: 441936000 Official number: JJR-103478	**5,546** 2,589 8,626 T/cm 17.7	Class: KR (NK)	**2004-04 Shin Kurushima Dockyard Co. Ltd. — Hashihama, Imabari** Yd No: 5281 Loa 113.98 (BB) Br ex 18.23 Dght 7.478 Lbp 108.05 Br md 18.20 Dpth 9.75 Welded, 1 dk	**(A12A2TC) Chemical Tanker** Double Hull (13F) Liq: 9,049 Cargo Heating Coils Compartments: 1 Ta, 16 Wing Ta, 2 Wing Slop Ta, ER 17 Cargo Pump (s): 12x250m^3/hr, 4x150m^3/hr, 1x100m^3/hr Manifold: Bow/CM: 58.2m	**1 oil engine** driving 1 FP propeller Total Power: 3,900kW (5,302hp) 14.2kn MAN-B&W 6L35MC 1 x 2 Stroke 6 Cy. 350 x 1050 3900kW (5302bhp) Makita Corp-Japan AuxGen: 3 x 480kW a.c Thrusters: 1 Tunnel thruster (f) Fuel: 102.0 (d.f.) 525.0 (r.f.)
9176383 9V8539 -	**SUNRISE EXPRESS** ex Orient Brave -2003 ex Westwind Bliss -2000 ex Hermano Naviera -1998 **Chorus Investment Pte Ltd** RCL Shipmanagement Pte Ltd Singapore Singapore MMSI: 565882000 Official number: 395931	**8,649** 3,394 9,575	Class: NK	**1998-10 Kwangyang Shipbuilding & Engineering Co Ltd — Janghang** Yd No: 141 Loa 118.87 (BB) Br ex - Dght 7.900 Lbp 108.00 Br md 19.60 Dpth 14.30 Welded, 1 dk	**(A31A2GA) General Cargo Ship (with Ro-Ro facility)** Trailers: 75 Grain: 19,036; Bale: 17,036 Compartments: 2 Ho, ER 2 Ha: (28.0 x 13.0) (28.7 x 13.0) Cranes: 2x30.7t; Derricks: 2x25t	**1 oil engine** driving 1 FP propeller Total Power: 3,884kW (5,281hp) 13.5kn B&W 6L35MC 1 x 2 Stroke 6 Cy. 350 x 1050 3884kW (5281bhp) Ssangyong Heavy Industries Co Ltd-South Korea AuxGen: 2 x 250kW a.c Fuel: 690.0
9628518 3FKF6 -	**SUNRISE-G** ex Cassandra 7 -2014 ex Sealink Cassandra 7 -2014 **Rederij Groen II BV** Rederij Groen BV Panama Panama MMSI: 354131000 Official number: 45671PEXT	**2,132** 639 2,057	Class: AB	**2014-02 Sealink Engineering & Slipway Sdn Bhd — Miri** Yd No: 170A Loa 59.90 Br ex - Dght 5.400 Lbp 52.80 Br md 16.50 Dpth 6.80 Welded, 1 dk	**(B21A20S) Platform Supply Ship**	**2 oil engines** reduction geared to sc. shafts driving 2 CP propellers Total Power: 3,282kW (4,462hp) 10.0kn Caterpillar 3516B 2 x Vee 4 Stroke 16 Cy. 170 x 190 each-1641kW (2231bhp) Caterpillar Inc-USA Thrusters: 1 Tunnel thruster (f)
7827586 - -	**SUNRISE III** ex Sunrise -1991 **Agropesquera Industrial Bahia Cupica SA** - Buenaventura Colombia Official number: MC-01-465	*105* 83 175		**1981 Steiner Shipyard, Inc. — Bayou La Batre, Al** Loa 22.81 Br ex - Dght 2.401 Lbp 20.12 Br md 6.70 Dpth 3.36 Welded, 1 dk	**(B11A2FT) Trawler**	**1 oil engine** reduction geared to sc. shaft driving 1 FP propeller Total Power: 268kW (364hp) Cummins KT-1150-M 1 x 4 Stroke 6 Cy. 159 x 159 268kW (364bhp) Cummins Engine Co Inc-USA
8302923 5VBH2 -	**SUNRISE III** ex Sunrise -2008 ex Alperen -2005 ex TCI Vijay -2004 ex Arktis Sun -1996 **Sunrise Shipping SAL** - Lome Togo MMSI: 671221000	**1,598** 956 2,301	Class: (LR) (TL) (IR) ✠ Classed LR until 21/11/96	**1985-05 A/S Nordsovaerftet — Ringkobing** Yd No: 176 Loa 74.33 Br ex 11.36 Dght 4.630 Lbp 70.16 Br md 11.20 Dpth 6.70 Welded, 2 dks	**(A31A2GX) General Cargo Ship** Grain: 3,355; Bale: 3,014 TEU 54 C.Ho 36/20' (40') C.Dk 18/20' (40') Compartments: 1 Ho, ER, 2 Tw Dk 2 Ha: 2 (18.7 x 8.0)ER Derricks: 2x22t; Winches: 2 Ice Capable	**1 oil engine** with clutches, flexible couplings & sr geared to sc. shaft driving 1 CP propeller Total Power: 810kW (1,101hp) 10.0kn Alpha 6L23/30 1 x 4 Stroke 6 Cy. 225 x 300 810kW (1101bhp) MAN B&W Diesel A/S-Denmark AuxGen: 3 x 84kW 380V 50Hz a.c Fuel: 34.5 (d.f.) 153.5 (r.f.)
7614288 - -	**SUNRISE INDEPENDENT** ex Independent -2004 ex Stephanie S -1990 ex Edward St. Philip -1981 ex Winnie -1974 ex Tern -1974 ex Smith Alpha -1974 **Industrial Transport Ltd** - Port of Spain Trinidad & Tobago	*153* 46 -		**1955 Smith Alpha — Morgan City, La** Yd No: 55 Loa 31.69 Br ex 8.22 Dght 3.012 Lbp 30.43 Br md 8.20 Dpth 3.40 Welded, 1 dk	**(B32A2ST) Tug**	**1 oil engine** reduction geared to sc. shaft driving 1 Propeller Total Power: 2,059kW (2,799hp) EMD (Electro-Motive) 16-645-E5 1 x Vee 2 Stroke 16 Cy. 230 x 254 2059kW (2799bhp) (new engine 1989) General Motors Corp.Electro-Motive Div.-La Grange
9209958 S6DT2 -	**SUNRISE LILY** - **Oxalis Shipping Co Pte Ltd** - Singapore Singapore Official number: 389379	**4,215** 1,683 5,999 T/cm 13.9	Class: NK	**1999-11 Naikai Zosen Corp — Onomichi HS (Setoda Shipyard)** Yd No: 656 Loa 109.60 Br ex - Dght 5.814 Lbp 103.00 Br md 18.00 Dpth 8.60 Welded, 1 dk	**(A13B2TP) Products Tanker** Double Hull (13F) Liq: 7,445; Liq (Oil): 7,445 Compartments: 10 Wing Ta, ER 2 Cargo Pump (s)	**1 oil engine** driving 1 FP propeller Total Power: 2,206kW (2,999hp) 12.1kn Hanshin LH38L 1 x 4 Stroke 6 Cy. 380 x 760 2206kW (2999bhp) The Hanshin Diesel Works Ltd-Japan AuxGen: 3 x a.c Thrusters: 1 Thwart. FP thruster (f) Fuel: 170.0 (d.f.)
9380427 3EKK4 -	**SUNRISE MIYAJIMA** - **Bright Carrier SA** Sugahara Kisen KK Panama Panama MMSI: 372746000 Official number: 3277807A	**11,681** 6,457 19,127 T/cm 30.7	Class: NK	**2007-06 Yamanishi Corp — Ishinomaki MG** Yd No: 1050 Loa 139.92 (BB) Br ex 25.00 Dght 8.496 Lbp 132.00 Br md 25.00 Dpth 11.50 Welded, 1 dk	**(A21A2BC) Bulk Carrier** Grain: 23,161; Bale: 22,563 Compartments: 4 Ho, ER 4 Ha: ER 4 (17.5 x 15.0) Cranes: 3x30.5t	**1 oil engine** driving 1 FP propeller Total Power: 5,200kW (7,070hp) 13.0kn MAN-B&W 7S35MC 1 x 2 Stroke 7 Cy. 350 x 1400 5200kW (7070bhp) Makita Corp-Japan AuxGen: 3 x 442kW a.c Fuel: 1070.0
8838025 - -	**SUNRISE No. 1** ex Obata Maru No. 28 -1994 - -	*108* 32 -		**1980-01 K.K. Murakami Zosensho — Ishinomaki** L reg 29.00 Br ex - Dght 2.100 Lbp - Br md 6.10 Dpth 2.60 Welded, 1 dk	**(B11B2FV) Fishing Vessel**	**1 oil engine** driving 1 FP propeller Total Power: 294kW (400hp) Hanshin 1 x 4 Stroke 6 Cy. 294kW (400bhp) The Hanshin Diesel Works Ltd-Japan

9550072 **SUNRISE ORIENT**
3WFD9
\-
Haiphong Sea Product Shipbuilding JSC
\-
Haiphong *Vietnam*
MMSI: 574001270

2,580 Class: VR
1,467
4,244

2011-11 Haiphong Fishery Shipbuilding JSC — Haiphong Yd No: HT-156
Loa 89.99 (BB) Br ex - Dght 6.150
Lbp 82.60 Br md 13.60 Dpth 7.66
Welded, 1 dk

(A31A2GX) General Cargo Ship
Grain: 5,360; Bale: 4,830
Compartments: 2 Ho, ER
2 Ha: (26.4 x 8.4)ER (14.4 x 8.4)
Cranes: 2x10t

1 oil engine reduction geared to sc. shaft driving 1 FP propeller
Total Power: 1,471kW (2,000hp) 10.0kn
Chinese Std. Type LB8250ZLC
1 x 4 Stroke 8 Cy. 250 x 320 1471kW (2000bhp)
Zibo Diesel Engine Factory-China
AuxGen: 2 x 150kW 400V a.c
Fuel: 250.0

7386946 **SUNRISE R**
9LD2205 *ex Little Miss -2008 ex Al Waleed -2007*
\- *ex Sevilla -1997 ex Widar -1989*
ex Wiking -1986
Focus Marine Co
SC Rezkozan Impex Srl
Freetown *Sierra Leone*
MMSI: 667904000
Official number: SL100904

2,767 Class: DR (GL)
1,597
3,311

1973-11 J.J. Sietas Schiffswerft — Hamburg
Yd No: 692
Loa 93.20 Br ex 14.76 Dght 5.520
Lbp 82.81 Br md 14.51 Dpth 7.95
Welded, 2 dks

(A31A2GX) General Cargo Ship
Grain: 5,802; Bale: 5,428
TEU 192 C. 192/20' incl. 16 ref C.
Compartments: 1 Ho, ER
1 Ha: (51.3 x 10.3)ER
Ice Capable

1 oil engine reduction geared to sc. shaft driving 1 FP propeller
Total Power: 2,207kW (3,001hp) 14.5kn
MaK 6M551AK
1 x 4 Stroke 6 Cy. 450 x 550 2207kW (3001bhp)
MaK Maschinenbau GmbH-Kiel
Fuel: 193.0

9288007 **SUNRISE SAMBU**
DSNR6
\- **Sambu Shipping Co Ltd**
\-
Jeju *South Korea*
MMSI: 440213000
Official number: JJR-040933

2,748 Class: KR
1,185
3,613
T/cm
10.7

2004-07 Nokbong Shipbuilding Co Ltd — Geoje
Yd No: 394
Loa 91.60 (BB) Br ex 14.20 Dght 5.813
Lbp 84.00 Br md 14.20 Dpth 7.50
Welded, 1 dk

(A12B2TR) Chemical/Products Tanker
Double Hull (13F)
Liq: 4,092; Liq (Oil): 4,092
Cargo Heating Coils
10 Cargo Pump (s): 10x200m³/hr
Manifold: Bow/CM: 48m

1 oil engine driving 1 FP propeller
Total Power: 2,427kW (3,300hp) 14.3kn
Hanshin LH41LA
1 x 4 Stroke 6 Cy. 410 x 800 2427kW (3300bhp)
The Hanshin Diesel Works Ltd-Japan
AuxGen: 3 x 320kW 4400V a.c
Fuel: 50.0 (d.f.) 120.0 (r.f.)

9227223 **SUNRISE SAMPAGUITA**
DUTQ9 *ex Anatolian -2006*
\- **Transnational Uyeno Corp**
Transnational Uyeno Maritime Inc
SatCom: Inmarsat C 454875110
Manila *Philippines*
MMSI: 548751000
Official number: 00-0000149

3,490 Class: NK (TL) (BV)
1,618
5,554
T/cm
14.2

2001-08 Celiktekne Sanayii ve Ticaret A.S. — Tuzla, Istanbul Yd No: 33
Loa 109.10 (BB) Br ex 16.19 Dght 5.768
Lbp 99.80 Br md 16.00 Dpth 7.25
Welded, 1 dk

(A12B2TR) Chemical/Products Tanker
Double Hull (13F)
Liq: 5,748; Liq (Oil): 5,748
Cargo Heating Coils
Compartments: 12 Ta, ER
3 Cargo Pump (s): 3x450m³/hr
Manifold: Bow/CM: 55m

1 oil engine reduction geared to sc. shaft driving 1 FP propeller
Total Power: 2,720kW (3,698hp) 12.5kn
MAN-B&W 8L27/38
1 x 4 Stroke 8 Cy. 270 x 380 2720kW (3698bhp)
MAN B&W Diesel A/S-Denmark
Fuel: 49.0 (d.f.) 205.0 (r.f.)

9345037 **SUNRISE SEA**
\-
\- **Shandong Weifang Shunyuan Shipping Co Ltd**
Wanzhou Shipping SA

2,885
1,983
5,000

2004-09 Shenjia Shipyard — Shanghai
Loa 96.30 Br ex - Dght 5.800
Lbp 89.80 Br md 15.80 Dpth 7.40
Welded, 1 dk

(A31A2GX) General Cargo Ship

1 oil engine geared to sc. shaft driving 1 FP propeller
Total Power: 1,765kW (2,400hp) 12.0kn
Chinese Std. Type 8300ZC
1 x 4 Stroke 8 Cy. 300 x 380 1765kW (2400bhp)
Wuxi Antai Power Machinery Co Ltd-China

9570462 **SUNRISE SERENITY**
3FWI4
\- **Alosa Maritima SA & Sur Maritima SA**
Asahi Shipping Co Ltd (Asahi Kaiun KK)
Panama *Panama*
MMSI: 372622000
Official number: 4171710

39,737 Class: NK
25,724
76,544
T/cm
66.6

2010-07 Shin Kasado Dockyard Co Ltd — Kudamatsu YC Yd No: K-014
Loa 224.94 (BB) Br ex - Dght 14.139
Lbp 217.00 Br md 32.26 Dpth 19.50
Welded, 1 dk

(A21A2BC) Bulk Carrier
Grain: 90,644
Compartments: 7 Ho, ER
7 Ha: 6 (17.1 x 15.6)ER (17.1 x 12.8)

1 oil engine driving 1 FP propeller
Total Power: 10,320kW (14,031hp) 15.3kn
MAN-B&W 6S60MC
1 x 2 Stroke 6 Cy. 600 x 2292 10320kW (14031bhp)
Mitsui Engineering & Shipbuilding CLtd-Japan
Fuel: 3269.0 (r.f.)

9520649 **SUNRISE SKY**
3FOA2
\- **Diamond Camellia SA**
MC Shipping Ltd
SatCom: Inmarsat C 437359810
Panama *Panama*
MMSI: 373598000
Official number: 4406412

32,319 Class: NK
19,458
58,120
T/cm
57.4

2012-07 Tsuneishi Heavy Industries (Cebu) Inc — Balamban Yd No: SC-170
Loa 189.99 (BB) Br ex - Dght 12.830
Lbp 185.60 Br md 32.26 Dpth 18.00
Welded, 1 dk

(A21A2BC) Bulk Carrier
Grain: 72,689; Bale: 70,122
Compartments: 5 Ho, ER
5 Ha: ER
Cranes: 4x30t

1 oil engine driving 1 FP propeller
Total Power: 8,400kW (11,421hp) 14.5kn
MAN-B&W 6S50MC-C
1 x 2 Stroke 6 Cy. 500 x 2000 8400kW (11421bhp)
Mitsui Engineering & Shipbuilding CLtd-Japan
Fuel: 2380.0

9384899 **SUNRISE SURABAYA**
3EII5 *ex Hanjin Surabaya -2013*
\- **Los Halillos Shipping Co SA**
Laurus Ship Management Co Ltd
Panama *Panama*
MMSI: 372310000
Official number: 35180PEXT1

17,225 Class: NK
7,875
21,978

2007-01 Imabari Shipbuilding Co Ltd — Imabari EH (Imabari Shipyard) Yd No: 672
Loa 171.99 (BB) Br ex 27.60 Dght 9.516
Lbp 160.00 Br md 27.60 Dpth 14.00
Welded, 1 dk

(A33A2CC) Container Ship (Fully Cellular)
TEU 1708 C Ho 610 TEU C Dk 1098 incl 202 ref C
Compartments: 5 Cell Ho, ER
8 Ha: 7 (12.6 x 23.4)ER (12.6 x 13.2)

1 oil engine driving 1 FP propeller
Total Power: 15,820kW (21,509hp) 19.7kn
MAN-B&W 7S60MC-C
1 x 2 Stroke 7 Cy. 600 x 2400 15820kW (21509bhp)
Mitsui Engineering & Shipbuilding CLtd-Japan
AuxGen: 3 x a.c
Thrusters: 1 Tunnel thruster (f)
Fuel: 2180.0

8987589 **SUNRISE TRINITY**
\- *ex Mary S -2004*
\- **Industrial Transport Ltd**
\-
Port of Spain *Trinidad & Tobago*

190
129
\-

1945 Gibbs Gas Engine Co. — Jacksonville, Fl
Loa 30.78 Br ex 7.92 Dght -
Lbp 29.35 Br md 7.90 Dpth 3.96
Welded, 1 dk

(B32A2ST) Tug

1 oil engine reduction geared to sc. shaft driving 1 Propeller
Total Power: 2,059kW (2,799hp)
EMD (Electro-Motive) 16-645-E5
1 x Vee 2 Stroke 16 Cy. 230 x 254 2059kW (2799bhp) (new engine 2004)
General Motors Corp.Electro-Motive Div.-La Grange

8014514 **SUNRISER**
\- *ex Ferry Kuroshima -1996*
\- **M Y Lines Inc**
\-
Cebu *Philippines*
Official number: CEB1002367

131
\-
36

1980-05 K.K. Mukai Zosensho — Nagasaki
Yd No: 380
Loa 29.35 Br ex 7.60 Dght 1.870
Lbp 24.50 Br md 7.00 Dpth 2.70
Welded, 1 dk

(A36A2PR) Passenger/Ro-Ro Ship (Vehicles)

1 oil engine reduction geared to sc. shaft driving 1 FP propeller
Total Power: 441kW (600hp)
Yanmar S185L-ST
1 x 4 Stroke 6 Cy. 185 x 230 441kW (600bhp)
Yanmar Diesel Engine Co Ltd-Japan

9592898 **SUNROAD MITOYA**
3FDJ2
\- **Million Comets SA**
KK Kyowa Sansho
SatCom: Inmarsat C 435537210
Panama *Panama*
MMSI: 355372000
Official number: 4264811

13,829 Class: NK
7,787
23,186

2011-04 Kurinoura Dockyard Co Ltd — Yawatahama EH Yd No: 413
Loa 154.00 (BB) Br ex - Dght 9.466
Lbp 144.50 Br md 24.60 Dpth 13.00
Welded, 1 dk

(A21A2BC) Bulk Carrier
Grain: 28,000; Bale: 27,386
Compartments: 4 Ho, ER
4 Ha: ER
Cranes: 3x30t

1 oil engine driving 1 FP propeller
Total Power: 5,180kW (7,043hp) 14.0kn
MAN-B&W 7S35MC
1 x 2 Stroke 7 Cy. 350 x 1400 5180kW (7043bhp)
The Hanshin Diesel Works Ltd-Japan

9317274 **SUNROAD YATSUKA**
3EAB
\- **Polar Star Line SA**
KK Kyowa Sansho
SatCom: Inmarsat C 435655311
Panama *Panama*
MMSI: 356553000
Official number: 32988PEXT2

14,941 Class: NK
8,472
24,989

2005-03 Kurinoura Dockyard Co Ltd — Yawatahama EH Yd No: 381
Loa 158.00 (BB) Br ex - Dght 9.616
Lbp 149.50 Br md 25.00 Dpth 13.50
Welded, 1 dk

(A21A2BC) Bulk Carrier
Grain: 32,526; Bale: 31,481
Compartments: 4 Ho, ER
4 Ha: 3 (20.3 x 17.4)ER (20.3 x 13.1)
Cranes: 4x30t

1 oil engine driving 1 FP propeller
Total Power: 5,200kW (7,070hp) 13.0kn
B&W 7S35MC
1 x 2 Stroke 7 Cy. 350 x 1400 5200kW (7070bhp)
The Hanshin Diesel Works Ltd-Japan
Fuel: 900.0

9497000 **SUNROSE E**
ICRD
\- **Ireos E Srl**
\-
SatCom: Inmarsat C 424703571
Genoa *Italy*
MMSI: 247299300
Official number: 166 RI

8,890 Class: BV
4,412
13,050

2011-03 China CYC Shipping Group Co Ltd — Yueqing ZJ Yd No: ZY1001
Loa 138.60 (BB) Br ex - Dght 8.000
Lbp 129.80 Br md 20.40 Dpth 11.00
Welded, 1 dk

(A21A2BC) Bulk Carrier
Grain: 16,917
Compartments: 4 Ho, ER
4 Ha: ER
Cranes: 2x25t
Ice Capable

1 oil engine reduction geared to sc. shafts driving 1 FP propeller
Total Power: 3,310kW (4,500hp) 12.0kn
Yanmar 8N330-EN
1 x 4 Stroke 8 Cy. 330 x 440 3310kW (4500bhp)
Qingdao Zichai Boyang Diesel EngineCo Ltd-China
AuxGen: 3 x 331kW 60Hz a.c

9402122 **SUNSET**
C6XY4
\- **Sashiko Maritime SA**
Samos Steamship Co
SatCom: Inmarsat C 431100542
Nassau *Bahamas*
MMSI: 311025800
Official number: 8001675

22,697 Class: AB
12,674
37,334

2009-07 Saiki Heavy Industries Co Ltd — Saiki OT
Yd No: 1178
Loa 177.85 (BB) Br ex - Dght 10.850
Lbp 169.80 Br md 28.60 Dpth 15.00
Welded, 1 dk

(A21A2BC) Bulk Carrier
Double Hull
Grain: 46,030; Bale: 45,707
Compartments: 5 Ho, ER
5 Ha: ER
Cranes: 4x30t

1 oil engine driving 1 FP propeller
Total Power: 7,080kW (9,626hp) 14.5kn
Mitsubishi 6UEC52LA
1 x 2 Stroke 6 Cy. 520 x 1600 7080kW (9626bhp)
Akasaka Tekkosho KK (Akasaka DieselLtd)-Japan
AuxGen: 3 x 440kW a.c
Fuel: 280.0 (d.f.) 1435.0 (r.f.)

7827598 **SUNSET**
\-
\- \-
\-

105
72
\-

1981 Steiner Shipyard, Inc. — Bayou La Batre, Al
Loa 22.81 Br ex - Dght 2.401
Lbp 20.12 Br md 6.71 Dpth 3.36
Welded, 1 dk

(B11A2FT) Trawler

1 oil engine reduction geared to sc. shaft driving 1 FP propeller
Total Power: 268kW (364hp)
Cummins KT-1150-M
1 x 4 Stroke 6 Cy. 159 x 159 268kW (364bhp)
Cummins Engine Co Inc-USA

IMO / Call sign	Name / Owner	Tonnage	Class	Builder / Dimensions	Type	Machinery
8943040 - -	**SUNSET '98** - -	**113** 77 -		**1998-08 Steiner Shipyard, Inc. — Bayou La Batre, Al** Loa 22.86 Br ex - Dght - Lbp 20.33 Br md 6.70 Dpth 3.35 Welded, 1 dk	**(B11A2FT) Trawler**	**1 oil engine** reduction geared to sc. shaft driving 1 FP propeller Total Power: 268kW (364hp) Cummins KT-19-M 1 x 4 Stroke 6 Cy. 159 x 159 268kW (364bhp) Cummins Engine Co Inc-USA
7820150 *WCZ6529* -	**SUNSET BAY** **Evening Star Inc** Icicle Seafoods Inc *Seattle, WA* *United States of America* MMSI: 338673000 Official number: 598484	**289** 86 -		**1978-10 Marine Construction & Design Co. (MARCO) — Seattle, Wa** Yd No: 371 Loa 32.95 Br ex 8.82 Dght 4.420 Lbp 29.27 Br md 8.60 Dpth 3.97 Welded, 1 dk	**(B11B2FV) Fishing Vessel** Ins: 212 Compartments: 3 Ho, ER Cranes: 1x8t	**1 oil engine** geared to sc. shaft driving 1 FP propeller Total Power: 625kW (850hp) 11.5kn Caterpillar D398SCAC 1 x Vee 4 Stroke 12 Cy. 159 x 203 625kW (850bhp) Caterpillar Tractor Co-USA AuxGen: 1 x 155kW, 1 x 135kW, 1 x 55kW
7807134 *DTBZ3* -	**SUNSHINE** *ex* Seo Jin No. 301 *-2011* *ex* Jaesung No. 801 *-2011* *ex* Kyung Dong No. 801 *-2000* *ex* Cheog Yang No. 81 *-1993* **Sunwoo Corp** - *Busan* *South Korea* MMSI: 440046000 Official number: 1101001-6261105	*416* 234 442	Class: (KR)	**1978-12 Dae Sun Shipbuilding & Engineering Co Ltd — Busan** Yd No: 213 Loa 55.17 Br ex - Dght 3.779 Lbp 49.03 Br md 8.62 Dpth 4.02 Welded, 1 dk	**(B11B2FV) Fishing Vessel** Ins: 543 2 Ha: (1.3 x 1.0) (1.7 x 1.7)	**1 oil engine** driving 1 FP propeller Total Power: 993kW (1,350hp) 13.8kn Akasaka AH28 1 x 4 Stroke 6 Cy. 280 x 440 993kW (1350bhp) Akasaka Tekkosho KK (Akasaka DieselLtd)-Japan AuxGen: 2 x 160kW 225V a.c
8517762 - -	**SUNSHINE** - **Rainbow Seafoods Pvt Ltd** - *Mormugao* *India* Official number: 2134	*104* 31 66	Class: (IR)	**1986-02 Chowgule & Co Pvt Ltd — Goa** Yd No: 88 Loa 23.09 Br ex 7.17 Dght 2.501 Lbp 20.02 Br md 6.99 Dpth 3.20 Welded, 1 dk	**(B11A2FS) Stern Trawler**	**1 oil engine** sr geared to sc. shaft driving 1 FP propeller Total Power: 313kW (426hp) Caterpillar 3412PCTA 1 x Vee 4 Stroke 12 Cy. 137 x 152 313kW (426bhp) Caterpillar Tractor Co-USA AuxGen: 2 x 13kW 240V 50Hz a.c Fuel: 43.5 (d.f.)
7307433 *WX7170* -	**SUNSHINE** *ex* Elizabeth I *-1993* *ex* Irene & Hilda II *-1978* *ex* New Orleans *-1974* **Rhode Island Recycled Metals LLC** - *Providence, RI* *United States of America* Official number: 505291	*126* 85 -		**1966 St Charles Steel Works Inc — Thibodaux, La** L reg 21.46 Br ex - Dght - Lbp - Br md 7.01 Dpth 3.31 Welded, 1 dk	**(B11B2FV) Fishing Vessel**	**1 oil engine** driving 1 FP propeller Total Power: 283kW (385hp)
1007392 - -	**SUNSHINE** *ex* Myanma Y-397 *-2002* **Corvette Shipping Co** - *Myanmar*	**500** - -		**2002-04 Myanma Shipyards — Yangon** Yd No: Y-397 Loa - Br ex - Dght - Lbp - Br md - Dpth - Welded, 1 dk	**(X11A2YP) Yacht**	**1 oil engine** driving 1 FP propeller
9043706 - -	**SUNSHINE** - **Char Pon Marine Co Ltd** - *Chinese Taipei*	*299* - 46		**1991-06 Mitsui Eng. & SB. Co. Ltd. — Tamano** Yd No: TH1618 Loa 43.20 Br ex - Dght 1.400 Lbp 37.80 Br md 10.80 Dpth 3.50 Welded, 1 dk	**(A37B2PS) Passenger Ship** Passengers: unberthed: 300	**2 oil engines** reduction geared to sc. shafts driving 2 FP propellers Total Power: 5,296kW (7,200hp) 36.5kn Pielstick 16PA4V200VGA 2 x Vee 4 Stroke 16 Cy. 200 x 210 each-2648kW (3600bhp) Niigata Engineering Co Ltd-Japan AuxGen: 2 x 400kW 225V 60Hz a.c
9393632 *C6X09* -	**SUNSHINE** **Jonquil International Co** Samos Steamship Co *Nassau* *Bahamas* MMSI: 311017800 Official number: 8001616	**22,697** 12,674 37,317	Class: AB	**2009-02 Saiki Heavy Industries Co Ltd — Saiki OT** Yd No: 1175 Loa 177.85 (BB) Br ex - Dght 10.850 Lbp 169.80 Br md 28.60 Dpth 15.00 Welded, 1 dk	**(A21A2BC) Bulk Carrier** Double Hull Grain: 46,030; Bale: 45,707 Compartments: 5 Ho, ER 5 Ha: ER Cranes: 4x30t	**1 oil engine** driving 1 FP propeller Total Power: 7,080kW (9,626hp) 14.5kn Mitsubishi 6UEC52LA 1 x 2 Stroke 6 Cy. 520 x 1600 7080kW (9626bhp) Akasaka Tekkosho KK (Akasaka DieselLtd)-Japan AuxGen: 3 x 440kW a.c
9473183 *9HA2255* -	**SUNSHINE** **Ceres Trading Inc** Alpha Sigma Shipping Corp *Valletta* *Malta* MMSI: 248215000 Official number: 9473183	**41,342** 25,325 76,000 T/cm 68.2	Class: BV	**2010-05 Jiangnan Shipyard (Group) Co Ltd — Shanghai** Yd No: H2456 Loa 225.00 (BB) Br ex - Dght 14.000 Lbp 217.00 Br md 32.26 Dpth 19.60 Welded, 1 dk	**(A21A2BC) Bulk Carrier** Grain: 90,362 Compartments: 7 Ho, ER 7 Ha: ER	**1 oil engine** driving 1 FP propeller Total Power: 8,833kW (12,009hp) 14.5kn MAN-B&W 5S60MC 1 x 2 Stroke 5 Cy. 600 x 2292 8833kW (12009bhp) Hudong Heavy Machinery Co Ltd-China AuxGen: 3 x 560kW 60Hz a.c Fuel: 2300.0
9569205 *5IXB87* -	**SUNSHINE** *ex* Carnation *-2013* *ex* Panda *-2012* *ex* Safe *-2012* **NITC** - *Zanzibar* *Tanzania (Zanzibar)* MMSI: 677008600	**164,680** 108,000 317,554 T/cm 181.2	Class: (LR) ✠ Classed LR until 7/9/12	**2012-09 Shanghai Waigaoqiao Shipbuilding Co Ltd — Shanghai** Yd No: 1220 Loa 333.00 (BB) Br ex 60.04 Dght 22.640 Lbp 320.00 Br md 60.00 Dpth 30.50 Welded, 1 dk	**(A13A2TV) Crude Oil Tanker** Double Hull (13F) Liq: 334,000; Liq (Oil): 335,000 Cargo Heating Coils Compartments: 5 Ta, 10 Wing Ta, ER, 2 Wing Slop Ta 3 Cargo Pump (s): 3x5500m³/hr Manifold: Bow/CM: 165.2m	**1 oil engine** driving 1 FP propeller Total Power: 31,640kW (43,018hp) 16.1kn Wartsila 7RT-flex82T 1 x 2 Stroke 7 Cy. 820 x 3375 31640kW (43018bhp) AuxGen: 3 x 1600kW 450V 60Hz a.c Boilers: e (ex.g.) 26.5kgf/cm² (26.0bar), WTAuxB (o.f.) 23.0kgf/cm² (22.6bar) Fuel: 480.0 (d.f.) 8440.0 (r.f.)
8928284 *T2NX4* -	**SUNSHINE 1** *ex* Toll Pluto *-2013* *ex* Kimtrans Pluto *-2010* **Oceansky Marine Shipping Pte Ltd** Chahaya Shipping & Trading Co Pte Ltd *Funafuti* *Tuvalu* Official number: 29789713	**258** 77 -	Class: GL KI (BV)	**1997-06 Nga Chai Shipyard Sdn Bhd — Sibu** Yd No: 9502 Loa 29.00 Br ex - Dght 3.600 Lbp 26.78 Br md 8.60 Dpth 4.20 Welded, 1 dk	**(B32A2ST) Tug**	**2 oil engines** geared to sc. shafts driving 2 FP propellers Total Power: 1,350kW (1,836hp) Cummins KTA-38-M0 2 x Vee 4 Stroke 12 Cy. 159 x 159 each-675kW (918bhp) (new engine 1996) Cummins Engine Co Ltd-United Kingdom Fuel: 201.0 (d.f.)
8749028 *3DNY* -	**SUNSHINE 801** *ex* Zhe Din Yuan No. 801 *-2011* **Sunshine Fisheries Co Ltd** - *Suva* *Fiji* Official number: 000564	**191** 57 -		**2006-01 Huanghai Shipbuilding Co Ltd — Rongcheng SD** Loa 36.60 Br ex - Dght 2.600 Lbp - Br md 6.60 Dpth 3.30 Welded, 1 dk	**(B11B2FV) Fishing Vessel**	**1 oil engine** reduction geared to sc. shaft driving 1 Propeller Total Power: 325kW (442hp)
8749004 *3DNZ* -	**SUNSHINE 802** *ex* Zhe Din Yuan No. 802 *-2009* **Sunshine Fisheries Co Ltd** - *Suva* *Fiji* Official number: 000753	**198** 65 -		**2002-01 Huanghai Shipbuilding Co Ltd — Rongcheng SD** Loa 34.52 Br ex - Dght 2.500 Lbp - Br md 7.00 Dpth 3.50 Welded, 1 dk	**(B11B2FV) Fishing Vessel**	**1 oil engine** reduction geared to sc. shaft driving 1 Propeller Total Power: 325kW (442hp)
9338852 *C6XN6* -	**SUNSHINE ACE** **Snowscape Car Carriers SA** New Asian Shipping Co Ltd *Nassau* *Bahamas* MMSI: 311015100 Official number: 8001606	**58,917** 18,167 18,858	Class: NK	**2009-02 Minaminippon Shipbuilding Co Ltd — Usuki OT** Yd No: 703 Loa 199.95 (BB) Br ex - Dght 9.816 Lbp 190.00 Br md 32.26 Dpth 14.70 Welded, 12 dks	**(A35B2RV) Vehicles Carrier** Side door/ramp (s) Quarter stern door/ramp (s. a.) Cars: 6,237	**1 oil engine** driving 1 FP propeller Total Power: 15,820kW (21,509hp) 20.0kn MAN-B&W 7S60MC-C 1 x 2 Stroke 7 Cy. 600 x 2400 15820kW (21509bhp) Mitsui Engineering & Shipbuilding CLtd-Japan Thrusters: 1 Tunnel thruster (f) Fuel: 2660.0
9401996 *9V8265* -	**SUNSHINE BLISS** **'K' Line Pte Ltd (KLPL)** Blue Marine Management Corp *Singapore* *Singapore* MMSI: 565778000 Official number: 395532	**40,070** 25,292 76,441 T/cm 67.1	Class: NK	**2010-02 Oshima Shipbuilding Co Ltd — Saikai NS** Yd No: 10534 Loa 225.00 (BB) Br ex - Dght 14.124 Lbp 220.00 Br md 32.26 Dpth 19.39 Welded, 1 dk	**(A21A2BC) Bulk Carrier** Grain: 89,918; Bale: 87,940 Compartments: 1 Wing Ho, 6 Ho, ER 7 Ha: ER	**1 oil engine** driving 1 FP propeller Total Power: 8,789kW (11,950hp) 14.5kn MAN-B&W 5S60MC-C 1 x 2 Stroke 5 Cy. 600 x 2400 8789kW (11950bhp) Kawasaki Heavy Industries Ltd-Japan AuxGen: 3 x a.c Fuel: 2370.0
9433808 *3FWP5* -	**SUNSHINE EXPRESS** **Sun God Navigation SA** Fuyo Kaiun Co Ltd SatCom: Inmarsat C 437129413 *Panama* *Panama* MMSI: 371294000 Official number: 41556KJ	**28,465** 14,372 50,077 T/cm 52.1	Class: NK	**2011-02 Onomichi Dockyard Co Ltd — Onomichi HS** Yd No: 558 Loa 182.50 Br ex - Dght 12.917 Lbp 175.00 Br md 32.20 Dpth 18.40 Welded, 1 dk	**(A13B2TP) Products Tanker** Double Hull (13F) Liq: 54,347; Liq (Oil): 55,000	**1 oil engine** driving 1 FP propeller Total Power: 8,580kW (11,665hp) 14.8kn MAN-B&W 6S50MC 1 x 2 Stroke 6 Cy. 500 x 1910 8580kW (11665bhp) Mitsui Engineering & Shipbuilding Co Ltd-Japan Fuel: 1907.0 (r.f.)

7122687 *DUOI* -	**SUNSHINE II** *ex* Trinity *-1989* *ex* Batore *-1985* *ex* Bucklaw *-1981* **Delsan Transport Lines Inc** - *Manila* *Philippines* Official number: MNLD000265	*966* 489 950	Class: (BV)	**1971 Boele's Scheepswerven en Machinefabriek N.V. — Bolnes** Yd No: 1042 Loa 64.70 Br ex 10.32 Dght 3.595 Lbp 59.47 Br md 10.24 Dpth 5.82 Welded, 1 dk	**(A11B2TG) LPG Tanker** Liq (Gas): 1,193 2 x Gas Tank (s); 2 (stl) cyl horizontal 4 Cargo Pump (s)	**1 oil engine** driving 1 FP propeller Total Power: 552kW (750hp) 11.6kn Blackstone E6 1 x 4 Stroke 6 Cy. 222 x 292 552kW (750bhp) Lister Blackstone MirrleesMarine Ltd.-Dursley AuxGen: 3 x 53kW 440V 60Hz a.c Fuel: 69.0 (d.f.) 3.5pd
7040982 *DZIH* -	**SUNSHINE III** *ex* Kabibe *-1989* *ex* James Cook *-1987* *ex* Athina *-1973* **Delsan Transport Lines Inc** - *Manila* *Philippines* Official number: 229309	*1,404* 809 1,530 T/cm 6.4	Class: (NV)	**1971-03 B.V. Scheepswerf "Waterhuizen" J. Pattje — Waterhuizen** Yd No: 293 Loa 68.79 Br ex 11.51 Dght 5.117 Lbp 62.84 Br md 11.49 Dpth 5.85 Welded, 1 dk	**(A11B2TG) LPG Tanker** Liq (Gas): 1,563 4 x Gas Tank (s); 4 independent (C.mn.stl) cyl horizontal 4 Cargo Pump (s): 4x50m³/hr Manifold: Bow/CM: 29m Ice Capable	**1 oil engine** sr geared to sc. shaft driving 1 FP propeller Total Power: 1,103kW (1,500hp) 12.0kn MWM TBD441V12 1 x Vee 4 Stroke 12 Cy. 230 x 270 1103kW (1500bhp) Motoren Werke Mannheim AG (MWM)-West Germany AuxGen: 3 x 160kW 440V 60Hz a.c Fuel: 148.5 (r.f.) 5.0pd
8748933 *3DZB* -	**SUNSHINE NO. 6** - **Sunshine Fisheries Co Ltd** - *Suva* *Fiji* Official number: 000564	**191** 57 -		**2006-01 Huanghai Shipbuilding Co Ltd — Rongcheng SD** Loa 36.60 Br ex - Dght 2.600 Lbp - Br md 6.60 Dpth 3.30 Welded, 1 dk	**(B11B2FV) Fishing Vessel**	**1 oil engine** reduction geared to sc. shaft driving 1 Propeller Total Power: 325kW (442hp)
9408114 *WDE4432* -	**SUNSHINE STATE** - **APT Sunshine State** Intrepid Ship Management Inc *Wilmington, DE* *United States of America* MMSI: 367353090 Official number: 1222406	**29,527** 12,859 48,633	Class: AB	**2009-12 National Steel & Shipbuilding Co. (NASSCO) — San Diego, Ca** Yd No: 503 Loa 183.00 (BB) Br ex - Dght 12.800 Lbp 174.00 Br md 32.20 Dpth 19.00 Welded, 1 dk	**(A12B2TR) Chemical/Products Tanker** Double Hull (13F) Liq: 51,301; Liq (Oil): 54,016 Compartments: 12 Wing Ta, 2 Wing Slop Ta, ER 12 Cargo Pump (s): 12x600m³/hr Manifold: Bow/CM: 88.3m	**1 oil engine** driving 1 FP propeller Total Power: 8,684kW (11,807hp) 15.0kn MAN-B&W 6S50MC 1 x 2 Stroke 6 Cy. 500 x 1910 8684kW (11807bhp) Doosan Engine Co Ltd-South Korea AuxGen: 3 x 900kW a.c Fuel: 170.0 (d.f.) 1000.0 (r.f.)
8978071 *6KCB* -	**SUNSTAR** *ex* Jupiter No. 1 *-2012* **Sunwoo Corp** - *Busan* *South Korea* MMSI: 441864000 Official number: 1206001-6261103	**910** 306 1,139	Class: KR	**2001-08 San Yang Shipbuilding Co., Ltd. — Kaohsiung** Yd No: 814 Loa 58.20 Br ex - Dght - Lbp 51.90 Br md 9.00 Dpth 3.95 Welded, 1 dk	**(B11B2FV) Fishing Vessel**	**1 oil engine** reduction geared to sc. shaft driving 1 Propeller 12.5kn
8861515 *HP6912* -	**SUNTAL No. 1** *ex* Sinowood No. 1 *-2012* **Suntal Maritime Corp** Yue Xiu United Transportation Corp *Panama* *Panama* Official number: 2044392	**674** 427 -		**1980 Kwong Hing Shipyards — Hong Kong** L reg 36.87 Br ex 13.72 Dght 3.960 Lbp - Br md - Dpth - Welded, 1 dk	**(B32A2ST) Tug**	**1 oil engine** driving 1 FP propeller
8861527 *HP6913* -	**SUNTAL No. 2** *ex* Sinowood No. 2 *-2012* **Suntal Maritime Corp** Yue Xiu United Transportation Corp *Panama* *Panama* Official number: 2044192	**451** 330 -		**1977 Kwong Hing Shipyards — Hong Kong** L reg 30.43 Br ex 12.80 Dght 3.660 Lbp - Br md - Dpth - Welded, 1 dk	**(B32A2ST) Tug**	**1 oil engine** driving 1 FP propeller
8861539 *HP6914* -	**SUNTAL No. 3** *ex* Sinowood No. 3 *-1980* **Suntal Maritime Corp** Yue Xiu United Transportation Corp *Panama* *Panama* Official number: 2044292	**457** 345 -		**1980 Guangzhou Shipyard — Guangzhou GD** L reg 30.01 Br ex 12.00 Dght 4.150 Lbp - Br md - Dpth - Welded, 1 dk	**(B32A2ST) Tug**	**1 oil engine** driving 1 FP propeller
8861541 *HP6915* -	**SUNTAL No. 4** *ex* Sinowood No. 4 *-1980* **Suntal Maritime Corp** Yue Xiu United Transportation Corp *Panama* *Panama* Official number: 2044492	**512** 376 -		**1980 Guangzhou Wenchong Shipyard — Guangzhou GD** L reg 31.01 Br ex 13.00 Dght 4.150 Lbp - Br md - Dpth - Welded, 1 dk	**(B32A2ST) Tug**	**1 oil engine** driving 1 FP propeller
8810504 *UIKL* -	**SUNTAR** *ex* Hobart *-2010* *ex* Proton *-2007* *ex* Suntar *-2007* *ex* Daikoku Maru No. 8 *-2006* *ex* Kashima Maru No. 56 *-2002* **Antey Co Ltd (TOO 'Antey')** - *Nevelsk* *Russia* MMSI: 273430790	**564** 309 295	Class: RS	**1989-02 Sanuki Shipbuilding & Iron Works Co Ltd — Mitoyo KG** Yd No: 1200 Loa 52.10 (BB) Br ex - Dght 3.200 Lbp 44.20 Br md 8.40 Dpth 3.55 Welded, 1 dk	**(B11B2FV) Fishing Vessel** Ins: 548	**1 oil engine** driving 1 FP propeller Total Power: 699kW (950hp) 13.0kn Niigata 6M28BFT 1 x 4 Stroke 6 Cy. 280 x 480 699kW (950bhp) Niigata Engineering Co Ltd-Japan
8938095 *YD4989* -	**SUNTER** *ex* Daya Gemilang *-2004* **PT Rig Tenders Indonesia Tbk** - *Jakarta* *Indonesia*	**171** 52 -	Class: KI (AB) (GL)	**1998-05 P.T. Dayakaltim Bahagia — Samarinda** Loa 28.00 Br ex - Dght 2.880 Lbp 24.50 Br md 7.50 Dpth 3.30 Welded, 1 dk	**(B32A2ST) Tug**	**2 oil engines** reduction geared to sc. shafts driving 2 FP propellers Total Power: 1,434kW (1,950hp) Caterpillar D398TA 2 x Vee 4 Stroke 12 Cy. 159 x 203 each-717kW (975bhp) (made 1996) Caterpillar Inc-USA
8976918 *DGUJ* -	**SUNTHORICE** *ex* White Shark *-1999* *ex* Aussenjade II *-1978* **Sunthorice** - *Rostock* *Germany* MMSI: 211362370	**376** - -		**1902 Jos L Meyer — Papenburg** Converted From: Lightship-1978 Lengthened-1932 Loa 56.90 Br ex - Dght - Lbp - Br md 8.20 Dpth 3.40 Riveted, 1 dk	**(A37B2PS) Passenger Ship**	**1 oil engine** driving 1 Propeller Total Power: 368kW (500hp) 11.0kn MWM 1 x 368kW (500bhp) (new engine 1932) Motorenwerk Mannheim AG (MWM)-Germany AuxGen: 1 x 55kW 380/220V
8513314 *DIXS* -	**SUNTIS** - **Frank Hagenah Schiffahrt** Warnecke Schiffahrt GbR *Itzehoe* *Germany* MMSI: 218005000 Official number: 1846	**1,564** 708 1,815	Class: GL	**1985-07 Schiffs. Hugo Peters Wewelsfleth Peters & Co. GmbH — Wewelsfleth** Yd No: 614 Loa 82.48 Br ex 11.33 Dght 3.850 Lbp 76.82 Br md 11.31 Dpth 5.41 Welded, 2 dks	**(A31A2GX) General Cargo Ship** Grain: 2,894; Bale: 2,881 TEU 48 C. 48/20' (40') Compartments: 1 Ho, ER 1 Ha: (49.8 x 9.0)ER Ice Capable	**1 oil engine** with flexible couplings & sr reverse geared to sc. shaft driving 1 FP propeller Total Power: 441kW (600hp) 10.5kn MWM TBD440-6K 1 x 4 Stroke 6 Cy. 230 x 270 441kW (600bhp) Motoren Werke Mannheim AG (MWM)-West Germany AuxGen: 2 x 92kW 380/220V 50Hz a.c, 1 x 46kW 380/220V 50Hz a.c Thrusters: 1 Thwart. FP thruster (f) Fuel: 110.0 (d.f.)
8920115 *3EXX7* -	**SUNWARD** *ex* Great Fish *-2013* *ex* Sunny Falcon *-2009* **Sunward Marine SA** Wills International Co Ltd SatCom: Inmarsat C 435293420 *Panama* *Panama* MMSI: 352934000 Official number: 1894290F	**3,778** 1,987 6,174 T/cm 13.9	Class: NK (KR)	**1990-03 Sanuki Shipbuilding & Iron Works Co Ltd — Mitoyo KG** Yd No: 1210 Converted From: Products Tanker-2007 Conv to DH-2007 Loa 105.50 (BB) Br ex - Dght 7.060 Lbp 96.50 Br md 16.00 Dpth 8.45 Welded, 1 dk	**(A13B2TP) Products Tanker** Double Hull (13F) Liq: 5,790; Liq (Oil): 6,910 Compartments: 10 Wing Ta, 1 Slop Ta, 2 Wing Slop Ta, ER 4 Cargo Pump (s): 2x1000m³/hr, 1x400m³/hr, 1x200m³/hr Manifold: Bow/CM: 48m	**1 oil engine** driving 1 FP propeller Total Power: 2,427kW (3,300hp) 12.0kn Hanshin 6EL40 1 x 4 Stroke 6 Cy. 400 x 800 2427kW (3300bhp) The Hanshin Diesel Works Ltd-Japan AuxGen: 2 x 280kW 445V 60Hz a.c Fuel: 89.3 (d.f.) (Heating Coils) 369.7 (r.f.) 10.0pd
7301697 *WDC9221* -	**SUNWAY** *ex* Tradewind *-2007* *ex* Sea Gull *-1989* **Scandia Fisheries Inc** - *Seattle, WA* *United States of America* MMSI: 367099160 Official number: 538730	*122* 87 -		**1972 Hatteras Yachts, Inc. — New Bern, NC** L reg 19.73 Br ex 6.71 Dght - Lbp - Br md - Dpth 3.15 Bonded, 1 dk	**(B11B2FV) Fishing Vessel** Hull Material: Reinforced Plastic	**1 oil engine** driving 1 FP propeller Total Power: 268kW (364hp)
7925027 *H3YV* -	**SUNWAY B** *ex* Spyros K *-2009* *ex* Bum Dong *-2004* **Sunway Navigation SA** - SatCom: Inmarsat C 435535910 *Panama* *Panama* MMSI: 355359000 Official number: 3008004B	**9,751** 5,127 17,823 T/cm 25.7	Class: (KR) (AB)	**1980-12 Korea Shipbuilding & Engineering Corp — Busan** Yd No: 1016 Loa 135.52 (BB) Br ex 23.04 Dght 9.432 Lbp 127.01 Br md 23.00 Dpth 12.12 Welded, 1 dk	**(A13B2TP) Products Tanker** Double Bottom Entire Compartment Length Liq: 17,823; Liq (Oil): 17,823 Cargo Heating Coils Compartments: 16 Ta, ER 3 Cargo Pump (s): 3x500m³/hr Manifold: Bow/CM: 69m	**1 oil engine** driving 1 FP propeller Total Power: 5,914kW (8,041hp) 14.8kn B&W 6L55GFC 1 x 2 Stroke 6 Cy. 550 x 1380 5914kW (8041bhp) Hitachi Zosen Corp-Japan AuxGen: 2 x 400kW 450V 60Hz a.c Fuel: 118.0 (d.f.) (Heating Coils) 1236.5 (r.f.) 36.0pd

8509882 *9LY2438* -	**SUNYIELD** *ex* B. P. P. 31 *-2011* *ex* Ohminesan Maru *-2007* **Treasure Creation Ltd** Ocean Grow International Shipmanagement Consultant Corp SatCom: Inmarsat C 466700523 *Freetown* *Sierra Leone* MMSI: 667003241 Official number: SL103241	**3,434** 1,595 5,321 T/cm 13.0	Class: (NK)	**1985-09 Fukuoka Shipbuilding Co Ltd — Fukuoka FO** Yd No: 1118 Loa 107.85 (BB) Br ex 15.04 Dght 6.298 Lbp 99.52 Br md 15.00 Dpth 7.52 Welded, 1 dk	**(A13B2TP) Products Tanker** Single Hull Liq: 5,549; Liq (Oil): 5,549 Compartments: 10 Ta, ER 3 Cargo Pump (s): 2x1000m³/hr, 1x300m³/hr Manifold: Bow/CM: 54m	**1 oil engine** driving 1 CP propeller Total Power: 2,206kW (2,999hp) 12.5kn Mitsubishi 6UEC37L 1 x 2 Stroke 6 Cy. 370 x 880 2206kW (2999bhp) Akasaka Tekkosho KK (Akasaka DieselLtd)-Japan AuxGen: 1 x 320kW 440V 60Hz a.c, 2 x 200kW 440V 60Hz a.c Thrusters: 1 Thwart. CP thruster (f) Fuel: 89.5 (d.f.) 391.0 (r.f.) 6.5pd
9644859 *JD3364* -	**SUO MARU** - **Seagate Corp** - *Shunan, Yamaguchi* *Japan* Official number: 141682	*219* - -		**2012-05 Kanagawa Zosen — Kobe** Yd No: 640 Loa 35.00 Br ex - Dght 3.100 Lbp 30.50 Br md 9.60 Dpth 4.17 Welded, 1 dk	**(B32A2ST) Tug**	**2 oil engines** reduction geared to sc. shafts driving 2 FP propellers Total Power: 3,676kW (4,998hp) Niigata 6L28HX 2 x 4 Stroke 6 Cy. 280 x 370 each-1838kW (2499bhp) Niigata Engineering Co Ltd-Japan
8130708 *JI3120* -	**SUO MARU No. 2** - **Fukada Salvage & Marine Works Co Ltd (Fukada Salvage Kensetsu KK)** - SatCom: Inmarsat B 343115010 *Osaka, Osaka* *Japan* MMSI: 431150000 Official number: 125136	*198* - 157		**1982-03 K.K. Odo Zosen Tekko — Shimonoseki** Yd No: 281 Loa 33.20 Br ex 8.44 Dght 3.001 Lbp 29.52 Br md 8.21 Dpth 3.61 Welded, 1 dk	**(B32A2ST) Tug** Derricks: 1x5t	**2 oil engines** sr geared to sc. shafts driving 2 FP propellers Total Power: 1,324kW (1,800hp) Daihatsu 6PSHTBM-26H 2 x 4 Stroke 6 Cy. 260 x 320 each-662kW (900bhp) Daihatsu Diesel Manufacturing Co Lt-Japan AuxGen: 1 x 120kW 220V 60Hz a.c, 1 x 50kW 220V 60Hz a.c
9460631 *7JPU* -	**SUOH PACIFIC** *ex* Initial Salute *-2013* **Nippon Yusen Kabushiki Kaisha (NYK Line)** - *Shunan, Yamaguchi* *Japan* MMSI: 432934000 Official number: 141992	**50,802** 28,719 92,266	Class: NK	**2011-03 Oshima Shipbuilding Co Ltd — Saikai NS** Yd No: 10592 Loa 235.00 (BB) Br ex - Dght 13.057 Lbp 226.00 Br md 43.00 Dpth 18.55 Welded, 1 dk	**(A21A2BC) Bulk Carrier** Double Hull Grain: 108,633 Compartments: 5 Ho, ER 5 Ha: ER	**1 oil engine** driving 1 FP propeller Total Power: 11,910kW (16,193hp) 14.3kn Mitsubishi 6UEC60LSII 1 x 2 Stroke 6 Cy. 600 x 2300 11910kW (16193bhp) Mitsubishi Heavy Industries Ltd-Japan Fuel: 3835.0 (r.f.)
9315408 *OJLE* -	**SUOMENLINNA II** - **Suomenlinnan Liikenne OY (Sveaborgs Trafik AB)** - *Helsinki* *Finland* MMSI: 230985490 Official number: 12330	**329** 127 72		**2004-04 Stocznia Marynarki Wojennej SA (Naval Shipyard Gdynia) — Gdynia** Yd No: NS301 Loa 33.80 Br ex - Dght 3.200 Lbp 31.22 Br md 8.50 Dpth 3.25 Welded, 1 dk	**(A37B2PS) Passenger Ship** Ice Capable	**3 diesel electric oil engines** driving 3 gen. each 360kW 690V a.c Connecting to 2 elec. motors each (500kW) driving 2 Azimuth electric drive units Total Power: 1,284kW (1,746hp) 8.0kn Volvo Penta TAMD165A 3 x 4 Stroke 6 Cy. 144 x 165 each-428kW (582bhp) AB Volvo Penta-Sweden
7416351 *XUNM8* -	**SUOMI** *ex* Ecopacific-2 *-2009* *ex* Ekopasifik-2 *-2005* *ex* Tae Chang No. 73 *-1993* **Jetbridge Ltd** - *Phnom Penh* *Cambodia* MMSI: 515159000 Official number: 0974130	**490** 239 476	Class: UB (RS) (KR)	**1974-11 KK Kanasashi Zosen — Shizuoka SZ** Yd No: 1167 Converted From: Fishing Vessel-1993 Loa 55.30 Br ex 8.60 Dght 3.480 Lbp 49.28 Br md 8.60 Dpth 3.92 Welded, 1 dk	**(B12B2FC) Fish Carrier**	**1 oil engine** driving 1 FP propeller Total Power: 809kW (1,100hp) 12.0kn Akasaka AH27R 1 x 4 Stroke 6 Cy. 270 x 420 809kW (1100bhp) Akasaka Tekkosho KK (Akasaka DieselLtd)-Japan AuxGen: 2 x 200kW 225V a.c Fuel: 301.0 (d.f.)
9288057 *PHBT* -	**SUOMIGRACHT** - **BV Beheer Maatschappij Klippergracht, BV Beheer Maatschappij Paleisgracht & BV Beheer Maatschappij Prinsengracht** Spliethoff's Bevrachtingskantoor BV *Amsterdam* *Netherlands* MMSI: 246100000 Official number: 42279	**18,321** 7,647 23,660	Class: LR ✠**100A1** SS 11/2009 strengthened for heavy cargoes, container cargoes in holds, on upper deck and upper deck hatch covers, timber deck cargoes tanktop suitable for discharge by grabs *IWS LI Finnish-Swedish Ice Class 1AS at draught of 10.832m Max/min draught fwd 10.47/4.22m Max/min draught aft 11.47/6.60m ✠**LMC** **UMS** Eq.Ltr: I†; Cable: 616.0/64.0 U3 (a)	**2004-11 Stocznia Szczecinska Nowa Sp z oo — Szczecin** Yd No: B587/IV/6 Loa 185.40 (BB) Br ex 25.66 Dght 10.587 Lbp 173.50 Br md 25.30 Dpth 14.60 Welded, 1 dk	**(A31A2GX) General Cargo Ship** Grain: 27,600 TEU 1291 C Ho 555 TEU C Dk 736 TEU incl 120 ref C. Compartments: 3 Ho, ER 3 Ha: ER Cranes: 3x120t Ice Capable	**1 oil engine** with flexible couplings & sr geared to sc. shaft driving 1 CP propeller Total Power: 12,060kW (16,397hp) 19.1kn Wartsila 6L64 1 x 4 Stroke 6 Cy. 640 x 900 12060kW (16397bhp) Wartsila Italia SpA-Italy AuxGen: 3 x 450kW 445V 60Hz a.c, 1 x 1000kW 445V 60Hz a.c Boilers: TOH (o.f.) 10.2kgf/cm² (10.0bar), TOH (ex.g.) 10.2kgf/cm² (10.0bar) Thrusters: 1 Thwart. CP thruster (f) Fuel: 240.0 (d.f.) 1591.0 (r.f.) 45.0pd
9116773 *UAEG* -	**SUOYARVI** - **CJSC 'Armator'** Neva Shipping Co (OOO Nevskaya Sudokhodnaya Kompaniya) *St Petersburg* *Russia* MMSI: 273334000	**1,596** 831 2,300	Class: RS	**1994-09 TOO Onega Arminius Shipbuilders — Petrozavodsk** Yd No: 10523/002 Loa 81.44 Br ex 11.46 Dght 4.233 Lbp 77.40 Br md 11.30 Dpth 5.40 Welded, 1 dk	**(A31A2GX) General Cargo Ship** Grain: 2,926 TEU 72 C. 72/20' Compartments: 1 Ho, ER 1 Ha: Ice Capable	**1 oil engine** reduction geared to sc. shaft driving 1 FP propeller Total Power: 1,000kW (1,360hp) 9.5kn MaK 6M332C 1 x 4 Stroke 6 Cy. 240 x 330 1000kW (1360bhp) Krupp MaK Maschinenbau GmbH-Kiel
9158757 *HSCE2*	**SUPA BHUM** *launched as* Santi Bhum *-1998* **Regional Container Lines Public Co Ltd** RCL Shipmanagement Pte Ltd SatCom: Inmarsat B 356703710 *Bangkok* *Thailand* MMSI: 567071000 Official number: 401001778	**6,393** 3,239 8,016 T/cm 21.6	Class: NK	**1998-03 Kyokuyo Shipyard Corp — Shimonoseki YC** Yd No: 416 Loa 121.90 (BB) Br ex 21.85 Dght 6.615 Lbp 115.00 Br md 21.80 Dpth 8.80 Welded, 1 dk	**(A33A2CC) Container Ship (Fully Cellular)** TEU 628 C Ho 260 TEU C Dk 368 TEU incl 60 ref C Compartments: 6 Cell Ho, ER 6 Ha: 2 (12.6 x 13.0)Tappered (12.6 x 18.4)Tappered 3 (12.6 x 18.4)ER Cranes: 2x36t	**1 oil engine** driving 1 FP propeller Total Power: 5,296kW (7,200hp) 16.0kn Mitsubishi 6UEC45LA 1 x 2 Stroke 6 Cy. 450 x 1350 5296kW (7200bhp) Mitsubishi Heavy Industries Ltd-Japan AuxGen: 3 x 560kW 450V 60Hz a.c Thrusters: 1 Thwart. CP thruster (f) Fuel: 66.2 (d.f.) (Heating Coils) 601.9 (r.f.) 24.0pd
7644192 - -	**SUPAT BAHARI** *ex* Osam Pride *-1985* *ex* Tokachi Maru *-1985* **PT Tytyan Samodra Shipping Co** - *Jakarta* *Indonesia*	*160* 49 -	Class: (NK)	**1967-07 Kanagawa Zosen — Kobe** Loa 27.13 Br ex - Dght 3.241 Lbp 24.49 Br md 7.60 Dpth 3.61 Welded, 1 dk	**(B32A2ST) Tug**	**2 oil engines** driving 2 FP propellers Total Power: 1,324kW (1,800hp) 12.0kn Nippon Hatsudoki HS6NV325 2 x 4 Stroke 6 Cy. 325 x 460 each-662kW (900bhp) Nippon Hatsudoki-Japan AuxGen: 3 x 14kW
6927119 - -	**SUPAT LAUT** *ex* Osam Talent *-1985* *ex* Tokiwa Maru *-1976* **PT Tytyan Samodra Shipping Co** - *Jakarta* *Indonesia*	*164* 43 49	Class: (NK)	**1969-02 Shimoda Dockyard Co. Ltd. — Shimoda** Yd No: 164 Loa 27.51 Br ex 7.62 Dght 3.322 Lbp 24.49 Br md 7.60 Dpth 3.61 Welded, 1 dk	**(B32A2ST) Tug**	**2 oil engines** driving 2 FP propellers Total Power: 1,324kW (1,800hp) 12.5kn Nippon Hatsudoki HS6NV325 2 x 4 Stroke 6 Cy. 325 x 460 each-662kW (900bhp) Nippon Hatsudoki-Japan AuxGen: 2 x 16kW
7012404 - -	**SUPE 1** *ex* Huascar 8 *-1976* - -	*200* - -	Class: (LR) ✠ Classed LR until 28/7/82	**1970-03 Fabricaciones Metallicas E.P.S. (FABRIMET) — Callao** Yd No: 399 Loa 30.18 Br ex 7.80 Dght 3.315 Lbp 26.45 Br md 7.68 Dpth 3.66 Welded	**(B11B2FV) Fishing Vessel**	**1 oil engine** reverse reduction geared to sc. shaft driving 1 FP propeller Total Power: 416kW (566hp) Caterpillar D379TA 1 x Vee 4 Stroke 8 Cy. 159 x 203 416kW (566bhp) Caterpillar Tractor Co-USA AuxGen: 1 x 1kW 24V d.c
9151606 - -	**SUPE 1** - - -	**356** 132 -		**1997-09 Astilleros Naves Industriales S.A. (NAVINSA) — Callao** Yd No: 20 Loa - Br ex - Dght - Lbp - Br md - Dpth - Welded, 1 dk	**(B11B2FV) Fishing Vessel** Liq: 530	**1 oil engine** geared to sc. shaft driving 1 FP propeller Total Power: 1,432kW (1,947hp) Caterpillar 3516TA 1 x Vee 4 Stroke 16 Cy. 170 x 190 1432kW (1947bhp) Caterpillar Inc-USA
7104764 - -	**SUPE 2** *ex* Huascar 16 *-1975* - -	*213* 99 274	Class: (LR) ✠ Classed LR until 28/7/82	**1971-04 Fabricaciones Metallicas E.P.S. (FABRIMET) — Callao** Yd No: 419 Loa 30.18 Br ex 7.80 Dght 3.315 Lbp 26.45 Br md 7.68 Dpth 3.69 Welded	**(B11B2FV) Fishing Vessel** Compartments: 1 Ho, ER 1 Ha: (3.5 x 2.6)	**1 oil engine** reverse reduction geared to sc. shaft driving 1 FP propeller Total Power: 496kW (674hp) 12.0kn Caterpillar D379SCAC 1 x Vee 4 Stroke 8 Cy. 159 x 203 496kW (674bhp) Caterpillar Tractor Co-USA AuxGen: 2 x 1kW 24V d.c Fuel: 11.0 (d.f.)

IMO / Call sign	Name / Owner / Manager / Port	Tonnage	Class	Built / Shipbuilder / Dimensions	Type	Machinery
7109300 - -	**SUPE 3** *ex* Huascar 17 *-1976* - -	*213* 99 274	Class: (LR) ✠ Classed LR until 28/7/82	**1971**-05 **Fabricaciones Metallicas E.P.S. (FABRIMET) — Callao** Yd No: 420 Loa 30.18 Br ex 7.80 Dght 3.315 Lbp 26.45 Br md 7.68 Dpth 3.69 Welded	**(B11B2FV) Fishing Vessel** Compartments: 1 Ho, ER 1 Ha: (3.5 x 2.6)	**1 oil engine** reverse reduction geared to sc. shaft driving 1 FP propeller Total Power: 496kW (674hp) 12.0kn Caterpillar D379SCAC 1 x Vee 4 Stroke 8 Cy. 159 x 203 496kW (674bhp) Caterpillar Tractor Co-USA AuxGen: 2 x 1kW 24V d.c Fuel: 11.0 (d.f.)
7004184 - -	**SUPE 9** *ex* Puerto Supe 9 *-1976* *ex* Celia *-1976* - -	*200* - 249	Class: (LR) ✠ Classed LR until 28/7/82	**1969**-11 **Fabricaciones Metallicas E.P.S. (FABRIMET) — Callao** Yd No: 392 Loa 30.18 Br ex 7.80 Dght 3.315 Lbp 26.45 Br md 7.68 Dpth 3.69 Welded	**(B11B2FV) Fishing Vessel** Compartments: 1 Ho, ER 1 Ha: (3.5 x 2.6) Cranes: 1x3t	**1 oil engine** reverse reduction geared to sc. shaft driving 1 FP propeller Total Power: 335kW (455hp) 11.0kn G.M. (Detroit Diesel) 16V-71 1 x Vee 2 Stroke 16 Cy. 108 x 127 335kW (455bhp) General Motors Corp-USA AuxGen: 1 x 1kW 24V d.c Fuel: 11.0 (d.f.)
7027332 - -	**SUPE 10** *ex* Puerto Supe 10 *-1976* *ex* Maru *-1975* - -	*213* 99 274	Class: (LR) ✠ Classed LR until 28/7/82	**1970**-08 **Fabricaciones Metallicas E.P.S. (FABRIMET) — Callao** Yd No: 405 Loa 30.18 Br ex 7.80 Dght 3.315 Lbp 26.45 Br md 7.68 Dpth 3.69 Welded	**(B11B2FV) Fishing Vessel** Compartments: 1 Ho, ER 1 Ha: (3.5 x 2.6)	**1 oil engine** sr reverse geared to sc. shaft driving 1 FP propeller Total Power: 515kW (700hp) 11.0kn G.M. (Detroit Diesel) 16V-71 1 x Vee 2 Stroke 16 Cy. 108 x 127 515kW (700bhp) General Motors Corp-USA AuxGen: 2 x 1kW 24V d.c Fuel: 11.0 (d.f.)
9173422 - -	**SUPE II** - -	**519** - -		**1998**-07 **Remesa Astilleros S.A. — Callao** Yd No: 107 Loa 42.45 Br ex - Dght 4.050 Lbp 37.29 Br md 8.85 Dpth 4.45 Welded, 1 dk	**(B11B2FV) Fishing Vessel**	**1 oil engine** reduction geared to sc. shaft driving 1 FP propeller Total Power: 1,177kW (1,600hp) 12.0kn Caterpillar 3512TA 1 x Vee 4 Stroke 12 Cy. 170 x 190 1177kW (1600bhp) Caterpillar Inc-USA
9643324 - -	**SUPER 98** - **PT Bunga Nusa Mahakam** - *Samarinda* *Indonesia*	**811** 244 -	Class: KI	**2011**-07 **C.V. Teknik Jaya Industri — Samarinda** Yd No: 45 Loa 70.77 Br ex - Dght 2.737 Lbp 65.29 Br md 12.70 Dpth 3.65 Welded, 1 dk	**(A35D2RL) Landing Craft** Bow ramp (centre)	**2 oil engines** reduction geared to sc. shafts driving 2 Propellers Yanmar 2 x 4 Stroke Yanmar Diesel Engine Co Ltd-Japan
9547738 *PMRD* -	**SUPER 99** **PT Aditya Aryaprawira Shipping** - *Samarinda* *Indonesia* MMSI: 525013680	**555** 167 -	Class: KI	**2008**-09 **C.V. Teknik Jaya Industri — Samarinda** Loa 64.95 Br ex - Dght 2.720 Lbp 57.73 Br md 11.00 Dpth 3.20 Welded, 1 dk	**(A35D2RL) Landing Craft**	**2 oil engines** reduction geared to sc. shafts driving 2 Propellers Total Power: 706kW (960hp) Mitsubishi 2 x 4 Stroke each-353kW (480bhp) Mitsubishi Heavy Industries Ltd-Japan
9140530 *3FQW6*	**SUPER CHALLENGE** *ex* IVS Super Challenge *-2003* *ex* Super Challenge *-2002* **Stove Rederi AS** Belships (Tianjin) Shipmanagement & Consultancy Co Ltd *Panama* *Panama* MMSI: 352603000 Official number: 2350297F	**17,977** 9,871 28,581	Class: NK	**1996**-11 **Tsuneishi Shipbuilding Co Ltd — Fukuyama HS** Yd No: 1083 Loa 172.00 (BB) Br ex - Dght 9.568 Lbp 165.00 Br md 27.00 Dpth 13.60 Welded, 1 dk	**(A21A2BC) Bulk Carrier** Grain: 38,472; Bale: 37,446 Compartments: 5 Ho, ER 5 Ha: (12.9 x 16.0)4 (19.8 x 17.6)ER Cranes: 4x30.5t	**1 oil engine** driving 1 FP propeller Total Power: 7,135kW (9,701hp) 14.0kn B&W 5S50MC 1 x 2 Stroke 5 Cy. 500 x 1910 7135kW (9701bhp) Kawasaki Heavy Industries Ltd-Japan Fuel: 1370.0 (r.f.)
7207918 *WYZ3566* -	**SUPER COON** *ex* Sidney *-1980* **Supercoon Inc** - *Brownsville, TX* *United States of America* Official number: 531553	*103* 70 -		**1971 Marine Mart, Inc. — Port Isabel, Tx** L reg 19.69 Br ex 6.13 Dght - Lbp - Br md - Dpth 3.46 Welded	**(B11B2FV) Fishing Vessel**	**1 oil engine** driving 1 FP propeller Total Power: 246kW (334hp)
9131515 *9HA3276* -	**SUPER-FAST ANDALUCIA** *ex* Bayard *-1998* **Cia Trasmediterranea SA (Acciona Trasmediterranea)** - *Valletta* *Malta* MMSI: 229369000 Official number: 9131515	**26,536** 16,740 12,488	Class: NV	**1997**-12 **Fincantieri-Cant. Nav. Italiani S.p.A. — Ancona** Yd No: 5994 Loa 185.00 (BB) Br ex 25.30 Dght 7.700 Lbp 170.00 Br md 25.20 Dpth 17.00 Welded, 2 dks	**(A35A2RR) Ro-Ro Cargo Ship** Passengers: driver berths: 12 Stern door/ramp (centre) Len: 13.00 Wid: 15.00 Swl: - Lane-Len: 3465 Trailers: 240 Ice Capable	**2 oil engines** with clutches, flexible couplings & sr geared to sc. shafts driving 2 CP propellers Total Power: 25,140kW (34,180hp) 22.0kn MAN 9L58/64 2 x 4 Stroke 9 Cy. 580 x 640 each-12570kW (17090bhp) MAN B&W Diesel AG-Augsburg AuxGen: 3 x 1200kW 220/440V 60Hz a.c Thrusters: 2 Thwart. FP thruster (f) Fuel: 60.0 (d.f.) (Heating Coils) 1400.0 (r.f.) 110.0pd
9263370 *9HA3525* -	**SUPER FAST GALICIA** *ex* Superfast Galicia *-2014* *ex* Atalaya de Alcudia *-2005* **Maritime Global Operator Ltd** V Ships Leisure SAM *Valletta* *Malta* MMSI: 229695000 Official number: 9263370	**16,686** 5,006 6,500	Class: LR ✠ **100A1** SS 11/2010 roll on - roll off passenger ship ✠ **LMC** **UMS** Eq.Ltr: G†; Cable: 577.5/60.0 U3 (a)	**2003**-05 **Hijos de J. Barreras S.A. — Vigo** Yd No: 1612 Loa 159.70 (BB) Br ex 24.16 Dght 6.500 Lbp 147.00 Br md 23.70 Dpth 15.60 Welded, 3 dks	**(A36A2PR) Passenger/Ro-Ro Ship (Vehicles)** Passengers: 120; cabins: 30 Stern door/ramp (p) Len: 15.00 Wid: - Swl: - Stern door/ramp (s) Len: 15.00 Wid: 6.00 Swl: - Stern door/ramp (centre) Len: 15.00 Wid: 11.00 Swl: - Lane-Len: 1750 Cars: 225	**2 oil engines** with flexible couplings & sr geared to sc. shafts driving 2 CP propellers Total Power: 25,200kW (34,262hp) 23.0kn Wartsila 12V46C 2 x Vee 4 Stroke 12 Cy. 460 x 580 each-12600kW (17131bhp) Wartsila Finland Oy-Finland AuxGen: 2 x 800kW 400V 50Hz a.c, 2 x 800kW 400V 50Hz a.c Boilers: AuxB (o.f.) 8.2kgf/cm² (8.0bar), WTAuxB (ex.g.) 8.2kgf/cm² (8.0bar) Thrusters: 2 Thwart. CP thruster (f) Fuel: 130.0 (d.f.) 1060.0 (r.f.) 43.0pd
9204362 *9HA3274* -	**SUPER-FAST LEVANTE** **Maritime Global Operator Ltd** - *Valletta* *Malta* MMSI: 229367000 Official number: 9204362	**17,391** 5,252 7,200	Class: BV	**2001**-03 **Union Naval Valencia SA (UNV) — Valencia** Yd No: 280 Loa 158.00 (BB) Br ex - Dght 6.500 Lbp 139.50 Br md 25.20 Dpth 8.40 Welded	**(A36A2PR) Passenger/Ro-Ro Ship (Vehicles)** Passengers: driver berths: 12 Stern door/ramp (p) Len: 8.60 Wid: 7.00 Swl: 66 Stern door/ramp (s) Len: 8.60 Wid: 7.00 Swl: 66 Lane-Len: 2000 Lane-Wid: 3.00 Lane-clr ht: 4.50 Cars: 117, Trailers: 102	**4 oil engines** geared to sc. shafts driving 2 CP propellers Total Power: 25,204kW (34,268hp) 22.0kn Wartsila 6L46C 4 x 4 Stroke 6 Cy. 460 x 580 each-6301kW (8567bhp) Wartsila Diesel S.A.-Bermeo AuxGen: 2 x 1500kW a.c Thrusters: 2 Thwart. FP thruster (f) Fuel: 905.3 (r.f.) (Heating Coils)
8867947 *IZSZ* -	**SUPER FLYTE** **Alilauro GRUSON SpA** MultiService Group Srl *Naples* *Italy* MMSI: 247097200	**464** 187 130	Class: RI	**1992 WaveMaster International Pty Ltd — Fremantle WA** Loa 44.90 Br ex 9.00 Dght 2.300 Lbp - Br md 8.98 Dpth 3.25 Welded, 1 dk	**(A37B2PS) Passenger Ship** Hull Material: Aluminium Alloy Passengers: unberthed: 525	**2 oil engines** geared to sc. shafts driving 2 FP propellers Total Power: 3,260kW (4,432hp) 28.0kn M.T.U. 16V396TE74 2 x Vee 4 Stroke 16 Cy. 165 x 185 each-1630kW (2216bhp) MTU Friedrichshafen GmbH-Friedrichshafen
9576272 *VRJ09* -	**SUPER GRACE** **Super Grace Enterprises Ltd** - *Hong Kong* *Hong Kong* MMSI: 477847200 Official number: HK-3309	**45,263** 26,562 81,629 T/cm 72.2	Class: CC	**2011**-12 **Guangzhou Longxue Shipbuilding Co Ltd — Guangzhou GD** Yd No: L0020 Loa 229.06 (BB) Br ex 32.31 Dght 14.450 Lbp 223.50 Br md 32.26 Dpth 20.20 Welded, 1 dk	**(A21A2BC) Bulk Carrier** Grain: 97,130 Compartments: 7 Ho, ER 7 Ha: 6 (16.7 x 15.0)ER (15.0 x 13.3)	**1 oil engine** driving 1 FP propeller Total Power: 10,260kW (13,949hp) 14.5kn MAN-B&W 5S60MC-C8 1 x 2 Stroke 5 Cy. 600 x 2400 10260kW (13949bhp) Hudong Heavy Machinery Co Ltd-China AuxGen: 3 x 620kW 450V a.c Fuel: 2953.0
7652060 *HP7664* -	**SUPER GREEN-6** *ex* Shanghai Maru No. 3 *-1994* *ex* Sumiyoshi Maru *-1990* **Super Green SA** Hansu Corp *Panama* *Panama* Official number: 23025SC	*478* 265 710		**1973**-10 **Asahi Zosen K.K. — Sumoto** Loa 53.29 Br ex - Dght 4.360 Lbp 49.00 Br md 10.00 Dpth 5.52 Welded, 2dks	**(A24D2BA) Aggregates Carrier** Grain: 920 1 Ha: ER	**1 oil engine** driving 1 FP propeller Total Power: 956kW (1,300hp) 10.5kn Daihatsu 6DS-26 1 x 4 Stroke 6 Cy. 260 x 320 956kW (1300bhp) Daihatsu Diesel Manufacturing Co Lt-Japan

IMO / Call sign	Name, owner, manager, port, flag	Tonnage	Class	Builder, dimensions	Type	Machinery
8863240 *HP7315* -	**SUPER GREEN I** *ex* Heiwa Maru *-1993* *ex* Yahata Maru No. 11 *-1993* **Super Green I** Hansu Trading Corp *Panama* *Panama* Official number: 22526SC	*450* 211 834		**1974 Higo Zosen — Kumamoto** Loa 51.00 Br ex - Dght - Lbp 48.00 Br md 11.00 Dpth 5.05 Welded, 1 dk	**(B33A2DG) Grab Dredger**	**1 oil engine** driving 1 FP propeller Total Power: 956kW (1,300hp) Makita KNLH6275 1 x 4 Stroke 6 Cy. 275 x 450 956kW (1300bhp) Makita Corp-Japan
8924666 *DUH2326* -	**SUPER ISLAND EXPRESS** *ex* Rosemaida *-1993* *ex* Manazuru *-1996* **Island Shipping Corp** - *Cebu* *Philippines* Official number: CEB1002035	*131* 88 -		**1972-02 Sumidagawa Zosen K.K. — Tokyo** Loa 29.00 Br ex - Dght 1.250 Lbp 26.50 Br md 5.40 Dpth 2.40 Welded, 1 dk	**(A37B2PS) Passenger Ship** Passengers: unberthed: 216	**2 oil engines** driving 2 FP propellers Total Power: 794kW (1,080hp) 15.0kn Niigata 6MG18X 2 x 4 Stroke 6 Cy. 180 x 200 each-397kW (540bhp) Niigata Engineering Co Ltd-Japan
8881644 *DUH2217* -	**SUPER ISLAND EXPRESS III** *ex* Maricar *-1996* *ex* Nagasaki No. 2 *-1994* **Island Shipping Corp** - *Cebu* *Philippines* Official number: CEB1000148	*169* 111 28		**1972 K.K. Mukai Zosensho — Nagasaki** Loa 32.25 Br ex - Dght 1.850 Lbp 29.00 Br md 6.60 Dpth 2.60 Welded, 1 dk	**(A37B2PS) Passenger Ship**	**1 oil engine** driving 1 FP propeller Total Power: 552kW (750hp) 11.5kn Yanmar 1 x 4 Stroke 552kW (750bhp) Yanmar Diesel Engine Co Ltd-Japan
9121077 *SX3772* -	**SUPER JET** *ex* Andreas Cat *-2004* *ex* Jet One *-2004* *ex* Seajet 1 *-2002* **Champion Jet Maritime Co** Seajets Catamaran Joint Venture *Piraeus* *Greece* MMSI: 239430000 Official number: 10328	**493** 337 50	Class: LR (HR) (NV) **100A1** SS 04/2010 SSC passenger, catamaran, HSC, G2 **UMS**	**1995-07 Oskarshamns Varv AB — Oskarshamn** Yd No: 535 Loa 42.00 Br ex 10.30 Dght 1.800 Lbp 37.37 Br md 10.00 Dpth 4.08 Welded, 1 dk	**(A37B2PS) Passenger Ship** Hull Material: Aluminium Alloy Passengers: unberthed: 386	**4 oil engines** with clutches, flexible couplings & sr geared to sc. shafts driving 4 Water jets Total Power: 5,940kW (8,076hp) 38.0kn M.T.U. 12V396TE74 4 x Vee 4 Stroke 12 Cy. 165 x 185 each-1485kW (2019bhp) MTU Friedrichshafen GmbH-Friedrichshafen AuxGen: 2 x 85kW a.c
8653138 *YB3608* -	**SUPER JET 19** - **PT Pelayaran Nasional Bahtera Bestari Shipping** - *Tanjungpinang* *Indonesia* Official number: 1535/GGA	**231** 70 -	Class: KI (Class contemplated)	**2010-04 PT Bintan Marina Shipyard — Tanjungpinang** Loa 38.00 Br ex - Dght - Lbp 34.75 Br md 5.50 Dpth 2.40 Welded, 1 dk	**(A37B2PS) Passenger Ship**	**2 oil engines** reduction geared to sc. shafts driving 2 Propellers Total Power: 2,984kW (4,058hp) Cummins KTA-50-M2 2 x Vee 4 Stroke 16 Cy. 159 x 159 each-1492kW (2029bhp) Cummins Engine Co Ltd-United Kingdom
8924484 - -	**SUPER JET 225** - **Tunas Rupat Follow Me Express Sdn Bhd** -	**198** 78 -	Class: (BV)	**1994 Far East Shipyard Co Sdn Bhd — Sibu** Yd No: 64/91 Loa 44.45 Br ex - Dght 1.300 Lbp 40.31 Br md 5.40 Dpth 2.00 Welded, 2 dks	**(A37B2PS) Passenger Ship** Hull Material: Aluminium Alloy Ice Capable	**2 oil engines** reduction geared to sc. shafts driving 2 FP propellers Total Power: 1,114kW (1,514hp) 30.0kn Yanmar 16LAK-ST1 2 x Vee 4 Stroke 16 Cy. 150 x 165 each-557kW (757bhp) Yanmar Diesel Engine Co Ltd-Japan
9201592 *9HJN9* -	**SUPER LADY** *ex* Young Lady *-2008* **EM Bulkers Co Ltd** Eastern Mediterranean Maritime Ltd *Valletta* *Malta* MMSI: 249064000 Official number: 9201592	**56,204** 32,082 105,528 T/cm 89.2	Class: LR ✠ **100A1** SS 05/2010 Double Hull oil tanker ESP LI **ShipRight** (SDA, FDA, CM) ✠ **LMC** **UMS IGS** Eq.Ltr: R†; Cable: 693.9/84.0 U3 (a)	**2000-05 Sumitomo Heavy Industries Ltd. — Yokosuka Shipyard, Yokosuka** Yd No: 1252 Lengthened-2010 Loa 240.10 (BB) Br ex 42.03 Dght 14.878 Lbp 229.00 Br md 42.00 Dpth 21.30 Welded, 1 dk	**(A13A2TW) Crude/Oil Products Tanker** Double Hull (13F) Liq: 115,572; Liq (Oil): 115,572 Cargo Heating Coils Compartments: 12 Wing Ta, ER, 2 Wing Slop Ta 3 Cargo Pump (s): 3x2500m³/hr Manifold: Bow/CM: 117.9m	**1 oil engine** driving 1 FP propeller Total Power: 12,000kW (16,315hp) 15.2kn Sulzer 6RTA58T 1 x 2 Stroke 6 Cy. 580 x 2416 12000kW (16315bhp) Diesel United Ltd.-Aioi AuxGen: 3 x 720kW 450V 60Hz a.c Boilers: e (ex.g.) 21.5kgf/cm² (21.1bar), AuxB (o.f.) 18.0kgf/cm² (17.7bar), AuxB (o.f.) 18.4kgf/cm² (18.0bar) Fuel: 261.0 (d.f.) (Heating Coils) 2792.0 (r.f.)
9251171 *S6NW6* -	**SUPER LEAGUE** - **Super League Maritime Co Pte Ltd** Interunity Management Corp SA SatCom: Inmarsat C 45460010 *Singapore* *Singapore* MMSI: 564600000 Official number: 389767	**5,812** 2,081 7,155 T/cm 18.3	Class: NK	**2002-05 Watanabe Zosen KK — Imabari EH** Yd No: 331 Loa 119.00 (BB) Br ex 18.84 Dght 6.759 Lbp 112.00 Br md 18.80 Dpth 8.80 Welded, 1 dk	**(A11B2TG) LPG Tanker** Double Bottom Entire Compartment Length Liq (Gas): 7,387 2 x Gas Tank (s); 2 membrane (C.mn.stl) pri horizontal 3 Cargo Pump (s): 3x450m³/hr Manifold: Bow/CM: 55.9m	**1 oil engine** driving 1 FP propeller Total Power: 4,192kW (5,699hp) 15.0kn B&W 6S35MC 1 x 2 Stroke 6 Cy. 350 x 1400 4192kW (5699bhp) Hitachi Zosen Corp-Japan AuxGen: 2 x a.c Fuel: 142.0 (d.f.) 635.0 (r.f.)
7100471 *WX7617* -	**SUPER LINER** *ex* Mississippi II *-2001* *ex* Sandra Lee *-1995* *ex* Miss Snow White *-1991* *ex* Chief White Hair *-1991* **Soi Van Nguyen** - *Ocean Springs, MS* *United States of America* Official number: 505953	*101* 69 -		**1966 Rockport Yacht & Supply Co. (RYSCO) — Rockport, Tx** L reg 21.37 Br ex 6.56 Dght - Lbp - Br md - Dpth 2.39 Welded	**(B11B2FV) Fishing Vessel**	**1 oil engine** driving 1 FP propeller Total Power: 294kW (400hp) Caterpillar D346SCAC 1 x Vee 4 Stroke 8 Cy. 137 x 165 294kW (400bhp) Caterpillar Tractor Co-USA
9094743 *JD2181* -	**SUPER LINER HAYATE** - **Hayate Kaiun** - *Miyakojima, Okinawa* *Japan* Official number: 140251	*145* - 30		**2006-01 Sanuki Shipbuilding & Iron Works Co Ltd — Mitoyo KG** Yd No: 121 Loa 32.80 Br ex - Dght 1.300 Lbp 26.00 Br md 8.40 Dpth 3.01 Welded, 1 dk	**(A36A2PR) Passenger/Ro-Ro Ship (Vehicles)** Hull Material: Aluminium Alloy Passengers: unberthed: 300	**2 oil engines** driving 2 Propellers Total Power: 3,088kW (4,198hp) 24.0kn Niigata 12V16FX 2 x Vee 4 Stroke 12 Cy. 165 x 185 each-1544kW (2099bhp) Niigata Engineering Co Ltd-Japan
8923789 - -	**SUPER MARINE** - - -	*161* - -		**1996-06 K.K. Miho Zosensho — Osaka** Loa 35.44 Br ex - Dght 1.200 Lbp 33.00 Br md 6.70 Dpth 2.95 Welded, 1 dk	**(A37B2PS) Passenger Ship** Hull Material: Aluminium Alloy Passengers: unberthed: 152	**2 oil engines** driving 2 FP propellers Total Power: 2,900kW (3,942hp) 30.0kn M.T.U. 2 x Vee 4 Stroke 16 Cy. 165 x 185 each-1450kW (1971bhp)
9227845 - -	**SUPER MARINE 1** - - -	*171* - 19		**2000-07 Sanuki Shipbuilding & Iron Works Co Ltd — Mitoyo KG** Yd No: 117A Loa 36.01 Br ex - Dght 1.024 Lbp 32.23 Br md 6.70 Dpth 2.95 Welded	**(A37B2PS) Passenger Ship** Passengers: unberthed: 152	**2 oil engines** reduction geared to sc. shafts driving 2 FP propellers Total Power: 2,898kW (3,940hp) 30.0kn M.T.U. 16V396TB83 2 x Vee 4 Stroke 16 Cy. 165 x 185 each-1449kW (1970bhp) MTU Friedrichshafen GmbH-Friedrichshafen AuxGen: 1 x 64kW a.c Fuel: 8.0 (d.f.)
7853389 *HP6094* -	**SUPER OIL 8** *ex* Bethany Mandiri *-1992* *ex* Hoei Maru No. 11 *-1990* - - *Panama* *Panama* Official number: 1971691	**291** 179 650		**1976 K.K. Fujishiro Zosen — Chiba** Loa 43.01 Br ex - Dght 2.901 Lbp 40.19 Br md 9.01 Dpth 3.00 Welded, 1 dk	**(A13B2TU) Tanker (unspecified)**	**1 oil engine** driving 1 FP propeller Total Power: 368kW (500hp) 9.0kn Matsui 1 x 4 Stroke 368kW (500bhp) Matsui Iron Works Co Ltd-Japan
7216713 *H08916* -	**SUPER RED** *ex* Toni Walker *-1973* **Merce D Rosado** - *Panama* *Panama* Official number: 431874	*147* 100 -		**1956 F.B. Walker & Sons, Inc. — Pascagoula, Ms** Yd No: 159 L reg 27.86 Br ex 6.81 Dght - Lbp - Br md 6.76 Dpth 2.87 Welded, 1 dk	**(B21A2OC) Crew/Supply Vessel**	**2 oil engines** driving 2 FP propellers Total Power: 442kW (600hp) General Motors 6-110 2 x 2 Stroke 6 Cy. 127 x 142 each-221kW (300bhp) General Motors Corp-USA
8982838 - -	**SUPER SEABUS III** - **Azam Marine Co Ltd** - *Zanzibar* *Tanzania* Official number: 100044	**319** 90 -	Class: (BV)	**1998-11 South Pacific Marine Pty Ltd — Burpengary QLD** Yd No: 98/006 Loa 31.00 Br ex 9.80 Dght 1.900 Lbp - Br md 9.50 Dpth 3.10 Welded, 1 dk	**(A37B2PS) Passenger Ship** Hull Material: Aluminium Alloy Passengers: unberthed: 284	**4 oil engines** geared to sc. shafts driving 2 CP propellers Total Power: 2,984kW (4,056hp) 35.0kn MAN D2842LE 4 x Vee 4 Stroke 12 Cy. 128 x 142 each-746kW (1014bhp) MAN Nutzfahrzeuge AG-Nuernberg
8025331 *PJPN* -	**SUPER SERVANT 3** - **Super Servant 3 NV** Dockwise Yacht Transport LLC SatCom: Inmarsat C 430615610 *Willemstad* *Curacao* MMSI: 306156000 Official number: 1993-C-1385	**10,224** 3,067 14,138	Class: AB	**1982-03 Oshima Shipbuilding Co Ltd — Saikai NS** Yd No: 10059 Loa 139.10 Br ex 32.31 Dght 6.260 Lbp 130.03 Br md 32.01 Dpth 8.51 Welded, 1 dk	**(A38C3GH) Heavy Load Carrier, semi submersible**	**2 oil engines** with flexible couplings & sr gearedto sc. shafts driving 2 CP propellers Total Power: 6,252kW (8,500hp) 13.0kn Werkspoor 6TM410 2 x 4 Stroke 6 Cy. 410 x 470 each-3126kW (4250bhp) Stork Werkspoor Diesel BV-Netherlands AuxGen: 2 x 400kW 450V 60Hz a.c, 4 x 190kW 450V 60Hz a.c Thrusters: 2 Thwart. CP thruster (f) Fuel: 201.0 (d.f.) 1439.5 (r.f.) 30.0pd

IMO / Call sign	Name / Owners	Tonnage	Class	Build / Dimensions	Type	Machinery
8025343 *PJPO* -	**SUPER SERVANT 4** **Shuttle Shipping NV** Spliethoff Transport BV SatCom: Inmarsat C 430615710 *Willemstad* *Curacao* MMSI: 306157000	**12,642** 3,792 14,138	Class: AB	**1982-06 Oshima Shipbuilding Co Ltd — Saikai NS** Yd No: 10060 Lengthened-1993 Loa 169.50 Br ex 32.31 Dght 6.260 Lbp 160.41 Br md 32.01 Dpth 8.59 Welded, 1 dk	**(A38C3GH) Heavy Load Carrier, semi submersible**	**2 oil engines** with flexible couplings & sr gearedto sc. shafts driving 2 CP propellers Total Power: 6,252kW (8,500hp) 14.0kn Werkspoor 6TM410 2 x 4 Stroke 6 Cy. 410 x 470 each-3126kW (4250bhp) Stork Werkspoor Diesel BV-Netherlands AuxGen: 2 x 400kW 450V 60Hz a.c, 4 x 190kW 450V 60Hz a.c Thrusters: 2 Thwart. CP thruster (f) Fuel: 201.0 (d.f.) 1439.5 (r.f.) 30.0pd
7633442 *C4YY* -	**SUPER SHUTTLE** *ex* Passat *-1997* *ex* Passat 1 *-1990* *ex* Passat *-1986* **Pepita Shipping Co Ltd** Malayan Towage & Salvage Corp (SALVTUG) *Limassol* *Cyprus* MMSI: 209419000 Official number: 7633442	**1,660** 670 2,030	Class: (GL)	**1977-09 J.J. Sietas Schiffswerft — Hamburg** Yd No: 819 Loa 72.27 (BB) Br ex 12.83 Dght 4.447 Lbp 65.51 Br md 12.81 Dpth 6.84 Welded, 2 dks	**(A31A2GX) General Cargo Ship** Grain: 3,174; Bale: 3,114 TEU 132 C. 132/20' (40') incl. 10 ref C. Compartments: 1 Ho, ER 1 Ha: (43.8 x 10.2)ER Ice Capable	**1 oil engine** reduction geared to sc. shaft driving 1 FP propeller Total Power: 1,280kW (1,740hp) 11.5kn Alpha 12V23L-VO 1 x Vee 4 Stroke 12 Cy. 225 x 300 1280kW (1740bhp) Alpha Diesel A/S-Denmark Thrusters: 1 Thwart. FP thruster (f)
8151659 *DUH2429* -	**SUPER SHUTTLE FERRY 1** *ex* Camiguin Star *-2002* *ex* Ferry Matsushima *-1999* *ex* Ehime No. 5 *-1988* **Asian Marine Transport Corp** - *Cebu* *Philippines* Official number: CEB1004436	*199* 109 94		**1971 Binan Senpaku Kogyo K.K. — Onomichi** Loa 33.00 Br ex - Dght 2.501 Lbp 29.01 Br md 7.80 Dpth 2.90 Welded, 1 dk	**(A37B2PS) Passenger Ship** Passengers: unberthed: 250	**1 oil engine** driving 1 FP propeller Total Power: 515kW (700hp) 11.5kn Daihatsu 1 x 4 Stroke 515kW (700bhp) Daihatsu Diesel Manufacturing Co Lt-Japan
8957106 *DUK2029* -	**SUPER SHUTTLE FERRY 3** *ex* Maito Maru No. 3 *-2000* *ex* Ganne No. 3 *-2000* **Asian Marine Transport Corp** - *Cagayan de Oro* *Philippines* Official number: CDO7003391	*192* 109 -		**1971-03 Binan Senpaku Kogyo K.K. — Onomichi** Loa 33.90 Br ex - Dght 2.500 Lbp 28.20 Br md 7.80 Dpth 2.80 Welded, 1 dk	**(A36A2PR) Passenger/Ro-Ro Ship (Vehicles)** Passengers: unberthed: 350	**1 oil engine** driving 1 FP propeller Total Power: 368kW (500hp) 10.5kn Daihatsu 1 x 4 Stroke 368kW (500bhp) Daihatsu Diesel Manufacturing Co Lt-Japan
7801518 *DUA2577* -	**SUPER SHUTTLE FERRY 6** *ex* Gigaventures *-2001* *ex* Ferry Kakeroma *-1995* **Asian Marine Transport Corp** - *Cebu* *Philippines* Official number: MNLD002541	*134* 66 58		**1978-11 Tokushima Zosen Sangyo K.K. — Komatsushima** Yd No: 550 Loa 33.24 Br ex - Dght 1.700 Lbp 29.00 Br md 7.00 Dpth 2.46 Riveted\Welded, 1 dk	**(A37B2PS) Passenger Ship**	**1 oil engine** driving 1 FP propeller Total Power: 294kW (400hp) Yanmar 6AL-UT 1 x 4 Stroke 6 Cy. 165 x 200 294kW (400bhp) Yanmar Diesel Engine Co Ltd-Japan
7322495 *DUND4* -	**SUPER SHUTTLE FERRY 7** *ex* Asia Taiwan *-1999* *ex* Geiyo *-1989* **Asian Marine Transport Corp** Super Shuttle Ferry *Cebu* *Philippines* Official number: CEB1000289	*730* 270 234	Class: (BV)	**1973-01 Matsuura Tekko Zosen K.K. — Osakikamijima** Yd No: 230 Loa 56.27 Br ex 11.13 Dght 2.591 Lbp 52.51 Br md 11.10 Dpth 3.12 Welded, 1 dk	**(A36A2PR) Passenger/Ro-Ro Ship (Vehicles)** Passengers: unberthed: 340 Stern ramp (a) Trailers: 18	**2 oil engines** geared to sc. shafts driving 2 FP propellers Total Power: 1,912kW (2,600hp) 14.0kn Daihatsu 6DS-26 2 x 4 Stroke 6 Cy. 260 x 320 each-956kW (1300bhp) Daihatsu Diesel Manufacturing Co Lt-Japan
7311185 *DUH2527* -	**SUPER SHUTTLE FERRY 9** *ex* Koun Maru No. 15 *-2003* *ex* Omishima *-1987* **Asian Marine Transport Corp** - *Cebu* *Philippines* Official number: CDO7011936	*189* 74 -		**1971-07 Fukumoto Zosensho — Onomichi** Yd No: 120 Loa 33.10 Br ex - Dght 2.501 Lbp 29.49 Br md 8.01 Dpth 3.10 Welded, 2 dks	**(A37B2PS) Passenger Ship**	**1 oil engine** driving 1 FP propeller Total Power: 515kW (700hp) 11.3kn Daihatsu 1 x 4 Stroke 515kW (700bhp) Daihatsu Diesel Manufacturing Co Lt-Japan
8840846 *DUH2534* -	**SUPER SHUTTLE FERRY 10** *ex* Seto *-2004* *ex* Takehara *-1997* **Asian Marine Transport Corp** - *Cagayan de Oro* *Philippines* Official number: CDO7012117	*354* 91 -		**1988-10 Kanbara Zosen K.K. — Onomichi** Yd No: 370 Loa 49.80 Br ex - Dght 2.650 Lbp 37.25 Br md 10.40 Dpth 3.61 Welded, 1 dk	**(A36A2PR) Passenger/Ro-Ro Ship (Vehicles)** Bow ramp (centre) Stern ramp (centre)	**2 oil engines** reduction geared to sc. shaft (s) driving 2 FP propellers Total Power: 2,060kW (2,800hp) Daihatsu 6DLM-26FSL 2 x 4 Stroke 6 Cy. 260 x 340 each-1030kW (1400bhp) Daihatsu Diesel Manufacturing Co Lt-Japan
8217817 *DUH2613* -	**SUPER SHUTTLE FERRY 12** *ex* Ferry Tarama *-2007* **Asian Marine Transport Corp** - *Cebu* *Philippines* Official number: CEB1006933	*324* 220 260		**1983-01 Usuki Iron Works Co Ltd — Usuki OT** Yd No: 1527 Loa 53.01 Br ex - Dght 3.801 Lbp 50.02 Br md 10.41 Dpth 6.00 Welded, 1 dk	**(A36A2PR) Passenger/Ro-Ro Ship (Vehicles)**	**2 oil engines** sr geared to sc. shafts driving 2 FP propellers Total Power: 2,060kW (2,800hp) Niigata 6MG25CXE 2 x 4 Stroke 6 Cy. 250 x 320 each-1030kW (1400bhp) Niigata Engineering Co Ltd-Japan
6811528 *DUE2163* -	**SUPER SHUTTLE FERRY 15** *ex* Joy Ruby *-2007* *ex* Viva Sto. Nino *-2007* *ex* Bisan Maru *-1982* **Asian Marine Transport Corp** - *Cebu* *Philippines* Official number: BAT5000381	*486* 128 262		**1967 Kanda Zosensho K.K. — Kure** Yd No: 127 Loa 49.99 Br ex - Dght 2.642 Lbp 44.96 Br md 11.80 Dpth 3.25 Welded, 1 dk	**(A36A2PR) Passenger/Ro-Ro Ship (Vehicles)** Passengers: 196	**2 oil engines** driving 2 FP propellers Total Power: 1,250kW (1,700hp) 13.0kn Daihatsu 8PSTBM-26D 2 x 4 Stroke 8 Cy. 260 x 320 each-625kW (850bhp) Daihatsu Kogyo-Japan AuxGen: 2 x 80kW Fuel: 22.0 6.0pd
8616960 *DUH2643* -	**SUPER SHUTTLE FERRY 18** *ex* Orange Princess *-2008* **Asian Marine Transport Corp** - *Cebu* *Philippines* Official number: CEB1008050	*695* 486 266		**1987-03 Nakamura Shipbuilding & Engine Works Co. Ltd. — Yanai** Yd No: 158 Loa 60.79 Br ex 14.00 Dght 2.801 Lbp 55.02 Br md 12.01 Dpth 3.81 Welded, 1 dk	**(A36A2PR) Passenger/Ro-Ro Ship (Vehicles)** Passengers: unberthed: 250 Trailers: 5	**2 oil engines** with clutches, flexible couplings & dr reverse geared to sc. shafts driving 2 FP propellers Total Power: 2,206kW (3,000hp) 15.0kn Daihatsu 6DLM-26 2 x 4 Stroke 6 Cy. 260 x 340 each-1103kW (1500bhp) Daihatsu Diesel Manufacturing Co Lt-Japan Thrusters: 1 Thwart. CP thruster (f)
8806319 *DUH2648* -	**SUPER SHUTTLE FERRY 19** *ex* Sakura *-2009* *ex* Shimotsui *-2000* **Asian Marine Transport Corp** - *Cebu* *Philippines* Official number: CEB1008069	*383* 268 139		**1988-03 Shin Kurushima Dockyard Co. Ltd. — Akitsu** Yd No: 2558 Loa 41.64 Br ex - Dght 2.801 Lbp 37.80 Br md 11.00 Dpth 3.81 Welded, 1 dk	**(A36A2PR) Passenger/Ro-Ro Ship (Vehicles)** Passengers: unberthed: 242 Trailers: 7	**2 oil engines** with flexible couplings & reverse reduction geared to sc. shafts driving 2 FP propellers Total Power: 1,250kW (1,700hp) 12.7kn Niigata 6M26BGT 2 x 4 Stroke 6 Cy. 260 x 460 each-625kW (850bhp) Niigata Engineering Co Ltd-Japan
8865341 - -	**SUPER SHUTTLE FERRY 20** *ex* Shuttle No. 3 *-2010* **Asian Marine Transport Corp** - *Cebu* *Philippines* Official number: CEB1008214	*353* 111 70		**1992-12 Kanbara Zosen K.K. — Onomichi** Yd No: 433 Loa 49.00 Br ex - Dght 3.000 Lbp 38.70 Br md 9.50 Dpth 3.60 Welded, 1 dk	**(A36A2PR) Passenger/Ro-Ro Ship (Vehicles)**	**2 oil engines** with clutches, flexible couplings & geared to sc. shafts driving 2 Propellers 1 fwd and 1 aft Total Power: 1,176kW (1,598hp) Daihatsu 6DLM-26FSL 2 x 4 Stroke 6 Cy. 260 x 340 each-588kW (799bhp) Daihatsu Diesel Manufacturing Co Lt-Japan
7935280 *DUH2670* -	**SUPER SHUTTLE FERRY 23** *ex* Oshima No. 3 *-2009* *ex* Oshima *-2001* **Asian Marine Transport Corp** - *Cebu* *Philippines* Official number: CEB1008186	*195* 137 105		**1979-11 K.K. Kawamoto Zosensho — Osakikamijima** Yd No: 83 Loa 40.01 Br ex 10.01 Dght 2.131 Lbp 35.01 Br md 8.60 Dpth 3.00 Welded, 1 dk	**(A36A2PR) Passenger/Ro-Ro Ship (Vehicles)**	**1 oil engine** driving 1 FP propeller Total Power: 588kW (799hp)
8319586 *DUH2871* -	**SUPER SHUTTLE FERRY 24** *ex* Hamatsubaki *-2010* **Asian Marine Transport Corp** - *Cebu* *Philippines* Official number: CEB1008250	*170* 119 55		**1984-03 Suzuki Shipyard Co. Ltd. — Yokkaichi** Yd No: 501 Loa 30.61 Br ex - Dght 1.878 Lbp 27.01 Br md 9.61 Dpth 3.08 Welded, 1 dk	**(A36A2PR) Passenger/Ro-Ro Ship (Vehicles)** Passengers: unberthed: 126	**2 oil engines** sr geared to sc. shafts driving 2 FP propellers Total Power: 486kW (660hp) Kubota M6D17BHCS 2 x 4 Stroke 6 Cy. 174 x 205 each-243kW (330bhp) Kubota Tekkosho-Japan
8211057 *DUH2385* -	**SUPER SHUTTLE FERRY V** *ex* Gothong Shuttle Ferry 1 *-2002* *ex* Dogo Maru *-1997* **Asian Marine Transport Corp** Super Shuttle Ferry *Cebu* *Philippines* Official number: CEB1003059	*565* 265 215		**1982-12 Wakamatsu Zosen K.K. — Kitakyushu** Yd No: 331 Loa 44.40 Br ex 11.51 Dght 2.801 Lbp 40.59 Br md 10.91 Dpth 3.71 Welded, 1 dk	**(A36A2PR) Passenger/Ro-Ro Ship (Vehicles)** Passengers: unberthed: 350 Cars: 50, Trailers: 14	**2 oil engines** with clutches, flexible couplings & dr reverse geared to sc. shafts driving 2 FP propellers Total Power: 1,104kW (1,500hp) 13.0kn Daihatsu 6PSHTCM-26H 2 x 4 Stroke 6 Cy. 260 x 320 each-552kW (750bhp) Daihatsu Diesel Manufacturing Co Lt-Japan

Identity	Name / Owner	Tonnage	Class	Build / Dimensions	Type / Capacity	Machinery
8615722 *DUH2676* -	**SUPER SHUTTLE RORO 2** *ex* Koyo Maru No. 23 *-2010* **Asian Marine Transport Corp** - *Cebu* *Philippines* Official number: CEB1008149	*1,737* 1,181 1,463		**1987**-03 **Imamura Zosen — Kure** Yd No: 317 Loa 90.02 (BB) Br ex 14.23 Dght 4.801 Lbp 81.72 Br md 14.20 Dpth 11.66 Welded, 2 dks	**(A35B2RV) Vehicles Carrier**	**1 oil engine** with flexible couplings & sr gearedto sc. shaft driving 1 CP propeller Total Power: 2,427kW (3,300hp) Hanshin 6EL40 1 x 4 Stroke 6 Cy. 400 x 800 2427kW (3300bhp) The Hanshin Diesel Works Ltd-Japan Thrusters: 1 Thwart. CP thruster (a)
8808173 *4DEH3* -	**SUPER SHUTTLE RORO 3** *ex* Atsuta Maru *-2009* **Asian Marine Transport Corp** - *Cebu* *Philippines* MMSI: 548370100 Official number: CEB1008216	**7,023** 4,795 4,621	Class: (NK)	**1989**-01 **Kanda Zosensho K.K. — Kawajiri** Yd No: 319 Lengthened-1998 Loa 128.80 (BB) Br ex 19.92 Dght 5.975 Lbp 120.30 Br md 19.90 Dpth 6.84 Welded	**(A35B2RV) Vehicles Carrier** Quarter stern door/ramp (p. a.) Quarter stern door/ramp (s. a.) Cars: 904	**1 oil engine** driving 1 CP propeller Total Power: 6,473kW (8,801hp) 18.0kn B&W 8L42MC 1 x 2 Stroke 8 Cy. 420 x 1360 6473kW (8801bhp) (made 1988) Hitachi Zosen Corp-Japan AuxGen: 3 x 480kW 450V 60Hz a.c Fuel: 475.0 (r.f.)
7822500 *DUH3289* -	**SUPER SHUTTLE RORO 5** *ex* Sandy III *-2012* *ex* Tajura *-2005* **Asian Marine Transport Corp** - *Cebu* *Philippines* Official number: CEB1008744	**6,105** 1,832 2,900	Class: GL	**1980**-05 **Schlichting-Werft GmbH — Luebeck** Yd No: 1413 Loa 111.16 (BB) Br ex 17.91 Dght 5.160 Lbp 98.51 Br md 17.70 Dpth 11.76 Welded, 2 dks	**(A35A2RR) Ro-Ro Cargo Ship** Passengers: driver berths: 12 Stern door/ramp (centre) Len: 15.00 Wid: 8.00 Swl: 92 Lane-Len: 1020 Lane-Wid: 13.00 Lane-clr ht: 6.26 Trailers: 63 Grain: 12,150; Bale: 11,133 TEU 199 C RoRo Dk 134 TEU C Dk 65 TEU Compartments: 1 Ho, ER Ice Capable	**2 oil engines** reduction geared to sc. shafts driving 2 CP propellers Total Power: 3,310kW (4,500hp) 16.0kn MaK 6M453AK 2 x 4 Stroke 6 Cy. 320 x 420 each-1655kW (2250bhp) Krupp MaK Maschinenbau GmbH-Kiel AuxGen: 3 x 446kW 450V 60Hz a.c, 1 x 56kW 450V 60Hz a.c Thrusters: 1 Thwart. FP thruster (f) Fuel: 77.0 (d.f.) 355.5 (r.f.) 18.5pd
9117727 *DUH3329* -	**SUPER SHUTTLE RORO 7** *ex* Asiana Breeze *-2013* *ex* Southern Breeze *-2009* *ex* Dia Ace *-2000* **Asian Marine Transport Corp** - *Cebu* *Philippines* Official number: CEB1008810	**13,540** 4,062 4,339	Class: NK	**1994**-11 **Mitsubishi Heavy Industries Ltd. — Shimonoseki** Yd No: 994 Loa 146.00 (BB) Br ex 23.40 Dght 5.719 Lbp 135.00 Br md 21.40 Dpth 13.20 Welded, 2 dks	**(A35A2RR) Ro-Ro Cargo Ship** Quarter bow door/ramp (s) Len: 20.00 Wid: 6.50 Swl: - Quarter stern door/ramp (s) Len: 20.00 Wid: 6.50 Swl: - Lane-Len: 1200 Cars: 524	**1 oil engine** with flexible couplings & sr geared to sc. shaft driving 1 FP propeller Total Power: 5,149kW (7,001hp) 15.0kn Pielstick 12PC2-6V-400 1 x Vee 4 Stroke 12 Cy. 400 x 460 5149kW (7001bhp) Nippon Kokan KK (NKK Corp)-Japan AuxGen: 2 x 809kW a.c Thrusters: 1 Thwart. CP thruster (f) Fuel: 485.0 (r.f.) 18.4pd
8413992 *DUH3322* -	**SUPER SHUTTLE RORO 8** *ex* Cimbria *-2012* *ex* Cimbria Seaways *-2011* *ex* Aquae *-2011* *ex* Tor Cimbria *-2006* *ex* Dana Cimbria *-2000* *launched as* Mercandian Express II *-1986* **Asian Marine Transport Corp** - *Cebu* *Philippines* Official number: CEB1008774	**12,189** 3,656 6,897	Class: NV	**1986**-04 **Frederikshavn Vaerft A/S — Frederikshavn** Yd No: 417 Loa 145.01 (BB) Br ex 21.59 Dght 6.620 Lbp 135.01 Br md 20.40 Dpth 12.15 Welded, 2 dks	**(A35A2RR) Ro-Ro Cargo Ship** Passengers: cabins: 6; berths: 12 Stern door/ramp (s) Len: 14.50 Wid: 6.50 Swl: 100 Stern door/ramp (p. lwr) Len: 7.60 Wid: 6.50 Swl: - Stern door/ramp (p. upr) Len: 7.20 Wid: 6.50 Swl: - Lane-Len: 2026 Lane-Wid: 6.50 Lane-clr ht: 4.50 Trailers: 160 Bale: 20,941 TEU 458 incl 360 ref C.	**1 oil engine** with flexible couplings & sr gearedto sc. shaft driving 1 CP propeller Total Power: 6,618kW (8,998hp) 17.0kn MaK 6M601AK 1 x 4 Stroke 6 Cy. 580 x 600 6618kW (8998bhp) Krupp MaK Maschinenbau GmbH-Kiel AuxGen: 1 x 1900kW 440V 60Hz a.c, 2 x 1136kW 440V 60Hz a.c Thrusters: 1 Thwart. CP thruster (f); 2 Thwart. CP thruster (a)
7902647 *DUH3407* -	**SUPER SHUTTLE RORO 9** *ex* Queen V *-2013* *ex* Medqueen *-2013* *ex* Norqueen *-2013* *ex* Bore Queen *-1991* **Asian Marine Transport Corp** Hermes Maritime Services Pvt Ltd *Cebu* *Philippines*	**17,884** 5,366 11,400	Class: LR ✠ **100A1** SS 12/2010 Ice Class 1A ✠ **LMC** **UMS** Eq.Ltr: (E†) ; Cable: 577.5/66.0 U2	**1980**-12 **Rauma-Repola Oy — Rauma** Yd No: 261 Lengthened-1995 Loa 170.93 (BB) Br ex 23.04 Dght 7.617 Lbp 158.80 Br md 23.00 Dpth 17.51 Welded, 2 dks, 1 movable dk (hoistable) in Tw dk	**(A35A2RR) Ro-Ro Cargo Ship** Passengers: driver berths: 12 Stern door/ramp (centre) Len: 14.20 Wid: 15.00 Swl: 60 Lane-Len: 2067 Lane-Wid: 2.70 Lane-clr ht: 7.10 Cars: 920, Trailers: 155 Bale: 23,874 TEU 572 incl 55 ref C. Compartments: 1 Ho, ER 1 Ha: ER Ice Capable	**2 oil engines** with clutches, flexible couplings & sr geared to sc. shafts driving 2 CP propellers Total Power: 12,000kW (16,316hp) 17.5kn MaK 8M552C 2 x 4 Stroke 8 Cy. 450 x 520 each-6000kW (8158bhp) (new engine 1996) Krupp MaK Maschinenbau GmbH-Kiel AuxGen: 1 x 800kW 400V 50Hz a.c, 3 x 568kW 400V 50Hz a.c Thrusters: 2 Thwart. FP thruster (f) Fuel: 255.0 (d.f.) 988.0 (r.f.) 45.0pd
7647845 *WYC2634* -	**SUPER STAR** **Pacific Emerald Seafoods Inc** - *Seattle, WA* *United States of America* Official number: 580199	*142* 96 -		**1977 Marine Builders, Inc. — Mobile, Al** L reg 23.47 Br ex 6.84 Dght - Lbp - Br md - Dpth 3.38 Welded, 1dk	**(B11B2FV) Fishing Vessel**	**1 oil engine** driving 1 FP propeller Total Power: 268kW (364hp)
9469247 *3ESQ3* -	**SUPER STAR** **Cypress Navigation Co SA** Lizstar (Singapore) Pte Ltd *Panama* *Panama* MMSI: 370393000 Official number: 3420208A	**9,932** 4,569 14,376 T/cm 22.0	Class: NK	**2008**-08 **Higaki Zosen K.K. — Imabari** Yd No: 616 Loa 127.66 (BB) Br ex - Dght 9.446 Lbp 119.50 Br md 19.60 Dpth 14.50 Welded, 1 dk	**(A31A2GX) General Cargo Ship** Grain: 20,085; Bale: 18,818 Cranes: 3x30.7t	**1 oil engine** driving 1 FP propeller Total Power: 4,200kW (5,710hp) 13.5kn MAN-B&W 6S35MC 1 x 2 Stroke 6 Cy. 350 x 1400 4200kW (5710bhp) Makita Corp-Japan Fuel: 740.0 (r.f.)
8122969 *H3MW*	**SUPER SUN** *ex* Hope 2 *-2002* *ex* Super Sun *-2001* *ex* Seven Pioneer *-2000* *ex* Roubini *-1997* *ex* Nordic Trader *-1992* *ex* Elm Trader *-1992* *ex* Scan Trader *-1982* **Sea Commander Shipping SA** Jui Zong Ship Management Co Ltd *Panama* *Panama* MMSI: 355569000 Official number: 3025004A	**11,256** 6,546 18,791 T/cm 28.2	Class: CR (LR) (KR) (BV) (NV) (NK) Classed LR until 31/7/97	**1982**-08 **Sasebo Heavy Industries Co. Ltd. — Sasebo Yard, Sasebo** Yd No: 309 Loa 146.07 (BB) Br ex 22.89 Dght 9.315 Lbp 137.01 Br md 22.86 Dpth 12.60 Welded, 1 dk	**(A21A2BC) Bulk Carrier** Grain: 23,197; Bale: 22,378 Compartments: 4 Ho, ER 4 Ha: (16.0 x 9.6)3 (19.2 x 11.2)ER Derricks: 4x25t	**1 oil engine** driving 1 FP propeller Total Power: 5,884kW (8,000hp) 13.5kn Mitsubishi 6UEC52/125H 1 x 2 Stroke 6 Cy. 520 x 1250 5884kW (8000bhp) Kobe Hatsudoki KK-Japan AuxGen: 2 x 340kW 440V 60Hz a.c Fuel: 180.0 (d.f.) 1621.5 (r.f.) 25.0pd
7340801 - -	**SUPER T** *ex* Super Trader *-1996* *ex* Todra *-1995* **Transportadora Maritima de Combustible (TRAMACO SA)** -	**1,807** 693 2,405	Class: (RI) (BV)	**1974**-07 **Cochrane & Sons Ltd. — Selby** Yd No: 1547 Loa 80.37 Br ex - Dght 4.701 Lbp 79.25 Br md 12.43 Dpth 5.29 Welded, 1 dk	**(A13B2TP) Products Tanker** Single Hull Liq: 2,584; Liq (Oil): 2,584 Compartments: 10 Ta, ER	**1 oil engine** driving 1 FP propeller Total Power: 1,765kW (2,400hp) 13.0kn MWM TBD500-8 1 x 4 Stroke 8 Cy. 360 x 450 1765kW (2400bhp) Motoren Werke Mannheim AG (MWM)-West Germany Fuel: 173.0 (d.f.)
7216658 - -	**SUPER TIDE** **Marine Welding Services** - *United Arab Emirates*	*198* 134 -	Class: (AB)	**1965 Burton Shipyard Co., Inc. — Port Arthur, Tx** Yd No: 382 Loa 50.30 Br ex - Dght 2.998 Lbp 47.00 Br md 11.59 Dpth 3.66 Welded, 1 dk	**(B21A20S) Platform Supply Ship**	**2 oil engines** sr geared to sc. shafts driving 2 FP propellers Total Power: 1,126kW (1,530hp) Caterpillar D398SCAC 2 x Vee 4 Stroke 12 Cy. 159 x 203 each-563kW (765bhp) Caterpillar Tractor Co-USA AuxGen: 2 x 60kW 240/480V 60Hz a.c Fuel: 110.5 (d.f.)
8739176 *9WHF8* -	**SUPER TOP 1** **Top Intergroup Sdn Bhd** - *Kuching* *Malaysia* MMSI: 533000753 Official number: 330929	**126** 38 -		**2007**-10 **Sapor Shipbuilding Industries Sdn Bhd — Sibu** Loa 23.22 Br ex - Dght 2.400 Lbp 21.14 Br md 6.70 Dpth 2.95 Welded, 1 dk	**(B32A2ST) Tug**	**2 oil engines** reduction geared to sc. shafts driving 2 FP propellers Total Power: 894kW (1,216hp) Cummins KTA-19-M3 2 x 4 Stroke 6 Cy. 159 x 159 each-447kW (608bhp) Chongqing Cummins Engine Co Ltd-China
9106663 *3FHX5* -	**SUPER ZEARTH** **Zearth Tanker Corp** Idemitsu Tanker Co Ltd SatCom: Inmarsat C 435534410 *Panama* *Panama* MMSI: 355344000 Official number: 2239495E	**148,362** 82,276 265,253 T/cm 171.0	Class: NK	**1995**-09 **Ishikawajima-Harima Heavy Industries Co Ltd (IHI) — Kure** Yd No: 3053 Loa 333.00 (BB) Br ex - Dght 19.530 Lbp 319.00 Br md 60.00 Dpth 28.65 Welded, 1 dk	**(A13A2TV) Crude Oil Tanker** Double Hull Liq: 319,942; Liq (Oil): 319,942 Compartments: 5 Ta, 10 Wing Ta, ER 3 Cargo Pump (s): 3x4500m³/hr	**1 oil engine** driving 1 FP propeller Total Power: 22,000kW (29,911hp) 15.6kn Sulzer 7RTA84T 1 x 2 Stroke 7 Cy. 840 x 3150 22000kW (29911bhp) Diesel United Ltd.-Aioi AuxGen: 1 x 900kW 450V 60Hz a.c, 2 x 920kW 450V 60Hz a.c, 1 x 430kW 450V 60Hz a.c Fuel: 5268.0 (r.f.) 81.3pd

9538165 *C6AR9* -	**SUPERBA** **Skylark Seacarriers Ltd** Super-Eco Tankers Management Inc *Nassau* Bahamas MMSI: 311000133 Official number: 700564	**25,269** 10,334 37,949 T/cm 47.5	Class: NV	**2014-03 Guangzhou Shipyard International Co Ltd — Guangzhou GD** Yd No: 08131014 Loa 183.00 (BB) Br ex 31.28 Dght 10.515 Lbp 178.50 Br md 31.00 Dpth 16.00 Welded, 1 dk	**(A12B2TR) Chemical/Products Tanker** Double Hull (13F) Liq: 39,900; Liq (Oil): 51,470 Compartments: 6 Wing Ta, 6 Wing Ta, 1 Wing Slop Ta, 1 Wing Slop Ta, ER 12 Cargo Pump (s): 12x500m^3/hr Manifold: Bow/CM: 88m	**1 oil engine** driving 1 FP propeller Total Power: 8,900kW (12,100hp) 14.2kn MAN-B&W 5S50ME-B9 1 x 2 Stroke 5 Cy. 500 x 2214 8900kW (12100bhp) Dalian Marine Diesel Co Ltd-China AuxGen: 3 x a.c Thrusters: 1 Tunnel thruster (f) Fuel: 130.0 (d.f.) 1180.0 (r.f.)
8982474 - -	**SUPERBOAT** **Yongyuth Hemjinda** - *Bangkok* Thailand Official number: 460003648	**295** 139 -		**2003-10 Mits Decisions Co., Ltd. — Samut Sakhon** Loa 36.20 Br ex - Dght - Lbp - Br md 7.50 Dpth 4.30 Welded, 1 dk	**(B12B2FC) Fish Carrier**	**1 oil engine** geared to sc. shaft driving 1 Propeller Total Power: 596kW (810hp) Cummins 1 x 4 Stroke 596kW (810bhp) Cummins Engine Co Inc-USA
7212511 *HP6467* -	**SUPERCARGO** *ex* Kyowa Maru No. 11 *-1991* *ex* Yutaka Maru *-1980* **Super Charter Ltd** - *Panama* Panama Official number: D4871789PEXT	*199* 111 650		**1970 Sasaki Shipbuilding Co Ltd — Osakikamijima HS** Yd No: 147 Loa 48.77 Br ex 8.03 Dght 3.201 Lbp 45.01 Br md 8.01 Dpth 3.31 Welded, 1 dk	**(A31A2GX) General Cargo Ship**	**1 oil engine** driving 1 FP propeller Total Power: 515kW (700hp) 11.0kn Niigata 6M26KCHS 1 x 4 Stroke 6 Cy. 260 x 400 515kW (700bhp) Niigata Engineering Co Ltd-Japan
8843331 - -	**SUPERCARGO No. 2** *ex* Takuho Maru No. 2 *-1991* *ex* Taiyo Maru No. 5 *-1991* - -	*194* 90 550		**1970 K.K. Watanabe Zosensho — Nagasaki** Loa 40.20 Br ex - Dght 3.100 Lbp 36.00 Br md 7.80 Dpth 4.50 Welded, 1 dk	**(A31A2GX) General Cargo Ship** 1 Ha: (18.5 x 6.2)ER	**1 oil engine** driving 1 FP propeller Total Power: 405kW (551hp) 10.0kn Hanshin 1 x 4 Stroke 405kW (551bhp) The Hanshin Diesel Works Ltd-Japan
8814134 *DUH2246* -	**SUPERCAT 2** *ex* Camoes *-1995* **Philippine Fast Ferry Corp** Supercat Fast Ferry Corp *Cebu* Philippines Official number: CEB1001053	**449** 152 110	Class: (NV)	**1990-07 FBM Marinteknik (S) Pte Ltd — Singapore** Yd No: 119 Loa 41.51 Br ex 11.04 Dght 1.196 Lbp 36.85 Br md 11.02 Dpth 3.77 Welded, 1 dk	**(A37B2PS) Passenger Ship** Hull Material: Aluminium Alloy Passengers: unberthed: 306	**2 oil engines** with clutches, flexible couplings & sr geared to sc. shafts driving 2 Water jets Total Power: 3,878kW (5,272hp) 38.0kn M.T.U. 16V396TB84 2 x Vee 4 Stroke 16 Cy. 165 x 185 each-1939kW (2636bhp) MTU Friedrichshafen GmbH-Friedrichshafen AuxGen: 2 x 52kW 220/380V 50Hz a.c
8745589 *DUH3123* -	**SUPERCAT 26** *ex* Seacat *-2011* **International Broking Services Pty Ltd** Supercat Fast Ferry Corp *Cebu* Philippines Official number: CEB1008342	**175** 123 -		**1998 West Boat Builders Pty Ltd — Fremantle WA** Yd No: 4 Loa 26.00 Br ex - Dght 1.600 Lbp - Br md 8.60 Dpth 2.50 Welded, 1 dk	**(A37B2PS) Passenger Ship** Hull Material: Aluminium Alloy	**2 oil engines** REDUCTION: reduction geared to sc. shafts driving 2 Propellers Total Power: 1,640kW (2,230hp) 25.0kn Caterpillar C32 2 x Vee 4 Stroke 12 Cy. 145 x 162 each-820kW (1115bhp) (new engine 2010) Caterpillar Inc-USA AuxGen: 2 x 60kW a.c
8911803 *DUH2679* -	**SUPERCAT 36** *ex* Blue Fin *-2010* **Supercat Fast Ferry Corp** - *Cebu* Philippines Official number: CEB1008200	**238** 167 50	Class: LR ✠ **100A1** SS 04/2010 catamaran, for Batangas to Calapan service in reasonable weather ✠ **LMC** Cable: 130.0/16.0 U2	**1990-04 North Queensland Engineers & Agents Pty Ltd — Cairns QLD** Yd No: 163 Loa 34.80 Br ex 10.00 Dght 2.500 Lbp 31.65 Br md 9.56 Dpth 3.25 Welded, 1 dk	**(A37B2PS) Passenger Ship** Hull Material: Aluminium Alloy Passengers: unberthed: 250	**2 oil engines** with clutches, flexible couplings & sr geared to sc. shafts driving 2 Water jets Total Power: 3,360kW (4,568hp) 34.0kn MWM TBD604V16 2 x Vee 4 Stroke 16 Cy. 170 x 195 each-1680kW (2284bhp) (new engine 2002) Deutz AG-Koeln AuxGen: 2 x 32kW 415V 50Hz a.c Fuel: 7.6 (d.f.)
8911815 *DUH2677* -	**SUPERCAT 38** *ex* Sir David Martin *-2009* **Supercat Fast Ferry Corp** - *Cebu* Philippines Official number: CEB1008197	*238* 167 50	Class: LR ✠ **100A1** SS 11/2009 catamaran, for Batangas to Calapan service in reasonable weather ✠ **LMC** Cable: 260.0/16.0 U2	**1990-12 North Queensland Engineers & Agents Pty Ltd — Cairns QLD** Yd No: 172 Loa 34.80 Br ex 10.00 Dght 2.390 Lbp 29.35 Br md 9.56 Dpth 3.18 Welded, 1 dk	**(A37B2PS) Passenger Ship** Hull Material: Aluminium Alloy	**2 oil engines** with clutches, flexible couplings & sr geared to sc. shafts driving 2 Water jets Total Power: 3,360kW (4,568hp) MWM TBD604BV16 2 x Vee 4 Stroke 16 Cy. 170 x 195 each-1680kW (2284bhp) (new engine 2002) Deutz AG-Koeln AuxGen: 2 x 32kW 415V 50Hz a.c
9622277 *XVRH* -	**SUPERDONG III** **Superdong - Kien Giang Fast Ferry Co Ltd** - *Saigon* Vietnam MMSI: 574012604 Official number: VNSG-2025-TK	**242** 100 91	Class: VR	**2010-06 Jana Seribu Shipbuilding (M) Sdn Bhd — Sibu** Yd No: TG0901 Loa 46.90 Br ex 6.70 Dght 1.250 Lbp 41.90 Br md 5.50 Dpth 2.30 Welded, 1 dk	**(A37B2PS) Passenger Ship** Hull Material: Aluminium Alloy Passengers: unberthed: 306	**2 oil engines** reduction geared to sc. shafts driving 2 FP propellers Total Power: 2,420kW (3,290hp) 27.0kn Mitsubishi S12R-MPTK 2 x Vee 4 Stroke 12 Cy. 170 x 180 each-1210kW (1645bhp) Mitsubishi Heavy Industries Ltd-Japan AuxGen: 2 x 68kW 380V a.c
9647265 *3WDS9* -	**SUPERDONG IV** **Superdong - Kien Giang Fast Ferry Co Ltd** - *Saigon* Vietnam Official number: VNSG-2089-TK	**242** 100 82	Class: VR	**2011-07 Kaibuok Shipyard (M) Sdn Bhd — Sibu** Yd No: TG02 Loa 46.95 Br ex 6.70 Dght 1.250 Lbp 41.90 Br md 5.50 Dpth 2.30 Welded, 1 dk	**(A37B2PS) Passenger Ship** Hull Material: Aluminium Alloy Passengers: unberthed: 306	**2 oil engines** reduction geared to sc. shafts driving 2 Propellers Total Power: 2,420kW (3,290hp) 27.0kn Mitsubishi S12R-MPTK 2 x Vee 4 Stroke 12 Cy. 170 x 180 each-1210kW (1645bhp) Mitsubishi Heavy Industries Ltd-Japan
9693044 *XVPQ9* -	**SUPERDONG V** **Superdong - Kien Giang Fast Ferry Co Ltd** - *Saigon* Vietnam Official number: 23/2012/TT	**157** 97 85	Class: VR	**2012-12 Jana Seribu Shipbuilding (M) Sdn Bhd — Sibu** Yd No: TG10 Loa 45.99 Br ex 6.20 Dght 1.250 Lbp 42.40 Br md 5.00 Dpth 2.30 Welded, 1 dk	**(A37B2PS) Passenger Ship** Hull Material: Aluminium Alloy	**2 oil engines** reduction geared to sc. shafts driving 2 FP propellers Total Power: 1,518kW (2,064hp) 27.0kn Mitsubishi S6R2-MTK3L 2 x 4 Stroke 6 Cy. 170 x 220 each-759kW (1032bhp) Mitsubishi Heavy Industries Ltd-Japan AuxGen: 2 x 69kW 380V a.c Fuel: 14.0
9702819 *3WLA* -	**SUPERDONG VI** **Superdong - Kien Giang Fast Ferry Co Ltd** - *Saigon* Vietnam Official number: VNSG-06/2013TT	**157** 74 85	Class: VR	**2013-05 Kaibuok Shipyard (M) Sdn Bhd — Sibu** Yd No: TG02 Loa 45.99 Br ex 6.20 Dght 1.250 Lbp 42.40 Br md 5.00 Dpth 2.30 Welded, 1 dk	**(A37B2PS) Passenger Ship** Hull Material: Aluminium Alloy Passengers: unberthed: 275	**2 oil engines** reduction geared to sc. shafts driving 2 FP propellers Total Power: 1,518kW (2,064hp) 27.0kn Mitsubishi S6R2-MTK3L 2 x 4 Stroke 6 Cy. 170 x 220 each-759kW (1032bhp) Mitsubishi Heavy Industries Ltd-Japan AuxGen: 2 x 65kW 380V a.c Fuel: 14.0
9399325 *EADD* -	**SUPERFAST BALEARES** **Naviera Ciboulette AIE** Cia Trasmediterranea SA (Acciona Trasmediterranea) *Santa Cruz de Tenerife* Spain (CSR) MMSI: 225430000	**30,998** 18,547 10,140	Class: BV	**2010-06 Navantia SA — Puerto Real** Yd No: 510 Loa 209.00 (BB) Br ex - Dght 7.100 Lbp 190.00 Br md 26.50 Dpth 23.55 Welded, 4 dks	**(A35A2RR) Ro-Ro Cargo Ship** Passengers: driver berths: 12 Stern door/ramp (centre) Len: 18.60 Wid: 15.00 Swl: - Lane-Len: 3530 Lane-clr ht: 6.80 Cars: 100, Trailers: 210	**4 oil engines** reduction geared to sc. shafts driving 2 CP propellers Total Power: 43,200kW (58,736hp) 26.0kn MAN-B&W 9L48/60B 4 x 4 Stroke 9 Cy. 480 x 600 each-10800kW (14684bhp) MAN B&W Diesel AG-Augsburg AuxGen: 3 x 1635kW 400V 50Hz a.c, 2 x 2000kW 400V 50Hz a.c Thrusters: 2 Tunnel thruster (f) Fuel: 150.0 (d.f.) 1050.0 (r.f.) 173.0pd
9131527 *9HA3275* -	**SUPERFAST CANARIAS** *ex* Brabant *-1998* **Cia Trasmediterranea SA (Acciona Trasmediterranea)** - *Valletta* Malta MMSI: 229368000 Official number: 9131527	**26,536** 16,740 11,600	Class: NV	**1998-04 Fincantieri-Cant. Nav. Italiani S.p.A. — Ancona** Yd No: 5995 Loa 185.00 (BB) Br ex - Dght 7.700 Lbp 170.00 Br md 25.30 Dpth 17.00 Welded, 2 dks	**(A35A2RR) Ro-Ro Cargo Ship** Passengers: berths: 12; driver berths: 12 Stern door/ramp (a) Len: 13.00 Wid: 15.00 Swl: - Lane-Len: 3465 Trailers: 240 Ice Capable	**2 oil engines** reduction geared to sc. shafts driving 2 CP propellers Total Power: 25,020kW (34,018hp) 22.0kn MAN 9L58/64 2 x 4 Stroke 9 Cy. 580 x 640 each-12510kW (17009bhp) MAN B&W Diesel AG-Augsburg AuxGen: 3 x 1200kW 220/440V 60Hz a.c Thrusters: 2 Thwart. FP thruster (f) Fuel: 1500.0 (r.f.) 105.0pd

IMO / Call sign	Name / Owner	Tonnage	Class	Builder / Dimensions	Type	Machinery
9350719 *SVAK2* -	**SUPERFAST I** **Superfast One Inc** SuperFast Ferries SA *Piraeus* *Greece* MMSI: 240815000 Official number: 11802	**25,757** 11,426 8,500	Class: RI	**2008-10 Nuovi Cantieri Apuania SpA — Carrara** Yd No: 1240 Loa 198.99 (BB) Br ex 27.00 Dght 6.400 Lbp 176.92 Br md 26.61 Dpth 15.30 Welded, 1 dk	**(A36A2PR) Passenger/Ro-Ro Ship (Vehicles)** Passengers: unberthed: 578; cabins: 103; berths: 375 Stern door/ramp (p. a.) Len: 13.00 Wid: 7.60 Swl: - Stern door/ramp (s. a.) Len: 13.00 Wid: 13.90 Swl: - Lane-Len: 2623 Cars: 120	**2 oil engines** reduction geared to sc. shafts driving 2 CP propellers Total Power: 24,000kW (32,630hp) 24.0kn Wartsila 12V46 2 x Vee 4 Stroke 12 Cy. 460 x 580 each-12000kW (16315bhp) Wartsila Italia SpA-Italy AuxGen: 3 x 1600kW a.c Thrusters: 2 Thwart. CP thruster (f) Fuel: 135.0 1085.0 87.0pd
9458511 *SVAU2* -	**SUPERFAST II** **Superfast Two Inc** SuperFast Ferries SA *Piraeus* *Greece* MMSI: 240951000 Official number: 11930	**25,518** 11,559 7,500	Class: RI	**2009-09 Nuovi Cantieri Apuania SpA — Carrara** (Aft section) Yd No: 1242 **2009-09 Fincantieri-Cant. Nav. Italiani S.p.A. — Ancona** (Fwd section) Loa 198.99 (BB) Br ex - Dght 6.400 Lbp 176.92 Br md 26.60 Dpth 9.60 Welded, 1 dk	**(A36A2PR) Passenger/Ro-Ro Ship (Vehicles)** Passengers: 950 Stern door/ramp (p. a.) Stern door/ramp (s. a.) Lorries: 140, Cars: 100	**2 oil engines** geared to sc. shafts driving 2 CP propellers Total Power: 25,200kW (34,262hp) 24.0kn Wartsila 12V46 2 x Vee 4 Stroke 12 Cy. 460 x 580 each-12600kW (17131bhp) Wartsila Italia SpA-Italy
9227417 *SYCF* -	**SUPERFAST XI** **SuperFast Endeka Inc** SuperFast Ferries SA *Piraeus* *Greece* MMSI: 239918000 Official number: 11026	**30,902** 11,667 6,574 T/cm 40.4	Class: AB	**2002-07 Flender Werft AG — Luebeck** Yd No: 682 Loa 199.90 (BB) Br ex - Dght 6.580 Lbp 186.00 Br md 25.00 Dpth 14.50 Welded, 11 dks	**(A36A2PR) Passenger/Ro-Ro Ship (Vehicles)** Passengers: 1550; unberthed: 760; cabins: 202; berths: 790 Stern door/ramp (p) Len: 12.00 Wid: 8.00 Swl: - Stern door/ramp (s) Len: 12.00 Wid: 5.00 Swl: - Lane-Len: 2000 Lorries: 130, Cars: 100	**4 oil engines** geared to sc. shafts driving 2 CP propellers Total Power: 48,000kW (65,260hp) 28.5kn Wartsila 12V46C 4 x Vee 4 Stroke 12 Cy. 460 x 580 each-12000kW (16315bhp) Wartsila Finland Oy-Finland AuxGen: 3 x 1472kW a.c, 2 x 1900kW 450/230V 60Hz a.c Thrusters: 2 Thwart. CP thruster (f); 1 Thwart. CP thruster (a) Fuel: 120.0 (d.f.) 1458.0 (r.f.)
9227429 *SYCD* -	**SUPERFAST XII** **Attica Ferries Maritime Co** *Piraeus* *Greece* MMSI: 239919000 Official number: 11052	**30,902** 11,831 6,578 T/cm 40.4	Class: AB	**2002-10 Flender Werft AG — Luebeck** Yd No: 683 Loa 199.90 (BB) Br ex - Dght 6.580 Lbp 186.00 Br md 25.00 Dpth 14.50 Welded, 11 dks	**(A36A2PR) Passenger/Ro-Ro Ship (Vehicles)** Passengers: 1550; unberthed: 729; cabins: 198; berths: 790 Stern door/ramp (p) Len: 9.40 Wid: 8.00 Swl: - Stern door/ramp (s) Len: 9.40 Wid: 8.00 Swl: - Lane-Len: 1915 Lane-Wid: 3.10 Lane-clr ht: 4.85 Lorries: 130, Cars: 100	**4 oil engines** with flexible coupling clutches & geared to sc. shafts driving 2 CP propellers Total Power: 48,000kW (65,260hp) 28.5kn Wartsila 12V46C 4 x Vee 4 Stroke 12 Cy. 460 x 580 each-12000kW (16315bhp) Wartsila Finland Oy-Finland AuxGen: 3 x 1772kW 450V 60Hz a.c, 2 x 1920kW 450V 60Hz a.c Thrusters: 2 Thwart. CP thruster (f); 1 Thwart. CP thruster (a) Fuel: 120.0 (d.f.) (Heating Coils) 1458.0 (r.f.) 125.0pd
7346221 *SWKV* -	**SUPERFERRY II** *ex* Ionian Express *-1992* *ex* Prince Laurent *-1992* **Golden Star Ferries Shipping Co** - *Piraeus* *Greece* MMSI: 237001000 Official number: 9939	*4,986* 2,406 1,029	Class: BV (LR) (HR) ✠ Classed LR until 12/92	**1974-07 N.V. Boelwerf S.A. — Temse** Yd No: 1477 Loa 121.70 (BB) Br ex 19.82 Dght 4.800 Lbp 111.61 Br md 19.21 Dpth 10.45 Welded, 2 dks 3rd dk clear of mchy. space (2nd dk light cargoes only)	**(A36A2PR) Passenger/Ro-Ro Ship (Vehicles)** Passengers: unberthed: 1945; cabins: 21; berths: 62 Bow door & ramp (centre) Stern door/ramp (centre) Len: 7.70 Wid: 6.00 Swl: - Lane-Len: 403 Lane-clr ht: 4.45 Cars: 271	**2 oil engines** reduction geared to sc. shafts driving 2 CP propellers Total Power: 13,240kW (18,002hp) 19.5kn Pielstick 18PC2V-400 2 x Vee 4 Stroke 18 Cy. 400 x 460 each-6620kW (9001bhp) Chantiers de l'Atlantique-France AuxGen: 3 x 504kW 380V 50Hz a.c Thrusters: 1 Thwart. FP thruster (f) Fuel: 1274.0 (d.f.)
8611520 *XCCB9* -	**SUPERFLEX TRADER** *ex* Difko Fyn *-2003* *ex* Superflex Echo *-1995* **Transbordadores del Caribe SA de CV** - SatCom: Inmarsat C 434500284 *Cozumel* *Mexico* MMSI: 345110008	**4,101** 1,230 1,291	Class: (LR) ✠ Classed LR until 4/7/01	**1989-02 North East Shipbuilders Ltd. — Pallion, Sunderland** Yd No: 5 Loa 95.81 Br ex 17.00 Dght 3.612 Lbp 90.02 Br md 15.02 Dpth 9.86 Welded, 2 dks	**(A36A2PR) Passenger/Ro-Ro Ship (Vehicles)** Passengers: unberthed: 253 Bow door/ramp Len: 4.50 Wid: 4.00 Swl: - Stern door/ramp Len: 4.50 Wid: 4.00 Swl: - Quarter bow ramp (s. upr) Len: 6.00 Wid: 3.50 Swl: - Quarter stern ramp (p. upr) Len: 6.00 Wid: 3.50 Swl: - Lane-Len: 608 Lane-Wid: 3.50 Lane-clr ht: 4.20 Lorries: 30, Cars: 36	**10 diesel electric oil engines** driving 10 gen. each 275kW 440V a.c Connecting to 4 elec. motors each (550kW) driving 4 Directional propellers Total Power: 3,420kW (4,650hp) 12.8kn Cummins NTA-855-M 10 x 4 Stroke 6 Cy. 140 x 152 each-342kW (465bhp) Cummins Engine Co Ltd-United Kingdom Fuel: 120.0 (d.f.) 12.0pd
9147368 *ZMA3029* -	**SUPERFLYTE** **Fullers Group Ltd** - *Auckland* *New Zealand* MMSI: 512000928 Official number: 876199	**578** 230 200	Class: BV	**1996-11 WaveMaster International Pty Ltd — Fremantle WA** Yd No: 140 Loa 41.00 Br ex 12.00 Dght 2.500 Lbp 35.80 Br md 12.00 Dpth 3.70 Welded, 1 dk	**(A37B2PS) Passenger Ship** Hull Material: Aluminium Alloy Passengers: unberthed: 640	**2 oil engines** geared to sc. shafts driving 2 FP propellers Total Power: 3,640kW (4,948hp) 26.0kn Deutz TBD620V16 2 x Vee 4 Stroke 16 Cy. 170 x 195 each-1820kW (2474bhp) Motoren Werke Mannheim AG (MWM)-Mannheim
8651867 *ZCCL5* -	**SUPERFUN** *ex* Bossanova *-2011* *ex* Mahogany *-2009* *ex* Winged Glory *-2005* *ex* Walmiki Ii *-2000* **Superfun Ltd** Ulrich Baer *George Town* *Cayman Islands (British)* MMSI: 319163000 Official number: 726716	**333** 100 -	Class: AB	**1993-08 Cantiere Navale Officine Meccaniche Rossato S.r.l. — Marghera** Yd No: 94 Loa 39.57 Br ex - Dght 1.800 Lbp - Br md 7.60 Dpth 3.75 Welded, 1 dk	**(X11A2YP) Yacht**	**2 oil engines** driving 2 Propellers Total Power: 1,420kW (1,930hp) Caterpillar 3508D 2 x Vee 4 Stroke 8 Cy. 170 x 190 each-710kW (965bhp) Caterpillar Inc-USA
7607651 *YHJK* -	**SUPERIN II** *ex* Elida *-2001* *ex* Kyokuho Maru No. 12 *-1991* - - *Belawan* *Indonesia*	**664** 217 1,098 T/cm 4.5	Class: (KI)	**1976-05 Imamura Zosen — Kure** Yd No: 215 Loa 56.32 Br ex 10.04 Dght 4.100 Lbp 52.02 Br md 10.01 Dpth 4.55 Welded, 1 dk	**(A12A2TC) Chemical Tanker**	**1 oil engine** driving 1 FP propeller Total Power: 809kW (1,100hp) Hanshin 6LU28 1 x 4 Stroke 6 Cy. 280 x 440 809kW (1100bhp) Hanshin Nainenki Kogyo-Japan
9149184 *9V5420* -	**SUPERIOR** **PSA Marine Pte Ltd** *Singapore* *Singapore* MMSI: 563000690 Official number: 387662	**291** 87 80	Class: LR ✠ **100A1** SS 06/2012 tug Singapore coastal & 30 miles seaward service ✠ **LMC** Eq.Ltr: F; Cable: 275.0/19.0 U2	**1997-06 Zhenjiang Shipyard — Zhenjiang JS** (Hull) Yd No: KR-96-110803 **1997-06 Kea Resources Pte Ltd — Singapore** Loa 31.00 Br ex 10.10 Dght 2.610 Lbp 28.40 Br md 9.50 Dpth 3.80 Welded, 1 dk	**(B32A2ST) Tug**	**2 oil engines** with clutches, flexible couplings & sr geared to sc. shafts driving 2 Directional propellers Total Power: 2,500kW (3,400hp) 12.0kn Deutz SBV6M628 2 x 4 Stroke 6 Cy. 240 x 280 each-1250kW (1700bhp) Motoren Werke Mannheim AG (MWM)-Mannheim AuxGen: 2 x 85kW 415V 50Hz a.c
9172038 *5IQP17* -	**SUPERIOR** *ex* Daisy *-2013* *ex* Susangird *-2012* *ex* Iran Susangird *-2008* **Daisy Shipping Co Ltd** NITC *Zanzibar* *Tanzania (Zanzibar)* MMSI: 677001600	**81,479** 50,676 159,681 T/cm 117.5	Class: (GL) (NV)	**1999-09 Daewoo Heavy Industries Ltd — Geoje** Yd No: 5131 Loa 274.00 (BB) Br ex 48.04 Dght 17.022 Lbp 264.00 Br md 48.00 Dpth 23.20 Welded, 1 dk	**(A13A2TV) Crude Oil Tanker** Double Hull (13F) Liq: 166,683; Liq (Oil): 169,880 Compartments: 12 Wing Ta, ER, 2 Wing Slop Ta 3 Cargo Pump (s): 3x3500m³/hr Manifold: Bow/CM: 129m	**1 oil engine** driving 1 FP propeller Total Power: 16,853kW (22,913hp) 15.2kn B&W 6S70MC 1 x 2 Stroke 6 Cy. 700 x 2674 16853kW (22913bhp) Korea Heavy Industries & ConstrCo Ltd (HANJUNG)-South Korea AuxGen: 3 x 970kW 450V 60Hz a.c Fuel: 281.6 (d.f.) (Heating Coils) 4491.0 (r.f.) 70.2pd
9553220 *D5AU4* -	**SUPERIOR** **Sea Transport Investments SA** Leros Management SA SatCom: Inmarsat C 463712355 *Monrovia* *Liberia* MMSI: 636015447 Official number: 15447	**32,987** 19,238 56,556 T/cm 58.8	Class: LR ✠ **100A1** SS 06/2012 bulk carrier CSR BC-A GRAB (20) Nos. 2 & 4 holds may be empty ESP **ShipRight** (CM) *IWS LI ✠ **LMC** **UMS** Eq.Ltr: M†; Cable: 632.5/73.0 U3 (a)	**2012-06 COSCO (Zhoushan) Shipyard Co Ltd — Zhoushan ZJ** Yd No: N193 Loa 189.99 (BB) Br ex 32.30 Dght 12.800 Lbp 185.60 Br md 32.26 Dpth 18.00 Welded, 1 dk	**(A21A2BC) Bulk Carrier** Grain: 71,634; Bale: 68,200 Compartments: 5 Ho, ER 5 Ha: ER Cranes: 4x30t	**1 oil engine** driving 1 FP propeller Total Power: 9,480kW (12,889hp) 14.2kn MAN-B&W 6S50MC-C 1 x 2 Stroke 6 Cy. 500 x 2000 9480kW (12889bhp) Hyundai Heavy Industries Co Ltd-South Korea AuxGen: 3 x 600kW 450V 60Hz a.c Boilers: AuxB (Comp) 9.2kgf/cm² (9.0bar)

8101472 **SUPERIOR GLORY**
9WEB *ex Swee Long Satu -1992*
\- **Superior Shipping Sdn Bhd**
Meling Trading Agencies
Labuan *Malaysia*
MMSI: 533553000
Official number: 324886

832 430 1,310 Class: (AB)

1981-02 Orion Tuas Shipyard Pte Ltd — Singapore Yd No: OTS-1
Loa - Br ex - Dght 3.760
Lbp 52.02 Br md 12.01 Dpth 4.53
Welded, 1 dk

(A31A2GX) General Cargo Ship
Compartments: 2 Ho, ER
2 Ha: ER

2 oil engines reverse reduction geared to sc. shafts driving 2 FP propellers
Total Power: 626kW (852hp) 9.0kn
Caterpillar 3406PCTA
2 x 4 Stroke 6 Cy. 137 x 165 each-313kW (426bhp)
Caterpillar Tractor Co-USA

9318840 **SUPERIOR PACESETTER**
YJUX3 *ex Sealink Maju 20 -2006*
\- **Wild Well Control Inc**
Port Vila *Vanuatu*
MMSI: 576067000
Official number: 1687

499 149 423 Class: AB

2006-03 Sealink Shipyard Sdn Bhd — Miri Yd No: 119
Loa 38.00 Br ex - Dght 3.800
Lbp 36.30 Br md 11.80 Dpth 4.80
Welded, 1 dk

(B21B20A) Anchor Handling Tug Supply

2 oil engines geared to sc. shafts driving 2 FP propellers
Total Power: 3,494kW (4,750hp) 12.0kn
Caterpillar 3516B
2 x Vee 4 Stroke 16 Cy. 170 x 190 each-1747kW (2375bhp)
Caterpillar Inc-USA
AuxGen: 2 x 145kW 415V 50Hz a.c
Thrusters: 1 Thwart. CP thruster (f)

9315484 **SUPERIOR PESCADORES**
3EBM2
\- **Superior Pescadores SA**
Shih Wei Navigation Co Ltd
Panama *Panama*
MMSI: 371164000
Official number: 3089705A

8,479 3,825 11,987 T/cm 20.0 Class: CR NK

2005-06 Higaki Zosen K.K. — Imabari Yd No: 582
Loa 116.99 Br ex - Dght 8.864
Lbp 109.01 Br md 19.60 Dpth 14.00
Welded, 1 dk

(A31A2GX) General Cargo Ship
Grain: 17,684; Bale: 16,716
Compartments: 2 Ho, ER
2 Ha: (32.2 x 14.0)ER (23.8 x 14.0)
Cranes: 2x30.7t; Derricks: 1x60t,1x30t

1 oil engine driving 1 FP propeller
Total Power: 3,900kW (5,302hp) 13.4kn
B&W 6L35MC
1 x 2 Stroke 6 Cy. 350 x 1050 3900kW (5302bhp)
Mitsui Engineering & Shipbuilding CLtd-Japan
Fuel: 810.0

7811513 **SUPERIOR REEFER**
HQXG9 *ex Choke Reefer 3 -2010 ex Reefer Cape -1998*
\- *ex Emmely -1984*
Kelona Marine SA
Sea Safe Services Co Ltd
San Lorenzo *Honduras*
MMSI: 334816000
Official number: L-0338381

2,243 984 2,769 Class: GL (LR) ✠ Classed LR until 4/85

1979-09 B.V. Scheepswerf Jonker & Stans — Hendrik-Ido-Ambacht Yd No: 346
Lengthened-1985
Loa 91.12 Br ex 13.09 Dght 4.865
Lbp 84.92 Br md 13.01 Dpth 7.57
Welded, 2 dks

(A34A2GR) Refrigerated Cargo Ship
Ins: 3,866
TEU 18 C.Dk 18/20' (40')
Compartments: 4 Ho, ER
4 Ha: ER
Derricks: 8x3t
Ice Capable

1 oil engine sr geared to sc. shaft driving 1 FP propeller
Total Power: 1,320kW (1,795hp) 12.5kn
MaK 6M452AK
1 x 4 Stroke 6 Cy. 320 x 450 1320kW (1795bhp)
MaK Maschinenbau GmbH-Kiel
AuxGen: 3 x 176kW 440V 60Hz a.c

8973916 **SUPERIOR SERVICE**
WDG9349 *ex Ryan Candies -2006*
\- **Genesis Marine LLC**
Houston, TX *United States of America*
MMSI: 338343000
Official number: 637601

389 116 433

1981 Halter Marine, Inc. — Lockport, La Yd No: 980
Loa 32.00 Br ex - Dght 5.020
Lbp - Br md 10.36 Dpth 5.27
Welded, 1 dk

(B32A2ST) Tug

2 oil engines reduction geared to sc. shafts driving 2 FP propellers
Total Power: 2,206kW (3,000hp) 12.5kn
EMD (Electro-Motive) 12-645-E2
2 x Vee 2 Stroke 12 Cy. 230 x 254 each-1103kW (1500bhp)
General Motors Corp.Electro-Motive Div.-La Grange

7533680 **SUPERIOR STAR**
9WCJ6 *ex Ocean Tramp -1996 ex Pep Sea -1984*
\- **Yong Hung Shipping Sdn Bhd**
Kuching *Malaysia*
MMSI: 533552000
Official number: 327906

1,523 518 1,424 Class: (BV)

1976-06 Orskov Christensens Staalskibsvaerft A/S — Frederikshavn Yd No: 97
Loa 71.89 (BB) Br ex 13.16 Dght 3.556
Lbp 66.20 Br md 12.98 Dpth 6.76
Welded, 2 dks

(A31A2GX) General Cargo Ship
Grain: 3,316; Bale: 3,143
TEU 54 C. 54/20'
Compartments: 1 Ho, ER
1 Ha: (37.8 x 8.4)ER
Cranes: 2x40t
Ice Capable

1 oil engine reduction geared to sc. shaft driving 1 CP propeller
Total Power: 736kW (1,001hp) 11.0kn
Alpha 10V23LU
1 x Vee 4 Stroke 10 Cy. 225 x 300 736kW (1001bhp) (new engine 1985)
MAN B&W Diesel A/S-Denmark
AuxGen: 3 x 120kW 380V 50Hz a.c
Fuel: 223.0 (d.f.)

9285201 **SUPERIORITY**
2GJZ8 *ex Seniority -2007*
\- **FSL-16 Inc**
James Fisher (Shipping Services) Ltd
London *United Kingdom*
MMSI: 235098061
Official number: 8001381

3,859 1,276 4,415 Class: LR
✠ **100A1** SS 02/2012
Double Hull oil and chemical tanker, Ship Type 2
ESP
LI
✠ **LMC** **UMS CCS**
Eq.Ltr: U;
Cable: 467.5/40.0 U3 (a)

2007-02 Qingshan Shipyard — Wuhan HB Yd No: 20020403
Converted From: Products Tanker-2010
Loa 95.15 (BB) Br ex 17.12 Dght 5.890
Lbp 87.13 Br md 17.00 Dpth 7.70
Welded, 1 dk

(A12B2TR) Chemical/Products Tanker
Double Hull (13F)
Liq: 4,510; Liq (Oil): 4,510
Compartments: 6 Ta, 1 Slop Ta, ER
6 Cargo Pump (s): 6x375m³/hr
Manifold: Bow/CM: 46.2m

6 diesel electric oil engines driving 6 gen. each 486kW 450V a.c Connecting to 2 elec. motors each (900kW) driving 2 FP propellers
Total Power: 3,090kW (4,200hp) 11.5kn
MAN D2840LE
6 x Vee 4 Stroke 10 Cy. 128 x 142 each-515kW (700bhp)
MAN Nutzfahrzeuge AG-Nuernberg
Boilers: HWH (o.f.) 3.9kgf/cm² (3.8bar)
Thrusters: 1 Thwart. FP thruster (f)

9578074 **SUPERIORITY**
4DEN7
\- **Sea Coast Maritime Shipping Corp**
Cebu *Philippines*
MMSI: 548439100
Official number: CEB1008377

3,097 1,252 4,000 Class: BV (AB)

2011-03 Samho Shipbuilding Co Ltd — Tongyeong Yd No: 1230
Loa 94.87 (BB) Br ex - Dght 5.840
Lbp 88.00 Br md 15.40 Dpth 7.60
Welded, 1 dk

(A13B2TP) Products Tanker
Double Hull (13F)
Liq: 4,560; Liq (Oil): 4,476
Compartments: 5 Wing Ta, 5 Wing Ta, ER

1 oil engine driving 1 Propeller
Total Power: 2,206kW (2,999hp)
Hanshin LH38L
1 x 4 Stroke 6 Cy. 380 x 760 2206kW (2999bhp)
The Hanshin Diesel Works Ltd-Japan
AuxGen: 3 x 400kW a.c
Fuel: 50.2 (d.f.) 211.2 (r.f.)

9206401 **SUPERJET**
IINO
\- **Navigazione Libera del Golfo Srl**
Naples *Italy*
MMSI: 247540000

497 196 56 Class: RI

1999-07 Marinteknik Shipbuilders (S) Pte Ltd — Singapore Yd No: 161
Loa 45.00 Br ex 9.00 Dght 1.259
Lbp - Br md 8.90 Dpth 3.35
Welded

(A37B2PS) Passenger Ship
Passengers: unberthed: 550

2 oil engines geared to sc. shafts driving 2 Water jets
Total Power: 4,000kW (5,438hp) 30.0kn
M.T.U. 16V396TE74L
2 x Vee 4 Stroke 16 Cy. 165 x 185 each-2000kW (2719bhp)
MTU Friedrichshafen GmbH-Friedrichshafen
Fuel: 26.0 (d.f.)

7918165 **SUPERJUMBO**
ITMC
\- **Snav SpA**
\-
Naples *Italy*
MMSI: 247165400
Official number: 225

263 174 30 Class: RI

1981-07 Navaltecnica — San Benedetto del Tronto Yd No: 192
Loa 33.10 Br ex 7.05 Dght 1.564
Lbp 30.10 Br md 7.00 Dpth 3.80
Welded, 2 dks

(A37B2PS) Passenger Ship
Hull Material: Aluminium Alloy
Passengers: unberthed: 256

2 oil engines reverse reduction geared to sc. shafts driving 2 CP propellers
Total Power: 3,472kW (4,720hp) 34.0kn
M.T.U. 16V652TB81
2 x Vee 4 Stroke 16 Cy. 190 x 230 each-1736kW (2360bhp)
MTU Friedrichshafen GmbH-Friedrichshafen
AuxGen: 2 x 88kW 220V 50Hz a.c
Fuel: 5.5 (d.f.)

8404965 **SUPERMAN**
WDA3482 *ex Sea Eagle -2012 ex Makandra No. 32 -1992*
\- **Superman LLC**
Grand Isle, LA *United States of America*
MMSI: 366798960
Official number: 1020019

132 90 -

1984-12 Master Marine, Inc. — Bayou La Batre, Al Yd No: 273
Loa 25.94 Br ex - Dght -
Lbp - Br md 6.72 Dpth 3.81
Welded, 1 dk

(B11A2FT) Trawler
Ins: 91

1 oil engine with clutches & sr geared to sc. shaft driving 1 FP propeller
Total Power: 331kW (450hp)
Caterpillar 3412T
1 x Vee 4 Stroke 12 Cy. 137 x 152 331kW (450bhp)
Caterpillar Tractor Co-USA

8635253 **SUPERNA**
VTSV
\- **Gees Marine Products Pvt Ltd**
\-
Mormugao *India*
Official number: F-MRH-004

127 38 70 Class: (IR)

1990-11 Chowgule & Co Pvt Ltd — Goa Yd No: 102
Loa 24.00 Br ex 7.38 Dght 2.600
Lbp 20.00 Br md 7.20 Dpth 3.40
Welded, 1 dk

(B11A2FT) Trawler

1 oil engine reduction geared to sc. shaft driving 1 FP propeller
Total Power: 352kW (479hp) 10.0kn
Caterpillar 3412TA
1 x Vee 4 Stroke 12 Cy. 137 x 152 352kW (479bhp)
Caterpillar Inc-USA
AuxGen: 2 x 50kW 415V 50Hz a.c

9610212 **SUPERNOVA**
3FEL5
Helmstar Shipping SA & Hakuyo Kisen Co Ltd
Hakuyo Kisen KK (Hakuyo Kisen Co Ltd)
Panama *Panama*
MMSI: 373563000
Official number: 4395312

21,699 12,253 36,367 Class: NK

2012-06 Shikoku Dockyard Co. Ltd. — Takamatsu Yd No: 1072
Loa 176.50 (BB) Br ex - Dght 10.720
Lbp 168.50 Br md 28.80 Dpth 15.20
Welded, 1 dk

(A21A2BC) Bulk Carrier
Grain: 47,089; Bale: 45,414
Compartments: 5 Ho, ER
5 Ha: ER
Cranes: 4x30.5t

1 oil engine driving 1 FP propeller
Total Power: 7,300kW (9,925hp) 14.5kn
MAN-B&W 6S46MC-C
1 x 2 Stroke 6 Cy. 460 x 1932 7300kW (9925bhp)
Mitsui Engineering & Shipbuilding CLtd-Japan
Fuel: 1950.0

9438303 **SUPERNOVA**
9V9518 *ex Onsys Leo -2013*
\- **Panoil Tankers Pte Ltd**
Panoil Petroleum Pte Ltd
Singapore *Singapore*
MMSI: 566241000
Official number: 397223

5,034 1,958 7,008 T/cm 15.6 Class: LR
✠ **100A1** SS 07/2009
Double Hull oil tanker carriage of oils with a FP exceeding 60 degree C
ESP
*IWS
LI
✠ **LMC**
Eq.Ltr: X;
Cable: 495.0/50.0 U2 (a)

2009-07 Titan Quanzhou Shipyard Co Ltd — Hui'an County FJ Yd No: H0014
Loa 99.36 (BB) Br ex 18.08 Dght 7.000
Lbp 94.00 Br md 18.00 Dpth 10.00
Welded, 1 dk

(A13B2TP) Products Tanker
Double Hull (13F)
Compartments: 10 Wing Ta, 2 Wing Slop Ta, ER

2 oil engines with clutches, flexible couplings & dr reverse geared to sc. shafts driving 2 FP propellers
Total Power: 2,940kW (3,998hp) 11.5kn
MAN-B&W 6L28/32A
2 x 4 Stroke 6 Cy. 280 x 320 each-1470kW (1999bhp)
Zhenjiang Marine Diesel Works-China
AuxGen: 2 x 360kW 400V 50Hz a.c
Boilers: AuxB (o.f.) 7.7kgf/cm² (7.6bar)
Thrusters: 1 Thwart. FP thruster (f)

9328687 **SUPERPESA XI**
\- -
\- -
\-

2,048 842 3,248 Class: AB

2005-06 Transnave Estaleiros Reparos eConstrucao Naval S/A Yd No: 18
Loa 72.40 Br ex - Dght 4.930
Lbp 70.10 Br md 16.46 Dpth 6.10
Welded, 1 dk

(B21A20S) Platform Supply Ship

2 oil engines geared to sc. shafts driving 2 Directional propellers
Total Power: 2,868kW (3,900hp)
Caterpillar 3516B
2 x Vee 4 Stroke 16 Cy. 170 x 190 each-1434kW (1950bhp)
Caterpillar Inc-USA

IMO / Call sign	Name / Owner	Tonnage	Class	Build / Dimensions	Type	Machinery
9309928 *PS6458* -	**SUPERPESA XIII** **Superpesa Companhia de Transportes Especiais e Intermodais** SatCom: Inmarsat C 471000092 *Rio de Janeiro* Brazil Official number: 3810512028	**264** 79 283	Class: (AB)	**2004-07 Transnave Estaleiros Reparos eConstrucao Naval S/A** Yd No: 16 Loa 34.98 Br ex - Dght 3.250 Lbp 30.05 Br md 8.60 Dpth 4.00 Welded, 1 dk	**(B34S2QM) Mooring Vessel**	**2 oil engines** geared to sc. shafts driving 2 Directional propellers Total Power: 1,268kW (1,724hp) Caterpillar 3508B 2 x Vee 4 Stroke 8 Cy. 170 x 190 each-634kW (862bhp) Caterpillar Inc-USA AuxGen: 2 x 99kW a.c
9318199 *PS6715* -	**SUPERPESA XIV** **Superpesa Companhia de Transportes Especiais e Intermodais** - *Rio de Janeiro* Brazil Official number: 3810512401	**264** 79 283	Class: (AB)	**2004-07 Transnave Estaleiros Reparos eConstrucao Naval S/A** Yd No: 17 Loa 34.98 Br ex - Dght 3.250 Lbp 30.05 Br md 8.60 Dpth 4.00 Welded, 1 dk	**(B34S2QM) Mooring Vessel**	**2 oil engines** geared to sc. shafts driving 2 Directional propellers Total Power: 1,268kW (1,724hp) Caterpillar 3508B 2 x Vee 4 Stroke 8 Cy. 170 x 190 each-634kW (862bhp) Caterpillar Inc-USA AuxGen: 2 x 99kW a.c
9374519 *JWNH* -	**SUPERSPEED 1** **Kristiansand Line AS** Color Line Marine AS *Kristiansand* Norway MMSI: 259490000	**36,822** 11,047 5,400	Class: NV	**2008-02 Aker Yards Oy — Rauma** Yd No: 1359 Loa 211.30 (BB) Br ex 30.60 Dght 6.700 Lbp 195.30 Br md 25.80 Dpth 20.40 Welded, 5 dks plus 6 non continuous.	**(A36A2PR) Passenger/Ro-Ro Ship (Vehicles)** Passengers: unberthed: 1928; cabins: 54 Bow door/ramp (centre) Stern door/ramp (centre) Lane-Len: 2034 Cars: 778 Ice Capable	**4 oil engines** reduction geared to sc. shafts driving 2 CP propellers Total Power: 38,400kW (52,208hp) 27.0kn Wartsila 9L46 4 x 4 Stroke 9 Cy. 460 x 580 each-9600kW (13052bhp) Wartsila Finland Oy-Finland AuxGen: 4 x 3000kW a.c Thrusters: 2 Tunnel thruster (f); 1 Tunnel thruster (a) Fuel: 181.2 (d.f.) 1228.5 (r.f.)
9378682 *JWNE* -	**SUPERSPEED 2** **Oslo Line AS** Color Group AS *Kristiansand* Norway MMSI: 258092000	**34,231** 10,269 5,400	Class: NV	**2008-06 Aker Yards Oy — Rauma** Yd No: 1360 Loa 212.80 (BB) Br ex 30.60 Dght 6.700 Lbp 195.30 Br md 25.80 Dpth 20.40 Welded, 6 dks plus 5 dks non continuous	**(A36A2PR) Passenger/Ro-Ro Ship (Vehicles)** Passengers: unberthed: 1928; cabins: 54 Bow door/ramp (centre) Stern door/ramp (centre) Lane-Len: 2030 Vehicles: 720 Ice Capable	**4 oil engines** reduction geared to sc. shafts driving 2 CP propellers Total Power: 38,400kW (52,208hp) 27.0kn Wartsila 9L46 4 x 4 Stroke 9 Cy. 460 x 580 each-9600kW (13052bhp) Wartsila Finland Oy-Finland AuxGen: 4 x 3000kW a.c Thrusters: 2 Tunnel thruster (f); 1 Tunnel thruster (a) Fuel: 181.2 (d.f.) 1228.5 (r.f.)
9365398 *ESIY* -	**SUPERSTAR** **Tallink Group Ltd (AS Tallink Grupp)** - *Tallinn* Estonia MMSI: 276747000 Official number: 5P08D01	**36,277** 14,073 5,000	Class: BV	**2008-04 Fincantieri-Cant. Nav. Italiani S.p.A. — Ancona** Yd No: 6140 Loa 176.95 (BB) Br ex - Dght 7.100 Lbp 162.84 Br md 27.60 Dpth 21.25 Welded, 6 dks	**(A36A2PR) Passenger/Ro-Ro Ship (Vehicles)** Passengers: unberthed: 1244; cabins: 186; berths: 736 Bow door/ramp (centre) Stern door/ramp (centre) Lane-Len: 1930 Cars: 660 Ice Capable	**4 oil engines** reduction geared to sc. shafts driving 2 CP propellers Total Power: 50,400kW (68,524hp) 27.5kn Wartsila 12V46C 4 x Vee 4 Stroke 12 Cy. 460 x 580 each-12600kW (17131bhp) Wartsila Italia SpA-Italy AuxGen: 3 x 786kW 50Hz a.c Thrusters: 2 Tunnel thruster (f)
8816065 - -	**SUPERSTAR** *ex* Tyrving *-2002* *ex* Draupner *-1999* **Evertrust Fast Ferry Co Ltd** - *Hualien* Chinese Taipei	**439** 138 50	Class: (NV)	**1989-05 Fjellstrand AS — Omastrand** Yd No: 1590 Loa 38.82 Br ex 9.44 Dght - Lbp - Br md - Dpth 3.91 Riveted	**(A37B2PS) Passenger Ship** Hull Material: Aluminium Alloy Passengers: unberthed: 243	**2 oil engines** geared to sc. shafts driving 2 Water jets Total Power: 4,078kW (5,544hp) 35.0kn M.T.U. 16V396TB84 2 x Vee 4 Stroke 16 Cy. 165 x 185 each-2039kW (2772bhp) MTU Friedrichshafen GmbH-Friedrichshafen AuxGen: 2 x 70kW 230V 50Hz a.c
9008421 *C6LG6* -	**SUPERSTAR AQUARIUS** *ex* Norwegian Wind *-2007* *ex* Windward *-1998* **Superstar Aquarius Ltd** Star Cruises Administrative Services Sdn Bhd (Star Cruises) SatCom: Inmarsat C 430800241 *Nassau* Bahamas MMSI: 308273000 Official number: 723124	**51,309** 28,920 6,731 T/cm 39.0	Class: NV (BV)	**1993-05 Chantiers de l'Atlantique — St-Nazaire** Yd No: D30 Lengthened-1998 Loa 229.84 (BB) Br ex 32.10 Dght 7.010 Lbp 199.80 Br md 28.50 Dpth 17.83 Welded, 14 dks	**(A37A2PC) Passenger/Cruise** Passengers: cabins: 765; berths: 2100 Ice Capable	**4 oil engines** with clutches, flexible couplings & sr geared to sc. shafts driving 2 CP propellers Total Power: 18,638kW (25,340hp) 18.5kn MAN 6L40/54 2 x 4 Stroke 6 Cy. 400 x 540 each-3994kW (5430bhp) MAN B&W Diesel AG-Augsburg MAN 8L40/54 2 x 4 Stroke 8 Cy. 400 x 540 each-5325kW (7240bhp) MAN B&W Diesel AG-Augsburg AuxGen: 2 x 3500kW 6600V 60Hz a.c, 2 x 2950kW 6600V 60Hz a.c Thrusters: 2 Thwart. CP thruster (f) Fuel: 111.0 (d.f.) 1124.0 (r.f.) 100.0pd
9008419 *C6LG5* -	**SUPERSTAR GEMINI** *ex* Norwegian Dream *-2012* *ex* Dreamward *-1998* **Ocean Dream Ltd** Star Cruises Administrative Services Sdn Bhd (Star Cruises) SatCom: Inmarsat C 430800164 *Nassau* Bahamas MMSI: 308272000 Official number: 723123	**50,764** 28,641 6,731 T/cm 39.0	Class: NV (BV)	**1992-11 Chantiers de l'Atlantique — St-Nazaire** Yd No: C30 Lengthened-1998 Loa 229.84 (BB) Br ex 32.10 Dght 7.000 Lbp 199.80 Br md 28.50 Dpth 17.83 Welded, 14 dks	**(A37A2PC) Passenger/Cruise** Passengers: cabins: 874; berths: 2100 Ice Capable	**4 oil engines** with clutches, flexible couplings & sr geared to sc. shafts driving 2 CP propellers Total Power: 18,638kW (25,340hp) 18.5kn MAN 6L40/54 2 x 4 Stroke 6 Cy. 400 x 540 each-3994kW (5430bhp) MAN B&W Diesel AG-Augsburg MAN 8L40/54 2 x 4 Stroke 8 Cy. 400 x 540 each-5325kW (7240bhp) MAN B&W Diesel AG-Augsburg AuxGen: 2 x 3500kW 6600V 60Hz a.c, 2 x 2950kW 6600V 60Hz a.c Thrusters: 2 Thwart. CP thruster (f) Fuel: 111.0 (d.f.) 1124.0 (r.f.) 100.0pd
8612134 *C6DM2* -	**SUPERSTAR LIBRA** *ex* Norwegian Sea *-2005* *ex* Seaward *-1997* **Superstar Libra Ltd** Star Cruises Administrative Services Sdn Bhd (Star Cruises) SatCom: Inmarsat C 430818810 *Nassau* Bahamas MMSI: 308188000 Official number: 715194	**42,285** 23,341 5,000	Class: NV	**1988-05 Wartsila Marine Industries Inc — Turku** Yd No: 1294 Loa 216.17 (BB) Br ex 32.64 Dght 7.020 Lbp 178.06 Br md 32.63 Dpth 9.40 Welded, 6 dks	**(A37A2PC) Passenger/Cruise** Passengers: cabins: 740; berths: 1796	**4 oil engines** with clutches, flexible couplings & sr geared to sc. shafts driving 2 CP propellers Total Power: 18,476kW (25,120hp) 20.0kn Sulzer 8ZAL40S 4 x 4 Stroke 8 Cy. 400 x 560 each-4619kW (6280bhp) Wartsila Diesel Oy-Finland AuxGen: 3 x 2840kW 6600V 60Hz a.c Thrusters: 2 Thwart. CP thruster (f) Fuel: 142.0 (d.f.) 1910.0 (r.f.)
9141077 *3FEL9* -	**SUPERSTAR VIRGO** **Superstar Virgo Ltd** Star Cruises Administrative Services Sdn Bhd (Star Cruises) SatCom: Inmarsat C 435727120 *Panama* Panama MMSI: 357271000 Official number: 2676000C	**75,338** 45,235 8,530	Class: NV	**1999-08 Jos L Meyer GmbH — Papenburg** Yd No: 647 Loa 268.60 (BB) Br ex - Dght 7.900 Lbp 235.60 Br md 32.20 Dpth 11.50 Welded, 14 decks	**(A37A2PC) Passenger/Cruise** Passengers: cabins: 902; berths: 3350	**4 diesel electric oil engines** driving 4 gen. Connecting to 2 elec. motors each (20000kW) driving 2 FP propellers Total Power: 58,800kW (79,944hp) 24.0kn MAN 14V48/60 4 x Vee 4 Stroke 14 Cy. 480 x 600 each-14700kW (19986bhp) MAN B&W Diesel AG-Augsburg Thrusters: 2 Thwart. FP thruster (f); 1 Tunnel thruster (a)
8914051 *VRIE6* -	**SUPERTEC** *ex* Dixiemaiden *-2011* *ex* Dixie Monarch *-2006* **Supertec Maritime Co Ltd** Shanghai Anrita Shipping Co Ltd SatCom: Inmarsat C 447703749 *Hong Kong* Hong Kong MMSI: 477266300 Official number: HK3023	**39,023** 19,550 44,679 T/cm 55.0	Class: NK	**1991-07 Sanoyas Corp — Kurashiki OY** Yd No: 1106 Loa 199.99 (BB) Br ex - Dght 10.717 Lbp 194.00 Br md 32.20 Dpth 22.35 Welded, 1 dk	**(A24B2BW) Wood Chips Carrier** Grain: 99,705 Compartments: 6 Ho, ER 6 Ha: (16.3 x 12.3) (14.8 x 17.2)3 (16.3 x 17.2) (13.3 x 17.2)ER Cranes: 3x14.7t	**1 oil engine** driving 1 FP propeller Total Power: 8,518kW (11,581hp) 14.3kn Sulzer 6RTA52 1 x 2 Stroke 6 Cy. 520 x 1800 8518kW (11581bhp) Diesel United Ltd.-Aioi AuxGen: 3 x 720kW 450V 60Hz a.c Fuel: 103.6 (d.f.) 1925.4 (r.f.) 27.7pd
8985907 *MXSA6* -	**SUPERTOY** **Beacon Estates (Chepstow) Ltd** - *London* United Kingdom MMSI: 234997000 Official number: 726481	**161** 48 -		**1993 Kha Shing Enterprises Co Ltd — Kaohsiung** Yd No: 106 Loa 27.90 Br ex - Dght 1.800 Lbp - Br md 6.78 Dpth - Bonded, 1 dk	**(X11A2YP) Yacht** Hull Material: Reinforced Plastic Passengers: cabins: 5; berths: 10	**2 oil engines** driving 2 Propellers Total Power: 1,618kW (2,200hp) 13.5kn MAN 2 x Vee 4 Stroke 12 Cy. each-809kW (1100bhp) MAN B&W Diesel AG-Augsburg AuxGen: 2 x 25kW Thrusters: 1 Thwart. FP thruster (f)

9328182 **SUPETAR**
9AA2127
-
Jadrolinija
-
Rijeka *Croatia*
MMSI: 238151740

2,438 Class: CS
781
855

2004-07 Brodosplit - Brodogradiliste Specijalnih Objekata doo — Split Yd No: 599
Loa 87.60 Br ex - Dght 2.400
Lbp 80.00 Br md 17.50 Dpth 3.70
Welded, 1 dk

(A36A2PR) Passenger/Ro-Ro Ship (Vehicles)
Bow ramp (f)
Len: 6.50 Wid: 8.50 Swl: 50
Stern ramp (a)
Len: 6.50 Wid: 8.50 Swl: 50
Lane-clr ht: 4.40
Cars: 100

4 oil engines geared to sc. shafts driving 4 Directional propellers 2 propellers aft, 2 fwd
Total Power: 1,600kW (2,176hp) 11.5kn
Caterpillar 3412E-TA
4 x Vee 4 Stroke 12 Cy. 137 x 152 each-400kW (544bhp)
Caterpillar Inc-USA

5386057 **SUPPER CLUBCRUISE 02**
HO4101
ex Helgoland *-2005* *ex* Alte Liebe *-1984*
ex Wappen *-1966*
ex Wappen von Hamburg *-1964*
Amstelaviv Investment BV
Supperclub Cruise BV
Panama *Panama*
MMSI: 371432000
Official number: 3126606C

3,464 Class: (GL)
1,233
2,494

1962-03 Blohm & Voss AG — Hamburg Yd No: 823
Loa 103.97 Br ex 15.12 Dght 4.103
Lbp 93.02 Br md 15.02 Dpth 8.01
Welded, 2 dks

(A37B2PS) Passenger Ship
Passengers: unberthed: 1980
Compartments: 1 Ho, ER
1 Ha: (3.5 x 2.5)ER
Cranes: 1x1t
Ice Capable

2 oil engines driving 2 CP propellers
Total Power: 6,590kW (8,960hp) 22.0kn
Pielstick 16PC2V-400
2 x Vee 4 Stroke 16 Cy. 400 x 460 each-3295kW (4480bhp)
Ottensener Eisenwerk AG-Hamburg
AuxGen: 3 x 330kW 380V 50Hz a.c
Thrusters: 1 Thwart. FP thruster (f)

8969290 **SUPPLIER**
-
-
ex Mermaid Supplier *-2009*
Tasmanian Seafoods Pty Ltd
-
Dampier, WA *Australia*
Official number: 852614

103
30
-

1985 in Australia
Loa - Br ex - Dght 1.275
Lbp 29.05 Br md 7.20 Dpth 1.68
Welded, 1 dk

(A35D2RL) Landing Craft
Bow ramp

2 oil engines reduction geared to sc. shafts driving 2 FP propellers
Total Power: 236kW (320hp) 9.0kn
Scania DS9
2 x 4 Stroke 6 Cy. 115 x 136 each-118kW (160bhp)
Saab Scania AB-Sweden
AuxGen: 1 x 38kW, 1 x 20kW

9513347 **SUPPORT I**
9V7532
-
ex Tekun 24269 *-2012*
East Marine Pte Ltd
-
Singapore *Singapore*
MMSI: 566729000
Official number: 398234

259 Class: GL
78
277

2011-06 Kian Juan Dockyard Sdn Bhd — Miri Yd No: 132
Loa 30.00 Br ex - Dght 3.500
Lbp 27.73 Br md 8.59 Dpth 4.11
Welded, 1 dk

(B32A2ST) Tug

2 oil engines reverse reduction geared to sc. shafts driving 2 FP propellers
Total Power: 2,238kW (3,042hp)
Cummins KTA-38-M2
2 x Vee 4 Stroke 12 Cy. 159 x 159 each-1119kW (1521bhp)
Cummins Engine Co Inc-USA
AuxGen: 2 x 80kW 415V a.c

9513359 **SUPPORT II**
9V7527
-
ex Tekun 24270 *-2012*
East Marine Pte Ltd
-
Singapore *Singapore*
MMSI: 566723000
Official number: 398235

259 Class: GL
78
281

2011-09 Kian Juan Dockyard Sdn Bhd — Miri Yd No: 133
Loa 30.00 Br ex - Dght 3.500
Lbp 27.73 Br md 8.59 Dpth 4.11
Welded, 1 dk

(B32A2ST) Tug

2 oil engines reverse reduction geared to sc. shafts driving 2 FP propellers
Total Power: 2,238kW (3,042hp)
Cummins KTA-38-M2
2 x Vee 4 Stroke 12 Cy. 159 x 159 each-1119kW (1521bhp)
Cummins Engine Co Inc-USA
AuxGen: 2 x 80kW 415V a.c

6409131 **SUPPORTER-G**
HO4806
ex Supporter *-2007* *ex* Stril Supporter *-2005*
ex Striltral *-1990* *ex* Loranso *-1990*
ex Anso *-1984* *ex* Torrand *-1982*
ex Ingar Iversen *-1978* *ex* Ronstad *-1971*
ex Rembakk *-1967*
Rederij Groen BV
-
Panama *Panama*
MMSI: 357536000
Official number: 3356108A

466 Class: NV
139
400

1964-07 Elektrosveis — Sagvaag (Hull launched by) Yd No: 10
1964-07 Gerh. Voldnes AS — Fosnavaag (Hull completed by) Yd No: 2
Converted From: Stern Trawler-1990
Converted From: Fishing Vessel-1982
Loa 43.74 Br ex 7.35 Dght 4.490
Lbp 32.91 Br md 7.31 Dpth 5.85
Welded, 1 dk

(B22G2OY) Standby Safety Vessel
Compartments: 2 Ho, ER
2 Ha: (1.6 x 1.9) (1.9 x 1.9)ER
Cranes: 1x2t; Winches: 1
Ice Capable

1 oil engine reduction geared to sc. shaft driving 1 CP propeller
Total Power: 883kW (1,201hp) 12.5kn
MaK 6MU451AK
1 x 4 Stroke 6 Cy. 320 x 450 883kW (1201bhp) (made 1974, fitted 1982)
MaK Maschinenbau GmbH-Kiel
AuxGen: 1 x a.c, 1 x a.c
Thrusters: 1 Directional thruster (f); 1 Thwart. FP thruster (a)
Fuel: 112.0

9457725 **SUPRAMAX VIVI**
9HN09
-
Happy Auntie SA
Chian Spirit Maritime Enterprises Inc
Valletta *Malta*
MMSI: 249235000
Official number: 9457725

32,474 Class: LR (NV)
17,790 **100A1** SS 08/2008
53,413 bulk carrier
T/cm BC-A
57.3 No. 3 hold or Nos. 2 & 4 holds may be empty
ESP
ESN
LI
upper deck and hatch covers strengthened for a load of 4.5 and 2.5 tonnes/m2
LMC **UMS**

2008-08 Chengxi Shipyard Co Ltd — Jiangyin JS Yd No: CX4246
Loa 190.04 (BB) Br ex - Dght 12.540
Lbp 183.09 Br md 32.26 Dpth 17.50
Welded, 1 dk

(A21A2BC) Bulk Carrier
Grain: 65,900; Bale: 64,000
Compartments: 5 Ho, ER
5 Ha: 4 (21.6 x 22.4)ER (19.2 x 20.8)
Cranes: 4x36t

1 oil engine driving 1 FP propeller
Total Power: 9,480kW (12,889hp) 14.2kn
MAN-B&W 6S50MC-C
1 x 2 Stroke 6 Cy. 500 x 2000 9480kW (12889bhp)
Dalian Marine Diesel Works-China
AuxGen: 3 x 680kW 60Hz a.c
Fuel: 215.0 (d.f.) 2000.0 (r.f.) 34.5pd

9521007 **SUPRASTAR**
V7UJ3
-
Serono Shipping Co
Midocean (IOM) Ltd
SatCom: Inmarsat C 453836051
Majuro *Marshall Islands*
MMSI: 538003959
Official number: 3959

33,044 Class: BV
19,231
57,000
T/cm
58.8

2011-01 Qingshan Shipyard — Wuhan HB Yd No: 20060369
Loa 189.99 (BB) Br ex - Dght 12.800
Lbp 185.00 Br md 32.26 Dpth 18.00
Welded, 1 dk

(A21A2BC) Bulk Carrier
Grain: 71,634; Bale: 68,200
Compartments: 5 Ho, ER
5 Ha: ER
Cranes: 4x30t

1 oil engine driving 1 FP propeller
Total Power: 9,480kW (12,889hp) 14.2kn
MAN-B&W 6S50MC-C
1 x 2 Stroke 6 Cy. 500 x 2000 9480kW (12889bhp)
STX Engine Co Ltd-South Korea
AuxGen: 2 x 770kW 60Hz a.c, 1 x 600kW 60Hz a.c

9590395 **SUPREME**
9V8717
-
Sino Tankers Pte Ltd
United Maritime Pte Ltd
Singapore *Singapore*
MMSI: 564412000
Official number: 396145

710 Class: CC
213
670

2010-10 Ocean Leader Shipbuilding Co Ltd — Zhongshan GD Yd No: 198
Loa 42.46 Br ex - Dght 3.200
Lbp 40.07 Br md 11.80 Dpth 5.20
Welded, 1 dk

(A13B2TP) Products Tanker
Double Hull (13F)
Liq: 810; Liq (Oil): 810

2 oil engines reduction geared to sc. shafts driving 2 FP propellers
Total Power: 894kW (1,216hp) 8.5kn
Cummins KTA-19-M3
2 x 4 Stroke 6 Cy. 159 x 159 each-447kW (608bhp)
Chongqing Cummins Engine Co Ltd-China
AuxGen: 2 x 80kW 400V a.c
Fuel: 33.0

9688984 **SUPREME**
AWCZ
-
ex Vijai 57 *-2013*
Jindal ITF Ltd
-
Mumbai *India*
MMSI: 419000799
Official number: 4101

1,231 Class: IR
557
2,100

2013-09 Vijai Marine Services — Goa Yd No: 57
Loa 69.40 (BB) Br ex - Dght 3.300
Lbp - Br md 13.40 Dpth 4.35
Welded, 1 dk

(A31A2GX) General Cargo Ship

2 oil engines reduction geared to sc. shafts driving 2 Propellers
Total Power: 588kW (800hp)
Cummins
2 x 4 Stroke each-294kW (400bhp)
Cummins India Ltd-India

8739786 **SUPREME**
-
-
Oriental Link Co Ltd
-
Bangkok *Thailand*
Official number: 441000306

142
96
-

2000-01 Thong Chansawang — Samut Sakhon
Loa 23.04 Br ex - Dght -
Lbp - Br md 6.82 Dpth 3.63
Welded, 1 dk

(B32A2ST) Tug

1 oil engine reduction geared to sc. shaft driving 1 Propeller
Total Power: 683kW (929hp)
Caterpillar
1 x 4 Stroke 683kW (929bhp)
Caterpillar Inc-USA

9610391 **SUPREME ACE**
3ETV4
-
Chloe Navigation SA
MOL Ship Management Singapore Pte Ltd
Panama *Panama*
MMSI: 357147000
Official number: 4328811

59,022 Class: NK
18,290
18,384

2011-12 Minaminippon Shipbuilding Co Ltd — Usuki OT Yd No: 718
Loa 199.95 (BB) Br ex - Dght 9.820
Lbp 190.00 Br md 32.20 Dpth 34.20
Welded, 12 dks

(A35B2RV) Vehicles Carrier
Side door/ramp (s)
Quarter stern door/ramp (s. a.)
Cars: 6,163

1 oil engine driving 1 FP propeller
Total Power: 15,130kW (20,571hp) 20.6kn
MAN-B&W 7S60MC-C
1 x 2 Stroke 7 Cy. 600 x 2400 15130kW (20571bhp)
Mitsui Engineering & Shipbuilding CLtd-Japan
Thrusters: 1 Tunnel thruster (f)
Fuel: 2860.0

8112500 **SUPREME EXPLORER**
C6DQ3
-
ex Beaufort Explorer *-2013*
ex CGG Laurentian *-2008* *ex* Laurentian *-2003*
ex Labrador Horizon *-2001*
ex Simon Labrador *-1998*
ex Seaway Labrador *-1991*
Supreme Hydro FZE
-
SatCom: Inmarsat C 430800186
Nassau *Bahamas*
MMSI: 308161000
Official number: 715224

3,375 Class: IR NV
1,013
3,060

1983-03 Brattvag Skipsinnredning AS — Brattvaag Yd No: 40
Converted From: Diving Support Vessel-1988
Lengthened-1991
Loa 80.50 Br ex 18.42 Dght 5.512
Lbp 72.00 Br md 16.81 Dpth 7.12
Welded, 1 dk

(B31A2SR) Research Survey Vessel

4 diesel electric oil engines driving 4 gen. each 1220kW 600V a.c Connecting to 2 elec. motors each (1471kW) driving 2 Directional propellers
Total Power: 5,120kW (6,960hp)
Wartsila 8R22
4 x 4 Stroke 8 Cy. 220 x 240 each-1280kW (1740bhp)
Oy Wartsila Ab-Finland
Thrusters: 2 Thwart. FP thruster (f); 2 Retract. directional thruster (f)

9335642 *EI7350* DA 38
SUPREME II
James Connoly
-
Drogheda *Irish Republic*
MMSI: 250102900
Official number: 403620
179 54 -
2004-04 SOCARENAM — Boulogne Yd No: 193
Loa 24.65 (BB) Br ex - Dght 3.650
Lbp - Br md 7.40 Dpth 3.90
Welded, 1 dk
(B11A2FS) Stern Trawler
1 oil engine reduction geared to sc. shafts driving 1 CP propeller
Total Power: 421kW (572hp) 10.5kn
A.B.C. 6MDXC
1 x 4 Stroke 6 Cy. 242 x 320 421kW (572bhp)
Anglo Belgian Corp NV (ABC)-Belgium

9070357 *AVDK* -
SUPREME VISION
ex Svitzer Cecile *-2009* *ex* Cecile *-2008*
ex Seri Mutiara 803 *-2003*
Supreme Global Services Pvt Ltd
Falcon Offshore Services (I) Pvt Ltd
Mumbai *India*
MMSI: 419094600
Official number: 3657
495 149 203
Class: IR (BV)
1994-01 Cheoy Lee Shipyards Ltd — Hong Kong Yd No: 4499
Loa 37.80 Br ex 11.02 Dght 3.500
Lbp 35.76 Br md 11.00 Dpth 4.70
Welded, 1 dk
(B32A2ST) Tug
2 oil engines with clutches, flexible couplings & dr geared to sc. shafts driving 2 CP propellers
Total Power: 3,700kW (5,030hp)
Caterpillar 3606TA
2 x 4 Stroke 6 Cy. 280 x 300 each-1850kW (2515bhp)
Caterpillar Inc-USA
AuxGen: 2 x 200kW 380V 50Hz a.c

8946286 *DUA2178* -
SUPREMO
Triple F Inter Island Corp
-
Manila *Philippines*
Official number: 00-0001322
995 627 -
1990 Padaco Marine Works & Shipbuilding Corp. — Manila
L reg 87.88 Br ex - Dght -
Lbp - Br md 17.01 Dpth 4.23
Welded, 1 dk
(A35D2RL) Landing Craft
2 oil engines driving 1 FP propeller , 1 Propeller
Total Power: 956kW (1,300hp)
MAN
2 x 4 Stroke each-478kW (650bhp)

8026505 *A4DH* -
SUR
Port Services Corp Ltd
-
Port Sultan Qaboos *Oman*
Official number: 61
168 - -
Class: AB
1981-10 Selco Shipyard Pte Ltd — Singapore Yd No: 300
Loa 26.50 Br ex - Dght 3.158
Lbp 25.81 Br md 7.99 Dpth 3.99
Welded, 1 dk
(B32A2ST) Tug
2 oil engines reverse reduction geared to sc. shafts driving 2 FP propellers
Total Power: 1,754kW (2,384hp) 11.3kn
M.T.U. 12V396TC62
2 x Vee 4 Stroke 12 Cy. 165 x 185 each-877kW (1192bhp)
MTU Friedrichshafen GmbH-Friedrichshafen
AuxGen: 2 x 68kW

7640017 - -
SUR ESTE 501
ex Southern Venture *-1997*
ex Asahi Maru No. 10 *-1993*
ex Shinmei Maru No. 38 *-1988*
Sur Este Argen SA
-
289 197 373
Class: (LR) (KR)
Classed LR until 15/6/98
1977-03 Niigata Engineering Co Ltd — Niigata NI Yd No: 1537
Loa 48.87 (BB) Br ex 8.52 Dght 3.353
Lbp 43.17 Br md 8.50 Dpth 4.63
Welded, 1 dk
(B11B2FV) Fishing Vessel
1 oil engine driving 1 CP propeller
Total Power: 736kW (1,001hp)
Niigata 6M28KEHS
1 x 4 Stroke 6 Cy. 280 x 440 736kW (1001bhp)
Niigata Engineering Co Ltd-Japan
AuxGen: 2 x 220kW 225V 60Hz a.c

7815258 *6NLF* -
SUR ESTE No. 305
ex Sur Este No. 302 *-1991* *ex* Saja-8 *-1989*
ex Tenryu Maru No. 6 *-1989*
Dong Nam Co Ltd
-
Busan *South Korea*
Official number: 9505057-6210008
359 - 383
Class: (KR)
1978-08 Miho Zosensho K.K. — Shimizu Yd No: 1090
Loa 50.15 Br ex 8.52 Dght 3.366
Lbp 43.50 Br md 8.50 Dpth 3.57
Welded, 1 dk
(B11B2FV) Fishing Vessel
1 oil engine driving 1 FP propeller
Total Power: 883kW (1,201hp)
Akasaka DM28AR
1 x 4 Stroke 6 Cy. 280 x 460 883kW (1201bhp)
Akasaka Tekkosho KK (Akasaka DieselLtd)-Japan

8025109 *6NLQ* -
SUR ESTE No. 306
ex Spica No. 8 *-1993*
ex Taiwa Maru No. 58 *-1992*
ex Usa Maru No. 18 *-1987*
Dong Nam Co Ltd
-
Busan *South Korea*
Official number: 9507056-6260005
370 - 357
Class: (KR)
1981-06 Kochi Jyuko (Kaisei Zosen) K.K. — Kochi Yd No: 1447
Loa 50.41 Br ex - Dght 3.417
Lbp 43.87 Br md 8.51 Dpth 3.56
Welded, 1 dk
(B11B2FV) Fishing Vessel
Ins: 356
1 oil engine geared to sc. shaft driving 1 FP propeller
Total Power: 956kW (1,300hp) 11.5kn
Akasaka DM30R
1 x 4 Stroke 6 Cy. 300 x 480 956kW (1300bhp)
Akasaka Tekkosho KK (Akasaka DieselLtd)-Japan
AuxGen: 2 x 216kW 225V a.c

7904451 *LW4645* -
SUR ESTE No. 502
ex Rebeca No. 7 *-1997*
ex Choko Maru No. 38 *-1996*
ex Fukuseki Maru No. 2 *-1991*
ex Hosei Maru No. 23 *-1989*
Dong Nam Co Ltd
Sur Este Argen SA
SatCom: Inmarsat C 470181161
Mar del Plata *Argentina*
MMSI: 701000945
Official number: 02201
695 247 643
Class: (KR)
1979-06 Yamanishi Shipbuilding Co Ltd — Ishinomaki MG Yd No: 856
Loa 58.91 Br ex - Dght 3.834
Lbp 49.81 Br md 9.30 Dpth 4.20
Welded, 1 dk
(B11B2FV) Fishing Vessel
1 oil engine driving 1 FP propeller
Total Power: 1,214kW (1,651hp) 12.8kn
Hanshin 6LU32G
1 x 4 Stroke 6 Cy. 320 x 510 1214kW (1651bhp)
Hanshin Nainenki Kogyo-Japan
AuxGen: 2 x 240kW 225V a.c

8217506 *DTAP6* -
SUR ESTE No. 700
ex Beacon No. 7 *-1989*
ex Tenyu Maru No. 57 *-1989*
Dong Nam Co Ltd
-
Busan *South Korea*
MMSI: 440759000
Official number: 0112002-6260005
271 - 455
Class: KR
1983-01 Niigata Engineering Co Ltd — Niigata NI Yd No: 1763
Loa 57.51 (BB) Br ex - Dght 4.115
Lbp 50.22 Br md 9.91 Dpth 6.00
Welded, 1 dk
(B11A2FS) Stern Trawler
Ins: 470
Compartments: 5 Ho, ER
12 Ha: ER
1 oil engine with flexible couplings & sr gearedto sc. shaft driving 1 CP propeller
Total Power: 1,912kW (2,600hp)
Niigata 6MG40CX
1 x 4 Stroke 6 Cy. 400 x 520 1912kW (2600bhp)
Niigata Engineering Co Ltd-Japan
AuxGen: 2 x 264kW 225V a.c

8312851 *DTAI8* -
SUR ESTE No. 707
ex Rouguimex V *-1992*
ex Nisshin Maru No. 51 *-1992*
Dong Nam Co Ltd
-
SatCom: Inmarsat C 431209010
Busan *South Korea*
MMSI: 441051000
Official number: 0112003-6260004
816 244 621
Class: KR
1983-12 K.K. Murakami Zosensho — Ishinomaki Yd No: 1137
Loa 58.20 (BB) Br ex 9.86 Dght 4.371
Lbp 50.40 Br md - Dpth 6.08
Welded, 2 dks
(B11A2FS) Stern Trawler
Ins: 489
Compartments: 5 Ho, ER
6 Ha: ER
1 oil engine driving 1 CP propeller
Total Power: 1,912kW (2,600hp)
Niigata 6M40CFX
1 x 4 Stroke 6 Cy. 400 x 600 1912kW (2600bhp)
Niigata Engineering Co Ltd-Japan

8414465 *DTAR6* -
SUR ESTE No. 709
ex Hokko Maru No. 137 *-1993*
Dong Nam Co Ltd
-
SatCom: Inmarsat C 431210010
Busan *South Korea*
MMSI: 440761000
Official number: 0112004-6260003
279 - 588
Class: KR
1984-10 Yamanishi Shipbuilding Co Ltd — Ishinomaki MG Yd No: 907
Loa 58.25 (BB) Br ex 9.83 Dght 4.760
Lbp 50.25 Br md 9.81 Dpth 6.13
Welded, 2 dks
(B11B2FV) Fishing Vessel
1 oil engine with flexible couplings & sr gearedto sc. shaft driving 1 CP propeller
Total Power: 1,912kW (2,600hp)
Niigata 6MG40CX
1 x 4 Stroke 6 Cy. 400 x 520 1912kW (2600bhp)
Niigata Engineering Co Ltd-Japan

8973227 - -
SUR NO. 1
ex Hayatomo Maru No. 1 *-2008*
ex Nikko Maru No. 26 *-2008*
ex Hoei Maru No. 50 *-2008*
-
-
188 - -
1975-01 Y.K. Tokai Zosensho — Tsukumi
Loa 25.00 Br ex - Dght 3.000
Lbp 21.00 Br md 8.20 Dpth 3.80
Welded, 1 dk
(B32B2SA) Articulated Pusher Tug
2 oil engines driving 2 FP propellers
Total Power: 736kW (1,001hp) 12.0kn
Hanshin
2 x 4 Stroke
The Hanshin Diesel Works Ltd-Japan

9351907 - -
SURABAYA
Government of The Republic of Indonesia (Markas Besar TNI Angkatan Laut - Indonesian Navy)
-
Indonesia
11,300 - 1,750
2007-09 Dae Sun Shipbuilding & Engineering Co Ltd — Busan Yd No: 459
Loa 122.00 Br ex - Dght 6.000
Lbp 109.20 Br md 22.00 Dpth 6.70
Welded, 1 dk
(B34U2QH) Hospital Vessel
2 oil engines reduction geared to sc. shafts driving 2 CP propellers
Total Power: 5,002kW (6,800hp) 15.0kn
MAN-B&W 12V28/32A
2 x Vee 4 Stroke 12 Cy. 280 x 320 each-2501kW (3400bhp)
MAN B&W Diesel AG-Augsburg

9554731 *VRML4* -
SURABAYA EXPRESS
Surabaya Express Ltd
Nova Shipping & Logistics Pte Ltd
Hong Kong *Hong Kong*
MMSI: 477242500
Official number: HK-3907
54,686 20,576 70,099
Class: AB
2013-09 Jiangsu Newyangzi Shipbuilding Co Ltd — Jingjiang JS Yd No: YZJ2010-975
Loa 215.40 (BB) Br ex 37.05 Dght 12.800
Lbp 210.60 Br md 37.00 Dpth 23.95
Welded, 1 dk
(A24B2BW) Wood Chips Carrier
Grain: 133,243
Compartments: 6 Ho, ER
6 Ha: ER
Cranes: 3x25t
1 oil engine driving 1 FP propeller
Total Power: 10,470kW (14,235hp) 14.5kn
Wartsila 6RT-flex50
1 x 2 Stroke 6 Cy. 500 x 2050 10470kW (14235bhp)
Doosan Engine Co Ltd-South Korea
AuxGen: 3 x 560kW a.c
Fuel: 580.0 (d.f.) 3080.0 (r.f.)

7709514 *YEDL* -
SURABAYA EXPRESS
ex Harfan Jaya *-1998* *ex* Palembang *-1998*
ex Armada Abadi *-1996* *ex* Golden Light *-1988*
ex Yamasachi Maru *-1987*
PT Pelayaran Sejahtera Bahtera Agung
-
Jakarta *Indonesia*
3,114 1,799 5,080
Class: (NK) (KI)
1977-08 Kurinoura Dockyard Co Ltd — Yawatahama EH Yd No: 126
Loa 95.69 Br ex - Dght 5.965
Lbp 89.52 Br md 16.01 Dpth 7.22
Welded, 1 dk
(A31A2GX) General Cargo Ship
Grain: 6,289; Bale: 5,784
2 Ha: (20.1 x 8.0) (31.7 x 8.0)ER
Derricks: 3x15t
1 oil engine driving 1 FP propeller
Total Power: 2,207kW (3,001hp) 12.0kn
Hanshin 6LUS40
1 x 4 Stroke 6 Cy. 400 x 640 2207kW (3001bhp)
Hanshin Nainenki Kogyo-Japan
AuxGen: 2 x 120kW 445V a.c

IMO / Call sign	Name / Owner	Tonnage	Class	Construction	Type	Machinery
7613806 *YHCY* -	**SURABAYA FORTUNE** *ex* Jaya Ceres *-2000* *ex* Trans-Port I *-1997* *ex* Seawell Sapphire *-1995* *ex* Don Faustino *-1994* *ex* Isla Serrana *-1988* *ex* San Juan II *-1987* *ex* Eleanora *-1984* *ex* Santa Cruz *-1981* *ex* Finnorient *-1981* *ex* Eleanora *-1979* **PT Dharma Laut Raharja** *Jakarta* *Indonesia*	**2,161** 648 2,573	Class: (LR) (KI) (RI) (BV) ✠ Classed LR until 7/1/97	**1978-01 Chung Wah Shipbuilding & Engineering Co. Ltd. — Hong Kong** Yd No: 158 Loa 76.51 Br ex 17.30 Dght 3.823 Lbp 71.07 Br md 17.07 Dpth 6.71 Welded, 1 dk	**(A31C2GD) Deck Cargo Ship** Stern ramp TEU 190 C.Dk 190/20' Cranes: 1x30t	**2 oil engines** reverse reduction geared to sc. shafts driving 2 FP propellers Total Power: 2,206kW (3,000hp) 11.0kn Deutz SBA12M528 2 x Vee 4 Stroke 12 Cy. 220 x 280 each-1103kW (1500bhp) Kloeckner Humboldt Deutz AG-West Germany AuxGen: 3 x 260kW 440V 60Hz a.c Fuel: 262.0 (d.f.)
9147772 *YD4536* -	**SURALAYA** *ex* T. B. Suralaya *-1998* **PT Arpeni Pratama Ocean Line Tbk** - *Jakarta* *Indonesia* Official number: 4536	**226** 68 420	Class: KI (AB)	**1997-06 Far East Shipyard Co Sdn Bhd — Sibu** Yd No: 03/96 Loa 29.27 Br ex 8.60 Dght 3.500 Lbp 27.08 Br md - Dpth 4.11 Welded, 1 dk	**(B32A2ST) Tug**	**2 oil engines** geared to sc. shafts driving 2 FP propellers Total Power: 1,766kW (2,402hp) Yanmar M220-EN 2 x 4 Stroke 6 Cy. 220 x 300 each-883kW (1201bhp) Yanmar Diesel Engine Co Ltd-Japan AuxGen: 2 x 60kW a.c
7927063 *YHKV* -	**SURAMADU NUSANTARA** *ex* Diamond Star 6 *-2003* *ex* Diamond Star 5 *-2003* *ex* Sakurajima Maru No. 8 *-2003* **PT Prima Eksekutif** PT Jembatan Nusantara *Semarang* *Indonesia* MMSI: 525002092	*672* 202 370	Class: KI	**1979-12 Kanda Zosensho K.K. — Kawajiri** Yd No: 246 Loa 53.25 Br ex - Dght 2.652 Lbp 47.04 Br md 13.01 Dpth 3.61 Welded, 2 dks	**(A36A2PR) Passenger/Ro-Ro Ship (Vehicles)** Passengers: unberthed: 738	**2 oil engines** geard to sc. shafts driving 2 FP propellers Total Power: 1,472kW (2,002hp) 10.5kn Hanshin 6LUD26G 2 x 4 Stroke 6 Cy. 260 x 440 each-736kW (1001bhp) The Hanshin Diesel Works Ltd-Japan
9323716 - -	**SURANIMALA** - **Government of The Democratic Socialist Republic of Sri Lanka (Ports Authority)** - *Colombo* *Sri Lanka*	**553** 165 273	Class: LR ✠ **100A1** SS 09/2009 tug Sri Lanka coastal service ✠ **LMC** Eq.Ltr: I; Cable: 330.0/24.0 U2 (a)	**2004-09 Colombo Dockyard Ltd. — Colombo** Yd No: 177 Loa 34.45 Br ex 12.32 Dght 4.400 Lbp 31.43 Br md 12.10 Dpth 6.90 Welded, 1 dk	**(B32A2ST) Tug**	**2 oil engines** gearing integral to driving 2 Z propellers Total Power: 4,600kW (6,254hp) 12.0kn Wartsila 8L26 2 x 4 Stroke 8 Cy. 260 x 320 each-2300kW (3127bhp) Wartsila Nederland BV-Netherlands AuxGen: 2 x 165kW 400V 50Hz a.c
9066930 *HSB4571* -	**SURATCHANYA** *ex* Core Amethyst *-2011* *ex* Kasei Maru *-2002* **VCC Inter Marine Service & Transport Co Ltd** - *Bangkok* *Thailand* Official number: 540001669	*2,148* 909 3,367 T/cm 9.4	Class: (NK)	**1993-06 Kanrei Zosen K.K. — Naruto** Yd No: 361 Loa 85.02 Br ex - Dght 6.013 Lbp 79.50 Br md 13.40 Dpth 6.80 Welded, 1 dk	**(A13B2TP) Products Tanker** Double Bottom Entire Compartment Length Liq: 3,260; Liq (Oil): 3,360 2 Cargo Pump (s): 2x1000m³/hr Manifold: Bow/CM: 44.2m	**1 oil engine** driving 1 FP propeller Total Power: 2,060kW (2,801hp) Hanshin 6EL38 1 x 4 Stroke 6 Cy. 380 x 760 2060kW (2801bhp) The Hanshin Diesel Works Ltd-Japan Thrusters: 1 Tunnel thruster (f) Fuel: 41.8 (d.f.) 151.6 (r.f.)
8817007 *HSB3658* -	**SURATCHARIN** *ex* Otaka Maru No. 11 *-2013* **VCC Inter Marine Service & Transport Co Ltd** - *Bangkok* *Thailand* MMSI: 567001407 Official number: 500052832	**1,009** 577 2,105		**1988-11 Asakawa Zosen K.K. — Imabari** Yd No: 341 Loa - Br ex - Dght 4.922 Lbp 66.02 Br md 12.01 Dpth 5.52 Welded, 1 dk	**(A13B2TP) Products Tanker**	**1 oil engine** geared to sc. shaft driving 1 FP propeller Total Power: 1,324kW (1,800hp) 12.5kn Hanshin 6LU35G 1 x 4 Stroke 6 Cy. 350 x 550 1324kW (1800bhp) The Hanshin Diesel Works Ltd-Japan
9094901 *9BCO* -	**SURAYA** *ex* Maroof *-2006* *ex* Farishtey *-2001* **A Mahmodnegad** Sea Hawk Trading & Shipping Services *Bushehr* *Iran* MMSI: 422384000 Official number: 17312	**488** 367 -	Class: AS	**1980-01 Sadra International — Bandar Abbas** Yd No: 2 Converted From: General Cargo Barge, Non-propelled-2001 Loa 47.80 Br ex - Dght 4.200 Lbp 45.89 Br md 9.00 Dpth 4.90 Welded, 1 dk	**(A31A2GX) General Cargo Ship**	**2 oil engines** geared to sc. shafts driving 2 FP propellers Total Power: 1,250kW (1,700hp) Yanmar 6LX-ET 2 x 4 Stroke 6 Cy. 150 x 165 each-625kW (850bhp) (new engine 2001, fitted 2001) Yanmar Diesel Engine Co Ltd-Japan
8023319 *9LD2366* -	**SURAYA-Y** *ex* Thuraya-Y *-2011* *ex* Sac Flix *-2009* **Suraya Shipping Co Ltd** Indicator Marine Co Ltd *Freetown* *Sierra Leone* MMSI: 667005066 Official number: SL105066	**9,099** 5,398 15,855 T/cm 25.3	Class: (LR) (TL) (BV) Classed LR until 8/9/09	**1982-01 Astilleros Espanoles SA (AESA) — Seville** Yd No: 242 Loa 146.24 (BB) Br ex - Dght 9.102 Lbp 134.00 Br md 21.40 Dpth 12.20 Welded, 1 dk	**(A21A2BC) Bulk Carrier** Grain: 20,966 Compartments: 5 Ho, ER 5 Ha: 2 (10.2 x 12.6)3 (10.4 x 12.6)ER Cranes: 3x16t	**1 oil engine** driving 1 FP propeller Total Power: 5,075kW (6,900hp) 16.0kn B&W 7L45GFCA 1 x 2 Stroke 7 Cy. 450 x 1200 5075kW (6900bhp) Astilleros Espanoles SA (AESA)-Spain AuxGen: 3 x 520kW 440V 60Hz a.c Boilers: e (Comp) 8.0kgf/cm² (7.8bar), AuxB (o.f.) 8.0kgf/cm² (7.8bar)
9614581 *2EAP3* -	**SURE SHAMAL** *ex* Marineco Shamal *-2013* **Sure Wind Marine Holdings Ltd** Sure Wind Marine Ltd *Newcastle upon Tyne* *United Kingdom* MMSI: 235083503 Official number: 917497	**126** 44 24	Class: BV	**2011-06 Scheepswerf Made B.V. — Made** (Hull) Yd No: (532501) **2011-06 B.V. Scheepswerf Damen — Gorinchem** Yd No: 532501 Loa 25.75 Br ex 10.40 Dght 1.800 Lbp 23.98 Br md 10.06 Dpth 3.50 Welded, 1 dk	**(B21A2OC) Crew/Supply Vessel** Hull Material: Aluminium Alloy Passengers: unberthed: 12 Cranes: 1	**2 oil engines** reduction geared to sc. shafts driving 2 FP propellers Total Power: 2,162kW (2,940hp) 22.0kn Caterpillar C32 ACERT 2 x Vee 4 Stroke 12 Cy. 145 x 162 each-1081kW (1470bhp) Caterpillar Inc-USA AuxGen: 2 x 22kW 400/230V 50Hz a.c Thrusters: 2 Tunnel thruster (f)
9698903 *J8B4858* -	**SURE STAR** - **Sure Wind Marine Ltd** - *Kingstown* *St Vincent & The Grenadines* MMSI: 375894000	**149** 45 25	Class: BV (Class contemplated)	**2014-01 Damen Shipyards Singapore Pte Ltd — Singapore** (Hull) Yd No: (532517) **2014-01 B.V. Scheepswerf Damen — Gorinchem** Yd No: 532517 Loa 25.75 Br ex - Dght 1.800 Lbp - Br md 10.40 Dpth 3.00 Welded, 1 dk	**(B21A2OC) Crew/Supply Vessel** Hull Material: Aluminium Alloy	**2 oil engines** reduction geared to sc. shafts driving 2 FP propellers Total Power: 1,492kW (2,028hp) 22.0kn Caterpillar C32 ACERT 2 x Vee 4 Stroke 12 Cy. 145 x 162 each-746kW (1014bhp) Caterpillar Inc-USA AuxGen: 2 x 22kW 400/230V 50Hz a.c Thrusters: 2 Tunnel thruster 1 (p) 1 (s) Fuel: 19.0 (d.f.)
9029669 - -	**SURENDRA SAI** - **Paradip Port Trust** - *Paradip* *India*	**115** 29 5	Class: IR	**2006-01 Corporated Consultancy & Eng Enterprise Pvt Ltd — Haora** Yd No: 256 Loa 25.00 Br ex 6.76 Dght 2.000 Lbp 23.00 Br md 6.50 Dpth 3.00 Welded, 1 dk	**(B34N2QP) Pilot Vessel**	**1 oil engine** reduction geared to sc. shaft driving 1 Directional propeller Total Power: 368kW (500hp) MWM TBD4V12M 1 x Vee 4 Stroke 12 Cy. 128 x 140 368kW (500bhp) Greaves Cotton Ltd-India
9559896 *V2FW6* -	**SURENES** *ex* Thorco Asia *-2012* *completed as* Victory Scan *-2012* **MarShip GmbH & Co KG ms 'Sinus Medii'** MarShip Bereederungs GmbH & Co KG *Saint John's* *Antigua & Barbuda* MMSI: 305825000	**6,351** 3,617 9,737	Class: BV	**2012-06 Jiangsu Yangzi Changbo Shipbuilding Co Ltd — Jingjiang JS** (Hull) Yd No: 07-019 **2012-06 Volharding Shipyards B.V. — Foxhol** Yd No: 701 Loa 132.20 (BB) Br ex 15.90 Dght 7.780 Lbp 124.56 Br md 15.87 Dpth 9.65 Welded, 1 dk	**(A31A2GX) General Cargo Ship** Grain: 12,822 Compartments: 2 Ho, ER 2 Ha: ER Cranes: 2x60t Ice Capable	**1 oil engine** reduction geared to sc. shaft driving 1 CP propeller Total Power: 4,000kW (5,438hp) 14.8kn Bergens B32: 40L8P 1 x 4 Stroke 8 Cy. 320 x 400 4000kW (5438bhp) Rolls Royce Marine AS-Norway AuxGen: 1 x 555kW 440V 60Hz a.c, 2 x 324kW 440V 60Hz a.c Fuel: 612.0
9400693 *WDF5385* -	**SURF CHALLENGER** *ex* Dmt Emerald *-2010* **Surf Subsea Inc** - *New Orleans, LA* *United States of America* MMSI: 366638000 Official number: 1190616	**4,193** 1,257 3,277	Class: AB	**2006-11 Bender Shipbuilding & Repair Co Inc — Mobile AL** Yd No: 7770 Loa 89.00 Br ex - Dght 4.980 Lbp 79.02 Br md 17.98 Dpth 7.38 Welded, 1 dk	**(B22A2OV) Diving Support Vessel** Cranes: 1x100t	**4 diesel electric oil engines** driving 4 gen. each 1825kW a.c Connecting to 2 elec. motors driving 2 Z propellers Total Power: 7,300kW (9,924hp) 10.0kn Caterpillar 3516B-HD 4 x Vee 4 Stroke 16 Cy. 170 x 215 each-1825kW (2481bhp) Caterpillar Inc-USA Thrusters: 2 Thwart. CP thruster (f) Fuel: 651.8 (d.f.)
9293038 *YJQS7* -	**SURF EXPRESS** - **Bourbon Supply Investissements SAS** Bourbon Offshore Surf SAS *Port Vila* *Vanuatu* Official number: 2106	**461** 138 263	Class: BV	**2003-09 Chantiers Piriou — Concarneau** Yd No: 253 Loa 53.55 Br ex - Dght 2.350 Lbp - Br md 10.00 Dpth 4.05 Welded, 1 dk	**(B21A2OC) Crew/Supply Vessel** Hull Material: Aluminium Alloy Passengers: unberthed: 50	**4 oil engines** geared to sc. shafts driving 4 Water jets Total Power: 5,300kW (7,204hp) 20.0kn Cummins KTA-50-M2 4 x Vee 4 Stroke 16 Cy. 159 x 159 each-1325kW (1801bhp) Cummins Engine Co Ltd-United Kingdom Thrusters: 1 Tunnel thruster (f)
9705691 *HP6705* -	**SURF LESTARI** - **Bourbon PS SASU** Bourbon Offshore Asia Pte Ltd *Panama* *Panama* MMSI: 373149000 Official number: 45455PEXT	**464** 139 440	Class: BV (Class contemplated)	**2014-04 South East Asia Shipyard — Ben Luc** Yd No: 66 Loa 53.40 Br ex 10.40 Dght 2.100 Lbp 50.45 Br md 10.00 Dpth 4.40 Welded, 1 dk	**(B21A2OC) Crew/Supply Vessel** Hull Material: Aluminium Alloy Passengers: unberthed: 60	**4 oil engines** reduction geared to sc. shafts driving 4 Water jets Total Power: 5,968kW (8,116hp) 20.0kn Cummins KTA-50-M2 4 x Vee 4 Stroke 16 Cy. 159 x 159 each-1492kW (2029bhp) Cummins Engine Co Ltd-United Kingdom Thrusters: 2 Tunnel thruster (f)

LR/IMO No. / Call sign / Flag	Name / Former names / Owner / Port	Tonnage	Class	Builder / Dimensions	Type	Machinery
9546564 *PNTA* -	**SURF MANDIRI** *ex* BOURBON LIBERTY 230 *-2010* **PT Surf Marine Indonesia** - *Jakarta* *Indonesia* MMSI: 525015776 Official number: 2738/PPM	**1,733** 519 1,456	Class: AB KI	**2010-08 Yangzhou Dayang Shipbuilding Co Ltd — Yangzhou JS** Yd No: DY1013 Loa 59.78 Br ex - Dght 4.880 Lbp 57.34 Br md 15.00 Dpth 5.50 Welded, 1 dk	**(B21B20A) Anchor Handling Tug Supply**	**3 diesel electric oil engines** driving 3 gen. each 1825kW 480V a.c Connecting to 6 elec. motors each (842kW) driving 3 Z propellers fixed unit only Total Power: 5,475kW (7,443hp) 12.0kn Cummins QSK60-M 3 x Vee 4 Stroke 16 Cy. 159 x 190 each-1825kW (2481bhp) Cummins Engine Co Inc-USA Thrusters: 2 Tunnel thruster (f)
9394662 *PNUI* -	**SURF MITRA** *ex* Bourbon Liberty 231 *-2010* **PT Surf Marine Indonesia** - *Jakarta* *Indonesia* MMSI: 525015788 Official number: 1906	**1,733** 519 1,464	Class: AB KI (BV)	**2010-10 Yangzhou Dayang Shipbuilding Co Ltd — Yangzhou JS** Yd No: DH2014 Loa 59.78 Br ex - Dght 4.880 Lbp 57.34 Br md 15.00 Dpth 5.50 Welded, 1 dk	**(B21B20A) Anchor Handling Tug Supply**	**3 diesel electric oil engines** driving 3 gen. each 1825kW 480V a.c Connecting to 6 elec. motors each (842kW) driving 3 Z propellers fixed unit only Total Power: 5,148kW (6,999hp) 12.0kn Cummins QSK60-M 3 x Vee 4 Stroke 16 Cy. 159 x 190 each-1716kW (2333bhp) Cummins Engine Co Inc-USA Thrusters: 2 Tunnel thruster (f) Fuel: 640.0
9571260 *PNYE* -	**SURF PANGLIMA** *ex* Bourbon Liberty 118 *-2012* **PT Surf Marine Indonesia** - *Surabaya* *Indonesia* MMSI: 525015939	**1,515** 455 1,529	Class: AB KI	**2010-05 Yangzhou Dayang Shipbuilding Co Ltd — Yangzhou JS** Yd No: DY818 Loa 57.90 Br ex - Dght 4.900 Lbp 54.90 Br md 14.00 Dpth 5.50 Welded, 1 dk	**(B21A20S) Platform Supply Ship**	**3 diesel electric oil engines** driving 2 gen. each 1235kW 480V a.c 1 gen. of 435kW 480V a.c Connecting to 3 elec. motors each (843kW) driving 3 Z propellers fixed unit Total Power: 3,364kW (4,575hp) 10.5kn Cummins KT-19-M 1 x 4 Stroke 6 Cy. 159 x 159 380kW (517bhp) Cummins Engine Co Inc-USA Cummins KTA-50-M2 2 x Vee 4 Stroke 16 Cy. 159 x 159 each-1492kW (2029bhp) Cummins Engine Co Inc-USA Thrusters: 2 Tunnel thruster (f) Fuel: 447.0 (d.f.)
9653903 *9V2590* -	**SURF PERDANA** *launched as* Bourbon Explorer 503 *-2014* **Bourbon Supply Asia Pte Ltd** Bourbon Offshore Asia Pte Ltd *Singapore* *Singapore*	**3,147** 1,126 3,600	Class: BV	**2014-03 Zhejiang Shipbuilding Co Ltd — Fenghua ZJ** Yd No: ZJ4003 Loa 78.25 (BB) Br ex 17.72 Dght 6.300 Lbp 71.62 Br md 17.20 Dpth 7.80 Welded, 1 dk	**(B21A20S) Platform Supply Ship**	**4 diesel electric oil engines** driving 4 gen. Connecting to 2 elec. motors driving 2 Z propellers Total Power: 7,060kW (9,600hp) 12.5kn Caterpillar 3512C 4 x Vee 4 Stroke 12 Cy. 170 x 215 each-1765kW (2400bhp) Caterpillar Inc-USA Thrusters: 2 Tunnel thruster (f)
9571258 *PNYD* -	**SURF PERWIRA** *ex* Bourbon Liberty 117 *-2012* **PT Surf Marine Indonesia** - *Jakarta* *Indonesia* MMSI: 525015938 Official number: 2679/KA	**1,515** 455 1,528	Class: AB KI	**2010-05 Yangzhou Dayang Shipbuilding Co Ltd — Yangzhou JS** Yd No: DY817 Loa 57.95 Br ex - Dght 4.300 Lbp 54.90 Br md 14.00 Dpth 5.50 Welded, 1 dk	**(B21A20S) Platform Supply Ship**	**3 diesel electric oil engines** driving 2 gen. each 1235kW 480V a.c 1 gen. of 435kW 480V a.c Connecting to 3 elec. motors each (843kW) driving 3 Z propellers fixed unit Total Power: 3,364kW (4,575hp) 10.5kn Cummins KT-19-M 1 x 4 Stroke 6 Cy. 159 x 159 380kW (517bhp) Cummins Engine Co Inc-USA Cummins KTA-50-M2 2 x Vee 4 Stroke 16 Cy. 159 x 159 each-1492kW (2029bhp) Cummins Engine Co Inc-USA Thrusters: 2 Tunnel thruster (f) Fuel: 447.0 (d.f.)
9092719 - -	**SURFER 1** *ex* Ernst Thalmann *-1995* *ex* Anklam *-1980* - -	*317* 95 -		**1969-05 VEB Peene-Werft — Wolgast** Yd No: 226 Converted From: Training Vessel-1995 Converted From: Minesweeper-1980 L reg 47.35 Br ex - Dght - Lbp - Br md 6.70 Dpth 4.10 Welded, 1 dk	**(X11A2YP) Yacht**	**2 oil engines** driving 2 Propellers Kolomna 12DRN23/30 2 x Vee 2 Stroke 12 Cy. 230 x 300 VEB Dieselmotorenwerk Rostock-Rostock
9134062 - -	**SURFER 251** - **Bourbon Offshore Surf SAS** -	*116* 53 15		**1996-03 Chantiers Piriou — Concarneau** Yd No: 179 Converted From: Ferry (Passenger only)-2009 Loa 25.80 Br ex - Dght 1.200 Lbp 21.83 Br md 6.20 Dpth 2.80 Welded, 1 dk	**(B21A20C) Crew/Supply Vessel** Passengers: unberthed: 70	**4 oil engines** geared to sc. shafts driving 4 Water jets Total Power: 2,440kW (3,316hp) 28.0kn M.T.U. 12V183TE72 4 x Vee 4 Stroke 12 Cy. 128 x 142 each-610kW (829bhp) MTU Friedrichshafen GmbH-Friedrichshafen AuxGen: 2 x 30kW 380V 50Hz a.c Fuel: 6.0 (d.f.)
9161780 *FQBG* -	**SURFER 252** - **Bourbon Offshore Surf SAS** - *Marseille* *France (FIS)* MMSI: 227084000 Official number: 894594K	**116** 53 15		**1997-06 Chantiers Piriou — Concarneau** Yd No: 185 Converted From: Ferry (Passenger only)-2009 Loa 25.80 Br ex - Dght 1.200 Lbp 21.83 Br md 6.20 Dpth 2.80 Welded, 1 dk	**(B21A20C) Crew/Supply Vessel** Hull Material: Aluminium Alloy Passengers: unberthed: 70	**4 oil engines** geared to sc. shafts driving 4 Water jets Total Power: 2,440kW (3,316hp) 28.0kn M.T.U. 12V183TE72 4 x Vee 4 Stroke 12 Cy. 128 x 142 each-610kW (829bhp) MTU Friedrichshafen GmbH-Friedrichshafen AuxGen: 2 x 30kW 380V 50Hz a.c Fuel: 6.0 (d.f.)
9161792 - -	**SURFER 253** - **Bourbon Interoil Nigeria Ltd** Bourbon Offshore Surf SAS *Port Harcourt* *Nigeria*	**116** 53 15	Class: (BV)	**1997-03 Chantiers Piriou — Concarneau** Yd No: 186 Converted From: Ferry (Passenger only)-2009 Loa 25.80 Br ex - Dght 1.200 Lbp 21.83 Br md 6.20 Dpth 2.80 Welded, 1 dk	**(B21A20C) Crew/Supply Vessel** Hull Material: Aluminium Alloy Passengers: unberthed: 70	**4 oil engines** geared to sc. shafts driving 4 Water jets Total Power: 2,440kW (3,316hp) 28.0kn M.T.U. 12V183TE72 4 x Vee 4 Stroke 12 Cy. 128 x 142 each-610kW (829bhp) MTU Friedrichshafen GmbH-Friedrichshafen AuxGen: 2 x 30kW 380V 50Hz a.c Fuel: 6.0 (d.f.)
9258583 *FOSS* -	**SURFER 254** - **Bourbon Offshore Surf SAS** - *Marseille* *France (FIS)* MMSI: 635000400 Official number: 924323Z	**116** 53 15		**2002-04 Chantiers Piriou — Concarneau** Yd No: 243 Loa 25.80 Br ex - Dght 1.200 Lbp 21.83 Br md 6.20 Dpth 2.80 Welded, 1 dk	**(B21A20C) Crew/Supply Vessel** Passengers: unberthed: 70	**4 oil engines** geared to sc. shafts driving 4 Water jets Total Power: 2,440kW (3,316hp) 28.0kn M.T.U. 12V183TE72 4 x Vee 4 Stroke 12 Cy. 128 x 142 each-610kW (829bhp) MTU Friedrichshafen GmbH-Friedrichshafen AuxGen: 2 x 30kW 380V 50Hz a.c Fuel: 6.0
8664022 *FQCT* -	**SURFER 255** - **Bourbon Offshore Surf SAS** - *Marseille* *France (FIS)* MMSI: 228147600	**121** 38 -		**2007-06 Chantiers Piriou — Concarneau** Loa 25.91 Br ex - Dght - Lbp 22.65 Br md 6.20 Dpth 2.60 Welded, 1 dk	**(B21A20C) Crew/Supply Vessel** Hull Material: Aluminium Alloy Passengers: unberthed: 70	**4 oil engines** reduction geared to sc. shafts driving 4 Water jets Total Power: 2,440kW (3,316hp) M.T.U. 12V183TE72 4 x Vee 4 Stroke 12 Cy. 128 x 142 each-610kW (829bhp) MTU Friedrichshafen GmbH-Friedrichshafen
9093282 - -	**SURFER 256** - **Bourbon Interoil Nigeria Ltd** - *Port Harcourt* *Nigeria* Official number: SR541	**121** 38 15	Class: BV	**2006-08 West Atlantic Shipyard — Port Harcourt** Yd No: WAS03 Converted From: Supply Tender-2009 Loa - Br ex - Dght 1.200 Lbp 25.90 Br md 6.20 Dpth - Welded, 1 dk	**(B21A20C) Crew/Supply Vessel** Hull Material: Aluminium Alloy Passengers: unberthed: 70	**4 oil engines** geared to sc. shafts driving 4 Water jets Total Power: 2,440kW (3,316hp) 28.0kn MAN 4 x Vee 4 Stroke 12 Cy. 128 x - each-610kW (829bhp) MAN B&W Diesel AG-Augsburg AuxGen: 2 x 30kW 380V 50Hz a.c Fuel: 6.0
8663614 - -	**SURFER 257** - **Bourbon Interoil Nigeria Ltd** - *Port Harcourt* *Nigeria*	**121** 38 16	Class: BV	**2009-01 West Atlantic Shipyard — Port Harcourt** Yd No: WAS09 Loa 24.95 Br ex - Dght 1.100 Lbp 21.81 Br md 6.20 Dpth - Welded, 1 dk	**(B21A20C) Crew/Supply Vessel** Hull Material: Aluminium Alloy Passengers: unberthed: 70	**4 oil engines** reduction geared to sc. shafts driving 4 Water jets Total Power: 2,440kW (3,316hp) 30.0kn MAN 4 x Vee 4 Stroke 12 Cy. 128 x 142 each-610kW (829bhp) MAN B&W Diesel AG-Augsburg AuxGen: 2 x 60kW 50Hz a.c Fuel: 6.0 (d.f.)
8661927 *FNNM* -	**SURFER 258** - **Bourbon Offshore Surf SAS** - *Marseille* *France (FIS)*	**121** 38 -	Class: BV	**2008-04 Chantiers Piriou — Concarneau** Yd No: C295 Loa 25.35 Br ex - Dght 1.000 Lbp 21.82 Br md 6.20 Dpth 2.55 Welded, 1 dk	**(B21A20C) Crew/Supply Vessel** Hull Material: Aluminium Alloy Passengers: unberthed: 70	**4 oil engines** reduction geared to sc. shafts driving 4 Water jets Total Power: 2,644kW (3,596hp) 35.0kn MAN 4 x Vee 4 Stroke 12 Cy. 127 x 142 each-661kW (899bhp) MAN Nutzfahrzeuge AG-Nuernberg

8664034 *FNNN* -	**SURFER 259** - **Bourbon Offshore Surf SAS** - *Marseille* *France (FIS)* MMSI: 635016700	**121** 38 -	Class: (BV)	**2008-06 Chantiers Piriou — Concarneau** Yd No: C296 Loa 25.91 Br ex - Dght - Lbp 22.65 Br md 6.20 Dpth 2.60 Welded, 1 dk	**(B21A20C) Crew/Supply Vessel** Hull Material: Aluminium Alloy Passengers: unberthed: 70	**4 oil engines** reduction geared to sc. shafts driving 4 Water jets Total Power: 2,648kW (3,600hp) MAN 4 x each-662kW (900bhp) MAN Nutzfahrzeuge AG-Nuernberg
9228693 *FHAK* -	**SURFER 320** - **Bourbon Offshore Surf SAS** - *Marseille* *France (FIS)* MMSI: 228073000 Official number: 924294T	**192** 59 23	Class: BV	**2000-09 Chantiers Piriou — Concarneau** Yd No: 221 Loa 33.50 Br ex - Dght 1.230 Lbp 28.71 Br md 6.70 Dpth 3.00 Welded, 1 dk	**(B21A20C) Crew/Supply Vessel** Hull Material: Aluminium Alloy Passengers: 93	**3 oil engines** with clutches, flexible couplings & sr geared to sc. shafts driving 3 Water jets Total Power: 4,362kW (5,931hp) 35.0kn M.T.U. 12V396TE74 3 x Vee 4 Stroke 12 Cy. 165 x 185 each-1454kW (1977bhp) MTU Friedrichshafen GmbH-Friedrichshafen AuxGen: 2 x 60kW 440/220V 50Hz a.c Fuel: 12.2 (d.f.)
9282766 *HP5731* -	**SURFER 321** - **Bourbon East Asia Pte Ltd** Bourbon Offshore Asia Pte Ltd *Panama* *Panama* MMSI: 373699000 Official number: 4442712A	**163** 48 38	Class: BV	**2003-01 Chantiers Piriou — Concarneau** Yd No: 249 Loa 33.50 Br ex - Dght 1.200 Lbp 29.10 Br md 6.70 Dpth 3.00 Welded, 1 dk	**(B21A20C) Crew/Supply Vessel** Hull Material: Aluminium Alloy Passengers: 60	**3 oil engines** geared to sc. shafts driving 3 Water jets Total Power: 4,359kW (5,925hp) 35.0kn M.T.U. 12V396TE74L 3 x Vee 4 Stroke 12 Cy. 165 x 185 each-1453kW (1975bhp) MTU Friedrichshafen GmbH-Friedrichshafen AuxGen: 2 x 60kW 380/220V 60Hz a.c
9466037 *5NFB9* -	**SURFER 322** *ex* Surfer 32 M *-2007* **Bourbon Interoil Nigeria Ltd** - *Port Harcourt* *Nigeria* MMSI: 657228000	**226** 67 29	Class: BV	**2007-07 West Atlantic Shipyard — Port Harcourt** Yd No: WAS04 Loa 34.33 Br ex - Dght 1.200 Lbp 29.60 Br md 6.70 Dpth 3.00 Welded, 1 dk	**(B21A20C) Crew/Supply Vessel** Hull Material: Aluminium Alloy Passengers: 90	**3 oil engines** reduction geared to sc. shafts driving 3 Water jets Total Power: 4,500kW (6,117hp) 35.0kn M.T.U. 12V396TE74L 3 x Vee 4 Stroke 12 Cy. 165 x 185 each-1500kW (2039bhp) MTU Friedrichshafen GmbH-Friedrichshafen
9377468 *FMHS* -	**SURFER 323** - **Bourbon Offshore Surf SAS** - *Marseille* *France (FIS)* MMSI: 228328700 Official number: 924672D	**201** 61 29	Class: BV	**2006-03 Chantiers Piriou — Concarneau** Yd No: C265 Loa 34.33 Br ex - Dght 1.200 Lbp 31.02 Br md 6.70 Dpth 3.00 Welded, 1 dk	**(B21A20C) Crew/Supply Vessel** Hull Material: Aluminium Alloy Passengers: 90	**3 oil engines** reduction geared to sc. shafts driving 3 Water jets Total Power: 4,359kW (5,925hp) 35.0kn M.T.U. 12V396TE74L 3 x Vee 4 Stroke 12 Cy. 165 x 185 each-1453kW (1975bhp) MTU Friedrichshafen GmbH-Friedrichshafen
9405174 *HP4891* -	**SURFER 324** - **Bourbon East Asia Pte Ltd** Bourbon Offshore Asia Pte Ltd *Panama* *Panama* MMSI: 355190000 Official number: 4465213A	**168** 50 29	Class: BV	**2007-04 Chantiers Piriou — Concarneau** Yd No: C288 Loa 34.33 Br ex - Dght 1.200 Lbp 29.60 Br md 6.70 Dpth 3.00 Welded, 1 dk	**(B21A20C) Crew/Supply Vessel** Hull Material: Aluminium Alloy Passengers: 90	**3 oil engines** reduction geared to sc. shafts driving 3 Water jets Total Power: 4,500kW (6,117hp) 35.0kn M.T.U. 12V396TE74L 3 x Vee 4 Stroke 12 Cy. 165 x 185 each-1500kW (2039bhp) MTU Friedrichshafen GmbH-Friedrichshafen
9425344 *FNLJ* -	**SURFER 325** - **Bourbon Offshore Surf SAS** - *Marseille* *France (FIS)* MMSI: 228328900 Official number: 926356J	**199** 60 29	Class: BV	**2007-10 Chantiers Piriou — Concarneau** Yd No: C290 Loa 34.33 Br ex - Dght 1.200 Lbp 29.60 Br md 6.70 Dpth 3.00 Welded, 1 dk	**(B21A20C) Crew/Supply Vessel** Hull Material: Aluminium Alloy Passengers: 90	**3 oil engines** reduction geared to sc. shafts driving 3 Water jets Total Power: 4,500kW (6,117hp) 35.0kn M.T.U. 12V396TE74L 3 x Vee 4 Stroke 12 Cy. 165 x 185 each-1500kW (2039bhp) MTU Friedrichshafen GmbH-Friedrichshafen
9499709 *FNSG* -	**SURFER 326** - **Bourbon Offshore Surf SAS** - *Marseille* *France (FIS)* MMSI: 228329600 Official number: 927781H	**168** 60 38	Class: BV	**2009-02 Chantiers Piriou — Concarneau** Yd No: C298 Loa 34.33 Br ex - Dght 1.400 Lbp 29.60 Br md 6.70 Dpth 2.97 Welded, 1 dk	**(B21A20C) Crew/Supply Vessel** Hull Material: Aluminium Alloy	**3 oil engines** reduction geared to sc. shafts driving 3 Water jets Total Power: 4,500kW (6,117hp) 34.0kn M.T.U. 12V396TE74L 3 x Vee 4 Stroke 12 Cy. 165 x 185 each-1500kW (2039bhp) MTU Friedrichshafen GmbH-Friedrichshafen AuxGen: 2 x 62kW 50Hz a.c
9499711 *FNJZ* -	**SURFER 327** - **Bourbon Offshore Surf SAS** - SatCom: Inmarsat C 422830591 *Marseille* *France (FIS)* MMSI: 228305900 Official number: 928442B	**168** 60 38	Class: BV	**2009-05 Chantiers Piriou — Concarneau** Yd No: C299 Loa 34.30 Br ex - Dght 1.400 Lbp 29.50 Br md 6.70 Dpth 3.00 Welded, 1 dk	**(B21A20C) Crew/Supply Vessel** Hull Material: Aluminium Alloy	**3 oil engines** reduction geared to sc. shafts driving 3 Water jets Total Power: 4,500kW (6,117hp) 34.0kn M.T.U. 12V396TE74L 3 x Vee 4 Stroke 12 Cy. 165 x 185 each-1500kW (2039bhp) MTU Friedrichshafen GmbH-Friedrichshafen AuxGen: 2 x 62kW 50Hz a.c
9601974 *5NUV9* -	**SURFER 328** - **Bourbon Offshore Surf SAS** - *Lagos* *Nigeria* MMSI: 657875000	**168** 50 37	Class: BV	**2011-08 West Atlantic Shipyard — Port Harcourt** Yd No: WAS31 Loa 34.33 Br ex 6.71 Dght 1.200 Lbp 29.60 Br md 6.70 Dpth 3.00 Welded, 1 dk	**(B21A20C) Crew/Supply Vessel** Hull Material: Aluminium Alloy	**3 oil engines** reduction geared to sc. shafts driving 3 Water jets Total Power: 4,500kW (6,117hp) 34.0kn M.T.U. 12V396TE74L 3 x Vee 4 Stroke 12 Cy. 165 x 185 each-1500kW (2039bhp) MTU Friedrichshafen GmbH-Friedrichshafen
9566899 *YB4722* -	**SURFER 2601** - **PT Surf Marine Indonesia** - *Jakarta* *Indonesia* MMSI: 525016650 Official number: 2010PST NO6166/L	**128** 39 56	Class: BV KI	**2009-03 South East Asia Shipyard — Ben Luc** Yd No: 12 Loa 26.20 Br ex - Dght 1.090 Lbp 24.77 Br md 6.20 Dpth 2.60 Welded, 1 dk	**(B21A20C) Crew/Supply Vessel** Hull Material: Aluminium Alloy Passengers: unberthed: 50	**4 oil engines** geared to sc. shafts driving 4 Water jets Total Power: 2,644kW (3,596hp) 26.0kn MAN D2842LE 4 x Vee 4 Stroke 12 Cy. 128 x 142 each-661kW (899bhp) MAN Nutzfahrzeuge AG-Nuernberg AuxGen: 2 x 44kW 50Hz a.c
9566904 *HP7213* -	**SURFER 2602** - **Bourbon Supply Investissements SAS** Bourbon Offshore Surf SAS *Panama* *Panama* MMSI: 371244000 Official number: 4042809A	**112** 34 56	Class: BV	**2009-03 South East Asia Shipyard — Ben Luc** Yd No: 13 Loa 26.20 Br ex - Dght 1.090 Lbp 24.00 Br md 6.20 Dpth 2.60 Welded, 1 dk	**(B21A20C) Crew/Supply Vessel** Hull Material: Aluminium Alloy Passengers: unberthed: 50	**4 oil engines** geared to sc. shafts driving 4 Water jets Total Power: 2,644kW (3,596hp) 26.0kn MAN D2842LE 4 x Vee 4 Stroke 12 Cy. 128 x 142 each-661kW (899bhp) MAN Nutzfahrzeuge AG-Nuernberg AuxGen: 2 x 44kW 50Hz a.c
9567300 *HP6508* -	**SURFER 2603** - **Bourbon Supply Investissements SAS** Bourbon Offshore Surf SAS *Panama* *Panama* MMSI: 371038000 Official number: 4177210	**112** 34 56	Class: BV	**2009-08 South East Asia Shipyard — Ben Luc** Yd No: 14 Loa 26.20 Br ex - Dght 1.090 Lbp 24.00 Br md 6.20 Dpth 2.60 Welded, 1 dk	**(B21A20C) Crew/Supply Vessel** Hull Material: Aluminium Alloy Passengers: unberthed: 50	**4 oil engines** geared to sc. shafts driving 4 Water jets Total Power: 2,644kW (3,596hp) 26.0kn MAN D2842LE 4 x Vee 4 Stroke 12 Cy. 128 x 142 each-661kW (899bhp) MAN Nutzfahrzeuge AG-Nuernberg AuxGen: 2 x 44kW 50Hz a.c
9567568 *HP2676* -	**SURFER 2604** - **Bourbon Supply Investissements SAS** Bourbon Offshore Surf SAS *Panama* *Panama* MMSI: 370875000 Official number: 4164510	**112** 34 56	Class: BV	**2009-11 South East Asia Shipyard — Ben Luc** Yd No: 15 Loa 26.20 Br ex - Dght 1.090 Lbp 24.00 Br md 6.20 Dpth 2.60 Welded, 1 dk	**(B21A20C) Crew/Supply Vessel** Hull Material: Aluminium Alloy Passengers: unberthed: 50	**4 oil engines** geared to sc. shafts driving 4 Water jets Total Power: 2,644kW (3,596hp) 26.0kn MAN D2842LE 4 x Vee 4 Stroke 12 Cy. 128 x 142 each-661kW (899bhp) MAN Nutzfahrzeuge AG-Nuernberg AuxGen: 2 x 44kW 50Hz a.c
9581100 *HP2700* -	**SURFER 2605** - **Bourbon Offshore Surf SAS** - *Panama* *Panama* MMSI: 355770000 Official number: 39965PEXT	**112** 34 56	Class: BV	**2009-11 South East Asia Shipyard — Ben Luc** Yd No: 27 Loa 26.20 Br ex - Dght 1.090 Lbp 24.00 Br md 6.20 Dpth 2.60 Welded, 1 dk	**(B21A20C) Crew/Supply Vessel** Hull Material: Aluminium Alloy Passengers: unberthed: 50	**4 oil engines** geared to sc. shafts driving 4 Water jets Total Power: 3,236kW (4,400hp) 26.0kn MAN D2842LE 4 x Vee 4 Stroke 12 Cy. 128 x 142 each-809kW (1100bhp) MAN Nutzfahrzeuge AG-Nuernberg AuxGen: 2 x 44kW 50Hz a.c
9588756 *H09438* -	**SURFER 2606** - **Bourbon Offshore Surf SAS** - *Panama* *Panama* MMSI: 353080000 Official number: 4192610	**112** 34 56	Class: BV	**2010-05 South East Asia Shipyard — Ben Luc** Yd No: 28 Loa 26.20 Br ex 6.70 Dght 1.090 Lbp 24.59 Br md 6.20 Dpth 2.60 Welded, 1 dk	**(B21A20C) Crew/Supply Vessel** Hull Material: Aluminium Alloy Passengers: unberthed: 50	**4 oil engines** recuction geared to sc. shafts driving 4 Water jets Total Power: 3,236kW (4,400hp) 26.0kn MAN D2842LE 4 x Vee 4 Stroke 12 Cy. 128 x 142 each-809kW (1100bhp) MAN Nutzfahrzeuge AG-Nuernberg AuxGen: 2 x 44kW 50Hz a.c

9592862 *HP7392* -	**SURFER 2607** **Bourbon Offshore Surf SAS** - *Panama* *Panama* Official number: 4207510	**112** 34 56	Class: BV	**2010-08 South East Asia Shipyard — Ben Luc** Yd No: 29 Loa 27.00 Br ex 6.70 Dght 1.090 Lbp 24.59 Br md 6.20 Dpth 2.60 Welded, 1 dk	**(B21A20C) Crew/Supply Vessel** Hull Material: Aluminium Alloy Passengers: unberthed: 50	**4 oil engines** reduction geared to sc. shafts driving 4 Water jets Total Power: 3,236kW (4,400hp) 26.0kn MAN D2842LE 4 x Vee 4 Stroke 12 Cy. 128 x 142 each-809kW (1100bhp) MAN Nutzfahrzeuge AG-Nuernberg AuxGen: 2 x 44kW 50Hz a.c
9604562 *HP5202* -	**SURFER 2608** **Bourbon Supply Investissements SAS** Bourbon Offshore Surf SAS *Panama* *Panama* Official number: 4246011	**111** 33 75	Class: BV	**2010-10 South East Asia Shipyard — Ben Luc** Yd No: 30 Loa 26.90 Br ex 6.70 Dght 1.090 Lbp 24.00 Br md 6.20 Dpth 2.60 Welded, 1 dk	**(B21A20C) Crew/Supply Vessel** Hull Material: Aluminium Alloy Passengers: unberthed: 50	**4 oil engines** reduction geared to sc. shafts driving 4 Water jets Total Power: 3,236kW (4,400hp) 26.0kn MAN D2842LE 4 x Vee 4 Stroke 12 Cy. 128 x 142 each-809kW (1100bhp) MAN Nutzfahrzeuge AG-Nuernberg AuxGen: 2 x 44kW 50Hz a.c
9610585 *HP7245* -	**SURFER 2609** *ex SEAS 31 -2011* **Bourbon Supply Investissements SAS** Bourbon Offshore Surf SAS *Panama* *Panama* MMSI: 352289000 Official number: 4257411	**112** 34 75	Class: BV	**2011-01 South East Asia Shipyard — Ben Luc** Yd No: 31 Loa 26.90 Br ex - Dght 1.090 Lbp 24.00 Br md 6.20 Dpth 2.60 Welded, 1 dk	**(B21A20C) Crew/Supply Vessel** Hull Material: Aluminium Alloy Passengers: unberthed: 50	**4 oil engines** geared to sc. shafts driving 4 Water jets Total Power: 2,648kW (3,600hp) 26.0kn MAN D2842LE 4 x Vee 4 Stroke 12 Cy. 128 x 142 each-662kW (900bhp) MAN Nutzfahrzeuge AG-Nuernberg AuxGen: 2 x 44kW 50Hz a.c
9611400 *YB4782* -	**SURFER 2610** **PT Surf Marine Indonesia** - *Tanjung Priok* *Indonesia* MMSI: 525015780 Official number: GT.128 NO.3205/PST	**128** 39 75	Class: BV KI	**2010-12 South East Asia Shipyard — Ben Luc** Yd No: 32 Loa 26.90 Br ex - Dght 1.090 Lbp 24.77 Br md 6.20 Dpth 2.60 Welded, 1 dk	**(B21A20C) Crew/Supply Vessel** Hull Material: Aluminium Alloy Passengers: unberthed: 50	**4 oil engines** geared to sc. shafts driving 4 Water jets Total Power: 3,236kW (4,400hp) 26.0kn MAN D2842LE 4 x Vee 4 Stroke 12 Cy. 128 x 142 each-809kW (1100bhp) MAN Nutzfahrzeuge AG-Nuernberg AuxGen: 2 x 44kW 50Hz a.c Fuel: 8.0 (d.f.)
9611412 *5NUV5* -	**SURFER 2611** **Bourbon Interoil Nigeria Ltd** - *Lagos* *Nigeria*	**112** 34 56	Class: BV (KI)	**2011-04 South East Asia Shipyard — Ben Luc** Yd No: 34 Loa 26.20 Br ex - Dght 1.090 Lbp 24.00 Br md 6.20 Dpth 2.60 Welded, 1 dk	**(B21A20C) Crew/Supply Vessel** Hull Material: Aluminium Alloy Passengers: unberthed: 50	**4 oil engines** geared to sc. shafts driving 4 Water jets Total Power: 3,236kW (4,400hp) 26.0kn MAN D2842LE 4 x Vee 4 Stroke 12 Cy. 128 x 142 each-809kW (1100bhp) MAN Nutzfahrzeuge AG-Nuernberg AuxGen: 2 x 44kW 50Hz a.c
9611424 *HP7094* -	**SURFER 2612** **Bourbon Supply Investissements SAS** Bourbon Offshore Asia Pte Ltd *Panama* *Panama* MMSI: 356978000 Official number: 4319111	**111** 33 56	Class: BV	**2011-04 South East Asia Shipyard — Ben Luc** Yd No: 35 Loa 26.20 Br ex - Dght 1.090 Lbp 24.00 Br md 6.20 Dpth 2.60 Welded, 1 dk	**(B21A20C) Crew/Supply Vessel** Hull Material: Aluminium Alloy Passengers: unberthed: 50	**4 oil engines** geared to sc. shafts driving 4 Water jets Total Power: 2,648kW (3,600hp) 26.0kn MAN D2842LE 4 x Vee 4 Stroke 12 Cy. 128 x 142 each-662kW (900bhp) MAN Nutzfahrzeuge AG-Nuernberg AuxGen: 2 x 44kW 50Hz a.c
9596557 - -	**SURFER 2621** **Bourbon Interoil Nigeria Ltd** - *Lagos* *Nigeria*	**112** - 52	Class: BV	**2010-03 West Atlantic Shipyard — Port Harcourt** Yd No: WAS27 Loa 26.90 Br ex - Dght 1.100 Lbp 26.20 Br md 6.20 Dpth 2.60 Welded, 1 dk	**(B21A20C) Crew/Supply Vessel** Hull Material: Aluminium Alloy Passengers: unberthed: 50	**4 oil engines** reduction geared to sc. shafts driving 4 Water jets Total Power: 2,648kW (3,600hp) 26.0kn MAN D2842LE 4 x Vee 4 Stroke 12 Cy. 128 x 142 each-662kW (900bhp) MAN Nutzfahrzeuge AG-Nuernberg AuxGen: 2 x 44kW 400V a.c
9605310 - -	**SURFER 2622** **Bourbon Interoil Nigeria Ltd** - *Lagos* *Nigeria*	**112** - 52	Class: BV	**2010-06 West Atlantic Shipyard — Port Harcourt** Yd No: WAS28 Loa 26.90 Br ex - Dght 1.100 Lbp 26.20 Br md 6.20 Dpth 2.60 Welded, 1 dk	**(B21A20C) Crew/Supply Vessel** Hull Material: Aluminium Alloy Passengers: unberthed: 50	**4 oil engines** reduction geared to sc. shafts driving 4 Water jets Total Power: 3,236kW (4,400hp) 26.0kn MAN D2842LE 4 x Vee 4 Stroke 12 Cy. 128 x 142 each-809kW (1100bhp) MAN Nutzfahrzeuge AG-Nuernberg AuxGen: 2 x 44kW 400V 50Hz a.c
8663664 *5NTU* -	**SURFER 2623** **Bourbon Interoil Nigeria Ltd** - *Lagos* *Nigeria* MMSI: 657602000	**112** - 52	Class: BV	**2010-09 West Atlantic Shipyard — Port Harcourt** Yd No: WAS29 Loa 26.90 Br ex - Dght 1.100 Lbp 26.20 Br md 6.20 Dpth 2.60 Welded, 1 dk	**(B21A20C) Crew/Supply Vessel** Hull Material: Aluminium Alloy Passengers: unberthed: 50	**4 oil engines** reduction geared to sc. shafts driving 4 Water jets Total Power: 2,648kW (3,600hp) 26.0kn MAN D2842LE 1 x Vee 4 Stroke 12 Cy. 128 x 142 662kW (900bhp) MAN Nutzfahrzeuge AG-Nuernberg MAN D2842LE 3 x Vee 4 Stroke 12 Cy. 128 x 142 each-662kW (900bhp) MAN Nutzfahrzeuge AG-Nuernberg AuxGen: 2 x 44kW 50Hz a.c Fuel: 6.0 (d.f.)
8663676 *5NG2* -	**SURFER 2624** **Bourbon Interoil Nigeria Ltd** - *Lagos* *Nigeria*	**112** - 52	Class: BV	**2011-01 West Atlantic Shipyard — Port Harcourt** Yd No: WAS30 Loa 26.90 Br ex Dght 1.100 Lbp 26.20 Br md 6.20 Dpth 2.60 Welded, 1 dk	**(B21A20C) Crew/Supply Vessel** Hull Material: Aluminium Alloy Passengers: unberthed: 50	**4 oil engines** reduction geared to sc. shafts driving 4 Water jets Total Power: 2,648kW (3,600hp) 26.0kn MAN D2842LE 1 x Vee 4 Stroke 12 Cy. 128 x 142 662kW (900bhp) MAN Nutzfahrzeuge AG-Nuernberg MAN D2842LE 3 x Vee 4 Stroke 12 Cy. 128 x 142 each-662kW (900bhp) MAN Nutzfahrzeuge AG-Nuernberg AuxGen: 2 x 44kW 50Hz a.c Fuel: 6.0 (d.f.)
9566320 *HP4939* -	**SURFER 3601** **Latin Quarter Servicios Maritimos Internacional Lda** Bourbon Offshore Surf SAS SatCom: Inmarsat C 435285910 *Panama* *Panama* MMSI: 352859000 Official number: 4170910	**211** 64 96	Class: BV	**2010-01 Chantiers Piriou — Concarneau** Yd No: C302 Loa 36.30 Br ex - Dght 1.260 Lbp 32.30 Br md 6.70 Dpth 3.00 Welded, 1 dk	**(B21A20C) Crew/Supply Vessel** Hull Material: Aluminium Alloy Passengers: unberthed: 50	**3 oil engines** reduction geared to sc. shafts driving 3 Water jets Total Power: 6,000kW (8,157hp) 40.0kn M.T.U. 16V396TE74L 3 x Vee 4 Stroke 16 Cy. 165 x 185 each-2000kW (2719bhp) MTU Friedrichshafen GmbH-Friedrichshafen AuxGen: 2 x 62kW 50Hz a.c Fuel: 15.0 (d.f.)
9566332 *HP5095* -	**SURFER 3602** **Latin Quarter Servicios Maritimos Internacional Lda** Bourbon Offshore Surf SAS *Panama* *Panama* MMSI: 357688000 Official number: 4195410	**211** 64 96	Class: BV	**2010-05 Chantiers Piriou — Concarneau** Yd No: C303 Loa 36.30 Br ex - Dght 1.260 Lbp 32.30 Br md 6.70 Dpth 3.00 Welded, 1 dk	**(B21A20C) Crew/Supply Vessel** Hull Material: Aluminium Alloy Passengers: unberthed: 50	**3 oil engines** reduction geared to sc. shafts driving 3 Water jets Total Power: 6,000kW (8,157hp) 40.0kn M.T.U. 16V396TE74L 3 x Vee 4 Stroke 16 Cy. 165 x 185 each-2000kW (2719bhp) MTU Friedrichshafen GmbH-Friedrichshafen AuxGen: 2 x 62kW 50Hz a.c Fuel: 15.0
9595541 *5BRP3* -	**SURFER 3603** **Bourbon Offshore Surf SAS** - *Limassol* *Cyprus* MMSI: 210584000	**211** 64 21	Class: BV	**2011-08 Chantiers Piriou — Concarneau** Yd No: C308 Loa 36.30 Br ex - Dght 1.260 Lbp 32.30 Br md 6.70 Dpth 3.00 Welded, 1 dk	**(B21A20C) Crew/Supply Vessel** Hull Material: Aluminium Alloy Passengers: unberthed: 50	**3 oil engines** reduction geared to sc. shafts driving 3 Water jets Total Power: 6,000kW (8,157hp) 40.0kn M.T.U. 16V396TE74L 3 x Vee 4 Stroke 16 Cy. 165 x 185 each-2000kW (2719bhp) MTU Friedrichshafen GmbH-Friedrichshafen AuxGen: 2 x 62kW 50Hz a.c Fuel: 18.0 (d.f.)
9276016 *9HTS7* -	**SURFER ROSA** *completed as Kazbek -2004* **Kiko Financing Ltd** Minerva Marine Inc *Valletta* *Malta* MMSI: 215555000 Official number: 8589	**29,327** 11,984 46,719 T/cm 52.3	Class: NV	**2004-02 Hyundai Mipo Dockyard Co Ltd — Ulsan** Yd No: 0202 Loa 183.21 (BB) Br ex 32.24 Dght 12.200 Lbp 174.00 Br md 32.20 Dpth 18.80 Welded, 1 dk	**(A12B2TR) Chemical/Products Tanker** Double Hull (13F) Liq: 51,470; Liq (Oil): 51,470 Cargo Heating Coils Compartments: 12 Wing Ta, 2 Wing Slop Ta, ER 12 Cargo Pump (s): 12x600m³/hr Manifold: Bow/CM: 90.8m Ice Capable	**1 oil engine** driving 1 FP propeller Total Power: 9,466kW (12,870hp) 14.6kn B&W 6S50MC-C 1 x 2 Stroke 6 Cy. 500 x 2000 9466kW (12870bhp) Hyundai Heavy Industries Co Ltd-South Korea AuxGen: 3 x 902kW a.c Fuel: 210.7 (d.f.) 1385.2 (r.f.)

IMO / Call sign	Name / Owner / Manager / Port	Tonnage	Class	Builder / Dimensions	Type	Machinery
7630517 *UGFL* -	**SURGAN** **Poseydon Co Ltd** - *Nevelsk* *Russia* Official number: 751615	**172** 51 89	Class: (RS)	**1976 Sretenskiy Sudostroitelnyy Zavod — Sretensk** Yd No: 85 Loa 33.96 Br ex 7.09 Dght 2.899 Lbp 30.00 Br md 7.00 Dpth 3.69 Welded, 1 dk	**(B11B2FV) Fishing Vessel** Bale: 96 Compartments: 1 Ho, ER 1 Ha: (1.6 x 1.3) Derricks: 2x2t; Winches: 2 Ice Capable	**1 oil engine** driving 1 FP propeller Total Power: 224kW (305hp) 9.3kn S.K.L. 8NVD36-1U 1 x 4 Stroke 8 Cy. 240 x 360 224kW (305bhp) VEB Schwermaschinenbau "KarlLiebknecht" (SKL)-Magdeburg AuxGen: 1 x 86kW, 1 x 60kW Fuel: 22.0 (d.f.)
9119361 *UBRB* -	**SURGUT** *ex* Aleksey Kortunov *-2004* **Temryuk Trans Marine Co Ltd** Marine Shipping Co Ltd (OOO 'Morskaya Sudokhodnaya Kompaniya') SatCom: Inmarsat C 427300873 *Temryuk* *Russia* MMSI: 273452000 Official number: 931327	**4,110** 1,358 4,916	Class: RS	**1994-08 Sudostroitelnyy Zavod "Krasnoye Sormovo" — Nizhniy Novgorod** Yd No: 19611/29 Loa 117.50 Br ex 16.56 Dght 4.770 Lbp 111.40 Br md 16.40 Dpth 6.70 Welded, 1 dk	**(A31A2GX) General Cargo Ship** Compartments: 3 Ho, ER 3 Ha: ER 3 (18.7 x 11.8)	**2 oil engines** driving 2 FP propellers Total Power: 1,940kW (2,638hp) 11.0kn S.K.L. 8NVDS48A-3U 2 x 4 Stroke 8 Cy. 320 x 480 each-970kW (1319bhp) SKL Motoren u. Systemtechnik AG-Magdeburg AuxGen: 3 x 150kW Thrusters: 1 Tunnel thruster (f) Fuel: 220.0 (d.f.) 240.0 (r.f.)
7722059 *V7MH7* -	**SURI** *ex* Fierce Contender *-2007* *ex* Rosanna Hebert *-1987* **Suri Holdings Ltd** - *Bikini* *Marshall Islands* MMSI: 538070349 Official number: 70349	**1,352** 405 845	Class: BV (RS) (AB)	**1978-02 Halter Marine, Inc. — Lockport, La** Yd No: 656 Converted From: Fishing Vessel-1987 Converted From: Offshore Supply Ship-1987 Loa 52.42 Br ex 11.61 Dght 3.350 Lbp - Br md 11.59 Dpth 3.97 Welded, 1 dk	**(X11A2YP) Yacht**	**2 oil engines** reverse reduction geared to sc. shafts driving 2 FP propellers Total Power: 1,368kW (1,860hp) 12.0kn G.M. (Detroit Diesel) 16V-149 2 x Vee 2 Stroke 16 Cy. 146 x 146 each-684kW (930bhp) General Motors Corp-USA AuxGen: 2 x 75kW Thrusters: 1 Thwart. FP thruster (f)
9086992 *V8V2041* -	**SURIA** **Seri Mutiara Express** - *Bandar Seri Begawan* *Brunei* Official number: 0122	**128** 47 20	Class: NK	**1993-10 Yong Choo Kui Shipyard Sdn Bhd — Sibu** Yd No: 0192 Loa 37.50 Br ex - Dght 1.306 Lbp 33.92 Br md 4.40 Dpth 2.30 Welded, 1 dk	**(A37A2PC) Passenger/Cruise**	**2 oil engines** geared to sc. shafts driving 2 FP propellers Total Power: 776kW (1,056hp) 25.0kn G.M. (Detroit Diesel) 12V-92-TA 2 x Vee 2 Stroke 12 Cy. 123 x 127 each-388kW (528bhp) General Motors Detroit DieselAllison Divn-USA AuxGen: 2 x 30kW a.c
9025302 - -	**SURIA 22** *ex* Dong Meng Ho *-2006* **Magadan Fishing Port (A/O 'Magadanskiy Morskoy Rybnyy Port')** - *South Korea* Official number: 906128	**208** 62 -		**1990-12 Daeyang Shipbuilding Co Ltd — Gunsan** Loa 33.41 Br ex - Dght 2.695 Lbp - Br md 6.50 Dpth 3.00 Welded, 1 dk	**(B11B2FV) Fishing Vessel**	**1 oil engine** driving 1 Propeller Alpha 6L23/30 1 x 4 Stroke 6 Cy. 225 x 300 Ssangyong Heavy Industries Co Ltd-South Korea
8845042 - -	**SURIATI** *ex* Ihin *-2000* *ex* Inti Nusantara No. 1 *-2000* **PT Suri Lines** - *Makassar* *Indonesia*	*447* 135 -	Class: (KI)	**1972 Fong Kuo Shipbuilding Co Ltd — Kaohsiung** Loa 41.30 Br ex - Dght 2.900 Lbp 36.00 Br md 7.60 Dpth 3.50 Welded, 1 dk	**(A31A2GX) General Cargo Ship**	**1 oil engine** driving 1 FP propeller Total Power: 809kW (1,100hp) Makita GNLH6275 1 x 4 Stroke 6 Cy. 275 x 450 809kW (1100bhp) Makita Diesel Co Ltd-Japan
7018745 *LW8572* -	**SURIMI I** *ex* Arko Fish No. 8 *-1993* *ex* Hachikiccho Maru *-1991* *ex* Kiccho Maru No. 8 *-1988* *ex* Showa Maru No. 21 *-1980* **Surimi SA** - *Buenos Aires* *Argentina* MMSI: 701000848 Official number: 0170	**363** 127 494	Class: (NK)	**1969 Miho Zosensho K.K. — Shimizu** Yd No: 714 Loa 53.29 Br ex 8.51 Dght 3.175 Lbp 47.50 Br md 8.49 Dpth 3.76 Welded, 1 dk	**(B11B2FV) Fishing Vessel**	**1 oil engine** driving 1 FP propeller Total Power: 883kW (1,201hp) Niigata 6M28X 1 x 4 Stroke 6 Cy. 280 x 440 883kW (1201bhp) Niigata Engineering Co Ltd-Japan
9366677 *UHRE* -	**SURKUM** **Vanino Marine Trading Port JSC (Vaninskiy Morskoy Torgovyy Port OAO)** - *Vanino* *Russia*	**198** 59 89	Class: RS (LR) ✠ Classed LR until 27/11/08	**2006-11 Damen Shipyards Changde Co Ltd — Changde HN** (Hull) **2006-11 B.V. Scheepswerf Damen — Gorinchem** Yd No: 510819 Loa 25.86 Br ex 8.94 Dght 3.300 Lbp 23.00 Br md 8.90 Dpth 4.30 Welded, 1 dk	**(B32A2ST) Tug** Ice Capable	**2 oil engines** gearing integral to driving 2 Directional propellers Total Power: 2,028kW (2,758hp) 11.0kn Caterpillar 3512B-HD 2 x Vee 4 Stroke 12 Cy. 170 x 215 each-1014kW (1379bhp) Caterpillar Inc-USA AuxGen: 2 x 84kW 400V 50Hz a.c Fuel: 74.0 (d.f.)
8209315 *CB2924* -	**SURMAR I** **Pesquera Coronel SA** - *Valparaiso* *Chile* MMSI: 725000199 Official number: 2304	*567* 233 -	Class: (GL)	**1981 Astilleros y Servicios Navales S.A. (ASENAV) — Valdivia** Yd No: 021 Loa 43.21 Br ex 10.04 Dght 4.501 Lbp 36.61 Br md 10.00 Dpth 6.71 Welded, 2 dks	**(B11B2FV) Fishing Vessel** Ins: 710	**1 oil engine** geared to sc. shaft driving 1 FP propeller Total Power: 813kW (1,105hp) 12.5kn Deutz SBV6M628 1 x 4 Stroke 6 Cy. 240 x 280 813kW (1105bhp) Kloeckner Humboldt Deutz AG-West Germany
9344588 *TCDA6* -	**SURMENE KA** *ex* Advance 8 *-2005* **Akbasoglu Foreign Trade & Ship Management Co Ltd (Akbasoglu Dis Ticaret ve Gemi Isletmeciligi Ltd Sti)** TRANS KA Tanker Management Co Ltd (TRANS KA Tanker Isletmeciligi Ltd Sti) *Istanbul* *Turkey* MMSI: 271000789 Official number: 1011	**2,983** 1,151 3,945 T/cm 12.0	Class: BV (CC)	**2005-03 Yangzhou Kejin Shipyard Co Ltd — Jiangdu JS** Yd No: QJ3600-01 Loa 95.80 (BB) Br ex - Dght 5.100 Lbp 88.00 Br md 15.20 Dpth 7.20 Welded, 1 dk	**(A12B2TR) Chemical/Products Tanker** Double Hull (13F) Liq: 4,598; Liq (Oil): 4,598 Compartments: 2 Wing Slop Ta, 10 Wing Ta, ER 2 Cargo Pump (s): 2x360m³/hr Manifold: Bow/CM: 46.5m Ice Capable	**1 oil engine** with flexible couplings & sr geared to sc. shaft driving 1 FP propeller Total Power: 2,060kW (2,801hp) 10.5kn Guangzhou 8320ZC 1 x 4 Stroke 8 Cy. 320 x 440 2060kW (2801bhp) Guangzhou Diesel Engine Factory CoLtd-China AuxGen: 3 x 200kW 400/220V 50Hz a.c
8741260 *MTJL2* PD 368	**SURMOUNT** *ex* Vela *-2011* **Secutus Fishing LLP** Peter & J Johnstone Ltd *Peterhead* *United Kingdom* MMSI: 233667000 Official number: B14303	**243** 81 -		**1995 Astilleros Armon SA — Navia** Loa 24.29 (BB) Br ex - Dght 2.960 Lbp - Br md 7.50 Dpth - Welded, 1 dk	**(B11B2FV) Fishing Vessel**	**1 oil engine** driving 1 Propeller Total Power: 439kW (597hp)
8007597 - -	**SURO No. 10** **Government of The Republic of South Korea (Ministry of Transportation)** - *South Korea*	*400* -		**1980-12 Daedong Shipbuilding Co Ltd — Busan** Loa - Br ex - Dght - Lbp - Br md - Dpth - Welded, 1 dk	**(B31A2SR) Research Survey Vessel**	**1 oil engine** geared to sc. shaft driving 1 FP propeller Total Power: 552kW (750hp) Niigata 6MG20AX 1 x 4 Stroke 6 Cy. 200 x 260 552kW (750bhp) Niigata Engineering Co Ltd-Japan
7831915 *UIAK* -	**SUROVSK** **Dalmoreprodukt Holding Co (Kholdingovaya Kompaniya 'Dalmoreprodukt')** - *Vladivostok* *Russia* Official number: 791345	**739** 221 332	Class: RS	**1980 Zavod "Leninskaya Kuznitsa" — Kiyev** Yd No: 244 Loa 53.75 (BB) Br ex 10.72 Dght 4.290 Lbp 47.92 Br md 10.50 Dpth 6.00 Welded, 1 dk	**(B11A2FS) Stern Trawler** Ins: 218 Compartments: 1 Ho, ER 1 Ha: (1.6 x 1.6) Derricks: 2x1.5t Ice Capable	**1 oil engine** driving 1 FP propeller Total Power: 971kW (1,320hp) 12.8kn S.K.L. 8NVD48A-2U 1 x 4 Stroke 8 Cy. 320 x 480 971kW (1320bhp) VEB Schwermaschinenbau "KarlLiebknecht" (SKL)-Magdeburg Fuel: 185.0 (d.f.)
8929563 - -	**SUROVYY** **Okeanrybflot JSC (A/O 'Okeanrybflot')** - *Petropavlovsk-Kamchatskiy* *Russia* Official number: 761937	**180** 54 46	Class: RS	**1976 Gorokhovetskiy Sudostroitelnyy Zavod — Gorokhovets** Yd No: 342 Loa 29.30 Br ex 8.49 Dght 3.090 Lbp 27.00 Br md 8.30 Dpth 4.30 Welded, 1 dk	**(B32A2ST) Tug** Ice Capable	**2 oil engines** driving 2 CP propellers Total Power: 882kW (1,200hp) 11.4kn Russkiy 6D30/50-4-3 2 x 2 Stroke 6 Cy. 300 x 500 each-441kW (600bhp) Mashinostroitelnyy Zavod"Russkiy-Dizel"-Leningrad AuxGen: 2 x 30kW a.c Fuel: 36.0 (d.f.)
9010008 *3EQA8* -	**SURPLUS** *ex* Merak *-2006* **Surplus Enterprises Inc** Harmony Transportation Co Ltd SatCom: Inmarsat C 435510810 *Panama* *Panama* MMSI: 355108000 Official number: 1945891E	**5,551** 2,351 7,055	Class: NK	**1991-01 Shin Kochi Jyuko K.K. — Kochi** Yd No: 7008 Loa 98.17 (BB) Br ex - Dght 7.429 Lbp 89.95 Br md 18.80 Dpth 12.90 Welded, 2 dks	**(A31A2GX) General Cargo Ship** Grain: 13,789; Bale: 12,611 Compartments: 2 Ho, ER 2 Ha: ER Derricks: 2x30t,2x25t	**1 oil engine** driving 1 FP propeller Total Power: 2,424kW (3,296hp) 12.4kn Hanshin 6EL40 1 x 4 Stroke 6 Cy. 400 x 800 2424kW (3296bhp) The Hanshin Diesel Works Ltd-Japan AuxGen: 3 x 164kW a.c Fuel: 525.0 (r.f.)

IMO / Call sign / Flag	Name / Owner	GT / NT / DWT	Class	Builder / Dimensions	Type	Machinery
5131567 - -	**SURPRISE** *ex* Thordis *-2006* *ex* Sandvikingur *-2006* *ex* Johanna *-2006* *ex* Njordur *-1993* *ex* Larus Sveinsson *-1974* *ex* Sigurdur Bjarni *-1968* *ex* Kristjan Valgeir *-1966* *ex* Gjafar *-1964* - -	127 38 -	Class: (BV)	**1960 Scheepswerf & Machinefabriek Fa A van Bennekum NV — Sliedrecht** Yd No: 32 Loa 27.27 Br ex 6.25 Dght 2.744 Lbp - Br md 6.23 Dpth 3.05 Welded, 1 dk	**(B11B2FV) Fishing Vessel** 2 Ha: 2 (2.6 x 1.4)ER Derricks: 1x2t; Winches: 1	**1 oil engine** driving 1 FP propeller Total Power: 416kW (566hp) Caterpillar D379SCAC 1 x Vee 4 Stroke 8 Cy. 159 x 203 416kW (566bhp) (new engine 1972) Caterpillar Tractor Co-USA
9239707 *WDA7276* -	**SURRIE MORAN** - **Moran Towing Corp** - *Wilmington, DE* *United States of America* MMSI: 366841550 Official number: 1104101	232 69 -	Class: AB	**2000-10 Washburn & Doughty Associates Inc — East Boothbay ME** Yd No: 71 Loa 28.04 Br ex - Dght 4.200 Lbp - Br md 9.75 Dpth - Welded, 1 dk	**(B32A2ST) Tug**	**2 oil engines** gearing integral to driving 2 Z propellers Total Power: 3,090kW (4,202hp) EMD (Electro-Motive) 16-645-E2 2 x Vee 2 Stroke 16 Cy. 230 x 254 each-1545kW (2101bhp) General Motors Corp.Electro-Motive Div.-La Grange
8119508 *YJVY5* -	**SURSUM CORDA** - **Sursum Corda Shipping Ltd** Pacific Blue Ltd *Port Vila* *Vanuatu* MMSI: 576015000 Official number: 1887	347 104 -	Class: (LR) (BV) Classed LR until 23/3/95	**1981 Scheepswerf Bodewes Gruno B.V. — Foxhol** Yd No: 251 Converted From: Trawler-2005 Loa 38.05 Br ex 8.02 Dght 3.740 Lbp 33.90 Br md 8.00 Dpth 4.40 Welded, 1 dk	**(B22G2OY) Standby Safety Vessel**	**1 oil engine** dr reverse geared to sc. shaft driving 1 FP propeller Total Power: 1,160kW (1,577hp) 12.0kn Kromhout 9FEHD240 1 x 4 Stroke 9 Cy. 240 x 260 1160kW (1577bhp) Stork Werkspoor Diesel BV-Netherlands AuxGen: 2 x 64kW 380/220V 50Hz a.c, 1 x 16kW 380/220V 50Hz a.c Thrusters: 1 Thwart. FP thruster (f)
9034119 *PHVB* UK 172	**SURSUM CORDA** - **Zeevisserijbedrijf Sursum Corda BV** - SatCom: Inmarsat C 424561210 *Urk* *Netherlands* MMSI: 245612000 Official number: 20947	**458** 137 -		**1992-01 Scheepswerf Metz B.V. — Urk** Yd No: 92 Loa 41.40 Br ex 8.60 Dght 3.750 Lbp 37.40 Br md 8.50 Dpth 5.00 Welded, 1 dk	**(B11A2FT) Trawler** Ins: 200	**1 oil engine** with flexible couplings & sr geared to sc. shaft driving 1 FP propeller Total Power: 1,471kW (2,000hp) 13.5kn Stork-Werkspoor 6SW280 1 x 4 Stroke 6 Cy. 280 x 300 1471kW (2000bhp) Stork Wartsila Diesel BV-Netherlands Thrusters: 1 Thwart. FP thruster (f) Fuel: 94.9 (d.f.)
9109263 *H3OD* -	**SURUGA 1** *ex* Suruga *-2000* **Sealand Trading Service Corp** Dongwon Industries Co Ltd SatCom: Inmarsat A 1206242 *Panama* *Panama* MMSI: 356065000 Official number: 2734100CH	**2,596** 1,052 2,392	Class: KR (NK)	**1994-10 KK Kanasashi — Shizuoka SZ** Yd No: 3351 Loa 88.94 (BB) Br ex - Dght 5.140 Lbp 82.60 Br md 14.50 Dpth 8.00 Welded, 2 dks	**(A34A2GR) Refrigerated Cargo Ship** Ins: 4,031 Compartments: 4 Ho, ER 4 Ha: 4 (3.2 x 3.2)ER Derricks: 8x5t	**1 oil engine** driving 1 FP propeller Total Power: 1,471kW (2,000hp) 12.7kn B&W 6S26MC 1 x 2 Stroke 6 Cy. 260 x 980 1471kW (2000bhp) The Hanshin Diesel Works Ltd-Japan AuxGen: 2 x 388kW 445V a.c Fuel: 700.0 (r.f.)
9118886 *JEGP* S01-1150	**SURUGA MARU** - **Shizuoka Prefectural Office** - SatCom: Inmarsat B 343171310 *Shizuoka, Shizuoka* *Japan* MMSI: 431713000 Official number: 133264	*134* - -		**1995-03 KK Kanasashi — Shizuoka SZ** Yd No: 3362 Loa 34.00 (BB) Br ex - Dght 2.700 Lbp 28.00 Br md 6.60 Dpth 3.10 Welded, 1 dk	**(B12D2FR) Fishery Research Vessel**	**1 oil engine** reduction geared to sc. shaft driving 1 CP propeller Total Power: 883kW (1,201hp) Akasaka T26FD 1 x 4 Stroke 6 Cy. 260 x 440 883kW (1201bhp) Akasaka Tekkosho KK (Akasaka DieselLtd)-Japan Thrusters: 1 Thwart. FP thruster (f); 1 Tunnel thruster (a)
9047659 *JI3489* -	**SURUGA MARU** - **YK Nakagawa Kaiun** - *Kasaoka, Okayama* *Japan* Official number: 133413	*297* - 724		**1992-06 Koa Sangyo KK — Takamatsu KG** Yd No: 566 Loa 52.83 Br ex - Dght 3.680 Lbp - Br md 8.60 Dpth 3.90 Welded, 1 dk	**(A12A2TC) Chemical Tanker** Liq: 521 Compartments: 6 Ta, ER 1 Cargo Pump (s): 1x150m³/hr	**1 oil engine** driving 1 FP propeller Total Power: 736kW (1,001hp) Yanmar MF26-HT 1 x 4 Stroke 6 Cy. 260 x 500 736kW (1001bhp) Yanmar Diesel Engine Co Ltd-Japan
8921432 *JH3157* -	**SURUGA MARU** - **KK Daito Corp & Shimizu Futo KK** Shimizu Futo KK *Shizuoka, Shizuoka* *Japan* Official number: 131546	*147* - 130	Class: NK	**1990-03 Sagami Zosen Tekko K.K. — Yokosuka** Yd No: 243 Loa 30.60 Br ex 8.82 Dght 2.991 Lbp 27.00 Br md 8.80 Dpth 3.50 Welded, 1 dk	**(B32A2ST) Tug**	**2 oil engines** with clutches & dr geared to sc. shafts driving 2 FP propellers Total Power: 2,206kW (3,000hp) 13.8kn Yanmar T260-ET 2 x 4 Stroke 6 Cy. 260 x 330 each-1103kW (1500bhp) Yanmar Diesel Engine Co Ltd-Japan Fuel: 33.0 (d.f.)
9498157 *JD2641* -	**SURUGA MARU** - **Yamanaka Zousen KK (Yamanaka Shipbuilding Corp)** - *Imabari, Ehime* *Japan* Official number: 140746	*498* - 1,570		**2008-03 Yamanaka Zosen K.K. — Imabari** Yd No: 760 Loa 76.38 Br ex - Dght 3.970 Lbp 70.18 Br md 12.30 Dpth 6.85 Welded, 1 dk	**(A31A2GX) General Cargo Ship** Grain: 2,401; Bale: 2,401 1 Ha: (40.1 x 10.0)	**1 oil engine** driving 1 FP propeller Total Power: 1,618kW (2,200hp) 12.8kn Hanshin LH34LAG 1 x 4 Stroke 6 Cy. 340 x 640 1618kW (2200bhp) The Hanshin Diesel Works Ltd-Japan
9674426 *JD3442* -	**SURUGA MARU** - **Tokyoto Kanko Kisen KK** - *Yokohama, Kanagawa* *Japan* MMSI: 431004067 Official number: 141809	*213* - -		**2012-11 Kanagawa Zosen — Kobe** Yd No: 651 Loa 38.40 Br ex - Dght 3.900 Lbp - Br md 9.40 Dpth - Welded, 1 dk	**(B32A2ST) Tug**	**2 oil engines** gearing integral to driving 2 Z propellers Total Power: 3,676kW (4,998hp) Niigata 6L28HX 2 x 4 Stroke 6 Cy. 280 x 370 each-1838kW (2499bhp) Niigata Engineering Co Ltd-Japan
8882985 - -	**SURVEYOR** - **TNY Shipping BV** Enka Insaat ve Sanayi AS *Aqtau* *Kazakhstan*	125 37 -	Class: BV	**1990-07 B.V. Scheepswerf Damen — Gorinchem** Yd No: 2025 Loa 24.00 Br ex 10.75 Dght 1.260 Lbp - Br md 10.00 Dpth 2.50 Welded, 1 dk	**(B34L2QU) Utility Vessel** Cranes: 1x26t,1x12t	**3 oil engines** with clutches & reduction geared to sc. shafts driving 3 FP propellers Total Power: 738kW (1,002hp) 8.7kn Caterpillar 3406B 3 x 4 Stroke 6 Cy. 137 x 165 each-246kW (334bhp) Caterpillar Inc-USA AuxGen: 1 x 32kW 220/380V 50Hz a.c Thrusters: 1 Directional thruster (f) Fuel: 128.0 (d.f.) 3.8pd
9666974 *FIFS* -	**SURVILLE** *ex* Hyundai Mipo 8098 *-2014* **SNC Surville Bail** Geogas Trading SA *Marseille* *France (FIS)* MMSI: 228032600	**23,160** 6,900 26,120	Class: BV	**2014-03 Hyundai Mipo Dockyard Co Ltd — Ulsan** Yd No: 8098 Loa 173.70 (BB) Br ex 28.04 Dght 10.400 Lbp 167.52 Br md 28.00 Dpth 17.80 Welded, 1 dk	**(A11B2TG) LPG Tanker** Liq (Gas): 35,000	**1 oil engine** driving 1 FP propeller 16.4kn
8941016 *WDD6817* -	**SURVIVOR** *ex* Lady Barbara *-2007* **Barbara H Inc** - *Pago Pago, AS* *United States of America* Official number: 1051462	**134** 92 -		**1997 Johnson Shipbuilding & Repair — Bayou La Batre, Al** Yd No: 139 L reg 20.18 Br ex - Dght - Lbp - Br md 7.01 Dpth 3.72 Welded, 1 dk	**(B11B2FV) Fishing Vessel**	**1 oil engine** driving 1 FP propeller
8970146 - -	**SURVIVOR II** *ex* Twin Sons *-2005* **Eno Percie Banks Wood** - *Roatan* *Honduras* Official number: U-1828149	**152** 45 -		**2001-08 Master Boat Builders, Inc. — Coden, Al** L reg 24.87 Br ex - Dght - Lbp - Br md 7.31 Dpth 3.81 Welded, 1 dk	**(B11B2FV) Fishing Vessel**	**1 oil engine** driving 1 FP propeller
8999348 - -	**SURYA 01** - **Muhammad Eliansyah** - *Samarinda* *Indonesia*	**166** 99 -	Class: KI	**2002-05 C.V. Karya Lestari Industri — Samarinda** L reg 22.75 Br ex - Dght - Lbp 21.45 Br md 6.50 Dpth 3.05 Welded, 1 dk	**(B32A2ST) Tug**	**2 oil engines** geared to sc. shafts driving 2 Propellers Total Power: 920kW (1,250hp) 8.0kn Caterpillar D379B 2 x Vee 4 Stroke 8 Cy. 159 x 203 each-460kW (625bhp) (made 1996, fitted 2002) Caterpillar Inc-USA

8657861 *AVWC* -	**SURYA 1** - **SVS Marine Services Pvt Ltd** - *Mumbai* *India* MMSI: 419000619 Official number: 4045	**1,330** 491 2,200	Class: IR (Class contemplated)	**2011**-01 **Shoft Shipyard Pvt Ltd — Bharuch** Yd No: 230 Loa 70.00 Br ex - Dght 3.200 Lbp 67.00 Br md 14.00 Dpth 4.50 Welded, 1 dk	**(A31A2GX) General Cargo Ship**	**2 oil engines** reduction geared to sc. shafts driving 2 Propellers Total Power: 824kW (1,120hp) Cummins 2 x each-412kW (560bhp) Cummins India Ltd-India
8657873 *AVWD* -	**SURYA 2** - **SVS Marine Services Pvt Ltd** - *Mumbai* *India* MMSI: 419000620 Official number: 4046	**1,330** 491 2,200	Class: IR (Class contemplated)	**2011**-02 **Shoft Shipyard Pvt Ltd — Bharuch** Yd No: 231 Loa 70.00 Br ex - Dght 3.200 Lbp 67.00 Br md 14.00 Dpth 4.50 Welded, 1 dk	**(A31A2GX) General Cargo Ship**	**2 oil engines** reduction geared to sc. shafts driving 2 Propellers Total Power: 824kW (1,120hp) Cummins 2 x each-412kW (560bhp) Cummins India Ltd-India
8999386 - -	**SURYA 02** - **Muhammad Eliansyah** - *Samarinda* *Indonesia*	**117** 70 -	Class: KI	**2003**-03 **C.V. Karya Lestari Industri — Samarinda** Loa 22.75 Br ex - Dght - Lbp 21.45 Br md 6.50 Dpth 3.05 Welded, 1 dk	**(B32A2ST) Tug**	**2 oil engines** reduction geared to sc. shafts driving 2 Propellers Total Power: 698kW (950hp) 8.0kn Caterpillar 3408TA 2 x Vee 4 Stroke 8 Cy. 137 x 152 each-349kW (475bhp) Caterpillar Inc-USA AuxGen: 1 x 74kW 400/380V a.c, 1 x 15kW 400/380V a.c, 1 x 10kW 400/380V a.c
8962072 *YD6479* -	**SURYA 2** - **PT Bahtera Dwiputra Mandiri** - *Banjarmasin* *Indonesia*	**125** 75 241	Class: KI (BV)	**1993**-01 **Xiamen Shipyard — Xiamen FJ** Yd No: Y-2057 Loa 25.20 Br ex - Dght 2.900 Lbp 23.26 Br md 7.20 Dpth 3.83 Welded, 1 dk	**(B32A2ST) Tug**	**1 oil engine** reduction geared to sc. shaft driving 1 FP propeller Total Power: 942kW (1,281hp) 11.2kn Caterpillar 3512TA 1 x Vee 4 Stroke 12 Cy. 170 x 190 942kW (1281bhp) Caterpillar Inc-USA AuxGen: 1 x 25kW 380/220V 50Hz a.c
9710672 *AWET* -	**SURYA 3** - **SVS Marine Services Pvt Ltd** - *Mumbai* *India* MMSI: 419000845 Official number: 4124	**2,263** 879 3,000	Class: IR	**2014**-02 **Nantong Tongde Shipyard Co Ltd — Nantong JS** Yd No: 083 Loa 82.00 Br ex - Dght 3.600 Lbp 79.30 Br md 16.00 Dpth 5.50 Welded, 1 dk	**(A31A2GX) General Cargo Ship**	**2 oil engines** reduction geared to sc. shafts driving 2 FP propellers Total Power: 1,490kW (2,026hp) Cummins 2 x each-745kW (1013bhp) Cummins Engine Co Inc-USA
8737075 *YD6937* -	**SURYA 07** - **PT Terang Dunia Agung** - *Samarinda* *Indonesia*	**125** 38 -	Class: (KI)	**2006 C.V. Karya Lestari Industri — Samarinda** Loa 23.00 Br ex - Dght - Lbp 21.40 Br md 6.50 Dpth 2.80 Welded, 1 dk	**(B32A2ST) Tug**	**2 oil engines** driving 2 Propellers Total Power: 912kW (1,240hp) Yanmar 6LAHM-STE3 2 x 4 Stroke 6 Cy. 150 x 165 each-456kW (620bhp) Yanmar Diesel Engine Co Ltd-Japan
9024190 *YD4507* -	**SURYA 33** *ex Sabang XXVII -2005* **PT Pelayaran Nasional Fajar Marindo Raya** Pt Sari Semesta Utama *Jambi* *Indonesia* Official number: 1996RRCNO485/L	**153** 46 -	Class: KI	**1996**-08 **P.T. Sabang Raya Indah — Jambi** Yd No: A-10 Loa 26.00 Br ex - Dght 2.990 Lbp 23.65 Br md 7.00 Dpth 3.50 Welded, 1 dk	**(B32A2ST) Tug**	**2 oil engines** geared to sc. shafts driving 2 Propellers Total Power: 918kW (1,248hp) 11.0kn Caterpillar 3412 2 x Vee 4 Stroke 12 Cy. 137 x 152 each-459kW (624bhp) (made 1996) Caterpillar Inc-USA AuxGen: 2 x 80kW 380/220V a.c
9263825 *YD6835* -	**SURYA 555** - **PT Trans Tirtajasa Gemilang** - *Banjarmasin* *Indonesia*	**148** 45 125	Class: KI (NK)	**2002**-02 **Tuong Aik (Sarawak) Sdn Bhd — Sibu** Yd No: 2108 L reg 21.30 Br ex - Dght 2.972 Lbp 21.85 Br md 7.60 Dpth 3.70 Welded, 1 dk	**(B32A2ST) Tug**	**2 oil engines** reduction geared to sc. shafts driving 2 FP propellers Total Power: 2,318kW (3,152hp) Caterpillar 3512TA 2 x Vee 4 Stroke 12 Cy. 170 x 190 each-1159kW (1576bhp) Caterpillar Inc-USA
9060534 *C6NT7* -	**SURYA AKI** - **MCGC International Ltd** PT Humpuss Intermoda Transportasi Tbk SatCom: Inmarsat C 430952110 *Nassau* *Bahamas* MMSI: 309521000 Official number: 727514	**20,524** 6,158 11,612	Class: NK	**1996**-02 **Kawasaki Heavy Industries Ltd — Sakaide KG** Yd No: 1440 Loa 151.00 (BB) Br ex - Dght 7.600 Lbp 140.00 Br md 28.00 Dpth 16.00 Welded, 1 dk	**(A11A2TN) LNG Tanker** Double Bottom Entire Compartment Length Liq (Gas): 19,538 3 x Gas Tank (s); 3 independent Kvaerner-Moss (alu) sph 6 Cargo Pump (s): 6x850m³/hr Manifold: Bow/CM: 83m	**1 Steam Turb** reduction geared to sc. shaft driving 1 FP propeller Total Power: 8,827kW (12,001hp) 18.5kn Kawasaki UA-120 1 x steam Turb 8827kW (12001shp) Kawasaki Heavy Industries Ltd-Japan AuxGen: 1 x 1300kW 450V a.c, 2 x 1300kW 450V a.c Fuel: 154.0 (d.f.) 1843.0 (r.f.) 68.0pd
9085766 *YDUS*	**SURYA CHANDRA** - **PT Suryandra Nusa** PT Arpeni Pratama Ocean Line Tbk *Jakarta* *Indonesia* MMSI: 525011097	**4,629** 2,124 6,868 T/cm 17.1	Class: KI (AB) (NV)	**1994**-08 **Jurong Shipyard Ltd — Singapore** Yd No: 1042 Loa 102.47 Br ex - Dght 6.010 Lbp 98.40 Br md 18.80 Dpth 8.50 Welded, 1 dk	**(A13B2TP) Products Tanker** Single Hull	**2 oil engines** geared to sc. shafts driving 2 FP propellers Total Power: 2,536kW (3,448hp) 12.0kn Yanmar 6Z280-EN 2 x 4 Stroke 6 Cy. 280 x 360 each-1268kW (1724bhp) Yanmar Diesel Engine Co Ltd-Japan
7607728 *YGRX* -	**SURYA EXPRESS** *ex Shuho Maru -1997* **PT Namsurya Citrasari Lines** - *Surabaya* *Indonesia*	*1,374* 791 2,139	Class: KI (NK)	**1976**-09 **Sasaki Shipbuilding Co Ltd — Osakikamijima HS** Yd No: 307 Loa 69.55 Br ex 11.43 Dght 5.023 Lbp 65.03 Br md 11.41 Dpth 6.81 Welded, 2 dks	**(A31A2GX) General Cargo Ship** Grain: 3,098; Bale: 2,557 Compartments: 1 Ho, ER 1 Ha: (38.4 x 8.4)ER	**1 oil engine** driving 1 FP propeller Total Power: 1,324kW (1,800hp) 11.0kn Hanshin 6EL32 1 x 4 Stroke 6 Cy. 320 x 640 1324kW (1800bhp) (made 1976) The Hanshin Diesel Works Ltd-Japan AuxGen: 2 x 128kW
9068158 - -	**SURYA FORTUNA** *ex Surya Jaya II -2004* **H Asro** - *Samarinda* *Indonesia*	**181** 55 -	Class: KI	**2001**-01 **C.V. Swadaya Utama — Samarinda** Loa 38.60 Br ex - Dght 1.750 Lbp 36.00 Br md 7.75 Dpth 2.20 Welded, 1 dk	**(A35D2RL) Landing Craft** Bow ramp (centre)	**2 oil engines** geared to sc. shafts driving 2 Propellers Total Power: 514kW (698hp) 7.0kn Nissan RD8 2 x Vee 4 Stroke 8 Cy. 135 x 125 each-257kW (349bhp) Nissan Diesel Motor Co. Ltd.-Ageo
8976695 *YB3345* -	**SURYA GEMILANG JAYA 8** - **PT Barelang Surya Gemilang** - *Batam* *Indonesia*	**144** 44 -	Class: (KI)	**2000**-11 **P.T. Sekip Hilir Shipyard — Batam** Loa 30.00 Br ex - Dght 1.050 Lbp 29.07 Br md 5.40 Dpth 2.44 Welded, 1 dk	**(A37B2PS) Passenger Ship** Hull Material: Aluminium Alloy	**2 oil engines** geared to sc. shafts driving 2 FP propellers Total Power: 2,100kW (2,856hp) 28.0kn M.T.U. 16V2000M70 2 x Vee 4 Stroke 16 Cy. 130 x 150 each-1050kW (1428bhp) (made 1999) MTU Friedrichshafen GmbH-Friedrichshafen AuxGen: 1 x 76kW 400/220V a.c
8106941 *VTDN* -	**SURYA I** - **Suraj Fisheries Pvt Ltd** - *Visakhapatnam* *India* Official number: 1934	*121* 75 -	Class: (IR)	**1981**-12 **Machinefabriek D.E. Gorter B.V. — Hoogezand** (Hull) Yd No: 81-7005 **1981**-12 **B.V. Scheepswerf Damen — Gorinchem** Yd No: 4102 Loa 23.50 Br ex 6.53 Dght 2.501 Lbp 21.01 Br md 6.51 Dpth 3.36 Welded	**(B11A2FT) Trawler**	**1 oil engine** geared to sc. shaft driving 1 FP propeller Total Power: 268kW (364hp) Caterpillar 3408TA 1 x Vee 4 Stroke 8 Cy. 137 x 152 268kW (364bhp) Caterpillar Tractor Co-USA
8106939 *VTDP* -	**SURYA II** - **Suraj Fisheries Pvt Ltd** - *Visakhapatnam* *India* Official number: 1935	*121* 75 -	Class: (IR)	**1981**-12 **Machinefabriek D.E. Gorter B.V. — Hoogezand** (Hull) Yd No: 81-7004 **1981**-12 **B.V. Scheepswerf Damen — Gorinchem** Yd No: 4101 Loa 23.50 Br ex 6.53 Dght 2.501 Lbp 21.01 Br md 6.51 Dpth 3.36 Welded	**(B11A2FT) Trawler**	**1 oil engine** geared to sc. shaft driving 1 FP propeller Total Power: 268kW (364hp) Caterpillar 3408TA 1 x Vee 4 Stroke 8 Cy. 137 x 152 268kW (364bhp) Caterpillar Tractor Co-USA
8649503 - -	**SURYA INDAH 2** - **PT Surya Indah Jaya** - *Samarinda* *Indonesia*	**1,097** 330 -	Class: KI	**2009**-09 **CV Sunjaya Abadi — Samarinda** Loa 75.50 Br ex - Dght 2.900 Lbp 69.10 Br md 13.50 Dpth 3.90 Welded, 1 dk	**(A35D2RL) Landing Craft**	**2 oil engines** reduction geared to sc. shafts driving 2 Propellers Total Power: 1,220kW (1,658hp) Yanmar 6AYM-ETE 2 x 4 Stroke 6 Cy. 155 x 180 each-610kW (829bhp) Yanmar Diesel Engine Co Ltd-Japan

8867806 - -	**SURYA INDAH I** *ex* Cong Nghiep 01 *-1998* **Surya Kalteng Indah Lines** - *Indonesia*	*160* 78 150	Class: (VR)	**1987 Kien An Shipbuilding Works — Haiphong** Loa 36.35 Br ex 7.46 Dght 1.700 Lbp - Br md 7.00 Dpth 2.50 Welded, 1 dk	**(A31A2GX) General Cargo Ship**	**1 oil engine** reduction geared to sc. shaft driving 1 FP propeller Total Power: 99kW (135hp) 9.0kn Skoda 6L160 1 x 4 Stroke 6 Cy. 160 x 225 99kW (135bhp) Skoda-Praha
8350188 *YFAE* -	**SURYA INDAH II** *ex* Raider II *-1994* *ex* Shinyo Maru No. 2 *-1993* **Surya Kalteng Indah Lines** - *Semarang* *Indonesia*	**572** 309 709	Class: (KI)	**1975-09 K.K. Mochizuki Zosensho — Osakikamijima** Loa 53.19 Br ex - Dght 3.310 Lbp 49.00 Br md 8.40 Dpth 5.01 Welded, 1 dk	**(A31A2GX) General Cargo Ship**	**1 oil engine** driving 1 FP propeller Total Power: 588kW (799hp) 11.0kn Niigata 6M28KGHS 1 x 4 Stroke 6 Cy. 280 x 440 588kW (799bhp) Niigata Engineering Co Ltd-Japan
9324708 *YD6975* -	**SURYA INDAH JAYA** *ex* Kaltim Dolphin 14-01 *-2007* **PT Surya Indah Jaya** - *Samarinda* *Indonesia*	**162** 49 -	Class: KI (GL)	**2004-06 Eastern Marine Shipbuilding Sdn Bhd — Sibu** Yd No: EM303 Loa 24.50 Br ex - Dght 2.720 Lbp 22.17 Br md 7.32 Dpth 3.20 Welded, 1 dk	**(B32A2ST) Tug**	**2 oil engines** geared to sc. shafts driving 2 FP propellers Total Power: 1,060kW (1,442hp) Caterpillar 3412TA 2 x Vee 4 Stroke 12 Cy. 137 x 152 each-530kW (721bhp) Caterpillar Inc-USA
9029293 - -	**SURYA IV** **PT Wahana Fajar Surya** - *Palembang* *Indonesia*	**297** 144 380	Class: KI	**2001-07 CV Buana Raya Utama — Palembang** Loa 39.00 Br ex - Dght 2.000 Lbp 37.50 Br md 8.90 Dpth 2.60 Welded, 1 dk	**(A13B2TU) Tanker (unspecified)**	**2 oil engines** geared to sc. shafts driving 2 Propellers Total Power: 486kW (660hp) Mitsubishi 8DC91 2 x Vee 4 Stroke 8 Cy. 141 x 152 each-243kW (330bhp) Mitsubishi Heavy Industries Ltd-Japan AuxGen: 1 x 118kW 380/220V a.c, 1 x 8kW 380/220V a.c
8737702 *PMRE* -	**SURYA JAYA** **PT Dian Bahari Sejati** - *Samarinda* *Indonesia* MMSI: 525003009 Official number: 2008 ILK NO. 4516/L	**357** 108 -	Class: KI	**2008-09 PT Muji Rahayu Shipyard — Tenggarong** Yd No: 11576 Loa 50.70 Br ex - Dght - Lbp 45.00 Br md 9.30 Dpth 3.00 Welded, 1 dk	**(A35D2RL) Landing Craft**	**2 oil engines** driving 2 Propellers Total Power: 514kW (698hp) Yanmar 6HA2M-HTE 2 x 4 Stroke 6 Cy. 130 x 165 each-257kW (349bhp) Yanmar Diesel Engine Co Ltd-Japan
8656063 - -	**SURYA JAYA** **Ng Swie Peng** - *Samarinda* *Indonesia*	**154** 47 -	Class: KI	**2011-04 Galangan Kapal Tunas Harapan — Samarinda** Loa - Br ex - Dght - Lbp 24.09 Br md 7.50 Dpth 3.00 Welded, 1 dk	**(B32A2ST) Tug**	**2 oil engines** reduction geared to sc. shafts driving 2 FP propellers
8998758 *YB6688* -	**SURYA JAYA 3** **PT Samudra Mandira Kaltim Prima** - *Samarinda* *Indonesia*	**294** 89 -	Class: KI	**2005-02 Galangan Kapal Tunas Harapan — Samarinda** Loa 45.00 Br ex - Dght - Lbp 42.75 Br md 8.98 Dpth 2.80 Welded, 1 dk	**(A35D2RL) Landing Craft** Bow door (centre)	**2 oil engines** driving 2 Propellers Total Power: 544kW (740hp) Nissan RE10 2 x Vee 4 Stroke 10 Cy. 135 x 132 each-272kW (370bhp) Nissan Diesel Motor Co. Ltd.-Ageo AuxGen: 2 x 37kW 280/220V a.c
8744248 *YB6418* -	**SURYA JAYA 8** **PT Mitra Swire CTM** Patricia Prasatya *Balikpapan* *Indonesia* Official number: 05032008	**204** 62 -	Class: KI	**2008-09 Galangan Kapal CV Karya Mulia — Balikpapan** Yd No: 12741 Loa 38.50 Br ex - Dght 1.875 Lbp 37.00 Br md 7.80 Dpth 2.50 Welded, 1 dk	**(A35D2RL) Landing Craft**	**2 oil engines** reduction geared to sc. shafts driving 2 Propellers Total Power: 514kW (698hp) Yanmar 6HA2M-DTE 2 x 4 Stroke 6 Cy. 130 x 165 each-257kW (349bhp) Yanmar Diesel Engine Co Ltd-Japan AuxGen: 2 x 80kW 400V a.c
7414547 *YGDG* -	**SURYA KARTIKA** *ex* Mermaid *-1999* *ex* Guang Da *-1997* *ex* Melon Queen *-1995* **PT Pelayaran Surya** - *Jakarta* *Indonesia* MMSI: 525019006	**4,833** 2,955 7,910	Class: (BV) (KI)	**1975-05 Watanabe Zosen KK — Imabari EH** Yd No: 171 Loa 115.65 Br ex 17.45 Dght 6.986 Lbp 107.09 Br md 17.40 Dpth 8.69 Welded, 1 dk	**(A31A2GX) General Cargo Ship** Grain: 10,695; Bale: 10,221 Compartments: 2 Ho, ER 2 Ha: (31.0 x 7.8) (30.7 x 7.8)ER Derricks: 4x15t	**1 oil engine** driving 1 FP propeller Total Power: 3,310kW (4,500hp) 12.0kn Mitsubishi 6UET45/80D 1 x 2 Stroke 6 Cy. 450 x 800 3310kW (4500bhp) Kobe Hatsudoki KK-Japan AuxGen: 1 x 400kW a.c Fuel: 569.6
7113040 *YCZV* -	**SURYA KARYA** *ex* Melton Viking *-1981* *ex* Ruth Graef *-1980* *ex* Tor Maas *-1974* *ex* Ruth *-1973* **PT Pelayaran Surya** - *Jakarta* *Indonesia*	**1,244** 438 1,150	Class: (KI) (GL)	**1971-07 Handel en Scheepsbouw Mij. Kramer & Booy N.V. — Kootstertille** Yd No: 170 Loa 64.15 Br ex 10.09 Dght 2.350 Lbp 61.31 Br md 10.03 Dpth 5.19 Welded, 2 dks	**(A31A2GX) General Cargo Ship** Grain: 2,362; Bale: 2,215 Compartments: 1 Ho, ER 1 Ha: (31.2 x 7.7)ER Derricks: 1x5t,1x3t; Winches: 2	**1 oil engine** reverse reduction geared to sc. shaft driving 1 FP propeller Total Power: 662kW (900hp) 11.5kn MWM TBD440-8 1 x 4 Stroke 8 Cy. 230 x 270 662kW (900bhp) Motoren Werke Mannheim AG (MWM)-West Germany AuxGen: 2 x 38kW 380V 50Hz a.c, 1 x 14kW 380V 50Hz a.c
8894794 *YD6578* -	**SURYA KARYA 1** *ex* SCM I *-2008* *ex* Amanda 1 *-2003* **PT Suryakarya Cipta Makmur** - *Banjarmasin* *Indonesia*	**122** 37 -	Class: KI (BV)	**1995-01 Zhuhai Xiangzhou Shipyard — Zhuhai GD** Yd No: 1-362 Loa 25.50 Br ex - Dght 3.050 Lbp 23.49 Br md 6.80 Dpth 3.60 Welded, 1 dk	**(B32A2ST) Tug**	**1 oil engine** reduction geared to screwshaft driving 1 FP propeller Total Power: 942kW (1,281hp) 10.0kn Caterpillar 3512TA 1 x Vee 4 Stroke 12 Cy. 170 x 190 942kW (1281bhp) Caterpillar Inc-USA AuxGen: 1 x 43kW 400V a.c, 1 x 22kW 400V a.c Fuel: 30.2 (d.f.)
8913617 *JVFW5* -	**SURYA KUBER** *ex* Pratibha Koyna *-2013* *ex* Sovereign *-2008* *ex* Presnya *-2004* - - *Ulaanbaatar* *Mongolia* MMSI: 457859000	**28,223** 13,568 47,071 T/cm 52.0	Class: (IR) (NV)	**1992-05 Halla Engineering & Heavy Industries Ltd — Incheon** Yd No: 176 Loa 183.20 (BB) Br ex 32.23 Dght 12.205 Lbp 174.00 Br md 32.20 Dpth 18.00 Welded, 1 dk	**(A13A2TW) Crude/Oil Products Tanker** Double Hull Liq: 54,079; Liq (Oil): 54,079 Cargo Heating Coils Compartments: 8 Ta, 2 Wing Slop Ta, ER 8 Cargo Pump (s): 8x850m³/hr Manifold: Bow/CM: 92.9m Ice Capable	**1 oil engine** driving 1 FP propeller Total Power: 7,466kW (10,151hp) 14.5kn B&W 6S50MC 1 x 2 Stroke 6 Cy. 500 x 1910 7466kW (10151bhp) Hyundai Heavy Industries Co Ltd-South Korea AuxGen: 3 x 600kW 440V 60Hz a.c Fuel: 178.3 (d.f.) (Heating Coils) 1404.8 (r.f.)
8999207 - -	**SURYA MAS** **PT Victoria Internusa Perkasa** - *Balikpapan* *Indonesia*	**261** 79 450	Class: KI	**2001-07 P.T. Galangan Kapal Mas Pioner — Samarinda** L reg 43.15 Br ex - Dght 2.170 Lbp 42.00 Br md 9.00 Dpth 2.70 Welded, 1 dk	**(A35D2RL) Landing Craft** Bow ramp (centre)	**2 oil engines** reduction geared to sc. shafts driving 2 FP propellers Total Power: 398kW (542hp) 7.0kn Mitsubishi S6BF-MTK 2 x 4 Stroke 6 Cy. 132 x 150 each-199kW (271bhp) (made 1974, fitted 2001) Mitsubishi Heavy Industries Ltd-Japan
8519198 *AVJT* -	**SURYA MUKHI** *ex* Thor Guardian *-2013* *ex* Amigo *-2007* *ex* Eugenio *-2006* *ex* Svendborg Guardian *-2003* **Amigo Shipping Corp** Royal Cruises & Allied Shipping Pvt Ltd *India* MMSI: 419000233	**2,200** 1,198 1,720	Class: IR IS (LR) ✠ Classed LR until 6/1/10	**1987-05 Danyard Aalborg A/S — Aalborg** (Hull launched by) **1987-05 Morso Vaerft A/S — Nykobing Mors** (Hull completed by) Yd No: 162 **1987-05 Monberg & Thorsen A/S — Aalborg** Loa 77.86 Br ex 13.49 Dght 3.706 Lbp 72.22 Br md 13.40 Dpth 7.29 Welded, 2 dks	**(A31A2GX) General Cargo Ship** Grain: 4,081; Bale: 4,042 TEU 160 C.Ho 84/20' (40') C.Dk 76/20' (40') incl. 24 ref C Compartments: 1 Ho, ER, 1 Tw Dk 1 Ha: (43.2 x 10.2)ER Cranes: 2x50t Ice Capable	**1 oil engine** with flexible couplings & sr gearedto sc. shaft driving 1 CP propeller Total Power: 1,320kW (1,795hp) 11.5kn MaK 6M452AK 1 x 4 Stroke 6 Cy. 320 x 450 1320kW (1795bhp) Krupp MaK Maschinenbau GmbH-Kiel AuxGen: 1 x 222kW 380V 50Hz a.c, 1 x 200kW 400V 60Hz a.c, 2 x 180kW 380V 50Hz a.c Fuel: 256.0 (d.f.) 7.7pd
9102875 *YDA4029* -	**SURYA OPINI** *ex* Pajero *-2005* *ex* Axon Baiduri *-1999* **PT Limabahari Pandunusa** - *Palembang* *Indonesia*	**119** 36 112	Class: KI (NK)	**1993-12 Super-Light Shipbuilding Contractor — Sibu** Yd No: 7 Loa 23.17 Br ex - Dght 2.388 Lbp 21.03 Br md 7.50 Dpth 2.90 Welded, 1 dk	**(B32A2ST) Tug**	**2 oil engines** reduction geared to sc. shafts driving 2 FP propellers Total Power: 706kW (960hp) 9.0kn Caterpillar 3408TA 2 x Vee 4 Stroke 8 Cy. 137 x 152 each-353kW (480bhp) Caterpillar Inc-USA AuxGen: 2 x 24kW a.c
8840195 *YDIO* -	**SURYA PAPUA** *ex* Surya Pratama *-2008* *ex* Asahi Maru *-2005* *ex* Tsukasa Maru *-1998* **PT Sarana Bahtera Irja** - *Surabaya* *Indonesia*	*1,305* 463 1,250	Class: KI	**1990-02 K.K. Yoshida Zosen Kogyo — Arida** Loa 71.97 Br ex 12.80 Dght 4.430 Lbp 65.50 Br md 11.00 Dpth 6.80 Welded, 1 dk	**(A31A2GX) General Cargo Ship** Grain: 2,247; Bale: 2,222 Compartments: 1 Ho, ER 1 Ha: (35.4 x 8.6)ER	**1 oil engine** geared to sc. shaft driving 1 FP propeller Total Power: 736kW (1,001hp) 10.5kn Hanshin LH28G 1 x 4 Stroke 6 Cy. 280 x 460 736kW (1001bhp) The Hanshin Diesel Works Ltd-Japan AuxGen: 1 x 120kW 225/130V a.c

IMO / Call sign	Name / Owner	Tonnage	Class	Builder / Dimensions	Type	Machinery
8912857 *POWO* -	**SURYA PEKIK** *ex* Ascension *-2012* *ex* Chekhov *-1998* **PT Sarana Bahtera Irja** - Indonesia	3,972 1,617 4,152	Class: (NV) (AB) (RS)	**1993-01 Sedef Gemi Endustrisi A.S. — Gebze** Yd No: 90 Loa 97.80 Br ex 17.34 Dght 5.620 Lbp 90.22 Br md 17.30 Dpth 7.00 Welded, 1 dk	**(A31A2GX) General Cargo Ship** Grain: 5,242; Bale: 5,227 TEU 221 C.Ho 111/20' C.Dk 110/20' incl. 12 ref C. Compartments: 2 Ho, ER 2 Ha: 2 (25.7 x 12.5)ER Cranes: 2x25t Ice Capable	**1 oil engine** driving 1 CP propeller Total Power: 3,354kW (4,560hp) 12.5kn B&W 6L35MC 1 x 2 Stroke 6 Cy. 350 x 1050 3354kW (4560bhp) H Cegielski Poznan SA-Poland AuxGen: 1 x 300kW 220/380V 50Hz a.c, 2 x 264kW 220/380V 50Hz a.c Fuel: 90.0 (d.f.) 275.0 (r.f.) 12.7pd
9015670 *PONM* -	**SURYA PELANGI** *ex* Thor Spring *-2012* *ex* CEC Spring *-2008* *ex* Sofrana Bligh *-2004* *ex* CEC Spring *-2003* *ex* Anking *-2002* *ex* CEC Spring *-2001* *ex* Arktis Spring *-2001* *ex* Mekong Spring *-1995* *ex* Arktis Spring *-1994* **PT Sarana Bahtera Irja** - *Jakarta* Indonesia	2,815 1,532 4,110 T/cm 11.2	Class: (LR) (BV) ✠ Classed LR until 30/6/98	**1993-05 A/S Nordsoevaerftet — Ringkobing** Yd No: 215 Loa 88.42 (BB) Br ex 15.15 Dght 6.010 Lbp 80.30 Br md 15.00 Dpth 7.50 Welded, 1 dk, 2nd portable deck in hold	**(A31A2GX) General Cargo Ship** Grain: 5,240; Bale: 4,907 TEU 247 C.Ho 93/20' (40') C.Dk 154/20' (40') incl. 25 ref C. Compartments: 1 Ho, ER, 1 Tw Dk 1 Ha: (50.0 x 11.8)ER Cranes: 2x50t Ice Capable	**1 oil engine** with flexible couplings & sr geared to sc. shaft driving 1 FP propeller Total Power: 2,200kW (2,991hp) 13.5kn MaK 6M453C 1 x 4 Stroke 6 Cy. 320 x 420 2200kW (2991bhp) Krupp MaK Maschinenbau GmbH-Kiel AuxGen: 3 x 223kW 380V 50Hz a.c, 1 x 208kW 380V 50Hz a.c Thrusters: 1 Thwart. CP thruster (f) Fuel: 338.8 (d.f.) 8.0pd
8909707 *PMMY* -	**SURYA PERSADA** *ex* Seiyo 8 *-2011* *ex* Seiyo *-2002* *ex* Sumitoku Maru No. 8 *-2001* **PT Sarana Bahtera Irja** - *Surabaya* Indonesia	1,245 727 1,767	Class: KI	**1989-12 Masui Zosensho K.K. — Nandan** Yd No: 212 Loa 63.95 (BB) Br ex - Dght 4.250 Lbp 59.00 Br md 12.50 Dpth 6.25 Welded, 1 dk	**(A31A2GX) General Cargo Ship** Grain: 780 Compartments: 1 Ho, ER 1 Ha: ER	**1 oil engine** driving 1 FP propeller Total Power: 736kW (1,001hp) Yanmar MF33-ST 1 x 4 Stroke 6 Cy. 330 x 620 736kW (1001bhp) Yanmar Diesel Engine Co Ltd-Japan AuxGen: 2 x 100kW 220/130V a.c
8844385 *PMFR* -	**SURYA PERTIWI** *ex* Seishin Maru *-2011* **PT Sarana Bahtera Irja** - *Surabaya* Indonesia	1,463 785 1,524	Class: KI	**1990-09 Mategata Zosen K.K. — Namikata** Yd No: 1027 Loa 76.50 Br ex - Dght 4.020 Lbp 71.65 Br md 12.00 Dpth 6.95 Welded, 1 dk	**(A31A2GX) General Cargo Ship** 1 Ha: (39.0 x 9.5)ER	**1 oil engine** geared to sc. shaft driving 1 FP propeller Total Power: 1,471kW (2,000hp) Hanshin 6LU35G 1 x 4 Stroke 6 Cy. 350 x 550 1471kW (2000bhp) The Hanshin Diesel Works Ltd-Japan AuxGen: 1 x 70kW 225V a.c, 1 x 137kW 225V a.c
9032977 *PNVX* -	**SURYA PESONA** *ex* Thor Falcon *-2011* *ex* Scan Falcon *-2002* **PT Sarana Bahtera Irja** - *Surabaya* Indonesia	1,969 1,131 2,784	Class: KI (BV)	**1992-11 Esbjerg Oilfield Services A/S — Esbjerg** Yd No: 63 Loa 83.20 Br ex - Dght 5.380 Lbp 77.20 Br md 13.20 Dpth 6.65 Welded, 1 dk	**(A31A2GX) General Cargo Ship** Grain: 3,792; Bale: 3,452 TEU 151 C. 151/20' Compartments: 1 Ho, ER 1 Ha: (49.8 x 10.2)ER Cranes: 2x50t Ice Capable	**1 oil engine** geared to sc. shaft driving 1 FP propeller Total Power: 1,596kW (2,170hp) 14.5kn Deutz SBV8M628 1 x 4 Stroke 8 Cy. 240 x 280 1596kW (2170bhp) Motoren Werke Mannheim AG (MWM)-Mannheim AuxGen: 2 x 140kW 380V a.c
9046148 *JZAC* -	**SURYA PIONEER** *ex* Thor Leader *-2013* *ex* CEC Leader *-2009* *ex* Arktis Crystal *-2003* *ex* CEC Crystal *-2002* *ex* Arktis Crystal *-2002* **PT Sarana Bahtera Irja** - Indonesia	3,810 2,055 5,394	Class: (LR) (BV) ✠ Classed LR until 21/12/12	**1994-05 A/S Nordsoevaerftet — Ringkobing** Yd No: 218 Loa 97.40 (BB) Br ex 16.36 Dght 6.710 Lbp 87.30 Br md 16.20 Dpth 8.50 Welded, 1 dk, 2nd portable deck in hold	**(A31A2GX) General Cargo Ship** Grain: 6,908; Bale: 6,318 TEU 350 C.Ho 126/20' C.Dk 224/20' incl. 50 ref C. Compartments: 1 Ho, ER, 1 Tw Dk 1 Ha: (56.6 x 12.8)ER Cranes: 2x50t	**1 oil engine** with flexible couplings & sr geared to sc. shaft driving 1 CP propeller Total Power: 3,300kW (4,487hp) 15.0kn MaK 9M453C 1 x 4 Stroke 9 Cy. 320 x 420 3300kW (4487bhp) Krupp MaK Maschinenbau GmbH-Kiel AuxGen: 1 x 413kW 440V 60Hz a.c, 3 x 323kW 440V 60Hz a.c Thrusters: 1 Thwart. CP thruster (f)
9376581 *HP4051* -	**SURYA PUTRA 5** **SMC Marine Services Pte Ltd** *Panama* Panama MMSI: 351906000 Official number: 41768PEXT	264 80 300	Class: AB NK	**2005-12 Hung Seng Shipbuilding Sdn Bhd — Sibu** Yd No: 038 Loa 30.00 Br ex - Dght 3.512 Lbp 28.08 Br md 8.60 Dpth 4.12 Welded, 1 dk	**(B32A2ST) Tug**	**2 oil engines** reduction geared to sc. shafts driving 2 FP propellers Total Power: 1,518kW (2,064hp) 12.0kn Mitsubishi S6R2-MTK3L 2 x 4 Stroke 6 Cy. 170 x 220 each-759kW (1032bhp) Mitsubishi Heavy Industries Ltd-Japan Fuel: 195.0 (d.f.)
9376646 *9V6853* -	**SURYA PUTRA 6** **SMC Offshore Services Pte Ltd** SMC Marine Services Pte Ltd *Singapore* Singapore MMSI: 563007310 Official number: 391825	255 77 231	Class: AB (NK)	**2006-01 Eastern Marine Shipbuilding Sdn Bhd — Sibu** Yd No: 60 Loa 30.10 Br ex - Dght 3.412 Lbp 27.79 Br md 8.60 Dpth 4.12 Welded, 1 dk	**(B32A2ST) Tug**	**2 oil engines** reduction geared to sc. shafts driving 2 FP propellers Total Power: 1,516kW (2,062hp) Mitsubishi S6R2-MPTK2 2 x 4 Stroke 6 Cy. 170 x 220 each-758kW (1031bhp) Mitsubishi Heavy Industries Ltd-Japan Fuel: 190.0 (d.f.)
9393888 *HP6860* -	**SURYA PUTRA 8** **Rosewood Ocean Shipping Inc** SMC Marine Services Pte Ltd *Panama* Panama MMSI: 373869000 Official number: 42725PEXT	263 79 273	Class: NK	**2006-11 Rajang Maju Shipbuilding Sdn Bhd — Sibu** Yd No: 65 Loa 30.00 Br ex - Dght 3.512 Lbp 27.73 Br md 8.60 Dpth 4.12 Welded, 1 dk	**(B32A2ST) Tug**	**2 oil engines** reduction geared to sc. shafts driving 2 FP propellers Total Power: 1,518kW (2,064hp) 12.0kn Mitsubishi S6R2-MPTK 2 x 4 Stroke 6 Cy. 170 x 220 each-759kW (1032bhp) Mitsubishi Heavy Industries Ltd-Japan AuxGen: 3 x 231kW a.c Fuel: 195.0 (d.f.)
9018426 *PNRP* -	**SURYA PUTRA JAYA** *ex* High Land *-2010* *ex* Melodia *-2003* **PT Cakra Bahana** - *Jakarta* Indonesia MMSI: 525017099 Official number: 2010 PST NO. 6570/L	25,808 11,224 41,460 T/cm 46.7	Class: KI NK	**1992-06 Imabari Shipbuilding Co Ltd — Marugame KG (Marugame Shipyard)** Yd No: 1194 Loa 181.61 Br ex 30.03 Dght 11.766 Lbp 172.00 Br md 30.00 Dpth 18.40 Welded, 1 dk	**(A13B2TP) Products Tanker** Double Hull Liq: 51,443; Liq (Oil): 51,443 Cargo Heating Coils Compartments: 8 Ta, ER 4 Cargo Pump (s): 4x950m³/hr Manifold: Bow/CM: 91m	**1 oil engine** driving 1 FP propeller Total Power: 7,135kW (9,701hp) 14.5kn B&W 5S60MC 1 x 2 Stroke 5 Cy. 600 x 2292 7135kW (9701bhp) Mitsui Engineering & Shipbuilding CLtd-Japan AuxGen: 3 x 360kW 450V 60Hz a.c Fuel: 108.1 (d.f.) (Part Heating Coils) 1445.7 (r.f.) 28.5pd
9399181 *9V6936* -	**SURYA RATNA 7** **International Bulk Trade Pte Ltd** SMC Marine Services Pte Ltd *Singapore* Singapore MMSI: 565181000 Official number: 392189	265 80 276	Class: NK	**2006-09 Hung Seng Shipbuilding Sdn Bhd — Sibu** Yd No: 041 Loa 30.00 Br ex 8.60 Dght 3.512 Lbp 28.08 Br md 8.60 Dpth 4.12 Welded, 1 dk	**(B32A2ST) Tug**	**2 oil engines** reduction geared to sc. shafts driving 2 FP propellers Total Power: 1,518kW (2,064hp) Mitsubishi S6R2-MPTK3 2 x 4 Stroke 6 Cy. 170 x 220 each-759kW (1032bhp) Mitsubishi Heavy Industries Ltd-Japan AuxGen: 2 x a.c Fuel: 200.0 (d.f.)
9488360 *9V7316* -	**SURYA RATNA 10** **International Bulk Trade Pte Ltd** SMC Marine Services Pte Ltd *Singapore* Singapore MMSI: 565805000 Official number: 393707	299 90 212	Class: NK	**2008-06 Tang Tiew Hee & Sons Sdn Bhd — Sibu** Yd No: 32 Loa 32.10 Br ex 9.02 Dght 3.616 Lbp 29.37 Br md 9.00 Dpth 4.20 Welded, 1 dk	**(B32A2ST) Tug**	**2 oil engines** reduction geared to sc. shafts driving 2 FP propellers Total Power: 2,380kW (3,236hp) Cummins KTA-50-M2 2 x Vee 4 Stroke 16 Cy. 159 x 159 each-1190kW (1618bhp) Cummins Engine Co Inc-USA Fuel: 205.0 (d.f.)
9542506 *9V7649* -	**SURYA RATNA 12** **International Bulk Trade Pte Ltd** - *Singapore* Singapore MMSI: 564455000 Official number: 394573	295 89 236	Class: NK	**2008-12 Hung Seng Shipbuilding Sdn Bhd — Sibu** Yd No: 01 Loa 32.10 Br ex - Dght 3.616 Lbp 29.63 Br md 9.00 Dpth 4.20 Welded, 1 dk	**(B32A2ST) Tug**	**2 oil engines** reduction geared to sc. shafts driving 2 Propellers Total Power: 2,386kW (3,244hp) Cummins KTA-50-M2 2 x Vee 4 Stroke 16 Cy. 159 x 159 each-1193kW (1622bhp) Cummins Engine Co Inc-USA Fuel: 200.0
9554444 *9V7935* -	**SURYA RATNA 20** **International Bulk Trade Pte Ltd** - *Singapore* Singapore MMSI: 563056000 Official number: 395065	204 62 204	Class: NK	**2009-06 Tang Tiew Hee & Sons Sdn Bhd — Sibu** Yd No: 41 Loa 27.56 Br ex 7.94 Dght 3.112 Lbp 25.69 Br md 7.93 Dpth 3.80 Welded, 1 dk	**(B32A2ST) Tug**	**2 oil engines** reduction geared to sc. shafts driving 2 Propellers Total Power: 1,302kW (1,770hp) Caterpillar 3412D 2 x Vee 4 Stroke 12 Cy. 145 x 162 each-651kW (885bhp) Caterpillar Inc-USA Fuel: 167.0
9637040 *9V8544* -	**SURYA RATNA 25** **International Bulk Trade Pte Ltd** - *Singapore* Singapore MMSI: 566147000 Official number: 395937	204 62 -	Class: NK	**2011-12 Hung Seng Shipbuilding Sdn Bhd — Sibu** Yd No: 17 Loa 27.56 Br ex 7.93 Dght 3.112 Lbp 24.18 Br md - Dpth 3.80 Welded, 1 dk	**(B32A2ST) Tug**	**2 oil engines** reduction geared to sc. shaft (s) driving 2 Propellers Total Power: 1,074kW (1,460hp) Caterpillar 2 x Vee 4 Stroke 16 Cy. 137 x 152 each-537kW (730bhp) Caterpillar Inc-USA AuxGen: 2 x 99kW a.c Fuel: 180.0 (d.f.)

IMO / Call sign / Flag	Name, former names, owner, manager, port	Tonnage	Class	Builder & dimensions	Type	Machinery
8107610 *YGNU* -	**SURYA SAMUDRA V** *ex* Avona Cargo II *-2002* *ex* Atlantic Mariner *-2000* *ex* Teysha *-1998* *ex* Bermuda Islander *-1995* *ex* Lux Hellenic *-1989* *ex* Mallorca *-1988* **PT Sinar Samudra Tripratama** PT Pelayaran Sinar Sanjaya Abadi SatCom: Inmarsat M 656385210 *Surabaya* *Indonesia* MMSI: 525290672	**1,828** 914 2,100	Class: KI (BV)	**1983**-07 **Ast. de Huelva S.A. — Huelva** Yd No: 139 Loa 79.97 Br ex - Dght 4.370 Lbp 73.32 Br md 13.21 Dpth 6.02 Welded, 1 dk	**(A33A2CC) Container Ship (Fully Cellular)** TEU 100 incl 39 ref C Compartments: 1 Cell Ho, ER 1 Ha: ER Cranes: 2	**1 oil engine** sr geared to sc. shaft driving 1 FP propeller Total Power: 1,493kW (2,030hp) 13.0kn Alpha 14V23L-VO 1 x Vee 4 Stroke 14 Cy. 225 x 300 1493kW (2030bhp) Construcciones Echevarria SA-Spain AuxGen: 4 x 512kW 380V a.c Fuel: 190.0 (d.f.)
9187356 *JFSA* -	**SURYA SATSUMA** **Mitsui OSK Lines Ltd & Nusantara Shipping Ltd** Humolco Trans Inc *Kagoshima, Kagoshima* *Japan* MMSI: 432275000 Official number: 136421	**20,017** 6,005 12,493 T/cm 34.4	Class: NK	**2000**-10 **Nippon Kokan KK (NKK Corp) — Tsu ME** Yd No: 192 Loa 151.03 (BB) Br ex 28.02 Dght 7.060 Lbp 143.50 Br md 28.00 Dpth 16.00 Welded, 1 dk	**(A11A2TN) LNG Tanker** Double Bottom Entire Compartment Length Liq (Gas): 23,096 3 x Gas Tank (s); 3 membrane (s.stl) pri horizontal 6 Cargo Pump (s): 6x850m³/hr Manifold: Bow/CM: 73m	**1 Steam Turb** reduction geared to sc. shaft driving 1 CP propeller Total Power: 7,796kW (10,599hp) 16.5kn Mitsubishi MS12-2 1 x steam Turb 7796kW (10599shp) Mitsubishi Heavy Industries Ltd-Japan AuxGen: 3 x 1300kW 450V 60Hz a.c Fuel: 285.7 (d.f.) (Heating Coils) 2524.5 (r.f.) 60.8pd
8651958 - -	**SURYA SEGARA** **PT Mitra Bahtera Segara Sejati Tbk** - *Bitung* *Indonesia*	**193** 58 -	Class: KI	**2010**-07 **P.T. Rejeki Abadi Sakti — Samarinda** Loa 28.50 Br ex - Dght 2.490 Lbp 27.16 Br md 8.20 Dpth 3.30 Welded, 1 dk	**(B32A2ST) Tug**	**2 oil engines** reduction geared to sc. shafts driving 2 Propellers AuxGen: 2 x 44kW 380/220V a.c
8328331 *YCXG* -	**SURYA SELARAS** *ex* Nusa Perintis *-1997* **PT Samudra Jayaniaga Perkasa** - *Jakarta* *Indonesia*	*481* 166 350	Class: (KI)	**1981 P.T. Adiguna Shipbuilding & Engineering — Jakarta** Yd No: 277 Loa 44.00 Br ex - Dght 2.720 Lbp 40.01 Br md 7.60 Dpth 3.20 Welded, 1 dk	**(A31A2GX) General Cargo Ship** Compartments: 2 Ho, ER	**1 oil engine** geared to sc. shaft driving 1 FP propeller Total Power: 409kW (556hp) Deutz SBA6M816 1 x 4 Stroke 6 Cy. 142 x 160 409kW (556bhp) Kloeckner Humboldt Deutz AG-West Germany
9244324 *AVGN* -	**SURYA SHAKTI** *ex* Qsa 9 *-2011* *ex* Cathay 9 *-2010* **SVS Marine Services Pvt Ltd** - *Mumbai* *India* MMSI: 419000147 Official number: 3722	**184** 56 163	Class: IR (NK)	**2000**-12 **Tuong Aik (Sarawak) Sdn Bhd — Sibu** Yd No: 2007 Loa 26.00 Br ex - Dght 3.012 Lbp 23.50 Br md 7.92 Dpth 3.65 Welded, 1 dk	**(B32A2ST) Tug**	**2 oil engines** reduction geared to sc. shafts driving 2 FP propellers Total Power: 1,074kW (1,460hp) Caterpillar 3412TA 2 x Vee 4 Stroke 12 Cy. 137 x 152 each-537kW (730bhp) Caterpillar Inc-USA Fuel: 129.0 (d.f.)
8032530 *YFIV* -	**SURYA TERANG ABADI** *ex* Jasmin *-2010* *ex* Kosei Maru No. 8 *-1995* *ex* Chiyo Maru No. 2 *-1990* *ex* Fuji Maru *-1988* **Albert Rumuy** - *Surabaya* *Indonesia*	**448** 267 700	Class: KI	**1980**-08 **Shin Nippon Jukogyo K.K. — Osakikamijima** Yd No: 163 Loa 46.70 Br ex - Dght 4.220 Lbp 43.21 Br md 8.01 Dpth 5.01 Welded, 1 dk	**(A31A2GX) General Cargo Ship**	**1 oil engine** driving 1 FP propeller Total Power: 353kW (480hp) Yanmar MF24-MT 1 x 4 Stroke 6 Cy. 240 x 440 353kW (480bhp) Yanmar Diesel Engine Co Ltd-Japan
7429578 - -	**SURYA TULUS** *ex* Sulut I *-1988* *ex* Ambassador 7 *-1990* *ex* Vigour Enterprise *-1988* *ex* Creces *-1987* *ex* Apollo I *-1986* *ex* Jics *-1985* **PT Pelayaran Surya** - *Jakarta* *Indonesia* MMSI: 525019012	**4,135** 2,878 5,543	Class: (NK) (KI)	**1975**-04 **Imamura Zosen — Kure** Yd No: 200 Loa 92.90 Br ex 16.02 Dght 7.011 Lbp 87.50 Br md 16.00 Dpth 11.60 Welded, 2 dks	**(A31A2GX) General Cargo Ship** Grain: 10,376; Bale: 9,600 Compartments: 2 Ho, ER 2 Ha: (19.5 x 8.0) (30.5 x 8.0)ER Derricks: 3x15t	**1 oil engine** driving 1 FP propeller Total Power: 2,795kW (3,800hp) 13.0kn Mitsubishi 6UET45/75C 1 x 2 Stroke 6 Cy. 450 x 750 2795kW (3800bhp) Akasaka Tekkosho KK (Akasaka DieselLtd)-Japan AuxGen: 2 x 190kW 110/440V 60Hz a.c Fuel: 84.0 (d.f.) 389.5 (r.f.) 11.0pd
9338462 *9V6580* -	**SURYA WIRA 2** **SMC Marine Services Pte Ltd** - *Singapore* *Singapore* MMSI: 563006160 Official number: 390888	**191** 58 188	Class: NK	**2005**-02 **Hung Seng Shipbuilding Sdn Bhd — Sibu** Yd No: 033 Loa 26.00 Br ex - Dght 3.062 Lbp 24.23 Br md 8.00 Dpth 3.65 Welded, 1 dk	**(B32A2ST) Tug**	**2 oil engines** geared to sc. shafts driving 2 FP propellers Total Power: 1,516kW (2,062hp) 9.0kn Mitsubishi S6R2-MPTK2 2 x 4 Stroke 6 Cy. 170 x 220 each-758kW (1031bhp) Mitsubishi Heavy Industries Ltd-Japan AuxGen: 2 x 50kW 60Hz a.c Fuel: 130.0 (d.f.)
9282211 *9V6254* -	**SURYA WIRA 5** **SMC Marine Services Pte Ltd** - *Singapore* *Singapore* MMSI: 563004180 Official number: 389912	**271** 81 -	Class: BV	**2002**-11 **Piasau Slipways Sdn Bhd — Miri** Yd No: 129 Loa 31.00 Br ex - Dght 3.000 Lbp 28.50 Br md 8.50 Dpth 3.80 Welded, 1 dk	**(B32A2ST) Tug**	**2 oil engines** geared to sc. shafts driving 2 FP propellers Total Power: 1,060kW (1,442hp) 10.0kn Caterpillar 3412TA 2 x Vee 4 Stroke 12 Cy. 137 x 152 each-530kW (721bhp) Caterpillar Inc-USA
9488372 *J8B4488* -	**SURYA WIRA 15** **Navimar Marine Enterprises Pte Ltd** Gulf Maritime Shipmanagement Co *Kingstown* *St Vincent & The Grenadines* MMSI: 376486000 Official number: 10961	**299** 90 208	Class: BV (NK)	**2008**-07 **Tang Tiew Hee & Sons Sdn Bhd — Sibu** Yd No: 33 Loa 32.10 Br ex 9.02 Dght 3.612 Lbp 29.61 Br md 9.00 Dpth 4.20 Welded, 1 dk	**(B32A2ST) Tug**	**2 oil engines** reduction geared to sc. shafts driving 2 FP propellers Total Power: 2,380kW (3,236hp) Cummins KTA-50-M2 2 x Vee 4 Stroke 16 Cy. 159 x 159 each-1190kW (1618bhp) Cummins Engine Co Inc-USA Fuel: 212.0 (d.f.)
9522570 *9V7504* -	**SURYA WIRA 19** **SMC Marine Services Pte Ltd** - SatCom: Inmarsat C 456596510 *Singapore* *Singapore* MMSI: 565965000 Official number: 394363	**299** 90 206	Class: NK	**2008**-11 **Tang Tiew Hee & Sons Sdn Bhd — Sibu** Yd No: 37 Loa 32.10 Br ex 9.19 Dght 3.612 Lbp 29.38 Br md 9.00 Dpth 4.20 Welded, 1 dk	**(B32A2ST) Tug**	**2 oil engines** reduction geared to sc. shafts driving 2 Propellers Total Power: 2,386kW (3,244hp) Cummins KTA-50-M2 2 x Vee 4 Stroke 16 Cy. 159 x 159 each-1193kW (1622bhp) Cummins Engine Co Inc-USA Fuel: 210.0
9554432 *9V7934* -	**SURYA WIRA 21** **SMC Marine Services Pte Ltd** - SatCom: Inmarsat C 456304810 *Singapore* *Singapore* MMSI: 563048000 Official number: 395064	**204** 62 208	Class: NK	**2009**-05 **Tang Tiew Hee & Sons Sdn Bhd — Sibu** Yd No: 40 Loa 27.56 Br ex 7.94 Dght 3.100 Lbp 24.18 Br md 7.93 Dpth 3.80 Welded, 1 dk	**(B32A2ST) Tug**	**2 oil engines** reduction geared to sc. shafts driving 2 Propellers Total Power: 1,302kW (1,770hp) Caterpillar 3412D 2 x Vee 4 Stroke 12 Cy. 145 x 162 each-651kW (885bhp) Caterpillar Inc-USA Fuel: 165.0
9556480 *9V7972* -	**SURYA WIRA 23** **SMC Marine Services Pte Ltd** - SatCom: Inmarsat C 456320810 *Singapore* *Singapore* MMSI: 563208000 Official number: 395310	**205** 62 207	Class: NK	**2009**-06 **Eastern Marine Shipbuilding Sdn Bhd — Sibu** Yd No: 86 Loa 27.56 Br ex - Dght 3.112 Lbp 25.69 Br md 7.93 Dpth 3.80 Welded, 1 dk	**(B32A2ST) Tug**	**2 oil engines** reduction geared to sc. shafts driving 2 FP propellers Total Power: 1,264kW (1,718hp) Caterpillar 3412D 2 x Vee 4 Stroke 12 Cy. 145 x 162 each-632kW (859bhp) Caterpillar Inc-USA AuxGen: 2 x 99kW a.c Fuel: 170.0
9646819 - -	**SURYA WIRA 26** **SMC Marine Services Pte Ltd** -	**198** 60 203	Class: NK	**2012**-10 **Moxen Shipyard Sdn Bhd — Sibu** Yd No: MS0108 Loa 27.56 Br ex 7.94 Dght 3.110 Lbp 25.69 Br md 7.93 Dpth 3.80 Welded, 1 dk	**(B32A2ST) Tug**	**2 oil engines** geared to sc.shafts driving 2 FP propellers Total Power: 1,264kW (1,718hp) Caterpillar 3412D 2 x Vee 4 Stroke 12 Cy. 145 x 162 each-632kW (859bhp) Caterpillar Inc-USA Fuel: 180.0
9637064 *9V8547* -	**SURYA WIRA 28** *ex* Surya Ratna 28 *-2012* **SMC Marine Services Pte Ltd** - *Singapore* *Singapore* Official number: 395940	**204** 62 203	Class: NK	**2012**-09 **Hung Seng Shipbuilding Sdn Bhd — Sibu** Yd No: 19 Loa 27.56 Br ex - Dght 3.112 Lbp 25.69 Br md 7.93 Dpth 3.80 Welded, 1 dk	**(B32A2ST) Tug**	**2 oil engines** reduction geared to sc. shaft (s) driving 2 FP propellers Total Power: 1,492kW (2,028hp) Caterpillar C32 ACERT 2 x Vee 4 Stroke 12 Cy. 145 x 162 each-746kW (1014bhp) Caterpillar Inc-USA Fuel: 180.0 (d.f.)

IMO / Call sign	Name / Owner	Tonnage	Class	Builder / Dimensions	Type	Machinery
9556492 *9V7971* -	**SURYA WIRA 29** **SMC Marine Services Pte Ltd** - SatCom: Inmarsat C 456320410 *Singapore* *Singapore* MMSI: 563204000 Official number: 395117	**205** 62 205	Class: NK	**2009-06 Eastern Marine Shipbuilding Sdn Bhd — Sibu** Yd No: 87 Loa 27.56 Br ex - Dght 3.112 Lbp 25.69 Br md 7.93 Dpth 3.80 Welded, 1 dk	**(B32A2ST) Tug**	**2 oil engines** reduction geared to sc. shafts driving 2 FP propellers Total Power: 1,264kW (1,718hp) Caterpillar 3412D 2 x Vee 4 Stroke 12 Cy. 145 x 162 each-632kW (859bhp) Caterpillar Inc-USA AuxGen: 2 x 99kW a.c Fuel: 165.0
9214824 *9V5781* -	**SURYA WIRA III** - **SMC Marine Services Pte Ltd** Hansar Corp Pte Ltd *Singapore* *Singapore* Official number: 388564	**121** 37 112	Class: NK	**1999-05 C E Ling Shipbuilding Sdn Bhd — Miri** Yd No: 018 Loa 23.17 Br ex - Dght 2.388 Lbp 21.03 Br md 7.00 Dpth 2.90 Welded, 1 dk	**(B32A2ST) Tug**	**2 oil engines** geared to sc. shafts driving 2 FP propellers Total Power: 794kW (1,080hp) Caterpillar 3412T 2 x Vee 4 Stroke 12 Cy. 137 x 152 each-397kW (540bhp) Caterpillar Inc-USA
7526766 *YDOK* -	**SURYANI LADJONI** *ex* Pulau Kalimantan *-2007* *ex* Erik Sif *-1984* **PT Pelayaran Surya Bintang Timur** - *Jakarta* *Indonesia* Official number: 6665/L	**2,226** 1,277 2,380	Class: KI (BV)	**1977-04 Bodewes' Scheepswerven B.V. — Hoogezand** Yd No: 529 Lengthened-1978 Loa 91.50 Br ex 13.06 Dght 5.160 Lbp 84.41 Br md 13.01 Dpth 7.50 Welded, 2 dks	**(A31A2GX) General Cargo Ship** Grain: 5,385; Bale: 4,859 Compartments: 2 Ho, ER, 2 Tw Dk 2 Ha: (21.5 x 9.5) (24.0 x 9.5)ER Derricks: 2x15t,1x10t,4x3t Ice Capable	**1 oil engine** driving 1 FP propeller Total Power: 1,324kW (1,800hp) 13.0kn MaK 8M452AK 1 x 4 Stroke 8 Cy. 320 x 450 1324kW (1800bhp) MaK Maschinenbau GmbH-Kiel AuxGen: 1 x 104kW 380V 50Hz a.c, 4 x 68kW 380V 50Hz a.c Fuel: 217.0 (r.f.)
8600210 *VVMB* -	**SURYATEJA I** - **Suvarna Rekha Marines Pvt Ltd** - *Visakhapatnam* *India* Official number: 2197	**136** 41 92	Class: (LR) (IR) ✠ Classed LR until 4/10/89	**1986-11 Kirim Shipbuilding Co Ltd — Koje** Yd No: 213 Loa 26.17 Br ex 6.84 Dght 2.640 Lbp 22.71 Br md 6.81 Dpth 3.13 Welded, 1 dk	**(B11A2FS) Stern Trawler**	**1 oil engine** with clutches & dr reverse geared to sc. shaft driving 1 FP propeller Total Power: 530kW (721hp) Caterpillar 3412TA 1 x Vee 4 Stroke 12 Cy. 137 x 152 530kW (721bhp) Caterpillar Tractor Co-USA AuxGen: 2 x 50kW 440V 60Hz a.c
8600222 *VVMC* -	**SURYATEJA II** - **Suvarna Rekha Marines Pvt Ltd** - *Visakhapatnam* *India* Official number: 2197	*136* 41 92	Class: (LR) (IR) ✠ Classed LR until 4/10/89	**1986-11 Kirim Shipbuilding Co Ltd — Koje** Yd No: 214 Loa 26.17 Br ex - Dght 2.640 Lbp 22.71 Br md 6.81 Dpth 3.13 Welded, 1 dk	**(B11A2FS) Stern Trawler** Ins: 95 Compartments: 1 Ho, ER 1 Ha: ER	**1 oil engine** dr reverse geared to sc. shaft driving 1 FP propeller Total Power: 530kW (721hp) Caterpillar 3412TA 1 x Vee 4 Stroke 12 Cy. 137 x 152 530kW (721bhp) Caterpillar Tractor Co-USA AuxGen: 2 x 50kW 440V 60Hz a.c
8603561 *VTRQ* -	**SURYATEJA III** - **Shrimp (India) Pvt Ltd** - *Mumbai* *India* Official number: 2364	**180** 57 138	Class: (IR) (AB)	**1988-09 Bharati Shipyard Ltd — Ratnagiri** Yd No: 192 Loa 27.00 (BB) Br ex 7.83 Dght 2.700 Lbp 23.50 Br md 7.50 Dpth 3.50 Welded, 1 dk	**(B11A2FT) Trawler** Ins: 100	**1 oil engine** with clutches & sr reverse geared to sc. shaft driving 1 FP propeller Total Power: 405kW (551hp) 10.0kn Caterpillar 3412TA 1 x Vee 4 Stroke 12 Cy. 137 x 152 405kW (551bhp) Caterpillar Inc-USA AuxGen: 2 x 50kW a.c
8603573 *VTRR* -	**SURYATEJA IV** - **Shrimp (India) Pvt Ltd** - *Mumbai* *India* Official number: 2365	**180** 57 138	Class: (IR) (AB)	**1989-02 Bharati Shipyard Ltd — Ratnagiri** Yd No: 193 Loa 27.00 (BB) Br ex 7.83 Dght 2.700 Lbp 23.50 Br md 7.50 Dpth 3.50 Welded, 1 dk	**(B11A2FT) Trawler** Ins: 100	**1 oil engine** with clutches & sr reverse geared to sc. shaft driving 1 FP propeller Total Power: 405kW (551hp) 10.0kn Caterpillar 3412TA 1 x Vee 4 Stroke 12 Cy. 137 x 152 405kW (551bhp) Caterpillar Inc-USA AuxGen: 2 x 50kW a.c
9159191 *YHFU* -	**SURYAWATI** *ex* Globe Unity *-2006* *ex* Brave Unity *-1997* **PT Bontang Maju Sejahtera** PT Arpeni Pratama Ocean Line Tbk *Jakarta* *Indonesia* MMSI: 525011095 Official number: 2006 PST NO. 4220/L	**36,175** 23,550 69,124 T/cm 64.4	Class: NK (KI)	**1996-12 Koyo Dockyard Co Ltd — Mihara HS** Yd No: 2076 Loa 224.98 (BB) Br ex - Dght 13.298 Lbp 215.00 Br md 32.20 Dpth 18.30 Welded, 1 dk	**(A21A2BC) Bulk Carrier** Double Bottom Entire Compartment Length Grain: 82,025 Compartments: 7 Ho, ER 7 Ha: (13.0 x 12.8)4 (17.9 x 14.4) (16.3 x 14.4) (14.7 x 14.4)ER	**1 oil engine** driving 1 FP propeller Total Power: 9,930kW (13,501hp) 14.8kn Sulzer 6RTA62 1 x 2 Stroke 6 Cy. 620 x 2150 9930kW (13501bhp) Mitsubishi Heavy Industries Ltd-Japan AuxGen: 3 x 440kW 450V 60Hz a.c Fuel: 157.0 (d.f.) (Heating Coils) 2569.0 (r.f.) 36.0pd
8991164 *VQKS7* FH 707	**SUSA UNO** - **Marjos Marin SL** Susa Fishing Ltd *Falmouth* *United Kingdom* MMSI: 235005640 Official number: C17795	**287** 86 143	Class: BV	**2003-08 Nodosa S.L. — Cangas** Yd No: 250 Loa 32.10 (BB) Br ex - Dght 3.460 Lbp - Br md 8.00 Dpth 5.70 Welded, 1 dk	**(B11A2FS) Stern Trawler**	**1 oil engine** reduction geared to sc. shaft driving 1 CP propeller Total Power: 719kW (978hp) 12.2kn A.B.C. 6DZC 1 x 4 Stroke 6 Cy. 256 x 310 719kW (978bhp) Anglo Belgian Corp NV (ABC)-Belgium AuxGen: 1 x 216kW
7634642 *9A6049* -	**SUSAC** - **Plovput doo** - *Split* *Croatia* Official number: 5T-307	*137* 44 40	Class: CS (JR)	**1948 Brodogradiliste 'Jozo Lozovina-Mosor' (Brodomosor) — Trogir** Yd No: 1 Converted From: Unknown Function-1970 Loa 31.12 Br ex 7.14 Dght 2.801 Lbp 26.50 Br md 6.81 Dpth 3.00 Welded, 1 dk	**(B34Q2QX) Lighthouse Tender** 1 Ha: (1.4 x 1.1) Derricks: 1x4t	**1 oil engine** driving 1 FP propeller Total Power: 250kW (340hp) 8.0kn Alpha 404-FO 1 x 2 Stroke 4 Cy. 230 x 400 250kW (340bhp) (new engine 1970) Titovi Zavodi 'Litostroj'-Yugoslavia AuxGen: 1 x 26kW 440V a.c Fuel: 13.0 (d.f.)
8917259 - -	**SUSAINAH** - **Agino Line** - *Nigeria*	*125* - -		**1991-05 Stocznia 'Wisla' — Gdansk** Yd No: WKR25/18 Loa - Br ex - Dght - Lbp 25.00 Br md - Dpth - Welded, 1 dk	**(B11A2FS) Stern Trawler**	**1 oil engine** geared to sc. shaft driving 1 FP propeller Total Power: 421kW (572hp) Caterpillar 3412T 1 x Vee 4 Stroke 12 Cy. 137 x 152 421kW (572bhp) Caterpillar Inc-USA
9032238 *JI3456* -	**SUSAKI MARU** - **Taiyo Shipping Co Ltd (Taiyo Kisen KK)** - *Osaka, Osaka* *Japan* MMSI: 431300557 Official number: 131706	*699* - 1,673	Class: NK	**1991-03 Sasaki Shipbuilding Co Ltd — Osakikamijima HS** Yd No: 555 Loa 66.57 Br ex - Dght 4.658 Lbp 62.00 Br md 11.00 Dpth 5.20 Welded, 1 dk	**(A24A2BT) Cement Carrier** Grain: 1,390 Compartments: 6 Ho, ER	**1 oil engine** reverse reduction geared to sc. shaft driving 1 FP propeller Total Power: 1,177kW (1,600hp) 10.5kn Akasaka K28SFD 1 x 4 Stroke 6 Cy. 280 x 500 1177kW (1600bhp) Akasaka Tekkosho KK (Akasaka DieselLtd)-Japan AuxGen: 3 x 152kW a.c Fuel: 65.0 (d.f.)
9115054 *JK5394* -	**SUSAKI MARU** *ex* Takayama Maru No. 3 *-1995* **KK Susaki Jyari** - *Susaki, Kochi* *Japan* Official number: 134747	*498* - 1,600		**1994-11 Hitachi Zosen Mukaishima Marine Co Ltd — Onomichi HS** Yd No: 86 Loa - Br ex - Dght 4.510 Lbp 61.50 Br md 13.00 Dpth 7.46 Welded, 1 dk	**(A31A2GX) General Cargo Ship**	**1 oil engine** driving 1 FP propeller Total Power: 736kW (1,001hp) Hanshin LH32LG 1 x 4 Stroke 6 Cy. 320 x 640 736kW (1001bhp) The Hanshin Diesel Works Ltd-Japan
9190365 *PHPY* -	**SUSAN** *ex* Sofie N *-2013* *ex* Alessia C *-2008* *ex* Alessia *-2008* **Miss Susan BV** Flagship Management Co BV *Delfzijl* *Netherlands* MMSI: 244101000 Official number: 52363	**2,999** 1,714 5,047 T/cm 11.5	Class: GL (LR) ✠ Classed LR until 26/8/09	**1999-08 B.V. Scheepswerf Damen Hoogezand — Foxhol** Yd No: 735 **1999-08 Santierul Naval Damen Galati S.A. — Galati** (Hull) Yd No: 933 Loa 94.99 (BB) Br ex 13.20 Dght 6.190 Lbp 90.25 Br md 13.17 Dpth 7.15 Welded, 1 dk	**(A31A2GX) General Cargo Ship** Grain: 6,196 TEU 224 C. 224/20' Compartments: 1 Ho, ER 1 Ha: (67.7 x 11.0)ER Ice Capable	**1 oil engine** with flexible couplings & sr gearedto sc. shaft driving 1 CP propeller Total Power: 2,400kW (3,263hp) 12.0kn MaK 8M25 1 x 4 Stroke 8 Cy. 255 x 400 2400kW (3263bhp) MaK Motoren GmbH & Co. KG-Kiel AuxGen: 1 x 210kW 400V 50Hz a.c, 2 x 140kW 400V 50Hz a.c Thrusters: 1 Thwart. FP thruster (f) Fuel: 38.0 (d.f.) (Heating Coils) 216.2 (r.f.) 10.0pd
6402236 *WCY5700* -	**SUSAN ANNE** *ex* Prince Nova *-1998* **Cross Sound Ferry Services Inc** - *New York, NY* *United States of America* MMSI: 367354350 Official number: 1067190	*2,855* 1,082 711	Class: (LR) ✠ Classed LR until 7/4/98	**1964-05 Ferguson Industries Ltd — Pictou NS** Yd No: 148 Loa 75.82 Br ex 16.79 Dght 3.753 Lbp 69.96 Br md 16.31 Dpth 5.49 Welded, 1 dk	**(A36A2PR) Passenger/Ro-Ro Ship (Vehicles)** Passengers: unberthed: 840 Bow door/ramp Lane-Len: 296 Lane-Wid: 3.81 Lane-clr ht: 4.26 Cars: 60	**2 oil engines** driving 2 CP propellers Total Power: 2,354kW (3,200hp) 15.0kn Fairbanks, Morse 10-38D8-1/8 2 x 2 Stroke 10 Cy. 207 x 254 each-1177kW (1600bhp) Canadian Locomotive Co Ltd-Canada AuxGen: 3 x 165kW 440V 60Hz a.c Thrusters: 1 Thwart. FP thruster (f) Fuel: 59.0 (d.f.)

9220782 *YJVA9* -	**SUSAN F. MCCALL** **Seabulk Global Transport Inc** SEACOR Marine LLC *Port Vila* *Vanuatu* MMSI: 576144000 Official number: 1717	**295** 88 165	Class: AB	**1999**-11 Yd No: 43 Loa 44.20 Br ex 8.53 Dght 1.900 Lbp 41.15 Br md 8.48 Dpth 3.56 Welded, 1 dk	**(B21A20C) Crew/Supply Vessel** Passengers: unberthed: 81	**5 oil engines** with clutches, flexible couplings & sr reverse geared to sc. shafts driving 5 FP propellers Total Power: 2,575kW (3,500hp) 16.0kn Cummins KTA-19-M 5 x 4 Stroke 6 Cy. 159 x 159 each-515kW (700bhp) Cummins Engine Co Inc-USA AuxGen: 2 x 50kW 120/208V 60Hz a.c Fuel: 59.5 (d.f.) 22.0pd
9048782 - -	**SUSAN IV** - -	*270* - -		**1992 Remesa Astilleros S.A. — Callao** Yd No: 022 Loa - Br ex - Dght - Lbp - Br md - Dpth - Welded, 1 dk	**(B11B2FV) Fishing Vessel**	**1 oil engine** reduction geared to sc. shaft driving 1 FP propeller Caterpillar 1 x 4 Stroke Caterpillar Inc-USA
7513240 *WDD6286* -	**SUSAN K** *ex* Sherri Ann *-2007* *ex* Dana Ann *-1994* *ex* Ladonna Luann *-1994* **Atlantic Vessels of New Jersey LLC** - *Ocean City, MD* *United States of America* MMSI: 367170870 Official number: 549645	*145* 105 -		**1973 F.B. Walker & Sons, Inc. — Pascagoula, Ms** L reg 21.86 Br ex 6.41 Dght - Lbp - Br md - Dpth 3.38 Welded, 1 dk	**(B11A2FT) Trawler**	**1 oil engine** driving 1 FP propeller Total Power: 257kW (349hp)
7421045 *ZR2940* -	**SUSAN KRUGER** *ex* White Lady *-1977* *ex* Jeppe Cimber *-1976* *ex* White Lady II *-1974* *ex* Sundbuss Jeppe *-1974* **Government of The Republic of South Africa (Department of Arts, Culture, Science & Technology - Robben Eiland Museum)** - *Cape Town* *South Africa* Official number: 350803	*143* 84 -	Class: (BV) (NV)	**1959 AS Westermoen Baatbyggeri & Mekaniske Verksted — Mandal** Yd No: 477 Loa 27.08 Br ex 6.61 Dght - Lbp - Br md - Dpth - Welded, 2 dks	**(A37B2PS) Passenger Ship** Passengers: unberthed: 160	**2 oil engines** driving 2 FP propellers Total Power: 272kW (370hp) Volvo Penta TMD96 2 x 4 Stroke 6 Cy. 121 x 140 each-136kW (185bhp) Volvo Pentaverken-Sweden AuxGen: 2 x 23kW 220V 50Hz a.c
7947697 *WQZ4631* -	**SUSAN L.** *ex* Alisa Andrea *-1974* **Five Fathoms Inc** - *Cape May, NJ* *United States of America* MMSI: 366211560 Official number: 610983	*178* 130 -		**1979 Harrison Boats, Inc. — Arapahoe, NC** L reg 25.70 Br ex 7.35 Dght - Lbp - Br md - Dpth 3.61 Welded, 1 dk	**(B11B2FV) Fishing Vessel**	**1 oil engine** driving 1 FP propeller Total Power: 496kW (674hp) G.M. (Detroit Diesel) 12V-149 1 x Vee 2 Stroke 12 Cy. 146 x 146 496kW (674bhp) General Motors Detroit DieselAllison Divn-USA
9120853 *OYIK2* -	**SUSAN MAERSK** **A P Moller - Maersk A/S** A P Moller SatCom: Inmarsat B 321913420 *Hellerup* *Denmark (DIS)* MMSI: 219134000 Official number: D3621	**92,198** 53,625 110,381 T/cm 124.0	Class: AB (LR) ✠ Classed LR until 3/12/08	**1997**-12 **Odense Staalskibsvaerft A/S — Munkebo (Lindo Shipyard)** Yd No: 161 Loa 347.00 (BB) Br ex 42.92 Dght 14.940 Lbp 331.54 Br md 42.80 Dpth 24.10 Welded, 1 dk	**(A33A2CC) Container Ship (Fully Cellular)** TEU 9578 incl 817 ref C Compartments: ER, 20 Cell Ho 20 Ha: ER	**1 oil engine** driving 1 FP propeller Total Power: 54,840kW (74,560hp) 24.6kn B&W 12K90MC 1 x 2 Stroke 12 Cy. 900 x 2550 54840kW (74560bhp) Mitsui Engineering & Shipbuilding CLtd-Japan AuxGen: 5 x 3000kW 6600V 60Hz a.c Boilers: AuxB (o.f.) 10.2kgf/cm² (10.0bar), AuxB (ex.g.) 10.2kgf/cm² (10.0bar) Thrusters: 1 Thwart. FP thruster (f); 2 Tunnel thruster (a)
8120155 *WBQ6742* -	**SUSAN MARIE II** *ex* Sea Fisher 10 *-2007* **Susan Marie Inc** - *Wildwood, NJ* *United States of America* MMSI: 366398180 Official number: 630313	*135* 91 -		**1980**-08 **Quality Marine, Inc. — Bayou La Batre, Al** Yd No: 144 Loa 25.33 Br ex - Dght - Lbp - Br md 7.01 Dpth 3.69 Welded, 1 dk	**(B11A2FS) Stern Trawler**	**1 oil engine** driving 1 FP propeller Total Power: 382kW (519hp) Caterpillar 3412TA 1 x Vee 4 Stroke 12 Cy. 137 x 152 382kW (519bhp) Caterpillar Tractor Co-USA
6604016 *WDB3025* -	**SUSAN MCALLISTER** *ex* Ybor *-2007* *ex* Leo *-2007* *ex* Vincent J. Robin IV *-2007* **McAllister Towing & Transportation Co Inc (MT & T)** - *New York, NY* *United States of America* MMSI: 366882530 Official number: 500035	*148* 70 -	Class: (AB)	**1965 Equitable Equipment Co. — Madisonville, La** Yd No: 1368 Loa 25.91 Br ex 7.37 Dght - Lbp 23.78 Br md 7.32 Dpth 3.15 Welded, 1 dk	**(B32A2ST) Tug**	**2 oil engines** sr reverse geared to sc. shafts driving 2 FP propellers Total Power: 1,126kW (1,530hp) Caterpillar D398B 2 x Vee 4 Stroke 12 Cy. 153 x 203 each-563kW (765bhp) Caterpillar Tractor Co-USA AuxGen: 2 x 40kW Fuel: 63.0
9227560 *WDA6881* -	**SUSAN MORAN** **Moran Towing Corp** - *Wilmington, DE* *United States of America* MMSI: 366837130 Official number: 1094074	**232** 69 -	Class: AB	**2000**-03 **Washburn & Doughty Associates Inc — East Boothbay ME** Yd No: 68 Loa 28.04 Br ex - Dght 3.200 Lbp 26.50 Br md 9.75 Dpth 4.20 Welded, 1 dk	**(B32A2ST) Tug**	**2 oil engines** gearing integral to driving 2 Z propellers Total Power: 3,162kW (4,300hp) EMD (Electro-Motive) 16-645-E6 2 x Vee 2 Stroke 16 Cy. 230 x 254 each-1581kW (2150bhp) General Motors Corp.Electro-Motive Div.-La Grange AuxGen: 2 x 50kW 440V 60Hz a.c
7730343 *WAQ8018* -	**SUSAN ROSE** *ex* Margaret Rose *-1980* **Joseph Lee Rose** - *North Cape May, NJ* *United States of America* MMSI: 366103960 Official number: 581472	*142* 96 -		**1977 Steiner Shipyard, Inc. — Bayou La Batre, Al** L reg 23.54 Br ex 7.01 Dght - Lbp - Br md - Dpth 3.48 Welded, 1dk	**(B11B2FV) Fishing Vessel**	**1 oil engine** driving 1 FP propeller Total Power: 416kW (566hp)
8660375 *5NQA2* -	**SUSAN T** *ex* Bonny Carrier *-2010* *ex* Herman G *-1997* **Riverman Nigeria Ltd** - *Lagos* *Nigeria* Official number: SR1502	**199** 92 -		**1975**-01 **Offshore Trawlers, Inc. — Bayou La Batre, Al** Yd No: 12 Loa 29.07 Br ex - Dght - Lbp - Br md 7.82 Dpth 2.30 Welded, 1 dk	**(B21A20S) Platform Supply Ship**	**2 oil engines** reduction geared to sc. shafts driving 2 Propellers Total Power: 1,060kW (1,442hp) 12.0kn G.M. (Detroit Diesel) 16V-92 2 x Vee 2 Stroke 16 Cy. 123 x 127 each-530kW (721bhp) General Motors Detroit DieselAllison Divn-USA
9296432 *XCRI1* -	**SUSAN TIDE** **Green Fleet Ltd** Tidewater de Mexico S de RL de CV *Ciudad del Carmen* *Mexico* MMSI: 345070274 Official number: 0401346331-6	**341** 102 438	Class: AB	**2003**-06 **Breaux Bay Craft, Inc. — Loreauville, La** Yd No: 1728 Loa 49.38 Br ex - Dght 2.530 Lbp 45.15 Br md 8.99 Dpth 3.66 Welded, 1 dk	**(B21A20C) Crew/Supply Vessel** Hull Material: Aluminium Alloy	**4 oil engines** geared to sc. shafts driving 4 FP propellers Total Power: 4,208kW (5,720hp) Caterpillar 3512B 4 x Vee 4 Stroke 12 Cy. 170 x 190 each-1052kW (1430bhp) Caterpillar Inc-USA AuxGen: 2 x 75kW a.c
9082257 - -	**SUSAN VI** **Copromar Srl** - *Peru*	*270* - 130		**1994**-12 **Remesa Astilleros S.A. — Callao** Yd No: 044 Loa - Br ex - Dght - Lbp - Br md - Dpth - Welded	**(B11B2FV) Fishing Vessel**	**1 oil engine** geared to sc. shaft driving 1 FP propeller Total Power: 372kW (506hp) Caterpillar D379TA 1 x Vee 4 Stroke 8 Cy. 159 x 203 372kW (506bhp) Caterpillar Inc-USA
8968789 *WCW4123* -	**SUSAN W** *ex* General Lee *-2004* **E N Bisso & Son Inc** - *New Orleans, LA* *United States of America* MMSI: 366925000 Official number: 648920	**377** 113 -	Class: (AB)	**1982**-06 **Modern Marine Power, Inc. — Houma, La** Yd No: 42 Loa - Br ex - Dght 3.616 Lbp 33.52 Br md 10.36 Dpth 4.21 Welded, 1 dk	**(B32A2ST) Tug**	**2 oil engines** reverse reduction geared to sc. shafts driving 2 FP propellers Total Power: 1,864kW (2,534hp) 12.0kn Caterpillar 3512TA 2 x Vee 4 Stroke 12 Cy. 170 x 190 each-932kW (1267bhp) (new engine 1999) Caterpillar Inc-USA AuxGen: 2 x 75kW a.c Fuel: 333.0 (d.f.)
6815017 - -	**SUSANA** **Jose Mendoza Alvarez** - *Callao* *Peru* Official number: CO-000192-PM	*225* 105 -		**1968 Ast. Picsa S.A. — Callao** L reg 26.83 Br ex 7.07 Dght - Lbp - Br md 7.04 Dpth 3.46 Welded, 1 dk	**(B11B2FV) Fishing Vessel**	**1 oil engine** driving 1 FP propeller Total Power: 279kW (379hp) Caterpillar D353SCAC 1 x 4 Stroke 6 Cy. 159 x 203 279kW (379bhp) Caterpillar Tractor Co-USA

IMO / Call sign	Name / Owner	Tonnage	Class	Builder / Dimensions	Type / Capacity	Machinery
5401833 - -	**SUSANA CRISTINA** *ex Bowqueen -1988* **Arimadeira-Extracao e Comercializacao de Areiras de Madeira Lda** *Funchal* *Portugal*	*1,238* 619 1,577	Class: (LR) ✠ Classed LR until 8/88	**1963-02 Ailsa Shipbuilding Co Ltd — Troon** Yd No: 515 Loa 78.52 Br ex 12.15 Dght 4.592 Lbp 73.16 Br md 11.89 Dpth 5.26 Riveted\Welded, 1 dk	**(B33A2DS) Suction Dredger** Liq: 1,049 Compartments: 1 Ho, ER 1 Ha: (23.1 x 8.5)ER Derricks: 1x10t,1x3t; Winches: 2	**1 oil engine** driving 1 FP propeller Total Power: 1,371kW (1,864hp) 12.5kn Mirrlees KLSSDM-8 1 x 4 Stroke 8 Cy. 381 x 508 1371kW (1864bhp) Mirrlees National Ltd.-Stockport AuxGen: 2 x 110kW 220V d.c Fuel: 56.0 (d.f.)
9406714 *LACF7* -	**SUSANA S** **Utkilen Shipinvest KS** Utkilen AS SatCom: Inmarsat C 425989010 *Bergen* *Norway (NIS)* MMSI: 259890000	**12,862** 6,639 19,540 T/cm 30.0	Class: GL	**2009-05 Qingshan Shipyard — Wuhan HB** Yd No: 20060408 Loa 164.34 (BB) Br ex 23.25 Dght 9.550 Lbp 155.40 Br md 23.20 Dpth 12.80 Welded, 1 dk	**(A12B2TR) Chemical/Products Tanker** Double Hull (13F) Liq: 22,384; Liq (Oil): 23,200 Cargo Heating Coils Compartments: 14 Wing Ta, 2 Wing Slop Ta, ER 14 Cargo Pump (s): 2x150m³/hr, 10x300m³/hr, 2x500m³/hr Manifold: Bow/CM: 79.4m Ice Capable	**1 oil engine** driving 1 CP propeller Total Power: 7,860kW (10,686hp) 15.5kn MAN-B&W 6S46MC-C 1 x 2 Stroke 6 Cy. 460 x 1932 7860kW (10686bhp) STX Engine Co Ltd-South Korea AuxGen: 3 x 910kW 440V a.c Thrusters: 1 Tunnel thruster (f) Fuel: 215.0 (d.f.) 1109.0 (r.f.)
9316488 *H02631* -	**SUSANNA** **International World Shipping Agencies SA** GAC Marine LLC *Panama* *Panama* MMSI: 352372000 Official number: 2988804B	**1,148** 344 975	Class: BV	**2004-05 GAC Marine Construction & Maintenance — Abu Dhabi** Yd No: 015 Loa 49.50 Br ex - Dght 5.600 Lbp 46.32 Br md 13.60 Dpth 6.40 Welded, 1 dk	**(B32A2ST) Tug** Passengers: 32	**2 oil engines** sr geared to sc. shafts driving 2 CP propellers Total Power: 5,884kW (8,000hp) 12.0kn Wartsila 6L32 2 x 4 Stroke 6 Cy. 320 x 400 each-2942kW (4000bhp) Wartsila Finland Oy-Finland AuxGen: 3 x 240kW 400/220V a.c Thrusters: 1 Tunnel thruster (f); 1 Tunnel thruster (a) Fuel: 674.0 (d.f.)
8020123 *YJTS8* -	**SUSANNA I** *ex Susanna -2008 ex Anke-Bettina -2000* *ex Pelikan -1992 ex Hammaburg -1989* **Granba Shipping & Trading Ltd** Wakes & Co Ltd *Port Vila* *Vanuatu* Official number: 2296	**1,512** 781 2,319	Class: TL (GL)	**1980-12 Schiffs. Hugo Peters Wewelsfleth Peters & Co. GmbH — Wewelsfleth** Yd No: 576 Loa 82.48 Br ex 11.38 Dght 4.218 Lbp 77.35 Br md 11.31 Dpth 5.41 Welded, 2 dks	**(A31A2GX) General Cargo Ship** Grain: 2,902; Bale: 2,898 TEU 48 C. 48/20' Compartments: 1 Ho, ER 1 Ha: (49.8 x 9.0)ER Ice Capable	**1 oil engine** reverse reduction geared to sc. shaft driving 1 FP propeller Total Power: 441kW (600hp) 10.5kn Deutz SBA8M528 1 x 4 Stroke 8 Cy. 220 x 280 441kW (600bhp) Kloeckner Humboldt Deutz AG-West Germany AuxGen: 2 x 92kW 220/380V 50Hz a.c, 1 x 45kW 220/380V 50Hz a.c Thrusters: 1 Thwart. FP thruster (f)
8303276 *DETY* NC 120	**SUSANNE** **Frischfisch GmbH 'Susanne'** - SatCom: Inmarsat C 421131085 *Cuxhaven* *Germany* MMSI: 211227510 Official number: 959	**492** 147 200	Class: (GL)	**1983-12 Motorenwerk Bremerhaven GmbH (MWB) — Bremerhaven** Yd No: 918 Loa 35.11 Br ex 9.61 Dght 4.201 Lbp 29.80 Br md 9.52 Dpth 6.71 Welded, 2 dks	**(B11A2FS) Stern Trawler** Ins: 216 Compartments: 2 Ho, ER 2 Ha: ER Ice Capable	**1 oil engine** with clutches, flexible couplings & sr geared to sc. shaft driving 1 CP propeller Total Power: 736kW (1,001hp) 11.5kn Deutz SBV6M628 1 x 4 Stroke 6 Cy. 240 x 280 736kW (1001bhp) Kloeckner Humboldt Deutz AG-West Germany
9279006 *PCBF* -	**SUSANNE** **JHM Van Dam & AW Kwakernaak** Scheepvaartbedrijf van Dam *Spijk* *Netherlands* MMSI: 244613000 Official number: 41451	**2,409** 993 3,200	Class: LR ✠ **100A1** SS 01/2009 strengthened for heavy cargoes, bottom strengthened for loading and unloading aground Ice Class 1C FS at a draught of 4.968m Max/min draught fwd 4.968/1.6m Max/min draught aft 4.968/3.2m Power required 748kw, power installed 1249kw ✠ **LMC** **UMS** Eq.Ltr: 0; Cable: 414.4/30.0 U3 (a)	**2004-01 Scheepswerf Peters B.V. — Kampen** Yd No: 1001 Loa 82.50 Br ex 12.52 Dght 4.850 Lbp 80.70 Br md 12.50 Dpth 8.00 Welded, 1 dk	**(A31A2GX) General Cargo Ship** Grain: 4,583 TEU 132 C Ho 96 TEU C Dk 36 TEU Compartments: 1 Ho, ER 1 Ha: ER Ice Capable	**1 oil engine** with flexible couplings & sr geared to sc. shaft driving 1 CP propeller Total Power: 1,349kW (1,834hp) 11.8kn Caterpillar 3512B-HD 1 x Vee 4 Stroke 12 Cy. 170 x 215 1349kW (1834bhp) Caterpillar Inc-USA AuxGen: 1 x 312kW 400V 50Hz a.c, 1 x 120kW 400V 50Hz a.c Thrusters: 1 Water jet (f)
9099183 *OZBE2* -	**SUSANNE A** *ex Schmarl -2008 ex Felicia -1997* *ex Farja 61/279 -1992* **Jens Alfastsen Rederiet** - *Horsens* *Denmark (DIS)* MMSI: 219012073 Official number: H1602	**348** 104 200		**1969-01 Kalmar Varv AB — Kalmar** Yd No: 426 Converted From: Deck Cargo Vessel-2008 Converted From: Ferry (Passenger/Vehicle)-2008 Loa 53.96 Br ex 11.72 Dght 1.580 Lbp - Br md 11.70 Dpth 2.40 Welded, 1 dk	**(B34P2QV) Salvage Ship** A-frames: 1x60t	**6 diesel electric oil engines** driving 6 gen. Connecting to 2 elec. motors driving 2 Voith-Schneider propellers Total Power: 708kW (960hp) 6.5kn Scania DN11 6 x 4 Stroke 6 Cy. 127 x 145 each-118kW (160bhp) Scania AB-Sweden
8310891 *VJT5724* -	**SUSANNE RICHEY II** **Southlander Fisheries Pty Ltd** - *Devonport, Tas* *Australia* Official number: 856009	*120* - -		**1982-10 J L & M J Mitchell — Dover TAS** Loa - Br ex - Dght 2.286 Lbp 22.56 Br md 7.01 Dpth - Welded, 1 dk	**(B11B2FV) Fishing Vessel**	**1 oil engine** driving 1 FP propeller Total Power: 268kW (364hp) Cummins 1 x 4 Stroke 268kW (364bhp) Cummins Engine Co Inc-USA
9215880 *9VPY4* -	**SUSANNE SCHULTE** *ex P&O Nedlloyd Aconcagua -2005* *launched as Susanne Schulte -2001* **Semakau Island Shipping Co Pte Ltd** Bernhard Schulte Shipmanagement (Bermuda) Ltd Partnership *Singapore* *Singapore* MMSI: 565475000 Official number: 393110	**26,718** 12,715 34,717 T/cm 51.1	Class: NV (LR) ✠ Classed LR until 23/4/01	**2001-04 Hyundai Heavy Industries Co Ltd — Ulsan** Yd No: 1298 Loa 210.07 (BB) Br ex - Dght 11.500 Lbp 199.00 Br md 30.20 Dpth 16.70 Welded, 1 dk	**(A33A2CC) Container Ship (Fully Cellular)** TEU 2556 C Ho 944 TEU C Dk 1612 TEU incl 600 ref C. Compartments: 5 Cell Ho, ER 10 Ha: (12.6 x 15.4)Tappered (12.6 x 20.4)Tappered (12.6 x 25.7)Tappered 7 (12.6 x 25.7)ER Cranes: 4x45t	**1 oil engine** driving 1 FP propeller Total Power: 21,572kW (29,329hp) 21.9kn Sulzer 7RTA72U 1 x 2 Stroke 7 Cy. 720 x 2500 21572kW (29329bhp) Hyundai Heavy Industries Co Ltd-South Korea AuxGen: 4 x 1600kW 220/450V 60Hz a.c Boilers: AuxB (Comp) 8.1kgf/cm² (7.9bar) Thrusters: 1 Thwart. CP thruster (f) Fuel: 150.0 (d.f.) (Heating Coils) 4100.0 (r.f.) 102.1pd
9334404 *OVJP2* -	**SUSANNE THERESA** *launched as Vanir -2006* **Herning Shipping A/S** - SatCom: Inmarsat C 422044710 *Struer* *Denmark (DIS)* MMSI: 220447000 Official number: D4223	**2,620** 1,136 3,464 T/cm 10.7	Class: BV	**2006-05 Dearsan Gemi Insaat ve Sanayii Koll. Sti. — Tuzla** (Hull) Yd No: 24 **2006-05 Yardimci Tersanesi A.S. — Tuzla** Yd No: (24) Loa 92.86 (BB) Br ex - Dght 5.700 Lbp 86.65 Br md 14.10 Dpth 7.20 Welded, 1 dk	**(A12B2TR) Chemical/Products Tanker** Double Hull (13F) Liq: 4,078; Liq (Oil): 4,101 Compartments: 10 Wing Ta, 2 Ta, ER 11 Cargo Pump (s): 10x150m³/hr, 1x100m³/hr Manifold: Bow/CM: 42m Ice Capable	**1 oil engine** reduction geared to sc. shaft driving 1 CP propeller Total Power: 1,980kW (2,692hp) 13.5kn MaK 6M25 1 x 4 Stroke 6 Cy. 255 x 400 1980kW (2692bhp) Caterpillar Motoren GmbH & Co. KG-Germany AuxGen: 3 x 292kW 380/220V 50Hz a.c, 1 x 540kW 380/220V 50Hz a.c Thrusters: 1 Thwart. FP thruster (f) Fuel: 29.0 (d.f.) 186.0 (r.f.) 9.0pd
9537379 *A8YF4* -	**SUSE** **ms 'Suse' Schiffahrtsgesellschaft mbH & Co KG** Reederei Hermann Wulff John-Peter Wulff GmbH & Co KG *Monrovia* *Liberia* MMSI: 636092191 Official number: 92191	**32,987** 19,288 56,925 T/cm 58.8	Class: LR ✠ **100A1** SS 05/2011 bulk carrier CSR BC-A GRAB (20) Nos. 2 & 4 holds may be empty ESP **ShipRight** (CM) *IWS LI ✠ **LMC** **UMS** Cable: 632.5/73.0 U3 (a)	**2011-05 Jiangsu Hantong Ship Heavy Industry Co Ltd — Tongzhou JS** Yd No: 043 Loa 188.65 (BB) Br ex 32.30 Dght 12.800 Lbp 185.00 Br md 32.26 Dpth 18.00 Welded, 1 dk	**(A21A2BC) Bulk Carrier** Grain: 71,634; Bale: 68,200 Compartments: 5 Ho, ER 5 Ha: 4 (21.3 x 18.3)ER (18.9 x 18.3) Cranes: 4x35t	**1 oil engine** driving 1 FP propeller Total Power: 9,480kW (12,889hp) 14.7kn MAN-B&W 6S50MC-C 1 x 2 Stroke 6 Cy. 500 x 2000 9480kW (12889bhp) Doosan Engine Co Ltd-South Korea AuxGen: 3 x 600kW 440V 60Hz a.c Boilers: AuxB (Comp) 7.9kgf/cm² (7.7bar) Fuel: 146.0 (d.f.) 2259.0 (r.f.)
7722334 *YFEP* -	**SUSEL PRIMA PERMAI III** *ex Super King -1995 ex Taiho Maru -1993* **PT Kurnia Kapuas Utama Tbk** - *Palembang* *Indonesia* MMSI: 525015553	*928* 591 1,821	Class: KI	**1978-04 Hakata Zosen K.K. — Imabari** Yd No: 186 Converted From: Chemical Tanker-1994 L reg 68.40 Br ex - Dght - Lbp 64.01 Br md 11.02 Dpth 5.01 Riveted\Welded, 1 dk	**(A13B2TP) Products Tanker** Compartments: 5 Ta, ER	**1 oil engine** driving 1 FP propeller Total Power: 1,324kW (1,800hp) Hanshin 6LU35 1 x 4 Stroke 6 Cy. 350 x 550 1324kW (1800bhp) Hanshin Nainenki Kogyo-Japan

IMO / Call sign	Name / Owner	Tonnage	Class	Build / Dimensions	Type	Machinery
8855798 - -	**SUSIE K** **New England Aquarium Corp** - *Boston, MA* *United States of America* Official number: 659673	*148* 111 -		**1983 at Woods Hole, Ma** Loa - Br ex - Dght - Lbp 23.29 Br md 6.89 Dpth 3.35 Welded, 1 dk	**(B11B2FV) Fishing Vessel**	**1 oil engine** driving 1 FP propeller
7940261 *WYD2944* -	**SUSITNA** **Michael Nakada** *Homer, AK* *United States of America* Official number: 603312	*166* 113 -		**1979 Raymond L. Bellamy — Hood River, Or** Converted From: Fishing Vessel-2010 L reg 24.39 Br ex 7.95 Dght - Lbp - Br md - Dpth 2.57 Welded, 1 dk	**(B31A2SR) Research Survey Vessel** Passengers: berths: 13	**2 oil engines** driving 1 FP propeller Total Power: 662kW (900hp) AuxGen: 1 x 106kW a.c
9577721 *WDF4361* -	**SUSITNA** **Matanuska-Susitna Borough** - *Port Mackenzie, AK* *United States of America* MMSI: 367450950 Official number: 1189367	**1,100** 313 47		**2011-08 Alaska Ship & Drydock Inc — Ketchikan AK** Yd No: 002 Loa 59.60 Br ex - Dght 3.810 Lbp 54.86 Br md 18.30 Dpth - Welded, 1 dk	**(A37B2PS) Passenger Ship** Passengers: unberthed: 134 Bow ramp (centre) Cars: 20	**4 oil engines** reduction geared to sc. shafts driving 4 Water jets Total Power: 6,960kW (9,464hp) 20.0kn M.T.U. 12V4000M 4 x Vee 4 Stroke 12 Cy. 165 x 190 each-1740kW (2366bhp) MTU Friedrichshafen GmbH-Friedrichshafen
9007245 *EHBT* -	**SUSO** **Antolin Perez Alonso** - *La Guardia* *Spain* MMSI: 224094500 Official number: 3-3557/	**209** 63 98		**1990-06 Astilleros Armon SA — Navia** Yd No: 236 Loa - Br ex - Dght 3.001 Lbp 22.26 Br md 7.01 Dpth 3.31 Welded	**(B11B2FV) Fishing Vessel**	**1 oil engine** geared to sc. shaft driving 1 FP propeller Total Power: 459kW (624hp) 10.5kn Caterpillar 3412PCTA 1 x Vee 4 Stroke 12 Cy. 137 x 152 459kW (624bhp) Caterpillar Inc-USA
9000845 *JH3138* -	**SUSQUEHANNA** **KK Izu Cruise** *Shimoda, Shizuoka* *Japan* Official number: 128483	*127* - 50		**1989-03 Ishida Zosen Kogyo YK — Onomichi HS** Yd No: 105 Loa 35.00 (BB) Br ex 7.55 Dght 1.750 Lbp 24.38 Br md 6.40 Dpth 2.50 Welded	**(A37B2PS) Passenger Ship**	**1 oil engine** with clutches, flexible couplings & reverse reduction geared to sc. shaft driving 1 FP propeller Total Power: 662kW (900hp) Yanmar 12LAAK-UT1 1 x Vee 4 Stroke 12 Cy. 148 x 165 662kW (900bhp) Yanmar Diesel Engine Co Ltd-Japan Thrusters: 1 Thwart. FP thruster (f)
9485112 *WDD9976* -	**SUSQUEHANNA** **Vane Line Bunkering Inc** *Baltimore, MD* *United States of America* MMSI: 367318750 Official number: 1205381	**327** 98 194		**2007-11 Thoma-Sea Boatbuilders Inc — Houma LA** Yd No: 132 Loa 29.13 Br ex - Dght - Lbp - Br md 10.36 Dpth 4.57 Welded, 1 dk	**(B32B2SP) Pusher Tug**	**2 oil engines** reverse reduction geared to sc. shafts driving 2 FP propellers Total Power: 3,090kW (4,202hp) Caterpillar 3516 2 x Vee 4 Stroke 16 Cy. 170 x 190 each-1545kW (2101bhp) Caterpillar Inc-USA
1006374 *ZCBR5*	**SUSSURRO** **Vesuvius International Ltd** Blue Ocean Management Ltd *Hamilton* *Bermuda (British)* MMSI: 310237000 Official number: 731231	**480** 144 -	Class: AB	**1998-11 de Vries Scheepsbouw B.V. — Aalsmeer** Yd No: 656 Loa 44.54 Br ex - Dght 2.200 Lbp 41.30 Br md 8.20 Dpth 4.20 Welded, 1 dk	**(X11A2YP) Yacht**	**2 oil engines & 1 Gas Turb** Gas Turbine geared to sc. shafts driving 3 Water jets Total Power: 11,000kW (14,956hp) Paxman 12VP185 2 x Vee 4 Stroke 12 Cy. 185 x 196 each-2500kW (3399bhp) Textron Lycoming TF80 1 x Gas Turb 6000kW (8158shp) Textron Lycoming-Stratford, Ct
8517530 *MHFX5* PD 378	**SUSTAIN** *ex Angela -2006* **Sustain (Peterhead) LLP** Peter & J Johnstone Ltd *Peterhead* *United Kingdom* MMSI: 235008690 Official number: C18459	**219** 86 111	Class: (GL)	**1986-03 Schiffs- u. Bootswerft Luebbe Voss — Westerende-Kirchloog** Yd No: 124 Loa 27.89 Br ex 6.38 Dght - Lbp 24.03 Br md 6.32 Dpth 3.61 Welded, 2 dks	**(B11B2FV) Fishing Vessel**	**1 oil engine** with flexible couplings & dr gearedto sc. shaft driving 1 CP propeller Total Power: 441kW (600hp) 11.0kn Callesen 6-427-FT 1 x 4 Stroke 6 Cy. 270 x 400 441kW (600bhp) Aabenraa Motorfabrik, HeinrichCallesen A/S-Denmark
9076806 *UVQM* -	**SUSU** *ex Sergieti -1998* **Lama Pivden Plus LLC** *Illichevsk* *Ukraine* MMSI: 272415000 Official number: 920178	**190** 57 70	Class: (RS)	**1992-09 OAO Astrakhanskaya Sudoverf — Astrakhan** Yd No: 101 Loa 31.85 Br ex - Dght 2.100 Lbp 27.80 Br md 7.08 Dpth 3.15 Welded, 1 dk	**(B12B2FC) Fish Carrier** Ins: 100 Ice Capable	**1 oil engine** geared to sc. shaft driving 1 FP propeller Total Power: 232kW (315hp) 10.3kn Daldizel 6CHSPN2A18-315 1 x 4 Stroke 6 Cy. 180 x 220 232kW (315bhp) Daldizel-Khabarovsk AuxGen: 2 x 25kW a.c Fuel: 14.0 (d.f.)
9012020 - -	**SUTLEJ** **Government of The Republic of India (Navy Department)** - *India*	*1,949* 535 1,189		**1993-02 Garden Reach Shipbuilders & Engineers Ltd. — Kolkata** Yd No: 2033 Loa 85.77 Br ex 12.82 Dght 3.430 Lbp 78.10 Br md 12.80 Dpth 5.86 Welded, 3 dks	**(B31A2SR) Research Survey Vessel**	**2 oil engines** with clutches, flexible couplings & sr geared to sc. shafts driving 2 FP propellers Total Power: 2,884kW (3,922hp) MAN G8V30/45ATL 2 x 4 Stroke 8 Cy. 300 x 450 each-1442kW (1961bhp) (made 1988, fitted 1993) Garden Reach Shipbuilders &Engineers Ltd-India Thrusters: 1 Thwart. FP thruster (a)
9564944 *9WHY3* -	**SUTRA 1** **Sutra Marine Sdn Bhd** - *Kuching* *Malaysia* MMSI: 533000863 Official number: 333040	**326** 97 285	Class: BV	**2010-03 Sarawak Land Shipyard Sdn Bhd — Miri** Yd No: 12 Loa 31.00 Br ex - Dght 3.500 Lbp 27.99 Br md 9.15 Dpth 4.30 Welded, 1 dk	**(B32A2ST) Tug**	**2 oil engines** reduction geared to sc. shafts driving 2 Propellers Total Power: 1,800kW (2,448hp) Chinese Std. Type 12V190 2 x Vee 4 Stroke 12 Cy. 190 x 210 each-900kW (1224bhp) Jinan Diesel Engine Co Ltd-China
9535553 *YDA4495* -	**SUTRA BHAKTI 1** **PT Foechs Sutra Bhakti** - *Jakarta* *Indonesia* Official number: 18660808	**260** 78 306	Class: KI (NK)	**2008-06 Jana Seribu Shipbuilding (M) Sdn Bhd — Sibu** Yd No: 23/07 Loa 30.00 Br ex - Dght 3.500 Lbp 28.01 Br md 8.60 Dpth 4.11 Welded, 1 dk	**(B32A2ST) Tug**	**2 oil engines** reduction geared to sc. shafts driving 2 FP propellers Total Power: 1,518kW (2,064hp) Mitsubishi S6R2-MPTK3 2 x 4 Stroke 6 Cy. 170 x 220 each-759kW (1032bhp) Mitsubishi Heavy Industries Ltd-Japan AuxGen: 2 x 78kW 415V 50Hz a.c Fuel: 200.0
9535565 *YDA4496* -	**SUTRA BHAKTI II** **PT Foechs Sutra Bhakti** - *Jakarta* *Indonesia*	**260** 78 301	Class: KI (NK)	**2007-06 Jana Seribu Shipbuilding (M) Sdn Bhd — Sibu** Yd No: 2030 Loa 30.00 Br ex - Dght 3.500 Lbp 28.01 Br md 8.60 Dpth 4.11 Welded, 1 dk	**(B32A2ST) Tug**	**2 oil engines** reduction geared to sc. shafts driving 2 FP propellers Total Power: 1,472kW (2,002hp) Mitsubishi S6R2-MPTK3 2 x 4 Stroke 6 Cy. 170 x 220 each-736kW (1001bhp) Mitsubishi Heavy Industries Ltd-Japan AuxGen: 2 x 78kW 415V 50Hz a.c Fuel: 196.0 (r.f.)
7713228 - -	**SUTTI REEFER** *ex Sierra Aracena -2001 ex Puerto Cadiz -1986* **Surin & Teelk Reefer Trading SA** -	**2,502** 1,019 2,703	Class: (LR) ✠ Classed LR until 1/5/11	**1979-01 Ast. del Cadagua W. E. Gonzalez S.A. — Bilbao** Yd No: 108 Loa 92.74 (BB) Br ex - Dght 5.146 Lbp 85.12 Br md 14.22 Dpth 7.73 Welded, 1 dk & S dk	**(A34A2GR) Refrigerated Cargo Ship** Ins: 3,809 Compartments: 4 Ho, ER, 4 Tw Dk 4 Ha: 4 (5.1 x 5.5) Cranes: 3x3t	**1 oil engine** sr geared to sc. shaft driving 1 FP propeller Total Power: 2,207kW (3,001hp) 12.0kn Deutz SBV8M358 1 x 4 Stroke 8 Cy. 400 x 580 2207kW (3001bhp) Hijos de J Barreras SA-Spain AuxGen: 3 x 360kW 380V 50Hz a.c Fuel: 120.0 (d.f.) 320.0 (r.f.) 9.5pd
9389461 *YJVE5* -	**SUTTON TIDE** **Vermillion Fleet Ltd** Tidewater Marine International Inc *Port Vila* *Vanuatu* MMSI: 576356000 Official number: 1744	**2,258** 677 2,094	Class: AB	**2007-11 Stocznia Polnocna SA (Northern Shipyard) — Gdansk** (Hull) Yd No: B844/04 **2007-11 Gdanska Stocznia 'Remontowa' SA — Gdansk** Yd No: 1674/04 Loa 70.00 Br ex - Dght 5.100 Lbp 63.60 Br md 15.50 Dpth 6.60 Welded, 1 dk	**(B21B20A) Anchor Handling Tug Supply**	**2 oil engines** reduction geared to sc. shafts driving 2 CP propellers Total Power: 5,970kW (8,116hp) 13.0kn EMD (Electro-Motive) 20-710-G7B 2 x Vee 2 Stroke 20 Cy. 230 x 279 each-2985kW (4058bhp) General Motors Corp.Electro-Motive Div.-La Grange AuxGen: 2 x 1500kW a.c, 1 x 250kW a.c, 1 x 150kW a.c Thrusters: 2 Tunnel thruster (f) Fuel: 821.5 (d.f.)

9267560 *OJKZ* -	**SUULA** - **Neste Shipping Oy** - *Porvoo* *Finland* MMSI: 230957000 Official number: 12364	**9,910** 4,596 14,665 T/cm 26.1	Class: LR (NV) **100A1** SS 02/2010 Double Hull oil and chemical tanker, Ship Type 2* SG 1.54 in all cargo tanks ESP LI Ice Class 1AS FS at a draught of 9.201m Max/min draughts fwd 9.201/4.40m Max/min draughts aft 9.201/5.90m Power required 7247kw, power installed 8400kw **LMC** **UMS** Cable: 577.5/56.0 U3 (a)	**2005-02 Estaleiros Navais de Viana do Castelo S.A. — Viana do Castelo** Yd No: 225 Loa 139.75 (BB) Br ex 21.71 Dght 8.700 Lbp 132.20 Br md 21.70 Dpth 11.85 Welded, 1 dk	**(A12B2TR) Chemical/Products Tanker** Double Hull (13F) Liq: 14,876; Liq (Oil): 14,876 Cargo Heating Coils Compartments: 12 Wing Ta, 2 Wing Slop Ta, ER 12 Cargo Pump (s): 12x350m^3/hr Manifold: Bow/CM: 71.3m Ice Capable	**1 oil engine** reduction geared to sc. shaft driving 1 CP propeller Total Power: 8,450kW (11,489hp) 15.3kn Wartsila 8L46C 1 x 4 Stroke 8 Cy. 460 x 580 8450kW (11489bhp) Wartsila Finland Oy-Finland AuxGen: 1 x 1200kW 440V 60Hz a.c, 2 x 1020kW 440V 60Hz a.c, 1 x 680kW 440V 60Hz a.c Boilers: e (ex.g.) 8.2kgf/cm^2 (8.0bar), AuxB (o.f.) 10.2kgf/cm^2 (10.0bar) Thrusters: 1 Thwart. CP thruster (f) Fuel: 125.0 (d.f.) 780.8 (r.f.)
7392854 *J2HU* -	**SUUNTA** - - - *Djibouti* *Djibouti* MMSI: 621819012	**422** 127 160		**1975-03 Rauma-Repola Oy — Savonlinna** Yd No: 150 Loa 39.76 Br ex 9.02 Dght 3.201 Lbp 35.62 Br md 9.00 Dpth 5.57 Welded, 1 dk	**(B31A2SR) Research Survey Vessel**	**1 diesel electric oil engine** Connecting to 1 elec. Motor driving 1 FP propeller Total Power: 883kW (1,201hp) Wartsila 824TS 1 x 4 Stroke 8 Cy. 240 x 310 883kW (1201bhp) Oy Wartsila Ab-Finland
9123245 *9HA3103* -	**SUURHUSEN S** *ex* Suurhusen *-2012* *ex* Saar Roma *-1996* **Velvet Marine Co Ltd** Rana Denizcilik Nakliyat Sanayi ve Ticaret Ltd Sti *Valletta* *Malta* MMSI: 229144000 Official number: 9123245	**2,805** 1,568 4,286	Class: GL NK (Class contemplated)	**1996-03 B.V. Scheepswerf Damen Hoogezand — Foxhol** Yd No: 711 Loa 89.90 (BB) Br ex - Dght 5.678 Lbp 84.90 Br md 13.17 Dpth 7.15 Welded, 1 dk	**(A31A2GX) General Cargo Ship** Double Hull Grain: 5,716 TEU 213 C. 213/20' Compartments: 1 Ho, ER 1 Ha: (62.5 x 11.0)ER Ice Capable	**1 oil engine** geared to sc. shaft driving 1 CP propeller Total Power: 1,800kW (2,447hp) 11.5kn Deutz SBV9M628 1 x 4 Stroke 9 Cy. 240 x 280 1800kW (2447bhp) Motoren Werke Mannheim AG (MWM)-Mannheim AuxGen: 2 x 136kW 380/220V 50Hz a.c, 1 x 264kW 380V 50Hz a.c Thrusters: 1 Thwart. FP thruster (f)
9682796 - -	**SUV 1** *ex* Xiang Yiyang Ji 5265 *-2013* *ex* Hunan Yiyang Hf 2023 *-2011* **PT Celebes Jaya Lines** - *Indonesia*	**988** 395 1,000	Class: ZC	**2011-01 Hunan Yiyang Anxing Shipyard — Yiyang HN** Yd No: HF 2023 Loa 68.80 Br ex 12.63 Dght 2.200 Lbp 65.02 Br md 12.60 Dpth 2.90 Welded, 1 dk	**(A24D2BA) Aggregates Carrier**	**2 oil engines** driving 2 Propellers
9682916 - -	**SUV 2** *ex* Chu Tian 1555 *-2013* *ex* Wanjiang Xinrong Hx-4326 *-2011* **PT Celebes Jaya Lines** - *Indonesia*	**1,051** 420 1,200	Class: ZC	**2011-01 in the People's Republic of China** Yd No: HX-4326 Loa 66.90 Br ex 12.53 Dght 2.300 Lbp - Br md 12.50 Dpth 3.00 Welded, 1 dk	**(A24D2BA) Aggregates Carrier**	**2 oil engines** reduction geared to sc. shafts driving 2 Propellers Chinese Std. Type Weichai Power Co Ltd-China
9682784 - -	**SUV 3** *ex* Chu Tian 1688 *-2013* **PT Celebes Jaya Lines** - *Indonesia*	**1,085** 434 1,250	Class: ZC	**2011-02 Hunan Yiyang Anxing Shipyard — Yiyang HN** Yd No: HF 2028 Loa 67.54 Br ex 12.83 Dght 2.400 Lbp - Br md 12.80 Dpth 3.10 Welded, 1 dk	**(A24D2BA) Aggregates Carrier**	**2 oil engines** driving 2 Propellers
8710027 *VO4961* -	**SUVAK** *ex* Genny And Doug *-2010* **Masiliit Corp** - *Iqaluit, NU* *Canada* Official number: 808324	*346* 199 -		**1987-05 Pictou Industries Ltd — Pictou NS** Yd No: 223 Loa 30.76 Br ex - Dght - Lbp 27.46 Br md 7.76 Dpth 3.92 Welded, 1 dk	**(B11B2FV) Fishing Vessel** Ins: 190	**1 oil engine** with flexible couplings & sr gearedto sc. shaft driving 1 FP propeller Total Power: 459kW (624hp) Caterpillar 3412TA 1 x Vee 4 Stroke 12 Cy. 137 x 152 459kW (624bhp) Caterpillar Inc-USA
9226449 *5BQW3* -	**SUVARNA** *ex* Skandi Hercules *-2008* *ex* Skandi PMS II *-2008* *ex* Boa Hercules *-2003* **Varun Cyprus Ltd** Varun Shipping Co Ltd *Limassol* *Cyprus* MMSI: 210577000	**4,820** 1,446 4,197	Class: NV (IR)	**2002-07 Dalian Shipyard Co Ltd — Dalian LN** Yd No: AH48-2 Loa 81.00 (BB) Br ex 20.04 Dght 8.200 Lbp 69.00 Br md 20.00 Dpth 9.00 Welded, 1 dk	**(B21B20A) Anchor Handling Tug Supply** Cranes: 1x15t	**2 oil engines** geared to sc. shafts driving 2 FP propellers Total Power: 12,000kW (16,316hp) 15.0kn Caterpillar 3616TA 2 x Vee 4 Stroke 16 Cy. 280 x 300 each-6000kW (8158bhp) Caterpillar Inc-USA AuxGen: 2 x 2000kW 440V 60Hz a.c, 1 x 1424kW 440V 60Hz a.c, 1 x 968kW 440V 60Hz a.c Thrusters: 1 Tunnel thruster (f); 1 Retract. directional thruster (f); 1 Tunnel thruster (a)
9170432 *VVFH* -	**SUVARNA SWARAJYA** - **The Shipping Corporation of India Ltd (SCI)** - SatCom: Inmarsat B 341903510 *Mumbai* *India* MMSI: 419212000 Official number: 2738	**21,827** 8,330 32,902 T/cm 40.0	Class: IR (BV)	**1998-11 Hyundai Heavy Industries Co Ltd — Ulsan** Yd No: 1103 Loa 172.95 (BB) Br ex 25.90 Dght 11.300 Lbp 166.40 Br md 25.87 Dpth 17.50 Welded, 1 dk	**(A13B2TP) Products Tanker** Double Hull (13F) Liq: 38,475; Liq (Oil): 38,475 Cargo Heating Coils Compartments: 12 Ta, 2 Slop Ta, ER 4 Cargo Pump (s): 4x1000m^3/hr Manifold: Bow/CM: 88.6m	**1 oil engine** driving 1 FP propeller Total Power: 6,630kW (9,014hp) 14.0kn MAN-B&W 5S50MC 1 x 2 Stroke 5 Cy. 500 x 1910 6630kW (9014bhp) Hyundai Heavy Industries Co Ltd-South Korea AuxGen: 3 x 650kW 450V 60Hz a.c Fuel: 219.0 (d.f.) 1075.0 (r.f.)
1008865 *ECDR* -	**SUVER** - **Naviera Pizarro SA** - SatCom: Inmarsat C 422432210 *Las Palmas* *Spain (CSR)* MMSI: 224322000 Official number: 2/2003	**441** - 65	Class: (LR) ✠ Classed LR until 10/6/08	**2005-06 Navantia SA — San Fernando (Sp)** Yd No: 398 Loa 41.75 (BB) Br ex 8.50 Dght 2.150 Lbp 36.29 Br md 8.20 Dpth 4.20 Welded, 1 dk	**(X11A2YP) Yacht**	**2 oil engines** with clutches, flexible couplings & sr reverse geared to sc. shafts driving 2 FP propellers Total Power: 1,880kW (2,556hp) 15.0kn Caterpillar 3512B 2 x Vee 4 Stroke 12 Cy. 170 x 190 each-940kW (1278bhp) Caterpillar Inc-USA AuxGen: 3 x 55kW 380V 50Hz a.c Thrusters: 1 Tunnel thruster (f)
7808293 *UHQP* -	**SUVOROVETS** - **Federal State Financed Institution 'Far-Eastern Expeditionary Division of Emergency & Rescue Operations'** - SatCom: Inmarsat C 427317310 *Vladivostok* *Russia* MMSI: 273384200 Official number: 802465	**3,121** 936 1,474	Class: RS	**1980-04 Oy Wartsila Ab — Helsinki** Yd No: 426 Lengthened Loa 74.41 Br ex 18.32 Dght 6.700 Lbp 65.00 Br md 17.62 Dpth 9.02 Welded, 2 dks	**(B32A2ST) Tug** Cranes: 2x5t,2x3t Ice Capable	**2 oil engines** driving 2 CP propellers Total Power: 5,590kW (7,600hp) Pielstick 6PC2-5L-400 2 x 4 Stroke 6 Cy. 400 x 460 each-2795kW (3800bhp) Oy Wartsila Ab-Finland Thrusters: 1 Thwart. FP thruster (f) Fuel: 1400.0 (r.f.)
9522324 *A8TH6* -	**SUVOROVSKY PROSPECT** - **Raintree Marine SA** SCF Unicom Singapore Pte Ltd 773135451 *Monrovia* *Liberia* MMSI: 636014356 Official number: 14356	**62,504** 35,399 113,905 T/cm 98.8	Class: NV	**2011-02 Hyundai Samho Heavy Industries Co Ltd — Samho** Yd No: S484 Loa 250.00 (BB) Br ex 44.04 Dght 15.000 Lbp 239.00 Br md 44.00 Dpth 21.00 Welded, 1 dk	**(A13A2TW) Crude/Oil Products Tanker** Double Hull (13F) Liq: 123,031; Liq (Oil): 123,030 Cargo Heating Coils Compartments: 12 Wing Ta, 2 Wing Slop Ta, ER 3 Cargo Pump (s): 3x3000m^3/hr Manifold: Bow/CM: 125.6m Ice Capable	**1 oil engine** driving 1 FP propeller Total Power: 13,560kW (18,436hp) 14.6kn MAN-B&W 6S60MC-C 1 x 2 Stroke 6 Cy. 600 x 2400 13560kW (18436bhp) MAN Diesel A/S-Denmark AuxGen: 3 x 720kW a.c Fuel: 275.0 (d.f.) 3315.0 (r.f.)
9408542 *SVAB6* -	**SUVRETTA** *ex* Nordic Bay *-2008* **Suvretta Transportation Special Maritime Enterprise (ENE)** Neda Maritime Agency Co Ltd SatCom: Inmarsat C 424077810 *Piraeus* *Greece* MMSI: 240778000 Official number: 11804	**62,856** 35,798 109,250 T/cm 99.7	Class: NV	**2008-10 STX Shipbuilding Co Ltd — Changwon (Jinhae Shipyard)** Yd No: 3003 Loa 249.99 (BB) Br ex 43.99 Dght 14.276 Lbp 239.00 Br md 43.96 Dpth 21.00 Welded, 1 dk	**(A13A2TW) Crude/Oil Products Tanker** Double Hull (13F) Liq: 126,238; Liq (Oil): 126,238 Cargo Heating Coils Compartments: 12 Wing Ta, 2 Wing Slop Ta, ER 3 Cargo Pump (s): 3x3000m^3/hr Manifold: Bow/CM: 126.4m	**1 oil engine** driving 1 FP propeller Total Power: 14,254kW (19,380hp) 15.0kn MAN-B&W 6S60MC-C 1 x 2 Stroke 6 Cy. 600 x 2400 14254kW (19380bhp) STX Engine Co Ltd-South Korea AuxGen: 3 x 900kW a.c Fuel: 250.0 (d.f.) 2855.0 (r.f.)
9094248 *JD2148* -	**SUWA MARU** - **Cosmo Kaiun KK** - *Yokkaichi, Mie* *Japan* Official number: 140208	*166* - -		**2005-09 Kanagawa Zosen — Kobe** Yd No: 535 Loa 31.25 Br ex - Dght 2.700 Lbp 27.50 Br md 9.00 Dpth 3.81 Welded, 1 dk	**(B32A2ST) Tug**	**2 oil engines** reduction geared to sc. shafts driving 2 Propellers Total Power: 2,058kW (2,798hp) 12.7kn Niigata 6L22HX 2 x 4 Stroke 6 Cy. 220 x 280 each-1029kW (1399bhp) Niigata Engineering Co Ltd-Japan

IMO / Call sign / Flag	Name / Owner / Port	Tonnage	Class	Build / Dimensions	Type	Machinery
8948583 *JM2308* -	**SUWA MARU** - - *Omuta, Fukuoka* *Japan* Official number: 98961	*131* - -		**1966-06 Fujinagata Zosensho — Osaka** Loa 27.00 Br ex - Dght 2.500 Lbp 24.00 Br md 7.50 Dpth 3.70 Welded, 1 dk	**(B32A2ST) Tug**	**2 oil engines** driving 2 FP propellers Total Power: 810kW (1,102hp) 12.0kn Fuji 6SD27.5BH 2 x 4 Stroke 6 Cy. 275 x 410 each-405kW (551bhp) Fuji Diesel Co Ltd-Japan
9606730 *JD3333* FS1-661	**SUWA MARU NO. 1** **KK Suya Shoten** - *Iwaki, Fukushima* *Japan* Official number: 141641	*250* - -		**2012-05 K.K. Watanabe Zosensho — Nagasaki** Yd No: 172 Loa 56.76 (BB) Br ex - Dght 3.500 Lbp 48.00 Br md 10.80 Dpth 5.64 Welded, 1 dk	**(B11B2FV) Fishing Vessel** Ins: 282	**1 oil engine** reduction geared to sc. shaft driving 1 Propeller Total Power: 2,647kW (3,599hp) Niigata 6MG34HX 1 x 4 Stroke 6 Cy. 340 x 450 2647kW (3599bhp) Niigata Engineering Co Ltd-Japan
7824211 - -	**SUWA MARU No. 11** - **Feng Pang Fishery Co Ltd** - *Chinese Taipei*	*160* - 200		**1979-04 Tokushima Zosen K.K. — Fukuoka** Yd No: 1320 Loa - Br ex - Dght 2.501 Lbp 34.80 Br md 6.71 Dpth 2.85 Welded	**(A34A2GR) Refrigerated Cargo Ship**	**1 oil engine** driving 1 FP propeller Total Power: 441kW (600hp) Fuji 1 x 4 Stroke 441kW (600bhp) Fuji Diesel Co Ltd-Japan
8809268 *JE2910* -	**SUWA MARU No. 22** - **KK Suya Shoten** - *Iwaki, Fukushima* *Japan* MMSI: 432032000 Official number: 130685	*305* - 500		**1988-06 Niigata Engineering Co Ltd — Niigata NI** Yd No: 2087 Loa 58.27 (BB) Br ex - Dght 3.730 Lbp 50.02 Br md 8.91 Dpth 4.20 Welded, 1 dk	**(B12B2FC) Fish Carrier** Ins: 430	**1 oil engine** with clutches, flexible couplings & sr geared to sc. shaft driving 1 CP propeller Total Power: 941kW (1,279hp) Pielstick 8PA5 1 x 4 Stroke 8 Cy. 255 x 270 941kW (1279bhp) Niigata Engineering Co Ltd-Japan
7920950 - -	**SUWA MARU No. 25** - **Kaohsiung Shih Feng Pang Fishing Co Ltd** - *Chinese Taipei*	*182* - 250		**1979-12 Tokushima Zosen K.K. — Fukuoka** Yd No: 1331 Loa 42.30 (BB) Br ex 6.71 Dght 2.593 Lbp 35.72 Br md - Dpth 2.93 Welded, 1 dk	**(B12B2FC) Fish Carrier**	**1 oil engine** driving 1 FP propeller Total Power: 699kW (950hp) 10.5kn Niigata 6MG28A 1 x 4 Stroke 6 Cy. 280 x 480 699kW (950bhp) Niigata Engineering Co Ltd-Japan
8921597 *JE3004* -	**SUWA MARU NO. 31** *ex* Koyo Maru No. 18 *-2005* *ex* Fukuyoshi Maru No. 1 *-2003* **Kanari Suisan KK** - SatCom: Inmarsat A 1205560 *Iwaki, Fukushima* *Japan* Official number: 130866	*135* - 344		**1990-03 K.K. Watanabe Zosensho — Nagasaki** Yd No: 1168 Loa 46.03 (BB) Br ex - Dght 2.900 Lbp 36.50 Br md 8.10 Dpth 3.30 Welded, 1 dk	**(B11B2FV) Fishing Vessel**	**1 oil engine** driving 1 CP propeller Total Power: 861kW (1,171hp) Niigata 6MG28HX 1 x 4 Stroke 6 Cy. 280 x 370 861kW (1171bhp) Niigata Engineering Co Ltd-Japan Thrusters: 1 Thwart. FP thruster (f)
8717166 - -	**SUWA MARU No. 33** - -	*300* - 552		**1987-12 Niigata Engineering Co Ltd — Niigata NI** Yd No: 2073 Loa 55.10 (BB) Br ex 8.72 Dght 3.641 Lbp 49.00 Br md 8.70 Dpth 4.09 Welded, 1 dk	**(B11B2FV) Fishing Vessel** Ins: 525 Compartments: 10 Ho, ER 10 Ha:	**1 oil engine** with clutches, flexible couplings & sr geared to sc. shaft driving 1 CP propeller Total Power: 861kW (1,171hp) Niigata 6MG28CX 1 x 4 Stroke 6 Cy. 280 x 350 861kW (1171bhp) Niigata Engineering Co Ltd-Japan Thrusters: 1 Thwart. FP thruster (f)
9015307 - -	**SUWA MARU No. 82** *ex* Hakuryo Maru No. 82 *-1992* **KK Suya Shoten** -	*299* - 582		**1989-01 Nichiro Zosen K.K. — Ishinomaki** Yd No: 531 Loa 57.12 (BB) Br ex - Dght 3.965 Lbp 49.50 Br md 8.80 Dpth 4.20 Welded	**(B11B2FV) Fishing Vessel** Ins: 459	**1 oil engine** with clutches, flexible couplings & reverse reduction geared to sc. shaft driving 1 FP propeller Total Power: 861kW (1,171hp) Niigata 6MG28HX 1 x 4 Stroke 6 Cy. 280 x 370 861kW (1171bhp) Niigata Engineering Co Ltd-Japan Thrusters: 1 Thwart. FP thruster (f)
8504612 - -	**SUWA MARU No. 258** *ex* Suwa Maru No. 58 *-1999* **Siam Bengal Fisheries Co Ltd** - *Thailand*	*135* - 137		**1985-05 Niigata Engineering Co Ltd — Niigata NI** Yd No: 1853 Loa 43.01 (BB) Br ex 8.31 Dght 2.710 Lbp 34.83 Br md 7.51 Dpth 3.08 Welded, 1 dk	**(B11B2FV) Fishing Vessel**	**1 oil engine** with clutches, flexible couplings & sr reverse geared to sc. shaft driving 1 FP propeller Total Power: 861kW (1,171hp) Niigata 6MG28BXF 1 x 4 Stroke 6 Cy. 280 x 350 861kW (1171bhp) Niigata Engineering Co Ltd-Japan
9380855 *J8B3299* -	**SUWAKO** **Suwako Shipping Co Ltd** Qingdao Harmony Shipping Co Ltd *Kingstown* *St Vincent & The Grenadines* MMSI: 375246000 Official number: 9771	**1,972** 1,395 3,385	Class: KR (CC)	**2006-05 Qingdao Shipyard — Qingdao SD** Yd No: QDZ427 Loa 81.00 Br ex - Dght 5.500 Lbp 76.00 Br md 13.60 Dpth 6.80 Welded, 1 dk	**(A31A2GX) General Cargo Ship** Compartments: 3 Ho 2 Ha: ER 2 (18.6 x 9.0)	**1 oil engine** reduction geared to sc. shaft driving 1 FP propeller Total Power: 1,324kW (1,800hp) 12.0kn Chinese Std. Type G6300ZC 1 x 4 Stroke 6 Cy. 300 x 380 1324kW (1800bhp) Ningbo CSI Power & Machinery GroupCo Ltd-China
8717958 - -	**SUWALL NO. 1** *ex* Pyung Jin *-2012* **Park Jeong Ok** Daesang Shipping Co Ltd *Ulsan* *South Korea* Official number: USR-886042	*286* - 252	Class: KR	**1988-10 ShinA Shipbuilding Co Ltd — Tongyeong** Yd No: 325 Loa 35.51 Br ex 9.28 Dght 3.710 Lbp 33.41 Br md 9.25 Dpth 4.50 Welded, 1 dk	**(B32B2SP) Pusher Tug**	**2 oil engines** reverse reduction geared to sc. shafts driving 2 CP propellers Total Power: 2,206kW (3,000hp) Hanshin 6LUN28G 2 x 4 Stroke 6 Cy. 280 x 480 each-1103kW (1500bhp) Ssangyong Heavy Industries Co Ltd-South Korea
9207912 *WCZ7163*	**SUWANNEE RIVER** **Banc of America Leasing & Capital LLC** Seabulk Towing Inc *Port Everglades, FL* *United States of America* MMSI: 366943490 Official number: 1095183	**330** 99 -	Class: (AB)	**2000-04 Halter Marine, Inc. — Lockport, La** Yd No: 1837 Loa 27.43 Br ex - Dght 4.760 Lbp 26.40 Br md 15.24 Dpth 3.30 Welded, 1 dk	**(B32A2ST) Tug**	**2 oil engines** gearing integral to driving 2 Z propellers Total Power: 2,970kW (4,038hp) Wartsila 9L20 2 x 4 Stroke 9 Cy. 200 x 280 each-1485kW (2019bhp) Wartsila NSD Finland Oy-Finland AuxGen: 2 x 65kW a.c
7303451 - -	**SUWE STAR** *ex* Princess Deborah *-2001* *ex* Barlinek *-1992* - *Lagos* *Nigeria*	*807* 362 1,079	Class: (PR)	**1973-07 Stocznia 'Wisla' — Gdansk** Yd No: B457/03 Loa 59.80 Br ex 10.22 Dght 4.201 Lbp 54.01 Br md - Dpth 4.81 Welded, 1 dk	**(A31A2GX) General Cargo Ship** Grain: 1,443; Bale: 1,420 Compartments: 1 Ho, ER 2 Ha: 2 (11.2 x 6.7)ER Ice Capable	**1 oil engine** driving 1 CP propeller Total Power: 662kW (900hp) 11.5kn Sulzer 6TD36 1 x 2 Stroke 6 Cy. 360 x 600 662kW (900bhp) Zaklady Urzadzen Technicznych'Zgoda' SA-Poland AuxGen: 2 x 72kW 400V a.c, 1 x 20kW 400V a.c Fuel: 53.0 (d.f.) 3.5pd
8024545 *5IM259* -	**SUWERTE** *ex* Binyass No. 1 *-2010* *ex* Jm Motor No. 3 *-2009* *ex* Sea Rock *-2008* *ex* Syalom I *-2007* *ex* Buana III *-2001* *ex* Iradat I *-1989* **China Harbour Engineering Co Ltd** - *Zanzibar* *Tanzania (Zanzibar)* MMSI: 677015900 Official number: 300022	*792* 238 1,412	Class: (KI) (AB)	**1981-08 Robin Shipyard Pte Ltd — Singapore** Yd No: 319 Loa 56.12 Br ex 14.30 Dght 2.710 Lbp 53.07 Br md 14.00 Dpth 3.73 Welded, 1 dk	**(A35D2RL) Landing Craft** Bow door/ramp Liq: 1,699; Liq (Oil): 1,699 Compartments: 8 Ta, ER	**2 oil engines** sr reverse geared to sc. shafts driving 2 FP propellers Total Power: 662kW (900hp) 7.5kn Niigata 6MG16X 2 x 4 Stroke 6 Cy. 160 x 200 each-331kW (450bhp) Niigata Engineering Co Ltd-Japan AuxGen: 2 x 52kW
7388231 *5VCH8* -	**SUXER S** *ex* Super Star K *-2014* *ex* Bdoor *-2011* *ex* Rapoca *-2006* *ex* Antonio Suardiaz *-1987* **Suliman Saeed Aljabri** Enamar Management Ltd *Lome* *Togo* MMSI: 671402000	**4,605** 1,550 4,243	Class: (LR) (CS) (JR) (BV) Classed LR until 28/11/06	**1976-02 Enrique Lorenzo y Cia SA — Vigo** Yd No: 378 Loa 106.30 (BB) Br ex 18.00 Dght 6.200 Lbp 96.50 Br md 17.50 Dpth 11.35 Welded, 2 dks	**(A35A2RR) Ro-Ro Cargo Ship** Stern door/ramp Bale: 9,450 Compartments: 1 Ho, ER, 1 Tw Dk 1 Ha: (11.5 x 12.9)ER	**1 oil engine** dr geared to sc. shaft driving 1 FP propeller Total Power: 4,413kW (6,000hp) 13.0kn Werkspoor 6TM410 1 x 4 Stroke 6 Cy. 410 x 470 4413kW (6000bhp) Fabrica de San Carlos SA-Spain AuxGen: 3 x 200kW 380V 50Hz a.c, 1 x 20kW 380V 50Hz a.c Thrusters: 1 Thwart. FP thruster (f) Fuel: 360.5 (d.f.) 27.5pd
9181326 *JM6589* -	**SUYO MARU** *ex* Shinai Maru *-2005* **Oita Kaiun KK** - *Tsukumi, Oita* *Japan* MMSI: 431600733 Official number: 135408	*445* - -		**1997-05 YK Furumoto Tekko Zosensho — Osakikamijima** Yd No: 626 Loa 59.32 Br ex - Dght - Lbp 53.00 Br md 9.40 Dpth 5.40 Welded, 1 dk	**(A31A2GX) General Cargo Ship** Bale: 1,160	**1 oil engine** driving 1 FP propeller Total Power: 736kW (1,001hp) 11.0kn Niigata 6M28BGT 1 x 4 Stroke 6 Cy. 280 x 480 736kW (1001bhp) Niigata Engineering Co Ltd-Japan

IMO / Call sign	Name / Owners / Flag	Tonnage	Class	Builder / Dimensions	Type	Machinery
9317377 *3EFH6* -	**SUZAKU** - **Kingship Lines SA** Santoku Senpaku Co Ltd *Panama* Panama MMSI: 355557000 Official number: 3194106A	**31,385** 17,161 54,881 T/cm 55.9	Class: NK	**2006-07 Oshima Shipbuilding Co Ltd — Saikai NS** Yd No: 10403 Loa 189.99 (BB) Br ex - Dght 12.515 Lbp 185.79 Br md 32.26 Dpth 17.62 Welded, 1 dk	**(A21A2BC) Bulk Carrier** Double Hull Grain: 64,824; Bale: 64,391 Compartments: 5 Ho, ER 5 Ha: ER Cranes: 4x30t	**1 oil engine** driving 1 FP propeller Total Power: 9,480kW (12,889hp) 14.5kn MAN-B&W 6S50MC-C 1 x 2 Stroke 6 Cy. 500 x 2000 9480kW (12889bhp) Kawasaki Heavy Industries Ltd-Japan Fuel: 1985.0
7702267 *9BDE* -	**SUZAN** - **Mohamed Reza Angali** - *Bandar Imam Khomeini* Iran MMSI: 422402000 Official number: 20283	*418* 225 590	Class: AS (AB)	**1977-09 S.K. Dhondy & Co. — Mumbai** Yd No: 128 Loa 47.02 Br ex - Dght 2.401 Lbp 43.44 Br md 10.01 Dpth 3.03 Welded, 1 dk	**(A14A2LO) Water Tanker**	**2 oil engines** driving 2 FP propellers Total Power: 548kW (746hp) MAN W8V175/22B 2 x 4 Stroke 8 Cy. 175 x 220 each-274kW (373bhp) Kirloskar Oil Engines Ltd-India AuxGen: 1 x 20kW a.c, 1 x 10kW a.c
9085596 *V2BD6*	**SUZANNE** *ex* Maersk Asia Decimo *-2007* *ex* Soochow *-1996* *ex* Micronesian Chief *-1995* *ex* Soochow *-1994* **ASG Funfte Altonaer Schifffahrts GmbH & Co KG** Reederei Harmstorf & Co Thomas Meier-Hedde GmbH & Co KG *Saint John's* Antigua & Barbuda MMSI: 304643000 Official number: 2830	**7,869** 4,270 10,747	Class: GL (LR) ✠ Classed LR until 30/12/05	**1994-10 Miho Zosensho K.K. — Shimizu** Yd No: 1431 Loa 129.78 (BB) Br ex 22.11 Dght 8.334 Lbp 119.98 Br md 22.00 Dpth 11.00 Welded, 1 dk	**(A33A2CC) Container Ship (Fully Cellular)** TEU 841 incl 100 ref C. Compartments: 5 Cell Ho, ER 6 Ha: ER Cranes: 2x37t	**1 oil engine** driving 1 FP propeller Total Power: 6,965kW (9,470hp) 17.0kn B&W 7L42MC 1 x 2 Stroke 7 Cy. 420 x 1360 6965kW (9470bhp) Hitachi Zosen Corp-Japan AuxGen: 3 x 550kW 445V 60Hz a.c Boilers: AuxB (Comp) 8.1kgf/cm² (7.9bar) Thrusters: 1 Thwart. CP thruster (f); 1 Tunnel thruster (a) Fuel: 846.0 (r.f.) 28.3pd
8036653 *WDC4720*	**SUZANNE BETH** *ex* Hope *-2005* *ex* Miss Heather II *-2001* *ex* Suzanne-Beth *-1992* **Oliver A Corp** - *Point Judith, RI* United States of America MMSI: 367029450 Official number: 622027	*168* 119 -		**1980 Washburn & Doughty Associates Inc — Woolwich ME** Yd No: 5 L reg 23.63 Br ex 7.07 Dght - Lbp - Br md - Dpth 3.56 Welded, 1 dk	**(B11A2FS) Stern Trawler**	**2 oil engines** geared to sc. shafts driving 2 FP propellers Total Power: 536kW (728hp) Cummins KT-1150-M 2 x 4 Stroke 6 Cy. 159 x 159 each-268kW (364bhp) Cummins Engine Co Inc-USA
9199763 *PFTC* -	**SUZANNE D** - **Stemat BV** - *Rotterdam* Netherlands MMSI: 245785000 Official number: 34266	**175** 52 -	Class: BV	**1998-05 Neptune Shipyards BV — Aalst (Nl)** Yd No: 224 Loa 25.99 Br ex - Dght 2.200 Lbp 24.98 Br md 9.50 Dpth 2.85 Welded, 1 dk	**(B34L2QU) Utility Vessel**	**2 oil engines** reduction geared to sc. shafts driving 2 FP propellers Total Power: 1,194kW (1,624hp) 9.0kn Cummins KT-38-M 2 x Vee 4 Stroke 12 Cy. 159 x 159 each-597kW (812bhp) Cummins Engine Co Ltd-United Kingdom AuxGen: 1 x 260kW 220/380V 50Hz a.c Fuel: 80.0 (d.f.)
8878958 - -	**SUZANNE M** *ex* Asahi Maru No. 18 *-1996* - -	**192** 66 -		**1980-11 Tonoura Dock Co. Ltd. — Miyazaki** L reg 26.60 Br ex - Dght - Lbp - Br md 5.90 Dpth 2.40 Welded, 1 dk	**(B11B2FV) Fishing Vessel**	**1 oil engine** driving 1 FP propeller Otsuka 1 x 4 Stroke KK Otsuka Diesel-Japan
8522389 - -	**SUZANNE SMITH** - - - Paraguay	**413** 281 -		**1971-03 Bludworth Shipyard Inc. — Houston, Tx** Loa - Br ex 10.39 Dght - Lbp 38.10 Br md 10.37 Dpth 3.51 Welded, 1 dk	**(B32A2ST) Tug**	**2 oil engines** driving 2 FP propellers Total Power: 3,310kW (4,500hp)
9288992 *UFZV* -	**SUZDAL** - **OOO Sudokhodnaya Kompaniya 'Astronavt' (Astronaut Shipping Co Ltd)** Navigator LLC *Astrakhan* Russia MMSI: 273444330 Official number: 020146	**4,378** 1,313 5,600 T/cm 22.0	Class: RS	**2003-07 Sudostroitelnyy Zavod "Krasnoye Sormovo" — Nizhniy Novgorod** Yd No: 19614/3 Loa 141.00 Br ex 16.90 Dght 3.730 Lbp 134.88 Br md 16.80 Dpth 6.10 Welded, 1 dk	**(A13B2TP) Products Tanker** Double Hull (13F) Liq: 6,587; Liq (Oil): 6,721 Compartments: 12 Wing Ta, ER, 1 Slop Ta 2 Cargo Pump (s): 2x250m³/hr Manifold: Bow/CM: 70m Ice Capable	**2 oil engines** geared to sc. shafts driving 2 FP propellers Total Power: 1,860kW (2,528hp) 10.0kn Wartsila 6L20 2 x 4 Stroke 6 Cy. 200 x 280 each-930kW (1264bhp) Wartsila Finland Oy-Finland Thrusters: 1 Thwart. FP thruster (f)
8939726 *WDB4252* -	**SUZEE Q** *ex* Capt. Lucky *-2007* **Suzee Q LLC** - *Poquoson, VA* United States of America MMSI: 366896420 Official number: 1043158	**135** 40 -		**1996 J & J Marine, Inc. — Bayou La Batre, Al** Yd No: 125 L reg 24.17 Br ex - Dght - Lbp - Br md 7.32 Dpth 3.84 Welded, 1 dk	**(B11B2FV) Fishing Vessel**	**1 oil engine** driving 1 FP propeller
8205204 *V2ZK4* -	**SUZIE Q** *ex* Johanna Trader *-2002* *ex* Vrouwe Johanna *-1995* **Amazon Shipping Ltd** - SatCom: Inmarsat C 430401292 *Saint John's* Antigua & Barbuda MMSI: 304010569 Official number: 2650	**1,980** 1,028 3,008	Class: BV	**1983-11 Scheepswerf Bijlholt B.V. — Foxhol** Yd No: 615 Loa 81.72 Br ex 14.10 Dght 5.360 Lbp 74.50 Br md 14.01 Dpth 6.46 Welded, 1 dk	**(A31A2GX) General Cargo Ship** Grain: 3,787; Bale: 3,645 TEU 95 C.Ho 55/20' C.Dk 40/20' Compartments: 1 Ho, ER 1 Ha: (41.2 x 10.2)ER Cranes: 2x12.5t	**1 oil engine** with flexible couplings & sr gearedto sc. shaft driving 1 CP propeller Total Power: 1,192kW (1,621hp) 13.4kn Caterpillar 3606TA 1 x 4 Stroke 6 Cy. 280 x 300 1192kW (1621bhp) (new engine 1989) Caterpillar Inc-USA AuxGen: 2 x 200kW 380V 50Hz a.c Fuel: 45.0 (d.f.) 211.0 (r.f.) 5.0pd
8210223 - -	**SUZU MARU** - - -	*498* - 1,598		**1982-08 Kinoura Zosen K.K. — Imabari** Yd No: 87 Loa 72.70 Br ex - Dght 4.144 Lbp 68.00 Br md 11.51 Dpth 6.30 Welded, 1 dk	**(A31A2GX) General Cargo Ship**	**1 oil engine** sr geared to sc. shaft driving 1 CP propeller Total Power: 1,030kW (1,400hp) Niigata 6M31AFT 1 x 4 Stroke 6 Cy. 310 x 530 1030kW (1400bhp) Niigata Engineering Co Ltd-Japan
8870102 *JE2697* -	**SUZU MARU NO. 21** *ex* Junyo Maru No. 21 *-2006* *ex* Suzu Maru No. 21 *-2005* *ex* Yamato Maru No. 8 *-2005* **YK Suzumaru Gyogyo** - *Matsumae, Hokkaido* Japan Official number: 124990	*138* - -		**1981-07 Kyowa Zosen — Kesennuma** L reg 28.70 Br ex - Dght - Lbp - Br md 6.10 Dpth 2.80 Welded, 1 dk	**(B11B2FV) Fishing Vessel**	**1 oil engine** driving 1 FP propeller Yanmar 1 x 4 Stroke Yanmar Diesel Engine Co Ltd-Japan
8630526 *JD2580* HK1-967	**SUZU MARU No. 36** *ex* Koei Maru No. 18 *-1997* **YK Suzumaru Gyogyo** - *Matsumae, Hokkaido* Japan Official number: 125623	*132* - -		**1983-01 KK Toyo Zosen Tekkosho — Kamaishi IW** Loa 28.60 Br ex - Dght 1.900 Lbp - Br md 5.70 Dpth 2.40 Welded, 1 dk	**(B11B2FV) Fishing Vessel**	**1 oil engine** driving 1 FP propeller Total Power: 338kW (460hp) Daihatsu 1 x 4 Stroke 338kW (460bhp) Daihatsu Diesel Manufacturing Co Lt-Japan
9032276 *JI3459* -	**SUZUKA** - **Kokoku Kaiun KK** - *Osaka, Osaka* Japan MMSI: 431300888 Official number: 131709	*2,919* - 2,817	Class: NK	**1991-05 Shin Kurushima Dockyard Co. Ltd. — Akitsu** Yd No: 2715 Loa 116.02 (BB) Br ex - Dght 4.513 Lbp 108.00 Br md 17.20 Dpth 12.00 Welded, 5 dks	**(A35B2RV) Vehicles Carrier** Quarter stern door/ramp (p. a.) Quarter stern door/ramp (s. a.) Cars: 574	**1 oil engine** dr reverse geared to sc. shaft driving 1 FP propeller Total Power: 4,413kW (6,000hp) 16.3kn Daihatsu 8DLM-40 1 x 4 Stroke 8 Cy. 400 x 480 4413kW (6000bhp) Daihatsu Diesel Manufacturing Co Lt-Japan AuxGen: 2 x 400kW a.c Thrusters: 1 Thwart. CP thruster (f) Fuel: 200.0 (r.f.)
9589906 *7JGJ* -	**SUZUKA** - **Government of Japan (Ministry of Land, Infrastructure & Transport) (The Coastguard)** - *Tokyo* Japan MMSI: 432741000 Official number: 141147	*1,320* - -		**2010-03 Mitsui Eng. & SB. Co. Ltd. — Tamano** Yd No: 1827 Loa 89.00 Br ex - Dght - Lbp - Br md 11.00 Dpth 5.00 Welded, 1 dk	**(B34H2SQ) Patrol Vessel**	**4 oil engines** reduction geared to sc. shafts driving 4 Water jets Total Power: 14,760kW (20,068hp)

IMO / Call sign / Flag	Name / Owner / Port	Tonnage	Class	Built / Dimensions	Type / Cargo	Machinery
9448073 *DUCC* -	**SUZUKA EXPRESS** - **PCTC Express VIII BV** Vroon BV *Manila* *Philippines* MMSI: 548824000 Official number: MNLA000741	**43,810** 13,143 15,154	Class: NK	2010-02 **Mitsubishi Heavy Industries Ltd. — Shimonoseki** Yd No: 1135 Loa 180.00 (BB) Br ex 30.03 Dght 9.222 Lbp 171.70 Br md 30.00 Dpth 33.52 Welded, 10 dks. incl. 2 liftable dks.	**(A35B2RV) Vehicles Carrier** Side door/ramp (s) Len: - Wid: - Swl: 25 Quarter stern door/ramp (s. a.) Len: - Wid: - Swl: 100 Cars: 3,205	**1 oil engine** driving 1 FP propeller Total Power: 11,560kW (15,717hp) 20.0kn Mitsubishi 8UEC50LSII 1 x 2 Stroke 8 Cy. 500 x 1950 11560kW (15717bhp) Mitsubishi Heavy Industries Ltd-Japan AuxGen: 3 x 875kW 450V 60Hz a.c Thrusters: 1 Thwart. CP thruster (f) Fuel: 2320.0 (r.f.)
9566215 *JD3012* -	**SUZUKA MARU** - **Nakata Kaiun KK** - *Kawasaki, Kanagawa* *Japan* MMSI: 431001206 Official number: 141169	*748* - 1,437		2010-03 **Kurinoura Dockyard Co Ltd — Yawatahama EH** Yd No: 412 Loa 69.98 Br ex - Dght 4.330 Lbp 66.00 Br md 11.30 Dpth 4.60 Welded, 1 dk	**(A13C2LA) Asphalt/Bitumen Tanker** Double Hull (13F) Asphalt: 1,417	**1 oil engine** driving 1 FP propeller Total Power: 1,323kW (1,799hp) Hanshin LH30L 1 x 4 Stroke 6 Cy. 300 x 600 1323kW (1799bhp) The Hanshin Diesel Works Ltd-Japan
7104075 - -	**SUZUKA MARU** - **Wha Sueng Co** - *South Korea*	*297* - 649		1971 **Hanasaki Zosensho K.K. — Yokosuka** Yd No: 143 Loa 42.93 Br ex 8.03 Dght 3.175 Lbp 40.01 Br md 8.01 Dpth 3.48 Welded, 1 dk	**(A13B2TU) Tanker (unspecified)** Compartments: 4 Ta, ER	**1 oil engine** driving 1 FP propeller Total Power: 331kW (450hp) 10.0kn Sumiyoshi S6MBHS 1 x 4 Stroke 6 Cy. 220 x 400 331kW (450bhp) Sumiyoshi Marine Diesel Co Ltd-Japan AuxGen: 1 x 15kW 100V d.c
9031806 *JI3467* -	**SUZUKA MARU No. 2** - - - *Uki, Kumamoto* *Japan* Official number: 131718	*198* - 512		1991-08 **Koa Sangyo KK — Takamatsu KG** Yd No: 561 Loa 49.59 Br ex - Dght 3.100 Lbp 45.00 Br md 7.80 Dpth 3.30 Welded, 1 dk	**(A12A2TC) Chemical Tanker** Liq: 393 Compartments: 6 Ta, ER 2 Cargo Pump (s): 2x150m³/hr	**1 oil engine** driving 1 FP propeller Total Power: 588kW (799hp) Yanmar MF26-ST 1 x 4 Stroke 6 Cy. 260 x 500 588kW (799bhp) Yanmar Diesel Engine Co Ltd-Japan
9172404 *JI3643* -	**SUZUKA MARU No. 3** - **Suzuka Kaiun KK** - *Osaka, Osaka* *Japan* Official number: 135940	*374* - 690		1997-11 **Koa Sangyo KK — Takamatsu KG** Yd No: 602 Loa 56.00 Br ex - Dght - Lbp 51.00 Br md 9.20 Dpth 4.00 Welded, 1 dk	**(A12A2TC) Chemical Tanker** Liq: 660 Compartments: 3 Ta, ER 2 Cargo Pump (s): 2x220m³/hr	**1 oil engine** driving 1 FP propeller Total Power: 736kW (1,001hp) 11.2kn Hanshin LH26G 1 x 4 Stroke 6 Cy. 260 x 440 736kW (1001bhp) The Hanshin Diesel Works Ltd-Japan
9213480 *JH3469* -	**SUZUKA MARU No. 3** - **Kawaki Kosan Kaisha Ltd** - *Yokkaichi, Mie* *Japan* Official number: 135657	*150* - -		1999-07 **Kanagawa Zosen — Kobe** Yd No: 474 Loa 31.25 Br ex - Dght 2.810 Lbp 29.00 Br md 8.20 Dpth 3.38 Welded, 1 dk	**(B34G2SE) Pollution Control Vessel**	**2 oil engines** reduction geared to sc. shafts driving 2 FP propellers Total Power: 1,472kW (2,002hp) 12.6kn Yanmar 6N18A-EN 2 x 4 Stroke 6 Cy. 180 x 280 each-736kW (1001bhp) Yanmar Diesel Engine Co Ltd-Japan
9046849 *JM6133* -	**SUZUKA MARU NO. 5** *ex Ryozan Maru -2005* **Suzuka Kaiun KK** - *Osaka, Osaka* *Japan* Official number: 133460	*489* - 1,232	Class: NK	1992-09 **Murakami Hide Zosen K.K. — Imabari** Yd No: 337 Loa 64.02 Br ex - Dght 4.194 Lbp 60.00 Br md 10.00 Dpth 4.50 Welded, 1 dk	**(A12A2TC) Chemical Tanker** Liq: 917 Compartments: 8 Wing Ta, ER 2 Cargo Pump (s): 2x300m³/hr	**1 oil engine** driving 1 FP propeller Total Power: 736kW (1,001hp) 10.5kn Hanshin 6LUN30AG 1 x 4 Stroke 6 Cy. 300 x 480 736kW (1001bhp) The Hanshin Diesel Works Ltd-Japan AuxGen: 3 x 80kW a.c Fuel: 37.0 (d.f.)
9511791 *JD2813* -	**SUZUKA MARU NO. 7** - **Suzuka Kaiun KK** - *Osaka, Osaka* *Japan* MMSI: 431000745 Official number: 140864	*749* - 1,646		2008-09 **Koa Sangyo KK — Marugame KG** Yd No: 637 Loa 69.02 Br ex - Dght 4.620 Lbp 65.00 Br md 11.00 Dpth 5.20 Welded, 1 dk	**(A12A2TC) Chemical Tanker** Double Hull (13F) Liq: 1,389 4 Cargo Pump (s): 4x250m³/hr	**1 oil engine** geared to sc. shaft driving 1 Propeller Total Power: 1,323kW (1,799hp) Hanshin LA28G 1 x 4 Stroke 6 Cy. 280 x 590 1323kW (1799bhp) The Hanshin Diesel Works Ltd-Japan
8731100 *JD2312* -	**SUZUKAZE** - **Matsusaka Municipal Office** - *Matsusaka, Mie* *Japan* Official number: 140394	*132* - -		2006-11 **in Japan** Yd No: CE-52 Loa 31.50 (BB) Br ex - Dght 0.960 Lbp 29.45 Br md 8.30 Dpth 2.65 Welded, 1 dk	**(A37B2PS) Passenger Ship** Hull Material: Aluminium Alloy Passengers: unberthed: 108	**2 oil engines** geared to sc. shafts driving 2 Propellers Total Power: 2,640kW (3,590hp) 30.0kn M.T.U. 12V4000M60 2 x Vee 4 Stroke 12 Cy. 165 x 190 each-1320kW (1795bhp) MTU Friedrichshafen GmbH-Friedrichshafen
9153082 *9V2581* -	**SUZURAN** - **Suzuran Shipping Pte Ltd** Asiatic Lloyd Shipping Pte Ltd *Singapore* *Singapore* MMSI: 564405000 Official number: 399195	**14,089** 7,023 17,704	Class: NK	1997-12 **Imabari Shipbuilding Co Ltd — Imabari EH (Imabari Shipyard)** Yd No: 537 Loa 163.66 (BB) Br ex - Dght 8.916 Lbp 152.00 Br md 26.00 Dpth 13.40 Welded, 1 dk	**(A33A2CC) Container Ship (Fully Cellular)** TEU 1177 incl 200 ref C. 16 Ha: 2 (12.6 x 8.0)2 (12.6 x 10.6)12 (12.7 x 10.9) Cranes: 2x40t	**1 oil engine** driving 1 FP propeller Total Power: 9,628kW (13,090hp) 18.0kn Mitsubishi 7UEC50LSII 1 x 2 Stroke 7 Cy. 500 x 1950 9628kW (13090bhp) Akasaka Tekkosho KK (Akasaka DieselLtd)-Japan AuxGen: 3 x a.c Thrusters: 1 Tunnel thruster (f) Fuel: 1880.0
9606895 *7JKO* -	**SUZURAN** - **Shin-Nihonkai Ferry Co Ltd** - *Otaru, Hokkaido* *Japan* MMSI: 431003496 Official number: 141565	**34,326** - 7,891		2012-06 **Mitsubishi Heavy Industries Ltd. — Nagasaki** Yd No: 2276 Loa 224.50 (BB) Br ex - Dght 7.400 Lbp 207.72 Br md 26.00 Dpth 18.61 Welded, 1 dk	**(A36A2PR) Passenger/Ro-Ro Ship (Vehicles)** Passengers: cabins: 128; berths: 613 Stern door/ramp (s. a.) Len: 7.80 Wid: 6.00 Swl: - Quarter stern door/ramp (s) Len: 16.00 Wid: 6.10 Swl: - Lorries: 158, Cars: 58	**2 diesel electric oil engines** driving 2 gen. each 8700kW a.c Connecting to 2 elec. motors each (6450kW) driving 2 Directional propellers Total Power: 17,400kW (23,658hp) 29.4kn Wartsila 12V38 2 x Vee 4 Stroke 12 Cy. 380 x 475 each-8700kW (11829bhp) Wartsila Finland Oy-Finland Thrusters: 2 Tunnel thruster (f) Fuel: 1050.0 (r.f.)
8961688 *JD2216* -	**SUZURAN MARU** - **Akan Kanko Kisen KK** - *Kushiro, Hokkaido* *Japan* Official number: 113178	*221* - -		1972-05 **Kushiro Senpaku Tekko K.K. — Kushiro** Loa 31.80 Br ex - Dght - Lbp 27.00 Br md 6.20 Dpth 1.90 Welded, 1 dk	**(A37B2PS) Passenger Ship** Passengers: unberthed: 480	**1 oil engine** driving 1 FP propeller Total Power: 191kW (260hp) 9.5kn Niigata 1 x 4 Stroke 191kW (260bhp) Niigata Engineering Co Ltd-Japan
6703068 *D6DV4* -	**SUZY** *ex Perla -2007 ex Omar A -2004* *ex Dina A -2001 ex Iman Billah -1996* *ex Maudi -1996 ex Nadine -1992* *ex Roselil -1976* - - *Moroni* *Union of Comoros*	*299* 166 726	Class: (BV)	1966 **A/S Nordsovaerftet — Ringkobing** Yd No: 27 Loa 49.71 Br ex 8.34 Dght 3.506 Lbp 44.30 Br md 8.31 Dpth 5.52 Welded, 1 dk & S dk	**(A31A2GX) General Cargo Ship** Grain: 1,303; Bale: 1,104 Compartments: 1 Ho, ER 2 Ha: (11.5 x 5.0) (11.9 x 5.0)ER Derricks: 2x2.5t; Winches: 2 Ice Capable	**1 oil engine** driving 1 CP propeller Total Power: 375kW (510hp) 11.0kn Alpha 406-24VO 1 x 2 Stroke 6 Cy. 240 x 400 375kW (510bhp) Alpha Diesel A/S-Denmark AuxGen: 2 x 8kW 220V a.c, 1 x 8kW 220V a.c Fuel: 35.5 (d.f.) 2.5pd
7643576 *WYN9901* -	**SUZY** *ex My Yvonne -1991* **Barry Carson** - *Pensacola, FL* *United States of America* Official number: 572383	*121* 82 -		1976 **Master Marine, Inc. — Bayou La Batre, Al** Yd No: 182 L reg 22.59 Br ex 6.71 Dght - Lbp - Br md - Dpth 3.41 Welded, 1 dk	**(B11B2FV) Fishing Vessel**	**1 oil engine** driving 1 FP propeller Total Power: 353kW (480hp)
9247601 *UBJI5* -	**SV. APOSTOL ANDREY** - **Valday-1 Ltd** JS North-Western Shipping Co (OAO 'Severo-Zapadnoye Parokhodstvo') *St Petersburg* *Russia* MMSI: 273355260 Official number: PMB4996	**4,974** 2,280 5,435	Class: GL (RS)	2002-12 **OAO Sudostroitelnyy Zavod "Severnaya Verf" — St.-Peterburg** Yd No: 901 Loa 128.20 (BB) Br ex 16.74 Dght 4.340 Lbp 122.80 Br md 16.50 Dpth 6.10 Welded, 1 dk	**(A31A2GX) General Cargo Ship** Grain: 8,340 TEU 267 C.Ho 180/20' C.Dk 87/20' incl. 20 ref C. Compartments: 3 Ho, ER Ice Capable	**2 oil engines** geared to sc. shafts driving 2 FP propellers Total Power: 2,160kW (2,936hp) 11.0kn Wartsila 6L20 2 x 4 Stroke 6 Cy. 200 x 280 each-1080kW (1468bhp) Wartsila Finland Oy-Finland AuxGen: 3 x 160kW a.c Thrusters: 1 Tunnel thruster (f)
7726392 *J8B4894* -	**SV CHAMPION** *ex Dms Champion -2013 ex Sutton Tide -2003* **AK Offshore & Marine Services Ltd** Sea & Vessel Offshore Marine Services Co LLC *Kingstown* *St Vincent & The Grenadines* MMSI: 376935000 Official number: 11367	**776** 213 839	Class: BV (AB)	1978-08 **Halter Marine, Inc. — Moss Point, Ms** Yd No: 684 Loa 54.87 Br ex - Dght 3.664 Lbp 51.82 Br md 12.19 Dpth 4.27 Welded, 1 dk	**(B21A2OS) Platform Supply Ship**	**2 oil engines** reverse reduction geared to sc. shafts driving 2 FP propellers Total Power: 1,626kW (2,210hp) 12.0kn Caterpillar D399TA 2 x Vee 4 Stroke 16 Cy. 159 x 203 each-813kW (1105bhp) Caterpillar Tractor Co-USA AuxGen: 2 x 125kW Thrusters: 1 Thwart. FP thruster (f)

IMO / Call sign	Name / Owner / Port	Tonnage	Class	Builder / Dimensions	Type	Machinery
9247637 *UBJI6* -	**SV. GEORGIY POBEDONOSETS** **Valday-3 Ltd** JS North-Western Shipping Co (OAO 'Severo-Zapadnoye Parokhodstvo') *St Petersburg* *Russia* MMSI: 273356260	**4,974** 2,280 5,440	Class: GL (RS)	**2003-08 OAO Sudostroitelnyy Zavod "Severnaya Verf" — St.-Peterburg** Yd No: 904 Loa 128.20 Br ex 16.74 Dght 4.340 Lbp 122.80 Br md 16.50 Dpth 6.10 Welded, 1 dk	**(A31A2GX) General Cargo Ship** Grain: 8,340 TEU 267 C.Ho 180/20' C.Dk 87/20' incl. 20 ref C. Ice Capable	**2 oil engines** geared to sc. shafts driving 2 FP propellers Total Power: 2,160kW (2,936hp) 11.0kn Wartsila 6L20C 2 x 4 Stroke 6 Cy. 200 x 280 each-1080kW (1468bhp) Wartsila Finland Oy-Finland
7912159 *9A2152* -	**SV. JURAJ** *ex* Jurjevo *-1991* **Jadrolinija** - *Rijeka* *Croatia* MMSI: 238113440 Official number: 2T-424	*759* 230 360	Class: CS	**1980-12 Brodogradiliste 'Titovo' — Kraljevica** Yd No: 431 Loa 49.92 Br ex 9.63 Dght 3.301 Lbp 45.60 Br md 9.61 Dpth 4.30 Welded, 1 dk	**(A36A2PR) Passenger/Ro-Ro Ship (Vehicles)** Passengers: unberthed: 300 Bow door/ramp Len: 4.00 Wid: 4.60 Swl: 18 Stern door/ramp Len: 4.00 Wid: 4.60 Swl: 18 Lane-Len: 46 Lane-Wid: 3.80 Lane-clr ht: 4.10 Lorries: 3, Cars: 20, Trailers: 4	**2 oil engines** geared to sc. shaft driving 2 Directional propellers aft, 1 fwd Total Power: 1,160kW (1,578hp) 12.0kn M.T.U. 8V4000M60 1 x Vee 4 Stroke 8 Cy. 165 x 190 580kW (789bhp) MTU Friedrichshafen GmbH-Friedrichshafen Fuel: 40.5 (d.f.) 7.2pd
9247613 *UBKI2* -	**SV. KNYAZ VLADIMIR** **Valday-2 Ltd** JS North-Western Shipping Co (OAO 'Severo-Zapadnoye Parokhodstvo') *St Petersburg* *Russia* MMSI: 273350360 Official number: 9780	**4,974** 2,280 5,440	Class: GL (RS)	**2003-03 OAO Sudostroitelnyy Zavod "Severnaya Verf" — St.-Peterburg** Yd No: 902 Loa 128.20 (BB) Br ex 16.74 Dght 4.340 Lbp 122.80 Br md 16.50 Dpth 6.10 Welded, 1 dk	**(A31A2GX) General Cargo Ship** Grain: 8,340 TEU 267 C.Ho 180/20' C.Dk 87/20' incl. 20 ref C. Compartments: 3 Ho, ER 3 Ha: ER 3 (25.6 x 12.6) Ice Capable	**2 oil engines** geared to sc. shafts driving 2 FP propellers Total Power: 2,160kW (2,936hp) 11.0kn Wartsila 6L20C 2 x 4 Stroke 6 Cy. 200 x 280 each-1080kW (1468bhp) Wartsila Finland Oy-Finland Thrusters: 1 Tunnel thruster (f) Fuel: 173.0 (d.f.)
9362504 *J8B4565* -	**SV MAHSHAHR** *ex* Svitzer Mahshahr *-2011* **Sea & Vessel Offshore Marine Services Co LLC** - *Kingstown* *St Vincent & The Grenadines* MMSI: 375787000 Official number: 11038	**436** 130 260	Class: LR ✠ **100A1** SS 12/2011 tug, fire fighting ship 1 (2400 m3/h) with water spray *IWS ✠ **LMC** **UMS** Eq.Ltr: G; Cable: 302.5/22.0 U2 (a)	**2006-12 ASL Shipyard Pte Ltd — Singapore** Yd No: 528 Loa 31.50 Br ex 11.50 Dght 4.400 Lbp 26.80 Br md 11.00 Dpth 6.10 Welded, 1 dk	**(B32A2ST) Tug**	**2 oil engines** gearing integral to driving 2 Z propellers Total Power: 3,676kW (4,998hp) 13.0kn Niigata 6L28HX 2 x 4 Stroke 6 Cy. 280 x 370 each-1838kW (2499bhp) Niigata Engineering Co Ltd-Japan AuxGen: 2 x 150kW 400V 50Hz a.c
5037412 - -	**SV MARINE VENTURE** *ex* SV Ocean Venture *-2001* *ex* Ara *-2000* *ex* Barsemeister Brehme *-1999* - -	**258** 77 328	Class: (GL)	**1959-12 Jadewerft Wilhelmshaven GmbH — Wilhelmshaven** Yd No: 64 Loa 41.46 Br ex 8.03 Dght 1.878 Lbp 37.55 Br md 8.01 Dpth 3.00 Welded, 1 dk	**(B34Q2QB) Buoy Tender** Cranes: 1x9t Ice Capable	**2 oil engines** reverse reduction geared to sc. shafts driving 2 Directional propellers Total Power: 514kW (698hp) 11.0kn MAN W8V175/22A 2 x 4 Stroke 8 Cy. 175 x 220 each-257kW (349bhp) Maschinenbau Augsburg Nuernberg (MAN)-Augsburg AuxGen: 1 x 15kW 220V d.c
8968882 *9AA7615* -	**SV. MARTIN** *ex* Dva Dida *-2013* *ex* Malta *-2009* *ex* Tethys-1 *-2005* *ex* Chefalu 4 *-1998* **Morski Rib Morska Lastavica** - *Split* *Croatia* Official number: 3T-160	**141** 42 38	Class: CS (RN)	**1985 Santierul Naval Tulcea — Tulcea** Yd No: N76 Loa 25.27 Br ex - Dght 2.400 Lbp 22.83 Br md 7.21 Dpth 3.43 Welded, 1 dk	**(B11B2FV) Fishing Vessel**	**1 oil engine** reduction geared to sc. shaft driving 1 FP propeller Total Power: 221kW (300hp) S.K.L. 6VD18/15AL-1 1 x 4 Stroke 6 Cy. 150 x 180 221kW (300bhp) VEB Elbe Werk-Rosslau AuxGen: 1 x 28kW 400V 50Hz a.c
5131220 *9A3386* -	**SV. NIKOLA** *ex* Zingara *-1998* *ex* Nova *-1989* *ex* Roye *-1987* *ex* Flint *-1980* *ex* Gisela Flint *-1974* **Denis Karlic** - *Zadar* *Croatia* MMSI: 238332440 Official number: 3T-231	**336** 164 488	Class: CS (BV) (RI) (GL)	**1961 Alfred Hagelstein Masch. u. Schiffswerft — Luebeck** Yd No: 604 Loa 45.39 Br ex 8.54 Dght 2.701 Lbp 43.54 Br md 8.53 Dpth 3.03 Riveted\Welded, 1 dk	**(A31A2GX) General Cargo Ship** Grain: 634; Bale: 583 Compartments: 1 Ho, ER 1 Ha: (21.3 x 5.4)ER Derricks: 2x2t; Winches: 2 Ice Capable	**1 oil engine** geared to sc. shaft driving 1 FP propeller Total Power: 272kW (370hp) 9.5kn Deutz SBA6M528 1 x 4 Stroke 6 Cy. 220 x 280 272kW (370bhp) Kloeckner Humboldt Deutz AG-West Germany AuxGen: 1 x 50kW 24V Fuel: 24.0 (d.f.)
8518077 *LZDY* -	**SV NIKOLAI** *ex* Burgas 3 *-2012* *ex* Burgas *-2010* **Northpool LLP** Seaborne Trade Ltd *Varna* *Bulgaria* MMSI: 207046000 Official number: 424	**7,455** 3,523 8,875	Class: (BR) (GL)	**1987-06 SA Juliana Constructora Gijonesa — Gijon** Yd No: 309 Loa 123.63 (BB) Br ex 21.06 Dght 8.016 Lbp 114.61 Br md 21.01 Dpth 10.52 Welded, 2 dks	**(A31A2GX) General Cargo Ship** Grain: 12,285; Bale: 11,318 TEU 446 Compartments: 3 Ho, ER, 3 Tw Dk 3 Ha: (12.6 x 9.9)2 (25.2 x 15.5)ER Cranes: 2x36t Ice Capable	**1 oil engine** driving 1 CP propeller Total Power: 4,472kW (6,080hp) 14.0kn B&W 8L35MC 1 x 2 Stroke 8 Cy. 350 x 1050 4472kW (6080bhp) Zaklady Przemyslu Metalowego 'HCegielski' SA-Poznan AuxGen: 1 x 500kW 380V a.c, 3 x 400kW 380V a.c Thrusters: 1 Thwart. CP thruster (f)
8315619 *V4WK2* -	**SV WAVE** *ex* Gulf Singa *-2013* *ex* Singa Hitam *-1995* **Sea & Vessel Offshore Marine Services Co LLC** - *Basseterre* *St Kitts & Nevis*	**549** 164 1,000	Class: BV (AB)	**1984-06 Southern Ocean Shipbuilding Co Pte Ltd — Singapore** Yd No: 152 Loa 40.01 Br ex 11.03 Dght 4.574 Lbp 36.50 Br md 11.00 Dpth 5.01 Welded, 1 dk	**(B21B20T) Offshore Tug/Supply Ship**	**2 oil engines** with clutches, flexible couplings & sr geared to sc. shafts driving 2 CP propellers Total Power: 2,648kW (3,600hp) 13.0kn Yanmar 6Z280L-ST 2 x 4 Stroke 6 Cy. 280 x 360 each-1324kW (1800bhp) Yanmar Diesel Engine Co Ltd-Japan AuxGen: 2 x 128kW Thrusters: 1 Thwart. CP thruster (f) Fuel: 385.0 (d.f.)
8640387 *LBSV* -	**SVALBARD** **Fosvarets Logistikkorganisasjon** Government of The Kingdom of Norway (Kystvakt) *Sortland* *Norway* MMSI: 259040000	*6,375* - 900	Class: NV	**2002-01 Langsten Slip & Baatbyggeri AS — Tomrefjord** Loa 103.70 Br ex 19.10 Dght 6.300 Lbp 89.00 Br md 19.08 Dpth 10.80 Welded, 1 dk	**(B34H2SQ) Patrol Vessel** Ice Capable	**4 diesel electric oil engines** driving 4 gen. each 3390kW a.c Connecting to 2 elec. motors each (5000kW) driving 2 Azimuth electric drive units Total Power: 14,120kW (19,196hp) Normo BRM-8 4 x 4 Stroke 8 Cy. 320 x 360 each-3530kW (4799bhp) Rolls Royce Marine AS-Norway
5330735 *SHJA* -	**SVALBARD** *ex* Sjoveien *-1984* **Briweha Shipping H/B** - *Stockholm* *Sweden*	**247** 93 -		**1936 Schiffbau Gesellschaft Unterweser AG — Bremerhaven** Lengthened-1966 L reg 33.35 Br ex 6.96 Dght 3.810 Lbp - Br md 6.91 Dpth - Riveted, 1 dk	**(B34K2QT) Training Ship**	**1 oil engine** driving 1 FP propeller Total Power: 294kW (400hp) 9.8kn Normo 1 x 4 Stroke 8 Cy. 220 x 320 294kW (400bhp) (new engine 1954) AS Bergens Mek Verksteder-Norway AuxGen: 1 x 40kW 110V d.c, 1 x 22kW 110V d.c Fuel: 35.5 (d.f.) 2.0pd
9251913 *LLRD* ST-019-F	**SVANAUG ELISE** **Kolbjorn Ervik & Sonner AS** - *Trondheim* *Norway* MMSI: 259130000	**1,514** 454 -	Class: NV	**2001-11 Stocznia Polnocna SA (Northern Shipyard) — Gdansk** (Hull) Yd No: B312/2 **2001-11 Eidsvik Skipsbyggeri AS — Uskedalen** Yd No: 68 Loa 64.00 Br ex - Dght 6.460 Lbp 56.40 Br md 13.00 Dpth 8.60 Welded, 1 dk	**(B11B2FV) Fishing Vessel**	**1 oil engine** reduction geared to sc. shaft driving 1 FP propeller Total Power: 3,460kW (4,704hp) 17.5kn Caterpillar 3612TA 1 x Vee 4 Stroke 12 Cy. 280 x 300 3460kW (4704bhp) Caterpillar Inc-USA
7905223 *LALN* -	**SVANAVAG** *ex* Dicada *-2007* *ex* Grenen *-2006* *ex* Accord *-2004* *ex* Serene *-1995* *ex* Altaire *-1987* **Sille Marie AS** - *Egersund* *Norway* MMSI: 257599600	**688** 206 858	Class: LR ✠ **100A1** SS 07/2010 fishing vessel ✠ **LMC** Eq.Ltr: I; Cable: U2 (a)	**1979-11 Myklebust Mek. Verksted AS — Gursken** Yd No: 9 Lengthened-1984 Loa 46.69 (BB) Br ex 9.02 Dght 6.500 Lbp 42.30 Br md 9.00 Dpth 7.20 Welded, 2 dks	**(B11A2FT) Trawler**	**1 oil engine** with clutches, flexible couplings & sr geared to sc. shaft driving 1 CP propeller Total Power: 1,320kW (1,795hp) Alpha 12V23/30A 1 x Vee 4 Stroke 12 Cy. 225 x 300 1320kW (1795bhp) (new engine 1996) MAN B&W Diesel A/S-Denmark AuxGen: 1 x 290kW 380V 50Hz a.c, 1 x 270kW 380V 50Hz a.c, 1 x 1000kW 380V 50Hz a.c Thrusters: 2 Thwart. FP thruster (f); 1 Tunnel thruster (a)

Identity / Owner / Registry	Tonnage	Class	Builder / Dimensions	Type / Cargo	Machinery
9007453 **SVANEN** *C6LA2* - **Ballast Nedam Equipment Services BV** - *Nassau* *Bahamas* MMSI: 308851000 Official number: 720778	**14,035** 4,210 7,871	Class: LR ✠ **100A1** SS 02/2011 crane pontoon LA coastal waters whereby the offshore distance does not exceed 50 miles and the sailing time to a suitable port, or to a recognized shelter, where no suitable port is available, does not exceed 12 hours. Operating condition (anchored or sailing) - main hoists starboard fore, portside fore and portside aft 600 tonnes SWL and main hoist starboard 1250 tonnes SWL in weather conditions not exceeding a two minutes average period 15 m/s wind speed and/or significant wave height (H1/3) of 1.5 m. Survival condition - anchored or sailing - unloaded in weather conditions not exceeding a 23 m/s mean (2 min) wind speed and/or significant wave height (H1/3) of 2.5 m ✠ **LMC** Eq.Ltr: B†; Cable: 550.0/0.0	**1991-02 Astilleros y Talleres del Noroeste SA (ASTANO) — Fene** (Hull) Yd No: 268 **1991-02 Grootint Zwijndrecht B.V. — Zwijndrecht** Yd No: 4058-7 Lengthened & Widened-1995 Loa 102.75 Br ex 72.31 Dght 4.322 Lbp 98.75 Br md 71.80 Dpth 6.00 Welded, 1 dk	**(B34B2SC) Crane Vessel** Gantry cranes: 1x8700t	**3 diesel electric oil engines** driving 3 gen. each 1336kW 660V a.c Connecting to 2 elec. motors each (1250kW) driving 2 Directional propellers Total Power: 5,400kW (7,341hp) 7.0kn Kromhout 9FEHD240 3 x 4 Stroke 9 Cy. 240 x 260 each-1800kW (2447bhp) Stork Wartsila Diesel BV-Netherlands Thrusters: 2 Thwart. FP thruster (f)
8918655 **SVANEN AV RORO** *SMFH* GG 840 **Svanen Fiskeri AB** - *Roro* *Sweden* MMSI: 266076000	**152** 31 -		**1989-01 AB Hasse Wester Mekaniska Verkstad — Uddevalla** Yd No: 55 Loa 19.39 Br ex 6.08 Dght - Lbp - Br md 6.00 Dpth 3.85 Welded, 1 dk	**(B11A2FS) Stern Trawler**	**1 oil engine** geared to sc. shaft driving 1 FP propeller Total Power: 386kW (525hp) Caterpillar 3412T 1 x Vee 4 Stroke 12 Cy. 137 x 152 386kW (525bhp) Caterpillar Inc-USA
8409070 **SVANHILD** *SFIB* *ex* Farja 323 *-1996* - **Government of The Kingdom of Sweden (Vagverket Farjerederiet)** - *Vaxholm* *Sweden* MMSI: 265577480	*373* 132 150		**1985-09 AB Asi-Verken — Amal** Yd No: 139 Loa 54.00 Br ex 13.90 Dght 3.500 Lbp - Br md - Dpth - Welded, 1 dk	**(A37B2PS) Passenger Ship**	**2 oil engines** driving 2 FP propellers Volvo Penta 2 x 4 Stroke AB Volvo Penta-Sweden
5418070 **SVANIC** *YL2636* *ex* Timor *-1973* *ex* Svanic *-1967* - **SIA Svanic** *Riga* *Latvia* MMSI: 275049032 Official number: 4360	**182** 54 -	Class: (BV)	**1962 VEB Ernst Thaelmann-Werft — Brandenburg** Yd No: 13115 Converted From: Trawler-1962 Loa 30.94 Br ex 6.61 Dght 3.090 Lbp - Br md 6.56 Dpth - Welded, 1 dk	**(X11A2YP) Yacht** 3 Ha: (0.6 x 0.9)2 (1.6 x 1.2)ER Derricks: 2x3.5t,1x1t	**1 oil engine** driving 1 FP propeller Total Power: 496kW (674hp) 12.0kn Polar SF16RS 1 x 4 Stroke 6 Cy. 250 x 300 496kW (674bhp) Nydqvist & Holm AB-Sweden AuxGen: 1 x 12kW 220V a.c Fuel: 18.0 (d.f.)
6500181 **SVANO AV VIDEBERG** - *ex* Krossfjord *-1999* *ex* Nordsnurp *-1998* - *ex* Krossfjord *-1997* - -	**379** 113 -		**1964-11 Skaalurens Skipsbyggeri AS — Rosendal** Yd No: 206/20 Lengthened-1967 Loa 40.37 Br ex 7.19 Dght 4.267 Lbp - Br md 7.17 Dpth 5.80 Welded, 1 dk	**(B11B2FV) Fishing Vessel**	**1 oil engine** driving 1 FP propeller Total Power: 607kW (825hp) 11.0kn Wichmann 5ACA 1 x 2 Stroke 5 Cy. 280 x 420 607kW (825bhp) (new engine 1976) Wichmann Motorfabrikk AS-Norway
9035163 **SVANOY** *LEVE* - **Fjord1 AS** - *Floro* *Norway* MMSI: 257390400	**2,631** 844 635	Class: (NV)	**1992-07 Johan Drage AS — Rognan** (Hull) Yd No: 393 **1992-07 Kaarboverkstedet AS — Harstad** Loa 83.30 Br ex 15.00 Dght 3.900 Lbp 70.80 Br md - Dpth 5.00 Welded	**(A36A2PR) Passenger/Ro-Ro Ship (Vehicles)** Passengers: unberthed: 399 Bow door Stern door Lane-clr ht: 3.50 Cars: 104, Trailers: 9	**2 oil engines** reduction geared to sc. shafts driving 2 FP propellers Total Power: 2,398kW (3,260hp) 15.0kn Wichmann 8V28B 2 x Vee 4 Stroke 8 Cy. 280 x 360 each-1199kW (1630bhp) Wartsila Wichmann Diesel AS-Norway
8116166 **SVANUR** *LAW04* *ex* Svanur II *-1995* *ex* Louise *-1995* - *ex* Lynx *-1994* *ex* Jette Dania *-1992* *ex* Skipper Most *-1992* *ex* Jette Dania *-1987* **Nes hf** - *Larvik* *Norway (NIS)* MMSI: 258982000	**1,516** 651 2,151	Class: GL (BV)	**1983-08 A/S Nordsovaerftet — Ringkobing** Yd No: 163 Loa 72.52 Br ex 11.70 Dght 4.530 Lbp 68.99 Br md 11.20 Dpth 6.70 Welded, 2 dks	**(A31A2GX) General Cargo Ship** Grain: 2,837; Bale: 2,642 TEU 67 C Ho 38 TEU C Dk 29 TEU incl 24 ref C Compartments: 1 Ho, ER 1 Ha: (40.6 x 7.6)ER Cranes: 2x15t Ice Capable	**1 oil engine** driving 1 FP propeller Total Power: 879kW (1,195hp) 10.0kn MaK 6M452AK 1 x 4 Stroke 6 Cy. 320 x 450 879kW (1195bhp) Krupp MaK Maschinenbau GmbH-Kiel AuxGen: 2 x 105kW 380V 50Hz a.c, 1 x 50kW 380V 50Hz a.c Fuel: 148.5 (d.f.) 3.5pd
5050397 **SVANVIK** *SGNM* *ex* Westland *-2009* *ex* Santos av Hono *-1978* GG 45 *ex* Brandenburg *-1977* **Roland Olsson** - *Vajern* *Sweden* MMSI: 265716000	**221** 66 -	Class: (BV)	**1961 VEB Ernst Thaelmann-Werft — Brandenburg** Loa 30.92 Br ex 6.63 Dght 3.660 Lbp 26.19 Br md 6.58 Dpth - Welded, 1 dk	**(B11A2FT) Trawler** 3 Ha: (0.9 x 0.5)2 (1.5 x 1.1)	**1 oil engine** driving 1 FP propeller Total Power: 706kW (960hp) Jonkopings 1 x 4 Stroke 8 Cy. 260 x 400 706kW (960bhp) (new engine 1967) AB Jonkopings Motorfabrik-Sweden
9323089 **SVARTFOSS** *V2PR3* *launched as* Kristian With *-2005* - **Frost Line Ltd** The Iceland Steamship Co Ltd (Eimskip Island Ehf) (Eimskip Ehf) *Saint John's* *Antigua & Barbuda* MMSI: 304882000 Official number: 2957	**2,990** 1,332 2,737	Class: NV	**2005-11 Stocznia Marynarki Wojennej SA (Naval Shipyard Gdynia) — Gdynia** (Hull) **2005-11 Vaagland Baatbyggeri AS — Vaagland** Yd No: 136 Loa 79.99 (BB) Br ex - Dght 5.950 Lbp 74.60 Br md 16.00 Dpth 6.10 Welded, 1 dk	**(A34A2GR) Refrigerated Cargo Ship** Ins: 4,150 TEU 58 incl 30 ref C. Cranes: 1x50t Ice Capable	**1 oil engine** geared to sc. shaft driving 1 CP propeller Total Power: 3,060kW (4,160hp) 16.0kn MAN-B&W 9L27/38 1 x 4 Stroke 9 Cy. 270 x 380 3060kW (4160bhp) MAN B&W Diesel AG-Augsburg AuxGen: 1 x 440/230V 60Hz a.c, 1 x 912kW 440/230V 60Hz a.c, 1 x 440/230V 60Hz a.c Thrusters: 1 Thwart. CP thruster (f); 1 Thwart. CP thruster (a) Fuel: 290.0 (d.f.)
6421048 **SVEA VIKING** *HPTB* - - - *Panama* *Panama* Official number: 06895PEXT2	**575** 203 -	Class: (GL) (NV)	**1964-01 Rolandwerft GmbH — Bremen** Yd No: 921 Loa 49.05 Br ex 9.50 Dght 2.032 Lbp 42.91 Br md 9.45 Dpth 5.21 Welded, 1 dk, pt 2nd dk	**(A37B2PS) Passenger Ship** Ice Capable	**1 oil engine** geared to sc. shaft driving 1 FP propeller Total Power: 675kW (918hp) 12.0kn Caterpillar 3508TA 1 x Vee 4 Stroke 8 Cy. 170 x 190 675kW (918bhp) (new engine 1992) Caterpillar Inc-USA AuxGen: 1 x 135kW 380V a.c
7818121 **SVEABULK** *LJBL* *ex* Euro Bulk *-1999* *ex* Quiescence *-1998* - **Seaworks AS** - SatCom: Inmarsat C 425995010 *Harstad* *Norway* MMSI: 259950000	**1,016** 500 1,465	Class: (LR) (BV) ✠ Classed LR until 25/10/84	**1979-10 A/S Nordsovaerftet — Ringkobing** Yd No: 137 Loa 72.29 Br ex 11.31 Dght 3.390 Lbp 68.66 Br md 11.21 Dpth 4.12 Welded, 1 dk	**(A31A2GX) General Cargo Ship** Grain: 1,874; Bale: 1,802 Compartments: 2 Ho, ER 2 Ha: (19.5 x 7.9) (17.5 x 7.9)ER	**1 oil engine** reverse reduction geared to sc. shaft driving 1 CP propeller Total Power: 912kW (1,240hp) 10.0kn Alpha 8V23L-VO 1 x Vee 4 Stroke 8 Cy. 225 x 300 912kW (1240bhp) Alpha Diesel A/S-Denmark AuxGen: 1 x 90kW 415V 50Hz a.c, 1 x 88kW 415V 50Hz a.c, 1 x 32kW 415V 50Hz a.c Fuel: 135.0 (r.f.)
7503594 **SVEAFJORD** *LCNI* *ex* Svealand *-2008* *ex* Frigo *-1993* - *ex* Trans Vik *-1993* **Eidshaug Rederi AS** Einar Eidshaug *Namsos* *Norway* MMSI: 258340000 Official number: 18756	**971** 360 1,066	Class: NV	**1976-05 Skaalurens Skipsbyggeri AS — Rosendal** Yd No: 226/39 Lengthened-1978 Loa 58.60 Br ex 11.03 Dght 3.770 Lbp 54.10 Br md 11.00 Dpth 6.71 Welded, 2 dks	**(A31A2GX) General Cargo Ship** Bale: 1,296 Derricks: 1x10t; Winches: 1 Ice Capable	**1 oil engine** driving 1 FP propeller Total Power: 515kW (700hp) 10.0kn Alpha 407-26VO 1 x 2 Stroke 7 Cy. 260 x 400 515kW (700bhp) Alpha Diesel A/S-Denmark AuxGen: 1 x a.c, 1 x a.c, 1 x a.c Fuel: 43.5 (d.f.) 4.0pd

IMO / Call sign	Name / Owner	Tonnage	Class	Builder / Dimensions	Type	Machinery
9390276 *LAZY* -	**SVEALAND** - **Eidshaug Rederi AS** - SatCom: Inmarsat C 425911910 *Namsos* *Norway* MMSI: 259119000	2,140 642 1,700	Class: NV	**2008-06 AS Rigas Kugu Buvetava (Riga Shipyard) — Riga** (Hull) **2008-06 Moen Slip AS — Kolvereid** Yd No: 64 Loa 62.00 Br ex Dght 5.000 Lbp 57.10 Br md 13.80 Dpth 9.60 Welded, 1 dk	**(A31B2GP) Palletised Cargo Ship** Ice Capable	**1 oil engine** reduction geared to sc. shaft driving 1 CP propeller Total Power: 1,942kW (2,640hp) A.B.C. 8DZC 1 x 4 Stroke 8 Cy. 256 x 310 1942kW (2640bhp) Anglo Belgian Corp NV (ABC)-Belgium AuxGen: 2 x a.c, 1 x a.c Thrusters: 1 Tunnel thruster (f); 1 Tunnel thruster (a)
7419248 *LHQR* -	**SVEANORD** *ex* Nordnes *-1996* *ex* Finnport I *-1994* *ex* Andramari *-1993* **Seaworks AS** Norbulk AS *Harstad* *Norway* MMSI: 258908000	834 465 1,068	Class: (LR) ✠ Classed LR until 7/5/11	**1976-02 Astilleros de Murueta S.A. — Gernika-Lumo** Yd No: 131 Loa 59.67 Br ex 10.34 Dght 3.893 Lbp 53.01 Br md 10.25 Dpth 4.40 Welded, 1 dk	**(A31A2GX) General Cargo Ship** Grain: 1,704; Bale: 1,520 Compartments: 1 Ho, ER 1 Ha: (31.3 x 7.6)ER	**1 oil engine** with flexible couplings & sr gearedto sc. shaft driving 1 FP propeller Total Power: 750kW (1,020hp) 12.0kn Caterpillar D399TA 1 x Vee 4 Stroke 16 Cy. 159 x 203 750kW (1020bhp) (new engine 1994) Caterpillar Inc-USA AuxGen: 2 x 40kW 380V 50Hz a.c, 1 x 16kW 380V 50Hz a.c Fuel: 119.0 (d.f.)
9229441 *LJTV* SF-8-A	**SVEBAS** *ex* Vestoey *-2010* *ex* Birgerson *-2006* **Ospa Rederi KS** - *Floro* *Norway* MMSI: 259660000	259 103 -	Class: (NV)	**2000-01 AS Rigas Kugu Buvetava (Riga Shipyard) — Riga** (Hull) **2000-01 Sletta Baatbyggeri AS — Mjosundet** Yd No: 90 Loa 23.99 (BB) Br ex - Dght 4.600 Lbp 21.50 Br md 8.00 Dpth 6.20 Welded, 1 dk	**(B11B2FV) Fishing Vessel** Bale: 150	**1 oil engine** geared to sc. shaft driving 1 FP propeller 10.0kn Caterpillar 1 x 4 Stroke Caterpillar Inc-USA AuxGen: 2 x a.c Thrusters: 1 Thwart. FP thruster (f); 1 Tunnel thruster (a)
6727208 *TFVG* SH 10	**SVEINBJORN JAKOBSSON** *ex* Saebjorg *-2009* *ex* Julius II *-1997* *ex* Julius *-1992* *ex* Andvari *-1992* *ex* Drifa *-1988* *ex* Manatindur *-1985* *ex* Hvalsnes *-1983* *ex* Sturlaugur *-1977* *ex* Drifa *-1972* **Utgerdarfelagid Dvergur hf** - *Olafsvik* *Iceland* MMSI: 251350110 Official number: 1054	176 53 -		**1967 Skipasmidastod Thorgeir & Ellert h/f — Akranes** Yd No: 19 Loa 26.22 Br ex 6.02 Dght - Lbp 22.81 Br md 6.00 Dpth 3.00 Welded, 1 dk	**(B11B2FV) Fishing Vessel**	**1 oil engine** reduction geared to sc. shaft driving 1 FP propeller Total Power: 465kW (632hp) Caterpillar 1 x 465kW (632bhp) (new engine 2001) Caterpillar Tractor Co-USA
7332476 *ZR3167* -	**SVEINN JONSSON** *ex* Dagstjarnan *-1980* *ex* Afjordsund *-1974* **Sentrawl Pty Ltd** - *Cape Town* *South Africa* MMSI: 601276000 Official number: 10008	576 173 -	Class: (NV)	**1973-11 AS Storviks Mek. Verksted — Kristiansund** Yd No: 53 Loa 46.36 Br ex 9.00 Dght 4.534 Lbp 39.83 Br md 8.97 Dpth 6.51 Welded, 2 dks	**(B11A2FS) Stern Trawler** Compartments: 1 Ho, ER 1 Ha: (2.2 x 1.9)ER Ice Capable	**1 oil engine** driving 1 FP propeller Total Power: 1,103kW (1,500hp) MaK 8M452AK 1 x 4 Stroke 8 Cy. 320 x 450 1103kW (1500bhp) MaK Maschinenbau GmbH-Kiel AuxGen: 2 x 99kW 220V 50Hz a.c
7407776 *LACK* -	**SVEIO** *ex* Roberg *-1996* **Norled AS** Tide ASA *Bergen* *Norway* MMSI: 257071700	662 221 -	Class: (NV)	**1975-06 AS Tromso Skipsverft & Mek. Verksted — Tromso** Yd No: 44 Loa 50.60 Br ex 11.28 Dght 3.404 Lbp 44.30 Br md 11.21 Dpth 4.22 Welded, 1 dk	**(A36A2PR) Passenger/Ro-Ro Ship (Vehicles)** Passengers: unberthed: 360 Bow door & ramp Stern door & ramp Lane-Len: 47 Lane-Wid: 2.50 Lane-clr ht: 4.50 Cars: 35, Trailers: 4	**1 oil engine** geared to sc. shaft driving 2 CP propellers aft, 1 fwd Total Power: 824kW (1,120hp) 11.0kn Normo LDM-8 1 x 4 Stroke 8 Cy. 250 x 300 824kW (1120bhp) AS Bergens Mek Verksteder-Norway AuxGen: 2 x 76kW 220V 50Hz a.c Fuel: 34.0 (d.f.) 3.5pd
6728355 *LLFW* -	**SVELA** *ex* Grip *-2005* **Frei Taubatservice AS** - *Kristiansund* *Norway*	167 56 -	Class: (NV)	**1967 AS Storviks Mek. Verksted — Kristiansund** Yd No: 28 Converted From: Ferry (Passenger/Vehicle)-1998 Loa 30.15 Br ex 9.56 Dght 2.672 Lbp 27.79 Br md 9.50 Dpth 3.51 Welded, 1 dk	**(B34R2QY) Supply Tender**	**1 oil engine** driving 2 CP propellers aft, 1 fwd Total Power: 254kW (345hp) Callesen 3-427-COT 1 x 4 Stroke 3 Cy. 270 x 400 254kW (345bhp) Aabenraa Motorfabrik, HeinrichCallesen A/S-Denmark AuxGen: 2 x 26kW 220V 50Hz a.c Fuel: 9.5 (d.f.)
9134139 *DGGW* -	**SVEN** *ex* Lucy Borchard *-2000* *ex* Solid *-1997* *ex* Sven *-1996* **ms 'Sven' Wilfried Rambow KG** Wilfried Rambow KG SatCom: Inmarsat M 621859310 *Hamburg* *Germany* MMSI: 211237900 Official number: 17975	6,362 3,998 7,223 T/cm 15.0	Class: GL	**1996-06 J.J. Sietas KG Schiffswerft GmbH & Co. — Hamburg** Yd No: 1126 Loa 121.94 (BB) Br ex 18.45 Dght 6.690 Lbp 114.90 Br md 18.20 Dpth 8.30 Welded, 1 dk	**(A33A2CC) Container Ship (Fully Cellular)** TEU 700 C Ho 108 TEU Open/Ho 324 TEU C Dk 268 TEU incl 70 ref. Compartments: 4 Cell Ho, ER 3 Ha: (12.4 x 12.9) (12.4 x 15.6) (12.6 x 15.6)ER	**1 oil engine** with flexible couplings & sr gearedto sc. shaft driving 1 CP propeller Total Power: 5,300kW (7,206hp) 16.5kn MAN 8L40/54 1 x 4 Stroke 8 Cy. 400 x 540 5300kW (7206bhp) MAN B&W Diesel AG-Augsburg AuxGen: 1 x 850kW 220/380V 50Hz a.c, 2 x 312kW 220/380V 50Hz a.c Thrusters: 1 Thwart. FP thruster (f)
9189574 *PBVV* -	**SVEN-D** *ex* Pride Of Sneek *-2013* *ex* Ute S *-2009* *ex* Ute *-2004* **Vof Orion** Visser Shipping BV *Sneek* *Netherlands* MMSI: 246636000 Official number: 53397	2,988 1,311 4,814	Class: GL	**1999-04 Societatea Comerciala Navol S.A. Oltenita — Oltenita** (Hull) **1999-04 Kroeger Werft GmbH & Co. KG — Schacht-Audorf** Yd No: 1545 Loa 99.63 (BB) Br ex - Dght 5.920 Lbp 91.45 Br md 16.90 Dpth 7.55 Welded, 1 dk	**(A31A2GX) General Cargo Ship** Double Hull Grain: 4,456; Bale: 4,166 TEU 366 C Ho 80 TEU C Dk 286 TEU incl 60 ref C. Compartments: 1 Ho, ER 3 Ha: ER Ice Capable	**1 oil engine** reduction geared to sc. shaft driving 1 CP propeller Total Power: 2,940kW (3,997hp) 15.5kn Alpha 12V28/32A 1 x Vee 4 Stroke 12 Cy. 280 x 320 2940kW (3997bhp) MAN B&W Diesel A/S-Denmark AuxGen: 1 x 783kW a.c Thrusters: 1 Thwart. FP thruster (f)
7229186 *DJSL* -	**SVEN JOHANNSEN** *ex* Friedrichsort *-1979* **Walter Johannsen** Juergen Johannsen *Travemuende* *Germany* MMSI: 211226990 Official number: 51872	*174* 112 51	Class: GL	**1972 Kroegerwerft GmbH & Co. KG — Schacht-Audorf** Yd No: 1379 Loa 37.44 Br ex 6.84 Dght 1.640 Lbp 29.27 Br md 6.81 Dpth 2.32 Welded, 1 dk	**(A37B2PS) Passenger Ship** Passengers: unberthed: 209	**1 oil engine** reduction geared to sc. shaft driving 1 FP propeller Total Power: 257kW (349hp) 12.0kn Volvo Penta D12 1 x 4 Stroke 6 Cy. 131 x 150 257kW (349bhp) (new engine 2007) AB Volvo Penta-Sweden
9166778 *OYJS2* -	**SVEND MAERSK** - **A P Moller - Maersk A/S** A P Moller SatCom: Inmarsat C 421979110 *Ribe* *Denmark (DIS)* MMSI: 219791000 Official number: D3732	92,198 53,625 110,381 T/cm 124.0	Class: AB	**1999-03 Odense Staalskibsvaerft A/S — Munkebo (Lindo Shipyard)** Yd No: 166 Loa 346.98 (BB) Br ex 42.92 Dght 14.940 Lbp 331.54 Br md 42.80 Dpth 24.10 Welded, 1 dk	**(A33A2CC) Container Ship (Fully Cellular)** TEU 9578 incl 817 ref C Compartments: ER, 20 Cell Ho 20 Ha: ER	**1 oil engine** driving 1 FP propeller Total Power: 54,840kW (74,560hp) 25.0kn B&W 12K90MC-C 1 x 2 Stroke 12 Cy. 900 x 2300 54840kW (74560bhp) Hitachi Zosen Corp-Japan AuxGen: 5 x 3000kW 6600V 60Hz a.c Thrusters: 1 Thwart. FP thruster (f); 2 Tunnel thruster (a)
9048263 *V2GC8* -	**SVENDBORG** *ex* BBC Colombia *-2009* *ex* CEC Svendborg *-2008* *ex* NDS Kuito *-2004* *ex* CEC Svendborg *-2003* *ex* Vedr *-2002* *ex* CEC Svendborg *-2002* *ex* Svendborg Governor *-2002* *ex* IAL Governor *-1994* *ex* Svendborg Governor *-1993* **Bischoff Schiffahrts GmbH & Co KG ms 'Svendborg'** Bischoff Schiffahrts Beteiligung GmbH *Saint John's* *Antigua & Barbuda* MMSI: 305892000 Official number: 4994	2,462 1,233 3,666	Class: NK (LR) ✠ Classed LR until 6/5/13	**1993-05 Svendborg Vaerft A/S — Svendborg** (Hull) Yd No: 201 **1993-05 Morso Vaerft A/S — Nykobing Mors** Yd No: 183 Loa 81.10 (BB) Br ex 13.79 Dght 5.890 Lbp 75.65 Br md 13.70 Dpth 7.30 Welded, 1 dk, 2nd portable dk in cargo space	**(A31A2GX) General Cargo Ship** Grain: 4,172 TEU 185 C.Ho 94/20' (40') C.Dk 91/20' (40') incl. 50 ref C. Compartments: 1 Ho, ER 1 Ha: (49.2 x 10.5)ER Cranes: 2x25t	**1 oil engine** with flexible couplings & sr geared to sc. shaft driving 1 CP propeller Total Power: 2,200kW (2,991hp) 13.5kn MaK 6M453C 1 x 4 Stroke 6 Cy. 320 x 420 2200kW (2991bhp) Krupp MaK Maschinenbau GmbH-Kiel AuxGen: 1 x 470kW 440V 60Hz a.c, 2 x 206kW 440V 60Hz a.c Fuel: 309.0 (d.f.) 10.5pd
9146467 *OZSK2* -	**SVENDBORG MAERSK** - **A P Moller - Maersk A/S** A P Moller SatCom: Inmarsat C 421914510 *Svendborg* *Denmark (DIS)* MMSI: 219145000 Official number: D3659	92,198 53,625 110,387 T/cm 124.0	Class: AB	**1998-09 Odense Staalskibsvaerft A/S — Munkebo (Lindo Shipyard)** Yd No: 164 Loa 346.98 (BB) Br ex - Dght 14.941 Lbp 331.54 Br md 42.80 Dpth 24.10 Welded	**(A33A2CC) Container Ship (Fully Cellular)** TEU 9578 incl 817 ref C Compartments: ER, 20 Cell Ho 20 Ha: ER	**1 oil engine** driving 1 FP propeller Total Power: 54,835kW (74,554hp) 25.0kn B&W 12K90MC 1 x 2 Stroke 12 Cy. 900 x 2550 54835kW (74554bhp) Hitachi Zosen Corp-Japan AuxGen: 5 x 3000kW 6600V 60Hz a.c Thrusters: 1 Thwart. FP thruster (f); 2 Thwart. FP thruster (a)

9454230 *V2FJ5* -	**SVENDBORG STRAIT** - **ms 'Svendborg Strait' GmbH & Co KG** Carsten Rehder Schiffsmakler und Reederei GmbH & Co KG *Saint John's* *Antigua & Barbuda* MMSI: 305694000	**12,514** 5,339 14,220	Class: GL	**2011-08 Nanjing Wujiazui Shipbuilding Co Ltd — Nanjing JS** Yd No: WJZ031 Loa 157.93 (BB) Br ex - Dght 8.600 Lbp 148.50 Br md 23.50 Dpth 11.90 Welded, 1 dk	**(A33A2CC) Container Ship (Fully Cellular)** TEU 1085 C Ho 372 TEU C Dk 713 incl 250 ref C Ice Capable	**1 oil engine** driving 1 CP propeller Total Power: 9,960kW (13,542hp) 18.5kn Wartsila 6RT-flex50 1 x 2 Stroke 6 Cy. 500 x 2050 9960kW (13542bhp) Hitachi Zosen Corp-Japan AuxGen: 1 x 1200kW 450V a.c, 2 x 900kW 450V a.c Thrusters: 1 Tunnel thruster (f)
9458901 *V2FV7* -	**SVENJA** - **SAL Heavy Lift GmbH** - *Saint John's* *Antigua & Barbuda* MMSI: 305815000	**15,026** 4,507 12,975	Class: GL	**2010-12 J.J. Sietas KG Schiffswerft GmbH & Co. — Hamburg** Yd No: 1279 Loa 160.50 (BB) Br ex 27.80 Dght 9.000 Lbp 149.38 Br md 27.50 Dpth 13.80 Welded, 1 dk	**(A31A2GX) General Cargo Ship** Grain: 17,735; Bale: 17,735 Compartments: 1 Ho, ER 1 Ha: ER Cranes: 2x1000t	**1 oil engine** reduction geared to sc. shaft driving 1 CP propeller Total Power: 12,604kW (17,136hp) 18.0kn MAN-B&W 9L58/64CD 1 x 4 Stroke 9 Cy. 580 x 640 12604kW (17136bhp) MAN B&W Diesel AG-Augsburg AuxGen: 1 x 1300kW 400V a.c, 2 x 1040kW 400V a.c, 1 x 560kW 400V a.c Thrusters: 1 Tunnel thruster (f); 1 Tunnel thruster (a)
9490674 *V7RM4* -	**SVENNER** - **Marvision Shipping Co Ltd** Scantank AS *Majuro* *Marshall Islands* MMSI: 538003540 Official number: 3540	**32,837** 19,559 58,000 T/cm 59.2	Class: BV	**2010-01 Yangzhou Dayang Shipbuilding Co Ltd — Yangzhou JS** Yd No: DY3006 Loa 189.99 (BB) Br ex - Dght 12.950 Lbp 185.00 Br md 32.26 Dpth 18.00 Welded, 1 dk	**(A21A2BC) Bulk Carrier** Grain: 71,549; Bale: 69,760 Compartments: 5 Ho, ER 5 Ha: ER Cranes: 4x35t	**1 oil engine** driving 1 FP propeller Total Power: 9,960kW (13,542hp) 14.3kn MAN-B&W 6S50MC-C 1 x 2 Stroke 6 Cy. 500 x 2000 9960kW (13542bhp)
7644087 - -	**SVERDLOVO** - **Pasifik Co Ltd** -	**825** 247 299	Class: (RS)	**1977-03 Zavod "Leninskaya Kuznitsa" — Kiyev** Yd No: 226 Loa 53.73 (BB) Br ex 10.71 Dght 4.290 Lbp 47.92 Br md 10.50 Dpth 6.02 Welded, 1 dk	**(B11A2FS) Stern Trawler** Ins: 220 Compartments: 1 Ho, ER 2 Ha: 2 (1.6 x 1.6) Derricks: 2x1.5t Ice Capable	**1 oil engine** driving 1 CP propeller Total Power: 971kW (1,320hp) 12.5kn S.K.L. 8NVD48A-2U 1 x 4 Stroke 8 Cy. 320 x 480 971kW (1320bhp) VEB Schwermaschinenbau "KarlLiebknecht" (SKL)-Magdeburg AuxGen: 1 x 300kW a.c, 3 x 160kW a.c Thrusters: 1 Thwart. FP thruster (f); 1 Tunnel thruster (a) Fuel: 185.0 (d.f.)
5139234 *LAOH* -	**SVERDRUPSON** *ex* Thorsteinson *-2009* *ex* H. U. Sverdrup *-1988* **Obsea AS** Obsea ApS SatCom: Inmarsat A 1311106 *Kristiansund* *Norway* MMSI: 257273000 Official number: 20510	**272** 81 -	Class: (NV)	**1960 Orens Mek. Verksted — Trondheim** Yd No: 26 Loa 38.89 Br ex 7.93 Dght 3.302 Lbp 34.02 Br md 7.61 Dpth 3.97 Welded, 1 dk	**(B31A2SR) Research Survey Vessel** Compartments: 1 Ho, ER 1 Ha: (1.8 x 2.2)ER Derricks: 2x3t; Winches: 2 Ice Capable	**1 oil engine** driving 1 CP propeller Total Power: 441kW (600hp) Wichmann 6ACA 1 x 2 Stroke 6 Cy. 280 x 420 441kW (600bhp) Wichmann Motorfabrikk AS-Norway AuxGen: 1 x 44kW 220V 50Hz a.c, 2 x 30kW 220V 50Hz a.c
7943299 *UBGD* -	**SVERKAYUSHCHIY** - **JSC Gals** - *Murmansk* *Russia*	**173** 51 88	Class: (RS)	**1981-06 Astrakhanskaya Sudoverf im. "Kirova" — Astrakhan** Yd No: 139 Loa 33.96 Br ex 7.09 Dght 2.899 Lbp 29.98 Br md 7.00 Dpth 3.69 Welded, 1 dk	**(B11B2FV) Fishing Vessel** Grain: 78 Compartments: 1 Ho, ER 1 Ha: (1.6 x 1.3) Derricks: 2x2t; Winches: 2 Ice Capable	**1 oil engine** driving 1 CP propeller Total Power: 290kW (394hp) 9.5kn Iveco Aifo 8210 SRM45 1 x 4 Stroke 6 Cy. 137 x 156 290kW (394bhp) (new engine 2005) IVECO AIFO S.p.A.-Pregnana Milanese AuxGen: 2 x 75kW a.c Fuel: 17.0 (d.f.)
9625956 *D5EQ7* -	**SVET** - **Caldy Maritime Ltd** SCF Novoship JSC (Novorossiysk Shipping Co) *Monrovia* *Liberia* MMSI: 636016137 Official number: 16137	**167,578** 110,083 321,039 T/cm 182.3	Class: NV RS	**2013-11 Bohai Shipbuilding Heavy Industry Co Ltd — Huludao LN** Yd No: BH518G1-7 Loa 331.76 (BB) Br ex 60.04 Dght 22.600 Lbp 319.75 Br md 60.00 Dpth 30.50 Welded, 1 dk	**(A13A2TV) Crude Oil Tanker** Double Hull (13F) Liq: 344,300; Liq (Oil): 340,000 Compartments: 5 Wing Ta, 5 Ta, 5 Wing Ta, 1 Wing Slop Ta, 1 Wing Slop Ta, ER 3 Cargo Pump (s): 3x5500m³/hr Manifold: Bow/CM: 165.4m	**1 oil engine** driving 1 FP propeller Total Power: 31,640kW (43,018hp) 15.5kn Wartsila 7RT-flex82T 1 x 2 Stroke 7 Cy. 820 x 3375 31640kW (43018bhp) AuxGen: 2 x 1200kW a.c Fuel: 808.0 (d.f.) 8864.0 (r.f.)
9519638 *9AA7459* -	**SVETI DUJAM** - **Radunica Maritime Inc** Jadroplov International Maritime Transport Ltd (Jadroplov dd) *Split* *Croatia* MMSI: 238293000	**30,092** 17,852 52,113	Class: BV CS	**2010-09 Brodosplit - Brodogradiliste doo — Split** Yd No: 467 Loa 189.99 (BB) Br ex 32.28 Dght 12.350 Lbp 182.00 Br md 32.24 Dpth 17.10 Welded, 1 dk	**(A21A2BC) Bulk Carrier** Double Hull Grain: 64,986 Compartments: 5 Ho, ER 5 Ha: ER Cranes: 4x35t	**1 oil engine** driving 1 FP propeller Total Power: 8,600kW (11,693hp) 14.3kn MAN-B&W 6S50MC-C 1 x 2 Stroke 6 Cy. 500 x 2000 8600kW (11693bhp) Brodosplit Tvornica Dizel Motoradoo-Croatia AuxGen: 3 x 620kW 60Hz a.c Fuel: 1660.0 (r.f.)
7919781 *9A9427* -	**SVETI DUJE** *ex* Pelflyer *-2004* *ex* Ibafon Flyer *-1987* **Corex Shipping Ltd** Splitska Plovidba dd *Split* *Croatia* MMSI: 238198000 Official number: 5T-797	**2,654** 1,613 2,850	Class: CS (NV) (HR)	**1982-01 Scheepswerven van Hemiksem N.V. — Hemiksem** Loa 93.60 Br ex 13.03 Dght 6.100 Lbp 85.60 Br md 13.01 Dpth 7.90 Welded, 1 dk	**(A31A2GX) General Cargo Ship** Grain: 5,567; Bale: 4,880 TEU 156 C. 156/20' (40') Compartments: 2 Ho, ER 2 Ha: (27.6 x 10.2) (24.6 x 10.2)ER Cranes: 2x10t,2x5t	**1 oil engine** driving 1 FP propeller Total Power: 1,848kW (2,513hp) Nohab 12V25 1 x Vee 4 Stroke 12 Cy. 250 x 300 1848kW (2513bhp) (new engine 1987) Wartsila Diesel AB-Sweden AuxGen: 2 x 170kW 380V 50Hz a.c, 1 x 85kW 380V 50Hz a.c
9281748 *9A8687* -	**SVETI KRISTOFOR** - **Rapska Plovidba dd** - *Rijeka* *Croatia* MMSI: 238118740 Official number: 2T-747	**427** 134 213	Class: CS	**2003-06 Shipyard 'Viktor Lenac' dd — Rijeka** Yd No: 129 Loa 42.00 Br ex - Dght 2.017 Lbp 35.20 Br md 15.30 Dpth 3.60 Welded	**(A36A2PR) Passenger/Ro-Ro Ship (Vehicles)** Passengers: 200 Cars: 48	**2 oil engines** geared to sc. shafts driving 2 FP propellers Total Power: 894kW (1,216hp) Cummins KTA-19-M3 2 x 4 Stroke 6 Cy. 159 x 159 each-447kW (608bhp) Cummins Engine Co Inc-USA
9326562 *9AA2126* -	**SVETI KRSEVAN** - **Jadrolinija** - *Rijeka* *Croatia* MMSI: 238151640 Official number: 2T-789	**2,438** 781 855	Class: CS	**2004-07 Brodogradiliste Kraljevica dd — Kraljevica** Yd No: 535 Loa 87.60 Br ex - Dght 2.400 Lbp 80.00 Br md 17.50 Dpth 3.70 Welded, 1 dk	**(A36A2PR) Passenger/Ro-Ro Ship (Vehicles)** Passengers: unberthed: 600 Bow ramp (f) Len: 6.50 Wid: 8.50 Swl: 50 Stern ramp (a) Len: 6.50 Wid: 8.50 Swl: 50 Lane-clr ht: 4.40 Cars: 100	**4 oil engines** geared to sc. shafts driving 4 Directional propellers Total Power: 1,600kW (2,176hp) 11.5kn Caterpillar 3412E-TA 4 x Vee 4 Stroke 12 Cy. 137 x 152 each-400kW (544bhp) Caterpillar Inc-USA AuxGen: 2 x 299kW 380/220V 50Hz a.c Fuel: 100.0 (d.f.)
9356933 *9AA2610* -	**SVETI MARIN** - **Rapska Plovidba dd** - *Rijeka* *Croatia* MMSI: 238200840 Official number: 2T-806	**496** 156 -	Class: CS	**2005-07 Shipyard 'Viktor Lenac' dd — Rijeka** Yd No: 131 Loa 49.20 Br ex - Dght 2.290 Lbp - Br md 15.30 Dpth 3.60 Welded, 1 dk	**(A36A2PR) Passenger/Ro-Ro Ship (Vehicles)** Passengers: 250	**2 oil engines** reduction geared to sc. shafts driving 2 FP propellers Total Power: 1,176kW (1,598hp) 10.0kn MAN D2842LE 2 x Vee 4 Stroke 12 Cy. 128 x 142 each-588kW (799bhp) MAN Nutzfahrzeuge AG-Nuernberg
9102966 *V7AL6* -	**SVETI NIKOLA I** - **Rosebank Maritime Inc** TST International SA *Majuro* *Marshall Islands* MMSI: 538005283 Official number: 5283	**25,600** 14,558 44,314 T/cm 51.3	Class: BV CS	**1997-06 'Uljanik' Brodogradiliste dd — Pula** Yd No: 405 Loa 183.00 (BB) Br ex 32.20 Dght 11.517 Lbp 175.00 Br md 32.00 Dpth 16.10 Welded, 1 dk	**(A21A2BC) Bulk Carrier** Grain: 54,771 Compartments: 5 Ho, ER 5 Ha: 5 (16.0 x 15.6)ER Cranes: 4x30t	**1 oil engine** driving 1 FP propeller Total Power: 8,580kW (11,665hp) 14.5kn B&W 6S50MC 1 x 2 Stroke 6 Cy. 500 x 1910 8580kW (11665bhp) 'Uljanik' Strojogradnja dd-Croatia AuxGen: 3 x 580kW 450V 60Hz a.c Fuel: 270.0 (d.f.) (Heating Coils) 1675.0 (r.f.) 31.5pd
7320332 *C6HD4* -	**SVETI STEFAN II** *ex* Nieborow *-2002* *ex* Stena Baltica *-1988* *ex* Prins Hamlet *-1988* *ex* Prinz Hamlet *-1987* **Adriatic Lines SA** - *Nassau* *Bahamas* MMSI: 309445000 Official number: 715383	**8,697** 3,629 1,080	Class: BV (NV) (PR) (GL)	**1973-11 Werft Nobiskrug GmbH — Rendsburg** Yd No: 679 Loa 118.83 (BB) Br ex 18.55 Dght 5.201 Lbp 107.85 Br md 18.34 Dpth 12.07 Welded, 3 dks	**(A36A2PR) Passenger/Ro-Ro Ship (Vehicles)** Passengers: unberthed: 474; berths: 626 Stern door/ramp (centre) Len: 4.89 Wid: 5.43 Swl: - Lane-Len: 645 Lane-Wid: 2.70 Lane-clr ht: 4.70 Cars: 225 Ice Capable	**4 oil engines** dr geared to sc. shafts driving 2 CP propellers Total Power: 11,768kW (16,000hp) 20.0kn Werkspoor 6TM410 4 x 4 Stroke 6 Cy. 410 x 470 each-2942kW (4000bhp) Stork Werkspoor Diesel BV-Netherlands AuxGen: 3 x 800kW 220/440V 60Hz a.c, 1 x 204kW 220/440V 60Hz a.c Thrusters: 1 Thwart. FP thruster (f) Fuel: 140.0 (d.f.) 202.0 (r.f.) 48.0pd

7505059 - -	**SVETIMATIJA** *ex* Frans van den Berg *-2003* *ex* Concordia Constans *-1997* *ex* Eben Haezer *-1991* **Mr Dragan Pavlicevic** -	*203* 60 -		**1975 Scheepswerf de Klerk B.V. — Walsoorden** Yd No: 56 Converted From: Fishing Vessel-1975 Lengthened-1987 Loa 32.52 Br ex - Dght - Lbp 29.57 Br md 7.04 Dpth 3.41 Welded, 1 dk	**(X11A2YP) Yacht**	**1 oil engine** driving 1 FP propeller Total Power: 992kW (1,349hp) Kromhout 6F240 1 x 4 Stroke 6 Cy. 240 x 260 992kW (1349bhp) (new engine 1985) Stork Werkspoor Diesel BV-Netherlands
7702322 *D6CG2* -	**SVETLA** *ex* Costis A *-2004* *ex* Anemos *-2002* *ex* Dina Jacoba *-2001* *ex* Anne *-1987* *ex* Dependent *-1982* **Pelagian Shipping Ltd** Sargem Denizcilik Gem Acenteligi Ticaret Ltd Sti *Moroni* *Union of Comoros* MMSI: 616249000 Official number: 1200296	**945** 602 1,473	Class: UA (BV)	**1977-08 Peters' Scheepsbouw B.V. — Kampen** Yd No: 118 Loa 64.42 Br ex - Dght 4.001 Lbp 59.46 Br md 10.71 Dpth 4.86 Welded, 1 dk	**(A31A2GX) General Cargo Ship** Grain: 1,961; Bale: 1,950 Compartments: 1 Ho, ER 1 Ha: (35.3 x 7.6)ER	**1 oil engine** reduction geared to sc. shaft driving 1 FP propeller Total Power: 736kW (1,001hp) 11.0kn Mitsubishi S12R-MPTA 1 x Vee 4 Stroke 12 Cy. 170 x 180 736kW (1001bhp) (new engine 1993) Mitsubishi Heavy Industries Ltd-Japan AuxGen: 2 x 28kW 380V 50Hz a.c Fuel: 84.5 (d.f.)
8606472 *4JGF* -	**SVETLAMOR-2** - **Caspian Basin Emergency Salvage Specialized Stock Society** - *Baku* *Azerbaijan* MMSI: 423094100 Official number: DGR-0094	**1,695** 509 1,000	Class: RS	**1987-09 Far East-Levingston Shipbuilding Ltd — Singapore** Yd No: B209 Converted From: Tug-2007 Loa 61.02 Br ex - Dght 4.501 Lbp 51.80 Br md 14.01 Dpth 6.02 Welded, 2 dks	**(B21B20T) Offshore Tug/Supply Ship**	**2 oil engines** with clutches, flexible couplings & sr geared to sc. shafts driving 2 CP propellers Total Power: 2,600kW (3,534hp) 12.6kn Wartsila 8R22 2 x 4 Stroke 8 Cy. 220 x 240 each-1300kW (1767bhp) Wartsila Diesel Oy-Finland AuxGen: 3 x 190kW a.c Thrusters: 1 Thwart. FP thruster (f)
7942154 *UCHP* -	**SVETLANA** *ex* Sorve *-1996* *ex* Metelitsa *-1992* **Saami Co Ltd (OOO Firma 'Saami')** - *Murmansk* *Russia* MMSI: 273427000 Official number: 800775	**795** 242 405	Class: RS	**1981-04 Zavod "Leninskaya Kuznitsa" — Kiyev** Yd No: 1490 Loa 54.82 Br ex 9.96 Dght 4.140 Lbp 50.29 Br md 9.80 Dpth 5.06 Welded, 1 dk	**(B11A2FS) Stern Trawler** Bale: 414 Compartments: 2 Ho, ER 3 Ha: 3 (1.5 x 1.6) Derricks: 2x1.3t Ice Capable	**1 oil engine** driving 1 FP propeller Total Power: 736kW (1,001hp) 12.0kn S.K.L. 8NVD48A-2U 1 x 4 Stroke 8 Cy. 320 x 480 736kW (1001bhp) VEB Schwermaschinenbau "KarlLiebknecht" (SKL)-Magdeburg Fuel: 154.0 (d.f.)
8969654 *WDG2135* -	**SVETLANA M** *ex* Big Corey *-2011* **Charca Fish V LLC** - *San Diego, CA* *United States of America* MMSI: 367512490 Official number: 1121787	**175** 52 -		**2001** Yd No: 230 L reg 26.15 Br ex - Dght - Lbp - Br md 7.92 Dpth 3.81 Welded, 1 dk	**(B11B2FV) Fishing Vessel**	**1 oil engine** driving 1 FP propeller
8606484 *UAKM* -	**SVETLOMOR-3** - **Murmansk Region Administration of Salvage & Special Operation (Murmanskoye Basseynovoye Avariyno-Spasatelnoye Upravleniye)** - *Vladivostok* *Russia* MMSI: 273132000 Official number: 861779	**1,695** 509 1,000	Class: RS	**1987-10 Far East-Levingston Shipbuilding Ltd — Singapore** Yd No: B210 Loa 61.02 Br ex - Dght 4.501 Lbp 51.80 Br md 14.00 Dpth 6.00 Welded, 2 dks	**(B32A2ST) Tug**	**2 oil engines** with clutches, flexible couplings & sr geared to sc. shafts driving 2 CP propellers Total Power: 2,600kW (3,534hp) 12.6kn Wartsila 8R22 2 x 4 Stroke 8 Cy. 220 x 240 each-1300kW (1767bhp) Wartsila Diesel Oy-Finland AuxGen: 3 x 190kW a.c Thrusters: 1 Thwart. FP thruster (f)
7740673 *UFAI* -	**SVETLOMORSK** - **Eridan Ltd** - *Petropavlovsk-Kamchatskiy* *Russia* MMSI: 273824220	**739** 221 322	Class: (RS)	**1978-09 Zavod "Leninskaya Kuznitsa" — Kiyev** Yd No: 237 Loa 53.73 (BB) Br ex 10.72 Dght 4.290 Lbp 47.92 Br md - Dpth 6.00 Welded, 1 dk	**(B11A2FS) Stern Trawler** Ins: 220 Compartments: 1 Ho, ER 2 Ha: 2 (1.6 x 1.6) Derricks: 2x3.3t Ice Capable	**1 oil engine** driving 1 CP propeller Total Power: 971kW (1,320hp) 12.5kn S.K.L. 8NVD48A-2U 1 x 4 Stroke 8 Cy. 320 x 480 971kW (1320bhp) VEB Schwermaschinenbau "KarlLiebknecht" (SKL)-Magdeburg Thrusters: 1 Thwart. FP thruster (f); 1 Tunnel thruster (a)
7945572 *UBMG* -	**SVETLOVODNYY** - **Transfish Co Ltd** - *Nevelsk* *Russia* MMSI: 273850200 Official number: 801424	**676** 233 495	Class: (RS)	**1981-08 Khabarovskiy Sudostroitelnyy Zavod im Kirova — Khabarovsk** Yd No: 831 Loa 55.01 Br ex 9.52 Dght 4.340 Lbp 50.04 Br md 9.30 Dpth 5.16 Welded, 1dk	**(B12B2FC) Fish Carrier** Ins: 632 Compartments: 2 Ho, ER 2 Ha: 2 (2.9 x 2.7) Derricks: 4x3.3t Ice Capable	**1 oil engine** driving 1 FP propeller 11.3kn S.K.L. 6NVD48-2U 1 x 4 Stroke 6 Cy. 320 x 480 VEB Schwermaschinenbau "KarlLiebknecht" (SKL)-Magdeburg Fuel: 105.0 (d.f.)
8971449 - -	**SVETLOVODSK** - **'Ukrrichflot' Joint Stock Shipping Co** - *Kiev* *Ukraine*	*993* 297 2,224		**1971 Kiyevskiy Sudostroitelnyy Sudoremontnyy Zavod — Kiyev** Yd No: 385 Loa 85.75 Br ex - Dght 2.100 Lbp - Br md 15.00 Dpth 2.80 Welded, 1 dk	**(A31A2GX) General Cargo Ship**	**2 oil engines** driving 2 FP propellers Total Power: 1,320kW (1,794hp) S.K.L. 6NVD48A-2U 2 x 4 Stroke 6 Cy. 320 x 480 each-660kW (897bhp) VEB Schwermaschinenbau "KarlLiebknecht" (SKL)-Magdeburg
8929501 - -	**SVETLYY** - **Franco-Trading JSC** - *Nakhodka* *Russia*	**189** 84 326	Class: RS	**1979-10 Bakinskiy Sudostroitelnyy Zavod im Vano Sturua — Baku** Yd No: 329 Loa 29.17 Br ex 8.01 Dght 3.120 Lbp 28.50 Br md 7.50 Dpth 3.60 Welded, 1 dk	**(B34G2SE) Pollution Control Vessel** Liq: 336; Liq (Oil): 336 Compartments: 8 Ta Ice Capable	**1 oil engine** geared to sc. shaft driving 1 FP propeller Total Power: 165kW (224hp) 7.5kn Daldizel 6CHNSP18/22 1 x 4 Stroke 6 Cy. 180 x 220 165kW (224bhp) Daldizel-Khabarovsk AuxGen: 1 x 50kW a.c, 1 x 30kW a.c Fuel: 10.0 (d.f.)
8953473 - -	**SVETLYY** - **Rybolovetskiy Kolkhoz 'Narody Severa'**	**117** 35 37	Class: (RS)	**1999-09 Sretenskiy Sudostroitelnyy Zavod — Sretensk** Yd No: 314 Loa 25.45 Br ex 6.80 Dght 2.390 Lbp 22.00 Br md - Dpth 3.30 Welded, 1 dk	**(B11A2FS) Stern Trawler** Grain: 64 Compartments: 1 Ho 1 Ha: (1.5 x 1.3) Ice Capable	**1 oil engine** driving 1 FP propeller Total Power: 220kW (299hp) 10.0kn S.K.L. 6NVD26A-2 1 x 4 Stroke 6 Cy. 180 x 260 220kW (299bhp) SKL Motoren u. Systemtechnik AG-Magdeburg AuxGen: 2 x 16kW Fuel: 12.0 (d.f.)
8728634 - -	**SVETLYY** - **Kord Co Ltd** - *Murmansk* *Russia*	**236** 121 442	Class: RS	**1981-09 Bakinskiy Sudostroitelnyy Zavod im Vano Sturua — Baku** Yd No: 349 Loa 35.17 Br ex 8.01 Dght 3.120 Lbp 33.25 Br md 7.58 Dpth 3.60 Welded, 1 dk	**(B34G2SE) Pollution Control Vessel** Liq: 460; Liq (Oil): 460 Compartments: 10 Ta Ice Capable	**1 oil engine** geared to sc. shaft driving 1 FP propeller Total Power: 166kW (226hp) 7.5kn Daldizel 6CHNSP18/22 1 x 4 Stroke 6 Cy. 180 x 220 166kW (226bhp) Daldizel-Khabarovsk AuxGen: 1 x 50kW a.c, 1 x 25kW Fuel: 11.0 (d.f.)
8728646 - -	**SVETLYY** - **State Enterprise 'Sevastopol Sea Fishing Port' (Derzhavne Pidpryyemstvo Sevastopolska Morskyy Rybnyy Port)** - *Sevastopol* *Ukraine* Official number: 850666	**191** 85 323	Class: (RS)	**1985-06 Svetlovskiy Sudoremontnyy Zavod — Svetlyy** Yd No: 24 Loa 29.45 Br ex 8.15 Dght 3.120 Lbp 28.50 Br md - Dpth 3.60 Welded, 1 dk	**(B34G2SE) Pollution Control Vessel** Liq: 332; Liq (Oil): 332 Compartments: 8 Ta Ice Capable	**1 oil engine** geared to sc. shaft driving 1 FP propeller Total Power: 166kW (226hp) 7.5kn Daldizel 6CHNSP18/22 1 x 4 Stroke 6 Cy. 180 x 220 166kW (226bhp) Daldizel-Khabarovsk AuxGen: 1 x 50kW a.c, 1 x 30kW Fuel: 13.0 (d.f.)
7832878 - -	**SVETLYY** - **NV Fesenko** - *Sevastopol* *Ukraine* Official number: 802709	*149* 101 20	Class: (RS)	**1980 Ilyichyovskiy Sudoremontnyy Zavod im. "50-letiya SSSR" — Ilyichyovsk** Yd No: 2 Loa 28.70 Br ex 6.35 Dght 1.480 Lbp 27.00 Br md - Dpth 2.50 Welded, 1 dk	**(A37B2PS) Passenger Ship** Passengers: unberthed: 250	**2 oil engines** driving 2 FP propellers Total Power: 220kW (300hp) 10.4kn Barnaultransmash 3D6C 2 x 4 Stroke 6 Cy. 150 x 180 each-110kW (150bhp) Barnaultransmash-Barnaul Fuel: 2.0 (d.f.)
7740685 - -	**SVETLYY** - -	*163* 39 88	Class: (RS)	**1978 Astrakhanskaya Sudoverf im. "Kirova" — Astrakhan** Yd No: 109 Loa 34.02 Br ex 7.09 Dght 2.899 Lbp 30.00 Br md - Dpth 3.66 Welded, 1 dk	**(B11B2FV) Fishing Vessel** Bale: 78 Compartments: 1 Ho, ER 1 Ha: (1.6 x 1.3) Derricks: 2x2t; Winches: 2 Ice Capable	**1 oil engine** driving 1 FP propeller Total Power: 224kW (305hp) 9.0kn S.K.L. 8NVD36-1U 1 x 4 Stroke 8 Cy. 240 x 360 224kW (305bhp) VEB Schwermaschinenbau "KarlLiebknecht" (SKL)-Magdeburg

IMO / Call sign	Name / Owner	Tonnage	Class	Builder / Dimensions	Type	Machinery
9356373 *UHJN* -	**SVETLYY** **OOO 'Global-Flot'** - *Kaliningrad* *Russia* MMSI: 273312050	**1,788** 536 980	Class: RS	**2006**-12 **Keppel Singmarine Pte Ltd — Singapore** Yd No: 300 Loa 65.00 Br ex 15.00 Dght 4.304 Lbp 62.36 Br md 15.00 Dpth 6.20 Welded, 1 dk	**(B21B20A) Anchor Handling Tug Supply** Cranes: 1x12t Ice Capable	**2 oil engines** geared to sc. shafts driving 2 CP propellers Total Power: 5,280kW (7,178hp) 13.0kn MaK 8M25 2 x 4 Stroke 8 Cy. 255 x 400 each-2640kW (3589bhp) Caterpillar Motoren GmbH & Co. KG-Germany AuxGen: 2 x 356kW 380V 50Hz a.c, 2 x 650kW 380V 50Hz a.c Thrusters: 1 Tunnel thruster (f) Fuel: 650.0 (d.f.)
8863343 *V3RH5* -	**SVETOSLAVA** *ex* Volgo-Don 5036 *-2000* **Saluta Shipping Ltd** Kent Shipping & Chartering Ltd SatCom: Inmarsat C 431240611 *Belize City* *Belize* MMSI: 312406000 Official number: 141120197	**3,994** 1,302 4,903	Class: IV (RR) (RS)	**1971 Santierul Naval Oltenita S.A. — Oltenita** Loa 138.40 Br ex 16.70 Dght 3.380 Lbp 129.60 Br md 16.50 Dpth 5.50 Welded, 1 dk	**(A31A2GX) General Cargo Ship** Grain: 6,270 Compartments: 2 Ho, ER 2 Ha: ER Ice Capable	**2 oil engines** driving 2 FP propellers Total Power: 1,324kW (1,800hp) 11.0kn Dvigatel Revolyutsii 6CHRNP36/45 2 x 4 Stroke 6 Cy. 360 x 450 each-662kW (900bhp) Zavod "Dvigatel Revolyutsii"-Gorkiy Fuel: 162.0 (d.f.)
9156539 *IBEU* -	**SVEVA** **Mediterranea di Navigazione SpA** - SatCom: Inmarsat B 324700452 *Ravenna* *Italy* MMSI: 247359000 Official number: 87	**11,270** 4,943 15,200 T/cm 27.2	Class: BV RI	**1999**-03 **Cant. Nav. de Poli S.p.A. — Pellestrina** Yd No: 163 Loa 136.00 (BB) Br ex 23.02 Dght 8.751 Lbp 126.50 Br md 23.00 Dpth 12.25 Welded, 1 dk	**(A12B2TR) Chemical/Products Tanker** Double Hull (13F) Liq: 16,409; Liq (Oil): 16,409 Cargo Heating Coils Compartments: 14 Wing Ta, 2 Wing Slop Ta, ER 14 Cargo Pump (s): 14x300m³/hr Manifold: Bow/CM: 66m Ice Capable	**1 oil engine** with clutches & geared to sc. shaft driving 1 CP propeller Total Power: 6,300kW (8,565hp) 15.0kn MAN 6L48/60 1 x 4 Stroke 6 Cy. 480 x 600 6300kW (8565bhp) MAN B&W Diesel AG-Augsburg AuxGen: 3 x 900kW 440V 60Hz a.c, 1 x 1500kW 450V 60Hz a.c Thrusters: 1 Thwart. CP thruster (f) Fuel: 175.0 (d.f.) (Heating Coils) 1123.0 (r.f.)
8521141 *PHAK* -	**SVEZIA** **Sleepdienst B Iskes & Zoon BV** - *Rotterdam* *Netherlands* MMSI: 246416000 Official number: 36125	**245** 73 140	Class: GL (RI)	**1988**-03 **Cant. Navale "Ferrari" S.p.A. — La Spezia** Yd No: 56 Loa 26.85 Br ex 9.50 Dght 3.200 Lbp 26.02 Br md 9.02 Dpth 3.70 Welded, 1 dk	**(B32A2ST) Tug**	**2 oil engines** with clutches, flexible couplings & sr geared to sc. shaft driving 2 Directional propellers Total Power: 2,370kW (3,222hp) 10.8kn Deutz SBV6M628 2 x 4 Stroke 6 Cy. 240 x 280 each-1185kW (1611bhp) Kloeckner Humboldt Deutz AG-West Germany AuxGen: 2 x 38kW 220/380V 50Hz a.c Fuel: 37.5 (d.f.) 5.5pd
9319014 *IQKS* -	**SVEZIA** **Rimorchiatori Riuniti Porto di Genova Srl** - *Genoa* *Italy* MMSI: 247130800 Official number: 3862	**335** 89 335	Class: RI	**2005**-09 **Cantieri Navali Termoli SpA — Termoli** Yd No: 195 Loa 27.50 Br ex - Dght 3.500 Lbp 26.75 Br md 11.50 Dpth 4.25 Welded, 1 dk	**(B32A2ST) Tug**	**2 oil engines** gearing integral to driving 2 Voith-Schneider propellers Total Power: 4,120kW (5,602hp) Wartsila 6L26 2 x 4 Stroke 6 Cy. 260 x 320 each-2060kW (2801bhp) Wartsila Finland Oy-Finland AuxGen: 3 x 116kW 380/220V 50Hz a.c Fuel: 157.0 (d.f.) 11.6pd
9490741 *V7RM5* -	**SVINOY** **Marfaction Shipping Co Ltd** Scantank AS *Majuro* *Marshall Islands* MMSI: 538003541 Official number: 3541	**32,837** 19,559 58,000 T/cm 59.2	Class: BV	**2010**-08 **Yangzhou Dayang Shipbuilding Co Ltd — Yangzhou JS** Yd No: DY3021 Loa 189.99 (BB) Br ex - Dght 12.950 Lbp 185.00 Br md 32.26 Dpth 18.00 Welded, 1 dk	**(A21A2BC) Bulk Carrier** Grain: 71,549; Bale: 69,760 Compartments: 5 Ho, ER 5 Ha: ER Cranes: 4x35t	**1 oil engine** driving 1 FP propeller Total Power: 8,700kW (11,829hp) 14.3kn MAN-B&W 6S50MC-C 1 x 2 Stroke 6 Cy. 500 x 2000 8700kW (11829bhp) Doosan Engine Co Ltd-South Korea AuxGen: 3 x 645kW 60Hz a.c
8228567 - -	**SVIR** **JSC Leasing-Ship** JSC 'Port Fleet Ltd' (ZAO 'Portovyy Flot') *St Petersburg* *Russia*	**235** 120 455	Class: (RS)	**1984 Bakinskiy Sudostroitelnyy Zavod im Vano Sturua — Baku** Yd No: 369 Loa 35.18 Br ex 8.01 Dght 3.120 Lbp 33.25 Br md - Dpth 3.61 Welded, 1 dk	**(B34G2SE) Pollution Control Vessel** Liq: 468; Liq (Oil): 468 Compartments: 10 Ta Ice Capable	**1 oil engine** geared to sc. shaft driving 1 FP propeller Total Power: 166kW (226hp) 8.0kn Daldizel 6CHNSP18/22 1 x 4 Stroke 6 Cy. 180 x 220 166kW (226bhp) Daldizel-Khabarovsk AuxGen: 1 x 50kW a.c, 1 x 30kW a.c Fuel: 13.0 (d.f.)
8866694 *UBII6* -	**SVIR** *ex* Svir-1 *-2012* *ex* Svir *-2001* *ex* Omskiy-9 *-1993* **High Seas Shipping Ltd** Dimar-Freight Co Ltd (OOO 'Dimar-Frakht') *Taganrog* *Russia* MMSI: 273356850	**2,426** 728 3,174	Class: RS UA	**1977**-10 **Krasnoyarskiy Sudostroitelnyy Zavod — Krasnoyarsk** Yd No: 13 Loa 108.40 Br ex 15.00 Dght 3.260 Lbp 101.80 Br md - Dpth 5.00 Welded, 1 dk	**(A31A2GX) General Cargo Ship**	**2 oil engines** driving 2 FP propellers Total Power: 1,030kW (1,400hp) S.K.L. 6NVD48A-2U 2 x 4 Stroke 6 Cy. 320 x 480 each-515kW (700bhp) VEB Schwermaschinenbau "KarlLiebknecht" (SKL)-Magdeburg
8852033 *XUEF6* -	**SVIR** *ex* Volgo-Don 5078 *-1992* **Arsenal Shipping Ltd** MD Shipping Co *Phnom Penh* *Cambodia* MMSI: 515291000 Official number: 1280834	**2,794** 1,078 4,060	Class: UA (RS)	**1980**-06 **Santierul Naval Oltenita S.A. — Oltenita** Loa 105.85 Br ex 16.70 Dght 3.850 Lbp 100.24 Br md 16.50 Dpth 5.50 Welded, 1 dk	**(A31A2GX) General Cargo Ship** Compartments: 2 Ho, ER 2 Ha: ER Ice Capable	**2 oil engines** driving 2 FP propellers Total Power: 1,324kW (1,800hp) 10.0kn Dvigatel Revolyutsii 6CHRNP36/45 2 x 4 Stroke 6 Cy. 360 x 450 each-662kW (900bhp) Zavod "Dvigatel Revolyutsii"-Gorkiy
6860294 *UGHW* -	**SVIRITSA** *ex* RR-1262 Sviritsa *-1975* **Yuzhno-Kurilskiy Rybokombinat Co Ltd** - *Nevelsk* *Russia* MMSI: 273564210	**248** 105 130	Class: RS	**1955**-01 **VEB Rosslauer Schiffswerft — Rosslau** Yd No: 1262 Loa 38.50 Br ex 7.28 Dght 2.760 Lbp 34.70 Br md 7.20 Dpth 3.50 Welded, 1 dk	**(B11B2FV) Fishing Vessel** Ice Capable	**1 oil engine** driving 1 FP propeller
9380116 *A7DD* -	**SVITZER AL SAFLIYA** **Nakilat SvitzerWijsmuller WLL** SvitzerWijsmuller Halul LLC *Doha* *Qatar* MMSI: 466501230	**171** 51 95	Class: LR (AB) **100A1** SS 06/2011 SSC work boat, mono, G6 HSC **LMC** Cable: 173.0/16.0 U2 (a)	**2006**-06 **Strategic Marine (S) Pte Ltd — Singapore** Yd No: H143 Loa 31.00 Br ex 7.50 Dght 1.380 Lbp 28.53 Br md 7.49 Dpth 3.02 Welded, 1 dk	**(B21A20C) Crew/Supply Vessel** Hull Material: Aluminium Alloy	**2 oil engines** gearing integral to driving 2 FP propellers Total Power: 2,262kW (3,075hp) 20.0kn Caterpillar C32 2 x Vee 4 Stroke 12 Cy. 145 x 162 each-1030kW (1400bhp) Caterpillar Inc-USA AuxGen: 2 x 69kW 415V 50Hz a.c Thrusters: 1 Thwart. FP thruster (f)
9380128 *A7DI* -	**SVITZER AL SHAMAL** **Nakilat SvitzerWijsmuller WLL** SvitzerWijsmuller Halul LLC *Doha* *Qatar* MMSI: 466501250 Official number: 306/10	**171** 51 45	Class: LR (AB) **100A1** SS 09/2011 SSC work boat, mono, G6 HSC **LMC** Cable: 173.0/16.0 U2 (a)	**2006**-09 **Strategic Marine (S) Pte Ltd — Singapore** Yd No: H144 Loa 31.00 Br ex 7.50 Dght 1.380 Lbp 28.53 Br md 7.49 Dpth 3.02 Welded, 1 dk	**(B21A20C) Crew/Supply Vessel** Hull Material: Aluminium Alloy	**2 oil engines** gearing integral to driving 2 FP propellers Total Power: 2,464kW (3,350hp) 20.0kn Caterpillar C32 2 x Vee 4 Stroke 12 Cy. 145 x 162 each-1232kW (1675bhp) Caterpillar Inc-USA AuxGen: 2 x 69kW 415V 50Hz a.c Thrusters: 1 Thwart. FP thruster (f)
9380130 *A7DH* -	**SVITZER AL SHAQAB** **Nakilat SvitzerWijsmuller WLL** SvitzerWijsmuller Halul LLC *Doha* *Qatar* MMSI: 466501240 Official number: 305/10	**171** 51 45	Class: LR (AB) **100A1** SS 10/2011 SSC work boat, mono, G6 HSC **LMC** Cable: 173.0/16.0 U2 (a)	**2006**-10 **Strategic Marine (S) Pte Ltd — Singapore** Yd No: H145 Loa 31.00 Br ex 7.50 Dght 1.380 Lbp 28.53 Br md 7.49 Dpth 3.02 Welded, 1 dk	**(B21A20C) Crew/Supply Vessel** Hull Material: Aluminium Alloy	**2 oil engines** gearing integral to driving 2 FP propellers Total Power: 2,464kW (3,350hp) 20.0kn Caterpillar C32 2 x Vee 4 Stroke 12 Cy. 145 x 162 each-1232kW (1675bhp) Caterpillar Inc-USA AuxGen: 2 x 69kW 415V 50Hz a.c Thrusters: 1 Thwart. FP thruster (f)
9554315 *VHDQ* -	**SVITZER ALBATROSS** **Svitzer Australia Pty Ltd (Svitzer Australasia)** - *Fremantle, WA* *Australia* MMSI: 503717000 Official number: 860161	**442** 132 273	Class: LR ✠ **100A1** SS 10/2011 tug, fire-fighting Ship 1 (2400m3/h) with water spray *IWS WDL (5t/m2 from aft to frame 15) ✠ **LMC** **UMS** Eq.Ltr: H; Cable: 302.5/22.0 U2 (a)	**2011**-10 **Jiangsu Zhenjiang Shipyard Co Ltd — Zhenjiang JS** Yd No: VZJ6173-0803 Loa 30.80 Br ex 11.32 Dght 5.300 Lbp 26.80 Br md 11.00 Dpth 6.10 Welded, 1 dk	**(B32A2ST) Tug**	**2 oil engines** gearing integral to driving 2 Z propellers Total Power: 3,676kW (4,998hp) Niigata 6L28HX 2 x 4 Stroke 6 Cy. 280 x 370 each-1838kW (2499bhp) Niigata Engineering Co Ltd-Japan AuxGen: 2 x 120kW 400V 50Hz a.c

9141144 *MWQN6* -	**SVITZER ALMA** *ex Lady Alma -2007* **Svitzer Humber Ltd** Svitzer Marine Ltd *Grimsby* *United Kingdom* MMSI: 232002712 Official number: 730051	**369** 110 320	Class: LR ✠**100A1** SS 12/2011 tug fire fighting ship 1 (2400 cubic metre/hr) limited European area service ✠**LMC** **UMS** Eq.Ltr: G; Cable: 302.5/22.0 U2	**1996-12 McTay Marine — Bromborough** Yd No: 118 Loa 29.31 Br ex 11.88 Dght 3.400 Lbp 28.50 Br md 11.00 Dpth 4.30 Welded, 1 dk	**(B32A2ST) Tug**	**2 oil engines** gearing integral to driving 2 Voith-Schneider propellers Total Power: 4,064kW (5,526hp) 13.3kn Ruston 6RK270M 2 x 4 Stroke 6 Cy. 270 x 305 each-2032kW (2763bhp) Ruston Paxman Diesels Ltd.-United Kingdom AuxGen: 2 x 70kW 415V 50Hz a.c Fuel: 85.0 (d.f.)
9409974 *HP3936* -	**SVITZER AMAZONAS** **Svitzer Canada Ltd** Svitzer (Caribbean) Ltd SatCom: Inmarsat C 435722310 *Panama* *Panama* MMSI: 357223000 Official number: 4040409B	**439** 131 260	Class: LR ✠**100A1** SS 01/2013 tug, fire fighting Ship 1 (2400m3/h) with water spray *IWS ✠**LMC** **UMS** Eq.Ltr: G; Cable: 302.5/22.0 U2 (a)	**2008-01 ASL Shipyard Pte Ltd — Singapore** Yd No: 557 Loa 31.50 Br ex 11.50 Dght 4.400 Lbp 26.80 Br md 11.00 Dpth 6.10 Welded, 1 dk	**(B32A2ST) Tug**	**2 oil engines** gearing integral to driving 2 Z propellers Total Power: 3,676kW (4,998hp) 12.5kn Niigata 6L28HX 2 x 4 Stroke 6 Cy. 280 x 370 each-1838kW (2499bhp) Niigata Engineering Co Ltd-Japan AuxGen: 2 x 150kW 400V 50Hz a.c
8415146 *ZQST9* -	**SVITZER ANGLIA** *ex Adsteam Anglia -2008 ex Sun Anglia -2006* **Svitzer Towage Ltd** Svitzer Marine Ltd *London* *United Kingdom* MMSI: 235000447 Official number: 709715	**339** 101 128 T/cm 2.4	✠**100A1** SS 12/2010 tug ✠**LMC** Eq.Ltr: G; Cable: 302.5/20.5 U2	**1985-11 McTay Marine Ltd. — Bromborough** Yd No: 59 Loa 33.79 Br ex 9.96 Dght 4.725 Lbp 31.02 Br md 9.50 Dpth 3.81 Welded, 1 dk	**(B32A2ST) Tug**	**2 oil engines** gearing integral to driving 2 Voith-Schneider propellers Total Power: 2,568kW (3,492hp) 12.0kn Ruston 6RK270M 2 x 4 Stroke 6 Cy. 270 x 305 each-1284kW (1746bhp) Ruston Diesels Ltd.-Newton-le-Willows AuxGen: 2 x 80kW 440V 50Hz a.c
9581564 *J8B4407* -	**SVITZER ANGOLA** **Svitzer Angola Shipowners (BVI) Ltd** Svitzer Angola Lda *Kingstown* *St Vincent & The Grenadines* MMSI: 377786000 Official number: 10880	**631** 189 473	Class: LR ✠**100A1** SS 05/2011 escort tug, fire fighting Ship 1 (2400m3/h) with water spray *IWS WDL (5t/m2 from frame 0 to frame 15) ✠**LMC** **UMS** Eq.Ltr: I*; Cable: 330.0/24.0 U2 (a)	**2011-05 Qingdao Qianjin Shipyard — Qingdao SD** Yd No: 8Z2026 Loa 33.30 Br ex 13.84 Dght 4.500 Lbp 28.60 Br md 13.00 Dpth 6.10 Welded, 1 dk	**(B32A2ST) Tug**	**2 oil engines** gearing integral to driving 2 Z propellers Total Power: 4,412kW (5,998hp) Niigata 8L28HX 2 x 4 Stroke 8 Cy. 280 x 370 each-2206kW (2999bhp) Niigata Engineering Co Ltd-Japan AuxGen: 3 x 224kW 400V 50Hz a.c
9369253 *UFHM* -	**SVITZER ANIVA** **Svitzer Sakhalin BV** Svitzer Sakhalin Terminal Towage *Korsakov* *Russia*	**663** 198 590	Class: RS (LR) ✠ Classed LR until 29/2/12	**2007-02 ASL Shipyard Pte Ltd — Singapore** Yd No: 510 Loa 35.30 Br ex 13.50 Dght 5.800 Lbp 34.50 Br md 13.00 Dpth 6.82 Welded, 1 dk	**(B32A2ST) Tug** Ice Capable	**2 oil engines** reduction geared to sc. shafts driving 2 CP propellers Total Power: 4,800kW (6,526hp) 12.0kn Bergens C25: 33L8P 2 x 4 Stroke 8 Cy. 250 x 330 each-2400kW (3263bhp) Rolls Royce Marine AS-Norway AuxGen: 2 x 225kW 415V 50Hz a.c Fuel: 248.0 (d.f.)
9334090 *XJAG* -	**SVITZER BEDFORD** **Svitzer Canada Ltd** Svitzer Marine Ltd *Halifax, NS* *Canada* MMSI: 316012760 Official number: 827735	**370** 111 207	Class: LR ✠**100A1** SS 08/2010 tug, fire fighting Ship 1 (2400 cubic m/hr) *IWS ✠**LMC** **UMS** Eq.Ltr: G†; Cable: 302.5/24.0 U2 (a)	**2005-08 Astilleros y Servicios Navales S.A. (ASENAV) — Valdivia** Yd No: 146 Loa 32.50 Br ex 11.00 Dght 4.200 Lbp 31.00 Br md 10.50 Dpth 4.80 Welded, 1 dk	**(B32A2ST) Tug**	**2 oil engines** gearing integral to driving 2 Directional propellers Total Power: 4,000kW (5,438hp) Caterpillar 3516B-TA 2 x Vee 4 Stroke 16 Cy. 170 x 190 each-2000kW (2719bhp) Caterpillar Inc-USA AuxGen: 2 x 260kW 450V 60Hz a.c
9127356 *MVZF8* -	**SVITZER BENTLEY** *ex Bentley -2009* **Svitzer Towage Ltd** Svitzer Marine Ltd *Felixstowe* *United Kingdom* MMSI: 232002594 Official number: 728875	**381** 114 200	Class: LR ✠**100A1** SS 06/2011 tug limited European area *IWS ✠**LMC** **UMS** Eq.Ltr: H; Cable: 302.5/22.0 U2	**1996-06 Stocznia Polnocna SA (Northern Shipyard) — Gdansk** (Hull) **1996-06 B.V. Scheepswerf Damen — Gorinchem** Yd No: 7907 Loa 32.72 Br ex 11.96 Dght 4.250 Lbp 29.00 Br md 10.60 Dpth 5.00 Welded, 1 dk	**(B32A2ST) Tug**	**2 oil engines** gearing integral to driving 2 Z propellers Total Power: 3,602kW (4,898hp) 13.7kn Ruston 6RK270M 2 x 4 Stroke 6 Cy. 270 x 305 each-1801kW (2449bhp) Ruston Paxman Diesels Ltd.-United Kingdom AuxGen: 2 x 70kW 415V 50Hz a.c
9592410 *9V9608* -	**SVITZER BETA** **Svitzer Asia Pte Ltd** *Singapore* *Singapore* MMSI: 566244000 Official number: 397347	**906** 271 -	Class: LR (BV) **100A1** SS 10/2011 tug, fire-fighting Ship 1 (2400m3/h) with water spray *IWS **LMC** **UMS**	**2011-10 Qingdao Qianjin Shipyard — Qingdao SD** Yd No: 6Z20802 Loa 45.64 Br ex - Dght 5.300 Lbp 42.38 Br md 13.20 Dpth 6.00 Welded, 1 dk	**(B32A2ST) Tug**	**2 oil engines** reduction geared to sc. shafts driving 2 Z propellers Total Power: 4,412kW (5,998hp) Niigata 8L28HX 2 x 4 Stroke 8 Cy. 280 x 370 each-2206kW (2999bhp) Niigata Engineering Co Ltd-Japan AuxGen: 2 x 425kW 50Hz a.c Fuel: 540.0
8414166 *MDWA8* -	**SVITZER BEVOIS** *ex Sir Bevois -2007* **Svitzer Towage Ltd** Svitzer Marine Ltd *Southampton* *United Kingdom* MMSI: 235064905 Official number: 710339	**250** 75 94	Class: LR ✠**100A1** SS 08/2010 tug harbour towage operations in UK harbours only, voyages between UK harbours only, not more than 30 nautical miles from a safe haven in the UK ✠**LMC** Cable: 125.0/16.0 U2	**1985-08 McTay Marine Ltd. — Bromborough** Yd No: 58 Loa 29.37 Br ex 9.12 Dght 4.580 Lbp 28.00 Br md 9.01 Dpth 3.71 Welded, 1 dk	**(B32A2ST) Tug**	**2 oil engines** with clutches, flexible couplings & sr geared to sc. shafts driving 2 Directional propellers Total Power: 2,000kW (2,720hp) Kromhout 6FHD240 2 x 4 Stroke 6 Cy. 240 x 260 each-1000kW (1360bhp) Stork Werkspoor Diesel BV-Netherlands AuxGen: 2 x 80kW 440V 50Hz a.c
9286695 *MCYT8* -	**SVITZER BIDSTON** **Svitzer A/S** Svitzer Marine Ltd *Liverpool* *United Kingdom* MMSI: 235014278 Official number: 908307	**366** 109 210	Class: LR ✠**100A1** SS 02/2014 tug fire fighting Ship 1 (2700 cubic m/h) with water spray *IWS ✠**LMC** **UMS** Eq.Ltr: G; Cable: 302.5/22.0 U2 (a)	**2004-02 Astilleros Zamakona SA — Santurtzi** Yd No: 515 Loa 29.50 Br ex 11.45 Dght 5.900 Lbp 28.00 Br md 11.00 Dpth 4.00 Welded, 1 dk	**(B32A2ST) Tug**	**2 oil engines** gearing integral to driving 2 Z propellers Total Power: 3,236kW (4,400hp) 12.3kn Niigata 6L28HX 2 x 4 Stroke 6 Cy. 280 x 370 each-1618kW (2200bhp) Niigata Engineering Co Ltd-Japan AuxGen: 2 x 184kW 415V 50Hz a.c
9008665 *OWOW2* -	**SVITZER BJORN** *ex Bjorn Af Goteborg -2013* **Svitzer Sverige AB** Em Z Svitzer AS *Copenhagen* *Denmark (DIS)* MMSI: 219018811 Official number: D4641	**356** 106 125	Class: LR ✠**100A1** SS 11/2011 tug Skagerrak, Kattegat, Baltic Sea, Gulfs of Finland and Bothnia coastal service, also North Sea coastal service between Esbjerg and lighthouse Blankenberge Ice Class 1C ✠**LMC** **UMS** Eq.Ltr: (E) ; Cable: 275.0/17.5 U2	**1991-11 Matsuura Tekko Zosen K.K. — Osakikamijima** Yd No: 367 Loa 32.89 Br ex 11.01 Dght 3.890 Lbp 26.40 Br md 10.23 Dpth 4.49 Welded, 1 dk	**(B32A2ST) Tug** Ice Capable	**2 oil engines** with clutches, flexible couplings & dr geared to sc. shafts driving 2 Directional propellers Contr. pitch Total Power: 2,942kW (4,000hp) Yanmar 8Z280-ET 2 x 4 Stroke 8 Cy. 280 x 360 each-1471kW (2000bhp) Yanmar Diesel Engine Co Ltd-Japan AuxGen: 2 x 128kW 385V 50Hz a.c Thrusters: 1 Thwart. CP thruster (f)
9286683 *MCSV5* -	**SVITZER BOOTLE** **Svitzer A/S** Svitzer Marine Ltd *Liverpool* *United Kingdom* MMSI: 235013782 Official number: 908160	**366** 109 210	Class: LR ✠**100A1** SS 12/2013 tug, fire fighting Ship 1 (2700 cubic m/hr) with water spray *IWS ✠**LMC** **UMS** Eq.Ltr: G; Cable: 302.5/22.0 U2 (a)	**2003-12 Astilleros Zamakona SA — Santurtzi** Yd No: 514 Loa 29.50 Br ex 11.45 Dght 5.900 Lbp 28.00 Br md 11.00 Dpth 4.00 Welded, 1 dk	**(B32A2ST) Tug**	**2 oil engines** gearing integral to driving 2 Z propellers Total Power: 3,236kW (4,400hp) 12.0kn Niigata 6L28HX 2 x 4 Stroke 6 Cy. 280 x 370 each-1618kW (2200bhp) Niigata Engineering Co Ltd-Japan AuxGen: 2 x 184kW 415V 50Hz a.c
9388455 *9V7122* -	**SVITZER BRANI** **Svitzer Asia Pte Ltd** - *Singapore* *Singapore* MMSI: 565424000 Official number: 392926	**855** 256 256	Class: LR (BV) **100A1** SS 10/2012 tug, fire fighting Ship 1 (2400m3/hr) with water spray *IWS **LMC** **UMS**	**2007-09 Unithai Shipyard & Engineering, Ltd. — Si Racha** Yd No: 115 Loa 45.64 Br ex - Dght 4.800 Lbp 42.36 Br md 13.20 Dpth 6.00 Welded, 1 dk	**(B32A2ST) Tug** Cranes: 1x6t	**2 oil engines** gearing integral to driving 2 Z propellers Total Power: 4,412kW (5,998hp) Niigata 6L28HX 2 x 4 Stroke 6 Cy. 280 x 370 each-2206kW (2999bhp) Niigata Engineering Co Ltd-Japan Thrusters: 1 Tunnel thruster (f)

8420945 *GFVD* -	**SVITZER BRENDA** *ex* Lady Brenda *-2008 ex* Kenley *-1991* *launched as* Yokosuka Maru No. 2 *-1985* **Svitzer Humber Ltd** Svitzer Marine Ltd *Rochester* *United Kingdom* MMSI: 232003492 Official number: 709291	**360** 108 -	Class: LR **100A1** SS 10/2008 tug near Continental trading area **LMC** Eq.Ltr: F; Cable: 306.0/28.0 U2 (a)	**1985**-06 **Hanasaki Zosensho K.K. — Yokosuka** Yd No: 198 Loa 38.00 Br ex 10.27 Dght 3.204 Lbp 30.89 Br md 10.00 Dpth 4.40 Welded, 1 dk	**(B32A2ST) Tug**	**2 oil engines** sr geared to sc. shafts driving 2 FP propellers Total Power: 2,354kW (3,200hp) 13.0kn Niigata 6L28BXE 2 x 4 Stroke 6 Cy. 280 x 320 each-1177kW (1600bhp) Niigata Engineering Co Ltd-Japan AuxGen: 3 x 64kW 445V 60Hz a.c
9280005 *MAPN5* -	**SVITZER BRISTOL** **Svitzer A/S** Svitzer Marine Ltd *Bristol* *United Kingdom* MMSI: 235011376 Official number: 907153	*366* 109 210	Class: LR ✠**100A1** SS 07/2013 tug fire fighting Ship 1 (2400 cubic m/hr) with water spray *IWS ✠**LMC** **UMS** Eq.Ltr: G; Cable: 302.5/22.0 U2 (a)	**2003**-07 **Astilleros Zamakona SA — Santurtzi** Yd No: 576 Loa 29.50 Br ex 11.45 Dght 5.900 Lbp 28.00 Br md 11.00 Dpth 4.00 Welded, 1 dk	**(B32A2ST) Tug**	**2 oil engines** gearing integral to driving 2 Z propellers Total Power: 3,236kW (4,400hp) Niigata 6L28HX 2 x 4 Stroke 6 Cy. 280 x 370 each-1618kW (2200bhp) Niigata Engineering Co Ltd-Japan AuxGen: 2 x 184kW 415/240V 50Hz a.c
9273753 *MBTT2* -	**SVITZER BRUNEL** **Svitzer A/S** Svitzer Marine Ltd *Bristol* *United Kingdom* MMSI: 235012605 Official number: 907873	**366** 109 210	Class: LR ✠**100A1** SS 09/2008 tug, fire fighting Ship 1 (2400 cubic m/hr) with water spray *IWS ✠**LMC** **UMS** Eq.Ltr: G; Cable: 302.5/22.0 U2 (a)	**2003**-09 **Astilleros Zamakona SA — Santurtzi** Yd No: 577 Loa 29.50 Br ex 11.45 Dght 5.900 Lbp 28.00 Br md 11.00 Dpth 4.00 Welded, 1 dk	**(B32A2ST) Tug**	**2 oil engines** gearing integral to driving 2 Z propellers Total Power: 3,236kW (4,400hp) 12.3kn Niigata 6L28HLX 2 x 4 Stroke 6 Cy. 280 x 400 each-1618kW (2200bhp) Niigata Engineering Co Ltd-Japan AuxGen: 2 x 184kW 415V 50Hz a.c
9389605 *UDTE* -	**SVITZER BUSSE** **Svitzer Sakhalin BV** Svitzer Asia Pte Ltd *Korsakov* *Russia* MMSI: 273325800 Official number: 060548	**663** 198 527	Class: RS (LR) ✠ Classed LR until 29/2/12	**2007**-12 **Admiralteyskiy Sudostroitelnyy Zavod — Sankt-Peterburg** Yd No: 02211 Loa 35.40 Br ex 13.50 Dght 6.590 Lbp 34.50 Br md 13.00 Dpth 6.82 Welded, 1 dk	**(B32A2ST) Tug** Ice Capable	**2 oil engines** reduction geared to sc. shafts driving 2 Directional propellers Total Power: 4,800kW (6,526hp) 12.0kn Bergens C25: 33L8P 2 x 4 Stroke 8 Cy. 250 x 330 each-2400kW (3263bhp) Rolls Royce Marine AS-Norway AuxGen: 2 x 225kW 400V 50Hz a.c Thrusters: 1 Tunnel thruster (a) Fuel: 248.0 (d.f.)
9440887 *2BPD3* -	**SVITZER CALDEY** **Santander Lease SA EFC (Bansalease SA)** Svitzer Marine Ltd *Milford Haven* *United Kingdom* MMSI: 235068112 Official number: 915424	**690** 207 393	Class: LR ✠**100A1** SS 04/2009 escort tug, ((82,64,8,91) (89,69,10,121)), fire-fighting Ship 1 (2400m3/h) with water spray *IWS ✠**LMC** **UMS** Eq.Ltr: J; Cable: 357.5/26.0 U2 (a)	**2009**-04 **Construcciones Navales P Freire SA — Vigo** Yd No: 654 Loa 34.00 (BB) Br ex - Dght 4.500 Lbp 32.20 Br md 14.50 Dpth 6.20 Welded, 1 dk	**(B32A2ST) Tug**	**2 oil engines** gearing integral to driving 2 Z propellers Total Power: 4,412kW (5,998hp) 13.0kn Niigata 8L28HLX 2 x 4 Stroke 8 Cy. 280 x 400 each-2206kW (2999bhp) Niigata Engineering Co Ltd-Japan AuxGen: 2 x 390kW 415V 50Hz a.c
9542300 *OA4802* -	**SVITZER CANETE** **Svitzer Peru SA** - *Callao* *Peru* MMSI: 760000250	**625** 189 415	Class: LR ✠**100A1** SS 12/2009 escort tug, fire fighting Ship 1 (2400m3/h) with water spray *IWS ✠**LMC** **UMS** Eq.Ltr: I; Cable: 330.0/26.0 U2 (a)	**2009**-12 **Qingdao Qianjin Shipyard — Qingdao SD** Yd No: 6Z2020 Loa 32.60 Br ex 13.40 Dght 4.500 Lbp 28.60 Br md 13.00 Dpth 5.70 Welded, 1 dk	**(B32A2ST) Tug**	**2 oil engines** geared to sc. shafts driving 2 Directional propellers Total Power: 4,412kW (5,998hp) Niigata 8L28HX 2 x 4 Stroke 8 Cy. 280 x 370 each-2206kW (2999bhp) Niigata Engineering Co Ltd-Japan AuxGen: 3 x 150kW 400V 50Hz a.c Thrusters: 2 Thwart. FP thruster
9354997 *J8B4528* -	**SVITZER CARONI** **Svitzer (Americas) Ltd** Svitzer (Caribbean) Ltd *Kingstown* *St Vincent & The Grenadines* MMSI: 377516000 Official number: 11001	**436** 130 260	Class: LR ✠**100A1** SS 07/2011 tug, fire fighting ship 1 (2400 m3/hr) with water spray *IWS Deck load of 5 tonnes/m2 ✠**LMC** **UMS** Eq.Ltr: G; Cable: 302.5/20.5 U2 (a)	**2006**-08 **ASL Shipyard Pte Ltd — Singapore** Yd No: 517 Loa 31.34 Br ex 11.02 Dght 4.400 Lbp 26.80 Br md 11.00 Dpth 6.11 Welded, 1 dk	**(B32A2ST) Tug**	**2 oil engines** gearing integral to driving 2 Z propellers Total Power: 3,676kW (4,998hp) 13.0kn Niigata 6L28HX 2 x 4 Stroke 6 Cy. 280 x 370 each-1838kW (2499bhp) Niigata Engineering Co Ltd-Japan AuxGen: 2 x 150kW 400V 50Hz a.c
9316397 - -	**SVITZER CASTLE** *ex* Castle Point *-2012* **Svitzer Marine Ltd** - *London* *United Kingdom* Official number: 737464	**374** 112 260	Class: LR ✠**100A1** SS 03/2010 escort tug, fire fighting ship 1 (2400 cubic m/h) with water spray *IWS ✠**LMC** **UMS** Eq.Ltr: H; Cable: 302.5/22.0 U2 (a)	**2005**-03 **Damen Shipyards Gdynia SA — Gdynia** (Hull) Yd No: 511210 **2005**-03 **B.V. Scheepswerf Damen — Gorinchem** Yd No: 511210 Loa 32.50 Br ex 10.64 Dght 4.250 Lbp 29.01 Br md 10.60 Dpth 5.00 Welded, 1 dk	**(B32A2ST) Tug**	**2 oil engines** geared to sc. shafts driving 2 Directional propellers Total Power: 3,960kW (5,384hp) 13.0kn MaK 6M25 2 x 4 Stroke 6 Cy. 255 x 400 each-1980kW (2692bhp) Caterpillar Motoren GmbH & Co. KG-Germany AuxGen: 3 x 85kW 400V 50Hz a.c
8919207 *MNXE5* -	**SVITZER CECILIA** *ex* Lady Cecilia *-2009* **Svitzer Humber Ltd** Svitzer Marine Ltd *Grimsby* *United Kingdom* MMSI: 232003119 Official number: 720303	**364** 109 205	Class: LR ✠**100A1** SS 06/2011 tug for near continental trading area service, fire fighting ship 1 (2400m3/hr) ✠**LMC** **UMS** Eq.Ltr: G; Cable: 302.5/20.5 U2	**1991**-06 **McTay Marine — Bromborough** Yd No: 93 Loa 30.58 Br ex 11.50 Dght 3.400 Lbp 28.50 Br md 11.00 Dpth 4.28 Welded, 1 dk	**(B32A2ST) Tug**	**2 oil engines** gearing integral to driving 2 Voith-Schneider propellers Total Power: 3,480kW (4,732hp) 12.8kn Ruston 6RK270M 2 x 4 Stroke 6 Cy. 270 x 305 each-1740kW (2366bhp) Ruston Diesels Ltd.-Newton-le-Willows AuxGen: 2 x 80kW 415V 50Hz a.c
9324409 *XCEP3* -	**SVITZER CHEMUL** **Svitzer Caribbean A/S** Svitzer (Caribbean) Ltd *Progreso* *Mexico* Official number: 3101339825-7	**318** 95 -	Class: LR (AB) **100A1** SS 06/2009 tug **LMC** Cable: 660.0/20.5 U3 (a)	**2004**-06 **Jiangsu Wuxi Shipyard Co Ltd — Wuxi JS** (Hull) Yd No: (1161) **2004**-06 **Pacific Ocean Engineering & Trading Pte Ltd (POET) — Singapore** Yd No: 1161 Loa 28.00 Br ex - Dght 3.500 Lbp 22.40 Br md 9.80 Dpth 4.80 Welded, 1 dk	**(B32A2ST) Tug**	**2 oil engines** gearing integral to driving 2 Z propellers Total Power: 2,648kW (3,600hp) Yanmar 8N21A-EN 2 x 4 Stroke 8 Cy. 210 x 290 each-1324kW (1800bhp) Yanmar Diesel Engine Co Ltd-Japan AuxGen: 2 x 99kW a.c
9412402 *OA2784* -	**SVITZER CHINCHA** *ex* Svitze *-2010* **Svitzer Peru SA** - *Callao* *Peru* MMSI: 760000340	**600** 189 415	Class: LR ✠**100A1** SS 12/2009 escort tug, fire fighting Ship 1 (2400m3/h) with water spray *IWS ✠**LMC** **UMS** Eq.Ltr: I; Cable: 330.0/26.0 U2 (a)	**2009**-12 **Qingdao Qianjin Shipyard — Qingdao SD** Yd No: 6Z2019 Loa 32.60 Br ex 13.40 Dght 4.600 Lbp 28.60 Br md 13.00 Dpth 6.10 Welded, 1 dk	**(B32A2ST) Tug**	**2 oil engines** gearing integral to driving 2 Z propellers Total Power: 4,412kW (5,998hp) Niigata 8L28HLX 2 x 4 Stroke 8 Cy. 280 x 400 each-2206kW (2999bhp) Niigata Engineering Co Ltd-Japan AuxGen: 3 x 150kW 440V 50Hz a.c
9366885 *VJN3166* -	**SVITZER COLMSLIE** *ex* Adsteam Colac *-2007* **Svitzer Australia Pty Ltd (Svitzer Australasia)** - *Brisbane, Qld* *Australia* MMSI: 503194500 Official number: 858119	**250** 75 150	Class: LR ✠**100A1** SS 04/2012 tug **LMC** **UMS** Eq.Ltr: F; Cable: 275.0/19.0 U2 (a)	**2007**-04 **Song Cam Shipyard — Haiphong** (Hull) **2007**-04 **B.V. Scheepswerf Damen — Gorinchem** Yd No: 512209 Loa 24.47 Br ex 11.33 Dght 3.650 Lbp 22.16 Br md 10.70 Dpth 4.60 Welded, 1 dk	**(B32A2ST) Tug**	**2 oil engines** gearing integral to driving 2 Z propellers Total Power: 4,200kW (5,710hp) Caterpillar 3516B-HD 2 x Vee 4 Stroke 16 Cy. 170 x 215 each-2100kW (2855bhp) Caterpillar Inc-USA AuxGen: 2 x 60kW 400V 50Hz a.c
9431094 *CA2902* -	**SVITZER CONDOR** **Svitzer Chile SA** - *Valparaiso* *Chile* MMSI: 725000721 Official number: 3243	**439** 131 125	Class: LR ✠**100A1** SS 04/2009 tug, fire-fighting Ship 1 (2400m3/h) with water spray *IWS ✠**LMC** **UMS** Eq.Ltr: G; Cable: 302.5/24.0 U2 (a)	**2009**-04 **ASL Shipyard Pte Ltd — Singapore** Yd No: 578 Loa 30.81 (BB) Br ex 11.04 Dght 4.400 Lbp 26.50 Br md 11.00 Dpth 6.10 Welded, 1 dk	**(B32A2ST) Tug**	**2 oil engines** gearing integral to driving 2 Z propellers Total Power: 3,675kW (4,997hp) 13.0kn Niigata 6L28HX 2 x 4 Stroke 6 Cy. 280 x 370 each-1837kW (2498bhp) Niigata Engineering Co Ltd-Japan AuxGen: 2 x 150kW 400V 50Hz a.c

8102141 *GCRY* -	**SVITZER CONSTANCE** *ex* Lady Constance *-2007* **Svitzer Humber Ltd** Svitzer Marine Ltd *Hull* *United Kingdom* MMSI: 235053755 Official number: 389072	285 85 170	Class: LR ✠ **100A1** SS 05/2012 tug near Continental trading area ✠ **LMC** **UMS** Eq.Ltr: F; Cable: 275.0/19.0 U2 (a)	1982-03 **Cochrane Shipbuilders Ltd. — Selby** Yd No: 115 Loa 30.21 Br ex 9.73 Dght 2.810 Lbp 28.30 Br md 9.20 Dpth 3.81 Welded, 1 dk	(B32A2ST) Tug	**2 oil engines** gearing integral to driving 2 Voith-Schneider propellers Total Power: 1,942kW (2,640hp) 12.5kn Ruston 6RKCM 2 x 4 Stroke 6 Cy. 254 x 305 each-971kW (1320bhp) Ruston Diesels Ltd.-Newton-le-Willows AuxGen: 2 x 78kW 415V 50Hz a.c Fuel: 56.0 (d.f.)
9300738 *AUGC* -	**SVITZER DAMKA** **Svitzer Hazira Pvt Ltd** Svitzer Middle East Ltd *Mumbai* *India* MMSI: 419053200 Official number: 4009	451 135 500	Class: IR (LR) ✠ Classed LR until 11/7/10	2004-09 **ASL Shipyard Pte Ltd — Singapore** Yd No: 327 Loa 31.80 Br ex 10.52 Dght 4.541 Lbp 30.45 Br md 10.50 Dpth 5.60 Welded, 1 dk	(B32A2ST) Tug	**2 oil engines** gearing integral to driving 2 Z propellers Total Power: 3,676kW (4,998hp) 12.0kn Niigata 6L28HX 2 x 4 Stroke 6 Cy. 280 x 370 each-1838kW (2499bhp) Niigata Engineering Co Ltd-Japan AuxGen: 2 x 174kW 415V 50Hz a.c
9314337 *6ADY* -	**SVITZER DELTA** **Svitzer Idku SAE** Svitzer Middle East Ltd *Alexandria* *Egypt* MMSI: 622166804 Official number: 7927	*439* - 297	Class: LR ✠ **100A1** SS 02/2010 escort tug, firefighting Ship 1 (2400 cubic m/hr) with water spray *IWS ✠ **LMC** **UMS** Eq.Ltr: H; Cable: 302.5/22.0 U2 (a)	2005-02 **ASL Shipyard Pte Ltd — Singapore** Yd No: 348 Loa 31.92 Br ex 10.54 Dght 4.550 Lbp 30.78 Br md 10.50 Dpth 5.60 Welded, 1 dk	(B32A2ST) Tug	**2 oil engines** gearing integral to driving 2 Z propellers Total Power: 3,676kW (4,998hp) 12.0kn Niigata 6L28HX 2 x 4 Stroke 6 Cy. 280 x 370 each-1838kW (2499bhp) Niigata Engineering Co Ltd-Japan AuxGen: 1 x 168kW 415V 50Hz a.c, 1 x 90kW 415V 50Hz a.c
9370123 *VLD2006* -	**SVITZER DOOLJA** *ex* Adsteam Doolja *-2007* **Svitzer Australia Pty Ltd (Svitzer Australasia)** - *Port Adelaide, SA* *Australia* MMSI: 503525000 Official number: 858259	482 144 452	Class: LR (BV) **100A1** SS 12/2011 Australian coastal services within 200 miles from the nearest port of refuge **LMC** Eq.Ltr: J; Cable: 357.5/26.0 U2 (a)	2006-12 **Shin Yang Shipyard Sdn Bhd — Miri** Yd No: 200 Loa 46.00 Br ex Dght 2.500 Lbp 42.95 Br md 10.90 Dpth 3.20 Welded, 1 dk	(A35D2RL) Landing Craft Bow ramp (centre)	**2 oil engines** sr geared to sc. shafts driving 2 FP propellers Total Power: 894kW (1,216hp) 10.0kn Cummins KTA-19-M3 2 x 4 Stroke 6 Cy. 159 x 159 each-447kW (608bhp) Cummins Engine Co Inc-USA AuxGen: 2 x 85kW 415V 50Hz a.c Thrusters: 1 Thwart. FP thruster (f)
9431070 *VHDF* -	**SVITZER EAGLE** **Svitzer Australia Pty Ltd (Svitzer Australasia)** - *Fremantle, WA* *Australia* MMSI: 503583000 Official number: 858948	439 131 125	Class: LR ✠ **100A1** SS 11/2008 tug fire-fighting Ship 1 (2400m3/h) with water spray *IWS ✠ **LMC** **UMS** Eq.Ltr: G; Cable: 302.5/24.0 U2 (a)	2008-11 **ASL Shipyard Pte Ltd — Singapore** Yd No: 568 Loa 30.81 Br ex 11.04 Dght 4.400 Lbp 26.50 Br md 11.00 Dpth 6.10 Welded, 1 dk	(B32A2ST) Tug	**2 oil engines** gearing integral to driving 2 Z propellers Total Power: 3,676kW (4,998hp) 13.0kn Niigata 6L28HX 2 x 4 Stroke 6 Cy. 280 x 370 each-1838kW (2499bhp) Niigata Engineering Co Ltd-Japan AuxGen: 2 x 150kW 400V 50Hz a.c
9592513 *AVVF* -	**SVITZER ECHO** **Svitzer Hazira Pvt Ltd** - *Mumbai* *India* MMSI: 419000596 Official number: 3999	906 271 250	Class: IR (BV)	2012-02 **Qingdao Qianjin Shipyard — Qingdao SD** Yd No: 7Z20803 Loa 45.64 Br ex - Dght 5.100 Lbp 42.38 Br md 13.20 Dpth 6.00 Welded, 1 dk	(B32A2ST) Tug	**2 oil engines** reduction geared to sc. shafts driving 2 Z propellers Total Power: 4,412kW (5,998hp) Niigata 2 x 4 Stroke each-2206kW (2999bhp) Niigata Engineering Co Ltd-Japan
9314325 *6ADZ* -	**SVITZER ELBEHEIRA** **Svitzer Idku SAE** Svitzer Middle East Ltd *Alexandria* *Egypt* MMSI: 622166801 Official number: 7926	*439* - 297	Class: LR ✠ **100A1** SS 02/2010 escort tug, firefighting Ship 1 (2400 cubic m/hr) with water spray *IWS ✠ **LMC** **UMS** Eq.Ltr: H; Cable: 302.5/22.0 U2 (a)	2005-02 **ASL Shipyard Pte Ltd — Singapore** Yd No: 347 Loa 31.92 Br ex 10.54 Dght 4.550 Lbp 30.78 Br md 10.50 Dpth 5.60 Welded, 1 dk	(B32A2ST) Tug	**2 oil engines** gearing integral to driving 2 Z propellers Total Power: 3,676kW (4,998hp) 12.0kn Niigata 6L28HX 2 x 4 Stroke 6 Cy. 280 x 370 each-1838kW (2499bhp) Niigata Engineering Co Ltd-Japan AuxGen: 1 x 168kW 415V 50Hz a.c, 1 x 90kW 415V 50Hz a.c
9185231 *MYSV5* -	**SVITZER ELLERBY** *ex* Adsteam Ellerby *-2007* *ex* Lady Emma H *-2005* *ex* Lady Emma *-1998* *ex* Chek Chau *-1998* **Svitzer Humber Ltd** Svitzer Marine Ltd *Rochester* *United Kingdom* MMSI: 232003503 Official number: 901550	267 80 180	Class: LR (BV) **100A1** SS 02/2013 tug coastal service **LMC** Cable: 302.5/22.0 U2 (a)	1998-02 **Imamura Zosen — Kure** Yd No: 398 Loa 29.70 Br ex 9.60 Dght 3.750 Lbp 23.50 Br md 9.00 Dpth 4.70 Welded, 1 dk	(B32A2ST) Tug	**2 oil engines** gearing integral to driving 2 Z propellers Total Power: 2,650kW (3,602hp) 13.1kn Niigata 6L25HX 2 x 4 Stroke 6 Cy. 250 x 350 each-1325kW (1801bhp) Niigata Engineering Co Ltd-Japan AuxGen: 2 x 80kW 385V 50Hz a.c Fuel: 96.7 (d.f.) 5.5pd
9355006 *YYV5049* -	**SVITZER ENDEAVOUR** *ex* SV Abadan *-2012* *ex* Svitzer Abadan *-2011* **Svitzer (Caribbean) Ltd** - *Puerto la Cruz* *Venezuela* Official number: AGSP3.514	436 130 260	Class: LR ✠ **100A1** SS 07/2011 tug fire fighting ship 1 (2400 m3/hr) with water spray *IWS Deck load of 5 tonnes/m2 ✠ **LMC** **UMS** Eq.Ltr: G; Cable: 302.5/20.5 U2 (a)	2006-07 **ASL Shipyard Pte Ltd — Singapore** Yd No: 518 Loa 31.34 Br ex 11.02 Dght 4.400 Lbp 26.80 Br md 11.00 Dpth 6.11 Welded, 1 dk	(B32A2ST) Tug	**2 oil engines** gearing integral to driving 2 Z propellers Total Power: 3,676kW (4,998hp) 13.0kn Niigata 6L28HX 2 x 4 Stroke 6 Cy. 280 x 370 each-1838kW (2499bhp) Niigata Engineering Co Ltd-Japan AuxGen: 2 x 150kW 400V 50Hz a.c
9362499 *J8B4561* -	**SVITZER ENDURANCE** *ex* SV Khoramshahr *-2013* *ex* Svitzer Khoramshahr *-2011* **Svitzer Middle East Ltd** - *Kingstown* *St Vincent & The Grenadines* MMSI: 377258000 Official number: 11034	436 130 260	Class: LR ✠ **100A1** SS 12/2011 tug, fire fighting Ship 1 (2400m3/h) with water spray *IWS ✠ **LMC** **UMS** Eq.Ltr: G; Cable: 302.5/22.0 U2 (a)	2006-12 **ASL Shipyard Pte Ltd — Singapore** Yd No: 527 Loa 31.50 Br ex 11.50 Dght 4.400 Lbp 26.80 Br md 11.00 Dpth 6.10 Welded, 1 dk	(B32A2ST) Tug	**2 oil engines** gearing integral to driving 2 Z propellers Total Power: 3,676kW (4,998hp) 13.0kn Niigata 6L28HX 2 x 4 Stroke 6 Cy. 280 x 370 each-1838kW (2499bhp) Niigata Engineering Co Ltd-Japan AuxGen: 2 x 150kW 400V 50Hz a.c
9362528 *J8B4563* -	**SVITZER ENTERPRISE** *ex* SV Kashan *-2013* *ex* Svitzer Kashan *-2012* **Svitzer Middle East Ltd** - *Kingstown* *St Vincent & The Grenadines* MMSI: 376893000 Official number: 11036	436 130 267	Class: LR ✠ **100A1** SS 02/2012 tug, fire fighting Ship 1 (2400 m3/h) with water spray *IWS ✠ **LMC** Eq.Ltr: G; Cable: 302.5/22.0 U2 (a)	2007-02 **ASL Shipyard Pte Ltd — Singapore** Yd No: 538 Loa 31.50 Br ex 11.50 Dght 4.400 Lbp 26.80 Br md 11.00 Dpth 6.10 Welded, 1 dk	(B32A2ST) Tug	**2 oil engines** reduction geared to sc. shafts driving 2 Directional propellers Total Power: 3,676kW (4,998hp) 13.0kn Niigata 6L28HX 2 x 4 Stroke 6 Cy. 280 x 370 each-1838kW (2499bhp) Niigata Engineering Co Ltd-Japan AuxGen: 2 x 150kW 400V 50Hz a.c
9431082 *VHDG* -	**SVITZER FALCON** **Svitzer Australia Pty Ltd (Svitzer Australasia)** - *Fremantle, WA* *Australia* MMSI: 503588000 Official number: 858982	439 131 249	Class: LR ✠ **100A1** SS 01/2009 tug, fire fighting Ship 1 (2400m3/h) with water spray *IWS ✠ **LMC** **UMS** Eq.Ltr: G; Cable: 302.5/24.0 U2 (a)	2009-01 **ASL Shipyard Pte Ltd — Singapore** Yd No: 577 Loa 31.50 Br ex 11.04 Dght 4.400 Lbp 26.50 Br md 11.00 Dpth 6.10 Welded, 1 dk	(B32A2ST) Tug	**2 oil engines** gearing integral to driving 2 Z propellers Total Power: 3,675kW (4,997hp) 13.0kn Niigata 6L28HX 2 x 4 Stroke 6 Cy. 280 x 370 each-1837kW (2498bhp) Niigata Engineering Co Ltd-Japan AuxGen: 2 x 150kW 400V 50Hz a.c
9277618 *MHMR3* -	**SVITZER FERRIBY** *ex* Adsteam Ferriby *-2007* **Svitzer SPC4 Pty Ltd** Svitzer Marine Ltd *Grimsby* *United Kingdom* MMSI: 235025323 Official number: 909914	207 72 150	Class: LR ✠ **100A1** SS 04/2010 tug **LMC** **UMS** Eq.Ltr: F; Cable: 275.0/17.5 U2 (a)	2005-04 **Damen Shipyards Changde Co Ltd — Changde HN** (Hull) Yd No: 512202 2005-04 **B.V. Scheepswerf Damen — Gorinchem** Yd No: 512202 Loa 24.55 Br ex 11.50 Dght 3.905 Lbp 22.16 Br md 10.70 Dpth 4.59 Welded, 1 dk	(B32A2ST) Tug	**2 oil engines** gearing integral to driving 2 Z propellers Total Power: 4,170kW (5,670hp) Caterpillar 3516B 2 x Vee 4 Stroke 16 Cy. 170 x 215 each-2085kW (2835bhp) Caterpillar Inc-USA AuxGen: 2 x 85kW 400V 50Hz a.c
9388467 *9V7125* -	**SVITZER FORTI** **Svitzer Asia Pte Ltd** - *Singapore* *Singapore* MMSI: 565447000 Official number: 392939	855 256 300	Class: LR (BV) **100A1** SS 11/2012 tug, fire fighting Ship 1 (2400m3/h) with water spray *IWS **LMC** **UMS**	2007-11 **Unithai Shipyard & Engineering, Ltd. — Si Racha** Yd No: 116 Loa 45.64 Br ex - Dght 4.800 Lbp 42.38 Br md 13.20 Dpth 6.00 Welded, 1 dk	(B32A2ST) Tug Cranes: 1x6t	**2 oil engines** gearing integral to driving 2 Z propellers Total Power: 4,412kW (5,998hp) Niigata 6L28HLX 2 x 4 Stroke 6 Cy. 280 x 400 each-2206kW (2999bhp) Niigata Engineering Co Ltd-Japan Thrusters: 1 Tunnel thruster (f)

IMO / Call sign	Name / Owner / Manager	Tonnage	Classification	Builder / Dimensions	Type	Machinery
9592525 *9VBD8* -	**SVITZER FOXTROT** **Svitzer Asia Pte Ltd** - *Singapore* *Singapore* MMSI: 566509000 Official number: 397848	**906** 271 250	Class: LR (BV) **100A1** SS 03/2012 tug, fire fighting Ship 1 (2400m3/hr) with water spray *IWS **LMC** **UMS**	**2012-03 Qingdao Qianjin Shipyard — Qingdao SD** Yd No: 7Z20804 Loa 45.64 Br ex - Dght 5.300 Lbp 42.78 Br md 13.20 Dpth 6.00 Welded, 1 dk	**(B32A2ST) Tug**	**2 oil engines** reduction geared to sc. shafts driving 2 Z propellers Total Power: 4,412kW (5,998hp) Niigata 8L28HX 2 x 4 Stroke 8 Cy. 280 x 370 each-2206kW (2999bhp) Niigata Engineering Co Ltd-Japan Thrusters: 1 Tunnel thruster (f)
8714255 *CSYR9* -	**SVITZER FUNCHAL** *ex* Lavan *-2013* *ex* SV Lavan *-2012* *ex* Lavan *-2011* *ex* Tenax *-2003* **Svitzer EuroMed BV** Svitzer Portugal - Reboques Maritimos SA *Lisbon* *Portugal* MMSI: 263602556 Official number: LX-121-RC	**429** 128 400	Class: LR (NV) **100A1** SS 06/2013 tug not exceeding 60 nautical miles coastal service upper deck strengthened for the carriage of heavy UDL, max. UDL not to exceed 5.0 tonne/square m *IWS **LMC** **UMS** Cable: 357.5/28.0 U2 (a)	**1988-07 Batservice Verft AS — Mandal** Yd No: 674 Loa 33.30 Br ex - Dght 5.020 Lbp 29.95 Br md 10.00 Dpth 5.60 Welded, 1 dk	**(B32A2ST) Tug**	**2 oil engines** with clutches, flexible couplings & sr geared to sc. shafts driving 2 Z propellers Total Power: 3,200kW (4,350hp) 13.3kn MaK 8M332AK 2 x 4 Stroke 8 Cy. 240 x 330 each-1600kW (2175bhp) (made 1987, fitted 1988) Krupp MaK Maschinenbau GmbH-Kiel AuxGen: 2 x 160kW 380V 50Hz a.c Thrusters: 1 Thwart. FP thruster (f) Fuel: 98.5 (d.f.) 6.0pd
9602447 *OZ2134* -	**SVITZER GAIA** **P/F Svitzer Faroe Islands** Svitzer Sverige AB *Torshavn* *Faeroes (FAS)* MMSI: 231846000	**433** 129 349	Class: LR ✠**100A1** SS 01/2012 tug, fire-fighting Ship 1 (2400 m3/h) with water spray *IWS EP (A, 0, S) main deck aft of frame 10, strengthened for load of 5 tonnes/m2 ✠**LMC** **UMS** Eq.Ltr: G; Cable: 302.5/24.0 U2 (a)	**2012-01 AB "Baltijos" Laivu Statykla — Klaipeda** Yd No: 901 Loa 31.50 Br ex 11.50 Dght 4.250 Lbp 26.80 Br md 11.00 Dpth 5.70 Welded, 1 dk	**(B32A2ST) Tug**	**3 diesel electric oil engines** driving 3 gen. each 1668kW 690V a.c Connecting to 2 elec. motors each (2100kW) reduction geared to sc. shafts driving 2 Directional propellers Total Power: 4,800kW (6,525hp) Wartsila 8L20 3 x 4 Stroke 8 Cy. 200 x 280 each-1600kW (2175bhp) Wartsila Finland Oy-Finland Thrusters: 1 Thwart. FP thruster (f)
9412373 *2AXZ5* -	**SVITZER GELLISWICK** **Svitzer Marine Ltd** - *Milford Haven* *United Kingdom* MMSI: 235063849 Official number: 914881	**490** 147 375	Class: LR ✠**100A1** SS 08/2013 escort tug, fire fighting Ship 1 (2400m3/h) with water sray *IWS ✠**LMC** **UMS** Eq.Ltr: H; Cable: 302.5/24.0 U2 (a)	**2008-08 Qingdao Qianjin Shipyard — Qingdao SD** Yd No: 6Z2016 Loa 32.60 Br ex 12.10 Dght 4.500 Lbp 28.60 Br md 11.60 Dpth 5.70 Welded, 1 dk	**(B32A2ST) Tug**	**2 oil engines** gearing integral to driving 2 Z propellers Total Power: 4,412kW (5,998hp) 12.0kn Niigata 8L28HX 2 x 4 Stroke 8 Cy. 280 x 370 each-2206kW (2999bhp) Niigata Engineering Co Ltd-Japan AuxGen: 2 x 150kW 400V 50Hz a.c Boilers: HWH (o.f.) 4.1kgf/cm² (4.0bar)
9602459 *OZ2142* -	**SVITZER GEO** **P/F Svitzer Faroe Islands** Svitzer Sverige AB *Torshavn* *Faeroes (FAS)* MMSI: 231848000	**433** 129 169	Class: LR ✠**100A1** SS 05/2012 tug, fire-fighting Ship 1 (2400m3/h) with water spray *IWS EP (A,0,S) main deck aft of frame 10, strengthened for load of 5 tonnes/m2 ✠**LMC** **UMS** Eq.Ltr: G; Cable: 302.5/24.0 U2 (a)	**2012-05 AB "Baltijos" Laivu Statykla — Klaipeda** Yd No: 902 Loa 31.50 Br ex 11.50 Dght 4.250 Lbp 26.80 Br md 11.00 Dpth 5.70 Welded, 1 dk	**(B32A2ST) Tug**	**3 diesel electric oil engines** driving 3 gen. each 1668kW 690V a.c Connecting to 2 elec. motors each (2100kW) driving 2 Directional propellers Total Power: 4,800kW (6,525hp) 10.5kn Wartsila 8L20 3 x 4 Stroke 8 Cy. 200 x 280 each-1600kW (2175bhp) Wartsila Finland Oy-Finland Thrusters: 1 Thwart. FP thruster (f)
9373682 *VNDC* -	**SVITZER GINGA** *ex* Adsteam Ginga *-2007* **Svitzer Australia Pty Ltd (Svitzer Australasia)** - *Darwin, NT* *Australia* MMSI: 503516000 Official number: 857812	**355** 106 210	Class: AB	**2006-02 PT Nanindah Mutiara Shipyard — Batam** Yd No: T152 Loa 30.00 Br ex - Dght - Lbp 28.67 Br md 10.80 Dpth 4.20 Welded, 1 dk	**(B32A2ST) Tug**	**2 oil engines** reduction geared to sc. shafts driving 2 Directional propellers Total Power: 3,372kW (4,584hp) Caterpillar 3516B-HD 2 x Vee 4 Stroke 16 Cy. 170 x 215 each-1686kW (2292bhp) Caterpillar Inc-USA AuxGen: 2 x 84kW a.c
9359430 *J8B4765* -	**SVITZER GRAND BAHAMA** **Freepoint Tug & Towing Services** Svitzer (Caribbean) Ltd *Kingstown* *St Vincent & The Grenadines* MMSI: 376256000 Official number: 11238	**330** 99 160	Class: LR (AB) **100A1** SS 06/2012 tug Bahamas coastal service **LMC**	**2007-06 Jiangsu Wuxi Shipyard Co Ltd — Wuxi JS** (Hull) Yd No: (1247) **2007-06 Pacific Ocean Engineering & Trading Pte Ltd (POET) — Singapore** Yd No: 1247 Loa 28.00 Br ex - Dght 4.000 Lbp 22.94 Br md 9.80 Dpth 4.90 Welded, 1 dk	**(B32A2ST) Tug**	**2 oil engines** reduction geared to sc. shafts driving 2 Z propellers Total Power: 2,648kW (3,600hp) Yanmar 8N21A-EV 2 x 4 Stroke 8 Cy. 210 x 290 each-1324kW (1800bhp) Yanmar Diesel Engine Co Ltd-Japan AuxGen: 2 x 99kW a.c
9366914 *VJSH* -	**SVITZER HAMILTON** *ex* Svitzer Kiama *-2007* *launched as* Adsteam Kiama *-2007* **Svitzer Australia Pty Ltd (Svitzer Australasia)** - *Newcastle, NSW* *Australia* MMSI: 503544000 Official number: 858278	**250** 75 123	Class: LR (BV) ✠**100A1** SS 07/2012 tug **LMC** **UMS** Eq.Ltr: F; Cable: 275.0/19.0 U2 (a)	**2007-07 Song Cam Shipyard — Haiphong** (Hull) **2007-07 B.V. Scheepswerf Damen — Gorinchem** Yd No: 512212 Loa 24.47 Br ex 11.33 Dght 3.650 Lbp 22.16 Br md 10.70 Dpth 4.60 Welded, 1 dk	**(B32A2ST) Tug**	**2 oil engines** gearing integral to driving 2 Z propellers Total Power: 4,200kW (5,710hp) Caterpillar 3516B-HD 2 x Vee 4 Stroke 16 Cy. 170 x 215 each-2100kW (2855bhp) Caterpillar Inc-USA AuxGen: 2 x 60kW 400V 50Hz a.c
9554327 *VHDR* -	**SVITZER HARRIER** **Svitzer Australia Pty Ltd (Svitzer Australasia)** - *Fremantle, WA* *Australia* MMSI: 503711000 Official number: 860160	**442** 132 270	Class: LR ✠**100A1** SS 10/2011 tug, fire-fighting Ship 1 (2400 m3/h) with water spray *IWS WDL (5t/m2 from aft to frame 15) ✠**LMC** **UMS** Eq.Ltr: H; Cable: 302.5/22.0 U2 (a)	**2011-10 Jiangsu Zhenjiang Shipyard Co Ltd — Zhenjiang JS** Yd No: VZJ6173-0804 Loa 30.80 Br ex 11.32 Dght 5.300 Lbp 26.80 Br md 11.00 Dpth 6.10 Welded, 1 dk	**(B32A2ST) Tug**	**2 oil engines** gearing integral to driving 2 Z propellers Total Power: 3,676kW (4,998hp) Niigata 6L28HX 2 x 4 Stroke 6 Cy. 280 x 370 each-1838kW (2499bhp) Niigata Engineering Co Ltd-Japan AuxGen: 2 x 120kW 400V 50Hz a.c
9366861 *MLES7* -	**SVITZER HARTY** *ex* Adsteam Harty *-2007* **Svitzer SPC4 Pty Ltd** Svitzer Marine Ltd *Rochester* *United Kingdom* MMSI: 235032474 Official number: 910990	**207** 207 150	Class: LR (BV) ✠**100A1** SS 02/2011 tug, fire fighting (2400 cubic m/h) with water spray limited European area service *IWS **LMC** **UMS** Eq.Ltr: F; Cable: 275.0/17.5 U2 (a)	**2006-02 Song Cam Shipyard — Haiphong** (Hull) Yd No: (512204) **2006-02 B.V. Scheepswerf Damen — Gorinchem** Yd No: 512204 Loa 24.55 Br ex 11.50 Dght 3.526 Lbp 22.16 Br md 10.70 Dpth 4.60 Welded, 1 dk	**(B32A2ST) Tug**	**2 oil engines** gearing integral to driving 2 Z propellers Total Power: 4,200kW (5,710hp) Caterpillar 3516B-HD 2 x Vee 4 Stroke 16 Cy. 170 x 215 each-2100kW (2855bhp) Caterpillar Inc-USA AuxGen: 2 x 50kW 400V 50Hz a.c Thrusters: 2 Thwart. FP thruster (f)
9440760 *2BOS5* -	**SVITZER HAVEN** **Santander Lease SA EFC (Bansalease SA)** Svitzer Marine Ltd *Milford Haven* *United Kingdom* MMSI: 235067991 Official number: 915405	**690** 207 -	Class: LR ✠**100A1** SS 03/2009 escort tug, fire fighting Ship 1 (2400 m3/h) with water spray *IWS ✠**LMC** **UMS** Eq.Ltr: J; Cable: 357.5/26.0 U2 (a)	**2009-03 Construcciones Navales P Freire SA — Vigo** Yd No: 653 Loa 34.00 Br ex 15.20 Dght 4.500 Lbp 32.20 Br md 14.50 Dpth 6.20 Welded, 1 dk	**(B32A2ST) Tug**	**2 oil engines** gearing integral to driving 2 Directional propellers Total Power: 5,754kW (7,824hp) 13.0kn General Electric 7FDM16 2 x Vee 4 Stroke 16 Cy. 229 x 267 each-2877kW (3912bhp) GE Marine Engines-Cincinnati, Oh AuxGen: 2 x 390kW 415V 50Hz a.c
9431068 *H9ZT* -	**SVITZER HAWK** **Svitzer Canada Ltd** Svitzer (Caribbean) Ltd *Panama* *Panama* MMSI: 370827000 Official number: 4001709C	**439** 131 249	Class: LR ✠**100A1** SS 09/2013 tug fire fighting Ship 1 (2400m3/h) with water spray *IWS ✠**LMC** **UMS** Eq.Ltr: G; Cable: 302.5/20.5 U2 (a)	**2008-09 ASL Shipyard Pte Ltd — Singapore** Yd No: 567 Loa 31.50 Br ex 11.50 Dght 4.400 Lbp 26.80 Br md 11.00 Dpth 6.10 Welded, 1 dk	**(B32A2ST) Tug**	**2 oil engines** gearing integral to driving 2 Z propellers Total Power: 3,676kW (4,998hp) 13.0kn Niigata 6L28HX 2 x 4 Stroke 6 Cy. 280 x 370 each-1838kW (2499bhp) Niigata Engineering Co Ltd-Japan AuxGen: 2 x 150kW 400V 50Hz a.c

7321659 *OULX2* -	**SVITZER HELIOS** *ex Arctic Helios -2008 ex Helios -1985* *ex Victoria -1981* **Svitzer Sverige AB** *Esbjerg* *Denmark (DIS)* MMSI: 219011629 Official number: D4387	304 91 -	Class: LR ✠100A1 SS 05/2010 tug Danish, Swedish and German Coastal Service Ice Class 1 Ice Class 1A ✠LMC Eq.Ltr: (e) ; Cable: U2	**1973-10 AB Asi-Verken — Amal** Yd No: 103 Loa 32.90 Br ex 9.76 Dght 4.331 Lbp 29.19 Br md 9.50 Dpth 5.31 Welded, 1 dk	**(B32A2ST) Tug** Ice Capable	**1 oil engine** driving 1 CP propeller Total Power: 2,354kW (3,200hp) Nohab F216V 1 x Vee 4 Stroke 16 Cy. 250 x 300 2354kW (3200bhp) AB NOHAB-Sweden AuxGen: 2 x 120kW 380V 50Hz a.c
9578581 *VJN4315* -	**SVITZER HERON** - **Svitzer Australia Pty Ltd (Svitzer Australasia)** *Port Adelaide, SA* *Australia* MMSI: 503784000 Official number: 860798	442 132 276	Class: LR ✠100A1 SS 06/2012 tug, fire-fighting Ship 1 (2400 m3/h) with water spray *IWS WDL (5t/m2 from aft to frame 15) ✠LMC UMS Eq.Ltr: H; Cable: 302.5/24.0 U2 (a)	**2012-06 Jiangsu Zhenjiang Shipyard Co Ltd — Zhenjiang JS** Yd No: VZJ6173-0810 Loa 31.57 Br ex 11.32 Dght 4.600 Lbp 26.73 Br md 11.00 Dpth 6.10 Welded, 1 dk	**(B32A2ST) Tug**	**2 oil engines** gearing integral to driving 2 Z propellers Total Power: 3,676kW (4,998hp) Niigata 6L28HX 2 x 4 Stroke 6 Cy. 280 x 370 each-1838kW (2499bhp) Niigata Engineering Co Ltd-Japan AuxGen: 2 x 150kW 400V 50Hz a.c
9517850 *J8B5010* -	**SVITZER HONESTY** *ex Fgm Honesty -2014 ex Posh Honesty -2011* **Svitzer (Caribbean) Ltd** Transport & Offshore Services BV (TOS) *Kingstown* *St Vincent & The Grenadines* Official number: 11483	472 141 345	Class: LR ✠100A1 SS 12/2010 tug ✠LMC Eq.Ltr: H; Cable: 302.5/22.0 U2 (a)	**2010-12 Yuexin Shipbuilding Co Ltd — Guangzhou GD** Yd No: 3117 Loa 32.00 Br ex 12.23 Dght 4.300 Lbp 25.85 Br md 11.59 Dpth 5.36 Welded, 1 dk	**(B32A2ST) Tug**	**2 oil engines** gearing integral to driving 2 Z propellers Total Power: 3,840kW (5,220hp) Caterpillar 3516B-HD 2 x Vee 4 Stroke 16 Cy. 170 x 215 each-1920kW (2610bhp) Caterpillar Inc-USA AuxGen: 2 x 136kW 415V 50Hz a.c
9517836 *J8B4992* -	**SVITZER HONOUR** *ex Fgm Honour -2014 ex Posh Honour -2011* **Svitzer (Caribbean) Ltd** Transport & Offshore Services Ship Delivery BV (TOS Ship Delivery) *Kingstown* *St Vincent & The Grenadines* MMSI: 376937000 Official number: 11465	472 141 346	Class: LR ✠100A1 SS 06/2010 tug ✠LMC Eq.Ltr: H; Cable: 302.5/22.0 U2 (a)	**2010-06 Yuexin Shipbuilding Co Ltd — Guangzhou GD** Yd No: 3115 Loa 32.00 Br ex 12.23 Dght 4.560 Lbp 25.93 Br md 11.60 Dpth 5.36 Welded, 1 dk	**(B32A2ST) Tug**	**2 oil engines** gearing integral to driving 2 Z propellers Total Power: 3,840kW (5,220hp) Caterpillar 3516B 2 x Vee 4 Stroke 16 Cy. 170 x 215 each-1920kW (2610bhp) Caterpillar Inc-USA AuxGen: 2 x 136kW 415V 50Hz a.c
9354973 *A4DQ8* -	**SVITZER HORMUZ** - **Svitzer Middle East Ltd** *Port Sultan Qaboos* *Oman* MMSI: 461000437 Official number: 1277	436 130 260	Class: LR ✠100A1 SS 05/2011 tug fire fighting ship 1 (2400 cubic m/hr) with water spray *IWS Deck load of 5 tonnes/M2 ✠LMC UMS Eq.Ltr: G; Cable: 302.5/22.0 U2 (a)	**2006-05 ASL Shipyard Pte Ltd — Singapore** Yd No: 507 Loa 31.34 Br ex 11.02 Dght 4.000 Lbp 26.80 Br md 11.00 Dpth 6.11 Welded, 1 dk	**(B32A2ST) Tug**	**2 oil engines** gearing integral to driving 2 Directional propellers Total Power: 3,676kW (4,998hp) 13.0kn Niigata 6L28HX 2 x 4 Stroke 6 Cy. 280 x 370 each-1838kW (2499bhp) Niigata Engineering Co Ltd-Japan AuxGen: 2 x 150kW 400V 50Hz a.c
9547855 *2FEW8* -	**SVITZER HUTTON** *ex Svitzer Nabi -2012 ex Stevns Breaker -2011* **Svitzer Marine Ltd** *Middlesbrough* *United Kingdom* MMSI: 235090671 Official number: D4421	381 114 190	Class: LR ✠100A1 SS 05/2010 tug, fire-fighting Ship 1 (2400m3/h) with water spray ✠LMC UMS Eq.Ltr: G; Cable: 330.0/20.0 U2 (a)	**2010-05 East Isle Shipyard Ltd — Georgetown PE** Yd No: 96 Loa 30.65 Br ex 11.72 Dght 3.940 Lbp 28.83 Br md 11.12 Dpth 5.25 Welded, 1 dk	**(B32A2ST) Tug**	**2 oil engines** gearing integral to driving 2 Directional propellers Total Power: 4,000kW (5,438hp) Caterpillar 3516B-HD 2 x Vee 4 Stroke 16 Cy. 170 x 190 each-2000kW (2719bhp) Caterpillar Inc-USA AuxGen: 2 x 165kW 400V 50Hz a.c Thrusters: 1 Tunnel thruster (f)
9495375 *OZ2135* -	**SVITZER HYMER** **P/F Svitzer Faroe Islands** Svitzer Sverige AB *Torshavn* *Faeroes (FAS)* MMSI: 231847000	575 172 150	Class: LR ✠100A1 SS 03/2010 escort tug, fire fighting Ship 1 (2400m3/h) with water spray *IWS Ice Class 1B FS at draught of 3.75m Max/min draught fwd 3.75/2.7m Max/min draught aft 3.75/2.7m Required power 1000kw, installed power 5280kw ✠LMC UMS Eq.Ltr: I; Cable: 330.0/86.0 U3 (a)	**2010-03 Astilleros Zamakona Pasaia SL — Pasaia** Yd No: 683 Loa 35.04 Br ex - Dght 4.040 Lbp 34.80 Br md 12.50 Dpth 4.75 Welded, 1 dk	**(B32A2ST) Tug** Ice Capable	**2 oil engines** gearing integral to driving 2 Voith-Schneider propellers Total Power: 5,280kW (7,178hp) GE Marine 16V228 2 x Vee 4 Stroke 16 Cy. 229 x 267 each-2640kW (3589bhp) GE Marine Engines-Cincinnati, Oh AuxGen: 2 x 294kW 400V 50Hz a.c
9314301 *6ADW* -	**SVITZER IDKU** - **Svitzer Idku SAE** Svitzer Middle East Ltd *Alexandria* *Egypt* MMSI: 622166803 Official number: 7925	436 130 293	Class: LR ✠100A1 SS 01/2010 tug, fire fighting Ship 1 (2400 cubic m/h) with water spray *IWS ✠LMC UMS Eq.Ltr: H; Cable: 302.5/22.0 U2 (a)	**2005-01 ASL Shipyard Pte Ltd — Singapore** Yd No: 337 Loa 31.92 Br ex 10.54 Dght 4.550 Lbp 30.78 Br md 10.50 Dpth 5.60 Welded, 1 dk	**(B32A2ST) Tug**	**2 oil engines** gearing integral to driving 2 Z propellers Total Power: 3,676kW (4,998hp) 12.0kn Niigata 6L28HX 2 x 4 Stroke 6 Cy. 280 x 370 each-1838kW (2499bhp) Niigata Engineering Co Ltd-Japan AuxGen: 1 x 168kW 415V 50Hz a.c, 1 x 90kW 415V 50Hz a.c
9342334 *MPQD* -	**SVITZER INTREPID** *ex Adsteam Intrepid -2007 ex Champion -2007* *ex Tadami Maru -2007* **Svitzer Towage Ltd** Svitzer Marine Ltd *London* *United Kingdom* MMSI: 235051992 Official number: 912723	*395* 119 250	Class: LR (NK) 100A1 SS 01/2010 tug U.K. coastal service *IWS LMC UMS Eq.Ltr: B; Cable: 331.0/25.0 U2 (a)	**2005-01 Kanagawa Zosen — Kobe** Yd No: 533 Loa 32.50 Br ex - Dght 3.715 Lbp 27.80 Br md 11.40 Dpth 4.40 Welded, 1 dk	**(B32A2ST) Tug**	**2 oil engines** gearing integral to driving 2 Z propellers Total Power: 3,236kW (4,400hp) 13.5kn Niigata 6L28HX 2 x 4 Stroke 6 Cy. 280 x 370 each-1618kW (2200bhp) Niigata Engineering Co Ltd-Japan AuxGen: 2 x 104kW 225V 60Hz a.c
8919219 *MPGP3* -	**SVITZER JOSEPHINE** *ex Adsteam Josephine -2007* *ex Lady Josephine -2007* **Svitzer Humber Ltd** Svitzer Marine Ltd *Grimsby* *United Kingdom* MMSI: 232003118 Official number: 720314	364 109 279	Class: LR ✠100A1 SS 08/2011 tug for near continental trading area service, fire fighting ship 1 (2400m3/hr) ✠LMC UMS Eq.Ltr: G; Cable: 302.5/20.5 U2	**1991-08 McTay Marine — Bromborough** Yd No: 94 Loa 30.58 Br ex 11.50 Dght 3.400 Lbp 28.50 Br md 11.00 Dpth 4.28 Welded, 1 dk	**(B32A2ST) Tug**	**2 oil engines** gearing integral to driving 2 Voith-Schneider propellers Total Power: 3,480kW (4,732hp) 12.8kn Ruston 6RK270M 2 x 4 Stroke 6 Cy. 270 x 305 each-1740kW (2366bhp) Ruston Diesels Ltd.-Newton-le-Willows AuxGen: 2 x 80kW 415V 50Hz a.c
9464194 *J8B5022* -	**SVITZER KALLANG** - **Svitzer Middle East Ltd** *Kingstown* *St Vincent & The Grenadines* MMSI: 375333000 Official number: 11495	493 147 280	Class: LR ✠100A1 SS 09/2009 tug, fire fighting Ship 1 (2400m3/h) with water spray *IWS ✠LMC UMS Eq.Ltr: I; Cable: 330.0/26.0 U2 (a)	**2009-09 Qingdao Qianjin Shipyard — Qingdao SD** Yd No: 6Z20511 Loa 36.80 Br ex 11.50 Dght 4.500 Lbp 31.10 Br md 11.50 Dpth 5.40 Welded, 1 dk	**(B32A2ST) Tug**	**2 oil engines** gearing integral to driving 2 Z propellers Total Power: 3,676kW (4,998hp) 13.0kn Niigata 6L28HX 2 x 4 Stroke 6 Cy. 280 x 370 each-1838kW (2499bhp) Niigata Engineering Co Ltd-Japan AuxGen: 3 x 150kW 400V 50Hz a.c
9396919 *A9D2928* -	**SVITZER KARAK** - **Svitzer Wijsmuller Bahrain** Svitzer Middle East Ltd *Bahrain* *Bahrain* MMSI: 408316000 Official number: BN 4097	318 95 162	Class: LR (AB) 100A1 SS 10/2011 tug LMC Cable: 302.0/20.5 SL	**2006-10 Jiangsu Wuxi Shipyard Co Ltd — Wuxi JS (Hull)** Yd No: H1221 **2006-10 Pacific Ocean Engineering & Trading Pte Ltd (POET) — Singapore** Yd No: 1221 Loa 27.70 Br ex - Dght 4.012 Lbp 22.94 Br md 9.80 Dpth 4.90 Welded, 1 dk	**(B32A2ST) Tug**	**2 oil engines** gearing integral to driving 2 Z propellers Total Power: 2,648kW (3,600hp) Yanmar 8N21A-EN 2 x 4 Stroke 8 Cy. 210 x 290 each-1324kW (1800bhp) Yanmar Diesel Engine Co Ltd-Japan AuxGen: 2 x 99kW 380V 50Hz a.c
8919180 *MMWE7* -	**SVITZER KATHLEEN** *ex Adsteam Kathleen -2007* *ex Lady Kathleen -2006* **Svitzer Humber Ltd** Svitzer Marine Ltd *Grimsby* *United Kingdom* MMSI: 232003120 Official number: 709341	364 109 279	Class: LR ✠100A1 SS 01/2011 tug for near continental trading area service, fire fighting ship 1 (2400m3/hr) *IWS ✠LMC UMS Eq.Ltr: G; Cable: 302.5/20.5 U2	**1991-01 McTay Marine — Bromborough** Yd No: 91 Loa 30.58 Br ex 11.50 Dght 3.400 Lbp 28.50 Br md 11.00 Dpth 4.28 Welded, 1 dk	**(B32A2ST) Tug**	**2 oil engines** gearing integral to driving 2 Voith-Schneider propellers Total Power: 3,480kW (4,732hp) 12.8kn Ruston 6RK270M 2 x 4 Stroke 6 Cy. 270 x 305 each-1740kW (2366bhp) Ruston Diesels Ltd.-Newton-le-Willows AuxGen: 2 x 80kW 415V 50Hz a.c

IMO / Call sign	Name / Owner	Tonnage	Classification	Builder / Dimensions	Type	Machinery
8501397 *MAYP7* -	**SVITZER KEELBY** *ex* Adsteam Keelby *-2007* *ex* Redcliffe *-2005* *ex* W. J. Trotter *-2003* **Svitzer Towage Ltd** Svitzer Marine Ltd *Grimsby* *United Kingdom* MMSI: 235006240 Official number: 907439	470 141 354	Class: LR (AB) **100A1** SS 05/2010 tug **LMC** **UMS** Cable: 440.0/25.0 U2 (a)	**1986**-05 **Carrington Slipways Pty Ltd — Newcastle NSW** Yd No: 181 Loa 33.91 Br ex 10.85 Dght 5.201 Lbp - Br md 10.83 Dpth 5.41 Welded, 1 dk	**(B32A2ST) Tug**	**2 oil engines** with clutches, flexible couplings & dr geared to sc. shafts driving 2 Z propellers Total Power: 3,532kW (4,802hp) 12.0kn Yanmar 8Z280-ET 2 x 4 Stroke 8 Cy. 280 x 360 each-1766kW (2401bhp) Yanmar Diesel Engine Co Ltd-Japan AuxGen: 2 x 140kW 415V 50Hz a.c
9440904 *2BIF8* -	**SVITZER KILROOM** **Santander Lease SA EFC (Bansalease SA)** Svitzer Marine Ltd *Milford Haven* *United Kingdom* MMSI: 235066353 Official number: 915204	819 245 -	Class: LR ✠**100A1** SS 12/2013 escort tug, fire fighting Ship 1 (2400m3/h) with water spray *IWS ✠**LMC** **UMS** Eq.Ltr: K; Cable: 357.5/28.0 U2 (a)	**2008**-12 **Construcciones Navales P Freire SA — Vigo** Yd No: 656 Loa 40.11 Br ex 15.40 Dght 6.550 Lbp 36.97 Br md 14.70 Dpth 6.10 Welded, 1 dk	**(B32A2ST) Tug**	**2 oil engines** reduction geared to sc. shafts driving 2 Directional propellers Total Power: 6,104kW (8,298hp) 13.0kn General Electric 7FDM16 2 x Vee 4 Stroke 16 Cy. 229 x 267 each-3052kW (4149bhp) GE Marine Engines-Cincinnati, Oh AuxGen: 2 x 390kW 415V 50Hz a.c
9389590 *UCUP* -	**SVITZER KORSAKOV** **Svitzer Sakhalin BV** Svitzer Asia Pte Ltd *Korsakov* *Russia* MMSI: 273324800	663 198 527	Class: RS (LR) ✠ Classed LR until 29/2/12	**2007**-12 **Admiralteyskiy Sudostroitelnyy Zavod — Sankt-Peterburg** Yd No: 02210 Loa 35.40 Br ex 13.50 Dght 5.500 Lbp 31.41 Br md 13.00 Dpth 6.82 Welded, 1 dk	**(B32A2ST) Tug** Ice Capable	**2 oil engines** reduction geared to sc. shafts driving 2 Directional propellers Total Power: 4,800kW (6,526hp) 12.0kn Bergens C25: 33L8P 2 x 4 Stroke 8 Cy. 250 x 330 each-2400kW (3263bhp) Rolls Royce Marine AS-Norway AuxGen: 2 x 225kW 400V 50Hz a.c Thrusters: 1 Tunnel thruster (a) Fuel: 248.0 (d.f.)
8919178 *MMHH9* -	**SVITZER LACEBY** *ex* Adsteam Laceby *-2007* *ex* Lady Anya *-2005* **Svitzer Humber Ltd** Svitzer Marine Ltd *Grimsby* *United Kingdom* MMSI: 232003117 Official number: 709339	364 109 279	Class: LR ✠**100A1** SS 12/2010 tug for near continental trading area service (fire fighting ship 1 (2400m3/hr) suspended) ✠**LMC** **UMS** Eq.Ltr: G; Cable: 302.5/20.5 U2	**1990**-12 **McTay Marine — Bromborough** Yd No: 90 Loa 30.58 Br ex 11.50 Dght 3.400 Lbp 28.50 Br md 11.00 Dpth 4.28 Welded, 1 dk	**(B32A2ST) Tug**	**2 oil engines** gearing integral to driving 2 Voith-Schneider propellers Total Power: 3,480kW (4,732hp) 12.8kn Ruston 6RK270M 2 x 4 Stroke 6 Cy. 270 x 305 each-1740kW (2366bhp) Ruston Diesels Ltd.-Newton-le-Willows AuxGen: 2 x 80kW 415V 50Hz a.c Fuel: 84.6 (d.f.)
9373670 *VNDD* -	**SVITZER LARRAKIA** *ex* Adsteam Larrakia *-2007* **Svitzer Australia Pty Ltd (Svitzer Australasia)** - *Darwin, NT* *Australia* MMSI: 503515000 Official number: 857813	355 106 210	Class: AB	**2006**-02 **PT Nanindah Mutiara Shipyard — Batam** Yd No: T151 Loa 30.00 Br ex - Dght - Lbp 28.67 Br md 10.80 Dpth 4.20 Welded, 1 dk	**(B32A2ST) Tug**	**2 oil engines** reduction geared to sc. shafts driving 2 Directional propellers Total Power: 3,324kW (4,520hp) Caterpillar 3516 2 x Vee 4 Stroke 16 Cy. 170 x 190 each-1662kW (2260bhp) Caterpillar Inc-USA
9234147 *ZQZV8* -	**SVITZER LAURA** *ex* Adsteam Laura *-2007* *ex* Lady Laura *-2006* **Svitzer Towage Ltd** Svitzer Marine Ltd *Grimsby* *United Kingdom* MMSI: 235001135 Official number: 904163	353 105 222	Class: LR ✠**100A1** SS 02/2011 tug limited European area ✠**LMC** **UMS** Eq.Ltr: G; Cable: 302.5/22.0 U2 (a)	**2001**-02 **Stocznia Polnocna SA (Northern Shipyard) — Gdansk** (Hull) **2001**-02 **B.V. Scheepswerf Damen — Gorinchem** Yd No: 511301 Loa 30.60 Br ex 11.20 Dght 4.050 Lbp 27.44 Br md 10.60 Dpth 5.00 Welded, 1 dk	**(B32A2ST) Tug**	**2 oil engines** reduction geared to sc. shafts driving 2 Directional propellers Total Power: 3,660kW (4,976hp) 12.0kn Niigata 6L28HX 2 x 4 Stroke 6 Cy. 280 x 370 each-1830kW (2488bhp) Niigata Engineering Co Ltd-Japan AuxGen: 2 x 80kW 380V 50Hz a.c
8000848 *CSXW6* -	**SVITZER LEIXOES** *ex* Groningen *-2005* **Svitzer Portugal - Reboques Maritimos SA** Svitzer Europe Holding BV *Lisbon* *Portugal* MMSI: 263622000	255 76 -	Class: BV	**1981**-01 **Tille Scheepsbouw B.V. — Kootstertille** Yd No: 221 Loa 28.70 Br ex 9.33 Dght 4.050 Lbp 26.19 Br md 9.00 Dpth 4.68 Welded, 1 dk	**(B32A2ST) Tug**	**2 oil engines** geared to sc. shafts driving 2 FP propellers Total Power: 1,766kW (2,402hp) 11.8kn Bolnes 8DNL150/600 2 x 2 Stroke 8 Cy. 190 x 350 each-883kW (1201bhp) 'Bolnes' Motorenfabriek BV-Netherlands AuxGen: 2 x 108kW 380V 50Hz a.c
9326110 - -	**SVITZER LEVTI** **Svitzer Hazira Pvt Ltd** Svitzer Middle East Ltd *Mumbai* *India*	300 - -		**2004**-08 **ASL Shipyard Pte Ltd — Singapore** Yd No: 359 Loa - Br ex - Dght - Lbp - Br md - Dpth - Welded, 1 dk	**(B34S2QM) Mooring Vessel**	**1 oil engine** driving 1 Propeller
9440758 *2BGW7* -	**SVITZER LINDSWAY** **Santander Lease SA EFC (Bansalease SA)** Svitzer Marine Ltd *Milford Haven* *United Kingdom* MMSI: 235066014 Official number: 914995	686 207 377	Class: LR ✠**100A1** SS 10/2013 escort tug, fire-fighting Ship 1 (2400m3/h) with water spray *IWS ✠**LMC** **UMS** Eq.Ltr: J; Cable: 357.5/26.0 U2 (a)	**2008**-10 **Construcciones Navales P Freire SA — Vigo** Yd No: 652 Loa 34.00 Br ex 15.20 Dght 4.500 Lbp 32.20 Br md 14.50 Dpth 6.20 Welded, 1 dk	**(B32A2ST) Tug**	**2 oil engines** reduction geared to sc. shafts driving 2 Z propellers Total Power: 5,754kW (7,824hp) 13.0kn General Electric 7FDM16 2 x Vee 4 Stroke 16 Cy. 229 x 267 each-2877kW (3912bhp) GE Marine Engines-Cincinnati, Oh AuxGen: 2 x 390kW 415V 50Hz a.c Fuel: 190.0 (d.f.)
8117495 *CSXW7* -	**SVITZER LISBOA** *ex* Brabant *-2005* *ex* Ajax *-1999* *ex* Brabant *-1990* **Svitzer Portugal - Reboques Maritimos SA** Svitzer Europe Holding BV *Lisbon* *Portugal* MMSI: 263623000	252 75 192	Class: BV	**1982**-05 **Tille Scheepsbouw B.V. — Kootstertille** Yd No: 229 Loa 28.53 Br ex - Dght 4.060 Lbp 26.19 Br md 9.33 Dpth 4.37 Welded, 1 dk	**(B32A2ST) Tug**	**2 oil engines** geared to sc. shafts driving 2 FP propellers Total Power: 1,766kW (2,402hp) 12.0kn Bolnes 8DNL150/600 2 x 2 Stroke 8 Cy. 190 x 350 each-883kW (1201bhp) 'Bolnes' Motorenfabriek BV-Netherlands
9554303 *J8B4526* -	**SVITZER LUCAYA** **Svitzer (Americas) Ltd** Freepoint Tug & Towing Services *Kingstown* *St Vincent & The Grenadines* MMSI: 376634000 Official number: 10999	442 132 276	Class: LR ✠**100A1** SS 07/2011 tug, fire-fighting Ship 1 (2400m3/h) with water spray *IWS WDL (5t/m2 from aft to frame 15) ✠**LMC** **UMS** Eq.Ltr: H; Cable: 302.5/22.0 U2 (a)	**2011**-07 **Jiangsu Zhenjiang Shipyard Co Ltd — Zhenjiang JS** Yd No: VZJ6173-0802 Loa 30.00 (BB) Br ex 11.32 Dght 4.600 Lbp 26.80 Br md 11.00 Dpth 6.10 Welded, 1 dk	**(B32A2ST) Tug**	**2 oil engines** gearing integral to driving 2 Z propellers Total Power: 3,676kW (4,998hp) Niigata 6L28HX 2 x 4 Stroke 6 Cy. 280 x 370 each-1838kW (2499bhp) Niigata Engineering Co Ltd-Japan AuxGen: 2 x 120kW 400V 50Hz a.c
9129495 *MVCY8* -	**SVITZER LYNDHURST** *ex* Adsteam Lyndhurst *-2009* *ex* Lyndhurst *-2006* **Svitzer Towage Ltd** Svitzer Marine Ltd *Southampton* *United Kingdom* MMSI: 232002565 Official number: 728779	379 113 174	Class: LR ✠**100A1** SS 05/2011 tug fire fighting ship 1 (2400 cubic metre/hr) U.K. coastal service ✠**LMC** **UMS** Eq.Ltr: G; Cable: 302.5/22.0 U2	**1996**-04 **McTay Marine — Bromborough** Yd No: 117 Loa 30.00 Br ex 11.60 Dght 3.400 Lbp 28.50 Br md 11.00 Dpth 4.30 Welded, 1 dk	**(B32A2ST) Tug**	**2 oil engines** gearing integral to driving 2 Voith-Schneider propellers Total Power: 2,954kW (4,016hp) 12.5kn Ruston 6RK270M 2 x 4 Stroke 6 Cy. 270 x 305 each-1477kW (2008bhp) Ruston Paxman Diesels Ltd.-United Kingdom AuxGen: 2 x 70kW 415V 50Hz a.c
9578555 *J8B4639* -	**SVITZER LYNX** **Svitzer Middle East Ltd** - *Kingstown* *St Vincent & The Grenadines* MMSI: 376224000 Official number: 11112	442 132 282	Class: LR ✠**100A1** SS 02/2012 tug, fire-fighting Ship 1 (2400 m/h) with water spray *IWS WDL (5t/m2 from aft to fr.15) ✠**LMC** **UMS** Eq.Ltr: H; Cable: 302.5/22.0 U2 (a)	**2012**-02 **Jiangsu Zhenjiang Shipyard Co Ltd — Zhenjiang JS** Yd No: VZJ6173-0807 Loa 31.50 (BB) Br ex 11.32 Dght 4.600 Lbp 26.73 Br md 11.00 Dpth 6.10 Welded, 1 dk	**(B32A2ST) Tug**	**2 oil engines** gearing integral to driving 2 Z propellers Total Power: 3,676kW (4,998hp) Niigata 6L28HX 2 x 4 Stroke 6 Cy. 280 x 370 each-1838kW (2499bhp) Niigata Engineering Co Ltd-Japan AuxGen: 2 x 120kW 400V 50Hz a.c
9581631 *VJN4277* -	**SVITZER MACQUARIE** *ex* Svitzer Neso *-2013* **Svitzer Australia Pty Ltd (Svitzer Australasia)** - *Newcastle, NSW* *Australia* MMSI: 503786000 Official number: 860743	630 189 484	Class: LR ✠**100A1** SS 05/2012 escort tug, fire-fighting Ship 1 (2400 m3/h) with water spray *IWS WDL (5t/m2 from fr 0 to fr 15) ✠**LMC** **UMS** Eq.Ltr: I; Cable: 330.0/24.0 U2 (a)	**2012**-05 **Qingdao Qianjin Shipyard — Qingdao SD** Yd No: 8Z2033 Loa 33.30 Br ex 13.86 Dght 5.000 Lbp - Br md 13.00 Dpth 5.70 Welded, 1 dk	**(B32A2ST) Tug**	**2 oil engines** gearing integral to driving 2 Z propellers Total Power: 4,412kW (5,998hp) Niigata 6L28HX 2 x 4 Stroke 6 Cy. 280 x 370 each-2206kW (2999bhp) Niigata Engineering Co Ltd-Japan AuxGen: 3 x 224kW 400V 50Hz a.c

9292905 *CSYR2* -	**SVITZER MADEIRA** *ex* Svitzer Medemblik *-2013* *ex* Svitzer Mull *-2009* **Svitzer EuroMed BV** Svitzer Portugal - Reboques Maritimos SA *Sines* *Portugal* MMSI: 263602554 Official number: SN 111 RC	**385** 115 226	Class: LR **✠100A1** SS 04/2010 escort tug (65,75,10,48) *IWS **✠LMC** **UMS** Eq.Ltr: g†; Cable: 303.1/22.0 U2 (a)	**2005-04 AB "Baltijos" Laivu Statykla — Klaipeda** (Hull) **2005-04 Odense Staalskibsvaerft A/S — Munkebo (Lindo Shipyard)** Yd No: 709 Loa 30.30 Br ex 11.50 Dght 4.100 Lbp 25.60 Br md 11.00 Dpth 5.30 Welded, 1 dk	**(B32A2ST) Tug**	**2 oil engines** gearing integral to driving 2 Directional propellers Total Power: 4,200kW (5,710hp) 11.0kn Caterpillar 3516B 2 x Vee 4 Stroke 16 Cy. 170 x 190 each-2100kW (2855bhp) Caterpillar Inc-USA AuxGen: 2 x 215kW 400V 50Hz a.c Boilers: HWH (o.f.) 3.1kgf/cm^2 (3.0bar) Thrusters: 1 Thwart. CP thruster (f)
9127368 *MWVH2* -	**SVITZER MADELEINE** *ex* Lady Madeleine *-2008* **Svitzer Humber Ltd** Svitzer Marine Ltd *Rochester* *United Kingdom* MMSI: 232002622 Official number: 728962	**381** 114 200	Class: LR **✠100A1** SS 07/2011 tug limited European trading area **✠LMC** **UMS** Eq.Ltr: H; Cable: 302.5/22.0 U2	**1996-07 Stocznia Polnocna SA (Northern Shipyard) — Gdansk** (Hull) **1996-07 B.V. Scheepswerf Damen — Gorinchem** Yd No: 7908 Loa 32.72 Br ex 11.96 Dght 3.800 Lbp 29.00 Br md 10.60 Dpth 5.00 Welded, 1 dk	**(B32A2ST) Tug**	**2 oil engines** gearing integral to driving 2 Z propellers Total Power: 3,600kW (4,894hp) 12.6kn Ruston 6RK270M 2 x 4 Stroke 6 Cy. 270 x 305 each-1800kW (2447bhp) Ruston Paxman Diesels Ltd.-United Kingdom AuxGen: 2 x 70kW 415V 50Hz a.c
9324796 *VHDK* -	**SVITZER MAITLAND** *ex* Svitzer Mercur *-2010* **Svitzer Australia Pty Ltd (Svitzer Australasia)** - *Newcastle, NSW* *Australia* MMSI: 503624000 Official number: 859487	**385** 115 218	Class: LR **✠100A1** SS 02/2011 escort tug (65,75,10,48) fire fighting Ship 1 with water spray *IWS **✠LMC** **UMS** Eq.Ltr: A†; Cable: 303.1/22.0 U2 (a)	**2006-02 AB "Baltijos" Laivu Statykla — Klaipeda** (Hull) **2006-02 Odense Staalskibsvaerft A/S — Munkebo (Lindo Shipyard)** Yd No: 713 Loa 30.30 Br ex 11.50 Dght 4.100 Lbp 25.60 Br md 11.00 Dpth 5.30 Welded, 1 dk	**(B32A2ST) Tug**	**2 oil engines** gearing integral to driving 2 Directional propellers Total Power: 4,200kW (5,710hp) 11.0kn Caterpillar 3516B 2 x Vee 4 Stroke 16 Cy. 170 x 215 each-2100kW (2855bhp) Caterpillar Inc-USA AuxGen: 2 x 215kW 400V 50Hz a.c Thrusters: 1 Thwart. CP thruster (f)
9317901 *PBJX* -	**SVITZER MALLAIG** - **Svitzer EuroMed BV** Svitzer Amsterdam BV *IJmuiden* *Netherlands* MMSI: 244630113	**385** 115 226	Class: LR **✠100A1** SS 09/2010 escort tug (65,75,10,48) fire fighting Ship 1 (2400m3/hr) with water spray *IWS **✠LMC** **UMS** Eq.Ltr: G; Cable: 302.3/22.0 U2 (a)	**2005-09 AB "Baltijos" Laivu Statykla — Klaipeda** (Hull) **2005-09 Odense Staalskibsvaerft A/S — Munkebo (Lindo Shipyard)** Yd No: 711 Loa 30.30 Br ex 11.50 Dght 4.800 Lbp 25.60 Br md 11.00 Dpth 5.30 Welded, 1 dk	**(B32A2ST) Tug**	**2 oil engines** gearing integral to driving 2 Directional propellers Total Power: 4,200kW (5,710hp) 11.0kn Caterpillar 3516B 2 x Vee 4 Stroke 16 Cy. 170 x 190 each-2100kW (2855bhp) Caterpillar Inc-USA AuxGen: 2 x 215kW 400/230V 50Hz a.c Thrusters: 1 Thwart. CP thruster (f) Fuel: 221.0 (d.f.) 20.0pd
9324784 *MKTS3* -	**SVITZER MALTBY** - **Svitzer Marine Ltd** - *Middlesbrough* *United Kingdom* MMSI: 235031351 Official number: 910971	**385** 115 218	Class: LR **✠100A1** SS 10/2010 fire fighting Ship 1 (2400m3/hr) with water spray *IWS **✠LMC** **UMS** Eq.Ltr: A†; Cable: 302.5/22.0 U2 (a)	**2005-10 AB "Baltijos" Laivu Statykla — Klaipeda** (Hull) **2005-11 Odense Staalskibsvaerft A/S — Munkebo (Lindo Shipyard)** Yd No: 712 Loa 30.30 Br ex 11.50 Dght 4.100 Lbp 25.60 Br md 11.00 Dpth 5.30 Welded, 1 dk	**(B32A2ST) Tug**	**2 oil engines** gearing integral to driving 2 Directional propellers Total Power: 4,200kW (5,710hp) 11.0kn Caterpillar 3516B 2 x Vee 4 Stroke 16 Cy. 170 x 190 each-2100kW (2855bhp) Caterpillar Inc-USA AuxGen: 2 x 215kW 400V 50Hz a.c Boilers: HWH (o.f.) 3.1kgf/cm^2 (3.0bar) Thrusters: 1 Thwart. CP thruster (f)
9292890 *PHCI* -	**SVITZER MARKEN** - **Svitzer A/S** Svitzer Amsterdam BV *IJmuiden* *Netherlands* MMSI: 245385000 Official number: 43794	**385** 115 226	Class: LR **✠100A1** SS 02/2010 escort tug *IWS **✠LMC** **UMS** Eq.Ltr: G†; Cable: 302.5/22.0 U2 (a)	**2005-02 AB "Baltijos" Laivu Statykla — Klaipeda** (Hull) **2005-02 Odense Staalskibsvaerft A/S — Munkebo (Lindo Shipyard)** Yd No: 708 Loa 30.30 Br ex 11.50 Dght 4.100 Lbp 25.60 Br md 11.00 Dpth 5.30 Welded, 1 dk	**(B32A2ST) Tug**	**2 oil engines** geared to sc. shafts driving 2 Directional propellers Total Power: 4,200kW (5,710hp) 11.0kn Caterpillar 3516B-HD 2 x Vee 4 Stroke 16 Cy. 170 x 215 each-2100kW (2855bhp) Caterpillar Inc-USA AuxGen: 2 x 215kW 400V 50Hz a.c Boilers: HWH (o.f.) 3.1kgf/cm^2 (3.0bar) Thrusters: 1 Thwart. CP thruster (f)
9391737 *VHDC* -	**SVITZER MARLOO** *ex* Adsteam Marloo *-2007* *launched as* Adsteam Calshot *-2006* **Svitzer Australia Pty Ltd (Svitzer Australasia)** - *Port Adelaide, SA* *Australia* MMSI: 503523000 Official number: 858209	**327** 98 127	Class: LR **✠100A1** SS 09/2011 tug **✠LMC** **UMS** Eq.Ltr: G; Cable: 32.0/20.5 U2 (a)	**2006-09 Hin Lee (Zhuhai) Shipyard Co Ltd — Zhuhai GD** (Hull) Yd No: 124 **2006-09 Cheoy Lee Shipyards Ltd — Hong Kong** Yd No: 4877 Loa 27.40 Br ex 11.52 Dght - Lbp 25.20 Br md 11.50 Dpth 5.03 Welded, 1 dk	**(B32A2ST) Tug**	**2 oil engines** gearing integral to driving 2 Z propellers Total Power: 3,728kW (5,068hp) Caterpillar 3516B-TA 2 x Vee 4 Stroke 16 Cy. 170 x 190 each-1864kW (2534bhp) Caterpillar Inc-USA AuxGen: 2 x 84kW 415V 50Hz a.c
9292852 *OVID2* -	**SVITZER MARS** - **Svitzer A/S** Svitzer Sverige AB *Fredericia* *Denmark (DIS)* MMSI: 220259000 Official number: D4025	**380** 114 175	Class: LR **✠100A1** SS 05/2009 escort tug (75, 65, 10, 48) fire fighting ship 1 (2400 cubic m/hr) with water spray *IWS Main deck aft of frame 10 strengthened for load of 5 tonnes/square m **✠LMC** **UMS** Eq.Ltr: G; Cable: 302.5/22.0 U2 (a)	**2004-05 AB "Baltijos" Laivu Statykla — Klaipeda** (Hull) **2004-05 Odense Staalskibsvaerft A/S — Munkebo (Lindo Shipyard)** Yd No: 704 Loa 30.30 Br ex 11.50 Dght 4.100 Lbp 25.60 Br md 11.00 Dpth 5.30 Welded, 1 dk	**(B32A2ST) Tug**	**2 oil engines** geared to sc. shafts driving 2 Directional propellers Total Power: 3,600kW (4,894hp) 11.0kn MaK 6M25 2 x 4 Stroke 6 Cy. 255 x 400 each-1800kW (2447bhp) Caterpillar Motoren GmbH & Co. KG-Germany AuxGen: 2 x 215kW 400V 50Hz a.c Boilers: HWH (o.f.) 3.1kgf/cm^2 (3.0bar) Thrusters: 1 Thwart. CP thruster (f) Fuel: 214.0 (d.f.)
9540443 *VHDP* -	**SVITZER MARYSVILLE** - **Svitzer Australia Pty Ltd (Svitzer Australasia)** - *Melbourne, Vic* *Australia* MMSI: 503546100 Official number: 859938	**250** 75 126	Class: LR **✠100A1** SS 09/2011 tug **LMC** **UMS** Eq.Ltr: F; Cable: 275.0/19.0 U2 (a)	**2011-09 Song Cam Shipyard — Haiphong** (Hull) Yd No: (512250) **2011-09 B.V. Scheepswerf Damen — Gorinchem** Yd No: 512250 Loa 24.47 Br ex 11.33 Dght 3.600 Lbp 22.16 Br md 10.70 Dpth 4.60 Welded, 1 dk	**(B32A2ST) Tug**	**2 oil engines** reduction geared to sc. shafts driving 2 Directional propellers Total Power: 4,200kW (5,710hp) Caterpillar 3516B-HD 2 x Vee 4 Stroke 16 Cy. 170 x 190 each-2100kW (2855bhp) Caterpillar Inc-USA AuxGen: 2 x 60kW 400V 50Hz a.c
9542324 *OA4804* -	**SVITZER MELCHORITA** - **Svitzer Peru SA** - *Callao* *Peru* MMSI: 760000260	**625** 189 415	Class: LR **✠100A1** SS 11/2009 escort tug, fire fighting Ship 1 (2400 m3/h) with water spray *IWS **✠LMC** **UMS** Eq.Ltr: I; Cable: 330.0/26.0 U2 (a)	**2009-11 Qingdao Qianjin Shipyard — Qingdao SD** Yd No: 7Z2022 Loa 32.60 Br ex 13.40 Dght 4.500 Lbp 28.60 Br md 13.00 Dpth 6.10 Welded, 1 dk	**(B32A2ST) Tug**	**2 oil engines** geared to sc. shafts driving 2 Directional propellers Total Power: 4,412kW (5,998hp) Niigata 8L28HX 2 x 4 Stroke 8 Cy. 280 x 370 each-2206kW (2999bhp) Niigata Engineering Co Ltd-Japan AuxGen: 3 x 150kW 440V 50Hz a.c
9127344 *MVZE8* -	**SVITZER MELTON** *ex* Melton *-2007* **Svitzer Towage Ltd** Svitzer Marine Ltd *Felixstowe* *United Kingdom* MMSI: 232002593 Official number: 728824	**381** 114 200	Class: LR **✠100A1** SS 05/2011 tug limited European area *IWS **✠LMC** **UMS** Eq.Ltr: H; Cable: 302.5/22.0 U2	**1996-05 Stocznia Polnocna SA (Northern Shipyard) — Gdansk** (Hull) **1996-05 B.V. Scheepswerf Damen — Gorinchem** Yd No: 7906 Loa 32.72 Br ex 11.96 Dght 3.800 Lbp 29.00 Br md 10.60 Dpth 5.00 Welded, 1 dk	**(B32A2ST) Tug**	**2 oil engines** gearing integral to driving 2 Z propellers Total Power: 3,600kW (4,894hp) 13.7kn Ruston 6RK270M 2 x 4 Stroke 6 Cy. 270 x 305 each-1800kW (2447bhp) Ruston Paxman Diesels Ltd.-United Kingdom AuxGen: 2 x 70kW 415V 50Hz a.c Fuel: 81.0 (d.f.) 19.0pd
8914685 *MMJY5* -	**SVITZER MERCIA** *ex* Adsteam Mercia *-2008* *ex* Sun Mercia *-2005* **Svitzer Towage Ltd** Svitzer Marine Ltd *London* *United Kingdom* MMSI: 232003233 Official number: 718767	**449** 134 200 T/cm 2.7	Class: LR **✠100A1** SS 07/2010 tug near continental trade only **✠LMC** Eq.Ltr: (H) ; Cable: 382.0/22.0 U2	**1990-07 McTay Marine — Bromborough** Yd No: 89 Loa 33.02 Br ex 10.45 Dght 3.300 Lbp 31.00 Br md 10.00 Dpth 4.20 Welded, 1 dk	**(B32A2ST) Tug**	**2 oil engines** gearing integral to driving 2 Voith-Schneider propellers Total Power: 2,840kW (3,862hp) 12.6kn Ruston 6RK270M 2 x 4 Stroke 6 Cy. 270 x 305 each-1420kW (1931bhp) Ruston Diesels Ltd.-Newton-le-Willows AuxGen: 2 x 108kW 440V 50Hz a.c Fuel: 119.1 (d.f.)
9357834 *VJN3054* -	**SVITZER MERINGA** *ex* Adsteam Meringa *-2007* **Svitzer Australia Pty Ltd (Svitzer Australasia)** - *Port Adelaide, SA* *Australia* Official number: 857814	**249** 74 -	Class: LR (BV) **100A1** SS 01/2011 tug, fire-fighting Ship 1 (2400m3/h) with water spray extended protected waters service at the Port of Newcastle, Australia **LMC** **UMS** Eq.Ltr: E; Cable: 135.0/17.5 U2 (a)	**2006-01 Damen Shipyards Changde Co Ltd — Changde HN** (Hull) **2006-01 B.V. Scheepswerf Damen — Gorinchem** Yd No: 512205 Loa 24.47 Br ex 11.33 Dght 5.350 Lbp 22.16 Br md 10.70 Dpth 4.60 Welded, 1 dk	**(B32A2ST) Tug**	**2 oil engines** gearing integral to driving 2 Z propellers Total Power: 4,170kW (5,670hp) Caterpillar 3516B-HD 2 x Vee 4 Stroke 16 Cy. 170 x 215 each-2085kW (2835bhp) Caterpillar Inc-USA AuxGen: 1 x 50kW 250V 50Hz a.c

IMO / Call sign	Name / Owner / Flag	GT / NT / DWT	Classification	Build / Dimensions	Type	Machinery
9292876 *MGCM4* -	**SVITZER MILFORD** **Svitzer Marine Ltd** Svitzer A/S *Milford Haven* *United Kingdom* MMSI: 235020899 Official number: 909437	**384** 115 226	Class: LR ✠ **100A1** SS 10/2009 escort tug (75, 65, 10, 48) fire fighting Ship 1 (2400 cubic m/h) with water spray *IWS Main deck aft of frame 10 strengthened for load of 5 tonnes/square m ✠ **LMC** **UMS** Eq.Ltr: G†; Cable: 302.5/22.0 U2 (a)	**2004-10 AB "Baltijos" Laivu Statykla — Klaipeda** (Hull) **2004-10 Odense Staalskibsvaerft A/S — Munkebo (Lindo Shipyard)** Yd No: 706 Loa 30.30 Br ex 11.50 Dght 4.100 Lbp 25.60 Br md 11.00 Dpth 5.30 Welded, 1 dk	**(B32A2ST) Tug**	**2 oil engines** gearing integral to driving 2 Z propellers Total Power: 3,600kW (4,894hp) 11.0kn MaK 6M25 2 x 4 Stroke 6 Cy. 255 x 400 each-1800kW (2447bhp) Caterpillar Motoren GmbH & Co. KG-Germany AuxGen: 2 x 215kW 400V 50Hz a.c Boilers: HWH (o.f.) Thrusters: 1 Thwart. CP thruster (f) Fuel: 214.0 (d.f.)
9292864 *OUVK2* -	**SVITZER MJOLNER** **Svitzer A/S** Svitzer Sverige AB *Copenhagen* *Denmark (DIS)* MMSI: 220272000 Official number: D4026	**380** 114 226	Class: LR ✠ **100A1** SS 07/2009 escort tug (65,75,10,48), fire fighting Ship 1 (2400m3/h) with water spray *IWS ✠ **LMC** **UMS** Eq.Ltr: G; Cable: 302.5/22.0 U2 (a)	**2004-07 AB "Baltijos" Laivu Statykla — Klaipeda** (Hull) **2004-07 Odense Staalskibsvaerft A/S — Munkebo (Lindo Shipyard)** Yd No: 705 Loa 30.30 Br ex 11.50 Dght 4.100 Lbp 25.60 Br md 11.00 Dpth 5.30 Welded, 1 dk	**(B32A2ST) Tug**	**2 oil engines** reduction geared to sc. shafts driving 2 Directional propellers Total Power: 3,600kW (4,894hp) 11.0kn MaK 6M25 2 x 4 Stroke 6 Cy. 255 x 400 each-1800kW (2447bhp) Caterpillar Motoren GmbH & Co. KG-Germany AuxGen: 2 x 215kW 400V 50Hz a.c Boilers: HWH (o.f.) 3.1kgf/cm² (3.0bar) Thrusters: 1 Thwart. CP thruster (f) Fuel: 214.0 (d.f.) 9.0pd
9185229 *MZDZ7* -	**SVITZER MOIRA** *ex* Lady Moira *-2007* *ex* Peng *-1999* *ex* Peng Chau *-1999* **Svitzer Humber Ltd** Svitzer Marine Ltd *Grimsby* *United Kingdom* MMSI: 235053752 Official number: 902685	**267** 80 180	Class: LR (BV) **100A1** SS 01/2013 tug United Kingdom coastal service **LMC**	**1998-01 Imamura Zosen — Kure** Yd No: 397 Loa 29.70 Br ex 9.60 Dght 3.750 Lbp 23.50 Br md 9.00 Dpth 4.70 Welded, 1 dk	**(B32A2ST) Tug**	**2 oil engines** gearing integral to driving 2 Z propellers Total Power: 2,650kW (3,602hp) 13.1kn Niigata 6L25HX 2 x 4 Stroke 6 Cy. 250 x 350 each-1325kW (1801bhp) Niigata Engineering Co Ltd-Japan AuxGen: 2 x 80kW 385V 50Hz a.c Fuel: 96.7 (d.f.) 5.5pd
9300740 *AUGD* -	**SVITZER MORA** **Svitzer Hazira Pvt Ltd** Svitzer Middle East Ltd *Mumbai* *India* MMSI: 419053600 Official number: 4010	**451** 135 500	Class: IR (LR) ✠ Classed LR until 11/7/10	**2004-09 ASL Shipyard Pte Ltd — Singapore** Yd No: 328 Loa 31.80 Br ex 10.52 Dght 4.541 Lbp 30.45 Br md 10.50 Dpth 5.60 Welded, 1 dk	**(B32A2ST) Tug**	**2 oil engines** geared to sc. shafts driving 2 Directional propellers Total Power: 3,676kW (4,998hp) 12.0kn Niigata 6L28HX 2 x 4 Stroke 6 Cy. 280 x 370 each-1838kW (2499bhp) Niigata Engineering Co Ltd-Japan AuxGen: 2 x 174kW 415V 50Hz a.c
8312007 *MNSJ2* -	**SVITZER MORAG** *ex* Lady Morag *-2008* *ex* Kestrel *-1991* *ex* Kuroshio *-1991* **Svitzer Towage Ltd** Svitzer Marine Ltd *Rochester* *United Kingdom* MMSI: 232004217 Official number: 704400	**365** 109 89	Class: LR **100A1** SS 04/2011 tug for service in the limited European trading area **LMC** Eq.Ltr: F; Cable: 300.0/28.0 U2 (a)	**1983-10 Hanasaki Zosensho K.K. — Yokosuka** Yd No: 192 Loa 36.28 Br ex 10.52 Dght 3.152 Lbp 30.80 Br md 10.00 Dpth 4.40 Welded, 1 dk	**(B32A2ST) Tug**	**2 oil engines** driving 2 Directional propellers Total Power: 2,500kW (3,400hp) Niigata 6L28BXE 2 x 4 Stroke 6 Cy. 280 x 320 each-1250kW (1700bhp) Niigata Engineering Co Ltd-Japan AuxGen: 2 x 88kW 220V 60Hz a.c
9370886 *A9D2917* -	**SVITZER MUHARRAQ** **Svitzer Wijsmuller Bahrain** Svitzer Middle East Ltd *Bahrain* *Bahrain* MMSI: 408315000 Official number: BN 4094	**332** 99 148	Class: LR (AB) **100A1** SS 02/2011 tug **LMC** Eq.Ltr: G; Cable: 137.0/20.0 U3 (a)	**2006-02 Jiangsu Wuxi Shipyard Co Ltd — Wuxi JS** (Hull) Yd No: (1204) **2006-02 Pacific Ocean Engineering & Trading Pte Ltd (POET) — Singapore** Yd No: 1204 Loa 28.00 Br ex - Dght 4.900 Lbp 22.94 Br md 9.80 Dpth 4.90 Welded, 1 dk	**(B32A2ST) Tug**	**2 oil engines** gearing integral to driving 2 Z propellers Total Power: 2,648kW (3,600hp) Yanmar 8N21A-EN 2 x 4 Stroke 8 Cy. 210 x 290 each-1324kW (1800bhp) Yanmar Diesel Engine Co Ltd-Japan AuxGen: 2 x 99kW 380V 50Hz a.c
9292888 *PBGX* -	**SVITZER MUIDEN** **Svitzer A/S** Svitzer Amsterdam BV *Amsterdam* *Netherlands* MMSI: 246115000 Official number: 43240	**384** 115 226	Class: LR ✠ **100A1** SS 12/2009 escort tug (75, 65, 10, 48) fire fighting Ship 1 (2400 cubic m/h) with water spray *IWS Main deck aft of frame 10 strengthened for load of 5 tonnes/square m ✠ **LMC** **UMS** Eq.Ltr: G†; Cable: 302.5/22.0 U2 (a)	**2004-12 AB "Baltijos" Laivu Statykla — Klaipeda** (Hull) **2004-12 Odense Staalskibsvaerft A/S — Munkebo (Lindo Shipyard)** Yd No: 707 Loa 30.30 Br ex 11.50 Dght 4.100 Lbp 25.60 Br md 11.00 Dpth 5.30 Welded, 1 dk	**(B32A2ST) Tug**	**2 oil engines** reduction geared to sc. shafts driving 2 Directional propellers Total Power: 3,600kW (4,894hp) 11.0kn MaK 6M25 2 x 4 Stroke 6 Cy. 255 x 400 each-1800kW (2447bhp) Caterpillar Motoren GmbH & Co. KG-Germany AuxGen: 2 x 215kW 400V 50Hz a.c Boilers: HWH (o.f.) 3.1kgf/cm² (3.0bar) Thrusters: 1 Thwart. CP thruster (f)
9354985 *A4DJ3* -	**SVITZER MUSCAT** **Svitzer Middle East Ltd** - *Port Sultan Qaboos* *Oman* MMSI: 461000048	**436** 130 260	Class: LR ✠ **100A1** SS 06/2011 tug fire fighting Ship 1 (2400 m3/h) with water spray *IWS ✠ **LMC** Eq.Ltr: G; Cable: 302.5/22.0 U2 (a)	**2006-06 ASL Shipyard Pte Ltd — Singapore** Yd No: 508 Loa 31.34 Br ex 11.02 Dght 4.000 Lbp 26.80 Br md 11.00 Dpth 6.11 Welded, 1 dk	**(B32A2ST) Tug**	**2 oil engines** gearing integral to driving 2 Z propellers Total Power: 3,676kW (4,998hp) 13.0kn Niigata 6L28HX 2 x 4 Stroke 6 Cy. 280 x 370 each-1838kW (2499bhp) Niigata Engineering Co Ltd-Japan AuxGen: 2 x 150kW 400V 50Hz a.c
9412385 *2AXZ7* -	**SVITZER MUSSELWICK** **Svitzer Marine Ltd** - *Milford Haven* *United Kingdom* MMSI: 235063852 Official number: 914882	**490** 147 375	Class: LR ✠ **100A1** SS 08/2013 escort tug, fire-fighting Ship 1 (2400m3/h with water spray) *IWS ✠ **LMC** **UMS** Eq.Ltr: H; Cable: 302.5/22.0 U2 (a)	**2008-08 Qingdao Qianjin Shipyard — Qingdao SD** Yd No: 6Z2017 Loa 32.60 Br ex 12.10 Dght 4.500 Lbp 28.60 Br md 11.60 Dpth 5.70 Welded, 1 dk	**(B32A2ST) Tug**	**2 oil engines** gearing integral to driving 2 Z propellers Total Power: 4,412kW (5,998hp) 12.0kn Niigata 8L28HX 2 x 4 Stroke 8 Cy. 280 x 370 each-2206kW (2999bhp) Niigata Engineering Co Ltd-Japan AuxGen: 2 x 150kW 400V 50Hz a.c Boilers: HWH (o.f.) 4.1kgf/cm² (4.0bar)
9317896 *VHDJ* -	**SVITZER MYALL** *ex* Svitzer Menja *-2010* **Svitzer Australia Pty Ltd (Svitzer Australasia)** - SatCom: Inmarsat C 450303956 *Newcastle, NSW* *Australia* MMSI: 503625000 Official number: 859486	**385** 115 233	Class: LR ✠ **100A1** SS 06/2010 escort tug fire fighting Ship 1 (2400 cubic m/h) with water spray *IWS ✠ **LMC** **UMS** Eq.Ltr: G; Cable: 303.1/22.0 U2 (a)	**2005-06 AB "Baltijos" Laivu Statykla — Klaipeda** (Hull) **2005-06 Odense Staalskibsvaerft A/S — Munkebo (Lindo Shipyard)** Yd No: 710 Loa 30.30 Br ex 11.50 Dght 4.100 Lbp 25.60 Br md 11.00 Dpth 5.30 Welded, 1 dk	**(B32A2ST) Tug**	**2 oil engines** gearing integral to driving 2 Directional propellers Total Power: 4,200kW (5,710hp) 11.0kn Caterpillar 3516B 2 x Vee 4 Stroke 16 Cy. 170 x 190 each-2100kW (2855bhp) Caterpillar Inc-USA AuxGen: 2 x 215kW 400V 50Hz a.c Boilers: HWH (o.f.) 3.1kgf/cm² (3.0bar) Thrusters: 1 Thwart. CP thruster (f)
9581629 *VJN4060* -	**SVITZER NAIAD** **Svitzer Australia Pty Ltd (Svitzer Australasia)** - *Townsville, Qld* *Australia* Official number: 860514	**630** 189 495	Class: LR ✠ **100A1** SS 04/2012 escort tug, fire-fighting Ship 1 (2400m3/h) with water spray *IWS WDL (5t/m2 from frame 0 to frame 15) ✠ **LMC** **UMS** Eq.Ltr: I; Cable: 330.0/24.0 U2 (a)	**2012-04 Qingdao Qianjin Shipyard — Qingdao SD** Yd No: 8Z2032 Loa 32.60 Br ex 13.86 Dght 5.000 Lbp 28.45 Br md 13.00 Dpth 6.10 Welded, 1 dk	**(B32A2ST) Tug**	**2 oil engines** gearing integral to driving 2 Z propellers Total Power: 3,676kW (4,998hp) Niigata 6L28HX 2 x 4 Stroke 6 Cy. 280 x 370 each-1838kW (2499bhp) Niigata Engineering Co Ltd-Japan AuxGen: 3 x 224kW 400V 50Hz a.c
9581643 *VJN4170* -	**SVITZER NANA** **Svitzer Australia Pty Ltd (Svitzer Australasia)** - *Townsville, Qld* *Australia* MMSI: 503771000 Official number: 860567	**630** 189 486	Class: LR ✠ **100A1** SS 05/2012 escort tug, fire-fighting Ship 1 (2400 m3/h) with water spray *IWS WDL (5t/m2 from fr 0 to fr 15) ✠ **LMC** **UMS** Eq.Ltr: I; Cable: 330.0/24.0 U2 (a)	**2012-05 Qingdao Qianjin Shipyard — Qingdao SD** Yd No: 8Z2034 Loa 32.60 Br ex 13.86 Dght 5.000 Lbp 28.85 Br md 13.00 Dpth 6.10 Welded, 1 dk	**(B32A2ST) Tug**	**2 oil engines** gearing integral to driving 2 Z propellers Total Power: 4,412kW (5,998hp) Niigata 6L28HX 2 x 4 Stroke 6 Cy. 280 x 370 each-2206kW (2999bhp) Niigata Engineering Co Ltd-Japan AuxGen: 3 x 224kW 400V 50Hz a.c

9547867 *2FEI4* -	**SVITZER NARI** *ex* Stevns Battler *-2011* **K/S Helle Stevns** Svitzer Marine Ltd *Liverpool* *United Kingdom* MMSI: 235090532	**381** 114 190	Class: LR **✠100A1** SS 09/2010 tug fire-fighting Ship 1 (2400m3/h) with water spray **✠LMC** **UMS** Eq.Ltr: G; Cable: 330.0/20.0 U2 (a)	**2010**-09 **East Isle Shipyard Ltd — Georgetown PE** Yd No: 97 Loa 30.65 Br ex 11.72 Dght 3.930 Lbp 28.83 Br md 11.12 Dpth 5.25 Welded, 1 dk	**(B32A2ST) Tug**	**2 oil engines** gearing integral to driving 2 Z propellers Total Power: 4,000kW (5,438hp) Caterpillar 3516B 2 x Vee 4 Stroke 16 Cy. 170 x 190 each-2000kW (2719bhp) Caterpillar Inc-USA AuxGen: 2 x 239kW 400V 50Hz a.c
9554298 *J8B4527* -	**SVITZER NASSAU** **Svitzer Australia Pty Ltd (Svitzer Australasia)** Svitzer (Caribbean) Ltd *Kingstown* *St Vincent & The Grenadines* MMSI: 377269000 Official number: 11000	**442** 132 276	Class: LR **✠100A1** SS 06/2011 tug, fire-fighting Ship 1 (2400 m3/h) with water spray *IWS WDL (5t/m2 from aft to frame 15) **✠LMC** **UMS** Eq.Ltr: H; Cable: 302.5/24.0 U2 (a)	**2011**-06 **Jiangsu Zhenjiang Shipyard Co Ltd — Zhenjiang JS** Yd No: VZJ6173-0801 Loa 30.00 (BB) Br ex 11.32 Dght 5.100 Lbp 26.80 Br md 11.00 Dpth 5.70 Welded, 1 dk	**(B32A2ST) Tug**	**2 oil engines** gearing integral to driving 2 Z propellers Total Power: 3,676kW (4,998hp) Niigata 6L28HX 2 x 4 Stroke 6 Cy. 280 x 370 each-1838kW (2499bhp) Niigata Engineering Co Ltd-Japan AuxGen: 2 x 120kW 400V 50Hz a.c
9533048 *OWBV2* -	**SVITZER NERTHUS** *ex* Stevns Iceflower *-2010* **Stevns Charter & Towage A/S, Skaarupsund A/S, Peter Lauritz Holmblad, Jorgen Schjerning Lundsgaard, Steen Lorenz Johan Hansen, Stevns Shipping A/S & Birgit Lundsgaard** Nordane Shipping A/S *Fredericia* *Denmark (DIS)* MMSI: 219075000 Official number: D4420	**381** 115 190	Class: LR **✠100A1** SS 12/2009 tug, fire-fighting Ship 1 (2400 m3/h) with water spray Ice Class 1A FS at a draught of 3.94m Max/min draughts fwd 3.94/2.70m Max/min draughts aft 3.94/3.50m Power required 1294kw, power installed 8730kw **✠LMC** **UMS** Eq.Ltr: G; Cable: 330.0/20.0 U2 (a)	**2009**-12 **East Isle Shipyard Ltd — Georgetown PE** Yd No: 95 Loa 30.65 Br ex 11.72 Dght 3.940 Lbp 28.83 Br md 11.12 Dpth 5.25 Welded, 1 dk	**(B32A2ST) Tug** Ice Capable	**2 oil engines** gearing integral to driving 2 Z propellers Total Power: 3,730kW (5,072hp) 12.0kn Caterpillar 3516B-HD 2 x Vee 4 Stroke 16 Cy. 170 x 190 each-1865kW (2536bhp) Caterpillar Inc-USA AuxGen: 2 x 239kW 400V 50Hz a.c
9366897 *VJN3167* -	**SVITZER NEWSTEAD** *ex* Adsteam Otway *-2007* **Svitzer Australia Pty Ltd (Svitzer Australasia)** - *Brisbane, Qld* *Australia* MMSI: 503194600 Official number: 858118	**250** 75 150	Class: LR **✠100A1** SS 04/2012 tug **LMC** **UMS** Eq.Ltr: F; Cable: 275.0/19.0 U2 (a)	**2007**-04 **Song Cam Shipyard — Haiphong** (Hull) **2007**-04 **B.V. Scheepswerf Damen — Gorinchem** Yd No: 512210 Loa 24.47 Br ex 11.33 Dght 3.650 Lbp 22.16 Br md 10.70 Dpth 4.60 Welded, 1 dk	**(B32A2ST) Tug**	**2 oil engines** gearing integral to driving 2 Z propellers Total Power: 4,200kW (5,710hp) 11.8kn Caterpillar 3516B-HD 2 x Vee 4 Stroke 16 Cy. 170 x 215 each-2100kW (2855bhp) Caterpillar Inc-USA AuxGen: 2 x 60kW 400V 50Hz a.c
9533036 *OWBT2* -	**SVITZER NJAL** *ex* Stevns Icequeen *-2010* **P/R Grete Stevns** Svitzer Sverige AB *Fredericia* *Denmark (DIS)* MMSI: 219072000 Official number: D4419	**381** 114 190	Class: LR **✠100A1** SS 09/2009 tug, fire fighting Ship 1 (2400m3/h) with water spray Ice Class 1A FS at draught of 3.94m Max/min draught fwd 3.94/2.70m Max/min draught aft 3.94/3.50m Required power 1294kw, installed power 3730kw **✠LMC** **UMS** Eq.Ltr: G; Cable: 330.0/20.0 U2 (a)	**2009**-09 **East Isle Shipyard Ltd — Georgetown PE** Yd No: 94 Loa 30.65 Br ex 11.72 Dght 3.930 Lbp 28.83 Br md 11.12 Dpth 5.25 Welded, 1 dk	**(B32A2ST) Tug** Passengers: berths: 6 Ice Capable	**2 oil engines** gearing integral to driving 2 Z propellers Total Power: 3,730kW (5,072hp) 12.0kn Caterpillar 3516B-HD 2 x Vee 4 Stroke 16 Cy. 170 x 190 each-1865kW (2536bhp) Caterpillar Inc-USA AuxGen: 2 x 239kW 400V 50Hz a.c Thrusters: 1 Tunnel thruster (f)
9342451 *OZ2116* -	**SVITZER ODEN** **P/F Svitzer Faroe Islands** Svitzer Sverige AB *Torshavn* *Faeroes (FAS)* MMSI: 231807000	**670** 201 170	Class: LR **✠100A1** SS 05/2011 escort tug (125,125,10,30), fire fighting Ship 1 (2400 m3/h) with water spray *IWS Ice Class 1C FS at draught 3.5m Max/min draught fwd 5.426/2.5m Max/min draught aft 5.426/3.5m Required power 4438kw, installed power 5280kw **✠LMC** **UMS** Eq.Ltr: i; Cable: 330.0/26.0 U2 (a)	**2006**-05 **ASL Shipyard Pte Ltd — Singapore** Yd No: 399 Loa 37.50 Br ex 14.00 Dght 6.050 Lbp 35.93 Br md 13.50 Dpth 5.30 Welded, 1 dk	**(B32A2ST) Tug** Ice Capable	**2 oil engines** gearing integral to driving 2 Voith-Schneider propellers Total Power: 5,280kW (7,178hp) 12.0kn MaK 8M25 2 x 4 Stroke 8 Cy. 255 x 400 each-2640kW (3589bhp) Caterpillar Motoren GmbH & Co. KG-Germany AuxGen: 2 x 211kW 400V 50Hz a.c
9554341 *J8B4638* -	**SVITZER ORYX** **Svitzer Middle East Ltd** - *Kingstown* *St Vincent & The Grenadines* MMSI: 376113000 Official number: 11111	**442** 132 276	Class: LR **✠100A1** SS 02/2012 tug, fire fighting Ship 1 (2400m3/h) with water spray *IWS WDL (5t/m2 from aft to fr. 15) **✠LMC** **UMS** Eq.Ltr: H; Cable: 302.5/24.0 U2 (a)	**2012**-02 **Jiangsu Zhenjiang Shipyard Co Ltd — Zhenjiang JS** Yd No: VZJ6173-0806 Loa 30.80 Br ex 11.32 Dght 5.300 Lbp 26.80 Br md 11.00 Dpth 6.10 Welded, 1 dk	**(B32A2ST) Tug**	**2 oil engines** gearing integral to driving 2 Z propellers Total Power: 3,676kW (4,998hp) Niigata 6L28HX 2 x 4 Stroke 6 Cy. 280 x 370 each-1838kW (2499bhp) Niigata Engineering Co Ltd-Japan AuxGen: 2 x 120kW 400V 50Hz a.c
9578567 *J8B4700* -	**SVITZER OWL** **Svitzer (Americas) Ltd** Svitzer (Caribbean) Ltd *Kingstown* *St Vincent & The Grenadines* MMSI: 376258000 Official number: 11173	**442** 132 285	Class: LR **✠100A1** SS 05/2012 tug, fire-fighting Ship 1 (2400m3/h) with water spray *IWS WDL (5t/m2 from aft to fr.15) **✠LMC** **UMS** Eq.Ltr: H; Cable: 302.5/22.0 U2 (a)	**2012**-05 **Jiangsu Zhenjiang Shipyard Co Ltd — Zhenjiang JS** Yd No: VZJ6173-0808 Loa 30.80 Br ex 11.32 Dght 4.600 Lbp 26.73 Br md 11.00 Dpth 6.10 Welded, 1 dk	**(B32A2ST) Tug**	**2 oil engines** gearing integral to driving 2 Z propellers Total Power: 3,676kW (4,998hp) Niigata 6L28HX 2 x 4 Stroke 6 Cy. 280 x 370 each-1838kW (2499bhp) Niigata Engineering Co Ltd-Japan AuxGen: 2 x 150kW 400V 50Hz a.c
9581590 *J8B4406* -	**SVITZER PADRAO** **Svitzer Angola Shipowners (BVI) Ltd** Svitzer Angola Lda *Kingstown* *St Vincent & The Grenadines* MMSI: 377208000 Official number: 10879	**631** 189 465	Class: LR **✠100A1** SS 06/2011 escort tug, fire-fighting Ship 1 (2400m3/h) with water spray *IWS WDL (5t/m2 from frame 0 to frame 15) **✠LMC** Eq.Ltr: I*; Cable: 330.0/24.0 U2 (a)	**2011**-06 **Qingdao Qianjin Shipyard — Qingdao SD** Yd No: 8Z2029 Loa 33.30 Br ex 13.84 Dght 5.000 Lbp 28.85 Br md 13.00 Dpth 6.10 Welded, 1 dk	**(B32A2ST) Tug**	**2 oil engines** gearing integral to driving 2 Z propellers Total Power: 4,412kW (5,998hp) Niigata 8L28HX 2 x 4 Stroke 8 Cy. 280 x 370 each-2206kW (2999bhp) Niigata Engineering Co Ltd-Japan AuxGen: 3 x 224kW 400V 50Hz a.c
9396907 *A9D2927* -	**SVITZER PELLA** **Svitzer Wijsmuller Bahrain** Svitzer Middle East Ltd *Bahrain* *Bahrain* MMSI: 408317000 Official number: BN 4098	**318** 95 165	Class: LR (AB) **100A1** SS 08/2011 tug **LMC** Cable: 302.0/20.5 SL	**2006**-08 **Jiangsu Wuxi Shipyard Co Ltd — Wuxi JS** (Hull) Yd No: H1220 **2006**-08 **Pacific Ocean Engineering & Trading Pte Ltd (POET) — Singapore** Yd No: 1220 Loa 27.70 Br ex - Dght 4.012 Lbp 22.94 Br md 9.80 Dpth 4.90 Welded, 1 dk	**(B32A2ST) Tug**	**2 oil engines** gearing integral to driving 2 Z propellers Total Power: 2,648kW (3,600hp) Yanmar 8N21A-EN 2 x 4 Stroke 8 Cy. 210 x 290 each-1324kW (1800bhp) Yanmar Diesel Engine Co Ltd-Japan AuxGen: 2 x 99kW 380V 50Hz a.c Fuel: 148.3 (r.f.)
9557927 *2DDS8* -	**SVITZER PEMBROKE** **Svitzer Marine Ltd** - *Milford Haven* *United Kingdom* MMSI: 235078115 Official number: 916815	**734** 220 232	Class: LR **✠100A1** SS 08/2010 escort tug, fire fighting Ship 1 (2400m3/h) with water spray *IWS **✠LMC** **UMS** Eq.Ltr: J; Cable: 357.5/30.0 U2 (a)	**2010**-08 **Astilleros Zamakona Pasaia SL — Pasaia** Yd No: 686 Loa 35.80 Br ex 15.30 Dght 4.839 Lbp 33.67 Br md 14.50 Dpth 6.20 Welded, 1 dk	**(B32A2ST) Tug** Cranes: 1x17t	**2 oil engines** gearing integral to driving 2 Directional propellers Total Power: 6,104kW (8,298hp) GE Marine 16V228 2 x Vee 4 Stroke 16 Cy. 229 x 267 each-3052kW (4149bhp) GE Marine Engines-Cincinnati, Oh AuxGen: 2 x 390kW 415V 50Hz a.c Fuel: 276.0 (r.f.)

9581605 *J8B4478* -	**SVITZER PINDA** **Svitzer Angola Shipowners (BVI) Ltd** Svitzer Angola Lda *Kingstown* *St Vincent & The Grenadines* MMSI: 377537000 Official number: 10951	**631** 189 490	Class: LR ✠ **100A1** SS 11/2011 escort tug, fire fighting Ship 1 (2400m3/h) with water spray *IWS WDL (5t/m2 from frame 0 to frame 15) ✠ **LMC** **UMS** Eq.Ltr: I; Cable: 330.0/24.0 U2 (a)	**2011-11 Qingdao Qianjin Shipyard — Qingdao SD** Yd No: 8Z2030 Loa 33.30 Br ex - Dght 3.700 Lbp 28.60 Br md 11.60 Dpth 5.70 Welded, 1 dk	**(B32A2ST) Tug**	**2 oil engines** gearing integral to driving 2 Z propellers Total Power: 4,412kW (5,998hp) Niigata 8L28HX 2 x 4 Stroke 8 Cy. 280 x 370 each-2206kW (2999bhp) Niigata Engineering Co Ltd-Japan AuxGen: 3 x 224kW 400V 50Hz a.c
9542312 *OA2786* -	**SVITZER PISCO** **Svitzer Peru SA** - *Callao* *Peru* MMSI: 760000350	**627** 189 415	Class: LR ✠ **100A1** SS 12/2009 escort tug, fire fighting Ship 1 (2400m3/h) with water spray *IWS ✠ **LMC** **UMS** Eq.Ltr: I; Cable: 330.0/26.0 U2 (a)	**2009-12 Qingdao Qianjin Shipyard — Qingdao SD** Yd No: 6Z2021 Loa 32.60 Br ex 13.40 Dght 4.600 Lbp 28.60 Br md 13.00 Dpth 6.10 Welded, 1 dk	**(B32A2ST) Tug**	**2 oil engines** geared to sc. shafts driving 2 Directional propellers Total Power: 4,412kW (5,998hp) Niigata 8L28HX 2 x 4 Stroke 8 Cy. 280 x 370 each-2206kW (2999bhp) Niigata Engineering Co Ltd-Japan AuxGen: 3 x 150kW 400V 50Hz a.c Thrusters: 2 Thwart. FP thruster
9440899 *2BPD2* -	**SVITZER RAMSEY** **Santander Lease SA EFC (Bansalease SA)** Svitzer Marine Ltd SatCom: Inmarsat C 423591563 *Milford Haven* *United Kingdom* MMSI: 235068109 Official number: 915550	**690** 207 377	Class: LR ✠ **100A1** SS 06/2009 escort tug EPN ((82,64,8,91) (89,69,10,121)), fire fighting Ship 1 (2400m3/h) with water spray *IWS ✠ **LMC** **UMS** Eq.Ltr: J; Cable: 357.5/26.0 U2 (a)	**2009-06 Construcciones Navales P Freire SA — Vigo** Yd No: 655 Loa 34.00 (BB) Br ex 15.20 Dght 4.500 Lbp 32.20 Br md 14.50 Dpth 6.20 Welded, 1 dk	**(B32A2ST) Tug**	**2 oil engines** gearing integral to driving 2 Z propellers Total Power: 4,412kW (5,998hp) 13.0kn Niigata 8L28HX 1 x 4 Stroke 8 Cy. 280 x 370 2206kW (2999bhp) Niigata Engineering Co Ltd-Japan Niigata 8MG28HX 1 x 4 Stroke 8 Cy. 280 x 370 2206kW (2999bhp) (made 2009) Niigata Engineering Co Ltd-Japan AuxGen: 2 x 390kW 415V 50Hz a.c
9314313 *6ADX* -	**SVITZER RASHEED** **Svitzer Idku SAE** Svitzer Middle East Ltd *Alexandria* *Egypt* MMSI: 622166802 Official number: 7924	*439* - 293	Class: LR ✠ **100A1** SS 01/2010 tug, fire fighting ship 1 (2400 cubic m/h) with water spray *IWS ✠ **LMC** **UMS** Eq.Ltr: H; Cable: 302.5/24.0 U2 (a)	**2005-01 ASL Shipyard Pte Ltd — Singapore** Yd No: 338 Loa 31.92 Br ex 10.54 Dght 4.550 Lbp 30.78 Br md 10.50 Dpth 5.50 Welded, 1 dk	**(B32A2ST) Tug**	**2 oil engines** gearing integral to driving 2 Z propellers Total Power: 3,676kW (4,998hp) 12.0kn Niigata 6L28HX 2 x 4 Stroke 6 Cy. 280 x 370 each-1838kW (2499bhp) Niigata Engineering Co Ltd-Japan AuxGen: 1 x 168kW 415V 50Hz a.c, 1 x 90kW 415V 50Hz a.c
9116888 *MVDF6* -	**SVITZER REDBRIDGE** *ex Adsteam Redbridge -2008* *ex Redbridge -2005* **Svitzer Towage Ltd** Svitzer Marine Ltd *Southampton* *United Kingdom* MMSI: 232002536 Official number: 728427	**399** 119 174	Class: LR ✠ **100A1** SS 08/2010 tug UK coastal service between the Thames Estuary and Lyme Bay within 21 nautical miles distance out to sea ✠ **LMC** Eq.Ltr: E; Cable: 302.5/17.5 U2 (a)	**1995-08 Yorkshire D.D. Co. Ltd. — Hull** Yd No: 339 Loa 33.00 Br ex 11.73 Dght 4.860 Lbp 30.50 Br md 11.20 Dpth - Welded, 1 dk	**(B32A2ST) Tug**	**2 oil engines** gearing integral to driving 2 Voith-Schneider propellers Total Power: 3,020kW (4,106hp) 12.5kn Kromhout 9FHD240 2 x 4 Stroke 9 Cy. 240 x 260 each-1510kW (2053bhp) Stork Wartsila Diesel BV-Netherlands AuxGen: 2 x 84kW 415V 50Hz a.c, 1 x 38kW 415V 50Hz a.c
9464209 *A4DQ2* -	**SVITZER SAHAM** *ex Svitzer Africa -2011* **Svitzer Middle East Ltd** - *Port Sultan Qaboos* *Oman* MMSI: 461000103 Official number: 1276	**493** 147 268	Class: LR ✠ **100A1** SS 11/2009 tug, fire-fighting Ship 1 (2400m3/h) with water spray *IWS ✠ **LMC** **UMS** Eq.Ltr: I; Cable: 330.0/26.0 U2 (a)	**2009-11 Qingdao Qianjin Shipyard — Qingdao SD** Yd No: 6Z20611 Loa 36.80 Br ex 11.50 Dght 4.500 Lbp 31.10 Br md 11.50 Dpth 5.40 Welded, 1 dk	**(B32A2ST) Tug**	**2 oil engines** gearing integral to driving 2 Z propellers Total Power: 3,676kW (4,998hp) Niigata 6L28HX 2 x 4 Stroke 6 Cy. 280 x 370 each-1838kW (2499bhp) Niigata Engineering Co Ltd-Japan AuxGen: 2 x 150kW 400V 50Hz a.c
9369241 *UFHN* -	**SVITZER SAKHALIN** **Svitzer Sakhalin BV** Svitzer Sakhalin Terminal Towage *Korsakov* *Russia* MMSI: 273315760	**663** 198 590	Class: RS (LR) ✠ Classed LR until 29/2/12	**2007-01 ASL Shipyard Pte Ltd — Singapore** Yd No: 509 Loa 35.30 Br ex 13.50 Dght 5.790 Lbp 34.50 Br md 13.00 Dpth 6.82 Welded, 1 dk	**(B32A2ST) Tug** Ice Capable	**2 oil engines** gearing integral to driving 2 Directional propellers Total Power: 4,800kW (6,526hp) 12.0kn Bergens C25: 33L8P 2 x 4 Stroke 8 Cy. 250 x 330 each-2400kW (3263bhp) Rolls Royce Marine AS-Norway AuxGen: 2 x 225kW 415V 50Hz a.c Fuel: 248.0 (d.f.)
8919192 *MNCR5* -	**SVITZER SARAH** *ex Adsteam Sarah -2007 ex Lady Sarah -2006* **Svitzer Humber Ltd** Svitzer Marine Ltd *Grimsby* *United Kingdom* MMSI: 232003121 Official number: 709350	**364** 109 279	Class: LR ✠ **100A1** SS 04/2011 tug for near continental trading area service, fire fighting ship 1 (2400m3/hr) ✠ **LMC** **UMS** Eq.Ltr: G; Cable: 302.5/20.5 U2	**1991-04 McTay Marine — Bromborough** Yd No: 92 Loa 30.58 Br ex 11.50 Dght 3.400 Lbp 28.50 Br md 11.00 Dpth 4.28 Welded, 1 dk	**(B32A2ST) Tug**	**2 oil engines** gearing integral to driving 2 Voith-Schneider propellers Total Power: 3,480kW (4,732hp) 12.8kn Ruston 6RK270M 2 x 4 Stroke 6 Cy. 270 x 305 each-1740kW (2366bhp) Ruston Diesels Ltd.-Newton-le-Willows AuxGen: 2 x 80kW 415V 50Hz a.c
9008653 *CSYQ7* -	**SVITZER SETUBAL** *ex Lars -2013* **Svitzer Portugal - Reboques Maritimos SA** - *Lisbon* *Portugal* MMSI: 263602553 Official number: LX-40-RC	**356** 106 118	Class: LR ✠ **100A1** SS 09/2011 tug Portugal coastal service Ice Class 1C ✠ **LMC** **UMS** Eq.Ltr: (E) ; Cable: 275.0/17.5 U2	**1991-09 Matsuura Tekko Zosen K.K. — Osakikamijima** Yd No: 366 Loa 32.89 Br ex 11.01 Dght 3.890 Lbp 26.40 Br md 10.23 Dpth 4.49 Welded, 1 dk	**(B32A2ST) Tug** Ice Capable	**2 oil engines** with clutches, flexible couplings & dr geared to sc. shafts, integral to Repxeller units driving 2 Directional propellers Total Power: 2,942kW (4,000hp) Yanmar 6Z280-EN 2 x 4 Stroke 6 Cy. 280 x 360 each-1471kW (2000bhp) Yanmar Diesel Engine Co Ltd-Japan AuxGen: 2 x 128kW 385V 50Hz a.c Thrusters: 1 Thwart. CP thruster (f)
9334650 *A4DL5* -	**SVITZER SHINAS** *ex Svitzer Duke -2009* **Svitzer Sohar LLC** Svitzer Middle East Ltd *Port Sultan Qaboos* *Oman* MMSI: 461000067 Official number: 365	**318** 95 151	Class: LR (AB) **100A1** SS 10/2009 tug **LMC** Cable: 302.5/20.5 U3 (a)	**2004-11 Jiangsu Wuxi Shipyard Co Ltd — Wuxi JS** (Hull) Yd No: (1166) **2004-11 Pacific Ocean Engineering & Trading Pte Ltd (POET) — Singapore** Yd No: 1166 Loa 28.00 Br ex - Dght 3.500 Lbp 22.40 Br md 9.80 Dpth 4.80 Welded, 1 dk	**(B32A2ST) Tug**	**2 oil engines** gearing integral to driving 2 Z propellers Total Power: 2,648kW (3,600hp) Yanmar 8N21A-EN 2 x 4 Stroke 8 Cy. 210 x 290 each-1324kW (1800bhp) Yanmar Diesel Engine Co Ltd-Japan AuxGen: 2 x 99kW 415V 60Hz a.c
9366873 *MNQJ6* -	**SVITZER SHOTLEY** *ex Adsteam Shotley -2007* **Svitzer SPC4 Pty Ltd** Svitzer Marine Ltd *Felixstowe* *United Kingdom* MMSI: 235037917 Official number: 911038	**243** 75 126	Class: LR ✠ **100A1** SS 05/2011 tug UK coastal service *IWS **LMC** **UMS** Eq.Ltr: F; Cable: 275.0/19.0 U2 (a)	**2006-05 Song Cam Shipyard — Haiphong** (Hull) Yd No: (512208) **2006-05 B.V. Scheepswerf Damen — Gorinchem** Yd No: 512208 Loa 24.55 Br ex 11.50 Dght 3.526 Lbp 22.16 Br md 10.70 Dpth 4.60 Welded, 1 dk	**(B32A2ST) Tug**	**2 oil engines** gearing integral to driving 2 Z propellers Total Power: 4,200kW (5,710hp) Caterpillar 3516B-HD 2 x Vee 4 Stroke 16 Cy. 170 x 215 each-2100kW (2855bhp) Caterpillar Inc-USA AuxGen: 2 x 50kW 400V 50Hz a.c
8513754 *CSYI4* -	**SVITZER SINES** *ex Svitzer Brightwell -2010 ex Brightwell -2007* **Svitzer Portugal - Reboques Maritimos SA** - *Lisbon* *Portugal* MMSI: 263601890 Official number: LX-38-RC	**256** 76 179	Class: LR ✠ **100A1** SS 10/2011 tug near Continental trading area service ✠ **LMC** Eq.Ltr: F; Cable: 275.0/19.0 U2 (a)	**1986-10 Richards (Shipbuilders) Ltd — Great Yarmouth** Yd No: 573 Loa 28.80 Br ex 9.05 Dght 4.060 Lbp 26.62 Br md 9.00 Dpth 4.67 Welded, 1 dk	**(B32A2ST) Tug**	**2 oil engines** with clutches & dr geared to sc. shafts driving 2 Directional propellers Total Power: 2,530kW (3,440hp) 12.5kn Ruston 6RK270M 2 x 4 Stroke 6 Cy. 270 x 305 each-1265kW (1720bhp) Ruston Diesels Ltd.-Newton-le-Willows AuxGen: 2 x 80kW 440V 50Hz a.c Fuel: 47.5 (d.f.)
9460708 *2BVO7* -	**SVITZER SKY** **Svitzer Marine Ltd** - *Bristol* *United Kingdom* MMSI: 235069704 Official number: 915467	**250** 75 150	Class: LR ✠ **100A1** SS 09/2013 tug *IWS **LMC** **UMS** Eq.Ltr: F; Cable: 275.0/19.0 U2 (a)	**2008-09 Song Cam Shipyard — Haiphong** (Hull) Yd No: (512226) **2008-09 B.V. Scheepswerf Damen — Gorinchem** Yd No: 512226 Loa 24.47 Br ex 11.33 Dght 3.650 Lbp 22.16 Br md 10.70 Dpth 4.60 Welded, 1 dk	**(B32A2ST) Tug**	**2 oil engines** reduction geared to sc. shafts driving 2 Directional propellers Total Power: 4,200kW (5,710hp) Caterpillar 3516B-HD 2 x Vee 4 Stroke 16 Cy. 170 x 215 each-2100kW (2855bhp) Caterpillar Inc-USA AuxGen: 2 x 60kW 400V 50Hz a.c

IMO / Call sign	Name / Owner	Tonnage	Classification	Builder / Dimensions	Type	Machinery
9324526 *A4DH3* -	**SVITZER SOHAR** **Svitzer Middle East Ltd** - *Port Sultan Qaboos* *Oman* MMSI: 461000040	**318** 95 150	Class: LR (AB) **100A1** SS 06/2009 tug **LMC** Cable: 302.5/20.5 U3 (a)	**2004-06 Jiangsu Wuxi Shipyard Co Ltd — Wuxi JS** (Hull) Yd No: (1155) **2004-06 Pacific Ocean Engineering & Trading Pte Ltd (POET) — Singapore** Yd No: 1155 Loa 28.00 Br ex - Dght 3.500 Lbp 22.40 Br md 9.80 Dpth 4.80 Welded, 1 dk	**(B32A2ST) Tug**	**2 oil engines** gearing integral to driving 2 Z propellers Total Power: 2,648kW (3,600hp) Yanmar 8N21A-EN 2 x 4 Stroke 8 Cy. 210 x 290 each-1324kW (1800bhp) Yanmar Diesel Engine Co Ltd-Japan AuxGen: 2 x 99kW 415V 60Hz a.c
9581588 *J8B4399* -	**SVITZER SOYO** **Svitzer Angola Shipowners (BVI) Ltd** Svitzer Angola Lda *Kingstown* *St Vincent & The Grenadines* MMSI: 377544000 Official number: 10872	**631** 189 475	Class: LR **✠100A1** SS 06/2011 escort tug, fire-fighting Ship 1 (2400m3/h) with water spray *IWS WDL (5t/m2 from frame 0 to frame 15) **✠LMC** **UMS** Eq.Ltr: I*; Cable: 330.0/24.0 U2 (a)	**2011-06 Qingdao Qianjin Shipyard — Qingdao SD** Yd No: 8Z2028 Loa 33.35 Br ex 13.84 Dght 5.000 Lbp 28.85 Br md 13.00 Dpth 6.10 Welded, 1 dk	**(B32A2ST) Tug**	**2 oil engines** gearing integral to driving 2 Z propellers Total Power: 4,412kW (5,998hp) Niigata 8L28HX 2 x 4 Stroke 8 Cy. 280 x 370 each-2206kW (2999bhp) Niigata Engineering Co Ltd-Japan AuxGen: 3 x 224kW 400V 50Hz a.c
9316402 *MGVF5* -	**SVITZER STANFORD** *ex Stanford -2012* **Svitzer Towage Ltd** Svitzer Marine Ltd *London* *United Kingdom* MMSI: 235023045 Official number: 737465	**374** 112 260	Class: LR **✠100A1** SS 02/2014 escort tug, fire fighting ship 1 (2400m3/h) with water spray **✠LMC** **UMS** Eq.Ltr: H; Cable: 302.5/22.0 U2 (a)	**2005-02 Damen Shipyards Gdynia SA — Gdynia** (Hull) Yd No: 511211 **2005-02 B.V. Scheepswerf Damen — Gorinchem** Yd No: 511211 Loa 32.50 Br ex 10.64 Dght 4.250 Lbp 29.01 Br md 10.60 Dpth 5.00 Welded, 1 dk	**(B32A2ST) Tug**	**2 oil engines** gearing integral to driving 2 Directional propellers Total Power: 3,960kW (5,384hp) 13.5kn MaK 6M25 2 x 4 Stroke 6 Cy. 255 x 400 each-1980kW (2692bhp) Caterpillar Motoren GmbH & Co. KG-Germany AuxGen: 3 x 85kW 400V 50Hz a.c
9352793 *MLNF7* -	**SVITZER STANLOW** **Svitzer A/S** Svitzer Marine Ltd *Liverpool* *United Kingdom* MMSI: 235010620 Official number: 911216	**656** 196 170	Class: LR **✠100A1** SS 05/2011 escort tug (140, 150, 10, 30), fire fighting Ship 1 (2400 m3/h) with water spray *IWS Ice Class 1C FS at draught 3.5m Max/min draught fwd 5.426/2.5m Max/min draught aft 5.426/3.5m Required power 4438kw, installed power 5280kw **✠LMC** **UMS** Eq.Ltr: i; Cable: 330.0/26.0 U2 (a)	**2006-05 ASL Shipyard Pte Ltd — Singapore** Yd No: 500 Loa 37.50 Br ex 14.00 Dght 3.512 Lbp 35.93 Br md 13.50 Dpth 5.30 Welded, 1 dk	**(B32A2ST) Tug** Ice Capable	**2 oil engines** gearing integral to driving 2 Voith-Schneider propellers Total Power: 5,280kW (7,178hp) MaK 8M25 2 x 4 Stroke 8 Cy. 255 x 400 each-2640kW (3589bhp) Caterpillar Motoren GmbH & Co. KG-Germany AuxGen: 2 x 211kW 400V 50Hz a.c
9581655 *VJN4269* -	**SVITZER STOCKTON** *ex Svitzer Nixie -2013* **Svitzer A/S** Svitzer Australia Pty Ltd (Svitzer Australasia) *Newcastle, NSW* *Australia* MMSI: 503787000 Official number: 860742	**630** 189 487	Class: LR **✠100A1** SS 06/2012 escort tug, fire-fighting Ship 1 (2400 m3/h) with water spray *IWS WDL (5t/m2 from fr 0 to fr 15) **✠LMC** **UMS** Eq.Ltr: I; Cable: 330.0/24.0 U2 (a)	**2012-06 Qingdao Qianjin Shipyard — Qingdao SD** Yd No: 8Z2035 Loa 32.60 Br ex 13.86 Dght 5.000 Lbp 28.80 Br md 13.00 Dpth 6.10 Welded, 1 dk	**(B32A2ST) Tug**	**2 oil engines** gearing integral to driving 2 Z propellers Total Power: 4,412kW (5,998hp) Niigata 6L28HX 2 x 4 Stroke 6 Cy. 280 x 370 each-2206kW (2999bhp) Niigata Engineering Co Ltd-Japan AuxGen: 3 x 224kW 400V 50Hz a.c
9460693 *2BOY7* -	**SVITZER SUN** **Svitzer Marine Ltd** *Hull* *United Kingdom* MMSI: 235068059 Official number: 915070	**250** 75 150	Class: LR **✠100A1** SS 07/2008 tug *IWS **LMC** **UMS** Eq.Ltr: F; Cable: 275.0/19.0 U2 (a)	**2008-07 Song Cam Shipyard — Haiphong** (Hull) Yd No: (512225) **2008-07 B.V. Scheepswerf Damen — Gorinchem** Yd No: 512225 Loa 24.47 Br ex 11.33 Dght 3.650 Lbp 22.16 Br md 10.70 Dpth 4.60 Welded, 1 dk	**(B32A2ST) Tug**	**2 oil engines** reduction geared to sc. shafts driving 2 Directional propellers Total Power: 4,200kW (5,710hp) Caterpillar 3516B-HD 2 x Vee 4 Stroke 16 Cy. 170 x 215 each-2100kW (2855bhp) Caterpillar Inc-USA AuxGen: 2 x 56kW 400V 50Hz a.c
9019468 *MPJV4* -	**SVITZER SURREY** *ex Adsteam Surrey -2010 ex Sun Surrey -2005* **Svitzer Towage Ltd** Svitzer Marine Ltd *London* *United Kingdom* MMSI: 232002812 Official number: 721990	**378** 113 143	Class: LR **✠100A1** SS 03/2012 tug near continental trading area service **✠LMC** Eq.Ltr: H; Cable: 302.5/22.0 U2	**1992-03 Richards (Shipbuilders) Ltd — Great Yarmouth** Yd No: 587 Loa 30.98 Br ex 10.97 Dght 4.676 Lbp 29.00 Br md 10.50 Dpth 3.50 Welded, 1 dk	**(B32A2ST) Tug**	**2 oil engines** gearing integral to driving 2 Voith-Schneider propellers Total Power: 2,814kW (3,826hp) 12.0kn Ruston 6RK270M 2 x 4 Stroke 6 Cy. 270 x 305 each-1407kW (1913bhp) Ruston Diesels Ltd.-Newton-le-Willows AuxGen: 2 x 85kW 440V 50Hz a.c Fuel: 59.0 (d.f.) 8.0pd
8224511 *GDBL* -	**SVITZER SUSAN** *ex Lady Susan -2009* **Yorlease Ltd** Svitzer Marine Ltd *Grimsby* *United Kingdom* MMSI: 235053756 Official number: 390360	**285** 85 145	Class: LR **✠100A1** SS 05/2009 tug **✠LMC** **UMS** Eq.Ltr: F; Cable: 560.0/20.5 U2 (a)	**1984-04 Soc. Argibay de Const. Navais e Mecanicas S.A.R.L. — Alverca** Yd No: 156 Loa 30.21 Br ex 9.73 Dght 4.615 Lbp 28.30 Br md 9.20 Dpth 3.81 Welded, 1 dk	**(B32A2ST) Tug**	**2 oil engines** gearing integral to driving 2 Voith-Schneider propellers Total Power: 1,942kW (2,640hp) 12.0kn Ruston 6RKCM 2 x 4 Stroke 6 Cy. 254 x 305 each-971kW (1320bhp) Ruston Diesels Ltd.-Newton-le-Willows AuxGen: 2 x 78kW 415V 50Hz a.c, 1 x 26kW 415V 50Hz a.c Fuel: 51.0 (d.f.)
9019470 *MQVW2* -	**SVITZER SUSSEX** *ex Adsteam Sussex -2007 ex Sun Sussex -2005* **Svitzer Towage Ltd** Svitzer Marine Ltd *London* *United Kingdom* MMSI: 232003804 Official number: 722109	**378** 113 143	Class: LR **✠100A1** SS 07/2012 tug near continental trading area service **✠LMC** Eq.Ltr: H; Cable: 302.5/22.0 U2	**1992-07 Richards (Shipbuilders) Ltd — Great Yarmouth** Yd No: 588 Loa 30.10 Br ex 10.96 Dght 4.676 Lbp 29.00 Br md 10.50 Dpth 3.50 Welded, 1 dk	**(B32A2ST) Tug**	**2 oil engines** gearing integral to driving 2 Voith-Schneider propellers Total Power: 2,814kW (3,826hp) 12.5kn Ruston 6RK270M 2 x 4 Stroke 6 Cy. 270 x 305 each-1407kW (1913bhp) Ruston Diesels Ltd.-Newton-le-Willows AuxGen: 2 x 85kW 440V 50Hz a.c Fuel: 59.0 (d.f.) 8.0pd
9578579 *VJN4314* -	**SVITZER SWIFT** **Svitzer A/S** Svitzer Australia Pty Ltd (Svitzer Australasia) *Port Adelaide, SA* *Australia* MMSI: 503783000 Official number: 860797	**442** 132 282	Class: LR **✠100A1** SS 06/2012 tug, fire-fighting Ship 1 (2400 m/h) with water spray *IWS WDL (5t/m2 from aft to fr. 15) **✠LMC** **UMS** Eq.Ltr: H; Cable: 302.5/24.0 U2 (a)	**2012-06 Jiangsu Zhenjiang Shipyard Co Ltd — Zhenjiang JS** Yd No: VZJ6173-0809 Loa 31.50 Br ex 11.53 Dght 4.600 Lbp 26.73 Br md 11.00 Dpth 6.10 Welded, 1 dk	**(B32A2ST) Tug**	**2 oil engines** driving 2 Directional propellers Total Power: 3,676kW (4,998hp) Niigata 6L28HX 2 x 4 Stroke 6 Cy. 280 x 370 each-1838kW (2499bhp) Niigata Engineering Co Ltd-Japan AuxGen: 2 x 150kW 400V 50Hz a.c
9548366 *OWDJ2* -	**SVITZER THOR** **Svitzer A/S** Svitzer Sverige AB SatCom: Inmarsat C 422000161 *Aarhus* *Denmark (DIS)* MMSI: 219015425 Official number: D4412	**635** 190 438	Class: LR **✠100A1** SS 01/2011 escort tug (95,10,30) (81,8,30), fire-fighting Ship 1 (2400m3/h) with water spray *IWS **✠LMC** Eq.Ltr: I*; Cable: 330.0/26.0 U2 (a)	**2011-01 Qingdao Qianjin Shipyard — Qingdao SD** Yd No: 7Z2025 Loa 33.30 Br ex 13.84 Dght 4.500 Lbp 28.04 Br md 13.00 Dpth 5.70 Welded, 1 dk	**(B32A2ST) Tug**	**2 oil engines** reduction geared to sc. shafts driving 2 Directional propellers Total Power: 4,044kW (5,498hp) Niigata 8L28HX 2 x 4 Stroke 8 Cy. 280 x 370 each-2022kW (2749bhp) Niigata Engineering Co Ltd-Japan AuxGen: 2 x 320kW 440V 50Hz a.c
9001693 *MMQU9* -	**SVITZER TRIMLEY** *ex Svitzer Trave -2014 ex Svitzer Trimley -2013* *ex Adsteam Trimley -2007 ex Trimley -2006* **Svitzer EuroMed BV** - *Harwich* *United Kingdom* MMSI: 232003889 Official number: 720139	**371** 111 -	Class: LR **✠100A1** SS 12/2010 tug U.K. near continental trading area service *IWS **✠LMC** Eq.Ltr: (E) ; Cable: 302.5/19.0 U2	**1991-03 Richards (Shipbuilders) Ltd — Great Yarmouth** Yd No: 584 Loa 30.64 Br ex 10.24 Dght 4.116 Lbp 25.00 Br md 9.60 Dpth 4.80 Welded, 1 dk	**(B32A2ST) Tug**	**2 oil engines** with flexible couplings & sr geared to sc. shafts driving 2 Directional propellers Total Power: 2,584kW (3,514hp) 12.0kn Ruston 6RK270M 2 x 4 Stroke 6 Cy. 270 x 305 each-1292kW (1757bhp) Ruston Diesels Ltd.-Newton-le-Willows AuxGen: 2 x 312kW 440V 50Hz a.c, 1 x 85kW 440V 50Hz a.c Thrusters: 1 Thwart. FP thruster (f) Fuel: 85.0 (d.f.)

9548354 *OWNB2* -	**SVITZER TRYM** **Em Z Svitzer AS** - *Fredericia* *Denmark (DIS)* MMSI: 219014875 Official number: D4411	**641** 192 448	Class: LR ✠**100A1** SS 10/2010 escort tug ((84, 10, 30), (64, 8, 30)) fire-fighting Ship 1 (2400m3/h) with water spray *IWS Ice Class 1B FS at a draught of 5.1m Max/min draughts fwd 5.1/3.2m Max/min draughts aft 5.1/3.2m Power required 1138kw, power installed 4044kw ✠**LMC** **UMS** Eq.Ltr: I; Cable: 330.0/26.0 U2 (a)	**2010-10 Qingdao Qianjin Shipyard — Qingdao SD** Yd No: 7Z2024 Loa 33.30 Br ex 13.84 Dght 5.300 Lbp 28.04 Br md 13.00 Dpth 5.70 Welded, 1 dk	**(B32A2ST) Tug**	**2 oil engines** reduction geared to sc. shafts driving 2 Directional propellers Total Power: 4,044kW (5,498hp) Niigata 8L28HX 2 x 4 Stroke 8 Cy. 280 x 370 each-2022kW (2749bhp) Niigata Engineering Co Ltd-Japan AuxGen: 2 x 320kW 440V 50Hz a.c
9548342 *OZ2118* -	**SVITZER TYR** **P/F Svitzer Faroe Islands** Svitzer Sverige AB *Torshavn* *Faeroes (FAS)* MMSI: 231809000	**641** 192 325	Class: LR ✠**100A1** SS 09/2010 escort tug ((84, 10, 30), (64, 8, 30)) fire fighting Ship 1 (2400m3/h) with water spray *IWS Ice Class 1B FS at draught of 5.10m Max/min draught fwd 5.10/3.20m Max/min draught aft 5.10/3.20m Required power 1138kw, installed power 4044kw ✠**LMC** **UMS** Eq.Ltr: I; Cable: 330.0/24.0 U2 (a)	**2010-09 Qingdao Qianjin Shipyard — Qingdao SD** Yd No: 7Z2023 Loa 32.60 (BB) Br ex 13.84 Dght 5.300 Lbp 28.60 Br md 13.00 Dpth 5.70 Welded, 1 dk	**(B32A2ST) Tug** Ice Capable	**2 oil engines** reduction geared to sc. shafts driving 2 Directional propellers Total Power: 4,044kW (5,498hp) Niigata 8L28HX 2 x 4 Stroke 8 Cy. 280 x 370 each-2022kW (2749bhp) Niigata Engineering Co Ltd-Japan AuxGen: 2 x 320kW 440V 50Hz a.c
9366902 *2AGX6* -	**SVITZER VALIANT** **Svitzer SPC4 Pty Ltd** Svitzer Marine Ltd *Grimsby* *United Kingdom* MMSI: 235059532 Official number: 913559	**250** 75 127	Class: LR ✠**100A1** SS 07/2012 tug **LMC** **UMS** Eq.Ltr: F; Cable: 275.0/19.0 U2 (a)	**2007-07 Song Cam Shipyard — Haiphong** (Hull) **2007-07 B.V. Scheepswerf Damen — Gorinchem** Yd No: 512211 Loa 24.47 Br ex 11.33 Dght 3.650 Lbp 22.16 Br md 10.70 Dpth 4.60 Welded, 1 dk	**(B32A2ST) Tug**	**2 oil engines** gearing integral to driving 2 Z propellers Total Power: 4,200kW (5,710hp) Caterpillar 3516B-HD 2 x Vee 4 Stroke 16 Cy. 170 x 215 each-2100kW (2855bhp) Caterpillar Inc-USA AuxGen: 2 x 60kW 400V 50Hz a.c
9193020 *MBQP9* -	**SVITZER VICTORY** *ex Adsteam Victory -2007 ex Gurrong -2005* **Svitzer Humber Ltd** Svitzer Marine Ltd *London* *United Kingdom* MMSI: 235011848 Official number: 907482	**495** 148 -	Class: LR (AB) **100A1** SS 05/2010 tug **LMC** **CCS** Cable: 327.5/25.0 U2 (a)	**2000-05 Oceanfast Marine Pty Ltd — Fremantle WA** (Hull launched by) Yd No: 29 **2000-05 in New Zealand** (Hull completed by) Loa 33.70 Br ex 11.50 Dght 5.400 Lbp 30.30 Br md 11.50 Dpth 5.85 Welded, 1 dk	**(B32A2ST) Tug**	**2 oil engines** gearing integral to driving 2 Z propellers Total Power: 3,654kW (4,968hp) 13.0kn Daihatsu 6DKM-28 2 x 4 Stroke 6 Cy. 280 x 390 each-1827kW (2484bhp) Daihatsu Diesel Manufacturing Co Lt-Japan AuxGen: 2 x 75kW 415V 50Hz a.c
9366689 *VJN3152* -	**SVITZER WARANG** *ex Adsteam Warang -2007* **Svitzer Australia Pty Ltd (Svitzer Australasia)** - *Port Adelaide, SA* *Australia* Official number: 858116	**294** 88 153	Class: LR ✠**100A1** SS 11/2011 tug **LMC** **UMS** Eq.Ltr: F; Cable: 275.0/19.0 U2 (a)	**2006-11 Song Cam Shipyard — Haiphong** (Hull) Yd No: (511521) **2006-11 B.V. Scheepswerf Damen — Gorinchem** Yd No: 511521 Loa 28.67 Br ex 10.42 Dght 3.610 Lbp 25.78 Br md 9.80 Dpth 4.60 Welded, 1 dk	**(B32A2ST) Tug**	**2 oil engines** reduction geared to sc. shafts driving 2 Directional propellers Total Power: 3,678kW (5,000hp) Caterpillar 3516B-HD 2 x Vee 4 Stroke 16 Cy. 170 x 215 each-1839kW (2500bhp) Caterpillar Inc-USA AuxGen: 2 x 85kW 400V 50Hz a.c
9366859 *MLEG9* -	**SVITZER WARDEN** *ex Adsteam Warden -2007* **Svitzer SPC4 Pty Ltd** Svitzer Marine Ltd *Rochester* *United Kingdom* MMSI: 235032469 Official number: 910991	**207** 207 150	Class: LR (BV) ✠**100A1** SS 02/2011 tug, fire fighting Ship 1 (2400 m3/h) with water spray limited European area service *IWS **LMC** **UMS** Eq.Ltr: F; Cable: 275.0/17.5 U2 (a)	**2006-02 Song Cam Shipyard — Haiphong** (Hull) Yd No: (512203) **2006-02 B.V. Scheepswerf Damen — Gorinchem** Yd No: 512203 Loa 24.55 Br ex 11.49 Dght 5.350 Lbp 22.16 Br md 10.70 Dpth 4.60 Welded, 1 dk	**(B32A2ST) Tug**	**2 oil engines** gearing integral to driving 2 Z propellers Total Power: 4,200kW (5,710hp) Caterpillar 3516B-HD 2 x Vee 4 Stroke 16 Cy. 170 x 215 each-2100kW (2855bhp) Caterpillar Inc-USA AuxGen: 2 x 50kW 400V 50Hz a.c
9366691 *VJN3151* -	**SVITZER WARRAWEE** *ex Adsteam Warrawee -2007* **Svitzer Australia Pty Ltd (Svitzer Australasia)** - *Port Adelaide, SA* *Australia* Official number: 858117	**294** 88 153	Class: LR ✠**100A1** SS 11/2011 tug **LMC** **UMS** Eq.Ltr: F; Cable: 275.0/19.0 U2 (a)	**2006-11 Song Cam Shipyard — Haiphong** (Hull) Yd No: (511522) **2006-11 B.V. Scheepswerf Damen — Gorinchem** Yd No: 511522 Loa 28.67 Br ex 10.42 Dght 3.610 Lbp 25.78 Br md 9.80 Dpth 4.60 Welded, 1 dk	**(B32A2ST) Tug**	**2 oil engines** reduction geared to sc. shafts driving 2 Directional propellers Total Power: 3,678kW (5,000hp) Caterpillar 3516B-HD 2 x Vee 4 Stroke 16 Cy. 170 x 215 each-1839kW (2500bhp) Caterpillar Inc-USA AuxGen: 2 x 84kW 400V 50Hz a.c
9440746 *2AXK6* -	**SVITZER WATERSTON** **Santander Lease SA EFC (Bansalease SA)** Svitzer Marine Ltd *Milford Haven* *United Kingdom* MMSI: 235063728 Official number: 914556	**690** 207 378	Class: LR ✠**100A1** SS 06/2013 fire fighting Ship 1 (2400 m3/h) with water spray *IWS escort tug EPN (40,90,8,57) ✠**LMC** **UMS** Eq.Ltr: J; Cable: 358.0/26.0 U2 (a)	**2008-06 Construcciones Navales P Freire SA — Vigo** Yd No: 651 Loa 34.00 Br ex - Dght 4.500 Lbp 32.20 Br md 14.50 Dpth 6.20 Welded, 1 dk	**(B32A2ST) Tug**	**2 oil engines** reduction geared to sc. shafts driving 2 Z propellers Total Power: 5,754kW (7,824hp) 13.0kn General Electric 7FDM16 2 x Vee 4 Stroke 16 Cy. 229 x 267 each-2877kW (3912bhp) GE Marine Engines-Cincinnati, Oh AuxGen: 2 x 390kW 415V 50Hz a.c Fuel: 182.0 (r.f.)
9412397 *2AXZ9* -	**SVITZER WATWICK** **Svitzer Marine Ltd** - *Milford Haven* *United Kingdom* MMSI: 235063854 Official number: 915188	**490** 147 375	Class: LR ✠**100A1** SS 12/2013 escort tug, fire fighting Ship 1 (2400m3/h) with water spray *IWS ✠**LMC** **UMS** Eq.Ltr: H; Cable: 302.5/24.0 U2 (a)	**2008-12 Qingdao Qianjin Shipyard — Qingdao SD** Yd No: 6Z2018 Loa 32.60 Br ex 12.10 Dght 4.500 Lbp 28.60 Br md 11.60 Dpth 5.70 Welded, 1 dk	**(B32A2ST) Tug**	**2 oil engines** gearing integral to driving 2 Z propellers Total Power: 4,412kW (5,998hp) 12.0kn Niigata 8L28HX 2 x 4 Stroke 8 Cy. 280 x 370 each-2206kW (2999bhp) Niigata Engineering Co Ltd-Japan AuxGen: 2 x 150kW 400V 50Hz a.c Boilers: HWH (o.f.) 4.1kgf/cm² (4.0bar)
9581576 *J8B4398* -	**SVITZER ZAIRE** **Svitzer Angola Shipowners (BVI) Ltd** Svitzer Angola Lda *Kingstown* *St Vincent & The Grenadines* MMSI: 376545000 Official number: 10871	**631** 189 483	Class: LR ✠**100A1** SS 05/2011 escort tug, fire-fighting Ship 1 (2400 m3/h) with water spray *IWS WDL (5t/m2 from frame 0 to frame 15) ✠**LMC** **UMS** Eq.Ltr: I*; Cable: 330.0/24.0 U2 (a)	**2011-05 Qingdao Qianjin Shipyard — Qingdao SD** Yd No: 8Z2027 Loa 33.35 Br ex 13.84 Dght 5.000 Lbp 28.85 Br md 13.00 Dpth 6.10 Welded, 1 dk	**(B32A2ST) Tug**	**2 oil engines** gearing integral to driving 2 Z propellers Total Power: 4,412kW (5,998hp) Niigata 8L28HX 2 x 4 Stroke 8 Cy. 280 x 370 each-2206kW (2999bhp) Niigata Engineering Co Ltd-Japan AuxGen: 3 x 224kW 400V 50Hz a.c
8991451 *9A2341* -	**SVJETIONIK** **Plovput doo** - *Split* *Croatia*	**306** 91 137	Class: CS	**1987 RO Inkobrod — Korcula** Yd No: 112 Loa 32.80 Br ex - Dght 2.094 Lbp 27.90 Br md 9.50 Dpth 3.20 Welded, 1 dk	**(B34T2QR) Work/Repair Vessel** 1 Ha: (2.8 x 6.0) Cranes: 1	**2 oil engines** geared to sc. shafts driving 2 Propellers Total Power: 522kW (710hp) 8.5kn Cummins NTA-855-M 2 x 4 Stroke 6 Cy. 140 x 152 each-261kW (355bhp) (new engine 1997) Cummins Engine Co Ltd-United Kingdom AuxGen: 2 x 157kW
9599353 *UBDL6* -	**SVL GLORY** **SVL Maritime B Ltd** SVL Marine Transit Services LLC SatCom: Inmarsat C 427306492 *Russia* MMSI: 273329070	**4,793** 1,851 7,102	Class: RS	**2011-05 Sudostroitelnyy Zavod "Krasnoye Sormovo" — Nizhniy Novgorod** Yd No: 09003 Loa 141.40 (BB) Br ex 16.84 Dght 4.600 Lbp 135.80 Br md 16.80 Dpth 6.82 Welded, 1 dk	**(A13B2TP) Products Tanker** Double Hull (13F) Liq: 8,256; Liq (Oil): 8,256 Compartments: 12 Wing Ta, 2 Wing Slop Ta, ER Ice Capable	**2 oil engines** reduction geared to sc. shafts driving 2 Directional propellers Total Power: 2,400kW (3,264hp) 10.5kn Wartsila 6L20 2 x 4 Stroke 6 Cy. 200 x 280 each-1200kW (1632bhp) Wartsila Finland Oy-Finland AuxGen: 3 x 296kW a.c Fuel: 240.0 (r.f.)

IMO / Call sign	Name / Owner	Tonnage / Class	Builder / Dimensions	Type / Cargo	Machinery
9645982 *UFNT* -	**SVL LIBERTY** **SVL Maritime C Ltd** SVL Marine Transit Services LLC *Novorossiysk* *Russia* MMSI: 273331440	**5,089** Class: RS 2,035 7,041	**2013-03 OAO Khersonskiy Sudostroitelnyy Zavod — Kherson** Yd No: 8001 Loa 140.85 (BB) Br ex 16.86 Dght 4.200 Lbp 137.10 Br md 16.70 Dpth 6.00 Welded, 1 dk	**(A13B2TP) Products Tanker** Double Hull (13F) Liq: 7,828; Liq (Oil): 7,828 Compartments: 6 Ta, ER	**2 oil engines** reduction geared to sc. shafts driving 2 Directional propellers Total Power: 2,400kW (3,264hp) 10.5kn Wartsila 6L20 2 x 4 Stroke 6 Cy. 200 x 280 each-1200kW (1632bhp) Wartsila Finland Oy-Finland AuxGen: 3 x 315kW a.c Thrusters: 1 Tunnel thruster (f) Fuel: 311.0 (d.f.)
9655468 *UBIK7* -	**SVL LOYALTY** **SVL Maritime D Ltd** SVL Marine Transit Services LLC *Novorossiysk* *Russia* MMSI: 273333570	**5,075** Class: RS 2,026 7,025	**2013-08 OAO Khersonskiy Sudostroitelnyy Zavod — Kherson** Yd No: 8002 Loa 140.85 Br ex 16.86 Dght 4.200 Lbp 137.10 Br md 16.70 Dpth 6.00 Welded, 1 dk	**(A13B2TP) Products Tanker** Double Hull (13F) Liq: 8,168; Liq (Oil): 8,168 Cargo Heating Coils Compartments: 6 Ta, ER Ice Capable	**2 oil engines** reduction geared to sc. shafts driving 2 Directional propellers Total Power: 2,400kW (3,264hp) 10.5kn Wartsila 6L20 2 x 4 Stroke 6 Cy. 200 x 280 each-1200kW (1632bhp) Wartsila Finland Oy-Finland AuxGen: 3 x 315kW a.c Fuel: 300.0 (d.f.)
9599341 *UBDL5* -	**SVL PRIDE** **SVL Maritime A Ltd** SVL Marine Transit Services LLC SatCom: Inmarsat C 427306489 *Russia* MMSI: 273324070	**4,793** Class: RS 1,851 7,111	**2010-11 Sudostroitelnyy Zavod "Krasnoye Sormovo" — Nizhniy Novgorod** Yd No: 09002 Loa 141.50 Br ex 16.84 Dght 4.600 Lbp 135.22 Br md 16.60 Dpth 6.82 Welded, 1 dk	**(A13A2TW) Crude/Oil Products Tanker** Double Hull (13F) Liq: 8,256; Liq (Oil): 8,256 Compartments: 12 Wing Ta, 2 Wing Slop Ta, ER Ice Capable	**2 oil engines** reduction geared to sc. shafts driving 2 Directional propellers Total Power: 2,160kW (2,936hp) 10.5kn Wartsila 6L20 2 x 4 Stroke 6 Cy. 200 x 280 each-1080kW (1468bhp) Wartsila Finland Oy-Finland Thrusters: 1 Tunnel thruster (f) Fuel: 240.0
9655470 *UHKU* -	**SVL UNITY** **SVL Maritime E Ltd** SVL Marine Transit Services LLC *Novorossiysk* *Russia* MMSI: 273337080	**5,075** Class: RS 2,023 7,023	**2013-10 OAO Khersonskiy Sudostroitelnyy Zavod — Kherson** Yd No: 8003 Loa 140.85 (BB) Br ex 16.86 Dght 4.200 Lbp 137.10 Br md 16.70 Dpth 6.00 Welded, 1 dk	**(A13B2TP) Products Tanker** Double Hull (13F) Liq: 7,938; Liq (Oil): 7,938 Cargo Heating Coils Compartments: 6 Wing Ta, 2 Wing Slop Ta, Wing ER Ice Capable	**2 oil engines** reduction geared to sc. shafts driving 2 Directional propellers Total Power: 2,400kW (3,264hp) 10.5kn Wartsila 6L20 2 x 4 Stroke 6 Cy. 200 x 280 each-1200kW (1632bhp) Wartsila Finland Oy-Finland AuxGen: 3 x 315kW a.c Thrusters: 1 Tunnel thruster (f) Fuel: 310.0
8964422 *WDG8015* -	**SVO MARINER** *ex* HOS Mariner *-2013* *ex* Candy Mariner *-2003* **Skansi Vessel Organization LLC** Skansi Marine LLC *New Orleans, LA* *United States of America* MMSI: 367573180 Official number: 1083977	**1,255** 376 1,656	**1999-09 Swiftships Shipbuilders LLC — Morgan City LA** Yd No: 495 Loa 67.06 Br ex - Dght 4.170 Lbp 67.05 Br md 14.02 Dpth 4.87 Welded, 1 dk	**(B21A20S) Platform Supply Ship**	**2 oil engines** reduction geared to sc. shafts driving 2 FP propellers Total Power: 2,868kW (3,900hp) 10.0kn EMD (Electro-Motive) 16-645-E2 2 x Vee 2 Stroke 16 Cy. 230 x 254 each-1434kW (1950bhp) General Motors Corp.Electro-Motive Div.-La Grange AuxGen: 2 x 125kW 480V 60Hz a.c Thrusters: 1 Thwart. FP thruster (f); 1 Tunnel thruster (a)
8929446 - -	**SVOYEVREMENNYY** **Uliss Co Ltd** Niko Co Ltd *Vostochnyy* *Russia* MMSI: 273434380 Official number: 791993	*187* Class: RS - 46	**1979-11 Gorokhovetskiy Sudostroitelnyy Zavod — Gorokhovets** Yd No: 381 Loa 29.30 Br ex 8.49 Dght 3.090 Lbp 27.00 Br md 8.30 Dpth 4.35 Welded, 1 dk	**(B32A2ST) Tug** Ice Capable	**2 oil engines** driving 2 CP propellers Total Power: 882kW (1,200hp) 11.4kn Russkiy 6D30/50-4-2 2 x 2 Stroke 6 Cy. 300 x 500 each-441kW (600bhp) Mashinostroitelnyy Zavod"Russkiy-Dizel"-Leningrad AuxGen: 2 x 30kW a.c Fuel: 36.0 (d.f.)
9664744 *J8B4706* -	**SVS AVERY** **Sandmore Ltd** Specialised Vessel Services (SVS) *Kingstown* *St Vincent & The Grenadines* MMSI: 376687000 Official number: 11179	**168** Class: BV 50 65	**2012-09 Damen Shipyards Singapore Pte Ltd — Singapore** (Hull) Yd No: 153 **2012-09 B.V. Scheepswerf Damen — Gorinchem** Yd No: 544821 Loa 34.30 Br ex 7.35 Dght 1.950 Lbp 32.00 Br md 6.80 Dpth 3.30 Welded, 1 dk	**(B21A20C) Crew/Supply Vessel** Hull Material: Aluminium Alloy	**3 oil engines** reduction geared to sc. shafts driving 3 FP propellers Total Power: 2,460kW (3,345hp) 25.5kn Caterpillar C32 3 x Vee 4 Stroke 12 Cy. 145 x 162 each-820kW (1115bhp) Caterpillar Inc-USA AuxGen: 2 x 58kW 415/240V 60Hz a.c Thrusters: 1 Tunnel thruster (f)
9047831 *5IM820* -	**SVS BONNY** *ex* Seikai No. 2 *-2013* **Specialised Vessel Services (SVS)** - *Zanzibar* *Tanzania* MMSI: 677072000 Official number: 100182	*131* - -	**1992-09 Hitachi Zosen Corp — Kawasaki KN** Yd No: 117304 Loa 38.00 Br ex - Dght 1.300 Lbp 33.50 Br md 8.80 Dpth 3.40 Welded, 1 dk	**(B12D2FP) Fishery Patrol Vessel**	**2 oil engines** with clutches, flexible couplings & sr reverse geared to sc. shaft driving 2 FP propellers Total Power: 4,090kW (5,560hp) 31.0kn M.T.U. 16V396TB94 2 x Vee 4 Stroke 16 Cy. 165 x 185 each-2045kW (2780bhp) MTU Friedrichshafen GmbH-Friedrichshafen
9676539 *J8B4987* -	**SVS CAVENDISH** **Specialised Vessel Services (SVS)** - *Kingstown* *St Vincent & The Grenadines* MMSI: 375017000 Official number: 11460	**472** Class: BV 141 350	**2014-03 189 Company — Haiphong** (Hull) **2014-03 B.V. Scheepswerf Damen — Gorinchem** Yd No: 547227 Loa 53.25 Br ex 10.20 Dght 33.200 Lbp 49.92 Br md 9.00 Dpth 4.70 Welded, 1 dk	**(B21A20C) Crew/Supply Vessel**	**4 oil engines** reduction geared to sc. shafts driving 4 Propellers Total Power: 7,060kW (9,600hp) 25.0kn Caterpillar 3512C 4 x Vee 4 Stroke 12 Cy. 170 x 215 each-1765kW (2400bhp) Caterpillar Inc-USA Thrusters: 2 Tunnel thruster (f)
9642239 - -	**SVS COCHRANE** **Kenya Marine Contractors EPZ Ltd** Specialised Vessel Services (SVS) *Dar es Salaam* *Tanzania*	**443** Class: BV 128 365	**2012-04 Song Thu Co. — Da Nang** (Hull) Yd No: (547213) **2012-04 B.V. Scheepswerf Damen — Gorinchem** Yd No: 547213 Loa 53.30 Br ex - Dght 3.200 Lbp 49.92 Br md 9.20 Dpth 4.70 Welded, 1 dk	**(B21A20C) Crew/Supply Vessel**	**4 oil engines** reduction geared to sc. shafts driving 4 FP propellers Total Power: 3,728kW (5,068hp) 25.0kn Caterpillar 3512TA 4 x Vee 4 Stroke 12 Cy. 170 x 190 each-932kW (1267bhp) Caterpillar Inc-USA AuxGen: 3 x 98kW 60Hz a.c Thrusters: 2 Tunnel thruster (f) Fuel: 160.0 (d.f.)
9650561 *J8B4908* -	**SVS CORNWALLIS** **Damen Shipyards Gorinchem** Specialised Vessel Services (SVS) *Kingstown* *St Vincent & The Grenadines* MMSI: 376991000 Official number: 11381	**443** Class: BV 132 -	**2013-09 189 Company — Haiphong** (Hull) **2013-09 B.V. Scheepswerf Damen — Gorinchem** Yd No: 547218 Loa 53.25 Br ex 10.10 Dght - Lbp 49.92 Br md 9.00 Dpth - Welded, 1 dk	**(B21A20C) Crew/Supply Vessel**	**4 oil engines** reduction geared to sc. shaft (s) driving 4 FP propellers Total Power: 4,472kW (6,080hp) 25.0kn Caterpillar 3512TA 4 x Vee 4 Stroke 12 Cy. 170 x 190 each-1118kW (1520bhp) Caterpillar Inc-USA AuxGen: 3 x 99kW 60Hz a.c
9581904 - -	**SVS DAMPIER** *ex* Sea Axe 544816 *-2011* **Kenya Marine Contractors EPZ Ltd** Specialised Vessel Services (SVS) *Zanzibar* *Tanzania*	**168** Class: (BV) 50 74	**2010-04 189 Company — Haiphong** (Hull) **2010-04 B.V. Scheepswerf Damen — Gorinchem** Yd No: 544816 Loa 34.40 Br ex - Dght 1.930 Lbp 32.00 Br md 6.50 Dpth 3.30 Welded, 1 dk	**(B21A20C) Crew/Supply Vessel** Hull Material: Aluminium Alloy Passengers: unberthed: 80	**3 oil engines** reduction geared to sc. shafts driving 3 FP propellers Total Power: 2,460kW (3,345hp) 25.5kn Caterpillar C32 3 x Vee 4 Stroke 12 Cy. 145 x 162 each-820kW (1115bhp) Caterpillar Inc-USA AuxGen: 2 x 65kW 60Hz a.c
8822002 *5IM412* -	**SVS DRAKE** *ex* New Investigator *-2011* *ex* Frank Cook *-1992* **Kenya Marine Contractors EPZ Ltd** Specialised Vessel Services (SVS) *Zanzibar* *Tanzania* MMSI: 677031200 Official number: 100114	*106* Class: (BV) 31 -	**1989-03 North Queensland Engineers & Agents Pty Ltd — Cairns QLD** Yd No: 171 Loa 24.95 Br ex 5.86 Dght - Lbp 21.00 Br md 5.62 Dpth 3.22 Welded	**(B34M2QS) Search & Rescue Vessel** Hull Material: Aluminium Alloy	**2 oil engines** with clutches, flexible couplings & sr geared to sc. shaft driving 2 Water jets Total Power: 898kW (1,220hp) Caterpillar 3412 2 x Vee 4 Stroke 12 Cy. 137 x 152 each-449kW (610bhp) (new engine 2011) Caterpillar Inc-USA
7394101 *5IM453* -	**SVS FROBISHER** *ex* Kaiko *-2011* *ex* Kaiko Maru *-2011* *ex* Kaiko Maru No. 3 *-2006* *ex* Keiten Maru *-2003* **Specialised Vessel Services (SVS)** - *Zanzibar* *Tanzania* MMSI: 677035300	**1,010** 303 697	**1974-06 Naikai Shipbuilding & Engineering Co Ltd — Onomichi HS (Taguma Shipyard)** Yd No: 391 Converted From: Stern Trawler-2011 Loa 61.90 Br ex 11.02 Dght 3.988 Lbp 55.00 Br md 11.00 Dpth 6.90 Riveted\Welded, 1 dk	**(B34H2SQ) Patrol Vessel**	**1 oil engine** driving 1 FP propeller Total Power: 1,471kW (2,000hp) Daihatsu 6DSM-32 1 x 4 Stroke 6 Cy. 320 x 380 1471kW (2000bhp) Daihatsu Diesel Manufacturing Co Lt-Japan

9013270 - -	**SVS GRENVILLE** *ex* Tosa Kaien Maru *-2012* **Specialised Vessel Services (SVS)** - *Zanzibar* *Tanzania*	*459* - 418		**1991**-03 **Miho Zosensho K.K. — Shimizu** Yd No: 1396 Converted From: Fishing Vessel-2012 Loa 53.99 (BB) Br ex 9.42 Dght 3.800 Lbp 46.00 Br md 9.40 Dpth 6.20 Welded	**(B34H2SQ) Patrol Vessel** Passengers: berths: 60 Cranes: 1x4t	**1 oil engine** with flexible couplings & sr geared to sc. shaft driving 1 CP propeller Total Power: 1,177kW (1,600hp) 10.0kn Hanshin LH28L 1 x 4 Stroke 6 Cy. 280 x 530 1177kW (1600bhp) The Hanshin Diesel Works Ltd-Japan Thrusters: 1 Thwart. CP thruster (f) Fuel: 245.0
9512159 *J8B3893* -	**SVS GUARDSMAN** *ex* Seaways 19 *-2011* **Specialised Vessel Services (SVS)** - *Kingstown* *St Vincent & The Grenadines* MMSI: 377346000 Official number: 10366	**168** 50 65	Class: BV	**2008**-09 **Damen Shipyards Singapore Pte Ltd — Singapore** (Hull) Yd No: (544806) **2008**-09 **B.V. Scheepswerf Damen — Gorinchem** Yd No: 544806 Loa 33.45 Br ex - Dght 2.650 Lbp 32.98 Br md 6.34 Dpth 3.30 Welded, 1 dk	**(B21A20C) Crew/Supply Vessel** Hull Material: Aluminium Alloy Passengers: unberthed: 63	**3 oil engines** reduction geared to sc. shafts driving 3 FP propellers Total Power: 2,460kW (3,345hp) 18.0kn Caterpillar C32 3 x Vee 4 Stroke 12 Cy. 145 x 162 each-820kW (1115bhp) Caterpillar Inc-USA Thrusters: 1 Tunnel thruster (f)
9657997 - -	**SVS HAWKINS** - **Kenya Marine Contractors EPZ Ltd** Specialised Vessel Services (SVS) *Zanzibar* *Tanzania (Zanzibar)*	**174** 52 40	Class: BV	**2012**-04 **Damen Shipyards Singapore Pte Ltd — Singapore** (Hull) Yd No: 152 **2012**-04 **B.V. Scheepswerf Damen — Gorinchem** Yd No: 544820 Loa 34.30 Br ex - Dght 1.950 Lbp 32.00 Br md 7.35 Dpth 3.30 Welded, 1 dk	**(B21A20C) Crew/Supply Vessel** Hull Material: Aluminium Alloy Passengers: unberthed: 80	**3 oil engines** reduction geared to sc. shafts driving 3 Propellers Total Power: 2,460kW (3,345hp) 25.5kn Caterpillar C32 3 x Vee 4 Stroke 12 Cy. 145 x 162 each-820kW (1115bhp) Caterpillar Inc-USA AuxGen: 2 x 58kW 60Hz a.c Thrusters: 1 Retract. directional thruster (f) Fuel: 50.0
8711435 *5IM801* -	**SVS KIDD** *ex* Miyako *-2012* **Specialised Vessel Services (SVS)** - *Zanzibar* *Tanzania* MMSI: 677070100 Official number: 100159	*136* - 100		**1988**-02 **Miho Zosensho K.K. — Shimizu** Yd No: 1292 Converted From: Stern Trawler-2012 Loa 38.77 (BB) Br ex - Dght 2.656 Lbp 32.20 Br md 6.60 Dpth 2.95 Welded, 1 dk	**(B34H2SQ) Patrol Vessel**	**1 oil engine** with clutches, flexible couplings & dr reverse geared to sc. shaft driving 1 CP propeller Total Power: 883kW (1,201hp) 12.0kn Yanmar 6T240-ET 1 x 4 Stroke 6 Cy. 240 x 310 883kW (1201bhp) Yanmar Diesel Engine Co Ltd-Japan AuxGen: 2 x 100kW 225V a.c Thrusters: 1 Thwart. FP thruster (f) Fuel: 62.0
9581916 - -	**SVS MONCK** *ex* Sea Axe 544817 *-2011* **Specialised Vessel Services (SVS)** - *Zanzibar* *Tanzania*	**168** 50 74	Class: BV	**2010**-04 **189 Company — Haiphong** (Hull) **2010**-04 **B.V. Scheepswerf Damen — Gorinchem** Yd No: 544817 Loa 34.40 Br ex - Dght 1.930 Lbp 32.00 Br md 6.50 Dpth 3.30 Welded, 1 dk	**(B21A20C) Crew/Supply Vessel** Hull Material: Aluminium Alloy Passengers: unberthed: 80	**3 oil engines** reduction geared to sc. shafts driving 3 FP propellers Total Power: 2,460kW (3,345hp) 25.5kn Caterpillar C32 3 x Vee 4 Stroke 12 Cy. 145 x 162 each-820kW (1115bhp) Caterpillar Inc-USA AuxGen: 2 x 65kW 60Hz a.c
8110538 *5IM544* -	**SVS MORGAN** *ex* Pacific Claymore *-2012* **Specialised Vessel Services (SVS)** - *Zanzibar* *Tanzania* MMSI: 677044400	**863** 258 1,053	Class: (AB)	**1982**-01 **Yokohama Zosen — Chiba** Yd No: 1397 Loa 57.70 Br ex - Dght 3.912 Lbp 52.51 Br md 12.21 Dpth 4.53 Welded, 1 dk	**(B21A20S) Platform Supply Ship** Passengers: berths: 32 Cranes: 1x26.8t	**2 oil engines** reverse reduction geared to sc. shafts driving 2 FP propellers Total Power: 2,060kW (2,800hp) 12.0kn Yanmar T260L-ST 2 x 4 Stroke 6 Cy. 260 x 330 each-1030kW (1400bhp) Yanmar Diesel Engine Co Ltd-Japan AuxGen: 3 x 160kW 440V 60Hz a.c Thrusters: 1 Thwart. CP thruster (f) Fuel: 290.8 (d.f.) 5.5pd
8838271 - -	**SVS RALEIGH** *ex* Express 23 *-2011* *ex* Abeer Eighteen *-2006* **Kenya Marine Contractors EPZ Ltd** Specialised Vessel Services (SVS) *Tanzania*	*169* 50 -	Class: BV (AB)	**1990**-05 **Aluminum Boats, Inc. — Crown Point, La** Yd No: 332 Loa - Br ex - Dght 1.890 Lbp 33.53 Br md 7.92 Dpth 3.81 Welded, 1 dk	**(B21A20C) Crew/Supply Vessel** Hull Material: Aluminium Alloy	**4 oil engines** reverse reduction geared to sc. shafts driving 4 FP propellers Total Power: 2,400kW (3,264hp) 20.0kn G.M. (Detroit Diesel) 12V-71 4 x Vee 2 Stroke 12 Cy. 108 x 127 each-600kW (816bhp) Detroit Diesel Corporation-Detroit, Mi AuxGen: 2 x 40kW a.c
9686534 *5NRL2* -	**SVS TEACH** - **MARTESE (Marine Technical Services) Ltd** Specialised Vessel Services (SVS) *Nigeria* MMSI: 657102300	**168** 50 -	Class: BV	**2013**-03 **Damen Shipyards Singapore Pte Ltd — Singapore** (Hull) Yd No: 154 **2013**-03 **B.V. Scheepswerf Damen — Gorinchem** Yd No: 544824 Loa 34.30 Br ex - Dght 1.950 Lbp 32.00 Br md 6.80 Dpth 3.30 Welded, 1 dk	**(B34H2SQ) Patrol Vessel** Hull Material: Aluminium Alloy	**3 oil engines** reduction geared to sc. shafts driving 3 FP propellers Total Power: 2,460kW (3,345hp) 25.5kn Caterpillar C32 3 x Vee 4 Stroke 12 Cy. 145 x 162 each-820kW (1115bhp) Caterpillar Inc-USA AuxGen: 2 x 70kW 60Hz a.c Fuel: 51.0 (d.f.)
7212078 *ENOQ* -	**SVYATA OLGA** *ex* Professor Minyayev *-2006* **Kiev State Academy of Water Transport** - SatCom: Inmarsat C 427310089 *Kherson* *Ukraine* Official number: 713007	**6,127** 1,838 5,495	Class: (RS)	**1972**-03 **Stocznia Szczecinska im A Warskiego — Szczecin** Yd No: B80/06 Loa 122.10 Br ex 17.02 Dght 7.360 Lbp 111.99 Br md 17.00 Dpth 9.94 Welded, 2 dks	**(B34K2QT) Training Ship** Bale: 5,175; Ins: 312; Liq: 223 Compartments: 2 Wing Dp Ta in Hold, ER, 3 Ho 5 Ha: (7.4 x 4.8) (8.8 x 5.9)2 (1.9 x 3.8)ER (8.0 x 8.9) Cranes: 1x5t; Derricks: 1x30t,1x10t,2x5t; Winches: 4 Ice Capable	**1 oil engine** driving 1 FP propeller Total Power: 4,045kW (5,500hp) 16.0kn Sulzer 5RND68 1 x 2 Stroke 5 Cy. 680 x 1250 4045kW (5500bhp) Zaklady Przemyslu Metalowego 'HCegielski' SA-Poznan
8980696 *UUCV* -	**SVYATAYA ANNA** *ex* Lenkoran *-2003* **JSC 'Agroexport'** - *Nikolayev* *Ukraine* MMSI: 272068800 Official number: 263	**1,659** 498 2,072	Class: RR	**1967 Santierul Naval Oltenita S.A. — Oltenita** Loa 93.86 Br ex 13.20 Dght 3.110 Lbp 90.00 Br md 13.00 Dpth 4.80 Welded, 1 dk	**(A31A2GX) General Cargo Ship** Grain: 2,966	**2 oil engines** driving 2 FP propellers Total Power: 736kW (1,000hp) 10.0kn S.K.L. 6NVD48 2 x 4 Stroke 6 Cy. 320 x 480 each-368kW (500bhp) VEB Schwermaschinenbau "KarlLiebknecht" (SKL)-Magdeburg
9247625 *UBJI8* -	**SVYATITEL ALEKSIY** - **Valday-4 Ltd** JS North-Western Shipping Co (OAO 'Severo-Zapadnoye Parokhodstvo') *St Petersburg* *Russia* MMSI: 273358260	**4,974** 2,280 5,440	Class: GL (RS)	**2003**-10 **OAO Sudostroitelnyy Zavod "Severnaya Verf" — St.-Peterburg** Yd No: 903 Loa 128.20 (BB) Br ex 16.74 Dght 4.340 Lbp 122.80 Br md 16.50 Dpth 6.10 Welded, 1 dk	**(A31A2GX) General Cargo Ship** Grain: 8,340 TEU 267 C.Ho 180/20' C.Dk 87/20' incl. 20 ref C.	**2 oil engines** geared to sc. shafts driving 2 FP propellers Total Power: 2,160kW (2,936hp) 11.0kn Wartsila 6L20C 2 x 4 Stroke 6 Cy. 200 x 280 each-1080kW (1468bhp) Wartsila Finland Oy-Finland Thrusters: 1 Tunnel thruster (f)
7811056 *UFAF* -	**SVYATITEL INNOKENTIY** *ex* Sibirskiy-2113 *-1997* *ex* Pan Rossa *-1994* *ex* Sibirskiy-2113 *-1992* **JSC LORP (A/O 'LORP' - Lena United River Shipping Co) (Lenskoye Obyedinyonnoye Rechnoye Parokhodstvo)** Orient Line Co Ltd SatCom: Inmarsat C 427305427 *Nakhodka* *Russia* MMSI: 273812010 Official number: 793622	**3,743** 1,122 4,409	Class: (RS)	**1980**-12 **Hollming Oy — Rauma** Yd No: 228 Loa 129.52 Br ex 15.80 Dght 3.720 Lbp 123.02 Br md 15.60 Dpth 6.02 Welded, 1 dk	**(A31A2GX) General Cargo Ship** Bale: 5,400 TEU 144 C. 144/20'	**2 oil engines** driving 2 FP propellers Total Power: 1,324kW (1,800hp) 10.2kn Dvigatel Revolyutsii 6CHRN36/45 2 x 4 Stroke 6 Cy. 360 x 450 each-662kW (900bhp) Zavod "Dvigatel Revolyutsii"-Gorkiy AuxGen: 2 x 126kW a.c Thrusters: 1 Thwart. FP thruster (f) Fuel: 210.0 (d.f.)
8843070 *UHRQ* -	**SVYATITEL NIKOLAY** *ex* 83 *-1992* **Litoral Co Ltd** - *Kholmsk* *Russia* MMSI: 273569400 Official number: 902095	**190** 57 70	Class: RS	**1991**-03 **Astrakhanskaya Sudoverf im. "Kirova" — Astrakhan** Yd No: 83 Loa 31.85 Br ex 7.08 Dght 2.100 Lbp 27.80 Br md 6.90 Dpth 3.15 Welded, 1 dk	**(B12B2FC) Fish Carrier** Ins: 100 Compartments: 2 Ho, ER 2 Ha: 2 (2.1 x 2.4)ER Derricks: 2x1t	**1 oil engine** geared to sc. shaft driving 1 FP propeller Total Power: 232kW (315hp) 10.2kn Daldizel 6CHSPN2A18-315 1 x 4 Stroke 6 Cy. 180 x 220 232kW (315bhp) Daldizel-Khabarovsk AuxGen: 2 x 25kW a.c Fuel: 14.0 (d.f.)
9024918 *UICV* -	**SVYATITEL PYOTR** *ex* Vus-431 *-1998* **LLC 'Kontur'** OOO 'Kontur-SPB' *St Petersburg* *Russia* MMSI: 273311340	**765** 229 540	Class: RS (RR)	**1964**-10 **Gorokhovetskiy Sudostroitelnyy Zavod — Gorokhovets** Loa 53.66 Br ex 9.30 Dght 3.390 Lbp - Br md 9.00 Dpth 4.00 Welded, 1 dk	**(B34G2SE) Pollution Control Vessel**	**1 oil engine** driving 1 FP propeller Total Power: 480kW (653hp) 10.0kn S.K.L. 6NVD48A-2U 1 x 4 Stroke 6 Cy. 320 x 480 480kW (653bhp) VEB Schwermaschinenbau "KarlLiebknecht" (SKL)-Magdeburg

8834782 *UCMB* -	**SVYATOGOR** **Collective Farm Fishery V Lenin (Rybolovetskiy Kolkhoz Imeni V I Lenina)** - *Petropavlovsk-Kamchatskiy* *Russia* MMSI: 273842300 Official number: 900051	**813** 243 332	Class: RS	**1990-09 Volgogradskiy Sudostroitelnyy Zavod — Volgograd** Yd No: 262 Loa 53.75 Br ex 10.72 Dght 4.041 Lbp 47.93 Br md 10.50 Dpth 6.02 Welded, 1 dk	**(B11A2FS) Stern Trawler** Ins: 218 Ice Capable	**1 oil engine** driving 1 CP propeller Total Power: 969kW (1,317hp) 12.7kn S.K.L. 8NVD48A-2U 1 x 4 Stroke 8 Cy. 320 x 480 969kW (1317bhp) VEB Schwermaschinenbau "KarlLiebknecht" (SKL)-Magdeburg AuxGen: 1 x 300kW a.c, 3 x 160kW a.c
8330700 *UIJO* -	**SVYATOY GEORGIY** *ex* Volodarskiy *-2011* **Zhemchuzhina Ltd** - SatCom: Inmarsat C 427310442 *Vladivostok* *Russia* MMSI: 273610200	**2,474** 742 911	Class: RS	**1985 Sudostroitelnyy Zavod "Baltiya" — Klaypeda** Yd No: 508 Converted From: Fishing Vessel Loa 85.10 Br ex 13.04 Dght 3.900 Lbp 76.80 Br md 13.00 Dpth 6.50 Welded, 1 dk	**(A34A2GR) Refrigerated Cargo Ship** Ins: 1,245 Cranes: 1x3.2t Ice Capable	**1 oil engine** driving 1 FP propeller Total Power: 852kW (1,158hp) 11.3kn S.K.L. 8NVD48A-2U 1 x 4 Stroke 8 Cy. 320 x 480 852kW (1158bhp) VEB Schwermaschinenbau "KarlLiebknecht" (SKL)-Magdeburg AuxGen: 2 x 320kW a.c, 1 x 150kW a.c Fuel: 254.0 (d.f.)
7418713 - -	**SVYATOY MIKHAIL** *ex* Kuchurgan *-2000* -	**748** 224 404	Class: (RS)	**1974-06 Zavod "Leninskaya Kuznitsa" — Kiyev** Yd No: 1391 Loa 54.82 Br ex 9.94 Dght 4.109 Lbp 50.29 Br md - Dpth 5.01 Welded, 1 dk	**(B11A2FS) Stern Trawler** Ins: 400 Compartments: 2 Ho, ER 3 Ha: 3 (1.6 x 1.4) Derricks: 2x1.3t; Winches: 2 Ice Capable	**1 oil engine** driving 1 CP propeller Total Power: 736kW (1,001hp) 12.0kn S.K.L. 8NVD48A-2U 1 x 4 Stroke 8 Cy. 320 x 480 736kW (1001bhp) VEB Schwermaschinenbau "KarlLiebknecht" (SKL)-Magdeburg
7338016 - -	**SVYATOY NIKOLAY** *ex* Opyt *-1995* *ex* RS-300 No. 2 *-1995* **OV Porozova** -	**173** 51 88	Class: (RS)	**1973-12 Astrakhanskaya Sudoverf im. "Kirova" — Astrakhan** Yd No: 2 Converted From: Research Vessel Loa 34.01 Br ex 7.10 Dght 2.900 Lbp 30.00 Br md - Dpth 3.68 Welded, 1 dk	**(B11A2FS) Stern Trawler** Grain: 78 Compartments: 1 Ho, ER 1 Ha: (1.7 x 1.3)ER Ice Capable	**1 oil engine** driving 1 FP propeller Total Power: 224kW (305hp) 9.0kn S.K.L. 8NVD36-1U 1 x 4 Stroke 8 Cy. 240 x 360 224kW (305bhp) VEB Schwermaschinenbau "KarlLiebknecht" (SKL)-Magdeburg AuxGen: 1 x 75kW a.c, 1 x 50kW a.c Fuel: 17.0 (d.f.)
9081447 *UCME* -	**SVYATOY NIKOLAY** **OOO 'Polluks' (Polluks Co Ltd)** - *Petropavlovsk-Kamchatskiy* *Russia* Official number: 913314	**448** 134 207	Class: RS	**1992-07 AO Zavod 'Nikolayevsk-na-Amure' — Nikolayevsk-na-Amure** Yd No: 1287 Loa 44.88 Br ex 9.47 Dght 3.770 Lbp 39.37 Br md 9.30 Dpth 5.13 Welded, 1 dk	**(B11A2FS) Stern Trawler** Ins: 210 Compartments: 1 Ho, ER 1 Ha: (2.1 x 2.1)ER Derricks: 4x3t Ice Capable	**1 oil engine** reduction geared to sc. shaft driving 1 FP propeller Total Power: 588kW (799hp) S.K.L. 6NVD48A-2U 1 x 4 Stroke 6 Cy. 320 x 480 588kW (799bhp) SKL Motoren u. Systemtechnik AG-Magdeburg
9035826 *UBSI7* -	**SVYATOY PAVEL** *ex* Weserstern *-2012* **Opair International Corp** LLC Valkur *Vladivostok* *Russia* MMSI: 273357270 Official number: 4428912	**6,441** 3,276 10,926 T/cm 19.5	Class: GL RS	**1992-08 MTW Schiffswerft GmbH — Wismar** Yd No: 121 Converted From: Chemical/Products Tanker-2012 Lengthened & Conv to DH-2001 Loa 127.20 (BB) Br ex 17.92 Dght 8.320 Lbp 121.10 Br md 17.70 Dpth 10.60 Welded, 1 dk	**(A13B2TP) Products Tanker** Double Hull (13F) Liq: 11,100; Liq (Oil): 11,098 Cargo Heating Coils Compartments: 12 Wing Ta, 2 Wing Slop Ta, ER 12 Cargo Pump (s): 12x220m³/hr Manifold: Bow/CM: 74m Ice Capable	**1 oil engine** driving 1 CP propeller Total Power: 3,792kW (5,156hp) 12.5kn B&W 6L35MC 1 x 2 Stroke 6 Cy. 350 x 1050 3792kW (5156bhp) MAN B&W Diesel A/S-Denmark AuxGen: 3 x 540kW 220/440V a.c, 1 x 500kW 220/440V a.c Thrusters: 1 Thwart. FP thruster (f)
9101417 *UEHJ* -	**SVYATOY PAVEL** **Morekhod Co Ltd (Morekhod OOO)** - *Petropavlovsk-Kamchatskiy* *Russia* MMSI: 273848300 Official number: 921645	**446** 133 207	Class: RS	**1993-08 AO Zavod 'Nikolayevsk-na-Amure' — Nikolayevsk-na-Amure** Yd No: 1294 Loa 44.88 Br ex 9.47 Dght 3.770 Lbp 39.37 Br md 9.30 Dpth 5.13 Welded, 1 dk	**(B11A2FS) Stern Trawler** Ins: 210 Compartments: 1 Ho 1 Ha: (2.1 x 2.1) Derricks: 4x3t Ice Capable	**1 oil engine** driving 1 FP propeller Total Power: 589kW (801hp) 11.5kn S.K.L. 6NVD48A-2U 1 x 4 Stroke 6 Cy. 320 x 480 589kW (801bhp) SKL Motoren u. Systemtechnik AG-Magdeburg
9100920 *UDDW* -	**SVYATOY PAVEL TAGANROGSKIY** *ex* Azov *-2001* **Larisa Anatolevna Grzhebina** - *Novorossiysk* *Russia*	**120** 35 48	Class: RS	**1993-08 Sosnovskiy Sudostroitelnyy Zavod — Sosnovka** Yd No: 844 Loa 25.50 Br ex 7.00 Dght 2.390 Lbp 22.00 Br md 6.80 Dpth 3.30 Welded, 1 dk	**(B11A2FS) Stern Trawler** Grain: 64 Compartments: 1 Ho 1 Ha: (1.4 x 1.5) Ice Capable	**1 oil engine** driving 1 FP propeller Total Power: 220kW (299hp) 9.5kn S.K.L. 6NVD26A-3 1 x 4 Stroke 6 Cy. 180 x 260 220kW (299bhp) SKL Motoren u. Systemtechnik AG-Magdeburg Fuel: 15.0 (d.f.)
9035838 *UBSI6* -	**SVYATOY PETR** *ex* Oderstern *-2012* **Opair International Corp** LLC Valkur SatCom: Inmarsat C 427305564 *Vladivostok* *Russia* MMSI: 273356270 Official number: 4431712	**6,441** 3,282 10,960 T/cm 19.5	Class: GL RS	**1992-09 MTW Schiffswerft GmbH — Wismar** Yd No: 122 Lengthened & Conv to DH-2001 Loa 127.20 (BB) Br ex 17.92 Dght 8.320 Lbp 121.10 Br md 17.70 Dpth 10.60 Welded, 1 dk	**(A12B2TR) Chemical/Products Tanker** Double Hull (13F) Liq: 11,098; Liq (Oil): 11,098 Cargo Heating Coils Compartments: 12 Wing Ta, 2 Wing Slop Ta, ER 12 Cargo Pump (s): 12x220m³/hr Manifold: Bow/CM: 74m Ice Capable	**1 oil engine** driving 1 CP propeller Total Power: 3,792kW (5,156hp) 12.5kn B&W 6L35MC 1 x 2 Stroke 6 Cy. 350 x 1050 3792kW (5156bhp) MAN B&W Diesel A/S-Denmark AuxGen: 3 x 540kW 220/440V a.c, 1 x 500kW 220/440V a.c Thrusters: 1 Thwart. FP thruster (f)
9101429 *UEGB* -	**SVYATOY PYOTR** **OOO 'Galis'** - *Petropavlovsk-Kamchatskiy* *Russia* Official number: 921128	**495** 149 207	Class: (RS)	**1993-05 AO Zavod 'Nikolayevsk-na-Amure' — Nikolayevsk-na-Amure** Yd No: 1292 Loa 44.88 Br ex 9.47 Dght 3.770 Lbp 39.37 Br md - Dpth 5.13 Welded, 1 dk	**(B11A2FS) Stern Trawler** Ins: 210 Compartments: 1 Ho 1 Ha: (2.1 x 2.1) Derricks: 4x3t Ice Capable	**1 oil engine** driving 1 FP propeller Total Power: 589kW (801hp) 11.5kn S.K.L. 6NVD48A-2U 1 x 4 Stroke 6 Cy. 320 x 480 589kW (801bhp) SKL Motoren u. Systemtechnik AG-Magdeburg
8138499 *UBNT* -	**SVYATOY PYOTR** *ex* Saint Peter *-2003* *ex* Berezino *-2001* **ZAO 'Ostrovnoye'** - *Kholmsk* *Russia*	**356** 107 138	Class: (RS)	**1983-07 Sudostroitelnyy Zavod "Avangard" — Petrozavodsk** Yd No: 410 Loa 35.74 Br ex - Dght 3.429 Lbp 29.62 Br md 8.92 Dpth 5.97 Welded, 1 dk	**(B11A2FS) Stern Trawler** Ins: 110 Compartments: 1 Ho, ER 1 Ha: (1.3 x 1.3) Derricks: 2x1.5t Ice Capable	**1 oil engine** geared to sc. shaft driving 1 FP propeller Total Power: 589kW (801hp) 10.5kn S.K.L. 6NVD48A-2U 1 x 4 Stroke 6 Cy. 320 x 480 589kW (801bhp) VEB Schwermaschinenbau "KarlLiebknecht" (SKL)-Magdeburg Fuel: 35.0 (d.f.)
9116979 *UDEN* -	**SVYATOY VLADIMIR** *ex* Sante Valderrana *-2001* *ex* Vladimir Gusenkov *-2001* *ex* Gintaras *-1997* **Bekerev Fishing Collective (Rybolovetskiy Kolkhoz im Bekereva)** - *Petropavlovsk-Kamchatskiy* *Russia* MMSI: 273421150 Official number: 920765	**2,416** 724 1,108	Class: RS (BV)	**1994-05 AB "Baltijos" Laivu Statykla — Klaipeda** Yd No: 820 Loa 85.06 Br ex 13.04 Dght 4.190 Lbp 76.80 Br md 13.00 Dpth 6.50 Welded, 1 dk	**(B12A2FF) Fish Factory Ship**	**1 oil engine** driving 1 FP propeller Total Power: 852kW (1,158hp) 10.7kn S.K.L. 8NVD48A-2U 1 x 4 Stroke 8 Cy. 320 x 480 852kW (1158bhp) SKL Motoren u. Systemtechnik AG-Magdeburg AuxGen: 4 x 311kW 220/380V 50Hz a.c Fuel: 236.0 (d.f.)
7903287 *JVYM4* -	**SW 1** *ex* Hai Soon 16 *-2011* *ex* Hua Fu *-2001* *ex* Kyrnikos *-2000* *ex* Eastern Navigator *-1996* *ex* Pacific Glory No. 1 *-1988* *ex* Pacific Glory *-1982* **Chen Yiquan** Yuantai Fuel Trading Pte Ltd *Ulaanbaatar* *Mongolia* MMSI: 457712000 Official number: 32261379	**3,521** 1,928 4,999 T/cm 14.6	Class: IS (LR) (NV) (NK) Classed LR until 6/1/11	**1979-07 Kurinoura Dockyard Co Ltd — Yawatahama EH** Yd No: 136 Loa 108.18 Br ex - Dght 6.945 Lbp 99.98 Br md 16.01 Dpth 8.01 Welded, 1 dk	**(A12B2TR) Chemical/Products Tanker** Double Bottom Entire Compartment Length Liq: 7,267; Liq (Oil): 7,267 Cargo Heating Coils Compartments: 4 Ta, 8 Wing Ta, ER, 2 Wing Slop Ta 5 Cargo Pump (s)	**1 oil engine** driving 1 FP propeller Total Power: 2,944kW (4,003hp) 12.8kn Akasaka DM47M 1 x 4 Stroke 6 Cy. 470 x 760 2944kW (4003bhp) Akasaka Tekkosho KK (Akasaka DieselLtd)-Japan AuxGen: 1 x 200kW 445V 60Hz a.c, 2 x 160kW 445V 60Hz a.c Boilers: e (ex.g.) 7.6kgf/cm² (7.5bar)
7913103 *JVBU5* -	**SW 2** *ex* Soon Wah *-2012* *ex* Marine Valour *-2003* *ex* Marine Spirit *-1999* *ex* Supreme Phoenix *-1999* *ex* Worldnet 1 *-1998* *ex* Global Success *-1998* *ex* Crane Ocean *-1995* *ex* Kakushin Maru *-1989* **Grand Ocean Shipping Line Inc** Yuantai Fuel Trading Pte Ltd *Ulaanbaatar* *Mongolia* MMSI: 457782000 Official number: 32881379	**3,053** 1,539 4,890	Class: IZ (NK) (NV)	**1979-10 Kurushima Dockyard Co. Ltd. — Onishi** Yd No: 2092 Loa 99.77 Br ex - Dght 6.594 Lbp 93.83 Br md 15.02 Dpth 7.83 Welded, 1 dk	**(A13B2TP) Products Tanker** Double Bottom Entire Compartment Length Liq: 5,527; Liq (Oil): 5,527	**1 oil engine** driving 1 FP propeller Total Power: 2,795kW (3,800hp) 13.0kn Hanshin 6LU50A 1 x 4 Stroke 6 Cy. 500 x 800 2795kW (3800bhp) The Hanshin Diesel Works Ltd-Japan AuxGen: 2 x 240kW 450V 60Hz a.c Fuel: 53.5 (d.f.) 183.5 (r.f.) 12.0pd

No. / Call sign	Name / Owner	Tonnage	Class	Builder / Dimensions	Type	Machinery
7009835 *H02698* -	**SW 11** *ex* Sango *-2007* *ex* I Hannah *-2007* *ex* Fiesta *-2007* *ex* Oshima Maru *-1983* **Sea Word Trade SA** - *Panama* *Panama* Official number: 35551PEXT	*243* 72 -		**1970**-02 **Narasaki Zosen KK — Muroran HK** Yd No: 704 Loa 44.30 Br ex 7.52 Dght 2.896 Lbp 38.82 Br md 7.50 Dpth 3.51 Welded, 1 dk	**(B11B2FV) Fishing Vessel**	**2 oil engines** geared to sc. shaft driving 1 FP propeller Total Power: 882kW (1,200hp) 11.5kn Daihatsu 6PSHT-26D 2 x 4 Stroke 6 Cy. 260 x 320 each-441kW (600bhp) Daihatsu Kogyo-Japan Fuel: 116.0 4.0pd
7509988 *YEIZ* -	**SWADAYA LESTARI** *ex* Armada Agung *-1997* *ex* LM Serene Lady *-1990* *ex* Justy *-1988* *ex* Golden Venture I *-1984* *ex* James Helm *-1981* *ex* Mercury Bell *-1980* **PT Swadaya Lestari Lines** - *Jakarta* *Indonesia* MMSI: 525019011 Official number: 1990 BA NO 8781/L	**5,797** 3,426 9,084	Class: KI (NK)	**1975**-11 **Minaminippon Shipbuilding Co Ltd — Usuki OT** Yd No: 502 Loa 126.07 Br ex 17.45 Dght 7.719 Lbp 117.99 Br md 17.40 Dpth 9.89 Welded, 1 dk	**(A31A2GX) General Cargo Ship** Grain: 12,891; Bale: 12,010 Compartments: 3 Ho, ER 3 Ha: (16.0 x 8.0) (24.0 x 8.0) (21.8 x 8.0)ER Derricks: 1x50t,5x20t; Winches: 5	**1 oil engine** driving 1 FP propeller Total Power: 4,266kW (5,800hp) 13.0kn Mitsubishi 8UET45/80D 1 x 2 Stroke 8 Cy. 450 x 800 4266kW (5800bhp) Kobe Hatsudoki KK-Japan AuxGen: 2 x 240kW 445V 60Hz a.c Fuel: 66.0 (d.f.) 851.5 (r.f.) 13.0pd
9161522 *PORT* -	**SWADAYA LESTARI I** *ex* Asian Rosalie *-2012* *ex* Tabah *-2003* **PT Swadaya Lestari Lines** - *Indonesia* MMSI: 525022093	**7,762** 2,646 8,905	Class: (NK)	**1997**-08 **Shin Kochi Jyuko K.K. — Kochi** Yd No: 7098 Loa 113.22 (BB) Br ex - Dght 7.309 Lbp 105.40 Br md 19.60 Dpth 13.20 Welded, 2 dks	**(A31A2GX) General Cargo Ship** Grain: 16,822; Bale: 15,176 Compartments: 2 Ho, 2 Tw Dk, ER 2 Ha: (20.3 x 14.8) (33.6 x 14.8)ER Cranes: 2x30t,1x25t	**1 oil engine** driving 1 FP propeller Total Power: 3,884kW (5,281hp) 13.3kn B&W 6L35MC 1 x 2 Stroke 6 Cy. 350 x 1050 3884kW (5281bhp) Makita Corp-Japan Fuel: 775.0
8138255 *PHVY* -	**SWAENSBORGH** *ex* Mira I *-2003* *ex* Adele Raap *-1985* *ex* Elenore *-1985* *ex* Anne *-1985* **Rood Boven Groen** - *Kampen* *Netherlands* MMSI: 245108000 Official number: 20137	*165* 78 -		**1907 J. Jacobs — Moorrege** Converted From: General Cargo Ship-1991 Lengthened-1957 Lengthened-1950 Loa 47.00 Br ex 5.85 Dght 1.920 Lbp 37.15 Br md 5.80 Dpth 2.56 Welded, 1 dk	**(X11A2YS) Yacht (Sailing)** Passengers: cabins: 13; berths: 30 2 Ha: 2 (14.4 x 3.7)	**1 oil engine** driving 1 FP propeller 9.0kn MaK MA423 1 x 4 Stroke 8 Cy. 290 x 420 Maschinenbau Kiel AG (MaK)-Kiel AuxGen: 1 x 24kW
8708581 - -	**SWAGATA** - **Kolkata Port Trust** - *Kolkata* *India*	**324** 97 89	Class: IR	**1991**-11 **Hooghly Dock & Port Engineers Ltd. — Haora** Yd No: 454 Loa 33.00 Br ex 9.16 Dght 2.820 Lbp 29.95 Br md 9.00 Dpth 4.50 Welded, 1 dk	**(B32A2ST) Tug**	**2 oil engines** with clutches, flexible couplings & sr reverse geared to sc. shafts driving 2 FP propellers Total Power: 730kW (992hp) MAN W8VBSLM 2 x 4 Stroke 8 Cy. 175 x 220 each-365kW (496bhp) Kirloskar Oil Engines Ltd-India
8861151 *VTSW* -	**SWAGATH** - **Swagath Marine Products Pvt Ltd** - *Mormugao* *India* Official number: F-MRH-003	**127** 38 71	Class: (IR)	**1991 Chowgule & Co Pvt Ltd — Goa** Yd No: 101 Loa 24.00 Br ex 7.36 Dght 2.500 Lbp 20.00 Br md 7.20 Dpth 3.30 Welded, 1 dk	**(B11A2FT) Trawler**	**1 oil engine** sr geared to sc. shaft driving 1 FP propeller Total Power: 353kW (480hp) 10.0kn Caterpillar 3412TA 1 x Vee 4 Stroke 12 Cy. 137 x 152 353kW (480bhp) (made 1988) Caterpillar Inc-USA AuxGen: 2 x 75kW 415V 50Hz a.c
9607447 *CQLT* -	**SWAKOP** - **ms 'Swakop' Schiffahrtsgesellschaft mbH & Co KG** John T Essberger GmbH & Co KG *Madeira* *Portugal (MAR)* MMSI: 255805350	**24,341** 11,521 34,274 T/cm 49.6	Class: GL	**2013**-01 **Yangfan Group Co Ltd — Zhoushan ZJ** Yd No: 2181 Loa 179.98 Br ex - Dght 10.100 Lbp 176.75 Br md 30.00 Dpth 14.70 Welded, 1 dk	**(A21A2BC) Bulk Carrier** Double Hull Grain: 46,700; Bale: 45,684 Compartments: 5 Ho, ER 5 Ha: 4 (19.2 x 20.3)ER (16.0 x 18.7) Cranes: 4x35t	**1 oil engine** driving 1 FP propeller Total Power: 6,900kW (9,381hp) 14.2kn Wartsila 5RT-flex50 1 x 2 Stroke 5 Cy. 500 x 2050 6900kW (9381bhp) Wartsila Hyundai Engine Co Ltd-South Korea AuxGen: 3 x 570kW 450V a.c Fuel: 160.0 (d.f.) 1700.0 (r.f.)
7637448 *PHYP* -	**SWALINGE** *ex* Tina H *-1996* *ex* Fenda *-1988* *ex* Tina Holwerda *-1987* *ex* Fenja *-1986* *ex* Tina Holwerda *-1977* **Swalinge Scheepvaart BV** - *Yerseke* *Netherlands* MMSI: 244209000 Official number: 988	**2,071** 621 3,064	Class: LR (BV) **100A1** SS 08/2012 hopper dredger **LMC** Eq.Ltr: O; Cable: 440.0/36.0 U2	**1977**-09 **Barkmeijer Stroobos B.V. — Stroobos** Yd No: 206 Converted From: General Cargo Ship-1995 Loa 81.70 (BB) Br ex 14.45 Dght 5.340 Lbp 74.56 Br md 14.01 Dpth 6.46 Welded, 1 dk	**(B33B2DU) Hopper/Dredger (unspecified)** Grain: 3,960 Compartments: 1 Ho, ER 1 Ha: (41.9 x 10.2)ER	**1 oil engine** sr geared to sc. shaft driving 1 CP propeller Total Power: 1,802kW (2,450hp) 12.5kn Alpha 16V23L-VO 1 x Vee 4 Stroke 16 Cy. 225 x 300 1802kW (2450bhp) Alpha Diesel A/S-Denmark AuxGen: 3 x 400kW 380V 50Hz a.c, 3 x 51kW 380V 50Hz a.c Thrusters: 1 Thwart. FP thruster (f) Fuel: 331.0 (d.f.) 7.0pd
7855698 - -	**SWALLOW** *ex* Sumiei Maru *-1994* - -	*199* 104 450		**1970 Ikeda Zosen K.K. — Osakikamijima** Loa 43.01 Br ex - Dght 3.401 Lbp 40.01 Br md 7.51 Dpth 5.36 Welded, 1 dk	**(A31A2GX) General Cargo Ship**	**1 oil engine** driving 1 FP propeller Total Power: 405kW (551hp) 10.0kn Sumiyoshi S6UCTHS 1 x 4 Stroke 6 Cy. 260 x 400 405kW (551bhp) Sumiyoshi Tekkosho-Japan
9171462 *5IQU22* -	**SWALLOW** *ex* Camellia *-2013* *ex* Saveh *-2012* *ex* Iran Saveh *-2008* **Camellia Shipping Co Ltd** NITC *Zanzibar* *Tanzania (Zanzibar)* MMSI: 677002100	**81,479** 50,676 159,758 T/cm 117.5	Class: (LR) (GL) (NV) ✠ Classed LR until 15/5/01	**2000**-05 **Daewoo Heavy Industries Ltd — Geoje** Yd No: 5135 Loa 274.00 (BB) Br ex 48.04 Dght 17.022 Lbp 264.00 Br md 48.00 Dpth 23.20 Welded, 1 dk	**(A13A2TV) Crude Oil Tanker** Double Hull (13F) Liq: 166,683; Liq (Oil): 166,683 Compartments: 12 Wing Ta, 2 Wing Slop Ta, ER 3 Cargo Pump (s): 3x3500m³/hr Manifold: Bow/CM: 129m	**1 oil engine** driving 1 FP propeller Total Power: 16,846kW (22,904hp) 15.2kn MAN-B&W 6S70MC 1 x 2 Stroke 6 Cy. 700 x 2674 16846kW (22904bhp) HSD Engine Co Ltd-South Korea AuxGen: 3 x 970kW 450V 60Hz a.c Fuel: 282.0 (d.f.) 4491.0 (r.f.)
9136125 *ECFX* -	**SWALLOW** *ex* Westerland *-2004* *ex* Swallow *-2003* **Logistica Integral Gallega SL** Naviera Sicar SL SatCom: Inmarsat C 422436310 *Santa Cruz de Tenerife* *Spain (CSR)* MMSI: 224363000 Official number: 4/2004	**2,848** 1,601 4,300	Class: GL (BV)	**1996**-05 **Bodewes' Scheepswerven B.V. — Hoogezand** Yd No: 571 Loa 90.46 (BB) Br ex - Dght 5.754 Lbp 84.39 Br md 13.20 Dpth 7.30 Welded, 1 dk	**(A31A2GX) General Cargo Ship** Grain: 5,798 TEU 206 C.Ho 114/20' (40') C.Dk 92/20' (40') Compartments: 1 Ho, ER 1 Ha: (64.6 x 10.8)ER Ice Capable	**1 oil engine** with clutches, flexible couplings & sr geared to sc. shafts driving 1 CP propeller Total Power: 1,840kW (2,502hp) 11.0kn Stork-Werkspoor 6SW280 1 x 4 Stroke 6 Cy. 280 x 300 1840kW (2502bhp) Stork Wartsila Diesel BV-Netherlands AuxGen: 1 x 290kW 220/380V 50Hz a.c, 1 x 136kW 220/380V 50Hz a.c Thrusters: 1 Thwart. FP thruster (f) Fuel: 178.0 (d.f.) 5.5pd
7110646 *DUH2076* -	**SWALLOW 1** *ex* Innoshima No. 8 *-1993* *ex* Shigei Maru No. 7 *-1984* **Daima Shipping Corp** - *Cagayan de Oro* *Philippines* Official number: CDO7000003	*185* 121 565		**1971 Kanbara Zosen K.K. — Onomichi** Yd No: 171 Loa 33.79 Br ex 10.04 Dght 1.804 Lbp 29.93 Br md 10.01 Dpth 2.90 Welded, 1 dk	**(A37B2PS) Passenger Ship** Passengers: 204	**1 oil engine** driving 1 FP propeller Total Power: 368kW (500hp) 7.5kn Mitsubishi 6SH20/26AC 1 x 4 Stroke 6 Cy. 200 x 260 368kW (500bhp) Mitsubishi Heavy Industries Ltd-Japan AuxGen: 1 x 48kW 225V d.c Fuel: 13.0 1.5pd
7409918 *DUH2294* -	**SWALLOW 2** *ex* Our Lady of Mediatrix *-1984* *ex* Tarumi *-1995* *ex* Shigei Maru No. 12 *-1984* **Daima Shipping Corp** - *Cagayan de Oro* *Philippines* Official number: 10-0000422	*203* 91 170		**1974**-06 **Kanbara Zosen K.K. — Onomichi** Yd No: 200 Loa 33.81 Br ex 10.02 Dght 2.693 Lbp 28.58 Br md 10.00 Dpth 2.90 Riveted\Welded, 1 dk	**(A36A2PR) Passenger/Ro-Ro Ship (Vehicles)** Passengers: unberthed: 239; berths: 24 Bow ramp (f) Stern ramp (a)	**1 oil engine** geared to sc. shaft driving 1 FP propeller Total Power: 441kW (600hp) 7.5kn Yanmar 6U-UT 1 x 4 Stroke 6 Cy. 200 x 240 441kW (600bhp) Yanmar Diesel Engine Co Ltd-Japan
9338620 *C6WR3* -	**SWALLOW ACE** - **Snowscape Car Carriers SA** MOL Ship Management Singapore Pte Ltd *Nassau* *Bahamas* MMSI: 309509000 Official number: 8001440	**58,685** 18,167 18,864	Class: NK	**2007**-11 **Minaminippon Shipbuilding Co Ltd — Usuki OT** Yd No: 697 Loa 199.95 (BB) Br ex - Dght 9.816 Lbp 190.00 Br md 32.26 Dpth 14.70 Welded, 12 dks	**(A35B2RV) Vehicles Carrier** Side door/ramp (s) Quarter stern door/ramp (s. a.) Cars: 6,237	**1 oil engine** driving 1 FP propeller Total Power: 15,540kW (21,128hp) 20.0kn Mitsubishi 8UEC60LSII 1 x 2 Stroke 8 Cy. 600 x 2300 15540kW (21128bhp) Mitsubishi Heavy Industries Ltd-Japan AuxGen: 4 x 975kW a.c Thrusters: 1 Tunnel thruster (f) Fuel: 2610.0
9100126 *C6WF8* -	**SWAMI** *ex* Arklow Swan *-2007* *ex* Swan *-2004* **Misje Rederi AS** - *Nassau* *Bahamas* MMSI: 308218000 Official number: 8001378	**2,839** 1,609 4,304	Class: BV	**1995**-01 **Bodewes' Scheepswerven B.V. — Hoogezand** Yd No: 570 Loa 90.46 (BB) Br ex - Dght 5.750 Lbp 84.60 Br md 13.20 Dpth 7.30 Welded	**(A31A2GX) General Cargo Ship** Grain: 5,799; Bale: 5,799 TEU 194 C.Ho 114/20' (40') C.Dk 80/20' (40') Compartments: 1 Ho, ER 1 Ha: (64.6 x 10.8)ER Ice Capable	**1 oil engine** geared to sc. shaft driving 1 FP propeller Total Power: 1,840kW (2,502hp) 12.3kn Stork-Werkspoor 6SW280 1 x 4 Stroke 6 Cy. 280 x 300 1840kW (2502bhp) Stork Wartsila Diesel BV-Netherlands AuxGen: 1 x 290kW 50Hz a.c, 1 x 136kW 50Hz a.c Thrusters: 1 Tunnel thruster (f) Fuel: 160.0 (d.f.)

9649940 *AVPI* -
SWAMI SAGAR
Shree Sagar Stevedores Pvt Ltd
-
Mormugao *India*
MMSI: 419000404
Official number: 3910
1,066 503 1,750
Class: IR
2012-01 **Vijai Marine Services — Goa** Yd No: 066
Loa 65.00 Br ex 12.02 Dght 3.300
Lbp - Br md 12.00 Dpth 4.35
Welded, 1 dk
(A31A2GX) General Cargo Ship
Bale: 1,875
Compartments: 1 Ho, ER
1 Ha: ER
2 oil engines reduction geared to sc. shafts driving 2 FP propellers
Total Power: 596kW (810hp) 10.0kn
Cummins NTA-855-M
2 x 4 Stroke 6 Cy. 140 x 152 each-298kW (405bhp)
Cummins India Ltd-India

8941585 - -
SWAMP WOMAN
Samuel E Korocy
-
Houston, TX *United States of America*
Official number: 949169
106 85 -
1989 Paul Inman — Anahuac, Tx
Loa - Br ex - Dght -
Lbp - Br md - Dpth 3.54
Bonded, 1 dk
(B11B2FV) Fishing Vessel
Hull Material: Reinforced Plastic
1 oil engine driving 1 FP propeller

8001000 *PJYI* -
SWAN
ex Sea Swan *-1996* *ex* Swan H. L. *-1989*
ex Dyvi Swan *-1988*
Swan BV
Dockwise Shipping BV
SatCom: Inmarsat A 1750552
Willemstad *Curacao*
MMSI: 306036000
Official number: 1996-C-1506
22,788 9,531 30,060 T/cm 50.4
Class: NV
1981-09 **Kaldnes Mek. Verksted AS — Tonsberg** Yd No: 217
Loa 180.50 Br ex - Dght 9.740
Lbp 170.97 Br md 32.28 Dpth 13.31
Welded, 1 dk
(A38C3GH) Heavy Load Carrier, semi submersible
Double Bottom Entire Compartment Length
Liq: 33,200; Liq (Oil): 33,200
Cargo Heating Coils
Compartments: 12 Ta, ER
Manifold: Bow/CM: 91m
1 oil engine driving 1 CP propeller
Total Power: 9,635kW (13,100hp) 16.0kn
B&W 6L67GFCA
1 x 2 Stroke 6 Cy. 670 x 1700 9635kW (13100bhp)
AS Fredriksstad Mek Verksted-Norway
AuxGen: 3 x 630kW 440V 60Hz a.c
Thrusters: 1 Thwart. CP thruster (f)
Fuel: 259.0 (d.f.) 1726.0 (r.f.)

9630183 *2ESC8* -
SWAN
ex Lyana *-2013*
Oleana Charters Ltd
Yacht Management Consultants Sarl (Hill Robinson Yacht Management Consultants)
Douglas *Isle of Man (British)*
MMSI: 235087703
Official number: 742860
1,008 302 187
Class: AB
2011-07 **Azimut-Benetti SpA — Livorno** Yd No: FB248
Loa 61.50 Br ex 10.60 Dght 3.080
Lbp 52.30 Br md 10.40 Dpth 5.45
Welded, 1 dk
(X11A2YP) Yacht
2 oil engines reduction geared to sc. shafts driving 2 Propellers
Total Power: 2,640kW (3,590hp) 13.0kn
M.T.U. 12V4000M60
2 x Vee 4 Stroke 12 Cy. 165 x 190 each-1320kW (1795bhp)
MTU Friedrichshafen GmbH-Friedrichshafen
AuxGen: 1 x 155kW a.c, 1 x 200kW a.c
Fuel: 145.0 (d.f.)

9502386 *9V7468* -
SWAN
GEA-Sierra Pte Ltd
Stellar Shipmanagement Services Pte Ltd
Singapore *Singapore*
MMSI: 565143000
Official number: 394269
4,724 2,239 7,310
Class: GL
2009-09 **Fujian Funing Shipyard Industry Co Ltd — Fu'an FJ** Yd No: 680-4
Loa 102.21 Br ex - Dght 7.100
Lbp 95.40 Br md 17.50 Dpth 9.50
Welded, 1 dk
(A13B2TP) Products Tanker
Double Hull (13F)
Liq: 7,526; Liq (Oil): 7,526
Ice Capable
2 oil engines reverse reduction geared to sc. shafts driving 2 FP propellers
Total Power: 2,942kW (4,000hp) 11.0kn
Yanmar 6EY26
2 x 4 Stroke 6 Cy. 260 x 385 each-1471kW (2000bhp)
Yanmar Diesel Engine Co Ltd-Japan
AuxGen: 3 x 280kW a.c
Thrusters: 1 Tunnel thruster (f)

9338826 *C6WV4* -
SWAN ACE
Snowscape Car Carriers SA
MOL Ship Management Singapore Pte Ltd
Nassau *Bahamas*
MMSI: 309369000
Official number: 8001469
58,685 18,167 18,867
Class: NK
2008-02 **Minaminippon Shipbuilding Co Ltd — Usuki OT** Yd No: 698
Loa 199.95 (BB) Br ex - Dght 9.816
Lbp 190.45 Br md 32.20 Dpth 14.70
Welded, 12 dks
(A35B2RV) Vehicles Carrier
Side door/ramp (s)
Quarter stern door/ramp (s. a.)
Cars: 6,237
1 oil engine driving 1 FP propeller
Total Power: 15,540kW (21,128hp) 20.0kn
Mitsubishi 8UEC60LSII
1 x 2 Stroke 8 Cy. 600 x 2300 15540kW (21128bhp)
Mitsubishi Heavy Industries Ltd-Japan
AuxGen: 3 x a.c
Thrusters: 1 Tunnel thruster (f)
Fuel: 2660.0

8512970 *C6TK9* -
SWAN ARROW
ex Norsul America *-2004*
ex Westwood Jago *-2003*
Swan Shipping Sarl
Gearbulk Ltd
Nassau *Bahamas*
MMSI: 311682000
Official number: 8000765
28,805 13,964 45,295
Class: NV
1987-07 **Ishikawajima-Harima Heavy Industries Co Ltd (IHI) — Aioi HG** Yd No: 2954
Loa 199.90 (BB) Br ex 30.59 Dght 11.720
Lbp 190.62 Br md 30.51 Dpth 16.21
Welded, 1 dk
(A31A2GO) Open Hatch Cargo Ship
Grain: 51,000; Bale: 50,000
TEU 2029
Compartments: 11 Ho, ER
11 Ha: (6.5 x 13.0)10 (13.1 x 25.3)ER
Gantry cranes: 2x40t
1 oil engine driving 1 FP propeller
Total Power: 8,076kW (10,980hp) 14.6kn
Sulzer 6RTA62
1 x 2 Stroke 6 Cy. 620 x 2150 8076kW (10980bhp)
Ishikawajima Harima Heavy IndustrieCo Ltd (IHI)-Japan
AuxGen: 4 x 520kW 450V 60Hz a.c, 1 x 80kW 450V 60Hz a.c

8907876 *C6TJ6* -
SWAN CHACABUCO
ex Chacabuco *-1997*
Blyth Shipholding SA
Chartworld Shipping Corp
Nassau *Bahamas*
MMSI: 311665000
Official number: 8000752
13,099 4,796 12,974 T/cm 26.8
Class: BV (LR) (NV)
✠ Classed LR until 9/11/97
1990-05 **Shin Kurushima Dockyard Co. Ltd. — Onishi** Yd No: 2665
Loa 152.00 (BB) Br ex 23.53 Dght 9.017
Lbp 144.00 Br md 23.50 Dpth 15.70
Welded, 5 dks
(A34A2GR) Refrigerated Cargo Ship
Side doors (p)
Lane-Wid: 1.70
Lane-clr ht: 2.20
Ins: 19,174
TEU 306 C Ho 138 TEU C Dk 168 TEU incl 54 ref C
Compartments: 4 Ho, 4 Tw Dk, ER
4 Ha: (12.7 x 7.9)3 (12.7 x 10.4)ER
Cranes: 2x30t,2x12.5t
1 oil engine driving 1 FP propeller
Total Power: 6,420kW (8,729hp) 18.5kn
B&W 6S50MC
1 x 2 Stroke 6 Cy. 500 x 1910 6420kW (8729bhp)
Mitsui Engineering & Shipbuilding CLtd-Japan
AuxGen: 3 x 680kW 450V 60Hz a.c, 1 x 400kW 450V 60Hz a.c
Fuel: 164.7 (d.f.) 1251.0 (r.f.) 36.0pd

9302841 *VRMD2* -
SWAN RIVER
ex Triton Lark *-2013*
Swan River Ltd
Pacific Basin Shipping (HK) Ltd
Hong Kong *Hong Kong*
MMSI: 477220600
Official number: HK-3840
31,275 18,504 56,025 T/cm 55.8
Class: NK
2005-05 **Mitsui Eng. & SB. Co. Ltd. — Tamano** Yd No: 1607
Loa 189.99 (BB) Br ex - Dght 12.575
Lbp 182.00 Br md 32.26 Dpth 17.90
Welded, 1 dk
(A21A2BC) Bulk Carrier
Grain: 70,811; Bale: 68,044
Compartments: 5 Ho, ER
5 Ha: 4 (21.1 x 18.9)ER (17.6 x 18.9)
Cranes: 4x30t
1 oil engine driving 1 FP propeller
Total Power: 9,480kW (12,889hp) 14.5kn
MAN-B&W 6S50MC-C
1 x 2 Stroke 6 Cy. 500 x 2000 9480kW (12889bhp)
Mitsui Engineering & Shipbuilding CLtd-Japan
Fuel: 2260.0

9550395 *9V8218* -
SWAN RIVER BRIDGE
'K' Line Pte Ltd (KLPL)
'K' Line (Singapore) Pte Ltd (KSP)
Singapore *Singapore*
MMSI: 565156000
Official number: 395466
17,237 7,875 21,918
Class: NK
2010-01 **Imabari Shipbuilding Co Ltd — Imabari EH (Imabari Shipyard)** Yd No: 693
Loa 171.99 (BB) Br ex 27.66 Dght 9.517
Lbp 160.00 Br md 27.60 Dpth 14.00
Welded, 1 dk
(A33A2CC) Container Ship (Fully Cellular)
TEU 1708 C Ho 610 TEU C Dk 1098 incl 145 ref C
1 oil engine driving 1 FP propeller
Total Power: 15,820kW (21,509hp) 19.7kn
MAN-B&W 7S60ME-C
1 x 2 Stroke 7 Cy. 600 x 2400 15820kW (21509bhp)
Kawasaki Heavy Industries Ltd-Japan
AuxGen: 3 x a.c
Thrusters: 1 Tunnel thruster (f)
Fuel: 2130.0

9691747 *9V7569* -
SWANSEA
ex Hkt No. 1 *-2014*
Tomiura Nippon Chartering Pte Ltd
Transocean Oil Pte Ltd
Singapore *Singapore*
MMSI: 563141000
Official number: 398253
498 208 795
Class: RI
2013-07 **Zhejiang Shenzhou Shipbuilding Co Ltd — Xiangshan County ZJ** Yd No: SZ12017
Loa 44.80 Br ex - Dght 3.250
Lbp 42.00 Br md 10.20 Dpth 4.22
Welded, 1 dk
(B35E2TF) Bunkering Tanker
Double Hull (13F)
2 oil engines geared to sc. shafts driving 2 FP propellers
Total Power: 746kW (1,014hp) 9.8kn
Cummins KT-19-M
2 x 4 Stroke 6 Cy. 159 x 159 each-373kW (507bhp)
Chongqing Cummins Engine Co Ltd-China
AuxGen: 2 x 50kW 400/220V 50Hz a.c

7740025 *YGOT* -
SWAPRI
ex Damai *-2002* *ex* Se Hwa No. 51 *-1999*
ex Tikonko No. 27 *-1999* *ex* Kowa Maru *-1999*
ex Kuromori Maru No. 32 *-1990*
PT Penida Citranusa
-
Surabaya *Indonesia*
499 309 -
Class: KI
1978-03 **KK Ouchi Zosensho — Matsuyama EH** Yd No: 153
L reg 50.00 Br ex - Dght 3.250
Lbp 44.72 Br md 8.50 Dpth 5.10
Welded, 1 dk
(B11B2FV) Fishing Vessel
1 oil engine driving 1 FP propeller
Total Power: 441kW (600hp)
Matsui 6M26KGHS
1 x 4 Stroke 6 Cy. 260 x 400 441kW (600bhp)
Matsui Iron Works Co Ltd-Japan

9101168 *VTZJ* -
SWARAJ DWEEP
Government of The Republic of India (Andaman & Nicobar Administration)
The Shipping Corporation of India Ltd (SCI)
SatCom: Inmarsat C 441947310
Mumbai *India*
MMSI: 419351000
Official number: 2494
14,239 4,741 4,701
Class: IR (LR)
✠ Classed LR until 13/4/05
1999-12 **Hindustan Shipyard Ltd — Visakhapatnam** Yd No: 11101
Loa 156.97 (BB) Br ex 21.03 Dght 6.700
Lbp 143.94 Br md 21.00 Dpth 12.80
Welded, 3 dks
(A32A2GF) General Cargo/Passenger Ship
Passengers: unberthed: 900; cabins: 63; berths: 300
Grain: 3,950; Bale: 3,772
Compartments: 2 Ho, ER
2 Ha: ER
Cranes: 2x25t
2 oil engines driving 2 FP propellers
Total Power: 5,280kW (7,178hp) 16.0kn
B&W 6L35MC
2 x 2 Stroke 6 Cy. 350 x 1050 each-2640kW (3589bhp)
MAN B&W Diesel A/S-Denmark
AuxGen: 5 x 1080kW 390V 50Hz a.c
Boilers: 2 e (ex.g.) 7.5kgf/cm² (7.4bar), 2 AuxB (o.f.) 7.3kgf/cm² (7.2bar)
Thrusters: 1 Thwart. FP thruster (f)
Fuel: 158.0 (d.f.) 828.0 (r.f.)

8111972 - -
SWARNA
Visakhapatnam Port Trust
-
Visakhapatnam *India*
Official number: 2037
368 110 177
Class: (IR)
1984-05 **Mazagon Dock Ltd. — Mumbai** Yd No: 726
Loa 32.97 Br ex 10.42 Dght 4.603
Lbp 31.53 Br md 10.00 Dpth 4.25
Welded, 1 dk
(B32A2ST) Tug
2 oil engines driving 2 Voith-Schneider propellers
Total Power: 2,162kW (2,940hp) 12.3kn
MAN G6V30/45ATL
2 x 4 Stroke 6 Cy. 300 x 450 each-1081kW (1470bhp)
Garden Reach Shipbuilders &Engineers Ltd-India
AuxGen: 2 x 88kW 415V 50Hz a.c, 1 x 32kW 415V 50Hz a.c
Fuel: 73.0 (d.f.)

IMO / Call sign	Name / Owner	Tonnage	Class	Builder / Dimensions	Type	Machinery
9217046 *VWH* -	**SWARNA** **New Mangalore Port Trust** - *Kochi* *India* MMSI: 419083200 Official number: 2777	**374** 112 147	Class: IR	**1999-07 Cochin Shipyard Ltd — Ernakulam** Yd No: BY-28 Loa 32.90 Br ex 10.02 Dght 3.200 Lbp 31.50 Br md 10.00 Dpth 4.25 Welded, 1 dk	**(B32A2ST) Tug**	**2 oil engines** gearing integral to driving 2 Voith-Schneider propellers Total Power: 2,540kW (3,454hp) 12.0kn Nohab 6R25 2 x 4 Stroke 6 Cy. 250 x 300 each-1270kW (1727bhp) Wartsila NSD Sweden AB-Sweden AuxGen: 2 x 100kW 415V 50Hz a.c Fuel: 50.0 (d.f.)
8905165 *POKG* -	**SWARNA BAHTERA** *ex* Toyo Maru No. 22 *-2012* - - *Indonesia*	*2,003* - 2,181	Class: (NK)	**1989-08 Imamura Zosen — Kure** Yd No: 343 Loa 93.60 (BB) Br ex - Dght 5.314 Lbp 85.00 Br md 16.00 Dpth 5.94 Welded, 2 dks	**(A35B2RV) Vehicles Carrier** Quarter stern door/ramp (p. a.) Quarter stern door/ramp (s. a.)	**1 oil engine** driving 1 CP propeller Total Power: 2,942kW (4,000hp) B&W 6L35MC 1 x 2 Stroke 6 Cy. 350 x 1050 2942kW (4000bhp) Hitachi Zosen Corp-Japan AuxGen: 3 x 235kW a.c Thrusters: 1 Tunnel thruster (a)
9414814 *AUYI* -	**SWARNA BRAHMAPUTRA** **The Shipping Corporation of India Ltd (SCI)** - *Mumbai* *India* MMSI: 419753000 Official number: 3527	**42,845** 21,337 73,595 T/cm 68.3	Class: IR LR ✠ **100A1** SS 09/2010 Double Hull oil tanker CSR ESP **ShipRight** (CM) *IWS LI SPM ✠ **LMC** **UMS IGS** Eq.Ltr: M†; Cable: 680.0/81.0 U3 (a)	**2010-09 STX Offshore & Shipbuilding Co Ltd — Changwon (Jinhae Shipyard)** Yd No: 1294 Loa 228.00 (BB) Br ex 32.26 Dght 14.200 Lbp 219.90 Br md 32.24 Dpth 20.65 Welded, 1 dk	**(A13B2TP) Products Tanker** Double Hull (13F) Liq: 80,300; Liq (Oil): 80,300 Compartments: 12 Wing Ta, 2 Wing Slop Ta, ER 12 Cargo Pump (s): 12x900m³/hr Manifold: Bow/CM: 112m	**1 oil engine** driving 1 FP propeller Total Power: 11,390kW (15,486hp) 15.0kn MAN-B&W 7S50MC-C 1 x 2 Stroke 7 Cy. 500 x 2000 11390kW (15486bhp) STX Engine Co Ltd-South Korea AuxGen: 3 x 1250kW 450V 60Hz a.c Boilers: e (ex.g.) 9.2kgf/cm² (9.0bar), WTAuxB (o.f.) 9.2kgf/cm² (9.0bar) Fuel: 200.0 (d.f.) 2100.0 (r.f.)
9414802 *AUYJ* -	**SWARNA GANGA** **The Shipping Corporation of India Ltd (SCI)** - *Mumbai* *India* MMSI: 419754000 Official number: 3528	**42,845** 21,337 73,580 T/cm 68.3	Class: IR LR ✠ **100A1** SS 08/2010 Double Hull oil tanker CSR ESP **ShipRight** (CM) *IWS LI SPM ✠ **LMC** **UMS IGS** Eq.Ltr: M†; Cable: 680.3/81.0 U3 (a)	**2010-08 STX Offshore & Shipbuilding Co Ltd — Changwon (Jinhae Shipyard)** Yd No: 1293 Loa 228.00 (BB) Br ex 32.26 Dght 14.200 Lbp 219.90 Br md 32.24 Dpth 20.65 Welded, 1 dk	**(A13B2TP) Products Tanker** Double Hull (13F) Liq: 80,300; Liq (Oil): 80,300 Compartments: 12 Wing Ta, 2 Wing Slop Ta, ER 12 Cargo Pump (s): 12x900m³/hr Manifold: Bow/CM: 112m	**1 oil engine** driving 1 FP propeller Total Power: 11,390kW (15,486hp) 15.0kn MAN-B&W 7S50MC-C 1 x 2 Stroke 7 Cy. 500 x 2000 11390kW (15486bhp) STX Engine Co Ltd-South Korea AuxGen: 3 x 1250kW 450V 60Hz a.c Boilers: e (ex.g.) 9.0kgf/cm² (8.8bar), WTAuxB (o.f.) 9.1kgf/cm² (8.9bar) Fuel: 200.0 (d.f.) 2100.0 (r.f.)
9414826 *AUYK* -	**SWARNA GODAVARI** **The Shipping Corporation of India Ltd (SCI)** - *Mumbai* *India* MMSI: 419755000 Official number: 3529	**42,845** 21,337 73,531 T/cm 68.3	Class: IR LR ✠ **100A1** SS 09/2010 Double Hull oil tanker CSR ESP **ShipRight** (CM) *IWS LI SPM ✠ **LMC** **UMS IGS** Eq.Ltr: M†; Cable: 680.3/81.0 U3 (a)	**2010-09 STX Offshore & Shipbuilding Co Ltd — Changwon (Jinhae Shipyard)** Yd No: 1295 Loa 228.00 (BB) Br ex 32.26 Dght 14.200 Lbp 219.90 Br md 32.24 Dpth 20.65 Welded, 1 dk	**(A13B2TP) Products Tanker** Double Hull (13F) Liq: 80,300; Liq (Oil): 80,300 Compartments: 12 Wing Ta, 2 Wing Slop Ta, ER 12 Cargo Pump (s): 12x900m³/hr Manifold: Bow/CM: 112m	**1 oil engine** driving 1 FP propeller Total Power: 11,390kW (15,486hp) 15.0kn MAN-B&W 7S50MC-C 1 x 2 Stroke 7 Cy. 500 x 2000 11390kW (15486bhp) STX Engine Co Ltd-South Korea AuxGen: 3 x 1250kW 450V 60Hz a.c Boilers: e (ex.g.) 9.2kgf/cm² (9.0bar), WTAuxB (o.f.) 9.2kgf/cm² (9.0bar) Fuel: 200.0 (d.f.) 2100.0 (r.f.)
9467720 *AUYL* -	**SWARNA JAYANTI** **The Shipping Corporation of India Ltd (SCI)** - *Mumbai* *India* MMSI: 419756000 Official number: 3530	**57,702** 32,638 105,000 T/cm 92.0	Class: AB IR	**2010-09 Hyundai Heavy Industries Co Ltd — Ulsan** Yd No: 2136 Loa 244.00 (BB) Br ex 42.03 Dght 14.900 Lbp 234.00 Br md 42.00 Dpth 21.00 Welded, 1 dk	**(A13A2TW) Crude/Oil Products Tanker** Double Hull (13F) Liq: 118,716; Liq (Oil): 105,000 Cargo Heating Coils Compartments: 12 Wing Ta, 2 Wing Slop Ta, ER 3 Cargo Pump (s): 3x3000m³/hr Manifold: Bow/CM: 121.5m	**1 oil engine** driving 1 FP propeller Total Power: 14,280kW (19,415hp) 14.5kn MAN-B&W 6S60MC-C8 1 x 2 Stroke 6 Cy. 600 x 2400 14280kW (19415bhp) Hyundai Heavy Industries Co Ltd-South Korea AuxGen: 3 x 880kW a.c Fuel: 110.0 (d.f.) 2500.0 (r.f.)
9431458 *AUYM* -	**SWARNA KALASH** **The Shipping Corporation of India Ltd (SCI)** - *Mumbai* *India* MMSI: 419757000 Official number: 3531	**29,845** 12,970 47,878 T/cm 53.4	Class: IR LR ✠ **100A1** SS 10/2009 Double Hull oil tanker CSR ESP *IWS LI SPM ✠ **LMC** **UMS IGS** Eq.Ltr: M†; Cable: 632.5/73.0 U3 (a)	**2009-10 Jinling Shipyard — Nanjing JS** Yd No: 07-0501 Loa 184.95 (BB) Br ex 32.23 Dght 11.000 Lbp 176.00 Br md 32.20 Dpth 18.20 Welded, 1 dk	**(A12B2TR) Chemical/Products Tanker** Double Hull (13F) Liq: 54,181; Liq (Oil): 54,181 Compartments: 12 Wing Ta, 2 Wing Slop Ta, ER	**1 oil engine** driving 1 FP propeller Total Power: 9,480kW (12,889hp) 14.5kn MAN-B&W 6S50MC-C 1 x 2 Stroke 6 Cy. 500 x 2000 9480kW (12889bhp) Yichang Marine Diesel Engine Co Ltd-China AuxGen: 3 x 800kW 440V 60Hz a.c Boilers: AuxB (o.f.) 9.2kgf/cm² (9.0bar), AuxB (Comp) 9.2kgf/cm² (9.0bar)
9467732 *AUYN* -	**SWARNA KAMAL** **The Shipping Corporation of India Ltd (SCI)** - SatCom: Inmarsat C 441922793 *Mumbai* *India* MMSI: 419758000 Official number: 3532	**57,702** 32,638 105,000 T/cm 92.0	Class: AB IR	**2010-11 Hyundai Heavy Industries Co Ltd — Ulsan** Yd No: 2137 Loa 244.00 (BB) Br ex 42.03 Dght 14.900 Lbp 234.00 Br md 42.00 Dpth 21.00 Welded, 1 dk	**(A13A2TW) Crude/Oil Products Tanker** Double Hull (13F) Liq: 118,385; Liq (Oil): 105,000 Cargo Heating Coils Compartments: 12 Wing Ta, 2 Wing Slop Ta, ER 3 Cargo Pump (s): 3x3000m³/hr Manifold: Bow/CM: 121.5m	**1 oil engine** driving 1 FP propeller Total Power: 14,280kW (19,415hp) 14.5kn MAN-B&W 6S60MC-C8 1 x 2 Stroke 6 Cy. 600 x 2400 14280kW (19415bhp) Hyundai Heavy Industries Co Ltd-South Korea AuxGen: 3 x 880kW a.c Fuel: 110.0 (d.f.) 2500.0 (r.f.)
9199505 *POQX* -	**SWARNA KARTIKA** *ex* Ferry Zamami *-2013* **PT Jembatan Nusantara** *Indonesia* MMSI: 525002124	*446* - 220		**1998-05 Yamanaka Zosen K.K. — Imabari** Yd No: 622 Loa 61.00 Br ex - Dght 3.200 Lbp 54.00 Br md 11.20 Dpth 6.70 Welded, 2 dks	**(A37B2PS) Passenger Ship**	**2 oil engines** geared to sc. shafts driving 2 FP propellers Total Power: 3,236kW (4,400hp) 17.0kn Niigata 6MG26HLX 2 x 4 Stroke 6 Cy. 260 x 350 each-1618kW (2200bhp) Niigata Engineering Co Ltd-Japan
9414840 *AUYO* -	**SWARNA KAVERI** **The Shipping Corporation of India Ltd (SCI)** - *Mumbai* *India* MMSI: 419759000 Official number: 3533	**42,845** 21,337 73,669 T/cm 68.3	Class: IR LR ✠ **100A1** SS 10/2010 Double Hull oil tanker CSR ESP **ShipRight** (CM) *IWS LI SPM ✠ **LMC** **UMS IGS** Eq.Ltr: M†; Cable: 680.3/81.0 U3 (a)	**2010-10 STX Offshore & Shipbuilding Co Ltd — Changwon (Jinhae Shipyard)** Yd No: 1297 Loa 228.00 (BB) Br ex 32.26 Dght 14.200 Lbp 219.90 Br md 32.24 Dpth 20.65 Welded, 1 dk	**(A13B2TP) Products Tanker** Double Hull (13F) Liq: 80,300; Liq (Oil): 80,300 Compartments: 12 Wing Ta, 2 Wing Slop Ta, ER 12 Cargo Pump (s): 12x900m³/hr Manifold: Bow/CM: 112m	**1 oil engine** driving 1 FP propeller Total Power: 11,390kW (15,486hp) 15.0kn MAN-B&W 7S50MC-C 1 x 2 Stroke 7 Cy. 500 x 2000 11390kW (15486bhp) STX Engine Co Ltd-South Korea AuxGen: 3 x 1250kW 450V 60Hz a.c Boilers: e (ex.g.) 9.2kgf/cm² (9.0bar), WTAuxB (o.f.) 9.2kgf/cm² (9.0bar) Fuel: 200.0 (d.f.) 2100.0 (r.f.)
9414838 *AUYP* -	**SWARNA KRISHNA** **The Shipping Corporation of India Ltd (SCI)** - *Mumbai* *India* MMSI: 419760000 Official number: 3534	**42,845** 21,337 73,655 T/cm 68.3	Class: IR LR ✠ **100A1** SS 10/2010 Double Hull oil tanker CSR ESP **ShipRight** (CM) *IWS LI SPM ✠ **LMC** **UMS IGS** Eq.Ltr: M†; Cable: 680.0/81.0 U3 (a)	**2010-10 STX Offshore & Shipbuilding Co Ltd — Changwon (Jinhae Shipyard)** Yd No: 1296 Loa 228.00 (BB) Br ex 32.26 Dght 14.200 Lbp 219.90 Br md 32.24 Dpth 20.65 Welded, 1 dk	**(A13B2TP) Products Tanker** Double Hull (13F) Liq: 80,300; Liq (Oil): 80,300 Compartments: 12 Wing Ta, 2 Wing Slop Ta, ER 12 Cargo Pump (s): 12x900m³/hr Manifold: Bow/CM: 112m	**1 oil engine** driving 1 FP propeller Total Power: 11,390kW (15,486hp) 15.0kn MAN-B&W 7S50MC-C 1 x 2 Stroke 7 Cy. 500 x 2000 11390kW (15486bhp) STX Engine Co Ltd-South Korea AuxGen: 3 x 1250kW 450V 60Hz a.c Boilers: e (ex.g.) 9.2kgf/cm² (9.0bar), WTAuxB (o.f.) 9.2kgf/cm² (9.0bar) Fuel: 200.0 (d.f.) 2100.0 (r.f.)

9421403 *AVEY* -	**SWARNA MALA** *completed as Zefiros -2010* **The Shipping Corporation of India Ltd (SCI)** - *Mumbai* India MMSI: 419000103 Official number: 3681	**29,993** 13,605 51,196 T/cm 52.0	Class: IR NV	**2010-01 STX Offshore & Shipbuilding Co Ltd — Changwon (Jinhae Shipyard)** Yd No: 1299 Loa 183.00 (BB) Br ex 32.23 Dght 13.147 Lbp 173.93 Br md 32.20 Dpth 19.10 Welded, 1 dk	**(A13B2TP) Products Tanker** Double Hull (13F) Liq: 52,092; Liq (Oil): 52,092 Cargo Heating Coils Compartments: 12 Wing Ta, 2 Wing Slop Ta, 1 Slop Ta, ER 12 Cargo Pump (s): 12x600m^3/hr Manifold: Bow/CM: 91.3m	**1 oil engine** driving 1 FP propeller Total Power: 9,480kW (12,889hp) 14.5kn MAN-B&W 6S50MC-C 1 x 2 Stroke 6 Cy. 500 x 2000 9480kW (12889bhp) STX Engine Co Ltd-South Korea AuxGen: 3 x 930kW a.c Fuel: 170.0 (d.f.) 1355.0 (r.f.)
9204257 *JZTP* -	**SWARNA NALINI** *ex Shimanami -2014* - - Indonesia MMSI: 525002129	*234* - -		**1998-05 Kanbara Zosen K.K. — Onomichi** Yd No: 502 Loa 49.80 Br ex - Dght - Lbp 34.60 Br md 11.10 Dpth 3.15 Welded	**(A36A2PR) Passenger/Ro-Ro Ship (Vehicles)**	**1 oil engine** driving 1 FP propeller Total Power: 736kW (1,001hp) 9.5kn Yanmar M220-UN 1 x 4 Stroke 6 Cy. 220 x 300 736kW (1001bhp) Yanmar Diesel Engine Co Ltd-Japan
9432672 *AUYQ* -	**SWARNA PUSHP** - **The Shipping Corporation of India Ltd (SCI)** - *Mumbai* India MMSI: 419761000 Official number: 3535	**29,845** 12,971 47,795 T/cm 54.0	Class: IR LR ✠ **100A1** SS 01/2010 Double Hull oil tanker CSR ESP *IWS LI SPM ✠ **LMC** **UMS IGS** Eq.Ltr: M†; Cable: 687.5/73.0 U3 (a)	**2010-01 Jinling Shipyard — Nanjing JS** Yd No: 07-0502 Loa 184.95 (BB) Br ex 32.23 Dght 12.317 Lbp 176.00 Br md 32.20 Dpth 18.20 Welded, 1 dk	**(A13B2TP) Products Tanker** Double Hull (13F) Liq: 50,473; Liq (Oil): 50,473 Compartments: 12 Wing Ta, 2 Wing Slop Ta, ER 12 Cargo Pump (s): 12x600m^3/hr Manifold: Bow/CM: 92.1m	**1 oil engine** driving 1 FP propeller Total Power: 9,480kW (12,889hp) 14.5kn MAN-B&W 6S50MC-C 1 x 2 Stroke 6 Cy. 500 x 2000 9480kW (12889bhp) Yichang Marine Diesel Engine Co Ltd-China AuxGen: 3 x 800kW 440V 60Hz a.c Boilers: AuxB (o.f.) 9.2kgf/cm^2 (9.0bar), AuxB (Comp) 9.2kgf/cm^2 (9.0bar) Fuel: 260.0 (d.f.) 1340.0 (r.f.)
9078775 *POKJ* -	**SWARNA PUTRI** *ex Rainbow Nomi -2012* **PT Jembatan Nusantara** - Indonesia MMSI: 525002121	*380* - 90		**1994-02 Nakatani Shipyard Co. Ltd. — Etajima** Yd No: 557 Loa 62.28 (BB) Br ex - Dght 2.600 Lbp 45.00 Br md 10.20 Dpth 3.60 Welded	**(A37B2PS) Passenger Ship**	**2 oil engines** sr geared to sc. shafts driving 2 FP propellers Total Power: 2,200kW (2,992hp) Yanmar T260-ST 2 x 4 Stroke 6 Cy. 260 x 330 each-1100kW (1496bhp) Yanmar Diesel Engine Co Ltd-Japan
9399818 *AUYR* -	**SWARNA SINDHU** - **The Shipping Corporation of India Ltd (SCI)** - *Mumbai* India MMSI: 419762000 Official number: 3536	**42,845** 21,337 73,650 T/cm 68.3	Class: IR LR ✠ **100A1** SS 07/2010 Double Hull oil tanker CSR ESP **ShipRight** (CM) *IWS LI SPM ✠ **LMC** **UMS IGS** Eq.Ltr: M†; Cable: 680.3/81.0 U3 (a)	**2010-07 STX Offshore & Shipbuilding Co Ltd — Changwon (Jinhae Shipyard)** Yd No: 1291 Loa 228.00 (BB) Br ex 32.26 Dght 14.200 Lbp 219.90 Br md 32.24 Dpth 20.65 Welded, 1 dk	**(A13B2TP) Products Tanker** Double Hull (13F) Liq: 80,300; Liq (Oil): 80,300 Compartments: 12 Wing Ta, 2 Wing Slop Ta, ER 12 Cargo Pump (s): 12x900m^3/hr Manifold: Bow/CM: 112m	**1 oil engine** driving 1 FP propeller Total Power: 11,390kW (15,486hp) 15.0kn MAN-B&W 7S50MC-C 1 x 2 Stroke 7 Cy. 500 x 2000 11390kW (15486bhp) STX Engine Co Ltd-South Korea AuxGen: 3 x 1250kW 450V 60Hz a.c Boilers: e (ex.g.) 13.3kgf/cm^2 (13.0bar), AuxB (o.f.) 9.2kgf/cm^2 (9.0bar) Fuel: 200.0 (d.f.) 2100.0 (r.f.)
7342134 *HP5545* -	**SWAT LINKS 9** *ex Sand Serin -2010* **Swat Links Ltd** - *Panama* Panama MMSI: 357838000 Official number: 019922543PE	**1,283** 384 2,120	Class: (LR) ✠ Classed LR until 4/8/09	**1974-12 Clelands Shipbuilding Co. Ltd. — Wallsend** (Hull) Yd No: 87 **1974-12 Ferguson Bros (Port Glasgow) Ltd — Port Glasgow** Loa 66.60 Br ex 12.22 Dght 4.827 Lbp 62.95 Br md 12.20 Dpth 5.54 Welded, 1 dk	**(B33A2DS) Suction Dredger** Hopper: 860	**1 oil engine** reverse reduction geared to sc. shaft driving 1 FP propeller Total Power: 846kW (1,150hp) 10.5kn Blackstone ESL8MK2 1 x 4 Stroke 8 Cy. 222 x 292 846kW (1150bhp) Mirrlees Blackstone (Stamford)Ltd.-Stamford AuxGen: 2 x 150kW 440V 50Hz a.c Thrusters: 1 Tunnel thruster (f) Fuel: 69.0 (d.f.)
9113783 *VVRC* -	**SWATANTRA** - **Visakhapatnam Port Trust** - *Visakhapatnam* India Official number: 2699	**359** 108 106	Class: (IR)	**1997-09 Hindustan Shipyard Ltd — Visakhapatnam** Yd No: 1167 Loa 33.50 Br ex 10.02 Dght 3.100 Lbp 32.02 Br md 10.00 Dpth 4.16 Welded, 1 dk	**(B32A2ST) Tug**	**2 oil engines** gearing integral to driving 2 Voith-Schneider propellers Total Power: 2,210kW (3,004hp) 10.0kn Normo KRMB-6 2 x 4 Stroke 6 Cy. 250 x 300 each-1105kW (1502bhp) Ulstein Bergen AS-Norway AuxGen: 2 x 140kW 390V 50Hz a.c Fuel: 60.0 (d.f.)
9152284 *A8VP2* -	**SWAZILAND** *ex MSC Swaziland -2012 ex NYK Castor -2010* **Shian Shipping Ltd** Zodiac Maritime Agencies Ltd SatCom: Inmarsat C 463707822 *Monrovia* Liberia MMSI: 636014642 Official number: 14642	**76,847** 30,006 82,275	Class: NK	**1998-01 Mitsubishi Heavy Industries Ltd. — Nagasaki** Yd No: 2134 Loa 299.90 (BB) Br ex - Dght 14.032 Lbp 287.00 Br md 40.00 Dpth 23.90 Welded, 1 dk	**(A33A2CC) Container Ship (Fully Cellular)** TEU 6208 C Ho 3156 TEU C Dk 3052 TEU incl 500 ref C. Compartments: ER, 8 Cell Ho 18 Ha: ER	**1 oil engine** driving 1 FP propeller Total Power: 52,960kW (72,004hp) 23.0kn B&W 12K90MC 1 x 2 Stroke 12 Cy. 900 x 2550 52960kW (72004bhp) Mitsui Engineering & Shipbuilding CLtd-Japan AuxGen: 4 x 2235kW 440V 60Hz a.c Thrusters: 2 Thwart. FP thruster (f) Fuel: 279.6 (d.f.) (Heating Coils) 8515.5 (r.f.) 183.0pd
9044932 *C4FJ2* -	**SWE-BULK** *ex Severnaya Dvina -2008 ex Ingo J -2005* *ex MF Levant -1999 ex Intermodal Levant -1996* *ex Diana J -1993 ex Queensee -1993* **Bora Wind Shipping Co Ltd** Rederi AB Swedish Bulk *Limassol* Cyprus MMSI: 210474000 Official number: 9044932	**2,480** 1,228 3,269	Class: RI (GL)	**1991-10 Estaleiros Navais de Viana do Castelo S.A. — Viana do Castelo** Yd No: 159 Loa 87.37 (BB) Br ex 13.02 Dght 4.700 Lbp 82.25 Br md 13.00 Dpth 7.10 Welded, 1 dk	**(A31A2GX) General Cargo Ship** Grain: 4,650 TEU 153 C.Ho 104/20' C.Dk 49/20' Compartments: 1 Ho, ER 1 Ha: (57.4 x 10.2)ER Ice Capable	**1 oil engine** with clutches & sr geared to sc. shaft driving 1 CP propeller Total Power: 1,320kW (1,795hp) 12.0kn Alpha 6L28/32A 1 x 4 Stroke 6 Cy. 280 x 320 1320kW (1795bhp) MAN B&W Diesel A/S-Denmark AuxGen: 1 x 250kW 220/380V a.c, 2 x 149kW 220/380V a.c Thrusters: 1 Thwart. FP thruster (f)
9194074 *5BWR3* -	**SWE-TRADER** *ex Singeldiep -2013 ex Salsa -2012* *ex Singeldiep -2011 ex Europa -2002* **Rederi AB Swedish Bulk** - *Limassol* Cyprus MMSI: 212179000 Official number: 9194074	**3,170** 1,876 4,555	Class: GL RI (BV)	**2000-07 Rousse Shipyard JSC — Rousse** Yd No: 405 Loa 98.90 Br ex - Dght 5.740 Lbp 92.50 Br md 13.80 Dpth 7.40 Welded, 1 dk	**(A31A2GX) General Cargo Ship** Grain: 6,255 TEU 282 C. 282/20' (40') 1 Ha: Cranes: 1x13t Ice Capable	**1 oil engine** reduction geared to sc. shaft driving 1 CP propeller Total Power: 2,880kW (3,916hp) 13.0kn MaK 6M32 1 x 4 Stroke 6 Cy. 320 x 480 2880kW (3916bhp) MaK Motoren GmbH & Co. KG-Kiel AuxGen: 3 x 216kW a.c
8605478 *C6VU6* -	**SWEDICA HAV** *ex Ophir -2006 ex Sea Weser -2001* *ex Jan Meeder -1997* **Hav Bulk AS** HAV Ship Management NorRus AS *Nassau* Bahamas MMSI: 309584000 Official number: 8001265	**1,616** 758 2,276	Class: GL (BV)	**1986-05 Schiffs. Hugo Peters Wewelsfleth Peters & Co. GmbH — Wewelsfleth** Yd No: 622 Loa 82.45 Br ex 11.33 Dght 4.168 Lbp 77.35 Br md 11.30 Dpth 5.40 Welded, 2 dks	**(A31A2GX) General Cargo Ship** Grain: 2,953; Bale: 2,945 TEU 76 C.Ho 44/20' C.Dk 32/20' Compartments: 1 Ho, ER 1 Ha: (49.8 x 9.0)ER Ice Capable	**1 oil engine** with clutches, flexible couplings & sr reverse geared to sc. shaft driving 1 FP propeller Total Power: 645kW (877hp) 10.5kn MWM TBD440-6K 1 x 4 Stroke 6 Cy. 230 x 270 645kW (877bhp) Motoren Werke Mannheim AG (MWM)-West Germany AuxGen: 1 x 190kW 380V 50Hz a.c, 2 x 82kW 380V 50Hz a.c Thrusters: 1 Thwart. FP thruster (f) Fuel: 96.0 (d.f.) 3.0pd
6826183 - -	**SWEE ANN SATU** *ex Septimus -1982* **Haiyuan Shipping Sdn Bhd** -	*399* 229 1,005	Class: (BV)	**1968 Frederikshavn Vaerft og Tordok A/S — Frederikshavn** Yd No: 280 Loa 59.34 Br ex 10.67 Dght 3.639 Lbp 53.01 Br md 10.60 Dpth 3.69 Welded, 2 dks	**(A31A2GX) General Cargo Ship** Grain: 2,168; Bale: 1,990 Compartments: 1 Ho, ER 2 Ha: (16.1 x 6.4) (9.2 x 6.4)ER Derricks: 3x5t; Winches: 3	**1 oil engine** driving 1 FP propeller Total Power: 588kW (799hp) 11.3kn Alpha 408-26VO 1 x 2 Stroke 8 Cy. 260 x 400 588kW (799bhp) Alpha Diesel A/S-Denmark AuxGen: 2 x 40kW 220V 50Hz a.c Fuel: 61.0 (d.f.) 3.0pd
7737339 - -	**SWEE KHENG SATU** - **MS Shipping Sdn Bhd** - *Kuching* Malaysia Official number: 671	*299* 140 296	Class: (NK)	**1978 Asian Welding Machinery Pte Ltd — Singapore** Loa 39.48 Br ex 8.01 Dght 2.591 Lbp 37.50 Br md 7.99 Dpth 3.00 Welded, 1 dk	**(A31A2GX) General Cargo Ship**	**2 oil engines** driving 2 FP propellers Total Power: 276kW (376hp) 8.5kn Isuzu E120-MF6R 2 x 4 Stroke 6 Cy. 135 x 140 each-138kW (188bhp) Isuzu Marine Engine Inc-Japan AuxGen: 2 x 24kW
9370795 *3ESN8* -	**SWEET BRIER** - **SS Harmony Shipping SA** Santoku Senpaku Co Ltd *Panama* Panama MMSI: 370370000 Official number: 3429108A	**39,895** 21,193 49,507	Class: NK	**2008-08 Tsuneishi Holdings Corp Tsuneishi Shipbuilding Co — Fukuyama HS** Yd No: 1370 Loa 199.90 Br ex - Dght 11.247 Lbp 191.50 Br md 32.20 Dpth 16.20 Welded, 1 dk	**(A24B2BW) Wood Chips Carrier** Grain: 102,130 Compartments: 6 Ho, ER 6 Ha: ER Cranes: 3x14.7t	**1 oil engine** driving 1 FP propeller Total Power: 8,360kW (11,366hp) 14.0kn MAN-B&W 6S50MC 1 x 2 Stroke 6 Cy. 500 x 1910 8360kW (11366bhp) Kawasaki Heavy Industries Ltd-Japan Fuel: 2820.0

IMO / Call sign / Flag	Name / Owner / Port	Tonnage	Class	Builder / Dimensions	Type	Machinery
8005185 *DUD6009* -	**SWEET BUNNY** *ex* Shoshin Maru No. 22 *-1993* **Sea Gold Fishing Corp** - *Manila* *Philippines* Official number: MNLD000100	*175* 96 -		**1980**-03 **K.K. Murakami Zosensho — Ishinomaki** Yd No: 1053 Loa 36.58 (BB) Br ex - Dght - Lbp 29.70 Br md 6.51 Dpth 2.54 Welded, 1 dk	**(B11B2FV) Fishing Vessel**	**1 oil engine** driving 1 FP propeller Total Power: 478kW (650hp) Niigata 6L25BXB 1 x 4 Stroke 6 Cy. 250 x 320 478kW (650bhp) Niigata Engineering Co Ltd-Japan
8745797 *ZCIU6* -	**SWEET DOLL** *ex* 11646 *-2003* **Golden Nights Ltd** Yacht Management Consultants Sarl (Hill Robinson Yacht Management Consultants) *George Town* *Cayman Islands (British)* MMSI: 319899000 Official number: 736834	**493** 147 -	Class: AB	**2003 Heesen Shipyards B.V. — Oss** Yd No: 11646 Loa 46.00 Br ex - Dght 2.780 Lbp 38.14 Br md 8.50 Dpth 3.80 Welded, 1 dk	**(X11A2YP) Yacht** Hull Material: Aluminium Alloy	**2 oil engines** reduction geared to sc. shafts driving 2 Propellers Total Power: 5,440kW (7,396hp) 24.0kn M.T.U. 16V4000M90 2 x Vee 4 Stroke 16 Cy. 165 x 190 each-2720kW (3698bhp) MTU Friedrichshafen GmbH-Friedrichshafen
9015993 *PNJQ* -	**SWEET ISTANBUL** *ex* Elegance *-2010* *ex* Bermuda Islander *-2007* *ex* Elegance *-2004* *ex* Zenit *-2004* *ex* Gracechurch Crown *-2002* *ex* Zenit *-1991* **PT Alken Abadi** - *Belawan* *Indonesia*	**3,815** 2,029 4,665 T/cm 15.0	Class: KI (GL)	**1991**-06 **J.J. Sietas KG Schiffswerft GmbH & Co. — Hamburg** Yd No: 1057 Loa 103.55 (BB) Br ex 16.22 Dght 6.074 Lbp 96.90 Br md 16.00 Dpth 8.00 Welded, 1 dk	**(A31A2GX) General Cargo Ship** Grain: 6,788; Bale: 6,615 TEU 372 C.Ho 134/20' (40') C.Dk 238/20' (40') incl. 50 ref C. Compartments: 3 Ho, ER 3 Ha: (12.4 x 10.3)2 (25.1 x 12.8)ER Ice Capable	**1 oil engine** with flexible couplings & sr geared to sc. shaft driving 1 CP propeller Total Power: 3,000kW (4,079hp) 14.5kn MaK 9M453C 1 x 4 Stroke 9 Cy. 320 x 420 3000kW (4079bhp) Krupp MaK Maschinenbau GmbH-Kiel AuxGen: 1 x 500kW 220/380V 50Hz a.c, 2 x 220kW 400/230V 50Hz a.c Thrusters: 1 Thwart. FP thruster (f) Fuel: 80.1 (d.f.) 399.5 (r.f.) 16.3pd
8708830 *E5U2672* -	**SWEET LADY** *ex* Nissei *-2013* **Dytamar Shipping Ltd** Rana Maritime Services SA *Avatiu* *Cook Islands* MMSI: 518725000 Official number: 1761	*6,429* - 3,845	Class: NK	**1988**-06 **Shin Kurushima Dockyard Co. Ltd. — Onishi** Yd No: 2523 Loa 138.00 (BB) Br ex - Dght 6.718 Lbp 132.43 Br md 21.00 Dpth 15.67 Welded	**(A35B2RV) Vehicles Carrier** Quarter stern door/ramp (p. a.) Quarter stern door/ramp (s. a.) Cars: 929	**1 oil engine** driving 1 FP propeller Total Power: 8,311kW (11,300hp) 20.0kn Mitsubishi 8UEC52LA 1 x 2 Stroke 8 Cy. 520 x 1600 8311kW (11300bhp) Mitsubishi Heavy Industries Ltd-Japan Thrusters: 1 Thwart. CP thruster (f); 1 Tunnel thruster (a) Fuel: 470.0 (r.f.)
7616078 *HQTT9* -	**SWEET LADY** *ex* Fast Lady *-1997* *ex* Stainless Hawk *-1996* *ex* Hinode Maru No. 2 *-1992* **Tango Bravo Maritime Services Ltd** - *San Lorenzo* *Honduras* MMSI: 334480000 Official number: L-1326915	**398** 302 1,188	Class: (BV)	**1977**-02 **Kyoei Zosen KK — Mihara HS** Yd No: 72 Loa 59.90 Br ex 9.83 Dght 3.910 Lbp 55.02 Br md 9.81 Dpth 4.35 Welded, 1 dk	**(A12A2TC) Chemical Tanker** Double Bottom Entire Compartment Length Liq: 1,158	**1 oil engine** geared to sc. shaft driving 1 FP propeller Total Power: 809kW (1,100hp) 11.7kn Hanshin 6LU28 1 x 4 Stroke 6 Cy. 280 x 440 809kW (1100bhp) Hanshin Nainenki Kogyo-Japan AuxGen: 1 x 76kW a.c
9316804 *9HA2289* -	**SWEET LADY III** *ex* Katrine Star *-2010* **Paradise Shipping Ltd** Eastern Mediterranean Maritime Ltd *Valletta* *Malta* MMSI: 248256000 Official number: 9316804	**30,822** 18,103 55,838 T/cm 56.1	Class: RI (NK)	**2006**-01 **Kawasaki Shipbuilding Corp — Kobe HG** Yd No: 1561 Loa 189.90 (BB) Br ex 32.26 Dght 12.522 Lbp 185.00 Br md 32.26 Dpth 17.80 Welded, 1 dk	**(A21A2BC) Bulk Carrier** Grain: 69,450; Bale: 66,368 Compartments: 5 Ho, ER 5 Ha: 4 (20.5 x 18.6)ER (17.8 x 18.6) Cranes: 4x30.5t	**1 oil engine** driving 1 FP propeller Total Power: 8,201kW (11,150hp) 14.6kn MAN-B&W 6S50MC-C 1 x 2 Stroke 6 Cy. 500 x 2000 8201kW (11150bhp) Kawasaki Heavy Industries Ltd-Japan AuxGen: 3 x a.c Fuel: 1790.0
8842947 *HP5661* -	**SWEET MIRI** *ex* Miri Glory *-2003* **Barington SA** Al Rafedain Marine Services LLC *Panama* *Panama* MMSI: 373547000 Official number: 43446PEXT	**1,042** 546 1,837 T/cm 7.4	Class: (BV) (AB)	**1990**-07 **Hong Leong-Lurssen Shipyard Bhd — Butterworth** Yd No: 1216 Loa 62.00 Br ex - Dght 3.662 Lbp 59.50 Br md 13.10 Dpth 4.35 Welded, 1 dk	**(B35E2TF) Bunkering Tanker** Single Hull Liq: 1,926; Liq (Oil): 1,968 Compartments: 8 Wing Ta, ER 2 Cargo Pump (s): 2x350m³/hr	**2 oil engines** reverse reduction geared to sc. shafts driving 2 FP propellers Total Power: 888kW (1,208hp) 10.0kn MWM TBD234V12 2 x Vee 4 Stroke 12 Cy. 128 x 140 each-444kW (604bhp) Motoren Werke Mannheim AG (MWM)-West Germany AuxGen: 3 x 80kW a.c
7333511 *DYSW* -	**SWEET SAIL** *ex* Mizushima Maru *-1978* **Sweet Lines Inc** - *Cebu* *Philippines* Official number: S1577	*844* 563 1,152	Class: (NK)	**1969 Fukushima Zosen Ltd. — Matsue** Loa 54.87 Br ex 9.33 Dght 4.509 Lbp 49.51 Br md 9.30 Dpth 6.91 Welded, 2 dks	**(A31A2GX) General Cargo Ship** Grain: 1,724; Bale: 1,656 TEU 50 C. 50/20' Compartments: 1 Ho, ER 1 Ha: (22.7 x 5.4)ER Derricks: 2x6t	**1 oil engine** driving 1 FP propeller Total Power: 1,103kW (1,500hp) 12.5kn Nippon Hatsudoki HS6NVA38 1 x 4 Stroke 6 Cy. 380 x 540 1103kW (1500bhp) Nippon Hatsudoki-Japan Fuel: 101.5 3.5pd
7315753 *DYST* -	**SWEET TIME** *ex* Carmelita *-1978* **Sweet Lines Inc** - *Cebu* *Philippines* Official number: S1103	*445* 203 1,003		**1971 Okayama Zosen K.K. — Hinase** Yd No: 218 Converted From: General Cargo Ship Loa 49.38 Br ex 7.93 Dght 3.963 Lbp - Br md - Dpth - Welded	**(A32A2GF) General Cargo/Passenger Ship** Passengers: 430	**1 oil engine** driving 1 FP propeller Total Power: 1,324kW (1,800hp)
9195901 *OJNF* -	**SWEGARD** *ex* Merwedelta *-2007* **Bore Ltd (Bore Oy Ab)** - SatCom: Inmarsat C 423099810 *Mariehamn* *Finland* MMSI: 230998000 Official number: 55228	**2,997** 1,707 4,956	Class: BV (LR) ✠	**2001**-04 **B.V. Scheepswerf Damen Hoogezand — Foxhol** Yd No: 756 **2001**-04 **Santierul Naval Damen Galati S.A. — Galati** (Hull) Yd No: 963 Loa 94.96 (BB) Br ex - Dght 6.200 Lbp 90.05 Br md 13.17 Dpth 7.15 Welded, 1 dk	**(A31A2GX) General Cargo Ship** Grain: 6,196 TEU 224 C.Ho 120 TEU C.Dk 104 TEU Compartments: 1 Ho, ER 1 Ha: (67.5 x 11.0)Tappered ER Ice Capable	**1 oil engine** reduction geared to sc. shaft driving 1 CP propeller Total Power: 2,400kW (3,263hp) 11.5kn MaK 8M25 1 x 4 Stroke 8 Cy. 255 x 400 2400kW (3263bhp) Caterpillar Motoren GmbH & Co. KG-Germany AuxGen: 1 x 452kW 400V 50Hz a.c, 2 x 145kW 400/220V 50Hz a.c Thrusters: 1 Water jet (f) Fuel: 31.9 (d.f.) 282.5 (r.f.)
7612008 *WDC7970* -	**SWELL RIDER** *ex* Polar Star *-2001* **Privateer LLC** - *Garibaldi, OR* *United States of America* MMSI: 367079690 Official number: 559907	*158* 107 -		**1974**-01 **Marine Power & Equipment Co. Ltd. — Seattle, Wa** L reg 22.35 Br ex 7.45 Dght - Lbp - Br md - Dpth 3.66 Welded, 1 dk	**(B11B2FV) Fishing Vessel**	**1 oil engine** driving 1 FP propeller Total Power: 500kW (680hp)
5028605 *VC8102* -	**SWELLMASTER** *ex* Irving Hemlock *-1996* *ex* Atherfield *-1972* **Atlantic Towing Ltd** Harbour Development Ltd *Saint John, NB* *Canada* MMSI: 316002592 Official number: 186491	*246* 102 417	Class: (LR) ✠ Classed LR until 10/93	**1956**-05 **John I Thornycroft & Co Ltd — Southampton** Yd No: 4163 Loa 34.14 Br ex 9.02 Dght 2.972 Lbp 30.48 Br md 8.23 Dpth 4.04 Riveted\Welded	**(B32A2ST) Tug**	**2 oil engines** reverse reduction geared to sc. shafts driving 2 FP propellers Total Power: 1,500kW (2,040hp) Caterpillar D398TA 2 x Vee 4 Stroke 12 Cy. 159 x 203 each-750kW (1020bhp) (new engine ,made 1973, fitted 1987) Caterpillar Tractor Co-USA AuxGen: 2 x 40kW 220V d.c, 1 x 25kW 220V d.c
9524798 *3FLY3* -	**SWERTIA** **Silver Arrow Maritime SA** Grow-Will Inc *Panama* *Panama* MMSI: 370666000 Official number: 4009209	**7,727** 2,819 9,037	Class: NK	**2008**-12 **Kanasashi Heavy Industries Co Ltd — Shizuoka SZ** Yd No: 8115 Loa 104.83 Br ex - Dght 8.216 Lbp 96.77 Br md 20.00 Dpth 13.80 Welded, 1 dk	**(A31A2GX) General Cargo Ship** Grain: 14,865; Bale: 15,738 Compartments: 2 Ho, ER 2 Ha: ER Cranes: 1x60t,2x30.7t	**1 oil engine** driving 1 Propeller Total Power: 3,309kW (4,499hp) 13.5kn Hanshin LH46LA 1 x 4 Stroke 6 Cy. 460 x 880 3309kW (4499bhp) The Hanshin Diesel Works Ltd-Japan
8709353 *VTSM* -	**SWETHA** **Surya Sea Foods Pvt Ltd** *Visakhapatnam* *India* Official number: VSP102	*179* 53 108	Class: (LR) (IR) ✠ Classed LR until 4/3/92	**1989**-03 **Chungmu Shipbuilding Co Inc — Tongyeong** Yd No: 192 Loa 27.40 Br ex 7.38 Dght 2.806 Lbp 23.02 Br md 7.21 Dpth 3.31 Welded, 1 Dk	**(B11A2FS) Stern Trawler** Ins: 120	**1 oil engine** with clutches, flexible couplings & sr reverse geared to sc. shaft driving 1 FP propeller Total Power: 416kW (566hp) MAN D2842ME 1 x Vee 4 Stroke 12 Cy. 128 x 141 416kW (566bhp) MAN Nutzfahrzeuge AG-Nuernberg AuxGen: 2 x 52kW 440V 60Hz a.c Fuel: 72.0 (d.f.)
7227839 *SPS2348* -	**SWI-7** *ex* Swi-3 *-2011* *ex* UST-94 *-2011* **Tadeusz Krupa** - *Swinoujscie* *Poland* MMSI: 261003090	*136* 34 43	Class: PR	**1972**-07 **Gdynska Stocznia Remontowa — Gdynia** (Hull) Yd No: B25s/A07 **1972**-07 **Stocznia Ustka SA — Ustka** Yd No: 344 Loa 24.57 Br ex 6.58 Dght 2.500 Lbp 21.85 Br md 6.56 Dpth 3.38 Welded, 1 dk	**(B11B2FV) Fishing Vessel**	**1 oil engine** driving 1 CP propeller Total Power: 257kW (349hp) 10.5kn Wola 22H12A 1 x Vee 4 Stroke 12 Cy. 135 x 155 257kW (349bhp) Zaklady Mechaniczne 'PZL Wola' im MNowotki-Poalnd AuxGen: 2 x 4kW 30V d.c

IMO / Call sign	Name / Owner / Flag	Tonnage	Class	Builder / Dimensions	Type	Machinery
7045877 - -	**SWI-33** *ex* DZI-109 *ex* WLA-151 *-1995* - -	*106* 39 33	Class: (PR)	**1963-06 Gdynska Stocznia Remontowa — Gdynia** Yd No: B25s/272 Loa 24.57 Br ex 6.61 Dght 2.361 Lbp 21.95 Br md 6.60 Dpth 3.38 Welded, 1 dk	**(B11B2FV) Fishing Vessel**	**1 oil engine** driving 1 FP propeller Total Power: 165kW (224hp) 9.5kn Volund DM-330 1 x 4 Stroke 3 Cy. 300 x 410 165kW (224bhp) A/S Volund-Denmark AuxGen: 1 x 3kW 24V d.c, 1 x 1kW 24V d.c
7405560 - -	**SWI-51** *ex* KOL-16 *-1995* *ex* KOL-27 *-1997* *ex* UST-89 *-1995* - -	*106* 29 35	Class: PR	**1974-09 Stocznia Ustka SA — Ustka** Yd No: B25s/A37 Loa 24.41 Br ex 6.58 Dght 2.501 Lbp 21.85 Br md 6.56 Dpth 3.38 Welded, 1 dk	**(B11B2FV) Fishing Vessel**	**1 oil engine** driving 1 CP propeller Total Power: 257kW (349hp) 10.0kn Wola 22H12A 1 x Vee 4 Stroke 12 Cy. 135 x 155 257kW (349bhp) Zaklady Mechaniczne 'PZL Wola' im MNowotki-Poalnd AuxGen: 2 x 4kW 30V d.c
9216779 *PNCD* -	**SWIBER 99** *ex* Swissco 99 *-2009* **PT Swiber Berjaya** - *Jakarta* *Indonesia*	**497** 149 -	Class: BV KI	**1999-01 Tuong Aik (Sarawak) Sdn Bhd — Sibu** Yd No: 9714 Loa 45.00 Br ex - Dght 4.000 Lbp 41.90 Br md 10.00 Dpth 5.00 Welded, 1 dk	**(B34L2QU) Utility Vessel**	**2 oil engines** with clutches & sr reverse geared to sc. shafts driving 2 FP propellers Total Power: 1,814kW (2,466hp) 10.0kn Caterpillar D399TA 2 x Vee 4 Stroke 16 Cy. 159 x 203 each-907kW (1233bhp) Caterpillar Inc-USA AuxGen: 2 x 200kW 415/220V 50Hz a.c Thrusters: 1 Tunnel thruster (f) Fuel: 309.0 (d.f.) 8.0pd
9502154 *V7QC8* -	**SWIBER ADA** - **Orchard Offshore AS** Newcruz Offshore Marine Pte Ltd *Majuro* *Marshall Islands* MMSI: 538003333 Official number: 3333	**1,537** 461 1,475	Class: BV	**2008-10 Guangzhou Hangtong Shipbuilding & Shipping Co Ltd — Jiangmen GD** Yd No: 062012 Loa 58.70 Br ex - Dght 4.750 Lbp 56.30 Br md 14.60 Dpth 5.50 Welded, 1 dk	**(B21B20A) Anchor Handling Tug Supply**	**2 oil engines** reduction geared to sc. shafts driving 2 CP propellers Total Power: 3,676kW (4,998hp) 13.5kn Niigata 6MG28HX 2 x 4 Stroke 6 Cy. 280 x 370 each-1838kW (2499bhp) Niigata Engineering Co Ltd-Japan
9466489 *YGIJ* -	**SWIBER ANNA** *ex* Intan AHT 1 *-2011* **PT Swiber Berjaya** Newcruz Offshore Marine Pte Ltd *Jakarta* *Indonesia* MMSI: 525012075	**497** 149 -	Class: BV KI	**2007-10 Berjaya Dockyard Sdn Bhd — Miri** Yd No: 42 Loa 45.00 Br ex - Dght 3.400 Lbp 40.00 Br md 11.00 Dpth 4.00 Welded, 1 dk	**(B21B20A) Anchor Handling Tug Supply**	**2 oil engines** reduction geared to sc. shafts driving 2 FP propellers Total Power: 2,612kW (3,552hp) 12.0kn Caterpillar 3516B 2 x Vee 4 Stroke 16 Cy. 170 x 190 each-1306kW (1776bhp) Caterpillar Inc-USA Thrusters: 1 Tunnel thruster (f) Fuel: 231.5
9555412 *V7RF6* -	**SWIBER ANNE-CHRISTINE** - **Bukit Timah Offshore AS** Vallianz Offshore Marine Pte Ltd *Majuro* *Marshall Islands* MMSI: 538003494 Official number: 3494	**2,708** 812 2,113	Class: AB	**2009-12 Fujian Southeast Shipyard — Fuzhou FJ** Yd No: DN70M-3 Loa 70.00 Br ex - Dght 6.100 Lbp 61.80 Br md 16.80 Dpth 7.50 Welded, 1 dk	**(B21B20A) Anchor Handling Tug Supply**	**2 oil engines** reduction geared to sc. shafts driving 2 CP propellers Total Power: 8,000kW (10,876hp) Wartsila 8L32 2 x 4 Stroke 8 Cy. 320 x 400 each-4000kW (5438bhp) Wartsila Finland Oy-Finland AuxGen: 2 x 1600kW a.c, 2 x 350kW a.c Thrusters: 2 Thwart. CP thruster (f); 1 Thwart. CP thruster (a) Fuel: 1220.0 (d.f.)
9574511 *V7SH6* -	**SWIBER ATLANTIS** - **Swiber Atlantis Pte Ltd** Newcruz Offshore Marine Pte Ltd *Majuro* *Marshall Islands* MMSI: 538003655 Official number: 3655	**3,389** 1,016 1,863	Class: AB (IR)	**2010-04 Guangzhou Hangtong Shipbuilding & Shipping Co Ltd — Jiangmen GD** Yd No: 072005 Loa 78.00 Br ex 20.02 Dght 4.800 Lbp 70.55 Br md 20.00 Dpth 6.50 Welded, 1 dk	**(B22A20V) Diving Support Vessel** Cranes: 1x100t	**2 oil engines** reduction geared to sc. shafts driving 2 Directional propellers Total Power: 3,240kW (4,406hp) 10.0kn Wartsila 9L20 2 x 4 Stroke 9 Cy. 200 x 280 each-1620kW (2203bhp) Wartsila Finland Oy-Finland AuxGen: 2 x 1300kW 415V 50Hz a.c, 3 x 534kW 415V 50Hz a.c Thrusters: 2 Thwart. CP thruster (f) Fuel: 1085.0 (d.f.)
9549994 *9V8993* -	**SWIBER BHANWAR** *ex* Asiastar 48279 *-2010* **Vallianz Marine Pte Ltd** Newcruz Offshore Marine Pte Ltd *Singapore* *Singapore* MMSI: 565522000	**735** 220 700	Class: BV	**2009-09 Guangzhou Panyu Lingshan Shipyard Ltd — Guangzhou GD** Yd No: 155 Loa 48.00 Br ex 12.86 Dght 3.800 Lbp 42.40 Br md 12.80 Dpth 4.60 Welded, 1 dk	**(B21B20A) Anchor Handling Tug Supply**	**2 oil engines** reduction geared to sc. shafts driving 2 CP propellers Total Power: 3,542kW (4,816hp) 12.0kn Caterpillar 3516B 2 x Vee 4 Stroke 16 Cy. 170 x 190 each-1771kW (2408bhp) Caterpillar Inc-USA AuxGen: 3 x 245kW 415V 50Hz a.c, 2 x 800kW 415V 50Hz a.c Thrusters: 1 Tunnel thruster (f) Fuel: 590.0
9530852 *9V9258* -	**SWIBER CARINA** *ex* Unistar 24278 *-2011* **Vallianz Marine Pte Ltd** Vallianz Offshore Marine Pte Ltd *Singapore* *Singapore* MMSI: 566023000 Official number: 396844	**531** 160 396	Class: NK (BV)	**2009-05 Guangzhou Panyu Lingshan Shipyard Ltd — Guangzhou GD** Yd No: 167 Loa 40.00 Br ex - Dght 3.810 Lbp 34.90 Br md 11.80 Dpth 4.60 Welded, 1 dk	**(B21B20T) Offshore Tug/Supply Ship**	**2 oil engines** reduction geared to sc. shafts driving 2 FP propellers Total Power: 1,790kW (2,434hp) Cummins KTA-38-M2 2 x Vee 4 Stroke 12 Cy. 159 x 159 each-895kW (1217bhp) Cummins Engine Co Ltd-United Kingdom AuxGen: 2 x 240kW 415V 50Hz a.c Thrusters: 1 Tunnel thruster (f) Fuel: 333.0
9408932 *JZIC* -	**SWIBER CHALLENGER** *ex* Swiwar Challenger *-2013* **PT Swiber Berjaya** - *Jakarta* *Indonesia* MMSI: 525012205	**1,470** 441 1,475	Class: BV KI	**2007-05 Guangzhou Hangtong Shipbuilding & Shipping Co Ltd — Jiangmen GD** Yd No: 052008 Loa 58.70 Br ex - Dght 4.750 Lbp 53.20 Br md 14.60 Dpth 5.50 Welded, 1 dk	**(B21B20A) Anchor Handling Tug Supply**	**2 oil engines** reduction geared to sc. shafts driving 2 CP propellers Total Power: 3,788kW (5,150hp) 13.5kn Caterpillar 3516B-HD 2 x Vee 4 Stroke 16 Cy. 170 x 215 each-1894kW (2575bhp) Caterpillar Inc-USA AuxGen: 3 x 320kW 415/220V 50Hz a.c
9535515 *9V8617* -	**SWIBER CHARLTON** - **Vallianz Marine Pte Ltd** Newcruz Offshore Marine Pte Ltd SatCom: Inmarsat C 456502312 *Singapore* *Singapore* MMSI: 565023000 Official number: 396024	**370** 111 -	Class: BV	**2010-12 Sapor Shipbuilding Industries Sdn Bhd — Sibu** Yd No: SAPOR 47 Loa 33.20 Br ex - Dght 3.800 Lbp 29.30 Br md 9.76 Dpth 4.30 Welded, 1 dk	**(B32A2ST) Tug**	**2 oil engines** reduction geared to sc. shafts driving 2 FP propellers Total Power: 2,386kW (3,244hp) Cummins KTA-50-M2 2 x Vee 4 Stroke 16 Cy. 159 x 159 each-1193kW (1622bhp) Cummins Engine Co Ltd-United Kingdom AuxGen: 2 x 80kW 50Hz a.c
9555395 *V7RF5* -	**SWIBER ELSE-MARIE** - **Bukit Timah Offshore AS** Vallianz Offshore Marine Pte Ltd SatCom: Inmarsat C 453834433 *Majuro* *Marshall Islands* MMSI: 538003493 Official number: 3493	**2,708** 812 2,135	Class: AB	**2009-08 Fujian Southeast Shipyard — Fuzhou FJ** Yd No: DN70M-1 Loa 70.00 Br ex - Dght 6.100 Lbp 61.80 Br md 16.80 Dpth 7.50 Welded, 1 dk	**(B21B20A) Anchor Handling Tug Supply**	**2 oil engines** reduction geared to sc. shaft (s) driving 2 Propellers Total Power: 8,000kW (10,876hp) Wartsila 8L32 2 x 4 Stroke 8 Cy. 320 x 400 each-4000kW (5438bhp) Wartsila Finland Oy-Finland AuxGen: 2 x 350kW a.c, 2 x 1600kW a.c Thrusters: 2 Tunnel thruster (f); 1 Tunnel thruster (a) Fuel: 1220.0 (d.f.)
9489182 *V7OH2* -	**SWIBER EXPLORER** - **Orchard Offshore AS** Newcruz Offshore Marine Pte Ltd *Majuro* *Marshall Islands* MMSI: 538003088 Official number: 3088	**618** 185 574	Class: BV	**2008-04 Borneo Shipping & Timber Agencies Sdn Ltd — Bintulu** Yd No: 88 Loa 45.00 Br ex - Dght 3.600 Lbp 41.77 Br md 11.80 Dpth 4.60 Welded, 1 dk	**(B21B20A) Anchor Handling Tug Supply**	**2 oil engines** geared to sc. shafts driving 2 FP propellers Total Power: 2,982kW (4,054hp) 10.0kn Caterpillar 3516B 2 x Vee 4 Stroke 16 Cy. 170 x 190 each-1491kW (2027bhp) Caterpillar Inc-USA
9435624 *9V7242* -	**SWIBER GALLANT** - **Sentosa Offshore AS** Newcruz Offshore Marine Pte Ltd *Singapore* *Singapore* MMSI: 565626000 Official number: 393400	**495** 149 353	Class: GL	**2007-11 PT Nanindah Mutiara Shipyard — Batam** Yd No: T177 Loa 40.00 Br ex - Dght 4.200 Lbp 36.80 Br md 11.40 Dpth 4.95 Welded, 1 dk	**(B21B20A) Anchor Handling Tug Supply**	**2 oil engines** reduction geared to sc. shafts driving 2 Propellers Total Power: 3,679kW (5,002hp) 12.0kn Yanmar 6EY26 2 x 4 Stroke 6 Cy. 260 x 385 each-1839kW (2500bhp) Yanmar Diesel Engine Co Ltd-Japan AuxGen: 3 x 270kW 415V a.c Thrusters: 1 Tunnel thruster (f)

IMO / Call sign / Flag	Name / Owner / Port	GT / NT / DWT	Class	Built / Builder / Dimensions	Type	Machinery
9598000 *9V8880* -	**SWIBER LINA** **Swiber Offshore Marine Pte Ltd** - *Singapore* *Singapore* MMSI: 564393000 Official number: 396349	**883** 265 611	Class: AB	**2011-05 Jiangsu Sunhoo Shipbuilding Co Ltd — Taixing JS** Yd No: SH008 Loa 45.00 Br ex - Dght 4.500 Lbp 43.50 Br md 12.60 Dpth 5.30 Welded, 1 dk	**(B32A2ST) Tug**	**2 oil engines** reverse reduction geared to sc. shafts driving 2 FP propellers Total Power: 3,840kW (5,220hp) Caterpillar 3516B-HD 2 x Vee 4 Stroke 16 Cy. 170 x 215 each-1920kW (2610bhp) Caterpillar Inc-USA AuxGen: 3 x 245kW a.c Fuel: 440.0 (d.f.)
9555424 *V7RF7* -	**SWIBER MARY-ANN** **Bukit Timah Offshore AS** Vallianz Offshore Marine Pte Ltd *Majuro* *Marshall Islands* MMSI: 538003495 Official number: 3495	**2,708** 812 2,096	Class: AB	**2010-07 Fujian Southeast Shipyard — Fuzhou FJ** Yd No: DN70M-5 Loa 70.00 Br ex - Dght 6.100 Lbp 61.80 Br md 16.80 Dpth 7.50 Welded, 1 dk	**(B21B20A) Anchor Handling Tug Supply**	**2 oil engines** reduction geared to sc. shaft (s) driving 2 CP propellers Total Power: 8,000kW (10,876hp) Wartsila 8L32 2 x 4 Stroke 8 Cy. 320 x 400 each-4000kW (5438bhp) Wartsila Finland Oy-Finland AuxGen: 2 x 1600kW a.c, 2 x 350kW a.c Thrusters: 2 Tunnel thruster (f) Fuel: 1220.0 (d.f.)
9476109 *9V7351* -	**SWIBER NAVIGATOR** **Orchard Offshore AS** Newcruz Offshore Marine Pte Ltd *Singapore* *Singapore* MMSI: 565834000 Official number: 393848	**618** 185 574	Class: BV	**2008-02 Borneo Shipping & Timber Agencies Sdn Ltd — Bintulu** Yd No: 89 Loa 45.00 Br ex - Dght 3.800 Lbp 39.40 Br md 11.80 Dpth 4.60 Welded, 1 dk	**(B21B20A) Anchor Handling Tug Supply**	**2 oil engines** geared to sc. shafts driving 2 FP propellers Total Power: 2,982kW (4,054hp) 10.0kn Caterpillar 3516B 2 x Vee 4 Stroke 16 Cy. 170 x 190 each-1491kW (2027bhp) Caterpillar Inc-USA AuxGen: 3 x 215kW a.c Thrusters: 1 Tunnel thruster (f) Fuel: 550.0 (d.f.)
9558529 *V7RN5* -	**SWIBER OSLO** **Sentosa Offshore AS** Newcruz Offshore Marine Pte Ltd *Majuro* *Marshall Islands* MMSI: 538003544 Official number: 3544	**1,537** 461 1,475	Class: BV	**2009-11 Guangzhou Hangtong Shipbuilding & Shipping Co Ltd — Jiangmen GD** Yd No: 072014 Loa 58.70 Br ex - Dght 4.750 Lbp 53.20 Br md 14.60 Dpth 5.50 Welded, 1 dk	**(B21B20A) Anchor Handling Tug Supply**	**2 oil engines** reduction geared to sc. shafts driving 2 CP propellers Total Power: 3,678kW (5,000hp) 13.5kn Niigata 6MG28HX 2 x 4 Stroke 6 Cy. 280 x 370 each-1839kW (2500bhp) Niigata Engineering Co Ltd-Japan AuxGen: 3 x 350kW 50Hz a.c
9027348 *YD4764* -	**SWIBER PHOENIX** *ex* Swisko Phoenix *-2006* **PT Swiber Berjaya** - *Cirebon* *Indonesia*	**181** 108 -	Class: (KI)	**2000-01 P.T. Jasa Wahana Tirta Samudera — Semarang** L reg 25.20 Br ex - Dght 2.290 Lbp 23.90 Br md 8.00 Dpth 3.00 Welded, 1 dk	**(B32A2ST) Tug**	**2 oil engines** reduction geared to sc. shafts driving 2 Propellers Total Power: 1,382kW (1,878hp) Cummins KTA-38-M 2 x Vee 4 Stroke 12 Cy. 159 x 159 each-691kW (939bhp) (made 1978, fitted 2000) Cummins Engine Co Inc-USA AuxGen: 2 x 40kW 380V a.c
9502116 *9V8069* -	**SWIBER RAVEN** **Vallianz Marine Pte Ltd** Newcruz Offshore Marine Pte Ltd SatCom: Inmarsat C 456596511 *Singapore* *Singapore* MMSI: 563965000 Official number: 395256	**298** 90 342	Class: GL	**2010-01 Forward Marine Enterprise Sdn Bhd — Sibu** Yd No: FM-51 Loa 31.10 Br ex - Dght 3.570 Lbp 28.72 Br md 9.50 Dpth 4.20 Welded, 1 dk	**(B32A2ST) Tug**	**2 oil engines** reverse reduction geared to sc. shafts driving 2 FP propellers Total Power: 2,386kW (3,244hp) Cummins KTA-50-M2 2 x Vee 4 Stroke 16 Cy. 159 x 159 each-1193kW (1622bhp) Cummins Engine Co Inc-USA AuxGen: 2 x 90kW a.c
9680475 *JZNG* -	**SWIBER RUBY** **PT Swiber Berjaya** - *Jakarta* *Indonesia* MMSI: 525005257	**1,678** 503 1,293	Class: AB	**2013-07 Fujian Southeast Shipyard — Fuzhou FJ** Yd No: DN59M-116 Loa 59.25 Br ex - Dght 4.950 Lbp 52.20 Br md 14.95 Dpth 6.10 Welded, 1 dk	**(B21B20A) Anchor Handling Tug Supply**	**2 oil engines** reduction geared to sc. shafts driving 2 CP propellers Total Power: 3,840kW (5,220hp) 11.0kn Caterpillar 3516C-HD 2 x Vee 4 Stroke 16 Cy. 170 x 215 each-1920kW (2610bhp) Caterpillar Inc-USA AuxGen: 2 x 800kW a.c, 2 x 350kW a.c Thrusters: 2 Tunnel thruster (f) Fuel: 520.0 (d.f.)
9558517 *9V8365* -	**SWIBER SANDEFJORD** **Sentosa Offshore AS** Vallianz Offshore Marine Pte Ltd *Singapore* *Singapore* MMSI: 565844000 Official number: 395659	**1,537** 461 1,475	Class: BV	**2009-08 Guangzhou Hangtong Shipbuilding & Shipping Co Ltd — Jiangmen GD** Yd No: 072013 Loa 58.70 Br ex - Dght 4.750 Lbp 53.20 Br md 14.60 Dpth 5.50 Welded, 1 dk	**(B21B20A) Anchor Handling Tug Supply**	**2 oil engines** reduction geared to sc. shafts driving 2 CP propellers Total Power: 3,678kW (5,000hp) 13.5kn Niigata 6MG28HX 2 x 4 Stroke 6 Cy. 280 x 370 each-1839kW (2500bhp) Niigata Engineering Co Ltd-Japan AuxGen: 3 x 350kW 50Hz a.c
9680487 *JZQO* -	**SWIBER SAPPHIRE** **PT Swiber Berjaya** Newcruz Offshore Marine Pte Ltd *Jakarta* *Indonesia* MMSI: 525012277	**1,678** 503 1,294	Class: AB	**2013-09 Fujian Southeast Shipyard — Fuzhou FJ** Yd No: DN59M-117 Loa 59.25 Br ex - Dght 4.950 Lbp 52.20 Br md 14.95 Dpth 6.10 Welded, 1 dk	**(B21B20A) Anchor Handling Tug Supply**	**2 oil engines** reduction geared to sc. shafts driving 2 CP propellers Total Power: 3,840kW (5,220hp) 11.0kn Caterpillar 3516C-HD 2 x Vee 4 Stroke 16 Cy. 170 x 215 each-1920kW (2610bhp) Caterpillar Inc-USA AuxGen: 2 x 800kW a.c, 2 x 350kW a.c Fuel: 520.0 (d.f.)
9430301 *9V6977* -	**SWIBER SINGAPORE** *ex* Swissco Singapore *-2008* **Swiber Offshore Marine Pte Ltd** Newcruz Offshore Marine Pte Ltd *Singapore* *Singapore* MMSI: 565415000 Official number: 392403	**977** 293 760	Class: BV	**2007-06 Guangdong Jiangmen Shipyard Co Ltd — Jiangmen GD** Yd No: GMG0513 Loa 48.00 Br ex - Dght 4.500 Lbp 43.77 Br md 13.20 Dpth 5.20 Welded, 1 dk	**(B21B20A) Anchor Handling Tug Supply**	**2 oil engines** reduction geared to sc. shafts driving 2 FP propellers Total Power: 3,282kW (4,462hp) Caterpillar 3516B-TA 2 x Vee 4 Stroke 16 Cy. 170 x 190 each-1641kW (2231bhp) Caterpillar Inc-USA AuxGen: 3 x 316kW 400/220V 50Hz a.c Thrusters: 1 Tunnel thruster (f) Fuel: 435.0 (d.f.)
9502166 *V7OX3* -	**SWIBER TORUNN** **Orchard Offshore AS** Newcruz Offshore Marine Pte Ltd *Majuro* *Marshall Islands* MMSI: 538003456 Official number: 3456	**1,537** 461 1,475	Class: BV	**2008-12 Guangzhou Hangtong Shipbuilding & Shipping Co Ltd — Jiangmen GD** Yd No: 062015 Loa 58.70 Br ex - Dght 4.750 Lbp 56.30 Br md 14.60 Dpth 5.50 Welded, 1 dk	**(B21B20A) Anchor Handling Tug Supply**	**2 oil engines** reduction geared to sc. shafts driving 2 CP propellers Total Power: 3,676kW (4,998hp) 13.5kn Niigata 6MG28HX 2 x 4 Stroke 6 Cy. 280 x 370 each-1838kW (2499bhp) Niigata Engineering Co Ltd-Japan
7623887 - -	**SWIBER TRADER** *ex* Dea Trader *-2006* *ex* Emerald Sand *-2001* *ex* Terra Nova Sea *-1989* *ex* Acadian Tempest *-1987* *ex* Offshore Trader *-1986* *ex* Normand Trader *-1984* **Swiber Offshore Marine Pte Ltd** -	**1,314** 395 1,947	Class: (LR) (NV) ✠ Classed LR until 24/10/80	**1979-06 Marystown Shipyard Ltd — Marystown NL** Yd No: 24 Loa 64.72 Br ex 14.13 Dght 5.914 Lbp 56.93 Br md 13.81 Dpth 6.91 Welded, 2 dks	**(B21B20A) Anchor Handling Tug Supply**	**2 oil engines** with clutches, flexible couplings & sr geared to sc. shafts driving 2 CP propellers Total Power: 4,414kW (6,002hp) 15.0kn Wichmann 9AXAG 2 x 2 Stroke 9 Cy. 300 x 450 each-2207kW (3001bhp) Wichmann Motorfabrikk AS-Norway AuxGen: 2 x 170kW 440V 60Hz a.c, 1 x 56kW 440V 60Hz a.c Thrusters: 1 Thwart. CP thruster (f) Fuel: 656.5 (d.f.)
9435636 *9V7243* -	**SWIBER VALIANT** **Sentosa Offshore AS** Newcruz Offshore Marine Pte Ltd *Singapore* *Singapore* MMSI: 565584000 Official number: 393401	**495** 149 365	Class: GL	**2007-09 PT Nanindah Mutiara Shipyard — Batam** Yd No: T178 Loa 40.00 Br ex - Dght 4.207 Lbp 34.82 Br md 11.40 Dpth 4.95 Welded, 1 dk	**(B21B20A) Anchor Handling Tug Supply**	**2 oil engines** reverse reduction geared to sc. shaft driving 2 FP propellers Total Power: 3,840kW (5,220hp) 12.0kn Yanmar 6EY26 2 x 4 Stroke 6 Cy. 260 x 385 each-1920kW (2610bhp) Yanmar Diesel Engine Co Ltd-Japan AuxGen: 3 x 270kW 415V 50Hz a.c Thrusters: 1 Tunnel thruster (f)
9422861 *JZJI* -	**SWIBER VENTURER** *ex* Swiwar Venturer *-2013* *ex* Swiber Venturer *-2010* *ex* Swiwar Venturer *-2008* **PT Swiber Berjaya** - *Jakarta* *Indonesia* MMSI: 525023210	**1,678** 503 1,392	Class: AB KI	**2007-04 Fujian Southeast Shipyard — Fuzhou FJ** Yd No: DN59M-11 Loa 59.25 Br ex - Dght 4.950 Lbp 52.20 Br md 14.95 Dpth 6.10 Welded, 1 dk	**(B21B20A) Anchor Handling Tug Supply**	**2 oil engines** reduction geared to sc. shafts driving 2 CP propellers Total Power: 3,840kW (5,220hp) 11.0kn Caterpillar 3516B-HD 2 x Vee 4 Stroke 16 Cy. 170 x 215 each-1920kW (2610bhp) Caterpillar Inc-USA AuxGen: 3 x 315kW a.c Thrusters: 1 Tunnel thruster (f) Fuel: 456.8 (r.f.)

IMO / Call sign	Name / Owner	Tonnage	Class	Builder / Dimensions	Type	Machinery
8113554 *PJYJ* -	**SWIFT** *ex* Sea Swift *-1996* *ex* Swift H. L. *-1989* *ex* Dyvi Swift *-1988* **Swift BV** Dockwise Shipping BV SatCom: Inmarsat C 430610910 *Willemstad* *Curacao* MMSI: 306109000 Official number: 1996-C-1512	**22,835** 9,573 32,187 T/cm 50.4	Class: NV	**1983-11 Samsung Shipbuilding & Heavy Industries Co Ltd — Geoje** Yd No: 1021 Loa 183.82 Br ex 32.31 Dght 9.490 Lbp 170.95 Br md 32.26 Dpth 13.31 Welded, 1 dk	**(A38C3GH) Heavy Load Carrier, semi submersible** Double Bottom Entire Compartment Length Liq: 32,924; Liq (Oil): 32,924 Cargo Heating Coils Compartments: 12 Ta, ER Manifold: Bow/CM: 91m	**1 oil engine** driving 1 CP propeller Total Power: 9,635kW (13,100hp) 15.7kn B&W 6L67GFCA 1 x 2 Stroke 6 Cy. 670 x 1700 9635kW (13100bhp) Mitsui Engineering & Shipbuilding CLtd-Japan AuxGen: 3 x 630kW 440V 60Hz a.c Thrusters: 1 Thwart. CP thruster (f) Fuel: 259.0 (d.f.) 1726.0 (r.f.)
8977015 - -	**SWIFT** *ex* Big Squall *-2003* *ex* Sea Dragon *-2003* **A R Singh Contractors Ltd** *Port of Spain* *Trinidad & Tobago*	**137** 41 -		**1974 Camcraft, Inc. — Crown Point, La** L reg 29.77 Br ex - Dght - Lbp - Br md 6.61 Dpth 2.13 Welded, 1 dk	**(B21A2OC) Crew/Supply Vessel** Hull Material: Aluminium Alloy	**1 oil engine** driving 1 Propeller
9149172 *9V5419* -	**SWIFT** **PSA Marine Pte Ltd** - *Singapore* *Singapore* MMSI: 563000680 Official number: 387661	**291** 87 80	Class: LR ✠ **100A1** SS 05/2012 tug Singapore coastal & 30 miles seaward service ✠ **LMC** Eq.Ltr: F; Cable: 275.0/19.0 U2	**1997-05 Zhenjiang Shipyard — Zhenjiang JS** (Hull) Yd No: KR-96-110802 **1997-05 Kea Resources Pte Ltd — Singapore** Loa 31.00 Br ex 10.10 Dght 2.610 Lbp 28.40 Br md 9.50 Dpth 3.80 Welded, 1 dk	**(B32A2ST) Tug**	**2 oil engines** with clutches, flexible couplings & sr geared to sc. shafts driving 2 Directional propellers Total Power: 2,500kW (3,400hp) 12.0kn Deutz SBV6M628 2 x 4 Stroke 6 Cy. 240 x 280 each-1250kW (1700bhp) Motoren Werke Mannheim AG (MWM)-Mannheim AuxGen: 2 x 85kW 415V 50Hz a.c
8804787 *MKZA7* -	**SWIFT** *ex* Hoo Swift *-2006* **Angel Shipping Ltd** Absolute Shipping Ltd *London* *United Kingdom* MMSI: 232002165 Official number: 717199	**794** 552 1,377	Class: BV	**1989-06 Yorkshire D.D. Co. Ltd. — Hull** Yd No: 318 Loa 58.27 Br ex 9.49 Dght 3.899 Lbp 54.72 Br md 9.40 Dpth 4.78 Welded, 1 dk	**(A31A2GX) General Cargo Ship** Grain: 1,770; Bale: 1,638 Compartments: 1 Ho, ER 1 Ha: ER	**2 oil engines** with flexible couplings & sr geared to sc. shafts driving 2 Directional propellers Total Power: 536kW (728hp) 9.0kn Cummins KT-19-M 2 x 4 Stroke 6 Cy. 159 x 159 each-268kW (364bhp) Cummins Charleston Inc-USA AuxGen: 3 x 6kW 24V d.c Fuel: 31.7 (d.f.) 2.5pd
8896015 *P2V4343* -	**SWIFT** **Golden Shipping Ltd** - *Port Moresby* *Papua New Guinea*	**531** 278 -	Class: (BV)	**1994-01 Tuong Aik (Sarawak) Sdn Bhd — Sibu** Yd No: 9301 Loa 43.24 Br ex - Dght 2.430 Lbp - Br md 13.10 Dpth 3.05 Welded, 1 dk	**(A35D2RL) Landing Craft**	**2 oil engines** reduction geared to sc. shafts driving 2 FP propellers Total Power: 780kW (1,060hp) 11.0kn Yanmar 6LAA-UTE 2 x 4 Stroke 6 Cy. 148 x 165 each-390kW (530bhp) Yanmar Diesel Engine Co Ltd-Japan AuxGen: 2 x 62kW 230/415V 50Hz a.c Fuel: 75.0 (d.f.)
9338838 *C6XB8* -	**SWIFT ACE** **Snowscape Car Carriers SA** Mitsui OSK Lines Ltd (MOL) *Nassau* *Bahamas* MMSI: 311004900 Official number: 8001508	**58,685** 18,167 18,865	Class: NK	**2008-05 Minaminippon Shipbuilding Co Ltd — Usuki OT** Yd No: 699 Loa 199.95 (BB) Br ex 32.26 Dght 9.816 Lbp 190.00 Br md 32.20 Dpth 14.70 Welded, 12 dks	**(A35B2RV) Vehicles Carrier** Side door/ramp (s) Quarter stern door/ramp (s. a.) Cars: 6,237	**1 oil engine** driving 1 FP propeller Total Power: 15,130kW (20,571hp) 20.0kn Mitsubishi 8UEC60LSII 1 x 2 Stroke 8 Cy. 600 x 2300 15130kW (20571bhp) Kobe Hatsudoki KK-Japan AuxGen: 4 x a.c Thrusters: 1 Tunnel thruster (f) Fuel: 2660.0
8918239 *C6NI7* -	**SWIFT ARROW** **Gearbulk Shipowning Ltd** Gearbulk Ltd SatCom: Inmarsat C 430937310 *Nassau* *Bahamas* MMSI: 309373000 Official number: 726184	**28,157** 8,841 42,276 T/cm 48.0	Class: NV	**1992-07 Mitsui Eng. & SB. Co. Ltd. — Tamano** Yd No: 1373 Loa 185.20 (BB) Br ex 30.40 Dght 12.220 Lbp 175.00 Br md 30.00 Dpth 18.20 Welded, 1 dk	**(A31A2GO) Open Hatch Cargo Ship** Grain: 46,976 Compartments: 8 Wing Ho, 2 Ho, ER 10 Ha: (15.6 x 16.2)8 (23.0 x 12.0) (15.4 x 19.2)ER Gantry cranes: 2x40t	**1 oil engine** driving 1 FP propeller Total Power: 9,378kW (12,750hp) 15.0kn B&W 5S60MC 1 x 2 Stroke 5 Cy. 600 x 2292 9378kW (12750bhp) Mitsui Engineering & Shipbuilding CLtd-Japan AuxGen: 3 x 990kW 450V 60Hz a.c Thrusters: 1 Thwart. CP thruster (f) Fuel: 195.9 (d.f.) (Heating Coils) 2147.1 (r.f.) 32.0pd
9206798 *P2V4126* -	**SWIFT No. 2** **Golden Shipping Ltd** - *Port Moresby* *Papua New Guinea*	**507** - 1,000	Class: (BV)	**2000-11 RH Trading — Port Moresby** Yd No: 9601 Loa - Br ex - Dght 2.420 Lbp 45.12 Br md 13.30 Dpth 3.05 Welded, 1 dk	**(A35D2RL) Landing Craft**	**2 oil engines** reduction geared to sc. shafts driving 2 FP propellers Total Power: 1,560kW (2,120hp) 10.0kn Yanmar 2 x 4 Stroke each-780kW (1060bhp) Yanmar Diesel Engine Co Ltd-Japan
9082130 *P2H3757* -	**SWIFT No. 3** *ex* Depan 6 *-2000* **Golden Shipping Ltd** - *Port Moresby* *Papua New Guinea* MMSI: 553111186	**710** 213 1,800	Class: BV (NK)	**1993-02 Fong Syn Shipyard Sdn Bhd — Sibu** Yd No: 6791 Loa 50.00 Br ex - Dght 2.655 Lbp 48.40 Br md 13.72 Dpth 3.35 Welded, 1 dk	**(A31A2GX) General Cargo Ship**	**2 oil engines** reduction geared to sc. shafts driving 2 FP propellers Total Power: 692kW (940hp) Caterpillar 3408TA 2 x Vee 4 Stroke 8 Cy. 137 x 152 each-346kW (470bhp) Caterpillar Inc-USA AuxGen: 2 x 100kW 415V 60Hz a.c Fuel: 126.9 (d.f.)
9049906 *P2V5083* -	**SWIFT NO. 5** *ex* Foxanne 1 *-2006* **Golden Shipping Ltd** - *Port Moresby* *Papua New Guinea* Official number: 000921	**442** 133 -		**2001-10 C E Ling Shipbuilding Sdn Bhd — Miri** Yd No: 032 Loa 44.90 Br ex 11.62 Dght 2.150 Lbp 43.84 Br md 11.60 Dpth 2.75 Welded, 1 dk	**(A35D2RL) Landing Craft**	**2 oil engines** driving 2 Propellers Cummins 2 x 4 Stroke Cummins Engine Co Inc-USA
9560338 *P2V5318* -	**SWIFT NO. 8** **Golden Shipping Ltd** - *Port Moresby* *Papua New Guinea* MMSI: 553111502 Official number: 000210	**1,442** 432 1,500	Class: BV	**2009-08 Straits Marine (PNG) Pty Ltd — Port Moresby** Yd No: 02 Loa 72.85 Br ex - Dght 3.500 Lbp 67.24 Br md 15.24 Dpth 4.50 Welded, 1 dk	**(A35D2RL) Landing Craft** Bow door/ramp (centre)	**2 oil engines** reduction geared to sc. shafts driving 2 FP propellers Total Power: 1,472kW (2,002hp) 12.0kn Yanmar 6RY17P-GV 2 x 4 Stroke 6 Cy. 165 x 219 each-736kW (1001bhp) Yanmar Diesel Engine Co Ltd-Japan
9536519 *9V7855* -	**SWIFT RESCUE** **First Response Marine Pte Ltd** Swire Pacific Offshore Operations Pte Ltd *Singapore* *Singapore* MMSI: 564314000 Official number: 394932	**4,290** 1,287 1,231	Class: AB	**2009-04 Singapore Technologies Marine Ltd — Singapore** Yd No: 618 Loa 83.70 (BB) Br ex 18.32 Dght 4.300 Lbp 73.20 Br md 18.30 Dpth 7.50 Welded, 1 dk	**(B22A2OR) Offshore Support Vessel** A-frames: 1	**2 oil engines** reduction geared to sc. shafts driving 2 CP propellers Total Power: 4,080kW (5,548hp) MAN-B&W 6L27/38 2 x 4 Stroke 6 Cy. 270 x 380 each-2040kW (2774bhp) MAN Diesel A/S-Denmark AuxGen: 2 x 1200kW a.c, 3 x 1360kW a.c Thrusters: 2 Tunnel thruster (f); 2 Thwart. CP thruster (a) Fuel: 634.0
8855865 - -	**SWIFT WATER '84** **Sahlman Seafoods Inc**	*101* 69 -		**1984 Steiner Shipyard, Inc. — Bayou La Batre, Al** Loa 22.86 Br ex - Dght - Lbp 20.33 Br md 6.71 Dpth 3.32 Welded, 1 dk	**(B11A2FT) Trawler**	**1 oil engine** geared to sc. shaft driving 1 FP propeller Total Power: 268kW (364hp) Cummins KT-1150-M 1 x 4 Stroke 6 Cy. 159 x 159 268kW (364bhp) Cummins Engine Co Inc-USA
9375226 *9V6818* -	**SWISSCO 48** **Swissco Offshore Pte Ltd** - *Singapore* *Singapore* MMSI: 565041000 Official number: 390165	**2,172** 651 2,395	Class: AB	**2006-04 Yangzhou Oceanus Shipbuilding Corp Ltd — Yizheng JS** (Hull) Yd No: 03-001 **2006-04 Singapore Marine Logistic Pte Ltd — Singapore** Yd No: (03-001) Loa 70.15 Br ex - Dght - Lbp 67.33 Br md 19.52 Dpth 4.27 Welded, 1 dk	**(B34L2QU) Utility Vessel** Cranes: 1x40t	**2 oil engines** reduction geared to sc. shafts driving 2 Propellers Total Power: 1,222kW (1,662hp) Caterpillar 3412D 2 x Vee 4 Stroke 12 Cy. 145 x 162 each-611kW (831bhp) Caterpillar Inc-USA
9206217 *YB8055* -	**SWISSCO 118** *ex* Slco Prosperity *-2000* **PT Surya Labuan Samudra** - *Bitung* *Indonesia*	**114** 39 -	Class: KI (BV)	**1998-12 Bonny Fair Development Ltd — Hong Kong** Yd No: XY-2093 Loa 26.00 Br ex - Dght 2.200 Lbp 23.85 Br md 6.80 Dpth 3.20 Welded, 1 dk	**(A13B2TU) Tanker (unspecified)**	**2 oil engines** geared to sc. shafts driving 2 FP propellers Total Power: 736kW (1,000hp) 10.0kn Cummins KTA-19-M 2 x 4 Stroke 6 Cy. 159 x 159 each-368kW (500bhp) Cummins Engine Co Inc-USA
8890982 *VKV6977* -	**SWISSCO 168** **Delmark Ship Management Pty Ltd** - *Melbourne, Vic* *Australia* MMSI: 503089600 Official number: 857966	**106** 31 114	Class: NK (BV)	**1995-01 Tuong Aik (Sarawak) Sdn Bhd — Sibu** Yd No: 9502 Loa 23.17 Br ex - Dght 2.350 Lbp 21.03 Br md 6.70 Dpth 2.90 Welded, 1 dk	**(B32A2ST) Tug**	**2 oil engines** driving 2 FP propellers Total Power: 700kW (952hp) 10.0kn Caterpillar 3408TA 2 x Vee 4 Stroke 8 Cy. 137 x 152 each-350kW (476bhp) Caterpillar Inc-USA AuxGen: 2 x 60kW 220V 50Hz a.c Fuel: 85.0 (d.f.)

IMO / Call sign / Flag	Name / Owner / Port	Tonnage	Class	Build / Dimensions	Type	Machinery
9179969 *YD6788* -	**SWISSCO 181** **PT Perusahaan Pelayaran Rusianto Bersaudara** - *Samarinda* *Indonesia*	**229** 68 -	Class: (BV)	**1997-08 Tuong Aik (Sarawak) Sdn Bhd — Sibu** Yd No: 1188 Loa 29.00 Br ex - Dght 3.520 Lbp 27.03 Br md 8.60 Dpth 4.30 Welded, 1 dk	**(B32A2ST) Tug**	**2 oil engines** geared to sc. shafts driving 2 FP propellers Total Power: 1,250kW (1,700hp) 11.0kn Caterpillar D398TA 2 x Vee 4 Stroke 12 Cy. 159 x 203 each-625kW (850bhp) Caterpillar Inc-USA
8838867 *HQOM6* -	**SWISSCO 188** *ex Hon Dat 02 -1995* **Swissco Marine Pte Ltd** - *San Lorenzo* *Honduras* Official number: L-1225494	*441* 219 400	Class: (VR)	**1988-01 at Haiphong** Loa 53.50 Br ex - Dght 2.550 Lbp - Br md 8.20 Dpth 3.20 Welded, 1 dk	**(A31A2GX) General Cargo Ship** Grain: 638 Compartments: 2 Ho, ER 2 Ha: 2 (9.0 x 4.5)ER	**1 oil engine** driving 1 FP propeller Total Power: 224kW (305hp) 10.0kn S.K.L. 6NVD36-1U 1 x 4 Stroke 6 Cy. 240 x 360 224kW (305bhp) VEB Schwermaschinenbau "KarlLiebknecht" (SKL)-Magdeburg AuxGen: 2 x 30kW a.c
9665205 *HP3279* -	**SWISSCO CHEETAH** **Swissco Offshore Pte Ltd** - *Panama* *Panama* MMSI: 353545000 Official number: 4507613	**249** 74 125	Class: AB	**2013-05 Hin Lee (Zhuhai) Shipyard Co Ltd — Zhuhai GD** (Hull) Yd No: 254 **2013-05 Cheoy Lee Shipyards Ltd — Hong Kong** Yd No: 5043 Loa 36.05 Br ex - Dght - Lbp 34.66 Br md 7.60 Dpth 3.56 Welded, 1 dk	**(B21A20C) Crew/Supply Vessel** Hull Material: Aluminium Alloy Passengers: unberthed: 70	**3 oil engines** reduction geared to sc. shafts driving 3 FP propellers Total Power: 3,357kW (4,563hp) 23.0kn Cummins KTA-38-M2 3 x Vee 4 Stroke 12 Cy. 159 x 159 each-1119kW (1521bhp) Cummins Engine Co Inc-USA Thrusters: 1 Tunnel thruster (f)
9696280 *9V2337* -	**SWISSCO EMERALD** **Swissco Energy Services Pte Ltd** Selat Marine Services Co Ltd *Singapore* *Singapore* MMSI: 563821000 Official number: 398908	**1,945** 583 1,500	Class: AB	**2014-01 Guangxin Shipbuilding & Heavy Industry Co Ltd — Zhongshan GD** Yd No: GS12136 Loa 60.50 Br ex 16.50 Dght 5.000 Lbp 54.30 Br md 15.80 Dpth 6.50 Welded, 1 dk	**(B21B20A) Anchor Handling Tug Supply**	**2 oil engines** reduction geared to sc. shafts driving 2 Z propellers Total Power: 4,708kW (6,400hp) Niigata 8L28HX 2 x 4 Stroke 8 Cy. 280 x 370 each-2354kW (3200bhp) Niigata Engineering Co Ltd-Japan
9637569 *9V9684* -	**SWISSCO JADE** **Swissco Offshore Pte Ltd** - *Singapore* *Singapore* MMSI: 566324000 Official number: 397472	**1,092** 327 760	Class: BV	**2012-01 Guangdong Jiangmen Shipyard Co Ltd — Jiangmen GD** Yd No: GMG0759 Loa 50.00 Br ex - Dght 4.500 Lbp 43.77 Br md 13.20 Dpth 5.20 Welded, 1 dk	**(B21B20A) Anchor Handling Tug Supply**	**2 oil engines** reduction geared to sc. shafts driving 2 CP propellers Total Power: 3,282kW (4,462hp) Caterpillar 3516B-HD 2 x Vee 4 Stroke 16 Cy. 170 x 215 each-1641kW (2231bhp) Caterpillar Inc-USA AuxGen: 3 x 350kW 50Hz a.c Thrusters: 1 Tunnel thruster (f) Fuel: 590.0
9676979 *9V2083* -	**SWISSCO NEPTUNE** **Swissco Offshore Pte Ltd** - *Singapore* *Singapore* MMSI: 566944000 Official number: 398599	**1,312** 393 -	Class: BV	**2013-09 Guangzhou Panyu Lingshan Shipyard Ltd — Guangzhou GD** Yd No: 231 Loa 57.20 Br ex - Dght 3.900 Lbp 52.50 Br md 13.80 Dpth 5.00 Welded, 1 dk	**(B21B20A) Anchor Handling Tug Supply** Cranes: 1x10t	**2 oil engines** reduction geared to sc. shafts driving 2 CP propellers Total Power: 3,530kW (4,800hp) Caterpillar 3512C 2 x Vee 4 Stroke 12 Cy. 170 x 215 each-1765kW (2400bhp) Caterpillar Inc-USA AuxGen: 3 x 300kW 50Hz a.c, 2 x 650kW 50Hz a.c Thrusters: 1 Tunnel thruster (f) Fuel: 550.0
9683166 *9V2150* -	**SWISSCO OPAL** **Swissco Offshore Pte Ltd** - *Singapore* *Singapore* MMSI: 563578000 Official number: 398677	**399** 119 -	Class: BV	**2013-11 Xin Yue Feng Shipyard Ltd — Jiangmen GD** Yd No: XYF110 Loa 34.00 Br ex 10.04 Dght 3.500 Lbp 31.80 Br md 10.00 Dpth 4.70 Welded, 1 dk	**(B21B20A) Anchor Handling Tug Supply** Cranes: 1x20t	**2 oil engines** reduction geared to sc. shafts driving 2 FP propellers Total Power: 2,354kW (3,200hp) Cummins KTA-50-M2 2 x Vee 4 Stroke 16 Cy. 159 x 159 each-1177kW (1600bhp) Cummins Engine Co Inc-USA AuxGen: 2 x 136kW 50Hz a.c Thrusters: 1 Tunnel thruster (f) Fuel: 310.0
9690119 *9V2084* -	**SWISSCO RUBY** **Swissco Ship Services Pte Ltd** Swissco Offshore Pte Ltd *Singapore* *Singapore* MMSI: 563297000 Official number: 398600	**1,182** 354 1,147	Class: BV	**2013-09 Guangzhou Panyu Lingshan Shipyard Ltd — Guangzhou GD** Yd No: 207 Loa 56.20 Br ex 13.86 Dght 4.750 Lbp 49.18 Br md 13.80 Dpth 5.50 Welded, 1 dk	**(B21B20A) Anchor Handling Tug Supply**	**2 oil engines** reduction geared to sc. shafts driving 2 FP propellers Total Power: 2,984kW (4,058hp) 12.5kn Caterpillar 3516C 2 x Vee 4 Stroke 16 Cy. 170 x 190 each-1492kW (2029bhp) Caterpillar Inc-USA AuxGen: 3 x 275kW 50Hz a.c Fuel: 620.0
9564669 *9V8226* -	**SWISSCO SABRE** **Swissco Offshore Pte Ltd** - *Singapore* *Singapore* MMSI: 565416000 Official number: 395477	**499** 149 560	Class: BV	**2010-07 Guangzhou Panyu Lingshan Shipyard Ltd — Guangzhou GD** Yd No: 174 Loa 40.00 Br ex - Dght 3.800 Lbp 34.90 Br md 11.80 Dpth 4.60 Welded, 1 dk	**(B21B20A) Anchor Handling Tug Supply**	**2 oil engines** reduction geared to sc. shafts driving 2 FP propellers Total Power: 3,090kW (4,202hp) Caterpillar 3516B 2 x Vee 4 Stroke 16 Cy. 170 x 190 each-1545kW (2101bhp) Caterpillar Inc-USA AuxGen: 2 x 200kW 415V 50Hz a.c Thrusters: 1 Tunnel thruster (f) Fuel: 300.0 (d.f.)
9425291 *9V7074* -	**SWISSCO SAPPHIRE** **Swissco Asia Pte Ltd** Swissco Offshore Pte Ltd *Singapore* *Singapore* MMSI: 565578000 Official number: 392759	**884** 265 1,000	Class: BV	**2007-12 Guangzhou Panyu Lingshan Shipyard Ltd — Guangzhou GD** Yd No: 150 Loa 48.00 Br ex - Dght 4.000 Lbp 44.52 Br md 12.80 Dpth 5.06 Welded, 1 dk	**(B21B20A) Anchor Handling Tug Supply**	**2 oil engines** reduction geared to sc. shafts driving 2 Z propellers Total Power: 3,282kW (4,462hp) 12.0kn Caterpillar 3516B 2 x Vee 4 Stroke 16 Cy. 170 x 190 each-1641kW (2231bhp) Caterpillar Inc-USA AuxGen: 3 x 245kW 415V 50Hz a.c Thrusters: 1 Tunnel thruster (f) Fuel: 680.0 (d.f.)
9559860 *POKX* -	**SWISSCO SEAHORSE** **PT Swissindo Marine** - *Indonesia* MMSI: 525015937	**375** 112 -	Class: BV	**2010-02 Guangzhou Panyu Lingshan Shipyard Ltd — Guangzhou GD** Yd No: 202 Loa 36.30 Br ex 10.50 Dght 3.500 Lbp 32.54 Br md 9.80 Dpth 4.30 Welded, 1 dk	**(B21B20A) Anchor Handling Tug Supply**	**2 oil engines** reduction geared to sc. shafts driving 2 FP propellers Total Power: 2,386kW (3,244hp) Cummins KTA-50-M2 2 x Vee 4 Stroke 16 Cy. 159 x 159 each-1193kW (1622bhp) Cummins Engine Co Ltd-United Kingdom AuxGen: 2 x 215kW 415V 50Hz a.c Thrusters: 1 Tunnel thruster (f)
9558438 *HP7448* -	**SWISSCO SEAL** **Swissco Offshore Pte Ltd** - *Panama* *Panama* MMSI: 370979000 Official number: 4065509	**115** 34 -	Class: BV	**2009-06 Lita Ocean Pte Ltd — Singapore** Yd No: H/81 Loa 26.00 Br ex - Dght 1.500 Lbp 24.68 Br md 6.70 Dpth 3.00 Welded, 1 dk	**(B21A20C) Crew/Supply Vessel** Hull Material: Aluminium Alloy Passengers: unberthed: 36	**2 oil engines** reduction geared to sc. shafts driving 2 FP propellers Total Power: 1,052kW (1,430hp) 18.5kn Caterpillar C18 2 x 4 Stroke 6 Cy. 145 x 183 each-526kW (715bhp) Caterpillar Inc-USA AuxGen: 2 x 36kW 400/115V 50Hz a.c Thrusters: 1 Tunnel thruster (f) Fuel: 15.0 (d.f.)
9515589 *9V7359* -	**SWISSCO SEARCHER** **Swissco Maritime Pte Ltd** Swissco Offshore Pte Ltd *Singapore* *Singapore* MMSI: 563010560 Official number: 393913	**235** 71 227	Class: GL	**2008-10 Berjaya Dockyard Sdn Bhd — Miri** Yd No: 58 Loa 26.00 Br ex - Dght 2.800 Lbp 23.56 Br md 9.20 Dpth 3.60 Welded, 1 dk	**(B32A2ST) Tug** Cranes: 1x5t	**2 oil engines** reverse reduction geared to sc. shafts driving 2 FP propellers Total Power: 1,302kW (1,770hp) Caterpillar 3412D 2 x Vee 4 Stroke 12 Cy. 145 x 162 each-651kW (885bhp) Caterpillar Inc-USA AuxGen: 2 x 78kW 415V a.c Fuel: 90.0 (d.f.)
9393890 *9V6930* -	**SWISSCO SENTOSA** *ex Berjaya 28 -2006* **Swissco Asia Pte Ltd** Swissco Offshore Pte Ltd *Singapore* *Singapore* MMSI: 565171000 Official number: 392156	**269** 81 298	Class: NK	**2006-05 Berjaya Dockyard Sdn Bhd — Miri** Yd No: 28 Loa 30.20 Br ex - Dght 3.612 Lbp 27.71 Br md 8.60 Dpth 4.30 Welded, 1 dk	**(B32A2ST) Tug**	**2 oil engines** reduction geared to sc. shafts driving 2 FP propellers Total Power: 1,492kW (2,028hp) Caterpillar 3508B 2 x Vee 4 Stroke 8 Cy. 170 x 190 each-746kW (1014bhp) Caterpillar Inc-USA AuxGen: 2 x 78kW 415/240V 50Hz a.c Fuel: 245.0 (r.f.)

9508500 *9V7447* -	**SWISSCO SENTRY** **Swissco Asia Pte Ltd** Swissco Offshore Pte Ltd *Singapore* *Singapore* MMSI: 563011510 Official number: 394202	**299** 90 -	Class: GL	**2008-10 Tuong Aik Shipyard Sdn Bhd — Sibu** Yd No: 2715 Loa 31.00 Br ex - Dght 3.000 Lbp 27.85 Br md 9.50 Dpth 3.80 Welded, 1 dk	**(B32A2ST) Tug** Ice Capable	**2 oil engines** reduction geared to sc. shafts driving 2 FP propellers Total Power: 896kW (1,218hp) Caterpillar 3412C 2 x Vee 4 Stroke 12 Cy. 137 x 152 each-448kW (609bhp) Caterpillar Inc-USA AuxGen: 2 x 160kW 50Hz a.c Thrusters: 1 Tunnel thruster (f) Fuel: 160.0 (d.f.)
9515577 *9V7358* -	**SWISSCO SERVER** **Swissco Maritime Pte Ltd** Swissco Offshore Pte Ltd *Singapore* *Singapore* MMSI: 563010550 Official number: 393912	**235** 71 228	Class: GL	**2008-10 Berjaya Dockyard Sdn Bhd — Miri** Yd No: 57 Loa 26.00 Br ex - Dght 2.800 Lbp 23.56 Br md 9.20 Dpth 3.60 Welded, 1 dk	**(B32A2ST) Tug** Cranes: 1x5t	**2 oil engines** reverse reduction geared to sc. shafts driving 2 FP propellers Total Power: 1,302kW (1,770hp) Caterpillar 3412D 2 x Vee 4 Stroke 12 Cy. 145 x 162 each-651kW (885bhp) Caterpillar Inc-USA AuxGen: 2 x 78kW a.c Fuel: 160.0 (d.f.)
9508495 *9V7448* -	**SWISSCO SHORE** **Swissco Asia Pte Ltd** Swissco Offshore Pte Ltd *Singapore* *Singapore* Official number: 394203	**229** 68 -	Class: BV (GL)	**2008-08 Tuong Aik Shipyard Sdn Bhd — Sibu** Yd No: 2713 Loa 26.00 Br ex - Dght 2.500 Lbp 24.00 Br md 11.00 Dpth 3.25 Welded, 1 dk	**(B34L2QU) Utility Vessel** Cranes: 1x9.5t	**2 oil engines** reduction geared to sc. shafts driving 2 FP propellers Total Power: 896kW (1,218hp) Caterpillar 3412C 2 x Vee 4 Stroke 12 Cy. 137 x 152 each-448kW (609bhp) Caterpillar Inc-USA AuxGen: 2 x 85kW 50Hz a.c Fuel: 90.0 (d.f.)
9536088 *YB4867* -	**SWISSCO SPEAR** **PT Swissindo Marine** Swissco Offshore Pte Ltd *Jakarta* *Indonesia*	**127** 38 42	Class: BV	**2008-12 SBF Shipbuilders (1977) Pty Ltd — Fremantle WA** Yd No: 281 Loa 30.10 Br ex - Dght 1.040 Lbp 27.00 Br md 6.80 Dpth 4.60 Welded, 1 dk	**(B21A2OC) Crew/Supply Vessel** Hull Material: Aluminium Alloy Passengers: unberthed: 50	**3 oil engines** reduction geared to sc. shafts driving 3 FP propellers Total Power: 1,323kW (1,800hp) 22.0kn Caterpillar 3406E-TA 3 x 4 Stroke 6 Cy. 137 x 165 each-441kW (600bhp) Caterpillar Inc-USA AuxGen: 2 x 36kW 415V 50Hz a.c Thrusters: 1 Tunnel thruster (f) Fuel: 25.0 (d.f.)
9479656 *YDA4689* -	**SWISSCO SPIRIT** **PT Swissindo Marine** - *Jakarta* *Indonesia* MMSI: 525015963	**128** 39 42	Class: BV KI	**2008-07 SBF Shipbuilders (1977) Pty Ltd — Fremantle WA** Yd No: 271 Loa 30.10 Br ex - Dght 1.040 Lbp 27.00 Br md 6.80 Dpth 2.55 Welded, 1 dk	**(B21A2OC) Crew/Supply Vessel** Hull Material: Aluminium Alloy Passengers: 50	**3 oil engines** geared to sc. shafts driving 3 FP propellers Total Power: 1,341kW (1,824hp) 22.0kn Caterpillar 3406E-TA 3 x 4 Stroke 6 Cy. 137 x 165 each-447kW (608bhp) Caterpillar Inc-USA AuxGen: 2 x 37kW 50Hz a.c Thrusters: 1 Thwart. FP thruster (f) Fuel: 22.0 (d.f.)
9438975 *YDA4581* -	**SWISSCO SPIRITS** *ex Swissco Swan -2010* **PT Swissindo Marine** Swissco Offshore Pte Ltd *Jakarta* *Indonesia* MMSI: 525015964	**113** 34 30	Class: BV KI	**2007-06 SBF Shipbuilders (1977) Pty Ltd — Fremantle WA** Yd No: 261 Loa 28.20 Br ex - Dght 1.500 Lbp 25.20 Br md 6.70 Dpth 5.00 Welded, 1 dk	**(B21A2OC) Crew/Supply Vessel** Hull Material: Aluminium Alloy Passengers: unberthed: 50	**3 oil engines** reverse reduction geared to sc. shafts driving 3 FP propellers Total Power: 1,341kW (1,824hp) 22.0kn Caterpillar 3406E-TA 3 x 4 Stroke 6 Cy. 137 x 165 each-447kW (608bhp) Caterpillar Inc-USA AuxGen: 2 x 24kW 50Hz a.c Thrusters: 1 Tunnel thruster (f) Fuel: 19.0 (d.f.)
9565819 *HO5800* -	**SWISSCO SPUR** **Swissco Offshore Pte Ltd** - *Panama* *Panama* Official number: 39532PEXT	**115** 34 -	Class: BV	**2009-08 Lita Ocean Pte Ltd — Singapore** Yd No: H/82 Loa 26.00 Br ex - Dght 1.500 Lbp 24.68 Br md 6.70 Dpth 3.00 Welded, 1 dk	**(B34J2SD) Crew Boat** Hull Material: Aluminium Alloy Passengers: unberthed: 36	**2 oil engines** reduction geared to sc. shafts driving 2 FP propellers Total Power: 1,066kW (1,450hp) 21.0kn Caterpillar C18 2 x 4 Stroke 6 Cy. 145 x 183 each-533kW (725bhp) Caterpillar Inc-USA AuxGen: 2 x 25kW 50Hz a.c Thrusters: 1 Tunnel thruster (f) Fuel: 14.0 (d.f.)
9412282 *9V9578* -	**SWISSCO SUCCESS** **Swissco Offshore Pte Ltd** - *Singapore* *Singapore* Official number: 397304	**299** 89 350	Class: BV KI	**2007-01 Guangzhou Panyu Lingshan Shipyard Ltd — Guangzhou GD** Yd No: 139 Loa 36.00 Br ex - Dght 3.250 Lbp 33.17 Br md 9.00 Dpth 4.00 Welded, 1 dk	**(B21B20T) Offshore Tug/Supply Ship**	**2 oil engines** reduction geared to sc. shafts driving 2 FP propellers Total Power: 1,258kW (1,710hp) 11.5kn Caterpillar 3508B 2 x Vee 4 Stroke 8 Cy. 170 x 190 each-629kW (855bhp) Caterpillar Inc-USA AuxGen: 2 x 136kW 415/220V 50Hz a.c Thrusters: 1 Tunnel thruster (f) Fuel: 200.0 (d.f.)
9616462 *9V8428* -	**SWISSCO SUMMIT** **Swissco Offshore Pte Ltd** *Singapore* *Singapore* MMSI: 566077000 Official number: 395772	**481** 144 100	Class: BV	**2011-06 Guangzhou Panyu Lingshan Shipyard Ltd — Guangzhou GD** Yd No: 227 Loa 40.62 Br ex 10.26 Dght 3.100 Lbp 36.80 Br md 10.00 Dpth 3.70 Welded, 1 dk	**(B21B20T) Offshore Tug/Supply Ship**	**2 oil engines** reduction geared to sc. shafts driving 2 FP propellers Total Power: 2,238kW (3,042hp) Cummins KTA-38-M2 2 x Vee 4 Stroke 12 Cy. 159 x 159 each-1119kW (1521bhp) Cummins Engine Co Ltd-United Kingdom AuxGen: 3 x 215kW 415V 50Hz a.c Thrusters: 1 Tunnel thruster (f)
9570321 *9V7769* -	**SWISSCO SUNRISE** **Swissco Ship Services Pte Ltd** Swissco Offshore Pte Ltd *Singapore* *Singapore* MMSI: 563013670 Official number: 394793	**256** 76 218	Class: BV	**2009-07 Swissco Structural Mechanical Pte Ltd — Singapore** Yd No: SW01/08 Loa 28.00 Br ex - Dght 2.500 Lbp - Br md 11.00 Dpth 3.25 Welded, 1 dk	**(B34L2QU) Utility Vessel**	**2 oil engines** reduction geared to sc. shafts driving 2 FP propellers Total Power: 896kW (1,218hp) Caterpillar 3412C 2 x Vee 4 Stroke 12 Cy. 137 x 152 each-448kW (609bhp) Caterpillar Inc-USA AuxGen: 2 x 83kW 415V 50Hz a.c Fuel: 160.0 (d.f.)
9397078 *PNTP* -	**SWISSCO SUPPLIER** **PT Swissindo Marine** - *Jakarta* *Indonesia* MMSI: 525015984	**1,123** 337 1,102	Class: BV	**2007-12 Guangzhou Panyu Lingshan Shipyard Ltd — Guangzhou GD** Yd No: 152 Loa 55.00 Br ex - Dght 4.750 Lbp 48.10 Br md 13.80 Dpth 5.50 Welded, 1 dk	**(B21B20A) Anchor Handling Tug Supply**	**2 oil engines** reduction geared to sc. shafts driving 2 FP propellers Total Power: 3,130kW (4,256hp) 12.5kn Caterpillar 3516B 2 x Vee 4 Stroke 16 Cy. 170 x 190 each-1565kW (2128bhp) Caterpillar Inc-USA AuxGen: 3 x 245kW 415V 50Hz a.c Thrusters: 1 Thwart. CP thruster (f) Fuel: 467.0 (d.f.)
7218759 - -	**SWISSCO SUPPLY** *ex H. J. Supply -1996 ex Bunker Tiger -1992* *ex Bunker SPC II -1985* - -	*277* 262 406	Class: (AB)	**1972 Westbank Shipyard Pte Ltd — Singapore** Yd No: 160 Converted From: Bunkering Vessel-1996 Loa 31.70 Br ex 9.20 Dght 2.774 Lbp 31.40 Br md 9.15 Dpth 3.97 Welded, 1 dk	**(A14A2LO) Water Tanker** Liq: 500; Liq (Oil): 500 Compartments: 10 Ta, ER 3 Cargo Pump (s): 3x80m³/hr Manifold: Bow/CM: 12m	**2 oil engines** reduction geared to sc. shafts driving 2 CP propellers Total Power: 692kW (940hp) 4.0kn Caterpillar 3408TA 2 x Vee 4 Stroke 8 Cy. 137 x 152 each-346kW (470bhp) Caterpillar Inc-USA Fuel: 20.0 (d.f.) 1.0pd
9495997 *9V7750* -	**SWISSCO SUPPORTER** **SW Maritime Pte Ltd** Swissco Offshore Pte Ltd *Singapore* *Singapore* MMSI: 564193000 Official number: 394772	**2,218** 665 1,505	Class: AB (BV)	**2009-09 Guangzhou Panyu Lingshan Shipyard Ltd — Guangzhou GD** Yd No: 160 Loa 70.16 Br ex 19.56 Dght 2.980 Lbp 68.54 Br md 19.52 Dpth 4.27 Welded, 1 dk	**(B34L2QU) Utility Vessel** Cranes: 1x27t	**2 oil engines** reduction geared to sc. shafts driving 2 Directional propellers Total Power: 1,566kW (2,130hp) 9.0kn Caterpillar 3508B 2 x Vee 4 Stroke 8 Cy. 170 x 190 each-783kW (1065bhp) Caterpillar Inc-USA AuxGen: 3 x 245kW 415V 50Hz a.c Thrusters: 1 Tunnel thruster (f) Fuel: 480.0 (r.f.)

9436288 *9V7052* -	**SWISSCO SURF** **Swissco Offshore Pte Ltd** Great Enquest Marine (GEM) *Singapore* *Singapore* Official number: 392696	**224** 68 -	Class: BV (IR) (GL)	**2007-06 Berjaya Dockyard Sdn Bhd — Miri** Yd No: 48 Loa 26.00 Br ex 9.22 Dght 2.800 Lbp - Br md 9.20 Dpth 3.60 Welded, 1 dk	**(B32A2ST) Tug** Cranes: 1x5t	**2 oil engines** reduction geared to sc. shafts driving 2 FP propellers Total Power: 1,060kW (1,442hp) Caterpillar 3412C 2 x Vee 4 Stroke 12 Cy. 137 x 152 each-530kW (721bhp) Caterpillar Inc-USA AuxGen: 2 x 78kW a.c Fuel: 86.0 (r.f.)
9550450 *9V8515* -	**SWISSCO SWIFT** **Swissco Asia Pte Ltd** Swissco Offshore Pte Ltd *Singapore* *Singapore* MMSI: 564925000 Official number: 395898	**499** 149 363	Class: BV	**2010-04 Guangzhou Panyu Lingshan Shipyard Ltd — Guangzhou GD** Yd No: 177 Loa 45.00 Br ex - Dght 3.400 Lbp 40.00 Br md 11.00 Dpth 4.00 Welded, 1 dk	**(B21B20A) Anchor Handling Tug Supply** Passengers: berths: 20	**2 oil engines** reduction geared to sc. shafts driving 2 FP propellers Total Power: 2,610kW (3,548hp) Caterpillar 3512B 2 x Vee 4 Stroke 12 Cy. 170 x 190 each-1305kW (1774bhp) Caterpillar Inc-USA AuxGen: 2 x 215kW 415V 50Hz a.c Thrusters: 1 Tunnel thruster (f) Fuel: 275.0 (d.f.)
9616474 *9V8429* -	**SWISSCO SYNERGY** **Swissco Offshore Pte Ltd** - *Singapore* *Singapore* MMSI: 566078000 Official number: 395773	**481** 144 100	Class: BV	**2011-07 Guangzhou Panyu Lingshan Shipyard Ltd — Guangzhou GD** Yd No: 228 Loa 40.62 Br ex 10.22 Dght 3.100 Lbp 36.80 Br md 10.00 Dpth 3.70 Welded, 1 dk	**(B21B20A) Anchor Handling Tug Supply**	**2 oil engines** reduction geared to sc. shafts driving 2 FP propellers Total Power: 2,238kW (3,042hp) Cummins KTA-38-M2 2 x Vee 4 Stroke 12 Cy. 159 x 159 each-1119kW (1521bhp) Cummins Engine Co Ltd-United Kingdom AuxGen: 3 x 215kW 415V 50Hz a.c Thrusters: 1 Tunnel thruster (f) Fuel: 240.0 (d.f.)
9684328 *9V6496* -	**SWISSCO TOPAZ** **Swissco Offshore Pte Ltd** - *Singapore* *Singapore* MMSI: 563146000 Official number: 398481	**499** 149 100	Class: BV	**2013-07 Guangzhou Panyu Lingshan Shipyard Ltd — Guangzhou GD** Yd No: 178 Loa 45.00 Br ex 11.27 Dght 3.400 Lbp 40.00 Br md 11.00 Dpth 4.00 Welded, 1 dk	**(B21B20A) Anchor Handling Tug Supply**	**2 oil engines** reduction geared to sc. shafts driving 2 FP propellers Total Power: 2,984kW (4,058hp) Caterpillar 3516C 2 x Vee 4 Stroke 16 Cy. 170 x 190 each-1492kW (2029bhp) Caterpillar Inc-USA AuxGen: 3 x 300kW 50Hz a.c Fuel: 260.0
9555400 *9V8058* -	**SWIWAR SURYA** *ex* Swiwar Crusader *-2011* **Oceanic Crusader Pte Ltd** Newcruz Offshore Marine Pte Ltd *Singapore* *Singapore* MMSI: 564286000 Official number: 395242	**2,708** 812 2,107	Class: AB	**2010-07 Fujian Southeast Shipyard — Fuzhou FJ** Yd No: DN70M-2 Loa 70.00 Br ex - Dght 6.100 Lbp 61.80 Br md 16.80 Dpth 7.50 Welded, 1 dk	**(B21B20A) Anchor Handling Tug Supply**	**2 oil engines** reduction geared to sc. shafts driving 2 CP propellers Total Power: 8,000kW (10,876hp) Wartsila 8L32 2 x 4 Stroke 8 Cy. 320 x 400 each-4000kW (5438bhp) Wartsila Finland Oy-Finland AuxGen: 2 x 1600kW a.c, 2 x 350kW a.c Fuel: 1220.0 (d.f.)
8518986 *9LD2461* -	**SWORD FISH** *ex* Island Navigator *-2012* *ex* Core Topaz *-2006* *ex* Kakuryo Maru No. 21 *-1998* **Combase Energy Ltd** - *Freetown* *Sierra Leone* MMSI: 667005161 Official number: SL105161	**729** 308 1,223	Class: (BV)	**1985-11 Sasaki Shipbuilding Co Ltd — Osakikamijima HS** Yd No: 395 Loa 64.75 Br ex - Dght 4.271 Lbp 60.03 Br md 9.52 Dpth 4.58 Welded, 1 dk	**(A13A2TV) Crude Oil Tanker** Compartments: 8 Ta, ER	**1 oil engine** with clutches, flexible couplings & reverse reduction geared to sc. shaft driving 1 FP propeller Total Power: 956kW (1,300hp) Akasaka DM28AKR 1 x 4 Stroke 6 Cy. 280 x 460 956kW (1300bhp) Akasaka Tekkosho KK (Akasaka DieselLtd)-Japan
8764755 *WDC4906* -	**SWORDFISH** **All Coast LLC** - *New Orleans, LA* *United States of America* MMSI: 367032580 Official number: 1091526	**637** 191 -		**2000 Conrad Industries, Inc. — Morgan City, La** Yd No: 665 Loa 34.44 Br ex - Dght - Lbp - Br md 19.65 Dpth 3.04 Welded, 1 dk	**(B22A2ZM) Offshore Construction Vessel, jack up**	**2 oil engines** geared to sc. shafts driving 2 Propellers Total Power: 1,618kW (2,200hp) Caterpillar 3412 2 x Vee 4 Stroke 12 Cy. 137 x 152 each-809kW (1100bhp) Caterpillar Inc-USA
9456317 *XCTI4* -	**SWORDFISH** **Naviera Petrolera Integral SA de CV** *Ciudad del Carmen* *Mexico* MMSI: 345070293 Official number: 04013571275	**455** 136 317	Class: AB	**2009-02 Island Boats Inc — Jeanerette LA** Yd No: 10113 Loa 53.35 Br ex - Dght 2.440 Lbp 48.78 Br md 9.75 Dpth 3.96 Welded, 1 dk	**(B21A20C) Crew/Supply Vessel** Hull Material: Aluminium Alloy Passengers: unberthed: 80	**4 oil engines** reduction geared to sc. shafts driving 4 Water jets Total Power: 5,296kW (7,200hp) 20.0kn Cummins KTA-50-M2 4 x Vee 4 Stroke 16 Cy. 159 x 159 each-1324kW (1800bhp) Cummins Engine Co Inc-USA AuxGen: 2 x 60Hz a.c Thrusters: 1 Tunnel thruster (f)
9385300 *V7BU2* -	**SWORDFISH** *ex* Siem Swordfish *-2012* **Swordfish Shipco Ltd** *Majuro* *Marshall Islands* MMSI: 538005198 Official number: 5198	**5,372** 1,611 4,386	Class: AB (NV)	**2007-09 Kleven Verft AS — Ulsteinvik** Yd No: 315 Loa 103.70 (BB) Br ex - Dght 6.150 Lbp 96.80 Br md 19.70 Dpth 7.70 Welded, 1 dk	**(B21A20S) Platform Supply Ship** Cranes: 1x150t Ice Capable	**4 diesel electric oil engines** driving 4 gen. each 2100kW a.c Connecting to 2 elec. motors each (2200kW) driving 2 Azimuth electric drive units Total Power: 8,632kW (11,736hp) 12.0kn Caterpillar 3616-HD 4 x Vee 4 Stroke 16 Cy. 170 x 215 each-2158kW (2934bhp) Caterpillar Inc-USA Thrusters: 2 Tunnel thruster (f); 1 Retract. directional thruster (f)
9572408 *9V8446* -	**SWORDFISH 5** *ex* Go Elnath *-2012* *ex* Swordfish 5 *-2012* **Swordfish 5 Pte Ltd** Go Offshore (Asia) Pte Ltd SatCom: Inmarsat C 456408311 *Singapore* *Singapore* MMSI: 564083000 Official number: 395793	**499** 149 353	Class: AB	**2010-11 Guangxi Guijiang Shipyard — Wuzhou GX** Yd No: H7059 Loa 40.00 Br ex - Dght 4.400 Lbp 36.80 Br md 11.40 Dpth 4.95 Welded, 1 dk	**(B21B20A) Anchor Handling Tug Supply** Cranes: 1x2t	**2 oil engines** reduction geared to sc. shafts driving 2 FP propellers Total Power: 2,942kW (4,000hp) 9.0kn Mitsubishi S8U-MPTK 2 x 4 Stroke 8 Cy. 240 x 260 each-1471kW (2000bhp) Mitsubishi Heavy Industries Ltd-Japan AuxGen: 3 x 300kW 440/220V a.c Thrusters: 1 Tunnel thruster (f) Fuel: 390.0
9031832 - -	**SWORDFISH 8** *ex* Koho Maru *-2013* **Nagasaki Shipping Pte Ltd**	*498* - 1,150	Class: IZ	**1991-08 Maebata Zosen Tekko K.K. — Sasebo** Yd No: 195 Loa 65.00 Br ex - Dght 4.040 Lbp 59.00 Br md 10.00 Dpth 4.50 Welded, 1 dk	**(A12A2TC) Chemical Tanker**	**1 oil engine** driving 1 FP propeller Total Power: 736kW (1,001hp) Niigata 6M28BGT 1 x 4 Stroke 6 Cy. 280 x 480 736kW (1001bhp) Niigata Engineering Co Ltd-Japan
6931017 *A6NY* -	**SWORDFISH ANN** *ex* Mac Tide 30 *-1997* *ex* Jaramac 30 *-1993* *ex* Nusa Tenggara *-1990* *ex* Jaramac 30 *-1984* *ex* John R. Ingram *-1972* **Linden Shipping International** - *Dubai* *United Arab Emirates* MMSI: 470582000 Official number: 4168	**268** 80 -	Class: AB (KI)	**1969 Adelaide Ship Construction Pty Ltd — Port Adelaide SA** Yd No: 51 Loa 32.00 Br ex 9.38 Dght 3.040 Lbp 29.22 Br md 9.15 Dpth 3.89 Welded, 1 dk	**(B32A2ST) Tug**	**2 oil engines** reverse reduction geared to sc. shafts driving 2 FP propellers Total Power: 2,486kW (3,380hp) Ruston 6ATCM 2 x 4 Stroke 6 Cy. 318 x 368 each-1243kW (1690bhp) Ruston & Hornsby Ltd.-Lincoln AuxGen: 2 x 70kW Fuel: 113.0
8735120 *2FGV5* -	**SWS THURROCK** *ex* Green Transient *-2012* *ex* Transient *-2009* *ex* Sirene *-2000* *ex* Windhorst *-1998* *ex* Irene *-1992* **S Walsh & Son Ltd** - *United Kingdom* MMSI: 235091147	**335** 161 558		**1964-01 Fa. Gebr. Geleijns — Moerdijk** Loa 55.00 Br ex 6.60 Dght 2.460 Lbp - Br md 6.50 Dpth 2.48 Welded, 1 dk	**(A31A2GX) General Cargo Ship**	**1 oil engine** reduction geared to sc. shaft driving 1 FP propeller Total Power: 425kW (578hp) Caterpillar 3408C 1 x Vee 4 Stroke 8 Cy. 137 x 152 425kW (578bhp) (new engine 1998) Caterpillar Inc-USA
9509504 *A6E3141* -	**SWYHAN 1** **Liwa Marine Services LLC** *Abu Dhabi* *United Arab Emirates* MMSI: 470987000	**202** 60 182	Class: BV	**2008-05 Eastern Marine Shipbuilding Sdn Bhd — Sibu** Yd No: 73 Loa 26.00 Br ex - Dght 3.000 Lbp 24.26 Br md 8.10 Dpth 3.60 Welded, 1 dk	**(B32A2ST) Tug**	**2 oil engines** reduction geared to sc. shafts driving 2 FP propellers Total Power: 1,060kW (1,442hp) 10.0kn Caterpillar 3412D 2 x Vee 4 Stroke 12 Cy. 145 x 162 each-530kW (721bhp) Caterpillar Inc-USA

IMO / Call sign	Name / Owner / Port	Tonnage	Class	Builder / Dimensions	Type	Machinery
8984032 *CQUV* -	**SY LOVE II** *ex* Goody *-1999* **Loxxiabail Slibail SA** Atlantic Madeira Yacht Management Lda *Madeira* *Portugal (MAR)* Official number: 1217	130 100 -		**1999 Cantieri Navali Versil Srl — Viareggio** Loa 26.10 Br ex - Dght 1.750 Lbp 22.20 Br md 6.26 Dpth 2.80 Welded, 1 dk	**(X11A2YP) Yacht** Passengers: cabins: 4; berths: 8	**2 oil engines** geared to sc. shafts driving 2 Propellers Total Power: 1,986kW (2,700hp) 23.0kn Caterpillar 3412 2 x Vee 4 Stroke 12 Cy. 137 x 152 each-993kW (1350bhp) Caterpillar Inc-USA
8995926 *MMZC2* -	**SY ROSEHEARTY** *ex* Audace *-2014* *ex* Rosehearty *-2014* **L'Audace Charters LP** - *Douglas* *Isle of Man (British)* MMSI: 235011240 Official number: 737888	499 149 83	Class: AB	**2006-02 Perini Navi SpA (Divisione Picchiotti) — Viareggio** Yd No: 2059 Loa 55.90 Br ex - Dght 3.972 Lbp 49.70 Br md 11.51 Dpth 5.55 Welded, 1 dk	**(X11A2YS) Yacht (Sailing)** Hull Material: Aluminium Alloy	**2 oil engines** reduction geared to sc. shafts driving 2 Propellers Total Power: 1,848kW (2,512hp) 15.0kn Deutz TBD616V12 2 x Vee 4 Stroke 12 Cy. 132 x 160 each-924kW (1256bhp) Deutz AG-Koeln
7736397 - - -	**SYAHHAIKAL III** *ex* Itakeru *-2013* *ex* Eishin Maru No. 1 *-1990* - - *Indonesia*	*177* - -		**1978-04 K.K. Mochizuki Zosensho — Osakikamijima** Yd No: 105 L reg 23.02 Br ex - Dght - Lbp - Br md 8.50 Dpth 3.51 Welded, 1 dk	**(B32B2SP) Pusher Tug**	**1 oil engine** driving 1 FP propeller
9066071 *UICW* -	**SYAM** **Baltasar Shipping SA** CJSC 'Onegoship' *St Petersburg* *Russia* MMSI: 273414060	1,596 831 2,300	Class: RS	**1993-05 Arminius Werke GmbH — Bodenwerder** (Hull) Yd No: 10527 **1993-05 Schiffswerft und Maschinenfabrik Cassens GmbH — Emden** Yd No: 197 Loa 81.44 Br ex 11.46 Dght 4.233 Lbp 77.40 Br md 11.30 Dpth 5.40 Welded, 1 dk	**(A31A2GX) General Cargo Ship** Grain: 2,926 TEU 72 C. 72/20' Compartments: 1 Ho, ER 1 Ha: (51.6 x 9.0)ER	**1 oil engine** with flexible couplings & sr reverse geared to sc. shaft driving 1 FP propeller Total Power: 1,000kW (1,360hp) 9.5kn MaK 6M332C 1 x 4 Stroke 6 Cy. 240 x 330 1000kW (1360bhp) Krupp MaK Maschinenbau GmbH-Kiel Thrusters: 1 Thwart. FP thruster (f)
8732128 - - -	**SYARASD I** **PT Multisari Bahari** - *Samarinda* *Indonesia*	152 46 -	Class: KI	**2008-05 C.V. Dok & Galangan Kapal Perlun — Samarinda** Loa 23.00 Br ex - Dght - Lbp 21.00 Br md 7.30 Dpth 3.20 Welded, 1 dk	**(B32A2ST) Tug**	**2 oil engines** geared to sc. shafts driving 2 FP propellers Total Power: 894kW (1,216hp) Cummins KTA-19-M3 2 x 4 Stroke 6 Cy. 159 x 159 each-447kW (608bhp) Cummins Engine Co Inc-USA
7616963 *YCGR* -	**SYARASD - V** *ex* Selat Sipura *-2010* **PT Multisari Bahari** - *Jakarta* *Indonesia*	157 48 -	Class: (KI) (NV)	**1977-09 Salthammer Baatbyggeri AS — Vestnes** (Hull) **1977-09 Bolsones Verft AS — Molde** Yd No: 249 Loa 26.01 Br ex - Dght 3.301 Lbp 24.01 Br md 8.01 Dpth 3.81 Welded, 1 dk	**(B32A2ST) Tug**	**1 oil engine** geared to sc. shaft driving 1 FP propeller Total Power: 883kW (1,201hp) 11.0kn Deutz SBA8M528 1 x 4 Stroke 8 Cy. 220 x 280 883kW (1201bhp) Kloeckner Humboldt Deutz AG-West Germany
7616975 *YDA4535* -	**SYARASD VI** *ex* Selat Sanding *-2010* **Government of The Republic of Indonesia (Direktorat Jenderal Perhubungan Laut - Ministry of Sea Communications)** PT (Persero) Pengerukan Indonesia *Jakarta* *Indonesia*	*157* 48 75	Class: (KI) (NV)	**1977-10 Salthammer Baatbyggeri AS — Vestnes** (Hull) **1977-10 Bolsones Verft AS — Molde** Yd No: 253 Loa 26.32 Br ex - Dght 3.301 Lbp 24.01 Br md 8.01 Dpth 3.81 Welded, 1 dk	**(B32A2ST) Tug**	**1 oil engine** geared to sc. shaft driving 1 FP propeller Total Power: 883kW (1,201hp) 11.0kn Deutz SBA8M528 1 x 4 Stroke 8 Cy. 220 x 280 883kW (1201bhp) Kloeckner Humboldt Deutz AG-West Germany
9033074 *3FDE4* -	**SYATT** *ex* Japan Tuna No. 3 *-2011* **Global Eminence Ltd** Ocean Grow International Shipmanagement Consultant Corp SatCom: Inmarsat C 437369810 *Panama* *Panama* MMSI: 373698000 Official number: 4386412	4,737 1,973 5,895	Class: PD (NK)	**1992-03 Hitachi Zosen Corp — Nagasu KM** Yd No: 4862 Loa 102.64 (BB) Br ex - Dght 7.013 Lbp 93.00 Br md 16.80 Dpth 8.50 Welded, 1 dk	**(A13B2TP) Products Tanker** Single Hull Liq: 5,632; Liq (Oil): 5,632 Cargo Heating Coils	**1 oil engine** driving 1 CP propeller Total Power: 3,604kW (4,900hp) 13.5kn Mitsubishi 7UEC37LA 1 x 2 Stroke 7 Cy. 370 x 880 3604kW (4900bhp) Akasaka Tekkosho KK (Akasaka DieselLtd)-Japan AuxGen: 3 x 420kW a.c Fuel: 475.0 (r.f.)
9565522 - - -	**SYBIL GRAHAM** **Graham Gulf Inc** - *New Orleans, LA* *United States of America* Official number: 1222116	427 - 432		**2009-12** Yd No: 95 Loa 56.38 Br ex - Dght 2.900 Lbp - Br md 10.33 Dpth 4.27 Welded, 1 dk	**(B21A2OC) Crew/Supply Vessel** Hull Material: Aluminium Alloy Passengers: unberthed: 80	**4 oil engines** reduction geared to sc. shafts driving 4 FP propellers Total Power: 5,368kW (7,300hp) 21.0kn Cummins QSK50-M 4 x Vee 4 Stroke 16 Cy. 159 x 159 each-1342kW (1825bhp) Cummins Engine Co Inc-USA AuxGen: 2 x 85kW a.c Thrusters: 1 Retract. directional thruster (f); 1 Tunnel thruster (f)
9198563 *LAOO5* -	**SYCAMORE** *ex* Jo Sycamore *-2011* **Zippora Pte Ltd** Jo Tankers A/S *Bergen* *Norway (NIS)* MMSI: 257568000	23,129 11,931 37,622 T/cm 50.1	Class: NV	**2000-09 Kleven Floro AS — Floro** Yd No: 140 Loa 183.10 (BB) Br ex 32.23 Dght 10.720 Lbp 176.90 Br md 32.20 Dpth 14.00 Welded, 1 dk	**(A12B2TR) Chemical/Products Tanker** Double Hull (13F) Liq: 39,240; Liq (Oil): 39,240 Cargo Heating Coils Compartments: 11 Ta (s.stl), 4 Wing Ta, 24 Wing Ta (s.stl), 2 Wing Slop Ta (s.stl), ER (s.stl) 39 Cargo Pump (s): 5x550m³/hr, 18x320m³/hr, 16x220m³/hr Manifold: Bow/CM: 95.3m	**1 oil engine** driving 1 CP propeller Total Power: 10,416kW (14,162hp) 15.5kn MAN-B&W 7S50MC-C 1 x 2 Stroke 7 Cy. 500 x 2000 10416kW (14162bhp) MAN B&W Diesel A/S-Denmark AuxGen: 1 x 1100kW 450V 60Hz a.c, 2 x 1260kW 450V 60Hz a.c Thrusters: 1 Tunnel thruster (f) Fuel: 246.0 (d.f.) (Heating Coils) 1694.0 (r.f.)
9259939 *NTGG* -	**SYCAMORE** **Government of The United States of America (US Coast Guard)** - *Cordova, AK* *United States of America* MMSI: 368014000	1,930 579 -	Class: (AB)	**2002-03 Marinette Marine Corp — Marinette WI** Yd No: 209 Loa 68.58 Br ex - Dght 3.960 Lbp 62.79 Br md - Dpth 6.00 Welded, 1 dk	**(B34Q2QB) Buoy Tender**	**2 oil engines** reduction geared to sc. shafts driving 2 FP propellers Total Power: 4,560kW (6,200hp) Caterpillar 3608 2 x 4 Stroke 8 Cy. 280 x 300 each-2280kW (3100bhp) Caterpillar Inc-USA
9123130 *4DEK3* -	**SYCAMORE GLOBAL 1** *ex* Beauty Juno *-2010* *ex* Beauty K *-2005* *ex* Rubin Falcon *-2003* **Sycamore Global Shipping Corp** - *Manila* *Philippines* MMSI: 548399100 Official number: 00-0000251	11,193 6,784 18,315 T/cm 28.1	Class: NK	**1996-07 Shikoku Dockyard Co. Ltd. — Takamatsu** Yd No: 880 Loa 148.17 (BB) Br ex - Dght 9.150 Lbp 135.95 Br md 22.80 Dpth 12.20 Welded, 1 dk	**(A21A2BC) Bulk Carrier** Grain: 23,212; Bale: 22,337 Compartments: 4 Ho, ER 4 Ha: (16.3 x 12.0)3 (19.5 x 12.0)ER Cranes: 3x30t	**1 oil engine** driving 1 FP propeller Total Power: 4,983kW (6,775hp) 13.5kn B&W 5L42MC 1 x 2 Stroke 5 Cy. 420 x 1360 4983kW (6775bhp) Mitsui Engineering & Shipbuilding CLtd-Japan AuxGen: 3 x 360kW a.c Fuel: 1005.0 (r.f.)
1009766 *ZGAX* -	**SYCARA V** **Sycara III Ltd** Vessel Safety Management LLC *George Town* *Cayman Islands (British)* MMSI: 319035600	1,566 469 300	Class: LR ✠ **100A1** SS 09/2010 SSC Yacht (P), mono, G6 ✠ **LMC** **UMS** Cable: 442.0/26.0 U2 (a)	**2010-09 Nobiskrug GmbH — Rendsburg** Yd No: 780 Loa 68.12 (BB) Br ex 12.50 Dght 3.700 Lbp 55.30 Br md 12.00 Dpth 6.60 Welded, 1 dk	**(X11A2YP) Yacht**	**2 oil engines** with clutches, flexible couplings & sr reverse geared to sc. shafts driving 2 FP propellers Total Power: 3,132kW (4,258hp) Caterpillar 3516B-HD 2 x Vee 4 Stroke 16 Cy. 170 x 190 each-1566kW (2129bhp) Caterpillar Inc-USA AuxGen: 3 x 248kW 440V 60Hz a.c Thrusters: 1 Thwart. FP thruster (f)
7832880 *UGEQ* -	**SYCHYOVO** **Dalmoreprodukt Holding Co (Kholdingovaya Kompaniya 'Dalmoreprodukt')** - *Vladivostok* *Russia* MMSI: 273817600 Official number: 791326	739 221 327	Class: RS	**1980-07 Volgogradskiy Sudostroitelnyy Zavod — Volgograd** Yd No: 890 Loa 53.75 (BB) Br ex 10.72 Dght 4.290 Lbp 47.92 Br md 10.50 Dpth 6.00 Welded, 1 dk	**(B11A2FS) Stern Trawler** Ins: 218 Compartments: 1 Ho, ER 1 Ha: (1.6 x 1.6) Derricks: 2x1.5t Ice Capable	**1 oil engine** driving 1 FP propeller Total Power: 971kW (1,320hp) 12.8kn S.K.L. 8NVD48A-2U 1 x 4 Stroke 8 Cy. 320 x 480 971kW (1320bhp) VEB Schwermaschinenbau "KarlLiebknecht" (SKL)-Magdeburg AuxGen: 1 x 300kW, 3 x 160kW, 2 x 135kW Fuel: 185.0 (d.f.)
5155109 - - -	**SYD-SYD I** *ex* Iles de Loos *-2003* *ex* Bramshorn *-1992* *ex* Hornelen *-1986* - -	298 161 427	Class: (NV)	**1952-05 AS Mjellem & Karlsen — Bergen** Yd No: 72 Loa 46.39 Br ex 8.64 Dght 3.501 Lbp - Br md 8.62 Dpth - Riveted\Welded, 2 dks	**(A37B2PS) Passenger Ship** Passengers: unberthed: 126; berths: 24 Bale: 668 Compartments: 1 Ho, ER 2 Ha: 2 (4.1 x 1.9)ER Derricks: 3x6t; Winches: 3	**1 oil engine** driving 1 FP propeller Total Power: 574kW (780hp) 12.0kn Normo LSMC-6 1 x 4 Stroke 6 Cy. 250 x 300 574kW (780bhp) (new engine 1966) AS Bergens Mek Verksteder-Norway

IMO / Call sign	Ship / Owner	Tonnage	Class	Builder / Dimensions	Type	Machinery
5262768 *SFWE* -	**SYDFART** *ex* Ann *-1977* *ex* Stigfjord *-1972* *ex* Hamnfjord *-1969* *ex* Olof Tratalja *-1965* **Sydfart AB** - *Grohogen* *Sweden* MMSI: 265586810	**176** 83 280		**1879** **P. Larsson — Torrskog** Yd No: 53 Loa 31.70 Br ex 6.53 Dght 3.226 Lbp - Br md 6.51 Dpth - Riveted, 1 dk	**(A31A2GX) General Cargo Ship** Hull Material: Iron Bale: 340 Compartments: 1 Ho, ER 1 Ha: (11.4 x 3.7)ER Derricks: 1x1.5t; Winches: 1	**1 oil engine** driving 1 FP propeller Total Power: 250kW (340hp) 8.5kn Alpha 404-24VO 1 x 2 Stroke 4 Cy. 240 x 400 250kW (340bhp) (new engine 1953) Frederikshavn Jernstoberi ogMaskinfabrik-Denmark Fuel: 9.0 (d.f.)
9196204 *PFBD* -	**SYDGARD** *ex* Griend *-2006* *ex* Polar Snow *-2003* **Bore Sydgard BV** Bore Ltd (Bore Oy Ab) SatCom: Inmarsat C 424490110 *Rotterdam* *Netherlands* MMSI: 244901000 Official number: 37045	**2,868** 1,613 3,780	Class: NV (LR) (BV) Classed LR until 9/9/11	**2000-10** **Scheepswerf Peters B.V. — Kampen** Yd No: 466 Loa 89.25 Br ex - Dght 5.660 Lbp 84.95 Br md 13.30 Dpth 7.15 Welded, 1 dk	**(A31A2GX) General Cargo Ship** Grain: 5,829 TEU 208 C.Ho 112 TEU C.Dk 96 TEU Compartments: 1 Ho, ER 1 Ha: (63.0 x 11.2)ER Ice Capable	**1 oil engine** with flexible couplings & reverse reduction geared to sc. shaft driving 1 CP propeller Total Power: 1,800kW (2,447hp) 12.5kn MaK 6M25 1 x 4 Stroke 6 Cy. 255 x 400 1800kW (2447bhp) MaK Motoren GmbH & Co. KG-Kiel AuxGen: 1 x 424kW 220/380V 50Hz a.c, 1 x 256kW 220/380V 50Hz a.c Thrusters: 1 Thwart. FP thruster (f) Fuel: 198.0 (d.f.) 8.0pd
9275385 *9VGN9* -	**SYDNEY** *ex* OOCL Sydney *-2011* **Singa Star Pte Ltd** Synergy Marine Pte Ltd *Singapore* *Singapore* MMSI: 563320000 Official number: 389936	**34,610** 16,865 43,093 T/cm 61.1	Class: NK	**2003-05** **Koyo Dockyard Co Ltd — Mihara HS** Yd No: 2145 Loa 234.62 (BB) Br ex 32.20 Dght 12.500 Lbp 218.00 Br md 32.20 Dpth 18.80 Welded, 1 dk	**(A33A2CC) Container Ship (Fully Cellular)** TEU 2762 C Ho 1216 TEU C Dk 1546 TEU incl 300 ref C.	**1 oil engine** driving 1 FP propeller Total Power: 28,879kW (39,264hp) 22.6kn B&W 8K80MC-C 1 x 2 Stroke 8 Cy. 800 x 2300 28879kW (39264bhp) Mitsui Engineering & Shipbuilding CLtd-Japan AuxGen: 4 x 1200kW a.c Thrusters: 1 Thwart. FP thruster (f) Fuel: 5255.0
7114745 *VL2270* -	**SYDNEY COVE** *ex* Barrier Cove *-1977* **Tasmanian Ports Corporation Pty Ltd (TasPorts)** - *Sydney, NSW* *Australia* MMSI: 503253500 Official number: 191905	*209* - -	Class: LR ✠ **100A1** SS 07/2010 Australian Offshore Operations, but not more than 200 Nautical Miles to Seaward from the Coast (USL Code 2B) ✠ **LMC** Eq.Ltr: (c) ; Cable: U1	**1971-09** **North Queensland Engineers & Agents Pty Ltd — Cairns QLD** Yd No: 37 Loa 29.42 Br ex 9.76 Dght 3.068 Lbp 26.32 Br md 9.40 Dpth 3.92 Welded, 1 dk	**(B32A2ST) Tug**	**2 oil engines** reverse reduction geared to sc. shafts driving 2 FP propellers Total Power: 1,472kW (2,002hp) 12.0kn Blackstone EWSL8 2 x 4 Stroke 8 Cy. 222 x 292 each-736kW (1001bhp) Lister Blackstone MirrleesMarine Ltd.-Dursley AuxGen: 2 x 41kW 415V 50Hz a.c Fuel: 27.5 (d.f.)
9062984 *VSXC4* -	**SYDNEY EXPRESS** *ex* CP Dynasty *-2006* *ex* Canmar Dynasty *-2005* *ex* TMM Guadalajara *-2003* *ex* P&O Nedlloyd Melbourne *-2001* *ex* Coral Seatel *-1998* *ex* Contship Sydney *-1998* *completed as* Coral Seatel *-1994* **Hapag-Lloyd Ships Ltd** Hapag-Lloyd AG *London* *United Kingdom* MMSI: 235003900 Official number: 905537	**23,540** 10,977 30,621 T/cm 47.0	Class: NV (GL)	**1994-12** **Stocznia Gdynia SA — Gdynia** Yd No: 8111/1 Loa 187.16 (BB) Br ex - Dght 11.500 Lbp 175.60 Br md 30.00 Dpth 16.75 Welded, 1 dk	**(A33A2CC) Container Ship (Fully Cellular)** TEU 2070 C Ho 836 TEU C Dk 1234 TEU incl 150 ref C. Compartments: 5 Cell Ho, ER 9 Ha: ER Cranes: 3x45t Ice Capable	**1 oil engine** driving 1 FP propeller Total Power: 17,940kW (24,391hp) 19.5kn Sulzer 6RTA72U 1 x 2 Stroke 6 Cy. 720 x 2500 17940kW (24391bhp) Korea Heavy Industries & ConstrCo Ltd (HANJUNG)-South Korea AuxGen: 3 x 1150kW 440V 60Hz a.c Thrusters: 1 Thwart. CP thruster (f) Fuel: 305.0 (d.f.) 2682.0 (r.f.) 79.3pd
7432317 *H3ZS* -	**SYDNEY MARIE** *ex* Torn Kristine *-2009* *ex* Astor S *-2002* *ex* Astor *-1996* **Caribbulk Shipping Ltd** - *Panama* *Panama* MMSI: 371942000 Official number: 4041009	**1,854** 1,145 3,100	Class: (NV) (BV)	**1976-09** **Batservice Verft AS — Mandal** Yd No: 648 Loa 80.07 Br ex 14.20 Dght 5.403 Lbp 74.58 Br md 13.77 Dpth 6.53 Welded, 1 dk	**(A31A2GX) General Cargo Ship** Grain: 3,941; Bale: 3,624 Compartments: 1 Ho, ER 2 Ha: 2 (20.8 x 10.1)ER Ice Capable	**1 oil engine** driving 1 CP propeller Total Power: 1,471kW (2,000hp) 12.8kn Deutz SBV6M358 1 x 4 Stroke 6 Cy. 400 x 580 1471kW (2000bhp) Kloeckner Humboldt Deutz AG-West Germany AuxGen: 2 x 120kW 380V 50Hz a.c, 1 x 40kW 380V 50Hz a.c Thrusters: 1 Thwart. FP thruster (f)
8707381 - -	**SYDNEY SHOWBOAT** - **Blue Line Cruises Pty Ltd** - *Sydney, NSW* *Australia* Official number: 852601	*735* 241 49	Class: (LR) ✠ Classed LR until 8/9/89	**1987-11** **Siong Huat Shipyard Pte Ltd — Singapore** Yd No: 242 Loa 41.31 Br ex 11.82 Dght 1.650 Lbp 33.46 Br md 9.50 Dpth 2.85 Welded, 1 dk	**(A37B2PS) Passenger Ship** Passengers: unberthed: 400	**2 oil engines** geared to sc. shaft driving 1 FP propeller Total Power: 352kW (478hp) Caterpillar 3406TA 2 x 4 Stroke 6 Cy. 137 x 165 each-176kW (239bhp) Caterpillar Inc-USA AuxGen: 2 x 155kW 415V 50Hz a.c Thrusters: 1 Water jet (f)
7405924 *JXWG* -	**SYKKYLVSFJORD** - **Fjord1 MRF AS** Fjord1 AS *Aalesund* *Norway* MMSI: 257393400	**765** 254 -	Class: (NV)	**1975-05** **Smedvik Mek. Verksted AS — Tjorvaag** Yd No: 48 Loa 64.37 Br ex 11.28 Dght 3.099 Lbp 56.01 Br md 11.23 Dpth 4.22 Welded, 1 dk	**(A36A2PR) Passenger/Ro-Ro Ship (Vehicles)** Passengers: unberthed: 300 Bow door/ramp Cars: 50	**1 oil engine** driving 2 CP propellers aft, 1 fwd Total Power: 883kW (1,201hp) MWM TBD484-6 1 x 4 Stroke 6 Cy. 320 x 480 883kW (1201bhp) Motoren Werke Mannheim AG (MWM)-West Germany AuxGen: 2 x 77kW 220V 50Hz a.c
8700137 *UBDF8* -	**SYLT** *ex* Svoboda *-2010* *ex* Svobodnyy *-2008* **HSH (Trading & Shipping) Ltd** JSC Rover *Nakhodka* *Russia* MMSI: 273337210	**2,966** 918 3,086 T/cm 11.7	Class: RS	**1989-05** **Wartsila Marine Industries Inc — Turku** Yd No: 1303 Loa 97.40 Br ex 14.23 Dght 5.100 Lbp 90.44 Br md 14.20 Dpth 6.50 Welded, 1 dk	**(A13B2TP) Products Tanker** Single Hull Liq: 3,258; Liq (Oil): 3,258 Compartments: 4 Ta, 4 Wing Ta, 1 Slop Ta, 2 Wing Slop Ta, ER 4 Cargo Pump (s): 4x130m³/hr Manifold: Bow/CM: 46m Ice Capable	**1 oil engine** with clutches, flexible couplings & sr geared to sc. shaft driving 1 CP propeller Total Power: 2,576kW (3,502hp) 13.5kn Russkiy 6CHN40/46 1 x 4 Stroke 6 Cy. 400 x 460 2576kW (3502bhp) Mashinostroitelnyy Zavod"Russkiy-Dizel"-Leningrad AuxGen: 1 x 400kW 50Hz a.c, 2 x 300kW 50Hz a.c Fuel: 59.0 (d.f.) (Heating Coils) 225.0 (r.f.) 13.0pd
9452103 *DF5118* -	**SYLT** - **Government of The Federal Republic of Germany (Wasserschuetzpolizei Schleswig-Holstein)** - *Kiel* *Germany* MMSI: 211429600	**198** 59 49	Class: (GL)	**2009-03** **Fr Fassmer GmbH & Co KG — Berne** Yd No: 06/1/3020 Loa 34.20 Br ex 7.20 Dght 1.600 Lbp 29.80 Br md 7.00 Dpth 3.60 Welded, 1 dk	**(B34H2SQ) Patrol Vessel** Hull Material: Aluminium Alloy Ice Capable	**2 oil engines** reverse reduction geared to sc. shafts driving 2 FP propellers Total Power: 2,880kW (3,916hp) 24.0kn M.T.U. 16V2000M72 2 x Vee 4 Stroke 16 Cy. 135 x 156 each-1440kW (1958bhp) MTU Friedrichshafen GmbH-Friedrichshafen AuxGen: 1 x 48kW 400V a.c, 1 x 44kW 400V a.c Thrusters: 1 Tunnel thruster (f)
9429273 *V2QJ8* -	**SYLT** - **mv 'Sylt' BV** Reederei Eckhoff GmbH & Co KG *Saint John's* *Antigua & Barbuda* MMSI: 305838000	**9,983** - 11,000	Class: GL	**2012-06** **Fujian Mawei Shipbuilding Ltd — Fuzhou FJ** Yd No: 431-10 Loa 140.66 (BB) Br ex - Dght 8.700 Lbp 130.57 Br md 23.20 Dpth 11.51 Welded, 1 dk	**(A33A2CC) Container Ship (Fully Cellular)** TEU 880 incl 231 ref C Compartments: 3 Cell Ho, ER 3 Ha: ER Ice Capable	**1 oil engine** reduction geared to sc. shaft driving 1 CP propeller Total Power: 9,000kW (12,236hp) 18.3kn MaK 9M43C 1 x 4 Stroke 9 Cy. 430 x 610 9000kW (12236bhp) Caterpillar Motoren GmbH & Co. KG-Germany Thrusters: 1 Tunnel thruster (f)
9321823 *5BFF3* -	**SYLT EXPRESS** - **Romo-Sylt-Linie GmbH & Co KG** Forde Reederei Seetouristik GmbH & Co KG *Limassol* *Cyprus* MMSI: 209392000	**3,652** 1,095 660	Class: GL	**2005-07** **UAB Vakaru Laivu Remontas (JSC Western Shiprepair) — Klaipeda** (Hull) Yd No: 19 **2005-07** **Fiskerstrand Verft AS — Fiskarstrand** Yd No: 51 Loa 88.16 Br ex 16.80 Dght 3.700 Lbp 83.10 Br md 16.10 Dpth 5.55 Welded, 1 dk	**(A36A2PR) Passenger/Ro-Ro Ship (Vehicles)** Passengers: unberthed: 600 Bow door/ramp (centre) Stern door/ramp (centre) Lane-Len: 166 Lane-Wid: 3.00 Lane-clr ht: 4.95 Cars: 80 Ice Capable	**4 diesel electric oil engines** driving 4 gen. each 1100kW 690V Connecting to 2 elec. motors driving 2 Azimuth electric drive units twin propellers Total Power: 4,400kW (5,984hp) 16.0kn Mitsubishi S12R-MPTK 4 x Vee 4 Stroke 12 Cy. 170 x 180 each-1100kW (1496bhp) Mitsubishi Heavy Industries Ltd-Japan
7115593 *FSBS* LR 318345	**SYLVANNA** *ex* Sylvana *-2007* **Mare Pesca Sarl** - *La Rochelle* *France* MMSI: 227588000 Official number: 318345	*197* 68 165	Class: (BV)	**1971** **Soc Industrielle et Commerciale de Consts Navales (SICCNa) — St-Malo** Yd No: 118 Loa 33.25 Br ex - Dght 3.560 Lbp 29.29 Br md 7.50 Dpth 3.89 Welded, 2 dks	**(B11A2FS) Stern Trawler** Ins: 150 Compartments: 1 Ho, ER	**1 oil engine** sr geared to sc. shaft driving 1 CP propeller Total Power: 574kW (780hp) 12.5kn Duvant 8VJS 1 x 4 Stroke 8 Cy. 255 x 300 574kW (780bhp) Moteurs Duvant-France Fuel: 52.5 (d.f.)
9219563 *LLDG* -	**SYLVARNES** - **Fjord1 AS** - *Floro* *Norway* MMSI: 259678000	**100** 40 10		**2000-04** **Lindstols Skips- & Baatbyggeri AS — Risor** Yd No: 316 Loa 25.45 Br ex - Dght - Lbp 22.50 Br md 8.00 Dpth - Welded	**(A36A2PR) Passenger/Ro-Ro Ship (Vehicles)** Hull Material: Aluminium Alloy Passengers: unberthed: 42 Cars: 7	**2 oil engines** geared to sc. shafts driving 2 FP propellers Total Power: 1,220kW (1,658hp) 30.0kn Mitsubishi S6R2-MPTK 2 x 4 Stroke 6 Cy. 170 x 220 each-610kW (829bhp) Mitsubishi Heavy Industries Ltd-Japan

8906286 *P3ZM8* -	**SYLVE** *ex* Vios *-2001* *ex* Morgenstond II *-1997* **Intermar Prosperity Shipping Co Ltd** Craftchart OU *Limassol* *Cyprus* MMSI: 210434000 Official number: 8906286	**1,999** 1,205 3,030	Class: RS (BV)	**1990-11 Scheepswerf Ferus Smit BV — Westerbroek** Yd No: 266 Loa 82.04 Br ex - Dght 4.941 Lbp 78.44 Br md 12.50 Dpth 6.60 Welded, 1 dk	**(A31A2GX) General Cargo Ship** Grain: 4,528 TEU 128 C. 128/20' Compartments: 1 Ho, ER 1 Ha: (54.1 x 10.5)ER Ice Capable	**1 oil engine** reduction geared to sc. shaft driving 1 CP propeller Total Power: 1,289kW (1,753hp) 12.0kn Caterpillar 3606TA 1 x 4 Stroke 6 Cy. 280 x 300 1289kW (1753bhp) Caterpillar Inc-USA AuxGen: 1 x a.c Thrusters: 1 Tunnel thruster (f) Fuel: 197.0 (d.f.)
8962917 *SJBF* -	**SYLVEIA** *ex* Lasse-Maja 2 *-1985* *ex* Farja 61/215 *-1984* **Vrango Transport AB** - *Vrango* *Sweden*	**112** 33 60		**1957 AB Asi-Verken — Amal** Yd No: 37 Loa 27.99 Br ex 8.14 Dght 2.410 Lbp - Br md 8.00 Dpth 2.68 Welded, 1 dk	**(A36A2PR) Passenger/Ro-Ro Ship (Vehicles)** Passengers: unberthed: 200	**3 oil engines** driving 3 FP propellers Total Power: 255kW (348hp) 8.0kn Volvo Penta MD96B 3 x 4 Stroke 6 Cy. 121 x 140 each-85kW (116bhp) Volvo Pentaverken-Sweden
5302219 *DNPN* -	**SYLVESTER** *ex* Esther-Jonny *-1989* *ex* Stromland *-1982* *ex* Ammy Vanggaard *-1977* *ex* Runmaro *-1969* **Cristall Seefischerei GmbH** - *Heiligenhafen* *Germany* Official number: 72896	**195** 98 -	Class: (BV)	**1962 VEB Ernst Thaelmann-Werft — Brandenburg** Loa 30.92 Br ex 6.63 Dght 2.701 Lbp 26.19 Br md 6.58 Dpth 3.10 Welded, 1 dk	**(B11A2FT) Trawler** 3 Ha: 2 (1.5 x 1.1) (0.9 x 0.5) Derricks: 1x3.5t,1x1.5t; Winches: 2	**1 oil engine** driving 1 CP propeller Total Power: 588kW (799hp) 11.0kn Alpha 408-26VO 1 x 2 Stroke 8 Cy. 260 x 400 588kW (799bhp) (new engine 1967) Alpha Diesel A/S-Denmark Fuel: 17.5 (d.f.)
9166467 *PEAX* -	**SYLVIA** **Rederij Rio Sal** Sam Shipping Vof *Krimpen a/d IJssel* *Netherlands* MMSI: 245752000 Official number: 33760	**3,999** 2,173 5,749 T/cm 14.3	Class: GL	**1999-05 Societatea Comerciala Severnav S.A. — Drobeta-Turnu Severin** Yd No: 5610001 Loa 107.05 Br ex 15.32 Dght 6.159 Lbp 100.32 Br md 15.00 Dpth 8.00 Welded, 1 dk	**(A31A2GX) General Cargo Ship** Grain: 7,800 TEU 325 C.Ho 159/20' C.Dk 166/20' incl.12 ref C. Compartments: 2 Ho, ER 2 Ha: (32.2 x 12.1)Tappered (38.5 x 12.1)Tappered ER Ice Capable	**1 oil engine** with flexible couplings & sr gearedto sc. shaft driving 1 CP propeller Total Power: 2,880kW (3,916hp) 12.0kn MaK 6M32 1 x 4 Stroke 6 Cy. 320 x 480 2880kW (3916bhp) MaK Motoren GmbH & Co. KG-Kiel AuxGen: 1 x 600kW 220/440V a.c, 2 x 164kW 220/440V 60Hz a.c Thrusters: 1 Thwart. CP thruster (f) Fuel: 57.0 (d.f.) 280.5 (d.f.) 10.5pd
9454383 *V2DP2* -	**SYLVIA** *launched as* Time *-2008* **Sylvia CV** Scheepvaartbedrijf van Dam *Saint John's* *Antigua & Barbuda* MMSI: 305288000	**1,917** 958 3,075	Class: BV	**2008-05 Umo Gemi Sanayi ve Ticaret Ltd — Karadeniz Eregli** Yd No: 03 Loa 80.28 Br ex - Dght 4.740 Lbp 77.29 Br md 12.50 Dpth 6.10 Welded, 1 dk	**(A31A2GX) General Cargo Ship** Grain: 3,537 Ice Capable	**1 oil engine** reduction geared to sc. shafts driving 1 CP propeller Total Power: 1,124kW (1,528hp) 11.0kn MaK 6M20C 1 x 4 Stroke 6 Cy. 200 x 300 1124kW (1528bhp) Caterpillar Motoren GmbH & Co. KG-Germany AuxGen: 2 x 150kW a.c
8836170 *ZQPD9* DS 8	**SYLVIA BOWERS** *ex* Emily Jayne *-2009* *ex* Blue Angel *-2001* **Scott Trawlers Ltd** - *Dumfries* *United Kingdom* MMSI: 235000480 Official number: C17098	**413** 123 -		**1988 N.V. Scheepswerven L. de Graeve — Zeebrugge** Loa 36.25 Br ex - Dght 4.050 Lbp - Br md 8.40 Dpth - Welded, 1 dk	**(B11B2FV) Fishing Vessel**	**1 oil engine** driving 1 FP propeller Total Power: 883kW (1,201hp) Kromhout 8FHD240 1 x 4 Stroke 8 Cy. 240 x 260 883kW (1201bhp) Stork Werkspoor Diesel BV-Netherlands
8845339 *WDE2527* -	**SYLVIA H** *ex* Mary Lou *-2006* **Ingram Barge Co** - *St Louis, MO* *United States of America* MMSI: 367100210 Official number: 685579	*514* 349 -		**1985 St Louis Ship Division of Pott Industries Inc — St Louis, Mo** Yd No: 1193 Loa - Br ex - Dght - Lbp 37.03 Br md 10.27 Dpth 3.20 Welded, 1 dk	**(B32A2ST) Tug**	**1 oil engine** driving 1 FP propeller
9150729 *OPUU* Z 525	**SYLVIA-MARY** *launched as* Ingrid *-1997* **Thor NV** - *Zeebrugge* *Belgium* MMSI: 205232000 Official number: 01 0366 1996	**138** 41 -		**1997-04 N.V. Scheepswerven L. de Graeve — Zeebrugge** Loa 23.85 Br ex - Dght - Lbp - Br md 6.56 Dpth 3.20 Welded, 1 dk	**(B11A2FT) Trawler**	**1 oil engine** geared to sc. shaft driving 1 FP propeller Total Power: 221kW (300hp) Caterpillar 1 x 4 Stroke 221kW (300bhp) Caterpillar Inc-USA
8330633 - -	**SYLVIA ONE** *ex* Mahe Geer *-1999* *ex* SCS-7044 *-1994* *ex* SCHS-7044 *-1991* - -	**104** 31 61	Class: (RS)	**1984 Azovskaya Sudoverf — Azov** Yd No: 7044 Loa 26.50 Br ex 6.58 Dght 2.340 Lbp 22.90 Br md - Dpth 3.05 Welded, 1 dk	**(B11B2FV) Fishing Vessel**	**1 oil engine** geared to sc. shaft driving 1 FP propeller Total Power: 165kW (224hp) 9.3kn Daldizel 6CHNSP18/22 1 x 4 Stroke 6 Cy. 180 x 220 165kW (224bhp) Daldizel-Khabarovsk AuxGen: 2 x 30kW a.c Fuel: 10.0 (d.f.)
9019389 *2ETK8* BM 112	**SYLVIA T** *ex* Becky Lou *-2013* *ex* Wikingbank *-2011* **Langdon & Philip Ltd** - *Brixham* *United Kingdom* MMSI: 235088014	**159** 47 -	Class: (GL)	**1992-03 Brodogradiliste 'Tisa' — Novi Becej** (Hull) Yd No: 78 **1992-03 B.V. Scheepswerf Maaskant — Stellendam** Yd No: 498 Loa 23.93 Br ex - Dght 3.400 Lbp - Br md 7.00 Dpth 3.65 Welded, 1 dk	**(B11B2FV) Fishing Vessel**	**1 oil engine** reverse reduction geared to sc. shaft driving 1 FP propeller Total Power: 221kW (300hp) 10.0kn MWM TBD604BL6 1 x 4 Stroke 6 Cy. 170 x 195 221kW (300bhp) Motoren Werke Mannheim AG (MWM)-Mannheim AuxGen: 3 x 254kW 220/380V a.c
8035300 *HO4098* -	**SYLVIE** *ex* Ailey 34 *-2011* *ex* Rebel *-1978* **Ailey Shipping Corp** - *Panama* *Panama* Official number: 08034PEXT2	*136* 92 -		**1978 Greenville SB. Corp. — Greenville, Ms** L reg 19.60 Br ex - Dght - Lbp - Br md 7.93 Dpth 2.21 Welded, 1 dk	**(B32A2ST) Tug**	**2 oil engines** driving 2 FP propellers Total Power: 882kW (1,200hp)
9332066 *VRCQ2* -	**SYLVIE** **Donati Shipping Corp SA** Unique Shipping (HK) Ltd *Hong Kong* *Hong Kong* MMSI: 477690200 Official number: HK-1863	**22,954** 6,886 26,348 T/cm 41.4	Class: LR ✠ **100A1** SS 03/2012 liquefied gas carrier Type 2G, Propane, butane, butylene, propylene, anhydrous ammonia and butadiene in independent tank Type A, maximum SG 0.70, partial loading VCM with maximum SG 0.97, maximum vapour pressure 0.25 bar (0.45 bar in harbour), minimum cargo temperature minus 50 degree C, **ShipRight** (SDA), *IWS LI ✠ **LMC UMS +Lloyd's RMC (LG)** Eq.Ltr: K†; Cable: 632.5/68.0 U3 (a)	**2007-03 Hyundai Heavy Industries Co Ltd — Ulsan** Yd No: 1762 Loa 174.00 (BB) Br ex 28.02 Dght 10.419 Lbp 165.00 Br md 28.00 Dpth 17.80 Welded, 1 dk	**(A11B2TG) LPG Tanker** Double Hull Liq (Gas): 34,513 3 x Gas Tank (s); 3 independent (C.mn.stl) pri horizontal 6 Cargo Pump (s): 6x400m³/hr Manifold: Bow/CM: 88.3m	**1 oil engine** driving 1 FP propeller Total Power: 9,981kW (13,570hp) 16.5kn MAN-B&W 7S50MC 1 x 2 Stroke 7 Cy. 500 x 1910 9981kW (13570bhp) Hyundai Heavy Industries Co Ltd-South Korea AuxGen: 4 x 615kW 450V 60Hz a.c Boilers: WTAuxB (Comp) 8.0kgf/cm² (7.8bar) Fuel: 158.6 (d.f.) 1764.8 (r.f.)

9406269 *SVBH3* -	**SYMI** **Symi II Special Maritime Enterprise (ENE)** Eletson Corp *Piraeus* *Greece* MMSI: 241107000 Official number: 12096	**22,977** 6,893 26,597 T/cm 41.5	Class: LR ✠ **100A1** SS 02/2012 liquefied gas carrier, Ship Type 2G Anhydrous ammonia, butane, butane and propane mixtures, butylene, butadiene, propane and propylene in independent tanks Type A, maximum SG 0.70, partial loading VCM with maximum SG 0.97, maximum vapour pressure 0.25 bar g (0.45 bar g in harbour), minimum cargo temperature minus 50 degree C **ShipRight** (ACS (B), SDA, FDA, CM) LI *IWS EP ✠ **LMC UMS +Lloyd's RMC (LG)** Eq.Ltr: K†; Cable: 632.5/68.0 U3 (a)	**2012-02 Hyundai Mipo Dockyard Co Ltd — Ulsan** Yd No: 8072 Loa 173.70 (BB) Br ex 28.03 Dght 10.419 Lbp 165.00 Br md 28.00 Dpth 17.80 Welded, 1 dk	**(A11B2TG) LPG Tanker** Double Bottom Entire Compartment Length Liq (Gas): 35,000 Manifold: Bow/CM: 88.7m	**1 oil engine** driving 1 FP propeller Total Power: 9,480kW (12,889hp) 16.0kn MAN-B&W 6S50MC-C 1 x 2 Stroke 6 Cy. 500 x 2000 9480kW (12889bhp) Hyundai Heavy Industries Co Ltd-South Korea AuxGen: 2 x 980kW 450V 60Hz a.c, 1 x 1150kW 450V 60Hz a.c Boilers: AuxB (Comp) 9.2kgf/cm² (9.0bar) Fuel: 444.0 (d.f.) 1497.0 (r.f.)
9418016 *A8WF8* -	**SYMI** **Symi Navigation SA** Aegean Bunkering Services Inc SatCom: Inmarsat C 463711392 *Monrovia* *Liberia* MMSI: 636014737 Official number: 14737	**4,580** 1,967 6,267 T/cm 15.5	Class: GL (NV)	**2012-04 Qingdao Hyundai Shipbuilding Co Ltd — Jiaonan SD** Yd No: 228 Loa 102.50 Br ex 17.82 Dght 6.600 Lbp 95.20 Br md 17.80 Dpth 8.80 Welded, 1 dk	**(A13B2TP) Products Tanker** Double Hull (13F) Liq: 6,882; Liq (Oil): 6,882 Cargo Heating Coils Compartments: 6 Wing Ta, 6 Wing Ta, ER 3 Cargo Pump (s): 2x750m³/hr, 1x300m³/hr	**1 oil engine** reverse reduction geared to sc. shaft driving 1 FP propeller Total Power: 2,160kW (2,937hp) 11.7kn Hyundai Himsen 9H25/33P 1 x 4 Stroke 9 Cy. 250 x 330 2160kW (2937bhp) Hyundai Heavy Industries Co Ltd-South Korea AuxGen: 3 x 400kW 450V a.c Thrusters: 1 Tunnel thruster (f)
7236165 *SV3524* -	**SYMI** *ex* Simi *-2012* *ex* Eftychia *-2005* *ex* Maria *-1984* **Aegean Shipping Co** - *Rhodes* *Greece* MMSI: 237025900 Official number: 45	**1,788** 784 -	Class: RS (AB)	**1974 D. Kamitsis & Co. — Piraeus** Yd No: 119 Converted From: Ferry (Passenger/Vehicle)-1977 Loa 61.32 Br ex 10.01 Dght 2.601 Lbp 52.35 Br md 9.20 Dpth 4.20 Welded, 1 dk	**(A37B2PS) Passenger Ship**	**2 oil engines** reverse reduction geared to sc. shafts driving 2 FP propellers Total Power: 2,384kW (3,242hp) 17.5kn MWM TBD441V12 2 x Vee 4 Stroke 12 Cy. 230 x 270 each-1192kW (1621bhp) Motoren Werke Mannheim AG (MWM)-West Germany AuxGen: 2 x 129kW
9131034 *V7GA5* -	**SYMI** *ex* Izola *-2013* *ex* Blue Zenith *-2004* **Saxony Navigation SA** Albamar Shipping Co SA *Majuro* *Marshall Islands* MMSI: 538002059 Official number: 2059	**26,341** 14,987 45,916 T/cm 49.0	Class: BV (KR)	**1997-09 Halla Engineering & Heavy Industries, Ltd. — Samho** Yd No: 1025 Loa 189.50 (BB) Br ex - Dght 11.610 Lbp 180.00 Br md 30.40 Dpth 16.50 Welded, 1 dk	**(A21A2BC) Bulk Carrier** Grain: 56,300; Bale: 53,589 Compartments: 5 Ho, Wing ER 5 Ha: ER 5 (20.0 x 15.4) Cranes: 4x30t	**1 oil engine** driving 1 FP propeller Total Power: 8,580kW (11,665hp) 14.0kn MAN-B&W 6S50MC 1 x 2 Stroke 6 Cy. 500 x 1910 8580kW (11665bhp) Hyundai Heavy Industries Co Ltd-South Korea
8951346 *V3OW8* -	**SYMPATHY** *ex* Simpati *-2006* *ex* Sympathy *-2005* *ex* Seaprincess *-2004* *ex* Kapitan Sherbakov *-2002* *ex* Volgo-Don 5037 *-2000* **Sympathy Maritime Co Ltd** LLC 'Shipping Agency Yug Rusi' *Belize City* *Belize* MMSI: 312658000 Official number: 371030060	**5,096** 2,728 5,295	Class: RS (RR)	**1972 Santierul Naval Oltenita S.A. — Oltenita** Yd No: 469 Loa 138.30 Br ex 16.70 Dght 3.520 Lbp 135.60 Br md 16.50 Dpth 5.50 Welded, 1 dk	**(A31A2GX) General Cargo Ship** Grain: 6,270 Compartments: 2 Ho, ER 2 Ha: (44.0 x 13.0) (45.0 x 13.0)ER	**2 oil engines** driving 2 FP propellers Total Power: 1,324kW (1,800hp) 11.0kn Dvigatel Revolyutsii 6CHRN36/45 2 x 4 Stroke 6 Cy. 360 x 450 each-662kW (900bhp) Zavod "Dvigatel Revolyutsii"-Gorkiy AuxGen: 2 x 100kW Fuel: 150.0 (d.f.)
9326055 *SVIQ* -	**SYMPHONIC** **Pontos Special Maritime Enterprise (ENE)** Nereus Shipping SA SatCom: Inmarsat C 424049410 *Piraeus* *Greece* MMSI: 240494000 Official number: 11471	**156,933** 98,886 298,522 T/cm 178.3	Class: AB	**2006-03 Universal Shipbuilding Corp — Nagasu KM (Ariake Shipyard)** Yd No: 029 Loa 329.99 (BB) Br ex 60.04 Dght 21.523 Lbp 316.00 Br md 60.00 Dpth 29.70 Welded, 1 dk	**(A13A2TV) Crude Oil Tanker** Double Hull (13F) Liq: 324,710; Liq (Oil): 324,710 Compartments: 5 Ta, 10 Wing Ta, 2 Wing Slop Ta, ER 3 Cargo Pump (s): 3x5500m³/hr Manifold: Bow/CM: 162.1m	**1 oil engine** driving 1 FP propeller Total Power: 25,090kW (34,112hp) 15.6kn MAN-B&W 7S80MC 1 x 2 Stroke 7 Cy. 800 x 3056 25090kW (34112bhp) Hitachi Zosen Corp-Japan AuxGen: 3 x 1000kW a.c Fuel: 335.4 (d.f.) 7091.9 (r.f.)
8016823 *FPSS* CC 544929	**SYMPHONIE** **Ramberfra Sarl** Cooperative Chingudy SatCom: Inmarsat C 422810410 *Concarneau* *France* MMSI: 228104000 Official number: 544929	*222* 79 300	Class: (BV)	**1981-10 Con. Mec. de Normandie — Cherbourg** Yd No: 34/05 Loa 34.02 Br ex 8.01 Dght 3.701 Lbp 31.02 Br md 7.92 Dpth 4.27 Welded, 1 dk	**(B11A2FS) Stern Trawler**	**1 oil engine** with clutches, flexible couplings & sr geared to sc. shaft driving 1 CP propeller Total Power: 588kW (799hp) 12.0kn Duvant 6VJMS 1 x 4 Stroke 6 Cy. 255 x 300 588kW (799bhp) Moteurs Duvant-France
7429267 *J8B4971* -	**SYMPHONY** *ex* South Michelle *-2010* *ex* Symphony *-2007* *ex* Bokelnburg *-1997* *ex* Kini Kersten *-1989* *ex* Bokelnburg *-1988* *ex* Isle of Man *-1983* *ex* Bokelnburg *-1981* *ex* Bourgogne *-1978* *ex* Bokelnburg *-1975* **Green Shipping OU** Atrica-Marine Ltd *Kingstown* *St Vincent & The Grenadines* MMSI: 375226000 Official number: 11444	**2,872** 1,366 3,336	Class: PR (GL)	**1975-12 Husumer Schiffswerft — Husum** Yd No: 1431 Lengthened-1978 Loa 99.29 Br ex 13.52 Dght 4.909 Lbp 90.12 Br md 13.49 Dpth 7.50 Welded, 2 dks	**(A31A2GX) General Cargo Ship** Grain: 4,870; Bale: 4,390 TEU 198 C. 198/20' Compartments: 1 Ho, ER 2 Ha: (37.3 x 10.2) (25.0 x 10.2)ER Ice Capable	**1 oil engine** geared to sc. shaft driving 1 FP propeller Total Power: 2,207kW (3,001hp) 14.0kn Deutz SBV6M540 1 x 4 Stroke 6 Cy. 370 x 400 2207kW (3001bhp) Kloeckner Humboldt Deutz AG-West Germany
7709100 *ERCG* -	**SYMPHONY** *ex* Aurelia M *-2012* *ex* Pelchaser *-2004* *ex* Lady Lienke *-1989* *ex* Sertan *-1987* **C&O Shipping Lines Co Ltd** Island Flag Shipping LLC *Giurgiulesti* *Moldova* MMSI: 214180307	**2,816** 1,589 3,168	Class: KC (BV) (HR) (GL)	**1978-03 Scheepswerf 'Friesland' BV — Lemmer** Yd No: 362 Lengthened-1984 Loa 95.81 Br ex 13.70 Dght 5.649 Lbp 88.96 Br md 13.61 Dpth 7.83 Welded, 2 dks	**(A31A2GX) General Cargo Ship** Grain: 4,716; Bale: 4,575 TEU 166 C.Ho 128/20' incl. 10 ref C. C.Dk 38/20' Compartments: 1 Ho, ER 1 Ha: (50.4 x 10.2)ER	**1 oil engine** reduction geared to sc. shaft driving 1 CP propeller Total Power: 1,765kW (2,400hp) 12.8kn Bolnes 16VDNL150/600 1 x Vee 2 Stroke 16 Cy. 190 x 350 1765kW (2400bhp) 'Bolnes' Motorenfabriek BV-Netherlands AuxGen: 1 x 200kW 380/220V 50Hz a.c, 3 x 198kW 380/220V 50Hz a.c Thrusters: 1 Thwart. FP thruster (f) Fuel: 263.0 (d.f.) 9.5pd
9449481 *9V7280* -	**SYMPHONY 5** *launched as* Danum 78 *-2008* **Seerak Offshore Pte Ltd** Regulus Ship Services Pte Ltd *Singapore* *Singapore* MMSI: 565764000 Official number: 393560	**475** 143 330	Class: NK	**2008-01 Piasau Slipways Sdn Bhd — Miri** Yd No: 257 Loa 37.00 Br ex - Dght 4.066 Lbp 34.69 Br md 11.40 Dpth 4.95 Welded, 1 dk	**(B32A2ST) Tug** Passengers: berths: 16	**2 oil engines** reduction geared to sc. shafts driving 2 FP propellers Total Power: 2,648kW (3,600hp) 10.0kn Cummins KTA-50-M2 2 x Vee 4 Stroke 16 Cy. 159 x 159 each-1324kW (1800bhp) Cummins Engine Co Inc-USA AuxGen: 2 x 150kW 415V 50Hz a.c Thrusters: 1 Thwart. FP thruster (f) Fuel: 280.0 (d.f.) 9.0pd
9549827 *9V7911* -	**SYMPHONY 14** **Regulus Ship Services Pte Ltd** - SatCom: Inmarsat C 456425310 *Singapore* *Singapore* MMSI: 564253000 Official number: 395036	**476** 143 202	Class: NK	**2009-06 Piasau Slipways Sdn Bhd — Miri** Yd No: 286 Loa 37.00 Br ex - Dght 4.066 Lbp 34.69 Br md 11.40 Dpth 4.95 Welded, 1 dk	**(B32A2ST) Tug** Passengers: 2	**2 oil engines** reduction geared to sc. shafts driving 2 FP propellers Total Power: 2,684kW (3,650hp) 11.0kn Cummins KTA-50-M2 2 x Vee 4 Stroke 16 Cy. 159 x 159 each-1342kW (1825bhp) Cummins Engine Co Inc-USA AuxGen: 2 x 150kW 50Hz a.c Thrusters: 1 Tunnel thruster (f) Fuel: 242.0 (d.f.)

IMO / Call sign	Name / Owner	Tonnage	Class	Built / Dimensions	Type	Machinery
8814005 *JG4838* -	**SYMPHONY CLASSICA** *ex Symphony -1998* **Sea Line Tokyo Co Ltd (KK Sea Line Tokyo)** - *Tokyo* *Japan* MMSI: 431000425 Official number: 131189	*1,084* - 160		**1989**-04 **Kanda Zosensho K.K. — Kawajiri** Yd No: 324 Loa 70.00 (BB) Br ex 10.52 Dght 2.570 Lbp 60.00 Br md 10.50 Dpth 3.60 Welded	**(A37B2PS) Passenger Ship** Passengers: unberthed: 600	**2 oil engines** with clutches, flexible couplings & sr reverse geared to sc. shafts driving 2 FP propellers Total Power: 1,176kW (1,598hp) 13.8kn Yanmar M200-SN 2 x 4 Stroke 6 Cy. 200 x 260 each-588kW (799bhp) (made 1988) Yanmar Diesel Engine Co Ltd-Japan AuxGen: 2 x 360kW 445V a.c Thrusters: 1 Thwart. CP thruster (f)
9032197 *JG5131* -	**SYMPHONY MODERNA** *ex Symphony II -1998* **Sea Line Tokyo Co Ltd (KK Sea Line Tokyo)** - *Tokyo* *Japan* MMSI: 431000424 Official number: 133158	*2,618* - 229		**1992**-07 **Kanda Zosensho K.K. — Kawajiri** Yd No: 336 Loa 83.20 (BB) Br ex 13.23 Dght 3.600 Lbp 70.00 Br md 13.00 Dpth 4.30 Welded, 1 dk	**(A37B2PS) Passenger Ship** Passengers: 550	**2 oil engines** sr geared to sc. shafts driving 2 CP propellers Total Power: 1,324kW (1,800hp) 12.8kn Yanmar M200-EN 2 x 4 Stroke 6 Cy. 200 x 260 each-662kW (900bhp) Yanmar Diesel Engine Co Ltd-Japan AuxGen: 2 x 680kW 445V 60Hz a.c, 1 x 120kW 445V 60Hz a.c Thrusters: 1 Thwart. CP thruster (f)
9251781 *IBGK* -	**SYN ACRAB** *ex Valderice -2006* **Synergas Srl** - *Naples* *Italy* MMSI: 247095300 Official number: 34RI	**7,605** 2,530 9,328 T/cm 20.6	Class: BV RI	**2003**-11 **Cantiere Navale di Pesaro SpA (CNP) — Pesaro** Yd No: 89 Loa 122.84 (BB) Br ex 19.05 Dght 8.000 Lbp 115.50 Br md 19.00 Dpth 9.51 Welded, 1 dk	**(A11B2TG) LPG Tanker** Double Sides Entire Compartment Length Liq (Gas): 8,852 2 x Gas Tank (s); 2 independent (5% Ni.stl) cyl horizontal 4 Cargo Pump (s): 4x250m³/hr Manifold: Bow/CM: 64.4m	**1 oil engine** geared to sc. shaft driving 1 CP propeller Total Power: 4,320kW (5,873hp) 15.0kn MaK 9M32 1 x 4 Stroke 9 Cy. 320 x 480 4320kW (5873bhp) Caterpillar Motoren GmbH & Co. KG-Germany AuxGen: 3 x 700kW 440V 60Hz a.c, 1 x 1100kW 440V 60Hz a.c Thrusters: 1 Tunnel thruster (f) Fuel: 157.3 (d.f.) 582.4 (r.f.)
9158240 *ICIV* -	**SYN ALTAIR** *ex Val Cadore -2006* **Synergas Srl** - SatCom: Inmarsat M 625584710 *Augusta* *Italy* MMSI: 247231000 Official number: 17	**5,778** 1,733 7,553 T/cm 16.8	Class: BV RI	**1998**-02 **Cantiere Navale di Pesaro SpA (CNP) — Pesaro** Yd No: 77 Loa 115.30 (BB) Br ex 16.80 Dght 8.100 Lbp 105.00 Br md 16.80 Dpth 11.80 Welded, 1 dk	**(A11B2TG) LPG Tanker** Double Bottom Entire Compartment Length Liq (Gas): 7,031 2 x Gas Tank (s); 2 independent (5% Ni.stl) dcy horizontal 6 Cargo Pump (s): 6x135m³/hr Manifold: Bow/CM: 56m	**1 oil engine** geared to sc. shaft driving 1 CP propeller Total Power: 3,960kW (5,384hp) 14.0kn Wartsila 6R38 1 x 4 Stroke 6 Cy. 380 x 475 3960kW (5384bhp) Wartsila NSD Nederland BV-Netherlands AuxGen: 1 x 1105kW 220/440V 60Hz a.c, 3 x 720kW 220/440V 60Hz a.c Thrusters: 1 Thwart. FP thruster (f) Fuel: 180.0 (d.f.) 568.0 (r.f.)
9003043 *IBVA* -	**SYN ATLAS** *ex Vallesina -2006* **Synergas Srl** - SatCom: Inmarsat A 1151601 *Augusta* *Italy* MMSI: 247265000 Official number: 11	**5,303** 1,590 6,396 T/cm 15.1	Class: BV RI	**1993**-01 **Cant. Nav. M. Morini & C. — Ancona** Yd No: 242 Loa 106.44 (BB) Br ex 16.80 Dght 7.800 Lbp 96.00 Br md 16.80 Dpth 11.80 Welded, 1 dk	**(A11B2TG) LPG Tanker** Double Bottom Entire Compartment Length Liq (Gas): 5,924 3 x Gas Tank (s); 3 independent (5% Ni.stl) dcy horizontal 6 Cargo Pump (s): 6x135m³/hr Manifold: Bow/CM: 52.3m	**1 oil engine** sr geared to sc. shaft driving 1 CP propeller Total Power: 4,480kW (6,091hp) 14.2kn Wartsila 12V32D 1 x Vee 4 Stroke 12 Cy. 320 x 350 4480kW (6091bhp) Wartsila Diesel Oy-Finland AuxGen: 3 x 586kW 220/440V 60Hz a.c, 1 x 1000kW 440V 60Hz a.c Thrusters: 1 Thwart. CP thruster (f) Fuel: 137.2 (d.f.) 437.5 (r.f.) 17.9pd
9003079 *ICVF* -	**SYN MAIA** *ex Val Foglia -2006* **Synergas Srl** - SatCom: Inmarsat A 1151651 *Augusta* *Italy* MMSI: 247093000 Official number: 99	**3,983** 1,195 4,444 T/cm 12.9	Class: BV RI	**1993**-04 **Cantiere Navale di Pesaro SpA (CNP) — Pesaro** Yd No: 66 Loa 98.50 (BB) Br ex 15.20 Dght 6.700 Lbp 90.00 Br md 15.20 Dpth 7.80 Welded, 1 dk	**(A11B2TG) LPG Tanker** Double Sides Entire Compartment Length Liq (Gas): 3,968 2 x Gas Tank (s); 2 independent (5% Ni.stl) cyl horizontal 2 Cargo Pump (s): 2x200m³/hr Manifold: Bow/CM: 55.5m	**1 oil engine** with clutches, flexible couplings & sr geared to sc. shaft driving 1 CP propeller Total Power: 3,000kW (4,079hp) 14.5kn Wartsila 8R32D 1 x 4 Stroke 8 Cy. 320 x 350 3000kW (4079bhp) Wartsila Diesel Oy-Finland AuxGen: 3 x 585kW 440V 60Hz a.c, 1 x 950kW 440V 60Hz a.c Thrusters: 1 Tunnel thruster (f) Fuel: 106.7 (d.f.) 395.0 (r.f.) 13.2pd
9003067 *ICFS* -	**SYN MARKAB** *ex Val di Fassa -2006 ex AGIP Sardegna -2000* **Synergas Srl** - SatCom: Inmarsat Mini-M 763257191 *Naples* *Italy* MMSI: 247199000 Official number: 1184	**3,983** 1,195 4,444 T/cm 12.9	Class: BV RI (AB)	**1992**-08 **Cantiere Navale di Pesaro SpA (CNP) — Pesaro** Yd No: 65 Loa 98.50 (BB) Br ex 15.20 Dght 6.710 Lbp 90.00 Br md 15.20 Dpth 7.80 Welded, 1 dk	**(A11B2TG) LPG Tanker** Double Sides Entire Compartment Length Liq (Gas): 3,967 2 x Gas Tank (s); 2 independent (5% Ni.stl) cyl horizontal 2 Cargo Pump (s): 2x200m³/hr Manifold: Bow/CM: 55.8m	**1 oil engine** with clutches, flexible couplings & sr geared to sc. shaft driving 1 CP propeller Total Power: 3,300kW (4,487hp) 13.5kn Wartsila 8R32E 1 x 4 Stroke 8 Cy. 320 x 350 3300kW (4487bhp) Wartsila Diesel Oy-Finland AuxGen: 1 x 800kW 220/440V 60Hz a.c, 3 x 580kW 220/440V 60Hz a.c Thrusters: 1 Thwart. FP thruster (f) Fuel: 92.6 (d.f.) 375.0 (r.f.) 11.5pd
9346902 *IBEK* -	**SYN TABIT** *ex Eleonora Lembo -2013* *ex Ocean Prima -2009* *launched as Ocean Pearl -2007* **Bomar One LLC** Synergas Srl *Naples* *Italy* MMSI: 247325500 Official number: 27	**3,827** 1,148 4,026 T/cm 123.0	Class: RI (LR) (AB) Classed LR until 17/12/08	**2007**-01 **Cantiere Navale di Pesaro SpA (CNP) — Pesaro** Yd No: 119 Loa 95.50 (BB) Br ex 15.54 Dght 6.500 Lbp 86.35 Br md 15.50 Dpth 8.00 Welded, 1 dk	**(A11B2TG) LPG Tanker** Double Bottom Entire Compartment Length Liq (Gas): 3,927 2 x Gas Tank (s); 2 independent (C.mn.stl) cyl horizontal 4 Cargo Pump (s): 4x250m³/hr Manifold: Bow/CM: 58.5m	**1 oil engine** with clutches, flexible couplings & sr geared to sc. shaft driving 1 CP propeller Total Power: 2,380kW (3,236hp) 14.3kn MAN-B&W 7L27/38 1 x 4 Stroke 7 Cy. 270 x 380 2380kW (3236bhp) MAN Diesel A/S-Denmark AuxGen: 3 x 509kW 440V 60Hz a.c, 1 x 700kW 450V a.c Boilers: TOH (o.f.), TOH (ex.g.) Thrusters: 1 Tunnel thruster (f) Fuel: 115.0 (d.f.) 321.0 (r.f.)
9346914 *IBEJ* -	**SYN TURAIS** *ex Margherita Iuliano -2013* *ex Ocean Primary -2009* *launched as Ocean Wind -2007* **Bomar Two LLC** Synergas Srl *Naples* *Italy* MMSI: 247325600 Official number: 28	**3,827** 1,148 4,026 T/cm 12.0	Class: RI (LR) (AB) Classed LR until 25/9/09	**2007**-07 **Cantiere Navale di Pesaro SpA (CNP) — Pesaro** Yd No: 120 Loa 95.50 (BB) Br ex 15.54 Dght 6.500 Lbp 86.35 Br md 15.50 Dpth 8.00 Welded, 1 dk	**(A11B2TG) LPG Tanker** Double Bottom Entire Compartment Length Liq (Gas): 3,927 2 x Gas Tank (s); 2 independent (C.mn.stl) cyl horizontal 4 Cargo Pump (s): 4x250m³/hr Manifold: Bow/CM: 58.5m	**1 oil engine** with clutches, flexible couplings & sr geared to sc. shaft driving 1 CP propeller Total Power: 2,380kW (3,236hp) 14.3kn MAN-B&W 7L27/38 1 x 4 Stroke 7 Cy. 270 x 380 2380kW (3236bhp) MAN Diesel A/S-Denmark AuxGen: 3 x 509kW 440V 60Hz a.c, 1 x 720kW 440V 60Hz a.c Boilers: TOH (o.f.) 7.1kgf/cm² (7.0bar), TOH (ex.g.) 7.1kgf/cm² (7.0bar) Thrusters: 1 Tunnel thruster (f) Fuel: 116.0 (d.f.) 321.0 (r.f.)
9346938 *ICKN* -	**SYN ZANIA** **Synergas Srl** - SatCom: Inmarsat Mini-M 761155094 *Naples* *Italy* MMSI: 247231200	**3,827** 1,150 4,026 T/cm 12.2	Class: BV RI	**2008**-05 **Cantiere Navale di Pesaro SpA (CNP) — Pesaro** Yd No: 122 Loa 95.50 (BB) Br ex 15.50 Dght 6.500 Lbp 86.35 Br md 15.00 Dpth 8.00 Welded, 1 dk	**(A11B2TG) LPG Tanker** Double Hull Liq (Gas): 3,927 2 x Gas Tank (s); 2 independent (C.mn.stl) cyl horizontal 4 Cargo Pump (s): 4x250m³/hr Manifold: Bow/CM: 54m	**1 oil engine** geared to sc. shaft driving 1 CP propeller Total Power: 2,720kW (3,698hp) 14.3kn MAN-B&W 7L27/38 1 x 4 Stroke 7 Cy. 270 x 380 2720kW (3698bhp) MAN Diesel A/S-Denmark AuxGen: 3 x a.c, 1 x a.c Thrusters: 1 Tunnel thruster (f) Fuel: 94.0 (d.f.) 318.0 (r.f.)
9187837 *IBJF* -	**SYN ZAURA** *ex Val Badia -2006* **Synergas Srl** - SatCom: Inmarsat M 624700291 *Augusta* *Italy* MMSI: 247602000	**3,850** 1,155 4,175 T/cm 12.3	Class: BV RI	**2000**-01 **Cantiere Navale di Pesaro SpA (CNP) — Pesaro** Yd No: 83 Loa 93.10 (BB) Br ex 15.50 Dght 6.500 Lbp 86.00 Br md 15.50 Dpth 8.00 Welded, 1 dk	**(A11B2TG) LPG Tanker** Double Sides Entire Compartment Length Liq (Gas): 3,924 2 x Gas Tank (s); 2 independent (C.mn.stl) cyl horizontal 2 Cargo Pump (s): 2x250m³/hr Manifold: Bow/CM: 54m	**1 oil engine** with flexible couplings & sr gearedto sc. shaft driving 1 CP propeller Total Power: 2,207kW (3,001hp) 14.5kn MAN-B&W 9L28/32A 1 x 4 Stroke 9 Cy. 280 x 320 2207kW (3001bhp) MAN B&W Diesel A/S-Denmark AuxGen: 3 x 360kW 440/220V 60Hz a.c Thrusters: 1 Thwart. CP thruster (f) Fuel: 95.0 (d.f.) (Heating Coils) 286.0 (r.f.) 13.8pd
9177466 *IBMV* -	**SYN ZOSMA** *ex Valle Aurora -2006* **Synergas Srl** - SatCom: Inmarsat M 624700187 *Augusta* *Italy* MMSI: 247354000	**3,819** 1,145 4,112 T/cm 12.3	Class: RI (BV)	**1999**-01 **Cantiere Navale di Pesaro SpA (CNP) — Pesaro** Yd No: 82 Loa 95.10 (BB) Br ex 15.50 Dght 6.500 Lbp 86.00 Br md 15.50 Dpth 8.00 Welded, 1 dk	**(A11B2TG) LPG Tanker** Double Sides Entire Compartment Length Liq (Gas): 3,927 2 x Gas Tank (s); 2 independent (9% Ni.stl) dcy horizontal 2 Cargo Pump (s): 2x250m³/hr Manifold: Bow/CM: 54m	**1 oil engine** geared to sc. shaft driving 1 CP propeller Total Power: 2,207kW (3,001hp) 12.0kn Alpha 9L28/32 1 x 4 Stroke 9 Cy. 280 x 320 2207kW (3001bhp) MAN B&W Diesel A/S-Denmark AuxGen: 3 x 360kW 440/220V 60Hz a.c Thrusters: 1 Tunnel thruster (f) Fuel: 75.7 (d.f.) 197.6 (r.f.)

9346940 *ICKM* -
SYN ZUBE
-
Synergas Srl
-
Naples *Italy*
MMSI: 247235100
3,827 1,150 4,027 T/cm 12.2
Class: BV RI
2008-11 Cantiere Navale di Pesaro SpA (CNP) — Pesaro Yd No: 123
Loa 95.47 (BB) Br ex - Dght 6.500
Lbp 86.35 Br md 15.50 Dpth 8.00
Welded, 1 dk
(A11B2TG) LPG Tanker
Double Bottom Entire Compartment Length
Liq (Gas): 3,927
3 x Gas Tank (s); 2 independent (C.mn.stl) cyl horizontal, ER
4 Cargo Pump (s): 4x250m³/hr
Manifold: Bow/CM: 54m
1 oil engine geared to sc. shaft driving 1 CP propeller
Total Power: 2,380kW (3,236hp) 14.3kn
MAN-B&W 7L27/38
1 x 4 Stroke 7 Cy. 270 x 380 2380kW (3236bhp)
MAN Diesel A/S-Denmark
AuxGen: 3 x 375kW 60Hz a.c
Thrusters: 1 Tunnel thruster (f)
Fuel: 90.0 (d.f.) 300.0 (r.f.)

8801515 *JVUT4* -
SYNERGY
ex Satsuki Maru *-1998*
Yong An Shipping SA
Yuantai Fuel Trading Pte Ltd
Ulaanbaatar *Mongolia*
MMSI: 457542000
Official number: 31001287
2,798 1,243 4,738 T/cm 11.5
Class: (NK)
1987-10 Iwagi Zosen Co Ltd — Kamijima EH Yd No: 118
Loa 91.93 Br ex - Dght 6.513
Lbp 85.60 Br md 16.01 Dpth 7.83
Welded, 1 dk
(A13B2TP) Products Tanker
Liq: 4,459; Liq (Oil): 4,550
2 Cargo Pump (s)
1 oil engine driving 1 FP propeller
Total Power: 2,427kW (3,300hp)
Hanshin 6EL40
1 x 4 Stroke 6 Cy. 400 x 800 2427kW (3300bhp)
The Hanshin Diesel Works Ltd-Japan
AuxGen: 3 x 213kW
Fuel: 299.0

8743878 *MJLZ4* -
SYNERGY
-
Oceanview Marine Ltd
Dominion Marine Corporate Services Ltd
Douglas *Isle of Man (British)*
MMSI: 235027917
Official number: 737519
144 43 -
Class: RN (Class contemplated)
2003-01 Falcon Yacht Service — Viareggio Yd No: 100/127
Loa 29.80 Br ex - Dght 2.330
Lbp 26.47 Br md 6.45 Dpth 3.10
Bonded, 1 dk
(X11A2YP) Yacht
Hull Material: Reinforced Plastic
2 oil engines reduction geared to sc. shafts driving 2 Propellers
Total Power: 2,982kW (4,054hp) 20.0kn
M.T.U. 12V2000M91
2 x Vee 4 Stroke 12 Cy. 130 x 150 each-1491kW (2027bhp)
MTU Friedrichshafen GmbH-Friedrichshafen
Fuel: 100.0 (d.f.)

9513763 *A8UO5* -
SYNERGY QUEEN
ex Sanko Queen *-2012*
Southern Route Maritime SA
Nissen Kaiun Co Ltd (Nissen Kaiun KK)
SatCom: Inmarsat C 463706828
Monrovia *Liberia*
MMSI: 636014529
Official number: 14529
160,102 103,297 309,741 T/cm 183.7
Class: AB
2010-01 Imabari Shipbuilding Co Ltd — Saijo EH (Saijo Shipyard) Yd No: 8065
Loa 333.00 (BB) Br ex 60.04 Dght 21.260
Lbp 324.00 Br md 60.00 Dpth 29.00
Welded, 1 dk
(A13A2TV) Crude Oil Tanker
Double Hull (13F)
Liq: 333,472; Liq (Oil): 333,472
Compartments: 5 Ta, 10 Wing Ta, 2 Wing Slop Ta, ER
3 Cargo Pump (s): 3x5500m³/hr
Manifold: Bow/CM: 164.1m
1 oil engine driving 1 FP propeller
Total Power: 31,040kW (42,202hp) 15.5kn
MAN-B&W 8S80MC-C
1 x 2 Stroke 8 Cy. 800 x 3200 31040kW (42202bhp)
AuxGen: 3 x a.c
Fuel: 480.0 (d.f.) 7430.0 (r.f.)

9430741 *9V6933* -
SYNERGY SUCCESS
-
Agility Project Logistics Pte Ltd
-
Singapore *Singapore*
MMSI: 563008840
Official number: 392171
142 43 259
Class: GL
2007-01 Yong Choo Kui Shipyard Sdn Bhd — Sibu Yd No: T32
Loa 23.50 Br ex - Dght 2.720
Lbp 21.07 Br md 7.32 Dpth 3.20
Welded, 1 dk
(B32A2ST) Tug
2 oil engines reduction geared to sc. shafts driving 2 FP propellers
Total Power: 894kW (1,216hp)
Cummins KTA-19-M3
2 x 4 Stroke 6 Cy. 159 x 159 each-447kW (608bhp)
Cummins Engine Co Inc-USA

9078165 *JL6166* -
SYOKEI
ex Kisaragi Maru No. 1 *-2012*
ex Kyokusho Maru *-2005*
ex Ai Maru No. 5 *-2004*
Shoho Kaiun KK
-
Osakikamijima, Hiroshima *Japan*
MMSI: 431500077
Official number: 132999
698 - 1,977
Class: NK
1993-05 Higaki Zosen K.K. — Imabari Yd No: 430
Loa 69.92 Br ex 12.02 Dght 4.875
Lbp 66.10 Br md 12.00 Dpth 5.35
Welded, 1 dk
(A13B2TP) Products Tanker
Liq: 2,167; Liq (Oil): 2,167
Compartments: 10 Ta, ER
1 oil engine reverse geared to sc. shaft driving 1 FP propeller
Total Power: 1,456kW (1,980hp)
B&W 4S26MC
1 x 2 Stroke 4 Cy. 260 x 980 1456kW (1980bhp)
Makita Corp-Japan
Thrusters: 1 Thwart. CP thruster (f)
Fuel: 80.0 (d.f.)

8819031 - -
SYONAN
ex Neptank VII *-2011*
Faber Marine Pte Ltd
Progressive Power Co Pte Ltd
1,937 1,389 3,863
Class: BV
1988-12 Greenbay Marine Pte Ltd — Singapore Yd No: 65
Loa 85.02 Br ex - Dght 4.901
Lbp 81.00 Br md 15.02 Dpth 6.23
Welded, 1 dk
(A13B2TP) Products Tanker
Liq: 4,200; Liq (Oil): 4,200
Compartments: 10 Wing Ta, ER
2 Cargo Pump (s): 2x650m³/hr
2 oil engines driving 2 FP propellers
Total Power: 530kW (720hp) 9.0kn
Mitsubishi S6R2-MTK
2 x 4 Stroke 6 Cy. 170 x 220 each-265kW (360bhp)
Mitsubishi Heavy Industries Ltd-Japan
AuxGen: 2 x 80kW 415V 50Hz a.c
Thrusters: 1 Thwart. FP thruster (f)

9594107 *JD3068* -
SYORYO MARU NO. 7
-
YK Shoryo Suisan
-
Kesennuma, Miyagi *Japan*
Official number: 141246
145 - 156
2010-06 Kidoura Shipyard Co Ltd — Kesennuma MG Yd No: 622
Loa 38.86 Br ex 7.10 Dght 2.750
Lbp 33.76 Br md 6.60 Dpth 3.06
Welded, 1 dk
(B11B2FV) Fishing Vessel
Bale: 121
1 oil engine driving 1 Propeller
Total Power: 882kW (1,199hp)
Niigata 6M26AFTE
1 x 4 Stroke 6 Cy. 260 x 460 882kW (1199bhp)
Niigata Engineering Co Ltd-Japan

9606352 *JD3210* -
SYORYU
-
Isewan Bosai KK
-
Toba, Mie *Japan*
Official number: 141460
118 - -
Class: NK
2011-05 Kanagawa Zosen — Kobe Yd No: 626
Loa 38.00 Br ex - Dght 3.300
Lbp 34.90 Br md 6.20 Dpth 3.30
Welded, 1 dk
(B32A2ST) Tug
2 oil engines reduction geared to sc. shafts driving 2 Propellers
Total Power: 2,440kW (3,318hp)
Yanmar 12AYM-WGT
2 x Vee 4 Stroke 12 Cy. 155 x 180 each-1220kW (1659bhp)
Yanmar Diesel Engine Co Ltd-Japan
AuxGen: 1 x 100kW a.c
Fuel: 13.0

9657985 - -
SYORYU
-
Nippon Shio Kaiso Co Ltd
-
Imabari, Ehime *Japan*
299 - 1,000
2012-07 Namikata Shipbuilding Co Ltd — Imabari EH Yd No: 237
Loa 62.78 Br ex - Dght 3.678
Lbp - Br md 10.30 Dpth -
Welded, 1 dk
(A31A2GX) General Cargo Ship
Double Hull
1 oil engine reduction geared to sc. shaft driving 1 Propeller
Total Power: 1,029kW (1,399hp) 9.5kn
Akasaka K28BR
1 x 4 Stroke 6 Cy. 280 x 480 1029kW (1399bhp)
Akasaka Tekkosho KK (Akasaka DieselLtd)-Japan

9087908 *T3CC2* -
SYOTA MARU
ex Terso *-2010* *ex* Musashi 3 *-2006*
ex Musashi *-2000*
Koo's Shipping Co SA
-
Tarawa *Kiribati*
MMSI: 529485000
Official number: K-15941219
4,491 2,125 5,103 T/cm 15.0
Class: NK
1994-06 Kyokuyo Shipyard Corp — Shimonoseki YC Yd No: 388
Loa 120.75 (BB) Br ex 16.63 Dght 6.914
Lbp 112.90 Br md 16.60 Dpth 10.00
Welded
(A34A2GR) Refrigerated Cargo Ship
Bale: 5,738; Ins: 5,738
TEU 1 incl 1 ref C
Compartments: 4 Ho, ER
4 Ha: 4 (4.7 x 4.4)ER
Derricks: 8x5t
1 oil engine driving 1 FP propeller
Total Power: 2,994kW (4,071hp) 14.5kn
B&W 6L35MC
1 x 2 Stroke 6 Cy. 350 x 1050 2994kW (4071bhp)
Makita Corp-Japan
Thrusters: 1 Thwart. CP thruster (f)
Fuel: 1240.0 (r.f.)

9594066 *JD3188* -
SYOUHAKU MARU
-
Reitaku Kaiun Co Ltd (Reitaku Kaiun KK)
-
Imabari, Ehime *Japan*
Official number: 141434
136 - 369
2011-04 Hakata Zosen K.K. — Imabari Yd No: 728
Loa 37.50 Br ex - Dght 3.008
Lbp 35.00 Br md 7.00 Dpth 3.25
Welded, 1 dk
(A13B2TP) Products Tanker
Double Hull
1 oil engine reduction geared to sc. shafts driving 1 Propeller
Total Power: 736kW (1,001hp) 8.0kn
Yanmar 6RY17P-GV
1 x 4 Stroke 6 Cy. 165 x 219 736kW (1001bhp)
Yanmar Diesel Engine Co Ltd-Japan
Thrusters: 1 Thwart. FP thruster (f)

9210165 - -
SYPHAX
-
Government of The Republic of Tunisia (Office des Ports Nationaux Tunisiens)
-
Sfax *Tunisia*
Official number: SF2323
406 121 -
Class: BV
1999-02 Alstom Leroux Naval SA — St-Malo Yd No: 627
Loa 31.00 Br ex - Dght 4.500
Lbp 29.60 Br md 11.00 Dpth 4.50
Welded, 1 dk
(B32A2ST) Tug
Passengers: berths: 12
2 oil engines gearing integral to driving 2 Voith-Schneider propellers
Total Power: 2,480kW (3,372hp) 12.0kn
Wartsila 8L20
2 x 4 Stroke 8 Cy. 200 x 280 each-1240kW (1686bhp)
Wartsila NSD Finland Oy-Finland
AuxGen: 2 x 177kW 380V 50Hz a.c

9150315 *LAJA7* -
SYPRESS
ex Jo Sypress *-2010*
Zippora Pte Ltd
Jo Tankers A/S
Bergen *Norway (NIS)*
MMSI: 257432000
22,626 11,688 36,677 T/cm 49.5
Class: NV (LR)
✠ Classed LR until 28/3/00
1998-04 Kvaerner Govan Ltd — Glasgow Yd No: 314
Loa 182.30 (BB) Br ex 32.05 Dght 10.731
Lbp 176.10 Br md 32.00 Dpth 14.00
Welded, 1 dk
(A12B2TR) Chemical/Products Tanker
Double Hull (13F)
Liq: 38,475; Liq (Oil): 38,475
Cargo Heating Coils
Compartments: 7 Wing Ta, 17 Wing Ta (s.stl), 13 Ta (s.stl), 2 Wing Slop Ta (s.stl), ER (s.stl)
37 Cargo Pump (s): 15x300m³/hr, 16x200m³/hr, 6x600m³/hr
Manifold: Bow/CM: 98.4m
1 oil engine driving 1 FP propeller
Total Power: 10,440kW (14,194hp) 15.5kn
B&W 6L60MC
1 x 2 Stroke 6 Cy. 600 x 1944 10440kW (14194bhp)
Kawasaki Heavy Industries Ltd-Japan
AuxGen: 1 x 1200kW 440V 60Hz a.c, 2 x 950kW 440V 60Hz a.c
Thrusters: 1 Thwart. CP thruster (f)
Fuel: 216.0 (d.f.) (Heating Coils) 2266.0 (r.f.) 46.0pd

IMO / Call sign	Name / Owner / Flag	Tonnage	Class	Builder / Dimensions	Type / Cargo	Machinery
9436941 9HA3455 -	**SYRA** *ex Stavanger Bell -2013* **Vari Shipping Ltd** Eastern Mediterranean Maritime Ltd *Valletta* *Malta* MMSI: 229619000 Official number: 9436941	**55,898** 29,810 105,309 T/cm 88.9	Class: LR **✠100A1** SS 03/2010 Double Hull oil tanker ESP **ShipRight** (SDA, FDA, CM) *IWS LI DSPM4 **✠LMC** **UMS IGS** Eq.Ltr: Rt; Cable: 687.5/84.0 U3 (a)	**2010-03 Sumitomo Heavy Industries Marine & Engineering Co., Ltd. — Yokosuka** Yd No: 1357 Loa 228.60 (BB) Br ex 42.03 Dght 14.808 Lbp 217.80 Br md 42.00 Dpth 21.50 Welded, 1 dk	**(A13A2TV) Crude Oil Tanker** Double Hull (13F) Liq: 98,688; Liq (Oil): 98,688 Cargo Heating Coils Compartments: 10 Wing Ta, 2 Wing Slop Ta, ER 3 Cargo Pump (s): 3x2500m^3/hr Manifold: Bow/CM: 116.6m	**1 oil engine** driving 1 FP propeller Total Power: 12,350kW (16,791hp) 14.8kn MAN-B&W 6S60MC-C 1 x 2 Stroke 6 Cy. 600 x 2400 12350kW (16791bhp) Mitsui Engineering & Shipbuilding CLtd-Japan AuxGen: 3 x 800kW 450V 60Hz a.c Boilers: e (ex.g.) 21.9kgf/cm^2 (21.5bar), AuxB (o.f.) 18.0kgf/cm^2 (17.7bar) Fuel: 200.0 (d.f.) 2300.0 (r.f.)
8651013 EI7600 DA41	**SYRACUSE** **Ivan Wilde** - *Drogheda* *Irish Republic* Official number: 403835	**119** 35 -		**1987 Ch. Pierre Glehen — Guilvinec** Loa 22.05 Br ex - Dght - Lbp - Br md - Dpth - Bonded, 1 dk	**(B11A2FS) Stern Trawler** Hull Material: Reinforced Plastic	**1 oil engine** driving 1 Propeller Total Power: 288kW (392hp)
9317810 5BWM3 -	**SYRIOTISSA** *ex Brilliant Trader -2013* **Syriotissa Maritime Co Ltd** Third Millenium Shipping Ltd *Limassol* *Cyprus* MMSI: 212168000	**47,051** 27,005 87,144 T/cm 79.7	Class: LR (NK) **100A1** SS 04/2011 bulk carrier BC-A Nos. 2, 4 & 6 holds may be empty ESP ESN *IWS LI **LMC** **UMS**	**2006-04 IHI Marine United Inc — Yokohama KN** Yd No: 3210 Loa 229.00 (BB) Br ex - Dght 14.135 Lbp 219.90 Br md 36.50 Dpth 19.90 Welded, 1 dk	**(A21A2BC) Bulk Carrier** Double Hull Grain: 98,961; Bale: 94,844 Compartments: 7 Ho, ER 7 Ha: (14.3 x 16.8)5 (17.1 x 16.8)ER (16.2 x 15.1)	**1 oil engine** driving 4 gen. driving 1 FP propeller Total Power: 10,300kW (14,004hp) 14.5kn Sulzer 6RTA58T 1 x 2 Stroke 6 Cy. 580 x 2416 10300kW (14004bhp) Diesel United Ltd.-Aioi Fuel: 3020.0
8863599 SPS2163 -	**SYRIUSZ** **Urzad Morski w Szczecinie (Szczecin Marine Board)** - *Szczecin* *Poland* MMSI: 261011190 Official number: 680114	*113* 34 -	Class: PR	**1992-04 Tczewska Stocznia Rzeczna — Tczew** Yd No: 287 Loa 23.16 Br ex - Dght - Lbp 21.64 Br md 6.80 Dpth 2.62 Welded, 1 dk	**(B34Q2QB) Buoy Tender**	**1 oil engine** reduction geared to sc. shaft driving 1 FP propeller Total Power: 309kW (420hp) Wola WOLA-H12 1 x Vee 4 Stroke 12 Cy. 135 x 155 309kW (420bhp) Zaklady Mechaniczne 'PZL Wola' SA-Poland AuxGen: 1 x 28kW 400V a.c
9371294 A8PW7 -	**SYROS** **Syros I Maritime Inc** Aegean Bunkering Services Inc *Monrovia* *Liberia* MMSI: 636013850 Official number: 13850	**3,220** 1,327 4,596	Class: AB	**2008-04 Fujian Southeast Shipyard — Fuzhou FJ** Yd No: 3500-6 Loa 90.22 (BB) Br ex - Dght 6.010 Lbp 85.00 Br md 15.60 Dpth 7.80 Welded, 1 dk	**(A13B2TP) Products Tanker** Double Hull (13F) Liq: 4,346; Liq (Oil): 4,346 3 Cargo Pump (s): 2x500m^3/hr, 1x300m^3/hr	**1 oil engine** reduction geared to sc. shaft driving 1 FP propeller Total Power: 2,480kW (3,372hp) Wartsila 8L26 1 x 4 Stroke 8 Cy. 260 x 320 2480kW (3372bhp) Wartsila Finland Oy-Finland AuxGen: 3 x 250kW a.c Thrusters: 1 Tunnel thruster (f) Fuel: 62.0 (d.f.) 298.0 (r.f.)
8707771 9HGQ9 -	**SYROS WIND** *ex Dan Supporter -2014 ex Mosa -2007* *ex Triton Loga -2006 ex Jan Becker -1998* **Syros Holdings Inc** Thetis Shipholding SA *Valletta* *Malta* MMSI: 256959000 Official number: 8707771	**2,749** 1,110 3,173	Class: GL	**1987-10 J.J. Sietas KG Schiffswerft GmbH & Co. — Hamburg** Yd No: 966 Loa 94.52 (BB) Br ex 16.16 Dght 4.980 Lbp 86.92 Br md 15.91 Dpth 7.55 Welded, 2 dks	**(A31A2GX) General Cargo Ship** Grain: 4,466; Bale: 4,269 TEU 262 C.Ho 82/20' (40') C.Dk 180/20' (40') incl. 40 ref C. Compartments: 1 Ho, ER 1 Ha: (57.6 x 12.8)ER	**1 oil engine** with flexible couplings & sr gearedto sc. shaft driving 1 CP propeller Total Power: 995kW (1,353hp) 14.0kn Wartsila 6R32 1 x 4 Stroke 6 Cy. 320 x 350 995kW (1353bhp) Wartsila Diesel Oy-Finland AuxGen: 1 x 180kW 220/380V 50Hz a.c, 1 x 110kW 220/380V 50Hz a.c, 1 x 21kW 220/380V 50Hz a.c
7110543 3VHJ -	**SYRTIS** **Government of The Republic of Tunisia (Office des Ports Nationaux Tunisiens)** - *Tunis* *Tunisia*	*187* - -	Class: (BV) (NV)	**1970 "Petrozavod" — Leningrad** Loa - Br ex 8.31 Dght 3.074 Lbp 28.20 Br md 7.95 Dpth 4.35 Welded, 1 dk	**(B32A2ST) Tug**	**2 oil engines** driving 2 CP propellers Total Power: 1,200kW (1,632hp) 10.0kn Russkiy 6DR30/50 2 x 2 Stroke 6 Cy. 300 x 500 each-600kW (816bhp) Mashinostroitelnyy Zavod"Russkiy-Dizel"-Leningrad AuxGen: 2 x 50kW 220V 50Hz a.c Fuel: 36.5 (d.f.)
7715393 YDPA -	**SYSTEMINDO PERDANA** *ex JTS Sentosa -2006 ex Melaka -2005* *ex Hub Melaka -1996* *ex Hyundai Malacca -1996* *ex Norasia Malacca -1994 ex Oxford -1993* *ex Bakkafoss -1987 ex City of Oxford -1983* **PT Systemindo Container Perdana** - *Batam* *Indonesia*	**3,981** 2,001 4,500	Class: (LR) (KI) ✠ Classed LR until 31/1/03	**1981-05 Appledore Shipbuilders Ltd — Bideford** Yd No: A.S.125 Loa 104.15 (BB) Br ex 16.77 Dght 5.950 Lbp 96.31 Br md 16.50 Dpth 8.11 Welded, 1 dk	**(A33A2CC) Container Ship (Fully Cellular)** Double Sides Entire Compartment Length Grain: 6,958; Bale: 6,720 TEU 300 C Ho 132 TEU C Dk 168 TEU incl 30 ref C. Compartments: 2 Ho, ER 2 Ha: (26.0 x 7.9)Tappered (39.2 x 13.0)ER	**1 oil engine** driving 1 FP propeller Total Power: 3,678kW (5,001hp) 12.0kn Doxford 58JS3 1 x 2 Stroke 3 Cy. 580 x 1220 3678kW (5001bhp) Doxford Engines Ltd.-Sunderland AuxGen: 3 x 350kW 440V 60Hz a.c Boilers: AuxB (Comp) 7.0kgf/cm^2 (6.9bar) Thrusters: 1 Thwart. FP thruster (f) Fuel: 60.5 (d.f.) 276.0 (r.f.) 16.5pd
8405775 PMBC -	**SYSTEMINDO PERMATA** *ex Dongjin Hakata -2007* *ex Tenreisan Maru -1998* **PT Systemindo Container Perdana** - *Tanjung Priok* *Indonesia* MMSI: 525016153	**4,288** 1,530 3,298	Class: KI (KR) (NK)	**1984-08 Imai Shipbuilding Co Ltd — Kochi KC** Yd No: 534 Loa 105.70 (BB) Br ex - Dght 5.829 Lbp 97.01 Br md 17.51 Dpth 8.72 Welded, 1 dk	**(A33A2CC) Container Ship (Fully Cellular)** TEU 180 C. 180/20' Compartments: 4 Ho, ER 4 Ha: (12.7 x 10.5)3 (12.7 x 13.2)ER	**1 oil engine** driving 1 CP propeller Total Power: 6,355kW (8,640hp) 17.5kn B&W 6L50MCE 1 x 2 Stroke 6 Cy. 500 x 1620 6355kW (8640bhp) Mitsui Engineering & Shipbuilding CLtd-Japan AuxGen: 3 x 360kW a.c Thrusters: 1 Thwart. CP thruster (f)
9197600 9V7992 -	**SYUKUR** **Cheviot Marine Services Pte Ltd** GL Pilot & Tug Services Pte Ltd *Singapore* *Singapore* Official number: 395141	**169** 50 123	Class: BV (LR) ✠ Classed LR until 9/12/09	**1998-12 Muhibbah Marine Engineering Sdn Bhd — Port Klang** Yd No: 5025 Loa 26.65 Br ex 7.62 Dght 3.196 Lbp 22.87 Br md 7.60 Dpth 3.60 Welded, 1 dk	**(B32A2ST) Tug**	**2 oil engines** reduction geared to sc. shafts driving 2 Z propellers Total Power: 930kW (1,264hp) 12.0kn Mitsubishi S6R2-MPTK 2 x 4 Stroke 6 Cy. 170 x 220 each-465kW (632bhp) Mitsubishi Heavy Industries Ltd-Japan AuxGen: 2 x 99kW 415V 50Hz a.c
9027350 - -	**SYUKUR 01** **PT Syukur Selamat Rima** - *Samarinda* *Indonesia*	**210** 63 -	Class: (KI)	**1998-04 CV Muji Rahayu — Tenggarong** L reg 29.50 Br ex - Dght - Lbp 26.75 Br md 8.50 Dpth 3.60 Welded, 1 dk	**(B32A2ST) Tug**	**2 oil engines** geared to sc. shafts driving 2 Propellers Total Power: 1,516kW (2,062hp) 12.0kn Yanmar 12LAAM-UTE 2 x Vee 4 Stroke 12 Cy. 148 x 165 each-758kW (1031bhp) (made 1996) Yanmar Diesel Engine Co Ltd-Japan
8742159 YB6215 -	**SYUKUR 05** **PT Matano Nusantara Line** - *Samarinda* *Indonesia*	**163** 45 -	Class: KI	**2002 CV Muji Rahayu — Tenggarong** Loa 28.45 Br ex - Dght - Lbp 27.02 Br md 8.00 Dpth 3.20 Welded, 1 dk	**(B32A2ST) Tug**	**2 oil engines** reduction geared to sc. shafts driving 2 Propellers Total Power: 1,686kW (2,292hp) Yanmar 12LAA-UTE1 2 x Vee 4 Stroke 12 Cy. 148 x 165 each-843kW (1146bhp) Yanmar Diesel Engine Co Ltd-Japan AuxGen: 2 x 81kW 440V a.c
9096246 YD6500 -	**SYUKUR 06** **PT Gema Bahari** - *Samarinda* *Indonesia*	**107** 64 -	Class: KI	**2002-12 CV Muji Rahayu — Tenggarong** Loa 23.50 Br ex - Dght - Lbp 21.80 Br md 6.50 Dpth 2.75 Welded, 1 dk	**(B32A2ST) Tug**	**2 oil engines** geared to sc. shaft driving 1 Propeller Total Power: 780kW (1,060hp) Yanmar 6LAAM-UTE 2 x 4 Stroke 6 Cy. 148 x 165 each-390kW (530bhp) Yanmar Diesel Engine Co Ltd-Japan
8658554 YD6580 -	**SYUKUR 10** **PT Daya Makmur Ocean** - *Samarinda* *Indonesia*	**122** 73 -	Class: KI	**2004-01 CV Muji Rahayu — Tenggarong** Loa 24.70 Br ex - Dght 1.990 Lbp 23.28 Br md 6.50 Dpth 2.60 Welded, 1 dk	**(B32A2ST) Tug**	**2 oil engines** reduction geared to sc. shafts driving 2 FP propellers AuxGen: 1 x 70kW 380V a.c, 1 x 88kW 380V a.c
8654704 YDA6081 -	**SYUKUR 12** **PT Bunga Teratai** - *Samarinda* *Indonesia*	**236** 71 -	Class: KI	**2009-08 PT Syukur Bersaudara — Samarinda** Loa 31.50 Br ex - Dght 2.750 Lbp 28.22 Br md 8.50 Dpth 3.60 Welded, 1 dk	**(B32A2ST) Tug**	**2 oil engines** reduction geared to sc. shafts driving 2 FP propellers Total Power: 1,686kW (2,292hp) Yanmar 12LAA-UTE1 2 x Vee 4 Stroke 12 Cy. 148 x 165 each-843kW (1146bhp) Yanmar Diesel Engine Co Ltd-Japan AuxGen: 2 x 88kW 380V a.c

IMO / Call sign / Flag	Name / Owner / Port	GT / NT / DWT	Class	Builder / Dimensions	Type	Machinery
9029384 - -	**SYUKUR 14** **Thomas Indriyatmo** *Samarinda* *Indonesia*	**212** 64 -	Class: KI	**2004**-07 **CV Muji Rahayu — Tenggarong** Loa - Br ex - Dght - Lbp 27.84 Br md 8.50 Dpth 2.50 Welded, 1 dk	**(B32A2ST) Tug**	**2 oil engines** driving 2 Propellers Total Power: 1,472kW (2,002hp) Yanmar 12LAAM-UTE 2 x Vee 4 Stroke 12 Cy. 148 x 165 each-736kW (1001bhp) Yanmar Diesel Engine Co Ltd-Japan AuxGen: 2 x 82kW 380/220V a.c
8743012 - -	**SYUKUR 15** **PT Bunga Teratai** - *Samarinda* *Indonesia*	**207** 63 -	Class: KI	**2005 PT Syukur Bersaudara — Samarinda** Loa 30.30 Br ex - Dght 2.900 Lbp 28.51 Br md 8.50 Dpth 3.60 Welded, 1 dk	**(B32A2ST) Tug**	**2 oil engines** reduction geared to sc. shafts driving 2 Propellers Total Power: 1,220kW (1,658hp) Yanmar 6AYM-ETE 2 x 4 Stroke 6 Cy. 155 x 180 each-610kW (829bhp) Yanmar Diesel Engine Co Ltd-Japan AuxGen: 2 x 88kW 380/220V a.c
9093476 *YD6806* -	**SYUKUR 16** **PT Citra Buana Bahari** - *Samarinda* *Indonesia*	**207** 63 -	Class: KI	**2005**-12 **CV Muji Rahayu — Tenggarong** Loa 30.30 Br ex - Dght - Lbp 26.50 Br md 8.50 Dpth 3.60 Welded, 1 dk	**(B32A2ST) Tug**	**2 oil engines** geared to sc. shafts driving 2 Propellers Total Power: 1,220kW (1,658hp) Yanmar 6AYM-ETE 2 x 4 Stroke 6 Cy. 155 x 180 each-610kW (829bhp) Yanmar Diesel Engine Co Ltd-Japan
8738433 *YDA6015* -	**SYUKUR 21** **Yanuar Perkasa Samudera CV** - *Samarinda* *Indonesia*	**187** 57 -	Class: KI	**2007**-09 **PT Syukur Bersaudara — Samarinda** Loa 29.50 Br ex - Dght 2.490 Lbp 27.69 Br md 8.10 Dpth 3.40 Welded, 1 dk	**(B32A2ST) Tug**	**2 oil engines** driving 2 Propellers Total Power: 1,472kW (2,002hp) Yanmar 6RY17P-GV 2 x 4 Stroke 6 Cy. 165 x 219 each-736kW (1001bhp) Yanmar Diesel Engine Co Ltd-Japan
8653798 - -	**SYUKUR 22** **PT Syukur Selamat Rima** - *Samarinda* *Indonesia*	**187** 62 -	Class: KI	**2007**-12 **PT Syukur Bersaudara — Samarinda** Loa - Br ex - Dght 2.740 Lbp 27.64 Br md 8.10 Dpth 3.60 Welded, 1 dk	**(B32A2ST) Tug**	**2 oil engines** reduction geared to sc. shafts driving 2 Propellers
8656788 - -	**SYUKUR 23** **PT Bunga Teratai** - *Samarinda* *Indonesia*	**196** 59 -	Class: KI	**2009**-06 **PT Syukur Bersaudara — Samarinda** Loa - Br ex - Dght 2.740 Lbp 27.64 Br md 8.10 Dpth 3.60 Welded, 1 dk	**(B32A2ST) Tug**	**2 oil engines** reduction geared to sc. shafts driving 2 FP propellers Total Power: 1,220kW (1,658hp) Yanmar 6AYM-ETE 2 x 4 Stroke 6 Cy. 155 x 180 each-610kW (829bhp) Yanmar Diesel Engine Co Ltd-Japan AuxGen: 2 x 88kW 380V a.c
8652495 - -	**SYUKUR 24** **PT Bunga Teratai** - *Samarinda* *Indonesia*	**203** 61 -	Class: KI	**2010**-02 **PT Syukur Bersaudara — Samarinda** Loa - Br ex - Dght - Lbp 27.55 Br md 8.10 Dpth 3.60 Welded, 1 dk	**(B32A2ST) Tug**	**2 oil engines** reduction geared to sc. shafts driving 2 Propellers
8652744 - -	**SYUKUR 25** **H Jufri Umar** - *Samarinda* *Indonesia*	**172** 52 -	Class: KI	**2006**-12 **PT Syukur Bersaudara — Samarinda** Loa 29.00 Br ex - Dght - Lbp 27.43 Br md 8.00 Dpth 3.60 Welded, 1 dk	**(B32A2ST) Tug**	**2 oil engines** reduction geared to sc. shafts driving 2 Propellers AuxGen: 2 x 88kW 380/220V a.c
8652500 - -	**SYUKUR 26** **PT Bunga Teratai** - *Samarinda* *Indonesia*	**192** 58 -	Class: KI	**2010**-05 **PT Syukur Bersaudara — Samarinda** Loa - Br ex - Dght 2.740 Lbp 27.64 Br md 8.10 Dpth 3.60 Welded, 1 dk	**(B32A2ST) Tug**	**2 oil engines** reduction geared to sc. shafts driving 2 Propellers Total Power: 1,220kW (1,658hp) Yanmar 6AYM-ETE 2 x 4 Stroke 6 Cy. 155 x 180 each-610kW (829bhp) Yanmar Diesel Engine Co Ltd-Japan AuxGen: 2 x 88kW 380V a.c
9049190 *YD.6729* -	**SYUKUR 27** **Yuliansyah Dan Muhammad Ridwan** - *Samarinda* *Indonesia*	**148** 88 -	Class: KI	**2004**-09 **CV Rio Utama Samarinda — Samarinda** Loa - Br ex - Dght 2.390 Lbp 25.00 Br md 7.00 Dpth 3.00 Welded, 1 dk	**(B32A2ST) Tug**	**2 oil engines** geared to sc. shafts driving 2 Propellers Total Power: 912kW (1,240hp) 8.0kn Yanmar 6LAH-STE3 2 x 4 Stroke 6 Cy. 150 x 165 each-456kW (620bhp) (made 2004) Yanmar Diesel Engine Co Ltd-Japan AuxGen: 2 x 90kW 220/130V a.c
8737180 *YD6497* -	**SYUKUR 28** **Yanuar Perkasa Samudera CV** - *Samarinda* *Indonesia*	**163** 49 -	Class: KI	**2002**-12 **CV Muji Rahayu — Tenggarong** Loa 28.50 Br ex - Dght 2.490 Lbp 26.00 Br md 8.00 Dpth 3.20 Welded, 1 dk	**(B32A2ST) Tug**	**2 oil engines** driving 2 Propellers Total Power: 1,472kW (2,002hp) Yanmar 12LAAM-UTE 2 x Vee 4 Stroke 12 Cy. 148 x 165 each-736kW (1001bhp) Yanmar Diesel Engine Co Ltd-Japan
8651544 - -	**SYUKUR 30** **PT Bunga Teratai** - *Samarinda* *Indonesia*	**187** 57 -	Class: KI	**2010**-07 **PT Syukur Bersaudara — Samarinda** Loa 27.00 Br ex - Dght 2.690 Lbp 25.63 Br md 7.75 Dpth 3.60 Welded, 1 dk	**(B32A2ST) Tug**	**2 oil engines** reduction geared to sc. shafts driving 2 Propellers
8649515 - -	**SYUKUR 32** **PT Bunga Teratai** - *Samarinda* *Indonesia*	**263** 79 -	Class: KI	**2010**-07 **PT Syukur Bersaudara — Samarinda** Loa 30.50 Br ex - Dght 2.710 Lbp 28.99 Br md 8.50 Dpth 3.60 Welded, 1 dk	**(B32A2ST) Tug**	**2 oil engines** reduction geared to sc. shafts driving 2 Propellers
8651661 - -	**SYUKUR 33** **PT Bunga Teratai** - *Samarinda* *Indonesia*	**234** 71 -	Class: KI	**2010**-05 **PT Syukur Bersaudara — Samarinda** Loa - Br ex - Dght 2.710 Lbp 28.99 Br md 8.50 Dpth 3.60 Welded, 1 dk	**(B32A2ST) Tug**	**2 oil engines** reduction geared to sc. shafts driving 2 Propellers AuxGen: 2 x 88kW 380V a.c
8659132 - -	**SYUKUR 35** **PT Bunga Teratai** - *Samarinda* *Indonesia*	**268** 81 -	Class: KI	**2011**-07 **PT Syukur Bersaudara — Samarinda** Loa 31.50 Br ex - Dght 2.850 Lbp 29.95 Br md 8.60 Dpth 3.80 Welded, 1 dk	**(B32A2ST) Tug**	**2 oil engines** reduction geared to sc. shafts driving 2 FP propellers Total Power: 1,518kW (2,064hp) Mitsubishi S6R2-MTK3L 2 x 4 Stroke 6 Cy. 170 x 220 each-759kW (1032bhp) Mitsubishi Heavy Industries Ltd-Japan AuxGen: 1 x 88kW 400V a.c
8734085 *YD6642* -	**SYUKUR 513** **H Jufri Umar** - *Samarinda* *Indonesia*	**163** 49 -	Class: KI	**2004 CV Muji Rahayu — Tenggarong** Loa 28.00 Br ex - Dght - Lbp 25.50 Br md 8.00 Dpth 3.25 Welded, 1 dk	**(B32A2ST) Tug**	**2 oil engines** driving 2 Propellers Total Power: 926kW (1,258hp) Yanmar 6LAAM-UTE 2 x 4 Stroke 6 Cy. 148 x 165 each-463kW (629bhp) Yanmar Diesel Engine Co Ltd-Japan
8703684 - -	**SYUWA NO. 12** *ex* Hokuto Maru *-2007* *ex* Taisei Maru *-1995* **Hongkong Syuwa Maritime Co Ltd** -	*222* - -		**1987**-05 **Sagami Zosen Tekko K.K. — Yokosuka** Yd No: 232A Loa 36.20 Br ex - Dght - Lbp 31.50 Br md 9.81 Dpth 4.37 Welded, 1 dk	**(B32A2ST) Tug**	**2 oil engines** geared integral to driving 2 Z propellers Total Power: 2,648kW (3,600hp) Niigata 6L28BXF 2 x 4 Stroke 6 Cy. 280 x 350 each-1324kW (1800bhp) Niigata Engineering Co Ltd-Japan AuxGen: 2 x 76kW 275V 60Hz a.c
8865511 - -	**SYUWA NO. 13** *ex* Tokai Maru *-2009* **Hongkong Syuwa Maritime Co Ltd**	*256* - -		**1992**-09 **Keihin Dock Co Ltd — Yokohama** Yd No: 229 Loa 31.90 Br ex - Dght 4.000 Lbp 30.85 Br md 9.60 Dpth 4.30 Welded, 1 dk	**(B32A2ST) Tug**	**2 oil engines** driving 2 FP propellers Total Power: 2,648kW (3,600hp) Yanmar 8Z280-EN 2 x 4 Stroke 8 Cy. 280 x 360 each-1324kW (1800bhp) Yanmar Diesel Engine Co Ltd-Japan
9011375 - -	**SYUWA NO. 15** *ex* Nagasaki Maru *-2009* **Hongkong Syuwa Maritime Co Ltd** -	*184* - -		**1990**-10 **Sagami Zosen Tekko K.K. — Yokosuka** Yd No: 245 Loa 33.20 Br ex 8.82 Dght 2.900 Lbp 29.00 Br md 8.80 Dpth 3.80 Welded, 1 dk	**(B32A2ST) Tug**	**2 oil engines** geared integral to driving 2 Z propellers Total Power: 2,280kW (3,100hp) 14.4kn Pielstick 6PA5 2 x 4 Stroke 6 Cy. 255 x 270 each-1140kW (1550bhp) Niigata Engineering Co Ltd-Japan AuxGen: 2 x 64kW 225V 60Hz a.c, 1 x 32kW 225V 60Hz a.c Fuel: 45.0 (d.f.) 11.1pd

IMO / Call sign	Name / Owner / Flag	Tonnage	Class	Builder / Dimensions	Type / Cargo	Machinery
9004504 *5BFC3* -	**SZAFIR** *ex* Socol 5 *-2011* *ex* Tauranga Chief *-2007* *ex* Socol 5 *-2002* *ex* Tasman Chief *-2002* *ex* Socol 5 *-2001* *ex* CMBT Zambezi *-2000* *ex* Socol 5 *-1995* **Voltaire Shipping Co Ltd** Euroafrica Services Ltd Sp z oo *Limassol* *Cyprus* MMSI: 209366000	**6,030** 3,602 9,597 T/cm 18.5	Class: PR (Class contemplated) (LR) ✠ Classed LR until 27/8/13	**1992**-07 **Miho Zosensho K.K. — Shimizu** Yd No: 1385 Loa 113.12 (BB) Br ex 19.22 Dght 8.541 Lbp 106.00 Br md 18.90 Dpth 11.28 Welded, 2 dks	**(A31A2GX) General Cargo Ship** Grain: 12,582; Bale: 11,528 TEU 564 C Ho 234 TEU C Dk 330 TEU incl 50 ref C. Compartments: 1 Ho, ER 2 Ha: (33.6 x 15.7) (35.7 x 15.7)ER Cranes: 2x50t	**1 oil engine** driving 1 CP propeller Total Power: 4,413kW (6,000hp) 12.5kn Hanshin 6LF58 1 x 4 Stroke 6 Cy. 580 x 1050 4413kW (6000bhp) The Hanshin Diesel Works Ltd-Japan AuxGen: 1 x 600kW 445V 60Hz a.c, 3 x 200kW 445V 60Hz a.c Boilers: TOH (o.f.) 10.2kgf/cm² (10.0bar), TOH (ex.g.) 10.2kgf/cm² (10.0bar)
7911284 *SPG2190* -	**SZAFIR** **Zegluga Gdanska Sp z oo (Marine Services Enterprise)** - *Gdansk* *Poland* MMSI: 261000330	**656** 213 81	Class: (PR)	**1982**-07 **Stocznia 'Wisla' — Gdansk** Yd No: KP2/3 Loa 37.60 Br ex 11.85 Dght 2.850 Lbp 35.79 Br md 11.50 Dpth 4.09 Welded, 1 dk	**(A37B2PS) Passenger Ship** Hull Material: Aluminium Alloy	**2 oil engines** driving 2 FP propellers Total Power: 838kW (1,140hp) 13.0kn Sulzer 6AL20/24 2 x 4 Stroke 6 Cy. 200 x 240 each-419kW (570bhp) Zaklady Przemyslu Metalowego 'HCegielski' SA-Poznan AuxGen: 2 x 90kW 400V 50Hz a.c, 2 x 50kW 400V 50Hz a.c Fuel: 19.5 (d.f.)
8813958 *YJZG3* -	**SZARE SZEREGI** **Saturn Three Shipping Ltd** Polska Zegluga Morska PP (POLSTEAM) *Port Vila* *Vanuatu* MMSI: 576050000 Official number: 731	**41,191** 25,556 73,470 T/cm 70.0	Class: NV PR	**1991**-08 **B&W Skibsvaerft A/S — Copenhagen** Yd No: 936 Loa 228.53 Br ex 32.27 Dght 14.100 Lbp 224.52 Br md 32.24 Dpth 19.00 Welded, 1 dk	**(A21A2BC) Bulk Carrier** Double Hull Grain: 84,960 Compartments: 9 Ho, ER 9 Ha: (11.2 x 9.0)8 (16.0 x 13.5)ER	**1 oil engine** driving 1 FP propeller Total Power: 7,995kW (10,870hp) 14.2kn B&W 5S60MC 1 x 2 Stroke 5 Cy. 600 x 2292 7995kW (10870bhp) Hyundai Heavy Industries Co Ltd-South Korea AuxGen: 3 x 550kW 440V 60Hz a.c Fuel: 297.7 (d.f.) 1852.0 (r.f.)
9594224 *C6ZH3* -	**SZCZECIN** **Ceres One Shipping Ltd** Polska Zegluga Morska PP (POLSTEAM) *Nassau* *Bahamas* MMSI: 311055400 Official number: 8001912	**24,145** 12,162 37,930	Class: AB PR	**2012**-03 **Tianjin Xingang Shipbuilding Industry Co Ltd — Tianjin** Yd No: 345-15 Loa 189.99 (BB) Br ex - Dght 10.400 Lbp 183.00 Br md 28.50 Dpth 15.10 Welded, 1 dk	**(A21A2BC) Bulk Carrier** Double Hull Grain: 48,935; Bale: 47,849 Compartments: 5 Ho, ER 5 Ha: ER Cranes: 4x30t Ice Capable	**1 oil engine** driving 1 FP propeller Total Power: 7,368kW (10,018hp) 14.0kn Wartsila 6RTA48T-B 1 x 2 Stroke 6 Cy. 480 x 2000 7368kW (10018bhp) Yichang Marine Diesel Engine Co Ltd-China AuxGen: 3 x 645kW a.c Fuel: 1753.0 (r.f.)
9130121 *D5DL6* -	**SZCZECIN TRADER** *ex* MOL Honesty *-2009* *ex* CMA CGM Kiwi *-2008* *ex* Szczecin Trader *-2003* *ex* Maruba Trader *-2003* *launched as* Szczecin Trader *-1998* **ms 'Szczecin Trader' Schiffahrts UG (haftungsbeschrankt) & Co KG** MCC Transport Singapore Pte Ltd *Monrovia* *Liberia* MMSI: 636092476 Official number: 92476	**16,803** 8,672 22,990 T/cm 37.1	Class: GL	**1998**-12 **Stocznia Szczecinska SA — Szczecin** Yd No: B170/1/17 Loa 183.95 (BB) Br ex - Dght 9.880 Lbp 171.94 Br md 25.30 Dpth 13.50 Welded, 1 dk	**(A33A2CC) Container Ship (Fully Cellular)** TEU 1730 C Ho 632 TEU C Dk 1096 TEU incl 200 ref C. Compartments: 4 Cell Ho, ER 9 Ha: ER Cranes: 3x40t	**1 oil engine** driving 1 FP propeller Total Power: 13,328kW (18,121hp) 19.0kn Sulzer 6RTA62U 1 x 2 Stroke 6 Cy. 620 x 2150 13328kW (18121bhp) H Cegielski Poznan SA-Poland AuxGen: 3 x 1232kW 220/440V a.c Thrusters: 1 Thwart. FP thruster (f)
9614749 *SNRF* -	**SZTORM** **Morska Sluzba Poszukiwania i Ratownictwa (Maritime Search & Rescue Service)** - *Gdynia* *Poland* Official number: RO/S-G-1268	**284** 85 70	Class: PR	**2012**-04 **Remontowa Shipbuilding SA — Gdansk** (Hull) Yd No: B812/1 **2012**-04 **Gdanska Stocznia 'Remontowa' SA — Gdansk** Yd No: 2436/1 Loa 36.90 Br ex - Dght 2.500 Lbp - Br md 8.10 Dpth - Welded, 1 dk	**(B34M2QS) Search & Rescue Vessel**	**3 oil engines** reduction geared to sc. shafts driving 3 Propellers M.T.U. MTU Friedrichshafen GmbH-Friedrichshafen
8821929 *P3EW4* -	**SZYMANOWSKI** **Szymanowski Shipping Co Ltd** Chinese-Polish JSC (Chinsko-Polskie Towarzystwo Okretowe SA) (CHIPOLBROK) SatCom: Inmarsat A 1101127 *Limassol* *Cyprus* MMSI: 212304000 Official number: 709361	**18,252** 9,106 22,313 T/cm 38.5	Class: LR (PR) ✠ **100A1** SS 06/2009 strengthened for heavy cargoes, container cargoes in holds Nos. 1, 2, 3 & 4 also on upper and poop decks and hatch covers LI Ice Class 1C FS at 9.30m draught Max/min draught fwd 9.158/5.012m Max/min draught aft 10.248/6.466m Required power 6403kw, installed power 9500kw ✠ **LMC** **UMS** Eq.Ltr: I†; Cable: 605.0/64.0 U3 (a)	**1991**-06 **Brodogradiliste '3 Maj' — Rijeka** Yd No: 657 Loa 169.75 (BB) Br ex 27.55 Dght 9.300 Lbp 162.20 Br md 27.50 Dpth 13.80 Welded, 1 dk, 2nd dk in Nos. 1 - 4 holds, 3rd dk in Nos. 2 - 4 holds	**(A31A2GX) General Cargo Ship** Grain: 36,808; Bale: 33,214 TEU 1094 C Ho 472 TEU C Dk 622 TEU incl 30 ref C. Compartments: 4 Ho, ER, 7 Tw Dk 7 Ha: (12.7 x 15.9)4 (25.5 x 10.3)2 (19.1 x 10.3)ER Cranes: 4x24.5t Ice Capable	**1 oil engine** driving 1 FP propeller Total Power: 9,500kW (12,916hp) 16.5kn Sulzer 5RTA62 1 x 2 Stroke 5 Cy. 620 x 2150 9500kW (12916bhp) Tvornica Dizel Motora '3 Maj'-Yugoslavia AuxGen: 3 x 704kW 450V 60Hz a.c Boilers: e (ex.g.) 8.2kgf/cm² (8.0bar), AuxB (o.f.) 8.2kgf/cm² (8.0bar) Fuel: 69.0 (d.f.) 1014.0 (r.f.) 39.1pd
9221372 - -	**T 6** **National Marine Dredging Co (NMDC)** - *United Arab Emirates*	**110** - -	Class: (BV)	**2000**-01 **IHC DeltaShipyard BV — Sliedrecht** Yd No: 977 Loa 19.50 Br ex 6.20 Dght 2.200 Lbp - Br md - Dpth 2.85 Welded, 1 dk	**(B32A2ST) Tug**	**2 oil engines** geared to sc. shafts driving 2 FP propellers Total Power: 1,120kW (1,522hp) 11.2kn Caterpillar 3412C-TA 2 x Vee 4 Stroke 12 Cy. 137 x 152 each-560kW (761bhp) Caterpillar Inc-USA
9065649 *YD4355* -	**T-32** **PT Gunung Raya Utama Timber Industries** - *Jakarta* *Indonesia*	*134* 80 95	Class: (KI) (NK)	**1992**-10 **Maju Layar Sdn Bhd — Sibu** Yd No: 6 L reg 22.70 Br ex - Dght 2.297 Lbp 21.34 Br md 7.50 Dpth 3.20 Welded, 1 dk	**(B32A2ST) Tug**	**2 oil engines** reduction geared to sc. shafts driving 2 FP propellers Total Power: 692kW (940hp) 11.0kn Caterpillar 3408TA 2 x Vee 4 Stroke 8 Cy. 137 x 152 each-346kW (470bhp) Caterpillar Inc-USA AuxGen: 2 x 21kW a.c
9066564 *DSPE7* -	**T-103 KUMYONG** *ex* Waka Maru No. 18 *-1993* **Kum Youg Development Co Ltd** - *Busan* *South Korea* MMSI: 440877000 Official number: BSR-070621	*187* - -	Class: KR	**1993**-02 **K.K. Watanabe Zosensho — Nagasaki** Yd No: 1218 Loa 36.54 Br ex - Dght 3.500 Lbp - Br md 10.00 Dpth 4.80 Welded, 1 dk	**(B32A2ST) Tug**	**2 oil engines** reduction geared to sc. shafts driving 2 FP propellers Total Power: 2,354kW (3,200hp) Yanmar 6Z280-EN 2 x 4 Stroke 6 Cy. 280 x 360 each-1177kW (1600bhp) Yanmar Diesel Engine Co Ltd-Japan
9144964 *D7MS* -	**T 301 KUMYONG** *ex* Hayase Maru *-2014* **Kum Youg Development Co Ltd** - *South Korea* MMSI: 440200000	*298* 138 289	Class: KR (Class contemplated)	**1996**-03 **Kanbara Zosen K.K. — Onomichi** Yd No: 481 Loa 39.30 Br ex - Dght 3.600 Lbp - Br md 9.40 Dpth 4.20 Welded, 1 dk	**(B32A2ST) Tug**	**2 oil engines** geared integral to driving 2 Z propellers Total Power: 3,090kW (4,202hp) Niigata 6L28HX 2 x 4 Stroke 6 Cy. 280 x 370 each-1545kW (2101bhp) Niigata Engineering Co Ltd-Japan
5347477 *S2YB* -	**T-1054** *ex* Shoyu Maru *-1975* **Bangladesh Inland Water Transport Corp** - *Chittagong* *Bangladesh* Official number: 317519	*741* 395 1,209	Class: (NK)	**1961 Mukaishima Dock Co. Ltd. — Onomichi** Yd No: 56 Loa 59.47 Br ex 9.15 Dght 4.352 Lbp 54.23 Br md 9.10 Dpth 4.50 Riveted\Welded, 1 dk	**(A13B2TP) Products Tanker** Liq: 1,392; Liq (Oil): 1,392 Compartments: 8 Ta, ER	**1 oil engine** driving 1 FP propeller Total Power: 559kW (760hp) 10.3kn Nippon Hatsudoki HS6NV325 1 x 4 Stroke 6 Cy. 325 x 460 559kW (760bhp) Nippon Hatsudoki-Japan AuxGen: 1 x 7kW 110V d.c, 1 x 5kW 110V d.c Fuel: 46.0
5237488 *S2YF* -	**T-1055** *ex* Miya Maru *-1975* **Bangladesh Inland Water Transport Corp** - *Chittagong* *Bangladesh* Official number: 317518	*784* 444 1,288	Class: (NK)	**1961 Mukaishima Dock Co. Ltd. — Onomichi** Yd No: 58 Loa 62.82 Br ex 9.15 Dght 4.292 Lbp 57.59 Br md 9.10 Dpth 4.50 Riveted\Welded, 1 dk	**(A13B2TP) Products Tanker** Liq: 1,548; Liq (Oil): 1,548 Compartments: 3 Ta, ER	**1 oil engine** driving 1 FP propeller Total Power: 559kW (760hp) 10.3kn Nippon Hatsudoki HS6NV325 1 x 4 Stroke 6 Cy. 325 x 460 559kW (760bhp) Nippon Hatsudoki-Japan AuxGen: 1 x 7kW 110V d.c, 1 x 5kW 110V d.c
7300679 *S2YD* -	**T-1057** *ex* Rakuyu Maru *-1975* **Bangladesh Inland Water Transport Corp** - *Chittagong* *Bangladesh* Official number: 317521	*575* 311 1,097	Class: (NK)	**1964 Sanuki Shipbuilding & Iron Works Co Ltd — Mitoyo KG** Yd No: 160 Loa 57.23 Br ex 8.51 Dght 4.111 Lbp 52.00 Br md 8.46 Dpth 4.27 Welded, 1 dk	**(A13B2TU) Tanker (unspecified)** Liq: 1,158; Liq (Oil): 1,158 Compartments: 3 Ta, ER	**1 oil engine** driving 1 FP propeller Total Power: 515kW (700hp) 10.0kn Hanshin 1 x 4 Stroke 6 Cy. 300 x 420 515kW (700bhp) The Hanshin Diesel Works Ltd-Japan

7424308 - -	T-1059 - **Bangladesh Inland Water Transport Corp** - *Chittagong* *Bangladesh* Official number: C.197	*859* 519 1,100		**1976**-04 **Khulna Shipyard Ltd — Khulna** Yd No: 428 Loa 64.62 Br ex 10.06 Dght 3.506 Lbp 59.44 Br md 9.77 Dpth 3.97 Welded, 1 dk	**(A13B2TU) Tanker (unspecified)**	**2 oil engines** driving 2 FP propellers Total Power: 810kW (1,102hp) Deutz RBV6M545 2 x 4 Stroke 6 Cy. 320 x 450 each-405kW (551bhp) Kloeckner Humboldt Deutz AG-West Germany
7228053 - -	**T 2000** *ex* Qabas 2 *-2000* *ex* Dehail *-1994* *ex* Oil Producer *-1978* **Tameem Shipping** -	*743* 288 1,092	Class: (LR) (HR) ✠ Classed LR until 19/6/96	**1972**-09 **van der Giessen-de Noord NV — Alblasserdam** Yd No: 892 Loa 56.44 Br ex 12.76 Dght 4.268 Lbp 51.36 Br md 12.50 Dpth 4.81 Welded, 1 dk	**(B21B20A) Anchor Handling Tug Supply** Derricks: 1x5t	**2 oil engines** reverse reduction geared to sc. shafts driving 2 FP propellers Total Power: 3,038kW (4,130hp) 14.5kn Allen 12PVBCS12-F 2 x Vee 4 Stroke 12 Cy. 242 x 305 each-1519kW (2065bhp) W. H. Allen, Sons & Co. Ltd.-Bedford AuxGen: 3 x 144kW 440V 60Hz a.c Thrusters: 2 Thwart. FP thruster (f) Fuel: 406.5 (d.f.)
8107751 - -	**T. C. D. D. I** - **Government of The Republic of Turkey (Turkiye Cumhuriyeti Devlet Demir Yollari - Haydarpasa Liman Isletmesi) (Turkish Republic State Railways - Haydarpasa Harbour Management)** - *Turkey*	*210* - -		**1983**-08 **Denizcilik Bankasi T.A.O. — Camialti, Istanbul** Yd No: 219 Loa - Br ex - Dght - Lbp 29.01 Br md 8.11 Dpth 3.92 Welded, 1 dk	**(B32A2ST) Tug**	**1 oil engine** driving 1 FP propeller Total Power: 1,103kW (1,500hp)
6829472 *HSCS* -	**T. C. P. 3** *ex* Siamsupachai *-1993* *ex* Siriwatana *-1988* *ex* Kodama *-1986* *ex* Toho Maru No. 1 *-1984* *ex* Shuko Maru *-1972* **VSP Marine Shipping Co Ltd** TCP Marine Shipping Co Ltd *Bangkok* *Thailand* Official number: 291040134	**2,570** 1,621 4,542 T/cm 10.0	Class: (NK)	**1968**-11 **Shin Naniwa Dock Co. Ltd. — Osaka** Yd No: 18 Loa 92.79 Br ex 13.24 Dght 6.630 Lbp 86.10 Br md 13.20 Dpth 7.00 Welded, 1 dk	**(A13A2TW) Crude/Oil Products Tanker** Liq: 5,384; Liq (Oil): 5,384 Cargo Heating Coils Compartments: 9 Ta, ER 2 Cargo Pump (s): 1x1200m³/hr, 1x500m³/hr Manifold: Bow/CM: 54m	**1 oil engine** driving 1 FP propeller Total Power: 1,839kW (2,500hp) 12.5kn Akasaka 6DH46SS 1 x 4 Stroke 6 Cy. 460 x 720 1839kW (2500bhp) Akasaka Tekkosho KK (Akasaka DieselLtd)-Japan AuxGen: 2 x 64kW 445V a.c Fuel: 20.0 (d.f.) (Heating Coils) 134.0 (r.f.) 8.0pd
7037064 *HSB2253* -	**T. C. P. 5** *ex* Sinothai *-1999* *ex* Propane Maru No. 7 *-1983* **Seangchalern Industry Co Ltd** - *Bangkok* *Thailand* Official number: 261032876	**1,168** 562 1,496		**1970**-12 **Tokushima Zosen Sangyo K.K. — Komatsushima** Yd No: 313 Converted From: LPG Tanker Loa 66.17 Br ex 11.03 Dght 5.200 Lbp 60.00 Br md 11.00 Dpth 5.75 Riveted\Welded, 1 dk	**(A13B2TP) Products Tanker** Ins: 1,411; Liq: 2,109; Liq (Oil): 2,109 Compartments: 6 Ta, ER	**1 oil engine** driving 1 FP propeller Total Power: 956kW (1,300hp) 11.5kn Nippon Hatsudoki HS6NV132 1 x 4 Stroke 6 Cy. 325 x 520 956kW (1300bhp) Nippon Hatsudoki-Japan Fuel: 66.0 5.0pd
7373767 *HSLJ* -	**T. C. P. 6** *ex* V. S. P. 1 *-1993* *ex* Suci *-1991* *ex* Eishin Maru No. 25 *-1985* **VSP Marine Shipping Co Ltd** - *Bangkok* *Thailand* MMSI: 567010200 Official number: 341003036	*2,814* 1,534 5,194 T/cm 11.6	Class: (NK)	**1974**-11 **Kochi Jyuko K.K. — Kochi** Yd No: 823 Loa 95.59 Br ex 15.04 Dght 6.759 Lbp 88.09 Br md 15.02 Dpth 7.98 Riveted\Welded, 1 dk	**(A12B2TR) Chemical/Products Tanker** Single Hull Liq: 5,448; Liq (Oil): 5,448 2 Cargo Pump (s)	**1 oil engine** driving 1 FP propeller Total Power: 2,795kW (3,800hp) 12.5kn Mitsubishi 6UET45/75C 1 x 2 Stroke 6 Cy. 450 x 750 2795kW (3800bhp) Akasaka Tekkosho KK (Akasaka DieselLtd)-Japan AuxGen: 2 x 160kW 445V 60Hz a.c Fuel: 164.5 13.0pd
7812505 *DSQB4* -	**T CAMELLIA** *ex* Hae Yuen *-2012* *ex* Hae Yune *-2005* *ex* Orient Star III *-2000* *ex* Hakuei Maru No. 2 *-1991* **Duck Ho Woo** - *Busan* *South Korea* MMSI: 441517000 Official number: BSR-922464	**140** 45 96	Class: KR	**1978**-09 **Wakamatsu Zosen K.K. — Kitakyushu** Yd No: 286 Loa 27.85 Br ex 8.00 Dght 2.809 Lbp 24.70 Br md 7.80 Dpth 3.60 Welded, 1 dk	**(B32B2SP) Pusher Tug**	**2 oil engines** reduction geared to sc. shaft driving 1 FP propeller Total Power: 1,324kW (1,800hp) 11.8kn Daihatsu 8PSHTB-26D 2 x 4 Stroke 8 Cy. 260 x 320 each-662kW (900bhp) Daihatsu Diesel Manufacturing Co Lt-Japan
9438688 *TCA2925* -	**T.DAMLA 1** *ex* T. Damla 1 *-2012* **T Damla Denizcilik AS** Ditas Deniz Isletmeciligi ve Tankerciligi AS *Istanbul* *Turkey* MMSI: 271010366	**430** 129 -	Class: TL (BV)	**2008**-05 **R.M.K. Tersanesi — Tuzla** Yd No: 69 Loa 30.45 Br ex - Dght 5.000 Lbp 30.19 Br md 10.50 Dpth 5.60 Welded, 1 dk	**(B32A2ST) Tug**	**2 oil engines** gearing integral to driving 2 Z propellers Total Power: 3,678kW (5,000hp) 12.0kn Niigata 6L28HX 2 x 4 Stroke 6 Cy. 280 x 370 each-1839kW (2500bhp) Niigata Engineering Co Ltd-Japan
9438705 *TCA2977* -	**T.DAMLA 2** *ex* T. Damla 2 *-2012* **T Damla Denizcilik AS** Ditas Deniz Isletmeciligi ve Tankerciligi AS *Istanbul* *Turkey* MMSI: 271002648	**430** 129 -	Class: TL (BV)	**2008**-09 **R.M.K. Tersanesi — Tuzla** Yd No: 72 Loa 32.70 Br ex - Dght 5.000 Lbp 30.19 Br md 10.50 Dpth 5.60 Welded, 1 dk	**(B32A2ST) Tug**	**2 oil engines** gearing integral to driving 2 Z propellers Total Power: 3,678kW (5,000hp) 12.0kn Niigata 6L28HX 2 x 4 Stroke 6 Cy. 280 x 370 each-1839kW (2500bhp) Niigata Engineering Co Ltd-Japan
9438119 *TCA2905* -	**T.DAMLA 3** *ex* T. Damla 3 *-2012* **T Damla Denizcilik AS** Ditas Deniz Isletmeciligi ve Tankerciligi AS *Istanbul* *Turkey* MMSI: 271002574	**430** 129 50	Class: TL (BV)	**2008**-03 **R.M.K. Tersanesi — Tuzla** Yd No: 67 Loa 33.00 Br ex - Dght 4.100 Lbp 29.35 Br md 10.50 Dpth 5.60 Welded, 1 dk	**(B32A2ST) Tug**	**2 oil engines** gearing integral to driving 2 Z propellers Total Power: 3,678kW (5,000hp) 12.0kn Niigata 6L28HX 2 x 4 Stroke 6 Cy. 280 x 370 each-1839kW (2500bhp) Niigata Engineering Co Ltd-Japan
9438690 *TCA2949* -	**T.DAMLA 4** *ex* T. Damla 4 *-2012* **T Damla Denizcilik AS** Ditas Deniz Isletmeciligi ve Tankerciligi AS *Istanbul* *Turkey* MMSI: 271010484	**430** 129 -	Class: TL (BV)	**2008**-07 **R.M.K. Tersanesi — Tuzla** Yd No: 71 Loa 32.70 Br ex - Dght 4.100 Lbp 30.18 Br md 10.50 Dpth 5.60 Welded, 1 dk	**(B32A2ST) Tug**	**2 oil engines** reduction geared to sc. shafts driving 2 Z propellers Total Power: 3,678kW (5,000hp) 12.0kn Niigata 6L28HX 2 x 4 Stroke 6 Cy. 280 x 370 each-1839kW (2500bhp) Niigata Engineering Co Ltd-Japan
8877514 - -	**T. F. 101** *ex* Tropic Fishery 101 *-2005* *ex* Azuma Maru No. 15 *-2005* *ex* Asahi Maru No. 18 *-2005* - -	*119* - -		**1980**-08 **Katsuura Dockyard Co. Ltd. — Nachi-Katsuura** L reg 28.20 Br ex - Dght - Lbp 28.12 Br md 6.00 Dpth 2.42 Welded, 1 dk	**(B11B2FV) Fishing Vessel**	**1 oil engine** driving 1 FP propeller Niigata 1 x 4 Stroke Niigata Engineering Co Ltd-Japan
9499838 *TCTP9* -	**T. GONUL** - **Kadikoy Tankercilik AS** Ditas Deniz Isletmeciligi ve Tankerciligi AS *Istanbul* *Turkey* MMSI: 271002726	**7,318** 3,651 10,873 T/cm 21.8	Class: NV (BV)	**2009**-04 **R.M.K. Tersanesi — Tuzla** Yd No: 75 Loa 123.72 (BB) Br ex - Dght 7.984 Lbp 117.60 Br md 18.90 Dpth 10.20 Welded, 1 dk	**(A12B2TR) Chemical/Products Tanker** Double Hull (13F) Liq: 12,637; Liq (Oil): 12,637 Cargo Heating Coils Compartments: 12 Wing Ta, 2 Wing Slop Ta, ER 12 Cargo Pump (s): 12x250m³/hr Manifold: Bow/CM: 67m Ice Capable	**1 oil engine** reduction geared to sc. shaft driving 1 CP propeller Total Power: 4,000kW (5,438hp) 14.1kn Wartsila 8L32 1 x 4 Stroke 8 Cy. 320 x 400 4000kW (5438bhp) Wartsila Finland Oy-Finland AuxGen: 3 x a.c, 1 x a.c Thrusters: 1 Tunnel thruster (f) Fuel: 101.0 (d.f.) 595.0 (r.f.)
8745319 - -	**T JAMES T** *ex* Casalinho *-2005* **Lynn-Dover Foods Ltd** - *Goderich, ON* *Canada* Official number: 122619	**104** 89 -		**1951 Mathieson's Boat Works — Goderich ON** L reg 19.02 Br ex - Dght - Lbp - Br md 6.37 Dpth 1.77 Welded, 1 dk	**(B11B2FV) Fishing Vessel**	**1 oil engine** driving 1 Propeller
8942072 *WDD7191* -	**T & L** *ex* Capt. Mai III *-2007* *ex* Hong Minh II *-2005* *ex* Capt. Phillip *-2001* *ex* Queen Annie *-1987* **Thomas & Sons inc** - *Galveston, TX* *United States of America* MMSI: 367183070 Official number: 923625	**157** 106 -		**1987 Master Boat Builders, Inc. — Coden, Al** Yd No: 126 L reg 24.96 Br ex - Dght - Lbp - Br md 7.35 Dpth 3.87 Welded, 1 dk	**(B11B2FV) Fishing Vessel**	**1 oil engine** driving 1 FP propeller

IMO / Call sign	Name / Owner	Tonnage	Class	Built / Dimensions	Type	Machinery	
8969472 *WDA6046* -	**T & L ELITE** *ex Gulf Challenger Iv -2012* **T & L Elite Inc** - *Port Bolivar, TX* *United States of America* MMSI: 366827090 Official number: 1117506	**174** 52 -		**2001** Yd No: 197A L reg 26.15 Br ex - Dght - Lbp - Br md 7.92 Dpth 3.81 Welded, 1 dk	**(B11B2FV) Fishing Vessel**	**1 oil engine** driving 1 FP propeller	
8939788 *WDD7358* -	**T & L II** *ex Vuong Vu -2009* **Master Thai Inc** - *Galveston, TX* *United States of America* MMSI: 367185370 Official number: 1042541	**168** 50 -		**1996 J & J Marine, Inc. — Bayou La Batre, Al** Yd No: 114 L reg 27.34 Br ex - Dght - Lbp - Br md 7.62 Dpth 3.84 Welded, 1 dk	**(B11B2FV) Fishing Vessel**	**1 oil engine** driving 1 FP propeller	
8037621 *WCJ6766* -	**T & L III** *ex Young King -2010 ex Miss Nancy -2001* *ex Miss Jennie -1995* **Thomas & Sons inc** - *Galveston, TX* *United States of America* MMSI: 366964160 Official number: 624430	*149* 101 -		**1980 Collier Shipbuilding, Inc. — Bayou La Batre, Al** Yd No: 7 L reg 23.66 Br ex 7.17 Dght - Lbp - Br md - Dpth 3.69 Welded, 1 dk	**(B11B2FV) Fishing Vessel**	**1 oil engine** driving 1 FP propeller Total Power: 346kW (470hp)	
8958112 *WDB9107* -	**T&L LEGEND** *ex Malibu -2012* **T&L Legend Inc** - *Port Bolivar, TX* *United States of America* Official number: 1085642	**141** 42 -		**1999 J-Built, Inc. — Bayou La Batre, Al** Yd No: 113 L reg 24.14 Br ex - Dght - Lbp - Br md 7.31 Dpth 3.81 Welded, 1 dk	**(B11B2FV) Fishing Vessel**	**1 oil engine** driving 1 FP propeller	
8941107 *WDH2810* -	**T & L PRIDE** *ex Kimmy II -2013* **Gulf Coast Harvest Inc** - *Port Bolivar, TX* *United States of America* MMSI: 367601420 Official number: 1050021	**148** 44 -		**1997 Master Boat Builders, Inc. — Coden, Al** Yd No: 240 L reg 24.87 Br ex - Dght - Lbp - Br md 7.32 Dpth 3.81 Welded, 1 dk	**(B11B2FV) Fishing Vessel**	**1 oil engine** driving 1 FP propeller	
9499553 *TCMJ3* -	**T. LEYLA** *ex Lady Ozge -2012* **Karsiyaka Tankercilik AS** Ditas Deniz Isletmeciligi ve Tankerciligi AS *Istanbul* *Turkey* MMSI: 271042693	**4,225** 2,039 6,271 T/cm 16.4	Class: NV (BV)	**2011-06 Sahin Celik Sanayi A.S. — Tuzla** Yd No: 47 Loa 121.62 (BB) Br ex - Dght 6.332 Lbp 111.86 Br md 16.00 Dpth 8.00 Welded, 1 dk	**(A12B2TR) Chemical/Products Tanker** Double Hull (13F) Liq: 6,548; Liq (Oil): 6,548 Cargo Heating Coils Compartments: 12 Wing Ta, ER 14 Cargo Pump (s): 2x100m³/hr, 12x200m³/hr	**1 oil engine** reduction geared to sc. shaft driving 1 CP propeller Total Power: 2,620kW (3,562hp) Hyundai Himsen 1 x 4 Stroke 9 Cy. 250 x 330 2620kW (3562bhp) Hyundai Heavy Industries Co Ltd-South Korea AuxGen: 3 x 465kW 60Hz a.c, 1 x 60Hz a.c Thrusters: 1 Tunnel thruster (f) Fuel: 50.0 (d.f.) 278.0 (r.f.)	14.0kn 9H25/33P
7643590 *WYH5812* -	**T. LUIS** *ex Navegante -1992 ex Tina & Maria -1992* **Milema Fishing Corp** - *New Bedford, MA* *United States of America* Official number: 572381	*134* 91 -		**1976 S & R Boat Builders, Inc. — Bayou La Batre, Al** Yd No: 21 L reg 21.98 Br ex 6.74 Dght - Lbp - Br md - Dpth 3.38 Welded, 1 dk	**(B11B2FV) Fishing Vessel**	**1 oil engine** driving 1 FP propeller Total Power: 313kW (426hp)	
8848379 - -	**T No. 103** *ex Hyundai No. 103 -1992* - -	*192* - 81	Class: (KR)	**1974-01 Hyundai Shipbuilding & Heavy Industries Co Ltd — Ulsan** Loa 28.80 Br ex - Dght - Lbp 25.92 Br md 8.60 Dpth 3.80 Welded, 1 dk	**(B32A2ST) Tug**	**2 oil engines** driving 2 FP propellers Total Power: 956kW (1,300hp) Niigata 2 x 4 Stroke 6 Cy. 250 x 320 each-478kW (650bhp) Niigata Engineering Co Ltd-Japan AuxGen: 2 x 48kW 225V a.c	10.8kn 6L25BX
7733280 *WCY7079* -	**T-ONE** *ex Captain Stephen -2001 ex Capt. Bui -1993* *ex Sea Wife -1993* **Trung Van Nguyen** - *Freeport, TX* *United States of America* Official number: 586504	*127* 87 -		**1977 Desco Marine — Saint Augustine, Fl** Yd No: 223-F L reg 20.97 Br ex - Dght - Lbp - Br md 6.74 Dpth 3.79 Bonded, 1 dk	**(B11B2FV) Fishing Vessel** Hull Material: Reinforced Plastic	**1 oil engine** driving 1 FP propeller Total Power: 268kW (364hp) Caterpillar 1 x 4 Stroke 268kW (364bhp) Caterpillar Tractor Co-USA	
8003319 - -	**T. P. S. 224** *ex Halliburton 224 -1995* - -	*199* 135 203	Class: (AB)	**1980-08 Rockport Yacht & Supply Co. (RYSCO) — Rockport, Tx** Yd No: 492 Loa 39.78 Br ex 10.09 Dght - Lbp 37.95 Br md 10.06 Dpth 2.16 Welded, 1 dk	**(A24A2BT) Cement Carrier**	**2 oil engines** reverse reduction geared to sc. shafts driving 2 FP propellers Total Power: 588kW (800hp) Caterpillar 2 x 4 Stroke 6 Cy. 159 x 203 each-294kW (400bhp) Caterpillar Tractor Co-USA AuxGen: 2 x 75kW	10.0kn D353TA
9611503 *3FFS4* -	**T PRIME** *ex STX Prime -2013* **STX Poseidon Shipping Co SA** STX Marine Service Co Ltd *Panama* *Panama* MMSI: 373837000 Official number: 4355112A	**20,867** 11,821 32,451 T/cm 46.1	Class: KR	**2011-12 Taizhou Maple Leaf Shipbuilding Co Ltd — Linhai ZJ** Yd No: LBC31800-040 Loa 179.90 (BB) Br ex - Dght 10.167 Lbp 171.50 Br md 28.40 Dpth 14.10 Welded, 1 dk	**(A21A2BC) Bulk Carrier** Grain: 42,565 Compartments: 5 Ho, ER 5 Ha: 3 (20.0 x 19.2) (18.4 x 19.2)ER (14.4 x 17.6) Cranes: 4x30.5t	**1 oil engine** driving 1 FP propeller Total Power: 6,480kW (8,810hp) MAN-B&W 1 x 2 Stroke 6 Cy. 420 x 1764 6480kW (8810bhp) STX (Dalian) Engine Co Ltd-China AuxGen: 3 x 465kW 450V a.c Fuel: 1638.0	13.6kn 6S42MC
8938928 *WDB4645* -	**T RAIN** *ex Catherine -2012 ex Angel Wings -2006* **Thach Van Tran** - *Houston, TX* *United States of America* MMSI: 366900760 Official number: 1032635	**132** 41 -		**1995 J & J Marine, Inc. — Bayou La Batre, Al** Yd No: 105 L reg 23.35 Br ex - Dght - Lbp - Br md 7.32 Dpth 3.84 Welded, 1 dk	**(B11B2FV) Fishing Vessel**	**1 oil engine** driving 1 FP propeller	
9248045 - -	**T. S. D1** - **Government of The Union of Myanmar (Ministry of Transport - Directorate of Water Resources & Improvement of River Systems)** - *Yangon* *Myanmar* Official number: 01W1014	**194** 58	Class: (CC)	**2001-04 Tianjin Xinhe Shipyard — Tianjin** Yd No: SB002 Loa 26.50 Br ex - Dght - Lbp 25.00 Br md 8.20 Dpth 2.50 Welded, 1 dk	**(B33A2DU) Dredger (unspecified)**	**2 oil engines** geared to sc. shafts driving 2 FP propellers Total Power: 350kW (476hp) Caterpillar 2 x 4 Stroke 6 Cy. 121 x 152 each-175kW (238bhp) Caterpillar Inc-USA AuxGen: 1 x 54kW 400V a.c, 1 x 27kW 400V a.c	7.2kn 3306TA
9242728 *AUCH* -	**T. S. H. D. CAUVERY** - **Chennai Port Trust** - *Chennai* *India* MMSI: 419483000 Official number: 3019	**2,326** 698 2,664	Class: IR	**2004-05 Cochin Shipyard Ltd — Ernakulam** Yd No: BY-42 Loa 74.45 Br ex 14.63 Dght 4.800 Lbp 69.94 Br md 14.60 Dpth 5.40 Welded, 1 dk	**(B33B2DT) Trailing Suction Hopper Dredger** Hopper: 1,700	**2 oil engines** geared to sc. shafts driving 2 CP propellers Total Power: 3,355kW (4,561hp) Caterpillar 2 x 4 Stroke 6 Cy. 280 x 300 each-1677kW (2280bhp) Caterpillar Inc-USA AuxGen: 3 x 210kW 415V 50Hz a.c, 2 x 360kW 415V 50Hz a.c Fuel: 105.0 (d.f.)	11.6kn 3606TA
9499826 *TCTC3* -	**T. SEVGI** - **Uskudar Tankercilik AS** Ditas Deniz Isletmeciligi ve Tankerciligi AS *Istanbul* *Turkey* MMSI: 271002688	**7,318** 3,651 10,983 T/cm 21.8	Class: NV (BV)	**2008-12 R.M.K. Tersanesi — Tuzla** Yd No: 74 Loa 123.72 (BB) Br ex - Dght 7.984 Lbp 117.60 Br md 18.90 Dpth 10.20 Welded, 1 dk	**(A12B2TR) Chemical/Products Tanker** Double Hull (13F) Liq: 12,247; Liq (Oil): 12,247 Compartments: 12 Wing Ta, 2 Wing Slop Ta, ER 12 Cargo Pump (s): 12x250m³/hr Manifold: Bow/CM: 67m Ice Capable	**1 oil engine** reduction geared to sc. shaft driving 1 CP propeller Total Power: 4,000kW (5,438hp) Wartsila 1 x 4 Stroke 8 Cy. 320 x 400 4000kW (5438bhp) Wartsila Finland Oy-Finland AuxGen: 3 x a.c, 1 x a.c Thrusters: 1 Tunnel thruster (f) Fuel: 101.0 (d.f.) 595.0 (r.f.)	14.1kn 8L32

IMO / Call sign	Name / Owner / Flag	Tonnage	Class	Builder / Dimensions	Type / Capacity	Machinery
9652911 *TCUY9* -	**T. SUNA** - **Sariyer Tankercilik AS** Ditas Deniz Isletmeciligi ve Tankerciligi AS *Istanbul* *Turkey* MMSI: 271043255	**29,754** 14,116 51,532	Class: NV	**2012-11 Hyundai Mipo Dockyard Co Ltd — Ulsan** Yd No: 2354 Loa 183.31 (BB) Br ex 32.22 Dght 13.300 Lbp 174.00 Br md 32.20 Dpth 19.10 Welded, 1 dk	**(A12B2TR) Chemical/Products Tanker** Double Hull (13F) Liq: 52,925; Liq (Oil): 52,925 Compartments: 12 Wing Ta, 2 Wing Slop Ta, ER	**1 oil engine** driving 1 FP propeller Total Power: 10,680kW (14,521hp) 15.2kn MAN-B&W 6S50ME-B9 1 x 2 Stroke 6 Cy. 500 x 2214 10680kW (14521bhp) Hyundai Heavy Industries Co Ltd-South Korea AuxGen: 3 x a.c
9611498 *3FYS2* -	**T SYMPHONY** *ex* STX Symphony *-2013* **STX Athena Shipping Co SA** STX Marine Service Co Ltd *Panama* *Panama* MMSI: 355352000 Official number: 4314711A	**20,867** 11,821 32,451 T/cm 46.1	Class: KR	**2011-08 Taizhou Maple Leaf Shipbuilding Co Ltd — Linhai ZJ** Yd No: LBC31800-039 Loa 179.90 (BB) Br ex - Dght 10.167 Lbp 171.50 Br md 28.40 Dpth 14.10 Welded, 1 dk	**(A21A2BC) Bulk Carrier** Grain: 42,565 Compartments: 5 Ho, ER 5 Ha: 3 (20.0 x 19.2) (18.4 x 19.2)ER (14.4 x 17.6) Cranes: 4x30t	**1 oil engine** driving 1 FP propeller Total Power: 6,480kW (8,810hp) 13.7kn MAN-B&W 6S42MC 1 x 2 Stroke 6 Cy. 420 x 1764 6480kW (8810bhp) STX (Dalian) Engine Co Ltd-China Fuel: 1630.0
9093880 *YD3410* -	**T T** *ex* Mitra Kencana II *-2013* *ex* Shokaku *-2007* **PT Sumber Surya Kencana** - *Tanjungpinang* *Indonesia*	**154** 47 -	Class: KI	**1998-08 YK Nakanoshima Zosensho — Kochi KC** L reg 23.00 Br ex - Dght 1.890 Lbp 21.25 Br md 8.00 Dpth 3.10 Welded, 1 dk	**(B32B2SP) Pusher Tug**	**1 oil engine** geared to sc. shaft driving 1 Propeller Total Power: 1,103kW (1,500hp) 8.0kn Fuji 6L32G 1 x 4 Stroke 6 Cy. 320 x 380 1103kW (1500bhp) (made 1987, fitted 1998) Fuji Diesel Co Ltd-Japan
9600736 *J8B4941* -	**T. T. ADDY** - **Government of The Republic of Ghana (Ports & Harbours Authority)** - *Kingstown* *St Vincent & The Grenadines* MMSI: 376052000 Official number: 11414	**294** 88 160	Class: LR (Class contemplated) **100A1** 11/2013 Class contemplated	**2013-11 Damen Shipyards Changde Co Ltd — Changde HN** (Hull) Yd No: (511577) **2013-11 B.V. Scheepswerf Damen — Gorinchem** Yd No: 511577 Loa 28.67 Br ex - Dght - Lbp - Br md 9.80 Dpth 4.60 Welded, 1 dk	**(B32A2ST) Tug**	**2 oil engines** reduction geared to sc. shafts driving 2 Z propellers Total Power: 3,372kW (4,584hp) Caterpillar 3516B-HD 2 x Vee 4 Stroke 16 Cy. 170 x 215 each-1686kW (2292bhp) Caterpillar Inc-USA
9280897 *9YGS* -	**T & T SPIRIT** *ex* Spearhead *-2007* **Port Authority of Trinidad & Tobago** Bay Ferries Ltd *Port of Spain* *Trinidad & Tobago* MMSI: 362029000	*6,558* 2,497 750	Class: NV	**2002-11 Incat Tasmania Pty Ltd — Hobart TAS** Yd No: 060 Converted From: Logistics Vessel (Naval Ro-Ro Cargo)-2007 Loa 97.22 (BB) Br ex 26.19 Dght 3.400 Lbp 81.60 Br md 26.17 Dpth 4.80 Welded	**(A36A2PR) Passenger/Ro-Ro Ship (Vehicles)** Hull Material: Aluminium Alloy Passengers: 881 Lane-Len: 380 Cars: 180	**4 oil engines** geared to sc. shafts driving 4 Water jets Total Power: 28,320kW (38,504hp) 38.0kn Ruston 20RK270 4 x Vee 4 Stroke 20 Cy. 270 x 305 each-7080kW (9626bhp) Paxman Diesels Ltd.-Colchester AuxGen: 4 x 265kW a.c
9522491 - -	**T1** - **QinetiQ Ltd** - *United Kingdom*	**115** - 67	Class: LR ✠ **100AN** SS 08/2010 SSC Cargo (A) SES CR G3 **LMC**	**2010-08 Aluminium Shipbuilders — Fareham** (Hull) Yd No: 121 **2010-08 Griffon Hoverwork Ltd — Southampton** Yd No: 094 Loa 29.67 Br ex - Dght 1.900 Lbp 27.40 Br md 7.40 Dpth 2.50 Welded, 1 dk	**(A35D2RL) Landing Craft** Hull Material: Aluminium Alloy Bow ramp (centre)	**2 oil engines** reduction geared to sc. shafts driving 2 Water jets Total Power: 5,440kW (7,396hp) M.T.U. 16V4000M90 2 x Vee 4 Stroke 16 Cy. 165 x 190 each-2720kW (3698bhp) MTU Friedrichshafen GmbH-Friedrichshafen
9236157 *YJRW2* -	**T1 ABIKE** *ex* Bennett Tide *-2013* **DTDW Holdings Ltd** Tidex Nigeria Ltd *Port Vila* *Vanuatu* MMSI: 576662000 Official number: 1308	**2,152** 1,089 3,350	Class: AB (NV)	**2001-05 Brevik Construction AS — Brevik** Yd No: 18 Loa 71.90 Br ex - Dght 5.900 Lbp 66.80 Br md 16.00 Dpth 7.00 Welded, 1 dk	**(B21A2OS) Platform Supply Ship**	**2 oil engines** reduction geared to sc. shafts driving 2 CP propellers Total Power: 4,016kW (5,460hp) Normo KRMB-9 2 x 4 Stroke 9 Cy. 250 x 300 each-2008kW (2730bhp) Rolls Royce Marine AS-Norway AuxGen: 2 x 250kW a.c, 2 x 1280kW a.c Thrusters: 1 Thwart. FP thruster (f); 1 Thwart. FP thruster (a) Fuel: 980.0
1006738 *ZCPQ3* -	**T6** *ex* Tytti *-2007* **Maritime Research Inc** Flyghtship Construction Ltd *George Town* *Cayman Islands (British)* MMSI: 319198000 Official number: 739710	**568** 170 130	Class: LR ✠ **100A1** SS 04/2012 SSC Yacht, mono, G6 ✠ **LMC** **UMS** Cable: 300.0/24.0 U2 (a)	**2007-04 Flyghtship Construction Ltd — Auckland** Yd No: 126 Loa 48.53 (BB) Br ex 10.00 Dght 3.500 Lbp 43.46 Br md 9.70 Dpth 5.83 Welded, 1 dk	**(X11A2YP) Yacht**	**2 oil engines** with clutches, flexible couplings & sr geared to sc. shafts driving 1 CP propeller Total Power: 2,160kW (2,936hp) 11.8kn Wartsila 6L20 2 x 4 Stroke 6 Cy. 200 x 280 each-1080kW (1468bhp) Wartsila Finland Oy-Finland AuxGen: 1 x 248kW 400V 50Hz a.c, 2 x 136kW 400V 50Hz a.c Thrusters: 1 Thwart. FP thruster (f); 1 Thwart. FP thruster (a)
8877760 - -	**TA** *ex* Taisho Maru No. 1 *-2013* **PT Indo Shipping Operator**	*181* - 370	Class: IZ	**1994-06 Hongawara Zosen K.K. — Fukuyama** Loa 42.80 Br ex - Dght 2.900 Lbp 38.50 Br md 7.50 Dpth 3.20 Welded, 1 dk	**(A12A2TC) Chemical Tanker** Liq: 173	**1 oil engine** driving 1 FP propeller Total Power: 353kW (480hp) 9.0kn Yanmar 6MAL-HTS 1 x 4 Stroke 6 Cy. 200 x 240 353kW (480bhp) Yanmar Diesel Engine Co Ltd-Japan
9126833 *BR3437* -	**TA CHENG** *ex* Korex Pusan *-2010* - - *Chinese Taipei* MMSI: 416004109	**2,919** 1,352 4,433 T/cm 12.0	Class: (KR)	**1995-09 Daedong Shipbuilding Co Ltd — Busan** Yd No: 400 Loa 99.00 (BB) Br ex - Dght 5.864 Lbp 92.00 Br md 15.00 Dpth 7.20 Welded, 1 dk	**(A31A2GX) General Cargo Ship** Grain: 4,622; Bale: 4,565 TEU 196 Compartments: 2 Ho, ER 2 Ha: ER Cranes: 2x20t	**1 oil engine** reduction geared to sc. shaft driving 1 FP propeller Total Power: 2,220kW (3,018hp) 12.0kn Wartsila 6R32D 1 x 4 Stroke 6 Cy. 320 x 350 2220kW (3018bhp) Ssangyong Heavy Industries Co Ltd-South Korea AuxGen: 2 x 600kW 440V 60Hz a.c Thrusters: 1 Thwart. FP thruster (f)
8628559 *BEBF* CT8-0062	**TA CHING 666** - **Ever Glory Fishery Co Ltd** - *Kaohsiung* *Chinese Taipei* MMSI: 416836000 Official number: 012169	**1,052** 359 800		**1991-12 Lien Ho Shipbuilding Co, Ltd — Kaohsiung** Loa 66.23 Br ex - Dght - Lbp 58.70 Br md 11.80 Dpth 4.55 Welded, 1 dk	**(B11B2FV) Fishing Vessel**	**1 oil engine** driving 1 Propeller Total Power: 2,206kW (2,999hp)
7041728 - -	**TA CHUAN No. 1** - **Chi Fong Fishing Co Ltd** - *Kaohsiung* *Chinese Taipei*	*200* 105 -		**1970 Taiwan Machinery Manufacturing Corp. — Kaohsiung** Loa 32.29 Br ex 6.35 Dght - Lbp - Br md 6.33 Dpth 2.95 Welded, 1 dk	**(B11A2FT) Trawler**	**1 oil engine** driving 1 FP propeller Total Power: 405kW (551hp) Matsui 1 x 4 Stroke 6 Cy. 270 x 420 405kW (551bhp) Matsui Iron Works Co Ltd-Japan
7041730 - -	**TA CHUAN No. 2** - **Chi Fong Fishing Co Ltd** - *Kaohsiung* *Chinese Taipei*	*200* 105 -		**1970 Taiwan Machinery Manufacturing Corp. — Kaohsiung** Loa 32.29 Br ex 6.35 Dght - Lbp - Br md 6.33 Dpth 2.95 Welded, 1 dk	**(B11A2FT) Trawler**	**1 oil engine** driving 1 FP propeller Total Power: 405kW (551hp) Matsui 1 x 4 Stroke 6 Cy. 270 x 420 405kW (551bhp) Matsui Iron Works Co Ltd-Japan
8749286 *BI2069* -	**TA CHUN 101** - **Shin Chun Fishery Co Ltd** - *Kaohsiung* *Chinese Taipei* MMSI: 416641000 Official number: 009450	**712** 218 -		**1985-07 Lien Ho Shipbuilding Co, Ltd — Kaohsiung** Yd No: 843 Loa 48.53 Br ex 8.59 Dght - Lbp - Br md - Dpth 3.75 Welded, 1 dk	**(B11B2FV) Fishing Vessel**	**1 oil engine** driving 1 FP propeller Daihatsu 1 x 4 Stroke 6 Cy. Daihatsu Diesel Manufacturing Co Lt-Japan
5184617 *BVHN* -	**TA FONG No. 1** *ex* Keifuku Maru No. 3 *-1966* **Ta Fong Fishery Co Ltd** - *Kaohsiung* *Chinese Taipei* Official number: 2157	*381* 277 -		**1960-12 KK Kanasashi Zosen — Shizuoka SZ** Yd No: 392 Loa 47.40 Br ex 7.83 Dght 3.252 Lbp 41.48 Br md 7.78 Dpth 3.81 Welded, 1 dk	**(B11B2FV) Fishing Vessel** Ins: 427 Compartments: 3 Ho, ER 3 Ha: ER Derricks: 4x1t; Winches: 2	**1 oil engine** driving 1 FP propeller Total Power: 515kW (700hp) 10.5kn Niigata M6F31HS 1 x 4 Stroke 6 Cy. 310 x 440 515kW (700bhp) Niigata Engineering Co Ltd-Japan AuxGen: 3 x 160kW 230V 60Hz a.c, 1 x 24kW 230V 60Hz a.c Fuel: 177.0
9259070 - -	**TA FU No. 1** - **Ching Tsuen Tsay Kuo**	**125** 49 -		**2001-08 in Chinese Taipei** Loa - Br ex - Dght - Lbp 25.80 Br md 5.50 Dpth - Welded, 1 dk	**(B11B2FV) Fishing Vessel**	**1 oil engine** driving 1 FP propeller
9259082 - -	**TA FU No. 2** - - -	**125** - -		**2001-09 in Chinese Taipei** Loa - Br ex - Dght - Lbp 25.80 Br md 5.50 Dpth - Welded, 1 dk	**(B11B2FV) Fishing Vessel**	**1 oil engine** driving 1 FP propeller

IMO / Call sign	Name / Owner / Port / Flag	Tonnage	Class	Builder / Dimensions	Type / Cargo	Machinery
9279824 *BNJH* -	**TA HO** - **Ta-Ho Maritime Corp** - *Keelung* *Chinese Taipei* MMSI: 416378000 Official number: 14341	**9,800** 3,636 13,638	Class: CR	**2004-01 China Shipbuilding Corp — Keelung** Yd No: 800 Loa 130.00 Br ex - Dght 7.100 Lbp 123.40 Br md 24.00 Dpth 10.00 Welded, 1 dk	**(A24A2BT) Cement Carrier** Double Hull Grain: 13,200 Compartments: 4 Ho, ER 4 Ha: ER	**3 diesel electric oil engines** driving 3 gen. each 1600kW a.c Connecting to 2 elec. motors each (2000kW) geared to sc. shafts driving 2 Z propellers Total Power: 5,100kW (6,933hp) 12.5kn Daihatsu 6DKM-26 3 x 4 Stroke 6 Cy. 260 x 380 each-1700kW (2311bhp) Daihatsu Diesel Manufacturing Co Lt-Japan Thrusters: 1 Tunnel thruster (f) Fuel: 100.0 (d.f.) 500.0 (r.f.)
7610892 - -	**TA KANG NO. 1** - **Ta Kang Petroleum Products Co Ltd** - *Hong Kong* *Hong Kong* Official number: 356574	*174* 107 -		**1974 Wong Cheong — Hong Kong** L reg 24.88 Br ex 7.93 Dght - Lbp - Br md - Dpth - Welded, 1 dk	**(A13B2TU) Tanker (unspecified)**	**1 oil engine** geared to sc. shaft driving 1 FP propeller Total Power: 184kW (250hp) 9.0kn Chinese Std. Type 6160A 1 x 4 Stroke 6 Cy. 160 x 225 184kW (250bhp) Weifang Diesel Engine Factory-China
9077824 *BCSY* -	**TA-KHUAN** - **Government of Taiwan (Ministry of Transportation & Communications)** - SatCom: Inmarsat A 1356236 *Chinese Taipei* Official number: 1601	**3,214** 964 2,400	Class: (AB)	**1995-07 Fincantieri-Cant. Nav. Italiani S.p.A. — La Spezia** Yd No: 5942 Loa 93.00 Br ex - Dght 5.090 Lbp 81.98 Br md 15.50 Dpth 8.70 Welded, 1 dk	**(B31A2SR) Research Survey Vessel** Compartments: 2 Ho 3 Ha: Cranes: 1x14.8t,1x12.8t	**4 diesel electric oil engines** driving 3 gen. each 1600kW 1 gen. of 450kW Connecting to 2 elec. motors each (1500kW) driving 2 FP propellers Total Power: 5,250kW (7,137hp) M.T.U. 12V183TE52 1 x Vee 4 Stroke 12 Cy. 128 x 142 450kW (612bhp) MTU Friedrichshafen GmbH-Friedrichshafen M.T.U. 16V396TE54 3 x Vee 4 Stroke 16 Cy. 165 x 185 each-1600kW (2175bhp) MTU Friedrichshafen GmbH-Friedrichshafen Thrusters: 1 Thwart. FP thruster (f); 1 Tunnel thruster (a)
9548184 *9H9334* -	**TA MATTEW II** - **Mako Distributors Ltd** - *Valletta* *Malta* Official number: 9548184	**115** 36 -		**2008-07 General Maintenance Ltd — Kirkop** Loa 28.00 Br ex - Dght - Lbp - Br md - Dpth - Welded, 1 dk	**(B12D2FM) Fish Farm Support Vessel** Cranes: 2	**2 oil engines** reduction geared to sc. shafts driving 2 Propellers
8430005 *HQFJ4* -	**TA MING No. 113** - **Tang I Chun** - *San Lorenzo* *Honduras* Official number: L-1823101	*174* 99 -		**1974 Kaohsiung Shipbuilding Co. Ltd. — Kaohsiung** L reg 27.31 Br ex - Dght 1.100 Lbp - Br md 6.22 Dpth 2.68 Welded, 1 dk	**(B11B2FV) Fishing Vessel**	**1 oil engine** driving 1 FP propeller Total Power: 515kW (700hp) 11.0kn Sumiyoshi 1 x 4 Stroke 6 Cy. 515kW (700bhp) Sumiyoshi Tekkosho-Japan
9176307 *9HHI6* -	**TA' PINU** - **Gozo Ferries Co Ltd** Gozo Channel Co Ltd *Valletta* *Malta* MMSI: 248692000 Official number: 6509	**4,893** 1,468 1,064	Class: NV	**2000-01 Malta Shipbuilding Co. Ltd. — Marsa** Yd No: 178 Loa 85.40 Br ex - Dght 4.000 Lbp 80.60 Br md 18.00 Dpth 6.20 Welded, 1 dk	**(A36A2PR) Passenger/Ro-Ro Ship (Vehicles)** Passengers: unberthed: 800 Bow door/ramp (centre) Len: 12.40 Wid: 7.50 Swl: - Stern door/ramp (centre) Len: 12.40 Wid: 7.50 Swl: - Lane-Len: 230 Lane-Wid: 2.50 Lane-clr ht: 4.90 Cars: 85	**4 diesel electric oil engines** driving 4 gen. each 1200kW 440V a.c Connecting to 4 elec. motors driving 4 Azimuth electric drive units 2 fwd and 2 aft Total Power: 5,300kW (7,204hp) 13.7kn Normo KRGB-6 4 x 4 Stroke 6 Cy. 250 x 300 each-1325kW (1801bhp) Ulstein Bergen AS-Norway Fuel: 110.0 (d.f.)
7220075 *BZFF* -	**TA SHENG No. 1** - **Ta Sheng Fishery Co Ltd** - *Kaohsiung* *Chinese Taipei*	*207* 100 -	Class: (CR)	**1970 Sen Koh Shipbuilding Corp — Kaohsiung** Loa 33.46 Br ex 6.35 Dght 2.464 Lbp 29.39 Br md 6.33 Dpth 2.57 Welded, 1 dk	**(B11B2FV) Fishing Vessel** Compartments: 3 Ho, ER 3 Ha: 2 (1.1 x 1.0) (1.9 x 1.0)ER	**1 oil engine** driving 1 FP propeller Total Power: 324kW (441hp) 10.0kn Alpha 404-26VO 1 x 2 Stroke 4 Cy. 260 x 400 324kW (441bhp) Taiwan Machinery ManufacturingCorp.-Kaohsiung AuxGen: 2 x 64kW 220V a.c
8210417 *BR3167* -	**TA YING** *ex* Green Ray *-1995* *ex* Kikou Maru *-1992* *ex* White Perla *-1991* **Ta Ying Steamship Co Ltd** Kaochin Steamship Co Ltd SatCom: Inmarsat C 441607180 *Kaohsiung* *Chinese Taipei* MMSI: 416071800 Official number: 012957	**2,659** 1,331 3,358	Class: (CR) (NK)	**1982-07 Matsuura Tekko Zosen K.K. — Osakikamijima** Yd No: 291 Loa 83.55 Br ex 14.03 Dght 5.798 Lbp 76.99 Br md 14.00 Dpth 8.51 Welded, 2 dks	**(A31A2GX) General Cargo Ship** Grain: 5,628; Bale: 4,964 Compartments: 2 Ho, ER 2 Ha: (11.9 x 9.5) (25.5 x 9.5)ER Derricks: 1x15t,2x10t	**1 oil engine** driving 1 FP propeller Total Power: 1,471kW (2,000hp) 11.5kn Makita GSLH637 1 x 4 Stroke 6 Cy. 370 x 590 1471kW (2000bhp) Makita Diesel Co Ltd-Japan AuxGen: 3 x 132kW a.c
7818949 - -	**TA YU** *ex* Taiyo Maru *-1997* **Ta Yu Navigation S de RL** - *Philippines*	**817** 418 998		**1979-04 Sasaki Shipbuilding Co Ltd — Osakikamijima HS** Yd No: 263 Loa 59.01 Br ex - Dght 3.901 Lbp 54.72 Br md 10.00 Dpth 5.69 Welded, 2 dks	**(A31A2GX) General Cargo Ship**	**1 oil engine** driving 1 FP propeller Total Power: 956kW (1,300hp) Hanshin 6LUN28A 1 x 4 Stroke 6 Cy. 280 x 480 956kW (1300bhp) The Hanshin Diesel Works Ltd-Japan
7041704 - -	**TA ZONG No. 1** - **Huong Cheng Fishing Co Ltd** - *Kaohsiung* *Chinese Taipei*	*200* - -		**1970 San Yang Shipbuilding Co., Ltd. — Kaohsiung** Loa 36.71 Br ex 6.33 Dght 2.591 Lbp 31.98 Br md 6.30 Dpth 3.00 Welded, 1 dk	**(B11A2FT) Trawler**	**1 oil engine** driving 1 FP propeller Total Power: 368kW (500hp) Niigata 6M26HS 1 x 4 Stroke 6 Cy. 260 x 400 368kW (500bhp) Niigata Engineering Co Ltd-Japan
7041716 - -	**TA ZONG No. 2** - **Huong Cheng Fishing Co Ltd** - *Kaohsiung* *Chinese Taipei*	*200* - -		**1970 San Yang Shipbuilding Co., Ltd. — Kaohsiung** Loa 36.71 Br ex 6.33 Dght 2.591 Lbp 31.98 Br md 6.30 Dpth 3.00 Welded, 1 dk	**(B11A2FT) Trawler**	**1 oil engine** driving 1 FP propeller Total Power: 368kW (500hp) Niigata 6M26HS 1 x 4 Stroke 6 Cy. 260 x 400 368kW (500bhp) Niigata Engineering Co Ltd-Japan
9546461 *PCSZ* -	**TAAGBORG** - **Taagborg Beheer BV** Wagenborg Shipping BV *Delfzijl* *Netherlands* MMSI: 246912000	**14,695** 6,695 21,338	Class: LR ✠ **100A1** SS 05/2013 strengthened for heavy cargoes and any holds may be empty, container cargoes in all holds and on upper deck and on all hatch covers **ShipRight** ACS (B) *IWS LI ✠ **LMC** **UMS** Eq.Ltr: H†; Cable: 576.9/60.0 U3 (a)	**2013-05 Hudong-Zhonghua Shipbuilding (Group) Co Ltd — Shanghai** Yd No: H1596A Loa 172.28 (BB) Br ex 21.74 Dght 9.380 Lbp 161.29 Br md 21.49 Dpth 13.31 Welded, 1 dk	**(A31A2GX) General Cargo Ship** Grain: 23,000; Bale: 23,000 TEU 1228 C Ho 586 TEU C Dk 642 TEU incl 72 ref C Compartments: 2 Ho, ER 2 Ha: (58.7 x 17.8)ER (55.4 x 17.8) Cranes: 4x60t Ice Capable	**1 oil engine** with clutches, flexible couplings & sr geared to sc. shafts driving 1 CP propeller Total Power: 7,500kW (10,197hp) 14.5kn Wartsila 6L46F 1 x 4 Stroke 6 Cy. 460 x 580 7500kW (10197bhp) Wartsila Italia SpA-Italy AuxGen: 3 x 450kW 450V 60Hz a.c, 1 x 800kW 450V 60Hz a.c Boilers: TOH (o.f.) 10.2kgf/cm² (10.0bar), TOH (ex.g.) 10.2kgf/cm² (10.0bar) Thrusters: 1 Thwart. CP thruster (f)
7398315 *WCF4794* -	**TAASINGE** - **M/V Defiant Inc** - *Kodiak, AK* *United States of America* MMSI: 303324000 Official number: 547210	*121* 82 -		**1973 Allied Shipyard, Inc. — Larose, La** Loa - Br ex - Dght - Lbp 19.89 Br md 6.71 Dpth - Welded, 1 dk	**(B11B2FV) Fishing Vessel**	**1 oil engine** driving 1 FP propeller Total Power: 243kW (330hp)
5348081 *SUJH* -	**TAAWON 2** - **Societe Cooperative des Petroles** - *Suez* *Egypt* MMSI: 622121215	*391* 192 500	Class: LR (BV) (PR) **A1** SS 09/2010 oil tanker FP 60~C & above Egyptiancoastal service mediterranean only,15 miles seaward, windforce not exceeding Beaufort 6 **LMC** Eq.Ltr: (g) ; Cable: 350.0/28.0 U1	**1959 Wroclawskie Stocznie 'Zacisze' — Wroclaw** Yd No: BMT500/01 Loa 53.29 Br ex 8.51 Dght 1.699 Lbp 49.99 Br md 8.20 Dpth 3.41 Welded, 1 dk	**(A13B2TU) Tanker (unspecified)** Compartments: 6 Ta, ER	**2 oil engines** driving 2 FP propellers Total Power: 448kW (610hp) 10.0kn S.K.L. 6NVD36 2 x 4 Stroke 6 Cy. 240 x 360 each-224kW (305bhp) (Re-engined ,made 1988, Reconditioned & fitted 1990) SKL Motoren u. Systemtechnik AG-Magdeburg AuxGen: 1 x 8kW 110V d.c, 1 x 6kW 110V d.c

5348093 *SUJP* -	**TAAWON 3** **Societe Cooperative des Petroles** - *Suez* *Egypt* MMSI: 622121214 Official number: 31	*392* 196 500	Class: BV	**1960 Wroclawskie Stocznie 'Zacisze' — Wroclaw** Yd No: BMT500/02 Loa 53.60 Br ex 8.49 Dght 2.500 Lbp 49.99 Br md 8.21 Dpth 3.41 Welded, 1 dk	**(A13B2TU) Tanker (unspecified)** Compartments: 6 Ta, ER	**2 oil engines** driving 2 FP propellers Total Power: 442kW (600hp) 11.0kn Halberstadt 6NVD36 2 x 4 Stroke 6 Cy. 240 x 360 each-221kW (300bhp) (made 1958, fitted 1960) VEB Maschinenbau Halberstadt-Halberstadt AuxGen: 1 x 6kW 110V d.c
5348108 *SUJQ* -	**TAAWON 4** **Societe Cooperative des Petroles** - *Alexandria* *Egypt* MMSI: 622121216 Official number: 44	*391* 197 500	Class: LR (BV) (PR) **A1** SS 11/2011 oil tanker FP exceeding 60~C Egyptian Mediterranean coastal service **LMC** Eq.Ltr: (g) ; Cable: 325.0/28.0 U1	**1959 Wroclawskie Stocznie 'Zacisze' — Wroclaw** Yd No: BMT500/03 Loa 53.29 Br ex 8.51 Dght 1.699 Lbp 49.99 Br md 8.20 Dpth 3.41 Welded, 1 dk	**(A13B2TU) Tanker (unspecified)** Compartments: 6 Ta, ER	**2 oil engines** driving 2 FP propellers Total Power: 448kW (610hp) S.K.L. 6NVD36-1U 2 x 4 Stroke 6 Cy. 240 x 360 each-224kW (305bhp) (new engine ,made 1982, fitted 1985) VEB Schwermaschinenbau "KarlLiebknecht" (SKL)-Magdeburg AuxGen: 2 x 20kW 380V 50Hz a.c
5348110 *SUJT* -	**TAAWON 5** **Societe Cooperative des Petroles** - *Port Said* *Egypt* MMSI: 622121217	*391* 194 500	Class: BV	**1961 Wroclawskie Stocznie 'Zacisze' — Wroclaw** Yd No: BMT500/04 Loa 53.35 Br ex 8.49 Dght 1.699 Lbp 49.99 Br md 8.21 Dpth 3.41 Welded, 1 dk	**(A13B2TU) Tanker (unspecified)** Compartments: 6 Ta, ER	**2 oil engines** driving 2 FP propellers Total Power: 442kW (600hp) 10.0kn Halberstadt 6NVD36 2 x 4 Stroke 6 Cy. 240 x 360 each-221kW (300bhp) (made 1960, fitted 1961) VEB Maschinenbau Halberstadt-Halberstadt AuxGen: 1 x 6kW 110V d.c
5348122 *SUJV* -	**TAAWON 6** **Societe Cooperative des Petroles** - *Suez* *Egypt* MMSI: 622121218 Official number: 202	*391* 194 500	Class: LR (BV) **A1** SS 04/2008 oil tanker extended protected water services from the ports of Alexandria, Damietta, Port Said and Suez up to 12 NM **LMC** Cable: 325.0/28.0 U1	**1959 Wroclawskie Stocznie 'Zacisze' — Wroclaw** Yd No: BMT500/05 Loa 53.37 Br ex 8.51 Dght 1.699 Lbp 49.99 Br md 8.21 Dpth 3.41 Welded, 1 dk	**(A13B2TU) Tanker (unspecified)** Compartments: 6 Ta, ER	**2 oil engines** driving 2 FP propellers Total Power: 442kW (600hp) S.K.L. 6VD36/24A-1 2 x 4 Stroke 6 Cy. 240 x 360 each-221kW (300bhp) (made 1982, fitted 1986) VEB Schwermaschinenbau "KarlLiebknecht" (SKL)-Magdeburg AuxGen: 2 x 26kW 400V 50Hz a.c
7600627 *SUCV* -	**TAAWON 8** **Societe Cooperative des Petroles** - SatCom: Inmarsat C 462211939 *Suez* *Egypt* MMSI: 622121220	*1,244* 546 1,829	Class: LR ✠**100A1** SS 10/2011 oil tanker Egyptian Coasting and Red Sea service and to Aden ESP ✠**LMC** Eq.Ltr: L; Cable: U2	**1977-06 "Naus" Shipyard Philippou Bros. S.A. — Piraeus** Yd No: 129 Loa 73.00 Br ex 11.26 Dght 4.426 Lbp 67.67 Br md 11.00 Dpth 5.11 Welded, 1 dk	**(A13B2TP) Products Tanker** Compartments: 8 Ta, ER	**2 oil engines** sr geared to sc. shafts driving 2 CP propellers Total Power: 1,824kW (2,480hp) 12.0kn Alpha 8V23L-VO 2 x Vee 4 Stroke 8 Cy. 225 x 300 each-912kW (1240bhp) Alpha Diesel A/S-Denmark AuxGen: 2 x 85kW 380V 50Hz a.c, 1 x 50kW 380V 50Hz a.c Boilers: 2 AuxB (o.f.) 12.0kgf/cm² (11.8bar)
7600639 *SUFA* -	**TAAWON 9** **Societe Cooperative des Petroles** - SatCom: Inmarsat C 462211940 *Suez* *Egypt* MMSI: 622121211 Official number: 1412	*1,244* 546 1,829	Class: LR ✠**100A1** SS 01/2011 oil tanker for cargoes with FP above 60~C Egyptian coasting and Red Sea service and to Aden ESP ✠**LMC** Eq.Ltr: L; Cable: U2	**1977-09 "Naus" Shipyard Philippou Bros. S.A. — Piraeus** Yd No: 130 Loa 73.00 Br ex 11.28 Dght 4.426 Lbp 67.67 Br md 11.00 Dpth 5.11 Welded, 1 dk	**(A13B2TP) Products Tanker** Compartments: 8 Ta, ER	**2 oil engines** sr geared to sc. shafts driving 2 CP propellers Total Power: 1,824kW (2,480hp) 12.0kn Alpha 8V23L-VO 2 x Vee 4 Stroke 8 Cy. 225 x 300 each-912kW (1240bhp) Alpha Diesel A/S-Denmark AuxGen: 2 x 85kW 380V 50Hz a.c, 1 x 50kW 380V 50Hz a.c Boilers: 2 AuxB (o.f.) 12.0kgf/cm² (11.8bar)
8112201 *SUCH* -	**TAAWON 11** **Societe Cooperative des Petroles** - *Port Said* *Egypt* MMSI: 622121221 Official number: 2066	*643* 315 1,085	Class: LR ✠**100A1** SS 06/2011 oil tanker FP 60~C and above ESP ✠**LMC** Eq.Ltr: K; Cable: 357.5/28.0 U2	**1982-04 B.V. Scheepswerven v/h H.H. Bodewes — Millingen a/d Rijn** Yd No: 763 Loa 60.13 Br ex 10.19 Dght 4.011 Lbp 54.62 Br md 9.91 Dpth 4.50 Welded, 1 dk	**(A13A2TV) Crude Oil Tanker** Liq: 1,100; Liq (Oil): 1,100 Cargo Heating Coils Compartments: 6 Ta, ER	**2 oil engines** driving 2 CP propellers Total Power: 648kW (882hp) Alpha 404-26VO 2 x 2 Stroke 4 Cy. 260 x 400 each-324kW (441bhp) B&W Alpha Diesel A/S-Denmark AuxGen: 2 x 76kW 400V 50Hz a.c, 1 x 47kW 400V 50Hz a.c Boilers: 2 db (o.f.) 13.7kgf/cm² (13.4bar) Fuel: 308.5 (d.f.) 737.0 (r.f.)
8112213 *SUYK* -	**TAAWON 12** **Societe Cooperative des Petroles** - SatCom: Inmarsat C 462211942 *Alexandria* *Egypt* MMSI: 622121212 Official number: 2097	*644* 315 1,084	Class: LR ✠**100A1** SS 01/2011 oil tanker FP 60~C & above ESP ✠**LMC** Eq.Ltr: K; Cable: 357.5/28.0 U2	**1982-06 B.V. Scheepswerven v/h H.H. Bodewes — Millingen a/d Rijn** Yd No: 764 Loa 60.13 Br ex 10.19 Dght 4.004 Lbp 54.62 Br md 9.91 Dpth 4.50 Welded, 1 dk	**(A13A2TV) Crude Oil Tanker** Liq: 1,100; Liq (Oil): 1,100 Cargo Heating Coils Compartments: 6 Ta, ER	**2 oil engines** driving 2 CP propellers Total Power: 648kW (882hp) Alpha 404-26VO 2 x 2 Stroke 4 Cy. 260 x 400 each-324kW (441bhp) B&W Alpha Diesel A/S-Denmark AuxGen: 2 x 76kW 400V 50Hz a.c, 1 x 47kW 400V 50Hz a.c Boilers: 2 db (o.f.) 13.7kgf/cm² (13.4bar) Fuel: 308.5 (d.f.) 737.0 (r.f.)
8316742 *SUSF* -	**TAAWON 14** **Societe Cooperative des Petroles** - SatCom: Inmarsat C 462211943 *Port Said* *Egypt* MMSI: 622121213 Official number: 2400	*643* 315 975	Class: LR ✠**100A1** SS 01/2009 oil tanker Mediterranean and Red Sea service, FP 60~C and above ESP ✠**LMC** Eq.Ltr: k; Cable: 357.5/28.0 U2	**1984-02 B.V. Scheepswerven v/h H.H. Bodewes — Millingen a/d Rijn** Yd No: 774 Loa 60.13 Br ex 10.19 Dght 4.004 Lbp 54.69 Br md 9.91 Dpth 4.53 Welded, 1 dk	**(B35E2TF) Bunkering Tanker** Liq: 1,100; Liq (Oil): 1,100 Cargo Heating Coils Compartments: 6 Ta, ER	**2 oil engines** driving 2 CP propellers Total Power: 648kW (882hp) 10.0kn Alpha 404-26VO 2 x 2 Stroke 4 Cy. 260 x 400 each-324kW (441bhp) B&W Alpha Diesel A/S-Denmark AuxGen: 2 x 76kW 400V 50Hz a.c, 1 x 47kW 400V 50Hz a.c Boilers: 2 db 13.7kgf/cm² (13.4bar) Fuel: 308.5 (d.f.) 737.0 (r.f.)
8611934 *SSCK* -	**TAAWON 15** **Societe Cooperative des Petroles** - *Port Said* *Egypt* Official number: 3599	*148* 49 120	Class: LR ✠**100A1** SS 10/2010 oil tanker FP exceeding 60~C, Egyptian coastal service ✠**LMC** Cable: U2	**1990-10 Canal Naval Construction Co. — Port Said (Port Fuad)** Yd No: 432 Loa 33.02 Br ex 6.30 Dght 2.182 Lbp 30.84 Br md 6.00 Dpth 2.75 Welded, 1 dk	**(A13B2TP) Products Tanker** Compartments: 4 Ta, ER	**1 oil engine** with clutches, flexible couplings & sr reverse geared to sc. shaft driving 1 FP propeller Total Power: 545kW (741hp) MWM TBD604V8 1 x Vee 4 Stroke 8 Cy. 160 x 185 545kW (741bhp) Motoren Werke Mannheim AG (MWM)-West Germany AuxGen: 2 x 45kW 380V 50Hz a.c
9631046 - -	**TAB 001** **PT Trada Dryship** - *Surabaya* *Indonesia*	**1,166** 350 -	Class: RI	**2012-11 PT Dewa Ruci Agung — Surabaya** Yd No: BIC-11.02 Loa 54.98 Br ex - Dght 2.250 Lbp 53.51 Br md 15.00 Dpth 3.22 Welded, 1 dk	**(B22A2ZA) Accommodation Ship**	**2 oil engines** reduction geared to sc. shafts driving 2 FP propellers Total Power: 894kW (1,216hp) 7.0kn Caterpillar C18 ACERT 2 x 4 Stroke 6 Cy. 145 x 183 each-447kW (608bhp) Caterpillar Inc-USA AuxGen: 3 x 300kW 400V 50Hz a.c
8318104 *6ADP* -	**TABA** **The Egyptian Navigation Co (ENC)** - *Alexandria* *Egypt* MMSI: 622120438 Official number: 2534	**6,650** 1,995 3,133	Class: GL	**1985-02 Schlichting-Werft GmbH — Luebeck** Yd No: 2011 Loa 112.71 (BB) Br ex 17.91 Dght 5.250 Lbp 101.10 Br md 17.51 Dpth 11.99 Welded, 2 dks	**(A35A2RR) Ro-Ro Cargo Ship** Passengers: driver berths: 12 Stern door & ramp (a) Len: 15.00 Wid: 8.00 Swl: 50 Lane-Len: 890 Lane-Wid: 13.00 Lane-clr ht: 6.00 Cars: 359 Bale: 11,430 TEU 257 C Ho 177 TEU C Dk 80 TEU Ice Capable	**2 oil engines** with flexible couplings & sr gearedto sc. shafts driving 2 CP propellers Total Power: 5,405kW (7,349hp) 17.0kn MaK 9M453AK 2 x 4 Stroke 9 Cy. 320 x 420 each-2702kW (3674bhp) Krupp MaK Maschinenbau GmbH-Kiel AuxGen: 3 x 486kW 440V 60Hz a.c Thrusters: 1 Thwart. FP thruster (f) Fuel: 131.0 (d.f.) 535.0 (r.f.)
9170054 *JYB203* -	**TABA** *ex* Lucky-2 *-2008* *ex* Bluewater Lady *-2002* **Sindbad For Marine Transport** - *Aqaba* *Jordan* Official number: 11	**124** 48 -	Class: IM RI (AB)	**1997-02 Sabre Catamarans Pty Ltd — Fremantle WA** Yd No: 134 Loa 22.00 Br ex - Dght 1.400 Lbp 18.70 Br md 7.56 Dpth 1.67 Welded, 1 dk	**(A37B2PS) Passenger Ship** Hull Material: Aluminium Alloy Passengers: unberthed: 129	**2 oil engines** driving 2 FP propellers Total Power: 1,544kW (2,100hp) 24.0kn Caterpillar 3412TA 2 x Vee 4 Stroke 12 Cy. 137 x 152 each-772kW (1050bhp) Caterpillar Inc-USA AuxGen: 1 x 29kW a.c, 1 x 19kW a.c
9111840 - -	**TABA** **Government of The Arab Republic of Egypt (Ministry of Maritime Transport - Ports & Lighthouses Administration)** - *Suez* *Egypt*	**280** - -	Class: LR ✠**100A1** SS 11/2001 tug Egyptian coastal service ✠**LMC** Eq.Ltr: C; Cable: 303.0/17.5 U2	**1996-11 Timsah SB. Co. — Ismailia** Yd No: 1234 Loa 29.00 Br ex 9.00 Dght 3.060 Lbp 27.50 Br md 8.60 Dpth 3.60 Welded, 1 dk	**(B32A2ST) Tug**	**2 oil engines** gearing integral to driving 2 Voith-Schneider propellers Total Power: 1,766kW (2,402hp) Yanmar M220-EN 2 x 4 Stroke 6 Cy. 220 x 300 each-883kW (1201bhp) Yanmar Diesel Engine Co Ltd-Japan AuxGen: 2 x 60kW 400V 50Hz a.c

IMO / Call sign	Name / Owner	Tonnage	Class	Builder / Dimensions	Type	Machinery
9253674 - -	**TABA 2** **Government of The Arab Republic of Egypt (Ministry of Maritime Transport - Ports & Lighthouses Administration)** - *Alexandria* Egypt	**280** - -	Class: LR ✠**100A1** SS 05/2003 tug Egyptian coastal service ✠**LMC** Eq.Ltr: C; Cable: 275.0/17.5 U2 (a)	**2003-05 Timsah SB. Co. — Abu Qir, Alexandria** Yd No: 1484 Loa 30.50 Br ex 9.00 Dght 4.476 Lbp 28.00 Br md 8.60 Dpth 3.60 Welded, 1 dk	**(B32A2ST) Tug**	**2 oil engines** gearing integral to driving 2 Voith-Schneider propellers Total Power: 1,764kW (2,398hp) Yanmar M220-EN 2 x 4 Stroke 6 Cy. 220 x 300 each-882kW (1199bhp) Yanmar Diesel Engine Co Ltd-Japan AuxGen: 2 x 60kW 380V 50Hz a.c
9373917 *A8NX8* -	**TABAGO BAY** *ex* Mell Serapong *-2011* *ex* Tabago Bay *-2009* *ex* Vega Amethyst *-2007* **ms 'Tabago Bay' Schifffahrtsges mbH & Co KG** NSC Schifffahrtsgesellschaft mbH & Cie KG *Monrovia* Liberia MMSI: 636091446 Official number: 91446	**9,957** 5,020 13,781 T/cm 28.0	Class: GL	**2007-11 Taizhou Kouan Shipbuilding Co Ltd — Taizhou JS** Yd No: KA407 Loa 147.87 (BB) Br ex 23.43 Dght 8.510 Lbp 140.30 Br md 23.25 Dpth 11.50 Welded, 1 dk	**(A33A2CC) Container Ship (Fully Cellular)** Grain: 16,067; Bale: 16,067 TEU 1118 C Ho 334 TEU C Dk 784 incl 240 ref C Compartments: 5 Ho, ER 7 Ha: ER Cranes: 2x45t	**1 oil engine** reduction geared to sc. shaft driving 1 CP propeller Total Power: 9,730kW (13,229hp) 19.6kn MAN-B&W 7L58/64 1 x 4 Stroke 7 Cy. 580 x 640 9730kW (13229bhp) MAN B&W Diesel AG-Augsburg AuxGen: 3 x 570kW 450V a.c, 1 x 1400kW 450V a.c Thrusters: 1 Tunnel thruster (f) Fuel: 199.8 (d.f.) 1306.3 (r.f.)
7920924 - - -	**TABAN** *ex* Shoyo *-2009* *ex* Ariho *-2008* - -	*127* - 44		**1979-12 K.K. Odo Zosen Tekko — Shimonoseki** Yd No: 260 Loa 26.30 Br ex 7.01 Dght 2.300 Lbp 24.58 Br md 7.00 Dpth 2.95 Welded, 1 dk	**(B34G2SE) Pollution Control Vessel**	**2 oil engines** reduction geared to sc. shafts driving 2 FP propellers Total Power: 514kW (698hp) 10.5kn Yanmar 6AL-HT 2 x 4 Stroke 6 Cy. 165 x 200 each-257kW (349bhp) Yanmar Diesel Engine Co Ltd-Japan
9420368 *9BTC* -	**TABAN 1** **Teu Feeder Ltd** Valfajre Shipping Co *Qeshm Island* Iran MMSI: 422814000	**9,957** 5,032 13,734 T/cm 28.0	Class: (GL)	**2009-01 Jinling Shipyard — Nanjing JS** Yd No: 04-0428 Loa 147.86 (BB) Br ex - Dght 8.500 Lbp 140.30 Br md 23.25 Dpth 11.50 Welded, 1 dk	**(A33A2CC) Container Ship (Fully Cellular)** Grain: 16,000; Bale: 16,000 TEU 1118 C Ho 334 TEU C Dk 784 incl 240 ref C Cranes: 2x45t Ice Capable	**1 oil engine** reduction geared to sc. shafts driving 1 CP propeller Total Power: 9,730kW (13,229hp) 19.6kn MAN-B&W 7L58/64 1 x 4 Stroke 7 Cy. 580 x 640 9730kW (13229bhp) Hudong Heavy Machinery Co Ltd-China AuxGen: 1 x 1400kW 450V a.c, 3 x 570kW 450V a.c Thrusters: 1 Tunnel thruster (f)
8320171 *EPCL9* -	**TABANDEH** *ex* Atrium *-2013* *ex* Iran Hamzeh *-2009* **Sparkle Brilliant Development Ltd** Rahbaran Omid Darya Ship Management Co Iran MMSI: 422050200	**25,768** 14,253 43,288 T/cm 50.0	Class: KR (LR) ✠ Classed LR until 9/2/12	**1986-03 Daewoo Shipbuilding & Heavy Machinery Ltd — Geoje** Yd No: 1025 Loa 190.00 (BB) Br ex 30.03 Dght 11.618 Lbp 181.01 Br md 30.00 Dpth 16.31 Welded, 1 dk	**(A21A2BC) Bulk Carrier** Grain: 52,560; Bale: 50,765 Compartments: 5 Ho, ER 5 Ha: (17.6 x 11.0)4 (17.6 x 14.5)ER Cranes: 4x25t	**1 oil engine** driving 1 FP propeller Total Power: 8,458kW (11,499hp) 14.5kn B&W 6L60MC 1 x 2 Stroke 6 Cy. 600 x 1944 8458kW (11499bhp) Hitachi Zosen Corp-Japan AuxGen: 4 x 500kW 450V 60Hz a.c Boilers: AuxB (o.f.) 8.0kgf/cm² (7.8bar), AuxB (ex.g.) 10.0kgf/cm² (9.8bar)rcv 8kgf/cm² (7.8bar) Fuel: 268.5 (d.f.) 2073.0 (r.f.)
7927403 *DUTC2* -	**TABANGAO** *ex* Nanyo Maru *-2003* *ex* Kansai Maru No. 33 *-2003* *ex* Hanyo Maru *-2000* **Malayan Towage & Salvage Corp (SALVTUG)** *Manila* Philippines MMSI: 548084100 Official number: 00-0001392	*199* 104 -		**1980-03 Shin Yamamoto Shipbuilding & Engineering Co Ltd — Kochi KC** Yd No: 302 Loa 31.49 Br ex 8.62 Dght 2.601 Lbp 28.71 Br md 8.60 Dpth 3.81 Welded, 1 dk	**(B32A2ST) Tug**	**2 oil engines** gearing integral to driving 2 Z propellers Total Power: 1,912kW (2,600hp) Niigata 6MG25BX 2 x 4 Stroke 6 Cy. 250 x 320 each-956kW (1300bhp) Niigata Engineering Co Ltd-Japan
7358652 *9LB2067* -	**TABARK** *ex* Fatheh Al Rahman *-2000* *ex* Ghazal 1 *-2006* *ex* Ghazal *-2005* *ex* Al Noor *-2004* *ex* Al Katheeria II *-2003* *ex* Ocean Executive *-2000* *ex* Siic Evo *-1998* *ex* Sang Thai Honor *-1997* *ex* Pico do Funcho *-1989* *ex* Sandra K *-1984* *ex* Fjallfoss *-1983* *ex* Mercandian Transporter *-1977* **Sheikh Mosa Mohammed Ayadaldeen & Basam Akram Gzal** - *Freetown* Sierra Leone MMSI: 667190000 Official number: SL100190	**1,861** 1,069 3,097	Class: (NV) (GL)	**1974-08 Frederikshavn Vaerft A/S — Frederikshavn** Yd No: 349 Loa 78.52 (BB) Br ex 13.09 Dght 4.140 Lbp 70.82 Br md 13.01 Dpth 7.01 Welded, 2 dks	**(A31A2GX) General Cargo Ship** Grain: 3,802; Bale: 3,378 TEU 74 C. 74/20' Compartments: 2 Ho, ER 2 Ha: (18.9 x 8.0) (19.5 x 8.0)ER Cranes: 1x5t; Derricks: 2x5t	**1 oil engine** driving 1 CP propeller Total Power: 1,379kW (1,875hp) Deutz SBV9M628 1 x 4 Stroke 9 Cy. 240 x 280 1379kW (1875bhp) (new engine 1998) Motoren Werke Mannheim AG (MWM)-Mannheim AuxGen: 1 x 240kW 220/440V 60Hz a.c, 2 x 72kW 220/440V 60Hz a.c Fuel: 221.5 (d.f.) 8.0pd
7423990 *5VBC5* -	**TABARK ALAAH** *ex* Katia *-2011* *ex* Pia V *-2008* *ex* Pia *-2007* *ex* Pia Theresa *-2006* *ex* Limfjord *-1984* *ex* Arroi *-1982* **Damas Shipholding Inc** - *Lome* Togo MMSI: 671189000	**563** 169 683	Class: (LR) (BV) Classed LR until 23/8/10	**1976-09 A/S Nordsovaerftet — Ringkobing** Yd No: 111 Converted From: General Cargo Ship-1985 Loa 49.69 Br ex 8.32 Dght 3.695 Lbp 44.45 Br md 8.30 Dpth 5.50 Welded, 1 dk	**(A12D2LV) Vegetable Oil Tanker** Double Hull Liq: 656 Cargo Heating Coils Compartments: 6 Ta (s.stl), ER 6 Cargo Pump (s): 6x54m³/hr Manifold: Bow/CM: 22.5m	**1 oil engine** driving 1 CP propeller Total Power: 441kW (600hp) 11.0kn Alpha 406-26VO 1 x 2 Stroke 6 Cy. 260 x 400 441kW (600bhp) Alpha Diesel A/S-Denmark AuxGen: 1 x 96kW 220/380V 50Hz a.c, 2 x 39kW 220/380V 50Hz a.c, 1 x 28kW 220/380V 50Hz a.c Fuel: 50.0 (d.f.) 3.0pd
8903454 - -	**TABAS 1** **Industrial Fishing Co** Kish Free Zone Organization (KFZO) *Bushehr* Iran	**171** 51 -	Class: (BV)	**1991-07 Stocznia 'Wisla' — Gdansk** Yd No: WKR25301 Loa 25.65 Br ex Dght 3.430 Lbp 22.32 Br md 7.40 Dpth 4.00 Welded	**(B11A2FS) Stern Trawler**	**1 oil engine** reduction geared to sc. shaft driving 1 FP propeller Total Power: 375kW (510hp) Caterpillar 3412T 1 x Vee 4 Stroke 12 Cy. 137 x 152 375kW (510bhp) Caterpillar Inc-USA
8903466 - -	**TABAS 2** **Industrial Fishing Co** Kish Free Zone Organization (KFZO) *Bushehr* Iran	**171** 51 -	Class: (BV)	**1991-07 Stocznia 'Wisla' — Gdansk** Yd No: WKR25302 Loa - Br ex - Dght - Lbp 25.00 Br md 7.40 Dpth 4.00 Welded	**(B11A2FS) Stern Trawler**	**1 oil engine** reduction geared to sc. shaft driving 1 FP propeller Total Power: 375kW (510hp) Caterpillar 3412T 1 x Vee 4 Stroke 12 Cy. 137 x 152 375kW (510bhp) Caterpillar Inc-USA
8903478 - -	**TABAS 3** **Industrial Fishing Co** Kish Free Zone Organization (KFZO) *Bushehr* Iran	**171** 51 -	Class: (BV)	**1992-09 Stocznia 'Wisla' — Gdansk** Yd No: WKR25303 Loa 25.65 Br ex - Dght 3.430 Lbp 22.32 Br md 7.40 Dpth 4.00 Welded	**(B11A2FS) Stern Trawler**	**1 oil engine** reduction geared to sc. shaft driving 1 FP propeller Total Power: 375kW (510hp) Caterpillar 3412T 1 x Vee 4 Stroke 12 Cy. 137 x 152 375kW (510bhp) Caterpillar Inc-USA
8903480 - -	**TABAS 4** **Industrial Fishing Co** Kish Free Zone Organization (KFZO) *Bushehr* Iran	**171** 51 -	Class: (BV)	**1992-09 Stocznia 'Wisla' — Gdansk** Yd No: WKR25304 Loa 25.65 Br ex - Dght - Lbp 22.32 Br md 7.40 Dpth 4.00 Welded	**(B11A2FS) Stern Trawler**	**1 oil engine** reduction geared to sc. shaft driving 1 FP propeller Total Power: 375kW (510hp) Caterpillar 3412T 1 x Vee 4 Stroke 12 Cy. 137 x 152 375kW (510bhp) Caterpillar Inc-USA
8903492 - -	**TABAS 5** - **Neptune Sayd Fishing Co** - *Bushehr* Iran	**171** 51 -	Class: (BV)	**1991 Stocznia 'Wisla' — Gdansk** Yd No: WKR25305 Loa 25.65 Br ex - Dght - Lbp 22.32 Br md 7.40 Dpth 4.00 Welded	**(B11A2FS) Stern Trawler**	**1 oil engine** reduction geared to sc. shaft driving 1 FP propeller Total Power: 375kW (510hp) Caterpillar 3412T 1 x Vee 4 Stroke 12 Cy. 137 x 152 375kW (510bhp) Caterpillar Inc-USA
8903507 *EPQL* -	**TABAS 6** **Mokhtari F** - *Bushehr* Iran Official number: 16845	**160** 48 -	Class: AS (BV)	**1991 Stocznia 'Wisla' — Gdansk** Yd No: WKR25306 Loa 25.65 Br ex - Dght - Lbp 22.32 Br md 7.40 Dpth 4.00 Welded	**(B11A2FS) Stern Trawler**	**1 oil engine** geared to sc. shaft driving 1 FP propeller Total Power: 375kW (510hp) Caterpillar 3412T 1 x Vee 4 Stroke 12 Cy. 137 x 152 375kW (510bhp) Caterpillar Inc-USA

IMO / Call sign / Flag	Name / Owner / Port	Tonnage	Class	Build / Dimensions	Type	Machinery
8903519 *EPQM* -	**TABAS 7** - **Farz A** - *Bandar Abbas* *Iran* MMSI: 422666000 Official number: 3.223	**160** 48 -	Class: AS (BV)	**1991 Stocznia 'Wisla' — Gdansk** Yd No: WKR25307 Loa 25.65 Br ex - Dght 3.000 Lbp 22.32 Br md 7.40 Dpth 4.00 Welded, 1 dk	**(B11A2FS) Stern Trawler**	**1 oil engine** geared to sc. shaft driving 1 FP propeller Total Power: 375kW (510hp) Caterpillar 3412T 1 x Vee 4 Stroke 12 Cy. 137 x 152 375kW (510bhp) Caterpillar Inc-USA
8903521 *EPQN* -	**TABAS 8** - **Amini A & Partners** - *Bushehr* *Iran* MMSI: 422677000 Official number: 17544	**160** 48 -	Class: AS (BV)	**1991**-09 **Stocznia 'Wisla' — Gdansk** Yd No: WKR25308 Loa 25.65 Br ex - Dght 3.000 Lbp 22.32 Br md 7.40 Dpth 4.00 Welded, 1 dk	**(B11A2FS) Stern Trawler**	**1 oil engine** geared to sc. shaft driving 1 FP propeller Total Power: 370kW (503hp) Caterpillar 3412 1 x Vee 4 Stroke 12 Cy. 137 x 152 370kW (503bhp) Caterpillar Inc-USA
8903533 *EPQO* -	**TABAS 9** - **Mahmoud Amini** - *Bandar Abbas* *Iran* MMSI: 422744000 Official number: 683	**171** 51 -	Class: AS (BV)	**1993**-03 **Stocznia 'Wisla' — Gdansk** Yd No: WKR25309 Loa 25.65 Br ex - Dght 3.000 Lbp 22.32 Br md 7.40 Dpth 4.00 Welded, 1 dk	**(B11A2FS) Stern Trawler**	**1 oil engine** geared to sc. shaft driving 1 FP propeller Total Power: 375kW (510hp) Caterpillar 3412 1 x Vee 4 Stroke 12 Cy. 137 x 152 375kW (510bhp) Caterpillar Inc-USA
8903545 - -	**TABAS 10** - **Neptune Sayd Fishing Co** - *Bandar Abbas* *Iran*	**171** 51 -	Class: (BV)	**1993**-03 **Stocznia 'Wisla' — Gdansk** Yd No: WKR25310 Loa 25.65 Br ex - Dght 3.000 Lbp 22.32 Br md 7.40 Dpth 4.00 Welded, 1 dk	**(B11A2FS) Stern Trawler**	**1 oil engine** geared to sc. shaft driving 1 FP propeller Total Power: 375kW (510hp) 9.2kn Caterpillar 3412 1 x Vee 4 Stroke 12 Cy. 137 x 152 375kW (510bhp) Caterpillar Inc-USA
7035250 - -	**TABASCO** - **Government of Mexico (Secretaria de Communicaciones y Transportes - Direccion General de Dragado)** - *Tampico* *Mexico*	*2,245* 1,049 2,459	Class: (BV)	**1970**-09 **Dubigeon-Normandie S.A. — Prairie-au-Duc, Nantes** Yd No: 121 Loa 79.81 Br ex 14.56 Dght 4.814 Lbp 73.11 Br md 14.25 Dpth 5.80 Welded, 1 dk	**(B33B2DT) Trailing Suction Hopper Dredger** Hopper: 1,400	**2 oil engines** reduction geared to sc. shafts driving 2 FP propellers Total Power: 2,184kW (2,970hp) 12.0kn MAN G7V30/45ATL 2 x 4 Stroke 7 Cy. 300 x 450 each-1092kW (1485bhp) Maschinenbau Augsburg Nuernberg (MAN)-Augsburg AuxGen: 3 x 260kW 440V 60Hz a.c Thrusters: 1 Thwart. FP thruster (f)
9294812 *A8IL9* -	**TABEA** *ex* MSC Turchia *-2010* *ex* Cholguan *-2006* **ms 'Tabea' Schiffahrtsgesellschaft mbh & Co KG** Peter Doehle Schiffahrts-KG *Monrovia* *Liberia* MMSI: 636091212 Official number: 91212	**66,280** 36,284 68,228	Class: LR ✠ **100A1** SS 02/2011 container ship *IWS LI **ShipRight** (SDA, FDA, CM) ✠ **LMC** **UMS** Eq.Ltr: X†; Cable: 742.5/97.0 U3 (a)	**2006**-02 **China Shipbuilding Corp (CSBC) — Kaohsiung** Yd No: 826 Loa 275.80 (BB) Br ex 40.10 Dght 14.000 Lbp 263.80 Br md 40.00 Dpth 24.20 Welded, 1 dk	**(A33A2CC) Container Ship (Fully Cellular)** TEU 5527 C Ho 2601 TEU C Dk 2926 TEU incl 500 ref C. Compartments: 7 Cell Ho, ER 7 Ha: ER	**1 oil engine** driving 1 FP propeller Total Power: 54,926kW (74,677hp) 25.6kn Sulzer 10RT-flex96C 1 x 2 Stroke 10 Cy. 960 x 2500 54926kW (74677bhp) Doosan Engine Co Ltd-South Korea AuxGen: 4 x 1980kW 450V 60Hz a.c Boilers: e (ex.g.) 12.2kgf/cm² (12.0bar), WTAuxB (o.f.) 8.2kgf/cm² (8.0bar) Thrusters: 1 Thwart. CP thruster (f)
8822430 *LW9317* -	**TABEIRON** *ex* Tabeirones *-2004* *ex* Esturion *-2004* **Vieira Argentina SA** Eduardo Vieira SA SatCom: Inmarsat C 470100739 *Puerto Deseado* *Argentina* Official number: 02233	*358* 115 261	Class: (LR) (BV) ✠ Classed LR until 23/10/02	**1990**-06 **Factoria Naval de Marin S.A. — Marin** Yd No: 39 Loa 35.50 (BB) Br ex 8.68 Dght 3.901 Lbp 30.51 Br md 8.62 Dpth 6.10 Welded, 2 dks	**(B11A2FS) Stern Trawler** Ins: 280	**1 oil engine** with clutches, flexible couplings & sr geared to sc. shaft driving 1 CP propeller Total Power: 662kW (900hp) 11.0kn A.B.C. 6MDXC 1 x 4 Stroke 6 Cy. 242 x 320 662kW (900bhp) Anglo Belgian Corp NV (ABC)-Belgium AuxGen: 2 x 160kW 380V 50Hz a.c, 1 x 80kW 380V 50Hz a.c
8616192 *LW7242* -	**TABEIRON DOS** *ex* Andvari *-2006* *ex* Unaaq *-1994* *ex* Ungaaq *-1989* **Vieira Argentina SA** Eduardo Vieira SA *Puerto Deseado* *Argentina* MMSI: 701006086 Official number: 02323	*437* 167 161	Class: (BV) (NV)	**1987**-05 **Danyard Aalborg A/S — Aalborg** (Hull) **1987**-05 **Johs Kristensen Skibsbyggeri A/S — Hvide Sande** Yd No: 182 Loa 35.01 Br ex - Dght 4.460 Lbp 28.81 Br md 9.61 Dpth 6.91 Welded, 1 dk	**(B11A2FS) Stern Trawler** Ice Capable	**1 oil engine** driving 1 CP propeller Total Power: 929kW (1,263hp) Wartsila 6R22 1 x 4 Stroke 6 Cy. 220 x 240 929kW (1263bhp) Wartsila Diesel Oy-Finland AuxGen: 3 x 220kW 380V d.c
8656556 *LW3149* -	**TABEIRON TRES** - **Pesquera Quara SA** - *Argentina* Official number: 2365	**107** - -		**2004 Coserena SA — Puerto Deseado** Loa 20.90 Br ex - Dght - Lbp - Br md 6.60 Dpth 3.35 Welded, 1 dk	**(B11B2FV) Fishing Vessel**	**1 oil engine** driving 1 Propeller Total Power: 404kW (549hp)
8401004 *4RAU* -	**TABERNACLE GRACE** *ex* Sailor *-2005* *ex* Fortuna Australia *-2003* *ex* Halim Mete *-1999* *ex* Maritime Peace *-1996* *ex* Ken Ann *-1989* *ex* Orion Queen *-1987* **Tokyo Cement Co (Lanka) PLC** Ocean Ship Management Pte Ltd *Colombo* *Sri Lanka* MMSI: 417222308 Official number: 1280	**15,473** 8,978 25,996	Class: NK	**1985**-01 **Hashihama Shipbuilding Co Ltd — Tadotsu KG** Yd No: 832 Loa 160.20 (BB) Br ex - Dght 10.229 Lbp 150.02 Br md 25.21 Dpth 14.03 Welded, 1 dk	**(A21A2BC) Bulk Carrier** Grain: 32,754; Bale: 31,565 Compartments: 4 Ho, ER 4 Ha: (18.4 x 12.8)3 (21.6 x 12.8)ER Cranes: 4x25t; Derricks: 1x25t	**1 oil engine** driving 1 FP propeller Total Power: 5,296kW (7,200hp) 13.5kn B&W 6L50MCE 1 x 2 Stroke 6 Cy. 500 x 1620 5296kW (7200bhp) Mitsui Engineering & Shipbuilding CLtd-Japan AuxGen: 2 x 400kW a.c Fuel: 1205.0 (r.f.)
8400579 *4RAL* -	**TABERNACLE PRINCE** *ex* Crio *-2003* *ex* Handy Samurai *-1990* *ex* Elegant C *-1988* *ex* Lake Suwa *-1988* **Fuji Cement Co (Lanka) Ltd** Ocean Ship Management Pte Ltd *Colombo* *Sri Lanka* MMSI: 417222299 Official number: 1259	**11,276** 4,648 18,520	Class: LR (NK) **100A1** SS 05/2012 ESP **LMC** Eq.Ltr: D†; Cable: 550.0/54.0 U2 (a)	**1984**-10 **Sasebo Heavy Industries Co. Ltd. — Sasebo Yard, Sasebo** Yd No: 333 Converted From: Bulk Carrier-2007 Loa 148.00 (BB) Br ex - Dght 9.318 Lbp 138.80 Br md 23.10 Dpth 12.70 Welded, 1 dk	**(A24A2BT) Cement Carrier** Grain: 23,790; Bale: 23,103 Compartments: 4 Ho, ER 4 Ha: (17.6 x 9.6)3 (19.2 x 11.2)ER Derricks: 4x25t	**1 oil engine** driving 1 FP propeller Total Power: 4,266kW (5,800hp) 13.5kn Mitsubishi 6UEC52HA 1 x 2 Stroke 6 Cy. 520 x 1250 4266kW (5800bhp) Kobe Hatsudoki KK-Japan AuxGen: 2 x 300kW 445V 60Hz a.c Boilers: e (ex.g.) 7.1kgf/cm² (7.0bar), AuxB (Comp) 7.1kgf/cm² (7.0bar)
9106699 *4RCC* -	**TABERNACLE STAR II** *ex* ID Symphony *-2011* *ex* Cynthia Crown *-2005* **Tokyo Cement Co (Lanka) PLC** Ocean Ship Management Pte Ltd *Colombo* *Sri Lanka* MMSI: 417222343 Official number: 1317	**14,431** 8,741 23,716 T/cm 33.5	Class: NK	**1995**-01 **KK Kanasashi — Toyohashi AI** Yd No: 3370 Loa 150.52 (BB) Br ex - Dght 9.560 Lbp 143.00 Br md 26.00 Dpth 13.20 Welded, 1 dk	**(A21A2BC) Bulk Carrier** Grain: 31,249; Bale: 30,169 Compartments: 4 Ho, ER 4 Ha: (17.9 x 12.8)3 (19.5 x 17.8)ER Cranes: 4x30t	**1 oil engine** driving 1 FP propeller Total Power: 5,296kW (7,200hp) 13.6kn B&W 6L42MC 1 x 2 Stroke 6 Cy. 420 x 1360 5296kW (7200bhp) Kawasaki Heavy Industries Ltd-Japan Fuel: 890.0 (r.f.)
7520281 *5AMN* -	**TABKAH** - **Government of Libya (Socialist Ports Co)** - *Derna* *Libya* Official number: BP209	*301* - -	Class: (LR) ✠ Classed LR until 11/9/96	**1977**-12 **Soc. Argibay de Const. Navais e Mecanicas S.A.R.L. — Alverca** Yd No: 140 Loa 35.01 Br ex 9.22 Dght 3.531 Lbp 32.01 Br md 9.01 Dpth 4.65 Welded, 1 dk	**(B32A2ST) Tug**	**2 oil engines** reverse reduction geared to sc. shafts driving 2 FP propellers Total Power: 2,400kW (3,264hp) MaK 6M332AK 2 x 4 Stroke 6 Cy. 240 x 330 each-1200kW (1632bhp) MaK Maschinenbau GmbH-Kiel AuxGen: 2 x 80kW 380V 50Hz a.c, 1 x 48kW 380V 50Hz a.c
9615810 *YJRB7* -	**TABLATE TIDE** - **Platinum Fleet Ltd** Tidewater Marine International Inc *Port Vila* *Vanuatu* MMSI: 576984000 Official number: 2038	**1,678** 503 1,338	Class: AB	**2011**-03 **Fujian Southeast Shipyard — Fuzhou FJ** Yd No: DN59M-90 Loa 59.25 Br ex - Dght 4.950 Lbp 52.20 Br md 14.95 Dpth 6.10 Welded, 1 dk	**(B21B20A) Anchor Handling Tug Supply**	**2 oil engines** reduction geared to sc. shafts driving 2 CP propellers Total Power: 3,840kW (5,220hp) 11.0kn Caterpillar 3516B-HD 2 x Vee 4 Stroke 16 Cy. 170 x 215 each-1920kW (2610bhp) Caterpillar Inc-USA AuxGen: 2 x 800kW a.c, 2 x 350kW a.c Thrusters: 2 Tunnel thruster (f) Fuel: 520.0
7921409 *YGPZ* -	**TABONGANEN 03** *ex* Puteri Dewi *-2000* *ex* Allwell Profile *-2000* *ex* Meisho Maru No. 18 *-1992* **PT Pelayaran Teladan Makmur Jaya** - *Surabaya* *Indonesia* MMSI: 525017080	**967** 632 1,798	Class: KI (NK)	**1980**-02 **Kurinoura Dockyard Co Ltd — Yawatahama EH** Yd No: 147 Loa 68.56 Br ex - Dght 4.701 Lbp 64.00 Br md 11.00 Dpth 5.00 Welded, 1 dk	**(A13B2TU) Tanker (unspecified)** Double Bottom Entire Compartment Length Liq: 2,147; Liq (Oil): 2,147	**1 oil engine** geared to sc. shaft driving 1 FP propeller Total Power: 1,324kW (1,800hp) Hanshin 6LU35G 1 x 4 Stroke 6 Cy. 350 x 550 1324kW (1800bhp) The Hanshin Diesel Works Ltd-Japan

IMO / Call sign	Name / Owner	Tonnage	Class	Builder / Dimensions	Type	Machinery
7825904 *H03187* -	**TABOR** **Banco Internacional de Panama SA** - *Panama* *Panama*	*119* 41 110		**1979-09 Ast. Picsa S.A. — Callao** Yd No: 118 Loa 21.70 Br ex 6.94 Dght - Lbp 19.61 Br md 6.71 Dpth 2.75 Welded, 1 dk	**(B11B2FV) Fishing Vessel**	**1 oil engine** driving 1 FP propeller Total Power: 202kW (275hp) Caterpillar 3406PCTA 1 x 4 Stroke 6 Cy. 137 x 165 202kW (275bhp) Caterpillar Tractor Co-USA
6710592 *H03076* -	**TABOS** *ex* Taler *-2003* *ex* Diana-2 *-2000* *ex* Nordmeer *-2000* **DMB International Co Ltd** - *Panama* *Panama* MMSI: 351023000 Official number: 30963PEXT	**615** 185 372	Class: (RS) (DS)	**1966-01 VEB Elbewerft — Boizenburg** Loa 48.95 Br ex 10.09 Dght 4.100 Lbp 44.29 Br md 9.99 Dpth 5.52 Welded, 1 dk	**(B11A2FG) Factory Stern Trawler** Ins: 540 Ice Capable	**1 oil engine** driving 1 CP propeller Total Power: 736kW (1,001hp) 12.0kn S.K.L. 8NVD48A-2U 1 x 4 Stroke 8 Cy. 320 x 480 736kW (1001bhp) VEB Schwermaschinenbau "KarlLiebknecht" (SKL)-Magdeburg AuxGen: 2 x 200kW 390V a.c, 1 x 45kW 390V a.c Fuel: 166.0 (d.f.)
8128406 *EQIV* -	**TABOUK** **Government of The Islamic Republic of Iran (Ports & Maritime Organisation)** - *Bandar Imam Khomeini* *Iran* MMSI: 422255000 Official number: 556	**235** 70 159	Class: AS (LR) ✠ Classed LR until 31/3/93	**1983-03 B.V. Scheepswerf Jonker & Stans — Hendrik-Ido-Ambacht** Yd No: 361 Loa 28.50 Br ex 9.15 Dght 3.250 Lbp 24.90 Br md 8.81 Dpth 4.25 Welded, 1 dk	**(B32A2ST) Tug**	**2 oil engines** with clutches, flexible couplings & sr reverse geared to sc. shafts driving 2 FP propellers Total Power: 1,678kW (2,282hp) Caterpillar D399SCAC 2 x Vee 4 Stroke 16 Cy. 159 x 203 each-839kW (1141bhp) Caterpillar Tractor Co-USA AuxGen: 2 x 73kW 220/380V 50Hz a.c Fuel: 81.0 (d.f.)
8601769 *4JGN* -	**TABRIZ KHALILBEYLI** *ex* Vikhr-12 *-1993* **Specialized Sea Oil Fleet Organisation, Caspian Sea Oil Fleet, State Oil Co of the Republic of Azerbaijan** - *Baku* *Azerbaijan* MMSI: 423071100 Official number: DGR-0087	**2,008** 602 382	Class: RS	**1987-02 Stocznia Polnocna im Bohaterow Westerplatte — Gdansk** Yd No: B98/12 Loa 72.30 Br ex 14.36 Dght 4.700 Lbp 63.00 Br md 14.01 Dpth 6.40 Welded	**(B34F2SF) Fire Fighting Vessel**	**2 oil engines** geared to sc. shafts driving 2 CP propellers Total Power: 4,320kW (5,874hp) 16.0kn Sulzer 16ASV25/30 2 x Vee 4 Stroke 16 Cy. 250 x 300 each-2160kW (2937bhp) Zaklady Przemyslu Metalowego 'HCegielski' SA-Poznan AuxGen: 2 x 600kW a.c, 3 x 400kW a.c Fuel: 167.0 (d.f.)
8855322 - -	**TABU SORO** *ex* Magic Dragon *-1993* **Bruce A Mounier Jr** -	*174* 118 -		**1981 Bayou Marine Builders, Inc. — Bayou La Batre, Al** Loa - Br ex - Dght - Lbp 24.51 Br md 7.32 Dpth 3.72 Welded, 1 dk	**(B11B2FV) Fishing Vessel**	**1 oil engine** driving 1 FP propeller Total Power: 338kW (460hp)
8729872 - -	**TABUADUA** *ex* LCT Tabuadua *-1995* *ex* CTW Alpha *-1989* *ex* Erik *-1989* **Ryan Shipping Ltd** - *Whangarei* *New Zealand* Official number: 876132	**331** 99 512	Class: (NV)	**1976 Scheepswerf Ravestein BV — Deest** Loa 45.00 Br ex 10.00 Dght 2.010 Lbp - Br md - Dpth 2.50 Welded, 1 dk	**(A31A2GX) General Cargo Ship**	**2 oil engines** driving 2 Water jets Total Power: 368kW (500hp) 7.5kn Caterpillar 2 x 4 Stroke each-184kW (250bhp) Caterpillar Tractor Co-USA AuxGen: 1 x 44kW a.c, 1 x 40kW a.c Thrusters: 2 Thwart. FP thruster (f)
7826439 *DUA2040* -	**TABUELAN NAVISTAR** *ex* Matimco 1 *-1989* **Tri-Star Megalink Corp** - *Cebu* *Philippines* Official number: CEB1000514	*247* - 500		**1979-07 L'Nor Marine Services Inc. — Mandaue** Yd No: 80 Loa 60.66 Br ex 10.70 Dght 2.032 Lbp 51.85 Br md 10.36 Dpth 2.54 Welded, 1 dk	**(A35D2RL) Landing Craft** Bow door/ramp	**2 oil engines** geared to sc. shafts driving 2 FP propellers Total Power: 552kW (750hp) Cummins VT-1710-M 2 x Vee 4 Stroke 12 Cy. 140 x 152 each-276kW (375bhp) Cummins Engine Co Inc-USA
7631846 *HZGP* -	**TABUK** *ex* Tebuk *-1999* **Government of The Kingdom of Saudi Arabia (General Directorate of Frontier Force, General Administration of Naval Affairs Maintenance & Supply Department)** - *Jeddah* *Saudi Arabia* Official number: 355	*684* 176 110	Class: (GL)	**1977-11 Bayerische Schiffbaug. mbH vorm. A. Schellenberger — Erlenbach** Yd No: 1050 Loa 60.05 Br ex 10.32 Dght 4.851 Lbp 56.04 Br md 10.02 Dpth 4.86 Welded, 1 dk	**(B34K2QT) Training Ship**	**2 oil engines** reverse reduction geared to sc. shafts driving 2 FP propellers Total Power: 3,530kW (4,800hp) 19.0kn M.T.U. 16V358TB82 2 x Vee 4 Stroke 16 Cy. 185 x 200 each-1765kW (2400bhp) MTU Friedrichshafen GmbH-Friedrichshafen AuxGen: 2 x 416kW 220/380V a.c, 2 x 160kW 220/380V a.c
8917467 *5VBZ6* -	**TABUK** *ex* Fasirus *-2011* *ex* Folegandros *-2010* **Tabuk Maritime Inc** Marian Ship Management & Consultancy Services Pvt Ltd *Lome* *Togo* MMSI: 671344000 Official number: TG00415	**29,506** 11,650 45,425 T/cm 51.8	Class: LR ✠ **100A1** SS 07/2012 Double Hull oil tanker MARPOL 20.1.3. ESP SPM ✠ **LMC** **UMS IGS** Eq.Ltr: M†; Cable: 632.5/73.0 U3 (a)	**1992-07 Hitachi Zosen Corp — Maizuru KY** Yd No: 4848 Loa 183.00 (BB) Br ex 32.23 Dght 12.016 Lbp 174.00 Br md 32.20 Dpth 19.00 Welded, 1 dk	**(A13A2TW) Crude/Oil Products Tanker** Double Hull (13F) Liq: 53,667; Liq (Oil): 53,667 Cargo Heating Coils Compartments: 7 Ta, 2 Wing Slop Ta, ER 4 Cargo Pump (s): 4x1200m³/hr Manifold: Bow/CM: 94m	**1 oil engine** driving 1 FP propeller Total Power: 6,765kW (9,198hp) 11.0kn B&W 6S50MC 1 x 2 Stroke 6 Cy. 500 x 1910 6765kW (9198bhp) Hitachi Zosen Corp-Japan AuxGen: 3 x 560kW 450V 60Hz a.c Boilers: 2 AuxB (o.f.) 18.0kgf/cm² (17.7bar) Fuel: 192.4 (d.f.) (Heating Coils) 1547.4 (r.f.) 28.0pd
7641281 *YBDK* -	**TABULARASA** **Lembaga Penelitian Perikanan Laut** - *Jakarta* *Indonesia*	*100* 62 -	Class: (KI)	**1961 P.T. Pakin — Jakarta** Loa - Br ex - Dght - Lbp 20.63 Br md 5.88 Dpth 3.61 Welded	**(B12D2FR) Fishery Research Vessel**	**1 oil engine** driving 1 FP propeller Total Power: 147kW (200hp) Alpha 344-FO 1 x 2 Stroke 4 Cy. 200 x 340 147kW (200bhp) Titovi Zavodi 'Litostroj'-Yugoslavia AuxGen: 1 x 5kW 110/220V
6929208 *3DOR* -	**TABUSORO** *ex* Heia *-1974* **Government of The Republic of The Fiji Islands (FIMSA)** - *Suva* *Fiji* Official number: 332630	*199* 118 398	Class: (NV)	**1969 VEB Rosslauer Schiffswerft — Rosslau** Yd No: 3271 Loa 40.42 Br ex 8.03 Dght 2.756 Lbp 37.09 Br md 8.01 Dpth 3.20 Welded, 1 dk	**(A34A2GR) Refrigerated Cargo Ship** Grain: 62; Ins: 343 TEU 2 C.Dk 2/20' Compartments: 1 Ho, ER 1 Ha: (19.8 x 3.9)ER Derricks: 1x5t,1x3t; Winches: 2	**1 oil engine** driving 1 CP propeller Total Power: 294kW (400hp) 9.0kn S.K.L. 8NVD26A-2 1 x 4 Stroke 8 Cy. 180 x 260 294kW (400bhp) (new engine 1972) VEB Schwermaschinenbau "KarlLiebknecht" (SKL)-Magdeburg AuxGen: 2 x 10kW 220V 50Hz a.c
8428832 - -	**TABUT** **Yemen Fishing Corp** - *Aden* *Yemen*	**286** 84 -		**1978 Guangzhou Fishing Vessel Shipyard — Guangzhou GD** Loa 44.82 Br ex 7.60 Dght 2.200 Lbp - Br md - Dpth 2.70 Welded, 1 dk	**(B11B2FV) Fishing Vessel**	**1 oil engine** geared to sc. shaft driving 1 FP propeller Total Power: 441kW (600hp) Chinese Std. Type 6300 1 x 4 Stroke 6 Cy. 300 x 380 441kW (600bhp) Guangzhou Diesel Engine Factory CoLtd-China
7028348 - -	**TABZCOOB 101** *ex* Western 101 *-1970* **Western Shellfish International** - *Panama* *Panama*	*200* - -	Class: (AB)	**1970-05 Astilleros de Veracruz S.A. — Veracruz** Yd No: 51 Loa - Br ex 6.79 Dght - Lbp 24.06 Br md 6.74 Dpth 3.71 Welded, 1 dk	**(B11B2FV) Fishing Vessel** Compartments: 1 Ho, ER 1 Ha:	**1 oil engine** reverse reduction geared to sc. shaft driving 1 FP propeller Total Power: 416kW (566hp) Caterpillar D379SCAC 1 x Vee 4 Stroke 8 Cy. 159 x 203 416kW (566bhp) Caterpillar Tractor Co-USA Fuel: 120.0 (d.f.)
1009857 *ZCYI5* -	**TACANUYASO. M.S.** **Lightstone Ltd** - *George Town* *Cayman Islands (British)* MMSI: 319003600 Official number: 741411	**1,354** 406 220	Class: LR ✠ **100A1** SS 02/2009 SSC Yacht (P), mono, G6 ✠ **LMC** **UMS** Cable: 385.0/28.0 U3 (a)	**2009-02 C.R.N. Cant. Nav. Ancona S.r.l. — Ancona** Yd No: 123 Loa 60.40 Br ex 11.50 Dght 3.200 Lbp 52.57 Br md 11.20 Dpth 6.00 Welded, 1 dk	**(X11A2YP) Yacht**	**2 oil engines** with clutches, flexible couplings & sr reverse geared to sc. shafts driving 2 FP propellers Total Power: 4,000kW (5,438hp) Caterpillar 3516B 2 x Vee 4 Stroke 16 Cy. 170 x 215 each-2000kW (2719bhp) Caterpillar Inc-USA AuxGen: 2 x 275kW 400V 50Hz a.c, 1 x 175kW 400V 50Hz a.c Thrusters: 1 Thwart. FP thruster (f)
9210177 - -	**TACAPES** **Government of The Republic of Tunisia (Office des Ports Nationaux Tunisiens)** - *Gabes* *Tunisia*	**540** 121 -	Class: BV	**1999-03 Alstom Leroux Naval SA — St-Malo** Yd No: 628 Loa 31.00 Br ex - Dght 2.910 Lbp - Br md 11.00 Dpth - Welded, 1 dk	**(B32A2ST) Tug** Passengers: berths: 12	**2 oil engines** gearing integral to driving 2 Voith-Schneider propellers Total Power: 2,480kW (3,372hp) 12.0kn Wartsila 8L20 2 x 4 Stroke 8 Cy. 200 x 280 each-1240kW (1686bhp) Wartsila NSD Finland Oy-Finland AuxGen: 2 x 156kW a.c

9280213 *LXTC* -	**TACCOLA** *ex* Francesco di Giorgio *-2006* **European Dredging Co SA** - SatCom: Inmarsat C 425345410 *Luxembourg* *Luxembourg* MMSI: 253454000	**4,683** 1,405 6,955	Class: BV	**2003-12 IZAR Construcciones Navales SA — Gijon** Yd No: 369 Loa 94.70 (BB) Br ex - Dght 7.200 Lbp 84.70 Br md 21.00 Dpth 8.50 Welded	**(B33B2DT) Trailing Suction Hopper Dredger** Hopper: 4,400	**2 diesel electric oil engines** driving 2 gen. each 2150kW 1760V a.c Connecting to 2 elec. motors each (2150kW) driving 2 Azimuth electric drive units Total Power: 5,300kW (7,206hp) 12.3kn A.B.C. 12VDZC 2 x Vee 4 Stroke 12 Cy. 256 x 310 each-2650kW (3603bhp) Anglo Belgian Corp NV (ABC)-Belgium Thrusters: 1 Tunnel thruster (f)
6920343 *VXRQ* -	**TACHEK** *ex* Texada Queen *-1977* **British Columbia Ferry Services Inc** - *Victoria, BC* *Canada* MMSI: 316001271 Official number: 330601	*798* 533 152		**1969-03 Allied Shipbuilders Ltd — North Vancouver BC** Yd No: 164 Loa 49.54 (BB) Br ex 14.69 Dght 2.413 Lbp 45.88 Br md 14.64 Dpth 4.45 Welded, 1 dk	**(A36A2PR) Passenger/Ro-Ro Ship (Vehicles)** Passengers: unberthed: 150 Bow door Stern door Cars: 30	**2 oil engines** driving 2 FP propellers Total Power: 882kW (1,200hp) 12.0kn Ruston 2 x 4 Stroke 6 Cy. 127 x 149 each-441kW (600bhp) Ruston & Hornsby Ltd.-Lincoln AuxGen: 2 x 60kW 450V 60Hz a.c, 1 x 30kW 450V 60Hz a.c
9213167 *7JLE* -	**TACHIBANA** - **Mitsui OSK Lines Ltd (MOL)** Universal Marine Corp *Ainan, Ehime* *Japan* MMSI: 432841000 Official number: 141588	**83,601** 46,652 154,324	Class: NK	**2000-09 Koyo Dockyard Co Ltd — Mihara HS** Yd No: 2117 Loa 274.93 (BB) Br ex - Dght 16.271 Lbp 266.00 Br md 47.00 Dpth 23.60 Welded, 1 dk	**(A21A2BC) Bulk Carrier** Grain: 182,127 Compartments: 7 Ho, ER 7 Ha: 7 (20.9 x 21.8)ER	**1 oil engine** driving 1 FP propeller Total Power: 15,666kW (21,299hp) 14.8kn B&W 6S70MC 1 x 2 Stroke 6 Cy. 700 x 2674 15666kW (21299bhp) Mitsui Engineering & Shipbuilding CLtd-Japan AuxGen: 3 x 615kW 450V 60Hz a.c Fuel: 3739.0 (r.f.)
9449807 *JD2357* -	**TACHIBANA** - **KK Daito Corp** - *Tokyo* *Japan* Official number: 140466	*239* - -		**2007-03 Hanasaki Zosensho K.K. — Yokosuka** Yd No: 280 Loa 36.06 Br ex - Dght 3.300 Lbp - Br md 10.00 Dpth 4.40 Welded, 1 dk	**(B32A2ST) Tug**	**2 oil engines** reduction geared to sc. shafts driving 2 Z propellers Total Power: 2,940kW (3,998hp) Niigata 6L28HX 2 x 4 Stroke 6 Cy. 280 x 370 each-1470kW (1999bhp) Niigata Engineering Co Ltd-Japan
7946007 *HP2702* -	**TACHIBANA MARU** - **Gan Beng** - *Panama* *Panama* Official number: 948579A	*119* 33 -	Class: (BV)	**1971 Kuwata Dock K.K. — Onomichi** Loa 27.01 Br ex - Dght 2.601 Lbp 25.00 Br md 6.51 Dpth 3.10 Welded, 1 dk	**(B32A2ST) Tug**	**1 oil engine** driving 1 FP propeller Total Power: 1,030kW (1,400hp) 12.0kn Hanshin 1 x 4 Stroke 1030kW (1400bhp) The Hanshin Diesel Works Ltd-Japan
7120108 - CE9011	**TACNA 7** *ex* Manua *-1976* **Pesquera Tacna SR Ltda** - *Chimbote* *Peru* Official number: CE-001851-PM	*310* 140 -	Class: (GL)	**1971 Ast. Picsa S.A. — Callao** Yd No: 366 Loa - Br ex 8.03 Dght - Lbp 33.81 Br md 8.01 Dpth 3.84 Welded, 1 dk	**(B11B2FV) Fishing Vessel**	**1 oil engine** reverse reduction geared to sc. shaft driving 1 FP propeller Total Power: 651kW (885hp) Baudouin DVX12 1 x Vee 4 Stroke 12 Cy. 185 x 200 651kW (885bhp) Societe des Moteurs Baudouin SA-France
7933880 *WDD8194* -	**TACOMA** *ex* Lady Faye *-2009* **Nga Thi Thuy Nguyen** - *Houston, TX* *United States of America* MMSI: 367196250 Official number: 612602	*178* 121 -		**1979-08 Marine Builders, Inc. — Mobile, Al** Yd No: 120 L reg 27.16 Br ex 7.93 Dght - Lbp - Br md - Dpth 2.29 Welded, 1 dk	**(B11A2FT) Trawler**	**2 oil engines** driving 2 FP propellers Total Power: 536kW (728hp) Caterpillar 3408TA 2 x Vee 4 Stroke 8 Cy. 137 x 152 each-268kW (364bhp) Caterpillar Tractor Co-USA
9133977 *KUS10525* -	**TACOMA** - **State of Washington (Department of Transportation)** Washington State Department of Transportation (Washington State Ferries) *Seattle, WA* *United States of America* MMSI: 366772760 Official number: 1052576	**12,684** 5,426 1,393		**1997-08 Todd Pacific Shipyards Corp. — Seattle, Wa** Yd No: 91 Loa 138.00 Br ex 27.00 Dght 5.334 Lbp 125.40 Br md 26.73 Dpth 7.51 Welded, 2 dks	**(A36A2PR) Passenger/Ro-Ro Ship (Vehicles)** Passengers: unberthed: 2500 Bow door Stern door Cars: 218	**4 diesel electric oil engines** driving 4 gen. each 3000kW 4160V a.c Connecting to 2 elec. motors each (4413kW) driving 2 Propellers 1 fwd and 1 aft Total Power: 10,592kW (14,400hp) 18.0kn EMD (Electro-Motive) 16-710-G7 4 x Vee 2 Stroke 16 Cy. 230 x 279 each-2648kW (3600bhp) General Motors Corp.Electro-Motive Div.-La Grange AuxGen: 2 x 455kW
5348421 *CXEO* -	**TACUAREMBO S-2** *launched as* Nuri *-1962* **Government of The Oriental Republic of Uruguay (Servicio Oceanografico y Pesca)** - *Montevideo* *Uruguay* MMSI: 770576118 Official number: 1757	*121* 53 -		**1962 Ast. de T. Ruiz de Velasco — Bilbao** Yd No: 72 Loa 27.89 Br ex 6.02 Dght 2.921 Lbp 24.01 Br md 6.00 Dpth 3.20 Riveted\Welded	**(B11A2FT) Trawler**	**1 oil engine** geared to sc. shaft driving 1 FP propeller Total Power: 320kW (435hp) Deutz RBA6M528 1 x 4 Stroke 6 Cy. 220 x 280 320kW (435bhp) Kloeckner Humboldt Deutz AG-West Germany Fuel: 37.5
9442811 *JD2444* -	**TADAMI MARU** - **Far East Towing Co Ltd** Fukushima Kisen KK *Soma, Fukushima* *Japan* Official number: 140568	*253* - 194	Class: NK	**2007-06 Kanagawa Zosen — Kobe** Yd No: 571 Loa 32.50 Br ex - Dght 3.615 Lbp 28.93 Br md 11.40 Dpth 4.40 Welded, 1 dk	**(B32A2ST) Tug**	**2 oil engines** reduction geared to sc. shafts driving 2 Propellers Total Power: 3,310kW (4,500hp) Niigata 6L28HX 2 x 4 Stroke 6 Cy. 280 x 370 each-1655kW (2250bhp) Niigata Engineering Co Ltd-Japan Fuel: 110.0 (d.f.)
5429110 *6VKM* DAK 602	**TADORNE** - **Armement SOPASEN** - *Dakar* *Senegal*	*228* 76 -	Class: (BV)	**1963 Ateliers et Chantiers de La Manche — Dieppe** Yd No: 1177 Loa 37.67 Br ex 7.24 Dght 3.537 Lbp 32.11 Br md 7.22 Dpth 3.92 Welded, 1 dk	**(B11A2FT) Trawler**	**1 oil engine** driving 1 FP propeller Total Power: 552kW (750hp) 12.0kn Crepelle 6SN 1 x 4 Stroke 6 Cy. 260 x 280 552kW (750bhp) Crepelle et Cie-France Fuel: 65.0 (d.f.)
8626836 *LW9109* -	**TAE BAEK No. 75** - - - *Argentina* MMSI: 701000962 Official number: 02364	*472* - 846	Class: (KR)	**1987 Pohang Shipbuilding Co Ltd — Pohang** Yd No: 22 Loa 57.51 Br ex - Dght 3.982 Lbp 49.51 Br md 10.20 Dpth 4.14 Welded, 1 dk	**(B11B2FV) Fishing Vessel**	**1 oil engine** driving 1 FP propeller Total Power: 956kW (1,300hp) Hanshin 6LUN28A 1 x 4 Stroke 6 Cy. 280 x 480 956kW (1300bhp) Ssangyong Heavy Industries Co Ltd-South Korea
8717829 *HLJH* -	**TAE BAEK No. 91** *ex* O Dae Yang No. 727 *-1993* **Ye Ram Co Ltd** - *Busan* *South Korea* MMSI: 440297000 Official number: 9512365-6260000	**495** - 607	Class: (KR)	**1988-10 Dae Sun Shipbuilding & Engineering Co Ltd — Busan** Yd No: 334 Loa 59.52 Br ex 9.52 Dght 4.130 Lbp 51.00 Br md 9.50 Dpth 4.53 Welded	**(B11B2FV) Fishing Vessel** Ins: 643 Compartments: 1 Wing Yes	**1 oil engine** with flexible couplings & sr geared to sc. shaft driving 1 FP propeller Total Power: 1,030kW (1,400hp) Niigata 6M28AFTE 1 x 4 Stroke 6 Cy. 280 x 480 1030kW (1400bhp) Ssangyong Heavy Industries Co Ltd-South Korea
5398414 *6MKU* -	**TAE BAEK No. 95** *ex* O Dae Yang No. 201 *-1993* *ex* Zenko Maru No. 30 *-1972* **Samho Co Ltd** - *Busan* *South Korea* Official number: 9512003-6260005	**410** - -	Class: (KR)	**1962 KK Kanasashi Zosen — Shizuoka SZ** Yd No: 440 Loa 54.46 Br ex 8.67 Dght 3.633 Lbp 48.93 Br md 8.60 Dpth 4.12 Welded, 1 dk	**(B11B2FV) Fishing Vessel** Ins: 637 3 Ha: 3 (1.7 x 1.6)ER	**1 oil engine** driving 1 FP propeller Total Power: 809kW (1,100hp) 12.0kn Akasaka YM6SS 1 x 4 Stroke 6 Cy. 370 x 520 809kW (1100bhp) Akasaka Tekkosho KK (Akasaka DieselLtd)-Japan AuxGen: 2 x 128kW 230V a.c
8827569 - -	**TAE BAEK No. 606** *ex* Jin Yang No. 107 *-2000* **Illex SA** - *Argentina* Official number: 02361	*435* 346 545	Class: (KR)	**1988-11 Banguhjin Engineering & Shipbuilding Co Ltd — Ulsan** Yd No: 72 Loa 59.50 Br ex - Dght 3.662 Lbp 51.00 Br md 9.50 Dpth 4.15 Welded, 1 dk	**(B11B2FV) Fishing Vessel**	**1 oil engine** driving 1 FP propeller Total Power: 1,030kW (1,400hp) 11.5kn Niigata 6M28AFTE 1 x 4 Stroke 6 Cy. 280 x 480 1030kW (1400bhp) Ssangyong Heavy Industries Co Ltd-South Korea AuxGen: 2 x 600kW 225V a.c
6804094 *HLBI* -	**TAE CHANG No. 7** *ex* Partera No. 7 *-1978* *ex* Seiju Maru No. 1 *-1977* **Kang Sung Luk** - *Busan* *South Korea* Official number: BS-A-1249	*251* 121 -	Class: (KR)	**1967 KK Kanasashi Zosen — Shizuoka SZ** Yd No: 800 Loa 43.69 Br ex 8.11 Dght 2.921 Lbp 38.38 Br md 8.08 Dpth 3.23 Welded, 1 dk	**(B12B2FC) Fish Carrier** Ins: 359 2 Ha: (1.5 x 2.6) (1.2 x 1.2)ER	**1 oil engine** driving 1 FP propeller Total Power: 699kW (950hp) 11.3kn Niigata 6M31HS 1 x 4 Stroke 6 Cy. 310 x 460 699kW (950bhp) Niigata Engineering Co Ltd-Japan AuxGen: 2 x 144kW 220V a.c

IMO / Call sign / Flag	Name / Owner / Port	Tonnage	Class	Built / Builder / Dimensions	Type	Machinery	Speed / Engine
5098533 *6NJS* -	**TAE CHANG No. 11** *ex* Eifuku Maru No. 15 *-1976* **Tae Chang Fisheries Co Ltd** - *Busan* *South Korea* Official number: BF38547	*293* 147 -	Class: (KR)	**1961 Yamanishi Shipbuilding Co Ltd — Ishinomaki MG** Yd No: 397 Loa 46.31 Br ex 7.65 Dght - Lbp 41.00 Br md 7.61 Dpth 3.61 Welded, 1 dk	**(B11B2FV) Fishing Vessel** Compartments: 3 Ho, ER 3 Ha: 3 (1.3 x 1.3)ER Derricks: 4x1t; Winches: 1	**1 oil engine** driving 1 FP propeller Total Power: 552kW (750hp) Akasaka 1 x 4 Stroke 6 Cy. 326 x 460 552kW (750bhp) Akasaka Tekkosho KK (Akasaka DieselLtd)-Japan AuxGen: 2 x 64kW 220V 50Hz a.c, 1 x 24kW 220V 50Hz a.c	11.5kn TR6SS
6413338 *6MHV* -	**TAE CHANG No. 23** *ex* Partera No. 23 *-1979* *ex* Hakujin Maru *-1971* **Tae Chang Fisheries Co Ltd** - *Busan* *South Korea* Official number: BS-A-1413	*293* 144 343	Class: (KR)	**1964 KK Kanasashi Zosen — Shizuoka SZ** Yd No: 553 Loa 47.93 Br ex 7.75 Dght 2.998 Lbp 42.55 Br md 7.70 Dpth 3.46 Welded, 1 dk	**(B11B2FV) Fishing Vessel** Ins: 391 5 Ha: 2 (1.0 x 0.7)3 (1.1 x 1.4)ER	**1 oil engine** driving 1 FP propeller Total Power: 736kW (1,001hp) Akasaka 1 x 4 Stroke 6 Cy. 350 x 500 736kW (1001bhp) Akasaka Tekkosho KK (Akasaka DieselLtd)-Japan AuxGen: 2 x 120kW 225V a.c	11.5kn SR6SS
5123869 *HLMM* -	**TAE CHANG No. 26** *ex* Partera No. 26 *-1978* *ex* Fukuyoshi Maru No. 35 *-1977* **Tae Chang Fisheries Co Ltd** - *Busan* *South Korea* Official number: BS-A-1280	*325* 181 405	Class: (KR)	**1962 KK Kanasashi Zosen — Shizuoka SZ** Yd No: 448 Loa 50.55 Br ex 7.85 Dght 3.440 Lbp 44.79 Br md 7.80 Dpth 3.81 Welded, 1 dk	**(B11B2FV) Fishing Vessel** Ins: 521 4 Ha: 4 (1.6 x 1.6)ER	**1 oil engine** driving 1 FP propeller Total Power: 736kW (1,001hp) Akasaka 1 x 4 Stroke 6 Cy. 350 x 500 736kW (1001bhp) Akasaka Tekkosho KK (Akasaka DieselLtd)-Japan AuxGen: 3 x 120kW 230V a.c	11.3kn SR6SS
6620383 *DTBF* -	**TAE CHANG No. 27** *ex* Partera No. 27 *-1978* *ex* Kasuga Maru No. 1 *-1977* **Tae Chang Fisheries Co Ltd** - *Busan* *South Korea* Official number: BS-A-1297	*278* 134 -	Class: (KR)	**1966 KK Kanasashi Zosen — Shizuoka SZ** Yd No: 752 Loa 46.31 Br ex 7.73 Dght 2.998 Lbp 40.95 Br md 7.70 Dpth 3.46 Welded, 1 dk	**(B11B2FV) Fishing Vessel** Ins: 322 4 Ha: 2 (1.0 x 8.9)2 (1.7 x 1.5)	**1 oil engine** driving 1 FP propeller Total Power: 603kW (820hp) Akasaka 1 x 4 Stroke 6 Cy. 300 x 440 603kW (820bhp) Akasaka Tekkosho KK (Akasaka DieselLtd)-Japan AuxGen: 2 x 104kW 230V a.c	11.3kn TM6SSI
6715580 *6MUX* -	**TAE CHANG No. 35** *ex* Nikko Maru No. 6 *-1977* **Tae Chang Fisheries Co Ltd** - *Busan* *South Korea* Official number: BS-A-767	*250* 79 -	Class: (KR)	**1967 Miho Zosensho K.K. — Shimizu** Yd No: 608 Loa 46.11 Br ex 7.24 Dght - Lbp 38.00 Br md 7.22 Dpth 3.48 Welded, 1 dk	**(B11B2FV) Fishing Vessel** 11 Ha: 5 (1.1 x 1.1)6 (1.1 x 0.8)ER	**1 oil engine** driving 1 FP propeller Total Power: 552kW (750hp) Niigata 1 x 4 Stroke 6 Cy. 280 x 440 552kW (750bhp) Niigata Engineering Co Ltd-Japan AuxGen: 2 x 80kW 230V a.c	
6615405 *6MUY* -	**TAE CHANG No. 36** *ex* Kairyu Maru No. 21 *-1976* **Tae Chang Fisheries Co Ltd** - *Busan* *South Korea* Official number: BF36306	*196* 77 -	Class: (KR)	**1966 KK Kanasashi Zosen — Shizuoka SZ** Yd No: 731 Loa 41.53 Br ex - Dght 2.794 Lbp 34.52 Br md 6.61 Dpth 3.18 Welded, 1 dk	**(B11B2FV) Fishing Vessel**	**1 oil engine** driving 1 FP propeller Total Power: 552kW (750hp) Akasaka 1 x 4 Stroke 6 Cy. 270 x 420 552kW (750bhp) Akasaka Tekkosho KK (Akasaka DieselLtd)-Japan	6DH27SS
6615388 *6KVV* -	**TAE CHANG No. 56** *ex* Partera No. 56 *-1979* *ex* Fukuyoshi Maru No. 5 *-1976* **Tae Chang Fisheries Co Ltd** - *Busan* *South Korea* Official number: BS-A-1749	*226* 112 -	Class: (KR)	**1966 KK Kanasashi Zosen — Shizuoka SZ** Yd No: 729 Loa 42.65 Br ex 7.55 Dght 2.896 Lbp 37.88 Br md 7.52 Dpth 3.38 Welded, 1 dk	**(B11B2FV) Fishing Vessel**	**1 oil engine** driving 1 FP propeller Total Power: 552kW (750hp) Niigata 1 x 4 Stroke 6 Cy. 280 x 440 552kW (750bhp) Niigata Engineering Co Ltd-Japan	
7394852 *6KXF* -	**TAE CHANG No. 76** *ex* Cipsa No. 10 *-1983* **Ah Jin Fisheries Co** - *Busan* *South Korea* Official number: BS02-A2073	*326* 164 404	Class: (KR)	**1974-05 Uchida Zosen — Ise** Yd No: 748 Loa 50.40 Br ex 8.36 Dght 3.455 Lbp 44.00 Br md 8.31 Dpth 3.61 Welded, 1 dk	**(B11B2FV) Fishing Vessel** Ins: 145 2 Ha: (1.3 x 1.0) (1.8 x 1.8)ER	**1 oil engine** driving 1 FP propeller Total Power: 736kW (1,001hp) Hanshin 1 x 4 Stroke 6 Cy. 260 x 440 736kW (1001bhp) Hanshin Nainenki Kogyo-Japan AuxGen: 2 x 200kW 225V a.c	11.8kn 6LUD26
8413710 *HLIL* -	**TAE CHANG No. 303** - **Choi Yung-Ja** - *Guryongpo* *South Korea* Official number: KN6865-A1524	*122* 38 67	Class: (KR)	**1983-12 Sungkwang Shipbuilding Co Ltd — Tongyeong** Yd No: 123 Loa 34.09 (BB) Br ex 6.30 Dght 2.301 Lbp 27.41 Br md 5.81 Dpth 2.72 Welded, 1 dk	**(B11B2FV) Fishing Vessel** Ins: 125	**1 oil engine** with clutches, flexible couplings & sr reverse geared to sc. shaft driving 1 FP propeller Total Power: 272kW (370hp) Yanmar 1 x 4 Stroke 6 Cy. 200 x 240 272kW (370bhp) Ssangyong Heavy Industries Co Ltd-South Korea AuxGen: 1 x 60kW 225V a.c	6ML-HT
8627804 *HMPS* -	**TAE DOK SAN** *ex* Son Gyong 7 *-2012* *ex* Ji Da *-2009* *ex* Chang Xin *-2006* *ex* Ai Ying *-2004* *ex* Ai Ge *-2001* *ex* Shoei Maru No. 37 *-1999* **Taedoksan Shipping Co** - *Nampho* *North Korea* MMSI: 445026000 Official number: 3504455	**1,254** 611 1,098	Class: KC	**1985-09 K.K. Yoshida Zosen Kogyo — Arida** Loa 71.40 Br ex - Dght 3.601 Lbp 65.99 Br md 11.00 Dpth 6.20 Welded, 1 dk	**(A31A2GX) General Cargo Ship**	**1 oil engine** driving 1 FP propeller Total Power: 956kW (1,300hp) Makita 1 x 4 Stroke 6 Cy. 310 x 600 956kW (1300bhp) Makita Diesel Co Ltd-Japan	11.0kn LS31
7738656 *HMBY* -	**TAE DONG GANG** - **Taedonggang Shipping Co** Taedonggang Sonbak Co Ltd SatCom: Inmarsat C 444513010 *Nampho* *North Korea* MMSI: 445130000 Official number: 2500791	*9,010* 5,657 13,550	Class: KC	**1976 Nampo Shipyard — Nampo** Loa 155.40 Br ex - Dght 9.230 Lbp - Br md 20.37 Dpth - Welded, 1 dk	**(A31A2GX) General Cargo Ship** Grain: 19,500; Bale: 17,900	**1 oil engine** driving 1 FP propeller	12.5kn
8949874 - -	**TAE GIL 3** *ex* Shinsei Maru No. 6 *-2009* - - *South Korea*	*116* - -		**1973-06 Shinyo Tekko K.K. — Kobe** Yd No: 1011 Loa 25.00 Br ex - Dght 1.500 Lbp 22.00 Br md 8.00 Dpth 2.48 Welded, 1 dk	**(B34X2QA) Anchor Handling Vessel**	**2 oil engines** driving 2 FP propellers Total Power: 736kW (1,000hp) Yanmar 2 x 4 Stroke 6 Cy. 200 x 240 each-368kW (500bhp) Yanmar Diesel Engine Co Ltd-Japan	11.0kn 6M-UT
6402339 *6MCX* -	**TAE HWA No. 1** *ex* Han Gil No. 1 *-1994* *ex* Seisho Maru No. 3 *-1976* **Tae Hwa Fishery Co Ltd** - *Tongyeong* *South Korea* Official number: KS7880-A5127	*183* 87 214	Class: (KR)	**1963 KK Kanasashi Zosen — Shizuoka SZ** Yd No: 510 Loa 39.04 Br ex 6.96 Dght 2.721 Lbp 33.53 Br md 6.91 Dpth 3.10 Welded, 1 dk	**(B11B2FV) Fishing Vessel** Ins: 212	**1 oil engine** driving 1 FP propeller Total Power: 456kW (620hp) Akasaka 1 x 4 Stroke 6 Cy. 270 x 400 456kW (620bhp) Akasaka Tekkosho KK (Akasaka DieselLtd)-Japan AuxGen: 2 x 48kW 230V a.c	10.5kn MA6SS
8626850 *6MVO* -	**TAE KWANG No. 101** - **Choi Hung-Son** - *Busan* *South Korea* Official number: BS-A-2572	*104* - 86	Class: (KR)	**1987 Kirim Shipbuilding Co Ltd — Koje** Loa 38.82 Br ex - Dght 2.401 Lbp 32.31 Br md 6.30 Dpth 2.95 Welded, 1 dk	**(B11A2FT) Trawler**	**1 oil engine** driving 1 FP propeller Total Power: 552kW (750hp) Hanshin 1 x 4 Stroke 6 Cy. 260 x 400 552kW (750bhp) Ssangyong Heavy Industries Co Ltd-South Korea	10.5kn 6L26BGSH
8626848 *6MVP* -	**TAE KWANG No. 102** - **Choi Hung-Son** - *Busan* *South Korea* Official number: BS-A-2573	*104* - 86	Class: (KR)	**1987 Kirim Shipbuilding Co Ltd — Koje** Loa 38.82 Br ex - Dght 2.401 Lbp 32.31 Br md 6.30 Dpth 2.95 Welded, 1 dk	**(B11A2FT) Trawler**	**1 oil engine** driving 1 FP propeller Total Power: 552kW (750hp) Hanshin 1 x 4 Stroke 6 Cy. 260 x 400 552kW (750bhp) Ssangyong Heavy Industries Co Ltd-South Korea	10.5kn 6L26BGSH
8963600 *HMYE6* -	**TAE SIN** *ex* Cho Dang *-2002* *ex* Dong Hae An *-2001* *ex* Chosei Maru No. 73 *-1991* **Korea Daesong Trading Sinuiju Branch Co** - *Sinuiju* *North Korea* Official number: 863005	**209** 69 119	Class: KC	**1973 Ofunato Zosen Tekko K.K. — Ofunato** Loa 35.93 Br ex - Dght 2.310 Lbp 29.25 Br md 6.20 Dpth 2.60 Welded, 1 dk	**(B11B2FV) Fishing Vessel**	**1 oil engine** driving 1 FP propeller Total Power: 552kW (750hp) Akasaka 1 x 4 Stroke 552kW (750bhp) Akasaka Tekkosho KK (Akasaka DieselLtd)-Japan	

8732037 *HMKD* -	**TAE SONG 1** *ex* Son Gyong 6 *-2012* *ex* Nam San 11 *-2008* *ex* Fu Lim 58 *-2008* *ex* Dong Qing *-2008* **Korea Namsan Shipping Corp** - *Nampho* *North Korea* MMSI: 445036000 Official number: 4502799	**1,150** 567 1,400	Class: KC	**1995**-09 **in the People's Republic of China** Loa 68.40 Br ex - Dght 3.900 Lbp 64.40 Br md 11.90 Dpth 5.00 Welded, 1 dk	**(A31A2GX) General Cargo Ship**	**1 oil engine** geared to sc. shaft driving 1 Propeller Total Power: 552kW (750hp) Chinese Std. Type 1 x 4 Stroke 6 Cy. 300 x 380 552kW (750bhp) in China	 6300ZC
8891857 *HMEI* -	**TAE SONG 117** *ex* Apollo 7 *-2008* **Korea Potonggang Shipping Co** - *Hungnam* *North Korea* Official number: 2104051	*285* 120 340	Class: KC	**1971 Oyama Zosen Tekko K.K. — Japan** Loa - Br ex - Dght 2.800 Lbp 35.40 Br md 7.40 Dpth - Welded, 1 dk	**(A31A2GX) General Cargo Ship**	**1 oil engine** driving 1 FP propeller	
8210699 *HMYE5* -	**TAE SONG 422** *ex* Dae Song 422 *-2012* *ex* Toyo Maru No. 11 *-1998* *ex* Yahata Maru *-1986* **Korea Daesong Shipping Co** - *Nampho* *North Korea* MMSI: 445051000 Official number: 3201606	**905** 381 1,082	Class: KC	**1982**-08 **Nakatani Shipyard Co. Ltd. — Etajima** Yd No: 478 Loa 60.70 Br ex - Dght 3.750 Lbp 56.01 Br md 10.51 Dpth 6.00 Welded, 1 dk	**(A31A2GX) General Cargo Ship** Grain: 2,105; Bale: 1,980 Compartments: 1 Ho, ER 1 Ha: ER	**1 oil engine** driving 1 FP propeller Total Power: 956kW (1,300hp) Hanshin 1 x 4 Stroke 6 Cy. 280 x 480 956kW (1300bhp) The Hanshin Diesel Works Ltd-Japan	 6LUN28A
7209095 *P7ZT* -	**TAE SONG SAN** *ex* Puk Dae Bong *-2013* *ex* Rui Feng *-2006* *ex* Sky 2 *-2005* *ex* Paramushir 102 *-2002* *ex* Vulkan 18 *-1992* *ex* Zuiho Maru No. 38 *-1992* *ex* Keifuku Maru No. 5 *-1984* **Sangmyong Trading General Corp** - *Nampho* *North Korea* MMSI: 445507000 Official number: 2200550	**495** 250 497	Class: (RS) (KR)	**1971 Miho Zosensho K.K. — Shimizu** Yd No: 810 Loa 54.79 Br ex 8.72 Dght 3.460 Lbp 49.00 Br md 8.70 Dpth 3.85 Welded, 1 dk	**(B11B2FV) Fishing Vessel** Ins: 485	**1 oil engine** driving 1 FP propeller Total Power: 1,103kW (1,500hp) Niigata 1 x 4 Stroke 6 Cy. 370 x 540 1103kW (1500bhp) Niigata Engineering Co Ltd-Japan	 12.7kn 6M37AHS
6817948 *HMDQ* -	**TAE SUNG 923** *ex* Daesong No. 201 *-2004* *ex* Tae Sung 923 *-2002* *ex* Dae Song 923 *-1997* *ex* Nankai Maru *-1997* *ex* Aki *-1979* *ex* Aki Maru No. 13 *-1979* **Korea Jangsaeng Trading Co Ltd** - *Chongjin* *North Korea* MMSI: 445081000 Official number: 1804000	*708* 441 820	Class: KC	**1968**-03 **Imamura Zosen — Kure** Yd No: 140 Loa 54.49 Br ex 9.02 Dght 4.039 Lbp 49.61 Br md 9.00 Dpth 4.50 Welded, 1 dk	**(A31A2GX) General Cargo Ship** Grain: 1,200; Bale: 950 Compartments: 1 Ho, ER 1 Ha: (26.9 x 5.0)ER	**1 oil engine** driving 1 FP propeller Total Power: 1,103kW (1,500hp) Niigata 1 x 4 Stroke 6 Cy. 370 x 540 1103kW (1500bhp) Niigata Engineering Co Ltd-Japan AuxGen: 2 x 12kW 225V a.c	 12.0kn 6M37AHS
7231672 *6LBY* -	**TAE WON No. 808** *ex* Duk Soo No. 305 *-1992* *ex* Calomex No. 12 *-1987* *ex* Yamasan Maru No. 85 *-1983* **Sung Kyung Fisheries Co Ltd** - *Busan* *South Korea* Official number: 9507083-6260002	*370* 187 516	Class: (KR)	**1972 Narasaki Zosen KK — Muroran HK** Yd No: 804 Loa 57.10 Br ex 9.02 Dght 3.830 Lbp 50.50 Br md 9.00 Dpth 5.69 Welded, 2 dks	**(B11B2FV) Fishing Vessel**	**1 oil engine** driving 1 FP propeller Total Power: 1,692kW (2,300hp) Fuji 1 x 4 Stroke 6 Cy. 400 x 620 1692kW (2300bhp) Fuji Diesel Co Ltd-Japan	 6S40CH
7408330 - -	**TAE WOONG No. 502** *ex* Hafna No. 502 *-1986* *ex* The Woong No. 502 *-1986* *ex* Tomi Maru No. 23 *-1986* **Tae Bong Ha Lee** - *Manta* *Ecuador* Official number: P-04-0381	*519* 141 143	Class: (KR)	**1974**-08 **Niigata Engineering Co Ltd — Niigata NI** Yd No: 1325 Loa 47.63 Br ex 8.21 Dght 3.251 Lbp 42.14 Br md 8.18 Dpth 3.59 Welded, 1 dk	**(B11B2FV) Fishing Vessel**	**1 oil engine** driving 1 FP propeller Total Power: 736kW (1,001hp) Niigata 1 x 4 Stroke 6 Cy. 280 x 440 736kW (1001bhp) Niigata Engineering Co Ltd-Japan AuxGen: 2 x 200kW 225V a.c	 11.5kn 6M28EX
7127091 *6NGE* -	**TAE WOONG No. 608** *ex* Orion No. 503 *-1989* *ex* Duk Soo No. 503 *-1988* *ex* Wonmex No. 701 *-1987* *ex* Duk Soo No. 51 *-1986* *ex* Nitto Maru No. 75 *-1984* **Seo Dong International Co Ltd** - *Busan* *South Korea* MMSI: 440649000 Official number: 9512038-6471109	*391* 203 437	Class: KR	**1971 Narasaki Zosen KK — Muroran HK** Yd No: 786 Loa 55.48 Br ex 9.02 Dght 3.561 Lbp 48.90 Br md 9.00 Dpth 5.72 Welded, 2 dks	**(B11A2FT) Trawler**	**1 oil engine** driving 1 FP propeller Total Power: 1,692kW (2,300hp) Hanshin 1 x 4 Stroke 6 Cy. 400 x 640 1692kW (2300bhp) Hanshin Nainenki Kogyo-Japan	 6LU40
7417707 *D8WY* -	**TAE YANG** *ex* Continental Partner No. 1 *-1993* *ex* Sam Jung *-1993* **ES Line Corp Co Ltd** - *Busan* *South Korea* Official number: BSR-755932	*998* 547 1,584	Class: (KR)	**1976**-01 **Daedong Shipbuilding Co Ltd — Busan** Yd No: 147 Loa 68.92 Br ex - Dght 4.522 Lbp 63.00 Br md 10.50 Dpth 5.30 Welded, 1 dk	**(A31A2GX) General Cargo Ship** Grain: 1,998; Bale: 1,902 Compartments: 3 Ho, ER 3 Ha: ER Derricks: 1x10t,1x5t	**1 oil engine** driving 1 FP propeller Total Power: 1,103kW (1,500hp) Makita 1 x 4 Stroke 6 Cy. 300 x 480 1103kW (1500bhp) Makita Diesel Co Ltd-Japan AuxGen: 2 x 80kW 445V a.c	 14.0kn GSLH630
7314553 *6MGM* -	**TAE YANG No. 21** *ex* Pacific No. 1 *-1996* *ex* Dong Bang No. 77 *-1993* *ex* Daitoku Maru No. 17 *-1993* **Nasung Shipping Co Ltd** - SatCom: Inmarsat C 444055412 *Busan* *South Korea* Official number: 9512445-6260003	*1,526* 821 2,493	Class: (KR) (NK)	**1973**-07 **Usuki Iron Works Co Ltd — Usuki OT** Yd No: 865 Loa 89.15 Br ex 12.83 Dght 5.665 Lbp 83.00 Br md 12.80 Dpth 6.50 Welded, 1 dk	**(B12B2FC) Fish Carrier** Ins: 2,550 3 Ha: 3 (5.6 x 4.1) Derricks: 6x3t	**1 oil engine** driving 1 FP propeller Total Power: 2,795kW (3,800hp) Mitsubishi 1 x 2 Stroke 6 Cy. 450 x 750 2795kW (3800bhp) Kobe Hatsudoki KK-Japan AuxGen: 2 x 240kW 445V a.c Fuel: 569.0 13.0pd	 15.5kn 6UET45/75C
6716340 - -	**TAE YANG No. 102** *ex* Kook Yang No. 102 *-1993* **Korea Marine Industry Development Corp** - *Busan* *South Korea* Official number: BF21639	*133* 41 113	Class: (KR)	**1967 Fukuoka Shipbuilding Co Ltd — Fukuoka FO** Yd No: 887 Loa 33.56 Br ex 6.15 Dght 2.401 Lbp 28.61 Br md 6.10 Dpth 2.75 Welded, 1 dk	**(B11B2FV) Fishing Vessel** Ins: 100 4 Ha: 4 (0.9 x 1.1)	**1 oil engine** driving 1 FP propeller Total Power: 331kW (450hp) Hanshin 1 x 4 Stroke 6 Cy. 270 x 400 331kW (450bhp) Hanshin Nainenki Kogyo-Japan AuxGen: 2 x 26kW 230V a.c	 9.0kn Z76
6716364 *6KWU* -	**TAE YANG No. 105** *ex* Kook Yang No. 105 *-1993* **Korea Marine Industry Development Corp** - *Busan* *South Korea* Official number: BF21641	*133* 41 113	Class: (KR)	**1967 Fukuoka Shipbuilding Co Ltd — Fukuoka FO** Yd No: 890 Loa 33.56 Br ex 6.15 Dght 2.401 Lbp 28.61 Br md 6.10 Dpth 2.75 Welded, 1 dk	**(B11B2FV) Fishing Vessel** Ins: 100 4 Ha: 4 (0.9 x 1.1)	**1 oil engine** driving 1 FP propeller Total Power: 331kW (450hp) Hanshin 1 x 4 Stroke 6 Cy. 270 x 400 331kW (450bhp) Hanshin Nainenki Kogyo-Japan AuxGen: 2 x 26kW 230V a.c	 9.0kn Z76
6716376 *6KWV* -	**TAE YANG No. 106** *ex* Kook Yang No. 106 *-1993* **Korea Marine Industry Development Corp** - *Busan* *South Korea* Official number: BF21642	*133* 41 113	Class: (KR)	**1967 Fukuoka Shipbuilding Co Ltd — Fukuoka FO** Yd No: 883 Loa 33.56 Br ex 6.15 Dght 2.401 Lbp 28.61 Br md 6.10 Dpth 2.75 Welded, 1 dk	**(B11B2FV) Fishing Vessel** Ins: 100 4 Ha: 4 (0.9 x 1.1)	**1 oil engine** driving 1 FP propeller Total Power: 331kW (450hp) Hanshin 1 x 4 Stroke 6 Cy. 270 x 400 331kW (450bhp) Hanshin Nainenki Kogyo-Japan AuxGen: 2 x 26kW 230V a.c	 9.0kn Z76
6919643 *6LQI* -	**TAE YANG No. 115** *ex* Kook Yang No. 115 *-1993* **Ahn Sang Mee** - *Busan* *South Korea* Official number: BS-A-437	*133* 41 113	Class: (KR)	**1969 Tokushima Zosen K.K. — Fukuoka** Yd No: 801 Loa 33.56 Br ex 6.13 Dght 2.388 Lbp 28.61 Br md 6.10 Dpth 2.75 Welded, 1 dk	**(B11B2FV) Fishing Vessel** Ins: 100 4 Ha: 4 (0.9 x 1.1)	**1 oil engine** driving 1 FP propeller Total Power: 331kW (450hp) Hanshin 1 x 4 Stroke 6 Cy. 240 x 400 331kW (450bhp) Hanshin Nainenki Kogyo-Japan AuxGen: 2 x 26kW 230V a.c	 9.0kn 6L24MS

6919667 *6LQK* -	**TAE YANG No. 117** *ex* Kook Yang No. 117 **Korea Marine Industry Development Corp** - *Busan* *South Korea* Official number: BF22322	*133* 41 113	Class: (KR)	**1969 Tokushima Zosen K.K. — Fukuoka** Yd No: 803 Loa 33.56 Br ex 6.13 Dght 2.388 Lbp 28.61 Br md 6.10 Dpth 2.75 Welded, 1 dk	**(B11B2FV) Fishing Vessel** Ins: 100 4 Ha: 4 (0.9 x 1.1)ER	**1 oil engine** driving 1 FP propeller Total Power: 331kW (450hp) 9.0kn Hanshin 6L24MS 1 x 4 Stroke 6 Cy. 240 x 400 331kW (450bhp) Hanshin Nainenki Kogyo-Japan AuxGen: 2 x 24kW 230V a.c
6919679 *6LQL* -	**TAE YANG No. 118** *ex* Kook Yang No. 118 **Korea Marine Industry Development Corp** - *Busan* *South Korea* Official number: BF22323	*133* 41 113	Class: (KR)	**1969 Tokushima Zosen K.K. — Fukuoka** Yd No: 805 Loa 33.56 Br ex 6.13 Dght 2.388 Lbp 28.61 Br md 6.10 Dpth 2.75 Welded, 1 dk	**(B11B2FV) Fishing Vessel** Ins: 100 4 Ha: 4 (0.9 x 1.1)ER	**1 oil engine** driving 1 FP propeller Total Power: 331kW (450hp) 9.0kn Kobe 1 x 4 Stroke 6 Cy. 250 x 400 331kW (450bhp) Hanshin Nainenki Kogyo-Japan AuxGen: 2 x 24kW 230V a.c
8805121 *DSPM8* -	**TAE YOUNG** *ex* C Blooming *-2011* *ex* Shoho Maru *-2007* **Sungwon Energy Co Ltd** Hanyu Shipping Co Ltd *Busan* *South Korea* MMSI: 441263000 Official number: BSR-071143	**736** 346 1,131	Class: KR	**1988-10 Mukaishima Zoki Co. Ltd. — Onomichi** Yd No: 251 Loa 64.33 Br ex 10.03 Dght 3.961 Lbp 60.00 Br md 10.00 Dpth 4.50 Welded, 1 dk	**(A12A2TC) Chemical Tanker** Liq: 1,300 Compartments: 8 Wing Ta	**1 oil engine** with clutches, flexible couplings & sr reverse geared to sc. shaft driving 1 FP propeller Total Power: 736kW (1,001hp) 11.8kn Niigata 6M28BFT 1 x 4 Stroke 6 Cy. 280 x 480 736kW (1001bhp) Niigata Engineering Co Ltd-Japan Fuel: 56.0
7831575 *6KWQ* -	**TAE YOUNG No. 62** - **Kim Kum An** - *Busan* *South Korea* Official number: BS-A-1729	*149* 29 167	Class: (KR)	**1979-01 ShinA Shipbuilding Co Ltd — Tongyeong** Loa 39.25 Br ex - Dght - Lbp 31.81 Br md 7.31 Dpth 2.90 Welded, 1 dk	**(B11B2FV) Fishing Vessel**	**1 oil engine** driving 1 FP propeller Total Power: 1,177kW (1,600hp) 12.5kn Niigata 6M31KEGS 1 x 4 Stroke 6 Cy. 310 x 460 1177kW (1600bhp) Niigata Engineering Co Ltd-Japan AuxGen: 2 x 70kW 225V a.c
9377872 - -	**TAEBAEK** - **Namsung Yesun Co Ltd** - *Pyeongtaek* *South Korea* MMSI: 440500175 Official number: PTR-053542	**277** - -	Class: KR	**2005-12 Yeunsoo Shipbuilding Co Ltd — Janghang** Yd No: 21 Loa 35.24 Br ex - Dght 3.100 Lbp 30.00 Br md 9.50 Dpth 4.10 Welded, 1 dk	**(B32A2ST) Tug**	**2 oil engines** reduction geared to sc. shafts driving 2 Z propellers Total Power: 3,310kW (4,500hp) M.T.U. 16V4000M60 2 x Vee 4 Stroke 16 Cy. 165 x 190 each-1655kW (2250bhp) MTU Friedrichshafen GmbH-Friedrichshafen
9135341 - -	**TAECHANG PEARL** *ex* Kyokutoku Maru *-2009* **Tae Chang Shipping Co Ltd** - *Yeosu* *South Korea* MMSI: 440315060 Official number: YSR-095662	*749* - 1,910	Class: KR	**1996-01 K.K. Miura Zosensho — Saiki** Yd No: 1151 Loa 77.00 Br ex - Dght 4.590 Lbp 72.00 Br md 11.50 Dpth 5.00 Welded, 1 dk	**(A13B2TP) Products Tanker** Liq: 2,199; Liq (Oil): 2,199	**1 oil engine** driving 1 FP propeller Total Power: 1,324kW (1,800hp) 11.5kn Hanshin LH30LG 1 x 4 Stroke 6 Cy. 300 x 600 1324kW (1800bhp) The Hanshin Diesel Works Ltd-Japan
9418107 - -	**TAECHONG NO. 2** - **Yong Nam Co Ltd** - *Incheon* *South Korea* MMSI: 440004570 Official number: ICR-062875	**275** - -	Class: KR	**2006-11 Samkwang Shipbuilding & Engineering Co Ltd — Incheon** Yd No: 06-02 Loa 36.50 Br ex - Dght 3.300 Lbp 31.15 Br md 10.00 Dpth 4.50 Welded, 1 dk	**(B32A2ST) Tug**	**2 oil engines** reduction geared to sc. shafts driving 2 Propellers Total Power: 3,384kW (4,600hp) Yanmar 6EY26 2 x 4 Stroke 6 Cy. 260 x 385 each-1692kW (2300bhp) Yanmar Diesel Engine Co Ltd-Japan
8741870 *HP6366* -	**TAEHUNG-TB1** *ex* 207 Sam Yang Ho *-2010* *ex* Suwa Maru *-2006* **Taehung Marine SA** - *Panama* *Panama* Official number: 4151410	**118** 35 -		**1985-09 Uchida Zosen — Ise** L reg 23.10 Br ex - Dght - Lbp - Br md 7.00 Dpth 3.00 Welded, 1 dk	**(B32A2ST) Tug**	**1 oil engine** reduction geared to sc. shaft driving 1 Propeller Total Power: 588kW (799hp) Niigata 6MG20CX 1 x 4 Stroke 6 Cy. 200 x 260 588kW (799bhp) Niigata Engineering Co Ltd-Japan
9115420 *DTBK9* -	**TAELIM IRIS** *ex* Sun Jin No. 555 *-2013* *ex* Kumage *-2002* **Taelim Shipping Co Ltd** - *Busan* *South Korea* MMSI: 440106610 Official number: 0207007-6261102	**1,475** - 600		**1994-11 Sanyo Zosen K.K. — Onomichi** Yd No: 1063 Loa 77.36 (BB) Br ex - Dght 3.800 Lbp 68.00 Br md 12.00 Dpth 8.17 Welded, 2 dks.	**(A35B2RV) Vehicles Carrier**	**2 oil engines** with clutches & reverse reduction geared to sc. shafts driving 2 FP propellers Total Power: 3,678kW (5,000hp) Akasaka 6U28AK 2 x 4 Stroke 6 Cy. 280 x 380 each-1839kW (2500bhp) Akasaka Tekkosho KK (Akasaka DieselLtd)-Japan
8708191 *DSPF5* -	**TAELIM JASMINE** *ex* Shotoku Maru No. 75 *-2007* **Taelim Shipping Co Ltd** Korean Society of Ship Inspection & Technology *Jeju* *South Korea* MMSI: 440906000 Official number: JJR-079401	**591** 380 520		**1987-06 Niigata Engineering Co Ltd — Niigata NI** Yd No: 2062 Loa 55.77 (BB) Br ex - Dght 3.850 Lbp 49.15 Br md 8.90 Dpth 3.85 Welded	**(B12B2FC) Fish Carrier** Ins: 573	**1 oil engine** with clutches, flexible couplings & sr geared to sc. shaft driving 1 CP propeller Total Power: 1,177kW (1,600hp) Niigata 6M31AFTE 1 x 4 Stroke 6 Cy. 310 x 530 1177kW (1600bhp) Niigata Engineering Co Ltd-Japan
8028814 *DTAA8* -	**TAELIM LOTUS** *ex* Jin Hae 7 *-2006* *ex* Orion No. 5 *-2004* *ex* Orion V *-1996* *ex* Tonina *-1982* **Taelim Shipping Co Ltd** - *Busan* *South Korea* MMSI: 440622000 Official number: BSR-031625	**586** 213 547	Class: (KR) (NK)	**1981-03 KK Kanasashi Zosen — Shizuoka SZ** Yd No: 2061 Loa 55.94 Br ex - Dght 3.052 Lbp 49.81 Br md 8.81 Dpth 4.20 Welded, 1 dk	**(B11B2FV) Fishing Vessel** Ins: 576 4 Ha: 2 (1.0 x 1.0) (1.9 x 1.9) (8.9 x 7.0)	**1 oil engine** driving 1 FP propeller Total Power: 993kW (1,350hp) 11.5kn Akasaka AH28 1 x 4 Stroke 6 Cy. 280 x 440 993kW (1350bhp) Akasaka Tekkosho KK (Akasaka DieselLtd)-Japan AuxGen: 2 x 200kW 225V a.c
7404413 *6MHP* -	**TAEWON NO. 607** *ex* O Yang No. 86 *-1982* *ex* Dairin Maru No. 28 *-1986* **Seo Dong International Co Ltd** - *Busan* *South Korea* Official number: 9507068-6260001	*341* 162 -	Class: (KR)	**1974-11 Goriki Zosensho — Ise** Yd No: 770 Loa 56.82 Br ex 9.07 Dght 3.487 Lbp 49.51 Br md 9.05 Dpth 3.54 Riveted\Welded, 1 dk	**(B11B2FV) Fishing Vessel** Ins: 399	**1 oil engine** driving 1 FP propeller Total Power: 1,692kW (2,300hp) 14.0kn Akasaka AH40 1 x 4 Stroke 6 Cy. 400 x 600 1692kW (2300bhp) Akasaka Tekkosho KK (Akasaka DieselLtd)-Japan AuxGen: 2 x 240kW 225V a.c
8206648 *CNJK* -	**TAFDNA** - **Omnium Marocaine de Peche** - SatCom: Inmarsat C 424237210 *Agadir* *Morocco* Official number: 8-627	*324* 142 405	Class: (BV)	**1983-02 Construcciones Navales Santodomingo SA — Vigo** Yd No: 484 Loa 38.31 Br ex 8.59 Dght 4.050 Lbp 34.78 Br md 8.51 Dpth 6.15 Welded, 1 dk	**(B11A2FS) Stern Trawler** Ins: 402 Compartments: 1 Ho, ER 2 Ha: ER	**1 oil engine** with clutches, flexible couplings & sr geared to sc. shaft driving 1 FP propeller Total Power: 853kW (1,160hp) 12.3kn Deutz SBA8M528 1 x 4 Stroke 8 Cy. 220 x 280 853kW (1160bhp) Hijos de J Barreras SA-Spain AuxGen: 2 x 140kW 380V 50Hz a.c
7403823 - -	**TAFELNAY** *ex* Antonito Pelayo *-1990* *launched as* El Canito *-1984* **Tafelnay Fisheries SA** - *Agadir* *Morocco*	*189* 61 -	Class: (BV)	**1974 Const. Nav. del Sureste S.A. — Alicante** Yd No: 07 Loa 30.99 Br ex 7.01 Dght - Lbp 28.15 Br md 6.99 Dpth 3.61 Welded, 1 dk	**(B11A2FS) Stern Trawler**	**1 oil engine** driving 1 FP propeller Total Power: 625kW (850hp) 10.8kn Caterpillar D398SCAC 1 x Vee 4 Stroke 12 Cy. 159 x 203 625kW (850bhp) Caterpillar Tractor Co-USA Fuel: 65.0 (d.f.)
5348512 *EBZP* -	**TAFIRA** - **Monte Ventoso SA** - *Las Palmas de Gran Canaria* *Spain* MMSI: 224166160 Official number: 3-2489/	**259** 78 -	Class: (BV)	**1960 Astilleros de Murueta S.A. — Gernika-Lumo** Yd No: 32 L reg 32.62 Br ex 6.91 Dght - Lbp 31.98 Br md - Dpth 3.99 Welded, 1 dk	**(B11A2FT) Trawler** 2 Ha: 2 (0.9 x 0.9)	**1 oil engine** driving 1 FP propeller Total Power: 427kW (581hp) 10.0kn Werkspoor 1 x 4 Stroke 8 Cy. 270 x 500 427kW (581bhp) NV Werkspoor-Netherlands
7230587 *7TAE* -	**TAFNA 1** - **Entreprise Portuaire de Skikda (EPS)** - *Alger* *Algeria*	*359* 104 139	Class: (BV)	**1973-01 D.W. Kremer Sohn — Elmshorn** Yd No: 1155 Loa 34.90 Br ex 9.66 Dght 3.703 Lbp 30.82 Br md 9.20 Dpth 4.70 Welded	**(B32A2ST) Tug**	**1 oil engine** reverse reduction geared to sc. shaft driving 1 CP propeller Total Power: 2,207kW (3,001hp) 13.0kn MaK 12M453AK 1 x Vee 4 Stroke 12 Cy. 320 x 420 2207kW (3001bhp) MaK Maschinenbau GmbH-Kiel

IMO / Call sign	Ship / Owner	Tonnage	Class	Build	Type	Machinery
7302835 *7TAF* -	**TAFNA 2** **Entreprise Portuaire de Skikda (EPS)** - *Skikda* *Algeria*	*359* 104 139	Class: BV	**1973-03 D.W. Kremer Sohn — Elmshorn** Yd No: 1156 Loa 34.90 Br ex 9.66 Dght 3.925 Lbp 30.82 Br md 9.20 Dpth 4.70 Welded	**(B32A2ST) Tug**	**1 oil engine** reverse reduction geared to sc. shaft driving 1 CP propeller Total Power: 2,207kW (3,001hp) 13.0kn MaK 12M453AK 1 x Vee 4 Stroke 12 Cy. 320 x 420 2207kW (3001bhp) MaK Maschinenbau GmbH-Kiel
8910550 *5WCX* -	**TAFOLA** **Government of The Independent State of Samoa** Samoa Port Authority *Apia* *Samoa* Official number: 0032	**120** 36 39 T/cm 1.4	Class: (NK)	**1989-11 Kanagawa Zosen — Kobe** Yd No: 332 Loa 25.90 Br ex - Dght 2.100 Lbp 23.85 Br md 6.80 Dpth 2.80 Welded, 1 dk	**(B32A2ST) Tug**	**2 oil engines** sr geared to sc. shafts driving 2 FP propellers Total Power: 1,176kW (1,598hp) 11.0kn Yanmar M200-SN 2 x 4 Stroke 6 Cy. 200 x 260 each-588kW (799bhp) Yanmar Diesel Engine Co Ltd-Japan AuxGen: 1 x 40kW 225V 50Hz a.c, 1 x 24kW 225V 50Hz a.c Fuel: 21.8 (d.f.) 3.9pd
9209178 *CNA4191* -	**TAFOUKT** *ex* Nuevo Harmanos Gonzalez *-2007* **Khalid Fisheries** - *Morocco* MMSI: 242891000	**158** - -	Class: (BV)	**1999-02 Astilleros Armon SA — Navia** Yd No: 466 Loa 23.00 Br ex - Dght 2.900 Lbp 18.80 Br md 7.00 Dpth 3.00 Welded, 1 dk	**(B11A2FT) Trawler**	**1 oil engine** geared to sc. shaft driving 1 FP propeller Total Power: 257kW (349hp) Cummins 1 x 4 Stroke 257kW (349bhp) Cummins Engine Co Ltd-United Kingdom
9292814 *CNA2487* -	**TAFRAOUT** **Royaume Du Maroc (Societe d'Exploitation des Ports (SODEP) - Marsa Maroc)** - *Agadir* *Morocco* MMSI: 242562000	**235** 80 162	Class: BV	**2004-07 Astilleros Zamakona SA — Santurtzi** Yd No: 605 Loa 27.00 Br ex - Dght 3.110 Lbp 25.85 Br md 9.70 Dpth 5.50 Welded, 1 dk	**(B32A2ST) Tug**	**2 oil engines** geared to sc. shafts driving 2 Directional propellers Total Power: 2,160kW (2,936hp) 12.0kn Wartsila 6L20 2 x 4 Stroke 6 Cy. 200 x 280 each-1080kW (1468bhp) Wartsila Diesel S.A.-Bermeo
8886589 *WBQ9253* -	**TAFT BEACH** **Gilmerton Tugs LLC** Norfolk Tug Co *Chesapeake, VA* *United States of America* MMSI: 367017010 Official number: 647773	*118* 80 -		**1982 Offshore Shipbuilders, Inc. — Houma, La** Yd No: 8 Loa 24.38 Br ex - Dght - Lbp - Br md 7.92 Dpth 3.25 Welded, 1 dk	**(B32A2ST) Tug**	**2 oil engines** reduction geared to sc. shafts driving 2 FP propellers Total Power: 1,324kW (1,800hp) G.M. (Detroit Diesel) 16V-149 2 x Vee 2 Stroke 16 Cy. 146 x 146 each-662kW (900bhp) General Motors Detroit DieselAllison Divn-USA
9075802 - -	**TAFTAN** - - *Bandar Anzali* *Iran*	**104** 31 58	Class: (RS)	**1992-05 AO Azovskaya Sudoverf — Azov** Yd No: 1056 Loa 26.50 Br ex 6.59 Dght 2.360 Lbp 22.90 Br md - Dpth 3.05 Welded, 1 dk	**(B11A2FS) Stern Trawler**	**1 oil engine** geared to sc. shaft driving 1 FP propeller Total Power: 165kW (224hp) 9.3kn Daldizel 6CHNSP18/22 1 x 4 Stroke 6 Cy. 180 x 220 165kW (224bhp) Daldizel-Khabarovsk AuxGen: 2 x 30kW Fuel: 9.0 (d.f.)
9428554 *AUZM* -	**TAG-4** *ex* PFS Energy *-2009* **Tag Offshore Ltd** - *Mumbai* *India* MMSI: 419773000 Official number: 3556	**1,922** 647 1,884	Class: IR (NV)	**2009-02 ABG Shipyard Ltd — Surat** Yd No: 281 Loa 63.40 Br ex - Dght 5.500 Lbp 56.53 Br md 15.80 Dpth 6.80 Welded, 1 dk	**(B21B20A) Anchor Handling Tug Supply**	**2 oil engines** reduction geared to sc. shafts driving 2 CP propellers Total Power: 4,516kW (6,140hp) 14.0kn General Electric 7FDM12 2 x Vee 4 Stroke 12 Cy. 229 x 267 each-2258kW (3070bhp) General Electric Co.-Lynn, Ma AuxGen: 2 x 350kW a.c, 2 x 1000kW a.c Thrusters: 2 Tunnel thruster (f); 1 Tunnel thruster (a)
9378993 *AUOG* -	**TAG-5** **Tag Offshore Ltd** - *Mumbai* *India* MMSI: 419789000 Official number: 3268	**1,904** 638 1,350	Class: IR NV	**2009-07 ABG Shipyard Ltd — Surat** Yd No: 261 Loa 63.40 Br ex - Dght 4.800 Lbp 56.46 Br md 15.80 Dpth 6.80 Welded, 1 dk	**(B21B20A) Anchor Handling Tug Supply**	**2 oil engines** reduction geared to sc. shafts driving 2 CP propellers Total Power: 4,708kW (6,400hp) 13.0kn Yanmar 8N280-EN 2 x 4 Stroke 8 Cy. 280 x 380 each-2354kW (3200bhp) Yanmar Diesel Engine Co Ltd-Japan AuxGen: 2 x 1000kW 440V 60Hz a.c, 2 x 350kW 440V 60Hz a.c Thrusters: 2 Tunnel thruster (f); 1 Tunnel thruster (a)
9641716 *AWDQ* -	**TAG 6** *ex* Heng Sheng Tuo 1hao *-2013* *ex* Heng Sheng 1 *-2012* **Zodiac Business Services Pte Ltd** Tag Offshore Ltd *India* MMSI: 419000816	**2,360** 708 2,437	Class: IR RI (CC)	**2012-01 Fujian Hengsheng Shipping Heavy Industry Co Ltd — Fu'an FJ** Yd No: HS001 Loa 68.60 Br ex 16.70 Dght 5.800 Lbp 61.00 Br md 16.20 Dpth 7.20 Welded, 1 dk	**(B21B20A) Anchor Handling Tug Supply** Ice Capable	**2 oil engines** reduction geared to sc. shafts driving 2 Propellers Total Power: 6,178kW (8,400hp) 13.4kn Chinese Std. Type 8320ZC 2 x 4 Stroke 8 Cy. 320 x 440 each-3089kW (4200bhp) Ningbo CSI Power & Machinery GroupCo Ltd-China AuxGen: 2 x 1000kW 400V a.c, 2 x 400kW 400V a.c
9379002 *AUOF* -	**TAG-7** **Tag Offshore Ltd** - *Mumbai* *India* MMSI: 419098100 Official number: 3267	**1,906** 650 1,350	Class: IR (NV)	**2010-07 ABG Shipyard Ltd — Surat** Yd No: 262 Loa 63.40 Br ex - Dght 4.800 Lbp 56.47 Br md 15.80 Dpth 6.80 Welded, 1 dk	**(B21B20A) Anchor Handling Tug Supply**	**2 oil engines** reduction geared to sc. shafts driving 2 CP propellers Total Power: 4,708kW (6,400hp) 11.0kn Yanmar 8N280-EN 2 x 4 Stroke 8 Cy. 280 x 380 each-2354kW (3200bhp) Yanmar Diesel Engine Co Ltd-Japan AuxGen: 2 x 1000kW 440V 60Hz a.c, 2 x 350kW 440V 60Hz a.c Thrusters: 2 Tunnel thruster (f); 1 Tunnel thruster (a)
9549554 *AVED* -	**TAG-8** *completed as* Kestrel K *-2009* *launched as* Al Amin *-2009* **Tag Offshore Ltd** - SatCom: Inmarsat C 441922634 *Mumbai* *India* MMSI: 419097600 Official number: 3666	**2,369** 710 3,023	Class: IR (AB)	**2009-12 Fujian Mawei Shipbuilding Ltd — Fuzhou FJ** Yd No: 618-12 Loa 70.00 Br ex 16.82 Dght 6.300 Lbp 61.80 Br md 16.80 Dpth 7.50 Welded, 1 dk	**(B21A20S) Platform Supply Ship**	**2 oil engines** reduction geared to sc. shafts driving 2 Directional propellers Total Power: 3,840kW (5,220hp) 12.0kn Caterpillar 3516B-HD 2 x Vee 4 Stroke 16 Cy. 170 x 215 each-1920kW (2610bhp) Caterpillar Inc-USA AuxGen: 3 x 1000kW a.c, 1 x 410kW a.c
9428592 *AVEE* -	**TAG-9** *ex* PFS Force *-2011* **Tag Offshore Ltd** - *Mumbai* *India* MMSI: 419097800 Official number: 3667	**1,922** 650 1,600	Class: IR (NV)	**2010-04 ABG Shipyard Ltd — Surat** Yd No: 286 Loa 63.40 Br ex 15.80 Dght 4.800 Lbp 56.53 Br md 15.60 Dpth 6.80 Welded, 1 dk	**(B21B20A) Anchor Handling Tug Supply**	**2 oil engines** reduction geared to sc. shafts driving 2 CP propellers Total Power: 4,516kW (6,140hp) 14.0kn General Electric 7FDM12 1 x Vee 4 Stroke 12 Cy. 229 x 267 2258kW (3070bhp) General Electric Co.-Lynn, Ma AuxGen: 2 x 1000kW a.c, 2 x 350kW a.c Thrusters: 2 Tunnel thruster (f); 1 Tunnel thruster (a)
9474474 *AVXB* -	**TAG-10** *ex* Sanko Bride *-2012* **Tag Offshore Ltd** - *Mumbai* *India* MMSI: 419000645 Official number: 4061	**2,430** 782 2,510	Class: IR (AB)	**2010-07 Universal Shipbuilding Corp — Yokohama KN (Keihin Shipyard)** Yd No: 0052 Loa 68.00 Br ex - Dght 6.010 Lbp 61.45 Br md 16.40 Dpth 7.20 Welded, 1 dk	**(B21B20A) Anchor Handling Tug Supply** Liq: 831	**2 oil engines** reduction geared to sc. shafts driving 2 CP propellers Total Power: 9,000kW (12,236hp) Wartsila 9L32 2 x 4 Stroke 9 Cy. 320 x 400 each-4500kW (6118bhp) Wartsila Finland Oy-Finland AuxGen: 2 x 320kW 440V 60Hz a.c, 2 x 1800kW 440V 60Hz a.c Thrusters: 2 Thwart. CP thruster (f); 1 Thwart. CP thruster (a) Fuel: 828.0 (r.f.)
8600002 *AVTA* -	**TAG 11** *ex* Lady Gerda *-2012* *ex* Shelf Ranger *-2001* **Tag Offshore Ltd** - *Mumbai* *India* MMSI: 419000539 Official number: 3992	**1,997** 599 2,060	Class: IR (NV)	**1987-07 Hudong Shipyard — Shanghai** Yd No: 1172 Loa 69.14 (BB) Br ex 15.02 Dght 6.101 Lbp 61.48 Br md 15.00 Dpth 7.01 Welded, 2 dks	**(B21B20A) Anchor Handling Tug Supply** Ice Capable	**4 oil engines** reduction geared to sc. shafts driving 2 CP propellers Total Power: 6,368kW (8,656hp) 11.0kn Deutz SBV9M628 4 x 4 Stroke 9 Cy. 240 x 280 each-1592kW (2164bhp) Kloeckner Humboldt Deutz AG-West Germany AuxGen: 2 x 900kW 440V 60Hz a.c, 2 x 500kW 440V 60Hz a.c, 1 x 250kW 440V 60Hz a.c Thrusters: 1 Tunnel thruster (f); 1 Tunnel thruster (a); 1 Retract. directional thruster (f) Fuel: 841.5 (d.f.)

IMO / Call sign / Flag	Name / Owner / Port	Tonnage	Class	Builder / Dimensions	Type	Machinery
9630456 *AWAA* -	**TAG 12** *ex* Xin Hai Gong *-2013* **Tag Offshore Ltd** - *Mumbai* *India* MMSI: 419000721 Official number: 4074	**2,772** 681 4,317	Class: IR (CC)	**2011-08 Fujian Baima Shipyard — Fu'an FJ** Yd No: BM2010T-1 Loa 69.00 Br ex 16.22 Dght 5.700 Lbp 61.00 Br md 16.20 Dpth 7.00 Welded, 1 dk	**(B21B20T) Offshore Tug/Supply Ship** Ice Capable	**2 oil engines** reduction geared to sc. shafts driving 2 Propellers Total Power: 3,530kW (4,800hp) 12.0kn Chinese Std. Type G8320ZC 2 x 4 Stroke 8 Cy. 320 x 440 each-1765kW (2400bhp) Ningbo CSI Power & Machinery GroupCo Ltd-China AuxGen: 2 x 1000kW 400V a.c, 2 x 400kW 400V a.c
9680827 *AWFH* -	**TAG 13** *ex* Excelsior *-2014* **Tag Offshore Ltd** - *Mumbai* *India* MMSI: 419000860 Official number: 4137	**2,267** 680 1,500	Class: AB IR	**2014-01 Fujian Southeast Shipyard — Fuzhou FJ** Yd No: DN65M-1 Loa 65.00 Br ex 16.00 Dght 4.950 Lbp 58.50 Br md 16.00 Dpth 6.20 Welded, 1 dk	**(B21B20A) Anchor Handling Tug Supply**	**2 oil engines** reduction geared to sc shafts driving 2 Propellers Niigata 1 x 4 Stroke Niigata Engineering Co Ltd-Japan
7827665 - -	**TAG-A-LONG** *ex* Capt. Mike *-1991* - -	*106* 72 -		**1981 Steiner Shipyard, Inc. — Bayou La Batre, Al** Yd No: 87 Loa 22.81 Br ex - Dght 2.401 Lbp 20.12 Br md 6.71 Dpth 3.36 Welded, 1 dk	**(B11A2FT) Trawler**	**1 oil engine** reduction geared to sc. shaft driving 1 FP propeller Total Power: 268kW (364hp) Cummins KT-1150-M 1 x 4 Stroke 6 Cy. 159 x 159 268kW (364bhp) Cummins Engine Co Inc-USA
9619359 *AVKZ* -	**TAG LAXMI** - **Tag Offshore Ltd** - *Mumbai* *India* MMSI: 419000285 Official number: 3825	**341** 102 190	Class: IR (AB)	**2011-05 Jiangsu Suyang Marine Co Ltd — Yangzhong JS** (Hull) Yd No: (1458) **2011-05 Pacific Ocean Engineering & Trading Pte Ltd (POET) — Singapore** Yd No: 1458 Loa 30.00 Br ex 9.82 Dght 3.800 Lbp 29.50 Br md 9.80 Dpth 4.88 Welded, 1 dk	**(B32A2ST) Tug**	**2 oil engines** reduction geared to sc. shafts driving 2 Directional propellers Total Power: 2,942kW (4,000hp) Niigata 6L26HLX 2 x 4 Stroke 6 Cy. 260 x 350 each-1471kW (2000bhp) Niigata Engineering Co Ltd-Japan AuxGen: 2 x 130kW a.c
9371880 *AULD* -	**TAG MAMTA** *ex* Wei Gang Tuo 18 *-2005* **Tag Offshore Ltd** - *Mumbai* *India* MMSI: 419060900 Official number: 3189	**435** 131 208	Class: IR (CC)	**2005-07 Yantai Salvage Bureau Shipyard — Yantai SD** Yd No: YJLZ04-09 Loa 36.10 Br ex 10.02 Dght 3.500 Lbp 32.25 Br md 10.00 Dpth 4.80 Welded, 1 dk	**(B32A2ST) Tug**	**2 oil engines** reduction geared to sc. shafts driving 2 Directional propellers Total Power: 3,944kW (5,362hp) Daihatsu 6DKM-26 2 x 4 Stroke 6 Cy. 260 x 380 each-1972kW (2681bhp) Daihatsu Diesel Manufacturing Co Lt-Japan AuxGen: 2 x 80kW 380V 50Hz a.c Fuel: 119.0 (d.f.)
9076428 *9MHS7* -	**TAG NUR DUA** *ex* Bertam *-2008* **T A G Marine Sdn Bhd** - *Port Klang* *Malaysia* Official number: 332494	**263** 78 120	Class: (LR) ✠ Classed LR until 25/1/13	**1994-06 Ironwoods Shipyard Sdn Bhd — Kuching** Yd No: 051 Loa 29.40 Br ex 9.52 Dght 3.300 Lbp 26.35 Br md 9.00 Dpth 4.35 Welded, 1 dk	**(B32A2ST) Tug**	**2 oil engines** with flexible couplings & sr geared to sc. shafts driving 2 Directional propellers Total Power: 2,642kW (3,592hp) Blackstone ESL8MK2 2 x 4 Stroke 8 Cy. 222 x 292 each-1321kW (1796bhp) Mirrlees Blackstone (Stockport)Ltd.-Stockport AuxGen: 3 x 79kW 415V 50Hz a.c
7708869 *9MAM5* -	**TAG NUR SATU** *ex* Penaga *-2008* **T A G Marine Sdn Bhd** - *Penang* *Malaysia* MMSI: 533000157 Official number: 324202	**279** 84 99	Class: (LR) ✠ Classed LR until 23/6/10	**1978-09 Penang Shipbuilding Corp Sdn Bhd — Penang** Yd No: 14428 Loa 32.80 Br ex 9.73 Dght 3.601 Lbp 29.00 Br md 9.10 Dpth 4.00 Welded, 1 dk	**(B32A2ST) Tug**	**2 oil engines** with clutches, flexible couplings & sr reverse geared to sc. shafts driving 2 FP propellers Total Power: 1,472kW (2,002hp) Kromhout 8FCHD240 2 x 4 Stroke 8 Cy. 240 x 260 each-736kW (1001bhp) Stork Werkspoor Diesel BV-Netherlands AuxGen: 3 x 48kW 440V 60Hz a.c
8019473 *9MQJ8* -	**TAG NUR TIGA** *ex* Sattahip 2 *-2013* **T A G Marine Sdn Bhd** - *Port Klang* *Malaysia* Official number: 334565	**333** 99 -	Class: (AB)	**1980-10 Sing Koon Seng Pte Ltd — Singapore** Yd No: SKS531 Loa - Br ex - Dght - Lbp 29.72 Br md 9.31 Dpth 4.63 Welded, 1 dk	**(B32A2ST) Tug**	**2 oil engines** geared to sc. shafts driving 2 FP propellers Total Power: 2,354kW (3,200hp) Yanmar 6Z-ST 2 x 4 Stroke 6 Cy. 280 x 340 each-1177kW (1600bhp) Yanmar Diesel Engine Co Ltd-Japan
9603582 *AVHZ* -	**TAG RAJVIR** *ex* You Lian 3 *-2010* **Tag Offshore Ltd** - SatCom: Inmarsat C 441922862 *Mumbai* *India* MMSI: 419000185 Official number: 3756	**451** 135 551	Class: IR (CC)	**2010-09 Yiu Lian Dockyards (Zhangzhou) Ltd — Zhangzhou FJ** Yd No: 09-19T/SK Loa 36.80 Br ex 10.02 Dght 3.600 Lbp 32.30 Br md 10.00 Dpth 4.60 Welded, 1 dk	**(B32A2ST) Tug**	**2 oil engines** reduction geared to sc. shafts driving 2 Z propellers Total Power: 2,942kW (4,000hp) Niigata 6L26HLX 2 x 4 Stroke 6 Cy. 260 x 350 each-1471kW (2000bhp) Niigata Engineering Co Ltd-Japan
9412268 *AUOU* -	**TAG SHIV** *ex* Yan Lao Tuo 7 *-2006* **Tag Offshore Ltd** - *Mumbai* *India* MMSI: 419065100 Official number: 3282	**431** 129 227	Class: IR (CC)	**2006-06 Yantai Salvage Bureau Shipyard — Yantai SD** Yd No: YJLZ05-14 Loa 36.10 Br ex 10.02 Dght 3.500 Lbp 33.60 Br md 10.00 Dpth 4.80 Welded, 1 dk	**(B32A2ST) Tug**	**2 oil engines** reduction geared to sc. shafts driving 2 Z propellers Total Power: 2,908kW (3,954hp) Niigata 6L26HLX 2 x 4 Stroke 6 Cy. 260 x 350 each-1454kW (1977bhp) Niigata Engineering Co Ltd-Japan AuxGen: 2 x 100kW 380V 50Hz a.c Fuel: 100.1 (d.f.)
9612193 *AVJY* -	**TAG SHWETA** *ex* You Lian 5 *-2011* **Tag Offshore Ltd** - *Mumbai* *India* MMSI: 419000238 Official number: 3806	**451** 135 551	Class: IR (CC)	**2011-01 Yiu Lian Dockyards (Zhangzhou) Ltd — Zhangzhou FJ** Yd No: 09-28T/SK Loa 36.80 Br ex 10.02 Dght 3.600 Lbp 32.30 Br md 10.00 Dpth 4.60 Welded, 1 dk	**(B32A2ST) Tug**	**2 oil engines** reduction geared to sc. shafts driving 2 Z propellers Total Power: 2,942kW (4,000hp) Niigata 6L26HLX 2 x 4 Stroke 6 Cy. 260 x 350 each-1471kW (2000bhp) Niigata Engineering Co Ltd-Japan
9412256 *AUOV* -	**TAG SIA** *ex* Yan Lao Tuo 6 *-2006* **Tag Offshore Ltd** - *Mumbai* *India* MMSI: 419065300 Official number: 3283	**431** 129 227	Class: IR	**2006-05 Yantai Salvage Bureau Shipyard — Yantai SD** Yd No: YJLZ05-13 Loa 36.10 Br ex 10.02 Dght 3.500 Lbp 33.60 Br md 10.00 Dpth 4.80 Welded, 1 dk	**(B32A2ST) Tug**	**2 oil engines** reduction geared to sc. shafts driving 2 Z propellers Total Power: 2,908kW (3,954hp) Niigata 6L26HLX 2 x 4 Stroke 6 Cy. 260 x 350 each-1454kW (1977bhp) Niigata Engineering Co Ltd-Japan AuxGen: 2 x 100kW 380V 50Hz a.c Fuel: 100.1 (d.f.)
9294563 *H8UX* -	**TAGA** - **Blue Tree Maritima SA** NYK Shipmanagement Pte Ltd SatCom: Inmarsat C 435501510 *Panama* *Panama* MMSI: 355015000 Official number: 3012904B	**160,007** 99,180 303,430 T/cm 180.1	Class: NK	**2004-07 Universal Shipbuilding Corp — Nagasu KM (Ariake Shipyard)** Yd No: 017 Loa 332.98 (BB) Br ex - Dght 21.024 Lbp 320.00 Br md 60.00 Dpth 29.40 Welded, 1 dk	**(A13A2TV) Crude Oil Tanker** Double Hull (13F) Liq: 349,796; Liq (Oil): 349,796 3 Cargo Pump (s): 3x5500m³/hr Manifold: Bow/CM: 164m	**1 oil engine** driving 1 FP propeller Total Power: 26,757kW (36,379hp) 15.7kn B&W 6S90MC-C 1 x 2 Stroke 6 Cy. 900 x 3188 26757kW (36379bhp) Hitachi Zosen Corp-Japan Fuel: 7420.0
6821444 *WCZ4449* -	**TAGA** *ex* Celtic *-1999* *ex* Uno Maru *-1994* *ex* Toho Maru *-1980* **Saipan Marine Corp** Cabras Marine Corp *Saipan, MP* *United States of America* Official number: 1076158	*192* 57 -	Class: RI	**1968 Osaka Shipbuilding Co Ltd — Osaka OS** Yd No: 280 Loa 25.20 Br ex 8.64 Dght 2.560 Lbp 24.49 Br md 8.62 Dpth 3.79 Riveted\Welded, 1 dk	**(B32A2ST) Tug**	**2 oil engines** driving 2 FP propellers Total Power: 1,544kW (2,100hp) 12.0kn Daihatsu 8PSHTBM-26D 2 x 4 Stroke 8 Cy. 260 x 320 each-772kW (1050bhp) Daihatsu Kogyo-Japan AuxGen: 1 x 80kW 225V a.c Fuel: 26.5 7.0pd
9373905 *A8NF9* -	**TAGA BAY** *launched as* Vega Aquamarin *-2007* **ms 'Taga Bay' GmbH & Co Containerschiff KG** NSC Schifffahrtsgesellschaft mbH & Cie KG *Monrovia* *Liberia* MMSI: 636091412 Official number: 91412	**9,957** 5,020 13,760 T/cm 28.0	Class: GL	**2007-08 Taizhou Kouan Shipbuilding Co Ltd — Taizhou JS** Yd No: KA406 Loa 147.87 (BB) Br ex 23.43 Dght 8.510 Lbp 140.30 Br md 23.25 Dpth 11.50 Welded, 1 dk	**(A33A2CC) Container Ship (Fully Cellular)** Grain: 16,067; Bale: 16,067 TEU 1118 C Ho 334 TEU C Dk 784 incl 240 ref C Compartments: 5 Ho, ER 7 Ha: ER Cranes: 2x45t	**1 oil engine** reduction geared to sc. shaft driving 1 CP propeller Total Power: 9,730kW (13,229hp) 19.6kn MAN-B&W 7L58/64 1 x 4 Stroke 7 Cy. 580 x 640 9730kW (13229bhp) MAN B&W Diesel AG-Augsburg AuxGen: 1 x 1400kW 450/230V a.c, 3 x 570kW 450/230V a.c Thrusters: 1 Tunnel thruster (f) Fuel: 199.8 (d.f.) 1306.3 (r.f.)

8878908 - - -	**TAGA MARU No. 3** *ex* Taga Maru No. 38 - - *Myanmar*	*108* - -		**1977 Sanuki Shipbuilding & Iron Works Co Ltd — Mitoyo KG** L reg 26.60 Br ex - Dght - Lbp - Br md 5.60 Dpth 2.20 Welded, 1 dk	**(B11B2FV) Fishing Vessel**	**1 oil engine** driving 1 FP propeller Niigata 1 x 4 Stroke Niigata Engineering Co Ltd-Japan
8935213 - -	**TAGANROG** **Intermar-2000 Marine Fishery Co Ltd** -	**104** 31 58	Class: (RS)	**1997-10 Sudoverf — Rybinsk** Yd No: 2905 Loa 26.50 Br ex 6.50 Dght 2.320 Lbp 23.61 Br md - Dpth 3.05 Welded, 1 dk	**(B11A2FS) Stern Trawler**	**1 oil engine** geared to sc. shaft driving 1 FP propeller Total Power: 232kW (315hp) 9.5kn Daldizel 6CHSP18/22 1 x 4 Stroke 6 Cy. 180 x 220 232kW (315bhp) Daldizel-Khabarovsk AuxGen: 2 x 25kW Fuel: 9.0 (d.f.)
8129606 *UBGF2* -	**TAGANROGA** *ex* Taganrog *-1992* **Inzer Ltd** Ost-Oil Co Ltd SatCom: Inmarsat C 427302235 *Vladivostok* *Russia* MMSI: 273331510	**5,154** 1,645 6,297 T/cm 16.4	Class: RS	**1983-11 Rauma-Repola Oy — Rauma** Yd No: 280 Loa 113.01 Br ex 18.33 Dght 7.201 Lbp 105.34 Br md 18.31 Dpth 8.51 Welded, 1 dk	**(A13B2TP) Products Tanker** Double Bottom Entire Compartment Length Liq: 5,943; Liq (Oil): 5,943 Part Cargo Heating Coils Compartments: 3 Ta, 8 Wing Ta, ER 11 Cargo Pump (s): 3x190m^3/hr, 8x145m^3/hr Manifold: Bow/CM: 50m Ice Capable	**1 oil engine** driving 1 FP propeller Total Power: 4,350kW (5,914hp) 13.0kn B&W 6L45GFCA 1 x 2 Stroke 6 Cy. 450 x 1200 4350kW (5914bhp) Bryanskiy Mashinostroitelnyy Zavod (BMZ)-Bryansk AuxGen: 4 x 200kW 380V 50Hz a.c Fuel: 623.0 (r.f.) 18.7pd
8935225 - -	**TAGANROGSKIY ZALIV** **Sekova A A Private Enterprise** - *Taganrog* *Russia*	**104** 31 58	Class: RS	**1997-10 Sudoverf — Rybinsk** Yd No: 2904 Loa 26.50 Br ex 6.50 Dght 2.320 Lbp 23.61 Br md - Dpth 3.05 Welded, 1 dk	**(B11A2FS) Stern Trawler**	**1 oil engine** geared to sc. shaft driving 1 FP propeller Total Power: 232kW (315hp) 9.5kn Daldizel 6CHSP18/22 1 x 4 Stroke 6 Cy. 180 x 220 232kW (315bhp) Daldizel-Khabarovsk AuxGen: 2 x 25kW Fuel: 9.0 (d.f.)
9016973 *A8UC4* -	**TAGANROGSKIY ZALIV** *ex* Tira *-2010* *ex* Anapa *-2009* *ex* Olympus *-1998* *ex* Kapitan Volchkovich *-1996* **Merlin Marine Corp** Lavinia Corp *Monrovia* *Liberia* MMSI: 636014471 Official number: 14471	**12,413** 4,903 10,984 T/cm 23.4	Class: AB (RS)	**1993-02 MTW Schiffswerft GmbH — Wismar** Yd No: 245 Loa 152.14 Br ex - Dght 9.000 Lbp 142.00 Br md 22.20 Dpth 13.60 Welded, 1 dk, 2nd & 3rd dk in holds only	**(A34A2GR) Refrigerated Cargo Ship** Ins: 13,300 Compartments: 4 Ho, ER, 4 Tw Dk 4 Ha: 4 (6.0 x 3.9)ER Derricks: 9x5t Ice Capable	**1 oil engine** driving 1 FP propeller Total Power: 7,600kW (10,333hp) 15.5kn MAN K5SZ70/125BL 1 x 2 Stroke 5 Cy. 700 x 1250 7600kW (10333bhp) Dieselmotorenwerk Rostock GmbH-Rostock
9374090 *9HA2995* -	**TAGANROGSKIY ZALIV** **Yustat Shipping 1 Ltd** JSC 'Yugreftransflot' SatCom: Inmarsat C 422901910 *Valletta* *Malta* MMSI: 229019000 Official number: 9374090	**4,970** 2,214 5,465	Class: RS	**2012-05 Saigon Shipbuilding Industry Co Ltd — Ho Chi Minh City** Yd No: SSIC-005 Loa 128.20 (BB) Br ex 16.74 Dght 4.340 Lbp 122.80 Br md 16.50 Dpth 6.10 Welded, 1 dk	**(A31A2GX) General Cargo Ship** Grain: 8,090 TEU 267 incl 20 ref C Compartments: 3 Ho, ER 3 Ha: ER 3 (25.5 x 12.6)	**2 oil engines** reduction geared to sc. shafts driving 2 FP propellers Total Power: 2,280kW (3,100hp) 11.0kn Wartsila 6L20C 2 x 4 Stroke 6 Cy. 200 x 280 each-1140kW (1550bhp) Wartsila Finland Oy-Finland AuxGen: 3 x 160kW a.c Thrusters: 1 Tunnel thruster (f) Fuel: 220.0 (d.f.)
6907858 - NDB 354	**TAGANT II** *ex* Sung Yang No. 2 *-1986* *ex* Daiei Maru No. 8 *-1977* **Ahmed of Sidi Baba** Parimco SA *Nouadhibou* *Mauritania*	*356* 159 -	Class: (RI) (KR)	**1968 Nishii Dock Co. Ltd. — Ise** Yd No: 176 Loa 48.39 Br ex 8.82 Dght - Lbp 43.90 Br md 8.62 Dpth 3.84 Riveted\Welded, 1 dk	**(B11A2FS) Stern Trawler** Ins: 392 4 Ha: 2 (1.8 x 1.8) (1.8 x 2.2) (1.0 x 1.9)ER	**1 oil engine** driving 1 CP propeller Total Power: 1,177kW (1,600hp) 10.3kn Akasaka 6DH38SS 1 x 4 Stroke 6 Cy. 380 x 560 1177kW (1600bhp) Akasaka Tekkosho KK (Akasaka DieselLtd)-Japan AuxGen: 2 x 104kW 230V a.c
7312206 - -	**TAGANT No. 1** *ex* Xeyxo *-1984* **Volyroc Trading SA** - *Nouadhibou* *Mauritania*	*263* 99 -	Class: (BV)	**1973 Ast. Celaya — Bilbao** Yd No: 137 Loa 33.46 Br ex - Dght - Lbp 29.49 Br md 7.50 Dpth 3.81 Welded, 1 dk	**(B11A2FT) Trawler** Grain: 214 Compartments: 1 Ho, ER	**1 oil engine** driving 1 FP propeller Total Power: 736kW (1,001hp) 12.0kn M.T.M. TI829C 1 x 4 Stroke 8 Cy. 295 x 420 736kW (1001bhp) La Maquinista Terrestre y Mar (MTM)-Spain Fuel: 69.0 (d.f.)
6620802 - -	**TAGAR** **Kolkata Port Trust** - *Kolkata* *India*	*156* - -	Class: IR (LR) ✠ Classed LR until 4/68	**1967-02 Richards (Shipbuilders) Ltd — Lowestoft** Yd No: 488 Loa 27.44 Br ex 8.03 Dght 2.979 Lbp 24.54 Br md 7.93 Dpth 3.66 Riveted\Welded, 1 dk	**(B32A2ST) Tug**	**2 oil engines** reverse reduction geared to sc. shafts driving 2 FP propellers Total Power: 736kW (1,000hp) 9.0kn MAN G5V235/330ATL 2 x 4 Stroke 5 Cy. 235 x 330 each-368kW (500bhp) Maschinenbau Augsburg Nuernberg (MAN)-Augsburg AuxGen: 2 x 55kW 400V 50Hz a.c Fuel: 25.5 (d.f.)
9644122 *PPMO* -	**TAGAZ** **Wilson Sons Offshore SA** - *Rio de Janeiro* *Brazil* MMSI: 710236000	**4,281** 2,377 4,500	Class: LR ✠**100A1** SS 02/2013 offshore supply ship *IWS EP ✠**LMC** **UMS** Eq.Ltr: U; Cable: 495.0/44.0 U3 (a)	**2013-02 Wilson, Sons SA — Guaruja** (Hull) Yd No: 128 **2013-02 B.V. Scheepswerf Damen — Gorinchem** Yd No: 552018 Loa 89.50 (BB) Br ex 16.04 Dght 6.150 Lbp 83.79 Br md 16.00 Dpth 7.80 Welded, 1 dk	**(B21A20S) Platform Supply Ship**	**4 diesel electric oil engines** driving 4 gen. each 1600kW 690V a.c Connecting to 2 elec. motors each (2500kW) driving 2 Directional propellers Total Power: 6,512kW (8,852hp) Caterpillar 3512C-HD 4 x Vee 4 Stroke 12 Cy. 170 x 215 each-1628kW (2213bhp) Caterpillar Inc-USA Thrusters: 2 Thwart. FP thruster (f)
8206686 *CNFY* -	**TAGHAZOUT** *launched as* Tamesna *-1983* **Omnium Marocaine de Peche** - *Laayoune* *Morocco*	*323* 142 405	Class: BV	**1983-12 Construcciones Navales Santodomingo SA — Vigo** Yd No: 488 Loa 38.31 Br ex 8.59 Dght 4.050 Lbp 34.78 Br md 8.50 Dpth 6.15 Welded, 1 dk	**(B11A2FS) Stern Trawler** Ins: 402 Compartments: 1 Ho, ER 2 Ha: ER	**1 oil engine** with clutches, flexible couplings & sr geared to sc. shaft driving 1 FP propeller Total Power: 853kW (1,160hp) 12.3kn Deutz SBA8M528 1 x 4 Stroke 8 Cy. 220 x 280 853kW (1160bhp) Hijos de J Barreras SA-Spain AuxGen: 2 x 140kW 380V 50Hz a.c
9444704 *5AGH* -	**TAGHREFT** **Government of Libya (Socialist Ports Co)** - *Homs* *Libya* Official number: 9444704	**176** 52 89	Class: (LR) (BV) ✠ Classed LR until 16/1/13	**2008-10 Stocznia Tczew Sp z oo — Tczew** (Hull) Yd No: (509822) **2008-10 B.V. Scheepswerf Damen — Gorinchem** Yd No: 509822 Loa 26.16 Br ex 7.94 Dght 3.090 Lbp 25.52 Br md 7.90 Dpth 4.05 Welded, 1 dk	**(B32A2ST) Tug**	**2 oil engines** with clutches, flexible couplings & sr geared to sc. shafts driving 2 FP propellers Total Power: 2,610kW (3,548hp) Caterpillar 3512B-HD 2 x Vee 4 Stroke 12 Cy. 170 x 190 each-1305kW (1774bhp) Caterpillar Inc-USA AuxGen: 2 x 51kW 400V 50Hz a.c
7512882 *DUH2122* -	**TAGOLOAN RIVER** **Philippine Sinter Corp** - *Cagayan de Oro* *Philippines* Official number: 10-0000158	*245* 126 76	Class: (NK)	**1975-12 Sanyo Zosen K.K. — Onomichi** Yd No: 720 Loa 32.01 Br ex 9.43 Dght 3.099 Lbp 30.26 Br md 9.40 Dpth 4.20 Welded, 1 dk	**(B32B2SP) Pusher Tug** Derricks: 1x6t	**2 oil engines** driving 2 FP propellers Total Power: 2,354kW (3,200hp) 12.0kn Niigata 8L25BX 2 x 4 Stroke 8 Cy. 250 x 320 each-1177kW (1600bhp) Niigata Engineering Co Ltd-Japan
7626164 *HO2099* -	**TAGOMAGO JET** *ex* Tunen *-1993* **Societe de Navigation Gabonaise (SONAGAB)** - *Panama* *Panama* Official number: 35102PEXT	**189** 67 40	Class: (RI) (NV)	**1977-05 Westermoen Hydrofoil AS — Mandal** Yd No: 52 Loa 30.03 Br ex 9.07 Dght 1.467 Lbp 27.12 Br md 9.05 Dpth 3.12 Welded, 1 dk	**(A37B2PS) Passenger Ship** Hull Material: Aluminium Alloy Passengers: unberthed: 180	**2 oil engines** geared to sc. shafts driving 2 FP propellers Total Power: 2,648kW (3,600hp) 22.0kn AGO 195V12CSHR 2 x Vee 4 Stroke 12 Cy. 195 x 180 each-1324kW (1800bhp) Societe Alsacienne de ConstructionsMecaniques (SACM)-France AuxGen: 2 x 27kW 220V 50Hz a.c
7236567 - -	**TAGOSHIMA MARU No. 6** **Arbata Jamore & Sons** -	*298* 153 405		**1972 Miho Zosensho K.K. — Shimizu** Yd No: 837 Loa 51.06 Br ex 8.03 Dght 3.468 Lbp 43.21 Br md 8.01 Dpth 3.71 Welded, 1 dk	**(B11B2FV) Fishing Vessel**	**1 oil engine** driving 1 FP propeller Total Power: 956kW (1,300hp) Niigata 6M28EX 1 x 4 Stroke 6 Cy. 280 x 440 956kW (1300bhp) Niigata Engineering Co Ltd-Japan
8326498 - -	**TAGRIFT** **Benino-Arabe Libyenne de Peche Maritime** - *Cotonou* *Benin*	*154* 43 -	Class: (BV)	**1983 Soc. Esercizio Cant. S.p.A. — Viareggio** Yd No: 666 Loa 25.81 Br ex - Dght 2.650 Lbp 20.40 Br md 7.03 Dpth 3.41 Welded, 1 dk	**(B11A2FS) Stern Trawler**	**1 oil engine** driving 1 FP propeller Total Power: 500kW (680hp) Baudouin 12P15.2SR 1 x Vee 4 Stroke 12 Cy. 150 x 150 500kW (680bhp) Societe des Moteurs Baudouin SA-France AuxGen: 2 x 88kW 220/380V 50Hz a.c

IMO / Call sign	Name / Owner / Port	Tonnage	Class	Builder / Dimensions	Type / Cargo	Machinery
9204166 *CB6640* -	**TAGUA** *ex* Sea Kent *-2001* **Sudamericana Agencias Aereas y Maritimas SA (SAAM)** - *Valparaiso* *Chile* MMSI: 725000530 Official number: 3022	**258** 63 -	Class: (BV)	**1998-12 Shanghai Fishing Vessel Shipyard — Shanghai** Yd No: XY-2094 Loa 26.00 Br ex - Dght 3.400 Lbp 23.30 Br md 9.40 Dpth 4.30 Welded, 1 dk	**(B32A2ST) Tug**	**2 oil engines** reduction geared to sc. shafts driving 2 FP propellers Total Power: 1,884kW (2,562hp) Caterpillar 3512TA 2 x Vee 4 Stroke 12 Cy. 170 x 190 each-942kW (1281bhp) Caterpillar Inc-USA
6725183 *3EXE* -	**TAGUA PIRE** *ex* Pispis *-2001* *ex* Mar Baltico *-1984* *ex* Hammersborg *-1981* *ex* Jojo *-1970* **Taguapire SA** - *Panama* *Panama* Official number: 09626PEXT2	*468* 324 778	Class: (GL) (NV)	**1967-10 Schiffswerft H. Rancke — Hamburg** Yd No: 211 Lengthened-1981 Loa 79.00 Br ex 10.11 Dght 3.322 Lbp 71.53 Br md 10.10 Dpth 5.01 Welded, 2 dks	**(A31A2GX) General Cargo Ship** Grain: 1,748; Bale: 1,528 Compartments: 1 Ho, ER 1 Ha: (28.0 x 6.0)ER Derricks: 2x3t Ice Capable	**1 oil engine** driving 1 FP propeller Total Power: 1,103kW (1,500hp) 11.8kn Wichmann 6AXA 1 x 2 Stroke 6 Cy. 300 x 450 1103kW (1500bhp) (new engine 1973) Wichmann Motorfabrikk AS-Norway AuxGen: 2 x 47kW 220/380V 50Hz a.c Fuel: 56.0 (d.f.) 4.5pd
8517152 - -	**TAGULA BAY** - **B A La Macchia Pty Ltd** - *Cairns, Qld* *Australia* Official number: 851693	*180* - -	Class: (NV)	**1985-06 North Queensland Engineers & Agents Pty Ltd — Cairns QLD** Loa 22.76 Br ex 6.81 Dght 2.750 Lbp - Br md 6.76 Dpth 3.15 Welded, 1 dk	**(B11B2FV) Fishing Vessel**	**1 oil engine** with clutches, flexible couplings & sr geared to sc. shaft driving 1 FP propeller Total Power: 351kW (477hp) Cummins KT-1150-M 1 x 4 Stroke 6 Cy. 159 x 159 351kW (477bhp) Cummins Engine Co Inc-USA AuxGen: 1 x 110kW 415V 50Hz a.c, 1 x 64kW 415V 50Hz a.c
8309579 *LAZA2* -	**TAGUS** *ex* Nosac Express *-1996* **Wilhelmsen Lines Shipowning AS** Wilhelmsen Lines Car Carrier Ltd SatCom: Inmarsat C 425883810 *Tonsberg* *Norway (NIS)* MMSI: 258838000	**48,357** 16,723 21,900	Class: NV	**1985-03 Daewoo Shipbuilding & Heavy Machinery Ltd — Geoje** Yd No: 4402 Loa 195.30 (BB) Br ex - Dght 11.058 Lbp 182.40 Br md 32.26 Dpth 21.70 Welded, 12 dks, incl. Nos.3, 5, 6, 8, 9 & 11 dks hoistable	**(A35B2RV) Vehicles Carrier** Side door/ramp (s) Len: 25.00 Wid: 7.00 Swl: 15 Quarter stern door/ramp (s) Len: 45.00 Wid: 10.50 Swl: 112 Lane-clr ht: 6.40 Cars: 5,409 Ice Capable	**1 oil engine** driving 1 FP propeller Total Power: 14,169kW (19,264hp) 19.0kn B&W 6L80GBE 1 x 2 Stroke 6 Cy. 800 x 1950 14169kW (19264bhp) Hyundai Engine & Machinery Co Ltd-South Korea AuxGen: 2 x 1205kW 450V 60Hz a.c, 1 x 800kW 450V 60Hz a.c, 1 x 670kW 450V 60Hz a.c Thrusters: 1 Thwart. CP thruster (f) Fuel: 225.0 (d.f.) 3262.0 (r.f.) 58.0pd
7921461 *3EFU6* -	**TAHA** *ex* Stah *-2006* *ex* Sunrise Shoun *-1986* **Aurora Boreal Shipmanagement SA** - *Panama* *Panama* MMSI: 354539000 Official number: 34397PEXT	**3,529** 1,909 6,165 T/cm 11.9	Class: (BV) (NK)	**1980-08 Kurinoura Dockyard Co Ltd — Yawatahama EH** Yd No: 153 Loa 105.39 Br ex - Dght 6.765 Lbp 97.19 Br md 16.01 Dpth 8.01 Welded, 1 dk	**(A12B2TR) Chemical/Products Tanker** Double Bottom Entire Compartment Length Liq: 6,481; Liq (Oil): 6,481 Cargo Heating Coils Compartments: 10 Wing Ta, ER 4 Cargo Pump (s): 4x400m³/hr Manifold: Bow/CM: 40m	**1 oil engine** driving 1 FP propeller Total Power: 2,648kW (3,600hp) 12.8kn Akasaka DM47 1 x 4 Stroke 6 Cy. 470 x 760 2648kW (3600bhp) Akasaka Tekkosho KK (Akasaka DieselLtd)-Japan AuxGen: 2 x 500kW 450V 60Hz a.c Fuel: 67.5 (d.f.) 477.5 (r.f.) 12.0pd
9195860 *9HA3252* -	**TAHA** *ex* Rosa *-2012* **Kamer Shipping Ltd** CVS Denizcilik Sanayi Ticaret Ltd Sti *Valletta* *Malta* MMSI: 229344000 Official number: 9195860	**2,998** 1,709 5,050 T/cm 11.5	Class: BV (LR) ✠ Classed LR until 16/11/10	**2000-11 B.V. Scheepswerf Damen Hoogezand — Foxhol** Yd No: 765 **2000-11 Santierul Naval Damen Galati S.A. — Galati** (Hull) Yd No: 959 Loa 95.16 (BB) Br ex 13.26 Dght 6.330 Lbp 90.25 Br md 13.17 Dpth 7.15 Welded, 1 dk	**(A31A2GX) General Cargo Ship** Double Hull Grain: 6,196 TEU 224 C Ho 120 TEU C Dk 104 TEU incl 4 ref C. Compartments: 1 Ho, ER 2 Ha: (38.3 x 11.0) (28.4 x 11.0)ER Ice Capable	**1 oil engine** with flexible couplings & sr gearedto sc. shaft driving 1 CP propeller Total Power: 2,200kW (2,991hp) 11.5kn MaK 8M25 1 x 4 Stroke 8 Cy. 255 x 400 2200kW (2991bhp) MaK Motoren GmbH & Co. KG-Kiel AuxGen: 2 x 145kW 400V 50Hz a.c Boilers: HWH (o.f.) 3.6kgf/cm² (3.5bar) Thrusters: 1 Thwart. FP thruster (f)
9565857 *9MLK5* -	**TAHA ASSAFA** *launched as* SK Line 109 *-2010* **TH Marine Sdn Bhd** TH Alam Management (M) Sdn Bhd *Port Klang* *Malaysia* MMSI: 533056500 Official number: 334256	**2,534** 760 2,362	Class: BV (AB)	**2010-07 Fujian Mawei Shipbuilding Ltd — Fuzhou FJ** Yd No: SK109 Loa 70.70 Br ex - Dght 5.400 Lbp 63.00 Br md 16.00 Dpth 7.20 Welded, 1 dk	**(B21B20A) Anchor Handling Tug Supply**	**2 oil engines** reduction geared to sc. shafts driving 2 CP propellers Total Power: 8,002kW (10,880hp) Bergens B32: 40L8P 2 x 4 Stroke 8 Cy. 320 x 400 each-4001kW (5440bhp) Rolls Royce Marine AS-Norway AuxGen: 2 x 1730kW a.c, 2 x 590kW a.c Thrusters: 2 Tunnel thruster (f); 1 Tunnel thruster (a) Fuel: 960.0
9565845 *9MLK4* -	**TAHA ASSALAM** *launched as* SK Line 108 *-2010* **TH Marine Sdn Bhd** - *Port Klang* *Malaysia* MMSI: 533056400 Official number: 334255	**2,534** 760 2,341	Class: BV (AB)	**2010-07 Fujian Mawei Shipbuilding Ltd — Fuzhou FJ** Yd No: SK108 Loa 70.70 Br ex - Dght 5.980 Lbp 63.00 Br md 16.00 Dpth 7.20 Welded, 1 dk	**(B21B20A) Anchor Handling Tug Supply**	**2 oil engines** reduction geared to sc. shafts driving 2 CP propellers Total Power: 8,002kW (10,880hp) Bergens B32: 40L8P 2 x 4 Stroke 8 Cy. 320 x 400 each-4001kW (5440bhp) Rolls Royce Marine AS-Norway AuxGen: 2 x 1730kW a.c, 2 x 590kW a.c Fuel: 960.0
9456056 *9MFK2* -	**TAHA DUA** - **Powertium Marine Sdn Bhd** - *Port Klang* *Malaysia* MMSI: 533015700 Official number: 332444	**168** 50 40	Class: BV	**2008-02 Damen Shipyards Singapore Pte Ltd — Singapore** (Hull) Yd No: (544805) **2008-02 B.V. Scheepswerf Damen — Gorinchem** Yd No: 544805 Loa 33.57 Br ex - Dght 1.950 Lbp - Br md 6.70 Dpth 3.30 Welded, 1 dk	**(B21A20C) Crew/Supply Vessel** Hull Material: Aluminium Alloy Passengers: unberthed: 80	**3 oil engines** reduction geared to sc. shafts driving 3 FP propellers Total Power: 2,460kW (3,345hp) Caterpillar C32 3 x Vee 4 Stroke 12 Cy. 145 x 162 each-820kW (1115bhp) Caterpillar Inc-USA Thrusters: 1 Tunnel thruster (f)
9456044 *9MFJ9* -	**TAHA SATU** - **Powertium Marine Sdn Bhd** - *Port Klang* *Malaysia* MMSI: 533015600 Official number: 332443	**168** 50 40	Class: BV	**2008-01 Damen Shipyards Singapore Pte Ltd — Singapore** (Hull) Yd No: (544804) **2008-01 B.V. Scheepswerf Damen — Gorinchem** Yd No: 544804 Loa 33.57 Br ex - Dght 1.950 Lbp - Br md 6.70 Dpth 3.30 Welded, 1 dk	**(B21A20C) Crew/Supply Vessel** Passengers: unberthed: 80	**3 oil engines** reduction geared to sc. shafts driving 3 FP propellers Total Power: 2,460kW (3,345hp) 18.0kn Caterpillar C32 3 x Vee 4 Stroke 12 Cy. 145 x 162 each-820kW (1115bhp) Caterpillar Inc-USA Thrusters: 1 Tunnel thruster (f)
8307947 *9LD2547* -	**TAHA-Y** *ex* Tia *-2013* *ex* Ciclope *-2012* *ex* Surenes *-2004* *ex* Hawk *-1999* *ex* Western Hawk *-1999* *ex* Surenes *-1995* **Delphina Shiptrade SA** - *Freetown* *Sierra Leone* MMSI: 667005247 Official number: SL105247	**18,977** 9,296 29,319 T/cm 40.4	Class: PR (Class contemplated) (LR) (NV) (AB) (NK) Classed LR until 1/6/13	**1985-03 Sumitomo Heavy Industries Ltd. — Oppama Shipyard, Yokosuka** Yd No: 1122 Loa 170.01 (BB) Br ex 27.54 Dght 10.002 Lbp 162.00 Br md 27.50 Dpth 14.20 Welded, 1 dk	**(A31A2GX) General Cargo Ship** Grain: 36,208; Bale: 36,035 TEU 514 C Ho 270 TEU C Dk 244 TEU Compartments: 6 Ho, ER 6 Ha: ER Cranes: 3x25t	**1 oil engine** driving 1 FP propeller Total Power: 5,033kW (6,843hp) 13.0kn Sulzer 6RTA58 1 x 2 Stroke 6 Cy. 580 x 1700 5033kW (6843bhp) Sumitomo Heavy Industries Ltd-Japan AuxGen: 3 x 500kW 450V 60Hz a.c Boilers: AuxB (Comp) 8.0kgf/cm² (7.8bar)
6614205 *EPNH* -	**TAHA86** *ex* Kheradmand *-2009* **NIOC Tug Boat Services** - *Bushehr* *Iran* MMSI: 422828000 Official number: 17220	*373* 59 -	Class: (LR) ✠ Classed LR until 20/3/96	**1966-10 Charles D. Holmes & Co. Ltd. — Beverley** Yd No: 1002 Loa 40.67 Br ex 10.11 Dght 3.493 Lbp 36.58 Br md 9.61 Dpth 4.35 Welded	**(B32A2ST) Tug**	**1 oil engine** sr reverse geared to sc. shaft driving 1 FP propeller Total Power: 1,214kW (1,651hp) 12.0kn Crossley CGL8 1 x 2 Stroke 8 Cy. 368 x 483 1214kW (1651bhp) Crossley Bros. Ltd.-Manchester AuxGen: 2 x 75kW 220V d.c
9605322 *7JLP* -	**TAHAROA DESTINY** - **Nippon Yusen Kabushiki Kaisha (NYK Line)** - SatCom: Inmarsat C 443285510 *Tokyo* *Japan* MMSI: 432855000 Official number: 141628	**90,267** 32,426 176,594	Class: NK	**2012-05 Mitsubishi Heavy Industries Ltd. — Nagasaki** Yd No: 2279 Loa 290.40 (BB) Br ex - Dght 18.310 Lbp 280.00 Br md 45.00 Dpth 24.70 Welded, 1 dk	**(A21B2BO) Ore Carrier** Grain: 110,134; Ore: 110,134 Compartments: 6 Ho, ER 6 Ha: ER	**1 oil engine** driving 1 FP propeller Total Power: 17,000kW (23,113hp) 15.0kn MAN-B&W 6S70ME-C8 1 x 2 Stroke 6 Cy. 700 x 2800 17000kW (23113bhp) Hitachi Zosen Corp-Japan Fuel: 6580.0
8224860 *CNOX* -	**TAHER** - **Omnium Marocaine de Peche** - SatCom: Inmarsat C 424237410 *Agadir* *Morocco*	*324* 142 337	Class: (BV)	**1984-05 Construcciones Navales Santodomingo SA — Vigo** Yd No: 493 Loa 38.31 Br ex 8.59 Dght 4.050 Lbp 34.78 Br md 8.51 Dpth 6.15 Welded, 2 dks	**(B11A2FS) Stern Trawler** Ins: 402 Compartments: 1 Ho, ER 2 Ha: ER	**1 oil engine** with clutches, flexible couplings & sr geared to sc. shaft driving 1 FP propeller Total Power: 853kW (1,160hp) 12.3kn Deutz SBA8M528 1 x 4 Stroke 8 Cy. 220 x 280 853kW (1160bhp) Hijos de J Barreras SA-Spain AuxGen: 2 x 140kW 380V 50Hz a.c

IMO / Call sign	Name / Owner / Port	Tonnage	Class	Built / Dimensions	Type	Machinery
9095931 *9BHA* -	**TAHER** **Shaker Rezaei** - *Bandar Imam Khomeini* *Iran* MMSI: 422417000 Official number: 20485	*382* 287 760	Class: AS	**1974**-01 **in Iran** Yd No: 2 L reg 44.46 Br ex - Dght 3.500 Lbp - Br md 8.15 Dpth 4.65 Welded, 1 dk	**(A31A2GX) General Cargo Ship**	**1 oil engine** driving 1 Propeller Total Power: 401kW (545hp) Mitsubishi 1 x 4 Stroke 401kW (545bhp) Mitsubishi Heavy Industries Ltd-Japan
9463798 *YDA6417* -	**TAHIR** **PT Maritim Barito Perkasa** *Banjarmasin* *Indonesia* Official number: 3195 / IIA	**249** 74 170	Class: AB	**2007**-09 **PT Perkasa Melati — Batam** Yd No: PM018 Loa 29.50 Br ex - Dght 3.500 Lbp 26.50 Br md 9.00 Dpth 4.16 Welded, 1 dk	**(B32A2ST) Tug**	**2 oil engines** reduction geared to sc. shafts driving 2 FP propellers Total Power: 2,080kW (2,828hp) Mitsubishi S12R-MTK 2 x Vee 4 Stroke 12 Cy. 170 x 180 each-1040kW (1414bhp) Mitsubishi Heavy Industries Ltd-Japan
8650643 *TCMC3* - -	**TAHIR KAPTAN 2** - - *Samsun* *Turkey* MMSI: 271009036 Official number: 1384	**174** 52 -		**2009**-01 **Basaran Gemi Sanayi — Trabzon** Yd No: 92 Loa 26.50 Br ex 9.20 Dght - Lbp - Br md 9.00 Dpth 3.39 Welded, 1 dk	**(B11B2FV) Fishing Vessel**	**2 oil engines** reduction geared to sc. shafts driving 2 Propellers
8908040 *FGQN* PY 1405	**TAHITI NUI** **Claude Cassel** - *Papeete* *France* MMSI: 228294000	*153* 69 120		**1990**-10 **Chantiers Piriou — Concarneau** Loa 24.80 Br ex - Dght - Lbp 22.50 Br md 7.40 Dpth 3.96 Welded, 1 dk	**(B11B2FV) Fishing Vessel** Ins: 90	**1 oil engine** sr geared to sc. shaft driving 1 FP propeller Total Power: 324kW (441hp) Unidiesel UD150V12M1 1 x Vee 4 Stroke 12 Cy. 150 x 180 324kW (441bhp) Poyaud S.S.C.M.-Surgeres
9240067 *FNGY* -	**TAHITI NUI** **Direction De L'Equipement, Flotille Administrative** - *Papeete* *France* MMSI: 546007000 Official number: 862767	**1,921** 576 1,300	Class: BV (NV)	**2001**-06 **Fujian Southeast Shipyard — Fuzhou FJ** Loa 69.50 Br ex 12.40 Dght 4.600 Lbp 64.00 Br md - Dpth 7.50 Welded	**(A37B2PS) Passenger Ship**	**2 oil engines** reduction geared to sc. shafts driving 2 FP propellers Total Power: 4,060kW (5,520hp) 15.5kn Caterpillar 3606TA 2 x 4 Stroke 6 Cy. 280 x 300 each-2030kW (2760bhp) Caterpillar Inc-USA
9309370 *FVFZ* -	**TAHITI NUI II** **Groupement d'Intervention de la Polynesie (GIP)** - *Papeete* *France* MMSI: 546003400	**403** 121 200	Class: (BV)	**2004**-01 **Fujian Southeast Shipyard — Fuzhou FJ** Yd No: 2002-04 Loa 43.00 Br ex - Dght 2.000 Lbp 38.41 Br md 9.00 Dpth 2.60 Welded, 1 dk	**(A35D2RL) Landing Craft** Bow ramp (f)	**2 oil engines** reduction geared to sc. shafts driving 2 FP propellers Total Power: 1,324kW (1,800hp) 12.0kn Baudouin 12M26SR 2 x Vee 4 Stroke 12 Cy. 150 x 150 each-662kW (900bhp) Societe des Moteurs Baudouin SA-France
9331438 *FVGK* -	**TAHITI NUI III** **Direction De L'Equipement, Flotille Administrative** - *Papeete* *France* MMSI: 546003500	**403** 121 200	Class: (BV)	**2005**-01 **Fujian Southeast Shipyard — Fuzhou FJ** Yd No: 2003-05 Loa 43.00 Br ex - Dght 2.000 Lbp 38.40 Br md 9.00 Dpth 2.60 Welded, 1 dk	**(A35D2RL) Landing Craft** Bow ramp (f)	**2 oil engines** reduction geared to sc. shafts driving 2 FP propellers Total Power: 1,324kW (1,800hp) 12.0kn Baudouin 12M26SR 2 x Vee 4 Stroke 12 Cy. 150 x 150 each-662kW (900bhp) Societe des Moteurs Baudouin SA-France
8964020 *FMCJ* -	**TAHITI NUI IX** *ex* Mehulina *-2003* *ex* Herlina *-2000* **Direction De L'Equipement, Flotille Administrative** - *Papeete* *France* MMSI: 546004800	**377** 114 500	Class: BV (KI)	**1997**-09 **Wonsan Shipyard — Wonsan** Yd No: 305-020 Loa 56.60 Br ex - Dght 1.850 Lbp 50.00 Br md 10.80 Dpth 2.60 Welded, 1 dk	**(A35D2RL) Landing Craft** Quarter bow door/ramp (f) Compartments: 1 Ho, ER 1 Ha: ER	**2 oil engines** driving 2 FP propellers Total Power: 486kW (660hp) 10.0kn Cummins NTA-350-M 2 x 4 Stroke 6 Cy. 117 x 140 each-243kW (330bhp) Cummins Engine Co Inc-USA
9028380 *F07149* -	**TAHITI NUI VII** *ex* Kaoha Nui *-1992* *ex* Keke III *-1982* **Direction De L'Equipement, Flotille Administrative** - *Papeete* *France* MMSI: 227007500	*155* 84 -	Class: BV	**1982**-01 **in French Polynesia** Yd No: 0401 Loa 30.40 Br ex - Dght - Lbp 26.50 Br md 6.54 Dpth 3.05 Welded, 1 dk	**(A37B2PS) Passenger Ship** Hull Material: Aluminium Alloy	**2 oil engines** geared to sc. shafts driving 2 FP propellers Total Power: 1,760kW (2,392hp) 21.0kn Wartsila 2 x Vee 4 Stroke 12 Cy. each-880kW (1196bhp) Societe Surgerienne de ConstructionMecaniques-France AuxGen: 2 x 166kW 60Hz a.c
9378060 *FMHM* -	**TAHITI NUI VIII** **Groupement d'Intervention de la Polynesie (GIP)** - *Papeete* *France* MMSI: 546009700	**1,224** 368 1,000	Class: BV	**2007**-08 **Fujian Southeast Shipyard — Fuzhou FJ** Yd No: 0401 Loa 73.00 Br ex - Dght 2.500 Lbp 68.80 Br md 16.00 Dpth 3.55 Welded, 1 dk	**(A35D2RL) Landing Craft**	**3 oil engines** reduction geared to sc. shafts driving 3 FP propellers Total Power: 2,430kW (3,303hp) 12.5kn Baudouin 12M26SR 3 x Vee 4 Stroke 12 Cy. 150 x 150 each-810kW (1101bhp) Societe des Moteurs Baudouin SA-France
9597032 *9HA3130* -	**TAHITI ONE** **Stavanger Navigation Ltd** Sea Traders SA *Valletta* *Malta* MMSI: 229177000 Official number: 9597032	**44,229** 27,068 81,353 T/cm 71.0	Class: LR ✠ **100A1** SS 09/2012 bulk carrier CSR BC-A GRAB (30) Nos. 2, 4 & 6 holds may be empty ESP **ShipRight** (CM,ACS (B)) *IWS LI ✠ **LMC** **UMS** Eq.Ltr: Q†; Cable: 687.5/81.0 U3 (a)	**2012**-09 **Hyundai Heavy Industries Co Ltd — Ulsan** Yd No: 2465 Loa 229.00 (BB) Br ex 32.29 Dght 14.500 Lbp 223.00 Br md 32.25 Dpth 20.10 Welded, 1 dk	**(A21A2BC) Bulk Carrier** Grain: 95,700 Compartments: 7 Ho, ER 7 Ha: ER	**1 oil engine** driving 1 FP propeller Total Power: 11,620kW (15,799hp) 14.5kn MAN-B&W 7S50MC-C8 1 x 2 Stroke 7 Cy. 500 x 2000 11620kW (15799bhp) Hyundai Heavy Industries Co Ltd-South Korea AuxGen: 3 x 640kW 450V 60Hz a.c Boilers: WTAuxB (Comp) 9.0kgf/cm² (8.8bar)
8611221 *3ETD3* -	**TAHSIN** *ex* Thamesteel 1 *-2014* *ex* Boklum *-2008* *ex* Lea *-2002* *ex* Sonja B *-1999* **Star Shipping Consulting Corp** Voda Denizcilik Ic ve Dis Ticaret Ltd Sti (Voda Shipping) *Panama* *Panama* MMSI: 353502000 Official number: 45550PEXT	**1,984** 1,056 3,217	Class: GL	**1989**-06 **IHC Holland NV Beaver Dredgers — Sliedrecht** (Hull) Yd No: 10297 **1989**-06 **B.V. Scheepswerf Damen — Gorinchem** Yd No: 8210 Loa 89.30 Br ex - Dght 4.332 Lbp 86.28 Br md 12.50 Dpth 6.35 Welded, 2 dks	**(A31A2GX) General Cargo Ship** Grain: 3,983 TEU 150 C. 150/20' Compartments: 1 Ho, ER 1 Ha: (63.4 x 10.1)ER Ice Capable	**1 oil engine** with flexible couplings & reverse reduction geared to sc. shaft driving 1 FP propeller Total Power: 927kW (1,260hp) 11.5kn Deutz SBV6M628 1 x 4 Stroke 6 Cy. 240 x 280 927kW (1260bhp) Kloeckner Humboldt Deutz AG-West Germany AuxGen: 2 x 84kW 220/380V a.c, 1 x 38kW 220/380V a.c Thrusters: 1 Thwart. FP thruster (f)
8515661 *TCWJ9* -	**TAHSIN KALKAVAN** *ex* Celtic Mariner *-2013* *ex* Muhlenberg *-2006* **TTT Denizcilik ve Ticaret Ltd Sti** Imamoglu Denizcilik ve Kara Nakliyat Ticaret AS *Istanbul* *Turkey* MMSI: 271043540	**1,957** 880 2,886	Class: BV (GL)	**1986**-01 **J.J. Sietas KG Schiffswerft GmbH & Co. — Hamburg** Yd No: 964 Loa 87.86 (BB) Br ex 11.54 Dght 4.668 Lbp 85.32 Br md 11.31 Dpth 6.76 Welded, 2 dks	**(A31A2GX) General Cargo Ship** Grain: 3,777; Bale: 3,753 TEU 90 C. 90/20' (40') Compartments: 1 Ho, ER 1 Ha: (55.9 x 9.3)ER	**1 oil engine** with flexible couplings & sr reverse geared to sc. shaft driving 1 FP propeller Total Power: 441kW (600hp) 11.0kn Deutz SBV6M628 1 x 4 Stroke 6 Cy. 240 x 280 441kW (600bhp) Kloeckner Humboldt Deutz AG-West Germany AuxGen: 1 x 180kW 220V 60Hz a.c, 1 x 60kW 220V 60Hz a.c, 1 x 32kW 220V 60Hz a.c Thrusters: 1 Thwart. FP thruster (f) Fuel: 190.0 (d.f.) 3.5pd
9027362 *YD4593* -	**TAHU** *ex* SDS 14 *-2000* **PT Harapan Bahtera Internusa** - *Jakarta* *Indonesia*	**215** 129 -	Class: KI	**1998**-07 **P.T. Indomarine — Jakarta** Loa 25.00 Br ex - Dght 2.800 Lbp 21.84 Br md 7.60 Dpth 3.50 Welded, 1 dk	**(B32A2ST) Tug**	**2 oil engines** driving 2 Propellers Total Power: 1,204kW (1,636hp) 11.0kn Mitsubishi S6R2-MPTK 2 x 4 Stroke 6 Cy. 170 x 220 each-602kW (818bhp) (made 1997) Mitsubishi Heavy Industries Ltd-Japan

Number / Call sign / Fishing no.	Name / Owners / Port / Flag	Tonnage	Class	Builder / Dimensions	Type / Capacity	Machinery
5128572 *MYBP* UL 666	**TAHUME** *ex* Angel Lady *-1998* *ex* Lord Ivan *-1994* *ex* Porfesa II *-1993* *ex* Viking Deeps *-1986* *ex* George Craig *-1973* *launched as* John Watterston *-1957* **Bexleyhill Ltd** Pesca Cruxeiras SL SatCom: Inmarsat C 423232610 *Ullapool* *United Kingdom* MMSI: 232326000 Official number: A13160	**315** 94 -	Class: GL (LR) ✠ Classed LR until 19/11/93	**1957-11 Livingstone & Co. Ltd. — Peterhead** Yd No: 3 Converted From: Standby Safety Vessel-1987 Converted From: Trawler-1976 Loa 35.69 Br ex 7.07 Dght - Lbp - Br md 7.01 Dpth 4.05 Riveted\Welded, 1 dk	**(B11A2FT) Trawler**	**1 oil engine** reduction geared to sc. shaft driving 1 CP propeller Total Power: 485kW (659hp) 10.0kn Blackstone ERS8M 1 x 4 Stroke 8 Cy. 222 x 292 485kW (659bhp) (made 1972, fitted 1973) Mirrlees Blackstone (Stamford)Ltd.-Stamford AuxGen: 1 x 15kW 110V d.c, 1 x 10kW 110V d.c, 1 x 9kW 110V d.c Fuel: 122.0 (d.f.)
8703581 - -	**TAI 1** *ex* Cheng I No. 201 *-2012* *ex* Hakko Maru No. 58 *-2004* *ex* Komine Maru No. 2 *-1999* **Ocean Empire Trading Inc** Ying Sheng Hsiang Fishery Co Ltd	*383* - 460		**1987-06 Miho Zosensho K.K. — Shimizu** Yd No: 1304 Loa 54.62 (BB) Br ex 8.64 Dght 3.391 Lbp 48.01 Br md 8.60 Dpth 3.76 Welded, 1 dk	**(B11B2FV) Fishing Vessel** Grain: 742; Bale: 665	**1 oil engine** with clutches, flexible couplings & sr geared to sc. shaft driving 1 FP propeller Total Power: 736kW (1,001hp) Niigata 6M28BFT 1 x 4 Stroke 6 Cy. 280 x 480 736kW (1001bhp) Niigata Engineering Co Ltd-Japan
8400529 *3FJR* -	**TAI AN** *ex* Fuat Bey *-2013* *ex* Sanko Splendour *-1997* **Tai An Shipping Co Ltd** Xiamen Lianghui Ship Management Co Ltd *Panama* *Panama* MMSI: 357571000 Official number: 44380PEXT	**16,582** 9,524 27,652 T/cm 38.8	Class: NK (TL)	**1985-07 Mitsubishi Heavy Industries Ltd. — Nagasaki** Yd No: 1962 Loa 165.50 (BB) Br ex 27.03 Dght 9.599 Lbp 158.02 Br md 27.01 Dpth 13.31 Welded, 1 dk	**(A21A2BC) Bulk Carrier** Grain: 34,811; Bale: 34,182 Compartments: 5 Ho, ER 5 Ha: (8.0 x 13.5)4 (19.2 x 13.5)ER Cranes: 4x25t	**1 oil engine** driving 1 FP propeller Total Power: 5,685kW (7,729hp) 13.5kn Mitsubishi 6UE52LA 1 x 2 Stroke 6 Cy. 520 x 1600 5685kW (7729bhp) Mitsubishi Heavy Industries Ltd-Japan AuxGen: 3 x 450kW 450V 60Hz a.c Fuel: 234.5 (d.f.) (Heating Coils) 1258.5 (r.f.) 21.0pd
8021593 *LQBU* -	**TAI AN** *ex* Daishin Maru No. 28 *-1999* **Prodesur SA** San Arawa SA *Ushuaia* *Argentina* MMSI: 701000627 Official number: 01530	*3,061* 1,164 3,490	Class: NK	**1981-07 Mitsubishi Heavy Industries Ltd. — Shimonoseki** Yd No: 836 Loa 102.50 Br ex - Dght 6.366 Lbp 94.72 Br md 15.71 Dpth 6.91 Welded, 2 dks	**(B11A2FS) Stern Trawler** Bale: 2,409; Liq: 247 3 Ha: 3 (2.3 x 2.8)ER Derricks: 6x3t	**1 oil engine** driving 1 FP propeller Total Power: 3,310kW (4,500hp) 13.5kn B&W 6K45GFC 1 x 2 Stroke 6 Cy. 450 x 900 3310kW (4500bhp) Hitachi Zosen Corp-Japan AuxGen: 3 x 880kW 450V 60Hz a.c Fuel: 145.0 (d.f.) 1188.0 (r.f.)
9015008 *BVIB* -	**TAI AN CHENG** **Xiamen Ocean Shipping Co (COSCO XIAMEN)** - *Xiamen, Fujian* *China* MMSI: 412442870	**16,703** 8,748 22,814 T/cm 36.0	Class: CC	**1992-12 Guangzhou Shipyard — Guangzhou GD** Yd No: 01004 Loa 174.00 (BB) Br ex - Dght 10.000 Lbp 162.00 Br md 25.60 Dpth 14.20 Welded, 2 dks	**(A31A2GX) General Cargo Ship** Grain: 32,973 Compartments: 4 Ho, ER	**1 oil engine** driving 1 FP propeller Total Power: 8,050kW (10,945hp) 16.5kn B&W 6L60MCE 1 x 2 Stroke 6 Cy. 600 x 1944 8050kW (10945bhp) Dalian Marine Diesel Works-China
8318312 *BONK* -	**TAI AN HAI** **Tianjin Yuanhua Shipping Co Ltd** - SatCom: Inmarsat A 1570312 *Tianjin* *China* MMSI: 412324000	**27,417** 14,944 47,663	Class: CC	**1986-10 Hudong Shipyard — Shanghai** Yd No: 1155 Loa 189.94 (BB) Br ex - Dght 11.700 Lbp 180.00 Br md 32.20 Dpth 16.60 Welded, 1 dk	**(A21A2BC) Bulk Carrier** Grain: 57,000; Bale: 56,100 Compartments: 5 Ho, ER 5 Ha: (16.0 x 15.0)4 (17.6 x 15.0)ER Cranes: 4x15t Ice Capable	**1 oil engine** driving 1 FP propeller Total Power: 6,789kW (9,230hp) 14.3kn B&W 6L60MCE 1 x 2 Stroke 6 Cy. 600 x 1944 6789kW (9230bhp) Hudong Shipyard-China
9223277 *BOKD* -	**TAI AN KOU** **Tianjin COSCO Shipping Co Ltd** COSCO Shipping Co Ltd (COSCOL) *Tianjin* *China* MMSI: 412023000	**15,840** 4,752 20,247	Class: CC (NV)	**2002-11 Guangzhou Shipyard International Co Ltd — Guangzhou GD** Yd No: 9130012 Loa 156.00 (BB) Br ex - Dght 7.400 Lbp 145.00 Br md 36.00 Dpth 10.00 Welded, 1 dk	**(A38C3GH) Heavy Load Carrier, semi submersible** Cranes: 2x15t Ice Capable	**3 diesel electric oil engines** driving 3 gen. Connecting to 2 elec. motors each (4710kW) driving 2 Azimuth electric drive units 14.0kn Wartsila 9R32 3 x 4 Stroke 9 Cy. 320 x 350 Wartsila Finland Oy-Finland Thrusters: 2 Tunnel thruster (f)
8876431 *BHOB* -	**TAI CANG HE** *ex* J. Glory *-2011* **Taicang Container Lines Co Ltd** JOSCO Yuansheng Shipping Management Co Ltd *Taicang, Jiangsu* *China* MMSI: 413364020	**4,879** 2,465 6,720 T/cm 16.5	Class: CC	**1994-12 Dae Sun Shipbuilding & Engineering Co Ltd — Busan** Yd No: 409 Loa 113.00 (BB) Br ex - Dght 6.440 Lbp 103.00 Br md 19.00 Dpth 8.50 Welded, 1 dk	**(A33A2CC) Container Ship (Fully Cellular)** TEU 357 C Ho 151 TEU C Dk 206 TEU Compartments: 5 Cell Ho, ER 6 Ha: ER	**1 oil engine** driving 1 FP propeller Total Power: 3,354kW (4,560hp) 14.0kn B&W 6L35MC 1 x 2 Stroke 6 Cy. 350 x 1050 3354kW (4560bhp) Ssangyong Heavy Industries Co Ltd-South Korea Thrusters: 1 Thwart. FP thruster (f)
9142423 *BHOB2* -	**TAI CANG HU** *ex* Jin Man Hu *-2012* *ex* Eagle Union *-2002* *ex* Jin Man Hu *-1997* **Taicang Container Lines Co Ltd** Jiangsu Ocean Shipping Co Ltd (JOSCO) SatCom: Inmarsat C 441243915 *Taicang, Jiangsu* *China* MMSI: 413360890	**2,900** 1,313 4,830	Class: CC (GL)	**1997-01 Kroeger Werft GmbH & Co. KG — Schacht-Audorf** Yd No: 1538 Loa 98.43 (BB) Br ex - Dght 5.910 Lbp 91.45 Br md 16.90 Dpth 7.55 Welded, 2 dks	**(A31A2GX) General Cargo Ship** Grain: 4,456; Bale: 4,166 TEU 366 C Ho 80 TEU C Dk 286 TEU incl 46 ref C. Compartments: 1 Ho, ER, 1 Tw Dk 3 Ha: (25.7 x 10.6)Tappered (25.7 x 13.2) (6.2 x 10.5)ER Ice Capable	**1 oil engine** reduction geared to sc. shaft driving 1 CP propeller Total Power: 2,940kW (3,997hp) 14.8kn MaK 8M453C 1 x 4 Stroke 8 Cy. 320 x 420 2940kW (3997bhp) MaK Motoren GmbH & Co. KG-Kiel AuxGen: 1 x 588kW 220/440V a.c, 2 x 256kW 220/440V a.c Thrusters: 1 Thwart. FP thruster (f)
9498872 *VRES4* -	**TAI CHANG** **Tai Chang Maritime Inc** Ocean Longevity Shipping & Management Co Ltd *Hong Kong* *Hong Kong* MMSI: 477728300	**50,697** 30,722 92,500 T/cm 80.9	Class: BV	**2010-04 Yangfan Group Co Ltd — Zhoushan ZJ** Yd No: 2109 Loa 230.00 (BB) Br ex - Dght 14.900 Lbp 222.00 Br md 38.00 Dpth 20.70 Welded, 1 dk	**(A21A2BC) Bulk Carrier** Grain: 110,330 Compartments: 7 Ho, ER 7 Ha: 5 (17.9 x 17.0)ER 2 (15.3 x 14.6)	**1 oil engine** driving 1 FP propeller Total Power: 12,240kW (16,642hp) 14.1kn MAN-B&W 6S60MC 1 x 2 Stroke 6 Cy. 600 x 2292 12240kW (16642bhp) Doosan Engine Co Ltd-South Korea AuxGen: 3 x 730kW 60Hz a.c Fuel: 3454.0
8430366 *HQHN5* -	**TAI CHENG No. 6** **Lubmain International SA** *San Lorenzo* *Honduras* Official number: L-1923671	**429** 203 -		**1986 Fong Kuo Shipbuilding Co Ltd — Kaohsiung** L reg 41.80 Br ex - Dght 2.260 Lbp - Br md 8.00 Dpth 3.50 Welded, 1 dk	**(B11B2FV) Fishing Vessel**	**1 oil engine** driving 1 FP propeller Total Power: 736kW (1,001hp) 13.0kn
8966377 - -	**TAI CHIN 101** **Taiwan Navigation Co Ltd** - *Taichung* *Chinese Taipei* Official number: 013070	**360** 108 127	Class: CR	**1996-10 Taiwan Machinery Manufacturing Corp. — Kaohsiung** Loa 30.20 Br ex 9.81 Dght 4.260 Lbp 28.40 Br md 9.80 Dpth 5.25 Welded, 1 dk	**(B32A2ST) Tug**	**2 oil engines** reduction geared to sc. shafts driving 2 FP propellers Total Power: 2,638kW (3,586hp) Wartsila 8L20 2 x 4 Stroke 8 Cy. 200 x 280 each-1319kW (1793bhp) Wartsila Diesel Oy-Finland AuxGen: 2 x 160kW 450V 60Hz a.c
8966389 - -	**TAI CHIN 102** **Taiwan Navigation Co Ltd** - *Taichung* *Chinese Taipei* Official number: 13070	**360** 108 127	Class: CR	**1996-11 Taiwan Machinery Manufacturing Corp. — Kaohsiung** Loa 30.20 Br ex 9.81 Dght 4.262 Lbp 28.40 Br md 9.80 Dpth 5.25 Welded, 1 dk	**(B32A2ST) Tug**	**2 oil engines** reduction geared to sc. shafts driving 2 FP propellers Total Power: 2,638kW (3,586hp) Wartsila 8L20 2 x 4 Stroke 8 Cy. 200 x 280 each-1319kW (1793bhp) Wartsila Diesel Oy-Finland AuxGen: 2 x 160kW 450V 60Hz a.c
8660387 *BR3296* -	**TAI CHIN 201** **Taiwan Navigation Co Ltd** - *Chinese Taipei* MMSI: 416003083	**433** - 156	Class: CR	**2007-01 Jong Shyn Shipbuilding Co., Ltd. — Kaohsiung** Loa 32.55 Br ex - Dght - Lbp - Br md 11.50 Dpth 4.30 Welded, 1 dk	**(B32A2ST) Tug**	**2 oil engines** reduction geared to sc. shafts driving 2 Voith-Schneider propellers 14.0kn Niigata Niigata Engineering Co Ltd-Japan
8660399 *BR3297* -	**TAI CHIN 202** **Taiwan Navigation Co Ltd** - *Chinese Taipei* MMSI: 416003084	**433** - 156	Class: CR	**2007-01 Jong Shyn Shipbuilding Co., Ltd. — Kaohsiung** Loa 32.55 Br ex - Dght - Lbp - Br md 11.50 Dpth 4.30 Welded, 1 dk	**(B32A2ST) Tug**	**2 oil engines** reduction geared to sc. shafts driving 2 Voith-Schneider propellers 14.0kn Niigata Niigata Engineering Co Ltd-Japan
8660404 *BR3299* -	**TAI CHIN 203** **Taiwan Navigation Co Ltd** - *Chinese Taipei* MMSI: 416003095	**433** - 134	Class: CR	**2007-01 Jong Shyn Shipbuilding Co., Ltd. — Kaohsiung** Loa 32.55 Br ex - Dght - Lbp - Br md 11.50 Dpth 4.30 Welded, 1 dk	**(B32A2ST) Tug**	**2 oil engines** reduction geared to sc. shafts driving 2 Voith-Schneider propellers 12.1kn Niigata Niigata Engineering Co Ltd-Japan

IMO / Call sign / Flag	Name / Owner / Manager / Port	Tonnage	Class	Builder / Dimensions	Type / Cargo	Machinery
8660416 *BR3300* -	**TAI CHIN 205** **Taiwan Navigation Co Ltd** - *Chinese Taipei* MMSI: 416003096	**433** - 134	Class: CR	**2007-01 Jong Shyn Shipbuilding Co., Ltd. — Kaohsiung** Loa 32.55 Br ex - Dght - Lbp - Br md 11.50 Dpth 4.30 Welded, 1 dk	**(B32A2ST) Tug**	**2 oil engines** reduction geared to sc. shafts driving 2 Voith-Schneider propellers 12.1kn Niigata Niigata Engineering Co Ltd-Japan
8966391 *BR3066* -	**TAI CHIN 803** *ex Tai Chin 103 -2013* **Taiwan Navigation Co Ltd** - *Taichung* *Chinese Taipei* Official number: 13072	**337** 101 167	Class: CR	**1996-09 Taiwan Machinery Manufacturing Corp. — Kaohsiung** Loa 34.30 Br ex 9.61 Dght 3.310 Lbp 33.00 Br md 9.60 Dpth 4.30 Welded, 1 dk	**(B32A2ST) Tug**	**2 oil engines** reduction geared to sc. shafts driving 2 FP propellers Total Power: 1,978kW (2,690hp) Wartsila 6L20 2 x 4 Stroke 6 Cy. 200 x 280 each-989kW (1345bhp) Wartsila Diesel Oy-Finland AuxGen: 2 x 107kW 450V 60Hz a.c
8430990 - - -	**TAI CHIN No. 12** - -	*718* 287 -		**1989 Sen Koh Shipbuilding Corp — Kaohsiung** L reg 50.60 Br ex - Dght - Lbp - Br md 8.90 Dpth 3.85 Welded, 1 dk	**(B11B2FV) Fishing Vessel**	**1 oil engine** driving 1 FP propeller Total Power: 883kW (1,201hp) 12.0kn
8860808 *XVCK* -	**TAI CHINH II** *ex Khanh Hung 07 -2000 ex Nha Trang-8 -1996* *ex Phu Khanh I -1989 ex Soon Hok -1985* **Tigi Shipping Transport & Commercial Services Co Ltd** - SatCom: Inmarsat C 457409312 *Saigon* *Vietnam* MMSI: 574093083 Official number: VNSG-1663-TH	**998** 574 1,620	Class: VR	**1934-07 in the United Kingdom** Lengthened-2002 Loa 71.84 Br ex 9.98 Dght 4.800 Lbp 65.90 Br md 9.96 Dpth 5.60 Welded, 1 dk	**(A31A2GX) General Cargo Ship** Grain: 1,291 Compartments: 2 Ho 2 Ha: 2 (6.4 x -)	**1 oil engine** driving 1 FP propeller Total Power: 721kW (980hp) Skoda 6L350IIPN 1 x 4 Stroke 6 Cy. 350 x 500 721kW (980bhp) (new engine 1985) CKD Praha-Praha
8890607 *BCGE* -	**TAI CHUAN** *ex Yu Quan -2003* **Shandong Province Land-Sea Transportation Corp** SDSC Ship Management Co Ltd SatCom: Inmarsat C 441273210 *Yantai, Shandong* *China* MMSI: 412320770	**1,528** 895 2,307	Class: (CC)	**1995-07 Shandong Weihai Shipyard — Weihai SD** Loa 73.80 Br ex - Dght 5.000 Lbp 68.00 Br md 12.80 Dpth 6.20 Welded, 1 dk	**(A31A2GX) General Cargo Ship** Grain: 3,156; Bale: 3,050 Compartments: 2 Ho, ER 2 Ha: ER 2 (13.0 x 7.0) Ice Capable	**1 oil engine** geared to sc. shaft driving 1 FP propeller Total Power: 749kW (1,018hp) 11.2kn Daihatsu 6DSM-22 1 x 4 Stroke 6 Cy. 220 x 280 749kW (1018bhp) Shaanxi Diesel Engine Factory-China AuxGen: 2 x 90kW 400V a.c
8889555 *XUNZ3* -	**TAI DA** *ex Lofty Hope -2011 ex Akitsu Maru No. 8 -2009* **Safety Shipping Co Ltd** - *Phnom Penh* *Cambodia* MMSI: 514237000 Official number: 0995336	*1,478* 693 1,500		**1995-02 Mategata Zosen K.K. — Namikata** Yd No: 1055 Loa 74.14 Br ex - Dght 4.020 Lbp 69.00 Br md 12.00 Dpth 6.90 Welded, 1 dk	**(A31A2GX) General Cargo Ship** Grain: 2,870; Bale: 2,567 Compartments: 1 Ho, ER 1 Ha: (40.2 x 9.5)ER	**1 oil engine** reverse geared to sc. shaft driving 1 FP propeller Total Power: 736kW (1,001hp) 11.5kn Akasaka A31R 1 x 4 Stroke 6 Cy. 310 x 600 736kW (1001bhp) Akasaka Tekkosho KK (Akasaka DieselLtd)-Japan
9334208 *3FKK7* -	**TAI DE SHENG** **Changsheng Shipping Co Ltd** Ocean Grow International Shipmanagement Consultant Corp *Panama* *Panama* MMSI: 356675000 Official number: 41807PEXTF2	**1,948** 865 3,041	Class: IB	**2004-09 Fujian Baima Shipyard — Fu'an FJ** Yd No: 1407-3 Loa 81.85 Br ex - Dght 4.950 Lbp 76.65 Br md 13.20 Dpth 6.20 Welded, 1 dk	**(A31A2GX) General Cargo Ship**	**1 oil engine** geared to sc. shaft driving 1 FP propeller Total Power: 736kW (1,001hp) 11.0kn Chinese Std. Type G6300ZCA 1 x 4 Stroke 6 Cy. 300 x 380 736kW (1001bhp) Ningbo CSI Power & Machinery GroupCo Ltd-China
8512140 - -	**TAI FAT** **Tai Fat Shipping (HK) Co Ltd** -	**273** 110 500		**1985-01 Yuezhong Shipyard — Zhongshan GD** Loa - Br ex - Dght 2.452 Lbp 33.30 Br md 8.01 Dpth 3.66 Welded, 1 dk	**(A31A2GX) General Cargo Ship**	**1 oil engine** geared to sc. shaft driving 1 FP propeller Total Power: 221kW (300hp) Caterpillar 1 x 4 Stroke 221kW (300bhp) Caterpillar Tractor Co-USA
7929580 - -	**TAI FAT** *ex Tai Sheng -1999 ex Sanko Maru -1994* **Tominaga Industry Corp** -	**1,304** 629 1,800		**1980-04 K.K. Matsuura Zosensho — Osakikamijima** Yd No: 276 Loa 69.86 Br ex 11.54 Dght 4.750 Lbp 65.03 Br md 11.51 Dpth 6.28 Welded, 1 dk	**(A31A2GX) General Cargo Ship**	**1 oil engine** driving 1 FP propeller Total Power: 1,177kW (1,600hp) 11.0kn Makita GSLH633 1 x 4 Stroke 6 Cy. 330 x 530 1177kW (1600bhp) Makita Diesel Co Ltd-Japan
7822158 *BIID* -	**TAI FENG** *ex Yin Chu -1994 ex Shi Ji Hao Yun -2006* *ex SMS Kartanegara II -2006* *ex Zhi Jiang Kou -2001* **Shandong Muping Shipping Co Ltd** - *China* MMSI: 413374660	**13,455** 4,067 7,374	Class: (LR) (CC) ✠ Classed LR until 18/12/81	**1979-12 Kawasaki Heavy Industries Ltd — Sakaide KG** Yd No: 1314 Converted From: Ro-Ro Cargo Ship-2006 Loa 146.55 (BB) Br ex 22.64 Dght 6.820 Lbp 130.00 Br md 22.60 Dpth 14.20 Welded, 2 dks	**(B33A2DS) Suction Dredger** Hopper: 5,500	**1 oil engine** sr geared to sc. shaft driving 1 CP propeller Total Power: 7,760kW (10,550hp) 13.5kn MAN 10V52/55A 1 x Vee 4 Stroke 10 Cy. 520 x 550 7760kW (10550bhp) Kawasaki Heavy Industries Ltd-Japan AuxGen: 1 x 740kW 390V 50Hz a.c, 2 x 720kW 390V 50Hz a.c Thrusters: 1 Thwart. FP thruster (f) Fuel: 126.0 (d.f.) 644.0 (r.f.) 35.0pd
7908615 *BIFB* -	**TAI FU** *ex Yusho Maru No. 25 -1989* **Venture Marine Corp** - *Keelung* *Chinese Taipei* Official number: 11330	*1,188* 603 1,530	Class: (CR)	**1979-08 Iwagi Zosen Co Ltd — Kamijima EH** Yd No: 12 Loa 68.33 Br ex - Dght 4.352 Lbp 63.81 Br md 11.51 Dpth 6.33 Welded, 1 dk	**(A31A2GX) General Cargo Ship** Compartments: 1 Ho, ER 1 Ha: (36.0 x 7.6)ER Derricks: 2x7t	**1 oil engine** driving 1 FP propeller Total Power: 1,103kW (1,500hp) 13.1kn Makita GSLH630 1 x 4 Stroke 6 Cy. 300 x 480 1103kW (1500bhp) Makita Diesel Co Ltd-Japan
9084231 *3FOU4* -	**TAI FU** *ex Oriente Prime -2013* **Gold Glory Shipping Ltd** Guangzhou Seaway International Ship Management Co Ltd SatCom: Inmarsat C 435416810 *Panama* *Panama* MMSI: 354168000 Official number: 23649PEXT1	**13,865** 7,738 21,955	Class: NK	**1994-10 Saiki Heavy Industries Co Ltd — Saiki OT** (Hull) Yd No: 1036 **1994-10 Onomichi Dockyard Co Ltd — Onomichi HS** Yd No: 382 Loa 157.79 (BB) Br ex - Dght 9.115 Lbp 148.00 Br md 25.00 Dpth 12.70 Welded, 1 dk	**(A21A2BC) Bulk Carrier** Grain: 29,254; Bale: 28,299 Compartments: 4 Ho, ER 4 Ha: (20.0 x 17.5)Tappered 3 (20.8 x 17.5)ER Cranes: 4x30t	**1 oil engine** driving 1 FP propeller Total Power: 5,296kW (7,200hp) 14.0kn Mitsubishi 6UEC45LA 1 x 2 Stroke 6 Cy. 450 x 1350 5296kW (7200bhp) Kobe Hatsudoki KK-Japan AuxGen: 3 x a.c Fuel: 1270.0 (r.f.)
8125088 *BZS08* -	**TAI FU 102** *ex Taishou -2002* *ex Capt. Cristiano da Rosa -2002* *ex Tunacores -1994* *launched as Tunamar II -1986* **Shandong Oceanic Fisheries Co Ltd** Shandong Zhonglu Oceanic Fisheries Co Ltd *Qingdao, Shandong* *China* MMSI: 412833000 Official number: YQ020J020027	**1,348** 404 1,320	Class: (RP)	**1986-02 Estaleiros Sao Jacinto S.A. — Aveiro** Yd No: 142 Loa 67.49 Br ex 12.27 Dght 5.819 Lbp 61.88 Br md 12.04 Dpth 8.29 Welded, 1 dk	**(B11B2FV) Fishing Vessel**	**1 oil engine** with clutches, flexible couplings & reverse reduction geared to sc. shaft driving 1 FP propeller Total Power: 2,648kW (3,600hp) EMD (Electro-Motive) 20-645-E7 1 x Vee 2 Stroke 20 Cy. 230 x 254 2648kW (3600bhp) General Motors Corp-USA AuxGen: 2 x 408kW a.c, 1 x 250kW a.c Thrusters: 1 Thwart. FP thruster (f)
7908976 *T3LY* -	**TAI FU No. 1** *ex Sun Big No. 1 -1999 ex Sky Reefer -1993* **Sun Big Reefer Shipping SA** Sun Victory Shipping SA SatCom: Inmarsat C 452909610 *Tarawa* *Kiribati* MMSI: 529096000 Official number: K-10790747	**6,049** 2,680 6,044	Class: IZ (NK)	**1979-10 Minaminippon Shipbuilding Co Ltd — Usuki OT** Yd No: 527 Loa 137.00 Br ex 17.56 Dght 7.164 Lbp 127.01 Br md 17.51 Dpth 10.01 Welded, 2 dks	**(A34A2GR) Refrigerated Cargo Ship** Ins: 7,049 Compartments: 4 Ho, ER 4 Ha: 4 (7.0 x 6.0)ER Derricks: 4x5t	**1 oil engine** driving 1 FP propeller Total Power: 5,884kW (8,000hp) 17.5kn Mitsubishi 6UEC52/125H 1 x 2 Stroke 6 Cy. 520 x 1250 5884kW (8000bhp) Kobe Hatsudoki KK-Japan AuxGen: 3 x 440kW 445V 60Hz a.c Fuel: 424.0 (d.f.) 1358.0 (r.f.)
7927453 *T3MH* -	**TAI FU No. 3** *ex Sun Big No. 66 -1999 ex Falcon II -1993* *ex Falcon -1991* **Sun Victory Shipping SA** - *Tarawa* *Kiribati* MMSI: 529105000 Official number: K-10800756	**3,505** 1,915 4,166	Class: CR (NK)	**1980-04 K.K. Taihei Kogyo — Akitsu** Yd No: 1357 Loa 99.58 Br ex - Dght 7.116 Lbp 91.75 Br md 15.80 Dpth 9.30 Welded, 2 dks	**(A34A2GR) Refrigerated Cargo Ship** Ins: 4,648 3 Ha: ER Derricks: 6x5t	**1 oil engine** driving 1 FP propeller Total Power: 3,678kW (5,001hp) 15.1kn Hanshin 6LU54A 1 x 4 Stroke 6 Cy. 540 x 850 3678kW (5001bhp) The Hanshin Diesel Works Ltd-Japan AuxGen: 2 x 570kW 450V 60Hz a.c Fuel: 180.5 (d.f.) 606.5 (r.f.) 17.0pd

9550462 *BVIV5* -	**TAI GANG** *ex Bao Ping -2012* **Fujian Quanzhou Fengze Shipping Co** *Quanzhou, Fujian* *China* MMSI: 412704040	**2,994** 1,636 4,631	Class: CC	**2008-12 Tongzhou Tongyang Shipyard Co Ltd — Tongzhou JS** Yd No: 4096 Loa 92.80 Br ex - Dght 6.250 Lbp 86.00 Br md 15.20 Dpth 7.70 Welded, 1 dk	**(A31A2GX) General Cargo Ship**	**1 oil engine** driving 1 Propeller Total Power: 2,059kW (2,799hp) Guangzhou 8320ZC 1 x 4 Stroke 8 Cy. 320 x 440 2059kW (2799bhp) Guangzhou Diesel Engine Factory CoLtd-China AuxGen: 2 x 250kW 400V a.c
8318300 *BONJ* -	**TAI GU HAI** **COSCO Bulk Carrier Co Ltd (COSCO BULK)** - SatCom: Inmarsat C 441232110 *Tianjin* *China* MMSI: 412303000	**22,050** 13,047 37,393 T/cm 39.4	Class: CC	**1985-12 Hudong Shipyard — Shanghai** Yd No: 1154 Loa 186.20 (BB) Br ex - Dght 11.240 Lbp 178.00 Br md 28.40 Dpth 15.60 Welded, 1 dk	**(A21A2BC) Bulk Carrier** Grain: 46,939; Bale: 46,068 Compartments: 5 Ho, ER 5 Ha: 2 (16.0 x 13.6)3 (16.8 x 13.6)ER Cranes: 4x25t	**1 oil engine** driving 1 FP propeller Total Power: 9,179kW (12,480hp) 14.0kn B&W 6L60MCE 1 x 2 Stroke 6 Cy. 600 x 1944 9179kW (12480bhp) Hudong Shipyard-China AuxGen: 3 x 470kW 450V 60Hz a.c Fuel: 80.0 (d.f.) 1961.5 (r.f.) 33.5pd
8890619 *BCGD* -	**TAI HAI** *ex Tai Cheng -2004* **Shandong Province Land-Sea Transportation Corp** SDSC Ship Management Co Ltd SatCom: Inmarsat C 441273110 *Yantai, Shandong* *China* MMSI: 412320760	**1,528** 895 2,419	Class: (CC)	**1996-02 Shandong Weihai Shipyard — Weihai SD** Loa 73.80 Br ex - Dght 5.100 Lbp 68.00 Br md 12.80 Dpth 6.20 Welded, 1 dk	**(A31A2GX) General Cargo Ship** Grain: 3,155; Bale: 3,050 Compartments: 2 Ho, ER 2 Ha: 2 (13.0 x 7.0)ER Ice Capable	**1 oil engine** reduction geared to sc. shaft driving 1 FP propeller Total Power: 746kW (1,014hp) 11.2kn Chinese Std. Type LB6250ZLC 1 x 4 Stroke 6 Cy. 250 x 320 746kW (1014bhp) Zibo Diesel Engine Factory-China AuxGen: 2 x 75kW 400V a.c
9137131 *BDTQ* -	**TAI HANG 1** *ex Global Challenger -2010* **Taihang Shipping Co Ltd** *Tangshan, Hebei* *China* MMSI: 413955000	**38,639** 24,551 73,218 T/cm 65.7	Class: CC (KR)	**1996-11 Samsung Heavy Industries Co Ltd — Geoje** Yd No: 1184 Loa 224.96 (BB) Br ex - Dght 13.913 Lbp 213.06 Br md 32.24 Dpth 19.10 Welded, 1 dk	**(A21A2BC) Bulk Carrier** Grain: 85,551 Compartments: 7 Ho, ER 7 Ha: (16.6 x 11.0)6 (16.6 x 14.1)ER	**1 oil engine** driving 1 FP propeller Total Power: 8,678kW (11,799hp) 14.5kn B&W 6S60MC 1 x 2 Stroke 6 Cy. 600 x 2292 8678kW (11799bhp) Samsung Heavy Industries Co Ltd-South Korea
9128257 *BTFH* -	**TAI HANG 3** *ex Makiki -2010 ex Attila -2006* *ex Aspen -2002 ex N O L Pollux -2000* **Taihang Shipping Co Ltd** *Tangshan, Hebei* *China* MMSI: 413271170	**38,520** 24,567 73,049 T/cm 65.7	Class: CC (LR) ✠ Classed LR until 25/5/10	**1997-04 Samsung Heavy Industries Co Ltd — Geoje** Yd No: 1179 Loa 224.98 (BB) Br ex 32.28 Dght 13.896 Lbp 216.00 Br md 32.24 Dpth 19.10 Welded, 1 dk	**(A21A2BC) Bulk Carrier** Grain: 85,552 Compartments: 7 Ho, ER 7 Ha: (16.6 x 11.0)6 (16.6 x 14.1)ER	**1 oil engine** driving 1 FP propeller Total Power: 8,679kW (11,800hp) 14.8kn B&W 6S60MC 1 x 2 Stroke 6 Cy. 600 x 2292 8679kW (11800bhp) Samsung Heavy Industries Co Ltd-South Korea AuxGen: 3 x 550kW 450V 60Hz a.c Boilers: AuxB (Comp) 8.2kgf/cm² (8.0bar) Fuel: 149.0 (d.f.) (Heating Coils) 2243.0 (r.f.) 35.0pd
9123647 *BDTK* -	**TAI HANG 6** *ex Iguana -2010 ex Pacific Carrier -2004* *ex Pacific Fortune -2001* **Taihang Shipping Co Ltd** *Tangshan, Hebei* *China* MMSI: 413974000	**36,559** 23,279 70,349 T/cm 64.0	Class: CC (NK)	**1996-04 Sanoyas Hishino Meisho Corp — Kurashiki OY** Yd No: 1136 Loa 225.00 (BB) Br ex 32.30 Dght 13.271 Lbp 217.00 Br md 32.20 Dpth 18.30 Welded, 1 dk	**(A21A2BC) Bulk Carrier** Grain: 81,838; Bale: 78,529 Compartments: 7 Ho, ER 7 Ha: (16.7 x 13.4)6 (16.7 x 15.0)ER	**1 oil engine** driving 1 FP propeller Total Power: 10,916kW (14,841hp) 14.0kn Sulzer 7RTA52 1 x 2 Stroke 7 Cy. 520 x 1800 10916kW (14841bhp) Diesel United Ltd.-Aioi Fuel: 2405.0 (r.f.)
9205823 *BTFY* -	**TAI HANG 8** *ex Xanadu -2010 ex CMB Daisy -2005* *ex Sea Daisy -2004* **Taihang Shipping Co Ltd** *Tangshan, Hebei* *China* MMSI: 413271250	**37,722** 24,219 72,270 T/cm 66.6	Class: CC (NK)	**1999-10 Imabari Shipbuilding Co Ltd — Marugame KG (Marugame Shipyard)** Yd No: 1314 Loa 224.94 (BB) Br ex - Dght 13.553 Lbp 217.00 Br md 32.20 Dpth 18.70 Welded, 1 dk	**(A21A2BC) Bulk Carrier** Grain: 85,467 Compartments: 7 Ho, ER 7 Ha: (16.3 x 14.4)5 (17.9 x 14.4) (13.0 x 12.8)ER	**1 oil engine** driving 1 FP propeller Total Power: 9,783kW (13,301hp) 14.5kn B&W 6S60MC 1 x 2 Stroke 6 Cy. 600 x 2292 9783kW (13301bhp) Mitsui Engineering & Shipbuilding CLtd-Japan AuxGen: 3 x 500kW 440V 60Hz a.c Fuel: 146.1 (d.f.) (Heating Coils) 3232.6 (r.f.) 37.8pd
9193850 *BTFG* -	**TAI HANG 9** *ex Ernst Salamon -2010* *ex Far Eastern Queen -2001* **Bank of Communications Finance Leasing Co Ltd** Taihang Shipping Co Ltd *Tangshan, Hebei* *China* MMSI: 413978000	**38,888** 25,413 74,002 T/cm 66.0	Class: CC (NK)	**1999-08 Imabari Shipbuilding Co Ltd — Marugame KG (Marugame Shipyard)** Yd No: 1312 Loa 224.97 (BB) Br ex - Dght 14.013 Lbp 215.00 Br md 32.20 Dpth 19.30 Welded, 1 dk	**(A21A2BC) Bulk Carrier** Grain: 86,557 Compartments: 7 Ho, ER 7 Ha: (13.0 x 12.8)6 (17.9 x 15.6)ER	**1 oil engine** driving 1 FP propeller Total Power: 8,827kW (12,001hp) 14.5kn B&W 7S50MC 1 x 2 Stroke 7 Cy. 500 x 1910 8827kW (12001bhp) Mitsui Engineering & Shipbuilding CLtd-Japan AuxGen: 3 x 360kW 450V a.c Fuel: 3105.0 (r.f.)
9604483 *BSCA* -	**TAI HANG 118** **Taihang Shipping Co Ltd** - SatCom: Inmarsat C 441206511 *China* MMSI: 412065000	**28,000** 47,500	Class: CC	**2012-03 China Shipping Industry (Jiangsu) Co Ltd — Jiangdu JS** Yd No: IS47500/B-04 Loa 199.99 (BB) Br ex - Dght 10.700 Lbp - Br md 32.26 Dpth 16.20 Welded, 1 dk	**(A21A2BC) Bulk Carrier** Grain: 57,200 Compartments: 5 Ho, ER 5 Ha: ER	**1 oil engine** driving 1 FP propeller Total Power: 6,450kW (8,769hp) 13.0kn MAN-B&W 6S46MC-C 1 x 2 Stroke 6 Cy. 460 x 1932 6450kW (8769bhp)
9604512 *BSCF* -	**TAI HANG 158** **Taihang Shipping Co Ltd** *Tangshan, Hebei* *China*	**30,334** 16,987 46,380	Class: CC	**2013-12 China Shipping Industry (Jiangsu) Co Ltd — Jiangdu JS** Yd No: IS47500/B-06 Loa 199.99 (BB) Br ex - Dght 10.700 Lbp 192.00 Br md 32.26 Dpth 16.20 Welded, 1 dk	**(A21A2BC) Bulk Carrier** Grain: 57,200 Compartments: 5 Ho, ER 5 Ha: ER	**1 oil engine** driving 1 FP propeller Total Power: 6,450kW (8,769hp) 13.0kn MAN-B&W 6S46MC-C 1 x 2 Stroke 6 Cy. 460 x 1932 6450kW (8769bhp)
9604524 *BSCT* -	**TAI HANG 188** **Taihang Shipping Co Ltd** *Tangshan, Hebei* *China*	**30,334** 16,987 47,500	Class: CC	**2012-09 China Shipping Industry (Jiangsu) Co Ltd — Jiangdu JS** Yd No: IS47500/B-07 Loa 199.99 (BB) Br ex - Dght 10.700 Lbp - Br md 32.26 Dpth 16.20 Welded, 1 dk	**(A21A2BC) Bulk Carrier** Grain: 57,200 Compartments: 5 Ho, ER 5 Ha: ER	**1 oil engine** driving 1 FP propeller Total Power: 6,450kW (8,769hp) 13.0kn MAN-B&W 6S46MC-C 1 x 2 Stroke 6 Cy. 460 x 1932 6450kW (8769bhp)
9278806 *H9FD* -	**TAI HAPPINESS** **Tai Shing Maritime Co SA** Taiwan Navigation Co Ltd *Panama* *Panama* MMSI: 352390000 Official number: 3033104B	**29,398** 17,662 52,686	Class: AB	**2004-11 Oshima Shipbuilding Co Ltd — Saikai NS** Yd No: 10382 Loa 189.00 (BB) Br ex - Dght 12.100 Lbp 179.00 Br md 32.26 Dpth 17.15 Welded, 1 Dk.	**(A21A2BC) Bulk Carrier** Double Hull Grain: 64,253; Bale: 63,132 Compartments: 5 Ho, ER 5 Ha: (21.0 x 18.6)2 (19.0 x 18.6) (22.0 x 18.6)ER (17.0 x 18.6) Cranes: 4x30t	**1 oil engine** driving 1 FP propeller Total Power: 9,466kW (12,870hp) 14.5kn B&W 6S50MC-C 1 x 2 Stroke 6 Cy. 500 x 2000 9466kW (12870bhp) Kawasaki Heavy Industries Ltd-Japan AuxGen: 3 x 520kW a.c Fuel: 179.0 (d.f.) 1851.0 (r.f.)
9216676 *H3WV* -	**TAI HARMONY** **Tai Shing Maritime Co SA** Taiwan Navigation Co Ltd *Panama* *Panama* MMSI: 357032000 Official number: 2792701B	**28,615** 17,654 51,008	Class: AB	**2001-03 Oshima Shipbuilding Co Ltd — Saikai NS** Yd No: 10291 Loa 189.99 (BB) Br ex - Dght 11.898 Lbp 182.00 Br md 32.26 Dpth 16.67 Welded, 1 dk	**(A21A2BC) Bulk Carrier** Grain: 65,000; Bale: 64,162 Compartments: 5 Ho, ER 5 Ha: (18.7 x 17.6) (19.5 x 17.6)2 (22.1 x 17.6) (21.2 x 17.6)ER Cranes: 4x30t	**1 oil engine** driving 1 FP propeller Total Power: 9,467kW (12,871hp) 14.5kn B&W 6S50MC-C 1 x 2 Stroke 6 Cy. 500 x 2000 9467kW (12871bhp) Kawasaki Heavy Industries Ltd-Japan
9233428 *H9ZB* -	**TAI HARVEST** **Tai Shing Maritime Co SA** Taiwan Navigation Co Ltd *Panama* *Panama* MMSI: 351134000 Official number: 2848302A	**28,615** 17,654 51,008	Class: AB	**2002-03 Oshima Shipbuilding Co Ltd — Saikai NS** Yd No: 10310 Loa 190.00 (BB) Br ex - Dght 11.920 Lbp 182.00 Br md 32.26 Dpth 16.67 Welded, 1 dk	**(A21A2BC) Bulk Carrier** Grain: 65,000 Compartments: 5 Ho, ER 5 Ha: (19.5 x 17.6)2 (22.1 x 17.6) (21.3 x 17.6)ER (18.7 x 17.6) Cranes: 4x30t	**1 oil engine** driving 1 FP propeller Total Power: 9,467kW (12,871hp) 14.5kn B&W 6S50MC-C 1 x 2 Stroke 6 Cy. 500 x 2000 9467kW (12871bhp) Mitsui Engineering & Shipbuilding CLtd-Japan
9284556 *HOXR* -	**TAI HAWK** **Tai Shing Maritime Co SA** Taiwan Navigation Co Ltd *Panama* *Panama* MMSI: 354740000 Official number: 3045805C	**29,398** 17,662 52,686	Class: AB	**2004-12 Oshima Shipbuilding Co Ltd — Saikai NS** Yd No: 10383 Loa 189.99 (BB) Br ex - Dght 12.100 Lbp 179.00 Br md 32.26 Dpth 17.15 Welded, 1 dk	**(A21A2BC) Bulk Carrier** Double Hull Grain: 64,253; Bale: 63,132 Compartments: 5 Ho, ER 5 Ha: (21.0 x 18.6)2 (19.0 x 18.6) (22.0 x 18.6)ER (17.0 x 18.6) Cranes: 4x30t	**1 oil engine** driving 1 FP propeller Total Power: 9,466kW (12,870hp) 14.5kn B&W 6S50MC-C 1 x 2 Stroke 6 Cy. 500 x 2000 9466kW (12870bhp) Mitsui Engineering & Shipbuilding CLtd-Japan AuxGen: 3 x 520kW a.c Fuel: 179.0 (d.f.) 1851.0 (r.f.)
9550333 *BERZ4* -	**TAI HE RONG 1** - *Yangpu, Hainan* *China* MMSI: 412592390	**10,823** 6,062 17,000	Class: ZC	**2009-05 Fu'an Huanao Shipbuilding Co Ltd — Fu'an FJ** Yd No: 2007W4300208 Loa 156.03 Br ex 22.80 Dght 8.000 Lbp 147.80 Br md 22.40 Dpth 11.50 Welded, 1 dk	**(A31A2GX) General Cargo Ship** Grain: 18,900	**1 oil engine** reduction geared to sc. shaft driving 1 Propeller Total Power: 3,824kW (5,199hp) 12.5kn Pielstick 8PC2-5L 1 x 4 Stroke 8 Cy. 400 x 460 3824kW (5199bhp) Shaanxi Diesel Heavy Industry Co Lt-China

9363077 *BVER7* -	**TAI HE WANG** *ex* Jin Min Jiang 16 *-2011* **Haistar Maritime Co Ltd** - *China* MMSI: 412454550	**2,813** 1,575 5,000	Class: UB	**2005-06 Yueqing Huanghuagang Shipyard — Yueqing ZJ** Loa 95.90 Br ex - Dght 6.100 Lbp 89.00 Br md 13.80 Dpth 7.40 Welded, 1 dk	**(A31A2GX) General Cargo Ship**	**1 oil engine** reduction geared to sc. shaft driving 1 FP propeller Total Power: 1,765kW (2,400hp) 11.0kn Chinese Std. Type G8300ZC 1 x 4 Stroke 8 Cy. 300 x 380 1765kW (2400bhp) Wuxi Antai Power Machinery Co Ltd-China
9216688 *H9DK* -	**TAI HEALTH** **Tai Shing Maritime Co SA** Taiwan Navigation Co Ltd *Panama* Panama MMSI: 356235000 Official number: 2796701B	**28,615** 17,654 51,008	Class: AB	**2001-05 Oshima Shipbuilding Co Ltd — Saikai NS** Yd No: 10292 Loa 189.99 (BB) Br ex 32.29 Dght 11.920 Lbp 182.00 Br md 32.26 Dpth 16.67 Welded, 1 dk	**(A21A2BC) Bulk Carrier** Grain: 65,414; Bale: 64,162 Compartments: 5 Ho 5 Ha: (18.7 x 17.6) (19.5 x 17.6)2 (22.1 x 17.6) (21.3 x 17.6)ER Cranes: 4x30t	**1 oil engine** driving 1 FP propeller Total Power: 9,467kW (12,871hp) 14.5kn B&W 6S50MC-C 1 x 2 Stroke 6 Cy. 500 x 2000 9467kW (12871bhp) Kawasaki Heavy Industries Ltd-Japan
9304370 *3EJF9* -	**TAI HONESTY** **Tai Shing Maritime Co SA** Taiwan Navigation Co Ltd *Panama* Panama MMSI: 372506000 Official number: 3256607A	**30,669** 18,498 55,418 T/cm 55.9	Class: BV (NK)	**2007-03 Oshima Shipbuilding Co Ltd — Saikai NS** Yd No: 10445 Loa 189.99 (BB) Br ex - Dght 12.480 Lbp 181.79 Br md 32.26 Dpth 17.62 Welded, 1 dk	**(A21A2BC) Bulk Carrier** Double Hull Grain: 69,872; Bale: 68,798 Compartments: 5 Ho, ER 5 Ha: 2 (22.3 x 18.6) (18.6 x 18.6) (21.3 x 18.6)ER (16.7 x 18.6) Cranes: 4x30t	**1 oil engine** driving 1 FP propeller Total Power: 8,208kW (11,160hp) 14.5kn MAN-B&W 6S50MC-C 1 x 2 Stroke 6 Cy. 500 x 2000 8208kW (11160bhp) Mitsui Engineering & Shipbuilding CLtd-Japan AuxGen: 3 x 520kW 450/110V 60Hz a.c
8011079 *HQQG8* -	**TAI HONG 1** *ex* Amber 9 *-1999* *ex* Amber *-1999* *ex* Kaho Maru No. 18 *-1999* *ex* Usa Maru No. 12 *-1987* **Shandong Ocean Fishery Co** - SatCom: Inmarsat M 633448211 *San Lorenzo* Honduras Official number: L-1925929	**522** 166 378	Class: (KR)	**1980-06 Kochi Jyuko (Kaisei Zosen) K.K. — Kochi** Yd No: 1393 Loa - Br ex - Dght 3.201 Lbp 43.87 Br md 8.51 Dpth 3.56 Welded, 1 dk	**(B11B2FV) Fishing Vessel**	**1 oil engine** driving 1 FP propeller Total Power: 956kW (1,300hp) Akasaka DM28R 1 x 4 Stroke 6 Cy. 280 x 460 956kW (1300bhp) Akasaka Tekkosho KK (Akasaka DieselLtd)-Japan
9033191 *V3TG* -	**TAI HONG 6** *ex* Fukuyo Maru No. 58 *-2014* **Fukuyo Suisan KK** - *Belize City* Belize MMSI: 312791000 Official number: 161410800	*379* - -		**1991-06 KK Kanasashi — Shizuoka SZ** Yd No: 3261 Loa 55.16 (BB) Br ex 8.73 Dght 3.401 Lbp 48.10 Br md 8.72 Dpth 3.75 Welded, 1 dk	**(B11B2FV) Fishing Vessel** Ins: 525	**1 oil engine** with clutches, flexible couplings & sr reverse geared to sc. shaft driving 1 FP propeller Total Power: 736kW (1,001hp) 10.0kn Niigata 6M28BFT 1 x 4 Stroke 6 Cy. 280 x 480 736kW (1001bhp) Niigata Engineering Co Ltd-Japan
9156632 - -	**TAI HONG NO. 7** *ex* Ryoei Maru No. 38 *-2010* **Shandong Zhonglu Oceanic Fisheries Co Ltd** -	**619** 258 -		**1997-02 KK Kanasashi — Shizuoka SZ** Yd No: 3398 Loa 57.00 (BB) Br ex - Dght 3.500 Lbp 50.60 Br md 9.00 Dpth 3.90 Welded, 1 dk	**(B11B2FV) Fishing Vessel** Ins: 533 Compartments: 5 Ho 4 Ha:	**1 oil engine** with flexible couplings & sr gearedto sc. shaft driving 1 FP propeller Total Power: 1,177kW (1,600hp) Hanshin LH31G 1 x 4 Stroke 6 Cy. 310 x 530 1177kW (1600bhp) The Hanshin Diesel Works Ltd-Japan
8431009 - -	**TAI HSING No. 11** - - SatCom: Inmarsat M 641673510	*720* 285 -		**1989 Sen Koh Shipbuilding Corp — Kaohsiung** L reg 50.60 Br ex - Dght - Lbp - Br md 8.90 Dpth 3.85 Welded, 1 dk	**(B11B2FV) Fishing Vessel**	**1 oil engine** driving 1 FP propeller Total Power: 883kW (1,201hp) 12.0kn
7815521 - -	**TAI HU** *ex* Tai Hui I *-2001* *ex* Jui Jhi No. 101 *-2001* *ex* Hsiang Chang No. 132 *-1999* *ex* Inari Maru No. 32 *-1997* *ex* Shinmei Maru No. 7 *-1989* **Shandong Zhonglu Oceanic Fisheries Co Ltd** -	**564** 207 371		**1978-09 Niigata Engineering Co Ltd — Niigata NI** Yd No: 1610 Loa 48.87 Br ex - Dght 3.610 Lbp 42.83 Br md 8.51 Dpth 3.64 Welded, 1 dk	**(B11B2FV) Fishing Vessel**	**1 oil engine** driving 1 FP propeller Total Power: 809kW (1,100hp) Niigata 6M28ZG 1 x 4 Stroke 6 Cy. 280 x 440 809kW (1100bhp) Niigata Engineering Co Ltd-Japan
9307932 *9VJZ2* -	**TAI HU** *launched as* Dalisia *-2007* **Da Xin Tankers (Pte) Ltd** Ocean Tankers (Pte) Ltd *Singapore* Singapore MMSI: 565620000 Official number: 393498	**42,010** 22,444 73,980 T/cm 67.2	Class: AB	**2007-08 New Century Shipbuilding Co Ltd — Jingjiang JS** Yd No: 0307329 Loa 228.60 (BB) Br ex - Dght 14.518 Lbp 219.70 Br md 32.26 Dpth 20.80 Welded, 1 dk	**(A13A2TW) Crude/Oil Products Tanker** Double Hull (13F) Liq: 81,640; Liq (Oil): 85,000 Cargo Heating Coils Compartments: 12 Wing Ta, 2 Wing Slop Ta, ER 3 Cargo Pump (s): 3x2300m³/hr Manifold: Bow/CM: 111.6m	**1 oil engine** driving 1 FP propeller Total Power: 11,300kW (15,363hp) 14.0kn MAN-B&W 5S60MC-C 1 x 2 Stroke 5 Cy. 600 x 2400 11300kW (15363bhp) Hudong Heavy Machinery Co Ltd-China AuxGen: 3 x 900kW 450/220V 60Hz a.c Fuel: 230.0 (d.f.) 2100.0
8405763 *BITP* -	**TAI HU 3** *ex* Golden Prosperity *-2002* *ex* Chivalry *-1995* *ex* Jaraconda *-1988* **CITIC Shipping Shanghai Co Ltd** China International Trust & Investment Corp (Holdings) Ltd (CITIC) SatCom: Inmarsat M 635291510 *China* MMSI: 412371740	**22,091** 12,671 38,883 T/cm 47.2	Class: (NK)	**1985-07 Ishikawajima-Harima Heavy Industries Co Ltd (IHI) — Kure** Yd No: 2918 Loa 180.80 (BB) Br ex 30.54 Dght 10.931 Lbp 171.00 Br md 30.50 Dpth 15.30 Welded, 1 dk	**(A21A2BC) Bulk Carrier** Grain: 46,112; Bale: 44,492 Compartments: 5 Ho, ER 5 Ha: (15.2 x 12.8)4 (19.2 x 15.2)ER Cranes: 4x25t	**1 oil engine** driving 1 FP propeller Total Power: 5,001kW (6,799hp) 14.3kn Sulzer 6RTA58 1 x 2 Stroke 6 Cy. 580 x 1700 5001kW (6799bhp) Ishikawajima Harima Heavy IndustrieCo Ltd (IHI)-Japan AuxGen: 3 x 450kW 450V 60Hz a.c Fuel: 86.5 (d.f.) (Heating Coils) 1626.5 (r.f.) 23.0pd
8822480 *BIPO* -	**TAI HU 6** *ex* Desert Sky *-2007* *ex* Desert Star *-2003* *ex* Promina *-1997* **CITIC Shipping Shanghai Co Ltd** China International Trust & Investment Corp (Holdings) Ltd (CITIC) SatCom: Inmarsat C 441300072 *China* MMSI: 413371620	**28,164** 14,909 48,320 T/cm 54.4	Class: (LR) (CS) (JR) ✠ Classed LR until 1/2/08	**1990-06 Brodogradiliste Split (Brodosplit) — Split** Yd No: 366 Loa 192.00 (BB) Br ex 32.05 Dght 11.723 Lbp 183.00 Br md 32.00 Dpth 16.70 Welded, 1 dk	**(A21A2BC) Bulk Carrier** Grain: 57,006; Bale: 55,408 Compartments: 5 Ho, ER 5 Ha: (15.4 x 14.4)4 (19.8 x 14.4)ER Cranes: 4x25t Ice Capable	**1 oil engine** driving 1 FP propeller Total Power: 9,180kW (12,481hp) 14.8kn B&W 6L60MC 1 x 2 Stroke 6 Cy. 600 x 1944 9180kW (12481bhp) Brodogradiliste Split (Brodosplit)-Yugoslavia AuxGen: 3 x 560kW 450V 60Hz a.c Boilers: e (ex.g.) 7.1kgf/cm² (7.0bar), AuxB (o.f.) 7.1kgf/cm² (7.0bar) Fuel: 186.0 (d.f.) 1379.0 (r.f.) 40.5pd
8896895 *BBQS* -	**TAI HUA** **Shandong Fisheries Marine Transportation Co** - SatCom: Inmarsat C 441227410 *Qingdao, Shandong* China	**297** 96 225	Class: (CC)	**1994 Qingdao Marine Fishery Co Fishing Vessel Shipyard — Qingdao SD** Loa 46.60 Br ex - Dght 2.950 Lbp 40.30 Br md 7.60 Dpth 3.80 Welded, 1 dk	**(A34A2GR) Refrigerated Cargo Ship** Grain: 270; Ins: 688 Compartments: 2 Ho, ER 2 Ha: ER Cranes: 1x2t	**1 oil engine** geared to sc. shaft driving 1 FP propeller Total Power: 400kW (544hp) 13.0kn Chinese Std. Type 6300 1 x 4 Stroke 6 Cy. 300 x 380 400kW (544bhp) Zibo Diesel Engine Factory-China AuxGen: 2 x 90kW 400V a.c
7816812 - -	**TAI HUA** *ex* Shuri *-1999* **Government of The People's Republic of China** - *Shanghai* China	*3,887* 1,707 4,346	Class: (NK)	**1979-01 Imabari Shipbuilding Co Ltd — Imabari EH (Imabari Shipyard)** Yd No: 380 Loa 129.95 (BB) Br ex - Dght 5.676 Lbp 120.02 Br md 20.01 Dpth 5.74 Welded, 2 dks	**(A35A2RR) Ro-Ro Cargo Ship** Side door/ramp (s. f.) Len: 12.50 Wid: 4.50 Swl: 38 Side door/ramp (s. a.) Len: 12.50 Wid: 4.50 Swl: 38 Lane-Wid: 4.50 Lane-clr ht: 5.20 Lorries: 55, Cars: 44	**1 oil engine** geared to sc. shaft driving 1 FP propeller Total Power: 7,649kW (10,400hp) 17.0kn Pielstick 16PC2-5V-400 1 x Vee 4 Stroke 16 Cy. 400 x 460 7649kW (10400bhp) Niigata Engineering Co Ltd-Japan AuxGen: 2 x 500kW 450V 60Hz a.c Fuel: 77.0 (d.f.) 424.5 (r.f.) 28.5pd
8919556 *BOND* -	**TAI HUA HAI** **COSCO Bulk Carrier Co Ltd (COSCO BULK)** - SatCom: Inmarsat B 341230010 *Tianjin* China MMSI: 412300000	**27,598** 15,047 47,377	Class: CC	**1991-06 Hudong Shipyard — Shanghai** Yd No: 1192A Loa 189.94 (BB) Br ex - Dght 11.700 Lbp 180.00 Br md 32.20 Dpth 16.60 Welded, 1 dk	**(A21A2BC) Bulk Carrier** Grain: 57,009; Bale: 56,142 Compartments: 5 Ho, ER 5 Ha: (16.0 x 15.0)4 (16.0 x 17.6)ER Cranes: 4x30t Ice Capable	**1 oil engine** driving 1 FP propeller Total Power: 6,178kW (8,400hp) 14.5kn B&W 6L60MCE 1 x 2 Stroke 6 Cy. 600 x 1944 6178kW (8400bhp) Hudong Shipyard-China
8890786 *BNIF* -	**TAI HUNG** *ex* Kyoyu Maru *-2008* **Taiwan Fuel & Energy Supply Co Ltd** - *Kaohsiung* Chinese Taipei MMSI: 416384000	**998** 576 1,822	Class: CR	**1995-11 Maebata Zosen Tekko K.K. — Sasebo** Yd No: 218 Loa 74.52 Br ex - Dght 4.865 Lbp 69.00 Br md 11.50 Dpth 5.25 Welded, 1 dk	**(A13B2TP) Products Tanker** Liq: 2,299; Liq (Oil): 2,299 2 Cargo Pump (s): 2x850m³/hr	**1 oil engine** driving 1 FP propeller Total Power: 1,471kW (2,000hp) 12.5kn Yanmar MF33-ST 1 x 4 Stroke 6 Cy. 330 x 620 1471kW (2000bhp) Yanmar Diesel Engine Co Ltd-Japan

9559406 *9VBC7* -	**TAI HUNG SAN** **Hua Xin Shipping (Pte) Ltd** Nova Tankers A/S SatCom: Inmarsat C 456535210 *Singapore* *Singapore* MMSI: 565352000 Official number: 391628	**163,882** 108,066 317,924 T/cm 181.2	Class: AB	**2010-02 Shanghai Waigaoqiao Shipbuilding Co Ltd — Shanghai** Yd No: 1104 Loa 333.00 (BB) Br ex 60.05 Dght 22.664 Lbp 320.00 Br md 60.00 Dpth 30.50 Welded, 1 dk	**(A13A2TV) Crude Oil Tanker** Double Hull (13F) Liq: 334,954; Liq (Oil): 334,954 Cargo Heating Coils Compartments: 5 Ta, 10 Wing Ta, 2 Wing Slop Ta, ER 3 Cargo Pump (s): 3x5000m³/hr Manifold: Bow/CM: 165.2m	**1 oil engine** driving 1 FP propeller Total Power: 29,340kW (39,891hp) MAN-B&W 1 x 2 Stroke 6 Cy. 900 x 3188 29340kW (39891bhp) CSSC MES Diesel Co Ltd-China AuxGen: 3 x 1150kW a.c Fuel: 475.0 (d.f.) 9000.0 (r.f.)	 16.1kn 6S90MC-C
9304382 *3ENM3* -	**TAI HUNTER** **Tai Shing Maritime Co SA** Taiwan Navigation Co Ltd *Panama* *Panama* MMSI: 357499000 Official number: 3339508A	**30,669** 18,498 55,418 T/cm 55.9	Class: BV (NK)	**2007-12 Oshima Shipbuilding Co Ltd — Saikai NS** Yd No: 10451 Loa 190.00 (BB) Br ex - Dght 12.460 Lbp 181.79 Br md 32.26 Dpth 17.61 Welded, 1 dk	**(A21A2BC) Bulk Carrier** Double Hull Grain: 69,872; Bale: 68,798 Compartments: 5 Ho, ER 5 Ha: 2 (22.3 x 18.6) (18.6 x 18.6) (21.3 x 18.6)ER (16.7 x 18.6) Cranes: 4x30t	**1 oil engine** driving 1 FP propeller Total Power: 8,208kW (11,160hp) MAN-B&W 1 x 2 Stroke 6 Cy. 500 x 2000 8208kW (11160bhp) Mitsui Engineering & Shipbuilding CLtd-Japan AuxGen: 3 x 520kW 450V 60Hz a.c	 14.5kn 6S50MC-C
8811027 *BHFO* -	**TAI HWA** **Taiwan Navigation Co Ltd** *Kaohsiung* *Chinese Taipei* MMSI: 416100010 Official number: 11553	*8,134* 2,722 2,296	Class: CR (AB)	**1989-09 Hayashikane Dockyard Co Ltd — Nagasaki NS** Yd No: 972 Loa 120.00 (BB) Br ex 19.50 Dght 5.600 Lbp 111.19 Br md 19.30 Dpth 12.85 Welded, 2 dks	**(A36A2PR) Passenger/Ro-Ro Ship (Vehicles)** Passengers: unberthed: 1126; cabins: 21; berths: 64; driver berths: 14	**2 oil engines** sr geared to sc. shafts driving 2 FP propellers Total Power: 10,924kW (14,852hp) MAN 2 x 4 Stroke 9 Cy. 400 x 450 each-5462kW (7426bhp) Mitsubishi Heavy Industries Ltd-Japan AuxGen: 3 x 680kW 450V 60Hz a.c Thrusters: 1 Tunnel thruster (f) Fuel: 352.0 (d.f.) 474.0 (r.f.) 20.0pd	 21.0kn 9L40/45
8804244 *3FYZ6* -	**TAI JI** *ex* Green Winter *-2011* *ex* Pacific Alaska *-2007* *ex* Green Winter *-2006* *ex* Frio Canarias *-1996* **Hong Kong (Liaoyu Group) Co Ltd** Liaoning Province Dalian Ocean Fishery Group Corp *Panama* *Panama* MMSI: 357497000 Official number: 4273511	**4,970** 3,118 6,526 T/cm 16.7	Class: LR (NV) (NK) **100A1** SS 03/2009 **LMC** **Lloyd's RMC** Eq.Ltr: W; Cable: 495.0/50.0 U2	**1989-03 Shin Kurushima Dockyard Co. Ltd. — Akitsu** Yd No: 2583 Loa 124.70 (BB) Br ex 17.83 Dght 7.325 Lbp 117.00 Br md 17.80 Dpth 9.85 Welded, 1 dk	**(A34A2GR) Refrigerated Cargo Ship** Ins: 7,646 Compartments: 4 Ho, ER, 4 Tw Dk 4 Ha: ER Derricks: 8x5t	**1 oil engine** driving 1 FP propeller Total Power: 5,222kW (7,100hp) Mitsubishi 1 x 2 Stroke 6 Cy. 450 x 1350 5222kW (7100bhp) Kobe Hatsudoki KK-Japan AuxGen: 3 x 450kW 440V 60Hz a.c Boilers: e (ex.g.) 9.7kgf/cm² (9.5bar), AuxB (o.f.) 7.1kgf/cm² (7.0bar) Fuel: 134.0 (d.f.) 1081.0 (r.f.) 19.6pd	 17.0kn 6UEC45LA
9140619 *XUAN4* -	**TAI JIA** *ex* Koun Maru *-2010* **Tai Da Shipping Co Ltd** Yuan Da Shipping Co Ltd *Phnom Penh* *Cambodia* MMSI: 514364000 Official number: 1096431	**1,495** 919 1,600	Class: UB	**1996-03 Watanabe Zosen KK — Imabari EH** Yd No: 293 Loa 76.99 (BB) Br ex 11.52 Dght 4.180 Lbp 71.50 Br md 11.50 Dpth 7.20 Welded, 1 dk	**(A31A2GX) General Cargo Ship** Bale: 2,507 Compartments: 1 Ho, ER 1 Ha: ER	**1 oil engine** with flexible couplings & reverse geared to sc. shaft driving 1 FP propeller Total Power: 735kW (999hp) Hanshin 1 x 4 Stroke 6 Cy. 340 x 640 735kW (999bhp) The Hanshin Diesel Works Ltd-Japan	 LH34LG
9161429 *BXOO* -	**TAI JIAN** **Humen Lung Wei Passenger Ferry Co Ltd** Chu Kong Shipping Enterprises (Holdings) Co Ltd *Dongguan, Guangdong* *China* MMSI: 412462270	**509** 169 40	Class: CC	**1997-06 Austal Ships Pty Ltd — Fremantle WA** Yd No: 120 Loa 40.10 (BB) Br ex 11.82 Dght 1.350 Lbp 35.60 Br md 11.50 Dpth 3.80 Welded, 1 dk	**(A37B2PS) Passenger Ship** Hull Material: Aluminium Alloy Passengers: unberthed: 318	**2 oil engines** geared to sc. shafts driving 2 Water jets Total Power: 3,960kW (5,384hp) M.T.U. 2 x Vee 4 Stroke 16 Cy. 165 x 185 each-1980kW (2692bhp) MTU Friedrichshafen GmbH-Friedrichshafen	 34.5kn 16V396TE74L
8838099 - -	**TAI JIN** *ex* Yung Chang No. 201 *-2001* *ex* Kofuku Maru No. 1 *-1997* *ex* Hofuku Maru No. 1 *-1992* *ex* Ichi Maru No. 36 *-1992* **Shandong Zhonglu Oceanic Fisheries Co Ltd**	**218** 73 -		**1979 Higashi Kyushu Shipbuilding Co Ltd — Usuki OT** L reg 30.40 Br ex - Dght 2.000 Lbp - Br md 6.20 Dpth 2.50 Welded, 1 dk	**(B11B2FV) Fishing Vessel**	**1 oil engine** driving 1 FP propeller Total Power: 331kW (450hp) Yanmar 1 x 4 Stroke 331kW (450bhp) Yanmar Diesel Engine Co Ltd-Japan	
6513281 - -	**TAI KEE No. 8** *ex* Myofuku Maru No. 1 *-1980* **Tak Hing Loong S de RL**	*130* 81 286	Class: (BV)	**1964 Nakamura Kogyo — Yokohama** Yd No: 175 Loa 30.20 Br ex 6.66 Dght 2.286 Lbp 28.00 Br md 6.61 Dpth 2.49 Welded, 1 dk	**(A13B2TU) Tanker (unspecified)**	**1 oil engine** driving 1 FP propeller	
9119282 *HP7142* -	**TAI KING** *ex* Tycoon *-2011* *ex* Kaisho Maru *-2011* **Tycoon Marine SA** Fu Sheng Shipping Safety Management Consultant Co Ltd SatCom: Inmarsat C 435774510 *Panama* *Panama* MMSI: 357745000 Official number: 4379112	*1,481* 444 1,600	Class: PD	**1994-12 Yamanaka Zosen K.K. — Imabari** Yd No: 566 Loa 74.95 Br ex - Dght 4.240 Lbp 70.00 Br md 11.50 Dpth 7.24 Welded, 1 dk	**(A31A2GX) General Cargo Ship**	**1 oil engine** driving 1 FP propeller Total Power: 1,324kW (1,800hp) Hanshin 1 x 4 Stroke 6 Cy. 300 x 600 1324kW (1800bhp) The Hanshin Diesel Works Ltd-Japan	 12.1kn LH30LG
7623564 - -	**TAI LEE 6** - - -	*332* 223 508		**1975 Hip Hing Cheung Shipyard Ltd. — Hong Kong** Yd No: 540 Loa 40.09 Br ex 8.84 Dght 2.744 Lbp 38.41 Br md 8.54 Dpth 3.66 Welded, 1 dk	**(A13B2TU) Tanker (unspecified)**	**2 oil engines** reverse reduction geared to sc. shafts driving 2 FP propellers Total Power: 272kW (370hp) Daimler 2 x 4 Stroke 6 Cy. 128 x 150 each-136kW (185bhp) (made 1972, fitted 1975) Daimler Benz AG-West Germany	 6.5kn OM355
8004545 *BZ70N* -	**TAI LI** *ex* Daito Maru No. 78 *-2011* *ex* Fukukyu Maru No. 27 *-1994* **Zhoushan Haixing Ocean Fisheries Co Ltd** *Zhoushan, Zhejiang* *China* Official number: 412968000	**742** 222		**1980-05 KK Kanasashi Zosen — Shizuoka SZ** Yd No: 2043 Loa 56.22 Br ex - Dght 3.601 Lbp 50.22 Br md 9.01 Dpth 6.08 Welded, 2 dks	**(B11B2FV) Fishing Vessel**	**1 oil engine** reverse geared to sc. shaft driving 1 FP propeller Total Power: 1,324kW (1,800hp) Akasaka 1 x 4 Stroke 6 Cy. 360 x 540 1324kW (1800bhp) Akasaka Tekkosho KK (Akasaka DieselLtd)-Japan	 DM36R
8748660 *BZYC7* -	**TAI LONG 1** *ex* Fong Kuo No. 708 *-2012* **Shandong Zhonglu Oceanic Fisheries Co Ltd** *Qingdao, Shandong* *China*	**1,203** 361 999		**1989-09 Fong Kuo Shipbuilding Co Ltd — Kaohsiung** Yd No: 278 Loa 64.70 Br ex - Dght 5.021 Lbp 55.90 Br md 12.20 Dpth 7.20 Welded, 1 dk	**(B11B2FV) Fishing Vessel**	**1 oil engine** driving 1 Propeller Total Power: 2,645kW (3,596hp) Daihatsu 1 x 4 Stroke 8 Cy. 320 x 360 2645kW (3596bhp) Daihatsu Diesel Manufacturing Co Lt-Japan	 8DKM-32
8748555 - -	**TAI LONG 2** *ex* Yung Hsing Fa No. 668 *-2012* **Shandong Zhonglu Oceanic Fisheries Co Ltd** *Qingdao, Shandong* *China*	**996** 572 -		**1990-03 Lien Ho Shipbuilding Co, Ltd — Kaohsiung** Loa 66.20 Br ex - Dght 4.550 Lbp 58.90 Br md 11.80 Dpth 4.80 Welded, 1 dk	**(B11B2FV) Fishing Vessel**	**1 oil engine** driving 1 Propeller Total Power: 2,206kW (2,999hp) Niigata 1 x 4 Stroke 6 Cy. 320 x 420 2206kW (2999bhp) Niigata Engineering Co Ltd-Japan	 6MG32CLX
8418320 *BHFP* -	**TAI MA** *ex* New Kyushu *-1998* **Lian Chiang Hsien (County) Government** Taiwan Navigation Co Ltd *Keelung* *Chinese Taipei* MMSI: 416100050	**4,717** 1,415 1,000	Class: CR	**1985-03 Usuki Iron Works Co Ltd — Usuki OT** Yd No: 1545 Loa 110.01 (BB) Br ex - Dght 4.500 Lbp 100.01 Br md 16.01 Dpth 5.82 Welded	**(A36A2PR) Passenger/Ro-Ro Ship (Vehicles)** Passengers: unberthed: 520; cabins: 12; berths: 24 Bow door & ramp Len: 5.70 Wid: 3.70 Swl: - Stern door/ramp Len: 5.50 Wid: 3.80 Swl: - Quarter stern door/ramp (p) Len: 12.80 Wid: 3.70 Swl: - Lorries: 30, Cars: 12	**2 oil engines** geared to sc. shafts driving 2 FP propellers Total Power: 6,620kW (9,000hp) Pielstick 2 x 4 Stroke 6 Cy. 400 x 460 each-3310kW (4500bhp) Ishikawajima Harima Heavy IndustrieCo Ltd (IHI)-Japan Thrusters: 1 Tunnel thruster (f)	 19.0kn 6PC2-6L-400
9210115 *BIDB* -	**TAI MIN STAR** *ex* King Tamatoa *-2012* *ex* NGV Liamone *-2010* **Ba Fwu Industry Co Ltd** - *Kaohsiung* *Chinese Taipei* MMSI: 416470000	**9,351** 2,805 869	Class: BV CR (Class contemplated)	**2000-05 Alstom Leroux Naval SA — Lanester** Yd No: 824 Loa 134.00 Br ex 19.80 Dght 3.350 Lbp 120.00 Br md 18.90 Dpth 6.20 Welded, 2 dks	**(A36A2PR) Passenger/Ro-Ro Ship (Vehicles)** Passengers: unberthed: 1116 Bow door/ramp Len: 11.00 Wid: 3.38 Swl: - Stern door/ramp (p) Len: 8.00 Wid: 4.30 Swl: - Stern door/ramp (s) Len: 8.00 Wid: 4.30 Swl: - Cars: 250	**2 oil engines & 2 Gas Turbs** geared to sc. shafts driving 4 Water jets Total Power: 63,000kW (85,654hp) M.T.U. 2 x Vee 4 Stroke 20 Cy. 230 x 280 each-6500kW (8837bhp) MTU Friedrichshafen GmbH-Friedrichshafen GE Marine 2 x Gas Turb each-25000kW (33990shp) GE Marine Engines-Cincinnati, Oh AuxGen: 5 x 418kW a.c Thrusters: 2 Thwart. CP thruster (f) Fuel: 312.0 (d.f.)	 42.0kn 20V1163TB73 LM2500+

IMO / Call sign	Name / Owner	Tonnage	Class	Built / Dimensions	Type / Cargo	Machinery
9637844 *BDAA* -	**TAI NAN** **Government of Taiwan (Coast Guard General Bureau, Maritime Patrol Directorate)** - *Kaohsiung* *Chinese Taipei* MMSI: 416445000 Official number: 014890	**2,462** 738 450	Class: (NV)	**2010-11 Jong Shyn Shipbuilding Co., Ltd. — Kaohsiung** Yd No: 178 Loa 98.50 Br ex 13.22 Dght 3.800 Lbp 87.30 Br md 13.20 Dpth 7.60 Welded, 1 dk	**(B34H2SQ) Patrol Vessel**	**2 oil engines** reduction geared to sc. shafts driving 2 CP propellers Total Power: 14,800kW (20,122hp) 15.0kn M.T.U. 20V1163TB93 2 x Vee 4 Stroke 20 Cy. 230 x 280 each-7400kW (10061bhp) MTU Friedrichshafen GmbH-Friedrichshafen Thrusters: 1 Thwart. FP thruster (f)
8217116 *BBQR* -	**TAI NING** *ex* Singapore Fontaine *-1993* **Shandong Zhonglu Fishery Shipping Co Ltd** - SatCom: Inmarsat C 441224715 *Qingdao, Shandong* *China* MMSI: 412322280 Official number: 010927	**3,260** 1,589 3,901	Class: CC (NK)	**1983-01 Kochi Jyuko K.K. — Kochi** Yd No: 2280 Loa 92.23 Br ex - Dght 6.568 Lbp 85.02 Br md 16.21 Dpth 9.50 Welded, 3 dks	**(A34A2GR) Refrigerated Cargo Ship** Ins: 4,326 Compartments: 3 Ho, ER 3 Ha: 3 (5.0 x 5.1)ER Derricks: 6x4t	**1 oil engine** sr geared to sc. shaft driving 1 FP propeller Total Power: 3,310kW (4,500hp) 14.0kn Pielstick 6PC2-6L-400 1 x 4 Stroke 6 Cy. 400 x 460 3310kW (4500bhp) Ishikawajima Harima Heavy IndustrieCo Ltd (IHI)-Japan AuxGen: 1 x 640kW 450V 60Hz a.c, 2 x 600kW 450V 60Hz a.c Fuel: 134.0 (d.f.) 590.0 (r.f.) 12.5pd
9617002 *VRJW7* -	**TAI O** **Hongkong United Dockyards Ltd** The Hongkong Salvage & Towage Co Ltd *Hong Kong* *Hong Kong* MMSI: 477765400	**481** 144 198	Class: LR ✠ **100A1** SS 04/2012 tug ✠ **LMC** Eq.Ltr: H; Cable: 275.0/22.0 U2 (a)	**2012-04 Hin Lee (Zhuhai) Shipyard Co Ltd — Zhuhai GD** (Hull) Yd No: 233 **2012-04 Cheoy Lee Shipyards Ltd — Hong Kong** Yd No: 5022 Loa 30.25 Br ex 11.90 Dght 4.200 Lbp 28.20 Br md 11.60 Dpth 5.39 Welded, 1 dk	**(B32A2ST) Tug**	**2 oil engines** gearing integral to driving 2 Z propellers Total Power: 3,676kW (4,998hp) Niigata 6L28HX 2 x 4 Stroke 6 Cy. 280 x 370 each-1838kW (2499bhp) Niigata Engineering Co Ltd-Japan AuxGen: 2 x 80kW 380V 50Hz a.c
9102411 - -	**TAI OON No. 3** **Tai Oon Transport Co** *Bandar Seri Begawan* *Brunei* Official number: 0151	**338** 102 528	Class: (NK)	**1993-10 Chiong Brothers Shipyard Co — Sibu** Yd No: 7292 Loa 36.60 Br ex - Dght - Lbp 34.78 Br md 12.20 Dpth 3.05 Welded, 1 dk	**(A31A2GX) General Cargo Ship**	**2 oil engines** reduction geared to sc. shafts driving 2 FP propellers Total Power: 522kW (710hp) 8.0kn Cummins NTA-855-M 2 x 4 Stroke 6 Cy. 140 x 152 each-261kW (355bhp) Cummins Engine Co Inc-USA
8720929 - -	**TAI PAN** - -	*930* 301 -		**1988 Sea Management Corp — Caboolture QLD** Yd No: V003 Loa 34.90 Br ex 13.70 Dght 3.000 Lbp - Br md 13.68 Dpth 3.98 Welded, 3 dks	**(A37B2PS) Passenger Ship**	**2 oil engines** driving 2 FP propellers Total Power: 504kW (686hp) MWM 2 x Vee 4 Stroke 12 Cy. each-252kW (343bhp) Motoren Werke Mannheim AG (MWM)-West Germany Thrusters: 1 Thwart. FP thruster (f)
7401978 - -	**TAI PING** *ex* Zhe Jiao Ji 601 *-2005* *ex* Hakuryu *-2005* *ex* Hakuryu Maru *-1999* **Eternal Star International Ltd** Shanghai Marukichi Ship Management Co Ltd	*1,142* 366 2,009		**1974-11 Honda Zosen — Saiki** Yd No: 625 Loa 71.18 Br ex 11.56 Dght 4.827 Lbp 65.79 Br md 11.54 Dpth 5.39 Welded, 1 dk	**(A24A2BT) Cement Carrier**	**1 oil engine** driving 1 FP propeller Total Power: 1,471kW (2,000hp) 11.5kn Hanshin 6LUD35 1 x 4 Stroke 6 Cy. 350 x 550 1471kW (2000bhp) Hanshin Nainenki Kogyo-Japan
7378377 *3FWN8* -	**TAI PING** *ex* Volissos Spirit *-2008* *ex* Gassam *-2007* *ex* Ocean Hope *-2007* *ex* Hope C *-2003* *ex* Toro *-1999* *ex* Amadeus *-1994* *ex* Sensei *-1993* *ex* Mare Dorico *-1991* *ex* Kingdom Venture *-1980* **Red Flag Heavy Industry Co Ltd & Zhong Yuan Shipping Co Ltd** Shanghai Marukichi Ship Management Co Ltd SatCom: Inmarsat C 435123110 *Panama* *Panama* MMSI: 351231000 Official number: 4077009	**18,858** 10,500 30,702	Class: KC (LR) (KR) (RI) ✠ Classed LR until 16/7/00	**1975-05 Usuki Iron Works Co Ltd — Saiki OT** Yd No: 1172 Loa 178.39 (BB) Br ex 26.88 Dght 10.662 Lbp 167.21 Br md 26.80 Dpth 14.71 Welded, 1 dk	**(A21A2BC) Bulk Carrier** Grain: 38,660; Bale: 37,237 Compartments: 5 Ho, ER 5 Ha: (9.6 x 15.0)4 (17.6 x 15.0)ER Derricks: 5x22t	**1 oil engine** driving 1 FP propeller Total Power: 8,495kW (11,550hp) 12.0kn Sulzer 7RND68 1 x 2 Stroke 7 Cy. 680 x 1250 8495kW (11550bhp) Ishikawajima Harima Heavy IndustrieCo Ltd (IHI)-Japan AuxGen: 3 x 420kW 445V 60Hz a.c Fuel: 172.5 (d.f.) 1666.0 (r.f.) 38.5pd
9504164 *VRDU4* -	**TAI PING** **Blue Ocean Merchant Marine Ltd** Dandong Marine Shipping Co Ltd *Hong Kong* *Hong Kong* MMSI: 477058700 Official number: HK-2106	**5,275** 2,309 7,991	Class: CC	**2008-04 Huanghai Shipbuilding Co Ltd — Rongcheng SD** Yd No: HCY-82 Loa 117.00 Br ex - Dght 6.400 Lbp 110.00 Br md 19.70 Dpth 8.50 Welded, 1 dk	**(A31A2GX) General Cargo Ship** Grain: 9,608; Bale: 9,608 TEU 629 C Ho 200 TEU C Dk 429 TEU. Compartments: 3 Ho, ER 3 Ha: (25.4 x 15.0) (31.9 x 15.0)ER (19.5 x 15.0) Ice Capable	**2 oil engines** reduction geared to sc. shafts driving 2 Propellers Total Power: 5,000kW (6,798hp) 13.8kn Daihatsu 8DKM-28 2 x 4 Stroke 8 Cy. 280 x 390 each-2500kW (3399bhp) Shaanxi Diesel Heavy Industry Co Lt-China AuxGen: 3 x 250kW 400V a.c
9408011 *3EID4* -	**TAI PING 8** *ex* An Quan Zhou No. 22 *-2006* **Jin Jing Biao** Shanghai Marukichi Ship Management Co Ltd *Panama* *Panama* MMSI: 372115000 Official number: 34991PEXTF2	**2,990** 1,353 5,000	Class: OM	**2006-02 Zhejiang Tenglong Shipyard — Wenling ZJ** Yd No: 3100167 Loa 97.17 Br ex - Dght - Lbp 90.00 Br md 15.60 Dpth 7.50 Welded, 1 dk	**(A24A2BT) Cement Carrier**	**1 oil engine** geared to sc. shaft driving 1 FP propeller Total Power: 2,060kW (2,801hp) 13.0kn Chinese Std. Type 8300ZC 1 x 4 Stroke 8 Cy. 300 x 380 2060kW (2801bhp) in China
9617961 *VRIG5* -	**TAI PING SHAN** **Yin Que Shipping Co Ltd** China Shipping International Shipmanagement Co Ltd SatCom: Inmarsat C 447703420 *Hong Kong* *Hong Kong* MMSI: 477013300 Official number: HK-3037	**32,962** 19,142 56,607 T/cm 58.8	Class: CC	**2011-09 China Shipping Industry (Jiangsu) Co Ltd — Jiangdu JS** Yd No: CIS57000-03 Loa 189.99 (BB) Br ex 32.30 Dght 12.800 Lbp 185.00 Br md 32.26 Dpth 18.00 Welded, 1 dk	**(A21A2BC) Bulk Carrier** Grain: 71,634; Bale: 68,200 Compartments: 5 Ho, ER 5 Ha: 4 (21.3 x 18.3)ER (18.9 x 18.3) Cranes: 4x30t	**1 oil engine** driving 1 FP propeller Total Power: 9,480kW (12,889hp) 14.2kn MAN-B&W 6S50MC-C 1 x 2 Stroke 6 Cy. 500 x 2000 9480kW (12889bhp) Yichang Marine Diesel Engine Co Ltd-China AuxGen: 3 x 600kW 450V a.c
7731426 *HO6249* -	**TAI PING SHAN** *ex* Tak On *-1981* *ex* Ginza *-1978* *ex* Kohnan Maru No. 1 *-1978* **Hang Hing Navigation Corp** - *Panama* *Panama* Official number: 821777A	*246* 109 457	Class: (BV)	**1964 Kochiken Zosen — Kochi** Yd No: 281 Loa 43.01 Br ex 7.40 Dght 3.161 Lbp 38.10 Br md - Dpth 3.41 Welded, 1 dk	**(A31A2GX) General Cargo Ship** Bale: 200 Compartments: 1 Ho, ER 1 Ha: (3.7 x 6.1)ER	**1 oil engine** driving 1 FP propeller Total Power: 515kW (700hp) 10.0kn Niigata 1 x 4 Stroke 6 Cy. 280 x 440 515kW (700bhp) Niigata Engineering Co Ltd-Japan
9218260 *H3TI* -	**TAI PLENTY** **Tai Shing Maritime Co SA** Taiwan Navigation Co Ltd *Panama* *Panama* MMSI: 352939000 Official number: 2777701C	**38,382** 24,691 73,060 T/cm 65.4	Class: AB	**2000-12 Sumitomo Heavy Industries Ltd. — Yokosuka Shipyard, Yokosuka** Yd No: 1271 Loa 225.00 (BB) Br ex 32.30 Dght 13.876 Lbp 216.00 Br md 32.26 Dpth 19.20 Welded, 1 dk	**(A21A2BC) Bulk Carrier** Grain: 87,179 Compartments: 7 Ho, ER 7 Ha: (16.3 x 13.4)6 (16.3 x 15.0)ER	**1 oil engine** driving 1 FP propeller Total Power: 10,185kW (13,848hp) 14.7kn Sulzer 7RTA48T-B 1 x 2 Stroke 7 Cy. 480 x 2000 10185kW (13848bhp) Diesel United Ltd.-Aioi AuxGen: 3 x 420kW 450V 60Hz a.c Fuel: 2600.0 (r.f.)
9225380 *H9EM* -	**TAI PRIZE** **Tai Shing Maritime Co SA** Taiwan Navigation Co Ltd *Panama* *Panama* MMSI: 352299000 Official number: 2797401B	**38,382** 24,691 73,000 T/cm 65.4	Class: AB	**2001-06 Sumitomo Heavy Industries Ltd. — Yokosuka Shipyard, Yokosuka** Yd No: 1278 Loa 225.00 (BB) Br ex 32.30 Dght 13.876 Lbp 216.00 Br md 32.26 Dpth 19.20 Welded, 1 dk	**(A21A2BC) Bulk Carrier** Grain: 87,180 Compartments: 7 Ho, ER 7 Ha: 6 (15.0 x 16.3)ER (13.4 x 16.3)	**1 oil engine** driving 1 FP propeller Total Power: 10,185kW (13,848hp) 14.5kn Sulzer 7RTA48T 1 x 2 Stroke 7 Cy. 480 x 2000 10185kW (13848bhp) Diesel United Ltd.-Aioi
9218272 *H3WU* -	**TAI PROFIT** **Tai Shing Maritime Co SA** Taiwan Navigation Co Ltd *Panama* *Panama* MMSI: 357071000 Official number: 2790201C	**38,382** 24,691 73,105 T/cm 65.4	Class: LR (AB) **100A1** SS 03/2011 bulk carrier strengthened for heavy cargoes, Nos. 2, 4 & 6 holds may be empty LI ESP **LMC** **UMS**	**2001-03 Sumitomo Heavy Industries Ltd. — Yokosuka Shipyard, Yokosuka** Yd No: 1272 Loa 225.00 (BB) Br ex 32.30 Dght 13.876 Lbp 216.00 Br md 32.26 Dpth 19.20 Welded, 1 dk	**(A21A2BC) Bulk Carrier** Double Bottom Entire Compartment Length Grain: 87,180 Compartments: 7 Ho, ER 7 Ha: (16.4 x 12.4)6 (16.4 x 15.0)ER	**1 oil engine** driving 1 FP propeller Total Power: 10,185kW (13,848hp) 14.2kn Sulzer 7RTA48T 1 x 2 Stroke 7 Cy. 480 x 2000 10185kW (13848bhp) Diesel United Ltd.-Aioi AuxGen: 3 x 420kW 450V 60Hz a.c Fuel: 169.0 (d.f.) (Heating Coils) 2404.3 (r.f.) 35.4pd
9281827 *HPTH* -	**TAI PROGRESS** **Tai Shing Maritime Co SA** Taiwan Navigation Co Ltd *Panama* *Panama* MMSI: 355432000 Official number: 2976404B	**41,378** 26,189 77,834	Class: AB CR	**2004-01 China Shipbuilding Corp (CSBC) — Kaohsiung** Yd No: 815 Loa 224.79 (BB) Br ex - Dght 14.100 Lbp 217.00 Br md 32.26 Dpth 19.50 Welded, 1 Dk.	**(A21A2BC) Bulk Carrier** Double Bottom Entire Compartment Length Grain: 92,151 Compartments: 7 Ho, ER 7 Ha: 5 (17.1 x 15.0) (17.1 x 15.0)ER (17.1 x 14.0)	**1 oil engine** driving 1 FP propeller Total Power: 10,002kW (13,599hp) 14.5kn MAN-B&W 5S60MC-C 1 x 2 Stroke 5 Cy. 600 x 2400 10002kW (13599bhp) Mitsui Engineering & Shipbuilding CLtd-Japan AuxGen: 3 x 480kW 60Hz a.c Fuel: 120.0 (d.f.) 2460.0 (r.f.) 35.6pd

9290696 *HPWT* -	**TAI PROMOTION** **Tai Shing Maritime Co SA** Taiwan Navigation Co Ltd *Panama* *Panama* MMSI: 356268000 Official number: 2972404B	**41,378** 26,189 77,000	Class: LR (AB) (CR) **100A1** SS 02/2014 bulk carrier strengthened for heavy cargoes, Nos. 2, 4 & 6 holds may be empty ESN *IWS ESP LI **LMC** **UMS** Eq.Ltr: P†; Cable: 660.0/78.0 U3 (a)	**2004-02 China Shipbuilding Corp (CSBC) — Kaohsiung** Yd No: 816 Loa 224.79 (BB) Br ex 32.61 Dght 14.100 Lbp 217.00 Br md 32.26 Dpth 19.50 Welded, 1 dk	**(A21A2BC) Bulk Carrier** Grain: 92,500 Compartments: 7 Ho, ER 7 Ha: 6 (17.1 x 15.0)ER (17.1 x 13.4)	**1 oil engine** driving 1 FP propeller Total Power: 10,006kW (13,604hp) 14.5kn MAN-B&W 5S60MC-C 1 x 2 Stroke 5 Cy. 600 x 2400 10006kW (13604bhp) Mitsui Engineering & Shipbuilding CLtd-Japan AuxGen: 3 x 440kW 440V 60Hz a.c, 1 x 99kW 440V 60Hz a.c Boilers: AuxB (Comp) 7.3kgf/cm^2 (7.2bar)
9303510 *3EDC4* -	**TAI PROSPERITY** **Tai Shing Maritime Co SA** Taiwan Navigation Co Ltd *Panama* *Panama* MMSI: 371545000 Official number: 3126106A	**41,372** 26,094 77,000	Class: BV	**2005-10 China Shipbuilding Corp — Keelung** Yd No: 847 Loa 225.00 (BB) Br ex - Dght 14.100 Lbp 217.00 Br md 32.26 Dpth 19.50 Welded, 1 dk	**(A21A2BC) Bulk Carrier** Grain: 92,500 Compartments: 7 Ho, ER 7 Ha: 6 (17.1 x 15.0)ER (17.1 x 13.4)	**1 oil engine** driving 1 FP propeller Total Power: 10,006kW (13,604hp) 14.5kn MAN-B&W 6S60MC 1 x 2 Stroke 6 Cy. 600 x 2292 10006kW (13604bhp) Mitsui Engineering & Shipbuilding CLtd-Japan
9109005 *BKWT4* -	**TAI RONG 9** *ex* Ru Yi Quan *-2009* **Zhejiang Huashun Marine Co Ltd** Union Rich Shipping Co Ltd SatCom: Inmarsat C 441301212 *Zhoushan, Zhejiang* *China* MMSI: 413433520 Official number: 070009000014	**6,577** 3,421 10,266 T/cm 19.2	Class: CC (GL)	**1995-12 Neue Brand Werft GmbH & Co. KG — Oldenburg** Yd No: 244 Loa 128.80 (BB) Br ex - Dght 8.177 Lbp 119.00 Br md 18.60 Dpth 10.90 Welded, 1 dk	**(A31A2GX) General Cargo Ship** Grain: 11,927 TEU 598 C. 598/20' incl. 50 ref C. Compartments: 3 Ho, ER 3 Ha: ER Ice Capable	**1 oil engine** with flexible couplings & sr gearedto sc. shaft driving 1 CP propeller Total Power: 5,400kW (7,342hp) 16.0kn MaK 8M552C 1 x 4 Stroke 8 Cy. 450 x 520 5400kW (7342bhp) Krupp MaK Maschinenbau GmbH-Kiel Thrusters: 1 Thwart. FP thruster (f)
8829505 - -	**TAI RONG 15** *ex* Jing Hai 3 *-2008* *ex* Bang Chui Dao *-2008* *ex* Jian She 21 *-2006* **Zhoushan Tairong International Marine Co Ltd** Winson Shipping (Taiwan) Co Ltd *Yangpu, Hainan* *China*	**2,992** 1,476 4,980	Class: IZ (CC)	**1988-03 Bohai Shipyard — Huludao LN** Loa 107.42 Br ex - Dght 6.180 Lbp 98.00 Br md 15.00 Dpth 7.49 Welded, 1 dk	**(A13B2TP) Products Tanker** Single Hull Liq: 6,050; Liq (Oil): 6,050 Compartments: 10 Wing Ta, ER	**1 oil engine** driving 1 FP propeller Total Power: 2,501kW (3,400hp) 13.7kn Sulzer 5RTA38 1 x 2 Stroke 5 Cy. 380 x 1100 2501kW (3400bhp) Shanghai Diesel Engine Co Ltd-China AuxGen: 2 x 250kW 400V a.c, 1 x 64kW 400V a.c
9373802 *BKSS6* -	**TAI RONG 16** *launched as* Xin An Da 29 *-2005* **Zhoushan Tairong International Marine Co Ltd** Yingkou Power Ship Management Co Ltd *Zhoushan, Zhejiang* *China* MMSI: 412426170	**1,575** 1,292 3,000	Class: UB	**2005-08 Taizhou Jiangbei Shipyard — Taizhou JS** Loa 82.00 Br ex - Dght 5.100 Lbp 78.75 Br md 12.80 Dpth 6.20 Welded, 1 dk	**(A31A2GX) General Cargo Ship**	**1 oil engine** driving 1 FP propeller Total Power: 735kW (999hp) Chinese Std. Type 1 x 4 Stroke 735kW (999bhp) Zibo Diesel Engine Factory-China
8991396 - -	**TAI RONG 18** *ex* Jinqian 16 *-2005* **Zhoushan Tairong International Marine Co Ltd** Union Rich Shipping Co Ltd	*1,666* 933 3,000		**1989-07 Wenzhou Dongfang Shipyard — Yueqing ZJ** Loa 80.00 Br ex 12.00 Dght 5.300 Lbp 73.50 Br md 11.80 Dpth 6.60 Welded, 1 dk	**(A31A2GX) General Cargo Ship**	**1 oil engine** driving 1 Propeller Total Power: 735kW (999hp) Hanshin 1 x 4 Stroke 735kW (999bhp) The Hanshin Diesel Works Ltd-Japan
9084217 *3FHT4* -	**TAI RUI** *ex* Oriente Grace *-2013* **Tai Rui Shipping Co Ltd** Shanghai Vasteast International Shipping Management Co Ltd SatCom: Inmarsat C 435355310 *Panama* *Panama* MMSI: 353553000 Official number: 2156394E	**13,725** 7,721 22,020	Class: NK	**1994-07 Saiki Heavy Industries Co Ltd — Saiki OT** (Hull) Yd No: 1033 **1994-07 Onomichi Dockyard Co Ltd — Onomichi HS** Yd No: 380 Loa 157.50 (BB) Br ex - Dght 9.109 Lbp 148.00 Br md 25.00 Dpth 12.70 Welded, 1 dk	**(A21A2BC) Bulk Carrier** Grain: 29,254; Bale: 28,299 Compartments: 4 Ho, ER 4 Ha: (20.0 x 17.5)3 (20.8 x 17.5)ER Cranes: 4x30t	**1 oil engine** driving 1 FP propeller Total Power: 5,296kW (7,200hp) 14.0kn Mitsubishi 6UEC45LA 1 x 2 Stroke 6 Cy. 450 x 1350 5296kW (7200bhp) Kobe Hatsudoki KK-Japan AuxGen: 3 x 290kW a.c Fuel: 1270.0 (r.f.)
9418066 *9VBC6* -	**TAI SAN** **Hua Kang Shipping Pte Ltd** Nova Tankers A/S SatCom: Inmarsat C 456404310 *Singapore* *Singapore* MMSI: 564043000 Official number: 391627	**164,680** 108,060 318,068 T/cm 181.2	Class: LR ✠ **100A1** SS 08/2009 Double Hull oil tanker ESP CSR **ShipRight** (CM) *IWS LI SPM ✠ **LMC** **UMS IGS** Eq.Ltr: E*; Cable: 770.0/117.0 U3 (a)	**2009-08 Shanghai Waigaoqiao Shipbuilding Co Ltd — Shanghai** Yd No: 1102 Loa 332.29 (BB) Br ex 60.03 Dght 22.640 Lbp 319.86 Br md 59.99 Dpth 30.50 Welded, 1 dk	**(A13A2TV) Crude Oil Tanker** Double Hull (13F) Liq: 334,956; Liq (Oil): 334,956 Cargo Heating Coils Compartments: 5 Ta, 10 Wing Ta, 2 Wing Slop Ta, ER 3 Cargo Pump (s): 3x5000m^3/hr Manifold: Bow/CM: 165.2m	**1 oil engine** driving 1 FP propeller Total Power: 29,340kW (39,891hp) 16.1kn MAN-B&W 6S90MC-C 1 x 2 Stroke 6 Cy. 900 x 3188 29340kW (39891bhp) CSSC MES Diesel Co Ltd-China AuxGen: 3 x 1270kW 450V 60Hz a.c Boilers: e (ex.g.) 19.4kgf/cm^2 (19.0bar), WTAuxB (o.f.) 18.4kgf/cm^2 (18.0bar) Fuel: 478.0 (d.f.) 8445.0 (r.f.)
9613068 *VRIU2* -	**TAI SHAN** **Maxson Shipping Inc** Oak Maritime (Canada) Inc *Hong Kong* *Hong Kong* MMSI: 477899200 Official number: HK-3149	**91,374** 57,770 176,000 T/cm 120.6	Class: BV	**2011-08 Shanghai Jiangnan Changxing Shipbuilding Co Ltd — Shanghai** Yd No: H1233 Loa 292.00 (BB) Br ex - Dght 18.300 Lbp 282.00 Br md 45.00 Dpth 24.80 Welded, 1 dk	**(A21A2BC) Bulk Carrier** Grain: 194,169; Bale: 183,425 Compartments: 9 Ho, ER 9 Ha: ER	**1 oil engine** driving 1 FP propeller Total Power: 16,860kW (22,923hp) 14.0kn MAN-B&W 6S70MC 1 x 2 Stroke 6 Cy. 700 x 2674 16860kW (22923bhp) CSSC MES Diesel Co Ltd-China AuxGen: 3 x 900kW 60Hz a.c Fuel: 3220.0
9067465 *BXBM* -	**TAI SHAN** **Shenzhen Xunlong Passenger Shipping Ltd** *Shenzhen, Guangdong* *China* MMSI: 412460920	*560* 184 42	Class: CC	**1993-06 Austal Ships Pty Ltd — Fremantle WA** Yd No: 101 Loa 39.90 Br ex 11.80 Dght 1.400 Lbp 35.00 Br md 11.50 Dpth 3.80 Welded, 1 dk	**(A37B2PS) Passenger Ship** Hull Material: Aluminium Alloy Passengers: unberthed: 354	**2 oil engines** reduction geared to sc. shafts driving 2 Water jets Total Power: 3,840kW (5,220hp) 32.5kn M.T.U. 16V396TE74L 2 x Vee 4 Stroke 16 Cy. 165 x 185 each-1920kW (2610bhp) MTU Friedrichshafen GmbH-Friedrichshafen AuxGen: 2 x 108kW 380V a.c
8513560 *C6AZ2* -	**TAI SHAN** *ex* Nosac Tai Shan *-1996* **Caiano Ship AS** Green Management Sp z oo *Nassau* *Bahamas* MMSI: 311000197 Official number: 7000612	**48,676** 14,603 15,577	Class: NV (NK)	**1986-12 Sumitomo Heavy Industries Ltd. — Oppama Shipyard, Yokosuka** Yd No: 1139 Loa 190.05 (BB) Br ex 32.29 Dght 8.920 Lbp 180.00 Br md 32.26 Dpth 13.75 Welded, 12 dks, incl. 4 dks hoistable	**(A35B2RV) Vehicles Carrier** Side door/ramp (s) Len: 20.00 Wid: 5.00 Swl: 16 Quarter stern door/ramp (s) Len: 35.00 Wid: 7.00 Swl: 100 Lane-Wid: 3.39 Lane-clr ht: 4.60 Cars: 5,720	**1 oil engine** driving 1 FP propeller Total Power: 8,715kW (11,849hp) 18.0kn Sulzer 7RTA58 1 x 2 Stroke 7 Cy. 580 x 1700 8715kW (11849bhp) Sumitomo Heavy Industries Ltd-Japan AuxGen: 3 x 780kW 220/440V 60Hz a.c Thrusters: 1 Thwart. CP thruster (f)
8310267 *BBRH* -	**TAI SHENG** *ex* Tokuko *-1996* *ex* Tokuko Maru *-1991* **Qingdao Haifeng Shipping Co** *Qingdao, Shandong* *China* MMSI: 412321260	**1,736** 615 1,710	Class: (CC) (NK)	**1983-09 Kochi Jyuko (Kaisei Zosen) K.K. — Kochi** Yd No: 1601 Loa 76.00 (BB) Br ex - Dght 4.652 Lbp 70.01 Br md 13.21 Dpth 7.52 Welded, 2 dks	**(A34A2GR) Refrigerated Cargo Ship** Ins: 2,012 Compartments: 2 Ho, ER 2 Ha: 2 (5.8 x 6.0)ER Derricks: 4x5t; Winches: 4	**1 oil engine** driving 1 FP propeller Total Power: 1,471kW (2,000hp) 12.8kn Hanshin 6EL32 1 x 4 Stroke 6 Cy. 320 x 640 1471kW (2000bhp) The Hanshin Diesel Works Ltd-Japan AuxGen: 2 x 320kW a.c
6928199 - -	**TAI SHIANG No. 1** **Tai Shiang Fishing Co Ltd** *Kaohsiung* *Chinese Taipei*	*250* 99 -		**1969 Tien Erh Shipbuilding Co., Ltd. — Kaohsiung** Loa 36.71 Br ex 6.63 Dght - Lbp 33.33 Br md 6.61 Dpth 3.05 Welded, 1 dk	**(B11B2FV) Fishing Vessel**	**1 oil engine** driving 1 FP propeller Makita 1 x 4 Stroke Makita Tekkosho-Japan
9633264 *3FUG6* -	**TAI SHINE** **Tai Shing Maritime Co SA** Taiwan Navigation Co Ltd *Panama* *Panama* MMSI: 371850000 Official number: 4428512	**34,775** 20,098 61,473 T/cm 61.4	Class: BV	**2012-10 Shin Kasado Dockyard Co Ltd — Kudamatsu YC** Yd No: K-040 Loa 199.90 (BB) Br ex - Dght 13.000 Lbp 195.00 Br md 32.24 Dpth 18.60 Welded, 1 dk	**(A21A2BC) Bulk Carrier** Grain: 77,674; Bale: 73,552 Compartments: 5 Ho, ER 5 Ha: 4 (23.5 x 19.0)ER (18.7 x 19.0) Cranes: 4x30.5t	**1 oil engine** driving 1 FP propeller Total Power: 8,459kW (11,501hp) 14.5kn MAN-B&W 6S50MC-C8 1 x 2 Stroke 6 Cy. 500 x 2000 8459kW (11501bhp) Mitsui Engineering & Shipbuilding CLtd-Japan AuxGen: 3 x 500kW 60Hz a.c Fuel: 2560.0
8919568 *BONE* -	**TAI SHUN HAI** **COSCO Bulk Carrier Co Ltd (COSCO BULK)** - SatCom: Inmarsat A 1571103 *Tianjin* *China* MMSI: 412301000	**27,958** 15,047 47,378	Class: CC	**1991-10 Hudong Shipyard — Shanghai** Yd No: 1193A Loa 189.94 (BB) Br ex - Dght 11.700 Lbp 180.00 Br md 32.20 Dpth 16.60 Welded, 1 dk	**(A21A2BC) Bulk Carrier** Grain: 57,009; Bale: 56,142 Compartments: 5 Ho, ER 5 Ha: (16.0 x 15.0)4 (16.0 x 17.6)ER Cranes: 4x30t Ice Capable	**1 oil engine** driving 1 FP propeller Total Power: 6,178kW (8,400hp) 14.5kn B&W 6L60MCE 1 x 2 Stroke 6 Cy. 600 x 1944 6178kW (8400bhp) Hudong Shipyard-China

8431190 *HQFI7* -	**TAI SHUN No. 1** - **Kuwei Chao** - *San Lorenzo* *Honduras* Official number: L-1823107	*180* 82 -		**1985 Suao Shipbuilding Co., Ltd. — Suao** L reg 28.18 Br ex - Dght 1.100 Lbp 33.15 Br md 6.00 Dpth 2.90 Welded, 1 dk	**(B11B2FV) Fishing Vessel**	**1 oil engine** driving 1 FP propeller Total Power: 625kW (850hp) 12.0kn
9642148 *3EUN4* -	**TAI SUCCESS** - **Tai Shing Maritime Co SA** Taiwan Navigation Co Ltd *Panama* *Panama* MMSI: 371651000 Official number: 44212TT	**34,775** 20,098 61,486 T/cm 61.4	Class: AB (BV)	**2013-03 Shin Kasado Dockyard Co Ltd — Kudamatsu YC** Yd No: K-041 Loa 199.98 (BB) Br ex - Dght 12.960 Lbp 195.00 Br md 32.24 Dpth 18.60 Welded, 1 dk	**(A21A2BC) Bulk Carrier** Grain: 77,674; Bale: 73,552 Compartments: 5 Ho, ER 5 Ha: 4 (23.5 x 19.0)ER (18.7 x 19.0) Cranes: 4x30.5t	**1 oil engine** driving 1 FP propeller Total Power: 8,450kW (11,489hp) 14.5kn MAN-B&W 6S50MC-C 1 x 2 Stroke 6 Cy. 500 x 2000 8450kW (11489bhp) Mitsui Engineering & Shipbuilding CLtd-Japan AuxGen: 3 x 550kW a.c Fuel: 210.0 (d.f.) 2437.0 (r.f.)
7853327 - -	**TAI WA** *ex* Taiwa Maru *-1993* - -	*499* 380 1,200		**1977 Kogushi Zosen K.K. — Okayama** Loa 62.90 Br ex - Dght 4.250 Lbp 57.99 Br md 10.00 Dpth 4.50 Welded, 1 dk	**(A12A2TC) Chemical Tanker**	**1 oil engine** driving 1 FP propeller Total Power: 883kW (1,201hp) 11.5kn Hanshin 6LU28 1 x 4 Stroke 6 Cy. 280 x 440 883kW (1201bhp) The Hanshin Diesel Works Ltd-Japan
9440227 *VRDE8* -	**TAI WO** - **Easy Sky Shipping Ltd** Shanghai Dongzhan Shipping Co Ltd *Hong Kong* *Hong Kong* MMSI: 477036900 Official number: HK-1982	**3,763** 1,227 4,999	Class: CC	**2008-02 Ningbo Dongfang Shipyard Co Ltd — Ningbo ZJ** Yd No: C06-022 Loa 101.90 Br ex - Dght 5.900 Lbp 96.00 Br md 16.00 Dpth 8.00 Welded, 1 dk	**(A13C2LA) Asphalt/Bitumen Tanker** Double Hull (13F) Liq (Gas): 4,525 Compartments: 10 Wing Ta, 2 Wing Slop Ta, ER Ice Capable	**1 oil engine** reduction geared to sc. shaft driving 1 FP propeller Total Power: 2,060kW (2,801hp) 11.5kn Guangzhou 8320ZC 1 x 4 Stroke 8 Cy. 320 x 440 2060kW (2801bhp) Guangzhou Diesel Engine Factory CoLtd-China AuxGen: 2 x 250kW 400V a.c
8966406 *BR2039* -	**TAI WU** - **Kinmen County Bus & Ferry Management Office** Wujiang Ferry Co Ltd *Kaohsiung* *Chinese Taipei* MMSI: 416900070 Official number: 13361	**198** 74 46	Class: CR	**1997-12 Jong Shyn Shipbuilding Co., Ltd. — Kaohsiung** Loa 32.95 Br ex 8.38 Dght 1.700 Lbp 29.60 Br md 8.20 Dpth 2.80 Welded, 1 dk	**(A37B2PS) Passenger Ship**	**2 oil engines** reduction geared to sc. shafts driving 2 FP propellers Total Power: 1,214kW (1,650hp) 13.0kn Caterpillar 3412TA 2 x Vee 4 Stroke 12 Cy. 137 x 152 each-607kW (825bhp) Caterpillar Inc-USA AuxGen: 2 x 99kW 220V a.c
9005625 *BAPI* -	**TAI XIANG** *ex* Maya *-2003* **Liaoning Province Dalian Ocean Fishery Group Corp** - *Dalian, Liaoning* *China* MMSI: 412203740	**1,950** 631 1,950	Class: CC (NK)	**1991-02 Nakatani Shipyard Co. Ltd. — Etajima** Yd No: 533 Loa 84.02 (BB) Br ex - Dght 4.271 Lbp 78.00 Br md 13.00 Dpth 4.30 Welded, 2 dks	**(A34A2GR) Refrigerated Cargo Ship** Ins: 2,586 Compartments: 2 Ho, ER, 2 Tw Dk	**1 oil engine** driving 1 FP propeller Total Power: 1,471kW (2,000hp) 12.1kn Hanshin 6EL32 1 x 4 Stroke 6 Cy. 320 x 640 1471kW (2000bhp) The Hanshin Diesel Works Ltd-Japan AuxGen: 2 x 320kW a.c
8514485 *XUJM7* -	**TAI XIANG** *ex* Seiun Maru No. 8 *-2002* **Yong Run Shipping Co Ltd** Dalian Yanping Shipping Management Co Ltd *Phnom Penh* *Cambodia* MMSI: 515863000 Official number: 0585132	**1,341** 717 1,580	Class: UB	**1985-10 Yamanaka Zosen K.K. — Imabari** Yd No: 316 Loa 73.31 (BB) Br ex - Dght 4.252 Lbp 68.00 Br md 11.51 Dpth 6.91 Welded, 2 dks	**(A31A2GX) General Cargo Ship** Grain: 2,636; Bale: 2,563 Compartments: 1 Ho, ER 1 Ha: ER	**1 oil engine** with clutches, flexible couplings & sr reverse geared to sc. shaft driving 1 FP propeller Total Power: 1,030kW (1,400hp) Hanshin 6LUN28ARG 1 x 4 Stroke 6 Cy. 280 x 480 1030kW (1400bhp) The Hanshin Diesel Works Ltd-Japan
8626719 *XUBT5* -	**TAI XIANG 2** *ex* Rich Star *-2014* *ex* Kyokuzan *-2009* **Zhongtai Shipping Ltd** Yan Ping Shipping (HK) Co Ltd *Phnom Penh* *Cambodia* MMSI: 515359000 Official number: 1085569	**1,385** 569 1,550	Class: UB (BV)	**1985 Yamanaka Zosen K.K. — Imabari** Loa 73.00 Br ex - Dght 4.231 Lbp 68.00 Br md 11.51 Dpth 6.91 Welded, 1 dk	**(A31A2GX) General Cargo Ship** Grain: 2,468; Bale: 2,419	**1 oil engine** reduction geared to sc. shaft driving 1 FP propeller Total Power: 1,030kW (1,400hp) 10.5kn Hanshin 6LUN28ARG 1 x 4 Stroke 6 Cy. 280 x 480 1030kW (1400bhp) The Hanshin Diesel Works Ltd-Japan
9088598 *XUQW7* -	**TAI XIN** *ex* Fukuyama Maru No. 31 *-2009* **XinHai Shipping Co Ltd** Yuan Da Shipping Co Ltd *Phnom Penh* *Cambodia* MMSI: 515185000 Official number: 0994243	**1,496** 845 1,600	Class: UB	**1994-06 Shinhama Dockyard Co. Ltd. — Anan** Yd No: 836 Loa 75.22 Br ex - Dght - Lbp 71.93 Br md 12.00 Dpth 7.10 Welded, 1 dk	**(A31A2GX) General Cargo Ship** Grain: 2,607; Bale: 2,596 Compartments: 1 Ho 1 Ha: (40.2 x 9.5)	**1 oil engine** reverse geared to sc. shaft driving 1 FP propeller Total Power: 736kW (1,001hp) 11.0kn Akasaka A31R 1 x 4 Stroke 6 Cy. 310 x 600 736kW (1001bhp) Akasaka Tekkosho KK (Akasaka DieselLtd)-Japan Fuel: 93.0 (d.f.)
8210273 *T3AL2* -	**TAI XING** *ex* World Mora *-1995* *ex* World Fontaine *-1992* **Shandong Zhonglu Fishery Shipping Co Ltd** - *Tarawa* *Kiribati* MMSI: 529445000	**3,218** 1,545 5,956	Class: CC (NK)	**1982-10 Kochi Jyuko (Eiho Zosen) K.K. — Kochi** Yd No: 1548 Loa 91.50 (BB) Br ex - Dght 6.550 Lbp 85.00 Br md 16.20 Dpth 9.50 Welded, 3 dks	**(A34A2GR) Refrigerated Cargo Ship** Ins: 4,332 Compartments: 3 Ho, ER 3 Ha: 3 (5.0 x 5.1)ER Derricks: 6x4t	**1 oil engine** driving 1 FP propeller Total Power: 3,310kW (4,500hp) 14.5kn Hanshin 6ELS44 1 x 4 Stroke 6 Cy. 440 x 880 3310kW (4500bhp) The Hanshin Diesel Works Ltd-Japan AuxGen: 2 x 560kW 450V 60Hz a.c Fuel: 116.0 (d.f.) 577.5 (r.f.) 13.5pd
8838465 - -	**TAI YANG No. 1** *ex* Koryo Maru No. 5 *-1996* *ex* Shinkai Maru No. 25 *-1992* *ex* Shinsei Maru No. 25 *-1992* **Chosei S de RL** - *San Lorenzo* *Honduras* Official number: L-0326609	**190** 57 -		**1978 Fujishin Zosen K.K. — Kamo** L reg 30.10 Br ex - Dght 2.100 Lbp 31.28 Br md 5.85 Dpth 2.65 Welded, 1 dk	**(B11B2FV) Fishing Vessel**	**1 oil engine** driving 1 FP propeller Total Power: 294kW (400hp) Hanshin 1 x 4 Stroke 294kW (400bhp) The Hanshin Diesel Works Ltd-Japan
9009592 *BNIE* -	**TAI YI** *ex* Ryuyo Maru *-2006* **Taiwan Fuel & Energy Supply Co Ltd** - SatCom: Inmarsat Mini-M 763931259 *Taichung* *Chinese Taipei* MMSI: 416382000 Official number: 14383	**738** 309 1,026	Class: CR	**1990-12 Ishii Zosen K.K. — Futtsu** Yd No: 267 Loa 65.00 (BB) Br ex - Dght 4.151 Lbp 60.05 Br md 10.00 Dpth 4.40 Welded, 1 dk	**(A13B2TP) Products Tanker** Liq: 1,187; Liq (Oil): 1,187 Compartments: 8 Ta, ER 1 Cargo Pump (s): 1x500m³/hr	**1 oil engine** with clutches & reverse geared to sc. shaft driving 1 FP propeller Total Power: 1,030kW (1,400hp) 11.4kn Yanmar MF29-UT 1 x 4 Stroke 6 Cy. 290 x 520 1030kW (1400bhp) Matsue Diesel KK-Japan Fuel: 14.0 (d.f.) 50.0 (r.f.)
9136503 *V3NW4* -	**TAI YIN** *ex* Calm Ocean *-2011* *ex* Kami Maru 1 *-2009* **Senior Master Shipping Co Ltd** Senior Master International Ship Management Co Ltd SatCom: Inmarsat C 431256910 *Belize City* *Belize* MMSI: 312569000 Official number: 610920001	**1,482** 824 1,415	Class: IT	**1995-11 Hitachi Zosen Mukaishima Marine Co Ltd — Onomichi HS** Yd No: 102 Loa 67.91 Br ex - Dght 4.040 Lbp 67.50 Br md 12.00 Dpth 7.00 Welded, 1 dk	**(A31A2GX) General Cargo Ship**	**1 oil engine** driving 1 FP propeller Total Power: 1,471kW (2,000hp) 10.0kn Makita LN33L 1 x 4 Stroke 6 Cy. 330 x 640 1471kW (2000bhp) Makita Corp-Japan
8838611 - -	**TAI YIN** *ex* Yung Chang No. 606 *-2001* *ex* Kosei Maru No. 36 *-1997* *ex* Ichi Maru No. 8 *-1997* **Shandong Zhonglu Oceanic Fisheries Co Ltd** -	**193** 69 -		**1979 Minami-Kyushu Zosen KK — Ichikikushikino KS** L reg 30.10 Br ex - Dght 2.000 Lbp - Br md 6.20 Dpth 2.50 Welded, 1 dk	**(B11B2FV) Fishing Vessel**	**1 oil engine** driving 1 FP propeller Total Power: 272kW (370hp) Otsuka 1 x 4 Stroke 272kW (370bhp) KK Otsuka Diesel-Japan
8303678 *DSDQ7* -	**TAI YOUNG JASMIN** *ex* Stork Voyager *-1994* **Han Il Leasing Co Ltd** Taiyoung Shipping Co Ltd *Busan* *South Korea* Official number: BSR-941136	**2,483** 1,568 4,503	Class: (KR) (NK)	**1983-08 Honda Zosen — Saiki** Yd No: 714 Loa 94.75 Br ex - Dght 5.503 Lbp 88.02 Br md 15.82 Dpth 6.91 Welded, 1 dk	**(A31A2GX) General Cargo Ship** Grain: 5,466; Bale: 4,904 Compartments: 2 Ho, ER 2 Ha: 2 (21.0 x 8.4)ER Derricks: 2x20t,2x15t; Winches: 4	**1 oil engine** driving 1 FP propeller Total Power: 2,059kW (2,799hp) 12.0kn Hanshin 6EL38 1 x 4 Stroke 6 Cy. 380 x 760 2059kW (2799bhp) The Hanshin Diesel Works Ltd-Japan AuxGen: 2 x 88kW
8810657 *BAIL* -	**TAI YU** *ex* Tairyu *-1998* *ex* Arizona Maru *-1993* **Liaoning Province Dalian Ocean Fishery Group Corp** - SatCom: Inmarsat C 450301950 *Dalian, Liaoning* *China* MMSI: 412202350	**1,912** 652 1,930	Class: CC (NK)	**1989-01 Teraoka Shipyard Co Ltd — Minamiawaji HG** Yd No: 275 Loa 84.33 Br ex - Dght 4.271 Lbp 78.00 Br md 13.00 Dpth 7.40 Welded	**(A34A2GR) Refrigerated Cargo Ship** Ins: 2,596 4 Ha: 4 (7.0 x 6.0)ER Derricks: 4x3t	**1 oil engine** driving 1 FP propeller Total Power: 1,471kW (2,000hp) 12.0kn Akasaka A34 1 x 4 Stroke 6 Cy. 340 x 660 1471kW (2000bhp) Akasaka Tekkosho KK (Akasaka DieselLtd)-Japan

8953095 - -	**TAI-YU 8** - **Desarrollo Pesquero SA** - *San Lorenzo* *Honduras* Official number: L-1927230	**528** 260 -		**1987 San Yang Shipbuilding Co., Ltd. — Kaohsiung** L reg 58.75 Br ex - Dght - Lbp - Br md 9.36 Dpth 4.36 Welded, 1 dk	**(B11B2FV) Fishing Vessel**	**1 oil engine** driving 1 FP propeller Total Power: 1,119kW (1,521hp) Daihatsu 1 x 4 Stroke 1119kW (1521bhp) Daihatsu Diesel Manufacturing Co Lt-Japan
9379222 *V3GH2* -	**TAI YUAN** - **Tai Yuan (Hong Kong) International Shipping Co Ltd** Yun Xing Shipping Co Ltd *Belize City* *Belize* MMSI: 312431000 Official number: 060620734	**1,972** 1,410 3,357	Class: BV (CC)	**2006-09 Rushan Shipbuilding Co Ltd — Rushan SD** Yd No: SRC8030-03 Loa 81.20 (BB) Br ex - Dght 5.500 Lbp 76.00 Br md 13.60 Dpth 6.80 Welded, 1 dk	**(A31A2GX) General Cargo Ship** Bale: 4,541 Compartments: 2 Ho, ER 2 Ha: ER 2 (18.6 x 9.0) Ice Capable	**1 oil engine** reduction geared to sc. shaft driving 1 FP propeller Total Power: 1,323kW (1,799hp) 12.0kn Hanshin LH31G 1 x 4 Stroke 6 Cy. 310 x 530 1323kW (1799bhp) The Hanshin Diesel Works Ltd-Japan AuxGen: 2 x 120kW 400V a.c Fuel: 160.0
8431011 - -	**TAI YUAN HUNG** - **Tai Shyun Fishery Co Ltd** - *San Lorenzo* *Honduras* Official number: L-1823004	*462* 163 -		**1989 Sen Koh Shipbuilding Corp — Kaohsiung** L reg 42.88 Br ex - Dght - Lbp - Br md 8.00 Dpth 3.50 Welded, 1 dk	**(B11B2FV) Fishing Vessel**	**1 oil engine** driving 1 FP propeller Total Power: 809kW (1,100hp) 13.0kn
7915993 *BXEQ* -	**TAI ZHOU** *ex Dynamic LP -1996* **Government of The People's Republic of China (The Chemical Industry & Petroleum Gas Co)** - *Shantou, Guangdong* *China*	**775** 434 721	Class: CC (NK)	**1979-11 Kochi Jyuko (Eiho Zosen) K.K. — Kochi** Yd No: 1334 Loa 58.32 Br ex 10.22 Dght 4.022 Lbp 53.52 Br md 10.20 Dpth 4.58 Welded, 1 dk	**(A11B2TG) LPG Tanker** Liq (Gas): 1,191 2 x Gas Tank (s);	**1 oil engine** geared to sc. shaft driving 1 FP propeller Total Power: 1,324kW (1,800hp) 12.0kn Hanshin 6LU35G 1 x 4 Stroke 6 Cy. 350 x 550 1324kW (1800bhp) The Hanshin Diesel Works Ltd-Japan AuxGen: 2 x 288kW
7708807 *D6A2018* -	**TAIBA** *ex African Warrior II -2008 ex Frio Ionian -2005* *ex Frio Monaco -1996 ex Souss -1994* - - *Union of Comoros*	**4,033** 1,209 4,193	Class: IS (BV)	**1978-03 Miho Zosensho K.K. — Shimizu** Yd No: 1070 Converted From: Refrigerated Cargo Ship-2010 Loa 105.01 (BB) Br ex - Dght 6.562 Lbp 97.01 Br md 16.01 Dpth 9.56 Welded, 1 dk	**(A38A2GL) Livestock Carrier**	**1 oil engine** driving 1 FP propeller Total Power: 4,781kW (6,500hp) 16.5kn Hanshin 6LUS58 1 x 4 Stroke 6 Cy. 580 x 1050 4781kW (6500bhp) The Hanshin Diesel Works Ltd-Japan AuxGen: 3 x 400kW 445V 60Hz a.c Fuel: 153.0 (d.f.) (Heating Coils) 76.0 (r.f.) 18.0pd
9036090 - -	**TAIBA** *ex Alica -1994* - - -	*171* 51 330	Class: (BV)	**1990 Stocznia 'Wisla' — Gdansk** Yd No: 1101 Loa 25.71 Br ex - Dght 3.682 Lbp 22.46 Br md 7.41 Dpth 4.02 Welded	**(B11A2FS) Stern Trawler**	**1 oil engine** driving 1 CP propeller Total Power: 420kW (571hp) 9.0kn MAN D2842LE 1 x Vee 4 Stroke 12 Cy. 128 x 142 420kW (571bhp) MAN Nutzfahrzeuge AG-Nuernberg AuxGen: 2 x 168kW 440V 50Hz a.c
9203930 *HZQJ* -	**TAIBAH** - **Al Tawba International Navigation Co** Bakri Navigation Co Ltd *Dammam* *Saudi Arabia* MMSI: 403545000	**28,981** 11,678 44,954 T/cm 51.1	Class: NV	**2000-05 Hanjin Heavy Industries & Construction Co Ltd — Busan** Yd No: 066 Loa 183.20 (BB) Br ex 32.23 Dght 12.167 Lbp 174.45 Br md 32.20 Dpth 18.90 Welded, 1 dk	**(A12A2TC) Chemical Tanker** Double Hull (13F) Liq: 53,498 Compartments: 23 Ta, 1 Slop Ta, ER 22 Cargo Pump (s): 20x600m³/hr, 2x300m³/hr Manifold: Bow/CM: 96.7m	**1 oil engine** driving 1 FP propeller Total Power: 9,480kW (12,889hp) 14.5kn B&W 6S50MC-C 1 x 2 Stroke 6 Cy. 500 x 2000 9480kW (12889bhp) Hyundai Heavy Industries Co Ltd-South Korea AuxGen: 3 x 1080kW Fuel: 278.0 (d.f.) 2015.0 (r.f.)
8921365 *JLJU* HK1-1167	**TAICHU MARU No. 28** - **Kurokawa Suisan KK** - *Wakkanai, Hokkaido* *Japan* Official number: 128593	*160* - -		**1990-02 Narasaki Zosen KK — Muroran HK** Yd No: 1112 Loa 38.12 (BB) Br ex - Dght 3.336 Lbp 31.50 Br md 7.40 Dpth 4.61 Welded, 1 dk	**(B11A2FS) Stern Trawler** Ins: 136	**1 oil engine** with clutches, flexible couplings & sr geared to sc. shaft driving 1 CP propeller Total Power: 1,030kW (1,400hp) Akasaka 6U28 1 x 4 Stroke 6 Cy. 280 x 340 1030kW (1400bhp) Akasaka Tekkosho KK (Akasaka DieselLtd)-Japan
9674505 *JD3518* -	**TAIEI MARU** - **Japan Railway Construction, Transport & Technology Agency & Eikichi Kaiun KK** Eikichi Kaiun KK *Tamano, Okayama* *Japan* Official number: 141925	**499** - 1,670		**2013-04 Yamanaka Zosen K.K. — Imabari** Yd No: 836 Loa 75.24 Br ex - Dght 4.150 Lbp - Br md 12.00 Dpth 7.12 Welded, 1 dk	**(A31A2GX) General Cargo Ship** Grain: 2,936; Bale: 2,852	**1 oil engine** driving 1 Propeller Total Power: 1,323kW (1,799hp) Niigata 6M31NT 1 x 4 Stroke 6 Cy. 310 x 600 1323kW (1799bhp) Niigata Engineering Co Ltd-Japan
9124811 *JL6390* -	**TAIEI MARU No. 11** - **Otsu Kaiun YK** - *Anan, Tokushima* *Japan* Official number: 135074	*499* - 1,490		**1995-06 K.K. Miura Zosensho — Saiki** Yd No: 1126 Loa 75.50 Br ex - Dght 4.030 Lbp 70.00 Br md 12.50 Dpth 6.90 Welded, 1 dk	**(A31A2GX) General Cargo Ship** Compartments: 1 Ho 1 Ha: (38.4 x 10.1)	**1 oil engine** driving 1 FP propeller Total Power: 736kW (1,001hp) 11.0kn Hanshin LH34LAG 1 x 4 Stroke 6 Cy. 340 x 640 736kW (1001bhp) The Hanshin Diesel Works Ltd-Japan
8748751 *BZS02* -	**TAIFU 101** *ex Hong Fu 308 -2011 ex Hong Fu 303 -2011* **Shandong Oceanic Fisheries Co Ltd** Shandong Zhonglu Fishery Shipping Co Ltd *Qingdao, Shandong* *China* Official number: YQ020J010133	**1,152** 345 -		**1987-09 Fong Kuo Shipbuilding Co Ltd — Kaohsiung** Yd No: 249 Loa 64.70 Br ex - Dght - Lbp - Br md 12.20 Dpth - Welded, 1 dk	**(B11B2FV) Fishing Vessel**	**1 oil engine** reduction geared to sc. shaft driving 1 Propeller Total Power: 2,645kW (3,596hp) Daihatsu 8DKM-32 1 x 4 Stroke 8 Cy. 320 x 360 2645kW (3596bhp) Daihatsu Diesel Manufacturing Co Lt-Japan
8663365 *BHUG* -	**TAIFU SHIPPING NO. 1** - **Zhangjiagang Zhongyou Futai Shipping Co Ltd** - *Zhangjiagang, Jiangsu* *China* Official number: 060211000005	**3,659** 2,049 5,000		**2011-01 Jiangsu Longhai Shipbuilding Co Ltd — Jiangdu JS** Yd No: 2011S0000060 Loa 104.60 Br ex - Dght 5.600 Lbp 96.58 Br md 17.40 Dpth 7.80 Welded, 1 dk	**(A13B2TP) Products Tanker**	**1 oil engine** driving 1 FP propeller Total Power: 2,206kW (2,999hp) Chinese Std. Type 1 x 2206kW (2999bhp) Ningbo CSI Power & Machinery GroupCo Ltd-China
8845171 *YQHJ* -	**TAIFUNS 1** *ex Taifuns -2012 ex Tayfun -1992* **SC Pro West Investment Srl** - *Romania* MMSI: 264900254	**180** 54 46	Class: (RS)	**1972 "Petrozavod" — Leningrad** Yd No: 815 Loa 29.30 Br ex 8.49 Dght 3.900 Lbp 27.65 Br md 8.30 Dpth 4.34 Welded, 1 dk	**(B32A2ST) Tug** Ice Capable	**2 oil engines** driving 2 CP propellers Total Power: 882kW (1,200hp) 11.4kn Russkiy 6D30/50-4-2 2 x 2 Stroke 6 Cy. 300 x 500 each-441kW (600bhp) Mashinostroitelnyy Zavod"Russkiy-Dizel"-Leningrad AuxGen: 2 x 25kW a.c Fuel: 43.0 (d.f.)
9339973 *3EJT8* -	**TAIGA** - **Esteem Maritime** MMS Co Ltd SatCom: Inmarsat Mini-M 761119561 *Panama* *Panama* MMSI: 372618000 Official number: 3265007A	**160,109** 103,527 311,141 T/cm 183.9	Class: NK	**2007-03 Mitsui Eng. & SB. Co. Ltd., Chiba Works — Ichihara** Yd No: 1669 Loa 333.00 (BB) Br ex 60.04 Dght 20.943 Lbp 324.00 Br md 60.00 Dpth 28.80 Welded, 1 dk	**(A13A2TV) Crude Oil Tanker** Double Hull (13F) Liq: 339,586; Liq (Oil): 347,656 Compartments: 5 Ta, 10 Wing Ta, 2 Wing Slop Ta, ER 3 Cargo Pump (s): 3x5500m³/hr Manifold: Bow/CM: 167.3m	**1 oil engine** driving 1 FP propeller Total Power: 27,160kW (36,927hp) 15.7kn MAN-B&W 7S80MC-C 1 x 2 Stroke 7 Cy. 800 x 3200 27160kW (36927bhp) Mitsui Engineering & Shipbuilding CLtd-Japan AuxGen: 2 x 1050kW 440V 60Hz a.c, 1 x 1050kW 440V 50Hz a.c Fuel: 525.0 (d.f.) 8100.0 (r.f.)
7950668 - -	**TAIGEN MARU No. 28** - - -	*433* 229 -		**1975-04 K.K. Murakami Zosensho — Ishinomaki** L reg 51.79 Br ex - Dght - Lbp - Br md 9.20 Dpth 4.02 Welded, 1 dk	**(B11B2FV) Fishing Vessel**	**1 oil engine** driving 1 FP propeller Total Power: 1,324kW (1,800hp) Hanshin 6LU35 1 x 4 Stroke 6 Cy. 350 x 550 1324kW (1800bhp) The Hanshin Diesel Works Ltd-Japan
8863604 *HO3922* -	**TAIHAI 6** *ex Min Hai 452 -2008* **Fuzhou Taihai Shipping Co Ltd** - *Panama* *Panama* MMSI: 371029000 Official number: 3461009A	**1,466** 815 2,145	Class: IT (CC)	**1992-01 Jiangsu Jiangyang Shipyard Group Co Ltd — Yangzhou JS** Loa 71.53 Br ex - Dght 4.800 Lbp 66.00 Br md 12.50 Dpth 6.00 Welded, 1 dk	**(A21A2BC) Bulk Carrier** Grain: 2,916; Bale: 2,738 Compartments: 2 Ho, ER 2 Ha: 2 (13.2 x 7.0)ER Cranes: 4x2t	**1 oil engine** geared to sc. shaft driving 1 FP propeller Total Power: 971kW (1,320hp) 10.5kn Chinese Std. Type 6320ZCD 1 x 4 Stroke 6 Cy. 320 x 440 971kW (1320bhp) (made 1990) Guangzhou Diesel Engine Factory CoLtd-China AuxGen: 3 x 75kW 400V a.c
7823475 *9V3943* -	**TAIHEI** *ex Taihei Maru -1997* **EM (Far East) Holdings Pte Ltd** East Marine Pte Ltd *Singapore* *Singapore* MMSI: 564887000 Official number: 385932	**312** 94 148	Class: BV (GL)	**1979-03 Kanrei Zosen K.K. — Naruto** Yd No: 278 Loa 33.10 Br ex - Dght 3.100 Lbp 29.49 Br md 8.21 Dpth 3.71 Riveted\Welded, 1 dk	**(B34P2QV) Salvage Ship**	**2 oil engines** reduction geared to sc. shafts driving 2 FP propellers Total Power: 1,912kW (2,600hp) 10.0kn Daihatsu 6DSM-26 2 x 4 Stroke 6 Cy. 260 x 320 each-956kW (1300bhp) Daihatsu Diesel Manufacturing Co Lt-Japan AuxGen: 1 x 118kW 50Hz a.c

8859287 **TAIHEI MARU** *158*
JI3425 -
- **Ikeda Shoji KK** 330
Katsuura, Chiba *Japan*
Official number: 131667
1991-12 **Hongawara Zosen K.K. — Fukuyama**
Yd No: 357
Loa 39.74 Br ex - Dght 2.990
Lbp 36.00 Br md 7.20 Dpth 3.10
Welded, 1 dk
(A13B2TU) Tanker (unspecified)
Liq: 376; Liq (Oil): 376
1 Cargo Pump (s): 1x300m³/hr
1 oil engine driving 1 FP propeller
Total Power: 353kW (480hp) 9.0kn
Yanmar 6MAL-HTS
1 x 4 Stroke 6 Cy. 200 x 240 353kW (480bhp)
Yanmar Diesel Engine Co Ltd-Japan

8890085 **TAIHEI MARU** *499*
JK5319 -
- **Daio Shoun KK** -
Nakano Lines Ltd (Nakano Kaiun KK)
Shunan, Yamaguchi *Japan*
Official number: 134782
1995-09 **Yamanaka Zosen K.K. — Imabari**
Yd No: 581
L reg 72.00 Br ex - Dght -
Lbp - Br md 12.00 Dpth 7.00
Welded, 1 dk
(A31A2GX) General Cargo Ship
1 oil engine driving 1 FP propeller
Total Power: 1,471kW (2,000hp) 13.0kn
Hanshin LH36LA
1 x 4 Stroke 6 Cy. 360 x 670 1471kW (2000bhp)
The Hanshin Diesel Works Ltd-Japan

9092472 **TAIHEI MARU** **146**
- 25
- **Mazuda International Inc** -
-
1986-11 **Sakamoto Zosensho — Nandan**
L reg 22.50 Br ex - Dght -
Lbp - Br md 6.50 Dpth 3.00
Welded, 1 dk
(B32A2ST) Tug
2 oil engines driving 2 Propellers
Total Power: 1,028kW (1,398hp)
Niigata 6MG20AX
2 x 4 Stroke 6 Cy. 200 x 260 each-514kW (699bhp)
Niigata Engineering Co Ltd-Japan

9042922 **TAIHEI MARU** *498*
JM6135 -
- **Ogata Kaiun YK** 1,326
-
Hofu, Yamaguchi *Japan*
Official number: 133463
1992-12 **K.K. Saidaiji Zosensho — Okayama**
Yd No: 182
Loa 72.70 Br ex - Dght 3.350
Lbp 70.00 Br md 12.70 Dpth 6.00
Welded, 1 dk
(A31A2GX) General Cargo Ship
1 oil engine driving 1 FP propeller
Total Power: 1,692kW (2,300hp)
Akasaka DM38AK
1 x 4 Stroke 6 Cy. 380 x 600 1692kW (2300bhp)
Akasaka Tekkosho KK (Akasaka DieselLtd)-Japan

9011430 **TAIHEI MARU** *199*
JI3452 -
- **Yoshiharu Ota** 700
-
Kaminoseki, Yamaguchi *Japan*
Official number: 131702
1991-02 **Taiyo Shipbuilding Co Ltd — Sanyoonoda YC** Yd No: 223
Loa - Br ex - Dght 3.301
Lbp 50.22 Br md 9.42 Dpth 5.52
Welded
(A31A2GX) General Cargo Ship
Bale: 1,148
Compartments: 1 Ho, ER
1 Ha: ER
1 oil engine with clutches & geared to sc. shaft driving 1 FP propeller
Total Power: 662kW (900hp)
Hanshin LH26G
1 x 4 Stroke 6 Cy. 260 x 440 662kW (900bhp)
The Hanshin Diesel Works Ltd-Japan

9197258 **TAIHEI MARU** *499*
JM6564 -
- **YK Nangoku Jari** 1,500
-
Kagoshima, Kagoshima *Japan*
Official number: 135432
1998-05 **Yamakawa Zosen Tekko K.K. — Kagoshima** Yd No: 758
Loa 67.75 Br ex - Dght 4.300
Lbp 62.00 Br md 13.30 Dpth 7.00
Welded, 1 dk
(A31A2GX) General Cargo Ship
1 oil engine driving 1 FP propeller
Total Power: 1,471kW (2,000hp) 11.5kn
Niigata 6M34BGT
1 x 4 Stroke 6 Cy. 340 x 620 1471kW (2000bhp)
Niigata Engineering Co Ltd-Japan

9207144 **TAIHEI MARU** *749* Class: NK
JG5546 -
- **Iino Gas Transport Co Ltd** 1,100
Kobe, Hyogo *Japan*
MMSI: 431301369
Official number: 136715
1999-04 **K.K. Miura Zosensho — Saiki** Yd No: 1218
Loa 61.95 Br ex - Dght 4.250
Lbp 58.00 Br md 11.50 Dpth 5.10
Welded, 1 dk
(A11B2TG) LPG Tanker
Liq (Gas): 1,310
2 x Gas Tank (s);
1 oil engine driving 1 FP propeller
Total Power: 1,471kW (2,000hp) 12.0kn
Hanshin LH34LG
1 x 4 Stroke 6 Cy. 340 x 640 1471kW (2000bhp)
The Hanshin Diesel Works Ltd-Japan
Fuel: 170.0 (d.f.) 8.3pd

9078957 **TAIHEIZAN MARU** *437*
JK5302 -
- **Taihei Kaiun YK** 1,254
-
Kaminoseki, Yamaguchi *Japan*
Official number: 134082
1994-03 **Taiyo Shipbuilding Co Ltd — Sanyoonoda YC** Yd No: 251
Loa 68.62 (BB) Br ex - Dght 4.000
Lbp 62.00 Br md 11.00 Dpth 6.30
Welded, 1 dk
(A31A2GX) General Cargo Ship
Grain: 2,002
Compartments: 1 Ho, ER
1 Ha: ER
1 oil engine driving 1 FP propeller
Total Power: 735kW (999hp)
Niigata 6M28BGT
1 x 4 Stroke 6 Cy. 280 x 480 735kW (999bhp)
Niigata Engineering Co Ltd-Japan
Thrusters: 1 Thwart. FP thruster (f)

8032762 **TAIHO GO No. 58** *483*
JH2902 *ex* Hashimoto Maru *-1999* -
- **Hirao Kensetsu KK** -
-
Iki, Nagasaki *Japan*
Official number: 124405
1980-11 **Yaizu Dock — Yaizu** Yd No: 53
Loa 36.00 Br ex - Dght -
Lbp 34.50 Br md 14.30 Dpth 2.80
Welded, 1 dk
(B34B2SC) Crane Vessel
2 oil engines driving 2 FP propellers
Total Power: 442kW (600hp) 7.5kn
Yanmar
2 x 4 Stroke each-221kW (300bhp)
Yanmar Diesel Engine Co Ltd-Japan

9047192 **TAIHO MARU** *3,542* Class: NK
JI3480 -
- **Taiyo Shipping Co Ltd (Taiyo Kisen KK)** 5,618
Osaka, Osaka *Japan*
MMSI: 431300536
Official number: 133391
1992-04 **Nishi Shipbuilding Co Ltd — Imabari EH**
Yd No: 370
Loa 93.05 Br ex - Dght 6.943
Lbp 88.00 Br md 16.30 Dpth 8.25
Welded, 1 dk
(A24A2BT) Cement Carrier
Grain: 4,690; Bale: 4,690
Compartments: 12 Ho, ER
1 oil engine reverse geared to sc. shaft driving 1 CP propeller
Total Power: 3,089kW (4,200hp) 12.5kn
Mitsubishi 6UEC37LA
1 x 2 Stroke 6 Cy. 370 x 880 3089kW (4200bhp)
Akasaka Tekkosho KK (Akasaka DieselLtd)-Japan
AuxGen: 3 x 300kW a.c
Fuel: 250.0 (r.f.)

9016208 **TAIHO MARU** *195*
JJ3687 *ex* Kiho Maru *-2010* -
- **Ueda Eisen Unyu KK** -
-
Tamano, Okayama *Japan*
Official number: 129273
1991-01 **Kanagawa Zosen — Kobe** Yd No: 353
L reg 29.00 Br ex - Dght -
Lbp - Br md 9.20 Dpth 4.10
Welded
(B32A2ST) Tug
2 oil engines driving 2 FP propellers
Total Power: 2,648kW (3,600hp)
Daihatsu 6DLM-28S
2 x 4 Stroke 6 Cy. 280 x 360 each-1324kW (1800bhp)
Daihatsu Diesel Manufacturing Co Lt-Japan

9093232 **TAIHO MARU** *498*
JD2242 -
- **Taiho Kaiun YK** 1,800
-
Minamiawaji, Hyogo *Japan*
Official number: 140311
2006-04 **Tokuoka Zosen K.K. — Naruto** Yd No: 288
Loa 74.95 Br ex - Dght 4.470
Lbp 69.00 Br md 11.80 Dpth 7.55
Welded, 1 dk
(A31A2GX) General Cargo Ship
Grain: 2,557
1 oil engine driving 1 Propeller
Total Power: 1,618kW (2,200hp) 12.0kn
Niigata 6M34BGT
1 x 4 Stroke 6 Cy. 340 x 620 1618kW (2200bhp)
Niigata Engineering Co Ltd-Japan

9136814 **TAIHO MARU** *498*
JM6358 -
- **Furukawa Kaiun YK** 1,550
-
Sasebo, Nagasaki *Japan*
Official number: 134596
1995-11 **Sanyo Zosen K.K. — Onomichi**
Yd No: 1068
Loa 72.10 (BB) Br ex - Dght 4.300
Lbp 65.00 Br md 12.70 Dpth 7.25
Welded, 1 dk
(A31A2GX) General Cargo Ship
Grain: 1,327
Compartments: 1 Ho, ER
1 Ha: ER
1 oil engine driving 1 FP propeller
Total Power: 736kW (1,001hp)
Akasaka A34
1 x 4 Stroke 6 Cy. 340 x 660 736kW (1001bhp)
Akasaka Tekkosho KK (Akasaka DieselLtd)-Japan
Thrusters: 1 Thwart. FP thruster (f)

9140358 **TAIHO MARU** **40,322** Class: NK
3FMP6 13,245
- **Ocean Woodland Shipping Co Ltd** 48,817
Universal Marine Corp
SatCom: Inmarsat C 435678110
Panama *Panama*
MMSI: 356781000
Official number: 2326296CH
1996-09 **Oshima Shipbuilding Co Ltd — Saikai NS**
Yd No: 10203
Loa 209.01 (BB) Br ex - Dght 10.825
Lbp 200.00 Br md 32.20 Dpth 22.10
Welded, 1 dk
(A24B2BW) Wood Chips Carrier
Grain: 102,155
Compartments: 6 Ho, ER
6 Ha: (16.0 x 12.5)4 (16.0 x 18.7) (12.8 x 18.7)ER
Cranes: 3x14.5t
1 oil engine driving 1 FP propeller
Total Power: 7,282kW (9,901hp) 14.2kn
Mitsubishi 6UEC50LSII
1 x 2 Stroke 6 Cy. 500 x 1950 7282kW (9901bhp)
Mitsubishi Heavy Industries Ltd-Japan
AuxGen: 3 x 580kW a.c
Fuel: 2298.0 (r.f.) 26.4pd

9459591 **TAIHO MARU** **3,858** Class: NK
YJRZ2 1,740
- **Princess Line SA** 4,393
Hayama Senpaku KK (Hayama Shipping Ltd)
Port Vila *Vanuatu*
MMSI: 577077000
Official number: 2143
2008-08 **Minamiawaji Zosen Co Ltd — Minamiawaji HG** Yd No: 401
Loa 98.28 Br ex - Dght 6.679
Lbp 88.50 Br md 16.80 Dpth 9.90
Welded, 1 dk
(A34A2GR) Refrigerated Cargo Ship
Ins: 4,920
1 oil engine driving 1 FP propeller
Total Power: 3,250kW (4,419hp) 15.1kn
MAN-B&W 5L35MC
1 x 2 Stroke 5 Cy. 350 x 1050 3250kW (4419bhp)
Makita Corp-Japan
Fuel: 755.0

8603664 **TAIHO MARU No. 3** *460*
JG4599 -
- **YK Taiho Maru Kaiun** 880
-
Minamiboso, Chiba *Japan*
Official number: 126001
1986-07 **Ishii Zosen K.K. — Futtsu** Yd No: 200
Loa 48.01 Br ex - Dght 3.852
Lbp 43.01 Br md 10.61 Dpth 5.52
Welded, 2 dks
(B33A2DG) Grab Dredger
Compartments: 1 Ho, ER
1 Ha: ER
1 oil engine driving 1 FP propeller
Total Power: 809kW (1,100hp)
Fuji 6S27.5G
1 x 4 Stroke 6 Cy. 275 x 410 809kW (1100bhp)
Fuji Diesel Co Ltd-Japan
Thrusters: 1 Thwart. FP thruster (f)

6903553 **TAIHO MARU No. 8** *111*
- *ex* Dairyo Maru No. 2 *-2010* 24
- - -
-
1968 **Hayashikane Shipbuilding & Engineering Co Ltd — Nagasaki NS** Yd No: 682
Loa 34.83 Br ex 6.63 Dght 2.388
Lbp 29.49 Br md 6.61 Dpth 2.80
Welded, 1 dk
(B11B2FV) Fishing Vessel
1 oil engine driving 1 FP propeller
Total Power: 699kW (950hp)
Niigata
1 x 4 Stroke 6 Cy. 280 x 440 699kW (950bhp)
Niigata Engineering Co Ltd-Japan

IMO / Call sign	Name / Owner	Tonnage	Class	Builder / Dimensions	Type	Machinery
8910689 *JISH* -	**TAIHO MARU NO. 8** *ex* Ryujin Maru No. 78 *-2005* *ex* Shoyu Maru No. 88 *-1995* **Ocean Fisheries YK** - SatCom: Inmarsat A 1205254 *Tokyo* *Japan* MMSI: 431702780 Official number: 130098	*409* - 503		**1989**-12 **Miho Zosensho K.K. — Shimizu** Yd No: 1361 Loa 55.45 (BB) Br ex - Dght 3.499 Lbp - Br md 8.70 Dpth 3.85 Welded, 1 dk	**(B11B2FV) Fishing Vessel** Ins: 687	**1 oil engine** with clutches & sr reverse geared to sc. shaft driving 1 FP propeller Total Power: 736kW (1,001hp) Akasaka K28SFD 1 x 4 Stroke 6 Cy. 280 x 500 736kW (1001bhp) Akasaka Tekkosho KK (Akasaka DieselLtd)-Japan
8633102 - -	**TAIHO MARU No. 32** - **Jih Fu Yuyeh Co Ltd** - *Chinese Taipei*	*233* - -		**1976 Maebata Zosen Tekko K.K. — Sasebo** L reg 41.70 Br ex - Dght 3.000 Lbp - Br md 7.70 Dpth 3.60 Welded, 1 dk	**(B11B2FV) Fishing Vessel**	**1 oil engine** driving 1 FP propeller
8415823 *JRJD* TK1-1362	**TAIHO MARU NO. 35** *ex* Shinsei Maru *-2002* **Ocean Fisheries YK** - *Tokyo* *Japan* MMSI: 431100890 Official number: 128119	*379* - -		**1984**-11 **KK Kanasashi Zosen — Shizuoka SZ** Yd No: 3045 Loa 53.50 (BB) Br ex 8.74 Dght 3.401 Lbp 46.89 Br md 8.70 Dpth 3.76 Welded, 1 dk	**(B11B2FV) Fishing Vessel**	**1 oil engine** with clutches, flexible couplings & sr reverse geared to sc. shaft driving 1 FP propeller Total Power: 736kW (1,001hp) Hanshin 6LUN28AG 1 x 4 Stroke 6 Cy. 280 x 480 736kW (1001bhp) The Hanshin Diesel Works Ltd-Japan
8805171 *T2PB4* -	**TAIHOZAN MARU** - **Harita Berlian Shipping Pte Ltd** - *Funafuti* *Tuvalu* Official number: 29848813	*225* - -	Class: IZ	**1989**-03 **K.K. Odo Zosen Tekko — Shimonoseki** Yd No: 353 Loa 29.50 Br ex Dght 3.400 Lbp 27.50 Br md 9.20 Dpth 4.00 Welded, 1 dk	**(B32B2SP) Pusher Tug**	**2 oil engines** geared to sc. shafts driving 2 FP propellers Total Power: 2,648kW (3,600hp) Hanshin 6EL30G 2 x 4 Stroke 6 Cy. 300 x 600 each-1324kW (1800bhp) The Hanshin Diesel Works Ltd-Japan
9457684 *JD2487* -	**TAIHOZAN MARU** - **Futaba Kisen KK** - *Hiroshima, Hiroshima* *Japan* Official number: 140616	*498* - 1,600		**2007**-10 **K.K. Watanabe Zosensho — Nagasaki** Yd No: 145 Loa 76.12 Br ex - Dght 4.030 Lbp 70.20 Br md 12.30 Dpth 7.00 Welded, 1 dk	**(A31A2GX) General Cargo Ship** Bale: 2,478 Compartments: 1 Ho, ER 1 Ha: ER (40.0 x 10.0)	**1 oil engine** geared to sc. shaft driving 1 FP propeller Total Power: 1,176kW (1,599hp) Akasaka K31SFD 1 x 4 Stroke 6 Cy. 310 x 530 1176kW (1599bhp) Akasaka Tekkosho KK (Akasaka DieselLtd)-Japan
9384851 *VRCT4* -	**TAIHUA STAR** - **Eaglehill Trading Ltd** Pacific Basin Shipping (HK) Ltd *Hong Kong* *Hong Kong* MMSI: 477768700 Official number: HK-1889	**16,951** 10,134 28,456 T/cm 39.6	Class: NK (LR) (AB) Classed LR until 18/1/13	**2007**-03 **Shimanami Shipyard Co Ltd — Imabari EH** Yd No: 506 Loa 169.26 (BB) Br ex 27.24 Dght 9.762 Lbp 160.40 Br md 27.20 Dpth 13.60 Welded, 1 dk	**(A21A2BC) Bulk Carrier** Grain: 37,523; Bale: 35,763 Compartments: 5 Ho, ER 5 Ha: 4 (19.2 x 17.6)ER (13.6 x 16.0) Cranes: 4x30.5t	**1 oil engine** driving 1 FP propeller Total Power: 5,850kW (7,954hp) 13.5kn MAN-B&W 6S42MC 1 x 2 Stroke 6 Cy. 420 x 1764 5850kW (7954bhp) Makita Corp-Japan AuxGen: 3 x 440kW 450V 60Hz a.c Boilers: WTAuxB (o.f.) Fuel: 134.0 (d.f.) 1205.7 (r.f.)
8100818 - -	**TAIJIN MARU No. 7** *ex* Ishida Maru No. 52 *-1985* **YL Square** - *Philippines*	*208* - 295		**1980**-09 **Daiwa Zosen K.K. — Choshi** Yd No: 233 Loa 46.36 (BB) Br ex 8.21 Dght 0.405 Lbp 38.00 Br md 7.51 Dpth 3.08 Welded, 1 dk	**(B11B2FV) Fishing Vessel**	**1 oil engine** reduction geared to sc. shaft driving 1 FP propeller Total Power: 875kW (1,190hp) Yanmar 6ZL-DT 1 x 4 Stroke 6 Cy. 280 x 340 875kW (1190bhp) Yanmar Diesel Engine Co Ltd-Japan
8130174 *T3EG* -	**TAIJIN NO. 18** *ex* Taijin Maru No. 18 *-2010* **Kiribati & Taijin Fishing Co Ltd** - *Tarawa* *Kiribati* Official number: KSR 090/10	**1,016** 304 1,531	Class: NK	**1982**-02 **Miho Zosensho K.K. — Shimizu** Yd No: 1203 Loa 61.90 (BB) Br ex 11.64 Dght 4.350 Lbp 56.30 Br md 11.41 Dpth 6.89 Welded, 1 dk	**(B11B2FV) Fishing Vessel**	**1 oil engine** with clutches, flexible couplings & dr reverse geared to sc. shaft driving 1 FP propeller Total Power: 1,839kW (2,500hp) 15.4kn Niigata 8MG31FZ 1 x 4 Stroke 8 Cy. 310 x 380 1839kW (2500bhp) Niigata Engineering Co Ltd-Japan Thrusters: 1 Thwart. FP thruster (f)
9148611 *7JQE* -	**TAIJU** - **Triumph Sea Ltd** Bernhard Schulte Shipmanagement (India) Pvt Ltd SatCom: Inmarsat C 443295310 *Kure, Hiroshima* *Japan* MMSI: 432953000 Official number: 142038	**87,441** 57,477 173,020 T/cm 119.0	Class: NK (LR) ✠ Classed LR until 11/4/12	**1997**-05 **Nippon Kokan KK (NKK Corp) — Tsu ME** Yd No: 162 Loa 289.00 (BB) Br ex 45.40 Dght 17.780 Lbp 279.00 Br md 45.00 Dpth 24.10 Welded, 1 dk	**(A21A2BC) Bulk Carrier** Grain: 191,582 Compartments: 9 Ho, ER 9 Ha: (15.2 x 18.8)7 (15.2 x 20.6) (15.2 x 17.5)ER	**1 oil engine** driving 1 FP propeller Total Power: 14,710kW (20,000hp) 14.5kn B&W 6S70MC 1 x 2 Stroke 6 Cy. 700 x 2674 14710kW (20000bhp) Mitsui Engineering & Shipbuilding CLtd-Japan AuxGen: 3 x 600kW 440V 60Hz a.c Boilers: AuxB (Comp) 6.9kgf/cm² (6.8bar) Fuel: 4530.0
8020381 - -	**TAIJUAN** - **Giuseppe & Coral Raye Rotondella** - *Cairns, Qld* *Australia* Official number: 385884	*112* 92 -		**1980**-07 **K Shipyard Construction Co — Fremantle WA** Yd No: 55 Loa 22.51 Br ex 6.13 Dght 2.806 Lbp 20.91 Br md 6.00 Dpth 3.15 Welded, 1 dk	**(B11B2FV) Fishing Vessel**	**1 oil engine** driving 1 FP propeller Total Power: 331kW (450hp) 10.0kn Caterpillar 3412PCTA 1 x Vee 4 Stroke 12 Cy. 137 x 152 331kW (450bhp) Caterpillar Tractor Co-USA
8936401 *JM6545* -	**TAIKAI MARU** *ex* Kunihiro Maru *-2011* **Osakawan Kaihatsu Kanri KK** - *Osaka, Osaka* *Japan* MMSI: 431600862 Official number: 135396	*134* - -		**1997**-11 **Kimura Zosen K.K. — Kure** Loa 29.70 Br ex - Dght - Lbp - Br md 9.00 Dpth 6.20 Welded, 1 dk	**(B32A2ST) Tug**	**2 oil engines** driving 2 FP propellers Total Power: 2,942kW (4,000hp) 10.0kn Yanmar 6N280-EN 2 x 4 Stroke 6 Cy. 280 x 380 each-1471kW (2000bhp) Yanmar Diesel Engine Co Ltd-Japan
7616535 - -	**TAIKAN MARU** *ex* Puerto No. 15 *-1989* *ex* Eizan Maru No. 66 *-1989* *ex* Shiretoko Maru *-1989* **Won Yeong Iron Co Ltd** - *South Korea*	*534* - 1,810		**1977**-01 **Sanyo Zosen K.K. — Onomichi** Yd No: 750 Loa - Br ex - Dght 4.501 Lbp 62.51 Br md 11.02 Dpth 5.06 Welded, 1 dk	**(A13B2TP) Products Tanker**	**1 oil engine** driving 1 FP propeller Total Power: 1,177kW (1,600hp) Akasaka DM33 1 x 4 Stroke 6 Cy. 330 x 500 1177kW (1600bhp) (new engine 1995) Akasaka Tekkosho KK (Akasaka DieselLtd)-Japan
8103901 *JJ3294* -	**TAIKASAN MARU No. 2** - **Iino Gas Transport Co Ltd** - *Kobe, Hyogo* *Japan* MMSI: 431336000 Official number: 125187	**1,660** 498 1,507	Class: NK	**1982**-01 **Sasebo Heavy Industries Co. Ltd. — Sasebo Yard, Sasebo** Yd No: 290 Loa 73.89 (BB) Br ex 12.63 Dght 4.512 Lbp 69.12 Br md 12.60 Dpth 6.33 Welded, 1 dk	**(A11B2TG) LPG Tanker** Liq (Gas): 1,498 3 x Gas Tank (s);	**1 oil engine** driving 1 CP propeller Total Power: 1,765kW (2,400hp) 13.5kn Hanshin 6EL35 1 x 4 Stroke 6 Cy. 350 x 700 1765kW (2400bhp) The Hanshin Diesel Works Ltd-Japan AuxGen: 2 x 350kW 450V 60Hz a.c Fuel: 36.5 (d.f.) 82.0 (r.f.) 8.5pd
9037953 *JRTG* -	**TAIKEI MARU No. 1** - **Taikei Gyogyo KK** - SatCom: Inmarsat B 343179610 *Ishinomaki, Miyagi* *Japan* MMSI: 431796000 Official number: 132202	*349* - -		**1991**-12 **Hayashikane Dockyard Co Ltd — Nagasaki NS** Yd No: 996 Loa 64.20 (BB) Br ex Dght 4.540 Lbp 55.00 Br md 12.00 Dpth 7.39 Welded	**(B11B2FV) Fishing Vessel**	**1 oil engine** reverse reduction geared to sc. shaft driving 1 FP propeller Total Power: 1,912kW (2,600hp) Yanmar 6N330-EN 1 x 4 Stroke 6 Cy. 330 x 440 1912kW (2600bhp) Yanmar Diesel Engine Co Ltd-Japan
8319419 *8LXK* -	**TAIKEI MARU No. 2** *ex* Iwaki Maru *-1999* **Taikei Gyogyo KK** - *Ishinomaki, Miyagi* *Japan* MMSI: 431338000 Official number: 126613	*196* - 87		**1984**-04 **Narasaki Zosen KK — Muroran HK** Yd No: 1049 Loa 42.41 Br ex 7.82 Dght 3.000 Lbp 35.70 Br md 7.80 Dpth 3.40 Welded, 1 dk	**(B12D2FR) Fishery Research Vessel** Ins: 75 Compartments: 6 Ho, ER 6 Ha: ER	**1 oil engine** with clutches, flexible couplings & sr geared to sc. shaft driving 1 CP propeller Total Power: 956kW (1,300hp) Niigata 6MG25CXE 1 x 4 Stroke 6 Cy. 250 x 320 956kW (1300bhp) Niigata Engineering Co Ltd-Japan
9150901 *JI3607* -	**TAIKEI MARU No. 5** - **Keishin Kaiun KK** - *Osaka, Osaka* *Japan* MMSI: 431300411 Official number: 135912	*748* - 2,010	Class: NK	**1996**-06 **Hakata Zosen K.K. — Imabari** Yd No: 601 Loa 77.00 Br ex - Dght 4.657 Lbp 73.20 Br md 11.50 Dpth 5.15 Welded, 1 dk	**(A13B2TP) Products Tanker** Liq: 2,243; Liq (Oil): 2,243	**1 oil engine** driving 1 FP propeller Total Power: 1,471kW (2,000hp) 12.6kn Hanshin LH32L 1 x 4 Stroke 6 Cy. 320 x 640 1471kW (2000bhp) The Hanshin Diesel Works Ltd-Japan Fuel: 60.0 (d.f.)

7827823 - -	**TAIKEI MARU No. 52** - **Philippine Aquatic Products Enterprises Inc** - *Philippines*	*214* - -		**1978**-11 **K.K. Murakami Zosensho — Ishinomaki** Yd No: 1025 Loa 36.50 Br ex - Dght - Lbp 34.57 Br md 7.01 Dpth 2.82 Welded, 1 dk	**(B11B2FV) Fishing Vessel**	**1 oil engine** driving 1 FP propeller Total Power: 662kW (900hp) Yanmar G250-E 1 x 4 Stroke 6 Cy. 250 x 290 662kW (900bhp) Yanmar Diesel Engine Co Ltd-Japan
7220403 *JMKC* -	**TAIKEI MARU No. 52** *ex* Wakamiya Maru No. 52 *-1998* *ex* Masa Maru No. 28 *-1984* - - SatCom: Inmarsat C 443166610 *Higashikagawa, Kagawa* *Japan* MMSI: 431666000 Official number: 111304	*385* 192 505		**1972**-07 **KK Kanasashi Zosen — Shizuoka SZ** Yd No: 1058 Loa 55.30 Br ex 8.64 Dght 3.404 Lbp 49.00 Br md 8.62 Dpth 3.89 Welded, 1 dk	**(B11B2FV) Fishing Vessel**	**1 oil engine** driving 1 FP propeller Total Power: 956kW (1,300hp) Daihatsu 6DSM-26 1 x 4 Stroke 6 Cy. 260 x 320 956kW (1300bhp) Daihatsu Diesel Manufacturing Co Lt-Japan
9032214 *JI3464* -	**TAIKI MARU** - **Taiyo Shipping Co Ltd (Taiyo Kisen KK)** - *Osaka, Osaka* *Japan* MMSI: 431300622 Official number: 131715	*3,322* - 5,620	Class: NK	**1991**-07 **Nishi Shipbuilding Co Ltd — Imabari EH** Yd No: 367 Loa 93.02 Br ex - Dght 6.905 Lbp 88.00 Br md 16.30 Dpth 8.20 Welded, 1 dk	**(A24A2BT) Cement Carrier** Grain: 4,652; Bale: 4,652 Compartments: 12 Ho, ER	**1 oil engine** driving 1 CP propeller Total Power: 3,089kW (4,200hp) 12.5kn Mitsubishi 6UEC37LA 1 x 2 Stroke 6 Cy. 370 x 880 3089kW (4200bhp) Akasaka Tekkosho KK (Akasaka DieselLtd)-Japan AuxGen: 3 x 300kW a.c Fuel: 250.0 (r.f.)
9200548 *JI3658* -	**TAIKI MARU** - **Taikai Marine YK** - *Osaka, Osaka* *Japan* Official number: 136781	*148* - -		**1999**-02 **Kanrei Zosen K.K. — Naruto** Yd No: 383 Loa 32.01 Br ex - Dght - Lbp - Br md 9.80 Dpth 6.00 Welded, 1 dk	**(B32A2ST) Tug**	**2 oil engines** reduction geared to sc. shafts driving 2 FP propellers Total Power: 2,942kW (4,000hp) 10.0kn Daihatsu 6DKM-26 2 x 4 Stroke 6 Cy. 260 x 380 each-1471kW (2000bhp) Daihatsu Diesel Manufacturing Co Lt-Japan
9651474 *JD3387* -	**TAIKI MARU NO. 3** - **Marui Suisan YK** - *Unzen, Nagasaki* *Japan* Official number: 141718	*199* - -		**2012**-08 **Kidoura Shipyard Co Ltd — Kesennuma MG** Yd No: 627 Loa 46.36 Br ex - Dght 2.920 Lbp - Br md 7.50 Dpth - Welded, 1 dk	**(B11B2FV) Fishing Vessel**	**1 oil engine** reduction geared to sc. shafts driving 1 Propeller Total Power: 1,840kW (2,502hp) Yanmar 6EY26W-4 1 x 4 Stroke 6 Cy. 260 x 385 1840kW (2502bhp) Yanmar Diesel Engine Co Ltd-Japan
8823874 *JJ3594* -	**TAIKI MARU No. 8** - **Taiki Kenzai KK** - *Ieshima, Hyogo* *Japan* Official number: 130808	*486* - 569		**1988**-08 **Masui Zosensho K.K. — Nandan** Loa 50.00 Br ex - Dght 3.220 Lbp 46.00 Br md 10.50 Dpth 5.35 Welded, 1 dk	**(B33A2DG) Grab Dredger**	**1 oil engine** driving 1 FP propeller Total Power: 515kW (700hp) Yanmar MF26-ST 1 x 4 Stroke 6 Cy. 260 x 500 515kW (700bhp) Yanmar Diesel Engine Co Ltd-Japan
9033244 - -	**TAIKI MARU No. 71** - **Taiki Suisan YK**	*119* - -		**1990**-11 **Kesennuma Tekko — Kesennuma** Yd No: 276 L reg 31.60 (BB) Br ex - Dght 2.300 Lbp 31.50 Br md 6.40 Dpth 2.80 Welded	**(B11B2FV) Fishing Vessel** Ins: 151	**1 oil engine** driving 1 CP propeller Total Power: 592kW (805hp) Niigata 6M26AFTE 1 x 4 Stroke 6 Cy. 260 x 460 592kW (805bhp) Niigata Engineering Co Ltd-Japan
5199832 - -	**TAIKI MARU No. 71** *ex* Choei Maru No. 35 *-1984* *ex* Kyowa Maru No. 8 *-1965* **Sho Ko Man** - *South Korea*	*164* 89 -		**1960 Kochiken Zosen — Kochi** Yd No: 212 L reg 30.76 Br ex 6.33 Dght - Lbp - Br md 6.30 Dpth 3.10 Welded, 1 dk	**(B11B2FV) Fishing Vessel**	**1 oil engine** driving 1 FP propeller Total Power: 316kW (430hp) 9.5kn Kobe 1 x 4 Stroke 6 Cy. 270 x 400 316kW (430bhp) Kobe Hatsudoki Seizosho-Japan Fuel: 93.5
9661924 *7JOB* -	**TAIKI MARU NO. 81** - **Kesennuma Enyo Gyogyo Seisau Kumiai (Kesennuma Pelagic Fishery Cooperative)** - *Kesennuma, Miyagi* *Japan* Official number: 141858	*119* - -		**2013**-03 **Kidoura Shipyard Co Ltd — Kesennuma MG** Yd No: 631 Loa 36.66 Br ex - Dght 2.500 Lbp - Br md 6.40 Dpth - Welded, 1 dk	**(B11B2FV) Fishing Vessel**	**1 oil engine** reduction geared to sc. shaft driving 1 Propeller Total Power: 882kW (1,199hp) Niigata 6M26AFTE 1 x 4 Stroke 6 Cy. 260 x 460 882kW (1199bhp) Niigata Engineering Co Ltd-Japan
9561629 *3EYR5* -	**TAIKLI** - **Unicorn Successor SA** Wisdom Marine Lines SA *Panama* *Panama* MMSI: 353921000 Official number: 4349512	**9,984** 4,443 13,139	Class: NK	**2011**-11 **Kegoya Dock K.K. — Kure** Yd No: 1132 Loa 124.55 Br ex - Dght 9.020 Lbp 115.00 Br md 20.50 Dpth 14.50 Welded, 1 dk	**(A31A2GA) General Cargo Ship (with Ro-Ro facility)** Quarter stern door/ramp (s. a.) Grain: 21,830; Bale: 19,679 Compartments: 2 Ho, ER 2 Ha: ER Cranes: 2x40t; Derricks: 2x30t	**1 oil engine** driving 1 FP propeller Total Power: 4,200kW (5,710hp) 13.2kn MAN-B&W 6S35MC 1 x 2 Stroke 6 Cy. 350 x 1400 4200kW (5710bhp) The Hanshin Diesel Works Ltd-Japan Fuel: 990.0
8204975 *LAQT4* -	**TAIKO** *ex* Barber Hector *-1988* **Wilhelmsen Lines Shipowning AS** Wilhelmsen Ship Management (Norway) AS SatCom: Inmarsat B 325869310 *Tonsberg* *Norway (NIS)* MMSI: 258693000	**66,635** 26,072 43,986	Class: LR ✠ **100A1** CS 06/2009 vehicle carrier roll on - roll off ship movable decks LI ✠ **LMC** **UMS** Eq.Ltr: T†; Cable: 715.0/87.0 U3 (a)	**1984**-04 **Hyundai Heavy Industries Co Ltd — Ulsan** Yd No: 250 Converted From: Ro-Ro Cargo Ship-2003 Loa 262.08 (BB) Br ex 32.31 Dght 11.729 Lbp 246.41 Br md 32.26 Dpth 21.01 Welded, 8 dks, incl. 2 hoistable dks	**(A35B2RV) Vehicles Carrier** Side door (s) Quarter stern door/ramp (s) Len: 45.20 Wid: 12.50 Swl: 420 Lane-clr ht: 6.30 Cars: 4,474 Bale: 72,500 Cranes: 1x40t	**1 oil engine** driving 1 FP propeller Total Power: 26,919kW (36,599hp) 20.5kn B&W 8L90GB 1 x 2 Stroke 8 Cy. 900 x 2180 26919kW (36599bhp) Hyundai Engine & Machinery Co Ltd-South Korea AuxGen: 3 x 1900kW 450V 60Hz a.c, 2 x 900kW 450V 60Hz a.c Boilers: AuxB (o.f.) 6.9kgf/cm^2 (6.8bar) 6.9kgf/cm^2 (6.8bar), AuxB (ex.g.) 11.9kgf/cm^2 (11.7bar) 6.0kgf/cm^2 (5.9bar)rcv 6,9kg/cm^2 (6,86bar) Thrusters: 1 Thwart. CP thruster (f); 1 Thwart. CP thruster (a) Fuel: 579.0 (d.f.) 7660.5 (r.f.) 110.5pd
9052886 *JM6141* -	**TAIKO** - **Nomo Shosen KK** - *Nagasaki, Nagasaki* *Japan* MMSI: 431600023 Official number: 133493	*1,272* - 600		**1992**-09 **Usuki Shipyard Co Ltd — Usuki OT** Yd No: 1617 Loa 86.97 (BB) Br ex - Dght 3.600 Lbp 73.00 Br md 13.80 Dpth 4.70 Welded	**(A36A2PR) Passenger/Ro-Ro Ship (Vehicles)** Passengers: 350 Quarter stern ramp (centre) Cars: 44, Trailers: 14	**2 oil engines** reduction geared to sc. shafts driving 2 CP propellers Total Power: 4,414kW (6,002hp) 19.0kn Daihatsu 8DLM-32 2 x 4 Stroke 8 Cy. 320 x 400 each-2207kW (3001bhp) Daihatsu Diesel Manufacturing Co Lt-Japan AuxGen: 1 x 450kW 450V 60Hz a.c Thrusters: 1 Tunnel thruster (f)
8844256 - -	**TAIKO** *ex* Taiko Maru No. 1 *-2013* **PT Indo Shipping Operator** -	*198* - 480	Class: IZ	**1990**-05 **Hongawara Zosen K.K. — Fukuyama** Loa 45.25 Br ex - Dght 3.300 Lbp 41.00 Br md 7.60 Dpth 3.40 Welded, 1 dk	**(A12A2TC) Chemical Tanker**	**1 oil engine** driving 1 FP propeller Total Power: 588kW (799hp) 10.0kn Niigata 6NSC-M 1 x 4 Stroke 6 Cy. 190 x 260 588kW (799bhp) Niigata Engineering Co Ltd-Japan
8626537 *9MLJ3* -	**TAIKO I** *ex* Capital 1 *-2011* *ex* Ryoka *-2011* *ex* Ryoka Maru No. 1 *-2006* **Marine Outsourcing Sdn Bhd** - *Port Klang* *Malaysia* MMSI: 533063900 Official number: 334242	**482** 145 792	Class: MY	**1985 Mukaishima Zoki Co. Ltd. — Onomichi** Loa 52.51 Br ex - Dght 3.750 Lbp 48.01 Br md 9.01 Dpth 4.09 Welded, 1 dk	**(A12A2TC) Chemical Tanker** Double Hull Liq: 419	**1 oil engine** geared to sc. shaft driving 1 FP propeller Total Power: 699kW (950hp) 10.5kn Hanshin 6LU26G 1 x 4 Stroke 6 Cy. 260 x 440 699kW (950bhp) The Hanshin Diesel Works Ltd-Japan
8421004 - -	**TAIKO MARU** *ex* Sumiyoshi Maru No. 52 *-2002* **PT Utama Mina Bahari** - *Indonesia*	*379* - 449		**1985**-03 **Miho Zosensho K.K. — Shimizu** Yd No: 1252 Loa 54.62 (BB) Br ex 8.62 Dght 3.406 Lbp 48.01 Br md 8.60 Dpth 3.76 Welded, 1 dk	**(B11B2FV) Fishing Vessel** Ins: 145	**1 oil engine** with clutches, flexible couplings & sr reverse geared to sc. shaft driving 1 FP propeller Total Power: 736kW (1,001hp) Niigata 6M28AFTE 1 x 4 Stroke 6 Cy. 280 x 480 736kW (1001bhp) Niigata Engineering Co Ltd-Japan
7855234 *JH2528* -	**TAIKO MARU** *ex* Koei Maru *-2005* *ex* Jinsho Maru *-1992* **Tamotsu Suzuki** - *Handa, Aichi* *Japan* Official number: 112275	*162* - 439		**1972**-02 **Hamajima Zosen K.K. — Japan** Loa 38.00 Br ex - Dght 3.101 Lbp 36.00 Br md 7.00 Dpth 3.31 Welded, 1 dk	**(A31A2GX) General Cargo Ship**	**1 oil engine** driving 1 FP propeller Total Power: 88kW (120hp) 6.5kn Mitsubishi 1 x 88kW (120bhp) Mitsubishi Heavy Industries Ltd-Japan

7735563 *JL4594* -	**TAIKO MARU** - **Nakashita Kaiun YK** - *Matsuyama, Ehime* Japan Official number: 122960	*176* - 255		**1978-09 KK Ouchi Zosensho — Matsuyama EH** Yd No: 152 Loa - Br ex - Dght 2.800 Lbp 26.12 Br md 7.51 Dpth 3.03 Welded, 1 dk	**(B33A2DG) Grab Dredger**	**1 oil engine** driving 1 FP propeller Total Power: 221kW (300hp) 8.5kn
8664060 *JD3453* -	**TAIKO MARU** - **Mukae Kensetsu KK** - *Hiroshima, Hiroshima* Japan Official number: 134758	*160* - -		**1995-11 Kegoya Dock K.K. — Kure** L reg 24.00 Br ex - Dght 3.500 Lbp - Br md 8.00 Dpth 4.50 Welded, 1 dk	**(B32B2SP) Pusher Tug**	**2 oil engines** reduction geared to sc. shafts driving 2 Propellers Total Power: 1,764kW (2,398hp) Hanshin LH26G 2 x 4 Stroke 6 Cy. 260 x 440 each-882kW (1199bhp) The Hanshin Diesel Works Ltd-Japan
8896132 - -	**TAIKO MARU** *ex* Ashu Maru **NHT Shipping & Trading Pte Ltd** -	*188* 103 521		**1976-04 K.K. Mochizuki Zosensho — Osakikamijima** Loa 46.00 Br ex - Dght 3.310 Lbp 41.00 Br md 7.50 Dpth 5.00 Welded, 1 dk	**(A31A2GX) General Cargo Ship** Grain: 954; Bale: 865 Compartments: 1 Ho, ER 1 Ha: (22.0 x 5.5)ER	**1 oil engine** driving 1 FP propeller Total Power: 441kW (600hp) 9.3kn Matsui 1 x 4 Stroke 441kW (600bhp) Matsui Iron Works Co Ltd-Japan
9054884 - -	**TAIKO MARU** - **Han Dong Shipbuilding Co Ltd** - South Korea	*448* - 906		**1992-04 Sasaki Shipbuilding Co Ltd — Osakikamijima HS** Yd No: 566 Loa 58.54 Br ex 9.62 Dght 3.875 Lbp 54.00 Br md 9.60 Dpth 4.50 Welded, 1 dk	**(A13B2TP) Products Tanker** Compartments: 8 Ta, ER	**1 oil engine** reverse geared to sc. shaft driving 1 FP propeller Total Power: 1,103kW (1,500hp) Akasaka A28 1 x 4 Stroke 6 Cy. 280 x 550 1103kW (1500bhp) Akasaka Tekkosho KK (Akasaka DieselLtd)-Japan Thrusters: 1 Thwart. CP thruster (f)
9147069 *JL6461* -	**TAIKO MARU** - **Saigu Kaiun KK** - *Imabari, Ehime* Japan Official number: 135532	*499* - 1,600		**1996-06 Yamanaka Zosen K.K. — Imabari** Yd No: 588 Loa 74.90 (BB) Br ex - Dght 4.080 Lbp 70.00 Br md 12.00 Dpth 7.01 Welded, 1 dk	**(A31A2GX) General Cargo Ship** Grain: 2,853; Bale: 2,792 Compartments: 1 Ho, ER 1 Ha: ER	**1 oil engine** driving 1 FP propeller Total Power: 736kW (1,001hp) Hanshin LH30L 1 x 4 Stroke 6 Cy. 300 x 600 736kW (1001bhp) The Hanshin Diesel Works Ltd-Japan Thrusters: 1 Thwart. FP thruster (f)
9134347 *JL6417* -	**TAIKO MARU** - **Koyo Kaiun KK** - SatCom: Inmarsat C 443191820 *Saiki, Oita* Japan MMSI: 431500395 Official number: 135096	*749* - 1,968	Class: NK	**1995-11 Shin Kochi Jyuko K.K. — Kochi** Yd No: 7073 Loa 76.61 Br ex - Dght 4.732 Lbp 72.00 Br md 11.40 Dpth 5.25 Welded, 1 dk	**(A13B2TP) Products Tanker** Liq: 2,200; Liq (Oil): 2,200	**1 oil engine** driving 1 FP propeller Total Power: 1,471kW (2,000hp) 12.4kn Niigata 6M34AET 1 x 4 Stroke 6 Cy. 340 x 620 1471kW (2000bhp) Niigata Engineering Co Ltd-Japan Fuel: 75.0 (d.f.)
9238557 *JI3683* -	**TAIKO MARU** - **Corporation for Advanced Transport & Technology & Taiyo Shipping Co Ltd (Unyu Shisetsu Seibi Jigyodan & Taiyo Kisen KK)** Taiyo Shipping Co Ltd (Taiyo Kisen KK) *Osaka, Osaka* Japan MMSI: 431301547 Official number: 137063	*5,389* - 8,549	Class: NK	**2001-01 Kanrei Zosen K.K. — Naruto** Yd No: 390 Loa 117.81 (BB) Br ex - Dght 7.015 Lbp 110.00 Br md 18.80 Dpth 9.10 Welded, 1 dk	**(A24A2BT) Cement Carrier** Grain: 6,925	**1 oil engine** driving 1 CP propeller Total Power: 3,900kW (5,302hp) 12.8kn B&W 6L35MC 1 x 2 Stroke 6 Cy. 350 x 1050 3900kW (5302bhp) Makita Corp-Japan Fuel: 244.0 (r.f.)
9251119 *JL6615* -	**TAIKO MARU** - **Taiyo Kisen KK** - *Imabari, Ehime* Japan MMSI: 431501702 Official number: 136539	*749* - 2,118	Class: NK	**2001-10 Murakami Hide Zosen K.K. — Imabari** Yd No: 518 Loa 75.52 Br ex - Dght 4.581 Lbp 72.55 Br md 12.00 Dpth 5.10 Welded, 1 dk	**(A13B2TP) Products Tanker** Double Hull (13F) Liq: 2,250; Liq (Oil): 2,250	**1 oil engine** Reduction geared to sc. shafts driving 1 FP propeller Total Power: 1,618kW (2,200hp) 13.0kn Daihatsu 6DKM-26 1 x 4 Stroke 6 Cy. 260 x 380 1618kW (2200bhp) Daihatsu Diesel Manufacturing Co Lt-Japan Fuel: 81.0
9651022 *JD3396* -	**TAIKO MARU** - **Sowa Kaiun YK** - *Kasaoka, Okayama* Japan Official number: 141735	*499* - 1,282		**2012-09 Koa Sangyo KK — Marugame KG** Yd No: 655 Loa 63.89 Br ex - Dght 4.200 Lbp - Br md 10.00 Dpth - Welded, 1 dk	**(A12A2TC) Chemical Tanker** Double Hull (13F) Liq: 1,206	**1 oil engine** reduction geared to sc. shaft driving 1 Propeller Total Power: 1,030kW (1,400hp) 10.5kn Hanshin LH28G 1 x 4 Stroke 6 Cy. 280 x 460 1030kW (1400bhp) The Hanshin Diesel Works Ltd-Japan
7535731 - -	**TAIKO MARU No. 1** *ex* Daikichi Maru No. 23 *-1987* - -	*142* - -		**1975-08 K.K. Izutsu Zosensho — Nagasaki** Yd No: 711 Loa 38.51 Br ex 7.70 Dght - Lbp 31.53 Br md 6.90 Dpth 2.77 Welded, 1 dk	**(B11B2FV) Fishing Vessel**	**1 oil engine** reduction geared to sc. shaft driving 1 FP propeller Total Power: 956kW (1,300hp) Niigata 6L25BX 1 x 4 Stroke 6 Cy. 250 x 320 956kW (1300bhp) Niigata Engineering Co Ltd-Japan
8823240 - -	**TAIKO MARU No. 3** - -	*449* - 604		**1989-01 Kimura Zosen K.K. — Kure** Loa 48.00 Br ex - Dght 3.020 Lbp 43.04 Br md 11.51 Dpth 5.31 Welded, 1 dk	**(A24D2BA) Aggregates Carrier**	**1 oil engine** driving 1 FP propeller Total Power: 588kW (799hp) Niigata 6M28GX 1 x 4 Stroke 6 Cy. 280 x 440 588kW (799bhp) Niigata Engineering Co Ltd-Japan
8817186 *JJPY* MG1-1677	**TAIKO MARU No. 7** *ex* Taiho Maru No. 7 *-1994* *ex* Taiko Maru No. 7 *-1990* **Murata Gyogyo KK** - SatCom: Inmarsat A 1202350 *Kesennuma, Miyagi* Japan MMSI: 431702840 Official number: 130753	*489* - 530		**1989-01 Miho Zosensho K.K. — Shimizu** Yd No: 1340 Loa 56.49 (BB) Br ex 8.92 Dght 3.612 Lbp 49.80 Br md 8.90 Dpth 3.97 Welded, 1 dk	**(B11B2FV) Fishing Vessel** Ins: 721	**1 oil engine** with clutches, flexible couplings & sr reverse geared to sc. shaft driving 1 FP propeller Total Power: 1,177kW (1,600hp) Niigata 6M31AFTE 1 x 4 Stroke 6 Cy. 310 x 530 1177kW (1600bhp) Niigata Engineering Co Ltd-Japan
8815035 - -	**TAIKO MARU No. 8** *ex* Ryusei Maru No. 8 *-1994* *ex* Taiko Maru No. 8 *-1990* - -	*469* - 536		**1988-09 Miho Zosensho K.K. — Shimizu** Yd No: 1335 Loa 56.49 (BB) Br ex 8.92 Dght 3.612 Lbp 49.80 Br md 8.90 Dpth 3.97 Welded, 1 dk	**(B11B2FV) Fishing Vessel** Ins: 721	**1 oil engine** with clutches, flexible couplings & sr reverse geared to sc. shaft driving 1 FP propeller Total Power: 1,177kW (1,600hp) Niigata 6M31AFTE 1 x 4 Stroke 6 Cy. 310 x 530 1177kW (1600bhp) Niigata Engineering Co Ltd-Japan
8820652 - -	**TAIKO MARU No. 8** - - - China	*100* - 176		**1988-10 Nakatani Shipyard Co. Ltd. — Etajima** Yd No: 522 Loa 27.00 Br ex - Dght 3.560 Lbp 24.00 Br md 9.20 Dpth 5.60 Welded, 1 dk	**(B32B2SP) Pusher Tug**	**2 oil engines** driving 1 FP propeller Total Power: 2,354kW (3,200hp) Hanshin 6LUN30AG 2 x 4 Stroke 6 Cy. 300 x 480 each-1177kW (1600bhp) The Hanshin Diesel Works Ltd-Japan
9709829 *7JQX* -	**TAIKO MARU NO. 8** *ex* Miho 1565 *-2014* **Murata Gyogyo KK** - *Kesennuma, Miyagi* Japan MMSI: 432971000	*479* - -	Class: FA	**2014-03 Miho Zosensho K.K. — Shimizu** Yd No: 1565 Loa 57.41 (BB) Br ex - Dght 3.900 Lbp - Br md 9.00 Dpth - Welded, 1 dk	**(B11B2FV) Fishing Vessel**	**1 oil engine** reduction geared to sc. shaft driving 1 Propeller Total Power: 1,029kW (1,399hp) Niigata 6M28BFT 1 x 4 Stroke 6 Cy. 280 x 480 1029kW (1399bhp) Niigata Engineering Co Ltd-Japan
7918294 - -	**TAIKO MARU No. 11** - - -	*254* - -		**1980-02 Sanuki Shipbuilding & Iron Works Co Ltd — Mitoyo KG** Yd No: 1052 Loa - Br ex - Dght - Lbp 37.80 Br md 7.41 Dpth 3.05 Welded, 1 dk	**(B11B2FV) Fishing Vessel**	**1 oil engine** driving 1 FP propeller Total Power: 552kW (750hp) Niigata 6M26ZE 1 x 4 Stroke 6 Cy. 260 x 400 552kW (750bhp) Niigata Engineering Co Ltd-Japan
8910665 *JKJC* MG1-1735	**TAIKO MARU No. 17** *ex* Taiho Maru No. 17 *-1994* *ex* Taiko Maru No. 17 *-1990* **Murata Gyogyo KK** - SatCom: Inmarsat A 1200523 *Kesennuma, Miyagi* Japan MMSI: 431703790 Official number: 130780	*465* - 532		**1989-11 Miho Zosensho K.K. — Shimizu** Yd No: 1358 Loa 49.98 (BB) Br ex - Dght 3.611 Lbp - Br md 8.90 Dpth 3.97 Welded, 1 dk	**(B11B2FV) Fishing Vessel** Ins: 722	**1 oil engine** sr reverse geared to sc. shaft driving 1 FP propeller Total Power: 1,177kW (1,600hp) Niigata 6M31AFTE 1 x 4 Stroke 6 Cy. 310 x 530 1177kW (1600bhp) Niigata Engineering Co Ltd-Japan

8423430 *7LAE* HK1-947	**TAIKO MARU NO. 28** *ex* Marunaka Maru No. 28 *-2005* *ex* Yahata Maru No. 21 *-1997* *ex* Koryo Maru No. 38 *-1993* **YK Daiko Suisan** - *Nemuro, Hokkaido* *Japan* Official number: 127141	*198* - -		**1985**-02 **K.K. Yoshida Zosen Tekko — Kesennuma** Yd No: 328 L reg 31.00 Br ex - Dght - Lbp - Br md 6.51 Dpth 2.70 Welded	**(B11B2FV) Fishing Vessel**	**1 oil engine** driving 1 FP propeller
8408507 - -	**TAIKO MARU NO. 38** *ex* Shinei Maru No. 28 *-1989* - -	*198* - 600		**1984**-10 **Hamamoto Zosensho K.K. — Tokushima** Yd No: 662 Loa 51.21 Br ex - Dght 3.201 Lbp 47.02 Br md 9.52 Dpth 3.31 Welded, 2 dks	**(A31A2GX) General Cargo Ship** Grain: 687 Compartments: 1 Ho, ER 1 Ha: ER	**1 oil engine** driving 1 FP propeller Total Power: 552kW (750hp) Hanshin 6LU26G 1 x 4 Stroke 6 Cy. 260 x 440 552kW (750bhp) The Hanshin Diesel Works Ltd-Japan
8864361 *JG4586* CB1-60041	**TAIKO MARU No. 58** **Kadoman Suisan YK** - *Choshi, Chiba* *Japan* MMSI: 432186000 Official number: 128938	*144* - -		**1988**-04 **Otsuchi Zosen Kogyo K.K. — Otsuchi** L reg 32.00 Br ex - Dght 2.200 Lbp - Br md 6.20 Dpth 2.70 Welded, 1 dk	**(B11B2FV) Fishing Vessel**	**1 oil engine** reduction geared to sc. shaft driving 1 FP propeller Yanmar 1 x 4 Stroke Yanmar Diesel Engine Co Ltd-Japan
9600504 *VRIG8* -	**TAIKOO** **Hongkong United Dockyards Ltd** The Hongkong Salvage & Towage Co Ltd *Hong Kong* *Hong Kong* MMSI: 477095700 Official number: HK-3040	**481** 144 198	Class: LR ✠ **100A1** SS 09/2011 tug ✠ **LMC** Eq.Ltr: H; Cable: 275.0/19.0 U2 (a)	**2011**-09 **Hin Lee (Zhuhai) Shipyard Co Ltd — Zhuhai GD** (Hull) Yd No: 229 **2011**-09 **Cheoy Lee Shipyards Ltd — Hong Kong** Yd No: 5019 Loa 30.25 Br ex - Dght 4.200 Lbp - Br md 11.60 Dpth 5.00 Welded, 1 dk	**(B32A2ST) Tug**	**2 oil engines** gearing integral to driving 2 Z propellers Total Power: 3,676kW (4,998hp) Niigata 6L28HX 2 x 4 Stroke 6 Cy. 280 x 370 each-1838kW (2499bhp) Niigata Engineering Co Ltd-Japan AuxGen: 2 x 80kW 380V 50Hz a.c
9567805 *JD2984* -	**TAIKOU MARU** **YK Sanko Kaiun** - *Kamiamakusa, Kumamoto* *Japan* MMSI: 431001073 Official number: 141123	*298* - 999		**2009**-10 **Taiyo Shipbuilding Co Ltd — Sanyoonoda YC** Yd No: 321 Loa 63.32 Br ex - Dght 6.150 Lbp - Br md 10.20 Dpth - Welded, 1 dk	**(A31A2GX) General Cargo Ship** Grain: 1,646; Bale: 1,642 1 Ha: ER (33.6 x 7.8)	**1 oil engine** reduction geared to sc. shaft driving 1 FP propeller Total Power: 1,030kW (1,400hp) Hanshin LH28G 1 x 4 Stroke 6 Cy. 280 x 460 1030kW (1400bhp) The Hanshin Diesel Works Ltd-Japan
6613380 - -	**TAILLEFER 2** *ex* Glencloy *-1978* - - *Nigeria*	**187** 88 259	Class: (LR) ✠ Classed LR until 2/11/05	**1966**-06 **Scott & Sons (Bowling) Ltd. — Bowling** Yd No: 434 Loa 33.33 Br ex 7.29 Dght 2.674 Lbp 30.59 Br md 7.01 Dpth 2.75 Riveted\Welded, 1 dk	**(A31A2GX) General Cargo Ship** Derricks: 1x5t	**1 oil engine** with hydraulic coupling driving 1 CP propeller Total Power: 228kW (310hp) 9.0kn Alpha 404-24VO 1 x 2 Stroke 4 Cy. 240 x 400 228kW (310bhp) Alpha Diesel A/S-Denmark AuxGen: 2 x 4kW 250V 50Hz a.c
9364409 *FGD5050* -	**TAILLEFER 3** *ex* Merre *-2004* **Transportes Maritimes Cotiers TMC** - *Vannes* *France* MMSI: 227566810 Official number: 894118	**400** - 600	Class: BV	**2004**-07 **Societe des Etablissemnets Merre (SEEM) — Nort-sur-Erdre** Yd No: 2000 Loa 40.00 Br ex - Dght 2.600 Lbp - Br md 7.80 Dpth 3.50 Welded, 1 dk	**(A31A2GX) General Cargo Ship**	**1 oil engine** reduction geared to sc. shaft driving 1 FP propeller Total Power: 447kW (608hp) Cummins KTA-19-M3 1 x 4 Stroke 6 Cy. 159 x 159 447kW (608bhp) Cummins Engine Co Ltd-United Kingdom
9091569 - -	**TAIMANE** *ex* Don Alfonso *-2007* **Longline Services Inc** - *Utulei, AS* *United States of America* Official number: 1108206	*104* 83 -		**1998**-12 **Ast. Pomares — Alicante** Loa 24.00 Br ex - Dght - Lbp - Br md 6.71 Dpth 2.74 Welded, 1 dk	**(B11B2FV) Fishing Vessel**	**1 oil engine** driving 1 Propeller
8803733 *UBNG4* -	**TAIMANIA** *ex* Newfoundland Breeze *-1995* **JSC 'Kurilskiy Rybak'** - *Nevelsk* *Russia* MMSI: 273356020	**703** 211 275	Class: RS (LR) (GL) Classed LR until 2/7/10	**1989**-06 **Marystown Shipyard Ltd — Marystown NL** Yd No: 45 Loa 42.02 Br ex 11.40 Dght 4.301 Lbp 36.60 Br md 11.02 Dpth 6.70 Welded	**(B11A2FS) Stern Trawler** Ins: 320	**1 oil engine** with flexible couplings & sr gearedto sc. shaft driving 1 CP propeller Total Power: 1,839kW (2,500hp) 11.5kn Deutz SBV9M628 1 x 4 Stroke 9 Cy. 240 x 280 1839kW (2500bhp) Kloeckner Humboldt Deutz AG-West Germany AuxGen: 2 x 412kW 460V 60Hz a.c, 1 x 180kW 460V 60Hz a.c Fuel: 137.0 (d.f.)
9678056 *VRLZ2* -	**TAIMIN 1** **Taimin Petroleum & Chemicals Ltd** - *Hong Kong* *Hong Kong* Official number: HK-3808	**1,191** 433 1,698	Class: CC	**2013**-05 **Zhongshan Jinhui Shipbuilding & Repair Yard Co Ltd — Zhongshan GD** Yd No: JH2016 Loa 48.00 Br ex - Dght 5.000 Lbp 44.50 Br md 13.80 Dpth 6.60 Welded, 1 dk	**(A13B2TP) Products Tanker** Double Hull (13F) Liq: 1,656; Liq (Oil): 1,656 Compartments: 4 Wing Ta, 4 Wing Ta, 1 Wing Slop Ta, 1 Wing Slop Ta, ER	**2 oil engines** reduction geared to sc. shafts driving 2 Propellers Total Power: 1,192kW (1,620hp) 9.0kn Cummins KT-38-M 2 x Vee 4 Stroke 12 Cy. 159 x 159 each-596kW (810bhp) Chongqing Cummins Engine Co Ltd-China AuxGen: 2 x 75kW 400V a.c
9695822 *VRMJ3* -	**TAIMIN 2** **Hill Power Development Ltd** Taimin Petroleum & Chemicals Ltd *Hong Kong* *Hong Kong* Official number: HK-3890	**1,165** 487 1,876	Class: CC	**2013**-08 **Guangzhou Fishing Vessel Shipyard — Guangzhou GD** Yd No: 12-002 Loa 48.00 Br ex - Dght 4.800 Lbp 45.80 Br md 13.80 Dpth 6.20 Welded, 1 dk	**(A13B2TP) Products Tanker** Double Hull (13F) Liq: 1,704; Liq (Oil): 1,704 Compartments: 4 Wing Ta, 4 Wing Ta, 1 Wing Slop Ta, 1 Wing Slop Ta, ER	**2 oil engines** reduction geared to sc. shafts driving 2 Propellers Total Power: 1,492kW (2,028hp) 10.5kn Cummins K38-M 2 x Vee 4 Stroke 12 Cy. 159 x 159 each-746kW (1014bhp) Chongqing Cummins Engine Co Ltd-China AuxGen: 2 x 75kW 400V a.c
8896572 - -	**TAIMIN 7** *ex* Advance No. 2 *-2011* **Taimin Petroleum & Chemicals Ltd** - *Hong Kong* *Hong Kong* Official number: HK-0280	**233** 81 268	Class: CC	**1995** **Lingnan Shipyard — Guangzhou GD** Loa 35.00 Br ex - Dght 2.450 Lbp 33.30 Br md 7.40 Dpth 2.96 Welded, 1 dk	**(A13B2TU) Tanker (unspecified)** Liq: 290; Liq (Oil): 146 Compartments: 4 Wing Ta, ER	**1 oil engine** geared to sc. shaft driving 1 FP propeller Total Power: 82kW (111hp) 9.2kn Gardner 8LXB 1 x 4 Stroke 8 Cy. 121 x 152 82kW (111bhp) L. Gardner & Sons Ltd.-Manchester AuxGen: 2 x 24kW 400V a.c
8995093 - -	**TAINO** *ex* Jackie B. *-1997* *ex* Waneta (YTM-384) *-1975* *ex* Waneta (YTB-384) *-1962* *ex* Waneta (YT-384) *-1944* **Remolcadores Dominicanos SA** - *Santo Domingo* *Dominican Rep.* Official number: R-0021SDG	*174* 118 -		**1944**-04 **Ira S. Bushey & Son, Inc. — New York, NY** L reg 29.87 Br ex - Dght - Lbp - Br md 7.62 Dpth 4.63 Welded, 1 dk	**(B32A2ST) Tug**	**1 oil engine** reduction geared to sc. shaft driving 1 Propeller Total Power: 1,692kW (2,300hp) 11.5kn Fairbanks, Morse 10-38TD-1/8 1 x 2 Stroke 10 Cy. 207 x 254 1692kW (2300bhp) (new engine 1986) Fairbanks Morse & Co.-New Orleans, La
7515860 - -	**TAINO** *ex* State King *-1976* **Lynam, Joseph & Ella Jackson** - *Roatan* *Honduras* Official number: RHT-25016	*110* 75 -		**1973** **Bender Welding & Machine Co Inc — Mobile AL** L reg 20.85 Br ex 6.71 Dght - Lbp - Br md - Dpth 3.38 Welded, 1 dk	**(B11A2FT) Trawler**	**1 oil engine** driving 1 FP propeller Total Power: 268kW (364hp) Caterpillar D353SCAC 1 x 4 Stroke 6 Cy. 159 x 203 268kW (364bhp) Caterpillar Tractor Co-USA
7719583 - -	**TAINO** - -	*669* 210 572	Class: RC (LR) ✠ Classed LR until 23/4/97	**1979**-05 **Maritima del Musel S.A. — Gijon** Yd No: 200 Loa 53.01 (BB) Br ex 10.37 Dght 3.512 Lbp 47.00 Br md 10.01 Dpth 4.50 Welded, 1 dk	**(B34Q2QB) Buoy Tender**	**2 oil engines** reverse reduction geared to sc. shafts driving 2 FP propellers Total Power: 1,140kW (1,550hp) Alpha 5V23LU 2 x 4 Stroke 5 Cy. 225 x 300 each-570kW (775bhp) Construcciones Echevarria SA-Spain AuxGen: 3 x 120kW 220V 60Hz a.c
8705993 *ELMA6*	**TAIO COSMOS** **Misuga SA** Misuga Kaiun Co Ltd SatCom: Inmarsat A 1241770 *Monrovia* *Liberia* MMSI: 636009085 Official number: 9085	**35,582** 17,794 43,524 T/cm 51.6	Class: NK	**1988**-07 **Mitsubishi Heavy Industries Ltd. — Kobe** Yd No: 1171 Loa 193.85 (BB) Br ex - Dght 11.021 Lbp 186.00 Br md 32.20 Dpth 18.30 Welded, 1 dk	**(A24B2BW) Wood Chips Carrier** Grain: 91,229 Compartments: 6 Ho, ER 6 Ha: ER Cranes: 3x12.5t	**1 oil engine** driving 1 FP propeller Total Power: 6,657kW (9,051hp) 14.6kn Sulzer 5RTA52 1 x 2 Stroke 5 Cy. 520 x 1800 6657kW (9051bhp) Mitsubishi Heavy Industries Ltd-Japan AuxGen: 3 x 600kW a.c Fuel: 1390.0 (r.f.)

IMO / Call sign	Name / Owner / Manager / Flag	Tonnage	Class	Builder / Dimensions	Type / Cargo	Machinery
8704432 *3EZF5* -	**TAIO FRONTIER** **Taio Frontier SA** Misuga Kaiun Co Ltd SatCom: Inmarsat A 1332475 *Panama* *Panama* MMSI: 355589000 Official number: 1753588E	**35,663** 16,221 41,205 T/cm 53.7	Class: NK	**1987-10 Sanoyas Corp — Kurashiki OY** Yd No: 1087 Loa 198.03 (BB) Br ex 32.26 Dght 10.026 Lbp 188.02 Br md 32.21 Dpth 18.29 Welded, 1 dk	**(A24B2BW) Wood Chips Carrier** Grain: 89,522 Compartments: 6 Ho, ER 6 Ha: ER	**1 oil engine** driving 1 FP propeller Total Power: 6,193kW (8,420hp) 14.2kn Sulzer 6RTA58 1 x 2 Stroke 6 Cy. 580 x 1700 6193kW (8420bhp) Sumitomo Heavy Industries Ltd-Japan AuxGen: 3 x 326kW Fuel: 1430.0 (r.f.)
8616374 *ELMA4* -	**TAIO RAINBOW** **Misuga SA** Misuga Kaiun Co Ltd SatCom: Inmarsat B 363614410 *Monrovia* *Liberia* MMSI: 636009083 Official number: 9083	**35,895** 17,037 42,071 T/cm 51.6	Class: NK	**1987-12 Sumitomo Heavy Industries Ltd. — Oppama Shipyard, Yokosuka** Yd No: 1147 Loa 198.03 (BB) Br ex 32.24 Dght 10.826 Lbp 188.02 Br md 32.21 Dpth 18.29 Welded, 1 dk	**(A24B2BW) Wood Chips Carrier** Grain: 90,450 Compartments: 6 Ho, ER 6 Ha: ER Cranes: 3x12.5t	**1 oil engine** driving 1 FP propeller Total Power: 6,193kW (8,420hp) 14.0kn Sulzer 6RTA58 1 x 2 Stroke 6 Cy. 580 x 1700 6193kW (8420bhp) Sumitomo Heavy Industries Ltd-Japan AuxGen: 4 x 530kW Fuel: 1440.0 (r.f.)
9615286 *JD3273* -	**TAIOU MARU** **Kimura Kaiun KK** - *Nagasaki, Nagasaki* *Japan* MMSI: 431003171 Official number: 141561	*749* - 1,874	Class: NK	**2011-12 Maebata Zosen Tekko K.K. — Sasebo** Yd No: 300 Loa 72.39 Br ex - Dght 4.910 Lbp 68.00 Br md 11.50 Dpth 5.35 Welded, 1 dk	**(A12B2TR) Chemical/Products Tanker** Double Hull (13F) Liq: 1,842; Liq (Oil): 1,880	**1 oil engine** reduction geared to sc. shaft driving 1 Propeller Total Power: 1,618kW (2,200hp) Hanshin LA32G 1 x 4 Stroke 6 Cy. 320 x 680 1618kW (2200bhp) The Hanshin Diesel Works Ltd-Japan Fuel: 90.0
8127701 *VRRM* -	**TAIPA** *ex Princesa Guacimara -1990* **Tak Sun International Ltd** Shun Tak-China Travel Ship Management Ltd (TurboJET) *Hong Kong* *Hong Kong* MMSI: 477026000 Official number: HK-0007	*267* 98 50	Class: AB	**1981-08 Boeing Marine Systems — Seattle, Wa** Yd No: 0021 Loa 27.44 Br ex 9.15 Dght 1.521 Lbp 23.93 Br md 8.55 Dpth 2.62 Welded, 1 dk	**(A37B2PS) Passenger Ship** Hull Material: Aluminium Alloy Passengers: unberthed: 250	**2 Gas Turbs** dr geared to sc. shafts driving 2 Water jets Total Power: 5,442kW (7,398hp) 43.0kn Allison 501-K20B 2 x Gas Turb each-2721kW (3699shp) General Motors Detroit DieselAllison Divn-USA AuxGen: 2 x 50kW 440V 60Hz a.c Thrusters: 1 Thwart. FP thruster (f)
9399478 *SVAL2* -	**TAIPAN** **Legato Maritime Co** Heidmar Inc SatCom: Inmarsat C 424082810 *Piraeus* *Greece* MMSI: 240828000 Official number: 11856	**83,545** 49,022 157,048 T/cm 112.7	Class: AB	**2009-03 Jiangsu Rongsheng Shipbuilding Co Ltd — Rugao JS** Yd No: 1011 Loa 274.50 (BB) Br ex 48.04 Dght 17.019 Lbp 264.00 Br md 48.00 Dpth 23.70 Welded, 1 dk	**(A13A2TV) Crude Oil Tanker** Double Hull (13F) Liq: 167,552; Liq (Oil): 167,552 Cargo Heating Coils Compartments: 12 Wing Ta, 2 Wing Slop Ta, ER 3 Cargo Pump (s): 3x3500m³/hr Manifold: Bow/CM: 138.8m	**1 oil engine** driving 1 FP propeller Total Power: 16,860kW (22,923hp) 15.1kn MAN-B&W 6S70MC-C 1 x 2 Stroke 6 Cy. 700 x 2800 16860kW (22923bhp) Doosan Engine Co Ltd-South Korea AuxGen: 3 x 940kW a.c Fuel: 257.0 (d.f.) 4493.0 (r.f.)
9349174 *A8VY2* -	**TAIPAN** **ms 'Taipan' Schiffahrtsgesellschaft mbH & Co KG** Amazsa Hamburg GmbH SatCom: Inmarsat C 463708050 *Monrovia* *Liberia* MMSI: 636092056 Official number: 92056	**10,965** 4,717 12,611 T/cm 28.4	Class: GL	**2007-03 Naval Gijon S.A. (NAGISA) — Gijon** Yd No: 700 Loa 140.55 (BB) Br ex 23.08 Dght 8.700 Lbp 131.00 Br md 22.80 Dpth 11.90 Welded, 1 dk	**(A33A2CC) Container Ship (Fully Cellular)** Double Bottom Entire Compartment Length TEU 925 C Ho 294 TEU C Dk 631 TEU incl 200 ref C. Compartments: 6 Cell Ho, ER 6 Ha: 5 (12.7 x 20.1)ER (12.7 x 12.7) Ice Capable	**1 oil engine** reduction geard to sc. shaft driving 1 CP propeller Total Power: 9,603kW (13,056hp) 18.3kn MAN-B&W 8L48/60B 1 x 4 Stroke 8 Cy. 480 x 600 9603kW (13056bhp) MAN B&W Diesel AG-Augsburg AuxGen: 1 x 1000kW a.c, 2 x 750kW a.c, 1 x 500kW a.c Thrusters: 1 Tunnel thruster (f) Fuel: 65.0 (d.f.) 950.0 (r.f.)
9311866 *C6VF2* -	**TAIPAN** *launched as Morning Countess -2006* **Taipan Maritime Ltd** Ray Car Carriers Ltd SatCom: Inmarsat C 430892110 *Nassau* *Bahamas* MMSI: 308921000 Official number: 8001180	**57,692** 21,037 21,021	Class: NV	**2006-12 Stocznia Gdynia SA — Gdynia** Yd No: 8168/15 Loa 199.90 (BB) Br ex - Dght 10.000 Lbp 187.90 Br md 32.26 Dpth 32.73 Welded, 11 dks. incl. Nos.1, 3, 5 & 7 dks hoistable	**(A35B2RV) Vehicles Carrier** Side door/ramp (s) Len: 25.00 Wid: 7.00 Swl: 22 Quarter stern door/ramp (s. a.) Len: 38.00 Wid: 7.00 Swl: 150 Cars: 6,658	**1 oil engine** driving 1 FP propeller Total Power: 15,539kW (21,127hp) 20.4kn MAN-B&W 7S60MC-C 1 x 2 Stroke 7 Cy. 600 x 2400 15539kW (21127bhp) H Cegielski Poznan SA-Poland AuxGen: 3 x 1450kW 440/220V 60Hz a.c Thrusters: 1 Tunnel thruster (f) Fuel: 135.0 (d.f.) 3800.0 (r.f.)
6924387 - -	**TAIPAN II** *ex Oceaneer -1998 ex San Pedro Sound -1992* **Metro Plating Pty Ltd** - *Cairns, Qld* *Australia* Official number: 855845	*326* 165 338		**1969 Carrington Slipways Pty Ltd — Newcastle NSW** Yd No: 50 Loa 36.58 Br ex 9.00 Dght 3.429 Lbp 34.68 Br md 8.84 Dpth 3.97 Welded, 1 dk	**(B21B20T) Offshore Tug/Supply Ship** Liq: 263 Compartments: 11 Ta, ER	**2 oil engines** reverse reduction geared to sc. shafts driving 2 FP propellers Total Power: 1,030kW (1,400hp) 12.5kn G.M. (Detroit Diesel) 16V-71 2 x Vee 2 Stroke 16 Cy. 108 x 127 each-515kW (700bhp) General Motors Corp-USA AuxGen: 2 x 100kW 415V 50Hz a.c Fuel: 22.5 (d.f.)
8924719 - -	**TAIPESAR 1** **Gin Jau Yang Fishery Production Co Ltd** -	**868** 411 -		**1996 Fong Kuo Shipbuilding Co Ltd — Kaohsiung** L reg 58.28 Br ex - Dght - Lbp - Br md 10.30 Dpth 4.50 Welded, 1 dk	**(B11B2FV) Fishing Vessel**	**1 oil engine** driving 1 FP propeller 11.0kn Akasaka 1 x 4 Stroke 6 Cy. Akasaka Tekkosho KK (Akasaka DieselLtd)-Japan
9200653 *BDAM* -	**TAIPOWER PROSPERITY I** **Taiwan Power Co** Yang Ming Marine Transport Corp *Taichung* *Chinese Taipei* MMSI: 416346000 Official number: 013772	**49,565** 29,067 88,005 T/cm 81.1	Class: AB CR	**2000-09 China Shipbuilding Corp (CSBC) — Kaohsiung** Yd No: 740 Loa 232.18 (BB) Br ex - Dght 13.520 Lbp 227.00 Br md 38.00 Dpth 19.40 Welded, 1 dk	**(A21A2BC) Bulk Carrier** Double Bottom Entire Compartment Length Grain: 105,796 Compartments: 6 Ho, ER 6 Ha: 5 (28.9 x 18.2) (28.9 x 18.2)ER	**1 oil engine** driving 1 FP propeller Total Power: 10,813kW (14,701hp) 14.5kn Sulzer 6RTA58T 1 x 2 Stroke 6 Cy. 580 x 2416 10813kW (14701bhp) Taiwan Machinery ManufacturingCorp.-Kaohsiung AuxGen: 3 x 615kW 110/450V 60Hz a.c Fuel: 2520.0 (r.f.) (Heating Coils) 36.0pd
9200665 *BDAR* -	**TAIPOWER PROSPERITY II** **Taiwan Power Co** Yang Ming Marine Transport Corp *Taichung* *Chinese Taipei* MMSI: 416347000 Official number: 013773	**49,565** 29,067 88,018 T/cm 81.1	Class: AB CR	**2000-12 China Shipbuilding Corp (CSBC) — Kaohsiung** Yd No: 741 Loa 232.18 (BB) Br ex - Dght 13.520 Lbp 227.00 Br md 38.00 Dpth 19.40 Welded, 1 dk	**(A21A2BC) Bulk Carrier** Double Bottom Entire Compartment Length Grain: 105,796 Compartments: 6 Ho, ER 6 Ha: 5 (28.9 x 18.2) (28.9 x 18.2)ER	**1 oil engine** driving 1 FP propeller Total Power: 8,937kW (12,151hp) 14.5kn Sulzer 6RTA58T 1 x 2 Stroke 6 Cy. 580 x 2416 8937kW (12151bhp) Taiwan Machinery ManufacturingCorp.-Kaohsiung AuxGen: 3 x 615kW 110/615V 60Hz a.c Fuel: 2520.0 (r.f.) (Heating Coils) 36.0pd
9567594 *BDAB* -	**TAIPOWER PROSPERITY V** **Taiwan Power Co** - *Kaohsiung* *Chinese Taipei* MMSI: 416440000 Official number: 17342C	**50,236** 30,616 93,774	Class: BV CR	**2011-03 CSBC Corp, Taiwan — Kaohsiung** Yd No: 983 Loa 234.80 (BB) Br ex - Dght 14.500 Lbp 226.20 Br md 38.00 Dpth 20.00 Welded, 1 dk	**(A21A2BC) Bulk Carrier** Grain: 107,033 Compartments: 7 Ho, ER 7 Ha: ER	**1 oil engine** driving 1 FP propeller Total Power: 11,290kW (15,350hp) 14.5kn Wartsila 6RT-flex58T 1 x 2 Stroke 6 Cy. 580 x 2416 11290kW (15350bhp) Hyundai Heavy Industries Co Ltd-South Korea AuxGen: 3 x 560kW 60Hz a.c Fuel: 2450.0 (r.f.)
9567609 *BDAK* -	**TAIPOWER PROSPERITY VI** **Taiwan Power Co** Taiwan Navigation Co Ltd *Kaohsiung* *Chinese Taipei* MMSI: 416441000 Official number: 015048	**50,236** 30,616 93,774	Class: CR LR ✠ **100A1** SS 05/2011 bulk carrier CSR BC-B maximum cargo density 1.266 tonnes/m3 GRAB (20) ESP **ShipRight** (CM, ACS (B)) *IWS LI ✠ **LMC** **UMS** Eq.Ltr: S†; Cable: 687.5/87.0 U3 (a)	**2011-05 CSBC Corp, Taiwan — Kaohsiung** Yd No: 984 Loa 234.80 (BB) Br ex 38.04 Dght 14.500 Lbp 226.20 Br md 38.00 Dpth 20.00 Welded, 1 dk	**(A21A2BC) Bulk Carrier** Grain: 107,033 Compartments: 7 Ho, ER 7 Ha: ER	**1 oil engine** driving 1 FP propeller Total Power: 11,290kW (15,350hp) 15.0kn Wartsila 6RTA58T 1 x 2 Stroke 6 Cy. 580 x 2416 11290kW (15350bhp) Hyundai Heavy Industries Co Ltd-South Korea AuxGen: 3 x 560kW 450V 60Hz a.c Boilers: AuxB (Comp) 8.1kgf/cm² (7.9bar)
9567611 *BDAV* -	**TAIPOWER PROSPERITY VII** **Taiwan Power Co** - SatCom: Inmarsat C 441644210 *Kaohsiung* *Chinese Taipei* MMSI: 416442000	**50,236** 30,616 93,300	Class: BV CR	**2011-08 CSBC Corp, Taiwan — Kaohsiung** Yd No: 985 Loa 234.80 (BB) Br ex - Dght 14.500 Lbp 226.20 Br md 38.00 Dpth 20.00 Welded, 1 dk	**(A21A2BC) Bulk Carrier** Grain: 107,033 Compartments: 7 Ho, ER 7 Ha: ER	**1 oil engine** driving 1 FP propeller Total Power: 11,290kW (15,350hp) 14.5kn Wartsila 6RT-flex58T 1 x 2 Stroke 6 Cy. 580 x 2416 11290kW (15350bhp) Hyundai Heavy Industries Co Ltd-South Korea AuxGen: 3 x 560kW 60Hz a.c

9567623 *BDAY* -	**TAIPOWER PROSPERITY VIII** **Taiwan Power Co** Taiwan Navigation Co Ltd SatCom: Inmarsat C 441644310 *Kaohsiung* *Chinese Taipei* MMSI: 416443000	**50,236** 30,616 93,773	Class: CR LR ✠ **100A1** SS 10/2011 bulk carrier CSR BC-B maximum cargo density 1.266 tonnes/m3 GRAB (20) ESP **ShipRight** (CM,ACS (B)) *IWS LI ✠ **LMC** **UMS** Eq.Ltr: S†; Cable: 687.5/87.0 U3 (a)	2011-10 **CSBC Corp, Taiwan — Kaohsiung** Yd No: 986 Loa 234.80 (BB) Br ex 38.04 Dght 14.500 Lbp 226.20 Br md 38.00 Dpth 20.00 Welded, 1 dk	**(A21A2BC) Bulk Carrier** Grain: 107,033 Compartments: 7 Ho, ER 7 Ha: ER	**1 oil engine** driving 1 FP propeller Total Power: 11,290kW (15,350hp) 15.0kn Wartsila 6RTA58T 1 x 2 Stroke 6 Cy. 580 x 2416 11290kW (15350bhp) Hyundai Heavy Industries Co Ltd-South Korea AuxGen: 3 x 560kW 450V 60Hz a.c Boilers: AuxB (Comp) 7.5kgf/cm^2 (7.4bar)
9553098 *JD2968* -	**TAIRA MARU** **Taira Kisen KK** - *Ozu, Ehime* *Japan* MMSI: 431001045 Official number: 141096	*748* - 1,435		**2009**-10 **Kurinoura Dockyard Co Ltd — Yawatahama EH** Yd No: 411 Loa 69.98 Br ex - Dght 4.300 Lbp 66.00 Br md 11.30 Dpth 5.20 Welded, 1 dk	**(A13C2LA) Asphalt/Bitumen Tanker** Double Hull (13F) Asphalt: 1,417	**1 oil engine** driving 1 FP propeller Total Power: 1,323kW (1,799hp) Hanshin LH30L 1 x 4 Stroke 6 Cy. 300 x 600 1323kW (1799bhp) The Hanshin Diesel Works Ltd-Japan
8228490 *UFPR* -	**TAIROVO** *ex* Kirovskiy *-1999* **Kamtramp Co Ltd (OOO 'Kamtramp')** - *Petropavlovsk-Kamchatskiy* *Russia* MMSI: 273829220 Official number: 832166	**677** 233 495	Class: RS	**1984 Khabarovskiy Sudostroitelnyy Zavod im Kirova — Khabarovsk** Yd No: 847 Loa 55.02 Br ex 9.53 Dght 4.341 Lbp 50.04 Br md 9.30 Dpth 5.19 Welded, 1 dk	**(B12B2FC) Fish Carrier** Ins: 632	**1 oil engine** driving 1 FP propeller Total Power: 588kW (799hp) 11.3kn S.K.L. 6NVD48A-2U 1 x 4 Stroke 6 Cy. 320 x 480 588kW (799bhp) VEB Schwermaschinenbau "KarlLiebknecht" (SKL)-Magdeburg AuxGen: 3 x 150kW Fuel: 114.0 (d.f.)
8111269 *3ELR8* -	**TAIS C** *ex* Annemarie B *-2007* *ex* L'Armorique *-2004* *ex* Bangor *-1997* *ex* Brabo *-1996* *ex* Norasia Adria *-1989* *ex* Brabo *-1987* **Nautic Shipowner Ltd** Chariot Global Shipmanagement Ltd SatCom: Inmarsat C 435440710 *Panama* *Panama* MMSI: 354407000 Official number: 3309207	**3,092** 1,575 4,800	Class: (LR) (BR) (NV) Classed LR until 8/7/09	**1984**-03 **Belgian Shipbuilders Corp. -Fulton Marine N.V. — Ruisbroek** Yd No: 148 Loa 89.90 (BB) Br ex 15.85 Dght 6.646 Lbp 83.60 Br md 15.80 Dpth 8.20 Welded, 1 dk & S dk	**(A31A2GX) General Cargo Ship** Grain: 5,235; Bale: 4,729 TEU 245 C.Ho 113/20' (40') C.Dk 132/20' (40') incl. 33 ref C. Compartments: 1 Ho, ER, 1 Tw Dk 1 Ha: (49.9 x 12.9)ER Cranes: 2x25t	**2 oil engines** with clutches, flexible couplings & sr geared to sc. shaft driving 1 CP propeller Total Power: 2,388kW (3,246hp) 13.0kn A.B.C. 6DZC 2 x 4 Stroke 6 Cy. 256 x 310 each-1194kW (1623bhp) Anglo Belgian Corp NV (ABC)-Belgium AuxGen: 1 x 367kW 380V 50Hz a.c, 1 x 274kW 380V 50Hz a.c Boilers: e (ex.g.) 7.1kgf/cm^2 (7.0bar)
8865092 *JG5146* -	**TAISEI** **Taisei Kaiun KK** - *Yokohama, Kanagawa* *Japan* Official number: 133456	*166* - 450		**1992**-07 **Toa Tekko K.K. — Yokohama** L reg 37.40 Br ex - Dght 2.600 Lbp - Br md 7.80 Dpth 3.10 Welded, 1 dk	**(A13B2TP) Products Tanker** 2 Cargo Pump (s): 2x250m^3/hr	**1 oil engine** driving 1 FP propeller Total Power: 478kW (650hp) Niigata 6NSD-M 1 x 4 Stroke 6 Cy. 160 x 210 478kW (650bhp) Niigata Engineering Co Ltd-Japan
9705378 *JD3386* -	**TAISEI** - - *Osakikamijima, Hiroshima* *Japan* MMSI: 431003739 Official number: 141717	*499* - 1,730		**2012**-07 **Koike Zosen Kaiun KK — Osakikamijima** Yd No: 551 Loa 69.71 (BB) Br ex - Dght 4.410 Lbp 63.00 Br md 13.20 Dpth 7.35 Welded, 1 dk	**(A31A2GX) General Cargo Ship** Compartments: 1 Ho, ER 1 Ha: ER (25.2 x 10.2)	**1 oil engine** reduction geared to sc. shaft driving 1 Propeller
8976700 *YD4668* -	**TAISEI MAJU NO. 9** *ex* Taisei Maru No. 27 *-2000* *ex* Serika *-2000* **PT Aneka Atlanticindo Nidyatama** - *Palembang* *Indonesia*	**164** 50 -	Class: KI	**1969**-11 **K.K. Izutsu Zosensho — Nagasaki** Loa 35.23 Br ex - Dght 2.450 Lbp 29.98 Br md 6.60 Dpth 2.85 Welded, 1 dk	**(B32A2ST) Tug**	**1 oil engine** driving 1 FP propeller Total Power: 956kW (1,300hp) Niigata 6MG25HX 1 x 4 Stroke 6 Cy. 250 x 350 956kW (1300bhp) (, fitted 1969) Niigata Engineering Co Ltd-Japan
8990134 *JG5748* -	**TAISEI MARU** **Wing Maritime Service Corp** - *Yokohama, Kanagawa* *Japan* Official number: 137220	*228* - -		**2004**-05 **Keihin Dock Co Ltd — Yokohama** Yd No: 265 Loa 36.20 Br ex - Dght - Lbp 32.00 Br md 9.80 Dpth 4.37 Welded, 1 dk	**(B32A2ST) Tug**	**2 oil engines** Geared Integral to driving 2 Z propellers Total Power: 2,942kW (4,000hp) 13.5kn Niigata 6L28HX 2 x 4 Stroke 6 Cy. 280 x 370 each-1471kW (2000bhp) Niigata Engineering Co Ltd-Japan
9016612 *VNW3716* 0644	**TAISEI MARU** *ex* Taisei Maru No. 28 *-1999* *ex* Tosa Maru *-1994* **Goldcrest Enterprises** - *Fremantle, WA* *Australia* MMSI: 503426000 Official number: 856440	*119* - 97		**1991**-04 **Sanuki Shipbuilding & Iron Works Co Ltd — Mitoyo KG** Yd No: 1220 Loa 35.70 (BB) Br ex - Dght 2.493 Lbp 30.00 Br md 6.50 Dpth 2.80 Welded	**(B11B2FV) Fishing Vessel** Ins: 37	**1 oil engine** sr geared to sc. shaft driving 1 FP propeller Total Power: 508kW (691hp) Niigata 6MG22HX 1 x 4 Stroke 6 Cy. 220 x 280 508kW (691bhp) Niigata Engineering Co Ltd-Japan
9136979 *JK5425* -	**TAISEI MARU** **Ohnishi Kaiun/Toyota** Ohnishi Kaiun KK *Kure, Hiroshima* *Japan* MMSI: 431400468 Official number: 134670	*2,997* - 4,999	Class: NK	**1995**-09 **Watanabe Zosen KK — Imabari EH** Yd No: 290 Loa 104.95 (BB) Br ex 15.53 Dght 6.560 Lbp 98.00 Br md 15.50 Dpth 7.70 Welded, 1 dk	**(A13A2TW) Crude/Oil Products Tanker** Liq: 5,557; Liq (Oil): 5,557 Compartments: 10 Ta, ER	**1 oil engine** with clutches & reverse geared to sc. shaft driving 1 CP propeller Total Power: 2,942kW (4,000hp) Akasaka A45S 1 x 4 Stroke 6 Cy. 450 x 880 2942kW (4000bhp) Akasaka Tekkosho KK (Akasaka DieselLtd)-Japan Fuel: 275.0 (r.f.)
9159048 *JL6483* -	**TAISEI MARU** **Taisei Kisen KK** - *Anan, Tokushima* *Japan* MMSI: 431500568 Official number: 135518	*749* - 2,000	Class: NK	**1997**-03 **Hitachi Zosen Mukaishima Marine Co Ltd — Onomichi HS** Yd No: 111 Loa 83.43 Br ex - Dght 4.352 Lbp 79.00 Br md 13.40 Dpth 7.63 Welded, 1 dk	**(A31A2GX) General Cargo Ship** Grain: 3,902; Bale: 3,547 Compartments: 1 Ho, ER 1 Ha: (43.8 x 10.5)ER	**1 oil engine** driving 1 FP propeller Total Power: 1,471kW (2,000hp) 12.3kn Hanshin LH38L 1 x 4 Stroke 6 Cy. 380 x 760 1471kW (2000bhp) The Hanshin Diesel Works Ltd-Japan AuxGen: 3 x a.c Fuel: 140.0 (d.f.)
8949032 *JM6634* -	**TAISEI MARU** - - *Nagasaki, Nagasaki* *Japan* Official number: 136383	*104* - -		**1998**-10 **Amakusa Zosen K.K. — Amakusa** Yd No: 126 L reg 20.08 Br ex - Dght - Lbp 20.00 Br md 8.20 Dpth 3.10 Welded, 1 dk	**(B32B2SP) Pusher Tug**	**1 oil engine** driving 1 FP propeller Total Power: 736kW (1,001hp) 10.0kn Yanmar 6N280-EN 1 x 4 Stroke 6 Cy. 280 x 380 736kW (1001bhp) Yanmar Diesel Engine Co Ltd-Japan
8713366 *JK4708* -	**TAISEI MARU** **Minato Kaiun Co Ltd** - *Sakaide, Kagawa* *Japan* Official number: 129530	*199* - 692		**1988**-02 **K.K. Miura Zosensho — Saiki** Yd No: 805 Loa - Br ex - Dght - Lbp 54.01 Br md 9.50 Dpth 5.57 Welded, 1 dk	**(A31A2GX) General Cargo Ship**	**1 oil engine** driving 1 FP propeller Total Power: 625kW (850hp) Hanshin 6LU26RG 1 x 4 Stroke 6 Cy. 260 x 440 625kW (850bhp) The Hanshin Diesel Works Ltd-Japan
8022274 - -	**TAISEI MARU** *ex* Tone Maru No. 22 *-1989* *ex* Shoei Maru No. 33 *-1984* - - *Chinese Taipei*	*498* - 1,600		**1981**-01 **K.K. Yoshida Zosen Kogyo — Arida** Yd No: 355 Loa - Br ex - Dght 4.601 Lbp 65.03 Br md 11.02 Dpth 6.41 Welded, 1 dk	**(A31A2GX) General Cargo Ship**	**1 oil engine** driving 1 FP propeller Total Power: 1,287kW (1,750hp) Hanshin 6LU38G 1 x 4 Stroke 6 Cy. 380 x 580 1287kW (1750bhp) Hanshin Nainenki Kogyo-Japan

Identity	Name / Owner	Tonnage	Class	Build / Dimensions	Type	Machinery
7924920 *JLPY* -	**TAISEI MARU** **Government of Japan (Ministry of Land, Infrastructure & Transport)** - SatCom: Inmarsat C 443149710 *Tokyo* *Japan* MMSI: 431497000 Official number: 123723	*5,886* 1,779 3,273		**1981-03 Nippon Kokan KK (NKK Corp) — Yokohama KN (Tsurumi Shipyard)** Yd No: 981 Loa 124.85 (BB) Br ex 17.02 Dght 5.819 Lbp 115.02 Br md 17.01 Dpth 10.52 Welded, 3 dks	**(B34K2QT) Training Ship**	**1 Steam Turb** dr geared to sc. shaft driving 1 FP propeller Total Power: 5,149kW (7,001hp) 18.0kn Kawasaki 1 x steam Turb 5149kW (7001shp) Kawasaki Heavy Industries Ltd-Japan AuxGen: 1 x 840kW 450V 60Hz a.c, 1 x 560kW 450V 60Hz a.c Thrusters: 1 Thwart. FP thruster (f) Fuel: 1791.5 (r.f.) 55.0 (d.f.) 47.5pd
6412035 - -	**TAISEI MARU** *ex* Isotoku Maru No. 2 **Shinyo Shoji** - *South Korea*	*165* - -		**1964 K.K. Ichikawa Zosensho — Ise** Yd No: 1230 Loa - Br ex 6.41 Dght 2.693 Lbp 30.99 Br md 6.35 Dpth 3.00 Riveted\Welded, 1 dk	**(B11B2FV) Fishing Vessel**	**1 oil engine** driving 1 FP propeller Fuji 1 x 4 Stroke 6 Cy. 300 x 430 Ikegai Tekkosho-Japan
5399406 - -	**TAISEI MARU** *ex* Zuiko Maru *-1986* - - *Chinese Taipei*	*198* - -		**1962 Osaka Shipbuilding Co Ltd — Osaka OS** Yd No: 185 Loa 31.70 Br ex 8.28 Dght 2.718 Lbp 27.74 Br md 8.21 Dpth 3.81 Welded, 1 dk	**(B32A2ST) Tug**	**2 oil engines** geared to sc. shafts driving 2 FP propellers Total Power: 1,398kW (1,900hp) 12.0kn Fuji 6MD32H 2 x 4 Stroke 6 Cy. 320 x 380 each-699kW (950bhp) Fuji Diesel Co Ltd-Japan AuxGen: 2 x 25kW 225V a.c Fuel: 44.5 7.0pd
9687784 *7JPO*	**TAISEI MARU** **National Institute for Sea Training, Independent Administrative Institution & Century Tokyo Leasing Corp** National Institute for Sea Training, Independent Administrative Institution *Japan* MMSI: 432968000	**3,990** - 1,350	Class: FA	**2014-03 Mitsui Eng. & SB. Co. Ltd. — Tamano** Yd No: TS-1890 Loa 91.28 (BB) Br ex - Dght 5.100 Lbp 80.00 Br md 15.50 Dpth 9.00 Welded, 1 dk	**(B34K2QT) Training Ship**	**1 oil engine** driving 1 FP propeller Total Power: 3,000kW (4,079hp) 14.5kn
9266786 *JI3702*	**TAISEI MARU** **Corporation for Advanced Transport & Technology, Tabuchi Kaiun Kaisha Ltd & Seiwa Kaiun KK** Tabuchi Kaiun Co Ltd *Osaka, Osaka* *Japan* MMSI: 431301631 Official number: 137089	*3,789* - 4,990	Class: NK	**2002-09 K.K. Miura Zosensho — Saiki** Yd No: 1253 Loa 104.45 Br ex - Dght 6.200 Lbp 99.20 Br md 16.00 Dpth 8.10 Welded, 1 dk	**(A13B2TP) Products Tanker** Double Hull (13F) Liq: 6,420; Liq (Oil): 6,420	**1 oil engine** driving 1 FP propeller Total Power: 3,883kW (5,279hp) 13.5kn B&W 6L35MC 1 x 2 Stroke 6 Cy. 350 x 1050 3883kW (5279bhp) Mitsui Engineering & Shipbuilding CLtd-Japan Fuel: 330.0
9365532 *JD2171* -	**TAISEI MARU** *ex* Midori Maru *-2008* **Matsue Kaiun YK** Sanyo Kaiun Shokai Co Ltd (KK Sanyo Kaiun Shokai) *Osaka, Osaka* *Japan* Official number: 140238	**499** - 1,240		**2005-10 Imura Zosen K.K. — Komatsushima** Yd No: 313 Loa 65.40 Br ex - Dght 4.200 Lbp 59.98 Br md 10.40 Dpth 4.50 Welded, 1 dk	**(A13B2TP) Products Tanker** Double Hull (13F)	**1 oil engine** reverse geared to sc. shaft driving 1 FP propeller Total Power: 736kW (1,001hp) Akasaka K28BR 1 x 4 Stroke 6 Cy. 280 x 480 736kW (1001bhp) Akasaka Tekkosho KK (Akasaka DieselLtd)-Japan
8617847 *JM5543* -	**TAISEI MARU No. 1** *ex* Hokusho Maru No. 8 *-1998* **Taisei Kaiun YK** *Hiroshima, Hiroshima* *Japan* Official number: 129352	*356* - 515		**1986-11 Yamakawa Zosen Tekko K.K. — Kagoshima** Yd No: 677 Loa 47.81 (BB) Br ex 9.58 Dght 3.161 Lbp 43.01 Br md 9.52 Dpth 3.51 Welded, 1 dk	**(B33A2DG) Grab Dredger** Grain: 513 Compartments: 1 Ho, ER 1 Ha: ER Cranes: 1	**1 oil engine** reverse reduction geared to sc. shaft driving 1 FP propeller Total Power: 478kW (650hp) Hanshin 6LU26G 1 x 4 Stroke 6 Cy. 260 x 440 478kW (650bhp) The Hanshin Diesel Works Ltd-Japan
9078971 *JM6284* -	**TAISEI MARU No. 1** - *Kitakyushu, Fukuoka* *Japan* Official number: 132740	*376* - 686		**1993-08 K.K. Watanabe Zosensho — Nagasaki** Yd No: 003 Loa - Br ex - Dght 3.800 Lbp 52.10 Br md 12.00 Dpth 6.05 Welded, 1 dk	**(A31A2GX) General Cargo Ship**	**1 oil engine** driving 1 FP propeller Total Power: 736kW (1,001hp) 11.1kn Hanshin 6LU32G 1 x 4 Stroke 6 Cy. 320 x 510 736kW (1001bhp) The Hanshin Diesel Works Ltd-Japan
9058115 *JG5212* -	**TAISEI MARU No. 1** **KK Ono Kaisoten** - *Tokyo* *Japan* Official number: 133851	*151* - 353		**1993-03 Suzuki Shipyard Co. Ltd. — Yokkaichi** Yd No: 607 Loa 36.20 Br ex - Dght 2.770 Lbp 33.00 Br md 7.80 Dpth 3.20 Welded, 1 dk	**(A12A2TC) Chemical Tanker** Compartments: 4 Ta, ER 2 Cargo Pump (s): 2x150m³/hr	**1 oil engine** sr geared to sc. shaft driving 1 FP propeller Total Power: 360kW (489hp) Yanmar 6LAH-ST 1 x 4 Stroke 6 Cy. 150 x 165 360kW (489bhp) Yanmar Diesel Engine Co Ltd-Japan
8817215 - -	**TAISEI MARU No. 3** **PT Karya Cemerlang** *Indonesia*	*498* - 500		**1988-09 Nakatani Shipyard Co. Ltd. — Etajima** Yd No: 520 Loa - Br ex - Dght 3.061 Lbp 42.02 Br md 11.02 Dpth 5.31 Welded, 1 dk	**(A24D2BA) Aggregates Carrier**	**1 oil engine** driving 1 FP propeller Total Power: 736kW (1,001hp) Yanmar MF28-UT 1 x 4 Stroke 6 Cy. 280 x 450 736kW (1001bhp) Yanmar Diesel Engine Co Ltd-Japan
9033579 - -	**TAISEI MARU No. 5** - -	*149* - 375		**1991-09 Suzuki Shipyard Co. Ltd. — Yokkaichi** Yd No: 587 Loa 35.56 Br ex - Dght 2.900 Lbp 33.00 Br md 7.80 Dpth 3.20 Welded, 1 dk	**(A12A2TC) Chemical Tanker** Liq: 220 Compartments: 4 Ta, ER	**1 oil engine** reduction geared to sc. shaft driving 1 FP propeller Total Power: 331kW (450hp) Yanmar 6LAK-ST1 1 x 4 Stroke 6 Cy. 150 x 165 331kW (450bhp) Yanmar Diesel Engine Co Ltd-Japan
8032633 - -	**TAISEI MARU No. 5** *ex* Kaifuku Maru No. 5 *-2000* - -	*148* - 260		**1980-10 K.K. Takagi Zosensho — Matsuzaki** Yd No: 186 Loa - Br ex - Dght 2.600 Lbp 29.90 Br md 6.71 Dpth 2.70 Welded, 1 dk	**(A13B2TU) Tanker (unspecified)**	**1 oil engine** driving 1 FP propeller Total Power: 191kW (260hp) 8.5kn Sumiyoshi 1 x 4 Stroke 191kW (260bhp) Sumiyoshi Marine Diesel Co Ltd-Japan
7608291 - -	**TAISEI MARU No. 5** - -	*116* 23 -		**1976-09 Tokushima Zosen K.K. — Fukuoka** Yd No: 1215 Loa 38.05 (BB) Br ex 6.99 Dght 2.744 Lbp 31.40 Br md 6.95 Dpth 2.80 Welded, 1 dk	**(B11B2FV) Fishing Vessel**	**1 oil engine** driving 1 FP propeller Total Power: 699kW (950hp) Yanmar 6Z-ST 1 x 4 Stroke 6 Cy. 280 x 340 699kW (950bhp) Yanmar Diesel Engine Co Ltd-Japan
8617720 - -	**TAISEI MARU No. 8** - - *South Korea*	*100* - -		**1986-11 Nakatani Shipyard Co. Ltd. — Etajima** Yd No: 507 Loa 26.00 Br ex - Dght 3.911 Lbp 24.00 Br md 9.20 Dpth 6.10 Welded, 1 dk	**(B32B2SP) Pusher Tug**	**1 oil engine** driving 1 FP propeller Total Power: 1,324kW (1,800hp) Niigata 6M34AGT 1 x 4 Stroke 6 Cy. 340 x 620 1324kW (1800bhp) Niigata Engineering Co Ltd-Japan
8403997 *JDRR* HK1-916	**TAISEI MARU No. 8** **Taisei Gyogyo KK** *Monbetsu, Hokkaido* *Japan* Official number: 127087	*161* - 155		**1984-05 Niigata Engineering Co Ltd — Niigata NI** Yd No: 1820 Loa 38.94 (BB) Br ex 7.40 Dght 2.539 Lbp 31.91 Br md 6.61 Dpth 2.87 Welded, 1 dk	**(B11B2FV) Fishing Vessel** Ins: 131 Compartments: 4 Ho, ER 11 Ha: ER	**1 oil engine** with clutches, flexible couplings & dr geared to sc. shaft driving 1 CP propeller Total Power: 736kW (1,001hp) Pielstick 6PA5 1 x 4 Stroke 6 Cy. 255 x 270 736kW (1001bhp) Niigata Engineering Co Ltd-Japan Thrusters: 1 Thwart. FP thruster (f); 1 Tunnel thruster (a)
8703531 *LW9578* -	**TAISEI MARU No. 8** *ex* Daian Maru No. 178 *-2002* *ex* Chidori Maru No. 58 *-1991* **Mattera Hermanos SA** - *Argentina* MMSI: 701000892 Official number: 02207	*950* - 1,090		**1987-09 Kitanihon Zosen K.K. — Hachinohe** Yd No: 222 Loa 71.00 (BB) Br ex - Dght 4.180 Lbp 61.02 Br md 10.61 Dpth 7.01 Welded, 2 dks	**(B11B2FV) Fishing Vessel**	**1 oil engine** geared to sc. shaft driving 1 CP propeller Total Power: 1,324kW (1,800hp) Akasaka K31FD 1 x 4 Stroke 6 Cy. 310 x 530 1324kW (1800bhp) Akasaka Tekkosho KK (Akasaka DieselLtd)-Japan
8823848 - -	**TAISEI MARU No. 11** *ex* Kowan Maru No. 11 *-1994* - -	*444* - 616		**1988-10 Yano Zosen K.K. — Imabari** Loa 50.00 Br ex - Dght 3.270 Lbp 45.00 Br md 11.00 Dpth 5.40 Welded, 1 dk	**(B33A2DG) Grab Dredger**	**1 oil engine** driving 1 FP propeller Total Power: 588kW (799hp) 10.0kn Niigata 6M28BFT 1 x 4 Stroke 6 Cy. 280 x 480 588kW (799bhp) Niigata Engineering Co Ltd-Japan

8005628 - -	TAISEI MARU No. 11 - Deepsea Fishing Ltd -	*344* 174 -		1980-07 Sanuki Shipbuilding & Iron Works Co Ltd — Mitoyo KG Yd No: 1066 Loa - Br ex - Dght - Lbp 47.17 Br md 8.72 Dpth 3.71 Welded, 1 dk	(B11B2FV) Fishing Vessel	1 oil engine driving 1 FP propeller Total Power: 1,103kW (1,500hp) Akasaka DM33 1 x 4 Stroke 6 Cy. 330 x 500 1103kW (1500bhp) Akasaka Tekkosho KK (Akasaka DieselLtd)-Japan
8710728 *YJTJ8* -	TAISEI MARU No. 15 - Ocho Dorado Shipping SA Taiseimaru Kaiun KK *Port Vila* *Vanuatu* MMSI: 577167000 Official number: 2230	4,993 2,628 6,374	Class: NK	1988-04 Mitsubishi Heavy Industries Ltd. — Shimonoseki Yd No: 908 Loa 124.25 (BB) Br ex - Dght 7.126 Lbp 115.00 Br md 17.80 Dpth 9.30 Welded, 1 dk	(A34A2GR) Refrigerated Cargo Ship Ins: 6,335 7 Ha: 6 (3.8 x 3.4) (3.5 x 3.4)ER Cranes: 4x5t,4x3t,1x3t,7x2t	1 oil engine reverse reduction geared to sc. shaft driving 1 FP propeller Total Power: 3,847kW (5,230hp) 16.0kn Mitsubishi 6UEC45LA 1 x 2 Stroke 6 Cy. 450 x 1350 3847kW (5230bhp) Mitsubishi Heavy Industries Ltd-Japan AuxGen: 3 x 750kW 450V 60Hz a.c Thrusters: 1 Thwart. CP thruster (f); 1 Tunnel thruster (a) Fuel: 2370.0 (r.f.)
8876869 *JD2572* -	TAISEI MARU No. 15 - YK Hori Gyogyobu - *Akkeshi, Hokkaido* *Japan* MMSI: 431639000 Official number: 125611	*179* - -		1982-08 K.K. Otsuchi Kogyo — Otsuchi L reg 28.80 Br ex - Dght 2.280 Lbp 27.34 Br md 6.20 Dpth 2.60 Welded, 1 dk	(B11B2FV) Fishing Vessel	1 oil engine driving 1 FP propeller Niigata 1 x 4 Stroke Niigata Engineering Co Ltd-Japan
9016478 *JL5866* -	TAISEI MARU No. 18 - YK Taisei Sangyo - *Matsuyama, Ehime* *Japan* MMSI: 431501257 Official number: 132064	*698* - 2,100		1991-04 Hitachi Zosen Mukaishima Marine Co Ltd — Onomichi HS Yd No: 38 Loa 75.12 Br ex 14.60 Dght 4.820 Lbp 69.00 Br md 14.50 Dpth 7.75 Welded	(A24D2BA) Aggregates Carrier Grain: 1,448 Compartments: 1 Ho, ER 1 Ha: ER	1 oil engine with clutches, flexible couplings & reverse geared to sc. shaft driving 1 FP propeller Total Power: 1,471kW (2,000hp) Hanshin 6LU38G 1 x 4 Stroke 6 Cy. 380 x 580 1471kW (2000bhp) The Hanshin Diesel Works Ltd-Japan
9033050 *JL6109* -	TAISEI MARU No. 21 - Shirakawa Kisen KK - *Tokushima, Tokushima* *Japan* Official number: 133003	*499* - 1,400		1992-10 Hamamoto Zosensho K.K. — Tokushima Yd No: 758 Loa 76.90 (BB) Br ex - Dght 4.073 Lbp 70.00 Br md 12.00 Dpth 7.00 Welded, 2 dks	(A31A2GX) General Cargo Ship Bale: 2,374 Compartments: 1 Ho, ER 1 Ha: ER	1 oil engine driving 1 FP propeller Total Power: 736kW (1,001hp) Niigata 6M34AGT 1 x 4 Stroke 6 Cy. 340 x 620 736kW (1001bhp) Niigata Engineering Co Ltd-Japan Thrusters: 1 Thwart. FP thruster (f)
8815578 - -	TAISEI MARU No. 21 - Han Dong Co Ltd - *South Korea*	*269* - 390		1989-03 Suzuki Shipyard Co. Ltd. — Yokkaichi Yd No: 562 Loa - Br ex - Dght 3.101 Lbp 44.02 Br md 8.51 Dpth 3.61 Welded, 1 dk	(A12A2TC) Chemical Tanker	1 oil engine driving 1 FP propeller Total Power: 331kW (450hp) Yanmar S165L-UT 1 x 4 Stroke 6 Cy. 165 x 210 331kW (450bhp) Yanmar Diesel Engine Co Ltd-Japan
9109196 *JL6202* -	TAISEI MARU No. 22 - YK Taisei Sangyo - *Matsuyama, Ehime* *Japan* MMSI: 431500281 Official number: 133979	*698* - 2,100		1994-12 Honda Zosen — Saiki Yd No: 870 Loa - Br ex - Dght 4.860 Lbp 68.00 Br md 14.60 Dpth 8.03 Welded, 1 dk	(B33A2DS) Suction Dredger	1 oil engine driving 1 FP propeller Total Power: 1,765kW (2,400hp) Hanshin LH36LG 1 x 4 Stroke 6 Cy. 360 x 670 1765kW (2400bhp) The Hanshin Diesel Works Ltd-Japan Thrusters: 1 Tunnel thruster (f)
9086758 *JILE* -	TAISEI MARU No. 24 - Taiseimaru Kaiun KK - SatCom: Inmarsat A 1206243 *Ise, Mie* *Japan* MMSI: 431678000 Official number: 134374	4,992 1,904 6,365	Class: NK	1994-10 Mitsubishi Heavy Industries Ltd. — Shimonoseki Yd No: 993 Loa 124.25 (BB) Br ex 17.84 Dght 7.127 Lbp 115.00 Br md 17.80 Dpth 9.30 Welded, 1 dk	(A34A2GR) Refrigerated Cargo Ship Ins: 6,348 7 Ha: (3.5 x 3.4)6 (3.8 x 3.4)ER Derricks: 8x5t	1 oil engine driving 1 FP propeller Total Power: 4,583kW (6,231hp) 16.8kn Mitsubishi 6UEC45LA 1 x 2 Stroke 6 Cy. 450 x 1350 4583kW (6231bhp) Kobe Hatsudoki KK-Japan AuxGen: 3 x 800kW a.c Thrusters: 1 Thwart. CP thruster (f); 1 Tunnel thruster (a) Fuel: 362.0 (d.f.) 1672.0 (r.f.) 18.0pd
9140516 *JG5461* -	TAISEI MARU No. 25 - KK Ono Kaisoten - *Tokyo* *Japan* Official number: 135822	*499* - 1,640		1996-05 Suzuki Shipyard Co. Ltd. — Yokkaichi Yd No: 625 Loa 60.40 (BB) Br ex - Dght 3.920 Lbp 55.50 Br md 10.20 Dpth 4.50 Welded, 1 dk	(A12A2TC) Chemical Tanker Compartments: 3 Ta, ER	1 oil engine driving 1 FP propeller Total Power: 1,177kW (1,600hp) 11.5kn Hanshin LH28LG 1 x 4 Stroke 6 Cy. 280 x 530 1177kW (1600bhp) The Hanshin Diesel Works Ltd-Japan
9227883 *JG5611* -	TAISEI MARU No. 27 - KK Ono Kaisoten - *Tokyo* *Japan* Official number: 136966	*266* - 600		2000-07 Suzuki Shipyard Co. Ltd. — Yokkaichi Yd No: 655 Loa 48.00 Br ex - Dght - Lbp 45.00 Br md 8.60 Dpth 3.60 Welded, 1 dk	(A12A2TC) Chemical Tanker	1 oil engine driving 1 FP propeller Total Power: 736kW (1,001hp) 11.5kn Hanshin LH26G 1 x 4 Stroke 6 Cy. 260 x 440 736kW (1001bhp) The Hanshin Diesel Works Ltd-Japan Fuel: 22.6 (d.f.)
8879483 *JM6351* -	TAISEI MARU No. 28 - YK Nakazato Zosensho - *Sasebo, Nagasaki* *Japan* Official number: 133632	*197* - 356		1994-10 Amakusa Zosen K.K. — Amakusa Yd No: 106 Loa 46.62 Br ex - Dght 2.770 Lbp 43.00 Br md 10.50 Dpth 5.40 Welded, 1 dk	(A31A2GX) General Cargo Ship	1 oil engine driving 1 FP propeller Total Power: 736kW (1,001hp) 10.5kn Niigata 6M26AGTE 1 x 4 Stroke 6 Cy. 260 x 460 736kW (1001bhp) Niigata Engineering Co Ltd-Japan
9047324 *JG5595* -	TAISEI MARU No. 32 *ex Eastern Calm -1999* KK Ono Kaisoten - *Tokyo* *Japan* MMSI: 431100849 Official number: 136769	*696* - 1,322	Class: (NK)	1992-07 Suzuki Shipyard Co. Ltd. — Yokkaichi Yd No: 600 Loa 65.70 (BB) Br ex - Dght 4.249 Lbp 60.50 Br md 10.80 Dpth 5.20 Welded, 1 dk	(A12A2LP) Molten Sulphur Tanker Liq: 624 Cargo Heating Coils Compartments: 6 Ta, ER	1 oil engine driving 1 FP propeller Total Power: 1,545kW (2,101hp) 11.5kn Hanshin 6EL32 1 x 4 Stroke 6 Cy. 320 x 640 1545kW (2101bhp) The Hanshin Diesel Works Ltd-Japan AuxGen: 2 x 144kW a.c
9115509 *JJ3822* -	TAISEI MARU No. 37 *ex Sanei Maru -2010* Sanei Unyu Kiko KK Tsurumaru Shipping Co Ltd *Matsuyama, Ehime* *Japan* MMSI: 431300239 Official number: 132326	*749* - 2,000		1995-01 Shitanoe Shipbuilding Co Ltd — Usuki OT Yd No: 1161 Loa 77.72 (BB) Br ex - Dght 5.090 Lbp 70.00 Br md 14.00 Dpth 8.45 Welded, 1 dk	(A31A2GX) General Cargo Ship Grain: 2,269; Bale: 2,235 Compartments: 1 Ho, ER 1 Ha: ER	1 oil engine with clutches & reverse geared to sc. shaft driving 1 FP propeller Total Power: 1,471kW (2,000hp) Hanshin LH41LAG 1 x 4 Stroke 6 Cy. 410 x 800 1471kW (2000bhp) The Hanshin Diesel Works Ltd-Japan
9601625 *JD3142* -	TAISEI MARU NO. 38 - Japan Railway Construction, Transport & Technology Agency & Ebisu Kaiun YK Ebisu Kaiun YK *Tokushima, Tokushima* *Japan* MMSI: 431002106 Official number: 141366	*498* - 1,630		2010-11 Tokuoka Zosen K.K. — Naruto L reg 72.44 (BB) Br ex - Dght 4.180 Lbp 70.20 Br md 12.00 Dpth 7.17 Welded, 1 dk	(A31A2GX) General Cargo Ship	1 oil engine driving 1 Propeller Total Power: 736kW (1,001hp)
9185803 *JG5532* -	TAISETSU MARU - Izumi Kisen Co Ltd & Maruwa Kaiun KK Izumi Kisen KK (Izumi Shipping Co Ltd) *Tokyo* *Japan* MMSI: 431100522 Official number: 136588	*14,188* - 20,150	Class: NK	1998-06 Kanda Zosensho K.K. — Kawajiri Yd No: 386 Loa 150.50 (BB) Br ex - Dght 9.692 Lbp 143.00 Br md 25.00 Dpth 13.30 Welded, 1 dk	(A24E2BL) Limestone Carrier Grain: 15,427 Compartments: 3 Ho, ER	1 oil engine driving 1 CP propeller Total Power: 5,980kW (8,130hp) 13.7kn B&W 6L42MC 1 x 2 Stroke 6 Cy. 420 x 1360 5980kW (8130bhp) Hitachi Zosen Corp-Japan AuxGen: 3 x 600kW 450V a.c Thrusters: 1 Thwart. FP thruster (f) Fuel: 340.0 (r.f.) 22.4pd
8747886 *JD2922* -	TAISHIN MARU - Kubo Kaiun YK - *Takamatsu, Kagawa* *Japan* Official number: 141028	*499* - 1,800		2009-07 Fukushima Zosen Ltd. — Matsue Yd No: 362 Loa 74.67 Br ex - Dght 4.350 Lbp 69.00 Br md 12.00 Dpth 7.38 Welded, 1 dk	(A31A2GX) General Cargo Ship Grain: 2,615; Bale: 2,615 1 Ha: ER (40.0 x 9.5)	1 oil engine reduction geared to sc. shaft driving 1 Propeller Total Power: 1,618kW (2,200hp) 12.0kn Niigata 6M34BGT 1 x 4 Stroke 6 Cy. 340 x 620 1618kW (2200bhp) Niigata Engineering Co Ltd-Japan

	Name / Owner	Tonnage	Class	Build	Type	Machinery
8028761 - -	**TAISHO** *ex Taisho Maru No. 16* **Nakane Marine S de RL** - *San Lorenzo* *Honduras* Official number: L-1326730	*158* - 330		**1981**-04 **Jyonan Zosen K.K. — Ube** Yd No: 137 Loa 38.00 Br ex 6.53 Dght 2.942 Lbp 34.02 Br md 6.51 Dpth 3.00 Welded, 1 dk	**(A12A2TC) Chemical Tanker**	**1 oil engine** reverse reduction geared to sc. shaft driving 1 FP propeller Total Power: 272kW (370hp) 9.5kn Yanmar 6M-HT 1 x 4 Stroke 6 Cy. 200 x 240 272kW (370bhp) Yanmar Diesel Engine Co Ltd-Japan
8844684 *JK5085* -	**TAISHO MARU** - **Shoichi Horikawa** - *Hiroshima, Hiroshima* *Japan* Official number: 132531	*332* - 336		**1990**-10 **Nagashima Zosen KK — Kihoku ME** Loa 45.50 Br ex - Dght 2.920 Lbp 39.50 Br md 9.50 Dpth 3.10 Welded, 1 dk	**(A31A2GX) General Cargo Ship**	**1 oil engine** driving 1 FP propeller Total Power: 368kW (500hp) 9.9kn Yanmar MF28-HT 1 x 4 Stroke 6 Cy. 280 x 450 368kW (500bhp) Matsue Diesel KK-Japan
8702525 *JI3307* -	**TAISHO MARU** - **Taiyo Shipping Co Ltd (Taiyo Kisen KK)** - *Osaka, Osaka* *Japan* MMSI: 431300084 Official number: 128708	*3,215* - 5,678	Class: NK	**1987**-07 **Imabari Shipbuilding Co Ltd — Imabari EH (Imabari Shipyard)** Yd No: 465 Loa 93.02 (BB) Br ex - Dght 6.904 Lbp 88.02 Br md 16.31 Dpth 8.21 Welded, 1 dk	**(A24A2BT) Cement Carrier** Grain: 4,652; Bale: 4,652	**1 oil engine** driving 1 FP propeller Total Power: 3,089kW (4,200hp) 12.5kn Mitsubishi 6UEC37LA 1 x 2 Stroke 6 Cy. 370 x 880 3089kW (4200bhp) Akasaka Tekkosho KK (Akasaka DieselLtd)-Japan AuxGen: 4 x 207kW a.c Thrusters: 1 Thwart. CP thruster (f) Fuel: 250.0 (r.f.)
9109299 *JH3336* -	**TAISHO MARU** - **Taisho Kaiun YK** - *Hazu, Aichi* *Japan* Official number: 133247	*466* - 437		**1994**-09 **Katsuura Dockyard Co. Ltd. — Nachi-Katsuura** Yd No: 330 Loa 50.30 Br ex - Dght 2.820 Lbp 44.20 Br md 10.50 Dpth 3.00 Welded, 1 dk	**(A31A2GX) General Cargo Ship**	**1 oil engine** driving 1 FP propeller Total Power: 736kW (1,001hp) 8.0kn Matsui ML627GSC 1 x 4 Stroke 6 Cy. 270 x 480 736kW (1001bhp) Matsui Iron Works Co Ltd-Japan
9242405 *BR3414* -	**TAISHO MARU** *ex Daisho Maru -2010* **Tehsin Shipping Co Ltd** Kaochin Steamship Co Ltd *Kaohsiung* *Chinese Taipei* MMSI: 416003985 Official number: 015031	*499* - 1,540		**2000**-07 **Yamanaka Zosen K.K. — Imabari** Yd No: 656 Loa 75.49 (BB) Br ex - Dght 4.042 Lbp 70.18 Br md 12.30 Dpth 6.95 Welded, 1 dk	**(A31A2GX) General Cargo Ship** Grain: 2,461 TEU 80 C. 80/20' Compartments: 1 Ho, ER 1 Ha: ER	**1 oil engine** reduction geared to sc. shaft driving 1 FP propeller Total Power: 1,324kW (1,800hp) 12.5kn Daihatsu 6DKM-26 1 x 4 Stroke 6 Cy. 260 x 380 1324kW (1800bhp) Daihatsu Diesel Manufacturing Co Lt-Japan AuxGen: 2 x 120kW 445V 60Hz a.c Thrusters: 1 Thwart. FP thruster (f) Fuel: 82.0 (d.f.) 5.4pd
8509868 *JJ3460* -	**TAISHO MARU No. 3** - **Seiwa Kaiun KK** - *Osaka, Osaka* *Japan* Official number: 125360	*198* - 555		**1985**-09 **Daiko Dockyard Co. Ltd. — Osaka** Yd No: 132 Loa 46.61 Br ex - Dght 3.350 Lbp 43.01 Br md 7.60 Dpth 3.61 Welded, 1 dk	**(A12A2TC) Chemical Tanker** Liq: 284 Compartments: 6 Ta, ER 1 Cargo Pump (s): 1x150m³/hr	**1 oil engine** driving 1 FP propeller Total Power: 441kW (600hp) Yanmar MF24-HT 1 x 4 Stroke 6 Cy. 240 x 420 441kW (600bhp) Yanmar Diesel Engine Co Ltd-Japan
8916724 - -	**TAISHO MARU No. 5** - - -	*154* - 340		**1990**-05 **K.K. Odo Zosen Tekko — Shimonoseki** Yd No: 370 Loa 40.08 Br ex 6.82 Dght 2.950 Lbp 36.00 Br md 6.80 Dpth 3.10 Welded, 1 dk	**(A12A2TC) Chemical Tanker** Liq: 167 Compartments: 4 Ta, ER	**1 oil engine** with clutches & reverse geared to sc. shaft driving 1 FP propeller Total Power: 331kW (450hp) Matsui ML624GS 1 x 4 Stroke 6 Cy. 240 x 400 331kW (450bhp) Matsui Iron Works Co Ltd-Japan
9485291 *JD2556* -	**TAISHO MARU NO. 6** - **Taiho Unyu KK (Taiho Shipping Co Ltd)** - *Osaka, Osaka* *Japan* Official number: 140685	*198* - 552		**2007**-11 **Hongawara Zosen K.K. — Fukuyama** Yd No: 608 Loa 49.72 Br ex 8.02 Dght 3.150 Lbp 45.00 Br md 8.00 Dpth 3.35 Welded, 1 dk	**(A12A2TC) Chemical Tanker** Double Hull (13F) Liq: 346 1 Cargo Pump (s): 1x200m³/hr	**1 oil engine** reduction geared to sc. shaft driving 1 Propeller Total Power: 588kW (799hp) 10.5kn Yanmar 1 x 4 Stroke 588kW (799bhp) Yanmar Diesel Engine Co Ltd-Japan
8844452 - -	**TAISHO MARU No. 8** - - -	*174* - 336		**1990**-08 **Hongawara Zosen K.K. — Fukuyama** Loa 41.70 Br ex - Dght 2.800 Lbp 37.00 Br md 7.20 Dpth 3.30 Welded, 1 dk	**(A12A2TC) Chemical Tanker**	**1 oil engine** driving 1 FP propeller Total Power: 331kW (450hp) 9.5kn Yanmar S165L-UT 1 x 4 Stroke 6 Cy. 165 x 210 331kW (450bhp) Yanmar Diesel Engine Co Ltd-Japan
8916578 - -	**TAISHO MARU No. 25** - - -	*451* - 650		**1989**-10 **Honda Zosen — Saiki** Yd No: 806 Loa 47.80 (BB) Br ex - Dght 3.450 Lbp 43.80 Br md 11.00 Dpth 5.35 Welded, 1 dk	**(A24D2BA) Aggregates Carrier** Compartments: 1 Ho, ER	**1 oil engine** with clutches & reverse geared to sc. shaft driving 1 FP propeller Total Power: 736kW (1,001hp) Niigata 6M26AGTE 1 x 4 Stroke 6 Cy. 260 x 460 736kW (1001bhp) Niigata Engineering Co Ltd-Japan Thrusters: 1 Thwart. FP thruster (f)
8865030 *JK5176* -	**TAISHO MARU No. 31** - **Miyazaki Kisen YK** - *Kagoshima, Kagoshima* *Japan* Official number: 133056	*487* - 1,188		**1992**-07 **Kimura Zosen K.K. — Kure** L reg 62.00 Br ex - Dght 4.400 Lbp - Br md 13.00 Dpth 7.20 Welded, 1 dk	**(A24D2BA) Aggregates Carrier**	**1 oil engine** driving 1 FP propeller Total Power: 736kW (1,001hp) Niigata 6M34AGT 1 x 4 Stroke 6 Cy. 340 x 620 736kW (1001bhp) Niigata Engineering Co Ltd-Japan
7378303 - -	**TAISHO No. 1** - **Taisho Jitsugyo** - *Keelung* *Chinese Taipei*	*499* - -		**1974**-03 **Usuki Iron Works Co Ltd — Usuki OT** Yd No: 932 Loa - Br ex 10.01 Dght 4.090 Lbp 53.80 Br md 9.99 Dpth - Welded, 1 dk	**(B11B2FV) Fishing Vessel**	**1 oil engine** driving 1 FP propeller Total Power: 2,059kW (2,799hp) Hanshin 6LUS40 1 x 4 Stroke 6 Cy. 400 x 640 2059kW (2799bhp) The Hanshin Diesel Works Ltd-Japan
9402366 *JD2355* -	**TAISHU MARU NO. 7** - **Taishu Kaiun KK** - *Fukuoka, Fukuoka* *Japan* Official number: 140464	*199* - 700		**2007**-01 **Taiyo Shipbuilding Co Ltd — Sanyoonoda YC** Yd No: 312 Loa 56.90 (BB) Br ex - Dght 3.120 Lbp 53.00 Br md 9.40 Dpth 5.30 Welded, 1 dk	**(A31A2GX) General Cargo Ship** Grain: 1,170; Bale: 1,170 Compartments: 1 Ho, ER 1 Ha: ER (30.8 x 7.0)	**1 oil engine** reduction geared to sc. shaft driving 1 FP propeller Total Power: 735kW (999hp) 11.0kn Hanshin LH26G 1 x 4 Stroke 6 Cy. 260 x 440 735kW (999bhp) The Hanshin Diesel Works Ltd-Japan
7103849 - -	**TAISIER II** *ex Golden Sand 3 -2000 ex Dargahan 5 -2000* **Saeed Ali Al Shamsi** -	*123* 60 107	Class: (LR) ✠ Classed LR until 21/11/75	**1971**-03 **Astilleros Luzuriaga SA — Pasaia** Yd No: 153 Loa 23.78 Br ex 7.45 Dght 2.794 Lbp 21.01 Br md 7.32 Dpth 3.66 Welded, 1 dk	**(B11A2FT) Trawler**	**1 oil engine** reverse reduction geared to sc. shaft driving 1 FP propeller Total Power: 400kW (544hp) Caterpillar D353TA 1 x 4 Stroke 6 Cy. 159 x 203 400kW (544bhp) Caterpillar Tractor Co-USA AuxGen: 2 x 20kW 216V 60Hz a.c
8971310 *BASS* -	**TAISING 805** *ex Guo Ji 805 -2003* **Taising Fishery (Singapore) Pte Ltd** - *Dalian, Liaoning* *China* Official number: 010021	**297** 89 208		**1998**-02 **Dalian Fishing Vessel Co — Dalian LN** Loa 47.50 Br ex - Dght 2.950 Lbp 37.00 Br md 7.80 Dpth 3.85 Welded, 1 dk	**(A34A2GR) Refrigerated Cargo Ship**	**1 oil engine** driving 1 FP propeller Total Power: 558kW (759hp)
8971322 - -	**TAISING 806** *ex Guo Ji 806 -2003* **Taising Fishery (Singapore) Pte Ltd** - *Dalian, Liaoning* *China* Official number: 010022	**297** 89 208		**1998**-02 **Dalian Fishing Vessel Co — Dalian LN** Loa 47.50 Br ex - Dght 2.950 Lbp 37.00 Br md 7.60 Dpth 3.85 Welded, 1 dk	**(A34A2GR) Refrigerated Cargo Ship**	**1 oil engine** driving 1 FP propeller Total Power: 558kW (759hp)
8966078 *CB6536* -	**TAITAO** *ex Transportier -2011* **Astilleros Kotesky SA** - *Valparaiso* *Chile* MMSI: 725001790 Official number: 3108	*124* - -		**1964 Astilleros Marco Chilena S.A. — Iquique** L reg 28.13 Br ex - Dght - Lbp - Br md 7.50 Dpth 3.83 Welded, 1 dk	**(B11B2FV) Fishing Vessel**	**1 oil engine** driving 1 FP propeller

IMO / Call sign / Fishing no.	Name / Owner / Manager	Tonnage	Class	Build / Dimensions	Type / Capacity	Machinery
9403669 *3FJB7* -	**TAITAR NO. 1** **NiMiC No 1 SA** NiMiC Ship Management Co Ltd SatCom: Inmarsat C 437184610 *Panama* *Panama* MMSI: 371846000 Official number: 4128910A	**118,634** 35,591 77,089 T/cm 111.1	Class: NK	**2009**-10 **Mitsubishi Heavy Industries Ltd. — Nagasaki** Yd No: 2241 Loa 289.50 (BB) Br ex - Dght 11.929 Lbp 277.00 Br md 49.00 Dpth 27.00 Welded, 1 dk	**(A11A2TN) LNG Tanker** Double Hull Liq (Gas): 144,627 4 x Gas Tank (s); 4 independent Kvaerner-Moss (s.stl) sph 8 Cargo Pump (s): 8x1500m³/hr Manifold: Bow/CM: 130.9m	**1 Steam Turb** reduction geared to sc. shaft driving 1 FP propeller Total Power: 26,919kW (36,599hp) 18.5kn Kawasaki UA-400 1 x steam Turb 26919kW (36599shp) Kawasaki Heavy Industries Ltd-Japan AuxGen: 2 x 3100kW 450V 60Hz a.c, 1 x 3100kW 450V 60Hz a.c Thrusters: 1 Tunnel thruster (f) Fuel: 350.0 (d.f.) 5413.0 (r.f.)
9403645 *3EXZ* -	**TAITAR NO. 2** **NiMiC No 2 SA** NiMiC Ship Management Co Ltd SatCom: Inmarsat C 437230710 *Panama* *Panama* MMSI: 372307000 Official number: 4121810A	**118,634** 35,591 77,089 T/cm 111.1	Class: NK	**2009**-12 **Kawasaki Shipbuilding Corp — Sakaide KG** Yd No: 1625 Loa 289.50 (BB) Br ex - Dght 11.929 Lbp 277.00 Br md 49.00 Dpth 27.00 Welded, 1 dk	**(A11A2TN) LNG Tanker** Double Hull Liq (Gas): 144,627 4 x Gas Tank (s); 4 independent Kvaerner-Moss (s.stl) sph 8 Cargo Pump (s): 8x1500m³/hr Manifold: Bow/CM: 130.9m	**1 Steam Turb** reduction geared to sc. shaft driving 1 FP propeller Total Power: 26,919kW (36,599hp) 19.5kn Kawasaki UA-400 1 x steam Turb 26919kW (36599shp) Kawasaki Heavy Industries Ltd-Japan AuxGen: 2 x 3100kW 450V 60Hz a.c, 1 x 3100kW 450V 60Hz a.c Thrusters: 1 Tunnel thruster (f) Fuel: 350.0 (d.f.) 5413.0 (r.f.)
9403671 *3FMD5* -	**TAITAR NO. 3** **NiMiC No 3 SA** NiMiC Ship Management Co Ltd SatCom: Inmarsat C 437219510 *Panama* *Panama* MMSI: 372195000 Official number: 39879PEXT1	**118,634** 35,591 77,089 T/cm 111.1	Class: NK	**2010**-01 **Mitsubishi Heavy Industries Ltd. — Nagasaki** Yd No: 2242 Loa 289.50 (BB) Br ex - Dght 11.929 Lbp 277.00 Br md 49.00 Dpth 27.00 Welded, 1 dk	**(A11A2TN) LNG Tanker** Double Hull Liq (Gas): 144,627 4 x Gas Tank (s); 4 independent Kvaerner-Moss (s.stl) sph 8 Cargo Pump (s): 8x1500m³/hr Manifold: Bow/CM: 130.9m	**1 Steam Turb** reduction geared to sc. shaft driving 1 FP propeller Total Power: 26,919kW (36,599hp) 18.5kn Kawasaki UA-400 1 x steam Turb 26919kW (36599shp) Kawasaki Heavy Industries Ltd-Japan AuxGen: 2 x 3100kW 450V 60Hz a.c, 1 x 3100kW 450V 60Hz a.c Thrusters: 1 Tunnel thruster (f) Fuel: 350.0 (d.f.) 5413.0 (r.f.)
9403657 *3EXA9* -	**TAITAR NO. 4** **NiMiC No 4 SA** NiMiC Ship Management Co Ltd SatCom: Inmarsat C 435176710 *Panama* *Panama* MMSI: 351767000 Official number: 4208810	**118,634** 35,591 77,053 T/cm 111.0	Class: NK	**2010**-10 **Kawasaki Heavy Industries Ltd — Sakaide KG** Yd No: 1626 Loa 289.50 (BB) Br ex - Dght 11.930 Lbp 277.00 Br md 49.00 Dpth 27.00 Welded, 1 dk	**(A11A2TN) LNG Tanker** Double Hull Liq (Gas): 144,596 4 x Gas Tank (s); 4 independent Kvaerner-Moss (alu) sph 8 Cargo Pump (s): 8x1500m³/hr Manifold: Bow/CM: 130.9m	**1 Steam Turb** reduction geared to sc. shaft driving 1 FP propeller Total Power: 26,919kW (36,599hp) 19.5kn Kawasaki UA-400 1 x steam Turb 26919kW (36599shp) Kawasaki Heavy Industries Ltd-Japan AuxGen: 2 x 3100kW a.c, 1 x 3100kW a.c Thrusters: 1 Tunnel thruster (f) Fuel: 370.0 (d.f.) 5950.0 (r.f.)
9253507 *ZQTW5* FR 227	**TAITS** **Klondyke Fishing Co Ltd** - *Fraserburgh* *United Kingdom* MMSI: 235118000 Official number: C17249	**1,965** 590 1,736	Class: NV	**2001**-02 **Societatea Comerciala Severnav S.A. — Drobeta-Turnu Severin** (Hull) **2001**-02 **Karmsund Maritime Service AS — Kopervik** Yd No: 11 Lengthened-2009 Loa 70.60 Br ex 13.03 Dght 7.111 Lbp 64.00 Br md 13.00 Dpth 8.00 Welded, 1 dk	**(B11B2FV) Fishing Vessel** Ins: 1,330	**1 oil engine** reduction geared to sc. shaft driving 1 CP propeller Total Power: 4,045kW (5,500hp) Bergens BVM-12 1 x Vee 4 Stroke 12 Cy. 320 x 360 4045kW (5500bhp) Rolls Royce Marine AS-Norway
9066382 *JM6283* -	**TAIWA MARU** **Wada Kaiun KK** - *Kitakyushu, Fukuoka* *Japan* Official number: 132739	*498* - 1,180		**1993**-04 **Sanyo Zosen K.K. — Onomichi** Yd No: 1053 Loa 64.98 Br ex 10.02 Dght 4.180 Lbp 60.40 Br md 10.00 Dpth 4.55 Welded, 1 dk	**(A12A2TC) Chemical Tanker** Liq: 1,229 Compartments: 8 Ta, ER 2 Cargo Pump (s): 2x300m³/hr	**1 oil engine** with clutches & reverse geared to sc. shaft driving 1 FP propeller Total Power: 736kW (1,001hp) Akasaka K28BFD 1 x 4 Stroke 6 Cy. 280 x 480 736kW (1001bhp) Akasaka Tekkosho KK (Akasaka DieselLtd)-Japan
9185384 *JNJY* K01-998	**TAIWA MARU No. 8** **KK Taiwa** - SatCom: Inmarsat B 343111610 *Tosa, Kochi* *Japan* MMSI: 431116000 Official number: 136492	*379* - -		**1998**-02 **KK Kanasashi — Shizuoka SZ** Yd No: 3458 Loa 56.00 (BB) Br ex 8.00 Dght - Lbp 49.00 Br md - Dpth 3.00 Welded, 1 dk	**(B11B2FV) Fishing Vessel** Ins: 483 Compartments: 3 Ho 3 Ha:	**1 oil engine** with clutches, flexible couplings & sr geared to sc. shaft driving 1 FP propeller Total Power: 736kW (1,001hp) Akasaka K28SFD 1 x 4 Stroke 6 Cy. 280 x 500 736kW (1001bhp) Akasaka Tekkosho KK (Akasaka DieselLtd)-Japan
7366271 - -	**TAIWA MARU No. 8** - -	*499* 321 1,199		**1974**-03 **K.K. Matsuo Tekko Zosensho — Matsue** Yd No: 280 Loa 58.12 Br ex 9.22 Dght - Lbp 53.50 Br md 9.20 Dpth 4.30 Riveted\Welded, 1 dk	**(A12A2TC) Chemical Tanker**	**1 oil engine** geared to sc. shaft driving 1 FP propeller Total Power: 956kW (1,300hp) Daihatsu 6DSM-26 1 x 4 Stroke 6 Cy. 260 x 320 956kW (1300bhp) Daihatsu Diesel Manufacturing Co Lt-Japan
9146675 - -	**TAIWA MARU No. 18** - -	**577** 231 -		**1996**-06 **KK Kanasashi — Shizuoka SZ** Yd No: 3367 Loa 56.00 (BB) Br ex - Dght - Lbp 49.00 Br md 8.00 Dpth 3.00 Welded, 1 dk	**(B11B2FV) Fishing Vessel** Ins: 483	**1 oil engine** with clutches, flexible couplings & sr reverse geared to sc. shaft driving 1 FP propeller Total Power: 736kW (1,001hp) 12.8kn Akasaka K28SFD 1 x 4 Stroke 6 Cy. 280 x 500 736kW (1001bhp) Akasaka Tekkosho KK (Akasaka DieselLtd)-Japan AuxGen: 2 x 320kW a.c Fuel: 289.0 (d.f.) 5.0pd
9250593 *JNKR* K01-978	**TAIWA MARU NO. 78** **KK Taiwa** - *Tosa, Kochi* *Japan* MMSI: 432306000 Official number: 136503	*409* - -		**2001**-07 **Kanasashi Heavy Industries Co Ltd — Shizuoka SZ** Yd No: 8007 Loa 57.69 Br ex - Dght - Lbp - Br md 9.00 Dpth 3.90 Welded, 1 dk	**(B11B2FV) Fishing Vessel**	**1 oil engine** geared to sc. shaft driving 1 FP propeller Total Power: 1,177kW (1,600hp) Akasaka K28SFD 1 x 4 Stroke 6 Cy. 280 x 500 1177kW (1600bhp) Akasaka Tekkosho KK (Akasaka DieselLtd)-Japan
9053488 *JPSY* K01-828	**TAIWA MARU No. 88** **KK Taiwa** - SatCom: Inmarsat A 1204520 *Tosa, Kochi* *Japan* MMSI: 431500470 Official number: 132914	*409* - -		**1992**-04 **KK Kanasashi — Shizuoka SZ** Yd No: 3297 Loa 56.70 (BB) Br ex 8.83 Dght 3.450 Lbp 49.60 Br md 8.80 Dpth 3.84 Welded, 1 dk	**(B11B2FV) Fishing Vessel**	**1 oil engine** with flexible couplings & sr reverse geared to sc. shaft driving 1 FP propeller Total Power: 1,177kW (1,600hp) Akasaka K31FD 1 x 4 Stroke 6 Cy. 310 x 530 1177kW (1600bhp) Akasaka Tekkosho KK (Akasaka DieselLtd)-Japan
9105281 - -	**TAIWA MARU No. 108** - - *China*	**405** 237 -		**1994**-05 **KK Kanasashi — Shizuoka SZ** Yd No: 3341 Loa 56.00 (BB) Br ex - Dght 3.450 Lbp 49.20 Br md 8.80 Dpth 3.85 Welded, 1 dk	**(B11B2FV) Fishing Vessel** Grain: 457; Bale: 410	**1 oil engine** with clutches, flexible couplings & sr reverse geared to sc. shaft driving 1 FP propeller Total Power: 736kW (1,001hp) 12.6kn Akasaka K28SFD 1 x 4 Stroke 6 Cy. 280 x 500 736kW (1001bhp) Akasaka Tekkosho KK (Akasaka DieselLtd)-Japan AuxGen: 2 x 320kW a.c Fuel: 272.0 (d.f.) 3.0pd
8934180 *BP3227* -	**TAIWAN FUEL** *ex* Kyosei Maru *-2006* **Taiwan Fuel & Energy Supply Co Ltd** - *Taichung* *Chinese Taipei* MMSI: 416179800 Official number: 14649	**1,068** 588 1,866	Class: CR	**1997 Kurinoura Dockyard Co Ltd — Yawatahama EH** Yd No: 340 Loa 77.00 Br ex - Dght 4.460 Lbp 72.00 Br md 11.50 Dpth 5.20 Welded, 1 dk	**(A13B2TP) Products Tanker** Liq: 2,205; Liq (Oil): 2,205 2 Cargo Pump (s): 2x750m³/hr	**1 oil engine** driving 1 FP propeller Total Power: 1,618kW (2,200hp) 12.0kn Akasaka A34C 1 x 4 Stroke 6 Cy. 340 x 620 1618kW (2200bhp) Akasaka Tekkosho KK (Akasaka DieselLtd)-Japan Fuel: 14.0 (d.f.) 60.0 (r.f.)
7110775 - -	**TAIWAN MACHY** **Ching Fa Fishing Co Ltd** - *Chinese Taipei*	*150* - -		**1970 Taiwan Machinery Manufacturing Corp. — Kaohsiung** Loa - Br ex - Dght - Lbp - Br md - Dpth - Welded	**(B11B2FV) Fishing Vessel**	**1 oil engine** driving 1 FP propeller 9.0kn

8883575 - -	**TAIWAN No. 8** **Taiwan Salvage Engineering Co Ltd** - *Kaohsiung* *Chinese Taipei* Official number: 7903	*221* 99 108	Class: CR	**1981 Lien Ho Shipbuilding Co, Ltd — Kaohsiung** Loa 29.00 Br ex 9.21 Dght 2.000 Lbp 26.00 Br md 9.00 Dpth 2.70 Welded, 1 dk	**(B34B2SC) Crane Vessel**	**2 oil engines** geared to sc. shafts driving 2 FP propellers Total Power: 316kW (430hp) 7.0kn Yanmar 6MA-HT 2 x 4 Stroke 6 Cy. 200 x 240 each-158kW (215bhp) Yanmar Diesel Engine Co Ltd-Japan AuxGen: 1 x 200kW 450V a.c
8883587 - -	**TAIWAN No. 10** **Taiwan Salvage Engineering Co Ltd** - *Kaohsiung* *Chinese Taipei* Official number: 7932	*221* 99 108	Class: CR	**1981 Lien Ho Shipbuilding Co, Ltd — Kaohsiung** Loa 29.00 Br ex 9.21 Dght 2.000 Lbp 26.00 Br md 9.00 Dpth 2.70 Welded, 1 dk	**(B34B2SC) Crane Vessel**	**2 oil engines** geared to sc. shafts driving 2 FP propellers Total Power: 316kW (430hp) 7.5kn Yanmar 6MA-HT 2 x 4 Stroke 6 Cy. 200 x 240 each-158kW (215bhp) Yanmar Diesel Engine Co Ltd-Japan AuxGen: 1 x 200kW 450V a.c
8877277 - -	**TAIWAN No. 11** **Taiwan Salvage Engineering Co Ltd** - *Kaohsiung* *Chinese Taipei*	*497* 149 -	Class: CR	**1990 Lien Ho Shipbuilding Co, Ltd — Kaohsiung** Loa 41.30 Br ex - Dght 3.200 Lbp 38.50 Br md 11.60 Dpth 4.50 Welded, 1 dk	**(B34T2QR) Work/Repair Vessel**	**2 oil engines** geared to sc. shafts driving 2 FP propellers Total Power: 882kW (1,200hp) Yanmar M220-EN 2 x 4 Stroke 6 Cy. 220 x 300 each-441kW (600bhp) Yanmar Diesel Engine Co Ltd-Japan AuxGen: 1 x 360kW 450V a.c, 1 x 100kW 450V a.c
8980488 *JL6490* -	**TAIYO** **Nippon Kaiun KK (Nippon Shipping Co Ltd)** - *Takamatsu, Kagawa* *Japan* MMSI: 431501747 Official number: 137032	*994* - 540		**2002-12 Yamanaka Zosen K.K. — Imabari** Yd No: 675 L reg 62.01 Br ex - Dght 2.800 Lbp - Br md 15.00 Dpth 4.20 Welded, 1 dk	**(A35A2RR) Ro-Ro Cargo Ship** Stern ramp (a) Angled bow ramp (f)	**2 oil engines** driving 2 Propellers Total Power: 1,472kW (2,002hp) Niigata 6MG19HX 2 x 4 Stroke 6 Cy. 190 x 260 each-736kW (1001bhp) Niigata Engineering Co Ltd-Japan Thrusters: 1 Thwart. FP thruster (f)
8631659 *JM5710* -	**TAIYO** **Yasuda Sangyo Kisen KK (Yasuda Ocean Line Co Ltd)** - *Sasebo, Nagasaki* *Japan* Official number: 130356	*106* - -		**1988-03 Nankai Zosen — Kochi** Loa 32.00 Br ex 6.62 Dght 1.800 Lbp 26.80 Br md 6.60 Dpth 2.78 Bonded, 1 dk	**(A37B2PS) Passenger Ship** Hull Material: Reinforced Plastic Passengers: 231	**2 oil engines** driving 1 FP propeller Total Power: 1,472kW (2,002hp) G.M. (Detroit Diesel) 16V-92-TI 2 x Vee 2 Stroke 16 Cy. 123 x 127 each-736kW (1001bhp) General Motors Corp-USA
9325726 *3EEU4* -	**TAIYO** **Baba Maritime SA** MK Shipmanagement Co Ltd *Panama* *Panama* MMSI: 371815000 Official number: 3145206A	**6,395** 3,658 10,080	Class: NK	**2006-02 Shin Kurushima Dockyard Co. Ltd. — Hashihama, Imabari** Yd No: 5413 Loa 100.59 Br ex - Dght 9.219 Lbp 93.50 Br md 18.80 Dpth 13.00 Welded, 2 dks	**(A31A2GX) General Cargo Ship** Grain: 13,999; Bale: 12,865 Compartments: 2 Ho, ER 2 Ha: (28.5 x 12.6)ER (19.5 x 12.6) Cranes: 2x30.7t; Derricks: 1x30t	**1 oil engine** driving 1 FP propeller Total Power: 2,390kW (3,249hp) 12.5kn MAN-B&W 5L35MC 1 x 2 Stroke 5 Cy. 350 x 1050 2390kW (3249bhp) Makita Corp-Japan AuxGen: 3 x 347kW a.c Fuel: 650.0
8859146 *3FVJ5* -	**TAIYO 6** *ex* Zhong He 18 *-2012* *ex* Suzu Maru No. 18 *-2011* **Taihai International Shipping Ltd** Dalian Chuangjie Shipping Co Ltd *Panama* *Panama* MMSI: 357394000 Official number: 4366512A	**2,035** 1,160 3,694	Class: IB	**1991-08 Shinwa Sangyo K.K. — Osakikamijima** Yd No: 483 Lengthened-2011 Loa 81.68 Br ex - Dght 3.270 Lbp 77.17 Br md 12.00 Dpth 7.20 Welded, 1 dk	**(A31A2GX) General Cargo Ship** Grain: 4,200; Bale: 3,890 Compartments: 1 Ho, ER 1 Ha: (19.2 x 9.6)ER Cranes: 1	**1 oil engine** driving 1 FP propeller Total Power: 662kW (900hp) 11.0kn Hanshin LH28LG 1 x 4 Stroke 6 Cy. 280 x 530 662kW (900bhp) The Hanshin Diesel Works Ltd-Japan
8864438 *JK5130* -	**TAIYO MARU** *ex* Kyokushin Maru *-2006* **YK Okamine Kaiun** - *Kure, Hiroshima* *Japan* Official number: 133038	*199* - 423		**1992-04 Hongawara Zosen K.K. — Fukuyama** Loa 47.65 Br ex - Dght 2.950 Lbp 43.00 Br md 7.80 Dpth 3.40 Welded, 1 dk	**(A12A2TC) Chemical Tanker** 2 Cargo Pump (s): 2x100m³/hr	**1 oil engine** driving 1 FP propeller Total Power: 478kW (650hp) 10.0kn Hanshin 1 x 4 Stroke 478kW (650bhp) The Hanshin Diesel Works Ltd-Japan
8944109 *JK5548* -	**TAIYO MARU** **Taiyo Kaiun YK** - *Kure, Hiroshima* *Japan* Official number: 135267	*199* - -		**1998-09 Y.K. Okajima Zosensho — Matsuyama** Yd No: 254 Loa 57.66 Br ex - Dght - Lbp 51.00 Br md 9.50 Dpth 5.50 Welded, 1 dk	**(A31A2GX) General Cargo Ship**	**1 oil engine** reverse geared to sc. shaft driving 1 FP propeller Total Power: 736kW (1,001hp) 11.9kn Akasaka K26SR 1 x 4 Stroke 6 Cy. 260 x 480 736kW (1001bhp) Akasaka Tekkosho KK (Akasaka DieselLtd)-Japan
8806436 - -	**TAIYO MARU** *ex* Tatsu Maru *-2003* **PT Akita Putera Lines** *Indonesia*	*199* - 700		**1988-03 Yamanaka Zosen K.K. — Imabari** Yd No: 362 Loa 56.01 (BB) Br ex - Dght 3.241 Lbp 52.00 Br md 9.40 Dpth 5.47 Welded, 2 dks	**(A31A2GX) General Cargo Ship** Grain: 1,330; Bale: 1,299 Compartments: 1 Ho, ER 1 Ha: (31.0 x 7.5)ER	**1 oil engine** with clutches & reverse geared to sc. shaft driving 1 FP propeller Total Power: 588kW (799hp) 9.9kn Hanshin 6LU26G 1 x 4 Stroke 6 Cy. 260 x 440 588kW (799bhp) The Hanshin Diesel Works Ltd-Japan
8713160 *JG4692* -	**TAIYO MARU** **YK Shiba Kaiun** - *Komatsushima, Tokushima* *Japan* Official number: 129753	*143* - 465		**1987-11 Iisaku Zosen K.K. — Nishi-Izu** Yd No: 87135 Loa 40.52 Br ex - Dght 2.471 Lbp 38.51 Br md 8.50 Dpth 2.80 Welded, 1 dk	**(A13B2TP) Products Tanker** Liq: 550; Liq (Oil): 550	**1 oil engine** with clutches, flexible couplings & reverse reduction geared to sc. shaft driving 1 FP propeller Total Power: 331kW (450hp) Matsui ML624GSC 1 x 4 Stroke 6 Cy. 240 x 400 331kW (450bhp) Matsui Iron Works Co Ltd-Japan Thrusters: 1 Thwart. FP thruster (f)
9100619 *JL6299* -	**TAIYO MARU** **Kokichi Umakoshi** - *Imabari, Ehime* *Japan* Official number: 134877	*351* - 917		**1994-10 Taiyo Shipbuilding Co Ltd — Sanyoonoda YC** Yd No: 255 Loa 69.02 (BB) Br ex - Dght 3.350 Lbp 62.00 Br md 10.70 Dpth 5.90 Welded, 1 dk	**(A31A2GX) General Cargo Ship** Grain: 1,758 Compartments: 1 Ho, ER 1 Ha: ER	**1 oil engine** driving 1 FP propeller Total Power: 735kW (999hp) Hanshin LH28G 1 x 4 Stroke 6 Cy. 280 x 460 735kW (999bhp) The Hanshin Diesel Works Ltd-Japan Thrusters: 1 Thwart. FP thruster (f)
8217037 *JI3156* -	**TAIYO MARU** **Shoyo Kisen Kaisha Ltd** - *Osaka, Osaka* *Japan* Official number: 126452	*159* - -		**1982-11 Kanagawa Zosen — Kobe** Yd No: 243 Loa 31.50 Br ex - Dght 2.601 Lbp 26.52 Br md 8.62 Dpth 3.81 Welded, 1 dk	**(B32A2ST) Tug**	**2 oil engines** Geared Integral to driving 2 Z propellers Total Power: 1,912kW (2,600hp) Niigata 6MG25BX 2 x 4 Stroke 6 Cy. 250 x 320 each-956kW (1300bhp) Niigata Engineering Co Ltd-Japan AuxGen: 2 x 80kW 220V a.c
6720597 - -	**TAIYO MARU** -	*547* 215 339		**1967 Hayashikane Shipbuilding & Engineering Co Ltd — Yokosuka KN** Yd No: 658 Loa 56.01 Br ex 9.61 Dght 3.963 Lbp 49.51 Br md 9.58 Dpth 6.66 Welded, 1 dk	**(B11B2FV) Fishing Vessel**	**1 oil engine** driving 1 FP propeller Total Power: 1,324kW (1,800hp) 11.5kn Niigata 16MGV25X 1 x Vee 4 Stroke 16 Cy. 250 x 320 1324kW (1800bhp) Niigata Engineering Co Ltd-Japan
9671280 *JD3583* -	**TAIYO MARU** **Taiyo Kisen KK** - *Imabari, Ehime* *Japan* MMSI: 431004884 Official number: 142027	*998* - 2,440	Class: NK	**2013-09 Murakami Hide Zosen K.K. — Imabari** Yd No: 597 Loa 79.92 Br ex - Dght 5.161 Lbp 76.10 Br md 12.20 Dpth 5.75 Welded, 1 dk	**(A13B2TP) Products Tanker** Double Hull (13F) Liq: 2,459; Liq (Oil): 2,459	**1 oil engine** reduction geared to sc. shaft driving 1 Propeller Total Power: 1,618kW (2,200hp) Daihatsu 6DKM-26 1 x 4 Stroke 6 Cy. 260 x 380 1618kW (2200bhp) Daihatsu Diesel Manufacturing Co Lt-Japan Fuel: 120.0
9219630 *JK5516* -	**TAIYO MARU No. 1** **YK Sumikin Kisen** - *Kure, Hiroshima* *Japan* Official number: 135324	*198* - -		**1999-06 Taiyo Shipbuilding Co Ltd — Sanyoonoda YC** Yd No: 277 Loa 45.93 Br ex - Dght - Lbp 42.00 Br md 7.80 Dpth 3.30 Welded, 1 dk	**(A13B2TU) Tanker (unspecified)** Double Hull 1 Cargo Pump (s): 1x500m³/hr	**1 oil engine** driving 1 FP propeller Total Power: 625kW (850hp) 11.0kn Niigata 6M26BGT 1 x 4 Stroke 6 Cy. 260 x 460 625kW (850bhp) Niigata Engineering Co Ltd-Japan Fuel: 22.0 (d.f.)
7930008 - -	**TAIYO MARU No. 1** *ex* Mankan Maru No. 5 *-1993* *ex* Matsuei Maru No. 88 *-1983* - -	*344* 165 432		**1980-05 Niigata Engineering Co Ltd — Niigata NI** Yd No: 1671 Loa 54.28 Br ex - Dght 3.391 Lbp 47.53 Br md 8.91 Dpth 3.76 Welded, 1 dk	**(B11B2FV) Fishing Vessel**	**1 oil engine** geared to sc. shaft driving 1 FP propeller Total Power: 736kW (1,001hp) Niigata 6M31AET 1 x 4 Stroke 6 Cy. 310 x 530 736kW (1001bhp) Niigata Engineering Co Ltd-Japan

Numbers	Name / Owner	Tonnage	Class	Builder / Dimensions	Type / Capacity	Machinery
7535717 - -	**TAIYO MARU No. 2** - -	*116* 24 -		**1975-07 K.K. Izutsu Zosensho — Nagasaki** Yd No: 710 Loa 38.51 Br ex 7.70 Dght - Lbp 31.53 Br md 6.90 Dpth 2.77 Welded, 1 dk	**(B11B2FV) Fishing Vessel**	**1 oil engine** reduction geared to sc. shaft driving 1 FP propeller Total Power: 956kW (1,300hp) Niigata 6L25BX 1 x 4 Stroke 6 Cy. 250 x 320 956kW (1300bhp) Niigata Engineering Co Ltd-Japan
9058866 *JK5209* -	**TAIYO MARU No. 2** **YK Kotobuki Shipping** - *Bizen, Okayama* Japan Official number: 133683	*498* - 1,217	Class: NK	**1993-01 Sanyo Zosen K.K. — Onomichi** Yd No: 1051 Loa 64.39 Br ex 10.02 Dght 4.120 Lbp 60.00 Br md 10.00 Dpth 4.50 Welded, 1 dk	**(A12B2TR) Chemical/Products Tanker** Liq: 1,300; Liq (Oil): 1,300 Compartments: 8 Wing Ta, ER	**1 oil engine** geared to sc. shaft driving 1 FP propeller Total Power: 736kW (1,001hp) 11.8kn Akasaka K28BFD 1 x 4 Stroke 6 Cy. 280 x 480 736kW (1001bhp) Akasaka Tekkosho KK (Akasaka DieselLtd)-Japan Fuel: 55.0 (d.f.)
9565364 *7JES* MG1-2033	**TAIYO MARU NO. 2** **Taiyo A&F Co Ltd (Taiyo A&F KK)** - *Tokyo* Japan MMSI: 432708000 Official number: 140940	*415* - 826		**2009-07 Miho Zosensho K.K. — Shimizu** Yd No: 1535 Loa 66.50 Br ex 12.20 Dght 4.700 Lbp 57.00 Br md 12.13 Dpth 4.75 Welded, 1 dk	**(B11B2FV) Fishing Vessel**	**1 oil engine** driving 1 CP propeller Total Power: 2,942kW (4,000hp) Akasaka AH41AK 1 x 4 Stroke 6 Cy. 410 x 640 2942kW (4000bhp) Akasaka Tekkosho KK (Akasaka DieselLtd)-Japan
9100554 - -	**TAIYO MARU No. 3** - - Bangladesh	*749* - 2,073		**1994-05 Shin Kurushima Dockyard Co. Ltd. — Hashihama, Imabari** Yd No: 2812 Loa 76.67 (BB) Br ex - Dght 4.830 Lbp 72.00 Br md 11.40 Dpth 5.35 Welded, 1 dk	**(A13B2TP) Products Tanker** Liq: 2,240; Liq (Oil): 2,240 Compartments: 10 Ta, ER	**1 oil engine** with clutches & reverse geared to sc. shaft driving 1 FP propeller Total Power: 1,471kW (2,000hp) Hanshin LH32LG 1 x 4 Stroke 6 Cy. 320 x 640 1471kW (2000bhp) The Hanshin Diesel Works Ltd-Japan
8625636 - -	**TAIYO MARU No. 3** - - South Korea	*171* - -		**1986 Azumi Zosen Kensetsu K.K. — Himeji** Loa 28.02 Br ex - Dght 3.001 Lbp 25.00 Br md 8.01 Dpth 3.31 Welded, 1 dk	**(B32B2SP) Pusher Tug**	**1 oil engine** geared to sc. shaft driving 1 FP propeller Total Power: 1,471kW (2,000hp) 8.0kn Hanshin 6LU35G 1 x 4 Stroke 6 Cy. 350 x 550 1471kW (2000bhp) The Hanshin Diesel Works Ltd-Japan
7912965 - -	**TAIYO MARU No. 5** - - *Noumea* France	*344* 173 -		**1979-10 KK Kanasashi Zosen — Shizuoka SZ** Yd No: 2027 Loa 53.68 Br ex - Dght 3.401 Lbp 47.71 Br md 8.81 Dpth 3.76 Welded, 1 dk	**(B11B2FV) Fishing Vessel**	**1 oil engine** driving 1 FP propeller Total Power: 883kW (1,201hp) Niigata 6MG28ZE 1 x 4 Stroke 6 Cy. 280 x 480 883kW (1201bhp) Niigata Engineering Co Ltd-Japan
9135389 *JBME* FS1-650	**TAIYO MARU No. 5** **KK Yoshida Kiyoshi Shoten** - SatCom: Inmarsat C 443179710 *Iwaki, Fukushima* Japan MMSI: 431797000 Official number: 133343	*432* - -		**1995-10 Niigata Engineering Co Ltd — Niigata NI** Yd No: 2300 Loa 57.00 (BB) Br ex - Dght - Lbp 49.00 Br md 9.00 Dpth 3.00 Welded, 1 dk	**(B11B2FV) Fishing Vessel** Ins: 559	**1 oil engine** with clutches, flexible couplings & sr reverse geared to sc. shaft driving 1 FP propeller Total Power: 699kW (950hp) Niigata 6M28MFT 1 x 4 Stroke 6 Cy. 280 x 480 699kW (950bhp) Niigata Engineering Co Ltd-Japan
9151474 *JM6508* -	**TAIYO MARU No. 5** **Taiyo Kaiun KK** - *Ube, Yamaguchi* Japan Official number: 134611	*392* - 1,150		**1996-11 Taiyo Shipbuilding Co Ltd — Sanyoonoda YC** Yd No: 267 Loa 70.68 (BB) Br ex - Dght 3.750 Lbp 67.20 Br md 11.00 Dpth 6.10 Welded, 1 dk	**(A31A2GX) General Cargo Ship** Liq: 2,243 Compartments: 1 Ho, ER 1 Ha: ER	**1 oil engine** driving 1 FP propeller Total Power: 736kW (1,001hp) Hanshin 6LC28LG 1 x 4 Stroke 6 Cy. 280 x 530 736kW (1001bhp) The Hanshin Diesel Works Ltd-Japan
7004720 - -	**TAIYO MARU No. 7** - -	*111* 22 -		**1969 K.K. Izutsu Zosensho — Nagasaki** Yd No: 526 Loa 35.46 Br ex 6.74 Dght 2.471 Lbp 30.21 Br md 6.71 Dpth 2.80 Welded, 1 dk	**(B11B2FV) Fishing Vessel**	**1 oil engine** driving 1 FP propeller Total Power: 736kW (1,001hp) Niigata 6L25BX 1 x 4 Stroke 6 Cy. 250 x 320 736kW (1001bhp) Niigata Engineering Co Ltd-Japan
9057977 *JDHW* KG1-38	**TAIYO MARU No. 8** **Hamazaki Suisan YK** - SatCom: Inmarsat A 1205232 *Ichikikushikino, Kagoshima* Japan MMSI: 432415000 Official number: 132761	*379* - 465		**1992-06 Miho Zosensho K.K. — Shimizu** Yd No: 1412 Loa 56.04 (BB) Br ex 8.82 Dght 3.452 Lbp 49.20 Br md 8.80 Dpth 3.80 Welded, 1 dk	**(B11B2FV) Fishing Vessel**	**1 oil engine** with clutches, flexible couplings & sr geared to sc. shaft driving 1 FP propeller Total Power: 736kW (1,001hp) Akasaka K28BFD 1 x 4 Stroke 6 Cy. 280 x 480 736kW (1001bhp) Akasaka Tekkosho KK (Akasaka DieselLtd)-Japan
9033488 *JJ3706* -	**TAIYO MARU No. 8** *ex Kamigumi Maru No. 3 -1999* **Taiyo Kaiun YK** - *Karatsu, Saga* Japan Official number: 132351	*199* - 699		**1991-12 Nippon Zosen Tekko K.K. — Kitakyushu** Yd No: 338 Loa 55.87 (BB) Br ex 9.52 Dght 3.290 Lbp 51.00 Br md 9.50 Dpth 5.50 Welded, 2 dks	**(A31A2GX) General Cargo Ship** Grain: 1,251; Bale: 1,105 Compartments: 1 Ho, ER 1 Ha: ER	**1 oil engine** with clutches & reverse geared to sc. shaft driving 1 FP propeller Total Power: 625kW (850hp) Akasaka T26SR 1 x 4 Stroke 6 Cy. 260 x 440 625kW (850bhp) Akasaka Tekkosho KK (Akasaka DieselLtd)-Japan
8849036 - -	**TAIYO MARU No. 8** - -	*138* - -		**1976 Minami-Nippon Zosen KK — Ichikikushikino KS** L reg 29.40 Br ex - Dght - Lbp - Br md 6.40 Dpth 2.50 Welded, 1 dk	**(B11B2FV) Fishing Vessel**	**1 oil engine** driving 1 FP propeller Total Power: 353kW (480hp)
9392262 *JD2246* -	**TAIYO MARU NO. 8** **Taiyo Kaiun KK** - *Yamaguchi, Yamaguchi* Japan MMSI: 431402047 Official number: 140315	**399** - 1,300		**2006-06 Taiyo Shipbuilding Co Ltd — Sanyoonoda YC** Yd No: 310 Loa 70.65 Br ex - Dght 3.640 Lbp 65.00 Br md 11.00 Dpth 6.10 Welded, 1 dk	**(A31A2GX) General Cargo Ship**	**1 oil engine** reduction geared to sc. shaft driving 1 FP propeller Total Power: 1,177kW (1,600hp) Niigata 6M28NT 1 x 4 Stroke 6 Cy. 280 x 480 1177kW (1600bhp) Niigata Engineering Co Ltd-Japan
8909927 - -	**TAIYO MARU No. 11** - - Indonesia	*397* - 1,145		**1990-01 Taiyo Shipbuilding Co Ltd — Sanyoonoda YC** Yd No: 216 Loa 67.72 Br ex - Dght 3.700 Lbp 62.00 Br md 11.00 Dpth 6.00 Welded, 2 dks	**(A31A2GX) General Cargo Ship** Compartments: 1 Ho, ER 1 Ha: ER	**1 oil engine** geared to sc. shaft driving 1 FP propeller Total Power: 809kW (1,100hp) Hanshin LH28G 1 x 4 Stroke 6 Cy. 280 x 460 809kW (1100bhp) The Hanshin Diesel Works Ltd-Japan
8921133 *JMSH* FS1-585	**TAIYO MARU No. 11** **KK Ichi Maru** - SatCom: Inmarsat A 1204473 *Iwaki, Fukushima* Japan MMSI: 431702640 Official number: 130744	*379* - -		**1990-03 KK Kanasashi Zosen — Shizuoka SZ** Yd No: 3218 Loa 54.71 (BB) Br ex 8.73 Dght 3.400 Lbp 48.10 Br md 8.70 Dpth 3.75 Welded, 1 dk	**(B11B2FV) Fishing Vessel** Ins: 540	**1 oil engine** with clutches, flexible couplings & sr reverse geared to sc. shaft driving 1 FP propeller Total Power: 736kW (1,001hp) Niigata 6M28BFT 1 x 4 Stroke 6 Cy. 280 x 480 736kW (1001bhp) Niigata Engineering Co Ltd-Japan
7935137 - -	**TAIYO MARU No. 15** **Char Pon Marine Co Ltd** - Chinese Taipei	*199* - 592		**1979 Hayashi Zosen — Osakikamijima** Yd No: 118 Loa - Br ex - Dght - Lbp 46.00 Br md 8.01 Dpth 5.01 Welded, 1 dk	**(A31A2GX) General Cargo Ship**	**1 oil engine** driving 1 FP propeller Total Power: 625kW (850hp) Hanshin 1 x 4 Stroke 625kW (850bhp) The Hanshin Diesel Works Ltd-Japan
9079509 *JL6090* -	**TAIYO MARU No. 18** **Taiyo Kaiun YK** - *Naruto, Tokushima* Japan Official number: 132980	*489* - 1,350		**1993-12 Hamamoto Zosensho K.K. — Tokushima** Yd No: 781 Loa 69.20 (BB) Br ex - Dght 4.382 Lbp 62.00 Br md 13.00 Dpth 7.10 Welded, 2 dks	**(A31A2GX) General Cargo Ship** Grain: 1,295 Compartments: 1 Ho, ER 1 Ha: ER	**1 oil engine** driving 1 FP propeller Total Power: 736kW (1,001hp) Niigata 6M34AGT 1 x 4 Stroke 6 Cy. 340 x 620 736kW (1001bhp) Niigata Engineering Co Ltd-Japan Thrusters: 1 Thwart. FP thruster (f)
9567817 *JD3050* -	**TAIYO MARU NO. 18** **Taiyo Kaiun KK** - *Ube, Yamaguchi* Japan MMSI: 431001326 Official number: 141222	*369* - 1,250		**2010-03 Taiyo Shipbuilding Co Ltd — Sanyoonoda YC** Yd No: 322 Loa 68.00 Br ex - Dght 3.740 Lbp 62.00 Br md 11.00 Dpth 6.30 Welded, 1 dk	**(A31A2GX) General Cargo Ship** Grain: 1,901; Bale: 1,901 1 Ha: ER (35.2 x 8.6)	**1 oil engine** reduction geared to sc. shaft driving 1 FP propeller Total Power: 1,176kW (1,599hp) Niigata 6M28NT 1 x 4 Stroke 6 Cy. 280 x 480 1176kW (1599bhp) Niigata Engineering Co Ltd-Japan

Identity	Name / Owner	Tonnage	Class	Builder / Dimensions	Type / Cargo	Machinery
9042776 *JREC* FS1-5	**TAIYO MARU No. 21** **KK Yoshida Kiyoshi Shoten** - SatCom: Inmarsat A 1204713 *Iwaki, Fukushima* *Japan* MMSI: 432269000 Official number: 132234	*435* - -		**1991-12 KK Kanasashi — Shizuoka SZ** Yd No: 3286 Loa 56.70 (BB) Br ex 8.83 Dght 3.450 Lbp 49.60 Br md 8.80 Dpth 3.84 Welded, 1 dk	**(B11B2FV) Fishing Vessel** Ins: 555	**1 oil engine** with clutches, flexible couplings & sr reverse geared to sc. shaft driving 1 FP propeller Total Power: 736kW (1,001hp) Niigata 6M28HFT 1 x 4 Stroke 6 Cy. 280 x 480 736kW (1001bhp) Niigata Engineering Co Ltd-Japan
8967357 *JPEZ* -	**TAIYO MARU No. 21** **Taiyo A&F Co Ltd (Taiyo A&F KK)** - *Tokyo* *Japan* MMSI: 431333000 Official number: 137000	*135* - -		**2001-04 K.K. Watanabe Zosensho — Nagasaki** Yd No: 088 Loa 47.17 (BB) Br ex - Dght 2.980 Lbp 37.50 Br md 8.10 Dpth 3.30 Welded, 1 dk	**(B11B2FV) Fishing Vessel**	**1 oil engine** driving 1 FP propeller Total Power: 2,206kW (2,999hp) Niigata 6MG28HLX 1 x 4 Stroke 6 Cy. 280 x 400 2206kW (2999bhp) Niigata Engineering Co Ltd-Japan
7231608 - -	**TAIYO MARU No. 25** **YK Maruju Gyogyo** -	*181* - 245		**1972 Tokushima Zosen K.K. — Fukuoka** Yd No: 1081 Loa 39.10 Br ex 6.74 Dght 2.801 Lbp 33.51 Br md 6.71 Dpth 3.28 Welded, 1 dk	**(B11B2FV) Fishing Vessel**	**1 oil engine** driving 1 FP propeller Total Power: 883kW (1,201hp) Niigata 6L25BX 1 x 4 Stroke 6 Cy. 250 x 320 883kW (1201bhp) Niigata Engineering Co Ltd-Japan
6706527 - -	**TAIYO MARU No. 26** - -	*199* 94 -		**1966 Fukuoka Shipbuilding Co Ltd — Fukuoka FO** Yd No: 837 Loa 38.00 Br ex 6.63 Dght 2.998 Lbp 35.18 Br md 6.61 Dpth 3.36 Welded, 1 dk	**(B11B2FV) Fishing Vessel**	**1 oil engine** driving 1 FP propeller Total Power: 552kW (750hp) Niigata 1 x 4 Stroke 6 Cy. 280 x 440 552kW (750bhp) Niigata Engineering Co Ltd-Japan
8708036 *7KLS* KG1-228	**TAIYO MARU No. 28** **Hamazaki Suisan YK** - SatCom: Inmarsat A 1201170 *Ichikikushikino, Kagoshima* *Japan* MMSI: 432380000 Official number: 129492	*367* - -		**1987-07 KK Kanasashi Zosen — Shizuoka SZ** Yd No: 3136 Loa 50.09 (BB) Br ex 8.44 Dght 3.252 Lbp 43.52 Br md 8.40 Dpth 3.61 Welded, 1 dk	**(B11B2FV) Fishing Vessel** Grain: 468; Bale: 417	**1 oil engine** with clutches, flexible couplings & sr reverse geared to sc. shaft driving 1 FP propeller Total Power: 736kW (1,001hp) Hanshin LH28G 1 x 4 Stroke 6 Cy. 280 x 460 736kW (1001bhp) The Hanshin Diesel Works Ltd-Japan
9115468 *JI3580* -	**TAIYO MARU No. 32** **Taiyo Tanker KK** - *Osaka, Osaka* *Japan* MMSI: 431300266 Official number: 135023	*749* - 2,060		**1995-05 Shin Kurushima Dockyard Co. Ltd. — Hashihama, Imabari** Yd No: 2813 Loa 76.67 (BB) Br ex 11.40 Dght 4.830 Lbp 72.00 Br md - Dpth 5.35 Welded, 1 dk	**(A13B2TP) Products Tanker** Liq: 2,319; Liq (Oil): 2,319 Compartments: 10 Ta, ER	**1 oil engine** reverse geared to sc. shaft driving 1 FP propeller Total Power: 1,471kW (2,000hp) Hanshin LH32LG 1 x 4 Stroke 6 Cy. 320 x 640 1471kW (2000bhp) The Hanshin Diesel Works Ltd-Japan
8717192 *JKRY* FS1-555	**TAIYO MARU No. 37** **KK Yoshida Kiyoshi Shoten** - SatCom: Inmarsat A 1204212 *Iwaki, Fukushima* *Japan* MMSI: 431875000 Official number: 130682	*379* - -		**1988-04 Niigata Engineering Co Ltd — Niigata NI** Yd No: 2076 Loa 54.06 (BB) Br ex - Dght 3.441 Lbp 47.91 Br md 8.70 Dpth 3.81 Welded, 1 dk	**(B11B2FV) Fishing Vessel** Ins: 516	**1 oil engine** with clutches, flexible couplings & sr geared to sc. shaft driving 1 CP propeller Total Power: 699kW (950hp) Niigata 6M28BFT 1 x 4 Stroke 6 Cy. 280 x 480 699kW (950bhp) Niigata Engineering Co Ltd-Japan
9146754 *JEKL* S01-1166	**TAIYO MARU No. 38** **Miho Maguro Gyogyo KK (Miho Tuna Fishery Co Ltd)** - SatCom: Inmarsat B 343186910 *Shizuoka, Shizuoka* *Japan* MMSI: 431869000 Official number: 133274	*408* - 455		**1996-06 Miho Zosensho K.K. — Shimizu** Yd No: 1475 Loa 56.00 (BB) Br ex - Dght 3.451 Lbp 49.00 Br md 8.00 Dpth 3.80 Welded, 1 dk	**(B11B2FV) Fishing Vessel** Ins: 678	**1 oil engine** with flexible couplings & sr gearedto sc. shaft driving 1 FP propeller Total Power: 736kW (1,001hp) 13.0kn Niigata 6M28HFT 1 x 4 Stroke 6 Cy. 280 x 480 736kW (1001bhp) Niigata Engineering Co Ltd-Japan AuxGen: 2 x 240kW 225V a.c Fuel: 293.0 (d.f.) 3.0pd
8921119 *JRII* S01-1278	**TAIYO MARU NO. 58** *ex* Fukutoku Maru No. 8 *-2013* **Miho Maguro Gyogyo KK (Miho Tuna Fishery Co Ltd)** - SatCom: Inmarsat A 1201144 *Kesennuma, Miyagi* *Japan* MMSI: 431703660 Official number: 130903	*379* - -		**1990-03 KK Kanasashi Zosen — Shizuoka SZ** Yd No: 3207 Loa 54.71 (BB) Br ex - Dght 3.400 Lbp 48.10 Br md 8.70 Dpth 3.75 Welded, 1 dk	**(B11B2FV) Fishing Vessel** Ins: 479	**1 oil engine** with clutches & sr reverse geared to sc. shaft driving 1 FP propeller Total Power: 736kW (1,001hp) Niigata 6M28BFT 1 x 4 Stroke 6 Cy. 280 x 480 736kW (1001bhp) Niigata Engineering Co Ltd-Japan
7118387 - -	**TAIYO MARU No. 73** **Nippon Senpaku Kogyo Co Ltd (Nippon Senpaku Kogyo KK)** -	*268* - -		**1971 Tokushima Zosen K.K. — Fukuoka** Yd No: 1013 Loa 49.33 Br ex 7.62 Dght 3.175 Lbp 42.98 Br md 7.60 Dpth 3.61 Welded, 1 dk	**(B11A2FT) Trawler**	**1 oil engine** driving 1 FP propeller Total Power: 1,103kW (1,500hp) Niigata 8MG25BX 1 x 4 Stroke 8 Cy. 250 x 320 1103kW (1500bhp) Niigata Engineering Co Ltd-Japan
7212676 - -	**TAIYO MARU No. 75** - -	*334* - 474		**1972 Tokushima Zosen K.K. — Fukuoka** Yd No: 1063 Loa 51.31 Br ex 7.83 Dght 3.760 Lbp 45.01 Br md 7.80 Dpth 3.92 Welded, 1 dk	**(B11B2FV) Fishing Vessel**	**1 oil engine** driving 1 FP propeller Total Power: 1,471kW (2,000hp) Niigata 6L31EZ 1 x 4 Stroke 6 Cy. 310 x 380 1471kW (2000bhp) Niigata Engineering Co Ltd-Japan
8627933 *JG4607*	**TAIYO No. 1** **Akihiko Suzuki** - *Yokohama, Kanagawa* *Japan* Official number: 128919	*156* - 460		**1985-09 Muneta Zosen K.K. — Akashi** Loa - Br ex - Dght 3.000 Lbp 34.60 Br md 8.01 Dpth 3.61 Welded, 1 dk	**(A31A2GX) General Cargo Ship**	**1 oil engine** driving 1 FP propeller
8603755 *V6PTP* -	**TAIYO POHNPEI** *ex* Fuji Maru *-2012* *ex* Nippon Maru *-2007* **Taiyo Micronesia Corp** Taiyo A&F Co Ltd (Taiyo A&F KK) *Kolonia, Pohnpei* *Micronesia* MMSI: 510054000 Official number: 129779	**1,788** 612 1,380	Class: KR	**1986-08 Miho Zosensho K.K. — Shimizu** Yd No: 1286 Loa 78.57 (BB) Br ex 14.03 Dght 5.562 Lbp 70.01 Br md 14.00 Dpth 8.28 Welded, 2 dks	**(B11A2FS) Stern Trawler**	**1 oil engine** with clutches, flexible couplings & reverse reduction geared to sc. shaft driving 1 FP propeller Total Power: 2,795kW (3,800hp) Akasaka AH40AK 1 x 4 Stroke 6 Cy. 400 x 640 2795kW (3800bhp) Akasaka Tekkosho KK (Akasaka DieselLtd)-Japan Thrusters: 1 Thwart. FP thruster (f)
9156591 *ERSW* -	**TAIYOH** *ex* Taiyoh III *-2012* **First Global Inc** Saud Shipping *Moldova* MMSI: 214181923	**52,618** 28,191 95,666 T/cm 89.7	Class: BV (Class contemplated) NK	**1997-06 Imabari Shipbuilding Co Ltd — Marugame KG (Marugame Shipyard)** Yd No: 1271 Loa 246.89 (BB) Br ex 42.34 Dght 13.470 Lbp 235.00 Br md 42.00 Dpth 19.50 Welded, 1 dk	**(A13A2TW) Crude/Oil Products Tanker** Double Hull (13F) Liq: 108,107; Liq (Oil): 108,107 Cargo Heating Coils Compartments: 4 Ta, 6 Wing Ta, ER 3 Cargo Pump (s): 3x2500m³/hr Manifold: Bow/CM: 125m	**1 oil engine** driving 1 FP propeller Total Power: 11,360kW (15,445hp) 14.5kn Sulzer 7RTA62 1 x 2 Stroke 7 Cy. 620 x 2150 11360kW (15445bhp) Diesel United Ltd.-Aioi AuxGen: 3 x 520kW 450V 60Hz a.c Fuel: 280.0 (d.f.) (Heating Coils) 3176.0 (r.f.) 44.7pd
9044176 *DSNQ7* -	**TAIYOUNG SKY** **Taiyoung Shipping Co Ltd** - *Jeju* *South Korea* MMSI: 440077000 Official number: JJR-049579	**2,483** 815 3,709 T/cm 10.5	Class: KR	**1992-07 Dae Sun Shipbuilding & Engineering Co Ltd — Busan** Yd No: 390 Loa 94.50 (BB) Br ex - Dght 5.691 Lbp 88.01 Br md 14.00 Dpth 7.00 Welded, 1 dk	**(A31A2GX) General Cargo Ship** Grain: 2,987 Compartments: 2 Ho, ER 2 Ha: 2 (25.0 x 9.5)ER	**1 oil engine** driving 1 FP propeller Total Power: 2,189kW (2,976hp) 12.7kn B&W 6S26MC 1 x 2 Stroke 6 Cy. 260 x 980 2189kW (2976bhp) Ssangyong Heavy Industries Co Ltd-South Korea AuxGen: 2 x 200kW 445V 60Hz a.c Thrusters: 1 Thwart. FP thruster (a) Fuel: 72.7 (d.f.) 211.5 (r.f.) 8.2pd
9071454 *DSON6* -	**TAIYOUNG STAR** **Taiyoung Shipping Co Ltd** - *Jeju* *South Korea* MMSI: 440970000 Official number: JJR-051644	**1,545** 545 2,163	Class: KR	**1993-11 ShinA Shipbuilding Co Ltd — Tongyeong** Yd No: 367 Loa 79.10 (BB) Br ex 12.24 Dght 5.012 Lbp 73.50 Br md 12.00 Dpth 6.20 Welded, 1 dk	**(A31A2GX) General Cargo Ship** Grain: 1,591 Compartments: 1 Ho, ER 1 Ha: ER	**1 oil engine** with clutches, flexible couplings & sr reverse geared to sc. shaft driving 1 FP propeller Total Power: 1,261kW (1,714hp) 12.0kn Alpha 6L28/32A 1 x 4 Stroke 6 Cy. 280 x 320 1261kW (1714bhp) Ssangyong Heavy Industries Co Ltd-South Korea AuxGen: 2 x 160kW 445V a.c

9044152 *DSNN5* -
TAIYOUNG SUN
Taiyoung Shipping Co Ltd
-
Jeju *South Korea*
MMSI: 441405000
Official number: JJR-049225

2,487 815 3,739
Class: KR

1992-02 Dae Sun Shipbuilding & Engineering Co Ltd — Busan Yd No: 388
Loa 94.50 (BB) Br ex - Dght 5.691
Lbp 88.00 Br md 14.00 Dpth 7.00
Welded, 1 dk

(A31A2GX) General Cargo Ship
Grain: 2,579; Bale: 2,579
Compartments: 2 Ho, ER
2 Ha: 2 (25.0 x 9.5)ER

1 oil engine driving 1 FP propeller
Total Power: 2,189kW (2,976hp) 12.7kn
B&W 6S26MC
1 x 2 Stroke 6 Cy. 260 x 980 2189kW (2976bhp)
Ssangyong Heavy Industries Co Ltd-South Korea
AuxGen: 2 x 200kW 445V 60Hz a.c
Thrusters: 1 Thwart. FP thruster (a)
Fuel: 72.7 (d.f.) 211.5 (r.f.) 8.2pd

8323276 *JL5225* -
TAIYU MARU NO. 17
Taiyu Gyogyo KK
-
Ainan, Ehime *Japan*
Official number: 126357

199 - -

1984-04 K.K. Izutsu Zosensho — Nagasaki Yd No: 882
Loa 47.55 (BB) Br ex - Dght 3.222
Lbp 39.81 Br md 7.56 Dpth 3.66
Welded, 1 dk

(B11B2FV) Fishing Vessel
Ins: 360

1 oil engine with clutches & sr reverse geared to sc. shaft driving 1 FP propeller
Total Power: 861kW (1,171hp)
Yanmar 6Z280-ET
1 x 4 Stroke 6 Cy. 280 x 360 861kW (1171bhp)
Yanmar Diesel Engine Co Ltd-Japan

9009619 *JL5972* -
TAIYU MARU NO. 25
Taiyu Gyogyo KK
-
Ainan, Ehime *Japan*
MMSI: 431186000
Official number: 131438

335 - -

1991-02 K.K. Izutsu Zosensho — Nagasaki Yd No: 1002
Loa - Br ex - Dght 3.901
Lbp 53.95 Br md 9.01 Dpth 4.42
Welded

(B11B2FV) Fishing Vessel

1 oil engine driving 1 FP propeller
Total Power: 1,147kW (1,559hp)
Daihatsu 6DKM-32
1 x 4 Stroke 6 Cy. 320 x 360 1147kW (1559bhp)
Daihatsu Diesel Manufacturing Co Lt-Japan

8889622 *JK5314* -
TAIZAN
Toshiyo Suetomi
-
Hofu, Yamaguchi *Japan*
MMSI: 431400439
Official number: 134095

199 - 639

1995-06 YK Furumoto Tekko Zosensho — Osakikamijima Yd No: 616
Loa 57.70 Br ex - Dght 3.300
Lbp 51.00 Br md 9.50 Dpth 5.55
Welded, 1 dk

(A31A2GX) General Cargo Ship
Compartments: 1 Ho, ER
1 Ha: (30.5 x 7.5)ER

1 oil engine driving 1 FP propeller
Total Power: 736kW (1,001hp) 11.0kn
Niigata 6M26AGTE
1 x 4 Stroke 6 Cy. 260 x 460 736kW (1001bhp)
Niigata Engineering Co Ltd-Japan

9244635 *HOMQ* -
TAIZAN
Ocean Link Maritime SA
Kyoei Tanker Co Ltd
SatCom: Inmarsat C 435550210
Panama *Panama*
MMSI: 355502000
Official number: 2876802B

160,084 95,718 300,405 T/cm 179.3
Class: NK

2002-09 Nippon Kokan KK (NKK Corp) — Tsu ME Yd No: 225
Loa 333.00 (BB) Br ex 60.04 Dght 20.865
Lbp 321.67 Br md 60.00 Dpth 29.60
Welded, 1 dk

(A13A2TV) Crude Oil Tanker
Double Hull (13F)
Liq: 334,336; Liq (Oil): 334,336
Compartments: 5 Ta, ER, 10 Wing Ta, 2 Wing Slop Ta
4 Cargo Pump (s): 3x5000m³/hr, 1x2500m³/hr
Manifold: Bow/CM: 164.2m

1 oil engine driving 1 FP propeller
Total Power: 27,160kW (36,927hp) 16.1kn
Sulzer 7RTA84T
1 x 2 Stroke 7 Cy. 840 x 3150 27160kW (36927bhp)
Diesel United Ltd.-Aioi
AuxGen: 3 x 1200kW 450V 60Hz a.c
Fuel: 401.0 (d.f.) (Heating Coils) 7960.0 (r.f.) 102.6pd

9207493 *JK5574* -
TAIZAN MARU
Daio Shoun KK
Nakano Lines Ltd (Nakano Kaiun KK)
Shunan, Yamaguchi *Japan*
MMSI: 431401616
Official number: 136113

499 - 1,593

1998-11 Yamanaka Zosen K.K. — Imabari Yd No: 630
Loa 76.23 Br ex - Dght 4.060
Lbp 70.00 Br md 12.00 Dpth 7.01
Welded, 1 dk

(A31A2GX) General Cargo Ship
Grain: 2,477
Compartments: 1 Ho, ER
1 Ha: (40.0 x 9.5)ER

1 oil engine driving 1 FP propeller
Total Power: 1,471kW (2,000hp) 13.5kn
Hanshin LH34LA
1 x 4 Stroke 6 Cy. 340 x 640 1471kW (2000bhp)
The Hanshin Diesel Works Ltd-Japan

9619892 *VRIJ9* -
TAIZHOU PIONEER
Maple Diamond Maritime Ltd
Maple Leaf Shipping Co Ltd
Hong Kong *Hong Kong*
MMSI: 477095800
Official number: HK-3065

20,954 11,781 32,453 T/cm 46.0
Class: NK (GL)

2011-09 Taizhou Maple Leaf Shipbuilding Co Ltd — Linhai ZJ Yd No: LBC31800-029
Loa 179.90 (BB) Br ex - Dght 10.170
Lbp 171.50 Br md 28.40 Dpth 14.10
Welded, 1 dk

(A21A2BC) Bulk Carrier
Grain: 43,496; Bale: 41,780
Compartments: 5 Ho, ER
5 Ha: 3 (20.0 x 19.2) (18.4 x 19.2)ER (14.4 x 17.6)
Cranes: 4x30t

1 oil engine driving 1 FP propeller
Total Power: 6,480kW (8,810hp) 13.7kn
MAN-B&W 6S42MC
1 x 2 Stroke 6 Cy. 420 x 1764 6480kW (8810bhp)
STX Engine Co Ltd-South Korea
Fuel: 120.0 (d.f.) 1200.0 (r.f.)

9559559 *YDA6420* -
TAJAM
PT Maritim Barito Perkasa
-
Banjarmasin *Indonesia*
MMSI: 525002008

180 54 114
Class: AB (NK)

2009-09 Fulsail Sdn Bhd — Sibu (Hull) Yd No: 7513
2009-09 Pacific Ocean Engineering & Trading Pte Ltd (POET) — Singapore Yd No: (7513)
Loa 27.00 Br ex - Dght 2.810
Lbp 24.95 Br md 8.20 Dpth 3.60
Welded, 1 dk

(B32A2ST) Tug

2 oil engines reduction geared to sc. shafts driving 2 Propellers
Total Power: 1,790kW (2,434hp)
Cummins KTA-38-M2
2 x Vee 4 Stroke 12 Cy. 159 x 159 each-895kW (1217bhp)
Cummins Engine Co Ltd-United Kingdom
AuxGen: 2 x 80kW a.c
Fuel: 110.0

9565821 *JD2915* -
TAJIMA
Hyogo Prefecture
-
Kobe, Hyogo *Japan*
Official number: 141018

199 - -

2009-07 Nagasaki Zosen K.K. — Nagasaki Yd No: 1220
Loa 44.50 Br ex 7.62 Dght 2.800
Lbp 36.00 Br md 7.60 Dpth 3.20
Welded, 1 dk

(B12D2FR) Fishery Research Vessel

1 oil engine reduction geared to sc. shaft driving 1 Propeller
Total Power: 1,471kW (2,000hp)
Niigata 6MG26HLX
1 x 4 Stroke 6 Cy. 260 x 350 1471kW (2000bhp)
Niigata Engineering Co Ltd-Japan

8910469 - -
TAJIMA MARU
Zhoushan Port Haitong Tug & Barge Co Ltd
-
China

205 - 103

1990-01 Imamura Zosen — Kure Yd No: 344
Loa 32.83 Br ex 9.52 Dght 3.200
Lbp 26.50 Br md 9.50 Dpth 4.30
Welded, 1 dk

(B32A2ST) Tug

2 oil engines with flexible couplings & dr geared to sc. shafts driving 2 CP propellers
Total Power: 2,574kW (3,500hp)
Yanmar 6Z280L-ET
2 x 4 Stroke 6 Cy. 280 x 360 each-1287kW (1750bhp)
Yanmar Diesel Engine Co Ltd-Japan

8731306 *JD2342* -
TAJIMA MARU
Sanyo Kaiji Co Ltd
-
Amagasaki, Hyogo *Japan*
Official number: 140435

233 - -

2007-02 Hatayama Zosen KK — Yura WK Yd No: 248
Loa 42.33 Br ex - Dght 3.090
Lbp 37.00 Br md 8.80 Dpth 3.99
Welded, 1 dk

(B32A2ST) Tug

2 oil engines geared to sc. shafts driving 2 Propellers
Total Power: 3,236kW (4,400hp) 14.7kn
Yanmar 6N280M-SV
2 x 4 Stroke 6 Cy. 280 x 380 each-1618kW (2200bhp)
Yanmar Diesel Engine Co Ltd-Japan

8005953 - -
TAJIMA MARU No. 1
Nakane Marine S de RL
-
Honduras

171 - 400

1980-11 KK Ura Kyodo Zosensho — Awaji HG Yd No: 206
Loa - Br ex - Dght -
Lbp 34.12 Br md 6.51 Dpth 2.80
Welded, 1 dk

(A13B2TU) Tanker (unspecified)

1 oil engine driving 1 FP propeller
Total Power: 294kW (400hp)
Matsui MU623CS
1 x 4 Stroke 6 Cy. 230 x 380 294kW (400bhp)
Matsui Iron Works Co Ltd-Japan

9133848 *9HA2672* -
TAJIMARE
ex Tajima *-2011*
Indochina Ltd
Dynacom Tankers Management Ltd
Valletta *Malta*
MMSI: 215215000
Official number: 9133848

148,330 82,276 265,539 T/cm 170.5
Class: NK

1996-09 Ishikawajima-Harima Heavy Industries Co Ltd (IHI) — Kure Yd No: 3069
Loa 333.00 (BB) Br ex - Dght 19.530
Lbp 319.00 Br md 60.00 Dpth 28.65
Welded, 1 dk

(A13A2TV) Crude Oil Tanker
Double Hull (13F)
Liq: 304,415; Liq (Oil): 304,415
4 Cargo Pump (s): 3x5000m³/hr, 1x2400m³/hr

1 oil engine driving 1 FP propeller
Total Power: 27,186kW (36,962hp) 16.0kn
Sulzer 7RTA84T
1 x 2 Stroke 7 Cy. 840 x 3150 27186kW (36962bhp)
Diesel United Ltd.-Aioi
AuxGen: 2 x 920kW a.c, 1 x 900kW a.c, 1 x 600kW a.c
Fuel: 5333.0 (r.f.) 92.4pd

7433804 *XCIF* -
TAJIN
ex Tender Puma *-1980*
ex Musketeer Friend *-1978*
Perforaciones Maritimas Mexicanas SA
Condux SA de CV
Ciudad del Carmen *Mexico*
MMSI: 345070019
Official number: 2707

456 158 -
Class: AB

1977-03 Mangone Shipbuilding Co. — Houston, Tx Yd No: 121
Loa 56.39 Br ex 11.61 Dght 3.814
Lbp 48.16 Br md 11.59 Dpth 4.91
Welded, 1 dk

(B32A2ST) Tug
Ice Capable

2 oil engines sr geared to sc. shafts driving 2 CP propellers
Total Power: 5,296kW (7,200hp) 15.0kn
EMD (Electro-Motive) 20-645-E5
2 x Vee 2 Stroke 20 Cy. 230 x 254 each-2648kW (3600bhp)
General Motors Corp.Electro-Motive Div.-La Grange
AuxGen: 2 x 125kW a.c
Thrusters: 1 Thwart. FP thruster (f)
Fuel: 468.5 (d.f.)

9258014 *XCLN3* -
TAJIN
ex Sea music *-2008*
TMM Division Maritima SA de CV
Petroleos Mexicanos SA (PEMEX) Refinacion
Gerencia de Transportacion Maritima
Coatzacoalcos *Mexico*
MMSI: 345030066

28,529 12,315 47,147 T/cm 50.6
Class: LR (BV)
100A1 SS 06/2013
Double Hull oil tanker
ESP
LI
*IWS
LMC **UMS IGS**

2003-06 Onomichi Dockyard Co Ltd — Onomichi HS Yd No: 491
Loa 182.50 (BB) Br ex 32.23 Dght 12.666
Lbp 172.00 Br md 32.20 Dpth 19.10
Welded, 1 dk

(A13B2TP) Products Tanker
Double Hull (13F)
Liq: 50,332; Liq (Oil): 50,332
Cargo Heating Coils
Compartments: 2 Ta, 12 Wing Ta, ER, 2 Wing Slop Ta
4 Cargo Pump (s): 4x1000m³/hr
Manifold: Bow/CM: 91.7m

1 oil engine driving 1 FP propeller
Total Power: 8,683kW (11,805hp) 14.5kn
B&W 6S50MC
1 x 2 Stroke 6 Cy. 500 x 1910 8683kW (11805bhp)
Mitsui Engineering & Shipbuilding CLtd-Japan
Fuel: 132.4 (d.f.) 1635.8 (r.f.)

8657469 *9AA4756* -
TAJNA MORA
Ivica Antisic
-
Split *Croatia*
Official number: 5T-970

169 50 -
Class: CS

2007-05 Poseidon - Obrt za Proizvodnju i Popravak Plovila — Kastel Stafilic
Loa 30.80 Br ex - Dght 1.880
Lbp 23.50 Br md 7.50 Dpth 3.31
Welded, 1 dk

(A37B2PS) Passenger Ship

2 oil engines reduction geared to sc. shafts driving 2 FP propellers
Total Power: 420kW (572hp) 10.0kn
Daewoo L086TIH
2 x 4 Stroke 6 Cy. 111 x 139 each-210kW (286bhp)
Doosan Infracore Co Ltd-South Korea

IMO / Call sign	Name / Owner	Tonnage	Class	Builder / Dimensions	Type	Machinery
7722827 - -	**TAJRI 1** *ex* Zhan Hai Gong 116 *-2012* *ex* Da An *-2012* *ex* Hai Jiu *-2012* *ex* Eisei Maru *-1990* **PT Pelayaran Tajri Samudera** -	**826** 462 1,498	Class: (NK)	**1978-09 Sasaki Shipbuilding Co Ltd — Osakikamijima HS** Yd No: 322 Loa 61.73 Br ex - Dght 4.712 Lbp 57.00 Br md 10.61 Dpth 5.11 Welded, 1 dk	**(A13B2TP) Products Tanker** Liq: 1,610; Liq (Oil): 1,610	**1 oil engine** geared to sc. shaft driving 1 FP propeller Total Power: 956kW (1,300hp) Daihatsu 6DSM-26F 1 x 4 Stroke 6 Cy. 260 x 320 956kW (1300bhp) Daihatsu Diesel Manufacturing Co Lt-Japan
8965141 *T3VA* -	**TAK** *ex* Daiun Maru No. 3 *-2013* **Ali Salemi Khouzani** *Tarawa* *Kiribati* MMSI: 529311000 Official number: K-12911292	*202* 129 -	Class: IZ	**2000-12 Yano Zosen K.K. — Imabari** Yd No: 181 Loa 58.30 Br ex - Dght - Lbp 52.00 Br md 9.60 Dpth 5.55 Welded, 1 dk	**(A31A2GX) General Cargo Ship**	**1 oil engine** driving 1 FP propeller Total Power: 736kW (1,001hp) 12.4kn Hanshin LH28G 1 x 4 Stroke 6 Cy. 280 x 460 736kW (1001bhp) The Hanshin Diesel Works Ltd-Japan Fuel: 40.0 (d.f.)
7403196 *LYJN* -	**TAK-1** *ex* Ise *-1997* *ex* Courageux *-1988* *ex* Ise *-1987* **Petersen & Alpers GmbH & Co KG** Towmar Baltic UAB *Klaipeda* *Lithuania* MMSI: 277145000 Official number: 838	**181** 54 -	Class: GL	**1975-01 Muetzelfeldtwerft GmbH — Cuxhaven** Yd No: 191 Loa 26.17 Br ex 8.84 Dght 2.801 Lbp 24.82 Br md 8.79 Dpth 3.61 Welded, 1 dk	**(B32A2ST) Tug** Ice Capable	**2 oil engines** geared to sc. shafts driving 2 Directional propellers Total Power: 1,280kW (1,740hp) Deutz SBA6M528 2 x 4 Stroke 6 Cy. 220 x 280 each-640kW (870bhp) Kloeckner Humboldt Deutz AG-West Germany
7818339 *LYJP* -	**TAK-3** *ex* John *-1997* **Neue Schleppdampfschiffsreederei Louis Meyer GmbH & Co KG** Towmar Baltic UAB *Klaipeda* *Lithuania* MMSI: 277147000 Official number: 816	**159** 48 34	Class: GL	**1978-12 Johann Oelkers KG — Hamburg** Yd No: 577 Loa 23.09 Br ex 8.56 Dght - Lbp 22.03 Br md 8.51 Dpth 3.61 Welded, 1 dk	**(B32A2ST) Tug**	**2 oil engines** reduction geared to sc. shafts driving 2 Directional propellers Total Power: 1,080kW (1,468hp) 10.5kn Deutz SBA12M816 2 x Vee 4 Stroke 12 Cy. 142 x 160 each-540kW (734bhp) Kloeckner Humboldt Deutz AG-West Germany
7920405 *LYJZ* -	**TAK-4** *ex* Johanna *-1997* **Petersen & Alpers GmbH & Co KG** Towmar Baltic UAB *Klaipeda* *Lithuania* MMSI: 277148000 Official number: 787	**207** 62 93	Class: GL	**1980-03 Muetzelfeldtwerft GmbH — Cuxhaven** Yd No: 198 Loa 26.75 Br ex 8.84 Dght 2.801 Lbp 24.82 Br md 8.81 Dpth 3.59 Welded, 1 dk	**(B32A2ST) Tug** Ice Capable	**2 oil engines** geared to sc. shafts driving 2 Directional propellers Total Power: 1,280kW (1,740hp) Deutz SBA6M528 2 x 4 Stroke 6 Cy. 220 x 280 each-640kW (870bhp) Kloeckner Humboldt Deutz AG-West Germany
7237262 *LYLT* -	**TAK-5** *ex* Jan *-1999* *ex* Bugsier 2 *-1997* **Neue Schleppdampfschiffsreederei Louis Meyer GmbH & Co KG** Towmar Baltic UAB *Klaipeda* *Lithuania* MMSI: 277149000 Official number: 822	**181** 54 105	Class: GL	**1972 Schiffswerft u. Maschinenfabrik Max Sieghold — Bremerhaven** Yd No: 159 Loa 26.07 Br ex 8.84 Dght 2.801 Lbp 23.80 Br md 8.79 Dpth 3.59 Welded, 1 dk	**(B32A2ST) Tug** Ice Capable	**2 oil engines** geared to sc. shafts driving 2 Directional propellers Total Power: 1,280kW (1,740hp) Deutz SBA6M528 2 x 4 Stroke 6 Cy. 220 x 280 each-640kW (870bhp) Kloeckner Humboldt Deutz AG-West Germany
9550917 *LY2456* -	**TAK-6** **Towmar Baltic UAB** - *Klaipeda* *Lithuania* MMSI: 277421000 Official number: 821	**277** 83 122	Class: RS	**2009-08 OAO Leningradskiy Sudostroitelnyy Zavod 'Pella' — Otradnoye** Yd No: 612 Loa 29.44 Br ex - Dght 3.120 Lbp 26.50 Br md 9.50 Dpth 4.82 Welded, 1 dk	**(B32A2ST) Tug** Ice Capable	**2 oil engines** reduction geared to sc. shafts driving 2 Directional propellers Total Power: 3,370kW (4,582hp) Caterpillar 3516B-HD 2 x Vee 4 Stroke 16 Cy. 170 x 215 each-1685kW (2291bhp) Caterpillar Inc-USA AuxGen: 2 x 84kW a.c Fuel: 60.0 (d.f.)
9166534 *LYQN* -	**TAK-7** *ex* Michel *-2011* **Towmar Baltic UAB** - *Klaipeda* *Lithuania* MMSI: 277461000 Official number: 841	**333** 100 156	Class: GL	**1998-07 Astilleros Zamakona SA — Santurtzi** Yd No: 418 Loa 29.99 Br ex - Dght 2.780 Lbp 27.65 Br md 11.00 Dpth 4.00 Welded, 1 dk	**(B32A2ST) Tug** Ice Capable	**2 oil engines** with clutches, flexible couplings & reduction geared to sc. shafts driving 2 Directional propellers Total Power: 3,000kW (4,078hp) 12.0kn MaK 8M20 2 x 4 Stroke 8 Cy. 200 x 300 each-1500kW (2039bhp) MaK Motoren GmbH & Co. KG-Kiel AuxGen: 2 x 156kW 380/220V 50Hz a.c Fuel: 95.0 (d.f.) 12.4pd
6800438 *YL2738* -	**TAK-8** *ex* Grifon-3 *-2006* *ex* Tak-8 *-2004* *ex* Gosta *-2004* **Liepaja Special Economic Zone Authority (SEZ) ('Liepajas Speciala Ekonomiska Zona')** - *Liepaja* *Latvia* Official number: 2145	**230** 64 113	Class: RS (LR) ✠ Classed LR until 30/1/04	**1968-01 Cochrane & Sons Ltd. — Selby** Yd No: 1516 Loa 29.52 Br ex 9.00 Dght 3.899 Lbp 26.72 Br md 8.50 Dpth 4.15 Welded, 1 dk	**(B32A2ST) Tug** Ice Capable	**1 oil engine** sr geared to sc. shaft driving 1 CP propeller Total Power: 1,809kW (2,460hp) 12.5kn Ruston 9ATCM 1 x 4 Stroke 9 Cy. 318 x 368 1809kW (2460bhp) Ruston & Hornsby Ltd.-Lincoln AuxGen: 1 x 75kW 220V d.c, 1 x 50kW 220V d.c Fuel: 76.0 (d.f.)
9126649 *LYRF* -	**TAK-9** *ex* Boa Tor *-2004* *ex* Birk *-2000* *ex* Boa Tor *-1998* **Towmar Baltic UAB** - *Klaipeda* *Lithuania* MMSI: 277296000 Official number: 814	**408** 122 689	Class: GL (NV) (AB)	**1995-02 President Marine Pte Ltd — Singapore** Yd No: 173 Loa 33.70 Br ex 11.30 Dght 4.006 Lbp 32.00 Br md 10.60 Dpth 4.96 Welded, 1 dk	**(B32A2ST) Tug**	**2 oil engines** reduction geared to sc. shafts driving 2 Directional propellers Total Power: 2,898kW (3,940hp) Nohab 6R25 2 x 4 Stroke 6 Cy. 250 x 300 each-1449kW (1970bhp) Wartsila Diesel AB-Sweden AuxGen: 2 x 120kW 220/400V 50Hz a.c Fuel: 200.0 (d.f.) 11.8pd
8014992 *D9FJ* -	**TAK YANG** **Ssangyong Shipping Co Ltd** - *Busan* *South Korea* MMSI: 440306000 Official number: BSR-806310	**4,678** 2,754 7,859	Class: KR	**1981-04 Shinhama Dockyard Co. Ltd. — Anan** Yd No: 726 Loa 111.05 Br ex - Dght 7.034 Lbp 106.03 Br md 17.81 Dpth 9.12 Welded, 1 dk	**(A24A2BT) Cement Carrier**	**1 oil engine** driving 1 FP propeller Total Power: 2,942kW (4,000hp) 12.5kn Hanshin 6LU50A 1 x 4 Stroke 6 Cy. 500 x 800 2942kW (4000bhp) Hanshin Nainenki Kogyo-Japan AuxGen: 2 x 269kW 445V a.c
9303613 - -	**TAKA** **Ecrolight Pty Ltd** - *Cairns, Qld* *Australia* Official number: 857465	**150** - -		**2003-12 Adelaide Ship Const International Pty Ltd — Port Adelaide SA** Yd No: 315 Loa 26.50 Br ex - Dght - Lbp - Br md 8.00 Dpth - Welded, 1 dk	**(A37B2PS) Passenger Ship**	**1 oil engine** driving 1 FP propeller Total Power: 600kW (816hp) 12.0kn M.T.U. 12V2000M 1 x Vee 4 Stroke 12 Cy. 130 x 150 600kW (816bhp) Detroit Diesel Corporation-Detroit, Mi
8898075 *YFFM* -	**TAKA BONERATE** *ex* Menumbar X *-2000* **PT Pelita Anugerah Bahari** - *Banjarmasin* *Indonesia*	**370** 195 600	Class: (KI)	**1995-06 P.T. Dok Rahmat — Banjarmasin** Loa 47.00 Br ex - Dght 2.200 Lbp 45.00 Br md 10.50 Dpth 2.75 Welded, 1 dk	**(A35D2RL) Landing Craft** Bow ramp (centre)	**2 oil engines** reduction geared to sc. shafts driving 2 FP propellers Total Power: 354kW (482hp) 8.0kn Yanmar 6BNGGE 2 x 4 Stroke 6 Cy. 155 x 180 each-177kW (241bhp) (made 1995) Yanmar Diesel Engine Co Ltd-Japan Fuel: 50.0 (d.f.)
8865456 *JJ3850* -	**TAKA MARU** **Sanyo Kaiji Co Ltd** - *Amagasaki, Hyogo* *Japan* Official number: 132376	*199* - 222	Class: (NK)	**1992-10 Hatayama Zosen KK — Yura WK** Yd No: 210 Loa 32.82 Br ex - Dght 3.724 Lbp 26.50 Br md 9.50 Dpth 4.29 Welded, 1 dk	**(B32A2ST) Tug**	**2 oil engines** Geared Integral to driving 2 Z propellers Total Power: 2,648kW (3,600hp) 14.4kn Yanmar 6N280-UN 2 x 4 Stroke 6 Cy. 280 x 380 each-1324kW (1800bhp) Yanmar Diesel Engine Co Ltd-Japan
8908789 *JNIK* -	**TAKACHIHO** *ex* Ferry Takachiho *-2007* **A' Line Ferry Co Ltd (Marue Ferry KK)** - *Tokyo* *Japan* MMSI: 431528000 Official number: 131951	*3,891* - 2,726		**1990-02 Yamanishi Shipbuilding Co Ltd — Ishinomaki MG** Yd No: 977 Loa 131.16 (BB) Br ex - Dght 5.412 Lbp 120.00 Br md 20.00 Dpth 9.00 Welded, 2 dks	**(A35A2RR) Ro-Ro Cargo Ship** Passengers: berths: 12 Quarter bow door/ramp (p) Len: - Wid: - Swl: 45 Quarter stern door/ramp (p) Len: - Wid: - Swl: 45 Lane-Len: 350 Trailers: 26 Bale: 6,057 68 TEU C. Dk. 68 TEU Cranes: 1x25t	**1 oil engine** driving 1 CP propeller Total Power: 9,930kW (13,501hp) 19.9kn Pielstick 18PC2-6V-400 1 x Vee 4 Stroke 18 Cy. 400 x 460 9930kW (13501bhp) Nippon Kokan KK (NKK Corp)-Japan AuxGen: 2 x 760kW 445V 60Hz a.c Thrusters: 1 Thwart. CP thruster (f) Fuel: 69.0 (d.f.)

IMO / Call sign	Name / Owner	Tonnage	Class	Build / Dimensions	Type	Machinery
9643427 *7JJO* -	**TAKACHIHO** **Government of Japan (Ministry of Land, Infrastructure & Transport) (The Coastguard)** - *Tokyo* *Japan* Official number: 141482	*209* - 40		**2011-08 Mitsubishi Heavy Industries Ltd. — Shimonoseki** Yd No: 1151 Loa 46.00 Br ex - Dght 1.500 Lbp - Br md 7.80 Dpth 4.13 Welded, 1 dk	**(B34H2SQ) Patrol Vessel** Hull Material: Aluminium Alloy	**3 oil engines** reduction geared to sc. shafts driving 3 Water jets 35.0kn
9183348 *3FXA8* -	**TAKACHIHO II** **Seaborn Enterprises SA** Nippon Yusen Kabushiki Kaisha (NYK Line) SatCom: Inmarsat B 335701610 *Panama* *Panama* MMSI: 357016000 Official number: 2599698C	**149,376** 91,210 280,889 T/cm 170.1	Class: NK	**1998-10 Ishikawajima-Harima Heavy Industries Co Ltd (IHI) — Kure** Yd No: 3101 Loa 330.00 (BB) Br ex 60.00 Dght 20.428 Lbp 316.60 Br md 60.00 Dpth 28.90 Welded, 1 dk	**(A13A2TV) Crude Oil Tanker** Double Hull (13F) Liq: 313,335; Liq (Oil): 313,335 Compartments: 5 Ta, 10 Wing Ta, 2 Wing Slop Ta, ER 3 Cargo Pump (s): 3x5000m³/hr Manifold: Bow/CM: 154.6m	**1 oil engine** driving 1 FP propeller Total Power: 27,160kW (36,927hp) 16.1kn Sulzer 7RTA84T 1 x 2 Stroke 7 Cy. 840 x 3150 27160kW (36927bhp) Diesel United Ltd.-Aioi AuxGen: 2 x 1100kW 450V a.c, 1 x 900kW 450V a.c, 1 x 550kW 450V a.c Fuel: 386.6 (d.f.) (Heating Coils) 6117.1 (r.f.) 94.8pd
8628016 *JL5447* -	**TAKACHIHO MARU** **YK Hamasaki Kaiun** - *Nakajima, Ehime* *Japan* Official number: 128384	*160* - 407		**1986-06 KK Ouchi Zosensho — Matsuyama EH** Loa 46.72 Br ex - Dght 3.110 Lbp 42.02 Br md 8.21 Dpth 4.91 Welded, 1 dk	**(A31A2GX) General Cargo Ship**	**1 oil engine** driving 1 FP propeller Total Power: 368kW (500hp) 8.5kn Matsui ML624GHS 1 x 4 Stroke 6 Cy. 240 x 400 368kW (500bhp) Matsui Iron Works Co Ltd-Japan
7378092 - -	**TAKACHIHO MARU** *ex* Shinei Maru No. 8 *-2003* *ex* Nagashima *-2002* *ex* Takachino Maru *-2001* *ex* Sansho Maru *-1998* *ex* Daiou *-1996* *ex* Daio *-1992* - -	*204* - -	Class: (BV)	**1973-12 Oura Dock — Imabari** Yd No: 89 Loa 44.00 Br ex 7.24 Dght 2.515 Lbp 41.00 Br md 7.22 Dpth 3.38 Riveted\Welded, 1 dk	**(B32A2ST) Tug**	**2 oil engines** driving 2 FP propellers Total Power: 2,354kW (3,200hp) Yanmar 2 x 4 Stroke 6 Cy. 250 x 320 each-1177kW (1600bhp) Yanmar Diesel Engine Co Ltd-Japan
9153757 *JL6513* -	**TAKAFUJI MARU** **Kanehiro Kisen YK & Kimoto Kisen KK** Kanehiro Kisen YK *Imabari, Ehime* *Japan* MMSI: 431500526 Official number: 135540	*3,331* - 4,925	Class: NK	**1996-10 Hakata Zosen K.K. — Imabari** Yd No: 603 Loa 103.75 Br ex - Dght 6.863 Lbp 96.00 Br md 15.50 Dpth 8.15 Welded, 1 dk	**(A13B2TP) Products Tanker** Liq: 5,292; Liq (Oil): 5,400	**1 oil engine** driving 1 FP propeller Total Power: 2,942kW (4,000hp) 13.5kn Hanshin LH46LG 1 x 4 Stroke 6 Cy. 460 x 880 2942kW (4000bhp) The Hanshin Diesel Works Ltd-Japan Fuel: 245.0
7824821 *JNAT* -	**TAKAHARU MARU** **Shinnihon Kinkai Kisen KK & Ube Shipping & Logistics Ltd** Ube Shipping & Logistics Ltd (Ube Kosan KK) *Ube, Yamaguchi* *Japan* MMSI: 431400924 Official number: 121080	*11,736* - 18,433	Class: NK	**1979-11 Kasado Dockyard Co Ltd — Kudamatsu YC** Yd No: 310 Loa 158.50 Br ex - Dght 9.502 Lbp 149.99 Br md 23.21 Dpth 12.02 Welded, 1 dk	**(A24A2BT) Cement Carrier** Grain: 14,321 Compartments: 4 Ho, ER Cranes: 1x3t; Derricks: 2x3t; Winches: 4	**2 oil engines** reduction geared to sc. shaft driving 1 FP propeller Total Power: 8,826kW (12,000hp) 15.3kn MaK 8M552AK 2 x 4 Stroke 8 Cy. 450 x 520 each-4413kW (6000bhp) Ube Industries Ltd-Japan AuxGen: 3 x 400kW 450V 60Hz a.c Fuel: 111.5 (d.f.) 1085.0 (r.f.) 38.0pd
9321304 *3EKN6* -	**TAKAHASHI** **Gios Maritima SA** NYK Shipmanagement Pte Ltd SatCom: Inmarsat C 437277110 *Panama* *Panama* MMSI: 372771000 Official number: 3280007B	**160,295** 103,233 314,020 T/cm 184.9	Class: NK	**2007-05 Nantong COSCO KHI Ship Engineering Co Ltd (NACKS) — Nantong JS** Yd No: 044 Loa 333.00 Br ex - Dght 21.064 Lbp 324.00 Br md 60.00 Dpth 29.00 Welded, 1 dk	**(A13A2TV) Crude Oil Tanker** Double Hull (13F) Liq: 342,240; Liq (Oil): 342,240 Compartments: 5 Ta, 10 Wing Ta, 2 Wing Slop Ta, ER 3 Cargo Pump (s): 3x5500m³/hr Manifold: Bow/CM: 166.5m	**1 oil engine** driving 1 FP propeller Total Power: 27,160kW (36,927hp) 14.5kn MAN-B&W 7S80MC-C 1 x 2 Stroke 7 Cy. 800 x 3200 27160kW (36927bhp) Kawasaki Heavy Industries Ltd-Japan Fuel: 6040.0
8888953 - -	**TAKAHIRO MARU No. 18** *ex* Sagakatsu Maru No. 28 *-1998* **An Mi Kyung** - *South Korea*	*115* - -		**1980-02 Nishii Dock Co. Ltd. — Ise** L reg 28.00 Br ex - Dght - Lbp - Br md 5.80 Dpth 2.50 Bonded, 1 dk	**(B11B2FV) Fishing Vessel** Hull Material: Reinforced Plastic	**1 oil engine** driving 1 FP propeller Yanmar 1 x 4 Stroke Yanmar Diesel Engine Co Ltd-Japan
9225213 *ZMR6821* -	**TAKAHIWAI** **North Tugz Ltd** - *Auckland* *New Zealand* Official number: 876336	**338** - -	Class: (LR) ✠ Classed LR until 5/10/05	**2000-09 North Port Engineering Ltd — Whangarei** Yd No: 133 Loa 22.20 Br ex 9.22 Dght 3.150 Lbp 20.80 Br md 9.20 Dpth 4.15 Welded, 1 dk	**(B32A2ST) Tug**	**2 oil engines** with clutches, flexible couplings & reduction geared to sc. shafts driving 2 FP propellers Total Power: 3,282kW (4,462hp) 12.0kn Caterpillar 3516TA 2 x Vee 4 Stroke 16 Cy. 170 x 190 each-1641kW (2231bhp) Caterpillar Inc-USA Fuel: 91.0 (d.f.)
8210120 *JE2789* -	**TAKAHOKO MARU NO. 1** **Government of Japan (Ministry of Economy, Trade & Industry)** Japan Oil Gas & Metals National Corp (JOGMEC) *Tokyo* *Japan* MMSI: 431700255 Official number: 126591	*495* - 297		**1983-07 Ishikawajima Ship & Chemical Plant Co Ltd — Tokyo** Yd No: 542 Loa 46.13 Br ex 11.51 Dght 3.601 Lbp 42.02 Br md 11.00 Dpth 5.01 Welded, 1 dk	**(B34T2QR) Work/Repair Vessel**	**2 oil engines** with clutches, flexible couplings & dr geared to sc. shafts driving 2 FP propellers Total Power: 2,354kW (3,200hp) Niigata 6L28BXE 2 x 4 Stroke 6 Cy. 280 x 320 each-1177kW (1600bhp) Niigata Engineering Co Ltd-Japan
8210534 *JE2788* -	**TAKAHOKO MARU No. 2** **Government of Japan (Ministry of Economy, Trade & Industry)** Japan Oil Gas & Metals National Corp (JOGMEC) *Tokyo* *Japan* Official number: 126589	*499* - 254		**1983-05 Mitsubishi Heavy Industries Ltd. — Shimonoseki** Yd No: 853 Loa 48.01 Br ex - Dght 4.060 Lbp 38.03 Br md 10.41 Dpth 4.22 Welded, 1 dk	**(B34G2SE) Pollution Control Vessel**	**2 oil engines** Geared Integral to driving 2 Z propellers Total Power: 1,912kW (2,600hp) 12.5kn Niigata 6L25BX 2 x 4 Stroke 6 Cy. 250 x 320 each-956kW (1300bhp) Niigata Engineering Co Ltd-Japan
8217087 *JE2787* -	**TAKAHOKO MARU No. 3** **Government of Japan (Ministry of Economy, Trade & Industry)** Japan Oil Gas & Metals National Corp (JOGMEC) *Tokyo* *Japan* Official number: 126588	*483* - 690		**1983-05 Kitanihon Zosen K.K. — Hachinohe** Yd No: 176 Loa 44.71 Br ex - Dght 3.801 Lbp 37.80 Br md 12.01 Dpth 4.53 Welded, 1 dk	**(B34G2SE) Pollution Control Vessel**	**2 oil engines** Geared Integral to driving 2 Z propellers Total Power: 1,912kW (2,600hp) 12.5kn Niigata 6L25BX 2 x 4 Stroke 6 Cy. 250 x 320 each-956kW (1300bhp) Niigata Engineering Co Ltd-Japan
9104237 *JK5338* -	**TAKAKI MARU** *ex* Sumiho Maru *-2012* **Sumiho Kisen YK** - *Karatsu, Saga* *Japan* Official number: 134695	*199* - 700		**1994-05 Kegoya Dock K.K. — Kure** Yd No: 961 Loa 56.30 (BB) Br ex 9.32 Dght 3.480 Lbp 51.00 Br md 9.30 Dpth 5.80 Welded, 2 dks	**(A31A2GX) General Cargo Ship** Compartments: 1 Ho, ER	**1 oil engine** reverse geared to sc. shaft driving 1 FP propeller Total Power: 736kW (1,001hp) Matsui ML627GSC 1 x 4 Stroke 6 Cy. 270 x 480 736kW (1001bhp) Matsui Iron Works Co Ltd-Japan
9478676 *7JJG* -	**TAKAMATSU MARU** **Nippon Yusen Kabushiki Kaisha (NYK Line)** - SatCom: Inmarsat C 443283110 *Tokyo* *Japan* MMSI: 432831000 Official number: 141453	**157,961** 107,082 311,087 T/cm 170.1	Class: NK	**2012-06 IHI Marine United Inc — Kure HS** Yd No: 3317 Converted From: Container Ship (Fully Cellular)-2012 Loa 333.00 (BB) Br ex 60.04 Dght 21.040 Lbp 322.00 Br md 60.00 Dpth 28.50 Welded, 1 dk	**(A13A2TV) Crude Oil Tanker** Double Hull (13F) Liq: 330,000; Liq (Oil): 330,000 Compartments: 5 Ta, 10 Wing Ta, ER, 2 Wing Slop Ta 3 Cargo Pump (s): 3x5500m³/hr Manifold: Bow/CM: 163.6m	**1 oil engine** driving 1 FP propeller Total Power: 27,160kW (36,927hp) 15.5kn Wartsila 7RT-flex84T 1 x 2 Stroke 7 Cy. 840 x 3150 27160kW (36927bhp) Diesel United Ltd.-Aioi Fuel: 730.0 (d.f.) 6630.0 (r.f.)
9295593 *7JKK* -	**TAKAMINE** **Nippon Yusen Kabushiki Kaisha (NYK Line)** - *Tokyo* *Japan* MMSI: 432832000 Official number: 141545	**159,903** 99,266 306,206 T/cm 182.0	Class: NK	**2004-06 Mitsubishi Heavy Industries Ltd. — Nagasaki** Yd No: 2189 Loa 333.00 (BB) Br ex 60.04 Dght 20.825 Lbp 324.00 Br md 60.00 Dpth 29.10 Welded, 1 dk	**(A13A2TV) Crude Oil Tanker** Double Hull (13F) Liq: 334,704; Liq (Oil): 350,035 Compartments: 5 Ta, 10 Wing Ta, 2 Wing Slop Ta, ER 3 Cargo Pump (s): 3x5500m³/hr Manifold: Bow/CM: 166m	**1 oil engine** driving 1 FP propeller Total Power: 27,022kW (36,739hp) 15.5kn Mitsubishi 7UEC85LSII 1 x 2 Stroke 7 Cy. 850 x 3150 27022kW (36739bhp) Mitsubishi Heavy Industries Ltd-Japan AuxGen: 2 x 1100kW a.c, 1 x 1200kW a.c Fuel: 7815.0
8990122 *JG5747* -	**TAKAO MARU** **Tokyo Kisen KK** - *Yokohama, Kanagawa* *Japan* MMSI: 431101077 Official number: 137219	*239* - -		**2004-05 Kanagawa Zosen — Kobe** Yd No: 528 Loa 37.20 Br ex - Dght 3.070 Lbp 32.70 Br md 9.80 Dpth 4.21 Welded, 1 dk	**(B32A2ST) Tug**	**2 oil engines** Geared Integral to driving 2 Z propellers Total Power: 2,942kW (4,000hp) 13.5kn Niigata 6L28HX 2 x 4 Stroke 6 Cy. 280 x 370 each-1471kW (2000bhp) Niigata Engineering Co Ltd-Japan

ID	Name / Owner	Tonnage	Class	Build / Dimensions	Type / Cargo	Machinery
8803941 *JVZM4* -	**TAKAO MARU No. 1** - - - *Ulaanbaatar* *Mongolia*	*478* - 484		**1988-08 Ishii Zosen K.K. — Futtsu** Yd No: 231 Loa 47.10 (BB) Br ex - Dght 3.452 Lbp 42.10 Br md 11.00 Dpth 3.51 Welded, 1 dk	**(A24D2BA) Aggregates Carrier** Grain: 830 Compartments: 1 Ho, ER 1 Ha: ER	**1 oil engine** with clutches & reverse reduction geared to sc. shaft driving 1 FP propeller Total Power: 736kW (1,001hp) 11.0kn Yanmar MF26-HT 1 x 4 Stroke 6 Cy. 260 x 500 736kW (1001bhp) Yanmar Diesel Engine Co Ltd-Japan
9478664 *9V8940* -	**TAKAOKA** - **Rebun Shipping Pte Ltd** Nippon Yusen Kabushiki Kaisha (NYK Line) SatCom: Inmarsat C 456625810 *Singapore* *Singapore* MMSI: 566152000 Official number: 396419	**158,051** 106,920 311,061 T/cm 170.1	Class: NK	**2011-09 IHI Marine United Inc — Kure HS** Yd No: 3316 Converted From: Container Ship (Fully Cellular)-2011 Loa 333.00 (BB) Br ex 60.04 Dght 21.040 Lbp 322.00 Br md 60.00 Dpth 28.50 Welded, 1 dk	**(A13A2TV) Crude Oil Tanker** Double Hull (13F) Liq: 330,400; Liq (Oil): 330,400 Cargo Heating Coils Compartments: 5 Ta, 10 Wing Ta, ER, 2 Wing Slop Ta 3 Cargo Pump (s): 3x5500m³/hr Manifold: Bow/CM: 163.6m	**1 oil engine** driving 1 FP propeller Total Power: 29,400kW (39,972hp) 15.5kn Wartsila 7RT-flex84T 1 x 2 Stroke 7 Cy. 840 x 3150 29400kW (39972bhp) Diesel United Ltd.-Aioi Fuel: 730.0 (d.f.) 6830.0 (r.f.)
8975639 *ZMY7599* -	**TAKAPU2** *ex Takapu (A 07) -1980* **Charter Now Ltd & Kiwi Cruising Ltd** - *Auckland* *New Zealand* Official number: 876348	**126** 51 -		**1980-07 Whangarei Eng. & Construction Co. Ltd. — Whangarei** Yd No: 159 Converted From: Research Vessel-2003 Loa 26.82 Br ex - Dght - Lbp - Br md 6.10 Dpth 2.25 Welded, 1 dk	**(A37B2PS) Passenger Ship**	**2 oil engines** geared to sc. shafts driving 2 Propellers Total Power: 444kW (604hp) 12.0kn Cummins KT-1150-M 2 x 4 Stroke 6 Cy. 159 x 159 each-222kW (302bhp) Cummins Engine Co Inc-USA Fuel: 11.0 (d.f.)
1005124 *6YRS4* -	**TAKAPUNA** *ex Baliceaux -2006* **Takapuna Sail Ltd** - *Jamaica* MMSI: 339329000	*182* - 165	Class: (LR) ✠ Classed LR until 14/7/97	**1994-07 Cant. Valdettaro Srl — Le Grazie** Yd No: 169 Loa 34.00 Br ex 7.95 Dght 2.800 Lbp 28.38 Br md 7.94 Dpth 4.93 Welded, 1 dk	**(X11A2YS) Yacht (Sailing)**	**1 oil engine** reverse reduction geared to sc. shaft driving 1 FP propeller Total Power: 354kW (481hp) M.T.U. 12V183AA91 1 x Vee 4 Stroke 12 Cy. 128 x 142 354kW (481bhp) MTU Friedrichshafen GmbH-Friedrichshafen AuxGen: 2 x 53kW 380V 50Hz a.c Thrusters: 1 Thwart. FP thruster (f)
8506749 *C6AY9* -	**TAKARA** *ex Nosac Takara -1996* **Caiano Ship AS** Green Management Sp z oo *Nassau* *Bahamas* MMSI: 311000196 Official number: 7000611	**48,547** 14,565 15,546	Class: NV (NK)	**1986-09 Sumitomo Heavy Industries Ltd. — Oppama Shipyard, Yokosuka** Yd No: 1138 Loa 190.05 (BB) Br ex 32.29 Dght 8.921 Lbp 180.02 Br md 32.26 Dpth 13.75 Welded, 12 dks, incl. 4 dks hoistable	**(A35B2RV) Vehicles Carrier** Side door/ramp (p) Len: 20.00 Wid: 5.00 Swl: 16 Side door/ramp (s) Len: 20.00 Wid: 5.00 Swl: 16 Quarter stern door/ramp (s) Len: 35.00 Wid: 7.00 Swl: 100 Lane-Wid: 3.39 Lane-clr ht: 4.60 Cars: 5,720	**1 oil engine** driving 1 FP propeller Total Power: 8,716kW (11,850hp) 18.0kn Sulzer 7RTA58 1 x 2 Stroke 7 Cy. 580 x 1700 8716kW (11850bhp) Sumitomo Heavy Industries Ltd-Japan AuxGen: 3 x 780kW 220/440V a.c Thrusters: 1 Tunnel thruster (f)
8859433 - -	**TAKARA** *ex Takara Maru No. 1 -2013* - - *Indonesia*	*462* - 500		**1991-11 Koike Zosen Kaiun KK — Osakikamijima** Loa 49.50 Br ex - Dght 3.270 Lbp 45.00 Br md 10.50 Dpth 5.30 Welded, 1 dk	**(B33A2DG) Grab Dredger** 1 Ha: (14.3 x 7.8)ER Cranes: 1x1.8t	**1 oil engine** driving 1 FP propeller Total Power: 588kW (799hp) 10.0kn Daihatsu 6DLM-24S 1 x 4 Stroke 6 Cy. 240 x 320 588kW (799bhp) Daihatsu Diesel Manufacturing Co Lt-Japan
8503266 *JL5088* -	**TAKARA MARU** - **Horiuchi Kisen YK** - *Matsuyama, Ehime* *Japan* Official number: 127492	*349* - 550		**1985-05 Shitanoe Shipbuilding Co Ltd — Usuki OT** Yd No: 1047 Loa 52.08 Br ex - Dght - Lbp 48.01 Br md 9.01 Dpth 3.92 Welded, 1 dk	**(A14H2LH) Alcohol Tanker**	**1 oil engine** geared to sc. shaft driving 1 FP propeller Total Power: 736kW (1,001hp) Akasaka DM28AKFD 1 x 4 Stroke 6 Cy. 280 x 460 736kW (1001bhp) Akasaka Tekkosho KK (Akasaka DieselLtd)-Japan
7909334 - -	**TAKARI** - **Menbar Pty Ltd** - *Darwin, NT* *Australia* Official number: 375138	*117* 76 -		**1978 K Shipyard Construction Co — Fremantle WA** Loa 22.81 Br ex 6.53 Dght 3.101 Lbp 21.42 Br md 6.41 Dpth 3.51 Welded, 1 dk	**(B11A2FT) Trawler**	**1 oil engine** reduction geared to sc. shaft driving 1 FP propeller Total Power: 265kW (360hp) 10.0kn Caterpillar 3408T 1 x Vee 4 Stroke 8 Cy. 137 x 152 265kW (360bhp) Caterpillar Tractor Co-USA
8848599 *JL5829* -	**TAKASAGO** *ex Toho No. 1 -2006* **Meiko Kisen KK** - *Bizen, Okayama* *Japan* Official number: 131487	*185* - 504		**1991-02 YK Furumoto Tekko Zosensho — Osakikamijima** Loa 52.57 Br ex - Dght 3.350 Lbp 45.80 Br md 8.60 Dpth 5.30 Welded, 1 dk	**(A31A2GX) General Cargo Ship** 1 Ha: (25.9 x 6.7)ER	**1 oil engine** driving 1 FP propeller Total Power: 478kW (650hp) 11.0kn Matsui 6M26KGHS 1 x 4 Stroke 6 Cy. 260 x 400 478kW (650bhp) Matsui Iron Works Co Ltd-Japan
8841149 - -	**TAKASAGO** *ex Takasago Maru No. 5 -2013* **PT Citra Baru Adinusantara**	*171* - 453		**1990-05 YK Furumoto Tekko Zosensho — Osakikamijima** Loa 49.96 Br ex - Dght 3.200 Lbp 45.00 Br md 8.30 Dpth 5.10 Welded, 1 dk	**(A31A2GX) General Cargo Ship** Compartments: 1 Ho, ER 1 Ha: (26.6 x 6.3)ER	**1 oil engine** driving 1 FP propeller Total Power: 405kW (551hp) 10.0kn Niigata 6M26KGHS 1 x 4 Stroke 6 Cy. 260 x 400 405kW (551bhp) Niigata Engineering Co Ltd-Japan
8967149 *JJ4029* -	**TAKASAGO** - **Imoto Shoun Kaisha** - *Kobe, Hyogo* *Japan* MMSI: 431501666 Official number: 135973	*499* - 1,599		**2001-01 Yamanaka Zosen K.K. — Imabari** Yd No: 660 Loa 77.08 (BB) Br ex - Dght - Lbp 71.30 Br md 13.00 Dpth 6.62 Welded, 1 dk	**(A31A2GX) General Cargo Ship**	**1 oil engine** reduction geared to sc. shaft driving 1 FP propeller Total Power: 1,765kW (2,400hp) 13.5kn Daihatsu 6DKM-28 1 x 4 Stroke 6 Cy. 280 x 390 1765kW (2400bhp) Daihatsu Diesel Manufacturing Co Lt-Japan Thrusters: 1 Tunnel thruster (f) Fuel: 107.0 (d.f.)
9134426 *JL6428* -	**TAKASAGO MARU** - **Takasago Kaiun YK** - *Anan, Tokushima* *Japan* Official number: 135132	*498* - 1,500		**1995-10 K.K. Tachibana Senpaku Tekko — Anan** Yd No: 848 Loa - Br ex - Dght - Lbp - Br md - Dpth - Welded, 1 dk	**(A31A2GX) General Cargo Ship**	**1 oil engine** driving 1 FP propeller Total Power: 736kW (1,001hp) 10.8kn Hanshin LH30LG 1 x 4 Stroke 6 Cy. 300 x 600 736kW (1001bhp) The Hanshin Diesel Works Ltd-Japan
9652363 *JD3504* -	**TAKASAGO MARU NO. 5** - **YK Yamamoto Kaiun** - *Amakusa, Kumamoto* *Japan* Official number: 141905	*237* - 780		**2013-04 Taiyo Shipbuilding Co Ltd — Sanyoonoda YC** Yd No: 333 Loa 59.90 Br ex - Dght 3.240 Lbp - Br md 9.80 Dpth 5.60 Welded, 1 dk	**(A31A2GX) General Cargo Ship** Grain: 1,220; Bale: 1,214	**1 oil engine** reduction geared to sc. shaft driving 1 Propeller Total Power: 882kW (1,199hp) 12.2kn Niigata 6M26AGTE 1 x 4 Stroke 6 Cy. 260 x 460 882kW (1199bhp) Niigata Engineering Co Ltd-Japan
8961808 *JH3470* -	**TAKASAGO MARU No. 11** - **Takasago Kaiun KK** - *Yokkaichi, Mie* *Japan* MMSI: 431200516 Official number: 135658	*749* - -		**2000-08 K.K. Miura Zosensho — Saiki** Yd No: 1126 Loa 80.00 Br ex - Dght - Lbp 74.00 Br md 14.30 Dpth 7.80 Welded, 1 dk	**(A31A2GX) General Cargo Ship**	**1 oil engine** driving 1 FP propeller Total Power: 2,574kW (3,500hp) 14.0kn Hanshin LH41LAG 1 x 4 Stroke 6 Cy. 410 x 800 2574kW (3500bhp) The Hanshin Diesel Works Ltd-Japan
8974867 *H03586* -	**TAKASAGO MARU NO. 21** - **Glorious Clamor Maritime Inc** Nakanishi Kikai Kogyosho Co Ltd *Panama* *Panama* Official number: 32522PEXT	**450** 135 -		**2001-07 Hangzhou Dongfeng Shipbuilding Co Ltd — Hangzhou ZJ** Yd No: 20101 Loa 26.53 Br ex 16.97 Dght 5.042 Lbp 25.02 Br md - Dpth 7.16 Welded, 1 dk	**(B32B2SA) Articulated Pusher Tug**	**2 oil engines** geared to sc. shafts driving 2 Propellers Total Power: 2,428kW (3,302hp) 12.0kn Akasaka 8U28AK 2 x 4 Stroke 8 Cy. 280 x 380 each-1214kW (1651bhp) Akasaka Tekkosho KK (Akasaka DieselLtd)-Japan
7855208 - -	**TAKASAKA MARU No. 3** - **Ever Star Shipping SA** -	*286* - 550		**1973 Shin Nikko Zosen K.K. — Onomichi** Yd No: 76 Loa 47.71 Br ex - Dght 3.301 Lbp 45.01 Br md 8.21 Dpth 3.61 Welded, 1 dk	**(B34E2SY) Effluent carrier**	**1 oil engine** driving 1 FP propeller Total Power: 736kW (1,001hp) Kubota M6D26BHCS 1 x 4 Stroke 6 Cy. 260 x 320 736kW (1001bhp) Kubota Tekkosho-Japan
9320831 *3EEB* -	**TAKASAKI** - **Violeta Maritima Lines SA** NYK Shipmanagement Pte Ltd SatCom: Inmarsat C 437175110 *Panama* *Panama* MMSI: 371751000 Official number: 3128906A	**159,939** 97,016 300,390 T/cm 170.1	Class: NK	**2005-12 IHI Marine United Inc — Kure HS** Yd No: 3215 Loa 333.00 Br ex - Dght 20.535 Lbp 324.00 Br md 60.00 Dpth 29.00 Welded, 1 dk	**(A13A2TV) Crude Oil Tanker** Double Hull (13F) Liq: 330,175; Liq (Oil): 349,779 Compartments: 5 Ta, 10 Wing Ta, 2 Wing Slop Ta, ER 3 Cargo Pump (s): 3x5500m³/hr Manifold: Bow/CM: 163.5m	**1 oil engine** driving 1 FP propeller Total Power: 27,161kW (36,928hp) 15.6kn Sulzer 7RTA84T-B 1 x 2 Stroke 7 Cy. 840 x 3150 27161kW (36928bhp) Diesel United Ltd.-Aioi AuxGen: 3 x 1150kW 440V 50Hz a.c Fuel: 7630.0

9624342 *JD3244* -	**TAKASHIMA** **KK Takashima Kisen** - *Kamiamakusa, Kumamoto* *Japan* Official number: 141519	*273* - 800		**2011-11 Yano Zosen K.K. — Imabari** Yd No: 252 Loa 63.72 (BB) Br ex - Dght 3.258 Lbp 58.00 Br md 10.00 Dpth 5.80 Welded, 1 dk	**(A31A2GX) General Cargo Ship** Double Hull Compartments: 1 Ho, ER 1 Ha: ER	**1 oil engine** reduction geared to sc. shaft driving 1 Propeller Total Power: 1,029kW (1,399hp) Niigata 6M28BGT 1 x 4 Stroke 6 Cy. 280 x 480 1029kW (1399bhp) Niigata Engineering Co Ltd-Japan Thrusters: 1 Thwart. FP thruster (f)
9062788 *JM6270* -	**TAKASHIMA** **YK Hashimura Kaiun** - *Tosa, Kochi* *Japan* Official number: 133548	*199* - 633		**1993-04 Y.K. Takasago Zosensho — Naruto** Yd No: 188 Loa 59.90 Br ex - Dght 3.180 Lbp 53.00 Br md 9.50 Dpth 5.42 Welded, 1 dk	**(A31A2GX) General Cargo Ship** Compartments: 1 Ho, ER 1 Ha: (31.0 x 7.5)ER	**1 oil engine** driving 1 FP propeller Total Power: 736kW (1,001hp) 12.1kn Niigata 6M28BGT 1 x 4 Stroke 6 Cy. 280 x 480 736kW (1001bhp) Niigata Engineering Co Ltd-Japan
9234939 *JL6600* -	**TAKASHO MARU** **Kurokawa Kisen KK** - *Imabari, Ehime* *Japan* Official number: 136524	*202* - -		**2000-02 Yano Zosen K.K. — Imabari** Yd No: 178 Loa 58.80 Br ex - Dght - Lbp 52.00 Br md 9.50 Dpth 5.63 Welded, 1 dk	**(A31A2GX) General Cargo Ship** Grain: 1,200 Compartments: 1 Ho, ER 1 Ha: (30.2 x 7.5)ER	**1 oil engine** driving 1 FP propeller Total Power: 736kW (1,001hp) 11.0kn Niigata 6M28BGT 1 x 4 Stroke 6 Cy. 280 x 480 736kW (1001bhp) Niigata Engineering Co Ltd-Japan Fuel: 24.0 (d.f.)
9066514 - -	**TAKASU** *ex* New Takasu *-2012* **PT Indo Shipping Operator**	*498* - 1,600		**1993-03 Shitanoe Shipbuilding Co Ltd — Usuki OT** Yd No: 1138 Loa - Br ex - Dght 4.080 Lbp 72.00 Br md 11.70 Dpth 7.03 Welded, 1 dk	**(A31A2GX) General Cargo Ship**	**1 oil engine** reverse geared to sc. shaft driving 1 FP propeller Total Power: 1,324kW (1,800hp) Akasaka A31R 1 x 4 Stroke 6 Cy. 310 x 600 1324kW (1800bhp) Akasaka Tekkosho KK (Akasaka DieselLtd)-Japan
9119830 *JJ3828* -	**TAKASUGAWA MARU** **YK Nisshin Kaiun** - *Himeji, Hyogo* *Japan* MMSI: 431100208 Official number: 134172	*629* - 1,328		**1995-12 Ishii Zosen K.K. — Futtsu** Yd No: 335 Loa 68.00 (BB) Br ex - Dght 3.670 Lbp 62.00 Br md 13.20 Dpth 7.00 Welded, 1 dk	**(A24D2BA) Aggregates Carrier** Grain: 1,590 Compartments: 1 Ho, ER 1 Ha: ER	**1 oil engine** with clutches & reverse geared to sc. shaft driving 1 FP propeller Total Power: 1,765kW (2,400hp) Akasaka A34 1 x 4 Stroke 6 Cy. 340 x 660 1765kW (2400bhp) Akasaka Tekkosho KK (Akasaka DieselLtd)-Japan Thrusters: 1 Thwart. FP thruster (f)
9177686 *3FT06* -	**TAKASUZU** **Sakura Shipholding SA & Burney Japan Co Ltd** Nippon Yusen Kabushiki Kaisha (NYK Line) *Panama* *Panama* MMSI: 370946000 Official number: 4485213	**152,145** 89,552 279,989 T/cm 173.0	Class: NK	**2000-06 Mitsubishi Heavy Industries Ltd. — Nagasaki** Yd No: 2154 Loa 329.99 (BB) Br ex 60.04 Dght 20.340 Lbp 319.00 Br md 60.00 Dpth 28.80 Welded, 1 dk	**(A13A2TV) Crude Oil Tanker** Double Hull (13F) Liq: 308,376; Liq (Oil): 318,681 Compartments: 5 Ta, 10 Wing Ta, ER, 2 Wing Slop Ta 4 Cargo Pump (s): 3x5000m³/hr, 1x2750m³/hr Manifold: Bow/CM: 154.6m	**1 oil engine** driving 1 FP propeller Total Power: 27,030kW (36,750hp) 15.9kn Mitsubishi 7UEC85LSII 1 x 2 Stroke 7 Cy. 850 x 3150 27030kW (36750bhp) Mitsubishi Heavy Industries Ltd-Japan AuxGen: 2 x 1100kW a.c Fuel: 398.0 (d.f.) (Heating Coils) 5653.0 (r.f.) 105.0pd
7903134 *JJ3169* -	**TAKATA MARU** **Naikai Eisen KK & KK Nissho Trade Marine Service** Naikai Eisen KK *Kobe, Hyogo* *Japan* Official number: 121072	*192* - -		**1979-07 Kanbara Zosen K.K. — Onomichi** Yd No: 237 Loa 31.50 Br ex - Dght 2.760 Lbp 27.00 Br md 8.80 Dpth 3.60 Welded, 1 dk	**(B32A2ST) Tug**	**2 oil engines** Geared Integral to driving 2 Z propellers Total Power: 2,648kW (3,600hp) Niigata 6L28HX 2 x 4 Stroke 6 Cy. 280 x 370 each-1324kW (1800bhp) Niigata Engineering Co Ltd-Japan
9714006 *JD3423* -	**TAKATAKI** **Government of Japan (Ministry of Land, Infrastructure & Transport) (The Coastguard)** - *Tokyo* *Japan* Official number: 141777	*126* - -		**2013-01 Niigata Shipbuilding & Repair Inc — Niigata NI** Loa 37.00 Br ex - Dght 1.480 Lbp - Br md 6.70 Dpth - Welded, 1 dk	**(B34H2SQ) Patrol Vessel**	**2 oil engines** reduction geared to sc. shafts driving 2 Water jets Total Power: 6,240kW (8,484hp) M.T.U. 16V4000M93 2 x Vee 4 Stroke 16 Cy. 170 x 190 each-3120kW (4242bhp) MTU Friedrichshafen GmbH-Friedrichshafen
9240574 *H04350* -	**TAKATORI** *ex* Takatori Maru *-2006* **KME Shipping SA** Jung Dong Shipping Co Ltd *Panama* *Panama* MMSI: 371996000 Official number: 3196306A	**381** 114 -		**2000-04 Kotobuki Kogyo KK — Ichikikushikino KS** Yd No: 115 Loa 35.15 Br ex - Dght 3.520 Lbp - Br md 9.40 Dpth 3.90 Welded, 1 dk	**(B32A2ST) Tug**	**2 oil engines** geared to sc. shafts driving 2 FP propellers Total Power: 2,354kW (3,200hp) 12.0kn Yanmar 6N260-EN 2 x 4 Stroke 6 Cy. 260 x 360 each-1177kW (1600bhp) Yanmar Diesel Engine Co Ltd-Japan Fuel: 86.0 (d.f.)
9219642 *JL6597* -	**TAKATORI** **Seiyo Kisen KK** - *Imabari, Ehime* *Japan* Official number: 136468	*499* - 1,566		**1999-06 Yamanaka Zosen K.K. — Imabari** Yd No: 631 Loa 76.68 Br ex - Dght 4.030 Lbp 71.30 Br md 13.00 Dpth 6.62 Welded, 1 dk	**(A31A2GX) General Cargo Ship** Compartments: 1 Ho, ER 1 Ha: (38.5 x 10.4)ER	**1 oil engine** driving 1 FP propeller Total Power: 1,471kW (2,000hp) 13.0kn Hanshin LH32L 1 x 4 Stroke 6 Cy. 320 x 640 1471kW (2000bhp) The Hanshin Diesel Works Ltd-Japan
7724928 *JQLG* -	**TAKATORI** **Government of Japan (Ministry of Land, Infrastructure & Transport) (The Coastguard)** - *Tokyo* *Japan* MMSI: 431100143 Official number: 121466	*468* - -		**1978-03 Naikai Shipbuilding & Engineering Co Ltd — Onomichi HS (Taguma Shipyard)** Yd No: 429 Loa 45.70 Br ex 9.22 Dght 2.960 Lbp 42.60 Br md 9.20 Dpth 4.30 Riveted\Welded, 1 dk	**(B34H2SQ) Patrol Vessel**	**2 oil engines** driving 2 CP propellers Total Power: 2,206kW (3,000hp) 15.0kn Fuji 6S32F 2 x 4 Stroke 6 Cy. 320 x 500 each-1103kW (1500bhp) Fuji Diesel Co Ltd-Japan
9276157 *JJ4044* -	**TAKATORI MARU** **Koun KK** - *Kamiamakusa, Kumamoto* *Japan* Official number: 135992	*499* - 1,526		**2002-10 K.K. Murakami Zosensho — Naruto** Yd No: 236 Loa 74.99 Br ex - Dght 4.070 Lbp 70.00 Br md 12.30 Dpth 7.00 Welded, 1 dk	**(A31A2GX) General Cargo Ship** Grain: 2,492	**1 oil engine** driving 1 FP propeller Total Power: 1,323kW (1,799hp) Hanshin LH30LG 1 x 4 Stroke 6 Cy. 300 x 600 1323kW (1799bhp) The Hanshin Diesel Works Ltd-Japan
7354577 - -	**TAKATORI MARU No. 33** **-**	*284* 145 228		**1973-11 KK Kanasashi Zosen — Shizuoka SZ** Yd No: 1137 Loa 48.19 Br ex 8.23 Dght 3.252 Lbp 42.30 Br md 8.21 Dpth 3.61 Welded, 1 dk	**(B11B2FV) Fishing Vessel**	**1 oil engine** driving 1 FP propeller Total Power: 736kW (1,001hp) Hanshin 6LU28 1 x 4 Stroke 6 Cy. 280 x 440 736kW (1001bhp) Hanshin Nainenki Kogyo-Japan
9011234 *JEZR* K01-811	**TAKATOYO MARU No. 38** **Iwao Yamamoto** - SatCom: Inmarsat A 1202115 *Muroto, Kochi* *Japan* MMSI: 431032000 Official number: 131494	*434* - 442		**1990-10 Miho Zosensho K.K. — Shimizu** Yd No: 1391 Loa 54.74 (BB) Br ex - Dght 3.407 Lbp 48.00 Br md 8.60 Dpth 3.75 Welded	**(B11B2FV) Fishing Vessel** Ins: 610	**1 oil engine** with flexible couplings & sr geared to sc. shaft driving 1 FP propeller Total Power: 736kW (1,001hp) Akasaka K28SFD 1 x 4 Stroke 6 Cy. 280 x 500 736kW (1001bhp) Akasaka Tekkosho KK (Akasaka DieselLtd)-Japan
9042831 *JG5095* -	**TAKATSUKI** **Government of Japan (Ministry of Land, Infrastructure & Transport) (The Coastguard)** - *Tokyo* *Japan* Official number: 133128	*114* - 19		**1992-03 Mitsubishi Heavy Industries Ltd. — Shimonoseki** Yd No: 967 Loa 37.41 Br ex 6.72 Dght 1.150 Lbp 31.50 Br md 6.70 Dpth 3.30 Welded, 1 dk	**(B34H2SQ) Patrol Vessel** Hull Material: Aluminium Alloy	**2 oil engines** with clutches & sr geared to sc. shafts driving 2 Water jets Total Power: 3,898kW (5,300hp) M.T.U. 16V396TB94 2 x Vee 4 Stroke 16 Cy. 165 x 185 each-1949kW (2650bhp) MTU Friedrichshafen GmbH-Friedrichshafen
9084841 *JI3576* -	**TAKATSURU MARU** **Bussan Kissen YK** - *Imabari, Ehime* *Japan* MMSI: 431300215 Official number: 135017	*498* - 1,199		**1994-09 Kyoei Zosen KK — Mihara HS** Yd No: 263 Loa 64.20 Br ex - Dght - Lbp - Br md 10.00 Dpth 4.50 Welded, 1 dk	**(A13B2TP) Products Tanker** 2 Cargo Pump (s): 2x500m³/hr	**1 oil engine** driving 1 FP propeller Total Power: 1,030kW (1,400hp) 11.5kn Hanshin LH28G 1 x 4 Stroke 6 Cy. 280 x 460 1030kW (1400bhp) The Hanshin Diesel Works Ltd-Japan

IMO / Call sign	Name / Owner	Tonnage	Class	Builder / Dimensions	Type	Machinery
6516805 *EPBB* -	**TAKAVAR** *ex* Banckert *-1989* *ex* Maasbank *-1977* **Goyaei H & partner** - *Bushehr* *Iran* Official number: 16538	**224** 67 -	Class: AS (LR) (AB) Classed LR until 6/12/00	**1965-08 N.V. Scheepswerven v/h H.H. Bodewes — Millingen a/d Rijn** Yd No: 641 Loa 32.85 Br ex 7.82 Dght 3.518 Lbp 30.20 Br md 7.50 Dpth 4.00 Welded, 1 dk	**(B32A2ST) Tug**	**2 oil engines** sr geared to sc. shaft driving 1 FP propeller Total Power: 970kW (1,318hp) Stork RH0218K 2 x 4 Stroke 8 Cy. 210 x 300 each-485kW (659bhp) Koninklijke Machinefabriek GebrStork & Co NV-Netherlands AuxGen: 2 x 40kW 220V d.c, 1 x 12kW 240V d.c Fuel: 86.5 (d.f.)
9314533 *EPAX*	**TAKAVAR 3** - **Bahregan Marine Services Co Ltd** - *Bushehr* *Iran* Official number: 0280	**284** 85 -	Class: (BV)	**2004-03 Piasau Slipways Sdn Bhd — Miri** Yd No: 170 Loa 31.00 Br ex - Dght 3.048 Lbp 27.88 Br md 9.50 Dpth 3.80 Welded, 1 dk	**(B32A2ST) Tug**	**2 oil engines** geared to sc. shafts driving 2 FP propellers Total Power: 1,516kW (2,062hp) Mitsubishi S6R2-MPTK2 2 x 4 Stroke 6 Cy. 170 x 220 each-758kW (1031bhp) Mitsubishi Heavy Industries Ltd-Japan
7378169 *EPPP* -	**TAKAVAR 5** *ex* Sistan *-1977* **Goyaei H & partner** - *Bushehr* *Iran* MMSI: 422811000 Official number: 17120	*167* 52 138	Class: AS (LR) ✠ Classed LR until 1/5/96	**1974-07 Towa Zosen K.K. — Shimonoseki** Yd No: 452 Loa 27.92 Br ex 7.35 Dght 3.074 Lbp 25.23 Br md 6.99 Dpth 3.51 Welded, 1 dk	**(B32A2ST) Tug**	**1 oil engine** reverse reduction geared to sc. shaft driving 1 FP propeller Total Power: 839kW (1,141hp) Caterpillar D399SCAC 1 x Vee 4 Stroke 16 Cy. 159 x 203 839kW (1141bhp) Caterpillar Tractor Co-USA AuxGen: 2 x 52kW 225V 50Hz a.c
6812792 *EPXA* -	**TAKAVAR 7** *ex* Kosar I *-2011* *ex* Pourandokht I *-1988* **Goyaei H & partner** - *Bandar Abbas* *Iran* MMSI: 422225000 Official number: 44	**461** 138 406	Class: AS (NV) (AB) (BV)	**1968 N.V. Scheepswerven v/h H.H. Bodewes — Millingen a/d Rijn** Yd No: 668 Loa 38.21 Br ex 10.37 Dght 4.973 Lbp 37.39 Br md 9.96 Dpth 5.47 Welded, 1 dk	**(B32A2ST) Tug**	**2 oil engines** driving 2 CP propellers Total Power: 4,582kW (6,230hp) 14.0kn De Industrie 6D8HD 2 x 4 Stroke 6 Cy. 400 x 600 each-2291kW (3115bhp) NV Motorenfabriek 'De Industrie'-Netherlands AuxGen: 2 x 124kW 440V 60Hz a.c Fuel: 177.0 (d.f.)
6812807 *EPXB* -	**TAKAVAR 8** *ex* Kosar II *-1988* *ex* Pourandokht II *-1988* **Goyaei H & partner** - *Bandar Abbas* *Iran* Official number: 45	*461* 138 406	Class: AS (NV) (AB)	**1968 N.V. Scheepswerven v/h H.H. Bodewes — Millingen a/d Rijn** Yd No: 669 Loa 38.21 Br ex 10.37 Dght 4.973 Lbp 37.39 Br md 9.96 Dpth 5.47 Welded, 1 dk	**(B32A2ST) Tug**	**2 oil engines** driving 2 CP propellers Total Power: 2,294kW (3,118hp) 14.0kn De Industrie 6D8HD 2 x 4 Stroke 6 Cy. 400 x 600 each-1147kW (1559bhp) NV Motorenfabriek 'De Industrie'-Netherlands AuxGen: 2 x 124kW 440V 60Hz a.c Fuel: 177.0 (d.f.)
8854146 - -	**TAKAYA MARU No. 20** - - - *China*	*136* - -		**1991 Fukui Zosen K.K. — Japan** Loa 29.50 Br ex - Dght 2.700 Lbp 25.00 Br md 8.00 Dpth 3.49 Welded, 1 dk	**(B32A2ST) Tug**	**1 oil engine** driving 1 FP propeller Total Power: 1,471kW (2,000hp) Yanmar MF33-UT 1 x 4 Stroke 6 Cy. 330 x 620 1471kW (2000bhp) Yanmar Diesel Engine Co Ltd-Japan
8103793 - -	**TAKAYAMA MARU** *ex* Kyoei Maru No. 21 *-1994* - - *South Korea*	*583* - 1,513	Class: (NK)	**1981-03 Mategata Zosen K.K. — Namikata** Yd No: 202 Loa 64.50 Br ex - Dght 4.311 Lbp 58.81 Br md 13.01 Dpth 6.02 Welded, 2 dks	**(A31A2GX) General Cargo Ship** Grain: 1,917; Bale: 1,902 1 Ha: (23.3 x 9.9)ER	**1 oil engine** driving 1 FP propeller Total Power: 1,324kW (1,800hp) 10.8kn Makita GSLH633 1 x 4 Stroke 6 Cy. 330 x 530 1324kW (1800bhp) Makita Diesel Co Ltd-Japan AuxGen: 2 x 72kW
8224846 *CNNA*	**TAKBIR** - **Omnium Marocaine de Peche** - SatCom: Inmarsat C 424237510 *Casablanca* *Morocco*	*324* 142 405	Class: (BV)	**1984-02 Construcciones Navales Santodomingo SA — Vigo** Yd No: 491 Loa 38.31 Br ex 8.59 Dght 4.050 Lbp 34.78 Br md 8.50 Dpth 6.15 Welded, 2 dks	**(B11A2FS) Stern Trawler** Ins: 402	**1 oil engine** with clutches, flexible couplings & sr geared to sc. shaft driving 1 FP propeller Total Power: 853kW (1,160hp) 12.3kn Deutz SBA8M528 1 x 4 Stroke 8 Cy. 220 x 280 853kW (1160bhp) Hijos de J Barreras SA-Spain AuxGen: 2 x 140kW 380V 50Hz a.c
8129876 *JJ3325* -	**TAKE MARU** - **Miura Kaiun KK** - *Kobe, Hyogo* *Japan* Official number: 125236	*197* - 72		**1982-09 Hikari Kogyo K.K. — Yokosuka** Yd No: 324 Loa 30.99 Br ex - Dght 2.741 Lbp 27.01 Br md 8.81 Dpth 3.51 Welded, 1 dk	**(B32A2ST) Tug**	**2 oil engines** with clutches, flexible couplings & reverse reduction geared to sc. shafts driving 2 FP propellers Total Power: 1,912kW (2,600hp) Yanmar 6T260L-ST 2 x 4 Stroke 6 Cy. 260 x 330 each-956kW (1300bhp) Yanmar Diesel Engine Co Ltd-Japan
7312969 - -	**TAKE MARU** *ex* Maiko Maru No. 2 *-1998* - - *South Korea*	*122* - -		**1973 Sanyo Zosen K.K. — Onomichi** Yd No: 662 Loa 25.80 Br ex 7.02 Dght 2.286 Lbp 23.00 Br md 7.00 Dpth 3.00 Riveted\Welded, 1 dk	**(B32A2ST) Tug**	**2 oil engines** driving 2 FP propellers Total Power: 1,104kW (1,500hp) Fuji 6M23CH 2 x 4 Stroke 6 Cy. 230 x 260 each-552kW (750bhp) Fuji Diesel Co Ltd-Japan
7312907 - -	**TAKE MARU No. 8** *ex* Hokuyo Maru *-1996* *ex* Kitakyushu Maru *-1996* **Hyundae Marine Co Ltd**	*192* - 79		**1973 Towa Zosen K.K. — Shimonoseki** Yd No: 433 Loa 30.48 Br ex 8.82 Dght 3.023 Lbp 26.98 Br md 8.79 Dpth 3.48 Welded, 1 dk	**(B32A2ST) Tug**	**2 oil engines** driving 2 FP propellers Total Power: 1,766kW (2,402hp) Niigata 6L25BX 2 x 4 Stroke 6 Cy. 250 x 320 each-883kW (1201bhp) Niigata Engineering Co Ltd-Japan
7203443 *JJ2730* -	**TAKE MARU No. 8** *ex* Yoshida Maru *-2001* **YK Takemaru Kaiun** - *Osaka, Osaka* *Japan* Official number: 112491	*199* - -		**1971-05 Towa Zosen K.K. — Shimonoseki** Yd No: 412 Loa 32.52 Br ex 8.84 Dght 2.598 Lbp 27.01 Br md 8.82 Dpth 3.51 Welded, 1 dk	**(B32A2ST) Tug**	**2 oil engines** driving 2 FP propellers Total Power: 1,766kW (2,402hp) Niigata 6L25BX 2 x 4 Stroke 6 Cy. 250 x 320 each-883kW (1201bhp) Niigata Engineering Co Ltd-Japan AuxGen: 2 x 40kW 225V a.c
7530688 - -	**TAKE MARU No. 18** - -	*101* 35 -		**1976-06 Sanyo Zosen K.K. — Onomichi** Yd No: 735 Loa 23.30 Br ex 6.62 Dght 2.300 Lbp 20.00 Br md 6.60 Dpth 3.00 Welded, 1 dk	**(B32A2ST) Tug**	**2 oil engines** Geared Integral to driving 2 Z propellers Total Power: 736kW (1,000hp) Niigata 6MG16HS 2 x 4 Stroke 6 Cy. 160 x 200 each-368kW (500bhp) Niigata Engineering Co Ltd-Japan
8890114 *JI3584*	**TAKE MARU No. 23** - **YK Takemaru Kaiun** - *Osaka, Osaka* *Japan* Official number: 135026	**279** - -		**1995-07 Kanbara Zosen K.K. — Onomichi** Yd No: 472 Loa 38.50 Br ex - Dght 3.400 Lbp 33.00 Br md 9.60 Dpth 4.50 Welded, 1 dk	**(B32A2ST) Tug**	**2 oil engines** Geared Integral to driving 2 Z propellers Total Power: 2,942kW (4,000hp) 14.4kn Niigata 6L28HX 2 x 4 Stroke 6 Cy. 280 x 370 each-1471kW (2000bhp) Niigata Engineering Co Ltd-Japan
7409932 *DUTL4* -	**TAKE MARU No. 28** *ex* Nagoya Maru *-1985* **North Harbor Tug Corp** - *Manila* *Philippines* Official number: 00-0001268	*124* 49 -		**1974-08 Kanagawa Zosen — Kobe** Yd No: 142 Loa 26.20 Br ex 8.01 Dght 2.591 Lbp 23.00 Br md 7.98 Dpth 3.61 Riveted\Welded, 1 dk	**(B32A2ST) Tug**	**2 oil engines** Geared Integral to driving 2 Z propellers Total Power: 1,220kW (1,658hp) Niigata 6L20AX 2 x 4 Stroke 6 Cy. 200 x 260 each-610kW (829bhp) Niigata Engineering Co Ltd-Japan
8028785 *JJ3267* -	**TAKE MARU NO. 33** *ex* Heiwa Maru *-2007* *ex* Katsuragi *-2003* *ex* Tosei Maru *-1991* **Kenichi Ishiba** - *Osaka, Osaka* *Japan* Official number: 121230	*195* - -		**1981-04 Kanagawa Zosen — Kobe** Yd No: 218 Loa 30.30 Br ex 8.62 Dght 2.601 Lbp 25.76 Br md 8.60 Dpth 3.77 Welded, 1 dk	**(B32A2ST) Tug**	**2 oil engines** geared integral to driving 2 Z propellers Total Power: 1,912kW (2,600hp) 12.5kn Niigata 6L25BX 2 x 4 Stroke 6 Cy. 250 x 320 each-956kW (1300bhp) Niigata Engineering Co Ltd-Japan
9172985 *JG5373* -	**TAKE MARU NO. 38** *ex* Takamatsu Maru *-2012* **Wing Maritime Service Corp** - *Osaka, Osaka* *Japan* Official number: 136609	*184* - -		**1997-11 Yokohama Yacht Co Ltd — Yokohama KN** Yd No: 9490 Loa 33.20 Br ex 8.80 Dght - Lbp 29.90 Br md - Dpth 3.80 Welded, 1 dk	**(B32A2ST) Tug**	**2 oil engines** with clutches, flexible couplings & reduction geared to sc. shafts driving 2 Directional propellers Total Power: 2,280kW (3,100hp) Yanmar 6N260-UN 2 x 4 Stroke 6 Cy. 260 x 360 each-1140kW (1550bhp) Yanmar Diesel Engine Co Ltd-Japan
7903081 *JJ3175* -	**TAKE MARU No. 51** *ex* Soun Maru *-1997* **Takeshi Yoshimine** - *Osaka, Osaka* *Japan* Official number: 121081	*296* - -		**1979-06 Kanagawa Zosen — Kobe** Yd No: 200 Loa 35.50 Br ex - Dght 3.101 Lbp 31.25 Br md 9.20 Dpth 4.20 Welded, 1 dk	**(B32A2ST) Tug**	**2 oil engines** Geared Integral to driving 2 Z propellers Total Power: 2,574kW (3,500hp) 12.9kn Fuji 6L27.5X 2 x 4 Stroke 6 Cy. 275 x 320 each-1287kW (1750bhp) Fuji Diesel Co Ltd-Japan

8221351 *JI3151* -	**TAKE MARU NO. 78** *ex* Konan Maru *-2007* *ex* Take Maru No. 78 *-2001* *ex* Yoshino Maru *-2001* **YK Takemaru Kaiun** - *Osaka, Osaka* *Japan* Official number: 126444	*281* - -		1982-10 **Hatayama Zosen KK — Yura WK** Yd No: 180 Loa 32.45 Br ex - Dght 3.501 Lbp 27.50 Br md 9.52 Dpth 4.12 Welded, 1 dk	**(B32A2ST) Tug**	**2 oil engines** Geared Integral to driving 2 Z propellers Total Power: 2,750kW (3,738hp) 13.5kn Niigata 6L28BX 2 x 4 Stroke 6 Cy. 280 x 320 each-1375kW (1869bhp) Niigata Engineering Co Ltd-Japan
9203033 *JI3650* -	**TAKE MARU No. 82** - **YK Takemaru Kaiun** - *Yokohama, Kanagawa* *Japan* MMSI: 431300812 Official number: 135949	*294* - -		1998-03 **Kanbara Zosen K.K. — Onomichi** Yd No: 470 Loa 38.50 Br ex - Dght - Lbp 33.00 Br md 9.60 Dpth 4.50 Welded, 1 dk	**(B32A2ST) Tug**	**2 oil engines** Geared Integral to driving 2 Z propellers Total Power: 2,942kW (4,000hp) 13.5kn Niigata 6L28HX 2 x 4 Stroke 6 Cy. 280 x 370 each-1471kW (2000bhp) Niigata Engineering Co Ltd-Japan
9088160 *JK5229* -	**TAKEHARA MARU** **Asia Pacific Marine Corp & Epdc Coal Tech Co Ltd & Shinwa Naiko Kaiun Kaisha Ltd** Asia Pacific Marine Corp *Tokyo* *Japan* MMSI: 431400325 Official number: 133080	**1,499** 2,349	Class: NK	1994-05 **Sasaki Shipbuilding Co Ltd — Osakikamijima HS** Yd No: 587 Loa 82.53 Br ex - Dght 5.219 Lbp 76.00 Br md 13.20 Dpth 6.00 Welded, 1 dk	**(A24E2BL) Limestone Carrier** Grain: 2,000	**1 oil engine** driving 1 FP propeller Total Power: 1,912kW (2,600hp) 12.5kn Akasaka A37 1 x 4 Stroke 6 Cy. 370 x 720 1912kW (2600bhp) Akasaka Tekkosho KK (Akasaka DieselLtd)-Japan Fuel: 100.0 (d.f.)
9184201 *3FFH9* -	**TAKEKO** - **North Star Shipholding SA** COSCO Container Lines Co Ltd (COSCON) SatCom: Inmarsat C 435729410 *Panama* *Panama* MMSI: 357294000 Official number: 2636699D	**8,957** 4,132 9,513 T/cm 24.6	Class: NK	1999-04 **Kyokuyo Shipyard Corp — Shimonoseki YC** Yd No: 422 Loa 138.03 (BB) Br ex - Dght 7.800 Lbp 128.00 Br md 22.40 Dpth 11.30 Welded, 1 dk	**(A33A2CC) Container Ship (Fully Cellular)** TEU 564 C Ho 214 TEU C Dk 350 incl 222 ref C Compartments: 6 Cell Ho, ER 11 Ha: (12.6 x 13.6)Tappered 2 (12.6 x 8.3)Tappered 8 (12.6 x 8.3)ER	**1 oil engine** driving 1 FP propeller Total Power: 7,208kW (9,800hp) 17.5kn B&W 6S46MC-C 1 x 2 Stroke 6 Cy. 460 x 1932 7208kW (9800bhp) Kawasaki Heavy Industries Ltd-Japan Fuel: 41.4 (d.f.) (Heating Coils) 924.1 (r.f.) 36.0pd
8863276 *HP7372* -	**TAKESHIMA MARU No. 2** - **Sinkobe Enterprise** - *Panama* *Panama* Official number: D7351789PEXT	*199* 131 550		1974 **Takeshima Zosen K.K. — Japan** Loa 47.50 Br ex - Dght 3.100 Lbp 44.01 Br md 7.80 Dpth 3.40 Welded, 1 dk	**(A13B2TU) Tanker (unspecified)** Liq: 666; Liq (Oil): 666 Cargo Heating Coils 1 Cargo Pump (s): 1x500m³/hr	**1 oil engine** driving 1 FP propeller Total Power: 552kW (750hp) 10.0kn Niigata 1 x 4 Stroke 552kW (750bhp) Niigata Engineering Co Ltd-Japan
9526162 *3FDZ5* -	**TAKESHIO** *completed as* Jin Yu *-2012* **Peony Shipholding SA** - SatCom: Inmarsat C 437357510 *Panama* *Panama* MMSI: 373575000 Official number: 4400512	**23,855** 11,814 38,494 T/cm 51.3	Class: NK	2012-06 **Naikai Zosen Corp — Onomichi HS (Setoda Shipyard)** Yd No: 752 Loa 184.75 (BB) Br ex - Dght 10.020 Lbp 177.00 Br md 30.60 Dpth 14.50 Welded, 1 dk	**(A31A2GO) Open Hatch Cargo Ship** Double Hull Grain: 47,235; Bale: 46,315 Compartments: 5 Ho, ER 5 Ha: 3 (20.8 x 20.8) (23.3 x 20.8)ER (15.5 x 17.6) Cranes: 4x30t	**1 oil engine** driving 1 FP propeller Total Power: 6,781kW (9,219hp) 14.3kn MAN-B&W 6S46MC-C 1 x 2 Stroke 6 Cy. 460 x 1932 6781kW (9219bhp) Hitachi Zosen Corp-Japan Fuel: 2230.0
7831927 *UCRC* -	**TAKHKURAND** *ex* Tahkurand *-2000* *ex* Takhkurand *-1992* **OOO 'Magadanmore'** AOZT 'Vostoktransservis' Marine Shipping Co *Magadan* *Russia* MMSI: 273455450 Official number: 790874	**747** 224 405	Class: RS	1980-06 **Zavod "Leninskaya Kuznitsa" — Kiyev** Yd No: 1478 Loa 54.82 Br ex 9.96 Dght 4.140 Lbp 50.29 Br md 9.80 Dpth 5.06 Welded, 1 dk	**(B11A2FS) Stern Trawler** Bale: 414 Compartments: 2 Ho, ER 3 Ha: 3 (1.5 x 1.6) Derricks: 2x1.3t Ice Capable	**1 oil engine** driving 1 FP propeller Total Power: 736kW (1,001hp) 12.0kn S.K.L. 8NVD48A-2U 1 x 4 Stroke 8 Cy. 320 x 480 736kW (1001bhp) VEB Schwermaschinenbau "KarlLiebknecht" (SKL)-Magdeburg Fuel: 154.0 (d.f.)
9101340 *URBA* -	**TAKIL** *ex* Karat *-2004* **Mayak Alfa Ltd** - *Kerch* *Ukraine* Official number: 922008	**190** 57 70	Class: (RS)	1993-08 **OAO Astrakhanskaya Sudoverf — Astrakhan** Yd No: 112 Loa 31.85 Br ex 7.08 Dght 2.100 Lbp 27.80 Br md - Dpth 3.15 Welded, 1 dk	**(B12B2FC) Fish Carrier** Ins: 100 Compartments: 2 Ho 2 Ha: 2 (2.1 x 2.4) Derricks: 2x1t Ice Capable	**1 oil engine** geared to sc. shaft driving 1 FP propeller Total Power: 232kW (315hp) 10.2kn Daldizel 6CHSPN2A18-315 1 x 4 Stroke 6 Cy. 180 x 220 232kW (315bhp) Daldizel-Khabarovsk AuxGen: 2 x 25kW Fuel: 14.0 (d.f.)
9316543 *3EAL5* -	**TAKIS** - **Lonok Shipping Co** Lotus Shipping Co Ltd *Panama* *Panama* MMSI: 355348000 Official number: 3095705A	**7,064** 3,430 10,813 T/cm 20.0	Class: AB	2005-05 **Nokbong Shipbuilding Co Ltd — Geoje** Yd No: 397 Loa 121.40 (BB) Br ex - Dght 8.300 Lbp 113.40 Br md 19.20 Dpth 10.80 Welded, 1 dk	**(A12B2TR) Chemical/Products Tanker** Double Hull (13F) Liq: 11,342; Liq (Oil): 11,342 Cargo Heating Coils Compartments: 10 Wing Ta, 2 Wing Slop Ta, ER 10 Cargo Pump (s): 10x300m³/hr Manifold: Bow/CM: 51m	**1 oil engine** driving 1 FP propeller Total Power: 4,519kW (6,144hp) 14.0kn MAN-B&W 6S35MC 1 x 2 Stroke 6 Cy. 350 x 1400 4519kW (6144bhp) STX Engine Co Ltd-South Korea AuxGen: 3 x 615kW a.c Thrusters: 1 Thwart. FP thruster (f) Fuel: 44.5 (d.f.) 453.4 (r.f.)
5393579 *SV4991* -	**TAKIS M II** *ex* Creta Salvor *-1989* *ex* Wrestler *-1979* **Evripos Tugs Shipping Co** Sirios Shipmanagement Co Ltd *Chalkis* *Greece* MMSI: 237107500 Official number: 414	*247* 43	Class: (LR) ✠ Classed LR until 10/12/86	1957-07 **James Lamont & Co. Ltd. — Port Glasgow** Yd No: 389 Loa 34.78 Br ex 9.10 Dght 3.626 Lbp 31.70 Br md 8.54 Dpth 3.89 Riveted\Welded, 1 dk	**(B32A2ST) Tug**	**1 oil engine** dr geared to sc. shaft driving 1 FP propeller Total Power: 783kW (1,065hp) 12.0kn Widdop GMB8 1 x 4 Stroke 8 Cy. 318 x 470 783kW (1065bhp) H. Widdop & Co. Ltd.-Keighley AuxGen: 1 x 70kW 110V d.c, 1 x 15kW 110V d.c Fuel: 67.0 (d.f.)
8007717 *3FQU4* -	**TAKLAMAKAN** *ex* Oryong No. 322 *-2009* *ex* Acacia No. 31 *-1993* **BHD Trading Co Ltd SA** - *Panama* *Panama* MMSI: 351267000 Official number: 38805PEXT	**614** 258 503	Class: (KR)	1980-08 **Dae Sun Shipbuilding & Engineering Co Ltd — Busan** Yd No: 243 Loa 55.17 Br ex 8.62 Dght 3.805 Lbp 49.69 Br md 8.60 Dpth 4.02 Welded, 1 dk	**(B11B2FV) Fishing Vessel** 2 Ha: (1.3 x 1.0) (1.8 x 1.8)	**1 oil engine** driving 1 FP propeller Total Power: 993kW (1,350hp) 13.5kn Hanshin 6LUN28 1 x 4 Stroke 6 Cy. 280 x 480 993kW (1350bhp) The Hanshin Diesel Works Ltd-Japan AuxGen: 2 x 200kW 225V a.c
7943392 *J7BQ9* -	**TAKLIFT 1** - **Smit Singapore Pte Ltd** - *Portsmouth* *Dominica*	**2,129** 638 -	Class: (BV)	1969-03 **De Rotterdamsche Droogdok Mij NV — Rotterdam** Yd No: 328 Loa 60.92 Br ex - Dght 3.900 Lbp 58.25 Br md 23.40 Dpth 5.60 Welded, 1 dk	**(Y11B4WL) Sheerlegs Pontoon** Derricks: 2x250t,2x150t	**2 oil engines** driving 2 FP propellers Total Power: 798kW (1,084hp) Cummins VTA-28-M2 2 x Vee 4 Stroke 12 Cy. 140 x 152 each-399kW (542bhp) (new engine 1990) Kirloskar Oil Engines Ltd-India Fuel: 146.5 (d.f.)
8010506 *PHWS* -	**TAKLIFT 4** - **Smit Shipping Singapore Pte Ltd** Smit Vessel Management Services BV *Rotterdam* *Netherlands* MMSI: 244394000 Official number: 707	**5,695** 1,708 4,625	Class: LR ✠ **100A1** SS 03/2010 pontoon with accommodation units extended protected waters service LA *IWS ✠ **LMC** Eq.Ltr: (S) ; Cable: 770.0/62.0 U2	1981-09 **Verolme Scheepswerf Heusden B.V. — Heusden** Yd No: 985 Loa 83.11 Br ex 35.25 Dght 6.001 Lbp 80.42 Br md 28.03 Dpth 7.00 Welded, 1 dk	**(Y11B4WL) Sheerlegs Pontoon** A-frames: 1x2200t; Cranes: 1x1400t	**2 oil engines** with flexible couplings & sr gearedto sc. shafts driving 2 CP propellers Total Power: 1,656kW (2,252hp) Caterpillar D399SCAC 2 x Vee 4 Stroke 16 Cy. 159 x 203 each-828kW (1126bhp) Caterpillar Tractor Co-USA AuxGen: 3 x 320kW 440V 60Hz a.c, 1 x 156kW 440V 60Hz a.c Thrusters: 2 Thwart. CP thruster (f)
7734806 *9V5979* -	**TAKLIFT 6** *ex* Hebe 2 *-1987* **Smit Shipping Singapore Pte Ltd** Smit Singapore Pte Ltd SatCom: Inmarsat M 624424110 *Singapore* *Singapore* MMSI: 563301000 Official number: 389059	**3,297** 989 -	Class: GL	1975-03 **Howaldtswerke-Deutsche Werft AG (HDW) — Kiel** Yd No: 530870 Loa 72.57 Br ex 30.03 Dght 4.111 Lbp - Br md 30.01 Dpth 5.49 Welded, 1 dk	**(Y11B4WL) Sheerlegs Pontoon** Derricks: 1x1200t	**2 oil engines** sr geared to sc. shafts driving 2 Directional propellers Total Power: 1,000kW (1,360hp) 6.0kn Deutz SBF16M716 2 x Vee 4 Stroke 16 Cy. 135 x 160 each-500kW (680bhp) Kloeckner Humboldt Deutz AG-West Germany Thrusters: 2 Thwart. FP thruster (f)

IMO / Call sign / Flag	Name / Former names / Owner / Manager / Port	Tonnage (GT / NT / DWT)	Class	Build / Dimensions	Ship type / Cargo	Machinery
7829273 *PHWN* -	**TAKLIFT 7** *ex* Hebelift 3 *-1987* **Smit Heavy Lift Europe BV** Smit Vessel Management Services BV *Rotterdam* *Netherlands* MMSI: 246385000 Official number: 33189	**3,343** 1,003 -	Class: GL	**1976**-03 **Howaldtswerke-Deutsche Werft AG (HDW) — Kiel** Yd No: 530902 Loa 71.99 Br ex 30.03 Dght 4.501 Lbp 69.12 Br md 30.01 Dpth 5.52 Welded, 1 dk	**(Y11B4WL) Sheerlegs Pontoon** Derricks: 1x800t	**3 oil engines** sr geared to sc. shafts driving 3 Directional propellers Total Power: 1,434kW (1,950hp) 6.0kn Deutz SBF16M716 3 x Vee 4 Stroke 16 Cy. 135 x 160 each-478kW (650bhp) Kloeckner Humboldt Deutz AG-West Germany AuxGen: 3 x 408kW 380/220V 50Hz a.c, 1 x 92kW 380/220V 50Hz a.c, 1 x 64kW 380/220V 50Hz a.c Thrusters: 2 Thwart. FP thruster (f)
8224884 *CNRS* -	**TAKMIL** **Omnium Marocaine de Peche** - SatCom: Inmarsat C 424237610 *Agadir* *Morocco*	*323* 142 405	Class: (BV)	**1984**-11 **Construcciones Navales Santodomingo SA — Vigo** Yd No: 495 Loa 38.31 Br ex 8.59 Dght 4.050 Lbp 34.78 Br md 8.51 Dpth 6.15 Welded, 1 dk	**(B11A2FS) Stern Trawler** Ins: 402	**1 oil engine** with clutches, flexible couplings & sr geared to sc. shaft driving 1 FP propeller Total Power: 853kW (1,160hp) 12.3kn Deutz SBA8M528 1 x 4 Stroke 8 Cy. 220 x 280 853kW (1160bhp) Hijos de J Barreras SA-Spain AuxGen: 2 x 140kW 380V 50Hz a.c
9041667 *EPCH5* -	**TAKNAVAZ** *ex* Yas *-2013* *ex* Hisashige Maru No. 1 *-2012* **Mohammad Mahmoud Nejad** - *Iran*	*199* - 655		**1991**-11 **K.K. Miura Zosensho — Saiki** Yd No: 1018 Loa 58.70 (BB) Br ex - Dght 3.120 Lbp 53.00 Br md 9.50 Dpth 5.30 Welded	**(A31A2GX) General Cargo Ship**	**1 oil engine** driving 1 FP propeller Total Power: 625kW (850hp) Niigata 6M26AGTE 1 x 4 Stroke 6 Cy. 260 x 460 625kW (850bhp) Niigata Engineering Co Ltd-Japan Thrusters: 1 Tunnel thruster (f)
9046796 *EPAT3* -	**TAKNAZ** *ex* Fukuhisa Maru *-2012* - - *Iran* MMSI: 422011200	*199* - 700		**1992**-02 **K.K. Miura Zosensho — Saiki** Yd No: 1020 L reg 54.50 Br ex - Dght 3.180 Lbp 52.40 Br md 9.60 Dpth 5.40 Welded, 1 dk	**(A31A2GX) General Cargo Ship**	**1 oil engine** driving 1 FP propeller Total Power: 625kW (850hp) Niigata 6M26AGTE 1 x 4 Stroke 6 Cy. 260 x 460 625kW (850bhp) Niigata Engineering Co Ltd-Japan
8815293 *5IM390* -	**TAKNIS** *ex* Montaser M *-2014* *ex* Princess Sira *-2011* *ex* Marti Pride *-2008* *ex* Vera *-2006* *ex* Gera *-2003* *ex* Arfell *-2003* *ex* Gera *-2001* *ex* Inishowen *-1998* *ex* Angela Jurgens *-1996* **Salahadden Ghit M Al Khtri** Lulu Shipping Co SA *Zanzibar* *Tanzania (Zanzibar)* MMSI: 677029000 Official number: 300140	**2,749** 1,110 3,376	Class: MG (GL)	**1988**-11 **J.J. Sietas KG Schiffswerft GmbH & Co. — Hamburg** Yd No: 967 Loa 94.50 (BB) Br ex 16.14 Dght 5.010 Lbp 87.00 Br md 15.91 Dpth 7.54 Welded, 2 dks	**(A31A2GX) General Cargo Ship** Grain: 4,466; Bale: 4,269 TEU 262 C Ho 82 TEU C dk 180 TEU incl 40 ref C Compartments: 1 Ho, ER 1 Ha: (57.8 x 12.8)ER Ice Capable	**1 oil engine** with flexible couplings & sr geared to sc. shaft driving 1 CP propeller Total Power: 995kW (1,353hp) 14.3kn Wartsila 6R32D 1 x 4 Stroke 6 Cy. 320 x 350 995kW (1353bhp) Wartsila Diesel Oy-Finland AuxGen: 1 x 400kW 220/380V 50Hz a.c, 2 x 220kW 220/380V 50Hz a.c, 1 x 20kW 220/380V 50Hz a.c Thrusters: 1 Thwart. FP thruster (f)
8029648 - -	**TAKOJIMA MARU No. 1** **East Food SA** -	*247* - -		**1981**-03 **Tokushima Zosen K.K. — Fukuoka** Yd No: 1358 Loa - Br ex - Dght 2.601 Lbp 38.10 Br md 7.59 Dpth 3.10 Welded, 1 dk	**(B11B2FV) Fishing Vessel**	**1 oil engine** driving 1 FP propeller Total Power: 1,030kW (1,400hp) Hanshin 6LU32 1 x 4 Stroke 6 Cy. 320 x 510 1030kW (1400bhp) Hanshin Nainenki Kogyo-Japan
8404082 *JH3031* -	**TAKOJIMA MARU No. 2** **Hamada Gyogyo KK** - *Suzu, Ishikawa* *Japan* Official number: 127592	*297* - 449		**1984**-07 **Wakamatsu Zosen K.K. — Kitakyushu** Yd No: 335 Loa 51.85 (BB) Br ex 8.34 Dght 3.090 Lbp 44.51 Br md 8.31 Dpth 4.00 Welded, 1 dk	**(B12B2FC) Fish Carrier**	**1 oil engine** with clutches & sr reverse geared to sc. shaft driving 1 FP propeller Total Power: 1,177kW (1,600hp) Hanshin 6LUN30RG 1 x 4 Stroke 6 Cy. 300 x 480 1177kW (1600bhp) The Hanshin Diesel Works Ltd-Japan Thrusters: 1 Thwart. FP thruster (f)
8702537 *JH3035* IK1-268	**TAKOJIMA MARU No. 3** **Hamada Gyogyo KK** - *Suzu, Ishikawa* *Japan* Official number: 127596	*110* - 92		**1987**-04 **K.K. Izutsu Zosensho — Nagasaki** Yd No: 930 Loa 41.61 (BB) Br ex 8.36 Dght 2.652 Lbp 33.00 Br md 7.51 Dpth 3.08 Welded, 1 dk	**(B11B2FV) Fishing Vessel**	**1 oil engine** geared to sc. shaft driving 1 CP propeller Total Power: 743kW (1,010hp) Daihatsu 6DLM-26FS 1 x 4 Stroke 6 Cy. 260 x 340 743kW (1010bhp) Daihatsu Diesel Manufacturing Co Lt-Japan
8804957 - -	**TAKOJIMA MARU No. 7** - -	*135* - 138		**1988**-06 **K.K. Izutsu Zosensho — Nagasaki** Yd No: 948 Loa 46.70 (BB) Br ex 8.75 Dght 2.801 Lbp 37.10 Br md 7.90 Dpth 3.26 Welded, 1 dk	**(B11B2FV) Fishing Vessel**	**1 oil engine** driving 1 CP propeller Total Power: 861kW (1,171hp) Niigata 6MG28CX 1 x 4 Stroke 6 Cy. 280 x 350 861kW (1171bhp) Niigata Engineering Co Ltd-Japan Thrusters: 1 Thwart. FP thruster (f)
8881632 - -	**TAKOJIMA MARU No. 77** **King Ford Co** - *Philippines*	*190* - -		**1977** **Kitanihon Zosen K.K. — Hachinohe** L reg 38.00 Br ex - Dght - Lbp - Br md 7.00 Dpth 3.40 Welded, 1 dk	**(B11B2FV) Fishing Vessel**	**1 oil engine** driving 1 FP propeller
7010860 *5VBE2* -	**TAKORADI** *ex* Agia Zoni VI *-2011* *ex* Leone III *-2009* *ex* Karthea *-1998* *ex* Shell Mariner *-1991* *ex* Bernard Lafitte *-1986* *ex* Ferton *-1980* *ex* Letizia Napoleone *-1978* **Danae Marine Ltd** Starwind Management Co *Togo* MMSI: 671202000	*1,375* 868 2,721	Class: (HR) (RI) (BV)	**1970**-07 **Cant. Nav. Sgorbini — La Spezia** Yd No: 60 Loa 81.49 Br ex 12.53 Dght 4.333 Lbp 76.61 Br md 12.50 Dpth 5.01 Welded, 1 dk	**(A13B2TP) Products Tanker** Liq: 3,389; Liq (Oil): 3,389 Compartments: 10 Ta, ER 4 Cargo Pump (s)	**2 oil engines** driving 2 FP propellers Total Power: 1,412kW (1,920hp) Deutz RBA8M528 2 x 4 Stroke 8 Cy. 220 x 280 each-706kW (960bhp) Kloeckner Humboldt Deutz AG-West Germany AuxGen: 2 x 38kW 220V 50Hz a.c Fuel: 112.0 (d.f.) 7.5pd
5351052 *WI9491* -	**TAKU** **State of Alaska (Department of Transportation & Public Facilities) (Alaska Marine Highways System)** - *Wrangell, AK* *United States of America* MMSI: 338697000 Official number: 290756	**7,302** 2,496 759 T/cm 13.3	Class: AB	**1963**-03 **Puget Sound Bridge & Drydock Co. — Seattle, Wa** Yd No: 112 Loa 107.30 Br ex 22.46 Dght 5.180 Lbp 95.71 Br md 22.41 Dpth 7.17 Welded, 2 dks	**(A36A2PR) Passenger/Ro-Ro Ship (Vehicles)** Passengers: unberthed: 270; cabins: 42; berths: 100 Stern door/ramp Side ramp (p) Side ramp (s) Lane-Wid: 3.00 Lane-clr ht: 4.26 Trailers: 69	**2 oil engines** with clutches, flexible couplings & sr geared to sc. shafts driving 2 CP propellers Total Power: 5,884kW (8,000hp) 16.5kn MaK 8M453C 2 x 4 Stroke 8 Cy. 320 x 420 each-2942kW (4000bhp) (new engine ,made 1992) Krupp MaK Maschinenbau GmbH-Kiel AuxGen: 2 x 400kW 460V 60Hz a.c Thrusters: 1 Thwart. FP thruster (f) Fuel: 1218.0 (d.f.) 15.0pd
9356220 *JD2153* -	**TAKUMI** **Muroran Tsusen KK** - *Muroran, Hokkaido* *Japan* MMSI: 431800698 Official number: 140218	*199* - -		**2005**-09 **Narasaki Zosen KK — Muroran HK** Yd No: 1183 Loa 34.01 Br ex - Dght 3.160 Lbp 29.50 Br md 9.20 Dpth 4.01 Welded, 1 dk	**(B32A2ST) Tug**	**2 oil engines** reduction geared to sc. shafts driving 2 CP propellers Total Power: 2,942kW (4,000hp) Yanmar 6EY26 2 x 4 Stroke 6 Cy. 260 x 385 each-1471kW (2000bhp) Yanmar Diesel Engine Co Ltd-Japan
9281126 *JL6593* -	**TAKUMI MARU** **Corporation for Advanced Transport & Technology & Iyo Kaiun KK** Iyo Kaiun KK *Ozu, Ehime* *Japan* MMSI: 431501744 Official number: 136566	*392* - 443	Class: NK	**2002**-11 **Chengxi Shipyard — Jiangyin JS** Yd No: 6011 Loa 32.11 Br ex - Dght 6.628 Lbp 29.76 Br md 17.50 Dpth 9.45 Welded, 1 Dk.	**(B32B2SP) Pusher Tug**	**1 oil engine** driving 1 FP propeller Total Power: 3,310kW (4,500hp) B&W 6L35MC 1 x 2 Stroke 6 Cy. 350 x 1050 3310kW (4500bhp) The Hanshin Diesel Works Ltd-Japan AuxGen: 3 x 710kW a.c Fuel: 240.0 (d.f.)
8202484 *7JWN* -	**TAKUYO** **Government of Japan (Ministry of Land, Infrastructure & Transport) (The Coastguard)** - *Tokyo* *Japan* MMSI: 431561000 Official number: 126752	*2,474* - -		**1983**-08 **Nippon Kokan KK (NKK Corp) — Yokohama KN (Tsurumi Shipyard)** Yd No: 1001 Loa 96.00 (BB) Br ex 14.23 Dght 4.591 Lbp 90.00 Br md 14.20 Dpth 7.30 Welded, 2 dks	**(B31A2SR) Research Survey Vessel**	**2 oil engines** driving 2 CP propellers Total Power: 3,824kW (5,200hp) 16.0kn Fuji 6S40B 2 x 4 Stroke 6 Cy. 400 x 580 each-1912kW (2600bhp) Fuji Diesel Co Ltd-Japan Thrusters: 1 Thwart. FP thruster (f)

9176498 *JI3647* -	**TAKUYO MARU** - **Japan Railway Construction, Transport & Technology Agency & Daiichi Senpaku Kaisha & Umewaka Kaiun Co Ltd** Daiichi Chuo Naiko Kaisha *Osaka, Osaka* *Japan* MMSI: 431300759 Official number: 135944	**8,566** - 10,750 T/cm 22.3	Class: NK	**1998-03 Tsuneishi Shipbuilding Co Ltd — Fukuyama HS** Yd No: 1141 Loa 123.17 (BB) Br ex - Dght 7.518 Lbp 117.00 Br md 20.40 Dpth 11.90 Welded, 1 dk	**(A24E2BL) Limestone Carrier** Grain: 7,866; Bale: 7,110	**1 oil engine** driving 1 CP propeller Total Power: 3,884kW (5,281hp) 13.0kn B&W 6L35MC 1 x 2 Stroke 6 Cy. 350 x 1050 3884kW (5281bhp) Makita Corp-Japan AuxGen: 3 x 450kW 450V 60Hz a.c Thrusters: 1 Thwart. FP thruster (f) Fuel: 59.4 (d.f.) (Heating Coils) 377.5 (r.f.) 15.4pd
9176888 *JQVA* MG1-2001	**TAKUYO MARU** - **Miyagi Prefecture** - *Ishinomaki, Miyagi* *Japan* MMSI: 431921000 Official number: 132254	*120* - -		**1997-03 K.K. Yoshida Zosen Tekko — Kesennuma** Yd No: 505 Loa 33.71 Br ex - Dght - Lbp 27.50 Br md 6.60 Dpth 3.00 Welded, 1 dk	**(B12D2FR) Fishery Research Vessel**	**1 oil engine** driving 1 FP propeller Total Power: 883kW (1,201hp) 11.5kn Niigata 6MG22HX 1 x 4 Stroke 6 Cy. 220 x 280 883kW (1201bhp) Niigata Engineering Co Ltd-Japan
7371587 - -	**TAKUYO MARU No. 2** - **GK Samejima Sekiyuten** -	*299* 138 -		**1973-12 Goriki Zosensho — Ise** Yd No: 758 Loa - Br ex 8.03 Dght 2.998 Lbp 43.82 Br md 8.01 Dpth 3.69 Riveted\Welded, 1 dk	**(B11B2FV) Fishing Vessel**	**1 oil engine** driving 1 FP propeller Total Power: 1,177kW (1,600hp) Akasaka AH33 1 x 4 Stroke 6 Cy. 330 x 500 1177kW (1600bhp) Akasaka Tekkosho KK (Akasaka DieselLtd)-Japan
7923081 - -	**TAKUZAN** *ex* Takusan Maru No. 3 *-1999* - -	*199* - 520	Class: KC	**1979-06 Maeno Zosen KK — Sanyoonoda YC** Yd No: 50 Loa 45.10 Br ex 7.82 Dght 3.300 Lbp 41.00 Br md 7.80 Dpth 3.40 Welded, 1 dk	**(A13B2TU) Tanker (unspecified)**	**1 oil engine** driving 1 FP propeller Total Power: 441kW (600hp) Hanshin 6L26BGSH 1 x 4 Stroke 6 Cy. 260 x 400 441kW (600bhp) The Hanshin Diesel Works Ltd-Japan
9373979 *YDA4598* -	**TAL ENDEAVOUR** - **PT Armada Rock Karunia Transshipment** - *Tanjung Priok* *Indonesia*	**254** 77 197	Class: KI (AB) (NK)	**2005-11 Yong Choo Kui Shipyard Sdn Bhd — Sibu** Yd No: 2499 Loa 27.00 Br ex - Dght 3.212 Lbp 25.09 Br md 8.60 Dpth 4.07 Welded, 1 dk	**(B32A2ST) Tug**	**2 oil engines** reduction geared to sc. shafts driving 2 FP propellers Total Power: 1,472kW (2,002hp) Caterpillar 3508B-TA 2 x Vee 4 Stroke 8 Cy. 170 x 190 each-736kW (1001bhp) Caterpillar Inc-USA AuxGen: 2 x 75kW 400V a.c Fuel: 185.0 (d.f.)
8350293 - -	**TAL JAWA** *ex* Shinsei Maru *-2005* *ex* Koto Maru *-1987* - -	*175* - -		**1970-06 Osaka Shipbuilding Co Ltd — Osaka OS** Yd No: 317 Loa 28.05 Br ex - Dght 2.810 Lbp 26.01 Br md 8.21 Dpth 3.92 Welded, 1 dk	**(B32A2ST) Tug**	**2 oil engines** geared to sc. shafts driving 2 FP propellers Total Power: 1,618kW (2,200hp) 12.0kn Fuji 6MD32H 2 x 4 Stroke 6 Cy. 320 x 380 each-809kW (1100bhp) Fuji Diesel Co Ltd-Japan
8012114 *3ERE3* -	**TALA** *ex* Lupigas *-2013* *ex* Berkine *-2008* *ex* Arago *-1995* *ex* Norgas Venture *-1990* *ex* North Venture *-1988* *ex* Marco Polo *-1986* **HDL Partners Corp** - SatCom: Inmarsat C 437002010 *Panama* *Panama* MMSI: 370020000 Official number: 3457209B	**4,165** 1,249 4,852 T/cm 12.1	Class: (BV) (NV)	**1982-06 Kristiansands Mek. Verksted AS — Kristiansand** Yd No: 237 Loa 95.66 (BB) Br ex - Dght 7.116 Lbp 88.02 Br md 17.20 Dpth 10.00 Welded, 1 dk	**(A11B2TG) LPG Tanker** Liq (Gas): 4,300 4 x Gas Tank (s); 4 independent (stl) dcy horizontal 8 Cargo Pump (s): 8x560m³/hr Manifold: Bow/CM: 43.8m Ice Capable	**1 oil engine** with flexible couplings & sr gearedto sc. shaft driving 1 CP propeller Total Power: 2,640kW (3,589hp) 13.0kn Alpha 12V28/32 1 x Vee 4 Stroke 12 Cy. 280 x 320 2640kW (3589bhp) (made 1982) MAN B&W Diesel A/S-Denmark AuxGen: 3 x 630kW 440V 60Hz a.c Thrusters: 1 Thwart. FP thruster (f) Fuel: 165.0 (d.f.) 394.0 (r.f.)
9181493 *V7XD7* -	**TALA** *ex* Bright Sky *-2011* **Multon Navigation Inc** Lydia Mar Shipping Co SA *Majuro* *Marshall Islands* MMSI: 538004454 Official number: 4454	**15,349** 8,111 24,175	Class: NK	**1998-09 Kanda Zosensho K.K. — Kawajiri** Yd No: 389 Loa 158.50 (BB) Br ex - Dght 9.417 Lbp 151.00 Br md 25.80 Dpth 13.30 Welded, 1 dk	**(A31A2GX) General Cargo Ship** Grain: 29,463; Bale: 28,768 Compartments: 4 Ho, ER 4 Ha: (22.4 x 20.2)3 (24.0 x 20.2)ER Cranes: 3x30t	**1 oil engine** driving 1 FP propeller Total Power: 5,980kW (8,130hp) 14.2kn B&W 6L42MC 1 x 2 Stroke 6 Cy. 420 x 1360 5980kW (8130bhp) Mitsui Engineering & Shipbuilding CLtd-Japan AuxGen: 2 x 400kW a.c Fuel: 1460.0
8328642 *CNA2852* -	**TALA 2** *ex* Okba *-1990* *ex* Soho Maru No. 32 *-1972* **Talab SA** - SatCom: Inmarsat C 424226510 *Agadir* *Morocco* Official number: 8-359	*299* 155 -	Class: (KR)	**1965 Usuki Iron Works Co Ltd — Usuki OT** L reg 37.80 Br ex - Dght - Lbp - Br md 8.01 Dpth 3.61 Welded, 1 dk	**(B11B2FV) Fishing Vessel**	**1 oil engine** driving 1 FP propeller Total Power: 736kW (1,001hp)
8828288 *CNCX* -	**TALA 9** - **Talab SA** - SatCom: Inmarsat C 424226610 *Kenitra* *Morocco* Official number: 5-97	**102** 50 132	Class: (KR)	**1989-02 Yongsung Shipbuilding Co Ltd — Geoje** Loa 27.90 Br ex - Dght 2.964 Lbp 23.50 Br md 7.20 Dpth 3.20 Welded, 1 dk	**(B11A2FT) Trawler**	**1 oil engine** driving 1 FP propeller Total Power: 441kW (600hp) 9.9kn Yanmar S165L-ET 1 x 4 Stroke 6 Cy. 165 x 210 441kW (600bhp) Yanmar Diesel Engine Co Ltd-Japan AuxGen: 2 x 209kW 225V a.c
8828276 *CNDX* -	**TALA 10** - **Talab SA** - SatCom: Inmarsat C 424226210 *Kenitra* *Morocco* Official number: 5-98	**102** 50 132	Class: (KR)	**1989-02 Yongsung Shipbuilding Co Ltd — Geoje** Loa 27.90 Br ex - Dght 2.976 Lbp 23.50 Br md 7.20 Dpth 3.20 Welded, 1 dk	**(B11A2FT) Trawler**	**1 oil engine** driving 1 FP propeller Total Power: 441kW (600hp) 10.1kn Yanmar S165L-ET 1 x 4 Stroke 6 Cy. 165 x 210 441kW (600bhp) Yanmar Diesel Engine Co Ltd-Japan AuxGen: 2 x 209kW 225V a.c
8828264 *CNA2661* -	**TALA 11** - **Talab SA** - *Kenitra* *Morocco* Official number: 5-99	**102** 50 132	Class: (KR)	**1989-12 Yongsung Shipbuilding Co Ltd — Geoje** Loa 27.90 Br ex - Dght 2.965 Lbp 23.50 Br md 7.20 Dpth 3.20 Welded, 1 dk	**(B11A2FT) Trawler**	**1 oil engine** driving 1 FP propeller Total Power: 441kW (600hp) 10.0kn Yanmar S165L-ET 1 x 4 Stroke 6 Cy. 165 x 210 441kW (600bhp) Yanmar Diesel Engine Co Ltd-Japan AuxGen: 2 x 209kW 225V a.c
8828290 *CNA2130* -	**TALA 12** - **Talab SA** - SatCom: Inmarsat C 424226310 *Kenitra* *Morocco* Official number: 5-104	**102** 50 132	Class: (KR)	**1989-05 Yongsung Shipbuilding Co Ltd — Geoje** Loa 27.90 Br ex - Dght 3.050 Lbp 23.50 Br md 7.20 Dpth 3.20 Welded, 1 dk	**(B11A2FT) Trawler**	**1 oil engine** driving 1 FP propeller Total Power: 441kW (600hp) 9.4kn Yanmar S165L-ET 1 x 4 Stroke 6 Cy. 165 x 210 441kW (600bhp) Yanmar Diesel Engine Co Ltd-Japan AuxGen: 2 x 209kW 225V a.c
8828305 *CNA2270* -	**TALA 15** - **Talab SA** - SatCom: Inmarsat C 424226410 *Kenitra* *Morocco* Official number: 5-101	**102** 50 132	Class: (KR)	**1989-05 Yongsung Shipbuilding Co Ltd — Geoje** Loa 27.90 Br ex - Dght 3.050 Lbp 23.50 Br md 7.20 Dpth 3.20 Welded, 1 dk	**(B11A2FT) Trawler**	**1 oil engine** driving 1 FP propeller Total Power: 441kW (600hp) 9.8kn Yanmar S165L-ET 1 x 4 Stroke 6 Cy. 165 x 210 441kW (600bhp) Yanmar Diesel Engine Co Ltd-Japan AuxGen: 2 x 209kW 225V a.c
8828317 - -	**TALA 16** - **Talab SA** - *Kenitra* *Morocco*	*102* 50 132	Class: (KR)	**1989-05 Yongsung Shipbuilding Co Ltd — Geoje** Loa 27.90 Br ex - Dght 3.050 Lbp 23.50 Br md 7.20 Dpth 3.20 Welded, 1 dk	**(B11A2FT) Trawler**	**1 oil engine** driving 1 FP propeller Total Power: 441kW (600hp) 9.6kn Yanmar S165L-ET 1 x 4 Stroke 6 Cy. 165 x 210 441kW (600bhp) Yanmar Diesel Engine Co Ltd-Japan AuxGen: 2 x 209kW 225V a.c
9323998 *CNA4111* -	**TALA 18** - **Finance Company of Souss SA (Fishing Port Agadir Morocco) SOFINAS SA** - *Kenitra* *Morocco* MMSI: 242085100	**292** 178 187	Class: BV	**2005-12 Astilleros La Parrilla S.A. — San Esteban de Pravia** Yd No: 201 Loa - Br ex - Dght 3.450 Lbp - Br md - Dpth - Welded, 1 dk	**(B11A2FS) Stern Trawler**	**1 oil engine** geared to sc. shaft driving 1 FP propeller Total Power: 728kW (990hp) Caterpillar 3512B 1 x Vee 4 Stroke 12 Cy. 170 x 190 728kW (990bhp) Caterpillar Inc-USA

IMO / Call sign	Name / Owner	Tonnage	Class	Builder / Dimensions	Type	Machinery
8869426 DUA2424 -	**TALABA** ex Maria Berlinda **Batangas Bay Carriers Inc** - Manila Philippines Official number: MNLD001806	163 91 251		**1981 Mayon Docks Inc. — Tabaco** Converted From: Oil Tanker-1995 Loa 34.44 Br ex - Dght 2.060 Lbp - Br md 6.71 Dpth 2.13 Welded, 1 dk	**(B34T2QR) Work/Repair Vessel**	**2 oil engines** driving 2 FP propellers Total Power: 352kW (478hp) 7.0kn G.M. (Detroit Diesel) 8V-71-N 2 x Vee 2 Stroke 8 Cy. 108 x 127 each-176kW (239bhp) Detroit Diesel Corporation-Detroit, Mi AuxGen: 1 x 27kW 220V a.c
7941588 IJIT -	**TALAFI** **Francesco Pignotti** - San Benedetto del Tronto Italy Official number: 610	105 39 -		**1972 Navaltecnica — San Benedetto del Tronto** Loa 24.52 Br ex 6.20 Dght 3.141 Lbp 20.99 Br md 6.18 Dpth 3.10 Welded, 1 dk	**(B11B2FV) Fishing Vessel**	**1 oil engine** geared to sc. shaft driving 1 FP propeller Total Power: 185kW (252hp) Blackstone EV6M 1 x 4 Stroke 6 Cy. 222 x 292 185kW (252bhp) Lister Blackstone Marine Ltd.-Dursley
8005680 WDE7273 -	**TALAFOFO** ex Trabajador -2008 ex Sioux -2002 ex Ryuko Maru -1993 **Cabras Marine Corp** Malayan Towage & Salvage Corp (SALVTUG) Piti, GU United States of America Official number: 1210931	295 88 209	Class: AB	**1980-06 Sanyo Zosen K.K. — Onomichi** Yd No: 808 Loa 34.70 Br ex - Dght 3.001 Lbp 30.03 Br md 9.21 Dpth 4.02 Welded, 1 dk	**(B32A2ST) Tug**	**2 oil engines** driving 2 FP propellers Total Power: 2,500kW (3,400hp) Niigata 6MG28BX 2 x 4 Stroke 6 Cy. 280 x 320 each-1250kW (1700bhp) Niigata Engineering Co Ltd-Japan
8648389 ZGAV7 -	**TALAL** **Mona Co Ltd** Safehaven International Ltd George Town Cayman Islands (British) MMSI: 319034600 Official number: 742913	397 119 -		**2010-06 Tecnomarine SpA — La Spezia** Loa 43.00 Br ex - Dght 2.920 Lbp 39.60 Br md 8.43 Dpth 3.89 Bonded, 1 dk	**(X11A2YP) Yacht** Hull Material: Reinforced Plastic	**2 oil engines** reduction geared to sc. shafts driving 2 FP propellers Total Power: 5,440kW (7,396hp) 24.0kn M.T.U. 16V4000M90 2 x Vee 4 Stroke 16 Cy. 165 x 190 each-2720kW (3698bhp) MTU Friedrichshafen GmbH-Friedrichshafen AuxGen: 2 x 50kW a.c
8323317 UDSK -	**TALAN** ex Sumiyoshi Maru No. 18 -2006 **JSC Vostok-1** - Nakhodka Russia MMSI: 273445180	798 336 513	Class: RS	**1983-12 KK Kanasashi Zosen — Shizuoka SZ** Yd No: 3018 Loa 57.70 (BB) Br ex 9.12 Dght 3.780 Lbp 51.00 Br md 9.10 Dpth 3.95 Welded, 1 dk	**(B11B2FV) Fishing Vessel** Compartments: 5 Ho, ER 5 Ha: ER	**1 oil engine** with clutches & sr geared to sc. shaft driving 1 FP propeller Total Power: 1,103kW (1,500hp) Niigata 6M31AGT 1 x 4 Stroke 6 Cy. 310 x 530 1103kW (1500bhp) Niigata Engineering Co Ltd-Japan Fuel: 222.0 (d.f.)
9141194 UAER -	**TALAN** ex Choko Maru No. 7 -2006 **MAG-SEA International** - Magadan Russia MMSI: 273314740	651 302 538	Class: RS	**1996-01 Kidoura Shipyard Co Ltd — Kesennuma MG** Yd No: 600 Loa 56.60 (BB) Br ex 8.82 Dght 3.450 Lbp 49.30 Br md 8.80 Dpth 3.82 Welded, 1 dk	**(B11B2FV) Fishing Vessel** Ins: 495	**1 oil engine** reduction geared to sc. shaft driving 1 FP propeller Total Power: 736kW (1,001hp) 12.7kn Akasaka K28SFD 1 x 4 Stroke 6 Cy. 280 x 500 736kW (1001bhp) Akasaka Tekkosho KK (Akasaka DieselLtd)-Japan AuxGen: 2 x 320kW a.c Fuel: 292.0 (d.f.) 3.0pd
5159569 VCMK -	**TALAPUS** ex Imperial Nanaimo -1974 ex Beeceelite -1946 **Cloverleaf Shipping Ltd** - Vancouver, BC Canada Official number: 170128	413 193 457	Class: (LR) ✠ Classed LR until 5/49	**1937-12 Marine Industries Ltee (MIL) — Sorel QC** Yd No: 56 Loa 38.87 Br ex 8.28 Dght 3.525 Lbp 36.58 Br md 8.23 Dpth 3.81 Welded, 1 dk	**(A13B2TU) Tanker (unspecified)** Liq: 422; Liq (Oil): 422 Cargo Heating Coils Compartments: 8 Ta, ER	**1 oil engine** driving 1 FP propeller Total Power: 423kW (575hp) 8.5kn Fairbanks, Morse 1 x 2 Stroke 5 Cy. 355 x 430 423kW (575bhp) Fairbanks Morse & Co.-New Orleans, La AuxGen: 2 x 35kW 220V d.c Fuel: 26.5 (d.f.) (Heating Coils) 2.5pd
8977821 - -	**TALARA** ex Stephanie Mccall -2010 **IMI Del Peru SAC**	201 100 184		**1991-11 Gulf Craft Inc — Patterson LA** Yd No: 362 Loa 40.00 Br ex - Dght 2.000 Lbp 37.00 Br md 8.00 Dpth 3.00 Welded, 1 dk	**(B21A2OC) Crew/Supply Vessel** Hull Material: Aluminium Alloy Passengers: 73; cabins: 4	**4 oil engines** driving 2 gen. each 50kW with clutches, flexible couplings & sr reverse geared to sc. shafts driving 4 FP propellers Total Power: 2,000kW (2,720hp) 20.0kn Cummins KTA-19-M 4 x 4 Stroke 6 Cy. 159 x 159 each-500kW (680bhp) Cummins Engine Co Inc-USA AuxGen: 2 x 50kW a.c Fuel: 32.0 (d.f.) 8.4pd
6819702 - -	**TALARA 1** ex Helland IV -1979 **Pesquera El Tiburon SCR Ltda** - Huacho Peru Official number: CE-0238-PM	235 122 -	Class: (GL)	**1968 Construcciones Navales SA (CONASA) — Callao** Yd No: 2 Loa 31.32 Br ex 7.68 Dght 3.607 Lbp 28.10 Br md 7.65 Dpth 3.99 Welded, 1 dk	**(B11A2FT) Trawler** Ins: 344 Compartments: 2 Ho, ER 1 Ha: (2.8 x 1.0) Derricks: 1x1t; Winches: 1	**1 oil engine** driving 1 FP propeller Total Power: 375kW (510hp) 12.0kn Caterpillar D379TA 1 x Vee 4 Stroke 8 Cy. 159 x 203 375kW (510bhp) Caterpillar Tractor Co-USA
6819714 - -	**TALARA 2** ex Helland V -1979 - - -	235 122 -	Class: (GL)	**1968 Construcciones Navales SA (CONASA) — Callao** Yd No: 3 Loa 31.32 Br ex 7.68 Dght 3.607 Lbp 28.10 Br md 7.65 Dpth 3.84 Welded, 1 dk	**(B11A2FT) Trawler** Ins: 344	**1 oil engine** reverse reduction geared to sc. shaft driving 1 FP propeller Total Power: 375kW (510hp) 12.0kn Caterpillar D379TA 1 x Vee 4 Stroke 8 Cy. 159 x 203 375kW (510bhp) Caterpillar Tractor Co-USA
6924026 - -	**TALARA 5** ex Trisa VIII -1979 - -	190 116 -		**1968 Maestranza y Astillero Delta S.A. — Callao** L reg 27.89 Br ex 7.68 Dght 3.582 Lbp - Br md 7.65 Dpth 3.97 Welded, 1 dk	**(B11A2FT) Trawler**	**1 oil engine** driving 1 FP propeller Total Power: 375kW (510hp) 10.0kn Caterpillar D379SCAC 1 x Vee 4 Stroke 8 Cy. 159 x 203 375kW (510bhp) Caterpillar Tractor Co-USA
7042693 - -	**TALARA 6** ex Himalaya -1979 **Pesquera Don Miguel SRL** - Chimbote Peru Official number: CE-002477-PM	350 - -		**1970 Maestranza y Astillero Delta S.A. — Callao** Yd No: 40 Loa - Br ex - Dght - Lbp - Br md - Dpth - Bonded, 1 dk	**(B11B2FV) Fishing Vessel** Hull Material: Reinforced Plastic	**1 oil engine** geared to sc. shaft driving 1 FP propeller Caterpillar 1 x 4 Stroke Caterpillar Tractor Co-USA
9335654 FMCM SB 907929	**TALARIANTE** **Armement Dahouetin** - Saint-Brieuc France Official number: 907929	172 - -		**2004-09 SOCARENAM — Boulogne** Yd No: 194 Loa 24.95 Br ex - Dght - Lbp - Br md 7.40 Dpth 3.90 Welded, 1 dk	**(B11A2FS) Stern Trawler**	**1 oil engine** geared to sc. shaft driving 1 CP propeller Caterpillar 1 x 4 Stroke Caterpillar Inc-USA
8429290 - -	**TALAS** ex Tong Un No. 308 -1998 - -	159 - 341	Class: (KR)	**1985 Pohang Shipbuilding Co Ltd — Pohang** Loa 37.22 Br ex 7.55 Dght 2.899 Lbp 34.02 Br md 7.51 Dpth 3.31 Welded, 1 dk	**(A31A2GX) General Cargo Ship**	**1 oil engine** driving 1 FP propeller Total Power: 493kW (670hp) 9.8kn Hanshin 6L26BGSH 1 x 4 Stroke 6 Cy. 260 x 400 493kW (670bhp) Ssangyong Heavy Industries Co Ltd-South Korea AuxGen: 1 x 20kW 225V a.c
9339210 ECBN 3-VILL-17-	**TALASA** **Talasa Barbanza SL** - Santa Eugenia de Ribeira Spain MMSI: 224581000 Official number: 3-7/2002	427 186 294		**2006-09 Astilleros Armon Vigo SA — Vigo** Yd No: 16 Loa 39.00 (BB) Br ex - Dght 3.310 Lbp 32.75 Br md 8.10 Dpth 3.80 Welded, 1 dk	**(B11B2FV) Fishing Vessel**	**1 oil engine** geared to sc. shaft driving 1 FP propeller Total Power: 316kW (430hp) 9.0kn Caterpillar 1 x 4 Stroke 316kW (430bhp) Caterpillar Inc-USA AuxGen: 1 x 300kW 380V 50Hz a.c, 1 x 150kW 380V 50Hz a.c, 1 x 400kW 380V 50Hz a.c
9290787 A8GA8 -	**TALASSA** ex MSC Malta -2010 ex Choapa -2006 **Peter Doehle Schiffahrts-KG** - Monrovia Liberia MMSI: 636091213 Official number: 91213	66,280 36,284 68,228	Class: LR ✠ **100A1** SS 02/2010 container ship *IWS LI **ShipRight** (SDA, FDA, CM) ✠ **LMC** **UMS** Eq.Ltr: X†; Cable: 742.5/97.0 U3 (a)	**2005-02 China Shipbuilding Corp (CSBC) — Kaohsiung** Yd No: 824 Loa 275.80 (BB) Br ex 40.10 Dght 14.000 Lbp 263.80 Br md 40.00 Dpth 24.20 Welded, 1 dk	**(A33A2CC) Container Ship (Fully Cellular)** TEU 5527 C Ho 2601 TEU C Dk 2926 TEU incl 500 ref C. Compartments: 7 Cell Ho, ER 7 Ha: ER	**1 oil engine** driving 1 FP propeller Total Power: 54,926kW (74,677hp) 25.6kn Sulzer 10RTA96C 1 x 2 Stroke 10 Cy. 960 x 2500 54926kW (74677bhp) Doosan Engine Co Ltd-South Korea AuxGen: 4 x 1980kW 450/230V 60Hz a.c Boilers: e (ex.g.) 12.2kgf/cm² (12.0bar), WTAuxB (o.f.) 8.2kgf/cm² (8.0bar) Thrusters: 1 Thwart. CP thruster (f)

6617582 - -	**TALAY MENDI** - - -	**259** 77 174	Class: (BV)	**1966 Astilleros de Murueta S.A. — Gernika-Lumo** Yd No: 75 Loa 36.66 Br ex 6.94 Dght 3.480 Lbp 32.01 Br md 6.91 Dpth 3.92 Welded, 1 dk	**(B11A2FT) Trawler** Ins: 182 Compartments: 2 Ho, ER 2 Ha: 2 (0.9 x 0.9)ER Derricks: 1x4t; Winches: 1	**1 oil engine** driving 1 FP propeller Total Power: 552kW (750hp) 11.0kn Deutz RV8M536 1 x 4 Stroke 8 Cy. 270 x 360 552kW (750bhp) Kloeckner Humboldt Deutz AG-West Germany Fuel: 95.0 (d.f.)
9244178 *LLQM* H-74-AV	**TALBOR** - **Talbor AS** BR Birkeland Fiskebatrederi AS *Bergen* *Norway* MMSI: 259129000	**1,514** 454 1,956	Class: NV	**2001-09 OAO Vyborgskiy Sudostroitelnyy Zavod — Vyborg** (Hull) Yd No: 922 **2001-09 Fitjar Mek. Verksted AS — Fitjar** Yd No: 22 Loa 64.10 Br ex - Dght 7.000 Lbp 56.56 Br md 13.00 Dpth 6.80 Welded, 1 dk	**(B11B2FV) Fishing Vessel** Grain: 1,550; Ins: 1,550	**1 oil engine** with clutches, flexible couplings & sr geared to sc. shaft driving 1 CP propeller Total Power: 3,457kW (4,700hp) 14.0kn Caterpillar 3612TA 1 x Vee 4 Stroke 12 Cy. 280 x 300 3457kW (4700bhp) Caterpillar Inc-USA AuxGen: 1 x 1500kW 440V 60Hz a.c, 2 x 590kW 440V 60Hz a.c Thrusters: 1 Thwart. FP thruster (f); 1 Tunnel thruster (a) Fuel: 380.0 (d.f.) (Heating Coils)
7122950 - -	**TALBOT III** *ex* Snow Reefer *-1986* *ex* Masa Maru No. 18 *-1982* - -	*299* 154 -		**1971 KK Kanasashi Zosen — Shizuoka SZ** Yd No: 1012 Loa 52.05 Br ex 8.54 Dght 3.404 Lbp 45.27 Br md 8.51 Dpth 5.80 Welded, 1 dk	**(B11B2FV) Fishing Vessel**	**1 oil engine** driving 1 FP propeller Total Power: 846kW (1,150hp) Hanshin 6LU32 1 x 4 Stroke 6 Cy. 320 x 510 846kW (1150bhp) Hanshin Nainenki Kogyo-Japan
7122027 *3BFN* -	**TALBOT V** *ex* Reef *-2006* *ex* Sea Reefer *-2006* *ex* Ice Reefer *-2006* *ex* Ryujin Maru No. 8 *-1982* *ex* Fukuseki Maru No. 5 *-1980* **Talbot Fishing Co** - *Port Louis* *Mauritius* Official number: 108659	*254* 128 -		**1970 KK Kanasashi Zosen — Shizuoka SZ** Yd No: 977 Loa 47.78 Br ex 8.13 Dght 3.302 Lbp 41.00 Br md 8.11 Dpth 5.69 Welded, 2 dks	**(B11B2FV) Fishing Vessel**	**1 oil engine** driving 1 FP propeller Total Power: 736kW (1,001hp) Niigata 1 x 4 Stroke 6 Cy. 280 x 440 736kW (1001bhp) Niigata Engineering Co Ltd-Japan
8808812 - -	**TALCAN** - **Pesquera del Estrecho SA** -	*289* 77 170	Class: (RI) (BV)	**1989-11 Polyships S.A. — Vigo** Yd No: 100007 Loa 30.00 Br ex 8.30 Dght 3.270 Lbp 26.00 Br md 8.00 Dpth 4.20 Bonded, 2 dks	**(B11B2FV) Fishing Vessel** Hull Material: Reinforced Plastic Ins: 196	**1 oil engine** with clutches, flexible couplings & sr reverse geared to sc. shaft driving 1 FP propeller Total Power: 519kW (706hp) 11.0kn Caterpillar 3508TA 1 x Vee 4 Stroke 8 Cy. 170 x 190 519kW (706bhp) Caterpillar Inc-USA AuxGen: 2 x 80kW 220V a.c
8834304 - BI652	**TALEB** *ex* Ittipesca Sesto *-2005* *ex* Kirki *-2000* **Nord Pesca** - *Bizerte* *Tunisia*	**444** 136 364	Class: (BV) (RI) (HR)	**1988 Homatas Brothers Shipyard — Thessaloniki** Loa 38.10 Br ex 9.30 Dght 3.700 Lbp 33.00 Br md - Dpth 4.60 Welded, 1 dk	**(B11B2FV) Fishing Vessel**	**1 oil engine** reduction geared to sc. shaft driving 1 FP propeller Total Power: 740kW (1,006hp) 12.0kn MaK 6M282AK 1 x 4 Stroke 6 Cy. 240 x 280 740kW (1006bhp) Krupp MaK Maschinenbau GmbH-Kiel AuxGen: 3 x 448kW 380V a.c
8919465 *FOVN* CC 911320	**TALENDUIC** *ex* Platon *-1996* **Compagnie Francaise Du Thon Oceanique** - *Concarneau* *France* MMSI: 226240000 Official number: 911320	**2,109** 633 1,650	Class: BV	**1992-05 Ast. de Huelva S.A. — Huelva** Yd No: 467 Loa 79.80 Br ex - Dght 6.500 Lbp 69.20 Br md 13.50 Dpth 8.90 Welded, 2 dks	**(B11B2FV) Fishing Vessel** Ins: 1,840	**1 oil engine** with clutches & sr reverse geared to sc. shaft driving 1 FP propeller Total Power: 3,641kW (4,950hp) 15.0kn Wartsila 9R32E 1 x 4 Stroke 9 Cy. 320 x 350 3641kW (4950bhp) Construcciones Echevarria SA-Spain Thrusters: 1 Thwart. CP thruster (f); 1 Tunnel thruster (a)
9123611 *DSPK9*	**TALENT** *ex* Maritime Talent *-2007* **KEB Capital Inc** Changsung Shipping Co Ltd *Jeju* *South Korea* MMSI: 441171000 Official number: JJR-079839	**26,381** 16,138 47,574	Class: KR (NK)	**1996-01 Oshima Shipbuilding Co Ltd — Saikai NS** Yd No: 10177 Loa 189.99 (BB) Br ex 30.53 Dght 11.829 Lbp 181.60 Br md 30.50 Dpth 16.50 Welded, 1 dk	**(A21A2BC) Bulk Carrier** Grain: 59,923; Bale: 58,763 Compartments: 5 Ho, ER 5 Ha: (16.8 x 15.3)4 (20.8 x 15.3)ER Cranes: 4x30t	**1 oil engine** driving 1 FP propeller Total Power: 8,871kW (12,061hp) 14.6kn Sulzer 6RTA52U 1 x 2 Stroke 6 Cy. 520 x 1800 8871kW (12061bhp) Diesel United Ltd.-Aioi
9578866 *9WKE6* -	**TALENT 1** - **Talent Shipping Sdn Bhd** - *Kuching* *Malaysia* MMSI: 533000881 Official number: 333171	**326** 97 285	Class: BV	**2010-08 Sarawak Land Shipyard Sdn Bhd — Miri** Yd No: 14 Loa 31.00 Br ex - Dght 3.500 Lbp 27.99 Br md 9.15 Dpth 4.30 Welded, 1 dk	**(B32A2ST) Tug**	**2 oil engines** reduction geared to sc. shafts driving 2 FP propellers Total Power: 1,518kW (2,064hp) Mitsubishi S6R2-MTK3L 2 x 4 Stroke 6 Cy. 170 x 220 each-759kW (1032bhp) Mitsubishi Heavy Industries Ltd-Japan AuxGen: 2 x 80kW 50Hz a.c
8729420 *UCQU* -	**TALER** *ex* Nuklon *-2011* **Sigma Marine Technology Co Ltd (OOO 'Sigma Marin Tekhnolodzhi')** - *Sovetskaya Gavan* *Russia* MMSI: 273421700 Official number: 890112	**806** 221 364	Class: RS	**1989-07 Zavod "Leninskaya Kuznitsa" — Kiyev** Yd No: 1613 Loa 54.84 Br ex 10.15 Dght 4.141 Lbp 50.32 Br md 9.80 Dpth 5.01 Welded, 1 dk	**(B11A2FS) Stern Trawler** Ins: 412	**1 oil engine** driving 1 CP propeller Total Power: 852kW (1,158hp) 12.0kn S.K.L. 8NVD48A-2U 1 x 4 Stroke 8 Cy. 320 x 480 852kW (1158bhp) VEB Schwermaschinenbau "KarlLiebknecht" (SKL)-Magdeburg AuxGen: 4 x 160kW a.c Fuel: 155.0 (d.f.)
8988765 *2DIS5* -	**TALES** *ex* Pegaso *-2010* *ex* Only 4 U *-2005* *ex* Petara *-2005* **Banque Populaire Cote d'Azur** - *London* *United Kingdom* MMSI: 235079322 Official number: 828338	**721** 216 -	Class: AB	**2002-05 Proteksan-Turquoise Yachts Inc — Tuzla** Yd No: 39 Loa 53.00 Br ex - Dght 2.850 Lbp 47.00 Br md 9.50 Dpth 4.85 Welded, 1 dk	**(X11A2YP) Yacht**	**2 oil engines** reduction geared to sc. shafts driving 2 FP propellers Total Power: 2,238kW (3,042hp) 16.0kn Caterpillar 3512B 2 x Vee 4 Stroke 12 Cy. 170 x 190 each-1119kW (1521bhp) Caterpillar Inc-USA
9482976 - -	**TALESAP** - **Imperial Grand Transport Co Ltd** - *Bangkok* *Thailand* Official number: 490002672	**148** 77 -		**2006-09 PSP Marine Co Ltd — Samut Sakhon** Loa 39.50 Br ex - Dght - Lbp - Br md 11.00 Dpth 3.00 Welded, 1 dk	**(A37B2PS) Passenger Ship**	**2 oil engines** driving 2 Propellers Total Power: 470kW (640hp) Hino 2 x 4 Stroke each-235kW (320bhp) Hino Motors Ltd.-Tokyo
9208253 *9BRT* -	**TALESH** *ex* Dalma Courageous *-2010* *ex* Jaya Courageous *-2004* **Ali Akbari** - *Bandar Abbas* *Iran* Official number: 11531	**113** 34 -	Class: AS (GL)	**1999-02 P.T. Jaya Asiatic Shipyard — Batam** Yd No: SP015 Loa 23.17 Br ex - Dght 2.400 Lbp 21.26 Br md 7.00 Dpth 2.90 Welded, 1 dk	**(B32A2ST) Tug**	**2 oil engines** reverse reduction geared to sc. shafts driving 2 FP propellers Total Power: 700kW (952hp) 12.0kn Caterpillar 3408TA 2 x Vee 4 Stroke 8 Cy. 137 x 152 each-350kW (476bhp) Caterpillar Inc-USA AuxGen: 2 x 32kW 220/380V a.c
9442055 *PPZF* -	**TALHA-MAR** - **Wilson Sons Offshore SA** - *Rio de Janeiro* *Brazil* MMSI: 710005030	**2,987** 1,023 4,394	Class: LR ✠**100A1** SS 10/2010 offshore supply ship *IWS **LMC** **UMS** Eq.Ltr: U; Cable: 495.0/44.0 U3 (a)	**2010-10 Wilson, Sons SA — Guaruja** (Hull) Yd No: 103 **2010-10 B.V. Scheepswerf Damen — Gorinchem** Yd No: 552009 Loa 87.40 (BB) Br ex 16.04 Dght 6.200 Lbp 81.56 Br md 16.00 Dpth 7.50 Welded, 1 dk	**(B21A20S) Platform Supply Ship**	**4 diesel electric oil engines** driving 4 gen. each 1360kW 690V a.c Connecting to 2 elec. motors each (2000kW) driving 2 Directional propellers Total Power: 5,696kW (7,744hp) 12.2kn Caterpillar 3512B-TA 4 x Vee 4 Stroke 12 Cy. 170 x 190 each-1424kW (1936bhp) Caterpillar Inc-USA Thrusters: 2 Directional thruster (f)

IMO / Call sign	Ship / Owners / Flag	Tonnage	Class	Builder / Dimensions	Type	Machinery
9173692 *OJIH* -	**TALI** **ESL Shipping Oy** - SatCom: Inmarsat C 423091611 *Helsinki* *Finland* MMSI: 230916000 Official number: 120026	**10,098** 4,597 13,340 T/cm 26.8	Class: LR ✠**100A1** SS 08/2013 strengthened for heavy cargoes, Nos . 1 & 2 holds may be empty LI strengthened for grab discharge, grab weight 26 tonnes Ice Class 1AS at 8.379m draught Max/min draught fwd 8.379/5.215m Max/min draught aft 8.379/5.715m Power required 5760kw, installed 6250kw ✠**LMC** **UMS** Eq.Ltr: C†; Cable: 550.0/52.0 U3	**1998-08 Aker Finnyards Oy — Rauma** Yd No: 422 Loa 137.10 Br ex 21.63 Dght 8.190 Lbp 129.02 Br md 21.60 Dpth 11.01 Welded, 1 dk	**(A31A2GX) General Cargo Ship** Double Hull Grain: 16,786; Bale: 16,786 Compartments: 2 Ho, ER 2 Ha: 2 (37.6 x 17.6)ER Cranes: 3x27.5t Ice Capable	**1 oil engine** with flexible couplings & sr gearedto sc. shaft driving 1 CP propeller Total Power: 6,250kW (8,498hp) 13.5kn Wartsila 8R46A 1 x 4 Stroke 8 Cy. 460 x 580 6250kW (8498bhp) Wartsila NSD Finland Oy-Finland AuxGen: 3 x 628kW 400V 50Hz a.c Boilers: e (ex.g.) 7.8kgf/cm² (7.6bar), AuxB (o.f.) 7.4kgf/cm² (7.3bar) Thrusters: 1 Thwart. CP thruster (f) Fuel: 85.0 (d.f.) (Heating Coils) 750.0 (r.f.) 20.0pd
5281049 *5VAA3* -	**TALI** *ex* Lavinia *-2008* *ex* Ingela *-1995* *ex* Ireen *-1990* *ex* Westlill *-1987* *ex* Ireen *-1983* *ex* Irene *-1978* *ex* Auguste Schulte *-1970* *ex* Polchow *-1969* **Tali Queen Shipping SA** Ocean Enterprises SA *Lome* *Togo* MMSI: 671002000	**1,458** 800 2,425	Class: (GL)	**1957-11 Schiffbau Gesellschaft Unterweser AG — Bremerhaven** Yd No: 400 Lengthened-1970 Loa 82.17 Br ex 10.88 Dght 5.220 Lbp 76.36 Br md 10.81 Dpth 6.58 Riveted\Welded, 1 dk	**(A31A2GX) General Cargo Ship** Grain: 2,080; Bale: 1,935 Compartments: 1 Ho, ER 2 Ha: 2 (19.1 x 5.4)ER Ice Capable	**1 oil engine** reduction geared to sc. shaft driving 1 FP propeller Total Power: 772kW (1,050hp) 12.0kn MaK MSU582A 1 x 4 Stroke 6 Cy. 385 x 580 772kW (1050bhp) Maschinenbau Kiel AG (MaK)-Kiel AuxGen: 1 x 35kW 220V d.c, 1 x 20kW 220V d.c, 1 x 15kW 220V d.c
8311338 - -	**TALI** - **Karachi Port Trust** -	*150* - 200		**1993-08 Khalil Marine Engineering Works — Karachi** Yd No: 150 Loa - Br ex - Dght 2.400 Lbp 25.00 Br md 6.20 Dpth 2.60 Welded, 1 dk	**(B35E2TF) Bunkering Tanker**	**1 oil engine** driving 1 FP propeller MAN 1 x 4 Stroke MAN B&W Diesel AG-Augsburg
9484699 *A8ZK2* -	**TALIA** **1 Westbulk BV** Marwave Shipmanagement BV *Monrovia* *Liberia* MMSI: 636092256 Official number: 15435	**51,253** 31,173 92,997 T/cm 80.9	Class: AB	**2011-10 Taizhou CATIC Shipbuilding Heavy Industry Ltd — Taizhou JS** Yd No: TK0205 Loa 230.00 (BB) Br ex - Dght 14.900 Lbp 222.00 Br md 38.00 Dpth 20.70 Welded, 1 dk	**(A21A2BC) Bulk Carrier** Grain: 110,330 Compartments: 7 Ho, ER 7 Ha: ER	**1 oil engine** driving 1 FP propeller Total Power: 13,560kW (18,436hp) 14.1kn MAN-B&W 6S60MC-C 1 x 2 Stroke 6 Cy. 600 x 2400 13560kW (18436bhp) AuxGen: 3 x 700kW a.c Fuel: 233.0 (d.f.) 3567.0 (r.f.)
9311854 *C6VJ6* -	**TALIA** **Talia Maritime Ltd** Ray Car Carriers Ltd *Nassau* *Bahamas* MMSI: 308599000 Official number: 8001179	**57,692** 21,037 21,021	Class: NV	**2006-08 Stocznia Gdynia SA — Gdynia** Yd No: 8168/14 Loa 199.90 (BB) Br ex - Dght 10.000 Lbp 187.90 Br md 32.26 Dpth 32.64 Welded, 11 dks. incl. Nos.1, 3, 5 & 7 dks hoistable	**(A35B2RV) Vehicles Carrier** Side door/ramp (s) Len: 25.00 Wid: 7.00 Swl: 22 Quarter stern door/ramp (s. a.) Len: 38.00 Wid: 7.00 Swl: 150 Cars: 6,658 Ice Capable	**1 oil engine** driving 1 FP propeller Total Power: 15,539kW (21,127hp) 20.4kn MAN-B&W 7S60MC-C 1 x 2 Stroke 7 Cy. 600 x 2400 15539kW (21127bhp) H Cegielski Poznan SA-Poland AuxGen: 3 x a.c Thrusters: 1 Thwart. CP thruster (f)
7724796 *YEXY* -	**TALIABU UTAMA** *ex* Toyofuku Maru No. 1 *-1969* - - *Banjarmasin* *Indonesia*	*444* 194 773	Class: (KI)	**1977-12 Kyoei Zosen KK — Mihara HS** Yd No: 78 Loa 50.53 Br ex - Dght 3.501 Lbp 45.88 Br md 8.41 Dpth 3.76 Welded, 1 dk	**(A12A2TC) Chemical Tanker**	**1 oil engine** driving 1 FP propeller Total Power: 588kW (799hp) Matsui 6M26KGHS 1 x 4 Stroke 6 Cy. 260 x 400 588kW (799bhp) Matsui Iron Works Co Ltd-Japan
8626109 *YGNS* -	**TALIAMAN** *ex* Tetsuryu Maru *-2003* **PT Taliaman Unggul Lines** - *Surabaya* *Indonesia*	*494* 325 520	Class: KI	**1984-10 K.K. Kanmasu Zosensho — Imabari** Loa 49.71 Br ex - Dght 3.101 Lbp 46.51 Br md 8.21 Dpth 5.01 Welded, 1 dk	**(A31A2GX) General Cargo Ship** Grain: 1,473; Bale: 1,347	**1 oil engine** driving 1 FP propeller Total Power: 368kW (500hp) 10.0kn Yanmar 6M-UT 1 x 4 Stroke 6 Cy. 200 x 240 368kW (500bhp) Yanmar Diesel Engine Co Ltd-Japan
8732518 *FQLZ* BA 7839937	**TALION** - - SatCom: Inmarsat C 422740910 *Bayonne* *France* MMSI: 227409000 Official number: 983937	**109** - -		**1991-01 in France** Loa 20.78 Br ex - Dght - Lbp 18.10 Br md 6.63 Dpth - Welded, 1 dk	**(B11A2FS) Stern Trawler**	**1 oil engine** driving 1 Propeller Total Power: 287kW (390hp)
7818195 *YHMD* -	**TALISAYAN PERMAI** *ex* Flausan *-2003* *ex* Marine Blue *-1997* *ex* Taiyo No. 11 *-1995* *ex* Taihei Hope *-1992* *ex* Shinho Hope *-1990* *ex* Shioji *-1990* **PT Samudra Alam Raya** - *Surabaya* *Indonesia*	**1,168** 559 1,391	Class: KI (KR)	**1978-09 Mategata Zosen K.K. — Namikata** Yd No: 158 Loa 69.40 Br ex - Dght 3.971 Lbp 64.40 Br md 11.50 Dpth 6.10 Riveted\Welded, 1 dk	**(A31A2GX) General Cargo Ship**	**1 oil engine** driving 1 FP propeller Total Power: 736kW (1,001hp) Hanshin 6LU35 1 x 4 Stroke 6 Cy. 350 x 550 736kW (1001bhp) Hanshin Nainenki Kogyo-Japan
8918942 *PJYK* -	**TALISMAN** *ex* Front Comor *-2008* *ex* Comor *-1999* **Talisman BV** Dockwise Shipping BV *Willemstad* *Curacao* MMSI: 306867000 Official number: 2008-C-1959	**42,515** 12,755 53,000 T/cm 108.0	Class: NV	**1993-07 Brodosplit - Brodogradiliste doo — Split** Yd No: 370 Converted From: Crude Oil Tanker-2008 Loa 216.00 (BB) Br ex 44.54 Dght 10.440 Lbp 207.85 Br md 44.44 Dpth 14.00 Welded, 1 dk	**(A38C3GH) Heavy Load Carrier, semi submersible**	**1 oil engine** driving 1 FP propeller Total Power: 13,368kW (18,175hp) 14.0kn B&W 6S70MC 1 x 2 Stroke 6 Cy. 700 x 2674 13368kW (18175bhp) Brodosplit Tvornica Dizel Motoradoo-Croatia AuxGen: 3 x 900kW 440V 60Hz a.c Fuel: 313.0 (d.f.) 4524.0 (r.f.)
9191319 *LAOW5* -	**TALISMAN** **Wilhelmsen Lines Shipowning AS** Wilhelmsen Ship Management (Norway) AS SatCom: Inmarsat C 425761310 *Tonsberg* *Norway (NIS)* MMSI: 257613000	**67,140** 23,674 38,300 T/cm 69.5	Class: NV	**2000-06 Daewoo Heavy Industries Ltd — Geoje** Yd No: 4424 Loa 240.60 (BB) Br ex 32.29 Dght 11.750 Lbp 226.00 Br md 32.26 Dpth 15.60 Welded, 8 dks, incl. 4 dks hoistable	**(A35B2RV) Vehicles Carrier** Quarter stern door/ramp (s. a.) Len: 44.50 Wid: 12.00 Swl: 320 Cars: 5,496 TEU 2340	**1 oil engine** driving 1 FP propeller Total Power: 20,940kW (28,470hp) 20.0kn B&W 8L70MC 1 x 2 Stroke 8 Cy. 700 x 2268 20940kW (28470bhp) HSD Engine Co Ltd-South Korea Thrusters: 1 Thwart. FP thruster (f); 1 Tunnel thruster (a)
8965830 *CB2197* -	**TALISMAN** **Pesquera Qurbosa Nicolaus Queirolo & Compania Ltda** - *Valparaiso* *Chile* MMSI: 725000254 Official number: 2523	*464* - -		**1987 Astilleros y Servicios Navales S.A. (ASENAV) — Valdivia** L reg 40.22 Br ex - Dght - Lbp - Br md 8.60 Dpth 6.80 Welded, 1 dk	**(B11B2FV) Fishing Vessel**	**1 oil engine** driving 1 FP propeller
1011070 *ZGBL8* -	**TALISMAN C** **Talisman Sea Ltd** Nigel Burgess Ltd (BURGESS) *George Town* *Cayman Islands (British)* MMSI: 319027500	**1,560** 468 200	Class: LR ✠**100A1** SS 06/2011 SSC Yacht, mono, G6 ✠**LMC** **UMS** Cable: 385.0/26.0 U3 (a)	**2011-06 Celikyat Insaa Sanayi ve Ticaret AS — Basiskele** (Hull) Yd No: (53) **2011-06 Proteksan-Turquoise Yachts Inc — Istanbul (Pendik)** Yd No: 53 Loa 70.54 Br ex 12.14 Dght 3.890 Lbp 59.82 Br md 12.00 Dpth 7.00 Welded, 1 dk	**(X11A2YP) Yacht** Hull Material: Aluminium Alloy	**2 oil engines** with clutches, flexible couplings & reverse reduction geared to sc. shafts driving 2 FP propellers Total Power: 3,650kW (4,962hp) 15.0kn Caterpillar 3516B-HD 2 x Vee 4 Stroke 16 Cy. 170 x 215 each-1825kW (2481bhp) Caterpillar Inc-USA AuxGen: 3 x 200kW 400V 50Hz a.c Thrusters: 1 Thwart. FP thruster (f)
9361005 *MJNN6* -	**TALISMAN MAITON** *ex* Talisman C1 *-2012* *ex* Talisman C *-2011* **Talisman Maiton Ltd** Nigel Burgess Ltd (BURGESS) *Douglas* *Isle of Man (British)* MMSI: 235009270 Official number: 737783	**692** 207 112	Class: AB	**2006-01 Proteksan-Turquoise Yachts Inc — Tuzla** Yd No: 41 Loa 54.20 Br ex - Dght 3.100 Lbp 47.64 Br md 9.30 Dpth 4.77 Welded, 1 dk	**(X11A2YP) Yacht**	**2 oil engines** reduction geared to sc. shafts driving 2 Propellers Total Power: 2,238kW (3,042hp) 16.0kn Caterpillar 3512B 2 x Vee 4 Stroke 12 Cy. 170 x 190 each-1119kW (1521bhp) Caterpillar Inc-USA

1004625 *ZCAN7* -	**TALITHA** *ex* Talitha G. *-2008* *ex* Jezebel *-1993* *ex* Elpetal *-1983* *ex* Beaumont *-1949* *ex* Carola *-1942* *ex* Chalena *-1939* *ex* Reveler *-1931* **Talitha Ltd** Royale Oceanic International Yacht Management Ltd SatCom: Inmarsat A 1105563 *Hamilton* *Bermuda (British)* MMSI: 310051000 Official number: 705670	**1,103** 330 -	Class: LR ✠**100A1** SS 01/2009 Yacht ✠**LMC** **UMS** Eq.Ltr: J; Cable: 330.0/26.0 U2 (a)	**1930**-10 **Fried. Krupp Germaniawerft AG — Kiel** Loa 80.00 Br ex 10.39 Dght 3.910 Lbp 62.90 Br md 10.36 Dpth 5.79 Welded, 1 dk	**(X11A2YP) Yacht**	**2 oil engines** with clutches, flexbile couplings & sr geared to sc. shafts driving 2 CP propellers Total Power: 2,100kW (2,856hp) Caterpillar 3516TA 2 x Vee 4 Stroke 16 Cy. 170 x 190 each-1050kW (1428bhp) (new engine 1992) Caterpillar Inc-USA AuxGen: 3 x 275kW 400V 50Hz a.c Thrusters: 1 Thwart. FP thruster (f)
8206662 *CNLD* -	**TALIWINE** **Omnium Marocaine de Peche** SatCom: Inmarsat C 424237710 *Agadir* *Morocco* Official number: 8-645	*323* 142 405	Class: (BV)	**1983**-08 **Construcciones Navales Santodomingo SA — Vigo** Yd No: 486 Loa 38.31 Br ex 8.59 Dght 4.050 Lbp 35.62 Br md 8.50 Dpth 6.15 Welded, 1 dk	**(B11A2FS) Stern Trawler** Ins: 402	**1 oil engine** with clutches, flexible couplings & sr geared to sc. shaft driving 1 FP propeller Total Power: 853kW (1,160hp) 12.3kn Deutz SBA8M528 1 x 4 Stroke 8 Cy. 220 x 280 853kW (1160bhp) Hijos de J Barreras SA-Spain AuxGen: 2 x 140kW 380V 50Hz a.c
9611046 *D5BK4*	**TALLAHASSEE** **Stronsay Shipping Ltd** Norwest Management Co Pte Ltd *Monrovia* *Liberia* MMSI: 636015539 Official number: 15539	**9,743** 4,597 12,574	Class: GL	**2012**-10 **Taizhou Kouan Shipbuilding Co Ltd — Taizhou JS** Yd No: TK0602 Loa 143.18 (BB) Br ex - Dght 8.300 Lbp 133.43 Br md 22.61 Dpth 11.30 Welded, 1 dk	**(A33A2CC) Container Ship (Fully Cellular)** TEU 1042 C Ho 316 TEU C Dk 726 TEU incl 119 ref C	**1 oil engine** driving 1 FP propeller Total Power: 8,730kW (11,869hp) 17.8kn Wartsila 6RT-flex48T 1 x 2 Stroke 6 Cy. 480 x 2000 8730kW (11869bhp) Qingdao Qiyao Wartsila MHI LinshanMarine Diesel Co Ltd (QMD)-China AuxGen: 3 x 730kW a.c Thrusters: 1 Tunnel thruster (f)
9130224 *V2PA1*	**TALLIN** **Bojen ms 'Tallin' KG** Kapitan Siegfried Bojen- Schiffahrtsbetrieb eK SatCom: Inmarsat C 430401829 *Saint John's* *Antigua & Barbuda* MMSI: 304010867	**2,810** 1,562 4,250	Class: GL	**1997**-09 **Santierul Naval Galati S.A. — Galati** (Hull) Yd No: 913 **1997**-09 **B.V. Scheepswerf Damen Hoogezand — Foxhol** Yd No: 721 Loa 89.74 (BB) Br ex - Dght 5.719 Lbp 84.99 Br md 13.17 Dpth 7.15 Welded, 1 dk	**(A31A2GX) General Cargo Ship** Grain: 5,718 TEU 221 C.Ho 117/20' C.Dk 104/20' Compartments: 1 Ho, ER 1 Ha: (62.5 x 11.0)ER Ice Capable	**1 oil engine** reduction geared to sc. shaft driving 1 CP propeller Total Power: 2,200kW (2,991hp) 10.5kn MWM TBD645L6 1 x 4 Stroke 6 Cy. 330 x 450 2200kW (2991bhp) Motoren Werke Mannheim AG (MWM)-Mannheim AuxGen: 1 x 600kW 220/380V a.c, 2 x 136kW 220/380V a.c Fuel: 200.0 (d.f.)
9150286 *YYKT* -	**TALLINK AUTOEXPRESS 2** *ex* Boomerang *-2001* **Hansalink Ltd** Consolidada de Ferrys CA (CONFERRY) *Pampatar* *Venezuela* MMSI: 775504000 Official number: ARSH-11994	**5,419** 1,626 361	Class: (NV)	**1997**-04 **Austal Ships Pty Ltd — Fremantle WA** Yd No: 53 Loa 82.30 Br ex 23.40 Dght 2.795 Lbp 69.60 Br md 23.10 Dpth 6.70 Welded, 1 dk	**(A36A2PR) Passenger/Ro-Ro Ship (Vehicles)** Hull Material: Aluminium Alloy Passengers: unberthed: 700 Stern door/ramp Cars: 175	**4 oil engines** with clutches, flexible couplings & sr geared to sc. shafts driving 4 Water jets Total Power: 24,000kW (32,632hp) 37.0kn M.T.U. 20V1163TB73 4 x Vee 4 Stroke 20 Cy. 230 x 280 each-6000kW (8158bhp) MTU Friedrichshafen GmbH-Friedrichshafen AuxGen: 4 x 269kW 380V 50Hz a.c Fuel: 67.5 (d.f.) 108.0pd
8616441 *SLOK* KA 15	**TALLONA** **Tallona A/B** *Sturko* *Sweden* MMSI: 266048000	**165** 49 90		**1986**-07 **Smogens Plat & Svetsindustri AB — Smogen** Yd No: 39 Loa 23.68 Br ex 7.07 Dght - Lbp 19.51 Br md 7.00 Dpth 3.51 Welded, 1 dk	**(B11A2FS) Stern Trawler**	**1 oil engine** driving 1 CP propeller Total Power: 382kW (519hp) MAN D2542MLE 1 x Vee 4 Stroke 12 Cy. 125 x 142 382kW (519bhp) MAN Nutzfahrzeuge AG-Nuernberg Thrusters: 1 Thwart. CP thruster (f)
9404039 *UBAF9* -	**TALNAKH** **JSC Mining & Metallurgical Company 'Norilsk Nickel'** Murmansk Transport Branch of JSC Mining & Metallurgical Company 'Norilsk Nickel' *Murmansk* *Russia* MMSI: 273348820	**17,031** 5,257 18,095	Class: RS	**2008**-12 **Wadan Yards MTW GmbH — Wismar** (Aft & pt cargo sections) Yd No: 160 **2008**-12 **Wadan Yards Warnow GmbH — Rostock** (Fwd & pt cargo sections) Loa 169.04 Br ex 26.45 Dght 10.000 Lbp 159.86 Br md 23.10 Dpth 14.20 Welded, 2 dks	**(A31A2GX) General Cargo Ship** TEU 738 C Ho 389 TEU C Dk 349 TEU incl 21 ref C Compartments: 4 Ho, ER 4 Ha: (19.2 x 18.1)2 (25.6 x 18.1)ER (10.4 x 11.8) Cranes: 2x45t Ice Capable	**3 diesel electric oil engines** driving 3 gen. each 5820kW a.c Connecting to 1 elec. Motor of (13000kW) driving 1 Azimuth electric drive unit Total Power: 19,950kW (27,123hp) 12.5kn Wartsila 12V32 3 x Vee 4 Stroke 12 Cy. 320 x 400 each-6650kW (9041bhp) Wartsila Finland Oy-Finland Thrusters: 1 Thwart. CP thruster (f) Fuel: 2500.0 (r.f.)
8223311 *YJRZ7* -	**TALOFA** *ex* Fortune Reefer *-2012* *ex* Fortune *-2011* *ex* Friend *-2008* *ex* Smart Reefer Satu *-2002* *ex* Bizen Reefer *-1999* **Kova Fishery Co Ltd** Dongwon Industries Co Ltd *Port Vila* *Vanuatu* MMSI: 577082000 Official number: 2147	**4,394** 1,893 4,942	Class: KR (NK)	**1983**-05 **Honda Zosen — Saiki** Yd No: 712 Loa 107.88 Br ex 17.15 Dght 6.741 Lbp 99.83 Br md 17.11 Dpth 10.11 Welded, 2 dks	**(A34A2GR) Refrigerated Cargo Ship** Ins: 5,737 Compartments: 3 Ho, ER 3 Ha: (6.4 x 5.0)2 (6.5 x 5.0)ER Derricks: 6x4t	**1 oil engine** driving 1 FP propeller Total Power: 4,413kW (6,000hp) 16.5kn Mitsubishi 6UEC45HA 1 x 2 Stroke 6 Cy. 450 x 1150 4413kW (6000bhp) Akasaka Tekkosho KK (Akasaka DieselLtd)-Japan AuxGen: 2 x 600kW 450V 60Hz a.c Fuel: 186.5 (d.f.) 776.5 (r.f.) 19.0pd
8110459 - -	**TALOFA 1** *ex* Lofa *-2006* **Got Fish Ltd** -	*188* 57 -		**1981**-11 **Uchida Zosen — Ise** Yd No: 819 Loa - Br ex - Dght 2.401 Lbp 37.01 Br md 7.01 Dpth 2.72 Welded, 1 dk	**(B11B2FV) Fishing Vessel**	**1 oil engine** driving 1 FP propeller Total Power: 368kW (500hp) Yanmar 6MAL-HT 1 x 4 Stroke 6 Cy. 200 x 240 368kW (500bhp) Yanmar Diesel Engine Co Ltd-Japan
8104010 *5IM812*	**TALON** *ex* Pacific Dart *-2013* **Comarco Mauritius Ltd** Kenya Marine Contractors EPZ Ltd *Zanzibar* *Tanzania* MMSI: 677071200 Official number: 100174	**863** 258 1,065	Class: AB	**1981**-07 **Yokohama Zosen — Chiba** Yd No: 1393 Loa 57.71 Br ex 12.22 Dght 3.912 Lbp 52.51 Br md 12.21 Dpth 4.50 Welded, 1 dk	**(B21B20T) Offshore Tug/Supply Ship** Passengers: berths: 23	**2 oil engines** reverse reduction geared to sc. shafts driving 2 FP propellers Total Power: 3,090kW (4,202hp) 12.5kn Yanmar 8Z-ST 2 x 4 Stroke 8 Cy. 280 x 340 each-1545kW (2101bhp) Yanmar Diesel Engine Co Ltd-Japan AuxGen: 3 x 160kW 440V 60Hz a.c Thrusters: 1 Thwart. FP thruster (f) Fuel: 287.4 (d.f.) 7.0pd
7043843 *SWST* -	**TALOS** *ex* Mykonos *-2013* *ex* Spheroid *-2001* *ex* Niekerk *-1987* *ex* RoRo Trader *-1985* *ex* Starmark *-1981* **Creta Cargo Lines Shipping Co (Kpeta Kaprko Aaine Naytikh Etaipha)** *Piraeus* *Greece* MMSI: 239786000 Official number: 10899	**7,171** 2,151 2,838	Class: (NV)	**1971**-07 **Langvik Sarpsborg Mek. Verksted — Sarpsborg** (Hull launched by) **1971**-07 **Nymo Mek. Verksted AS — Grimstad** (Hull completed by) **1971**-07 **Ankerlokken Verft Floro AS — Floro** Yd No: 85 Lengthened-1990 Loa 124.20 Br ex - Dght 4.954 Lbp 100.03 Br md 19.21 Dpth 13.21 Welded, 2 dks	**(A35A2RR) Ro-Ro Cargo Ship** Passengers: driver berths: 12 Stern door/ramp Lane-Len: 728 Trailers: 52 Grain: 8,860	**2 oil engines** driving 2 FP propellers Total Power: 5,884kW (8,000hp) 19.0kn Pielstick 8PC2L-400 2 x 4 Stroke 8 Cy. 400 x 460 each-2942kW (4000bhp) Lindholmen Motor AB-Sweden AuxGen: 1 x 552kW 440V 60Hz a.c, 1 x 420kW 440V 60Hz a.c Thrusters: 1 Thwart. FP thruster (f) Fuel: 656.5 (d.f.) 24.5pd
8834835 *UIHK* -	**TALYCHA** **Trans Flot Service Co Ltd** - SatCom: Inmarsat C 427300822 *Murmansk* *Russia* MMSI: 273415810 Official number: 891971	**2,342** 702 901	Class: RS (Class contemplated)	**1990**-09 **Sudostroitelnyy Zavod "Baltiya" — Klaypeda** Yd No: 805 Loa 85.07 (BB) Br ex 13.05 Dght 4.041 Lbp 76.97 Br md 13.04 Dpth 6.50 Welded, 1 dk	**(B11B2FV) Fishing Vessel** Ins: 1,245 Ice Capable	**1 oil engine** driving 1 FP propeller Total Power: 852kW (1,158hp) 11.3kn S.K.L. 8NVD48A-2U 1 x 4 Stroke 8 Cy. 320 x 480 852kW (1158bhp) VEB Schwermaschinenbau "KarlLiebknecht" (SKL)-Magdeburg AuxGen: 2 x 534kW a.c, 1 x 220kW a.c
8868824 *XVBR* -	**TAM BAC 01** **Khuyen Luong Port (Cang Khuyen Luong Hanoi)** - *Haiphong* *Vietnam*	**327** 184 400	Class: (VR)	**1985 Tam Bac Shipyard — Haiphong** Loa 53.55 Br ex - Dght 2.550 Lbp - Br md 7.60 Dpth 3.20 Welded, 1 dk	**(A31A2GX) General Cargo Ship** Grain: 714 Compartments: 2 Ho, ER 2 Ha: 2 (9.0 x 5.0)ER	**1 oil engine** driving 1 FP propeller Total Power: 224kW (305hp) 9.0kn S.K.L. 6NVD36-1U 1 x 4 Stroke 6 Cy. 240 x 360 224kW (305bhp) VEB Schwermaschinenbau "KarlLiebknecht" (SKL)-Magdeburg AuxGen: 2 x 30kW a.c
7737626 *D7PQ* -	**TAM HAE** **Korea Institute of Geoscience & Mineral Resources** - *Pohang* *South Korea* Official number: PHR-776007	*173* 32 93	Class: (KR)	**1977 Busan Shipbuilding Co Ltd — Busan** Loa 33.99 Br ex - Dght - Lbp 30.03 Br md 6.63 Dpth 2.77 Welded, 1 dk	**(B31A2SR) Research Survey Vessel**	**1 oil engine** driving 1 FP propeller Total Power: 151kW (205hp) 12.5kn G.M. (Detroit Diesel) 16V-71-N 1 x Vee 2 Stroke 16 Cy. 108 x 127 151kW (205bhp) Detroit Diesel Eng. Co.-Detroit, Mi AuxGen: 2 x 60kW 225V d.c

9027037 **TAM HUNG**
-
- **Nam Trieu Shipbuilding Industry Corp (NASICO)**
Nam Trieu Shipping Co Ltd
SatCom: Inmarsat C 457499963
Haiphong *Vietnam*
MMSI: 574012547
Official number: VN-1708-VT

498 Class: (VR)
308
938

2003-10 Saigon Shipbuilding & Marine Ind One Member Co Ltd — Ho Chi Minh City
Yd No: HT-25
Loa 58.00 Br ex 9.02 Dght 3.200
Lbp 55.00 Br md 9.00 Dpth 3.90
Welded, 1 dk

(A31A2GX) General Cargo Ship

1 oil engine reverse reduction geared to sc. shaft driving 1 Propeller
Total Power: 382kW (519hp) 8.0kn
Weifang X6170ZC
1 x 4 Stroke 6 Cy. 170 x 200 382kW (519bhp)
Weifang Diesel Engine Factory-China

7417989 **TAM RA**
D8WK
- **Gun Hae Shipping Co Ltd**
Busan *South Korea*
Official number: BSR-755781

999 Class: (KR)
506
1,659

1975 Busan Shipbuilding Co Ltd — Busan
Yd No: 127
Loa 69.42 Br ex - Dght 4.620
Lbp 63.00 Br md 10.49 Dpth 5.31
Welded, 1 dk

(A31A2GX) General Cargo Ship
Grain: 2,129; Bale: 2,000
Derricks: 2x5t

1 oil engine driving 1 FP propeller
Total Power: 956kW (1,300hp) 13.5kn
Matsui MS28FSC
1 x 4 Stroke 6 Cy. 280 x 420 956kW (1300bhp)
Matsui Iron Works Co Ltd-Japan
AuxGen: 2 x 80kW 220V a.c

8875906 **TAM YANG**
DSAA6
- **Bukyong National University (PKNU)**
SatCom: Inmarsat A 1660636
Busan *South Korea*
MMSI: 440311000
Official number: BSR-930082

653 Class: KR
282
503

1993-06 Dae Sun Shipbuilding & Engineering Co Ltd — Busan Yd No: 396
Loa 58.10 Br ex - Dght 4.150
Lbp 53.00 Br md 11.00 Dpth 4.80
Welded, 1 dk

(B31A2SR) Research Survey Vessel

1 oil engine reverse reduction geared to sc. shaft driving 1 FP propeller
Total Power: 1,324kW (1,800hp) 12.7kn
Alpha 6L28/32A
1 x 4 Stroke 6 Cy. 280 x 320 1324kW (1800bhp)
Ssangyong Heavy Industries Co Ltd-South Korea
AuxGen: 2 x 336kW 450V a.c
Fuel: 252.0 (d.f.)

8517346 **TAMA HOPE**
C6MB8
ex Lamitan -1993 ex Tama Hope -1992
- **Tama Hope Shipping Co Ltd**
Seatrade Groningen BV
SatCom: Inmarsat C 430800396
Nassau *Bahamas*
MMSI: 308765000
Official number: 723497

6,579 Class: BV (NK)
3,615
7,690

1986-12 Nipponkai Heavy Ind. Co. Ltd. — Toyama
Yd No: 239
Loa 145.55 (BB) Br ex - Dght 7.416
Lbp 138.00 Br md 18.70 Dpth 10.52
Welded, 3 dks

(A34A2GR) Refrigerated Cargo Ship
Bale: 9,937; Ins: 9,937
TEU 24 incl 24 ref C
Compartments: 4 Ho, ER
4 Ha: 4 (8.3 x 6.0)ER
Derricks: 8x5t

1 oil engine driving 1 FP propeller
Total Power: 6,841kW (9,301hp) 18.0kn
B&W 6L50MC
1 x 2 Stroke 6 Cy. 500 x 1620 6841kW (9301bhp)
Mitsui Engineering & Shipbuilding CLtd-Japan
AuxGen: 4 x 560kW 450/230V 60Hz a.c
Fuel: 45.0 (d.f.) 1160.0 (r.f.) 27.0pd

7326465 **TAMA MARU**
ex Hayafuji Maru -1991
-
-
South Korea

196
-
-

1973-08 Kanagawa Zosen — Kobe Yd No: 130
Loa 29.65 Br ex 8.64 Dght 2.591
Lbp 24.21 Br md 8.62 Dpth 3.79
Riveted\Welded, 1 dk

(B32A2ST) Tug

2 oil engines driving 2 FP propellers
Total Power: 2,294kW (3,118hp)
Niigata 6L25BX
2 x 4 Stroke 6 Cy. 250 x 320 each-1147kW (1559bhp)
Niigata Engineering Co Ltd-Japan

8517358 **TAMA STAR**
C6MA6
ex Bulan -1993 ex Tama Star -1992
- **Tama Star Shipping Co Ltd**
Seatrade Groningen BV
SatCom: Inmarsat C 430800397
Nassau *Bahamas*
MMSI: 308743000
Official number: 723487

6,579 Class: BV (NK)
3,615
7,685

1987-02 Nipponkai Heavy Ind. Co. Ltd. — Toyama
Yd No: 240
Loa 145.55 (BB) Br ex 18.71 Dght 7.416
Lbp 138.00 Br md 18.70 Dpth 10.52
Welded, 3 dks

(A34A2GR) Refrigerated Cargo Ship
Ins: 9,937
TEU 24 incl 24 ref C
Compartments: 4 Ho, ER
4 Ha: 4 (8.3 x 6.0)ER
Derricks: 8x5t

1 oil engine driving 1 FP propeller
Total Power: 6,841kW (9,301hp) 18.0kn
B&W 6L50MC
1 x 2 Stroke 6 Cy. 500 x 1620 6841kW (9301bhp)
Mitsui Engineering & Shipbuilding CLtd-Japan
AuxGen: 4 x 560kW 450/230V 60Hz a.c
Fuel: 45.0 (d.f.) 1160.0 (r.f.) 27.0pd

9313149 **TAMAGAWA**
3EKV8
- **KAW1573 Shipping SA**
Kawasaki Kisen Kaisha Ltd (Kawasaki Kisen KK) ('K' Line)
SatCom: Inmarsat Mini-M 761116344
Panama *Panama*
MMSI: 372848000
Official number: 3306307A

160,231 Class: AB
103,096
314,237
T/cm
185.0

2007-06 Kawasaki Shipbuilding Corp — Sakaide KG Yd No: 1573
Loa 333.00 (BB) Br ex 60.04 Dght 21.082
Lbp 324.00 Br md 60.00 Dpth 29.30
Welded, 1 dk

(A13A2TV) Crude Oil Tanker
Double Hull (13F)
Liq: 337,222; Liq (Oil): 337,222
Compartments: 5 Ta, 10 Wing Ta, 2 Wing Slop Ta, ER
3 Cargo Pump (s): 3x5500m³/hr
Manifold: Bow/CM: 166.5m

1 oil engine driving 1 FP propeller
Total Power: 25,480kW (34,643hp) 15.6kn
MAN-B&W 7S80MC
1 x 2 Stroke 7 Cy. 800 x 3056 25480kW (34643bhp)
Kawasaki Heavy Industries Ltd-Japan
AuxGen: 3 x 1325kW a.c
Fuel: 615.1 (d.f.) 7415.3 (r.f.)

7226550 **TAMAKI**
-
- **Ports of Auckland Ltd**
-
Auckland *New Zealand*
Official number: 349012

221 Class: (LR)
66 ✠ Classed LR until 28/2/98
340

1972-09 Whangarei Eng. & Construction Co. Ltd. — Whangarei Yd No: 130
Loa 29.67 Br ex 8.97 Dght 2.934
Lbp 27.44 Br md 8.55 Dpth 3.59
Welded, 1 dk

(B32A2ST) Tug

2 oil engines reduction geared to sc. shafts driving 2 Directional propellers
Total Power: 1,324kW (1,800hp)
Ruston 6RKCM
2 x 4 Stroke 6 Cy. 254 x 305 each-662kW (900bhp)
English Electric Co. Ltd.-Newton-le-Willows
AuxGen: 2 x 60kW 400V 50Hz a.c

9522831 **TAMAKI PRINCESS**
3FXM4
- **Oriental Pearl Maritime SA**
Fair Field Shipping Co Ltd (Fair Field Shipping KK)
SatCom: Inmarsat C 437038510
Panama *Panama*
MMSI: 370385000
Official number: 4044609

6,736 Class: NK
3,335
10,024

2009-05 Sanuki Shipbuilding & Iron Works Co Ltd — Mitoyo KG Yd No: 1338
Loa 103.64 (BB) Br ex - Dght 9.065
Lbp 96.50 Br md 18.80 Dpth 13.20
Welded, 1 dk

(A31A2GX) General Cargo Ship
Double Sides Partial, Double Bottom Partial
Grain: 13,658; Bale: 12,696
Compartments: 2 Ho, ER
2 Ha: ER
Cranes: 2x30t; Derricks: 1x30t

1 oil engine driving 1 FP propeller
Total Power: 3,120kW (4,242hp) 13.0kn
Mitsubishi 6UEC37LA
1 x 2 Stroke 6 Cy. 370 x 880 3120kW (4242bhp)
Akasaka Tekkosho KK (Akasaka DieselLtd)-Japan
Fuel: 660.0

7416624 **TAMAMIZU MARU**
JI2811
ex Wakamiyo Maru No. 1 -2004
ex Tamamizu Maru -2002
- **Aichi Kaiun Sangyo KK**
Tahara, Aichi *Japan*
Official number: 115749

174
-
220

1974-08 Yokohama Yacht Co Ltd — Yokohama KN
Yd No: 702
Loa 28.00 Br ex - Dght 2.590
Lbp 26.00 Br md 7.70 Dpth 3.10
Welded, 1 dk

(A14A2LO) Water Tanker

1 oil engine driving 1 FP propeller
Total Power: 221kW (300hp) 7.0kn
Kubota M6D20BS
1 x 4 Stroke 6 Cy. 200 x 240 221kW (300bhp)
Kubota Corp-Japan

8884622 **TAMAN**
4JKS
ex MSK-10 -1979
- **Specialized Sea Oil Fleet Organisation, Caspian Sea Oil Fleet, State Oil Co of the Republic of Azerbaijan**
Baku *Azerbaijan*
MMSI: 423170100
Official number: DGR-0302

817 Class: RS
81
343

1979 Sudostroitelnyy Zavod "Krasnyye Barrikady" — Krasnyye Barrikady Yd No: 10
Loa 54.49 Br ex 14.78 Dght 2.160
Lbp 51.50 Br md 14.00 Dpth 3.70
Welded, 1 dk

(B34B2SC) Crane Vessel
Cranes: 1x25t

2 oil engines driving 2 FP propellers
Total Power: 1,030kW (1,400hp) 11.0kn
Russkiy 6DR30/50-6-3
2 x 2 Stroke 6 Cy. 300 x 500 each-515kW (700bhp)
Mashinostroitelnyy Zavod"Russkiy-Dizel"-Leningrad
AuxGen: 3 x 100kW a.c
Fuel: 118.0 (d.f.)

9402158 **TAMAN**
-
- **Portservice 'Zhelezni Rog' LLC**
Oteko-Terminal LLC
SatCom: Inmarsat C 427301788
Temryuk *Russia*
MMSI: 273331010

277 Class: RS
83
118

2007-11 OAO Leningradskiy Sudostroitelnyy Zavod 'Pella' — Otradnoye Yd No: 605
Loa 28.50 Br ex 9.50 Dght 4.600
Lbp 26.66 Br md 9.28 Dpth 4.82
Welded, 1 dk

(B32A2ST) Tug
Ice Capable

2 oil engines reduction geared to sc. shafts driving 2 Z propellers
Total Power: 2,484kW (3,378hp) 12.0kn
Caterpillar 3516
2 x Vee 4 Stroke 16 Cy. 170 x 190 each-1242kW (1689bhp)
Caterpillar Inc-USA
AuxGen: 2 x 84kW a.c
Fuel: 82.0 (d.f.)

9552501 **TAMANACO**
YYME
- **Panavenflot Corp**
PDV Marina SA
Las Piedras *Venezuela*
MMSI: 775094000
Official number: AMMT-2930

56,326 Class: LR
29,819 ✠ **100A1** SS 04/2012
104,636 Double Hull oil tanker
T/cm CSR
88.9 ESP
ShipRight (CM, ACS (B))
*IWS
LI
DSPM4
✠ **LMC** **UMS IGS**
Eq.Ltr: T†;
Cable: 715.0/87.0 U3 (a)

2012-04 Sumitomo Heavy Industries Marine & Engineering Co., Ltd. — Yokosuka
Yd No: 1374
Loa 228.60 (BB) Br ex 42.04 Dght 14.780
Lbp 217.80 Br md 42.00 Dpth 21.50
Welded, 1 dk

(A13A2TV) Crude Oil Tanker
Double Hull (13F)
Liq: 98,700; Liq (Oil): 98,700
Cargo Heating Coils
Compartments: 10 Wing Ta, 2 Wing Slop Ta, 1 Slop Ta, ER
3 Cargo Pump (s): 3x2500m³/hr
Manifold: Bow/CM: 116.6m

1 oil engine driving 1 FP propeller
Total Power: 12,350kW (16,791hp) 14.8kn
MAN-B&W 6S60MC-C
1 x 2 Stroke 6 Cy. 600 x 2400 12350kW (16791bhp)
Mitsui Engineering & Shipbuilding CLtd-Japan
AuxGen: 3 x 640kW 450V 60Hz a.c
Boilers: e (ex.g.) 22.3kgf/cm² (21.9bar), WTAuxB (o.f.) 18.4kgf/cm² (18.0bar)
Fuel: 250.0 (d.f.) 2170.0 (r.f.)

8014461 **TAMANAMI**
JG4134
ex Hanayuki -1999
- **Government of Japan (Ministry of Land, Infrastructure & Transport) (The Coastguard)**
-
Tokyo *Japan*
MMSI: 431100433
Official number: 123728

123
-
76

1981-03 Mitsubishi Heavy Industries Ltd. — Shimonoseki Yd No: 831
Loa 26.00 Br ex 6.30 Dght 1.130
Lbp 24.50 Br md 6.29 Dpth 3.04
Welded, 1 dk

(B34H2SQ) Patrol Vessel
Hull Material: Aluminium Alloy

3 oil engines driving 3 FP propellers
Total Power: 2,208kW (3,003hp) 22.0kn
Mitsubishi 12DM20TK
3 x Vee 4 Stroke 12 Cy. 160 x 200 each-736kW (1001bhp)
Mitsubishi Heavy Industries Ltd-Japan
Fuel: 5.0 (d.f.)

No. / Call sign	Name, owner, port	Tonnage	Class	Built, dimensions	Type, capacity	Machinery
8206636 *CNKB* -	**TAMANAR** **Omnium Marocaine de Peche** - SatCom: Inmarsat C 424237810 *Agadir* *Morocco* Official number: 8-633	*323* 142 405	Class: (BV)	**1983**-03 **Construcciones Navales Santodomingo SA — Vigo** Yd No: 483 Loa 38.31 Br ex 8.59 Dght 4.050 Lbp 35.62 Br md 8.50 Dpth 4.04 Welded, 1 dk	**(B11A2FS) Stern Trawler** Ins: 402	**1 oil engine** with clutches, flexible couplings & sr geared to sc. shaft driving 1 FP propeller Total Power: 853kW (1,160hp) 12.3kn Deutz SBA8M528 1 x 4 Stroke 8 Cy. 220 x 280 853kW (1160bhp) Hijos de J Barreras SA-Spain AuxGen: 2 x 140kW 380V 50Hz a.c
6928553 *UDWM* -	**TAMANGO** **Antey Co Ltd (TOO 'Antey')** - *Vladivostok* *Russia* MMSI: 273848600	**680** 284 257	Class: RS	**1967**-12 **Khabarovskiy Sudostroitelnyy Zavod im Kirova — Khabarovsk** Yd No: 154 Loa 54.23 Br ex 9.38 Dght 3.590 Lbp 48.76 Br md 9.33 Dpth 4.75 Welded, 1 dk	**(B11A2FT) Trawler** Ins: 361 Compartments: 2 Ho, ER 2 Ha: 2 (1.5 x 1.6) Derricks: 1x2t,1x1.5t; Winches: 2 Ice Capable	**1 oil engine** driving 1 FP propeller Total Power: 588kW (799hp) 12.0kn S.K.L. 8NVD48AU 1 x 4 Stroke 8 Cy. 320 x 480 588kW (799bhp) VEB Schwermaschinenbau "KarlLiebknecht" (SKL)-Magdeburg AuxGen: 3 x 100kW Fuel: 137.0 (d.f.)
9279355 *JK5611* -	**TAMANO MARU** **Eikichi Kaiun KK & Nippon Eisen KK** Nihon Tug-Boat Co Ltd *Tamano, Okayama* *Japan* Official number: 136164	*193* - -		**2002**-11 **Kanagawa Zosen — Kobe** Yd No: 511 L reg 33.30 Br ex - Dght - Lbp - Br md 8.80 Dpth 3.91 Welded, 1 Dk.	**(B32A2ST) Tug**	**2 oil engines** Geared Integral to driving 2 Z propellers Total Power: 2,942kW (4,000hp) 13.5kn Niigata 6L28HX 2 x 4 Stroke 6 Cy. 280 x 370 each-1471kW (2000bhp) Niigata Engineering Co Ltd-Japan
9203667 *FOOV* -	**TAMANOU** **SNC Nouminvest** Societe Oceanienne de Remorquage et d'Assistance (SORA) *Noumea* *France* MMSI: 540111000 Official number: 899347	**258** 77 487	Class: BV	**1998**-12 **President Marine Pte Ltd — Singapore** Yd No: 250 Loa 29.40 Br ex - Dght 3.600 Lbp - Br md 8.70 Dpth 4.10 Welded, 1 dk	**(B32A2ST) Tug**	**2 oil engines** with clutches, flexible couplings & sr reverse geared to sc. shafts driving 2 FP propellers Total Power: 2,060kW (2,800hp) 12.0kn Yanmar T240A-ET 2 x 4 Stroke 6 Cy. 240 x 310 each-1030kW (1400bhp) Yanmar Diesel Engine Co Ltd-Japan AuxGen: 2 x 177kW 415V 50Hz a.c Fuel: 160.0 (d.f.) 9.6pd
8727044 *UZUY* -	**TAMANSKIY** **State Enterprise Kerch Sea Fishing Port** - SatCom: Inmarsat C 427228310 *Kerch* *Ukraine* MMSI: 272283000 Official number: 852642	**1,904** 767 3,079	Class: RS	**1985**-12 **Shipbuilding & Shiprepairing Yard 'Ivan Dimitrov' — Rousse** Yd No: 445 Converted From: Chemical Tanker-2012 Converted From: Products Tanker-2007 Converted From: Bunkering Vessel-1990 Loa 77.53 Br ex 14.34 Dght 5.350 Lbp 73.24 Br md 14.00 Dpth 6.50 Welded, 1 dk	**(A12B2TR) Chemical/Products Tanker** Liq: 2,818; Liq (Oil): 2,818 Compartments: 10 Wing Ta, ER Ice Capable	**1 oil engine** driving 1 FP propeller Total Power: 883kW (1,201hp) 10.5kn S.K.L. 8NVD48A-2U 1 x 4 Stroke 8 Cy. 320 x 480 883kW (1201bhp) VEB Schwermaschinenbau "KarlLiebknecht" (SKL)-Magdeburg AuxGen: 2 x 150kW a.c
6602824 - - -	**TAMAR** *ex Uskgarth -1996* - -	*161* - -	Class: (LR) ✠ Classed LR until 23/2/00	**1966**-03 **Richards (Shipbuilders) Ltd — Lowestoft** Yd No: 484 Loa 28.96 Br ex 7.60 Dght 3.150 Lbp 26.22 Br md 7.17 Dpth 3.66 Riveted\Welded, 1 dk	**(B32A2ST) Tug**	**1 oil engine** sr reverse geared to sc. shaft driving 1 FP propeller Total Power: 625kW (850hp) Blackstone ETS8 1 x 4 Stroke 8 Cy. 222 x 292 625kW (850bhp) Lister Blackstone Marine Ltd.-Dursley AuxGen: 2 x 30kW 220V d.c
8034772 *WTM6207* -	**TAMAR** **Tamar Inc** - *Cordova, AK* *United States of America* MMSI: 367181950 Official number: 617170	*129* 116 -		**1979 Bob Pluss Welding — Chula Vista, Ca** L reg 23.11 Br ex 7.32 Dght - Lbp - Br md - Dpth 2.24 Welded, 1 dk	**(B11B2FV) Fishing Vessel**	**1 oil engine** driving 1 FP propeller Total Power: 346kW (470hp)
9256638 *2GLT4* -	**TAMAR** *ex Torm Tamar -2010 ex Tamar -2008* **Fidelity Shipping AS** MTM Ship Management Pte Ltd *Douglas* *Isle of Man (British)* MMSI: 235098484	**42,771** 19,807 70,362 T/cm 67.6	Class: GL NV	**2003**-07 **Daewoo Shipbuilding & Marine Engineering Co Ltd — Geoje** Yd No: 5234 Loa 228.00 (BB) Br ex 32.23 Dght 13.820 Lbp 219.00 Br md 32.20 Dpth 20.90 Welded, 1 dk	**(A13B2TP) Products Tanker** Double Hull (13F) Liq: 82,054; Liq (Oil): 82,054 Cargo Heating Coils Compartments: 12 Wing Ta, 2 Wing Slop Ta, ER 12 Cargo Pump (s): 12x900m³/hr Manifold: Bow/CM: 112.8m	**1 oil engine** driving 1 FP propeller Total Power: 11,287kW (15,346hp) 14.6kn MAN-B&W 5S60MC-C 1 x 2 Stroke 5 Cy. 600 x 2400 11287kW (15346bhp) Doosan Engine Co Ltd-South Korea AuxGen: 3 x 900kW a.c
9456226 *V7SQ6* -	**TAMAR** *ex Turandot -2010* **Genshipping Corp** Splosna Plovba doo (Splosna plovba International Shipping & Chartering Ltd) *Majuro* *Marshall Islands* MMSI: 538003703 Official number: 3703	**32,987** 19,231 56,563 T/cm 58.8	Class: LR ✠ **100A1** SS 05/2010 bulk carrier CSR BC-A GRAB (20) Nos. 2 & 4 holds may be empty ESP **ShipRight** (CM) *IWS LI ✠ **LMC** **UMS** Cable: 634.7/73.0 U3 (a)	**2010**-05 **Jiangsu Hantong Ship Heavy Industry Co Ltd — Tongzhou JS** Yd No: 023 Loa 189.99 (BB) Br ex 32.30 Dght 12.800 Lbp 185.00 Br md 32.26 Dpth 18.00 Welded, 1 dk	**(A21A2BC) Bulk Carrier** Grain: 71,634; Bale: 68,200 Compartments: 5 Ho, ER 5 Ha: ER Cranes: 4x35t	**1 oil engine** driving 1 FP propeller Total Power: 9,480kW (12,889hp) 14.2kn MAN-B&W 6S50MC-C 1 x 2 Stroke 6 Cy. 500 x 2000 9480kW (12889bhp) Doosan Engine Co Ltd-South Korea AuxGen: 3 x 600kW 440V 60Hz a.c Boilers: AuxB (Comp) 7.9kgf/cm² (7.7bar)
9310939 - -	**TAMAR II** **Tamar Bridge & Torpoint Ferry Joint Committee** - *United Kingdom*	**748** 229 245	Class: LR ✠ **AT** SS 05/2011 ferry Tamar Estuary service **LMC**	**2005**-03 **Ferguson Shipbuilders Ltd — Port Glasgow** Yd No: 718 Loa 73.00 Br ex 20.37 Dght 1.600 Lbp 48.00 Br md 19.75 Dpth 3.10 Welded, 1 dk	**(A36A2PR) Passenger/Ro-Ro Ship (Vehicles)** Passengers: unberthed: 320 Bow ramp (centre) Len: - Wid: 16.70 Swl: 44 Stern ramp (centre) Len: - Wid: 16.70 Swl: 44 Cars: 73	**3 diesel electric oil engines** driving 3 gen. each 294kW 450V a.c Connecting to 2 elec. motors each (250kW) Total Power: 930kW (1,263hp) 5.0kn Volvo Penta D12 3 x 4 Stroke 6 Cy. 131 x 150 each-310kW (421bhp) AB Volvo Penta-Sweden
9260366 *HOEH* -	**TAMARA** **LPG Transportation Shipping & Trading Co SA** Star Management Associates *Panama* *Panama* MMSI: 353900000 Official number: 2850902B	**5,286** 1,995 6,017 T/cm 17.5	Class: BV (NK)	**2002**-05 **Kyokuyo Shipyard Corp — Shimonoseki YC** Yd No: 438 Loa 117.02 (BB) Br ex 18.23 Dght 6.814 Lbp 110.00 Br md 18.20 Dpth 8.90 Welded, 1 dk	**(A11B2TG) LPG Tanker** Double Sides Entire Compartment Length Liq (Gas): 7,077 2 x Gas Tank (s); 2 independent (C.mn.stl) cyl horizontal 5 Cargo Pump (s): 2x400m³/hr, 1x300m³/hr, 2x215m³/hr Manifold: Bow/CM: 54.7m Ice Capable	**1 oil engine** driving 1 FP propeller Total Power: 3,900kW (5,302hp) 14.8kn B&W 6L35MC 1 x 2 Stroke 6 Cy. 350 x 1050 3900kW (5302bhp) Mitsui Engineering & Shipbuilding CLtd-Japan AuxGen: 2 x 400kW 440V 60Hz a.c Thrusters: 1 Thwart. CP thruster (f) Fuel: 109.8 (d.f.) (Heating Coils) 610.0 (r.f.) 16.3pd
7001364 *ERKT* -	**TAMARA** *ex Adriane -2010 ex Cito -1997 ex Adria -1990* *ex Adriana -1986* **Island Flag Shipping LLC** - *Giurgiulesti* *Moldova* MMSI: 214181120	**1,371** 428 1,307	Class: (GL)	**1970**-10 **Bayerische Schiffbaug. mbH vorm. A. Schellenberger — Erlenbach** Yd No: 1011 Loa 69.83 (BB) Br ex 11.61 Dght 3.591 Lbp 65.46 Br md 11.52 Dpth 6.91 Welded, 2 dks	**(A31A2GX) General Cargo Ship** Grain: 3,229; Bale: 2,965 TEU 45 C.45/20' Compartments: 1 Ho, ER 1 Ha: (31.2 x 7.6)ER Ice Capable	**1 oil engine** sr geared to sc. shaft driving 1 FP propeller Total Power: 1,214kW (1,651hp) 12.5kn MWM RHS345SU 1 x 4 Stroke 6 Cy. 360 x 450 1214kW (1651bhp) Motoren Werke Mannheim AG (MWM)-West Germany AuxGen: 2 x 42kW 380V 50Hz a.c, 1 x 30kW 380V 50Hz a.c Fuel: 142.0 (d.f.)
7105706 *YCSE* -	**TAMARA** *ex Niaga XXXI -1986 ex Prinsenwal -1980* *ex Prinsenbeek -1979 ex Jettie -1972* **PT Berlian Tirta Lestari** - *Jakarta* *Indonesia* MMSI: 525019512	**1,592** 1,056 2,854	Class: KI (BV)	**1971**-06 **Bodewes' Scheepswerven N.V. — Hoogezand** Yd No: 509 Loa 81.41 Br ex 12.02 Dght 5.601 Lbp 74.50 Br md 11.92 Dpth 6.76 Welded, 1 dk	**(A31A2GX) General Cargo Ship** Grain: 3,770; Bale: 3,535 Compartments: 1 Ho, ER 2 Ha: 2 (19.2 x 8.6)ER Derricks: 4x5t; Winches: 4 Ice Capable	**1 oil engine** driving 1 FP propeller Total Power: 1,103kW (1,500hp) 12.5kn MaK 8M451AK 1 x 4 Stroke 8 Cy. 320 x 450 1103kW (1500bhp) Atlas MaK Maschinenbau GmbH-Kiel AuxGen: 2 x 85kW 380V 50Hz a.c, 1 x 36kW 380V 50Hz a.c, 1 x 16kW 380V 50Hz a.c
8880523 *UAJV* -	**TAMARA** **Marine Line Co Ltd** - SatCom: Inmarsat C 427320833 *Vladivostok* *Russia* MMSI: 273459400 Official number: 930201	**683** 233 520	Class: RS	**1995**-07 **AO Oston — Khabarovsk** Yd No: 897 Loa 54.99 Br ex 9.49 Dght 4.460 Lbp 50.04 Br md - Dpth 5.16 Welded, 1 dk	**(B12B2FC) Fish Carrier** Ice Capable	**1 oil engine** driving 1 FP propeller Total Power: 589kW (801hp) 11.3kn S.K.L. 6NVD48A-2U 1 x 4 Stroke 6 Cy. 320 x 480 589kW (801bhp) SKL Motoren u. Systemtechnik AG-Magdeburg

IMO / Call sign / Flag	Name / Owner / Port	Tonnage	Class	Builder / Dimensions	Type	Machinery
8939063 *WDB9324* -	**TAMARA ALANE** *ex* Anna Bell *-2006* *ex* Ashley Le Tran *-2000* **Vessel Tamara Alane Inc** - *Lowland, NC* *United States of America* MMSI: 366973830 Official number: 1029425	**135** 41 -		**1995 La Force Shipyard Inc — Coden AL** Yd No: 59 L reg 23.81 Br ex - Dght - Lbp - Br md 7.32 Dpth 3.75 Welded, 1 dk	**(B11B2FV) Fishing Vessel**	**1 oil engine** driving 1 FP propeller
9223978 *EAQB* 3-CO-65-99	**TAMARA E YAIZA** **Pesquera O Redero SL** - *Muros* *Spain* Official number: 3-5/1999	*217* - -		**2000-06 Astilleros y Talleres Ferrolanos S.A. (ASTAFERSA) — Ferrol** Yd No: 353 Loa - Br ex - Dght - Lbp - Br md - Dpth - Welded, 1 dk	**(B11B2FV) Fishing Vessel**	**1 oil engine** driving 1 FP propeller GUASCOR 1 x 4 Stroke Gutierrez Ascunce Corp (GUASCOR)-Spain
9233143 *4LNL2* -	**TAMARA I** *ex* Dogancay II *-2003* **Batumi Oil Terminal Ltd** - *Georgia* MMSI: 213981000 Official number: C-00417	**205** 61 -	Class: MG (AB)	**2001-01 Sahin Celik Sanayi A.S. — Tuzla** Yd No: 19 Loa - Br ex - Dght 3.250 Lbp 24.50 Br md 8.60 Dpth 4.30 Welded, 1 dk	**(B32A2ST) Tug**	**2 oil engines** with clutches, flexible couplings & sr reverse geared to sc. shafts driving 2 FP propellers Total Power: 2,206kW (3,000hp) 13.0kn Caterpillar 3512B-TA 2 x Vee 4 Stroke 12 Cy. 170 x 190 each-1103kW (1500bhp) Caterpillar Inc-USA AuxGen: 2 x 59kW 380V 50Hz a.c
9237826 *4LNM2* -	**TAMARA II** *ex* Dogancay III *-2003* **Batumi Oil Terminal Ltd** - *Georgia* MMSI: 213982000 Official number: C-00418	**205** 61 72	Class: (AB)	**2001-05 Sahin Celik Sanayi A.S. — Tuzla** Yd No: 20 Loa 25.33 Br ex - Dght 3.250 Lbp 24.00 Br md 8.60 Dpth 4.30 Welded, 1 dk	**(B32A2ST) Tug**	**2 oil engines** with clutches, flexible couplings & sr geared to sc. shafts driving 2 FP propellers Total Power: 2,236kW (3,040hp) 12.5kn Caterpillar 3512TA 2 x Vee 4 Stroke 12 Cy. 170 x 190 each-1118kW (1520bhp) Caterpillar Inc-USA AuxGen: 2 x 68kW 380V 50Hz a.c Fuel: 70.0 (d.f.)
8005939 *HQME8* -	**TAMARA No. 8** *ex* Matsuei Maru No. 5 *-2003* **Marinex S de RL** - *San Lorenzo* *Honduras* Official number: L-1924900	*299* 154 -		**1980-08 Uchida Zosen — Ise** Yd No: 807 Loa - Br ex - Dght - Lbp 43.64 Br md 8.51 Dpth 3.59 Welded, 1 dk	**(B11B2FV) Fishing Vessel**	**1 oil engine** driving 1 FP propeller Total Power: 883kW (1,201hp) Niigata 6MG25BX 1 x 4 Stroke 6 Cy. 250 x 320 883kW (1201bhp) Niigata Engineering Co Ltd-Japan
8976279 - -	**TAMARACK** *ex* Wagl 248 *-2003* **Carib Marine** - *Georgetown* *Guyana* Official number: 0000160	*360* 245 -		**1934 Manitowoc Shipbuilding Co — Manitowoc WI** Converted From: Buoy Tender L reg 35.35 Br ex - Dght - Lbp - Br md 8.83 Dpth 2.80 Welded, 1 dk	**(B11B2FV) Fishing Vessel**	**1 oil engine** driving 1 Propeller Total Power: 883kW (1,201hp)
9261970 *D5EY8* -	**TAMARACK** *ex* Spring Progress *-2013* **Delano Shipping LLC** TST International SA *Monrovia* *Liberia* MMSI: 636016198 Official number: 16198	**27,989** 17,077 50,344 T/cm 53.5	Class: NK	**2003-01 Kawasaki Shipbuilding Corp — Kobe HG** Yd No: 1533 Loa 189.80 (BB) Br ex - Dght 11.925 Lbp 181.00 Br md 32.26 Dpth 16.90 Welded, 1 dk	**(A21A2BC) Bulk Carrier** Double Bottom Entire Compartment Length Grain: 63,198; Bale: 60,713 Compartments: 5 Ho, ER 5 Ha: (20.2 x 18.0)3 (20.2 x 18.0)ER (17.6 x 18.0) Cranes: 4x30.5t	**1 oil engine** driving 1 FP propeller Total Power: 8,090kW (10,999hp) 14.5kn MAN-B&W 6S50MC-C 1 x 2 Stroke 6 Cy. 500 x 2000 8090kW (10999bhp) (made 2003) Kawasaki Heavy Industries Ltd-Japan AuxGen: 3 x 550kW a.c Fuel: 109.0 (d.f.) (Heating Coils) 1782.0 (r.f.) 28.0pd
8429850 *WDF6478* -	**TAMARAW** *ex* Island Warrior *-2011* *ex* Ocean Warrior *-2002* *ex* Marine Constructor *-1993* *ex* Tatnuck *-1982* *ex* ATA 195 *-1948* *ex* Tatnuck *-1945* **Seabridge Inc** - *Apra Harbor, GU* *United States of America* MMSI: 369613000 Official number: 646126	**471** - -		**1945-02 Levingston SB. Co. — Orange, Tx** Yd No: 362 Loa - Br ex - Dght 4.632 Lbp 41.00 Br md 10.06 Dpth 5.19 Welded, 1 dk	**(B32A2ST) Tug**	**1 oil engine** driving 1 FP propeller
7851393 - -	**TAMARII EIMO** *ex* Moorea Ferry *-1987* *ex* Tosa *-1980* **Societe Nerii** - *Tahiti* *France*	*480* 273 -	Class: (BV)	**1968 Nakamura Shipbuilding & Engine Works Co. Ltd. — Matsue** Loa 43.69 Br ex - Dght 2.771 Lbp 40.01 Br md 11.37 Dpth 3.61 Welded, 1 dk	**(A36A2PR) Passenger/Ro-Ro Ship (Vehicles)** Passengers: 300	**2 oil engines** driving 2 FP propellers Total Power: 1,250kW (1,700hp) 13.5kn Daihatsu 8PSTM-26D 2 x 4 Stroke 8 Cy. 260 x 320 each-625kW (850bhp) Daihatsu Diesel Manufacturing Co Lt-Japan
9573880 *JD3079* -	**TAMARIKI MARU** **Tamariki Kisen KK** - *Kure, Hiroshima* *Japan* MMSI: 431001417 Official number: 141266	*499* - 1,200		**2010-06 Hakata Zosen K.K. — Imabari** Yd No: 727 Loa 64.50 Br ex - Dght 4.190 Lbp 60.00 Br md 10.00 Dpth 4.50 Welded, 1 dk	**(A13B2TP) Products Tanker** Double Hull (13F) Liq: 1,200; Liq (Oil): 1,200	**1 oil engine** reverse geared to sc. shaft driving 1 FP propeller Total Power: 1,176kW (1,599hp) Akasaka K28S 1 x 4 Stroke 6 Cy. 280 x 500 1176kW (1599bhp) Akasaka Tekkosho KK (Akasaka DieselLtd)-Japan
9652624 *JD3400* -	**TAMARIKI MARU NO. 1** **Tamariki Kisen KK** - *Kure, Hiroshima* *Japan* MMSI: 431003767 Official number: 141747	*998* - 2,316	Class: NK	**2012-09 Hakata Zosen K.K. — Imabari** Yd No: 750 Loa 79.90 (BB) Br ex - Dght 5.050 Lbp 76.00 Br md 12.00 Dpth 5.70 Welded, 1 dk	**(A13B2TP) Products Tanker** Double Hull (13F) Liq: 2,253; Liq (Oil): 2,253	**1 oil engine** reverse geared to sc. shaft driving 1 FP propeller Total Power: 1,618kW (2,200hp) 12.9kn Akasaka AX33BR 1 x 4 Stroke 6 Cy. 330 x 620 1618kW (2200bhp) Akasaka Tekkosho KK (Akasaka DieselLtd)-Japan Fuel: 115.0
9072472 - -	**TAMARIKI MARU No. 8** - -	*497* - 1,258	Class: (NK)	**1993-05 Hakata Zosen K.K. — Imabari** Yd No: 550 Loa 65.40 Br ex - Dght 4.176 Lbp 60.90 Br md 10.00 Dpth 4.50 Welded, 1 dk	**(A13B2TP) Products Tanker** Liq: 1,266; Liq (Oil): 1,266	**1 oil engine** reverse geared to sc. shaft driving 1 FP propeller Total Power: 736kW (1,001hp) 11.0kn Hanshin LH28G 1 x 4 Stroke 6 Cy. 280 x 460 736kW (1001bhp) The Hanshin Diesel Works Ltd-Japan Fuel: 65.0 (d.f.)
9078268 - -	**TAMARIKI MARU No. 37** - -	*999* - 2,340		**1993-12 Imamura Zosen — Kure** Yd No: 367 Loa 79.00 (BB) Br ex - Dght 5.220 Lbp 74.00 Br md 12.00 Dpth 5.75 Welded, 1 dk	**(A13B2TP) Products Tanker** Compartments: 10 Ta, ER	**1 oil engine** driving 1 FP propeller Total Power: 1,618kW (2,200hp) Akasaka A34 1 x 4 Stroke 6 Cy. 340 x 660 1618kW (2200bhp) Akasaka Tekkosho KK (Akasaka DieselLtd)-Japan Thrusters: 1 Thwart. CP thruster (f)
8805987 - -	**TAMARIN** *ex* Bonfi *-2000* - -	**275** 83 205	Class: (KR) (BV)	**1989-12 Metalurgia e Construcao Naval S.A. (CORENA) — Itajai** Yd No: 227 Loa 32.50 Br ex - Dght 3.725 Lbp 25.80 Br md 8.41 Dpth 4.60 Welded	**(B11A2FS) Stern Trawler**	**1 oil engine** driving 1 FP propeller Total Power: 629kW (855hp) 11.0kn MWM TBD604BL6 1 x 4 Stroke 6 Cy. 170 x 195 629kW (855bhp) Motoren Werke Mannheim AG (MWM)-West Germany
5351521 - -	**TAMARIN** **Jailing Forestry Industries Inc** - *Georgetown* *Guyana* Official number: 0000437	*181* 84 -	Class: (AB)	**1953 Gulfport Shipbuilding Corp. — Port Arthur, Tx** Yd No: 411 Loa - Br ex 7.68 Dght 3.547 Lbp 29.47 Br md 7.65 Dpth 3.94 Welded, 1 dk	**(B32A2ST) Tug**	**1 oil engine** with clutches & sr geared to sc. shaft driving 1 FP propeller Total Power: 1,206kW (1,640hp) 10.5kn General Motors 16-278-A 1 x Vee 2 Stroke 16 Cy. 222 x 267 1206kW (1640bhp) General Motors Corp-USA AuxGen: 2 x 30kW Fuel: 40.5
9391531 *FNQG* -	**TAMARIN** **GIE Tamarin** Socatra Reunion *Marseille* *France (FIS)* MMSI: 228329800 Official number: 927779F	**29,995** 13,358 50,129 T/cm 52.0	Class: BV (AB)	**2008-11 SPP Plant & Shipbuilding Co Ltd — Sacheon** Yd No: S1014 Loa 183.16 (BB) Br ex 32.24 Dght 13.076 Lbp 174.00 Br md 32.20 Dpth 19.10 Welded, 1 dk	**(A13B2TP) Products Tanker** Double Hull (13F) Liq: 52,108; Liq (Oil): 53,509 Cargo Heating Coils Compartments: 12 Wing Ta, 2 Wing Slop Ta, ER 12 Cargo Pump (s): 12x600m³/hr Manifold: Bow/CM: 90.8m	**1 oil engine** driving 1 FP propeller Total Power: 9,480kW (12,889hp) 14.9kn MAN-B&W 6S50MC-C 1 x 2 Stroke 6 Cy. 500 x 2000 9480kW (12889bhp) Doosan Engine Co Ltd-South Korea AuxGen: 3 x 900kW 60Hz a.c Fuel: 300.0 (d.f.) 1200.0 (r.f.)

IMO / Call sign	Name / Owner	Tonnage	Class	Build / Dimensions	Type	Machinery
8888355 *YD4652* -	**TAMARIN I** *ex* QM Pioneer 808 *-2000* **PT Ekanuri Indra Pratama** - *Jakarta* *Indonesia*	**132** 79 100	Class: (KI) (NK)	**1995 Rajang Maju Shipbuilding Sdn Bhd — Sibu** Yd No: 7194 Loa 21.00 Br ex - Dght 2.350 Lbp 19.49 Br md 6.70 Dpth 2.90 Welded, 1 dk	**(B32A2ST) Tug**	**2 oil engines** reduction geared to sc. shafts driving 2 FP propellers Total Power: 474kW (644hp) 10.0kn Caterpillar 3406T 2 x 4 Stroke 6 Cy. 137 x 165 each-237kW (322bhp) Caterpillar Inc-USA
9153147 *YD4653* -	**TAMARIN III** *ex* QM Pioneer 888 *-2000* **PT Tamarin Samudra** - *Jakarta* *Indonesia*	**162** 95 103	Class: KI (NK)	**1996-04 Yong Choo Kui Shipyard Sdn Bhd — Sibu** Yd No: 2395 Loa 23.17 Br ex - Dght 2.388 Lbp 21.03 Br md 7.00 Dpth 2.90 Welded, 1 dk	**(B32A2ST) Tug**	**2 oil engines** reduction geared to sc. shafts driving 2 FP propellers Total Power: 794kW (1,080hp) 10.0kn Caterpillar 3412T 2 x Vee 4 Stroke 12 Cy. 137 x 152 each-397kW (540bhp) Caterpillar Inc-USA
9182887 *YD4654* -	**TAMARIN IV** *ex* QM Pioneer 8113 *-2000* **PT Tamarin Samudra** - *Jakarta* *Indonesia*	**156** 93 113	Class: KI (NK)	**1997-07 Super-Light Shipbuilding Contractor — Sibu** Yd No: 29 Loa 23.17 Br ex - Dght 2.388 Lbp 21.03 Br md 7.00 Dpth 2.90 Welded, 1 dk	**(B32A2ST) Tug**	**2 oil engines** reduction geared to sc. shafts driving 2 FP propellers Total Power: 794kW (1,080hp) 12.0kn Caterpillar 3412TA 2 x Vee 4 Stroke 12 Cy. 137 x 152 each-397kW (540bhp) Caterpillar Inc-USA
9171723 *YD4655* -	**TAMARIN V** *ex* Arena 3388 *-2000* **PT Sumatra Putra** - *Jakarta* *Indonesia*	**181** 50 129	Class: KI (NK)	**1997-06 C E Ling Shipbuilding Sdn Bhd — Miri** Yd No: 007 Loa 25.00 Br ex - Dght 2.712 Lbp 22.88 Br md 7.62 Dpth 3.30 Welded, 1 dk	**(B32A2ST) Tug**	**2 oil engines** reduction geared to sc. shafts driving 2 FP propellers Total Power: 988kW (1,344hp) 10.0kn Caterpillar 3412TA 2 x Vee 4 Stroke 12 Cy. 137 x 152 each-494kW (672bhp) Caterpillar Inc-USA
1004235 - -	**TAMARINDO** *ex* Alta *-2008* *ex* Talon *-2002* *ex* Ginnylou *-2002* **Tamarindo Yachting Ltd** -	**317** 95 -	✠ **100A1** SS 11/2006 Yacht ✠ **LMC**	**1987-07 Cant. Nav. Picchiotti SpA — Viareggio** Loa 37.70 Br ex 7.65 Dght 2.470 Lbp 32.50 Br md - Dpth 4.33 Welded, 1 dk	**(X11A2YP) Yacht**	**2 oil engines** geared to sc. shafts driving 2 FP propellers Total Power: 920kW (1,250hp) Caterpillar 3412TA 2 x Vee 4 Stroke 12 Cy. 137 x 152 each-460kW (625bhp) Caterpillar Inc-USA
9223980 *LADV6* -	**TAMARITA** **Ugland Shipping AS** Ugland Marine Services AS *Grimstad* *Norway (NIS)* MMSI: 257512000	**30,053** 18,207 52,292 T/cm 55.5	Class: NV (NK)	**2001-08 Tsuneishi Heavy Industries (Cebu) Inc — Balamban** Yd No: SC-025 Loa 190.00 Br ex - Dght 12.024 Lbp 182.00 Br md 32.26 Dpth 17.00 Welded, 1 dk	**(A21A2BC) Bulk Carrier** Double Bottom Entire Compartment Length Grain: 67,756; Bale: 65,601 Compartments: 5 Ho, ER 5 Ha: (20.4 x 18.4)4 (21.3 x 18.4)ER Cranes: 4x30t	**1 oil engine** driving 1 FP propeller Total Power: 7,800kW (10,605hp) 14.5kn B&W 6S50MC 1 x 2 Stroke 6 Cy. 500 x 1910 7800kW (10605bhp) Mitsui Engineering & Shipbuilding CLtd-Japan AuxGen: 3 x 440kW 450V 60Hz a.c Fuel: 159.0 (d.f.) (Heating Coils) 2100.0 (r.f.) 28.7pd
7303047 *IQJN* -	**TAMARIX** *ex* Tulipano *-1982* *ex* Mazarpesca Quarto *-1982* **Cooperativa Mazarpesca** - *Mazara del Vallo* *Italy* Official number: 58	*199* 90 -		**1973 Cant. Nav. M. Morini & C. — Ancona** Yd No: 134 Loa 32.72 Br ex 7.01 Dght - Lbp 25.00 Br md - Dpth 3.66 Welded, 1 dk	**(B11B2FV) Fishing Vessel**	**1 oil engine** driving 1 FP propeller Total Power: 441kW (600hp) Deutz RBV6M545 1 x 4 Stroke 6 Cy. 320 x 450 441kW (600bhp) Kloeckner Humboldt Deutz AG-West Germany
9016193 *JK5026* -	**TAMASHIMA MARU** **Seagate Corp** - *Kure, Hiroshima* *Japan* Official number: 131760	*187* - -		**1990-12 Kanagawa Zosen — Kobe** Yd No: 352 Loa 35.00 Br ex - Dght - Lbp 31.00 Br md 8.60 Dpth 3.60 Welded	**(B32A2ST) Tug**	**2 oil engines** driving 2 FP propellers Total Power: 2,280kW (3,100hp) Yanmar T260A-GN 2 x 4 Stroke 6 Cy. 260 x 330 each-1140kW (1550bhp) Yanmar Diesel Engine Co Ltd-Japan
8889127 *JH3341* -	**TAMASHIO** **Green Kaiji KK** - *Nagoya, Aichi* *Japan* Official number: 133255	*167* - -		**1995-05 Kanbara Zosen K.K. — Onomichi** Yd No: 471 Loa 31.52 Br ex - Dght 2.700 Lbp 27.00 Br md 8.80 Dpth 3.60 Welded, 1 dk	**(B32A2ST) Tug**	**2 oil engines** Geared Integral to driving 2 Z propellers Total Power: 1,766kW (2,402hp) 13.0kn Niigata 6L25HX 2 x 4 Stroke 6 Cy. 250 x 350 each-883kW (1201bhp) Niigata Engineering Co Ltd-Japan
8904939 *JL5809* -	**TAMATAKA MARU No. 82** **Shikoku Ferry KK** - *Takamatsu, Kagawa* *Japan* MMSI: 431000617 Official number: 131417	*855* - 350		**1989-07 Sanuki Shipbuilding & Iron Works Co Ltd — Mitoyo KG** Yd No: 1206 Loa 71.83 Br ex - Dght 2.700 Lbp 66.55 Br md 14.30 Dpth 3.70 Welded	**(A36A2PR) Passenger/Ro-Ro Ship (Vehicles)** Passengers: unberthed: 300 Cars: 55	**2 oil engines** driving 2 FP propellers Total Power: 1,912kW (2,600hp) 12.0kn Makita GNLH630 2 x 4 Stroke 6 Cy. 300 x 480 each-956kW (1300bhp) Makita Diesel Co Ltd-Japan
9009968 *JL5822* -	**TAMATAKA MARU No. 85** **Shikoku Ferry KK** - *Takamatsu, Kagawa* *Japan* MMSI: 431000293 Official number: 131480	*852* - 350		**1990-10 Sanuki Shipbuilding & Iron Works Co Ltd — Mitoyo KG** Yd No: 1217 Loa 71.83 (BB) Br ex - Dght 2.700 Lbp 66.55 Br md 14.30 Dpth 3.70 Welded	**(A36A2PR) Passenger/Ro-Ro Ship (Vehicles)** Passengers: unberthed: 300 Bow door/ramp (centre) Stern door/ramp (centre) Cars: 55	**2 oil engines** driving 2 FP propellers Total Power: 1,912kW (2,600hp) Makita GNLH630 2 x 4 Stroke 6 Cy. 300 x 480 each-956kW (1300bhp) Makita Diesel Co Ltd-Japan
9047702 *JL6077* -	**TAMATAKA MARU No. 87** **Shikoku Ferry KK** - *Takamatsu, Kagawa* *Japan* MMSI: 431000294 Official number: 132966	*853* - 350		**1992-09 Sanuki Shipbuilding & Iron Works Co Ltd — Mitoyo KG** Yd No: 1227 Loa 71.83 (BB) Br ex - Dght 2.700 Lbp 66.55 Br md 14.30 Dpth 3.70 Welded, 1 dk	**(A36A2PR) Passenger/Ro-Ro Ship (Vehicles)** Passengers: unberthed: 300 Cars: 55	**2 oil engines** sr geared to sc. shafts driving 2 FP propellers Total Power: 1,912kW (2,600hp) Makita GNLH630 2 x 4 Stroke 6 Cy. 300 x 480 each-956kW (1300bhp) Makita Corp-Japan
9134103 *FODY* -	**TAMATIA** **SCP Tamatia** - *Papeete* *France* MMSI: 227122900	**154** - 116	Class: BV	**1999-02 Shipbuilding (Fiji) Ltd. (SFL) — Suva** Yd No: 03 Loa - Br ex - Dght 2.500 Lbp 24.80 Br md 7.40 Dpth 3.96 Welded, 1 dk	**(B11B2FV) Fishing Vessel** Ins: 80	**1 oil engine** geared to sc. shaft driving 1 FP propeller Total Power: 332kW (451hp) 10.0kn Wartsila UD25L6M4 1 x 4 Stroke 6 Cy. 150 x 180 332kW (451bhp) Wartsila NSD France SA-France
7927178 *H02434* -	**TAMAYA 1** *ex* Michalis *-2007* *ex* Vemachem III *-2003* *ex* Irene VII *-1996* *ex* Tenryu Maru No. 5 *-1992* *ex* Kinu Maru *-1982* **Tamaya Shipping Offshore SAL** Societe Dakaroise de Transit (SODATRA) *Panama* *Panama* MMSI: 372509000 Official number: 3325707A	**922** 383 1,441 T/cm 5.4	Class: (NV) (NK)	**1980-02 Kitanihon Zosen K.K. — Hachinohe** Yd No: 162 Loa 63.91 (BB) Br ex 10.80 Dght 4.463 Lbp 58.43 Br md 10.41 Dpth 5.01 Welded, 1 dk	**(A13B2TP) Products Tanker** Liq: 1,458; Liq (Oil): 1,458 Cargo Heating Coils Compartments: 8 Ta, ER 2 Cargo Pump (s): 2x400m³/hr Manifold: Bow/CM: 26m	**1 oil engine** driving 1 FP propeller Total Power: 1,618kW (2,200hp) 11.0kn Akasaka DM38AR 1 x 4 Stroke 6 Cy. 380 x 600 1618kW (2200bhp) Akasaka Tekkosho KK (Akasaka DieselLtd)-Japan AuxGen: 2 x 256kW 110/220V 60Hz a.c Fuel: 32.5 (d.f.) (Part Heating Coils) 130.0 (r.f.)
6711625 *HIRD264* -	**TAMAYO** *ex* Howard H *-2004* *ex* Gulf King *-1969* **Remolcadores Dominicanos SA** - *Santo Domingo* *Dominican Rep.* MMSI: 327770014 Official number: RM-T9-074SDG	*190* 129 -	Class: (AB)	**1967 Southern SB. Corp. — Slidell, La** Yd No: 71 Loa 38.10 Br ex - Dght 4.582 Lbp 36.23 Br md 9.76 Dpth 5.24 Welded, 1 dk	**(B32A2ST) Tug**	**2 oil engines** reverse reduction geared to sc. shafts driving 2 FP propellers Total Power: 2,354kW (3,200hp) Fairbanks, Morse 8-38D8-1/8 2 x 2 Stroke 8 Cy. 207 x 254 each-1177kW (1600bhp) Fairbanks Morse & Co.-New Orleans, La AuxGen: 2 x 60kW a.c Fuel: 456.0
9142241 *JL6464* -	**TAMAYOSHI MARU No. 5** **YK Tamai Kaiun** - *Imabari, Ehime* *Japan* Official number: 135535	*199* - 550		**1996-09 Sanuki Shipbuilding & Iron Works Co Ltd — Mitoyo KG** Yd No: 1267 Loa 49.03 (BB) Br ex - Dght 3.150 Lbp 44.00 Br md 8.20 Dpth 3.40 Welded, 1 dk	**(A13B2TP) Products Tanker** Liq: 600; Liq (Oil): 600 Compartments: 8 Ta, ER	**1 oil engine** geared to sc. shaft driving 1 FP propeller Total Power: 625kW (850hp) Hanshin 6LC26G 1 x 4 Stroke 6 Cy. 260 x 440 625kW (850bhp) The Hanshin Diesel Works Ltd-Japan
9011210 *JK4909* -	**TAMAYOSHI MARU No. 18** **Wako Kensetsu KK** - *Takehara, Hiroshima* *Japan* Official number: 132475	*494* - 1,600		**1990-11 Matsuura Tekko Zosen K.K. — Osakikamijima** Yd No: 361 Loa 66.19 Br ex 13.80 Dght 4.780 Lbp 60.00 Br md 13.20 Dpth 7.80 Welded, 1 dk	**(A24D2BA) Aggregates Carrier** Grain: 925 Compartments: 1 Ho, ER 1 Ha: ER	**1 oil engine** reverse geared to sc. shaft driving 1 FP propeller Total Power: 736kW (1,001hp) Hanshin 6EL32G 1 x 4 Stroke 6 Cy. 320 x 640 736kW (1001bhp) The Hanshin Diesel Works Ltd-Japan Thrusters: 1 Thwart. CP thruster (f)

IMO / Call sign	Name / Owner	Tonnage	Class	Build	Type	Machinery
9033531 - - -	**TAMAYOSHI MARU No. 21** - - South Korea	*168* - -		**1992-07 Shin Yamamoto Shipbuilding & Engineering Co Ltd — Kochi KC** Yd No: 339 Loa 31.00 Br ex - Dght - Lbp - Br md 10.00 Dpth 7.00 Welded, 1 dk	**(B32B2SP) Pusher Tug**	**1 oil engine** driving 1 FP propeller Total Power: 1,471kW (2,000hp) Niigata 6M38HFT 1 x 4 Stroke 6 Cy. 380 x 700 1471kW (2000bhp) Niigata Engineering Co Ltd-Japan
9343405 *3FXV6* -	**TAMBA** **Rafflesia Shipholding SA** NYK Shipmanagement Pte Ltd SatCom: Inmarsat Mini-M 764893229 *Panama* Panama MMSI: 353424000 Official number: 4018209	**159,927** 97,999 302,107 T/cm 182.5	Class: NK	**2009-01 IHI Marine United Inc — Kure HS** Yd No: 3222 Loa 333.00 (BB) Br ex 60.04 Dght 20.635 Lbp 324.00 Br md 60.00 Dpth 29.00 Welded, 1 dk	**(A13A2TV) Crude Oil Tanker** Double Hull (13F) Liq: 342,771; Liq (Oil): 342,771 Cargo Heating Coils Compartments: 10 Wing Ta, 5 Ta, 2 Wing Slop Ta, ER 4 Cargo Pump (s): 3x5500m³/hr, 1x2500m³/hr Manifold: Bow/CM: 163.6m	**1 oil engine** driving 1 FP propeller Total Power: 27,160kW (36,927hp) 15.7kn Wartsila 7RT-flex84T 1 x 2 Stroke 7 Cy. 840 x 3150 27160kW (36927bhp) Diesel United Ltd.-Aioi AuxGen: 3 x 1100kW a.c Fuel: 463.0 (d.f.) 6900.0 (r.f.)
9413729 *9WGU6* -	**TAMBAH MAJU** **Neopetro Venture Sdn Bhd** Neopetro Sdn Bhd *Kuching* Malaysia MMSI: 533000514 Official number: 330795	**495** 146 550	Class: BV	**2007-01 Eastern Marine Shipbuilding Sdn Bhd — Sibu** Yd No: 67 Loa 47.00 Br ex - Dght 2.480 Lbp 43.21 Br md 11.00 Dpth 3.20 Welded, 1 dk	**(A35D2RL) Landing Craft** Bow ramp (centre)	**2 oil engines** reduction geared to sc. shafts driving 2 FP propellers Total Power: 882kW (1,200hp) 10.0kn Cummins KTA-19-M3 2 x 4 Stroke 6 Cy. 159 x 159 each-441kW (600bhp) Cummins Engine Co Inc-USA AuxGen: 2 x 80kW a.c
7321879 *VL3375* -	**TAMBAI II** **Polaris Marine Pty Ltd** *Brisbane, Qld* Australia Official number: 852341	*106* 32 80		**1973 North Queensland Engineers & Agents Pty Ltd — Cairns QLD** Yd No: 47 Loa 27.44 Br ex 6.33 Dght 1.501 Lbp 23.93 Br md 6.10 Dpth 2.14 Welded, 1 dk	**(A35D2RL) Landing Craft** Bow door/ramp	**2 oil engines** reduction geared to sc. shafts driving 2 FP propellers Total Power: 294kW (400hp) 9.0kn Caterpillar D333TA 2 x 4 Stroke 6 Cy. 114 x 140 each-147kW (200bhp) Caterpillar Tractor Co-USA Fuel: 20.5 (d.f.) 1.5pd
9463762 *YDA6421* -	**TAMBAT** **PT Maritim Barito Perkasa** *Banjarmasin* Indonesia MMSI: 525002009 Official number: 3181 / IIA	**249** 74 171	Class: AB	**2007-08 PT Perkasa Melati — Batam** Yd No: PM017 Loa 29.50 Br ex - Dght 3.500 Lbp 26.50 Br md 9.00 Dpth 4.16 Welded, 1 dk	**(B32A2ST) Tug**	**2 oil engines** reduction geared to sc. shafts driving 2 Propellers Total Power: 2,080kW (2,828hp) Mitsubishi S12R-MPTK 2 x Vee 4 Stroke 12 Cy. 170 x 180 each-1040kW (1414bhp) Mitsubishi Heavy Industries Ltd-Japan AuxGen: 2 x 80kW a.c Fuel: 69.0 (r.f.)
7015080 *CB2202* -	**TAMBO** *ex* Epesa 3 *-2011* *ex* Tumbes 9 *-2011* *ex* PA 27 *-1976* **Corpesca SA** Chile Official number: 2354	*310* 140 -	Class: (GL)	**1969 Ast. Picsa S.A. — Callao** Yd No: 305 L reg 35.09 Br ex 8.03 Dght - Lbp - Br md 8.01 Dpth 3.84 Welded, 1 dk	**(B11B2FV) Fishing Vessel**	**1 oil engine** reverse reduction geared to sc. shaft driving 1 FP propeller Total Power: 530kW (721hp) 12.0kn MAN G6V235/330ATL 1 x 4 Stroke 6 Cy. 235 x 330 530kW (721bhp) Maschinenbau Augsburg Nuernberg (MAN)-Augsburg
6710267 - -	**TAMBO 1** *ex* Tasa 24 *-1976* **Pesquera Arantas SCR Ltda** - *Callao* Peru Official number: CE-0065-PM	*150* - -	Class: (AB)	**1966 Promecan Ingenieros S.A. — Callao** Yd No: 68 Loa - Br ex 6.74 Dght - Lbp 21.49 Br md 6.71 Dpth 3.51 Welded, 1 dk	**(B11A2FT) Trawler** Compartments: 1 Ho, ER 1 Ha: (1.9 x 3.3)	**1 oil engine** driving 1 CP propeller Total Power: 221kW (300hp) Normo Z4 1 x 2 Stroke 4 Cy. 300 x 360 221kW (300bhp) AS Bergens Mek Verksteder-Norway Fuel: 12.0 (d.f.)
6615170 - -	**TAMBO 3** *ex* Tasa 20 *-1976* - -	*105* - -	Class: (AB)	**1965 Promecan Ingenieros S.A. — Callao** Yd No: 39 Loa - Br ex - Dght - Lbp 21.49 Br md 6.71 Dpth 3.51 Welded, 1 dk	**(B11A2FT) Trawler** Compartments: 1 Ho, ER 1 Ha: (1.9 x 3.3)	**1 oil engine** driving 1 CP propeller Total Power: 221kW (300hp) Normo Z4 1 x 2 Stroke 4 Cy. 300 x 360 221kW (300bhp) AS Bergens Mek Verksteder-Norway Fuel: 12.0 (d.f.)
6921684 - -	**TAMBO 7** *ex* Palmira *-1976* - -	*105* - -	Class: (AB)	**1967 Promecan Ingenieros S.A. — Callao** Yd No: 85 Loa - Br ex 6.74 Dght - Lbp 21.47 Br md 6.71 Dpth 3.51 Welded	**(B11A2FT) Trawler** Compartments: 1 Ho, ER 1 Ha: (3.3 x 1.9)	**1 oil engine** driving 1 FP propeller Total Power: 386kW (525hp) G.M. (Detroit Diesel) 12V-71-N 1 x Vee 2 Stroke 12 Cy. 108 x 127 386kW (525bhp) General Motors Corp-USA
6608830 - -	**TAMBO 8** *ex* Rosita 9 *-1979* - -	*120* - -	Class: (LR) ✠ Classed LR until 3/70	**1966-03 Fabricaciones Metallicas E.P.S. (FABRIMET) — Callao** Yd No: 315 Loa 25.20 Br ex 7.14 Dght 2.998 Lbp 21.49 Br md 7.01 Dpth 3.46 Welded	**(B11B2FV) Fishing Vessel**	**1 oil engine** reverse reduction geared to sc. shaft driving 1 FP propeller Total Power: 386kW (525hp) G.M. (Detroit Diesel) 12V-71-N 1 x Vee 2 Stroke 12 Cy. 108 x 127 386kW (525bhp) General Motors Corp-USA
6615247 - -	**TAMBO 9** *ex* Rosita 10 *-1979* **Pesquera Tintorera SR Ltda** *Ilo* Peru Official number: IO-000956-PM	*164* 62 -	Class: (LR) ✠ Classed LR until 8/70	**1966-08 Fabricaciones Metallicas E.P.S. (FABRIMET) — Callao** Yd No: 316 Loa 25.20 Br ex 7.14 Dght 2.693 Lbp 21.49 Br md 7.01 Dpth 3.46 Welded, 1 dk	**(B11B2FV) Fishing Vessel**	**1 oil engine** reverse reduction geared to sc. shaft driving 1 FP propeller Total Power: 386kW (525hp) G.M. (Detroit Diesel) 12V-71-N 1 x Vee 2 Stroke 12 Cy. 108 x 127 386kW (525bhp) General Motors Corp-USA
9064970 - -	**TAMBOR** **Navieras Tambor SA** Simon Barcelo Costa Rica	*250* - 100	Class: (AB)	**1992-10 Atlantic Marine — Jacksonville, Fl** Yd No: 223 Loa 39.62 Br ex - Dght - Lbp - Br md 13.72 Dpth - Welded	**(A36A2PR) Passenger/Ro-Ro Ship (Vehicles)**	**2 oil engines** reduction geared to sc. shafts driving 2 FP propellers Total Power: 988kW (1,344hp) Caterpillar 3412TA 2 x Vee 4 Stroke 12 Cy. 137 x 152 each-494kW (672bhp) Caterpillar Inc-USA
9407732 - -	**TAMBOR II** *launched as* Paralos *-2006* **Navieras Tambor SA** - *Puntarenas* Costa Rica	**998** 642 300		**2006-12 Panagiotakis Bros. — Salamina** Loa 82.40 Br ex - Dght 2.800 Lbp - Br md 17.50 Dpth 3.90 Welded, 1 dk	**(A36A2PR) Passenger/Ro-Ro Ship (Vehicles)** Passengers: unberthed: 900 Bow door (f) Stern door (a) Cars: 160	**2 oil engines** driving 2 Propellers 12.0kn
9620839 - -	**TAMBOR III** **Marina Punta Piedra Amarilla SA** Naviera Tambor SA *Puntarenas* Costa Rica	**1,337** 455 1,067		**2011-08 Construcciones A Maggiolo SA — Callao** Yd No: 30 Loa 82.40 Br ex - Dght 2.800 Lbp 81.20 Br md 17.56 Dpth 3.90 Welded, 1 dk	**(A36A2PR) Passenger/Ro-Ro Ship (Vehicles)** Passengers: unberthed: 850 Bow ramp (centre) Stern ramp (centre) Cars: 160	**4 oil engines** reduction geared to sc. shafts driving 4 Z propellers Total Power: 1,764kW (2,400hp) 12.0kn Caterpillar 4 x 4 Stroke each-441kW (600bhp) Caterpillar Inc-USA
9251896 *A8ED6* -	**TAMBOURIN** **Rederi AB Vastergarn & Dionysos Maritime Co Ltd** Laurin Maritime (America) Inc *Monrovia* Liberia MMSI: 636012227 Official number: 12227	**26,914** 14,288 46,764 T/cm 52.8	Class: NV	**2004-11 Brodotrogir dd - Shipyard Trogir — Trogir** Yd No: 307 Loa 182.74 (BB) Br ex 32.21 Dght 12.180 Lbp 176.75 Br md 32.18 Dpth 17.20 Welded, 1 dk	**(A12B2TR) Chemical/Products Tanker** Double Hull (13F) Liq: 51,910; Liq (Oil): 53,900 Compartments: 14 Wing Ta, 2 Wing Slop Ta, ER 16 Cargo Pump (s): 6x400m³/hr, 10x250m³/hr Manifold: Bow/CM: 91.5m	**2 oil engines** reduction geared to sc. shaft driving 1 CP propeller Total Power: 7,700kW (10,468hp) 14.5kn MaK 8M32C 2 x 4 Stroke 8 Cy. 320 x 480 each-3850kW (5234bhp) Caterpillar Motoren GmbH & Co. KG-Germany AuxGen: 2 x a.c Fuel: 90.0 (d.f.) 1350.0 (r.f.)
8225723 *UIMH* -	**TAMBOV** *ex* Guadalajara *-2009* *ex* Tambov *-2004* **Daltransflot Co Ltd** Murmantransflot Co Ltd *Vladivostok* Russia MMSI: 273512400	**12,527** 4,895 12,243	Class: RS	**1982-12 VEB Mathias-Thesen-Werft — Wismar** Yd No: 221 Converted From: Fish Carrier-2009 Loa 152.69 Br ex 22.26 Dght 9.000 Lbp 142.02 Br md 22.23 Dpth 13.62 Welded, 1 dk, 2nd & 3rd dk in holds only	**(A34A2GR) Refrigerated Cargo Ship** Ins: 13,326 Compartments: 4 Ho, ER, 8 Tw Dk 4 Ha: 4 (6.0 x 3.9)ER Derricks: 2x10t,7x5t Ice Capable	**1 oil engine** driving 1 FP propeller Total Power: 6,620kW (9,001hp) 13.5kn MAN K9Z60/105E 1 x 2 Stroke 9 Cy. 600 x 1050 6620kW (9001bhp) VEB Maschinenbau Halberstadt-Halberstadt Fuel: 5606.0 (r.f.)
8428052 *DZWY* -	**TAMBULI** **Majestic Shipping Corp** *Manila* Philippines Official number: BAT5000086	*244* 123 200		**1977 at Manila** Loa - Br ex 9.17 Dght - Lbp 51.85 Br md 9.16 Dpth 2.32 Welded, 1 dk	**(A35D2RL) Landing Craft**	**1 oil engine** driving 1 FP propeller Total Power: 184kW (250hp) Cummins 1 x 4 Stroke 184kW (250bhp) Cummins Engine Co Inc-USA

IMO / Call sign	Name / Owner	Tonnage	Class	Build	Type	Machinery
5367673 *JXBO* -	**TAMBUR** *ex* Traust *-1975* **Boa Shipping AS** Boa Offshore AS *Trondheim* *Norway* MMSI: 258198000	**142** 56 -	Class: (NV)	**1958 Ankerlokken Slipper & Mek Verksted — Floro** Yd No: 19 Loa 25.51 Br ex 7.19 Dght 3.598 Lbp 22.05 Br md 7.14 Dpth 4.07 Welded, 1 dk	**(B32A2ST) Tug** Compartments: 1 Ho, ER Derricks: 1x3t; Winches: 1 Ice Capable	**1 oil engine** driving 1 CP propeller Total Power: 588kW (799hp) Wichmann 8ACA 1 x 2 Stroke 8 Cy. 280 x 420 588kW (799bhp) Wichmann Motorfabrikk AS-Norway AuxGen: 2 x 18kW 230V 50Hz a.c
1004247 - -	**TAMER II** - **Tamer II** - *Jeddah* *Saudi Arabia*	**231** - -	Class: LR ✠**100A1** SS 05/2011 Yacht ***LMC**	**1986-10 Jachtwerf Jongert B.V. — Medemblik** Loa 33.15 Br ex 7.70 Dght 3.800 Lbp 26.80 Br md - Dpth 5.70 Welded, 1 dk	**(X11A2YS) Yacht (Sailing)**	**1 oil engine** geared to sc. shaft driving 1 FP propeller Total Power: 478kW (650hp) MWM TBD234V12 1 x Vee 4 Stroke 12 Cy. 128 x 140 478kW (650bhp) MTU Friedrichshafen GmbH-Friedrichshafen
8113281 *TCDN* -	**TAMER KIRAN** **Kirden Denizcilik ve Ticaret AS** Pasifik Gemi Isletmeciligi ve Ticaret AS *Istanbul* *Turkey* MMSI: 271000032 Official number: 5127	**3,996** 2,575 6,468	Class: BV (AB)	**1983-06 Atilim Gemi Insaat Sanayii ve Ticaret A.S. — Istanbul** Yd No: 4 Loa 107.65 (BB) Br ex 16.51 Dght 6.927 Lbp 99.35 Br md 15.51 Dpth 8.79 Welded, 1 dk	**(A31A2GX) General Cargo Ship** Grain: 8,835; Bale: 8,013 Compartments: 3 Ho, ER 3 Ha: ER Derricks: 2x10t,2x5t; Winches: 4	**1 oil engine** sr geared to sc. shaft driving 1 FP propeller Total Power: 2,648kW (3,600hp) 13.5kn MaK 9M453AK 1 x 4 Stroke 9 Cy. 320 x 420 2648kW (3600bhp) Krupp MaK Maschinenbau GmbH-Kiel AuxGen: 2 x 188kW a.c, 1 x 80kW a.c
9218648 *LAQU5* -	**TAMERLANE** **Wilhelmsen Lines Shipowning AS** Wilhelmsen Ship Management (Norway) AS SatCom: Inmarsat C 425775810 *Tonsberg* *Norway (NIS)* MMSI: 257758000	**67,140** 23,674 38,500 T/cm 69.5	Class: NV	**2001-02 Daewoo Shipbuilding & Marine Engineering Co Ltd — Geoje** Yd No: 4430 Loa 240.60 (BB) Br ex - Dght 11.750 Lbp 226.00 Br md 32.26 Dpth 15.60 Welded	**(A35B2RV) Vehicles Carrier** Quarter stern door/ramp (s. a.) Len: 44.50 Wid: 12.00 Swl: 320 Cars: 5,496 TEU 2340	**1 oil engine** driving 1 FP propeller Total Power: 20,940kW (28,470hp) 20.0kn B&W 8L70MC 1 x 2 Stroke 8 Cy. 700 x 2268 20940kW (28470bhp) HSD Engine Co Ltd-South Korea Thrusters: 1 Tunnel thruster (f); 1 Tunnel thruster (a)
9191307 *LAOL5* -	**TAMESIS** **Wilhelmsen Lines Shipowning AS** Wilhelmsen Ship Management (Norway) AS SatCom: Inmarsat C 425756510 *Tonsberg* *Norway (NIS)* MMSI: 257565000	**67,140** 23,674 39,516 T/cm 69.5	Class: NV	**2000-04 Daewoo Heavy Industries Ltd — Geoje** Yd No: 4423 Loa 240.60 (BB) Br ex 32.29 Dght 11.750 Lbp 226.54 Br md 32.26 Dpth 15.60 Welded, 8 dks, incl. 4 hoistable	**(A35B2RV) Vehicles Carrier** Quarter stern door/ramp (s) Len: 44.50 Wid: 12.00 Swl: 320 Cars: 5,496 Grain: 125,620 TEU 2392	**1 oil engine** driving 1 FP propeller Total Power: 20,941kW (28,471hp) 20.0kn B&W 8L70MC 1 x 2 Stroke 8 Cy. 700 x 2268 20941kW (28471bhp) HSD Engine Co Ltd-South Korea AuxGen: 3 x 1580kW 440V 60Hz a.c, 2 x 1216kW 440V 60Hz a.c Thrusters: 1 Thwart. CP thruster (f); 1 Tunnel thruster (a) Fuel: 311.6 (d.f.) (Heating Coils) 4796.2 (r.f.) 82.0pd
8206674 *CNFF* -	**TAMESNA** **Omnium Marocaine de Peche** SatCom: Inmarsat C 424237910 *Agadir* *Morocco*	*323* 143 405	Class: BV	**1984-01 Construcciones Navales Santodomingo SA — Vigo** Yd No: 487 Loa 38.31 Br ex 8.59 Dght 4.050 Lbp 34.78 Br md 8.50 Dpth 6.15 Welded, 2 dks	**(B11A2FS) Stern Trawler** Ins: 402	**1 oil engine** with clutches, flexible couplings & sr geared to sc. shaft driving 1 FP propeller Total Power: 853kW (1,160hp) 12.3kn Deutz SBA8M528 1 x 4 Stroke 8 Cy. 220 x 280 853kW (1160bhp) Hijos de J Barreras SA-Spain AuxGen: 2 x 140kW 380V 50Hz a.c
9120425 *7TZK* -	**TAMGOUT** *ex* Hyun Yang *-2001* **Nolis-Spa** - *Alger* *Algeria* MMSI: 605266120	**3,116** 1,753 4,999	Class: BV (KR)	**1995-01 Banguhjin Engineering & Shipbuilding Co Ltd — Ulsan** Yd No: 96 Loa 101.00 Br ex - Dght 6.274 Lbp 93.30 Br md 15.40 Dpth 7.60 Welded, 1 dk	**(A12B2TR) Chemical/Products Tanker** Liq: 6,053; Liq (Oil): 6,053 Compartments: 10 Ta, ER	**1 oil engine** driving 1 FP propeller Total Power: 2,427kW (3,300hp) 13.0kn Akasaka A41 1 x 4 Stroke 6 Cy. 410 x 800 2427kW (3300bhp) Hyundai Heavy Industries Co Ltd-South Korea AuxGen: 3 x 720kW 200/445V 60Hz a.c Fuel: 207.5 (r.f.)
9063823 *6LTV* -	**TAMGU 5** *ex* Kyung Buk No. 885 *-2001* **Government of The Republic of South Korea (National Fisheries Research & Development Agency, East Sea Fisheries Supervision Offfice)** - *Pohang* *South Korea* Official number: 9512041-6471104	**262** - 175	Class: (KR)	**1993-08 Chungmu Shipbuilding Co Inc — Tongyeong** Yd No: 234 Loa 45.50 Br ex - Dght 3.350 Lbp 39.00 Br md 8.00 Dpth 3.50 Welded, 1 dk	**(B12D2FR) Fishery Research Vessel** Ins: 57	**1 oil engine** geared to sc. shaft driving 1 FP propeller Total Power: 1,275kW (1,733hp) 12.3kn Caterpillar 3516TA 1 x Vee 4 Stroke 16 Cy. 170 x 190 1275kW (1733bhp) Caterpillar Inc-USA AuxGen: 2 x 300kW 240V a.c
9435882 *DSPX2* -	**TAMGU 20** **Government of The Republic of South Korea (National Fisheries Research & Development Agency, East Sea Fisheries Supervision Offfice)** - *Busan* *South Korea* MMSI: 441476000 Official number: 0802002-6267103	**885** 367 466	Class: KR	**2008-05 Ilheung Shipbuilding & Engineering Co Ltd — Mokpo** Yd No: 06-137 Loa 63.26 Br ex - Dght 4.516 Lbp 56.50 Br md 11.80 Dpth 7.00 Welded, 1 dk	**(B31A2SR) Research Survey Vessel**	**2 oil engines** reduction geared to sc. shafts driving 2 FP propellers Total Power: 1,500kW (2,040hp) 15.2kn Hyundai Himsen 6H21/32P 2 x 4 Stroke 6 Cy. 210 x 320 each-750kW (1020bhp) Hyundai Heavy Industries Co Ltd-South Korea AuxGen: 3 x 80kW 450V a.c Fuel: 251.0 (d.f.)
9065120 *6LTA* -	**TAMGU NO. 3** *ex* Busan No. 881 *-2009* **Government of The Republic of South Korea (National Fisheries Research & Development Agency, East Sea Fisheries Supervision Offfice)** - SatCom: Inmarsat A 1660613 *Gijang* *South Korea* MMSI: 440134000 Official number: KS8773-A1458	**369** 240 275	Class: (KR)	**1992-07 Daesin Shipbuilding Co Ltd — Gunsan** Loa 51.54 (BB) Br ex - Dght 3.981 Lbp 44.00 Br md 9.40 Dpth 4.21 Welded, 1 dk	**(B12D2FR) Fishery Research Vessel**	**1 oil engine** sr geared to sc. shaft driving 1 CP propeller Total Power: 1,177kW (1,600hp) 14.8kn Wartsila 8R22 1 x 4 Stroke 8 Cy. 220 x 240 1177kW (1600bhp) Ssangyong Heavy Industries Co Ltd-South Korea
9126821 *6NLI* -	**TAMGU NO. 8** *ex* Inchon No. 888 *-2009* **Government of The Republic of South Korea (West Sea Fisheries Institute, National Fisheries Research & Development Institute)** - SatCom: Inmarsat C 444068112 *Incheon* *South Korea* MMSI: 440063000 Official number: 9510003-6231104	**280** - -		**1995-10 Chungmu Shipbuilding Co Inc — Tongyeong** Yd No: 243 Loa 47.20 Br ex - Dght 3.000 Lbp 40.00 Br md 8.60 Dpth 3.70 Welded, 1 dk	**(B12D2FR) Fishery Research Vessel**	**1 oil engine** driving 1 FP propeller Total Power: 1,300kW (1,767hp) Wartsila 8R22 1 x 4 Stroke 8 Cy. 220 x 240 1300kW (1767bhp) Ssangyong Heavy Industries Co Ltd-South Korea
9131175 *DSE08* -	**TAMHAE II** **Korea Institute of Geoscience & Mineral Resources** - SatCom: Inmarsat B 344026410 *Jinhae* *South Korea* MMSI: 440238000 Official number: MSR-976518	**2,091** 625 1,099	Class: KR	**1996-12 Ulstein Verft AS — Ulsteinvik** Yd No: 246 Loa 64.40 (BB) Br ex - Dght 5.262 Lbp 54.80 Br md 15.00 Dpth 6.50 Welded, 1 dk	**(B31A2SR) Research Survey Vessel**	**2 oil engines** geared to sc. shafts driving 2 FP propellers Total Power: 3,236kW (4,400hp) 13.5kn Normo KRM-8 2 x 4 Stroke 8 Cy. 250 x 300 each-1618kW (2200bhp) Ulstein Bergen AS-Norway AuxGen: 2 x 1280kW 440/220V 60Hz a.c, 1 x 435kW 440/220V 60Hz a.c Thrusters: 1 Thwart. FP thruster (f); 1 Thwart. FP thruster (a)
8855815 - -	**TAMI DARLENE** - -	*137* 41 -		**1989 at Coden, Al** Loa - Br ex - Dght - Lbp 21.82 Br md 6.64 Dpth 3.35 Welded, 1 dk	**(B11B2FV) Fishing Vessel**	**1 oil engine** driving 1 FP propeller
8013895 *CB2678* -	**TAMI S** *ex* Miho Maru No. 11 *-1992* *ex* Daikoku Maru *-1985* **Pesquera Omega Ltd** - *Valparaiso* *Chile* MMSI: 725000326 Official number: 2770	**478** 151 -	Class: (BV)	**1980-06 KK Kanasashi Zosen — Shizuoka SZ** Yd No: 2048 Loa 48.90 Br ex - Dght 3.630 Lbp 42.96 Br md 8.50 Dpth 3.64 Bonded, 1 dk	**(B11B2FV) Fishing Vessel** Hull Material: Reinforced Plastic	**1 oil engine** driving 1 FP propeller Total Power: 956kW (1,300hp) Akasaka DM28R 1 x 4 Stroke 6 Cy. 280 x 460 956kW (1300bhp) Akasaka Tekkosho KK (Akasaka DieselLtd)-Japan

8325080 *XCLS8* -	**TAMIAHUA** *ex* Wahoo 4 *-2009* *ex* Smit Noorwegen *-1984* **Marinoil Servicios Maritimos SA de CV** *Tampico* *Mexico* MMSI: 345010059	**160** 48 63	Class: GL (BV)	**1984-06 Scheepswerf Bijlholt B.V. — Foxhol** Yd No: 618 Loa 25.81 Br ex 8.06 Dght 2.701 Lbp 23.50 Br md 7.80 Dpth 3.71 Welded, 1 dk	**(B32A2ST) Tug**	**2 oil engines** with flexible couplings & sr gearedto sc. shafts driving 2 CP propellers Total Power: 1,472kW (2,002hp) 12.3kn Kromhout 6FHD240 2 x 4 Stroke 6 Cy. 240 x 260 each-736kW (1001bhp) Stork Werkspoor Diesel BV-Netherlands AuxGen: 2 x 35kW 380V 50Hz a.c Fuel: 57.0 (d.f.) 7.0pd
9422237 *3EVA5* -	**TAMIAT NAVIGATOR** **Pacific Transport Trading SA** Iino Marine Service Co Ltd *Panama* *Panama* MMSI: 356150000 Official number: 4183910	**29,151** 12,241 46,625 T/cm 52.0	Class: AB	**2010-08 Hyundai Mipo Dockyard Co Ltd — Ulsan** Yd No: 2105 Loa 183.31 (BB) Br ex 32.24 Dght 12.318 Lbp 174.00 Br md 32.00 Dpth 18.80 Welded, 1 dk	**(A12B2TR) Chemical/Products Tanker** Double Hull (13F) Liq: 53,362; Liq (Oil): 53,362 Part Cargo Heating Coils Compartments: 12 Wing Ta, 2 Wing Slop Ta, 1 Slop Ta, ER 12 Cargo Pump (s): 12x600m³/hr Manifold: Bow/CM: 91.2m	**1 oil engine** driving 1 FP propeller Total Power: 9,480kW (12,889hp) 14.8kn MAN-B&W 6S50MC-C 1 x 2 Stroke 6 Cy. 500 x 2000 9480kW (12889bhp) Hyundai Heavy Industries Co Ltd-South Korea AuxGen: 3 x 1030kW a.c Fuel: 209.0 (d.f.) 1340.0 (r.f.)
8221416 *ATML* -	**TAMIL ANNA** **Poompuhar Shipping Corp Ltd** - SatCom: Inmarsat C 441951610 *Chennai* *India* MMSI: 419416000 Official number: 2141	**27,986** 11,934 39,985 T/cm 57.3	Class: IR (LR) ✠ Classed LR until 1/9/02	**1985-08 Hitachi Zosen Corp — Maizuru KY** Yd No: 4730 Loa 210.00 (BB) Br ex 29.95 Dght 9.551 Lbp 200.00 Br md 29.90 Dpth 14.80 Welded, 1 dk	**(A21A2BC) Bulk Carrier** Grain: 54,719 Compartments: 6 Ho, ER 6 Ha: 6 (17.0 x 15.6)ER Cranes: 6x25t	**1 oil engine** driving 1 FP propeller Total Power: 8,606kW (11,701hp) 16.0kn B&W 6L60MC 1 x 2 Stroke 6 Cy. 600 x 1944 8606kW (11701bhp) Hitachi Zosen Corp-Japan AuxGen: 4 x 780kW 450V 60Hz a.c Boilers: e (ex.g.) 12.0kgf/cm² (11.8bar), AuxB (o.f.) 7.0kgf/cm² (6.9bar) Fuel: 178.5 (d.f.) 1523.5 (r.f.)
8221430 *VWMG* -	**TAMIL KAMARAJ** **Poompuhar Shipping Corp Ltd** - SatCom: Inmarsat C 441951410 *Chennai* *India* MMSI: 419418000 Official number: 2208	**27,997** 11,962 39,990 T/cm 57.3	Class: IR (LR) ✠ Classed LR until 3/10/02	**1987-01 Hitachi Zosen Corp — Maizuru KY** Yd No: 4732 Loa 210.00 (BB) Br ex 29.95 Dght 9.557 Lbp 200.00 Br md 29.90 Dpth 14.80 Welded, 1 dk	**(A21A2BC) Bulk Carrier** Grain: 54,719 Compartments: 6 Ho, ER 6 Ha: 6 (17.0 x 15.6)ER Cranes: 6x25t	**1 oil engine** driving 1 FP propeller Total Power: 8,605kW (11,699hp) 14.7kn B&W 6L60MC 1 x 2 Stroke 6 Cy. 600 x 1944 8605kW (11699bhp) Hitachi Zosen Corp-Japan AuxGen: 4 x 780kW 450V 60Hz a.c Boilers: e (ex.g.) 12.0kgf/cm² (11.8bar), AuxB (o.f.) 7.0kgf/cm² (6.9bar) Fuel: 178.5 (d.f.) 1523.5 (r.f.)
9107631 *VVMA* -	**TAMIL NADU** **The Shipping Corporation of India Ltd (SCI)** *Mumbai* *India* MMSI: 419446000 Official number: 2757	**28,029** 16,154 45,792 T/cm 52.2	Class: BV IR	**2000-09 Hindustan Shipyard Ltd — Visakhapatnam** Yd No: 1135 Loa 193.50 (BB) Br ex 30.45 Dght 11.822 Lbp 185.96 Br md 30.40 Dpth 16.40 Welded, 1 dk	**(A21A2BC) Bulk Carrier** Grain: 54,671 Compartments: 5 Ho, ER 5 Ha: (19.2 x 12.8)4 (19.2 x 14.4)ER Cranes: 5x25t	**1 oil engine** driving 1 FP propeller Total Power: 8,030kW (10,918hp) 14.0kn Sulzer 5RTA62U 1 x 2 Stroke 5 Cy. 620 x 2150 8030kW (10918bhp) H Cegielski Poznan SA-Poland AuxGen: 3 x 650kW 390V 50Hz a.c Fuel: 270.0 (d.f.) (Heating Coils) 2073.0 (r.f.) 28.0pd
8221428 *VVKG* -	**TAMIL PERIYAR** **Poompuhar Shipping Corp Ltd** - SatCom: Inmarsat C 441951510 *Chennai* *India* MMSI: 419417000 Official number: 2167	**27,997** 11,962 39,990 T/cm 57.3	Class: IR (LR) ✠ Classed LR until 1/9/02	**1986-09 Hitachi Zosen Corp — Maizuru KY** Yd No: 4731 Loa 210.00 (BB) Br ex 29.95 Dght 9.559 Lbp 200.00 Br md 29.90 Dpth 14.80 Welded, 1 dk	**(A21A2BC) Bulk Carrier** Grain: 54,719 Compartments: 6 Ho, ER 6 Ha: 6 (17.0 x 15.6)ER Cranes: 6x25t	**1 oil engine** driving 1 FP propeller Total Power: 8,606kW (11,701hp) 16.0kn B&W 6L60MC 1 x 2 Stroke 6 Cy. 600 x 1944 8606kW (11701bhp) Hitachi Zosen Corp-Japan AuxGen: 4 x 780kW 450V 60Hz a.c Boilers: e (ex.g.) 12.0kgf/cm² (11.8bar), AuxB (o.f.) 7.0kgf/cm² (6.9bar) Fuel: 178.5 (d.f.) 1523.5 (r.f.)
9580388 *A6E2230* -	**TAMIM ALDAR** *ex* Pacific Prince *-2013* **Elite Way Marine Services Est** *Abu Dhabi* *United Arab Emirates* MMSI: 470417000	**5,770** 1,731 10,000	Class: BV	**2009-12 Nanjing Hathaway Runqi Marine Engineering Co Ltd — Nanjing JS** Yd No: HR2008018 Loa 106.02 Br ex - Dght 5.900 Lbp 101.60 Br md 25.00 Dpth 8.00 Welded, 1 dk	**(A31C2GD) Deck Cargo Ship**	**2 oil engines** reduction geared to sc. shafts driving 2 Propellers Total Power: 2,942kW (4,000hp) 10.0kn Chinese Std. Type LB8250ZLC 2 x 4 Stroke 8 Cy. 250 x 320 each-1471kW (2000bhp) Zibo Diesel Engine Factory-China
9667552 *A9KM* -	**TAMIMI 3** **High Seas Marine & Industrial Services Co Ltd** Gagasan Offshore Fleet Sdn Bhd *Bahrain* *Bahrain* MMSI: 408535000 Official number: BN6097	**290** 87 81	Class: AB	**2013-06 Sam Aluminium Engineering Pte Ltd — Singapore** Yd No: H100 Loa 40.38 Br ex - Dght 1.300 Lbp 38.93 Br md 7.80 Dpth 3.64 Welded, 1 dk	**(B21A20C) Crew/Supply Vessel** Hull Material: Aluminium Alloy	**3 oil engines** reduction geared to sc. shafts driving 3 Propellers Total Power: 3,243kW (4,410hp) 18.0kn Caterpillar C32 ACERT 3 x Vee 4 Stroke 12 Cy. 145 x 162 each-1081kW (1470bhp) Caterpillar Inc-USA AuxGen: 2 x 98kW a.c Fuel: 95.0 (d.f.)
9290945 *D5BM8* -	**TAMINA** *ex* MSC France *-2010* *ex* Copiapo *-2006* **ms 'Tamina' Schiffahrtsgesellschaft mbH & Co KG** Peter Doehle Schiffahrts-KG *Monrovia* *Liberia* MMSI: 636092392 Official number: 92392	**66,280** 36,284 68,228	Class: LR ✠ **100A1** SS 10/2009 container ship *IWS LI **ShipRight** (SDA, FDA, CM) ✠ **LMC** **UMS** Eq.Ltr: X†; Cable: 742.5/97.0 U3 (a)	**2004-10 China Shipbuilding Corp (CSBC) — Kaohsiung** Yd No: 823 Loa 275.80 (BB) Br ex 40.10 Dght 14.000 Lbp 263.80 Br md 40.00 Dpth 24.20 Welded, 1 dk	**(A33A2CC) Container Ship (Fully Cellular)** TEU 5527 C Ho 2601 TEU C Dk 2926 TEU incl 500 ref C. Compartments: ER, 7 Cell Ho 15 Ha: (12.7 x 30.5)ER 13 (12.7 x 36.0) (12.7 x 20.6)	**1 oil engine** driving 1 FP propeller Total Power: 54,926kW (74,677hp) 25.6kn Sulzer 10RTA96C 1 x 2 Stroke 10 Cy. 960 x 2500 54926kW (74677bhp) Doosan Engine Co Ltd-South Korea AuxGen: 4 x 1980kW 450/230V 60Hz a.c Boilers: e (ex.g.) 12.2kgf/cm² (12.0bar), WTAuxB (o.f.) 8.2kgf/cm² (8.0bar) Thrusters: 1 Thwart. CP thruster (f) Fuel: 314.4 (d.f.) 7653.5 (r.f.) 198.0pd
7805150 *SIPT* -	**TAMINA** *ex* Triton Av Goteborg *-2008* *ex* Trondenes *-1997* *ex* Esso Harstad *-1995* **Tamina Shipping AB** *Gothenburg* *Sweden* MMSI: 266321000	**996** 492 1,536 T/cm 4.4	Class: RI (NV)	**1979-07 Skaalurens Skipsbyggeri AS — Rosendal** Yd No: 231/44 Lengthened-1998 Loa 67.50 Br ex 10.62 Dght 4.350 Lbp 63.00 Br md 10.42 Dpth 5.50 Welded, 1 dk	**(A13B2TP) Products Tanker** Liq: 752; Liq (Oil): 752; Asphalt: 752 Cargo Heating Coils Compartments: 12 Wing Ta, ER 4 Cargo Pump (s): 4x175m³/hr Manifold: Bow/CM: 30m Ice Capable	**1 oil engine** sr geared to sc. shaft driving 1 FP propeller Total Power: 754kW (1,025hp) 12.0kn Normo LDM-6 1 x 4 Stroke 6 Cy. 250 x 300 754kW (1025bhp) AS Bergens Mek Verksteder-Norway AuxGen: 2 x 118kW 220V 50Hz a.c Thrusters: 1 Thwart. FP thruster (f) Fuel: 44.5 (d.f.) 4.0pd
8209339 *VHS3178* -	**TAMINGA** **Svitzer Australia Pty Ltd (Svitzer Australasia)** *Port Adelaide, SA* *Australia* MMSI: 503582000 Official number: 850474	**425** 128 -	Class: (AB)	**1983-05 Carrington Slipways Pty Ltd — Newcastle NSW** Yd No: 156 Loa 32.01 Br ex 10.93 Dght 4.250 Lbp 29.60 Br md 10.61 Dpth 5.36 Welded, 1 dk	**(B32A2ST) Tug**	**2 oil engines** with clutches, flexible couplings & dr geared to sc. shafts driving 2 Directional propellers Total Power: 2,648kW (3,600hp) 12.5kn Daihatsu 6DSM-28 2 x 4 Stroke 6 Cy. 280 x 340 each-1324kW (1800bhp) Daihatsu Diesel Manufacturing Co Lt-Japan AuxGen: 2 x 125kW
8905658 *CNA2486* -	**TAMLALT 1** *ex* Targa *-2008* **Societe des Peches du Sud de l'Atlas** - SatCom: Inmarsat C 424213810 *Agadir* *Morocco*	**207** 75 159	Class: (LR) (BV) ✠ Classed LR until 1/10/98	**1989-12 Astilleros Armon SA — Navia** Yd No: 206 Loa 29.50 Br ex 7.87 Dght 4.050 Lbp 27.11 Br md 7.76 Dpth 4.20 Welded, 1 dk	**(B11A2FS) Stern Trawler** Ins: 150	**1 oil engine** with clutches, flexible couplings & sr reverse geared to sc. shaft driving 1 FP propeller Total Power: 570kW (775hp) 10.5kn Caterpillar 3508TA 1 x Vee 4 Stroke 8 Cy. 170 x 190 570kW (775bhp) Caterpillar Inc-USA AuxGen: 2 x 80kW 380V 50Hz a.c
8905646 *CNA2485* -	**TAMLALT 2** *ex* Anfa *-2008* **Societe des Peches du Sud de l'Atlas** - SatCom: Inmarsat C 424211410 *Agadir* *Morocco*	**207** 75 159	Class: (LR) (BV) ✠ Classed LR until 28/10/98	**1989-11 Astilleros Armon SA — Navia** Yd No: 205 Loa 29.50 Br ex 7.87 Dght 4.050 Lbp 27.11 Br md 7.76 Dpth 4.20 Welded, 1 dk	**(B11A2FS) Stern Trawler** Ins: 150	**1 oil engine** with clutches, flexible couplings & sr reverse geared to sc. shaft driving 1 FP propeller Total Power: 570kW (775hp) 10.5kn Caterpillar 3508TA 1 x Vee 4 Stroke 8 Cy. 170 x 190 570kW (775bhp) Caterpillar Inc-USA AuxGen: 2 x 80kW 380V 50Hz a.c
9006057 *CNA2583* -	**TAMLALT 3** *ex* Al Doha *-2013* *ex* Doha *-2006* **Societe des Peches du Sud de l'Atlas** - SatCom: Inmarsat C 424231310 *Agadir* *Morocco*	**406** 121 289	Class: BV	**1990-08 S.A. Balenciaga — Zumaya** Yd No: 345 Loa 39.60 Br ex - Dght 4.010 Lbp 32.60 Br md 8.81 Dpth 5.85 Welded, 2 dks	**(B11A2FS) Stern Trawler** Ins: 320	**1 oil engine** with clutches, flexible couplings & reduction geared to sc. shaft driving 1 FP propeller Total Power: 736kW (1,001hp) MaK 6M282AK 1 x 4 Stroke 6 Cy. 240 x 280 736kW (1001bhp) Krupp MaK Maschinenbau GmbH-Kiel

9006045 *CNA2582* -	**TAMLALT 4** *ex* Fajr *-2013* **Societe des Peches du Sud de l'Atlas** - *Agadir* *Morocco*	**406** 121 289	Class: (BV)	**1990**-05 **S.A. Balenciaga — Zumaya** Yd No: 344 Loa 39.60 Br ex - Dght 4.010 Lbp 32.62 Br md 8.81 Dpth 5.85 Welded	**(B11A2FS) Stern Trawler** Ins: 320	**1 oil engine** with clutches, flexible couplings & reduction geared to sc. shaft driving 1 FP propeller Total Power: 739kW (1,005hp) 12.0kn MaK 6M282AK 1 x 4 Stroke 6 Cy. 240 x 280 739kW (1005bhp) Krupp MaK Maschinenbau GmbH-Kiel AuxGen: 2 x 144kW 220/380V a.c Fuel: 214.0 (d.f.)
9018866 *CNA2658* -	**TAMLALT 5** *ex* Watr *-2013* *launched as* Goizaldi *-1990* **Societe des Peches du Sud de l'Atlas** - SatCom: Inmarsat C 424231510 *Agadir* *Morocco*	**406** 121 289	Class: BV	**1990**-12 **S.A. Balenciaga — Zumaya** Yd No: 348 Loa 39.60 Br ex - Dght 3.701 Lbp 32.62 Br md 8.81 Dpth 3.85 Welded	**(B11A2FS) Stern Trawler** Ins: 320	**1 oil engine** with clutches, flexible couplings & reduction geared to sc. shaft driving 1 FP propeller Total Power: 736kW (1,001hp) 13.3kn MaK 6M282AK 1 x 4 Stroke 6 Cy. 240 x 280 736kW (1001bhp) Krupp MaK Maschinenbau GmbH-Kiel AuxGen: 2 x 144kW 220/380V a.c Fuel: 214.0 (d.f.)
8808989 - -	**TAMLUK** - **Government of The Republic of India (Central Inland Water Transport Corp Ltd)** - *Kolkata* *India*	**200** - 53	Class: (IR)	**1992**-03 **Central Inland Water Transport Corp. Ltd. — Kolkata** Yd No: 399 Loa 29.55 Br ex 8.41 Dght 1.700 Lbp 27.50 Br md 8.00 Dpth 2.60 Welded, 1 dk	**(B32B2SP) Pusher Tug**	**2 oil engines** with clutches & sr reverse geared to sc. shafts driving 2 FP propellers Total Power: 698kW (950hp) 9.7kn Cummins KTA-1150-M 2 x 4 Stroke 6 Cy. 159 x 159 each-349kW (475bhp) Kirloskar Cummins Ltd-India AuxGen: 2 x 72kW 415V 50Hz a.c
8310580 *VLTN* -	**TAMMAR** - **DMS Maritime Pty Ltd** - *Fremantle, WA* *Australia*	*163* - -	Class: LR ✠**100A1** SS 03/2008 tug ✠**LMC** Eq.Ltr: C; Cable: 247.5/16.0 U2	**1984**-02 **Australian Shipbuilding Industries (WA) Pty Ltd — Fremantle WA** Yd No: 216 Loa 26.40 Br ex 8.79 Dght 3.123 Lbp 23.63 Br md 8.23 Dpth 4.20 Welded, 1 dk	**(B32A2ST) Tug**	**2 oil engines** with clutches, flexible couplings & dr reverse geared to sc. shafts driving 2 FP propellers Total Power: 1,882kW (2,558hp) G.M. (Detroit Diesel) 16V-149-TI 2 x Vee 2 Stroke 16 Cy. 146 x 146 each-941kW (1279bhp) General Motors Detroit DieselAllison Divn-USA AuxGen: 1 x 45kW 415V 50Hz a.c, 1 x 26kW 415V 50Hz a.c Fuel: 41.5 (d.f.)
7200207 *HP9719* -	**TAMMY** *ex* Rio Yaracuy *-1999* *ex* El Venado Grande *-1972* **Neighborhood Shipping Inc** - *Panama* *Panama* Official number: 28462PEXT	*147* 81 -		**1966 Universal Iron Works — Houma, La** L reg 24.56 Br ex 7.62 Dght - Lbp 23.47 Br md - Dpth 3.10 Welded, 1 dk	**(B32A2ST) Tug**	**1 oil engine** driving 1 FP propeller Total Power: 956kW (1,300hp) 11.0kn Caterpillar 1 x 4 Stroke 956kW (1300bhp) Caterpillar Tractor Co-USA
8851089 - -	**TAMMY** *ex* Rock Hill *-2006* **Seiya Ltd** - *Nigeria* Official number: SR588	*110* 74 -		**1981 LAD Construction Co Inc — Gibson, La** Loa - Br ex - Dght - Lbp 17.37 Br md 7.65 Dpth 2.62 Welded, 1 dk	**(B32A2ST) Tug**	**1 oil engine** driving 1 FP propeller
8521359 *WAI6569* -	**TAMPA** *launched as* Paz *-1985* **Seabulk Towing Inc** - *Tampa, FL* *United States of America* MMSI: 366943510 Official number: 689860	*190* 129 -		**1985**-10 **Gulf-Tampa Drydock Co. — Tampa, Fl** Loa 30.48 Br ex - Dght 3.496 Lbp 28.66 Br md 9.15 Dpth 4.58 Welded, 1 dk	**(B32A2ST) Tug**	**2 oil engines** with clutches & reverse reduction geared to sc. shafts driving 2 FP propellers Total Power: 4,414kW (6,002hp) EMD (Electro-Motive) 16-645-E5 2 x Vee 2 Stroke 16 Cy. 230 x 254 each-2207kW (3001bhp) General Motors Corp.Electro-Motive Div.-La Grange AuxGen: 2 x 99kW 60Hz a.c
8207020 *3FYW4* -	**TAMPA** *ex* Scotia Wind *-2010* *ex* Atair Star *-2006* *ex* Makatsarija *-2000* *ex* Kapitan Makatsariya *-1994* **SMY Shipping & Trading Co Ltd** Overseas Shipping & Stevedoring Co (OSSCO) *Panama* *Panama* MMSI: 352195000 Official number: 38646HOC	**10,937** 5,887 17,550 T/cm 27.9	Class: PX (NV) (RS)	**1984**-12 **Brodogradiliste Split (Brodosplit) — Split** Yd No: 327 Loa 151.30 (BB) Br ex 22.43 Dght 9.468 Lbp 142.94 Br md 22.40 Dpth 12.15 Welded, 1 dk	**(A13B2TP) Products Tanker** Double Bottom Entire Compartment Length Liq: 20,092; Liq (Oil): 20,092 Compartments: 10 Wing Ta, 6 Ta, ER, 2 Wing Slop Ta 16 Cargo Pump (s) Ice Capable	**1 oil engine** driving 1 CP propeller Total Power: 5,296kW (7,200hp) 14.5kn MAN K6SZ52/105CL 1 x 2 Stroke 6 Cy. 520 x 1050 5296kW (7200bhp) Brodogradiliste Split (Brodosplit)-Yugoslavia AuxGen: 1 x 720kW 400V 50Hz a.c, 2 x 560kW 400V 50Hz a.c Thrusters: 1 Thwart. CP thruster (f) Fuel: 133.7 (d.f.) 1002.4 (r.f.)
9363027 *9HHA9* -	**TAMPA** - **Erwina Shipping Ltd** TMS Dry Ltd SatCom: Inmarsat Mini-M 761145345 *Valletta* *Malta* MMSI: 256974000 Official number: 9363027	**91,373** 58,745 177,987 T/cm 120.6	Class: AB	**2008**-04 **Shanghai Waigaoqiao Shipbuilding Co Ltd — Shanghai** Yd No: 1061 Loa 291.95 (BB) Br ex 45.04 Dght 18.300 Lbp 282.00 Br md 45.00 Dpth 24.80 Welded, 1 dk	**(A21A2BC) Bulk Carrier** Grain: 194,179; Bale: 183,425 Compartments: 9 Ho, ER 9 Ha: 7 (15.5 x 20.0)ER 2 (15.5 x 16.5)	**1 oil engine** driving 1 FP propeller Total Power: 16,860kW (22,923hp) 14.0kn MAN-B&W 6S70MC 1 x 2 Stroke 6 Cy. 700 x 2674 16860kW (22923bhp) Hudong Heavy Machinery Co Ltd-China AuxGen: 3 x 900kW a.c Fuel: 327.0 (d.f.) 4131.0 (r.f.)
9325104 *VRLQ9* -	**TAMPA BAY** - **Tampa Bay Ltd** Pacific Basin Shipping (HK) Ltd *Hong Kong* *Hong Kong* MMSI: 477250400 Official number: HK-3743	**17,979** 10,748 29,671 T/cm 40.5	Class: NK	**2007**-07 **Shikoku Dockyard Co. Ltd. — Takamatsu** Yd No: 1028 Loa 170.70 Br ex 27.00 Dght 9.716 Lbp 163.50 Br md 27.00 Dpth 13.80 Welded, 1 dk	**(A21A2BC) Bulk Carrier** Grain: 40,031; Bale: 38,422 Compartments: 5 Ho, ER 5 Ha: 4 (20.0 x 17.8)ER (12.8 x 16.2) Cranes: 4x30.5t	**1 oil engine** driving 1 FP propeller Total Power: 6,150kW (8,362hp) 14.3kn MAN-B&W 6S42MC 1 x 2 Stroke 6 Cy. 420 x 1764 6150kW (8362bhp) Mitsui Engineering & Shipbuilding CLtd-Japan AuxGen: 4 x 395kW a.c Fuel: 1675.0
8009947 *WDC5373* -	**TAMPA SEAHORSE** - **RP/PHL Marine Leasing LLC** - *New Orleans, LA* *United States of America* MMSI: 367040110 Official number: 638867	*197* 134 852	Class: (AB)	**1981**-07 **Houma Fabricators Inc — Houma LA** Yd No: 70 Loa 47.55 Br ex 11.74 Dght 3.752 Lbp 45.73 Br md 11.60 Dpth 4.35 Welded, 1 dk	**(B21A20S) Platform Supply Ship**	**2 oil engines** sr reverse geared to sc. shafts driving 2 FP propellers Total Power: 1,250kW (1,700hp) 10.0kn Caterpillar D398SCAC 2 x Vee 4 Stroke 12 Cy. 159 x 203 each-625kW (850bhp) Caterpillar Tractor Co-USA AuxGen: 2 x 75kW 450/225V 60Hz a.c Thrusters: 1 Thwart. FP thruster (f) Fuel: 112.0 (d.f.)
8743098 *YGNJ* -	**TAMPAKAN** - **PT Panca Prima Prakarsa** - *Semarang* *Indonesia*	**322** 97 -	Class: KI	**2003 in Indonesia** Loa 34.10 Br ex - Dght 3.750 Lbp 31.05 Br md 8.68 Dpth 4.42 Welded, 1 dk	**(B32A2ST) Tug**	**2 oil engines** reduction geared to sc. shafts driving 2 Propellers Total Power: 1,986kW (2,700hp) Ruston 6ARM 2 x 4 Stroke 6 Cy. 260 x 368 each-993kW (1350bhp) (Re-engined ,made 1972, refitted 2003) Ruston & Hornsby Ltd.-Lincoln AuxGen: 2 x 220kW 415/240V a.c
9258284 *YDA6415* -	**TAMPAN** - **PT Maritim Barito Perkasa** - *Banjarmasin* *Indonesia* Official number: GT245NO3220/IIA	**245** 74 -	Class: AB (BV)	**2001**-09 **Tuong Aik (Sarawak) Sdn Bhd — Sibu** Yd No: 2101 Loa 29.00 Br ex - Dght 3.640 Lbp 26.50 Br md 9.00 Dpth 4.25 Welded, 1 dk	**(B32A2ST) Tug**	**2 oil engines** geared to sc. shafts driving 2 FP propellers Total Power: 1,766kW (2,402hp) Yanmar M220-EN 2 x 4 Stroke 6 Cy. 220 x 300 each-883kW (1201bhp) Yanmar Diesel Engine Co Ltd-Japan
9391309 *XCKO5* -	**TAMPICO** *ex* Topaz *-2008* **Petroleos Mexicanos SA (PEMEX) Refinacion Gerencia de Transportacion Maritima** - *Salina Cruz* *Mexico* MMSI: 345200010 Official number: 2003142432-5	**29,832** 13,306 50,463 T/cm 52.0	Class: LR (AB) **100A1** SS 10/2008 Double Hull oil and chemical tanker, Ship Type 2 ESP *IWS LI SPM **LMC** **UMS IGS**	**2008**-10 **SPP Plant & Shipbuilding Co Ltd — Sacheon** Yd No: S1018 Loa 183.09 (BB) Br ex 32.24 Dght 13.100 Lbp 174.00 Br md 32.20 Dpth 19.10 Welded, 1 dk	**(A12B2TR) Chemical/Products Tanker** Double Hull (13F) Liq: 52,150; Liq (Oil): 53,540 Cargo Heating Coils Compartments: 12 Wing Ta, 2 Wing Slop Ta, ER 12 Cargo Pump (s): 12x600m³/hr Manifold: Bow/CM: 92m	**1 oil engine** driving 1 FP propeller Total Power: 9,480kW (12,889hp) 14.9kn MAN-B&W 6S50MC-C 1 x 2 Stroke 6 Cy. 500 x 2000 9480kW (12889bhp) Doosan Engine Co Ltd-South Korea AuxGen: 3 x 900kW a.c Fuel: 100.0 (d.f.) 1300.0 (r.f.)
7653222 - -	**TAMPO MAS** *ex* Moro Jaya *-1983* *ex* Hokusei Maru *-1978* **Berjaya Tankers (M) Sdn Bhd** -	*474* 245 860		**1966 Kanto Kogyo K.K. — Hakodate** Loa 47.76 Br ex - Dght 3.501 Lbp 44.00 Br md 9.50 Dpth 4.09 Welded, 1 dk	**(A13B2TU) Tanker (unspecified)** Liq: 400; Liq (Oil): 400 Compartments: 3 Ta, ER	**1 oil engine** driving 1 FP propeller Total Power: 405kW (551hp) 7.0kn Matsui 1 x 4 Stroke 6 Cy. 270 x 400 405kW (551bhp) Matsui Iron Works Co Ltd-Japan

8318520 - -	**TAMRALIPTA** **Government of The Republic of India (Central Inland Water Transport Corp Ltd)** - *Kolkata* *India*	*218* - 62	Class: (LR) ✠ Classed LR until 15/12/87	**1986-10 Central Inland Water Transport Corp. Ltd. — Kolkata** Yd No: 395 Loa 29.70 Br ex 7.93 Dght 1.696 Lbp 27.41 Br md 7.61 Dpth 2.52 Welded, 1 dk	**(B32B2SP) Pusher Tug**	**2 oil engines** with clutches, flexible couplings & sr reverse geared to sc. shafts driving 2 FP propellers Total Power: 994kW (1,352hp) MAN R8V16/18TL 2 x 4 Stroke 8 Cy. 160 x 180 each-497kW (676bhp) Garden Reach Shipbuilders &Engineers Ltd-India AuxGen: 2 x 24kW 415V 50Hz a.c

9204520 *VWKE* -	**TAMRALIPTA** - **Kolkata Port Trust** - *Kolkata* *India* Official number: 2814	**462** 139 159	Class: (IR)	**2000-06 Bharati Shipyard Ltd — Ratnagiri** Yd No: 275 Loa 33.00 Br ex 10.72 Dght 3.970 Lbp 31.00 Br md 10.70 Dpth 5.50 Welded, 1 dk	**(B32A2ST) Tug**	**2 oil engines** driving 2 gen. each 100kW a.c geared to sc. shafts driving 2 Directional propellers Total Power: 3,240kW (4,406hp) 11.0kn Wartsila 9L20 2 x 4 Stroke 9 Cy. 200 x 280 each-1620kW (2203bhp) Wartsila Finland Oy-Finland AuxGen: 2 x 100kW 415V 50Hz a.c Fuel: 88.0 (d.f.)

8518651 *TCUK8* -	**TAMREY** *ex* Arabella *-2012* *ex* Global Ambition *-1998* *ex* Alaska Trader *-1994* **Tamrey Denizcilik Ltd Sti** T ve O Denizcilik Ltd Sti (T & O Denizcilik Ltd Sti) *Istanbul* *Turkey* MMSI: 271043138	**14,877** 8,942 25,758 T/cm 35.2	Class: BV (KR) (NK)	**1986-03 Imabari Shipbuilding Co Ltd — Imabari EH (Imabari Shipyard)** Yd No: 455 Loa 159.43 (BB) Br ex - Dght 9.918 Lbp 149.80 Br md 26.00 Dpth 13.60 Welded, 1 dk	**(A21A2BC) Bulk Carrier** Grain: 32,461; Bale: 31,095 Compartments: 4 Ho, ER 4 Ha: (18.4 x 12.8)3 (21.6 x 12.8)ER Cranes: 3x25t; Derricks: 1x25t	**1 oil engine** driving 1 FP propeller Total Power: 4,965kW (6,750hp) 13.2kn B&W 5L50MC 1 x 2 Stroke 5 Cy. 500 x 1620 4965kW (6750bhp) Mitsui Engineering & Shipbuilding CLtd-Japan AuxGen: 4 x 267kW a.c

8428064 - -	**TAMSI** *ex* Oil Queen *-1994* **Batangas Bay Carriers Inc** - *Manila* *Philippines* Official number: MNLD000682	**122** 70 170		**1965 Sandoval Shipyards Inc. — Manila** L reg 26.66 Br ex 6.25 Dght 1.950 Lbp 25.59 Br md 6.10 Dpth 2.44 Welded, 1 dk	**(A13B2TP) Products Tanker** Liq: 210; Liq (Oil): 210 Compartments: 8 Ta, ER	**2 oil engines** with clutches & reverse reduction geared to sc. shafts driving 2 FP propellers Total Power: 226kW (308hp) 5.0kn Isuzu E120 2 x 4 Stroke 6 Cy. 135 x 140 each-113kW (154bhp) Isuzu Marine Engine Inc-Japan

6709165 *WCG5899* -	**TAMUNO-IBI** *ex* Clean Waters I *-2009* *ex* Response 1 *-1984* *ex* Stacey Tide *-1983* *ex* Martha Theriot *-1983* **GFL Marine Services Ltd** - *Long Beach, CA* *United States of America* MMSI: 366929360 Official number: 293858	*195* 125 -		**1964 American Marine Corp. — New Orleans, La** Yd No: 862 Loa - Br ex - Dght 2.868 Lbp 41.48 Br md 10.67 Dpth 3.43 Welded, 1 dk	**(B34G2SE) Pollution Control Vessel**	**1 oil engine** driving 1 FP propeller Total Power: 978kW (1,330hp)

8764456 - -	**TAMUNO-ISELEGHA** *ex* Nicole Eymard *-2012* *ex* Arapaho *-2004* **Associated Gas & Oil Co Ltd** - *Lagos* *Nigeria* Official number: SR1476	**547** 164 -	Class: (AB)	**1998-10 Hope Services, Inc. — Houma, La** Yd No: 131 Loa 31.69 Br ex - Dght - Lbp 27.43 Br md 15.24 Dpth 2.99 Welded, 1 dk	**(B22A2ZM) Offshore Construction Vessel, jack up**	**2 oil engines** reverse reduction geared to sc. shafts driving 2 Propellers Total Power: 678kW (922hp) G.M. (Detroit Diesel) 16V-71 2 x Vee 2 Stroke 16 Cy. 108 x 127 each-339kW (461bhp) Detroit Diesel Corporation-Detroit, Mi AuxGen: 2 x 99kW a.c

8656685 *YD3520* -	**TAN 5** *ex* Iwagi Maru No. 11 *-2009* *ex* Kami Maru No. 8 *-2000* **PT Tanker Armada Nusantara** - *Jakarta* *Indonesia*	**127** 39 -	Class: KI	**1984-04 Nippon Zosen Tekko K.K. — Kitakyushu** Loa - Br ex - Dght 2.300 Lbp 23.04 Br md 7.10 Dpth 3.10 Welded, 1 dk	**(B32A2ST) Tug**	**1 oil engine** reduction geared to sc. shaft driving 1 Propeller 10.0kn Niigata Niigata Engineering Co Ltd-Japan

7714375 *BXCW* -	**TAN BAO HAO** *ex* Western Reliance *-1994* *ex* T. W. Nelson *-1985* **Government of The People's Republic of China (Guangzhou Marine Geological Survey Shipping Co)** - SatCom: Inmarsat A 1572364 *Guangzhou, Guangdong* *China* MMSI: 412461570	**2,619** 785 889	Class: CC (AB)	**1978-09 Mitsubishi Heavy Industries Ltd. — Shimonoseki** Yd No: 792 Loa 86.64 (BB) Br ex 14.03 Dght 4.820 Lbp 77.02 Br md 14.01 Dpth 7.47 Welded, 2 dks	**(B31A2SR) Research Survey Vessel** Ice Capable	**4 oil engines** geared to sc. shafts driving 2 CP propellers Total Power: 4,192kW (5,698hp) 15.8kn Daihatsu 6DSM-26 2 x 4 Stroke 6 Cy. 260 x 320 each-919kW (1249bhp) Daihatsu Diesel Manufacturing Co Lt-Japan Daihatsu 8DSM-26 2 x 4 Stroke 8 Cy. 260 x 320 each-1177kW (1600bhp) Daihatsu Diesel Manufacturing Co Lt-Japan AuxGen: 3 x 700kW Thrusters: 1 Thwart. FP thruster (f)

9133575 *JVSG3* -	**TAN BINH 22** *ex* Benny *-2007* *ex* Melta *-2003* *ex* Fair Fountain *-1999* *ex* Brother Fountain *-1997* **Tan Binh Co Ltd** - *Ulaanbaatar* *Mongolia* MMSI: 457990000 Official number: 21990795	**4,667** 2,188 6,243 T/cm 13.4	Class: VR (NK)	**1995-08 Sanyo Zosen K.K. — Onomichi** Yd No: 1067 Loa 96.70 (BB) Br ex - Dght 7.330 Lbp 85.78 Br md 17.40 Dpth 11.60 Welded, 1 dk	**(A31A2GX) General Cargo Ship** Grain: 10,383; Bale: 9,867 Compartments: 2 Ho, ER 2 Ha: (14.7 x 10.5) (28.0 x 10.5)ER Derricks: 3x25t	**1 oil engine** driving 1 FP propeller Total Power: 2,427kW (3,300hp) 11.8kn Akasaka A41 1 x 4 Stroke 6 Cy. 410 x 800 2427kW (3300bhp) Akasaka Tekkosho KK (Akasaka DieselLtd)-Japan

9016167 *JVVG4* -	**TAN BINH 24** *ex* Lucky Diamond *-2007* *ex* Luna White *-2000* **Tan Binh Co Ltd** - *Ulaanbaatar* *Mongolia* MMSI: 457601000 Official number: 31131291	**4,405** 2,806 7,194	Class: VR (NK)	**1991-04 Iwagi Zosen Co Ltd — Kamijima EH** Yd No: 138 Loa 106.86 (BB) Br ex - Dght 6.868 Lbp 100.00 Br md 17.60 Dpth 8.70 Welded	**(A31A2GX) General Cargo Ship** Grain: 9,701; Bale: 8,903 Compartments: 2 Ho, ER 2 Ha: 2 (28.7 x 10.4)ER Derricks: 4x25t	**1 oil engine** driving 1 FP propeller Total Power: 2,942kW (4,000hp) 13.0kn Mitsubishi 6UEC37LA 1 x 2 Stroke 6 Cy. 370 x 880 2942kW (4000bhp) Akasaka Tekkosho KK (Akasaka DieselLtd)-Japan

9175858 *JVVG3* -	**TAN BINH 28** *ex* Lucky Pioneer *-2008* *ex* Woody King *-2006* **Tan Binh Co Ltd** - *Ulaanbaatar* *Mongolia* MMSI: 457093000 Official number: 23270897	**6,448** 3,114 7,547	Class: VR (CR) (NK)	**1997-12 Higaki Zosen K.K. — Imabari** Yd No: 488 Loa 100.33 Br ex - Dght 7.514 Lbp 93.50 Br md 19.60 Dpth 13.00 Welded, 1 dk	**(A31A2GX) General Cargo Ship** Grain: 14,756; Bale: 13,390 Compartments: 2 Ho, ER 2 Ha: (29.4 x 14.0) (19.6 x 14.0)ER Cranes: 3x25t	**1 oil engine** driving 1 FP propeller Total Power: 3,884kW (5,281hp) 13.0kn B&W 6L35MC 1 x 2 Stroke 6 Cy. 350 x 1050 3884kW (5281bhp) The Hanshin Diesel Works Ltd-Japan AuxGen: 2 x 320kW 450V a.c Fuel: 686.0 (r.f.) 15.5pd

8612964 *JVRD4* -	**TAN BINH 30** *ex* Pan Ace *-2008* *ex* Marine Jeju *-2005* *ex* Mandiri Jaya *-2003* *ex* Asian Queen *-1995* **Tan Binh Co Ltd** - *Ulaanbaatar* *Mongolia* MMSI: 457481000 Official number: 30091286	**5,607** 2,404 7,009	Class: VR (KR) (NK)	**1986-08 Higaki Zosen K.K. — Imabari** Yd No: 345 Loa 98.18 (BB) Br ex 18.04 Dght - Lbp 89.95 Br md 18.01 Dpth 13.00 Welded, 2 dks	**(A31A2GX) General Cargo Ship** Grain: 13,732; Bale: 12,188 Compartments: 2 Ho, ER, 2 Tw Dk 2 Ha: (24.1 x 11.2) (24.1 x 11.2)ER Cranes: 2x25t; Derricks: 2x15t	**1 oil engine** driving 1 FP propeller Total Power: 2,795kW (3,800hp) 12.6kn Mitsubishi 6UEC37LA 1 x 2 Stroke 6 Cy. 370 x 880 2795kW (3800bhp) Kobe Hatsudoki KK-Japan AuxGen: 2 x 280kW 450V 60Hz a.c

8920103 *JVWE4* -	**TAN BINH 36** *ex* Ching Ho *-2009* *ex* Ken Ryu *-1997* **Tan Binh Co Ltd** - *Ulaanbaatar* *Mongolia* MMSI: 457632000 Official number: 31391290	**13,706** 7,738 22,256 T/cm 32.9	Class: VR (CR) (NK)	**1990-07 Saiki Heavy Industries Co Ltd — Saiki OT** Yd No: 1010 Loa 157.50 (BB) Br ex - Dght 9.115 Lbp 148.00 Br md 25.00 Dpth 12.70 Welded, 1 dk	**(A21A2BC) Bulk Carrier** Grain: 29,301; Bale: 28,299 Compartments: 4 Ho, ER 4 Ha: (20.0 x 11.7)Tappered 3 (20.8 x 17.5)ER Cranes: 4x30t	**1 oil engine** driving 1 FP propeller Total Power: 4,590kW (6,241hp) 13.0kn Mitsubishi 6UEC45LA 1 x 2 Stroke 6 Cy. 450 x 1350 4590kW (6241bhp) Akasaka Tekkosho KK (Akasaka DieselLtd)-Japan AuxGen: 2 x 400kW 445V 60Hz a.c Fuel: 80.6 (d.f.) 804.9 (r.f.) 16.0pd

9122875 *3FXZ7* -	**TAN BINH 39** *ex* Venus Frontier *-2012* *ex* C. S. Valiant *-2006* **Tan Binh Co Ltd** - *Panama* *Panama* MMSI: 357085000 Official number: 4536213	**15,438** 8,180 23,956	Class: NK VR	**1996-06 Kanda Zosensho K.K. — Kawajiri** Yd No: 375 Loa 158.50 (BB) Br ex - Dght 9.417 Lbp 151.00 Br md 25.80 Dpth 13.30 Welded, 1 dk	**(A31A2GX) General Cargo Ship** Grain: 29,463; Bale: 28,768 Compartments: 4 Ho, ER 4 Ha: ER Cranes: 4x30t	**1 oil engine** driving 1 FP propeller Total Power: 5,980kW (8,130hp) 15.2kn B&W 6L42MC 1 x 2 Stroke 6 Cy. 420 x 1360 5980kW (8130bhp) Mitsui Engineering & Shipbuilding CLtd-Japan Fuel: 1465.0 (r.f.)

9140229 *3FGF6* -	**TAN BINH 45** *ex* Global Ace *-2012* *ex* California Rainbow II *-2001* **Tan Binh Co Ltd** - *Panama* *Panama* MMSI: 356461000 Official number: 2308096E	**15,500** 7,901 23,483	Class: NK	**1996-06 Mitsubishi Heavy Industries Ltd. — Nagasaki** Yd No: 2116 Loa 164.50 (BB) Br ex - Dght 9.600 Lbp 157.00 Br md 24.00 Dpth 13.40 Welded, 1 dk	**(A31A2GO) Open Hatch Cargo Ship** Grain: 29,873; Bale: 29,561 TEU 720 Compartments: 5 Ho, ER 5 Ha: (12.6 x 10.8)2 (25.2 x 19.8)2 (13.5 x 19.8)ER Cranes: 3x30t	**1 oil engine** driving 1 FP propeller Total Power: 5,149kW (7,001hp) 14.0kn Mitsubishi 5UEC52LA 1 x 2 Stroke 5 Cy. 520 x 1600 5149kW (7001bhp) Mitsubishi Heavy Industries Ltd-Japan AuxGen: 3 x 440kW 450V a.c Fuel: 948.0 (r.f.) 17.3pd

IMO / Call sign	Name, owner, port	Tonnage	Class	Builder / Dimensions	Type / Capacity	Machinery
9191436 *3FJK9* -	**TAN BINH 69** *ex* Cosmos Verde *-2013* **Tan Binh Co Ltd** - *Panama* *Panama* MMSI: 357457000 Official number: 28102PEXT4	**15,137** 8,906 24,838	Class: NK (BV)	**1999-06 Shikoku Dockyard Co. Ltd. — Takamatsu** Yd No: 891 Loa 153.50 Br ex - Dght 9.701 Lbp 146.00 Br md 26.20 Dpth 13.30 Welded, 1 dk	**(A21A2BC) Bulk Carrier** Grain: 32,341; Bale: 31,387 Compartments: 4 Ho, ER 4 Ha: (20.3 x 12.8)3 (20.3 x 17.6)ER Cranes: 4x30t	**1 oil engine** driving 1 FP propeller Total Power: 5,517kW (7,501hp) 15.8kn B&W 6L42MC 1 x 2 Stroke 6 Cy. 420 x 1360 5517kW (7501bhp) Mitsui Engineering & Shipbuilding CLtd-Japan AuxGen: 2 x 440kW 450V 60Hz a.c Fuel: 1220.0
9158111 - -	**TAN CANG 01** - **Sai Gon New Port Co** - *Saigon* *Vietnam* Official number: VNSG-1415-TK	**159** 48 106	Class: VR (NK)	**1996-10 Sapor Shipyard Sdn Bhd — Sibu** Yd No: 30/94 Loa 25.00 Br ex 7.92 Dght 2.850 Lbp 22.99 Br md 7.60 Dpth 3.50 Welded, 1 dk	**(B32A2ST) Tug**	**2 oil engines** driving 2 FP propellers Total Power: 988kW (1,344hp) Caterpillar 3412TA 2 x Vee 4 Stroke 12 Cy. 137 x 152 each-494kW (672bhp) Caterpillar Inc-USA
8954233 - -	**TAN CANG 06** - **Sai Gon New Port Co** - *Saigon* *Vietnam* Official number: VNSG-1466-TK	**129** 39 -	Class: VR	**1975 in the United States of America** Loa 30.88 Br ex 7.62 Dght 3.000 Lbp 27.50 Br md 7.60 Dpth 4.22 Welded, 1 dk	**(B32A2ST) Tug**	**1 oil engine** driving 1 FP propeller Total Power: 1,324kW (1,800hp) 10.0kn General Motors 16-278-A 1 x Vee 2 Stroke 16 Cy. 222 x 267 1324kW (1800bhp) General Motors Corp-USA
9023548 - -	**TAN CANG 12** - **Sai Gon New Port Co** - *Saigon* *Vietnam* Official number: VNSG-1553-TK	**368** 110 -	Class: VR	**1988-01 Brodogradiliste 'Tito' — Belgrade** Yd No: 192A Loa 36.31 Br ex 9.70 Dght 3.570 Lbp 34.14 Br md 9.43 Dpth 4.70 Welded, 1 dk	**(B32A2ST) Tug**	**2 oil engines** geared to sc. shafts driving 2 Propellers Total Power: 2,221kW (3,019hp) Sulzer 6ASL25D 2 x 4 Stroke 6 Cy. 250 x 300 each-927kW (1260bhp) Tvornica Dizel Motora '3 Maj'-Yugoslavia
8517645 *H09089* -	**TAN CANG 69** *ex* SMS Odyssey *-2013* *ex* VOS Odyssey *-2011* *ex* DEA Odyssey *-2009* *ex* Smit-Lloyd 57 *-2004* **Dang Development Investment Ltd** Hai Duong Co Ltd (HADUCO) *Panama* *Panama* MMSI: 370389000 Official number: 4544013	**1,256** 377 1,000	Class: AB	**1987-07 Scheepswerf en Mfbk. Ysselwerf B.V. — Capelle a/d IJssel** Yd No: 330 Loa 58.04 Br ex - Dght 4.801 Lbp 50.00 Br md 13.20 Dpth 6.15 Welded, 1 dk	**(B21B20A) Anchor Handling Tug Supply**	**4 oil engines** with clutches, flexible couplings & sr geared to sc. shafts driving 2 CP propellers Total Power: 3,918kW (5,326hp) 11.0kn Wartsila 6R22 2 x 4 Stroke 6 Cy. 220 x 240 each-840kW (1142bhp) Wartsila Diesel Oy-Finland Wartsila 8R22 2 x 4 Stroke 8 Cy. 220 x 240 each-1119kW (1521bhp) Wartsila Diesel Oy-Finland AuxGen: 2 x 800kW 440V 60Hz a.c Thrusters: 2 Thwart. CP thruster (f); 1 Tunnel thruster (a) Fuel: 503.0 (d.f.) 26.5pd
7633428 *HMYJ4* -	**TAN GYOL BONG** *ex* Lu Sheng *-2008* *ex* Diana D *-1992* *ex* Tatiana *-1990* *ex* Levern *-1987* *ex* Zim Alexandria *-1987* *ex* Akak Express *-1985* *ex* Levern *-1983* **Korea Kumbyol Trading Co** - *Nampho* *North Korea* MMSI: 445268000 Official number: 2707117	**1,592** 671 2,044	Class: (CC) (GL)	**1977-09 J.J. Sietas Schiffswerft — Hamburg** Yd No: 814 Loa 72.07 Br ex 12.83 Dght 4.447 Lbp 65.51 Br md 12.81 Dpth 6.81 Welded, 2 dks	**(A31A2GX) General Cargo Ship** Grain: 3,199; Bale: 3,143 TEU 127 C.Ho 53/20' (40') C.Dk 74/20' (40') Compartments: 1 Ho, ER 1 Ha: (43.8 x 10.2)ER Ice Capable	**1 oil engine** driving 1 FP propeller Total Power: 736kW (1,001hp) 12.0kn MaK 6M452AK 1 x 4 Stroke 6 Cy. 320 x 450 736kW (1001bhp) MaK Maschinenbau GmbH-Kiel
7000126 *YD3162* -	**TAN I** *ex* Aec I *-2002* *ex* Taiyo No. 1 *-2001* *ex* Taiyo Maru No. 1 *-1981* **PT Tanker Armada Nusantara** - *Dumai* *Indonesia*	**247** 75 -	Class: KI (NK)	**1969-08 Shimoda Dockyard Co. Ltd. — Shimoda** Yd No: 170 Loa 29.01 Br ex 8.51 Dght 2.794 Lbp 26.50 Br md 8.50 Dpth 3.90 Welded, 1 dk	**(B32A2ST) Tug**	**2 oil engines** geared to sc. shafts driving 2 FP propellers Total Power: 736kW (1,000hp) Daihatsu 8PSHTCM-26D 2 x 4 Stroke 8 Cy. 260 x 320 each-368kW (500bhp) Daihatsu Kogyo-Japan AuxGen: 2 x 50kW 225V a.c
7856290 *YDA4052* -	**TAN III** *ex* Hotoku No. 1 *-2005* *ex* Hotoku Maru No. 1 *-1992* **PT Tanker Armada Nusantara** - *Jakarta* *Indonesia*	**261** 79 -	Class: KI	**1972-10 Yamanaka Zosen K.K. — Imabari** Yd No: 118 Loa 32.50 Br ex - Dght 3.050 Lbp 28.50 Br md 9.01 Dpth 3.81 Welded, 1 dk	**(B32A2ST) Tug**	**2 oil engines** driving 2 FP propellers Total Power: 2,354kW (3,200hp) 12.0kn Niigata 8MG25BX 2 x 4 Stroke 8 Cy. 250 x 320 each-1177kW (1600bhp) Niigata Engineering Co Ltd-Japan
8830554 - -	**TAN JIANG** - **Guangdong Sanfu Passenger & Cargo Transport Associate Co** - *Kaiping, Guangdong* *China*	*1,578* 573 -	Class: (CC)	**1984-01 Guangdong Jiangmen Shipyard — Jiangmen GD** Loa 66.73 Br ex - Dght 2.660 Lbp 57.90 Br md 12.40 Dpth 6.30 Welded, 1 dk	**(A37B2PS) Passenger Ship**	**2 oil engines** geared to sc. shafts driving 2 FP propellers Total Power: 882kW (1,200hp) 12.0kn Chinese Std. Type 6300 2 x 4 Stroke 6 Cy. 300 x 380 each-441kW (600bhp) Guangzhou Diesel Engine Factory CoLtd-China AuxGen: 3 x 160kW 390V a.c
7122273 *3WSO* -	**TAN PHU** *ex* Geneco-01 *-1992* *ex* Inari Maru No. 16 *-1992* *ex* Nikko Maru No. 15 *-1982* **Branch of Vinafco Saigon (Chi Nhanh Vinafco Saigon)** - *Saigon* *Vietnam*	**495** 219 350	Class: (VR)	**1970 KK Kanasashi Zosen — Shizuoka SZ** Yd No: 978 Loa 50.47 Br ex 8.34 Dght 3.296 Lbp 44.51 Br md 8.31 Dpth 3.71 Welded, 1 dk	**(B11B2FV) Fishing Vessel** Ins: 445 Compartments: 3 Ho	**1 oil engine** driving 1 FP propeller Total Power: 736kW (1,001hp) Niigata 6M28KHS 1 x 4 Stroke 6 Cy. 280 x 440 736kW (1001bhp) Niigata Engineering Co Ltd-Japan AuxGen: 2 x 250kW a.c
8985490 - -	**TAN PHUNG** *ex* Su Sam *-2010* - -	**584** 269 1,060	Class: KC	**1987-12 Nampo Shipyard — Nampo** Loa 60.00 Br ex - Dght 4.200 Lbp 55.00 Br md 9.30 Dpth 4.90 Welded, 1 dk	**(A31A2GX) General Cargo Ship**	**1 oil engine** driving 1 Propeller Total Power: 588kW (799hp)
9023093 - -	**TAN VIET 27-ALCI** *ex* Thinh Long 27-Alci *-2012* *ex* Huu Nghi 09 *-2004* **Agriculture Leasing Co I** Thien Anh River Sea Transport JSC *Haiphong* *Vietnam* MMSI: 574012078 Official number: VN-1724-VT	**999** 605 2,028	Class: VR	**2003-11 Nam Ha Shipyard — Nam Ha** Yd No: HT-27 Loa 69.40 Br ex 10.82 Dght 4.500 Lbp 65.80 Br md 10.80 Dpth 5.50 Welded, 1 dk	**(A31A2GX) General Cargo Ship** Bale: 2,265 Compartments: 2 Ho, ER 3 Ha: (15.0 x 7.4) (16.9 x 7.4)	**1 oil engine** driving 1 FP propeller Total Power: 552kW (750hp) 9.0kn S.K.L. 8NVD48-1U 1 x 4 Stroke 8 Cy. 320 x 480 552kW (750bhp) (made 1991, fitted 2003) SKL Motoren u. Systemtechnik AG-Magdeburg
7232236 *YDA4074* -	**TAN VII** *ex* Shinkai Maru No. 11 *-2005* **PT Tanker Armada Nusantara** - *Jakarta* *Indonesia*	**255** 77 -	Class: KI (NK)	**1972-04 Shimoda Dockyard Co. Ltd. — Shimoda** Yd No: 203 Loa 29.00 Br ex 8.54 Dght 2.800 Lbp 26.50 Br md 8.50 Dpth 3.90 Welded, 1 dk	**(B32B2SP) Pusher Tug**	**2 oil engines** driving 2 FP propellers Total Power: 1,912kW (2,600hp) 12.3kn Daihatsu 6DSM-26 2 x 4 Stroke 6 Cy. 260 x 320 each-956kW (1300bhp) Daihatsu Diesel Manufacturing Co Lt-Japan AuxGen: 2 x 60kW
7125665 - -	**TAN VINH TV 5555** *ex* Khanh Hoi 7 *-2002* *ex* Palat *-2002* *ex* Binh Chanh *-1997* *ex* Morgol *-1991* *ex* Somio *-1990* **Ba Toan Co Ltd** - *Saigon* *Vietnam* Official number: VNSG-1605-TH	**740** 480 1,181	Class: VR (GL)	**1972-01 Ast. Celaya — Bilbao** Yd No: 127 Loa 57.54 Br ex 10.44 Dght 4.139 Lbp 54.01 Br md 10.42 Dpth 4.70 Welded, 1 dk	**(A31A2GX) General Cargo Ship** Grain: 1,803; Bale: 1,596 TEU 141 C. 141/20' (40') incl. 18 ref C. Compartments: 1 Ho, ER 1 Ha: (33.0 x 7.6)ER	**1 oil engine** driving 1 FP propeller Total Power: 919kW (1,249hp) 15.0kn MAN V8V-16/18TL 1 x Vee 4 Stroke 16 Cy. 160 x 180 919kW (1249bhp) EN Bazan de Construcciones NavalesMilitares SA-Spain AuxGen: 1 x 72kW 380V 50Hz a.c, 2 x 32kW 380V 50Hz a.c Fuel: 65.0 (d.f.)
9525584 *9HA2992* -	**TANA** - **Desan Deniz Insaat Sanayi AS** K Tankering & Shipmanagement Co (K Tankercilik ve Gemi Isletmeciligi AS) *Valletta* *Malta* MMSI: 229015000 Official number: 9525584	**4,242** 1,992 6,480 T/cm 15.7	Class: BV	**2011-11 Desan Tersanesi — Tuzla, Istanbul** Yd No: 22 Loa 109.00 (BB) Br ex - Dght 6.650 Lbp 101.60 Br md 16.80 Dpth 8.30 Welded, 1 dk	**(A12B2TR) Chemical/Products Tanker** Double Hull (13F) Liq: 6,888; Liq (Oil): 6,888 Cargo Heating Coils Compartments: 10 Wing Ta, 2 Wing Slop Ta, ER 10 Cargo Pump (s): 10x220m³/hr Manifold: Bow/CM: 33.9m Ice Capable	**1 oil engine** reduction geared to sc. shaft driving 1 CP propeller Total Power: 2,640kW (3,589hp) 13.5kn MAN-B&W 8L27/38 1 x 4 Stroke 8 Cy. 270 x 380 2640kW (3589bhp) MAN Diesel A/S-Denmark AuxGen: 3 x 416kW 400V 60Hz a.c Thrusters: 1 Tunnel thruster (f) Fuel: 66.0 (d.f.) 320.0 (r.f.)

9498846 *A8YF9* -	**TANA SEA** **Ostracion Seaway Corp** NSC Shipping GmbH & Cie KG *Monrovia* *Liberia* MMSI: 636015044 Official number: 15044	**50,729** 30,722 93,246 T/cm 80.8	Class: GL (NV) (BV)	**2011-04 Yangfan Group Co Ltd — Zhoushan ZJ** Yd No: 2100 Loa 229.20 (BB) Br ex - Dght 14.900 Lbp 222.00 Br md 38.00 Dpth 20.70 Welded, 1 dk	**(A21A2BC) Bulk Carrier** Grain: 110,300 Compartments: 7 Ho, ER 7 Ha: 5 (17.9 x 17.0)ER 2 (15.3 x 14.6)	**1 oil engine** driving 1 FP propeller Total Power: 12,240kW (16,642hp) 14.1kn MAN-B&W 6S60MC 1 x 2 Stroke 6 Cy. 600 x 2292 12240kW (16642bhp) Hyundai Heavy Industries Co Ltd-South Korea AuxGen: 3 x a.c Fuel: 180.0 (d.f.) 3100.0 (r.f.) 40.5pd
9423578 *2EKP2* -	**TANAGER BULKER** **Lauritzen Bulkers A/S** J Lauritzen Singapore Pte Ltd SatCom: Inmarsat C 423597649 *Douglas* *Isle of Man (British)* MMSI: 235085919 Official number: 742810	**32,309** 19,458 57,991 T/cm 57.4	Class: NK	**2011-05 Tsuneishi Heavy Industries (Cebu) Inc — Balamban** Yd No: SC-131 Loa 189.99 (BB) Br ex - Dght 12.826 Lbp 185.60 Br md 32.26 Dpth 18.00 Welded, 1 dk	**(A21A2BC) Bulk Carrier** Grain: 72,689; Bale: 70,122 Compartments: 5 Ho, ER 5 Ha: 4 (21.1 x 18.6)ER (17.2 x 17.0) Cranes: 4x30t	**1 oil engine** driving 1 FP propeller Total Power: 8,400kW (11,421hp) 14.5kn MAN-B&W 6S50MC-C 1 x 2 Stroke 6 Cy. 500 x 2000 8400kW (11421bhp) Mitsui Engineering & Shipbuilding CLtd-Japan Fuel: 160.0 (d.f.) 2220.0 (r.f.)
8936229 - -	**TANAIR I** **PT Multitrans Raya** - *Samarinda* *Indonesia*	*270* 81 -	Class: KI	**1994-06 C.V. Bina Karya Sejahtera — Samarinda** Loa - Br ex - Dght - Lbp 43.00 Br md 9.30 Dpth 2.80 Welded, 1 dk	**(A35D2RL) Landing Craft** Bow ramp (centre)	**2 oil engines** reduction geared to sc. shafts driving 2 FP propellers Total Power: 560kW (762hp) 9.5kn Caterpillar 3406B 2 x 4 Stroke 6 Cy. 137 x 165 each-280kW (381bhp) Caterpillar Inc-USA
8898001 - -	**TANAIR II** **PT Tanair Pratama Nusantara** - *Samarinda* *Indonesia*	**216** 129 -	Class: KI	**1995-12 C.V. Swadaya Utama — Samarinda** Loa 24.45 Br ex - Dght - Lbp - Br md 7.00 Dpth 3.30 Welded, 1 dk	**(B32A2ST) Tug**	**2 oil engines** reduction geared to sc. shafts driving 2 FP propellers Total Power: 882kW (1,200hp) Cummins KTA-19-M3 2 x 4 Stroke 6 Cy. 159 x 159 each-441kW (600bhp) Cummins Engine Co Inc-USA
8936607 - -	**TANAIR IV** *ex* SSM 1202 *-2001* **PT Tanair Pratama Nusantara** - *Jakarta* *Indonesia*	**123** 73 -	Class: (KI) (BV)	**1997-12 Tuong Aik (Sarawak) Sdn Bhd — Sibu** Yd No: 9707 Loa 23.26 Br ex - Dght 2.220 Lbp 21.96 Br md 7.00 Dpth 2.90 Welded, 1 dk	**(B32A2ST) Tug**	**2 oil engines** geared to sc. shafts driving 2 FP propellers Total Power: 794kW (1,080hp) 10.8kn Caterpillar 3412TA 2 x Vee 4 Stroke 12 Cy. 137 x 152 each-397kW (540bhp) Caterpillar Inc-USA Fuel: 73.0 (d.f.)
9099937 *YDA6065* -	**TANAIR IX** **PT Tanair Pratama Nusantara** - *Jakarta* *Indonesia*	**237** 72 -	Class: KI	**2007-12 C.V. Dok & Galangan Kapal Perlun — Samarinda** Loa 29.50 Br ex - Dght - Lbp 25.20 Br md 8.60 Dpth 3.80 Welded, 1 dk	**(B32A2ST) Tug**	**2 oil engines** reduction geared to sc. shafts driving 2 Propellers Total Power: 2,238kW (3,042hp) Cummins KTA-38-M2 2 x Vee 4 Stroke 12 Cy. 159 x 159 each-1119kW (1521bhp) Cummins Engine Co Inc-USA
9192246 *YD4825* -	**TANAIR V** *ex* SSM 1501 *-2001* **PT Tanair Pratama Nusantara** - *Jakarta* *Indonesia*	**146** 87 -	Class: KI (BV)	**1998-03 Tuong Aik (Sarawak) Sdn Bhd — Sibu** Yd No: 9708 Loa 25.30 Br ex - Dght - Lbp 23.62 Br md 7.30 Dpth 3.50 Welded, 1 dk	**(B32A2ST) Tug**	**2 oil engines** geared to sc. shafts driving 2 FP propellers Total Power: 988kW (1,344hp) 8.0kn Caterpillar 3412TA 2 x Vee 4 Stroke 12 Cy. 137 x 152 each-494kW (672bhp) Caterpillar Inc-USA
9028988 *YD6708* -	**TANAIR VII** **PT Tanair Pratama Nusantara** - *Jakarta* *Indonesia*	**141** 43 -	Class: KI (GL)	**2005-05 Tuong Aik Shipyard Sdn Bhd — Sibu** Yd No: 2411 Loa 23.50 Br ex - Dght 2.699 Lbp - Br md 7.32 Dpth 3.20 Welded, 1 dk	**(B32A2ST) Tug**	**2 oil engines** geared to sc. shafts driving 2 Propellers Total Power: 1,074kW (1,460hp) Caterpillar 3412TA 2 x Vee 4 Stroke 12 Cy. 137 x 152 each-537kW (730bhp) Caterpillar Inc-USA AuxGen: 2 x 42kW 400V a.c
9028990 *YDA4126* -	**TANAIR VIII** **PT Tanair Pratama Nusantara** - *Jakarta* *Indonesia*	**143** 43 -	Class: (KI) (GL)	**2005-10 Tuong Aik Shipyard Sdn Bhd — Sibu** Yd No: 2423 Loa 23.50 Br ex - Dght 2.699 Lbp 21.35 Br md 7.32 Dpth 3.20 Welded, 1 dk	**(B32A2ST) Tug**	**2 oil engines** geared to sc. shafts driving 2 Propellers Total Power: 1,074kW (1,460hp) Caterpillar 3412TA 2 x Vee 4 Stroke 12 Cy. 137 x 152 each-537kW (730bhp) Caterpillar Inc-USA
8740515 - -	**TANAIR X** **PT Tanair Pratama Nusantara** - *Batam* *Indonesia*	**218** 66 -	Class: KI	**2009-06 C.V. Mercusuar Mandiri — Batam** Loa 29.00 Br ex - Dght - Lbp 27.07 Br md 8.00 Dpth 3.70 Welded, 1 dk	**(B32A2ST) Tug**	**2 oil engines** driving 2 Propellers Total Power: 2,238kW (3,042hp) Cummins KTA-38-M2 2 x Vee 4 Stroke 12 Cy. 159 x 159 each-1119kW (1521bhp) Cummins Engine Co Inc-USA
8652627 - -	**TANAIR XI** **PT Tanair Pratama Nusantara** - *Batam* *Indonesia*	**189** 57 -	Class: KI	**2011-01 C.V. Mercusuar Mandiri — Batam** Loa 25.00 Br ex - Dght - Lbp 23.52 Br md 7.32 Dpth 3.20 Welded, 1 dk	**(B32A2ST) Tug**	**2 oil engines** reduction geared to sc. shafts driving 2 Propellers AuxGen: 2 x 69kW 380V a.c
6721008 *SPG2714* -	**TANAIS** *ex* Myrgrunn *-2004* *ex* Lars-Arild *-1993* *ex* Seines *-1990* *ex* Kargit Bagenkop *-1974* **Istpol Sp z oo** - *Gdansk* *Poland* Official number: 101112	*313* 162 493	Class: PR (BV)	**1967 Martin Jansen GmbH & Co. KG Schiffsw. u. Masch. — Leer** Yd No: 81 Loa 44.96 Br ex 7.52 Dght 2.769 Lbp 41.00 Br md 7.50 Dpth 3.15 Welded, 1 dk	**(A31A2GX) General Cargo Ship** Grain: 649; Bale: 621 Compartments: 1 Ho, ER 1 Ha: (20.5 x 4.9)ER Derricks: 2x2t; Winches: 2 Ice Capable	**1 oil engine** driving 1 CP propeller Total Power: 250kW (340hp) 9.5kn Alpha 404-24VO 1 x 2 Stroke 4 Cy. 240 x 400 250kW (340bhp) Alpha Diesel A/S-Denmark Fuel: 15.0 (d.f.)
9305336 *UBLF2* -	**TANAIS** **Don River Shipping JSC (OAO 'Donrechflot')** - *Taganrog* *Russia* MMSI: 273330220	**5,723** 3,353 7,078	Class: RS	**2008-03 OAO Okskaya Sudoverf — Navashino** Yd No: 1901 Loa 139.63 Br ex 16.73 Dght 4.600 Lbp 133.84 Br md 16.51 Dpth 6.00 Welded, 1 dk	**(A31A2GX) General Cargo Ship** Double Hull Grain: 10,871 TEU 280 C Ho 210 TEU C Dk 70 TEU Compartments: 2 Ho, ER 2 Ha: (26.7 x 14.4)ER (20.7 x 13.4) Ice Capable	**2 oil engines** geared to sc. shafts driving 2 FP propellers Total Power: 2,300kW (3,128hp) 10.5kn Wartsila 6L20 2 x 4 Stroke 6 Cy. 200 x 280 each-1150kW (1564bhp) Wartsila Finland Oy-Finland AuxGen: 3 x 150kW 50Hz a.c
9283899 *V3RX4* -	**TANAIS DREAM** *ex* Ja Aladdin Dream II *-2013* **Tanais Shipping Ltd** Rosshipcom Marine Ltd *Belize City* *Belize* MMSI: 312288000 Official number: 371330076	**16,980** 10,098 28,611 T/cm 39.7	Class: NK	**2003-02 Imabari Shipbuilding Co Ltd — Imabari EH (Imabari Shipyard)** Yd No: 587 Loa 169.26 (BB) Br ex - Dght 9.778 Lbp 160.40 Br md 27.20 Dpth 13.60 Welded, 1 dk	**(A21A2BC) Bulk Carrier** Grain: 37,523; Bale: 35,762 Compartments: 5 Ho, ER 5 Ha: 4 (19.2 x 17.6)ER (13.6 x 16.0) Cranes: 4x30.5t	**1 oil engine** driving 1 FP propeller Total Power: 5,850kW (7,954hp) 14.0kn B&W 6S42MC 1 x 2 Stroke 6 Cy. 420 x 1764 5850kW (7954bhp) Makita Corp-Japan Fuel: 1245.0
8306852 *V3OQ8* -	**TANAIS EXPRESS** *ex* Lord Byron *-2011* *ex* Blue Star *-2007* *ex* Refioglu *-2005* *ex* Fortuna America *-1999* *ex* Golden Ruby *-1998* *ex* Astoria Trader *-1993* **Tanais Shipping Ltd** Rosshipcom Marine Ltd *Belize City* *Belize* MMSI: 312655000 Official number: 371130066	**14,889** 8,920 25,694 T/cm 36.4	Class: NK	**1985-12 Imabari Shipbuilding Co Ltd — Imabari EH (Imabari Shipyard)** Yd No: 453 Loa 159.43 (BB) Br ex 26.04 Dght 9.908 Lbp 149.82 Br md 26.00 Dpth 13.62 Welded, 1 dk	**(A21A2BC) Bulk Carrier** Grain: 32,461; Bale: 31,095 Compartments: 4 Ho, ER 4 Ha: (18.4 x 12.8)3 (21.6 x 12.8)ER Cranes: 3x25t; Derricks: 1x25t	**1 oil engine** driving 1 FP propeller Total Power: 4,708kW (6,401hp) 13.4kn B&W 5L50MC 1 x 2 Stroke 5 Cy. 500 x 1620 4708kW (6401bhp) Hitachi Zosen Corp-Japan AuxGen: 4 x 267kW a.c Fuel: 1085.0 (r.f.)
9186479 *V3RM5* -	**TANAIS FLYER** *ex* Rabee *-2013* *ex* Atlantic Queen *-2009* **Tanais Shipping Ltd** Rosshipcom Marine Ltd *Belize City* *Belize* MMSI: 312629000 Official number: 371330078	**18,061** 9,616 28,674	Class: NK	**1998-11 Imabari Shipbuilding Co Ltd — Imabari EH (Imabari Shipyard)** Yd No: 545 Loa 169.54 (BB) Br ex - Dght 9.748 Lbp 160.40 Br md 27.20 Dpth 13.80 Welded, 1 dk	**(A21A2BC) Bulk Carrier** Grain: 37,181; Bale: 35,401 Compartments: 5 Ho, ER 5 Ha: (12.8 x 18.2)3 (20.8 x 22.8) (17.6 x 22.8)ER Cranes: 4x30.5t	**1 oil engine** driving 1 FP propeller Total Power: 7,987kW (10,859hp) 12.5kn B&W 6L50MC 1 x 2 Stroke 6 Cy. 500 x 1620 7987kW (10859bhp) Mitsui Engineering & Shipbuilding CLtd-Japan AuxGen: 2 x 410kW a.c Fuel: 1933.0
8400206 *V3RJ3* -	**TANAIS LEADER** *ex* Adventurer *-2011* *ex* Sea Rose *-2001* *ex* Handy Rose *-1993* *ex* Sun Rose *-1993* *ex* Hellespont Daring *-1988* *ex* Sanko Daring *-1985* **Tanais Shipping Ltd** Rosshipcom Marine Ltd *Belize City* *Belize* MMSI: 312067000 Official number: 371130069	**16,605** 9,208 27,622 T/cm 37.5	Class: RS (LR) (GL) (NK) (NV) Classed LR until 1/8/12	**1984-11 Mitsui Eng. & SB. Co. Ltd. — Tamano** Yd No: 1308 Loa 168.15 (BB) Br ex 26.31 Dght 9.760 Lbp 160.00 Br md 26.00 Dpth 13.63 Welded, 1 dk	**(A21A2BC) Bulk Carrier** Grain: 34,665; Bale: 33,417 Compartments: 5 Ho, ER 5 Ha: (9.5 x 13.3)4 (18.9 x 13.3)ER Cranes: 4x25t	**1 oil engine** driving 1 FP propeller Total Power: 5,520kW (7,505hp) 14.4kn B&W 6L50MCE 1 x 2 Stroke 6 Cy. 500 x 1620 5520kW (7505bhp) Mitsui Engineering & Shipbuilding CLtd-Japan AuxGen: 3 x 400kW 450V 60Hz a.c Boilers: AuxB (Comp) 6.0kgf/cm² (5.9bar) Fuel: 102.0 (d.f.) (Heating Coils) 1360.0 (r.f.) 21.5pd

IMO / Call sign / Flag	Name / Owner	Tonnage	Class	Builder / Dimensions	Type	Machinery
9079365 *HZG5859* -	**TANAJIB** **Saudi Arabian Oil Co (SAUDI ARAMCO)** - *Dammam* *Saudi Arabia* MMSI: 403701310 Official number: 837	**842** 252 280	Class: AB	**1996**-08 **N.V. Scheepswerf van Rupelmonde — Rupelmonde** (Hull launched by) Yd No: 2191 **1996**-08 **Belgian Shipbuilders Corp. -Fulton Marine N.V. — Ruisbroek** (Hull completed by) Yd No: 2191 Loa 41.07 Br ex 12.73 Dght 5.110 Lbp 37.52 Br md 12.70 Dpth 6.35 Welded, 1 dk	**(B32A2ST) Tug**	**2 oil engines** with clutches, flexible couplings & reduction geared to sc. shafts driving 2 Directional propellers Total Power: 4,600kW (6,254hp) 13.0kn Caterpillar 3608TA 2 x 4 Stroke 8 Cy. 280 x 300 each-2300kW (3127bhp) Caterpillar Inc-USA Thrusters: 1 Thwart. CP thruster (f)
5351868 - -	**TANAKAWA MARU** - **Jeffrey Rogers (S) Pte Ltd** -	*192* - -		**1944 Yamamoto Zosen KK — Kochi KC** Loa 32.44 Br ex 8.01 Dght 3.201 Lbp 28.81 Br md 7.98 Dpth 3.61 Welded, 1 dk	**(B32A2ST) Tug**	**2 oil engines** driving 2 FP propellers Total Power: 1,288kW (1,752hp) Hanshin 2 x 4 Stroke each-644kW (876bhp) (new engine 0000) The Hanshin Diesel Works Ltd-Japan
7915541 *OZ2084* -	**TANANGER** *ex* Forest Swan *-1995* *ex* Jerome B *-1993* *ex* Canis *-1991* **Skipafelagid Nor Lines Sp/f** Norresundby Shipping A/S SatCom: Inmarsat C 423120110 *Torshavn* *Faeroe Islands (Danish)* MMSI: 231201000	**4,636** 1,755 4,380	Class: BV (Class contemplated) NV	**1980**-11 **Fosen Mek. Verksteder AS — Rissa** Yd No: 27 Loa 102.49 (BB) Br ex - Dght 6.063 Lbp 93.30 Br md 16.51 Dpth 11.16 Welded, 3 dks	**(A35A2RR) Ro-Ro Cargo Ship** Stern door/ramp (centre) Side door (s) Lane-Len: 348 Grain: 9,973; Bale: 8,360; Ins: 680 TEU 86 incl 30 ref C. Compartments: 1 Ho, ER 1 Ha: (13.5 x 5.2)ER Cranes: 1x25t,1x5t Ice Capable	**1 oil engine** reduction geared to sc. shaft driving 1 FP propeller Total Power: 2,880kW (3,916hp) 14.0kn MaK 6M32 1 x 4 Stroke 6 Cy. 320 x 480 2880kW (3916bhp) (new engine 1999) MaK Motoren GmbH & Co. KG-Kiel AuxGen: 3 x 179kW 380V 50Hz a.c Fuel: 244.0 (r.f.) 13.0pd
5317094 *HP7255* -	**TANANO** *ex* Secil Grande *-1993* *ex* Secil Novo *-1953* **World Travelling Shipping Corp** - *Panama* *Panama* MMSI: 352016000 Official number: 22439LP	*715* 336 864	Class: (LR) ✠ Classed LR until 19/8/92	**1951**-11 **George Brown & Co. (Marine) Ltd. — Greenock** Yd No: 254 Loa 56.19 Br ex 9.58 Dght 3.944 Lbp 51.82 Br md 9.53 Dpth 4.02 Riveted\Welded, 1 dk	**(A31A2GX) General Cargo Ship** Grain: 1,069; Bale: 1,003 Compartments: 2 Ho, ER 2 Ha: ER Derricks: 1x14.8t; Winches: 2	**1 oil engine** driving 1 FP propeller Total Power: 633kW (861hp) 10.0kn Polar M46M 1 x 2 Stroke 6 Cy. 340 x 570 633kW (861bhp) British Polar Engines Ltd.-Glasgow Fuel: 38.5
9714094 *JD3443* -	**TANBA MARU** **Sanyo Kaiji KK** - *Amagasaki, Hyogo* *Japan* MMSI: 431004171 Official number: 141810	**199** - -		**2013**-02 **Hatayama Zosen KK — Yura WK** Loa 36.00 Br ex - Dght - Lbp - Br md 9.00 Dpth - Welded, 1 dk	**(B32A2ST) Tug**	**2 oil engines** reduction geared to sc. shafts driving 2 Propellers Total Power: 3,680kW (5,004hp) Yanmar 6EY26 2 x 4 Stroke 6 Cy. 260 x 385 each-1840kW (2502bhp) Yanmar Diesel Engine Co Ltd-Japan
9125360 *T2VT3* -	**TANBINH 38** *ex* Clipper Lancaster *-2011* *ex* Paclogger *-2004* *ex* Sea Dream *-1999* **Tan Binh Co Ltd** - *Funafuti* *Tuvalu* MMSI: 572255210 Official number: 24689611	**17,209** 10,714 28,249 T/cm 39.6	Class: NK VR (LR) (AB) Classed LR until 20/1/06	**1996**-05 **KK Kanasashi — Toyohashi AI** Yd No: 3411 Loa 169.93 (BB) Br ex 27.24 Dght 9.538 Lbp 162.00 Br md 27.20 Dpth 13.40 Welded, 1 dk	**(A21A2BC) Bulk Carrier** Grain: 37,752; Bale: 36,517 Compartments: 5 Ho, ER 5 Ha: (12.0 x 12.8)4 (20.0 x 17.8)ER Cranes: 4x30t	**1 oil engine** driving 1 FP propeller Total Power: 5,884kW (8,000hp) 14.0kn Mitsubishi 5UEC52LA 1 x 2 Stroke 5 Cy. 520 x 1600 5884kW (8000bhp) Kobe Hatsudoki KK-Japan AuxGen: 3 x 441kW 450V 60Hz a.c Fuel: 105.0 (d.f.) (Heating Coils) 1031.0 (r.f.) 24.5pd
9567740 *C6AY5* -	**TANCHOU ARROW** **Gearbulk Shipowning Ltd** Gearbulk Norway AS *Nassau* *Bahamas* MMSI: 311000193 Official number: 7000608	**45,500** 22,100 72,400	Class: NV	**2014**-03 **Oshima Shipbuilding Co Ltd — Saikai NS** Yd No: 10664 Loa 210.00 (BB) Br ex - Dght 13.730 Lbp 206.00 Br md 36.00 Dpth 19.54 Welded, 1 dk	**(A31A2GO) Open Hatch Cargo Ship** Grain: 85,000 TEU 445 C Dk Compartments: 8 Ho, ER 8 Ha: ER Cranes: 4x45t	**1 oil engine** driving 1 FP propeller Total Power: 9,390kW (12,767hp) 14.5kn MAN-B&W 5S60ME-C8 1 x 2 Stroke 5 Cy. 600 x 2400 9390kW (12767bhp) Mitsui Engineering & Shipbuilding CLtd-Japan AuxGen: 2 x a.c, 1 x a.c Thrusters: 1 Tunnel thruster (f)
9654127 *VJN3977* -	**TANCRED** **National Australia Bank Ltd** DMS Maritime Pty Ltd *Fremantle, WA* *Australia* MMSI: 503678700 Official number: 860260	**217** 65 -	Class: LR (BV) **100A1** SS 06/2012 tug *IWS **UMS**	**2012**-06 **Damen Shipyards Changde Co Ltd — Changde HN** (Hull) Yd No: (512904) **2012**-06 **B.V. Scheepswerf Damen — Gorinchem** Yd No: 512904 Loa 22.73 Br ex - Dght 3.400 Lbp 20.38 Br md 9.80 Dpth 4.50 Welded, 1 dk	**(B32A2ST) Tug**	**2 oil engines** reduction geared to sc. shaft (s) driving 2 FP propellers Total Power: 3,530kW (4,800hp) Caterpillar 3512C 2 x Vee 4 Stroke 12 Cy. 170 x 215 each-1765kW (2400bhp) AuxGen: 2 x 51kW 50Hz a.c Fuel: 48.0 (d.f.)
8605167 *LALX4* -	**TANCRED** *ex* Nosac Sea *-1996* *ex* Nosac Tancred *-1989* **Wilhelmsen Lines Shipowning AS** Wilhelmsen Lines Car Carrier Ltd SatCom: Inmarsat C 425878710 *Tonsberg* *Norway (NIS)* MMSI: 258787000	**48,676** 14,603 15,577	Class: NV (NK)	**1987**-04 **Sumitomo Heavy Industries Ltd. — Oppama Shipyard, Yokosuka** Yd No: 1142 Loa 190.05 (BB) Br ex 32.29 Dght 8.921 Lbp 180.02 Br md 32.26 Dpth 13.75 Welded, 12 dks incl 4 hoistable	**(A35B2RV) Vehicles Carrier** Side door/ramp (s) Len: 20.00 Wid: 5.00 Swl: 16 Quarter stern door/ramp (s) Len: 35.00 Wid: 7.00 Swl: 100 Lane-Wid: 3.39 Lane-clr ht: 4.60 Cars: 5,720	**1 oil engine** driving 1 FP propeller Total Power: 8,716kW (11,850hp) 18.0kn Sulzer 7RTA58 1 x 2 Stroke 7 Cy. 580 x 1700 8716kW (11850bhp) Sumitomo Heavy Industries Ltd-Japan AuxGen: 2 x 780kW 440V 60Hz a.c Thrusters: 1 Thwart. CP thruster (f)
9396725 *V7PB5* -	**TANDARA SPIRIT** *ex* Helcion *-2011* *launched as* Mexico *-2008* **Energetic Tank Inc** Teekay Shipping (Australia) Pty Ltd *Majuro* *Marshall Islands* MMSI: 538003202 Official number: 3202	**30,040** 13,312 50,760 T/cm 51.9	Class: NV (LR) ✠ Classed LR until 29/4/08	**2008**-04 **SPP Shipbuilding Co Ltd — Tongyeong** Yd No: H1013 Loa 183.00 (BB) Br ex 32.24 Dght 13.016 Lbp 174.00 Br md 32.20 Dpth 19.10 Welded, 1 dk	**(A12B2TR) Chemical/Products Tanker** Double Hull (13F) Liq: 52,179; Liq (Oil): 52,126 Cargo Heating Coils Compartments: 12 Wing Ta, 2 Wing Slop Ta, ER 12 Cargo Pump (s): 12x600m³/hr Manifold: Bow/CM: 92m	**1 oil engine** driving 1 FP propeller Total Power: 9,480kW (12,889hp) 14.9kn MAN-B&W 6S50MC-C 1 x 2 Stroke 6 Cy. 500 x 2000 9480kW (12889bhp) Doosan Engine Co Ltd-South Korea AuxGen: 3 x 900kW 450V 60Hz a.c Fuel: 235.0 (d.f.) 1530.0 (r.f.)
9028926 - -	**TANDAY** *ex* Kursun-53 *-2011* *ex* Kervansaray-1 *-2006* *ex* Bolunmez-1 *-1990* **Batys Munai Trans LLP** - *Aqtau* *Kazakhstan*	**125** 62 137	Class: RS	**1981**-05 **Cemalettin Oyar — Istanbul** Loa 34.00 Br ex 5.62 Dght 2.150 Lbp 32.25 Br md 5.51 Dpth 2.78 Welded, 1 dk	**(A13B2TU) Tanker (unspecified)**	**1 oil engine** geared to sc. shaft driving 1 FP propeller Total Power: 342kW (465hp) 10.0kn Volvo Penta TD162FL 1 x 4 Stroke 6 Cy. 144 x 165 342kW (465bhp) AB Volvo Penta-Sweden
6708147 *LGJD* -	**TANDBERG POLAR** *ex* Khan *-2013* *ex* Argus *-2000* *ex* Mor *-1997* *ex* Coburg *-1993* *ex* Alfred Lamey *-1970* **Tandberg Eiendom AS** - *Oslo* *Norway* MMSI: 257370500	**235** 70 -	Class: (LR) ✠ Classed LR until 17/2/93	**1967**-04 **James Lamont & Co. Ltd. — Port Glasgow** Yd No: 406 Loa 32.14 Br ex 8.56 Dght 3.353 Lbp 29.88 Br md 8.08 Dpth 4.12 Riveted\Welded	**(B32A2ST) Tug**	**1 oil engine** dr geared to sc. shaft driving 1 CP propeller Total Power: 1,250kW (1,700hp) 11.0kn MWM 1 x 4 Stroke 6 Cy. 360 x 450 1250kW (1700bhp) Motoren Werke Mannheim AG (MWM)-West Germany AuxGen: 2 x 25kW 220V d.c Thrusters: 1 Thwart. FP thruster (f)
9027386 *YEOX* -	**TANDE'MAND** **PT ASDP Indonesia Ferry (Persero) - Angkutan Sungai Danau & Penyeberangan** - *Jakarta* *Indonesia*	**646** 194 -	Class: KI	**1991**-06 **P.T. Dok & Galangan Kapal Nusantara — Semarang** Loa 44.30 Br ex - Dght 2.000 Lbp 37.50 Br md 12.00 Dpth 3.00 Welded, 1 dk	**(A37B2PS) Passenger Ship**	**2 oil engines** geared to sc. shafts driving 2 Propellers Total Power: 1,472kW (2,002hp) 11.7kn Yanmar 12LAA-UTE1 2 x Vee 4 Stroke 12 Cy. 148 x 165 each-736kW (1001bhp) Yanmar Diesel Engine Co Ltd-Japan
9096521 *9BQP* -	**TANDIS 11** **M Abkhoo** Setareh Sahabi Marine Safety Equipment Service Co *Bandar Imam Khomeini* *Iran* MMSI: 422740000 Official number: 20677	**197** 59 -	Class: AS	**1989**-01 **Sadra International — Bandar Abbas** Yd No: 10MM Converted From: Fishing Vessel-2008 Loa 27.40 Br ex - Dght 2.300 Lbp - Br md 7.20 Dpth 4.00 Welded, 1 dk	**(B21B20T) Offshore Tug/Supply Ship**	**2 oil engines** geared to sc. shafts driving 2 Propellers Total Power: 1,040kW (1,414hp) Cummins 2 x 4 Stroke each-520kW (707bhp) (new engine 2008) Cummins Engine Co Inc-USA
8207537 *EPB07* -	**TANDIS 21** *ex* Gazelle *-2012* *ex* Shamrock Gazelle *-2003* *ex* Seabulk Gazelle *-2000* *ex* Selat Hope *-1997* *ex* Mansal 29 *-1995* *ex* Reja *-1986* **Sealantic Co FZC** - *Iran* MMSI: 422029400	**348** 105 356	Class: (CC) (AB) (NV)	**1982**-05 **Eastern Marine, Inc. — Panama City, Fl** Yd No: 61 Loa 39.63 Br ex - Dght 3.247 Lbp 34.60 Br md 9.15 Dpth 3.51 Welded, 1 dk	**(B22A20V) Diving Support Vessel**	**2 oil engines** reverse reduction geared to sc. shafts driving 2 FP propellers Total Power: 882kW (1,200hp) 12.0kn G.M. (Detroit Diesel) 16V-92 2 x Vee 2 Stroke 16 Cy. 123 x 127 each-441kW (600bhp) General Motors Detroit DieselAllison Divn-USA AuxGen: 2 x 90kW 380V 60Hz a.c Thrusters: 1 Thwart. FP thruster (f)

IMO / Call sign	Name / Owner / Port	Tonnage	Class	Build / Dimensions	Type	Machinery
7367768 - -	**TANDOR** *ex* De Vrouw Jannetje *ex* Concordia *-1984* **NV Tasda Fish** - *Paramaribo* *Suriname* Official number: SA-102	**244** 73 -		**1974**-03 **W. Visser & Zoon B.V. Werf "De Lastdrager" — Den Helder** Yd No: 75 Loa 35.34 Br ex 7.65 Dght 3.080 Lbp 31.12 Br md 7.50 Dpth 4.12 Welded, 1 dk	**(B11A2FT) Trawler**	**1 oil engine** driving 1 FP propeller Total Power: 1,103kW (1,500hp) Bolnes 10DNL150/600 1 x 2 Stroke 10 Cy. 190 x 350 1103kW (1500bhp) 'Bolnes' Motorenfabriek BV-Netherlands
8935304 *HP5963* -	**TANDOR** *ex* Hessel SR *-2013* *ex* Limanda *-2001* **NV Holsu** - *Panama* *Panama* MMSI: 354312000 Official number: D19922805PEXT	**130** 39 -		**1994 Zeebrugse Scheepswerven N.V. — Zeebrugge** Loa 23.93 Br ex 6.45 Dght - Lbp - Br md - Dpth - Welded, 1 dk	**(B11B2FV) Fishing Vessel**	**1 oil engine** driving 1 FP propeller
9614464 *YDB4145* -	**TANDUR** *ex* TS Adventure *-2012* **PT Pelayaran Citramaritimindo Pratama** - *Jakarta* *Indonesia*	**251** 75 -	Class: BV	**2012**-07 **Bengbu Shenzhou Machinery Co Ltd — Bengbu AH** (Hull) Yd No: (1447) **2012**-07 **Pacific Ocean Engineering & Trading Pte Ltd (POET) — Singapore** Yd No: 1447 Loa 29.50 Br ex 9.60 Dght 3.500 Lbp 28.36 Br md 9.00 Dpth 4.16 Welded, 1 dk	**(B32A2ST) Tug**	**2 oil engines** reduction geared to sc. shafts driving 2 FP propellers Total Power: 1,856kW (2,524hp) Chinese Std. Type XCW8200ZC 2 x 4 Stroke 8 Cy. 200 x 270 each-928kW (1262bhp) Weichai Power Co Ltd-China AuxGen: 2 x 100kW 50Hz a.c Fuel: 190.0 (d.f.)
9178381 *WDF2025* -	**TAN'ERLIQ** - **Vessel Management Services Inc** - *Valdez, AK* *United States of America* MMSI: 366760670 Official number: 1074362	**1,046** 313 -	Class: AB	**1999**-05 **Dakota Creek Industries Inc — Anacortes WA** Yd No: 34 Loa 46.63 Br ex 14.63 Dght 5.500 Lbp 46.60 Br md - Dpth 6.09 Welded, 1 dk	**(B32A2ST) Tug**	**2 oil engines** gearing integral to driving 2 Voith-Schneider propellers Total Power: 7,496kW (10,192hp) 14.0kn Caterpillar 3612TA 2 x Vee 4 Stroke 12 Cy. 280 x 300 each-3748kW (5096bhp) Caterpillar Inc-USA AuxGen: 2 x 190kW a.c
8307272 *BJLM* -	**TANG QUAN** - **COSCO Yinggang Shipping Co Ltd** - SatCom: Inmarsat A 1570623 *Haikou, Hainan* *China* MMSI: 412523350	**8,848** 4,966 11,200	Class: CC	**1984**-07 **Kyokuyo Shipyard Corp — Shimonoseki YC** Yd No: 322 Loa 138.00 (BB) Br ex 20.63 Dght 9.316 Lbp 129.00 Br md 20.60 Dpth 12.40 Welded, 1 dk	**(A34A2GR) Refrigerated Cargo Ship** Grain: 8,133; Bale: 7,579; Ins: 5,971 TEU 35 Compartments: ER, 4 Ho 4 Ha: ER Cranes: 3x6t	**1 oil engine** driving 1 FP propeller Total Power: 5,516kW (7,500hp) 16.7kn B&W 5L60MC 1 x 2 Stroke 5 Cy. 600 x 1944 5516kW (7500bhp) Mitsui Engineering & Shipbuilding CLtd-Japan
8915847 - -	**TANGALOOMA JET** *ex* Seacom I *-2001* **Betty Joan Osborne, Brian George Osborne & Tisad Building Pty Ltd** - *Brisbane, Qld* *Australia* MMSI: 503405300 Official number: 857046	*376* - 50	Class: (NK)	**1990**-06 **North Queensland Engineers & Agents Pty Ltd — Cairns QLD** Yd No: 170 Loa 40.17 Br ex - Dght 1.600 Lbp 33.77 Br md 15.60 Dpth 4.54 Welded	**(A37B2PS) Passenger Ship** Hull Material: Aluminium Alloy Passengers: unberthed: 430	**2 oil engines** with clutches, flexible couplings & geared to sc. shafts driving 2 Water jets Total Power: 2,870kW (3,902hp) G.M. (Detroit Diesel) 16V-149-TI 2 x Vee 2 Stroke 16 Cy. 146 x 146 each-1435kW (1951bhp) General Motors Detroit DieselAllison Divn-USA
7510456 *PS5568* -	**TANGARA** - **Petroleo Brasileiro SA (PETROBRAS)** Petrobras Transporte SA (TRANSPETRO) - Fronape SatCom: Inmarsat A 1550252 *Rio de Janeiro* *Brazil* MMSI: 710000000 Official number: 3810248266	*2,358* 707 1,920	Class: AB	**1976**-04 **Mitsui SB. & Eng. Co. Ltd. — Tamano** Yd No: F437 Loa 86.01 Br ex 14.64 Dght 6.001 Lbp 79.02 Br md 14.61 Dpth 7.22 Welded, 1 dk	**(B32A2ST) Tug** Derricks: 2x5t	**2 oil engines** reverse reduction geared to sc. shafts driving 2 CP propellers Total Power: 8,826kW (12,000hp) 18.8kn Pielstick 12PC2-2V-400 2 x Vee 4 Stroke 12 Cy. 400 x 460 each-4413kW (6000bhp) Niigata Engineering Co Ltd-Japan AuxGen: 2 x 500kW a.c, 1 x 240kW a.c Thrusters: 1 Thwart. FP thruster (f) Fuel: 1998.0 (d.f.)
9189691 *YJVJ6* -	**TANGAROA** *ex* Faro Villano *-2008* **Tangaroa Fishing Ltd** - *Port Vila* *Vanuatu* MMSI: 576375000 Official number: 5032	**472** 141 400	Class: BV	**1999**-07 **Astilleros Zamakona SA — Santurtzi** Yd No: 450 Loa - Br ex - Dght 4.080 Lbp 37.50 Br md 9.50 Dpth 4.80 Welded, 1 dk	**(B11B2FV) Fishing Vessel**	**1 oil engine** reduction geared to sc. shaft driving 1 FP propeller Total Power: 1,177kW (1,600hp) 12.0kn Caterpillar 3516TA 1 x Vee 4 Stroke 16 Cy. 170 x 190 1177kW (1600bhp) Caterpillar Inc-USA AuxGen: 3 x 275kW 380V 50Hz a.c
9011571 *ZMFR* -	**TANGAROA** - **NIWA Vessel Management Ltd** - SatCom: Inmarsat A 1663313 *Wellington* *New Zealand* MMSI: 512000058 Official number: 875871	**2,291** 687	Class: NV	**1991**-05 **Mjellem & Karlsen Verft AS — Bergen** Yd No: 142 Loa 70.01 (BB) Br ex - Dght 5.790 Lbp 61.83 Br md 13.81 Dpth 8.50 Welded, 1 dk	**(B12D2FR) Fishery Research Vessel** Ice Capable	**1 oil engine** geared to sc. shaft driving 1 CP propeller Total Power: 2,998kW (4,076hp) Wartsila 8R32D 1 x 4 Stroke 8 Cy. 320 x 350 2998kW (4076bhp) Wartsila Diesel Oy-Finland Thrusters: 1 Tunnel thruster (f)
8008759 *V5TB* L919	**TANGENI BAY** *ex* Libertas *-2003* **Tangeni Investments (Pty) Ltd** - *Luderitz* *Namibia* Official number: 98LB004	*304* 175 -		**1980 Ornelas Fishing Co. (Pty.) Ltd. — Cape Town** Loa 29.95 Br ex 8.36 Dght - Lbp - Br md - Dpth 3.23 Welded, 1 dk	**(B11B2FV) Fishing Vessel**	**2 oil engines** driving 2 FP propellers Total Power: 312kW (424hp) Caterpillar D353TA 2 x 4 Stroke 6 Cy. 159 x 203 each-156kW (212bhp) Caterpillar Tractor Co-USA
9112777 *CNA4608* -	**TANGER EXPRESS** *ex* Mette Mols *-2011* **Tanger Jet Shipping Cie** FRS Iberia SLU *Tangier* *Morocco* MMSI: 242127100	**14,221** 4,313 4,030	Class: BV	**1996**-06 **Orskov Christensens Staalskibsvaerft A/S — Frederikshavn** Yd No: 192 Loa 136.40 (BB) Br ex 24.60 Dght 6.000 Lbp 125.30 Br md 24.00 Dpth 13.85 Welded, 2 dks	**(A36A2PR) Passenger/Ro-Ro Ship (Vehicles)** Passengers: unberthed: 600 Bow door/ramp (centre) Len: 5.30 Wid: 8.00 Swl: - Stern door (p) Len: 5.15 Wid: 7.58 Swl: - Stern door (s) Len: 5.15 Wid: 7.58 Swl: - Lane-Len: 1240 Cars: 344 Ice Capable	**2 oil engines** driving 2 CP propellers Total Power: 11,700kW (15,908hp) 19.2kn B&W 9L35MC 2 x 2 Stroke 9 Cy. 350 x 1050 each-5850kW (7954bhp) MAN B&W Diesel A/S-Denmark AuxGen: 2 x 1108kW a.c, 3 x 935kW a.c Thrusters: 2 Thwart. CP thruster (f)
7931674 *DUA6538* -	**TANGERINE 88** *ex* Yuan Feng *-2008* *ex* Chrissi *-2004* *ex* Argomar *-2004* *ex* Emerald Light *-1994* *ex* Emerald Tathum *-1990* *ex* Extremar *-1988* **Yuan Feng Shipping Inc** Ningbo Merchant Refrigeration Shipping Co SatCom: Inmarsat C 454800035 *Philippines*	**1,792** 682 2,257	Class: (PR) (BV)	**1981**-03 **Ast. del Cadagua W. E. Gonzalez S.A. — Bilbao** Yd No: 114 Loa 83.70 (BB) Br ex 12.40 Dght 5.201 Lbp 76.03 Br md 12.02 Dpth 6.81 Welded, 2 dks	**(A34A2GR) Refrigerated Cargo Ship** Ins: 2,545 Compartments: 3 Ho, ER, 3 Tw Dk 3 Ha: 3 (7.8 x 6.0)ER Derricks: 6x3t; Winches: 6	**1 oil engine** driving 1 FP propeller Total Power: 1,545kW (2,101hp) 13.9kn Deutz RBV6M358 1 x 4 Stroke 6 Cy. 400 x 580 1545kW (2101bhp) Hijos de J Barreras SA-Spain AuxGen: 3 x 320kW 380V 50Hz a.c Fuel: 90.0 (d.f.) 280.0 (r.f.) 6.0pd
9512355 *V7XG9* -	**TANGERINE ISLAND** - **Nico Shipping Inc** Funada Kaiun KK *Majuro* *Marshall Islands* MMSI: 538004478 Official number: 4478	**43,013** 27,239 82,265 T/cm 70.2	Class: NK	**2012**-01 **Tsuneishi Shipbuilding Co Ltd — Fukuyama HS** Yd No: 1475 Loa 228.99 (BB) Br ex - Dght 14.429 Lbp 222.00 Br md 32.26 Dpth 20.05 Welded, 1 dk	**(A21A2BC) Bulk Carrier** Grain: 97,381 Compartments: 7 Ho, ER 7 Ha: ER	**1 oil engine** driving 1 FP propeller Total Power: 9,710kW (13,202hp) 14.5kn MAN-B&W 6S60MC-C 1 x 2 Stroke 6 Cy. 600 x 2400 9710kW (13202bhp) Mitsui Engineering & Shipbuilding CLtd-Japan Fuel: 3180.0
9463803 *YDA6418* -	**TANGGON** - **PT Maritim Barito Perkasa** - *Jakarta* *Indonesia* MMSI: 525002006 Official number: 3223/IIA	**249** 74 172	Class: AB	**2007**-11 **PT Perkasa Melati — Batam** Yd No: PM019 Loa 29.50 Br ex - Dght 3.500 Lbp 26.50 Br md 9.00 Dpth 4.16 Welded, 1 dk	**(B32A2ST) Tug**	**2 oil engines** reduction geared to sc. shafts driving 2 FP propellers Total Power: 2,080kW (2,828hp) Mitsubishi S12R-MTK 2 x Vee 4 Stroke 12 Cy. 170 x 180 each-1040kW (1414bhp) Mitsubishi Heavy Industries Ltd-Japan AuxGen: 2 x 80kW a.c Fuel: 61.7 (d.f.)

IMO / Call sign	Name / Owner / Manager / Registry	Tonnage	Classification	Builder / Dimensions	Type / Cargo	Machinery
9029372 - -	**TANGGUH** **PT Bandar Niaga Raya** - *Cirebon* *Indonesia*	**139** 42 -	Class: KI	**2006**-04 **P.T. Pantai Mulia Semesta — Tegal** Loa 25.00 Br ex - Dght 2.400 Lbp 21.00 Br md 8.00 Dpth 3.25 Welded, 1 dk	**(B32A2ST) Tug**	**2 oil engines** geared to sc. shafts driving 2 Propellers Total Power: 1,220kW (1,658hp) 7.5kn Yanmar 6AYM-ETE 2 x 4 Stroke 6 Cy. 155 x 180 each-610kW (829bhp) (made 2005) Yanmar Diesel Engine Co Ltd-Japan AuxGen: 1 x 44kW 380/220V a.c, 2 x 18kW 380/220V a.c
9334284 *9V7631* -	**TANGGUH BATUR** **LNG North-South Shipping Co (Singapore) Pte Ltd** NYK LNG Shipmanagement Ltd SatCom: Inmarsat C 456409010 *Singapore* *Singapore* MMSI: 564090000 Official number: 394535	**97,432** 29,230 84,980 T/cm 104.3	Class: LR (NV) **100A1** SS 12/2008 liquified gas tanker, Ship Type 2G methane (LNG) in membrane tanks, maximum vapour pressure 0.25 bar, minimum temperature 163 degree C *IWS LI ECO (TOC) **LMC** **UMS**	**2008**-12 **Daewoo Shipbuilding & Marine Engineering Co Ltd — Geoje** Yd No: 2242 Loa 285.40 (BB) Br ex 43.44 Dght 12.500 Lbp 274.39 Br md 43.40 Dpth 26.00 Welded, 1 dk	**(A11A2TN) LNG Tanker** Double Bottom Entire Compartment Length Liq (Gas): 142,988 4 x Gas Tank (s); 4 membrane (36% Ni.stl) pri horizontal 8 Cargo Pump (s): 8x1700m³/hr Manifold: Bow/CM: 141.6m	**1 Steam Turb** reduction geared to sc. shaft driving 1 FP propeller Total Power: 28,464kW (38,700hp) 19.5kn Kawasaki UA-400 1 x steam Turb 28464kW (38700shp) Kawasaki Heavy Industries Ltd-Japan AuxGen: 3 x 3500kW a.c Thrusters: 1 Tunnel thruster (f) Fuel: 505.0 (d.f.) 6915.0 (r.f.)
9422316 *YEZG* -	**TANGGUH EWAKO** **PT KBRI Joint Operation** PT BP Tangguh *Manokwari* *Indonesia* MMSI: 525015835	**491** 185 194	Class: KI LR ✠ **100A1** SS 04/2011 escort tug, fire fighting Ship 1 (2400m3/h) ✠ **LMC** **UMS** Eq.Ltr: G; Cable: 302.5/22.0 U2 (a)	**2011**-04 **P.T. PAL Indonesia — Surabaya** Yd No: 265 Loa 32.60 Br ex 12.22 Dght 4.900 Lbp 30.20 Br md 11.60 Dpth 5.36 Welded, 1 dk	**(B32A2ST) Tug**	**2 oil engines** gearing integral to driving 2 Z propellers Total Power: 3,236kW (4,400hp) Niigata 6L28HX 2 x 4 Stroke 6 Cy. 280 x 370 each-1618kW (2200bhp) Niigata Engineering Co Ltd-Japan AuxGen: 2 x 160kW 380V 50Hz a.c
9349007 *3ERT7* -	**TANGGUH FOJA** **Ocean 1919 Shipping No 1 SA** Kawasaki Kisen Kaisha Ltd (Kawasaki Kisen KK) ('K' Line) SatCom: Inmarsat C 437016810 *Panama* *Panama* MMSI: 370168000 Official number: 3456609	**97,897** 30,877 82,338 T/cm 104.8	Class: AB	**2008**-11 **Samsung Heavy Industries Co Ltd — Geoje** Yd No: 1619 Loa 285.10 (BB) Br ex - Dght 11.500 Lbp 274.00 Br md 43.40 Dpth 26.00 Welded, 1 dk	**(A11A2TN) LNG Tanker** Double Bottom Entire Compartment Length Liq (Gas): 154,948 5 x Gas Tank (s); 4 membrane (s.stl) pri horizontal, ER 8 Cargo Pump (s): 8x1850m³/hr Manifold: Bow/CM: 142.7m	**4 diesel electric oil engines** driving 3 gen. each 11000kW 6600V a.c 1 gen. of 5500kW 6600V a.c Connecting to 2 elec. motors each (12650kW) driving 1 FP propeller Total Power: 39,900kW (54,247hp) 19.5kn Wartsila 12V50DF 3 x Vee 4 Stroke 12 Cy. 500 x 580 each-11400kW (15499bhp) Wartsila France SA-France Wartsila 6L50DF 1 x 4 Stroke 6 Cy. 500 x 580 5700kW (7750bhp) Wartsila France SA-France Thrusters: 1 Tunnel thruster (f) Fuel: 5915.0 (d.f.)
9422299 *PMRZ* -	**TANGGUH GAROPA** **PT KBRI Joint Operation** PT BP Tangguh *Manokwari* *Indonesia* MMSI: 525015398	**450** - 194	Class: KI LR ✠ **100A1** SS 12/2010 escort tug, fire fighting ship 1 (2400 m3/h) ✠ **LMC** **UMS** Eq.Ltr: G; Cable: 302.5/22.0 U2 (a)	**2010**-12 **P.T. PAL Indonesia — Surabaya** Yd No: 263 Loa 32.60 Br ex 12.22 Dght 4.100 Lbp 30.20 Br md 11.60 Dpth 5.36 Welded, 1 dk	**(B32A2ST) Tug**	**2 oil engines** gearing integral to driving 2 Z propellers Total Power: 3,236kW (4,400hp) Niigata 6L28HX 2 x 4 Stroke 6 Cy. 280 x 370 each-1618kW (2200bhp) Niigata Engineering Co Ltd-Japan AuxGen: 2 x 160kW 380V 50Hz a.c
9333632 *C6XC2* -	**TANGGUH HIRI** **Tangguh Hiri Finance Ltd** Teekay Shipping (Glasgow) Ltd SatCom: Inmarsat C 430978711 *Nassau* *Bahamas* MMSI: 309787000 Official number: 9000271	**101,957** 31,576 84,467 T/cm 106.5	Class: LR ✠ **100A1** SS 11/2013 liquefied gas tanker, Ship Type 2G methane (LNG) in membrane tanks maximum vapour pressure 0.25 bar minimum temperature minus 163 degree C **ShipRight** (SDA) *IWS LI EP (B,P,N) ✠ **LMC** **UMS CCS** Eq.Ltr: A*; Cable: 742.5/102.0 U3 (a)	**2008**-11 **Hyundai Heavy Industries Co Ltd — Ulsan** Yd No: 1780 Loa 288.43 (BB) Br ex 44.24 Dght 12.200 Lbp 275.00 Br md 44.20 Dpth 26.00 Welded, 1 dk	**(A11A2TN) LNG Tanker** Double Hull Liq (Gas): 151,885 4 x Gas Tank (s); 4 membrane (s.stl) pri horizontal 8 Cargo Pump (s): 8x1800m³/hr Manifold: Bow/CM: 146.2m	**4 diesel electric oil engines** driving 2 gen. each 1100kW 6600V a.c 2 gen. each 8250kW 6600V a.c Connecting to 2 elec. motors each (14860kW) driving 1 FP propeller Total Power: 39,900kW (54,248hp) 20.0kn Wartsila 12V50DF 2 x Vee 4 Stroke 12 Cy. 500 x 580 each-11400kW (15499bhp) Wartsila Italia SpA-Italy Wartsila 9L50DF 2 x 4 Stroke 9 Cy. 500 x 580 each-8550kW (11625bhp) Wartsila Italia SpA-Italy Boilers: e (ex.g.) 15.3kgf/cm² (15.0bar), WTAuxB (o.f.) 11.9kgf/cm² (11.7bar) Thrusters: 1 Thwart. FP thruster (f) Fuel: 5648.0 (d.f.)
9349019 *3ETB6* -	**TANGGUH JAYA** **Ocean1919 Shipping No 2 SA** Kawasaki Kisen Kaisha Ltd (Kawasaki Kisen KK) ('K' Line) SatCom: Inmarsat C 437050210 *Panama* *Panama* MMSI: 370502000 Official number: 3457409A	**97,897** 30,877 82,313 T/cm 104.8	Class: AB	**2008**-12 **Samsung Heavy Industries Co Ltd — Geoje** Yd No: 1620 Loa 285.10 (BB) Br ex - Dght 11.500 Lbp 274.00 Br md 43.40 Dpth 26.00 Welded, 1 dk	**(A11A2TN) LNG Tanker** Double Bottom Entire Compartment Length Liq (Gas): 154,948 5 x Gas Tank (s); 4 membrane (s.stl) pri horizontal, ER 8 Cargo Pump (s): 8x1850m³/hr Manifold: Bow/CM: 142.7m	**4 diesel electric oil engines** driving 3 gen. each 11000kW 6600V a.c 1 gen. of 5500kW 6600V a.c Connecting to 2 elec. motors each (12650kW) driving 1 FP propeller Total Power: 39,900kW (54,247hp) 19.5kn Wartsila 12V50DF 3 x Vee 4 Stroke 12 Cy. 500 x 580 each-11400kW (15499bhp) Wartsila France SA-France Wartsila 6L50DF 1 x 4 Stroke 6 Cy. 500 x 580 5700kW (7750bhp) Wartsila France SA-France Thrusters: 1 Tunnel thruster (f) Fuel: 5435.0 (d.f.)
9422287 *PMMK* -	**TANGGUH MANGIWANG** **PT KBRI Joint Operation** BP Berau Ltd *Manokwari* *Indonesia* MMSI: 525015328 Official number: 2575	**481** 145 194	Class: KI LR ✠ **100A1** SS 09/2010 escort tug, fire fighting Ship 1 (2400m3/h) ✠ **LMC** **UMS** Eq.Ltr: G; Cable: 302.5/20.5 U2 (a)	**2010**-09 **P.T. PAL Indonesia — Surabaya** Yd No: 262 Loa 32.00 Br ex 12.22 Dght 4.100 Lbp 30.20 Br md 11.60 Dpth 5.36 Welded, 1 dk	**(B32A2ST) Tug**	**2 oil engines** gearing integral to driving 2 Z propellers Total Power: 3,236kW (4,400hp) Niigata 6L28HLX 2 x 4 Stroke 6 Cy. 280 x 400 each-1618kW (2200bhp) Niigata Engineering Co Ltd-Japan AuxGen: 2 x 160kW 380V 50Hz a.c
9355379 *H9NH* -	**TANGGUH PALUNG** **Ocean1919 Shipping No 3 SA** Kawasaki Kisen Kaisha Ltd (Kawasaki Kisen KK) ('K' Line) SatCom: Inmarsat C 437076610 *Panama* *Panama* MMSI: 370766000 Official number: 4012009	**97,897** 30,877 82,407 T/cm 104.8	Class: AB	**2009**-03 **Samsung Heavy Industries Co Ltd — Geoje** Yd No: 1634 Loa 285.10 (BB) Br ex - Dght 11.500 Lbp 274.00 Br md 43.40 Dpth 26.00 Welded, 1 dk	**(A11A2TN) LNG Tanker** Double Bottom Entire Compartment Length Liq (Gas): 154,948 4 x Gas Tank (s); 4 membrane (s.stl) pri horizontal 8 Cargo Pump (s): 8x1850m³/hr Manifold: Bow/CM: 142.7m	**4 diesel electric oil engines** driving 3 gen. each 11000kW 6600V a.c 1 gen. of 5500kW 6600V a.c Connecting to 2 elec. motors each (12650kW) driving 1 FP propeller Total Power: 39,900kW (54,247hp) 19.5kn Wartsila 12V50DF 3 x Vee 4 Stroke 12 Cy. 500 x 580 each-11400kW (15499bhp) Wartsila France SA-France Wartsila 6L50DF 1 x 4 Stroke 6 Cy. 500 x 580 5700kW (7750bhp) Wartsila France SA-France Thrusters: 1 Tunnel thruster (f) Fuel: 5435.0 (d.f.)
9422304 *PLXR* -	**TANGGUH PAURU** **PT KBRI Joint Operation** PT BP Tangguh *Manokwari* *Indonesia* MMSI: 525015834	**481** 145 194	Class: KI LR ✠ **100A1** SS 04/2011 escort tug, fire fighting Ship 1 (2400m3/h) ✠ **LMC** **UMS** Eq.Ltr: G; Cable: 302.5/20.5 U2 (a)	**2011**-04 **P.T. PAL Indonesia — Surabaya** Yd No: 264 Loa 32.00 Br ex 12.22 Dght 4.100 Lbp 30.20 Br md 11.60 Dpth 5.36 Welded, 1 dk	**(B32A2ST) Tug**	**2 oil engines** gearing integral to driving 2 Z propellers Total Power: 3,236kW (4,400hp) Niigata 6L28HX 2 x 4 Stroke 6 Cy. 280 x 370 each-1618kW (2200bhp) Niigata Engineering Co Ltd-Japan AuxGen: 2 x 160kW 380V 50Hz a.c

9361990 C6XC3 -
TANGGUH SAGO
Tangguh Sago Finance Ltd
Teekay Shipping (Glasgow) Ltd
SatCom: Inmarsat C 430874110
Nassau *Bahamas*
MMSI: 308741000
Official number: 9000272

101,957 31,576 84,484 T/cm 106.5

Class: LR
✠ **100A1** SS 03/2014
liquefied gas tanker, Type 2G
methane (LNG) in membrane tanks
maximum vapour pressure 0.25 bar
minimum cargo temperature minus 163 degress C
ShipRight (SDA)
*IWS
LI
EP (B,P,N)
✠ **LMC** **UMS CCS**
Eq.Ltr: A*;
Cable: 742.5/102.0 U3 (a)

2009-03 Hyundai Samho Heavy Industries Co Ltd — Samho Yd No: S298
Loa 288.43 (BB) Br ex 44.24 Dght 12.200
Lbp 275.00 Br md 44.20 Dpth 26.00
Welded, 1 dk

(A11A2TN) LNG Tanker
Double Hull
Liq (Gas): 151,872
5 x Gas Tank (s); 4 membrane (s.stl) pri horizontal, ER
8 Cargo Pump (s): 8x1800m³/hr
Manifold: Bow/CM: 146.2m

4 diesel electric oil engines driving 2 gen. each 11000kW 6600V a.c 2 gen. each 8250kW 6600V a.c Connecting to 2 elec. motors each (14860kW) driving 1 FP propeller
Total Power: 39,900kW (54,248hp) 20.0kn
Wartsila 12V50DF
2 x Vee 4 Stroke 12 Cy. 500 x 580 each-11400kW (15499bhp)
Wartsila Italia SpA-Italy
Wartsila 9L50DF
2 x 4 Stroke 9 Cy. 500 x 580 each-8550kW (11625bhp)
Wartsila Italia SpA-Italy
Boilers: e (ex.g.) 15.3kgf/cm² (15.0bar), WTAuxB (o.f.) 11.9kgf/cm² (11.7bar)
Thrusters: 1 Thwart. FP thruster (f)
Fuel: 5800.0 (d.f.)

9325893 9V7630 -
TANGGUH TOWUTI
LNG East-West Shipping Co (Singapore) Pte Ltd
NYK LNG Shipmanagement Ltd
SatCom: Inmarsat C 456321410
Singapore *Singapore*
MMSI: 563214000
Official number: 394534

97,432 29,230 84,992 T/cm 104.3

Class: LR (NV)
100A1 SS 10/2013
liquefied gas tanker, Ship Type 2G
methane (LNG) in membrane tanks, maximum vapour pressure 0.25 bar, minimum temperature minus 163 degree C
*IWS
LI
ECO (TOC)
LMC **UMS**

2008-10 Daewoo Shipbuilding & Marine Engineering Co Ltd — Geoje Yd No: 2241
Loa 285.40 (BB) Br ex 43.44 Dght 12.500
Lbp 274.40 Br md 43.40 Dpth 26.00
Welded, 1 dk

(A11A2TN) LNG Tanker
Double Bottom Entire Compartment Length
Liq (Gas): 142,988
4 x Gas Tank (s); 4 membrane (36% Ni.stl) pri horizontal
8 Cargo Pump (s): 8x1700m³/hr
Manifold: Bow/CM: 141.6m

1 Steam Turb reduction geared to sc. shaft driving 1 FP propeller
Total Power: 28,460kW (38,694hp) 19.5kn
Kawasaki UA-400
1 x steam Turb 28460kW (38694shp)
Kawasaki Heavy Industries Ltd-Japan
AuxGen: 1 x 3450kW 6600V 60Hz a.c, 2 x 3450kW 6600V 60Hz a.c
Thrusters: 1 Tunnel thruster (f)
Fuel: 505.0 (d.f.) 6915.0 (r.f.)

8905543 9HA3127 -
TANGIER
ex Maersk Tangier *-2013*
ex Torben Maersk *-2007*
Hera Marine LLC
Technomar Shipping Inc
Valletta *Malta*
MMSI: 229174000
Official number: 8905543

17,700 7,244 21,238 T/cm 38.7

Class: RI (LR)
✠ Classed LR until 24/3/11

1990-10 Tsuneishi Shipbuilding Co Ltd — Fukuyama HS Yd No: 640
Loa 161.02 (BB) Br ex 28.23 Dght 10.022
Lbp 152.00 Br md 28.20 Dpth 15.30
Welded, 1 dk

(A33A2CC) Container Ship (Fully Cellular)
TEU 1316 C Ho 554 TEU C Dk 762 TEU incl 118 ref C.
Compartments: 4 Cell Ho, ER
8 Ha: (6.5 x 12.9) (12.6 x 17.8)6 (14.2 x 22.8)ER
Gantry cranes: 1x40t

1 oil engine driving 1 FP propeller
Total Power: 10,480kW (14,249hp) 18.0kn
B&W 8S50MC
1 x 2 Stroke 8 Cy. 500 x 1910 10480kW (14249bhp)
Mitsui Engineering & Shipbuilding CLtd-Japan
AuxGen: 3 x 1160kW 450V 60Hz a.c
Boilers: AuxB (o.f.) 7.0kgf/cm² (6.9bar), AuxB (ex.g.) 10.5kgf/cm² (10.3bar)
Thrusters: 1 Thwart. CP thruster (f); 1 Thwart. CP thruster (a)
Fuel: 225.2 (d.f.) 38.0pd

6408993 WYR2928 -
TANGIER ISLAND
ex Carlos Miguel *-1979* *ex* T-Akl 32 *-1979*
ex FS 548 *-1957*
Omega Protein Inc
-
Reedville, VA *United States of America*
MMSI: 367108890
Official number: 565268

538 365 -

Class: (AB)

1944 United Concrete Pipe Corp. — Long Beach, Ca Yd No: 109
Converted From: Replenishment Dry Cargo Vessel
L reg 50.72 Br ex 9.83 Dght 3.061
Lbp 50.30 Br md 9.76 Dpth 4.37
Welded

(B11A2FT) Trawler

2 oil engines driving 2 FP propellers
Total Power: 1,324kW (1,800hp)
G.M. (Detroit Diesel) 16V-149
2 x Vee 2 Stroke 16 Cy. 146 x 146 each-662kW (900bhp) (new engine 1972)
General Motors Corp-USA
Fuel: 75.0

9665504 WDH2080 -
TANGIER ISLAND
Vane Line Bunkering Inc
-
Baltimore, MD *United States of America*
MMSI: 367594190
Official number: 1248549

270 81 212

Class: AB (Class contemplated)

2013-12 Chesapeake Shipbuilding, Inc. — Salisbury, Md Yd No: 106
Loa 28.65 Br ex - Dght -
Lbp - Br md 9.75 Dpth 4.04
Welded, 1 dk

(B32B2SP) Pusher Tug

2 oil engines reduction geared to sc. shafts driving 2 Propellers
Total Power: 3,530kW (4,800hp)
Caterpillar 3512C
2 x Vee 4 Stroke 12 Cy. 170 x 215 each-1765kW (2400bhp)
Caterpillar Inc-USA

9559561 YDA6431 -
TANGKAS
PT Maritim Barito Perkasa
-
Banjarmasin *Indonesia*
MMSI: 525002011

180 54 120

Class: AB (NK)

2009-11 Fulsail Sdn Bhd — Sibu (Hull) Yd No: 7514
2009-11 Pacific Ocean Engineering & Trading Pte Ltd (POET) — Singapore Yd No: (7514)
Loa 27.00 Br ex - Dght 2.810
Lbp 24.95 Br md 8.20 Dpth 3.60
Welded, 1 dk

(B32A2ST) Tug

2 oil engines reduction geared to sc. shafts driving 2 Propellers
Total Power: 1,790kW (2,434hp)
Cummins KTA-38-M2
2 x Vee 4 Stroke 12 Cy. 159 x 159 each-895kW (1217bhp)
Cummins Engine Co Ltd-United Kingdom
AuxGen: 2 x 80kW a.c
Fuel: 110.0 (d.f.)

9072252 POLH -
TANGKAS
ex Queen Arrow II *-2012* *ex* Cyber I *-2009*
ex Kwang Sung *-1999*
PT Indobaruna Bulk Transport
-
Jakarta *Indonesia*
MMSI: 525019599

5,979 2,659 10,640

Class: NK (KR)

1993-04 ShinA Shipbuilding Co Ltd — Tongyeong Yd No: 359
Loa 122.00 (BB) Br ex 19.03 Dght 7.885
Lbp 115.00 Br md 19.00 Dpth 10.30
Welded, 1 dk

(A24A2BT) Cement Carrier
Grain: 9,896
Compartments: 2 Ho, ER

1 oil engine driving 1 FP propeller
Total Power: 3,913kW (5,320hp) 15.5kn
B&W 7L35MC
1 x 2 Stroke 7 Cy. 350 x 1050 3913kW (5320bhp)
Ssangyong Heavy Industries Co Ltd-South Korea
AuxGen: 2 x 400kW 445V a.c
Thrusters: 1 Thwart. CP thruster (f); 1 Tunnel thruster (a)
Fuel: 480.0

9123403 V7ZX4 -
TANGO
ex Matilde *-2012*
Delos Shipholding SA
Unimar Success SA
Majuro *Marshall Islands*
MMSI: 538004935
Official number: 4935

81,329 52,339 160,013 T/cm 113.8

Class: AB

1997-01 Hyundai Heavy Industries Co Ltd — Ulsan Yd No: 980
Loa 280.28 (BB) Br ex - Dght 17.519
Lbp 270.00 Br md 45.00 Dpth 23.80
Welded, 1 dk

(A21A2BC) Bulk Carrier
Grain: 176,176; Bale: 167,346
Compartments: 9 Ho, ER
9 Ha: (14.5 x 15.2)8 (14.5 x 20.0)ER

1 oil engine driving 1 FP propeller
Total Power: 15,172kW (20,628hp) 14.5kn
MAN-B&W 6S70MC
1 x 2 Stroke 6 Cy. 700 x 2674 15172kW (20628bhp)
Hyundai Heavy Industries Co Ltd-South Korea

1010703 ZGBM2 -
TANGO
Arinter Management Inc
Edmiston Yacht Management Ltd
George Town *Cayman Islands (British)*
MMSI: 319028500
Official number: 743537

2,083 624 380

Class: LR
✠ **100A1** SS 07/2011
SSC
Yacht, mono, G6
✠ **LMC** **UMS**
Cable: 446.2/28.0 U3 (a)

2011-07 NMC Alblasserdam BV — Alblasserdam (Hull) Yd No: (802)
2011-07 Jacht- en Scheepswerf C. van Lent & Zonen B.V. — Kaag Yd No: 802
Loa 69.29 Br ex 12.50 Dght 3.700
Lbp 61.00 Br md 11.80 Dpth 6.25
Welded, 1 dk

(X11A2YP) Yacht

2 oil engines with flexible couplings & sr reverse geared to sc. shafts driving 2 CP propellers
Total Power: 4,640kW (6,308hp) 22.0kn
M.T.U. 16V4000M70
2 x Vee 4 Stroke 16 Cy. 165 x 190 each-2320kW (3154bhp)
MTU Friedrichshafen GmbH-Friedrichshafen
AuxGen: 3 x 308kW 400V 50Hz a.c
Thrusters: 1 Tunnel thruster (f)

5017656 - -
TANGO
ex Ango *-1972*
Almaric Shipping Inc
-
Georgetown *Guyana*
Official number: 0000291

274 160 445

Class: (BV)

1948 Karlstads Varv AB — Karlstad
Lengthened-1963
Loa 43.95 Br ex 7.35 Dght 3.200
Lbp 40.54 Br md 7.29 Dpth 3.43
Riveted\Welded, 1 dk

(A31A2GX) General Cargo Ship
2 Ha: 2 (10.9 x 3.9)ER
Derricks: 1x1.5t,1x1t; Winches: 2

1 oil engine driving 1 CP propeller
Total Power: 250kW (340hp) 9.0kn
Alpha 404-24VO
1 x 2 Stroke 4 Cy. 240 x 400 250kW (340bhp)
Frederikshavn Jernstoberi ogMaskinfabrik-Denmark
AuxGen: 2 x 25kW 110V d.c

7612216 SDHJ -
TANGO
ex Nordking *-2008*
Petersen & Sorensen Motorvaerksted A/S
-
Trollhattan *Sweden*
MMSI: 265211000

1,155 569 1,472

Class: (LR)
✠ Classed LR until 29/11/11

1976-12 Tokushima Zosen Sangyo K.K. — Komatsushima Yd No: 513
Loa 67.01 Br ex 11.69 Dght 4.263
Lbp 60.03 Br md 11.66 Dpth 5.62
Welded, 1 dk

(A31A2GX) General Cargo Ship
Grain: 2,271; Bale: 1,997
Compartments: 1 Ho, ER
1 Ha: (37.1 x 8.3)ER

1 oil engine reverse reduction geared to sc. shaft driving 1 FP propeller
Total Power: 736kW (1,001hp) 11.0kn
Niigata 6MG25BX
1 x 4 Stroke 6 Cy. 250 x 320 736kW (1001bhp)
Niigata Engineering Co Ltd-Japan
AuxGen: 2 x 80kW 445V 60Hz a.c
Fuel: 76.0 (d.f.) 4.0pd

7901100 - -
TANGO
Pescas SAIC
-

110 83 165

Class: (AB)

1979-09 SANYM S.A. — Buenos Aires Yd No: 23
Loa - Br ex - Dght 2.990
Lbp 22.31 Br md 6.51 Dpth 3.31
Welded, 1 dk

(B11A2FS) Stern Trawler
Compartments: 1 Ho, ER

1 oil engine reverse reduction geared to sc. shaft driving 1 FP propeller
Total Power: 386kW (525hp) 10.0kn
Caterpillar D353SCAC
1 x 4 Stroke 6 Cy. 159 x 203 386kW (525bhp)
Caterpillar Tractor Co-USA
AuxGen: 2 x 24kW a.c

9454486 3FIQ -
TANGO
Trek Maritima SA
NYK Shipmanagement Pte Ltd
SatCom: Inmarsat C 435152911
Panama *Panama*
MMSI: 351529000
Official number: 4091209

159,927 97,999 301,662 T/cm 182.6

Class: NK

2009-10 IHI Marine United Inc — Kure HS Yd No: 3244
Loa 333.00 (BB) Br ex 60.04 Dght 20.635
Lbp 324.00 Br md 60.00 Dpth 29.00
Welded, 1 dk

(A13A2TV) Crude Oil Tanker
Double Hull (13F)
Liq: 333,000; Liq (Oil): 333,000
Compartments: 5 Ta, 10 Wing Ta, 2 Wing Slop Ta, ER
3 Cargo Pump (s): 3x5500m³/hr
Manifold: Bow/CM: 163.6m

1 oil engine driving 1 FP propeller
Total Power: 27,160kW (36,927hp) 15.7kn
Wartsila 7RTA84T
1 x 2 Stroke 7 Cy. 840 x 3150 27160kW (36927bhp)
Diesel United Ltd.-Aioi
AuxGen: 4 x a.c
Fuel: 728.0 (d.f.) 6829.0 (r.f.)

9262003 *V2BG4* -	**TANGO** *ex* Caribbean Sina *-2013* *ex* Colca *-2009* *ex* Caribbean Sina *-2008* *ex* CMA CGM Maroni *-2006* *ex* Caribbean Sina *-2005* *launched as* Atlantic Voyager *-2004* **Klaus Eilbrecht Schiffahrts GmbH & Co KG ms 'Caribbean Sina'** Reederei Eilbrecht GmbH & Co KG *Saint John's* *Antigua & Barbuda* MMSI: 304578000 Official number: 3998	**4,462** 1,988 5,608	Class: BV (LR) (GL) Classed LR until 1/12/13	**2004-01 Qingshan Shipyard — Wuhan HB** Yd No: KS990308 Loa 99.99 (BB) Br ex - Dght 6.654 Lbp 95.80 Br md 18.80 Dpth 8.40 Welded, 1 dk	**(A31A2GX) General Cargo Ship** Grain: 7,177 TEU 502 C Ho 141 TEU C Dk 361 TEU incl 84 ref C Compartments: 3 Ho, ER 3 Ha: 2 (25.2 x 15.7)ER (6.5 x 7.8) Cranes: 2x40t	**1 oil engine** reduction geared to sc. shaft driving 1 CP propeller Total Power: 4,320kW (5,873hp) 15.0kn MaK 9M32C 1 x 4 Stroke 9 Cy. 320 x 480 4320kW (5873bhp) Caterpillar Motoren GmbH & Co. KG-Germany AuxGen: 1 x 700kW 450/230V a.c, 2 x 570kW 450/230V a.c Thrusters: 1 Tunnel thruster (f)
9686261 *9MSM9* -	**TANGO 5** **Tang Wee Loke** - *Langkawi* *Malaysia* MMSI: 533130093	**285** 85 -	Class: BV	**2013-03 Horizon Yacht Co Ltd — Kaohsiung** Yd No: 115E101 Loa 34.80 Br ex 7.75 Dght 2.400 Lbp 30.72 Br md 7.66 Dpth 3.75 Welded, 1 dk	**(X11A2YP) Yacht**	**2 oil engines** reduction geared to sc. shafts driving 2 FP propellers Total Power: 1,618kW (2,200hp) 13.0kn MAN D2842LE 2 x Vee 4 Stroke 12 Cy. 128 x 142 each-809kW (1100bhp) MAN Nutzfahrzeuge AG-Nuernberg AuxGen: 2 x 50kW 50Hz a.c Fuel: 40.0 (d.f.)
9402378 *8QGK* -	**TANGO 6** *ex* Taiping 10193 *-2012* **Maldives Transport & Contracting Co Pvt Ltd** - *Male* *Maldives* MMSI: 455323000	**114** 20 116	Class: GL (NK)	**2006-11 Bonafile Shipbuilders & Repairs Sdn Bhd — Sandakan** Yd No: 35/05 Loa 23.17 Br ex - Dght 2.412 Lbp 21.39 Br md 7.02 Dpth 2.90 Welded, 1 dk	**(B32A2ST) Tug**	**2 oil engines** reduction geared to sc. shafts driving 2 FP propellers Total Power: 706kW (960hp) Caterpillar 3408C 2 x Vee 4 Stroke 8 Cy. 137 x 152 each-353kW (480bhp) Caterpillar Inc-USA AuxGen: 2 x 36kW a.c
9550046 *9V7274* -	**TANGO 7** **Raven Pte Ltd** POSH Maritime Pte Ltd *Singapore* *Singapore* MMSI: 563090000 Official number: 393535	**249** 74 138	Class: AB	**2009-01 Bengbu Shenzhou Machinery Co Ltd — Bengbu AH** (Hull) Yd No: (1303) **2009-01 Pacific Ocean Engineering & Trading Pte Ltd (POET) — Singapore** Yd No: 1303 Loa 29.50 Br ex - Dght 3.500 Lbp 27.00 Br md 9.00 Dpth 4.16 Welded, 1 dk	**(B32A2ST) Tug**	**2 oil engines** reduction geared to sc. shafts driving 2 Propellers Total Power: 2,354kW (3,200hp) Yanmar 8N21A-SV 2 x 4 Stroke 8 Cy. 210 x 290 each-1177kW (1600bhp) Yanmar Diesel Engine Co Ltd-Japan AuxGen: 2 x 130kW a.c Thrusters: 1 Tunnel thruster (f) Fuel: 200.0
9148049 *8QEW* -	**TANGO 575** *ex* Sinar Sentosa *-2005* **Maldives Transport & Contracting Co Pvt Ltd** - *Male* *Maldives* MMSI: 455285000 Official number: C7754A	**106** 31 -	Class: (GL) (BV)	**1996-01 Tuong Aik (Sarawak) Sdn Bhd — Sibu** Yd No: 9503 Loa 23.17 Br ex - Dght 2.367 Lbp 22.06 Br md 6.70 Dpth 2.90 Welded, 1 dk	**(B32A2ST) Tug**	**2 oil engines** geared to sc. shafts driving 2 FP propellers Total Power: 746kW (1,014hp) 10.0kn Cummins KTA-19-M 2 x 4 Stroke 6 Cy. 159 x 159 each-373kW (507bhp) (made 1995) Cummins Engine Co Inc-USA AuxGen: 2 x 60kW 220V 50Hz a.c Fuel: 85.0 (d.f.)
7048128 *L2EE* -	**TANGO I** *ex* Tango *-2001* *ex* Seismic Surveyor *-1996* **Bentonicos De Argentina SA** - *Argentina* Official number: 02724	**635** 463 -		**1969 Mangone Shipbuilding Co. — Houston, Tx** Yd No: 91 Converted From: Research Vessel-2005 L reg 50.01 Br ex 10.98 Dght 3.683 Lbp 47.60 Br md - Dpth 4.58 Welded, 1 dk	**(B34M2QS) Search & Rescue Vessel** A-frames: 1x15t; Cranes: 1	**2 oil engines** sr geared to sc. shafts driving 2 FP propellers Total Power: 1,766kW (2,402hp) 12.0kn EMD (Electro-Motive) 12-567-BC 2 x Vee 2 Stroke 12 Cy. 216 x 254 each-883kW (1201bhp) General Motors Corp-USA
9402665 *3EUB9* -	**TANGO I** *ex* Tango *-2012* *ex* Las Palmas *-2010* *ex* OW Las Palmas *-2010* *ex* MK Maju *-2008* **Exotic Waves Marine SA** Mare Maritime Co SA SatCom: Inmarsat C 437333010 *Panama* *Panama* MMSI: 373330000 Official number: 4364612XT	**4,445** 1,963 6,893	Class: AB	**2008-03 Jiangmen Yinxing Shipbuilding Co Ltd — Jiangmen GD** Yd No: GMG0509 Loa 100.50 (BB) Br ex 18.02 Dght 6.800 Lbp 95.10 Br md 18.00 Dpth 9.50 Welded, 1 dk	**(A13B2TP) Products Tanker** Double Hull (13F) Liq: 7,066; Liq (Oil): 7,066 Compartments: 10 Wing Ta, 2 Wing Slop Ta, ER	**2 oil engines** geared to sc. shafts driving 2 FP propellers Total Power: 3,236kW (4,400hp) 12.0kn Daihatsu 6DKM-26 2 x 4 Stroke 6 Cy. 260 x 380 each-1618kW (2200bhp) Anqing Marine Diesel Engine Works-China AuxGen: 3 x 320kW a.c Fuel: 155.0 (d.f.) 260.7 (r.f.)
9075888 - -	**TANGO II** *ex* Avachinskiy *-2009* **Bentonicos De Argentina SA** -	**861** 258 332	Class: (RS)	**1992-09 OAO Volgogradskiy Sudostroitelnyy Zavod — Volgograd** Yd No: 274 Loa 53.74 Br ex 10.71 Dght 4.040 Lbp 47.92 Br md - Dpth 6.00 Welded, 1 dk	**(B11A2FS) Stern Trawler** Ice Capable	**1 oil engine** geared to sc. shaft driving 1 CP propeller Total Power: 971kW (1,320hp) 10.0kn S.K.L. 8NVD48A-2U 1 x 4 Stroke 8 Cy. 320 x 480 971kW (1320bhp) SKL Motoren u. Systemtechnik AG-Magdeburg AuxGen: 1 x 300kW a.c, 3 x 160kW Fuel: 154.0 (d.f.)
9484704 *D5AZ7* -	**TANGO SEA** **Ost One Shipping Co Ltd** NSC Shipping GmbH & Cie KG *Monrovia* *Liberia* MMSI: 636015478 Official number: 15478	**51,253** 31,173 93,028 T/cm 80.8	Class: GL (AB)	**2011-12 Taizhou CATIC Shipbuilding Heavy Industry Ltd — Taizhou JS** Yd No: TK0206 Loa 229.20 (BB) Br ex - Dght 14.900 Lbp 222.00 Br md 38.00 Dpth 20.70 Welded, 1 dk	**(A21A2BC) Bulk Carrier** Grain: 110,330 Compartments: 7 Ho, ER 7 Ha: 5 (17.9 x 17.0)ER 2 (15.3 x 14.6)	**1 oil engine** driving 1 FP propeller Total Power: 13,560kW (18,436hp) 14.1kn MAN-B&W 6S60MC-C 1 x 2 Stroke 6 Cy. 600 x 2400 13560kW (18436bhp) Hyundai Heavy Industries Co Ltd-South Korea AuxGen: 3 x 700kW 450V a.c Fuel: 233.0 (d.f.) 3567.0 (r.f.) 41.0pd
9188922 *9HSH8* -	**TANGRA** **Tangra Maritime Ltd** Bulcom Ltd *Valletta* *Malta* MMSI: 256366000 Official number: 9188922	**7,617** 3,520 9,643	Class: NK (LR) ✠ Classed LR until 12/2/12	**2007-01 Bulyard Shipbuilding Industry AD — Varna** Yd No: 287 Loa 126.08 (BB) Br ex 20.04 Dght 8.080 Lbp 113.75 Br md 20.00 Dpth 10.40 Welded, 1 dk	**(A31A2GX) General Cargo Ship** Double Hull Grain: 11,833; Bale: 11,542 TEU 533 Compartments: 3 Ho, ER 3 Ha: 2 (25.5 x 15.5)ER (12.8 x 9.0)	**1 oil engine** with flexible couplings & sr geared to sc. shaft driving 1 CP propeller Total Power: 5,400kW (7,342hp) 14.0kn MaK 6M43C 1 x 4 Stroke 6 Cy. 430 x 610 5400kW (7342bhp) Caterpillar Motoren GmbH & Co. KG-Germany AuxGen: 2 x 450kW 380V 50Hz a.c, 1 x 544kW 380V 50Hz a.c Boilers: e (ex.g.) 7.3kgf/cm² (7.2bar), WTAuxB (o.f.) 7.3kgf/cm² (7.2bar) Thrusters: 1 Thwart. FP thruster (f) Fuel: 175.0 (d.f.) 770.0 (r.f.)
9000924 *BDXE* -	**TANGSHANHAI 3** *ex* Tolhuaca *-2006* *ex* Konamar *-2005* *ex* Kayax *-1999* *launched as* J. Jessica *-1991* **Tang Shan Hua Xing Shipping Co Ltd** - *Tangshan, Hebei* *China* MMSI: 412271280	**23,277** 13,807 42,226 T/cm 47.6	Class: (NK)	**1991-09 Oshima Shipbuilding Co Ltd — Saikai NS** Yd No: 10139 Loa 180.00 (BB) Br ex - Dght 11.228 Lbp 172.00 Br md 30.50 Dpth 15.80 Welded, 1 dk	**(A21A2BC) Bulk Carrier** Grain: 52,125; Bale: 51,118 Compartments: 5 Ho, ER 5 Ha: (14.4 x 15.3)4 (19.2 x 15.3)ER Cranes: 4x25t	**1 oil engine** driving 1 FP propeller Total Power: 6,230kW (8,470hp) 14.0kn Sulzer 6RTA52 1 x 2 Stroke 6 Cy. 520 x 1800 6230kW (8470bhp) Diesel United Ltd.-Aioi AuxGen: 4 x 323kW a.c
7629427 *EQGB* -	**TANGSIR** *ex* Tangestan *-1982* *ex* Fujii Maru *-1977* *ex* Hiyoshi Maru No. 7 *-1977* **Malihe Motraghi** Iran Julius *Abadan* *Iran*	*497* 265 950	Class: (GL) (NK)	**1968 Wakayama Zosen — Kainan** Yd No: 403 Loa 53.80 Br ex 9.53 Dght 3.815 Lbp 49.51 Br md 9.50 Dpth 4.30 Welded, 1 dk	**(A31A2GX) General Cargo Ship** Bale: 624 1 Ha: (21.4 x 6.3)ER	**1 oil engine** driving 1 FP propeller Total Power: 883kW (1,201hp) 9.5kn Kobe 6EEFSS 1 x 4 Stroke 6 Cy. 330 x 520 883kW (1201bhp) Kobe Hatsudoki KK-Japan AuxGen: 1 x 40kW 380V a.c
7324041 *WDA8720* -	**TANI RAE** **Westport Seafood Inc** - *Westport, WA* *United States of America* MMSI: 366857350 Official number: 542076	*161* 130 -		**1972 Bender Welding & Machine Co Inc — Mobile AL** Yd No: 341 L reg 25.06 Br ex 7.32 Dght - Lbp - Br md - Dpth 3.41 Welded	**(B11B2FV) Fishing Vessel**	**1 oil engine** driving 1 FP propeller Total Power: 496kW (674hp)
5131139 *9GKT* -	**TANIA** *ex* Keta I *-1995* *ex* Tania *-1994* *ex* Giralda *-1985* **UT Bank Ltd** - *Takoradi* *Ghana* Official number: 316827	**221** 77 226	Class: (HR) (BV)	**1961-08 Ateliers & Chantiers de La Rochelle-Pallice — La Rochelle** Yd No: 5060 Loa 34.73 Br ex 7.22 Dght 3.852 Lbp 31.73 Br md 6.91 Dpth 3.97 Riveted\Welded, 1 dk	**(B11A2FT) Trawler** Ins: 140 Compartments: 1 Ho, ER 2 Ha: 2 (1.0 x 1.3) Derricks: 1x1t; Winches: 1	**1 oil engine** driving 1 FP propeller Total Power: 552kW (750hp) 11.0kn Sulzer 8BAH22 1 x 2 Stroke 8 Cy. 220 x 320 552kW (750bhp) Cie de Constructions Mecaniques (CCM), procede Sulzer-France AuxGen: 1 x 100kW 100V d.c, 1 x 24kW 100V d.c Fuel: 40.5 (d.f.)

6520210 - -	**TANIA** *ex* Menia *-2005* *ex* Nina II *-2004* *ex* Agios Nektarios K *-2004* - -	*336* 169 -	Class: KC	**1964 N. Savvas Shipyard — Piraeus** Loa 33.00 Br ex 9.30 Dght 1.800 Lbp - Br md - Dpth - Welded, 1 dk	**(A36A2PR) Passenger/Ro-Ro Ship (Vehicles)**	**2 oil engines** driving 2 FP propellers Total Power: 176kW (240hp) Mercedes Benz 2 x 4 Stroke 4 Cy. each-88kW (120bhp) Daimler Benz AG-West Germany
9194218 *EA3308* 3-VI-75-98	**TANIA MARIA** - **Pesqueras Javimar SL** - *La Guardia* *Spain* MMSI: 224081430 Official number: 3-5/1998	**143** 58 -		**1998-03 Montajes Cies S.L. — Vigo** Yd No: 37 Loa - Br ex - Dght 4.210 Lbp 24.00 Br md 6.40 Dpth 2.90 Welded, 1 dk	**(B11A2FS) Stern Trawler**	**1 oil engine** driving 1 FP propeller Total Power: 530kW (721hp) Mitsubishi S6R2-MPTK 1 x 4 Stroke 6 Cy. 170 x 220 530kW (721bhp) Mitsubishi Heavy Industries Ltd-Japan
1005746 *2FEP7* -	**TANIA T** *ex* Zaliv Ii *-2012* **Gumby Ltd** - *London* *United Kingdom* MMSI: 235090601 Official number: 918043	*361* 108 -	Class: LR ✠ **100A1** SS 01/2013 (PC) Yacht **LMC** Cable: 300.0/18.0	**2003-01 Mondo Marine SpA — Savona** Yd No: 40/2 Loa 41.50 Br ex - Dght 1.700 Lbp 35.06 Br md 7.80 Dpth 4.00 Bonded, 1 dk	**(X11A2YP) Yacht** Hull Material: Reinforced Plastic	**2 oil engines** with clutches, flexible couplings & sr reverse geared to sc. shafts driving 2 FP propellers Total Power: 3,360kW (4,568hp) 23.0kn Deutz TBD620V12 2 x Vee 4 Stroke 12 Cy. 170 x 195 each-1680kW (2284bhp) Deutz AG-Koeln AuxGen: 2 x 80kW 380V 50Hz a.c
9667899 *3FGT4* -	**TANIKAZE** - **Olamar Navegacion SA** Usui Kaiun KK (Usui Kaiun Co Ltd) *Panama* *Panama* MMSI: 373100000 Official number: 4464813	**31,753** 18,647 56,064	Class: NK	**2013-03 Minaminippon Shipbuilding Co Ltd — Usuki OT** Yd No: 738 Loa 189.99 (BB) Br ex 32.29 Dght 12.720 Lbp 182.00 Br md 32.25 Dpth 18.10 Welded, 1 dk	**(A21A2BC) Bulk Carrier** Grain: 71,345; Bale: 68,733 Compartments: 5 Ho, ER 5 Ha: ER Cranes: 4x30t	**1 oil engine** driving 1 FP propeller Total Power: 9,480kW (12,889hp) 14.5kn MAN-B&W 6S50MC-C 1 x 2 Stroke 6 Cy. 500 x 2000 9480kW (12889bhp) Mitsui Engineering & Shipbuilding CLtd-Japan Fuel: 2230.0
9734824 - -	**TANIMAS** - **PT Tanimas Maritim Indonesia** - *Batam* *Indonesia* Official number: 2014 PPm No.3436/L	**148** 45 -	Class: KI (Class contemplated) RI	**2014-02 PT Citra Shipyard — Batam** Yd No: TB 045 Loa 21.74 Br ex - Dght - Lbp - Br md 7.32 Dpth 3.20 Welded, 1 dk	**(B32A2ST) Tug**	**2 oil engines** reduction geared to sc. ahafts driving 2 FP propellers Total Power: 894kW (1,216hp) Caterpillar C18 ACERT 2 x 4 Stroke 6 Cy. 145 x 183 each-447kW (608bhp) Caterpillar Inc-USA
8403117 *YB5220* -	**TANIMBAR BAHARI** *ex* Kanzaki Maru No. 2 *-2002* **PT Citra Baru Adinusantara** - *Surabaya* *Indonesia*	*551* 240 570	Class: KI	**1984-03 Kochi Jyuko (Kaisei Zosen) K.K. — Kochi** Yd No: 1681 Loa 46.74 Br ex - Dght 3.650 Lbp 42.86 Br md 9.45 Dpth 4.91 Welded, 1 dk	**(A31A2GX) General Cargo Ship** Grain: 1,229; Bale: 969 Compartments: 1 Ho, ER 1 Ha: ER	**1 oil engine** geared to sc. shaft driving 1 FP propeller Total Power: 441kW (600hp) Akasaka A24R 1 x 4 Stroke 6 Cy. 240 x 450 441kW (600bhp) Akasaka Tekkosho KK (Akasaka DieselLtd)-Japan
8627660 *YGVW* -	**TANIMBAR PERMAI** *ex* K K 24 *-2004* *ex* Hanei Maru No. 15 *-2000* **Go John Santiago** PT Citra Baru Adinusantara *Cirebon* *Indonesia*	*644* 194 700	Class: KI	**1986-05 Yano Zosen K.K. — Imabari** Converted From: Grab Dredger-2006 Loa 52.61 Br ex - Dght 3.900 Lbp 48.48 Br md 10.51 Dpth 5.20 Welded, 1 dk	**(A31A2GX) General Cargo Ship**	**1 oil engine** driving 1 FP propeller Total Power: 405kW (551hp) 8.5kn Niigata 6M28AGTE 1 x 4 Stroke 6 Cy. 280 x 480 405kW (551bhp) Niigata Engineering Co Ltd-Japan
8602505 *YGWI* -	**TANIMBAR SEHATI** *ex* Sumiwaka Maru No. 15 *-2000* - - *Surabaya* *Indonesia*	**1,007** 313 1,333	Class: KI	**1985-12 K.K. Murakami Zosensho — Naruto** Yd No: 165 Loa 57.18 (BB) Br ex - Dght 4.571 Lbp 52.02 Br md 12.01 Dpth 6.20 Welded, 2 dks	**(A31A2GX) General Cargo Ship** Grain: 900; Bale: 860 Compartments: 1 Ho, ER 1 Ha: ER	**1 oil engine** with clutches & reverse reduction geared to sc. shaft driving 1 FP propeller Total Power: 662kW (900hp) 10.0kn Niigata 6M28AGTE 1 x 4 Stroke 6 Cy. 280 x 480 662kW (900bhp) Niigata Engineering Co Ltd-Japan
8708787 - -	**TANIMBAR SEJAHTERA** *ex* K K 15 *-2006* *ex* Shimeta Maru No. 8 *-1999* **PT Cakrawala Nusa Bahari** - *Surabaya* *Indonesia*	**848** 255 1,200	Class: (KI)	**1987-08 Honda Zosen — Saiki** Yd No: 765 Lengthened-2006 L reg 59.17 (BB) Br ex 11.03 Dght 3.250 Lbp 54.60 Br md 11.00 Dpth 5.35 Welded	**(A31A2GX) General Cargo Ship** Compartments: 2 Ho, ER 2 Ha: ER	**1 oil engine** driving 1 FP propeller Total Power: 625kW (850hp) 8.5kn Niigata 6M26AGTE 1 x 4 Stroke 6 Cy. 260 x 460 625kW (850bhp) Niigata Engineering Co Ltd-Japan AuxGen: 1 x 64kW 225V 60Hz a.c
8864347 *9BNK* -	**TANIN** *ex* Sada Maru No. 1 *-2006* **A Zare** - *Bushehr* *Iran* MMSI: 422360000 Official number: 17584	*390* - 398	Class: AS	**1992-01 Nagashima Zosen KK — Kihoku ME** Yd No: 311 Loa 47.35 (BB) Br ex - Dght 2.970 Lbp 42.00 Br md 10.00 Dpth 3.15 Welded, 1 dk	**(A24D2BA) Aggregates Carrier**	**1 oil engine** driving 1 FP propeller Total Power: 956kW (1,300hp) 9.8kn Matsui ML627GSC 1 x 4 Stroke 6 Cy. 270 x 480 956kW (1300bhp) Matsui Iron Works Co Ltd-Japan
8711318 *UBJG8* -	**TANIR** *ex* Ice Queen *-2010* *ex* MSC Trader *-1998* *ex* Good Fast *-1995* *ex* MSC Trader *-1994* *ex* Good Fast *-1994* **Chukotka Trading Co (A/O 'Chukotskaya Torgovaya Kompaniya')** Norfes-Marine Service Co Ltd *Vladivostok* *Russia* MMSI: 273351700	**7,085** 2,937 7,346 T/cm 20.2	Class: RS (NK) (BV)	**1994-06 Ast. Reunidos del Nervion S.A. — Bilbao** Yd No: 564 Loa 132.70 Br ex 19.86 Dght 6.891 Lbp 122.06 Br md 19.62 Dpth 8.80 Welded, 1 dk	**(A31A2GX) General Cargo Ship** Grain: 10,474; Bale: 10,022 TEU 294 C Compartments: 4 Ho, ER 4 Ha: (12.6 x 10.2) (19.2 x 15.4)2 (18.8 x 15.4)ER Cranes: 4x20t Ice Capable	**1 oil engine** driving 1 CP propeller Total Power: 5,119kW (6,960hp) 14.6kn B&W 6L42MC 1 x 2 Stroke 6 Cy. 420 x 1360 5119kW (6960bhp) AO Bryanskiy MashinostroitelnyyZavod (BMZ)-Bryansk AuxGen: 1 x 400kW 380V 50Hz a.c, 2 x 440kW 380V 50Hz a.c Fuel: 66.5 (d.f.) 585.1 (r.f.)
8407383 *AUNV* -	**TANISHQ** *ex* Nabard *-2008* *ex* Kaabeh *-1987* **Cambay Marine International Pvt Ltd** - *Mumbai* *India* MMSI: 419064600 Official number: 3255	**456** 137 350	Class: AS IR (NV)	**1984-11 Wakamatsu Zosen K.K. — Kitakyushu** Yd No: 338 Loa 38.00 Br ex 10.01 Dght 3.644 Lbp 35.01 Br md 10.00 Dpth 3.97 Welded, 1 dk	**(B34L2QU) Utility Vessel**	**2 oil engines** with clutches, flexible couplings & sr reverse geared to sc. shafts driving 2 FP propellers Total Power: 2,060kW (2,800hp) 10.0kn Yanmar T260-ST 2 x 4 Stroke 6 Cy. 260 x 330 each-1030kW (1400bhp) Yanmar Diesel Engine Co Ltd-Japan AuxGen: 2 x 240kW 380V 50Hz a.c, 1 x 100kW 380V 50Hz a.c Thrusters: 1 Thwart. CP thruster (f)
1004297 *2DYL7* -	**TANIT** *ex* Terancar Nadine *-2004* *ex* Terancar-Nitani *-2004* **Mercantile Leasing SpA** - *United Kingdom* MMSI: 235083004 Official number: 917143	**364** 109 -	Class: (LR) ✠ Classed LR until 18/4/06	**1967-09 Camper & Nicholsons (Yachts) Ltd. — Southampton** Yd No: 921 Loa 45.56 Br ex 7.83 Dght 2.650 Lbp 41.17 Br md - Dpth 3.41 Welded, 1 dk	**(X11A2YP) Yacht**	**2 oil engines** driving 2 FP propellers Total Power: 882kW (1,200hp) MAN G6V235/330ATL 2 x 4 Stroke 6 Cy. 235 x 330 each-441kW (600bhp) Maschinenbau Augsburg Nuernberg (MAN)-Augsburg
9598579 *TSNC* -	**TANIT** - **Compagnie Tunisienne de Navigation SA (COTUNAV)** - SatCom: Inmarsat C 467274810 *La Goulette* *Tunisia* MMSI: 672748000	**52,645** 32,581 6,189	Class: BV	**2012-05 Daewoo Shipbuilding & Marine Engineering Co Ltd — Geoje** Yd No: 7511 Loa 210.00 (BB) Br ex 35.30 Dght 7.590 Lbp 189.69 Br md 30.00 Dpth 10.50 Welded, 1 dk	**(A36A2PR) Passenger/Ro-Ro Ship (Vehicles)** Passengers: unberthed: 800; berths: 2400 Bow door/ramp (centre) Len: 22.80 Wid: 7.40 Swl: - Stern door/ramp (p. a.) Len: 20.90 Wid: 9.80 Swl: - Stern door/ramp (s. a.) Len: 20.90 Wid: 9.80 Swl: - Cars: 1,060 Ice Capable	**4 oil engines** driving 4 gen. each 14000kW a.c Connecting to 2 elec. motors driving 2 CP propellers Total Power: 57,600kW (78,312hp) 27.5kn MAN-B&W 12V48/60CR 4 x Vee 4 Stroke 12 Cy. 480 x 600 each-14400kW (19578bhp) MAN B&W Diesel AG-Augsburg Thrusters: 2 Tunnel thruster (f) Fuel: 290.0 (d.f.) 1780.0 (r.f.)
7939511 *WYA2866* -	**TANITA** - **Tana Inc** - *Brownsville, TX* *United States of America* Official number: 601131	*119* 81 -		**1978 Julio Gonzalez Boat Builders, Inc. — Brownsville, Tx** L reg 21.98 Br ex 6.76 Dght - Lbp - Br md - Dpth 3.38 Welded, 1 dk	**(B11B2FV) Fishing Vessel**	**1 oil engine** driving 1 FP propeller Total Power: 268kW (364hp)
8603547 *PHWV* -	**TANJA** *ex* Kate *-1996* *ex* Containerships II *-1990* *launched as* Kate *-1986* **Rederi AB Lillgaard** Holwerda Shipmanagement BV *Rotterdam* *Netherlands* MMSI: 244115000 Official number: 33759	**3,801** 2,050 4,647	Class: GL	**1986-12 J.J. Sietas KG Schiffswerft GmbH & Co. — Hamburg** Yd No: 977 Loa 103.89 Br ex 16.24 Dght 6.070 Lbp 96.60 Br md 16.01 Dpth 8.01 Welded, 2 dks	**(A31A2GX) General Cargo Ship** Grain: 6,861; Bale: 6,366 TEU 341 C.Dk 207/20' (40') C.Ho 134/20' (40') incl. 25 ref C. Compartments: 2 Ho, ER 3 Ha: (12.6 x 10.3)2 (25.1 x 12.8)ER Ice Capable	**1 oil engine** with flexible couplings & sr gearedto sc. shaft driving 1 CP propeller Total Power: 1,633kW (2,220hp) 14.0kn Wartsila 8R32D 1 x 4 Stroke 8 Cy. 320 x 350 1633kW (2220bhp) Oy Wartsila Ab-Finland

IMO / Call sign	Name / Owner / Manager	Tonnage	Class	Builder / Dimensions	Type / Cargo	Machinery
8657043 *DKOA* -	**TANJA** **Jorg Nagel** - *Heiligenhafen* *Germany* MMSI: 211224970 Official number: 51702	203 100 -		**1951 VEB Boddenwerft Damgarten — Ribnitz-Damgarten** Converted From: Fishing Vessel-1951 Loa 24.00 Br ex - Dght - Lbp - Br md 7.00 Dpth - Welded, 1 dk	**(X11A2YP) Yacht**	**1 oil engine** driving 1 Propeller
8722525 - -	**TANJA** *ex* MRTK-0690 *-1997* **Krediidipanga Liisingu Ltd (Krediidipanga Liisingu AS)** JSC Gertron (Gertron OU)	117 35 30	Class: (RS)	**1985-12 Sosnovskiy Sudostroitelnyy Zavod — Sosnovka** Yd No: 690 Loa 25.50 Br ex 7.00 Dght 2.390 Lbp 22.00 Br md - Dpth 3.30 Welded, 1 dk	**(B11A2FS) Stern Trawler** Ice Capable	**1 oil engine** driving 1 FP propeller Total Power: 221kW (300hp) 9.5kn S.K.L. 6NVD26A-2 1 x 4 Stroke 6 Cy. 180 x 260 221kW (300bhp) VEB Schwermaschinenbau "KarlLiebknecht" (SKL)-Magdeburg
8818623 *V2PM5* -	**TANJA** **Marlen Shipping Co Ltd** UAB Juru Agentura 'Forsa' *Saint John's* *Antigua & Barbuda* MMSI: 305068000 Official number: 2914	2,190 1,051 3,292	Class: GL	**1989-12 Schiffswerft und Maschinenfabrik Cassens GmbH — Emden** Yd No: 184 Loa 82.50 Br ex - Dght 5.280 Lbp 79.10 Br md 12.60 Dpth 6.65 Welded, 1 dk	**(A31A2GX) General Cargo Ship** Grain: 4,078 TEU 138 C.Ho 93/20' (40') C.Dk 45/20' (40') Compartments: 1 Ho, ER 1 Ha: (54.0 x 10.3)ER Ice Capable	**1 oil engine** sr geared to sc. shaft driving 1 CP propeller Total Power: 1,100kW (1,496hp) 11.0kn Deutz SBV8M628 1 x 4 Stroke 8 Cy. 240 x 280 1100kW (1496bhp) Kloeckner Humboldt Deutz AG-West Germany AuxGen: 1 x 502kW 380V 50Hz a.c, 1 x 200kW 380V 50Hz a.c, 1 x 80kW 380V 50Hz a.c Thrusters: 1 Thwart. FP thruster (f)
9437206 *C4YA2* -	**TANJA A.** *ex* Medbaykal *-2013* **Faroe Shipping Co Ltd** Marlow Ship Management Deutschland GmbH & Co KG *Limassol* *Cyprus* MMSI: 210379000 Official number: 9437206	9,946 4,900 12,001	Class: GL	**2007-10 Zhejiang Ouhua Shipbuilding Co Ltd — Zhoushan ZJ** Yd No: 507 Loa 139.10 (BB) Br ex - Dght 8.800 Lbp 129.00 Br md 22.60 Dpth 11.80 Welded, 1 dk	**(A33A2CC) Container Ship (Fully Cellular)** TEU 990 C incl 254 ref C.	**1 oil engine** reduction geared to sc. shaft driving 1 CP propeller Total Power: 9,600kW (13,052hp) 19.0kn MAN-B&W 8L48/60B 1 x 4 Stroke 8 Cy. 480 x 600 9600kW (13052bhp) MAN B&W Diesel AG-Augsburg AuxGen: 1 x 2000kW 450/230V a.c, 2 x 910kW 450/230V a.c Thrusters: 1 Tunnel thruster (f); 1 Tunnel thruster (f)
9257503 *A8YR7* -	**TANJA JACOB** *ex* Four Ketch *-2007* **Panamax Schiffahrts GmbH & Co KG** Ernst Jacob GmbH & Co KG *Monrovia* *Liberia* MMSI: 636092217 Official number: 92217	40,037 20,900 73,004 T/cm 66.0	Class: AB	**2003-01 Samsung Heavy Industries Co Ltd — Geoje** Yd No: 1423 Loa 228.50 (BB) Br ex - Dght 14.020 Lbp 219.00 Br md 32.24 Dpth 20.20 Welded, 1 dk	**(A13B2TP) Products Tanker** Double Hull (13F) Liq: 75,783; Liq (Oil): 75,783 Cargo Heating Coils Compartments: 12 Wing Ta, 2 Wing Slop Ta, ER 3 Cargo Pump (s): 3x2000m³/hr Manifold: Bow/CM: 112.3m	**1 oil engine** driving 1 FP propeller Total Power: 12,268kW (16,680hp) 15.0kn MAN-B&W 6S60MC 1 x 2 Stroke 6 Cy. 600 x 2292 12268kW (16680bhp) Doosan Engine Co Ltd-South Korea AuxGen: 3 x 700kW 60Hz a.c Fuel: 178.0 (d.f.) 2545.0 (r.f.)
9174361 *ZIQT6* -	**TANJA KOSAN** *ex* Tarquin Vale *-2002* **Lauritzen Kosan A/S** - *Douglas* *Isle of Man (British)* MMSI: 235509000 Official number: 734745	4,693 1,754 5,996 T/cm 15.0	Class: BV	**1999-04 Hyundai Heavy Industries Co Ltd — Ulsan** Yd No: 1124 Loa 106.98 (BB) Br ex 15.72 Dght 7.254 Lbp 98.40 Br md 15.70 Dpth 8.25 Welded, 1 dk	**(A11B2TG) LPG Tanker** Double Bottom Entire Compartment Length Liq (Gas): 6,259 2 x Gas Tank (s); 2 independent (stl) cyl horizontal 3 Cargo Pump (s): 2x350m³/hr, 1x300m³/hr Manifold: Bow/CM: 53.8m Ice Capable	**1 oil engine** driving 1 CP propeller Total Power: 3,500kW (4,759hp) 15.0kn B&W 5S35MC 1 x 2 Stroke 5 Cy. 350 x 1400 3500kW (4759bhp) Hyundai Heavy Industries Co Ltd-South Korea AuxGen: 1 x 400kW 440/220V 60Hz a.c, 3 x 472kW 440/220V 60Hz a.c Thrusters: 1 Thwart. FP thruster (f) Fuel: 136.0 (d.f.) 530.0 (r.f.)
5352161 *9MSX* -	**TANJONG DUNGUN** **Government of Malaysia (Director of Marine - West Malaysia)** - *Penang* *Malaysia* Official number: 199563	*183* 84 245		**1961 United Engineers Ltd — Singapore** Yd No: 82 Loa 33.08 Br ex 8.69 Dght 1.982 Lbp 31.32 Br md 8.54 Dpth 2.21 Riveted\Welded, 1 dk	**(B33B2DG) Grab Hopper Dredger** Compartments: 1 Ho, ER 1 Ha: Cranes: 1x4t	**1 oil engine** geared to sc. shaft driving 1 FP propeller Total Power: 364kW (495hp) 10.0kn Blackstone ERS6 1 x 4 Stroke 6 Cy. 222 x 292 364kW (495bhp) Lister Blackstone Marine Ltd.-Dursley AuxGen: 1 x 5kW 110V d.c Fuel: 14.0 (d.f.)
6616473 *9MUI* -	**TANJONG GEMUROH** **Sumai Engineering Sdn Bhd** - *Penang* *Malaysia* Official number: 324039	*450* 152 356	Class: MY	**1966 Syarikat Perkapalan Kris Tanah Melayu Ltd — Penang** Loa 44.43 Br ex 10.88 Dght 2.286 Lbp 42.68 Br md 10.67 Dpth 2.92 Welded, 1 dk	**(B33B2DS) Suction Hopper Dredger**	**2 oil engines** geared to sc. shafts driving 2 FP propellers Total Power: 530kW (720hp) 9.5kn Blackstone EV8M 2 x 4 Stroke 8 Cy. 222 x 292 each-265kW (360bhp) Lister Blackstone Marine Ltd.-Dursley AuxGen: 2 x 60kW 220V d.c, 1 x 10kW 220V d.c Fuel: 30.5 (d.f.)
7944360 *9MAB8* -	**TANJONG PINANG** **Government of Malaysia (Director of Marine Peninsular Malaysia)** - *Penang* *Malaysia* Official number: 324196	*551* 367 135	Class: (NK)	**1980 Malaysia Shipyard & Engineering Sdn Bhd — Pasir Gudang** Loa - Br ex - Dght 1.809 Lbp 42.52 Br md 12.01 Dpth 2.90 Welded, 1 dk	**(B33A2DC) Cutter Suction Dredger**	**2 oil engines** sr geared to sc. shafts driving 2 FP propellers Total Power: 500kW (680hp) 9.0kn Caterpillar 3408T 2 x Vee 4 Stroke 8 Cy. 137 x 152 each-250kW (340bhp) Caterpillar Tractor Co-USA AuxGen: 3 x 60kW
8318518 - -	**TANJORE** **Government of The Republic of India (Central Inland Water Transport Corp Ltd)** - *Kolkata* *India* Official number: WB1188	*218* - 62	Class: (LR) ✠ Classed LR until 15/12/87	**1986-05 Central Inland Water Transport Corp. Ltd. — Kolkata** Yd No: 394 Loa 28.53 Br ex 7.62 Dght 1.601 Lbp 27.41 Br md 7.61 Dpth 2.52 Welded, 1 dk	**(B32B2SP) Pusher Tug**	**2 oil engines** with clutches, flexible couplings & sr reverse geared to sc. shafts driving 2 FP propellers Total Power: 994kW (1,352hp) 6.5kn MAN R8V16/18TL 2 x 4 Stroke 8 Cy. 160 x 180 each-497kW (676bhp) Garden Reach Shipbuilders &Engineers Ltd-India AuxGen: 2 x 24kW 415V 50Hz a.c Fuel: 40.5 (d.f.)
8659364 - -	**TANJUNG API** **Government of The Republic of Indonesia (Direktorat Jenderal Perhubungan Darat - Ministry of Land Communications)** PT ASDP Indonesia Ferry (Persero) - Angkutan Sungai Danau & Penyeberangan *Tanjung Priok* *Indonesia*	616 185 -	Class: KI	**2011-05 PT Dumas — Surabaya** Loa - Br ex - Dght 2.150 Lbp 40.60 Br md 12.00 Dpth 3.20 Welded, 1 dk	**(A36A2PR) Passenger/Ro-Ro Ship (Vehicles)** Bow ramp (centre) Stern ramp (centre)	**2 oil engines** reduction geared to sc. shafts driving 2 Propellers 11.0kn AuxGen: 2 x 83kW 400V a.c
9205304 - -	**TANJUNG ARA** **Government of Malaysia (Director of Marine - Sabah)** - *Malaysia*	110 - -		**2001-04 Kay Marine Sdn Bhd — Kuala Terengganu** (Hull) **2001-04 B.V. Scheepswerf Damen — Gorinchem** Yd No: 5647 Loa 24.00 Br ex - Dght - Lbp - Br md 6.00 Dpth 3.00 Welded, 1 dk	**(B34H2SQ) Patrol Vessel**	**2 oil engines** geared to sc. shafts driving 2 FP propellers Total Power: 2,340kW (3,182hp) Deutz TBD620V12 2 x Vee 4 Stroke 12 Cy. 170 x 195 each-1170kW (1591bhp) Deutz AG-Koeln
8935471 *YD4836* -	**TANJUNG BAHARI 8** *ex* Seacoral Tetra *-2002* **PT Pelayaran Nasional Sandico Ocean Line** - *Jakarta* *Indonesia* MMSI: 525012084	125 38 -	Class: KI (BV)	**1997 Huten Marine Sdn Bhd — Kuching** Yd No: 06/97 Loa 23.26 Br ex - Dght 2.360 Lbp 21.96 Br md 7.00 Dpth 2.90 Welded, 1 dk	**(B32A2ST) Tug**	**2 oil engines** geared to sc. shafts driving 2 FP propellers Total Power: 738kW (1,004hp) Cummins KTA-19-M 2 x 4 Stroke 6 Cy. 159 x 159 each-369kW (502bhp) Cummins Engine Co Inc-USA AuxGen: 1 x 16kW 220V 50Hz a.c, 1 x 21kW 220V a.c Fuel: 72.0 (d.f.)
9247998 *YD4770* -	**TANJUNG BAHARI 9** *ex* SDS 22 *-2008* **PT Tanjung Bahari Perkasa** - *Jakarta* *Indonesia*	131 40 -	Class: KI (NK)	**2001-03 Tuong Aik (Sarawak) Sdn Bhd — Sibu** Yd No: 2008 L reg 23.50 Br ex - Dght 1.950 Lbp 21.76 Br md 7.32 Dpth 3.20 Welded, 1 dk	**(B32B2SP) Pusher Tug**	**2 oil engines** geared to sc. shafts driving 2 FP propellers Total Power: 942kW (1,280hp) 10.0kn Yanmar 6LAHM-STE3 2 x 4 Stroke 6 Cy. 150 x 165 each-471kW (640bhp) Yanmar Diesel Engine Co Ltd-Japan
8957924 - -	**TANJUNG BAHARI 10** *ex* Barito Perkasa *-2008* **PT Tanjung Bahari Perkasa** - *Batam* *Indonesia* Official number: PST 1740/L	117 70 -	Class: KI	**1999-05 P.T. Sentosa Mulia Shipyard — Batam** Loa 22.80 Br ex - Dght 2.390 Lbp 20.84 Br md 6.70 Dpth 2.90 Welded, 1 dk	**(B32A2ST) Tug**	**2 oil engines** reduction geared to sc. shafts driving 2 FP propellers Total Power: 942kW (1,280hp) 10.0kn Yanmar 6LAHM-STE 2 x 4 Stroke 6 Cy. 150 x 165 each-471kW (640bhp) Yanmar Diesel Engine Co Ltd-Japan

IMO / Call sign	Name / Owner / Port	Tonnage	Class	Builder / Dimensions	Type	Machinery
9506631 *YDA4529* -	**TANJUNG BAHARI 11** *completed as SG 30 -2009* **PT Tanjung Bahari Perkasa** - *Jakarta* *Indonesia*	**192** 58 188	Class: KI (GL)	**2009-11 Rajang Maju Shipbuilding Sdn Bhd — Sibu** Yd No: 75 Loa 26.00 Br ex - Dght 3.000 Lbp 24.24 Br md 8.00 Dpth 3.65 Welded, 1 dk	**(B32A2ST) Tug**	**2 oil engines** reverse reduction geared to sc. shafts driving 2 FP propellers Total Power: 1,220kW (1,658hp) Yanmar 6AYM-ETE 2 x 4 Stroke 6 Cy. 155 x 180 each-610kW (829bhp) Yanmar Diesel Engine Co Ltd-Japan
9594975 *YDA4749* -	**TANJUNG BAHARI 12** **PT Pelayaran Nasional Tanjung Bahari Perkasa** - *Jakarta* *Indonesia*	**200** 60 188	Class: KI	**2010-12 Rajang Maju Shipbuilding Sdn Bhd — Sibu** Yd No: RMM0010 Loa 26.00 Br ex - Dght 3.000 Lbp 24.28 Br md 8.00 Dpth 3.65 Welded, 1 dk	**(B32A2ST) Tug**	**2 oil engines** reverse reduction geared to sc. shafts driving 2 FP propellers Total Power: 1,220kW (1,658hp) Yanmar 6AYM-ETE 2 x 4 Stroke 6 Cy. 155 x 180 each-610kW (829bhp) Yanmar Diesel Engine Co Ltd-Japan AuxGen: 2 x 49kW a.c
9665310 *YDB4184* -	**TANJUNG BAHARI 15** **PT Tanjung Bahari Perkasa** - *Jakarta* *Indonesia*	**217** 66 188	Class: NK	**2012-12 Rajang Maju Shipbuilding Sdn Bhd — Sibu** Yd No: RMM0028 Loa 26.00 Br ex - Dght 3.012 Lbp 24.19 Br md 8.00 Dpth 3.65 Welded, 1 dk	**(B32A2ST) Tug**	**2 oil engines** reduction geared to sc. shafts driving 2 FP propellers Total Power: 1,220kW (1,658hp) Yanmar 6AYM-WET 2 x 4 Stroke 6 Cy. 155 x 180 each-610kW (829bhp) Yanmar Diesel Engine Co Ltd-Japan Fuel: 150.0
9666730 *YDB4185* -	**TANJUNG BAHARI 16** **PT Tanjung Bahari Perkasa** - *Jakarta* *Indonesia*	**217** 66 187	Class: NK	**2012-12 Rajang Maju Shipbuilding Sdn Bhd — Sibu** Yd No: RMM0029 Loa 26.00 Br ex - Dght 3.012 Lbp 24.19 Br md 8.00 Dpth 3.65 Welded, 1 dk	**(B32A2ST) Tug**	**2 oil engines** reduction geared to sc. shafts driving 2 FP propellers Total Power: 1,220kW (1,658hp) Yanmar 6AYM-WET 2 x 4 Stroke 6 Cy. 155 x 180 each-610kW (829bhp) Yanmar Diesel Engine Co Ltd-Japan Fuel: 150.0
9678240 *YDB4186* -	**TANJUNG BAHARI 17** **PT Tanjung Bahari Perkasa** - *Jakarta* *Indonesia*	**143** 43 159	Class: NK	**2012-11 East Oceanic Shipyard Sdn Bhd — Sibu** Yd No: 007 Loa 23.90 Br ex - Dght 2.912 Lbp 22.43 Br md 7.60 Dpth 3.50 Welded, 1 dk	**(B32A2ST) Tug**	**2 oil engines** reduction geared to sc. shafts driving 2 FP propellers Total Power: 894kW (1,216hp) Cummins KTA-19-M3 2 x 4 Stroke 6 Cy. 159 x 159 each-447kW (608bhp) Cummins Engine Co Inc-USA Fuel: 109.0 (d.f.)
9605920 *YDA4731* -	**TANJUNG BAHARI 18** *ex Vitawani Vt4 -2010* **PT Pelayaran Nasional Tanjung Bahari Perkasa** - *Jakarta* *Indonesia*	**217** 65 -	Class: BV KI	**2010-11 Vitawani Shipbuilding Sdn Bhd — Sibu** Yd No: VT4 Loa 26.00 Br ex 8.18 Dght 3.000 Lbp 23.98 Br md 8.00 Dpth 3.65 Welded, 1 dk	**(B32A2ST) Tug**	**2 oil engines** reduction geared to sc. shafts driving 2 FP propellers Total Power: 1,302kW (1,770hp) Caterpillar 3412D 2 x Vee 4 Stroke 12 Cy. 145 x 162 each-651kW (885bhp) Caterpillar Inc-USA AuxGen: 2 x 40kW 50Hz a.c
9607552 *YDA4878* -	**TANJUNG BAHARI 19** **PT Pelayaran Nasional Tanjung Bahari Perkasa** - *Jakarta* *Indonesia*	**194** 59 192	Class: GL KI	**2011-08 Rajang Maju Shipbuilding Sdn Bhd — Sibu** Yd No: RMM0022 Loa 26.00 Br ex - Dght 3.000 Lbp 23.86 Br md 8.00 Dpth 3.65 Welded, 1 dk	**(B32A2ST) Tug**	**2 oil engines** reduction geared to sc. shafts driving 1 Propeller Total Power: 1,220kW (1,658hp) Yanmar 6AYM-WET 2 x 4 Stroke 6 Cy. 155 x 180 each-610kW (829bhp) Yanmar Diesel Engine Co Ltd-Japan
9609172 *YDA4792* -	**TANJUNG BAHARI 20** **PT Pelayaran Nasional Tanjung Bahari Perkasa** - *Jakarta* *Indonesia*	**204** 62 206	Class: KI (NK)	**2011-03 Eastern Marine Shipbuilding Sdn Bhd — Sibu** Yd No: 94 Loa 27.56 Br ex - Dght 3.112 Lbp 24.18 Br md 7.93 Dpth 3.80 Welded, 1 dk	**(B32A2ST) Tug**	**2 oil engines** reduction geared to sc. shafts driving 2 Propellers Total Power: 1,220kW (1,658hp) Yanmar 6AYM-ETE 2 x 4 Stroke 6 Cy. 155 x 180 each-610kW (829bhp) Yanmar Diesel Engine Co Ltd-Japan
9634361 *YDA4924* -	**TANJUNG BAHARI 21** **PT Pelayaran Nasional Tanjung Bahari Perkasa** - *Jakarta* *Indonesia*	**266** 80 270	Class: GL KI	**2011-11 Tang Tiew Hee & Sons Sdn Bhd — Sibu** Yd No: 56 Loa 30.00 Br ex 8.61 Dght 3.500 Lbp 28.06 Br md 8.60 Dpth 4.11 Welded, 1 dk	**(B32A2ST) Tug**	**2 oil engines** reduction geared to sc. shafts driving 2 FP propellers Total Power: 1,518kW (2,064hp) Mitsubishi S6R2-MTK3L 2 x 4 Stroke 6 Cy. 170 x 220 each-759kW (1032bhp) Mitsubishi Heavy Industries Ltd-Japan AuxGen: 2 x 91kW 415V a.c
9634373 *YDA4923* -	**TANJUNG BAHARI 22** **PT Pelayaran Nasional Tanjung Bahari Perkasa** - *Jakarta* *Indonesia*	**266** 80 274	Class: KI (GL)	**2011-11 Tang Tiew Hee & Sons Sdn Bhd — Sibu** Yd No: 57 Loa 30.00 Br ex 8.61 Dght 3.440 Lbp 28.06 Br md 8.60 Dpth 4.11 Welded, 1 dk	**(B32A2ST) Tug**	**2 oil engines** reduction geared to sc. shafts driving 2 FP propellers Total Power: 1,518kW (2,064hp) Mitsubishi S6R2-MTK3L 2 x 4 Stroke 6 Cy. 170 x 220 each-759kW (1032bhp) Mitsubishi Heavy Industries Ltd-Japan
9690274 *YDB4328* -	**TANJUNG BAHARI 23** **PT Tanjung Bahari Perkasa** - *Jakarta* *Indonesia*	**219** 66 197	Class: NK	**2013-07 East Oceanic Shipyard Sdn Bhd — Sibu** Yd No: 008 Loa 26.00 Br ex - Dght 3.012 Lbp 24.46 Br md 8.40 Dpth 3.60 Welded, 1 dk	**(B32A2ST) Tug**	**2 oil engines** reduction geared to sc. shafts driving 2 FP propellers Total Power: 1,220kW (1,658hp) Yanmar 6AYM-WET 2 x 4 Stroke 6 Cy. 155 x 180 each-610kW (829bhp) Yanmar Diesel Engine Co Ltd-Japan AuxGen: 1 x 40kW a.c Fuel: 163.0
8807911 *V8V2203* -	**TANJUNG BAKARANG** **Government of The State of Brunei** - *Bandar Seri Begawan* *Brunei* Official number: 0104	*164* 73 20	Class: BV (Class contemplated) (LR) ✠ Classed LR until 9/1/12	**1988-04 Cheoy Lee Shipyards Ltd — Hong Kong** Yd No: 4261 Loa 25.84 Br ex 6.48 Dght 1.600 Lbp 21.78 Br md 6.25 Dpth 3.43 Bonded, 1 dk	**(B34L2QU) Utility Vessel** Hull Material: Reinforced Plastic	**2 oil engines** with clutches, flexible couplings & sr reverse geared to sc. shafts driving 2 FP propellers Total Power: 1,324kW (1,800hp) MAN D2842LXE 2 x Vee 4 Stroke 12 Cy. 128 x 142 each-662kW (900bhp) MAN Nutzfahrzeuge AG-Nuernberg AuxGen: 2 x 56kW 380V 50Hz a.c
8621862 *YB4414* -	**TANJUNG BARU** *ex Taiki Maru No. 3 -2004* **PT Lima Utama Wisesa** - *Jakarta* *Indonesia*	**666** 376 669	Class: KI	**1984-03 K.K. Miura Zosensho — Saiki** Yd No: 701 Converted From: Grab Dredger-2006 Loa 50.60 Br ex - Dght 3.201 Lbp 46.06 Br md 11.00 Dpth 5.41 Welded, 1 dk	**(A31A2GX) General Cargo Ship** Grain: 419 Compartments: 1 Ho, ER 1 Ha: (8.8 x 8.8)ER Cranes: 1x1t,1	**1 oil engine** geared to sc. shaft driving 1 FP propeller Total Power: 883kW (1,201hp) 9.5kn Niigata 6M28AGT 1 x 4 Stroke 6 Cy. 280 x 480 883kW (1201bhp) Niigata Engineering Co Ltd-Japan
9562128 *9MIR8* -	**TANJUNG BIRU 1** **Icon Ship Management Sdn Bhd** - *Port Klang* *Malaysia* MMSI: 533040500 Official number: 334108	**1,669** 500 1,650	Class: BV	**2009-10 Muhibbah Marine Engineering Sdn Bhd — Port Klang** Yd No: 20073 Loa 60.00 Br ex - Dght 4.850 Lbp 58.74 Br md 16.00 Dpth 5.50 Welded, 1 dk	**(B21B20A) Anchor Handling Tug Supply**	**2 oil engines** reduction geared to sc. shafts driving 2 CP propellers Total Power: 3,840kW (5,220hp) 11.0kn Yanmar 6EY26 2 x 4 Stroke 6 Cy. 260 x 385 each-1920kW (2610bhp) Yanmar Diesel Engine Co Ltd-Japan AuxGen: 2 x 675kW 415V 50Hz a.c, 2 x 245kW 415V 50Hz a.c Thrusters: 1 Thwart. CP thruster (f) Fuel: 470.0
9562130 *9MIR9* -	**TANJUNG BIRU 2** **Icon Ship Management Sdn Bhd** - *Port Klang* *Malaysia* MMSI: 533040600 Official number: 334109	**1,669** 500 1,650	Class: BV	**2009-12 Muhibbah Marine Engineering Sdn Bhd — Port Klang** Yd No: 20074 Loa 60.00 Br ex - Dght 4.850 Lbp 58.74 Br md 16.00 Dpth 5.50 Welded, 1 dk	**(B21B20A) Anchor Handling Tug Supply**	**2 oil engines** reduction geared to sc. shafts driving 2 CP propellers Total Power: 3,840kW (5,220hp) 11.0kn Yanmar 6EY26 2 x 4 Stroke 6 Cy. 260 x 385 each-1920kW (2610bhp) Yanmar Diesel Engine Co Ltd-Japan AuxGen: 2 x 675kW 415V 50Hz a.c, 2 x 245kW 415V 50Hz a.c Thrusters: 1 Thwart. CP thruster (f) Fuel: 470.0
8864919 - -	**TANJUNG BUNGA UTAMA** *ex Meitoku Maru No. 2 -2012* - - *Indonesia*	*186* - 544		**1992-08 Maekawa Zosensho — Japan** L reg 46.60 Br ex - Dght 3.270 Lbp - Br md 8.60 Dpth 5.10 Welded, 1 dk	**(A31A2GX) General Cargo Ship**	**1 oil engine** driving 1 FP propeller Total Power: 515kW (700hp) Matsui 6M26KGHS 1 x 4 Stroke 6 Cy. 260 x 400 515kW (700bhp) Matsui Iron Works Co Ltd-Japan

IMO / Call sign	Name / Owner	Tonnage	Class	Build / Dimensions	Type	Machinery
9027398 *YFAD* -	**TANJUNG BURANG** **Government of The Republic of Indonesia (Direktorat Jenderal Perhubungan Darat - Ministry of Land Communications)** PT ASDP Indonesia Ferry (Persero) - Angkutan Sungai Danau & Penyeberangan *Jakarta* *Indonesia* MMSI: 525019432	**507** 152 -	Class: KI	**1993-08 PT Dumas — Surabaya** Loa 45.30 Br ex - Dght 2.000 Lbp 39.50 Br md 12.00 Dpth 3.00 Welded, 1 dk	**(A37B2PS) Passenger Ship**	**2 oil engines** driving 2 Propellers Total Power: 956kW (1,300hp) 10.5kn Niigata 6NSD-M 2 x 4 Stroke 6 Cy. 160 x 210 each-478kW (650bhp) (made 1992) Niigata Engineering Co Ltd-Japan
8208177 *PKAH* -	**TANJUNG BUTON** *ex* Fathimah *-2010* *ex* Central Success *-2007* *ex* West Gold *-2006* *ex* New Energy *-2005* *ex* Pro Kingborn *-2005* *ex* Azalea I *-2005* *ex* Delfini I *-2003* *ex* Abdoun Symphony *-1998* *ex* Chemical Symphony *-1997* *ex* Gogo Chemsun *-1990* **PT Tanjung Buton Makmur Sejahtera** PT Kreasi Mas Marine *Jakarta* *Indonesia* MMSI: 525011105	**5,205** 2,386 9,093 T/cm 17.0	Class: KI (RS) (NK) (NV)	**1983-01 Higaki Zosen K.K. — Imabari** Yd No: 282 Loa 110.11 (BB) Br ex 18.34 Dght 8.070 Lbp 102.40 Br md 18.30 Dpth 10.00 Welded, 1 dk	**(A12B2TR) Chemical/Products Tanker** Liq: 9,428; Liq (Oil): 9,428 Compartments: 18 Ta, ER 18 Cargo Pump (s) Manifold: Bow/CM: 53.4m	**1 oil engine** driving 1 FP propeller Total Power: 4,413kW (6,000hp) 13.0kn Mitsubishi 6UEC45/115H 1 x 2 Stroke 6 Cy. 450 x 1150 4413kW (6000bhp) Kobe Hatsudoki KK-Japan AuxGen: 3 x 320kW 450V 60Hz a.c
9577197 - -	**TANJUNG BUYUT 1-206** **PT Pelabuhan Indonesia II (Persero) (Indonesia Port Corp II) (PELINDO II)** - *Palembang* *Indonesia*	**204** 62 78	Class: KI	**2009-10 P.T. Daya Radar Utama — Jakarta** Yd No: 126 Loa 23.50 Br ex - Dght 2.400 Lbp 21.68 Br md 7.00 Dpth 3.15 Welded, 1 dk	**(B32A2ST) Tug**	**2 oil engines** reduction geared to sc. shafts driving 2 Propellers Total Power: 882kW (1,200hp) 11.0kn Yanmar 6AYM-STE 2 x 4 Stroke 6 Cy. 155 x 180 each-441kW (600bhp) Yanmar Diesel Engine Co Ltd-Japan
9588196 - -	**TANJUNG BUYUT 2-212** **PT Pelabuhan Indonesia II (Persero) (Indonesia Port Corp II) (PELINDO II)** - *Panjang* *Indonesia*	**291** 88 145	Class: KI	**2011-05 P.T. Daya Radar Utama — Jakarta** Yd No: 127 Loa 29.00 Br ex - Dght 3.500 Lbp 25.50 Br md 9.40 Dpth 4.58 Welded, 1 dk	**(B32A2ST) Tug**	**2 oil engines** reduction geared to sc. shafts driving 2 Propellers Total Power: 1,600kW (2,176hp) Yanmar 6N21AL-SV 2 x 4 Stroke 6 Cy. 210 x 290 each-800kW (1088bhp) Yanmar Diesel Engine Co Ltd-Japan
9588201 - -	**TANJUNG BUYUT 3-212** **PT Pelabuhan Indonesia II (Persero) (Indonesia Port Corp II) (PELINDO II)** - *Panjang* *Indonesia*	**291** 88 145	Class: KI	**2011-07 P.T. Daya Radar Utama — Jakarta** Yd No: 128 Loa 29.00 Br ex - Dght 3.500 Lbp 25.50 Br md 9.40 Dpth 4.58 Welded, 1 dk	**(B32A2ST) Tug**	**2 oil engines** reduction geared to sc. shafts driving 2 Propellers Total Power: 1,600kW (2,176hp) Yanmar 6N21AL-SV 2 x 4 Stroke 6 Cy. 210 x 290 each-800kW (1088bhp) Yanmar Diesel Engine Co Ltd-Japan
9548134 *9MIR6* -	**TANJUNG DAHAN 1** **Icon Ship Management Sdn Bhd** - *Port Klang* *Malaysia* MMSI: 533040700 Official number: 334106	**1,706** 511 1,708	Class: AB	**2010-02 Grade One Marine Shipyard Sdn Bhd — Sitiawan** Yd No: G003 Loa 60.00 Br ex 16.02 Dght 5.100 Lbp 54.00 Br md 16.00 Dpth 6.00 Welded, 1 dk	**(B21B20A) Anchor Handling Tug Supply** Cranes: 1x5t	**2 oil engines** reduction geared to sc. shafts driving 2 CP propellers Total Power: 4,060kW (5,520hp) 13.0kn Caterpillar C280-6 2 x 4 Stroke 6 Cy. 280 x 300 each-2030kW (2760bhp) Caterpillar Inc-USA AuxGen: 1 x 1000kW 415V 50Hz a.c, 2 x 275kW 415V 50Hz a.c Thrusters: 1 Tunnel thruster (f)
9548146 *9MIR7* -	**TANJUNG DAHAN 2** **Icon Ship Management Sdn Bhd** - *Port Klang* *Malaysia* MMSI: 533040800 Official number: 334107	**1,706** 511 1,790	Class: AB	**2010-05 Grade One Marine Shipyard Sdn Bhd — Sitiawan** Yd No: G005 Loa 60.00 Br ex 16.02 Dght 5.100 Lbp 53.90 Br md 16.00 Dpth 6.00 Welded, 1 dk	**(B21B20A) Anchor Handling Tug Supply** Cranes: 1x5t	**2 oil engines** reduction geared to sc. shafts driving 2 CP propellers Total Power: 4,060kW (5,520hp) 13.0kn Caterpillar C280-6 2 x 4 Stroke 6 Cy. 280 x 300 each-2030kW (2760bhp) Caterpillar Inc-USA AuxGen: 1 x 1000kW 415V 50Hz a.c, 2 x 275kW 415V 50Hz a.c Thrusters: 1 Tunnel thruster (f) Fuel: 467.0
9410375 *9MFH7* -	**TANJUNG DAWAI** **Icon Ship Management Sdn Bhd** - *Port Klang* *Malaysia* MMSI: 533013000 Official number: 332421	**953** 367 1,279	Class: BV	**2007-10 Muhibbah Marine Engineering Sdn Bhd — Port Klang** Yd No: 20063 Loa 59.20 Br ex - Dght 4.750 Lbp 52.30 Br md 13.80 Dpth 5.50 Welded, 1 dk	**(B21B20A) Anchor Handling Tug Supply** Double Hull	**2 oil engines** reduction geared to sc. shafts driving 2 CP propellers Total Power: 4,004kW (5,444hp) 13.0kn Caterpillar 3606 2 x 4 Stroke 6 Cy. 280 x 300 each-2002kW (2722bhp) Caterpillar Inc-USA
9256341 *YD4780* -	**TANJUNG ENIM** **PT Arpeni Pratama Ocean Line Tbk** - *Jakarta* *Indonesia* MMSI: 525011050	**166** 50 159	Class: (NK)	**2001-07 Far East Shipyard Co Sdn Bhd — Sibu** Yd No: 03/97 Loa - Br ex - Dght 2.872 Lbp 23.22 Br md 7.60 Dpth 3.50 Welded, 1 dk	**(B32A2ST) Tug**	**2 oil engines** driving 2 FP propellers Total Power: 1,176kW (1,598hp)
9522453 *9MID7* -	**TANJUNG GAYA** **Icon Ship Management Sdn Bhd** - *Port Klang* *Malaysia* MMSI: 533020700 Official number: 333968	**1,031** 309 -	Class: BV	**2008-12 Muhibbah Marine Engineering Sdn Bhd — Port Klang** Yd No: 20069 Loa 49.00 Br ex - Dght 4.000 Lbp 47.50 Br md 13.20 Dpth 5.30 Welded, 1 dk	**(B21B20A) Anchor Handling Tug Supply**	**2 oil engines** reduction geared to sc. shafts driving 2 CP propellers Total Power: 2,648kW (3,600hp) Yanmar 8N21A-EV 2 x 4 Stroke 8 Cy. 210 x 290 each-1324kW (1800bhp) Yanmar Diesel Engine Co Ltd-Japan AuxGen: 2 x 200kW 50Hz a.c Thrusters: 1 Tunnel thruster (f)
9528689 *9MIC4* -	**TANJUNG GELANG** **Icon Ship Management Sdn Bhd** - *Port Klang* *Malaysia* MMSI: 533038800 Official number: 333909	**1,536** 461 1,121	Class: AB	**2009-05 Boustead Naval Shipyard Sdn Bhd — Lumut** Yd No: 025 Loa 60.80 Br ex - Dght 4.300 Lbp 54.00 Br md 14.78 Dpth 5.75 Welded, 1 dk	**(B22F20W) Well Stimulation Vessel** Cranes: 1	**2 oil engines** reduction geared to sc. shafts driving 2 Propellers Total Power: 4,060kW (5,520hp) Caterpillar 3606 2 x 4 Stroke 6 Cy. 280 x 300 each-2030kW (2760bhp) Caterpillar Inc-USA AuxGen: 3 x 405kW a.c, 2 x a.c Thrusters: 1 Tunnel thruster (f) Fuel: 426.0 (r.f.)
8631142 *YHCU* -	**TANJUNG GLORY DUA** *ex* Tropic *-2001* **PT Tanjung Glory Shipping** - *Jakarta* *Indonesia* MMSI: 525019137	**732** 232 1,100	Class: KI (NK)	**1987-09 Kurinoura Dockyard Co Ltd — Yawatahama EH** Yd No: 245 Loa 64.95 Br ex 10.02 Dght 4.250 Lbp 60.00 Br md 10.00 Dpth 4.50 Welded, 1 dk	**(A12A2TC) Chemical Tanker** Liq: 920	**1 oil engine** driving 1 FP propeller Total Power: 956kW (1,300hp) 10.6kn Hanshin 6LU28G 1 x 4 Stroke 6 Cy. 280 x 440 956kW (1300bhp) The Hanshin Diesel Works Ltd-Japan
7823669 *YFAS* -	**TANJUNG GLORY SATU** *ex* Kinpuku Maru No. 18 *-1993* **PT Tanjung Glory Shipping** - *Makassar* *Indonesia*	**604** 160 1,000	Class: (KI)	**1979-02 Ito Senpaku K.K. — Japan** Yd No: 166 Loa - Br ex 9.22 Dght 3.901 Lbp 48.01 Br md 9.20 Dpth 4.09 Riveted\Welded, 1 dk	**(A13B2TU) Tanker (unspecified)**	**1 oil engine** driving 1 FP propeller Total Power: 956kW (1,300hp) 10.5kn Yanmar MF28-UT 1 x 4 Stroke 6 Cy. 280 x 450 956kW (1300bhp) Matsue Diesel KK-Japan
9352638 *9MGK9* -	**TANJUNG HUMA** **Icon Ship Management Sdn Bhd** - *Port Klang* *Malaysia* MMSI: 533001500 Official number: 330447	**1,601** 480 1,619	Class: AB	**2005-09 MSET Shipbuilding Corp Sdn Bhd — Kuala Terengganu** Yd No: 5688 Loa 60.00 Br ex 16.96 Dght 4.830 Lbp 54.00 Br md 16.00 Dpth 5.50 Welded, 1 dk	**(B21B20A) Anchor Handling Tug Supply**	**2 oil engines** reduction geared to sc. shafts driving 2 CP propellers Total Power: 4,050kW (5,506hp) Deutz SBV9M628 2 x 4 Stroke 9 Cy. 240 x 280 each-2025kW (2753bhp) Deutz AG-Koeln AuxGen: 2 x 260kW a.c, 2 x 700kW a.c Thrusters: 1 Thwart. CP thruster (f)

7514737 *YCFF*	**TANJUNG II** **PT PERTAMINA (PERSERO)** - *Balikpapan* *Indonesia* Official number: 606+2D	*231* 70 -	Class: KI (AB)	**1976-06 Sing Koon Seng Pte Ltd — Singapore** Yd No: SKS295 Loa 29.51 Br ex 8.71 Dght 3.436 Lbp 26.98 Br md 8.60 Dpth 4.17 Welded, 1 dk	**(B32A2ST) Tug**	**2 oil engines** reverse reduction geared to sc. shafts driving 2 FP propellers Total Power: 1,066kW (1,450hp) 12.0kn Caterpillar D348TA 2 x Vee 4 Stroke 12 Cy. 137 x 165 each-533kW (725bhp) Caterpillar Tractor Co-USA AuxGen: 2 x 40kW Fuel: 95.0 (d.f.)
9379997 *YDA4135* -	**TANJUNG JATI** **PT Buana Jaya Pratama** PT Arpeni Pratama Ocean Line Tbk *Jakarta* *Indonesia*	**253** 76 165	Class: KI (AB)	**2006-07 Qingdao Shipyard — Qingdao SD** Yd No: QDZ433 Loa 29.50 Br ex - Dght 3.500 Lbp 27.49 Br md 9.00 Dpth 4.16 Welded, 1 dk	**(B32A2ST) Tug**	**2 oil engines** reduction geared to sc. shafts driving 2 Propellers Total Power: 1,766kW (2,402hp) Yanmar 6N21A-SV 2 x 4 Stroke 6 Cy. 210 x 290 each-883kW (1201bhp) Yanmar Diesel Engine Co Ltd-Japan AuxGen: 2 x 90kW 400V a.c
7733369 - -	**TANJUNG JOHOR XV** *ex Sam Hong V -1984 ex Zuisho -1979* **PT Tanjung Johor Wood Industry** - *Jambi* *Indonesia*	*119* 34 66	Class: KI (NK)	**1978-02 K.K. Miura Zosensho — Oseto** Loa 28.33 Br ex - Dght 2.728 Lbp 25.58 Br md 7.01 Dpth 3.13 Welded, 1 dk	**(B32A2ST) Tug**	**1 oil engine** driving 1 FP propeller Total Power: 846kW (1,150hp) 11.0kn Hanshin Z6WBSH 1 x 4 Stroke 6 Cy. 350 x 500 846kW (1150bhp) Hanshin Nainenki Kogyo-Japan AuxGen: 2 x 40kW
9130664 *YD4900* -	**TANJUNG JOHOR XXV** *ex LM Super -2003* **PT Tanjung Johor Wood Industry** - *Jakarta* *Indonesia*	**115** 69 81	Class: KI (NK)	**1995-05 Eastern Marine Shipbuilding Sdn Bhd — Sibu** Yd No: 7594 Loa 21.30 Br ex - Dght 2.412 Lbp 19.94 Br md 6.70 Dpth 2.75 Welded, 1 dk	**(B32A2ST) Tug**	**2 oil engines** with clutches, flexible couplings & sr reverse geared to sc. shafts driving 2 CP propellers Total Power: 692kW (940hp) 10.0kn Caterpillar 3408TA 2 x Vee 4 Stroke 8 Cy. 137 x 152 each-346kW (470bhp) Caterpillar Inc-USA AuxGen: 4 x 16kW 415V 50Hz a.c Fuel: 42.7 (d.f.) 2.6pd
9086174 *YD4998* -	**TANJUNG JOHOR XXVII** *ex Bintang Ocean II -2006* **PT Tanjung Johor Wood Industry** - *Jakarta* *Indonesia*	**115** 69 112	Class: KI (NK)	**1993-07 Rajang Maju Shipbuilding Sdn Bhd — Sibu** Yd No: 11 Loa 23.17 Br ex - Dght 2.388 Lbp 21.03 Br md 7.00 Dpth 2.90 Welded, 1 dk	**(B32A2ST) Tug**	**2 oil engines** reduction geared to sc. shafts driving 2 FP propellers Total Power: 692kW (940hp) 10.0kn Caterpillar 3408B 2 x Vee 4 Stroke 8 Cy. 137 x 152 each-346kW (470bhp) Caterpillar Inc-USA AuxGen: 2 x 16kW a.c
9691711 - -	**TANJUNG KABAT** **Government of The Republic of Indonesia (Direktorat Jenderal Perhubungan Darat - Ministry of Land Communications)** PT ASDP Indonesia Ferry (Persero) - Angkutan Sungai Danau & Penyeberangan *Ambon* *Indonesia*	**660** 198 353	Class: KI	**2013-01 P.T. Adiluhung Sarana Segara Industri — Bangkalan** Yd No: A.035 Loa 45.50 Br ex 12.20 Dght 2.150 Lbp 40.15 Br md 12.00 Dpth 3.20 Welded, 1 dk	**(A36A2PR) Passenger/Ro-Ro Ship (Vehicles)**	**2 oil engines** reduction geared to sc. shafts driving 2 Propellers Total Power: 1,220kW (1,658hp) Yanmar 6AYM-WET 2 x 4 Stroke 6 Cy. 155 x 180 each-610kW (829bhp) Yanmar Diesel Engine Co Ltd-Japan AuxGen: 2 x 91kW 380V a.c
8917857 - -	**TANJUNG KEMARONG** **Government of Malaysia (Director of Marine & Ministry of Transport)** -	**714** 214 450	Class: (BV)	**1990-10 Malaysia Shipyard & Engineering Sdn Bhd — Pasir Gudang** Yd No: 043 Loa 57.40 Br ex - Dght 2.010 Lbp 53.63 Br md 12.00 Dpth 3.00 Welded, 1 dk	**(B33B2DT) Trailing Suction Hopper Dredger** Hopper: 500	**2 oil engines** geared to sc. shafts driving 2 FP propellers Total Power: 530kW (720hp) 7.0kn Cummins NTA-855-M 2 x 4 Stroke 6 Cy. 140 x 152 each-265kW (360bhp) Cummins Engine Co Ltd-United Kingdom AuxGen: 2 x 40kW 230/415V 50Hz a.c Fuel: 66.5 (d.f.) 1.2pd
8616740 *V8V2201* -	**TANJUNG KERAMAT** **Government of The State of Brunei** - *Bandar Seri Begawan* *Brunei* Official number: 0100	**123** 37 -	Class: (AB) (BV)	**1987-06 Singapore Slipway & Engineering Co. Pte Ltd — Singapore** Yd No: 165 Loa - Br ex - Dght 2.512 Lbp 20.22 Br md 7.01 Dpth 3.20 Welded, 1 dk	**(B32A2ST) Tug**	**2 oil engines** geared to sc. shafts driving 2 FP propellers Total Power: 1,060kW (1,442hp) Caterpillar 3412TA 2 x Vee 4 Stroke 12 Cy. 137 x 152 each-530kW (721bhp) Caterpillar Inc-USA
9050204 - -	**TANJUNG KINDANA** **Government of The State of Brunei (Department of Marine - Ministry of Communication)** - *Brunei*	**177** 53 -	Class: (LR) ✠ Classed LR until 26/2/09	**1992-11 Guangzhou Huangpu Shipyard — Guangzhou GD** (Hull) **1992-11 Cheoy Lee Shipyards Ltd — Hong Kong** Yd No: 4471 Loa 28.24 Br ex 8.22 Dght - Lbp 27.13 Br md 8.00 Dpth 2.50 Welded, 1 dk	**(B34B2SO) Pile Driving Vessel**	**2 oil engines** with clutches, flexible couplings & sr reverse geared to sc. shafts driving 2 FP propellers Total Power: 442kW (600hp) Cummins NT-855-M 2 x 4 Stroke 6 Cy. 140 x 152 each-221kW (300bhp) Cummins Engine Co Inc-USA AuxGen: 2 x 40kW 380V 50Hz a.c
9290256 *9WE05* -	**TANJUNG KLIAS** **Government of Malaysia (Director of Marine - Sabah)** - *Labuan* *Malaysia* Official number: 329912	**169** 51 44		**2004-03 Kay Marine Sdn Bhd — Kuala Terengganu** Yd No: J59/1 Loa 26.70 Br ex - Dght 1.500 Lbp 25.20 Br md 8.15 Dpth 2.80 Welded, 1 dk	**(B34G2SE) Pollution Control Vessel** Hull Material: Aluminium Alloy	**2 oil engines** driving 2 gen. each 80kW geared to sc. shafts driving 2 Water jets Total Power: 1,640kW (2,230hp) 14.0kn Caterpillar 3412E-TA 2 x Vee 4 Stroke 12 Cy. 137 x 152 each-820kW (1115bhp) Caterpillar Inc-USA AuxGen: 2 x 60kW a.c
8652512 *PNGH* -	**TANJUNG KOAKO** **Government of The Republic of Indonesia (Direktorat Jenderal Perhubungan Darat - Ministry of Land Communications)** - *Ambon* *Indonesia*	**1,148** 432 432	Class: KI	**2010-06 P.T. Sanur Marindo Shipyard — Tegal** Loa 45.50 Br ex - Dght 2.140 Lbp 40.65 Br md 12.00 Dpth 3.20 Welded, 1 dk	**(A36A2PR) Passenger/Ro-Ro Ship (Vehicles)**	**2 oil engines** reduction geared to sc. shafts driving 2 Propellers Total Power: 1,220kW (1,658hp) Yanmar 6AYM-ETE 2 x 4 Stroke 6 Cy. 155 x 180 each-610kW (829bhp) Yanmar Diesel Engine Co Ltd-Japan
9612337 *V8V3106* -	**TANJUNG LUMBA-LUMBA** **Government of The State of Brunei (Port Department - Ministry of Communications)** - *Muara* *Brunei* MMSI: 508038000 Official number: 0051	**445** 133 278	Class: BV (Class contemplated) (AB)	**2011-07 Fujian Funing Shipyard Industry Co Ltd — Fu'an FJ** Yd No: 602-1 Loa 33.70 Br ex - Dght 4.000 Lbp 30.20 Br md 10.60 Dpth 4.96 Welded, 1 dk	**(B32A2ST) Tug**	**2 oil engines** reduction geared to sc. shafts driving 2 FP propellers Total Power: 3,282kW (4,462hp) Caterpillar 3516B 2 x Vee 4 Stroke 16 Cy. 170 x 190 each-1641kW (2231bhp) Caterpillar Inc-USA AuxGen: 2 x 150kW a.c
9618472 - -	**TANJUNG MADLAHAR** **Government of The Republic of Indonesia (Direktorat Jenderal Perhubungan Darat - Ministry of Land Communications)** - *Ambon* *Indonesia*	**500** 150 182	Class: KI	**2011-03 P.T. Daya Radar Utama — Jakarta** Yd No: 150 Loa 40.00 Br ex - Dght 2.000 Lbp 34.50 Br md 10.50 Dpth 2.80 Welded, 1 dk	**(A36A2PR) Passenger/Ro-Ro Ship (Vehicles)**	**2 oil engines** reduction geared to sc. shafts driving 2 Propellers Total Power: 980kW (1,332hp) Mitsubishi S6A3-MPTK 2 x 4 Stroke 6 Cy. 150 x 175 each-490kW (666bhp) Mitsubishi Heavy Industries Ltd-Japan AuxGen: 2 x 90kW a.c
9352626 *9MGL2* -	**TANJUNG MANIS** **Tanjung Offshore Services Sdn Bhd** Icon Ship Management Sdn Bhd *Port Klang* *Malaysia* MMSI: 533002200 Official number: 330448	**915** 274 750	Class: AB	**2005-07 Muhibbah Marine Engineering Sdn Bhd — Port Klang** Yd No: 20055 Loa 45.00 Br ex - Dght 4.200 Lbp 41.25 Br md 12.60 Dpth 5.20 Welded	**(B21A2OS) Platform Supply Ship**	**2 oil engines** reduction geared to sc. shafts driving 2 CP propellers Total Power: 4,050kW (5,506hp) 11.5kn Deutz SBV9M628 2 x 4 Stroke 9 Cy. 240 x 280 each-2025kW (2753bhp) Deutz AG-Koeln Thrusters: 1 Tunnel thruster (f)
9027403 - -	**TANJUNG MAS** **PT Alur Hijau** - *Balikpapan* *Indonesia*	**101** 31 -	Class: KI	**2002-08 P.T. Telaga Nirmala Sejahtera — Samarinda** L reg 29.00 Br ex - Dght - Lbp 27.00 Br md 6.60 Dpth 2.00 Welded, 1 dk	**(A35D2RL) Landing Craft** Bow ramp (centre)	**2 oil engines** geared to sc. shafts driving 2 Propellers Total Power: 280kW (380hp) 7.0kn Mitsubishi 6D15 2 x 4 Stroke 6 Cy. 113 x 115 each-140kW (190bhp) Mitsubishi Heavy Industries Ltd-Japan
9305233 *9WE06* -	**TANJUNG NOSONG** **Government of Malaysia (Director of Marine - Sabah)** - *Labuan* *Malaysia* Official number: 329913	**169** 51 44		**2004-03 Kay Marine Sdn Bhd — Kuala Terengganu** Yd No: J59/2 Loa 26.70 Br ex - Dght 1.500 Lbp 25.20 Br md 8.15 Dpth 2.80 Welded, 1 dk	**(B34G2SE) Pollution Control Vessel** Hull Material: Aluminium Alloy Bow ramp (f)	**2 oil engines** driving 2 gen. each 80kW a.c geared to sc. shafts driving 2 Water jets Total Power: 1,640kW (2,230hp) 14.0kn Caterpillar 3412E-TA 2 x Vee 4 Stroke 12 Cy. 137 x 152 each-820kW (1115bhp) Caterpillar Inc-USA AuxGen: 2 x 60kW a.c

IMO / Call sign / Flag	Name / Former names / Owner / Port	Tonnage	Class	Builder / Dimensions	Type	Machinery
7409906 *YCBS* -	**TANJUNG PAKAR** *ex* Tambang IX *-1989* *ex* Permina Tunda I *-1989* **PT Bestindo Citra Samudera** - *Jakarta* *Indonesia*	**3,498** 1,238 -	Class: (KI) (NK)	**1974-08 Mitsui SB. & Eng. Co. Ltd. — Tamano** Yd No: HF1391 L reg 102.00 Br ex - Dght 5.340 Lbp 99.50 Br md 17.00 Dpth 7.00 Welded, 1 dk	**(B32B2SP) Pusher Tug**	**2 oil engines** driving 2 FP propellers Total Power: 2,354kW (3,200hp) 10.5kn Hanshin 6LUD32 2 x 4 Stroke 6 Cy. 320 x 510 each-1177kW (1600bhp) Hanshin Nainenki Kogyo-Japan AuxGen: 1 x 144kW 450V a.c Fuel: 66.0 12.5pd
8865327 - -	**TANJUNG PENGHARAPAN-2** *ex* Fujisan *-2013* *ex* Fujisan Maru No. 2 *-2012* **PT Indo Shipping Operator** - *Indonesia*	*199* - 639		**1992-10 Kimura Zosen K.K. — Kure** L reg 52.50 Br ex - Dght 3.220 Lbp - Br md 9.40 Dpth 5.40 Welded, 1 dk	**(A31A2GX) General Cargo Ship**	**1 oil engine** geared to sc. shaft driving 1 FP propeller Total Power: 736kW (1,001hp) Hanshin LH26G 1 x 4 Stroke 6 Cy. 260 x 440 736kW (1001bhp) The Hanshin Diesel Works Ltd-Japan
8351091 - -	**TANJUNG PERKASA** *ex* Hiromi *-1982* *ex* Kyosho Maru No. 20 *-1993* **PT Pelayaran Tanjung Redep Indah Perkasa** - *Surabaya* *Indonesia*	**771** 232 653	Class: KI	**1982-11 Shinwa Sangyo K.K. — Osakikamijima** Yd No: 405 Loa - Br ex - Dght 3.350 Lbp 53.50 Br md 9.50 Dpth 5.52 Welded, 1 dk	**(A31A2GX) General Cargo Ship**	**1 oil engine** driving 1 FP propeller Total Power: 956kW (1,300hp) Fuji 6S32F 1 x 4 Stroke 6 Cy. 320 x 500 956kW (1300bhp) Fuji Diesel Co Ltd-Japan
7352036 *YFCF* -	**TANJUNG PERMAI** *ex* Sea Rex *-1993* *ex* Rex I *-1992* *ex* Koyo 7 *-1992* *ex* Shinyo Maru No. 13 *-1991* **PT Samudra Alam Raya** - *Surabaya* *Indonesia*	*737* 260 800	Class: KI	**1973-10 Sasaki Shipbuilding Co Ltd — Osakikamijima HS** Yd No: 183 Converted From: Bulk Aggregates Carrier-1995 Loa 53.19 Br ex 11.00 Dght 4.496 Lbp 48.49 Br md 10.98 Dpth 5.49 Welded, 2 dks	**(A31A2GX) General Cargo Ship**	**1 oil engine** driving 1 FP propeller Total Power: 736kW (1,001hp) 12.0kn Hanshin 1 x 4 Stroke 6 Cy. 736kW (1001bhp) (, fitted 1973) The Hanshin Diesel Works Ltd-Japan AuxGen: 2 x 51kW 220V a.c
9651905 *9MQE4* -	**TANJUNG PIAI 1** **Icon Ship Management Sdn Bhd** - *Port Klang* *Malaysia* MMSI: 533130959 Official number: 334516	**3,396** 1,019 3,500	Class: BV	**2013-06 Muhibbah Marine Engineering Sdn Bhd — Port Klang** Yd No: 20099 Loa 77.00 (BB) Br ex - Dght 6.400 Lbp 68.40 Br md 17.60 Dpth 8.00 Welded, 1 dk	**(B21A20S) Platform Supply Ship**	**4 diesel electric oil engines** driving 4 gen. each 1600kW a.c Connecting to 2 elec. motors driving 2 Azimuth electric drive units Total Power: 6,564kW (8,924hp) 14.2kn Caterpillar 3516B 4 x Vee 4 Stroke 16 Cy. 170 x 190 each-1641kW (2231bhp) Caterpillar Inc-USA Thrusters: 2 Tunnel thruster (f) Fuel: 1070.0
9369930 *9MGU7* -	**TANJUNG PINANG 1** **Icon Ship Management Sdn Bhd** - *Port Klang* *Malaysia* MMSI: 533000136 Official number: 330558	**1,617** 485 1,787	Class: AB	**2006-08 Muhibbah Marine Engineering Sdn Bhd — Port Klang** Yd No: 20058 Loa 60.00 Br ex - Dght 4.850 Lbp 54.00 Br md 16.00 Dpth 5.50 Welded, 1 dk	**(B21B20T) Offshore Tug/Supply Ship**	**2 oil engines** reduction geared to sc. shafts driving 2 CP propellers Total Power: 3,650kW (4,962hp) 10.0kn Caterpillar 3606 2 x 4 Stroke 6 Cy. 280 x 300 each-1825kW (2481bhp) Caterpillar Inc-USA AuxGen: 2 x 260kW a.c, 2 x 700kW 60Hz a.c Thrusters: 1 Thwart. CP thruster
9369942 *9MGU8* -	**TANJUNG PINANG 2** **Icon Ship Management Sdn Bhd** - *Port Klang* *Malaysia* MMSI: 533000137 Official number: 330559	**1,617** 485 1,768	Class: AB	**2006-10 Muhibbah Marine Engineering Sdn Bhd — Port Klang** Yd No: 20059 Loa 60.00 Br ex - Dght 4.850 Lbp 53.90 Br md 16.00 Dpth 5.50 Welded, 1 dk	**(B21B20T) Offshore Tug/Supply Ship**	**2 oil engines** reduction geared to sc. shafts driving 2 CP propellers Total Power: 3,700kW (5,030hp) 12.0kn Caterpillar 3606 2 x 4 Stroke 6 Cy. 280 x 300 each-1850kW (2515bhp) Caterpillar Inc-USA AuxGen: 2 x 260kW a.c, 2 x 700kW a.c Thrusters: 1 Thwart. CP thruster Fuel: 520.0
9394856 *9MGV5* -	**TANJUNG PINANG 3** **Icon Ship Management Sdn Bhd** - *Port Klang* *Malaysia* MMSI: 533000138 Official number: 330570	**1,629** 488 1,744	Class: AB BV (Class contemplated)	**2007-03 MSET Shipbuilding Corp Sdn Bhd — Kuala Terengganu** Yd No: 5705 Loa 60.00 Br ex - Dght 4.850 Lbp 53.90 Br md 16.00 Dpth 5.50 Welded, 1 dk	**(B21B20T) Offshore Tug/Supply Ship**	**2 oil engines** reduction geared to sc. shafts driving 2 CP propellers Total Power: 3,700kW (5,030hp) Caterpillar 3606 2 x 4 Stroke 6 Cy. 280 x 300 each-1850kW (2515bhp) Caterpillar Inc-USA AuxGen: 2 x 700kW a.c, 2 x 260kW a.c Thrusters: 1 Tunnel thruster (f) Fuel: 444.4 (r.f.)
9394868 *9MGV6* -	**TANJUNG PINANG 4** **Icon Ship Management Sdn Bhd** - *Port Klang* *Malaysia* MMSI: 533000139 Official number: 330571	**1,629** 488 1,650	Class: AB BV (Class contemplated)	**2007-05 MSET Shipbuilding Corp Sdn Bhd — Kuala Terengganu** Yd No: 5706 Loa 60.00 Br ex - Dght 4.850 Lbp 53.90 Br md 16.00 Dpth 5.50 Welded, 1 dk	**(B21B20T) Offshore Tug/Supply Ship**	**2 oil engines** reduction geared to sc. shafts driving 2 CP propellers Total Power: 3,700kW (5,030hp) Caterpillar 3606 2 x 4 Stroke 6 Cy. 280 x 300 each-1850kW (2515bhp) Caterpillar Inc-USA AuxGen: 2 x 700kW a.c, 2 x 260kW a.c Thrusters: 1 Tunnel thruster (f)
8999130 - -	**TANJUNG PURA II** **PT Putra Tanjungpura** - *Balikpapan* *Indonesia*	**329** 99 -	Class: KI	**2002-12 C.V. Mercusuar Mandiri — Batam** L reg 32.00 Br ex - Dght 3.490 Lbp 28.80 Br md 9.00 Dpth 4.28 Welded, 1 dk	**(B32A2ST) Tug**	**2 oil engines** reduction geared to sc. shafts driving 2 Propellers Total Power: 1,838kW (2,498hp) 12.0kn Cummins KTA-50-M 2 x Vee 4 Stroke 16 Cy. 159 x 159 each-919kW (1249bhp) Cummins Engine Co Inc-USA
9068457 - -	**TANJUNG PURA III** **PT Putra Tanjungpura** - *Samarinda* *Indonesia*	**108** 64 -	Class: KI	**2003-04 C.V. Dok Swarga — Samarinda** Loa 23.50 Br ex - Dght 2.160 Lbp 21.79 Br md 6.50 Dpth 2.70 Welded, 1 dk	**(B32A2ST) Tug**	**2 oil engines** geared to sc. shafts driving 2 Propellers Total Power: 794kW (1,080hp) 8.0kn Nissan RF10 2 x Vee 4 Stroke 10 Cy. 138 x 142 each-397kW (540bhp) Nissan Diesel Motor Co. Ltd.-Ageo
8654089 - -	**TANJUNG PURA IX** **PT Putra Tanjungpura** - *Samarinda* *Indonesia*	**133** 40 -	Class: KI	**2011-01 PT Galangan Putra Tanjungpura — Samarinda** Loa 23.75 Br ex - Dght 2.240 Lbp 22.27 Br md 7.00 Dpth 3.00 Welded, 1 dk	**(B32A2ST) Tug**	**2 oil engines** reduction geared to sc. shafts driving 2 FP propellers AuxGen: 2 x 54kW 380V a.c
8652524 - -	**TANJUNG PURA VI** **PT Putra Tanjungpura** - *Samarinda* *Indonesia*	**255** 77 -	Class: KI	**2010-11 C.V. Swadaya Utama — Samarinda** Loa 31.00 Br ex - Dght 3.070 Lbp 29.13 Br md 9.00 Dpth 3.65 Welded, 1 dk	**(B32A2ST) Tug**	**2 oil engines** reduction geared to sc. shafts driving 2 Propellers
8652548 - -	**TANJUNG PURA VII** **PT Putra Tanjungpura** - *Samarinda* *Indonesia*	**256** 77 -	Class: KI	**2010-11 C.V. Swadaya Utama — Samarinda** Loa 31.00 Br ex - Dght 3.010 Lbp 29.13 Br md 9.00 Dpth 3.65 Welded, 1 dk	**(B32A2ST) Tug**	**2 oil engines** reduction geared to sc. shafts driving 2 Propellers Total Power: 1,220kW (1,658hp) Mitsubishi S6R2-MPTK 2 x 4 Stroke 6 Cy. 170 x 220 each-610kW (829bhp) Mitsubishi Heavy Industries Ltd-Japan
8658528 - -	**TANJUNG PURA VIII** **PT Putra Tanjungpura** - *Samarinda* *Indonesia*	**357** 108 -	Class: KI	**2011-01 PT Galangan Putra Tanjungpura — Samarinda** Loa - Br ex - Dght 3.490 Lbp 31.44 Br md 9.10 Dpth 4.30 Welded, 1 dk	**(B32A2ST) Tug**	**2 oil engines** reduction geared to sc. shafts driving 2 FP propellers Total Power: 1,472kW (2,002hp) Chinese Std. Type 6210ZLC 2 x 4 Stroke 6 Cy. 210 x 290 each-736kW (1001bhp) Zibo Diesel Engine Factory-China AuxGen: 2 x 81kW 380V a.c
8655265 - -	**TANJUNG PURA X** **PT Putra Tanjungpura** - *Samarinda* *Indonesia*	**133** 40 -	Class: KI	**2011-01 PT Galangan Putra Tanjungpura — Samarinda** Loa 23.75 Br ex - Dght 2.240 Lbp 22.75 Br md 7.00 Dpth 3.00 Welded, 1 dk	**(B32A2ST) Tug**	**2 oil engines** reduction geared to sc. shafts driving 2 FP propellers Total Power: 1,060kW (1,442hp) Daewoo V222TIH 2 x Vee 4 Stroke 12 Cy. 128 x 142 each-530kW (721bhp) Doosan Infracore Co Ltd-South Korea

IMO / Call sign	Name / Owner / Port	Tonnage	Class	Builder / Dimensions	Type	Machinery
8659534 - -	**TANJUNG PURA XI** **PT Putra Tanjungpura** *Samarinda* *Indonesia*	**170** 51 -	Class: KI	**2011-07 PT Galangan Putra Tanjungpura — Samarinda** Loa 25.75 Br ex - Dght - Lbp 24.28 Br md 7.50 Dpth 3.35 Welded, 1 dk	**(B32A2ST) Tug**	**2 oil engines** reduction geared to sc. shafts driving 2 FP propellers Total Power: 1,220kW (1,658hp) Mitsubishi S6R2-MPTK 2 x 4 Stroke 6 Cy. 170 x 220 each-610kW (829bhp) Mitsubishi Heavy Industries Ltd-Japan AuxGen: 2 x 59kW 380V a.c
8659522 - -	**TANJUNG PURA XII** **PT Putra Tanjungpura** *Samarinda* *Indonesia*	**167** 51 -	Class: KI	**2011-07 PT Galangan Putra Tanjungpura — Samarinda** Loa 25.75 Br ex - Dght - Lbp 24.28 Br md 7.50 Dpth 3.35 Welded, 1 dk	**(B32A2ST) Tug**	**2 oil engines** reduction geared to sc. shafts driving 2 FP propellers Total Power: 1,220kW (1,658hp) Mitsubishi S6R2-MPTK 2 x 4 Stroke 6 Cy. 170 x 220 each-610kW (829bhp) Mitsubishi Heavy Industries Ltd-Japan AuxGen: 2 x 59kW 380V a.c
9485540 *9MHW6* -	**TANJUNG PUTERI 1** **Icon Ship Management Sdn Bhd** - *Port Klang* *Malaysia* MMSI: 533019100 Official number: 333857	**1,669** 500 1,790	Class: BV	**2008-07 Muhibbah Marine Engineering Sdn Bhd — Port Klang** Yd No: 20066 Loa 60.00 Br ex - Dght 4.850 Lbp 54.00 Br md 16.00 Dpth 5.50 Welded, 1 dk	**(B21B20A) Anchor Handling Tug Supply** Double Hull	**2 oil engines** reduction geared to sc. shafts driving 2 CP propellers Total Power: 4,004kW (5,444hp) 13.0kn Caterpillar 3606 2 x 4 Stroke 6 Cy. 280 x 300 each-2002kW (2722bhp) Caterpillar Inc-USA Thrusters: 1 Tunnel thruster (f)
9485552 *9MHW7* -	**TANJUNG PUTERI 2** **Icon Ship Management Sdn Bhd** - *Port Klang* *Malaysia* MMSI: 533019200 Official number: 333858	**1,669** 500 1,790	Class: BV	**2008-09 Muhibbah Marine Engineering Sdn Bhd — Port Klang** Yd No: 20067 Loa 60.00 Br ex - Dght 4.850 Lbp 54.00 Br md 16.00 Dpth 5.50 Welded, 1 dk	**(B21B20A) Anchor Handling Tug Supply** Double Hull	**2 oil engines** reduction geared to sc. shafts driving 2 CP propellers Total Power: 4,004kW (5,444hp) 13.0kn Caterpillar 3606 2 x 4 Stroke 6 Cy. 280 x 300 each-2002kW (2722bhp) Caterpillar Inc-USA Thrusters: 1 Tunnel thruster (f)
7344857 - -	**TANJUNG SANTAN** *ex* Prima Mariner *-1990* **PT PERTAMINA (PERSERO)** - *Jakarta* *Indonesia*	*205* 62 305	Class: (KI) (AB)	**1973-11 Asia-Pacific Shipyard Pte Ltd — Singapore** Yd No: 107 L reg 34.14 Br ex 10.67 Dght 1.194 Lbp 34.12 Br md 10.65 Dpth 1.96 Welded, 1 dk	**(A35D2RL) Landing Craft** Bow door/ramp	**2 oil engines** reverse reduction geared to sc. shafts driving 2 FP propellers Total Power: 514kW (698hp) 8.0kn Cummins NTA-855-M 2 x 4 Stroke 6 Cy. 140 x 152 each-257kW (349bhp) (, fitted 1973) Cummins Engine Co Inc-USA AuxGen: 1 x 28kW a.c, 1 x 10kW a.c Fuel: 53.0 (d.f.)
9331971 *9MIR5* -	**TANJUNG SARI** **Icon Ship Management Sdn Bhd** - *Port Klang* *Malaysia* MMSI: 533040900 Official number: 334105	**1,673** 501 1,650	Class: BV	**2009-11 Boustead Naval Shipyard Sdn Bhd — Lumut** Yd No: 023 Loa 60.00 Br ex - Dght 4.850 Lbp 58.74 Br md 16.00 Dpth 5.50 Welded, 1 dk	**(B21B20A) Anchor Handling Tug Supply**	**2 oil engines** reduction geared to sc. shafts driving 2 CP propellers Total Power: 4,060kW (5,520hp) Caterpillar 3606 2 x 4 Stroke 6 Cy. 280 x 300 each-2030kW (2760bhp) Caterpillar Inc-USA AuxGen: 2 x 675kW 415V a.c, 2 x 280kW a.c Thrusters: 1 Tunnel thruster (f) Fuel: 475.0
9097654 *YB6222* -	**TANJUNG SELE** **H Mustari** - *Samarinda* *Indonesia*	**193** 58 -	Class: KI	**2002-06 P.T. Kaltim Shipyard — Samarinda** Loa 37.75 Br ex - Dght 1.950 Lbp 34.60 Br md 7.50 Dpth 2.40 Welded, 1 dk	**(A35D2RL) Landing Craft**	**2 oil engines** reduction geared to sc. shafts driving 2 Propellers Total Power: 470kW (640hp) Mitsubishi 8DC90A 2 x Vee 4 Stroke 8 Cy. 135 x 140 each-235kW (320bhp) Mitsubishi Heavy Industries Ltd-Japan
8829775 *V8SW* -	**TANJUNG SEMASTA** **Government of The State of Brunei (Department of Marine - Ministry of Communication)** - *Bandar Seri Begawan* *Brunei* Official number: 0103	**182** 54 -	Class: (AB)	**1988 Brooke Dockyard & Engineering Works Corp — Kuching** Yd No: 140 Loa - Br ex - Dght 2.600 Lbp 23.00 Br md 8.80 Dpth 2.90 Welded, 1 dk	**(B33B2DG) Grab Hopper Dredger**	**2 oil engines** reverse reduction geared to sc. shaft driving 2 FP propellers Total Power: 640kW (870hp) 7.0kn Caterpillar 3406TA 2 x 4 Stroke 6 Cy. 137 x 165 each-320kW (435bhp) Caterpillar Inc-USA AuxGen: 2 x 50kW a.c
9283447 *9WE08* -	**TANJUNG TRANG** **Government of Malaysia (Director of Marine - Sabah)** - SatCom: Inmarsat C 453381410 *Labuan* *Malaysia* MMSI: 533814000 Official number: 329925	**1,060** 318 300	Class: (LR) ✠ Classed LR until 29/7/09	**2004-09 Far East Shipyard Co Sdn Bhd — Sibu** Yd No: 08/02 Loa 52.00 Br ex 12.22 Dght 3.500 Lbp 48.00 Br md 12.00 Dpth 5.00 Welded, 1 dk	**(B34Q2QB) Buoy Tender**	**2 oil engines** with clutches, flexible couplings & sr geared to sc. shafts driving 2 Directional propellers Total Power: 3,900kW (5,302hp) 15.0kn Wartsila 6L26A 2 x 4 Stroke 6 Cy. 260 x 320 each-1950kW (2651bhp) Wartsila Finland Oy-Finland AuxGen: 3 x 248kW 415V 50Hz a.c Thrusters: 1 Thwart. FP thruster (f)
8652536 *PMOU* -	**TANJUNG TUNGKOR** **Government of The Republic of Indonesia (Direktorat Jenderal Perhubungan Darat - Ministry of Land Communications)** - *Ambon* *Indonesia*	**1,220** 366 947	Class: (KI)	**2008-11 P.T. Sanur Marindo Shipyard — Tegal** Loa 58.50 Br ex - Dght 2.740 Lbp 52.32 Br md 12.20 Dpth 4.50 Welded, 1 dk	**(A32A2GF) General Cargo/Passenger Ship** Passengers: berths: 447	**2 oil engines** reduction geared to sc. shafts driving 2 Propellers Total Power: 1,220kW (1,658hp) 12.0kn Yanmar 2 x each-610kW (829bhp) Yanmar Diesel Engine Co Ltd-Japan
7928548 - -	**TANKER 231** **Suez Canal Authority** - *Ismailia* *Egypt*	*300* - 400	Class: (GL)	**1986-10 Timsah SB. Co. — Ismailia** Yd No: 373 Loa 42.77 Br ex - Dght 2.652 Lbp - Br md 7.75 Dpth 3.00 Welded, 1 dk	**(A14A2LO) Water Tanker**	**2 oil engines** geared to sc. shafts driving 2 FP propellers Total Power: 448kW (610hp) S.K.L. 6NVD36-1U 2 x 4 Stroke 6 Cy. 240 x 360 each-224kW (305bhp) VEB Schwermaschinenbau "KarlLiebknecht" (SKL)-Magdeburg
8219700 - -	**TANKER No. 10** **Alexandria General Water Authority** - *Alexandria* *Egypt*	*207* 101 300	Class: (LR) ✠ Classed LR until 4/10/88	**1984-07 Alexandria Shipyard — Alexandria** Yd No: 10117 Loa 35.95 Br ex 7.01 Dght - Lbp 33.51 Br md 7.00 Dpth 2.85 Welded, 1 dk	**(A14A2LO) Water Tanker** Liq: 300 Compartments: 4 Ta, ER	**1 oil engine** with clutches, flexible couplings & sr reverse geared to sc. shaft driving 1 FP propeller Total Power: 342kW (465hp) MAN D2542MLE 1 x Vee 4 Stroke 12 Cy. 125 x 142 342kW (465bhp) Maschinenbau Augsburg Nuernberg (MAN)-Augsburg AuxGen: 2 x 25kW 220V 50Hz a.c
8215388 - -	**TANKER No. 11** **Alexandria General Water Authority** - *Alexandria* *Egypt* Official number: 2551	*352* 181 550	Class: (LR) ✠ Classed LR until 4/10/88	**1985-06 Rashid Co for Nile Constructions — Rashid** Yd No: 37 Loa 42.37 Br ex 7.83 Dght 2.823 Lbp 40.01 Br md 7.61 Dpth 3.76 Welded, 1 dk	**(A14A2LO) Water Tanker** Liq: 540 Compartments: 6 Ta, ER	**1 oil engine** with clutches & sr reverse geared to sc. shaft driving 1 FP propeller Total Power: 530kW (721hp) Caterpillar 3412TA 1 x Vee 4 Stroke 12 Cy. 137 x 152 530kW (721bhp) Caterpillar Tractor Co-USA AuxGen: 2 x 46kW 380V 50Hz a.c
8215390 - -	**TANKER No. 12** **Alexandria General Water Authority** - *Alexandria* *Egypt* Official number: 2579	*352* 181 550	Class: (LR) ✠ Classed LR until 4/10/88	**1985-07 Rashid Co for Nile Constructions — Rashid** Yd No: 38 Loa 42.37 Br ex 7.83 Dght 2.901 Lbp 40.01 Br md 7.61 Dpth 3.76 Welded, 1 dk	**(A14A2LO) Water Tanker** Liq: 540 Compartments: 6 Ta, ER	**1 oil engine** with clutches & sr reverse geared to sc. shaft driving 1 FP propeller Total Power: 530kW (721hp) Caterpillar 3412TA 1 x Vee 4 Stroke 12 Cy. 137 x 152 530kW (721bhp) Caterpillar Tractor Co-USA AuxGen: 2 x 46kW 380V 50Hz a.c
8215405 - -	**TANKER No. 13** **Alexandria General Water Authority** - *Alexandria* *Egypt* Official number: 2580	*352* 181 550	Class: (LR) ✠ Classed LR until 4/10/88	**1985-09 Rashid Co for Nile Constructions — Rashid** Yd No: 39 Loa 42.37 Br ex 7.83 Dght 2.823 Lbp 40.01 Br md 7.61 Dpth 3.76 Welded, 1 dk	**(A14A2LO) Water Tanker** Liq: 540 Compartments: 6 Ta, ER	**1 oil engine** with clutches & sr reverse geared to sc. shaft driving 1 FP propeller Total Power: 530kW (721hp) Caterpillar 3412TA 1 x Vee 4 Stroke 12 Cy. 137 x 152 530kW (721bhp) Caterpillar Tractor Co-USA AuxGen: 2 x 46kW 380V 50Hz a.c

IMO / Call sign	Name / Owner / Port	Tonnage	Class	Builder / Dimensions	Type / Capacity	Machinery
7944748 - -	**TANKER No. 230** - **Suez Canal Authority** - *Ismailia* *Egypt*	*300* - -	Class: (GL)	**1978 Timsah SB. Co. — Ismailia** Yd No: 227 Loa 42.78 Br ex 7.75 Dght 2.661 Lbp - Br md - Dpth 3.00 Welded, 1 dk	**(A13B2TU) Tanker (unspecified)** Compartments: 2 Ta, ER	**2 oil engines** driving 2 FP propellers Total Power: 330kW (448hp) 10.0kn S.K.L. 6NVD36-1U 2 x 4 Stroke 6 Cy. 240 x 360 each-165kW (224bhp) VEB Schwermaschinenbau "KarlLiebknecht" (SKL)-Magdeburg AuxGen: 2 x 72kW 380/220V a.c
8316089 - -	**TANKOIL** *ex* Sino Kin *-1999* *ex* Carol *-1996* *ex* Chloe II *-1996* *ex* Sun Cypress *-1989* **Divine Marine Shipping Nigeria Ltd** - *Nigeria*	**3,757** 2,093 6,242 T/cm 13.7	Class: (CC) (NV) (NK)	**1983-10 Higaki Zosen K.K. — Imabari** Yd No: 303 Loa 102.49 (BB) Br ex 15.52 Dght 6.880 Lbp 95.81 Br md 15.51 Dpth 8.10 Welded, 1 dk	**(A12B2TR) Chemical/Products Tanker** Liq: 6,598; Liq (Oil): 6,598 Cargo Heating Coils Compartments: 10 Ta, ER 4 Cargo Pump (s)	**1 oil engine** driving 1 FP propeller Total Power: 2,869kW (3,901hp) 12.5kn Mitsubishi 6UEC37L 1 x 2 Stroke 6 Cy. 370 x 880 2869kW (3901bhp) Kobe Hatsudoki KK-Japan AuxGen: 2 x 220kW 100/440V 60Hz a.c
5422203 *OITW* -	**TANKOS** *ex* Regitze *-1991* *ex* Regitze Tholstrup *-1984* **Destination Line Oy** - *Naantali* *Finland* MMSI: 230212000 Official number: 10161	**326** 131 349	Class: (BV)	**1963-07 A/S Svendborg Skibsvaerft — Svendborg** Yd No: 102 Loa 46.92 Br ex 8.13 Dght 2.706 Lbp 42.02 Br md 8.11 Dpth 3.03 Welded, 1 dk	**(A11B2TG) LPG Tanker** Liq (Gas): 387 2 x Gas Tank (s); 2 independent (stl) cyl horizontal Ice Capable	**1 oil engine** geared to sc. shaft driving 1 FP propeller Total Power: 486kW (661hp) 11.5kn Grenaa 6F24 1 x 4 Stroke 6 Cy. 240 x 300 486kW (661bhp) (new engine 1974) A/S Grenaa Motorfabrik-Denmark Fuel: 28.5 (d.f.)
8327105 *SHXY* -	**TANKSKAR** *ex* Sjobjorn X *-1999* *ex* Monstank *-1995* *ex* Haugland *-1984* *ex* Blaskjell *-1977* *ex* Shell N. 64 *-1971* **Tankskar Rederi AB** - *Styrso* *Sweden* MMSI: 265550210	**181** 103 330	Class: (NV)	**1955 Frednes Slip & Mek. Verksted — Porsgrunn** Yd No: 2 Loa 36.30 Br ex 7.01 Dght 2.710 Lbp 33.56 Br md - Dpth 2.87 Welded, 1 dk	**(A13B2TU) Tanker (unspecified)** Liq: 390; Liq (Oil): 390	**1 oil engine** driving 1 FP propeller Total Power: 268kW (364hp) Cummins 1 x 4 Stroke 6 Cy. 159 x 159 268kW (364bhp) Cummins Engine Co Inc-USA
5352458 *TUN2042* -	**TANOE** **Boluda France SAS** Les Abeilles CI *Abidjan* *Cote d'Ivoire*	*130* 84 -	Class: (LR) (BV) ✠	**1962-01 N.V. Scheepswerf "Alphen" P. de Vries Lentsch — Alphen a/d Rijn** Yd No: 412 Loa 25.00 Br ex 7.14 Dght 2.794 Lbp 23.02 Br md 6.81 Dpth 3.56 Welded, 1 dk	**(B32A2ST) Tug**	**1 oil engine** driving 1 FP propeller Total Power: 552kW (750hp) Deutz RBV6M545 1 x 4 Stroke 6 Cy. 320 x 450 552kW (750bhp) Kloeckner Humboldt Deutz AG-West Germany
9537410 *XCSL5* -	**TANOK** **Intertug Mexico SAPI de CV** *Manzanillo* *Mexico* MMSI: 345140401	**484** 145 252	Class: LR ✠ **100A1** SS 10/2011 escort tug, fire fighting Ship 1 with water spray **LMC** **UMS** Eq.Ltr: G; Cable: 275.0/19.0 U2 (a)	**2011-10 Song Cam Shipyard — Haiphong** (Hull) **2011-10 B.V. Scheepswerf Damen — Gorinchem** Yd No: 513016 Loa 32.14 Br ex 13.29 Dght 3.970 Lbp 31.64 Br md 12.50 Dpth 5.40 Welded, 1 dk	**(B32A2ST) Tug** Cranes: 1x5t	**2 oil engines** gearing integral to driving 2 Directional propellers Total Power: 5,420kW (7,370hp) Caterpillar C280-8 2 x 4 Stroke 8 Cy. 280 x 300 each-2710kW (3685bhp) Caterpillar Inc-USA AuxGen: 2 x 162kW 400V 50Hz a.c
6907743 *HSCA* -	**TANON** *ex* Aris *-2005* *ex* Bangkhunprom *-2005* *ex* Nisshin Trader *-1981* *ex* Akakura Maru *-1979* **Krung Dhana Nava Co Ltd** - *Bangkok* *Thailand* Official number: 321005686	**3,398** 2,140 5,687	Class: (NK)	**1968-12 Imabari Shipbuilding Co Ltd — Imabari EH (Imabari Shipyard)** Yd No: 192 Loa 101.58 Br ex 15.73 Dght 6.590 Lbp 94.01 Br md 15.70 Dpth 8.01 Riveted\Welded, 1 dk	**(A31A2GX) General Cargo Ship** Grain: 7,323; Bale: 7,002 Compartments: 2 Ho, ER 2 Ha: (24.6 x 8.3) (28.1 x 8.3)ER Derricks: 3x15t,1x10t	**1 oil engine** driving 1 FP propeller Total Power: 2,427kW (3,300hp) 12.0kn Mitsubishi 6UD45 1 x 2 Stroke 6 Cy. 450 x 720 2427kW (3300bhp) Mitsubishi Heavy Industries Ltd-Japan AuxGen: 2 x 128kW 445V 60Hz a.c Fuel: 44.5 (d.f.) 336.0 (r.f.) 8.5pd
9474620 *A8ZY8* -	**TANSANIT** *ex* POS Tansanit *-2013* **Conti 178 Schifffahrt-GmbH & Co KG Nr 1** BBG-Bremer Bereederungsgesellschaft mbH & Co KG SatCom: Inmarsat C 463710860 *Monrovia* *Liberia* MMSI: 636092284 Official number: 92284	**51,195** 31,136 92,776 T/cm 80.9	Class: AB	**2011-09 COSCO (Zhoushan) Shipyard Co Ltd — Zhoushan ZJ** Yd No: N304 Loa 229.20 (BB) Br ex - Dght 14.900 Lbp 222.00 Br md 38.00 Dpth 20.70 Welded, 1 dk	**(A21A2BC) Bulk Carrier** Grain: 110,330 Compartments: 7 Ho, ER 7 Ha: ER	**1 oil engine** driving 1 FP propeller Total Power: 12,240kW (16,642hp) 14.1kn MAN-B&W 6S60MC 1 x 2 Stroke 6 Cy. 600 x 2292 12240kW (16642bhp) Doosan Engine Co Ltd-South Korea AuxGen: 3 x 730kW a.c Fuel: 233.0 (d.f.) 3597.0 (r.f.)
8992728 *TC7890* -	**TANSEL-M** **Mercan Petrol Ve Den Tas Hc Ve Ltd Sti** - *Istanbul* *Turkey* MMSI: 271010475 Official number: 6934	**296** 156 490		**1996-07 Torlak Gemi Insaat Sanayi ve Ticaret A.S. — Tuzla** Yd No: 06 Loa 49.40 Br ex - Dght 2.090 Lbp 43.80 Br md 7.50 Dpth 3.40 Welded, 1 dk	**(B35E2TF) Bunkering Tanker**	**1 oil engine** driving 1 Propeller Total Power: 522kW (710hp) 13.0kn MAN 1 x 4 Stroke 522kW (710bhp) MAN B&W Diesel AG-Augsburg
9115262 *JMRV* -	**TANSHU MARU** **Hyogo Prefecture** SatCom: Inmarsat C 443171710 *Kobe, Hyogo* *Japan* MMSI: 431717000 Official number: 132433	*499* 222 341		**1995-03 Miho Zosensho K.K. — Shimizu** Yd No: 1446 Loa 56.00 (BB) Br ex - Dght 3.750 Lbp 49.00 Br md 9.50 Dpth 6.12 Welded, 1 dk	**(B11A2FS) Stern Trawler** Ins: 38	**1 oil engine** with flexible couplings & sr geared to sc. shaft driving 1 CP propeller Total Power: 1,324kW (1,800hp) Hanshin LH31G 1 x 4 Stroke 6 Cy. 310 x 530 1324kW (1800bhp) The Hanshin Diesel Works Ltd-Japan
9172521 - -	**TANSHU MARU** - -	*142* - 400		**1997-06 Imura Zosen K.K. — Komatsushima** Yd No: 285 Loa 37.00 Br ex - Dght - Lbp 34.00 Br md 8.00 Dpth 3.10 Welded, 1 dk	**(A24A2BT) Cement Carrier**	**1 oil engine** driving 1 FP propeller Total Power: 441kW (600hp) 11.9kn Yanmar S185L-ET 1 x 4 Stroke 6 Cy. 185 x 230 441kW (600bhp) Yanmar Diesel Engine Co Ltd-Japan
7735678 - -	**TANSHU MARU** - -	*199* - 360		**1978 Yutaka Sangyo K.K. — Aioi** Yd No: 8 Loa 36.00 Br ex - Dght 2.600 Lbp 33.23 Br md 7.51 Dpth 3.03 Welded, 1 dk	**(A24A2BT) Cement Carrier**	**1 oil engine** driving 1 FP propeller Total Power: 250kW (340hp) 8.0kn Yanmar 6AL-HT 1 x 4 Stroke 6 Cy. 165 x 200 250kW (340bhp) Yanmar Diesel Engine Co Ltd-Japan
9385697 *JWNJ* -	**TANSOY** **Fjord1 AS** - *Floro* *Norway* MMSI: 258119500	**181** 57 25		**2007-01 Batservice Mandal AS — Mandal** Yd No: 57 Loa 29.45 Br ex - Dght 1.850 Lbp 26.50 Br md 9.00 Dpth 2.85 Welded, 1 dk	**(A36A2PR) Passenger/Ro-Ro Ship (Vehicles)** Hull Material: Aluminium Alloy Double Hull Passengers: unberthed: 96 Cars: 10	**2 oil engines** reduction geared to sc. shafts driving 2 CP propellers Total Power: 2,090kW (2,842hp) 28.0kn Caterpillar C32 2 x Vee 4 Stroke 12 Cy. 145 x 162 each-1045kW (1421bhp) Caterpillar Inc-USA
9497086 *V7VE4* -	**TANTA T.** **Kallithea Capital Ltd** Tsangaris Bros Ltd SatCom: Inmarsat C 453835918 *Majuro* *Marshall Islands* MMSI: 538004100 Official number: 4100	**20,218** 11,367 32,500	Class: BV	**2011-03 Zhejiang Hongxin Shipbuilding Co Ltd — Taizhou ZJ** Yd No: 2008-09 Loa 177.50 (BB) Br ex - Dght 10.217 Lbp 169.02 Br md 28.20 Dpth 14.20 Welded, 1 dk	**(A21A2BC) Bulk Carrier** Grain: 40,161; Bale: 38,849 Compartments: 5 Ho, ER 5 Ha: 4 (19.2 x 21.0)ER (14.4 x 15.2) Cranes: 4x30t Ice Capable	**1 oil engine** driving 1 FP propeller Total Power: 6,386kW (8,682hp) 14.2kn MAN-B&W 6S42MC 1 x 2 Stroke 6 Cy. 420 x 1764 6386kW (8682bhp) STX Engine Co Ltd-South Korea AuxGen: 3 x 500kW 60Hz a.c
7740697 - -	**TANTAL** **Dagestan Hydrometeorological Centre (Dagestanskiy Tsentr po Gidrometeorologii Monitoringu Okruzhayushchey Sredu)** - *Makhachkala* *Russia*	*166* 18 40	Class: RS	**1978-02 Sretenskiy Sudostroitelnyy Zavod — Sretensk** Yd No: 10 Loa 33.96 Br ex 7.09 Dght 2.680 Lbp 30.00 Br md - Dpth 3.65 Welded, 1 dk	**(B31A2SR) Research Survey Vessel** Derricks: 2x2t Ice Capable	**1 oil engine** driving 1 FP propeller Total Power: 221kW (300hp) 9.0kn S.K.L. 8NVD36-1U 1 x 4 Stroke 8 Cy. 240 x 360 221kW (300bhp) VEB Schwermaschinenbau "KarlLiebknecht" (SKL)-Magdeburg
8907670 *UBOH6* -	**TANTAL** *ex* Keoyoung Ace *-2011* *ex* Seokwang Ace *-2005* *ex* Kyokuho Maru No. 16 *-2000* **OOO 'Prim Port Bunker'** - *Vostochnyy* *Russia* MMSI: 273354630	**737** 334 1,191	Class: RS (KR) (NK)	**1989-06 Teraoka Shipyard Co Ltd — Minamiawaji HG** Yd No: 282 L reg 62.03 (BB) Br ex - Dght 3.932 Lbp 62.00 Br md 10.00 Dpth 4.50 Welded, 1 dks	**(A12B2TR) Chemical/Products Tanker** Liq: 1,225; Liq (Oil): 1,225 Compartments: 7 Ta, ER	**1 oil engine** driving 1 FP propeller Total Power: 736kW (1,001hp) 19.0kn Hanshin LH28G 1 x 4 Stroke 6 Cy. 280 x 460 736kW (1001bhp) The Hanshin Diesel Works Ltd-Japan

IMO / Call sign / Flag	Name / Former names / Owner / Manager / Port	Tonnage	Class	Builder / Dimensions	Type / Capacity	Machinery
7421980 *C6NP9* -	**TANTAWAN FPSO** *ex* Tantawan Explorer *-2008* *ex* Bayern *-1995* **Chevron Block B8/32 (Thailand) Ltd, Chevron Offshore (Thailand) Ltd, Palang Sophon Ltd & Orange Energy Ltd** Chevron Offshore (Thailand) Ltd SatCom: Inmarsat B 330948310 *Nassau* *Bahamas* MMSI: 309483000 Official number: 727484	**67,408** 50,030 136,960 T/cm 108.8	Class: AB (GL)	**1976**-10 **Howaldtswerke-Deutsche Werft AG (HDW) — Hamburg** Yd No: 93 Converted From: Crude Oil Tanker-1996 Loa 284.01 Br ex 43.46 Dght 15.701 Lbp 272.02 Br md 43.41 Dpth 20.63 Welded, 1 dk	**(B22E2OF) FPSO, Oil** Liq: 160,897; Liq (Oil): 160,897	**1 Steam Turb** geared to sc. shaft driving 1 FP propeller Total Power: 17,652kW (24,000hp) 16.0kn AEG 1 x steam Turb 17652kW (24000shp) BV Koninklijke Mij 'De Schelde'-Netherlands AuxGen: 2 x 900kW 450V 60Hz a.c
9070278 *PMIU* -	**TANTO ABADI** *ex* Blue Lake *-2008* **PT Tanto Intim Line** - *Jakarta* *Indonesia* MMSI: 525016244	**3,577** 1,520 4,323 T/cm 13.1	Class: KI (LR) ✠ Classed LR until 1/7/08	**1994**-09 **Jiangxi Jiangzhou Shipyard — Ruichang JX** Yd No: A435 Loa 93.50 (BB) Br ex 17.63 Dght 5.800 Lbp 84.90 Br md 17.60 Dpth 7.60 Welded, 1 dk	**(A33A2CC) Container Ship (Fully Cellular)** TEU 270 C Ho 106 TEU C Dk 164 TEU incl 40 ref C. Compartments: 2 Cell Ho, ER 4 Ha: (12.6 x 8.1)Tappered 3 (12.6 x 13.5)ER Cranes: 1x36t	**1 oil engine** driving 1 FP propeller Total Power: 2,800kW (3,807hp) 13.5kn B&W 5L35MC 1 x 2 Stroke 5 Cy. 350 x 1050 2800kW (3807bhp) Yichang Marine Diesel Engine Co Ltd-China AuxGen: 3 x 200kW 450V 60Hz a.c Boilers: AuxB (Comp) 9.2kgf/cm² (9.0bar)
9085699 *JZEA* -	**TANTO ALAM** *ex* Jin Teng *-2013* **PT Tanto Intim Line** - *Indonesia* MMSI: 525013027	**3,994** 2,017 5,962	Class: CC (NK)	**1994**-06 **Dae Sun Shipbuilding & Engineering Co Ltd — Busan** Yd No: 411 Loa 107.00 (BB) Br ex - Dght 6.200 Lbp 97.50 Br md 17.20 Dpth 8.30 Welded, 1 dk	**(A33A2CC) Container Ship (Fully Cellular)** TEU 338 C Ho 132 TEU C Dk 206 TEU incl 25 ref C Compartments: 5 Cell Ho, ER 6 Ha: ER	**1 oil engine** driving 1 FP propeller Total Power: 3,912kW (5,319hp) 14.8kn B&W 7L35MC 1 x 2 Stroke 7 Cy. 350 x 1050 3912kW (5319bhp) Ssangyong Heavy Industries Co Ltd-South Korea AuxGen: 2 x 320kW a.c
9085704 *JZEB* -	**TANTO AMAN** *ex* Jin Da *-2013* **PT Tanto Intim Line** - *Indonesia* MMSI: 525013028	**3,994** 2,017 5,962	Class: (CC) (NK)	**1994**-10 **Dae Sun Shipbuilding & Engineering Co Ltd — Busan** Yd No: 412 Loa 107.00 (BB) Br ex 17.22 Dght 6.530 Lbp 97.50 Br md 17.20 Dpth 8.30 Welded, 1 dk	**(A33A2CC) Container Ship (Fully Cellular)** TEU 338 C Ho 132 TEU C Dk 206 TEU incl 25 ref C Compartments: 5 Cell Ho, ER 5 Ha: (12.5 x 8.0)4 (12.5 x 13.2)ER	**1 oil engine** driving 1 FP propeller Total Power: 3,913kW (5,320hp) 14.9kn B&W 7L35MC 1 x 2 Stroke 7 Cy. 350 x 1050 3913kW (5320bhp) Ssangyong Heavy Industries Co Ltd-South Korea
7425297 *YFKP* -	**TANTO ANDA** *ex* Blue Shark *-1996* **PT Pelayaran Sejahtera Bahtera Agung** - *Jakarta* *Indonesia*	**3,907** 2,394 6,364	Class: KI (KR) (NK)	**1975**-10 **Asakawa Zosen K.K. — Imabari** Yd No: 252 Loa 106.46 Br ex - Dght 6.725 Lbp 97.95 Br md 16.29 Dpth 8.36 Welded, 1 dk	**(A31A2GX) General Cargo Ship** Grain: 8,403; Bale: 7,699 2 Ha: 2 (28.5 x 8.3)ER Derricks: 4x15t	**1 oil engine** driving 1 FP propeller Total Power: 2,795kW (3,800hp) 12.8kn Hanshin 6LU50A 1 x 4 Stroke 6 Cy. 500 x 800 2795kW (3800bhp) The Hanshin Diesel Works Ltd-Japan AuxGen: 2 x 132kW 445V a.c
8906664 *PNYU* -	**TANTO BERKAT** *ex* Tiger River *-2011* *ex* Sima Shirin *-2003* *ex* Tiger River *-2002* *ex* Dragon Sentosa *-1998* *ex* Mekong Sentosa *-1997* *ex* Dragon Sentosa *-1996* **PT Tanto Intim Line** - *Jakarta* *Indonesia* MMSI: 525016694	**5,203** 2,182 6,425 T/cm 18.2	Class: KI (LR) ✠ Classed LR until 28/3/11	**1991**-03 **Qiuxin Shipyard — Shanghai** Yd No: 1202 Loa 119.32 (BB) Br ex 18.04 Dght 6.500 Lbp 110.00 Br md 18.00 Dpth 8.50 Welded, 1 dk	**(A33A2CC) Container Ship (Fully Cellular)** TEU 319 C Ho 134 TEU C Dk 185 TEU incl 40 ref C. Compartments: 3 Cell Ho, ER 5 Ha: ER Cranes: 2x36t	**1 oil engine** driving 1 FP propeller Total Power: 4,410kW (5,996hp) 14.6kn B&W 6L42MC 1 x 2 Stroke 6 Cy. 420 x 1360 4410kW (5996bhp) Hudong Shipyard-China AuxGen: 3 x 480kW 450V 60Hz a.c Boilers: AuxB (Comp) 9.2kgf/cm² (9.0bar) Fuel: 145.0 (d.f.) 505.0 (r.f.) 14.5pd
9003196 *PNXP* -	**TANTO BERSAMA** *ex* Asian Trader *-2011* *ex* Asian Pollux *-2003* **PT Tanto Intim Line** - *Jakarta* *Indonesia* MMSI: 525013014	**16,731** 8,251 22,735 T/cm 39.2	Class: KI (LR) (GL) (NK) Classed LR until 13/4/11	**1991**-04 **Shin Kurushima Dockyard Co. Ltd. — Onishi** Yd No: 2701 Loa 184.51 (BB) Br ex 27.60 Dght 9.528 Lbp 174.78 Br md 27.60 Dpth 14.00 Welded, 1 dk	**(A33A2CC) Container Ship (Fully Cellular)** TEU 1404 C Ho 634 TEU C Dk 770 TEU incl 200 ref C. Compartments: ER, 5 Cell Ho 17 Ha: (12.8 x 11.1)2 (12.8 x 8.4)ER 14 (12.8 x 11.0)	**1 oil engine** driving 1 FP propeller Total Power: 10,590kW (14,398hp) 19.0kn Mitsubishi 6UEC60LS 1 x 2 Stroke 6 Cy. 600 x 2200 10590kW (14398bhp) Kobe Hatsudoki KK-Japan AuxGen: 3 x 680kW 450V 60Hz a.c Fuel: 132.7 (d.f.) 1803.9 (r.f.) 41.0pd
9035515 *POBV* -	**TANTO BERSATU** *ex* Terra Bona *-2011* *ex* La Bonita *-2003* **PT Tanto Intim Line** - *Jakarta* *Indonesia* MMSI: 525013016	**16,869** 8,531 22,308	Class: KI (NK)	**1993**-03 **Shin Kurushima Dockyard Co. Ltd. — Onishi** Yd No: 2755 Loa 184.51 (BB) Br ex - Dght 9.628 Lbp 174.78 Br md 27.60 Dpth 14.00 Welded, 1 dk	**(A33A2CC) Container Ship (Fully Cellular)** TEU 1304 incl 100 ref C. Compartments: ER, 5 Cell Ho 17 Ha: (12.8 x 11.1)2 (12.8 x 8.4)ER 14 (12.8 x 11.0) Cranes: 3x40t	**1 oil engine** driving 1 FP propeller Total Power: 10,592kW (14,401hp) 19.1kn Mitsubishi 6UEC60LS 1 x 2 Stroke 6 Cy. 600 x 2200 10592kW (14401bhp) Kobe Hatsudoki KK-Japan AuxGen: 3 x 1006kW 440V a.c Fuel: 2020.0 (r.f.)
8807569 *PMUN* -	**TANTO CAHAYA** *ex* Kota Cahaya *-2009* **PT Tanto Intim Line** - *Jakarta* *Indonesia* MMSI: 525016160	**9,877** 4,696 13,453	Class: KI (BV)	**1992**-01 **Shanghai Shipyard — Shanghai** Yd No: 144 Loa 147.50 (BB) Br ex - Dght 8.060 Lbp 138.52 Br md 22.20 Dpth 10.90 Welded, 1 dk	**(A31A2GX) General Cargo Ship** Grain: 16,567; Bale: 15,999 TEU 784 incl 96 ref C. Compartments: 3 Ho, ER 4 Ha: (25.5 x 11.2) (38.3 x 16.0)2 (25.5 x 16.0)ER Cranes: 2x35t	**1 oil engine** driving 1 FP propeller Total Power: 4,899kW (6,661hp) 15.0kn Sulzer 6RTA48 1 x 2 Stroke 6 Cy. 480 x 1400 4899kW (6661bhp) Shanghai Diesel Engine Co Ltd-China AuxGen: 3 x 444kW 450V a.c
8910328 *PNEN* -	**TANTO CERIA** *ex* Infinity *-2009* **PT Tanto Intim Line** - *Jakarta* *Indonesia* MMSI: 525016576	**3,461** 1,903 4,419	Class: KI (NK) (BV)	**1989**-09 **Hakata Zosen K.K. — Imabari** Yd No: 320 Loa 98.85 (BB) Br ex 16.04 Dght 5.736 Lbp 89.90 Br md 16.00 Dpth 7.10 Welded, 1 dk	**(A31A2GX) General Cargo Ship** Grain: 6,078; Bale: 6,078 TEU 361 Compartments: 2 Ho, ER 2 Ha: (25.4 x 12.6) (37.1 x 12.6)ER Cranes: 2x30.5t	**1 oil engine** driving 1 CP propeller Total Power: 3,089kW (4,200hp) 13.5kn Mitsubishi 6UEC37LA 1 x 2 Stroke 6 Cy. 370 x 880 3089kW (4200bhp) Akasaka Tekkosho KK (Akasaka DieselLtd)-Japan AuxGen: 2 x 200kW 445V a.c Fuel: 365.0 (r.f.)
7709497 *YCQC* -	**TANTO CITRA** *ex* Citrowati *-2009* *ex* Tekad *-1992* **PT Pelayaran Sejahtera Bahtera Agung** - *Jakarta* *Indonesia*	**3,910** 2,357 6,302	Class: KI (NK)	**1977**-09 **Kochiken Zosen — Kochi** Yd No: 652 Loa 106.43 Br ex 16.44 Dght 6.703 Lbp 97.95 Br md 16.40 Dpth 8.16 Welded, 1 dk	**(A31A2GX) General Cargo Ship** Grain: 8,389; Bale: 7,696 2 Ha: (28.5 x 8.3) (28.6 x 8.3)ER Derricks: 4x15t	**1 oil engine** driving 1 FP propeller Total Power: 2,795kW (3,800hp) 12.4kn Mitsubishi 6UET45/75C 1 x 2 Stroke 6 Cy. 450 x 750 2795kW (3800bhp) Akasaka Tekkosho KK (Akasaka DieselLtd)-Japan AuxGen: 2 x 160kW
7372531 *YEMA* -	**TANTO DELI** *ex* Ma Fatima *-1991* *ex* Nautilus Primo *-1989* *ex* Arya Permata *-1985* *ex* Andhika Permata *-1983* *ex* Kalimantan *-1975* **PT Haji Saifuddin Timur Raya** - *Jakarta* *Indonesia*	*3,701* 2,506 6,587	Class: (KI) (NK)	**1974**-07 **Imai Shipbuilding Co Ltd — Kochi KC** Yd No: 335 Loa 104.03 Br ex 16.39 Dght 6.816 Lbp 98.60 Br md 16.36 Dpth 8.35 Welded, 1 dk	**(A31A2GX) General Cargo Ship** Grain: 8,632; Bale: 8,100 Compartments: 2 Ho, ER 2 Ha: (28.1 x 8.3) (28.5 x 8.3)ER Derricks: 4x15t; Winches: 4	**1 oil engine** driving 1 FP propeller Total Power: 2,795kW (3,800hp) 12.3kn Mitsubishi 6UET45/75C 1 x 2 Stroke 6 Cy. 450 x 750 2795kW (3800bhp) Akasaka Tekkosho KK (Akasaka DieselLtd)-Japan AuxGen: 2 x 144kW a.c Fuel: 547.5 (r.f.) 13.0pd
9103154 *PNCT* -	**TANTO EXPRESS** *ex* Cocopalm Isle *-2009* **PT Tanto Intim Line** - *Jakarta* *Indonesia* MMSI: 525016549	**9,179** 3,970 11,244	Class: KI (NK)	**1994**-07 **Shin Kurushima Dockyard Co. Ltd. — Akitsu** Yd No: 2798 Loa 144.02 (BB) Br ex - Dght 7.728 Lbp 135.10 Br md 21.80 Dpth 10.70 Welded, 1 dk	**(A33A2CC) Container Ship (Fully Cellular)** TEU 662 incl. 150 ref C. Compartments: 7 Cell Ho, ER 13 Ha: (12.6 x 8.3)12 (12.6 x 8.0)ER Cranes: 2x40t,2x35t	**1 oil engine** driving 1 FP propeller Total Power: 7,943kW (10,799hp) 18.0kn Mitsubishi 6UEC52LS 1 x 2 Stroke 6 Cy. 520 x 1850 7943kW (10799bhp) Kobe Hatsudoki KK-Japan Thrusters: 1 Thwart. CP thruster (f) Fuel: 1055.0 (r.f.)
8912833 *PNMA* -	**TANTO FAJAR I** *ex* Fansipan *-2010* *ex* ST Fidelity *-2009* *ex* Louise *-2005* *ex* Nogliki *-2000* *ex* Madison Colombo *-1997* *ex* Nogliki *-1997* **PT Tanto Intim Line** - *Jakarta* *Indonesia* MMSI: 525016661	**3,976** 1,618 4,168	Class: KI (RS) (BV) (NV)	**1992**-07 **Sedef Gemi Endustrisi A.S. — Gebze** Yd No: 88 Loa 97.80 Br ex 17.34 Dght 5.620 Lbp 90.22 Br md 17.30 Dpth 7.00 Welded, 1 dk	**(A31A2GX) General Cargo Ship** Grain: 5,242; Bale: 5,227 TEU 221 C.Ho 111/20' C.Dk 110/20' incl. 12 ref C. Compartments: 2 Ho, ER 2 Ha: 2 (25.7 x 12.5)ER Cranes: 2x25t Ice Capable	**1 oil engine** driving 1 CP propeller Total Power: 3,354kW (4,560hp) 12.5kn B&W 6L35MC 1 x 2 Stroke 6 Cy. 350 x 1050 3354kW (4560bhp) H Cegielski Poznan SA-Poland AuxGen: 2 x 450kW 400V a.c Fuel: 90.0 (d.f.) 275.0 (r.f.) 12.7pd
8901004 *PNMB* -	**TANTO FAJAR II** *ex* Bernina *-2010* *ex* St Spirit *-2009* *ex* Nikolay Kantemir *-2002* *launched as* Baykovo *-1992* **PT Tanto Intim Line** - *Jakarta* *Indonesia* MMSI: 525016662	**3,972** 1,617 4,705	Class: KI (RS)	**1992**-11 **Sedef Gemi Endustrisi A.S. — Gebze** Yd No: 81 Loa 97.80 Br ex - Dght 5.620 Lbp 90.22 Br md 17.30 Dpth 7.00 Welded, 1 dk	**(A31A2GX) General Cargo Ship** Grain: 5,242; Bale: 5,227 TEU 221 C.Ho 111/20' C.Dk 110/20' incl. 12 ref C. Compartments: 2 Ho, ER 2 Ha: 2 (25.7 x 12.5)ER Cranes: 2x25t Ice Capable	**1 oil engine** driving 1 CP propeller Total Power: 3,354kW (4,560hp) 12.5kn B&W 6L35MC 1 x 2 Stroke 6 Cy. 350 x 1050 3354kW (4560bhp) H Cegielski Poznan SA-Poland AuxGen: 2 x 450kW 400V a.c Fuel: 90.0 (d.f.) 275.0 (r.f.) 12.7pd

8900995 *PNMM* -	**TANTO FAJAR III** *ex* Pacific Laila *-2010* *ex* Andes *-2010* *ex* St Brilliance *-2009* *ex* Novokubansk *-2002* *launched as* Shelikhovo *-1992* **PT Tanto Intim Line** - *Jakarta* *Indonesia* MMSI: 525016663	**3,988** 1,618 4,705	Class: KI (RS)	**1992**-11 **Sedef Gemi Endustrisi A.S. — Gebze** Yd No: 80 Loa 97.80 Br ex 17.30 Dght 5.620 Lbp 90.22 Br md - Dpth 7.00 Welded, 1 dk	**(A31A2GX) General Cargo Ship** Grain: 5,242; Bale: 5,227 TEU 221 C.Ho 111/20' C.Dk 110/20' incl. 12 ref C. Compartments: 2 Ho, ER 2 Ha: 2 (25.7 x 12.5)ER Cranes: 2x25t Ice Capable	**1 oil engine** driving 1 CP propeller Total Power: 3,354kW (4,560hp) 12.5kn B&W 6L35MC 1 x 2 Stroke 6 Cy. 350 x 1050 3354kW (4560bhp) H Cegielski Poznan SA-Poland AuxGen: 2 x 328kW 400V a.c Fuel: 90.0 (d.f.) 275.0 (r.f.) 12.7pd
8419506 *YHDL* -	**TANTO HANDAL** *ex* Baltra Express *-2004* *ex* Ultra Orient *-2000* *ex* Ultraflex Orient *-1999* *ex* Vega V *-1996* *ex* Vega *-1995* **PT Tanto Intim Line** Bauhinia Marine Pte Ltd *Jakarta* *Indonesia* MMSI: 525016080	**3,814** 1,970 5,063	Class: KI (NK)	**1985**-08 **Kochi Jyuko (Eiho Zosen) K.K. — Kochi** Yd No: 1795 Loa 98.35 (BB) Br ex - Dght 5.762 Lbp 89.97 Br md 17.21 Dpth 7.88 Welded, 2 dks	**(A31A2GX) General Cargo Ship** Grain: 7,019; Bale: 6,538 TEU 300 C. 300/20' (40') Compartments: 2 Ho, ER 2 Ha: 2 (25.9 x 12.7)ER Cranes: 2x25t	**1 oil engine** driving 1 CP propeller Total Power: 2,207kW (3,001hp) 12.0kn Akasaka A41 1 x 4 Stroke 6 Cy. 410 x 800 2207kW (3001bhp) Akasaka Tekkosho KK (Akasaka DieselLtd)-Japan AuxGen: 3 x 240kW a.c
8104474 *PMGW* -	**TANTO HARI** *ex* Hari Bhum *-2008* *ex* Ville de Mascate *-1994* *ex* Champion *-1992* *ex* Ville de Mascate *-1991* *ex* Woermann Sanaga *-1991* *ex* Nedlloyd Zaire *-1990* *ex* Champion *-1988* *ex* Contship Champion *-1988* *ex* Cape Race *-1988* *ex* Contship Champion *-1987* *ex* Australian Eagle *-1985* *ex* Champion *-1982* **PT Tanto Intim Line** - SatCom: Inmarsat C 452500988 *Jakarta* *Indonesia* MMSI: 525016220	**5,931** 3,092 7,754	Class: KI (GL)	**1981**-09 **Rickmers Rhederei GmbH Rickmers Werft — Bremerhaven** Yd No: 404 Loa 126.29 (BB) Br ex 20.43 Dght 6.562 Lbp 117.20 Br md 20.01 Dpth 8.72 Welded, 2 dks	**(A31A2GX) General Cargo Ship** Grain: 11,106; Bale: 10,539 TEU 584 C.Ho 200/20' (40') C.Dk 384/20' (40') incl. 50 ref C. Compartments: 2 Ho, ER 2 Ha: 2 (37.8 x 15.6)ER Cranes: 2x35t Ice Capable	**1 oil engine** driving 1 CP propeller Total Power: 4,413kW (6,000hp) 15.5kn Mitsubishi 6UEC45/115H 1 x 2 Stroke 6 Cy. 450 x 1150 4413kW (6000bhp) Akasaka Tekkosho KK (Akasaka DieselLtd)-Japan AuxGen: 1 x 440kW 440V 60Hz a.c, 3 x 240kW 440V 60Hz a.c Thrusters: 1 Thwart. FP thruster (f) Fuel: 82.0 (d.f.) 612.0 (r.f.) 18.5pd
8419491 *YGUR* -	**TANTO HARMONI** *ex* Pulsar *-2000* **PT Tanto Intim Line** - *Jakarta* *Indonesia* MMSI: 525016056	**3,666** 1,870 4,546	Class: KI (NK)	**1985**-03 **Kochi Jyuko (Eiho Zosen) K.K. — Kochi** Yd No: 1766 Loa 97.06 (BB) Br ex 17.23 Dght 5.217 Lbp 89.97 Br md 17.20 Dpth 7.85 Welded, 2 dks	**(A31A2GX) General Cargo Ship** Grain: 7,398; Bale: 6,827 TEU 300 C.300/20' (40') Compartments: 2 Ho, ER 2 Ha: 2 (26.6 x 12.7)ER	**1 oil engine** driving 1 FP propeller Total Power: 2,133kW (2,900hp) 12.0kn Akasaka A41 1 x 4 Stroke 6 Cy. 410 x 800 2133kW (2900bhp) Akasaka Tekkosho KK (Akasaka DieselLtd)-Japan AuxGen: 3 x 240kW a.c
9683506 *JZDL* -	**TANTO HARUM** *ex* Bo Da 7 *-2013* **PT Tanto Intim Line** - *Jakarta* *Indonesia* MMSI: 525013029	**6,616** 3,704 7,716	Class: (CC)	**2013**-04 **Ningbo Boda Shipbuilding Co Ltd — Xiangshan County ZJ** Yd No: BD1207 Loa 119.90 (BB) Br ex - Dght 5.191 Lbp 115.00 Br md 21.80 Dpth 7.30 Welded, 1 dk	**(A31A2GX) General Cargo Ship** Double Hull (13F)	**1 oil engine** reduction geared to sc. shaft driving 1 Propeller Total Power: 2,500kW (3,399hp) 10.5kn Daihatsu 8DKM-28 1 x 4 Stroke 8 Cy. 280 x 390 2500kW (3399bhp) Anqing Marine Diesel Engine Works-China
8419477 *YGOI* -	**TANTO HAWARI** *ex* Weser Star *-1998* *ex* Tiger Shark *-1998* *ex* Weser Star *-1998* *ex* Dragon Seraya *-1996* *ex* Weser Star *-1995* *ex* Mekong Star *-1995* *ex* Weser Star *-1994* *ex* Menkar *-1991* *ex* Royal Star *-1989* **PT Tanto Intim Line** - SatCom: Inmarsat C 421045511 *Jakarta* *Indonesia* MMSI: 525016059	**3,666** 1,870 4,584	Class: KI (NK)	**1985**-01 **Kochi Jyuko (Eiho Zosen) K.K. — Kochi** Yd No: 1763 Loa 97.08 (BB) Br ex - Dght 5.417 Lbp 89.97 Br md 17.20 Dpth 7.85 Welded, 2 dks	**(A31A2GX) General Cargo Ship** Grain: 7,432; Bale: 6,827 TEU 300 C. 300/20' (40') incl. 20 ref C. Compartments: 2 Ho, ER 2 Ha: 2 (26.6 x 12.7)ER Cranes: 2x25.4t	**1 oil engine** driving 1 FP propeller Total Power: 2,133kW (2,900hp) 12.0kn Akasaka A41 1 x 4 Stroke 6 Cy. 410 x 800 2133kW (2900bhp) Akasaka Tekkosho KK (Akasaka DieselLtd)-Japan AuxGen: 2 x 240kW a.c
8419465 *YGVO* -	**TANTO HORAS** *ex* Elbe Star *-2004* *ex* Pul Sejahtera *-1992* *ex* Rex Star *-1990* **PT Tanto Intim Line** - *Jakarta* *Indonesia* MMSI: 525016057	**3,666** 1,870 4,596	Class: KI (NK)	**1984**-12 **Kochi Jyuko (Eiho Zosen) K.K. — Kochi** Yd No: 1753 Loa 97.08 (BB) Br ex - Dght 5.217 Lbp 89.95 Br md 17.20 Dpth 7.85 Welded, 2 dks	**(A31A2GX) General Cargo Ship** Grain: 7,432; Bale: 6,827 TEU 259 C.259/20' (40) incl. 20 ref C. Compartments: 2 Ho, ER 2 Ha: 2 (26.6 x 12.7)ER Cranes: 2x25t	**1 oil engine** driving 1 FP propeller Total Power: 2,133kW (2,900hp) 12.0kn Akasaka A41 1 x 4 Stroke 6 Cy. 410 x 800 2133kW (2900bhp) Akasaka Tekkosho KK (Akasaka DieselLtd)-Japan AuxGen: 3 x 240kW a.c
7425625 *YFKO* -	**TANTO INDAH** *ex* Black Whale *-1997* **PT Pelayaran Sejahtera Bahtera Agung** - *Jakarta* *Indonesia*	**3,907** 2,394 6,363	Class: KI (KR) (NK)	**1975**-08 **Asakawa Zosen K.K. — Imabari** Yd No: 250 Loa 106.43 (BB) Br ex - Dght 6.725 Lbp 97.95 Br md 16.30 Dpth 8.13 Welded, 1 dk	**(A31A2GX) General Cargo Ship** Grain: 8,403; Bale: 7,699 2 Ha: (28.4 x 8.3) (28.5 x 8.3)ER Derricks: 4x15t	**1 oil engine** driving 1 FP propeller Total Power: 2,795kW (3,800hp) 12.5kn Hanshin 6LU50A 1 x 4 Stroke 6 Cy. 500 x 800 2795kW (3800bhp) Hanshin Nainenki Kogyo-Japan AuxGen: 2 x 132kW 445V a.c
9179505 *PNFP* -	**TANTO JAYA** *ex* Sinar Bali *-2009* **PT Tanto Intim Line** - *Jakarta* *Indonesia* MMSI: 525016584	**12,471** 5,336 15,237 T/cm 28.7	Class: KI (GL) (BV)	**1998**-02 **Hakata Zosen K.K. — Imabari** Yd No: 608 Loa 147.00 (BB) Br ex - Dght 8.950 Lbp 136.57 Br md 25.00 Dpth 13.70 Welded, 1 dk	**(A33A2CC) Container Ship (Fully Cellular)** TEU 1060 C Ho 444 TEU C Dk 616 TEU incl 104 ref C. Compartments: 4 Cell Ho, ER 7 Ha: 6 (12.6 x 21.4)ER	**1 oil engine** driving 1 FP propeller Total Power: 9,989kW (13,581hp) 17.5kn B&W 7S50MC 1 x 2 Stroke 7 Cy. 500 x 1910 9989kW (13581bhp) Mitsui Engineering & Shipbuilding CLtd-Japan AuxGen: 3 x 560kW 445V 60Hz a.c Thrusters: 1 Thwart. FP thruster (f) Fuel: 133.0 (d.f.) 1300.0 (r.f.) 39.8pd
7105794 *YDNO* -	**TANTO KARUNIA** *ex* Satu Bangsa *-2009* *ex* Tenkomaru *-2009* *ex* Wayo Maru *-1984* **PT Cahaya Lautan Kumala** - *Jakarta* *Indonesia*	**1,873** 1,143 3,048	Class: KI	**1971**-03 **Imabari Shipbuilding Co Ltd — Imabari EH (Imabari Shipyard)** Yd No: 270 Loa 81.99 Br ex 12.53 Dght 5.639 Lbp 77.02 Br md 12.50 Dpth 7.62 Riveted\Welded, 1 dk	**(A31A2GX) General Cargo Ship** Grain: 4,630; Bale: 4,289 Compartments: 2 Ho, ER 2 Ha: 2 (22.0 x 7.0)ER	**1 oil engine** driving 1 FP propeller Total Power: 1,471kW (2,000hp) Hanshin 6LU38 1 x 4 Stroke 6 Cy. 380 x 580 1471kW (2000bhp) Hanshin Nainenki Kogyo-Japan AuxGen: 2 x 48kW 445V a.c Fuel: 207.5
8129943 *YHPH* -	**TANTO KARUNIA II** *ex* Oriental Pearl *-2003* *ex* Sin Hai *-2003* *ex* Annapurna *-1996* *ex* Ocean Crown *-1994* *ex* Moana Pacific *-1990* *ex* Seahawk *-1985* *ex* Atlantic Carrier *-1983* *ex* Ruth Drescher *-1983* **PT Tanto Intim Line** - *Jakarta* *Indonesia* MMSI: 525016101	**10,359** 5,221 14,495	Class: KI (GL)	**1983**-06 **Ishikawajima-Harima Heavy Industries Co Ltd (IHI) — Aioi HG** Yd No: 2808 Loa 148.39 (BB) Br ex 22.76 Dght 8.249 Lbp 140.60 Br md 22.71 Dpth 11.10 Welded, 1 dk	**(A31A2GX) General Cargo Ship** Grain: 17,443; Bale: 16,905 TEU 812 incl 60 ref C. Compartments: 4 Ho, ER 4 Ha: ER Cranes: 3x36t	**1 oil engine** sr geared to sc. shaft driving 1 CP propeller Total Power: 5,737kW (7,800hp) 12.0kn Pielstick 12PC2-5V-400 1 x Vee 4 Stroke 12 Cy. 400 x 460 5737kW (7800bhp) Ishikawajima Harima Heavy IndustrieCo Ltd (IHI)-Japan
8204901 *YGZC* -	**TANTO KITA** *ex* Elpis *-2004* *ex* Joint Gratia *-2000* *ex* Do Nam No. 8 *-1997* **PT Tanto Intim Line** - *Jakarta* *Indonesia* MMSI: 525016081	**4,942** 3,043 7,185	Class: KI (KR)	**1983**-04 **Daedong Shipbuilding Co Ltd — Busan** Yd No: 261 Loa 117.99 (BB) Br ex 18.24 Dght 6.532 Lbp 108.51 Br md 18.20 Dpth 8.51 Welded, 1 dk	**(A31A2GX) General Cargo Ship** Grain: 10,428; Bale: 9,692 TEU 288 C. 288/20' (40') Compartments: 2 Ho, ER 2 Ha: 2 (31.5 x 13.1)ER Derricks: 4x20t	**1 oil engine** driving 1 FP propeller Total Power: 3,310kW (4,500hp) 13.5kn Hanshin 6ELS44 1 x 4 Stroke 6 Cy. 440 x 880 3310kW (4500bhp) Ssangyong Heavy Industries Co Ltd-South Korea AuxGen: 2 x 249kW 445V a.c
8812746 *PMZI* -	**TANTO LESTARI** *ex* Da Lian *-2009* *ex* Fair Fortune *-2001* *ex* Maersk Asia Quarto *-1994* *ex* Excellence Container *-1992* **PT Tanto Intim Line** - *Jakarta* *Indonesia* MMSI: 525016495	**6,979** 3,592 9,918	Class: KI (CC) (NK)	**1989**-09 **Shin Kurushima Dockyard Co. Ltd. — Akitsu** Yd No: 2626 Loa 124.02 (BB) Br ex - Dght 7.614 Lbp 115.00 Br md 20.90 Dpth 10.20 Welded, 1 dk	**(A33A2CC) Container Ship (Fully Cellular)** TEU 569 incl 120 ref C Compartments: 6 Ho, ER 6 Ha: 5 (12.6 x 8.1) (12.6 x 5.4)ER Cranes: 2x40t	**1 oil engine** driving 1 FP propeller Total Power: 4,855kW (6,601hp) 15.0kn B&W 6L42MC 1 x 2 Stroke 6 Cy. 420 x 1360 4855kW (6601bhp) Innoshima Machinery Co Ltd-Japan AuxGen: 3 x 400kW 450V 60Hz a.c Fuel: 94.0 (d.f.) 626.0 (r.f.)
8130928 *YEGG* -	**TANTO LUMOSO** *ex* Lumoso Express *-2006* *ex* Royal Accord *-1996* **PT Tanto Intim Line** - *Jakarta* *Indonesia* MMSI: 525016138	**8,147** 4,282 11,973	Class: KI (GL) (NK)	**1982**-04 **K.K. Taihei Kogyo — Akitsu** Yd No: 1526 Loa 137.50 (BB) Br ex - Dght 7.913 Lbp 128.00 Br md 20.01 Dpth 10.62 Welded, 1 dk	**(A33A2CC) Container Ship (Fully Cellular)** TEU 538 incl 50 ref C Compartments: 4 Cell Ho, ER 7 Ha: ER Cranes: 2x35t	**1 oil engine** driving 1 FP propeller Total Power: 5,149kW (7,001hp) 16.0kn Mitsubishi 7UEC45/115H 1 x 2 Stroke 7 Cy. 450 x 1150 5149kW (7001bhp) Kobe Hatsudoki KK-Japan

IMO / Call Sign	Name / Owner	Tonnage	Class	Builder / Dimensions	Type / Cargo	Machinery
7506534 *YEWH* -	**TANTO MANDIRI** *ex* Bunga Gelang *-1993* **PT Tanto Intim Line** - *Jakarta* *Indonesia* MMSI: 525016120	**2,975** 1,719 3,900	Class: (AB) (KI)	**1976-05 Murakami Hide Zosen K.K. — Imabari** Yd No: 127 Loa 85.10 Br ex - Dght 7.200 Lbp 79.94 Br md 15.63 Dpth 8.82 Welded, 2 dks	**(A31A2GX) General Cargo Ship** Grain: 5,805; Bale: 5,578 TEU 81 C.Ho 69/20' (40') C.Dk 12/20' (40') Compartments: 2 Ho, ER 2 Ha: ER Cranes: 1x30t,2x5t	**1 oil engine** driving 1 FP propeller Total Power: 2,648kW (3,600hp) 14.3kn Hanshin 6LU50 1 x 4 Stroke 6 Cy. 500 x 800 2648kW (3600bhp) The Hanshin Diesel Works Ltd-Japan AuxGen: 2 x 200kW Fuel: 46.0 (d.f.) 298.0 (r.f.) 12.5pd
9683520 *JZDM* -	**TANTO MANIS** *ex* Bo Da 10 *-2013* **PT Tanto Intim Line** - *Indonesia*	**6,616** 3,704 7,716	Class: (CC)	**2013-04 Ningbo Boda Shipbuilding Co Ltd — Xiangshan County ZJ** Yd No: BD1208 Loa 119.90 (BB) Br ex - Dght 5.200 Lbp 115.00 Br md 21.80 Dpth 7.30 Welded, 1 dk	**(A31A2GX) General Cargo Ship** Double Hull (13F)	**1 oil engine** reduction geared to sc. shaft driving 1 Propeller Total Power: 2,500kW (3,399hp) 10.5kn Daihatsu 8DKM-28 1 x 4 Stroke 8 Cy. 280 x 390 2500kW (3399bhp) Anqing Marine Diesel Engine Works-China
7412616 *YCKC* -	**TANTO MURNI** *ex* Bineka No. 7 *-1988* *ex* Maravillano II *-1979* **PT Berkah Samudra Line** - *Jakarta* *Indonesia* Official number: 6470+BA	**3,372** 2,115 5,934	Class: KI (NK)	**1975-03 Oshima Dock KK — Imabari EH** Yd No: 567 Loa 101.12 Br ex 16.24 Dght 6.585 Lbp 95.18 Br md 16.21 Dpth 8.21 Welded, 1 dk	**(A31A2GX) General Cargo Ship** Grain: 7,454; Bale: 6,931 2 Ha: (27.9 x 8.0) (29.4 x 8.0) Derricks: 4x15t	**1 oil engine** driving 1 FP propeller Total Power: 2,795kW (3,800hp) 12.8kn Mitsubishi 6UET45/75C 1 x 2 Stroke 6 Cy. 450 x 750 2795kW (3800bhp) Akasaka Tekkosho KK (Akasaka DieselLtd)-Japan AuxGen: 2 x 128kW Fuel: 567.0 13.0pd
9088641 *PNCU* -	**TANTO PERMAI** *ex* Hibiscus Isle *-2009* **PT Tanto Intim Line** - *Jakarta* *Indonesia* MMSI: 525016550	**8,652** 3,956 11,250	Class: (NK)	**1994-04 Shin Kurushima Dockyard Co. Ltd. — Akitsu** Yd No: 2797 Loa 144.02 (BB) Br ex 21.86 Dght 7.728 Lbp 135.00 Br md 21.80 Dpth 10.70 Welded, 1 dk	**(A33A2CC) Container Ship (Fully Cellular)** TEU 662 C incl. 150 ref C. 13 Ha: (12.6 x 8.3)12 (12.6 x 8.0)ER Cranes: 2x40t,2x35t	**1 oil engine** driving 1 FP propeller Total Power: 7,943kW (10,799hp) 18.9kn Mitsubishi 6UEC52LS 1 x 2 Stroke 6 Cy. 520 x 1850 7943kW (10799bhp) Kobe Hatsudoki KK-Japan Thrusters: 1 Thwart. CP thruster (f) Fuel: 79.1 (d.f.) 941.8 (r.f.) 29.8pd
9118408 *POYQ* -	**TANTO PRATAMA** *ex* Far Colombo *-2012* *ex* Tiger Wave *-2010* *ex* Box Wave *-2004* *ex* Intelligence Container *-2002* **PT Tanto Intim Line** - *Jakarta* *Indonesia* MMSI: 525013026	**17,613** 8,215 24,134 T/cm 39.7	Class: KI (BV) (AB)	**1995-06 Shin Kurushima Dockyard Co. Ltd. — Onishi** Yd No: 2840 Loa 182.83 (BB) Br ex - Dght 9.530 Lbp 170.33 Br md 28.00 Dpth 14.00 Welded, 1 dk	**(A33A2CC) Container Ship (Fully Cellular)** TEU 1510 C Ho 558 TEU C Dk 952 TEU incl 60 ref C. Compartments: 6 Cell Ho 9 Ha: (12.8 x 11.1) (12.8 x 7.9)7 (12.8 x 10.6)	**1 oil engine** driving 1 FP propeller Total Power: 11,681kW (15,881hp) 20.9kn B&W 6S60MC 1 x 2 Stroke 6 Cy. 600 x 2292 11681kW (15881bhp) Mitsui Engineering & Shipbuilding CLtd-Japan AuxGen: 2 x 560kW 440V a.c Fuel: 134.0 (d.f.) 2744.0 (r.f.) 43.8pd
9167526 *POET* -	**TANTO RAYA** *ex* Da Xin *-2010* *ex* Richmond *-2002* **PT Tanto Intim Line** - *Jakarta* *Indonesia* MMSI: 525013018	**6,867** 3,479 9,114	Class: KI (NK)	**1998-07 Shin Kochi Jyuko K.K. — Kochi** Yd No: 7105 Loa 120.84 (BB) Br ex - Dght 7.528 Lbp 111.60 Br md 20.20 Dpth 10.40 Welded, 1 dk	**(A33A2CC) Container Ship (Fully Cellular)** TEU 588 C.Ho 252 C.Dk 336 incl. 100 ref. C Compartments: 4 Cell Ho, ER 6 Ha: (12.6 x 10.7)5 (12.6 x 15.9)ER Cranes: 2x36t	**1 oil engine** driving 1 FP propeller Total Power: 5,590kW (7,600hp) 15.6kn B&W 8S35MC 1 x 2 Stroke 8 Cy. 350 x 1400 5590kW (7600bhp) Makita Corp-Japan AuxGen: 3 x 485kW 450V 60Hz a.c Thrusters: 1 Tunnel thruster (f) Fuel: 147.9 (d.f.) (Heating Coils) 680.9 (r.f.) 26.3pd
8401729 *YHBE* -	**TANTO REJEKI** *ex* Kwaichung Express *-2001* *ex* Tricolor Song *-1994* *ex* Annapurna *-1992* *ex* Pul Adil *-1989* *ex* Flex America *-1988* **PT Tanto Intim Line** - *Jakarta* *Indonesia* MMSI: 525016082	**2,662** 1,819 3,827	Class: KI (BV)	**1984-05 Hakata Zosen K.K. — Imabari** Yd No: 287 Loa 91.39 (BB) Br ex - Dght 5.750 Lbp 84.00 Br md 14.80 Dpth 7.01 Welded, 1 dk	**(A31A2GX) General Cargo Ship** Grain: 5,658; Bale: 5,459 Compartments: 2 Ho, ER 2 Ha: ER Cranes: 1x25t	**1 oil engine** driving 1 CP propeller Total Power: 1,692kW (2,300hp) Akasaka A34FD 1 x 4 Stroke 6 Cy. 340 x 660 1692kW (2300bhp) Akasaka Tekkosho KK (Akasaka DieselLtd)-Japan
9240940 *POBU* -	**TANTO SAKTI I** *ex* Glory 1 *-2011* *ex* Ramitha *-2011* **Global Glory Shipping Ltd** PT Tanto Intim Line *Jakarta* *Indonesia* MMSI: 525013015	**6,361** 2,984 5,600	Class: (LR) ✠ Classed LR until 29/8/11	**2003-09 Qingshan Shipyard — Wuhan HB** Yd No: 20000302 Loa 125.30 (BB) Br ex - Dght 5.900 Lbp 118.00 Br md 20.60 Dpth 8.70 Welded, 1 dk	**(A31A2GX) General Cargo Ship** TEU 665 C.Ho 169/20' C.Dk 496/20' incl. 60 ref C. Compartments: 3 Ho, ER Cranes: 2x45t Ice Capable	**1 oil engine** driving 1 CP propeller Total Power: 5,970kW (8,117hp) 16.5kn B&W 6L42MC 1 x 2 Stroke 6 Cy. 420 x 1360 5970kW (8117bhp) Hudong Heavy Machinery Co Ltd-China AuxGen: 1 x 600kW 440V 60Hz a.c, 2 x 616kW 440V 60Hz a.c Boilers: AuxB (Comp) 8.4kgf/cm² (8.2bar), HWH 4.5kgf/cm² (4.4bar) Thrusters: 1 Thwart. FP thruster (f) Fuel: 152.0 (d.f.) 572.0 (r.f.)
9240938 *POKA* -	**TANTO SAKTI II** *ex* Glory 2 *-2011* *ex* Antaradus *-2011* *ex* CMA CGM Mashrek *-2004* *ex* Antaradus *-2003* **PT Tanto Intim Line** - *Jakarta* *Indonesia* MMSI: 525013020	**6,361** 2,984 5,664	Class: KI (LR) ✠ Classed LR until 24/1/12	**2003-01 Qingshan Shipyard — Wuhan HB** Yd No: 20000301 Loa 125.30 (BB) Br ex 19.60 Dght 5.900 Lbp 118.20 Br md 20.60 Dpth 8.70 Welded, 1 dk	**(A31A2GX) General Cargo Ship** TEU 665 C.Ho 169/20' C.Dk 496/20' incl 60 ref C. Cranes: 2x45t	**1 oil engine** driving 1 CP propeller Total Power: 5,970kW (8,117hp) 16.5kn MAN-B&W 6L42MC 1 x 2 Stroke 6 Cy. 420 x 1360 5970kW (8117bhp) Hudong Heavy Machinery Co Ltd-China AuxGen: 1 x 600kW 440V 60Hz a.c, 2 x 550kW 440V 60Hz a.c Boilers: AuxB (Comp) 8.2kgf/cm² (8.0bar), HWH 4.5kgf/cm² (4.4bar) Thrusters: 1 Thwart. FP thruster (f)
8104498 *YHTQ* -	**TANTO SATRIA** *ex* Da Li *-2004* *ex* Tiger Stream *-2003* *ex* Sea Success I *-2001* *ex* Eagle Success *-1997* *ex* Sea Laurel *-1995* *ex* Marivia *-1994* *ex* Eagle Nova *-1994* *ex* Marivia *-1989* *ex* EA Endeavour *-1988* *ex* Husa II *-1985* *ex* Marivia *-1985* *ex* Mississippi *-1984* *ex* Marivia *-1984* *ex* European Eagle *-1983* *ex* Marivia *-1983* **PT Tanto Intim Line** - *Jakarta* *Indonesia* MMSI: 525016100	**5,974** 3,092 7,612	Class: KI (BV) (RS) (GL)	**1982-12 Rickmers Rhederei GmbH Rickmers Werft — Bremerhaven** Yd No: 406 Loa 127.51 (BB) Br ex 20.05 Dght 6.580 Lbp 117.23 Br md 20.01 Dpth 8.72 Welded, 2 dks	**(A31A2GX) General Cargo Ship** Grain: 11,331; Bale: 10,522 TEU 584 C Ho 200 TEU C Dk 384 TEU incl 50 ref C. Compartments: 2 Ho, ER 2 Ha: 2 (37.8 x 15.5)ER Cranes: 2x35t Ice Capable	**1 oil engine** driving 1 CP propeller Total Power: 4,413kW (6,000hp) 15.5kn Mitsubishi 6UEC45/115H 1 x 2 Stroke 6 Cy. 450 x 1150 4413kW (6000bhp) Akasaka Tekkosho KK (Akasaka DieselLtd)-Japan AuxGen: 1 x 440kW 440V 60Hz a.c, 3 x 240kW 440V 60Hz a.c Thrusters: 1 Thwart. FP thruster (f) Fuel: 80.5 (d.f.) 599.5 (r.f.) 20.0pd
9036416 *YHDN* -	**TANTO SAYANG** *ex* Korean Pearl *-2001* **PT Tanto Intim Line** - *Jakarta* *Indonesia* MMSI: 525016079	**4,937** 2,414 7,207	Class: KI (KR)	**1990-08 Dae Sun Shipbuilding & Engineering Co Ltd — Busan** Yd No: 361 Loa 115.02 (BB) Br ex 19.60 Dght 6.713 Lbp 105.01 Br md 19.02 Dpth 8.51 Welded, 1 dk	**(A33A2CC) Container Ship (Fully Cellular)** TEU 333 incl 25 ref C. Compartments: 3 Cell Ho, ER 6 Ha: ER Cranes: 2	**1 oil engine** driving 1 FP propeller Total Power: 3,354kW (4,560hp) 14.3kn B&W 6L35MC 1 x 2 Stroke 6 Cy. 350 x 1050 3354kW (4560bhp) Ssangyong Heavy Industries Co Ltd-South Korea
9714197 *BKAD5* -	**TANTO SEHAT** *ex* Bo Da 11 *-2014* **PT Tanto Intim Line** - *Ningbo, Zhejiang* *China* MMSI: 413452760	**6,659** 3,729 8,180	Class: ZC (Class contemplated)	**2014-02 Ningbo Boda Shipbuilding Co Ltd — Xiangshan County ZJ** Yd No: BD1307 Loa 119.90 Br ex - Dght 5.200 Lbp 115.00 Br md 21.80 Dpth 7.30 Welded, 1 dk	**(A31A2GX) General Cargo Ship**	**1 oil engine** reduction geared to sc. shafts driving 1 FP propeller Total Power: 2,561kW (3,482hp) Daihatsu 8DKM-28 1 x 4 Stroke 8 Cy. 280 x 390 2561kW (3482bhp) Anqing Marine Diesel Engine Works-China
9168570 *POSY* -	**TANTO SEMANGAT** *ex* Bunga Mas 12 *-2012* **PT Tanto Intim Line** - *Jakarta* *Indonesia* MMSI: 525013024	**8,612** 1,400 10,313 T/cm 24.2	Class: KI (AB)	**1999-01 Hanjin Heavy Industries Co Ltd — Busan** Yd No: 060 Loa 140.00 (BB) Br ex - Dght 7.510 Lbp 132.93 Br md 20.50 Dpth 10.50 Welded, 1 dk	**(A33A2CC) Container Ship (Fully Cellular)** TEU 710 C Ho 278 TEU C Dk 432 TEU incl 60 ref C Compartments: 5 Cell Ho, ER 7 Ha: ER Cranes: 2x40t	**1 oil engine** driving 1 FP propeller Total Power: 6,510kW (8,851hp) 17.1kn Sulzer 5RTA48T 1 x 2 Stroke 5 Cy. 480 x 2000 6510kW (8851bhp) Samsung Heavy Industries Co Ltd-South Korea AuxGen: 3 x 600kW 450V 60Hz a.c Fuel: 80.5 (d.f.) (Heating Coils) 672.0 (r.f.) 28.4pd
9168582 *POSX* -	**TANTO SENANG** *ex* Bunga Mas 11 *-2012* **PT Tanto Intim Line** - *Jakarta* *Indonesia* MMSI: 525013023	**8,612** 1,400 10,325 T/cm 24.2	Class: KI (AB)	**1998-09 Hanjin Heavy Industries Co Ltd — Busan** Yd No: 059 Loa 140.00 (BB) Br ex - Dght 7.513 Lbp 132.94 Br md 20.50 Dpth 10.50 Welded, 1 dk	**(A33A2CC) Container Ship (Fully Cellular)** TEU 710 C Ho 278 TEU C Dk 432 TEU incl 60 ref C Compartments: 5 Cell Ho, ER 7 Ha: ER Cranes: 2x40t	**1 oil engine** driving 1 FP propeller Total Power: 6,510kW (8,851hp) 17.1kn Sulzer 5RTA48T 1 x 2 Stroke 5 Cy. 480 x 2000 6510kW (8851bhp) Samsung Heavy Industries Co Ltd-South Korea AuxGen: 3 x 600kW 450V 60Hz a.c Fuel: 80.5 (d.f.) (Heating Coils) 672.0 (r.f.) 28.4pd

IMO / Call sign / Flag	Name / Former names / Owner / Port / MMSI	GT / NT / DWT	Class	Built / Dimensions	Type	Machinery
8324270 *YGFO* -	**TANTO SENTOSA** *ex* Thuban *-1999* *ex* Chung Lie *-1988* **PT Tanto Intim Line** - *Jakarta* *Indonesia* MMSI: 525016111	**4,870** 2,802 6,829	Class: CR KI (NK)	**1984**-04 **K.K. Taihei Kogyo — Akitsu** Yd No: 1670 Loa 105.00 (BB) Br ex - Dght 6.715 Lbp 96.00 Br md 20.00 Dpth 8.70 Welded, 1 dk	**(A33A2CC) Container Ship (Fully Cellular)** TEU 256 Compartments: 9 Ho, ER 9 Ha: ER Cranes: 2x35t	**1 oil engine** driving 1 FP propeller Total Power: 4,046kW (5,501hp) 14.3kn Mitsubishi 6UEC45HA 1 x 2 Stroke 6 Cy. 450 x 1150 4046kW (5501bhp) Kobe Hatsudoki KK-Japan AuxGen: 3 x 480kW a.c
8115538 *YHGI* -	**TANTO SEPAKAT** *ex* ATL Endurance *-2002* *ex* Katania *-1998* *ex* Canterbury Express *-1996* *ex* Scol Carrier *-1985* *ex* Katania *-1984* **PT Tanto Intim Line** - *Jakarta* *Indonesia* MMSI: 525016086	**4,460** 2,412 6,163	Class: KI (GL)	**1983**-12 **Zhonghua Shipyard — Shanghai** Yd No: 8101 Loa 105.95 (BB) Br ex 17.56 Dght 6.989 Lbp 96.02 Br md 17.51 Dpth 9.02 Welded, 2 dks	**(A31A2GX) General Cargo Ship** Grain: 7,930 TEU 310 C. 310/20' (40') Compartments: 1 Ho, ER 2 Ha: (25.8 x 13.9) (38.4 x 13.9)ER Cranes: 2x36t Ice Capable	**1 oil engine** driving 1 CP propeller Total Power: 2,870kW (3,902hp) 13.5kn Mitsubishi 6UEC37/88H 1 x 2 Stroke 6 Cy. 370 x 880 2870kW (3902bhp) Akasaka Tekkosho KK (Akasaka DieselLtd)-Japan Thrusters: 1 Thwart. FP thruster (f)
9056519 *PNUS* -	**TANTO SETIA** *ex* London Tower *-2010* *ex* Nantai Queen *-1999* **PT Tanto Intim Line** - *Jakarta* *Indonesia* MMSI: 525013013	**17,651** 8,135 23,884 T/cm 39.7	Class: KI (NK)	**1994**-03 **Shin Kurushima Dockyard Co. Ltd. — Onishi** Yd No: 2776 Loa 182.84 (BB) Br ex - Dght 9.530 Lbp 170.33 Br md 28.00 Dpth 14.00 Welded, 1 dk	**(A33A2CC) Container Ship (Fully Cellular)** TEU 1525 C Ho 546 TEU C Dk 979 TEU incl 133 ref C. Compartments: ER, 5 Cell Ho 17 Ha: (12.8 x 11.1)2 (12.8 x 7.9)ER 14 (12.8 x 10.6) Cranes: 2x40.6t	**1 oil engine** driving 1 FP propeller Total Power: 11,681kW (15,881hp) 19.0kn B&W 6S60MC 1 x 2 Stroke 6 Cy. 600 x 2292 11681kW (15881bhp) Hitachi Zosen Corp-Japan AuxGen: 3 x 485kW 440V a.c Fuel: 94.5 (d.f.) 2741.0 (r.f.) 45.7pd
8104486 *YGSE* -	**TANTO SINERGI** *ex* Antares *-2000* *ex* Martrader *-2000* *ex* EWL Venezuela *-1997* *ex* Merzario Francia *-1991* *ex* Premier *-1991* *ex* Woermann Sankuru *-1990* *ex* City of Rotterdam *-1989* *ex* Noble *-1986* *ex* Sanna *-1986* *ex* Premier *-1985* *ex* Singapore Eagle *-1985* *ex* Premier *-1982* **PT Tanto Intim Line** - *Jakarta* *Indonesia* MMSI: 525016055	**5,931** 3,092 7,754	Class: KI (GL)	**1982**-03 **Rickmers Rhederei GmbH Rickmers Werft — Bremerhaven** Yd No: 405 Loa 126.47 (BB) Br ex 20.27 Dght 6.571 Lbp 117.20 Br md 20.01 Dpth 8.72 Welded, 2 dks	**(A31A2GX) General Cargo Ship** Grain: 11,106; Bale: 10,539 TEU 584 C Ho 200 TEU C Dk 384 TEU incl 50 ref C. Compartments: 2 Ho, ER 2 Ha: 2 (37.8 x 15.6)ER Cranes: 2x35t Ice Capable	**1 oil engine** driving 1 CP propeller Total Power: 4,413kW (6,000hp) 15.5kn Mitsubishi 6UEC45/115H 1 x 2 Stroke 6 Cy. 450 x 1150 4413kW (6000bhp) Akasaka Tekkosho KK (Akasaka DieselLtd)-Japan AuxGen: 1 x 440kW 440V 60Hz a.c, 3 x 240kW 440V 60Hz a.c Thrusters: 1 Thwart. FP thruster (f) Fuel: 82.0 (d.f.) 612.0 (r.f.) 18.5pd
8115590 *YDKI* -	**TANTO STAR** *ex* New Sea Star *-2006* *ex* QC Star *-2006* *ex* New Sea Star *-2003* *ex* Tiger Cliff *-2003* *ex* Nordsino *-1999* *ex* Maersk Bravo *-1990* *ex* Nordsino *-1987* *ex* Ville du Levant *-1986* *ex* Nordsino *-1983* **PT Tanto Intim Line** - *Tanjung Priok* *Indonesia* MMSI: 525016131	**9,909** 4,895 13,193	Class: KI (GL)	**1982**-12 **Shanghai Shipyard — Shanghai** Yd No: 118 Loa 147.50 (BB) Br ex 22.23 Dght 8.084 Lbp 138.03 Br md 22.20 Dpth 10.93 Welded, 1 dk	**(A33A2CC) Container Ship (Fully Cellular)** Grain: 16,567; Bale: 15,999 TEU 846 C Ho 304 TEU C Dk 542 TEU incl 50 ref C. Compartments: 3 Cell Ho, ER 3 Ha: (25.5 x 11.2) (38.3 x 16.0) (25.5 x 16.0)ER Cranes: 2x36t Ice Capable	**1 oil engine** driving 1 FP propeller Total Power: 5,504kW (7,483hp) 15.0kn B&W 5L55GFCA 1 x 2 Stroke 5 Cy. 550 x 1380 5504kW (7483bhp) Hitachi Zosen Corp-Japan AuxGen: 3 x 400kW 450V 60Hz a.c Thrusters: 1 Thwart. FP thruster (f) Fuel: 260.0 (d.f.) 800.0 (r.f.) 23.5pd
9055498 *JZGM* -	**TANTO SUBUR I** *ex* Trade Worlder *-2013* **PT Tanto Intim Line** - *Indonesia* MMSI: 525013031	**4,811** 2,410 6,796 T/cm 16.5	Class: (CC) (AB)	**1993**-04 **Dae Sun Shipbuilding & Engineering Co Ltd — Busan** Yd No: 397 Loa 112.96 (BB) Br ex - Dght 6.513 Lbp 103.78 Br md 18.99 Dpth 8.47 Welded, 1 dk	**(A33A2CC) Container Ship (Fully Cellular)** TEU 385 Compartments: 5 Cell Ho, ER 6 Ha: ER	**1 oil engine** driving 1 FP propeller Total Power: 3,354kW (4,560hp) 14.5kn B&W 6L35MC 1 x 2 Stroke 6 Cy. 350 x 1050 3354kW (4560bhp) Ssangyong Heavy Industries Co Ltd-South Korea AuxGen: 3 x 400kW 445V 60Hz a.c Thrusters: 1 Thwart. FP thruster (f) Fuel: 39.7 (d.f.) 407.3 (r.f.) 14.7pd
9055503 *JZKS* -	**TANTO SUBUR II** *ex* Trade Hope *-2013* **PT Tanto Intim Line** - *Indonesia* MMSI: 525013033	**4,811** 2,410 6,810 T/cm 16.5	Class: (CC) (AB)	**1993**-06 **Dae Sun Shipbuilding & Engineering Co Ltd — Busan** Yd No: 398 Loa 112.96 (BB) Br ex - Dght 6.513 Lbp 103.78 Br md 18.99 Dpth 8.47 Welded, 1 dk	**(A33A2CC) Container Ship (Fully Cellular)** TEU 385 Compartments: 5 Cell Ho, ER 5 Ha: 5 (12.6 x 13.0)ER	**1 oil engine** driving 1 FP propeller Total Power: 3,354kW (4,560hp) 14.0kn B&W 6L35MC 1 x 2 Stroke 6 Cy. 350 x 1050 3354kW (4560bhp) Ssangyong Heavy Industries Co Ltd-South Korea AuxGen: 3 x 320kW 445V 60Hz a.c Thrusters: 1 Thwart. FP thruster (f) Fuel: 39.7 (d.f.) 407.3 (r.f.) 14.7pd
8504674 *YDQW* -	**TANTO SURYA** *ex* Da Fa *-2006* *ex* Isra Bhum *-1998* *ex* Da Fa *-1997* *ex* Isra Bhum *-1997* *ex* Da Fa *-1992* *ex* St. Louis *-1992* *ex* Margaletta *-1990* *ex* Kuo Hsiung *-1990* **PT Tanto Intim Line** - *Jakarta* *Indonesia* MMSI: 525016130	**8,142** 3,406 8,995	Class: KI (CC) (AB) (NK)	**1985**-08 **Towa Zosen K.K. — Shimonoseki** Yd No: 563 Loa 130.00 (BB) Br ex - Dght 8.980 Lbp 120.00 Br md 21.01 Dpth 11.16 Welded, 1 dk	**(A33A2CC) Container Ship (Fully Cellular)** TEU 480 C Ho 238 TEU C Dk 242 TEU incl 30 ref C Compartments: 3 Cell Ho, ER 9 Ha: (12.6 x 10.8)4 (6.7 x 5.5)4 (26.2 x 8.1)ER Cranes: 2x40t	**1 oil engine** driving 1 FP propeller Total Power: 3,530kW (4,799hp) 12.0kn Mitsubishi 6UEC45LA 1 x 2 Stroke 6 Cy. 450 x 1350 3530kW (4799bhp) Kobe Hatsudoki KK-Japan AuxGen: 3 x 430kW 445V 60Hz a.c Fuel: 89.0 (d.f.) 483.5 (r.f.) 18.5pd
9169665 *POSW* -	**TANTO TANGGUH** *ex* Bunga Mas 10 *-2012* *ex* Bunga Mas Sepuloh *-2003* *ex* Bunga Mas 10 *-2003* **PT Tanto Intim Line** - *Jakarta* *Indonesia* MMSI: 525013022	**9,380** 5,558 12,288 T/cm 15.0	Class: KI (Class contemplated) (AB)	**1998**-09 **Kyokuyo Shipyard Corp — Shimonoseki YC** Yd No: 420 Loa 144.83 (BB) Br ex 22.42 Dght 8.216 Lbp 134.00 Br md 22.40 Dpth 11.00 Welded, 1 dk	**(A33A2CC) Container Ship (Fully Cellular)** TEU 736 C Ho 314 TEU C Dk 422 TEU incl 60 ref C Compartments: 7 Cell Ho, ER 7 Ha: ER Cranes: 2x40t	**1 oil engine** driving 1 FP propeller Total Power: 7,988kW (10,860hp) 17.0kn B&W 6S50MC 1 x 2 Stroke 6 Cy. 500 x 1910 7988kW (10860bhp) Kawasaki Heavy Industries Ltd-Japan AuxGen: 3 x 600kW 440V 60Hz a.c Fuel: 95.0 (d.f.) (Heating Coils) 1027.0 (r.f.) 29.0pd
9169653 *POSV* -	**TANTO TERANG** *ex* Bunga Mas 9 *-2012* **PT Tanto Intim Line** - *Jakarta* *Indonesia* MMSI: 525013021	**9,380** 5,558 12,250 T/cm 15.0	Class: (AB)	**1998**-07 **Kyokuyo Shipyard Corp — Shimonoseki YC** Yd No: 418 Loa 144.83 (BB) Br ex - Dght 8.216 Lbp 134.00 Br md 22.40 Dpth 11.00 Welded, 1 dk	**(A33A2CC) Container Ship (Fully Cellular)** TEU 736 C Ho 314 TEU C Dk 422 TEU incl 60 ref C Compartments: 7 Cell Ho, ER 7 Ha: ER Cranes: 2x40t	**1 oil engine** driving 1 FP propeller Total Power: 7,988kW (10,860hp) 17.0kn B&W 6L50MC 1 x 2 Stroke 6 Cy. 500 x 1620 7988kW (10860bhp) Kawasaki Heavy Industries Ltd-Japan AuxGen: 3 x 600kW 440V 60Hz a.c Fuel: 95.0 (d.f.) (Heating Coils) 1027.0 (r.f.) 29.0pd
6817754 *CGBY* -	**TANU** **Government of Canada (Canadian Coast Guard)** - *Ottawa, ON* *Canada* MMSI: 316091000 Official number: 330370	*754* 204 -	Class: (LR) ✠ Classed LR until 6/1/98	**1968**-09 **Yarrows Ltd — Victoria BC** Yd No: 324 Loa 54.69 Br ex 9.96 Dght 3.277 Lbp 50.17 Br md 9.76 Dpth 4.58 Welded, 1 dk	**(B12D2FP) Fishery Patrol Vessel**	**2 oil engines** geared to sc. shaft driving 1 FP propeller Total Power: 1,930kW (2,624hp) 12.0kn Fairbanks, Morse 8-38D8-1/8 2 x 2 Stroke 8 Cy. 207 x 254 each-965kW (1312bhp) Fairbanks Morse (Canada) Ltd-Canada AuxGen: 3 x 150kW 460V 60Hz a.c
7110024 *VM2181* -	**TANUNDA** *ex* Harman *-1986* **South Sea Towage Ltd** - *Melbourne, Vic* *Australia* Official number: 343998	*159* 2 143	Class: (LR) ✠ Classed LR until 22/3/99	**1971**-09 **Carrington Slipways Pty Ltd — Newcastle NSW** Yd No: 63 Loa 25.81 Br ex 8.11 Dght 3.810 Lbp 23.25 Br md 7.78 Dpth 4.07 Welded, 1 dk	**(B32A2ST) Tug** 2 Ha: (1.2 x 1.2) (0.4 x 0.4)	**2 oil engines** geared to sc. shafts driving 2 FP propellers Total Power: 1,176kW (1,598hp) 11.0kn Blackstone ESS8 2 x 4 Stroke 8 Cy. 222 x 292 each-588kW (799bhp) Lister Blackstone MirrleesMarine Ltd.-Dursley AuxGen: 2 x 28kW 415V 50Hz a.c Fuel: 39.5 (d.f.)
9589463 *ZGAO5* -	**TANUSHA** **Murray Marketing Inc** Fraser Worldwide SAM *George Town* *Cayman Islands (British)* Official number: 742456	**299** 89 65	Class: AB	**2010**-04 **Azimut-Benetti SpA — Viareggio** Yd No: BC123 Loa 35.80 Br ex - Dght 2.220 Lbp 30.80 Br md 7.86 Dpth 3.93 Bonded, 1 dk	**(X11A2YP) Yacht** Hull Material: Reinforced Plastic	**2 oil engines** reduction geared to sc. shafts driving 2 Propellers Total Power: 2,206kW (3,000hp) 15.0kn M.T.U. 12V2000M91 2 x Vee 4 Stroke 12 Cy. 130 x 150 each-1103kW (1500bhp) MTU Friedrichshafen GmbH-Friedrichshafen AuxGen: 2 x 80kW a.c
9374600 *V7NE8* -	**TANUX I** *ex* Zamil 35 *-2006* **Tanux Shipping KS** - *Majuro* *Marshall Islands* MMSI: 538002949 Official number: 2949	**1,161** 348 949	Class: AB	**2006**-07 **Hin Lee (Zhuhai) Shipyard Co Ltd — Zhuhai GD** (Hull) Yd No: 104 **2006**-07 **Cheoy Lee Shipyards Ltd — Hong Kong** Yd No: 4882 Loa 53.80 Br ex - Dght 3.600 Lbp 48.80 Br md 13.80 Dpth 4.50 Welded, 1 dk	**(B22A2OR) Offshore Support Vessel**	**2 oil engines** reverse reduction geared to sc. shafts driving 2 FP propellers Total Power: 2,316kW (3,148hp) Caterpillar 3512B-TA 2 x Vee 4 Stroke 12 Cy. 170 x 190 each-1158kW (1574bhp) Caterpillar Inc-USA AuxGen: 3 x 260kW a.c Thrusters: 1 Tunnel thruster (f)

IMO / Call sign	Name / Owner / Port	Tonnage	Class	Builder / Dimensions	Type / Cargo	Machinery
9318826 *V7NE7* -	**TANUX II** *ex Sealink Vanessa 3 -2006* **Tanux Shipping KS** - SatCom: Inmarsat C 453832745 *Majuro* *Marshall Islands* MMSI: 538002948 Official number: 2948	**496** 148 527	Class: AB	**2004-12 Sealink Shipyard Sdn Bhd — Miri** Yd No: 110 Loa 48.00 Br ex - Dght 2.500 Lbp 46.20 Br md 11.00 Dpth 3.50 Welded, 1 dk	**(B21A2OS) Platform Supply Ship**	**2 oil engines** geared to sc. shafts driving 2 FP propellers Total Power: 1,790kW (2,434hp) Cummins KTA-38-M2 2 x Vee 4 Stroke 12 Cy. 159 x 159 each-895kW (1217bhp) Cummins Engine Co Inc-USA
9392406 *V7MP4* -	**TANUX III** *ex Sealink Vanessa 5 -2007* **Tanux Shipping KS** - *Majuro* *Marshall Islands* MMSI: 538002884 Official number: 2884	**496** 149 438	Class: AB	**2006-09 Sealink Shipyard Sdn Bhd — Miri** Yd No: 128 Loa 48.00 Br ex - Dght 2.500 Lbp 46.20 Br md 11.00 Dpth 3.50 Welded, 1 dk	**(B21A2OS) Platform Supply Ship**	**2 oil engines** reduction geared to sc. shafts driving 2 Propellers Total Power: 2,500kW (3,400hp) Cummins KTA-50-M2 2 x Vee 4 Stroke 16 Cy. 159 x 159 each-1250kW (1700bhp) Cummins Engine Co Inc-USA AuxGen: 2 x 150kW a.c Thrusters: 1 Tunnel thruster (f) Fuel: 150.1 (d.f.) 119.6 (r.f.)
8606379 *CNSV* -	**TANWACA 1** *ex Hala -2008* **Societe des Peches du Sud de l'Atlas** - SatCom: Inmarsat C 424232210 *Agadir* *Morocco*	*375* 151 400	Class: (BV)	**1989-02 Saint-Malo Naval — St-Malo** Yd No: 601 Loa 39.90 Br ex - Dght - Lbp 36.80 Br md 9.01 Dpth 3.95 Welded, 2 dks	**(B11A2FS) Stern Trawler**	**1 oil engine** reduction geared to sc. shaft driving 1 CP propeller Total Power: 929kW (1,263hp) 12.0kn Wartsila 6R22 1 x 4 Stroke 6 Cy. 220 x 240 929kW (1263bhp) Moteurs Duvant Crepelle-France AuxGen: 3 x 101kW 380V a.c
8606367 - -	**TANWACA 2** *ex Wassane -2008* **Societe des Peches du Sud de l'Atlas** - SatCom: Inmarsat C 424232510 *Agadir* *Morocco*	*375* 151 400	Class: (BV)	**1989-02 Ateliers et Chantiers de La Manche — Dieppe** Yd No: 501 Loa 39.91 Br ex 9.30 Dght 3.550 Lbp 35.32 Br md 9.00 Dpth 3.95 Welded, 2 dks	**(B11A2FS) Stern Trawler** Ins: 350	**1 oil engine** with clutches, flexible couplings & sr reverse geared to sc. shaft driving 1 FP propeller Total Power: 930kW (1,264hp) 12.0kn Wartsila 6R22 1 x 4 Stroke 6 Cy. 220 x 240 930kW (1264bhp) Moteurs Duvant Crepelle-France AuxGen: 2 x 280kW 380V a.c Fuel: 276.0 (d.f.)
8606381 *CNBM* -	**TANWACA 3** *ex Marouf -2008* **Societe des Peches du Sud de l'Atlas** - *Agadir* *Morocco*	*375* 151 400	Class: (BV)	**1989-04 Ateliers et Chantiers de La Manche — Dieppe** Yd No: 502 Loa 39.90 Br ex 9.30 Dght 3.550 Lbp 34.80 Br md 9.01 Dpth 6.25 Welded	**(B11A2FS) Stern Trawler** Ins: 350	**1 oil engine** with clutches, flexible couplings & sr reverse geared to sc. shaft driving 1 FP propeller Total Power: 684kW (930hp) 12.0kn Wartsila 6R22 1 x 4 Stroke 6 Cy. 220 x 240 684kW (930bhp) Wartsila Diesel Normed SA-France AuxGen: 3 x 101kW 220/380V a.c Fuel: 276.2
8606393 *CNTF* -	**TANWACA 4** *ex Imade -1989* **Societe des Peches du Sud de l'Atlas** - SatCom: Inmarsat C 424232310 *Agadir* *Morocco*	*375* 151 400	Class: (BV)	**1989-04 Ateliers et Chantiers de La Manche — Dieppe** (Hull launched by) Yd No: 1344 **1989-04 Saint-Malo Naval — St-Malo** (Hull completed by) Yd No: 602 Loa 39.91 Br ex - Dght - Lbp 36.81 Br md 9.01 Dpth 3.97 Welded	**(B11A2FS) Stern Trawler**	**1 oil engine** dr geared to sc. shaft driving 1 FP propeller Total Power: 930kW (1,264hp) 12.0kn Wartsila 6R22 1 x 4 Stroke 6 Cy. 220 x 240 930kW (1264bhp) Wartsila Diesel Normed SA-France AuxGen: 3 x 101kW 220/380V a.c Fuel: 276.0
8842648 *WDC8005* -	**TANYA KAIT** *ex Captain Kelly -2004* **C T Scallop Ventures LLC** - *Atlantic City, NJ* *United States of America* MMSI: 367080190 Official number: 907393	*137* 110 -		**1986 Horton Boats, Inc. — Bayou La Batre, Al** Yd No: 239 Loa - Br ex - Dght - Lbp 23.77 Br md 6.71 Dpth 3.66 Welded, 1 dk	**(B11A2FT) Trawler**	**1 oil engine** driving 1 FP propeller
8959269 *ISWY* -	**TANZANIA II** *ex Rubiera -2004* **Allibo Adriatico SpA** - *Chioggia* *Italy* Official number: CI 3576	*139* 66 100	Class: RI	**1967-10 Cant. Nav. Vittoria — Adria** Yd No: 120 Loa 23.58 Br ex - Dght - Lbp 21.86 Br md 6.79 Dpth 2.30 Welded, 1 dk	**(B32A2ST) Tug**	**2 oil engines** driving 2 FP propellers Total Power: 782kW (1,064hp) Deutz SBA8M816 1 x 4 Stroke 8 Cy. 142 x 160 391kW (532bhp) (, fitted 2008) Kloeckner Humboldt Deutz AG-West Germany AuxGen: 1 x 40kW 220V 50Hz a.c
9306122 *OT3354* -	**TANZANITE** - **Tank Reederei II SA** - *Antwerpen* *Belgium* MMSI: 205014600 Official number: 6004034	**2,011** - 4,165	Class: LR ✠ **A1** SS 07/2009 inland waterways chemical tanker, Type 'N' closed in association with a list of defined cargoes SG 1.0 pv+25kPa L.S.'T'. also for estuary service between Antwerp, Zeebrugge/Oostende, maximum 5 miles seaward, for a maximum significant wave height of 1.60 metres **LMC** **UMS** Cable: 330.0/36.0 U2 (a)	**2004-07 Hangzhou Dongfeng Shipbuilding Co Ltd — Hangzhou ZJ** (Hull) Yd No: 2002-38 **2004-07 de Gerlien-van Tiem B.V. — Druten** Yd No: 255 Loa 110.00 Br ex 13.60 Dght 4.200 Lbp 106.90 Br md 13.50 Dpth 5.32 Welded, 1 dk	**(A13B2TP) Products Tanker** Double Hull (13F) Liq: 4,700; Liq (Oil): 4,700 Compartments: 12 Wing Ta, ER	**1 oil engine** with clutches, flexible couplings & sr reverse geared to sc. shaft driving 1 FP propeller Total Power: 1,471kW (2,000hp) A.B.C. 8MDZC 1 x 4 Stroke 8 Cy. 256 x 310 1471kW (2000bhp) Anglo Belgian Corp NV (ABC)-Belgium AuxGen: 1 x 100kW 400V 50Hz a.c, 1 x 60kW 400V 50Hz a.c Boilers: TOH (o.f.) 10.2kgf/cm² (10.0bar) Thrusters: 2 Water jet (f)
9639696 *3FQQ6* -	**TAO ACE** - **Tao Ace SA** Wisdom Marine Lines SA *Panama* *Panama* MMSI: 353399000 Official number: 4504013	**15,289** 8,932 25,064	Class: NV (NK)	**2013-05 Murakami Hide Zosen K.K. — Imabari** Yd No: 590 Loa 158.15 (BB) Br ex 24.04 Dght 9.990 Lbp 149.80 Br md 24.00 Dpth 13.80 Welded, 1 dk	**(A21A2BC) Bulk Carrier** Grain: 33,154; Bale: 31,300 Compartments: 4 Ho, ER 4 Ha: ER Cranes: 4x25t	**1 oil engine** driving 1 FP propeller Total Power: 5,180kW (7,043hp) 13.2kn MAN-B&W 7S35MC 1 x 2 Stroke 7 Cy. 350 x 1400 5180kW (7043bhp) MAN Diesel A/S-Denmark AuxGen: 3 x a.c
9487586 *3FLN4* -	**TAO BRAVE** - **Tao Brave SA** Wisdom Marine Lines SA SatCom: Inmarsat C 435783910 *Panama* *Panama* MMSI: 357839000 Official number: 4245211	**15,243** 8,954 25,064	Class: GL (BV)	**2011-01 Murakami Hide Zosen K.K. — Imabari** Yd No: 577 Loa 158.15 (BB) Br ex - Dght 9.981 Lbp 149.81 Br md 24.00 Dpth 13.80 Welded, 1 dk	**(A21A2BC) Bulk Carrier** Grain: 33,154; Bale: 31,300 Compartments: 4 Ho, ER 5 Ha: Cranes: 4x30.7t	**1 oil engine** driving 1 FP propeller Total Power: 5,180kW (7,043hp) 13.2kn MAN-B&W 7S35MC 1 x 2 Stroke 7 Cy. 350 x 1400 5180kW (7043bhp) The Hanshin Diesel Works Ltd-Japan AuxGen: 3 x 400kW 445V a.c
9620504 *BOUE* -	**TAO HUA HAI** - **COSCO Bulk Carrier Co Ltd (COSCO BULK)** - SatCom: Inmarsat C 441407010 *Tianjin* *China* MMSI: 414070000 Official number: 020012000033	**64,654** 37,347 115,184	Class: CC	**2012-05 Shanghai Jiangnan Changxing Heavy Industry Co Ltd — Shanghai** Yd No: H1001A Loa 254.00 (BB) Br ex - Dght 14.500 Lbp 249.83 Br md 43.00 Dpth 20.80 Welded, 1 dk	**(A21A2BC) Bulk Carrier** Grain: 137,792; Bale: 132,246 Compartments: 7 Ho, ER 7 Ha: (18.3 x 21.0)4 (19.2 x 21.0) (16.5 x 21.0)ER (14.6 x 18.0)	**1 oil engine** driving 1 FP propeller Total Power: 13,080kW (17,784hp) 14.5kn Wartsila 6RT-flex58T 1 x 2 Stroke 6 Cy. 580 x 2416 13080kW (17784bhp) Doosan Engine Co Ltd-South Korea AuxGen: 3 x 720kW 450V a.c Fuel: 286.0 (d.f.) 3355.0 (r.f.)
9614062 *BPGO* -	**TAO LIN WAN** - **China Shipping Tanker Co Ltd** - *Shanghai* *China* MMSI: 414728000	**60,166** 34,623 110,929	Class: CC	**2012-09 Dalian Shipbuilding Industry Co Ltd — Dalian LN (No 2 Yard)** Yd No: PC1100-38 Loa 244.70 (BB) Br ex 42.03 Dght 12.000 Lbp 234.00 Br md 42.00 Dpth 21.60 Welded, 1 dk	**(A13A2TW) Crude/Oil Products Tanker** Double Hull (13F) Liq: 118,683; Liq (Oil): 118,000 Compartments: 6 Wing Ta, 6 Wing Ta, 1 Wing Slop Ta, 1 Wing Slop Ta, 1 Slop Ta, ER 3 Cargo Pump (s): 3x3000m³/hr Ice Capable	**1 oil engine** driving 1 FP propeller Total Power: 14,283kW (19,419hp) 15.3kn MAN-B&W 6S60ME-C 1 x 2 Stroke 6 Cy. 600 x 2400 14283kW (19419bhp) Dalian Marine Diesel Co Ltd-China Fuel: 185.0 (d.f.) 3365.0 (r.f.)

IMO / Call sign	Name / Owner / Manager / Flag	Tonnage	Class	Builder / Dimensions	Type / Cargo	Machinery
9487574 *3FBK* -	**TAO MARINER** **Tao Mariner SA** Wisdom Marine Lines SA *Panama* *Panama* MMSI: 356158000 Official number: 4218411	**15,243** 8,954 25,064	Class: GL (BV)	**2010**-10 **Murakami Hide Zosen K.K. — Imabari** Yd No: 576 Loa 158.15 (BB) Br ex - Dght 9.981 Lbp 149.81 Br md 24.00 Dpth 13.80 Welded, 1 dk	**(A21A2BC) Bulk Carrier** Grain: 33,154; Bale: 31,300 Compartments: 4 Ho, ER 4 Ha: ER Cranes: 4x30.7t	**1 oil engine** driving 1 FP propeller Total Power: 5,180kW (7,043hp) 13.2kn MAN-B&W 7S35MC 1 x 2 Stroke 7 Cy. 350 x 1400 5180kW (7043bhp) The Hanshin Diesel Works Ltd-Japan AuxGen: 3 x 400kW 445V a.c
9487562 *3FLP2* -	**TAO STAR** **Hakushin Kisen Co Ltd & Hakushin Panama SA** Wisdom Marine Lines SA SatCom: Inmarsat C 435592710 *Panama* *Panama* MMSI: 355927000 Official number: 4188410	**15,243** 8,954 25,064	Class: GL (BV)	**2010**-08 **Murakami Hide Zosen K.K. — Imabari** Yd No: 575 Loa 158.15 (BB) Br ex - Dght 9.990 Lbp 149.80 Br md 24.00 Dpth 13.80 Welded, 1 dk	**(A21A2BC) Bulk Carrier** Grain: 33,154; Bale: 31,300 Compartments: 4 Ho, ER 4 Ha: ER Cranes: 4x30.7t	**1 oil engine** driving 1 FP propeller Total Power: 5,180kW (7,043hp) 13.2kn MAN-B&W 7S35MC 1 x 2 Stroke 7 Cy. 350 x 1400 5180kW (7043bhp) The Hanshin Diesel Works Ltd-Japan AuxGen: 3 x 400kW 445V 60Hz a.c
9639701 *3FXS5* -	**TAO TREASURE** **Tao Treasure SA** Wisdom Marine Lines SA *Panama* *Panama* MMSI: 355690000 Official number: 44859TT	**15,289** 8,932 25,035	Class: NK	**2013**-08 **Murakami Hide Zosen K.K. — Imabari** Yd No: 591 Loa 158.15 (BB) Br ex - Dght 9.990 Lbp 149.80 Br md 24.00 Dpth 13.80 Welded, 1 dk	**(A21A2BC) Bulk Carrier** Grain: 33,154; Bale: 31,300 Compartments: 4 Ho, ER 4 Ha: ER Cranes: 4x25t	**1 oil engine** driving 1 FP propeller Total Power: 5,180kW (7,043hp) 13.2kn MAN-B&W 7S35MC 1 x 2 Stroke 7 Cy. 350 x 1400 5180kW (7043bhp) The Hanshin Diesel Works Ltd-Japan AuxGen: 3 x 400kW a.c Fuel: 1171.0
7738058 - -	**TAO YU** **Chinese Petroleum Corp -Taoyuan Refinery** - *Keelung* *Chinese Taipei* Official number: 7179	*114* 33 -	Class: CR	**1978 Taiwan Machinery Manufacturing Corp. — Kaohsiung** Loa 24.20 Br ex 7.51 Dght 1.842 Lbp 23.00 Br md 7.50 Dpth 2.60 Welded, 1 dk	**(B32A2ST) Tug**	**2 oil engines** driving 2 FP propellers Total Power: 570kW (774hp) MWM TBD601-6K 2 x 4 Stroke 6 Cy. 160 x 165 each-285kW (387bhp) Motoren Werke Mannheim AG (MWM)-West Germany AuxGen: 2 x 32kW 230/130V a.c
8417106 - -	**TAO YU No. 2** **Chinese Petroleum Corp -Taoyuan Refinery** - *Keelung* *Chinese Taipei* Official number: 9565	**114** 34 -	Class: CR	**1985**-10 **Taiwan Machinery Manufacturing Corp. — Kaohsiung** Yd No: 6394 Loa 24.20 Br ex 7.70 Dght 1.720 Lbp 23.00 Br md 7.50 Dpth 2.60 Welded, 1 dk	**(B32A2ST) Tug**	**2 oil engines** with clutches, flexible couplings & sr geared to sc. shafts driving 2 Directional propellers Total Power: 570kW (774hp) 10.0kn MWM TBD601-6K 2 x 4 Stroke 6 Cy. 160 x 165 each-285kW (387bhp) Motoren Werke Mannheim AG (MWM)-West Germany AuxGen: 2 x 42kW 220V 60Hz a.c Fuel: 83.5 (d.f.) 4.5pd
9078024 *BP3001* -	**TAO YU No. 3** **CPC Corp Taiwan** - *Keelung* *Chinese Taipei* MMSI: 416900040 Official number: 12625	**471** 141 223	Class: CR	**1994**-08 **Lien Ho Shipbuilding Co, Ltd — Kaohsiung** Yd No: 057 Loa 33.00 Br ex - Dght 3.700 Lbp 32.00 Br md 11.70 Dpth 5.20 Welded, 1 dk	**(B32A2ST) Tug**	**2 oil engines** with clutches, flexible couplings & sr geared to sc. shafts driving 2 Directional propellers Total Power: 2,648kW (3,600hp) Nohab 6R25 2 x 4 Stroke 6 Cy. 250 x 300 each-1324kW (1800bhp) Wartsila Diesel AB-Sweden
9108893 *BRVJ* -	**TAO YUAN** **Shanghai Inchon International Ferry Co Ltd** Shanghai Puhai Shipping Co Ltd *Shanghai* *China* MMSI: 412051430	**7,065** 3,322 9,946	Class: CC	**1995**-11 **Qiuxin Shipyard — Shanghai** Yd No: 1234 Loa 121.20 (BB) Br ex - Dght 7.970 Lbp 112.00 Br md 20.80 Dpth 10.50 Welded, 1 dk	**(A33A2CC) Container Ship (Fully Cellular)** TEU 504 C Ho 238 TEU C Dk 266 TEU incl 30 ref C. Cranes: 5	**1 oil engine** reduction geared to sc. shaft driving 1 FP propeller Total Power: 5,400kW (7,342hp) 15.5kn MaK 8M552C 1 x 4 Stroke 8 Cy. 450 x 520 5400kW (7342bhp) Krupp MaK Maschinenbau GmbH-Kiel
7210939 *BVAM* -	**TAO YUAN No. 31** **Tao Yuan Marine Products Co Ltd** - *Kaohsiung* *Chinese Taipei*	*269* 184 -	Class: (CR)	**1972 Chung Yi Shipbuilding Corp. — Kaohsiung** Loa 38.00 Br ex 6.94 Dght 2.750 Lbp 33.00 Br md 6.91 Dpth 3.15 Welded, 1 dk	**(B11B2FV) Fishing Vessel** Ins: 261 Compartments: 3 Ho, ER 4 Ha: 2 (1.2 x 0.9)2 (1.2 x 1.2)ER Derricks: 1x1t	**1 oil engine** driving 1 FP propeller Total Power: 478kW (650hp) 10.0kn Hanshin 6L26ASH 1 x 4 Stroke 6 Cy. 260 x 400 478kW (650bhp) Hanshin Nainenki Kogyo-Japan AuxGen: 2 x 80kW 230V a.c
7211024 *BECF* -	**TAO YUAN No. 51** **Tao Yuan Marine Products Co Ltd** - *Kaohsiung* *Chinese Taipei*	*269* 184 -	Class: (CR)	**1972 Chung Yi Shipbuilding Corp. — Kaohsiung** Loa 38.00 Br ex 6.94 Dght 2.750 Lbp 33.00 Br md 6.91 Dpth 3.15 Welded, 1 dk	**(B11B2FV) Fishing Vessel** Ins: 261 Compartments: 3 Ho, ER 5 Ha: 2 (1.2 x 0.9)2 (1.2 x 1.2) (0.9 x 0.9)ER Derricks: 1x1t	**1 oil engine** driving 1 FP propeller Total Power: 478kW (650hp) 10.0kn Akasaka 6MH25SSR 1 x 4 Stroke 6 Cy. 250 x 400 478kW (650bhp) Akasaka Tekkosho KK (Akasaka DieselLtd)-Japan AuxGen: 2 x 80kW 230V a.c
9338577 *3EQV2* -	**TAOKAS WISDOM** **Taokas Wisdom SA** Wisdom Marine Lines SA SatCom: Inmarsat C 437105010 *Panama* *Panama* MMSI: 371050000 Official number: 3398408A	**19,822** 10,514 31,943 T/cm 45.1	Class: NK	**2008**-04 **The Hakodate Dock Co Ltd — Hakodate HK** Yd No: 818 Loa 175.53 (BB) Br ex - Dght 9.640 Lbp 167.00 Br md 29.40 Dpth 13.70 Welded, 1 dk	**(A21A2BC) Bulk Carrier** Double Hull Grain: 42,620; Bale: 39,627 Compartments: 5 Ho, ER 5 Ha: ER Cranes: 4x30t	**1 oil engine** driving 1 FP propeller Total Power: 6,840kW (9,300hp) 14.5kn Mitsubishi 6UEC52LA 1 x 2 Stroke 6 Cy. 520 x 1600 6840kW (9300bhp) Akasaka Tekkosho KK (Akasaka DieselLtd)-Japan AuxGen: 4 x 316kW a.c Fuel: 1450.0
9277917 *VRYP8* -	**TAP MUN** **Hongkong United Dockyards Ltd** The Hongkong Salvage & Towage Co Ltd *Hong Kong* *Hong Kong* Official number: HK-1030	**231** - 102	Class: LR ✠ **100A1** SS 07/2013 Hong Kong harbour service ✠ **LMC** Eq.Ltr: E; Cable: 302.5/22.0 U2 (a)	**2003**-07 **Kegoya Dock K.K. — Kure** Yd No: 1080 Loa 25.20 Br ex 9.12 Dght 3.750 Lbp 19.80 Br md 8.50 Dpth 4.70 Welded, 1 dk	**(B32A2ST) Tug**	**2 oil engines** gearing integral to driving 2 Z propellers Total Power: 2,354kW (3,200hp) 12.4kn Niigata 6L25HX 2 x 4 Stroke 6 Cy. 250 x 350 each-1177kW (1600bhp) Niigata Engineering Co Ltd-Japan AuxGen: 2 x 64kW 385V 50Hz a.c
8325729 *D3R2336* -	**TAPADO** **Empresa Nacional de Abastecimiento Tecnico Material a Industria de Pesca (ENATIP)** - *Luanda* *Angola* Official number: 671	*162* 51 -	Class: (BV)	**1985**-11 **Soc. Esercizio Cant. S.p.A. — Viareggio** Yd No: 671 Loa 30.10 Br ex - Dght 2.801 Lbp 23.91 Br md 7.21 Dpth 5.47 Welded, 1 dk	**(B11B2FV) Fishing Vessel**	**1 oil engine** with flexible couplings & sr reverse geared to sc. shaft driving 1 FP propeller Total Power: 625kW (850hp) 11.8kn Caterpillar D398SCAC 1 x Vee 4 Stroke 12 Cy. 159 x 203 625kW (850bhp) Caterpillar Tractor Co-USA Thrusters: 1 Thwart. FP thruster (f)
7039139 *FIPO* -	**TAPATAI** *ex Silver Fish -1980* **Government of The Republic of France (Direction Centre Exp Nucleaire)** - *France*	*240* 69 203	Class: (BV)	**1971 Chantiers et Ateliers de La Perriere — Lorient** Yd No: 365 Loa 41.15 Br ex 7.57 Dght 3.001 Lbp 38.51 Br md 7.51 Dpth 3.79 Welded, 1 dk	**(B21B20A) Anchor Handling Tug Supply**	**2 oil engines** reduction geared to sc. shafts driving 2 CP propellers Total Power: 1,544kW (2,100hp) 14.5kn Polar SF16RS-F 2 x 4 Stroke 6 Cy. 250 x 300 each-772kW (1050bhp) AB NOHAB-Sweden AuxGen: 2 x 102kW 220/380V 50Hz a.c Thrusters: 1 Thwart. FP thruster (f) Fuel: 63.0 (d.f.)
9239977 *A8NW6* -	**TAPATIO** **Partankers VII AS** Laurin Maritime (America) Inc *Monrovia* *Liberia* MMSI: 636011885 Official number: 13575	**26,914** 14,228 46,764 T/cm 52.8	Class: NV	**2003**-10 **Brodotrogir dd - Shipyard Trogir — Trogir** Yd No: 304 Loa 182.90 (BB) Br ex 32.22 Dght 12.180 Lbp 176.00 Br md 32.20 Dpth 17.20 Welded, 1 dk	**(A12B2TR) Chemical/Products Tanker** Double Hull (13F) Liq: 52,969; Liq (Oil): 52,969 Compartments: 14 Wing Ta, 2 Wing Slop Ta, ER 14 Cargo Pump (s): 6x400m³/hr, 8x250m³/hr Manifold: Bow/CM: 91.5m	**2 oil engines** with clutches, flexible couplings & dr geared to sc. shaft driving 1 CP propeller Total Power: 7,680kW (10,442hp) 14.5kn MaK 8M32C 2 x 4 Stroke 8 Cy. 320 x 480 each-3840kW (5221bhp) Caterpillar Motoren GmbH & Co. KG-Germany AuxGen: 2 x a.c, 1 x a.c
6913534 *ATOM* -	**TAPI** **Government of The Republic of India (Ministry of Industry & Civil Supplies)** Mazagon Dock Ltd *Mumbai* *India* Official number: 1681	*179* 36 70	Class: IR (LR) ✠ Classed LR until 21/7/93	**1976**-10 **Alcock, Ashdown & Co. Ltd. — Bhavnagar** (Hull launched by) Yd No: B607/63 **1976**-10 **Mazagon Dock Ltd. — Mumbai** (Hull completed by) Yd No: B607/63 Loa 32.31 Br ex 8.67 Dght 3.283 Lbp 28.66 Br md 8.03 Dpth 3.81 Riveted\Welded, 1 dk	**(B32A2ST) Tug**	**2 oil engines** reverse reduction geared to sc. shafts driving 2 FP propellers Total Power: 824kW (1,120hp) MAN G6V30/45ATL 2 x 4 Stroke 6 Cy. 300 x 450 each-412kW (560bhp) Dok en Werf Mij. Wilton FijenoordB.V.-Schiedam AuxGen: 1 x 52kW 115V d.c, 1 x 15kW 115V d.c Fuel: 45.5
8617550 *DUA2909* -	**TAPILON** *ex Arrows Maru No. 3 -2000* **Delsan Transport Lines Inc** Astra Shipmanagement Corp *Manila* *Philippines* Official number: 00-0001374	*793* 573 2,060	Class: (NK)	**1986**-11 **Iwagi Zosen Co Ltd — Kamijima EH** Yd No: 115 Loa 74.30 Br ex - Dght 4.770 Lbp 70.01 Br md 11.21 Dpth 5.41 Welded, 1 dk	**(A13B2TP) Products Tanker** Liq: 2,027; Liq (Oil): 2,027	**1 oil engine** driving 1 FP propeller Total Power: 1,177kW (1,600hp) Akasaka A28FD 1 x 4 Stroke 6 Cy. 280 x 550 1177kW (1600bhp) Akasaka Tekkosho KK (Akasaka DieselLtd)-Japan Fuel: 75.0 (r.f.)

7940766 - -	**TAPILU I** *ex* Garrapatero I **Pesquera Tapilu SA de CV** - *Mazatlan* *Mexico*	*104* 53 -	Class: (AB)	**1976 Astilleros Monarca S.A. — Guaymas** Yd No: 570 Loa - Br ex - Dght - Lbp 20.93 Br md 6.05 Dpth 3.10 Welded, 1 dk	**(B11A2FT) Trawler** Compartments: 1 Ho, ER 1 Ha: (2.1 x 1.3)	**1 oil engine** reverse reduction geared to sc. shaft driving 1 FP propeller Total Power: 268kW (364hp) 9.0kn Caterpillar D343TA 1 x 4 Stroke 6 Cy. 137 x 165 268kW (364bhp) Caterpillar Tractor Co-USA AuxGen: 1 x 3kW d.c, 1 x 1kW d.c
7521912 *FNNA* -	**TAPORO IX** *ex* Coast Trader *-2007* *ex* Nordvik *-2006* *ex* Stenfjell *-2004* *ex* Fjell *-1985* **Compagnie Francaise Maritime de Tahiti** - *Papeete* *France* MMSI: 546012200	**2,818** 1,031 2,818	Class: BV (GL)	**1976-06 Fosen Mek. Verksteder AS — Rissa** Yd No: 17 Lengthened-1989 Loa 87.00 Br ex 14.53 Dght 5.090 Lbp 80.40 Br md 14.51 Dpth 9.40 Welded, 2 dks pt 3rd dk	**(A31B2GP) Palletised Cargo Ship** Side door (s) Grain: 6,962; Bale: 6,597; Ins: 566 TEU 90 C. 90/20' Compartments: 1 Ho, ER 1 Ha: (13.2 x 6.2)ER Cranes: 1x40t; Derricks: 1x40t Ice Capable	**1 oil engine** driving 1 CP propeller Total Power: 2,207kW (3,001hp) 13.0kn Wichmann 9AXAG 1 x 2 Stroke 9 Cy. 300 x 450 2207kW (3001bhp) Wichmann Motorfabrikk AS-Norway AuxGen: 2 x 168kW 380V 50Hz a.c Thrusters: 1 Thwart. FP thruster (f) Fuel: 188.5 (d.f.)
7521948 *FQXB* -	**TAPORO VI** *ex* Nordic *-1992* *ex* Nordvaer *-1988* **Compagnie Francaise Maritime de Tahiti** - *Papeete* *France* MMSI: 227007200	*497* 246 1,200	Class: (NV) (BV)	**1977-10 Fosen Mek. Verksteder AS — Rissa** Yd No: 20 Loa 69.60 Br ex 14.51 Dght 4.471 Lbp 63.00 Br md - Dpth 9.40 Welded, 3 dks	**(A31B2GP) Palletised Cargo Ship** Side door (s) Grain: 4,176; Bale: 4,174; Ins: 425 TEU 38 C. 38/20' Compartments: 1 Ho, ER 1 Ha: (13.3 x 6.3)ER Cranes: 1x8t; Derricks: 1x40t; Winches: 1 Ice Capable	**1 oil engine** driving 1 FP propeller Total Power: 2,207kW (3,001hp) 13.5kn Normo KVM-16 1 x Vee 4 Stroke 16 Cy. 250 x 300 2207kW (3001bhp) AS Bergens Mek Verksteder-Norway AuxGen: 2 x 168kW 380V 50Hz a.c Thrusters: 1 Thwart. FP thruster (f)
7525360 *FNPF* -	**TAPORO VII** *ex* Rogaland *-2001* **Compagnie Francaise Maritime de Tahiti** - *Papeete* *France* MMSI: 228139800 Official number: 862768	**2,420** 726 1,533	Class: BV (NV)	**1978-07 Fosen Mek. Verksteder AS — Rissa** Yd No: 21 Lengthened-1981 Loa 80.40 (BB) Br ex 14.53 Dght 4.471 Lbp 63.00 Br md 14.48 Dpth 9.38 Welded, 3 dks	**(A31B2GP) Palletised Cargo Ship** Side door (s) Grain: 4,245; Bale: 4,177; Ins: 566 TEU 58 C. 58/20' Compartments: 1 Ho, ER 1 Ha: (13.1 x 6.1)ER Cranes: 1x8t; Derricks: 1x40t; Winches: 2 Ice Capable	**1 oil engine** sr geared to sc. shaft driving 1 CP propeller Total Power: 2,207kW (3,001hp) 14.0kn Wichmann 9AXA 1 x 2 Stroke 9 Cy. 300 x 450 2207kW (3001bhp) Wichmann Motorfabrikk AS-Norway AuxGen: 3 x 168kW 380V 50Hz a.c Thrusters: 1 Thwart. FP thruster (f) Fuel: 200.0 (d.f.) 8.0pd
8115100 *FMAP* -	**TAPORO VIII** *ex* Highland Carrier *-2004* *ex* Trinity Bay *-1998* *ex* Leichhardt *-1990* **Compagnie Francaise Maritime de Tahiti** - *Papeete* *France* MMSI: 546006000 Official number: 925677	**1,832** 549 1,266	Class: BV (LR) (NV) ✠ Classed LR until 30/4/04	**1981-12 Ube Dockyard Co. Ltd. — Ube** (Hull) Yd No: 169 **1981-12 Kasado Dockyard Co Ltd — Kudamatsu YC** Yd No: 325 Loa 64.01 Br ex 14.53 Dght 3.712 Lbp 59.39 Br md 14.51 Dpth 8.01 Welded, 2 dks	**(A35A2RR) Ro-Ro Cargo Ship** Stern ramp (a) Len: 3.58 Wid: 5.00 Swl: - Stern door & ramp (a) Len: 13.70 Wid: 5.50 Swl: - Grain: 2,311; Bale: 2,039 TEU 46 C.Ho 10/20' C.Dk 36/20' incl. 16 ref C. Compartments: 1 Ho, ER 1 Ha: (13.5 x 5.8)ER Cranes: 1x25t	**2 oil engines** dr geared to sc. shafts driving 2 Directional propellers Total Power: 1,324kW (1,800hp) 11.0kn Daihatsu 6DSM-22 2 x 4 Stroke 6 Cy. 220 x 280 each-662kW (900bhp) Daihatsu Diesel Manufacturing Co Lt-Japan AuxGen: 3 x 240kW 420V 50Hz a.c Thrusters: 2 Directional thruster (f) Fuel: 140.0 (d.f.) 6.0pd
9647435 *ZMG2705* -	**TAPUHI** - **CentrePort Ltd** - *Wellington* *New Zealand* MMSI: 512003558 Official number: 11256	**250** 75 125	Class: LR ✠ **100A1** SS 03/2013 tug *IWS **LMC** **UMS** Eq.Ltr: F; Cable: 275.0/19.0 U2 (a)	**2013-03 Damen Shipyards Changde Co Ltd — Changde HN** (Hull) Yd No: (512264) **2013-03 B.V. Scheepswerf Damen — Gorinchem** Yd No: 512264 Loa 24.47 Br ex 11.33 Dght 5.350 Lbp 22.16 Br md 10.70 Dpth 4.59 Welded, 1 dk	**(B32A2ST) Tug**	**2 oil engines** gearing integral to driving 2 Directional propellers Total Power: 4,200kW (5,710hp) 11.8kn Caterpillar 3516C 2 x Vee 4 Stroke 16 Cy. 170 x 190 each-2100kW (2855bhp) Caterpillar Inc-USA AuxGen: 2 x 68kW 400V 50Hz a.c
9501174 *V7Z14*	**TAQAH** - **Taqah Maritime Transportation Co Ltd** Oman Shipping Co SAOC *Majuro* *Marshall Islands* MMSI: 538004833 Official number: 4833	**162,960** 107,929 316,373 T/cm 178.1	Class: AB (LR) ✠ Classed LR until 15/10/12	**2012-10 Hyundai Heavy Industries Co Ltd — Ulsan** Yd No: 2250 Loa 333.14 (BB) Br ex 60.05 Dght 22.625 Lbp 319.00 Br md 60.00 Dpth 30.40 Welded, 1 dk	**(A13A2TV) Crude Oil Tanker** Double Hull (13F) Liq: 337,180; Liq (Oil): 317,000 Compartments: 5 Ta, 10 Wing Ta, ER, 2 Wing Slop Ta 3 Cargo Pump (s): 3x5000m³/hr Manifold: Bow/CM: 166m	**1 oil engine** driving 1 FP propeller Total Power: 31,640kW (43,018hp) 15.5kn Wartsila 7RT-flex82T 1 x 2 Stroke 7 Cy. 820 x 3375 31640kW (43018bhp) Wartsila Hyundai Engine Co Ltd-South Korea AuxGen: 3 x 1400kW 450V 60Hz a.c Boilers: e (ex.g.) 24.3kgf/cm² (23.8bar), WTAuxB (o.f.) 20.3kgf/cm² (19.9bar) Fuel: 1049.8 (d.f.) 9296.0 (r.f.)
7718400 *YEUK*	**TAQWA** *ex* Oleochem 1 *-1994* *ex* Asean Maru *-1993* *ex* Geinan Maru *-1992* *ex* Shuko Maru *-1983* **PT Tankindo Perdana** - *Jakarta* *Indonesia*	**746** 230 1,164	Class: (KI) (BV)	**1977-09 Kyoei Zosen KK — Mihara HS** Yd No: 77 Loa 61.42 Br ex - Dght 3.940 Lbp 56.00 Br md 9.80 Dpth 4.45 Welded, 1 dk	**(A12A2TC) Chemical Tanker** Liq: 877 Cargo Heating Coils 4 Cargo Pump (s): 4x220m³/hr	**1 oil engine** driving 1 FP propeller Total Power: 1,324kW (1,800hp) Akasaka DM36 1 x 4 Stroke 6 Cy. 360 x 540 1324kW (1800bhp) Akasaka Tekkosho KK (Akasaka DieselLtd)-Japan
8026969 - -	**TAR SHIEH** - **China Merchants Steam Navigation Co Ltd** - *Kaohsiung* *Chinese Taipei*	*109* 78 -		**1980-07 Taiwan Machinery Manufacturing Corp. — Kaohsiung** Loa 26.52 Br ex - Dght 2.101 Lbp 24.29 Br md 6.01 Dpth 2.49 Welded, 1 dk	**(B34J2SD) Crew Boat**	**2 oil engines** driving 2 FP propellers Total Power: 280kW (380hp) 9.0kn Isuzu E120-MF6R 2 x 4 Stroke 6 Cy. 135 x 140 each-140kW (190bhp) Isuzu Marine Engine Inc-Japan
7607417 *XUAB3* -	**TARA** *ex* Ranim *-2003* *ex* Gudrun Danielsen *-2003* *ex* Kaloum *-1984* *ex* Gudrun Danielsen *-1982* **Mariposa Maritime Co** Hamza Shipping Co SatCom: Inmarsat C 451541010 *Phnom Penh* *Cambodia* MMSI: 515410000 Official number: 0377006	**2,622** 1,637 3,705	Class: IV (BV)	**1977-11 E.J. Smit & Zoon's Scheepswerven B.V. — Westerbroek** Yd No: 815 Loa 82.81 Br ex - Dght 6.111 Lbp 74.53 Br md 15.02 Dpth 8.82 Welded, 2 dks	**(A31A2GX) General Cargo Ship** Grain: 5,945; Bale: 5,377 Compartments: 1 Ho, ER 2 Ha: 2 (19.2 x 10.5)ER Derricks: 2x25t,2x10t Ice Capable	**1 oil engine** dr geared to sc. shaft driving 1 FP propeller Total Power: 1,765kW (2,400hp) 13.8kn MaK 8M452AK 1 x 4 Stroke 8 Cy. 320 x 450 1765kW (2400bhp) MaK Maschinenbau GmbH-Kiel AuxGen: 4 x 81kW 380V 50Hz a.c
7344247 *AVPX*	**TARA** - **Zeba & Sabah Associates** - *Kolkata* *India* MMSI: 419000419 Official number: 1416	*511* - -		**1977-01 Garden Reach Workshops Ltd. — Kolkata** Yd No: 870 Loa 37.80 Br ex - Dght 3.722 Lbp 36.94 Br md 10.09 Dpth 4.27 Welded, 1 dk	**(B32A2ST) Tug**	**2 oil engines** reverse reduction geared to sc. shaft driving 1 FP propeller Total Power: 992kW (1,348hp) MAN G5V30/45ATL 2 x 4 Stroke 5 Cy. 300 x 450 each-496kW (674bhp) Garden Reach Shipbuilders &Engineers Ltd-India
8817552 *FVNM* -	**TARA** *ex* Tara V *-2009* *ex* Seamaster *-2004* *ex* Antartica *-2000* *ex* U. A. P. *-1991* **Fonds Tara** - *Marseille* *France (FIS)* MMSI: 226070000 Official number: 748443A	**168** 50 -	Class: BV	**1989-05 Soc. Francaise de Cons. Nav. — Villeneuve-la-Garenne** Yd No: 857 Loa 34.29 Br ex 9.75 Dght 1.150 Lbp 28.80 Br md 7.20 Dpth 2.95 Welded, 1 dk	**(B31A2SR) Research Survey Vessel** Hull Material: Aluminium Alloy	**2 oil engines** with flexible couplings & dr reverse geared to sc. shafts driving 2 FP propellers Total Power: 550kW (748hp) 10.0kn MWM TBD234V8 2 x Vee 4 Stroke 8 Cy. 128 x 140 each-275kW (374bhp) Motoren Werke Mannheim AG (MWM)-West Germany AuxGen: 1 x 30kW 220V 50Hz a.c
8960153 *UFQZ* -	**TARA-1** *ex* Kola Beldy *-2002* *ex* Volgoneft-161 *-2002* **Palmali Co Ltd** - *Taganrog* *Russia* MMSI: 273448030	**3,515** 1,150 4,889	Class: RS (RR)	**1982-03 Shipbuilding & Shiprepairing Yard 'Ivan Dimitrov' — Rousse** Yd No: 096 Loa 132.60 Br ex 16.90 Dght 3.510 Lbp 125.50 Br md 16.52 Dpth 5.52 Welded, 1 dk	**(A13B2TP) Products Tanker** Double Hull Liq: 6,775; Liq (Oil): 6,775 Compartments: 12 Ta, ER 2 Cargo Pump (s): 2x500m³/hr Ice Capable	**2 oil engines** driving 2 FP propellers Total Power: 1,472kW (2,002hp) S.K.L. 8NVD48AU 2 x 4 Stroke 8 Cy. 320 x 480 each-736kW (1001bhp) VEB Schwermaschinenbau "KarlLiebknecht" (SKL)-Magdeburg AuxGen: 3 x 300kW a.c Fuel: 75.0 (d.f.)
7503544 *EPAT7* -	**TARA 1** *ex* 1 Hurizan *-2002* **Mohsen Najafian** - *Khorramshahr* *Iran* MMSI: 422011600 Official number: 20679	*486* 292 1,000	Class: (LR) (IN) ✠ Classed LR until 26/8/92	**1975-08 Yamanishi Shipbuilding Co Ltd — Ishinomaki MG** Yd No: 796 Converted From: Oil Tanker-1975 Rebuilt Loa 50.30 Br ex 12.37 Dght 2.700 Lbp 49.30 Br md 12.01 Dpth 3.30 Welded, 1 dk	**(A35D2RL) Landing Craft** Liq: 1,872; Liq (Oil): 1,872 Compartments: 8 Ta, ER	**1 oil engine** driving 1 FP propeller Total Power: 809kW (1,100hp) Akasaka AH27 1 x 4 Stroke 6 Cy. 270 x 420 809kW (1100bhp) Akasaka Tekkosho KK (Akasaka DieselLtd)-Japan AuxGen: 2 x 60kW 225V 50Hz a.c Fuel: 56.0 (d.f.)

7011369 *DZXP* -	**TARA 1** *ex* Central Luzon *-1989* *ex* Birka *-1981* **DMC Construction Equipment Resources Inc** - *Batangas* *Philippines* Official number: ZAM2000117	*1,130* 738 2,530	Class: (LR) (BV) ✠ Classed LR until 7/84	**1970-04 N.V. Scheepswerf en Machinefabriek "De Biesbosch" — Dordrecht** Yd No: 530 Converted From: Container Ship (Fully Cellular)-1977 Loa 81.60 Br ex 14.28 Dght 5.028 Lbp 74.35 Br md 14.20 Dpth 7.70 Welded, 2 dks	**(A31A2GX) General Cargo Ship** Grain: 3,646; Bale: 3,541 Compartments: 1 Ho, ER 1 Ha: (50.6 x 10.5)Tappered ER Cranes: 1x360t; Derricks: 2x16t	**1 oil engine** driving 1 FP propeller Total Power: 1,765kW (2,400hp) 13.6kn MaK 6M551AK 1 x 4 Stroke 6 Cy. 450 x 550 1765kW (2400bhp) Atlas MaK Maschinenbau GmbH-Kiel AuxGen: 3 x 120kW 380V 50Hz a.c Fuel: 203.0 (r.f.)
9088988 - -	**TARA BAI** - **Government of The Republic of India (Coast Guard)** - *Chennai* *India*	*273* 71 56	Class: (AB) (IR)	**1987 Singapore Slipway & Engineering Co. Pte Ltd — Singapore** Yd No: B0192 Loa 44.90 Br ex - Dght 2.600 Lbp 42.30 Br md 7.00 Dpth 3.90 Welded, 1 dk	**(B34H2SQ) Patrol Vessel**	**2 oil engines** sr geared to sc. shafts driving 2 FP propellers Total Power: 2,960kW (4,024hp) 24.0kn M.T.U. 12V538TB82 2 x Vee 4 Stroke 12 Cy. 185 x 200 each-1480kW (2012bhp) MTU Friedrichshafen GmbH-Friedrichshafen AuxGen: 2 x 100kW 415V 50Hz a.c Fuel: 30.0 (d.f.)
8648468 *WDD4446* -	**TARA CROSBY** *ex* El Pato Grande *-2010* **Crosby Marine Transportation LLC** Crosby Tugs LLC *New Orleans, LA* *United States of America* MMSI: 367144810 Official number: 542118	**332** 99 -		**1972-08 Houma Welders Inc — Houma LA** Yd No: 27 Rebuilt-2009 Loa 30.46 Br ex - Dght 4.300 Lbp - Br md 8.99 Dpth 4.84 Welded, 1 dk	**(B32A2ST) Tug**	**2 oil engines** reduction geared to sc. shafts driving 2 FP propellers Total Power: 1,790kW (2,434hp) EMD (Electro-Motive) 12-645 BC 1 x Vee 2 Stroke 12 Cy. 230 x 254 895kW (1217bhp) General Motors Corp-USA EMD (Electro-Motive) 12-645-C 1 x Vee 2 Stroke 12 Cy. 230 x 254 895kW (1217bhp) General Motors Corp-USA AuxGen: 2 x 75kW 60Hz a.c
7232597 *WYZ7255* -	**TARA DARLENE** *ex* Lady Ashley *-2005* *ex* Capt. Ca *-2004* *ex* Mr. Tom *-1992* **Edward D Ross Jr** - *New Orleans, LA* *United States of America* Official number: 538544	*125* 85 -		**1972 Desco Marine — Saint Augustine, Fl** Yd No: 109-F L reg 20.97 Br ex 6.74 Dght - Lbp - Br md - Dpth 3.81 Bonded, 1 dk	**(B11B2FV) Fishing Vessel** Hull Material: Reinforced Plastic Ins: 45	**1 oil engine** driving 1 FP propeller Total Power: 268kW (364hp) Caterpillar 3408TA 1 x Vee 4 Stroke 8 Cy. 137 x 152 268kW (364bhp) Caterpillar Tractor Co-USA
8647830 - -	**TARA EAGLE** *ex* Pingvinen *-2009* **Ekoh Consulting Services Inc & Great Eagle Maritime International Ltd** Great Eagle Maritime International Ltd *Lagos* *Nigeria*	**143** 42 -		**1975-03 Lunde Varv & Verkstads AB — Ramvik** Yd No: 147 Converted From: Torpedo Recovery Vessel-2011 Loa 33.00 Br ex 6.50 Dght 3.380 Lbp 31.35 Br md 6.10 Dpth - Welded, 1 dk	**(X11A2YP) Yacht**	**2 oil engines** reduction geared to sc. shafts driving 2 Propellers Total Power: 1,442kW (1,960hp) M.T.U. 8V331TC92 2 x Vee 4 Stroke 8 Cy. 165 x 155 each-721kW (980bhp) (new engine 2011) MTU Friedrichshafen GmbH-Friedrichshafen
9198757 - -	**TARA HIJAU I** *ex* Many No. 1 *-2006* **PT Taruna Cipta Kencana** *Indonesia*	**119** 35 241	Class: (CC)	**1998-09 Guangdong Jiangmen Shipyard Co Ltd — Jiangmen GD** Yd No: 61 Loa 23.80 Br ex 7.22 Dght 3.089 Lbp 22.34 Br md 6.82 Dpth 3.64 Welded, 1 dk	**(B32A2ST) Tug**	**1 oil engine** geared to sc. shaft driving 1 FP propeller Total Power: 883kW (1,201hp) Cummins KTA-38-M2 1 x Vee 4 Stroke 12 Cy. 159 x 159 883kW (1201bhp) Chongqing Cummins Engine Co Ltd-China
7424009 *VWLC* -	**TARA KIRAN** *ex* Bhoruka 2 *-2005* *ex* Bente Folmer *-1986* *ex* Bente Frem *-1982* **Sapthagiri Shipping Co Ltd** Mak Lines *Mumbai* *India* MMSI: 419022200 Official number: 2184	**539** 245 710	Class: IR (BV)	**1976-11 A/S Nordsovaerftet — Ringkobing** Yd No: 113 Loa 49.75 Br ex 8.32 Dght 3.404 Lbp 44.45 Br md 8.30 Dpth 5.50 Welded, 2 dks	**(A31A2GX) General Cargo Ship** Grain: 1,312; Bale: 1,159 Compartments: 1 Ho, ER 1 Ha: (24.3 x 4.8)ER Derricks: 2x5t; Winches: 2	**1 oil engine** driving 1 CP propeller Total Power: 441kW (600hp) 10.5kn Alpha 406-26VO 1 x 2 Stroke 6 Cy. 260 x 400 441kW (600bhp) Alpha Diesel A/S-Denmark AuxGen: 2 x 39kW 380V 50Hz a.c
7313470 - -	**TARA LEE** *ex* Barbados 11 *-1992* **Henry & Ingrid Meyer** - *Bridgetown* *Barbados* Official number: 356708	**127** 85 -		**1973 Desco Marine — Saint Augustine, Fl** Yd No: 134-F Loa 22.86 Br ex 6.71 Dght 2.744 Lbp - Br md - Dpth - Bonded, 1 dk	**(B11B2FV) Fishing Vessel** Hull Material: Reinforced Plastic	**1 oil engine** geared to sc. shaft driving 1 FP propeller Total Power: 268kW (364hp) 9.0kn Caterpillar 3406PCTA 1 x 4 Stroke 6 Cy. 137 x 165 268kW (364bhp) Caterpillar Tractor Co-USA
8998007 *WDC7091* -	**TARA LOUISA** *ex* Lyons Gerald *-2007* *ex* Chesapeake Energy *-2000* *ex* S. S. Midway *-2000* **Rodan Marine Service II LLC** - *Cut Off, LA* *United States of America* Official number: 600097	**160** 48 -		**1978-01 Offshore Trawlers, Inc. — Bayou La Batre, Al** Yd No: 58 L reg 25.45 Br ex - Dght - Lbp - Br md 7.31 Dpth 2.13 Welded, 1 dk	**(B21A20S) Platform Supply Ship**	**1 oil engine** driving 1 Propeller
8034409 - -	**TARA RENITA** - **Renita Enterprise Ltd** - *Trinidad & Tobago*	*105* 71 -		**1981 Steiner Shipyard, Inc. — Bayou La Batre, Al** Loa 22.81 Br ex - Dght 2.401 Lbp 20.12 Br md 6.71 Dpth 3.36 Welded, 1 dk	**(B11A2FT) Trawler**	**1 oil engine** reduction geared to sc. shaft driving 1 FP propeller Total Power: 268kW (364hp) Cummins KT-1150-M 1 x 4 Stroke 6 Cy. 159 x 159 268kW (364bhp) Cummins Engine Co Inc-USA
8901353 *5ARS* -	**TARABULUS** - **National Fishing & Marketing Co (NAFIMCO)** - *Tripoli* *Libya*	*173* 54 -	Class: (LR) ✠ Classed LR until 29/1/97	**1992-03 Chungmu Shipbuilding Co Inc — Tongyeong** Yd No: 229 Loa 31.15 (BB) Br ex 7.72 Dght - Lbp 25.25 Br md 7.70 Dpth 3.50 Welded, 1 dk	**(B11A2FS) Stern Trawler** Ins: 100	**1 oil engine** with flexible couplings & sr geared to sc. shaft driving 1 CP propeller Total Power: 704kW (957hp) Blackstone ESL6MK2 1 x 4 Stroke 6 Cy. 222 x 292 704kW (957bhp) Mirrlees Blackstone (Stamford)Ltd.-Stamford AuxGen: 2 x 72kW 380V 50Hz a.c
9071674 *TCBN7* -	**TARABYA-E** *ex* Bora-Can *-2009* **Alasonya Denizcilik Ticaret Ltd Sti** - *Istanbul* *Turkey* MMSI: 271002176 Official number: 6462	**389** 194 671	Class: (TL)	**1994-07 Yildirim Gemi Insaat Sanayii A.S. — Tuzla** Loa 53.25 Br ex - Dght 3.210 Lbp 49.25 Br md 7.00 Dpth 3.85 Welded, 1 dk	**(A13B2TP) Products Tanker** Compartments: 6 Ta, ER	**1 oil engine** with flexible couplings & sr geared to sc. shaft driving 1 FP propeller Total Power: 313kW (426hp) 9.2kn S.K.L. 6NVD36A-1U 1 x 4 Stroke 6 Cy. 240 x 360 313kW (426bhp) SKL Motoren u. Systemtechnik AG-Magdeburg
9245304 *EPAH3* -	**TARADIS** *ex* Iran Darya *-2011* *ex* Volodymyr Ukrainets *-2009* **Western Surge Shipping Co Ltd** Khazar Sea Shipping Lines *Bandar Anzali* *Iran* MMSI: 422887000	**2,842** 1,414 3,850	Class: IN (GL)	**2002-10 Societatea Comerciala Navol S.A. Oltenita — Oltenita** Yd No: 395 Loa 98.00 (BB) Br ex - Dght 4.000 Lbp 93.50 Br md 16.00 Dpth 5.70 Welded, 1 dk	**(A31A2GX) General Cargo Ship** Double Bottom Entire Compartment Length Grain: 4,936 TEU 228 c. 228/20' Compartments: 3 Ho, ER 3 Ha: (12.6 x 10.5)2 (25.5 x 13.2)ER Ice Capable	**2 oil engines** with clutches and reverse reduction to sc. shaft (s) driving 2 FP propellers Total Power: 1,700kW (2,312hp) 11.5kn S.K.L. 6VD29/24AL-2 2 x 4 Stroke 6 Cy. 240 x 290 each-850kW (1156bhp) SKL Motoren u. Systemtechnik AG-Magdeburg AuxGen: 2 x 140kW 380V a.c Thrusters: 1 Thwart. FP thruster (f) Fuel: 250.0 (d.f.) 8.1pd
9177741 - -	**TARAFDAR** - **Government of The Republic of India (Navy Department)** - *India*	**260** 78 55	Class: (IR)	**1999-01 Tebma Shipyards Ltd — Chengalpattu** Yd No: 63 Loa - Br ex - Dght 2.600 Lbp - Br md - Dpth - Welded, 1 dk	**(B32A2ST) Tug**	**1 oil engine** driving 1 FP propeller Cummins KTA-3067-M 1 x Vee 4 Stroke 16 Cy. 159 x 159 Cummins India Ltd-India
9191321 *LAPN5* -	**TARAGO** - **Wilhelmsen Lines AS** Wilhelmsen Ship Management (Norway) AS SatCom: Inmarsat C 425767210 *Tonsberg* *Norway (NIS)* MMSI: 257672000	**67,140** 23,674 39,516 T/cm 69.5	Class: NV	**2000-09 Daewoo Heavy Industries Ltd — Geoje** Yd No: 4425 Loa 240.60 (BB) Br ex 32.29 Dght 11.750 Lbp 226.00 Br md 32.26 Dpth 15.60 Welded, 8 dks, incl. 4 dks hoistable	**(A35B2RV) Vehicles Carrier** Quarter stern door/ramp (s) Len: 44.50 Wid: 12.00 Swl: 320 Cars: 5,496 TEU 2340	**1 oil engine** driving 1 FP propeller Total Power: 20,940kW (28,470hp) 20.0kn B&W 8L70MC 1 x 2 Stroke 8 Cy. 700 x 2268 20940kW (28470bhp) HSD Engine Co Ltd-South Korea Thrusters: 1 Tunnel thruster (f); 1 Tunnel thruster (a)
9071349 *YD4719* -	**TARAHAN JAYA** *ex* Tarahan *-2000* *ex* TS 29-4 *-2000* **PT Arpeni Pratama Ocean Line Tbk** - *Jakarta* *Indonesia*	**234** 71 -	Class: KI RI (BV)	**1992-12 Universal Dockyard Ltd. — Hong Kong** Yd No: 295 Loa 29.00 Br ex 8.20 Dght 3.110 Lbp 24.04 Br md - Dpth 4.07 Welded	**(B32A2ST) Tug**	**2 oil engines** geared to sc. shafts driving 2 FP propellers Total Power: 736kW (1,000hp) 11.5kn Cummins KTA-19-M500 2 x 4 Stroke 6 Cy. 159 x 159 each-368kW (500bhp) Cummins Engine Co Ltd-United Kingdom

IMO / Call sign	Name / Owner	Tonnage	Class	Built	Type	Machinery
8224872 *CNPB* -	**TARAJI** - **Omnium Marocaine de Peche** - SatCom: Inmarsat C 424238010 *Agadir* *Morocco*	*324* 142 405	Class: BV	**1984-09 Construcciones Navales Santodomingo SA — Vigo** Yd No: 494 Loa 38.31 Br ex - Dght 4.091 Lbp 34.78 Br md 8.51 Dpth 4.04 Welded, 2 dks	**(B11A2FS) Stern Trawler** Ins: 402	**1 oil engine** with clutches, flexible couplings & sr geared to sc. shaft driving 1 FP propeller Total Power: 853kW (1,160hp) 12.3kn Deutz SBA8M528 1 x 4 Stroke 8 Cy. 220 x 280 853kW (1160bhp) Hijos de J Barreras SA-Spain AuxGen: 2 x 140kW 380V 50Hz a.c
8956578 *EPCH8* -	**TARAK 1** *ex* Liliya-S *-2013* *ex* Martunya *-2012* *ex* Agidel *-2005* *ex* ST-1358 *-2001* **Tarak Khazar Shipping Co** - *Bandar Anzali* *Iran* MMSI: 422046400	**1,928** 696 2,970	Class: IN UA (RS) (RR)	**1988-11 Sudostroitelnyy Zavod im. "40-aya Godovshchina Oktyabrya"-Bor** Yd No: 316 Loa 86.26 Br ex 12.30 Dght 4.100 Lbp 82.64 Br md 12.00 Dpth 5.80 Welded, 1 dk	**(A31A2GX) General Cargo Ship** Grain: 2,545	**2 oil engines** driving 2 FP propellers Total Power: 882kW (1,200hp) 10.0kn S.K.L. 8VDS36/24A-1 2 x 4 Stroke 8 Cy. 240 x 360 each-441kW (600bhp) VEB Schwermaschinenbau "KarlLiebknecht" (SKL)-Magdeburg AuxGen: 3 x 50kW a.c
8934491 *EPBO5* -	**TARAK 2** *ex* Samur 17 *-2012* *ex* Sky Walker *-2004* *ex* Millenium *-2000* *ex* Fort *-1999* *ex* Nastya *-1998* *ex* Vermont *-1998* *ex* ST-1323 *-1998* **Tarak Khazar Shipping Co** - *Bandar Anzali* *Iran* MMSI: 422029200 Official number: 1061	**1,846** 554 2,755	Class: IN (RS)	**1986-01 Volgogradskiy Sudostroitelnyy Zavod — Volgograd** Yd No: 132 Loa 88.80 Br ex 12.00 Dght 4.100 Lbp 83.90 Br md 12.00 Dpth 6.00 Welded, 1 dk	**(A31A2GX) General Cargo Ship**	**2 oil engines** driving 2 FP propellers Total Power: 1,030kW (1,400hp) 10.0kn S.K.L. 6NVD48A-2U 2 x 4 Stroke 6 Cy. 320 x 480 each-515kW (700bhp) VEB Schwermaschinenbau "KarlLiebknecht" (SKL)-Magdeburg Fuel: 95.0 (d.f.)
9539999 *VRMC6* -	**TARAKAN EXPRESS** - **Tarakan Express Ltd** Nova Shipping & Logistics Pte Ltd *Hong Kong* *Hong Kong* MMSI: 477030900 Official number: HK-3836	**54,550** 20,576 70,382	Class: AB	**2013-06 Jiangsu Newyangzi Shipbuilding Co Ltd — Jingjiang JS** Yd No: YZJ2010-974 Loa 215.40 (BB) Br ex 37.05 Dght 12.800 Lbp 210.60 Br md 37.00 Dpth 23.95 Welded, 1 dk	**(A24B2BW) Wood Chips Carrier** Grain: 133,243 Compartments: 6 Ho, ER 6 Ha: ER Cranes: 3x27.5t	**1 oil engine** driving 1 FP propeller Total Power: 10,470kW (14,235hp) 14.5kn Wartsila 6RT-flex50 1 x 2 Stroke 6 Cy. 500 x 2050 10470kW (14235bhp) Doosan Engine Co Ltd-South Korea AuxGen: 3 x 560kW a.c Fuel: 580.0 (d.f.) 3080.0 (r.f.)
7614226 *TCZH* -	**TARAMA 2** *ex* 0642 *-2011* *ex* Dunarea *-2011* **Dalsan Sualti Ve Liman Hizmetleri Sanayi Ticaret Ltd Sti** - *Istanbul* *Turkey*	**823** 225 1,320	Class: TL (RN)	**1967-03 Santierul Naval Oltenita S.A. — Oltenita** Loa 61.80 Br ex 10.83 Dght 2.450 Lbp 58.00 Br md 10.82 Dpth 4.50 Welded, 1 dk	**(B33A2DB) Bucket Ladder Dredger**	**4 diesel electric oil engines** driving 4 gen. each 200kW 220V d.c Connecting to 2 elec. motors driving 2 FP propellers Total Power: 696kW (948hp) 7.0kn S.K.L. 6NVD36 4 x 4 Stroke 6 Cy. 240 x 360 each-174kW (237bhp) VEB Schwermaschinenbau "KarlLiebknecht" (SKL)-Magdeburg AuxGen: 1 x 64kW 220V d.c, 1 x 16kW 220V d.c
8120246 - -	**TARAMATI** - **Ocean Fisheries (Nigeria) Ltd** - *Lagos* *Nigeria*	*148* - -		**1982-01 Quality Marine, Inc. — Bayou La Batre, Al** Yd No: 156 Loa 27.16 Br ex - Dght 2.744 Lbp 24.69 Br md 7.01 Dpth 3.69 Welded, 1 dk	**(B11A2FT) Trawler**	**1 oil engine** driving 1 FP propeller Total Power: 382kW (519hp) Caterpillar 3412TA 1 x Vee 4 Stroke 12 Cy. 137 x 152 382kW (519bhp) Caterpillar Tractor Co-USA
9524762 *LAMI7* -	**TARANGER** - **Westfal-Larsen & Co AS** Westfal-Larsen Management AS *Bergen* *Norway (NIS)* MMSI: 259982000	**29,712** 12,289 45,372 T/cm 52.3	Class: NV	**2011-07 Hyundai Mipo Dockyard Co Ltd — Ulsan** Yd No: 2277 Loa 183.00 (BB) Br ex 32.23 Dght 12.320 Lbp 174.00 Br md 32.20 Dpth 18.80 Welded, 1 dk	**(A12B2TR) Chemical/Products Tanker** Double Hull (13F) Liq: 51,612; Liq (Oil): 53,458 Compartments: 20 Wing Ta, 2 Wing Slop Ta, ER 20 Cargo Pump (s): 20x600m³/hr Manifold: Bow/CM: 91m	**1 oil engine** driving 1 FP propeller Total Power: 9,480kW (12,889hp) 14.5kn MAN-B&W 6S50MC-C 1 x 2 Stroke 6 Cy. 500 x 2000 9480kW (12889bhp) Hyundai Heavy Industries Co Ltd-South Korea AuxGen: 3 x 730kW 60Hz a.c Thrusters: 1 Tunnel thruster (f) Fuel: 223.0 (d.f.) 1471.0 (r.f.)
1005253 - -	**TARANGINI** - **Government of The Republic of India (Navy Department)** - *Kochi* *India*	**360** - 132	Class: (LR) ✠ Classed LR until 26/11/03	**1997-11 Goa Shipyard Ltd. — Goa** Yd No: 1170 Loa 54.00 Br ex 8.53 Dght 4.200 Lbp 37.20 Br md 8.52 Dpth 6.25 Welded, 2 dks	**(X11A2YS) Yacht (Sailing)**	**2 oil engines** sr reverse geared to sc. shafts driving 2 FP propellers Total Power: 478kW (650hp) 9.6kn Cummins NTA-855-M 2 x 4 Stroke 6 Cy. 140 x 152 each-239kW (325bhp) Kirloskar Cummins Ltd-India AuxGen: 2 x 80kW 415V 50Hz a.c
9048940 - -	**TARANGINI** - **Government of The Republic of India (National Institute of Fisheries Post Harvest Technology & Training)** - *Kochi* *India* Official number: F-CHN-015	**151** 45 45	Class: (IR)	**1995-05 Bharati Shipyard Ltd — Ratnagiri** Yd No: 236 Loa 24.00 Br ex 7.54 Dght - Lbp 21.00 Br md 7.40 Dpth 3.50 Welded, 1 dk	**(B11A2FS) Stern Trawler**	**1 oil engine** sr geared to sc. shaft driving 1 FP propeller Total Power: 373kW (507hp) 10.0kn MWM TBD234V12 1 x Vee 4 Stroke 12 Cy. 128 x 140 373kW (507bhp) Motoren Werke Mannheim AG (MWM)-Mannheim AuxGen: 2 x 40kW 415V a.c Fuel: 40.0 (d.f.)
9644081 *FFZT* PL 929533	**TARANIS** - **Armement Porcher SAS** - *Paimpol* *France* MMSI: 228004600	**207** - -		**2011-04 SOCARENAM — Boulogne** Loa 25.20 (BB) Br ex - Dght - Lbp 23.00 Br md 7.10 Dpth - Welded, 1 dk	**(B11A2FS) Stern Trawler**	**1 oil engine** reduction geared to sc. shaft driving 1 Propeller Total Power: 738kW (1,003hp)
9234587 *A8AI5* -	**TARANTELLA** - **Whitefin Shipping Co Ltd** Laurin Maritime (America) Inc *Monrovia* *Liberia* MMSI: 636011604 Official number: 11604	**26,914** 14,288 46,764 T/cm 52.8	Class: NV	**2002-09 Brodotrogir dd - Shipyard Trogir — Trogir** Yd No: 302 Loa 182.90 (BB) Br ex 32.23 Dght 12.180 Lbp 176.00 Br md 32.20 Dpth 17.10 Welded, 1 Dk.	**(A12B2TR) Chemical/Products Tanker** Double Hull (13F) Liq: 51,910; Liq (Oil): 51,910 Cargo Heating Coils Compartments: 14 Wing Ta, 2 Wing Slop Ta, ER 14 Cargo Pump (s): 8x250m³/hr, 6x400m³/hr Manifold: Bow/CM: 92m	**2 oil engines** with clutches, flexible couplings & reduction geared to sc. shaft driving 1 CP propeller Total Power: 7,680kW (10,442hp) 14.5kn MaK 8M32C 2 x 4 Stroke 8 Cy. 320 x 480 each-3840kW (5221bhp) Caterpillar Motoren GmbH & Co. KG-Germany AuxGen: 1 x 3200kW a.c, 2 x 682kW 60Hz a.c
9133513 *V2AK2* -	**TARANTO** - **Siegfried Bojen ms 'Ibiza' GmbH & Co KG** Kapitan Siegfried Bojen- Schiffahrtsbetrieb eK SatCom: Inmarsat C 430401355 *Saint John's* *Antigua & Barbuda* MMSI: 304010614 Official number: 2457	**2,061** 1,161 3,005	Class: GL	**1995-11 Slovenske Lodenice a.s. — Komarno** Yd No: 1707 Loa 88.45 (BB) Br ex - Dght 4.950 Lbp - Br md 11.35 Dpth 6.40 Welded, 1 dk	**(A31A2GX) General Cargo Ship** Double Hull Grain: 4,165 TEU 118 C.Ho 40/20' (40') C.Dk 78/20' (40') incl. 6 ref C. Compartments: 1 Ho, ER 1 Ha: (57.5 x 9.0)ER Ice Capable	**1 oil engine** reverse reduction geared to sc. shaft driving 1 FP propeller Total Power: 1,125kW (1,530hp) 10.5kn Deutz SBV6M628 1 x 4 Stroke 6 Cy. 240 x 280 1125kW (1530bhp) Motoren Werke Mannheim AG (MWM)-Mannheim AuxGen: 2 x 68kW 380/220V 50Hz a.c Thrusters: 1 Thwart. FP thruster (f) Fuel: 124.0 (d.f.) 5.0pd
7515353 - -	**TARASCO** - **Administracion Portuaria Integral de Lazaro Cardenas, SA de CV Pronlongacion** - *Lazaro Cardenas* *Mexico*	*139* 52 110	Class: (AB)	**1976-07 Astilleros de Marina — Tampico** Yd No: 40 Loa 26.07 Br ex 6.00 Dght 2.439 Lbp 25.30 Br md 5.80 Dpth 3.05 Welded, 1 dk	**(B32A2ST) Tug**	**2 oil engines** geared to sc. shafts driving 2 FP propellers Total Power: 1,250kW (1,700hp) Caterpillar D398SCAC 2 x Vee 4 Stroke 12 Cy. 159 x 203 each-625kW (850bhp) Caterpillar Tractor Co-USA
7647467 *XCRA* -	**TARASCO** *ex* Talisman *-1981* **Condux SA de CV** - *Ciudad del Carmen* *Mexico* MMSI: 345070021 Official number: 2617	*4,377* 562 -	Class: (BV) (AB)	**1976-07 Siong Huat Shipyard Pte Ltd — Singapore** Loa 86.26 Br ex 18.29 Dght 3.585 Lbp 76.38 Br md - Dpth 4.27 Welded, 1 dk	**(B34B2SC) Crane Vessel** Cranes: 1x250t	**4 oil engines** sr geared to sc. shafts driving 2 Directional propellers , 2 fwd Total Power: 2,208kW (3,000hp) 9.0kn Poyaud A12V85M 4 x Vee 4 Stroke 12 Cy. 150 x 180 each-552kW (750bhp) Societe Surgerienne de ConstructionMecaniques-France AuxGen: 4 x 240kW a.c Fuel: 739.5 (d.f.)
8964393 *E5U2755* -	**TARASKA** *ex* Diosa Josephine *-2005* *ex* Sea Express *-2000* **Erongo Fishing Pty Ltd** - *Avatiu* *Cook Islands* MMSI: 518808000 Official number: 1842	**370** 111 -	Class: AB (Class contemplated) (BV)	**2000-05** Yd No: 303 Loa 34.67 Br ex - Dght 2.360 Lbp 34.13 Br md 9.75 Dpth 3.96 Welded, 1 dk	**(B22A2OV) Diving Support Vessel**	**2 oil engines** reduction geared to sc. shafts driving 2 FP propellers Total Power: 1,790kW (2,434hp) 11.0kn Cummins KTA-38-M2 2 x Vee 4 Stroke 12 Cy. 159 x 159 each-895kW (1217bhp) Cummins Engine Co Inc-USA AuxGen: 2 x 370kW 440/220V 60Hz a.c

6916782 - CE8512	**TARATA 2** *ex* Miguel Angel *-1976* **Pesqueria Rescate SRL** - *Chimbote* *Peru*	*235* 122 -	Class: (GL)	**1969 Construcciones Navales SA (CONASA) — Callao** Yd No: 4 Loa - Br ex 7.62 Dght - Lbp 28.10 Br md 7.60 Dpth 3.81 Welded, 1 dk	**(B11B2FV) Fishing Vessel**	**1 oil engine** reduction geared to sc.shaft driving 1 FP propeller Total Power: 375kW (510hp) 11.8kn Caterpillar D379SCAC 1 x Vee 4 Stroke 8 Cy. 159 x 203 375kW (510bhp) Caterpillar Tractor Co-USA
7008556 - -	**TARATA 3** *ex* Santona IV *-1975* **Pesquera Don Miguel SRL** - *Chimbote* *Peru* Official number: CE-004830-PM	*258* 132 142	Class: (BV)	**1969 Construcciones Navales SA (CONASA) — Callao** Loa 31.70 Br ex 7.65 Dght 3.633 Lbp - Br md 7.62 Dpth 4.02 Welded, 1 dk	**(B11A2FT) Trawler** Ins: 374 Compartments: 2 Ho, ER 2 Ha: 2 (2.6 x 1.3)	**1 oil engine** driving 1 FP propeller Total Power: 416kW (566hp) 12.0kn Caterpillar D398SCAC 1 x Vee 4 Stroke 12 Cy. 159 x 203 416kW (566bhp) Caterpillar Tractor Co-USA
6915958 - -	**TARATA 4** *ex* Bosna III *-1979* - -	*196* 117 334	Class: (BV)	**1968 Maestranza y Astillero Delta S.A. — Callao** L reg 27.89 Br ex 7.78 Dght 3.302 Lbp - Br md 7.75 Dpth 3.69 Welded	**(B11A2FT) Trawler** Grain: 334 Compartments: 2 Ho, ER 2 Ha: (2.5 x 2.1) (1.4 x 2.1) Derricks: 1x1.5t; Winches: 1	**1 oil engine** driving 1 FP propeller Total Power: 313kW (426hp) 9.5kn Caterpillar D353SCAC 1 x 4 Stroke 6 Cy. 159 x 203 313kW (426bhp) Caterpillar Tractor Co-USA
7014957 - -	**TARATA 7** *ex* Dimona II *-1975* - -	*215* 127 240	Class: (BV)	**1970 Maestranza y Astillero Delta S.A. — Callao** Yd No: 34 Loa 27.82 Br ex 7.90 Dght 3.645 Lbp - Br md 7.88 Dpth 4.02 Welded, 1 dk	**(B11B2FV) Fishing Vessel** Compartments: 1 Ho, ER 2 Ha: (3.1 x 2.6) (1.7 x 2.6)ER	**1 oil engine** driving 1 FP propeller Total Power: 313kW (426hp) 10.0kn Caterpillar D353SCAC 1 x 4 Stroke 6 Cy. 159 x 203 313kW (426bhp) Caterpillar Tractor Co-USA AuxGen: 1 x 2kW Fuel: 11.0 (d.f.)
7102132 - -	**TARATA 8** *ex* Milo *-1979* - -	*215* - -		**1970 Maestranza y Astillero Delta S.A. — Callao** Yd No: 41 Loa - Br ex - Dght - Lbp - Br md - Dpth - Bonded, 1 dk	**(B11B2FV) Fishing Vessel** Hull Material: Reinforced Plastic	**1 oil engine** geared to sc. shaft driving 1 FP propeller General Motors 1 x 2 Stroke General Motors Corp-USA
7109829 - -	**TARATA 9** *ex* Santelmo *-1976* - -	*238* 126 142	Class: (BV)	**1969 Construcciones Navales SA (CONASA) — Callao** Loa 31.70 Br ex 7.68 Dght 3.633 Lbp - Br md 7.65 Dpth 4.02 Welded, 1 dk	**(B11B2FV) Fishing Vessel** Grain: 345 Compartments: 2 Ho, ER 1 Ha: (2.2 x 1.0) Derricks: 1x1t; Winches: 1	**1 oil engine** driving 1 FP propeller Total Power: 416kW (566hp) 12.0kn Caterpillar D398SCAC 1 x Vee 4 Stroke 12 Cy. 159 x 203 416kW (566bhp) Caterpillar Tractor Co-USA Fuel: 17.5 (d.f.)
6817651 - -	**TARATA 10** *ex* Helland III *-1979* - -	*236* 123 -		**1968 Construcciones Navales SA (CONASA) — Callao** L reg 31.28 Br ex 7.68 Dght 3.607 Lbp - Br md 7.65 Dpth 3.99 Welded, 1 dk	**(B11A2FT) Trawler** Ins: 344 Compartments: 2 Ho, ER 1 Ha: (2.8 x 1.0) Derricks: 1x1t; Winches: 1	**1 oil engine** driving 1 FP propeller Total Power: 375kW (510hp) 12.0kn Caterpillar D379SCAC 1 x Vee 4 Stroke 8 Cy. 159 x 203 375kW (510bhp) Caterpillar Tractor Co-USA
8805224 *J8B4836* -	**TARAZARA** *ex* Vassilios Xx *-2013* *ex* Aida *-2001* *ex* Seiwa Maru *-2001* **Florence Navigation Inc** 8 Balls Resources Ltd *Kingstown* *St Vincent & The Grenadines* MMSI: 376971000 Official number: 11309	**992** 590 1,896 T/cm 6.2	Class: (BV)	**1988-02 Sasaki Shipbuilding Co Ltd — Osakikamijima HS** Yd No: 516 Loa 68.38 (BB) Br ex - Dght 4.853 Lbp 64.01 Br md 12.01 Dpth 5.31 Welded, 1 dk	**(A13B2TP) Products Tanker** Double Bottom Entire Compartment Length Liq: 2,213; Liq (Oil): 2,213 Compartments: 10 Ta, ER 3 Cargo Pump (s)	**1 oil engine** with clutches, flexible couplings & reduction geared to sc. shaft driving 1 CP propeller Total Power: 1,324kW (1,800hp) Hanshin 6EL30 1 x 4 Stroke 6 Cy. 300 x 600 1324kW (1800bhp) The Hanshin Diesel Works Ltd-Japan
9408322 *9V7787* -	**TARBET SPIRIT** *ex* Phoenix Ambition *-2014* **TIL V LLC** Teekay Shipping (UK) Ltd SatCom: Inmarsat C 456378810 *Singapore* *Singapore* MMSI: 563788000 Official number: 394813	**60,205** 32,143 107,529 T/cm 91.9	Class: AB	**2009-06 Tsuneishi Holdings Corp Tsuneishi Shipbuilding Co — Tadotsu KG** Yd No: 1418 Loa 243.80 (BB) Br ex - Dght 14.920 Lbp 237.00 Br md 42.00 Dpth 21.30 Welded, 1 dk	**(A13A2TW) Crude/Oil Products Tanker** Double Hull (13F) Liq: 115,778; Liq (Oil): 120,650 Cargo Heating Coils Compartments: 12 Wing Ta, 2 Wing Slop Ta, ER 3 Cargo Pump (s): 3x3000m³/hr Manifold: Bow/CM: 121.7m	**1 oil engine** driving 1 FP propeller Total Power: 13,560kW (18,436hp) 15.0kn MAN-B&W 6S60MC-C 1 x 2 Stroke 6 Cy. 600 x 2400 13560kW (18436bhp) Mitsui Engineering & Shipbuilding CLtd-Japan AuxGen: 3 x 640kW a.c Fuel: 270.0 (d.f.) 3800.0 (r.f.)
7038680 *JXIE3* -	**TARCO SEA** *ex* Esdorp *-1986* *ex* Ostediek *-1982* *ex* Catriona *-1972* *launched as* Ostediek *-1971* **Rederiaktieselskabet Nyborg** A K Aagesen & Partners AS *Kristiansand* *Norway (NIS)* MMSI: 258243000	**1,300** 390 1,263	Class: NV (GL)	**1971-03 Scheepswerf Hoogezand N.V. — Bergum** Yd No: 159 Converted From: General Cargo Ship-1986 Loa 75.72 Br ex 11.10 Dght 3.761 Lbp 70.06 Br md 11.00 Dpth 6.05 Welded, 2 dks	**(A12A2TC) Chemical Tanker** Grain: 2,885; Bale: 2,620; Liq: 1,083 Ice Capable	**1 oil engine** driving 1 FP propeller Total Power: 971kW (1,320hp) 12.0kn Deutz RBV8M545 1 x 4 Stroke 8 Cy. 320 x 450 971kW (1320bhp) Kloeckner Humboldt Deutz AG-West Germany AuxGen: 2 x 60kW 220/380V 50Hz a.c, 1 x 30kW 220/380V 50Hz a.c
9316452 *VHLN* -	**TARCOOLA** **Svitzer Australia Pty Ltd (Svitzer Australasia)** - *Port Adelaide, SA* *Australia* MMSI: 503480000 Official number: 857555	**294** 88 -	Class: LR ✠ **100A1** SS 12/2009 tug ✠ **LMC** **UMS** Eq.Ltr: F; Cable: 275.0/19.0 U2 (a)	**2004-12 PT Nanindah Mutiara Shipyard — Batam** Yd No: T120 Loa 28.50 Br ex 10.30 Dght 5.200 Lbp 26.50 Br md 10.30 Dpth 3.80 Welded, 1 dk	**(B32A2ST) Tug**	**2 oil engines** gearing integral to driving 2 Directional propellers Total Power: 2,984kW (4,058hp) 12.0kn Caterpillar 3516B-TA 2 x Vee 4 Stroke 16 Cy. 170 x 190 each-1492kW (2029bhp) Caterpillar Inc-USA AuxGen: 2 x 160kW 415V 50Hz a.c
8991487 *9A3598* -	**TAREJ** *ex* Pipi Mali I *-2011* **Peter Pan doo** - *Rijeka* *Croatia* MMSI: 238337540 Official number: 2R-101	**155** 46 -	Class: CS	**1996 Tehnomont Brodogradiliste Pula doo — Pula** Loa 24.94 Br ex - Dght 2.510 Lbp 20.20 Br md 7.35 Dpth 3.67 Welded, 1 dk	**(B11B2FV) Fishing Vessel**	**1 oil engine** geared to sc. shaft driving 1 Propeller Total Power: 625kW (850hp) Caterpillar D398 1 x Vee 4 Stroke 12 Cy. 159 x 203 625kW (850bhp) Caterpillar Inc-USA AuxGen: 1 x 30kW 230V 50Hz a.c
6720614 - -	**TAREK** - **Government of Libya** - *Benghazi* *Libya*	*129* - -	Class: (LR) ✠ Classed LR until 4/2/87	**1967-09 R. Dunston (Hessle) Ltd. — Hessle** Yd No: S847 Loa 28.50 Br ex 7.65 Dght 3.004 Lbp 25.91 Br md 7.32 Dpth 3.43 Welded, 1 dk	**(B32A2ST) Tug**	**2 oil engines** sr reverse geared to sc. shafts driving 2 CP propellers Total Power: 992kW (1,348hp) Blackstone ERS8M 2 x 4 Stroke 8 Cy. 222 x 292 each-496kW (674bhp) Lister Blackstone Marine Ltd.-Dursley AuxGen: 2 x 35kW 220V 50Hz a.c
5411565 - -	**TAREK** *ex* Hilal *-1989* - -	*393* - -	Class: (LR) ✠ Classed LR until 3/12/82	**1963-04 Scott & Sons (Bowling) Ltd. — Bowling** Yd No: 428 Loa 40.24 Br ex 10.09 Dght 4.255 Lbp 36.58 Br md 9.61 Dpth 4.35 Riveted\Welded	**(B32A2ST) Tug** 2 Ha: (0.4 x 0.6) (0.9 x 0.9)	**1 oil engine** with flexible couplings & sr reverse geared to sc. shaft driving 1 FP propeller Total Power: 1,103kW (1,500hp) 11.0kn Crossley CGL8 1 x 2 Stroke 8 Cy. 368 x 483 1103kW (1500bhp) Crossley Bros. Ltd.-Manchester AuxGen: 2 x 60kW 110V d.c Fuel: 124.0 (d.f.)
7301295 *9WAD*	**TAREK** **Government of Malaysia (Director of Marine - Sabah)** - *Labuan* *Malaysia* Official number: M47	*120* 50 71		**1973 Chung Wah Shipbuilding & Engineering Co. Ltd. — Hong Kong** Yd No: 140 Loa 24.39 Br ex 6.94 Dght 2.286 Lbp 21.95 Br md 6.71 Dpth 3.05 Welded, 1 dk	**(B32A2ST) Tug**	**2 oil engines** reverse reduction geared to sc. shafts driving 2 FP propellers Total Power: 596kW (810hp) Blackstone ESL6MK2 2 x 4 Stroke 6 Cy. 222 x 292 each-298kW (405bhp) Mirrlees Blackstone (Stamford)Ltd.-Stamford
7408744 *5ANM* -	**TAREK BENZIAD** **National Fishing & Marketing Co (NAFIMCO)** - *Tripoli* *Libya*	*200* 92 -	Class: (LR) Classed LR until 9/6/93	**1975 Cant. Nav. M. Morini & C. — Ancona** Yd No: 153 Loa 32.64 Br ex 6.99 Dght - Lbp 25.25 Br md 6.80 Dpth 3.64 Welded	**(B11B2FV) Fishing Vessel**	**1 oil engine** reverse reduction geared to sc. shaft driving 1 FP propeller Total Power: 1,100kW (1,496hp) MaK 8M451AK 1 x 4 Stroke 8 Cy. 320 x 450 1100kW (1496bhp) MaK Maschinenbau GmbH-Kiel

8417845 *IMJW* -	**TARENTUM** **Rimorchiatori Napoletani Srl** - *Taranto* *Italy* Official number: 146	**273** 81 129 T/cm 2.3	Class: RI	**1985-09 Cantiere Navale di Pesaro SpA (CNP) — Pesaro** Yd No: 56 Loa 33.53 Br ex 9.28 Dght 3.898 Lbp 29.01 Br md 8.58 Dpth 4.27 Welded, 1 dk	**(B32A2ST) Tug**	**1 oil engine** with flexible couplings & sr gearedto sc. shaft driving 1 CP propeller Total Power: 1,622kW (2,205hp) 12.5kn MAN G9V30/45ATL 1 x 4 Stroke 9 Cy. 300 x 450 1622kW (2205bhp) MAN B&W Diesel GmbH-Augsburg AuxGen: 2 x 80kW 380V 50Hz a.c, 1 x 25kW 380V 50Hz a.c Fuel: 80.0 (d.f.) 8.5pd
6621088 - -	**TAREQ II** *ex* Louis Caubriere *-1971* **Government of The Republic of Tunisia (Office Nationale des Peches)** - *Tunis* *Tunisia*	*200* 65 -	Class: (BV)	**1966 Ch. de Normandie — Grand Quevilly** Yd No: 292 Loa 33.00 Br ex 8.16 Dght 3.607 Lbp 28.50 Br md 7.95 Dpth 4.02 Welded, 2 dks	**(B11A2FS) Stern Trawler** Ins: 130 Compartments: 3 Ho, ER 3 Ha: 2 (0.9 x 0.9) (0.4 x 0.6)ER Derricks: 1x0.3t	**2 oil engines** geared to sc. shaft driving 1 CP propeller Total Power: 662kW (900hp) 12.0kn Caterpillar D353SCAC 2 x 4 Stroke 6 Cy. 159 x 203 each-331kW (450bhp) Caterpillar Tractor Co-USA Fuel: 58.5 (d.f.)
7648083 *YERM* -	**TAREUMAN JAYA** *ex* Bahtera Pacific *-2002* *ex* Eifuku Maru No. 18 *-1990* **PT Tareuman Sejati Sejahtera** - *Makassar* *Indonesia*	**910** 337 800	Class: (KI)	**1975-01 Azumi Zosen Kensetsu K.K. — Himeji** Loa 57.99 Br ex - Dght 4.500 Lbp 54.01 Br md 11.51 Dpth 5.85 Welded, 1dk	**(A24D2BA) Aggregates Carrier** 1 Ha: ER	**1 oil engine** driving 1 FP propeller Total Power: 1,177kW (1,600hp) 11.0kn Yanmar 6Z-ET 1 x 4 Stroke 6 Cy. 280 x 340 1177kW (1600bhp) Yanmar Diesel Engine Co Ltd-Japan
8732465 *PNAD* -	**TAREX I** *ex* Crusader 05 *-2010* *ex* Ye Shan 5 *-2010* *ex* Min Tai 5 Hao *-2005* **PT Pelayaran Taruna Kusan Explosive (TAREXSHIP)** - *Pontianak* *Indonesia*	**1,020** 497 2,309	Class: KI	**1996-03 Fujian Fishing Vessel Shipyard — Fuzhou FJ** Loa 72.22 Br ex - Dght 2.800 Lbp 66.42 Br md 11.50 Dpth 5.00 Welded, 1 dk	**(A31A2GX) General Cargo Ship**	**1 oil engine** geared to sc. shaft driving 1 Propeller Total Power: 552kW (750hp) Chinese Std. Type 6300ZC 1 x 4 Stroke 6 Cy. 300 x 380 552kW (750bhp) Ningbo Zhonghua Dongli PowerMachinery Co Ltd -China
6923278 *CNLP* -	**TARFAYA** *ex* Richelieu *-1975* **MAROPECHE SA** - *Casablanca* *Morocco* Official number: 6-602	*579* 292 676	Class: (BV)	**1969 Ateliers et Chantiers de La Manche — Dieppe** Yd No: 1210 Loa 47.00 Br ex 10.90 Dght 4.827 Lbp 41.00 Br md 10.60 Dpth 5.11 Welded, 2 dks	**(B11B2FV) Fishing Vessel** Ins: 500	**1 oil engine** reverse reduction geared to sc. shaft driving 1 FP propeller Total Power: 1,287kW (1,750hp) 13.0kn AGO 240G12VS 1 x Vee 4 Stroke 12 Cy. 240 x 220 1287kW (1750bhp) Societe Alsacienne de ConstructionsMecaniques (SACM)-France AuxGen: 2 x 206kW 380V d.c Fuel: 149.5 (d.f.)
9313369 *CNA3983* -	**TARFAYA VI** **Finance Company of Souss SA (Fishing Port Agadir Morocco) SOFINAS SA** - *Agadir* *Morocco* MMSI: 242572000	**316** 94 200	Class: BV	**2004-05 Francisco Cardama, SA — Vigo** Yd No: 213 Loa 32.00 Br ex - Dght - Lbp 27.00 Br md 8.20 Dpth 5.80 Welded, 1 dk	**(B11A2FS) Stern Trawler**	**1 oil engine** geared to sc. shaft driving 1 FP propeller Total Power: 662kW (900hp) 11.0kn GUASCOR F360TA-SP 1 x Vee 4 Stroke 12 Cy. 152 x 165 662kW (900bhp) Gutierrez Ascunce Corp (GUASCOR)-Spain
9323340 *V7LN9* -	**TARGALE** **Stende Navigation Inc** Latvian Shipping Co (Latvijas Kugnieciba) *Majuro* *Marshall Islands* MMSI: 538002775 Official number: 2775	**30,641** 15,306 52,660 T/cm 56.8	Class: NV	**2007-03 '3 Maj' Brodogradiliste dd — Rijeka** Yd No: 698 Loa 195.19 (BB) Br ex 32.24 Dght 12.500 Lbp 187.30 Br md 32.20 Dpth 17.80 Welded, 1 dk	**(A12B2TR) Chemical/Products Tanker** Double Hull (13F) Liq: 56,190; Liq (Oil): 56,190 Compartments: 12 Wing Ta, 2 Wing Slop Ta, ER 12 Cargo Pump (s): 12x550m³/hr Manifold: Bow/CM: 97.1m Ice Capable	**1 oil engine** driving 1 FP propeller Total Power: 9,650kW (13,120hp) 14.0kn Sulzer 7RTA48T-B 1 x 2 Stroke 7 Cy. 480 x 2000 9650kW (13120bhp) '3 Maj' Motori i Dizalice dd-Croatia AuxGen: 3 x 960kW 450V 60Hz a.c Fuel: 193.0 (d.f.) 1551.0 (r.f.) 39.0pd
9419448 *9HA2149* -	**TARGET** **Target Shipping Ltd** Ursa Shipping Ltd *Valletta* *Malta* MMSI: 248057000 Official number: 9419448	**61,341** 35,396 115,804 T/cm 99.0	Class: NV	**2009-11 Samsung Heavy Industries Co Ltd — Geoje** Yd No: 1739 Loa 248.96 (BB) Br ex 43.83 Dght 14.925 Lbp 239.00 Br md 43.80 Dpth 21.00 Welded, 1 dk	**(A13A2TV) Crude Oil Tanker** Double Hull (13F) Liq: 123,644; Liq (Oil): 127,542 Cargo Heating Coils Compartments: 12 Wing Ta, 2 Wing Slop Ta, ER 3 Cargo Pump (s): 3x2800m³/hr Manifold: Bow/CM: 125.2m	**1 oil engine** driving 1 FP propeller Total Power: 13,560kW (18,436hp) 15.3kn MAN-B&W 6S60MC-C 1 x 2 Stroke 6 Cy. 600 x 2400 13560kW (18436bhp) Doosan Engine Co Ltd-South Korea AuxGen: 3 x 800kW a.c Fuel: 240.0 (d.f.) 3200.0 (r.f.)
8617938 *PJLL*	**TARGET** *ex* Front Target *-2007* *ex* Genmar Centaur *-2004* *ex* Crude Target *-2003* *ex* Nord-Jahre Target *-2000* *ex* Jahre Target *-1993* **Target BV** Dockwise Shipping BV *Willemstad* *Curacao* MMSI: 306869000 Official number: 2008-C-1957	**42,515** 12,755 53,806 T/cm 108.0	Class: NV	**1990-02 Brodogradiliste Split (Brodosplit) — Split** Yd No: 361 Converted From: Crude Oil/Products Tanker-2007 Shortened-2007 Loa 216.86 (BB) Br ex 44.50 Dght 10.440 Lbp 207.86 Br md 44.44 Dpth 14.00 Welded, 1 dk	**(A38C3GH) Heavy Load Carrier, semi submersible** Single Hull	**1 oil engine** driving 1 FP propeller Total Power: 13,368kW (18,175hp) 14.0kn B&W 6S70MC 1 x 2 Stroke 6 Cy. 700 x 2674 13368kW (18175bhp) Brodogradiliste Split (Brodosplit)-Yugoslavia AuxGen: 3 x 900kW 440V 60Hz a.c, 1 x 160kW 440V 60Hz a.c Fuel: 264.0 (d.f.) 4256.0 (r.f.) 4.8pd
9089360 *9WFQ5*	**TARGET** **Wang Nieng Lee Holdings Bhd** - *Kuching* *Malaysia* MMSI: 533761000 Official number: 329582	**220** 66 -	Class: NK (NV)	**2003-11 Sapor Shipyard Sdn Bhd — Sibu** Yd No: S46/2000 Loa 27.00 Br ex 7.83 Dght 3.200 Lbp 24.92 Br md 7.80 Dpth 4.00 Welded, 1 dk	**(B32A2ST) Tug**	**2 oil engines** driving 2 Propellers Total Power: 1,472kW (2,002hp) Cummins 2 x 4 Stroke each-736kW (1001bhp) Cummins Engine Co Inc-USA
7322330 - -	**TARGET 1** *ex* Kinsei *-1996* *ex* Kinsei Maru *-1994* **Megahijau Sdn Bhd** - *San Lorenzo* *Honduras* Official number: L-3828060	**151** 45 -		**1973-06 Kochi Jyuko K.K. — Kochi** Yd No: 762 Loa 27.92 Br ex 7.83 Dght - Lbp 25.00 Br md 7.80 Dpth 3.50 Welded, 1 dk	**(B32A2ST) Tug**	**2 oil engines** driving 2 FP propellers Total Power: 736kW (1,000hp) Makita 2 x 4 Stroke 6 Cy. 290 x 440 each-368kW (500bhp) Makita Tekkosho-Japan
9121390 - -	**TARHUNAH** **Government of Libya (Socialist Ports Co)** - *Tripoli* *Libya*	**627** 188 550	Class: BV (LR) ✠	**1995-06 Scheepswerf Slob B.V. — Papendrecht** (Hull) Yd No: 400 **1995-06 B.V. Scheepswerf Damen — Gorinchem** Yd No: 2159 Loa 46.00 Br ex 11.04 Dght 3.300 Lbp 43.70 Br md 11.00 Dpth 4.00 Welded, 1 dk	**(B33B2DT) Trailing Suction Hopper Dredger** Hopper: 500	**2 oil engines** geared to sc. shafts driving 2 Directional propellers Total Power: 540kW (734hp) MWM TBD234V8 2 x Vee 4 Stroke 8 Cy. 128 x 140 each-270kW (367bhp) Motoren Werke Mannheim AG (MWM)-Mannheim AuxGen: 2 x 80kW 380V 50Hz a.c
9327748 *C6VT6*	**TARIFA** *ex* Morning Charisma *-2007* *launched as* Tarifa *-2007* **Tarifa Maritime Ltd** Ray Car Carriers Ltd *Nassau* *Bahamas* MMSI: 309847000 Official number: 8001254	**57,692** 21,037 21,120	Class: NV	**2007-04 Stocznia Gdynia SA — Gdynia** Yd No: 8168/16 Loa 199.90 (BB) Br ex - Dght 10.000 Lbp 187.90 Br md 32.26 Dpth 32.73 Welded, 11 dks. incl. Nos.1, 3, 5 & 7 dks hoistable	**(A35B2RV) Vehicles Carrier** Side door/ramp (s) Len: 25.00 Wid: 7.00 Swl: 22 Quarter stern door/ramp (s. a.) Len: 38.00 Wid: 7.00 Swl: 150 Cars: 6,658 Ice Capable	**1 oil engine** driving 1 FP propeller Total Power: 15,539kW (21,127hp) 20.4kn MAN-B&W 7S60MC-C 1 x 2 Stroke 7 Cy. 600 x 2400 15539kW (21127bhp) H Cegielski Poznan SA-Poland AuxGen: 3 x a.c Thrusters: 1 Tunnel thruster (f)
9285598 *EHSC*	**TARIFA** **Remolcadores y Barcazas de Tenerife SA** - SatCom: Inmarsat C 422419510 *Seville* *Spain* MMSI: 224195000 Official number: 1-1/2004	**1,500** - 748		**2004-04 Construcciones Navales P Freire SA — Vigo** Yd No: 527 Loa 68.50 (BB) Br ex - Dght 4.500 Lbp 59.00 Br md 11.00 Dpth 7.20 Welded, 1 dk	**(B34H2SQ) Patrol Vessel** Ice Capable	**1 oil engine** geared to sc. shaft driving 1 CP propeller Total Power: 2,400kW (3,263hp) MaK 8M25 1 x 4 Stroke 8 Cy. 255 x 400 2400kW (3263bhp) Caterpillar Motoren GmbH & Co. KG-Germany AuxGen: 2 x 350kW a.c Thrusters: 1 Tunnel thruster (f) Fuel: 710.0 (d.f.)
9150999 *C4NX2* -	**TARIFA JET** *ex* Pescara Jet *-2006* *ex* Sardinia Jet *-2005* *ex* Sicilia Jet *-2004* **Forde Reederei Seetouristik SL** FRS Iberia SLU *Limassol* *Cyprus* MMSI: 209375000 Official number: P546	**4,995** 2,008 350	Class: NV (RI)	**1997-05 Incat Tasmania Pty Ltd — Hobart TAS** Yd No: 043 Loa 86.62 Br ex - Dght 3.628 Lbp 71.80 Br md 26.00 Dpth 4.12 Welded, 1 dk	**(A36A2PR) Passenger/Ro-Ro Ship (Vehicles)** Hull Material: Aluminium Alloy Passengers: unberthed: 800 Cars: 175	**4 oil engines** reduction geared to sc. shafts driving 4 Water jets Total Power: 28,304kW (38,484hp) 35.0kn Ruston 20RK270 4 x Vee 4 Stroke 20 Cy. 270 x 305 each-7076kW (9621bhp) Ruston Paxman Diesels Ltd.-United Kingdom AuxGen: 4 x 240kW 220/380V 50Hz a.c

IMO / Call sign / Flag	Name / Owner / Port	Tonnage	Class	Builder / Dimensions	Type	Machinery
7053393 *CNA4070* -	**TARIK** **Royaume Du Maroc (Societe d'Exploitation des Ports (SODEP) - Marsa Maroc)** - *Safi* *Morocco* MMSI: 242068100	*136* - 48	Class: BV	**1970 Gutehoffnungshuette Sterkrade AG Rheinwerft Walsum — Duisburg** Loa 27.11 Br ex 8.41 Dght 2.998 Lbp 24.26 Br md 7.80 Dpth 3.66 Welded, 1 dk	**(B32A2ST) Tug**	**1 oil engine** driving 1 FP propeller Total Power: 1,092kW (1,485hp) 12.0kn MAN G7V30/45ATL 1 x 4 Stroke 7 Cy. 300 x 450 1092kW (1485bhp) Maschinenbau Augsburg Nuernberg (MAN)-Augsburg AuxGen: 2 x 52kW 220/380V 50Hz a.c Fuel: 88.0 (d.f.)
8413473 *TCSZ7* -	**TARIK 3** *ex* Arisbe *-2008* *ex* Hasil *-1992* *ex* Kota Hasil *-1990* **Garanti Finansal Kiralama AS (Garanti Leasing)** Horizon Gemi Isletmeciligi Sanayi ve Ticaret AS *Istanbul* *Turkey* MMSI: 271001030 Official number: TUGS 1467	**19,602** 10,920 34,142 T/cm 41.8	Class: NK (LR) ✠ Classed LR until 25/9/10	**1986-03 Hayashikane Shipbuilding & Engineering Co Ltd — Shimonoseki YC** Yd No: 1286 Loa 181.01 (BB) Br ex 27.03 Dght 10.718 Lbp 172.02 Br md 27.01 Dpth 15.12 Welded, 1 dk	**(A21A2BC) Bulk Carrier** Grain: 41,771; Bale: 40,986 Compartments: 5 Ho, ER 5 Ha: 5 (16.8 x 11.9)ER Cranes: 4x25t	**1 oil engine** driving 1 FP propeller Total Power: 9,540kW (12,971hp) 14.1kn Sulzer 6RTA58 1 x 2 Stroke 6 Cy. 580 x 1700 9540kW (12971bhp) Ishikawajima Harima Heavy IndustrieCo Ltd (IHI)-Japan AuxGen: 3 x 400kW 450V 60Hz a.c Boilers: e 11.0kgf/cm² (10.8bar), AuxB (o.f.) 8.0kgf/cm² (7.8bar) Fuel: 174.0 (d.f.) 1253.0 (r.f.)
8846400 - -	**TARIK EL KHAIR** *ex* Triton *-1990* - -	**117** 98 30	Class: RP (RS)	**1989 Sosnovskiy Sudostroitelnyy Zavod — Sosnovka** Yd No: 742 Loa 25.50 Br ex 6.80 Dght 2.390 Lbp 22.00 Br md - Dpth 3.30 Welded, 1 dk	**(B11A2FS) Stern Trawler**	**1 oil engine** driving 1 FP propeller Total Power: 220kW (299hp) S.K.L. 6NVD26A-2 1 x 4 Stroke 6 Cy. 180 x 260 220kW (299bhp) VEB Schwermaschinenbau "KarlLiebknecht" (SKL)-Magdeburg
8001517 *3EPM4* -	**TARIK EMIR** *ex* S Naz *-2008* *ex* Naftobulk IV *-2007* *ex* Yellow Blue *-2004* *ex* Apollonia Naiad *-2000* *ex* Aditya Rashmi *-1993* *ex* Helene *-1987* *ex* Eighteen Venture *-1986* **Mina Shipping & Trading Co Ltd** Mina Denizcilik ve Ticaret Ltd Sti SatCom: Inmarsat C 435649910 *Panama* *Panama* MMSI: 356499000 Official number: 3458909A	**4,052** 2,391 6,623	Class: (TL) (RI) (NV) (IR) (NK) (BV)	**1980-10 Iwagi Zosen Co Ltd — Kamijima EH** Yd No: 18 Loa 106.41 Br ex 16.36 Dght 6.854 Lbp 98.61 Br md 16.34 Dpth 8.41 Welded, 1 dk	**(A31A2GX) General Cargo Ship** Grain: 8,581; Bale: 7,913 Compartments: 2 Ho, ER 2 Ha: (27.2 x 8.3) (28.5 x 8.3)ER Derricks: 2x25t,2x15t	**1 oil engine** driving 1 FP propeller Total Power: 2,796kW (3,801hp) 12.5kn Mitsubishi 6UET45/75C 1 x 2 Stroke 6 Cy. 450 x 750 2796kW (3801bhp) Akasaka Tekkosho KK (Akasaka DieselLtd)-Japan AuxGen: 2 x 160kW 445V 60Hz a.c, 1 x 186kW 445V 60Hz a.c Fuel: 88.0 (d.f.) 494.5 (r.f.) 12.5pd
5345986 *TCBT3* -	**TARIK GUNER** *ex* Tamanlar *-1990* *ex* Hizir Kaptan *-1977* *ex* Sutluce *-1975* *ex* Bosphorus No. 63 *-1954* **Husnu Guner ve Ortlar** - *Istanbul* *Turkey* MMSI: 271002421 Official number: 19	**489** 295 908	Class: (LR) (GL) ✠	**1909-12 Ateliers et Chantiers de France — Dunkirk** Yd No: 69 Converted From: Ferry (Passenger only)-1975 Loa 49.99 Br ex 8.01 Dght 3.490 Lbp 44.30 Br md - Dpth 3.87 Riveted, 1 dk	**(A24D2BA) Aggregates Carrier**	**1 oil engine** driving 1 FP propeller Total Power: 224kW (305hp) S.K.L. 6NVD36-1U 1 x 4 Stroke 6 Cy. 240 x 360 224kW (305bhp) (new engine 1975) VEB Schwermaschinenbau "KarlLiebknecht" (SKL)-Magdeburg
9559937 *AVDH* -	**TARINI** **Paradip Port Trust** - *Kolkata* *India* Official number: 3654	**284** 85 107	Class: IR	**2011-05 Bharati Shipyard Ltd — Ratnagiri** Yd No: 400 Loa 30.10 Br ex 10.22 Dght 3.900 Lbp 29.50 Br md 9.60 Dpth 4.80 Welded, 1 dk	**(B32A2ST) Tug**	**2 oil engines** reduction geared to sc. shafts driving 2 Directional propellers Total Power: 2,880kW (3,916hp) Wartsila 8L20 2 x 4 Stroke 8 Cy. 200 x 280 each-1440kW (1958bhp) Wartsila Finland Oy-Finland
7035054 *9KGD* -	**TARIQ** *ex* Asaka Maru No. 2 *-1976* **Alghunaim Trading Co** - *Kuwait* *Kuwait* Official number: KT134	*484* 267 649	Class: (AB)	**1970 Akitsu Dock K.K. — Akitsu** Yd No: 379 Loa 55.40 Br ex 12.04 Dght 3.582 Lbp 49.51 Br md 12.02 Dpth 3.76 Welded, 2 dks	**(A35A2RR) Ro-Ro Cargo Ship** Compartments: 1 Ho, ER 1 Ha: (1.9 x 3.5)ER	**2 oil engines** geared to sc. shaft driving 1 FP propeller Total Power: 1,104kW (1,500hp) 13.0kn Niigata 6MMG25BX 2 x 4 Stroke 6 Cy. 250 x 320 each-552kW (750bhp) Niigata Engineering Co Ltd-Japan AuxGen: 2 x 40kW 225V a.c
9109768 *7TXO* -	**TARIQ IBN ZIYAD** **Entreprise Nationale de Transport Maritime des Voyageurs (ENTMV)** - SatCom: Inmarsat C 460500610 *Alger* *Algeria* MMSI: 605246160 Official number: 2942	**21,659** 8,826 5,125 T/cm 30.0	Class: BV	**1995-11 Union Naval de Levante SA (UNL) — Valencia** Yd No: 211 Loa 153.27 (BB) Br ex - Dght 6.000 Lbp 138.00 Br md 25.20 Dpth 8.70 Welded, 2 dks	**(A36A2PR) Passenger/Ro-Ro Ship (Vehicles)** Passengers: unberthed: 508; cabins: 178; berths: 804 Bow door/ramp Len: 13.00 Wid: 5.00 Swl: - Stern door/ramp Len: 10.50 Wid: 8.00 Swl: - Side door/ramp (p. a.) Len: 6.50 Wid: 5.00 Swl: - Lane-Len: 780 Cars: 446	**2 oil engines** with flexible couplings & sr gearedto sc. shafts driving 2 CP propellers Total Power: 22,186kW (30,164hp) 21.5kn Wartsila 12V46 2 x Vee 4 Stroke 12 Cy. 460 x 580 each-11093kW (15082bhp) Wartsila Diesel S.A.-Bermeo AuxGen: 4 x 1300kW 220/380V 50Hz a.c Thrusters: 2 Thwart. CP thruster (f) Fuel: 845.0 (d.f.)
8742147 *YB6288* -	**TARJUN** **PT Benua Raya Katulistiwa** - *Balikpapan* *Indonesia*	**299** 90 -	Class: KI	**2005 C.V. Mercusuar Mandiri — Batam** Loa 42.00 Br ex - Dght - Lbp 39.60 Br md 10.00 Dpth 2.50 Welded, 1 dk	**(A37B2PS) Passenger Ship**	**2 oil engines** reduction geared to sc. shafts driving 2 Propellers Total Power: 470kW (640hp) Mitsubishi 8DC9 2 x Vee 4 Stroke 8 Cy. 135 x 140 each-235kW (320bhp) Mitsubishi Heavy Industries Ltd-Japan AuxGen: 2 x 77kW 380/220V a.c
8659792 - -	**TARJUN 07** **Sdr Effendi** - *Balikpapan* *Indonesia*	**195** 59 -	Class: KI	**2011-06 C.V. Mercusuar Mandiri — Batam** Loa 41.75 Br ex - Dght 1.790 Lbp 35.50 Br md 7.50 Dpth 2.50 Welded, 1 dk	**(A35D2RL) Landing Craft** Bow ramp (centre)	**2 oil engines** reduction geared to sc. shafts driving 2 Propellers AuxGen: 1 x 88kW 380V a.c
9295622 *HP8912* -	**TARKA** *launched as* DMS Blackbird *-2004* **Stardazz Pte Ltd** - *Panama* *Panama* MMSI: 371568000	**212** 63 200	Class: BV	**2004-04 Stocznia Kozle Serwis Sp z oo — Kedzierzyn-Kozle** (Hull) Yd No: 1072 **2004-04 B.V. Scheepswerf Damen Hardinxveld — Hardinxveld-Giessendam** Yd No: 1556 Loa 26.00 Br ex 9.38 Dght 2.650 Lbp 23.36 Br md 9.10 Dpth 3.60 Welded, 1 dk	**(B32A2ST) Tug** Cranes: 1	**2 oil engines** geared to sc. shafts driving 2 Propellers Total Power: 1,650kW (2,244hp) 10.0kn Caterpillar 3508B-TA 2 x Vee 4 Stroke 8 Cy. 170 x 190 each-825kW (1122bhp) Caterpillar Inc-USA AuxGen: 2 x 70kW a.c Thrusters: 1 Tunnel thruster (f) Fuel: 130.0 (d.f.)
8725149 - -	**TARKHAN** *ex* PTR-50 No. 39 *-1994* **Ukrainian Fishing Co Ltd** -	**187** 56 77	Class: (RS)	**1988-03 Astrakhanskaya Sudoverf im. "Kirova" — Astrakhan** Yd No: 39 Loa 31.85 Br ex 7.08 Dght 2.100 Lbp 27.80 Br md - Dpth 3.15 Welded, 1 dk	**(B12B2FC) Fish Carrier** Ins: 100	**1 oil engine** geared to sc. shaft driving 1 FP propeller Total Power: 221kW (300hp) 10.2kn Daldizel 6CHNSP18/22-300 1 x 4 Stroke 6 Cy. 180 x 220 221kW (300bhp) Daldizel-Khabarovsk AuxGen: 2 x 25kW Fuel: 14.0 (d.f.)
6872871 *UZYI* -	**TARKHANKUT** *ex* Ural *-1994* **G V Abuladze** - *Kherson* *Ukraine* Official number: 520102	*255* 88 125	Class: (RS)	**1952 VEB Elbewerft — Boizenburg** Yd No: 193 Converted From: Fishing Vessel Loa 38.51 Br ex 7.37 Dght 2.701 Lbp 34.70 Br md - Dpth 3.41 Welded, 1 dk	**(B12B2FC) Fish Carrier** Ins: 267 Compartments: 2 Ho, ER 2 Ha: 2 (1.2 x 1.2) Derricks: 1x1t Ice Capable	**1 oil engine** driving 1 FP propeller Total Power: 221kW (300hp) 9.5kn S.K.L. R8DV136 1 x 4 Stroke 8 Cy. 240 x 360 221kW (300bhp) VEB Schwermaschinenbau "KarlLiebknecht" (SKL)-Magdeburg AuxGen: 1 x 57kW a.c, 1 x 39kW a.c Fuel: 20.0 (d.f.)
5352886 *ESZA* -	**TARMO** **Government of The Republic of Estonia (Estonian Maritime Administration) (Eesti Veeteede Amet)** - *Tallinn* *Estonia* MMSI: 276158000 Official number: 5R00L24	**3,916** 1,174 1,585		**1963-03 Wartsila-Koncernen, Ab Sandvikens Skeppsdocka & MV — Helsinki** Yd No: 373 Loa 84.51 Br ex 21.21 Dght 7.300 Lbp 78.52 Br md 21.11 Dpth 9.50 Welded, 3 dks	**(B34C2SI) Icebreaker** Ice Capable	**4 diesel electric oil engines** driving 4 gen. each 2400kW 800V d.c Connecting to 4 elec. motors driving 2 Propellers , 2 fwd Total Power: 10,120kW (13,760hp) Sulzer 8MH51 4 x 2 Stroke 8 Cy. 510 x 550 each-2530kW (3440bhp) Wartsila Koncernen, Ab SandvikensSkeppsdocka & MV-Finland AuxGen: 4 x 340kW 450V 60Hz a.c Fuel: 880.0 (d.f.) 50.0pd

IMO / Call sign	Name / Owner	Tonnage	Class	Builder / Dimensions	Type / Cargo	Machinery
6925056 - -	**TARMUGLI** **Government of The Republic of India (Ministry of Home Affairs)** - *Kolkata* *India* Official number: 1353	*338* 134 -		**1969 Garden Reach Workshops Ltd. — Kolkata** Yd No: 598 Loa 37.50 Br ex 8.36 Dght 2.515 Lbp 33.23 Br md 8.08 Dpth 2.90 Welded, 1 dk	**(A37B2PS) Passenger Ship**	**2 oil engines** driving 2 FP propellers Total Power: 382kW (520hp) MAN W6V175/22A 2 x 4 Stroke 6 Cy. 175 x 220 each-191kW (260bhp) Kirloskar Oil Engines Ltd-India
9372652 *OZDU2* -	**TARNBRIS** **Tarnshipping A/S** Tarntank Rederi AB *Skagen* *Denmark (DIS)* MMSI: 219015298 Official number: D4517	**7,315** 3,589 11,289 T/cm 22.2	Class: NV (BV)	**2007-07 Selah Makina Sanayi ve Ticaret A.S. — Tuzla, Istanbul** Yd No: 49 Loa 129.50 (BB) Br ex - Dght 8.150 Lbp 123.00 Br md 19.80 Dpth 10.40 Welded, 1 dk	**(A12B2TR) Chemical/Products Tanker** Double Hull (13F) Liq: 12,215; Liq (Oil): 12,250 Cargo Heating Coils Compartments: 12 Wing Ta, 2 Wing Slop Ta, ER 12 Cargo Pump (s): 12x250m³/hr Manifold: Bow/CM: 65m Ice Capable	**1 oil engine** reduction geared to sc. shaft driving 1 CP propeller Total Power: 4,500kW (6,118hp) 14.5kn MaK 9M32C 1 x 4 Stroke 9 Cy. 320 x 480 4500kW (6118bhp) Caterpillar Motoren GmbH & Co. KG-Germany AuxGen: 3 x 620kW a.c, 1 x a.c Thrusters: 1 Tunnel thruster (f) Fuel: 78.0 (d.f.) 515.0 (r.f.)
9151890 *OWQA2* -	**TARNDAL** *ex Dicksi -2005* **Tarnshipping A/S** Tarntank Rederi AB *Skagen* *Denmark (DIS)* MMSI: 219514000 Official number: D 4654	**5,685** 2,630 8,269 T/cm 16.7	Class: NV	**1998-07 Qiuxin Shipyard — Shanghai** Yd No: 1253 Loa 115.10 (BB) Br ex - Dght 7.200 Lbp 107.83 Br md 18.25 Dpth 9.88 Welded, 1 dk	**(A12A2TC) Chemical Tanker** Double Hull (13F) Liq: 9,007 Compartments: 10 Wing Ta, ER, 2 Wing Slop Ta 10 Cargo Pump (s): 10x350m³/hr Manifold: Bow/CM: 51m Ice Capable	**1 oil engine** geared to sc. shaft driving 1 CP propeller Total Power: 3,960kW (5,384hp) 13.5kn Wartsila 6L38 1 x 4 Stroke 6 Cy. 380 x 475 3960kW (5384bhp) Wartsila NSD Nederland BV-Netherlands AuxGen: 1 x 1300kW 220/450V 60Hz a.c, 2 x 715kW 220/450V 60Hz a.c Thrusters: 1 Thwart. FP thruster (f) Fuel: 116.0 (d.f.) (Heating Coils) 426.0 (r.f.) 14.0pd
9167930 *OWQG2* -	**TARNFORS** *launched as Guervik -1998* **Tarntank Rederi AB** *Skagen* *Denmark (DIS)* MMSI: 219529000 Official number: D 4655	**5,698** 2,607 8,245 T/cm 17.6	Class: NV	**1998-12 Qiuxin Shipyard — Shanghai** Yd No: 1254 Loa 115.10 (BB) Br ex 18.33 Dght 7.500 Lbp 107.83 Br md 18.25 Dpth 9.88 Welded, 1 dk	**(A12B2TR) Chemical/Products Tanker** Double Hull (13F) Liq: 9,009; Liq (Oil): 9,009 Cargo Heating Coils Compartments: 10 Wing Ta, ER 10 Cargo Pump (s): 10x350m³/hr Ice Capable	**1 oil engine** Connecting to 1 elec. Motor reduction geared to sc. shaft driving 1 CP propeller Total Power: 3,960kW (5,384hp) 14.0kn Wartsila 6R38 1 x 4 Stroke 6 Cy. 380 x 475 3960kW (5384bhp) Wartsila NSD Nederland BV-Netherlands AuxGen: 1 x 1300kW 220/450V 60Hz a.c, 2 x 720kW 220/450V 60Hz a.c, 1 x 350kW 220/450V 60Hz a.c Thrusters: 1 Thwart. FP thruster (f) Fuel: 129.5 (d.f.) 388.2 (r.f.) 14.0pd
7041560 *UBWT* -	**TARNICA** **Maritime Projects & Technologies Ltd** *Russia* MMSI: 273317840	**564** 182 641	Class: (PR)	**1970 Wroclawska Stocznia Rzeczna — Wroclaw** Yd No: ZB700/04 Loa 57.35 Br ex 9.05 Dght 3.280 Lbp 54.00 Br md 9.01 Dpth 3.74 Welded, 1 dk	**(B34E2SW) Waste Disposal Vessel** Liq: 692; Liq (Oil): 692 Cargo Heating Coils Compartments: 8 Ta, ER 3 Cargo Pump (s): 3x215m³/hr Manifold: Bow/CM: 24m Ice Capable	**1 oil engine** driving 1 FP propeller Total Power: 294kW (400hp) 8.0kn Sulzer 8BAH22 1 x 2 Stroke 8 Cy. 220 x 320 294kW (400bhp) Zaklady Przemyslu Metalowego 'HCegielski' SA-Poznan AuxGen: 3 x 120kW 400V 50Hz a.c Fuel: 24.0 (d.f.) (Heating Coils)
9168386 *3FBV2* -	**TAROKO** *ex Shichigahama Maru -2009* **TG Finance Co Ltd** Wisdom Marine Lines SA *Panama* *Panama* MMSI: 351725000 Official number: 4100810A	**4,814** 2,938 7,984	Class: NK	**1997-06 Nishi Shipbuilding Co Ltd — Imabari EH** Yd No: 404 Loa 99.99 Br ex - Dght 7.213 Lbp 94.50 Br md 18.80 Dpth 9.20 Welded, 1 dk	**(A31A2GX) General Cargo Ship** Grain: 10,211; Bale: 9,500 2 Ha: (17.8 x 10.5) (30.4 x 10.5) Derricks: 2x30t,1x25t	**1 oil engine** driving 1 FP propeller Total Power: 3,236kW (4,400hp) 12.5kn Mitsubishi 6UEC33LSII 1 x 2 Stroke 6 Cy. 330 x 1050 3236kW (4400bhp) Akasaka Tekkosho KK (Akasaka DieselLtd)-Japan Fuel: 480.0
9275397 *A8ZK7* -	**TAROKO** *ex OOCL Melbourne -2011* **Little Pine Key Ltd** Seachange Maritime LLC *Monrovia* *Liberia* MMSI: 636015233 Official number: 15233	**34,610** 16,865 43,093 T/cm 61.1	Class: NK	**2003-06 Koyo Dockyard Co Ltd — Mihara HS** Yd No: 2146 Loa 234.62 (BB) Br ex 32.23 Dght 12.520 Lbp 218.00 Br md 32.20 Dpth 18.80 Welded, 1 dk	**(A33A2CC) Container Ship (Fully Cellular)** TEU 2762 C Ho 1216 TEU C Dk 1546 TEU incl 300 ref C. Compartments: ER, 6 Cell Ho	**1 oil engine** driving 1 FP propeller Total Power: 28,880kW (39,265hp) 22.6kn B&W 8K80MC-C 1 x 2 Stroke 8 Cy. 800 x 2300 28880kW (39265bhp) Mitsui Engineering & Shipbuilding CLtd-Japan AuxGen: 4 x 1200kW 450/225V 60Hz a.c Thrusters: 1 Thwart. FP thruster (f) Fuel: 141.0 (d.f.) 4725.0 (r.f.) 108.0pd
9486996 *UPX* -	**TARPAN** *ex Caspian Mover 1 -2009* **Arzalk Shipping Ltd** Albros Shipping & Trading Ltd Co (Albros Denizcilik ve Ticaret Ltd Sti) *Aqtau* *Kazakhstan* MMSI: 436000076	**712** 213 574	Class: BV	**2009-02 Gelibolu Gemi Insa Sanayi ve Ticaret AS — Gelibolu** Yd No: 43 Loa 42.00 Br ex - Dght 3.500 Lbp 40.49 Br md 12.50 Dpth 4.83 Welded, 1 dk	**(B21B20A) Anchor Handling Tug Supply** Passengers: berths: 18	**3 oil engines** reduction geared to sc. shafts driving 3 CP propellers Total Power: 3,642kW (4,953hp) Cummins KTA-50-M2 3 x Vee 4 Stroke 16 Cy. 159 x 159 each-1214kW (1651bhp) Cummins Engine Co Inc-USA AuxGen: 3 x 150kW 400V 50Hz a.c Thrusters: 1 Tunnel thruster (f) Fuel: 330.0 (d.f.)
8880509 - -	**TARPAN** **Formant Co Ltd** -	**353** 111 155	Class: (RS)	**1994-11 Sretenskiy Sudostroitelnyy Zavod — Sretensk** Yd No: 208 Loa 39.90 Br ex 8.90 Dght 3.200 Lbp 36.23 Br md - Dpth 4.60 Welded, 1 dk	**(B11B2FV) Fishing Vessel** Grain: 95 Ice Capable	**1 oil engine** geared to sc. shaft driving 1 CP propeller Total Power: 441kW (600hp) 9.5kn Daldizel 6CHNSP18/22-600 1 x 4 Stroke 6 Cy. 180 x 220 441kW (600bhp) Daldizel-Khabarovsk AuxGen: 3 x 75kW Fuel: 60.0 (d.f.)
7629037 - -	**TARPAN** - -	*184* - 46	Class: (PR)	**1975 "Petrozavod" — Leningrad** Yd No: 848 Loa 29.29 Br ex 8.31 Dght 3.080 Lbp 25.43 Br md - Dpth 4.35 Welded, 1 dk	**(B32A2ST) Tug** Ice Capable	**2 oil engines** driving 2 FP propellers Total Power: 882kW (1,200hp) 10.5kn Russkiy 6DR30/50-4-2 2 x 2 Stroke 6 Cy. 300 x 500 each-441kW (600bhp) Mashinostroitelnyy Zavod"Russkiy-Dizel"-Leningrad AuxGen: 2 x 20kW 380V a.c
8317502 *VJAH* -	**TARPAN** **Svitzer Australia Pty Ltd (Svitzer Australasia)** SatCom: Inmarsat C 450301980 *Port Adelaide, SA* *Australia* MMSI: 503079000 Official number: 851326	*426* 128 420	Class: LR (AB) **100A1** SS 12/2009 tug **LMC** **UMS** Eq.Ltr: H; Cable: 302.5/22.0 U2	**1984-12 Tamar Shipbuilding Pty Ltd — Launceston TAS** Yd No: 41 Loa 32.31 Br ex 10.90 Dght 4.560 Lbp 30.31 Br md 10.61 Dpth 5.36 Welded, 1 dk	**(B32A2ST) Tug**	**2 oil engines** with clutches & sr geared to sc. shafts driving 2 Directional propellers Total Power: 2,648kW (3,600hp) 12.0kn Daihatsu 6DSM-28 2 x 4 Stroke 6 Cy. 280 x 340 each-1324kW (1800bhp) Daihatsu Diesel Manufacturing Co Lt-Japan AuxGen: 2 x 150kW 415V 50Hz a.c
7390923 *WYT8695* -	**TARPON** *ex Morania No. 1 -1993* *ex Miriam M. Defelice -1986* **Penn Maritime Inc** *Philadelphia, PA* *United States of America* MMSI: 366920940 Official number: 556953	**448** 134 -	Class: AB	**1974-05 McDermott Shipyards Inc — Morgan City LA** Yd No: 191 Converted From: Tug-2006 Loa - Br ex 10.37 Dght 4.242 Lbp 36.63 Br md 10.34 Dpth 5.01 Welded, 1 dk	**(B32B2SA) Articulated Pusher Tug**	**2 oil engines** reverse reduction geared to sc. shafts driving 2 FP propellers Total Power: 3,162kW (4,300hp) 12.0kn EMD (Electro-Motive) 12-645-E5 2 x Vee 2 Stroke 12 Cy. 230 x 254 each-1581kW (2150bhp) General Motors Corp.Electro-Motive Div.-La Grange AuxGen: 2 x 75kW a.c Fuel: 457.0 (d.f.)
9055292 *UADV* -	**TARPON** **Akros Fishing Co Ltd (A/O Akros)** SatCom: Inmarsat A 1407262 *Petropavlovsk-Kamchatskiy* *Russia* MMSI: 273845700	**1,315** 395 857	Class: RS (NV)	**1994-10 Elbewerft Boizenburg GmbH — Boizenburg** Yd No: 111 Loa 52.50 (BB) Br ex 11.59 Dght 5.426 Lbp 45.00 Br md 11.50 Dpth 8.05 Welded, 2 dks	**(B11B2FV) Fishing Vessel** Ins: 850 Ice Capable	**1 oil engine** with flexible couplings & reduction geared to sc. shaft driving 1 CP propeller Total Power: 1,060kW (1,441hp) MAN-B&W 8L23/30A 1 x 4 Stroke 8 Cy. 225 x 300 1060kW (1441bhp) MAN B&W Diesel AG-Augsburg AuxGen: 2 x 291kW a.c, 1 x 560kW a.c Thrusters: 1 Thwart. FP thruster (f)
7325162 *HC2615* -	**TARQUI** *ex Maria -1986* **Inepaca CA** *Manta* *Ecuador* Official number: P-04-0020	**444** 162 159		**1973 Astilleros de Veracruz S.A. — Veracruz** Yd No: 94 Loa 31.48 Br ex 8.79 Dght 3.963 Lbp 28.76 Br md 8.62 Dpth 4.68 Welded, 2 dks	**(B11B2FV) Fishing Vessel**	**1 oil engine** driving 1 FP propeller Total Power: 372kW (506hp) Caterpillar D379TA 1 x Vee 4 Stroke 8 Cy. 159 x 203 372kW (506bhp) Caterpillar Tractor Co-USA

6807357 **TARRAFAL**
D4ER *ex* Buganvilla *-2004* *ex* Betula *-1992*
- **Sociedad de Transportes Maritimos Ltda (STM)**
Sao Vicente *Cape Verde*

3,686
1,308
868

Class: (LR)
✠ Classed LR until 25/4/07

1968-04 Jos L Meyer — Papenburg Yd No: 532
Loa 71.30 Br ex 16.74 Dght 4.001
Lbp 64.17 Br md 16.31 Dpth 5.41
Welded, 1 dk, 2nd dk clear of mchy. spaces spaces

(A36A2PR) Passenger/Ro-Ro Ship (Vehicles)
Passengers: unberthed: 900
Bow door & ramp
Stern door/ramp
Lane-Len: 216
Lane-clr ht: 4.30
Cars: 105
Ice Capable

4 oil engines sr geared to sc. shafts + NE (p inboard & outboard) 2/83 + NE (s outer) made 67 fitted 9/82 driving 2 CP propellers
Total Power: 3,236kW (4,400hp) 14.5kn
Deutz SBA8M528
4 x 4 Stroke 8 Cy. 220 x 280 each-809kW (1100bhp) (new engine ,made 1967, fitted 1982)
Kloeckner Humboldt Deutz AG-West Germany
AuxGen: 1 x 148kW 380V 50Hz a.c, 4 x 115kW 380V 50Hz a.c
Thrusters: 1 Thwart. FP thruster (f)

8820212 **TARRAGONA**
A8NH4 *ex* Maersk Tarragona *-2013*
- *ex* Tobias Maersk *-2007* *ex* TRSL Antares *-1996*
ex Tobias Maersk *-1995*
Hermes Marine LLC (MI)
Technomar Shipping Inc
SatCom: Inmarsat C 463700975
Monrovia *Liberia*
MMSI: 636013480
Official number: 13480

17,700
7,244
21,229
T/cm
38.7

Class: RI (LR) (AB)
✠ Classed LR until 22/3/11

1990-07 Tsuneishi Shipbuilding Co Ltd — Fukuyama HS Yd No: 628
Loa 161.02 (BB) Br ex 28.23 Dght 10.000
Lbp 152.00 Br md 28.20 Dpth 15.30
Welded, 1 dk

(A33A2CC) Container Ship (Fully Cellular)
TEU 1316 C Ho 554 TEU C Dk 762 TEU incl 118 ref C.
Compartments: 4 Cell Ho, ER
8 Ha: (6.5 x 12.9) (12.6 x 17.8)6 (14.2 x 22.8)ER
Gantry cranes: 1x40t

1 oil engine driving 1 CP propeller
Total Power: 10,480kW (14,249hp) 18.5kn
B&W 8S50MC
1 x 2 Stroke 8 Cy. 500 x 1910 10480kW (14249bhp)
Mitsui Engineering & Shipbuilding CLtd-Japan
AuxGen: 3 x 1160kW 450V 60Hz a.c
Boilers: AuxB (ex.g.), AuxB (o.f.) 7.0kgf/cm² (6.9bar)
Thrusters: 1 Thwart. CP thruster (f); 1 Thwart. CP thruster (a)

7123394 **TARRAO EXPRESS**
3FLL6 *ex* Anclamar *-1998* *ex* Venus II *-1998*
- *ex* Venusia *-1996* *ex* Vittoria *-1994*
ex Domenico Scotto *-1993* *ex* Aiden *-1981*
ex Jackie Silvana *-1980*
ex Thea Danielsen *-1978*
Baineivy-N Corp
-
Panama *Panama*
MMSI: 356715000
Official number: 25455PEXT4

1,596
996
2,816

Class: (RI) (BV)

1972-01 Bodewes' Scheepswerven N.V. — Hoogezand Yd No: 511
Loa 87.46 Br ex 11.94 Dght 5.360
Lbp 79.18 Br md 11.89 Dpth 6.51
Welded, 1 dk

(A31A2GX) General Cargo Ship
Grain: 3,475; Bale: 3,242
Compartments: 1 Ho, ER
2 Ha: 2 (18.5 x 8.5)ER
Derricks: 4x3t; Winches: 4

1 oil engine driving 1 FP propeller
Total Power: 1,177kW (1,600hp) 12.5kn
MaK 8M451AK
1 x 4 Stroke 8 Cy. 320 x 450 1177kW (1600bhp)
MaK Maschinenbau GmbH-Kiel
AuxGen: 2 x 105kW 380V 50Hz a.c, 1 x 42kW 380V 50Hz a.c
Fuel: 154.5 (d.f.) 6.0pd

7930620 **TARSAN I**
YB5202 *ex* Eben *-2004* *ex* Tong Un No. 303 *-2001*
- **PT Pelayaran Bina Usaha Surya**
-
Surabaya *Indonesia*

291
141
400

Class: KI (KR)

1980-11 Donghae Shipbuilding Co Ltd — Ulsan Yd No: 7925
Loa 43.21 Br ex 7.83 Dght 2.720
Lbp 38.00 Br md 7.80 Dpth 3.70
Welded, 1 dk

(A31A2GX) General Cargo Ship
Grain: 446; Bale: 405
1 Ha: (16.9 x 3.9)ER
Derricks: 3x2t

1 oil engine driving 1 FP propeller
Total Power: 368kW (500hp) 10.8kn
Matsui MU623CGHS
1 x 4 Stroke 6 Cy. 230 x 380 368kW (500bhp)
Matsui Iron Works Co Ltd-Japan
AuxGen: 2 x 14kW 220V a.c

7727358 **TARSANA 1**
-
- **Suez Canal Authority**
-
Suez *Egypt*

106
-
-

Class: (NV)

1978-12 Salthammer Baatbyggeri AS — Vestnes (Hull)
1978-10 Bolsones Verft AS — Molde Yd No: 260
Loa 22.51 Br ex 6.71 Dght 3.244
Lbp 20.17 Br md 6.68 Dpth 3.54
Welded, 1 dk

(B32A2ST) Tug
Ice Capable

1 oil engine reduction geared to sc. shaft driving 1 FP propeller
Total Power: 1,250kW (1,700hp)
Deutz SBA12M528
1 x Vee 4 Stroke 12 Cy. 220 x 280 1250kW (1700bhp)
Kloeckner Humboldt Deutz AG-West Germany
AuxGen: 2 x 50kW 380V 50Hz a.c, 1 x 32kW 380V 50Hz a.c
Thrusters: 1 Thwart. FP thruster (f)

7727360 **TARSANA 2**
SUOY
- **Suez Canal Authority**
-
Suez *Egypt*

106
-
-

Class: (NV)

1978-12 Salthammer Baatbyggeri AS — Vestnes (Hull)
1978-12 Bolsones Verft AS — Molde Yd No: 261
Loa 22.51 Br ex 6.71 Dght 3.244
Lbp 20.17 Br md 6.68 Dpth 3.54
Welded, 1 dk

(B32A2ST) Tug
Ice Capable

1 oil engine reduction geared to sc. shaft driving 1 FP propeller
Total Power: 1,250kW (1,700hp)
Deutz SBA12M528
1 x Vee 4 Stroke 12 Cy. 220 x 280 1250kW (1700bhp)
Kloeckner Humboldt Deutz AG-West Germany
AuxGen: 2 x 50kW 380V 50Hz a.c, 1 x 32kW 380V 50Hz a.c
Thrusters: 1 Thwart. FP thruster (f)

6718257 **TARSO**
- *ex* Zapata *-1996*
- **Tarso Peche Sarl**
-
Dakar *Senegal*

131
39
242

Class: (BV)

1967 Construcciones Navales P Freire SA — Vigo Yd No: 42
Loa 26.62 Br ex 6.33 Dght 3.125
Lbp 23.02 Br md 6.30 Dpth 3.41
Welded, 1 dk

(B11A2FT) Trawler
Ins: 8,334
2 Ha: 2 (1.0 x 1.3)ER
Derricks: 1x3t

1 oil engine reduction geared to sc. shaft driving 1 FP propeller
Total Power: 325kW (442hp) 10.3kn
GUASCOR E318T-SP
1 x Vee 4 Stroke 12 Cy. 150 x 150 325kW (442bhp) (new engine 1982)
Gutierrez Ascunce Corp (GUASCOR)-Spain
Fuel: 36.5 (d.f.)

9487213 **TARSUS**
9HTR9
- **Tarsus Shipping Ltd**
Genel Denizcilik Nakliyati AS (GEDEN LINES)
Valletta *Malta*
MMSI: 249419000
Official number: 9487213

31,117
18,159
53,208

Class: NV (BV)

2008-11 Zhejiang Shipbuilding Co Ltd — Ningbo ZJ Yd No: 07-171
Loa 189.90 (BB) Br ex - Dght 12.490
Lbp 182.00 Br md 32.26 Dpth 17.20
Welded, 1 dk

(A21A2BC) Bulk Carrier
Grain: 65,049
Compartments: 5 Ho, ER
5 Ha: ER
Cranes: 4x35t

1 oil engine driving 1 CP propeller
Total Power: 9,480kW (12,889hp) 14.7kn
MAN-B&W 6S50MC-C
1 x 2 Stroke 6 Cy. 500 x 2000 9480kW (12889bhp)
Doosan Engine Co Ltd-South Korea
AuxGen: 3 x a.c

8890293 **TARTI**
SX4333 *ex* Falcon III *-2005* *ex* Meteor 29 *-1995*
- **Olympus Sea Lines Shipping Co**
-
Piraeus *Greece*
MMSI: 237022200
Official number: 10372

136
96
-

Class: (AB)

1974 Zelenodolskiy Sudostroitelnyy Zavod im. "Gorkogo" — Zelenodolsk Yd No: 015
Loa 34.60 Br ex 9.50 Dght -
Lbp 28.00 Br md 9.48 Dpth 2.62
Welded, 1 dk

(A37B2PS) Passenger Ship
Hull Material: Aluminium Alloy

2 oil engines driving 2 FP propellers
Total Power: 1,618kW (2,200hp)
Zvezda M400
2 x Vee 4 Stroke 12 Cy. 180 x 200 each-809kW (1100bhp)
"Zvezda"-Leningrad

7408782 **TARTOUS**
-
- **Syrian Petroleum Co**
-

300
-
-

Class: (BV)

1976 Diesel Workshop — Lebanon Yd No: B44
Loa - Br ex - Dght 1.400
Lbp 41.52 Br md 10.00 Dpth 3.50
Welded

(B22A2OR) Offshore Support Vessel

2 oil engines driving 2 FP propellers

7013252 **TARU II**
HKRV *ex* Jenlil *-1991* *ex* Afro Star *-1985*
- *ex* Amigo Star *-1979* *ex* Tove Lonborg *-1976*
ex Marag Star *-1973* *ex* Vibeke Dania *-1970*
-
-
Isla de San Andres *Colombia*
Official number: MC-07-133

299
167
848

Class: (BV) (NV)

1970 Batservice Verft AS — Mandal Yd No: 588
Loa 55.00 Br ex 9.33 Dght 3.512
Lbp 50.02 Br md 9.30 Dpth 4.61
Welded, 2 dks

(A31A2GX) General Cargo Ship
Grain: 1,548; Bale: 1,398
TEU 28 C. 28/20'
Compartments: 1 Ho, ER
2 Ha: 2 (13.3 x 6.0)ER
Derricks: 2x5t; Winches: 2
Ice Capable

1 oil engine driving 1 CP propeller
Total Power: 441kW (600hp) 10.0kn
Alpha 406-26VO
1 x 2 Stroke 6 Cy. 260 x 400 441kW (600bhp)
Alpha Diesel A/S-Denmark
AuxGen: 2 x 35kW 220V 50Hz a.c
Fuel: 40.5 (d.f.) 2.5pd

7711115 **TARU III**
- *ex* Maasmond *-1994* *ex* Atap *-1993*
- *ex* Pia Arre *-1992* *ex* Jackson Bay *-1992*
ex Pia Arre *-1992*
-
-
Isla de San Andres *Colombia*
Official number: MC-07-140

399
276
746

Class: (BV)

1977-06 Soby Motorfabrik og Staalskibsvaerft A/S — Soby Yd No: 57
Loa 62.18 Br ex 11.26 Dght 3.556
Lbp 57.00 Br md 11.21 Dpth 3.61
Welded, 2 dks

(A31A2GX) General Cargo Ship
Grain: 2,442; Bale: 2,250
Compartments: 2 Ho, ER
1 Ha: (34.2 x 7.7)ER
Derricks: 2x5t
Ice Capable

1 oil engine driving 1 CP propeller
Total Power: 662kW (900hp) 11.0kn
Alpha 409-26VO
1 x 2 Stroke 9 Cy. 260 x 400 662kW (900bhp) (made 1976)
Alpha Diesel A/S-Denmark
AuxGen: 3 x 60kW 220/380V 50Hz a.c
Fuel: 118.0 (d.f.)

6705743 **TARUA 6**
-
- **Port Authority of Thailand (Marine Department)**
-
Bangkok *Thailand*
Official number: 101019118

171
-
-

1967-02 Theodor Buschmann Schiffswerft GmbH & Co. — Hamburg Yd No: 118
Loa 27.51 Br ex 8.16 Dght 3.404
Lbp 24.77 Br md 7.65 Dpth 3.76
Welded, 1 dk

(B32A2ST) Tug

1 oil engine driving 1 Directional propeller
Total Power: 736kW (1,001hp)
MWM
1 x 4 Stroke 8 Cy. 320 x 480 736kW (1001bhp)
Motoren Werke Mannheim AG (MWM)-West Germany

6821860 **TARUA 7**
-
- **Port Authority of Thailand (Marine Department)**
-
Bangkok *Thailand*

175
-
-

1968-08 Elsflether Werft AG — Elsfleth Yd No: 359
Loa 28.38 Br ex 8.28 Dght 3.810
Lbp 25.48 Br md 7.90 Dpth 3.87
Welded, 1 dk

(B32A2ST) Tug

1 oil engine driving 1 Directional propeller
MWM
1 x 4 Stroke 6 Cy. 360 x 450
Motoren Werke Mannheim AG (MWM)-West Germany

7723560 **TARUA 10**
-
- **Port Authority of Thailand (Marine Department)**
-
Bangkok *Thailand*

178
46
160

Class: (AB)

1977 Sing Koon Seng Pte Ltd — Singapore Yd No: SKS423
Loa 25.51 Br ex - Dght -
Lbp 23.91 Br md 7.62 Dpth 3.84
Welded, 1 dk

(B32A2ST) Tug

2 oil engines geared to sc. shafts driving 2 FP propellers
Total Power: 1,104kW (1,500hp) 10.0kn
Caterpillar D398TA
2 x Vee 4 Stroke 12 Cy. 159 x 203 each-552kW (750bhp)
Caterpillar Tractor Co-USA

LR/IMO No. / Call sign	Ship name / Owner / Manager / Port / Flag	Tonnage	Class	Built / Builder / Dimensions	Type / Cargo	Machinery
8112768 - -	**TARUA 12** **Port Authority of Thailand (Marine Department)** - *Bangkok* *Thailand*	*220* 183 -	Class: (AB)	**1981-09 Sing Koon Seng Pte Ltd — Singapore** Yd No: 578 Loa 32.42 Br ex - Dght 3.601 Lbp 29.70 Br md 9.30 Dpth 4.60 Welded, 1 dk	**(B32A2ST) Tug**	**1 oil engine** sr geared to sc. shaft driving 1 FP propeller Total Power: 1,324kW (1,800hp) Yanmar 6Z-ET 1 x 4 Stroke 6 Cy. 280 x 340 1324kW (1800bhp) Yanmar Diesel Engine Co Ltd-Japan
8706507 - -	**TARUA 113** **Port Authority of Thailand (Marine Department)** - *Bangkok* *Thailand*	*193* 131 -	Class: (GL)	**1986-08 The Sahaisant Co., Ltd. — Bangkok** Yd No: 198 Loa - Br ex - Dght - Lbp 27.01 Br md 7.92 Dpth 4.12 Welded, 1 dk	**(B32A2ST) Tug**	**1 oil engine** geared to sc. shaft driving 1 FP propeller Total Power: 914kW (1,243hp) Blackstone ESL6MK2 1 x 4 Stroke 6 Cy. 222 x 292 914kW (1243bhp) Mirrlees Blackstone (Stamford)Ltd.-Stamford
8706519 - -	**TARUA 114** **Port Authority of Thailand (Marine Department)** - *Bangkok* *Thailand*	*193* 131 -	Class: (GL)	**1986-08 The Sahaisant Co., Ltd. — Bangkok** Yd No: 199 Loa - Br ex - Dght - Lbp 27.01 Br md 7.92 Dpth 4.12 Welded, 1 dk	**(B32A2ST) Tug**	**1 oil engine** geared to sc. shaft driving 1 FP propeller Total Power: 914kW (1,243hp) Blackstone ESL6MK2 1 x 4 Stroke 6 Cy. 222 x 292 914kW (1243bhp) Mirrlees Blackstone (Stamford)Ltd.-Stamford
9040261 - -	**TARUA 115** **Port Authority of Thailand (Marine Department)** - *Thailand* Official number: 351002781	**302** 90 -	Class: (AB)	**1992-08 The Sahaisant Co., Ltd. — Bangkok** Yd No: 228 Loa - Br ex - Dght - Lbp 25.00 Br md 9.80 Dpth 3.85 Welded, 1 dk	**(B32A2ST) Tug**	**2 oil engines** reduction geared to sc. shaft driving 1 Voith-Schneider propeller Total Power: 3,600kW (4,894hp) Yanmar 2 x 4 Stroke 6 Cy. 220 x 300 each-1800kW (2447bhp) Yanmar Diesel Engine Co Ltd-Japan
9040273 - -	**TARUA 116** **Port Authority of Thailand (Marine Department)** - *Thailand* Official number: 351002799	**302** 90 -	Class: (AB)	**1992-08 The Sahaisant Co., Ltd. — Bangkok** Yd No: 229 Loa - Br ex - Dght - Lbp 25.00 Br md 9.80 Dpth 3.85 Welded, 1 dk	**(B32A2ST) Tug**	**2 oil engines** reduction geared to sc. shaft driving 1 Voith-Schneider propeller Total Power: 3,600kW (4,894hp) Yanmar 2 x 4 Stroke 6 Cy. 220 x 300 each-1800kW (2447bhp) Yanmar Diesel Engine Co Ltd-Japan
9579975 - -	**TARUA 119** **Port Authority of Thailand (Marine Department)** - *Bangkok* *Thailand* Official number: 5400-02924	**418** - 170	Class: (LR) ✠ Classed LR until 30/11/11	**2011-11 Asian Marine Services Public Co Ltd (ASIMAR) — Phra Samut Chedi** Yd No: 51 Loa 32.00 (BB) Br ex 10.54 Dght 3.100 Lbp 30.80 Br md 10.50 Dpth 4.50 Welded, 1 dk	**(B32A2ST) Tug**	**2 oil engines** gearing integral to driving 2 Directional propellers Total Power: 2,060kW (2,800hp) Yanmar 8N21A-EN 2 x 4 Stroke 8 Cy. 210 x 290 each-1030kW (1400bhp) Yanmar Diesel Engine Co Ltd-Japan AuxGen: 2 x 151kW 380V 50Hz a.c
9621388 - -	**TARUA 120** **Port Authority of Thailand (Marine Department)** - *Bangkok* *Thailand* Official number: 5500-01645	**424** 128 172	Class: (LR) ✠ Classed LR until 5/10/13	**2012-07 Italthai Marine Co., Ltd. — Samut Prakan** Yd No: 162 Loa 28.20 Br ex 11.81 Dght 3.750 Lbp 22.50 Br md 11.50 Dpth 5.34 Welded, 1 dk	**(B32A2ST) Tug**	**2 oil engines** gearing integral to driving 2 Z propellers Total Power: 2,120kW (2,882hp) Daihatsu 6DKM-20 2 x 4 Stroke 6 Cy. 200 x 300 each-1060kW (1441bhp) Daihatsu Diesel Manufacturing Co Lt-Japan AuxGen: 2 x 132kW 380V 50Hz a.c Fuel: 63.0 (d.f.)
9005651 *HSFV* -	**TARUA 203** **Port Authority of Thailand (Marine Department)** Government of The Kingdom of Thailand (Marine Department) *Bangkok* *Thailand* Official number: 331002363	**300** 90 93	Class: (NK)	**1990-12 K.K. Odo Zosen Tekko — Shimonoseki** Yd No: 383 Loa 34.30 Br ex - Dght 2.662 Lbp 31.68 Br md 9.00 Dpth 3.80 Welded, 1 dk	**(B32A2ST) Tug**	**2 oil engines** with clutches, flexible couplings & dr geared to sc. shafts driving 2 Directional propellers Total Power: 2,206kW (3,000hp) Yanmar T260-ET 2 x 4 Stroke 6 Cy. 260 x 330 each-1103kW (1500bhp) Yanmar Diesel Engine Co Ltd-Japan AuxGen: 2 x 96kW a.c
9005663 *HSFW* -	**TARUA 204** **Port Authority of Thailand (Marine Department)** Government of The Kingdom of Thailand (Marine Department) *Bangkok* *Thailand* Official number: 331002371	**299** 90 93	Class: (NK)	**1991-03 K.K. Odo Zosen Tekko — Shimonoseki** Yd No: 384 Loa 34.30 Br ex - Dght 2.662 Lbp 31.68 Br md 9.00 Dpth 3.80 Welded	**(B32A2ST) Tug**	**2 oil engines** with clutches, flexible couplings & dr geared to sc. shafts driving 2 Directional propellers Total Power: 2,206kW (3,000hp) 12.5kn Yanmar T260-ET 2 x 4 Stroke 6 Cy. 260 x 330 each-1103kW (1500bhp) Yanmar Diesel Engine Co Ltd-Japan AuxGen: 2 x 96kW a.c
9005675 *HSFX* -	**TARUA 205** **Port Authority of Thailand (Marine Department)** Government of The Kingdom of Thailand (Marine Department) *Bangkok* *Thailand* Official number: 331002389	**299** 90 93	Class: (NK)	**1991-03 K.K. Odo Zosen Tekko — Shimonoseki** Yd No: 385 Loa 34.30 Br ex 9.29 Dght 2.662 Lbp 31.68 Br md 9.00 Dpth 3.80 Welded, 1 dk	**(B32A2ST) Tug**	**2 oil engines** with clutches, flexible couplings & dr geared to sc. shafts driving 2 Directional propellers Total Power: 2,206kW (3,000hp) 12.5kn Yanmar T260-ET 2 x 4 Stroke 6 Cy. 260 x 330 each-1103kW (1500bhp) Yanmar Diesel Engine Co Ltd-Japan AuxGen: 2 x 96kW a.c
9005687 *HSFY* -	**TARUA 206** **Port Authority of Thailand (Marine Department)** Government of The Kingdom of Thailand (Marine Department) *Bangkok* *Thailand* Official number: 341001246	**108** 33 67	Class: (NK)	**1991-03 K.K. Odo Zosen Tekko — Shimonoseki** Yd No: 386 Loa 22.50 Br ex 6.78 Dght 2.201 Lbp 20.22 Br md 6.60 Dpth 3.00 Welded, 1 dk	**(B32A2ST) Tug**	**2 oil engines** geared to sc. shafts driving 2 FP propellers Total Power: 736kW (1,000hp) 10.4kn Yanmar 6KHK-ST 2 x 4 Stroke 6 Cy. 133 x 160 each-368kW (500bhp) Yanmar Diesel Engine Co Ltd-Japan AuxGen: 2 x 30kW a.c
9005699 *HSFZ* -	**TARUA 207** **Port Authority of Thailand (Marine Department)** Government of The Kingdom of Thailand (Marine Department) *Bangkok* *Thailand* Official number: 341001254	**108** 33 67	Class: (NK)	**1991-03 K.K. Odo Zosen Tekko — Shimonoseki** Yd No: 387 Loa 22.50 Br ex 6.78 Dght 2.201 Lbp 20.22 Br md 6.60 Dpth 3.00 Welded, 1 dk	**(B32A2ST) Tug**	**2 oil engines** with clutches, flexible couplings & dr geared to sc. shafts driving 2 CP propellers Total Power: 736kW (1,000hp) 10.4kn Yanmar 6KHK-ST 2 x 4 Stroke 6 Cy. 133 x 160 each-368kW (500bhp) Yanmar Diesel Engine Co Ltd-Japan AuxGen: 2 x 30kW a.c
9579987 - -	**TARUA 301** **Port Authority of Thailand (Marine Department)** - *Bangkok* *Thailand* Official number: 5400-02916	**418** - 170	Class: (LR) ✠ Classed LR until 30/11/11	**2011-11 Asian Marine Services Public Co Ltd (ASIMAR) — Phra Samut Chedi** Yd No: 52 Loa 32.00 Br ex 10.54 Dght 3.100 Lbp 30.80 Br md 10.50 Dpth 4.50 Welded, 1 dk	**(B32A2ST) Tug**	**2 oil engines** gearing integral to driving 2 Directional propellers Total Power: 2,060kW (2,800hp) Yanmar 8N21A-UN 2 x 4 Stroke 8 Cy. 210 x 290 each-1030kW (1400bhp) Yanmar Diesel Engine Co Ltd-Japan AuxGen: 2 x 151kW 380V 50Hz a.c
9639127 - -	**TARUA 302** **Port Authority of Thailand (Marine Department)** - *Bangkok* *Thailand* Official number: 5500-03401	**424** - 133	Class: (LR) ✠ Classed LR until 5/10/13	**2012-11 Italthai Marine Co., Ltd. — Samut Prakan** Yd No: 163 Loa 28.20 Br ex 11.81 Dght 4.400 Lbp 22.50 Br md 11.50 Dpth 5.34 Welded, 1 dk	**(B32A2ST) Tug**	**2 oil engines** gearing integral to driving 2 Z propellers Total Power: 3,236kW (4,400hp) Daihatsu 6DKM-26 2 x 4 Stroke 6 Cy. 260 x 380 each-1618kW (2200bhp) Daihatsu Diesel Manufacturing Co Lt-Japan AuxGen: 2 x 132kW 380V 50Hz a.c Fuel: 106.0 (r.f.)
9331402 *3EBF6* -	**TARUCA** *ex Cedar Galaxy -2012* **Gem Shipping Inc** Naviera Ultranav Ltda *Panama* *Panama* MMSI: 371094000 Official number: 3082905B	**11,728** 6,349 19,983 T/cm 29.8	Class: NK	**2005-06 Fukuoka Shipbuilding Co Ltd — Fukuoka FO** Yd No: 1251 Loa 144.09 (BB) Br ex 24.23 Dght 9.666 Lbp 136.00 Br md 24.19 Dpth 12.90 Welded, 1 dk	**(A12B2TR) Chemical/Products Tanker** Double Hull (13F) Liq: 20,971; Liq (Oil): 20,971 Cargo Heating Coils Compartments: 20 Ta (s.stl), 2 Slop Ta (s.stl), ER (s.stl) 20 Cargo Pump (s): 14x300m³/hr, 6x200m³/hr Manifold: Bow/CM: 80.5m	**1 oil engine** driving 1 FP propeller Total Power: 6,230kW (8,470hp) 14.5kn Mitsubishi 7UEC45LA 1 x 2 Stroke 7 Cy. 450 x 1350 6230kW (8470bhp) Akasaka Tekkosho KK (Akasaka DieselLtd)-Japan AuxGen: 3 x 450kW a.c Thrusters: 1 Tunnel thruster (f) Fuel: 126.0 (d.f.) 993.0 (r.f.)
9267625 *7JQZ* -	**TARUMAESAN MARU** **Mitsui OSK Lines Ltd (MOL)** MOL Ship Management Co Ltd (MOLSHIP) *Tomakomai, Hokkaido* *Japan* MMSI: 432978000 Official number: 142122	**52,981** 27,015 91,438	Class: NK	**2003-04 Imabari Shipbuilding Co Ltd — Marugame KG (Marugame Shipyard)** Yd No: 1378 Loa 234.94 (BB) Br ex - Dght 12.832 Lbp 226.00 Br md 43.00 Dpth 19.30 Welded, 1 dk	**(A21A2BC) Bulk Carrier** Grain: 112,883 Compartments: 7 Ho, ER 7 Ha: 6 (15.8 x 20.8)ER (15.8 x 19.2)	**1 oil engine** driving 1 FP propeller Total Power: 13,199kW (17,945hp) 15.0kn Mitsubishi 7UEC60LS 1 x 2 Stroke 7 Cy. 600 x 2200 13199kW (17945bhp) Kobe Hatsudoki KK-Japan Fuel: 3290.0

IMO / Call sign / Flag	Name / Former names / Owner / Port	GT / NT / DWT	Class	Builder / Dimensions	Type	Machinery
7394060 *YDLW* -	**TARUNA PUTRA II** *ex* Isabella Indah *-1995* *ex* Armada Irian *-1990* *ex* Armada Jaya *-1990* *ex* Chuo Maru *-1983* **PT Triputra Taruna Lines** - *Jakarta* *Indonesia* MMSI: 525015193 Official number: 6655/L	**1,312** 779 2,154	Class: KI	**1974**-05 **Sanyo Zosen K.K. — Onomichi** Yd No: 677 Loa 69.25 Br ex 11.43 Dght 5.290 Lbp 65.00 Br md 11.41 Dpth 7.17 Riveted\Welded, 1 dk	**(A31A2GX) General Cargo Ship**	**1 oil engine** driving 1 FP propeller Total Power: 1,471kW (2,000hp) Hanshin 6LUD35G 1 x 4 Stroke 6 Cy. 350 x 550 1471kW (2000bhp) Hanshin Nainenki Kogyo-Japan
7715159 *YESI* -	**TARUNA PUTRA III** *ex* Ika Permai *-1996* *ex* Koei Maru *-1994* **PT Cahaya Lautan Kumala** - *Surabaya* *Indonesia*	**1,127** 605 1,533	Class: KI	**1977**-08 **K.K. Uno Zosensho — Imabari** Yd No: 103 Loa - Br ex - Dght 4.550 Lbp 60.00 Br md 11.02 Dpth 6.51 Riveted\Welded, 2 dks	**(A31A2GX) General Cargo Ship**	**1 oil engine** driving 1 FP propeller Total Power: 1,177kW (1,600hp) Hanshin 6LUD32G 1 x 4 Stroke 6 Cy. 320 x 510 1177kW (1600bhp) Hanshin Nainenki Kogyo-Japan
8125727 *YHUG* -	**TARUNA PUTRA IX** *ex* New Ocean 1 *-2006* *ex* Amethyst *-2002* *ex* Genie *-1998* *ex* Daikoku Maru No. 38 *-1996* **PT Fajar Timur Baru Jaya** - *Palembang* *Indonesia* MMSI: 525015035	**1,257** 817 1,581	Class: KI	**1982**-06 **Kurinoura Dockyard Co Ltd — Yawatahama EH** Yd No: 170 Loa 70.30 Br ex - Dght 4.523 Lbp 65.03 Br md 11.02 Dpth 6.41 Welded, 1 dk	**(A31A2GX) General Cargo Ship** Grain: 2,830; Bale: 2,482 Compartments: 1 Ho, ER 1 Ha: ER	**1 oil engine** with clutches, flexible couplings & sr reverse geared to sc. shaft driving 1 FP propeller Total Power: 1,214kW (1,651hp) 14.0kn Hanshin 6LU32G 1 x 4 Stroke 6 Cy. 320 x 510 1214kW (1651bhp) The Hanshin Diesel Works Ltd-Japan
8816546 *YGVC* -	**TARUNA PUTRA VIII** *ex* In Sung *-2001* *ex* Keum Yang Birdie *-1998* **PT Triputra Taruna Lines** - *Palembang* *Indonesia* MMSI: 525019090	**1,240** 568 2,257	Class: KI (KR)	**1988**-03 **Pohang Shipbuilding Co Ltd — Pohang** Yd No: 23 Loa 70.49 Br ex - Dght 4.581 Lbp 65.03 Br md 12.01 Dpth 5.41 Welded, 1 dk	**(A31A2GX) General Cargo Ship**	**1 oil engine** driving 1 FP propeller Total Power: 956kW (1,300hp) 11.0kn Hanshin 6LUN28G 1 x 4 Stroke 6 Cy. 280 x 480 956kW (1300bhp) Ssangyong Heavy Industries Co Ltd-South Korea
8328769 *UAAN* -	**TARUTINO** **Marshal Zhukov Co Ltd** - *Petropavlovsk-Kamchatskiy* *Russia* MMSI: 273454940	**356** 107 138	Class: RS	**1984**-10 **Sudostroitelnyy Zavod "Avangard" — Petrozavodsk** Yd No: 417 Loa 35.74 Br ex 8.92 Dght 3.429 Lbp 29.62 Br md 8.80 Dpth 5.95 Welded, 1 dk	**(B11A2FS) Stern Trawler** Ins: 110 Compartments: 1 Ho, ER 1 Ha: (1.3 x 1.3) Derricks: 2x1.5t Ice Capable	**1 oil engine** driving 1 FP propeller Total Power: 589kW (801hp) 10.9kn S.K.L. 6NVD48A-2U 1 x 4 Stroke 6 Cy. 320 x 480 589kW (801bhp) VEB Schwermaschinenbau "KarlLiebknecht" (SKL)-Magdeburg AuxGen: 2 x 160kW Fuel: 35.0 (d.f.)
8994362 *V3OY2* -	**TARZAN III** **Wang Ming-Fa** - *Belize City* *Belize* MMSI: 312171000 Official number: 020310169	*105* 30 -		**1998**-01 **Astilleros Tecnonaval S.A. — Tigre** Loa 23.80 Br ex - Dght - Lbp - Br md 6.80 Dpth 3.25 Bonded, 1 dk	**(B11B2FV) Fishing Vessel** Hull Material: Reinforced Plastic	**1 oil engine** driving 1 Propeller 7.5kn Cummins 1 x 4 Stroke Cummins Engine Co Inc-USA
8994374 - -	**TARZAN VIII** **Wang Ming-Fa** - *Nicaragua*	*113* 71 -		**1997**-01 **Astilleros Tecnonaval S.A. — Tigre** Loa 23.10 Br ex - Dght - Lbp - Br md 5.45 Dpth 4.50 Bonded, 1 dk	**(B11B2FV) Fishing Vessel** Hull Material: Reinforced Plastic	**1 oil engine** geared to sc. shaft driving 1 Propeller Total Power: 478kW (650hp) 7.5kn Caterpillar 3412 1 x Vee 4 Stroke 12 Cy. 137 x 152 478kW (650bhp) Caterpillar Inc-USA
8994386 - -	**TARZAN XII** **Wang Ming-Fa** - *Nicaragua*	*113* 71 -		**1997**-01 **Astilleros Tecnonaval S.A. — Tigre** Loa 23.10 Br ex - Dght - Lbp - Br md 5.45 Dpth 4.50 Bonded, 1 dk	**(B11B2FV) Fishing Vessel** Hull Material: Reinforced Plastic	**1 oil engine** geared to sc. shaft driving 1 Propeller 7.5kn Caterpillar 3412 1 x Vee 4 Stroke 12 Cy. 137 x 152 Caterpillar Inc-USA
6728795 - -	**TASA 24** *ex* San Pedro III *-2012* *ex* Tortuga 10 *-2010* *ex* Golden Rose VII *-1975* **Pesquera Uglan SA** - *Guayaquil* *Ecuador* Official number: P-00-00876	*133* 40 -	Class: (GL)	**1967 Ast. Picsa S.A. — Callao** Loa 26.80 Br ex 7.07 Dght - Lbp - Br md 7.04 Dpth 3.43 Welded, 1 dk	**(B11B2FV) Fishing Vessel**	**1 oil engine** reverse reduction geared to sc. shaft driving 1 FP propeller Total Power: 279kW (379hp) Caterpillar D353SCAC 1 x 4 Stroke 6 Cy. 159 x 203 279kW (379bhp) (made 1966, fitted 1980) Caterpillar Tractor Co-USA AuxGen: 1 x 4kW 24V a.c
7022095 - -	**TASA 31** **Peruana de Pesca SA (PEPESCA)** - *Callao* *Peru*	*200* - 249	Class: (LR) ✠ Classed LR until 2/76	**1970**-06 **Fabricaciones Metallicas E.P.S. (FABRIMET) — Callao** Yd No: 382 Loa 30.18 Br ex 7.80 Dght 3.696 Lbp 26.45 Br md 7.68 Dpth - Welded	**(B11B2FV) Fishing Vessel**	**1 oil engine** sr reverse geared to sc. shaft driving 1 FP propeller Total Power: 416kW (566hp) Caterpillar D379TA 1 x Vee 4 Stroke 8 Cy. 159 x 203 416kW (566bhp) Caterpillar Tractor Co-USA AuxGen: 1 x 1kW 24V d.c
9383053 - -	**TASA 41** **Tecnologica de Alimentos SA** - *Peru*	**590** - -		**2005**-10 **SIMA Serv. Ind. de la Marina Chimbote (SIMACH) — Chimbote** Yd No: 504 Loa - Br ex - Dght - Lbp 43.00 Br md 8.84 Dpth 4.50 Welded, 1 dk	**(B11B2FV) Fishing Vessel**	**1 oil engine** driving 1 Propeller
9319284 - -	**TASA 43** **Tecnologica de Alimentos SA** - *Callao* *Peru*	**500** - -	Class: GL	**2004**-08 **SIMA Serv. Ind. de la Marina Chimbote (SIMACH) — Chimbote** Yd No: 488 Loa 44.70 Br ex - Dght - Lbp - Br md 10.30 Dpth 5.00 Welded, 1 dk	**(B11B2FV) Fishing Vessel** Ins: 400	**1 oil engine** geared to sc. shaft driving 1 CP propeller Total Power: 960kW (1,305hp) MAN-B&W 6L23/30A 1 x 4 Stroke 6 Cy. 225 x 300 960kW (1305bhp) MAN B&W Diesel A/S-Denmark
9319296 - -	**TASA 44** **Tecnologica de Alimentos SA** - *Callao* *Peru*	**500** - -	Class: GL	**2004**-08 **SIMA Serv. Ind. de la Marina Chimbote (SIMACH) — Chimbote** Yd No: 489 Loa 44.70 Br ex - Dght - Lbp - Br md 10.30 Dpth 5.00 Welded, 1 dk	**(B11B2FV) Fishing Vessel** Ins: 400	**1 oil engine** geared to sc. shaft driving 1 CP propeller Total Power: 960kW (1,305hp) MAN-B&W 6L23/30A 1 x 4 Stroke 6 Cy. 225 x 300 960kW (1305bhp) MAN B&W Diesel A/S-Denmark
9319301 - -	**TASA 45** **Tecnologica de Alimentos SA** - *Callao* *Peru*	**500** - -	Class: GL	**2004**-08 **SIMA Serv. Ind. de la Marina Chimbote (SIMACH) — Chimbote** Yd No: 490 Loa 44.70 Br ex - Dght - Lbp - Br md 10.30 Dpth 5.00 Welded, 1 dk	**(B11B2FV) Fishing Vessel** Ins: 400	**1 oil engine** geared to sc. shaft driving 1 CP propeller Total Power: 960kW (1,305hp) MAN-B&W 6L23/30A 1 x 4 Stroke 6 Cy. 225 x 300 960kW (1305bhp)
9184964 - -	**TASA 51** *ex* Sipesa 63 *-2005* **Tecnologica de Alimentos SA** - *Callao* *Peru* Official number: CO-20761-PM	**565** 153 700	Class: GL (LR) ✠ Classed LR until 6/10/03	**2002**-04 **SIMA Serv. Ind. de la Marina Callao (SIMAC) — Callao** Yd No: 63 Loa 51.50 (BB) Br ex 10.80 Dght 4.480 Lbp 47.40 Br md 10.60 Dpth 5.05 Welded, 1 dk	**(B11B2FV) Fishing Vessel** Grain: 630 Compartments: 5 Ho, ER	**1 oil engine** with clutches, flexible couplings & sr geared to sc. shaft driving 1 CP propeller Total Power: 1,845kW (2,508hp) 12.3kn Caterpillar 3606TA 1 x 4 Stroke 6 Cy. 280 x 300 1845kW (2508bhp) Caterpillar Inc-USA AuxGen: 1 x 590kW 440V 60Hz a.c, 1 x 190kW 440V 60Hz a.c
9184952 - -	**TASA 52** *ex* Sipesa 62 *-2005* **Tecnologica de Alimentos SA** - *Callao* *Peru* Official number: CO-20777-PM	**565** 153 700	Class: GL (LR) ✠ Classed LR until 10/12/03	**2002**-04 **SIMA Serv. Ind. de la Marina Callao (SIMAC) — Callao** Yd No: 62 Loa 51.50 (BB) Br ex 10.80 Dght 4.480 Lbp 47.40 Br md 10.60 Dpth 5.05 Welded, 1 dk	**(B11B2FV) Fishing Vessel** Grain: 600 Compartments: 5 Ho, ER	**1 oil engine** with flexible couplings & sr geared to sc. shafts driving 1 CP propeller Total Power: 1,845kW (2,508hp) 12.3kn Caterpillar 3606TA 1 x 4 Stroke 6 Cy. 280 x 300 1845kW (2508bhp) Caterpillar Inc-USA AuxGen: 1 x 590kW 440V 60Hz a.c, 1 x 190kW 440V 60Hz a.c
9133604 - -	**TASA 53** *ex* Maru 2 *-2005* **Tecnologica de Alimentos SA** - *Chimbote* *Peru* Official number: CO-13918-PM	**635** 221 449	Class: GL	**1996**-03 **Andina de Desarrollo S.A. — Callao** Yd No: 136 Loa 47.00 Br ex - Dght 4.340 Lbp 41.75 Br md 9.95 Dpth 4.88 Welded, 1 dk	**(B11B2FV) Fishing Vessel**	**1 oil engine** reduction geared to sc. shaft driving 1 FP propeller Total Power: 1,037kW (1,410hp) 12.7kn Caterpillar 3516TA 1 x Vee 4 Stroke 16 Cy. 170 x 190 1037kW (1410bhp) Caterpillar Inc-USA
9453004 - -	**TASA-54** **Tecnologica de Alimentos SA** - *Peru* Official number: CO-13008-PM	**200** - -		**2007**-04 **SIMA Serv. Ind. de la Marina Chimbote (SIMACH) — Chimbote** Yd No: 516 Loa - Br ex - Dght - Lbp - Br md 7.92 Dpth - Welded, 1 dk	**(B11B2FV) Fishing Vessel**	**1 oil engine** driving 1 Propeller

IMO / Call sign / Reg.	Name, former names, owner, manager, port, flag	GT / NT / DWT	Classification	Build, shipyard, dimensions	Ship type, cargo	Machinery
9348039 - -	**TASA 55** - **Tecnologica de Alimentos SA** *Callao* *Peru*	*500* 127 611	Class: GL	**2005-05 SIMA Serv. Ind. de la Marina Chimbote (SIMACH) — Chimbote** Yd No: 491 Loa 48.75 (BB) Br ex - Dght 4.745 Lbp 44.70 Br md 10.50 Dpth 5.17 Welded, 1 dk	**(B11B2FV) Fishing Vessel**	**1 oil engine** geared to sc. shaft driving 1 FP propeller Total Power: 1,280kW (1,740hp) 13.0kn MAN-B&W 8L23/30A 1 x 4 Stroke 8 Cy. 225 x 300 1280kW (1740bhp) MAN B&W Diesel A/S-Denmark
9140712 - -	**TASA 57** *ex* Copetsa 4 **Tecnologica de Alimentos SA** - *Callao* *Peru* Official number: CO-17359-PM	*457* 146 643	Class: GL	**1997-09 Andina de Desarrollo S.A. — Callao** Yd No: 165 Loa 46.00 Br ex - Dght 4.360 Lbp 40.30 Br md 9.95 Dpth 4.88 Welded, 1 dk	**(B11B2FV) Fishing Vessel**	**1 oil engine** reduction geared to sc. shaft driving 1 FP propeller Total Power: 1,030kW (1,400hp) 13.5kn Caterpillar 3516TA 1 x Vee 4 Stroke 16 Cy. 170 x 190 1030kW (1400bhp) Caterpillar Inc-USA AuxGen: 2 x 65kW 220V a.c
9140683 - -	**TASA 58** *ex* Copetsa 2 **Tecnologica de Alimentos SA** - *Callao* *Peru* Official number: CO-17057-PM	*489* 150 550	Class: GL	**1997-06 Andina de Desarrollo S.A. — Callao** Yd No: 156 Loa 46.00 Br ex - Dght 4.360 Lbp 40.30 Br md 9.95 Dpth 4.88 Welded, 1 dk	**(B11B2FV) Fishing Vessel**	**1 oil engine** reduction geared to sc. shaft driving 1 FP propeller Total Power: 1,030kW (1,400hp) 13.5kn Caterpillar 3516TA 1 x Vee 4 Stroke 16 Cy. 170 x 190 1030kW (1400bhp) Caterpillar Inc-USA AuxGen: 2 x 65kW 220V a.c
7042473 - -	**TASA 217** *ex* Bravo 2 *-2013* *ex* Chimbote 7 *-2013* *ex* Alcatraz 3 *-1976* **Pesquera Uglan SA** - *Guayaquil* *Ecuador* Official number: P-00-00875	**179** 54 274	Class: (LR) (GL) ✠ Classed LR until 1/5/81	**1971-01 Fabricaciones Metallicas E.P.S. (FABRIMET) — Callao** Yd No: 415 Loa 32.59 Br ex 7.80 Dght 3.315 Lbp 26.45 Br md 7.68 Dpth 3.69 Welded, 1 dk	**(B11B2FV) Fishing Vessel** Compartments: 1 Ho, ER 1 Ha: (3.5 x 2.6)ER	**1 oil engine** sr reverse geared to sc. shaft driving 1 FP propeller Total Power: 496kW (674hp) 11.0kn Caterpillar D379SCAC 1 x Vee 4 Stroke 8 Cy. 159 x 203 496kW (674bhp) Caterpillar Tractor Co-USA AuxGen: 2 x 1kW 24V d.c Fuel: 11.0 (d.f.)
7008518 - -	**TASA 311** *ex* Junin 8 *-2013* *ex* Nelson *-1975* **Pesquera Monticristi SA** - *Manta* *Ecuador* Official number: P-04-00936	**250** 75 -	Class: (GL)	**1969 Ast. Picsa S.A. — Callao** Yd No: 281 Loa 36.44 Br ex 8.03 Dght 3.250 Lbp 32.80 Br md 8.00 Dpth 4.05 Welded	**(B11B2FV) Fishing Vessel**	**1 oil engine** reverse reduction geared to sc. shaft driving 1 FP propeller Total Power: 625kW (850hp) Caterpillar D398SCAC 1 x Vee 4 Stroke 12 Cy. 159 x 203 625kW (850bhp) Caterpillar Tractor Co-USA
9064308 - -	**TASA 411** *ex* Sipan *-2009* **Tecnologica de Alimentos SA** - *Chimbote* *Peru* Official number: CE-011080-PM	*378* 174 430	Class: LR ✠ **100A1** SS 04/2009 fishing vessel Peruvian coastal service *IWS ✠ **LMC** Cable: 305.0/24.0 U1 (a)	**1993-12 Andina de Desarrollo S.A. — Callao** Yd No: 123 Loa 38.75 Br ex 8.47 Dght 3.700 Lbp 33.30 Br md 8.30 Dpth 4.15 Welded, 1 dk	**(B11B2FV) Fishing Vessel**	**1 oil engine** with clutches, flexible couplings & sr reverse geared to sc. shaft driving 1 FP propeller Total Power: 791kW (1,075hp) 12.0kn Caterpillar 3512TA 1 x Vee 4 Stroke 12 Cy. 170 x 190 791kW (1075bhp) Caterpillar Inc-USA AuxGen: 1 x 5kW 24V d.c
9062946 - -	**TASA 416** *ex* Salkantay *-2009* **Tecnologica de Alimentos SA** - *Huacho* *Peru* Official number: HO-010722-PM	*364* 153 436	Class: LR ✠ **100A1** SS 04/2006 fishing vessel Peruvian coastal service *IWS ✠ **LMC** Cable: 137.5/22.0 U2 (a)	**1993-11 Astilleros Naves Industriales S.A. (NAVINSA) — Callao** Yd No: 06 Loa 36.60 Br ex 8.77 Dght 3.900 Lbp 32.53 Br md 8.60 Dpth 4.27 Welded, 1 dk	**(B11B2FV) Fishing Vessel**	**1 oil engine** with clutches, flexible couplings & dr reverse geared to sc. shaft driving 1 FP propeller Total Power: 1,118kW (1,520hp) Caterpillar 3512TA 1 x Vee 4 Stroke 12 Cy. 170 x 190 1118kW (1520bhp) Caterpillar Inc-USA AuxGen: 1 x 5kW 24V d.c, 1 x 20kW 24V d.c
9064310 - -	**TASA 417** *ex* Inansa *-2009* **Tecnologica de Alimentos SA** - *Chimbote* *Peru* Official number: CE-011079-PM	*398* 148 430	Class: LR ✠ **100A1** SS 03/2014 fishing vessel Peruvian coastal services *IWS **LMC** Cable: 305.0/24.0 U1 (a)	**1993-12 Andina de Desarrollo S.A. — Callao** Yd No: 124 Loa 38.75 Br ex 8.47 Dght 3.700 Lbp 33.30 Br md 8.30 Dpth 4.15 Welded, 1 dk	**(B11B2FV) Fishing Vessel**	**1 oil engine** with clutches, flexible couplings & sr reverse geared to sc. shaft driving 1 FP propeller Total Power: 791kW (1,075hp) 12.0kn Caterpillar 3512TA 1 x Vee 4 Stroke 12 Cy. 170 x 190 791kW (1075bhp) Caterpillar Inc-USA AuxGen: 1 x 5kW 24V d.c, 1 x 5kW 24V d.c
9130016 - -	**TASA 419** *ex* Dona Beila *-2009* *ex* Esther 6 *-2000* **Tecnologica de Alimentos SA** - *Callao* *Peru* Official number: CO-12974-PM	**447** 201 545	Class: GL	**1995-10 Andina de Desarrollo S.A. — Callao** Yd No: 142 Loa 42.69 Br ex 9.09 Dght 3.900 Lbp 37.16 Br md 9.05 Dpth 4.35 Welded, 1 dk	**(B11B2FV) Fishing Vessel**	**1 oil engine** reduction geared to sc. shaft driving 1 FP propeller Total Power: 1,037kW (1,410hp) 13.0kn Caterpillar 3516TA 1 x Vee 4 Stroke 16 Cy. 170 x 190 1037kW (1410bhp) Caterpillar Inc-USA AuxGen: 2 x 18kW a.c
9156319 - -	**TASA 420** *ex* Guillermo *-2010* **Tecnologica de Alimentos SA** - *Callao* *Peru* Official number: CO-17299-PM	**350** - 590	Class: LR ✠ **100A1** SS 06/2010 fishing vessel Peruvian coastal service ✠ **LMC** Eq.Ltr: H; Cable: 371.2/22.0 U2 (a)	**1998-02 Astilleros Naves Industriales S.A. (NAVINSA) — Callao** Yd No: 23 Loa 40.86 Br ex - Dght 3.900 Lbp 38.60 Br md 8.60 Dpth 4.40 Welded, 1 dk	**(B11B2FV) Fishing Vessel**	**1 oil engine** with clutches, flexible couplings & sr reverse geared to sc. shaft driving 1 FP propeller Total Power: 900kW (1,224hp) 12.5kn Caterpillar 3512TA 1 x Vee 4 Stroke 12 Cy. 170 x 190 900kW (1224bhp) Caterpillar Inc-USA AuxGen: 1 x 300kW 220/440V 60Hz a.c, 1 x 30kW 220/440V 60Hz a.c
9133628 - -	**TASA 427** *ex* Esther 7 *-2011* **Cridani SAC** Tecnologica de Alimentos SA *Callao* *Peru* Official number: CO-14971-PM	**447** 201 510	Class: GL	**1996-11 Andina de Desarrollo S.A. — Callao** Yd No: 143 Loa 42.70 Br ex - Dght 3.900 Lbp 37.16 Br md 9.05 Dpth 4.35 Welded, 1 dk	**(B11B2FV) Fishing Vessel**	**1 oil engine** reduction geared to sc. shaft driving 1 FP propeller Total Power: 1,037kW (1,410hp) 13.0kn Caterpillar 3516TA 1 x Vee 4 Stroke 16 Cy. 170 x 190 1037kW (1410bhp) Caterpillar Inc-USA AuxGen: 2 x 18kW a.c
9235581 *9V8253* -	**TASANEE** *ex* POS Long Beach *-2011* *ex* Tasanee *-2010* *ex* Engiadina *-2009* *ex* Norasia Engiadina *-2003* *ex* Engiadina *-2002* **Shark Key Pte Ltd** Seachange Maritime (Singapore) Pte Ltd *Singapore* *Singapore* MMSI: 564985000 Official number: 395519	**27,779** 14,769 39,418 T/cm 56.7	Class: NK (LR) (GL) Classed LR until 12/3/13	**2002-07 Hyundai Mipo Dockyard Co Ltd — Ulsan** Yd No: 0034 Loa 222.17 (BB) Br ex - Dght 12.020 Lbp 210.00 Br md 30.00 Dpth 16.80 Welded, 1 dk	**(A33A2CC) Container Ship (Fully Cellular)** TEU 2824 C Ho 1026 C Dk 1798 incl 554 ref C. Compartments: 6 Cell Ho, ER 6 Ha: ER	**1 oil engine** driving 1 FP propeller Total Power: 25,270kW (34,357hp) 22.0kn MAN-B&W 7K80MC-C 1 x 2 Stroke 7 Cy. 800 x 2300 25270kW (34357bhp) Hyundai Heavy Industries Co Ltd-South Korea AuxGen: 4 x 1500kW 450/230V 60Hz a.c Boilers: AuxB (Comp) 8.7kgf/cm² (8.5bar) Thrusters: 1 Thwart. CP thruster (f) Fuel: 215.0 (d.f.) 3241.0 (r.f.)
7385356 *EGVH* VI-5-9604	**TASARTE** - **Pesquera Montelor SA** - SatCom: Inmarsat C 422491720 *Vigo* *Spain* MMSI: 224917000 Official number: 3-9604/	**696** 255 100	Class: (RI) (BV)	**1976-03 Ast. de Mallorca S.A. — Palma de Mallorca** Yd No: 212 Lengthened-1982 Loa 53.22 Br ex 9.50 Dght 4.067 Lbp 46.06 Br md - Dpth 6.51 Welded, 2 dks	**(B11A2FS) Stern Trawler**	**1 oil engine** driving 1 FP propeller Total Power: 1,177kW (1,600hp) 12.0kn Deutz RBV6M358 1 x 4 Stroke 6 Cy. 400 x 580 1177kW (1600bhp) (new engine 1976) Kloeckner Humboldt Deutz AG-West Germany
8309581 *LAON2* -	**TASCO** *ex* Nosac Explorer *-1996* *ex* Nosac Tasco *-1989* **Wilhelmsen Lines Shipowning AS** Wilhelmsen Lines Car Carrier Ltd SatCom: Inmarsat C 425879810 *Tonsberg* *Norway (NIS)* MMSI: 258798000	**48,393** 16,723 22,067	Class: NV	**1985-02 Daewoo Shipbuilding & Heavy Machinery Ltd — Geoje** Yd No: 4401 Loa 195.30 (BB) Br ex - Dght 11.058 Lbp 182.40 Br md 32.26 Dpth 30.97 Welded, 12 dks, incl. Nos.3, 5, 6, 8, 9 & 11 dks hoistable	**(A35B2RV) Vehicles Carrier** Side door/ramp (s) Len: 25.00 Wid: 7.00 Swl: 25 Quarter stern door/ramp (s) Len: 45.00 Wid: 10.50 Swl: 112 Lane-Len: 5018 Lane-clr ht: 6.40 Cars: 5,409 Ice Capable	**1 oil engine** driving 1 FP propeller Total Power: 14,169kW (19,264hp) 19.0kn B&W 6L80GBE 1 x 2 Stroke 6 Cy. 800 x 1950 14169kW (19264bhp) Hyundai Engine & Machinery Co Ltd-South Korea AuxGen: 2 x 1205kW 450V 60Hz a.c, 1 x 800kW 450V 60Hz a.c, 1 x 670kW 450V 60Hz a.c Thrusters: 1 Thwart. CP thruster (f) Fuel: 225.0 (d.f.) 3262.0 (r.f.) 58.0pd
9125346 *HSDZ2* -	**TASCO 1** *ex* Tasco I *-2004* **Tipco Asphalt Public Co Ltd** Tipco Maritime Co Ltd *Bangkok* *Thailand* MMSI: 567286000 Official number: 470003137	**4,063** 1,219 4,685 T/cm 14.0	Class: NK	**1995-07 KK Kanasashi — Shizuoka SZ** Yd No: 3372 Loa 104.23 (BB) Br ex - Dght 5.768 Lbp 97.00 Br md 17.00 Dpth 8.80 Welded, 1 dk	**(A13B2TP) Products Tanker** Liq: 4,354; Liq (Oil): 4,354; Asphalt: 4,354 Cargo Heating Coils Compartments: 4 Ta, ER 3 Cargo Pump (s): 1x500m³/hr, 2x400m³/hr	**1 oil engine** driving 1 FP propeller Total Power: 2,589kW (3,520hp) 13.5kn B&W 4L35MC 1 x 2 Stroke 4 Cy. 350 x 1050 2589kW (3520bhp) Makita Corp-Japan AuxGen: 3 x 320kW a.c Thrusters: 1 Thwart. FP thruster (f) Fuel: 70.0 (d.f.) 290.0 (r.f.) 9.7pd

9615999 **TASCO AMARIT**
HSB4699
-
Tasco Shipping Co Ltd
Tipco Maritime Co Ltd
Bangkok *Thailand*
MMSI: 567463000
Official number: TG55026

6,106
1,832
7,532
T/cm
17.3

Class: NK

2012-07 **Shin Kurushima Dockyard Co. Ltd. — Hashihama, Imabari** Yd No: 5698
Loa 104.98 (BB) Br ex - Dght 6.977
Lbp 99.95 Br md 19.60 Dpth 11.00
Welded, 1 dk

(A13C2LA) Asphalt/Bitumen Tanker
Double Hull (13F)
Liq: 6,830; Liq (Oil): 6,970; Asphalt: 6,970

1 oil engine driving 1 FP propeller
Total Power: 3,900kW (5,302hp) 13.7kn
MAN-B&W 6L35MC
1 x 2 Stroke 6 Cy. 350 x 1050 3900kW (5302bhp)
Makita Corp-Japan
Fuel: 560.0

9279680 **TASCO AMATA**
HSB2978
-
Bitumen Marine Co Ltd
Tipco Maritime Co Ltd
Bangkok *Thailand*
MMSI: 567226000
Official number: 460000585

6,035
1,811
7,146
T/cm
17.3

Class: NK

2003-06 **Shin Kurushima Dockyard Co. Ltd. — Hashihama, Imabari** Yd No: 5226
Loa 105.00 (BB) Br ex - Dght 6.727
Lbp 99.95 Br md 19.60 Dpth 11.00
Welded, 1 Dk.

(A13B2TP) Products Tanker
Double Hull (13F)
Liq: 6,976; Liq (Oil): 6,976; Asphalt: 6,976
Cargo Heating Coils
2 Cargo Pump (s)

1 oil engine driving 1 FP propeller
Total Power: 3,906kW (5,311hp) 13.7kn
MAN-B&W 6L35MC
1 x 2 Stroke 6 Cy. 350 x 1050 3906kW (5311bhp)
Makita Corp-Japan
AuxGen: 3 x 315kW a.c
Thrusters: 1 Tunnel thruster (f)
Fuel: 600.0

9118800 **TASCO AMORN**
HSB4569
-
ex Prime Success *-2011* *ex* Black Road *-2007*
ex Osco Phoenix *-2006*
ex Bitumen Busan *-2004*
ex Kinko Maru No. 21 *-2003*
Alpha Maritime Co Ltd
Tipco Maritime Co Ltd
Bangkok *Thailand*
MMSI: 567426000
Official number: TG 54012

1,354
469
2,005

Class: NK (KR)

1995-02 **Hitachi Zosen Mukaishima Marine Co Ltd — Onomichi HS** Yd No: 87
Lengthened-2003
Loa 83.45 Br ex - Dght 4.722
Lbp 77.74 Br md 11.00 Dpth 6.04
Welded, 1 dk

(A13B2TP) Products Tanker
Double Hull (13F)
Liq: 1,762; Liq (Oil): 1,762; Asphalt: 1,762
Compartments: 10 Ta, ER
2 Cargo Pump (s): 2x500m³/hr

1 oil engine reverse geared to sc. shaft driving 1 FP propeller
Total Power: 1,324kW (1,800hp) 11.0kn
Akasaka A31R
1 x 4 Stroke 6 Cy. 310 x 600 1324kW (1800bhp)
Akasaka Tekkosho KK (Akasaka DieselLtd)-Japan
AuxGen: 3 x 116kW a.c
Fuel: 130.0 (d.f.)

9279642 **TASCO ANAN**
HSB4561
-
ex Kakusho 1 *-2011*
Tasco Shipping Co Ltd
Tipco Maritime Co Ltd
Bangkok *Thailand*
MMSI: 567423000
Official number: TG54007

3,525
1,058
3,851
T/cm
14.0

Class: NK

2003-07 **Murakami Hide Zosen K.K. — Imabari** Yd No: 532
Loa 102.95 (BB) Br ex - Dght 4.800
Lbp 97.00 Br md 17.80 Dpth 7.25
Welded, 1 Dk.

(A13C2LA) Asphalt/Bitumen Tanker
Double Hull
Liq: 3,595; Liq (Oil): 3,668; Asphalt: 3,595
Compartments: 12 Wing Ta, ER
2 Cargo Pump (s): 2x400m³/hr
Manifold: Bow/CM: 50.8m

1 oil engine driving 1 FP propeller
Total Power: 2,206kW (2,999hp) 12.5kn
Hanshin LH38L
1 x 4 Stroke 6 Cy. 380 x 760 2206kW (2999bhp)
The Hanshin Diesel Works Ltd-Japan
AuxGen: 2 x 250kW a.c
Thrusters: 1 Tunnel thruster (f)
Fuel: 115.0 (d.f.) 280.0 (r.f.)

8857978 **TASE**
ERMY
-
ex Torstar *-1996* *ex* Evelyn *-1995*
ex Omskiy-101 *-1993*
Partner Shipping Ltd
Patra Ltd
Giurgiulesti *Moldova*
MMSI: 214181325

1,836
849
2,800

Class: UA (BV)

1979 Santierul Naval Oltenita S.A. — Oltenita Yd No: 114
Shortened-1996
Loa 84.78 Br ex 15.00 Dght 3.720
Lbp 78.10 Br md 14.80 Dpth 5.00
Welded, 1 dk

(A31A2GX) General Cargo Ship
Compartments: 3 Ho, ER
3 Ha: 2 (15.5 x 10.9) (9.0 x 10.3)ER

2 oil engines driving 2 FP propellers
Total Power: 1,030kW (1,400hp)
S.K.L. 6NVD48A-2U
2 x 4 Stroke 6 Cy. 320 x 480 each-515kW (700bhp)
VEB Schwermaschinenbau "KarlLiebknecht" (SKL)-Magdeburg

7322067 **TASHA MARIE**
-
-
ex Miss Maryellen *-1980*
John Fernandez
-
Galveston, TX *United States of America*
Official number: 549412

125
85
-

1973 Desco Marine — Saint Augustine, Fl Yd No: 125-F
L reg 20.97 Br ex - Dght -
Lbp - Br md 6.75 Dpth 3.81
Bonded, 1 dk

(B11A2FT) Trawler
Hull Material: Reinforced Plastic

1 oil engine driving 1 FP propeller
Total Power: 268kW (364hp)

8521775 **TASHINA I**
VVMD
-
East Coast Boatbuilders & Engineering Ltd
-
Visakhapatnam *India*

115
-
151

Class: (LR) (IR)
✠ Classed LR until 12/87

1986-09 **VSR BV — Made** (Hull)
1986-09 **B.V. Scheepswerf Damen — Gorinchem** Yd No: 4139
Loa 24.01 Br ex 6.61 Dght 2.852
Lbp 21.70 Br md 6.51 Dpth 3.36
Welded, 1 dk

(B11A2FS) Stern Trawler
Ins: 70

1 oil engine with clutches & sr reverse geared to sc. shaft driving 1 FP propeller
Total Power: 405kW (551hp)
Caterpillar 3408TA
1 x Vee 4 Stroke 8 Cy. 137 x 152 405kW (551bhp)
Caterpillar Tractor Co-USA
AuxGen: 1 x 14kW 220V 50Hz a.c

9029152 **TASIK GEMILANG**
-
-
Pemerintah Kabupaten Bengkalis
-
Palembang *Indonesia*

563
169
-

Class: KI

2005-04 **P.T. Dok & Perkapalan Kodja Bahari — Palembang**
Loa 41.00 Br ex - Dght 2.100
Lbp 35.80 Br md 10.60 Dpth 2.90
Welded, 1 dk

(A36A2PR) Passenger/Ro-Ro Ship (Vehicles)

2 oil engines geared to sc. shafts driving 2 Propellers
Total Power: 912kW (1,240hp) 12.0kn
Yanmar 6LAH-STE3
2 x 4 Stroke 6 Cy. 150 x 165 each-456kW (620bhp)
Yanmar Diesel Engine Co Ltd-Japan
AuxGen: 2 x 68kW 380V a.c

9670274 **TASIK MAS**
POYL
-
PT Pelayaran Tempuran Emas Tbk (TEMAS Line)
-
Jakarta *Indonesia*
MMSI: 525019381

6,659
3,729
8,180

Class: CC (Class contemplated) KI

2012-12 **Lianyungang Wuzhou Shipbuilding Co Co Ltd — Guanyun County JS** Yd No: WZ-38
Loa 119.90 (BB) Br ex - Dght 5.200
Lbp 115.00 Br md 21.80 Dpth 7.30
Welded, 1 dk

(A33A2CC) Container Ship (Fully Cellular)
TEU 537

1 oil engine reduction geared to sc. shaft driving 1 FP propeller
Total Power: 1,765kW (2,400hp) 11.5kn
Chinese Std. Type 8320ZC
1 x 4 Stroke 8 Cy. 320 x 440 1765kW (2400bhp)
Guangzhou Diesel Engine Factory CoLtd-China
Thrusters: 1 Tunnel thruster (f)

9403891 **TASING SWAN**
OUYQ2
-
ex Erria Mie *-2012* *ex* Hamza Efe Bey *-2008*
Uni-Tankers mt 'Tasing Swan' ApS
Uni-Tankers A/S (UNI-TANKERS)
Middelfart *Denmark (DIS)*
MMSI: 219432000
Official number: D4588

7,232
3,643
11,347
T/cm
22.0

Class: GL (BV)

2007-05 **Istanbul Shipyard — Istanbul (Tuzla)** Yd No: 13
Loa 129.75 (BB) Br ex - Dght 8.000
Lbp 121.25 Br md 19.60 Dpth 10.40
Welded, 1 dk

(A12B2TR) Chemical/Products Tanker
Double Hull (13F)
Liq: 12,396; Liq (Oil): 12,396
Cargo Heating Coils
Compartments: 14 Wing Ta, 2 Wing Slop Ta, ER
14 Cargo Pump (s): 14x300m³/hr
Manifold: Bow/CM: 68m
Ice Capable

1 oil engine reduction geared to sc. shaft driving 1 CP propeller
Total Power: 4,500kW (6,118hp) 13.0kn
MAN-B&W 9L32/40
1 x 4 Stroke 9 Cy. 320 x 400 4500kW (6118bhp)
MAN B&W Diesel AG-Augsburg
AuxGen: 2 x 494kW 400/220V 50Hz a.c, 1 x 1032kW 400/220V 50Hz a.c
Thrusters: 1 Tunnel thruster (f)
Fuel: 114.0 (d.f.) 535.0 (r.f.)

9064384 **TASINGE MAERSK**
OUSX2
-
ex Maersk California *-2002*
ex Caroline Maersk *-1997*
A P Moller - Maersk A/S
A P Moller
Svendborg *Denmark (DIS)*
MMSI: 220157000
Official number: D4012

20,842
10,298
28,550

Class: AB (LR)
✠ Classed LR until 9/10/96

1994-01 **Odense Staalskibsvaerft A/S — Munkebo (Lindo Shipyard)** Yd No: 151
Loa 190.48 (BB) Br ex 27.83 Dght 10.320
Lbp 180.15 Br md 27.80 Dpth 15.23
Welded, 1 dk

(A33A2CC) Container Ship (Fully Cellular)
TEU 1827 C Ho 719 TEU C Dk 1108 TEU incl 164 ref C.
Compartments: 5 Cell Ho, ER
10 Ha: ER
Gantry cranes: 1x35t

1 oil engine driving 1 FP propeller
Total Power: 11,415kW (15,520hp) 18.7kn
Mitsubishi 9UEC50LSII
1 x 2 Stroke 9 Cy. 500 x 1950 11415kW (15520bhp)
Mitsubishi Heavy Industries Ltd-Japan
AuxGen: 3 x 1250kW 450V 60Hz a.c
Thrusters: 1 Thwart. FP thruster (f); 1 Tunnel thruster (a)

6615699 **TASIR 6**
TC5724
-
ex Murat Turgut *-2011*
Turkiye Taskomuru Kuruma Genel Mudurlugu
-
Zonguldak *Turkey*
Official number: 520

230
119
300

Class: (LR)
✠ Classed LR until 7/68

1966-06 **Celiktrans Deniz Insaat Kizaklari Ltd. Sti — Tuzla,Ist** Yd No: 25
Loa 32.52 Br ex 9.02 Dght 1.800
Lbp 30.79 Br md 9.01 Dpth 2.80
Welded, 1 dk

(B34A2SH) Hopper, Motor
Compartments: 1 Ho, ER

1 oil engine reverse geared to sc. shaft driving 1 FP propeller
Total Power: 250kW (340hp) 9.0kn
Alpha 404-24VO
1 x 2 Stroke 4 Cy. 240 x 400 250kW (340bhp)
Alpha Diesel A/S-Denmark
AuxGen: 1 x 15kW 220V d.c
Fuel: 8.0 (d.f.)

7347330 **TASK ONE**
-
-
ex Hi Heidyn *-2011* *ex* Hoy Head II *-2011*
ex Hoy Head *-1994* *ex* Geira *-1987*
-
-
-

147
76
54

Class: (LR)
✠ Classed LR until 14/3/75

1973-11 **p/f Torshavnar Skipasmidja — Torshavn** Yd No: 19
Converted From: Ferry (Passenger/Vehicle)-1996
Loa 25.23 Br ex 7.88 Dght 1.982
Lbp 22.64 Br md 7.85 Dpth 3.20
Welded, 1 dk

(B34T2QR) Work/Repair Vessel

2 oil engines sr geared to sc. shafts driving 2 CP propellers
Total Power: 264kW (358hp) 8.5kn
Kelvin TA6
2 x 4 Stroke 6 Cy. 165 x 184 each-132kW (179bhp)
GEC Diesels Ltd.Kelvin Marine Div.-Glasgow
AuxGen: 2 x 29kW 240V 50Hz a.c
Fuel: 6.0 (d.f.)

8973978 **TASKENT-I**
YM3836
-
Taskent Turizm ve Deniz Hizmetleri Ticaret Ltd Sti
-
Istanbul *Turkey*
Official number: 5102

109
33
-

1983 Gemsan Gemi Sanayii Koll. Sti. — Tuzla
Loa 31.05 Br ex - Dght 1.400
Lbp - Br md 5.60 Dpth 2.70
Welded, 1 dk

(A37B2PS) Passenger Ship
Passengers: unberthed: 150

2 oil engines geared to sc. shafts driving 2 FP propellers
Total Power: 346kW (470hp) 11.0kn
Volvo Penta
2 x 4 Stroke each-173kW (235bhp)
AB Volvo Penta-Sweden
AuxGen: 2 x a.c

8973980 **TASKENT-II**
TC4990
-
Taskent Turizm ve Deniz Hizmetleri Ticaret Ltd Sti
-
Istanbul *Turkey*
MMSI: 271010581
Official number: 5566

209
132
-

1987-06 **Gamsar Shipyard — Istanbul**
Loa 43.90 Br ex - Dght -
Lbp - Br md 7.50 Dpth 2.50
Welded, 1 dk

(A37B2PS) Passenger Ship
Passengers: unberthed: 290

2 oil engines geared to sc. shafts driving 2 FP propellers
Total Power: 550kW (748hp) 15.0kn
Volvo Penta
2 x 4 Stroke each-275kW (374bhp)
AB Volvo Penta-Sweden
AuxGen: 2 x a.c

Ship	Tonnage	Class	Builder / Dimensions	Type / Capacity	Machinery
9361342 *ZDKI2* - **TASMAN** **A Broersma, A R Brouwer & Pitrans BV** Rederij Tasman *Gibraltar* *Gibraltar (British)* MMSI: 236617000 Official number: 9361342	**2,999** 1,643 4,537	Class: BV	**2007-11 Scheepswerf Ferus Smit BV — Westerbroek** Yd No: 377 Loa 89.78 (BB) Br ex - Dght 5.950 Lbp 84.99 Br md 14.00 Dpth 7.50 Welded, 1 dk	**(A31A2GX) General Cargo Ship** Grain: 6,088 TEU 146 C Ho 102 TEU C Dk 44 TEU incl 10 ref C Compartments: 1 Ho, ER 1 Ha: ER (61.5 x 11.5) Ice Capable	**1 oil engine** geared to sc. shaft driving 1 CP propeller Total Power: 2,320kW (3,154hp) 13.0kn MaK 8M25 1 x 4 Stroke 8 Cy. 255 x 400 2320kW (3154bhp) Caterpillar Motoren GmbH & Co. KG-Germany AuxGen: 2 x 140kW 400V 50Hz a.c, 1 x 340kW 400V 50Hz a.c Thrusters: 1 Tunnel thruster (f)
9452854 *9HA3163* - **TASMAN CASTLE** **ms 'Tasman Castle' GmbH & Co KG** Norddeutsche Reederei H Schuldt GmbH & Co KG *Valletta* *Malta* MMSI: 229237000 Official number: 9452854	**32,987** 19,231 56,868 T/cm 58.8	Class: GL (LR) ✠ Classed LR until 25/1/11	**2011-01 Jiangsu Hantong Ship Heavy Industry Co Ltd — Tongzhou JS** Yd No: 024 Loa 190.01 (BB) Br ex 32.32 Dght 12.800 Lbp 185.00 Br md 32.28 Dpth 18.00 Welded, 1 dk	**(A21A2BC) Bulk Carrier** Grain: 71,634; Bale: 68,200 Compartments: 5 Ho, ER 5 Ha: 4 (21.3 x 18.3)ER (18.9 x 18.3) Cranes: 4x35t	**1 oil engine** driving 1 FP propeller Total Power: 9,480kW (12,889hp) 14.2kn MAN-B&W 6S50MC-C 1 x 2 Stroke 6 Cy. 500 x 2000 9480kW (12889bhp) Doosan Engine Co Ltd-South Korea AuxGen: 3 x 600kW 450V 60Hz a.c Boilers: AuxB (Comp) 8.0kgf/cm² (7.8bar)
8002925 - - **TASMAN EXPLORER** **Jo Dimento & U Mahi** -	*118* 39 -		**1980-08 Marine Structures Ltd** Yd No: 2 Loa 23.53 Br ex - Dght 2.591 Lbp 22.03 Br md 6.40 Dpth 3.50 Welded, 1 dk	**(B11A2FS) Stern Trawler**	**1 oil engine** driving 1 FP propeller Total Power: 382kW (519hp) Caterpillar 3412PCTA 1 x Vee 4 Stroke 12 Cy. 137 x 152 382kW (519bhp) Caterpillar Tractor Co-USA
9045950 *A8JI6* - **TASMAN MERMAID** *ex Antarctic Mermaid -2006 ex Skausund -2004* *ex Tasman Mermaid -2001* **'Tasman Mermaid' Schiffahrtsgesellschaft mbH & Co KG** Triton Schiffahrts GmbH SatCom: Inmarsat A 1262345 *Monrovia* *Liberia* MMSI: 636091099 Official number: 91099	**9,829** 3,538 10,457 T/cm 18.5	Class: BV	**1993-01 Iwagi Zosen Co Ltd — Kamijima EH** Yd No: 148 Loa 141.80 (BB) Br ex - Dght 8.816 Lbp 133.00 Br md 22.80 Dpth 13.00 Welded, 3 dks, 4th dk in Nos. 2, 3 & 4 holds	**(A34A2GR) Refrigerated Cargo Ship** Ins: 15,281 TEU 138 incl 49 ref C Compartments: 4 Ho, ER, 11 Tw Dk 4 Ha: ER Cranes: 2x30t,2x10t	**1 oil engine** driving 1 FP propeller Total Power: 9,165kW (12,461hp) 19.0kn B&W 7S50MC 1 x 2 Stroke 7 Cy. 500 x 1910 9165kW (12461bhp) Hitachi Zosen Corp-Japan AuxGen: 3 x 800kW 450V 60Hz a.c Fuel: 92.2 (d.f.) 1568.8 (r.f.) 39.0pd
7617151 *WDB5559* - **TASMAN SEA** *ex Ambassador -2000* **K-Sea Operating LLC** - *New York, NY* *United States of America* MMSI: 366910960 Official number: 578207	**499** 149 -	Class: AB	**1976-11 Main Iron Works, Inc. — Houma, La** Yd No: 311 Loa 37.65 Br ex - Dght 4.700 Lbp 36.10 Br md 10.37 Dpth 4.98 Welded, 1 dk	**(B32B2SA) Articulated Pusher Tug**	**2 oil engines** geared to sc. shafts driving 2 FP propellers Total Power: 2,868kW (3,900hp) 12.0kn EMD (Electro-Motive) 16-645-E6 2 x Vee 2 Stroke 16 Cy. 230 x 254 each-1434kW (1950bhp) General Motors Corp.Electro-Motive Div.-La Grange AuxGen: 2 x 98kW Fuel: 416.5 (d.f.)
7026900 *WY9501* - **TASMAN SEA** *ex Lollie R -2000 ex Tasman Seal -2000* *ex Dresser Explorer -1978* *ex Aquatic Explorer -1976* - - *Pago Pago, AS* *United States of America* Official number: 522186	**371** 252 -		**1969 Burton Shipyard Co., Inc. — Port Arthur, Tx** Yd No: 453 Loa 50.30 Br ex 11.66 Dght 3.383 Lbp 47.30 Br md 11.60 Dpth 3.97 Welded, 1 dk	**(B11B2FV) Fishing Vessel**	**2 oil engines** reduction geared to sc. shafts driving 2 FP propellers Total Power: 1,654kW (2,248hp) 13.0kn Caterpillar D399SCAC 2 x Vee 4 Stroke 16 Cy. 159 x 203 each-827kW (1124bhp) Caterpillar Tractor Co-USA AuxGen: 2 x 150kW 120V 60Hz a.c
9218064 *VRWX4* - **TASMAN SEA** **Bernard (BVI) Ltd** Pacific Basin Shipping (HK) Ltd SatCom: Inmarsat C 447786410 *Hong Kong* *Hong Kong* MMSI: 477864000 Official number: HK-0670	**17,433** 9,829 28,456 T/cm 35.0	Class: NK	**2001-02 Kanda Zosensho K.K. — Kawajiri** Yd No: 406 Loa 170.00 (BB) Br ex - Dght 9.767 Lbp 162.00 Br md 27.00 Dpth 13.80 Welded, 1 dk	**(A21A2BC) Bulk Carrier** Double Bottom Entire Compartment Length Grain: 37,732; Bale: 36,683 Compartments: 5 Ho, ER 5 Ha: (14.1 x 15.0)4 (19.2 x 18.0)ER Cranes: 4x30.5t	**1 oil engine** driving 1 FP propeller Total Power: 5,884kW (8,000hp) 13.5kn Mitsubishi 5UEC52LA 1 x 2 Stroke 5 Cy. 520 x 1600 5884kW (8000bhp) Kobe Hatsudoki KK-Japan AuxGen: 2 x 400kW 100/450V 60Hz a.c, 1 x 300kW a.c Fuel: 126.0 (d.f.) (Heating Coils) 1134.0 (r.f.) 21.0pd
8706480 *ZMDM* - **TASMAN VIKING** *ex Halfdan I Bud -1995* **Endurance Fishing Co Ltd** - *Nelson* *New Zealand* Official number: 876147	**372** 112 181	Class: LR (NV) **100A1** SS 04/2009 stern trawler Ice Class 1D **LMC** Cable: 302.5/20.5 U3	**1989-04 Lunde Varv & Verkstads AB — Ramvik** Yd No: 227 Loa 36.60 (BB) Br ex 8.51 Dght - Lbp 30.22 Br md 8.17 Dpth 6.20 Welded, 2 dks	**(B11A2FS) Stern Trawler** Ins: 250 Ice Capable	**1 oil engine** with clutches, flexible couplings & sr geared to sc. shaft driving 1 CP propeller Total Power: 993kW (1,350hp) Normo LDM-6 1 x 4 Stroke 6 Cy. 250 x 300 993kW (1350bhp) Bergen Diesel AS-Norway AuxGen: 1 x 580kW 380V 50Hz a.c, 1 x 212kW 380V 50Hz a.c Thrusters: 1 Thwart. FP thruster (f)
9180190 *VHAF* - **TASMANIAN ACHIEVER** **Commonwealth Bank of Australia** Toll Transport Pty Ltd SatCom: Inmarsat C 450301661 *Melbourne, Vic* *Australia* MMSI: 503087000 Official number: 856087	**20,343** 6,103 11,000 T/cm 28.7	Class: NV	**1999-05 Samsung Heavy Industries Co Ltd — Geoje** Yd No: 1249 Lengthened-2004 Loa 184.40 (BB) Br ex 23.64 Dght 6.350 Lbp 172.37 Br md 23.60 Dpth 8.10 Welded, 2 dks, incl. 1 hoistable dk	**(A35A2RR) Ro-Ro Cargo Ship** Passengers: cabins: 6; berths: 12; driver berths: 12 Stern ramp (a) Len: 17.00 Wid: 18.60 Swl: - Lane-Len: 2378 Lane-Wid: 3.00 Lane-clr ht: 6.80 Trailers: 177 TEU 592 C RoRo Dk 383 TEU C Dk 209 TEU incl 153 ref C.	**4 oil engines** reduction geared to sc. shaft (s) driving 2 CP propellers Total Power: 15,360kW (20,884hp) 19.5kn Wartsila 8L32 4 x 4 Stroke 8 Cy. 320 x 400 each-3840kW (5221bhp) Wartsila NSD Finland Oy-Finland AuxGen: 2 x 1200kW 440V 60Hz a.c, 2 x 1000kW 440V 60Hz a.c Thrusters: 2 Tunnel thruster (f) Fuel: 156.0 (d.f.) (Heating Coils) 755.0 (r.f.) 63.5pd
9265419 *7TDN* - **TASSILI II** **Entreprise Nationale de Transport Maritime des Voyageurs (ENTMV)** - *Alger* *Algeria* MMSI: 605046150	**20,024** 7,858 3,520	Class: BV	**2004-10 IZAR Construcciones Navales SA — Seville** Yd No: 293 Loa 142.92 (BB) Br ex - Dght 6.300 Lbp 129.59 Br md 24.00 Dpth 14.65 Welded	**(A36A2PR) Passenger/Ro-Ro Ship (Vehicles)** Passengers: 1300; cabins: 209 Bow door & ramp (f) Stern door/ramp (a) Len: 8.20 Wid: 14.60 Swl: - Lane-Len: 1350 Cars: 300	**2 oil engines** reduction geared to sc. shafts driving 2 CP propellers Total Power: 25,200kW (34,262hp) 22.0kn Wartsila 12V46C 2 x Vee 4 Stroke 12 Cy. 460 x 580 each-12600kW (17131bhp) Wartsila Finland Oy-Finland AuxGen: 4 x 1369kW 60Hz a.c Thrusters: 2 Tunnel thruster (f)
9278313 *7TZU* - **TASSINA 1** **Entreprise Portuaire d'Arzew (EPA)** - *Arzew* *Algeria*	**309** 92 -	Class: BV	**2002-11 PO SevMash Predpriyatiye — Severodvinsk** (Hull) **2002-11 B.V. Scheepswerf Damen — Gorinchem** Yd No: 511713 Loa 30.82 Br ex 10.20 Dght 4.080 Lbp 28.03 Br md 9.40 Dpth 4.70 Welded	**(B32A2ST) Tug**	**2 oil engines** geared to sc. shafts driving 2 Directional propellers Total Power: 2,280kW (3,100hp) 12.5kn MaK 6M20 2 x 4 Stroke 6 Cy. 200 x 300 each-1140kW (1550bhp) Caterpillar Motoren GmbH & Co. KG-Germany AuxGen: 2 x 180kW 400/220V 50Hz a.c
9278375 *7TZV* - **TASSINA 2** **Entreprise Portuaire d'Arzew (EPA)** - *Arzew* *Algeria*	**309** 92 245	Class: (BV)	**2003-03 PO SevMash Predpriyatiye — Severodvinsk** (Hull) Yd No: (511716) **2003-03 B.V. Scheepswerf Damen — Gorinchem** Yd No: 511716 Loa 30.82 Br ex 10.20 Dght 3.750 Lbp 29.80 Br md 9.44 Dpth 4.80 Welded	**(B32A2ST) Tug**	**2 oil engines** geared to sc. shafts driving 2 Directional propellers Total Power: 2,160kW (2,936hp) 12.0kn MaK 6M20 2 x 4 Stroke 6 Cy. 200 x 300 each-1080kW (1468bhp) Caterpillar Motoren GmbH & Co. KG-Germany AuxGen: 2 x 180kW 400/220V 50Hz a.c
9278387 *7TZW* - **TASSINA 3** **Entreprise Portuaire d'Arzew (EPA)** - *Arzew* *Algeria* MMSI: 605266425	*309* 92 -	Class: BV	**2003-04 PO SevMash Predpriyatiye — Severodvinsk** (Hull) Yd No: (511717) **2003-04 B.V. Scheepswerf Damen — Gorinchem** Yd No: 511717 Loa 30.82 Br ex 10.20 Dght 3.750 Lbp 29.80 Br md 9.40 Dpth 4.80 Welded	**(B32A2ST) Tug**	**2 oil engines** geared to sc. shafts driving 2 Directional propellers Total Power: 2,160kW (2,936hp) 12.0kn MaK 6M20 2 x 4 Stroke 6 Cy. 200 x 300 each-1080kW (1468bhp) Caterpillar Motoren GmbH & Co. KG-Germany AuxGen: 2 x 180kW 400/220V 50Hz a.c
9278404 *7TZX* - **TASSINA 4** **Entreprise Portuaire d'Arzew (EPA)** - *Arzew* *Algeria* MMSI: 605266426	**313** 93 -	Class: BV	**2003-09 PO SevMash Predpriyatiye — Severodvinsk** (Hull) Yd No: (511719) **2003-09 B.V. Scheepswerf Damen — Gorinchem** Yd No: 511719 Loa 30.82 Br ex 10.20 Dght 4.080 Lbp 28.03 Br md 9.40 Dpth 4.70 Welded, 1 dk	**(B32A2ST) Tug**	**2 oil engines** geared to sc. shafts driving 2 Directional propellers Total Power: 2,280kW (3,100hp) 12.5kn MaK 6M20 2 x 4 Stroke 6 Cy. 200 x 300 each-1140kW (1550bhp) Caterpillar Motoren GmbH & Co. KG-Germany

8663652 *SX3845* -	**TASSOS II** *ex* Dimitrios I *-1994* *ex* Sofia *-1993* *ex* Epidendron *-1990* *ex* Mau *-1990* **North Aegean Slops** - *Thessaloniki* *Greece* MMSI: 237144200 Official number: 217	218 149 400		**1959 Zavod No. 490 — Ilyichyovsk** Converted From: General Cargo Ship-1995 Loa 41.10 Br ex - Dght - Lbp 38.20 Br md 6.50 Dpth - Welded, 1 dk	**(B34E2SW) Waste Disposal Vessel**	**1 oil engine** reduction geared to sc. shaft driving 1 FP propeller Total Power: 450kW (612hp) M.T.U. 1 x Vee 4 Stroke 12 Cy. 150 x 180 450kW (612bhp) (new engine 1994) MTU Friedrichshafen GmbH-Friedrichshafen
7723235 *CNDG* -	**TASSOUMITE** **Park Peche Maroc** - SatCom: Inmarsat C 424246910 *Casablanca* *Morocco* Official number: 6-718	*307* 93 480	Class: (BV)	**1979-07 Ateliers et Chantiers de La Manche — St-Malo** Yd No: 1274 Loa 34.90 Br ex 8.36 Dght 3.641 Lbp 30.36 Br md 8.32 Dpth 4.45 Welded, 1 dk	**(B11A2FS) Stern Trawler**	**1 oil engine** reduction geared to sc. shaft driving 1 CP propeller Total Power: 706kW (960hp) 12.5kn MaK 6M332AK 1 x 4 Stroke 6 Cy. 240 x 330 706kW (960bhp) MaK Maschinenbau GmbH-Kiel Fuel: 75.0 (d.f.)
8205084 *EQIT* -	**TASUA** **Government of The Islamic Republic of Iran (Ports & Maritime Organisation)** - *Bushehr* *Iran* Official number: 17135	*208* 63 135	Class: AS (LR) ✠ Classed LR until 1/5/96	**1983-04 Scheepsbouw Alblas B.V. — Krimpen a/d IJssel** (Hull) **1983-04 B.V. Scheepswerf Damen — Gorinchem** Yd No: 3140 Loa 30.21 Br ex 8.06 Dght 3.301 Lbp 26.95 Br md 7.80 Dpth 4.04 Welded, 1 dk	**(B32A2ST) Tug**	**2 oil engines** with clutches, flexible couplings & sr reverse geared to sc. shafts driving 2 FP propellers Total Power: 1,800kW (2,448hp) MWM TBD440-6 2 x 4 Stroke 6 Cy. 230 x 270 each-900kW (1224bhp) Motoren Werke Mannheim AG (MWM)-West Germany AuxGen: 2 x 64kW 380V 50Hz a.c Fuel: 78.0 (d.f.)
7430577 *CNJM* -	**TATA 2** *ex* Britania B M *-1982* **Omnium Marocaine de Peche** - *Agadir* *Morocco* Official number: 8-593	*314* 151 -	Class: (BV)	**1977-03 Construcciones Navales Santodomingo SA — Vigo** Yd No: 447 Loa 38.31 Br ex 8.62 Dght 4.006 Lbp 35.13 Br md 8.50 Dpth 6.15 Welded, 2 dks	**(B11A2FS) Stern Trawler**	**1 oil engine** geared to sc. shaft driving 1 FP propeller Total Power: 853kW (1,160hp) 12.0kn Deutz SBA8M528 1 x 4 Stroke 8 Cy. 220 x 280 853kW (1160bhp) Hijos de J Barreras SA-Spain Fuel: 193.5 (d.f.)
7922635 *CNJA* -	**TATA 3** *ex* Casablanca IV *-1982* **Omnium Marocaine de Peche** - *Agadir* *Morocco* Official number: 8-593	*268* 66 284	Class: (BV)	**1981-05 Construcciones Navales P Freire SA — Vigo** Yd No: 213 Loa 35.64 Br ex 8.46 Dght 3.950 Lbp 31.20 Br md 8.30 Dpth 6.10 Welded, 2 dks	**(B11A2FS) Stern Trawler** Ins: 265 Compartments: 1 Ho, ER 1 Ha:	**1 oil engine** geared to sc. shaft driving 1 CP propeller Total Power: 640kW (870hp) 11.0kn Volund DMTK630 1 x 4 Stroke 6 Cy. 300 x 410 640kW (870bhp) Larsconti Olsen e Hijos-Alicante Fuel: 191.5 (d.f.)
7226782 *ATJE* -	**TATA JYOTI** **Samak Food Corp** - *Mumbai* *India* Official number: 1522	*104* 65 54	Class: (IR) (AB)	**1972 Astilleros Unidos del Pacifico S.A. (AUPSA) — Mazatlan** Yd No: 445 Loa 21.95 Br ex - Dght 2.562 Lbp 20.30 Br md 6.09 Dpth 3.66 Welded, 1 dk	**(B11A2FT) Trawler**	**1 oil engine** sr reverse geared to sc. shaft driving 1 FP propeller Total Power: 268kW (364hp) Caterpillar D343SCAC 1 x 4 Stroke 6 Cy. 137 x 165 268kW (364bhp) Caterpillar Tractor Co-USA AuxGen: 2 x 3kW
7226794 *ATJF* -	**TATA SIDDHI** **Samak Food Corp** - *Mumbai* *India* Official number: 1523	*104* 65 54	Class: (IR) (AB)	**1972 Astilleros Unidos del Pacifico S.A. (AUPSA) — Mazatlan** Yd No: 467 Loa 21.95 Br ex - Dght 2.562 Lbp 20.03 Br md 6.09 Dpth 3.66 Welded, 1 dk	**(B11A2FT) Trawler**	**1 oil engine** sr geared to sc. shaft driving 1 FP propeller Total Power: 268kW (364hp) Caterpillar D343SCAC 1 x 4 Stroke 6 Cy. 137 x 165 268kW (364bhp) Caterpillar Tractor Co-USA AuxGen: 2 x 3kW
9410210 *A8SM5* -	**TATAKI** **Equitrust Inc** Dynacom Tankers Management Ltd SatCom: Inmarsat C 463705925 *Monrovia* *Liberia* MMSI: 636014250 Official number: 14250	**85,362** 47,371 149,992 T/cm 122.3	Class: AB	**2010-01 New Times Shipbuilding Co Ltd — Jingjiang JS** Yd No: 0316302 Loa 274.20 (BB) Br ex 50.04 Dght 16.000 Lbp 264.00 Br md 50.00 Dpth 23.20 Welded, 1 dk	**(A13A2TV) Crude Oil Tanker** Double Hull (13F) Liq: 173,378; Liq (Oil): 182,178 Cargo Heating Coils Compartments: 12 Wing Ta, 2 Wing Slop Ta, ER 3 Cargo Pump (s): 3x4000m³/hr Manifold: Bow/CM: 139.6m	**1 oil engine** driving 1 FP propeller Total Power: 18,660kW (25,370hp) 15.3kn MAN-B&W 6S70MC-C 1 x 2 Stroke 6 Cy. 700 x 2800 18660kW (25370bhp) Hyundai Heavy Industries Co Ltd-South Korea AuxGen: 3 x 950kW a.c Fuel: 243.0 (d.f.) 4414.0 (r.f.)
8915639 *YEIT* -	**TATAMAILAU** **Government of The Republic of Indonesia (Direktorat Jenderal Perhubungan Laut - Ministry of Sea Communications)** PT Pelayaran Nasional Indonesia (PELNI) *Kupang* *Indonesia* MMSI: 525005012	**6,041** 1,812 1,399	Class: KI (GL)	**1990-11 Jos L Meyer GmbH & Co — Papenburg** Yd No: 628 Loa 99.80 (BB) Br ex 18.30 Dght 4.200 Lbp 90.50 Br md 18.00 Dpth 9.40 Welded, 3 dks	**(A37B2PS) Passenger Ship** Passengers: unberthed: 915; cabins: 17; berths: 54 Grain: 530; Bale: 490 Compartments: 1 Ho 1 Ha: (7.0 x 5.5) Cranes: 2x5t	**2 oil engines** with flexible couplings & dr geared to sc. shafts driving 2 FP propellers Total Power: 3,200kW (4,350hp) 15.0kn MaK 6M453C 2 x 4 Stroke 6 Cy. 320 x 420 each-1600kW (2175bhp) Krupp MaK Maschinenbau GmbH-Kiel AuxGen: 4 x 420kW 220/380V a.c, 1 x 168kW 220/380V a.c Thrusters: 1 Thwart. CP thruster (f)
8918394 *UZAR* -	**TATARBUNARY** **Ukrainian Danube Shipping Co** - SatCom: Inmarsat A 1406204 *Izmail* *Ukraine* MMSI: 272145000 Official number: 930409	**2,977** 1,490 4,039	Class: RS	**1993-10 Estaleiros Navais de Viana do Castelo S.A. — Viana do Castelo** Yd No: 177 Loa 88.15 (BB) Br ex 15.52 Dght 5.670 Lbp 82.30 Br md 15.50 Dpth 7.10 Welded, 1 dk	**(A31A2GX) General Cargo Ship** Grain: 5,076 TEU 178 C. 178/20' Compartments: 2 Ho, ER 2 Ha: 2 (25.2 x 12.6)ER Cranes: 2x8t Ice Capable	**1 oil engine** with flexible couplings & sr gearedto sc. shaft driving 1 CP propeller Total Power: 1,985kW (2,699hp) 12.0kn Wartsila 6R32 1 x 4 Stroke 6 Cy. 320 x 350 1985kW (2699bhp) Wartsila Diesel Oy-Finland Thrusters: 1 Thwart. FP thruster (f) Fuel: 210.0
7730159 *UCLX* -	**TATARSTAN** **Svelna Trade PLC (OOO 'Svelna Treyd')** - SatCom: Inmarsat C 427320860 *Vladivostok* *Russia* MMSI: 273848200	**2,683** 918 1,961	Class: RS	**1977-12 Zelenodolskiy Sudostroitelnyy Zavod im. "Gorkogo" — Zelenodolsk** Yd No: 601 Loa 95.13 Br ex 13.85 Dght 5.487 Lbp 84.00 Br md - Dpth 7.60 Welded, 1 dk	**(B12B2FC) Fish Carrier** Ins: 2,500 Compartments: 3 Ho, ER 3 Ha: 3 (3.5 x 2.9)ER Derricks: 6x5t Ice Capable	**1 oil engine** driving 1 FP propeller Total Power: 1,839kW (2,500hp) 13.5kn Skoda 6L525IIPS 1 x 4 Stroke 6 Cy. 525 x 720 1839kW (2500bhp) CKD Praha-Praha Fuel: 136.0 (r.f.)
8733330 *EBRN* 3-VI-520-0	**TATAY** **Pesquerias Hersumar SL** - *Vigo* *Spain* Official number: 3-20/2000	**283** 85 -		**2001-11 Montajes Cies S.L. — Vigo** Loa 32.00 (BB) Br ex - Dght - Lbp 26.00 Br md 7.20 Dpth 3.60 Welded, 1 dk	**(B11B2FV) Fishing Vessel**	**1 oil engine** driving 1 Propeller Total Power: 368kW (500hp)
9482770 *V7SO3* -	**TATE J** **Seven Navigation Co LLC** Apex Bulk Carriers LLC *Majuro* *Marshall Islands* MMSI: 538003692 Official number: 3692	**23,456** 11,522 34,439	Class: NK (AB)	**2012-01 SPP Shipbuilding Co Ltd — Tongyeong** Yd No: H4043 Loa 180.00 (BB) Br ex - Dght 9.920 Lbp 172.00 Br md 30.00 Dpth 14.70 Welded, 1 dk	**(A21A2BC) Bulk Carrier** Single Hull Grain: 48,765; Bale: 46,815 Compartments: 5 Ho, ER 5 Ha: ER Cranes: 4x35t	**1 oil engine** driving 1 FP propeller Total Power: 7,900kW (10,741hp) 14.0kn MAN-B&W 5S50MC-C 1 x 2 Stroke 5 Cy. 500 x 2000 7900kW (10741bhp) Doosan Engine Co Ltd-South Korea AuxGen: 3 x 600kW a.c Fuel: 198.0 (d.f.) 1701.0 (r.f.)
7218876 - -	**TATEGAMI MARU** *ex* Eitai Maru *-1982* - -	*199* - 63		**1972-04 Towa Zosen K.K. — Shimonoseki** Yd No: 424 Loa 30.61 Br ex 8.84 Dght 2.598 Lbp 27.01 Br md 8.82 Dpth 3.51 Welded, 1 dk	**(B32A2ST) Tug**	**2 oil engines** Geared Integral to driving 2 Z propellers Total Power: 2,132kW (2,898hp) 12.5kn Niigata 6L25BX 2 x 4 Stroke 6 Cy. 250 x 320 each-1066kW (1449bhp) Niigata Engineering Co Ltd-Japan
9004035 *JL5909* -	**TATEISHI** **Oshima Kisen KK** - *Kamijima, Ehime* *Japan* Official number: 130664	*144* - 102		**1990-03 Naikai Shipbuilding & Engineering Co Ltd — Onomichi HS (Taguma Shipyard)** Yd No: 561 Loa 32.80 Br ex 10.60 Dght 2.058 Lbp 23.90 Br md 9.60 Dpth 3.00 Welded	**(A36A2PR) Passenger/Ro-Ro Ship (Vehicles)**	**1 oil engine** reduction geared to sc. shafts driving 2 FP propellers Total Power: 368kW (500hp) 8.5kn Yanmar M200-DN 1 x 4 Stroke 6 Cy. 200 x 260 368kW (500bhp) Yanmar Diesel Engine Co Ltd-Japan
8617562 *JH3088* -	**TATEIWA MARU** *ex* Akiba Maru *-2006* **Nihon Tug-Boat Co Ltd** - *Otaru, Hokkaido* *Japan* Official number: 128458	*194* - -		**1987-01 Kanagawa Zosen — Kobe** Yd No: 293 Loa 33.91 Br ex - Dght 3.101 Lbp 29.52 Br md 9.42 Dpth 4.02 Welded, 1 dk	**(B32A2ST) Tug**	**2 oil engines** with clutches & dr geared to sc. shafts driving 2 Z propellers Total Power: 2,574kW (3,500hp) Niigata 6L28BXE 2 x 4 Stroke 6 Cy. 280 x 320 each-1287kW (1750bhp) Niigata Engineering Co Ltd-Japan

Number	Name / Owner	Tonnage	Class	Built / Dimensions	Type / Cargo	Machinery
9244623 *HSB4749* -	**TATEYAMA** - **Srithai Marine Co Ltd** NYK Shipmanagement Pte Ltd *Bangkok* *Thailand* MMSI: 567473000 Official number: TG 55037	**160,072** 95,718 300,373 T/cm 179.3	Class: NK	**2002-04 Nippon Kokan KK (NKK Corp) — Tsu ME** Yd No: 222 Loa 333.00 (BB) Br ex 60.04 Dght 20.863 Lbp 320.00 Br md 60.00 Dpth 29.60 Welded, 1 dk	**(A13A2TV) Crude Oil Tanker** Double Hull (13F) Liq: 334,232; Liq (Oil): 341,260 Compartments: 5 Ta, 10 Wing Ta, 2 Wing Slop Ta, ER 3 Cargo Pump (s): 3x5000m^3/hr Manifold: Bow/CM: 163.5m	**1 oil engine** driving 1 FP propeller Total Power: 26,777kW (36,406hp) 16.1kn Sulzer 7RTA84T 1 x 2 Stroke 7 Cy. 840 x 3150 26777kW (36406bhp) Diesel United Ltd.-Aioi AuxGen: 3 x 1200kW a.c Fuel: 350.0 (d.f.) 7100.0 (r.f.)
9199189 *JH3193* TYT-1	**TATEYAMA MARU** - **Toyama Prefecture** - *Toyama, Toyama* *Japan* MMSI: 431266000 Official number: 134415	*160* - -		**1998-10 Nagasaki Zosen K.K. — Nagasaki** Yd No: 1161 Loa 40.51 (BB) Br ex 7.02 Dght 3.020 Lbp 33.50 Br md 7.00 Dpth 3.00 Welded, 1 dk	**(B12D2FR) Fishery Research Vessel**	**1 oil engine** reduction geared to sc. shaft driving 1 CP propeller Total Power: 1,103kW (1,500hp) 14.0kn Niigata 6MG25HX 1 x 4 Stroke 6 Cy. 250 x 350 1103kW (1500bhp) Niigata Engineering Co Ltd-Japan AuxGen: 2 x 240kW a.c Thrusters: 1 Thwart. FP thruster (f)
7916600 - -	**TATEYAMA MARU** - - -	*156* - -		**1980-03 Nipponkai Heavy Ind. Co. Ltd. — Toyama** Yd No: 207 Loa - Br ex - Dght 2.552 Lbp 30.03 Br md 6.91 Dpth 2.93 Welded, 1 dk	**(B12D2FR) Fishery Research Vessel**	**1 oil engine** driving 1 FP propeller Total Power: 736kW (1,001hp) Niigata 6MG25BX 1 x 4 Stroke 6 Cy. 250 x 320 736kW (1001bhp) Niigata Engineering Co Ltd-Japan
7722683 - -	**TATEYAMA MARU** - **Ocean Fisheries Co (Pte) Ltd** - *Sri Lanka*	*149* - -		**1977-11 Nagasaki Zosen K.K. — Nagasaki** Yd No: 631 Loa 37.75 Br ex - Dght 2.452 Lbp 32.01 Br md 6.71 Dpth 2.93 Welded, 1 dk	**(B11B2FV) Fishing Vessel**	**1 oil engine** driving 1 FP propeller Total Power: 368kW (500hp) Daihatsu 6DSM-26 1 x 4 Stroke 6 Cy. 260 x 320 368kW (500bhp) Daihatsu Diesel Manufacturing Co Lt-Japan
7014919 - -	**TATI** - **Industrial Pesquera Monteverde CA (INPECA)** - *Guayaquil* *Ecuador* Official number: P-00-0527	*240* 128 -	Class: (BV)	**1970 Construcciones Navales SA (CONASA) — Callao** L reg 31.70 Br ex 7.60 Dght - Lbp 30.21 Br md - Dpth 3.89 Welded, 1 dk	**(B11A2FT) Trawler**	**1 oil engine** geared to sc. shaft driving 1 FP propeller Total Power: 382kW (519hp) 12.0kn Caterpillar 3408PCTA 1 x Vee 4 Stroke 8 Cy. 137 x 152 382kW (519bhp) (made 1977, fitted 1980) Caterpillar Tractor Co-USA Fuel: 17.5 (d.f.)
9677416 *J8Y4434* -	**TATIANA** *ex* Princess Yachts Pyi Y8036 D212 *-2012* **Tatiana Cruising Co Ltd** LLC 'Aston Enterprise Agency' *Kingstown* *St Vincent & The Grenadines* Official number: 40904	**114** 91 -		**2012-04 Princess Yachts International Plc — Plymouth** Yd No: Y8036 D212 Loa 23.99 Br ex 6.24 Dght - Lbp - Br md 6.24 Dpth 3.20 Welded, 1 dk	**(X11A2YP) Yacht**	**2 oil engines** reduction geared to sc. shaft (s) driving 2 Propellers Total Power: 1,640kW (2,230hp) Caterpillar C32 2 x Vee 4 Stroke 12 Cy. 145 x 162 each-820kW (1115bhp) Caterpillar Inc-USA
9406972 *FNOE* -	**TATIANA-B** - **CFT Location** Maritima SA *Martigues* *France* MMSI: 228287600 Official number: 925847	**2,158** 986 3,536	Class: BV	**2008-05 SC Aker Braila SA — Braila** (Hull) Yd No: 110 **2008-05 Aker Yards AS Brevik — Brevik** Yd No: 60 Loa 89.20 Br ex - Dght 5.000 Lbp 86.00 Br md 13.80 Dpth 6.45 Welded, 1 dk	**(A12B2TR) Chemical/Products Tanker** Double Hull (13F) Liq: 3,500; Liq (Oil): 3,500	**2 oil engines** reduction geared to sc. shafts driving 2 CP propellers Total Power: 2,080kW (2,828hp) 12.0kn Mitsubishi S6U2-MPTK 2 x 4 Stroke 6 Cy. 240 x 260 each-1040kW (1414bhp) Mitsubishi Heavy Industries Ltd-Japan Thrusters: 1 Tunnel thruster (f)
8655916 *2GXU5* -	**TATIANA PER SEMPRE** - **Arielstar Ltd** Resag Ltd *United Kingdom* MMSI: 235101408	**381** 114 -	Class: RI	**2007-05 Baglietto S.p.A. — Varazze** Yd No: 10194 Loa 44.00 Br ex - Dght 1.800 Lbp 39.70 Br md 8.14 Dpth 4.00 Welded, 1 dk	**(X11A2YP) Yacht** Hull Material: Aluminium Alloy	**2 oil engines** reduction geared to sc. shafts driving 2 Propellers Total Power: 5,440kW (7,396hp) 27.0kn M.T.U. 16V4000M90 2 x Vee 4 Stroke 16 Cy. 165 x 190 each-2720kW (3698bhp) MTU Friedrichshafen GmbH-Friedrichshafen Thrusters: 1 Tunnel thruster (f)
7326635 *HCTA* -	**TATIANA V** *ex* Atsuta Maru *-1986* **Acotramar CA** - *Guayaquil* *Ecuador* Official number: CN-00-0060	*1,016* 799 1,929	Class: (KI) (AB)	**1973-08 Asakawa Zosen K.K. — Imabari** Yd No: 228 Loa 68.36 (BB) Br ex 12.02 Dght 5.398 Lbp 68.00 Br md 11.99 Dpth 5.57 Riveted\Welded, 1 dk	**(A13C2LA) Asphalt/Bitumen Tanker** Liq: 1,834; Liq (Oil): 1,834; Asphalt: 1,834 Compartments: 1 Ho, ER, 6 Wing Ta	**1 oil engine** driving 1 FP propeller Total Power: 1,618kW (2,200hp) 12.0kn Akasaka AH38 1 x 4 Stroke 6 Cy. 380 x 560 1618kW (2200bhp) Akasaka Tekkosho KK (Akasaka DieselLtd)-Japan AuxGen: 2 x 80kW a.c
7629673 *HCTT* -	**TATIANA VI** *ex* Alexia *-1996* *ex* Filergos *-1989* *ex* Yuyo Maru *-1987* *ex* Tenryu Maru No. 25 *-1983* **Acotramar CA** - *Guayaquil* *Ecuador* Official number: TN-00-0163	*842* 555 2,022	Class: (BV)	**1973-07 Shirahama Zosen K.K. — Honai** Yd No: 55 Loa 77.73 Br ex 10.83 Dght 4.573 Lbp 71.89 Br md 10.80 Dpth 5.01 Welded, 1 dk	**(A13B2TP) Products Tanker** Liq: 2,147; Liq (Oil): 2,147 Compartments: 4 Ta, ER	**1 oil engine** driving 1 FP propeller Total Power: 1,177kW (1,600hp) 12.6kn Hanshin 6LUD32 1 x 4 Stroke 6 Cy. 320 x 510 1177kW (1600bhp) Hanshin Nainenki Kogyo-Japan AuxGen: 2 x 96kW 225V a.c
9678185 *YGBV* -	**TATIHU** - **Government of The Republic of Indonesia (Direktorat Jenderal Perhubungan Darat - Ministry of Land Communications)** - *Ambon* *Indonesia* MMSI: 525007195 Official number: 1291/DDA	**820** 246 -	Class: KI	**2013-02 P.T. Mariana Bahagia — Palembang** Yd No: 61 Loa 56.02 Br ex - Dght 2.700 Lbp 49.15 Br md 14.00 Dpth 3.80 Welded, 1 dk	**(A36A2PR) Passenger/Ro-Ro Ship (Vehicles)** Passengers: unberthed: 196 Cars: 25	**2 oil engines** reduction geared to sc. ahafts driving 2 Propellers Total Power: 1,716kW (2,334hp) 12.0kn Mitsubishi S12A2-MPTK 2 x Vee 4 Stroke 12 Cy. 150 x 160 each-858kW (1167bhp) Mitsubishi Heavy Industries Ltd-Japan AuxGen: 2 x 91kW 380V a.c
9562776 *ZGCI5* -	**TATII** - **Tamsen Yachts International Ltd** Dominion Marine Corporate Services Ltd *United Kingdom*	**358** 107 -	Class: RI	**2009-07 in Turkey** Yd No: 177 Loa 40.50 Br ex 8.44 Dght 1.650 Lbp 33.85 Br md - Dpth 3.50 Bonded, 1 dk	**(X11A2YP) Yacht** Hull Material: Reinforced Plastic	**2 oil engines** reduction geared to sc. shafts driving 2 Propellers Total Power: 3,580kW (4,868hp) M.T.U. 16V2000M93 2 x Vee 4 Stroke 16 Cy. 135 x 156 each-1790kW (2434bhp) MTU Friedrichshafen GmbH-Friedrichshafen AuxGen: 2 x 90kW a.c
8312772 *CBTT* -	**TATIO** *ex* Western Andes *-2000* *ex* Pacific Andes *-1996* *ex* Western Andes *-1992* *ex* Endurance *-1988* *ex* Endurance I *-1985* **Andes International Shipping Inc** Administradora de Naves Humboldt Ltda SatCom: Inmarsat A 1360563 *Valparaiso* *Chile* MMSI: 725009700 Official number: 3025	**22,208** 13,837 37,715 T/cm 46.8	Class: LR ✠ **100A1** SS 03/2010 bulk carrier strengthened for heavy cargoes, Nos. 2 & 4 holds may be empty ESP ESN-Hold 1 ✠ **LMC** **UMS** Eq.Ltr: I†; Cable: 605.0/64.0 U3	**1985-05 Mitsubishi Heavy Industries Ltd. — Nagasaki** Yd No: 1948 Loa 182.81 (BB) Br ex 28.45 Dght 10.789 Lbp 174.02 Br md 28.41 Dpth 15.22 Welded, 1 dk	**(A21A2BC) Bulk Carrier** Grain: 51,199; Bale: 46,099 TEU 168 Compartments: 5 Ho, ER 5 Ha: (12.8 x 15.0)4 (19.2 x 15.0)ER Cranes: 4x25t	**1 oil engine** driving 1 FP propeller Total Power: 9,540kW (12,971hp) 14.5kn Sulzer 6RTA58 1 x 2 Stroke 6 Cy. 580 x 1700 9540kW (12971bhp) Mitsubishi Heavy Industries Ltd-Japan AuxGen: 3 x 480kW 450V 60Hz a.c Boilers: e 12.0kgf/cm^2 (11.8bar), AuxB (o.f.) 6.9kgf/cm^2 (6.8bar) Fuel: 182.0 (d.f.) 1631.0 (r.f.) 24.0pd
9456135 *A8TK9* -	**TATJANA** - **ms 'Tatjana' Schiffahrtsgesellschaft mbH & Co KG** Uwe Von Allworden Shipping GmbH & Co KG SatCom: Inmarsat C 463706447 *Monrovia* *Liberia* MMSI: 636091830 Official number: 91830	**32,987** 19,231 56,758 T/cm 58.8	Class: LR ✠ **100A1** SS 11/2009 bulk carrier CSR BC-A GRAB (20) Nos. 2, 4 holds may be empty ESP **ShipRight** (CM) *IWS LI ✠ **LMC** **UMS** Cable: 633.9/73.0 U3 (a)	**2009-11 Jiangsu Hantong Ship Heavy Industry Co Ltd — Tongzhou JS** Yd No: 018 Loa 189.99 (BB) Br ex 32.30 Dght 12.800 Lbp 185.00 Br md 32.26 Dpth 18.00 Welded, 1 dk	**(A21A2BC) Bulk Carrier** Grain: 71,634; Bale: 68,200 Compartments: 5 Ho, ER 5 Ha: ER Cranes: 4x35t	**1 oil engine** driving 1 FP propeller Total Power: 9,480kW (12,889hp) 14.2kn MAN-B&W 6S50MC-C 1 x 2 Stroke 6 Cy. 500 x 2000 9480kW (12889bhp) Doosan Engine Co Ltd-South Korea AuxGen: 3 x 600kW 450V 60Hz a.c Boilers: AuxB (Comp) 9.1kgf/cm^2 (8.9bar)
9075498 *TCBE6* -	**TATLISUM** - **Bahri Ticaret Ltd Sti** - *Istanbul* *Turkey* MMSI: 271002181 Official number: 6364	**373** 214 750		**1993 Rota Denizcilik Ticaret A.S. — Tuzla, Istanbul** Yd No: 19 Loa 49.51 Br ex - Dght 3.110 Lbp 44.84 Br md 8.00 Dpth 3.60 Welded, 1 dk	**(A14A2LO) Water Tanker** Compartments: 8 Ta, ER	**1 oil engine** with flexible couplings & sr geared to sc. shaft driving 1 FP propeller Total Power: 405kW (551hp) Volvo Penta TAMD162 1 x 4 Stroke 6 Cy. 144 x 165 405kW (551bhp) AB Volvo Penta-Sweden

1006336 *ZCIF8* -	**TATOOSH** **Fowler Sea Inc** Fraser Yachts Florida Inc *George Town* *Cayman Islands (British)* MMSI: 319801000 Official number: 731293	**3,229** 968 550	Class: LR ✠ **100A1** SS 06/2010 SSC Yacht (P) mono G6 service area ✠ **LMC** **UMS** Cable: 440.0/42.0 U3 (a)	**2000-06 HDW-Nobiskrug GmbH — Rendsburg** Yd No: 757 Loa 92.10 (BB) Br ex 15.49 Dght 4.800 Lbp 79.20 Br md 14.95 Dpth 8.00 Welded, 2 dks	**(X11A2YP) Yacht**	**2 oil engines** with clutches, flexible couplings & sr reverse geared to sc. shafts driving 2 FP propellers Total Power: 6,602kW (8,976hp) 19.0kn Deutz SBV16M628 2 x Vee 4 Stroke 16 Cy. 240 x 280 each-3301kW (4488bhp) Motoren Werke Mannheim AG (MWM)-Mannheim AuxGen: 3 x 600kW 400V 50Hz a.c, 2 x 320kW 400V 60Hz a.c Thrusters: 1 Thwart. FP thruster (f); 1 Tunnel thruster (a)
7048300 - -	**TATOSO** **Government of American Samoa** - *Pago Pago, AS* *United States of America*	*148* 99 -	Class: (AB)	**1968 Equitable Equipment Co. — Madisonville, La** Yd No: 1513 Loa 25.94 Br ex 7.55 Dght 2.439 Lbp 23.78 Br md 7.32 Dpth 3.08 Welded, 1 dk	**(B32A2ST) Tug**	**2 oil engines** reverse reduction geared to sc. shafts driving 2 FP propellers Total Power: 1,126kW (1,530hp) Caterpillar D398TA 2 x Vee 4 Stroke 12 Cy. 159 x 203 each-563kW (765bhp) Caterpillar Tractor Co-USA AuxGen: 2 x 40kW
9582960 *D5CZ6* -	**TATRY** **Galatea Four Navigation Ltd** Polska Zegluga Morska PP (POLSTEAM) *Monrovia* *Liberia* MMSI: 636015818 Official number: 15818	**43,025** 27,217 82,138 T/cm 70.2	Class: PR (Class contemplated) (NK)	**2013-10 Tadotsu Shipbuilding Co Ltd — Tadotsu KG** Yd No: 1509 Loa 228.99 Br ex - Dght 14.430 Lbp 222.00 Br md 32.26 Dpth 20.05 Welded, 1 dk	**(A21A2BC) Bulk Carrier** Grain: 97,000 Compartments: 7 Ho, ER 7 Ha: 6 (17.8 x 15.4)ER (16.2 x 13.8)	**1 oil engine** driving 1 FP propeller Total Power: 13,560kW (18,436hp) 14.5kn MAN-B&W 6S60MC-C 1 x 2 Stroke 6 Cy. 600 x 2400 13560kW (18436bhp) Mitsui Engineering & Shipbuilding CLtd-Japan
1010260 *ZCYJ* -	**TATS** *ex* Loretta Anne IV *-2012* *ex* Loretta Anne *-2011* *ex* Allogante *-2009* **Fejoca Ltd** - SatCom: Inmarsat C 431900232 *George Town* *Cayman Islands (British)* MMSI: 319003500 Official number: 741416	**299** 89 45	Class: LR ✠ **100A1** SS 06/2009 SSC Yacht, mono, G6 Cable: 280.0/16.0 SH	**2009-06 Alloy Yachts — Auckland** Yd No: 38 Loa 40.00 Br ex 8.50 Dght 1.860 Lbp 35.42 Br md 8.46 Dpth 3.90 Welded, 1 dk	**(X11A2YP) Yacht** Hull Material: Aluminium Alloy	**2 oil engines** with clutches, flexible couplings & sr reverse geared to sc. shafts driving 2 FP propellers Total Power: 2,088kW (2,838hp) 15.0kn Caterpillar C32 2 x Vee 4 Stroke 12 Cy. 145 x 162 each-1044kW (1419bhp) Caterpillar Inc-USA AuxGen: 2 x 69kW 400V 50Hz a.c Thrusters: 1 Thwart. FP thruster (f); 1 Thwart. FP thruster (a)
8949783 - -	**TATSU MARU No. 5** **Yun Song Foundation Co Ltd** - *South Korea*	*107* - -		**1971-08 Ando Shipbuilding Co. Ltd. — Tokyo** Loa 21.50 Br ex - Dght 2.050 Lbp 19.50 Br md 9.00 Dpth 2.70 Welded, 1 dk	**(B34X2QA) Anchor Handling Vessel**	**2 oil engines** driving 2 FP propellers Total Power: 442kW (600hp) 9.0kn Daihatsu 2 x 4 Stroke each-221kW (300bhp) Daihatsu Diesel Manufacturing Co Lt-Japan
8625131 *JG4672* -	**TATSU MARU No. 38** **Kocho Bussan KK** - *Kamogawa, Chiba* *Japan* Official number: 126005	*199* - 408		**1987-04 KK Ouchi Zosensho — Matsuyama EH** L reg 38.50 Br ex - Dght 2.800 Lbp - Br md 8.21 Dpth 3.00 Welded, 1 dk	**(A24A2BT) Cement Carrier**	**1 oil engine** driving 1 FP propeller Total Power: 478kW (650hp) 11.0kn Hanshin 1 x 4 Stroke 478kW (650bhp) The Hanshin Diesel Works Ltd-Japan
9036399 *JM6075* -	**TATSU MARU No. 61** *ex* Koei Maru No. 53 *-2000* **Mitsushio Bussan KK** - *Kamogawa, Chiba* *Japan* Official number: 132679	*499* - 1,500		**1991-09 Honda Zosen — Saiki** Yd No: 828 Loa 76.58 Br ex - Dght 4.050 Lbp 70.00 Br md 12.00 Dpth 7.00 Welded, 1 dk	**(A31A2GX) General Cargo Ship** Compartments: 1 Ho, ER 1 Ha: ER	**1 oil engine** reduction geared to sc. shaft driving 1 FP propeller Total Power: 1,177kW (1,600hp) 11.5kn Niigata 6M28HFT 1 x 4 Stroke 6 Cy. 280 x 480 1177kW (1600bhp) Niigata Engineering Co Ltd-Japan AuxGen: 1 x 100kW 445V a.c, 1 x 96kW 445V a.c
8944147 *JCGP* MG1-1958	**TATSU MARU No. 68** **Kodama Gyogyo YK** - *Shiogama, Miyagi* *Japan* MMSI: 431053000 Official number: 136264	*379* - -		**1998-09 K.K. Yoshida Zosen Tekko — Kesennuma** Yd No: 510 L reg 49.65 Br ex - Dght - Lbp - Br md 8.80 Dpth 3.82 Welded, 1 dk	**(B11B2FV) Fishing Vessel**	**1 oil engine** driving 1 FP propeller
8620909 - -	**TATSUFUKU MARU No. 8** - -	*108* - -		**1982 K.K. Kinan Zosensho — Nachi-Katsuura** L reg 24.10 Br ex - Dght 2.000 Lbp - Br md 5.60 Dpth 2.20 Welded, 1 dk	**(B11B2FV) Fishing Vessel**	**1 oil engine** driving 1 FP propeller Total Power: 250kW (340hp)
9132870 *JL6336* -	**TATSUHIRO MARU No. 8** **KM Marine Co Ltd** - *Tokyo* *Japan* MMSI: 431500394 Official number: 135113	*748* - 1,850		**1995-10 Sasaki Shipbuilding Co Ltd — Osakikamijima HS** Yd No: 600 Loa - Br ex - Dght 4.750 Lbp 66.00 Br md 12.00 Dpth 5.25 Welded, 1 dk	**(A13B2TP) Products Tanker**	**1 oil engine** driving 1 FP propeller Total Power: 1,471kW (2,000hp) Hanshin LH34LAG 1 x 4 Stroke 6 Cy. 340 x 640 1471kW (2000bhp) The Hanshin Diesel Works Ltd-Japan
9250244 *HOBS* -	**TATSUKI MARU** **Laodameia Shipholding SA** Hachiuma Steamship Co Ltd (Hachiuma Kisen KK) *Panama* *Panama* MMSI: 352992000 Official number: 2845102CH	**52,964** 27,188 91,765	Class: NK	**2002-04 Imabari Shipbuilding Co Ltd — Marugame KG (Marugame Shipyard)** Yd No: 1379 Loa 234.94 (BB) Br ex - Dght 12.868 Lbp 226.00 Br md 43.00 Dpth 19.30 Welded, 1 dk	**(A21A2BC) Bulk Carrier** Grain: 112,883 Compartments: 7 Ho, ER 7 Ha: 6 (15.8 x 20.8)ER (15.8 x 19.2)	**1 oil engine** driving 1 FP propeller Total Power: 11,732kW (15,951hp) 15.4kn Mitsubishi 7UEC60LS 1 x 2 Stroke 7 Cy. 600 x 2200 11732kW (15951bhp) Akasaka Tekkosho KK (Akasaka DieselLtd)-Japan Fuel: 3060.0
9216896 *JBTC* -	**TATSUMAI** **KK Soho Enterprise** - *Kesennuma, Miyagi* *Japan* MMSI: 431535000 Official number: 133360	*499* - -		**1999-09 Sanuki Shipbuilding & Iron Works Co Ltd — Mitoyo KG** Yd No: 1287 Loa 63.01 Br ex - Dght 4.060 Lbp 55.60 Br md 9.30 Dpth 5.35 Welded, 1 dk	**(B12D2FP) Fishery Patrol Vessel**	**1 oil engine** reduction geared to sc. shaft driving 1 FP propeller Total Power: 1,912kW (2,600hp) 15.2kn Daihatsu 6DKM-28 1 x 4 Stroke 6 Cy. 280 x 390 1912kW (2600bhp) Daihatsu Diesel Manufacturing Co Lt-Japan
9041576 *JI3479* -	**TATSUMI MARU** **KK Tatsumi Shokai** - *Osaka, Osaka* *Japan* MMSI: 431400942 Official number: 133390	*699* - 1,730	Class: NK	**1992-02 Kanmon Zosen K.K. — Shimonoseki** Yd No: 532 Loa 69.30 (BB) Br ex 11.52 Dght 4.509 Lbp 65.00 Br md 11.50 Dpth 5.00 Welded, 1 dk	**(A24A2BT) Cement Carrier** Grain: 1,408; Bale: 1,363 Compartments: 3 Ho, ER	**1 oil engine** with clutches, flexible couplings & sr geared to sc. shaft driving 1 FP propeller Total Power: 1,030kW (1,400hp) 11.0kn Hanshin LH28G 1 x 4 Stroke 6 Cy. 280 x 460 1030kW (1400bhp) The Hanshin Diesel Works Ltd-Japan AuxGen: 3 x 146kW a.c Fuel: 45.0 (d.f.)
8963363 *JH2179* -	**TATSUMI MARU** **Gamagori Kanko Kisen KK** - *Gamagori, Aichi* *Japan* Official number: 101367	*188* - -		**1967-08 Ito Zosen K.K. — Tobishima** Loa 26.50 Br ex - Dght 2.850 Lbp 24.00 Br md 10.00 Dpth 3.00 Welded, 1 dk	**(A37B2PS) Passenger Ship** Passengers: unberthed: 715	**2 oil engines** driving 2 FP propellers Total Power: 662kW (900hp) 11.0kn Nippon Hatsudoki 2 x 4 Stroke each-331kW (450bhp) Nippon Hatsudoki-Japan
8808159 *JMOI* FS1-560	**TATSUMI MARU No. 56** **Tatsumi Suisan KK** - SatCom: Inmarsat A 1204371 *Iwaki, Fukushima* *Japan* MMSI: 431704220 Official number: 130687	*379* - 455		**1988-07 KK Kanasashi Zosen — Toyohashi AI** Yd No: 3171 Loa 53.62 (BB) Br ex - Dght 3.401 Lbp 47.20 Br md 8.70 Dpth 3.76 Welded, 1 dk	**(B11B2FV) Fishing Vessel**	**1 oil engine** with clutches, flexible couplings & sr reverse geared to sc. shaft driving 1 FP propeller Total Power: 736kW (1,001hp) Niigata 6M28BFT 1 x 4 Stroke 6 Cy. 280 x 480 736kW (1001bhp) Niigata Engineering Co Ltd-Japan
9036612 *JRDV* FS1-607	**TATSUMI MARU No. 57** **Tatsumi Suisan KK** - SatCom: Inmarsat A 1204542 *Iwaki, Fukushima* *Japan* MMSI: 431700660 Official number: 132232	*379* - -		**1991-08 KK Kanasashi — Shizuoka SZ** Yd No: 3263 Loa 55.16 (BB) Br ex 8.73 Dght 3.400 Lbp 48.40 Br md 8.70 Dpth 3.75 Welded, 1 dk	**(B11B2FV) Fishing Vessel** Ins: 586	**1 oil engine** with clutches, flexible couplings & sr reverse geared to sc. shaft driving 1 FP propeller Total Power: 736kW (1,001hp) Niigata 6M28BFT 1 x 4 Stroke 6 Cy. 280 x 480 736kW (1001bhp) Niigata Engineering Co Ltd-Japan

IMO / Call sign	Name / Owner / Port	Tonnage	Class	Builder / Dimensions	Type	Machinery
9157375 - -	**TATSUMI NO. 8** *ex Seisho -2003* - - *China*	*194* - -		**1997-02 K.K. Izutsu Zosensho — Nagasaki** Yd No: 1070 Loa 30.50 Br ex - Dght - Lbp 29.90 Br md 11.00 Dpth 6.20 Welded, 1 dk	**(B32B2SP) Pusher Tug**	**1 oil engine** geared to sc. shaft driving 1 FP propeller Total Power: 2,574kW (3,500hp) 10.5kn Yanmar 6N330-EN 1 x 4 Stroke 6 Cy. 330 x 440 2574kW (3500bhp) Yanmar Diesel Engine Co Ltd-Japan
9063524 *JK5161* -	**TATSURYO MARU** **Fuji Kisen YK** Ube Shipping & Logistics Ltd (Ube Kosan KK) *Hofu, Yamaguchi* *Japan* MMSI: 431400121 Official number: 133024	*699* - 1,500	Class: NK	**1993-03 K.K. Miura Zosensho — Saiki** Yd No: 1063 Loa 70.00 Br ex - Dght 4.386 Lbp 65.00 Br md 11.50 Dpth 4.90 Welded	**(A24H2BZ) Powder Carrier** Grain: 1,437	**1 oil engine** reduction geared to sc. shaft driving 1 FP propeller Total Power: 1,412kW (1,920hp) 10.5kn Daihatsu 6DLM-28 1 x 4 Stroke 6 Cy. 280 x 360 1412kW (1920bhp) Daihatsu Diesel Manufacturing Co Lt-Japan AuxGen: 4 x 200kW a.c Fuel: 45.0 (d.f.)
7810375 *JJ3136* -	**TATSUTA MARU** **Naikai Eisen KK** - *Kobe, Hyogo* *Japan* Official number: 118879	*354* - -		**1978-11 Kanbara Zosen K.K. — Onomichi** Yd No: 234 Loa 43.69 Br ex - Dght - Lbp 36.50 Br md 9.01 Dpth 4.17 Riveted\Welded, 1 dk	**(B32A2ST) Tug**	**2 oil engines** gearing integral to driving 2 Z propellers Total Power: 1,838kW (2,498hp) Niigata 6L28BX 2 x 4 Stroke 6 Cy. 280 x 320 each-919kW (1249bhp) Niigata Engineering Co Ltd-Japan
8894653 *JH3244* -	**TATSUYOSHI MARU** *ex Koei Maru -1999* **YK Takamaru Suisan** - *Nichinan, Miyazaki* *Japan* MMSI: 431200010 Official number: 133205	*116* - -		**1992-12 Higashi Kyushu Shipbuilding Co Ltd — Usuki OT** L reg 29.70 Br ex - Dght - Lbp - Br md 5.48 Dpth 2.48 Bonded, 1 dk	**(B11B2FV) Fishing Vessel** Hull Material: Reinforced Plastic	**1 oil engine** driving 1 FP propeller Niigata 1 x 4 Stroke Niigata Engineering Co Ltd-Japan
9682722 - -	**TATUTA MARU** - **Naikai Eisen KK** - *Japan*	*240* - 100	Class: FA	**2014-01 Keihin Dock Co Ltd — Yokohama** Yd No: 309 Loa 43.00 Br ex - Dght 4.000 Lbp - Br md 9.00 Dpth - Welded, 1 dk	**(B32A2ST) Tug**	**2 oil engines** reduction geared to sc. shafts driving 2 Propellers Total Power: 3,676kW (4,998hp) Niigata 6L28HX 2 x 4 Stroke 6 Cy. 280 x 370 each-1838kW (2499bhp) Niigata Engineering Co Ltd-Japan
8035075 *UHMW* -	**TATYANA** *ex Korfu -2003* **Kaminari LLC** - *Vladivostok* *Russia* MMSI: 273877200	**777** 224 405	Class: (RS)	**1982-05 Zavod "Leninskaya Kuznitsa" — Kiyev** Yd No: 1509 Loa 54.80 Br ex 9.80 Dght 4.140 Lbp 49.40 Br md 9.50 Dpth 5.00 Welded, 1 dk	**(B11A2FS) Stern Trawler** Ins: 414 Compartments: 2 Ho, ER 3 Ha: 3 (1.5 x 1.6) Derricks: 2x1.5t; Winches: 2 Ice Capable	**1 oil engine** driving 1 CP propeller Total Power: 736kW (1,001hp) 12.0kn S.K.L. 8NVD48AU 1 x 4 Stroke 8 Cy. 320 x 480 736kW (1001bhp) VEB Schwermaschinenbau "KarlLiebknecht" (SKL)-Magdeburg AuxGen: 4 x 150kW a.c Fuel: 154.0 (d.f.)
5419244 *DDTC* -	**TAUCHER O. WULF 3** *ex Castor -1993* **Otto Wulf GmbH & Co KG** - *Cuxhaven* *Germany* MMSI: 211331920 Official number: 908	**181** 54 114	Class: GL	**1963 F Schichau GmbH — Bremerhaven** Yd No: 1721 Loa 28.81 Br ex 8.36 Dght 3.750 Lbp 26.42 Br md 8.01 Dpth 3.48 Welded, 1 dk	**(B32A2ST) Tug** Ice Capable	**2 oil engines** sr geared to sc. shafts driving 2 Voith-Schneider propellers Total Power: 994kW (1,352hp) Deutz SBV6M536 2 x 4 Stroke 6 Cy. 270 x 360 each-497kW (676bhp) Kloeckner Humboldt Deutz AG-West Germany AuxGen: 1 x 75kW 380/220V a.c Fuel: 14.0 (d.f.)
6907169 *DGDA* -	**TAUCHER O. WULF 5** *ex Accurat -1994* **Otto Wulf GmbH & Co KG** - *Rostock* *Germany* MMSI: 211327150 Official number: 3330	**154** 46 99	Class: GL	**1968 Muetzelfeldtwerft GmbH — Cuxhaven** Yd No: 179 Loa 29.37 Br ex 7.93 Dght 3.210 Lbp 26.09 Br md 7.90 Dpth 3.69 Welded, 1 dk	**(B32A2ST) Tug** Ice Capable	**1 oil engine** driving 1 FP propeller Total Power: 883kW (1,201hp) Deutz SBV8M545 1 x 4 Stroke 8 Cy. 320 x 450 883kW (1201bhp) Kloeckner Humboldt Deutz AG-West Germany AuxGen: 2 x 37kW 24V d.c Fuel: 49.0 (d.f.)
7722528 *ZMA3783* -	**TAUDRE** *ex Albert Sanford -2011* **E & B Management Ltd** - *Auckland* *New Zealand* Official number: 349499	**227** 68 178	Class: (LR) ✠ Classed LR until 8/6/79	**1978-01 Kanmon Zosen K.K. — Shimonoseki** Yd No: 336 Loa 29.01 Br ex 8.08 Dght 3.328 Lbp 25.51 Br md 8.07 Dpth 3.95 Welded, 1 dk	**(B11A2FS) Stern Trawler**	**1 oil engine** reverse reduction geared to sc. shaft driving 1 FP propeller Total Power: 552kW (750hp) 10.5kn Daihatsu 6PSHTCM-26E 1 x 4 Stroke 6 Cy. 260 x 320 552kW (750bhp) Daihatsu Diesel Manufacturing Co Lt-Japan AuxGen: 2 x 48kW 405V 50Hz a.c
5190202 *CA2405* -	**TAUMA** *ex Tauranga -2001 ex Klorina -1995* **Naviera El Navegante Ltda** - *Valparaiso* *Chile* MMSI: 725000637 Official number: 3225	*172* 79 234		**1954 Glommens Mek Verksted — Fredrikstad** Yd No: 145 Lengthened-1956 Loa 30.00 Br ex 6.05 Dght 2.642 Lbp - Br md 6.00 Dpth - Welded, 1 dk	**(A12A2TC) Chemical Tanker** Liq: 201	**1 oil engine** driving 1 FP propeller Total Power: 239kW (325hp) 7.0kn Wichmann 4DCT 1 x 2 Stroke 4 Cy. 200 x 300 239kW (325bhp) (new engine 1969) Wichmann Motorfabrikk AS-Norway AuxGen: 1 x 6kW 220V 50Hz a.c
8648494 *T2FA3* -	**TAUMOANA** - **Tuvalu Tuna FH Co Ltd** - *Funafuti* *Tuvalu* MMSI: 572735000 Official number: 19930909	**1,738** 522 -		**2009-06 Ching Fu Shipbuilding Co Ltd — Kaohsiung** Yd No: 073 Loa 75.34 Br ex 13.60 Dght - Lbp - Br md - Dpth 7.70 Welded, 1 dk	**(B11B2FV) Fishing Vessel**	**1 oil engine** driving 1 Propeller Daihatsu 1 x 4 Stroke Daihatsu Diesel Manufacturing Co Lt-Japan
7804974 *XYNL* -	**TAUNG-GYI** *ex Taung-Gyee -1989* **Myanma Five Star Line** - *Yangon* *Myanmar* MMSI: 506162000	**1,595** 478 947	Class: (NV)	**1980-02 Salthammer Baatbyggeri AS — Vestnes** (Hull) Yd No: 120 **1980-02 Bolsones Verft AS — Molde** Yd No: 268 Loa 72.34 Br ex - Dght 3.960 Lbp 68.03 Br md 12.01 Dpth 6.51 Welded, 1 dk & S dk	**(A32A2GF) General Cargo/Passenger Ship** Passengers: unberthed: 295; cabins: 7; berths: 20 Bale: 990 Compartments: ER, 3 Ho 3 Ha: 2 (6.5 x 2.8)ER (3.2 x 2.8) Derricks: 5x5t; Winches: 5	**1 oil engine** reduction geared to sc. shaft driving 1 CP propeller Total Power: 2,427kW (3,300hp) 15.3kn Normo KVMB-16 1 x Vee 4 Stroke 16 Cy. 250 x 300 2427kW (3300bhp) AS Bergens Mek Verksteder-Norway AuxGen: 3 x 136kW 440V 60Hz a.c Fuel: 200.0 (d.f.)
9688661 *J8B4942* -	**TAUPO** - **Damen Marine Services BV** Thong Yong Offshore Pte Ltd *Kingstown* *St Vincent & The Grenadines* MMSI: 375068000 Official number: 11415	**327** 98 -	Class: BV (Class contemplated)	**2013-12 Damen Shipyards Kozle Sp z oo — Kedzierzyn-Kozle** (Hull) Yd No: 1187 **2013-12 B.V. Scheepswerf Damen Hardinxveld — Hardinxveld-Giessendam** Yd No: 571697 Loa 32.27 Br ex 9.50 Dght 3.320 Lbp 30.52 Br md 9.10 Dpth 4.40 Welded, 1 dk	**(B32A2ST) Tug**	**2 oil engines** reduction geared to sc. shafts driving 2 Propellers Total Power: 3,530kW (4,800hp) Caterpillar 3512C 2 x Vee 4 Stroke 12 Cy. 170 x 215 each-1765kW (2400bhp) Caterpillar Inc-USA Thrusters: 1 Tunnel thruster (f)
9368522 *ZMZN* -	**TAUPO** - **Government of New Zealand (Royal New Zealand Navy)** - *New Zealand* MMSI: 512158000 Official number: P3570	**551** 165 75	Class: LR ✠ **100A1** SS 05/2009 SSC patrol mono HSC G3 ✠ **LMC** **UMS** Cable: 197.0/17.5 U2 (a)	**2009-05 Tenix Shipbuilding New Zealand Ltd — Whangarei** Yd No: 358 Loa 55.00 Br ex 9.06 Dght 2.320 Lbp 49.30 Br md 9.00 Dpth 5.45 Welded, 1 dk	**(B34H2SQ) Patrol Vessel**	**2 oil engines** with clutches, flexible couplings & sr reverse geared to sc. shafts driving 2 CP propellers Total Power: 5,000kW (6,798hp) Paxman 12VP185 2 x Vee 4 Stroke 12 Cy. 185 x 196 each-2500kW (3399bhp) Paxman Diesels Ltd.-Colchester AuxGen: 2 x 103kW 440V 60Hz a.c
9211224 *IJRK* -	**TAUR** *ex Taurus -2004* **Tripmare Srl** - *Trieste* *Italy* MMSI: 247111500 Official number: 780	**452** 135 100	Class: RI	**2000-10 Astilleros Armon SA — Navia** Yd No: 498 Loa 32.50 Br ex - Dght 3.650 Lbp 30.50 Br md 11.00 Dpth 4.50 Welded, 1 dk	**(B32A2ST) Tug**	**2 oil engines** gearing integral to driving 2 Voith-Schneider propellers Total Power: 3,742kW (5,088hp) A.B.C. 8DZC 2 x 4 Stroke 8 Cy. 256 x 310 each-1871kW (2544bhp) Anglo Belgian Corp NV (ABC)-Belgium AuxGen: 2 x 160kW a.c Fuel: 142.4 (d.f.)
9134086 *FKVU* PY 1678	**TAURAA-TUA** - **Armement Cooperatif Polynesien** - *Papeete* *France* MMSI: 228180000	**154** - 116	Class: (BV)	**1996-05 United Engineers — Suva** Yd No: 091 Loa 24.80 Br ex - Dght 3.210 Lbp - Br md 7.40 Dpth 3.50 Welded, 1 dk	**(B11B2FV) Fishing Vessel** Ins: 80	**1 oil engine** with clutches, flexible couplings & sr reverse geared to sc. shaft driving 1 FP propeller Total Power: 332kW (451hp) Wartsila UD25L6M4 1 x 4 Stroke 6 Cy. 150 x 180 332kW (451bhp) Wartsila SACM Diesel SA-France

IMO / Call sign	Name / Owner / Port	Tonnage	Class	Builder / Dimensions	Type	Machinery
9294719 *FTCF* -	**TAURAA-TUA II** **SEML Tahiti Nui Rava'ai** - *Papeete* *France* MMSI: 546002500	**163** 49 -	Class: (BV)	**2003-10 Fujian Southeast Shipyard — Fuzhou FJ** Yd No: 2002-06 Loa 23.90 Br ex - Dght 2.900 Lbp 21.33 Br md 7.40 Dpth 3.80 Welded, 1 dk	**(B11B2FV) Fishing Vessel**	**1 oil engine** geared to sc. shaft driving 1 FP propeller Total Power: 405kW (551hp) Wartsila UD25L6M5D 1 x 4 Stroke 6 Cy. 150 x 180 405kW (551bhp) Wartsila Finland Oy-Finland
9340178 *FMDE* -	**TAURAA-TUA IV** **SEML Tahiti Nui Rava'ai** - *Papeete* *France* MMSI: 546007100	**166** 50 -	Class: (BV)	**2005-03 Fujian Southeast Shipyard — Fuzhou FJ** Yd No: 2004-5 Loa 23.90 Br ex - Dght 2.830 Lbp 20.60 Br md 7.40 Dpth 3.80 Welded, 1 dk	**(B11B2FV) Fishing Vessel**	**1 oil engine** reduction geared to sc. shaft driving 1 Propeller Total Power: 405kW (551hp) Wartsila UD25L6M5D 1 x 4 Stroke 6 Cy. 150 x 180 405kW (551bhp) Wartsila France SA-France
9340180 *FMDF* -	**TAURAA-TUA V** **SEML Tahiti Nui Rava'ai** - *Papeete* *France* MMSI: 546007200	**166** 50 -	Class: (BV)	**2005-03 Fujian Southeast Shipyard — Fuzhou FJ** Yd No: 2004-6 Loa 23.90 Br ex - Dght 2.830 Lbp 20.60 Br md 7.40 Dpth 3.80 Welded, 1 dk	**(B11B2FV) Fishing Vessel**	**1 oil engine** reduction geared to sc. shaft driving 1 Propeller Total Power: 405kW (551hp) Wartsila UD25L6M5D 1 x 4 Stroke 6 Cy. 150 x 180 405kW (551bhp) Wartsila France SA-France
9249714 *LLLV* -	**TAURANGA** **Napier AS** - *Haugesund* *Norway* MMSI: 258232000	**886** 265 800		**2001-04 Bommeloy Mek. Verksted AS — Bomlo** Yd No: 1 Loa 46.50 Br ex - Dght - Lbp - Br md 9.50 Dpth 4.20 Welded, 1 dk	**(B12C2FL) Live Fish Carrier (Well Boat)**	**1 oil engine** reduction geared to sc. shaft driving 1 FP propeller Total Power: 1,324kW (1,800hp) Caterpillar 3512B-HD 1 x Vee 4 Stroke 12 Cy. 170 x 215 1324kW (1800bhp) Caterpillar Inc-USA
9138367 *D5AY2* -	**TAURANGA** *ex* WEC Frans Hals *-2011* *ex* Petuja *-2010* *ex* Joanna Borchard *-2000* *launched as* Petuja *-1997* **ms 'Tauranga' Schiffahrts GmbH & Co KG** Coral Shipmanagement GmbH & Co KG *Monrovia* *Liberia* MMSI: 636092531 Official number: 92531	**6,362** 3,998 7,200 T/cm 15.0	Class: GL	**1997-04 J.J. Sietas KG Schiffswerft GmbH & Co. — Hamburg** Yd No: 1150 Loa 121.94 (BB) Br ex - Dght 6.690 Lbp 114.90 Br md 18.20 Dpth 8.30 Welded, 1 dk	**(A33A2CC) Container Ship (Fully Cellular)** TEU 700 C Ho 432 TEU C Dk 268 TEU incl 72 ref. Compartments: 4 Cell Ho, ER 2 Ha: (12.4 x 15.6) (12.6 x 15.6)ER	**1 oil engine** reduction geared to sc. shaft driving 1 CP propeller Total Power: 5,300kW (7,206hp) 16.5kn MAN 8L40/54 1 x 4 Stroke 8 Cy. 400 x 540 5300kW (7206bhp) MAN B&W Diesel AG-Augsburg AuxGen: 1 x 850kW a.c, 2 x 312kW 220/380V 50Hz a.c Thrusters: 1 Thwart. FP thruster (f)
9286736 *YD4951* -	**TAURIANS ONE** *ex* SDS 34 *-2003* **PT Trada Maritime** - *Palembang* *Indonesia*	**132** 79 116	Class: KI (NK)	**2003-03 C E Ling Shipbuilding Sdn Bhd — Miri** Yd No: 3402 Loa 25.10 Br ex - Dght 2.712 Lbp 22.82 Br md 7.32 Dpth 3.20 Welded, 1 dk	**(B32A2ST) Tug**	**2 oil engines** geared to sc. shafts driving 2 FP propellers Total Power: 1,204kW (1,636hp) 10.0kn Mitsubishi S6R2-MPTK 2 x 4 Stroke 6 Cy. 170 x 220 each-602kW (818bhp) (made 2002) Mitsubishi Heavy Industries Ltd-Japan AuxGen: 2 x 26kW a.c
9023330 *YD4953* -	**TAURIANS THREE** **PT Trada Maritime** - *Palembang* *Indonesia*	**171** 51 -	Class: KI	**2003-12 Bonafile Shipbuilders & Repairs Sdn Bhd — Sandakan** Loa 26.20 Br ex - Dght 2.900 Lbp 24.67 Br md 8.00 Dpth 3.80 Welded, 1 dk	**(B32A2ST) Tug**	**2 oil engines** geared to sc. shafts driving 2 Propellers Total Power: 1,204kW (1,636hp) Mitsubishi S6R2-MTK 2 x 4 Stroke 6 Cy. 170 x 220 each-602kW (818bhp) Mitsubishi Heavy Industries Ltd-Japan AuxGen: 2 x 24kW 450/240V a.c
9023328 *YD4952* -	**TAURIANS TWO** **PT Trada Maritime** - *Palembang* *Indonesia*	**171** 51 -	Class: KI	**2003-12 Bonafile Shipbuilders & Repairs Sdn Bhd — Sandakan** Loa 26.20 Br ex - Dght - Lbp 24.67 Br md 8.00 Dpth 3.80 Welded, 1 dk	**(B32A2ST) Tug**	**2 oil engines** driving 1 Propeller Total Power: 1,204kW (1,636hp) Mitsubishi S6R2-MPTK 2 x 4 Stroke 6 Cy. 170 x 220 each-602kW (818bhp) Mitsubishi Heavy Industries Ltd-Japan AuxGen: 2 x 48kW 400V a.c
7943873 *HP4618* -	**TAURO** *ex* Damas *-1977* **Tauro Fishing Inc** - *Panama* *Panama* Official number: 0850678D	*246* 82 -	Class: (GL)	**1976 Intermar S.A. — Callao** Yd No: 05 Loa 34.55 Br ex 7.95 Dght - Lbp 30.61 Br md - Dpth 4.30 Welded, 1 dk	**(B11B2FV) Fishing Vessel**	**1 oil engine** driving 1 FP propeller Total Power: 532kW (723hp) 13.5kn Caterpillar D399SCAC 1 x Vee 4 Stroke 16 Cy. 159 x 203 532kW (723bhp) (made 1972) Caterpillar Tractor Co-USA
9539717 *XCMV1* -	**TAURO** *ex* Blue Ocean *-2009* **Cotemar SA de CV** - SatCom: Inmarsat C 434507090 *Ciudad del Carmen* *Mexico* MMSI: 345070239	**2,428** 728 2,866	Class: NV (AB)	**2008-12 Jingjiang Nanyang Shipbuilding Co Ltd — Jingjiang JS** (Hull) Yd No: (1297) **2008-12 Pacific Ocean Engineering & Trading Pte Ltd (POET) — Singapore** Yd No: 1297 Loa 70.00 Br ex - Dght 5.600 Lbp 61.20 Br md 16.60 Dpth 6.80 Welded, 1 dk	**(B21A20S) Platform Supply Ship**	**2 oil engines** reduction geared to sc. shafts driving 2 Directional propellers Total Power: 3,676kW (4,998hp) Niigata 6L28HX 2 x 4 Stroke 6 Cy. 280 x 370 each-1838kW (2499bhp) Niigata Engineering Co Ltd-Japan AuxGen: 3 x 475kW a.c Fuel: 727.0
7908249 - -	**TAURO II** *ex* Gulf Fleet No. 37 *-1986* **Zapata Gulf Marine International Ltd** Tidewater de Mexico S de RL de CV	**1,063** 318 1,449	Class: AB	**1979-12 Quality Equipment Inc — Houma LA** Yd No: 157 Loa 62.49 Br ex 12.83 Dght 4.574 Lbp 55.58 Br md 12.81 Dpth 5.34 Welded, 1 dk	**(B21B20A) Anchor Handling Tug Supply**	**2 oil engines** reverse reduction geared to sc. shafts driving 2 FP propellers Total Power: 4,516kW (6,140hp) 13.0kn EMD (Electro-Motive) 16-645-E7 2 x Vee 2 Stroke 16 Cy. 230 x 254 each-2258kW (3070bhp) General Motors Corp.Electro-Motive Div.-La Grange AuxGen: 2 x 99kW 440V 60Hz a.c Thrusters: 1 Thwart. FP thruster (f)
9031985 *3FPC7* -	**TAUROGAS** *ex* Ocean Primate *-2009* *ex* Coral Actinia *-2007* **Norton Marine SA** Transgas Shipping Lines SAC SatCom: Inmarsat C 435676311 *Panama* *Panama* MMSI: 356763000 Official number: 4122610	**3,096** 928 3,566 T/cm 12.6	Class: LR (BV) **100A1** SS 05/2013 liquefied gas carrier, Ship Type 2PG Ammonia anhydrous, butadiene, butane-propane mixtures, butylenes, diethyl ether, dimethylamine, ethyl chloride, methyl chloride, propane, propylene, vinyl chloride, in independent tanks Type C, max SG 0.97, max vapour pressure 9.3 bar, min temp minus 48 degree C, max temp 50 degree C, *IWS **LMC** **UMS**	**1993-05 YVC Ysselwerf B.V. — Capelle a/d IJssel** Yd No: 260 Lengthened-1995 Loa 101.48 (BB) Br ex 14.00 Dght 4.960 Lbp 96.79 Br md 13.80 Dpth 7.20 Welded, 1 dk	**(A11B2TG) LPG Tanker** Liq (Gas): 3,220 2 x Gas Tank (s); 2 independent (C.mn.stl) cyl horizontal 2 Cargo Pump (s): 1x400m³/hr, 1x200m³/hr Manifold: Bow/CM: 56.7m	**1 oil engine** with flexible couplings & sr geared to sc. shaft driving 1 CP propeller Total Power: 1,521kW (2,068hp) 12.3kn Deutz SBV9M628 1 x 4 Stroke 9 Cy. 240 x 280 1521kW (2068bhp) Motoren Werke Mannheim AG (MWM)-Mannheim AuxGen: 3 x 292kW 440V 60Hz a.c Thrusters: 1 Thwart. FP thruster (f) Fuel: 310.0 (d.f.) 7.2pd
9038969 *UBKJ6* -	**TAURUS** *ex* Tarnsjo *-2012* **Aldebaran Maritime Ltd** Prime Shipping LLC *St Petersburg* *Russia* MMSI: 273350980	**6,534** 3,468 10,908 T/cm 20.1	Class: RS (NV) (GL)	**1993-06 Kvaerner Kleven Leirvik AS — Leirvik i Sogn** Yd No: 254 Loa 129.05 (BB) Br ex 18.36 Dght 8.100 Lbp 122.46 Br md 18.33 Dpth 10.40 Welded, 1 dk	**(A12B2TR) Chemical/Products Tanker** Double Hull Liq: 10,531; Liq (Oil): 10,531 Cargo Heating Coils Compartments: 14 Wing Ta, ER 7 Cargo Pump (s): 7x400m³/hr Manifold: Bow/CM: 58m Ice Capable	**1 oil engine** with flexible couplings & sr geared to sc. shaft driving 1 CP propeller Total Power: 3,300kW (4,487hp) 12.0kn MaK 9M453C 1 x 4 Stroke 9 Cy. 320 x 420 3300kW (4487bhp) Krupp MaK Maschinenbau GmbH-Kiel AuxGen: 3 x 650kW 440V 60Hz a.c, 1 x 500kW 440V 60Hz a.c Thrusters: 1 Thwart. CP thruster (f) Fuel: 54.6 (d.f.) (Part Heating Coils) 241.1 (r.f.) 11.0pd
9015395 *9V3499* -	**TAURUS** *ex* HLTaurus *-2009* *ex* SPC Taurus *-2001* **Tomiura Nippon Chartering Pte Ltd** Transocean Oil Pte Ltd *Singapore* *Singapore* MMSI: 563001810 Official number: 384530	**2,924** 1,912 6,011 T/cm 12.6	Class: NK	**1990-10 Dynamic Marine Pte Ltd — Singapore** Yd No: 033 Loa 89.00 Br ex - Dght 6.399 Lbp 83.60 Br md 16.30 Dpth 7.75 Welded, 1 dk	**(A13B2TP) Products Tanker** Single Hull Liq: 6,432; Liq (Oil): 6,432 2 Cargo Pump (s): 2x750m³/hr	**2 oil engines** sr geared to sc. shafts driving 2 FP propellers Total Power: 1,766kW (2,402hp) 10.5kn Yanmar M220-EN 2 x 4 Stroke 6 Cy. 220 x 300 each-883kW (1201bhp) Yanmar Diesel Engine Co Ltd-Japan AuxGen: 2 x 165kW 440V 50Hz a.c Thrusters: 1 Thwart. FP thruster (f) Fuel: 130.0 (d.f.) 3.5pd

IMO / Call sign / Flag	Name / Owners	Tonnage	Class	Builder / Dimensions	Type	Machinery
8969317 *WDB5562* -	**TAURUS** - **Kirby Offshore Marine LLC** K-Sea Operating LLC *New York, NY* *United States of America* MMSI: 366910990 Official number: 602379	**168** 50 -	Class: AB	**1979**-04 **Modern Marine Power, Inc. — Houma, La** Yd No: 27 Loa 25.60 Br ex - Dght 3.510 Lbp 24.05 Br md 7.62 Dpth 3.65 Welded, 1 dk	**(B32A2ST) Tug**	**2 oil engines** reverse reduction geared to sc. shafts driving 2 FP propellers Total Power: 1,508kW (2,050hp) 12.0kn G.M. (Detroit Diesel) 16V-149-NA 2 x Vee 2 Stroke 16 Cy. 146 x 146 each-754kW (1025bhp) General Motors Detroit DieselAllison Divn-USA AuxGen: 2 x 50kW 225/450V 60Hz a.c
9134593 *V7LZ7* -	**TAURUS** *ex* CMA CGM Castilla *-2009* *ex* Cap Victor *-2006* *ex* Columbus Waikato *-2006* *ex* Taurus *-2002* *ex* Kota Perabu *-2001* *ex* Taurus *-1999* **Alpha Ship GmbH ms 'Taurus' & Co KG** Alpha Shipmanagement GmbH & Co KG *Majuro* *Marshall Islands* MMSI: 538090285 Official number: 90285	**23,722** 9,843 29,260 T/cm 45.1	Class: GL	**1998**-12 **Stocznia Gdynia SA — Gdynia** Yd No: 8138/6 Loa 194.00 (BB) Br ex - Dght 11.500 Lbp 180.20 Br md 28.20 Dpth 16.80 Welded, 1 dk	**(A33A2CC) Container Ship (Fully Cellular)** TEU 1835 C Ho 780 TEU C Dk 1055 TEU incl 325 ref C. Compartments: 4 Cell Ho, ER 9 Ha: (18.5 x 13.2)Tappered 8 (12.8 x 23.6)ER Cranes: 3x45t	**1 oil engine** driving 1 FP propeller Total Power: 17,200kW (23,385hp) 21.3kn B&W 6L70MC 1 x 2 Stroke 6 Cy. 700 x 2268 17200kW (23385bhp) H Cegielski Poznan SA-Poland AuxGen: 2 x 1184kW 440/220V 60Hz a.c, 1 x 884kW 440/220V 60Hz a.c Thrusters: 1 Tunnel thruster (f) Fuel: 220.0 (d.f.) 2740.0 (r.f.) 85.0pd
8858673 *J8B4244* -	**TAURUS** *ex* Dobrogast *-2011* *ex* Fratzis *-2001* *ex* Island of Inousse *-1998* *ex* Maris Louiza *-1994* *ex* Volzhskiy-51 *-1994* **Toro Shipping & Trading Ltd** Almar Denizcilik Ticaret Ltd Sti *Kingstown* *St Vincent & The Grenadines* MMSI: 375568000 Official number: 10717	**2,975** 1,125 3,983	Class: RS (IV) (GL)	**1992**-08 **OAO Navashinskiy Sudostroitelnyy Zavod 'Oka' — Navashino** Yd No: 1053 Shortened-1999 Loa 105.80 Br ex - Dght 3.820 Lbp 99.23 Br md 16.50 Dpth 5.50 Welded, 1 dk	**(A31A2GX) General Cargo Ship** Grain: 4,477 Compartments: 2 Ho, ER 2 Ha: (19.9 x 12.5) (36.0 x 12.5)ER	**2 oil engines** driving 2 FP propellers Total Power: 1,766kW (2,402hp) 9.0kn Dvigatel Revolyutsii 6CHRNP36/45 2 x 4 Stroke 6 Cy. 360 x 450 each-883kW (1201bhp) Zavod "Dvigatel Revolyutsii"-Nizhniy Novgorod AuxGen: 2 x 100kW 380V a.c, 1 x 50kW 380V a.c Fuel: 163.0 (d.f.)
8846199 *WDE2531* -	**TAURUS** *ex* Laurie Becnel *-2011* *ex* Abby S *-2009* *ex* Anita M *-2006* **Ingram Barge Co** - *St Louis, MO* *United States of America* MMSI: 367031730 Official number: 663777	*684* 619 -		**1983 St Louis Ship Division of Pott Industries Inc — St Louis, Mo** Yd No: 5063 Loa - Br ex - Dght - Lbp 51.82 Br md 13.72 Dpth 2.38 Welded, 1 dk	**(B32A2ST) Tug**	**1 oil engine** driving 1 FP propeller
7819498 *WDB6361* -	**TAURUS** *ex* Casey Marie *-2005* *ex* Miss Nicole Rene *-1988* **Taurus Marine Inc** Cross Link Inc (Westar Marine Services) *San Francisco, CA* *United States of America* MMSI: 303200000 Official number: 599924	*116* 79 -		**1978 Service Machine & Shipbuilding Co — Amelia LA** Yd No: 125 Loa - Br ex - Dght - Lbp 22.86 Br md 7.32 Dpth 2.98 Welded, 1 dk	**(B32A2ST) Tug**	**1 oil engine** geared to sc. shaft driving 1 FP propeller Total Power: 883kW (1,201hp) G.M. (Detroit Diesel) 16V-92 1 x Vee 2 Stroke 16 Cy. 123 x 127 883kW (1201bhp) General Motors Detroit DieselAllison Divn-USA
7941021 *WYH6499* -	**TAURUS** *ex* Corey Chouest *-1988* **Dunlap Towing Co** - *La Conner, WA* *United States of America* MMSI: 303398000 Official number: 571411	*199* 135 -		**1975 North American Shipbuilding Inc — Larose LA** Yd No: 104 Loa - Br ex - Dght 3.048 Lbp 27.28 Br md 8.23 Dpth 3.59 Welded, 1 dk	**(B32A2ST) Tug**	**1 oil engine** driving 1 FP propeller Total Power: 1,765kW (2,400hp)
8018479 - -	**TAURUS** *ex* Chia Hong 22 *-1988* **Olympic Marine Ltd** - *Mumbai* *India* Official number: F-BOM0047	*328* 151 -	Class: (HR)	**1980 Taiwan Machinery Manufacturing Corp. — Kaohsiung** Yd No: 707 Loa 42.58 Br ex - Dght - Lbp 36.56 Br md 7.60 Dpth 3.61 Welded, 1 dk	**(B11A2FS) Stern Trawler**	**1 oil engine** driving 1 FP propeller Total Power: 809kW (1,100hp) Niigata 6M28AGT 1 x 4 Stroke 6 Cy. 280 x 480 809kW (1100bhp) Niigata Engineering Co Ltd-Japan
8215584 *HC4470* -	**TAURUS** - **Transportes Navieros Ecuatorianos (TRANSNAVE)** - *Guayaquil* *Ecuador* MMSI: 735057583 Official number: TN-00-0502	*802* 514 1,175	Class: (AB)	**1985 Astilleros Navales Ecuatorianos (ASTINAVE) — Guayaquil** Yd No: 410D Loa 53.07 Br ex 10.98 Dght 4.417 Lbp 48.80 Br md 10.76 Dpth 4.88 Welded, 1 dk	**(A13B2TP) Products Tanker** Compartments: 8 Ta, ER	**1 oil engine** geared to sc. shaft driving 1 FP propeller Total Power: 772kW (1,050hp) 11.0kn EMD (Electro-Motive) 8-645-E6 1 x Vee 2 Stroke 8 Cy. 230 x 254 772kW (1050bhp) General Motors Corp.Electro-Motive Div.-La Grange AuxGen: 3 x 90kW 240V 60Hz a.c Fuel: 60.0 (d.f.)
8133011 - -	**TAURUS** *ex* Don Guillo *-1995* *ex* Miss Lee *-1995* **Agropesquera Industrial Bahia Cupica Ltda Cl** - *Buenaventura* *Colombia* Official number: MC-01-0609	*118* 81 -		**1980 Steiner Shipyard, Inc. — Bayou La Batre, Al** Loa 22.85 Br ex 6.71 Dght 2.100 Lbp - Br md - Dpth 3.32 Welded, 1 dk	**(B11B2FV) Fishing Vessel**	**1 oil engine** driving 1 FP propeller Total Power: 268kW (364hp)
8411023 *ESPO* EK-9914	**TAURUS** *ex* Hvilvtenni *-1999* **Reyktal Ltd (AS Reyktal)** Eri Ehf *Tallinn* *Estonia* MMSI: 276388000 Official number: 199FJ38	**1,780** 571 770	Class: NV	**1985**-01 **AS Tangen Verft Kragero — Kragero** Yd No: 105 Loa 60.00 (BB) Br ex - Dght 5.620 Lbp 51.75 Br md 13.00 Dpth 8.12 Welded, 2 dks	**(B11A2FS) Stern Trawler** Ice Capable	**1 oil engine** geared to sc. shaft driving 1 CP propeller Total Power: 2,220kW (3,018hp) Wartsila 6R32 1 x 4 Stroke 6 Cy. 320 x 350 2220kW (3018bhp) Oy Wartsila Ab-Finland AuxGen: 1 x 1200kW 380V 50Hz a.c, 1 x 330kW 380V 50Hz a.c, 1 x 380V 50Hz a.c
8332629 *WDF2370* -	**TAURUS** *ex* Taurus Cenac *-2010* *ex* Taurus *-2009* *ex* Marie Cenac *-2005* *ex* R. I. Trahan *-1991* *ex* Ray Pater *-1991* *ex* Poseidon *-1991* **Enterprise Marine Services LLC** - *Houston, TX* *United States of America* MMSI: 367000560 Official number: 507262	*143* 97 -		**1967 Main Iron Works, Inc. — Houma, La** Yd No: 186 L reg 21.71 Br ex - Dght - Lbp - Br md 7.38 Dpth 3.10 Welded, 1 dk	**(B32A2ST) Tug**	**2 oil engines** geared to sc. shafts driving 2 FP propellers Total Power: 2,236kW (3,040hp) Caterpillar 3512TA 2 x Vee 4 Stroke 12 Cy. 170 x 190 each-1118kW (1520bhp) (new engine 1986) Caterpillar Tractor Co-USA
5354573 *SMPI* -	**TAURUS** *ex* Straume *-2000* *ex* Telemark I *-1972* *ex* Svein *-1945* *ex* Graasten *-1945* *ex* Emilie *-1945* **Rederiservice i Landskrona AB** - *Landskrona* *Sweden* MMSI: 265625930	**107** 47 152		**1907 Kobenhavns Flydedok og Skibsvaerft — Copenhagen** Yd No: 64 Loa 27.64 Br ex 5.49 Dght - Lbp - Br md 5.47 Dpth 2.60 Riveted, 1 dk	**(A31A2GX) General Cargo Ship** Compartments: 1 Ho, ER 1 Ha: (8.0 x 2.4)ER Derricks: 1; Winches: 1	**1 oil engine** driving 1 FP propeller Total Power: 257kW (349hp) G.M. (Detroit Diesel) 8V-71-N 1 x Vee 2 Stroke 8 Cy. 108 x 127 257kW (349bhp) (new engine 1973) General Motors Corp-USA
6620149 *DCJA* -	**TAURUS** *ex* Emstank 10 *-2010* **Broering Feuerschutztechnik GmbH** Empting Mineralole GmbH *Cuxhaven* *Germany* MMSI: 211286380 Official number: 3580	**152** 71 236 T/cm 1.8	Class: GL	**1966 Julius Diedrich Schiffswerft GmbH & Co KG — Moormerland** Yd No: 94 Loa 34.98 Br ex 6.51 Dght 2.071 Lbp 32.11 Br md 6.20 Dpth 2.37 Welded, 1 dk	**(A13B2TP) Products Tanker** Liq: 250; Liq (Oil): 250 Compartments: 6 Ta, ER 1 Cargo Pump (s): 1x90m³/hr Manifold: Bow/CM: 21m Ice Capable	**1 oil engine** reverse reduction geared to sc. shaft driving 1 FP propeller Total Power: 213kW (290hp) 10.5kn Deutz SBA6M816 1 x 4 Stroke 6 Cy. 142 x 160 213kW (290bhp) (new engine 1980) Kloeckner Humboldt Deutz AG-West Germany Fuel: 5.5 (d.f.) 1.5pd
6522543 - -	**TAURUS** *ex* Lady Cecilia *-2001* **Taipan Shipping Ltd** - *Port of Spain* *Trinidad & Tobago* Official number: TTP2021	**212** 63 -	Class: (LR) ✠ Classed LR until 24/8/06	**1966**-01 **Appledore Shipbuilders Ltd — Bideford** Yd No: A.S. 9 Loa 32.39 Br ex 9.05 Dght 3.506 Lbp 28.96 Br md 8.54 Dpth 4.12 Welded, 1 dk	**(B32A2ST) Tug**	**2 oil engines** sr reverse geared to sc. shafts driving 2 FP propellers Total Power: 1,488kW (2,024hp) 11.5kn Ruston 7VEBCM 2 x 4 Stroke 7 Cy. 260 x 368 each-744kW (1012bhp) Ruston & Hornsby Ltd.-Lincoln AuxGen: 2 x 55kW 440V 50Hz a.c, 1 x 77kW 400V 50Hz a.c Fuel: 51.0 (d.f.)
7714507 - -	**TAURUS** *ex* Todai *-2005* *ex* Appolo No. 12 *-2004* *ex* Masu Maru No. 3 *-2002* **Eijick Shipping Ltd** Shida Senpaku Co Ltd	**179** 53 -		**1977**-10 **Nagasaki Zosen K.K. — Nagasaki** Yd No: 620 Loa 35.56 Br ex - Dght 2.401 Lbp 29.62 Br md 6.32 Dpth 2.82 Welded, 1 dk	**(B11B2FV) Fishing Vessel**	**1 oil engine** driving 1 FP propeller Total Power: 515kW (700hp) Niigata 6L25BXB 1 x 4 Stroke 6 Cy. 250 x 320 515kW (700bhp) Niigata Engineering Co Ltd-Japan

IMO / Call sign	Name / Owner / Manager	Tonnage	Class	Builder / Dimensions	Type	Machinery
7334125 *CPB850* -	**TAURUS** *ex* New Wave *-2012* *ex* Cala Galdana *-2009* *ex* Rivamahon *-1982* **Nova Assets Corp** Ocean Marine Management Inc *La Paz* *Bolivia* MMSI: 720733000 Official number: 0001-07 09 2 35	**1,961** 589 1,283	Class: (BV)	**1974**-03 **Sociedad Metalurgica Duro Felguera — Gijon** Yd No: 101 Loa 75.01 (BB) Br ex 13.01 Dght 4.274 Lbp 68.03 Br md 13.00 Dpth 8.79 Welded, 2 dks	**(A35A2RR) Ro-Ro Cargo Ship** Stern door/ramp Bale: 3,842	**1 oil engine** driving 1 FP propeller Total Power: 1,765kW (2,400hp) 14.0kn MWM TBD500-8 1 x 4 Stroke 8 Cy. 360 x 450 1765kW (2400bhp) Fabrica de San Carlos SA-Spain AuxGen: 2 x 132kW 380V 50Hz a.c
7223297 *YYP2022* -	**TAURUS** **Atun CA** - *Venezuela* Official number: APNN-4886	*195* 62 -		**1972 Campbell Industries — San Diego, Ca** Yd No: 86 L reg 27.47 Br ex 7.62 Dght - Lbp - Br md - Dpth 2.77 Welded	**(B12B2FC) Fish Carrier**	**1 oil engine** driving 1 FP propeller Total Power: 533kW (725hp) General Motors 1 x 2 Stroke 533kW (725bhp) General Motors Corp-USA
9550773 *WDF3127* -	**TAURUS** *ex* Nichols *-2010* **San Francisco Bay Area Water Emergency Transportation Authority (WETA)** - *San Francisco, CA* *United States of America* MMSI: 367436230 Official number: 1215087	**317** - -		**2010**-04 **Nichols Bros. Boat Builders, Inc. — Freeland, Wa** (Hull) Yd No: S-158 **2010**-04 **Kvichak Marine Industries — Seattle, Wa** Yd No: 421 Loa 36.00 Br ex 8.73 Dght 1.880 Lbp 34.60 Br md 8.70 Dpth 3.80 Welded, 1 dk	**(A37B2PS) Passenger Ship** Hull Material: Aluminium Alloy Passengers: unberthed: 149	**2 oil engines** reduction geared to sc. shafts driving 2 FP propellers Total Power: 2,100kW (2,856hp) 25.0kn M.T.U. 16V2000M70 2 x Vee 4 Stroke 16 Cy. 130 x 150 each-1050kW (1428bhp) MTU Friedrichshafen GmbH-Friedrichshafen
9294783 *DSQW7* -	**TAURUS** **KDB Capital Corp** Shinsung Shipping Co Ltd *Jeju* *South Korea* MMSI: 441737000 Official number: JJR-102276	**4,562** 2,166 6,763	Class: KR	**2005**-02 **21st Century Shipbuilding Co Ltd — Tongyeong** Yd No: 206 Loa 109.50 (BB) Br ex - Dght 6.763 Lbp 102.01 Br md 16.60 Dpth 8.70 Welded, 1 dk	**(A31A2GX) General Cargo Ship** 2 Ha: ER 2 (29.4 x 11.1)	**1 oil engine** driving 1 FP propeller Total Power: 2,800kW (3,807hp) 13.0kn B&W 7S26MC 1 x 2 Stroke 7 Cy. 260 x 980 2800kW (3807bhp) STX Engine Co Ltd-South Korea AuxGen: 2 x 280kW 450V a.c
9240354 *SPG2952* -	**TAURUS** **'WUZ' Port & Maritime Services Co Ltd ('WUZ' Sp z oo Przedsiebiorstwo Uslug Portowych i Morskich)** - *Gdansk* *Poland* MMSI: 261003330	**332** 99 125	Class: PR	**2001**-04 **Stocznia Polnocna SA (Northern Shipyard) — Gdansk** Yd No: B830/1 Loa 30.00 Br ex 10.80 Dght 2.700 Lbp 28.80 Br md 10.50 Dpth 3.95 Welded, 1 dk	**(B32A2ST) Tug**	**2 oil engines** gearing integral to driving 2 Z propellers Total Power: 2,460kW (3,344hp) 11.4kn Caterpillar 3512B 2 x Vee 4 Stroke 12 Cy. 170 x 190 each-1230kW (1672bhp) Caterpillar Inc-USA AuxGen: 2 x 85kW a.c Fuel: 86.3 (d.f.)
9344978 *V2CK7* -	**TAURUS** **Harms Offshore AHT 'Taurus' GmbH & Co KG** Harms Bergung Transport & Heavylift GmbH & Co KG *Saint John's* *Antigua & Barbuda* MMSI: 305030000 Official number: 4262	**1,767** 530 1,494	Class: GL	**2007**-03 **Muetzelfeldtwerft GmbH — Cuxhaven** Yd No: 253 Loa 58.47 Br ex - Dght 6.600 Lbp 52.57 Br md 14.80 Dpth 7.65 Welded, 1 dk	**(B32A2ST) Tug** Ice Capable	**2 oil engines** reduction geared to sc. shafts driving 2 CP propellers Total Power: 14,004kW (19,040hp) 18.0kn MAN-B&W 14V32/40 2 x Vee 4 Stroke 14 Cy. 320 x 400 each-7002kW (9520bhp) AuxGen: 2 x 1200kW 400/230V 50Hz a.c Thrusters: 2 Thwart. CP thruster (f); 1 Thwart. CP thruster (a) Fuel: 100.0 (d.f.) 1060.0 (r.f.)
9314791 *PS6296* -	**TAURUS** *ex* Taurus I *-2012* *ex* Taurus *-2010* **Saveiros Camuyrano - Servicos Maritimos SA** - *Santos* *Brazil* Official number: 4010814462	**270** 81 209	Class: LR ✠**100A1** SS 07/2009 tug Brazilian coastal service ✠**LMC** **UMS** Eq.Ltr: F; Cable: 275.0/17.5 U2 (a)	**2004**-07 **Wilson, Sons SA — Guaruja** (Hull) Yd No: 078 **2004**-07 **B.V. Scheepswerf Damen — Gorinchem** Yd No: 512305 Loa 28.70 Br ex 10.60 Dght 3.650 Lbp 25.57 Br md 9.40 Dpth 4.40 Welded, 1 dk	**(B32A2ST) Tug**	**2 oil engines** geared to sc. shafts driving 2 Directional propellers Total Power: 2,610kW (3,548hp) 12.4kn Caterpillar 3512B-HD 2 x Vee 4 Stroke 12 Cy. 170 x 215 each-1305kW (1774bhp) Caterpillar Inc-USA AuxGen: 2 x 48kW 450V 60Hz a.c
9403530 *2CPB4* -	**TAURUS** **Newry Universal Inc** Enterprises Shipping & Trading SA *Douglas* *Isle of Man (British)* MMSI: 235074621 Official number: 741915	**93,196** 59,298 179,067	Class: BV	**2011**-09 **Sungdong Shipbuilding & Marine Engineering Co Ltd — Tongyeong** Yd No: 1031 Loa 292.00 (BB) Br ex - Dght 18.320 Lbp 283.50 Br md 45.00 Dpth 24.80 Welded, 1 dk	**(A21A2BC) Bulk Carrier** Grain: 198,193; Bale: 182,071 Compartments: 9 Ho, ER 9 Ha: ER	**1 oil engine** driving 1 FP propeller Total Power: 18,660kW (25,370hp) 14.6kn MAN-B&W 6S70MC-C 1 x 2 Stroke 6 Cy. 700 x 2800 18660kW (25370bhp) Hyundai Heavy Industries Co Ltd-South Korea AuxGen: 3 x 730kW 60Hz a.c
9657961 *UBTI* -	**TAURUS** **Taurus CJSC** Murmansk Trawl Fleet Co (OAO 'Murmanskiy Tralovyy Flot') *Murmansk* *Russia* MMSI: 273332880 Official number: 120791	**2,403** 780 2,881	Class: NV RS	**2013**-12 **'Uljanik' Brodogradiliste dd — Pula** Yd No: 493 Loa 63.85 Br ex - Dght 6.600 Lbp 57.55 Br md 13.50 Dpth 8.40 Welded, 1 dk	**(B11A2FS) Stern Trawler** Ins: 1,424 Compartments: 2 Ho, ER 2 Ha: (2.5 x 2.5)ER (2.7 x 2.7) Ice Capable	**1 oil engine** reduction geared to sc. shaft driving 1 CP propeller Total Power: 4,500kW (6,118hp) 14.5kn Wartsila 9L32 1 x 4 Stroke 9 Cy. 320 x 400 4500kW (6118bhp) Wartsila Finland Oy-Finland AuxGen: 2 x 781kW a.c, 1 x 1800kW a.c Thrusters: 1 Tunnel thruster (f) Fuel: 460.0
7806295 *YYAB* -	**TAURUS I** *ex* El Rifle *-1995* **Atunera Caribe SA (ATUNCASA)** - *Las Piedras* *Venezuela* Official number: AMMT-1252	**943** - -		**1980 Campbell Industries — San Diego, Ca** Yd No: 125 Loa 67.52 Br ex 12.81 Dght 5.792 Lbp 59.70 Br md 12.20 Dpth 5.85 Welded, 1 dk	**(B11B2FV) Fishing Vessel**	**1 oil engine** geared to sc. shaft driving 1 FP propeller Total Power: 2,648kW (3,600hp) 16.0kn EMD (Electro-Motive) 12-645-E5 1 x Vee 2 Stroke 12 Cy. 230 x 254 2648kW (3600bhp) General Motors Corp.Electro-Motive Div.-La Grange
8119546 *5BFH2* -	**TAURUS II** *ex* Taurus *-2005* **Baggermaatschappij Boskalis BV** - *Limassol* *Cyprus* MMSI: 212490000	**4,345** 1,303 1,500	Class: BV	**1983**-04 **BV Scheepswerf & Mfbk 'De Merwede' v/h van Vliet & Co — Hardinxveld** Yd No: 630 Loa 94.96 Br ex - Dght 4.811 Lbp 91.55 Br md 19.02 Dpth 7.62 Welded, 1 dk	**(B33A2DC) Cutter Suction Dredger**	**2 diesel electric oil engines** driving 1 gen. of 5040kW 660V a.c 1 gen. of 3440kW 660V a.c Connecting to 2 elec. motors each (2500kW) driving 2 FP propellers Total Power: 8,459kW (11,501hp) 11.5kn Werkspoor 6TM410 1 x 4 Stroke 6 Cy. 410 x 470 3384kW (4601bhp) Stork Werkspoor Diesel BV-Netherlands Werkspoor 9TM410 1 x 4 Stroke 9 Cy. 410 x 470 5075kW (6900bhp) Stork Werkspoor Diesel BV-Netherlands
9248916 *V2CM5* -	**TAURUS J** *ex* Delmas Lisboa *-2010* *completed as* Maersk Rostock *-2007* *ex* Taurus J *-2002* **Mare Schiffahrts GmbH & Co KG ms 'Taurus J'** Jungerhans Maritime Services GmbH & Co KG *Saint John's* *Antigua & Barbuda* MMSI: 304462000 Official number: 4276	**14,062** 5,525 18,832 T/cm 32.8	Class: GL	**2002**-11 **Peene-Werft GmbH — Wolgast** Yd No: 501 Loa 154.53 (BB) Br ex - Dght 9.500 Lbp 146.70 Br md 24.50 Dpth 14.20 Welded, 1 dk	**(A33A2CC) Container Ship (Fully Cellular)** TEU 1200 C Ho 476 TEU C Dk 724 TEU incl 289 ref C. Compartments: 4 Cell Ho, ER 7 Ha: (12.6 x 10.5)6 (12.6 x 20.4)ER Cranes: 2x45t	**1 oil engine** driving 1 FP propeller Total Power: 11,060kW (15,037hp) 18.3kn B&W 7S50MC-C 1 x 2 Stroke 7 Cy. 500 x 2000 11060kW (15037bhp) MAN B&W Diesel A/S-Denmark AuxGen: 4 x 740kW 440V 60Hz a.c Thrusters: 1 Thwart. FP thruster (f) Fuel: 224.4 (d.f.) (Heating Coils) 1472.0 (r.f.)
7740192 *HQHY7* -	**TAURUS No. 7** *ex* Ompharos *-1994* *ex* Sanko Maru No. 8 *-1994* *ex* Nikko Maru *-1987* **Seacomet Shipping Ltd** - *San Lorenzo* *Honduras* Official number: L-0323763	*403* 243 863		**1978**-02 **K.K. Yoshida Zosen Kogyo — Arida** Yd No: 275 L reg 53.50 Br ex - Dght 3.600 Lbp - Br md 10.00 Dpth 5.62 Welded, 1 dk	**(A31A2GX) General Cargo Ship**	**1 oil engine** driving 1 FP propeller
9370185 *9VBT7* -	**TAURUS OCEAN** *ex* Giant Sky *-2013* **Diamond Star Shipping Pte Ltd** Thome Ship Management Pte Ltd *Singapore* *Singapore* MMSI: 563135000 Official number: 398040	**41,668** 25,647 78,819	Class: NK	**2008**-02 **Sanoyas Hishino Meisho Corp — Kurashiki OY** Yd No: 1264 Loa 225.00 (BB) Br ex - Dght 14.380 Lbp 219.00 Br md 32.24 Dpth 19.90 Welded, 1 dk	**(A21A2BC) Bulk Carrier** Grain: 91,188 Compartments: 7 Ho, ER 7 Ha: ER	**1 oil engine** driving 1 FP propeller Total Power: 9,560kW (12,998hp) 14.5kn MAN-B&W 7S50MC-C 1 x 2 Stroke 7 Cy. 500 x 2000 9560kW (12998bhp) Mitsui Engineering & Shipbuilding CLtd-Japan AuxGen: 3 x a.c Fuel: 2480.0

Ship	Tonnage	Class	Builder / Dimensions	Type / Capacity	Machinery
9332822 *D5FI4* - **TAURUS SUN** *ex* Pacific Brave *-2013* **Holtev Shipping Inc** Zodiac Maritime Agencies Ltd *Monrovia* *Liberia* MMSI: 636016273 Official number: 16273	**59,164** 36,052 115,577 T/cm 93.3	Class: LR (AB) **100A1** SS 05/2012 Double Hull oil tanker ESP *IWS LI **LMC** **UMS IGS**	**2007-05 Sasebo Heavy Industries Co. Ltd. — Sasebo Yard, Sasebo** Yd No: 741 Loa 243.80 (BB) Br ex 42.04 Dght 15.620 Lbp 234.00 Br md 42.00 Dpth 21.50 Welded, 1 dk	**(A13A2TV) Crude Oil Tanker** Double Hull (13F) Liq: 124,074; Liq (Oil): 124,074 Cargo Heating Coils Compartments: 12 Wing Ta, 2 Wing Slop Ta, ER 3 Cargo Pump (s): 3x2500m³/hr Manifold: Bow/CM: 120m	**1 oil engine** driving 1 FP propeller Total Power: 11,700kW (15,907hp) 15.0kn MAN-B&W 6S60MC-C 1 x 2 Stroke 6 Cy. 600 x 2400 11700kW (15907bhp) Mitsui Engineering & Shipbuilding CLtd-Japan AuxGen: 3 x 700kW a.c Fuel: 72.9 (d.f.) 3228.1 (r.f.)
7230422 *YYEK* - **TAURUS TUNA** *ex* Pan Pacific *-1999* **Sociedad Mercantil Atunera (COASA)** - *Puerto Sucre* *Venezuela* MMSI: 775628000 Official number: APNN-6082	*1,082* 487 -		**1972-12 Campbell Industries — San Diego, Ca** Yd No: 87 Lengthened-2006 Loa 68.60 Br ex 12.86 Dght - Lbp - Br md 12.20 Dpth 5.87 Welded, 1 dk	**(B11B2FV) Fishing Vessel**	**1 oil engine** driving 1 FP propeller Total Power: 2,648kW (3,600hp) EMD (Electro-Motive) 20-645-E5 1 x Vee 2 Stroke 20 Cy. 230 x 254 2648kW (3600bhp) General Motors Corp-USA
9330111 *3ELY6* - **TAURUS TWO** *ex* Delzoukre *-2008* **Brandon Maritime SA** Maritime Enterprises Management SA *Panama* *Panama* MMSI: 354992000 Official number: 3328407B	**31,261** 18,291 53,630 T/cm 56.4	Class: NK	**2006-08 Yangzhou Dayang Shipbuilding Co Ltd — Yangzhou JS** Yd No: DY104 Loa 189.99 (BB) Br ex - Dght 12.508 Lbp 182.00 Br md 32.26 Dpth 17.20 Welded, 1 dk	**(A21A2BC) Bulk Carrier** Double Hull Grain: 65,751; Bale: 64,332 Compartments: 5 Ho, ER 5 Ha: 4 (21.3 x 18.3)ER (18.9 x 18.3) Cranes: 4x35t	**1 oil engine** driving 1 FP propeller Total Power: 9,480kW (12,889hp) 15.7kn MAN-B&W 6S50MC-C 1 x 2 Stroke 6 Cy. 500 x 2000 9480kW (12889bhp) STX Engine Co Ltd-South Korea AuxGen: 3 x 600kW a.c Fuel: 2020.0
8402838 *KVZW* - **TAUTUA** **Pago Pago Harbor Board** - *Pago Pago, AS* *United States of America*	*185* 55 143		**1985-03 Industrial & Marine Engineering Ltd — Suva** Yd No: 32 Loa 26.01 Br ex 8.34 Dght 3.761 Lbp 23.50 Br md 8.01 Dpth 4.07 Welded, 1 dk	**(B32A2ST) Tug**	**2 oil engines** with clutches & reverse reduction geared to sc. shafts driving 2 FP propellers Total Power: 1,140kW (1,550hp) Caterpillar 3508TA 2 x Vee 4 Stroke 8 Cy. 170 x 190 each-570kW (775bhp) Caterpillar Tractor Co-USA
7425821 *EPPZ* - **TAVANA** **Government of The Islamic Republic of Iran (Ministry of Finance)** - *Khorramshahr* *Iran*	*167* 48 71	Class: (LR) ✠ Classed LR until 19/11/82	**1975-08 Towa Zosen K.K. — Shimonoseki** Yd No: 480 Loa 27.92 Br ex 7.35 Dght 2.750 Lbp 25.10 Br md 7.00 Dpth 3.51 Welded, 1 dk	**(B32A2ST) Tug**	**1 oil engine** reverse reduction geared to sc. shaft driving 1 FP propeller Total Power: 853kW (1,160hp) Blackstone ESL8MK2 1 x 4 Stroke 8 Cy. 222 x 292 853kW (1160bhp) Mirrlees Blackstone (Stamford)Ltd.-Stamford AuxGen: 2 x 52kW 220V 50Hz a.c Fuel: 24.5 (d.f.)
9222027 *EQXI* - **TAVOUS 1** **Tavous Beheshti Kish Co** - *Bandar Abbas* *Iran* MMSI: 422207000 Official number: 11269	**505** 164 502	Class: AS (NV)	**2000-08 Batservice Mandal AS — Mandal** Yd No: 24 Loa 40.05 Br ex 11.46 Dght 2.350 Lbp 34.50 Br md 11.20 Dpth 3.90 Welded, 1 dk	**(A36A2PR) Passenger/Ro-Ro Ship (Vehicles)** Hull Material: Aluminium Alloy Passengers: unberthed: 317 Stern ramp Cars: 6	**4 oil engines** geared to sc. shafts driving 2 CP propellers Total Power: 3,196kW (4,344hp) 33.0kn M.T.U. 12V2000M70 4 x Vee 4 Stroke 12 Cy. 130 x 150 each-799kW (1086bhp) MTU Friedrichshafen GmbH-Friedrichshafen AuxGen: 2 x 80kW a.c
9222039 *EQXJ* - **TAVOUS 2** **Tavous Beheshti Kish Co** - *Bandar Abbas* *Iran* MMSI: 422208000 Official number: 11286	**518** 166 45	Class: AS (NV)	**2001-09 Batservice Mandal AS — Mandal** Yd No: 25 Loa 40.05 Br ex - Dght 2.350 Lbp 36.10 Br md 11.46 Dpth 3.90 Welded, 1 dk	**(A36A2PR) Passenger/Ro-Ro Ship (Vehicles)** Hull Material: Aluminium Alloy Passengers: unberthed: 289 Stern ramp Cars: 6	**4 oil engines** geared to sc. shafts driving 2 CP propellers Total Power: 3,196kW (4,344hp) 33.0kn M.T.U. 12V2000M70 4 x Vee 4 Stroke 12 Cy. 130 x 150 each-799kW (1086bhp) MTU Friedrichshafen GmbH-Friedrichshafen AuxGen: 2 x 80kW a.c
8838544 *UUAM6* - **TAVR** *ex* MYS Adamtash *-2007* **Private Enterprise 'Lartis'** - *Ukraine* MMSI: 272554000 Official number: I-305897	**2,342** 1,165 901	Class: (RS)	**1991-02 Sudostroitelnyy Zavod "Baltiya" — Klaypeda** Yd No: 807 Loa 85.07 Br ex 13.05 Dght 4.041 Lbp 76.97 Br md 13.02 Dpth 6.50 Welded, 1 dk	**(B11B2FV) Fishing Vessel** Ins: 1,245 Ice Capable	**1 oil engine** driving 1 FP propeller Total Power: 852kW (1,158hp) 11.3kn S.K.L. 8NVD48A-2U 1 x 4 Stroke 8 Cy. 320 x 480 852kW (1158bhp) SKL Motoren u. Systemtechnik AG-Magdeburg AuxGen: 2 x 534kW a.c, 1 x 220kW a.c
8826759 *UBIH4* - **TAVRIA** *ex* Sevastopolskaya Bukhta *-2010* **OOO Vostokflot (Private Co Ltd Vostokflot)** - *Vladivostok* *Russia* MMSI: 273359920	**6,989** 3,114 5,250	Class: RS	**1989-12 GP Sudostroitelnyy Zavod im. "61 Kommunara" — Nikolayev** Yd No: 1130 Loa 133.95 (BB) Br ex 18.00 Dght 6.480 Lbp 119.90 Br md - Dpth 10.70 Welded, 1 dk	**(A34A2GR) Refrigerated Cargo Ship** Ins: 7,050 Derricks: 4x5t,4x3.2t Ice Capable	**1 oil engine** driving 1 FP propeller Total Power: 3,960kW (5,384hp) 14.9kn B&W 6DKRN45/120 1 x 2 Stroke 6 Cy. 450 x 1200 3960kW (5384bhp) Bryanskiy Mashinostroitelnyy Zavod (BMZ)-Bryansk AuxGen: 3 x 500kW a.c Fuel: 2250.0
7418957 - - **TAVRIA** *ex* Cape Chidley *-2008* *ex* Esther Boyd *-1987* **Andy Bears Inc** -	*791* 374 -	Class: (LR) ✠	**1976-06 Ferguson Industries Ltd — Pictou NS** Yd No: 200 Loa 45.95 Br ex 11.16 Dght 4.268 Lbp 39.48 Br md 10.98 Dpth 6.74 Welded, 2 dks	**(B11A2FS) Stern Trawler** Compartments: ER, 1 Ho	**1 oil engine** sr geared to sc. shaft driving 1 CP propeller Total Power: 1,765kW (2,400hp) 10.0kn Nohab F212V 1 x Vee 4 Stroke 12 Cy. 250 x 300 1765kW (2400bhp) AB Bofors NOHAB-Sweden AuxGen: 2 x 200kW 230V 60Hz a.c, 1 x 65kW 230V 60Hz a.c Fuel: 173.0 (d.f.)
8924513 *UHTI* - **TAVRICHESKIY** **FCF Vskhody Kommunizma (Rybolovetskiy Kolkhoz 'Vskhody Kommunizma')** - *Murmansk* *Russia* MMSI: 273421600 Official number: 930678	**740** 222 414	Class: RS	**1993-12 ATVT Zavod "Leninska Kuznya" — Kyyiv** Yd No: 1675 Loa 54.82 Br ex 10.15 Dght 4.140 Lbp 50.30 Br md 9.80 Dpth 5.00 Welded, 1 dk	**(B11A2FS) Stern Trawler** Ins: 400 Ice Capable	**1 oil engine** driving 1 CP propeller Total Power: 852kW (1,158hp) 12.0kn S.K.L. 8NVD48A-2U 1 x 4 Stroke 8 Cy. 320 x 480 852kW (1158bhp) SKL Motoren u. Systemtechnik AG-Magdeburg AuxGen: 4 x 160kW a.c Fuel: 155.0 (d.f.)
9292060 *A8IZ6* - **TAVRICHESKY BRIDGE** **Edgerton Shipping Ltd** Unicom Management Services (Cyprus) Ltd SatCom: Inmarsat Mini-M 764647267 *Monrovia* *Liberia* MMSI: 636012908 Official number: 12908	**27,725** 13,762 46,697 T/cm 52.3	Class: LR ✠ **100A1** SS 10/2011 Double Hull oil tanker ESP **ShipRight** (SDA, FDA, CM) *IWS LI SPM EP ✠ **LMC** **UMS IGS** Eq.Ltr: M†; Cable: 632.5/73.0 U3 (a)	**2006-10 Admiralteyskiy Sudostroitelnyy Zavod — Sankt-Peterburg** Yd No: 02745 Loa 182.50 (BB) Br ex 32.34 Dght 12.197 Lbp 174.80 Br md 32.20 Dpth 17.50 Welded, 1 dk	**(A13B2TP) Products Tanker** Double Hull (13F) Liq: 51,910; Liq (Oil): 51,910 Compartments: 10 Wing Ta, 2 Wing Slop Ta, ER 10 Cargo Pump (s): 10x550m³/hr Manifold: Bow/CM: 90.9m	**1 oil engine** driving 1 FP propeller Total Power: 8,310kW (11,298hp) 14.3kn MAN-B&W 6S50MC-C 1 x 2 Stroke 6 Cy. 500 x 2000 8310kW (11298bhp) AO Bryanskiy MashinostroitelnyyZavod (BMZ)-Bryansk AuxGen: 2 x 1280kW 450V 60Hz a.c, 1 x 680kW 450V 60Hz a.c Boilers: e (ex.g.) 11.7kgf/cm² (11.5bar), WTAuxB (o.f.) 11.2kgf/cm² (11.0bar) Fuel: 99.0 (d.f.) 1419.0 (r.f.)
8931700 *UVIB* - **TAVRIDA** **Velton Ltd** - *Sevastopol* *Ukraine* Official number: 640484	**314** 94 276	Class: (RS)	**1965-03 Tuapsinskiy Sudomekhanicheskiy Zavod — Tuapse** Yd No: 23 Loa 48.25 Br ex 6.51 Dght 2.050 Lbp 44.40 Br md - Dpth 2.60 Welded, 1 dk	**(A31A2GX) General Cargo Ship** Grain: 247 Compartments: 1 Ho, ER 1 Ha: (21.0 x 4.0)ER	**2 oil engines** driving 2 FP propellers Total Power: 440kW (598hp) 10.5kn Barnaultransmash 3D12A 2 x Vee 4 Stroke 12 Cy. 150 x 180 each-220kW (299bhp) (new engine 1984) Barnaultransmash-Barnaul AuxGen: 1 x 12kW Fuel: 16.0 (d.f.)
7312282 *ENVD* - **TAVRIDA** *ex* MSB-21 *-1990* **Krymmorgidstroy Trust** - *Sevastopol* *Ukraine* Official number: 641951	*219* 96 236	Class: (RS)	**1964 Tuapsinskiy Sudomekhanicheskiy Zavod — Tuapse** Yd No: 21 Loa 48.21 Br ex 6.53 Dght 2.001 Lbp 45.45 Br md - Dpth 2.60 Welded, 1 dk	**(A31A2GX) General Cargo Ship** Bale: 247 Compartments: 1 Ho, ER 1 Ha: (21.0 x 3.9)ER	**2 oil engines** geared to sc. shafts driving 2 FP propellers Total Power: 442kW (600hp) 10.8kn Barnaultransmash 3D12A 2 x Vee 4 Stroke 12 Cy. 150 x 180 each-221kW (300bhp) Barnaultransmash-Barnaul Fuel: 18.0 (d.f.)
7644099 *EOTY* - **TAVRIYA** **State Enterprise 'Yalta Sea Trade Port'** - *Sevastopol* *Ukraine* MMSI: 272162000	**2,357** 928 3,136	Class: (RS)	**1977-07 Sudostroitelnyy Zavod im Volodarskogo — Rybinsk** Yd No: 73 Loa 114.03 Br ex 13.21 Dght 3.650 Lbp 108.01 Br md 12.98 Dpth 5.52 Welded, 1 dk	**(A31A2GX) General Cargo Ship** Grain: 4,297; Bale: 4,296 Compartments: 4 Ho, ER 4 Ha: (17.6 x 9.3)3 (17.9 x 9.3)ER Ice Capable	**2 oil engines** driving 2 FP propellers Total Power: 970kW (1,318hp) 10.8kn S.K.L. 6NVD48A-2U 2 x 4 Stroke 6 Cy. 320 x 480 each-485kW (659bhp) VEB Schwermaschinenbau "KarlLiebknecht" (SKL)-Magdeburg AuxGen: 3 x 50kW Fuel: 112.0 (d.f.)

7324297 - -	**TAVROVO** **Far-Eastern Fisherman Co Ltd (OOO Dalnevostochnyy Rybak)** -	**172** 51 100	Class: (RS)	**1973-05 Astrakhanskaya Sudoverf im. "Kirova" — Astrakhan** Yd No: 45 Loa 34.02 Br ex 7.09 Dght 2.890 Lbp 29.98 Br md - Dpth 3.69 Welded, 1 dk	**(B11B2FV) Fishing Vessel** Bale: 95 Compartments: 1 Ho, ER 1 Ha: (1.6 x 1.3) Derricks: 2x2t; Winches: 2 Ice Capable	**1 oil engine** driving 1 FP propeller Total Power: 224kW (305hp) 9.0kn S.K.L. 8NVD36-1U 1 x 4 Stroke 8 Cy. 240 x 360 224kW (305bhp) VEB Schwermaschinenbau "KarlLiebknecht" (SKL)-Magdeburg Fuel: 19.0 (d.f.)
9401879 *3ER04* -	**TAWA ARROW** **Glory Ocean Shipping SA** P&F Marine Co Ltd *Panama* *Panama* MMSI: 370117000 Official number: 3400108A	**30,983** 15,721 54,274	Class: NK	**2008-06 Oshima Shipbuilding Co Ltd — Saikai NS** Yd No: 10519 Loa 189.99 (BB) Br ex - Dght 12.447 Lbp 185.79 Br md 32.26 Dpth 17.62 Welded, 1 dk	**(A31A2GO) Open Hatch Cargo Ship** Grain: 60,106; Bale: 59,811 TEU 256 C.Dk 256/20' Compartments: 5 Ho, ER 5 Ha: ER Cranes: 4x36t	**1 oil engine** driving 1 FP propeller Total Power: 8,208kW (11,160hp) 14.5kn MAN-B&W 6S50MC-C 1 x 2 Stroke 6 Cy. 500 x 2000 8208kW (11160bhp) (new engine 2008) Kawasaki Heavy Industries Ltd-Japan AuxGen: 3 x 520kW a.c Fuel: 2032.0
7420998 - -	**TAWA No. 1** - - -	*172* 100 -		**1974 Lee Hing Shipyard Ltd. — Hong Kong** L reg 25.09 Br ex 7.93 Dght - Lbp - Br md - Dpth - Welded, 1 dk	**(A13B2TU) Tanker (unspecified)** Liq: 294; Liq (Oil): 294 Compartments: 4 Ta, ER	**1 oil engine** geared to sc. shaft driving 1 FP propeller Total Power: 184kW (250hp) 7.5kn Chinese Std. Type 6160A 1 x 4 Stroke 6 Cy. 160 x 225 184kW (250bhp) Weifang Diesel Engine Factory-China
8951669 *HP8074* -	**TAWAKKALI** *ex* Al Riyaz *-1994* **Muhammad Qasim Hafeez** - *Panama* *Panama* Official number: 23851PEXT	*337* 291 -		**1993 Veraval Shipbuilding — Veraval** L reg 28.95 Br ex - Dght - Lbp - Br md 8.43 Dpth 6.40 Welded, 1 dk	**(A31A2GX) General Cargo Ship**	**1 oil engine** driving 1 FP propeller Total Power: 1,030kW (1,400hp) 9.0kn Mitsubishi 1 x 1030kW (1400bhp) Mitsubishi Heavy Industries Ltd-Japan
9016557 *A4DH5* -	**TAWARIQ-3** *ex* Breave No. 1 *-2006* *ex* Yung Chan 1 *-2005* *ex* Dairin Maru No. 68 *-2004* *ex* Yamato Maru No. 21 *-1999* **Seas Tawariq Co LLC** - *Port Sultan Qaboos* *Oman*	**449** 182 320	Class: IS	**1990-11 Niigata Engineering Co Ltd — Niigata NI** Yd No: 2205 Loa 49.29 (BB) Br ex - Dght 3.205 Lbp 43.00 Br md 8.30 Dpth 3.55 Welded	**(B11B2FV) Fishing Vessel** Ins: 370	**1 oil engine** with flexible couplings & sr geared to sc. shaft driving 1 CP propeller Total Power: 699kW (950hp) Niigata 6M28BFT 1 x 4 Stroke 6 Cy. 280 x 480 699kW (950bhp) Niigata Engineering Co Ltd-Japan
7825112 *JVGJ4* -	**TAWAU** *ex* Scorpio *-2013* *ex* Hai Soon XII *-2008* *ex* Arun 1 *-2000* *ex* Fong Chiuen *-2000* *ex* Haiyin II *-1998* *ex* Yamae Maru *-1993* - - *Ulaanbaatar* *Mongolia* MMSI: 457872000	**1,861** 921 3,285	Class: IZ (NK)	**1979-12 Sasaki Shipbuilding Co Ltd — Osakikamijima HS** Yd No: 331 Loa 88.70 Br ex 12.63 Dght 5.808 Lbp 82.00 Br md 12.60 Dpth 6.41 Welded, 1 dk	**(A13B2TP) Products Tanker** Liq: 3,301; Liq (Oil): 3,301	**1 oil engine** driving 1 FP propeller Total Power: 2,059kW (2,799hp) 13.0kn Akasaka AH40 1 x 4 Stroke 6 Cy. 400 x 600 2059kW (2799bhp) Akasaka Tekkosho KK (Akasaka DieselLtd)-Japan AuxGen: 2 x 120kW 445V 60Hz a.c Fuel: 53.0 (d.f.) 159.5 (r.f.) 8.5pd
6917839 *HSAE* -	**TAWEECHOK MARINE** *ex* Poonsri Marine *-1986* *ex* Chang Chun *-1979* **Madam Poonsri Sutharom** - *Bangkok* *Thailand* Official number: 231025530	**3,054** 2,057 5,125	Class: (CR)	**1969-05 Kurushima Dockyard Co. Ltd. — Imabari** Yd No: 531 Loa 97.21 Br ex 15.63 Dght 6.376 Lbp 90.00 Br md 15.60 Dpth 7.78 Riveted\Welded, 1 dk	**(A31A2GX) General Cargo Ship** Grain: 6,527; Bale: 6,314 Compartments: 2 Ho, ER 2 Ha: (27.0 x 7.2) (25.9 x 7.2)ER Derricks: 2x15t,2x10t; Winches: 4	**1 oil engine** driving 1 FP propeller Total Power: 2,207kW (3,001hp) 13.0kn Akasaka 6DM51SS 1 x 4 Stroke 6 Cy. 510 x 840 2207kW (3001bhp) Akasaka Tekkosho KK (Akasaka DieselLtd)-Japan AuxGen: 2 x 160kW 450V 60Hz a.c Fuel: 434.0 (r.f.)
8013326 - -	**TAWES** - **PT Pasca Dana Sundari** - *Jakarta* *Indonesia*	*270* 81 50	Class: KI	**1980-11 P.T. Kodja (Unit I) — Jakarta** Yd No: 669 Loa 38.41 Br ex - Dght 1.501 Lbp 32.01 Br md 10.00 Dpth 2.49 Welded, 1 dk	**(A37B2PS) Passenger Ship**	**2 oil engines** geared to sc. shafts driving 2 FP propellers Total Power: 530kW (720hp) Nissan RD10 2 x Vee 4 Stroke 10 Cy. 135 x 125 each-265kW (360bhp) (, fitted 1980) Nissan Diesel Motor Co. Ltd.-Ageo
8022638 - -	**TAWFIK ELDEEB** - **Canal Harbour Works Co** - *Port Said* *Egypt*	*167* 5 330	Class: BV	**1981-06 Scheepswerf Bodewes Gruno B.V. — Foxhol** (Hull) Yd No: 249 **1981-06 B.V. Scheepswerf Damen — Gorinchem** Yd No: 3120 Loa 26.01 Br ex 8.03 Dght 3.250 Lbp 24.01 Br md 7.82 Dpth 4.04 Welded, 1 dk	**(B32A2ST) Tug**	**2 oil engines** geared to sc. shafts driving 2 FP propellers Total Power: 1,368kW (1,860hp) 12.0kn G.M. (Detroit Diesel) 16V-149-TI 2 x Vee 2 Stroke 16 Cy. 146 x 146 each-684kW (930bhp) General Motors Detroit DieselAllison Divn-USA
8224858 *CNOW* -	**TAWHID** *launched as* Takbir *-1984* **Omnium Marocaine de Peche** - SatCom: Inmarsat C 424238210 *Casablanca* *Morocco*	*324* 143 405	Class: BV	**1984-03 Construcciones Navales Santodomingo SA — Vigo** Yd No: 492 Loa 38.31 Br ex - Dght 4.050 Lbp 37.47 Br md 8.21 Dpth 6.15 Welded, 2 dks	**(B11A2FS) Stern Trawler** Ins: 402 Compartments: 1 Ho, ER 2 Ha: ER	**1 oil engine** with clutches, flexible couplings & sr geared to sc. shaft driving 1 FP propeller Total Power: 853kW (1,160hp) 12.3kn Deutz SBA8M528 1 x 4 Stroke 8 Cy. 220 x 280 853kW (1160bhp) Hijos de J Barreras SA-Spain AuxGen: 2 x 140kW 380V 50Hz a.c
7502112 *DUA2742* -	**TAWI TAWI PEARL I** *ex* New Manila 1 *-1997* *ex* Wespal 1 *-1997* **New Manila International Shipping Corp** - *Manila* *Philippines* Official number: MNLD007784	*415* 273 625		**1975-09 Sandoval Shipyards Inc. — Manila** Yd No: 10 Loa 42.98 Br ex 9.78 Dght - Lbp 39.60 Br md 9.76 Dpth 2.72 Welded, 1 dk	**(A35D2RL) Landing Craft** Bow door/ramp	**2 oil engines** reverse reduction geared to sc. shafts driving 2 FP propellers Total Power: 354kW (482hp) Yanmar 6KDAL-T 2 x 4 Stroke 6 Cy. 145 x 170 each-177kW (241bhp) Yanmar Diesel Engine Co Ltd-Japan
8982400 *9WEG3* -	**TAWINDO NO. 2** - **Osin Motor Sdn Bhd** - *Kota Kinabalu* *Malaysia* Official number: 329803	**116** 49 -		**2002-04 Hung Seng Shipbuilding Sdn Bhd — Sibu** Yd No: 022 Loa 39.02 Br ex 4.07 Dght 1.300 Lbp 34.65 Br md 4.05 Dpth 1.50 Welded, 1 dk	**(A37B2PS) Passenger Ship**	**2 oil engines** driving 2 Propellers Total Power: 1,176kW (1,598hp) Mitsubishi S6H-MTKL 2 x 4 Stroke 6 Cy. 150 x 175 each-588kW (799bhp) Mitsubishi Heavy Industries Ltd-Japan
5159349 - -	**TAXIARCHES** *ex* Panormitis *-1989* *ex* Imbrim *-1970* **Taxiarchis Fishing Co** -	*302* 96 224	Class: (BV)	**1956 S.A. des Ancien Chantiers Dubigeon — Nantes-Chantenay** Yd No: 763 Loa 36.89 Br ex 7.12 Dght 4.011 Lbp 32.44 Br md 7.01 Dpth 4.37 Riveted\Welded, 1 dk	**(B11A2FT) Trawler** 3 Ha: 3 (1.1 x 1.1) Derricks: 1x1.5t,1x0.8t	**1 oil engine** driving 1 FP propeller Total Power: 463kW (629hp) 12.0kn Sulzer 6BCA29 1 x 4 Stroke 6 Cy. 290 x 360 463kW (629bhp) Cie de Constructions Mecaniques (CCM), procede Sulzer-France AuxGen: 1 x 20kW 110V a.c Fuel: 76.0 (d.f.)
6930946 - -	**TAXIARCHIS** - - -	*180* 99 -		**1968 Th. Zervas & Sons — Piraeus** Loa 27.01 Br ex 6.10 Dght - Lbp 23.78 Br md 5.80 Dpth 2.60 Welded	**(A37B2PS) Passenger Ship**	**2 oil engines** driving 2 FP propellers Total Power: 514kW (698hp)
6913340 *SY6961* -	**TAXIARCHIS** *ex* Nordgard *-2006* *ex* Heimvik *-1989* *ex* Gerd *-1986* *ex* Klaus Block *-1983* **Kapetanikolas Shipping Co** - *Leros* *Greece* MMSI: 237989800 Official number: 7	**1,428** 815 1,464	Class: (GL)	**1969-07 J.J. Sietas Schiffswerft — Hamburg** Yd No: 654 Loa 77.02 Br ex 11.82 Dght 4.045 Lbp 70.62 Br md 11.21 Dpth 6.25 Welded, 2 dks	**(A31A2GX) General Cargo Ship** Grain: 2,747; Bale: 2,676 TEU 73 C. 73/20' Compartments: 1 Ho, ER 1 Ha: (44.3 x 8.5)ER Ice Capable	**1 oil engine** driving 1 FP propeller Total Power: 1,250kW (1,700hp) 12.5kn Deutz RBV6M358 1 x 4 Stroke 6 Cy. 400 x 580 1250kW (1700bhp) Kloeckner Humboldt Deutz AG-West Germany
6714536 *SV8566* -	**TAXIARCHIS** *ex* Taxiarchis Karapiperis 9 *-1997* *ex* Taxiarchis *-1991* *ex* Abeille No. 16 *-1984* **Lyboussakis Taxiarchis Naftiki Eteria** Tugboat Union - Lyboussakis Naftiki Eteria SatCom: Inmarsat C 423964210 *Piraeus* *Greece* MMSI: 239642000 Official number: 8582	**281** 84 -	Class: (BV) (HR)	**1967 At. & Forg. de l'Ouest — St. Nazaire** Yd No: RA8 Loa 32.19 Br ex 9.25 Dght 4.115 Lbp 31.91 Br md 8.72 Dpth 4.63 Welded, 1 dk	**(B32A2ST) Tug**	**1 oil engine** reverse reduction geared to sc. shaft driving 1 FP propeller Total Power: 1,471kW (2,000hp) 13.0kn Deutz SBV8M358 1 x 4 Stroke 8 Cy. 400 x 580 1471kW (2000bhp) Kloeckner Humboldt Deutz AG-West Germany AuxGen: 3 x 95kW 220V d.c Fuel: 61.0 (d.f.)

7431090 *SWYM* -	**TAXIARCHIS** *ex* Euromantique *-1999* *ex* Agia Methodia *-1995* *ex* Seaway I *-1994* *ex* Seaway Hobart *-1993* *ex* Union Hobart *-1984* **C-Link Ferries MC** NEL Lines (Maritime Co of Lesvos SA) SatCom: Inmarsat C 423962910 *Mytilene* *Greece* MMSI: 239629000 Official number: 10644	*5,088* 3,237 4,333	Class: RI (HR) (NV)	1976-06 **AS Framnaes Mek. Vaerksted — Sandefjord** Yd No: 186 Converted From: Ro-Ro Cargo Ship-1994 Loa 135.79 (BB) Br ex 26.73 Dght 6.165 Lbp 120.00 Br md 20.60 Dpth 14.71 Welded, 1 dk & S dk	**(A36A2PR) Passenger/Ro-Ro Ship (Vehicles)** Passengers: unberthed: 602; cabins: 57; berths: 198 Stern door/ramp (a) Len: 8.00 Wid: 8.00 Swl: - Lane-Len: 1050 Lane-clr ht: 6.17 Cars: 300 Bale: 17,089	**2 oil engines** geared to sc. shafts driving 2 CP propellers Total Power: 8,826kW (12,000hp) 18.5kn Pielstick 12PC2-2V-400 2 x Vee 4 Stroke 12 Cy. 400 x 460 each-4413kW (6000bhp) Lindholmen Motor AB-Sweden AuxGen: 3 x 450kW 440V 60Hz a.c Thrusters: 1 Thwart. FP thruster (f)
9117806 *SX9512* -	**TAXIARCHIS** *ex* Shin A No. 7 *-2001* *ex* Chang Il No. 7 *-1997* **Med Sea Tankers Shipping Co** - SatCom: Inmarsat C 423985810 *Piraeus* *Greece* MMSI: 239858000 Official number: 10902	**1,321** 771 2,547 T/cm 7.3	Class: GL (HR) (KR)	1994-02 **Haeyang Shipbuilding Co Ltd — Tongyeong** Yd No: 105 Converted From: Chemical/Products Tanker-2009 Loa 72.40 Br ex - Dght 5.520 Lbp 65.01 Br md 12.00 Dpth 6.00 Welded, 1 dk	**(A13B2TP) Products Tanker** Liq: 2,867; Liq (Oil): 2,867 2 Cargo Pump (s)	**1 oil engine** driving 1 FP propeller Total Power: 1,471kW (2,000hp) 11.8kn Alpha 6L28/32A 1 x 4 Stroke 6 Cy. 280 x 320 1471kW (2000bhp) Ssangyong Heavy Industries Co Ltd-South Korea AuxGen: 1 x 104kW 445V a.c
8736045 - - -	**TAXIARHIS** *ex* Taxiarchis *-2012* *ex* Ifigenia *-2008* *ex* Idion *-2008* *ex* Admiral 12 *-2008* *ex* OM-27 *-1995* **Oceania Shiptrade Ltd** -	**122** 36 -		1982-01 **Ilyichyovskiy Sudoremontnyy Zavod im. "50-letiya SSSR" — Ilyichyovsk** Loa 30.48 Br ex - Dght - Lbp - Br md 5.30 Dpth 2.55 Welded, 1 dk	**(A37B2PS) Passenger Ship**	**2 oil engines** reduction geared to sc. shafts driving 2 FP propellers Total Power: 530kW (720hp) 15.0kn Daewoo 2 x 4 Stroke each-265kW (360bhp) Daewoo Heavy Industries Ltd-South Korea
8867260 *XVBV* -	**TAY DO 04** *ex* An Giang 06 *-2005* *ex* Angkorvath 01 *-2001* **Mekong Shipping JSC (Cong Ty Co Phan Van Tai Song Bien Can Tho)** - SatCom: Inmarsat C 457432110 *Saigon* *Vietnam* MMSI: 574321000 Official number: VNSG-1753-VT	**2,534** 1,450 3,230	Class: (VR)	1988 **Ha Long Shipbuilding Co Ltd — Ha Long** Loa 91.82 Br ex - Dght 5.500 Lbp 84.99 Br md 14.00 Dpth 7.80 Welded, 1 dk	**(A31A2GX) General Cargo Ship** Grain: 5,380; Bale: 4,844 Compartments: 2 Ho, ER 2 Ha: 2 (18.2 x 8.5)ER	**1 oil engine** driving 1 FP propeller Total Power: 721kW (980hp) 10.0kn Skoda 6L350IIPN 1 x 4 Stroke 6 Cy. 350 x 500 721kW (980bhp) Skoda-Praha AuxGen: 3 x 80kW a.c
7916076 *XVJS* -	**TAY DO 06** *ex* Ben Thanh *-2006* *ex* Princess Toyo *-2006* **Mekong Shipping JSC (Cong Ty Co Phan Van Tai Song Bien Can Tho)** - SatCom: Inmarsat C 457407010 *Saigon* *Vietnam* MMSI: 574350000 Official number: VNSG-171-TH	**1,536** 1,069 2,534	Class: VR (NK)	1979-09 **Higaki Zosen K.K. — Imabari** Yd No: 232 Loa 77.04 Br ex 12.03 Dght 5.270 Lbp 71.50 Br md 12.00 Dpth 7.40 Welded, 2 dks	**(A31A2GX) General Cargo Ship** Grain: 4,012; Bale: 3,846 Compartments: 1 Ho, ER 1 Ha: (37.1 x 8.5)ER Derricks: 2x10t	**1 oil engine** driving 1 FP propeller Total Power: 1,471kW (2,000hp) 11.5kn Hanshin 6LUD35 1 x 4 Stroke 6 Cy. 350 x 550 1471kW (2000bhp) The Hanshin Diesel Works Ltd-Japan AuxGen: 2 x 76kW 220V a.c
9409687 *3WPU* -	**TAY DO STAR** - **Mekong Shipping JSC (Cong Ty Co Phan Van Tai Song Bien Can Tho)** - SatCom: Inmarsat C 457445910 *Saigon* *Vietnam* MMSI: 574459000 Official number: VNSG-1832-TH	**4,086** 2,472 6,485	Class: NK VR	2007-08 **Saigon Shipbuilding Industry Co Ltd — Ho Chi Minh City** Yd No: 007 Loa 102.79 (BB) Br ex - Dght 6.957 Lbp 94.50 Br md 17.00 Dpth 8.80 Welded, 1 dk	**(A31A2GX) General Cargo Ship** Grain: 8,610; Bale: 8,159 Derricks: 4x25t	**1 oil engine** driving 1 FP propeller Total Power: 2,648kW (3,600hp) 12.5kn Hanshin LH41LA 1 x 4 Stroke 6 Cy. 410 x 800 2648kW (3600bhp) The Hanshin Diesel Works Ltd-Japan AuxGen: 3 x 610kW a.c Fuel: 410.0
9329980 *XVFS* -	**TAY SON 1** - **Vietnam National Shipping Lines (VINALINES) (Tong Cong Ty Hang Hai Viet Nam)** Vinalines Shipping Co (VLC) *Haiphong* *Vietnam* MMSI: 574277000 Official number: VN-1927-VT	**8,216** 5,295 13,394	Class: NK VR	2004-12 **Ha Long Shipbuilding Co Ltd — Ha Long** Yd No: HL-08 Loa 136.40 (BB) Br ex - Dght 8.365 Lbp 126.00 Br md 20.20 Dpth 11.30 Welded, 1 dk	**(A31A2GX) General Cargo Ship** Grain: 18,601; Bale: 17,744 Compartments: 4 Ho, ER 4 Ha: (18.7 x 11.4) (19.4 x 11.4) (19.4 x 11.4)ER (18.3 x 10.8) Derricks: 4x25t	**1 oil engine** driving 1 FP propeller Total Power: 3,965kW (5,391hp) 13.2kn Mitsubishi 7UEC33LSII 1 x 2 Stroke 7 Cy. 330 x 1050 3965kW (5391bhp) Akasaka Tekkosho KK (Akasaka DieselLtd)-Japan Fuel: 710.0
9343041 *3WLS* -	**TAY SON 2** - **Vietnam National Shipping Lines (VINALINES) (Tong Cong Ty Hang Hai Viet Nam)** Vinalines Shipping Co (VLC) *Haiphong* *Vietnam* MMSI: 574294000 Official number: VN1957-VT	**8,216** 5,295 13,311	Class: NK VR	2005-03 **Ha Long Shipbuilding Co Ltd — Ha Long** Yd No: HL-09 Loa 136.40 (BB) Br ex - Dght 8.365 Lbp 126.00 Br md 20.20 Dpth 11.30 Welded, 1 dk	**(A31A2GX) General Cargo Ship** Grain: 18,601; Bale: 17,744 4 Ha: (18.7 x 11.4)2 (19.4 x 11.4)ER (18.3 x 10.8) Derricks: 4x25t	**1 oil engine** driving 1 FP propeller Total Power: 3,965kW (5,391hp) 13.2kn Mitsubishi 7UEC33LSII 1 x 2 Stroke 7 Cy. 330 x 1050 3965kW (5391bhp) Akasaka Tekkosho KK (Akasaka DieselLtd)-Japan Fuel: 710.0
9355599 *3WMV* -	**TAY SON 3** - **Vietnam National Shipping Lines (VINALINES) (Tong Cong Ty Hang Hai Viet Nam)** Vinalines Shipping Co (VLC) *Haiphong* *Vietnam* MMSI: 574624000 Official number: VN-14TT-VT	**8,216** 5,295 13,286	Class: NK VR	2005-09 **Ha Long Shipbuilding Co Ltd — Ha Long** Yd No: HL-10 Loa 136.40 (BB) Br ex - Dght 8.365 Lbp 126.67 Br md 20.20 Dpth 11.30 Welded, 1 dk	**(A31A2GX) General Cargo Ship** Grain: 18,601; Bale: 17,744 Compartments: 4 Ho, ER 4 Ha: (18.7 x 11.4)2 (19.4 x 11.4)ER (18.3 x 18.7) Derricks: 4x25t	**1 oil engine** driving 1 FP propeller Total Power: 3,965kW (5,391hp) 13.2kn Mitsubishi 7UEC33LSII 1 x 2 Stroke 7 Cy. 330 x 1050 3965kW (5391bhp) Akasaka Tekkosho KK (Akasaka DieselLtd)-Japan Fuel: 710.0
9370587 *3WNE* -	**TAY SON 4** - **Vietnam National Shipping Lines (VINALINES) (Tong Cong Ty Hang Hai Viet Nam)** Vinalines Shipping Co (VLC) *Haiphong* *Vietnam* MMSI: 574338000 Official number: VN-1927-VT	**8,216** 5,295 13,303	Class: NK VR	2005-11 **Ha Long Shipbuilding Co Ltd — Ha Long** Yd No: HL-11 Loa 136.40 (BB) Br ex 20.23 Dght 8.365 Lbp 126.00 Br md 20.20 Dpth 11.30 Welded, 1 dk	**(A31A2GX) General Cargo Ship** Grain: 18,601; Bale: 17,744 4 Ha: (18.7 x 11.4)2 (19.4 x 11.4)ER (18.3 x 10.8) Derricks: 4x25t	**1 oil engine** driving 1 FP propeller Total Power: 3,965kW (5,391hp) 13.2kn Mitsubishi 7UEC33LSII 1 x 2 Stroke 7 Cy. 330 x 1050 3965kW (5391bhp) Akasaka Tekkosho KK (Akasaka DieselLtd)-Japan AuxGen: 2 x 350kW 450V a.c Fuel: 710.0
9418676 *A6E3067* -	**TAYBAH-1** - **Khalid Faraj Shipping (UAE)** - *Abu Dhabi* *United Arab Emirates* MMSI: 470906000 Official number: 5333	**869** 260 600	Class: BV	2007-01 **Piasau Slipways Sdn Bhd — Miri** Yd No: 245 Loa 64.00 Br ex - Dght 2.700 Lbp 60.30 Br md 14.00 Dpth 3.65 Welded, 1 dk	**(A35D2RL) Landing Craft** Bow ramp (centre)	**2 oil engines** reduction geared to sc. shafts driving 2 FP propellers Total Power: 942kW (1,280hp) 10.0kn Cummins KTA-19-M3 2 x 4 Stroke 6 Cy. 159 x 159 each-471kW (640bhp) Cummins Engine Co Inc-USA
9571935 - -	**TAYCO AMPATO** - **Ian Taylor Peru SAC** - *Callao* *Peru*	**343** 103 178	Class: AB	2010-01 **Jiangsu Wuxi Shipyard Co Ltd — Wuxi JS** (Hull) Yd No: (1384) 2010-01 **Pacific Ocean Engineering & Trading Pte Ltd (POET) — Singapore** Yd No: 1384 Loa 30.00 Br ex - Dght 3.760 Lbp 29.29 Br md 9.80 Dpth 4.88 Welded, 1 dk	**(B32A2ST) Tug**	**2 oil engines** reduction geared to sc. shafts driving 2 Z propellers Total Power: 3,236kW (4,400hp) Niigata 6L28HX 2 x 4 Stroke 6 Cy. 280 x 370 each-1618kW (2200bhp) Niigata Engineering Co Ltd-Japan AuxGen: 2 x 130kW a.c Fuel: 115.0 (r.f.)
9258636 *OA4734* -	**TAYCO SACANTAY** *ex* Tayco Iv *-2011* **Ian Taylor y Compania SA** - *Callao* *Peru*	**218** 65 70	Class: BV	2002-08 **Detroit Chile SA — Puerto Montt** Yd No: 77 Loa 26.71 Br ex 8.72 Dght 3.400 Lbp 24.15 Br md 8.50 Dpth 4.00 Welded, 1 dk	**(B32A2ST) Tug**	**2 oil engines** geared to sc. shafts driving 2 FP propellers Total Power: 2,640kW (3,590hp) 12.0kn M.T.U. 12V4000M60 2 x Vee 4 Stroke 12 Cy. 165 x 190 each-1320kW (1795bhp) MTU Friedrichshafen GmbH-Friedrichshafen AuxGen: 2 x 80kW 380/220V 50Hz a.c
9258648 *CB7441* -	**TAYCO V** - **Ian Taylor y Compania SA** - *Valparaiso* *Chile* MMSI: 725000149 Official number: 3058	**218** 65 89	Class: BV	2002-08 **Detroit Chile SA — Puerto Montt** Yd No: 78 Loa 26.75 Br ex 8.72 Dght 3.440 Lbp 24.15 Br md 8.50 Dpth 4.20 Welded, 1 dk	**(B32A2ST) Tug**	**2 oil engines** geared to sc. shafts driving 2 FP propellers Total Power: 2,640kW (3,590hp) 12.0kn M.T.U. 12V4000M60 2 x Vee 4 Stroke 12 Cy. 165 x 190 each-1320kW (1795bhp) MTU Friedrichshafen GmbH-Friedrichshafen AuxGen: 2 x 80kW 380/220V 50Hz a.c Fuel: 65.0 (d.f.)

9654593 **TAYEB 1** **183** Class: BV
CNA4681 52
\- **Offshore Maroc SA** 110
\-
Casablanca *Morocco*
MMSI: 242134100

2013-01 Song Cam Shipyard — Haiphong (Hull) Yd No: (509844)
2013-01 B.V. Scheepswerf Damen — Gorinchem Yd No: 509844
Loa 26.09 Br ex 8.54 Dght 2.150
Lbp 23.96 Br md 7.94 Dpth 4.05
Welded, 1 dk

(B32A2ST) Tug

2 oil engines reduction geared to sc. shafts driving 2 FP propellers
Total Power: 2,428kW (3,302hp)
Caterpillar 3512C
2 x Vee 4 Stroke 12 Cy. 170 x 215 each-1214kW (1651bhp)
Caterpillar Inc-USA
AuxGen: 2 x 103kW 50Hz a.c
Fuel: 74.0 (d.f.)

9412361 **TAYFA** **5,372** Class: BV (TL)
PJVX 2,923
\- **Tayfa Denizcilik Ltd Sti** 8,300
Astas Denizcilik ve Ticaret Ltd Sti
Willemstad *Curacao*
MMSI: 306833000
Official number: 2007-C-1927

2006-12 Linhai Jianghai Shipbuilding Co Ltd — Linhai ZJ Yd No: 1
Loa 120.80 Br ex 17.92 Dght 6.350
Lbp 113.50 Br md 17.60 Dpth 8.30
Welded, 1 dk

(A31A2GX) General Cargo Ship
Grain: 10,642; Bale: 10,642

1 oil engine driving 1 FP propeller
Total Power: 2,868kW (3,899hp) 12.5kn
Pielstick 6PC2-5L
1 x 4 Stroke 6 Cy. 400 x 460 2868kW (3899bhp)
Shaanxi Diesel Heavy Industry Co Lt-China

8027183 **TAYFUN** **728** Class: RS
UBDZ 218
\- **Vostochny Port JSC** 245
\-
Vostochnyy *Russia*
MMSI: 273432650
Official number: 822666

1983-03 Hollming Oy — Rauma Yd No: 246
Loa 39.90 Br ex 12.48 Dght 4.900
Lbp 36.48 Br md 12.01 Dpth 7.00
Welded, 1 dk

(B32A2ST) Tug
Ice Capable

2 oil engines dr geared to sc. shafts driving 2 CP propellers
Total Power: 3,706kW (5,038hp) 14.3kn
Wartsila 6R32
2 x 4 Stroke 6 Cy. 320 x 350 each-1853kW (2519bhp)
Oy Wartsila Ab-Finland
Fuel: 224.0 (r.f.)

7407829 **TAYFUN** **179** Class: GL
UBQK5 *ex* Fairplay Xv *-2013* 53
\- **Morservis Co Ltd** -
\-
Kaliningrad *Russia*
MMSI: 273330290
Official number: RM-22-45

1975-02 Schiffswerft u. Maschinenfabrik Max Sieghold — Bremerhaven Yd No: 168
Loa 26.65 Br ex 8.84 Dght 2.801
Lbp 23.80 Br md 8.79 Dpth 3.59
Welded, 1 dk

(B32A2ST) Tug
Ice Capable

2 oil engines geared to sc. shafts driving 2 Directional propellers
Total Power: 1,280kW (1,740hp)
Deutz SBA6M528
2 x 4 Stroke 6 Cy. 220 x 280 each-640kW (870bhp)
Kloeckner Humboldt Deutz AG-West Germany

7391678 **TAYFUN** **272** Class: RS
\- 81
\- **Krasnodar Kray Committee for State Property (Komitet po Upravleniyu Gosimushchestvom Krasnodarskogo Kraya)** 83
\-
Novorossiysk *Russia*

1975-04 Brodogradiliste 'Tito' Beograd - Brod 'Tito' — Belgrade Yd No: 918
Loa 35.43 Br ex 9.21 Dght 3.140
Lbp 30.00 Br md 9.00 Dpth 4.52
Welded, 1 dk

(B32A2ST) Tug
Ice Capable

2 oil engines geared to sc. shaft driving 1 FP propeller
Total Power: 1,700kW (2,312hp)
B&W 7-26MTBF-40
2 x 4 Stroke 7 Cy. 260 x 400 each-850kW (1156bhp)
Titovi Zavodi 'Litostroj'-Yugoslavia
Fuel: 58.0 (d.f.)

6874996 **TAYFUN** **122** Class: (RS)
\- *ex* MB-6129 *-2013* 36
\- **OOO 'Balt-Shtok'** 43
\-

1966 VEB Schiffswerft "Edgar Andre" — Magdeburg Yd No: 6129
Loa 28.88 Br ex 6.76 Dght 2.800
Lbp 25.62 Br md 6.50 Dpth 3.02
Welded, 1 dk

(B32A2ST) Tug
Ice Capable

1 oil engine driving 1 FP propeller
Total Power: 294kW (400hp) 9.7kn
S.K.L. 6NVD48
1 x 4 Stroke 6 Cy. 320 x 480 294kW (400bhp)
VEB Schwermaschinenbau "KarlLiebknecht" (SKL)-Magdeburg
AuxGen: 2 x 27kW
Fuel: 25.0 (d.f.)

8727525 **TAYFUN** **109** Class: RS
UBAL 33
\- **Sergey Alexandrovich Frolov** 19
Pacific Network JSC (A/O 'Pasifik Netvork')
Petropavlovsk-Kamchatskiy *Russia*
Official number: 820035

1984-07 Astrakhan. SSZ im 10-iy God Oktyabrskoy Revolyutsii — Astrakhan Yd No: 8
Loa 27.15 Br ex 6.81 Dght 1.600
Lbp 23.50 Br md 6.64 Dpth 3.41
Welded, 1 dk

(B34M2QS) Search & Rescue Vessel

1 oil engine reduction geared to sc. shaft driving 1 FP propeller
Total Power: 240kW (326hp) 11.0kn
Caterpillar 3406
1 x 4 Stroke 6 Cy. 137 x 165 240kW (326bhp)
Caterpillar Inc-USA
AuxGen: 2 x 30kW
Fuel: 8.0 (d.f.)

9083225 **TAYFUN BAYRAKTAR** **3,557** Class: AB
TCTU 2,111
\- **Bayraktar Denizcilik ve Ticaret AS** 5,248
Bayraktar Gemi Isletmeciligi ve Kiralama AS (Bayraktar Shipmanagement & Chartering SA)
Istanbul *Turkey*
MMSI: 271000253
Official number: 6250

1992-08 Gisan Gemi Ins. San — Istanbul Yd No: 6
Lengthened-1995
Loa 109.80 (BB) Br ex - Dght 6.186
Lbp 99.20 Br md 14.00 Dpth 7.50
Welded, 1 dk

(A31A2GX) General Cargo Ship
Grain: 7,391; Bale: 7,035
Compartments: 2 Ho, ER
2 Ha: (28.2 x 9.5) (27.6 x 9.5)ER
Derricks: 2x5t,2x3t

1 oil engine driving 1 FP propeller
Total Power: 1,984kW (2,697hp) 12.5kn
S.K.L. 6VDS48/42AL-2
1 x 4 Stroke 6 Cy. 420 x 480 1984kW (2697bhp)
SKL Motoren u. Systemtechnik AG-Magdeburg

7714571 **TAYFUN-II** **397** Class: (RS)
\- *ex* Vremya M No. 1 *-1997* 130
\- *ex* Shotoku Maru No. 73 *-1992* 334
ex Yakushi Maru No. 7 *-1986*
Rybak-5 Ltd (OOO 'Rybak-5')

1977-09 Niigata Engineering Co Ltd — Niigata NI Yd No: 1567
Loa 48.32 Br ex 8.23 Dght 3.260
Lbp 42.52 Br md 8.21 Dpth 3.61
Welded, 1 dk

(B11B2FV) Fishing Vessel

1 oil engine driving 1 CP propeller
Total Power: 882kW (1,199hp) 11.0kn
Niigata 6M28KEHS
1 x 4 Stroke 6 Cy. 280 x 440 882kW (1199bhp)
Niigata Engineering Co Ltd-Japan
AuxGen: 1 x 310kW a.c, 1 x 250kW a.c
Fuel: 191.0 (d.f.)

9005857 **TAYLAN KALKAVAN** **3,169** Class: TL (AB)
TCTL 1,806
\- **OK Denizcilik Ltd Sti** 4,737
\- T/cm
Istanbul *Turkey* 11.5
MMSI: 271000302
Official number: 6513

1994-05 Torgem Gemi Insaat Sanayii ve Ticaret a.s. — Tuzla, Istanbul Yd No: 51
Loa 97.45 (BB) Br ex - Dght 6.231
Lbp 87.20 Br md 14.00 Dpth 7.60
Welded, 1 dk

(A31A2GX) General Cargo Ship
Grain: 5,400; Bale: 4,250
Compartments: 2 Ho, ER
2 Ha: ER

1 oil engine with flexible couplings & sr geared to sc. shaft driving 1 CP propeller
Total Power: 1,839kW (2,500hp) 12.6kn
Normo KRMB-9
1 x 4 Stroke 9 Cy. 250 x 300 1839kW (2500bhp)
Ulstein Bergen AS-Norway
AuxGen: 2 x 200kW 400V 50Hz a.c
Fuel: 215.0 (d.f.) 6.8pd

8745369 **TAYLOR MAID** **105**
\- *ex* Arlene *-1986* 93
\- **James Taylor Fishery Ltd** -
\-
Chatham, ON *Canada*
Official number: 176524

1946-01 Erieau Shipbuilding & Dry Dock Co Ltd — Erieau ON
L reg 16.09 Br ex - Dght -
Lbp - Br md 6.71 Dpth 1.43
Welded, 1 dk

(B11B2FV) Fishing Vessel

1 oil engine driving 1 Propeller
Total Power: 169kW (230hp) 11.0kn

7814644 **TAYLOR TIDE** **522** Class: (AB)
YYV2717 *ex* Clipper Grand Cayman *-1990* 159
\- **Twenty Grand Offshore Inc** 450
Tidewater Marine Service CA (SEMARCA)
Maracaibo *Venezuela*
MMSI: 775000214
Official number: AJZL-T-011

1980-01 Houma Fabricators Inc — Houma LA Yd No: 64
Loa 48.80 Br ex - Dght 3.753
Lbp 47.55 Br md 11.60 Dpth 4.35
Welded, 1 dk

(B21A2OS) Platform Supply Ship

2 oil engines reverse reduction geared to sc. shafts driving 2 FP propellers
Total Power: 1,368kW (1,860hp) 12.0kn
G.M. (Detroit Diesel) 16V-149
2 x Vee 2 Stroke 16 Cy. 146 x 146 each-684kW (930bhp)
General Motors Detroit DieselAllison Divn-USA
AuxGen: 2 x 75kW
Thrusters: 1 Thwart. FP thruster (f)

7733319 **TAYLORS CREEK** *150*
WBS6448 115
\- **JB Bait Co LLC** -
\-
Abbeville, LA *United States of America*
Official number: 586159

1977 at New Bern, NC
L reg 25.43 Br ex - Dght -
Lbp - Br md 8.11 Dpth 2.01
Welded, 1 dk

(B11B2FV) Fishing Vessel

1 oil engine driving 1 FP propeller
Total Power: 537kW (730hp)

9525895 **TAYMA** **141,077** Class: LR (GL)
9HA2989 75,670 **100A1** SS 03/2012
\- **Tayma Ltd** 145,451 container ship
United Arab Shipping Co (UASC) **ShipRight** (SDA, FDA)
Valletta *Malta* *IWS
MMSI: 229009000 LI
Official number: 9525895 ECO (TOC)
LMC **UMS**
Cable: 770.0/122.0 U3 (a)

2012-03 Samsung Heavy Industries Co Ltd — Geoje Yd No: 1880
Loa 366.05 (BB) Br ex 48.33 Dght 15.500
Lbp 349.50 Br md 48.20 Dpth 29.80
Welded, 1 dk

(A33A2CC) Container Ship (Fully Cellular)
TEU 13296 C Ho 6428 Teu C Dk 6868 TEU incl 1000 ref C
Compartments: 7 Cell Ho, ER

1 oil engine driving 1 FP propeller
Total Power: 71,770kW (97,578hp) 24.1kn
MAN-B&W 12K98ME7
1 x 2 Stroke 12 Cy. 980 x 2660 71770kW (97578bhp)
Doosan Engine Co Ltd-South Korea
AuxGen: 4 x 4250kW 6600V 60Hz a.c, 1 x 3800kW 6600V 60Hz a.c, 2 x 7000kW 6600V 60Hz a.c
Boilers: e (ex.g.) 7.6kgf/cm² (7.5bar), e (ex.g.) 13.8kgf/cm² (13.5bar), WTAuxB (o.f.) 8.2kgf/cm² (8.0bar)
Thrusters: 1 Thwart. CP thruster (f)
Fuel: 344.0 (d.f.) 12258.0 (r.f.)

9556507 **TAYMEN** **272** Class: RS
UBVF3 81
\- **JSC 'Transportno-Logisticheskiy Kompleks'** 118
\-
St Petersburg *Russia*
MMSI: 273336230

2009-09 OAO Leningradskiy Sudostroitelnyy Zavod 'Pella' — Otradnoye Yd No: 611
Loa 28.50 Br ex 9.80 Dght 3.500
Lbp 26.50 Br md 9.50 Dpth 4.80
Welded, 1 dk

(B32A2ST) Tug
Ice Capable

2 oil engines reduction geared to sc. shafts driving 2 Directional propellers
Total Power: 2,982kW (4,054hp)
Caterpillar 3516B
2 x Vee 4 Stroke 16 Cy. 170 x 190 each-1491kW (2027bhp)
Caterpillar Inc-USA
AuxGen: 2 x 83kW a.c

7640885 *UGQB* -	**TAYMEN** - **JSC Yuzhmorryblot** - *Nakhodka* *Russia* Official number: 762427	**172** 51 88	Class: RS	**1976-09 Zavod 'Nikolayevsk-na-Amure' — Nikolayevsk-na-Amure** Yd No: 145 Loa 33.97 Br ex 7.09 Dght 2.900 Lbp 29.97 Br md 7.00 Dpth 3.65 Welded, 1 dk	**(B11B2FV) Fishing Vessel** Bale: 115 Compartments: 1 Ho, ER 1 Ha: (1.3 x 1.6) Derricks: 2x2t; Winches: 2 Ice Capable	**1 oil engine** driving 1 FP propeller Total Power: 224kW (305hp) 9.5kn S.K.L. 8NVD36-1U 1 x 4 Stroke 8 Cy. 240 x 360 224kW (305bhp) VEB Schwermaschinenbau "KarlLiebknecht" (SKL)-Magdeburg AuxGen: 1 x 86kW, 1 x 60kW Fuel: 20.0 (d.f.)
6862319 - -	**TAYMEN** *ex* RS-5299 Taymen *-1972* - -	*120* 32 72	Class: (RS)	**1958 VEB Ernst Thaelmann-Werft — Brandenburg** Yd No: 5299 Loa 29.35 Br ex 6.29 Dght 2.440 Lbp 25.50 Br md - Dpth 3.00 Welded	**(B11B2FV) Fishing Vessel** Ice Capable	**1 oil engine** driving 1 FP propeller
8417481 *UEMM* -	**TAYMYR** **Government of The Russian Federation** Federal State Unitary Enterprise 'Atomflot' SatCom: Inmarsat A 1400635 *Murmansk* *Russia* MMSI: 273135100	**20,791** 6,237 3,581	Class: RS	**1989-06 Wartsila Marine Industries Inc — Helsinki (Helsingin Telakka)** Yd No: 474 Loa 149.70 Br ex 29.20 Dght 9.000 Lbp 136.32 Br md 28.87 Dpth 15.68 Welded	**(B34C2SI) Icebreaker** Cranes: 1x20t,1x16t,1x12t,1x10t Ice Capable	**3 diesel electric oil engines & 2 turbo electric Steam Turbs** driving 2 gen. each 18400kW 6300V a.c 3 gen. each 2320kW 6300V a.c Connecting to 3 elec. motors each (12000kW) driving 3 FP propellers Total Power: 43,880kW (59,661hp) 18.2kn Wartsila 6R22 3 x 4 Stroke 6 Cy. 220 x 240 each-2360kW (3209bhp) Wartsila Diesel Oy-Finland Russkiy 2 x steam Turb each-18400kW (25017shp) in the U.S.S.R. AuxGen: 3 x 2432kW 400V 50Hz a.c, 2 x 2000kW 400V 50Hz a.c Boilers: NR 30.0kgf/cm² (29.4bar) Superheater 300°C 30.0kgf/cm² (29.4bar) Thrusters: 3 Thwart. FP thruster (a) Fuel: 900.0 (d.f.)
8931762 *UCSQ* -	**TAYMYR** **MASCO JSC (ZAO 'Malaya Sudokhodnaya Kompaniya')** - *Murmansk* *Russia*	**277** 83 83	Class: RS	**1969-05 Brodogradiliste 'Tito' — Belgrade** Yd No: 235 Loa 35.43 Br ex 9.21 Dght 3.170 Lbp 30.00 Br md 9.00 Dpth 4.50 Welded, 1 dk	**(B32A2ST) Tug** Ice Capable	**2 oil engines** geared to sc. shaft driving 1 CP propeller Total Power: 1,704kW (2,316hp) 13.7kn B&W 7-26MTBF-40 2 x 4 Stroke 7 Cy. 260 x 400 each-852kW (1158bhp) Titovi Zavodi 'Litostroj'-Yugoslavia AuxGen: 2 x 100kW a.c, 1 x 20kW Fuel: 51.0 (d.f.)
7127730 *UAYI* -	**TAYOZHNIK** **OOO 'Nemusco'** - *Nakhodka* *Russia* MMSI: 273434560	**177** 53 112	Class: (RS)	**1971 Sretenskiy Sudostroitelnyy Zavod — Sretensk** Yd No: 32 Loa 33.91 Br ex 7.09 Dght 2.901 Lbp 30.00 Br md - Dpth 3.69 Welded, 1 dk	**(B11B2FV) Fishing Vessel** Bale: 114 Compartments: 1 Ho, ER 1 Ha: (1.6 x 1.3) Derricks: 2x2t Ice Capable	**1 oil engine** driving 1 FP propeller 9.0kn S.K.L. 1 x 4 Stroke 8 Cy. 240 x 360 VEB Schwermaschinenbau "KarlLiebknecht" (SKL)-Magdeburg Fuel: 17.0 (d.f.)
7829144 - - -	**TAYRONA** *ex* Tona *-2003* *ex* Skareholmen *-2003* *ex* Proef 11 *-2003* *ex* Hinrich Popp *-2003* *ex* Paul Radmann *-2003* - -	*249* 113 -		**1906 Schiffswerft, Maschinenfabrik und Trockendok G Seebeck AG — Bremerhaven** Yd No: 235 Lengthened-1961 Loa 42.40 Br ex 6.71 Dght - Lbp - Br md - Dpth - Welded, 1 dk	**(B11B2FV) Fishing Vessel**	**1 oil engine** driving 1 FP propeller Total Power: 364kW (495hp) Normo RTG-8 1 x 4 Stroke 8 Cy. 250 x 360 364kW (495bhp) (made 1957, fitted 1967) AS Bergens Mek Verksteder-Norway
9675236 *HO9047*	**TAYRONA** **Remolcadores Ultratug Ltda** - *Panama* *Panama* Official number: 44531PEXT	**455** 136 285	Class: AB	**2014-01 SIMA Serv. Ind. de la Marina Callao (SIMAC) — Callao** Yd No: 1251 Loa 30.00 Br ex - Dght 3.800 Lbp 28.00 Br md 12.00 Dpth 5.50 Welded, 1 dk	**(B32A2ST) Tug**	**2 oil engines** reduction geared to sc. shafts driving 2 Propellers Total Power: 3,788kW (5,150hp) 12.0kn Caterpillar 3516C-HD 2 x Vee 4 Stroke 16 Cy. 170 x 215 each-1894kW (2575bhp) Caterpillar Inc-USA
9140126 *5ATK* -	**TAZERBO** **General National Maritime Transport Co (GNMTC)** - SatCom: Inmarsat B 364200010 *Tripoli* *Libya* MMSI: 642136026 Official number: TP913	**2,928** 894 3,210	Class: NK	**1996-12 Kanrei Zosen K.K. — Naruto** Yd No: 372 Loa 96.00 (BB) Br ex - Dght 5.200 Lbp 89.50 Br md 15.00 Dpth 7.00 Welded, 1 dk	**(A11B2TG) LPG Tanker** Double Bottom Entire Compartment Length Liq (Gas): 3,312 Cargo Heating Coils 2 x Gas Tank (s); 2 independent (C.mn.stl) cyl horizontal 2 Cargo Pump (s): 2x300m³/hr Manifold: Bow/CM: 42m	**1 oil engine** driving 1 FP propeller Total Power: 2,405kW (3,270hp) 13.5kn B&W 6S26MC 1 x 2 Stroke 6 Cy. 260 x 980 2405kW (3270bhp) Makita Corp-Japan AuxGen: 3 x 240kW 445V a.c Fuel: 82.8 (d.f.) (Heating Coils) 354.4 (r.f.) 8.3pd
7304467 *CNME* -	**TAZIA 1** *ex* Tisli *-1994* *ex* Playa del Ingles *-1979* **Societe Pecatlan SA** Fomento del Mar (FOMAR) SatCom: Inmarsat C 424223810 *Agadir* *Morocco* Official number: 8-510	*229* 109 -	Class: (BV)	**1973-07 Ast. Neptuno — Valencia** Yd No: 52 Loa 31.63 Br ex 6.99 Dght 3.180 Lbp 26.95 Br md 6.82 Dpth 3.71 Welded, 1 dk	**(B11A2FS) Stern Trawler**	**1 oil engine** driving 1 CP propeller Total Power: 485kW (659hp) 10.5kn Poyaud A12150SRHM 1 x Vee 4 Stroke 12 Cy. 150 x 180 485kW (659bhp) Societe Surgerienne de ConstructionMecaniques-France Fuel: 76.5 (d.f.)
7424205 *CNNM*	**TAZIA 2** *ex* Tildi *-1995* *ex* Playa de Arinaga *-1980* **Societe Pecatlan SA** Fomento del Mar (FOMAR) SatCom: Inmarsat C 424223910 *Agadir* *Morocco* Official number: 8-511	*219* 89 157	Class: (BV)	**1975-11 Ast. de Huelva S.A. — Huelva** Yd No: 71 Loa 33.18 Br ex - Dght 3.420 Lbp 28.50 Br md 6.96 Dpth 3.70 Welded, 2 dks	**(B11A2FS) Stern Trawler**	**1 oil engine** reduction geared to sc. shaft driving 1 FP propeller Total Power: 515kW (700hp) 10.5kn GUASCOR E318TA.2-SP 1 x Vee 4 Stroke 12 Cy. 150 x 150 515kW (700bhp) (new engine 1990) Gutierrez Ascunce Corp (GUASCOR)-Spain Fuel: 100.0 (d.f.)
8600234 *5TTDB* -	**TAZIAZET - 1** *ex* Sjannoy *-2012* *ex* Sjarmor *-2008* *ex* Linholm Junior *-1993* *ex* Sea Star *-1989* *ex* Frisco Star *-1988* **IPR Mauritania SARL** - *Nouadhibou* *Mauritania* MMSI: 654045800	**190** 76 -	Class: (NV)	**1985-08 E. Furnes & Sonner Baatservice — Sovik** (Hull) Yd No: 8 **1985-08 Orjavik Industrier AS — Lyngstad** Yd No: 2 Loa 27.28 Br ex - Dght 3.900 Lbp 22.20 Br md 6.61 Dpth - Welded, 2 dks	**(B11B2FV) Fishing Vessel**	**2 oil engines** geared to sc. shafts driving 2 FP propellers Total Power: 588kW (800hp) Fiat 8281SRM 2 x Vee 4 Stroke 8 Cy. 145 x 130 each-294kW (400bhp) SA Fiat SGM-Torino AuxGen: 2 x 232kW 380V 50Hz a.c Thrusters: 1 Thwart. CP thruster (f); 1 Tunnel thruster (a)
7512284 *CNED* -	**TAZZEKA** *ex* Almudena Rosal *-1987* **Societe Shrimps Fisheries** - *Morocco*	*286* 135 155	Class: (BV)	**1976-12 Ast. de Huelva S.A. — Huelva** Yd No: 19 Loa 38.66 Br ex 7.24 Dght 3.450 Lbp 33.30 Br md 7.23 Dpth 3.92 Welded, 1 dk	**(B11A2FS) Stern Trawler**	**1 oil engine** driving 1 FP propeller Total Power: 861kW (1,171hp) 11.5kn S.K.L. 8NVD48A-2 1 x 4 Stroke 8 Cy. 320 x 480 861kW (1171bhp) VEB Schwermaschinenbau "KarlLiebknecht" (SKL)-Magdeburg Fuel: 125.0 (d.f.)
8660832 *YD3831* -	**TB. AME II** *ex* Ame II *-2013* **PT Anggun Maritim Esajaya** - *Batam* *Indonesia*	**259** 78 248	Class: RI (GL)	**2011-04 P.T. Bandar Victory Shipyard — Batam** Yd No: H-259 Loa 29.00 Br ex - Dght 3.590 Lbp 27.18 Br md 8.60 Dpth 4.10 Welded, 1 dk	**(B32A2ST) Tug**	**2 oil engines** reduction geared to sc. shaft (s) driving 2 FP propellers Total Power: 1,492kW (2,028hp) Caterpillar C32 ACERT 2 x Vee 4 Stroke 12 Cy. 145 x 162 each-746kW (1014bhp) Caterpillar Inc-USA
9674957 - -	**TB BUMA OPALS** *ex* Berjaya 80 *-2013* **PT Surya Bahau Mandiri** - *Samarinda* *Indonesia*	**253** 76 276	Class: KI (Class contemplated)	**2013-09 Berjaya Dockyard Sdn Bhd — Miri** Yd No: 80 Loa 28.09 Br ex - Dght 3.600 Lbp 25.47 Br md 8.54 Dpth 4.30 Welded, 1 dk	**(B32A2ST) Tug**	**2 oil engines** reduction geared to sc. shafts driving 2 Propellers Total Power: 1,640kW (2,230hp) Caterpillar C32 2 x Vee 4 Stroke 12 Cy. 145 x 162 each-820kW (1115bhp) Caterpillar Inc-USA

IMO / Call sign	Name / Owner	Tonnage	Class	Builder / Dimensions	Type	Machinery
9662784 - -	**TB FLORES 1** - **PT Andalan Mitra Bahari** - *Batam* *Indonesia*	**265** 78 287	Class: NK	**2012**-09 **SL Shipbuilding Contractor Sdn Bhd — Sibu** Yd No: 153 Loa 30.20 Br ex 8.62 Dght 3.510 Lbp 27.82 Br md 8.60 Dpth 4.20 Welded, 1 dk	**(B32A2ST) Tug**	**2 oil engines** reduction geared to sc. shafts driving 2 Propellers Total Power: 1,518kW (2,064hp) Mitsubishi S6R2-MTK3L 2 x 4 Stroke 6 Cy. 170 x 220 each-759kW (1032bhp) Mitsubishi Heavy Industries Ltd-Japan Fuel: 220.0 (d.f.)
9662772 *YDA3152* -	**TB NUNUKAN 1** - **PT Andalan Mitra Bahari** - *Batam* *Indonesia*	**260** 78 287	Class: NK	**2012**-09 **SL Shipbuilding Contractor Sdn Bhd — Sibu** Yd No: 152 Loa 30.20 Br ex 8.62 Dght 3.510 Lbp 27.21 Br md 8.60 Dpth 4.20 Welded, 1 dk	**(B32A2ST) Tug**	**2 oil engines** reduction geared to sc. shafts driving 2 Propellers Total Power: 1,518kW (2,064hp) Mitsubishi S6R2-MTK3L 2 x 4 Stroke 6 Cy. 170 x 220 each-759kW (1032bhp) Mitsubishi Heavy Industries Ltd-Japan Fuel: 220.0 (d.f.)
9662796 *YDA3245* -	**TB NUSA PENINDA 1** - **PT Andalan Mitra Bahari** - *Batam* *Indonesia*	**263** 79 288	Class: NK	**2012**-11 **SL Shipbuilding Contractor Sdn Bhd — Sibu** Yd No: 154 Loa 30.20 Br ex 8.62 Dght 3.512 Lbp 27.82 Br md 8.60 Dpth 4.20 Welded, 1 dk	**(B32A2ST) Tug**	**2 oil engines** reduction geared to sc. shafts driving 2 FP propellers Total Power: 1,518kW (2,064hp) Mitsubishi S6R2-MTK3L 2 x 4 Stroke 6 Cy. 170 x 220 each-759kW (1032bhp) Mitsubishi Heavy Industries Ltd-Japan AuxGen: 2 x 155kW a.c Fuel: 225.0
6408228 *HO6268* -	**TB SAROSA** *ex* Aspa Power 16 *-2000* *ex* Su Ying *-1983* *ex* Fuji III *-1980* *ex* Seika Maru *-1980* **Andalas Sarosa Line SA** - *Panama* *Panama* Official number: 8963PEXT4	*299* 76 -	Class: (BV)	**1964 Mitsubishi Zosen K.K. — Shimonoseki** Yd No: 595 Loa 32.21 Br ex 9.68 Dght 3.150 Lbp 30.23 Br md 9.61 Dpth 4.40 Welded	**(B32A2ST) Tug**	**2 oil engines** driving 2 CP propellers Total Power: 2,206kW (3,000hp) 12.5kn Ito A2216VIS 2 x Vee 4 Stroke 16 Cy. 220 x 340 each-1103kW (1500bhp) Ito Tekkosho-Japan Fuel: 43.5
9662576 *YDA3246* -	**TB SINGKAWANG 1** - **PT Andalan Mitra Bahari** - *Batam* *Indonesia*	**263** 79 292	Class: NK	**2012**-12 **Tang Tiew Hee & Sons Sdn Bhd — Sibu** Yd No: 63 Loa 30.20 Br ex 8.62 Dght 3.512 Lbp 27.82 Br md 8.60 Dpth 4.20 Welded, 1 dk	**(B32A2ST) Tug**	**2 oil engines** reduction geared to sc. shafts driving 2 FP propellers Total Power: 1,518kW (2,064hp) Mitsubishi S6R2-MTK3L 2 x 4 Stroke 6 Cy. 170 x 220 each-759kW (1032bhp) Mitsubishi Heavy Industries Ltd-Japan Fuel: 220.0
9662588 *YDA3244* -	**TB TAYAN 1** - **PT Andalan Mitra Bahari** - *Batam* *Indonesia*	**263** 79 292	Class: NK	**2013**-01 **Tang Tiew Hee & Sons Sdn Bhd — Sibu** Yd No: 64 Loa 30.20 Br ex 8.62 Dght 3.512 Lbp 27.82 Br md 8.60 Dpth 4.20 Welded, 1 dk	**(B32A2ST) Tug**	**2 oil engines** reduction geared to sc. shafts driving 2 FP propellers Total Power: 1,518kW (2,064hp) Mitsubishi S6R2-MTK3L 2 x 4 Stroke 6 Cy. 170 x 220 each-759kW (1032bhp) Mitsubishi Heavy Industries Ltd-Japan Fuel: 220.0
5160219 *HP7773* -	**TB VIRGINIA** *ex* Muria *-2012* *ex* GP America *-2002* *ex* Independent II *-2002* **Virginia Towage Inc** Total Ship BV (Sim Scheepvaart NV) *Panama* *Panama* MMSI: 373726000 Official number: 43611PEXT	**128** 38 45	Class: (BV)	**1960 Scheepsw. en Ghbw. v/h Jonker & Stans N.V. — Hendrik-Ido-Ambacht** Yd No: 288 Loa 29.21 Br ex 6.94 Dght 3.010 Lbp 27.01 Br md 6.90 Dpth 3.51 Welded, 1 dk	**(B32A2ST) Tug**	**2 oil engines** geared to sc. shaft driving 1 FP propeller Total Power: 662kW (900hp) 12.0kn Bolnes 6DL75/475 2 x 2 Stroke 6 Cy. 190 x 350 each-331kW (450bhp) NV Machinefabriek 'Bolnes' v/h JHvan Cappellen-Netherlands AuxGen: 1 x 3kW 24V d.c, 1 x 1kW 24V d.c
9489833 *3FUE5* -	**TBC PRESTIGE** *ex* Oel Prestige *-2014* **Orient Express Lines Inc** Orient Express Ship Management Ltd *Panama* *Panama* MMSI: 372812000 Official number: 45431PEXT	**19,999** 10,443 31,956 T/cm 45.3	Class: NV	**2014**-01 **Guangzhou Wenchong Shipyard Co Ltd — Guangzhou GD** Yd No: 402 Loa 176.50 (BB) Br ex 27.05 Dght 10.000 Lbp 171.00 Br md 27.00 Dpth 14.20 Welded, 1 dk	**(A21A2BC) Bulk Carrier** Grain: 40,442; Bale: 39,882 Cranes: 4x30t	**1 oil engine** driving 1 FP propeller Total Power: 6,386kW (8,682hp) 14.0kn MAN-B&W 6S42MC7 1 x 2 Stroke 6 Cy. 420 x 1764 6386kW (8682bhp) Hudong Heavy Machinery Co Ltd-China AuxGen: 3 x 560kW 450V 60Hz a.c
9606871 *3FM09* -	**TBC PRINCESS** - **Orient Express Lines Inc** Orient Express Ship Management Ltd *Panama* *Panama* MMSI: 370215000 Official number: 45003PEXT	**19,999** 10,443 31,963 T/cm 45.3	Class: NV	**2013**-11 **Guangzhou Wenchong Shipyard Co Ltd — Guangzhou GD** Yd No: 422 Loa 176.50 Br ex 27.05 Dght 10.000 Lbp 171.00 Br md 27.00 Dpth 14.20 Welded, 1 dk	**(A21A2BC) Bulk Carrier** Grain: 40,442; Bale: 39,882 Compartments: 5 Ho, ER 5 Ha: 4 (15.6 x 20.0)ER (15.6 x 16.5) Cranes: 4x30t	**1 oil engine** driving 1 FP propeller Total Power: 6,480kW (8,810hp) 14.3kn MAN-B&W 6S42MC7 1 x 2 Stroke 6 Cy. 420 x 1764 6480kW (8810bhp) AuxGen: 3 x a.c
9489821 *3FKB2* -	**TBC PROGRESS** *ex* Oel Progress *-2012* **Orient Express Lines Inc** Orient Express Ship Management Ltd *Panama* *Panama* MMSI: 373605000 Official number: 4457713	**19,999** 10,443 32,306 T/cm 45.3	Class: NV	**2012**-10 **Guangzhou Wenchong Shipyard Co Ltd — Guangzhou GD** Yd No: 401 Loa 176.50 (BB) Br ex - Dght 10.000 Lbp 171.00 Br md 27.00 Dpth 14.20 Welded, 1 dk	**(A21A2BC) Bulk Carrier** Grain: 40,442; Bale: 39,882 Compartments: 5 Ho, ER 5 Ha: (18.4 x 16.2)3 (19.2 x 16.2)ER (15.2 x 14.6) Cranes: 4x30t	**1 oil engine** driving 1 FP propeller Total Power: 6,480kW (8,810hp) 14.3kn MAN-B&W 6S42MC 1 x 2 Stroke 6 Cy. 420 x 1764 6480kW (8810bhp) Hudong Heavy Machinery Co Ltd-China AuxGen: 3 x 560kW 450V 60Hz a.c
9084358 *YDII* -	**TBI JAYA** *ex* Teruho Maru No. 12 *-2012* *ex* A Coop No. 8 *-2004* **PT Nusantara Jaya Line** - *Jakarta* *Indonesia*	**643** 239 700	Class: KI	**1994**-06 **Shinhama Dockyard Co. Ltd. — Tamano** Yd No: 262 Loa 57.60 Br ex - Dght 3.300 Lbp 53.65 Br md 9.50 Dpth 5.58 Welded, 1 dk	**(A31A2GX) General Cargo Ship** Grain: 1,353; Bale: 1,317 Compartments: 1 Ho, ER 1 Ha: (30.3 x 7.2)ER	**1 oil engine** driving 1 FP propeller Total Power: 662kW (900hp) 12.0kn Hanshin LH28G 1 x 4 Stroke 6 Cy. 280 x 460 662kW (900bhp) The Hanshin Diesel Works Ltd-Japan
9666687 *YDA3158* -	**TBM 1** - **PT Trisakti Bahari Mandiri** - *Batam* *Indonesia* MMSI: 525003160 Official number: GT.194 No.4200Ppm	**194** 159 -	Class: BV KI	**2012**-08 **PT BH Marine & Offshore Engineering — Batam** Yd No: T004 Loa 29.00 Br ex - Dght 3.100 Lbp 26.00 Br md 8.00 Dpth 3.70 Welded, 1 dk	**(B32A2ST) Tug**	**2 oil engines** reduction geared to sc. shafts driving 2 FP propellers Total Power: 970kW (1,318hp) Yanmar 6AYM-WST 1 x 4 Stroke 6 Cy. 155 x 180 485kW (659bhp) Yanmar Diesel Engine Co Ltd-Japan AuxGen: 2 x 26kW 50Hz a.c Fuel: 150.0 (d.f.)
8127385 - -	**TBS STONEBRIGHT** *ex* Hamilton Tide *-1989* **Point Marine LLC** Tidewater Marine International Inc	*744* 223 1,200	Class: AB	**1982**-01 **Halter Marine, Inc. — Moss Point, Ms** Yd No: 1004 Loa 58.68 Br ex - Dght 3.901 Lbp 54.11 Br md 12.20 Dpth 4.58 Welded, 1 dk	**(B21B20A) Anchor Handling Tug Supply**	**2 oil engines** dr reverse geared to sc. shafts driving 2 FP propellers Total Power: 3,390kW (4,610hp) 13.0kn EMD (Electro-Motive) 12-645-E7B 2 x Vee 2 Stroke 12 Cy. 230 x 254 each-1695kW (2305bhp) General Motors Corp.Electro-Motive Div.-La Grange AuxGen: 2 x 150kW 450V 60Hz a.c Thrusters: 1 Thwart. FP thruster (f) Fuel: 349.0 (d.f.) 16.0pd
8893221 - -	**TC-61** - - - *China*	**168** 55 -	Class: (VR)	**1987 in the People's Republic of China** Loa - Br ex - Dght 2.850 Lbp 27.70 Br md 6.90 Dpth 3.90 Welded, 1 dk	**(B11B2FV) Fishing Vessel**	**3 oil engines** reduction geared to sc. shafts driving 3 FP propellers Total Power: 209kW (284hp)
8893219 - -	**TC-62** - - - *China*	**168** 55 -	Class: (VR)	**1986 in the People's Republic of China** Loa - Br ex - Dght 2.850 Lbp 29.86 Br md 6.95 Dpth 3.85 Welded, 1 dk	**(B11B2FV) Fishing Vessel**	**3 oil engines** reduction geared to sc. shafts driving 3 FP propellers Total Power: 209kW (284hp)
8893269 - -	**TC-66** - - - *China*	**171** 60 -	Class: (VR)	**1986 in the People's Republic of China** Loa - Br ex - Dght 2.500 Lbp 28.00 Br md 7.20 Dpth 3.50 Welded, 1 dk	**(B11B2FV) Fishing Vessel**	**3 oil engines** reduction geared to sc. shafts driving 3 FP propellers Total Power: 426kW (580hp) AuxGen: 1 x 72kW a.c

Ship	Tonnage / Class	Build & Dimensions	Type & Capacity	Machinery
8893207 **TC-68** - - - - - *China*	**196** Class: (VR) 69 -	**1984 in the People's Republic of China** Loa - Br ex - Dght - Lbp 33.20 Br md 7.00 Dpth 3.90 Welded, 1 dk	**(B11B2FV) Fishing Vessel**	**3 oil engines** reduction geared to sc. shafts driving 3 FP propellers Total Power: 209kW (284hp)
8893192 **TC-69** - - - - - *China*	**152** Class: (VR) 53 -	**1981 in the People's Republic of China** Loa - Br ex - Dght 2.800 Lbp 27.10 Br md 6.80 Dpth 3.70 Welded, 1 dk	**(B11B2FV) Fishing Vessel**	**3 oil engines** reduction geared to sc. shafts driving 3 FP propellers Total Power: 209kW (284hp) AuxGen: 1 x 79kW a.c
8116556 **TC 81** - - **Marine Dredging Co No II (MADREDCO No 2) (Cong Ty Nao Vet Duong Bien So II)** - *Haiphong* *Vietnam*	**1,098** Class: VR (BV) 329 410	**1983-01 Dubigeon-Normandie S.A. — Prairie-au-Duc, Nantes** (Hull launched by) Yd No: 2568 **1983-01 Soc. des At. Francais de l'Ouest — Grand Quevilly** (Hull completed by) Loa 71.30 Br ex 13.52 Dght 2.400 Lbp 58.70 Br md 13.21 Dpth 4.02 Welded, 1 dk	**(B33A2DB) Bucket Ladder Dredger**	**2 oil engines** with clutches, flexible couplings & sr reverse geared to sc. shafts driving 2 FP propellers Total Power: 1,088kW (1,480hp) Crepelle 8PSN3L 2 x 4 Stroke 8 Cy. 260 x 320 each-544kW (740bhp) Crepelle et Cie-France AuxGen: 2 x 560kW 380V a.c, 1 x 250kW 380V a.c Fuel: 240.0
8116568 **TC 82** *XVHI* - **Vietnam Waterway Construction Corp (VINAWACO)** - *Haiphong* *Vietnam* Official number: VN-1232-VT	**1,098** Class: VR (BV) 329 410	**1983-06 Soc. des At. Francais de l'Ouest — Grand Quevilly** Yd No: 2569 Loa 69.80 Br ex 13.52 Dght 2.400 Lbp 58.70 Br md 13.21 Dpth 4.02 Welded, 1 dk	**(B33A2DB) Bucket Ladder Dredger**	**2 oil engines** with clutches, flexible couplings & sr reverse geared to sc. shafts driving 2 FP propellers Total Power: 1,088kW (1,480hp) Crepelle 8PSN3L 2 x 4 Stroke 8 Cy. 260 x 320 each-544kW (740bhp) Crepelle et Cie-France AuxGen: 2 x 376kW 380V a.c, 2 x 216kW 380V a.c Fuel: 240.0
9425942 **TC GOLD** *3FJG9* - **Hakuyo Kisen Co Ltd & Helmstar Shipping SA** Filharmony Shipmanagement Inc SatCom: Inmarsat C 435297011 *Panama* *Panama* MMSI: 352970000 Official number: 4236111	**32,287** Class: NK 19,458 58,096 T/cm 57.4	**2011-01 Tsuneishi Heavy Industries (Cebu) Inc — Balamban** Yd No: SC-127 Loa 189.99 (BB) Br ex - Dght 12.830 Lbp 185.60 Br md 32.26 Dpth 18.00 Welded, 1 dk	**(A21A2BC) Bulk Carrier** Grain: 72,689; Bale: 70,122 Compartments: 5 Ho, ER 5 Ha: ER Cranes: 4x30t	**1 oil engine** driving 1 FP propeller Total Power: 8,450kW (11,489hp) 14.5kn MAN-B&W 6S50MC-C 1 x 2 Stroke 6 Cy. 500 x 2000 8450kW (11489bhp) Mitsui Engineering & Shipbuilding CLtd-Japan Fuel: 2389.0 (r.f.)
9010527 **TCHILASSI** - - - *Pointe Noire* *Congo*	*120* - -	**1989-08 Master Marine, Inc. — Bayou La Batre, Al** Loa - Br ex - Dght - Lbp 23.47 Br md 6.72 Dpth - Welded	**(B11A2FS) Stern Trawler**	**1 oil engine** geared to sc. shaft driving 1 FP propeller Total Power: 530kW (721hp) Caterpillar 3412T 1 x Vee 4 Stroke 12 Cy. 137 x 152 530kW (721bhp) Caterpillar Inc-USA
8429989 **TCHING YE No. 236** *HQHH5* - **Lubmain International SA** - *San Lorenzo* *Honduras* Official number: L-1923616	**726** 275 -	**1990 Jong Shyn Shipbuilding Co., Ltd. — Kaohsiung** L reg 47.80 Br ex - Dght 2.270 Lbp - Br md 8.90 Dpth 3.85 Welded, 1 dk	**(B11B2FV) Fishing Vessel**	**1 oil engine** driving 1 FP propeller Total Power: 1,030kW (1,400hp) 13.0kn
9195236 **TCI PRABHU** *AVLD* - *ex* Ann-Sofie Scan *-2011* *ex* Forum Avarua *-2010* *ex* Ann-Sofie Scan *-2009* *ex* Skagen *-2005* *launched as* Ile de France *-1999* **TCI Seaways (A Division of Transport Corp of India Ltd)** - SatCom: Inmarsat C 441923133 *Mumbai* *India* MMSI: 419000289 Official number: 3829	**2,545** Class: IR (GL) 1,372 3,490	**1999-03 Slovenske Lodenice a.s. — Komarno** Yd No: 1421 Loa 86.40 (BB) Br ex 13.00 Dght 5.546 Lbp - Br md 12.80 Dpth 7.10 Welded, 1 dk	**(A31A2GX) General Cargo Ship** Double Hull Grain: 4,677; Bale: 4,620 TEU 167 C Ho 105 TEU C Dk 62 TEU. Compartments: 1 Ho, ER 1 Ha: (56.6 x 10.2)ER Cranes: 2x35t Ice Capable	**1 oil engine** reduction geared to sc. shaft driving 1 CP propeller Total Power: 1,800kW (2,447hp) 12.0kn MaK 6M25 1 x 4 Stroke 6 Cy. 255 x 400 1800kW (2447bhp) MaK Motoren GmbH & Co. KG-Kiel AuxGen: 1 x 376kW 220/380V a.c, 2 x 210kW 220/380V a.c Thrusters: 1 Tunnel thruster (f) Fuel: 170.0 (d.f.)
9148245 **TCI SURYA** *AURC* - *ex* Merwediep *-2007* *ex* Santa Luzia *-2002* *ex* Merwediep *-1998* **TCI Seaways (A Division of Transport Corp of India Ltd)** - *Mumbai* *India* MMSI: 419659000 Official number: 3339	**3,620** Class: IR (LR) 1,920 ✠ Classed LR until 22/4/08 4,513 T/cm 13.5	**1998-04 Scheepswerf Pattje B.V. — Waterhuizen** Yd No: 398 Loa 98.25 (BB) Br ex 15.66 Dght 5.650 Lbp 92.08 Br md 15.40 Dpth 7.35 Welded, 1 dk	**(A31A2GX) General Cargo Ship** Grain: 6,796 TEU 323 C.Ho 137/20' (40') C.Dk 186/20' (40') incl. 60 ref C. Compartments: 1 Ho, ER 2 Ha: (39.0 x 12.9)Tappered (25.5 x 12.9)ER Cranes: 2x40t	**1 oil engine** with flexible couplings & sr gearedto sc. shaft driving 1 CP propeller Total Power: 3,000kW (4,079hp) 15.0kn MaK 8M32C 1 x 4 Stroke 8 Cy. 320 x 480 3000kW (4079bhp) MaK Motoren GmbH & Co. KG-Kiel AuxGen: 1 x 560kW 440V 60Hz a.c, 3 x 300kW 440V 60Hz a.c Boilers: HWH (o.f.) 4.1kgf/cm² (4.0bar) Thrusters: 1 Thwart. FP thruster (f) Fuel: 52.0 (d.f.) 352.0 (r.f.)
8331962 **TCI XPS** *AUCA* - *ex* Tavake Oma *-2002* *ex* Southern Moana II *-2001* *ex* Tavake Oma *-1999* *ex* Princess Cathryn *-1999* *ex* Campbell *-1997* *ex* Feng Shun *-1994* *ex* Alex *-1993* **TCI Seaways (A Division of Transport Corp of India Ltd)** - *Mumbai* *India* MMSI: 419466000 Official number: 3012	**2,887** Class: IR (LR) (RI) (CC) 1,588 Classed LR until 28/1/04 4,463	**1984-06 Cant. Nav. Ugo Codecasa S.p.A. — Viareggio** Yd No: 42 Loa 83.32 (BB) Br ex 14.81 Dght 7.180 Lbp 75.90 Br md 14.80 Dpth 8.80 Welded, 1 dk	**(A31A2GX) General Cargo Ship** Grain: 5,238; Bale: 4,530 Compartments: 1 Ho, ER 1 Ha: ER	**1 oil engine** with flexible couplings & sr geared to sc. shaft driving 1 CP propeller Total Power: 2,729kW (3,710hp) Wartsila 8R32 1 x 4 Stroke 8 Cy. 320 x 350 2729kW (3710bhp) Oy Wartsila Ab-Finland AuxGen: 3 x 232kW 380V 50Hz a.c, 1 x 260kW 380V 50Hz a.c Boilers: e (ex.g.), AuxB (o.f.) Thrusters: 1 Thwart. FP thruster (f) Fuel: 7.0 (d.f.)
9559121 **TCL 4401** *9V8287* - **Daiho Energy Services Pte Ltd** - *Singapore* *Singapore* MMSI: 564907000 Official number: 395566	**472** Class: AB (BV) 141 -	**2009-09 Sapor Shipbuilding Industries Sdn Bhd — Sibu** Yd No: S26/2007 Loa 37.00 Br ex - Dght 4.050 Lbp 34.66 Br md 11.40 Dpth 4.95 Welded, 1 dk	**(B32A2ST) Tug**	**2 oil engines** reduction geared to sc. shafts driving 2 FP propellers Total Power: 3,432kW (4,666hp) Cummins QSK60-M 2 x Vee 4 Stroke 16 Cy. 159 x 190 each-1716kW (2333bhp) Cummins Engine Co Ltd-United Kingdom AuxGen: 2 x 150kW 50Hz a.c
9699543 **TCP 205** - **PT Transcoal Pacific** - *Samarinda* *Indonesia* Official number: 2013IIkNo.6607/L	**234** Class: KI (Class contemplated) 71 -	**2013-06 PT Mangkapulas Maju Jaya — Samarinda** Yd No: 20-19 Loa 27.01 Br ex - Dght - Lbp - Br md 8.50 Dpth - Welded, 1 dk	**(B32A2ST) Tug**	**2 oil engines** reduction geared to sc. shafts driving 2 Propellers Total Power: 1,518kW (2,064hp) Mitsubishi S6R2-MTK3L 2 x 4 Stroke 6 Cy. 170 x 220 each-759kW (1032bhp) Mitsubishi Heavy Industries Ltd-Japan
9668221 **TCP 1601** - **PT Transcoal Pacific** - *Samarinda* *Indonesia* Official number: GT.175 NO.4974/IIK	**175** Class: KI 53 -	**2012-06 CV Daya Raya Perkasa — Samarinda** Loa 24.94 Br ex - Dght - Lbp - Br md 7.00 Dpth 3.30 Welded, 1 dk	**(B32A2ST) Tug**	**2 oil engines** reduction geared to sc. shafts driving 2 FP propellers Total Power: 1,220kW (1,658hp) Yanmar 2 x each-610kW (829bhp) Yanmar Diesel Engine Co Ltd-Japan
9532434 **TCS DREAM** *DSQH5* - **Transchem Shipping Co Ltd** KS Shipping Co Ltd *Jeju* *South Korea* MMSI: 441578000 Official number: JJR-092127	**2,819** Class: KR 1,042 3,553 T/cm 11.1	**2009-03 Yangzhou Longchuan Shipbuilding Co Ltd — Jiangdu JS** Yd No: LH200701 Loa 93.00 (BB) Br ex 15.02 Dght 5.410 Lbp 87.00 Br md 15.00 Dpth 7.40 Welded, 1 dk	**(A12A2TC) Chemical Tanker** Double Hull (13F) Liq: 3,814 Cargo Heating Coils Compartments: 10 Wing Ta, ER 10 Cargo Pump (s): 10x120m³/hr Manifold: Bow/CM: 47m	**1 oil engine** reduction geared to sc. shaft driving 1 FP propeller Total Power: 1,760kW (2,393hp) 12.7kn MAN-B&W 8L28/32A 1 x 4 Stroke 8 Cy. 280 x 320 1760kW (2393bhp) Zhenjiang Marine Diesel Works-China AuxGen: 3 x 204kW 400V a.c Fuel: 61.0 (d.f.) 205.0 (r.f.)
9138903 **TCT GLORY** *D8BQ* - *ex* KEN Ann Maru *-2012* *ex* Ken Ann *-1998* **TCT Maritime Co Ltd** Se Ha Co Ltd *Jeju* *South Korea* MMSI: 441963000 Official number: JJR-121054	**19,495** Class: KR (NK) 10,622 32,115	**1997-04 Onomichi Dockyard Co Ltd — Onomichi HS** Yd No: 412 Loa 171.60 (BB) Br ex - Dght 10.421 Lbp 163.60 Br md 27.00 Dpth 14.80 Welded, 1 dk	**(A21A2BC) Bulk Carrier** Grain: 41,086; Bale: 39,923 Compartments: 5 Ho, ER 5 Ha: (13.4 x 15.0)4 (19.8 x 18.0)ER Cranes: 4x30t	**1 oil engine** driving 1 FP propeller Total Power: 7,061kW (9,600hp) 14.4kn Mitsubishi 6UEC52LA 1 x 2 Stroke 6 Cy. 520 x 1600 7061kW (9600bhp) Akasaka Tekkosho KK (Akasaka DieselLtd)-Japan Fuel: 1335.0 (r.f.)

IMO / Call sign	Name / Owner	Tonnage	Class	Builder / Dimensions	Type	Machinery
9418810 *TCWN8* -	**TDT-2** **Turker Deniz Tasimaciligi ve Ticaret AS** - SatCom: Inmarsat C 427100754 *Istanbul* *Turkey* MMSI: 271040020	**7,254** 3,653 10,901 T/cm 21.9	Class: BV	**2009-06 Turker Gemi Yapim Sanayi ve Ticaret AS — Basiskele** Yd No: 14 Loa 131.85 (BB) Br ex - Dght 8.100 Lbp 123.99 Br md 18.90 Dpth 10.20 Welded, 1 dk	**(A12B2TR) Chemical/Products Tanker** Double Hull (13F) Liq: 12,685; Liq (Oil): 12,685 Cargo Heating Coils Compartments: 12 Wing Ta, 2 Wing Slop Ta, ER 12 Cargo Pump (s): 12x300m³/hr Manifold: Bow/CM: 65m Ice Capable	**1 oil engine** reduction geared to sc. shaft driving 1 CP propeller Total Power: 4,445kW (6,043hp) 14.5kn MAN-B&W 9L32/40CD 1 x 4 Stroke 9 Cy. 320 x 400 4445kW (6043bhp) MAN B&W Diesel AG-Augsburg AuxGen: 3 x 590kW 440V 60Hz a.c, 1 x 1440kW 440V 60Hz a.c Thrusters: 1 Tunnel thruster (f) Fuel: 95.0 (d.f.) 563.0 (r.f.)
9458119 *TCWY3* -	**TDT-3** *completed as* Ozay-7 *-2009* **Ozayturker Denizcilik AS** - *Istanbul* *Turkey* MMSI: 271040131	**8,197** 3,753 11,490 T/cm 22.0	Class: BV	**2009-09 Dentas Gemi Insaat ve Onarim Sanayii A.S. — Istanbul** Yd No: 92 Loa 130.12 (BB) Br ex - Dght 8.350 Lbp 123.28 Br md 19.60 Dpth 10.90 Welded, 1 dk	**(A12B2TR) Chemical/Products Tanker** Double Hull (13F) Liq: 13,019; Liq (Oil): 13,003 Cargo Heating Coils Compartments: 18 Wing Ta, 2 Wing Slop Ta, ER 18 Cargo Pump (s): 12x200m³/hr, 6x300m³/hr Manifold: Bow/CM: 61.5m Ice Capable	**1 oil engine** reduction geared to sc. shaft driving 1 CP propeller Total Power: 5,400kW (7,342hp) 15.0kn MaK 6M43C 1 x 4 Stroke 6 Cy. 430 x 610 5400kW (7342bhp) Caterpillar Motoren GmbH & Co. KG-Germany AuxGen: 1 x 800kW 450V 60Hz a.c, 3 x 600kW 60Hz a.c Thrusters: 1 Tunnel thruster (f) Fuel: 50.0 (d.f.) 550.0 (r.f.)
9290701 *H3MG* -	**TE HO** **THC International SA** Ta-Ho Maritime Corp *Panama* *Panama* MMSI: 353837000 Official number: 2995604B	**41,372** 26,094 77,000	Class: BV	**2004-06 China Shipbuilding Corp — Keelung** Yd No: 809 Loa 225.00 (BB) Br ex - Dght 14.100 Lbp 217.00 Br md 32.26 Dpth 19.50 Welded, 1 dk	**(A21A2BC) Bulk Carrier** Grain: 92,500 Compartments: 7 Ho, ER 7 Ha: 6 (17.1 x 15.0)ER (17.1 x 13.3)	**1 oil engine** driving 1 FP propeller Total Power: 10,002kW (13,599hp) 14.4kn B&W 6S60MC 1 x 2 Stroke 6 Cy. 600 x 2292 10002kW (13599bhp) Mitsui Engineering & Shipbuilding CLtd-Japan
7356991 - -	**TE KOTUKU** - - *Apia* *Samoa*	*170* 128 -		**1974-09 Whangarei Eng. & Construction Co. Ltd. — Whangarei** Yd No: 143 L reg 27.55 Br ex 6.11 Dght 0.839 Lbp - Br md - Dpth - Welded, 2 dks	**(A37B2PS) Passenger Ship** Passengers: 150	**2 oil engines** driving 2 FP propellers Total Power: 756kW (1,028hp) 15.0kn Cummins VT12-800-M 2 x Vee 4 Stroke 12 Cy. 140 x 152 each-378kW (514bhp) Cummins Engine Co Inc-USA
8976293 *E5WJ* -	**TE KUKUPA** **Government of The Cook Islands (Police Department)** - *Avatiu* *Cook Islands* MMSI: 518000014 Official number: CI 0004/89	**165** 59 -		**1989-09 Australian Shipbuilding Industries (WA) Pty Ltd — Fremantle WA** Yd No: 283 Loa 33.02 Br ex 8.20 Dght 1.750 Lbp 28.20 Br md 8.10 Dpth 4.20 Welded, 1 dk	**(B34H2SQ) Patrol Vessel**	**2 oil engines** geared to sc. shafts driving 2 FP propellers Total Power: 2,074kW (2,820hp) Caterpillar 3516TA 2 x Vee 4 Stroke 16 Cy. 170 x 190 each-1037kW (1410bhp) Caterpillar Inc-USA
1006269 *ZCRJ6* -	**TE MANU** *ex* Andale *-2002* **Portos Marine Ltd** Wilson Yacht Management Ltd SatCom: Inmarsat C 431931510 *George Town* *Cayman Islands (British)* MMSI: 319315000 Official number: 731896	**612** 183 110	Class: LR ✠ **100A1** SS 07/2008 SSC Yacht mono G6 service area ✠ **LMC** Cable: 302.0/22.0 U2 (a)	**1998-07 Cant. Nav. Ugo Codecasa S.p.A. — Viareggio** Yd No: 61 Loa 49.35 (BB) Br ex - Dght 2.180 Lbp 41.70 Br md 9.50 Dpth 5.10 Welded, 2 dks	**(X11A2YP) Yacht**	**2 oil engines** with clutches, flexible couplings & sr reverse geared to sc. shafts driving 2 FP propellers Total Power: 3,280kW (4,460hp) 18.0kn Caterpillar 3516TA 2 x Vee 4 Stroke 16 Cy. 170 x 190 each-1640kW (2230bhp) Caterpillar Inc-USA AuxGen: 2 x 125kW 380V 50Hz a.c Thrusters: 1 Thwart. FP thruster (f)
8404006 *ZMA3763* -	**TE MARU** *ex* Sanuki Maru *-1984* **PrimePort Timaru Ltd** - *Timaru* *New Zealand* MMSI: 512004173 Official number: 380336	**245** 73 -	Class: LR **100A1** SS 02/2012 tug harbour service at Timaru Port, with occasional voyages to Lyttleton *IWS **LMC** Eq.Ltr: E; Cable: 250.0/24.0 U2	**1984-09 Sagami Zosen Tekko K.K. — Yokosuka** Yd No: 226 Loa 32.52 Br ex 9.00 Dght - Lbp 28.33 Br md 8.80 Dpth 2.47 Welded, 1 dk	**(B32A2ST) Tug**	**2 oil engines** with clutches, flexible couplings & dr geared to sc. shafts driving 2 Directional propellers Total Power: 2,206kW (3,000hp) 13.5kn Niigata 6L25CXE 2 x 4 Stroke 6 Cy. 250 x 320 each-1103kW (1500bhp) Niigata Engineering Co Ltd-Japan AuxGen: 2 x 64kW 225V 60Hz a.c Fuel: 25.0 (d.f.)
9563598 *ZMA2370* -	**TE MATA** **Port of Napier Ltd** - *Napier* *New Zealand* Official number: 876157	**331** - 86	Class: LR ✠ **100A1** SS 06/2011 tug, port of Napier harbour service *IWS ✠ **LMC** **UMS** Eq.Ltr: G; Cable: 30.0/20.5 U2 (a)	**2011-06 Strategic Marine (V) Co Ltd — Vung Tau** Yd No: H333 Loa 23.80 (BB) Br ex - Dght 3.200 Lbp 22.80 Br md 11.00 Dpth 4.50 Welded, 1 dk	**(B32A2ST) Tug**	**2 oil engines** gearing integral to driving 2 Voith-Schneider propellers Total Power: 4,080kW (5,548hp) Wartsila 6L26 2 x 4 Stroke 6 Cy. 260 x 320 each-2040kW (2774bhp) Wartsila Finland Oy-Finland AuxGen: 2 x 86kW 400V 50Hz a.c
9032460 *ZM2873* -	**TE MATUA** **Port of Tauranga Ltd** - *Tauranga* *New Zealand* Official number: 875974	**320** 96 -	Class: LR ✠ **100A1** SS 04/2012 tug New Zealand home trade ✠ **LMC** **UMS** Eq.Ltr: F; Cable: 247.5/17.5 U2	**1992-04 Marine Steel Ltd. — Auckland** Yd No: 103 Loa 30.48 Br ex 11.03 Dght 3.143 Lbp 28.61 Br md 10.97 Dpth 4.27 Welded, 1 dk	**(B32A2ST) Tug**	**2 oil engines** gearing integral to driving 2 Voith-Schneider propellers Total Power: 2,824kW (3,840hp) 12.0kn Caterpillar 3606TA 2 x 4 Stroke 6 Cy. 280 x 300 each-1412kW (1920bhp) Caterpillar Inc-USA AuxGen: 1 x 50kW 415V 50Hz a.c, 1 x 46kW 415V 50Hz a.c
7407087 - -	**TE-SITO** **Government of The Republic of Gambia (Ports Authority)** - *Banjul* *Gambia*	*146* 34 243	Class: (LR) ✠ Classed LR until 24/1/01	**1977-03 Soc. Argibay de Const. Navais e Mecanicas S.A.R.L. — Alverca** Yd No: 133 Loa 27.56 Br ex 7.73 Dght 2.761 Lbp 24.54 Br md 7.41 Dpth 3.76 Welded, 1 dk	**(B32A2ST) Tug**	**1 oil engine** sr geared to sc. shaft driving 1 CP propeller Total Power: 706kW (960hp) Deutz SBA8M528 1 x 4 Stroke 8 Cy. 220 x 280 706kW (960bhp) Kloeckner Humboldt Deutz AG-West Germany AuxGen: 2 x 56kW 380V 50Hz a.c Fuel: 33.0 (d.f.)
7342055 *EIHK8* S 73	**TEA ROSE** *ex* Sunlight *-1984* *ex* Alert *-1984* **Anthony Sheehy** - *Skibbereen* *Irish Republic* MMSI: 250001767 Official number: 404509	**152** 71 -		**1974 Campbeltown Shipyard Ltd. — Campbeltown** Yd No: 019 Loa 24.39 Br ex - Dght - Lbp - Br md 6.71 Dpth 2.80 Welded, 1 dk	**(B11A2FS) Stern Trawler**	**1 oil engine** geared to sc. shaft driving 1 FP propeller Total Power: 605kW (823hp) Caterpillar 3508B 1 x Vee 4 Stroke 8 Cy. 170 x 190 605kW (823bhp) (new engine 2002) Caterpillar Inc-USA
8958552 *WCZ4029* -	**TEACHER'S PET** **Trawler Teacher's Pet** - *Bayou La Batre, AL* *United States of America* Official number: 1081639	**160** 48 -		**1999 Ocean Marine, Inc. — Bayou La Batre, Al** Yd No: 352 L reg 25.35 Br ex - Dght - Lbp - Br md 7.62 Dpth 4.05 Welded, 1 dk	**(B11B2FV) Fishing Vessel**	**1 oil engine** driving 1 FP propeller
7301271 *H07977* -	**TEAGUE BAY** **Hess Oil Virgin Islands Corp** HOVENSA LLC SatCom: Inmarsat A 1330440 *Panama* *Panama* MMSI: 352653000 Official number: 0355273G	**1,348** 404 -	Class: AB	**1973-07 Yarrows Ltd — Victoria BC** Yd No: 353 Loa 45.09 Br ex 14.48 Dght 7.317 Lbp 44.51 Br md 13.72 Dpth 8.34 Welded, 1 dk	**(B32A2ST) Tug**	**2 oil engines** reverse reduction geared to sc. shafts driving 2 FP propellers Total Power: 5,296kW (7,200hp) EMD (Electro-Motive) 20-645-E7B 2 x Vee 2 Stroke 20 Cy. 230 x 254 each-2648kW (3600bhp) General Motors Corp-USA AuxGen: 2 x 225kW
8113566 *PJWD* -	**TEAL** *ex* Sea Teal *-1996* *ex* Teal H. L. *-1989* *ex* Dyvi Teal *-1988* **Teal BV** Dockwise Shipping BV SatCom: Inmarsat A 1750561 *Willemstad* *Curacao* MMSI: 306122000 Official number: 1996-C-1519	**22,835** 9,573 32,101 T/cm 50.4	Class: NV	**1984-01 Samsung Shipbuilding & Heavy Industries Co Ltd — Geoje** Yd No: 1022 Loa 180.83 Br ex - Dght 9.991 Lbp 171.43 Br md 32.28 Dpth 13.31 Welded, 1 dk	**(A38C3GH) Heavy Load Carrier, semi submersible** Double Bottom Entire Compartment Length	**1 oil engine** driving 1 CP propeller Total Power: 9,635kW (13,100hp) 15.7kn B&W 6L67GFCA 1 x 2 Stroke 6 Cy. 670 x 1700 9635kW (13100bhp) Mitsui Engineering & Shipbuilding CLtd-Japan AuxGen: 3 x 630kW 440V 60Hz a.c Thrusters: 1 Thwart. CP thruster (f) Fuel: 259.0 (d.f.) 1726.0 (r.f.)

IMO / Call sign	Name / Owner / Manager / Flag	Tonnage	Class	Builder / Dimensions	Type	Machinery
9219173 *VTXP* -	**TEAL** **Government of The Republic of India (Andaman & Nicobar Administration)** The Shipping Corporation of India Ltd (SCI) *Mumbai* *India* Official number: 2918	**449** 135 135	Class: (IR)	**2003-11 Hindustan Shipyard Ltd — Visakhapatnam** Yd No: 11106 Loa 40.40 Br ex 8.62 Dght 2.660 Lbp 36.50 Br md 8.40 Dpth 4.00 Welded, 1 dk	**(A37B2PS) Passenger Ship** Passengers: unberthed: 100	**2 oil engines** geared to sc. shafts driving 2 FP propellers Total Power: 1,324kW (1,800hp) 12.0kn Yanmar M200-EN 2 x 4 Stroke 6 Cy. 200 x 260 each-662kW (900bhp) Yanmar Diesel Engine Co Ltd-Japan AuxGen: 2 x 80kW 415V 50Hz a.c Fuel: 43.0 (d.f.)
9186780 *3FAQ9*	**TEAL ARROW** *ex* Pan Pac Spirit *-2013* **Gearbulk Shipowning Ltd** Gearbulk Ltd *Panama* *Panama* MMSI: 357142000 Official number: 2618399CH	**22,073** 9,929 36,466	Class: NK	**1999-02 Oshima Shipbuilding Co Ltd — Saikai NS** Yd No: 10254 Loa 173.00 (BB) Br ex - Dght 10.975 Lbp 165.00 Br md 29.00 Dpth 15.50 Welded, 1 dk	**(A21A2BC) Bulk Carrier** Double Hull Grain: 38,174 Compartments: 5 Ho, ER 5 Ha: 5 (22.6 x 22.0)ER Gantry cranes: 2x22.4t	**1 oil engine** driving 1 FP propeller Total Power: 7,047kW (9,581hp) 14.5kn B&W 6S46MC-C 1 x 2 Stroke 6 Cy. 460 x 1932 7047kW (9581bhp) Kawasaki Heavy Industries Ltd-Japan AuxGen: 3 x 600kW 450V 60Hz a.c Fuel: 123.8 (d.f.) (Heating Coils) 1741.8 (r.f.) 27.5pd
9343637 *2HDY3* -	**TEAL BAY** *ex* Beacon Sw *-2014* *ex* Beacon Sw Bulker *-2009* **PNR Marine Trading VIII LLC** Pioneer Marine Advisers Pte Ltd *Douglas* *Isle of Man (British)* MMSI: 235102851 Official number: 744963	**20,236** 10,947 32,327 T/cm 43.8	Class: CR NK	**2007-11 Kanda Zosensho K.K. — Kawajiri** Yd No: 482 Loa 177.13 (BB) Br ex 28.40 Dght 10.020 Lbp 168.50 Br md 28.40 Dpth 14.25 Welded, 1 dk	**(A31A2GO) Open Hatch Cargo Ship** Double Hull Grain: 42,595; Bale: 41,124 Compartments: 5 Ho, ER 5 Ha: 3 (20.8 x 24.0) (19.2 x 24.0)ER (13.6 x 15.8) Cranes: 4x30.5t	**1 oil engine** driving 1 FP propeller Total Power: 5,627kW (7,650hp) 14.3kn Mitsubishi 6UEC52LA 1 x 2 Stroke 6 Cy. 520 x 1600 5627kW (7650bhp) Kobe Hatsudoki KK-Japan AuxGen: 3 x 440kW a.c Fuel: 71.0 (d.f.) 1533.0 (r.f.) 24.5pd
9157052 *9VGW2* -	**TEAM ACE** *ex* Sam Yang No. 1 *-2005* **Uniline Marine Pte Ltd** JR Orion Services Pte Ltd *Singapore* *Singapore* MMSI: 564843000 Official number: 391353	**3,182** 1,789 4,998 T/cm 13.0	Class: KR	**1996-10 Haedong Shipbuilding Co Ltd — Tongyeong** Yd No: 1015 Loa 99.80 (BB) Br ex 15.72 Dght 6.328 Lbp 93.70 Br md 15.40 Dpth 7.80 Welded, 1 dk	**(A12B2TR) Chemical/Products Tanker** Double Bottom Entire Compartment Length Liq: 6,179; Liq (Oil): 6,179 Cargo Heating Coils 12 Cargo Pump (s) Manifold: Bow/CM: 56m	**1 oil engine** driving 1 FP propeller Total Power: 2,574kW (3,500hp) 14.0kn Hanshin LH41LA 1 x 4 Stroke 6 Cy. 410 x 800 2574kW (3500bhp) The Hanshin Diesel Works Ltd-Japan AuxGen: 3 x 240kW 445V a.c Fuel: 290.0 (d.f.)
9186273 *9VCS6* -	**TEAM BEE** *ex* On Yang *-2005* **Yujin Bravo Pte Ltd** JR Orion Services Pte Ltd SatCom: Inmarsat Mini-M 764549225 *Singapore* *Singapore* MMSI: 563834000 Official number: 391704	**3,166** 1,531 4,998 T/cm 12.9	Class: BV (LR) (KR) Classed LR until 1/11/12	**1998-02 Haedong Shipbuilding Co Ltd — Tongyeong** Yd No: 1022 Conv to DH-2007 Loa 99.90 (BB) Br ex 15.72 Dght 6.280 Lbp 93.06 Br md 15.40 Dpth 7.80 Welded, 1 dk	**(A12B2TR) Chemical/Products Tanker** Double Hull (13F) Liq: 6,080; Liq (Oil): 6,080 Compartments: 10 Wing Ta, 2 Wing Slop Ta, ER 10 Cargo Pump (s): 10x160m³/hr Manifold: Bow/CM: 53.5m	**1 oil engine** driving 1 FP propeller Total Power: 2,574kW (3,500hp) 12.5kn Hanshin LH41LA 1 x 4 Stroke 6 Cy. 410 x 800 2574kW (3500bhp) The Hanshin Diesel Works Ltd-Japan AuxGen: 3 x 240kW 440V 60Hz a.c Boilers: e (ex.g.) 13.0kgf/cm² (12.7bar), AuxB (o.f.) 10.0kgf/cm² (9.8bar) Fuel: 58.1 (d.f.) 215.2 (r.f.)
7932238 - -	**TEAM LIWA** *ex* Gulf Frontier *-2005* *ex* Seacor Frontier *-2003* *ex* Acadian Commander *-1996* **Global Spectrum Energy Services Ltd** Nico Middle East Ltd (Topaz Marine)	**1,530** 459 1,334	Class: AB	**1981-05 Halter Marine, Inc. — New Orleans, La** Yd No: 836 Converted From: Research Vessel-1996 Converted From: Offshore Tug/Supply Ship-1981 Rebuilt-1996 Loa 69.37 Br ex - Dght 3.852 Lbp 67.54 Br md 13.42 Dpth 4.88 Welded, 1 dk	**(B21A20S) Platform Supply Ship** Ice Capable	**4 diesel electric oil engines** driving 4 gen. each 900kW 600V a.c Connecting to 2 elec. motors driving 2 FP propellers Total Power: 3,400kW (4,624hp) 12.0kn G.M. (Detroit Diesel) 16V-149-TI 1 x Vee 2 Stroke 16 Cy. 146 x 146 850kW (1156bhp) (made 1981, fitted 1989) General Motors Detroit DieselAllison Divn-USA G.M. (Detroit Diesel) 16V-149-TI 3 x Vee 2 Stroke 16 Cy. 146 x 146 each-850kW (1156bhp) General Motors Detroit DieselAllison Divn-USA AuxGen: 1 x 120kW a.c Thrusters: 1 Thwart. FP thruster (f) Fuel: 725.0 (d.f.) 12.5pd
9291030 *J8B3273* -	**TEAM MUSCAT** **Team VIII Ltd** Nico Middle East Ltd (Topaz Marine) *Kingstown* *St Vincent & The Grenadines* MMSI: 375196000 Official number: 9745	**2,124** 638 3,000	Class: NV	**2003-02 Jiangsu Wuxi Shipyard Co Ltd — Wuxi JS** Yd No: 7000HP-1 Loa 65.91 Br ex - Dght 4.500 Lbp 58.44 Br md 16.99 Dpth 6.50 Welded, 1 dk	**(B21B20A) Anchor Handling Tug Supply**	**2 oil engines** reduction geared to sc. shafts driving 2 CP propellers Total Power: 5,148kW (7,000hp) 12.0kn Wartsila 6L32 2 x 4 Stroke 6 Cy. 320 x 400 each-2574kW (3500bhp) Wartsila Finland Oy-Finland AuxGen: 3 x a.c, 2 x a.c Thrusters: 1 Retract. directional thruster (f); 1 Tunnel thruster (f); 1 Tunnel thruster (a)
9125566 *V7VF4* -	**TEAM PROGRESS** *ex* Star Polaris *-2010* **Progress Marine SA** Team Fuel Corp *Majuro* *Marshall Islands* MMSI: 538004108 Official number: 4108	**26,897** 13,874 43,775 T/cm 51.6	Class: NK (AB)	**1996-10 Daewoo Heavy Industries Ltd — Geoje** Yd No: 1102 Loa 190.00 (BB) Br ex - Dght 11.220 Lbp 181.00 Br md 30.50 Dpth 16.60 Welded, 1 dk	**(A21A2BC) Bulk Carrier** Grain: 56,667; Bale: 54,931 Compartments: 5 Ho, ER 5 Ha: 5 (19.3 x 16.3)ER Cranes: 4x30t	**1 oil engine** driving 1 FP propeller Total Power: 8,290kW (11,271hp) 14.5kn B&W 6S50MC 1 x 2 Stroke 6 Cy. 500 x 1910 8290kW (11271bhp) Korea Heavy Industries & ConstrCo Ltd (HANJUNG)-South Korea AuxGen: 3 x 500kW a.c Fuel: 1850.0
9143714 *V7CR6* -	**TEAM QUEST** *ex* Voge Felix *-2013* *ex* Andros *-2006* *ex* Sea Wisdom *-2003* **Quest Marine Ltd** Team Fuel Corp *Majuro* *Marshall Islands* MMSI: 538005311 Official number: 5311	**14,599** 8,429 24,279	Class: LR (GL) (NK) **100A1** SS 01/2012 bulk carrier ESP LI ESN-Hold 1 timber deck cargo **LMC**	**1997-01 The Hakodate Dock Co Ltd — Hakodate HK** Yd No: 764 Loa 157.20 (BB) Br ex - Dght 9.530 Lbp 149.00 Br md 26.00 Dpth 13.30 Welded, 1 dk	**(A21A2BC) Bulk Carrier** Grain: 31,000; Bale: 29,800 Compartments: 4 Ho, ER 4 Ha: 3 (21.6 x 13.1) (18.5 x 13.1)ER Cranes: 4x30.5t	**1 oil engine** driving 1 FP propeller Total Power: 5,296kW (7,200hp) 14.0kn Mitsubishi 6UEC45LA 1 x 2 Stroke 6 Cy. 450 x 1350 5296kW (7200bhp) Akasaka Tekkosho KK (Akasaka DieselLtd)-Japan AuxGen: 2 x 400kW 440/220V a.c
9137753 *V2GI8* -	**TEAM SPIRIT** *ex* Thor Ingeborg *-2013* *ex* BBC Argentina *-2007* *ex* S. Gabriel *-2004* *ex* Industrial Unity *-1999* *ex* Odin *-1999* *ex* Industrial Unity *-1998* *ex* Odin *-1998* **ms 'Team Spirit' Schiffahrts GmbH & Co KG** Bischoff Schiffahrts Beteiligung GmbH *Saint John's* *Antigua & Barbuda* MMSI: 305952000 Official number: 5035	**4,078** 2,009 4,822	Class: NK (BV) (GL)	**1997-06 Stocznia Polnocna SA (Northern Shipyard) — Gdansk** Yd No: B196/2/4 Loa 101.32 (BB) Br ex 16.78 Dght 6.416 Lbp 93.80 Br md 16.60 Dpth 8.10 Welded, 1 dk	**(A31A2GX) General Cargo Ship** Grain: 6,800 TEU 390 C Ho 127 C Dk 263 TEU incl 50 ref C. Compartments: 1 Ho, ER 1 Ha: (57.8 x 13.4)ER Cranes: 2x60t Ice Capable	**1 oil engine** with flexible couplings & sr gearedto sc. shaft driving 1 CP propeller Total Power: 3,960kW (5,384hp) 15.5kn MAN 9L32/40 1 x 4 Stroke 9 Cy. 320 x 400 3960kW (5384bhp) MAN B&W Diesel AG-Augsburg AuxGen: 1 x 640kW 400V 50Hz a.c, 2 x 378kW 400V 50Hz a.c Thrusters: 1 Thwart. FP thruster (f) Fuel: 103.0 (d.f.) 442.0 (r.f.) 15.5pd
9346421 *9HPG8* -	**TEAM SPIRIT** *ex* Team Bremen *-2012* *ex* Normed Bremen *-2011* *launched as* Team Spirit *-2006* **ms 'Team Spirit' GmbH & Co KG** TEAM SHIP Management GmbH & Co KG *Valletta* *Malta* MMSI: 256240000 Official number: 9346421	**8,407** 4,215 11,142	Class: GL (NV)	**2006-11 Daehan Shipbuilding Co Ltd — Yeosu** Yd No: H501 Loa 129.50 (BB) Br ex - Dght 8.700 Lbp 120.60 Br md 19.00 Dpth 11.65 Welded, 1 dk	**(A31A2GX) General Cargo Ship** Double Bottom Entire Compartment Length Grain: 14,237; Bale: 13,565 TEU 697 C Ho 282 TEU C Dk 415 TEU incl 60 ref C. Compartments: 2 Ho, ER 2 Ha: (58.2 x 15.6)ER (18.9 x 15.6) Cranes: 2x60t	**1 oil engine** reduction geared to sc. shaft driving 1 CP propeller Total Power: 6,000kW (8,158hp) 16.0kn MaK 6M43C 1 x 4 Stroke 6 Cy. 430 x 610 6000kW (8158bhp) Caterpillar Motoren GmbH & Co. KG-Germany AuxGen: 3 x 400kW 450/220V a.c, 1 x 700kW 450/220V a.c Thrusters: 1 Tunnel thruster (f) Fuel: 200.0 (d.f.) 890.0 (r.f.)
7423976 *OUNW* L 227	**TEAM-WORK** *ex* Mette-Lotte *-1988* *ex* Breton *-1983* **Borge Jensen, Jorgen Kristensen & Jorgen Ruby Nielsen** Borge Jensen SatCom: Inmarsat C 421955310 *Thyboron* *Denmark* MMSI: 219553000 Official number: H713	**203** 78 -		**1976-07 Esmadan ApS — Esbjerg** Yd No: 90 Loa 31.55 Br ex 6.91 Dght 3.048 Lbp 27.49 Br md 6.89 Dpth 3.46 Welded, 1 dk	**(B11A2FT) Trawler**	**1 oil engine** geared to sc. shaft driving 1 FP propeller Total Power: 405kW (551hp) Grenaa 6F24T 1 x 4 Stroke 6 Cy. 240 x 300 405kW (551bhp) A/S Grenaa Motorfabrik-Denmark
9574729 *A8ZB2* -	**TEAMWORTH NO. 1** *launched as* Mimika *-2011* **Teamworth No 1 Co Ltd** Teamworth Shipping GmbH *Monrovia* *Liberia* MMSI: 636015172 Official number: 15172	**15,392** 7,641 22,733	Class: AB (LR) Classed LR until 26/10/13	**2011-05 Jiangsu Yangzi Changbo Shipbuilding Co Ltd — Jingjiang JS** Yd No: 06S-001 Loa 158.90 (BB) Br ex - Dght 9.700 Lbp 149.60 Br md 24.60 Dpth 14.00 Welded, 1 dk	**(A21A2BC) Bulk Carrier** Grain: 30,415 Compartments: 4 Ho, ER 4 Ha: ER Cranes: 3x30.5t	**1 oil engine** driving 1 FP propeller Total Power: 5,180kW (7,043hp) 14.2kn MAN-B&W 7S35MC 1 x 2 Stroke 7 Cy. 350 x 1400 5180kW (7043bhp) STX Engine Co Ltd-South Korea AuxGen: 3 x 563kW a.c Fuel: 190.0 (d.f.) 860.0 (r.f.)

IMO / Call sign	Name / Owner	Tonnage	Class	Builder / Dimensions	Type	Machinery
9643477 *D5BW6* -	**TEAMWORTH NO. 2** **Teamworth No 2 Co Ltd** Teamworth Shipping GmBH *Monrovia* *Liberia* MMSI: 636015620 Official number: 15620	**15,486** 7,695 22,631	Class: AB (LR) Classed LR until 3/10/13	**2012-05 Jiangsu Yangzijiang Shipbuilding Co Ltd — Jiangyin JS** Yd No: YZJ2006-835 Loa 158.90 (BB) Br ex - Dght 9.000 Lbp 149.60 Br md 24.60 Dpth 14.00 Welded, 1 dk	**(A21A2BC) Bulk Carrier** Grain: 30,763 Compartments: 4 Ho, ER 4 Ha: ER Cranes: 3x30.5t	**1 oil engine** driving 1 FP propeller Total Power: 5,180kW (7,043hp) 14.2kn MAN-B&W 7S35MC 1 x 2 Stroke 7 Cy. 350 x 1400 5180kW (7043bhp) STX Engine Co Ltd-South Korea AuxGen: 3 x 450kW a.c Fuel: 190.0 (d.f.) 860.0 (r.f.)
5375333 *SDZX* -	**TEATERSKEPPET** *ex* August Strindberg *-1988* *ex* Bjarnoy II *-1980* *ex* Vagbingur *-1974* **ms Teaterskeppet AB** - *Stockholm* *Sweden* MMSI: 265535300	**962** 288 612	Class: (LR) ✠ Classed LR until 6/3/81	**1959-11 Estaleiros Navais de Viana do Castelo S.A. — Viana do Castelo** Yd No: 45 Loa 61.02 Br ex 9.86 Dght 4.668 Lbp 56.01 Br md 9.76 Dpth 5.03 Riveted\Welded	**(B11A2FT) Trawler** Ice Capable	**1 oil engine** with flexible coupling driving 1 CP propeller Total Power: 1,081kW (1,470hp) MAN G7V40/60 1 x 4 Stroke 7 Cy. 400 x 600 1081kW (1470bhp) Maschinenbau Augsburg Nuernberg (MAN)-Augsburg
9292058 *A8HA9* -	**TEATRALNY BRIDGE** **Canfield Marine Co Ltd** Unicom Management Services (Cyprus) Ltd SatCom: Inmarsat C 463790973 *Monrovia* *Liberia* MMSI: 636012691 Official number: 12691	**27,725** 13,762 46,697 T/cm 52.3	Class: LR ✠ **100A1** SS 05/2011 Double Hull oil tanker ESP *IWS LI SPM EP **ShipRight** (SDA, FDA, CM) ✠ **LMC** **UMS IGS** Eq.Ltr: M†; Cable: 632.5/73.0 U3 (a)	**2006-05 Admiralteyskiy Sudostroitelnyy Zavod — Sankt-Peterburg** Yd No: 02744 Loa 182.50 (BB) Br ex 32.24 Dght 12.200 Lbp 174.80 Br md 32.20 Dpth 17.50 Welded, 1 dk	**(A13B2TP) Products Tanker** Double Hull (13F) Liq: 51,910; Liq (Oil): 51,910 Compartments: 10 Wing Ta, 2 Wing Slop Ta, ER 10 Cargo Pump (s): 10x550m³/hr Manifold: Bow/CM: 90m	**1 oil engine** driving 1 FP propeller Total Power: 8,310kW (11,298hp) 15.0kn MAN-B&W 6S50MC-C 1 x 2 Stroke 6 Cy. 500 x 2000 8310kW (11298bhp) AO Bryanskiy MashinostroitelnyyZavod (BMZ)-Bryansk AuxGen: 2 x 1280kW 450V 60Hz a.c, 1 x 680kW 450V 60Hz a.c Boilers: e (ex.g.) 11.7kgf/cm² (11.5bar), WTAuxB (o.f.) 11.2kgf/cm² (11.0bar)
9181778 *5NXA* -	**TEBAH** *ex* Ajax *-2013* **Petromarine Nigeria Ltd** - *Lagos* *Nigeria* MMSI: 657979000	**1,587** 324 1,274	Class: BV	**1998-01 Halter Marine, Inc. — Lockport, La** Yd No: 1660 Loa 66.57 Br ex - Dght 5.182 Lbp 63.50 Br md 14.02 Dpth 6.10 Welded, 1 dk	**(B21B20A) Anchor Handling Tug Supply**	**2 oil engines** with clutches, flexible couplings & sr reverse geared to sc. shafts driving 2 CP propellers Total Power: 8,402kW (11,424hp) 13.5kn Caterpillar 3612TA 2 x Vee 4 Stroke 12 Cy. 280 x 300 each-4201kW (5712bhp) Caterpillar Inc-USA AuxGen: 3 x 350kW 440V 60Hz a.c Thrusters: 1 Thwart. CP thruster (f) Fuel: 554.0 (d.f.) 17.5pd
9074846 *DSQA8* -	**TEBAH** *ex* Yusho Queen *-2008* **Shipping Imperial Co Ltd** - *Jeju* *South Korea* MMSI: 441513000 Official number: JJR-088567	**3,884** 2,150 5,318	Class: KR (BV) (NK)	**1993-12 Sanyo Zosen K.K. — Onomichi** Yd No: 1058 Loa 94.40 Br ex - Dght 6.600 Lbp 84.90 Br md 16.00 Dpth 10.60 Welded, 2 dks	**(A31A2GX) General Cargo Ship** Grain: 8,710; Bale: 8,290 Compartments: 2 Ho, ER 2 Ha: (15.4 x 10.2) (25.9 x 10.2)ER Derricks: 3x25t	**1 oil engine** driving 1 FP propeller Total Power: 1,471kW (2,000hp) 11.0kn Akasaka A41 1 x 4 Stroke 6 Cy. 410 x 800 1471kW (2000bhp) Akasaka Tekkosho KK (Akasaka DieselLtd)-Japan AuxGen: 3 x 140kW a.c
9614452 *YDB4146* -	**TEBAR** *ex* TS Advance *-2012* **PT Pelayaran Citramaritimindo Pratama** - *Jakarta* *Indonesia*	**251** 75 -	Class: BV	**2012-07 Bengbu Shenzhou Machinery Co Ltd — Bengbu AH** (Hull) Yd No: (1446) **2012-07 Pacific Ocean Engineering & Trading Pte Ltd (POET) — Singapore** Yd No: 1446 Loa 29.50 Br ex 9.60 Dght 3.500 Lbp 28.36 Br md 9.00 Dpth 4.16 Welded, 1 dk	**(B32A2ST) Tug**	**2 oil engines** reduction geared to sc. shafts driving 2 FP propellers Total Power: 1,856kW (2,524hp) Chinese Std. Type XCW8200ZC 2 x 4 Stroke 8 Cy. 200 x 270 each-928kW (1262bhp) Weichai Power Co Ltd-China AuxGen: 2 x 100kW 50Hz a.c Fuel: 190.0
7309273 *WCY2888* -	**TEBENKOF** **Doumit Marine Services LLC** - *Cathlamet, Wa* *United States of America* Official number: 249682	*122* 83 -		**1946 Weldit Tank & Steel Co. — Bellingham, Wa** L reg 23.02 Br ex 7.50 Dght - Lbp - Br md - Dpth 1.73 Welded, 1 dk	**(B11B2FV) Fishing Vessel**	**1 oil engine** driving 1 FP propeller Total Power: 227kW (309hp)
7531266 *7THF* -	**TEBESSA** **CNAN Med SpA** CNAN Group SpA *Alger* *Algeria* MMSI: 605086060 Official number: 2939	**8,393** 2,517 3,499	Class: BV	**1977-09 Towa Zosen K.K. — Shimonoseki** Yd No: 498 Loa 130.99 (BB) Br ex 18.52 Dght 6.217 Lbp 120.00 Br md 18.51 Dpth 13.52 Welded, 2 dks	**(A35A2RR) Ro-Ro Cargo Ship** Passengers: driver berths: 12 Stern door/ramp (a) Len: 10.50 Wid: 7.00 Swl: - Lane-Len: 2590 Lane-Wid: 3.50 Lorries: 45, Cars: 600 Bale: 11,200 2 Ha: (21.9 x 5.4) (10.5 x 5.4)ER Cranes: 1x5t	**2 oil engines** reduction geared to sc. shafts driving 2 CP propellers Total Power: 8,826kW (12,000hp) 18.3kn Pielstick 12PC2V-400 2 x Vee 4 Stroke 12 Cy. 400 x 460 each-4413kW (6000bhp) Nippon Kokan KK (NKK Corp)-Japan AuxGen: 3 x 640kW 220V 50Hz a.c Thrusters: 1 Thwart. FP thruster (f) Fuel: 87.5 (d.f.) 508.0 (r.f.) 42.0pd
9475662 *AUXW* -	**TEBMA TEAM 2** *ex* QSA Arwana *-2008* *ex* Arwana 3 *-2008* **Tebma Shipyards Ltd** Seachart Shipping Pvt Ltd *Chennai* *India* MMSI: 419081100 Official number: 3515	**151** 46 138	Class: IR (NK)	**2007-09 Sapor Shipbuilding Industries Sdn Bhd — Sibu** (Hull) Yd No: (120) **2007-09 SC Yii Brothers Shipyard Sdn Bhd — Sibu** (Hull completed by) Yd No: 120 Loa 23.90 Br ex - Dght 2.862 Lbp 22.31 Br md 7.32 Dpth 3.35 Welded, 1 dk	**(B32A2ST) Tug**	**2 oil engines** reduction geared to sc. shafts driving 2 FP propellers Total Power: 894kW (1,216hp) Cummins KTA-19-M3 2 x 4 Stroke 6 Cy. 159 x 159 each-447kW (608bhp) Cummins Engine Co Inc-USA AuxGen: 2 x 56kW a.c Fuel: 100.0
7407350 *C9QD* Q-22	**TEBO** *ex* Ifcor III *-1978* **Empresa Mocambicana de Pesca EE (EMOPESCA)** - *Maputo* *Mozambique*	*109* 74 -	Class: (AB)	**1975-03 Sandock-Austral Ltd. — Durban** Yd No: 64 Loa 22.89 Br ex 6.48 Dght 2.464 Lbp 20.73 Br md 6.38 Dpth 3.33 Welded, 1 dk	**(B11A2FS) Stern Trawler**	**1 oil engine** reverse reduction geared to sc. shaft driving 1 FP propeller Total Power: 313kW (426hp) 8.5kn Caterpillar D353SCAC 1 x 4 Stroke 6 Cy. 159 x 203 313kW (426bhp) Caterpillar Tractor Co-USA AuxGen: 2 x 20kW a.c Fuel: 26.5 (d.f.)
8919881 *3FUC* -	**TEBRA** *ex* Oriental Chemi *-2012* *ex* Sun Pine *-2010* *ex* Sutra Satu *-2006* *ex* Bariki *-2000* **Tebra Marine Inc** Aurum Ship Management FZE *Panama* *Panama* MMSI: 356262000 Official number: 43945PEXT	**4,808** 2,412 8,416 T/cm 15.8	Class: KR (NK)	**1990-08 Asakawa Zosen K.K. — Imabari** Yd No: 351 Loa 106.50 (BB) Br ex - Dght 7.814 Lbp 99.00 Br md 18.20 Dpth 9.60 Welded, 1 dk	**(A12A2TC) Chemical Tanker** Double Hull Liq: 8,594 Cargo Heating Coils Compartments: 1 Ta, 12 Wing Ta, ER 14 Cargo Pump (s): 14x150m³/hr Manifold: Bow/CM: 51.1m	**1 oil engine** driving 1 FP propeller Total Power: 3,090kW (4,201hp) 13.0kn Mitsubishi 6UEC37LA 1 x 2 Stroke 6 Cy. 370 x 880 3090kW (4201bhp) Akasaka Tekkosho KK (Akasaka DieselLtd)-Japan AuxGen: 2 x 320kW 450V 60Hz a.c Fuel: 69.8 (d.f.) 426.7 (r.f.) 10.0pd
8847832 *YL2272* -	**TEBRA** **Blackwood Group Ltd** Juri Vassiljev *Liepaja* *Latvia* MMSI: 275419000 Official number: 2045	**193** 86 326	Class: (RS)	**1980 Svetlovskiy Sudoremontnyy Zavod — Svetlyy** Yd No: 4 Loa 29.17 Br ex 8.01 Dght 3.240 Lbp 28.50 Br md 7.58 Dpth 3.60 Welded, 1 dk	**(B34G2SE) Pollution Control Vessel** Liq: 348; Liq (Oil): 348 Compartments: 8 Ta Ice Capable	**1 oil engine** geared to sc. shaft driving 1 FP propeller Total Power: 165kW (224hp) 7.5kn Daldizel 6CHNSP18/22 1 x 4 Stroke 6 Cy. 180 x 220 165kW (224bhp) Daldizel-Khabarovsk AuxGen: 1 x 50kW a.c, 1 x 25kW a.c Fuel: 13.0 (d.f.)
6701682 *IKDL* -	**TEBRO** *ex* Lady Thelma *-1985* **Servizi Marittimi e Portuali Srl (SEMARPO)** - *Palermo* *Italy* Official number: 1176	*213* 51 -	Class: (LR) (RI) ✠ Classed LR until 20/6/86	**1967-02 Appledore Shipbuilders Ltd — Bideford** Yd No: A.S. 20 Loa 33.05 Br ex 9.05 Dght 3.504 Lbp 28.96 Br md 8.54 Dpth 4.12 Welded, 1 dk	**(B32A2ST) Tug**	**2 oil engines** driving 2 FP propellers Total Power: 1,488kW (2,024hp) 12.0kn Ruston 2 x 4 Stroke 6 Cy. 260 x 368 each-744kW (1012bhp) Ruston & Hornsby Ltd.-Lincoln AuxGen: 2 x 35kW 400V 50Hz a.c, 1 x 12kW 400V 50Hz a.c
9648685 *UUAY7* -	**TEC-I** **LLC Tes-Terminal** - *Ukraine* MMSI: 272731000	**5,473** 2,711 8,840	Class: UA	**2012-07 DAHK Chernomorskyi Sudnobudivnyi Zavod — Mykolayiv** Yd No: 208 Loa 128.96 Br ex 17.53 Dght 7.122 Lbp 119.20 Br md 17.50 Dpth 9.20 Welded, 1 dk	**(A13B2TP) Products Tanker** Double Hull (13F)	**2 oil engines** reduction geared to sc. shafts driving 1 Propeller Total Power: 1,470kW (1,998hp) MaK 5M453 2 x 4 Stroke 5 Cy. 320 x 420 each-735kW (999bhp)

IMO / Call sign	Name / Owners	Tonnages	Class	Builder / Dimensions	Type	Machinery
9172337 *JK5344* -	**TECHNOS** **Chuden Kankyo Technos KK & Nippon Eisen KK** Nihon Tug-Boat Co Ltd *Hamada, Shimane* *Japan* MMSI: 431400803 Official number: 136132	*195* - -		**1997-08 Kanagawa Zosen — Kobe** Yd No: 446 Loa 33.90 Br ex - Dght - Lbp 29.50 Br md 9.40 Dpth 4.00 Welded, 1 dk	**(B32A2ST) Tug**	**2 oil engines** gearing integral to driving 2 Z propellers Total Power: 2,648kW (3,600hp) 14.6kn Niigata 6L28HX 2 x 4 Stroke 6 Cy. 280 x 370 each-1324kW (1800bhp) Niigata Engineering Co Ltd-Japan AuxGen: 2 x 104kW 225V 60Hz a.c Fuel: 56.0 (d.f.) 10.5pd
9217486 *J8XK5* -	**TECK** **Ivoirienne de Remorquage et de Sauvetage (IRES)** *Kingstown* *St Vincent & The Grenadines* MMSI: 375242000 Official number: 8323	**331** 99 385	Class: BV	**2000-01 Austal Ships Pty Ltd — Fremantle WA** Yd No: 142 Loa 29.50 Br ex 10.30 Dght 4.000 Lbp 27.80 Br md 10.00 Dpth 4.80 Welded, 1 dk	**(B32A2ST) Tug**	**2 oil engines** geared to sc. shafts driving 2 CP propellers Total Power: 2,206kW (3,000hp) 11.0kn Yanmar T260-ET 2 x 4 Stroke 6 Cy. 260 x 330 each-1103kW (1500bhp) Yanmar Diesel Engine Co Ltd-Japan AuxGen: 2 x 134kW 220/380V 50Hz a.c
5426649 - -	**TECO 2** *ex* Bunnie M *ex* Jim Kelly *-1979* *ex* John Palmer *-1976* *ex* W. F. Fredeman, Jr. *-1974* *ex* Captain W. F. Fredeman *-1970* *ex* Larry W. Stephenson *-1970* *ex* ST-874 *-1970* - *Venezuela*	*147* 100 -	Class: (AB)	**1945 Kewaunee Engineering Corp. — Kewaunee, Wi** Yd No: 78 Loa - Br ex 7.07 Dght - Lbp 24.67 Br md 7.01 Dpth 3.15 Welded, 1 dk	**(B32A2ST) Tug**	**1 oil engine** driving 1 FP propeller Total Power: 478kW (650hp) Sulzer 1 x 4 Stroke 6 Cy. 330 x 432 478kW (650bhp) Busch Sulzer Bros.-St. Louis, Mo
9137519 *YD4802* -	**TECTONA** **PT Tjipta Rimba Djaja** *Palembang* *Indonesia*	**129** 77 110	Class: KI (NK)	**1995-07 Perkapalan Rentas Sdn Bhd — Sibu** Yd No: 02 L reg 23.00 Br ex - Dght 2.360 Lbp 21.76 Br md 7.00 Dpth 2.90 Welded, 1 dk	**(B32A2ST) Tug**	**2 oil engines** reduction geared to sc. shafts driving 2 FP propellers Total Power: 794kW (1,080hp) 10.0kn Caterpillar 3412T 2 x Vee 4 Stroke 12 Cy. 137 x 152 each-397kW (540bhp) Caterpillar Inc-USA
9433016 *A8RE3* -	**TECTUS** *ex* FPMC P Duke *-2012* **FPMC Duke Marine Corp** Formosa Plastics Marine Corp (FPMC) SatCom: Inmarsat C 463705466 *Monrovia* *Liberia* MMSI: 636014081 Official number: 14081	**42,340** 21,747 74,862 T/cm 68.0	Class: AB	**2009-07 STX Offshore & Shipbuilding Co Ltd — Changwon (Jinhae Shipyard)** Yd No: 4001 Loa 228.00 (BB) Br ex 32.28 Dght 14.300 Lbp 219.00 Br md 32.24 Dpth 20.65 Welded, 1 dk	**(A13B2TP) Products Tanker** Double Hull (13F) Liq: 80,370; Liq (Oil): 80,370 Compartments: 12 Wing Ta, 2 Wing Slop Ta, ER 3 Cargo Pump (s): 3x2000m³/hr Manifold: Bow/CM: 113.1m	**1 oil engine** driving 1 FP propeller Total Power: 11,060kW (15,037hp) 15.0kn MAN-B&W 7S50MC-C 1 x 2 Stroke 7 Cy. 500 x 2000 11060kW (15037bhp) STX Engine Co Ltd-South Korea AuxGen: 3 x 900kW a.c Fuel: 152.0 (d.f.) 2520.0 (r.f.)
7225855 *CFN5905* -	**TECUMSEH** *ex* Tina Litrico *-2011* *ex* Judy Litrico *-2006* *ex* Islander *-1996* *ex* Sugar Islander *-1996* **Lower Lakes Towing Ltd** SatCom: Inmarsat C 431622713 *Port Dover, ON* *Canada* MMSI: 316021177 Official number: 836045	**18,049** 9,488 29,984 T/cm 40.2	Class: LR (AB) **100A1** SS 04/2008 bulk carrier ESP ESN hold No. 1 **LMC**	**1973-08 Lockheed Shipbuilding & Construction Co. — Seattle, Wa** Yd No: 139 Loa 195.38 Br ex 23.78 Dght 10.281 Lbp 188.98 Br md 23.47 Dpth 13.80 Welded, 1 dk	**(A21A2BC) Bulk Carrier** Grain: 33,346 Compartments: 6 Ho, ER 6 Ha: (14.0 x 12.8)5 (17.1 x 12.8)ER	**2 oil engines** dr geared to sc. shaft driving 1 CP propeller Total Power: 8,826kW (12,000hp) 14.0kn Pielstick 12PC2V-400 2 x Vee 4 Stroke 12 Cy. 400 x 460 each-4413kW (6000bhp) Fairbanks Morse & Co.-New Orleans, La AuxGen: 2 x 500kW, 1 x 450kW Fuel: 226.5 (d.f.) (Heating Coils) 2423.5 (r.f.) 31.5pd
7511503 - -	**TECUMSEH** *ex* El Gato Grande *-2006* *ex* Gulf Thor *-1981* **Sause Bros Inc** *Portland, OR* *United States of America* Official number: 616065	**466** 139 -	Class: (AB)	**1980-01 Avondale Shipyards Inc. — Harvey, La** Yd No: 130 Loa 37.34 Br ex - Dght 4.217 Lbp - Br md 10.37 Dpth 5.03 Welded, 1 dk	**(B32A2ST) Tug**	**2 oil engines** sr geared to sc. shafts driving 2 Directional propellers Total Power: 2,566kW (3,488hp) 12.0kn Alpha 12V23L-VO 2 x Vee 4 Stroke 12 Cy. 225 x 300 each-1283kW (1744bhp) B&W Alpha Diesel A/S-Denmark AuxGen: 2 x 99kW
5354327 *SIFG* -	**TED** *ex* Retu *-1999* *ex* Ted *-1996* **Marin & Hamnservice KA AB** Marin & Haverikonsult KA AB *Stockholm* *Sweden* MMSI: 265510630	**153** 45 153	Class: (LR) (NV) ✠ Classed LR until 22/4/83	**1961-12 AB Asi-Verken — Amal** Yd No: 56 Loa 26.52 Br ex 7.88 Dght 3.650 Lbp 24.01 Br md 7.65 Dpth 4.20 Welded, 1 dk	**(B32A2ST) Tug** Passengers: 37 Ice Capable	**1 oil engine** driving 1 CP propeller Total Power: 956kW (1,300hp) MaK 8Z421AK 1 x 4 Stroke 8 Cy. 290 x 420 956kW (1300bhp) Maschinenbau Kiel AG (MaK)-Kiel AuxGen: 1 x 65kW 220V 50Hz a.c, 1 x 12kW 220V 50Hz a.c
8618970 *VKN4840* -	**TED NOFFS** **Sydney Ports Corp** *Sydney, NSW* *Australia* MMSI: 503010100 Official number: 852858	*156* 46 -		**1987-09 Carrington Slipways Pty Ltd — Newcastle NSW** Yd No: 201 Loa 24.52 Br ex - Dght 3.001 Lbp 22.00 Br md 8.01 Dpth 4.02 Welded, 1 dk	**(B32A2ST) Tug**	**2 oil engines** with clutches & dr reverse geared to sc. shafts driving 2 CP propellers Total Power: 1,030kW (1,400hp) 11.5kn G.M. (Detroit Diesel) 12V-92-TA 2 x Vee 2 Stroke 12 Cy. 123 x 127 each-515kW (700bhp) General Motors Detroit DieselAllison Divn-USA Thrusters: 1 Thwart. FP thruster (f) Fuel: 28.5 (d.f.)
9670315 *WDG6554* -	**TED SMITH** *ex* Gulf Ship 273 *-2013* **Legacy Leader LLC** Galliano Marine Service LLC *Galliano, LA* *United States of America* MMSI: 369356000 Official number: 1244383	**3,242** 1,399 4,927	Class: AB	**2013-01 Gulf Ship LLC — Gulfport MS** Yd No: 273 Loa 91.14 Br ex - Dght 5.820 Lbp 84.70 Br md 18.29 Dpth 7.32 Welded, 1 dk	**(B21B20T) Offshore Tug/Supply Ship**	**2 oil engines** reduction geared to sc. shafts driving 2 CP propellers Total Power: 4,920kW (6,690hp) Caterpillar C280-8 2 x 4 Stroke 8 Cy. 280 x 300 each-2460kW (3345bhp) Caterpillar Inc-USA AuxGen: 2 x 2000kW a.c, 2 x 910kW a.c
9037070 *UBXF* -	**TEDDY BEAR** *ex* Argun *-2005* **Marinstar Co Ltd** - *Korsakov* *Russia* MMSI: 273148310	**1,552** 618 1,772	Class: RS	**1992-02 Santierul Naval Galati S.A. — Galati** Yd No: 820 Loa 72.50 Br ex 13.00 Dght 3.200 Lbp 65.60 Br md - Dpth 4.40 Welded, 1 dk	**(A35A2RR) Ro-Ro Cargo Ship** Bow door & ramp Bale: 1,640 TEU 65 C Ho 30 TEU C Dk 35 TEU Compartments: 1 Ho, ER 2 Ha: (12.6 x 8.7) (18.6 x 8.7)ER Cranes: 1x12.5t Ice Capable	**2 oil engines** reduction geared to sc. shafts driving 2 FP propellers Total Power: 1,280kW (1,740hp) 10.5kn S.K.L. 6NVDS48A-2U 2 x 4 Stroke 6 Cy. 320 x 480 each-640kW (870bhp) SKL Motoren u. Systemtechnik AG-Magdeburg AuxGen: 3 x 100kW 380V 50Hz a.c Fuel: 95.0 (d.f.) 123.0 (r.f.)
9392494 *JWQH* -	**TEDNO** **Norled AS** Tide ASA *Bergen* *Norway* MMSI: 258506000	**118** 47 10		**2007-04 Oma Baatbyggeri AS — Stord** Yd No: 523 Loa 22.50 Br ex - Dght - Lbp 21.75 Br md 7.60 Dpth 2.67 Welded, 1 dk	**(A37B2PS) Passenger Ship** Hull Material: Aluminium Alloy Passengers: unberthed: 85	**2 oil engines** reduction geared to sc. shafts driving 2 CP propellers Total Power: 2,160kW (2,936hp) 35.0kn M.T.U. 12V2000M72 2 x Vee 4 Stroke 12 Cy. 135 x 156 each-1080kW (1468bhp) MTU Friedrichshafen GmbH-Friedrichshafen
7337232 - -	**TEE CLAUDE** **Pesquera Continental SA** - *Cartagena de Indias* *Colombia* Official number: MC-05-558	*140* 112 -		**1972 Edward N. Horton Builders, Inc. — Mobile, Al** L reg 25.84 Br ex 6.84 Dght - Lbp 23.47 Br md - Dpth 3.38 Welded	**(B11B2FV) Fishing Vessel**	**1 oil engine** with clutches, flexible couplings & reduction geared to sc. shaft driving 1 FP propeller Total Power: 313kW (426hp) 9.0kn Caterpillar D353TA 1 x 4 Stroke 6 Cy. 159 x 203 313kW (426bhp) Caterpillar Tractor Co-USA AuxGen: 2 x 20kW 230V 60Hz a.c
9101649 - -	**TEEN** *ex* Oriental Dream *-2003* *ex* Eun Ji *-1997* **Alicia Marine Co Ltd** IranoHind Shipping Co Ltd	**26,828** 13,921 43,671	Class: BV (NV) (KR)	**1995-06 Hanjin Heavy Industries Co Ltd — Busan** Yd No: 021 Loa 190.00 (BB) Br ex 30.54 Dght 11.221 Lbp 181.00 Br md 30.50 Dpth 16.60 Welded, 1 dk	**(A21A2BC) Bulk Carrier** Grain: 56,673; Bale: 54,973 Compartments: 5 Ho, ER 5 Ha: 5 (18.9 x 16.0)ER Cranes: 4x30t	**1 oil engine** driving 1 FP propeller Total Power: 8,290kW (11,271hp) 14.5kn B&W 6S50MC 1 x 2 Stroke 6 Cy. 500 x 1910 8290kW (11271bhp) Hyundai Heavy Industries Co Ltd-South Korea AuxGen: 3 x 500kW 60Hz a.c
8736277 *VNW5929* -	**TEENA B** **Clipper Assets Pty Ltd** - *Fremantle, WA* *Australia* MMSI: 503088000 Official number: 853459	**210** 63 134		**1988-01 B Bailey — St Helens TAS** Yd No: 1 Loa 35.00 Br ex - Dght 4.890 Lbp - Br md 7.72 Dpth - Welded, 1 dk	**(B11A2FS) Stern Trawler**	**1 oil engine** driving 1 CP propeller Total Power: 736kW (1,001hp) Blackstone ESL6 1 x 4 Stroke 6 Cy. 222 x 292 736kW (1001bhp) Mirrlees Blackstone (Stockport)Ltd.-Stockport

9300130 *9VBE2* -	**TEERA BHUM** **Teera Thana Pte Ltd** RCL Shipmanagement Pte Ltd *Singapore* *Singapore* MMSI: 563912000 Official number: 391016	**21,932** 8,588 24,238	Class: GL	**2005-01 Jiangsu Yangzijiang Shipbuilding Co Ltd — Jiangyin JS** Yd No: 2003-661C Loa 196.89 (BB) Br ex - Dght 11.000 Lbp 185.10 Br md 27.80 Dpth 16.60 Welded, 1 dk	**(A33A2CC) Container Ship (Fully Cellular)** TEU 1858 C Ho 738 TEU C Dk 1120 TEU incl 300 ref C.	**1 oil engine** driving 1 FP propeller Total Power: 21,660kW (29,449hp) 22.0kn MAN-B&W 6K80MC-C 1 x 2 Stroke 6 Cy. 800 x 2300 21660kW (29449bhp) Hudong Heavy Machinery Co Ltd-China AuxGen: 3 x 1200kW 450/230V 60Hz a.c, 1 x 900kW 450/230V 60Hz a.c Thrusters: 1 Thwart. FP thruster (f)
9283722 *C6WK3* -	**TEESTA SPIRIT** *ex* Jeanette *-2007* *launched as* Athenian Harmony *-2004* **Teesta Spirit LLC** Teekay Marine (Singapore) Pte Ltd *Nassau* *Bahamas* MMSI: 308894000 Official number: 9000230	**29,242** 11,926 46,921 T/cm 52.3	Class: LR (AB) **100A1** SS 10/2009 Double Hull oil & chemical tanker, Ship Type 3 ESP *IWS LI **LMC** **UMS IGS** Eq.Ltr: N†; Cable: 660.0/76.0 U3 (a)	**2004-10 Hyundai Mipo Dockyard Co Ltd — Ulsan** Yd No: 0235 Loa 183.20 (BB) Br ex 32.22 Dght 12.216 Lbp 174.00 Br md 32.20 Dpth 18.80 Welded, 1 dk	**(A12B2TR) Chemical/Products Tanker** Double Hull (13F) Liq: 51,593; Liq (Oil): 52,732 Compartments: 12 Wing Ta, 2 Wing Slop Ta, ER 12 Cargo Pump (s): 12x600m³/hr Manifold: Bow/CM: 92.3m	**1 oil engine** driving 1 FP propeller Total Power: 9,466kW (12,870hp) 14.6kn B&W 6S50MC-C 1 x 2 Stroke 6 Cy. 500 x 2000 9466kW (12870bhp) Hyundai Heavy Industries Co Ltd-South Korea AuxGen: 3 x 730kW 440V 60Hz a.c Boilers: e (ex.g.) 12.0kgf/cm² (11.8bar), AuxB (o.f.) 9.2kgf/cm² (9.0bar) Fuel: 188.0 (d.f.) 1222.0 (r.f.)
9263497 *YDA6416* -	**TEGAP** **PT Maritim Barito Perkasa** - *Banjarmasin* *Indonesia* MMSI: 525002004	**254** 76 -	Class: BV	**2002-02 Tuong Aik (Sarawak) Sdn Bhd — Sibu** Yd No: 2103 Loa 29.00 Br ex - Dght 3.950 Lbp 26.50 Br md 9.00 Dpth 4.25 Welded, 1 dk	**(B32A2ST) Tug**	**2 oil engines** reduction geared to sc. shafts driving 2 FP propellers Total Power: 1,766kW (2,402hp) Yanmar M220-EN 2 x 4 Stroke 6 Cy. 220 x 300 each-883kW (1201bhp) Yanmar Diesel Engine Co Ltd-Japan
9512082 *YDA6516* -	**TEGAR** **PT Maritim Barito Perkasa** - *Banjarmasin* *Indonesia* MMSI: 525012054	**249** 74 168	Class: AB	**2009-05 PT Perkasa Melati — Batam** Yd No: PM025 Loa 29.50 Br ex 9.75 Dght 3.500 Lbp 27.00 Br md 9.00 Dpth 4.16 Welded, 1 dk	**(B32A2ST) Tug**	**2 oil engines** reverse reduction geared to sc. shafts driving 2 FP propellers Total Power: 2,080kW (2,828hp) Mitsubishi S12R-MPTK 2 x Vee 4 Stroke 12 Cy. 170 x 180 each-1040kW (1414bhp) Mitsubishi Heavy Industries Ltd-Japan
7622546 *PLQP* -	**TEGAR MULIA** *ex* Pulau Sebatik *-2005* *ex* Nila Samudra I *-1990* **PT Sumber Sarana Niaga Lines** - *Palembang* *Indonesia*	**576** 291 625	Class: (KI)	**1974 P.T. Nila Kandi — Palembang** Loa - Br ex - Dght - Lbp 49.31 Br md 8.49 Dpth 4.32 Welded, 1 dk	**(A31A2GX) General Cargo Ship**	**1 oil engine** driving 1 FP propeller Total Power: 530kW (721hp) Enterprise DMG6 1 x 4 Stroke 6 Cy. 305 x 381 530kW (721bhp) (made 1941, fitted 1974) Enterprise Engine & Foundry Co-USA AuxGen: 1 x 80kW 110/220V a.c
9164005 *UBDI7* -	**TEGEN** *ex* Dutch Pearl *-2008* **Silverburn Shipping Isle of Man Ltd** Ark Shipping Co Ltd *Novorossiysk* *Russia*	*141* 42 -	Class: RS (LR) ✠ Classed LR until 5/2/12	**1999-01 Scheepswerf "De Plaete" B.V. — Ooltgensplaat** Yd No: 9701 Loa 22.30 Br ex 7.90 Dght 2.550 Lbp 19.36 Br md 7.60 Dpth 3.00 Welded, 1 dk	**(B32A2ST) Tug** Ice Capable	**2 oil engines** with clutches, flexible couplings & dr reverse geared to sc. shafts driving 2 FP propellers Total Power: 1,308kW (1,778hp) Deutz TBD616V12 2 x Vee 4 Stroke 12 Cy. 132 x 160 each-654kW (889bhp) Deutz AG-Koeln AuxGen: 3 x 20kW 400V 50Hz a.c
9065015 - -	**TEGRANT** *ex* Oil Calabar *-2013* **Multiplan Nigeria Ltd** - *Lagos* *Nigeria*	**135** 40 64	Class: AB (GL)	**1993-06 Gulf Craft Inc — Patterson LA** Yd No: 385 Loa 30.50 Br ex - Dght 1.319 Lbp 27.90 Br md 7.00 Dpth 2.97 Welded, 1 dk	**(B21A2OC) Crew/Supply Vessel**	**2 oil engines** with clutches, flexible couplings & sr reverse geared to sc. shafts driving 2 FP propellers Total Power: 1,124kW (1,528hp) 20.0kn Caterpillar 3412TA 2 x Vee 4 Stroke 12 Cy. 137 x 152 each-562kW (764bhp) Caterpillar Inc-USA AuxGen: 2 x 40kW 220V 50Hz a.c Fuel: 20.8 (r.f.)
7648306 - -	**TEGUH** *ex* Tsunemi Maru *-2007* **Camar Layar Sdn Bhd** SMS Ship Management Services Sdn Bhd	*499* 284 1,000		**1973-04 KK Izumi Zosensho — Kitakyushu** Loa 54.31 Br ex - Dght 3.501 Lbp 50.02 Br md 11.00 Dpth 3.81 Welded, 1dk	**(A31A2GX) General Cargo Ship**	**1 oil engine** driving 1 FP propeller Total Power: 500kW (680hp) 10.0kn Yanmar 1 x 4 Stroke 500kW (680bhp) Yanmar Diesel Engine Co Ltd-Japan
9487342 *YDA6515* -	**TEGUH** **PT Maritim Barito Perkasa** - *Banjarmasin* *Indonesia* MMSI: 525012053	**249** 74 172	Class: AB	**2008-08 PT Perkasa Melati — Batam** Yd No: PM020 Loa 29.50 Br ex 9.75 Dght 3.500 Lbp 27.00 Br md 9.00 Dpth 4.16 Welded, 1 dk	**(B32A2ST) Tug**	**2 oil engines** reduction geared to sc. shafts driving 2 Propellers Total Power: 2,080kW (2,828hp) Mitsubishi S12R-MPTK 2 x Vee 4 Stroke 12 Cy. 170 x 180 each-1040kW (1414bhp) Mitsubishi Heavy Industries Ltd-Japan AuxGen: 2 x 80kW a.c
9585716 *9WIV9* -	**TEGUH 16501** **Fast Meridian Sdn Bhd** - *Kota Kinabalu* *Malaysia* Official number: 332626	**176** 53 145	Class: NK	**2012-03 Pleasant Engineering Sdn Bhd — Sandakan** Yd No: 08/08 Loa 26.20 Br ex - Dght 2.910 Lbp 24.00 Br md 8.00 Dpth 3.83 Welded, 1 dk	**(B32A2ST) Tug**	**2 oil engines** reduction geared to sc. shafts driving 2 FP propellers Total Power: 1,220kW (1,658hp) Yanmar 6AYM-ETE 2 x 4 Stroke 6 Cy. 155 x 180 each-610kW (829bhp) Yanmar Diesel Engine Co Ltd-Japan Fuel: 130.0 (d.f.)
9641936 *T2YD3* -	**TEGUH 20558** **Thaumas Marine Ltd** - *Funafuti* *Tuvalu* Official number: 27521312	**292** 88 281	Class: NK	**2014-01 Kian Juan Dockyard Sdn Bhd — Miri** Yd No: 152 Loa 30.00 Br ex - Dght 3.512 Lbp 27.70 Br md 8.60 Dpth 4.12 Welded, 1 dk	**(B32A2ST) Tug**	**2 oil engines** reduction geared to sc. shafts driving 2 Propellers Total Power: 1,472kW (2,002hp) Yanmar 6RY17P-GV 2 x 4 Stroke 6 Cy. 165 x 219 each-736kW (1001bhp) Yanmar Diesel Engine Co Ltd-Japan
9641948 *T2YE3* -	**TEGUH 20559** **Thaumas Marine Ltd** - *Funafuti* *Tuvalu* Official number: 27531312	**292** 88 278	Class: NK	**2014-01 Kian Juan Dockyard Sdn Bhd — Miri** Yd No: 153 Loa 30.00 Br ex - Dght 3.512 Lbp 27.70 Br md 8.60 Dpth 4.12 Welded, 1 dk	**(B32A2ST) Tug**	**2 oil engines** reduction geared to sc. shafts driving 2 Propellers Total Power: 1,472kW (2,002hp) Yanmar 6RY17P-GV 2 x 4 Stroke 6 Cy. 165 x 219 each-736kW (1001bhp) Yanmar Diesel Engine Co Ltd-Japan
8880303 - -	**TEGUH PERKASA** - -	*109* 33 -	Class: (GL)	**1992 Sanmarine Engineering Sdn Bhd — Sandakan** Yd No: 009 Loa - Br ex - Dght 2.833 Lbp 20.31 Br md 6.80 Dpth 3.43 Welded, 1 dk	**(B32A2ST) Tug**	**2 oil engines** reduction geared to sc. shafts driving 2 FP propellers Total Power: 522kW (710hp) 10.0kn Cummins NTA-855-M 2 x 4 Stroke 6 Cy. 140 x 152 each-261kW (355bhp) Cummins Engine Co Ltd-United Kingdom AuxGen: 2 x 15kW 220/380V a.c
7026211 - -	**TEH LUNG No. 3** **Teh Lung Fishing Co Ltd** - *Keelung* *Chinese Taipei*	*150* - -		**1970 Suao Shipbuilding Co., Ltd. — Suao** Loa 32.42 Br ex 6.33 Dght - Lbp 27.28 Br md 6.30 Dpth 3.10 Welded, 1 dk	**(B11A2FT) Trawler**	**1 oil engine** driving 1 FP propeller Total Power: 331kW (450hp)
9284659 *VRAC8* -	**TEH MAY** **Teh May Maritime Corp Ltd** Foremost Maritime Corp SatCom: Inmarsat C 447700067 *Hong Kong* *Hong Kong* MMSI: 477480500 Official number: HK-1340	**88,955** 58,078 175,085 T/cm 119.0	Class: AB	**2004-08 Shanghai Waigaoqiao Shipbuilding Co Ltd — Shanghai** Yd No: 1008 Loa 289.00 (BB) Br ex 45.05 Dght 18.119 Lbp 278.20 Br md 45.00 Dpth 24.65 Welded, 1 dk	**(A21A2BC) Bulk Carrier** Grain: 193,134; Bale: 183,425 Compartments: 9 Ho, ER 9 Ha: (15.5 x 20.0)6 (15.5 x 20.0)ER 2 (15.5 x 16.5)	**1 oil engine** driving 1 FP propeller Total Power: 16,860kW (22,923hp) 14.5kn MAN-B&W 6S70MC 1 x 2 Stroke 6 Cy. 700 x 2674 16860kW (22923bhp) Hudong Heavy Machinery Co Ltd-China AuxGen: 3 x 750kW a.c
9051997 *ZPRE* -	**TEHIA** *ex* Rasill *-2011* *ex* Bass *-2004* *ex* Cast Bass *-2000* *ex* Mirka *-1992* *launched as* Nevskiy-37 *-1992* **Naviship Paraguay SA** - *Asuncion* *Paraguay* MMSI: 755009822	**2,882** 1,509 2,250	Class: (HR)	**1992-06 Nevskiy Sudostroitelnyy i Sudorem. Zavod — Shlisselburg** (Hull) Yd No: 37 **1992-06 Instalho Scheepsreparatiebedrijf K C Hoogendoorn — Werkendam** Loa 108.90 Br ex 15.05 Dght 2.790 Lbp - Br md 14.80 Dpth 6.05 Welded, 1 dk	**(A31A2GX) General Cargo Ship** TEU 200 C. 200/20'	**2 oil engines** driving 2 FP propellers Total Power: 1,030kW (1,400hp) 9.0kn S.K.L. 6NVD48A-2U 2 x 4 Stroke 6 Cy. 320 x 480 each-515kW (700bhp) SKL Motoren u. Systemtechnik AG-Magdeburg AuxGen: 3 x 50kW 380V 50Hz a.c

IMO / Call sign / Fishing no.	Name / Owner	Tonnage	Class	Builder / Dimensions	Type	Machinery
7383621 *AQOB* -	**TEHKIK** **Government of The Islamic Republic of Pakistan (Marine Fisheries Department)** - *Karachi* *Pakistan*	*199* 32 83	Class: (GL)	**1976-06 Karachi Shipyard & Engineering Works Ltd. — Karachi** Yd No: 90 Loa 28.99 Br ex 7.68 Dght 3.001 Lbp 25.81 Br md 7.61 Dpth 3.51 Welded, 1 dk	**(B12D2FR) Fishery Research Vessel**	**1 oil engine** driving 1 FP propeller Total Power: 313kW (426hp) 10.0kn Alpha 405-24VO 1 x 2 Stroke 5 Cy. 240 x 400 313kW (426bhp) A/S B&W Motor? og Machinefabrikaf 1971-Denmark
9154799 *FKYI* -	**TEHORO III** - - - *Noumea* *France* MMSI: 540006500	**156** - -	Class: (BV)	**1996 Chantier Naval du Pacifique Sud (CNPS) — Papeete** Yd No: 951 Loa 24.80 Br ex - Dght 3.250 Lbp 21.79 Br md 7.40 Dpth 3.96 Welded, 1 dk	**(B11B2FV) Fishing Vessel**	**1 oil engine** geared to sc. shaft driving 1 FP propeller Total Power: 331kW (450hp) 10.0kn Wartsila UD25L6M4 1 x 4 Stroke 6 Cy. 150 x 180 331kW (450bhp) Wartsila SACM Diesel SA-France
8632275 *CB3769* -	**TEHUELCHE** **Government of The Republic of Chile (Ministero de Obras Publicas)** - *Valparaiso* *Chile* MMSI: 725001110 Official number: 2592	*187* 56 163	Class: (GL)	**1988-07 Astilleros y Servicios Navales S.A. (ASENAV) — Valdivia** Loa 34.55 Br ex 10.30 Dght 2.200 Lbp - Br md - Dpth - Welded, 1 dk	**(A36A2PR) Passenger/Ro-Ro Ship (Vehicles)**	**3 oil engines** tr geared to sc. shafts driving 3 Directional propellers Total Power: 360kW (489hp) 8.8kn Wizeman WM422SAS 3 x Vee 4 Stroke 8 Cy. 128 x 142 each-120kW (163bhp) J. Wizemann GmbH & Co.-Remseck AuxGen: 1 x 60kW 380V a.c
9423372 *LW3933* -	**TEHUELCHE I** **Antares Naviera SA** - *Buenos Aires* *Argentina* MMSI: 701006184 Official number: 02641	*268* 89 48	Class: (BV)	**2007-08 Guangdong Jiangmen Shipyard Co Ltd — Jiangmen GD** (Hull) Yd No: GMG0618 **2007-08 Greenbay Marine Pte Ltd — Singapore** Yd No: 159 Loa 30.00 Br ex - Dght 3.750 Lbp 28.16 Br md 9.50 Dpth 4.70 Welded, 1 dk	**(B32A2ST) Tug**	**2 oil engines** reduction geared to sc. shafts driving 2 Z propellers Total Power: 2,942kW (4,000hp) Niigata 6L26HLX 2 x 4 Stroke 6 Cy. 260 x 350 each-1471kW (2000bhp) Niigata Engineering Co Ltd-Japan AuxGen: 2 x 96kW 50Hz a.c
9259135 *OWBM* L 155	**TEIDE** **Tommy Bach** - *Denmark* MMSI: 220109000 Official number: H1343	**269** 80 -		**2002-06 AS Rigas Kugu Buvetava (Riga Shipyard) — Riga** (Hull) **2002-06 Vestvaerftet ApS — Hvide Sande** Yd No: 227 Loa 24.30 Br ex - Dght - Lbp 21.50 Br md 8.50 Dpth 6.40 Welded, 1 dk	**(B11B2FV) Fishing Vessel**	**1 oil engine** driving 1 FP propeller
7423598 - -	**TEIDE 7** *ex Hokuko No. 17 ex Ain-Es-Sfa -1988*	*216* 104 -	Class: (KR) (RI)	**1976-03 Cant. Nav. Catasta — San Benedetto del Tronto** Yd No: 9 Loa 34.19 Br ex 7.01 Dght - Lbp 31.75 Br md 7.00 Dpth 3.76 Welded, 2 dks	**(B11A2FT) Trawler**	**1 oil engine** driving 1 FP propeller Total Power: 574kW (780hp) 12.0kn MAN G6V235/330ATL 1 x 4 Stroke 6 Cy. 235 x 330 574kW (780bhp) Maschinenbau Augsburg Nuernberg (MAN)-Augsburg AuxGen: 2 x 108kW 220V a.c
9283241 *ECHE* -	**TEIDE SPIRIT** **Teekay Shipping Spain SL** Teekay Shipping Ltd SatCom: Inmarsat C 422479410 *Santa Cruz de Tenerife* *Spain (CSR)* MMSI: 224794000 Official number: 8/2004	**83,594** 48,940 159,426 T/cm 118.2	Class: NV	**2004-10 Daewoo Shipbuilding & Marine Engineering Co Ltd — Geoje** Yd No: 5197 Loa 274.00 (BB) Br ex 48.04 Dght 16.950 Lbp 264.00 Br md 48.00 Dpth 23.70 Welded, 1 dk	**(A13A2TV) Crude Oil Tanker** Double Hull (13F) Liq: 167,809; Liq (Oil): 171,089 Cargo Heating Coils Compartments: 12 Wing Ta, 2 Wing Slop Ta, ER 3 Cargo Pump (s): 3x3500m³/hr Manifold: Bow/CM: 134m	**1 oil engine** driving 1 FP propeller Total Power: 15,173kW (20,629hp) 15.2kn MAN-B&W 6S70MC 1 x 2 Stroke 6 Cy. 700 x 2674 15173kW (20629bhp) AuxGen: 3 x a.c Fuel: 550.0 (d.f.) 4200.0 (r.f.)
9286841 *LNTY* M-1-HO	**TEIGENES** **A/S Teigenes** Sigurd Teige *Fosnavaag* *Norway* MMSI: 259390000	**2,883** 864 2,444	Class: NV	**2005-11 Societatea Comerciala Navol S.A. Oltenita — Oltenita** (Hull) Yd No: 402 **2005-11 Stocznia Polnocna SA (Northern Shipyard) — Gdansk** Yd No: 336/1 Loa 75.40 (BB) Br ex - Dght 7.200 Lbp 66.40 Br md 15.60 Dpth 9.00 Welded	**(B11A2FS) Stern Trawler**	**1 diesel electric oil engine** driving 1 gen. of 912kW 690V a.c 2 gen. each 1360kW 690V a.c Connecting to 1 elec. Motor of (2000kW) geared to sc. shaft driving 1 CP propeller Total Power: 3,801kW (5,168hp) Caterpillar 3612TA 1 x Vee 4 Stroke 12 Cy. 280 x 300 3801kW (5168bhp) Caterpillar Inc-USA AuxGen: 1 x 2320kW 690V a.c Thrusters: 1 Tunnel thruster (f); 1 Tunnel thruster (a)
6700781 *CB2569* -	**TEIGENES** **Compania Pesquera Camanchaca SA** - *Valparaiso* *Chile* MMSI: 725000184 Official number: 2397	*499* 219 -	Class: (NV)	**1966-12 Hatlo Verksted AS — Ulsteinvik** Yd No: 30 Lengthened-1972 Loa 47.48 Br ex 8.54 Dght 3.988 Lbp 42.60 Br md 8.51 Dpth 4.60 Welded, 2 dks	**(B11B2FV) Fishing Vessel** Compartments: 1 Ho, 6 Ta, ER 7 Ha: (2.5 x 3.5)6 (2.5 x 1.6)ER Derricks: 1x3t; Winches: 1	**1 oil engine** driving 1 CP propeller Total Power: 1,368kW (1,860hp) Alpha 12V23L-VO 1 x Vee 4 Stroke 12 Cy. 225 x 300 1368kW (1860bhp) (new engine 1974) Alpha Diesel A/S-Denmark AuxGen: 1 x 180kW 220V 50Hz a.c, 1 x 166kW 220V 50Hz a.c, 1 x 75kW 220V 50Hz a.c Thrusters: 1 Thwart. FP thruster (f); 1 Tunnel thruster (a)
8227393 *YL2245* LA-0034	**TEIKA** *ex Riva -1992* **'OVI' Ltd** - *Riga* *Latvia* Official number: 1537	**195** 89 323	Class: (RS)	**1984 Svetlovskiy Sudoremontnyy Zavod — Svetlyy** Yd No: 18 Loa 29.45 Br ex 8.15 Dght 3.120 Lbp 27.50 Br md 7.58 Dpth 3.60 Welded	**(B34G2SE) Pollution Control Vessel** Ice Capable	**1 oil engine** geared to sc. shaft driving 1 FP propeller Total Power: 165kW (224hp) 7.5kn Daldizel 6CHNSP18/22 1 x 4 Stroke 6 Cy. 180 x 220 165kW (224bhp) Daldizel-Khabarovsk AuxGen: 1 x 50kW, 1 x 30kW Fuel: 11.0 (d.f.)
5032204 - -	**TEIMOSO** *ex Wellington -2005 ex Gurnard -1986* *ex Aziebank -1982 ex Azie -1973* **Lutamar-Prestacao de Servicos a Navegacao Lda** - *Setubal* *Portugal* Official number: S-51-RL	**168** 50 -		**1961 N.V. Scheepswerven v/h H.H. Bodewes — Millingen a/d Rijn** Yd No: 553 Loa 28.86 Br ex 8.39 Dght 3.801 Lbp 25.94 Br md 8.34 Dpth 3.48 Welded, 1 dk	**(B32A2ST) Tug**	**2 oil engines** reduction geared to sc. shafts driving 2 Directional propellers Total Power: 1,692kW (2,300hp) 11.5kn Stork 2 x 4 Stroke 8 Cy. 210 x 300 each-846kW (1150bhp) Koninklijke Machinefabriek GebrStork & Co NV-Netherlands Fuel: 32.0
9099389 *LNGY* H-92-S	**TEINESKJAER** **Teineskjaer AS** - *Bergen* *Norway* MMSI: 258015500	**161** 64 -		**2005-04 Stocznia Polnocna SA (Northern Shipyard) — Gdansk** Yd No: B335/1 Loa 20.12 (BB) Br ex - Dght - Lbp - Br md 7.04 Dpth 3.50 Welded, 1 dk	**(B11B2FV) Fishing Vessel**	**1 oil engine** geared to sc. shaft driving 1 Propeller Total Power: 447kW (608hp) Cummins KTA-19-M3 1 x 4 Stroke 6 Cy. 159 x 159 447kW (608bhp) Cummins Engine Co Inc-USA AuxGen: 2 x 115kW Thrusters: 1 Thwart. FP thruster (f); 1 Thwart. FP thruster (a)
9382437 *JWNM* -	**TEISTEN** **Norled AS** Tide ASA *Bergen* *Norway* MMSI: 259479000	**278** 92 30		**2006-12 Fjellstrand AS — Omastrand** Yd No: 1675 Loa 33.00 Br ex - Dght 1.400 Lbp - Br md 10.60 Dpth 3.35 Welded, 1 dk	**(A37B2PS) Passenger Ship** Hull Material: Aluminium Alloy Passengers: unberthed: 180	**4 diesel electric oil engines** driving 3 gen. each 500kW 690V Connecting to 2 elec. motors each (630kW) reduction geared to sc. shafts driving 2 Azimuth electric drive units Total Power: 3,600kW (4,896hp) 35.0kn M.T.U. 10V2000M72 4 x Vee 4 Stroke 10 Cy. 135 x 156 each-900kW (1224bhp) MTU Friedrichshafen GmbH-Friedrichshafen AuxGen: 2 x 57kW a.c
9226102 *OW2190* -	**TEISTIN** **Foroyar Landsstyri** Strandfaraskip Landsins *Skopun* *Faeroe Islands (Danish)* MMSI: 231130000	**1,260** 378 300	Class: NV	**2001-04 Porta Odra Sp z oo — Szczecin** (Hull) **2001-04 p/f Skipasmidjan a Skala — Skali** Yd No: 55 Loa 45.00 Br ex - Dght 3.100 Lbp 38.74 Br md 12.50 Dpth 4.60 Welded	**(A36A2PR) Passenger/Ro-Ro Ship (Vehicles)** Passengers: unberthed: 300 Cars: 33	**3 diesel electric oil engines** driving 3 gen. Connecting to 2 elec. motors driving 2 Directional propellers Total Power: 1,389kW (1,887hp) Deutz TBD616V12 3 x Vee 4 Stroke 12 Cy. 132 x 160 each-463kW (629bhp) Deutz AG-Koeln Thrusters: 1 Thwart. FP thruster (f)
9460784 *3FFL5* -	**TEIZAN** **Olamar Navegacion SA** Usui Kaiun KK (Usui Kaiun Co Ltd) *Panama* *Panama* MMSI: 356433000 Official number: 4296111	**29,104** 15,554 50,448	Class: NK	**2011-08 Oshima Shipbuilding Co Ltd — Saikai NS** Yd No: 10610 Loa 182.98 (BB) Br ex - Dght 12.150 Lbp 179.30 Br md 32.26 Dpth 17.15 Welded, 1 dk	**(A21A2BC) Bulk Carrier** Double Hull Grain: 59,117; Bale: 58,700 Compartments: 5 Ho, ER 5 Ha: 4 (20.5 x 25.8)ER (14.8 x 19.8) Cranes: 4x30t	**1 oil engine** driving 1 FP propeller Total Power: 7,760kW (10,550hp) 14.5kn MAN-B&W 6S50MC-C 1 x 2 Stroke 6 Cy. 500 x 2000 7760kW (10550bhp) Mitsui Engineering & Shipbuilding CLtd-Japan Fuel: 2000.0

IMO / Call sign	Name / Owner / Port	Tonnage	Class	Builder / Dimensions	Type	Machinery
9185176 *JE3144* -	**TEIZAN MARU** - **Miyagi Marine Service KK & Wing Maritime Service Corp** - *Shiogama, Miyagi* *Japan* Official number: 133365	*192* - -		**1998-04 Kanagawa Zosen — Kobe** Yd No: 461 Loa 33.30 Br ex - Dght - Lbp 29.00 Br md 9.20 Dpth 3.88 Welded, 1 dk	**(B32A2ST) Tug**	**2 oil engines** Geared Integral to driving 2 Z propellers Total Power: 2,354kW (3,200hp) 13.7kn Niigata 6MG25HX 2 x 4 Stroke 6 Cy. 250 x 350 each-1177kW (1600bhp) Niigata Engineering Co Ltd-Japan
6820488 - - -	**TEIZAN MARU No. 2** - - -	*177* - -		**1967 Tohoku Shipbuilding Co Ltd — Shiogama MG** Yd No: 106 Loa 29.30 Br ex 7.80 Dght 2.515 Lbp 26.00 Br md 7.78 Dpth 3.40 Welded, 1 dk	**(B32B2SP) Pusher Tug**	**2 oil engines** geared to sc. shafts driving 2 FP propellers Total Power: 882kW (1,200hp) 11.8kn Makita DSH633 2 x 4 Stroke 6 Cy. 330 x 470 each-441kW (600bhp) Makita Tekkosho-Japan AuxGen: 1 x 40kW 105V a.c, 1 x 15kW 105V a.c
8666434 *AUHP* -	**TEJA** - **P Suryarao** - *Visakhapatnam* *India* MMSI: 419576000 Official number: 3114	**159** 48 -	Class: IR	**2005-11 Santosh Fabricators — Kakinada** Yd No: 1008 Loa 24.00 Br ex - Dght - Lbp 21.86 Br md 7.80 Dpth 3.20 Welded, 1 dk	**(B21B20T) Offshore Tug/Supply Ship**	**2 oil engines** reduction geared to sc. shafts driving 2 Propellers Total Power: 596kW (810hp) Cummins NTA-855-M 2 x 4 Stroke 6 Cy. 140 x 152 each-298kW (405bhp) Cummins Engine Co Inc-USA
8917120 *YFWA* -	**TEK GLORY 1** *ex* Pontianak Caraka Jaya Niaga Iii-34 *-2011* **PT Tunas Eratama Karya Line** - *Jakarta* *Indonesia* MMSI: 525003144	**3,401** 1,895 4,180	Class: KI	**1997-11 P.T. PAL Indonesia — Surabaya** Yd No: 112 Loa 98.00 Br ex - Dght 5.500 Lbp 92.80 Br md 16.50 Dpth 7.80 Welded, 1 dk	**(A31A2GX) General Cargo Ship** TEU 178 C. 178/20'	**1 oil engine** geared to sc. shaft driving 1 FP propeller Total Power: 1,498kW (2,037hp) 11.9kn Pielstick 8PA5L 1 x 4 Stroke 8 Cy. 255 x 270 1498kW (2037bhp) Niigata Engineering Co Ltd-Japan
8627983 - -	**TEKAD** *ex* Kinei Maru No. 22 *-2001* **PT Jasa Bahtera Mulia** - *Indonesia*	**645** 248 692		**1986-07 K.K. Saidaiji Zosensho — Okayama** Loa 55.20 Br ex - Dght 3.371 Lbp 49.51 Br md 9.01 Dpth 5.52 Welded, 1 dk	**(A31A2GX) General Cargo Ship**	**1 oil engine** geared to sc. shaft driving 1 FP propeller Total Power: 405kW (551hp) 10.0kn Hanshin 6LU26G 1 x 4 Stroke 6 Cy. 260 x 440 405kW (551bhp) The Hanshin Diesel Works Ltd-Japan
9512070 *YDA6514* -	**TEKAD** - **PT Maritim Barito Perkasa** - *Banjarmasin* *Indonesia* MMSI: 525012052 Official number: 3265/IIA	**249** 74 168	Class: AB	**2009-05 PT Perkasa Melati — Batam** Yd No: PM024 Loa 29.50 Br ex 9.75 Dght 3.500 Lbp 27.00 Br md 9.00 Dpth 4.16 Welded, 1 dk	**(B32A2ST) Tug**	**2 oil engines** reverse reduction geared to sc. shafts driving 2 FP propellers Total Power: 2,080kW (2,828hp) Mitsubishi S12R-MPTK 2 x Vee 4 Stroke 12 Cy. 170 x 180 each-1040kW (1414bhp) Mitsubishi Heavy Industries Ltd-Japan
8819122 *ETKZ* -	**TEKEZE** *ex* Lim *-1999* *ex* Norviken *-1997* *ex* Moraca *-1995* **Ethiopian Shipping & Logistics Services Enterprise** - *Addis Ababa* *Ethiopia* MMSI: 624111000 Official number: 12/91	**13,651** 7,468 18,235 T/cm 34.6	Class: GL (AB) (BV)	**1990-04 VEB Warnowwerft Warnemuende — Rostock** Yd No: 280 Loa 165.50 (BB) Br ex - Dght 10.070 Lbp 152.40 Br md 23.05 Dpth 13.40 Welded, 1 dk	**(A31A2GX) General Cargo Ship** Grain: 24,634; Bale: 22,937 TEU 670 C Ho 360 TEU C Dk 310 TEU incl 45 ref C. Compartments: 4 Ho, ER, 4 Tw Dk 7 Ha: (12.6 x 12.6)4 (25.1 x 7.8)2 (19.2 x 7.8)ER Cranes: 1x40t,3x25t,1x5t Ice Capable	**1 oil engine** driving 1 CP propeller Total Power: 7,000kW (9,517hp) 15.9kn Sulzer 5RTA58 1 x 2 Stroke 5 Cy. 580 x 1700 7000kW (9517bhp) VEB Dieselmotorenwerk Rostock-Rostock AuxGen: 3 x 684kW 380V 50Hz a.c Thrusters: 1 Thwart. CP thruster (f) Fuel: 78.0 (d.f.) 1209.8 (r.f.) 34.5pd
8228775 - -	**TEKHFLOTETS** - **Government of The Russian Federation** - *Novorossiysk* *Russia* MMSI: 273421970	**182** 54 69	Class: RS	**1984-10 Pribaltiyskiy Sudostroitelnyy Zavod "Yantar" — Kaliningrad** Yd No: 804 Loa 29.32 Br ex 8.60 Dght 3.401 Lbp 27.00 Br md 8.30 Dpth 4.30 Welded, 1 dk	**(B32A2ST) Tug** Ice Capable	**2 oil engines** driving 2 CP propellers Total Power: 1,180kW (1,604hp) Pervomaysk 8CHNP25/34 2 x 4 Stroke 8 Cy. 250 x 340 each-590kW (802bhp) Pervomaydizelmash (PDM)-Pervomaysk AuxGen: 2 x 50kW a.c Fuel: 49.0 (d.f.)
7704710 - -	**TEKHNOLOG** *ex* Silver Harvester *-2006* *ex* Silver Harvester I *-2000* *ex* Silver Harvester *-1999* *ex* Saida *-1997* *ex* Osan *-1994* - -	**3,825** 1,147 2,690	Class: (LR) (RS) ✠ Classed LR until 21/4/00	**1980-09 Georg Eides Sonner AS — Hoylandsbygd** (Hull) Yd No: 107 **1980-09 Soviknes Verft AS — Sovik** Yd No: 85 Converted From: Fish Factory Ship-2008 Loa 87.71 Br ex 15.24 Dght 6.358 Lbp 76.99 Br md 15.00 Dpth 10.52 Welded, 2 dks	**(A34A2GR) Refrigerated Cargo Ship** Ins: 2,150 Derricks: 4x5t	**1 oil engine** sr geared to sc. shaft driving 1 CP propeller Total Power: 2,648kW (3,600hp) Deutz SBV8M540 1 x 4 Stroke 8 Cy. 370 x 400 2648kW (3600bhp) Kloeckner Humboldt Deutz AG-West Germany AuxGen: 3 x 640kW 440V 60Hz a.c, 1 x 240kW 440V 60Hz a.c Thrusters: 1 Thwart. FP thruster (f); 1 Tunnel thruster (a) Fuel: 600.0 (d.f.)
9101053 *UGRB* -	**TEKHNOLOG SARKISOV** *ex* Zaliv Vladimira *-1996* **JSC 'Dalrybprom'** - *Vladivostok* *Russia* MMSI: 273814900 Official number: 921728	**779** 223 414	Class: RS	**1993-07 ATVT Zavod "Leninska Kuznya" — Kyyiv** Yd No: 1668 Loa 54.82 Br ex 10.15 Dght 4.140 Lbp 50.30 Br md 9.80 Dpth 5.00 Welded, 1 dk	**(B11A2FS) Stern Trawler** Ins: 412 Compartments: 2 Ho 3 Ha: 3 (1.5 x 1.6) Derricks: 2x1t Ice Capable	**1 oil engine** driving 1 CP propeller Total Power: 852kW (1,158hp) 12.0kn S.K.L. 8NVD48A-2U 1 x 4 Stroke 8 Cy. 320 x 480 852kW (1158bhp) SKL Motoren u. Systemtechnik AG-Magdeburg
7368011 *YGNE* -	**TEKI SWETJA SATU** *ex* Telaga Mas *-2010* *ex* Kanal Mas *-2000* *ex* Straits Glory *-1999* *ex* Yong An *-1996* *ex* Junior Longo *-1984* *ex* Punta Arenas *-1984* *ex* Junior Longo *-1982* *ex* Junior Lilo *-1979* **PT Tri Praya Utama Line (TPUL)** - *Jakarta* *Indonesia*	**3,289** 1,553 6,520	Class: (LR) (KI) (CC) (BV) Classed LR until 1/5/00	**1974-05 Handel en Scheepsbouw Mij. Kramer & Booy B.V. — Kootstertille** Yd No: 184 Lengthened-1979 Loa 106.42 (BB) Br ex - Dght 5.700 Lbp 97.92 Br md 13.60 Dpth 5.90 Welded, 2 dks	**(A31A2GX) General Cargo Ship** Grain: 4,870; Bale: 4,814 TEU 186 C Ho 96 TEU C Dk 90 TEU incl 20 ref C Compartments: 2 Ho, ER 1 Ha: (51.8 x 10.3)ER Cranes: 2x80t	**1 oil engine** sr geared to sc. shaft driving 1 CP propeller Total Power: 2,137kW (2,905hp) 12.0kn Alpha 12U28L-VO 1 x Vee 4 Stroke 12 Cy. 280 x 320 2137kW (2905bhp) (new engine 1984) B&W Alpha Diesel A/S-Denmark AuxGen: 2 x 128kW 380V 50Hz a.c, 2 x 173kW 380V 50Hz a.c Thrusters: 1 Thwart. FP thruster (f) Fuel: 315.0 (d.f.) 9.0pd
8317825 *OIRR* -	**TEKLA I** *ex* Skarpen *-1996* **Suomenlahden Yhteysliikenne Oy** - *Kotka* *Finland* Official number: 10679	**120** 36 34		**1983-12 Rauma-Repola Oy — Savonlinna** Yd No: 460 Loa 23.91 Br ex 6.61 Dght 2.701 Lbp 20.71 Br md - Dpth 3.51 Welded, 1 dk	**(A36A2PR) Passenger/Ro-Ro Ship (Vehicles)** Passengers: unberthed: 37 Bow door/ramp Lorries: 1, Cars: 4	**1 oil engine** with clutches, flexible couplings & sr reverse geared to sc. shaft driving 1 FP propeller Total Power: 636kW (865hp) 10.0kn Wartsila 624TS 1 x 4 Stroke 6 Cy. 240 x 310 636kW (865bhp) Oy Wartsila Ab-Finland AuxGen: 1 x 44kW 380V 50Hz a.c Thrusters: 1 Thwart. FP thruster (f) Fuel: 10.0 (d.f.) 2.0pd
9199983 *9WEP9* -	**TEKNIK ALPHA** *ex* Oilserve Alpha *-2010* *ex* Britoil 32 *-2004* **Oilserve (L) Bhd** Scomi Oilserve Sdn Bhd *Port Klang* *Malaysia* MMSI: 533000096 Official number: 329950	**443** 133 350	Class: (BV) (AB)	**1998-10 Fujian Southeast Shipyard — Fuzhou FJ** Yd No: H8018 Loa 37.00 Br ex - Dght 4.640 Lbp 34.69 Br md 10.60 Dpth 4.95 Welded, 1 dk	**(B21B20A) Anchor Handling Tug Supply** Passengers: berths: 14	**2 oil engines** with clutches, flexible couplings & reverse reduction geared to sc. shafts driving 2 FP propellers Total Power: 2,984kW (4,058hp) 11.5kn Yanmar 8Z280-EN 2 x 4 Stroke 8 Cy. 280 x 360 each-1492kW (2029bhp) Yanmar Diesel Engine Co Ltd-Japan AuxGen: 2 x 300kW 220/380V 50Hz a.c Thrusters: 1 Thwart. FP thruster (f) Fuel: 200.0 (d.f.) 8.0pd
9204386 *9WEQ1* -	**TEKNIK BETA** *ex* Oilserve Beta *-2010* *ex* Britoil 35 *-2005* **Oilserve (L) Bhd** Scomi Oilserve Sdn Bhd *Port Klang* *Malaysia* MMSI: 533000107 Official number: 329951	**443** 133 350	Class: (BV) (AB)	**1999-03 Fujian Southeast Shipyard — Fuzhou FJ** Yd No: H8021 Loa 34.70 Br ex - Dght 4.360 Lbp 34.69 Br md 10.60 Dpth 4.95 Welded, 1 dk	**(B21B20A) Anchor Handling Tug Supply**	**2 oil engines** with clutches, flexible couplings & reverse reduction geared to sc. shafts driving 2 FP propellers Total Power: 2,984kW (4,058hp) 12.0kn Yanmar 8Z280-EN 2 x 4 Stroke 8 Cy. 280 x 360 each-1492kW (2029bhp) Yanmar Diesel Engine Co Ltd-Japan AuxGen: 2 x 300kW 380/220V 50Hz a.c Thrusters: 1 Thwart. FP thruster (f) Fuel: 200.0 (d.f.) 8.0pd
7907893 *9MEX8* -	**TEKNIK KEMBARA** *ex* Western Odyssey *-1993* **Maritime Mineral Resources Sdn Bhd** Giat Marin Sdn Bhd SatCom: Inmarsat C 453392110 *Port Klang* *Malaysia* Official number: 330330	**935** 280 -	Class: (AB)	**1980-04 Sing Koon Seng Pte Ltd — Singapore** Yd No: SKS506 Loa 56.32 Br ex 12.45 Dght 4.212 Lbp 53.29 Br md 12.01 Dpth 4.88 Welded, 1 dk	**(B31A2SR) Research Survey Vessel**	**2 oil engines** reverse reduction geared to sc. shafts driving 2 CP propellers Total Power: 1,604kW (2,180hp) 13.0kn Caterpillar D399TA 2 x Vee 4 Stroke 16 Cy. 159 x 203 each-802kW (1090bhp) Caterpillar Tractor Co-USA AuxGen: 2 x 100kW a.c Thrusters: 1 Thwart. FP thruster (f)

IMO / Call sign	Name / Owners	Tonnage	Class	Builder / Dimensions	Type	Machinery
7353999 *H3RN* -	**TEKNIK PERDANA** *ex* Hakurei Maru *-2000* **TL Geohydrographics Sdn Bhd** TL Geohydrographics Pte Ltd SatCom: Inmarsat B 343107210 *Panama* *Panama* MMSI: 352116000 Official number: 2779301C	**2,270** 681 1,057	Class: NK	**1974-03 Mitsubishi Heavy Industries Ltd. — Shimonoseki** Yd No: 727 Loa 86.95 Br ex 13.42 Dght 5.264 Lbp 77.02 Br md 13.39 Dpth 5.31 Welded, 2 dks	**(B31A2SR) Research Survey Vessel** 2 Ha: (1.3 x 2.5) (3.5 x 1.4) Ice Capable	**1 oil engine** driving 1 CP propeller Total Power: 2,795kW (3,800hp) 15.0kn Mitsubishi 6UET45/75C 1 x 2 Stroke 6 Cy. 450 x 750 2795kW (3800bhp) Akasaka Tekkosho KK (Akasaka DieselLtd)-Japan AuxGen: 3 x 600kW 450V 60Hz a.c Thrusters: 1 Thwart. CP thruster (f) Fuel: 442.0 (d.f.) 15.0pd
7803334 *HP9101* -	**TEKNIK PUTRA** *ex* Lowland Searcher *-1997* *ex* Auricula *-1995* **TL Geohydrographics Sdn Bhd** TL Geohydrographics Pte Ltd SatCom: Inmarsat A 1361415 *Panama* *Panama* MMSI: 351579000 Official number: 2513398C	**1,009** 302 181	Class: LR ✠ **100A1** SS 07/2010 ✠ **LMC** Eq.Ltr: L; Cable: 504.0/32.0 U2	**1980-11 Ferguson Bros (Port Glasgow) Ltd — Port Glasgow** Yd No: 482 Converted From: Weapons Trials Vessel-1995 Loa 59.65 Br ex 11.32 Dght 3.450 Lbp 52.00 Br md 11.00 Dpth 6.00 Welded, 2 dks	**(B31A2SR) Research Survey Vessel**	**2 oil engines** with clutches, flexible couplings & sr geared to sc. shafts driving 2 CP propellers Total Power: 956kW (1,300hp) 12.0kn Blackstone ESL6 2 x 4 Stroke 6 Cy. 222 x 292 each-478kW (650bhp) Mirrlees Blackstone (Stamford)Ltd.-Stamford AuxGen: 3 x 192kW 440/220V 60Hz a.c Thrusters: 1 Thwart. FP thruster (f)
7396692 *9MBD4* -	**TEKNIK SAMUDRA** *ex* Smit Maassluis *-1990* *ex* Smit-Lloyd 23 *-1984* *ex* Broco Pearl *-1979* **TL Geosciences Sdn Bhd** SatCom: Inmarsat A 1710352 *Port Klang* *Malaysia* MMSI: 533528000 Official number: 326085	**1,061** 319 915	Class: NV	**1975-06 B.V. Scheepswerf "Waterhuizen" J. Pattje — Waterhuizen** Yd No: 310 Loa 58.85 Br ex 12.03 Dght 4.120 Lbp 51.31 Br md 11.99 Dpth 5.90 Welded, 2 dks	**(B21B20T) Offshore Tug/Supply Ship** Passengers: berths: 12	**2 oil engines** driving 2 CP propellers Total Power: 2,132kW (2,898hp) 12.0kn Alpha 10V23L-VO 2 x Vee 4 Stroke 10 Cy. 225 x 300 each-1066kW (1449bhp) Alpha Diesel A/S-Denmark AuxGen: 2 x 169kW 440V 60Hz a.c Thrusters: 1 Thwart. FP thruster (f) Fuel: 400.0 (d.f.) 12.0pd
6511855 *HP9060* -	**TEKNIK SATRIA** *ex* Kommandor Therese *-1997* *ex* Husum *-1981* **TL Geohydrographics Sdn Bhd** TL Geohydrographics Pte Ltd SatCom: Inmarsat C 435152710 *Panama* *Panama* MMSI: 351527000 Official number: 2511898B	**1,145** 343 884	Class: (BV) (GL)	**1965-06 Luebecker Flender-Werke AG — Luebeck** Yd No: 552 Converted From: Stern Trawler-1981 Loa 64.22 Br ex 10.27 Dght 4.598 Lbp 55.02 Br md 10.09 Dpth 7.24 Welded, 2 dks	**(B22A20V) Diving Support Vessel** Passengers: berths: 40 Ice Capable	**1 oil engine** driving 1 CP propeller Total Power: 1,397kW (1,899hp) 13.0kn MaK MA582AK 1 x 4 Stroke 8 Cy. 385 x 580 1397kW (1899bhp) Maschinenbau Kiel AG (MaK)-Kiel AuxGen: 2 x 120kW 380V 50Hz a.c, 1 x 56kW 380V 50Hz a.c Thrusters: 1 Thwart. FP thruster (f) Fuel: 267.0 (d.f.) 5.5pd
9577202 *9MLJ2* -	**TEKNIK WIRA** **TL Geotechnics Sdn Bhd** TL Geosciences Sdn Bhd *Port Klang* *Malaysia* MMSI: 533067200 Official number: 334239	**1,988** 596 1,736	Class: BV (AB)	**2010-06 Sapor Shipbuilding Industries Sdn Bhd — Sibu** Yd No: SAPOR 66 Loa 61.25 Br ex - Dght 4.500 Lbp 53.90 Br md 16.00 Dpth 6.00 Welded, 1 dk	**(B21B20A) Anchor Handling Tug Supply** Cranes: 1x5t	**2 oil engines** reduction geared to sc. shafts driving 2 CP propellers Total Power: 2,984kW (4,058hp) 11.0kn Cummins KTA-50-M2 2 x Vee 4 Stroke 16 Cy. 159 x 159 each-1492kW (2029bhp) Cummins Engine Co Inc-USA AuxGen: 2 x 300kW a.c, 3 x 500kW a.c Thrusters: 1 Tunnel thruster (f); 1 Tunnel thruster (a)
8914300 *9MQT6* -	**TEKNOGAS** *ex* Alstergas *-2014* **Silverline Maritime Sdn Bhd** - *Malaysia* MMSI: 533180064	**4,200** 1,260 4,999 T/cm 13.8	Class: BV (GL)	**1991-02 B.V. Scheepswerf "Waterhuizen" J. Pattje — Waterhuizen** Yd No: 377 Loa 99.91 (BB) Br ex 15.93 Dght 6.690 Lbp 92.60 Br md 15.90 Dpth 9.00 Welded, 1 dk	**(A11B2TG) LPG Tanker** Double Bottom Entire Compartment Length Liq (Gas): 4,234 3 x Gas Tank (s); 2 independent (stl) dcy horizontal, ER 4 Cargo Pump (s): 4x150m³/hr Manifold: Bow/CM: 46.2m Ice Capable	**1 oil engine** reduction geared to sc. shaft driving 1 CP propeller Total Power: 3,000kW (4,079hp) 14.0kn MaK 9M453C 1 x 4 Stroke 9 Cy. 320 x 420 3000kW (4079bhp) Krupp MaK Maschinenbau GmbH-Kiel AuxGen: 1 x 1400kW 220/440V 60Hz a.c, 2 x 715kW 220/440V 60Hz a.c Thrusters: 1 Thwart. FP thruster (f)
7005982 *ERMR* -	**TEKOS** *ex* Arctic Swan *-2010* *ex* Nordstar *-1996* *ex* Lindtank *-1991* *ex* Ottawa *-1989* *ex* Jessica *-1988* *ex* Ottawa *-1984* **Urancal Trading SA** Marine Standard Ltd (OOO 'Morskoy Standart') *Chisinau* *Moldova* MMSI: 214181318	**2,428** 1,235 4,237 T/cm 10.6	Class: UA (NV)	**1970-03 Lodose Varv AB — Lodose** Yd No: 155 Loa 99.00 Br ex 12.53 Dght 6.427 Lbp 92.20 Br md 12.50 Dpth 7.60 Welded, 1 dk	**(A12A2TC) Chemical Tanker** Double Bottom Entire Compartment Length Liq: 4,829 Part Cargo Heating Coils Compartments: 10 Ta, 2 Slop Ta, ER 6 Cargo Pump (s): 2x325m³/hr, 4x125m³/hr Manifold: Bow/CM: 18m Ice Capable	**1 oil engine** sr geared to sc. shaft driving 1 FP propeller Total Power: 2,000kW (2,719hp) 12.0kn MaK 6M453C 1 x 4 Stroke 6 Cy. 320 x 420 2000kW (2719bhp) (new engine 1988) Krupp MaK Maschinenbau GmbH-Kiel Fuel: 190.0 (d.f.)
9047063 *V7NF2* -	**TEKTONEOS** *ex* Grand Festival *-2007* **Empress Marine Co** Odysea Carriers SA *Majuro* *Marshall Islands* MMSI: 538002950 Official number: 2950	**25,899** 13,673 43,620 T/cm 49.0	Class: RI (LR) (NK) Classed LR until 31/1/11	**1993-01 Tsuneishi Shipbuilding Co Ltd — Fukuyama HS** Yd No: 1011 Loa 185.84 (BB) Br ex 30.44 Dght 11.319 Lbp 177.00 Br md 30.40 Dpth 16.20 Welded, 1 dk	**(A21A2BC) Bulk Carrier** Grain: 53,594; Bale: 52,280 Compartments: 5 Ho, ER 5 Ha: (19.2 x 15.3)4 (20.8 x 15.3)ER Cranes: 4x30t	**1 oil engine** driving 1 FP propeller Total Power: 7,120kW (9,680hp) 14.0kn B&W 6L60MCE 1 x 2 Stroke 6 Cy. 600 x 1944 7120kW (9680bhp) Mitsui Engineering & Shipbuilding CLtd-Japan AuxGen: 2 x 575kW 450V 60Hz a.c Boilers: AuxB (Comp) 7.0kgf/cm² (6.9bar)
9436604 *9WIJ9* -	**TEKUN 12262** **Bonafile Shipbuilders & Repairs Sdn Bhd** *Kota Kinabalu* *Malaysia* MMSI: 533000242 Official number: 332261	**142** 43 -	Class: GL	**2007-06 Forward Marine Enterprise Sdn Bhd — Sibu** Yd No: FM-19 Loa 23.50 Br ex - Dght - Lbp 21.32 Br md 7.32 Dpth 3.20 Welded, 1 dk	**(B32A2ST) Tug**	**2 oil engines** reduction geared to sc. shafts driving 2 FP propellers Total Power: 894kW (1,216hp) Cummins KTA-19-M3 2 x 4 Stroke 6 Cy. 159 x 159 each-447kW (608bhp) Cummins Engine Co Inc-USA
9520510 - -	**TEKUN 12326** - -	**140** 42 125	Class: (GL)	**2009-03 Jana Seribu Shipbuilding (M) Sdn Bhd — Sibu** (Hull) Yd No: (78/07) **2009-03 Bonafile Shipbuilders & Repairs Sdn Bhd — Sandakan** Yd No: 78/07 Loa 23.50 Br ex Dght 2.700 Lbp 21.96 Br md 7.32 Dpth 3.20 Welded, 1 dk	**(B32A2ST) Tug**	**2 oil engines** reduction geared to sc. shafts driving 2 FP propellers Total Power: 894kW (1,216hp) 10.0kn Cummins KTA-19-M3 2 x 4 Stroke 6 Cy. 159 x 159 each-447kW (608bhp) Cummins Engine Co Inc-USA
9520522 - -	**TEKUN 12330** **PT Fajar Bumi Sakti**	**140** 42 104	Class: (GL)	**2009-06 Jana Seribu Shipbuilding (M) Sdn Bhd — Sibu** (Hull) Yd No: (81/07) **2009-06 Bonafile Shipbuilders & Repairs Sdn Bhd — Sandakan** Yd No: 81/07 Loa 23.50 Br ex - Dght 2.700 Lbp 21.96 Br md 7.32 Dpth 3.20 Welded, 1 dk	**(B32A2ST) Tug**	**2 oil engines** reverse reduction geared to sc. shafts driving 2 FP propellers Total Power: 894kW (1,216hp) Cummins KTA-19-M3 2 x 4 Stroke 6 Cy. 159 x 159 each-447kW (608bhp) Cummins Engine Co Inc-USA AuxGen: 2 x 30kW 415V a.c
9489663 *YDA4365* -	**TEKUN 16216** **PT Prima Armada Nusantara** - *Jakarta* *Indonesia* Official number: 2008 PST NO 5216/L	**163** 49 135	Class: KI NK	**2008-01 Bonafile Shipbuilders & Repairs Sdn Bhd — Sandakan** Yd No: 21/06 Loa 26.10 Br ex - Dght 2.762 Lbp 24.22 Br md 7.32 Dpth 3.35 Welded, 1 dk	**(B32A2ST) Tug**	**2 oil engines** reduction geared to sc. shafts driving 2 Propellers Total Power: 1,220kW (1,658hp) Yanmar 6AYM-ETE 2 x 4 Stroke 6 Cy. 155 x 180 each-610kW (829bhp) (new engine 2008) Yanmar Diesel Engine Co Ltd-Japan Fuel: 105.0
9517862 *9WIK4* -	**TEKUN 16217** **Perusahaan Sinar Jaya Sdn Bhd** *Kota Kinabalu* *Malaysia* MMSI: 533845000 Official number: 332264	**163** 49 136	Class: NK	**2008-08 Bonafile Shipbuilders & Repairs Sdn Bhd — Sandakan** Yd No: 22/06 Loa 26.10 Br ex - Dght 2.750 Lbp 24.22 Br md 7.32 Dpth 3.35 Welded, 1 dk	**(B32A2ST) Tug**	**2 oil engines** reduction geared to sc. shafts driving 2 FP propellers Total Power: 1,220kW (1,658hp) Yanmar 6AYM-ETE 2 x 4 Stroke 6 Cy. 155 x 180 each-610kW (829bhp) Yanmar Diesel Engine Co Ltd-Japan AuxGen: 2 x 50kW a.c Fuel: 100.0
9469156 *9V7646* -	**TEKUN 20267** **Coastal Marine Pte Ltd** - *Singapore* *Singapore* MMSI: 563333000 Official number: 394568	**254** 77 264	Class: NK	**2007-11 Bonafile Shipbuilders & Repairs Sdn Bhd — Sandakan** Yd No: 08/07 Loa 30.00 Br ex - Dght 3.500 Lbp 28.06 Br md 8.60 Dpth 4.12 Welded, 1 dk	**(B32A2ST) Tug**	**2 oil engines** reduction geared to sc. shafts driving 2 FP propellers Total Power: 1,220kW (1,658hp) Mitsubishi S6R2-MTK3L 2 x 4 Stroke 6 Cy. 170 x 220 each-610kW (829bhp) Mitsubishi Heavy Industries Ltd-Japan AuxGen: 2 x 97kW a.c Fuel: 225.0 (d.f.)

9582087 *9WIV3* -	**TEKUN 24395** **Pleasant Engineering Sdn Bhd** - *Kota Kinabalu* *Malaysia* Official number: 332620	**274** 82 -	Class: BV	**2012-03 Pleasant Engineering Sdn Bhd — Sandakan** Yd No: 01/08 Loa 29.20 Br ex - Dght 3.840 Lbp 27.46 Br md 9.00 Dpth 4.85 Welded, 1 dk	**(B32A2ST) Tug**	**2 oil engines** reduction geared to sc. shafts driving 2 FP propellers Total Power: 2,238kW (3,042hp) Cummins KTA-38-M2 2 x Vee 4 Stroke 12 Cy. 159 x 159 each-1119kW (1521bhp) Cummins Engine Co Inc-USA AuxGen: 2 x 78kW 50Hz a.c Fuel: 230.0
9582099 *9WKL5* -	**TEKUN 24396** **Pleasant Engineering Sdn Bhd** - *Kota Kinabalu* *Malaysia* Official number: 332621	**274** 82 -	Class: BV	**2012-03 Pleasant Engineering Sdn Bhd — Sandakan** Yd No: 02/08 Loa 29.20 Br ex - Dght 3.840 Lbp 27.46 Br md 9.00 Dpth 4.85 Welded, 1 dk	**(B32A2ST) Tug**	**2 oil engines** reduction geared to sc. shafts driving 2 FP propellers Total Power: 2,238kW (3,042hp) Cummins KTA-38-M2 2 x Vee 4 Stroke 12 Cy. 159 x 159 each-1119kW (1521bhp) Cummins Engine Co Ltd-United Kingdom AuxGen: 2 x 78kW 50Hz a.c Fuel: 230.0 (d.f.)
9574640 *9WIV6* -	**TEKUN 24398** **Pleasant Engineering Sdn Bhd** - *Kota Kinabalu* *Malaysia* MMSI: 533002490 Official number: 332623	**274** 82 -	Class: BV	**2011-09 Pleasant Engineering Sdn Bhd — Sandakan** Yd No: 05/08 Loa 29.20 Br ex - Dght 3.840 Lbp 27.46 Br md 9.00 Dpth 4.85 Welded, 1 dk	**(B32A2ST) Tug**	**2 oil engines** reduction geared to sc. shafts driving 2 FP propellers Total Power: 2,238kW (3,042hp) Cummins KTA-38-M2 2 x Vee 4 Stroke 12 Cy. 159 x 159 each-1119kW (1521bhp) Cummins Engine Co Ltd-United Kingdom AuxGen: 2 x 78kW 50Hz a.c Fuel: 230.0 (d.f.)
9574676 *9WIV7* -	**TEKUN 24505** **Pleasant Engineering Sdn Bhd** - *Kota Kinabalu* *Malaysia* MMSI: 533002510 Official number: 332624	**274** 82 -	Class: BV	**2011-09 Pleasant Engineering Sdn Bhd — Sandakan** Yd No: 11/08 Loa 29.20 Br ex - Dght 3.840 Lbp 27.46 Br md 9.00 Dpth 4.85 Welded, 1 dk	**(B32A2ST) Tug**	**2 oil engines** reduction geared to sc. shafts driving 2 FP propellers Total Power: 2,238kW (3,042hp) Cummins KTA-38-M2 2 x Vee 4 Stroke 12 Cy. 159 x 159 each-1119kW (1521bhp) Cummins Engine Co Ltd-United Kingdom AuxGen: 2 x 78kW 50Hz a.c Fuel: 230.0 (d.f.)
9519420 *T2BH3* -	**TEKUN 32338** **Thaumas Marine Ltd** - *Funafuti* *Tuvalu* Official number: 27381212	**298** 90 244	Class: NK	**2014-03 Rajang Maju Shipbuilding Sdn Bhd — Sibu** Yd No: RMM0077 Loa 32.00 Br ex - Dght 3.500 Lbp - Br md 9.14 Dpth 4.20 Welded, 1 dk	**(B32A2ST) Tug**	**2 oil engines** geared to sc. shafts driving 2 Propellers Total Power: 2,354kW (3,200hp) Cummins KTA-50-M2 2 x Vee 4 Stroke 16 Cy. 159 x 159 each-1177kW (1600bhp) Cummins Engine Co Inc-USA
9519468 *T2BM3* -	**TEKUN 32352** **Thaumas Marine Ltd** - *Funafuti* *Tuvalu* Official number: 24721111	**298** 90 249	Class: NK	**2011-08 Rajang Maju Shipbuilding Sdn Bhd — Sibu** Yd No: RMM0007 Loa 32.00 Br ex - Dght 3.500 Lbp 29.23 Br md 9.14 Dpth 4.20 Welded, 1 dk	**(B32A2ST) Tug**	**2 oil engines** reduction geared to sc. shafts driving 2 FP propellers Total Power: 2,386kW (3,244hp) Cummins KTA-50-M2 2 x Vee 4 Stroke 16 Cy. 159 x 159 each-1193kW (1622bhp) Cummins Engine Co Inc-USA Fuel: 240.0 (d.f.)
9519470 *T2BN3* -	**TEKUN 32353** **Thaumas Marine Ltd** - *Funafuti* *Tuvalu* Official number: 27391212	**298** 90 249	Class: NK	**2014-03 Rajang Maju Shipbuilding Sdn Bhd — Sibu** Yd No: RMM0008 Loa 32.00 Br ex - Dght 3.500 Lbp - Br md 9.14 Dpth 4.20 Welded, 1 dk	**(B32A2ST) Tug**	**2 oil engines** geared to sc. shafts driving 2 FP propellers Total Power: 2,984kW (4,058hp) Cummins KTA-50-M2 2 x Vee 4 Stroke 16 Cy. 159 x 159 each-1492kW (2029bhp) Cummins Engine Co Inc-USA
8992974 *YFDR* -	**TELAGA EXPRESS** **PT Telaga Citra Abadi** - *Tanjungpinang* *Indonesia*	**326** 98 -	Class: (KI)	**1997-03 P.T. Marina Indah Shipyard — Tanjungpinang** Loa 39.50 Br ex - Dght - Lbp 34.20 Br md 6.80 Dpth 3.10 Bonded, 1 dk	**(A37B2PS) Passenger Ship** Hull Material: Reinforced Plastic	**3 oil engines** geared to sc. shafts driving 3 Propellers Total Power: 1,347kW (1,830hp) M.T.U. 12V183 3 x Vee 4 Stroke 12 Cy. 128 x 142 each-449kW (610bhp) (made 1996) MTU Friedrichshafen GmbH-Friedrichshafen
9672375 *POYI* -	**TELAGA MAS** *ex Boda 4 -2012* **PT Pelayaran Tempuran Emas Tbk (TEMAS Line)** - *Indonesia* MMSI: 525019050	**6,640** 3,718 8,180	Class: (CC)	**2012-12 Ningbo Boda Shipbuilding Co Ltd — Xiangshan County ZJ** Yd No: BD1204 Loa 119.90 (BB) Br ex - Dght 5.200 Lbp 115.00 Br md 21.80 Dpth 7.30 Welded, 1 dk	**(A33A2CC) Container Ship (Fully Cellular)** TEU 537	**1 oil engine** reduction geared to sc. shaft driving 1 FP propeller Total Power: 2,060kW (2,801hp) 10.5kn Thrusters: 1 Tunnel thruster (f)
9390147 *V2FQ8* -	**TELAMON** **Argonauten Holding GmbH & Co KG** Wessels Reederei GmbH & Co KG *Saint John's* *Antigua & Barbuda* MMSI: 305760000 Official number: 4904	**2,452** 1,369 3,664	Class: GL	**2009-06 Slovenske Lodenice a.s. — Komarno** Yd No: 2977 Loa 87.83 (BB) Br ex - Dght 5.490 Lbp 81.32 Br md 12.80 Dpth 7.10 Welded, 1 dk	**(A31A2GX) General Cargo Ship** Grain: 4,585 TEU 176 incl. 6 ref. Compartments: 1 Ho, ER 1 Ha: ER Ice Capable	**1 oil engine** reduction geared to sc. shaft driving 1 CP propeller Total Power: 1,520kW (2,067hp) 11.7kn MaK 8M20C 1 x 4 Stroke 8 Cy. 200 x 300 1520kW (2067bhp) Caterpillar Motoren GmbH & Co. KG-Germany AuxGen: 1 x 240kW 400/220V a.c, 2 x 184kW 400/220V a.c Thrusters: 1 Tunnel thruster (f) Fuel: 155.0 (d.f.)
8969070 *SX8404* -	**TELAMON** **Karaiskakis Naftiki Eteria** Koinopraxia Epivatochimatagogon Salaminos *Piraeus* *Greece* MMSI: 237294700 Official number: 10581	*664* 391 614		**2000 in Greece** Loa 75.80 Br ex - Dght 2.200 Lbp 64.80 Br md 16.40 Dpth 3.20 Welded, 1 dk	**(A36A2PR) Passenger/Ro-Ro Ship (Vehicles)** Bow ramp (centre) Stern ramp (centre) Lane-clr ht: 4.40 Cars: 104	**2 oil engines** reduction geared to sc. shafts driving 2 Directional propellers Total Power: 1,600kW (2,176hp) MAN 1 x 4 Stroke 800kW (1088bhp) MAN B&W Diesel AG-Augsburg MAN 1 x 4 Stroke 800kW (1088bhp) (new engine 2000) MAN B&W Diesel AG-Augsburg AuxGen: 2 x 120kW a.c
8329725 - -	**TELANG** **PT PERTAMINA (PERSERO)** - *Banjarmasin* *Indonesia*	*153* 46 150	Class: KI	**1969 Scheepsreparatiebedrijf A. Swets — Hardinxveld-Giessendam** Loa 36.61 Br ex - Dght 1.500 Lbp 35.13 Br md 7.95 Dpth 2.04	**(A37B2PS) Passenger Ship**	**1 oil engine** geared to sc. shaft driving 1 FP propeller Total Power: 110kW (150hp) 8.0kn Cummins NH-220-IP 1 x 4 Stroke 6 Cy. 130 x 152 110kW (150bhp) Cummins Engine Co Inc-USA
8332760 *9A6359* -	**TELASCICA** **Ivan Juresko** - *Pula* *Croatia* Official number: 1T-189	*123* 53 130	Class: CS	**1952 Brodogradiliste 'Vicko Krstulovic' — Split** Loa 30.00 Br ex - Dght 2.407 Lbp 27.82 Br md 5.50 Dpth 2.49 Welded	**(A31A2GX) General Cargo Ship** 2 Ha: 2 (3.9 x 2.4) Derricks: 2x1t; Winches: 2	**1 oil engine** driving 1 FP propeller Total Power: 99kW (135hp) 7.5kn Alpha 343-F 1 x 2 Stroke 3 Cy. 200 x 340 99kW (135bhp) A/S Burmeister & Wain's Maskin ogSkibsbyggeri-Denmark
7708297 *7THR* -	**TELEGHMA** **CNAN Med SpA** CNAN Group SpA *Alger* *Algeria* MMSI: 605086190 Official number: 2906	**8,393** 2,517 3,517	Class: BV	**1978-12 Towa Zosen K.K. — Shimonoseki** Yd No: 502 Loa 131.02 (BB) Br ex 18.52 Dght 6.217 Lbp 120.00 Br md 18.50 Dpth 13.49 Welded, 2 dks	**(A35A2RR) Ro-Ro Cargo Ship** Passengers: cabins: 12; berths: 12 Stern ramp (a) Len: 7.50 Wid: 7.00 Swl: - Stern door/ramp (a) Len: 10.50 Wid: 7.00 Swl: - Lane-Len: 853 Lane-Wid: 3.50 Lane-clr ht: 1.80 Cars: 600 Bale: 11,370 2 Ha: (21.9 x 5.4) (10.5 x 5.4)ER Cranes: 1x5t	**2 oil engines** geared to sc. shafts driving 2 CP propellers Total Power: 8,826kW (12,000hp) 21.0kn Pielstick 12PC2-2V-400 2 x Vee 4 Stroke 12 Cy. 400 x 460 each-4413kW (6000bhp) Nippon Kokan KK (NKK Corp)-Japan AuxGen: 3 x 640kW 220V 50Hz a.c Thrusters: 1 Thwart. FP thruster (f)

IMO / Call sign / Fishing No.	Name / Owner / Manager / Port / Flag	GT / NT / DWT	Classification	Builder / Dimensions	Type / Cargo	Machinery
8112378 - -	**TELEMACHUS** *ex Calabar Seahorse -2004* **Coloured Fin Ltd (CFL)** - *Port of Spain* *Trinidad & Tobago*	**175** 53 84	Class: (AB)	**1982-06 Machinefabriek en Scheepswerf Vervako B.V. — Heusden** (Hull) **1982-06 B.V. Scheepswerf Damen — Gorinchem** Yd No: 2711 Loa 25.68 Br ex 6.81 Dght 2.690 Lbp 22.89 Br md 6.80 Dpth 3.42 Welded, 1 dk	**(B32A2ST) Tug**	**2 oil engines** sr reverse geared to sc. shafts driving 2 FP propellers Total Power: 842kW (1,144hp) Caterpillar D379SCAC 2 x Vee 4 Stroke 8 Cy. 159 x 203 each-421kW (572bhp) Caterpillar Tractor Co-USA AuxGen: 2 x 50kW 110/220V 60Hz a.c Fuel: 28.5 (d.f.) 6.0pd
9412086 *SVAP3*	**TELENDOS** **Telendos II Special Maritime Enterprise (ENE)** Eletson Corp *Piraeus* *Greece* MMSI: 240903000 Official number: 11952	**22,971** 6,891 26,634 T/cm 41.5	Class: LR **✠100A1** SS 01/2010 liquefied gas carrier, Ship Type 2G Anhydrous ammonia, butane, butane and propane mixtures, butadiene, butylene, propane and propylene in independent tanks Type A, maximum SG 0.70, partial loading VCM with maximum SG 0.97, maximum vapour pressure 0.25 bar (0.45 bar in harbour), minimum cargo temperature minus 50 degree C LI *IWS **ShipRight** (SDA, FDA, CM) EP **✠LMC UMS +Lloyd's RMC (LG)** Eq.Ltr: K†; Cable: 632.5/68.0 U3 (a)	**2010-01 Hyundai Mipo Dockyard Co Ltd — Ulsan** Yd No: 8014 Loa 173.70 (BB) Br ex 28.03 Dght 10.400 Lbp 165.00 Br md 28.00 Dpth 17.80 Welded, 1 dk	**(A11B2TG) LPG Tanker** Double Bottom Entire Compartment Length Liq (Gas): 35,128 3 x Gas Tank (s); 3 independent (C.mn.stl) pri horizontal 8 Cargo Pump (s): 8x400m³/hr Manifold: Bow/CM: 88.7m	**1 oil engine** driving 1 FP propeller Total Power: 9,480kW (12,889hp) 16.7kn MAN-B&W 6S50MC-C 1 x 2 Stroke 6 Cy. 500 x 2000 9480kW (12889bhp) Hyundai Heavy Industries Co Ltd-South Korea AuxGen: 2 x 900kW 450V 60Hz a.c, 1 x 760kW 450V 60Hz a.c Boilers: AuxB (Comp) 9.2kgf/cm² (9.0bar) Fuel: 131.0 (d.f.) 1497.0 (r.f.)
1006219 *ZCRQ7* -	**TELEOST** *ex Ulysses -2000* **Teleost (Cayman) Ltd** - *George Town* *Cayman Islands (British)* MMSI: 319451000 Official number: 731955	**487** 146 -	Class: LR **✠100A1** SS 02/2013 SSC Yacht mono, G6 **LMC UMS** Cable: 284.7/20.5 U2	**1998-11 Eltink's Scheeps- en Jachtwerf B.V. — Katwijk a/d Maas** (Hull) Yd No: 159 **1998-11 Jacht- en Scheepswerf C. van Lent & Zonen B.V. — Kaag** Yd No: 781 Loa 48.80 Br ex 8.65 Dght 2.430 Lbp 40.70 Br md 8.15 Dpth 4.55 Welded, 1 dk	**(X11A2YP) Yacht**	**2 oil engines** with flexible couplings & sr reverse geared to sc. shafts driving 2 FP propellers Total Power: 1,350kW (1,836hp) 14.5kn Caterpillar 3508TA 2 x Vee 4 Stroke 8 Cy. 170 x 190 each-675kW (918bhp) Caterpillar Inc-USA AuxGen: 1 x 125kW 400V 50Hz a.c, 1 x 145kW 400V 50Hz a.c Thrusters: 1 Thwart. FP thruster (f)
8714346 *CGCB* -	**TELEOST** *ex Atlantic Champion -1995* **Government of Canada (Canadian Coast Guard)** - SatCom: Inmarsat A 1562545 *Ottawa, ON* *Canada* MMSI: 316002140 Official number: 808657	**2,405** 1,216 -	Class: (NV)	**1988-07 Tangen Verft AS — Kragero** (Hull) Yd No: 93 **1988-07 Langsten Slip & Baatbyggeri AS — Tomrefjord** Yd No: 137 Converted From: Stern Trawler-1994 Loa 63.00 (BB) Br ex - Dght 6.240 Lbp 55.71 Br md 14.33 Dpth 8.89 Welded, 2 dks	**(B12D2FR) Fishery Research Vessel** Ins: 1,200 Ice Capable	**1 oil engine** with clutches, flexible couplings & sr geared to sc. shaft driving 1 CP propeller Total Power: 2,944kW (4,003hp) 14.5kn Caterpillar 3612TA 1 x Vee 4 Stroke 12 Cy. 280 x 300 2944kW (4003bhp) Caterpillar Inc-USA AuxGen: 1 x 1456kW 440V 60Hz a.c, 1 x 1070kW 440V 60Hz a.c, 1 x 560kW 440V 60Hz a.c Thrusters: 1 Thwart. CP thruster (f)
7636341 *OF3100* -	**TELEPAATTI** **Relacom Finland Oy** - *Turku* *Finland* MMSI: 230234000 Official number: 10683	**376** 117 320	Class: NV	**1978-11 Rauma-Repola Oy — Savonlinna** Yd No: 414 Loa 36.61 Br ex 7.73 Dght 3.100 Lbp 31.55 Br md 7.71 Dpth 3.87 Welded, 1 dk	**(B34D2SL) Cable Layer** Hull Material: Aluminium Alloy Ice Capable	**1 oil engine** with clutches, flexible couplings & sr geared to sc. shaft driving 1 CP propeller Total Power: 736kW (1,001hp) 10.0kn Wartsila 624TS 1 x 4 Stroke 6 Cy. 240 x 310 736kW (1001bhp) Oy Wartsila Ab-Finland AuxGen: 2 x 88kW 380V 50Hz a.c Thrusters: 1 Thwart. FP thruster (f); 1 Tunnel thruster (a)
9573153 *PQ7990* -	**TELESCOPIUM** **Saveiros Camuyrano - Servicos Maritimos SA** - *Santos* *Brazil* MMSI: 710013540 Official number: 3813889572	**374** 112 273	Class: LR **✠100A1** SS 04/2013 tug, fire-fighting Ship 1 (2400m3/hr) with water spray *IWS **LMC** **UMS** Eq.Ltr: H; Cable: 302.5/22.0 U2 (a)	**2013-04 Wilson, Sons SA — Guaruja** (Hull) Yd No: 123 **2013-04 B.V. Scheepswerf Damen — Gorinchem** Yd No: 511224 Loa 32.22 Br ex 11.70 Dght 5.000 Lbp 29.01 Br md 10.60 Dpth 5.00 Welded, 1 dk	**(B32A2ST) Tug**	**2 oil engines** gearing integral to driving 2 Directional propellers Total Power: 4,200kW (5,710hp) Caterpillar 3516B 2 x Vee 4 Stroke 16 Cy. 170 x 215 each-2100kW (2855bhp) Caterpillar Inc-USA AuxGen: 2 x 100kW 440V 60Hz a.c
8403478 - -	**TELFORD CORAL SUB** **Telford Property Fund Ltd** Telford South Molle Island Pty Ltd *Shute Harbour, Qld* *Australia*	*180* - 50		**1984-07 North Queensland Engineers & Agents Pty Ltd — Cairns QLD** Yd No: 117 Loa 18.01 Br ex 5.31 Dght 1.501 Lbp - Br md 5.01 Dpth 2.49 Welded, 1 dk	**(A37B2PS) Passenger Ship**	**1 oil engine** driving 4 hydraulic pumps connected to thruster units driving 1 FP propeller Total Power: 118kW (160hp) 3.0kn General Motors 8-21-T 1 x Vee 4 Stroke 8 Cy. 108 x 112 118kW (160bhp) General Motors Detroit DieselAllison Divn-USA Thrusters: 1 Thwart. FP thruster (f); 2 Directional thruster (a); 1 Thwart. CP thruster (a) Fuel: 1.0 (d.f.)
9105889 *IBBT* -	**TELIRI** **Elettra Tlc SpA** - SatCom: Inmarsat C 424707810 *Catania* *Italy* MMSI: 247057000 Official number: 1	**8,345** 2,503 3,400	Class: RI (BV)	**1996-03 Fincantieri-Cant. Nav. Italiani SpA — Livorno** Yd No: 5951 Loa 111.50 Br ex - Dght 6.513 Lbp 95.00 Br md 19.00 Dpth 12.50 Welded, 1 dk	**(B34D2SL) Cable Layer** Cranes: 1x23t,2x10t	**3 diesel electric oil engines** driving 3 gen. Connecting to 2 elec. motors each (2200kW) driving 2 Directional propellers Total Power: 10,128kW (13,769hp) 14.5kn Nohab 12V25 1 x Vee 4 Stroke 12 Cy. 250 x 300 2768kW (3763bhp) Wartsila Diesel Oy-Finland Nohab 16V25 2 x Vee 4 Stroke 16 Cy. 250 x 300 each-3680kW (5003bhp) Wartsila Diesel Oy-Finland Thrusters: 2 Thwart. CP thruster (f) Fuel: 529.0 (d.f.)
8877928 *ES2031* EK-9201	**TELISNA** **AS Caroline** - *Haapsalu* *Estonia* MMSI: 276379000 Official number: 198FH05	**117** 35 30	Class: (RS)	**1983 Sosnovskiy Sudostroitelnyy Zavod — Sosnovka** Yd No: 639 Loa 25.50 Br ex 7.00 Dght 2.390 Lbp 22.00 Br md 6.80 Dpth 3.30 Welded, 1 dk	**(B11B2FV) Fishing Vessel**	**1 oil engine** driving 1 FP propeller Total Power: 221kW (300hp) 9.5kn S.K.L. 6NVD26A-2 1 x 4 Stroke 6 Cy. 180 x 260 221kW (300bhp) VEB Schwermaschinenbau "KarlLiebknecht" (SKL)-Magdeburg AuxGen: 2 x 12kW a.c Fuel: 15.0 (d.f.)
5012606 *SDAW* -	**TELL AV DONSO** *ex Tell -2011 ex Tell Av Donso -2008* *ex Tellus av Donso -1996 ex Koptra -1994* *ex Gullmartank -1988 ex Reno -1985* *ex Alssund -1972 ex Inger -1962* **Bunkertell Rederi AB** - *Donso* *Sweden* MMSI: 265504570	**309** 199 673	Class: (BV)	**1959-07 Broderna Jonssons Torrdocka — Lidkoping** Yd No: 5 Lengthened-1994 Loa 44.70 Br ex - Dght 3.860 Lbp 41.80 Br md 6.84 Dpth 4.41 Riveted\Welded, 1 dk	**(A13B2TP) Products Tanker** Liq: 770; Liq (Oil): 770 Cargo Heating Coils Compartments: 10 Ta, ER 1 Cargo Pump (s): 1x240m³/hr Manifold: Bow/CM: 20m	**1 oil engine** driving 1 FP propeller Total Power: 213kW (290hp) 9.0kn Caterpillar D353TA 1 x 4 Stroke 6 Cy. 159 x 203 213kW (290bhp) Caterpillar Tractor Co-USA AuxGen: 1 x 8kW 110V d.c, 1 x 5kW 110V d.c Fuel: 12.0 (d.f.) 1.0pd
5354602 *IURL* -	**TELLARO** **Morfini SpA** - *Bari* *Italy* Official number: 218	*737* 585 1,146 T/cm 2.8	Class: (RI)	**1962-07 INMA SpA — La Spezia** Yd No: 45 Loa 68.26 Br ex 9.53 Dght 3.000 Lbp 64.50 Br md 9.50 Dpth 3.41 Riveted\Welded, 1 dk	**(A13B2TU) Tanker (unspecified)** Liq: 1,630; Liq (Oil): 1,630 Cargo Heating Coils Compartments: 6 Ta, ER 3 Cargo Pump (s)	**2 oil engines** driving 2 FP propellers Total Power: 706kW (960hp) 9.5kn Fiat L230.6S 2 x 4 Stroke 6 Cy. 230 x 350 each-353kW (480bhp) SA Fiat SGM-Torino Fuel: 18.5
9285835 *C6ZI7* -	**TELLEVIKEN** *ex Tanea -2011 launched as Ganstar -2005* **Telleviken LLC** Taurus Tankers Ltd *Nassau* *Bahamas* MMSI: 311056700 Official number: 8001925	**62,806** 34,551 115,340 T/cm 99.8	Class: AB (NV)	**2005-05 Samsung Heavy Industries Co Ltd — Geoje** Yd No: 1473 Loa 249.87 (BB) Br ex 43.84 Dght 14.900 Lbp 239.00 Br md 43.84 Dpth 21.30 Welded, 1 dk	**(A13B2TP) Products Tanker** Double Hull (13F) Liq: 124,259; Liq (Oil): 130,000 Cargo Heating Coils Compartments: 12 Wing Ta, 2 Wing Slop Ta, ER 3 Cargo Pump (s): 3x3000m³/hr Manifold: Bow/CM: 124m	**1 oil engine** driving 1 FP propeller Total Power: 13,560kW (18,436hp) 15.3kn MAN-B&W 6S60MC-C 1 x 2 Stroke 6 Cy. 600 x 2400 13560kW (18436bhp) Doosan Engine Co Ltd-South Korea AuxGen: 3 x 740kW a.c Fuel: 139.0 (d.f.) 3258.0 (r.f.)

7374436 *TCMK* -	**TELLI-I** *ex* Esden *-1994* *ex* Sapen I *-1985* *ex* Blue Sky *-1977* - - SatCom: Inmarsat C 427112310 *Samsun* *Turkey* MMSI: 271000217 Official number: 6608	**3,577** 1,947 6,343	Class: (TL) (NK)	**1974**-05 **Miyoshi Shipbuilding Co Ltd — Uwajima EH** Yd No: 218 Loa 105.67 Br ex 15.83 Dght 6.400 Lbp 98.00 Br md 15.80 Dpth 7.80 Welded, 1 dk	**(A13B2TP) Products Tanker** Double Sides Entire Compartment Length Liq: 6,928; Liq (Oil): 6,928 Part Cargo Heating Coils Compartments: 14 Ta, ER 4 Cargo Pump (s): 1x800m^3/hr, 1x500m^3/hr, 2x300m^3/hr Manifold: Bow/CM: 50m	**1 oil engine** driving 1 FP propeller Total Power: 2,795kW (3,800hp) 13.0kn Akasaka 6DM51SS 1 x 4 Stroke 6 Cy. 510 x 840 2795kW (3800bhp) Akasaka Tekkosho KK (Akasaka DieselLtd)-Japan AuxGen: 2 x 160kW Fuel: 100.0 (d.f.) (Heating Coils) 455.0 (r.f.) 12.0pd
7946760 *TC7276* -	**TELLIOGLU-1** *ex* Isakali Karaman *-2011* *ex* Baser-I *-1995* *ex* Tornaci 1 *-1995* - - *Trabzon* *Turkey* MMSI: 271041064 Official number: 746	*286* 185 350		**1960 Ilyas Koksal ve Ort. — Istanbul** Loa 36.53 Br ex - Dght 2.850 Lbp 33.25 Br md 7.10 Dpth 2.87 Welded, 1 dk	**(A31A2GX) General Cargo Ship**	**1 oil engine** driving 1 FP propeller Total Power: 368kW (500hp) 8.0kn Deutz 1 x 4 Stroke 6 Cy. 368kW (500bhp) Kloeckner Humboldt Deutz AG-West Germany
5354638 *TC5623* -	**TELLITABYA** - **TDI Liman Isletmesi** - *Istanbul* *Turkey* Official number: 3223	*108* 30 -	Class: (GL)	**1961 D.W. Kremer Sohn — Elmshorn** Yd No: 1076 Loa 26.17 Br ex 6.71 Dght 2.579 Lbp - Br md - Dpth 3.46 Welded, 1 dk	**(B32A2ST) Tug**	**1 oil engine** driving 1 FP propeller Total Power: 588kW (799hp) Deutz SBV8M536 1 x 4 Stroke 8 Cy. 270 x 360 588kW (799bhp) Kloeckner Humboldt Deutz AG-West Germany AuxGen: 1 x 60kW 220V d.c
9321615 *OXQC2* -	**TELLUS** *ex* Kungsvik *-2006* **P/R mt 'Tellus'** Sirius Shipping ApS SatCom: Inmarsat C 421917510 *Laeso* *Denmark (DIS)* MMSI: 219175000 Official number: D4474	**7,515** 3,031 9,181 T/cm 19.5	Class: NV (LR) ✠ Classed LR until 3/3/10	**2006**-11 **R.M.K. Tersanesi — Tuzla** Yd No: 64 Loa 124.50 (BB) Br ex 18.13 Dght 8.120 Lbp 115.70 Br md 18.00 Dpth 10.85 Welded, 1 dk	**(A12B2TR) Chemical/Products Tanker** Double Hull (13F) Liq: 10,475; Liq (Oil): 10,446 Cargo Heating Coils Compartments: 1 Ta, 10 Wing Ta, 2 Wing Slop Ta, ER 11 Cargo Pump (s): 11x330m^3/hr Manifold: Bow/CM: 62.5m Ice Capable	**1 oil engine** with clutches, flexible couplings & sr reverse geared to sc. shaft driving 1 CP propeller Total Power: 4,320kW (5,873hp) 15.0kn MaK 9M32C 1 x 4 Stroke 9 Cy. 320 x 480 4320kW (5873bhp) Caterpillar Motoren GmbH & Co. KG-Germany AuxGen: 3 x 728kW 440V 60Hz a.c, 1 x 1200kW 440V 60Hz a.c Boilers: e (ex.g.) 10.2kgf/cm^2 (10.0bar), TOH (o.f.) 10.2kgf/cm^2 (10.0bar) Thrusters: 1 Thwart. FP thruster (f) Fuel: 70.0 (d.f.) 300.0 (r.f.)
9050187 *9HA3442* -	**TELMA KOSAN** *ex* Tarquin Ranger *-2002* **Gasnaval SA** Lauritzen Kosan A/S *Valletta* *Malta* MMSI: 229606000 Official number: 9050187	**4,317** 1,549 5,771 T/cm 15.1	Class: BV	**1994**-03 **Appledore Shipbuilders Ltd — Bideford** Yd No: A.S.154 Loa 105.14 (BB) Br ex 15.90 Dght 6.900 Lbp 96.40 Br md 15.70 Dpth 8.25 Welded, 1 dk	**(A11B2TG) LPG Tanker** Liq (Gas): 5,532 2 x Gas Tank (s); 2 independent cyl horizontal 4 Cargo Pump (s): 4x175m^3/hr Manifold: Bow/CM: 48.4m Ice Capable	**1 oil engine** with clutches, flexible couplings & sr geared to sc. shaft driving 1 CP propeller Total Power: 3,450kW (4,691hp) 15.0kn MaK 6M551AK 1 x 4 Stroke 6 Cy. 450 x 550 3450kW (4691bhp) Krupp MaK Maschinenbau GmbH-Kiel AuxGen: 4 x 292kW 220/440V a.c Thrusters: 1 Thwart. CP thruster (f) Fuel: 578.0 (d.f.)
7534971 *9MYS* -	**TELOK INTAN** *ex* Fujiasu Maru No. 7 *-1982* **Mashaha Holdings Sdn Bhd** - *Penang* *Malaysia* Official number: 325269	*695* 460 1,126		**1970 Asakawa Zosen K.K. — Imabari** Loa 61.70 Br ex 9.53 Dght 4.192 Lbp 57.00 Br md 9.50 Dpth 4.60 Welded, 1 dk	**(A12A2TC) Chemical Tanker** Liq: 1,138 Compartments: 3 Ta, ER	**1 oil engine** driving 1 FP propeller Total Power: 883kW (1,201hp) 11.5kn Daihatsu 6DSM-26 1 x 4 Stroke 6 Cy. 260 x 320 883kW (1201bhp) Daihatsu Diesel Manufacturing Co Lt-Japan AuxGen: 2 x 48kW 225V a.c
7022411 *PKAB* -	**TELOK PATIPI** *ex* Barat *-1982* **Government of The Republic of Indonesia (Pemerintah Daerah Irian Jaya - Regional Govt)** - *Jakarta* *Indonesia*	*209* 200 203	Class: (KI)	**1969**-10 **P.T. Djantra Dock & Shipbuilding — Jakarta** Yd No: 40BC/64 Loa 36.99 Br ex 6.30 Dght 2.299 Lbp 32.49 Br md 6.25 Dpth 2.75 Welded, 1 dk	**(A31A2GX) General Cargo Ship**	**1 oil engine** driving 1 FP propeller Total Power: 202kW (275hp) 10.0kn MAN G6V235/33MA 1 x 4 Stroke 6 Cy. 235 x 330 202kW (275bhp) (made 1960, fitted 1969) Maschinenbau Augsburg Nuernberg (MAN)-Augsburg
7022423 *PKAA* -	**TELOK SERUI** - **Government of The Republic of Indonesia (Pemerintah Daerah Irian Jaya - Regional Govt)** - *Jakarta* *Indonesia*	*144* 137 203	Class: (KI)	**1969**-12 **P.T. Djantra Dock & Shipbuilding — Jakarta** Yd No: 40BC/65 Loa 36.99 Br ex 6.35 Dght 2.299 Lbp 32.49 Br md 6.30 Dpth 2.75 Welded, 1 dk	**(A31A2GX) General Cargo Ship**	**1 oil engine** driving 1 FP propeller Total Power: 202kW (275hp) MAN G6V235/330ATL 1 x 4 Stroke 6 Cy. 235 x 330 202kW (275bhp) (made 1960, fitted 1969) Maschinenbau Augsburg Nuernberg (MAN)-Augsburg
8606240 - -	**TELSTAR** - - - *Honduras*	*101* - -		**1985**-06 **Steiner Shipyard, Inc. — Bayou La Batre, Al** Loa 22.86 Br ex - Dght - Lbp 20.12 Br md 6.71 Dpth 3.36 Welded, 1 dk	**(B11A2FT) Trawler**	**1 oil engine** geared to sc. shaft driving 1 FP propeller Total Power: 276kW (375hp) Cummins KT-19-M 1 x 4 Stroke 6 Cy. 159 x 159 276kW (375bhp) Cummins Diesel International Ltd-USA
8521127 *PCEN* -	**TELSTAR** *ex* Tumak *-2011* *ex* Germania *-1994* **Amsterdam Tugs BV** Sleepdienst B Iskes & Zoon BV *IJmuiden* *Netherlands* MMSI: 245462000 Official number: 34446	**245** 73 445	Class: GL (RI)	**1987**-06 **Cant. Navale "Ferrari" S.p.A. — La Spezia** Yd No: 54 Loa 27.58 Br ex 9.12 Dght 3.200 Lbp 25.34 Br md 9.10 Dpth 3.70 Welded, 1 dk	**(B32A2ST) Tug**	**2 oil engines** with clutches & sr geared to sc. shafts driving 2 Directional propellers Total Power: 2,370kW (3,222hp) 10.8kn Deutz SBV6M628 2 x 4 Stroke 6 Cy. 240 x 280 each-1185kW (1611bhp) (made 1986) Kloeckner Humboldt Deutz AG-West Germany AuxGen: 2 x 38kW 220/380V 50Hz a.c Fuel: 37.5 (d.f.) 5.5pd
8652550 *PNJG* -	**TELUK AMBON** - **Government of The Republic of Indonesia (Direktorat Jenderal Perhubungan Darat - Ministry of Land Communications)** - *Tanjung Priok* *Indonesia*	**392** 118 -	Class: KI	**2010**-03 **P.T. Indomarine — Jakarta** Loa 40.00 Br ex - Dght 2.000 Lbp 36.10 Br md 10.50 Dpth 2.80 Welded, 1 dk	**(A36A2PR) Passenger/Ro-Ro Ship (Vehicles)**	**2 oil engines** reduction geared to sc. shafts driving 2 Propellers Total Power: 736kW (1,000hp) Yanmar 6HYM-ETE 2 x 4 Stroke 6 Cy. 133 x 165 each-368kW (500bhp) Yanmar Diesel Engine Co Ltd-Japan
9680322 *YDB6000* -	**TELUK BAJAU ALPHA** - **PT Agus Suta Lines** - *Samarinda* *Indonesia* Official number: 6164/IIk	**162** 49 -	Class: KI (Class contemplated)	**2012**-06 **P.T. Galangan Teluk Bajau Kaltim — Samarinda** Loa 23.06 Br ex - Dght 2.590 Lbp 22.73 Br md 7.20 Dpth 3.35 Welded, 1 dk	**(B32A2ST) Tug**	**2 oil engines** reduction geared to sc. shafts driving 2 FP propellers Total Power: 760kW (1,034hp) Cummins KT-19-M 2 x 4 Stroke 6 Cy. 159 x 159 each-380kW (517bhp) Cummins Engine Co Inc-USA
8731576 - -	**TELUK BAJAU BAHAGIA** - **PT Pelayaran Teluk Bajau Cipta Sejahtera** - *Samarinda* *Indonesia* Official number: 3589/IIK	**276** 83 -	Class: KI	**2007**-07 **P.T. Galangan Teluk Bajau Kaltim — Samarinda** Yd No: 06/GTBK Loa 31.00 Br ex - Dght 3.000 Lbp 27.50 Br md 8.50 Dpth 3.80 Welded, 1 dk	**(B32A2ST) Tug**	**2 oil engines** driving 2 FP propellers Total Power: 1,518kW (2,064hp) Mitsubishi S6R2-MTK3L 2 x 4 Stroke 6 Cy. 170 x 220 each-759kW (1032bhp) Mitsubishi Heavy Industries Ltd-Japan Fuel: 80.0 (d.f.)
9678018 - -	**TELUK BAJAU BRAVO** - **PT Pelayaran Teluk Bajau Cipta Sejahtera** - *Samarinda* *Indonesia* Official number: 2012 IIK No. 6223/L	**162** 49 -	Class: KI	**2012**-07 **P.T. Galangan Teluk Bajau Kaltim — Samarinda** Loa 23.75 Br ex 7.50 Dght 2.590 Lbp 21.50 Br md 7.20 Dpth 3.05 Welded, 1 dk	**(B32A2ST) Tug**	**2 oil engines** reduction geared to sc. shafts driving 2 FP propellers Total Power: 894kW (1,216hp) Cummins KTA-19-M3 2 x 4 Stroke 6 Cy. 159 x 159 each-447kW (608bhp) Cummins Engine Co Inc-USA AuxGen: 2 x 162kW 380/220V a.c
9286530 *YD6498* -	**TELUK BAJAU HARAPAN** - **PT Titian Mahakam Line** - *Samarinda* *Indonesia* Official number: IIK/3032/L	**143** 85 111	Class: KI (NK)	**2003**-01 **Yong Choo Kui Shipyard Sdn Bhd — Sibu** Yd No: 6721 Loa 23.50 Br ex - Dght 2.712 Lbp 21.37 Br md 7.32 Dpth 3.20 Welded, 1 dk	**(B32A2ST) Tug**	**2 oil engines** geared to sc. shafts driving 2 FP propellers Total Power: 940kW (1,278hp) Yanmar 6LAH-STE3 2 x 4 Stroke 6 Cy. 150 x 165 each-470kW (639bhp) Yanmar Diesel Engine Co Ltd-Japan AuxGen: 2 x 28kW a.c

8743024 **TELUK BAJAU MAKMUR** **339** Class: KI
- - 102
- **PT Pelayaran Teluk Bajau Cipta Sejahtera** -
Samarinda *Indonesia*

2009-11 PT Syukur Bersaudara — Samarinda
Loa 36.50 Br ex - Dght 2.600
Lbp 33.67 Br md 9.50 Dpth 3.60
Welded, 1 dk

(B32A2ST) Tug

2 oil engines reduction geared to sc. shafts driving 2 FP propellers
Total Power: 1,516kW (2,062hp)
Mitsubishi S6R2-MTK3L
2 x 4 Stroke 6 Cy. 170 x 220 each-758kW (1031bhp)
Mitsubishi Heavy Industries Ltd-Japan
AuxGen: 2 x 77kW 415V a.c
Fuel: 120.0

8738809 **TELUK BAJAU MULIA** **276** Class: KI
YDA6048 84
- **PT Pelayaran Teluk Bajau Cipta Sejahtera** -
Samarinda *Indonesia*

2007 P.T. Galangan Teluk Bajau Kaltim — Samarinda
Loa 31.00 Br ex - Dght 3.000
Lbp 28.03 Br md 8.50 Dpth 3.80
Welded, 1 dk

(B32A2ST) Tug

2 oil engines reduction geared to sc. shafts driving 2 FP propellers
Total Power: 1,518kW (2,064hp)
Mitsubishi S6R2-MTK3L
2 x 4 Stroke 6 Cy. 170 x 220 each-759kW (1032bhp)
Mitsubishi Heavy Industries Ltd-Japan
Fuel: 80.0 (d.f.)

9662966 **TELUK BAJAU SEJAHTERA** **456** Class: KI
POBT 137
- **PT Pelayaran Teluk Bajau Cipta Sejahtera** -
Samarinda *Indonesia*

2011-08 P.T. Galangan Teluk Bajau Kaltim — Samarinda
Loa 37.50 Br ex - Dght 3.560
Lbp 34.65 Br md 10.00 Dpth 4.20
Welded, 1 dk

(B32A2ST) Tug

2 oil engines reduction geared to sc. shafts driving 2 FP propellers
Total Power: 1,518kW (2,064hp)
Mitsubishi S6R2-MTK3L
2 x 4 Stroke 6 Cy. 170 x 220 each-759kW (1032bhp)
Mitsubishi Heavy Industries Ltd-Japan
Thrusters: 1 Tunnel thruster (f)

8650435 **TELUK BAJAU SEJATI** **601** Class: KI
- - 181
- **PT Pelayaran Teluk Bajau Cipta Sejahtera** -
Samarinda *Indonesia*

2010-12 P.T. Galangan Teluk Bajau Kaltim — Samarinda Yd No: 1-57-3-DK-10
Loa 38.11 Br ex - Dght 4.080
Lbp 35.32 Br md 11.00 Dpth 4.80
Welded, 1 dk

(B32A2ST) Tug

2 oil engines reduction geared to sc. shafts driving 2 FP propellers
Total Power: 2,354kW (3,200hp)
Cummins KTA-50-M2
2 x Vee 4 Stroke 16 Cy. 159 x 159 each-1177kW (1600bhp)
Cummins Engine Co Inc-USA
AuxGen: 2 x 80kW a.c
Thrusters: 1 Tunnel thruster (f)
Fuel: 230.0

8734061 **TELUK BAJAU SENTOSA** **276** Class: KI
- - 84
- **PT Pelayaran Teluk Bajau Cipta Sejahtera** -
Samarinda *Indonesia*

2005 P.T. Galangan Teluk Bajau Kaltim — Samarinda
Loa 31.00 Br ex - Dght -
Lbp 27.50 Br md 8.50 Dpth 3.80
Welded, 1 dk

(B32A2ST) Tug

2 oil engines driving 2 FP propellers
Total Power: 1,472kW (2,002hp)
Mitsubishi S6R2-MTK3L
2 x 4 Stroke 6 Cy. 170 x 220 each-736kW (1001bhp)
Mitsubishi Heavy Industries Ltd-Japan
Fuel: 80.0 (d.f.)

9684251 **TELUK BAYUR I** **236** Class: KI
- - 71
- **PT Pelabuhan Indonesia II (Persero) Cabang Teluk Bayur (Indonesia Port Corp II, Teluk Bayur)** 72
PT Pelabuhan Indonesia II (Persero) (Indonesia Port Corp II) (PELINDO II)
Semarang *Indonesia*

2013-02 PT Janata Marina Indah — Semarang Yd No: 062
Loa 26.50 Br ex 10.50 Dght -
Lbp 24.34 Br md 10.30 Dpth 3.80
Welded, 1 dk

(B32A2ST) Tug

2 oil engines reduction geared to sc. shafts driving 2 Propellers
Total Power: 2,942kW (4,000hp)
Niigata 6L26HLX
2 x 4 Stroke 6 Cy. 260 x 350 each-1471kW (2000bhp)
Niigata Engineering Co Ltd-Japan
AuxGen: 2 x 160kW 380V a.c

9563976 **TELUK BERAU** **4,374** Class: KI
PMVR *ex* Hongpu 67 *-2009* 2,616
- **PT Salam Pacific Indonesia Lines** 6,792
Jakarta *Indonesia*
MMSI: 525015473

2009-05 Linhai Jianghai Shipbuilding Co Ltd — Linhai ZJ Yd No: JH0907-1
Loa 114.30 Br ex - Dght 6.100
Lbp 107.60 Br md 16.00 Dpth 7.80
Welded, 1 dk

(A31A2GX) General Cargo Ship

1 oil engine geared to sc. shaft driving 1 FP propeller
Total Power: 2,059kW (2,799hp) 11.0kn
Guangzhou 8320ZC
1 x 4 Stroke 8 Cy. 320 x 440 2059kW (2799bhp)
Guangzhou Diesel Engine Factory CoLtd-China

9551076 **TELUK BINTUNI** **4,365** Class: KI
PMRG *ex* Hongpu 59 *-2008* 2,615
- **PT Salam Pacific Indonesia Lines** 6,792
Jakarta *Indonesia*
MMSI: 525015399

2008-12 Linhai Jianghai Shipbuilding Co Ltd — Linhai ZJ Yd No: JH0808
Loa 114.30 Br ex - Dght 6.100
Lbp 107.60 Br md 16.00 Dpth 7.80
Welded, 1 dk

(A33A2CC) Container Ship (Fully Cellular)
TEU 500

1 oil engine reduction geared to sc. shaft driving 1 Propeller
Total Power: 2,060kW (2,801hp) 13.0kn
Guangzhou 8320ZC
1 x 4 Stroke 8 Cy. 320 x 440 2060kW (2801bhp)
Guangzhou Diesel Engine Factory CoLtd-China
AuxGen: 2 x 240kW 400V a.c

8873661 **TELUK CENDERAWASIH I** **478** Class: KI
- - 158
- **Government of The Republic of Indonesia (Direktorat Jenderal Perhubungan Darat - Ministry of Land Communications)** -
PT ASDP Indonesia Ferry (Persero) - Angkutan Sungai Danau & Penyeberangan
Jakarta *Indonesia*

1993-02 P.T. Indomarine — Jakarta
Loa 38.30 Br ex - Dght 1.800
Lbp 32.50 Br md 10.50 Dpth 2.90
Welded, 1 dk

(A36A2PR) Passenger/Ro-Ro Ship (Vehicles)
Bow ramp (centre)
Stern ramp (centre)

2 oil engines reduction geared to sc. shafts driving 2 FP propellers
Total Power: 780kW (1,060hp)
Yanmar 6LAAM-UTE
2 x 4 Stroke 6 Cy. 148 x 165 each-390kW (530bhp) (made 1992)
Yanmar Diesel Engine Co Ltd-Japan
AuxGen: 2 x 11kW 220/380V a.c

8873673 **TELUK CENDERAWASIH II** **478** Class: KI
YDQK 158
- **Government of The Republic of Indonesia (Direktorat Jenderal Perhubungan Darat - Ministry of Land Communications)** -
PT ASDP Indonesia Ferry (Persero) - Angkutan Sungai Danau & Penyeberangan
Jakarta *Indonesia*

1993-03 P.T. Indomarine — Jakarta
Loa 38.30 Br ex - Dght 1.800
Lbp 32.50 Br md 10.50 Dpth 2.90
Welded, 1 dk

(A36A2PR) Passenger/Ro-Ro Ship (Vehicles)
Bow ramp (centre)
Stern ramp (centre)

2 oil engines reduction geared to sc. shafts driving 2 FP propellers
Total Power: 780kW (1,060hp)
Yanmar 6LAAM-UTE
2 x 4 Stroke 6 Cy. 148 x 165 each-390kW (530bhp) (made 1992)
Yanmar Diesel Engine Co Ltd-Japan
AuxGen: 2 x 11kW 220/380V a.c

9049944 **TELUK DAMAI** **198** Class: KI
- - 98
- **PT Pelayaran Teluk Bajau Cipta Sejahtera** -
Samarinda *Indonesia*

2003-01 P.T. Galangan Teluk Bajau Kaltim — Samarinda
Loa 38.50 Br ex - Dght 1.600
Lbp 36.75 Br md 8.50 Dpth 2.05
Welded, 1 dk

(A35D2RL) Landing Craft
Bow ramp (centre)

2 oil engines geared to sc. shafts driving 2 FP propellers
Total Power: 514kW (698hp)
Nissan RD10
2 x Vee 4 Stroke 10 Cy. 135 x 125 each-257kW (349bhp)
Nissan Diesel Motor Co. Ltd.-Ageo
AuxGen: 2 x 111kW 380/220V a.c
Fuel: 34.0

9551088 **TELUK FLAMINGGO** **4,365** Class: KI
PMQI *ex* Hongpu 60 *-2008* 2,615
- **PT Salam Pacific Indonesia Lines** 6,792
Jakarta *Indonesia*
MMSI: 525015393

2008-12 Linhai Jianghai Shipbuilding Co Ltd — Linhai ZJ Yd No: JH0809
Loa 114.30 Br ex - Dght 6.100
Lbp 107.60 Br md 16.00 Dpth 7.80
Welded, 1 dk

(A33A2CC) Container Ship (Fully Cellular)
TEU 500

1 oil engine reduction geared to sc. shaft driving 1 FP propeller
Total Power: 2,060kW (2,801hp) 13.0kn
Chinese Std. Type 8320ZC
1 x 4 Stroke 8 Cy. 320 x 440 2060kW (2801bhp)
Guangzhou Diesel Engine Factory CoLtd-China
AuxGen: 2 x 240kW 400V a.c

8102672 **TELUK JODOH I** *131* Class: (KI) (AB)
- - 2
- **Batam Industrial Development Authority** 87
Jakarta *Indonesia*

1982-01 Pan-Asia Shipyard & Engineering Co Pte Ltd — Singapore Yd No: PA/66
Loa 23.22 Br ex - Dght 2.263
Lbp 22.31 Br md 7.41 Dpth 2.87
Welded, 1 dk

(B32A2ST) Tug

2 oil engines sr reverse geared to sc. shafts driving 2 FP propellers
Total Power: 764kW (1,038hp) 10.0kn
Caterpillar 3412TA
2 x Vee 4 Stroke 12 Cy. 137 x 152 each-382kW (519bhp)
Caterpillar Tractor Co-USA
AuxGen: 2 x 40kW

7106695 **TELUK KABUI** *147* Class: (KI) (NK)
PKCG *ex* Kabui *-1973* 59
- **PT Pelayaran Nasional Indonesia (PELNI)** 191
Jakarta *Indonesia*

1970-12 KK Izumi Zosensho — Kitakyushu Yd No: 117
Loa 31.37 Br ex 6.41 Dght 2.100
Lbp 27.49 Br md 6.38 Dpth 2.67
Welded, 1 dk

(A31A2GX) General Cargo Ship
Grain: 209; Bale: 197
2 Ha: 2 (4.5 x 2.9)ER
Derricks: 4x2t

1 oil engine geared to sc. shaft driving 1 FP propeller
Total Power: 221kW (300hp) 9.8kn
Yanmar 6M-T
1 x 4 Stroke 6 Cy. 200 x 240 221kW (300bhp)
Yanmar Diesel Engine Co Ltd-Japan
Fuel: 18.5 1.5pd

5090995 **TELUK MAS** *1,118* Class: (KI) (GL)
PKUH *ex* Latowa *-1990* *ex* Djambu *-1990* 556
- **PT Pelayaran Tempuran Emas Tbk (TEMAS Line)** 960
Jakarta *Indonesia*
Official number: 1230/L

1962-02 Cantiere Navale M & B Benetti — Viareggio Yd No: 44
Loa 68.03 Br ex 10.06 Dght 4.242
Lbp 63.90 Br md 10.04 Dpth 6.10
Riveted\Welded, 2 dks

(A31A2GX) General Cargo Ship
2 Ha: (9.1 x 5.0) (11.5 x 5.0)ER
Derricks: 4x3t

1 oil engine driving 1 FP propeller
Total Power: 691kW (939hp) 9.0kn
Werkspoor TMABS336
1 x 4 Stroke 6 Cy. 330 x 600 691kW (939bhp)
NV Werkspoor-Netherlands
AuxGen: 1 x 60kW 220V d.c
Fuel: 114.0

8731150 *PMFT* -	**TELUK SINABANG** **Government of The Republic of Indonesia (Direktorat Jenderal Hubla)** - *Jakarta* *Indonesia* MMSI: 525016186	**750** 212 -	Class: KI	**2007**-12 **P.T. Daya Radar Utama — Jakarta** Loa 54.50 Br ex - Dght 2.430 Lbp 47.25 Br md 14.00 Dpth 3.40 Welded, 1 dk	**(A36A2PR) Passenger/Ro-Ro Ship (Vehicles)** Bow ramp (centre) Stern ramp (centre)	**2 oil engines** reduction geared to sc. shafts driving 2 Propellers Total Power: 1,516kW (2,062hp) Mitsubishi S6R2-MPTK2 2 x 4 Stroke 6 Cy. 170 x 220 each-758kW (1031bhp) Mitsubishi Heavy Industries Ltd-Japan AuxGen: 2 x 99kW 380V a.c
8849581 *YD5055* -	**TELUK SUNGKUN 08** *ex* Trisakti Setia *-2000* **PT Lintas Samudra Borneo Line** - *Surabaya* *Indonesia*	**185** 111 -	Class: (KI) (AB)	**1991**-05 **Jiangsu Wuxi Shipyard Co Ltd — Wuxi JS** Yd No: VEN1003 Loa 22.50 Br ex - Dght 2.400 Lbp 21.00 Br md 7.50 Dpth 3.20 Welded	**(B32A2ST) Tug**	**2 oil engines** sr geared to sc. shafts driving 2 FP propellers Total Power: 736kW (1,000hp) Cummins KTA-19-M 2 x 4 Stroke 6 Cy. 159 x 159 each-368kW (500bhp) Cummins Engine Co Inc-USA AuxGen: 2 x 88kW 400V a.c
7106700 *PKCH* -	**TELUK UTUMBUE** *ex* Utumbue *-1974* **PT Perusahaan Pelayaran Nusantara Jaya Wijaya Shipping Lines** - *Jayapura* *Indonesia*	*147* 59 191	Class: (KI) (NK)	**1970**-12 **KK Izumi Zosensho — Kitakyushu** Yd No: 118 Loa 31.37 Br ex 6.41 Dght 2.439 Lbp 27.49 Br md 6.38 Dpth 2.67 Welded, 1 dk	**(A31A2GX) General Cargo Ship** Grain: 209; Bale: 197 2 Ha: 2 (4.5 x 2.9)ER Derricks: 4x2t	**1 oil engine** geared to sc. shaft driving 1 FP propeller Total Power: 221kW (300hp) 9.8kn Yanmar 6M-T 1 x 4 Stroke 6 Cy. 200 x 240 221kW (300bhp) Yanmar Diesel Engine Co Ltd-Japan AuxGen: 1 x 22kW 115V Fuel: 18.5 1.5pd
9066588 *9GRW* -	**TEMA MANHEAN** *ex* Manhean *-2012* **Government of The Republic of Ghana (Ports & Harbours Authority)** - *Takoradi* *Ghana* Official number: 316861	**209** 62 183	Class: (GL)	**1995**-11 **Stocznia Tczew Sp z oo — Tczew** (Hull) **1995**-11 **B.V. Scheepswerf Damen — Gorinchem** Yd No: 3182 Loa 30.20 Br ex 8.03 Dght 3.300 Lbp 27.80 Br md 7.80 Dpth 4.05 Welded	**(B32A2ST) Tug**	**2 oil engines** reduction geared to sc. shafts driving 2 FP propellers Total Power: 1,866kW (2,538hp) 12.0kn Cummins KTA-50-M 2 x Vee 4 Stroke 16 Cy. 159 x 159 each-933kW (1269bhp) Cummins Engine Co Inc-USA AuxGen: 2 x 50kW 220/380V 50Hz a.c Fuel: 96.0 (d.f.)
6513475 - -	**TEMACO** *ex* Tempest *-2000* **Continental Offshore Pte Ltd** -	**284** 85 -		**1965 Adelaide Ship Construction Pty Ltd — Port Adelaide SA** Yd No: 26 Loa 31.86 Br ex 8.28 Dght 4.125 Lbp 29.24 Br md 8.11 Dpth 4.47 Welded, 1 dk	**(B32A2ST) Tug** Passengers: 100	**1 oil engine** reduction geared to sc. shaft driving 1 CP propeller Total Power: 1,193kW (1,622hp) 11.5kn General Motors 16-278-A 1 x Vee 2 Stroke 16 Cy. 222 x 267 1193kW (1622bhp) (made 1946, fitted 1965) General Motors Corp-USA AuxGen: 1 x 35kW 220V d.c, 1 x 25kW 220V d.c Fuel: 24.0 (d.f.)
7207920 *WDD4228* -	**TEMAN** **Diamond Services Corp** - *Morgan City, LA* *United States of America* MMSI: 367141940 Official number: 531995	*167* 113 -		**1971 Diamond Services Corp. — Bayou Sorrel, La** L reg 26.52 Br ex 8.84 Dght - Lbp - Br md 8.79 Dpth 2.01 Welded, 1 dk	**(B21A2OC) Crew/Supply Vessel**	**2 oil engines** driving 2 FP propellers Total Power: 882kW (1,200hp)
8844490 *YHFJ* -	**TEMAN NIAGA** *ex* Karya 9 *-2002* *ex* Myoei Maru *-2002* **PT Nusa Indo Lines** - *Jakarta* *Indonesia*	**666** 200 700	Class: KI	**1990**-06 **Azumi Zosen Kensetsu K.K. — Himeji** Converted From: Bulk Aggregates Carrier-2008 Loa 51.00 Br ex - Dght 4.000 Lbp 46.00 Br md 11.00 Dpth 5.30 Welded, 1 dk	**(A31A2GX) General Cargo Ship**	**1 oil engine** driving 1 FP propeller Total Power: 515kW (700hp) Matsui ML628GSC 1 x 4 Stroke 6 Cy. 280 x 520 515kW (700bhp) Matsui Iron Works Co Ltd-Japan AuxGen: 2 x 120kW 225V a.c
8654716 - -	**TEMAN SEJATI** **PT Artha Buana** - *Samarinda* *Indonesia*	**214** 65 -	Class: KI	**2008**-03 **PT Syukur Bersaudara — Samarinda** Loa - Br ex - Dght - Lbp 28.56 Br md 8.50 Dpth 3.60 Welded, 1 dk	**(B32A2ST) Tug**	**2 oil engines** reduction geared to sc. shafts driving 2 FP propellers Total Power: 1,220kW (1,658hp) Yanmar 6AYM-ETE 2 x 4 Stroke 6 Cy. 155 x 180 each-610kW (829bhp) Yanmar Diesel Engine Co Ltd-Japan AuxGen: 2 x 32kW 380/220V a.c
8738627 *YDA6322* -	**TEMAN SEJATI II** **PT Artha Buana** - *Samarinda* *Indonesia* Official number: 4605	**211** 64 -	Class: KI	**2008**-11 **PT Candi Pasifik — Samarinda** Yd No: 151108 Loa 29.00 Br ex - Dght - Lbp 26.78 Br md 8.00 Dpth 3.80 Welded, 1 dk	**(B32A2ST) Tug**	**2 oil engines** driving 2 Propellers Total Power: 1,716kW (2,334hp) Mitsubishi S12A2-MPTK 2 x Vee 4 Stroke 12 Cy. 150 x 160 each-858kW (1167bhp) Mitsubishi Heavy Industries Ltd-Japan
8662385 *YDA6606* -	**TEMAN SEJATI III** **PT Artha Buana** - *Samarinda* *Indonesia* Official number: 5000	**225** 68 -	Class: KI	**2009**-12 **PT Bunga Nusa Mahakam — Samarinda** Yd No: 261009 Loa 29.15 Br ex - Dght - Lbp 27.02 Br md 8.50 Dpth 3.70 Welded, 1 dk	**(B32A2ST) Tug**	**2 oil engines** reduction geared to sc. shafts driving 2 Propellers Total Power: 1,716kW (2,334hp) Mitsubishi S12A2-MPTK 2 x Vee 4 Stroke 12 Cy. 150 x 160 each-858kW (1167bhp) Mitsubishi Heavy Industries Ltd-Japan
9735311 *YB4911* -	**TEMANGGUNG** **PT Baruna Raya Logistics** - *Jakarta* *Indonesia* MMSI: 525019660	**100** 30 -	Class: BV (Class contemplated)	**2014**-02 **P.T. Batam Expressindo Shipyard — Batam** Yd No: 857 Loa 26.70 Br ex - Dght - Lbp - Br md 6.00 Dpth 1.40 Welded, 1 dk	**(B34H2SQ) Patrol Vessel** Hull Material: Aluminium Alloy	**2 oil engines** reduction geared to sc. shafts driving 2 Propellers Total Power: 1,492kW (2,028hp) Caterpillar C32 ACERT 2 x Vee 4 Stroke 12 Cy. 145 x 162 each-746kW (1014bhp) Caterpillar Inc-USA
9333929 *CQKO* -	**TEMARA** *ex* Shanghai Venture *-2011* **CIMSHIP Transportes Maritimos SA** Ership SAU *Madeira* *Portugal (MAR)* MMSI: 255804590	**32,505** 17,674 53,410 T/cm 57.3	Class: BV	**2007**-04 **Chengxi Shipyard Co Ltd — Jiangyin JS** Yd No: CX4214 Loa 189.89 (BB) Br ex - Dght 12.540 Lbp 183.25 Br md 32.26 Dpth 17.50 Welded, 1 dk	**(A21A2BC) Bulk Carrier** Double Hull Grain: 65,781; Bale: 64,000 Compartments: 5 Ho, ER 5 Ha: 4 (21.6 x 22.4)ER (19.2 x 20.8) Cranes: 4x36t	**1 oil engine** driving 1 FP propeller Total Power: 9,480kW (12,889hp) 14.2kn MAN-B&W 6S50MC-C 1 x 2 Stroke 6 Cy. 500 x 2000 9480kW (12889bhp) Hudong Heavy Machinery Co Ltd-China AuxGen: 3 x 650kW a.c Fuel: 230.0 (d.f.) (Heating Coils) 2000.0 (r.f.) 36.0pd
9242780 *PNPQ* -	**TEMASEK ATTAKA** **PT Bahtera Nusantara Indonesia** PT Bahtera Niaga Internasional *Jakarta* *Indonesia* MMSI: 525016315	**1,319** 446 1,300 T/cm 7.6	Class: KI NV	**2002**-02 **Pan-United Shipyard Pte Ltd — Singapore** Yd No: 137 Loa 58.00 Br ex 15.03 Dght 4.300 Lbp 51.55 Br md 15.00 Dpth 5.50 Welded, 1 dk	**(B21B20A) Anchor Handling Tug Supply**	**2 oil engines** with clutches, flexible couplings & sr geared to sc. shafts driving 2 CP propellers Total Power: 4,050kW (5,506hp) 14.0kn Wartsila 6L26 2 x 4 Stroke 6 Cy. 260 x 320 each-2025kW (2753bhp) Wartsila Finland Oy-Finland AuxGen: 2 x 1280kW 440V 60Hz a.c, 2 x 260kW 440V 60Hz a.c Thrusters: 2 Thwart. CP thruster (f) Fuel: 300.0 (d.f.) 20.0pd
9246255 *PNUR* -	**TEMASEK SEPINGGAN** **PT Bahtera Nusantara Indonesia** PT Bahtera Niaga Internasional *Jakarta* *Indonesia* MMSI: 525015814	**1,302** 391 1,300	Class: AB KI (NV)	**2002**-08 **Pan-United Shipyard Pte Ltd — Singapore** Yd No: 138 Loa 58.00 Br ex - Dght 4.300 Lbp 51.50 Br md 15.00 Dpth 5.50 Welded, 1 dk	**(B21B20A) Anchor Handling Tug Supply**	**2 oil engines** geared to sc. shafts driving 2 CP propellers Total Power: 4,050kW (5,506hp) 14.0kn Wartsila 6L26 2 x 4 Stroke 6 Cy. 260 x 320 each-2025kW (2753bhp) Wartsila Finland Oy-Finland AuxGen: 2 x 264kW a.c Thrusters: 2 Thwart. CP thruster (f)
9175547 *YGGS* -	**TEMBAGA 3** **PT Kuala Pelabuhan Indonesia** - *Jakarta* *Indonesia* MMSI: 525015058	**603** 181 -	Class: AB	**1998**-07 **Keppel Singmarine Dockyard Pte Ltd — Singapore** Yd No: 221 Loa 32.00 Br ex - Dght 4.000 Lbp - Br md 11.00 Dpth 6.00 Welded, 1 dk	**(B32B2SP) Pusher Tug**	**2 oil engines** geared to Sc. shafts driving 2 Directional propellers Total Power: 4,058kW (5,518hp) 12.0kn Caterpillar 3606TA 2 x 4 Stroke 6 Cy. 280 x 300 each-2029kW (2759bhp) Caterpillar Inc-USA AuxGen: 3 x 170kW a.c
9175559 *YGGT* -	**TEMBAGA 4** **PT Kuala Pelabuhan Indonesia** - *Jakarta* *Indonesia* MMSI: 525015056 Official number: 200 PST NO.1918/L	**603** 181 -	Class: AB	**1997**-11 **Keppel Singmarine Dockyard Pte Ltd — Singapore** Yd No: 222 Loa 32.00 Br ex - Dght 4.000 Lbp 32.00 Br md 11.00 Dpth 5.20 Welded, 1 dk	**(B32B2SP) Pusher Tug**	**2 oil engines** geared to sc. shafts driving 2 Directional propellers Total Power: 4,004kW (5,444hp) 14.5kn Caterpillar 3606TA 2 x 4 Stroke 6 Cy. 280 x 300 each-2002kW (2722bhp) Caterpillar Inc-USA AuxGen: 3 x 170kW a.c

IMO / Call sign	Name / Owner / Manager / Port / Flag	Tonnage	Class	Builder / Dimensions	Type / Capacity	Machinery
9337731 *V7MX8* -	**TEMBEK** *launched as* Tenbek *-2007* **Overseas LNG S1 Corp** Qatar Gas Transport Co Ltd (Nakilat) SatCom: Inmarsat C 453800475 *Majuro* *Marshall Islands* MMSI: 538002921 Official number: 2921	**136,410** 40,924 107,514 T/cm 133.1	Class: NV	**2007-11 Samsung Heavy Industries Co Ltd — Geoje** Yd No: 1605 Loa 315.16 (BB) Br ex 50.04 Dght 12.500 Lbp 303.00 Br md 50.00 Dpth 27.00 Welded, 1 dk	**(A11A2TN) LNG Tanker** Double Hull Liq (Gas): 211,885 6 x Gas Tank (s); 5 membrane (s.stl) pri horizontal, ER 10 Cargo Pump (s): 10x1400m³/hr Manifold: Bow/CM: 155.2m	**2 oil engines** driving 2 FP propellers Total Power: 37,320kW (50,740hp) 19.5kn MAN-B&W 6S70ME-C 2 x 2 Stroke 6 Cy. 700 x 2800 each-18660kW (25370bhp) Doosan Engine Co Ltd-South Korea AuxGen: 5 x 3210kW 6600V 60Hz a.c Fuel: 738.0 (d.f.) (Heating Coils) 7757.0 (r.f.)
9153202 *TCCU2* -	**TEMEL REIS II** **Istanbul Deniz Otobusleri Sanayi ve Ticaret AS (IDO)** - *Istanbul* *Turkey* MMSI: 271002342 Official number: 599	**395** 119 39	Class: TL (NV)	**1998-03 Kvaerner Fjellstrand AS — Omastrand** Yd No: 1640 Loa 35.00 Br ex - Dght 1.420 Lbp 32.22 Br md 10.10 Dpth 3.91 Welded, 2 dks	**(A37B2PS) Passenger Ship** Passengers: unberthed: 341	**4 oil engines** geared to sc. shafts driving 2 CP propellers Total Power: 2,404kW (3,268hp) 32.0kn M.T.U. 12V183TE72 4 x Vee 4 Stroke 12 Cy. 128 x 142 each-601kW (817bhp) MTU Friedrichshafen GmbH-Friedrichshafen AuxGen: 2 x 80kW 400V 50Hz a.c
7414705 *J8PX6* -	**TEMERAIRE** *ex* Cecrops *-2003* **Coloured Fin Ltd (CFL)** - *Kingstown* *St Vincent & The Grenadines* Official number: 400661	**295** 88 -	Class: LR ✠ **100A1** SS 05/2011 tug ✠ **LMC** Eq.Ltr: H; Cable: U2	**1976-02 Beliard-Murdoch S.A. — Oostende** Yd No: 226 Loa 29.98 Br ex 10.16 Dght 4.261 Lbp 27.11 Br md 10.01 Dpth 4.81 Welded, 1 dk	**(B32A2ST) Tug**	**2 oil engines** reverse reduction geared to sc. shafts driving 2 FP propellers Total Power: 3,162kW (4,300hp) EMD (Electro-Motive) 12-645-E5 2 x Vee 2 Stroke 12 Cy. 230 x 254 each-1581kW (2150bhp) General Motors Corp.Electro-Motive Div.-La Grange AuxGen: 2 x 76kW 440V 60Hz a.c, 1 x 36kW 440V 60Hz a.c Thrusters: 1 Tunnel thruster (f) Fuel: 159.5 (d.f.)
8740395 *PMOE* -	**TEMI** **Government of The Republic of Indonesia (Direktorat Jenderal Perhubungan Darat - Ministry of Land Communications)** PT ASDP Indonesia Ferry (Persero) - Angkutan Sungai Danau & Penyeberangan *Jakarta* *Indonesia* MMSI: 525015302	**1,148** 436 432	Class: KI	**2008-10 P.T. Sanur Marindo Shipyard — Tegal** Loa 45.50 Br ex - Dght 2.140 Lbp 40.65 Br md 12.00 Dpth 3.20 Welded, 1 dk	**(A36A2PR) Passenger/Ro-Ro Ship (Vehicles)**	**2 oil engines** driving 2 Propellers Total Power: 1,220kW (1,658hp) Yanmar 6AYM-ETE 2 x 4 Stroke 6 Cy. 155 x 180 each-610kW (829bhp) Yanmar Diesel Engine Co Ltd-Japan
9668257 *5NXO* -	**TEMILE** **E A Temile & Sons Development Co Ltd** CS Offshore DMCCO *Lagos* *Nigeria* MMSI: 657101100 Official number: SR2047	**3,602** 1,271 5,076	Class: AB	**2013-06 Fujian Mawei Shipbuilding Ltd — Fuzhou FJ** Yd No: 619-38 Loa 87.08 (BB) Br ex - Dght 6.060 Lbp 83.00 Br md 18.80 Dpth 7.40 Welded, 1 dk	**(B21A2OS) Platform Supply Ship** Cranes: 1x2t	**4 diesel electric oil engines** driving 4 gen. Connecting to 2 elec. motors each (2000kW) driving 2 Azimuth electric drive units Total Power: 6,864kW (9,332hp) 12.0kn Cummins QSK60-M 4 x Vee 4 Stroke 16 Cy. 159 x 190 each-1716kW (2333bhp) Cummins Diesel International Ltd-USA Thrusters: 1 Tunnel thruster (f); 1 Retract. directional thruster (f) Fuel: 1130.0 (d.f.)
7740831 *3EHG3* -	**TEMIRA** *ex* Bulgaria *-2006* **Plamar Navigation Ltd** Bulcom Ltd *Panama* *Panama* MMSI: 372068000 Official number: 3313107	**30,596** 18,041 52,975 T/cm 58.0	Class: (BR) (RS)	**1978 Sudostroitelnyy Zavod 'Okean' — Nikolayev** Loa 215.40 (BB) Br ex 31.86 Dght 12.250 Lbp 201.63 Br md 31.78 Dpth 16.84 Welded, 1 dk	**(A21A2BC) Bulk Carrier** Grain: 62,900 Compartments: 8 Ho, ER 8 Ha: (12.8 x 13.4)7 (12.8 x 16.7)ER	**1 oil engine** driving 1 FP propeller Total Power: 10,076kW (13,699hp) 14.3kn B&W 8DKRN74/160 1 x 2 Stroke 8 Cy. 740 x 1600 10076kW (13699bhp) Bryanskiy Mashinostroitelnyy Zavod (BMZ)-Bryansk Fuel: 671.0 (d.f.) (Heating Coils) 2563.0 (r.f.) 45.0pd
9374947 *3EDY8* -	**TEMIT** **Central Noble International Ltd** Tianjin Pennon International Shipping Management Co Ltd *Panama* *Panama* MMSI: 371732000 Official number: 3193306A	**1,972** 1,393 3,423	Class: CC	**2006-04 Rongcheng Xixiakou Shipyard Co Ltd — Rongcheng SD** Yd No: 009 Loa 81.00 (BB) Br ex - Dght 5.500 Lbp 76.00 Br md 13.60 Dpth 6.80 Welded, 1 dk	**(A31A2GX) General Cargo Ship** Grain: 4,487 Compartments: 2 Ho, ER 2 Ha: ER 2 (18.6 x 9.0) Ice Capable	**1 oil engine** reduction geared to sc. shaft driving 1 FP propeller Total Power: 1,618kW (2,200hp) 12.3kn Daihatsu 6DKM-26 1 x 4 Stroke 6 Cy. 260 x 380 1618kW (2200bhp) Anqing Marine Diesel Engine Works-China AuxGen: 2 x 150kW 400V a.c
8880456 *EROH* -	**TEMIXRON 1** *ex* Polenovo *-2007* **Temixron SA** Krystal Marine Ltd (OOO 'Krystall Marin') *Moldova* MMSI: 214181508	**1,652** 604 2,083	Class: (RS) (RR)	**1964-02 Slovenske Lodenice — Komarno** Yd No: 2028 Loa 103.62 Br ex 12.40 Dght 2.840 Lbp 97.30 Br md 12.20 Dpth 4.90 Welded, 1 dk	**(A31A2GX) General Cargo Ship** Grain: 3,415 Compartments: 4 Ho, ER 4 Ha: 4 (15.3 x 8.0)ER	**2 oil engines** driving 2 FP propellers Total Power: 772kW (1,050hp) 10.0kn Skoda 6L275PN 2 x 4 Stroke 6 Cy. 275 x 360 each-386kW (525bhp) (new engine 1990) CKD Praha-Praha AuxGen: 3 x 45kW a.c Fuel: 63.0 (d.f.)
8925311 *EROI* -	**TEMIXRON 2** *ex* Petrishchevo *-2007* **Temixron SA** Krystal Marine Ltd (OOO 'Krystall Marin') *Moldova* MMSI: 214181509	**1,843** 633 2,072	Class: IS (RS) (RR)	**1964-03 Slovenske Lodenice — Komarno** Yd No: 2029 Loa 103.50 Br ex 12.20 Dght 2.840 Lbp 100.05 Br md - Dpth 4.90 Welded, 1 dk	**(A31A2GX) General Cargo Ship**	**2 oil engines** driving 2 FP propellers Total Power: 772kW (1,050hp) Skoda 6L275PN 2 x 4 Stroke 6 Cy. 275 x 360 each-386kW (525bhp) CKD Praha-Praha
8925323 *ERLJ* -	**TEMIXRON 3** *ex* Astrakhan *-2008* **Temixron SA** Krystal Marine Ltd (OOO 'Krystall Marin') *Moldova* MMSI: 214181210	**1,843** 633 2,083	Class: IS (RS) (RR)	**1965-10 Zavody Tazkeho Strojarstva (ZTS) — Komarno** Yd No: 2052 Loa 103.60 Br ex 12.20 Dght 2.840 Lbp 100.05 Br md - Dpth 4.90 Welded, 1 dk	**(A31A2GX) General Cargo Ship**	**2 oil engines** driving 2 FP propellers Total Power: 772kW (1,050hp) Skoda 6L275PN 2 x 4 Stroke 6 Cy. 275 x 360 each-386kW (525bhp) CKD Praha-Praha
9447897 *A8VP9* -	**TEMPANOS** **Hull 1798 Co Ltd** Compania SudAmericana de Vapores SA (CSAV) *Monrovia* *Liberia* MMSI: 636014648 Official number: 14648	**88,586** 42,897 94,649	Class: GL	**2011-11 Samsung Heavy Industries Co Ltd — Geoje** Yd No: 1798 Loa 299.96 (BB) Br ex - Dght 13.500 Lbp 285.00 Br md 45.60 Dpth 24.60 Welded, 1 dk	**(A33A2CC) Container Ship (Fully Cellular)** TEU 8004 C Ho 3574 TEU C Dk 4430 TEU incl 1500 ref C.	**1 oil engine** driving 1 FP propeller Total Power: 43,610kW (59,292hp) 23.0kn MAN-B&W 7K98ME7 1 x 2 Stroke 7 Cy. 980 x 2660 43610kW (59292bhp) Doosan Engine Co Ltd-South Korea AuxGen: 2 x 2880kW 6600/450V a.c, 3 x 3360kW 6600/450V a.c Thrusters: 1 Tunnel thruster (f) Fuel: 290.0 (d.f.) 8600.0 (r.f.) 162.0pd
9130418 *YDA6412* -	**TEMPE** *ex* Keras *-2001* *ex* Regal 8 *-1998* **PT Maritim Barito Perkasa** - *Banjarmasin* *Indonesia* MMSI: 525002001	**177** 53 100	Class: KI (BV) (AB)	**1995-05 Hangzhou Dongfeng Shipyard — Hangzhou ZJ** Yd No: TS25-4 Loa 25.20 Br ex 8.30 Dght 2.300 Lbp 23.90 Br md 8.00 Dpth 3.00 Welded, 1 dk	**(B32A2ST) Tug**	**2 oil engines** reduction geared to sc. shafts driving 2 FP propellers Total Power: 1,184kW (1,610hp) 10.0kn MWM TBD234V16 2 x Vee 4 Stroke 16 Cy. 128 x 140 each-592kW (805bhp) (made 1992, fitted 1995) Motoren Werke Mannheim AG (MWM)-Mannheim AuxGen: 2 x 400kW 380V 50Hz a.c Fuel: 80.0 (d.f.) 4.8pd
8861412 - -	**TEMPEL** *ex* Cometa-IX *-1998* - -	*142* 92 14	Class: (RS)	**1977 Zavod im. "Ordzhonikidze" — Poti** Loa 35.10 Br ex 11.00 Dght 1.140 Lbp - Br md - Dpth - Welded, 1 dk	**(A37B2PS) Passenger Ship** Hull Material: Aluminium Alloy Passengers: unberthed: 102	**2 oil engines** driving 2 FP propellers Total Power: 1,324kW (1,800hp) 30.0kn Zvezda M400 2 x Vee 4 Stroke 12 Cy. 180 x 200 each-662kW (900bhp) "Zvezda"-Leningrad
7117553 - -	**TEMPELLAC** - -	*285* 75 318	Class: (GL)	**1971-10 Ast. Picsa S.A. — Callao** Yd No: 340 L reg 30.48 Br ex 7.62 Dght - Lbp - Br md - Dpth 3.66 Welded, 1 dk	**(B11B2FV) Fishing Vessel**	**1 oil engine** driving 1 FP propeller Total Power: 588kW (799hp) G.M. (Detroit Diesel) 12V-149 1 x Vee 2 Stroke 12 Cy. 146 x 146 588kW (799bhp) General Motors Corp-USA

IMO / Call sign	Name / Owner	Tonnage	Class	Builder / Dimensions	Type	Machinery
9235880 *OJKD* -	**TEMPERA** **SEB Leasing Oy** Neste Shipping Oy SatCom: Inmarsat C 423094410 *Porvoo* *Finland* MMSI: 230944000 Official number: 12236	**64,259** 30,846 106,034 T/cm 95.2	Class: LR ✠ **100A1** SS 08/2012 Double Hull oil tanker ESP **ShipRight** (SDA, FDA, CM) *IWS LI SPM Ice Class 1AS at 15.655m draught Max/min draught fwd 15.655/7.680m Max/min draught aft 15.655/8.950m Power required 16,000kw, installed power 16,000kw ✠ **LMC** **UMS IGS** Eq.Ltr: W†; Cable: 742.5/95.0 U3 (a)	**2002-08 Sumitomo Heavy Industries Ltd. — Yokosuka Shipyard, Yokosuka** Yd No: 1285 Loa 252.00 (BB) Br ex 44.05 Dght 15.319 Lbp 230.00 Br md 44.00 Dpth 22.50 Welded, 1 dk	**(A13A2TV) Crude Oil Tanker** Double Hull (13F) Liq: 116,562; Liq (Oil): 116,562 Cargo Heating Coils Compartments: 12 Wing Ta, ER, 2 Wing Slop Ta 3 Cargo Pump (s): 3x3500m³/hr Manifold: Bow/CM: 123m Ice Capable	**4 diesel electric oil engines** driving 2 gen. each 6000kW 6600V a.c 2 gen. each 4000kW 6600V a.c Connecting to 1 elec. Motor of (16000kW) driving 1 Azimuth electric drive unit Total Power: 21,080kW (28,662hp) 14.5kn Wartsila 6L38B 2 x 4 Stroke 6 Cy. 380 x 475 each-4220kW (5738bhp) Diesel United Ltd.-Aioi Wartsila 9L38B 2 x 4 Stroke 9 Cy. 380 x 475 each-6320kW (8593bhp) Diesel United Ltd.-Aioi AuxGen: 1 x 1700kW 6600/450V 60Hz a.c Boilers: e (ex.g.) 15.6kgf/cm² (15.3bar), e (ex.g.) 15.6kgf/cm² (15.3bar), WTAuxB (o.f.) 10.7kgf/cm² (10.5bar) Thrusters: 2 Thwart. CP thruster (f) Fuel: 260.0 (d.f.) 2663.0 (r.f.)
9320271 *ZFU5869* -	**TEMPEST** **Government of Bermuda (Department of Marine & Ports Services)** - *Hamilton* *Bermuda (British)*	*174* 118 18	Class: LR ✠ **100A1** SS 06/2009 SSC passenger catamaran HSC G2 for inter island service in Bermuda **LMC** **UMS** Cable: 110.0/14.0 U1	**2004-06 North West Bay Ships Pty Ltd — Margate TAS** Yd No: 7 Loa 23.56 Br ex 7.87 Dght 0.940 Lbp 20.77 Br md 7.66 Dpth 2.45 Welded, 1 dk	**(A37B2PS) Passenger Ship** Hull Material: Aluminium Alloy Passengers: unberthed: 177	**4 oil engines** geared to sc. shafts driving 4 Water jets Total Power: 2,100kW (2,856hp) 30.0kn M.T.U. 8V2000M70 4 x Vee 4 Stroke 8 Cy. 130 x 150 each-525kW (714bhp) MTU Friedrichshafen GmbH-Friedrichshafen AuxGen: 2 x 25kW 230V 60Hz a.c
9424754 *PHOT*	**TEMPEST** **Chemgas Shipping BV** - *Rotterdam* *Netherlands* MMSI: 244285000 Official number: 49402	**2,294** 688 1,809 T/cm 10.0	Class: BV	**2008-09 Societatea Comerciala Severnav S.A. — Drobeta-Turnu Severin** (Hull) Yd No: (680) **2008-09 Machinefabriek Breko B.V. — Papendrecht** Yd No: 680 Loa 99.90 Br ex 11.45 Dght 3.660 Lbp 96.79 Br md 11.40 Dpth 6.50 Welded, 1 dk	**(A11B2TG) LPG Tanker** Liq (Gas): 5,000 3 x Gas Tank (s); independent 3 Cargo Pump (s): 3x200m³/hr Manifold: Bow/CM: 50m	**2 oil engines** reduction geared to sc. shafts driving 2 FP propellers Total Power: 2,206kW (3,000hp) Mitsubishi S6U-MPTK 2 x 4 Stroke 6 Cy. 240 x 260 each-1103kW (1500bhp) Mitsubishi Heavy Industries Ltd-Japan Thrusters: 1 Tunnel thruster (f) Fuel: 55.0 (d.f.) 124.0 (d.f.)
9675846 - -	**TEMPEST** **JL Marine Pty Ltd** International Maritime Services Pty Ltd	**167** 73 40		**2013-08 Strategic Marine (S) Pte Ltd — Singapore** Yd No: H395 Loa 23.95 Br ex - Dght 1.850 Lbp - Br md 8.80 Dpth 3.80 Welded, 1 dk	**(B21A20C) Crew/Supply Vessel** Hull Material: Aluminium Alloy	**2 oil engines** reduction geared to sc. shafts driving 2 Propellers Total Power: 1,766kW (2,402hp) Yanmar 12AYM-WST 2 x Vee 4 Stroke 12 Cy. 155 x 180 each-883kW (1201bhp) Yanmar Diesel Engine Co Ltd-Japan
7390648 *5NBDJ* -	**TEMPEST** *ex* Veesea Tempest *-2001* *ex* Cozumel Island *-1991* **Phenix Associates Ltd** - *Nigeria* Official number: 377313	**877** 189 1,021	Class: (AB)	**1974-08 American Marine Corp. — New Orleans, La** Yd No: 1117 Converted From: Offshore Tug/Supply Ship-1991 Loa 55.58 Br ex 11.59 Dght 3.912 Lbp 53.45 Br md 11.56 Dpth 4.58 Welded, 1 dk	**(B21A20S) Platform Supply Ship**	**2 oil engines** reverse reduction geared to sc. shafts driving 2 FP propellers Total Power: 2,206kW (3,000hp) 12.5kn EMD (Electro-Motive) 16-645-E2 2 x Vee 2 Stroke 16 Cy. 230 x 254 each-1103kW (1500bhp) (Re-engined ,made 1950, Reconditioned & fitted 1974) General Motors Corp-USA AuxGen: 2 x 75kW Thrusters: 1 Thwart. FP thruster (f) Fuel: 394.0 (d.f.)
7309314 *WDE8510* -	**TEMPEST** **Northwest Tempest Inc** - *Seattle, WA* *United States of America* MMSI: 367093490 Official number: 506261	**187** 68 -		**1966 Pacific Fishermen, Inc. — Seattle, Wa** L reg 25.18 Br ex 7.93 Dght - Lbp - Br md - Dpth 2.87 Welded	**(B11B2FV) Fishing Vessel**	**1 oil engine** driving 1 FP propeller Total Power: 368kW (500hp)
8003216 *H04221* -	**TEMPLARIO I** *ex* Templario *-2005* *ex* Asturias *-2001* *ex* Shyri *-1998* *ex* Nambug Pioneer *-1998* *ex* Chance No. 1 *-1991* *ex* Brenda Jolene *-1990* **Tuna Liner Corp SA** - *Panama* *Panama* MMSI: 371696000 Official number: 3181306A	*1,245* 373 1,674	Class: (KR)	**1980-08 J M Martinac Shipbuilding Corp — Tacoma WA** Yd No: 221 Loa 69.26 Br ex 13.26 Dght 5.310 Lbp 61.15 Br md 12.80 Dpth 5.58 Welded, 2 dks	**(B11B2FV) Fishing Vessel**	**1 oil engine** geared to sc. shaft driving 1 FP propeller Total Power: 2,648kW (3,600hp) 14.0kn MaK 9M453AK 1 x 4 Stroke 9 Cy. 320 x 420 2648kW (3600bhp) Krupp MaK Maschinenbau GmbH-Kiel
8732776 *JXCH* VA-16-S	**TEMPO** *ex* Spleis *-2007* **Tempofisk AS** - *Kristiansand* *Norway* MMSI: 257802500	**125** 50 -		**1986-01 Bentsen & Sonner Slip & Mek. Verksted — Sogne** Yd No: 41 Loa 26.16 Br ex - Dght - Lbp - Br md 6.75 Dpth 3.44 Welded, 1 dk	**(B11A2FS) Stern Trawler**	**1 oil engine** geared to sc. shaft driving 1 Propeller Caterpillar 3508 1 x Vee 4 Stroke 8 Cy. 170 x 190 Caterpillar Tractor Co-USA
7378121 - -	**TEMPO No. 303** *ex* Tenyo Maru No. 35 *-1988* - -	*114* - 146		**1974-04 Tokushima Zosen K.K. — Fukuoka** Yd No: 1132 Loa 35.69 Br ex 6.13 Dght 2.388 Lbp 29.11 Br md 6.10 Dpth 2.87 Welded, 1 dk	**(B11B2FV) Fishing Vessel**	**1 oil engine** driving 1 FP propeller Total Power: 530kW (721hp) Yanmar 6GL-HT 1 x 4 Stroke 6 Cy. 240 x 290 530kW (721bhp) Yanmar Diesel Engine Co Ltd-Japan
7378133 - -	**TEMPO No. 305** *ex* Tenyo Maru No. 36 *-1988* - -	*114* - 146		**1974-04 Tokushima Zosen K.K. — Fukuoka** Yd No: 1133 Loa 35.69 Br ex 6.13 Dght 2.388 Lbp 29.11 Br md 6.10 Dpth 2.87 Welded, 1 dk	**(B11B2FV) Fishing Vessel**	**1 oil engine** driving 1 FP propeller Total Power: 530kW (721hp) Yanmar 6GL-HT 1 x 4 Stroke 6 Cy. 240 x 290 530kW (721bhp) Yanmar Diesel Engine Co Ltd-Japan
8030491 *WDC5705* -	**TEMPO SEA** *ex* Blue Aleutian *-2005* *ex* Tempo Sea *-2001* *ex* Constance *-1990* **f/v Tempo Sea LLC** - *Juneau, AK* *United States of America* MMSI: 367045260 Official number: 620538	**333** 99 -		**1980 Columbia Shipbuilders — The Dalles, Or** Lengthened-1991 Loa 35.36 Br ex 9.15 Dght - Lbp 35.23 Br md 9.14 Dpth 3.96 Welded, 1 dk	**(B11B2FV) Fishing Vessel**	**2 oil engines** driving 2 FP propellers Total Power: 478kW (650hp) G.M. (Detroit Diesel) 12V-71-N 2 x Vee 2 Stroke 12 Cy. 108 x 127 each-239kW (325bhp) General Motors Detroit DieselAllison Divn-USA
8827088 *YD4177* -	**TEMPOA** *ex* Wade Hampton *-1986* **PT Baruna Raya Logistics** - *Jakarta* *Indonesia* MMSI: 525017012	**204** 62	Class: KI	**1974 Breaux Bay Craft, Inc. — Loreauville, La** Yd No: 1299 Loa 36.60 Br ex - Dght 2.130 Lbp - Br md 8.50 Dpth 3.40 Welded, 1 dk	**(B21A20C) Crew/Supply Vessel**	**2 oil engines** driving 2 FP propellers Total Power: 1,250kW (1,700hp) Caterpillar D398SCAC 2 x Vee 4 Stroke 12 Cy. 159 x 203 each-625kW (850bhp) Caterpillar Tractor Co-USA AuxGen: 1 x 80kW 240V a.c
9158343 - -	**TEMPSA** **Government of Abu Dhabi** - *United Arab Emirates*	**120** - -	Class: (LR) ✠	**1997-06 Abu Dhabi Ship Building PJSC — Abu Dhabi** (Assembled by) Yd No: 032C **1997-06 B.V. Scheepswerf Damen — Gorinchem** (Parts for assembly by) Yd No: 6127 Loa 19.70 (BB) Br ex 6.04 Dght 2.020 Lbp 17.32 Br md 6.00 Dpth 2.80 Welded, 1 dk	**(B32A2ST) Tug**	**2 oil engines** with clutches, flexible couplings & sr reverse geared to sc. shafts driving 2 FP propellers Total Power: 1,060kW (1,442hp) 10.8kn Caterpillar 3412TA 2 x Vee 4 Stroke 12 Cy. 137 x 152 each-530kW (721bhp) Caterpillar Inc-USA AuxGen: 2 x 22kW 440V 50Hz a.c
9111931 *A8VI5* -	**TEMPTATION** *ex* Vergo *-2010* *ex* Arhimidis SB *-2008* *ex* Bright Halo *-2003* **Sailing Shipmanagement Inc** PL Shipping Co *Monrovia* *Liberia* MMSI: 636014614 Official number: 14614	**25,074** 15,145 45,320 T/cm 50.6	Class: NK	**1995-09 Oshima Shipbuilding Co Ltd — Saikai NS** Yd No: 10181 Loa 189.60 (BB) Br ex 30.53 Dght 11.276 Lbp 181.60 Br md 30.50 Dpth 15.80 Welded, 1 dk	**(A21A2BC) Bulk Carrier** Grain: 56,457; Bale: 55,364 Compartments: 5 Ho, ER 5 Ha: 4 (20.0 x 15.3) (16.0 x 15.3)ER Cranes: 4x30t	**1 oil engine** driving 1 FP propeller Total Power: 7,392kW (10,050hp) 15.2kn Mitsubishi 6UEC50LSII 1 x 2 Stroke 6 Cy. 500 x 1950 7392kW (10050bhp) Mitsubishi Heavy Industries Ltd-Japan Fuel: 1540.0 (r.f.)

IMO / Call sign	Name / Owner	Tonnage	Class	Builder / Dimensions	Type	Machinery
8028254 - -	**TEMPTATION** *ex Fir -2004 ex Silverthorn -2002* *ex Shamrock Enterprise -1990* **Howard & Compania Sociedad en Comandita Simple** - *Isla de San Andres* *Colombia* Official number: MC-07-0163	950 491 1,694	Class: (LR) ✠ Classed LR until 3/3/04	**1982-04 Scheepswerf Bodewes Gruno B.V. — Foxhol** Yd No: 252 Loa 69.30 Br ex 11.10 Dght 4.292 Lbp 63.91 Br md 11.00 Dpth 5.11 Welded, 1 dk	**(A31A2GX) General Cargo Ship** Grain: 1,993 TEU 60 C.Ho 36/20' (40') C.Dk 24/20' (40') Compartments: 1 Ho, ER 1 Ha: (37.2 x 7.8)ER	**1 oil engine** with clutches, flexible couplings & sr geared to sc. shaft driving 1 CP propeller Total Power: 912kW (1,240hp) 11.0kn Alpha 8V23L-VO 1 x Vee 4 Stroke 8 Cy. 225 x 300 912kW (1240bhp) B&W Alpha Diesel A/S-Denmark AuxGen: 3 x 44kW 220/380V 50Hz a.c Fuel: 95.0 (d.f.) 4.0pd
8985141 *PBFH* ARM 33	**TEMPUS FUGIT** *ex Sola Gratia -2009* **Visserijbedrijf Van Belzen VOF** - *Arnemuiden* *Netherlands* MMSI: 245331000 Official number: 40230	152 45 -		**2002-05 Stal-Rem SA — Gdansk** (Hull) Yd No: B320/1 **2002-05 Machinefabriek Padmos Stellendam B.V. — Stellendam** Yd No: 140 Loa 23.97 Br ex - Dght - Lbp 21.13 Br md 6.85 Dpth 3.63 Welded, 1 dk	**(B11B2FV) Fishing Vessel**	**1 oil engine** driving 1 Propeller Total Power: 221kW (300hp) Mitsubishi S6A-300-3 1 x 4 Stroke 6 Cy. 150 x 175 221kW (300bhp) Mitsubishi Heavy Industries Ltd-Japan
8934192 *EZCP* -	**TEMRYUK** - **OOO 'Arsko-Don'** - *Turkmenbashy* *Turkmenistan*	978 293 348	Class: RS	**1980-06 Sudostroitelnyy Zavod "Krasnyye Barrikady" — Krasnyye Barrikady** Yd No: 12 Loa 54.49 Br ex 14.78 Dght 2.160 Lbp 51.50 Br md - Dpth 3.70 Welded, 1 dk	**(A31A2GX) General Cargo Ship** Grain: 131 TEU 20 Compartments: 1 Ho 1 Ha: (5.6 x 3.5) Cranes: 1x25t	**2 oil engines** driving 2 FP propellers Total Power: 1,030kW (1,400hp) 11.0kn Russkiy 6DR30/50-6-3 2 x 2 Stroke 6 Cy. 300 x 500 each-515kW (700bhp) Mashinostroitelnyy Zavod"Russkiy-Dizel"-Leningrad AuxGen: 2 x 150kW a.c Fuel: 118.0 (d.f.)
9638991 *UBWI2* -	**TEMRYUK** *ex Grizli -2012* **JSC Tamanneftegaz** Oteko-Terminal LLC *Novorossiysk* *Russia* MMSI: 273354670	499 149 168	Class: RS	**2012-08 DP Craneship — Kerch** Yd No: 701 Loa 33.45 Br ex 13.05 Dght 4.100 Lbp 30.15 Br md 12.20 Dpth 5.98 Welded, 1 dk	**(B32A2ST) Tug** Ice Capable	**2 oil engines** reduction geared to sc. shafts driving 2 Directional propellers Total Power: 3,650kW (4,962hp) Caterpillar 3516C-HD 2 x Vee 4 Stroke 16 Cy. 170 x 215 each-1825kW (2481bhp) Caterpillar Inc-USA AuxGen: 2 x 86kW a.c Fuel: 130.0 (d.f.)
9005156 *XUTD9* -	**TEMTAI** *ex Daishin Maru -2009* **Temtai Shipping Ltd** Yantai Sky Harmony Shipping Management Co Ltd *Phnom Penh* *Cambodia* MMSI: 514207000 Official number: 0990302	1,494 634 1,600	Class: UM	**1990-06 Shin Yamamoto Shipbuilding & Engineering Co Ltd — Kochi KC** Yd No: 327 L reg 74.20 Br ex - Dght - Lbp - Br md 11.00 Dpth 7.00 Welded	**(A31A2GX) General Cargo Ship**	**1 oil engine** driving 1 FP propeller Total Power: 1,177kW (1,600hp) Niigata 6M34AFT 1 x 4 Stroke 6 Cy. 340 x 620 1177kW (1600bhp) Niigata Engineering Co Ltd-Japan
9520833 *2EMA9* -	**TEN JIN MARU** - **Chijin Shipping SA** NEOM Maritime (Singapore) Pte Ltd SatCom: Inmarsat C 423592769 *Douglas* *Isle of Man (British)* MMSI: 235086274 Official number: 742845	52,186 32,423 98,681 T/cm 14.4	Class: NK	**2011-05 Tsuneishi Group (Zhoushan) Shipbuilding Inc — Daishan County ZJ** Yd No: SS-090 Loa 239.99 (BB) Br ex - Dght 14.479 Lbp 236.00 Br md 38.00 Dpth 19.95 Welded, 1 dk	**(A21A2BC) Bulk Carrier** Grain: 113,237 Compartments: 7 Ho, ER 7 Ha: ER	**1 oil engine** driving 1 FP propeller Total Power: 12,700kW (17,267hp) 14.5kn MAN-B&W 6S60MC-C 1 x 2 Stroke 6 Cy. 600 x 2400 12700kW (17267bhp) Mitsui Engineering & Shipbuilding CLtd-Japan Fuel: 4000.0
9599119 *2FCE5* -	**TEN JO MARU** - **Chijin Shipping SA** NEOM Maritime (Singapore) Pte Ltd SatCom: Inmarsat C 423592993 *Douglas* *Isle of Man (British)* MMSI: 235090031 Official number: 742886	52,186 32,423 98,681 T/cm 14.4	Class: NK	**2011-12 Tsuneishi Group (Zhoushan) Shipbuilding Inc — Daishan County ZJ** Yd No: SS-114 Loa 239.99 (BB) Br ex 38.04 Dght 14.480 Lbp 236.00 Br md 38.00 Dpth 19.95 Welded, 1 dk	**(A21A2BC) Bulk Carrier** Grain: 113,237 Compartments: 7 Ho, ER 7 Ha: ER	**1 oil engine** driving 1 FP propeller Total Power: 12,700kW (17,267hp) 14.5kn MAN-B&W 6S60MC-C 1 x 2 Stroke 6 Cy. 600 x 2400 12700kW (17267bhp) Mitsui Engineering & Shipbuilding CLtd-Japan Fuel: 4000.0
7051644 *WR7485* -	**TEN NINETY ONE** *ex Bering Sea -2009 ex LSI (L)-1091 -2009* **Ralph L Davis** - *McKinleyville, CA* *United States of America* Official number: 285125	331 99 -		**1944 Defoe Shipbuilding Co. — Bay City, Mi** Yd No: 344 Loa 46.09 Br ex 7.12 Dght - Lbp - Br md - Dpth 3.46 Welded	**(B11B2FV) Fishing Vessel**	**1 oil engine** driving 1 FP propeller Total Power: 331kW (450hp)
9520912 *3EVN9* -	**TEN YOSHI MARU** - **Chijin Shipping SA** Union Marine Management Services Pte Ltd SatCom: Inmarsat C 435770712 *Panama* *Panama* MMSI: 357707000 Official number: 4235511	32,305 19,458 58,110 T/cm 57.4	Class: NV (NK)	**2011-01 Tsuneishi Group (Zhoushan) Shipbuilding Inc — Daishan County ZJ** Yd No: SS-070 Loa 189.99 (BB) Br ex - Dght 12.830 Lbp 185.60 Br md 32.26 Dpth 18.00 Welded, 1 dk	**(A21A2BC) Bulk Carrier** Grain: 72,689; Bale: 70,122 Compartments: 5 Ho, ER 5 Ha: ER Cranes: 4x30t	**1 oil engine** driving 1 FP propeller Total Power: 8,400kW (11,421hp) 14.5kn MAN-B&W 6S50MC-C 1 x 2 Stroke 6 Cy. 500 x 2000 8400kW (11421bhp) Mitsui Engineering & Shipbuilding CLtd-Japan AuxGen: 3 x a.c
9520900 *3FKB* -	**TEN YU MARU** - **Chijin Shipping SA** Union Marine Management Services Pte Ltd SatCom: Inmarsat C 435414110 *Panama* *Panama* MMSI: 354141000 Official number: 4222811	32,305 19,458 58,110 T/cm 57.4	Class: NK	**2010-11 Tsuneishi Group (Zhoushan) Shipbuilding Inc — Daishan County ZJ** Yd No: SS-069 Loa 189.99 (BB) Br ex - Dght 12.826 Lbp 185.60 Br md 32.26 Dpth 18.00 Welded, 1 dk	**(A21A2BC) Bulk Carrier** Grain: 72,689; Bale: 70,122 Compartments: 5 Ho, ER 5 Ha: ER Cranes: 4x30t	**1 oil engine** driving 1 FP propeller Total Power: 8,400kW (11,421hp) 14.5kn MAN-B&W 6S50MC-C 1 x 2 Stroke 6 Cy. 500 x 2000 8400kW (11421bhp) Mitsui Engineering & Shipbuilding CLtd-Japan
9546057 *9HA2184* -	**TENACE** - **Armamento Setramar Malta Ltd** Jolane SA SatCom: Inmarsat C 424812010 *Valletta* *Malta* MMSI: 248120000 Official number: 9546057	9,286 4,398 14,600	Class: RI	**2011-01 Tuzla Gemi Endustrisi A.S. — Tuzla** Yd No: 43 Loa 139.95 (BB) Br ex - Dght 7.780 Lbp 134.70 Br md 21.00 Dpth 10.60 Welded, 1 dk	**(A31A2GX) General Cargo Ship** Double Hull Grain: 16,200 Compartments: 2 Ho, ER 2 Ha: ER	**1 oil engine** reduction geared to sc. shaft driving 1 CP propeller Total Power: 4,350kW (5,914hp) 14.5kn Wartsila 6L38 1 x 4 Stroke 6 Cy. 380 x 475 4350kW (5914bhp) Wartsila Italia SpA-Italy
6622109 *IUTI* -	**TENACE** - **Rimorchiatori Sardi SpA** - *Cagliari* *Italy* Official number: 218	229 68 -	Class: (RI)	**1966 Cantiere Navale M & B Benetti — Viareggio** Yd No: 70 Loa 33.84 Br ex 8.13 Dght 3.728 Lbp 30.00 Br md 8.01 Dpth 4.20 Riveted\Welded, 1 dk	**(B32A2ST) Tug**	**1 oil engine** geared to sc. shaft driving 1 FP propeller Total Power: 1,250kW (1,700hp) MAN G8V30/45ATL 1 x 4 Stroke 8 Cy. 300 x 450 1250kW (1700bhp) Maschinenbau Augsburg Nuernberg (MAN)-Augsburg
5062584 *ILBH* -	**TENACE II** *ex Capocaccia -2001* **EMRR SAM** - *Genoa* *Italy* Official number: 8662	*125* 27 -	Class: (RI)	**1962 Cant. Nav. Solimano — Savona** Yd No: 31 Loa 24.01 Br ex 6.63 Dght 3.200 Lbp 21.37 Br md 6.61 Dpth 3.81 Riveted\Welded, 1 dk	**(B32A2ST) Tug**	**1 oil engine** driving 1 FP propeller Total Power: 736kW (1,001hp) Deutz RBV8M545 1 x 4 Stroke 8 Cy. 320 x 450 736kW (1001bhp) Kloeckner Humboldt Deutz AG-West Germany
9350707 *ICGA* -	**TENACIA** - **Grandi Navi Veloci (GRANNAVI) SpA** - *Palermo* *Italy* MMSI: 247230200	25,993 11,426 8,500	Class: RI	**2008-03 Nuovi Cantieri Apuania SpA — Carrara** Yd No: 1239 Loa 198.99 (BB) Br ex - Dght 6.400 Lbp 177.00 Br md 26.60 Dpth 15.30 Welded, 1 dk	**(A36A2PR) Passenger/Ro-Ro Ship (Vehicles)** Passengers: 473; cabins: 67 Stern door/ramp (p) Stern door/ramp (s) Lane-Len: 3000	**2 oil engines** reduction geared to sc. shafts driving 2 CP propellers Total Power: 25,200kW (34,262hp) 24.0kn Wartsila 12V46 2 x Vee 4 Stroke 12 Cy. 460 x 580 each-12600kW (17131bhp) Wartsila Italia SpA-Italy
5238004 *WDC9450* -	**TENACIOUS** *ex Nan McKay -2005 ex Tatarrax -1993* *ex Mobil 8 -1991* **C & T Equipment LLC** Morrish-Wallace Construction Inc (Ryba Marine Construction Co) *Cheboygan, MI* *United States of America* MMSI: 367102450 Official number: 281119	177 53 -	Class: (AB)	**1960 Ingalls SB. Corp. — Pascagoula, Ms** Yd No: 135 Loa 27.36 Br ex 7.80 Dght 3.525 Lbp 26.01 Br md 7.78 Dpth 3.81 Riveted\Welded, 1 dk	**(B32A2ST) Tug**	**1 oil engine** sr & reverse geared to sc. shaft driving 1 FP propeller Total Power: 1,177kW (1,600hp) EMD (Electro-Motive) 16-567 1 x Vee 2 Stroke 16 Cy. 216 x 254 1177kW (1600bhp) General Motors Corp-USA AuxGen: 2 x 40kW 110V d.c Fuel: 56.0 (d.f.)

IMO / Call sign	Name / Owner	Tonnage	Class	Builder / Dimensions	Type	Machinery
5354987 *VKBC* -	**TENACIOUS** - **Coral Coast Oceaneering Pty Ltd** - *Port Adelaide, SA* *Australia* MMSI: 503012900 Official number: 315306	*161* - -	Class: (LR) ✠ Classed LR until 19/12/00	**1961-06 Adelaide Ship Construction Pty Ltd — Port Adelaide SA** Yd No: 7 Loa 28.96 Br ex 7.57 Dght 3.487 Lbp 26.78 Br md 7.17 Dpth 3.66 Welded, 1 dk	**(B32A2ST) Tug** Passengers: 100	**1 oil engine** reduction geared to sc. shaft driving 1 FP propeller Total Power: 675kW (918hp) 11.0kn Ruston 1 x 4 Stroke 5 Cy. 318 x 368 675kW (918bhp) Ruston & Hornsby Ltd.-Lincoln AuxGen: 2 x 30kW 220V d.c Fuel: 21.5 (d.f.)
7009861 *9YES* -	**TENACIOUS** *ex* Keston *-2000* **Coloured Fin Ltd (CFL)** *Port of Spain* *Trinidad & Tobago*	**323** 96 -	Class: LR ✠ **100A1** SS 02/2007 tug Caribbean Sea service ✠ **LMC** Eq.Ltr: (e) ;	**1970-03 Richards (Shipbuilders) Ltd — Lowestoft** Yd No: 500 Loa 35.67 Br ex 9.53 Dght 3.772 Lbp 30.64 Br md 9.15 Dpth 4.42 Welded, 1 dk	**(B32A2ST) Tug**	**3 oil engines** reverse reduction geared to sc. shafts driving 3 FP propellers Total Power: 2,208kW (3,003hp) Blackstone EWSL8 3 x 4 Stroke 8 Cy. 222 x 292 each-736kW (1001bhp) Lister Blackstone MirrleesMarine Ltd.-Dursley AuxGen: 2 x 35kW 440V 50Hz a.c, 1 x 11kW 440V 50Hz a.c Fuel: 71.0 (d.f.)
7216294 *HQOQ8* -	**TENACIOUS** *ex* Cope *-1998* *ex* Wrahanala *-1998* *ex* Geomar I *-1985* *ex* Pointe Coupee *-1979* **Tenacious Shipping Corp** - *San Lorenzo* *Honduras* MMSI: 334832000 Official number: L-0325525	**797** 398 -	Class: (AB)	**1964 American Marine Corp. — New Orleans, La** Yd No: 896 Converted From: Offshore Supply Ship Loa - Br ex - Dght 3.074 Lbp 43.24 Br md 10.67 Dpth 3.66 Welded, 1 dk	**(A31C2GD) Deck Cargo Ship** Stern ramp (a)	**2 oil engines** geared to sc. shafts driving 2 FP propellers Total Power: 1,126kW (1,530hp) Caterpillar D398TA 2 x Vee 4 Stroke 12 Cy. 159 x 203 each-563kW (765bhp) Caterpillar Tractor Co-USA AuxGen: 2 x 40kW Fuel: 129.0 (d.f.)
7328994 - - -	**TENACIOUS** *ex* Salvenom *-1986* *ex* Asiatic Stamina *-1982* - -	*168* 25 -	Class: (AB)	**1973 Sing Koon Seng Pte Ltd — Singapore** Yd No: 78 Loa 24.39 Br ex - Dght - Lbp 23.02 Br md 7.29 Dpth 3.99 Welded, 1 dk	**(B32A2ST) Tug**	**1 oil engine** reverse reduction geared to sc. shaft driving 1 FP propeller Total Power: 713kW (969hp) Caterpillar D349TA 1 x Vee 4 Stroke 16 Cy. 137 x 165 713kW (969bhp) (made 1971, fitted 1973) Caterpillar Tractor Co-USA AuxGen: 1 x 32kW, 1 x 22kW Fuel: 90.5 (d.f.)
7927776 - -	**TENACIOUS** - **Morreau Fishing Ltd** - *Prince Rupert, BC* *Canada* Official number: 392896	*149* 43 120		**1980-06 Allied Shipbuilders Ltd — North Vancouver BC** Yd No: 222 Loa 22.84 Br ex 7.78 Dght 3.001 Lbp 20.81 Br md 7.62 Dpth 3.79 Welded, 1 dk	**(B11A2FS) Stern Trawler**	**1 oil engine** driving 1 FP propeller Total Power: 368kW (500hp) Alpha 405-26VO 1 x 2 Stroke 5 Cy. 260 x 400 368kW (500bhp) B&W Alpha Diesel A/S-Denmark
8820872 *ES2665* EK-0602	**TENACIOUS** *ex* Suecia *-1993* **Hiiu Kalur Ltd (AS Hiiu Kalur)** Dagomar Ltd (AS Dagomar) *Lehtma* *Estonia* MMSI: 276659000 Official number: 3F06F02	**183** 55 85	Class: (RS)	**1989-11 Smogens Plat & Svetsindustri AB — Smogen** Yd No: 44 Loa 23.95 Br ex 7.07 Dght 3.750 Lbp 21.11 Br md 7.02 Dpth 4.78 Welded, 1 dk	**(B11A2FS) Stern Trawler**	**1 oil engine** sr reverse geared to sc. shaft driving 1 FP propeller Total Power: 638kW (867hp) Caterpillar 3508TA 1 x Vee 4 Stroke 8 Cy. 170 x 190 638kW (867bhp) Caterpillar Inc-USA Thrusters: 1 Tunnel thruster (f)
9647887 *V7BR5* -	**TENACITY** - **Tenacity Shipping Co LLC** Doris Maritime Services SA *Majuro* *Marshall Islands* MMSI: 538005191 Official number: 5191	**19,999** 10,419 29,970 T/cm 43.5	Class: RI (AB)	**2013-07 Tsuji Heavy Industries (Jiangsu) Co Ltd — Zhangjiagang JS** Yd No: NB0027 Loa 178.70 (BB) Br ex - Dght 9.740 Lbp 170.00 Br md 28.00 Dpth 14.00 Welded, 1 dk	**(A21A2BC) Bulk Carrier** Grain: 40,633; Bale: 38,602 Compartments: 5 Ho, ER 5 Ha: 4 (20.8 x 21.0)ER (16.6 x 15.0) Cranes: 4x30t	**1 oil engine** driving 1 FP propeller Total Power: 6,232kW (8,473hp) 14.0kn MAN-B&W 6S42MC 1 x 2 Stroke 6 Cy. 420 x 1764 6232kW (8473bhp) STX Engine Co Ltd-South Korea AuxGen: 3 x 550kW a.c Fuel: 123.0 (d.f.) 1324.0 (r.f.)
6719392 *VC8125* -	**TENACITY I** *ex* Senator Don *-1986* *ex* Scotia Point *-1982* **CS Manpar Inc** Clearwater Seafoods Ltd Partnership *Lunenburg, NS* *Canada* MMSI: 316003990 Official number: 328503	*303* 91 -	Class: (LR) ✠ Classed LR until 15/6/73	**1967-08 Saint John Shipbuilding & Dry Dock Co Ltd — Saint John NB** Yd No: 1088 Loa 35.97 Br ex 8.64 Dght 3.353 Lbp 29.57 Br md 8.54 Dpth 4.12 Welded, 1 dk	**(B11A2FS) Stern Trawler**	**1 oil engine** sr reverse geared to sc. shaft driving 1 FP propeller Total Power: 750kW (1,020hp) 11.0kn Caterpillar D398TA 1 x Vee 4 Stroke 12 Cy. 159 x 203 750kW (1020bhp) Caterpillar Tractor Co-USA AuxGen: 2 x 55kW 220V 60Hz a.c Thrusters: 1 Thwart. FP thruster (f); 1 Tunnel thruster (a)
7428469 *9MSM* -	**TENAGA DUA** - **MISC Bhd** - SatCom: Inmarsat B 353319010 *Penang* *Malaysia* MMSI: 533190000 Official number: 324214	**80,510** 24,104 72,087 T/cm 97.2	Class: AB (BV)	**1981-08 Societe Metallurgique et Navale Dunkerque-Normandie — Dunkirk** Yd No: 302 Loa 280.63 (BB) Br ex 41.64 Dght 11.724 Lbp 266.00 Br md 41.61 Dpth 27.51 Welded, 1 dk	**(A11A2TN) LNG Tanker** Double Bottom Entire Compartment Length Liq (Gas): 127,400 5 x Gas Tank (s); 5 membrane Gas Transport (36% Ni.stl) pri horizontal 10 Cargo Pump (s): 10x1250m³/hr Manifold: Bow/CM: 142.2m	**1 Steam Turb** tr & dr geared to sc. shaft driving 1 FP propeller Total Power: 33,098kW (45,000hp) 20.0kn Stal-Laval 1 x steam Turb 33098kW (45000shp) Alsthom Atlantique-France AuxGen: 3 x 2600kW 440V 60Hz a.c Fuel: 430.0 (d.f.) (Heating Coils) 7920.0 (r.f.) 250.0pd
7428433 *9MUG* -	**TENAGA EMPAT** - **MISC Bhd** PETRONAS (Petroleum Nasional Bhd) SatCom: Inmarsat B 353319210 *Penang* *Malaysia* MMSI: 533192000 Official number: 324216	**80,510** 24,153 71,818 T/cm 159.8	Class: AB (BV)	**1981-03 Constructions Navales et Inds de La Mediterranee (CNIM) — La Seyne** Yd No: 1428 Converted From: LNG Tanker-2012 Loa 280.63 (BB) Br ex 41.64 Dght 11.724 Lbp 266.00 Br md 41.61 Dpth 27.51 Welded, 1 dk	**(B22E20G) Gas Processing Vessel** Double Bottom Entire Compartment Length Liq (Gas): 130,000 5 x Gas Tank (s); 5 membrane Gas Transport (36% Ni.stl) pri horizontal 10 Cargo Pump (s): 10x1125m³/hr Manifold: Bow/CM: 142m	**1 Steam Turb** tr & dr geared to sc. shaft driving 1 FP propeller Total Power: 33,098kW (45,000hp) 20.0kn Stal-Laval 1 x steam Turb 33098kW (45000shp) Alsthom Atlantique-France AuxGen: 2 x 2600kW 440V 60Hz a.c, 1 x 1400kW 440V 60Hz a.c Fuel: 6708.0 (r.f.) (Heating Coils) 372.0 (d.f.) 250.0pd
7428445 *9MTS* -	**TENAGA LIMA** - **MISC Bhd** - SatCom: Inmarsat B 353319310 *Penang* *Malaysia* MMSI: 533193000 Official number: 324217	**80,510** 24,153 72,083 T/cm 97.2	Class: AB (BV)	**1981-09 Constructions Navales et Inds de La Mediterranee (CNIM) — La Seyne** Yd No: 1429 Loa 280.63 (BB) Br ex 41.64 Dght 11.724 Lbp 266.00 Br md 41.61 Dpth 27.51 Welded, 1 dk	**(A11A2TN) LNG Tanker** Double Bottom Entire Compartment Length Liq (Gas): 127,409 5 x Gas Tank (s); 5 membrane Gas Transport (36% Ni.stl) pri horizontal 10 Cargo Pump (s): 10x1250m³/hr Manifold: Bow/CM: 142.1m	**1 Steam Turb** tr & dr geared to sc. shaft driving 1 FP propeller Total Power: 33,098kW (45,000hp) 20.0kn Stal-Laval 1 x steam Turb 33098kW (45000shp) Alsthom Atlantique-France AuxGen: 3 x 2600kW 440V 60Hz a.c Fuel: 470.0 (d.f.) (Heating Coils) 7770.0 (r.f.) 250.0pd
9080871 *YDA4725* -	**TENAGA MAJU** *ex* Greenville 12 *-2010* **PT Mandiri Abadi Maritim** - *Jakarta* *Indonesia* MMSI: 525004096	**220** 66 18	Class: KI (AB)	**1993-11 President Marine Pte Ltd — Singapore** Yd No: 153 Loa - Br ex - Dght 3.720 Lbp 29.00 Br md 8.60 Dpth 4.11 Welded, 1 dk	**(B32A2ST) Tug**	**2 oil engines** driving 2 FP propellers Total Power: 1,790kW (2,434hp) Yanmar M220-EN 2 x 4 Stroke 6 Cy. 220 x 300 each-895kW (1217bhp) Yanmar Diesel Engine Co Ltd-Japan
9115822 *YDA4187* -	**TENAGA MANDIRI** *ex* Q. S. Success *-2006* **PT Mandiri Abadi Maritim** PT Mandiri Abadi Santosa Ship Management Jakarta *Jakarta* *Indonesia* MMSI: 525025040	**118** 36 74	Class: KI (NK)	**1994-08 Sapor Shipyard Sdn Bhd — Sibu** (Hull) **1994-08 Pacific Ocean Engineering & Trading Pte Ltd (POET) — Singapore** Yd No: 1041 Loa 21.00 Br ex - Dght 2.409 Lbp 19.86 Br md 7.00 Dpth 3.30 Welded, 1 dk	**(B32A2ST) Tug**	**2 oil engines** reduction geared to sc. shafts driving 2 FP propellers Total Power: 626kW (852hp) Cummins KT-19-M 2 x 4 Stroke 6 Cy. 159 x 159 each-313kW (426bhp) Cummins Engine Co Inc-USA AuxGen: 2 x 30kW a.c Fuel: 65.0 (d.f.)
7428457 *9MUQ* -	**TENAGA SATU** - **MISC Bhd** PETRONAS (Petroleum Nasional Bhd) SatCom: Inmarsat B 353318915 *Penang* *Malaysia* MMSI: 533189000 Official number: 324213	**80,510** 24,153 71,814 T/cm 97.2	Class: AB (BV)	**1982-09 Soc Ind et Financiere des Chantiers de France-Dunkerque — Dunkirk** Yd No: 301 Converted From: LNG Tanker-2012 Loa 280.63 (BB) Br ex 41.64 Dght 11.726 Lbp 266.00 Br md 41.61 Dpth 27.50 Welded, 1 dk	**(B22E20G) Gas Processing Vessel** Double Bottom Entire Compartment Length Liq (Gas): 130,000 5 x Gas Tank (s); 5 membrane Gas Transport (36% Ni.stl) pri horizontal 10 Cargo Pump (s) Manifold: Bow/CM: 142.1m	**1 Steam Turb** tr & dr geared to sc. shaft driving 1 FP propeller Total Power: 33,098kW (45,000hp) 20.0kn Stal-Laval 1 x steam Turb 33098kW (45000shp) Alsthom Atlantique-France AuxGen: 2 x 2600kW 440V 60Hz a.c, 1 x 1400kW 440V 60Hz a.c Fuel: 6708.0 (r.f.) (Heating Coils) 372.0 (d.f.) 250.0pd

IMO / Call sign	Name / Owner / Port	Tonnage / Class	Builder / Dimensions	Type	Machinery
7428471 *9MTE* -	**TENAGA TIGA** **MISC Bhd** - SatCom: Inmarsat C 453327310 *Penang* *Malaysia* MMSI: 533191000 Official number: 324215	**80,510** 24,153 71,787 Class: AB (BV)	**1981-12 Societe Metallurgique et Navale Dunkerque-Normandie — Dunkirk** Yd No: 303 Loa 280.63 (BB) Br ex 41.64 Dght 11.724 Lbp 266.00 Br md 41.61 Dpth 27.51 Welded, 1 dk	**(A11A2TN) LNG Tanker** Double Bottom Entire Compartment Length Liq (Gas): 130,000 5 x Gas Tank (s); 5 membrane Gas Transport (36% Ni.stl) pri horizontal 10 Cargo Pump (s)	**1 Steam Turb** tr & dr geared to sc. shaft driving 1 FP propeller Total Power: 33,098kW (45,000hp) 20.0kn Stal-Laval 1 x steam Turb 33098kW (45000shp) Alsthom Atlantique-France AuxGen: 2 x 2600kW 440V 60Hz a.c, 1 x 1400kW 440V 60Hz a.c Thrusters: 1 Thwart. FP thruster (f) Fuel: 6708.0 (r.f.) (Heating Coils) 372.0 (d.f.) 250.0pd
6501850 *CY7449* -	**TENAKA** *ex* Comox Queen *-1977* **British Columbia Ferry Services Inc** - *Victoria, BC* *Canada* MMSI: 316001272 Official number: 322969	*651* 435 41	**1964-03 Victoria Machinery Depot Co Ltd — Victoria BC** Yd No: 107 Loa 46.18 Br ex 13.21 Dght 2.591 Lbp 41.20 Br md 13.11 Dpth 4.27 Welded, 1 dk	**(A36A2PR) Passenger/Ro-Ro Ship (Vehicles)** Passengers: unberthed: 206 Cars: 18	**2 oil engines** driving 2 FP propellers Total Power: 1,104kW (1,500hp) 12.0kn Paxman 2 x Vee 4 Stroke 12 Cy. 178 x 197 each-552kW (750bhp) Davey, Paxman & Co. Ltd.-Colchester AuxGen: 2 x 60kW 230V 60Hz a.c
8996619 *YD5129* -	**TENANG 1601** *ex* Highline 29 *-2008* **PT Trans Lintas Segara** - *Tanjung Priok* *Indonesia*	**290** 87 312 Class: KI (GL)	**2003-05 Rajang Maju Shipbuilding Sdn Bhd — Sibu** Yd No: 46 Loa 30.00 Br ex - Dght 3.470 Lbp - Br md 8.60 Dpth 4.12 Welded, 1 dk	**(B32A2ST) Tug**	**2 oil engines** geared to sc. shafts driving 2 Propellers Total Power: 1,204kW (1,636hp) Mitsubishi S6R2-MPTK 2 x 4 Stroke 6 Cy. 170 x 220 each-602kW (818bhp) (made 2002) Mitsubishi Heavy Industries Ltd-Japan AuxGen: 2 x 64kW 415/240V a.c
8996621 *YDA6388* -	**TENANG 1602** *ex* Highline 35 *-2010* **PT Trans Lintas Segara** - *Tanjung Priok* *Indonesia*	**179** 54 - Class: KI (GL)	**2003-10 Rajang Maju Shipbuilding Sdn Bhd — Sibu** Yd No: 50 Loa 27.20 Br ex - Dght 2.750 Lbp 25.40 Br md 7.32 Dpth 3.35 Welded, 1 dk	**(B32A2ST) Tug**	**2 oil engines** geared to sc. shafts driving 2 Propellers Total Power: 1,204kW (1,636hp) 11.0kn Mitsubishi S6R2-MPTK 2 x 4 Stroke 6 Cy. 170 x 220 each-602kW (818bhp) (made 2002) Mitsubishi Heavy Industries Ltd-Japan AuxGen: 2 x 60kW 415/240V a.c
9098177 *YDA6037* -	**TENANG 2001** *ex* Ps 03 *-2010* **Makkaraka** - *Samarinda* *Indonesia*	**174** 53 - Class: KI	**2005-01 C.V. Swadaya Utama — Samarinda** Loa 27.15 Br ex - Dght - Lbp 24.80 Br md 7.50 Dpth 3.20 Welded, 1 dk	**(B32A2ST) Tug**	**2 oil engines** reduction geared to sc. shafts driving 2 Propellers Total Power: 1,472kW (2,002hp) Caterpillar D398 2 x Vee 4 Stroke 12 Cy. 159 x 203 each-736kW (1001bhp) Caterpillar Inc-USA AuxGen: 2 x 80kW 400V a.c
8911621 *YDRL* -	**TENANG JAYA 1** *ex* Hosei Maru *-2006* **PT Ligita Jaya** PT Pelayaran Internusa Bahari Persada *Jakarta* *Indonesia*	*599* 375 700 Class: KI	**1990-02 Nippon Zosen Tekko K.K. — Kitakyushu** Yd No: 332 Loa 50.10 (BB) Br ex 9.08 Dght 4.090 Lbp 46.00 Br md 9.00 Dpth 5.20 Welded, 2 dks	**(A31A2GX) General Cargo Ship** Grain: 1,072; Bale: 1,067 Compartments: 1 Ho, ER 1 Ha: ER	**1 oil engine** driving 1 FP propeller Total Power: 478kW (650hp) Matsui MS26GSC-3 1 x 4 Stroke 6 Cy. 260 x 470 478kW (650bhp) Matsui Iron Works Co Ltd-Japan AuxGen: 1 x 55kW 225/130V a.c
9641699 *YD3956* -	**TENAU 1** *ex* Tb Tenau 1 *-2012* **PT Andalan Mitra Bahari** - *Batam* *Indonesia* Official number: 120986	**275** 83 289 Class: NK	**2012-02 Rajang Maju Shipbuilding Sdn Bhd — Sibu** Yd No: RMM0017 Loa 30.00 Br ex - Dght 3.510 Lbp 27.71 Br md 8.60 Dpth 4.12 Welded, 1 dk	**(B32A2ST) Tug**	**2 oil engines** reduction geared to sc. shafts driving 2 FP propellers Total Power: 1,518kW (2,064hp) Mitsubishi S6R2-MTK3L 2 x 4 Stroke 6 Cy. 170 x 220 each-759kW (1032bhp) Mitsubishi Heavy Industries Ltd-Japan Fuel: 220.0
9432995 *IIYN2* -	**TENAX** *ex* Anna Cosentino *-2012* *ex* Sanmar Eskort 80-V *-2010* **Impresa Fratelli Barretta Domenico e Giovanni SNC** - *Bari* *Italy* MMSI: 247294900	**490** 146 170 Class: RI (AB)	**2010-07 Gemsan Gemi Insa ve Gemi Isletmeciligi San. Ltd. — Tuzla** Yd No: 39 Loa 33.10 Br ex - Dght 6.100 Lbp 30.10 Br md 12.00 Dpth 5.36 Welded, 1 dk	**(B32A2ST) Tug**	**2 oil engines** reduction geared to sc. shafts driving 2 Propellers Total Power: 5,200kW (7,070hp) 13.0kn Wartsila 8L26 2 x 4 Stroke 8 Cy. 260 x 320 each-2600kW (3535bhp) Wartsila Italia SpA-Italy AuxGen: 2 x 120kW a.c Thrusters: 1 Tunnel thruster (f)
9348716 *MKSF5* -	**TENAX** **Boreas Shipping Ltd** Ostensjo Rederi AS *Southampton* *United Kingdom* MMSI: 235031241 Official number: 911142	**643** 193 444 Class: NV	**2006-01 Astilleros Gondan SA — Castropol** Yd No: 429 Loa 38.27 (BB) Br ex 14.72 Dght 3.700 Lbp 33.29 Br md 14.00 Dpth 5.42 Welded, 1 dk	**(B32A2ST) Tug** Passengers: cabins: 6	**2 oil engines** geared to sc. shafts driving 2 Voith-Schneider propellers Total Power: 5,040kW (6,852hp) 12.0kn Bergens C25: 33L9P 2 x 4 Stroke 9 Cy. 250 x 330 each-2520kW (3426bhp) Rolls Royce Marine AS-Norway AuxGen: 2 x 128kW 400/220V 50Hz a.c Fuel: 194.0 (d.f.)
9342358 *XCHG9* -	**TENAZ** **Hoteleria y Servicios Petroleros SA de CV (HSP)** Consultoria y Servicios Petroleros SA de CV (CSP) *Ciudad del Carmen* *Mexico* MMSI: 345070158	**494** 149 40 Class: NV	**2006-07 FBMA Marine Inc — Balamban** Yd No: 1022 Loa 28.50 Br ex 18.00 Dght 3.050 Lbp 23.80 Br md 16.20 Dpth 6.09 Welded, 1 dk	**(B21A20C) Crew/Supply Vessel** Passengers: unberthed: 150	**2 oil engines** geared to sc. shafts driving 2 CP propellers Total Power: 2,984kW (4,058hp) 20.0kn Cummins KTA-50-M2 2 x Vee 4 Stroke 16 Cy. 159 x 159 each-1492kW (2029bhp) Cummins Engine Co Inc-USA AuxGen: 2 x a.c Thrusters: 1 Tunnel thruster (f); 1 Tunnel thruster (a)
9385489 *C6YC3* -	**TENCA ARROW** **United Sea Shipping SA** Gearbulk Ltd SatCom: Inmarsat C 431100528 *Nassau* *Bahamas* MMSI: 311029200 Official number: 8001700	**44,684** 22,141 69,990 Class: NV	**2009-11 Oshima Shipbuilding Co Ltd — Saikai NS** Yd No: 10523 Loa 225.00 (BB) Br ex 32.27 Dght 14.007 Lbp 221.00 Br md 32.26 Dpth 20.56 Welded, 1 dk	**(A31A2GO) Open Hatch Cargo Ship** Grain: 85,028 TEU 445 C Dk Compartments: 8 Ho, ER 8 Ha: 7 (21.2 x 27.4)ER (12.4 x 20.6) Gantry cranes: 2x70t	**1 oil engine** driving 1 FP propeller Total Power: 12,577kW (17,100hp) 15.5kn MAN-B&W 6S60ME-C8 1 x 2 Stroke 6 Cy. 600 x 2400 12577kW (17100bhp) Kawasaki Heavy Industries Ltd-Japan AuxGen: 2 x 1199kW a.c, 1 x 750kW a.c Thrusters: 1 Tunnel thruster (f) Fuel: 120.0 (d.f.) 2860.0 (r.f.)
8870229 *JM6281* -	**TENCHO MARU** **YK Yamahata Unso** - *Kagoshima, Kagoshima* *Japan* Official number: 133557	*171* - 208	**1993-05 Toyo Zosen Tekko KK — Kitakyushu FO** Yd No: 310 Loa 38.60 Br ex - Dght 2.030 Lbp 29.90 Br md 9.00 Dpth 2.79 Welded, 1 dk	**(A36A2PR) Passenger/Ro-Ro Ship (Vehicles)**	**2 oil engines** driving 2 FP propellers Total Power: 736kW (1,000hp) 11.2kn Niigata 6NSE-M 2 x 4 Stroke 6 Cy. 150 x 165 each-368kW (500bhp) Niigata Engineering Co Ltd-Japan
8841101 *JI3413* -	**TENCHO MARU** *ex* Koho Maru *-2008* **Hideyuki Ryogo** - *Sumoto, Hyogo* *Japan* Official number: 131657	*165* - 449	**1990-04 Maekawa Zosensho — Japan** Loa 48.89 Br ex - Dght 3.160 Lbp 44.00 Br md 8.40 Dpth 5.00 Welded, 1 dk	**(A31A2GX) General Cargo Ship** Compartments: 1 Ho, ER 1 Ha: (25.0 x 6.2)ER	**1 oil engine** driving 1 FP propeller Total Power: 405kW (551hp) 10.0kn Matsui 6M26KGHS 1 x 4 Stroke 6 Cy. 260 x 400 405kW (551bhp) Matsui Iron Works Co Ltd-Japan
8869830 *JM6268* -	**TENCHO MARU No. 2** **Sanwa Shosen KK** - *Amakusa, Kumamoto* *Japan* MMSI: 431000511 Official number: 133546	*577* - 120	**1993-02 Fujiwara Zosensho — Imabari** Yd No: 122 Loa 53.35 Br ex - Dght 2.850 Lbp 46.20 Br md 12.50 Dpth 3.80 Welded, 1 dk	**(A36A2PR) Passenger/Ro-Ro Ship (Vehicles)** Passengers: unberthed: 350	**1 oil engine** geared to sc. shaft driving 1 FP propeller Total Power: 1,177kW (1,600hp) 12.7kn Daihatsu 6DLM-26FS 1 x 4 Stroke 6 Cy. 260 x 340 1177kW (1600bhp) Daihatsu Diesel Manufacturing Co Lt-Japan
5056133 - -	**TENDER** *ex* Terningen *-1983* *ex* Byfjorden *-1965* **Scheepvaartbedrijf R P Feenstra BV (Feenstra Shipping)** -	*213* 124 274 Class: (LR) (BV) ✠ Classed LR until 5/57	**1956-04 Donso Varv, Slip & Verkstad — Donso** Yd No: 4 Lengthened-1957 Loa 44.48 Br ex 6.53 Dght 2.623 Lbp 40.80 Br md 6.51 Dpth 2.85 Welded, 1 dk	**(A31A2GX) General Cargo Ship** Grain: 425 Compartments: 2 Ho, ER 2 Ha: (1.2 x 1.9) (21.4 x 3.6)ER Derricks: 1x5t,1x2t; Winches: 2	**1 oil engine** driving 1 FP propeller Total Power: 313kW (426hp) 10.0kn Alpha 405-24VO 1 x 2 Stroke 5 Cy. 240 x 400 313kW (426bhp) Alpha Diesel A/S-Denmark Fuel: 14.0 (d.f.)
8879897 *OZGJ2* -	**TENDER HOJ** *ex* Tandaren *-1965* **Rederiet Hoj A/S** - *Horsens* *Denmark (DIS)* MMSI: 219001725 Official number: H1192	**127** 38 - Class: FA	**1961 Karlskronavarvet AB — Karlskrona** Converted From: LNG Tanker-1979 Loa 27.60 Br ex 6.50 Dght - Lbp - Br md 6.48 Dpth 3.10 Welded, 1 dk	**(B22A20V) Diving Support Vessel**	**1 oil engine** driving 1 FP propeller Total Power: 177kW (241hp) 9.0kn Scania 1 x 4 Stroke 177kW (241bhp) AB Scania Vabis-Sweden

8134039 - - - - -	**TENDER I** *ex* Polaris I *-1995* *ex* Polaris *-1982* *ex* Terneuzen *-1981* - -	**237** 71 -	Class: (BV)	**1954 Haarlemsche Scheepsbouw Mij. N.V. — Haarlem** Yd No: 512 Converted From: Research Vessel-1986 Loa 39.20 Br ex - Dght 2.850 Lbp 36.88 Br md 7.52 Dpth 3.71 Welded, 1 dk	**(B22G20Y) Standby Safety Vessel**	**1 oil engine** driving 1 FP propeller Total Power: 316kW (430hp) 11.5kn Werkspoor TMAS276 1 x 4 Stroke 6 Cy. 270 x 500 316kW (430bhp) NV Werkspoor-Netherlands AuxGen: 3 x 170kW 220V a.c
9591595 *3FUI5* -	**TENDER SALUTE** **Misuga SA** Misuga Kaiun Co Ltd SatCom: Inmarsat C 435265512 *Panama* *Panama* MMSI: 352655000 Official number: 4309011	**50,617** 31,470 95,695	Class: NK	**2011-09 Imabari Shipbuilding Co Ltd — Marugame KG (Marugame Shipyard)** Yd No: 1574 Loa 234.98 (BB) Br ex - Dght 14.466 Lbp 227.00 Br md 38.00 Dpth 19.90 Welded, 1 dk	**(A21A2BC) Bulk Carrier** Grain: 109,476 Compartments: 7 Ho, ER 7 Ha: ER	**1 oil engine** driving 1 FP propeller Total Power: 12,950kW (17,607hp) 14.5kn MAN-B&W 6S60MC-C 1 x 2 Stroke 6 Cy. 600 x 2400 12950kW (17607bhp) Hitachi Zosen Corp-Japan Fuel: 3920.0
8727020 *UVFW* -	**TENDROVSKAYA** **JSC Chernomortekhflot** - *Odessa* *Ukraine* MMSI: 272244000	**915** 274 1,068	Class: (RS)	**1986-10 Santierul Naval Drobeta-Turnu Severin S.A. — Drobeta-Turnu S.** Yd No: 1240004 Loa 56.19 Br ex 11.21 Dght 3.700 Lbp 53.20 Br md 11.00 Dpth 4.44 Welded, 1 dk	**(B34A2SH) Hopper, Motor** Ice Capable	**2 oil engines** driving 2 FP propellers Total Power: 574kW (780hp) 8.9kn S.K.L. 6NVD26A-3 2 x 4 Stroke 6 Cy. 180 x 260 each-287kW (390bhp) VEB Schwermaschinenbau "KarlLiebknecht" (SKL)-Magdeburg AuxGen: 2 x 100kW a.c Fuel: 123.0 (d.f.)
9134373 *JL6368* -	**TENEI MARU** **Shoei Kisen KK** - *Ozu, Ehime* *Japan* MMSI: 431500438 Official number: 135172	*499* - 1,600	Class: NK	**1996-04 Shin Kochi Jyuko K.K. — Kochi** Yd No: 7078 Loa 74.43 Br ex - Dght 3.930 Lbp 70.00 Br md 12.50 Dpth 6.80 Welded, 1 dk	**(A31A2GX) General Cargo Ship** Grain: 2,976; Bale: 2,906 Compartments: 1 Ho, ER 1 Ha: (39.0 x 10.2)ER	**1 oil engine** driving 1 FP propeller Total Power: 736kW (1,001hp) 11.0kn Hanshin LH30LG 1 x 4 Stroke 6 Cy. 300 x 600 736kW (1001bhp) The Hanshin Diesel Works Ltd-Japan Fuel: 70.0 (r.f.)
8630332 *JL5545* -	**TENEI MARU No. 38** **Katsura Kaiun KK** - *Ieshima, Hyogo* *Japan* Official number: 129051	*392* - 1,224		**1986-09 K.K. Yoshida Zosen Kogyo — Arida** Loa 58.90 Br ex 12.22 Dght 4.260 Lbp 53.00 Br md 12.20 Dpth 6.10 Welded, 1 dk	**(B33A2DG) Grab Dredger** Cranes: 1	**1 oil engine** driving 1 FP propeller Total Power: 736kW (1,001hp) 10.5kn Fuji 6S32G 1 x 4 Stroke 6 Cy. 320 x 610 736kW (1001bhp) Fuji Diesel Co Ltd-Japan
9016686 *JJ3775* -	**TENEI MARU No. 60** **Tenei Kogyo KK** - *Himeji, Hyogo* *Japan* Official number: 132274	*488* - 1,356		**1991-07 Shinhama Dockyard Co. Ltd. — Tamano** Yd No: 253 Loa 65.94 (BB) Br ex - Dght - Lbp 60.00 Br md 13.20 Dpth 7.20 Welded, 2 dks	**(A24D2BA) Aggregates Carrier** Compartments: 1 Ho, ER 1 Ha: ER	**1 oil engine** reverse geared to sc. shaft driving 1 FP propeller Total Power: 736kW (1,001hp) Niigata 6M34AGT 1 x 4 Stroke 6 Cy. 340 x 620 736kW (1001bhp) Niigata Engineering Co Ltd-Japan
9019602 *EAHL* -	**TENEO** **TE Connectivity SubCom SL** - SatCom: Inmarsat C 422461720 *Santa Cruz de Tenerife* *Spain (CSR)* MMSI: 224632000 Official number: 2/1995	**3,112** 933 1,563	Class: BV	**1992-12 Hijos de J. Barreras S.A. — Vigo** Yd No: 1542 Loa 81.00 Br ex 14.02 Dght 5.700 Lbp 71.50 Br md 14.00 Dpth 6.80 Welded, 1 dk	**(B34D2SL) Cable Layer** A-frames: 1x5t; Cranes: 1x2.5t	**4 diesel electric oil engines** driving 4 gen. each 1130kW 660V a.c Connecting to 2 elec. motors each (1250kW) driving 1 FP propeller Total Power: 4,708kW (6,400hp) 14.5kn Normo KRGB-6 4 x 4 Stroke 6 Cy. 250 x 300 each-1177kW (1600bhp) Bergen Diesel AS-Norway Thrusters: 1 Directional thruster (f); 1 Tunnel thruster (f); 1 Tunnel thruster (a) Fuel: 207.1 (d.f.) 17.2pd
9249984 *EBYO* -	**TENERIFE CAR** **Navicar SA** Flota Suardiaz SL SatCom: Inmarsat C 422413111 *Santa Cruz de Tenerife* *Spain (CSR)* MMSI: 224131000 Official number: 5/2002	**13,112** 3,934 3,325	Class: LR ✠ **100A1** SS 07/2012 roll on - roll off cargo ship *IWS ✠ **LMC** **UMS** Eq.Ltr: D†; Cable: 550.0/54.0 U3 (a)	**2002-07 Hijos de J. Barreras S.A. — Vigo** Yd No: 1591 Loa 132.45 (BB) Br ex 21.63 Dght 5.514 Lbp 118.00 Br md 21.20 Dpth 15.40 Welded, 6 dks	**(A35B2RV) Vehicles Carrier** Stern door/ramp (centre) Len: 15.00 Wid: 10.00 Swl: - Side door/ramp (s) Len: 14.00 Wid: 2.50 Swl: - Cars: 1,350	**2 oil engines** with clutches, flexible couplings & sr geared to sc. shafts driving 2 CP propellers Total Power: 13,050kW (17,742hp) 20.0kn Wartsila 9L38 2 x 4 Stroke 9 Cy. 380 x 475 each-6525kW (8871bhp) Wartsila Diesel S.A.-Bermeo AuxGen: 2 x 648kW 400V 50Hz a.c, 2 x 648kW 400V 50Hz a.c Boilers: AuxB (Comp) 7.5kgf/cm² (7.4bar) Thrusters: 2 Thwart. CP thruster (f) Fuel: 105.0 (d.f.) 795.0 (r.f.) 47.0pd
9306720 *BPCY* -	**TENG CHI** **China Shipping Tanker Co Ltd** - *Shanghai* *China* MMSI: 413124000	**26,955** 11,381 42,047 T/cm 51.5	Class: CC	**2005-01 Guangzhou Shipyard International Co Ltd — Guangzhou GD** Yd No: 03130015 Loa 187.80 (BB) Br ex 31.53 Dght 11.300 Lbp 178.00 Br md 31.50 Dpth 16.80 Welded, 1 dk	**(A13B2TP) Products Tanker** Double Hull (13F) Liq: 45,895; Liq (Oil): 45,895 Cargo Heating Coils Compartments: 12 Wing Ta, 2 Wing Slop Ta, ER 3 Cargo Pump (s): 3x1200m³/hr Manifold: Bow/CM: 93m Ice Capable	**1 oil engine** driving 1 FP propeller Total Power: 8,580kW (11,665hp) 14.5kn MAN-B&W 6S50MC 1 x 2 Stroke 6 Cy. 500 x 1910 8580kW (11665bhp) Dalian Marine Diesel Works-China AuxGen: 3 x 664kW 450V a.c Fuel: 82.0 (d.f.) 1341.0 (r.f.)
9056935 *BOHE* -	**TENG FEI HAI** **COSCO Bulk Carrier Co Ltd (COSCO BULK)** - SatCom: Inmarsat C 441208410 *Tianjin* *China* MMSI: 412203000	**38,603** 24,351 69,967	Class: CC	**1995-12 Jiangnan Shipyard — Shanghai** Yd No: 2209 Loa 225.00 Br ex - Dght 13.622 Lbp 215.00 Br md 32.20 Dpth 18.70 Welded	**(A21A2BC) Bulk Carrier** Grain: 84,019; Bale: 81,365 Compartments: 7 Ho, ER 7 Ha: 5 (14.6 x 15.0) (14.7 x 15.0)ER (14.6 x 13.2)	**1 oil engine** driving 1 FP propeller Total Power: 8,459kW (11,501hp) 14.0kn B&W 6S60MC 1 x 2 Stroke 6 Cy. 600 x 2292 8459kW (11501bhp) Dalian Marine Diesel Works-China AuxGen: 3 x 616kW 450V a.c
9554884 *VRHV4* -	**TENG HANG** **HongKong Teng Hang Int'l Marine Transportation Ltd** Sino Far East Ship Management Co Ltd SatCom: Inmarsat C 447701891 *Hong Kong* *Hong Kong* MMSI: 477892600	**21,904** 11,919 35,000	Class: BV	**2011-02 Ningbo Dongfang Shipyard Co Ltd — Ningbo ZJ** Yd No: DFC08-068 Loa 179.98 Br ex - Dght 10.550 Lbp 172.25 Br md 28.40 Dpth 14.70 Welded, 1 dk	**(A21A2BC) Bulk Carrier** Grain: 44,433 Compartments: 5 Ho, ER 5 Ha: ER Cranes: 4x36t	**1 oil engine** driving 1 FP propeller Total Power: 6,480kW (8,810hp) 14.0kn MAN-B&W 6S42MC 1 x 2 Stroke 6 Cy. 420 x 1764 6480kW (8810bhp) STX Engine Co Ltd-South Korea AuxGen: 3 x 600kW 60Hz a.c
9525601 *3FKF5* -	**TENG XIN 1** *ex* Hong Xin 2 *-2013* *ex* Bin Dong Shan 32 *-2008* **Shanghai Ya Wa Industrial Co Ltd** - *Panama* *Panama* MMSI: 370396000 Official number: 44684PEXTF	**2,999** 1,787 4,500	Class: IS	**2008-04 Mindong Congmao Ship Industry Co Ltd — Fu'an FJ** Loa 96.68 Br ex - Dght 6.080 Lbp 89.88 Br md 15.20 Dpth 7.60 Welded, 1 dk	**(A31A2GX) General Cargo Ship** Grain: 6,410	**1 oil engine** reduction geared to sc. shaft driving 1 FP propeller Total Power: 1,325kW (1,801hp) 11.0kn Guangzhou 6320ZCD 1 x 4 Stroke 6 Cy. 320 x 440 1325kW (1801bhp) Guangzhou Diesel Engine Factory CoLtd-China
9211523 *BAGO* -	**TENG YUAN** **Dandong Daludao Haixing Enterprise (Group) Co Ltd** - *Dalian, Liaoning* *China* MMSI: 412202730 Official number: 030001000028	**289** 93 400	Class: CC	**1999-05 Huanghai Shipbuilding Co Ltd — Rongcheng SD** Yd No: A402-1/1 Loa 49.95 Br ex - Dght - Lbp 46.00 Br md 7.40 Dpth 3.70 Welded, 1 dk	**(A34A2GR) Refrigerated Cargo Ship** Ins: 338	**1 oil engine** reduction geared to sc. shaft driving 1 FP propeller Total Power: 1,324kW (1,800hp) 14.5kn Chinese Std. Type LB8250ZC 1 x 4 Stroke 8 Cy. 250 x 320 1324kW (1800bhp) Zibo Diesel Engine Factory-China AuxGen: 2 x 64kW 390V a.c
9223758 *BOTV* -	**TENG YUN HE** **COSCO Container Lines Co Ltd (COSCON)** - *Shanghai* *China* MMSI: 412277000	**20,569** 9,379 25,648 T/cm 42.0	Class: CC	**2000-04 Shanghai Shipyard — Shanghai** Yd No: 178 Loa 179.70 (BB) Br ex - Dght 10.640 Lbp 167.00 Br md 27.60 Dpth 15.90 Welded, 1 dk	**(A33A2CC) Container Ship (Fully Cellular)** TEU 1702 C Ho 776 TEU C Dk 926 TEU incl 200 ref C. Ice Capable	**1 oil engine** driving 1 FP propeller Total Power: 16,980kW (23,086hp) 20.0kn B&W 6L70MC 1 x 2 Stroke 6 Cy. 700 x 2268 16980kW (23086bhp) HHM Shangchuan Diesel Co Ltd-China AuxGen: 3 x 960kW 450V 60Hz a.c Thrusters: 1 Thwart. CP thruster (f) Fuel: 110.5 (d.f.) (Heating Coils) 2257.3 (r.f.) 70.0pd

IMO / Call sign	Name / Owner	Tonnage	Class	Builder / Dimensions	Type	Machinery
7816214 *ZMVH* -	**TENGAWAI** - **Sanford Ltd** - *Timaru* *New Zealand* Official number: 349395	133 40 -		**1979-02 Scheepsw. en Mfbk."De Biesbosch-Dordrecht" B.V. — Dordrecht** (Hull) **1979-02 B.V. Scheepswerf Damen — Gorinchem** Yd No: 3603 Loa 26.01 Br ex - Dght 2.891 Lbp 24.01 Br md 7.02 Dpth 2.98 Welded, 1 dk	**(B11A2FS) Stern Trawler**	**1 oil engine** reverse reduction geared to sc. shaft driving 1 FP propeller Total Power: 588kW (799hp) G.M. (Detroit Diesel) 12V-149-TI 1 x Vee 2 Stroke 12 Cy. 146 x 146 588kW (799bhp) General Motors Detroit DieselAllison Divn-USA
9465904 *YB5308* -	**TENGGARA EXPLORER** - **PT Indonusa Tenggara Marine** - *Benoa* *Indonesia*	179 54 80	Class: KI (BV)	**2007-10 SBF Shipbuilders (1977) Pty Ltd — Fremantle WA** Yd No: 262 Loa 32.40 Br ex 8.20 Dght 1.800 Lbp 29.49 Br md 7.90 Dpth 3.25 Welded, 1 dk	**(B34L2QU) Utility Vessel** Hull Material: Aluminium Alloy A-frames: 1	**2 oil engines** reverse reduction geared to sc. shafts driving 2 FP propellers Total Power: 882kW (1,200hp) Caterpillar C18 2 x 4 Stroke 6 Cy. 145 x 183 each-441kW (600bhp) Caterpillar Inc-USA Thrusters: 2 Tunnel thruster (f)
9281085 *YB5354* -	**TENGGARA SATU** - **PT Surya Samudra Jaya Perkasa** - *Benoa* *Indonesia*	*149* 45 26	Class: KI (BV)	**2002-11 SBF Shipbuilders (1977) Pty Ltd — Fremantle WA** Yd No: 227 Loa 29.90 Br ex 6.50 Dght 0.910 Lbp 26.60 Br md 6.26 Dpth 1.66 Welded, 2 dks	**(A37B2PS) Passenger Ship** Hull Material: Aluminium Alloy	**2 oil engines** with clutches & sr reverse geared to sc. shafts driving 2 FP propellers Total Power: 1,472kW (2,002hp) 25.0kn Caterpillar 3412E 2 x Vee 4 Stroke 12 Cy. 137 x 152 each-736kW (1001bhp) Caterpillar Inc-USA AuxGen: 2 x 38kW 380V a.c
7345162 *YBNI* -	**TENGGER** - **PT PERTAMINA (PERSERO)** - *Jakarta* *Indonesia*	*395* 119 -	Class: KI (AB)	**1974-12 Robin Shipyard Pte Ltd — Singapore** Yd No: 113 Loa 40.58 Br ex - Dght 3.963 Lbp 36.00 Br md 8.82 Dpth 4.53 Welded	**(B32A2ST) Tug**	**2 oil engines** driving 2 FP propellers Total Power: 2,354kW (3,200hp) 12.5kn Niigata 8MG25BX 2 x 4 Stroke 8 Cy. 250 x 320 each-1177kW (1600bhp) Niigata Engineering Co Ltd-Japan AuxGen: 2 x 80kW
7227449 *YB4299* -	**TENGGIRI** *ex Ferry Ponte -1980* **Government of The Republic of Indonesia (Direktorat Jenderal Perhubungan Darat - Ministry of Land Communications)** PT ASDP Indonesia Ferry (Persero) - Angkutan Sungai Danau & Penyeberangan *Jakarta* *Indonesia*	*267* 95 111	Class: KI	**1972-06 Matsuura Tekko Zosen K.K. — Osakikamijima** Yd No: 220 Loa 41.20 Br ex 10.22 Dght 2.312 Lbp 36.28 Br md 8.92 Dpth 3.10 Welded, 1 dk	**(A36A2PR) Passenger/Ro-Ro Ship (Vehicles)** Passengers: unberthed: 350	**2 oil engines** driving 2 Propellers fwd and 2 aft Total Power: 544kW (740hp) 10.0kn Yanmar 6M-HT 2 x 4 Stroke 6 Cy. 200 x 240 each-272kW (370bhp) Yanmar Diesel Engine Co Ltd-Japan Fuel: 9.0 1.0pd
9108518 - -	**TENGGIRI** *launched as* Lumba Lumba *-1995* **Government of The State of Brunei (Fisheries Department - Ministry of Industry & Primary Sources)** - *Bandar Seri Begawan* *Brunei* Official number: 0161	223 66 79	Class: (LR) (BV) ✠ Classed LR until 31/5/97	**1995-06 Cheoy Lee Shipyards Ltd — Hong Kong** Yd No: 4575 Loa 27.60 Br ex 7.59 Dght 2.100 Lbp 24.00 Br md 7.50 Dpth 3.40 Welded, 1 dk	**(B12D2FR) Fishery Research Vessel**	**1 oil engine** with clutches, flexible couplings & reverse reduction geared to sc. shaft driving 1 FP propeller Total Power: 1,119kW (1,521hp) 11.0kn Caterpillar 3508TA 1 x Vee 4 Stroke 8 Cy. 170 x 190 1119kW (1521bhp) Caterpillar Inc-USA AuxGen: 2 x 64kW 415V 50Hz a.c Thrusters: 1 Thwart. FP thruster (f)
9103075 *JL6086* -	**TENGU MARU** - **Mori Kaiun YK** - *Ikeda, Kagawa* *Japan* Official number: 132976	*199* - 570		**1993-07 Maekawa Zosensho — Japan** Yd No: 265 Loa 54.85 Br ex - Dght 3.300 Lbp 49.00 Br md 9.20 Dpth 5.25 Welded	**(A31A2GX) General Cargo Ship**	**1 oil engine** driving 1 FP propeller Total Power: 736kW (1,001hp) 10.5kn Hanshin LH26G 1 x 4 Stroke 6 Cy. 260 x 440 736kW (1001bhp) The Hanshin Diesel Works Ltd-Japan
7706445 - -	**TENGU MARU** - **Dragon Express** -	*179* - 395		**1977-03 Takebe Zosen — Takamatsu** Yd No: 67 Loa - Br ex - Dght - Lbp 41.00 Br md 7.80 Dpth 3.15 Welded, 1 dk	**(A31A2GX) General Cargo Ship**	**1 oil engine** driving 1 FP propeller Total Power: 243kW (330hp) Sumiyoshi 1 x 4 Stroke 6 Cy. 200 x 240 243kW (330bhp) Sumiyoshi Tekkosho-Japan
9128764 *YJQE5* -	**TENHO MARU** - **Princess Line SA** Hayama Senpaku KK (Hayama Shipping Ltd) *Port Vila* *Vanuatu* MMSI: 576414000 Official number: 1926	3,496 1,587 3,959	Class: NK	**1995-09 Miyoshi Shipbuilding Co Ltd — Uwajima EH** Yd No: 330 Loa 94.65 (BB) Br ex 16.42 Dght 6.664 Lbp 84.90 Br md 16.40 Dpth 9.90 Welded, 2 dks	**(A34A2GR) Refrigerated Cargo Ship** Ins: 4,561 Compartments: 4 Ho, ER 4 Ha: ER Cranes: 6x5t	**1 oil engine** driving 1 FP propeller Total Power: 2,942kW (4,000hp) 14.1kn B&W 5L35MC 1 x 2 Stroke 5 Cy. 350 x 1050 2942kW (4000bhp) Makita Corp-Japan Fuel: 725.0 (r.f.)
8877033 *JK5389* -	**TENJIN MARU** - **Offshore Operation Co Ltd** - *Etajima, Hiroshima* *Japan* Official number: 134118	*199* - 497		**1994-03 Hongawara Zosen K.K. — Fukuyama** Loa 47.33 Br ex - Dght 2.830 Lbp 43.00 Br md 7.80 Dpth 3.20 Welded, 1 dk	**(A13B2TU) Tanker (unspecified)** Liq: 547; Liq (Oil): 547	**1 oil engine** driving 1 FP propeller Total Power: 588kW (799hp) 9.5kn Matsui 1 x 4 Stroke 588kW (799bhp) Matsui Iron Works Co Ltd-Japan
8032255 - -	**TENJIN MARU** - **Nakane Marine S de RL** - *Honduras*	*181* 110 350		**1980-08 Ishida Zosen Kogyo YK — Onomichi HS** Yd No: 142 Loa - Br ex - Dght 2.900 Lbp 36.00 Br md 7.00 Dpth 3.00 Welded, 1 dk	**(A13B2TU) Tanker (unspecified)**	**1 oil engine** driving 1 FP propeller
8609228 - -	**TENJIN MARU No. 1** - **PT Pelayaran Bahari Maju** -	*490* - 1,188	Class: IZ	**1986-09 Tokushima Zosen Sangyo K.K. — Komatsushima** Yd No: 1936 Converted From: General Cargo Ship-2013 Loa 62.34 (BB) Br ex - Dght 3.461 Lbp 56.01 Br md 13.01 Dpth 5.62 Welded, 2 dks	**(B33A2DU) Dredger (unspecified)** Compartments: 1 Ho, ER 1 Ha: ER	**1 oil engine** driving 1 FP propeller Total Power: 736kW (1,001hp) Hanshin 6LUN28AG 1 x 4 Stroke 6 Cy. 280 x 480 736kW (1001bhp) The Hanshin Diesel Works Ltd-Japan
8890487 *JJ3829* -	**TENJIN MARU No. 8** *ex Yoshishige Maru No. 68 -2010* **Tamura Sekizai KK** - *Himeji, Hyogo* *Japan* Official number: 134173	*489* - -		**1995-07 Nagashima Zosen KK — Kihoku ME** Yd No: 385 Loa 66.80 Br ex - Dght - Lbp - Br md 13.50 Dpth 6.80 Welded, 1 dk	**(A24D2BA) Aggregates Carrier**	**1 oil engine** driving 1 FP propeller Total Power: 1,471kW (2,000hp) 13.0kn Akasaka A37 1 x 4 Stroke 6 Cy. 370 x 720 1471kW (2000bhp) Akasaka Tekkosho KK (Akasaka DieselLtd)-Japan
8821424 *JL5780* -	**TENJIN MARU No. 8** - **Kawasaki Kaiun YK** - *Tokushima, Tokushima* *Japan* Official number: 130599	*492* - 570		**1989-05 K.K. Saidaiji Zosensho — Okayama** Yd No: 162 L reg 47.10 Br ex - Dght - Lbp - Br md 10.50 Dpth 5.40 Welded, 1 dk	**(B33A2DG) Grab Dredger**	**1 oil engine** driving 1 FP propeller Total Power: 544kW (740hp) Hanshin 6LUN28AG 1 x 4 Stroke 6 Cy. 280 x 480 544kW (740bhp) The Hanshin Diesel Works Ltd-Japan
9142356 *JM6531* -	**TENJIN MARU No. 8** - **YK Shunki Kaiun** - *Kamiamakusa, Kumamoto* *Japan* Official number: 134635	*199* - 650		**1996-05 Yamakawa Zosen Tekko K.K. — Kagoshima** Yd No: 736 Loa - Br ex - Dght 3.120 Lbp 52.40 Br md 9.60 Dpth 5.40 Welded, 1 dk	**(A31A2GX) General Cargo Ship**	**1 oil engine** driving 1 FP propeller Total Power: 736kW (1,001hp) 10.5kn Niigata 6M26AGTE 1 x 4 Stroke 6 Cy. 260 x 460 736kW (1001bhp) Niigata Engineering Co Ltd-Japan
9209881 *JL6577* -	**TENJIN MARU No. 8** - **Okumoto Kaiun YK** - *Anan, Tokushima* *Japan* Official number: 135598	*499* - 1,577		**1999-03 K.K. Matsuura Zosensho — Osakikamijima** Yd No: 531 Loa 71.34 Br ex - Dght 4.000 Lbp 65.40 Br md 12.50 Dpth 7.00 Welded, 1 dk	**(A31A2GX) General Cargo Ship** Grain: 2,518 Compartments: 1 Ho, ER 1 Ha: (21.0 x 10.0)ER	**1 oil engine** driving 1 FP propeller Total Power: 1,471kW (2,000hp) 11.5kn Hanshin LH34LAG 1 x 4 Stroke 6 Cy. 340 x 640 1471kW (2000bhp) The Hanshin Diesel Works Ltd-Japan
9676670 *JD3353* -	**TENJIN MARU NO. 11** - **Daiju Kaiun KK** - *Anan, Tokushima* *Japan* Official number: 141668	*499* - 1,750		**2012-04 K.K. Murakami Zosensho — Naruto** Yd No: 288 L reg 71.61 Br ex - Dght 4.280 Lbp 70.00 Br md 12.00 Dpth 7.30 Welded, 1 dk	**(A31A2GX) General Cargo Ship** 1 Ha: ER (40.0 x 9.5)	**1 oil engine** reverse geared to sc. shaft driving 1 Propeller Total Power: 1,323kW (1,799hp) Akasaka AX31R 1 x 4 Stroke 6 Cy. 310 x 620 1323kW (1799bhp) Akasaka Tekkosho KK (Akasaka DieselLtd)-Japan

8805016 **TENJIN MARU No. 15** *431*
- -
- **China World Best Group Co Ltd** 1,115
-
China

1988-07 **Kyokuyo Shipyard Corp — Shimonoseki YC** Yd No: 2592
Loa 51.17 (BB) Br ex 12.52 Dght 5.021
Lbp 46.95 Br md 12.50 Dpth 6.80
Welded, 1 dk

(B33A2DS) Suction Dredger
Grain: 652
Compartments: 1 Ho, ER

1 oil engine geared to sc. shaft driving 1 FP propeller
Total Power: 736kW (1,001hp)
Hanshin 6LU35G
1 x 4 Stroke 6 Cy. 350 x 550 736kW (1001bhp)
The Hanshin Diesel Works Ltd-Japan
Thrusters: 1 Thwart. CP thruster (f)

8713110 **TENJIN MARU No. 28** *457*
- -
- **OG Marine Sdn Bhd** 1,246
-
Malaysia

1988-06 **Hamamoto Zosensho K.K. — Tokushima** Yd No: 710
Loa 61.14 (BB) Br ex - Dght 4.622
Lbp 54.01 Br md 11.51 Dpth 6.23
Welded, 2 dks

(A24D2BA) Aggregates Carrier
Grain: 800
Compartments: 1 Ho, ER
1 Ha: ER

1 oil engine driving 1 FP propeller
Total Power: 736kW (1,001hp)
Yanmar MF33-ST
1 x 4 Stroke 6 Cy. 330 x 620 736kW (1001bhp)
Yanmar Diesel Engine Co Ltd-Japan
Thrusters: 1 Thwart. FP thruster (f)

9152387 **TENJIN MARU No. 47** *881*
JJ3838 -
- **Tenjin Kaiun KK** 1,900
Himeji, Hyogo *Japan*
MMSI: 431300491
Official number: 134183

1996-12 **K.K. Miura Zosensho — Saiki** Yd No: 1176
Loa 82.00 Br ex - Dght -
Lbp 76.00 Br md 14.30 Dpth 7.60
Welded, 1 dk

(A31A2GX) General Cargo Ship

1 oil engine driving 1 FP propeller
Total Power: 1,471kW (2,000hp) 12.8kn
Hanshin LH41LAG
1 x 4 Stroke 6 Cy. 410 x 800 1471kW (2000bhp)
The Hanshin Diesel Works Ltd-Japan

9197234 **TENJIN MARU No. 65** *997*
JJ3950 -
- **Tenjin Kaiun KK** 2,500
Himeji, Hyogo *Japan*
MMSI: 431301101
Official number: 134205

1998-07 **K.K. Watanabe Zosensho — Nagasaki** Yd No: 064
Loa 85.55 Br ex - Dght 4.950
Lbp 78.00 Br md 15.00 Dpth 7.90
Welded, 1 dk

(A31A2GX) General Cargo Ship

1 oil engine driving 1 FP propeller
Total Power: 1,471kW (2,000hp) 15.6kn
Hanshin LH46LG
1 x 4 Stroke 6 Cy. 460 x 880 1471kW (2000bhp)
The Hanshin Diesel Works Ltd-Japan

8839536 **TENJO MARU NO. 8** *127*
JK4897 -
- **Kambara Logistics Co Ltd** -
Fukuyama, Hiroshima *Japan*
Official number: 131009

1989-12 **Hongawara Zosen K.K. — Fukuyama**
Loa 30.40 Br ex - Dght 2.750
Lbp 26.50 Br md 7.50 Dpth 3.38
Welded, 1 dk

(B32A2ST) Tug

1 oil engine driving 1 FP propeller
Total Power: 1,177kW (1,600hp) 12.7kn
Niigata 6M34AGT
1 x 4 Stroke 6 Cy. 340 x 620 1177kW (1600bhp)
Niigata Engineering Co Ltd-Japan

9343390 **TENJUN** **159,927** Class: NK
3ETD4 97,999
- **Magnolia Shipholding SA** 302,107
NYK Shipmanagement Pte Ltd T/cm
SatCom: Inmarsat Mini-M 764871611 182.5
Panama *Panama*
MMSI: 370526000
Official number: 3435408A

2008-09 **IHI Marine United Inc — Kure HS** Yd No: 3221
Loa 333.00 (BB) Br ex 60.04 Dght 20.635
Lbp 324.00 Br md 60.00 Dpth 29.00
Welded, 1 dk

(A13A2TV) Crude Oil Tanker
Double Hull (13F)
Liq: 330,189; Liq (Oil): 342,850
Cargo Heating Coils
Compartments: 5 Ta, 10 Wing Ta, 2 Wing Slop Ta, ER
3 Cargo Pump (s): 3x5500m³/hr
Manifold: Bow/CM: 163.6m

1 oil engine driving 1 FP propeller
Total Power: 27,160kW (36,927hp) 15.7kn
Wartsila 7RTA84T
1 x 2 Stroke 7 Cy. 840 x 3150 27160kW (36927bhp)
Diesel United Ltd.-Aioi
AuxGen: 3 x 1150kW 440V 50Hz a.c
Fuel: 630.0 (d.f.) 6970.0 (r.f.)

9357066 **TENKAI MARU** *498*
JD2075 -
- **Shinyo Kisen KK** 1,301
Bizen, Okayama *Japan*
Official number: 140124

2005-03 **KK Ura Kyodo Zosensho — Awaji HG** Yd No: 323
Loa 62.98 Br ex 10.02 Dght 4.278
Lbp 60.00 Br md 10.00 Dpth 5.00
Welded, 1 dk

(A12A2TC) Chemical Tanker
Double Hull (13F)

1 oil engine driving 1 FP propeller
Total Power: 736kW (1,001hp)
Niigata
1 x 4 Stroke 736kW (1001bhp)
Niigata Engineering Co Ltd-Japan

9152404 **TENKAKU** *748*
JM6537 -
- **Daio Kaiun Co Ltd (Daio Kaiun YK)** 2,025
Kamiamakusa, Kumamoto *Japan*
MMSI: 431600647
Official number: 134652

1996-11 **K.K. Miura Zosensho — Saiki** Yd No: 1181
Loa - Br ex - Dght -
Lbp 74.00 Br md 14.30 Dpth 7.80
Welded, 1 dk

(A31A2GX) General Cargo Ship

1 oil engine driving 1 FP propeller
Total Power: 1,471kW (2,000hp)
Hanshin LH41LAG
1 x 4 Stroke 6 Cy. 410 x 800 1471kW (2000bhp)
The Hanshin Diesel Works Ltd-Japan

9321299 **TENKI** **160,295** Class: NK
3EJE9 104,336
- **Colnago Maritima SA** 316,021
NYK Shipmanagement Pte Ltd T/cm
SatCom: Inmarsat C 437249510 184.9
Panama *Panama*
MMSI: 372495000
Official number: 3258407B

2007-03 **Nantong COSCO KHI Ship Engineering Co Ltd (NACKS) — Nantong JS** Yd No: 043
Loa 333.00 (BB) Br ex 60.04 Dght 21.176
Lbp 324.00 Br md 60.00 Dpth 29.00
Welded, 1 dk

(A13A2TV) Crude Oil Tanker
Double Hull (13F)
Liq: 352,809; Liq (Oil): 352,809
Compartments: 5 Ta, 10 Wing Ta, 2 Wing Slop Ta, ER
3 Cargo Pump (s): 3x5500m³/hr
Manifold: Bow/CM: 166.5m

1 oil engine driving 1 FP propeller
Total Power: 25,480kW (34,643hp) 14.5kn
MAN-B&W 7S80MC-C
1 x 2 Stroke 7 Cy. 800 x 3200 25480kW (34643bhp)
Kawasaki Heavy Industries Ltd-Japan
AuxGen: 3 x a.c
Fuel: 341.2 (d.f.) 5550.5 (r.f.)

9440978 **TENKI MARU** **32,415** Class: NV (NK)
3FSU 19,353
- **Chijin Shipping SA** 58,693
Union Marine Management Services Pte Ltd T/cm
Panama *Panama* 57.4
MMSI: 370078000
Official number: 4037509

2009-04 **Tsuneishi Group (Zhoushan) Shipbuilding Inc — Daishan County ZJ** Yd No: SS-040
Loa 189.99 (BB) Br ex - Dght 12.828
Lbp 185.78 Br md 32.26 Dpth 18.00
Welded, 1 dk

(A21A2BC) Bulk Carrier
Grain: 72,360; Bale: 70,557
Compartments: 5 Ho, ER
5 Ha: ER
Cranes: 4x30t

1 oil engine driving 1 FP propeller
Total Power: 8,400kW (11,421hp) 14.5kn
MAN-B&W 6S50MC-C
1 x 2 Stroke 6 Cy. 500 x 2000 8400kW (11421bhp)
Mitsui Engineering & Shipbuilding CLtd-Japan
AuxGen: 3 x 480kW a.c
Fuel: 2537.0

9440928 **TENKO MARU** **32,415** Class: NK
HPRN 19,353
- **Chijin Shipping SA** 58,732
NEOM Maritime (Singapore) Pte Ltd T/cm
Panama *Panama* 57.4
MMSI: 370715000
Official number: 4014309

2008-12 **Tsuneishi Group (Zhoushan) Shipbuilding Inc — Daishan County ZJ** Yd No: SS-037
Loa 189.99 (BB) Br ex - Dght 12.828
Lbp 185.60 Br md 32.26 Dpth 18.00
Welded, 1 dk

(A21A2BC) Bulk Carrier
Grain: 72,360; Bale: 70,557
Compartments: 5 Ho, ER
5 Ha: ER
Cranes: 4x30t

1 oil engine driving 1 FP propeller
Total Power: 8,400kW (11,421hp) 14.5kn
MAN-B&W 6S50MC-C
1 x 2 Stroke 6 Cy. 500 x 2000 8400kW (11421bhp)
Mitsui Engineering & Shipbuilding CLtd-Japan
AuxGen: 3 x 480kW a.c
Fuel: 2537.0 (r.f.)

8859603 **TENKO MARU** *198*
- 106
- **Asahi Line SA** 519
-

1970 **Shin Nikko Zosen K.K. — Onomichi**
Loa 40.50 Br ex - Dght 3.400
Lbp 36.00 Br md 8.00 Dpth 5.60
Welded, 1 dk

(A31A2GX) General Cargo Ship

1 oil engine driving 1 FP propeller
Total Power: 368kW (500hp) 8.0kn
Kubota
1 x 4 Stroke 368kW (500bhp)
Kubota Corp-Japan

7233979 **TENKO MARU** *284*
- *ex* Ryuo Maru No. 1 *-1989* 144
- *ex* Kyoshin Maru No. 51 *-1983* -
-
-

1972 **KK Kanasashi Zosen — Shizuoka SZ** Yd No: 1081
Loa 48.24 Br ex 8.23 Dght 3.252
Lbp 42.45 Br md 8.21 Dpth 3.61
Welded, 1 dk

(B11B2FV) Fishing Vessel

1 oil engine driving 1 FP propeller
Total Power: 736kW (1,001hp)
Niigata 6M28KHS
1 x 4 Stroke 6 Cy. 280 x 440 736kW (1001bhp)
Niigata Engineering Co Ltd-Japan

9125499 **TENKO MARU No. 5** *199*
JM6312 -
- **YK Tenko Shoji** 650
Bungo-Takada, Oita *Japan*
Official number: 134586

1995-10 **Taiyo Shipbuilding Co Ltd — Sanyoonoda YC** Yd No: 260
Loa 55.68 (BB) Br ex - Dght 3.289
Lbp 52.77 Br md 9.40 Dpth 5.50
Welded, 1 dk

(A31A2GX) General Cargo Ship
Grain: 1,118; Bale: 1,115

1 oil engine driving 1 FP propeller
Total Power: 735kW (999hp) 11.0kn
Niigata 6M28BGT
1 x 4 Stroke 6 Cy. 280 x 480 735kW (999bhp)
Niigata Engineering Co Ltd-Japan

9099248 **TENMA** *499*
JD2303 -
- **Shinei Kaiun YK** 1,438
Imoto Shoun Kaisha
Hofu, Yamaguchi *Japan*
MMSI: 431402072
Official number: 140385

2007-04 **Nagashima Zosen KK — Kihoku ME** Yd No: 707
Loa 80.00 (BB) Br ex - Dght 3.680
Lbp 72.80 Br md 13.20 Dpth 6.60
Welded, 1 dk

(A33A2CC) Container Ship (Fully Cellular)
TEU 140
Compartments: 1 Cell Ho, ER
1 Ha: ER (38.3 x 10.5)

1 oil engine driving 1 Propeller
Total Power: 1,839kW (2,500hp) 14.0kn
Niigata 6M34NT-G
1 x 4 Stroke 6 Cy. 340 x 620 1839kW (2500bhp)
Niigata Engineering Co Ltd-Japan
Thrusters: 1 Tunnel thruster (f)

9115341 **TENMA MARU** *739*
JM6451 -
- **Daio Kaiun Co Ltd (Daio Kaiun YK)** 2,011
Daiichi Chuo Kisen Kaisha
Kamiamakusa, Kumamoto *Japan*
MMSI: 431600632
Official number: 134543

1995-03 **K.K. Miura Zosensho — Saiki** Yd No: 1118
Loa 80.00 (BB) Br ex - Dght 4.758
Lbp 75.00 Br md 12.80 Dpth 7.65
Welded, 1 dk

(A31A2GX) General Cargo Ship
Grain: 2,773
Compartments: 1 Ho, ER
1 Ha: ER

1 oil engine driving 1 FP propeller
Total Power: 1,471kW (2,000hp)
Hanshin 6EL38
1 x 4 Stroke 6 Cy. 380 x 760 1471kW (2000bhp)
The Hanshin Diesel Works Ltd-Japan
Thrusters: 1 Thwart. FP thruster (f)

9440916 **TENMYO MARU** **32,415** Class: NV (NK)
9V2182 19,353
- **Kambara Kisen Singapore Pte Ltd** 58,749
Union Marine Management Services Pte Ltd T/cm
Singapore *Singapore* 57.4
MMSI: 563618000
Official number: 398713

2008-11 **Tsuneishi Group (Zhoushan) Shipbuilding Inc — Daishan County ZJ** Yd No: SS-036
Loa 189.99 Br ex - Dght 12.828
Lbp 185.60 Br md 32.26 Dpth 18.00
Welded, 1 dk

(A21A2BC) Bulk Carrier
Grain: 72,360; Bale: 70,557
Compartments: 5 Ho, ER
5 Ha: ER
Cranes: 4x30t

1 oil engine driving 1 FP propeller
Total Power: 8,400kW (11,421hp) 14.5kn
MAN-B&W 6S50MC-C
1 x 2 Stroke 6 Cy. 500 x 2000 8400kW (11421bhp)
Mitsui Engineering & Shipbuilding CLtd-Japan
AuxGen: 3 x 480kW a.c
Fuel: 2537.0

IMO / Call sign	Name / Owner	Tonnage	Class	Builder / Dimensions	Type / Cargo	Machinery
9666065 *LDKA* -	**TENNA** **Boreal Transport Nord AS** *Sandnessjoen* *Norway* MMSI: 258696000 Official number: 14	**2,357** 707 360	Class: NV	**2014-01 Ada Denizcilik ve Tersane Isletmeciligi AS — Istanbul (Tuzla)** (Hull) Yd No: (108) **2014-01 Fiskerstrand Verft AS — Fiskarstrand** Yd No: 14 Loa 71.20 Br ex 14.20 Dght 3.600 Lbp 65.00 Br md 14.20 Dpth 5.55 Welded, 1 dk	**(A36A2PR) Passenger/Ro-Ro Ship (Vehicles)**	**1 oil engine** driving 1 Propeller Total Power: 820kW (1,115hp) Caterpillar C32 1 x Vee 4 Stroke 12 Cy. 145 x 162 820kW (1115bhp)
9322736 *9VPC2* -	**TENNA BULKER** *ex Sat Trinity -2010 ex Yusho Trinity -2007* **J Lauritzen Singapore Pte Ltd** New Century Overseas Management Inc *Singapore* *Singapore* MMSI: 565499000 Official number: 393133	**16,960** 10,498 28,391 T/cm 39.7	Class: NK	**2005-01 Imabari Shipbuilding Co Ltd — Imabari EH (Imabari Shipyard)** Yd No: 595 Loa 169.26 (BB) Br ex - Dght 9.800 Lbp 160.40 Br md 27.20 Dpth 13.60 Welded, 1 dk	**(A21A2BC) Bulk Carrier** Grain: 37,523; Bale: 35,762 Compartments: 5 Ho, ER 5 Ha: 4 (19.2 x 17.6)ER (13.6 x 16.0) Cranes: 4x30.5t	**1 oil engine** driving 1 FP propeller Total Power: 5,850kW (7,954hp) 14.0kn MAN-B&W 6S42MC 1 x 2 Stroke 6 Cy. 420 x 1764 5850kW (7954bhp) Makita Corp-Japan Fuel: 1250.0
9160475 *MCBU4* -	**TENNA KOSAN** **Lauritzen Kosan Ship Owners A/S** Lauritzen Kosan A/S *Douglas* *Isle of Man (British)* MMSI: 235006490 Official number: 736378	**5,103** 1,623 6,095 T/cm 16.0	Class: BV	**1998-09 Hyundai Heavy Industries Co Ltd — Ulsan** Yd No: HP89 Loa 112.56 (BB) Br ex 16.02 Dght 7.224 Lbp 105.00 Br md 16.00 Dpth 8.25 Welded, 1 dk	**(A11B2TG) LPG Tanker** Double Sides Entire Compartment Length Liq (Gas): 5,777 2 x Gas Tank (s); 2 independent (C.mn.stl) cyl horizontal 3 Cargo Pump (s): 2x450m³/hr, 1x300m³/hr Manifold: Bow/CM: 58.9m Ice Capable	**1 oil engine** with flexible couplings & sr gearedto sc. shaft driving 1 CP propeller Total Power: 4,500kW (6,118hp) 16.0kn MaK 6M552C 1 x 4 Stroke 6 Cy. 450 x 520 4500kW (6118bhp) MaK Motoren GmbH & Co. KG-Kiel AuxGen: 3 x 360kW 440/220V 50Hz a.c, 1 x 700kW 440/220V 60Hz a.c Thrusters: 1 Thwart. FP thruster (f) Fuel: 113.0 (d.f.) (Heating Coils) 604.0 (r.f.) 19.8pd
6611083 *2CHQ9* -	**TENNAHERDHYA** *ex Bargarth -2010* **Tennaherdhya Shipping Ltd** Keynvor Morlift Ltd *Scilly* *United Kingdom* Official number: 916412	**161** 48 -	Class: (LR) ✠ Classed LR until 20/11/01	**1966-07 Richards (Shipbuilders) Ltd — Lowestoft** Yd No: 486 Loa 28.96 Br ex 7.60 Dght 3.150 Lbp 26.22 Br md 7.17 Dpth 3.66 Riveted\Welded, 1 dk	**(B32A2ST) Tug**	**1 oil engine** sr reverse geared to sc. shaft driving 1 FP propeller Total Power: 625kW (850hp) 10.3kn Blackstone ETS8 1 x 4 Stroke 8 Cy. 222 x 292 625kW (850bhp) Lister Blackstone Marine Ltd.-Dursley AuxGen: 2 x 30kW 220V d.c Fuel: 36.5 (d.f.)
9440966 *H3DT* -	**TENNEI MARU** **Chijin Shipping SA** NEOM Maritime (Singapore) Pte Ltd *Panama* *Panama* MMSI: 357550000 Official number: 4017509	**32,415** 19,353 58,743 T/cm 57.4	Class: NK	**2009-01 Tsuneishi Group (Zhoushan) Shipbuilding Inc — Daishan County ZJ** Yd No: SS-039 Loa 189.99 (BB) Br ex - Dght 12.828 Lbp 185.60 Br md 32.26 Dpth 18.00 Welded, 1 dk	**(A21A2BC) Bulk Carrier** Grain: 72,360; Bale: 70,557 Compartments: 5 Ho, ER 5 Ha: ER Cranes: 4x30t	**1 oil engine** driving 1 FP propeller Total Power: 8,400kW (11,421hp) 14.5kn MAN-B&W 6S50MC-C 1 x 2 Stroke 6 Cy. 500 x 2000 8400kW (11421bhp) Mitsui Engineering & Shipbuilding CLtd-Japan AuxGen: 3 x 480kW a.c Fuel: 2537.0
7046120 *WCP9680* -	**TENNER C** *ex Gulf Seas -1992* **Rainbow Marine Contractors Inc** Gulf Oceanic Marine Contractors Inc *Houma, LA* *United States of America* MMSI: 367004450 Official number: 527695	**226** 67 -	Class: (AB)	**1970 Main Iron Works, Inc. — Houma, La** Yd No: 233 Loa - Br ex 8.39 Dght 3.639 Lbp 29.32 Br md 8.23 Dpth 4.20 Welded, 1 dk	**(B32A2ST) Tug**	**2 oil engines** reverse reduction geared to sc. shafts driving 2 FP propellers Total Power: 1,434kW (1,950hp) EMD (Electro-Motive) 8-645-E5 2 x Vee 2 Stroke 8 Cy. 230 x 254 each-717kW (975bhp) General Motors Corp-USA AuxGen: 2 x 60kW Fuel: 191.0
8836584 *WDE21224* -	**TENNESSEE** *ex S/R Tennessee -2001* *ex Exxon Tennessee -1992* *ex Esso Tennessee -1992* **Amherst Madison Inc** *Charleston, WV* *United States of America* MMSI: 367320740 Official number: 502171	*760* 517 -		**1966 Dravo Corp. — Pittsburgh, Pa** Yd No: 4842 Loa - Br ex - Dght - Lbp 42.52 Br md 12.83 Dpth 2.44 Welded, 1 dk	**(B32A2ST) Tug**	**2 oil engines** reduction geared to sc. shafts driving 2 FP propellers Total Power: 3,178kW (4,320hp) Fairbanks, Morse 12-38D8-1/8 2 x 2 Stroke 12 Cy. 207 x 254 each-1589kW (2160bhp) Fairbanks Morse & Co.-New Orleans, La AuxGen: 2 x 100kW a.c Fuel: 481.0 (d.f.)
8859536 *JK5121* -	**TENNON MARU** **YK Sakata Kaiun** *Tokushima, Tokushima* *Japan* Official number: 132526	*182* - 494		**1991-12 KK Ouchi Zosensho — Matsuyama EH** Loa 50.00 Br ex - Dght 3.220 Lbp 46.00 Br md 8.50 Dpth 5.00 Welded, 1 dk	**(A31A2GX) General Cargo Ship**	**1 oil engine** driving 1 FP propeller Total Power: 441kW (600hp) Niigata 6M26BGT 1 x 4 Stroke 6 Cy. 260 x 460 441kW (600bhp) Niigata Engineering Co Ltd-Japan
9447859 *A8VP7* -	**TENO** **Hull 1794 Co Ltd** Southern Shipmanagement Co SA *Monrovia* *Liberia* MMSI: 636014646 Official number: 14545	**88,586** 42,897 94,526	Class: GL	**2011-08 Samsung Heavy Industries Co Ltd — Geoje** Yd No: 1794 Loa 299.96 (BB) Br ex - Dght 13.500 Lbp 285.00 Br md 45.60 Dpth 24.60 Welded, 1 dk	**(A33A2CC) Container Ship (Fully Cellular)** TEU 8004 C Ho 3574 TEU C Dk 4430 TEU incl 1500 ref C.	**1 oil engine** driving 1 FP propeller Total Power: 43,610kW (59,292hp) 23.0kn MAN-B&W 7K98ME7 1 x 2 Stroke 7 Cy. 980 x 2660 43610kW (59292bhp) Doosan Engine Co Ltd-South Korea AuxGen: 2 x 2880kW 6600/450V a.c, 3 x 3360kW 6600/450V a.c Thrusters: 1 Tunnel thruster (f) Fuel: 290.0 (d.f.) 8600.0 (r.f.) 162.0pd
9176541 *JM6583* -	**TENO MARU** **Daio Kaiun Co Ltd (Daio Kaiun YK)** *Kamiamakusa, Kumamoto* *Japan* MMSI: 431600768 Official number: 135443	*749* - 2,088		**1997-05 Yamakawa Zosen Tekko K.K. — Kagoshima** Yd No: 752 Loa 80.20 Br ex - Dght 4.650 Lbp 74.00 Br md 14.30 Dpth 7.94 Welded, 1 dk	**(A31A2GX) General Cargo Ship**	**1 oil engine** Geared to sc. shaft driving 1 FP propeller Total Power: 1,471kW (2,000hp) 12.0kn Hanshin LH41LAG 1 x 4 Stroke 6 Cy. 410 x 800 1471kW (2000bhp) The Hanshin Diesel Works Ltd-Japan
8904654 *JL5835* -	**TENO MARU No. 71** **Ohama Gyogyo KK** *Ainan, Ehime* *Japan* MMSI: 431133000 Official number: 131421	*320* - -		**1989-08 K.K. Izutsu Zosensho — Nagasaki** Yd No: 971 Loa - Br ex - Dght 3.901 Lbp 50.02 Br md 8.91 Dpth 4.42 Welded, 1 dk	**(B12B2FC) Fish Carrier** Ins: 510	**1 oil engine** reduction geared to sc. shaft driving 1 CP propeller Total Power: 1,147kW (1,559hp) Daihatsu 6DKM-32 1 x 4 Stroke 6 Cy. 320 x 360 1147kW (1559bhp) Daihatsu Diesel Manufacturing Co Lt-Japan
9597707 *7JIP* -	**TENO MARU NO. 73** **Taiyu Gyogyo KK** *Ainan, Ehime* *Japan* Official number: 141360	*245* - -		**2011-01 K.K. Izutsu Zosensho — Nagasaki** Yd No: 1143 Loa 49.85 Br ex - Dght 3.350 Lbp - Br md 8.60 Dpth 3.85 Welded, 1 dk	**(B11B2FV) Fishing Vessel**	**1 oil engine** driving 1 Propeller Total Power: 1,914kW (2,602hp) Daihatsu 6DKM-28 1 x 4 Stroke 6 Cy. 280 x 390 1914kW (2602bhp) Daihatsu Diesel Manufacturing Co Lt-Japan
9238961 *7JPB* -	**TENO MARU No. 75** **Taiyu Gyogyo KK** *Ainan, Ehime* *Japan* MMSI: 431471000 Official number: 136517	*339* - 150		**2001-04 Miho Zosensho K.K. — Shimizu** Yd No: 1493 Loa 60.49 (BB) Br ex - Dght - Lbp 52.00 Br md 8.90 Dpth 4.40 Welded, 1 dk	**(B12B2FC) Fish Carrier** Grain: 511; Bale: 477 Compartments: 9 Ho, ER Derricks: 2	**1 oil engine** reduction geared to sc. shaft driving 1 CP propeller Total Power: 1,339kW (1,821hp) 14.3kn Daihatsu 6DKM-36 1 x 4 Stroke 6 Cy. 360 x 480 1339kW (1821bhp) Daihatsu Diesel Manufacturing Co Lt-Japan AuxGen: 2 x 320kW 225V 60Hz a.c Fuel: 190.0 (d.f.)
6410958 - -	**TENO MARU No. 75** **Nahar Shipping Lines Ltd** - *Bangladesh*	*199* 96 -		**1964 K.K. Uwajima Zosensho — Uwajima** Yd No: 1106 L reg 33.99 Br ex 6.66 Dght 2.794 Lbp 33.51 Br md 6.61 Dpth 3.20 Riveted\Welded, 1 dk	**(B11B2FV) Fishing Vessel**	**1 oil engine** driving 1 FP propeller Total Power: 405kW (551hp) Makita 1 x 4 Stroke 6 Cy. 290 x 430 405kW (551bhp) Makita Tekkosho-Japan
8604993 - - -	**TENO MARU No. 81** - -	*135* - -		**1986-04 K.K. Izutsu Zosensho — Nagasaki** Yd No: 915 Loa - (BB) Br ex - Dght 2.952 Lbp 35.01 Br md 7.61 Dpth 3.08 Welded, 1 dk	**(B11B2FV) Fishing Vessel**	**1 oil engine** reverse reduction geared to sc. shaft driving 1 FP propeller Total Power: 861kW (1,171hp) Daihatsu 6DLM-28FSL 1 x 4 Stroke 6 Cy. 280 x 360 861kW (1171bhp) Daihatsu Diesel Manufacturing Co Lt-Japan

IMO / Call sign	Name / Owner	Tonnage	Class	Build / Dimensions	Type	Machinery
6416304 - -	**TENO MARU No. 82** - **Nahar Shipping Lines Ltd** - *Bangladesh*	*199* 101 -		**1964 Nagasaki Zosen K.K. — Nagasaki** Yd No: 79 Loa 37.83 Br ex 6.68 Dght 2.693 Lbp 33.51 Br md 6.63 Dpth 3.20 Welded, 1 dk	**(B11B2FV) Fishing Vessel**	**1 oil engine** driving 1 FP propeller Total Power: 405kW (551hp) Makita 1 x 4 Stroke 6 Cy. 290 x 430 405kW (551bhp) Makita Tekkosho-Japan
6416316 - -	**TENO MARU No. 83** - **Nahar Shipping Lines Ltd** - *Bangladesh*	*199* 101 -		**1964 Nagasaki Zosen K.K. — Nagasaki** Yd No: 80 Loa 37.83 Br ex 6.68 Dght 2.693 Lbp 33.51 Br md 6.61 Dpth 3.20 Welded, 1 dk	**(B11B2FV) Fishing Vessel**	**1 oil engine** driving 1 FP propeller Total Power: 405kW (551hp) Makita 1 x 4 Stroke 6 Cy. 290 x 430 405kW (551bhp) Makita Tekkosho-Japan Fuel: 35.5
8904666 *JL5836* -	**TENO MARU No. 85** - **Ohama Gyogyo KK** - *Ainan, Ehime* *Japan* MMSI: 431387000 Official number: 131422	*320* - 607		**1989-09 K.K. Izutsu Zosensho — Nagasaki** Yd No: 972 Loa 58.00 (BB) Br ex - Dght 3.901 Lbp 49.90 Br md 8.91 Dpth 4.40 Welded, 1 dk	**(B12B2FC) Fish Carrier** Ins: 510	**1 oil engine** driving 1 CP propeller Total Power: 1,147kW (1,559hp) Daihatsu 6DKM-32 1 x 4 Stroke 6 Cy. 320 x 360 1147kW (1559bhp) Daihatsu Diesel Manufacturing Co Lt-Japan Thrusters: 1 Thwart. CP thruster (f)
8604981 *JL5501* -	**TENO MARU No. 88** - **Ohama Gyogyo KK** - *Ainan, Ehime* *Japan* MMSI: 431240000 Official number: 128320	*135* - -		**1986-03 K.K. Izutsu Zosensho — Nagasaki** Yd No: 912 Loa - (BB) Br ex - Dght 2.952 Lbp 35.01 Br md 7.61 Dpth 3.08 Welded, 1 dk	**(B11B2FV) Fishing Vessel**	**1 oil engine** reverse reduction geared to sc. shaft driving 1 FP propeller Total Power: 861kW (1,171hp) Yanmar 6Z280L-ET 1 x 4 Stroke 6 Cy. 280 x 360 861kW (1171bhp) Yanmar Diesel Engine Co Ltd-Japan
9036727 *7JOM* EH1-443	**TENOH MARU NO. 7** - **Ohama Gyogyo KK** - SatCom: Inmarsat B 343135510 *Ainan, Ehime* *Japan* MMSI: 431501404 Official number: 132084	*1,093* 327 820		**1991-10 Miho Zosensho K.K. — Shimizu** Yd No: 1407 Loa 63.51 (BB) Br ex 12.02 Dght 4.440 Lbp 55.65 Br md 12.00 Dpth 7.26 Welded	**(B11B2FV) Fishing Vessel**	**1 oil engine** with flexible couplings & sr geared to sc. shaft driving 1 FP propeller Total Power: 1,949kW (2,650hp) Daihatsu 8DLM-32 1 x 4 Stroke 8 Cy. 320 x 400 1949kW (2650bhp) Daihatsu Diesel Manufacturing Co Lt-Japan Thrusters: 1 Thwart. FP thruster (a)
8742599 *JD2810* EH1-453	**TENOH MARU NO. 81** - **Taiyu Gyogyo KK** - *Ainan, Ehime* *Japan* Official number: 140860	*199* - -		**2008-11 K.K. Izutsu Zosensho — Nagasaki** Yd No: 1135 Loa 48.44 Br ex - Dght 3.510 Lbp - Br md 8.60 Dpth 3.70 Welded, 1 dk	**(B11B2FV) Fishing Vessel**	**1 diesel electric oil engine** reduction geared to sc. shaft driving 1 Propeller Total Power: 1,914kW (2,602hp) Daihatsu 6DKM-28 1 x 4 Stroke 6 Cy. 280 x 390 1914kW (2602bhp) Daihatsu Diesel Manufacturing Co Lt-Japan
8709846 *LLBR3* -	**TENOR** *ex* Remoy Fjord *-2004* *ex* Kaassassuk *-1999* *ex* Abel Egede *-1990* **Ole Mikal Saetremyr AS** Maritim Management AS *Aalesund* *Norway (NIS)* MMSI: 259663000	**2,111** 634 1,000	Class: NV	**1988-04 Tangen Verft AS — Kragero** (Hull) Yd No: 92 **1988-04 Langsten Slip & Baatbyggeri AS — Tomrefjord** Yd No: 134 Converted From: Stern Trawler-2007 Loa 59.01 (BB) Br ex - Dght 5.800 Lbp 51.41 Br md 13.01 Dpth 5.85 Welded, 3 dks	**(B31A2SR) Research Survey Vessel** Ice Capable	**1 oil engine** with flexible couplings & reductiongeared to sc. shaft driving 1 CP propeller Total Power: 2,998kW (4,076hp) 14.5kn Wichmann WX28V10 1 x Vee 4 Stroke 10 Cy. 280 x 360 2998kW (4076bhp) Wartsila Wichmann Diesel AS-Norway AuxGen: 1 x 1520kW 440V 60Hz a.c, 2 x 516kW 440V 60Hz a.c Thrusters: 1 Thwart. FP thruster (f)
9316696 *JD2032* -	**TENPAIZAN MARU** - **Tsurumaru Shipping Co Ltd** - *Kitakyushu, Fukuoka* *Japan* MMSI: 431602283 Official number: 140067	*7,664* - 10,564	Class: NK	**2004-10 Kanda Zosensho K.K. — Kawajiri** Yd No: 469 Loa 126.00 Br ex - Dght 7.418 Lbp 119.00 Br md 21.00 Dpth 10.60 Welded, 1 dk	**(A24A2BT) Cement Carrier** Grain: 9,328	**1 oil engine** driving 1 FP propeller Total Power: 4,635kW (6,302hp) 14.6kn Mitsubishi 6UEC37LSII 1 x 2 Stroke 6 Cy. 370 x 1290 4635kW (6302bhp) Akasaka Tekkosho KK (Akasaka DieselLtd)-Japan Fuel: 300.0
9063392 *JG5150* -	**TENPO MARU NO. 8** *ex* Shohei Maru No. 8 *-2010* **Seiho Kaiun KK** - *Nagoya, Aichi* *Japan* Official number: 133722	*148* - 465		**1992-11 Iisaku Zosen K.K. — Nishi-Izu** Yd No: 92164 Loa 40.50 Br ex - Dght 2.550 Lbp 38.50 Br md 8.50 Dpth 2.80 Welded, 1 dk	**(A13B2TP) Products Tanker** Compartments: 7 Ta, ER	**1 oil engine** with clutches & reverse geared to sc. shaft driving 1 FP propeller Total Power: 405kW (551hp) Matsui ML624GHS-1 1 x 4 Stroke 6 Cy. 240 x 400 405kW (551bhp) Matsui Iron Works Co Ltd-Japan Thrusters: 1 Thwart. FP thruster (f)
9109201 - -	**TENRYU** *ex* Horai Maru No. 10 *-2008* **PT Indo Shipping Operator** - *Indonesia*	*499* - 1,252	Class: IZ	**1994-11 Ishii Zosen K.K. — Futtsu** Yd No: 328 Loa 59.09 (BB) Br ex - Dght 4.725 Lbp 52.00 Br md 13.50 Dpth 6.80 Welded, 2 dks	**(A24D2BA) Aggregates Carrier** Grain: 738 Compartments: 1 Ho, ER 1 Ha: ER	**1 oil engine** reverse geared to sc. shaft driving 1 FP propeller Total Power: 736kW (1,001hp) Niigata 6M31BFT 1 x 4 Stroke 6 Cy. 310 x 530 736kW (1001bhp) Niigata Engineering Co Ltd-Japan Thrusters: 1 Thwart. FP thruster (f)
7818987 - -	**TENRYU** *ex* Hakuwa Maru No. 2 *-1990* **Pan Asian Shipping & Trading Co SA** - *Panama* *Panama* Official number: D3901789PEXT1	*499* - 1,179		**1978-11 Setouchi Zosen K.K. — Osakikamijima** Yd No: 472 Loa 59.10 Br ex 9.63 Dght 4.182 Lbp 55.00 Br md 9.60 Dpth 4.40 Welded, 1 dk	**(A13B2TU) Tanker (unspecified)** Liq: 1,400; Liq (Oil): 1,400	**1 oil engine** driving 1 FP propeller Total Power: 883kW (1,201hp) Hanshin 6LU28 1 x 4 Stroke 6 Cy. 280 x 440 883kW (1201bhp) The Hanshin Diesel Works Ltd-Japan
7737212 - -	**TENRYU** *ex* Crux *-1996* *ex* Aoki Maru No. 22 *-1994* *ex* Bulldozer Maru No. 22 *-1994* **Seitoku Marine S de RL** - *San Lorenzo* *Honduras* Official number: L-1725688	**272** 81 -		**1970 Kanawa Dockyard Co. Ltd. — Hiroshima** Loa 29.01 Br ex - Dght 2.701 Lbp 26.50 Br md 8.50 Dpth 3.92 Welded, 1 dk	**(B32B2SP) Pusher Tug**	**2 oil engines** driving 2 FP propellers Total Power: 1,766kW (2,402hp) 10.0kn Daihatsu 6DSM-26 2 x 4 Stroke 6 Cy. 260 x 320 each-883kW (1201bhp) Daihatsu Diesel Manufacturing Co Lt-Japan
6702492 - -	**TENRYU MARU** - **Taishin Kaihatsu KK** - *South Korea*	*160* - -		**1966 Kanagawa Zosen — Kobe** Yd No: 72 Loa 27.00 Br ex 7.65 Dght 2.794 Lbp 24.49 Br md 7.60 Dpth 3.61 Riveted\Welded, 1 dk	**(B32A2ST) Tug**	**2 oil engines** driving 2 FP propellers Total Power: 1,544kW (2,100hp) Nippon Hatsudoki HS6NV325 2 x 4 Stroke 6 Cy. 325 x 460 each-772kW (1050bhp) Nippon Hatsudoki-Japan
9168453 *JM4164* -	**TENRYU MARU** - **Toa Unyu KK** - *Naha, Okinawa* *Japan* MMSI: 431680087 Official number: 133758	*749* - 1,550		**1997-09 Sasaki Shipbuilding Co Ltd — Osakikamijima HS** Yd No: 613 Loa 70.00 Br ex - Dght 4.300 Lbp - Br md 11.20 Dpth 5.10 Welded, 1 dk	**(A13B2TP) Products Tanker**	**1 oil engine** driving 1 FP propeller Total Power: 1,765kW (2,400hp) Hanshin LH36L 1 x 4 Stroke 6 Cy. 360 x 670 1765kW (2400bhp) The Hanshin Diesel Works Ltd-Japan
9403750 *JD2289* -	**TENRYU MARU** - **Chiyoda Kaiji KK** - *Tokyo* *Japan* Official number: 140362	*228* - -		**2006-07 Kanagawa Zosen — Kobe** Yd No: 557 Loa 37.20 Br ex - Dght 3.100 Lbp 32.70 Br md 9.80 Dpth 4.17 Welded, 1 dk	**(B32A2ST) Tug**	**2 oil engines** reduction geared to sc. shafts driving 2 Propellers Total Power: 3,310kW (4,500hp) Niigata 6L28HX 2 x 4 Stroke 6 Cy. 280 x 370 each-1655kW (2250bhp) Niigata Engineering Co Ltd-Japan
9031868 *JNQC* KG1-302	**TENRYU MARU No. 2** - **Tenryu Sangyo YK** - SatCom: Inmarsat A 1204411 *Ichikikushikino, Kagoshima* *Japan* MMSI: 431602830 Official number: 132642	*379* - 451		**1991-05 Miho Zosensho K.K. — Shimizu** Yd No: 1405 Loa 54.04 (BB) Br ex 8.82 Dght 3.452 Lbp 49.20 Br md 8.80 Dpth 3.80 Welded, 1 dk	**(B11B2FV) Fishing Vessel** Ins: 704	**1 oil engine** with clutches, flexible couplings & sr geared to sc. shaft driving 1 FP propeller Total Power: 736kW (1,001hp) Akasaka K28BFD 1 x 4 Stroke 6 Cy. 280 x 480 736kW (1001bhp) Akasaka Tekkosho KK (Akasaka DieselLtd)-Japan

IMO / Call sign	Name / Owner	Tonnage	Class	Builder / Dimensions	Type	Machinery
9361433 *JD2142* -	**TENRYU MARU NO. 3** **Toa Unyu KK** - *Naha, Okinawa* *Japan* MMSI: 431680228 Official number: 140200	*746* - 1,650		**2005-07 Suzuki Shipyard Co. Ltd. — Yokkaichi** Yd No: 703 Loa 72.00 Br ex 11.55 Dght - Lbp 68.00 Br md 11.50 Dpth 5.40 Welded, 1 dk	**(A13B2TP) Products Tanker** Double Hull (13F)	**1 oil engine** driving 1 FP propeller Total Power: 1,910kW (2,597hp) Akasaka A37 1 x 4 Stroke 6 Cy. 370 x 720 1910kW (2597bhp) Akasaka Tekkosho KK (Akasaka DieselLtd)-Japan
9517953 *JD2801* -	**TENRYU MARU NO. 5** **Toa Unyu KK** - *Naha, Okinawa* *Japan* MMSI: 431000715 Official number: 140850	*748* - 1,559		**2008-10 Suzuki Shipyard Co. Ltd. — Yokkaichi** Yd No: 720 Loa 72.00 Br ex - Dght 4.500 Lbp 68.00 Br md 11.50 Dpth 5.40 Welded, 1 dk	**(A13B2TP) Products Tanker** Double Hull (13F)	**1 oil engine** driving 1 FP propeller Total Power: 1,471kW (2,000hp) Akasaka A34S 1 x 4 Stroke 6 Cy. 340 x 660 1471kW (2000bhp) Akasaka Tekkosho KK (Akasaka DieselLtd)-Japan
7718759 *HP7515* -	**TENRYU MARU No. 5** **Sinkobe Enterprise** - *Panama* *Panama* Official number: D7771789PEXT	*499* 282 1,081		**1977-08 Shimoda Dockyard Co. Ltd. — Shimoda** Yd No: 278 Loa 59.80 Br ex 9.53 Dght 4.214 Lbp 55.02 Br md 9.50 Dpth 4.53 Welded, 1 dk	**(A13B2TU) Tanker (unspecified)**	**1 oil engine** driving 1 FP propeller Total Power: 883kW (1,201hp) Hanshin 6LU28 1 x 4 Stroke 6 Cy. 280 x 440 883kW (1201bhp) Hanshin Nainenki Kogyo-Japan
9220469 *JM4168* -	**TENRYU MARU No. 7** **Toa Unyu KK** - *Naha, Okinawa* *Japan* MMSI: 431680176 Official number: 133764	*749* - 2,000	Class: (NK)	**1999-12 Sasaki Shipbuilding Co Ltd — Osakikamijima HS** Yd No: 625 Loa 71.91 Br ex - Dght 4.450 Lbp 67.00 Br md 11.40 Dpth 5.15 Welded, 1 dk	**(A13B2TP) Products Tanker** Double Hull Liq: 1,700; Liq (Oil): 1,700	**1 oil engine** driving 1 FP propeller Total Power: 1,471kW (2,000hp) 12.5kn Hanshin LH36L 1 x 4 Stroke 6 Cy. 360 x 670 1471kW (2000bhp) The Hanshin Diesel Works Ltd-Japan
9088172 *JM4152* -	**TENRYU MARU No. 8** **Toa Unyu KK** - *Naha, Okinawa* *Japan* MMSI: 431680026 Official number: 133744	**1,568** - 2,994	Class: (NK)	**1994-07 Sasaki Shipbuilding Co Ltd — Osakikamijima HS** Yd No: 588 Loa - Br ex - Dght 5.513 Lbp 85.00 Br md 13.20 Dpth 6.50 Welded, 1 dk	**(A13B2TP) Products Tanker** Liq: 3,189; Liq (Oil): 3,189	**1 oil engine** driving 1 FP propeller Total Power: 2,427kW (3,300hp) 13.5kn Akasaka A41 1 x 4 Stroke 6 Cy. 410 x 800 2427kW (3300bhp) Akasaka Tekkosho KK (Akasaka DieselLtd)-Japan AuxGen: 3 x 187kW a.c
8706923 *JHIO* KG1-551	**TENRYU MARU No. 18** *ex Kotoku Maru No. 1 -1999* **Tenryu Sangyo YK** SatCom: Inmarsat A 1200764 *Ichikikushikino, Kagoshima* *Japan* MMSI: 431600970 Official number: 129435	*379* - 484		**1987-05 Miho Zosensho K.K. — Shimizu** Yd No: 1307 Loa 54.80 Br ex 8.62 Dght 3.441 Lbp 48.00 Br md 8.60 Dpth 3.80 Welded, 1 dk	**(B11B2FV) Fishing Vessel** Grain: 688; Bale: 619	**1 oil engine** with clutches, flexible couplings & dr geared to sc. shaft driving 1 FP propeller Total Power: 736kW (1,001hp) Hanshin LH28G 1 x 4 Stroke 6 Cy. 280 x 460 736kW (1001bhp) The Hanshin Diesel Works Ltd-Japan
9420746 *JD2346* -	**TENRYU MARU NO. 18** **Toa Unyu KK** - *Naha, Okinawa* *Japan* MMSI: 431680236 Official number: 140444	*747* - 1,598		**2006-12 Suzuki Shipyard Co. Ltd. — Yokkaichi** Yd No: 710 Loa 72.00 Br ex 11.55 Dght - Lbp 68.00 Br md 11.50 Dpth 5.40 Welded, 1 dk	**(A13B2TP) Products Tanker** Double Hull (13F) Liq: 1,850; Liq (Oil): 1,850	**1 oil engine** driving 1 FP propeller Total Power: 1,765kW (2,400hp) 13.0kn Akasaka A34S 1 x 4 Stroke 6 Cy. 340 x 660 1765kW (2400bhp) Akasaka Tekkosho KK (Akasaka DieselLtd)-Japan
9272826 *JM4175* -	**TENRYU MARU NO. 21** **Toa Unyu KK** - *Naha, Okinawa* *Japan* MMSI: 431680213 Official number: 133773	*748* - 1,650		**2002-10 Kurinoura Dockyard Co Ltd — Yawatahama EH** Yd No: 371 Loa 71.95 Br ex - Dght - Lbp - Br md 11.50 Dpth 5.35 Welded, 1 dk	**(A13B2TP) Products Tanker** Double Hull (13F) Liq: 1,950; Liq (Oil): 1,950	**1 oil engine** driving 1 FP propeller Total Power: 1,765kW (2,400hp) Akasaka A37 1 x 4 Stroke 6 Cy. 370 x 720 1765kW (2400bhp) Akasaka Tekkosho KK (Akasaka DieselLtd)-Japan
8870126 *JD2577* -	**TENRYU MARU No. 38** **YK Sansen Kishida Gyogyobu** - *Hiroo, Hokkaido* *Japan* MMSI: 431807000 Official number: 125619	*131* - -		**1982-11 Fukui Zosen K.K. — Japan** Yd No: 192 Loa 36.07 (BB) Br ex - Dght - Lbp 28.80 Br md 5.65 Dpth 2.39 Welded, 1 dk	**(B11B2FV) Fishing Vessel** Ins: 91	**1 oil engine** reverse reduction geared to sc. shaft driving 1 FP propeller Total Power: 617kW (839hp) Yanmar T240-ET2 1 x 4 Stroke 6 Cy. 240 x 310 617kW (839bhp) Yanmar Diesel Engine Co Ltd-Japan
9089932 *WDE9365* -	**TENSAW** *ex Coastal Tensaw -2008* **Enterprise Marine Services LLC** - *Houma, LA* *United States of America* MMSI: 367127050 Official number: 1186668	*127* 102 -		**2006-11** Yd No: 86 L reg 19.81 Br ex - Dght - Lbp - Br md 7.92 Dpth 2.74 Welded, 1 dk	**(B32B2SP) Pusher Tug**	**1 oil engine** driving 1 Propeller
8859081 - -	**TENSEI MARU** - - - *Indonesia*	*488* - 1,567		**1991-09 K.K. Yoshida Zosen Kogyo — Arida** Loa 73.10 Br ex - Dght 4.320 Lbp 68.00 Br md 11.50 Dpth 7.10 Welded, 1 dk	**(A31A2GX) General Cargo Ship**	**1 oil engine** driving 1 FP propeller Total Power: 1,324kW (1,800hp) 11.5kn Hanshin 6EL30 1 x 4 Stroke 6 Cy. 300 x 600 1324kW (1800bhp) The Hanshin Diesel Works Ltd-Japan
8877605 *JJ3890* -	**TENSEI MARU** **Katayama Kaiun YK** - *Kobe, Hyogo* *Japan* Official number: 132421	*159* - 468		**1994-06 Maekawa Zosensho — Japan** Loa 48.27 Br ex - Dght 3.260 Lbp 43.00 Br md 8.30 Dpth 5.10 Welded, 1 dk	**(A31A2GX) General Cargo Ship** Compartments: 1 Ho, ER 1 Ha: (24.4 x 6.2)ER	**1 oil engine** geared to sc. shaft driving 1 FP propeller Total Power: 625kW (850hp) 11.6kn Hanshin 6LC26G 1 x 4 Stroke 6 Cy. 260 x 440 625kW (850bhp) The Hanshin Diesel Works Ltd-Japan
7736579 - -	**TENSEI MARU** *ex Goko Maru -1988* - -	*180* 106 410		**1978 Y.K. Okajima Zosensho — Matsuyama** Yd No: 183 L reg 38.20 Br ex - Dght 3.220 Lbp - Br md 7.50 Dpth 5.00 Welded, 1 dk	**(A31A2GX) General Cargo Ship**	**1 oil engine** driving 1 FP propeller Kubota 1 x 4 Stroke Kubota Tekkosho-Japan
9317169 *3EMS7* -	**TENSEI MARU** **Chijin Shipping SA** Union Marine Management Services Pte Ltd *Panama* *Panama* MMSI: 352421000 Official number: 3335107A	**30,046** 18,207 52,454 T/cm 55.5	Class: NK	**2007-09 Tsuneishi Holdings Corp Tsuneishi Shipbuilding Co — Fukuyama HS** Yd No: 1340 Loa 189.90 (BB) Br ex 32.26 Dght 12.022 Lbp 182.00 Br md 32.26 Dpth 17.00 Welded, 1 dk	**(A21A2BC) Bulk Carrier** Grain: 67,756; Bale: 65,601 Compartments: 5 Ho, ER 5 Ha: 4 (21.3 x 18.4)ER (20.4 x 18.4) Cranes: 4x30t	**1 oil engine** driving 1 FP propeller Total Power: 7,800kW (10,605hp) 14.5kn MAN-B&W 6S50MC 1 x 2 Stroke 6 Cy. 500 x 1910 7800kW (10605bhp) Mitsui Engineering & Shipbuilding CLtd-Japan AuxGen: 3 x a.c Fuel: 2315.0
8351481 *JL5157* -	**TENSEI MARU NO. 3** *ex Tencho Maru -2008 ex Joei Maru -1990* **Tetsuo Yamamoto** - *Mihara, Hiroshima* *Japan* Official number: 126305	*123* - 384		**1983-01 Tokuoka Zosen K.K. — Naruto** Yd No: 115 Loa 44.00 Br ex - Dght 2.910 Lbp 39.00 Br md 7.70 Dpth 4.60 Welded, 1 dk	**(A31A2GX) General Cargo Ship**	**1 oil engine** driving 1 FP propeller Total Power: 331kW (450hp) Matsui ML624GHS 1 x 4 Stroke 6 Cy. 240 x 400 331kW (450bhp) Matsui Iron Works Co Ltd-Japan
9440849 *3FMU2* -	**TENSHIN MARU** **Chijin Shipping SA** Union Marine Management Services Pte Ltd *Panama* *Panama* MMSI: 370732000 Official number: 4003409A	**43,158** 27,291 82,687 T/cm 70.2	Class: NV (NK)	**2008-09 Tsuneishi Group (Zhoushan) Shipbuilding Inc — Daishan County ZJ** Yd No: SS-035 Loa 228.99 Br ex - Dght 14.430 Lbp 222.00 Br md 32.26 Dpth 20.03 Welded, 1 dk	**(A21A2BC) Bulk Carrier** Grain: 97,186 Compartments: 7 Ho, ER 7 Ha: ER	**1 oil engine** driving 1 FP propeller Total Power: 11,060kW (15,037hp) 14.5kn MAN-B&W 7S50MC-C 1 x 2 Stroke 7 Cy. 500 x 2000 11060kW (15037bhp) Mitsui Engineering & Shipbuilding CLtd-Japan AuxGen: 3 x a.c Fuel: 2870.0
8910615 *JL5816* -	**TENSHO** *ex Yashima Maru No. 11 -2012* - - *Uki, Kumamoto* *Japan* Official number: 131474	*198* - 521		**1990-03 Koa Sangyo KK — Takamatsu KG** Yd No: 552 Loa 49.59 Br ex - Dght 3.103 Lbp 45.00 Br md 7.80 Dpth 3.30 Welded, 1 dk	**(A12A2TC) Chemical Tanker** Liq: 323 Compartments: 6 Ta, ER	**1 oil engine** driving 1 FP propeller Total Power: 588kW (799hp) Niigata 6M26BGT 1 x 4 Stroke 6 Cy. 260 x 460 588kW (799bhp) Niigata Engineering Co Ltd-Japan

IMO / Call sign	Name / Owner / Port	Tonnage	Class	Built / Builder / Dimensions	Type / Cargo	Machinery
8905464 - -	**TENSHO MARU** *ex Eishin Maru No. 2 -2002* **Coastaline Investment Pvt Ltd** *Male* *Maldives*	*498* - 1,198		**1989-05 Sasaki Shipbuilding Co Ltd — Osakikamijima HS** Yd No: 531 Loa 64.39 Br ex - Dght 4.120 Lbp 60.00 Br md 10.00 Dpth 4.50 Welded, 1 dk	**(A12A2TC) Chemical Tanker** Compartments: 8 Ta, ER	**1 oil engine** with clutches, flexible couplings & sr reverse geared to sc. shaft driving 1 FP propeller Total Power: 736kW (1,001hp) Niigata 6M28BFT 1 x 4 Stroke 6 Cy. 280 x 480 736kW (1001bhp) Niigata Engineering Co Ltd-Japan
9088794 *JK5304* -	**TENSHO MARU** **YK Ueno Kisen** - *Hofu, Yamaguchi* *Japan* Official number: 134085	*498* - 1,600		**1994-04 Watanabe Zosen KK — Imabari EH** Yd No: 280 Loa - Br ex - Dght 4.250 Lbp 70.90 Br md 12.00 Dpth 7.20 Welded, 1 dk	**(A31A2GX) General Cargo Ship**	**1 oil engine** driving 1 FP propeller Total Power: 736kW (1,001hp) Niigata 6M31AFTE 1 x 4 Stroke 6 Cy. 310 x 530 736kW (1001bhp) Niigata Engineering Co Ltd-Japan
9110004 *JK5232* -	**TENSHO MARU** **Kambara Logistics Co Ltd** - *Fukuyama, Hiroshima* *Japan* Official number: 134723	*172* - 213		**1994-12 Kambara Marine Development & Shipbuilding Co Ltd — Fukuyama HS** Yd No: OE-186 Loa 29.72 Br ex - Dght 3.550 Lbp 27.00 Br md 8.20 Dpth 4.10 Welded, 1 dk	**(B32A2ST) Tug**	**2 oil engines** with clutches, flexible couplings & reduction geared to sc. shafts driving 2 CP propellers Total Power: 1,104kW (1,500hp) 11.2kn Daihatsu 6DLM-22 2 x 4 Stroke 6 Cy. 220 x 300 each-552kW (750bhp) Daihatsu Diesel Manufacturing Co Lt-Japan Fuel: 79.0 (d.f.) 5.5pd
8631116 *JG4718* -	**TENSHO MARU** **Izu Shichito Kaiun KK** - *Tokyo* *Japan* Official number: 130176	*432* - 956		**1987-07 Hitachi Zosen Mukaishima Marine Co Ltd — Onomichi HS** Yd No: 1 Loa 54.30 Br ex 9.22 Dght 4.030 Lbp 50.00 Br md 9.20 Dpth 4.50 Welded, 1 dk	**(A31A2GX) General Cargo Ship**	**1 oil engine** driving 1 FP propeller Total Power: 1,030kW (1,400hp) Niigata 6M28BGT 1 x 4 Stroke 6 Cy. 280 x 480 1030kW (1400bhp) Niigata Engineering Co Ltd-Japan
8627323 - -	**TENSHO MARU** - - *South Korea*	*137* - 320		**1984 Kinoura Zosen K.K. — Imabari** Yd No: 122 Loa 36.00 Br ex - Dght 2.500 Lbp 35.00 Br md 6.70 Dpth 3.00 Welded, 1 dk	**(A13B2TU) Tanker (unspecified)** Liq: 360; Liq (Oil): 360 1 Cargo Pump (s): 1x300m³/hr	**1 oil engine** driving 1 FP propeller Total Power: 272kW (370hp) 8.0kn Niigata 1 x 4 Stroke 272kW (370bhp) Niigata Engineering Co Ltd-Japan
9720158 - -	**TENSHO MARU** **Izu Shichito Kaiun KK** - *Japan*	*459* - 957		**2013-11 Koike Zosen Kaiun KK — Osakikamijima** Yd No: 558 Loa - Br ex - Dght - Lbp - Br md - Dpth - Welded, 1 dk	**(A31A2GX) General Cargo Ship**	**1 oil engine** reduction geared to sc. shaft driving 1 Propeller Total Power: 1,324kW (1,800hp)
9105437 *JL6376* -	**TENSHO MARU No. 1** **Kosei Marine KK** - *Hofu, Yamaguchi* *Japan* Official number: 134850	*498* - 1,600		**1995-02 K.K. Murakami Zosensho — Naruto** Yd No: 216 Loa 75.42 (BB) Br ex 12.02 Dght 4.060 Lbp 70.00 Br md 12.00 Dpth 7.00 Welded, 1 dk	**(A31A2GX) General Cargo Ship** Grain: 2,458; Bale: 2,352 Compartments: 1 Ho, ER 1 Ha: ER	**1 oil engine** driving 1 FP propeller Total Power: 736kW (1,001hp) Hanshin LH30LG 1 x 4 Stroke 6 Cy. 300 x 600 736kW (1001bhp) The Hanshin Diesel Works Ltd-Japan
9191993 *JK5585* -	**TENSHO MARU NO. 5** *ex Shoyo Maru -2002* **Kambara Logistics Co Ltd** - *Fukuyama, Hiroshima* *Japan* Official number: 135290	*239* - 237	Class: (NK)	**2001-10 Donghai Shipyard — Shanghai** Yd No: 00385 Loa 36.75 Br ex - Dght 3.582 Lbp 33.09 Br md 9.20 Dpth 4.20 Welded, 1 dk	**(B32A2ST) Tug**	**1 oil engine** driving 1 FP propeller Total Power: 4,700kW (6,390hp) 14.5kn
8936451 *JM6609* -	**TENSHO MARU No. 8** **Nakamura Kaiun YK** - *Kitakyushu, Fukuoka* *Japan* Official number: 135486	*265* - -		**1997-12 K.K. Kamishima Zosensho — Osakikamijima** Yd No: 607 Loa 27.31 Br ex - Dght - Lbp 23.00 Br md 9.30 Dpth 6.10 Welded, 1 dk	**(A31A2GX) General Cargo Ship**	**2 oil engines** reduction geared to sc. shafts driving 2 FP propellers Total Power: 2,942kW (4,000hp) 7.8kn Daihatsu 6DKM-26 2 x 4 Stroke 6 Cy. 260 x 380 each-1471kW (2000bhp) Daihatsu Diesel Manufacturing Co Lt-Japan
8742733 *JD2836* -	**TENSHO MARU NO. 8** **KK Nakatosa Kaiun** - *Anan, Tokushima* *Japan* Official number: 140888	*499* - 1,830		**2008-10 YK Nakanoshima Zosensho — Kochi KC** Yd No: 257 Loa 74.71 Br ex - Dght 4.330 Lbp 69.00 Br md 12.00 Dpth 7.35 Welded, 1 dk	**(A31A2GX) General Cargo Ship** Bale: 2,467 1 Ha: ER (40.0 x 9.5)	**1 oil engine** reduction geared to sc. shaft driving 1 Propeller Total Power: 1,618kW (2,200hp) 12.0kn Niigata 6M34BGT 1 x 4 Stroke 6 Cy. 340 x 620 1618kW (2200bhp) Niigata Engineering Co Ltd-Japan
8609266 - -	**TENSHO MARU No. 16** **Dong Yang Co Ltd** - *South Korea*	*112* - 295		**1986-06 Uchida Zosen — Ise** Yd No: 845 Loa 37.60 Br ex - Dght 3.000 Lbp 33.00 Br md 7.00 Dpth 3.10 Welded, 1 dk	**(B34E2SY) Effluent carrier** Liq: 310 Compartments: 6 Ta, ER	**1 oil engine** geared to sc. shaft driving 1 FP propeller Total Power: 221kW (300hp) Yanmar 6M-T 1 x 4 Stroke 6 Cy. 200 x 240 221kW (300bhp) Yanmar Diesel Engine Co Ltd-Japan
8850712 *JD2594* HK1-968 -	**TENSHO MARU No. 28** *ex Seian Maru No. 71 -1995* *ex Kyosei Maru No. 128 -1995* **YK Yasuda Gyogyobu** - *Hiroo, Hokkaido* *Japan* Official number: 125627	*138* - -		**1983-04 Ishimura Zosen — Kimaishi** L reg 28.50 Br ex - Dght - Lbp - Br md 6.00 Dpth 2.60 Welded, 1 dk	**(B11B2FV) Fishing Vessel**	**1 oil engine** driving 1 FP propeller Total Power: 338kW (460hp) Daihatsu 1 x 4 Stroke 338kW (460bhp) Daihatsu Diesel Manufacturing Co Lt-Japan
9526629 *JD2841* -	**TENSHO NO. 2** **Tanba Kisen YK** - *Bizen, Okayama* *Japan* MMSI: 431000826 Official number: 140896	*749* - 1,950		**2008-12 Maebata Zosen Tekko K.K. — Sasebo** Yd No: 289 Loa 74.18 Br ex - Dght 4.800 Lbp 69.00 Br md 11.40 Dpth 5.35 Welded, 1 dk	**(A13B2TP) Products Tanker** Single Hull Liq: 2,180; Liq (Oil): 2,180	**1 oil engine** geared to sc. shaft driving 1 FP propeller Total Power: 1,618kW (2,200hp) 12.0kn Daihatsu 6DKM-26 1 x 4 Stroke 6 Cy. 260 x 380 1618kW (2200bhp) Daihatsu Diesel Manufacturing Co Lt-Japan
9324631 *S6BX8* -	**TENSHOU MARU** **Kambara Kisen Singapore Pte Ltd** Union Marine Management Services Pte Ltd *Singapore* *Singapore* MMSI: 566744000 Official number: 398191	**30,046** 18,207 52,450 T/cm 55.5	Class: NK	**2006-01 Tsuneishi Heavy Industries (Cebu) Inc — Balamban** Yd No: SC-068 Loa 189.99 (BB) Br ex - Dght 12.000 Lbp 182.00 Br md 32.26 Dpth 17.00 Welded, 1 dk	**(A21A2BC) Bulk Carrier** Grain: 67,756; Bale: 65,601 Compartments: 5 Ho, ER 5 Ha: 4 (21.3 x 18.4)ER (20.4 x 18.4) Cranes: 4x30t	**1 oil engine** driving 1 FP propeller Total Power: 7,796kW (10,599hp) 14.3kn B&W 6S50MC 1 x 2 Stroke 6 Cy. 500 x 1910 7796kW (10599bhp) Mitsui Engineering & Shipbuilding CLtd-Japan Fuel: 2150.0
9558294 *9V7512* -	**TENSHU MARU** **Kambara Kisen Singapore Pte Ltd** Kambara Kisen Co Ltd *Singapore* *Singapore* MMSI: 566714000 Official number: 398230	**92,379** 60,235 179,993	Class: NK	**2010-11 Tsuneishi Heavy Industries (Cebu) Inc — Balamban** Yd No: SC-185 Loa 291.90 (BB) Br ex - Dght 18.016 Lbp 286.90 Br md 45.00 Dpth 24.50 Welded, 1 dk	**(A21A2BC) Bulk Carrier** Grain: 200,998 Compartments: 9 Ho, ER 9 Ha: ER	**1 oil engine** driving 1 FP propeller Total Power: 17,690kW (24,051hp) 14.5kn MAN-B&W 7S65ME-C 1 x 2 Stroke 7 Cy. 650 x 2730 17690kW (24051bhp) Mitsui Engineering & Shipbuilding CLtd-Japan AuxGen: 3 x 550kW a.c
8708127 - -	**TENSHU MARU NO. 5** *ex Yokei Maru No. 5 -2007* *ex Kaiyo Maru No. 3 -2004* *ex Taisei Maru No. 21 -1992*	*291* - 692		**1987-10 K.K. Murakami Zosensho — Ishinomaki** Yd No: 1210 Loa 59.59 (BB) Br ex 10.27 Dght 3.860 Lbp 51.52 Br md 10.20 Dpth 6.20 Welded, 1 dk	**(B11A2FS) Stern Trawler**	**1 oil engine** sr geared to sc. shaft driving 1 CP propeller Total Power: 1,912kW (2,600hp) Hanshin 6LU40 1 x 4 Stroke 6 Cy. 400 x 640 1912kW (2600bhp) The Hanshin Diesel Works Ltd-Japan
9105229 *JM6276* -	**TENSHUN MARU** *ex Eiwa Maru No. 6 -2011* - - *Hirado, Nagasaki* *Japan* Official number: 133554	*455* - 1,182		**1994-08 Honda Zosen — Saiki** Yd No: 866 Loa 67.35 Br ex - Dght 3.950 Lbp 60.00 Br md 13.50 Dpth 6.80 Welded, 1 dk	**(A31A2GX) General Cargo Ship**	**1 oil engine** driving 1 FP propeller Total Power: 736kW (1,001hp) 10.5kn Niigata 6M31BGT 1 x 4 Stroke 6 Cy. 310 x 530 736kW (1001bhp) Niigata Engineering Co Ltd-Japan Thrusters: 1 Tunnel thruster (f) Fuel: 73.0 (d.f.)
9641390 *D5FO8*	**TENSO** **TDC Shipping SA** Daiichi Chuo Kisen Kaisha *Monrovia* *Liberia* MMSI: 636016329 Official number: 16329	**60,876** 25,481 97,102	Class: NK	**2014-01 Japan Marine United Corp (JMU) — Kure HS** Yd No: 3338 Loa 239.90 (BB) Br ex - Dght 13.053 Lbp 234.50 Br md 43.00 Dpth 20.50 Welded, 1 dk	**(A21A2BC) Bulk Carrier** Grain: 109,500 Compartments: 5 Ho, ER 5 Ha: ER	**1 oil engine** driving 1 FP propeller 14.0kn AuxGen: 4 x a.c

IMO / Call sign	Name / Owner	Tonnage	Class	Construction	Type	Machinery
9630248 *V7YY7* -	**TENTEN** **Rover Enterprises Inc** KBS Ltd *Majuro* *Marshall Islands* MMSI: 538004767 Official number: 4767	**44,009** 27,671 81,336 T/cm 71.9	Class: LR ✠ **100A1** SS 09/2012 bulk carrier CSR BC-A GRAB (30) Nos. 2, 4 & 6 holds may be empty ESP **ShipRight** (CM,ACS (B)) *IWS LI EP ✠ **LMC** **UMS** Eq.Ltr: Q†; Cable: 700.8/81.0 U3 (a)	**2012-09 New Century Shipbuilding Co Ltd — Jingjiang JS** Yd No: 0108216 Loa 228.87 (BB) Br ex 32.32 Dght 14.450 Lbp 225.34 Br md 32.27 Dpth 20.06 Welded, 1 dk	**(A21A2BC) Bulk Carrier** Grain: 97,000; Bale: 90,784 Compartments: 7 Ho, ER 7 Ha: 5 (18.3 x 15.0) (15.7 x 15.1)ER (13.1 x 13.2)	**1 oil engine** driving 1 FP propeller Total Power: 11,900kW (16,179hp) 14.1kn MAN-B&W 5S60MC-C8 1 x 2 Stroke 5 Cy. 600 x 2400 11900kW (16179bhp) STX Engine Co Ltd-South Korea AuxGen: 3 x 710kW 450V 60Hz a.c Boilers: AuxB (Comp) 8.8kgf/cm² (8.6bar)
9094573 *JD2204* -	**TENWA MARU** **Taiho Unyu KK (Taiho Shipping Co Ltd)** - *Osaka, Osaka* *Japan* Official number: 140275	*368* - 853		**2006-02 Hongawara Zosen K.K. — Fukuyama** Yd No: 580 Loa 53.33 Br ex - Dght 3.700 Lbp 48.50 Br md 9.20 Dpth 4.10 Welded, 1 dk	**(A12A2TC) Chemical Tanker** Double Hull (13F) Liq: 610	**1 oil engine** driving 1 Propeller Total Power: 735kW (999hp) 10.5kn Yanmar DY26-SN 1 x 4 Stroke 6 Cy. 260 x 440 735kW (999bhp) Yanmar Diesel Engine Co Ltd-Japan
8602799 *JBBC* -	**TENYO** **Government of Japan (Ministry of Land, Infrastructure & Transport) (The Coastguard)** - *Tokyo* *Japan* Official number: 129790	*435* - 224		**1986-11 Sumitomo Heavy Industries Ltd. — Uraga Shipyard, Yokosuka** Yd No: 1145 Loa 56.02 Br ex 9.82 Dght 3.080 Lbp 51.69 Br md 9.80 Dpth 5.00 Welded, 1 dk	**(B31A2SR) Research Survey Vessel**	**2 oil engines** driving 2 CP propellers Total Power: 956kW (1,300hp) 13.0kn Akasaka MH23R 2 x 4 Stroke 6 Cy. 230 x 390 each-478kW (650bhp) Akasaka Tekkosho KK (Akasaka DieselLtd)-Japan
9253985 *HOVG* -	**TENYO** **Forward Gloria Navigation SA** Daiwa Kisen KK (Daiwa Kisen Co Ltd) *Panama* *Panama* MMSI: 356758000 Official number: 2893503B	**43,347** 23,297 78,236	Class: NK	**2003-02 Mitsui Eng. & SB. Co. Ltd. — Tamano** Yd No: 1556 Loa 229.00 (BB) Br ex - Dght 12.889 Lbp 218.00 Br md 36.50 Dpth 18.50 Welded, 1 dk	**(A21A2BC) Bulk Carrier** Grain: 90,493 Compartments: 5 Ho, ER 5 Ha: 4 (17.8 x 16.0)ER (15.4 x 14.4)	**1 oil engine** driving 1 FP propeller Total Power: 10,224kW (13,901hp) 14.5kn B&W 5S60MC 1 x 2 Stroke 5 Cy. 600 x 2292 10224kW (13901bhp) Mitsui Engineering & Shipbuilding CLtd-Japan Fuel: 3040.0
9222443 *9V9366* -	**TENYO** **TOP-NYK MarineOne Pte Ltd** Thaioil Marine Co Ltd SatCom: Inmarsat C 456357111 *Singapore* *Singapore* MMSI: 563571000 Official number: 396972	**152,139** 90,099 281,050 T/cm 174.2	Class: NK	**2000-08 Mitsubishi Heavy Industries Ltd. — Nagasaki** Yd No: 2200 Loa 330.00 (BB) Br ex 60.04 Dght 20.401 Lbp 319.00 Br md 60.00 Dpth 28.80 Welded, 1 dk	**(A13A2TV) Crude Oil Tanker** Double Hull (13F) Liq: 308,376; Liq (Oil): 308,376 Compartments: 5 Ta, 10 Wing Ta, 2 Wing Slop Ta, ER 3 Cargo Pump (s): 3x5000m³/hr Manifold: Bow/CM: 155.5m	**1 oil engine** driving 1 FP propeller Total Power: 27,030kW (36,750hp) 15.9kn Mitsubishi 7UEC85LSII 1 x 2 Stroke 7 Cy. 850 x 3150 27030kW (36750bhp) Mitsubishi Heavy Industries Ltd-Japan AuxGen: 2 x 1050kW 450V 60Hz a.c, 1 x 900kW 450V 60Hz a.c Fuel: 410.0 (d.f.) 6260.0 (r.f.)
8323874 *JIFH* -	**TENYO MARU** **Suisan Daigakko (National Fisheries University)** SatCom: Inmarsat C 443103010 *Shimonoseki, Yamaguchi* *Japan* MMSI: 431030000 Official number: 127041	*1,020* 306 492		**1985-05 Mitsubishi Heavy Industries Ltd. — Shimonoseki** Yd No: 871 Lengthened-1996 Loa 62.60 Br ex 10.42 Dght 4.409 Lbp 56.50 Br md 10.41 Dpth 6.46 Welded, 2 dks	**(B11A2FS) Stern Trawler**	**1 oil engine** driving 1 CP propeller Total Power: 1,618kW (2,200hp) 12.5kn Hanshin 6ELS32 1 x 4 Stroke 6 Cy. 320 x 640 1618kW (2200bhp) The Hanshin Diesel Works Ltd-Japan Thrusters: 1 Thwart. CP thruster (f)
9124093 *JM6309* -	**TENYO MARU** **GK Nakatsuru Gumi** - *Tsukumi, Oita* *Japan* MMSI: 431600374 Official number: 133588	*749* - 2,100		**1995-05 K.K. Miura Zosensho — Saiki** Yd No: 1121 Loa 84.00 Br ex - Dght 4.590 Lbp 78.50 Br md 12.80 Dpth 7.80 Welded, 1 dk	**(A31A2GX) General Cargo Ship**	**1 oil engine** driving 1 FP propeller Total Power: 1,471kW (2,000hp) 12.0kn Niigata 6M34AFT 1 x 4 Stroke 6 Cy. 340 x 620 1471kW (2000bhp) Niigata Engineering Co Ltd-Japan
9142370 *JG5242* -	**TENYO MARU** **Japan Railway Construction, Transport & Technology Agency & Asia Pacific Marine Corp** Asia Pacific Marine Corp *Tokyo* *Japan* MMSI: 431100216 Official number: 134950	*4,342* - 6,686 T/cm 16.3	Class: NK	**1996-01 Kambara Marine Development & Shipbuilding Co Ltd — Fukuyama HS** Yd No: OE-205 Loa 114.13 (BB) Br ex 17.63 Dght 6.618 Lbp 107.00 Br md 17.60 Dpth 8.30 Welded, 1 dk	**(A24A2BT) Cement Carrier** Grain: 5,403 Compartments: 8 Ho, ER	**1 oil engine** driving 1 CP propeller Total Power: 2,648kW (3,600hp) 12.5kn Akasaka A41S 1 x 4 Stroke 6 Cy. 410 x 800 2648kW (3600bhp) Akasaka Tekkosho KK (Akasaka DieselLtd)-Japan AuxGen: 1 x 450kW 450V 60Hz a.c, 1 x 200kW 450V 60Hz a.c Thrusters: 1 Thwart. CP thruster (f) Fuel: 44.0 (d.f.) 132.0 (r.f.) 15.0pd
8014538 - -	**TENYO MARU No. 1** **Yung Hao Yu Yeh** - *Chinese Taipei*	*116* 27 144		**1980-08 K.K. Murakami Zosensho — Ishinomaki** Yd No: 1060 Loa 36.68 Br ex 7.40 Dght 2.961 Lbp 30.41 Br md 7.09 Dpth 2.82 Welded, 1 dk	**(B11B2FV) Fishing Vessel**	**1 oil engine** geared to sc. shaft driving 1 FP propeller Total Power: 1,324kW (1,800hp) 10.5kn Daihatsu 6DSM-28 1 x 4 Stroke 6 Cy. 280 x 340 1324kW (1800bhp) Daihatsu Diesel Manufacturing Co Lt-Japan AuxGen: 1 x 100kW 225V a.c, 1 x 80kW 225V a.c
7830612 - -	**TENYO MARU No. 2** **Makie Takatani**	*125* - -		**1967-02 Yamaoka Zosen K.K. — Japan** L reg 25.79 Br ex - Dght 1.900 Lbp - Br md 5.90 Dpth 2.50 Welded, 1 dk	**(A31A2GX) General Cargo Ship**	**1 oil engine** driving 1 FP propeller
7118715 - -	**TENYO MARU No. 2** *ex* Daiko Maru *-2001* *ex* Tenyo Maru *-2000* *ex* Komaki Maru *-1999* **Sea Green Co Ltd** - *South Korea*	*199* - -		**1971-10 Kanagawa Zosen — Kobe** Yd No: 111 Loa 26.73 Br ex 8.67 Dght 2.515 Lbp 26.01 Br md 8.62 Dpth 3.79 Riveted\Welded, 1 dk	**(B32A2ST) Tug**	**2 oil engines** driving 2 FP propellers Total Power: 1,766kW (2,402hp) 12.6kn Niigata 6L25BX 2 x 4 Stroke 6 Cy. 250 x 320 each-883kW (1201bhp) Niigata Engineering Co Ltd-Japan AuxGen: 2 x 48kW 225V a.c Thrusters: 2 Thwart. FP thruster (f)
7709655 - -	**TENYO MARU No. 3** **Sal Fishing Corp** - *Philippines*	*156* - -		**1977-04 K.K. Murakami Zosensho — Ishinomaki** Yd No: 992 Loa 37.39 Br ex - Dght 2.401 Lbp 30.76 Br md 6.32 Dpth 2.72 Welded, 1 dk	**(B11B2FV) Fishing Vessel**	**1 oil engine** driving 1 FP propeller Total Power: 515kW (700hp) Niigata 6L25BX 1 x 4 Stroke 6 Cy. 250 x 320 515kW (700bhp) Niigata Engineering Co Ltd-Japan
6909040 - -	**TENYO MARU No. 11** *ex* Daiei Maru No. 3 *-1999* **Tenyo Suisan KK**	*114* - -		**1968 Hakata Dock K.K. — Fukuoka** Yd No: 108 Loa 34.60 Br ex 6.13 Dght - Lbp 29.93 Br md 6.10 Dpth 2.95 Welded, 1 dk	**(B11B2FV) Fishing Vessel**	**1 oil engine** driving 1 FP propeller Total Power: 478kW (650hp) Akasaka 6MH25SSR 1 x 4 Stroke 6 Cy. 250 x 400 478kW (650bhp) Akasaka Tekkosho KK (Akasaka DieselLtd)-Japan
7213060 - -	**TENYO MARU No. 31** *ex* Daiyu Maru No. 25 *-1982* **Taiko Tsusho KK** -	*146* 76 -		**1972 Sanuki Shipbuilding & Iron Works Co Ltd — Mitoyo KG** Yd No: 622 Loa - Br ex 7.04 Dght 2.540 Lbp 30.92 Br md 7.01 Dpth 2.80 Riveted\Welded, 1 dk	**(B11B2FV) Fishing Vessel**	**1 oil engine** driving 1 FP propeller Total Power: 478kW (650hp) Hanshin 6L26AGSH 1 x 4 Stroke 6 Cy. 260 x 400 478kW (650bhp) Hanshin Nainenki Kogyo-Japan
7621243 *T2UX3* -	**TENYU MARU** *ex* Sam Yeong 5 *-2011* *ex* Kem Young 7 *-2007* *ex* Dong Chang Korea *-2005* *ex* Tensho Maru No. 8 *-2002* *ex* Shinsei Maru No. 5 *-1992* **Hozun Oil & Trading Pte Ltd** - *Funafuti* *Tuvalu* MMSI: 572234210 Official number: 24397711	**330** 246 650		**1977-01 KK Ura Kyodo Zosensho — Awaji HG** Yd No: 174 Loa 41.98 Br ex - Dght 3.366 Lbp - Br md 7.50 Dpth 3.40 Welded, 1 dk	**(A13B2TU) Tanker (unspecified)**	**1 oil engine** driving 1 FP propeller Total Power: 552kW (750hp) Matsui 6M26KGHS 1 x 4 Stroke 6 Cy. 260 x 400 552kW (750bhp) Matsui Iron Works Co Ltd-Japan

IMO / Call sign / Flag	Name / Former names / Owner / Manager / Port	Tonnage	Class	Builder / Dimensions	Type / Cargo	Machinery
7932965 - -	**TENYU MARU** - -	*199* - 699		**1979 Shin Nippon Jukogyo K.K. — Osakikamijima** Yd No: 157 L reg 49.72 Br ex - Dght 3.270 Lbp - Br md 9.01 Dpth 5.01 Welded, 1 dk	**(A31A2GX) General Cargo Ship**	**1 oil engine** driving 1 FP propeller
9042790 *JL6063* -	**TENYU MARU** *ex* Union *-2004* **Sugahara Jeneralist Co Ltd** - *Marugame, Kagawa* Japan Official number: 132152	*420* - 877		**1992-05 Maebata Zosen Tekko K.K. — Sasebo** Yd No: 199 Loa 57.72 (BB) Br ex - Dght 3.800 Lbp 52.00 Br md 9.40 Dpth 4.30 Welded, 1 dk	**(A12A2TC) Chemical Tanker** Liq: 659 Compartments: 3 Ta, ER 2 Cargo Pump (s): 2x200m³/hr	**1 oil engine** driving 1 FP propeller Total Power: 736kW (1,001hp) 10.9kn Hanshin LH28G 1 x 4 Stroke 6 Cy. 280 x 460 736kW (1001bhp) The Hanshin Diesel Works Ltd-Japan AuxGen: 2 x 64kW a.c
9067154 *JL6140* -	**TENYU MARU** - **Fukusho Kisen KK** - *Ube, Yamaguchi* Japan Official number: 133895	*499* - 1,199	Class: NK	**1993-05 Shitanoe Shipbuilding Co Ltd — Usuki OT** Yd No: 1140 Loa 64.85 Br ex - Dght 4.111 Lbp 61.00 Br md 10.30 Dpth 4.50 Welded, 1 dk	**(A12A2TC) Chemical Tanker** Liq: 1,230	**1 oil engine** driving 1 FP propeller Total Power: 736kW (1,001hp) 10.2kn Niigata 6M28BGT 1 x 4 Stroke 6 Cy. 280 x 480 736kW (1001bhp) Niigata Engineering Co Ltd-Japan AuxGen: 3 x 94kW a.c Fuel: 40.0 (d.f.)
9134402 *JH3346* -	**TENYU MARU NO. 1** *ex* Shinpo Maru No. 21 *-2002* **Ise Kaiun YK** Kansei Kaiun KK *Yokohama, Kanagawa* Japan Official number: 133285	*117* - 300		**1995-11 Suzuki Shipyard Co. Ltd. — Yokkaichi** Yd No: 623 Loa 35.61 Br ex - Dght - Lbp 33.00 Br md 6.80 Dpth 3.25 Welded, 1 dk	**(A13B2TP) Products Tanker** Liq: 323; Liq (Oil): 323 2 Cargo Pump (s): 2x200m³/hr	**1 oil engine** driving 1 FP propeller Total Power: 294kW (400hp) 8.0kn Matsui ML624GS 1 x 4 Stroke 6 Cy. 240 x 400 294kW (400bhp) Matsui Iron Works Co Ltd-Japan
8815566 *JK4889* -	**TENYU MARU No. 3** - **Masaharu Tanioka** - *Hiroshima, Hiroshima* Japan Official number: 131062	*450* - 463		**1989-01 Shitanoe Shipbuilding Co Ltd — Usuki OT** Yd No: 1091 Loa 47.02 (BB) Br ex 11.02 Dght 3.121 Lbp 42.00 Br md 11.00 Dpth 5.41 Welded, 1 dk	**(B33A2DG) Grab Dredger** Compartments: 1 Ho, ER 1 Ha: ER	**1 oil engine** driving 1 FP propeller Total Power: 736kW (1,001hp) Yanmar MF28-UT 1 x 4 Stroke 6 Cy. 280 x 450 736kW (1001bhp) (made 1988) Yanmar Diesel Engine Co Ltd-Japan
8801565 *JK4735* -	**TENYU MARU No. 8** - - *Himeji, Hyogo* Japan Official number: 129573	*494* - 1,348		**1987-10 Matsuura Tekko Zosen K.K. — Osakikamijima** Yd No: 335 Loa 65.66 (BB) Br ex 13.29 Dght 4.474 Lbp 59.92 Br md 13.20 Dpth 7.01 Welded, 2 dks	**(B33A2DG) Grab Dredger** Grain: 782 Compartments: 1 Ho, ER 1 Ha: ER	**1 oil engine** with clutches & reverse reduction geared to sc. shaft driving 1 FP propeller Total Power: 736kW (1,001hp) Hanshin 6LU35G 1 x 4 Stroke 6 Cy. 350 x 550 736kW (1001bhp) The Hanshin Diesel Works Ltd-Japan Thrusters: 1 Thwart. CP thruster (f)
9084982 *JG5158* -	**TENYU MARU No. 8** - **Ise Kaiun YK** Kansei Kaiun KK *Yokohama, Kanagawa* Japan Official number: 133731	*138* - 361		**1993-05 K.K. Tago Zosensho — Nishi-Izu** Yd No: 252 Loa 39.72 Br ex 7.90 Dght 2.500 Lbp 36.40 Br md 7.70 Dpth 2.75 Welded, 1 dk	**(A13B2TP) Products Tanker** Liq: 348; Liq (Oil): 348	**1 oil engine** geared to sc. shaft driving 1 FP propeller Total Power: 331kW (450hp) Sumiyoshi S23G 1 x 4 Stroke 6 Cy. 230 x 400 331kW (450bhp) Sumiyoshi Marine Diesel Co Ltd-Japan
7355105 - -	**TENYU MARU No. 8** *ex* Koei Maru No. 5 *-2002* **Fisheries Project Implementation Department Stats Trading Organization** - *Male* Maldives	*299* 150 -		**1974-03 Niigata Engineering Co Ltd — Niigata NI** Yd No: 1256 Loa 48.90 Br ex 8.34 Dght 3.252 Lbp 43.21 Br md 8.31 Dpth 3.66 Welded, 1 dk	**(B11B2FV) Fishing Vessel**	**1 oil engine** driving 1 FP propeller Total Power: 736kW (1,001hp) Niigata 6L28X 1 x 4 Stroke 6 Cy. 280 x 440 736kW (1001bhp) Niigata Engineering Co Ltd-Japan
7815519 - -	**TENYU MARU No. 18** - - -	*299* 143 369		**1978-09 Niigata Engineering Co Ltd — Niigata NI** Yd No: 1608 Loa 48.87 Br ex - Dght 3.260 Lbp 42.80 Br md 8.51 Dpth 3.61 Welded, 1 dk	**(B11B2FV) Fishing Vessel**	**1 oil engine** driving 1 FP propeller Total Power: 809kW (1,100hp) Niigata 6M28ZG 1 x 4 Stroke 6 Cy. 280 x 440 809kW (1100bhp) Niigata Engineering Co Ltd-Japan
6716041 - -	**TENYU MARU No. 28** *ex* Choko Maru No. 25 *-2002* *ex* Nitto Maru No. 5 *-2002* **Kiomasa Enterprise** - Indonesia	*271* 132 745		**1967-03 Niigata Engineering Co Ltd — Niigata NI** Yd No: 682 Loa 47.48 Br ex 7.80 Dght 3.125 Lbp 42.98 Br md 7.78 Dpth 3.51 Welded, 1 dk	**(B11B2FV) Fishing Vessel**	**1 oil engine** driving 1 FP propeller Total Power: 699kW (950hp) Niigata 6M31HS 1 x 4 Stroke 6 Cy. 310 x 460 699kW (950bhp) Niigata Engineering Co Ltd-Japan
6713702 - -	**TENYU MARU No. 38** - **Societe Malgache de Pecherie** - *Mahajanga* Madagascar	*314* 154 -		**1967 Yamanishi Shipbuilding Co Ltd — Ishinomaki MG** Yd No: 533 Loa 46.49 Br ex 8.26 Dght 3.201 Lbp 41.53 Br md 8.23 Dpth 3.66 Welded, 2 dks	**(B11A2FT) Trawler**	**1 oil engine** driving 1 FP propeller Total Power: 919kW (1,249hp) Niigata 6MG31X 1 x 4 Stroke 6 Cy. 310 x 380 919kW (1249bhp) Niigata Engineering Co Ltd-Japan
7314292 - -	**TENYU MARU NO. 38** - - - Malaysia	*284* 142 -		**1973 Niigata Engineering Co Ltd — Niigata NI** Yd No: 1203 Loa 47.68 Br ex 8.23 Dght 3.201 Lbp 42.55 Br md 8.21 Dpth 3.61 Welded, 1 dk	**(B11A2FT) Trawler**	**1 oil engine** driving 1 FP propeller Total Power: 736kW (1,001hp) Niigata 6L28X 1 x 4 Stroke 6 Cy. 280 x 440 736kW (1001bhp) Niigata Engineering Co Ltd-Japan
7935606 - -	**TENYU MARU No. 53** *ex* Shofuku Maru No. 73 *-1986* **Damalerio Fishing Enterprise** - Philippines	*123* - -		**1977 K.K. Watanabe Zosensho — Nagasaki** Yd No: 732 Loa 38.99 Br ex 6.61 Dght - Lbp 32.06 Br md 6.51 Dpth 2.95 Welded, 1 dk	**(B12B2FC) Fish Carrier**	**1 oil engine** reduction geared to sc. shaft driving 1 FP propeller Total Power: 809kW (1,100hp) Hanshin 6LU28 1 x 4 Stroke 6 Cy. 280 x 440 809kW (1100bhp) The Hanshin Diesel Works Ltd-Japan
8423789 *JG4478* -	**TENYU MARU No. 62** *ex* Kotatsu Maru No. 62 *-1995* *ex* Koshin Maru No. 62 *-1986* **YK Tenyu Maru** - *Okinoshima, Shimane* Japan Official number: 126879	*189* - -		**1985-09 K.K. Watanabe Zosensho — Nagasaki** Yd No: 1081 L reg 36.49 Br ex - Dght - Lbp - Br md 7.41 Dpth 3.71 Welded	**(B12B2FC) Fish Carrier**	**1 oil engine** driving 1 FP propeller
9179921 *JG5522* -	**TENZAN** - **KK Daito Corp** - *Tokyo* Japan Official number: 135904	*233* - -		**1997-11 Hanasaki Zosensho K.K. — Yokosuka** Yd No: 256 Loa 36.30 Br ex - Dght 3.180 Lbp 30.80 Br md 10.00 Dpth 4.40 Welded, 1 dk	**(B32A2ST) Tug**	**2 oil engines** with clutches, flexible couplings & reduction geared to sc. shafts driving 2 Z propellers Total Power: 2,648kW (3,600hp) Niigata 6L28HX 2 x 4 Stroke 6 Cy. 280 x 370 each-1324kW (1800bhp) Niigata Engineering Co Ltd-Japan
9066150 *JM6271* -	**TENZAN MARU No. 5** - **YK Tazaki Kisen** - *Kamiamakusa, Kumamoto* Japan Official number: 133549	*499* - 1,543		**1993-05 Honda Zosen — Saiki** Yd No: 847 Loa - Br ex - Dght 4.100 Lbp 70.00 Br md 12.00 Dpth 7.00 Welded, 1 dk	**(A31A2GX) General Cargo Ship**	**1 oil engine** reverse geared to sc. shaft driving 1 FP propeller Total Power: 1,324kW (1,800hp) Hanshin LH31G 1 x 4 Stroke 6 Cy. 310 x 530 1324kW (1800bhp) The Hanshin Diesel Works Ltd-Japan
9082283 - -	**TEO** - **Pesquera Rocio SR Ltda** - *Callao* Peru Official number: CO-010440-PM	*266* 101 130		**1994-02 Remesa Astilleros S.A. — Callao** Yd No: 047 Loa - Br ex - Dght - Lbp - Br md - Dpth - Welded	**(B11B2FV) Fishing Vessel**	**1 oil engine** driving 1 FP propeller
9588380 *V7UP5* -	**TEO** - **Ricchi Navigation Ltd** Meadway Shipping & Trading Inc *Majuro* Marshall Islands MMSI: 538003995 Official number: 3995	**23,460** 12,924 35,829 T/cm 49.6	Class: BV	**2011-05 Qidong Daoda Marine Heavy Industry — Qidong JS** Yd No: DD008 Loa 179.96 Br ex - Dght 10.517 Lbp 172.44 Br md 31.00 Dpth 14.60 Welded, 1 dk	**(A21A2BC) Bulk Carrier** Grain: 47,388; Bale: 46,545 Compartments: 5 Ho, ER 5 Ha: (19.2 x 21.0)3 (20.0 x 21.0)ER (16.0 x 17.5) Cranes: 4x30t	**1 oil engine** driving 1 FP propeller Total Power: 7,900kW (10,741hp) 14.2kn MAN-B&W 5S50MC-C 1 x 2 Stroke 5 Cy. 500 x 2000 7900kW (10741bhp) AuxGen: 3 x 600kW 60Hz a.c Fuel: 220.0 (d.f.) 1400.0 (r.f.) 23.0pd

7907415 *IRTD* -	**TEODORO BARRETTA** **Impresa Fratelli Barretta Domenico e Giovanni SNC** - SatCom: Inmarsat C 424745120 *Brindisi* *Italy* MMSI: 247607000 Official number: 53	**435** 130 100	Class: RI	**1981-01 Cant. Nav. A. Giorgetti — Viareggio** Yd No: 31 Loa 37.32 Br ex 10.32 Dght 4.660 Lbp 34.02 Br md 10.30 Dpth 5.11 Welded, 1 dk	**(B32A2ST) Tug** Ice Capable	**1 oil engine** driving 1 CP propeller Total Power: 2,713kW (3,689hp) MaK 9M453AK 1 x 4 Stroke 9 Cy. 320 x 420 2713kW (3689bhp) Krupp MaK Maschinenbau GmbH-Kiel
7911404 *CUYY* -	**TEOMAR** *ex* Todos Oceanos *-1989* **Alpe-Mar Pescas e Comercio de Peixe Lda** - *Sesimbra* *Portugal*	*201* - 120	Class: (LR) Classed LR until 6/3/91	**1981-10 Estaleiros Navais do Mondego S.A. — Figueira da Foz** Yd No: 192 Loa 34.50 Br ex 7.82 Dght 3.122 Lbp 29.32 Br md 7.61 Dpth 3.61 Welded, 1 dk	**(B11B2FV) Fishing Vessel**	**1 oil engine** sr geared to sc. shaft driving 1 FP propeller Total Power: 883kW (1,201hp) Nohab F26R 1 x 4 Stroke 6 Cy. 250 x 300 883kW (1201bhp) Nohab Diesel AB-Sweden AuxGen: 2 x 84kW 380V 50Hz a.c, 1 x 72kW 380V 50Hz a.c
9512068 *YDA6419* -	**TEPAT** **PT Maritim Barito Perkasa** - *Banjarmasin* *Indonesia* MMSI: 525002007	**249** 74 169	Class: AB	**2009-01 PT Perkasa Melati — Batam** Yd No: PM023 Loa 29.50 Br ex 9.75 Dght 3.500 Lbp 28.36 Br md 9.00 Dpth 4.16 Welded, 1 dk	**(B32A2ST) Tug**	**2 oil engines** reverse reduction geared to sc. shafts driving 2 FP propellers Total Power: 2,420kW (3,290hp) Mitsubishi S12R-MPTK 2 x Vee 4 Stroke 12 Cy. 170 x 180 each-1210kW (1645bhp) Mitsubishi Heavy Industries Ltd-Japan AuxGen: 2 x 80kW a.c
7343700 - -	**TEPERU** **Government of The Republic of Guyana (Ministry of Communications)** - *Georgetown* *Guyana* Official number: 356432	*101* 84 -		**1974 Sprostons (Guyana) Ltd. — Georgetown, Demerara** Loa 24.69 Br ex 6.51 Dght 2.134 Lbp 22.84 Br md 6.41 Dpth 2.75 Welded, 1 dk	**(B32A2ST) Tug**	**1 oil engine** reverse reduction geared to sc. shaft driving 1 FP propeller Total Power: 364kW (495hp) 12.0kn Blackstone ESL6MK2 1 x 4 Stroke 6 Cy. 222 x 292 364kW (495bhp) Mirrlees Blackstone (Stamford)Ltd.-Stamford
8864074 *UDCU* -	**TEPLOOZYORSKIY** *ex* RS-300 No. 60 *-1974* **OOO 'Amurrybprom'** - *Sovetskaya Gavan* *Russia* Official number: 731645	**172** 51 88	Class: (RS)	**1974 Astrakhanskaya Sudoverf im. "Kirova" — Astrakhan** Yd No: 60 Loa 34.01 Br ex 7.09 Dght 2.901 Lbp 29.98 Br md - Dpth 3.69 Welded, 1 dk	**(B11B2FV) Fishing Vessel** Ice Capable	**1 oil engine** driving 1 FP propeller Total Power: 224kW (305hp) 9.0kn S.K.L. 8NVD36-1U 1 x 4 Stroke 8 Cy. 240 x 360 224kW (305bhp) VEB Schwermaschinenbau "KarlLiebknecht" (SKL)-Magdeburg AuxGen: 1 x 75kW a.c, 1 x 50kW a.c, 1 x 28kW a.c Fuel: 19.0 (d.f.)
7431325 - -	**TEPOCA** *ex* Guadalupe Victoria *-1974* **Government of Mexico (Secretaria de Communicaciones y Transportes - Direccion General de Dragado)** - *Mexico*	*3,604* 1,608 -	Class: (BV)	**1975-04 Dubigeon-Normandie S.A. — Grand Quevilly** Yd No: 2531 Loa 114.00 Br ex 17.61 Dght 5.868 Lbp 98.02 Br md 17.53 Dpth 7.50 Welded, 1 dk	**(B33B2DT) Trailing Suction Hopper Dredger** Hopper: 3,000	**2 oil engines** driving 2 FP propellers Total Power: 2,162kW (2,940hp) 12.0kn MAN G6V30/45ATL 2 x 4 Stroke 6 Cy. 300 x 450 each-1081kW (1470bhp) Maschinenbau Augsburg Nuernberg (MAN)-Augsburg AuxGen: 3 x 260kW 440V 60Hz a.c
9147849 *CB5990* -	**TEPUAL** **CPT Empresas Maritimas SA** - *Valparaiso* *Chile* MMSI: 725000780 Official number: 2931	**245** 73 458	Class: AB	**1997-01 President Marine Pte Ltd — Singapore** Yd No: 213 Loa 29.00 Br ex - Dght 3.600 Lbp 27.00 Br md 8.93 Dpth 4.24 Welded, 1 dk	**(B32A2ST) Tug**	**2 oil engines** geared to sc. shafts driving 2 FP propellers Total Power: 2,060kW (2,800hp) Yanmar T240A-ET 2 x 4 Stroke 6 Cy. 240 x 310 each-1030kW (1400bhp) Yanmar Diesel Engine Co Ltd-Japan AuxGen: 2 x 60kW a.c
9345219 *V7MP3* -	**TEQUILA** **Barker Hill Enterprises SA** NGM Energy SA *Majuro* *Marshall Islands* MMSI: 538002883 Official number: 2883	**8,539** 4,117 13,085 T/cm 23.2	Class: AB	**2007-09 21st Century Shipbuilding Co Ltd — Tongyeong** Yd No: 220 Loa 128.60 (BB) Br ex - Dght 8.714 Lbp 120.40 Br md 20.40 Dpth 11.50 Welded, 1 dk	**(A12B2TR) Chemical/Products Tanker** Double Hull (13F) Liq: 13,395; Liq (Oil): 14,094 Cargo Heating Coils Compartments: 12 Wing Ta, 2 Wing Slop Ta, ER 12 Cargo Pump (s): 12x300m³/hr Manifold: Bow/CM: 60.7m	**1 oil engine** driving 1 FP propeller Total Power: 4,440kW (6,037hp) 13.5kn MAN-B&W 6S35MC 1 x 2 Stroke 6 Cy. 350 x 1400 4440kW (6037bhp) STX Engine Co Ltd-South Korea AuxGen: 3 x 550kW a.c Thrusters: 1 Tunnel thruster (f) Fuel: 76.0 (d.f.) 674.0 (r.f.)
9402110 *V7RJ5* -	**TEQUILA SUNRISE** **Hawk Marine Corp SA** Daiichi Chuo Marine Co Ltd (DC Marine) *Majuro* *Marshall Islands* MMSI: 538003520 Official number: 3520	**19,800** 10,370 31,612 T/cm 41.0	Class: NK	**2009-04 Saiki Heavy Industries Co Ltd — Saiki OT** Yd No: 1176 Loa 171.59 (BB) Br ex - Dght 10.400 Lbp 163.60 Br md 27.00 Dpth 14.80 Welded, 1 dk	**(A21A2BC) Bulk Carrier** Double Hull Grain: 40,298; Bale: 39,814 Compartments: 5 Ho, ER 5 Ha: ER Cranes: 4x30t	**1 oil engine** driving 1 FP propeller Total Power: 7,061kW (9,600hp) 14.5kn Mitsubishi 6UEC52LA 1 x 2 Stroke 6 Cy. 520 x 1600 7061kW (9600bhp) Akasaka Tekkosho KK (Akasaka DieselLtd)-Japan Fuel: 1590.0
7032935 - -	**TER YDE** - -	*101* 34 -		**1971 Beliard-Murdoch S.A. — Oostende** Yd No: 211 Loa 25.58 Br ex - Dght 2.502 Lbp 22.10 Br md 6.40 Dpth 3.20 Welded, 1 dk	**(B11A2FT) Trawler**	**1 oil engine** reduction geared to sc. shaft driving 1 FP propeller Total Power: 276kW (375hp) 10.5kn A.B.C. 6MDX 1 x 4 Stroke 6 Cy. 242 x 320 276kW (375bhp) Anglo Belgian Co NV (ABC)-Belgium
8411566 *J8B4857* -	**TERA** *ex* Mega *-2007* *ex* Baltic Sun *-2006* *ex* Atlantic Sun *-2005* *ex* Marrow Star *-2000* *ex* Waddenzee *-1999* **Link Shipping Ltd** Atrica-Marine Ltd *Kingstown* *St Vincent & The Grenadines* MMSI: 375891000 Official number: 11330	**1,861** 1,024 3,035	Class: IV (BV)	**1985-04 Scheepswerf- en Reparatiebedrijf "Harlingen" B.V. — Harlingen** Yd No: 70 Loa 91.01 Br ex 11.36 Dght 4.690 Lbp 86.82 Br md 11.31 Dpth 6.02 Welded, 1 dk	**(A31A2GX) General Cargo Ship** Grain: 3,552; Bale: 3,488 TEU 67 C. 67/20' (40') Compartments: 1 Ho, ER 1 Ha: (49.0 x 9.1)ER	**1 oil engine** with clutches, flexible couplings & sr geared to sc. shaft driving 1 CP propeller Total Power: 750kW (1,020hp) 10.0kn MWM TBD444-6 1 x 4 Stroke 6 Cy. 230 x 320 750kW (1020bhp) Motoren Werke Mannheim AG (MWM)-West Germany AuxGen: 1 x 176kW 220/440V a.c, 2 x 123kW 220/440V a.c Thrusters: 1 Thwart. FP thruster (f) Fuel: 123.0 (d.f.)
7815600 *HO6617* -	**TERA I** *ex* Greville *-2010* *ex* Daehyun No. 205 *-2007* *ex* Gaviota *-2005* *ex* Dong Won No. 615 *-1990* *ex* Sumi Maru No. 15 *-1987* **Xibro SA** - *Panama* *Panama* Official number: 39410PEXT1	**339** 209 332	Class: (KR)	**1978-09 Uchida Zosen — Ise** Yd No: 786 Loa 50.75 Br ex - Dght 3.395 Lbp 44.35 Br md 8.41 Dpth 3.54 Riveted\Welded, 1 dk	**(B11B2FV) Fishing Vessel**	**1 oil engine** reduction geared to sc. shaft driving 1 FP propeller Total Power: 956kW (1,300hp) 11.5kn Daihatsu 6DSM-26 1 x 4 Stroke 6 Cy. 260 x 320 956kW (1300bhp) Daihatsu Diesel Manufacturing Co Lt-Japan AuxGen: 1 x 200kW 225V a.c
5263853 - -	**TERAAKA** *ex* Ninikoria *-1975* *ex* Opatija *-1968* **Edgar Sebastian Roberts** - *San Francisco, CA* *United States of America* Official number: 676693	*900* 720 628	Class: (BV)	**1959-07 Brodogradiliste 'Titovo' — Kraljevica** Yd No: 361 Converted From: General Cargo/Passenger Ship-2000 Converted From: Yacht-1975 Loa 64.42 Br ex 9.71 Dght 3.950 Lbp 59.21 Br md 9.35 Dpth 6.15 Riveted\Welded, 2 dks	**(X11A2YP) Yacht** 3 Ha: (3.0 x 2.0) (3.5 x 5.4) (2.5 x 3.5) Derricks: 2x5t,4x2.5t	**1 oil engine** driving 1 FP propeller Total Power: 1,324kW (1,800hp) 15.0kn Sulzer 6TD48 1 x 2 Stroke 6 Cy. 480 x 700 1324kW (1800bhp) Tvornica Dizel Motora 'Jugoturbina'-Yugoslavia
9206152 *T3JC* -	**TERAKA 8** *ex* Shojin Maru No. 8 *-2011* **Marine Marawa Fisheries Ltd** - *Kiribati* MMSI: 529413000	*439* - 434		**1999-01 KK Kanasashi — Shizuoka SZ** Yd No: 3501 L reg 49.20 Br ex - Dght - Lbp - Br md 8.80 Dpth 3.85 Welded, 1 dk	**(B11B2FV) Fishing Vessel** Ins: 492	**1 oil engine** reverse reduction geared to sc. shaft driving 1 FP propeller Total Power: 1,176kW (1,599hp) Hanshin LH28G 1 x 4 Stroke 6 Cy. 280 x 460 1176kW (1599bhp) The Hanshin Diesel Works Ltd-Japan
9223215 *T3JD* -	**TERAKA 18** *ex* Shojin Maru No. 18 *-2011* **Marine Marawa Fisheries Ltd** - *Kiribati* MMSI: 529414000	*439* - 577		**2000-03 Kanasashi Heavy Industries Co Ltd — Shizuoka SZ** Yd No: 8002 Loa 56.17 (BB) Br ex 8.80 Dght - Lbp 49.00 Br md - Dpth 3.85 Welded, 1 dk	**(B11B2FV) Fishing Vessel**	**1 oil engine** geared to sc. shaft driving 1 FP propeller Total Power: 736kW (1,001hp) 12.9kn Hanshin LH28 1 x 4 Stroke 6 Cy. 280 x 460 736kW (1001bhp) The Hanshin Diesel Works Ltd-Japan AuxGen: 2 x 240kW 225V a.c

IMO / Call sign	Name / Owner	Tonnage	Class	Build	Type	Machinery
9258038 *T3JE* -	**TERAKA NO. 28** *ex* Shojin Maru No. 28 *-2011* **Marin Marawa Fisheries** - *Tarawa* *Kiribati* MMSI: 529415000 Official number: K-14011138	*660* - -		**2001**-11 **Kanasashi Heavy Industries Co Ltd — Shizuoka SZ** Yd No: 8010 Loa 56.17 Br ex - Dght - Lbp 49.20 Br md 8.80 Dpth 3.85 Welded, 1 dk	**(B11B2FV) Fishing Vessel**	**1 oil engine** driving 1 FP propeller Total Power: 736kW (1,001hp) Hanshin LH28 1 x 4 Stroke 6 Cy. 280 x 460 736kW (1001bhp) The Hanshin Diesel Works Ltd-Japan
8976712 - -	**TERANG DUNIA AGUNG** - **PT Bahar Budi Raya** - *Samarinda* *Indonesia*	**175** 53 -	Class: (KI)	**1996**-07 **C.V. Bina Karya Sejahtera — Samarinda** Loa 33.00 Br ex - Dght - Lbp - Br md 7.50 Dpth 2.00 Welded, 1 dk	**(A35D2RL) Landing Craft** Bow door (centre)	**2 oil engines** geared to sc. shafts driving 2 FP propellers Total Power: 324kW (440hp) Nissan RD8 2 x Vee 4 Stroke 8 Cy. 135 x 125 each-162kW (220bhp) (made 1996) Nissan Diesel Motor Co. Ltd.-Ageo
7650232 *YGZT* -	**TERANG MENTARI** *ex* Farida *-2008* *ex* Rajah Mas III *-2002* *ex* Harvest Victoria *-1995* *ex* Ever Green *-1994* *ex* Tomoe Maru *-1992* **PT Sarana Bahari Prima** - *Semarang* *Indonesia*	**1,100** 441 1,500	Class: KI	**1973**-06 **Taisei Zosen K.K. — Osakikamijima** Loa 64.74 Br ex 12.50 Dght 5.001 Lbp 60.26 Br md - Dpth 6.00 Welded, 1dk	**(A31A2GX) General Cargo Ship** Bale: 1,500 2 Ha: 2 (9.9 x 8.0)ER	**1 oil engine** driving 1 FP propeller Total Power: 1,177kW (1,600hp) 10.0kn Niigata 8MG25BX 1 x 4 Stroke 8 Cy. 250 x 320 1177kW (1600bhp) Niigata Engineering Co Ltd-Japan
8004076 *YGDD* 349NO247/O	**TERANG SURYA** *ex* Tuna Indah No. 03 *-1997* *ex* Katsuei Maru No. 88 *-1995* **PT Bali Ocean Anugrah Linger Indonesia** - *Kupang* *Indonesia* Official number: 199800K NO247/O	*349* 190 -		**1980**-07 **Fujishin Zosen K.K. — Kamo** Yd No: 355 Loa 51.16 Br ex 8.80 Dght 3.400 Lbp 43.46 Br md 8.51 Dpth 3.70 Welded, 1 dk	**(B11B2FV) Fishing Vessel**	**1 oil engine** driving 1 FP propeller Total Power: 809kW (1,100hp) Niigata 1 x 4 Stroke 6 Cy. 280 x 460 809kW (1100bhp) Niigata Engineering Co Ltd-Japan
7102247 *5VAG3* -	**TERANGA** *ex* Captain Jad *-2009* *ex* Haj Jamil *-2009* *ex* Mariam *-2007* *ex* Anntoro *-2006* *ex* Cap Carrier *-1978* *ex* Nes Carrier *-1977* *ex* Gullsund *-1976* *ex* Jodur *-1973* **B & I Shipping SAL (Offshore)** Breadbox Shipping Lines BV *Lome* *Togo* MMSI: 671047000 Official number: TG-00050L	**689** 341 914	Class: (BV) (NV)	**1971**-07 **VEB Elbewerften Boizenburg/Rosslau — Rosslau** Yd No: 3333 Loa 49.59 Br ex 10.11 Dght 3.900 Lbp 44.00 Br md 10.09 Dpth 5.62 Welded, 2 dks	**(A31A2GX) General Cargo Ship** Grain: 1,478; Bale: 1,346 TEU 27 C. 27/20' Compartments: 1 Ho, ER 1 Ha: (22.2 x 7.0)ER Derricks: 1x5t,1x3t; Winches: 2 Ice Capable	**1 oil engine** reduction geared to sc. shaft driving 1 CP propeller Total Power: 629kW (855hp) 10.0kn Normo LDMC-6 1 x 4 Stroke 6 Cy. 250 x 300 629kW (855bhp) (new engine 1983) AS Bergens Mek Verksteder-Norway AuxGen: 3 x 34kW 220V 50Hz a.c
9161534 - -	**TERAOKA 3** *ex* Teraoka No. 3 *-2002* *ex* Kinei Maru No. 28 *-2002* **Haedong Co Ltd** Hae Dong Shipping Co Ltd *South Korea*	**353** 105 -		**2002**-06 **Suzuki Shipyard Co. Ltd. — Yokkaichi** Yd No: 637 Loa 26.50 Br ex 9.52 Dght - Lbp 25.00 Br md 9.50 Dpth 5.50 Welded, 1 dk	**(B32B2SP) Pusher Tug**	**2 oil engines** driving 1 FP propeller Total Power: 1,472kW (2,002hp) Matsui MA29GSC-31 2 x 4 Stroke 6 Cy. 290 x 540 each-736kW (1001bhp) Matsui Iron Works Co Ltd-Japan
9659971 *9V2012* -	**TERAS ARIEL** **Teras Oranda Pte Ltd** Teras Offshore Pte Ltd *Singapore* *Singapore* MMSI: 566808000 Official number: 398408	**1,022** 306 872	Class: AB	**2013**-03 **Hin Lee (Zhuhai) Shipyard Co Ltd — Zhuhai GD** (Hull) Yd No: 265 **2013**-03 **Cheoy Lee Shipyards Ltd — Hong Kong** Yd No: 5041 Loa 50.00 Br ex - Dght 4.500 Lbp 43.60 Br md 12.60 Dpth 5.75 Welded, 1 dk	**(B32A2ST) Tug**	**2 oil engines** reduction geared to sc. shafts driving 2 CP propellers Total Power: 3,840kW (5,220hp) 13.5kn Yanmar 6EY26 2 x 4 Stroke 6 Cy. 260 x 385 each-1920kW (2610bhp) Yanmar Diesel Engine Co Ltd-Japan AuxGen: 3 x 350kW a.c Thrusters: 1 Thwart. CP thruster (f) Fuel: 670.0
9594391 *VJN4513* -	**TERAS BANDICOOT** **Teras Maritime Pty Ltd** Teras Australia Pty Ltd *Darwin, NT* *Australia* MMSI: 503006170 Official number: 860971	**1,369** 414 1,552	Class: AB	**2010**-11 **Nanjing Yonghua Ship Co Ltd — Nanjing JS** Yd No: YHSC-0908-02 Loa 54.47 Br ex - Dght 3.000 Lbp 51.78 Br md 18.00 Dpth 4.50 Welded, 1 dk	**(A35D2RL) Landing Craft** Bow ramp (centre)	**2 oil engines** reduction geared to sc. shafts driving 2 FP propellers Total Power: 942kW (1,280hp) Cummins KTA-19-M3 2 x 4 Stroke 6 Cy. 159 x 159 each-471kW (640bhp) Cummins Engine Co Inc-USA AuxGen: 3 x 80kW a.c
9659983 *9V2013* -	**TERAS BETHEL** **Teras Oranda Pte Ltd** Teras Offshore Pte Ltd *Singapore* *Singapore* MMSI: 566809000 Official number: 398409	**1,022** 306 872	Class: AB	**2013**-07 **Hin Lee (Zhuhai) Shipyard Co Ltd — Zhuhai GD** (Hull) Yd No: 266 **2013**-05 **Cheoy Lee Shipyards Ltd — Hong Kong** Yd No: 5042 Loa 50.00 Br ex - Dght 4.500 Lbp 43.60 Br md 12.60 Dpth 5.75 Welded, 1 dk	**(B32A2ST) Tug**	**2 oil engines** reduction geared to sc. shafts driving 2 CP propellers Total Power: 3,840kW (5,220hp) 13.5kn Yanmar 6EY26 2 x 4 Stroke 6 Cy. 260 x 385 each-1920kW (2610bhp) Yanmar Diesel Engine Co Ltd-Japan AuxGen: 3 x 350kW a.c Thrusters: 1 Thwart. CP thruster (f) Fuel: 544.0
9625982 *9V9425* -	**TERAS CAESAR** **Teras Progress Pte Ltd** Teras Offshore Pte Ltd *Singapore* *Singapore* MMSI: 566033000 Official number: 397059	**883** 265 547	Class: AB	**2012**-04 **CCCC BOMESC Marine Industry Co Ltd — Tianjin** Yd No: S21 Loa 45.00 Br ex - Dght 4.500 Lbp 38.70 Br md 12.60 Dpth 5.30 Welded, 1 dk	**(B32A2ST) Tug**	**2 oil engines** reduction geared to sc. shafts driving 2 FP propellers Total Power: 3,840kW (5,220hp) Caterpillar 3516B-HD 2 x Vee 4 Stroke 16 Cy. 170 x 215 each-1920kW (2610bhp) Caterpillar Inc-USA AuxGen: 2 x 180kW 415V 50Hz a.c, 1 x 390kW 415V 50Hz a.c Thrusters: 1 Thwart. FP thruster (f) Fuel: 440.0 (d.f.)
9664316 *9V2014* -	**TERAS CENTURION** **Meridian Maritime Pte Ltd** Teras Offshore Pte Ltd *Singapore* *Singapore* MMSI: 566810000 Official number: 398410	**1,022** 306 877	Class: AB	**2013**-08 **Hin Lee (Zhuhai) Shipyard Co Ltd — Zhuhai GD** (Hull) Yd No: 267 **2013**-09 **Cheoy Lee Shipyards Ltd — Hong Kong** Yd No: 5053 Loa 50.00 Br ex - Dght 4.500 Lbp 43.60 Br md 12.60 Dpth 5.75 Welded, 1 dk	**(B32A2ST) Tug**	**2 oil engines** reduction geared to sc. shafts driving 2 CP propellers Total Power: 3,680kW (5,004hp) 13.5kn Yanmar 6EY26 2 x 4 Stroke 6 Cy. 260 x 385 each-1840kW (2502bhp) Yanmar Diesel Engine Co Ltd-Japan AuxGen: 3 x 350kW a.c Thrusters: 1 Thwart. CP thruster (f) Fuel: 544.0
9567855 *9V9416* -	**TERAS CONQUEST** *ex* Teras Conquest 4 *-2011* **Teras Conquest 4 Pte Ltd** Teras Offshore Pte Ltd *Singapore* *Singapore* MMSI: 566027000 Official number: 397044	**5,097** 1,528 860	Class: AB	**2011**-06 **Saigon Shipyard Co Ltd — Ho Chi Minh City** Yd No: H0706A Loa 56.40 Br ex - Dght 3.660 Lbp - Br md 44.20 Dpth 6.86 Welded, 1 dk	**(B22A2ZM) Offshore Construction Vessel, jack up** Cranes: 1x213t,1x181t	**4 diesel electric oil engines** driving 4 gen. each 1285kW a.c Connecting to 3 elec. motors each 1500snp (1100kW) driving 3 Z propellers Total Power: 5,140kW (6,988hp) 6.0kn Caterpillar 3516B 4 x Vee 4 Stroke 16 Cy. 170 x 190 each-1285kW (1747bhp) Caterpillar Inc-USA Thrusters: 1 Tunnel thruster (f) Fuel: 550.0
8770546 *9V8356* -	**TERAS CONQUEST 1** *ex* Lewek Leader *-2013* **Teras Conquest 1 Pte Ltd** Teras Offshore Pte Ltd *Singapore* *Singapore* MMSI: 565985000 Official number: 395647	**5,097** 1,528 3,165	Class: AB	**2010**-01 **Saigon Shipyard Co Ltd — Ho Chi Minh City** Yd No: H0702 Loa 57.00 Br ex 44.00 Dght 3.660 Lbp 56.43 Br md - Dpth 6.86 Welded, 1 dk	**(B22A2ZM) Offshore Construction Vessel, jack up** Cranes: 2x250t	**4 diesel electric oil engines** driving 4 gen. each 1285kW a.c Connecting to 3 elec. motors each 1500snp reduction geared to sc. shafts driving 3 Z propellers Total Power: 5,140kW (6,988hp) 6.0kn Caterpillar 3516B 4 x Vee 4 Stroke 16 Cy. 170 x 190 each-1285kW (1747bhp) Caterpillar Inc-USA Thrusters: 1 Tunnel thruster (f)
9609782 *9V9841* -	**TERAS CONQUEST 5** *ex* Lewek Lifter *-2013* **Teras Conquest 5 Pte Ltd** Teras Offshore Pte Ltd *Singapore* *Singapore* MMSI: 566438000 Official number: 397650	**5,097** 1,528 3,165	Class: AB	**2012**-04 **Saigon Shipyard Co Ltd — Ho Chi Minh City** Yd No: H1005 Loa 57.00 Br ex - Dght 3.360 Lbp 56.43 Br md 44.00 Dpth 6.86 Welded, 1 dk	**(B22A2ZM) Offshore Construction Vessel, jack up** Cranes: 2x250t	**4 diesel electric oil engines** driving 4 gen. Connecting to 3 elec. motors each (1100kW) driving 3 Azimuth electric drive units Total Power: 6,564kW (8,924hp) 6.0kn Caterpillar 3516B 4 x Vee 4 Stroke 16 Cy. 170 x 190 each-1641kW (2231bhp) Caterpillar Inc-USA Thrusters: 1 Tunnel thruster (f)

IMO / Call sign	Name / Owner / Manager / Flag	Tonnage	Class	Built / Dimensions	Type	Machinery
9616228 *9V9688* -	**TERAS CONQUEST 6** **Teras Conquest 6 Pte Ltd** Teras Offshore Pte Ltd *Singapore* *Singapore* MMSI: 566604000 Official number: 397477	**5,097** 1,528 1,126	Class: AB	**2012-07 Triyards SSY — Ho Chi Minh City** Yd No: H0706B Loa 57.00 Br ex 44.20 Dght 3.360 Lbp - Br md 40.52 Dpth 6.86 Welded, 1 dk	**(B22A2ZM) Offshore Construction Vessel, jack up** Cranes: 2x250t	**4 diesel electric oil engines** driving 4 gen. each 1285kW a.c Connecting to 3 elec. motors driving 3 Azimuth electric drive units Total Power: 5,140kW (6,988hp) 6.0kn Caterpillar 3516B 4 x Vee 4 Stroke 16 Cy. 170 x 190 each-1285kW (1747bhp) Caterpillar Inc-USA Thrusters: 1 Tunnel thruster (f) Fuel: 550.0
9625994 *9V9426* -	**TERAS CONSTANTINE** **Teras Progress Pte Ltd** Teras Offshore Pte Ltd *Singapore* *Singapore* MMSI: 566034000 Official number: 397060	**883** 265 551	Class: AB	**2012-04 CCCC BOMESC Marine Industry Co Ltd — Tianjin** Yd No: S22 Loa 45.00 Br ex - Dght 4.500 Lbp 38.70 Br md 12.60 Dpth 5.30 Welded, 1 dk	**(B32A2ST) Tug**	**2 oil engines** reduction geared to sc. shafts driving 2 FP propellers Total Power: 3,840kW (5,220hp) Caterpillar 3516B-HD 2 x Vee 4 Stroke 16 Cy. 170 x 215 each-1920kW (2610bhp) Caterpillar Inc-USA AuxGen: 2 x 180kW 415V 50Hz a.c, 1 x 390kW 415V 50Hz a.c Thrusters: 1 Tunnel thruster (f) Fuel: 470.0 (d.f.)
9664328 *9V2015* -	**TERAS DARIUS** **Meridian Maritime Pte Ltd** Teras Offshore Pte Ltd *Singapore* *Singapore* MMSI: 566811000 Official number: 398411	**1,022** 306 862	Class: AB	**2013-10 Hin Lee (Zhuhai) Shipyard Co Ltd — Zhuhai GD** (Hull) Yd No: 268 **2013-10 Cheoy Lee Shipyards Ltd — Hong Kong** Yd No: 5054 Loa 49.98 Br ex - Dght 4.500 Lbp 43.85 Br md 12.60 Dpth 5.75 Welded, 1 dk	**(B32A2ST) Tug**	**2 oil engines** reduction geared to sc. shafts driving 2 CP propellers Total Power: 3,840kW (5,220hp) 13.5kn Yanmar 6EY26 2 x 4 Stroke 6 Cy. 260 x 385 each-1920kW (2610bhp) Yanmar Diesel Engine Co Ltd-Japan AuxGen: 3 x 350kW a.c Thrusters: 1 Thwart. CP thruster (f) Fuel: 670.0
9664330 *9V2016* -	**TERAS EDEN** **Meridian Maritime Pte Ltd** Teras Offshore Pte Ltd *Singapore* *Singapore* MMSI: 566812000 Official number: 398412	**962** 288 -	Class: AB	**2013-12 Hin Lee (Zhuhai) Shipyard Co Ltd — Zhuhai GD** (Hull) Yd No: 269 **2013-12 Cheoy Lee Shipyards Ltd — Hong Kong** Yd No: 5055 Loa 50.00 Br ex - Dght 4.500 Lbp 43.60 Br md 12.60 Dpth 5.75 Welded, 1 dk	**(B32A2ST) Tug**	**2 oil engines** reduction geared to sc. shafts driving 2 CP propellers Total Power: 3,840kW (5,220hp) 13.5kn Yanmar 6EY26 2 x 4 Stroke 6 Cy. 260 x 385 each-1920kW (2610bhp) Yanmar Diesel Engine Co Ltd-Japan AuxGen: 3 x 350kW a.c Thrusters: 1 Thwart. CP thruster (f) Fuel: 544.0
9636620 *9V9890* -	**TERAS GENESIS** **Teras Oranda Pte Ltd** Teras Offshore Pte Ltd *Singapore* *Singapore* MMSI: 566470000 Official number: 397710	**1,330** 399 1,361	Class: AB	**2012-04 Hin Lee (Zhuhai) Shipyard Co Ltd — Zhuhai GD** (Hull) Yd No: 174 **2012-04 Cheoy Lee Shipyards Ltd — Hong Kong** Yd No: 4944 Loa 58.00 Br ex - Dght 4.750 Lbp 51.70 Br md 13.80 Dpth 5.50 Welded, 1 dk	**(B21B20A) Anchor Handling Tug Supply**	**2 oil engines** reduction geared to sc. shafts driving 2 Propellers Total Power: 3,676kW (4,998hp) 12.0kn Niigata 6L28HX 2 x 4 Stroke 6 Cy. 280 x 370 each-1838kW (2499bhp) Niigata Engineering Co Ltd-Japan AuxGen: 3 x 320kW a.c Fuel: 490.0
9531296 *9V7501* -	**TERAS HYDRA** *ex* Hako 22 *-2009* **Teras Atlantic Pte Ltd** Teras Offshore Pte Ltd *Singapore* *Singapore* MMSI: 564049000 Official number: 394360	**486** 145 -	Class: AB (Class contemplated) (BV)	**2009-01 Yangzhou Oceanus Shipbuilding Corp Ltd — Yizheng JS** Yd No: YZC-2007-002 Loa 36.00 Br ex - Dght 4.200 Lbp 31.70 Br md 10.97 Dpth 4.90 Welded, 1 dk	**(B32A2ST) Tug**	**2 oil engines** reduction geared to sc. shafts driving 2 FP propellers Total Power: 2,388kW (3,246hp) 12.0kn Cummins KTA-50-M2 2 x Vee 4 Stroke 16 Cy. 159 x 159 each-1194kW (1623bhp) Cummins Engine Co Inc-USA
9531284 *9V7500* -	**TERAS HYDRA 2** *ex* Hako 20 *-2013* **Teras Atlantic Pte Ltd** Teras Offshore Pte Ltd *Singapore* *Singapore* MMSI: 564048000 Official number: 394359	**486** 145 -	Class: AB (BV)	**2009-01 Yangzhou Oceanus Shipbuilding Corp Ltd — Yizheng JS** Yd No: YZC-2007-001 Loa 36.00 Br ex - Dght 4.200 Lbp 31.70 Br md 10.97 Dpth 4.90 Welded, 1 dk	**(B32A2ST) Tug**	**2 oil engines** reduction geared to sc. shafts driving 2 FP propellers Total Power: 2,388kW (3,246hp) 12.0kn Cummins KTA-50-M2 2 x Vee 4 Stroke 16 Cy. 159 x 159 each-1194kW (1623bhp) Cummins Engine Co Inc-USA
9520302 *9V7496* -	**TERAS HYDRA 3** *ex* Hako 18 *-2013* **Teras Pacific Pte Ltd** Teras Offshore Pte Ltd *Singapore* *Singapore* MMSI: 565945000 Official number: 394350	**370** 111 -	Class: BV	**2008-09 Yong Choo Kui Shipyard Sdn Bhd — Sibu** Yd No: 26120 Loa 33.00 Br ex - Dght - Lbp 29.30 Br md 9.76 Dpth 4.30 Welded, 1 dk	**(B32A2ST) Tug**	**2 oil engines** reduction geared to sc. shafts driving 2 FP propellers Total Power: 2,354kW (3,200hp) 10.0kn Cummins KTA-50-M2 2 x Vee 4 Stroke 16 Cy. 159 x 159 each-1177kW (1600bhp) Cummins Engine Co Inc-USA AuxGen: 2 x 78kW a.c
9572135 - -	**TERAS PEGASUS 1** **Ezion Maritime Pte Ltd** Seahorse Heavy Transport Pte Ltd	**282** 84 234	Class: BV	**2009-10 Weihai Xinghai Shipyard Co Ltd — Weihai SD** Yd No: EH05 Loa 32.00 Br ex - Dght 3.800 Lbp 30.04 Br md 9.20 Dpth 4.60 Welded, 1 dk	**(B32A2ST) Tug**	**2 oil engines** reduction geared to sc. shafts driving 2 Propellers Total Power: 2,386kW (3,244hp) Cummins KTA-50-M2 2 x Vee 4 Stroke 16 Cy. 159 x 159 each-1193kW (1622bhp) Cummins Engine Co Ltd-United Kingdom
9572173 - -	**TERAS PEGASUS 2** **Ezion Maritime Pte Ltd** Seahorse Heavy Transport Pte Ltd	**282** 84 234	Class: BV	**2010-01 Weihai Xinghai Shipyard Co Ltd — Weihai SD** Yd No: EH06 Loa 32.00 Br ex - Dght 3.800 Lbp 29.50 Br md 9.20 Dpth 4.60 Welded, 1 dk	**(B32A2ST) Tug**	**2 oil engines** reduction geared to sc. shafts driving 2 FP propellers Total Power: 2,984kW (4,058hp) 12.0kn Cummins KTA-50-M2 2 x Vee 4 Stroke 16 Cy. 159 x 159 each-1492kW (2029bhp) Cummins Engine Co Ltd-United Kingdom AuxGen: 2 x 100kW 50Hz a.c Fuel: 242.0 (r.f.)
9506942 *9V7716* -	**TERAS PEGASUS 3** *ex* Hako 60 *-2011* *completed as* Teras Progress *-2009* **Teras Progress Pte Ltd** Hako Offshore Pte Ltd *Singapore* *Singapore* MMSI: 563409000 Official number: 394692	**317** 96 283	Class: AB (Class contemplated) GL HZ	**2009-02 Sapor Shipbuilding Industries Sdn Bhd — Sibu** Yd No: S29/2007 Loa 31.00 Br ex - Dght 3.500 Lbp 28.59 Br md 9.50 Dpth 4.20 Welded, 1 dk	**(B32A2ST) Tug**	**2 oil engines** reverse reduction geared to sc. shafts driving 2 FP propellers Total Power: 2,388kW (3,246hp) Cummins KTA-50-M2 2 x Vee 4 Stroke 16 Cy. 159 x 159 each-1194kW (1623bhp) Cummins Engine Co Inc-USA AuxGen: 2 x 80kW 415V a.c
9658252 *9V9966* -	**TERASEA EAGLE** **Terasea Pte Ltd** Posh Fleet Services Pte Ltd *Singapore* *Singapore* MMSI: 566514000 Official number: 397799	**3,513** 1,053 3,372	Class: AB	**2013-11 Japan Marine United Corp (JMU) — Yokohama KN (Tsurumi Shipyard)** Yd No: 0078 Loa 75.30 (BB) Br ex - Dght 6.600 Lbp 65.00 Br md 18.00 Dpth 8.16 Welded, 1 dk	**(B32A2ST) Tug**	**2 oil engines** reduction geared to sc. shafts driving 2 CP propellers Total Power: 12,000kW (16,316hp) 15.0kn Wartsila 12V32 2 x Vee 4 Stroke 12 Cy. 320 x 400 each-6000kW (8158bhp) Wartsila Finland Oy-Finland AuxGen: 2 x 1200kW 420V 50Hz a.c, 2 x 400kW 420V 50Hz a.c Thrusters: 1 Tunnel thruster (f); 1 Tunnel thruster (a) Fuel: 300.0 (d.f.) 2200.0 (r.f.)
9624586 *9V9964* -	**TERASEA FALCON** **Posh Terasea (II) Pte Ltd** Posh Fleet Services Pte Ltd *Singapore* *Singapore* MMSI: 566512000 Official number: 397797	**3,513** 1,053 3,369	Class: AB	**2013-03 Japan Marine United Corp (JMU) — Yokohama KN (Tsurumi Shipyard)** Yd No: 0074 Loa 75.30 (BB) Br ex - Dght 6.600 Lbp 65.00 Br md 18.00 Dpth 8.16 Welded, 1 dk	**(B32A2ST) Tug**	**2 oil engines** reduction geared to sc. shafts driving 2 CP propellers Total Power: 12,000kW (16,316hp) Wartsila 12V32 2 x Vee 4 Stroke 12 Cy. 320 x 400 each-6000kW (8158bhp) Wartsila Finland Oy-Finland AuxGen: 2 x 1200kW 420V 50Hz a.c, 2 x 400kW 420V 50Hz a.c Thrusters: 1 Tunnel thruster (f); 1 Tunnel thruster (a) Fuel: 300.0 (d.f.) 2200.0 (r.f.)

IMO / Call sign	Name / Owner / Port	Tonnage	Class	Built	Type	Machinery
9624598 *9V9965* -	**TERASEA HAWK** - **Posh Terasea (II) Pte Ltd** Posh Fleet Services Pte Ltd *Singapore* *Singapore* MMSI: 566513000 Official number: 397798	**3,513** 1,053 3,381	Class: AB	**2013-05 Japan Marine United Corp (JMU) — Yokohama KN (Tsurumi Shipyard)** Yd No: 0075 Loa 75.30 (BB) Br ex - Dght 6.600 Lbp 65.00 Br md 18.00 Dpth 8.16 Welded, 1 dk	**(B32A2ST) Tug**	**2 oil engines** reduction geared to sc. shafts driving 2 CP propellers Total Power: 12,000kW (16,316hp) Wartsila 12V32 2 x Vee 4 Stroke 12 Cy. 320 x 400 each-6000kW (8158bhp) Wartsila Finland Oy-Finland AuxGen: 2 x 1200kW 420V 50Hz a.c, 2 x 600kW 420V 50Hz a.c Thrusters: 1 Tunnel thruster (f); 1 Tunnel thruster (a) Fuel: 300.0 (d.f.) 2200.0 (r.f.)
9658264 *9V9967* -	**TERASEA OSPREY** - **Terasea Pte Ltd** - *Singapore* *Singapore* MMSI: 566515000 Official number: 397800	**3,513** 1,053 3,371	Class: AB (Class contemplated)	**2014-03 Japan Marine United Corp (JMU) — Yokohama KN (Tsurumi Shipyard)** Yd No: 0079 Loa 75.30 (BB) Br ex - Dght 8.100 Lbp 65.00 Br md 18.00 Dpth 8.10 Welded, 1 dk	**(B32A2ST) Tug**	**2 oil engines** reduction geared to sc. shafts driving 2 CP propellers Total Power: 12,000kW (16,316hp) Wartsila 12V32 2 x Vee 4 Stroke 12 Cy. 320 x 400 each-6000kW (8158bhp) Wartsila Finland Oy-Finland AuxGen: 2 x 1200kW 420V 50Hz a.c, 2 x 400kW 420V 50Hz a.c Thrusters: 1 Tunnel thruster (f); 1 Tunnel thruster (a) Fuel: 300.0 (d.f.) 2200.0 (r.f.)
8737374 - -	**TERATAI** - **Government of The Republic of Indonesia (Direktorat Jenderal Perhubungan Laut - Ministry of Sea Communications)** - *Jakarta* *Indonesia*	**518** 156 909	Class: KI	**1998-09 in Indonesia** Loa 47.63 Br ex - Dght 3.200 Lbp 44.64 Br md 9.75 Dpth 3.66 Welded, 1 dk	**(B33A2DU) Dredger (unspecified)**	**2 oil engines** reduction geared to sc. shafts driving 2 Propellers Total Power: 706kW (960hp) Caterpillar 3408C 2 x Vee 4 Stroke 8 Cy. 137 x 152 each-353kW (480bhp) Caterpillar Inc-USA AuxGen: 2 x 40kW 400/230V a.c
8957962 - -	**TERATAI** - **PT Pelayaran Nusantara 'Putra Samudra'** - *Palembang* *Indonesia*	**213** 64 -	Class: KI	**1999-09 PT PD & Industri Kenten Djaja — Palembang** Loa 30.50 Br ex - Dght 3.000 Lbp 26.50 Br md 8.60 Dpth 3.70 Welded, 1 dk	**(B32A2ST) Tug**	**2 oil engines** reduction geared to sc. shafts driving 2 FP propellers Total Power: 1,472kW (2,002hp) 11.0kn Niigata 6MG25BX 2 x 4 Stroke 6 Cy. 250 x 320 each-736kW (1001bhp) Niigata Engineering Co Ltd-Japan
7825916 *HO3237* -	**TERBIS** - **Naviera Terbis SA** - *Panama* *Panama* Official number: 1190982CH	*141* 94 110		**1979-11 Ast. Picsa S.A. — Callao** Yd No: 432 Loa 21.72 Br ex - Dght - Lbp 19.54 Br md 6.71 Dpth 2.75 Welded, 1 dk	**(B11B2FV) Fishing Vessel**	**1 oil engine** driving 1 FP propeller Total Power: 202kW (275hp) Caterpillar 3406PCTA 1 x 4 Stroke 6 Cy. 137 x 165 202kW (275bhp) Caterpillar Tractor Co-USA
7910008 *VRLZ* -	**TERCEIRA** *ex Normandy Princess -1981* **Bigrand International Ltd** Shun Tak-China Travel Ship Management Ltd (TurboJET) *Hong Kong* *Hong Kong* MMSI: 477037000 Official number: 379818	**267** 97 -	Class: AB	**1979-02 Boeing Marine Systems — Seattle, Wa** Yd No: 0012 Loa 30.10 Br ex 9.50 Dght 1.505 Lbp 23.93 Br md 8.54 Dpth 2.60 Welded, 2 dks	**(A37B2PS) Passenger Ship** Hull Material: Aluminium Alloy Passengers: unberthed: 278	**2 Gas Turbs** dr geared to sc. shafts driving 2 Water jets Total Power: 5,442kW (7,398hp) 43.0kn Allison 501-K20B 2 x Gas Turb each-2721kW (3699shp) General Motors Detroit DieselAllison Divn-USA AuxGen: 2 x 50kW 440V 60Hz a.c Thrusters: 1 Thwart. FP thruster (f)
9159830 *C6ZL7* -	**TERE MOANA** *ex Le Levant -2012* **Moana Cruise Line Ltd** Wilhelmsen Ship Management (Norway) AS *Nassau* *Bahamas* MMSI: 311058800	**3,504** 1,051 1,380	Class: BV	**1998-11 Alstom Leroux Naval SA — Lanester** Yd No: 625 Loa 100.26 (BB) Br ex 13.90 Dght 3.000 Lbp 88.50 Br md 13.10 Dpth 7.80 Welded, 5 dks	**(A37A2PC) Passenger/Cruise** Passengers: cabins: 45; berths: 95 Ice Capable	**2 oil engines** with clutches, flexible couplings & sr geared to sc. shafts driving 2 CP propellers Total Power: 2,970kW (4,038hp) 16.0kn Wartsila 9L20 2 x 4 Stroke 9 Cy. 200 x 280 each-1485kW (2019bhp) Wartsila NSD Finland Oy-Finland AuxGen: 3 x 413kW 380V 50Hz a.c Thrusters: 1 Thwart. CP thruster (f) Fuel: 200.0 (d.f.) 14.0pd
8878570 *UITC* -	**TEREK** *ex Ruslan -2000* **OOO 'Terek'** - SatCom: Inmarsat C 427301830 *Makhachkala* *Russia* MMSI: 273312420	**343** 102 170	Class: RS (Class contemplated)	**1993-06 OAO Astrakhanskaya Sudoverf — Astrakhan** Yd No: 12 Loa 39.10 Br ex 8.27 Dght 2.910 Lbp 34.45 Br md 7.80 Dpth 3.60 Welded, 1 dk	**(B11B2FV) Fishing Vessel** Ins: 120	**1 oil engine** driving 1 FP propeller Total Power: 425kW (578hp) 10.0kn S.K.L. 8VD36/24A-1U 1 x 4 Stroke 8 Cy. 240 x 360 425kW (578bhp) SKL Motoren u. Systemtechnik AG-Magdeburg AuxGen: 2 x 75kW a.c Fuel: 53.0 (d.f.)
8666654 - -	**TEREKHOL** - **Sesa Sterlite Ltd** - *Dahej* *India* Official number: GMB/DAHEJ/111	**1,568** 1,371 2,500	Class: IR	**2012-01 Waterways Shipyard Pvt Ltd — Udupi** Yd No: 145 Loa 74.00 Br ex - Dght 3.300 Lbp 71.30 Br md 14.30 Dpth 4.55 Welded, 1 dk	**(A31A2GX) General Cargo Ship**	**2 oil engines** reduction geared to sc. shafts driving 2 Propellers Total Power: 810kW (1,102hp) Volvo Penta D12MH 2 x 4 Stroke 6 Cy. 131 x 150 each-405kW (551bhp) AB Volvo Penta-Sweden
9552496 *YYLY* -	**TEREPAIMA** - **PDV Marina SA** - *Las Piedras* *Venezuela* MMSI: 775093000 Official number: AMMT-2918	**56,326** 29,819 104,736 T/cm 88.9	Class: LR ✠ **100A1** SS 10/2011 Double Hull oil tanker CSR ESP **ShipRight** (CM,ACS (B)) *IWS LI DSPM4 ✠ **LMC** **UMS IGS** Eq.Ltr: T†; Cable: 715.0/87.0 U3 (a)	**2011-10 Sumitomo Heavy Industries Marine & Engineering Co., Ltd. — Yokosuka** Yd No: 1373 Loa 228.60 (BB) Br ex 42.04 Dght 14.800 Lbp 217.80 Br md 42.00 Dpth 21.50 Welded, 1 dk	**(A13A2TV) Crude Oil Tanker** Double Hull (13F) Liq: 98,700; Liq (Oil): 98,700 Cargo Heating Coils Compartments: 10 Wing Ta, 2 Wing Slop Ta, ER 3 Cargo Pump (s): 3x2500m³/hr Manifold: Bow/CM: 116.6m	**1 oil engine** driving 1 FP propeller Total Power: 12,350kW (16,791hp) 14.8kn MAN-B&W 6S60MC-C 1 x 2 Stroke 6 Cy. 600 x 2400 12350kW (16791bhp) Mitsui Engineering & Shipbuilding CLtd-Japan AuxGen: 3 x 640kW 450V 60Hz a.c Boilers: e (ex.g.) 21.4kgf/cm² (21.0bar), WTAuxB (o.f.) 17.8kgf/cm² (17.5bar) Fuel: 250.0 (d.f.) 2170.0 (r.f.)
9175016 *WCX6417* -	**TERESA** - **Penn ATB Inc** Penn Maritime Inc *Philadelphia, PA* *United States of America* MMSI: 368133000 Official number: 1056534	**656** 196 -	Class: AB	**1997-08 Moss Point Marine, Inc. — Escatawpa, Ms** Yd No: 133 Loa 38.70 Br ex - Dght - Lbp 38.35 Br md 11.58 Dpth 6.09 Welded, 1 dk	**(B32B2SA) Articulated Pusher Tug**	**2 oil engines** reverse reduction geared to sc. shafts driving 2 FP propellers Total Power: 5,156kW (7,010hp) 12.0kn EMD (Electro-Motive) 16-645-F7B 2 x Vee 2 Stroke 16 Cy. 230 x 254 each-2578kW (3505bhp) General Motors Detroit DieselAllison Divn-USA AuxGen: 3 x 99kW a.c
9373577 *9VJY7* -	**TERESA COSULICH** - **Fratelli Cosulich Pte Ltd** JR Orion Services Pte Ltd *Singapore* *Singapore* MMSI: 565081000 Official number: 391831	**4,969** 1,859 6,956	Class: AB	**2006-05 Zhenjiang Sopo Shiprepair & Building Co Ltd — Zhenjiang JS** Yd No: SP0402 Loa 99.80 Br ex 18.02 Dght 6.990 Lbp 94.00 Br md 18.00 Dpth 10.00 Welded, 1 dk	**(A13B2TP) Products Tanker** Double Hull (13F) Liq: 7,135; Liq (Oil): 7,135 Compartments: 12 Wing Ta, ER 2 Cargo Pump (s): 2x750m³/hr	**2 oil engines** reduction geared to sc. shafts driving 2 FP propellers Total Power: 2,500kW (3,400hp) 11.9kn Daihatsu 6DLM-26S 2 x 4 Stroke 6 Cy. 260 x 340 each-1250kW (1700bhp) Shaanxi Diesel Heavy Industry Co Lt-China AuxGen: 3 x 260kW Fuel: 250.4 (d.f.)
8712415 - -	**TERESA MARIA** - **670154 Ontario Ltd** - *Chatham, ON* *Canada* Official number: 801796	*121* 108 80		**1987-07 Hike Metal Products Ltd — Wheatley ON** Loa 24.41 Br ex - Dght 1.524 Lbp 21.04 Br md 7.32 Dpth 2.49 Welded, 1 dk	**(B11B2FV) Fishing Vessel**	**1 oil engine** with clutches, flexible couplings & sr geared to sc. shaft driving 1 FP propeller Total Power: 270kW (367hp) Volvo Penta 1 x 4 Stroke 6 Cy. 270kW (367bhp) AB Volvo Penta-Sweden
7641683 *WYT9980* -	**TERESA MARIE** *ex Rush -1978* **S S N Corp** - *New Bedford, MA* *United States of America* Official number: 568670	*127* 86 -		**1975 S & R Boat Builders, Inc. — Bayou La Batre, Al** L reg 21.98 Br ex 6.76 Dght - Lbp - Br md - Dpth 3.38 Welded, 1 dk	**(B11A2FT) Trawler**	**1 oil engine** driving 1 FP propeller Total Power: 313kW (426hp) Caterpillar D353SCAC 1 x 4 Stroke 6 Cy. 159 x 203 313kW (426bhp) Caterpillar Tractor Co-USA

8507884 *WDC7823* -	**TERESA MARIE III** **Teresa Marie III Inc** - *Dover, DE* *United States of America* MMSI: 367077480 Official number: 677998	*192* 141 -		**1984-12 Eastern Marine, Inc. — Panama City, Fl** Yd No: 88 Loa - Br ex - Dght 2.744 Lbp 25.61 Br md 7.01 Dpth 3.97 Welded, 1 dk	**(B11A2FS) Stern Trawler**	**1 oil engine** geared to sc. shaft driving 1 FP propeller Total Power: 460kW (625hp) Caterpillar 3412PCTA 1 x Vee 4 Stroke 12 Cy. 137 x 152 460kW (625bhp) Caterpillar Tractor Co-USA
8605961 - -	**TERESA MARIE IV** - -	*197* 146 -		**1985-12 Eastern Marine, Inc. — Panama City, Fl** Yd No: 93 Loa - Br ex - Dght 2.744 Lbp 26.83 Br md 7.01 Dpth 3.97 Welded, 1 dk	**(B11A2FS) Stern Trawler**	**1 oil engine** geared to sc. shaft driving 1 FP propeller Total Power: 530kW (721hp) Caterpillar 3412PCTA 1 x Vee 4 Stroke 12 Cy. 137 x 152 530kW (721bhp) Caterpillar Tractor Co-USA
8957766 *WDC2114* -	**TERESA MARIE IV** *ex Princess Diana -2004* **Teresa Marie IV Inc** - *Portland, ME* *United States of America* MMSI: 366988130 Official number: 1089264	**188** 56 -		**1999** Yd No: 167 L reg 24.74 Br ex - Dght - Lbp - Br md 7.62 Dpth 3.41 Welded, 1 dk	**(B11B2FV) Fishing Vessel**	**1 oil engine** driving 1 FP propeller
5355955 *WDC6818* -	**TERESA MCALLISTER** *ex Marie S. Moran -1963* **McAllister Towing & Transportation Co Inc (MT & T)** - *New York, NY* *United States of America* MMSI: 367061730 Official number: 285087	*223* 151 -	Class: (AB)	**1961 Dravo Corp. — Wilmington, De** Yd No: 4120 Loa - Br ex 8.28 Dght 4.042 Lbp 29.47 Br md 8.23 Dpth 4.53 Welded, 1 dk	**(B32A2ST) Tug**	**1 oil engine** sr reverse geared to sc. shaft driving 1 FP propeller Total Power: 1,206kW (1,640hp) EMD (Electro-Motive) 16-567-BC 1 x Vee 2 Stroke 16 Cy. 216 x 254 1206kW (1640bhp) General Motors Corp-USA AuxGen: 1 x 40kW, 1 x 25kW Fuel: 101.5
5283554 - -	**TERESAMAR** *ex Praia de Paco d'Arcos -1985* -	**465** 139 343	Class: (LR) (RP) ✠ Classed LR until 8/72	**1959-02 Companhia Uniao Fabril — Lisbon** Yd No: 167 Loa 52.50 Br ex 8.48 Dght 4.109 Lbp 46.25 Br md - Dpth 4.35 Riveted\Welded, 1 dk	**(B11A2FT) Trawler**	**1 oil engine** driving 1 FP propeller Total Power: 809kW (1,100hp) 11.5kn Werkspoor TMAS398 1 x 4 Stroke 8 Cy. 390 x 680 809kW (1100bhp) NV Werkspoor-Netherlands Fuel: 110.0 (d.f.) 4.5pd
9336529 *FMER* -	**TEREVAU** *ex Silver Express -2012* **SNGV 2 Moorea** - *Papeete* *France* MMSI: 329001300 Official number: 919680	**739** 222 73	Class: BV	**2005-10 Austal Ships Pty Ltd — Fremantle WA** Yd No: 284 Loa 45.24 (BB) Br ex 12.50 Dght 1.800 Lbp 40.20 Br md 12.30 Dpth 4.00 Welded, 1 dk	**(A36A2PR) Passenger/Ro-Ro Ship (Vehicles)** Hull Material: Aluminium Alloy Passengers: unberthed: 360 Cars: 10	**4 oil engines** geared to sc. shafts driving 4 Water jets Total Power: 7,808kW (10,616hp) 38.0kn M.T.U. 16V396TE74L 4 x Vee 4 Stroke 16 Cy. 165 x 185 each-1952kW (2654bhp) MTU Friedrichshafen GmbH-Friedrichshafen
7048001 *WY7601* -	**TERI M** **Michael Silva** - *Provincetown, MA* *United States of America* Official number: 521738	*102* 72 -		**1969 Toche Enterprises, Inc. — Ocean Springs, Ms** L reg 20.88 Br ex 6.74 Dght - Lbp - Br md - Dpth 3.46 Welded	**(B11B2FV) Fishing Vessel**	**1 oil engine** driving 1 FP propeller Total Power: 368kW (500hp)
9551569 *HP7619* -	**TERIBE** **Panama Canal Authority** - SatCom: Inmarsat C 435659311 *Balboa* *Panama* MMSI: 356593000 Official number: 4324811	**359** 107 138	Class: (LR) ✠ Classed LR until 29/3/12	**2010-12 Hin Lee (Zhuhai) Shipyard Co Ltd — Zhuhai GD** (Hull) Yd No: 202 **2010-12 Cheoy Lee Shipyards Ltd — Hong Kong** Yd No: 4990 Loa 27.40 Br ex - Dght 3.740 Lbp 25.20 Br md 12.20 Dpth 5.05 Welded, 1 dk	**(B32A2ST) Tug**	**2 oil engines** gearing integral to driving 2 Z propellers Total Power: 3,924kW (5,336hp) GE Marine 12V228 2 x Vee 4 Stroke 12 Cy. 229 x 267 each-1962kW (2668bhp) General Electric Co.-Lynn, Ma AuxGen: 2 x 103kW 208V 60Hz a.c Fuel: 110.0 (d.f.)
7646607 *UAZQ* -	**TERIBERKA** *ex Hiiurand -1994 ex Khiyurand -1993* **Skumur Co Ltd** - *Murmansk* *Russia* MMSI: 273517500	**797** 239 395	Class: RS	**1977-11 Zavod "Leninskaya Kuznitsa" — Kiyev** Yd No: 1442 Loa 54.82 Br ex 9.96 Dght 4.139 Lbp 50.29 Br md 9.80 Dpth 5.01 Welded, 1 dk	**(B11A2FS) Stern Trawler** Ins: 414 Compartments: 2 Ho, ER 3 Ha: 3 (1.5 x 1.6) Derricks: 2x1.3t; Winches: 2 Ice Capable	**1 oil engine** driving 1 CP propeller Total Power: 736kW (1,001hp) 12.0kn S.K.L. 8NVD48A-2U 1 x 4 Stroke 8 Cy. 320 x 480 736kW (1001bhp) VEB Schwermaschinenbau "KarlLiebknecht" (SKL)-Magdeburg Fuel: 154.0 (d.f.)
8931748 *UFAX* -	**TERIBERKA** **Joint Stock Northern Shipping Co (A/O 'Severnoye Morskoye Parokhodstvo') (NSC ARKHANGELSK)** - *Arkhangelsk* *Russia* MMSI: 273913200	**643** 192 888	Class: RS	**1974-11 Santierul Naval Drobeta-Turnu Severin S.A. — Drobeta-Turnu S.** Yd No: 985 Loa 55.55 Br ex 10.42 Dght 3.500 Lbp 52.48 Br md 10.00 Dpth 4.30 Welded, 1 dk	**(B34A2SH) Hopper, Motor** Hopper: 500 Compartments: 1 Ho, ER 1 Ha: (23.9 x 6.9)ER Ice Capable	**2 oil engines** driving 2 FP propellers Total Power: 442kW (600hp) 8.8kn Pervomaysk 6CH25/34 2 x 4 Stroke 6 Cy. 250 x 340 each-221kW (300bhp) Pervomaydizelmash (PDM)-Pervomaysk AuxGen: 2 x 64kW Fuel: 60.0 (d.f.)
5354731 *YB4399* -	**TERIGAS 1** *ex Kota Silat X -2006 ex Telok X -2006* **PT Mitra Nusantara Raya** - *Jakarta* *Indonesia* Official number: 630/L	**327** 101 254	Class: KI	**1959-04 P.T. Pakin — Jakarta** Yd No: 451 Loa 40.29 Br ex 7.01 Dght 2.337 Lbp 34.03 Br md 6.99 Dpth 2.80 Welded, 1 dk	**(A32A2GF) General Cargo/Passenger Ship** Passengers: unberthed: 105 Grain: 312; Bale: 304 2 Ha: 2 (4.8 x 3.9)ER Derricks: 2x2.5t; Winches: 2	**1 oil engine** reduction geared to sc. shaft driving 1 FP propeller Total Power: 250kW (340hp) 12.0kn Deutz RV6M536 1 x 4 Stroke 6 Cy. 270 x 360 250kW (340bhp) Kloeckner Humboldt Deutz AG-West Germany AuxGen: 1 x 9kW 110V d.c Fuel: 12.0 (d.f.)
8622763 *YB5234* -	**TERIGAS 3** *ex Koei Maru No. 3 -2003 ex Shinai Maru -2003* **PT Anugerah Terigas Bahari** - *Surabaya* *Indonesia*	**484** 197 440	Class: KI	**1983-10 YK Furumoto Tekko Zosensho — Osakikamijima** Yd No: 525 Loa 43.36 Br ex - Dght 3.100 Lbp 42.00 Br md 8.01 Dpth 4.91 Welded, 1 dk	**(A31A2GX) General Cargo Ship**	**1 oil engine** geared to sc. shaft driving 1 FP propeller Total Power: 405kW (551hp) 9.0kn Matsui ML624GHS 1 x 4 Stroke 6 Cy. 240 x 400 405kW (551bhp) Matsui Iron Works Co Ltd-Japan
8626135 *YHTC* -	**TERIGAS 5** *ex Kinzan Maru No. 11 -2003* **PT Mitra Nusantara Raya** - *Surabaya* *Indonesia*	**482** 186 685	Class: KI	**1984-10 Hayashi Zosen — Osakikamijima** Loa 45.80 Br ex - Dght 4.200 Lbp 41.00 Br md 7.80 Dpth 4.80 Welded, 1 dk	**(A31A2GX) General Cargo Ship**	**1 oil engine** driving 1 FP propeller Total Power: 368kW (500hp) 9.0kn Matsui ML624GS 1 x 4 Stroke 6 Cy. 240 x 400 368kW (500bhp) Matsui Iron Works Co Ltd-Japan
6825024 *YESJ* -	**TERIGAS 6** *ex Puspitasari I -2007 ex Bintang Pacific -1993* *ex Far East Trader No. 1 -1992* *ex Kotoku Maru No. 8 -1991* **PT Anugerah Terigas Bahari** - *Makassar* *Indonesia*	*482* 223 850	Class: KI	**1968-08 K.K. Matsuura Zosensho — Osakikamijima** Yd No: 120 Loa 53.12 Br ex 8.54 Dght 3.709 Lbp 47.66 Br md 8.51 Dpth 4.02 Welded, 1 dk	**(A31A2GX) General Cargo Ship** Compartments: 1 Ho, ER 1 Ha: (26.0 x 5.9)ER	**1 oil engine** driving 1 FP propeller Total Power: 515kW (700hp) 9.5kn Matsui 6M26KGHS 1 x 4 Stroke 6 Cy. 260 x 400 515kW (700bhp) (, fitted 1968) Matsui Iron Works Co Ltd-Japan AuxGen: 2 x 24kW 100V d.c
9487354 *YDA6513* -	**TERIK** **PT Maritim Barito Perkasa** - *Banjarmasin* *Indonesia* MMSI: 525012051	**249** 74 167	Class: AB	**2008-10 PT Perkasa Melati — Batam** Yd No: PM021 Loa 29.50 Br ex 9.75 Dght 3.500 Lbp 27.00 Br md 9.00 Dpth 4.16 Welded, 1 dk	**(B32A2ST) Tug**	**2 oil engines** reverse reduction geared to sc. shafts driving 2 Propellers Total Power: 2,420kW (3,290hp) Mitsubishi S12R-MPTK 2 x Vee 4 Stroke 12 Cy. 170 x 180 each-1210kW (1645bhp) Mitsubishi Heavy Industries Ltd-Japan AuxGen: 2 x 80kW a.c
8991669 *WDB5141* -	**TERILYN** **Taurus Marine Inc** Cross Link Inc (Westar Marine Services) *San Francisco, CA* *United States of America* MMSI: 366906350 Official number: 530049	**148** 100 -		**1970 Industrial Steel & Machine Works — Gulfport, Ms** Yd No: 100 L reg 17.47 Br ex - Dght - Lbp - Br md 7.92 Dpth 3.26 Welded, 1 dk	**(B32A2ST) Tug**	**1 oil engine** driving 1 Propeller

IMO / Call sign	Name / Owner	Tonnage	Class	Builder / Dimensions	Type	Machinery
9309760 *VMQ9958* -	**TERLAK** **Pacific Marine Group Pty Ltd (PMG)** - *Townsville, Qld* *Australia* MMSI: 503697000 Official number: 860079	**404** 121 700	Class: LR ✠ **100A1** SS 12/2010 tug ✠ **LMC** Eq.Ltr: 0; Cable: 144.0/24.0 U3 (a)	**2005-12 Jiangsu Wuxi Shipyard Co Ltd — Wuxi JS** (Hull) Yd No: (1162) **2005-12 Pacific Ocean Engineering & Trading Pte Ltd (POET) — Singapore** Yd No: 1162 Loa 31.95 Br ex 10.04 Dght 3.800 Lbp 28.40 Br md 9.80 Dpth 4.80 Welded, 1 dk	**(B32A2ST) Tug**	**2 oil engines** with clutches, flexible couplings & sr geared to sc. shafts driving 2 FP propellers Total Power: 2,354kW (3,200hp) Yanmar 8N21A-EN 2 x 4 Stroke 8 Cy. 210 x 290 each-1177kW (1600bhp) Yanmar Diesel Engine Co Ltd-Japan AuxGen: 2 x 150kW 415V 50Hz a.c
8632457 *LGVR* -	**TERMAR II** *ex* Kristoffer Jr *-2010* *ex* Thales *-2008* *ex* Alsvagfrakt *-2008* *ex* Skrovabulk *-1999* *ex* Tommeliten *-1992* **Termar Sea Farm ASA** - *Sandnessjoen* *Norway* MMSI: 258207000	**148** 50 240		**1969 Kr.K. Frostad & Sonner — Tomrefjord** Loa 30.30 Br ex - Dght 3.180 Lbp 28.20 Br md 6.50 Dpth 3.20 Welded, 1 dk	**(B12C2FL) Live Fish Carrier (Well Boat)** Liq: 225	**1 oil engine** reverse geared to sc. shaft driving 1 Directional propeller Total Power: 268kW (364hp) Caterpillar D343 1 x 4 Stroke 6 Cy. 137 x 165 268kW (364bhp) (new engine 1973) Caterpillar Tractor Co-USA
8805975 *3XC29T* -	**TERMINETAYA** **Government of The People's Revolutionary Republic of Guinea (Secretariat Detat a la Peche de la Republique)** - *Conakry* *Guinea*	*300* - -	Class: (BV)	**1989-06 Metalurgia e Construcao Naval S.A. (CORENA) — Itajai** Yd No: 226 Loa 32.50 Br ex - Dght 4.200 Lbp 25.80 Br md 8.41 Dpth 4.60 Welded	**(B11A2FS) Stern Trawler**	**1 oil engine** driving 1 FP propeller Total Power: 629kW (855hp) 11.0kn MWM TBD604BL6 1 x 4 Stroke 6 Cy. 170 x 195 629kW (855bhp) Motoren Werke Mannheim AG (MWM)-West Germany
9258399 *IRVH* -	**TERMOLI JET** *ex* Flying Viking *-2003* **LTM SpA (Logistica Trasporti Molisana)** - *Naples* *Italy* MMSI: 247157700 Official number: 315	**672** 215 50	Class: RI (NV)	**2002-03 Fjellstrand AS — Omastrand** Yd No: 1661 Loa 44.00 Br ex - Dght 1.480 Lbp 40.50 Br md 11.20 Dpth 4.10 Welded, 1 dk	**(A37B2PS) Passenger Ship** Hull Material: Aluminium Alloy Passengers: unberthed: 354	**4 oil engines** reduction geared to sc. shafts driving 4 Water jets Total Power: 2,944kW (4,004hp) 33.0kn Caterpillar 3508B-TA 4 x Vee 4 Stroke 8 Cy. 170 x 190 each-736kW (1001bhp) Caterpillar Inc-USA AuxGen: 2 x 50Hz a.c
9266190 *V7EQ5* -	**TERN** *ex* Ida Selmer *-2006* **Tern Shipping LLC** Eagle Shipping International (USA) LLC *Majuro* *Marshall Islands* MMSI: 538002657 Official number: 2657	**27,986** 17,077 50,209 T/cm 53.3	Class: LR (NV) (NK) **100A1** SS 08/2013 bulk carrier strengthened for heavy cargoes, Nos. 2 & 4 holds may be empty ESN ESP LI *IWS **LMC** **UMS** Eq.Ltr: L†; Cable: 632.5/70.0 U3 (a)	**2003-08 Mitsui Eng. & SB. Co. Ltd. — Tamano** Yd No: 1575 Loa 189.80 (BB) Br ex - Dght 11.930 Lbp 181.90 Br md 32.26 Dpth 16.90 Welded, 1 dk	**(A21A2BC) Bulk Carrier** Grain: 63,198; Bale: 60,713 Compartments: 5 Ho, ER 5 Ha: ER 4 (20.2 x 18.0) (17.6 x 18.0) Cranes: 4x30t	**1 oil engine** driving 1 FP propeller Total Power: 8,800kW (11,964hp) 14.6kn MAN-B&W 6S50MC-C 1 x 2 Stroke 6 Cy. 500 x 2000 8800kW (11964bhp) Mitsui Engineering & Shipbuilding CLtd-Japan AuxGen: 3 x 480kW 450V 60Hz a.c Boilers: AuxB (Comp) 7.1kgf/cm² (7.0bar)
8000977 *PJXY* -	**TERN** *ex* Sea Tern *-1996* *ex* Tern H. L. *-1989* *ex* Dyvi Tern *-1988* **Tern BV** Dockwise Shipping BV SatCom: Inmarsat A 1750550 *Willemstad* *Curacao* MMSI: 306029000 Official number: 1996-C-1505	**22,788** 9,531 30,060 T/cm 50.4	Class: NV	**1982-02 Kaldnes Mek. Verksted AS — Tonsberg** Yd No: 218 Loa 180.50 Br ex - Dght 9.970 Lbp 170.97 Br md 32.28 Dpth 13.31 Welded, 1 dk	**(A38C3GH) Heavy Load Carrier, semi submersible** Double Bottom Entire Compartment Length	**1 oil engine** driving 1 CP propeller Total Power: 9,635kW (13,100hp) 16.0kn B&W 6L67GFCA 1 x 2 Stroke 6 Cy. 670 x 1700 9635kW (13100bhp) AS Nye Fredriksstad Mek Verksted-Norway AuxGen: 3 x 630kW 440V 60Hz a.c Thrusters: 1 Thwart. FP thruster (f) Fuel: 259.0 (d.f.) 1726.0 (r.f.)
8626757 *AUUL* -	**TERNA** *ex* Borcos 107 *-2008* *ex* Zakat *-1989* **ARC Marine Pvt Ltd** - *Mumbai* *India* MMSI: 419076100 Official number: 3426	**122** 36 20	Class: IR (GL)	**1986-07 Marinteknik Shipbuilders (S) Pte Ltd — Singapore** Yd No: 104 Loa 30.80 Br ex - Dght 0.820 Lbp 28.06 Br md 6.41 Dpth 2.57 Welded, 1 dk	**(B21A20C) Crew/Supply Vessel** Passengers: unberthed: 49	**2 oil engines** driving 2 Water jets Total Power: 888kW (1,208hp) 18.0kn MWM TBD234V12 2 x Vee 4 Stroke 12 Cy. 128 x 140 each-444kW (604bhp) Motoren Werke Mannheim AG (MWM)-West Germany
7947154 *OW2264* -	**TERNAN** **Foroyar Landsstyri** Strandfaraskip Landsins *Klaksvik* *Faeroe Islands (Danish)* MMSI: 231093000 Official number: A366	**927** 284 -	Class: NV	**1980-07 p/f Torshavnar Skipasmidja — Torshavn** Yd No: 24 Loa 43.29 Br ex - Dght - Lbp 37.01 Br md 11.00 Dpth 8.72 Welded, 2 dks	**(A36A2PR) Passenger/Ro-Ro Ship (Vehicles)** Bow door/ramp Len: 4.30 Wid: 3.60 Swl: - Stern door/ramp Len: 4.30 Wid: 3.60 Swl: - Lane-Len: 190 Lane-Wid: 3.50 Lane-clr ht: 4.20 Cars: 36	**2 oil engines** geared to sc. shafts driving 2 FP propellers Total Power: 926kW (1,258hp) 12.0kn Deutz SBA6M528 2 x 4 Stroke 6 Cy. 220 x 280 each-463kW (629bhp) Kloeckner Humboldt Deutz AG-West Germany AuxGen: 2 x 96kW 380V 50Hz a.c, 1 x 93kW 380V 50Hz a.c Thrusters: 1 Thwart. FP thruster (f)
7347029 *YFEF* -	**TERNATE JAYA** *ex* Universe Admiral *-1997* *ex* Sea Star *-1993* *ex* Atlantic Star *-1987* *ex* Artis *-1984* *ex* Gibtwo *-1983* *ex* Kantara K *-1983* *ex* Koerier *-1980* *ex* Lita Bewa *-1978* **PT Barru Bahari Lines** - *Jakarta* *Indonesia*	*1,597* 970 2,666	Class: (KI) (BV)	**1973-12 Orskovs Staalskibsvaerft A/S — Frederikshavn** Yd No: 67 Loa 71.50 Br ex - Dght 5.700 Lbp 65.60 Br md 13.00 Dpth 6.75 Welded, 2 dks	**(A31A2GX) General Cargo Ship** Grain: 3,278; Bale: 2,890 TEU 64 C. 64/20' Compartments: 1 Ho, ER 2 Ha: 2 (18.8 x 8.5)ER Cranes: 1x5t; Derricks: 2x5t Ice Capable	**1 oil engine** driving 1 CP propeller Total Power: 1,471kW (2,000hp) 12.0kn Alpha 16V23HU 1 x Vee 4 Stroke 16 Cy. 225 x 300 1471kW (2000bhp) Alpha Diesel A/S-Denmark AuxGen: 3 x 120kW 380V 50Hz a.c
7369027 *LMXY* -	**TERNESKJAER** *ex* Sveafjord 1 *-2008* *ex* Sveafjord *-2008* *ex* Risvaer *-2003* *ex* Heggholmen *-1995* *ex* Trans Sund *-1993* **Bio Feeder AS** Maritime Management AS *Bergen* *Norway* MMSI: 258435000	**882** 461 950	Class: NV (GL)	**1974-01 Fosen Mek. Verksteder AS — Rissa** Yd No: 11 Lengthened-1979 Loa 55.55 Br ex 11.03 Dght 3.771 Lbp 50.81 Br md 11.00 Dpth 5.62 Welded, 2 dks	**(A31A2GX) General Cargo Ship** Grain: 1,303; Bale: 1,133 Compartments: 1 Ho, ER 1 Ha: (14.2 x 9.5) Derricks: 1x10t; Winches: 1 Ice Capable	**1 oil engine** driving 1 CP propeller Total Power: 441kW (600hp) 10.0kn Alpha 406-26VO 1 x 2 Stroke 6 Cy. 260 x 400 441kW (600bhp) Alpha Diesel A/S-Denmark AuxGen: 2 x 50kW 220V 50Hz a.c, 1 x 40kW 220V 50Hz a.c
8915469 *ORMT* -	**TERNEUZEN** *ex* Fairplay XVI *-2010* *ex* Terneuzen *-2004* **URS Belgie NV** - *Ghent* *Belgium* MMSI: 205063000 Official number: 01 00299 1996	*249* 74 134	Class: LR ✠ **100A1** SS 08/2011 tug for service in Baltic Sea, North Sea, Irish Sea and English Channel between 61~North and 48~North ✠ **LMC** Eq.Ltr: (D) ; Cable: 275.0/19.0 U2	**1991-08 N.V. Scheepswerf van Rupelmonde — Rupelmonde** Yd No: 464 Loa 31.99 Br ex 9.05 Dght 3.950 Lbp 27.28 Br md 8.70 Dpth 4.67 Welded, 1 dk	**(B32A2ST) Tug**	**1 oil engine** with clutches, flexible couplings & dr reverse geared to sc. shaft driving 1 FP propeller Total Power: 1,470kW (1,999hp) 13.5kn A.B.C. 8MDZC 1 x 4 Stroke 8 Cy. 256 x 310 1470kW (1999bhp) Anglo Belgian Corp NV (ABC)-Belgium AuxGen: 2 x 108kW 380V 50Hz a.c Thrusters: 1 Retract. directional thruster (f) Fuel: 60.0 (d.f.)
8943480 *UFAK* -	**TERNEY** *ex* Kirensk *-2001* **Ardis Co Ltd** - *Vladivostok* *Russia* MMSI: 273452560 Official number: 825404	**2,463** 979 3,197	Class: RS	**1982 Santierul Naval Oltenita S.A. — Oltenita** Yd No: 136/31 Loa 108.40 Br ex 15.00 Dght 3.264 Lbp 105.00 Br md 14.80 Dpth 5.00 Welded, 1 dk	**(A31A2GX) General Cargo Ship** Grain: 4,370; Bale: 4,120 Compartments: 4 Ho, ER 4 Ha: ER 4 (15.5 x 10.9) Ice Capable	**2 oil engines** driving 2 FP propellers Total Power: 1,030kW (1,400hp) 9.0kn S.K.L. 6NVD48A-2U 2 x 4 Stroke 6 Cy. 320 x 480 each-515kW (700bhp) VEB Schwermaschinenbau "KarlLiebknecht" (SKL)-Magdeburg
8015233 *UAIF* -	**TERNEY-1** *ex* Take Maru No. 32 *-1994* **Vostok-Japan (S/P 'Vostok-Dzhapan')** - SatCom: Inmarsat C 427320698 *Vladivostok* *Russia*	**374** 131 218	Class: RS	**1981-02 Uchida Zosen — Ise** Yd No: 812 Loa 41.80 Br ex - Dght 2.831 Lbp 35.98 Br md 7.51 Dpth 3.18 Welded, 1 dk	**(B11B2FV) Fishing Vessel** Ins: 352	**1 oil engine** driving 1 FP propeller Total Power: 589kW (801hp) 11.0kn Hanshin 6LUD24G 1 x 4 Stroke 6 Cy. 240 x 410 589kW (801bhp) Hanshin Nainenki Kogyo-Japan AuxGen: 2 x 220kW a.c Fuel: 137.0 (d.f.)

9232955 *OWIR2* -	**TERNHAV** *ex* Tarnhav *-2009* **Tarntank Rederi AB** Brostrom AB *Skagen* *Denmark (DIS)* MMSI: 219082000 Official number: D4457	**9,980** 4,581 14,796 T/cm 25.2	Class: NV (GL)	**2002-05 Shanghai Edward Shipbuilding Co Ltd — Shanghai** Yd No: 122 Loa 141.20 (BB) Br ex 21.94 Dght 9.000 Lbp 133.00 Br md 21.60 Dpth 11.50 Welded, 1 dk	**(A12B2TR) Chemical/Products Tanker** Double Hull (13F) Liq: 15,807; Liq (Oil): 15,979 Cargo Heating Coils Compartments: 14 Wing Ta, 2 Wing Slop Ta, ER 7 Cargo Pump (s): 7x450m^3/hr Manifold: Bow/CM: 71m Ice Capable	**1 oil engine** geared to sc. shaft driving 1 CP propeller Total Power: 6,300kW (8,565hp) 14.8kn Wartsila 6L46C 1 x 4 Stroke 6 Cy. 460 x 580 6300kW (8565bhp) Wartsila Finland Oy-Finland AuxGen: 1 x 1500kW 440V 60Hz a.c, 3 x 750kW 440V 60Hz a.c Thrusters: 1 Tunnel thruster (f) Fuel: 81.0 (d.f.) (Heating Coils) 546.0 (r.f.) 25.0pd
9300829 *OWIM2* -	**TERNHOLM** *ex* Tarnholm *-2009* **Tarntank Rederi AB** Brostrom AB *Skagen* *Denmark (DIS)* MMSI: 219076000 Official number: D4459	**9,993** 4,581 14,825 T/cm 25.2	Class: NV (GL)	**2005-03 Shanghai Edward Shipbuilding Co Ltd — Shanghai** Yd No: 131 Loa 141.20 (BB) Br ex 21.94 Dght 9.000 Lbp 133.00 Br md 21.60 Dpth 11.50 Welded, 1 dk	**(A12B2TR) Chemical/Products Tanker** Double Hull (13F) Liq: 15,979; Liq (Oil): 15,979 Cargo Heating Coils Compartments: 14 Wing Ta, ER, 2 Wing Slop Ta 7 Cargo Pump (s): 7x450m^3/hr Manifold: Bow/CM: 71m Ice Capable	**1 oil engine** reduction geared to sc. shaft driving 1 CP propeller Total Power: 6,300kW (8,565hp) 14.0kn Wartsila 6L46C 1 x 4 Stroke 6 Cy. 460 x 580 6300kW (8565bhp) Wartsila Finland Oy-Finland AuxGen: 3 x 750kW 450V 60Hz a.c, 1 x a.c Thrusters: 1 Tunnel thruster (f) Fuel: 81.0 (d.f.) (Heating Coils) 368.0 (r.f.)
9693848 *LGJQ* -	**TERNINGEN** **Partrederiet Kystekspressen ANS** FosenNamsos Sjo AS *Trondheim* *Norway* MMSI: 257333000	**492** 159 -	Class: NV	**2014-03 Brodrene Aa AS — Hyen** Yd No: 274 Loa 40.80 Br ex - Dght 1.077 Lbp 40.00 Br md 10.80 Dpth 3.65 Welded, 1 dk	**(A37B2PS) Passenger Ship** Hull Material: Carbon Fibre Sandwich Passengers: unberthed: 275	**2 oil engines** reduction geared to sc. shafts driving 2 Water jets Total Power: 2,880kW (3,916hp) 33.5kn M.T.U. 16V2000M72 2 x Vee 4 Stroke 16 Cy. 135 x 156 each-1440kW (1958bhp) MTU Friedrichshafen GmbH-Friedrichshafen AuxGen: 2 x a.c
9121699 *OWIT2* -	**TERNLAND** *ex* Tarnland *-2009* **Tarntank Rederi AB** *Skagen* *Denmark (DIS)* MMSI: 219084000 Official number: D4455	**6,534** 3,481 10,877 T/cm 19.6	Class: NV (GL)	**1996-06 Kvaerner Kleven Leirvik AS — Leirvik i Sogn** Yd No: 255 Loa 129.22 (BB) Br ex 18.40 Dght 8.100 Lbp 123.13 Br md 18.37 Dpth 10.40 Welded, 1 dk	**(A12B2TR) Chemical/Products Tanker** Double Hull Liq: 12,153; Liq (Oil): 12,153 Cargo Heating Coils Compartments: 14 Wing Ta, ER 7 Cargo Pump (s): 7x400m^3/hr Ice Capable	**1 oil engine** reduction geared to sc. shaft driving 1 CP propeller Total Power: 3,960kW (5,384hp) 14.0kn MaK 9M32 1 x 4 Stroke 9 Cy. 320 x 480 3960kW (5384bhp) Krupp MaK Maschinenbau GmbH-Kiel AuxGen: 1 x 500kW a.c, 3 x 650kW a.c Thrusters: 1 Thwart. FP thruster (f) Fuel: 63.0 (d.f.) 183.0 (r.f.) 14.0pd
9277371 *OWIP2* -	**TERNVAG** *ex* Tarnvag *-2009* **Tarntank Rederi AB** Brostrom AB *Skagen* *Denmark (DIS)* MMSI: 219081000 Official number: D4458	**9,993** 4,581 14,803 T/cm 25.2	Class: NV (GL)	**2003-11 Shanghai Edward Shipbuilding Co Ltd — Shanghai** Yd No: 127 Loa 141.20 (BB) Br ex 21.94 Dght 9.000 Lbp 133.00 Br md 21.60 Dpth 11.50 Welded	**(A12B2TR) Chemical/Products Tanker** Double Hull (13F) Liq: 15,806; Liq (Oil): 15,797 Cargo Heating Coils Compartments: 14 Wing Ta, ER 7 Cargo Pump (s): 7x450m^3/hr Manifold: Bow/CM: 71m Ice Capable	**1 oil engine** geared to sc. shaft driving 1 CP propeller Total Power: 6,300kW (8,565hp) 15.8kn Wartsila 6L46C 1 x 4 Stroke 6 Cy. 460 x 580 6300kW (8565bhp) Wartsila Finland Oy-Finland AuxGen: 3 x 750kW 450V 60Hz a.c, 1 x a.c Thrusters: 1 Thwart. CP thruster (f) Fuel: 96.0 (d.f.) 576.0 (r.f.) 26.0pd
9221267 *OWIS2* -	**TERNVIK** *ex* Tarnvik *-2009* **Tarntank Rederi AB** Brostrom AB SatCom: Inmarsat B 326584510 *Skagen* *Denmark (DIS)* MMSI: 219083000 Official number: D4456	**9,980** 4,581 14,796 T/cm 25.2	Class: NV (GL)	**2001-05 Shanghai Edward Shipbuilding Co Ltd — Shanghai** Yd No: 119 Loa 141.20 (BB) Br ex 21.90 Dght 9.000 Lbp 133.00 Br md 21.60 Dpth 11.50 Welded, 1 dk	**(A12B2TR) Chemical/Products Tanker** Double Hull (13F) Liq: 15,806; Liq (Oil): 15,806 Cargo Heating Coils Compartments: 14 Wing Ta, ER 7 Cargo Pump (s): 7x450m^3/hr Manifold: Bow/CM: 71m Ice Capable	**1 oil engine** geared to sc. shaft driving 1 CP propeller Total Power: 6,300kW (8,565hp) 14.7kn Wartsila 6L46C 1 x 4 Stroke 6 Cy. 460 x 580 6300kW (8565bhp) Wartsila Finland Oy-Finland AuxGen: 3 x 750kW 450V 60Hz a.c, 1 x 1500kW 450V 60Hz a.c Thrusters: 1 Thwart. FP thruster (f) Fuel: 83.0 (d.f.) (Heating Coils) 523.0 (r.f.) 26.0pd
8668171 *OH3747* -	**TERRA 1** *ex* HH 201 *-2014* *ex* C O 1104 *-2000* *ex* M 20 *-1990* **Terramare Oy** *Helsinki* *Finland* MMSI: 230942790 Official number: 12795	**533** 170 810	Class: GL	**1977-09 Stocznia 'Wisla' — Gdansk** Yd No: 1104 Loa 59.97 Br ex - Dght 2.395 Lbp - Br md 9.50 Dpth 3.35 Welded, 1 dk	**(B34A2SH) Hopper, Motor**	**2 oil engines** driving 2 Rudder propellers 6.0kn Scania DS14 2 x 4 Stroke 8 Cy. 127 x 140 Saab Scania AB-Sweden
8668183 - -	**TERRA 2** *ex* HH 69 *-2014* *ex* CO-846 *-2000* **Terramare Oy** *Helsinki* *Finland* Official number: 12796	**538** 162 810	Class: GL	**1974-08 Plocka Stocznia Rzeczna — Plock** Yd No: 846 Loa 59.64 Br ex - Dght 2.400 Lbp - Br md 9.55 Dpth 3.35 Welded, 1 dk	**(B34A2SH) Hopper, Motor**	**2 oil engines** reduction geared to sc. shafts driving 2 Rudder propellers Caterpillar 3406 2 x 4 Stroke 6 Cy. 137 x 165 Caterpillar Inc-USA
5230040 - -	**TERRA NOVA** *ex* 1991-02 *-1992* *ex* Maxwell *-1991* **Puddister Shipping Co Ltd** Puddister Trading Co Ltd *Ottawa, ON* *Canada* Official number: 318511	*262* 107 -		**1961 Halifax Shipyards Ltd — Halifax NS** Yd No: 29 Loa 35.06 Br ex 7.62 Dght 2.134 Lbp - Br md - Dpth - Welded, 2 dks	**(B31A2SR) Research Survey Vessel**	**2 oil engines** driving 2 FP propellers Total Power: 514kW (698hp) Rolls Royce C8TFLM 2 x 4 Stroke 8 Cy. 130 x 152 each-257kW (349bhp) Rolls Royce Ltd.-Shrewsbury AuxGen: 1 x 40kW 120V 60Hz a.c, 1 x 15kW 120V 60Hz a.c
9183532 *VCXF* -	**TERRA NOVA FPSO** **Suncor Energy Inc** *St John's, NL* *Canada* MMSI: 316298000 Official number: 820771	**110,720** - 120,000	Class: LR ✠ **OI100AT (1)** CS 07/2011 floating production and oil storage installation for service at Terra Nova field, offshore Newfoundland OIWS LI PMT3 ✠ **LMC** **IGS CCS**	**2000-03 Daewoo Heavy Industries Ltd — Geoje** Yd No: 5901 Loa 292.25 Br ex 45.55 Dght 20.000 Lbp 277.00 Br md 45.50 Dpth 28.20 Welded, 1 dk	**(B22E2OF) FPSO, Oil** Double Hull (13F) Liq: 155,000; Liq (Oil): 155,000 Compartments: 14 Wing Ta, ER	**2 diesel electric oil engines & 2 turbo electric Gas Turbs** driving 2 gen. each 46410kW 13800V a.c 2 gen. each 6500kW 13800V a.c Connecting to 3 elec. motors each (5000kW) driving 3 Directional propellers Total Power: 111,480kW (151,568hp) Wartsila 18V32 2 x Vee 4 Stroke 18 Cy. 320 x 350 each-6840kW (9300bhp) Wartsila Finland Oy-Finland Thomassen PG6551B 2 x Gas Turb each-48900kW (66484shp) Thomassen International B.V.-Rheden Boilers: WTAuxB (o.f.) 14.5kgf/cm^2 (14.2bar) Thrusters: 2 Thwart. FP thruster (f)
7936698 - T 15	**TERRA NOVA II** *ex* Terra Nova *-1992* **Hugh Flannery** *Tralee* *Irish Republic* Official number: 402049	*206* 116 -		**1975 N.V. Scheepswerven L. de Graeve — Zeebrugge** Loa 33.53 Br ex - Dght - Lbp - Br md 7.58 Dpth 3.65 Welded, 1 dk	**(B11B2FV) Fishing Vessel**	**1 oil engine** driving 1 FP propeller Total Power: 736kW (1,001hp) MaK 6M452AK 1 x 4 Stroke 6 Cy. 320 x 450 736kW (1001bhp) MaK Maschinenbau GmbH-Kiel
9658276 *5BUG3* -	**TERRAMARE 1** **Baggermaatschappij Boskalis BV** BW Marine (Cyprus) Ltd *Limassol* *Cyprus* MMSI: 209808000 Official number: 9658276	**341** 99 -	Class: BV	**2012-12 Safe Co Ltd Sp z oo — Gdynia** (Hull) Yd No: (571679) **2012-12 B.V. Scheepswerf Damen Hardinxveld — Hardinxveld-Giessendam** Yd No: 571679 Loa 29.73 Br ex - Dght 3.200 Lbp 29.38 Br md 9.10 Dpth 4.40 Welded, 1 dk	**(B32A2ST) Tug**	**2 oil engines** reduction geared to sc. shafts driving 2 FP propellers Total Power: 2,464kW (3,350hp) Caterpillar 3512C 2 x Vee 4 Stroke 12 Cy. 170 x 215 each-1232kW (1675bhp) Caterpillar Inc-USA AuxGen: 1 x 85kW 50Hz a.c, 1 x 85kW 50Hz a.c Thrusters: 1 Tunnel thruster (f) Fuel: 160.0 (d.f.)
8843329 *ZQWK3* -	**TERRAMARE I** **Offshore Marine Solutions** *Penzance* *United Kingdom* MMSI: 235000681 Official number: 904285	*115* 34 -	Class: (GL)	**1960 Schiffs- u. Maschinenbau Mannheim AG — Mannheim** Yd No: 813 L reg 24.51 Br ex - Dght 1.500 Lbp - Br md 7.00 Dpth 2.20 Welded, 1 dk	**(B31A2SR) Research Survey Vessel** Bow ramp (f) Len: 4.60 Wid: 4.50 Swl: -	**2 oil engines** dr reverse geared to sc. shafts driving 2 FP propellers Total Power: 318kW (432hp) 9.6kn MWM RHS518A 2 x 4 Stroke 8 Cy. 140 x 180 each-159kW (216bhp) Motoren Werke Mannheim AG (MWM)-West Germany AuxGen: 1 x 40kW 220/380V a.c, 1 x 6kW 24V d.c
9092666 *DURA5* -	**TERRANOVA** *ex* Maria Priscilla *-2007* *ex* Isogas *-2004* **Shogun Ships Co Inc** *Manila* *Philippines* Official number: 00-0001279	*498* 292 1,415		**2002-01 Santiago Shipyard & Shipbuilding Corp — Manila** Yd No: 08-02 Loa 65.43 Br ex - Dght 3.100 Lbp 63.20 Br md 12.20 Dpth 3.70 Welded, 1 dk	**(A13B2TP) Products Tanker** Double Hull (13F)	**2 oil engines** geared to sc. shafts driving 2 Propellers Total Power: 882kW (1,200hp) Caterpillar 3412 2 x Vee 4 Stroke 12 Cy. 137 x 152 each-441kW (600bhp) Caterpillar Inc-USA

IMO / Call sign	Name / Owner	Tonnage	Class	Builder / Dimensions	Type	Machinery
9048213 *CB4956* -	**TERRANOVA** **Banestado Leasing SA** SatCom: Inmarsat A 1563232 *Valparaiso* *Chile* MMSI: 725000800 Official number: 2795	*919* 224 950	Class: (LR) ✠ Classed LR until 11/10/97	**1993-07 Ast. y Maestranzas de la Armada (ASMAR Chile) — Talcahuano** Yd No: 53 Loa 48.42 Br ex 10.22 Dght 6.000 Lbp 42.00 Br md 10.20 Dpth 7.30 Welded, 2 dks	**(B11B2FV) Fishing Vessel** Ins: 750	**1 oil engine** with clutches, flexible couplings & sr geared to sc. shaft driving 1 CP propeller Total Power: 1,600kW (2,175hp) 13.0kn MaK 8M332C 1 x 4 Stroke 8 Cy. 240 x 330 1600kW (2175bhp) Krupp MaK Maschinenbau GmbH-Kiel AuxGen: 1 x 296kW 380V 50Hz a.c, 1 x 160kW 380V 50Hz a.c Thrusters: 1 Thwart. CP thruster (f); 1 Tunnel thruster (a)
7819539 *KGDS* -	**TERRAPIN ISLAND** *ex* Eagle I *-2007* **GATX Third Aircraft Corp** Great Lakes Dredge & Dock Co LLC *New York, NY* *United States of America* MMSI: 366692000 Official number: 630823	*5,922* 1,776 4,940	Class: AB	**1981-03 Avondale Shipyards Inc. — Avondale, La** Yd No: 2320 Loa 103.64 Br ex 20.86 Dght 6.109 Lbp 94.80 Br md 20.81 Dpth 7.40 Welded, 1 dk	**(B33B2DT) Trailing Suction Hopper Dredger** Hopper: 4,893 Cranes: 1x25t	**2 oil engines** reverse reduction geared to sc. shafts driving 2 FP propellers Total Power: 5,486kW (7,458hp) 14.0kn Alco 16V251F 2 x Vee 4 Stroke 16 Cy. 229 x 267 each-2743kW (3729bhp) Alco Power Inc-USA AuxGen: 2 x 750kW 227/480V a.c Thrusters: 2 Thwart. CP thruster (f)
7309338 *WX9280* -	**TERREBONNE BAY** **Omega Protein Inc** - *New Orleans, LA* *United States of America* MMSI: 367108940 Official number: 508200	*537* 366 -		**1967 Burton Shipyard Co., Inc. — Port Arthur, Tx** Yd No: 424 L reg 49.57 Br ex 10.09 Dght - Lbp - Br md - Dpth 3.61 Welded	**(B11B2FV) Fishing Vessel**	**1 oil engine** driving 1 FP propeller Total Power: 1,125kW (1,530hp) Caterpillar D398SCAC 1 x Vee 4 Stroke 12 Cy. 159 x 203 1125kW (1530bhp) Caterpillar Tractor Co-USA
9418523 *WQAU* -	**TERREL TIDE** **Twenty Grand Marine Service LLC** Tidewater Marine LLC *New Orleans, LA* *United States of America* MMSI: 368503000 Official number: 1223124	**2,326** 697 3,644	Class: AB	**2009-12 Quality Shipyards LLC — Houma LA** Yd No: 1271 Loa 81.08 Br ex - Dght 5.030 Lbp 74.74 Br md 17.07 Dpth 5.95 Welded, 1 dk	**(B21A20S) Platform Supply Ship**	**2 oil engines** reduction geared to sc. shafts driving 2 FP propellers Total Power: 3,372kW (4,584hp) Caterpillar 3516C-HD 2 x Vee 4 Stroke 16 Cy. 170 x 215 each-1686kW (2292bhp) Caterpillar Inc-USA AuxGen: 3 x 340kW a.c
7618155 *WDC3034* -	**TERRI L. BRUSCO** *ex* Marne S *-1991* *ex* Red Shindi *-1991* **Brusco Tug & Barge Inc** - *Longview, WA* *United States of America* MMSI: 367001830 Official number: 299403	*108* 73 -		**1965 Universal Iron Works — Houma, La** Loa - Br ex 7.01 Dght - Lbp 21.95 Br md 6.96 Dpth 2.75 Welded, 1 dk	**(B32A2ST) Tug**	**2 oil engines** driving 2 FP propellers Total Power: 876kW (1,192hp) Caterpillar D353SCAC 2 x 4 Stroke 6 Cy. 159 x 203 each-438kW (596bhp) Caterpillar Tractor Co-USA
7219117 - -	**TERRIBLE** **Government of The Republic of Tunisia (Office des Ports Nationaux Tunisiens)** - *Tunis* *Tunisia*	*108* - -		**1972 Enrique Lorenzo y Cia SA — Vigo** Yd No: 358 Loa 23.22 Br ex - Dght 2.401 Lbp 22.03 Br md 6.41 Dpth 3.05 Welded, 1 dk	**(B32A2ST) Tug**	**1 oil engine** driving 1 FP propeller Total Power: 662kW (900hp) Baudouin DVX12SRJM 1 x Vee 4 Stroke 12 Cy. 185 x 200 662kW (900bhp) Societe des Moteurs Baudouin SA-France
7629623 *DUAC7* -	**TERRIER** *ex* Shinsei Maru *-1988* **Loadstar Shipping Co Inc** - *Manila* *Philippines* Official number: 00-0000571	**999** 545 2,601	Class: (NK)	**1975-02 Wakayama Zosen — Kainan** Yd No: 500 Loa 81.79 Br ex 11.61 Dght 5.284 Lbp 74.99 Br md 11.59 Dpth 7.12 Welded, 2 dks	**(A31A2GX) General Cargo Ship** Grain: 3,167; Bale: 2,860 Compartments: 2 Ho, ER 2 Ha: (14.4 x 8.0) (16.2 x 8.0)ER Derricks: 2x15t,1x10t	**1 oil engine** driving 1 FP propeller Total Power: 1,545kW (2,101hp) 12.0kn Hanshin 6LU38 1 x 4 Stroke 6 Cy. 380 x 580 1545kW (2101bhp) The Hanshin Diesel Works Ltd-Japan
6825036 *3FQZ9* -	**TERRIFIC** *ex* Hai Shun Oil *-1999* *ex* Kam Shum *-1999* *ex* Tong Mun *-1995* *ex* Koyo Maru No. 22 *-1992* **Terrific Shipping & Trading Co SA** - SatCom: Inmarsat M 635557410 *Panama* *Panama* MMSI: 357700000 Official number: 28347PEXT3	**1,149** 652 664		**1968-06 K.K. Taihei Kogyo — Akitsu** Yd No: 210 Converted From: Ro-Ro Cargo Ship-1998 Loa 76.94 Br ex 10.83 Dght 4.014 Lbp 66.10 Br md 10.80 Dpth 4.32 Welded, 1 dk	**(A13B2TU) Tanker (unspecified)**	**1 oil engine** driving 1 FP propeller Total Power: 1,103kW (1,500hp) 13.0kn Hanshin 6LU35 1 x 4 Stroke 6 Cy. 350 x 550 1103kW (1500bhp) Hanshin Nainenki Kogyo-Japan AuxGen: 1 x 64kW
7808217 *VM6058* -	**TERRITORY CHIEF** **Territory Chief Fishing Company Pty Ltd** - *Darwin, NT* *Australia* Official number: 355892	*117* 76 -		**1977 K Shipyard Construction Co — Fremantle WA** Yd No: 27 Loa 22.81 Br ex 6.68 Dght - Lbp 21.65 Br md 6.18 Dpth 2.19 Welded, 1 dk	**(B11B2FV) Fishing Vessel**	**1 oil engine** reduction geared to sc. shaft driving 1 FP propeller Total Power: 268kW (364hp) 9.5kn Caterpillar D343SCAC 1 x 4 Stroke 6 Cy. 137 x 165 268kW (364bhp) Caterpillar Tractor Co-USA
7909310 - -	**TERRITORY COMMANDER** **M G Kailis Pty Ltd** - *Fremantle, WA* *Australia* Official number: 355891	*117* 76 -		**1978-04 K Shipyard Construction Co — Fremantle WA** Loa 22.81 Br ex 6.53 Dght 3.101 Lbp 21.42 Br md 6.41 Dpth 3.51 Welded, 1 dk	**(B11A2FT) Trawler**	**1 oil engine** reduction geared to sc. shaft driving 1 FP propeller Total Power: 221kW (300hp) 9.5kn Caterpillar 3406T 1 x 4 Stroke 6 Cy. 137 x 165 221kW (300bhp) Caterpillar Tractor Co-USA
7437836 - -	**TERRITORY LEADER** **Australia Bay Seafoods Pty Ltd** - *Fremantle, WA* *Australia* Official number: 857105	*232* 73 -		**1975 K Shipyard Construction Co — Fremantle WA** Yd No: 18 Loa 23.47 Br ex 6.23 Dght 2.439 Lbp 22.97 Br md 6.10 Dpth 3.66 Welded, 1 dk	**(B11B2FV) Fishing Vessel**	**1 oil engine** driving 1 FP propeller Total Power: 302kW (411hp) M.T.U. 1 x 4 Stroke 6 Cy. 178 x 203 302kW (411bhp) MTU Friedrichshafen GmbH-Friedrichshafen
8222484 *VL6352* -	**TERRITORY PEARL** **A Raptis & Sons Pty Ltd** SatCom: Inmarsat C 450300284 *Darwin, NT* *Australia* Official number: 850695	*206* 62 111	Class: (NV)	**1983-08 North Arm Slipway Pty Ltd — Port Adelaide SA** Yd No: 10 Loa 27.65 Br ex 8.31 Dght 3.420 Lbp 25.00 Br md 8.11 Dpth 4.02 Welded, 1 dk	**(B11A2FT) Trawler** Ins: 128 Compartments: 1 Ho, ER 1 Ha: ER	**1 oil engine** with clutches & sr geared to sc. shaft driving 1 CP propeller Total Power: 441kW (600hp) G.M. (Detroit Diesel) 8V-149-TI 1 x Vee 2 Stroke 8 Cy. 146 x 146 441kW (600bhp) General Motors Detroit DieselAllison Divn-USA AuxGen: 2 x 105kW 415V 50Hz a.c
8812899 *YHZM* -	**TERRITORY TRADER** *ex* Multi Star *-2007* *ex* Unicorn Express *-2005* *ex* Southern Queen *-2001* *ex* CEC Thrust *-2000* *ex* Multiflex Thrust *-2000* *ex* Mint Thrust *-1999* *ex* Industrial Wave *-1999* *ex* Mint Thrust *-1998* *ex* Baltimar Boreas *-1995* **PT Meratus Line** - *Surabaya* *Indonesia* MMSI: 525025028	**2,826** 1,716 3,194	Class: KI LR ✠ **100A1** SS 04/2011 certified container securing arrangements ✠ **LMC** Eq.Ltr: S; Cable: 467.5/36.0 U3 (a)	**1991-04 Zhonghua Shipyard — Shanghai** Yd No: 8816 Loa 91.22 (BB) Br ex 15.06 Dght 5.000 Lbp 84.00 Br md 14.70 Dpth 7.60 Welded, 2 dks	**(A31A2GX) General Cargo Ship** Grain: 4,755 TEU 256 C.Ho 96/20' (40') C.Dk 160/20' (40') Compartments: 1 Ho, ER 1 Ha: (53.0 x 10.4)ER Cranes: 2x50t	**1 oil engine** driving 1 FP propeller Total Power: 1,692kW (2,300hp) 12.0kn B&W 4L35MC 1 x 2 Stroke 4 Cy. 350 x 1050 1692kW (2300bhp) Hudong Shipyard-China AuxGen: 3 x 188kW 390/225V 50Hz a.c Boilers: TOH New 10.2kgf/cm² (10.0bar) Fuel: 51.9 (d.f.) 225.7 (r.f.) 7.3pd
9169782 *9HJY8* -	**TERRY** *ex* Skledros *-2012* *ex* Murovdag *-2007* *ex* Murmansk *-2006* *launched as* Pochary *-1999* **Terry Shipping Corp** Halkidon Shipping Corp SatCom: Inmarsat C 425606510 *Valletta* *Malta* MMSI: 256065000 Official number: 9893	**10,321** 5,054 15,441 T/cm 29.0	Class: NV (RS)	**1999-10 Aker MTW Werft GmbH — Wismar** Yd No: 277 Loa 145.88 Br ex 22.53 Dght 8.700 Lbp 135.94 Br md 22.50 Dpth 11.25 Welded, 1 dk	**(A12B2TR) Chemical/Products Tanker** Double Hull (13F) Liq: 16,942; Liq (Oil): 16,947 Cargo Heating Coils Compartments: 7 Ta, 14 Wing Ta, 2 Wing Slop Ta, ER 3 Cargo Pump (s): 1x684m³/hr, 2x472m³/hr Manifold: Bow/CM: 81m Ice Capable	**1 oil engine** driving 1 CP propeller Total Power: 5,300kW (7,206hp) 14.4kn B&W 8S35MC 1 x 2 Stroke 8 Cy. 350 x 1400 5300kW (7206bhp) MAN B&W Diesel A/S-Denmark AuxGen: 3 x 670kW a.c Thrusters: 1 Tunnel thruster (f) Fuel: 50.0 (d.f.) 845.0 (r.f.)
9260744 *WDA5140* -	**TERRY BORDELON** **Bordelon Marine Inc** - *New Orleans, LA* *United States of America* MMSI: 366816910 Official number: 1111784	**435** 136 -		**2001-07 Bollinger Machine Shop & Shipyard, Inc. — Lockport, La** Yd No: 401 Loa 44.19 Br ex - Dght 3.016 Lbp 39.80 Br md 10.97 Dpth 3.50 Welded, 1 dk	**(B21A20S) Platform Supply Ship**	**2 oil engines** reduction geared to sc. shafts driving 2 FP propellers Total Power: 1,104kW (1,500hp) 12.0kn Cummins KTA-38-M0 2 x Vee 4 Stroke 12 Cy. 159 x 159 each-552kW (750bhp) Cummins Engine Co Inc-USA AuxGen: 2 x 60Hz a.c Thrusters: 1 Tunnel thruster (f)

IMO / Call sign	Name / Owner	Tonnage	Class	Build / Dimensions	Type	Machinery
7225295 *DUA6178* -	**TERRY D J** *ex* Choei Maru *-1991* **Irma Fishing & Trading Inc** - *Manila* *Philippines* Official number: MNLD001826	*432* 181 -		**1972 Nishii Dock Co. Ltd. — Ise** Yd No: 238 Loa 50.70 Br ex 8.13 Dght - Lbp 43.26 Br md 8.11 Dpth 3.56 Riveted\Welded, 1 dk	**(B11B2FV) Fishing Vessel**	**1 oil engine** driving 1 FP propeller Total Power: 736kW (1,001hp) Akasaka UHS27 1 x 4 Stroke 6 Cy. 270 x 420 736kW (1001bhp) Akasaka Tekkosho KK (Akasaka DieselLtd)-Japan
8127799 *CGTF* -	**TERRY FOX** **Government of Canada (Canadian Coast Guard)** - SatCom: Inmarsat C 431612220 *Vancouver, BC* *Canada* MMSI: 316122000 Official number: 803579	*4,233* 1,955 2,113	Class: (LR) ✠ Classed LR until 30/3/94	**1983-09 Burrard Yarrows Corp — North Vancouver BC** Yd No: 107 Converted From: Offshore Tug/Supply Ship-1994 Loa 88.02 Br ex 17.94 Dght 8.289 Lbp 75.39 Br md 17.51 Dpth 10.01 Welded, 1 dk	**(B34C2SI) Icebreaker** Liq: 102 Cranes: 1x5t Ice Capable	**4 oil engines** with clutches, flexible couplings & sr geared to sc. shafts driving 2 CP propellers Total Power: 16,176kW (21,992hp) 15.4kn Werkspoor 8TM410 4 x 4 Stroke 8 Cy. 410 x 470 each-4044kW (5498bhp) Stork Werkspoor Diesel BV-Netherlands AuxGen: 2 x 1000kW 460V 60Hz a.c, 2 x 750kW 460V 60Hz a.c Thrusters: 1 Thwart. CP thruster (a); 1 Water jet (f) Fuel: 1650.0 (d.f.)
7939418 *WDC2498* -	**TERRY LYNN** *ex* Lil Thomas *-2001* **Terry Lynn Inc** - *Magnolia Springs, AL* *United States of America* MMSI: 366993960 Official number: 601446	*142* 96 -		**1978 Marine Builders, Inc. — Mobile, Al** Yd No: 114 L reg 23.47 Br ex 6.81 Dght - Lbp - Br md - Dpth 3.41 Welded, 1 dk	**(B11B2FV) Fishing Vessel**	**1 oil engine** driving 1 FP propeller Total Power: 335kW (455hp)
7604154 - -	**TERRY & MARK** - -	*191* 130 -		**1974 at Pascagoula, Ms** L reg 24.30 Br ex - Dght - Lbp - Br md 7.32 Dpth 3.81 Welded	**(B11B2FV) Fishing Vessel**	**1 oil engine** driving 1 FP propeller Total Power: 368kW (500hp)
8802662 *PBVC* -	**TERSCHELLING** **Government of The Kingdom of The Netherlands (Rijkswaterstaat Directie Noordzee)** - *Terschelling* *Netherlands* MMSI: 245384000 Official number: 2460	**514** 154 -	Class: BV	**1988-10 Scheepswerf- en Reparatiebedrijf "Harlingen" B.V. — Harlingen** (Hull) Yd No: 81 **1988-10 B.V. Scheepswerf Damen — Gorinchem** Yd No: 8633 Loa 44.43 Br ex - Dght 3.100 Lbp 40.00 Br md 9.60 Dpth 5.00 Welded, 1 dk	**(B34Q2QB) Buoy Tender** Cranes: 1x10t Ice Capable	**2 diesel electric oil engines** driving 2 gen. each 1680kW Connecting to 2 elec. motors each (860kW) driving 2 CP propellers Total Power: 860kW (1,170hp) 11.0kn MAN 7L20/27 2 x 4 Stroke 7 Cy. 200 x 270 each-430kW (585bhp) Brons Industrie NV-Netherlands Thrusters: 1 Tunnel thruster (f)
8862973 *HO2450* -	**TERSCHELLING** **Nigel J Boston** - *Panama* *Panama* MMSI: 371306000 Official number: 3433308	**238** 71 -		**1964 N.V. Zaanlandse Scheepsbouw Mij. — Zaandam** Yd No: 500 Loa 40.56 Br ex 7.93 Dght 2.660 Lbp 38.00 Br md 7.90 Dpth 3.70 Welded	**(B34Q2QB) Buoy Tender**	**1 oil engine** driving 1 FP propeller Total Power: 480kW (653hp) 10.0kn Bolnes 1 x 2 Stroke 8 Cy. 480kW (653bhp) NV Machinefabriek 'Bolnes' v/h JHvan Cappellen-Netherlands
9313826 *PHBA* -	**TERSCHELLING** **Terschelling Shipping CV** Kustvaart Harlingen BV *Harlingen* *Netherlands* MMSI: 246507000 Official number: 42946	**3,990** 2,208 6,000	Class: BV	**2005-12 Scheepswerf Ferus Smit BV — Westerbroek** Yd No: 362 Loa 110.78 (BB) Br ex - Dght 6.090 Lbp 105.45 Br md 14.00 Dpth 8.13 Welded, 1 dk	**(A31A2GX) General Cargo Ship** Grain: 7,946; Bale: 7,946 TEU 252 C. Compartments: 2 Ho, ER 2 Ha: (50.8 x 11.5)ER (27.5 x 11.5) Ice Capable	**1 oil engine** geared to sc. shaft driving 1 CP propeller Total Power: 2,640kW (3,589hp) 13.0kn MaK 8M25 1 x 4 Stroke 8 Cy. 255 x 400 2640kW (3589bhp) Caterpillar Motoren GmbH & Co. KG-Germany AuxGen: 2 x 120kW 400/230V 50Hz a.c, 1 x 352kW 400/230V 50Hz a.c Thrusters: 1 Thwart. FP thruster (f) Fuel: 380.0 (r.f.) 10.0pd
7210109 - -	**TERSEN II** *ex* Ebisu Maru *-1983* - -	*499* 180 517		**1972 Usuki Iron Works Co Ltd — Usuki OT** Yd No: 821 Loa 60.76 Br ex 9.73 Dght 3.798 Lbp 54.01 Br md 9.71 Dpth 6.56 Welded, 2 dks	**(B11A2FT) Trawler**	**1 oil engine** driving 1 FP propeller Total Power: 1,545kW (2,101hp) Akasaka AH38 1 x 4 Stroke 6 Cy. 380 x 560 1545kW (2101bhp) Akasaka Tekkosho KK (Akasaka DieselLtd)-Japan
8137184 - -	**TERTIUS** - -	*148* 38 -		**1977 Evers-Werft — Niendorf/Ostsee** Yd No: 520 Loa 24.92 Br ex 7.04 Dght - Lbp 22.03 Br md 7.01 Dpth 3.10 Welded, 1 dk	**(B31A2SR) Research Survey Vessel**	**2 oil engines** reverse geared to sc. shafts driving 2 FP propellers Total Power: 242kW (330hp) MAN D2530MTE 2 x Vee 4 Stroke 10 Cy. 125 x 130 each-121kW (165bhp) Maschinenbau Augsburg Nuernberg (MAN)-Augsburg AuxGen: 1 x 70kW 220/380V a.c
8315554 *PGAN* -	**TERTNES** **CSL Pacific Shipping Ltd** CSL Australia Pty Ltd SatCom: Inmarsat C 424569610 *Rotterdam* *Netherlands* MMSI: 245696000 Official number: 35639	**7,857** 3,031 11,546	Class: NV	**1985-01 Kleven Mek Verksted AS — Ulsteinvik** Yd No: 92 Converted From: Bulk Cargo Carrier, Self-discharging -1992 Lengthened-1992 Loa 129.04 (BB) Br ex - Dght 8.680 Lbp 121.80 Br md 20.50 Dpth 11.60 Welded, 1 dk	**(B22K2OB) Pipe Burying Vessel** Passengers: berths: 46 Grain: 9,370 Compartments: 4 Ho, ER 4 Ha: 2 (14.7 x 10.0)2 (15.4 x 10.0)ER	**1 oil engine** with flexible couplings & reduction geared to sc. shaft driving 1 CP propeller Total Power: 2,795kW (3,800hp) 13.0kn Wartsila 8R32D 1 x 4 Stroke 8 Cy. 320 x 350 2795kW (3800bhp) Oy Wartsila Ab-Finland AuxGen: 2 x 290kW 440V 60Hz a.c Thrusters: 2 Thwart. CP thruster (f); 1 Thwart. CP thruster (a); 1 Thwart. CP thruster (a) Fuel: 181.1 (d.f.) 481.0 (r.f.)
8220943 *JJ3305* -	**TERU MARU No. 27** **KK Moricho Gumi** - *Minamiawaji, Hyogo* *Japan* Official number: 125205	*195* - -		**1982-03 Tajiri — Japan** Yd No: 115 Loa 30.80 Br ex - Dght - Lbp 27.72 Br md 8.62 Dpth 3.79 Welded, 1 dk	**(B32A2ST) Tug**	**2 oil engines** Geared Integral to driving 1 Propeller , 1 Z propeller Total Power: 1,912kW (2,600hp) Niigata 6M28AFTE 2 x 4 Stroke 6 Cy. 280 x 480 each-956kW (1300bhp) Niigata Engineering Co Ltd-Japan
7602869 *JJ3034* -	**TERU MARU No. 28** *ex* Hayaseto Maru *-1992* **KK Morinagagumi** - *Minamiawaji, Hyogo* *Japan* Official number: 118742	*188* - -		**1976-05 Kanagawa Zosen — Kobe** Yd No: 166 Loa 29.65 Br ex 8.64 Dght 2.693 Lbp 24.50 Br md 8.62 Dpth 3.81 Welded, 1 dk	**(B32A2ST) Tug**	**2 oil engines** Geared Integral to driving 2 Z propellers Total Power: 1,912kW (2,600hp) Niigata 6L25BX 2 x 4 Stroke 6 Cy. 250 x 320 each-956kW (1300bhp) Niigata Engineering Co Ltd-Japan
9027427 - -	**TERUBUK** **Government of The Republic of Indonesia (Direktorat Jenderal Perhubungan Darat - Ministry of Land Communications)** PT ASDP Indonesia Ferry (Persero) - Angkutan Sungai Danau & Penyeberangan *Jakarta* *Indonesia*	**322** 96 -	Class: KI	**1991-11 P.T. Najatim Dockyard — Surabaya** L reg 38.30 Br ex - Dght 1.800 Lbp 32.50 Br md 10.50 Dpth 2.90 Welded, 1 dk	**(A37B2PS) Passenger Ship** Bow ramp (centre) Stern ramp (centre)	**2 oil engines** geared to sc. shafts driving 2 Propellers Total Power: 780kW (1,060hp) 9.0kn Yanmar 6LAA-UTE 2 x 4 Stroke 6 Cy. 148 x 165 each-390kW (530bhp) Showa Precision Mchy. Co. Ltd.-Amagasaki
9027439 - -	**TERUBUK I** **Government of The Republic of Indonesia (Direktorat Jenderal Perhubungan Darat - Ministry of Land Communications)** PT ASDP Indonesia Ferry (Persero) - Angkutan Sungai Danau & Penyeberangan *Palembang* *Indonesia*	**399** 120 -	Class: KI	**2001-11 P.T. Dok & Perkapalan Kodja Bahari (Unit I) — Jakarta** L reg 40.00 Br ex - Dght 1.990 Lbp 34.50 Br md 10.50 Dpth 2.80 Welded, 1 dk	**(A36A2PR) Passenger/Ro-Ro Ship (Vehicles)** Bow ramp (centre) Stern ramp (centre)	**2 oil engines** geared to sc. shafts driving 2 Propellers Total Power: 736kW (1,000hp) 9.0kn Yanmar 6LAAM-UTE 2 x 4 Stroke 6 Cy. 148 x 165 each-368kW (500bhp) Yanmar Diesel Engine Co Ltd-Japan
8135382 - -	**TERUHO MARU** *ex* Tenho Maru *-1985* **Century Product Inc** - *Indonesia*	*168* - 413		**1982-09 Tokuoka Zosen K.K. — Naruto** Yd No: 110 Loa - Br ex - Dght 2.190 Lbp 40.01 Br md 8.01 Dpth 4.60 Welded, 1 dk	**(A31A2GX) General Cargo Ship**	**1 oil engine** driving 1 FP propeller Total Power: 368kW (500hp) Matsui ML624GHS 1 x 4 Stroke 6 Cy. 240 x 400 368kW (500bhp) Matsui Iron Works Co Ltd-Japan

IMO / Call sign	Name / Owner / Port	GT / NT / DWT	Class	Built / Dimensions	Type	Machinery
9611149 *JD3202* -	**TERUHO MARU NO. 22** **Teruei Kisen YK** - *Bizen, Okayama* *Japan* MMSI: 431002552 Official number: 141448	*498* - 1,595		**2011-04 Tokuoka Zosen K.K. — Naruto** Loa 76.00 Br ex - Dght 4.090 Lbp 70.20 Br md 12.00 Dpth 7.17 Welded, 1 dk	**(A31A2GX) General Cargo Ship**	**1 oil engine** driving 1 Propeller Total Power: 1,471kW (2,000hp) Hanshin 1 x 1471kW (2000bhp) The Hanshin Diesel Works Ltd-Japan
9049035 *YHJS* -	**TERUN NARNITU MTB EXPRESS** *ex* An Tian *-2004* **BUMD Kidabela-Kalwedo & PEMDA Maluku Tenggara Barat** - *Jakarta* *Indonesia*	**1,076** 323 -	Class: (KI)	**2002-01 Jiangsu Xinhua Shipyard Co Ltd — Nanjing JS** L reg 60.00 Br ex - Dght 3.000 Lbp 53.28 Br md 11.00 Dpth 4.50 Welded, 1 dk	**(A37B2PS) Passenger Ship**	**2 oil engines** geared to sc. shafts driving 2 Propellers Total Power: 2,126kW (2,890hp) Caterpillar 3512TA 2 x Vee 4 Stroke 12 Cy. 170 x 190 each-1063kW (1445bhp) Caterpillar Inc-USA
9334806 *YD3311* -	**TERUS DAYA 11** *ex* Marco Polo 227 *-2005* *launched as* Everlight 9 *-2005* **PT Mega Sumatera Lines** - *Tanjungpinang* *Indonesia*	**242** 73 -	Class: KI (GL) (BV)	**2004-12 Sterling Bay Shipbuilding Sdn Bhd — Sibu** Yd No: 005 Loa 27.00 Br ex - Dght 3.353 Lbp 24.98 Br md 8.52 Dpth 4.11 Welded, 1 dk	**(B32A2ST) Tug**	**2 oil engines** reduction geared to sc. shafts driving 2 Propellers Total Power: 1,516kW (2,062hp) Mitsubishi S6R2-MPTK2 2 x 4 Stroke 6 Cy. 170 x 220 each-758kW (1031bhp) (made 2004) Mitsubishi Heavy Industries Ltd-Japan AuxGen: 2 x 59kW 380/220V a.c
8738548 - -	**TERUS DAYA 17** **PT Pelayaran Teguh Persada Kencana** - *Batam* *Indonesia*	**259** 78 -	Class: KI	**2009-01 PT Bandar Abadi — Batam** Yd No: 017 Loa 28.05 Br ex - Dght 3.300 Lbp 26.07 Br md 8.60 Dpth 4.30 Welded, 1 dk	**(B32A2ST) Tug**	**2 oil engines** reduction geared to sc. shafts driving 2 Propellers Total Power: 1,516kW (2,062hp) Mitsubishi S6R2-MPTK3 2 x 4 Stroke 6 Cy. 170 x 220 each-758kW (1031bhp) Mitsubishi Heavy Industries Ltd-Japan AuxGen: 2 x 59kW 400V a.c
9574937 - -	**TERUS DAYA 19** **PT Asia Mega Lines** - *Batam* *Indonesia*	**259** 78 -	Class: KI	**2009-10 PT Bandar Abadi — Batam** Yd No: 025 Loa 28.05 Br ex — Dght 3.300 Lbp 26.07 Br md 8.60 Dpth 4.30 Welded, 1 dk	**(B32A2ST) Tug**	**2 oil engines** reduction geared to sc. shafts driving 2 Propellers Total Power: 912kW (1,240hp) Mitsubishi 2 x 4 Stroke each-456kW (620bhp) Mitsubishi Heavy Industries Ltd-Japan AuxGen: 2 x 129kW 380V a.c
9416343 *YD3371* -	**TERUS DAYA 21** **PT Pelayaran Sinar Gratia Nusantara** Eng Lee Shipping Co Pte Ltd *Tanjungpinang* *Indonesia* MMSI: 525004078 Official number: 5331L	**227** 69 -	Class: KI	**2006-09 PT Karya Teknik Utama — Batam** Yd No: 121 Loa 27.00 Br ex - Dght 3.000 Lbp 26.33 Br md 8.20 Dpth 4.10 Welded, 1 dk	**(B32A2ST) Tug**	**2 oil engines** reduction geared to sc. shafts driving 2 Propellers Total Power: 1,516kW (2,062hp) 10.0kn Mitsubishi S6R2-MPTK3L 2 x 4 Stroke 6 Cy. 170 x 220 each-758kW (1031bhp) Mitsubishi Heavy Industries Ltd-Japan AuxGen: 2 x 120kW 400V a.c
8737348 - -	**TERUS DAYA 23** **PT Pelayaran Sinar Gratia Nusantara** - *Batam* *Indonesia* MMSI: 525004045	**259** 78 -	Class: KI	**2009-03 PT Bandar Abadi — Batam** Yd No: 018 Loa 28.05 (BB) Br ex - Dght 3.300 Lbp 26.07 Br md 8.60 Dpth 4.30 Welded, 1 dk	**(B32A2ST) Tug**	**2 oil engines** driving 2 Propellers Total Power: 1,516kW (2,062hp) Mitsubishi S6R2-MTK3L 2 x 4 Stroke 6 Cy. 170 x 220 each-758kW (1031bhp) Mitsubishi Heavy Industries Ltd-Japan AuxGen: 2 x 56kW 380V a.c
9584073 - -	**TERUS DAYA 25** **PT Asia Mega Lines** - *Batam* *Indonesia*	**261** 78 -	Class: BV	**2010-06 PT Bandar Abadi — Batam** Yd No: 055 Loa 28.05 Br ex - Dght 3.300 Lbp 25.13 Br md 8.60 Dpth 4.30 Welded, 1 dk	**(B32A2ST) Tug**	**2 oil engines** reduction geared to sc. shafts driving 2 FP propellers Total Power: 1,518kW (2,064hp) Mitsubishi S6R2-MTK3L 2 x 4 Stroke 6 Cy. 170 x 220 each-759kW (1032bhp) Mitsubishi Heavy Industries Ltd-Japan AuxGen: 2 x 50kW 50Hz a.c
9574949 - -	**TERUS DAYA 27** **PT Pelayaran Sinar Gratia Nusantara** - *Batam* *Indonesia*	**254** 77 212	Class: KI	**2009-12 PT Bandar Abadi — Batam** Yd No: 032 Loa 28.00 Br ex — Dght 3.290 Lbp 26.07 Br md 8.60 Dpth 4.30 Welded, 1 dk	**(B32A2ST) Tug**	**2 oil engines** reduction geared to sc. shafts driving 2 Propellers Total Power: 1,518kW (2,064hp) Mitsubishi S6R2-MTK3L 2 x 4 Stroke 6 Cy. 170 x 220 each-759kW (1032bhp) Mitsubishi Heavy Industries Ltd-Japan AuxGen: 2 x 56kW 380V a.c
9584085 *YD3730* -	**TERUS DAYA 29** **PT Asia Mega Lines** - *Batam* *Indonesia*	**261** 78 -	Class: BV	**2010-06 PT Bandar Abadi — Batam** Yd No: 056 Loa 28.05 Br ex - Dght 3.300 Lbp 25.13 Br md 8.60 Dpth 4.30 Welded, 1 dk	**(B32A2ST) Tug**	**2 oil engines** reduction geared to sc. shafts driving 2 FP propellers Total Power: 1,518kW (2,064hp) Mitsubishi S6R2-MTK3L 2 x 4 Stroke 6 Cy. 170 x 220 each-759kW (1032bhp) Mitsubishi Heavy Industries Ltd-Japan AuxGen: 2 x 50kW 50Hz a.c Fuel: 150.0 (d.f.)
9655418 *YDA3099* -	**TERUS DAYA 31** **PT Pelayaran Asia Lestari Lines** - *Batam* *Indonesia* MMSI: 525020041 Official number: GT.254 No.3804/PPm	**254** 77 212	Class: BV	**2012-04 PT Bandar Abadi — Batam** Yd No: 112 Loa 28.05 Br ex - Dght 3.350 Lbp 25.13 Br md 8.60 Dpth 4.30 Welded, 1 dk	**(B32A2ST) Tug**	**2 oil engines** reduction geared to sc. shafts driving 2 FP propellers Total Power: 1,450kW (1,972hp) Chinese Std. Type 6190ZLC 2 x 4 Stroke 6 Cy. 190 x 210 each-725kW (986bhp) Jinan Diesel Engine Co Ltd-China Fuel: 150.0 (d.f.)
9618953 - -	**TERUS DAYA 33** **PT Pelayaran Asia Lestari Lines** - *Batam* *Indonesia*	**259** 78 212	Class: BV (Class contemplated) KI	**2011-05 PT Bandar Abadi — Batam** Yd No: 062 Loa 28.05 Br ex - Dght 3.350 Lbp 26.20 Br md 8.60 Dpth 4.30 Welded, 1 dk	**(B32A2ST) Tug**	**2 oil engines** reduction geared to sc. shafts driving 2 FP propellers Total Power: 1,500kW (2,040hp) Chinese Std. Type 12V190 2 x Vee 4 Stroke 12 Cy. 190 x 210 each-750kW (1020bhp) Jinan Diesel Engine Co Ltd-China AuxGen: 2 x 58kW 380V a.c
9656589 - -	**TERUS DAYA 35** **PT Pelayaran Asia Lestari Lines** - *Batam* *Indonesia* Official number: GT.254 NO. 3887/PPm	**254** 77 -	Class: BV	**2012-05 PT Bandar Abadi — Batam** Yd No: 128 Loa 28.05 Br ex - Dght 3.300 Lbp 25.13 Br md 8.60 Dpth 4.30 Welded, 1 dk	**(B32A2ST) Tug**	**2 oil engines** reduction geared to sc. shafts driving 2 FP propellers Total Power: 1,500kW (2,040hp) Chinese Std. Type 12V190 2 x Vee 4 Stroke 12 Cy. 190 x 210 each-750kW (1020bhp) Jinan Diesel Engine Co Ltd-China AuxGen: 2 x 40kW 50Hz a.c Fuel: 150.0 (d.f.)
9637208 - -	**TERUS DAYA 39** **PT Pelayaran Asia Lestari Lines** - *Batam* *Indonesia* Official number: GT.254 No. 3345/PPm	**254** 77 -	Class: BV	**2011-09 PT Bandar Abadi — Batam** Yd No: 082 Loa 28.05 Br ex - Dght 3.350 Lbp 25.13 Br md 8.60 Dpth 4.30 Welded, 1 dk	**(B32A2ST) Tug**	**2 oil engines** reduction geared to sc. shafts driving 2 FP propellers Total Power: 1,500kW (2,040hp) Chinese Std. Type 12V190 2 x Vee 4 Stroke 12 Cy. 190 x 210 each-750kW (1020bhp) Jinan Diesel Engine Co Ltd-China AuxGen: 2 x 50kW 50Hz a.c Fuel: 150.0 (d.f.)
9410117 *YD3868* -	**TERUS DAYA 47** *ex* Bintang Bahari *-2007* **PT Sinar Sumatera Lines** - *Batam* *Indonesia*	**256** 77 274	Class: KI (GL) (NK)	**2006-09 Berjaya Dockyard Sdn Bhd — Miri** Yd No: 32 Loa 28.09 Br ex 8.54 Dght 3.612 Lbp 25.47 Br md 8.53 Dpth 4.30 Welded, 1 dk	**(B32A2ST) Tug**	**2 oil engines** reduction geared to sc. shafts driving 2 FP propellers Total Power: 1,220kW (1,658hp) Mitsubishi S6R2-MPTK2 2 x 4 Stroke 6 Cy. 170 x 220 each-610kW (829bhp) Mitsubishi Heavy Industries Ltd-Japan AuxGen: 2 x 50kW 220V a.c Fuel: 250.0 (r.f.)

IMO / Call sign	Name / Owner / Port	Tonnage	Class	Build	Type	Machinery
9645994 - -	**TERUS DAYA 51** **PT Pelayaran Asia Lestari Lines** - *Batam* *Indonesia* Official number: GT.254 No. 3471/PPm	**254** 77 195	Class: BV	**2011-11 in Indonesia** (Hull) Yd No: (083) **2011-11 PT Bandar Abadi — Batam** Yd No: 083 Loa 28.05 Br ex - Dght 3.350 Lbp 25.13 Br md 8.60 Dpth 4.30 Welded, 1 dk	**(B32A2ST) Tug**	**2 oil engines** reduction geared to sc. shafts driving 2 FP propellers Total Power: 1,516kW (2,062hp) Chinese Std. Type 12V190 2 x Vee 4 Stroke 12 Cy. 190 x 210 each-758kW (1031bhp) Jinan Diesel Engine Co Ltd-China AuxGen: 2 x 50kW 50Hz a.c Fuel: 148.0 (d.f.)
9664847 - -	**TERUS DAYA 53** **PT Pelayaran Teguh Persada Kencana** - *Batam* *Indonesia* Official number: GT.254 NO.4131/PPM	**254** 77 -	Class: BV	**2012-06 PT Bandar Abadi — Batam** Yd No: 141 Loa 28.05 Br ex - Dght 3.300 Lbp 25.13 Br md 8.60 Dpth 4.30 Welded, 1 dk	**(B32A2ST) Tug**	**2 oil engines** reduction geared to sc. shafts driving 2 FP propellers Total Power: 1,500kW (2,040hp) Chinese Std. Type 12V190 2 x Vee 4 Stroke 12 Cy. 190 x 210 each-750kW (1020bhp) Jinan Diesel Engine Co Ltd-China AuxGen: 2 x 50kW 50Hz a.c Fuel: 150.0 (d.f.)
9669677 - -	**TERUS DAYA 55** **PT Asia Mega Lines** - *Batam* *Indonesia*	**254** 77 -	Class: BV	**2012-09 PT Bandar Abadi — Batam** Yd No: 142 Loa 28.05 Br ex - Dght 3.300 Lbp 25.13 Br md 8.60 Dpth 4.30 Welded, 1 dk	**(B32A2ST) Tug**	**2 oil engines** reduction geared to sc. shafts driving 2 FP propellers Total Power: 1,500kW (2,040hp) Chinese Std. Type 12V190 2 x Vee 4 Stroke 12 Cy. 190 x 210 each-750kW (1020bhp) Jinan Diesel Engine Co Ltd-China AuxGen: 2 x 40kW 50Hz a.c Fuel: 150.0 (d.f.)
9687825 - -	**TERUS DAYA 57** **PT Sinar Sumatera Lines** - *Batam* *Indonesia* Official number: GT185No4905/PPm	**254** 77 -	Class: BV	**2013-01 PT Bandar Abadi — Batam** Yd No: 182 Loa 28.05 Br ex - Dght 3.300 Lbp 25.13 Br md 8.60 Dpth 4.30 Welded, 1 dk	**(B32A2ST) Tug**	**2 oil engines** reduction geared to sc. shafts driving 2 FP propellers Total Power: 1,544kW (2,100hp) Mitsubishi S12A2-MPTK 2 x Vee 4 Stroke 12 Cy. 150 x 160 each-772kW (1050bhp) Mitsubishi Heavy Industries Ltd-Japan AuxGen: 2 x 40kW 50Hz a.c Fuel: 150.0 (d.f.)
8659560 *YDA4946* -	**TERUS JAYA** **PT Victoria Internusa Perkasa** - *Tanjung Priok* *Indonesia*	**201** 61 -	Class: KI	**2011-10 PT Mangkupalas Mitra Makmur — Samarinda** Loa 27.00 Br ex - Dght - Lbp 25.39 Br md 8.00 Dpth 3.60 Welded, 1 dk	**(B32A2ST) Tug**	**2 oil engines** reduction geared to sc. shafts driving 2 FP propellers Total Power: 1,220kW (1,658hp) Mitsubishi S6R2-MPTK 2 x 4 Stroke 6 Cy. 170 x 220 each-610kW (829bhp) Mitsubishi Heavy Industries Ltd-Japan AuxGen: 2 x 40kW 400V a.c
9204348 *3FGZ9*	**TERVE** *ex* Balsa 71 *-2012* **Gulka Shipping & Trading Co** TGS Shipping Services Ltd SatCom: Inmarsat C 435735110 *Panama* *Panama* MMSI: 357351000 Official number: 2639499CH	**4,362** 2,492 6,687	Class: NK	**1999-03 Sasebo Heavy Industries Co. Ltd. — Sasebo Yard, Sasebo** Yd No: 457 Loa 105.50 Br ex - Dght 6.916 Lbp 99.00 Br md 16.80 Dpth 8.80 Welded, 1 dk	**(A31A2GX) General Cargo Ship** Grain: 8,838; Bale: 8,193 Compartments: 3 Ho, ER 3 Ha: (15.4 x 8.4)2 (17.5 x 9.8)ER Cranes: 2x15.5t,1x15t	**1 oil engine** driving 1 FP propeller Total Power: 2,795kW (3,800hp) 12.5kn B&W 5L35MC 1 x 2 Stroke 5 Cy. 350 x 1050 2795kW (3800bhp) Mitsui Engineering & Shipbuilding CLtd-Japan Fuel: 430.0
9038866 *3FMP3*	**TESEO** **Venfleet Ltd** Bernhard Schulte Shipmanagement (Cyprus) Ltd SatCom: Inmarsat C 435233210 *Panama* *Panama* MMSI: 352332000 Official number: 2098193F	**54,827** 29,295 99,477 T/cm 99.5	Class: BV (AB)	**1993-07 Hyundai Heavy Industries Co Ltd — Ulsan** Yd No: 794 Loa 243.97 (BB) Br ex 45.68 Dght 11.580 Lbp 235.00 Br md 45.64 Dpth 18.40 Welded, 1 dk	**(A13A2TW) Crude/Oil Products Tanker** Double Hull (13F) Liq: 106,200; Liq (Oil): 106,200 Cargo Heating Coils Compartments: 8 Ta, ER 3 Cargo Pump (s): 3x2500m³/hr Manifold: Bow/CM: 121m	**1 oil engine** driving 1 FP propeller Total Power: 15,403kW (20,942hp) 16.0kn B&W 6S70MC 1 x 2 Stroke 6 Cy. 700 x 2674 15403kW (20942bhp) Hyundai Heavy Industries Co Ltd-South Korea AuxGen: 3 x 750kW 440V 60Hz a.c
6519041 *IPAX* -	**TESEO** *ex* Dalsfjord *-1994* **Medmar Navi SpA** *Naples* *Italy* MMSI: 247071700 Official number: 3836	*319* 141 -	Class: RI (NV)	**1965-06 Hasund Smie & Sveiseverk AS — Ulsteinvik** (Hull) Yd No: 2 **1965-06 Hatlo Verksted AS — Ulsteinvik** Yd No: 27 Loa 39.53 Br ex 10.11 Dght 2.909 Lbp 35.97 Br md 10.09 Dpth 3.81 Welded, 1 dk	**(A36A2PR) Passenger/Ro-Ro Ship (Vehicles)** Passengers: unberthed: 250 Lane-Len: 120 Cars: 29, Trailers: 2	**2 oil engines** driving 2 CP propellers Total Power: 588kW (800hp) 11.2kn Wichmann 4ACA 2 x 2 Stroke 4 Cy. 280 x 420 each-294kW (400bhp) (new engine 1970) Wichmann Motorfabrikk AS-Norway
7824704 *IPWJ*	**TESEO PRIMO** *ex* Teseo *-2001* *ex* Ecate *-2000* *ex* Marianna Asaro *-1998* *ex* Segugio *-1991* **Giacalone Vito, Matteo e Antonino** *Mazara del Vallo* *Italy* Official number: 314	**186** 55 -	Class: (RI)	**1981-01 Cant. Nav. M. Morini & C. — Ancona** Yd No: 169 Loa 32.67 Br ex 7.04 Dght 3.114 Lbp 25.28 Br md 7.01 Dpth 3.66 Welded, 1 dk	**(B11A2FS) Stern Trawler**	**1 oil engine** reverse reduction geared to sc. shaft driving 1 FP propeller Total Power: 736kW (1,001hp) MaK 6M331AK 1 x 4 Stroke 6 Cy. 240 x 330 736kW (1001bhp) Krupp MaK Maschinenbau GmbH-Kiel
9081526 *UDBO*	**TESEY** **Okeanrybflot JSC (A/O 'Okeanrybflot')** *Petropavlovsk-Kamchatskiy* *Russia* MMSI: 273846410 Official number: 920055	**683** 233 529	Class: (RS)	**1992-11 Khabarovskiy Sudostroitelnyy Zavod im Kirova — Khabarovsk** Yd No: 890 Loa 54.99 Br ex 9.49 Dght 4.460 Lbp 50.44 Br md 9.30 Dpth 5.16 Welded	**(B12B2FC) Fish Carrier** Ice Capable	**1 oil engine** driving 1 FP propeller Total Power: 588kW (799hp) 11.3kn S.K.L. 6NVD48A-2U 1 x 4 Stroke 6 Cy. 320 x 480 588kW (799bhp) SKL Motoren u. Systemtechnik AG-Magdeburg
9112404 *JGVJ* -	**TESHIO** **Government of Japan (Ministry of Land, Infrastructure & Transport) (The Coastguard)** - *Tokyo* *Japan* MMSI: 431800056 Official number: 135193	*563* - 500		**1995-10 Nippon Kokan KK (NKK Corp) — Yokohama KN (Tsurumi Shipyard)** Yd No: 1062 Loa 54.88 Br ex - Dght - Lbp 48.00 Br md 10.20 Dpth 5.00 Welded, 1 dk	**(B34H2SQ) Patrol Vessel** Ice Capable	**2 oil engines** reduction geared to sc. shafts driving 2 CP propellers Total Power: 2,648kW (3,600hp) 14.5kn Niigata 6MG25HX 2 x 4 Stroke 6 Cy. 250 x 350 each-1324kW (1800bhp) Niigata Engineering Co Ltd-Japan AuxGen: 2 x 160kW a.c, 2 x 100kW a.c Fuel: 54.0 (d.f.) 9.8pd
9004889 *LW9896*	**TESON** **Sallustro, Cicciotti, Ritorno** - SatCom: Inmarsat C 470113210 *Buenos Aires* *Argentina* MMSI: 701000534 Official number: 01541	*136* 71 20	Class: (RI)	**1990-11 Ast. Naval Federico Contessi y Cia. S.A. — Mar del Plata** Yd No: 59 Loa 26.50 Br ex - Dght 3.000 Lbp 24.85 Br md 7.00 Dpth 3.45 Welded	**(B11B2FV) Fishing Vessel**	**1 oil engine** geared to sc. shaft driving 1 FP propeller Total Power: 584kW (794hp) 8.5kn Caterpillar 3508TA 1 x Vee 4 Stroke 8 Cy. 170 x 190 584kW (794bhp) Caterpillar Inc-USA
9575436 *3FUU8*	**TESORO** **Glomax Shipping SA** Samsun Logix Corp *Panama* *Panama* MMSI: 371669000 Official number: 4214510	**20,939** 11,800 32,631	Class: KR (AB)	**2010-09 Liaoning Hongguan Ship Industry Co Ltd — Panjin LN** Yd No: HG802 Loa 179.90 (BB) Br ex - Dght 10.168 Lbp 171.50 Br md 28.40 Dpth 14.10 Welded, 1 dk	**(A21A2BC) Bulk Carrier** Grain: 43,679 Compartments: 5 Ho, ER 5 Ha: 3 (20.0 x 19.2) (18.4 x 19.2)ER (14.4 x 17.6) Cranes: 4x30.5t	**1 oil engine** driving 1 FP propeller Total Power: 6,480kW (8,810hp) 13.7kn MAN-B&W 6S42MC 1 x 2 Stroke 6 Cy. 420 x 1764 6480kW (8810bhp) STX Engine Co Ltd-South Korea AuxGen: 3 x 465kW a.c Fuel: 163.0 (d.f.) 1645.0 (r.f.)
7918177 - -	**TESORO 168** *ex* Chien Chang No. 66 *-2000* *ex* Zuisho Maru No. 8 *-2000* *ex* Daikatsu Maru No. 7 *-1994* *ex* Yamato Maru No. 1 *-1988* - -	**492** 181 -		**1979-11 Goriki Zosensho — Ise** Yd No: 826 L reg 47.09 Br ex - Dght 3.101 Lbp 40.70 Br md 8.01 Dpth 3.46 Welded, 1 dk	**(B11B2FV) Fishing Vessel** Ins: 302	**1 oil engine** driving 1 FP propeller Total Power: 736kW (1,001hp) 12.8kn Niigata 6M28ZG 1 x 4 Stroke 6 Cy. 280 x 440 736kW (1001bhp) Niigata Engineering Co Ltd-Japan

IMO / Call sign	Name / Owner	Tonnage	Class	Builder / Dimensions	Type / Cargo	Machinery
8913564 *V4VP2* -	**TESS** *ex* Eagle Bay *-2013* *ex* Angel No. 61 *-2012* *ex* Dominique *-2011* *ex* Spotless *-2011* *ex* Arbat *-2004* **Agile Maritime Services Corp** Lissome Marine Services LLC *Basseterre* *St Kitts & Nevis* MMSI: 341681000 Official number: SKN 1002589	**28,223** 13,568 47,084 T/cm 52.0	Class: NV (LR) Classed LR until 7/11/11	**1991-04 Halla Engineering & Heavy Industries Ltd — Incheon** Yd No: 171 Loa 183.20 (BB) Br ex 32.36 Dght 12.210 Lbp 174.00 Br md 32.20 Dpth 18.00 Welded, 1 dk	**(A13A2TW) Crude/Oil Products Tanker** Double Hull (13F) Liq: 54,079; Liq (Oil): 54,079 Cargo Heating Coils Compartments: 8 Ta, 2 Wing Slop Ta, ER 8 Cargo Pump (s): 8x850m^3/hr Manifold: Bow/CM: 92.9m	**1 oil engine** driving 1 FP propeller Total Power: 7,466kW (10,151hp) 14.0kn B&W 6S50MC 1 x 2 Stroke 6 Cy. 500 x 1910 7466kW (10151bhp) Hyundai Heavy Industries Co Ltd-South Korea Fuel: 178.3 (d.f.) (Heating Coils) 1404.8 (r.f.)
9423255 *2ECK6* -	**TESS BULKER** **Lauritzen Bulkers A/S** J Lauritzen Singapore Pte Ltd *Douglas* *Isle of Man (British)* MMSI: 235083944 Official number: 742809	**32,309** 19,458 57,991 T/cm 57.4	Class: NK	**2011-02 Tsuneishi Heavy Industries (Cebu) Inc — Balamban** Yd No: SC-130 Loa 189.99 (BB) Br ex - Dght 12.830 Lbp 185.60 Br md 32.26 Dpth 18.00 Welded, 1 dk	**(A21A2BC) Bulk Carrier** Grain: 72,690; Bale: 70,122 Compartments: 5 Ho, ER 5 Ha: ER Cranes: 4x30t	**1 oil engine** driving 1 FP propeller Total Power: 8,400kW (11,421hp) 14.5kn MAN-B&W 6S50MC-C 1 x 2 Stroke 6 Cy. 500 x 2000 8400kW (11421bhp) Mitsui Engineering & Shipbuilding CLtd-Japan Fuel: 2388.0 (r.f.)
9290799 *A8SD3* -	**TESSA** *ex* MSC Egypt *-2010* *ex* Chillan *-2006* **ms 'Tessa' Schiffahrtsgesellschaft mbH & Co KG** Peter Doehle Schiffahrts-KG *Monrovia* *Liberia* MMSI: 636091739 Official number: 91739	**66,280** 36,284 68,228	Class: LR ✠ **100A1** SS 05/2010 container ship *IWS LI **ShipRight** (SDA, FDA, CM) ✠ **LMC** **UMS** Eq.Ltr: X†; Cable: 742.5/97.0 U3 (a)	**2005-05 China Shipbuilding Corp (CSBC) — Kaohsiung** Yd No: 825 Loa 275.80 (BB) Br ex 40.10 Dght 14.023 Lbp 263.80 Br md 40.00 Dpth 24.20 Welded, 1 dk	**(A33A2CC) Container Ship (Fully Cellular)** TEU 5527 C Ho 2601 TEU C Dk 2926 TEU incl 500 ref C. Compartments: 7 Cell Ho, ER 7 Ha: ER	**1 oil engine** driving 1 FP propeller Total Power: 54,926kW (74,677hp) 25.6kn Sulzer 10RTA96C 1 x 2 Stroke 10 Cy. 960 x 2500 54926kW (74677bhp) Doosan Engine Co Ltd-South Korea AuxGen: 4 x 1980kW 450/230V 60Hz a.c Boilers: e (ex.g.) 12.2kgf/cm^2 (12.0bar), WTAuxB (o.f.) 8.2kgf/cm^2 (8.0bar) Thrusters: 1 Thwart. CP thruster (f)
7628447 *XUJD9* -	**TESSA** *ex* Stingray *-2007* *ex* Eleonora *-2006* *ex* Emerald *-2005* *ex* Emeralda *-2004* *ex* Solhav *-1999* *ex* Emerald *-1999* **Whitley Management Corp** Inter-Trans Co Ltd *Phnom Penh* *Cambodia* MMSI: 515847000 Official number: 0578109	**2,795** 1,434 4,300	Class: (LR) (RS) ✠ Classed LR until 21/5/03	**1978-04 Clelands Shipbuilding Co. Ltd — Wallsend** Yd No: 339 Loa 91.27 Br ex 14.58 Dght 5.449 Lbp 84.31 Br md 14.51 Dpth 7.78 Welded, 2 dks	**(A31A2GX) General Cargo Ship** Grain: 4,983; Bale: 4,616 Compartments: 2 Ho, ER, 2 Tw Dk 2 Ha: (24.9 x 10.9) (25.6 x 10.9)ER Ice Capable	**1 oil engine** with flexible couplings & sr gearedto sc. shaft driving 1 CP propeller Total Power: 2,427kW (3,300hp) 14.0kn Mirrlees KMR-6 1 x 4 Stroke 6 Cy. 381 x 457 2427kW (3300bhp) Mirrlees Blackstone (Stockport)Ltd.-Stockport AuxGen: 1 x 220kW 440V 60Hz a.c, 2 x 165kW 440V 60Hz a.c Boilers: TOH (o.f.) 8.1kgf/cm^2 (7.9bar) Thrusters: 1 Thwart. FP thruster (f)
5305235 - -	**TESSA KATHLEEN** *ex* Saguenay *-1990* - -	*429* 253 122	Class: (LR) ✠ Classed LR until 8/5/81	**1958-05 Davie Shipbuilding Ltd — Levis QC** Yd No: 618 Loa 45.90 Br ex 11.49 Dght 2.718 Lbp 40.70 Br md 11.28 Dpth 4.40 Welded, 1 dk	**(A36A2PR) Passenger/Ro-Ro Ship (Vehicles)** Passengers: unberthed: 200 Ice Capable	**2 oil engines** with hydraulic coupling driving 2 CP propellers 1 fwd and 1 aft Total Power: 500kW (680hp) 9.0kn Alpha 404-24VO 2 x 2 Stroke 4 Cy. 240 x 400 each-250kW (340bhp) A/S Burmeister & Wain's Maskin ogSkibsbyggeri-Denmark AuxGen: 2 x 8kW 120V 60Hz a.c
9160487 *MCRC4* -	**TESSA KOSAN** **Lauritzen Kosan Ship Owners A/S** Lauritzen Kosan A/S *Douglas* *Isle of Man (British)* MMSI: 235006740 Official number: 726379	**5,103** 1,623 6,049 T/cm 16.0	Class: BV	**1999-01 Hyundai Heavy Industries Co Ltd — Ulsan** Yd No: HP90 Loa 112.56 (BB) Br ex 16.02 Dght 7.224 Lbp 105.36 Br md 16.00 Dpth 8.25 Welded, 1 dk	**(A11B2TG) LPG Tanker** Double Sides Entire Compartment Length Liq (Gas): 5,777 2 x Gas Tank (s); 2 independent (C.mn.stl) cyl horizontal 3 Cargo Pump (s): 2x450m^3/hr, 1x300m^3/hr Manifold: Bow/CM: 58.9m Ice Capable	**1 oil engine** reduction geared to sc. shaft driving 1 FP propeller Total Power: 4,500kW (6,118hp) 16.0kn MaK 6M552C 1 x 4 Stroke 6 Cy. 450 x 520 4500kW (6118bhp) MaK Motoren GmbH & Co. KG-Kiel AuxGen: 3 x 360kW 440/220V 60Hz a.c, 1 x 700kW 440/220V 60Hz a.c Thrusters: 1 Tunnel thruster (f) Fuel: 113.0 (d.f.) 604.0 (r.f.)
9268265 *MJBU6* -	**TESSA PG** *ex* Evanne *-2005* *launched as* Irem Kalkavan *-2004* **Partrederiet Tessa PG DA** Pritchard-Gordon Tankers Ltd *Douglas* *Isle of Man (British)* MMSI: 235009020 Official number: 737516	**4,666** 2,233 7,010 T/cm 16.7	Class: LR (BV) **100A1** SS 03/2010 Double Hull oil & chemical tanker ESP *IWS LI Ice Class 1C at draught of 6.80m Max/min draught fwd 6.8/3.1m Max/min draught aft 6.8/4.7m Required power 1771kw, installed power 3840kw **LMC** **UMS** Cable: 385.0/50.0 U2 (a)	**2005-03 Sedef Gemi Endustrisi A.S. — Tuzla** Yd No: 127 Converted From: Products Tanker-2008 Converted From: Chemical/Products Tanker-2007 Loa 119.60 (BB) Br ex - Dght 6.720 Lbp 106.30 Br md 16.90 Dpth 8.40 Welded, 1 dk	**(A12B2TR) Chemical/Products Tanker** Double Hull (13F) Liq: 7,709; Liq (Oil): 7,709 Cargo Heating Coils Compartments: 14 Wing Ta, 1 Slop Ta, ER 14 Cargo Pump (s): 14x200m^3/hr Manifold: Bow/CM: 64.7m Ice Capable	**1 oil engine** reduction geared to sc. shaft driving 1 CP propeller Total Power: 3,840kW (5,221hp) 14.5kn MaK 8M32C 1 x 4 Stroke 8 Cy. 320 x 480 3840kW (5221bhp) Caterpillar Motoren GmbH & Co. KG-Germany AuxGen: 1 x 1140kW 400/230V 50Hz a.c, 3 x 420kW 400/230V 50Hz a.c Boilers: sg (o.f.) 4.1kgf/cm^2 (4.0bar), TOH (o.f.) 10.2kgf/cm^2 (10.0bar), TOH (ex.g.) 10.2kgf/cm^2 (10.0bar) Thrusters: 1 Tunnel thruster (f) Fuel: 64.0 (d.f.) 346.0 (r.f.)
9503794 *PHNC* -	**TESSA W** **Stemat BV** - *Rotterdam* *Netherlands* MMSI: 245154000 Official number: 50908	**213** 63 -	Class: BV	**2008-03 Neptune Shipyards BV — Aalst (Nl)** Yd No: 307 Loa 25.10 Br ex - Dght 2.400 Lbp - Br md 9.90 Dpth 3.50 Welded, 1 dk	**(B34T2QR) Work/Repair Vessel** Cranes: 1x10t	**2 oil engines** reduction geared to sc. shafts driving 2 Propellers Total Power: 1,492kW (2,028hp) 10.0kn Caterpillar 3508B 2 x Vee 4 Stroke 8 Cy. 170 x 190 each-746kW (1014bhp) Caterpillar Inc-USA AuxGen: 2 x 144kW a.c Thrusters: 1 Directional thruster (f) Fuel: 79.1 (d.f.)
7205465 *7TEL* -	**TESSALA II** *ex* Soummam-1 *-1989* **Societe des Travaux Maritimes de l'Ouest (SOTRAMO)** - *Alger* *Algeria*	*235* - -	Class: (BV)	**1971 Towa Zosen K.K. — Shimonoseki** Yd No: 394 Loa 32.31 Br ex 8.44 Dght 3.201 Lbp 29.01 Br md 8.41 Dpth 4.02 Welded, 1 dk	**(B32A2ST) Tug**	**2 oil engines** driving 2 CP propellers Total Power: 1,472kW (2,002hp) 12.9kn Pielstick 8PA4V185 2 x Vee 4 Stroke 8 Cy. 185 x 210 each-736kW (1001bhp) Chantiers de l'Atlantique-France AuxGen: 2 x 70kW 220/380V 50Hz a.c Fuel: 69.0 (d.f.)
9105061 *3FZM4* -	**TESSALINA** *ex* Voyager 1 *-2012* *ex* Taman *-2010* **Octavia Shipping Company SA** - *Panama* *Panama* MMSI: 373995000 Official number: 43854PEXT	**26,218** 11,273 40,727 T/cm 51.3	Class: (LR) (BV) ✠ Classed LR until 7/3/12	**1996-02 'Uljanik' Brodogradiliste dd — Pula** Yd No: 414 Loa 181.00 (BB) Br ex 32.03 Dght 11.017 Lbp 173.80 Br md 32.00 Dpth 17.00 Welded, 1 dk	**(A12B2TR) Chemical/Products Tanker** Double Hull (13F) Liq: 49,168; Liq (Oil): 49,168 Cargo Heating Coils Compartments: 10 Wing Ta, 2 Wing Slop Ta, ER 10 Cargo Pump (s): 10x550m^3/hr Manifold: Bow/CM: 90.4m	**1 oil engine** driving 1 FP propeller Total Power: 8,310kW (11,298hp) 14.8kn B&W 6S50MC 1 x 2 Stroke 6 Cy. 500 x 1910 8310kW (11298bhp) 'Uljanik' Strojogradnja dd-Croatia AuxGen: 3 x 1080kW 450V 60Hz a.c Boilers: e (ex.g.) 10.2kgf/cm^2 (10.0bar), AuxB (o.f.) 10.2kgf/cm^2 (10.0bar) Fuel: 146.0 (d.f.) 1599.0 (r.f.)
9572549 *JD3071* -	**TESSHO MARU** **Nittetsu Butsuryu KK** - *Tokyo* *Japan* Official number: 141251	*499* - 1,670		**2010-04 Yamanaka Zosen K.K. — Imabari** Yd No: 788 Loa 76.23 Br ex - Dght 4.060 Lbp 70.00 Br md 12.00 Dpth 7.01 Welded, 1 dk	**(A31A2GX) General Cargo Ship** Grain: 2,814; Bale: 2,778 1 Ha: ER (40.0 x 9.5)	**1 oil engine** driving 1 FP propeller Total Power: 1,618kW (2,200hp) Hanshin LA32G 1 x 4 Stroke 6 Cy. 320 x 680 1618kW (2200bhp) The Hanshin Diesel Works Ltd-Japan
8835413 *ZACF* -	**TESSTA ROSSA** *ex* Rajfi G *-2006* *ex* Dario 1 *-2002* *ex* Regi *-2000* *ex* Kapiten Ahmet Luli *-1998* - - *Durres* *Albania* MMSI: 201100035 Official number: P-450	*438* 181 500		**1983 Kantieri Detar "Durres" — Durres** Loa 46.13 Br ex - Dght 2.680 Lbp - Br md 8.00 Dpth 3.10 Welded, 1 dk	**(A31A2GX) General Cargo Ship**	**1 oil engine** driving 1 FP propeller Total Power: 425kW (578hp) S.K.L. 8NVD36A-1U 1 x 4 Stroke 8 Cy. 240 x 360 425kW (578bhp) VEB Schwermaschinenbau "KarlLiebknecht" (SKL)-Magdeburg
7917721 *J7AK3* -	**TESSY T** *ex* Truckee River *-2012* **Riverman Nigeria Ltd** - *Portsmouth* *Dominica* MMSI: 325310000 Official number: 50310	**666** 199 750	Class: (AB)	**1980-09 Halter Marine, Inc. — Lockport, La** Yd No: 857 Loa - Br ex - Dght 3.658 Lbp 54.87 Br md 12.20 Dpth 4.27 Welded, 1 dk	**(B21A2OS) Platform Supply Ship**	**2 oil engines** reverse reduction geared to sc. shafts driving 2 FP propellers Total Power: 1,368kW (1,860hp) 12.0kn G.M. (Detroit Diesel) 16V-149 2 x Vee 2 Stroke 16 Cy. 146 x 146 each-684kW (930bhp) General Motors Detroit DieselAllison Divn-USA AuxGen: 2 x 75kW Thrusters: 1 Thwart. FP thruster (f)

8963038 *FIWV* SB 899633	**TESTA ROSSA** *ex* Ange des Mers *-2005* **Armement AEF Sarl** - *Saint-Brieuc* *France* MMSI: 227143500 Official number: 899833	**133** 39 -		**2000-08 SOCARENAM — Boulogne** Yd No: 178 Loa 21.00 Br ex - Dght 3.198 Lbp 19.76 Br md 7.20 Dpth 3.60 Welded, 1 dk	**(B11B2FV) Fishing Vessel** Compartments: 1 Ho 2 Ha:	**1 oil engine** with clutches, flexible couplings & sr geared to sc. shaft driving 1 CP propeller Total Power: 316kW (430hp) Cummins 1 x 4 Stroke 316kW (430bhp) Cummins Engine Co Inc-USA Thrusters: 1 Thwart. FP thruster (f)
8323989 *YHRX* -	**TETAP JAYA** *ex* Daisei *-2005* *ex* Daisei Maru *-2003* **PT Pelayaran Internusa Bahari Persada** - *Surabaya* *Indonesia*	**1,254** 486 1,600	Class: KI	**1984-06 K.K. Miura Zosensho — Saiki** Yd No: 687 Loa 72.00 Br ex - Dght 4.201 Lbp 67.01 Br md 11.51 Dpth 6.40 Welded, 1 dk	**(A31A2GX) General Cargo Ship**	**1 oil engine** geared to sc. shaft driving 1 FP propeller Total Power: 956kW (1,300hp) 10.0kn Niigata 6M28AET 1 x 4 Stroke 6 Cy. 280 x 480 956kW (1300bhp) Niigata Engineering Co Ltd-Japan
7821764 *HOTV* -	**TETAUU** *ex* Crane South *-1995* *ex* Hikari Maru No. 5 *-1990* **Coam Trading Overseas Co Ltd SA** Coam Co Ltd *Panama* *Panama* MMSI: 354460000 Official number: 30388PEXT1	**1,967** 944 3,048	Class: (NK)	**1979-02 Naikai Shipbuilding & Engineering Co Ltd — Onomichi HS (Taguma Shipyard)** Yd No: 440 Loa 82.44 Br ex 13.24 Dght 5.974 Lbp 75.00 Br md 13.20 Dpth 6.60 Riveted\Welded, 1 dk	**(A13B2TP) Products Tanker** Liq: 3,437; Liq (Oil): 3,437	**2 oil engines** geared to sc. shaft driving 1 FP propeller Total Power: 1,912kW (2,600hp) 12.3kn Daihatsu 6DSM-26F 2 x 4 Stroke 6 Cy. 260 x 320 each-956kW (1300bhp) Daihatsu Diesel Manufacturing Co Lt-Japan AuxGen: 2 x 192kW 445V 60Hz a.c Fuel: 29.5 (d.f.) 86.0 (r.f.) 9.0pd
8325482 *EDYT* -	**TETHIS** *ex* Tetys *-1999* *launched as* Juan de Capapuig *-1984* **Servicios y Concesiones Maritimas Ibicencas SA (Sercomisa)** - *Las Palmas* *Spain (CSR)* MMSI: 224201000	**127** 63 38		**1984-10 Ast. y Varaderos de Tarragona S.A. — Tarragona** Yd No: 253 Loa 25.56 Br ex - Dght 1.851 Lbp 21.62 Br md 7.01 Dpth 2.87 Welded, 1 dk	**(A37B2PS) Passenger Ship**	**2 oil engines** sr geared to sc. shafts driving 2 FP propellers Total Power: 648kW (882hp) Baudouin 12F11SRM 2 x Vee 4 Stroke 12 Cy. 115 x 105 each-324kW (441bhp) Societe des Moteurs Baudouin SA-France AuxGen: 2 x 2kW 24V d.c
8210340 *UBLG5* -	**TETHYS** *ex* M S Chonburi *-2010* *ex* Roo Kaa 2 *-2009* *ex* Yano Maru No. 15 *-2003* **Majena Shipping Co Ltd** Krystal Marine Ltd (OOO 'Krystall Marin') SatCom: Inmarsat C 427303943 *Taganrog* *Russia* MMSI: 273355900	*825* 247 610	Class: RS	**1982-06 Kochi Jyuko (Kaisei Zosen) K.K. — Kochi** Yd No: 1541 Loa 51.74 Br ex - Dght 2.901 Lbp 49.51 Br md 16.01 Dpth 3.31 Welded, 1 dk	**(B34T2QR) Work/Repair Vessel**	**1 oil engine** driving 1 FP propeller Total Power: 883kW (1,201hp) Yanmar MF28-UT 1 x 4 Stroke 6 Cy. 280 x 450 883kW (1201bhp) Matsue Diesel KK-Japan
9053830 *J7CG9* -	**TETHYS** *ex* Benita *-2013* *ex* Anglia *-2007* *ex* Arabia *-1996* **Redford Invest Ltd** - *Portsmouth* *Dominica* MMSI: 325574000	**4,927** 2,941 6,918 T/cm 60.3	Class: BV GL	**1995-06 Alexandria Shipyard — Alexandria** Yd No: 10045 Loa 107.10 (BB) Br ex - Dght 6.155 Lbp 103.00 Br md 18.20 Dpth 8.00 Welded, 1 dk	**(A31A2GX) General Cargo Ship** Grain: 9,369; Bale: 9,245 TEU 260 C. 260/20' Compartments: 3 Ho, ER 3 Ha: ER Ice Capable	**1 oil engine** driving 1 FP propeller Total Power: 2,190kW (2,978hp) 12.0kn B&W 6S26MC 1 x 2 Stroke 6 Cy. 260 x 980 2190kW (2978bhp) MAN B&W Diesel A/S-Denmark AuxGen: 3 x 345kW 440V 60Hz a.c Thrusters: 1 Thwart. FP thruster (f) Fuel: 87.2 (d.f.) 464.3 (r.f.) 9.3pd
9517109 *UBTG5* -	**TETHYS** - **PB Norge AS** Prime Shipping LLC SatCom: Inmarsat C 427303943 *Taganrog* *Russia* MMSI: 273359090	**4,378** 1,313 5,530 T/cm 22.0	Class: RS	**2010-08 Sudostroitelnyy Zavod "Krasnoye Sormovo" — Nizhniy Novgorod** Yd No: 19614/17 Loa 141.00 Br ex 16.90 Dght 3.740 Lbp 134.88 Br md 16.80 Dpth 6.10 Welded, 1 dk	**(A13B2TP) Products Tanker** Double Hull (13F) Liq: 6,587; Liq (Oil): 6,721 Compartments: 12 Wing Ta, 1 Slop Ta, ER	**2 oil engines** reduction geared to sc. shafts driving 2 FP propellers Total Power: 1,860kW (2,528hp) 10.0kn Wartsila 6L20 2 x 4 Stroke 6 Cy. 200 x 280 each-930kW (1264bhp) Wartsila Finland Oy-Finland AuxGen: 3 x 150kW a.c Thrusters: 1 Tunnel thruster (f) Fuel: 174.0 (d.f.)
9406594 - -	**TETHYS** - - *Valletta* *Malta*	**149** - 90	Class: (BV)	**2006-07 Guy Couach-Plascoa — Gujan-Mestras** Yd No: 33002A606 Loa 35.00 Br ex - Dght 2.400 Lbp 28.40 Br md 6.80 Dpth 3.20 Bonded, 1 dk	**(X11A2YP) Yacht** Hull Material: Reinforced Plastic	**2 oil engines** reduction geared to sc. shafts driving 2 Propellers Total Power: 3,532kW (4,802hp) 23.0kn M.T.U. 16V2000M91 2 x Vee 4 Stroke 16 Cy. 130 x 150 each-1766kW (2401bhp) MTU Friedrichshafen GmbH-Friedrichshafen
8741765 *S7L2785* -	**TETHYS SUPPORTER** *ex* Husvik Supporter *-2013* *ex* KBV 004 *-2010* **Tethys Support Ltd** - *Victoria* *Seychelles* MMSI: 664000055	*290* 87 139	Class: RI	**1978-01 Lunde Varv & Verkstads AB — Ramvik** Yd No: 26 Loa 35.59 Br ex 8.18 Dght 3.000 Lbp 31.50 Br md 8.00 Dpth 4.20 Welded, 1 dk	**(B34G2SE) Pollution Control Vessel**	**2 oil engines** driving 1 CP propeller , 1 Propeller Total Power: 970kW (1,318hp) 10.0kn Alpha 406-26VO 2 x 2 Stroke 6 Cy. 260 x 400 each-485kW (659bhp) Alpha Diesel A/S-Denmark Thrusters: 1 Thwart. FP thruster (f)
9540352 *UCTQ* -	**TETI** - **Prime Shipping LLC** - *Taganrog* *Russia* MMSI: 273359070	**5,123** 1,757 7,509	Class: RS (RI)	**2010-08 Yangzhou Haichuan Shipyard — Yangzhou JS** Yd No: HCR0803 Loa 139.90 (BB) Br ex 16.94 Dght 4.650 Lbp 136.60 Br md 16.70 Dpth 7.00 Welded, 1 dk	**(A12B2TR) Chemical/Products Tanker** Double Hull (13F) Liq: 8,203; Liq (Oil): 7,830 Compartments: 12 Wing Ta, ER Ice Capable	**2 oil engines** reduction geared to sc. shafts driving 2 FP propellers Total Power: 2,206kW (3,000hp) 10.0kn Chinese Std. Type G6300ZC 2 x 4 Stroke 6 Cy. 300 x 380 each-1103kW (1500bhp) Weifang Diesel Engine Factory-China AuxGen: 2 x 372kW a.c Thrusters: 1 Tunnel thruster (f) Fuel: 367.0 (r.f.)
8809074 *IVTN* -	**TETIDE** - **Laziomar SpA** MultiService Group Srl *Naples* *Italy* MMSI: 247043100 Official number: 1708	*1,571* 826 500	Class: RI	**1989-06 Cant. Nav. de Poli S.p.A. — Pellestrina** Yd No: 128 Loa 71.15 (BB) Br ex 14.02 Dght 3.600 Lbp 64.30 Br md 14.00 Dpth 4.80 Welded	**(A36A2PR) Passenger/Ro-Ro Ship (Vehicles)** Passengers: unberthed: 1250	**2 oil engines** sr geared to sc. shafts driving 2 CP propellers Total Power: 4,264kW (5,798hp) GMT BL230.12V 2 x Vee 4 Stroke 12 Cy. 230 x 310 each-2132kW (2899bhp) Fincantieri Cantieri Navalitaliani SpA-Italy Thrusters: 1 Thwart. CP thruster (f)
9221437 *SYDU* -	**TETIEN TRADER** - **Julia Venture Maritime Ltd** Alnav Naftiliaki SA *Piraeus* *Greece* MMSI: 239875000 Official number: 10930	**39,213** 25,246 73,910 T/cm 66.3	Class: LR ✠ **100A1** SS 09/2011 bulk carrier strengthened for heavy cargoes, Nos. 2, 4 & 6 holds may be empty ESP ESN LI EP **ShipRight** (SDA, FDA, CM) ✠ **LMC** **UMS** Eq.Ltr: N†; Cable: 660.0/75.0	**2001-09 Namura Shipbuilding Co Ltd — Imari SG** Yd No: 211 Loa 224.90 (BB) Br ex 32.24 Dght 13.962 Lbp 215.00 Br md 32.20 Dpth 19.30 Welded, 1 dk	**(A21A2BC) Bulk Carrier** Grain: 89,040 Compartments: 7 Ho, ER 7 Ha: (16.8 x 13.2)6 (16.8 x 14.8)ER	**1 oil engine** driving 1 FP propeller Total Power: 10,371kW (14,100hp) 14.9kn B&W 7S50MC-C 1 x 2 Stroke 7 Cy. 500 x 2000 10371kW (14100bhp) Hitachi Zosen Corp-Japan AuxGen: 3 x 600kW 450V 60Hz a.c Boilers: AuxB (Comp) 7.0kgf/cm² (6.9bar)
7638909 - - -	**TETORA MARU No. 2** - -	*499* - 650		**1977-05 Kochi Jyuko (Eiho Zosen) K.K. — Kochi** Yd No: 215 Loa - Br ex - Dght 2.720 Lbp 43.01 Br md 16.01 Dpth 3.46 Welded, 1 dk	**(B21A20S) Platform Supply Ship**	**1 oil engine** driving 1 FP propeller Total Power: 441kW (600hp) Niigata 6L20AX 1 x 4 Stroke 6 Cy. 200 x 260 441kW (600bhp) Niigata Engineering Co Ltd-Japan
8021086 *PMAC* -	**TETRA** *ex* RMM 4 *-2008* *ex* Inlaco *-2000* *ex* Hoang Ngan 09 *-1996* *ex* Hue *-1994* *ex* Toho Maru *-1984* **PT Armada Siantan** - *Pontianak* *Indonesia*	**1,612** 1,046 2,223	Class: (KI) (VR) (NK)	**1981-01 Kinoura Zosen K.K. — Imabari** Yd No: 66 Loa 73.06 Br ex - Dght 4.850 Lbp 68.00 Br md 13.01 Dpth 7.00 Welded, 2 dks	**(A31A2GX) General Cargo Ship** Grain: 3,578; Bale: 3,177 1 Ha: (35.9 x 8.6)ER Derricks: 2x7t	**1 oil engine** driving 1 FP propeller Total Power: 1,324kW (1,800hp) 11.0kn Makita GSLH633 1 x 4 Stroke 6 Cy. 330 x 530 1324kW (1800bhp) Makita Diesel Co Ltd-Japan AuxGen: 2 x 80kW a.c
9412115 *9V6956* -	**TETRA I** - **Madura Lines Pte Ltd** Thong Yong 2000 Marine Pte Ltd *Singapore* *Singapore* MMSI: 565319000 Official number: 392296	**444** 133 420	Class: AB	**2007-01 Berjaya Dockyard Sdn Bhd — Miri** Yd No: 33 Loa 33.70 Br ex - Dght 4.000 Lbp 30.20 Br md 10.60 Dpth 4.96 Welded, 1 dk	**(B32A2ST) Tug**	**2 oil engines** reverse reduction geared to sc. shafts driving 2 FP propellers Total Power: 2,648kW (3,600hp) Niigata 6MG25HX 2 x 4 Stroke 6 Cy. 250 x 350 each-1324kW (1800bhp) Niigata Engineering Co Ltd-Japan AuxGen: 2 x 99kW a.c

IMO / Call sign / Flag	Name / Owner / Manager / Port	Tonnage	Class	Built / Builder / Dimensions	Type	Machinery
9412127 *9V6957* -	**TETRA II** **Madura Lines Pte Ltd** Thong Yong 2000 Marine Pte Ltd *Singapore* *Singapore* MMSI: 565320000 Official number: 392297	**444** 133 420	Class: AB	**2007-01 Berjaya Dockyard Sdn Bhd — Miri** Yd No: 35 Loa 33.70 Br ex - Dght 4.000 Lbp 29.60 Br md 10.60 Dpth 4.96 Welded, 1 dk	**(B32A2ST) Tug**	**2 oil engines** reduction geared to sc. shafts driving 2 FP propellers Total Power: 2,648kW (3,600hp) Niigata 6MG25HX 2 x 4 Stroke 6 Cy. 250 x 350 each-1324kW (1800bhp) Niigata Engineering Co Ltd-Japan AuxGen: 2 x 99kW a.c Fuel: 298.9 (r.f.)
9412139 *9V6958* -	**TETRA III** **Tetra III Pte Ltd** Otto Marine Ltd *Singapore* *Singapore* MMSI: 565379000 Official number: 392298	**444** 133 420	Class: AB	**2007-04 Berjaya Dockyard Sdn Bhd — Miri** Yd No: 36 Loa 33.70 Br ex - Dght 4.000 Lbp 29.60 Br md 10.60 Dpth 4.96 Welded, 1 dk	**(B32A2ST) Tug**	**2 oil engines** reduction geared to sc. shafts driving 2 FP propellers Total Power: 2,648kW (3,600hp) Niigata 6MG25HX 2 x 4 Stroke 6 Cy. 250 x 350 each-1324kW (1800bhp) Niigata Engineering Co Ltd-Japan AuxGen: 2 x 99kW a.c Fuel: 298.9 (r.f.)
7649556 - -	**TETRA SENTOSA** *ex* Shin Pung *-2008* *ex* Okura Maru *-2008* - - *Indonesia*	**1,278** 719 1,755	Class: (KR)	**1977-03 K.K. Yoshida Zosen Kogyo — Arida** Loa 69.91 Br ex - Dght 4.236 Lbp 65.00 Br md 11.51 Dpth 6.10 Welded, 2dks	**(A31A2GX) General Cargo Ship** Grain: 2,900; Bale: 2,450 1 Ha: (36.5 x 8.6)ER	**1 oil engine** driving 1 FP propeller Total Power: 1,324kW (1,800hp) 12.0kn Makita GSLH633 1 x 4 Stroke 6 Cy. 330 x 530 1324kW (1800bhp) Makita Diesel Co Ltd-Japan
9412153 *9V6960* -	**TETRA V** **Tetra V Pte Ltd** Otto Marine Ltd *Singapore* *Singapore* MMSI: 565381000 Official number: 392300	**444** 133 420	Class: AB	**2007-04 Berjaya Dockyard Sdn Bhd — Miri** Yd No: 38 Loa 33.70 Br ex - Dght 4.000 Lbp 29.60 Br md 10.60 Dpth 4.96 Welded, 1 dk	**(B32A2ST) Tug**	**2 oil engines** reduction geared to sc. shafts driving 2 Propellers Total Power: 2,648kW (3,600hp) Niigata 6MG25HX 2 x 4 Stroke 6 Cy. 250 x 350 each-1324kW (1800bhp) Niigata Engineering Co Ltd-Japan AuxGen: 2 x 99kW a.c Fuel: 298.9 (r.f.)
8944123 *JL6557* -	**TETSUEI MARU No. 7** **Kyoei Kisen KK** - *Imabari, Ehime* *Japan* Official number: 135608	*199* - -		**1998-08 Yano Zosen K.K. — Imabari** Yd No: 177 L reg 55.07 Br ex - Dght - Lbp 52.00 Br md 9.50 Dpth 5.63 Welded, 1 dk	**(A31A2GX) General Cargo Ship**	**1 oil engine** driving 1 FP propeller Total Power: 736kW (1,001hp) Matsui ML627GSC 1 x 4 Stroke 6 Cy. 270 x 480 736kW (1001bhp) Matsui Iron Works Co Ltd-Japan
7232157 - -	**TETSUHO MARU** - - *South Korea*	*277* - 87		**1971-12 Towa Zosen K.K. — Shimonoseki** Yd No: 421 Loa 34.02 Br ex 9.83 Dght 3.150 Lbp 32.80 Br md 9.81 Dpth 4.40 Welded, 1 dk	**(B32A2ST) Tug**	**2 oil engines** driving 2 FP propellers Total Power: 2,354kW (3,200hp) 13.5kn Fuji 6M32H3A 2 x 4 Stroke 6 Cy. 320 x 380 each-1177kW (1600bhp) Fuji Diesel Co Ltd-Japan AuxGen: 1 x 40kW 225V a.c Fuel: 183.0 (d.f.)
8899653 - -	**TETSUNN MARU** *ex* Tetsunn Maru No. 1 *-1996* - -	*140* 62 -		**1968-02 Daiko Dockyard Co. Ltd. — Osaka** Loa 24.50 Br ex - Dght 2.450 Lbp 20.15 Br md 8.00 Dpth 3.60 Welded, 1 dk	**(B32B2SP) Pusher Tug**	**1 oil engine** driving 1 FP propeller Total Power: 912kW (1,240hp) 8.0kn Daihatsu 6PSTBM-26D 1 x 4 Stroke 6 Cy. 260 x 320 912kW (1240bhp) Daihatsu Diesel Manufacturing Co Lt-Japan
8878154 *JL6290* -	**TETSURYU MARU** **Yoshu Kisen KK & Kowa Kisen YK** Yoshu Kisen KK *Imabari, Ehime* *Japan* MMSI: 431500242 Official number: 134865	*748* - 2,000		**1994-08 Namikata Shipbuilding Co Ltd — Imabari EH** Yd No: 186 Loa - Br ex - Dght - Lbp 78.00 Br md 13.00 Dpth 7.65 Welded, 1 dk	**(A31A2GX) General Cargo Ship**	**1 oil engine** driving 1 FP propeller Total Power: 1,471kW (2,000hp) 11.5kn Akasaka A37 1 x 4 Stroke 6 Cy. 370 x 720 1471kW (2000bhp) Akasaka Tekkosho KK (Akasaka DieselLtd)-Japan
8869878 - -	**TETSURYU MARU** *ex* Asa Maru *-2006* **PT Lima Srikandi Jaya** - *Indonesia*	*195* - 557		**1993-02 KK Ouchi Zosensho — Matsuyama EH** Loa 53.75 Br ex - Dght 3.200 Lbp 49.00 Br md 8.50 Dpth 5.00 Welded, 1 dk	**(A31A2GX) General Cargo Ship**	**1 oil engine** driving 1 FP propeller Total Power: 736kW (1,001hp) 10.5kn Yanmar 1 x 4 Stroke 736kW (1001bhp) Yanmar Diesel Engine Co Ltd-Japan
9633616 *JD3253* -	**TETSURYU MARU** **Fukushima Kaiun KK** - *Kanda, Fukuoka* *Japan* MMSI: 431002936 Official number: 141528	*229* - 800		**2011-10 K.K. Watanabe Zosensho — Nagasaki** Yd No: 180 Loa 60.81 Br ex - Dght 3.230 Lbp 55.00 Br md 9.80 Dpth 5.50 Welded, 1 dk	**(A31A2GX) General Cargo Ship**	**1 oil engine** reduction geared to sc. shaft driving 1 Propeller Total Power: 882kW (1,199hp) Hanshin LH26G 1 x 4 Stroke 6 Cy. 260 x 440 882kW (1199bhp) The Hanshin Diesel Works Ltd-Japan
9715232 *JD3524* -	**TETSURYU MARU** **YK Tetsuryu Kaiun** - *Kure, Hiroshima* *Japan* MMSI: 431004505 Official number: 141932	*267* - 900		**2013-06 Y.K. Okajima Zosensho — Matsuyama** Loa 60.00 Br ex - Dght - Lbp - Br md 10.00 Dpth - Welded, 1 dk	**(A31A2GX) General Cargo Ship**	**1 oil engine** reduction geared to sc. shaft driving 1 FP propeller Total Power: 735kW (999hp) Hanshin LH28G 1 x 4 Stroke 6 Cy. 280 x 460 735kW (999bhp) The Hanshin Diesel Works Ltd-Japan
8876704 *JK5401* -	**TETSURYU MARU No. 3** - - *Kure, Hiroshima* *Japan* Official number: 134698	*199* - 626		**1994-07 Shinwa Sangyo K.K. — Osakikamijima** Yd No: 520 L reg 50.90 (BB) Br ex - Dght 3.390 Lbp 49.50 Br md 9.20 Dpth 5.50 Welded, 1 dk	**(A31A2GX) General Cargo Ship**	**1 oil engine** driving 1 FP propeller Total Power: 735kW (999hp) 11.0kn Hanshin LH26G 1 x 4 Stroke 6 Cy. 260 x 440 735kW (999bhp) The Hanshin Diesel Works Ltd-Japan Thrusters: 1 Directional thruster (f)
8889775 *JK5412* -	**TETSUSHIN MARU** - - *Tokushima, Tokushima* *Japan* Official number: 134709	*131* - 450		**1995-05 KK Ouchi Zosensho — Matsuyama EH** Loa 42.75 Br ex - Dght 3.110 Lbp 38.00 Br md 8.00 Dpth 4.90 Welded, 1 dk	**(A31A2GX) General Cargo Ship**	**1 oil engine** reverse reduction geared to sc. shaft driving 1 FP propeller Total Power: 588kW (799hp) 10.0kn Yanmar 6N165-EN 1 x 4 Stroke 6 Cy. 165 x 232 588kW (799bhp) Yanmar Diesel Engine Co Ltd-Japan
9298624 *JL6712* -	**TETSUUN MARU NO. 1** **Tetsuun Kisen KK** - *Imabari, Ehime* *Japan* Official number: 137054	*499* - 1,587	Class: NK	**2003-09 Yamanaka Zosen K.K. — Imabari** Yd No: 681 Loa 76.38 Br ex - Dght 3.972 Lbp 70.18 Br md 12.30 Dpth 6.85 Welded, 2 dks	**(A31A2GX) General Cargo Ship** Grain: 2,423; Bale: 2,423 1 Ha: ER (40.1 x 10.0)	**1 oil engine** driving 1 Propeller Total Power: 1,471kW (2,000hp) Hanshin LH34LG 1 x 4 Stroke 6 Cy. 340 x 640 1471kW (2000bhp) The Hanshin Diesel Works Ltd-Japan Fuel: 100.0
9614268 *JD3206* -	**TETSUUN MARU NO. 5** **Tetsuun Kisen KK** - *Imabari, Ehime* *Japan* MMSI: 431002501 Official number: 141452	*499* - 1,825	Class: NK	**2011-04 Yamanaka Zosen K.K. — Imabari** Yd No: 811 Loa 74.22 (BB) Br ex - Dght 4.350 Lbp 68.00 Br md 12.10 Dpth 7.34 Welded, 1 dk	**(A31A2GX) General Cargo Ship** Double Hull (13F) Grain: 2,873; Bale: 2,795 1 Ha: ER (40.0 x 9.5)	**1 oil engine** driving 1 FP propeller Total Power: 1,618kW (2,200hp) 12.1kn Hanshin LH34LA 1 x 4 Stroke 6 Cy. 340 x 640 1618kW (2200bhp) The Hanshin Diesel Works Ltd-Japan Thrusters: 1 Thwart. FP thruster (f)
7432680 - -	**TETSUUN MARU No. 8** **Bookchun Co Ltd** - *South Korea*	*250* - -		**1975-10 K.K. Ichikawa Zosensho — Ise** Yd No: 1327 Loa 29.01 Br ex - Dght 2.794 Lbp 26.50 Br md 8.49 Dpth 3.89 Riveted\Welded, 1 dk	**(B32B2SP) Pusher Tug**	**2 oil engines** driving 2 FP propellers Total Power: 1,472kW (2,002hp) 11.1kn Daihatsu 8PSHTCM-26D 2 x 4 Stroke 8 Cy. 260 x 320 each-736kW (1001bhp) Daihatsu Diesel Manufacturing Co Lt-Japan
8915196 *JG4922* -	**TETSUYO MARU** **Sanyo Kaiun Co Ltd & Nittetsu Transport Service Co Ltd** Nittetsu Transport Service Co Ltd *Tokyo* *Japan* MMSI: 431100698 Official number: 131949	*4,112* - 5,476	Class: NK	**1989-12 Nishi Shipbuilding Co Ltd — Imabari EH** Yd No: 357 Loa 96.12 Br ex 18.72 Dght 5.810 Lbp 89.99 Br md 18.70 Dpth 8.45 Welded, 1 dk	**(A24E2BL) Limestone Carrier** Grain: 3,839 Compartments: 1 Ho, ER 1 Ha: (51.4 x 12.0)ER	**1 oil engine** driving 1 CP propeller Total Power: 2,427kW (3,300hp) 12.5kn Akasaka A41 1 x 4 Stroke 6 Cy. 410 x 800 2427kW (3300bhp) Akasaka Tekkosho KK (Akasaka DieselLtd)-Japan AuxGen: 3 x 213kW a.c Thrusters: 1 Thwart. FP thruster (f) Fuel: 180.0 (r.f.)

IMO / Call sign	Name / Owner / Flag	Tonnage	Class	Build / Dimensions	Type	Machinery
9250115 *PCUY* UK 145	**TEUNIS VAN ATJE** **Gebroeders Pasterkamp** - *Urk* *Netherlands* MMSI: 245316000 Official number: 37887	200 60 -		**2001-01 Celiktrans Deniz Insaat Kizaklari Ltd. Sti — Tuzla,Ist** (Hull) Yd No: B002 **2001-01 Luyt BV Machinefabriek en Dokbedrijf — Den Oever** Yd No: JT-02 Loa 27.10 (BB) Br ex - Dght 2.200 Lbp 23.75 Br md 7.00 Dpth 3.80 Welded, 1 dk	**(B11A2FS) Stern Trawler**	**1 oil engine** reduction geared to sc. shaft driving 1 CP propeller Total Power: 367kW (499hp) 10.0kn Caterpillar 3508B-TA 1 x Vee 4 Stroke 8 Cy. 170 x 190 367kW (499bhp) Caterpillar Inc-USA AuxGen: 1 x 80kW 220/360V 50Hz a.c, 1 x 80kW 220/360V 50Hz a.c
8026622 *EEPK* -	**TEUTA** *ex Zabal -2013* **Anijet Sherbimit Detar** - *Bilbao* *Spain*	*124* 32 79		**1982-12 S.L. Ardeag — Bilbao** (Hull) Yd No: 133 **1982-12 Ast. y Talleres Celaya S.A. — Bilbao** Yd No: 179 Loa 24.01 Br ex - Dght 2.752 Lbp 21.52 Br md 7.15 Dpth 3.51 Welded, 1 dk	**(B32A2ST) Tug**	**1 oil engine** driving 1 FP propeller Total Power: 1,044kW (1,419hp) Waukesha L6670DSIM 1 x Vee 4 Stroke 12 Cy. 232 x 216 1044kW (1419bhp) Waukesha Engine Div. DresserIndustries Inc.-Waukesha, Wi
7407221 *TCBJ4* -	**TEVABIL KALKAVAN** *ex Dogruyol II -1993* **Murteza-Seher-Tevabil Kalkavan** - *Istanbul* *Turkey* Official number: 4383	*424* 239 756		**1975-12 Torlaklar Tersanesi — Istanbul** Yd No: 32 Loa 57.83 Br ex 7.55 Dght 3.440 Lbp 53.40 Br md 7.50 Dpth 4.04 Welded, 2 dks	**(A31A2GX) General Cargo Ship**	**1 oil engine** driving 1 FP propeller Total Power: 559kW (760hp) 6.0kn M.T.U. 1 x Vee 4 Stroke 8 Cy. 559kW (760bhp) MTU Friedrichshafen GmbH-Friedrichshafen
9383326 *9HQY9* -	**TEVFIK BEY** *ex Aylish -2008* **Eurasia International Shipping Ltd** Unimarin Denizcilik Sanayi ve Ticaret Ltd Sti *Valletta* *Malta* MMSI: 249392000 Official number: 9383326	**5,287** 3,144 8,317	Class: BV (RI)	**2007-03 Linhai Hongsheng Shipbuilding Co Ltd — Linhai ZJ** Yd No: 012 Loa 120.80 Br ex - Dght 6.200 Lbp 113.50 Br md 17.60 Dpth 8.30 Welded, 1 dk	**(A31A2GX) General Cargo Ship** Grain: 10,642; Bale: 10,642 Compartments: 3 Ho, ER 3 Ha: ER 3 (25.0 x 12.5)	**1 oil engine** reduction geared to sc. shaft driving 1 FP propeller Total Power: 3,850kW (5,234hp) 12.5kn Pielstick 6PC2-6 1 x 4 Stroke 6 Cy. 400 x 460 3850kW (5234bhp) Shaanxi Diesel Heavy Industry Co Lt-China AuxGen: 2 x 200kW 400V 50Hz a.c, 1 x 120kW 400V 50Hz a.c Fuel: 261.0
8836986 *TCAN8* -	**TEVFIK KUYUMCU** *ex Ayturk -2005 ex Alemdar 1 -2003* *ex Demet Akbasoglu -1996* **Alpagul Deniz Hizmetleri ve Tasimacilik Ticaret Ltd Sti** - *Istanbul* *Turkey* MMSI: 271002164 Official number: 6004	**881** 520 1,114	Class: TL	**1990-07 at Istanbul** Lengthened Loa 73.25 Br ex - Dght 3.830 Lbp 65.80 Br md 9.50 Dpth 4.45 Welded, 1 dk	**(A13B2TP) Products Tanker** Compartments: 8 Ta, ER	**1 oil engine** driving 1 FP propeller Total Power: 970kW (1,319hp) S.K.L. 8NVD48A-2U 1 x 4 Stroke 8 Cy. 320 x 480 970kW (1319bhp) SKL Motoren u. Systemtechnik AG-Magdeburg
7304510 *5ZVN* -	**TEWA** *ex Lady Howard II -1975* - - *Mombasa* *Kenya* Official number: 10043	*217* - 118	Class: (LR) ✠ Classed LR until 6/6/88	**1973-05 Fellows & Co Ltd — Great Yarmouth** Yd No: 511 Loa 32.95 Br ex 8.67 Dght 3.429 Lbp 28.96 Br md 8.23 Dpth 4.04 Welded, 1 dk	**(B32A2ST) Tug**	**1 oil engine** reverse reduction geared to sc. shaft driving 1 FP propeller Total Power: 1,295kW (1,761hp) 11.0kn Ruston 8RKCM 1 x Vee 4 Stroke 8 Cy. 254 x 305 1295kW (1761bhp) Ruston Paxman Diesels Ltd.-Colchester AuxGen: 2 x 65kW 440V 50Hz a.c, 1 x 16kW 440V 50Hz a.c
7722073 *WDB6315* -	**TEXAN** - **Martin Operating Partnership LP** Martin Midstream Partners LP SatCom: Inmarsat C 430357010 *Houston, TX* *United States of America* MMSI: 366922150 Official number: 611687	**541** 162 -	Class: AB	**1979 Modern Marine Power, Inc. — Houma, La** Yd No: 24 Loa 30.48 Br ex - Dght 6.554 Lbp 30.48 Br md 10.62 Dpth 6.94 Welded, 1 dk	**(B32B2SA) Articulated Pusher Tug**	**2 oil engines** reverse reduction geared to sc. shafts driving 2 FP propellers Total Power: 3,678kW (5,000hp) 10.0kn Alco 16V251E 2 x Vee 4 Stroke 16 Cy. 229 x 267 each-1839kW (2500bhp) (Re-engined ,made 1980) Auburn Technology Inc-USA AuxGen: 2 x 75kW Fuel: 228.0 (d.f.)
7525097 *WX8357* -	**TEXAS** - **M L Bosworth** - *Galveston, TX* *United States of America* Official number: 507520	*118* 80 -		**1967 Bishop Shipbuilding Corp. — Aransas Pass, Tx** Yd No: 27 Loa - Br ex 6.76 Dght - Lbp 21.75 Br md 6.75 Dpth 3.13 Welded, 1 dk	**(B34N2QP) Pilot Vessel**	**1 oil engine** driving 1 FP propeller Total Power: 375kW (510hp) Caterpillar 1 x 4 Stroke 8 Cy. 375kW (510bhp) Caterpillar Tractor Co-USA
7309352 *WH2312* -	**TEXAS** - **Omega Protein Inc** - *Morgan City, LA* *United States of America* Official number: 270533	*269* 183 -		**1955 Burton Construction & Shipbuilding Corp. — Port Arthur, Tx** L reg 49.63 Br ex - Dght - Lbp - Br md 8.39 Dpth 2.42 Welded	**(B11B2FV) Fishing Vessel**	**1 oil engine** driving 1 FP propeller Total Power: 736kW (1,001hp)
8110942 *YJSV6* -	**TEXAS** *ex Texas Horizon -2008 ex Sea Wrangler -2006* *ex Midnight Wrangler -2005* *ex Wave Alert -2003 ex CSO Installer -2000* *ex Flex Installer -1998* *ex Northern Installer -1995* *ex ITM Installer -1986 ex Ugland Comex I -1985* **Cal Dive Offshore Contractors Inc** Cal Dive International Inc SatCom: Inmarsat C 457684410 *Port Vila* *Vanuatu* MMSI: 576844000 Official number: 1480	**4,759** 1,428 6,200	Class: NV	**1983-04 FEAB-Marstrandverken — Marstrand** Yd No: 160 Converted From: Cable-layer-2003 Converted From: Offshore Supply Ship-2000 Lengthened-1989 Loa 102.70 Br ex 19.42 Dght 6.780 Lbp 95.85 Br md 19.40 Dpth 8.36 Welded, 1 dk	**(B21A20S) Platform Supply Ship** Cranes: 1x25t,1x5t	**2 oil engines** with flexible couplings & sr gearedto sc. shafts driving 2 CP propellers Total Power: 5,520kW (7,504hp) 11.0kn Wartsila 8R32 2 x 4 Stroke 8 Cy. 320 x 350 each-2760kW (3752bhp) Oy Wartsila Ab-Finland AuxGen: 1 x 1904kW 440V 60Hz a.c, 1 x 1430kW 440V 60Hz a.c Thrusters: 3 Thwart. CP thruster (f); 3 Tunnel thruster (a) Fuel: 612.0 (d.f.) 830.0 (r.f.) 15.0pd
8204963 *LMWR3* -	**TEXAS** *ex Barber Texas -1989* **Wilhelmsen Lines Shipowning AS** Wilhelmsen Ship Management (Norway) AS SatCom: Inmarsat B 325759410 *Tonsberg* *Norway (NIS)* MMSI: 257594000	**66,635** 26,072 44,080	Class: (LR) ✠ Classed LR until 5/3/14	**1984-03 Hyundai Heavy Industries Co Ltd — Ulsan** Yd No: 249 Converted From: Ro-Ro Cargo Ship-2003 Loa 262.08 (BB) Br ex 32.31 Dght 11.729 Lbp 246.41 Br md 32.26 Dpth 21.01 Welded, 8 dks, incl. 2 hoistable dks	**(A35B2RV) Vehicles Carrier** Side door (s) Quarter stern door/ramp (s) Len: 45.20 Wid: 12.50 Swl: 420 Lane-clr ht: 6.30 Cars: 4,474 Bale: 72,500 Cranes: 1x40t	**1 oil engine** driving 1 FP propeller Total Power: 26,921kW (36,602hp) 21.0kn B&W 8L90GB 1 x 2 Stroke 8 Cy. 900 x 2180 26921kW (36602bhp) Hyundai Engine & Machinery Co Ltd-South Korea AuxGen: 3 x 1900kW 450V 60Hz a.c, 2 x 900kW 450V 60Hz a.c Boilers: AuxB (o.f.) 7.0kgf/cm² (6.9bar) 7.0kgf/cm² (6.9bar), AuxB (ex.g.) 12.0kgf/cm² (11.8bar) 7.0kgf/cm² (6.9bar)rcv 7kg/cm² (6,86bar) Thrusters: 1 Thwart. CP thruster (f); 1 Tunnel thruster (a) Fuel: 579.0 (d.f.) 7660.0 (r.f.) 110.5pd
8945074 - -	**TEXAS** - **Philippine Rigid Construction Corp** - *Cebu* *Philippines* Official number: T0051	*102* 30 -		**1972 at Cebu** L reg 26.67 Br ex - Dght - Lbp - Br md 6.09 Dpth 3.05 Welded, 1 dk	**(B32A2ST) Tug**	**1 oil engine** driving 1 FP propeller Total Power: 441kW (600hp)
9623685 *9HA3095* -	**TEXAS** - **Chinotrans Shipping Ltd** Dynacom Tankers Management Ltd *Valletta* *Malta* MMSI: 229132000 Official number: 9623685	**160,534** 110,387 318,563 T/cm 178.0	Class: AB	**2012-09 Hyundai Heavy Industries Co Ltd — Ulsan** Yd No: 2520 Loa 333.02 (BB) Br ex 60.04 Dght 22.500 Lbp 319.04 Br md 60.00 Dpth 30.40 Welded, 1 dk	**(A13A2TV) Crude Oil Tanker** Double Hull (13F) Liq: 330,600; Liq (Oil): 330,600 Compartments: 5 Wing Ta, 5 Ta, 5 Wing Ta, 1 Wing Slop Ta, 1 Wing Slop Ta, ER 3 Cargo Pump (s): 3x5500m³/hr	**1 oil engine** driving 1 FP propeller Total Power: 31,640kW (43,018hp) 15.5kn Wartsila 7RT-flex82T 1 x 2 Stroke 7 Cy. 820 x 3375 31640kW (43018bhp) Hyundai Heavy Industries Co Ltd-South Korea AuxGen: 3 x 1100kW a.c Fuel: 750.0 (d.f.) 8521.0 (r.f.)
8958186 *WCY8462* -	**TEXAS 1** - **Trawler Shrimp Texas 1 Inc** - *Port Lavaca, TX* *United States of America* Official number: 1074885	**137** 41 -		**1998 T.M. Jemison Construction Co., Inc. — Bayou La Batre, Al** Yd No: 124 L reg 24.14 Br ex - Dght - Lbp - Br md 7.31 Dpth 3.62 Welded, 1 dk	**(B11B2FV) Fishing Vessel**	**1 oil engine** driving 1 FP propeller

IMO / Call sign / Flag	Name / Owner / Manager	Tonnage	Class	Builder / Dimensions	Type	Machinery
7309364 *WY8201* -	**TEXAS CARIBBEAN** *ex* Shrimp Catcher *ex* Capt. Nini **David Lee Davis** - *Corpus Christi, TX* *United States of America* Official number: 523309	*164* 127 -		**1969 Toche Enterprises, Inc. — Ocean Springs, Ms** L reg 25.39 Br ex 7.32 Dght - Lbp - Br md - Dpth 3.56 Welded	**(B11B2FV) Fishing Vessel**	**1 oil engine** driving 1 FP propeller Total Power: 588kW (799hp)
8037528 - -	**TEXAS GOLD** - - -	*101* 86 -		**1980 Fashion Blacksmith, Inc. — Crescent City, Ca** L reg 17.41 Br ex 6.71 Dght - Lbp - Br md - Dpth 3.10 Welded, 1 dk	**(B11B2FV) Fishing Vessel**	**1 oil engine** driving 1 FP propeller Total Power: 257kW (349hp)
9272890 *JMVY* -	**TEXAS HIGHWAY** **Kawasaki Kisen Kaisha Ltd & Taiyo Nippon Kisen Co Ltd** Taiyo Nippon Kisen Co Ltd *Kobe, Hyogo* *Japan* MMSI: 432440000 Official number: 136005	**55,458** 16,637 17,481 T/cm 51.5	Class: NK	**2003-12 Imabari Shipbuilding Co Ltd — Marugame KG (Marugame Shipyard)** Yd No: 1400 Loa 199.94 (BB) Br ex - Dght 9.616 Lbp 190.00 Br md 32.20 Dpth 33.74 Welded, 12 dks	**(A35B2RV) Vehicles Carrier** Side door/ramp1 (p) 1 (s) Len: 17.00 Wid: 4.50 Swl: 20 Quarter stern door/ramp (s. a.) Len: 32.55 Wid: 7.00 Swl: 100 Cars: 6,043	**1 oil engine** driving 1 FP propeller Total Power: 13,940kW (18,953hp) 20.0kn Mitsubishi 8UEC60LSII 1 x 2 Stroke 8 Cy. 600 x 2300 13940kW (18953bhp) Kobe Hatsudoki KK-Japan AuxGen: 3 x 1280kW 450/110V 60Hz a.c Thrusters: 1 Thwart. CP thruster (f) Fuel: 150.0 (d.f.) 3370.0 (r.f.) 53.0pd
7743481 - -	**TEXAS LADY** **Jack E Yardley** - *Corpus Christi, TX* *United States of America* Official number: 594894	*129* 87 -		**1978 Desco Marine — Saint Augustine, Fl** Loa 20.83 Br ex 6.74 Dght - Lbp - Br md - Dpth 3.74 Bonded, 1 dk	**(B11A2FT) Trawler** Hull Material: Reinforced Plastic	**1 oil engine** driving 1 FP propeller Cummins 1 x 4 Stroke Cummins Engine Co Inc-USA
7647950 *WYG6929* -	**TEXAS LADY** **Zimco Marine Inc** - *Port Isabel, TX* *United States of America* Official number: 579997	*126* 85 -		**1977 Marine Mart, Inc. — Port Isabel, Tx** Yd No: 153 L reg 20.82 Br ex 6.15 Dght - Lbp - Br md - Dpth 3.76 Welded, 1dk	**(B11B2FV) Fishing Vessel**	**1 oil engine** driving 1 FP propeller Total Power: 268kW (364hp)
9044669 *WBO8579* -	**TEXAS RESPONDER** **Marine Spill Response Corp** - *Norfolk, VA* *United States of America* MMSI: 366595000 Official number: 983116	**1,322** 396 1,300	Class: AB	**1993-09 Bender Shipbuilding & Repair Co Inc — Mobile AL** Yd No: 1033 Loa 63.55 Br ex - Dght 4.368 Lbp 58.46 Br md 13.41 Dpth 5.18 Welded	**(B34G2SE) Pollution Control Vessel**	**2 oil engines** with clutches, flexible couplings & sr geared to sc. shafts driving 2 FP propellers Total Power: 2,238kW (3,042hp) 12.0kn Caterpillar 3512TA 2 x Vee 4 Stroke 12 Cy. 170 x 190 each-1119kW (1521bhp) Caterpillar Inc-USA AuxGen: 3 x 250kW a.c Thrusters: 1 Thwart. FP thruster (f) Fuel: 109.0
8956853 *HO2188* -	**TEXAS STAR** *ex* PBR/220 *-2000* **Cusack Investment SA** Bourbon Offshore Maritima SA *Panama* *Panama* Official number: 29146PEXT1	**269** 80 415	Class: (AB)	**1980 Service Machine & Shipbuilding Co — Amelia LA** Yd No: 134 L reg 35.96 Br ex - Dght 3.150 Lbp - Br md 8.53 Dpth 3.51 Welded, 1 dk	**(B21A20S) Platform Supply Ship**	**2 oil engines** driving 2 FP propellers Total Power: 1,838kW (2,498hp) 10.0kn General Motors 2 x each-919kW (1249bhp) General Motors Detroit DieselAllison Divn-USA
7722047 - -	**TEXAS STAR** *ex* Texas Star Casino *-2005* *ex* Millionaire's Casino *-2005* *ex* Stardancer V *-2003* *ex* Europa Star *-2001* *ex* Walter M *-1987* *ex* Southern Prince *-1986* **Texas Star LLC** Wanchese Fish Co Inc *Wanchese, NC* *United States of America* MMSI: 367131590	**169** 115 450	Class: (AB)	**1977-12 Halter Marine, Inc. — Lockport, La** Yd No: 655 Converted From: Day-excursion Passenger Ship-2013 Converted From: Offshore Supply Ship-1987 Loa 50.60 Br ex 11.89 Dght 3.353 Lbp 47.33 Br md 11.60 Dpth 3.97 Welded, 1 dk	**(B12A2FF) Fish Factory Ship**	**2 oil engines** reverse reduction geared to sc. shafts driving 2 FP propellers Total Power: 1,368kW (1,860hp) 12.0kn G.M. (Detroit Diesel) 16V-149 2 x Vee 2 Stroke 16 Cy. 146 x 146 each-684kW (930bhp) General Motors Detroit DieselAllison Divn-USA AuxGen: 2 x 75kW Thrusters: 1 Thwart. FP thruster (f)
9256860 *ELUP9* -	**TEXAS STAR** *ex* Herm *-2012* *ex* Montiron *-2012* **Bandera Marine Ltd** Atlas Maritime Ltd SatCom: Inmarsat B 363701238 *Monrovia* *Liberia* MMSI: 636010736 Official number: 10736	**61,991** 34,668 115,338 T/cm 98.1	Class: AB	**2003-07 Sanoyas Hishino Meisho Corp — Kurashiki OY** Yd No: 1206 Loa 249.00 (BB) Br ex 44.04 Dght 14.825 Lbp 238.00 Br md 44.00 Dpth 21.20 Welded, 1 dk	**(A13A2TV) Crude Oil Tanker** Double Hull (13F) Liq: 124,636; Liq (Oil): 126,595 Cargo Heating Coils Compartments: 12 Wing Ta, 2 Wing Slop Ta, ER 3 Cargo Pump (s): 3x2800m³/hr Manifold: Bow/CM: 126.2m	**1 oil engine** driving 1 FP propeller Total Power: 13,530kW (18,395hp) 14.8kn MAN-B&W 6S60MC-C 1 x 2 Stroke 6 Cy. 600 x 2400 13530kW (18395bhp) Kawasaki Heavy Industries Ltd-Japan AuxGen: 3 x 700kW 450/110V 60Hz a.c Fuel: 252.8 (d.f.) (Heating Coils) 3614.0 (r.f.)
8134481 - -	**TEXCLIPP III** **Societe Ivoirienne d'Avitaillement Portuaire** - *Abidjan* *Cote d'Ivoire*	*300* - 150	Class: (BV)	**1971 Ch. Carena — Abidjan** Loa 26.95 Br ex - Dght - Lbp - Br md 7.00 Dpth 2.11 Welded, 1 dk	**(A13B2TU) Tanker (unspecified)** Liq: 192; Liq (Oil): 192 Compartments: 8 Ta, ER	**2 oil engines** driving 2 FP propellers Total Power: 156kW (212hp) 8.5kn Perkins 6.354 (M) 2 x 4 Stroke 6 Cy. 98 x 127 each-78kW (106bhp) Perkins Engines Ltd.-Peterborough
9238363 *PBFC* -	**TEXEL** *ex* Onego Merchant *-2013* *ex* Texel *-2011* *ex* Dewi Parwati *-2008* *ex* Beluga Spirit *-2003* *ex* Dewi Parwati *-2003* **SO Texel CV** Kustvaart Harlingen BV *Harlingen* *Netherlands* MMSI: 245064000 Official number: 38963	**6,301** 3,582 8,930	Class: BV	**2002-03 Bodewes Scheepswerf "Volharding" Foxhol B.V. — Foxhol** Yd No: 348 Loa 132.20 (BB) Br ex - Dght 7.160 Lbp 123.84 Br md 15.87 Dpth 9.65 Welded, 1 dk	**(A31A2GX) General Cargo Ship** Grain: 12,855 TEU 552 C. 552/20' (40') incl. 25 ref C. Compartments: 2 Ho, ER 2 Ha: (52.5 x 13.2)ER (40.0 x 13.2) Cranes: 2x40t	**1 oil engine** reduction geared to sc. shaft driving 1 FP propeller Total Power: 3,840kW (5,221hp) 15.0kn MaK 8M32C 1 x 4 Stroke 8 Cy. 320 x 480 3840kW (5221bhp) Caterpillar Motoren GmbH & Co. KG-Germany Thrusters: 1 Tunnel thruster (f)
9060699 *PHXY* -	**TEXELBANK** **Smit Harbour Towage Rotterdam BV** - *Rotterdam* *Netherlands* MMSI: 245907000 Official number: 21951	**321** 96 169	Class: BV	**1992-06 Saint-Malo Naval — St-Malo** Yd No: 615 Loa 30.60 Br ex 9.95 Dght 3.060 Lbp 27.86 Br md 9.70 Dpth 4.02 Welded, 1 dk	**(B32A2ST) Tug**	**2 oil engines** with clutches, flexible couplings & dr geared to sc. shafts driving 2 Directional propellers Total Power: 2,470kW (3,358hp) 11.5kn Deutz SBV6M628 2 x 4 Stroke 6 Cy. 240 x 280 each-1235kW (1679bhp) Motoren Werke Mannheim AG (MWM)-Mannheim Fuel: 66.0 (d.f.)
8851338 *WBU2522* -	**TEXIAN** *ex* Osage *-1992* **Empty Barge Lines II Inc** - *Houston, TX* *United States of America* Official number: 625691	*138* 94 -		**1980 Thrift Shipbuilding & Repair, Inc. — Sulphur, La** Yd No: 25 Loa - Br ex - Dght - Lbp 19.81 Br md 7.92 Dpth 2.74 Welded, 1 dk	**(B32A2ST) Tug**	**1 oil engine** driving 1 FP propeller Total Power: 1,030kW (1,400hp)
9642916 *XCUY6* -	**TEXISTEPEC** **Petroleos Mexicanos SA (PEMEX) Refinacion Gerencia de Transportacion Maritima** - *Tampico* *Mexico* MMSI: 345010500 Official number: 2804506232-2	**30,159** 13,438 50,110	Class: NV	**2013-02 SPP Shipbuilding Co Ltd — Donghae (Goseong Shipyard)** Yd No: S5114 Loa 183.00 (BB) Br ex 32.23 Dght 13.060 Lbp 174.00 Br md 32.20 Dpth 19.10 Welded, 1 dk	**(A12B2TR) Chemical/Products Tanker** Double Hull (13F)	**1 oil engine** driving 1 FP propeller Total Power: 9,960kW (13,542hp) 15.0kn MAN-B&W 6S50MC-C8 1 x 2 Stroke 6 Cy. 500 x 2000 9960kW (13542bhp) AuxGen: 3 x a.c
8702226 *4JIG* -	**TEYMUR EHMEDOV** *ex* Buniyat Sardarov *-1994* *launched as* Sormovskiy-3061 *-1988* **Azerbaijan State Caspian Shipping Co (ASCSS)** - SatCom: Inmarsat C 442301210 *Baku* *Azerbaijan* MMSI: 423012100 Official number: DGR-0023	**3,048** 1,112 3,391 T/cm 13.2	Class: RS	**1988-10 Estaleiros Navais de Viana do Castelo S.A. — Viana do Castelo** Yd No: 142 Loa 118.70 Br ex 13.40 Dght 3.940 Lbp 112.50 Br md 13.20 Dpth 6.00 Welded, 1 dk	**(A31A2GX) General Cargo Ship** Grain: 4,751; Bale: 3,000 TEU 90 C. 90/20' (40') Compartments: 4 Ho, ER 4 Ha: 2 (18.7 x 9.2)2 (12.6 x 9.2)ER Ice Capable	**2 oil engines** driving 2 FP propellers Total Power: 1,280kW (1,740hp) 10.5kn S.K.L. 6NVD48A-2U 2 x 4 Stroke 6 Cy. 320 x 480 each-640kW (870bhp) VEB Schwermaschinenbau "KarlLiebknecht" (SKL)-Magdeburg AuxGen: 3 x 100kW 400V 50Hz a.c Thrusters: 1 Thwart. CP thruster (f)

IMO / Call sign	Name / Owner / Flag	GT / NT / DWT	Class	Built / Dimensions	Type	Machinery
8942333 *UGIY* -	**TEZEY** **Vostok Construction Cooperative (Staratelnaya Artel 'Vostok')** - *Nikolayevsk-na-Amure* *Russia*	**436** 130 295	Class: RS	**1970 Zavod 'Nikolayevsk-na-Amure' — Nikolayevsk-na-Amure** Yd No: 8 Loa 54.50 Br ex 7.70 Dght 2.020 Lbp 48.74 Br md - Dpth 3.50 Welded, 1 dk	**(A35A2RR) Ro-Ro Cargo Ship**	**2 oil engines** driving 2 FP propellers Total Power: 440kW (598hp) 10.5kn Barnaultransmash 3D12A 2 x Vee 4 Stroke 12 Cy. 150 x 180 each-220kW (299bhp) (new engine 1993) AO Barnaultransmash-Barnaul AuxGen: 3 x 30kW a.c Fuel: 22.0 (d.f.)
9082295 *UAEV* -	**TEZEY** *ex* Ekarma-1 *-2007* *ex* Grand East *-1994* **Vega JSC** - SatCom: Inmarsat A 1407412 *Murmansk* *Russia* MMSI: 273891300 Official number: 920820	**877** 226 384	Class: RS	**1993-08 AO Yaroslavskiy Sudostroitelnyy Zavod — Yaroslavl** Yd No: 388 Loa 53.74 Br ex 10.72 Dght 4.650 Lbp 47.92 Br md 10.50 Dpth 6.00 Welded	**(B11A2FS) Stern Trawler** Ice Capable	**1 oil engine** driving 1 CP propeller Total Power: 969kW (1,317hp) 12.6kn S.K.L. 8NVD48A-2U 1 x 4 Stroke 8 Cy. 320 x 480 969kW (1317bhp) SKL Motoren u. Systemtechnik AG-Magdeburg AuxGen: 3 x 150kW a.c, 1 x 300kW a.c Fuel: 192.0 (d.f.)
9203409 *9WD02* -	**TG. EMBANG** **Government of Malaysia (Director of Marine - Sarawak)** - *Kuching* *Malaysia* MMSI: 533494000 Official number: 329024	**233** 69 71	Class: (LR) ✠ Classed LR until 25/2/04	**1999-11 Brooke Dockyard & Engineering Works Corp — Kuching** Yd No: 148 Loa 34.00 Br ex 7.76 Dght 2.010 Lbp 30.00 Br md 7.00 Dpth 4.25 Welded, 1 dk	**(B34H2SQ) Patrol Vessel**	**2 oil engines** with clutches, flexible couplings & sr reverse geared to sc. shafts driving 2 FP propellers Total Power: 3,260kW (4,432hp) 19.0kn M.T.U. 12V396TE94 2 x Vee 4 Stroke 12 Cy. 165 x 185 each-1630kW (2216bhp) MTU Friedrichshafen GmbH-Friedrichshafen AuxGen: 2 x 72kW 415V 50Hz a.c Fuel: 40.0 (d.f.)
9203411 *9WD03* -	**TG. MANIS** **Government of Malaysia (Director of Marine - Sarawak)** - *Kuching* *Malaysia* MMSI: 533495000 Official number: 329144	**233** 69 71	Class: (LR) ✠ Classed LR until 25/2/04	**1999-11 Brooke Dockyard & Engineering Works Corp — Kuching** Yd No: 149 Loa 34.00 Br ex 7.76 Dght 2.000 Lbp 30.00 Br md 7.00 Dpth 4.25 Welded, 1 dk	**(B34H2SQ) Patrol Vessel**	**2 oil engines** with clutches, flexible couplings & sr reverse geared to sc. shafts driving 2 FP propellers Total Power: 3,260kW (4,432hp) 19.0kn M.T.U. 12V396TE94 2 x Vee 4 Stroke 12 Cy. 165 x 185 each-1630kW (2216bhp) MTU Friedrichshafen GmbH-Friedrichshafen AuxGen: 2 x 72kW 415V 50Hz a.c Fuel: 40.0 (d.f.)
8868903 - -	**TH-02** **Marine Dredging Co No II (MADREDCO No 2) (Cong Ty Nao Vet Duong Bien So II)** - *Haiphong* *Vietnam*	**370** 111 510	Class: VR	**1986-01 Bach Dang Shipyard — Haiphong** Yd No: 51 Converted From: General Cargo Ship-1999 Loa 42.75 Br ex 10.20 Dght 2.400 Lbp 41.00 Br md 10.00 Dpth 3.00 Welded, 1 dk	**(B33B2DS) Suction Hopper Dredger**	**1 oil engine** reduction geared to sc. shaft driving 1 FP propeller Total Power: 221kW (300hp) 11.0kn Barnaultransmash 3D12A 1 x Vee 4 Stroke 12 Cy. 150 x 180 221kW (300bhp) (made 1980) Barnaultransmash-Barnaul AuxGen: 1 x 6kW a.c
8934300 - -	**TH 04** **Marine Dredging Co No II (MADREDCO No 2) (Cong Ty Nao Vet Duong Bien So II)** - *Haiphong* *Vietnam*	**370** 111 510	Class: VR	**1986-01 Song Cam Shipyard — Haiphong** Loa 42.70 Br ex 10.02 Dght 2.400 Lbp 41.00 Br md 10.00 Dpth 3.00 Welded, 1 dk	**(B33B2DU) Hopper/Dredger (unspecified)** Hopper: 300 Compartments: 1 Ho, ER 1 Ha: (24.0 x 4.0)ER	**1 oil engine** reduction geared to sc. shaft driving 1 FP propeller Total Power: 221kW (300hp) 8.0kn Barnaultransmash 3D12A 1 x Vee 4 Stroke 12 Cy. 150 x 180 221kW (300bhp) Barnaultransmash-Barnaul
8925634 - -	**TH-04** **Machine Construction & Service JSC (Cong Ty Co Phan Thi Cong Co Gioi Va Dich Vu)** - *Haiphong* *Vietnam* Official number: VN-1233-SL	**372** 113 546	Class: VR	**1988-01 Song Cam Shipyard — Haiphong** Loa 42.80 Br ex 10.02 Dght 2.400 Lbp 39.36 Br md 10.00 Dpth 3.00 Welded, 1 dk	**(B34A2SH) Hopper, Motor**	**1 oil engine** reduction geared to sc. shaft driving 1 FP propeller Total Power: 221kW (300hp) 8.0kn Barnaultransmash 3D12A 1 x Vee 4 Stroke 12 Cy. 150 x 180 221kW (300bhp) Barnaultransmash-Barnaul
8934336 - -	**TH-05** **Vietnam Waterway Construction Corp (VINAWACO)** - *Haiphong* *Vietnam* Official number: VN-1233-SL	**372** 113 300	Class: VR	**1989-01 Song Cam Shipyard — Haiphong** Loa 42.80 Br ex 10.02 Dght 2.400 Lbp 41.00 Br md 10.00 Dpth 3.00 Welded, 1 dk	**(B34A2SH) Hopper, Motor** Hopper: 190 Compartments: 1 Ho, ER 1 Ha:	**1 oil engine** driving 1 FP propeller Total Power: 224kW (305hp) 9.0kn S.K.L. 6NVD36-1U 1 x 4 Stroke 6 Cy. 240 x 360 224kW (305bhp) SKL Motoren u. Systemtechnik AG-Magdeburg
9026734 - -	**TH-08-ALCI** *ex* Cong Huan 05-Alci *-2012* **Agriculture Leasing Co I** - *Haiphong* *Vietnam* MMSI: 574704000 Official number: VN-1874-VT	**499** 339 977	Class: VR	**2004-10 Nam Ha Shipyard — Nam Ha** Yd No: TB-07E Loa 56.00 Br ex 9.27 Dght 3.280 Lbp 53.21 Br md 9.25 Dpth - Welded, 1 dk	**(A31A2GX) General Cargo Ship**	**1 oil engine** geared to sc. shaft driving 1 Propeller Total Power: 382kW (519hp) 10.4kn Weifang X6170ZC 1 x 4 Stroke 6 Cy. 170 x 200 382kW (519bhp) Weifang Diesel Engine Factory-China
8868939 - -	**TH-12** **Thach Ha-Ha Tinh Transport Enterprise (Cong Ty Van Tai Thach Ha-Ha Tinh)** - *Vietnam*	*168* - 150	Class: (VR)	**1989 at Nghe An** Loa 36.55 Br ex - Dght 1.710 Lbp - Br md 7.20 Dpth 2.50 Welded, 1 dk	**(A31A2GX) General Cargo Ship** Grain: 262 Compartments: 2 Ho, ER 2 Ha: 2 (7.0 x 4.0)ER	**1 oil engine** reduction geared to sc. shaft driving 1 FP propeller Total Power: 99kW (135hp) 9.0kn Skoda 6L160 1 x 4 Stroke 6 Cy. 160 x 225 99kW (135bhp) (made 1985) CKD Praha-Praha AuxGen: 1 x 5kW a.c
8868927 - -	**TH-96-05** **Quang Xuong Breeding Plant Co (Cong Ty Giong Cay Quang Xuong)** - *Haiphong* *Vietnam*	**166** 86 200	Class: (VR)	**1989 at Haiphong** Loa 36.36 Br ex - Dght 1.900 Lbp - Br md 7.00 Dpth 2.50 Welded, 1 dk	**(A31A2GX) General Cargo Ship** Grain: 375 Compartments: 2 Ho, ER 2 Ha: 2 (7.0 x 4.0)ER	**1 oil engine** reduction geared to sc. shaft driving 1 FP propeller Total Power: 99kW (135hp) 8.0kn Skoda 6L160 1 x 4 Stroke 6 Cy. 160 x 225 99kW (135bhp) CKD Praha-Praha
9370848 *3FP04*	**TH SERENADE** **Sun Lanes Shipping SA** Synergy Maritime Pvt Ltd SatCom: Inmarsat C 437090310 *Panama* *Panama* MMSI: 370903000 Official number: 4023409	**60,205** 32,143 107,593 T/cm 95.2	Class: AB	**2009-02 Tsuneishi Holdings Corp Tsuneishi Shipbuilding Co — Fukuyama HS** Yd No: 1388 Loa 243.80 (BB) Br ex 42.03 Dght 14.578 Lbp 237.76 Br md 42.00 Dpth 21.30 Welded, 1 dk	**(A13A2TV) Crude Oil Tanker** Double Hull (13F) Liq: 121,065; Liq (Oil): 120,650 Cargo Heating Coils Compartments: 12 Wing Ta, 2 Wing Slop Ta, ER 3 Cargo Pump (s): 3x3000m³/hr Manifold: Bow/CM: 121.3m	**1 oil engine** driving 1 FP propeller Total Power: 13,560kW (18,436hp) 15.4kn MAN-B&W 6S60MC-C 1 x 2 Stroke 6 Cy. 600 x 2400 13560kW (18436bhp) Mitsui Engineering & Shipbuilding CLtd-Japan AuxGen: 3 x 640kW a.c Fuel: 270.0 (d.f.) 3800.0 (r.f.)
9370836 *9V2078* -	**TH SONATA** **Pusaka Laut Pte Ltd** Synergy Marine Pte Ltd *Singapore* *Singapore* MMSI: 563224000 Official number: 398595	**60,195** 32,143 107,510 T/cm 95.2	Class: AB	**2008-10 Tsuneishi Holdings Corp Tsuneishi Shipbuilding Co — Fukuyama HS** Yd No: 1387 Loa 243.80 (BB) Br ex - Dght 14.578 Lbp 237.00 Br md 42.00 Dpth 21.30 Welded, 1 dk	**(A13A2TV) Crude Oil Tanker** Double Hull (13F) Liq: 121,065; Liq (Oil): 120,650 Cargo Heating Coils Compartments: 12 Wing Ta, 2 Wing Slop Ta, ER 3 Cargo Pump (s): 3x3000m³/hr Manifold: Bow/CM: 121.3m	**1 oil engine** driving 1 FP propeller Total Power: 13,560kW (18,436hp) 15.4kn MAN-B&W 6S60MC-C 1 x 2 Stroke 6 Cy. 600 x 2400 13560kW (18436bhp) Mitsui Engineering & Shipbuilding CLtd-Japan AuxGen: 3 x 640kW a.c Fuel: 270.0 (d.f.) 3800.0 (r.f.)
9370850 *9VHM2* -	**TH SOUND** **Pusaka Laut Pte Ltd** Synergy Maritime Pvt Ltd SatCom: Inmarsat C 456407310 *Singapore* *Singapore* MMSI: 564073000 Official number: 393983	**60,205** 32,143 107,687 T/cm 95.2	Class: AB	**2009-05 Tsuneishi Holdings Corp Tsuneishi Shipbuilding Co — Fukuyama HS** Yd No: 1389 Loa 243.80 (BB) Br ex 42.03 Dght 14.578 Lbp 237.00 Br md 42.00 Dpth 21.30 Welded, 1 dk	**(A13A2TV) Crude Oil Tanker** Double Hull (13F) Liq: 121,065; Liq (Oil): 120,650 Cargo Heating Coils Compartments: 12 Wing Ta, 2 Wing Slop Ta, ER 3 Cargo Pump (s): 3x3000m³/hr Manifold: Bow/CM: 121.3m	**1 oil engine** driving 1 FP propeller Total Power: 13,560kW (18,436hp) 15.4kn MAN-B&W 6S60MC-C 1 x 2 Stroke 6 Cy. 600 x 2400 13560kW (18436bhp) Mitsui Engineering & Shipbuilding CLtd-Japan AuxGen: 3 x 640kW a.c Fuel: 270.0 (d.f.) 3800.0 (r.f.)
9403475 *3EPE9* -	**TH SYMPHONY** **Keishin Kaiun Co Ltd & Ever Bright Shipping SA** Keishin Kaiun Co Ltd SatCom: Inmarsat Mini-M 764820583 *Panama* *Panama* MMSI: 351018000 Official number: 3358108A	**57,458** 32,077 106,246 T/cm 91.5	Class: NK	**2008-02 Tsuneishi Holdings Corp Tsuneishi Shipbuilding Co — Tadotsu KG** Yd No: 1412 Loa 240.50 (BB) Br ex - Dght 14.878 Lbp 230.00 Br md 42.00 Dpth 21.20 Welded, 1 dk	**(A13A2TV) Crude Oil Tanker** Double Hull (13F) Liq: 114,413; Liq (Oil): 120,650 Cargo Heating Coils Compartments: ER, 14 Wing Ta 3 Cargo Pump (s): 3x2500m³/hr Manifold: Bow/CM: 123.2m	**1 oil engine** driving 1 FP propeller Total Power: 12,240kW (16,642hp) 15.0kn MAN-B&W 6S60MC 1 x 2 Stroke 6 Cy. 600 x 2292 12240kW (16642bhp) Mitsui Engineering & Shipbuilding CLtd-Japan Fuel: 195.0 (d.f.) 2437.0 (r.f.)

IMO / Call sign	Name / Owner	Tonnage	Class	Build / Dimensions	Type	Machinery
9297046 *9KDL* -	**THAFIR** **Government of The State of Kuwait (Coast Guard)** - *Kuwait* MMSI: 447117000	**185** 55 15	Class: (LR) ✠ 21/7/04	**2004-06 OCEA SA — St-Nazaire** Yd No: 313 Loa 35.20 Br ex 7.17 Dght 1.280 Lbp 29.85 Br md 6.80 Dpth 3.80 Welded, 1 dk	**(B34H2SQ) Patrol Vessel** Hull Material: Aluminium Alloy	**2 oil engines** with clutches, flexible coulpings & sr reverse geared to sc. shafts driving 2 Water jets Total Power: 3,480kW (4,732hp) M.T.U. 12V4000M70 2 x Vee 4 Stroke 12 Cy. 165 x 190 each-1740kW (2366bhp) MTU Friedrichshafen GmbH-Friedrichshafen AuxGen: 2 x 78kW 400V 50Hz a.c
8667098 *XVMD* -	**THAI ANH 06** *ex* Hai Van 36 *-2013* - - *Haiphong* *Vietnam* Official number: VN-2699-VT	**999** 656 1,965	Class: VR	**2008-09 Haiphong Mechanical & Trading Co. — Haiphong** Yd No: TQT-01 Loa 70.10 Br ex 10.82 Dght 4.680 Lbp 65.80 Br md 10.80 Dpth 5.55 Welded, 1 dk	**(A31A2GX) General Cargo Ship** Grain: 2,196 Compartments: 2 Ho, ER 2 Ha: ER 2 (15.0 x 7.0)	**1 oil engine** driving 1 FP propeller Total Power: 441kW (600hp) 10.0kn Chinese Std. Type 6300ZC 1 x 4 Stroke 6 Cy. 300 x 380 441kW (600bhp) Ningbo CSI Power & Machinery GroupCo Ltd-China
8868915 *3WEV* -	**THAI BINH 01** **Thai Binh River Transport Co (Cong Ty Van Tai Song Bien Thai Binh)** - *Haiphong* *Vietnam*	**130** 75 200	Class: (VR)	**1990 Song Lo Shipyard — Vinh Phu** Loa 40.25 Br ex - Dght 2.200 Lbp - Br md 6.20 Dpth 2.80 Welded, 1 dk	**(A31A2GX) General Cargo Ship** 2 Ha: 2 (9.0 x 4.0)ER	**1 oil engine** reduction geared to sc. shaft driving 1 FP propeller Total Power: 99kW (135hp) 8.0kn Skoda 6L160 1 x 4 Stroke 6 Cy. 160 x 225 99kW (135bhp) (made 1987) CKD Praha-Praha AuxGen: 1 x 6kW a.c
9568627 *XVLV* -	**THAI BINH 01** **Hoa Ngoc Lan Shipping Co Ltd** Binh Minh International Sunrise Shipping JSC *Haiphong* *Vietnam* MMSI: 574000550	**8,216** 5,295 13,298	Class: VR	**2010-07 TKV Shipbuilding & Mechanical Co — Ha Long** Yd No: S07-019 Loa 136.40 Br ex 20.23 Dght 8.350 Lbp 126.00 Br md 20.20 Dpth 11.30 Welded, 1 dk	**(A21A2BC) Bulk Carrier** Grain: 18,600; Bale: 17,744 Compartments: 4 Ho, ER 4 Ha: (18.7 x 11.4)2 (18.4 x 11.4)ER (18.3 x 10.8) Derricks: 4x25t	**1 oil engine** driving 1 FP propeller Total Power: 3,964kW (5,389hp) 13.2kn Mitsubishi 7UEC33LSII 1 x 2 Stroke 7 Cy. 330 x 1050 3964kW (5389bhp) Akasaka Tekkosho KK (Akasaka DieselLtd)-Japan AuxGen: 2 x 355kW 450V a.c
8988923 - -	**THAI BINH 07** *ex* Huu Nghi 15 *-1999* *ex* TB 0803-H *-1999* **Hong Son Trading Co Ltd (Cong Ty Tnhh Thuong Mai Dich Vu Hong Son)** - *Haiphong* *Vietnam* MMSI: 574794000 Official number: VN-1623-VT	**338** 211 557	Class: VR	**1994 Song Dao Shipyard — Nam Dinh** Loa 50.50 Br ex 8.15 Dght 2.650 Lbp 47.45 Br md 7.98 Dpth 3.45 Welded, 1 dk	**(A31A2GX) General Cargo Ship**	**2 oil engines** geared to sc. shafts driving 2 Propellers Total Power: 200kW (272hp) Skoda 6L160 1 x 4 Stroke 6 Cy. 160 x 225 99kW (135bhp) Skoda-Praha Yanmar 5KDGGE 1 x 4 Stroke 5 Cy. 145 x 170 101kW (137bhp) Yanmar Diesel Engine Co Ltd-Japan
8954283 - -	**THAI BINH 08** *ex* Tuan Chau *-2012* *ex* Dong Tien *-2004* *ex* Yet Kieu 01 *-1999* *ex* Min Hai 06 *-2000* **Yet Kieu Shipping Co Ltd (Cong Ty Trach Nhiem Huu Han van Tai Bien Yet Kieu)** - *Saigon* *Vietnam* Official number: VNSG-1487-TD	**341** 227 650	Class: (VR)	**1979 in Japan** Loa 48.47 Br ex 8.22 Dght 3.500 Lbp 44.03 Br md 8.20 Dpth 4.10 Welded, 1 dk	**(A13B2TU) Tanker (unspecified)**	**1 oil engine** driving 1 FP propeller Total Power: 294kW (400hp) S.K.L. 8NVD26A-2 1 x 4 Stroke 8 Cy. 180 x 260 294kW (400bhp) VEB Schwermaschinenbau "KarlLiebknecht" (SKL)-Magdeburg
9338515 - -	**THAI BINH 18** *ex* Hoang Loc 15 *-2007* *ex* Hoang Phat 02 *-2006* **Hong Son Trading Co Ltd (Cong Ty Tnhh Thuong Mai Dich Vu Hong Son)** - SatCom: Inmarsat C 457450810 *Haiphong* *Vietnam* MMSI: 574508000 Official number: VN-1879-VT	**499** 295 945	Class: VR	**2004-10 Haiphong Mechanical & Trading Co. — Haiphong** Loa 56.45 Br ex 9.02 Dght 3.380 Lbp 52.70 Br md 9.00 Dpth 4.12 Welded, 1 dk	**(A31A2GX) General Cargo Ship**	**1 oil engine** geared to sc. shaft driving 1 FP propeller Total Power: 441kW (600hp) Chinese Std. Type Z8170ZL 1 x 4 Stroke 8 Cy. 170 x 200 441kW (600bhp) Zibo Diesel Engine Factory-China
9561710 *3WHB9* -	**THAI BINH 28** *launched as* Anh Tu 09 *-2012* **Ngoc Hieu Shipping Co Ltd** Hoang Anh Trading Service JSC *Haiphong* *Vietnam* MMSI: 574001480 Official number: VN-3473-VT	**4,353** 2,679 7,060	Class: VR	**2012-06 Vu Hat Duong JSC — Hai Duong** Yd No: S72-06 Loa 105.67 Br ex 16.84 Dght 6.880 Lbp 98.50 Br md 16.80 Dpth 8.80 Welded, 1 dk	**(A31A2GX) General Cargo Ship** Compartments: 2 Ho, ER 2 Ha: ER 2 (26.6 x 10.0) Cranes: 1x20t,2x15t	**1 oil engine** reduction geared to sc. shaft driving 1 FP propeller Total Power: 2,501kW (3,400hp) 10.0kn Chinese Std. Type GN8320ZC 1 x 4 Stroke 8 Cy. 320 x 380 2501kW (3400bhp) Ningbo CSI Power & Machinery GroupCo Ltd-China AuxGen: 2 x 276kW 400V a.c Fuel: 470.0
9600009 *3WHG9* -	**THAI BINH 35** **Agriculture Leasing Co I** Hongson Trading Service Co Ltd *Haiphong* *Vietnam* MMSI: 574001530 Official number: VN-3450-VT	**1,660** 1,054 3,040	Class: VR	**2012-08 Huy Van Private Enterprise — Kim Thanh** Yd No: HT-160.02 Loa 79.99 Br ex 12.63 Dght 5.300 Lbp 74.80 Br md 12.60 Dpth 6.48 Welded, 1 dk	**(A31A2GX) General Cargo Ship** Grain: 3,964 Compartments: 2 Ho, ER 2 Ha: ER 2 (18.6 x 7.6)	**1 oil engine** reduction geared to sc. shaft driving 1 FP propeller Total Power: 1,324kW (1,800hp) 10.0kn Chinese Std. Type G6300ZC 1 x 4 Stroke 6 Cy. 300 x 380 1324kW (1800bhp) Ningbo CSI Power & Machinery GroupCo Ltd-China AuxGen: 2 x 90kW 400V a.c Fuel: 110.0
9557020 *3WDU* -	**THAI BINH 36** *launched as* Thai Binh 36-Alci *-2011* **Agriculture Leasing Co I** Hongson Trading Service Co Ltd SatCom: Inmarsat C 457495210 *Haiphong* *Vietnam* MMSI: 574952000	**1,599** 1,021 3,085	Class: VR	**2009-08 Huy Van Private Enterprise — Kim Thanh** Yd No: HT-160.01 Loa 79.99 Br ex 12.63 Dght 5.300 Lbp 74.80 Br md 12.60 Dpth 6.48 Welded, 1 dk	**(A21A2BC) Bulk Carrier** Grain: 3,964 Compartments: 2 Ho, ER 2 Ha: ER 2 (18.6 x 7.6)	**1 oil engine** geared to sc. shaft driving 1 FP propeller Total Power: 735kW (999hp) 12.0kn Chinese Std. Type G6300ZCA 1 x 4 Stroke 6 Cy. 300 x 380 735kW (999bhp) Weifang Diesel Engine Factory-China AuxGen: 2 x 60kW 400V a.c Fuel: 100.0
9573309 *3WAR9* -	**THAI BINH BAY** **Anh Tu Shipping JSC** Binh Minh International Sunrise Shipping JSC *Haiphong* *Vietnam* MMSI: 574000680	**8,333** 5,330 12,843	Class: VR	**2010-10 Hanoi Shipyard — Hanoi** Yd No: HT-170-A Loa 135.27 Br ex 20.24 Dght 8.200 Lbp 126.00 Br md 20.20 Dpth 11.30 Welded, 1 dk	**(A21A2BC) Bulk Carrier** Grain: 17,000 Compartments: 4 Ho, ER 4 Ha: (18.7 x 11.4) (18.3 x 10.8)ER 2 (19.4 x 11.4) Derricks: 2x25t	**1 oil engine** driving 1 FP propeller Total Power: 3,309kW (4,499hp) 13.2kn Hanshin LH46LA 1 x 4 Stroke 6 Cy. 460 x 880 3309kW (4499bhp) The Hanshin Diesel Works Ltd-Japan AuxGen: 2 x 330kW 450V a.c
9283344 *3WHS* -	**THAI BINH DUONG** **Waterway Dredging & Construction Co No 1 (Cong Ty Nao Vet Va Xay Dung Duong Thuy So 1)** - *Haiphong* *Vietnam* MMSI: 574786000 Official number: VN-1836-HB	**1,509** 453 1,916	Class: VR (GL)	**2004-03 B.V. Scheepswerf Damen Hoogezand — Foxhol** Yd No: 9109 Loa 64.00 Br ex - Dght 4.600 Lbp 60.00 Br md 13.00 Dpth 6.30 Welded, 1 dk	**(B33B2DT) Trailing Suction Hopper Dredger** Hopper: 1,500	**2 oil engines** reverse reduction geared to sc. shafts driving 2 CP propellers Total Power: 2,240kW (3,046hp) 10.0kn Deutz TBD620V12 2 x Vee 4 Stroke 12 Cy. 170 x 195 each-1120kW (1523bhp) Deutz AG-Koeln AuxGen: 1 x 520kW 440/220V a.c, 1 x 288kW 400/220V a.c Thrusters: 1 Tunnel thruster (f)
9647306 *3WHO* -	**THAI BINH DUONG 06** **Thai Binh Duong Investment & Transport Service JSC** - *Haiphong* *Vietnam*	**1,599** 970 3,040	Class: VR	**2011-09 Dai Nguyen Duong Co Ltd — Xuan Truong** Yd No: TKT140M1 Loa 79.57 Br ex 12.62 Dght 5.270 Lbp 75.37 Br md 12.60 Dpth 6.20 Welded, 1 dk	**(A31A2GX) General Cargo Ship** Grain: 3,579; Bale: 3,224 Compartments: 2 Ho, ER 2 Ha: (18.2 x 8.0)ER (19.3 x 8.0)	**1 oil engine** reduction geared to sc. shaft driving 1 FP propeller Total Power: 900kW (1,224hp) 10.0kn Chinese Std. Type 12V190 1 x Vee 4 Stroke 12 Cy. 190 x 210 900kW (1224bhp) Weifang Diesel Engine Factory-China AuxGen: 1 x 84kW 400V a.c Fuel: 76.0
9536260 *XVRJ* -	**THAI BINH STAR 01** *ex* Thai Binh Star *-2012* **Anh Tu Shipping JSC** Binh Minh International Sunrise Shipping JSC SatCom: Inmarsat C 457443710 *Haiphong* *Vietnam* MMSI: 574437000 Official number: VN-2881-VT	**5,444** 3,470 8,822	Class: VR	**2009-05 Vinacoal Shipbuilding Co — Ha Long** Yd No: S07-004 Loa 113.20 Br ex 17.63 Dght 7.200 Lbp 105.07 Br md 17.60 Dpth 9.50 Welded, 1 dk	**(A31A2GX) General Cargo Ship** Grain: 11,242; Bale: 8,993 Compartments: 3 Ho, ER 3 Ha: (18.9 x 11.0) (20.3 x 11.0)ER (19.4 x 11.0) Cranes: 3x20t	**1 oil engine** driving 1 FP propeller Total Power: 2,648kW (3,600hp) 12.0kn Hanshin LH41LA 1 x 4 Stroke 6 Cy. 410 x 800 2648kW (3600bhp) The Hanshin Diesel Works Ltd-Japan AuxGen: 2 x 265kW 450V a.c

8310944 *V7E07* -	**THAI BRIGHT** *ex* Candia *-2003* *ex* Cape York *-2001* *ex* Candia *-2000* *ex* Red Sea Encounter *-1992* *ex* Candia *-1991* *ex* Hanjin Candia *-1990* *ex* Candia *-1990* *ex* Red Sea Encounter *-1990* *ex* Lyme Bay *-1989* *ex* Candia *-1988* **Awards Shipping Co Ltd** MSI Ship Management Pte Ltd SatCom: Inmarsat C 453807820 *Majuro* *Marshall Islands* MMSI: 538001842 Official number: 1842	**18,723** 8,596 26,140	Class: BV (GL)	**1984-09 Howaldtswerke-Deutsche Werft AG (HDW) — Kiel** Yd No: 200 Loa 169.40 (BB) Br ex 25.51 Dght 10.183 Lbp 160.00 Br md 25.40 Dpth 15.50 Welded, 1 dk	**(A31A2GX) General Cargo Ship** Grain: 37,228; Bale: 36,492 TEU 1328 C Ho 712 TEU C Dk 616 TEU incl 70 ref C. Compartments: 2 Ho (comb), 4 Ho, ER 8 Ha: (12.7 x 10.3)5 (12.7 x 20.1) (12.5 x 20.1) (12.9 x 20.1)ER Cranes: 4x40t Ice Capable	**1 oil engine** driving 1 FP propeller Vane wheel Total Power: 6,803kW (9,249hp) 15.8kn Sulzer 6RLB66 1 x 2 Stroke 6 Cy. 660 x 1400 6803kW (9249bhp) Sulzer Bros Ltd-Switzerland AuxGen: 3 x 550kW 450V 60Hz a.c Fuel: 197.0 (d.f.) 1746.0 (r.f.) 37.0pd
8310956 *V7E06* -	**THAI DAWN** *ex* Caria *-2003* *ex* Victoria Bay *-1998* *ex* Caria *-1995* *ex* Santa Fe de Bogota *-1994* *ex* Caria *-1993* *ex* Lanka Abhaya *-1990* *ex* Norasia Caria *-1987* *launched as* Caria *-1985* **Harvest Shipping Co Ltd** - SatCom: Inmarsat C 453807811 *Majuro* *Marshall Islands* MMSI: 538001841 Official number: 1841	**18,722** 8,596 26,140	Class: BV (GL)	**1985-03 Howaldtswerke-Deutsche Werft AG (HDW) — Kiel** Yd No: 201 Loa 169.20 (BB) Br ex 25.94 Dght 10.202 Lbp 160.03 Br md 25.40 Dpth 15.52 Welded, 1 dk	**(A31A2GX) General Cargo Ship** Grain: 37,228; Bale: 36,492 TEU 1328 C Ho 712 TEU C Dk 616 TEU incl 70 ref C. Compartments: 2 Ho (comb), 4 Ho, ER 8 Ha: (12.7 x 10.3)5 (12.7 x 20.2)2 (12.9 x 20.2)ER Cranes: 4x40t Ice Capable	**1 oil engine** driving 1 FP propeller Total Power: 6,803kW (9,249hp) 15.8kn Sulzer 6RLB66 1 x 2 Stroke 6 Cy. 660 x 1400 6803kW (9249bhp) Sulzer Bros Ltd-Switzerland AuxGen: 3 x 550kW 450V 60Hz a.c Fuel: 197.0 (d.f.) 1746.0 (r.f.) 37.0pd
8941145 *WDE7836* -	**THAI EXPRESS 1** *ex* Dolphin *-2009* **Thai Express Inc** - *Galveston, TX* *United States of America* Official number: 1052205	**149** 44 -		**1997 Master Boat Builders, Inc. — Coden, Al** Yd No: 244 L reg 24.87 Br ex - Dght - Lbp - Br md 7.32 Dpth 3.81 Welded, 1 dk	**(B11B2FV) Fishing Vessel**	**1 oil engine** driving 1 FP propeller
7238101 - -	**THAI GULF** *ex* Hozan Maru *-1993* *ex* Tsukuba *-1993* **Thai Gulf Fish Meal Industry Co Ltd** - *Thailand* Official number: 367400010	*1,767* 1,249 3,176		**1973-04 Imabari Shipbuilding Co Ltd — Imabari EH (Imabari Shipyard)** Yd No: 276 Loa 82.00 Br ex 12.53 Dght 5.690 Lbp 77.02 Br md 12.50 Dpth 5.74 Riveted\Welded, 1 dk	**(A31A2GX) General Cargo Ship** Grain: 4,600; Bale: 4,250	**1 oil engine** driving 1 FP propeller Total Power: 1,618kW (2,200hp) Makita ESHC640 1 x 4 Stroke 6 Cy. 400 x 600 1618kW (2200bhp) Makita Tekkosho-Japan
7631793 *HSB2000* -	**THAI GULF KHONSONG 2** *ex* Siam Vanich 1 *-2000* **Siam Merchant Marine Co Ltd** - *Bangkok* *Thailand* Official number: 231013509	*469* 386 800		**1980-10 Bangkok Shipbuilding Co. — Bangkok** Yd No: 028 Loa 49.03 Br ex 9.00 Dght 3.752 Lbp 46.00 Br md - Dpth 4.27 Welded, 1 dk	**(A31A2GX) General Cargo Ship**	**1 oil engine** geared to sc. shaft driving 1 FP propeller Total Power: 405kW (551hp) Yanmar 6ML-DT 1 x 4 Stroke 6 Cy. 200 x 240 405kW (551bhp) Yanmar Diesel Engine Co Ltd-Japan
8667189 *XVRU* -	**THAI HA 18** - **Thai Ha Comercial & Transport JSC** - *Haiphong* *Vietnam* Official number: VN-2361-VT	**1,599** 1,057 3,149	Class: VR	**2007-11 Haiphong Mechanical & Trading Co. — Haiphong** Yd No: THB-11-25 Loa 79.80 Br ex 12.82 Dght 5.100 Lbp 74.80 Br md 12.80 Dpth 6.08 Welded, 1 dk	**(A31A2GX) General Cargo Ship** Grain: 3,471 Compartments: 2 Ho, ER 2 Ha: ER 2 (20.4 x 8.4)	**1 oil engine** driving 1 FP propeller 10.0kn Chinese Std. Type CW8200ZC 1 x 4 Stroke 8 Cy. 200 x 270 Zibo Diesel Engine Factory-China
8667191 *XVBD* -	**THAI HA 19** - **Thai Ha Comercial & Transport JSC** - *Haiphong* *Vietnam* Official number: VN-2628-VT	**1,599** 1,088 3,147	Class: VR	**2008-07 Haiphong Mechanical & Trading Co. — Haiphong** Yd No: THB-30-28 Loa 79.80 Br ex 12.82 Dght 5.060 Lbp 74.80 Br md 12.80 Dpth 6.20 Welded, 1 dk	**(A31A2GX) General Cargo Ship** Grain: 3,653 Compartments: 2 Ho, ER 2 Ha: (29.8 x 8.0)ER (20.4 x 8.0)	**1 oil engine** driving 1 FP propeller Total Power: 1,100kW (1,496hp) 10.0kn Chinese Std. Type 8300ZLCZA 1 x 4 Stroke 8 Cy. 300 x 380 1100kW (1496bhp) Zibo Diesel Engine Factory-China
9405356 *3WRC* -	**THAI HA 26** *ex* Hodasco 09 *-2014* **Vietnam Bank for Industry & Trade (VietinBank)** Hoang Dat Co Ltd (Cong Ty Tnhh Hoang Dat) SatCom: Inmarsat C 457437310 *Haiphong* *Vietnam* MMSI: 574373000 Official number: VN-2108-VT	**2,546** 1,427 4,281	Class: VR	**2006-07 Song Cam Shipyard — Haiphong** Yd No: H-175 Loa 93.27 Br ex - Dght 6.050 Lbp 84.95 Br md 13.60 Dpth 7.30 Welded, 1 dk	**(A31A2GX) General Cargo Ship**	**1 oil engine** reduction geared to sc. shaft driving 1 FP propeller Total Power: 1,765kW (2,400hp) Guangzhou 8320ZC 1 x 4 Stroke 8 Cy. 320 x 440 1765kW (2400bhp) Guangzhou Diesel Engine Factory CoLtd-China
8606305 *V7XQ5* -	**THAI HARVEST** *ex* Belo Oriente *-2011* **Greenfield Ltd** MSI Ship Management Pte Ltd *Majuro* *Marshall Islands* MMSI: 538004544 Official number: 4544	**23,124** 9,776 34,507	Class: NK	**1987-02 Sanoyas Corp — Kurashiki OY** Yd No: 1082 Loa 174.50 (BB) Br ex - Dght 11.018 Lbp 165.00 Br md 28.11 Dpth 16.31 Welded, 1 dk	**(A31A2GO) Open Hatch Cargo Ship** Grain: 41,150; Bale: 39,988 Compartments: 6 Ho, ER 6 Ha: ER Gantry cranes: 2x27.2t	**1 oil engine** driving 1 FP propeller Total Power: 5,406kW (7,350hp) 13.5kn Mitsubishi 5UEC60LA 1 x 2 Stroke 5 Cy. 600 x 1900 5406kW (7350bhp) Kobe Hatsudoki KK-Japan Fuel: 1610.0 (r.f.)
8225840 *9WEF* -	**THAI HO No. 1** - **Complete Logistic Services Bhd (CLSB)** - *Kuching* *Malaysia* MMSI: 533000113 Official number: 324910	*701* 454 900		**1982-09 Ocean Shipyard Co Sdn Bhd — Sibu** Loa 55.02 Br ex - Dght - Lbp - Br md 10.98 Dpth 4.27 Welded, 1 dk	**(A31A2GX) General Cargo Ship** Cranes: 2	**2 oil engines** driving 2 FP propellers Total Power: 698kW (950hp) 8.0kn Caterpillar D353SCAC 2 x 4 Stroke 6 Cy. 159 x 203 each-349kW (475bhp) Caterpillar Tractor Co-USA
7632785 - -	**THAI LAEM THONG 2** *ex* Chi Feng 8 *-1999* *ex* Acmes I *-1994* *ex* Fukuho *-1990* **Thai Laemthong Supply & Service Co Ltd** - *Bangkok* *Thailand* Official number: 421000247	**698** 296 1,102	Class: (NK)	**1976-11 Murakami Hide Zosen K.K. — Imabari** Yd No: 136 Loa 61.25 Br ex - Dght 4.000 Lbp 56.00 Br md 9.50 Dpth 4.50 Welded, 1 dk	**(B35E2TF) Bunkering Tanker** Liq: 1,147; Liq (Oil): 1,147	**1 oil engine** driving 1 FP propeller Total Power: 883kW (1,201hp) Makita GSLH6275 1 x 4 Stroke 6 Cy. 275 x 450 883kW (1201bhp) Makita Diesel Co Ltd-Japan AuxGen: 2 x 60kW a.c
9109940 *3FKS4* -	**THAI LAKER** *ex* Brave Pescadores *-2011* **Thai Laker Shipping Ltd** Grand Shipping Ltd SatCom: Inmarsat C 435378610 *Panama* *Panama* MMSI: 353786000 Official number: 2169394E	**5,471** 2,212 6,730	Class: NK	**1994-08 Higaki Zosen K.K. — Imabari** Yd No: 447 Loa 98.18 Br ex - Dght 7.544 Lbp 89.95 Br md 18.00 Dpth 13.00 Welded, 1 dk	**(A31A2GX) General Cargo Ship** Grain: 12,902; Bale: 11,974 Compartments: 2 Ho, ER 2 Ha: (21.7 x 10.2) (22.1 x 10.2)ER Derricks: 2x30t,2x25t	**1 oil engine** driving 1 FP propeller Total Power: 2,942kW (4,000hp) 13.0kn Hanshin LH46L 1 x 4 Stroke 6 Cy. 460 x 880 2942kW (4000bhp) The Hanshin Diesel Works Ltd-Japan AuxGen: 3 x 163kW a.c Fuel: 570.0 (r.f.)
9536569 *3WXX* -	**THAI LONG** - **Agribank Leasing Co II** Thai Long Trading-Transport JSC SatCom: Inmarsat C 457442310 *Saigon* *Vietnam* MMSI: 574423000 Official number: VNSG-1938-TH	**2,551** 1,497 4,375	Class: VR	**2008-12 Dai Duong Shipbuilding Co Ltd — Haiphong** Yd No: HP703-09 Loa 90.72 Br ex 13.00 Dght 6.160 Lbp 84.90 Br md 12.98 Dpth 7.60 Welded, 1 dk	**(A31A2GX) General Cargo Ship** Grain: 4,850 Compartments: 2 Ho, ER 2 Ha: ER 2 (21.0 x 8.0) Cranes: 2x10t	**1 oil engine** reduction geared to sc. shaft driving 1 FP propeller Total Power: 1,500kW (2,039hp) 11.0kn Chinese Std. Type G8300ZC 1 x 4 Stroke 8 Cy. 300 x 380 1500kW (2039bhp) Wuxi Antai Power Machinery Co Ltd-China AuxGen: 2 x 170kW 400V a.c Fuel: 210.0
8987046 *9WBB5* -	**THAI LUNG** *ex* Luconia No. 2 *-1994* **Complete Logistic Services Bhd (CLSB)** - *Labuan* *Malaysia* MMSI: 533000098 Official number: 325747	**672** 386 -		**1969-07 Wong Shipbuilding Contractor — Sibu** Loa 68.60 Br ex 11.43 Dght 2.590 Lbp 64.63 Br md 11.31 Dpth 3.35 Welded, 1 dk	**(A31A2GX) General Cargo Ship**	**2 oil engines** driving 2 Propellers Total Power: 736kW (1,000hp) Cummins 2 x 4 Stroke each-368kW (500bhp) Cummins Engine Co Inc-USA
9159000 *3FZG6* -	**THAI RIVER** *ex* Ocean Express *-2013* **Thai River Shipping Ltd** Grand Shipping Ltd SatCom: Inmarsat M 635647810 *Panama* *Panama* MMSI: 356478000 Official number: 25865PEXT2	**6,058** 2,745 8,474	Class: NK	**1997-02 Higaki Zosen K.K. — Imabari** Yd No: 476 Loa 100.48 Br ex - Dght 8.514 Lbp 92.80 Br md 18.60 Dpth 13.10 Welded, 1 dk	**(A31A2GX) General Cargo Ship** Grain: 12,529; Bale: 12,025 Compartments: 4 Ho, ER 4 Ha: (21.0 x 11.2) (26.5 x 11.2) (18.9 x 11.2) (18.0 x 11.2)ER Derricks: 2x30t,2x25t	**1 oil engine** driving 1 FP propeller Total Power: 2,942kW (4,000hp) 12.3kn Hanshin LH46L 1 x 4 Stroke 6 Cy. 460 x 880 2942kW (4000bhp) The Hanshin Diesel Works Ltd-Japan Fuel: 530.0

IMO / Call sign	Name / Owner / Port	Tonnage	Class	Build / Dimensions	Type	Machinery
5369841 *HSB2675* -	**THAI SAWAN** *ex* Dong Bang 04 *ex* Ninh Co *-1993* *ex* Shun Sang *-1984* *ex* Trans Reefer *-1975* *ex* Tsukishima Maru *-1972* **Mid Thongdee** - *Samut Prakan* *Thailand* Official number: 432300016	**1,338** 682 1,606	Class: (VR) (NK)	**1956**-01 **Shioyama Dockyard Co. Ltd. — Osaka** Yd No: 223 Loa 73.72 Br ex 10.83 Dght 4.812 Lbp 67.01 Br md 10.80 Dpth 5.69 Riveted\Welded, 1 dk	**(A31A2GX) General Cargo Ship** Grain: 1,636; Ins: 1,490 Compartments: 2 Ho, ER 4 Ha: 4 (2.3 x 2.3)ER Derricks: 4x1.5t; Winches: 4	**1 oil engine** driving 1 FP propeller Total Power: 993kW (1,350hp) 9.0kn Niigata M6F43AS 1 x 4 Stroke 6 Cy. 430 x 540 993kW (1350bhp) Niigata Tekkosho-Japan AuxGen: 2 x 120kW 230V a.c Fuel: 399.5
8821577 *3EYS2* -	**THAI SHAN** *ex* Dojun Ace *-2010* *ex* Bao He *-2004* *ex* Golden Harvest *-1996* **Thai Shan Shipping Ltd** Grand Shipping Ltd *Panama* *Panama* MMSI: 352632000 Official number: 4194710	**4,717** 2,486 6,467	Class: KR (NK)	**1989**-10 **Dae Sun Shipbuilding & Engineering Co Ltd — Busan** Yd No: 355 Loa 100.25 (BB) Br ex - Dght 6.639 Lbp 91.25 Br md 17.50 Dpth 10.50 Welded, 2 dks	**(A31A2GX) General Cargo Ship** Grain: 10,850; Bale: 10,077 Compartments: 2 Ho, ER, 2 Tw Dk 2 Ha: (25.4 x 12.5) (26.6 x 12.5)ER Derricks: 2x30t,2x20t	**1 oil engine** sr geared to sc. shaft driving 1 FP propeller Total Power: 2,501kW (3,400hp) 12.3kn Makita LS42L 1 x 4 Stroke 6 Cy. 420 x 840 2501kW (3400bhp) Makita Diesel Co Ltd-Japan AuxGen: 2 x 200kW a.c
9409596 *3WPM* -	**THAI SON 01** - **Nghia Thai Son Trading Ocean JSC** - *Haiphong* *Vietnam* MMSI: 574444000 Official number: VN-2223-VT	**1,598** 1,051 3,000	Class: VR	**2006**-08 **in Vietnam** Yd No: HT-106 Loa 79.15 Br ex - Dght 5.300 Lbp 74.80 Br md 12.60 Dpth 6.48 Welded, 1 dk	**(A31A2GX) General Cargo Ship**	**1 oil engine** geared to sc. shaft driving 1 Propeller Total Power: 1,103kW (1,500hp) Chinese Std. Type 8300ZLC 1 x 4 Stroke 8 Cy. 300 x 380 1103kW (1500bhp) Zibo Diesel Engine Factory-China
8836883 *XVWY* -	**THAI SON 02** *ex* Thang Loi *-2009* *ex* Duy Tan *-2001* *ex* Huan Luyen 108 *-1994* *ex* Bach Dang 10 *-1994* **Agribank Leasing Co II** Hai Long Trading Shipping Co Ltd *Haiphong* *Vietnam* MMSI: 574113103 Official number: VNSG-1476-TH	**967** 414 1,653	Class: VR	**1986** **Bach Dang Shipyard — Haiphong** Loa 80.75 Br ex 10.53 Dght 3.500 Lbp 75.00 Br md 10.50 Dpth 4.50 Welded, 1 dk	**(A31A2GX) General Cargo Ship** Grain: 1,740	**1 oil engine** driving 1 FP propeller Total Power: 883kW (1,201hp) 10.0kn Dvigatel Revolyutsii 6CHN36/45 1 x 4 Stroke 6 Cy. 360 x 450 883kW (1201bhp) Zavod "Dvigatel Revolyutsii"-Gorkiy AuxGen: 2 x 50kW a.c
9533775 *XVQC* -	**THAI SON 18** - **Nghia Thai Son Trading Ocean JSC** Thuan Nghia Maritime Co Ltd SatCom: Inmarsat C 457442610 *Haiphong* *Vietnam* MMSI: 574426000 Official number: VN-36DD-VT	**2,999** 2,010 5,368	Class: VR	**2009**-01 **Vu Hat Duong JSC — Hai Duong** Yd No: HT-40D-1 Loa 97.12 Br ex 15.63 Dght 6.450 Lbp 90.20 Br md 15.60 Dpth 8.10 Welded, 1 dk	**(A21A2BC) Bulk Carrier** Grain: 6,664; Bale: 6,003 Compartments: 2 Ho, ER 2 Ha: (23.4 x 9.0)ER (23.1 x 9.0) Derricks: 2x10t	**1 oil engine** reduction geared to sc. shaft driving 1 FP propeller Total Power: 1,765kW (2,400hp) 12.0kn Chinese Std. Type G8300ZC 1 x 4 Stroke 8 Cy. 300 x 380 1765kW (2400bhp) Ningbo CSI Power & Machinery GroupCo Ltd-China AuxGen: 2 x 198kW 400V 50Hz a.c
8666329 *XVYI* -	**THAI THUY 88** *ex* Huong Dien 36-ALCI *-2011* **18 Maritime Transport JSC** - *Haiphong* *Vietnam* Official number: VN-2868-VT	**1,599** 1,051 3,212 T/cm 839.0	Class: VR	**2009**-05 **Nam Trieu Shipbuilding Industry Co. Ltd. — Haiphong** Yd No: S07-002.20 Loa 78.63 Br ex 12.62 Dght 5.350 Lbp 73.60 Br md 12.60 Dpth 6.48 Welded, 1 dk	**(A31A2GX) General Cargo Ship** Grain: 3,313 Compartments: 2 Ho, ER 2 Ha: ER 2 (19.8 x 8.4)	**1 oil engine** driving 1 FP propeller Total Power: 928kW (1,262hp) 10.0kn Chinese Std. Type XCW8200ZC 1 x 4 Stroke 8 Cy. 200 x 270 928kW (1262bhp) Weichai Power Co Ltd-China
9023017 - -	**THAI TUAN 16** *ex* Song Diem 16 *-2005* **Thai Tuan Co Ltd** - *Haiphong* *Vietnam* Official number: VN-1543-VT	**488** 349 978	Class: VR	**2002**-09 **Nam Ha Shipyard — Nam Ha** Loa 54.40 Br ex 8.82 Dght 3.400 Lbp 50.50 Br md 8.80 Dpth 4.05 Welded, 1 dk	**(A31A2GX) General Cargo Ship**	**1 oil engine** reduction geared to sc. shaft driving 1 Propeller Total Power: 331kW (450hp) 8.5kn Weifang X6170ZC 1 x 4 Stroke 6 Cy. 170 x 200 331kW (450bhp) Weifang Diesel Engine Factory-China
8738873 - -	**THAI TUG** - **Asia Transpark Co Ltd** - *Bangkok* *Thailand* Official number: 451001192	**146** 44 -		**2002**-09 **Thai International Dockyard Co. Ltd. — Samut Prakan** Yd No: A 07191 Loa 24.00 Br ex - Dght - Lbp 22.30 Br md 7.10 Dpth 3.20 Welded, 1 dk	**(B32A2ST) Tug**	**2 oil engines** reduction geared to sc shafts. driving 2 Propellers Total Power: 302kW (410hp) Caterpillar 2 x 4 Stroke each-151kW (205bhp) Caterpillar Inc-USA
8662919 - -	**THAILAND AGGRESSOR** *ex* Star Dancer *-2005* *ex* Sun Dancer *-1997* *ex* Eurma Jane *-1994* **Elegance Travel & Transport Co Ltd** - *Phuket* *Thailand* Official number: 565100640	**250** 82 -		**1977** **Camcraft, Inc. — Crown Point, La** Yd No: 159 Converted From: Crewboat-1993 Loa 35.45 Br ex - Dght - Lbp - Br md 6.55 Dpth 2.76 Welded, 1 dk	**(A37A2PC) Passenger/Cruise** Hull Material: Aluminium Alloy	**2 oil engines** reduction geared to sc. shafts driving 2 Propellers
8938148 *9WCA2* -	**THAILINE** *ex* Jua Hong Dua *-1997* **Thailine Sdn Bhd** Shinline Sdn Bhd *Kuching* *Malaysia* MMSI: 533257000 Official number: 327076	**2,712** 1,579 4,000	Class: BV	**1994** **Moxen Shipyard Sdn Bhd — Sibu** Yd No: PR8201 Loa 84.60 Br ex - Dght 5.210 Lbp 79.80 Br md 16.46 Dpth 6.55 Welded, 1 dk	**(A31A2GX) General Cargo Ship** Grain: 4,912; Bale: 4,421 Compartments: 2 Ho, ER 2 Ha: ER Cranes: 2x12t	**2 oil engines** geared to sc. shafts driving 2 FP propellers Total Power: 1,980kW (2,692hp) 12.0kn Wartsila 6R20 2 x 4 Stroke 6 Cy. 200 x 280 each-990kW (1346bhp) Wartsila Diesel Oy-Finland AuxGen: 2 x 184kW a.c
9010046 *9WDY3* -	**THAILINE 2** *ex* Calayan Iris *-2001* **Thailine Sdn Bhd** Shinline Sdn Bhd *Kuching* *Malaysia* MMSI: 533513000 Official number: 329335	**5,555** 2,350 7,063	Class: NK	**1991**-01 **Shin Kurushima Dockyard Co. Ltd. — Hashihama, Imabari** Yd No: 2706 Loa 98.17 (BB) Br ex - Dght 7.427 Lbp 89.95 Br md 18.80 Dpth 12.90 Welded, 2 dks	**(A31A2GX) General Cargo Ship** Grain: 13,789; Bale: 12,611 Compartments: 2 Ho, ER 2 Ha: 2 (20.3 x 12.7)ER Derricks: 2x30t,2x25t	**1 oil engine** sr geared to sc. shaft driving 1 FP propeller Total Power: 2,424kW (3,296hp) 12.4kn Hanshin 6EL40 1 x 4 Stroke 6 Cy. 400 x 800 2424kW (3296bhp) The Hanshin Diesel Works Ltd-Japan AuxGen: 3 x 164kW a.c Fuel: 445.0 (r.f.)
9107253 *9WFE9* -	**THAILINE 3** *ex* Sun Rose *-2002* **Thailine Sdn Bhd** Shinline Sdn Bhd *Kuching* *Malaysia* MMSI: 533391000 Official number: 329430	**5,585** 2,791 7,919	Class: NK	**1995**-01 **Shin Kurushima Dockyard Co. Ltd. — Akitsu** Yd No: 2842 Loa 98.17 (BB) Br ex - Dght 8.080 Lbp 89.95 Br md 18.80 Dpth 12.90 Welded, 2 dks	**(A31A2GX) General Cargo Ship** Grain: 13,751; Bale: 12,822 Compartments: 2 Ho, ER 2 Ha: (21.0 x 12.7) (24.5 x 12.7)ER Derricks: 2x30t,2x25t	**1 oil engine** driving 1 FP propeller Total Power: 2,427kW (3,300hp) 12.4kn Akasaka A41 1 x 4 Stroke 6 Cy. 410 x 800 2427kW (3300bhp) Akasaka Tekkosho KK (Akasaka DieselLtd)-Japan Fuel: 440.0 (r.f.)
9084293 *9WFF5* -	**THAILINE 5** *ex* Vista *-2002* **Thailine Sdn Bhd** Shinline Sdn Bhd *Kuching* *Malaysia* MMSI: 533399000 Official number: 329453	**5,604** 2,301 6,984	Class: NK	**1994**-01 **Shin Kochi Jyuko K.K. — Kochi** Yd No: 7042 Loa 98.17 (BB) Br ex - Dght 7.429 Lbp 89.95 Br md 18.80 Dpth 12.90 Welded, 2 dks	**(A31A2GX) General Cargo Ship** Grain: 13,473; Bale: 12,472 Compartments: 2 Ho, ER 2 Ha: 2 (20.3 x 12.7)ER Cranes: 1x30t; Derricks: 2x25t	**1 oil engine** driving 1 FP propeller Total Power: 2,427kW (3,300hp) 12.4kn Hanshin 6EL40 1 x 4 Stroke 6 Cy. 400 x 800 2427kW (3300bhp) The Hanshin Diesel Works Ltd-Japan Fuel: 520.0 (r.f.)
9100530 *9WFN6* -	**THAILINE 6** *ex* Surabaya Queen *-2003* **Thailine Sdn Bhd** Shinline Sdn Bhd *Kuching* *Malaysia* MMSI: 533453000 Official number: 329586	**7,636** 2,336 9,118	Class: NK	**1994**-11 **Shin Kochi Jyuko K.K. — Kochi** Yd No: 7052 Loa 113.22 (BB) Br ex - Dght 7.309 Lbp 105.40 Br md 19.60 Dpth 13.20 Welded, 2 dks	**(A31A2GX) General Cargo Ship** Grain: 16,578; Bale: 15,141 Compartments: 2 Ho, ER 2 Ha: (20.3 x 12.6) (33.6 x 12.6)ER Cranes: 2x25t; Derricks: 1x25t	**1 oil engine** driving 1 FP propeller Total Power: 3,884kW (5,281hp) 13.3kn B&W 6L35MC 1 x 2 Stroke 6 Cy. 350 x 1050 3884kW (5281bhp) Mitsui Engineering & Shipbuilding CLtd-Japan Fuel: 630.0 (r.f.)
9181845 *9WFY8* -	**THAILINE 8** *ex* Asian Cosmos *-2004* **Thailine Sdn Bhd** Shinline Sdn Bhd *Kuching* *Malaysia* MMSI: 533766000 Official number: 329708	**6,181** 3,057 8,523	Class: NK	**1998**-08 **Nishi Shipbuilding Co Ltd — Imabari EH** Yd No: 412 Loa 100.64 Br ex - Dght 8.189 Lbp 92.75 Br md 18.80 Dpth 13.00 Welded, 1 dk	**(A31A2GX) General Cargo Ship** Grain: 14,711; Bale: 13,536 Compartments: 2 Ho, ER 2 Ha: (21.7 x 12.8) (25.2 x 12.8)ER Cranes: 1x30.5t; Derricks: 2x25t	**1 oil engine** driving 1 FP propeller Total Power: 3,236kW (4,400hp) 12.5kn B&W 5L35MC 1 x 2 Stroke 5 Cy. 350 x 1050 3236kW (4400bhp) Makita Corp-Japan Fuel: 550.0

9100542 *9WGP9* -	**THAILINE 9** *ex* Friendly Ace *-2006* *ex* Bandung Ace *-2003* **Thailine Sdn Bhd** Shinline Sdn Bhd *Kuching* *Malaysia* MMSI: 533791000 Official number: 330739	**7,636** 2,336 9,083	Class: NK	**1995-01 Shin Kochi Jyuko K.K. — Kochi** Yd No: 7053 Loa 113.22 (BB) Br ex - Dght 7.309 Lbp 105.40 Br md 19.60 Dpth 13.20 Welded, 2 dks	**(A31A2GX) General Cargo Ship** Grain: 16,578; Bale: 14,925 TEU 40 Compartments: 2 Ho, ER 2 Ha: (20.3 x 12.6) (33.6 x 12.6)ER Cranes: 2x25t; Derricks: 1x25t	**1 oil engine** driving 1 FP propeller Total Power: 3,884kW (5,281hp) 13.5kn B&W 6L35MC 1 x 2 Stroke 6 Cy. 350 x 1050 3884kW (5281bhp) Makita Corp-Japan Fuel: 630.0 (r.f.)
6507593 - -	**THAIRUNG RUAMMIT** *ex* B. P. P. 7 *-2005* *ex* C. P. 18 *-1989* *ex* Oversea 8 *-1989* *ex* Summit 20 *-1982* **Lao Saengcharoen Steel Co Ltd** -	*567* 320 1,016	Class: (LR) ✠ Classed LR until 2/2/83	**1965-01 Yamanishi Shipbuilding Co Ltd — Ishinomaki MG** Yd No: 464 Loa 48.49 Br ex 9.53 Dght 4.039 Lbp 45.01 Br md 9.49 Dpth 4.40 Welded, 1 dk	**(A13B2TU) Tanker (unspecified)**	**1 oil engine** driving 1 FP propeller Total Power: 368kW (500hp) Sumiyoshi S6NDTE 1 x 4 Stroke 6 Cy. 270 x 400 368kW (500bhp) Sumiyoshi Marine Diesel Co Ltd-Japan
8223098 *5IM511* -	**THALASSA** *ex* Chloe *-2011* *ex* Claudia Trader *-2007* *ex* Claudia L *-1996* **Thalassa Navigation SA** Coasters Maritime SA *Zanzibar* *Tanzania (Zanzibar)* MMSI: 677041100 Official number: 300251	**989** 446 1,758	Class: MB (BR) (GL)	**1983-06 Hermann Suerken GmbH & Co. KG — Papenburg** Yd No: 317 Loa 74.81 (BB) Br ex 10.60 Dght 3.665 Lbp 70.52 Br md 10.50 Dpth 5.70 Welded, 2 dks	**(A31A2GX) General Cargo Ship** Grain: 2,351; Bale: 2,310 Compartments: 1 Ho, ER 1 Ha: (46.8 x 8.2)ER	**1 oil engine** with clutches, flexible couplings & sr reverse geared to sc. shaft driving 1 FP propeller Total Power: 441kW (600hp) 10.3kn Deutz RBA6M528 1 x 4 Stroke 6 Cy. 220 x 280 441kW (600bhp) Kloeckner Humboldt Deutz AG-West Germany AuxGen: 3 x 93kW 380V 50Hz a.c Thrusters: 1 Thwart. FP thruster (f)
8101276 *PHYD* -	**THALASSA** *ex* Relinquenda *-1996* **Sailing Charter Thalassa BV** Stichting BBZ-ISM *Harlingen* *Netherlands* MMSI: 246329000 Official number: 2140	**257** 120 -		**1980-11 Scheepswerf Haak B.V. — Zaandam** Yd No: 956 Converted From: Fishing Vessel-1995 Loa 37.17 Br ex - Dght 3.330 Lbp 32.57 Br md 8.01 Dpth 4.42 Welded, 1 dk	**(A37A2PC) Passenger/Cruise** Passengers: unberthed: 120; cabins: 18; berths: 36	**1 oil engine** reduction geared to sc. shaft driving 1 FP propeller Total Power: 530kW (721hp) G.M. (Detroit Diesel) 16V-92 1 x Vee 2 Stroke 16 Cy. 123 x 127 530kW (721bhp) Detroit Diesel Corporation-Detroit, Mi Thrusters: 1 Tunnel thruster (f)
9070307 *FNFP*	**THALASSA** **Government of The Republic of France (Institut Francais de Recherche Pour l'Exploitation de la Mer) (IFREMER)** GIE Genavir Centre Ifremer de Brest SatCom: Inmarsat B 322729750 *Nantes* *France* MMSI: 227297000 Official number: 968095	**2,803** 840 955	Class: BV	**1995-12 Saint-Malo Naval — St-Malo** (Hull launched by) Yd No: 620 **1995-12 Manche Industrie Marine — Dieppe** (Hull completed by) Yd No: 520 Loa 74.00 Br ex - Dght 6.000 Lbp 64.90 Br md 14.90 Dpth 11.30 Welded	**(B12D2FR) Fishery Research Vessel** A-frames: 1 Ice Capable	**4 diesel electric oil engines** driving 4 gen. each 1000kW 380V Connecting to 1 elec. Motor of (2000kW) driving 1 FP propeller Total Power: 4,400kW (5,984hp) 15.0kn MWM TBD604BV12 4 x Vee 4 Stroke 12 Cy. 170 x 195 each-1100kW (1496bhp) Motoren Werke Mannheim AG (MWM)-Mannheim Fuel: 460.0
9258545 *VRZM7* -	**THALASSA** *ex* Adrastea *-2003* **Adrastea Maritima SA** Taiyo Nippon Kisen Co Ltd *Hong Kong* *Hong Kong* MMSI: 477807000 Official number: HK-1212	**39,966** 25,503 76,945	Class: NK	**2003-01 Oshima Shipbuilding Co Ltd — Saikai NS** Yd No: 10337 Loa 225.00 (BB) Br ex - Dght 14.126 Lbp 215.00 Br md 32.26 Dpth 19.39 Welded, 1 dk	**(A21A2BC) Bulk Carrier** Grain: 90,475; Bale: 88,871 Compartments: 7 Ho, ER 7 Ha: 6 (16.9 x 15.9)ER (16.0 x 14.1)	**1 oil engine** driving 1 FP propeller Total Power: 8,789kW (11,950hp) 14.5kn MAN-B&W 5S60MC-C 1 x 2 Stroke 5 Cy. 600 x 2400 8789kW (11950bhp) Kawasaki Heavy Industries Ltd-Japan Fuel: 2240.0
7382988 *VORX*	**THALASSA DESGAGNES** *ex* Rio Orinoco *-1993* *ex* Orinoco *-1982* *ex* Joasla *-1979* **Transport Desgagnes Inc** SatCom: Inmarsat C 431605410 *Quebec, QC* *Canada* MMSI: 316188000 Official number: 399944	**5,746** 3,048 9,748 T/cm 18.7	Class: LR (NV) **100A1** SS 12/2013 oil & chemical tanker maximum asphalt cargo temperature 170 degrees C, maximum oil cargo temperature 80 degrees C, in association with a list of defined cargoes TC ESP Ice Class 1A **LMC** **UMS** Eq.Ltr: X; Cable: 495.0/46.0 U3	**1976-05 Ankerlokken Verft Glommen AS — Fredrikstad** Yd No: 189 Loa 134.54 Br ex 17.23 Dght 7.916 Lbp 127.20 Br md 17.20 Dpth 10.00 Welded, 1 dk	**(A13C2LA) Asphalt/Bitumen Tanker** Double Hull Liq: 10,480; Liq (Oil): 10,480; Asphalt: 10,480 Part Cargo Heating Coils Compartments: 16 Wing Ta, ER 3 Cargo Pump (s): 3x300m³/hr Manifold: Bow/CM: 67m Ice Capable	**1 oil engine** driving 1 CP propeller Total Power: 3,678kW (5,001hp) 14.3kn B&W 8K42EF 1 x 2 Stroke 8 Cy. 420 x 900 3678kW (5001bhp) Hitachi Zosen Corp-Japan AuxGen: 3 x 500kW 440V 60Hz a.c Boilers: 2 TOH 10.2kgf/cm² (10.0bar), TOH (ex.g.) 4.1kgf/cm² (4.0bar) Fuel: 8.7 (d.f.) (Heating Coils) 788.0 (r.f.) 18.0pd
9665621 *9V2231* -	**THALASSA ELPIDA** **Thalassa Elpida Pte Ltd** Evergreen Marine Corp (Taiwan) Ltd (EVERGREEN LINE) *Singapore* *Singapore* MMSI: 564388000	**148,667** 66,853 152,344	Class: GL	**2014-03 Hyundai Heavy Industries Co Ltd — Ulsan** Yd No: 2617 Loa 368.48 (BB) Br ex - Dght 15.800 Lbp 352.00 Br md 51.00 Dpth 29.85 Welded, 1 dk	**(A33A2CC) Container Ship (Fully Cellular)** TEU 13806 incl 800 ref C	**1 oil engine** driving 1 FP propeller Total Power: 63,910kW (86,892hp) 23.0kn MAN-B&W 11S90ME-C9 1 x 2 Stroke 11 Cy. 900 x 3260 63910kW (86892bhp) Thrusters: 2 Tunnel thruster (f)
9665592 *9V2228* -	**THALASSA HELLAS** **Thalassa Hellas Pte Ltd** Evergreen Marine Corp (Taiwan) Ltd (EVERGREEN LINE) *Singapore* *Singapore* MMSI: 563377000 Official number: 398773	**148,667** 66,853 152,344	Class: GL	**2013-09 Hyundai Heavy Industries Co Ltd — Ulsan** Yd No: 2614 Loa 368.45 (BB) Br ex - Dght 15.800 Lbp 352.00 Br md 51.00 Dpth 29.85 Welded, 1 dk	**(A33A2CC) Container Ship (Fully Cellular)** TEU 13806 incl 800 ref C	**1 oil engine** driving 1 FP propeller Total Power: 53,250kW (72,399hp) 23.0kn MAN-B&W 11S90ME-C9 1 x 2 Stroke 11 Cy. 900 x 3260 53250kW (72399bhp) Thrusters: 2 Tunnel thruster (f)
8989288 *IN3406* -	**THALASSA II** *ex* Azur *-2011* *ex* Classico Conto Spese *-2005* **A-Leasing SpA** *Imperia* *Italy*	**132** 39 -	Class: RI	**2000-12 Cant. Nav. San Lorenzo SpA — Viareggio** Yd No: 406 Loa 26.75 Br ex 6.76 Dght 1.230 Lbp 24.42 Br md 6.75 Dpth 3.22 Bonded, 1 dk	**(X11A2YP) Yacht** Hull Material: Reinforced Plastic Passengers: cabins: 4; berths: 8	**2 oil engines** reduction geared to sc. shafts driving 2 FP propellers Total Power: 2,686kW (3,652hp) 20.0kn M.T.U. 16V2000M90 2 x Vee 4 Stroke 16 Cy. 130 x 150 each-1343kW (1826bhp) MTU Friedrichshafen GmbH-Friedrichshafen
9665607 *9V2229* -	**THALASSA PATRIS** **Thalassa Patris Pte Ltd** Enesel Pte Ltd *Singapore* *Singapore* MMSI: 563672000 Official number: 398774	**148,667** 152,344	Class: GL	**2013-11 Hyundai Heavy Industries Co Ltd — Ulsan** Yd No: 2615 Loa 368.47 (BB) Br ex - Dght 15.800 Lbp 351.99 Br md 51.00 Dpth 29.85 Welded, 1 dk	**(A33A2CC) Container Ship (Fully Cellular)** TEU 13806 incl 800 ref C	**1 oil engine** driving 1 FP propeller Total Power: 53,250kW (72,399hp) 23.0kn MAN-B&W 11S90ME-C9 1 x 2 Stroke 11 Cy. 900 x 3260 53250kW (72399bhp) Thrusters: 2 Tunnel thruster (f)
9665619 *9V2230* -	**THALASSA PISTIS** **Thalassa Patris Pte Ltd** Enesel SA *Singapore* *Singapore* MMSI: 564019000	**148,667** 152,343	Class: GL	**2014-01 Hyundai Heavy Industries Co Ltd — Ulsan** Yd No: 2616 Loa 368.47 (BB) Br ex - Dght 15.800 Lbp 352.00 Br md 51.00 Dpth 29.85 Welded, 1 dk	**(A33A2CC) Container Ship (Fully Cellular)** TEU 13806 incl 800 ref C	**1 oil engine** driving 1 FP propeller Total Power: 53,250kW (72,399hp) 23.0kn MAN-B&W 11S90ME-C9 1 x 2 Stroke 11 Cy. 900 x 3260 53250kW (72399bhp) Thrusters: 2 Tunnel thruster (f)
8709004 *HSB3341* -	**THALASSIC** *ex* Kotoku Maru *-2006* **Ayudhya Development Leasing Co Ltd (ADLC)** World Wide Transport Co Ltd *Bangkok* *Thailand* MMSI: 567000670 Official number: 480003367	*1,088* 327 1,021	Class: (NK)	**1987-11 Shitanoe Shipbuilding Co Ltd — Usuki OT** Yd No: 1068 Loa 63.00 Br ex 11.82 Dght 4.361 Lbp 57.10 Br md 11.80 Dpth 5.21 Welded, 1 dk	**(A11B2TG) LPG Tanker** Liq (Gas): 1,214 2 x Gas Tank (s);	**1 oil engine** driving 1 FP propeller Total Power: 1,177kW (1,600hp) 11.5kn Akasaka A31 1 x 4 Stroke 6 Cy. 310 x 600 1177kW (1600bhp) Akasaka Tekkosho KK (Akasaka DieselLtd)-Japan AuxGen: 3 x 204kW
9286592 *9HA3445* -	**THALASSINI** *ex* Ocean Lord *-2013* **Argo Shiptrade SA** Thenamaris (Ships Management) Inc *Valletta* *Malta* MMSI: 229609000 Official number: 9286592	**42,887** 27,547 82,977 T/cm 70.2	Class: NK	**2005-07 Tsuneishi Corp — Fukuyama HS** Yd No: 1303 Loa 228.99 Br ex - Dght 14.429 Lbp 222.00 Br md 32.26 Dpth 19.90 Welded, 1 dk	**(A21A2BC) Bulk Carrier** Grain: 97,233 Compartments: 7 Ho, ER 7 Ha: 6 (17.8 x 15.4)ER (16.0 x 13.8)	**1 oil engine** driving 1 FP propeller Total Power: 9,800kW (13,324hp) 14.5kn B&W 7S50MC-C 1 x 2 Stroke 7 Cy. 500 x 2000 9800kW (13324bhp) Fuel: 2590.0

9217656 *SXGP* -	**THALIA** **Thalia Transportation Corp** Neda Maritime Agency Co Ltd SatCom: Inmarsat C 423975610 *Piraeus* *Greece* MMSI: 239756000 Official number: 10835	**39,783** 25,329 75,120 T/cm 67.3	Class: LR ✠ **100A1** SS 01/2011 bulk carrier strengthened for heavy cargoes, Nos. 2, 4 & 6 holds may be empty ESP ESN *IWS LI **ShipRight** (SDA, FDA, CM) ✠ **LMC** **UMS** Eq.Ltr: P†; Cable: 664.1/78.0 U3 (a)	**2001-01 Hitachi Zosen Corp — Maizuru KY** Yd No: 4958 Loa 225.00 (BB) Br ex 32.24 Dght 13.841 Lbp 217.40 Br md 32.20 Dpth 19.15 Welded, 1 dk	**(A21A2BC) Bulk Carrier** Grain: 89,422; Bale: 86,925 Compartments: 7 Ho, ER 7 Ha: (16.3 x 13.5)6 (17.2 x 14.6)ER	**1 oil engine** driving 1 FP propeller Total Power: 10,750kW (14,616hp) 14.0kn B&W 6S60MC 1 x 2 Stroke 6 Cy. 600 x 2292 10750kW (14616bhp) Hitachi Zosen Corp-Japan AuxGen: 3 x 400kW 450V 60Hz a.c Boilers: AuxB (Comp) 7.0kgf/cm² (6.9bar) Fuel: 182.3 (d.f.) (Heating Coils) 2467.9 (r.f.)
8813556 *YDSS* -	**THALIA** *ex* New Soya *-2006* **PT Citra Niaga Mandiri** - *Makassar* *Indonesia* MMSI: 525024013 Official number: 2548	*2,987* 897 850	Class: KI	**1989-05 Naikai Shipbuilding & Engineering Co Ltd — Onomichi HS (Setoda Shipyard)** Yd No: 535 Loa 95.70 (BB) Br ex 15.14 Dght 4.000 Lbp 84.30 Br md 15.00 Dpth 5.40 Welded	**(A36A2PR) Passenger/Ro-Ro Ship (Vehicles)** Passengers: unberthed: 650 Stern door/ramp Cars: 56, Trailers: 21	**2 oil engines** with clutches, flexible couplings & sr reverse geared to sc. shaft driving 2 FP propellers Total Power: 4,414kW (6,002hp) 19.5kn Daihatsu 8DLM-32 2 x 4 Stroke 8 Cy. 320 x 400 each-2207kW (3001bhp) Daihatsu Diesel Manufacturing Co Lt-Japan AuxGen: 2 x 488kW 445V a.c Thrusters: 1 Thwart. CP thruster (f)
7650268 *HQKY2* -	**THALIA** *ex* Macsail *-1999* *ex* Pomegranat *-1996* *ex* Cosmo Ray I *-1992* *ex* Capita *-1990* *ex* Sun Po XI *-1990* *ex* Chin Shiang *-1990* *ex* Tonoura Maru *-1988* **Gold Strategic Ltd** - SatCom: Inmarsat C 433458810 *San Lorenzo* *Honduras* MMSI: 334588000 Official number: L-0334580	**1,350** 817 2,161	Class: (CC) (BV) (CR)	**1976-04 Toura Zosen — Japan** Loa 72.12 Br ex 11.41 Dght 5.010 Lbp 66.50 Br md 11.40 Dpth 6.81 Welded, 1dk	**(A31A2GX) General Cargo Ship** Grain: 2,654; Bale: 2,264 Compartments: 1 Ho, ER 1 Ha: (34.2 x 8.0)ER	**1 oil engine** driving 1 FP propeller Total Power: 1,471kW (2,000hp) 11.5kn Hanshin 6LUD35 1 x 4 Stroke 6 Cy. 350 x 550 1471kW (2000bhp) The Hanshin Diesel Works Ltd-Japan AuxGen: 2 x 80kW 220/445V 60Hz a.c
7700013 *FPCS* BR 385975	**THALIA** **Government of The Republic of France (Institut Francais de Recherche Pour l'Exploitation de la Mer) (IFREMER)** GIE Genavir Centre Ifremer de Brest *Brest* *France* MMSI: 227270000 Official number: 385975	*135* 34 370		**1978-05 Con. Mec. de Normandie — Cherbourg** Yd No: 24 Loa 24.52 Br ex 7.40 Dght 2.552 Lbp 22.41 Br md 7.04 Dpth 3.71 Welded, 1 dk	**(B12D2FR) Fishery Research Vessel**	**2 oil engines** geared to sc. shaft driving 1 FP propeller Total Power: 530kW (720hp) 10.5kn Poyaud A12150SRHM 2 x Vee 4 Stroke 12 Cy. 150 x 180 each-265kW (360bhp) Societe Surgerienne de ConstructionMecaniques-France
9590278 *2DBT3* -	**THALIMA** **Selmabipiemme Leasing SpA** - *London* *United Kingdom* MMSI: 235077622	**114** 34 -	Class: RI	**2010-04 Southern Wind Shipyard Pty Ltd — Cape Town** Yd No: 36 Loa 33.70 Br ex 7.30 Dght 4.200 Lbp 31.60 Br md 6.80 Dpth 3.15 Bonded, 1 dk	**(X11A2YS) Yacht (Sailing)** Hull Material: Reinforced Plastic	**1 oil engine** reduction geared to sc. shaft driving 1 Propeller Total Power: 265kW (360hp) Cummins QSB5.9 1 x 4 Stroke 6 Cy. 102 x 120 265kW (360bhp) Cummins Engine Co Inc-USA Fuel: 5.0 (d.f.)
5357836 *XYCZ* -	**THAMADA** **Board of Management for The Port of Yangon** - *Yangon* *Myanmar* Official number: 1108	*778* 207 -	Class: (LR) ✠ Classed LR until 6/60	**1958-12 Pacific Islands Shipbuilding Co. Ltd. — Hong Kong** Yd No: 201 Loa 61.40 Br ex 10.39 Dght 3.525 Lbp 56.29 Br md 10.37 Dpth 4.88 Riveted\Welded, 1 dk	**(B34N2QP) Pilot Vessel**	**2 oil engines** driving 2 CP propellers Total Power: 1,236kW (1,680hp) Alpha 497R 2 x 2 Stroke 7 Cy. 290 x 490 each-618kW (840bhp) Alpha Diesel A/S-Denmark
9011040 *XYZL* -	**THAMEE HLA** *ex* Cosmic Leader *-2010* *ex* Sun Dance *-2003* *ex* Cosmic Leader *-1995* **Myanma Five Star Line** - *Yangon* *Myanmar* MMSI: 506114000	**8,889** 3,645 9,801	Class: (NK)	**1991-05 Fukuoka Shipbuilding Co Ltd — Fukuoka FO** Yd No: 1161 Loa 124.20 (BB) Br ex 20.42 Dght 7.479 Lbp 114.00 Br md 20.40 Dpth 8.05 Welded, 2 dks	**(A31A2GA) General Cargo Ship (with Ro-Ro facility)** Quarter stern door/ramp (s. a.) Lorries: 78 Grain: 21,139; Bale: 19,771 Compartments: 2 Ho, ER 2 Ha: ER	**1 oil engine** driving 1 FP propeller Total Power: 4,472kW (6,080hp) 13.8kn B&W 8L35MC 1 x 2 Stroke 8 Cy. 350 x 1050 4472kW (6080bhp) Hitachi Zosen Corp-Japan AuxGen: 2 x 320kW 450V 60Hz a.c
9554286 *9V7701* -	**THAMES** **GEA-Tango Pte Ltd** Stellar Shipmanagement Services Pte Ltd *Singapore* *Singapore* MMSI: 565282000 Official number: 394652	**4,758** 2,321 7,393 T/cm 16.9	Class: BV	**2011-07 Nanjing Tianshun Shipbuilding Co Ltd — Nanjing JS** Yd No: 0606 Loa 115.00 (BB) Br ex - Dght 6.800 Lbp 109.00 Br md 17.60 Dpth 8.80 Welded, 1 dk	**(A13B2TP) Products Tanker** Double Hull (13F) Liq: 7,793; Liq (Oil): 7,793 Cargo Heating Coils Compartments: 5 Wing Ta, 5 Wing Ta, 2 Wing Slop Ta, ER 2 Cargo Pump (s): 2x1000m³/hr Manifold: Bow/CM: 58.7m	**1 oil engine** reduction geared to sc. shaft driving 1 FP propeller Total Power: 3,310kW (4,500hp) 12.0kn Yanmar 8N330-EN 1 x 4 Stroke 8 Cy. 330 x 440 3310kW (4500bhp) Qingdao Zichai Boyang Diesel EngineCo Ltd-China AuxGen: 3 x 280kW 60Hz a.c Thrusters: 1 Tunnel thruster (f) Fuel: 93.0 (d.f.) 347.0 (r.f.)
9145011 *MXFP4* -	**THAMES FISHER** **James Fisher & Sons Plc** James Fisher (Shipping Services) Ltd SatCom: Inmarsat C 423478911 *Barrow-in-Furness* *United Kingdom* MMSI: 234789000 Official number: 900460	**2,760** 1,464 4,765 T/cm 11.6	Class: LR ✠ **100A1** SS 10/2012 Double Hull oil tanker ESP LI ✠ **LMC** **UMS** Eq.Ltr: R; Cable: 441.3/40.0 U2	**1997-10 Vickers Shipbuilding & Engineering Ltd — Barrow-in-Furness** Yd No: 1115 Loa 91.40 Br ex 15.56 Dght 6.020 Lbp 85.22 Br md 15.50 Dpth 8.00 Welded, 1 dk	**(A13B2TP) Products Tanker** Double Hull (13F) Liq: 5,028; Liq (Oil): 5,028 Cargo Heating Coils Compartments: 10 Wing Ta, 2 Wing Slop Ta, ER 10 Cargo Pump (s): 10x175m³/hr Manifold: Bow/CM: 48m	**1 oil engine** with clutches, flexible couplings & sr geared to sc. shaft driving 1 CP propeller Total Power: 2,300kW (3,127hp) 12.0kn Ruston 8RK270M 1 x 4 Stroke 8 Cy. 270 x 305 2300kW (3127bhp) Ruston Paxman Diesels Ltd.-United Kingdom AuxGen: 1 x 600kW 450V 60Hz a.c, 2 x 400kW 450V 60Hz a.c Thrusters: 1 Thwart. FP thruster (f) Fuel: 182.0 (d.f.)
9316294 *C6UR4* -	**THAMES HIGHWAY** **Thames Maritime Ltd** Ray Car Carriers Ltd *Nassau* *Bahamas* MMSI: 311996000 Official number: 8001030	**23,498** 7,050 7,750	Class: NV	**2005-12 Stocznia Gdynia SA — Gdynia** Yd No: 8245/2 Loa 147.93 (BB) Br ex 26.40 Dght 7.900 Lbp 134.00 Br md 25.00 Dpth 25.20 Welded, 7 dks	**(A35B2RV) Vehicles Carrier** Stern door/ramp (p. a.) Len: 18.80 Wid: 6.00 Swl: 70 Quarter stern door/ramp (s. a.) Len: 27.50 Wid: 6.00 Swl: 70 Lane-clr ht: 4.80 Cars: 2,130 Ice Capable	**1 oil engine** driving 1 FP propeller Total Power: 9,170kW (12,468hp) 18.9kn MAN-B&W 7S46MC-C 1 x 2 Stroke 7 Cy. 460 x 1932 9170kW (12468bhp) H Cegielski Poznan SA-Poland AuxGen: 3 x 1120kW a.c Thrusters: 1 Thwart. CP thruster (f); 1 Thwart. CP thruster (a) Fuel: 170.0 (d.f.) 1400.0
9060704 *PHYE* -	**THAMESBANK** **Smit Harbour Towage Rotterdam BV** - *Rotterdam* *Netherlands* MMSI: 245906000 Official number: 21953	**321** 96 169	Class: BV	**1992-11 Saint-Malo Naval — St-Malo** Yd No: 616 Loa 30.60 Br ex 9.95 Dght 3.060 Lbp 27.86 Br md 9.70 Dpth 4.02 Welded, 1 dk	**(B32A2ST) Tug**	**2 oil engines** with clutches, flexible couplings & dr geared to sc. shafts driving 2 Directional propellers Total Power: 2,470kW (3,358hp) 11.5kn Deutz SBV6M628 2 x 4 Stroke 6 Cy. 240 x 280 each-1235kW (1679bhp) Motoren Werke Mannheim AG (MWM)-Mannheim AuxGen: 2 x 80kW 380/220V 50Hz a.c Fuel: 66.0 (d.f.)

IMO / Call sign	Name / Owner / Manager / Port	Tonnage	Class	Builder / Dimensions	Type / Cargo	Machinery
9546459 *PCRE* -	**THAMESBORG** **Thamesborg Beheer BV** Wagenborg Shipping BV *Delfzijl* Netherlands MMSI: 246887000 Official number: 23505Z2013	14,695 6,695 21,359	Class: LR ✠100A1 SS 01/2013 strengthened for heavy cargoes and any holds may be empty, container cargoes in all holds and upper deck and on all hatch covers **ShipRight** ACS (B) *IWS LI Ice class 1A FS at draught of 9.535m Max/min draught fwd 9.535/4.015m Max/min draught aft 9.535/5.715m Required power 7500kw, installed power 7500kw ✠**LMC** **UMS** Eq.Ltr: H†; Cable: 579.6/60.0 U3 (a)	2013-01 **Hudong-Zhonghua Shipbuilding (Group) Co Ltd — Shanghai** Yd No: H1595A Loa 172.28 (BB) Br ex 21.74 Dght 9.380 Lbp 161.34 Br md 21.49 Dpth 13.31 Welded, 1 dk	**(A31A2GX) General Cargo Ship** Grain: 23,000; Bale: 23,000 TEU 1228 C Ho 586 TEU C Dk 642 TEU incl 72 ref C Compartments: 2 Ho, ER 2 Ha: (58.7 x 17.8)ER (55.4 x 17.8) Cranes: 4x60t Ice Capable	**1 oil engine** with clutches, flexible couplings & sr geared to sc. shaft driving 1 CP propeller Total Power: 7,500kW (10,197hp) 14.5kn Wartsila 6L46F 1 x 4 Stroke 6 Cy. 460 x 580 7500kW (10197bhp) Wartsila Italia SpA-Italy AuxGen: 1 x 800kW 450V 60Hz a.c, 3 x 450kW 450V 60Hz a.c Boilers: TOH (o.f.) 10.2kgf/cm^2 (10.0bar), TOH (ex.g.) 10.2kgf/cm^2 (10.0bar) Thrusters: 1 Thwart. CP thruster (f)
9069712 *WYC3675* -	**THAMESHIP** *ex* Mahaska (YT-730) *-1970* *ex* Crusader (YNT-4) *-1970* **Thames Towboat Co Inc** - *New York, NY* United States of America MMSI: 367311220 Official number: 545979	187 127 -		1940-01 **Ira S. Bushey & Son, Inc. — New York, NY** Yd No: 473 L reg 29.57 Br ex - Dght - Lbp - Br md 7.74 Dpth 3.96 Welded, 1 dk	**(B32A2ST) Tug**	**1 oil engine** driving 1 Propeller
9300142 *9VBE3* -	**THANA BHUM** *launched as* Upa Bhum *-2005* **Teera Thana Pte Ltd** RCL Shipmanagement Pte Ltd *Singapore* Singapore MMSI: 564603000 Official number: 391017	21,932 8,588 24,225	Class: GL	2005-06 **Jiangsu Yangzijiang Shipbuilding Co Ltd — Jiangyin JS** Yd No: 2003-662C Loa 196.87 (BB) Br ex - Dght 11.000 Lbp 185.10 Br md 27.80 Dpth 16.60 Welded, 1 dk	**(A33A2CC) Container Ship (Fully Cellular)** TEU 1858 C Ho 738 TEU C Dk 1120 TEU incl 300 ref C.	**1 oil engine** driving 1 FP propeller Total Power: 21,660kW (29,449hp) 22.0kn MAN-B&W 6K80MC-C 1 x 2 Stroke 6 Cy. 800 x 2300 21660kW (29449bhp) Hudong Heavy Machinery Co Ltd-China AuxGen: 3 x 1200kW 450/230V 60Hz a.c, 1 x 900kW 450/230V 60Hz a.c Thrusters: 1 Thwart. CP thruster (f)
9125865 - -	**THANAA HAMDY** **Government of The Arab Republic of Egypt (Ministry of Maritime Transport - Ports & Lighthouses Administration)** - *Suez* Egypt	280 - -	Class: LR ✠100A1 SS 08/2006 tug Egyptian coastal service ✠**LMC** Eq.Ltr: (D) ; Cable: 275.0/17.5 U2	1997-11 **Port Said Engineering Works — Port Said** (Hull) Yd No: 663 1997-11 **Timsah SB. Co. — Ismailia** Yd No: 1262 Loa 28.00 Br ex 9.22 Dght 3.260 Lbp 25.18 Br md 8.80 Dpth 4.25 Welded, 1 dk	**(B32A2ST) Tug**	**2 oil engines** with clutches, flexible couplings & sr reverse geared to sc. shafts driving 2 FP propellers Total Power: 1,766kW (2,402hp) Yanmar M220-EN 2 x 4 Stroke 6 Cy. 220 x 300 each-883kW (1201bhp) Yanmar Diesel Engine Co Ltd-Japan AuxGen: 2 x 60kW 400V 50Hz a.c
9211963 - -	**THANAA HAMDY 2** **Government of The Arab Republic of Egypt (Ministry of Maritime Transport - Ports & Lighthouses Administration)** - *Suez* Egypt	280 - 370	Class: LR ✠100A1 SS 11/2011 tug Egyptian coastal service ✠**LMC** Eq.Ltr: F; Cable: 275.0/17.5 U2 (a)	2001-11 **Timsah SB. Co. — Egypt** Yd No: 1430 Loa 28.00 Br ex 9.22 Dght 3.250 Lbp 25.18 Br md 8.80 Dpth 4.25 Welded, 1 dk	**(B32A2ST) Tug**	**2 oil engines** with clutches, flexible couplings & sr reverse geared to sc. shafts driving 2 FP propellers Total Power: 1,766kW (2,402hp) 12.0kn Yanmar M220-EN 2 x 4 Stroke 6 Cy. 220 x 300 each-883kW (1201bhp) Yanmar Diesel Engine Co Ltd-Japan AuxGen: 2 x 80kW 380V 50Hz a.c
8982424 - -	**THANACHOTE** **Chaiyos Htongkhao-On** -	343 198 -		2003-03 **Thong Chansawang — Samut Sakhon** Loa 44.00 Br ex - Dght - Lbp - Br md 8.10 Dpth 4.40 Welded, 1 dk	**(B12B2FC) Fish Carrier**	**1 oil engine** geared to sc. shaft driving 1 Propeller Total Power: 1,078kW (1,466hp) Caterpillar 3512 1 x Vee 4 Stroke 12 Cy. 170 x 190 1078kW (1466bhp) Caterpillar Inc-USA
8313087 *HSB2620* -	**THANAPA** *ex* C. P. 34 *-2010* *ex* CPK 2 *-1999* *ex* Casa Satu *-1994* *ex* Kiyotama Maru *-1994* **PRS Pro Logistics Co Ltd** - *Bangkok* Thailand MMSI: 567012500 Official number: 421000409	1,892 917 2,988 T/cm 9.5	Class: (BV) (NK)	1983-07 **Nishi Shipbuilding Co Ltd — Imabari EH** Yd No: 326 Loa 88.63 (BB) Br ex - Dght 5.280 Lbp 81.90 Br md 13.01 Dpth 6.41 Welded, 1 dk	**(A13B2TP) Products Tanker** Liq: 3,392; Liq (Oil): 3,392 Cargo Heating Coils Compartments: 5 Ta, ER 2 Cargo Pump (s): 2x1000m^3/hr Manifold: Bow/CM: 42m	**1 oil engine** driving 1 FP propeller Total Power: 1,912kW (2,600hp) 12.0kn Hanshin 6ELS35 1 x 4 Stroke 6 Cy. 350 x 700 1912kW (2600bhp) The Hanshin Diesel Works Ltd-Japan AuxGen: 1 x 180kW 445V 60Hz a.c, 1 x 128kW 445V 60Hz a.c, 1 x 64kW 445V 60Hz a.c Fuel: 20.0 (d.f.) (Part Heating Coils) 105.0 (r.f.) 8.0pd
8311455 *HO4645* -	**THANASIS** *ex* Kyriaki I *-2008* *ex* RoRo Trader *-2005* *ex* Espalmador *-2005* **Pargo Maritime SA** Archipelagos Sea Lines Shipping Co *Panama* Panama MMSI: 371918000 Official number: 3235907A	530 165 263	Class: (BV) (RI)	1985-06 **Factoria Naval de Marin S.A. — Marin** Yd No: 12 Loa 33.02 Br ex - Dght 2.571 Lbp 28.02 Br md 10.51 Dpth 3.51 Welded, 3 dks	**(A36A2PR) Passenger/Ro-Ro Ship (Vehicles)**	**2 oil engines** with flexible couplings & sr reverse geared to sc. shafts driving 2 FP propellers Total Power: 1,104kW (1,500hp) 11.0kn GUASCOR E318TAO-SP 2 x Vee 4 Stroke 12 Cy. 150 x 150 each-552kW (750bhp) Gutierrez Ascunce Corp (GUASCOR)-Spain AuxGen: 2 x 49kW 220/380V 50Hz a.c Thrusters: 1 Thwart. FP thruster (f) Fuel: 28.0 (d.f.) 6.0pd
5174789 *SV7753* -	**THANASIS** *ex* Veronique I *-1987* *ex* Telis A *-1980* *ex* Ginevra 1 *-1977* *ex* Ginevra *-1975* *ex* Jole Binelli *-1967* *ex* Vindex *-1961* *launched as* Ferax *-1958* **Constantinos Demetriou** - *Piraeus* Greece Official number: 8385	*489* 309 827	Class: (AB) (RI)	1959-01 **"Navalmeccanica" Cant. Nav. — Senigallia** Yd No: 19 Loa 55.43 Br ex 9.63 Dght 3.579 Lbp 51.01 Br md 9.61 Dpth 3.97 Riveted\Welded, 1 dk	**(A31A2GX) General Cargo Ship** Grain: 1,019; Bale: 934 Compartments: 1 Ho, ER 3 Ha: ER Derricks: 5x2.5t; Winches: 5	**1 oil engine** driving 1 FP propeller Total Power: 515kW (700hp) 11.5kn Deutz RBV6M545 1 x 4 Stroke 6 Cy. 320 x 450 515kW (700bhp) Kloeckner Humboldt Deutz AG-West Germany AuxGen: 1 x 14kW d.c, 1 x 13kW d.c, 1 x 5kW d.c Fuel: 40.5
8868941 *XVGF* -	**THANG 10-01** **October Co-Operative (Hop Tac Xa Thang Muoi)** - *Haiphong* Vietnam	*150* - 200	Class: (VR)	1989 **Kien An Shipbuilding Works — Haiphong** Loa 36.35 Br ex - Dght 1.950 Lbp - Br md 7.46 Dpth 2.50 Welded, 1 dk	**(A31A2GX) General Cargo Ship** Grain: 264 Compartments: 2 Ho, ER 2 Ha: 2 (7.0 x 4.0)ER	**1 oil engine** reduction geared to sc. shaft driving 1 FP propeller Total Power: 99kW (135hp) 7.0kn Skoda 6L160 1 x 4 Stroke 6 Cy. 160 x 225 99kW (135bhp) CKD Praha-Praha
9344447 - -	**THANG DAT 06-ALCI** *ex* Thuy An 10 *-2005* **Agriculture Leasing Co I** Thang Dat River-Sea Transport Co Ltd *Haiphong* Vietnam MMSI: 574565000	469 294 770	Class: (VR)	2004-12 **Vinacoal Shipbuilding Co — Ha Long** Yd No: TKC-64-2 Loa 52.20 Br ex 9.02 Dght 2.950 Lbp 49.30 Br md 9.00 Dpth 3.60 Welded, 1 dk	**(A31A2GX) General Cargo Ship**	**1 oil engine** reduction geared to sc. shaft driving 1 FP propeller Total Power: 300kW (408hp) S.K.L. 8NVD36A-1U 1 x 4 Stroke 8 Cy. 240 x 360 300kW (408bhp) VEB Schwermaschinenbau "KarlLiebknecht" (SKL)-Magdeburg
8667854 - -	**THANG LOI 16** **Hoang Loc Shipping JSC** - *Haiphong* Vietnam Official number: VN-2247-Vt	499 281 942	Class: VR	2007-07 **Thang Loi Enterprise — Kim Thanh** Yd No: TKT457 Loa 57.07 Br ex 9.02 Dght 3.380 Lbp 53.32 Br md 9.00 Dpth 4.05 Welded, 1 dk	**(A31A2GX) General Cargo Ship** Compartments: 2 Ho, ER	**1 oil engine** driving 1 FP propeller 9.2kn Komatsu SA6D170-1 1 x 4 Stroke 6 Cy. 170 x 170 Komatsu Ltd-Japan
9181998 *3FTS8* -	**THANG LONG** *ex* Perseus *-2010* **Transport & Chartering Corp (VIETFRACHT)** SatCom: Inmarsat B 335372310 *Panama* Panama MMSI: 353723000 Official number: 2588298CH	6,715 2,885 8,934	Class: NK	1998-09 **Shin Kurushima Dockyard Co. Ltd. — Hashihama, Imabari** Yd No: 2977 Loa 99.97 Br ex - Dght 8.226 Lbp 93.50 Br md 19.60 Dpth 13.60 Welded, 1 dk	**(A31A2GX) General Cargo Ship** Grain: 15,691; Bale: 14,508 Compartments: 2 Ho, ER 2 Ha: (21.0 x 12.6) (27.0 x 12.6)ER Cranes: 2x30.5t; Derricks: 1x30t	**1 oil engine** driving 1 FP propeller Total Power: 3,884kW (5,281hp) 13.2kn B&W 6L35MC 1 x 2 Stroke 6 Cy. 350 x 1050 3884kW (5281bhp) Makita Corp-Japan Fuel: 610.0

IMO / Call sign / Flag	Name / Former names / Owner / Port	Tonnage	Class	Builder / Dimensions	Type / Capacity	Machinery
8005238 *BNHE* -	**THANG LONG** *ex* Seiko Maru *-1985* **Chin Ma Navigation Corp Ltd** - *Keelung* *Chinese Taipei* Official number: 012512	*1,217* 583 1,550	Class: CR (BV)	**1980-06 Nakatani Shipyard Co. Ltd. — Etajima** Yd No: 460 Loa 69.40 Br ex 11.51 Dght 4.252 Lbp 65.00 Br md 11.02 Dpth 6.33 Welded, 2 dks	**(A31A2GX) General Cargo Ship** Grain: 2,790; Bale: 2,600 Compartments: 1 Ho, ER 1 Ha: (36.0 x 8.5)ER Derricks: 1x10t,1x5t	**1 oil engine** driving 1 FP propeller Total Power: 1,177kW (1,600hp) 13.0kn Akasaka DM33 1 x 4 Stroke 6 Cy. 330 x 500 1177kW (1600bhp) Akasaka Tekkosho KK (Akasaka DieselLtd)-Japan
8930457 - -	**THANG LONG 20** *ex* Hai Long 01 *-1985* *ex* Hai Long *-1996* **Hai Long Transport Co (Cong Ty Van Tai Hai Long)** - *Quang Ninh* *Vietnam*	**171** 70 200	Class: (VR)	**1986 at Quang Ninh** Loa 33.50 Br ex - Dght 1.900 Lbp - Br md 7.00 Dpth 2.50 Welded, 1 dk	**(A31A2GX) General Cargo Ship** Bale: 257 Compartments: 1 Ho, ER 1 Ha: (6.0 x 4.0)ER	**1 oil engine** reduction geared to sc. shaft driving 1 FP propeller Total Power: 103kW (140hp) 7.0kn Yanmar 6KDE 1 x 4 Stroke 6 Cy. 145 x 170 103kW (140bhp) Yanmar Diesel Engine Co Ltd-Japan AuxGen: 1 x 3kW a.c
9024310 - -	**THANG LONG 79** *ex* Thuan Hai 01 *-2007* **Thang Long Trading JSC** - *Saigon* *Vietnam* MMSI: 574999637	**498** 328 1,022	Class: VR	**2002-01 Ha Long Shipbuilding Engineering JSC — Haiphong** Loa 55.60 Br ex 9.02 Dght 3.800 Lbp 51.50 Br md 9.00 Dpth 4.50 Welded, 1 dk	**(A31A2GX) General Cargo Ship**	**1 oil engine** driving 1 FP propeller Total Power: 425kW (578hp) 10.0kn S.K.L. 8NVD36A-1U 1 x 4 Stroke 8 Cy. 240 x 360 425kW (578bhp) SKL Motoren u. Systemtechnik AG-Magdeburg
8868628 - -	**THANG TAM 02** *ex* VT-102 *-1993* **Thang Tam Quang Ninh Co-operative (Hop Tac Xa Thang Tam - Quang Ninh)** - *Quang Ninh* *Vietnam*	**175** 72 295	Class: (VR)	**1969-01 in the People's Republic of China** Converted From: Fishing Vessel-1993 Lengthened-1993 Loa 37.84 Br ex - Dght 2.800 Lbp - Br md 6.72 Dpth 3.38 Welded, 1 dk	**(A31A2GX) General Cargo Ship** Grain: 299 2 Ha: (7.5 x 3.5) (6.8 x 3.5)ER	**1 oil engine** driving 1 FP propeller Total Power: 184kW (250hp) 10.0kn Chinese Std. Type 6267 1 x 4 Stroke 6 Cy. 267 x 330 184kW (250bhp) in China AuxGen: 1 x 9kW d.c, 1 x 3kW d.c
8894043 - -	**THANG TAM 06** - **Thang Tam Quang Ninh Co-operative (Hop Tac Xa Thang Tam - Quang Ninh)** - *Quang Ninh* *Vietnam*	**198** 94 230	Class: (VR)	**1993 Ha Long Shipbuilding Co Ltd — Ha Long** Loa - Br ex - Dght 2.600 Lbp 31.05 Br md 6.70 Dpth 3.50 Welded, 1 dk	**(A31A2GX) General Cargo Ship** Grain: 360 Compartments: 2 Ho, ER 2 Ha: ER	**1 oil engine** reduction geared to sc. shaft driving 1 FP propeller Total Power: 132kW (179hp) S.K.L. 6NVD26-2 1 x 4 Stroke 6 Cy. 180 x 260 132kW (179bhp) (made 1975) VEB Schwermaschinenbau "KarlLiebknecht" (SKL)-Magdeburg AuxGen: 1 x 5kW a.c
9287675 *8UAB* -	**THANGAM** - **Chennai Port Trust** - *Chennai* *India* Official number: 2967	**1,948** 584 300	Class: (IR)	**2002-11 Tianjin Shipyard — Tianjin** Yd No: 2000/38-27 Loa 55.03 Br ex 22.42 Dght 2.640 Lbp 53.10 Br md 22.00 Dpth 5.00 Welded, 1 dk	**(B34B2SC) Crane Vessel** Cranes: 1x150t	**3 diesel electric oil engines** driving 2 gen. each 815kW 415V a.c 1 gen. of 108kW 415V a.c Connecting to 2 elec. motors driving 2 Propellers Total Power: 1,713kW (2,328hp) 6.0kn Cummins 3 x 4 Stroke each-571kW (776bhp) Cummins Engine Co Inc-USA
8667206 *XVPL* -	**THANH AN 09-BIDV** - **BIDV Financial Leasing Co Ltd** Thanh An Shipping JSC *Haiphong* *Vietnam* Official number: VN-2764-VT	**999** 666 1,941	Class: VR	**2008-11 Haiphong Mechanical & Trading Co. — Haiphong** Yd No: THB12-02 Loa 69.85 Br ex 10.82 Dght 4.500 Lbp 65.95 Br md 10.80 Dpth 5.40 Welded, 1 dk	**(A31A2GX) General Cargo Ship** Bale: 2,201 Compartments: 2 Ho, ER 2 Ha: ER 2 (18.2 x 7.0)	**1 oil engine** driving 1 FP propeller 10.0kn Chinese Std. Type CW6200ZC 1 x 4 Stroke 6 Cy. 200 x 270 Weichai Power Co Ltd-China
9170107 *3WHC* -	**THANH BA** *ex* Asian Queen *-2004* **International Shipping & Labour Cooperation JSC (INLACO Saigon) (Cong Ty Co Phan Van Tai Bien Va Hop Tac Lao Dong Quoc Te)** - *Saigon* *Vietnam* MMSI: 574248000 Official number: VNSG-1695-TH	**4,769** 2,682 7,445	Class: NK VR	**1997-06 Kanawa Dockyard Co. Ltd. — Hiroshima** Yd No: 1015 Loa 98.52 Br ex 18.03 Dght 7.714 Lbp 89.95 Br md 18.00 Dpth 11.00 Welded, 1 dk	**(A31A2GX) General Cargo Ship** Grain: 10,761; Bale: 9,934 Compartments: 2 Ho, ER 2 Ha: (24.5 x 10.5) (39.9 x 10.5)ER Derricks: 2x30t,1x25t	**1 oil engine** driving 1 FP propeller Total Power: 2,427kW (3,300hp) 12.0kn Akasaka A41 1 x 4 Stroke 6 Cy. 410 x 800 2427kW (3300bhp) Akasaka Tekkosho KK (Akasaka DieselLtd)-Japan Fuel: 600.0
8847363 *XVAR* -	**THANH BINH 16** *ex* Hoang Phuong 18 *-2009* *ex* Hoan Kiem 06 *-2001* **Thanh Binh Shipping Co Ltd (Cong Ty Tnhh VTB Thanh Binh)** - *Haiphong* *Vietnam* MMSI: 574793000 Official number: VN-732-VT	**497** 276 916	Class: VR	**1986 Hanoi Shipyard — Hanoi** Loa 54.91 Br ex 8.46 Dght 3.850 Lbp 51.36 Br md 8.24 Dpth 4.55 Welded, 1 dk	**(A31A2GX) General Cargo Ship** Grain: 714 Compartments: 2 Ho, ER 2 Ha: 2 (9.0 x 4.5)ER Cranes: 1x1t	**1 oil engine** driving 1 FP propeller Total Power: 224kW (305hp) S.K.L. 6NVD36-1U 1 x 4 Stroke 6 Cy. 240 x 360 224kW (305bhp) VEB Schwermaschinenbau "KarlLiebknecht" (SKL)-Magdeburg
9026693 *3WHW* -	**THANH BINH 26-ALCI** - **Agriculture Leasing Co I** Thanh Binh Shipping Co Ltd (Cong Ty Tnhh VTB Thanh Binh) *Haiphong* *Vietnam* MMSI: 574710000 Official number: VN-1859-VT	**862** 557 1,516	Class: VR	**2004-08 Mechanical Shipbuilding Aquatic Product Enterprise — Haiphong** Yd No: SF-03-10 Loa 64.13 Br ex 10.52 Dght 3.950 Lbp 60.50 Br md 10.50 Dpth 4.60 Welded, 1 dk	**(A31A2GX) General Cargo Ship** Bale: 1,685 Compartments: 2 Ho, ER 2 Ha: ER 2 (17.3 x 7.0)	**1 oil engine** geared to sc. shaft driving 1 FP propeller Total Power: 530kW (721hp) 8.5kn Chinese Std. Type 8170ZCA 1 x 4 Stroke 8 Cy. 170 x 200 530kW (721bhp) (new engine 2004) Weichai Power Co Ltd-China
8665363 *3WTH* -	**THANH CHUONG 05** *ex* Thien Nhat 05 *-2009* **Thanh Chuong Shipping & Trading JSC** - *Haiphong* *Vietnam* Official number: VN-3040-VT	**1,598** 1,062 3,146	Class: VR	**2007-11 Hoang Anh Shipbuilding Industry Joint Stock Co. — Vietnam** Yd No: THB11-16 Loa 79.80 Br ex 12.82 Dght 5.100 Lbp 74.80 Br md 12.80 Dpth 6.08 Welded, 1 dk	**(A31A2GX) General Cargo Ship** Grain: 4,432; Bale: 3,993 Compartments: 2 Ho, ER 2 Ha: ER 2 (20.4 x 8.4)	**1 oil engine** reduction geared to sc. shaft driving 1 FP propeller Total Power: 720kW (979hp) 10.0kn Chinese Std. Type CW8200ZC 1 x 4 Stroke 8 Cy. 200 x 270 720kW (979bhp) Weichai Power Co Ltd-China Fuel: 44.0
8665636 *XVQR* -	**THANH CONG 09-ALCI** - **Agriculture Leasing Co I** Thanh Cong Shipping Co Ltd *Haiphong* *Vietnam* Official number: VN-2772-VT	**1,599** 1,095 3,182	Class: VR	**2008-12 Song Dao Shipyard — Nam Dinh** Yd No: THB-30-15 Loa 79.80 Br ex 12.82 Dght 5.060 Lbp 74.80 Br md 12.80 Dpth 6.20 Welded, 1 dk	**(A31A2GX) General Cargo Ship** Grain: 4,025; Bale: 3,659 Compartments: 2 Ho, ER 2 Ha: ER 2 (20.4 x 8.0)	**1 oil engine** reduction geared to sc. shaft driving 1 FP propeller Total Power: 1,100kW (1,496hp) 11.0kn Chinese Std. Type 8300ZLC 1 x 4 Stroke 8 Cy. 300 x 380 1100kW (1496bhp) Zibo Diesel Engine Factory-China AuxGen: 2 x 33kW 400V a.c Fuel: 58.0
8665765 *XVDC* -	**THANH CONG 18-ALCI** - **Chung Nghia JSC** - *Haiphong* *Vietnam* Official number: VN-2962-VT	**1,599** 1,084 3,185	Class: VR	**2009-08 Trung Bo Co Ltd — Giao Thuy** Yd No: THB-30-08 Loa 79.80 Br ex 12.82 Dght 5.060 Lbp 74.80 Br md 12.80 Dpth 6.20 Welded, 1 dk	**(A31A2GX) General Cargo Ship** Grain: 3,986; Bale: 3,591 Compartments: 2 Ho, ER 2 Ha: ER 2 (20.4 x 8.0)	**1 oil engine** reduction geared to sc. shaft driving 1 FP propeller Total Power: 736kW (1,001hp) 11.0kn S.K.L. 8NVD48A-2U 1 x 4 Stroke 8 Cy. 320 x 480 736kW (1001bhp) (made 1991, fitted 2009) SKL Motoren u. Systemtechnik AG-Magdeburg AuxGen: 2 x 30kW 400V a.c Fuel: 46.0
9557460 *3WAN* -	**THANH CONG 36** - **Thanh Cong Trade Co Ltd** - SatCom: Inmarsat C 457494710 *Haiphong* *Vietnam* MMSI: 574947000	**1,599** 1,017 3,020	Class: VR	**2009-11 Trung Bo Co Ltd — Giao Thuy** Yd No: HT-159 Loa 79.20 Br ex - Dght 5.300 Lbp 74.80 Br md 12.60 Dpth 6.48 Welded, 1 dk	**(A21A2BC) Bulk Carrier** Grain: 3,746; Bale: 3,374 Compartments: 2 Ho, ER 2 Ha: ER 2 (18.6 x 7.6)	**1 oil engine** reduction geared to sc. shaft driving 1 FP propeller Total Power: 736kW (1,001hp) 10.6kn Chinese Std. Type G6300ZCA 1 x 4 Stroke 6 Cy. 300 x 380 736kW (1001bhp) Ningbo CSI Power & Machinery GroupCo Ltd-China AuxGen: 2 x 77kW 400V a.c
9596600 *3WAF9* -	**THANH CONG 45** - **Thanh Cong Trade Co Ltd** - SatCom: Inmarsat C 457499917 *Haiphong* *Vietnam* MMSI: 574000570	**1,599** 1,027 3,031	Class: VR	**2010-11 Nguyen Van Tuan Mechanical Shipbuilding IPE — Kien Xuong** Yd No: HT-159-01 Loa 79.20 Br ex 12.62 Dght 5.300 Lbp 74.80 Br md 12.60 Dpth 6.48 Welded, 1 dk	**(A21A2BC) Bulk Carrier** Grain: 3,780 Compartments: 2 Ho, ER 2 Ha: ER 2 (18.6 x 7.6)	**1 oil engine** reduction geared to sc. shafts driving 1 FP propeller Total Power: 735kW (999hp) 10.0kn Chinese Std. Type G6300ZCA 1 x 4 Stroke 6 Cy. 300 x 380 735kW (999bhp) Ningbo CSI Power & Machinery GroupCo Ltd-China AuxGen: 2 x 90kW 400V a.c

IMO / Call sign	Ship / Owner	Tonnage	Class	Built / Dimensions	Type	Machinery
8838726 *XVAJ* -	**THANH CUONG** *ex Dong A 01 -2007 ex Bach Dang 22 -2003* **Thanh Cuong Transport Co Ltd** - SatCom: Inmarsat C 457415511 *Haiphong* *Vietnam* MMSI: 574155145 Official number: VN-951-VT	**1,247** 646 2,115	Class: VR	**1988 Bach Dang Shipyard — Haiphong** Deepened-2003 Loa 71.60 Br ex 11.66 Dght 5.300 Lbp 65.99 Br md 11.64 Dpth 6.10 Welded, 1 dk	**(A31A2GX) General Cargo Ship** Grain: 1,655 Compartments: 2 Ho, ER 2 Ha: 2 (13.2 x 7.0)ER	**1 oil engine** driving 1 FP propeller Total Power: 736kW (1,001hp) 11.0kn Hanshin 6LU26 1 x 4 Stroke 6 Cy. 260 x 440 736kW (1001bhp) The Hanshin Diesel Works Ltd-Japan AuxGen: 2 x 64kW 380V a.c
9023562 - -	**THANH CUONG 01** *ex Quang Huy 01 -2007* **Thanh Cuong Transport Co Ltd** - *Haiphong* *Vietnam* Official number: VN-2195-VT	**298** 188 -	Class: VR	**1993-01 LISEMCO — Haiphong** Loa 45.30 Br ex 7.92 Dght 2.920 Lbp 43.00 Br md 7.74 Dpth 3.60 Welded, 1 dk	**(A31A2GX) General Cargo Ship**	**1 oil engine** driving 1 Propeller Total Power: 147kW (200hp) 9.0kn S.K.L. 6NVD26-2 1 x 4 Stroke 6 Cy. 180 x 260 147kW (200bhp) SKL Motoren u. Systemtechnik AG-Magdeburg
7236397 *XVJG* -	**THANH DA** *ex Takezono Maru -1985* - - SatCom: Inmarsat C 457409010 *Saigon* *Vietnam* MMSI: 574090080 Official number: VNSG-11721-TH	**1,066** 441 1,312	Class: (VR) (NK)	**1972-09 Imamura Zosen — Kure** Yd No: 182 Loa 66.88 Br ex 11.03 Dght 4.450 Lbp 60.00 Br md 11.00 Dpth 4.50 Welded, 2 dks	**(A31A2GX) General Cargo Ship** Grain: 2,212 Compartments: 1 Ho, ER 1 Ha: (26.4 x 7.0)ER Derricks: 2x3t; Winches: 2	**1 oil engine** driving 1 FP propeller Total Power: 1,324kW (1,800hp) 10.0kn Hanshin 6LUD35 1 x 4 Stroke 6 Cy. 350 x 550 1324kW (1800bhp) Hanshin Nainenki Kogyo-Japan AuxGen: 2 x 80kW a.c
8666331 *3WWP* -	**THANH DAT 18** - **BIDV Financial Leasing Co II** Thanh Dat Shipping Co Ltd *Haiphong* *Vietnam* Official number: VN-2815-VT	**1,599** 1,035 3,068	Class: VR	**2008-06 Nam Trieu Shipbuilding Industry Co. Ltd. — Haiphong** Yd No: TKT140A8 Loa 79.57 Br ex 12.62 Dght 5.300 Lbp 75.37 Br md 12.60 Dpth 6.12 Welded, 1 dk	**(A31A2GX) General Cargo Ship** Bale: 3,412 Compartments: 2 Ho, ER 2 Ha: (19.3 x 8.0)ER (18.2 x 8.0)	**1 oil engine** driving 1 FP propeller Total Power: 1,100kW (1,496hp) 9.6kn Chinese Std. Type 8300ZLCZA 1 x 4 Stroke 8 Cy. 300 x 380 1100kW (1496bhp) Zibo Diesel Engine Factory-China
9026916 *3WLG* -	**THANH DAT 27-ALCI** - **Agriculture Leasing Co I** Thanh Dat Co Ltd (Cong Ty Tnhh Thanh Dat) *Haiphong* *Vietnam* MMSI: 574554000 Official number: VN-1936-VT	**910** 552 1,605	Class: VR	**2005-03 Nam Ha Shipyard — Nam Ha** Yd No: HT-36A Loa 64.80 Br ex 11.02 Dght 3.700 Lbp 60.85 Br md 11.00 Dpth 4.70 Welded, 1 dk	**(A31A2GX) General Cargo Ship**	**2 oil engines** geared to sc. shafts driving 2 Propellers Total Power: 1,266kW (1,722hp) 10.0kn Weifang X6170ZC 2 x 4 Stroke 6 Cy. 170 x 200 each-633kW (861bhp) Weifang Diesel Engine Factory-China
8667218 *XVTS* -	**THANH DAT 28-ALCI** *ex Thanh Luan 27-ALCI -2009* **Agriculture Leasing Co I** Thanh Luan Private Co *Haiphong* *Vietnam* Official number: VN-2756-VT	**1,599** 1,075 3,089	Class: VR	**2008-11 Haiphong Mechanical & Trading Co. — Haiphong** Yd No: TKT535 Loa 79.80 Br ex 12.82 Dght 5.040 Lbp 74.80 Br md 12.80 Dpth 6.08 Welded, 1 dk	**(A31A2GX) General Cargo Ship** Grain: 3,493 Compartments: 2 Ho, ER 2 Ha: ER 2 (20.4 x 8.4)	**1 oil engine** driving 1 FP propeller Total Power: 1,199kW (1,630hp) 10.0kn Chinese Std. Type CW12V200ZC 1 x Vee 4 Stroke 12 Cy. 200 x 270 1199kW (1630bhp) Weichai Power Co Ltd-China
8666795 *XVZQ* -	**THANH DO** *ex Thanh Thong 03 -2012* **Ha Trung River-Sea Transport Co Ltd (Cong Ty Tnhh Van Song Bien Ha Trung)** - *Haiphong* *Vietnam* Official number: VN-3498-VT	**692** 353 1,191	Class: VR	**2006-05 Huy Hoang Co Ltd — Nam Dinh** Yd No: TKC35-07 Loa 63.70 Br ex 10.70 Dght 3.000 Lbp 59.90 Br md 10.50 Dpth 3.70 Welded, 1 dk	**(A31A2GX) General Cargo Ship** Grain: 1,346; Bale: 1,213 Compartments: 2 Ho, ER 2 Ha: (15.5 x 7.5)ER (14.0 x 7.5)	**1 oil engine** driving 1 FP propeller Total Power: 400kW (544hp) 11.0kn Chinese Std. Type Z8170ZLC 1 x 4 Stroke 8 Cy. 170 x 200 400kW (544bhp) Weifang Diesel Engine Factory-China Fuel: 36.5
8941391 *WCX8257* -	**THANH HAI** *ex Mayflower II -2004* **Thanh Hai Inc** - *D'Iberville, MS* *United States of America* MMSI: 367307040 Official number: 1058673	**183** 54 -		**1997 T.M. Jemison Construction Co., Inc. — Bayou La Batre, Al** Yd No: 112 L reg 26.30 Br ex - Dght - Lbp - Br md 7.92 Dpth 3.96 Welded, 1 dk	**(B11B2FV) Fishing Vessel**	**1 oil engine** driving 1 FP propeller
9511208 *3WWZ* -	**THANH HAI 07** - **Thanh Hai Trading & Transport Co Ltd** - *Haiphong* *Vietnam* MMSI: 574921000	**499** 309 884	Class: VR	**2008-12 Nam Tien Co Ltd — Xuan Truong** Yd No: THB-21-01 Loa 56.77 Br ex 9.02 Dght 3.140 Lbp 53.00 Br md 9.00 Dpth 3.80 Welded, 1 dk	**(A31A2GX) General Cargo Ship** Grain: 1,181; Bale: 1,064 Compartments: 1 Ho, ER 1 Ha: ER (29.0 x 5.0)	**1 oil engine** reduction geared to sc. shaft driving 1 FP propeller Total Power: 441kW (600hp) 11.0kn Chinese Std. Type Z8170ZL 1 x 4 Stroke 8 Cy. 170 x 200 441kW (600bhp) Zibo Diesel Engine Factory-China AuxGen: 1 x 18kW 400V a.c
9511210 *3WWY* -	**THANH HAI 08** - **Thanh Hai Trading & Transport Co Ltd** - *Haiphong* *Vietnam* MMSI: 574922000	**499** 309 881	Class: VR	**2009-04 Nam Tien Co Ltd — Xuan Truong** Yd No: THB-21-02 Loa 56.77 Br ex 9.02 Dght 3.140 Lbp 53.00 Br md 9.00 Dpth 3.80 Welded, 1 dk	**(A31A2GX) General Cargo Ship** Grain: 1,181; Bale: 1,064 Compartments: 2 Ho, ER 1 Ha: ER (29.0 x 5.0)	**1 oil engine** reduction geared to sc. shaft driving 1 FP propeller Total Power: 441kW (600hp) 11.0kn Chinese Std. Type Z8170ZL 1 x 4 Stroke 8 Cy. 170 x 200 441kW (600bhp) Zibo Diesel Engine Factory-China AuxGen: 1 x 18kW 400/220V a.c
9511222 *XVMN* -	**THANH HAI 09** - **Thanh Hai Trading & Transport Co Ltd** - SatCom: Inmarsat C 457492310 *Haiphong* *Vietnam* MMSI: 574923000	**499** 309 884	Class: VR	**2009-05 Nam Tien Co Ltd — Xuan Truong** Yd No: THB-21-03 Loa 56.77 Br ex 9.02 Dght 3.140 Lbp 53.00 Br md 9.00 Dpth 3.80 Welded, 1 dk	**(A31A2GX) General Cargo Ship** Grain: 1,181; Bale: 1,064 Compartments: 1 Ho, ER 1 Ha: ER (29.0 x 5.0)	**1 oil engine** reduction geared to sc. shaft driving 1 FP propeller Total Power: 441kW (600hp) 11.0kn Chinese Std. Type Z8170ZL 1 x 4 Stroke 8 Cy. 170 x 200 441kW (600bhp) Zibo Diesel Engine Factory-China
9369837 *3WNO* -	**THANH HAI 18** *ex Victory 10 -2008* **Thanh Hai Transportation Sea Co Ltd** - SatCom: Inmarsat C 457433910 *Haiphong* *Vietnam* MMSI: 574339000 Official number: VN-2021-VT	**2,359** 1,498 3,897	Class: VR	**2006-02 LISEMCO — Haiphong** Yd No: H-144D Loa 86.20 Br ex - Dght 6.040 Lbp 80.10 Br md 13.60 Dpth 7.30 Welded, 1 dk	**(A31A2GX) General Cargo Ship** Grain: 5,452; Bale: 5,000 Compartments: 2 Ho, ER 2 Ha: (17.1 x 9.4)ER (17.5 x 9.4) Cranes: 2x8t	**1 oil engine** driving 1 FP propeller Total Power: 1,471kW (2,000hp) Hanshin 6LUD35 1 x 4 Stroke 6 Cy. 350 x 550 1471kW (2000bhp) The Hanshin Diesel Works Ltd-Japan AuxGen: 2 x 130kW 440V a.c Fuel: 890.0
8649761 *XVOD* -	**THANH HAI 58** *ex Hung Dat 27 -2009* **Agribank Leasing Co II** Thanh Hai Transportation Sea Co Ltd *Haiphong* *Vietnam* MMSI: 574012329 Official number: VN-2813-VT	**1,598** 1,059 3,200	Class: VR	**2008-10 Nam Ha Shipyard — Nam Ha** Yd No: HT-133.TM Loa 79.14 Br ex 12.62 Dght 5.450 Lbp 74.80 Br md 12.60 Dpth 6.48 Welded, 1 dk	**(A31A2GX) General Cargo Ship** Grain: 3,897; Bale: 3,543 Compartments: 2 Ho, ER 2 Ha: ER 2 (18.6 x 7.6)	**1 oil engine** reduction geared to sc. shaft driving 1 FP propeller Total Power: 720kW (979hp) 10.0kn Chinese Std. Type CW8200ZC 1 x 4 Stroke 8 Cy. 200 x 270 720kW (979bhp) Weichai Power Co Ltd-China AuxGen: 2 x 50kW 400V a.c Fuel: 53.0
8664993 *3WBK* -	**THANH HUNG 45** - **Thanh Hung Shipping Co Ltd** - *Haiphong* *Vietnam* Official number: VN-3039-VT	**999** 649 1,970	Class: VR	**2009-12 Nam Ha Shipyard — Nam Ha** Yd No: TKT129X1 Loa 69.86 Br ex 10.82 Dght 4.550 Lbp 65.85 Br md 10.80 Dpth 5.40 Welded, 1 dk	**(A31A2GX) General Cargo Ship** Grain: 2,423; Bale: 2,182 Compartments: 2 Ho, ER 2 Ha: ER 2 (17.1 x 7.2)	**1 oil engine** reduction geared to sc. shaft driving 1 FP propeller Total Power: 698kW (949hp) 10.0kn Chinese Std. Type XCW6200ZC 1 x 4 Stroke 6 Cy. 200 x 270 698kW (949bhp) Weichai Power Co Ltd-China AuxGen: 1 x 33kW 400V a.c
9024920 - -	**THANH HUY 126** *ex Thanh Dat 15 -2003* **Thanh Huy JSC** - SatCom: Inmarsat C 457481810 *Haiphong* *Vietnam* MMSI: 574818000 Official number: VN-1611-VT	**499** 327 934	Class: VR	**2003-03 Nam Ha Shipyard — Nam Ha** Yd No: ND-09B Loa 55.43 Br ex 8.52 Dght 3.480 Lbp 52.70 Br md 8.50 Dpth 4.25 Welded, 1 dk	**(A31A2GX) General Cargo Ship**	**1 oil engine** geared to sc. shaft driving 1 Propeller Total Power: 316kW (430hp) 9.0kn Weifang X6170ZC 1 x 4 Stroke 6 Cy. 170 x 200 316kW (430bhp) (made 2002) Weifang Diesel Engine Factory-China

9386029 *3WNY* -	**THANH HUYEN 07** *ex* Long Mon 01 *-2010* **Thanh Huyen Co Ltd** - SatCom: Inmarsat C 457436110 *Da Nang* *Vietnam* MMSI: 574631000 Official number: VNDN-248-TH	**1,404** 820 2,315	Class: VR	**2006**-08 **Da Nang Shipyard — Da Nang** Loa 69.50 Br ex - Dght 5.000 Lbp 64.20 Br md 12.00 Dpth 6.20 Welded, 1 dk	**(A31A2GX) General Cargo Ship**	**1 oil engine** reverse reduction geared to sc. shaft driving 1 FP propeller Total Power: 721kW (980hp) Chinese Std. Type CW6200ZC 1 x 4 Stroke 6 Cy. 200 x 270 721kW (980bhp) Weifang Diesel Engine Factory-China
8940012 - -	**THANH LAM** **Kien Mau Lam** - *North Richland Hills, TX* *United States of America* Official number: 1048406	**140** 42 -		**1996 La Force Shipyard Inc — Coden AL** Yd No: 79 L reg 24.90 Br ex - Dght - Lbp - Br md 7.32 Dpth 3.75 Welded, 1 dk	**(B11B2FV) Fishing Vessel**	**1 oil engine** driving 1 FP propeller
9622148 *3WAI9* -	**THANH LIEM 08** **Thanh Liem Co Ltd** - *Haiphong* *Vietnam* MMSI: 574012609	**1,599** 1,032 3,234	Class: VR	**2010**-11 **An Dong Shipbuilding Industry JSC — Haiphong** Yd No: DKTB02-14 Loa 78.68 Br ex 12.62 Dght 5.350 Lbp 73.60 Br md 12.60 Dpth 6.48 Welded, 1 dk	**(A31A2GX) General Cargo Ship** Grain: 3,799; Bale: 3,423 Compartments: 2 Ho, ER 2 Ha: ER 2 (19.8 x 8.4)	**1 oil engine** reduction geared to sc. shaft driving 1 FP propeller Total Power: 735kW (999hp) 10.0kn Chinese Std. Type 8300ZLC 1 x 4 Stroke 8 Cy. 300 x 380 735kW (999bhp) Zibo Diesel Engine Factory-China AuxGen: 2 x 56kW a.c Fuel: 89.0
9610846 *XVWO* -	**THANH LIEM 09** **Thanh Liem Co Ltd** - *Haiphong* *Vietnam*	**1,599** 1,032 3,234	Class: VR	**2010**-06 **An Dong Shipbuilding Industry JSC — Haiphong** Yd No: DKTB02-12 Loa 78.68 Br ex 12.62 Dght 5.350 Lbp 73.60 Br md 12.60 Dpth 6.48 Welded, 1 dk	**(A31A2GX) General Cargo Ship** Grain: 3,799; Bale: 3,423 Compartments: 2 Ho, ER 2 Ha: ER 2 (19.8 x 8.4)	**1 oil engine** driving 1 FP propeller Total Power: 735kW (999hp) 10.0kn Chinese Std. Type 8300ZLC 1 x 4 Stroke 8 Cy. 300 x 380 735kW (999bhp) Zibo Diesel Engine Factory-China AuxGen: 2 x 54kW 400V a.c
8665868 *XVWG* -	**THANH LONG 08** *ex* Anh Bang 08 *-2008* **359 Growth Stock Co** - *Haiphong* *Vietnam*	**786** 450 1,368	Class: VR	**2008**-03 **Truong Xuan Shipbuilding Industry JSC — Xuan Truong** Yd No: SKB05 Loa 64.00 Br ex 10.72 Dght 3.300 Lbp 59.90 Br md 10.50 Dpth 4.10 Welded, 1 dk	**(A31A2GX) General Cargo Ship** Grain: 1,700; Bale: 1,531 Compartments: 2 Ho, ER 2 Ha: ER 2 (20.0 x 7.6)	**2 oil engines** reduction geared to sc. shafts driving 2 FP propellers Total Power: 440kW (598hp) 11.0kn Chinese Std. Type Z6150ZLC 2 x 4 Stroke 6 Cy. 150 x 190 each-220kW (299bhp) Nantong Diesel Engine Co Ltd-China AuxGen: 1 x 16kW 230V a.c Fuel: 19.0
9022946 - -	**THANH LUYEN 45** *ex* Hoang Phuong 45 *-2004* **Thanh Luyen Co Ltd** - *Haiphong* *Vietnam*	**499** 339 1,018	Class: VR	**2001**-11 **Trung Hai Private Enterprise — Haiphong** Loa 55.60 Br ex 9.22 Dght 3.800 Lbp 51.50 Br md 9.00 Dpth 4.50 Welded, 1 dk	**(A31A2GX) General Cargo Ship**	**1 oil engine** driving 1 Propeller Total Power: 315kW (428hp) 10.0kn S.K.L. 6NVD36A-1U 1 x 4 Stroke 6 Cy. 240 x 360 315kW (428bhp) SKL Motoren u. Systemtechnik AG-Magdeburg
9379533 *3WMB* -	**THANH MINH 09** *ex* Van Kieu 09 *-2012* **Thanh Minh Transport Co Ltd** - *Haiphong* *Vietnam* MMSI: 574949000 Official number: VN-1949-VT	**499** 350 914	Class: VR	**2005**-08 **Song Dao Shipyard — Nam Dinh** Yd No: HT-90A Loa 57.23 Br ex 9.28 Dght 3.000 Lbp 54.20 Br md 9.26 Dpth 3.70 Welded, 1 dk	**(A31A2GX) General Cargo Ship** Grain: 1,268; Bale: 1,150 Compartments: 2 Ho, ER 2 Ha: ER 2 (12.5 x 5.0)	**1 oil engine** reduction geared to sc. shaft driving 1 FP propeller Total Power: 425kW (578hp) 9.0kn S.K.L. 8NVD36A-1U 1 x 4 Stroke 8 Cy. 240 x 360 425kW (578bhp) SKL Motoren u. Systemtechnik AG-Magdeburg
9026849 *3WIQ* -	**THANH MINH 27-ALCI** **Agriculture Leasing Co I** - *Haiphong* *Vietnam*	**491** 329 980	Class: VR	**2004**-12 **Nam Ha Shipyard — Nam Ha** Yd No: HT-51 Loa 55.00 Br ex 8.72 Dght 3.460 Lbp 51.84 Br md 8.70 Dpth 4.15 Welded, 1 dk	**(A31A2GX) General Cargo Ship**	**1 oil engine** driving 1 Propeller Total Power: 300kW (408hp) 10.5kn S.K.L. 8NVD36-1U 1 x 4 Stroke 8 Cy. 240 x 360 300kW (408bhp) SKL Motoren u. Systemtechnik AG-Magdeburg
9469663 - -	**THANH NHAN 05** *ex* Quy Hai 06 *-2012* **Quy Hai Co Ltd** - *Haiphong* *Vietnam*	**235** 71 -	Class: VR	**2007**-10 **Hai Long Co. — Haiphong** Yd No: DH-06-10 Loa 26.86 Br ex 9.20 Dght 2.800 Lbp 24.59 Br md 9.00 Dpth 4.19 Welded, 1 dk	**(B32A2ST) Tug**	**2 oil engines** geared to sc. shafts driving 2 FP propellers Total Power: 736kW (1,000hp) 9.0kn Volvo Penta TAMD162C 2 x 4 Stroke 6 Cy. 144 x 165 each-368kW (500bhp) AB Volvo Penta-Sweden AuxGen: 2 x 58kW 400V 50Hz a.c
9026825 *3WVC* -	**THANH PHAT 01** *ex* Imextrans 16 *-2014* *ex* Dai Duong 27-ALCI *-2007* **Thanh Phat Shipping Co Ltd** - SatCom: Inmarsat C 457451210 *Saigon* *Vietnam* MMSI: 574512000 Official number: VNSG-2165-THC	**1,080** 583 1,987	Class: VR	**2004**-12 **Hoang Anh Shipbuilding Industry Joint Stock Co. — Vietnam** Yd No: SCV-04 Converted From: General Cargo Ship-2008 Loa 69.85 Br ex 10.82 Dght 4.650 Lbp 65.85 Br md 10.80 Dpth 5.40 Welded, 1 dk	**(A12A2TC) Chemical Tanker** Double Hull (13F) Liq: 2,202 Compartments: 8 Wing Ta, ER	**1 oil engine** reduction geared to sc. shaf driving 1 FP propeller Total Power: 720kW (979hp) 8.4kn Chinese Std. Type CW8200ZC 1 x 4 Stroke 6 Cy. 200 x 270 720kW (979bhp) Weichai Power Co Ltd-China
8953992 - -	**THANH PHAT 26** *ex* Hong Hoa 09 *-2007* **Thanh Phat Shipping Co Ltd** - *Haiphong* *Vietnam*	**392** 249 735	Class: VR	**1997**-01 **An Duong Shipyard Co-operative — Haiphong** Rebuilt-2002 Loa 51.78 Br ex 7.94 Dght 3.200 Lbp 47.50 Br md 7.92 Dpth 3.91 Welded, 1 dk	**(A31A2GX) General Cargo Ship** Grain: 960 Compartments: 2 Ho, ER 2 Ha: (9.5 x 4.4) (14.5 x 4.4)ER	**2 oil engines** driving 2 FP propellers Total Power: 198kW (270hp) Skoda 6L160 2 x 4 Stroke 6 Cy. 160 x 225 each-99kW (135bhp) CKD Praha-Praha AuxGen: 1 x 8kW 380V a.c Fuel: 19.0 (d.f.)
8665777 *3WTK* -	**THANH PHAT 36** *ex* Hong Phuoc 36-ALCI *-2011* **Thanh Phat Shipping Co Ltd** - *Haiphong* *Vietnam* Official number: VN-3359-VT	**499** 369 983	Class: VR	**2008**-01 **Trung Bo Co Ltd — Giao Thuy** Yd No: S07-022 Loa 56.30 Br ex 9.02 Dght 3.330 Lbp 53.02 Br md 9.00 Dpth 3.97 Welded, 1 dk	**(A31A2GX) General Cargo Ship** Grain: 1,403; Bale: 1,237 Compartments: 2 Ho, ER 2 Ha: ER 2 (13.5 x 5.0)	**1 oil engine** reduction geared to sc. shaft driving 1 FP propeller Total Power: 425kW (578hp) 11.0kn Chinese Std. Type 8170ZC 1 x 4 Stroke 8 Cy. 170 x 200 425kW (578bhp) Zibo Diesel Engine Factory-China Fuel: 20.0
9023990 - -	**THANH PHONG 19** **Thanh Phong Shipping Co Ltd (Cong Ty Tnhh Van Tai Bien Thanh Phong)** - *Haiphong* *Vietnam* Official number: VN-1441-VT	**499** 339 1,018	Class: VR	**2001**-11 **Ha Long Shipbuilding Engineering JSC — Haiphong** Loa 55.60 Br ex 9.22 Dght 3.800 Lbp 51.50 Br md 9.00 Dpth 4.50 Welded, 1 dk	**(A31A2GX) General Cargo Ship**	**1 oil engine** geared to sc. shaft driving 1 Propeller Total Power: 405kW (551hp) 11.0kn Caterpillar D379 1 x Vee 4 Stroke 8 Cy. 159 x 203 405kW (551bhp) Caterpillar Inc-USA
9026019 - -	**THANH PHONG 27** **Thanh Phong Shipping Co Ltd (Cong Ty Tnhh Van Tai Bien Thanh Phong)** - *Haiphong* *Vietnam* MMSI: 574661000 Official number: VN-1725-VT	**918** 617 1,524	Class: VR	**2003**-12 **LISEMCO — Haiphong** Yd No: SVC-02 Loa 64.50 Br ex 10.83 Dght 4.200 Lbp 60.50 Br md 10.80 Dpth 5.10 Welded, 1 dk	**(A31A2GX) General Cargo Ship**	**1 oil engine** driving 1 FP propeller Total Power: 425kW (578hp) 10.0kn S.K.L. 8NVD36A-1U 1 x 4 Stroke 8 Cy. 240 x 360 425kW (578bhp) SKL Motoren u. Systemtechnik AG-Magdeburg
9026071 - -	**THANH PHONG 45** **Thanh Phong Trading & Shipping Co Ltd** - *Haiphong* *Vietnam* Official number: VN-2096-VT	**480** 302 852	Class: VR	**2003**-12 **Mechanical Shipbuilding Aquatic Product Enterprise — Haiphong** Loa 54.06 Br ex 9.02 Dght 3.150 Lbp 49.80 Br md 9.00 Dpth 3.80 Welded, 1 dk	**(A31A2GX) General Cargo Ship**	**1 oil engine** geared to sc. shaft driving 1 Propeller Total Power: 331kW (450hp) Yanmar 6MA-HT 1 x 4 Stroke 6 Cy. 200 x 240 331kW (450bhp) Yanmar Diesel Engine Co Ltd-Japan
8915184 *3WFO* -	**THANH SON** *ex* Never On Sunday *-2003* **International Shipping & Labour Cooperation JSC (INLACO Saigon) (Cong Ty Co Phan Van Tai Bien Va Hop Tac Lao Dong Quoc Te)** - *Saigon* *Vietnam* MMSI: 574216000 Official number: VNSG-22/10/02-TC	**4,405** 2,806 7,165	Class: VR (NK)	**1990**-02 **Nishi Shipbuilding Co Ltd — Imabari EH** Yd No: 356 Loa 106.86 (BB) Br ex - Dght 6.868 Lbp 100.00 Br md 17.60 Dpth 8.70 Welded, 1 dk	**(A31A2GX) General Cargo Ship** Grain: 9,701; Bale: 9,701 Compartments: 2 Ho, ER 2 Ha: ER Cranes: 4x25t	**1 oil engine** driving 1 FP propeller Total Power: 2,942kW (4,000hp) 12.5kn Mitsubishi 6UEC37LA 1 x 2 Stroke 6 Cy. 370 x 880 2942kW (4000bhp) Akasaka Tekkosho KK (Akasaka DieselLtd)-Japan AuxGen: 2 x 275kW 450V 60Hz a.c, 2 x 220kW 450V 60Hz a.c Fuel: 114.0 (d.f.) 476.0 (r.f.)

8667610 *XVSL* -	**THANH THANG 18** *ex* Trung Thang 18 *-2013* **Thanh Thang Trading Shipping Co Ltd** - *Haiphong* *Vietnam* Official number: VN-3512-VT	**999** 661 1,970	Class: VR	**2008-11 Truong Xuan Shipbuilding Industry JSC — Xuan Truong** Yd No: TKT129Q Loa 69.86 Br ex 10.82 Dght 4.550 Lbp 65.85 Br md 10.80 Dpth 5.40 Welded, 1 dk	**(A31A2GX) General Cargo Ship** Grain: 2,181; Bale: 2,400 Compartments: 2 Ho, ER 2 Ha: ER 2 (17.1 x 7.2)	**1 oil engine** driving 1 FP propeller Total Power: 600kW (816hp) 11.0kn Chinese Std. Type Z8170ZLC 1 x 4 Stroke 8 Cy. 170 x 200 600kW (816bhp) Zibo Diesel Engine Factory-China
8741806 *3WWE* -	**THANH THANH DAT 06** *ex* Hai Long 26 *-2013* **Thanh Thanh Dat Co Ltd** - *Haiphong* *Vietnam* MMSI: 574000230	**499** 337 952	Class: VR	**2008-06 Long Son Co Ltd — Tam Diep** Yd No: VNB01-02B Loa 59.50 Br ex 10.02 Dght 2.800 Lbp 55.75 Br md 10.00 Dpth 3.60 Welded, 1 dk	**(A31A2GX) General Cargo Ship** Grain: 1,301; Bale: 1,172 Compartments: 2 Ho, ER 2 Ha: ER 2 (14.3 x 6.0)	**1 oil engine** reduction geared to sc. shaft driving 1 FP propeller Total Power: 401kW (545hp) 10.0kn Chinese Std. Type Z8170ZL 1 x 4 Stroke 8 Cy. 170 x 200 401kW (545bhp) Zibo Diesel Engine Factory-China AuxGen: 2 x 40kW 400V a.c
9335082 *3WIF* -	**THANH THANH DAT 08** *ex* Hoang Bao 27 *-2011* *ex* DA NANG 45 *-2010* **Thanh Dat Co Ltd (Cong Ty Tnhh Thanh Dat)** - SatCom: Inmarsat C 457476010 *Haiphong* *Vietnam* MMSI: 574760000 Official number: VNDN-209-VT	**499** 316 885	Class: VR	**2004-10 Da Nang Shipyard — Da Nang** Loa 57.00 Br ex 9.17 Dght 3.300 Lbp 53.00 Br md 9.15 Dpth 4.05 Welded, 1 dk	**(A31A2GX) General Cargo Ship** Compartments: 2 Ho, ER 2 Ha: ER 2 (13.2 x 5.0)	**1 oil engine** reverse reduction geared to sc. shaft driving 1 FP propeller Total Power: 316kW (430hp) Weifang X6170ZC 1 x 4 Stroke 6 Cy. 170 x 200 316kW (430bhp) Weifang Diesel Engine Factory-China
9510175 *3WXP* -	**THANH THANH DAT 09** *ex* Dang Khoa 01 *-2011* **Thanh Thanh Dat Co Ltd** - *Haiphong* *Vietnam* MMSI: 574012239 Official number: VN-2558-VT	**499** 316 928	Class: VR	**2008-04 in Vietnam** Yd No: S-07-033-01 Loa 56.30 Br ex 9.02 Dght 3.280 Lbp 53.02 Br md 9.00 Dpth 3.97 Welded, 1 dk	**(A31A2GX) General Cargo Ship** Compartments: 2 Ho, ER 2 Ha: (13.0 x 5.0)ER (14.0 x 5.0)	**1 oil engine** reduction geared to sc. shaft driving 1 FP propeller Total Power: 401kW (545hp) 10.0kn Chinese Std. Type Z8170ZL 1 x 4 Stroke 8 Cy. 170 x 200 401kW (545bhp) Zibo Diesel Engine Factory-China AuxGen: 2 x 16kW 400V a.c
9532240 *XVMV8* -	**THANH THANH DAT 17** *ex* Thai Binh 16 *-2013* *ex* Thai Binh 16-Alci *-2011* **Thanh Dat Co Ltd (Cong Ty Tnhh Thanh Dat)** - SatCom: Inmarsat C 457469910 *Haiphong* *Vietnam* MMSI: 574699000	**499** 322 918	Class: VR	**2008-10 Song Ninh Co-operative — Vietnam** Yd No: THB-23-01 Loa 57.00 Br ex 9.16 Dght 3.270 Lbp 53.48 Br md 9.00 Dpth 3.97 Welded, 1 dk	**(A31A2GX) General Cargo Ship** Grain: 1,227; Bale: 1,105 Compartments: 2 Ho, ER 2 Ha: (16.5 x 5.0)ER (14.5 x 5.0)	**1 oil engine** reduction geared to sc. shaft driving 1 FP propeller Total Power: 441kW (600hp) Chinese Std. Type Z8170ZL 1 x 4 Stroke 8 Cy. 170 x 200 441kW (600bhp) Zibo Diesel Engine Factory-China
9548512 *3WXK* -	**THANH THANH DAT 18** *ex* HANG HA 05 *-2010* **Thanh Thanh Dat Co Ltd** - SatCom: Inmarsat C 457499921 *Haiphong* *Vietnam* MMSI: 574012332	**499** 373 887	Class: VR	**2008-11 Duc Manh Co Ltd — Kinh Mon** Yd No: HT-141-05 Loa 55.88 Br ex 9.52 Dght 3.200 Lbp 52.98 Br md 9.50 Dpth 3.85 Welded, 1 dk	**(A31A2GX) General Cargo Ship** Compartments: 2 Ho, ER 2 Ha: (12.5 x 5.6)ER (13.0 x 5.6)	**1 oil engine** reduction geared to sc. shaft driving 1 FP propeller Total Power: 441kW (600hp) 10.0kn Weifang 8170ZC 1 x 4 Stroke 8 Cy. 170 x 200 441kW (600bhp) (made 2007) Weifang Diesel Engine Factory-China AuxGen: 2 x 18kW 400V a.c
9511997 *XVSP* -	**THANH THANH DAT 26** *ex* Quang Anh 45 *-2012* **Quang Anh Trading & Shipping Co** - *Haiphong* *Vietnam* MMSI: 574012280	**499** 302 930	Class: VR	**2008-05 Vinashin Hoang Long Shipbuilding JSC — Thanh Hoa** Yd No: TH712-01 Loa 57.60 Br ex 9.10 Dght 2.960 Lbp 54.20 Br md 9.10 Dpth 3.60 Welded, 1 dk	**(A31A2GX) General Cargo Ship** Compartments: 2 Ho, ER 2 Ha: ER 2 (13.0 x 5.0)	**1 oil engine** reduction geared to sc. shaft driving 1 FP propeller Total Power: 331kW (450hp) 11.0kn Chinese Std. Type Z6170ZL 1 x 4 Stroke 6 Cy. 170 x 200 331kW (450bhp) Zibo Diesel Engine Factory-China
8985581 *XVEH* -	**THANH THANH DAT 27** *ex* Truong Phat 06 *-2010* *ex* Hai Phuong 18 *-2010* *ex* Phu An 18 *-2005* *ex* Hoang Dung 18 *-2002* *ex* Nghia Hong 09 *-2002* **Thanh Thanh Dat Co Ltd** - *Haiphong* *Vietnam* MMSI: 574012619 Official number: VN-1992-VT	**498** 321 905	Class: VR	**1997 Marine Service Co. No. 1 — Haiphong** Loa 58.30 Br ex 9.00 Dght 3.300 Lbp 54.96 Br md 8.58 Dpth 4.15 Welded, 1 dk	**(A31A2GX) General Cargo Ship** Grain: 1,225 Compartments: 2 Ho, ER 2 Ha: (14.5 x 5.5)ER (16.0 x 5.5)	**1 oil engine** driving 1 FP propeller Total Power: 224kW (305hp) 8.0kn S.K.L. 8NVD36 1 x 4 Stroke 8 Cy. 240 x 360 224kW (305bhp) (Re-engined ,made 1969, refitted 1997) SKL Motoren u. Systemtechnik AG-Magdeburg Fuel: 16.0 (d.f.)
9399246 *XVZA* -	**THANH THANH DAT 35** *ex* Khanh Viet *-2013* *ex* Longthinh Star 01 *-2009* *ex* Thien Toan 36-Alcii *-2008* *ex* Hai Thinh 36-ALCI *-2007* **Thanh Dat Co Ltd (Cong Ty Tnhh Thanh Dat)** - SatCom: Inmarsat C 457436710 *Haiphong* *Vietnam* MMSI: 574367000	**1,597** 1,042 3,021	Class: VR	**2006-11 Nam Ha Shipyard — Nam Ha** Yd No: THB-15-01 Loa 79.50 Br ex 12.32 Dght 5.120 Lbp 75.45 Br md 12.30 Dpth 6.30 Welded, 1 dk	**(A31A2GX) General Cargo Ship** Grain: 3,834; Bale: 3,454	**1 oil engine** reduction geared to sc. shaft driving 1 FP propeller Total Power: 1,103kW (1,500hp) 12.0kn Chinese Std. Type 8300ZLC 1 x 4 Stroke 8 Cy. 300 x 380 1103kW (1500bhp) Zibo Diesel Engine Factory-China
9353151 *3WLF* -	**THANH THANH DAT 36** *ex* Hung Thinh 36 *-2011* **Thanh Thanh Dat Co Ltd** - SatCom: Inmarsat C 457429510 *Haiphong* *Vietnam* MMSI: 574295000 Official number: VN-1961-VT	**1,595** 968 2,762	Class: VR	**2005-09 LISEMCO — Haiphong** Yd No: TKT-140 Loa 79.57 Br ex 12.62 Dght 5.000 Lbp 75.37 Br md 12.60 Dpth 6.00 Welded, 1 dk	**(A31A2GX) General Cargo Ship** Grain: 3,715	**1 oil engine** reduction geared to sc. shaft driving 1 Propeller Total Power: 735kW (999hp) 10.0kn Chinese Std. Type 8300ZLC 1 x 4 Stroke 8 Cy. 300 x 380 735kW (999bhp) Weifang Diesel Engine Factory-China
9548720 *XVNY* -	**THANH THANH DAT 45** *ex* VIET HUNG 05 *-2011* **Thanh Thanh Dat Co Ltd** - SatCom: Inmarsat C 457443610 *Haiphong* *Vietnam* MMSI: 574436000 Official number: VN-2659-VT	**1,599** 1,086 3,074	Class: VR	**2008-07 Huy Van Private Enterprise — Kim Thanh** Yd No: VNB-02-05 Loa 79.60 Br ex - Dght 5.050 Lbp 74.80 Br md 12.80 Dpth 6.10 Welded, 1 dk	**(A31A2GX) General Cargo Ship** Grain: 3,992 Compartments: 2 Ho, ER 2 Ha: ER 2 (20.4 x 8.4)	**1 oil engine** reduction geared to sc. shaft driving 1 FP propeller Total Power: 736kW (1,001hp) 9.0kn Chinese Std. Type 8300ZLC 1 x 4 Stroke 8 Cy. 300 x 380 736kW (1001bhp) Zibo Diesel Engine Factory-China AuxGen: 1 x 84kW 400V a.c Fuel: 80.0
9329241 *3WKY* -	**THANH THANH DAT 68** *ex* Dai Duong Sailor *-2013* *ex* Minh Phat 02 *-2012* **Thanh Dat Co Ltd (Cong Ty Tnhh Thanh Dat)** - SatCom: Inmarsat C 457429310 *Haiphong* *Vietnam* MMSI: 574293000 Official number: VN-1937-VT	**1,407** 836 2,336	Class: VR	**2005-05 Trung Hai Private Enterprise — Haiphong** Loa 76.00 Br ex 11.62 Dght 4.640 Lbp 71.67 Br md 11.60 Dpth 5.67 Welded, 1 dk	**(A31A2GX) General Cargo Ship**	**1 oil engine** driving 1 FP propeller Total Power: 750kW (1,020hp) 10.0kn S.K.L. 8NVD48A-1U 1 x 4 Stroke 8 Cy. 320 x 480 750kW (1020bhp) VEB Schwermaschinenbau "KarlLiebknecht" (SKL)-Magdeburg
9545821 *XVRC* -	**THANH THANH DAT 69** *ex* Tien Giang 07 *-2013* **Thanh Thanh Dat Co Ltd** - SatCom: Inmarsat C 457496610 *Haiphong* *Vietnam* MMSI: 574966000	**1,599** 1,049 3,045	Class: VR	**2009-12 Nam Tien Co Ltd — Xuan Truong** Yd No: DKTB-02.07 Loa 79.60 Br ex 12.82 Dght 5.050 Lbp 74.80 Br md 12.80 Dpth 6.10 Welded, 1 dk	**(A31A2GX) General Cargo Ship** Grain: 3,944; Bale: 3,535 Compartments: 2 Ho, ER 2 Ha: ER 2 (20.4 x 8.4)	**1 oil engine** reduction geared to sc. shaft driving 1 FP propeller Total Power: 720kW (979hp) 11.0kn Chinese Std. Type 8300ZLC 1 x 4 Stroke 8 Cy. 300 x 380 720kW (979bhp) (made 2008) Weichai Power Co Ltd-China
9520326 *XVJU* -	**THANH THONG 09** - **Thanh Thong Waterway Transport JSC** - *Haiphong* *Vietnam*	**499** 256 890	Class: VR	**2008-06 Huy Hoang Co Ltd — Nam Dinh** Yd No: TKC-31-07 Loa 54.84 Br ex 10.22 Dght 2.810 Lbp 51.78 Br md 10.00 Dpth 3.50 Welded, 1 dk	**(A31A2GX) General Cargo Ship** Grain: 787; Bale: 709 Compartments: 2 Ho, ER 2 Ha: (13.0 x 6.0)ER (11.5 x 6.0)	**1 oil engine** reduction geared to sc. shaft driving 1 FP propeller Total Power: 440kW (598hp) 11.0kn Chinese Std. Type Z8170ZL 1 x 4 Stroke 8 Cy. 170 x 200 440kW (598bhp) Zibo Diesel Engine Factory-China

IMO / Call sign	Name / Owner	Tonnage	Class	Builder / Dimensions	Type	Machinery
9314404 *3WGI* -	**THANH THUY** **International Shipping & Labour Cooperation JSC (INLACO Saigon) (Cong Ty Co Phan Van Tai Bien Va Hop Tac Lao Dong Quoc Te)** - *Saigon* *Vietnam* MMSI: 574244000 Official number: VNSG-1693-TH	**4,095** 2,448 6,596	Class: NK VR	**2004**-02 **Bach Dang Shipyard — Haiphong** Yd No: 207 Loa 102.79 Br ex 17.24 Dght 6.957 Lbp 94.50 Br md 17.00 Dpth 8.80 Welded, 1 dk	**(A31A2GX) General Cargo Ship** Grain: 8,610; Bale: 8,159 Derricks: 4x25t	**1 oil engine** driving 3 gen. driving 1 FP propeller Total Power: 2,647kW (3,599hp) 13.8kn Hanshin LH41LA 1 x 4 Stroke 6 Cy. 410 x 800 2647kW (3599bhp) The Hanshin Diesel Works Ltd-Japan Fuel: 375.0
7022784 - -	**THANH TO** *ex* Taisei Maru No. 41 *-1984* **Haiphong Maritime Transportation Co (MARITRANSCO) (Cong Ty Van Tai Bien Hai Phong)** - *Haiphong* *Vietnam*	*1,498* 784 3,008	Class: (VR) (NK)	**1970**-05 **Hayashikane Shipbuilding & Engineering Co Ltd — Nagasaki NS** Yd No: 767 Loa 80.32 Br ex 13.44 Dght 5.744 Lbp 74.00 Br md 13.42 Dpth 8.16 Welded, 2 dks	**(B12B2FC) Fish Carrier** Ins: 859; Liq: 2,231 4 Ha: (4.5 x 4.4)3 (4.6 x 4.4)ER Derricks: 8x3t	**1 oil engine** driving 1 FP propeller Total Power: 2,207kW (3,001hp) 12.0kn Mitsubishi 6UET39/65 1 x 2 Stroke 6 Cy. 390 x 650 2207kW (3001bhp) Kobe Hatsudoki Seizosho-Japan AuxGen: 2 x 160kW 440V 60Hz a.c Fuel: 71.0 (d.f.) 376.5 (r.f.) 11.0pd
8666343 *3WSX* -	**THANH TRUNG 27** **Thanh Trung Shipping Co Ltd** - *Haiphong* *Vietnam* Official number: VN-2298-VT	**998** 654 1,986	Class: VR	**2007**-09 **Nam Trieu Shipbuilding Industry Co. Ltd. — Haiphong** Yd No: TKT129N Loa 69.86 Br ex 10.82 Dght 4.550 Lbp 65.85 Br md 10.80 Dpth 5.40 Welded, 1 dk	**(A31A2GX) General Cargo Ship** Bale: 2,383 Compartments: 2 Ho, ER 2 Ha: ER 2 (17.1 x 7.2)	**1 oil engine** driving 1 FP propeller Total Power: 748kW (1,017hp) 10.0kn Chinese Std. Type 6210ZLC 1 x 4 Stroke 6 Cy. 210 x 290 748kW (1017bhp) Zibo Diesel Engine Factory-China
9601479 - -	**THANH TRUNG 36** **Thanh Trung Transport Co Ltd** - *Haiphong* *Vietnam* MMSI: 574012564	**1,348** 854 2,656	Class: VR	**2010**-05 **in Vietnam** Yd No: TKT534A Loa 74.50 Br ex 11.62 Dght 4.550 Lbp 70.74 Br md 11.60 Dpth 5.40 Welded, 1 dk	**(A31A2GX) General Cargo Ship** Bale: 3,221 Compartments: 2 Ho, ER 2 Ha: ER 2 (19.2 x 7.6)	**2 oil engines** reduction geared to sc. shafts driving 2 FP propellers Total Power: 660kW (898hp) 10.0kn Weifang X6170ZC 2 x 4 Stroke 6 Cy. 170 x 200 each-330kW (449bhp) Weichai Power Co Ltd-China AuxGen: 2 x 60kW 400V a.c
8666874 *XVRG* -	**THANH TUAN 18** **Ngoc Mai Trading Transport Service JSC** - *Haiphong* *Vietnam* Official number: VN-3078-VT	**1,599** 1,073 3,199	Class: VR	**2009**-03 **Diem Dien Shipbuilding Industry Co — Thai Thuy** Yd No: THB-30-59 Loa 79.80 Br ex 12.82 Dght 5.060 Lbp 74.80 Br md 12.80 Dpth 6.20 Welded, 1 dk	**(A31A2GX) General Cargo Ship** Compartments: 2 Ho, ER 2 Ha: ER 2 (20.4 x 8.0)	**1 oil engine** driving 1 FP propeller Total Power: 720kW (979hp) 11.0kn Chinese Std. Type CW8200ZC 1 x 4 Stroke 8 Cy. 200 x 270 720kW (979bhp) Weichai Power Co Ltd-China AuxGen: 2 x 24kW 400V a.c Fuel: 59.0
8893037 - -	**THANH VAN 27** *ex* Tuan Hung 27 *-2008* *ex* Sam Son 19 *-2004* *ex* Quang Minh 25 *-2001* *ex* Quang Minh 18 *-1995* *ex* Dinh Vu 02 *-1995* **Thanh Van Sea Transport Co-operative** - *Haiphong* *Vietnam* Official number: VN-1403-VT	**355** 243 709	Class: VR	**1989 Kien An Shipbuilding Works — Haiphong** Rebuilt-2004 Loa 49.90 Br ex 7.80 Dght 3.200 Lbp 47.13 Br md 7.56 Dpth 3.90 Welded, 1 dk	**(A31A2GX) General Cargo Ship** Grain: 375 Compartments: 2 Ho, ER 2 Ha: 2 (7.0 x 4.0)ER	**1 oil engine** reduction geared to sc. shaft driving 1 FP propeller Total Power: 132kW (179hp) 9.0kn S.K.L. 6NVD26-2 1 x 4 Stroke 6 Cy. 180 x 260 132kW (179bhp) (made 1967) VEB Schwermaschinenbau "KarlLiebknecht" (SKL)-Magdeburg AuxGen: 1 x 19kW a.c
8666238 - -	**THANH VINH 01-BIDV** **BIDV Financial Leasing Co Ltd** Vuong Thanh Vinh Shipping JSC *Haiphong* *Vietnam* Official number: VN-3005-VT	**1,599** 1,014 3,212	Class: VR	**2009**-11 **Cat Tuong Shipyard — Truc Ninh** Yd No: S07-008.09 Loa 78.63 Br ex 12.62 Dght 5.350 Lbp 73.60 Br md 12.60 Dpth 6.48 Welded, 1 dk	**(A31A2GX) General Cargo Ship** Grain: 3,231; Bale: 2,911 Compartments: 2 Ho, ER 2 Ha: (19.2 x 8.4)ER (19.8 x 8.4)	**1 oil engine** driving 1 FP propeller Total Power: 1,324kW (1,800hp) 10.0kn Chinese Std. Type G6300ZC 1 x 4 Stroke 6 Cy. 300 x 380 1324kW (1800bhp) Ningbo CSI Power & Machinery GroupCo Ltd-China
9476214 *3WQA* -	**THANH VINH 68** *ex* Trung Nguyen 09 *-2012* **Agribank Leasing Co II** Dai Trung Nguyen Trading & Construction Co Ltd *Haiphong* *Vietnam* MMSI: 574012089	**1,599** 1,009 3,080	Class: VR	**2007**-05 **Vinashin Casting Industry** Yd No: TKC-48A Loa 74.36 Br ex - Dght 5.340 Lbp 70.90 Br md 12.60 Dpth 6.30 Welded, 1 dk	**(A31A2GX) General Cargo Ship** Grain: 3,341 Compartments: 2 Ho, ER 2 Ha: (17.0 x 8.0)ER (19.3 x 8.0)	**1 oil engine** driving 1 FP propeller Total Power: 721kW (980hp) 10.0kn Skoda 6L350PN 1 x 4 Stroke 6 Cy. 350 x 500 721kW (980bhp) (made 1987, fitted 2007) CKD Praha-Praha AuxGen: 2 x 20kW 400V a.c
8741741 *3WVK* -	**THANH VINH 88** *ex* Trung Nguyen 36 *-2012* *ex* Hai Phuong 135 *-2007* **Agriculture Leasing Co II** Dai Trung Nguyen Trading & Construction Co Ltd *Saigon* *Vietnam*	**1,599** 1,004 3,079	Class: VR	**2007**-07 **Fishipco — Vietnam** Yd No: TKC48A-02 Loa 74.36 Br ex 12.62 Dght 5.340 Lbp 70.90 Br md 12.60 Dpth 6.30 Welded, 1 dk	**(A31A2GX) General Cargo Ship** Grain: 3,341; Bale: 3,341 2 Ha: (17.0 x 8.0)ER (19.3 x 8.0)	**1 oil engine** driving 1 FP propeller Total Power: 970kW (1,319hp) 9.0kn S.K.L. 8NVD48A-2U 1 x 4 Stroke 8 Cy. 320 x 480 970kW (1319bhp) (made 1989) SKL Motoren u. Systemtechnik AG-Magdeburg
9154763 *XYXA* -	**THANLWIN** **Myanma Five Star Line** - *Yangon* *Myanmar* Official number: 4578	**2,420** 729 592	Class: LR ✠ **100A1** SS 02/2005 passenger ship Myanmar, Thailand, Malaysia & Singapore coastal service ✠ **LMC**	**2000**-02 **Wusong Shipyard — Shanghai** Yd No: 96-1-5A Loa 77.00 Br ex - Dght 3.462 Lbp 69.00 Br md 13.60 Dpth 7.00 Welded, 1 dk	**(A37B2PS) Passenger Ship** Passengers: unberthed: 440	**1 oil engine** with clutches & sr reverse geared to sc. shaft driving 1 FP propeller Total Power: 2,940kW (3,997hp) 14.5kn MAN-B&W 12V28/32A 1 x Vee 4 Stroke 12 Cy. 280 x 320 2940kW (3997bhp) MAN B&W Diesel AG-Augsburg AuxGen: 3 x 250kW 400V 50Hz a.c
8613736 *TSNT* -	**THAPSUS** *ex* Karratha Spirit *-2011* *ex* Pioneer Spirit *-2002* **SAROST SA** - SatCom: Inmarsat C 467270810 *La Goulette* *Tunisia* MMSI: 672708000	**59,289** 35,989 106,672 T/cm 91.5	Class: BV (LR) (AB) ✠ Classed LR until 7/4/01	**1988**-02 **Hyundai Heavy Industries Co Ltd — Ulsan** Yd No: 474 Converted From: Crude Oil Tanker-2001 Loa 257.00 (BB) Br ex - Dght 14.670 Lbp 234.02 Br md 42.68 Dpth 21.52 Welded, 1 dk	**(B22H2OF) FSO, Oil** Single Hull Liq: 108,634; Liq (Oil): 108,634 Cargo Heating Coils Compartments: 6 Wing Ta, 5 Ta, 2 Wing Slop Ta, ER 3 Cargo Pump (s): 3x3500m³/hr Manifold: Bow/CM: 122.2m	**1 oil engine** driving 1 FP propeller Total Power: 10,165kW (13,820hp) 14.0kn B&W 6S60MC 1 x 2 Stroke 6 Cy. 600 x 2292 10165kW (13820bhp) Hyundai Engine & Machinery Co Ltd-South Korea AuxGen: 3 x 680kW 440V 60Hz a.c Fuel: 296.8 (d.f.) 2773.3 (r.f.)
9016832 *HSB3447* -	**THARERATANA 1** *ex* Nissho Maru *-2006* **AI Logistics Co Ltd** - *Thailand* MMSI: 567050400 Official number: 490001189	**997** 573 1,842	Class: (NK)	**1990**-11 **Yamanaka Zosen K.K. — Imabari** Yd No: 505 Loa 69.95 (BB) Br ex - Dght 4.850 Lbp 65.60 Br md 11.40 Dpth 5.45 Welded, 1 dk	**(A13B2TP) Products Tanker** Liq: 2,149; Liq (Oil): 2,149 Compartments: 12 Ta, ER	**1 oil engine** geared to sc. shaft driving 1 FP propeller Total Power: 1,471kW (2,000hp) Hanshin 6LU35G 1 x 4 Stroke 6 Cy. 350 x 550 1471kW (2000bhp) The Hanshin Diesel Works Ltd-Japan Thrusters: 1 Thwart. CP thruster (f)
9031820 - -	**THARERATANA 2** *ex* Fujishiro Maru *-2006* **AI Logistics Co Ltd** - *Thailand* Official number: 490003327	**315** 139 500		**1991**-07 **Kurinoura Dockyard Co Ltd — Yawatahama EH** Yd No: 289 Loa 47.94 Br ex 8.02 Dght 3.274 Lbp 44.10 Br md 8.00 Dpth 3.35 Welded, 1 dk	**(A13B2TP) Products Tanker**	**1 oil engine** geared to sc. shaft driving 1 FP propeller Total Power: 441kW (600hp) Sumiyoshi S23G 1 x 4 Stroke 6 Cy. 230 x 400 441kW (600bhp) Sumiyoshi Marine Diesel Co Ltd-Japan
9036832 *HSB3637* -	**THARERATANA 3** *ex* Wakamatsu Maru No. 2 *-2007* **AI Logistics Co Ltd** - *Bangkok* *Thailand* MMSI: 567052300 Official number: 500052337	**2,037** 947 2,998	Class: (NK)	**1991**-06 **Sasaki Shipbuilding Co Ltd — Osakikamijima HS** Yd No: 557 Loa 89.92 (BB) Br ex 13.23 Dght 5.503 Lbp 85.00 Br md 13.20 Dpth 6.50 Welded, 1 dk	**(A13B2TP) Products Tanker** Double Bottom Entire Compartment Length Liq: 3,450; Liq (Oil): 3,450 Compartments: 10 Wing Ta, ER 2 Cargo Pump (s): 2x1000m³/hr Manifold: Bow/CM: 45m	**1 oil engine** driving 1 CP propeller Total Power: 2,060kW (2,801hp) 13.0kn Hanshin 6EL38 1 x 4 Stroke 6 Cy. 380 x 760 2060kW (2801bhp) Hanshin Nainenki Kogyo-Japan AuxGen: 2 x 240kW 440V 60Hz a.c, 1 x 200kW 440V 60Hz a.c Thrusters: 1 Thwart. CP thruster (f) Fuel: 35.6 (d.f.) 156.4 (r.f.) 9.5pd
9106742 *HSPG2* -	**THARINEE NAREE** *ex* Cynthia Pioneer *-1997* **Precious Capitals Ltd** Great Circle Shipping Agency Ltd SatCom: Inmarsat A 1567157 *Bangkok* *Thailand* MMSI: 567038000 Official number: 401000691	**14,431** 8,741 23,724 T/cm 33.6	Class: NK	**1994**-11 **KK Kanasashi — Toyohashi AI** Yd No: 3365 Loa 150.50 (BB) Br ex - Dght 9.566 Lbp 143.00 Br md 26.00 Dpth 13.20 Welded, 1 dk	**(A21A2BC) Bulk Carrier** Grain: 31,249; Bale: 30,169 Compartments: 4 Ho, ER 4 Ha: (17.9 x 12.8)3 (19.5 x 17.8)ER Cranes: 4x30.5t	**1 oil engine** driving 1 FP propeller Total Power: 5,296kW (7,200hp) 13.9kn B&W 6L42MC 1 x 2 Stroke 6 Cy. 420 x 1360 5296kW (7200bhp) Kawasaki Heavy Industries Ltd-Japan AuxGen: 2 x 360kW 450V 60Hz a.c Fuel: 734.0 (r.f.) 19.8pd

IMO / Call sign	Name / Owner	Tonnage	Class	Build / Dimensions	Type / Capacity	Machinery
9649196 *PBLC* -	**THARSIS** **Banier Scheepvaart BV** Scheepvaartonderneming Tharsis CV *Delfzijl* *Netherlands* MMSI: 246091000 Official number: 4037833	**1,801** 675 2,300	Class: BV	**2012-09 B.V. Scheepswerf De Kaap — Meppel** Yd No: 253 Loa 87.95 (BB) Br ex 11.40 Dght 3.703 Lbp 84.57 Br md 11.31 Dpth 5.80 Welded, 1 dk	**(A31A2GX) General Cargo Ship** Grain: 3,272 TEU 78 C Ho 54 TEU C Dk 24 TEU Compartments: 1 Ho, ER 1 Ha: ER	**3 diesel electric oil engines** driving 3 gen. each 400kW a.c Connecting to 2 elec. motors each (375kW) driving 2 FP propellers Total Power: 1,764kW (2,397hp) 10.0kn Volvo Penta D13MG 1 x 4 Stroke 6 Cy. 131 x 158 588kW (799bhp) AB Volvo Penta-Sweden Volvo Penta D13MG 2 x 4 Stroke 6 Cy. 131 x 158 each-588kW (799bhp) AB Volvo Penta-Sweden Thrusters: 1 Tunnel thruster Fuel: 90.0
8814407 *HSUJ* -	**THARUA PHUKET 1** **Government of The Kingdom of Thailand (Ministry of Transport & Communications)** Chaophaya Terminal International Co Ltd *Bangkok* *Thailand* Official number: 311004280	**193** 131 69	Class: LR ✠**100A1** SS 04/2009 tug Thailand home trade limited area ✠**LMC** Eq.Ltr: (B) ; Cable: 247.5/16.0 U2	**1989-04 Singapore Slipway & Engineering Co. Pte Ltd — Singapore** Yd No: 173 Loa 25.02 Br ex 8.67 Dght - Lbp 21.70 Br md 8.40 Dpth 4.00 Welded, 1 dk	**(B32A2ST) Tug**	**2 oil engines** with flexible couplings & dr geared to sc. shafts driving 2 Directional propellers Total Power: 1,176kW (1,598hp) 11.0kn Blackstone ESL5MK2 2 x 4 Stroke 5 Cy. 222 x 292 each-588kW (799bhp) Mirrlees Blackstone (Stamford)Ltd.-Stamford AuxGen: 2 x 100kW 400V 50Hz a.c
8814380 *HSUH* -	**THARUA SONGKHLA 1** **Government of The Kingdom of Thailand (Ministry of Transport & Communications)** Chaophaya Terminal International Co Ltd *Bangkok* *Thailand* Official number: 311004264	*193* - 69	Class: LR ✠**100A1** SS 04/2009 tug Thailand home trade limited area ✠**LMC** Eq.Ltr: (B) ; Cable: 247.5/16.0 U2	**1989-04 Singapore Slipway & Engineering Co. Pte Ltd — Singapore** Yd No: 171 Loa 25.02 Br ex 8.67 Dght - Lbp 21.70 Br md 8.40 Dpth 4.00 Welded, 1 dk	**(B32A2ST) Tug**	**2 oil engines** with flexible couplings & dr geared to sc. shafts driving 2 Directional propellers Total Power: 1,176kW (1,598hp) 11.0kn Blackstone ESL5MK2 2 x 4 Stroke 5 Cy. 222 x 292 each-588kW (799bhp) Mirrlees Blackstone (Stamford)Ltd.-Stamford AuxGen: 2 x 100kW 400V 50Hz a.c
8814392 *HSUI* -	**THARUA SONGKHLA 2** **Government of The Kingdom of Thailand (Ministry of Transport & Communications)** Chaophaya Terminal International Co Ltd *Bangkok* *Thailand* Official number: 311004272	*193* - 69	Class: LR ✠**100A1** SS 04/2009 tug Thailand home trade limited area ✠**LMC** Eq.Ltr: (B) ; Cable: 247.5/16.0 U2	**1989-04 Singapore Slipway & Engineering Co. Pte Ltd — Singapore** Yd No: 172 Loa 25.02 Br ex 8.67 Dght - Lbp 21.70 Br md 8.40 Dpth 4.00 Welded, 1 dk	**(B32A2ST) Tug**	**2 oil engines** with flexible couplings & dr geared to sc. shafts driving 2 Directional propellers Total Power: 1,176kW (1,598hp) 11.0kn Blackstone ESL5MK2 2 x 4 Stroke 5 Cy. 222 x 292 each-588kW (799bhp) Mirrlees Blackstone (Stamford)Ltd.-Stamford AuxGen: 2 x 100kW 400V 50Hz a.c
9166651 *A8CQ5* -	**THASOS** *ex* Gallia *-2013* *ex* Alianca Shanghai *-2009* *ex* P&O Nedlloyd Eagle *-2003* *ex* Columbus Texas *-2001* *ex* Gallia *-1998* **Ailsa Shipping Corp** Goldenport Shipmanagement Ltd *Monrovia* *Liberia* MMSI: 636016014 Official number: 16014	**25,499** 12,450 34,116 T/cm 49.9	Class: GL	**1998-06 Thyssen Nordseewerke GmbH — Emden** Yd No: 520 Loa 199.93 (BB) Br ex - Dght 11.550 Lbp 187.90 Br md 29.80 Dpth 16.50 Welded, 1 dk	**(A33A2CC) Container Ship (Fully Cellular)** TEU 2452 C Ho 986 TEU C Dk 1466 TEU incl 300 ref C. Compartments: 6 Cell Ho, ER 10 Ha: (12.8 x 15.5)9 (12.8 x 25.7)ER Cranes: 3x40t	**1 oil engine** driving 1 CP propeller Total Power: 16,000kW (21,754hp) 21.0kn Mitsubishi 8UEC60LS 1 x 2 Stroke 8 Cy. 600 x 2200 16000kW (21754bhp) Mitsubishi Heavy Industries Ltd-Japan AuxGen: 1 x 1400kW 220/440V 60Hz a.c, 3 x 750kW 220/440V 60Hz a.c Thrusters: 1 Thwart. CP thruster (f) Fuel: 302.1 (d.f.) (Heating Coils) 2000.0 (r.f.) 63.5pd
9636709 *SVA3807* -	**THASOS II** *ex* Filotheos *-2012* **Livadas SC** Agios Nikolaos - Salamina Shipping Co *Piraeus* *Greece* MMSI: 239691400 Official number: 11836	**999** 642 -		**2011-07 Theodoropoulos General Marine Repairs — Ampelakia** Yd No: 158 Loa 107.03 Br ex - Dght 2.400 Lbp 84.11 Br md 18.08 Dpth - Welded, 1 dk	**(A36A2PR) Passenger/Ro-Ro Ship (Vehicles)** Bow ramp (centre) Stern ramp (centre)	**4 oil engines** reduction geared to sc. shafts driving 4 Propellers Total Power: 1,912kW (2,600hp) GUASCOR F240TAB-SP 4 x 4 Stroke 8 Cy. 152 x 165 each-478kW (650bhp) Gutierrez Ascunce Corp (GUASCOR)-Spain
8742692 *SVA2081* -	**THASSOS I** *ex* Protoporos III *-2008* **Thassos Shipping Co SA** Anonymos Naftiliaki Eteria Thassou (ANETH) *Piraeus* *Greece* MMSI: 239361400 Official number: 11657	**995** 634 -		**2008-05 in Greece** Loa 97.85 Br ex - Dght - Lbp - Br md 16.00 Dpth - Welded, 1 dk	**(A36A2PR) Passenger/Ro-Ro Ship (Vehicles)**	**4 oil engines** reduction geared to sc. shafts driving 4 Directional propellers Total Power: 2,000kW (2,720hp) Caterpillar 3412E 4 x Vee 4 Stroke 12 Cy. 137 x 152 each-500kW (680bhp) Caterpillar Inc-USA
7422867 - -	**THASSOS I** **SGE Shipping Co**	**999** 189 100	Class: (HR) (AB)	**1975-12 United Shipping Yard Co — Piraeus** Yd No: 78 Loa 59.49 Br ex 11.28 Dght 2.083 Lbp 52.48 Br md 9.91 Dpth 3.28 Welded, 1 dk	**(A36A2PR) Passenger/Ro-Ro Ship (Vehicles)** Bow door & ramp Cars: 105	**2 oil engines** reverse reduction geared to sc. shafts driving 2 FP propellers Total Power: 1,224kW (1,664hp) 13.0kn Waukesha L5792DSM 2 x Vee 4 Stroke 12 Cy. 216 x 216 each-612kW (832bhp) Waukesha Engine Div. DresserIndustries Inc.-Waukesha, Wi AuxGen: 2 x 40kW a.c
7924413 - -	**THASSOS IV** **SGE Shipping Co**	*724* 415 200	Class: (HR) (AB)	**1980-06 Nafpigokastaskevastiki Nafiliaki — Piraeus** Yd No: 407 Loa - Br ex - Dght 2.312 Lbp 58.78 Br md 13.61 Dpth 3.51 Welded, 1 dk	**(A36A2PR) Passenger/Ro-Ro Ship (Vehicles)** Passengers: unberthed: 314 Bow door & ramp (centre) Vehicles: 72	**2 oil engines** reverse reduction geared to sc. shafts driving 2 FP propellers Total Power: 1,654kW (2,248hp) 13.0kn Caterpillar D399TA 2 x Vee 4 Stroke 16 Cy. 159 x 203 each-827kW (1124bhp) Caterpillar Tractor Co-USA AuxGen: 2 x 85kW Fuel: 35.5 (d.f.)
8969123 *SX8565* -	**THASSOS VI** **Thassos Shipping Co SA** Anonymos Naftiliaki Eteria Thassou (ANETH) *Piraeus* *Greece* MMSI: 237325200 Official number: 10647	**885** 568 -	Class: RI	**2000-12 at Piraeus** Loa 81.50 Br ex - Dght 2.960 Lbp - Br md 14.20 Dpth 4.00 Welded, 1 dk	**(A37B2PS) Passenger Ship** Passengers: unberthed: 400 Cars: 135	**2 oil engines** reduction geared to sc. shafts driving 2 CP propellers Total Power: 3,280kW (4,460hp) 14.2kn Cummins QSK60-M 2 x Vee 4 Stroke 16 Cy. 159 x 190 each-1640kW (2230bhp) (new engine 2004) Cummins Engine Co Inc-USA
7238670 *HSB2027* -	**THATHONG** *ex* Fuji Maru No. 18 *-1985* **Prachak Pakdi Co Ltd** *Thailand* Official number: 288402301	*697* 504 1,934		**1972-12 Nishi Shipbuilding Co Ltd — Imabari EH** Yd No: 144 Loa - Br ex 11.00 Dght 4.801 Lbp 62.01 Br md 10.98 Dpth 5.21 Riveted\Welded, 1 dk	**(A13B2TP) Products Tanker**	**1 oil engine** reverse geared to sc. shaft driving 1 FP propeller Total Power: 1,214kW (1,651hp) Akasaka 6DH36SS 1 x 4 Stroke 6 Cy. 360 x 540 1214kW (1651bhp) Akasaka Tekkosho KK (Akasaka DieselLtd)-Japan
5357939 *XYUR* -	**THAUNG NAING YAY** **Board of Management for The Port of Yangon** - *Yangon* *Myanmar* Official number: 1153	*1,234* 574	Class: (LR) ✠ Classed LR until 7/64	**1962-11 Simons-Lobnitz Ltd. — Renfrew** Yd No: 1163 Loa 70.01 Br ex 11.92 Dght 4.500 Lbp 66.15 Br md 11.59 Dpth 5.47 Welded, 1 dk	**(B33B2DT) Trailing Suction Hopper Dredger** Hopper: 750	**2 oil engines** with fluid couplings & sr reverse geared to sc. shafts driving 2 FP propellers Total Power: 728kW (990hp) 10.0kn Blackstone ERS6 2 x 4 Stroke 6 Cy. 222 x 292 each-364kW (495bhp) Lister Blackstone Marine Ltd.-Dursley
9628362 *XYTX* -	**THAW DAR DAE WE** **Thuriya Sandar Win Co Ltd** *Yangon* *Myanmar* Official number: 6436 (A)	**1,067** 635 -		**2010-12 Myanma Port Authority — Yangon (Theinphyu Dockyard)** Yd No: 31MPA Loa 63.70 Br ex 18.30 Dght 3.660 Lbp - Br md - Dpth 4.27 Welded, 1 dk	**(A31A2GX) General Cargo Ship**	**1 oil engine** driving 1 Propeller
7377919 *HSB2223* -	**THAWORNSIN** *ex* Fortune II *-1992* *ex* Tenyo Maru *-1986* *ex* Daiju Maru No. 1 *-1981* **VSP Marine Shipping Co Ltd** - *Bangkok* *Thailand* MMSI: 567010300 Official number: 351001298	*1,287* 662 2,225	Class: (NK)	**1974-05 Kyokuyo Shipbuilding & Iron Works Co Ltd — Shimonoseki YC** Yd No: 269 Loa 77.27 Br ex 12.02 Dght 4.747 Lbp 71.00 Br md 11.99 Dpth 5.49 Welded, 1 dk	**(A13B2TP) Products Tanker** Liq: 2,412; Liq (Oil): 2,412	**1 oil engine** driving 1 FP propeller Total Power: 1,471kW (2,000hp) 11.4kn Hanshin 6LUD35 1 x 4 Stroke 6 Cy. 350 x 550 1471kW (2000bhp) The Hanshin Diesel Works Ltd-Japan AuxGen: 3 x 55kW a.c
9062221 *H04570* -	**THE AMERICAN CORVEL-I** *ex* Seitoku No. 3 *-2006* *ex* Seifuku Maru No. 21 *-2005* **Corvel Marine Corp SA** *Panama* *Panama* MMSI: 371301000 Official number: 3229207A	**629** 392 1,250		**1992-09 Hakata Zosen K.K. — Imabari** Yd No: 538 L reg 61.00 Br ex - Dght 4.250 Lbp 60.90 Br md 10.00 Dpth 4.50 Welded, 1 dk	**(A13B2TP) Products Tanker**	**1 oil engine** driving 1 FP propeller Total Power: 736kW (1,001hp) 10.0kn Hanshin LH28G 1 x 4 Stroke 6 Cy. 280 x 460 736kW (1001bhp) The Hanshin Diesel Works Ltd-Japan

7423914 *HP7562* -	**THE ARROW** *ex* Arrow *-2012* *ex* Danish Arrow *-2002* **Jorge Cordero** - *Panama* *Panama* Official number: 43932PEXT	**926** 277 759 T/cm 5.0	Class: IS (LR) ✠ Classed LR until 11/10/06	**1976**-06 **A/S Svendborg Skibsvaerft — Svendborg** Yd No: 151 Loa 66.50 (BB) Br ex 10.67 Dght 3.277 Lbp 59.14 Br md 10.51 Dpth 5.16 Welded, 1 dk	**(A11B2TG) LPG Tanker** Liq (Gas): 922 4 x Gas Tank (s); 4 independent (stl) ccy horizontal 2 Cargo Pump (s): 2x90m³/hr Manifold: Bow/CM: 36.5m Ice Capable	**1 oil engine** sr geared to sc. shaft driving 1 CP propeller Total Power: 670kW (911hp) 6.0kn Alpha 8V23L-VO 1 x Vee 4 Stroke 8 Cy. 225 x 300 670kW (911bhp) Alpha Diesel A/S-Denmark AuxGen: 3 x 104kW 380V 50Hz a.c Fuel: 71.5 (d.f.)
9695339 *KBEG* -	**THE BELLATOR** **CS Liftboats Inc** - *Abbeville, LA* *United States of America* MMSI: 367599110 Official number: 1250359	**2,031** 609 -	Class: AB	**2013**-12 **Gulf Island Marine Fabricators LLC — Houma LA** Yd No: 6018 Loa 45.72 Br ex 35.96 Dght - Lbp - Br md - Dpth - Welded, 1 dk	**(B22A2ZM) Offshore Construction Vessel, jack up** Cranes: 1x250t,1x40t	**2 oil engines** reduction geared to sc. shafts driving 2 Propellers Total Power: 1,640kW (2,230hp) Caterpillar C32 2 x Vee 4 Stroke 12 Cy. 145 x 162 each-820kW (1115bhp) Caterpillar Inc-USA Thrusters: 1 Tunnel thruster (f)
8421119 *HOLM* -	**THE BENEFACTOR** *ex* Veroika *-2005* *ex* Alam Baru *-2002* *ex* Doric Armour *-1994* **Kurosaki Shipping Inc** Sea Lion Shipmanagement Pvt Ltd *Panama* *Panama* MMSI: 355312000 Official number: 2905803B	**34,620** 21,177 65,117 T/cm 64.0	Class: LR ✠ **100A1** SS 05/2011 bulk carrier strengthened for heavy cargoes, Nos. 2, 4 & 6 holds may be empty ESP ESN-Hold 1 LI ✠ **LMC** **UMS** Eq.Ltr: N†; Cable: 660.0/76.0 U3	**1986**-05 **Nippon Kokan KK (NKK Corp) — Yokohama KN (Tsurumi Shipyard)** Yd No: 1031 Loa 222.00 (BB) Br ex 32.29 Dght 12.910 Lbp 212.00 Br md 32.25 Dpth 17.81 Welded, 1 dk	**(A21A2BC) Bulk Carrier** Grain: 74,938; Bale: 71,442 Compartments: 7 Ho, ER 7 Ha: (13.4 x 11.0)6 (14.6 x 14.3)ER	**1 oil engine** driving 1 FP propeller Total Power: 11,130kW (15,132hp) 14.5kn Sulzer 7RTA58 1 x 2 Stroke 7 Cy. 580 x 1700 11130kW (15132bhp) Nippon Kokan KK (NKK Corp)-Japan AuxGen: 3 x 500kW 450V 60Hz a.c Boilers: e 10.5kgf/cm² (10.3bar), AuxB (o.f.) 7.0kgf/cm² (6.9bar) Fuel: 157.0 (d.f.) 1896.0 (r.f.) 31.0pd
8664450 *V7YG9* -	**THE BIG BLUE** *ex* Imbros *-2013* **The Big Blue Ltd** - *Bikini* *Marshall Islands* MMSI: 538070838 Official number: 70838	**399** 119 344	Class: BV	**2010**-12 **Troy Marine Yatcilik Turizm Paz ve Tic Ltd Sti — Basiskele** Yd No: 1 Loa 42.00 (BB) Br ex - Dght 2.440 Lbp 37.18 Br md 8.40 Dpth 4.00 Welded, 1 dk	**(X11A2YP) Yacht**	**2 oil engines** reduction geared to sc. shafts driving 2 FP propellers Total Power: 1,104kW (1,500hp) 11.0kn Volvo Penta D16 2 x 4 Stroke 6 Cy. 144 x 165 each-552kW (750bhp) AB Volvo Penta-Sweden AuxGen: 1 x 86kW 50Hz a.c, 1 x 86kW 50Hz a.c Thrusters: 1 Tunnel thruster (f) Fuel: 59.0 (d.f.)
7031759 - -	**THE BIG BOSS** *ex* Vollsoy *-1996* *ex* Nordkappferja *-1982* **Sogemer SA** - *Libreville* *Gabon*	*258* 117 -	Class: (NV)	**1970 Ejnar S. Nielsen Mek. Verksted AS — Harstad** Yd No: 16 Loa 35.82 Br ex 9.17 Dght 3.048 Lbp 32.77 Br md 9.00 Dpth 3.87 Welded, 1 dk & S dk	**(A36A2PR) Passenger/Ro-Ro Ship (Vehicles)** Passengers: unberthed: 200 Bow door & ramp Stern ramp Cars: 16	**1 oil engine** driving 1 FP propeller Total Power: 397kW (540hp) Normo RSP6 1 x 4 Stroke 6 Cy. 250 x 360 397kW (540bhp) AS Bergens Mek Verksteder-Norway AuxGen: 2 x 32kW 220V 50Hz a.c Thrusters: 1 Thwart. FP thruster (f)
8416499 *S9B18* -	**THE BROTHERS V** *ex* Altamar *-2012* *ex* Franchesca I *-2009* *ex* Lion *-2007* - - *Sao Tome* *Sao Tome & Principe* MMSI: 668124342	**1,044** 448 1,294	Class: (LR) (NV) Classed LR until 1/10/08	**1985**-12 **A/S Nordsovaerftet — Ringkobing** Yd No: 180 Loa 65.51 Br ex - Dght 3.352 Lbp 62.01 Br md 10.01 Dpth 5.92 Welded, 2 dks	**(A31A2GX) General Cargo Ship** Grain: 2,161; Bale: 1,892 TEU 44 C.Ho 30/20' C.Dk 14/20' Compartments: 2 Ho, ER, 2 Tw Dk 2 Ha: (16.8 x 8.5) (20.4 x 8.5)ER Derricks: 2x8t; Winches: 2 Ice Capable	**1 oil engine** driving 1 CP propeller Total Power: 596kW (810hp) 10.0kn Callesen 6-427-FOTK 1 x 4 Stroke 6 Cy. 270 x 400 596kW (810bhp) Aabenraa Motorfabrik, HeinrichCallesen A/S-Denmark AuxGen: 3 x 50kW 380V 50Hz a.c, 1 x 25kW 380V 50Hz a.c
9242194 *WDD2572* -	**THE CHIEF** *ex* Queen Leslie II *-2005* **CC Scalloping Inc** - *New Bedford, MA* *United States of America* MMSI: 367117020 Official number: 1099995	**151** 45 -		**2000** Yd No: 172A Loa 25.17 Br ex 7.31 Dght - Lbp - Br md - Dpth 3.81 Welded, 1 dk	**(B11B2FV) Fishing Vessel**	**1 oil engine** driving 1 FP propeller
9429625 *VRDM6* -	**THE COTAI STRIP EXPO** **Venetian Macau Ltd** Chu Kong High-Speed Ferry Co Ltd *Hong Kong* *Hong Kong* MMSI: 477937300 Official number: HK-2044	**700** 240 84	Class: NV	**2007**-11 **Austal Ships Pty Ltd — Fremantle WA** Yd No: 313 Loa 47.50 Br ex 12.10 Dght 1.660 Lbp 43.80 Br md 11.80 Dpth 3.80 Welded, 1 dk	**(A37B2PS) Passenger Ship** Hull Material: Aluminium Alloy Passengers: 411	**4 oil engines** reduction geared to sc. shafts driving 4 Water jets Total Power: 9,148kW (12,436hp) M.T.U. 16V4000M70 4 x Vee 4 Stroke 16 Cy. 165 x 190 each-2287kW (3109bhp) MTU Friedrichshafen GmbH-Friedrichshafen AuxGen: 2 x a.c
8835205 *WAK9812* -	**THE DEACON** **Suderman & Young Towing Co LP** - *Houston, TX* *United States of America* MMSI: 366922110 Official number: 956938	**343** 102 -	Class: (AB)	**1990 Main Iron Works, Inc. — Houma, La** Yd No: 385 Loa - Br ex - Dght 4.874 Lbp 26.52 Br md 10.39 Dpth 5.64 Welded, 1 dk	**(B32A2ST) Tug**	**2 oil engines** sr geared to sc. shafts driving 2 FP propellers Total Power: 2,868kW (3,900hp) 12.5kn EMD (Electro-Motive) 16-645-E2 2 x Vee 2 Stroke 16 Cy. 230 x 254 each-1434kW (1950bhp) General Motors Corp.Electro-Motive Div.-La Grange AuxGen: 2 x 75kW a.c
7904932 *J8B3625* -	**THE EXPLORER** *ex* Sampler Setter *-2009* *ex* Sea Installer *-2007* *ex* Trenchsetter *-2005* *ex* Condock II *-1989* **International Underwater Sampling Ltd** ARGO Ship Management & Services Srl *Kingstown* *St Vincent & The Grenadines* MMSI: 376639000 Official number: 10098	**4,677** 1,403 1,980	Class: RI (LR) (GL) Classed LR until 13/1/09	**1979**-12 **Werft Nobiskrug GmbH — Rendsburg** Yd No: 697 Converted From: Barge Carrier-1989 Lengthened-1984 Loa 130.30 (BB) Br ex 20.02 Dght 4.600 Lbp 94.00 Br md 19.60 Dpth 4.90 Welded, 2 dks	**(B22J20E) Trenching Support Vessel** A-frames: 1x104t; Cranes: 2x63t	**2 oil engines** with flexible couplings & sr geared to sc. shafts driving 2 CP propellers Total Power: 2,170kW (2,950hp) 12.3kn MaK 6M452AK 2 x 4 Stroke 6 Cy. 320 x 450 each-1085kW (1475bhp) MaK Maschinenbau GmbH-Kiel AuxGen: 2 x 920kW 440V 50Hz a.c, 2 x 200kW 440V 50Hz a.c, 2 x 212kW 380V 50Hz a.c, 1 x 350kW 380V 60Hz a.c Thrusters: 2 Directional thruster (f); 1 Tunnel thruster (a)
9055620 *3FZE3* -	**THE FORGIVER** *ex* Pioneer Pacific *-2013* *ex* Cedar 3 *-2009* *ex* Dawn Voyager *-2009* *ex* Endurance II *-2008* *ex* Estepona *-2007* *ex* Bulk Patriot *-2006* *ex* CIC Horizon *-2006* *ex* Fareast Victory *-2000* **Goldbell Business Corp** SNP Shipping Services Pvt Ltd *Panama* *Panama* MMSI: 354739000 Official number: 45102PEXT	**38,267** 23,975 70,003 T/cm 65.6	Class: NK (LR) (RI) ✠ Classed LR until 19/4/07	**1994**-10 **Hudong Shipyard — Shanghai** Yd No: 1208A Loa 225.00 (BB) Br ex 32.25 Dght 13.620 Lbp 215.00 Br md 32.20 Dpth 18.70 Welded, 1 dk	**(A21A2BC) Bulk Carrier** Grain: 85,055; Bale: 81,564 Compartments: 7 Ho, ER 7 Ha: (14.4 x 13.2)6 (14.6 x 15.0)ER	**1 oil engine** driving 1 FP propeller Total Power: 9,021kW (12,265hp) 14.5kn B&W 6S60MC 1 x 2 Stroke 6 Cy. 600 x 2292 9021kW (12265bhp) Hudong Shipyard-China AuxGen: 3 x 510kW 450V 60Hz a.c Boilers: e (ex.g.) 12.0kgf/cm² (11.8bar), AuxB (o.f.) 8.0kgf/cm² (7.8bar) Fuel: 2490.0 (r.f.)
8709626 - -	**THE GOLDEN CRUISE** *ex* Havana Princess *-2001* *ex* Canima *-2000* - - *Mexico*	*480* 192 -	Class: (LR) (AB) Classed LR until 16/12/98	**1988**-05 **Atlantic Marine — Jacksonville, Fl** Yd No: 4210 Loa 32.01 Br ex 9.48 Dght - Lbp 31.01 Br md 9.47 Dpth 3.01 Welded, 1 dk	**(A37B2PS) Passenger Ship**	**2 oil engines** sr reverse geared to sc. shafts driving 2 FP propellers Total Power: 712kW (968hp) 12.0kn G.M. (Detroit Diesel) 12V-71 2 x Vee 2 Stroke 12 Cy. 108 x 127 each-356kW (484bhp) General Motors Detroit DieselAllison Divn-USA AuxGen: 2 x 40kW 480V 60Hz a.c Thrusters: 1 Thwart. FP thruster (f)
9429601 *VRDI3* -	**THE GRAND CANAL SHOPPES** **Venetian Macau Ltd** Chu Kong High-Speed Ferry Co Ltd *Hong Kong* *Hong Kong* MMSI: 477937100 Official number: HK-2009	**700** 240 84	Class: NV	**2007**-09 **Austal Ships Pty Ltd — Fremantle WA** Yd No: 311 Loa 47.50 Br ex 12.10 Dght 1.640 Lbp 43.80 Br md 11.80 Dpth 3.80 Welded, 1 dk	**(A37B2PS) Passenger Ship** Hull Material: Aluminium Alloy Passengers: 411	**4 oil engines** reduction geared to sc. shafts driving 4 Water jets Total Power: 9,148kW (12,436hp) M.T.U. 16V4000M70 4 x Vee 4 Stroke 16 Cy. 165 x 190 each-2287kW (3109bhp) MTU Friedrichshafen GmbH-Friedrichshafen AuxGen: 2 x a.c
7228041 - -	**THE GUARDIAN** *ex* Sea Guardian *-2001* *ex* Colo Colo *-1999* *ex* Lenga *-1990* *ex* Smit-Lloyd 46 *-1985* **Oil & Marine Agencies (GH) Ltd** - *Takoradi* *Ghana* Official number: GSR 0089	*786* 331 874	Class: (AB)	**1972 Scheepswerf "De Waal" N.V. — Zaltbommel** Yd No: 695 Loa 54.82 Br ex 12.30 Dght 4.439 Lbp 50.86 Br md 12.02 Dpth 4.96 Welded, 1 dk	**(B21B20A) Anchor Handling Tug Supply**	**2 oil engines** driving 2 CP propellers Total Power: 2,942kW (4,000hp) 13.0kn De Industrie 8D7HD 2 x 4 Stroke 8 Cy. 305 x 460 each-1471kW (2000bhp) NV Motorenfabriek 'De Industrie'-Netherlands AuxGen: 4 x 220V d.c Thrusters: 1 Thwart. FP thruster (f) Fuel: 259.0 (d.f.)

9124902 3FNG6 -
THE GUIDE
ex Rubin Power *-2011*
Tutbury Trading SA
SNP Shipping Services Pvt Ltd
SatCom: Inmarsat C 435680810
Panama *Panama*
MMSI: 356808000
Official number: 2321996E
37,846 23,677 72,326 T/cm 66.9
Class: NK
1996-09 **Sasebo Heavy Industries Co. Ltd. — Sasebo Yard, Sasebo** Yd No: 406
Loa 225.00 (BB) Br ex - Dght 13.500
Lbp 218.00 Br md 32.20 Dpth 18.70
Welded, 1 dk
(A21A2BC) Bulk Carrier
Grain: 84,790
Compartments: 7 Ho, ER
7 Ha: (15.3 x 12.8)6 (17.0 x 14.4)ER
1 oil engine driving 1 FP propeller
Total Power: 8,827kW (12,001hp) 14.5kn
B&W 6S60MC
1 x 2 Stroke 6 Cy. 600 x 2292 8827kW (12001bhp)
Mitsui Engineering & Shipbuilding CLtd-Japan
Fuel: 2230.0 (r.f.)

8856340 WDA4411 -
THE JAKE M
ex Remona Cruz *-2005*
G & S Trawlers Inc
Brownsville, TX *United States of America*
MMSI: 366809120
Official number: 910748
118 94 -
1987 Roca Construction Co. — Brownsville, Tx Yd No: 3
Loa - Br ex - Dght -
Lbp 21.95 Br md 6.25 Dpth 3.66
Bonded, 1 dk
(B11B2FV) Fishing Vessel
Hull Material: Reinforced Plastic
1 oil engine driving 1 FP propeller

8885573 - -
THE JOCKA
ex Sea King *-2000*
Jordan Lynn Inc
-
Harpswell, ME *United States of America*
Official number: 939745
110 88 -
1988 DMR Yachts, Inc. — Kennebunkport, Me
L reg 20.40 Br ex - Dght -
Lbp - Br md 5.79 Dpth 3.96
Welded, 1 dk
(B11B2FV) Fishing Vessel
1 oil engine driving 1 FP propeller

7502370 WYG7458 -
THE JUDGE
Suderman & Young Towing Co LP
-
Houston, TX *United States of America*
MMSI: 366920260
Official number: 585206
197 134 -
Class: (AB)
1977-10 **Todd Shipyards Corp. — Galveston, Tx** Yd No: 48
Loa 29.29 Br ex 9.81 Dght 4.931
Lbp 28.22 Br md 9.77 Dpth 5.74
Welded, 1 dk
(B32A2ST) Tug
2 oil engines reverse reduction geared to sc. shafts driving 2 FP propellers
Total Power: 2,354kW (3,200hp) 15.0kn
Nohab F28V
2 x Vee 4 Stroke 8 Cy. 250 x 300 each-1177kW (1600bhp)
AB Bofors NOHAB-Sweden
AuxGen: 2 x 100kW

9102344 3ETX9 -
THE JUST
ex Voshod 2 *-2012* *ex* Turicum *-2010*
ex Western Ocean *-1995*
Rougemont Worldwide SA
SNP Shipping Services Pvt Ltd
Panama *Panama*
MMSI: 353203000
Official number: 4453713
26,449 16,181 47,639 T/cm 50.9
Class: NK (NV)
1995-08 **Oshima Shipbuilding Co Ltd — Saikai NS** Yd No: 10185
Loa 189.99 (BB) Br ex - Dght 11.804
Lbp 182.83 Br md 30.50 Dpth 16.50
Welded, 1 dk
(A21A2BC) Bulk Carrier
Grain: 58,025; Bale: 55,474
Compartments: 5 Ho, ER
5 Ha: (16.0 x 15.3)4 (20.8 x 15.3)ER
Cranes: 4x25t
1 oil engine driving 1 FP propeller
Total Power: 7,333kW (9,970hp) 14.3kn
B&W 6S50MC
1 x 2 Stroke 6 Cy. 500 x 1910 7333kW (9970bhp)
Kawasaki Heavy Industries Ltd-Japan
AuxGen: 3 x 440kW 450V 60Hz a.c
Fuel: 114.0 (d.f.) (Part Heating Coils) 1767.0 (r.f.) 26.3pd

9017472 AULY -
THE LEELA
ex Kingfisher *-2006* *ex* Equator Dream II *-1998*
ex Equator Triangle *-1997*
Golden Globe Hotels Pvt Ltd
Ind-Aust Maritime Pvt Ltd
Mumbai *India*
MMSI: 419062900
Official number: 3210
722 216 60
Class: IR (NV)
1991-06 **Austal Ships Pty Ltd — Fremantle WA** Yd No: 14
Loa 38.03 Br ex 12.91 Dght 1.700
Lbp 35.33 Br md 12.90 Dpth 3.90
Welded
(A37B2PS) Passenger Ship
Hull Material: Aluminium Alloy
Passengers: unberthed: 216
2 oil engines geared to sc. shafts driving 2 FP propellers
Total Power: 2,862kW (3,892hp) 25.5kn
Caterpillar 3516TA
2 x Vee 4 Stroke 16 Cy. 170 x 190 each-1431kW (1946bhp)
Caterpillar Inc-USA
AuxGen: 2 x 145kW 400V 50Hz a.c
Fuel: 20.0 (d.f.)

5205784 WDC5836 -
THE LEGEND
ex Leland James *-1990* *ex* LSM 310 *-1990*
Tidewater Barge Lines Inc
-
Portland, OR *United States of America*
Official number: 262975
412 280 -
1944-05 **Pullman Standard Car Manufacturing Co. — Chicago, Il**
Loa - Br ex 10.37 Dght -
Lbp 35.72 Br md - Dpth -
Welded
(B32A2ST) Tug
2 oil engines driving 2 FP propellers
Total Power: 2,648kW (3,600hp)
Fairbanks, Morse
2 x 2 Stroke 5 Cy. 205 x 255 each-1324kW (1800bhp)
Fairbanks Morse & Co.-New Orleans, La

9140578 3FTR7 -
THE MERCIFUL
ex Coral Sea *-2011* *ex* Southern Cross *-2004*
Nelson Associated Ltd SA
Sea Lion Shipmanagement Pvt Ltd
SatCom: Inmarsat B 335164410
Panama *Panama*
MMSI: 351644000
Official number: 2509997D
38,469 25,048 73,939 T/cm 66.1
Class: NK
1997-10 **Tsuneishi Shipbuilding Co Ltd — Fukuyama HS** Yd No: 1108
Loa 225.00 (BB) Br ex - Dght 13.870
Lbp 216.00 Br md 32.26 Dpth 19.10
Welded, 1 dk
(A21A2BC) Bulk Carrier
Grain: 88,361
Compartments: 7 Ho, ER
7 Ha: (15.3 x 12.8)6 (17.0 x 15.4)ER
1 oil engine driving 1 FP propeller
Total Power: 8,900kW (12,100hp) 14.5kn
B&W 6S60MC
1 x 2 Stroke 6 Cy. 600 x 2292 8900kW (12100bhp)
Mitsui Engineering & Shipbuilding CLtd-Japan
AuxGen: 3 x 400kW a.c
Fuel: 2248.0 (r.f.) 32.5pd

1002627 9HA2770 -
THE MERCY BOYS
ex Shandor *-2012* *ex* Griff *-2002*
ex Louisianna *-1999* *ex* Margaux Rose *-1999*
Adonia Shipping Ltd
Yacht Management Consultants Sarl (Hill Robinson Yacht Management Consultants)
Valletta *Malta*
MMSI: 215607000
Official number: 1002627
530 159 -
Class: LR
✠ **100A1** SS 11/2008
Yacht
LMC
1986-04 **Fr Schweers Schiffs- und Bootswerft GmbH & Co KG — Berne**
Loa 46.42 Br ex 9.10 Dght 3.210
Lbp 43.22 Br md - Dpth 4.72
Welded, 1 dk
(X11A2YP) Yacht
1 oil engine driving 1 FP propeller
Total Power: 1,700kW (2,311hp)
MaK 8M332AK
1 x 4 Stroke 8 Cy. 240 x 330 1700kW (2311bhp)
Krupp MaK Maschinenbau GmbH-Kiel

8983686 - -
THE MEXICAN
Anna Maria Garcia
-
Port Lavaca, TX *United States of America*
Official number: 1133469
140
2002 T.M. Jemison Construction Co., Inc. — Bayou La Batre, Al Yd No: 187
L reg 24.14 Br ex - Dght -
Lbp - Br md 7.31 Dpth 3.65
Welded, 1 dk
(B11B2FV) Fishing Vessel
1 oil engine driving 1 Propeller

7407752 H04152 -
THE ODYSSEY
ex Gulmar Eagle *-2012* *ex* DP Eagle *-2005*
ex Anfitrite *-1998* *ex* Seaway Eagle *-1984*
ex Seaway Trias *-1976*
Oryx International Inc
Dulam International Ltd
SatCom: Inmarsat C 437148210
Panama *Panama*
MMSI: 371482000
Official number: 3132706B
1,598 479 1,036
Class: RI (NV)
1975-09 **Kaarbos Mek. Verksted AS — Harstad** Yd No: 81
Loa 63.45 Br ex 13.01 Dght 5.784
Lbp 55.93 Br md 12.98 Dpth 6.66
Welded, 2 dks
(B21B20T) Offshore Tug/Supply Ship
A-frames: 1x40t; Cranes: 1x15t
Ice Capable
2 diesel electric oil engines driving 2 gen. each 800kW 440V driving 2 CP propellers
Total Power: 3,090kW (4,202hp) 10.0kn
MaK 6M453AK
2 x 4 Stroke 6 Cy. 320 x 420 each-1545kW (2101bhp)
MaK Maschinenbau GmbH-Kiel
AuxGen: 1 x 800kW 440V 60Hz a.c, 2 x 170kW 440V 60Hz a.c, 1 x 400kW 440V 60Hz a.c
Thrusters: 1 Thwart. FP thruster (f); 1 Thwart. FP thruster (f); 1 Tunnel thruster (a)
Fuel: 500.0 (d.f.) 14.0pd

1001142 CRXU7 -
THE ONE
ex Carinthia VI *-2003*
Advanced Technical Research Ltd
Nuova Naviservice Srl
Madeira *Portugal (MAR)*
MMSI: 255906680
853 256 -
Class: RI (LR)
✠ Classed LR until 26/5/06
1973-09 **Fr. Luerssen Werft GmbH & Co. — Bremen** Yd No: 13434
Loa 71.06 Br ex 9.36 Dght 2.920
Lbp 66.70 Br md - Dpth 5.12
Welded, 1 dk
(X11A2YP) Yacht
2 oil engines with hydraulic clutches & reverse reduction geared to sc. shafts shafts driving 2 FP propellers
Total Power: 8,238kW (11,200hp)
M.T.U. 20V538TB93
2 x Vee 4 Stroke 20 Cy. 185 x 200 each-4119kW (5600bhp) (new engine 1994)
MTU Friedrichshafen GmbH-Friedrichshafen
AuxGen: 3 x 200kW 380V 50Hz a.c

9052604 3FRM2 -
THE OPENER
ex Id Red Sea *-2013* *ex* Cedar 2 *-2009*
ex Freyja Divine *-2009* *ex* Endeavour II *-2008*
ex Delray *-2007* *ex* Bulk Phoenix *-2006*
ex SD Triumph *-2006* *ex* Fareast Triumph *-1999*
Nilsar Trading Inc
SNP Shipping Services Pvt Ltd
Panama *Panama*
MMSI: 356994000
Official number: 45192PEXT
38,267 23,975 70,029 T/cm 65.6
Class: NK (LR) (RI)
✠ Classed LR until 11/5/07
1994-07 **Hudong Shipyard — Shanghai** Yd No: 1207A
Loa 225.00 (BB) Br ex 32.25 Dght 13.620
Lbp 215.00 Br md 32.20 Dpth 18.70
Welded, 1 dk
(A21A2BC) Bulk Carrier
Grain: 85,055; Bale: 81,564
Compartments: 7 Ho, ER
7 Ha: (14.4 x 13.2)6 (14.6 x 15.0)ER
1 oil engine driving 1 FP propeller
Total Power: 9,021kW (12,265hp) 14.4kn
B&W 6S60MC
1 x 2 Stroke 6 Cy. 600 x 2292 9021kW (12265bhp)
Hudong Shipyard-China
AuxGen: 3 x 510kW 450V 60Hz a.c
Boilers: e (ex.g.) 12.0kgf/cm² (11.8bar), AuxB (o.f.) 8.1kgf/cm² (7.9bar)
Fuel: 2500.0 (r.f.)

9429687 VRDV5 -
THE PLAZA
Cotaijet 317 Ltd
Chu Kong High-Speed Ferry Co Ltd
Hong Kong *Hong Kong*
MMSI: 477937700
Official number: HK-2115
700 203 84
Class: NV
2008-03 **Austal Ships Pty Ltd — Fremantle WA** Yd No: 317
Loa 47.50 (BB) Br ex 12.10 Dght 1.640
Lbp 44.11 Br md 11.80 Dpth 3.80
Welded, 1 dk
(A37B2PS) Passenger Ship
Hull Material: Aluminium Alloy
Passengers: 417
4 oil engines reduction geared to sc. shafts driving 4 Water jets
Total Power: 9,148kW (12,436hp)
M.T.U. 16v4000M70
4 x Vee 4 Stroke 16 Cy. 165 x 190 each-2287kW (3109bhp)
MTU Friedrichshafen GmbH-Friedrichshafen
AuxGen: 2 x a.c

9284568 *JYFD* -	**THE PRINCESS** **Arab Bridge Maritime Co** Arab Ship Management Ltd (ASM) *Aqaba* *Jordan* MMSI: 438607000 Official number: 55	**2,552** 765 255	Class: BV	**2003-07 Rodriquez Cantieri Navali SpA — Pietra Ligure** Yd No: 323 Loa 83.35 Br ex - Dght 2.020 Lbp 70.75 Br md 13.50 Dpth 8.80 Welded, 1 dk	**(A36A2PR) Passenger/Ro-Ro Ship (Vehicles)** Hull Material: Aluminium Alloy Passengers: unberthed: 654 Stern ramp (centre) Len: 7.00 Wid: 4.00 Swl: - Cars: 58	**4 oil engines** geared to sc. shafts driving 4 Water jets Total Power: 15,700kW (21,344hp) 33.0kn M.T.U. 16V595TE70 4 x Vee 4 Stroke 16 Cy. 190 x 210 each-3925kW (5336bhp) MTU Friedrichshafen GmbH-Friedrichshafen AuxGen: 3 x 211kW 400/220V 50Hz a.c Thrusters: 1 Retract. directional thruster (f)
7621645 *C6CX5* -	**THE PROVIDENCE** *ex* The Performer *-2010* *ex* V. S. O. Performer *-1989* *ex* Arctic Seal *-1987* **Dulam International Ltd** - SatCom: Inmarsat C 430800150 *Nassau* *Bahamas* MMSI: 308215000 Official number: 711118	**4,230** 1,269 2,012	Class: NV	**1977-11 Nylands Verksted — Oslo** Yd No: 784 Loa 96.04 Br ex 19.99 Dght 6.300 Lbp 82.73 Br md 18.00 Dpth 9.00 Welded, 2 dks	**(B22A20V) Diving Support Vessel** Passengers: berths: 109 Cranes: 1x130t,1x100t,2x5t,1x2t; Derricks: 1x160t; Winches: 1 Ice Capable	**4 oil engines** with clutches, flexible couplings & sr geared to sc. shafts driving 2 CP propellers Total Power: 4,500kW (6,120hp) 10.0kn Normo LDMB-8 4 x 4 Stroke 8 Cy. 250 x 300 each-1125kW (1530bhp) AS Bergens Mek Verksteder-Norway AuxGen: 4 x 1072kW 440V 60Hz a.c, 1 x 1072kW 440V 60Hz a.c Thrusters: 2 Thwart. CP thruster (f); 2 Tunnel thruster (a) Fuel: 876.0
7515793 - -	**THE QUEEN** *ex* Lady America *-2013* *ex* Queen Jean *-2013* **Marco Antonio Bonilla Castillo** - *Roatan* *Honduras* Official number: U-1822065	*105* 71 -		**1973 Sun Contractors, Inc. — Harvey, La** L reg 21.95 Br ex 6.96 Dght - Lbp - Br md - Dpth 3.48 Welded, 1 dk	**(B11A2FT) Trawler**	**1 oil engine** driving 1 FP propeller Total Power: 386kW (525hp)
8619546 *CYBP* -	**THE RANDELL DOMINAUX** *ex* Nunatsiavut Nanuk *-2013* *ex* Mikol L *-2006* *ex* Polar Viking *-2002* *ex* San Aotea *-2000* *ex* Midvingur *-1992* **CS Manpar Inc** Clearwater Seafoods Ltd Partnership *Iqaluit, NU* *Canada* MMSI: 316013590 Official number: 829727	**599** 179 -	Class: (NV)	**1988-08 Molde Verft AS — Hjelset** (Hull launched by) **1988-08 p/f Vags Skipasmidja — Vagur** (Hull completed by) Yd No: 8 **1988-08 Solstrand Slip & Baatbyggeri AS — Tomrefjord** Yd No: 44 Loa 40.60 Br ex - Dght 4.600 Lbp 40.60 Br md 9.00 Dpth 4.25 Welded	**(B11B2FV) Fishing Vessel** Ins: 280 Ice Capable	**1 oil engine** geared to sc. shaft driving 1 FP propeller Total Power: 819kW (1,114hp) MWM TBD440-6 1 x 4 Stroke 6 Cy. 230 x 270 819kW (1114bhp) Motoren Werke Mannheim AG (MWM)-West Germany AuxGen: 2 x 172kW 380V 50Hz a.c
8890346 - -	**THE RICHARD GEORGE** - **MacKenzie Forest Products Inc** - *Thunder Bay, ON* *Canada* Official number: 803829	*284* 193 -		**1993-07 Port Arthur Shipbuilding Co — Thunder Bay ON** Loa 27.74 Br ex - Dght - Lbp - Br md 12.19 Dpth 2.40 Welded, 1 dk	**(A31A2GX) General Cargo Ship**	**1 oil engine** driving 1 FP propeller Total Power: 416kW (566hp) 6.0kn
7938232 - -	**THE SAGA** *ex* Our Mama *-2013* *ex* Mama Jo *-1998* **John Bartlett Borden & Charles Gerkie** - *Roatan* *Honduras* Official number: U-1826659	*129* 88 -		**1978 Shrimp Trawlers Construction Co. — Amelia, La** L reg 22.32 Br ex 6.79 Dght - Lbp - Br md - Dpth 3.66 Welded, 1 dk	**(B11B2FV) Fishing Vessel**	**1 oil engine** driving 1 FP propeller Total Power: 301kW (409hp)
8321620 - -	**THE SEA PORCUPINE** - **Federal Military Government of Nigeria (Department of Fisheries - Federal Ministry of Agriculture)** - *Lagos* *Nigeria*	*114* 51 -	Class: (LR) ✠ Classed LR until 8/11/85	**1984-05 Schiffs- u. Bootswerft Luebbe Voss — Westerende-Kirchloog** Yd No: 114 Loa 23.19 Br ex 6.33 Dght 2.891 Lbp 19.99 Br md 6.20 Dpth 3.41 Welded, 1 dk	**(B11A2FS) Stern Trawler** Ins: 78	**1 oil engine** with clutches & sr reverse geared to sc. shaft driving 1 FP propeller Total Power: 530kW (721hp) Caterpillar 3412T 1 x Vee 4 Stroke 12 Cy. 137 x 152 530kW (721bhp) Caterpillar Tractor Co-USA AuxGen: 2 x 16kW 380V 50Hz a.c Fuel: 34.0 (d.f.)
7743027 *WDD3892* -	**THE SEEKER II** *ex* Tiffany H *-1998* **Seeker Fisheries Inc** - *Barnegat Light, NJ* *United States of America* MMSI: 367137680 Official number: 588768	*142* 96 -		**1977 Marine Builders, Inc. — Mobile, Al** L reg 23.47 Br ex 6.81 Dght - Lbp - Br md - Dpth 3.38 Welded, 1 dk	**(B11A2FT) Trawler**	**1 oil engine** driving 1 FP propeller Total Power: 386kW (525hp) G.M. (Detroit Diesel) 12V-71-TI 1 x Vee 2 Stroke 12 Cy. 108 x 127 386kW (525bhp) General Motors Detroit DieselAllison Divn-USA
8036574 *WDD8759* -	**THE SHOOTIST** *ex* Linda Christine *-1996* *ex* Roll Tide *-1980* **Cieutat Trawlers Inc** - *Mobile, AL* *United States of America* MMSI: 367302430 Official number: 621952	*128* 87 -		**1980 Gulf Coast Marine Builders, Inc. — Bayou La Batre, Al** Yd No: 32 L reg 23.69 Br ex 6.76 Dght - Lbp - Br md - Dpth 3.54 Welded, 1 dk	**(B11B2FV) Fishing Vessel**	**1 oil engine** driving 1 FP propeller Total Power: 382kW (519hp)
9583718 *MQPT5* -	**THE SNAPPER** - **Fastnet Ltd** Dominion Marine Corporate Services Ltd *Douglas* *Isle of Man (British)* MMSI: 235053244 Official number: 737870	**331** 99 -	Class: RI	**2007-04 Sunseeker International Ltd — Poole** Yd No: 50207121 Loa 36.89 Br ex - Dght 1.730 Lbp - Br md 7.87 Dpth 3.66 Bonded, 1 dk	**(X11A2YP) Yacht** Hull Material: Reinforced Plastic	**2 oil engines** reduction geared to sc. shafts driving 2 Propellers Total Power: 4,080kW (5,548hp) M.T.U. 12V4000M90 2 x Vee 4 Stroke 12 Cy. 165 x 190 each-2040kW (2774bhp) MTU Friedrichshafen GmbH-Friedrichshafen Fuel: 24.0 (d.f.)
8892576 *YB5124* -	**THE SPIRIT OF PURA** *ex* Francesca *-1995* **PT Purawisata Baruna** - *Semarang* *Indonesia*	*128* 76 -	Class: KI	**1991-01 in New Zealand** L reg 21.25 Br ex - Dght 0.700 Lbp 20.80 Br md 8.70 Dpth 1.90 Welded, 1 dk	**(A37B2PS) Passenger Ship** Hull Material: Reinforced Plastic	**2 oil engines** geared to sc. shafts driving 2 FP propellers Total Power: 552kW (750hp) 22.0kn Caterpillar 3408TA 2 x Vee 4 Stroke 8 Cy. 137 x 152 each-276kW (375bhp) Caterpillar Inc-USA
8989812 *J8Y4245* -	**THE STORM I** *ex* Sun Glider *-2010* **Storm Shipping Ltd** Navilux Management Sarl *Kingstown* *St Vincent & The Grenadines* MMSI: 376294000 Official number: 40715	**167** 50	Class: BV	**2005-05 Overmarine SpA — Viareggio** Yd No: 105/23 Loa 29.50 Br ex - Dght 1.100 Lbp 26.30 Br md 6.90 Dpth 3.80 Bonded, 1 dk	**(X11A2YP) Yacht** Hull Material: Reinforced Plastic	**2 oil engines** geared to sc. shafts driving 2 Propellers Total Power: 3,360kW (4,568hp) M.T.U. 12V396TE94 2 x Vee 4 Stroke 12 Cy. 165 x 185 each-1680kW (2284bhp) MTU Friedrichshafen GmbH-Friedrichshafen
9327542 *TCA2982* -	**THE THREE ANGELS** *ex* Tr 45 *-2009* **Bodrum Yolcu Limani Isletmeleri AS (Bodrum Cruise Port)** - *Istanbul* *Turkey* Official number: TUGS 1587	**168** 97 252	Class: AB	**2009-06 Yardimci Tersanesi A.S. — Tuzla** Yd No: 45 Loa 21.30 Br ex - Dght 2.400 Lbp 18.85 Br md 7.80 Dpth 3.30 Welded, 1 dk	**(B32A2ST) Tug**	**2 oil engines** reduction geared to sc. shafts driving 2 Propellers Total Power: 1,566kW (2,130hp) 12.5kn Caterpillar 3508B-TA 2 x Vee 4 Stroke 8 Cy. 170 x 190 each-783kW (1065bhp) Caterpillar Inc-USA AuxGen: 2 x 45kW a.c Fuel: 45.0 (d.f.)
9429613 *VRDM5* -	**THE VENETIAN** - **Venetian Macau Ltd** Chu Kong High-Speed Ferry Co Ltd *Hong Kong* *Hong Kong* MMSI: 477937200 Official number: HK-2043	**700** 240 84	Class: NV	**2007-11 Austal Ships Pty Ltd — Fremantle WA** Yd No: 312 Loa 47.50 Br ex 12.10 Dght 1.660 Lbp 43.80 Br md 11.80 Dpth 3.80 Welded, 1 dk	**(A37B2PS) Passenger Ship** Hull Material: Aluminium Alloy Passengers: 411	**4 oil engines** reduction geared to sc. shafts driving 4 Water jets Total Power: 9,148kW (12,436hp) M.T.U. 16V4000M70 4 x Vee 4 Stroke 16 Cy. 165 x 190 each-2287kW (3109bhp) MTU Friedrichshafen GmbH-Friedrichshafen AuxGen: 2 x a.c
7418878 *VY3791* -	**THE WALTER GRAY** *ex* Joshua Slocum *-2007* **Gray's Aqua Management Ltd** - *St Andrews, NB* *Canada* MMSI: 316017204 Official number: 345865	*240* 224 -		**1973 Halifax Metal Workers Ltd — Dartmouth NS** L reg 29.11 Br ex 11.89 Dght - Lbp - Br md - Dpth - Welded, 1 dk	**(A36A2PR) Passenger/Ro-Ro Ship (Vehicles)** Bow door/ramp Len: 6.09 Wid: 4.26 Swl: - Stern door/ramp Len: 6.09 Wid: 4.26 Swl: - Lane-Len: 27 Lane-Wid: 4.00 Lane-clr ht: 5.00 Cars: 15	**2 oil engines** driving 2 Propellers aft, 1 fwd Total Power: 264kW (358hp) 8.0kn Caterpillar 3306T 2 x 4 Stroke 6 Cy. 121 x 152 each-132kW (179bhp) Caterpillar Tractor Co-USA Fuel: 27.5 (d.f.) 0.5pd

8903234 *3EUJ2* -	**THE WATCHFUL** *ex* Marina Wave *-2013* *ex* Torm Gerd *-2000* **Flagstaff Developments Ltd Corp** SNP Shipping Services Pvt Ltd *Panama* *Panama* MMSI: 370359000 Official number: 4457513	**36,999** 22,656 69,451 T/cm 65.6	Class: LR (NV) **100A1** SS 01/2012 bulk carrier strengthened for heavy cargoes, Nos. 2, 4 & 6 holds may be empty ESP ESN-Hold 1 **LMC** **UMS**	**1992-01 Hashihama Shipbuilding Co Ltd — Tadotsu KG** (Hull) Yd No: 880 **1992-01 Tsuneishi Shipbuilding Co Ltd — Fukuyama HS** Yd No: 659 Loa 225.00 (BB) Br ex 32.24 Dght 13.200 Lbp 215.00 Br md 32.20 Dpth 18.30 Welded, 1 dk	**(A21A2BC) Bulk Carrier** Grain: 81,839 Compartments: 7 Ho, ER 7 Ha: (14.2 x 12.8)6 (16.8 x 14.4)ER	**1 oil engine** driving 1 FP propeller Total Power: 8,910kW (12,114hp) 14.0kn B&W 6S60MC 1 x 2 Stroke 6 Cy. 600 x 2292 8910kW (12114bhp) (made 1991) Kawasaki Heavy Industries Ltd-Japan AuxGen: 3 x 400kW 440V 60Hz a.c Boilers: AuxB (Comp) 7.1kgf/cm^2 (7.0bar) Fuel: 187.0 (d.f.) 2335.0 (r.f.) 30.0pd
8732166 *9HB3581* -	**THE WELLESLEY** *ex* New Life *-2013* **Saba Shipping Ltd** - *Valletta* *Malta* Official number: 8732166	**146** 43 -	Class: RI	**2002-01 in Italy** Yd No: 124 Loa 29.80 Br ex - Dght 2.400 Lbp 27.00 Br md 6.40 Dpth 3.17 Bonded, 1 dk	**(X11A2YP) Yacht** Hull Material: Reinforced Plastic	**2 oil engines** geared to sc. shafts driving 2 FP propellers Total Power: 2,686kW (3,652hp) 26.0kn M.T.U. 16V2000M90 2 x Vee 4 Stroke 16 Cy. 130 x 150 each-1343kW (1826bhp) MTU Friedrichshafen GmbH-Friedrichshafen
9219331 *C6RW4* -	**THE WORLD** **The World of ResidenSea II Ltd** Wilhelmsen Ship Management Ltd *Nassau* *Bahamas* MMSI: 311213000 Official number: 8000325	**43,188** 15,444 4,558	Class: NV	**2002-02 Bruces Verkstad AB — Landskrona** (Hull) Yd No: 247 **2002-02 Fosen Mek. Verksteder AS — Rissa** Yd No: 71 Loa 196.35 (BB) Br ex 29.80 Dght 6.900 Lbp 173.00 Br md 29.20 Dpth 9.10 Welded	**(A37A2PC) Passenger/Cruise** Passengers: cabins: 198; berths: 699 Ice Capable	**2 oil engines** geared to sc. shafts driving 2 CP propellers Total Power: 11,880kW (16,152hp) Wartsila 12V32 2 x Vee 4 Stroke 12 Cy. 320 x 350 each-5940kW (8076bhp) Wartsila Finland Oy-Finland AuxGen: 2 x 2800kW a.c, 3 x 1150kW a.c Thrusters: 2 Thwart. FP thruster (f); 1 Thwart. FP thruster (a) Fuel: 1276.0 (d.f.)
9107394 *V2IA3* -	**THEA II** *ex* Thea B *-2013* *ex* Bell Astron *-1997* *launched as* Thea B *-1995* **ms Thea II Schiffahrts GmbH & Co KG** Reederei Thekla Schepers GmbH & Co KG SatCom: Inmarsat C 430424710 *Saint John's* *Antigua & Barbuda* MMSI: 304247000	**2,899** 1,390 3,950	Class: GL	**1995-06 Elbewerft Boizenburg GmbH — Boizenburg** Yd No: 226 Lengthened-1995 Loa 99.33 (BB) Br ex 16.20 Dght 4.901 Lbp 92.89 Br md 16.00 Dpth 6.40 Welded, 1 dk	**(A31A2GX) General Cargo Ship** Double Bottom Entire Compartment Length Grain: 4,440 TEU 340 Compartments: 2 Ho, ER 2 Ha: ER Ice Capable	**1 oil engine** with flexible couplings & reduction geared to sc. shaft driving 1 CP propeller Total Power: 2,950kW (4,011hp) 14.5kn MAN 7L32/40 1 x 4 Stroke 7 Cy. 320 x 400 2950kW (4011bhp) MAN B&W Diesel AG-Augsburg AuxGen: 2 x 140kW 380/220V 50Hz a.c, 1 x 380kW 380/220V 50Hz a.c Thrusters: 1 Thwart. CP thruster (f)
8309438 *3FUA5* -	**THEA K** *ex* Dorothea *-2008* *ex* Garnet Star *-1994* **Palstek Shipping Inc** Nova Marine Carriers SA *Panama* *Panama* MMSI: 370712000 Official number: 4033809A	**13,021** 7,428 22,025 T/cm 30.0	Class: BV (GL) (NK)	**1984-03 Tohoku Shipbuilding Co Ltd — Shiogama MG** Yd No: 207 Loa 155.20 (BB) Br ex 22.89 Dght 9.945 Lbp 145.70 Br md 22.86 Dpth 13.59 Welded, 1 dk	**(A21A2BC) Bulk Carrier** Grain: 26,613; Bale: 25,556 Compartments: 4 Ho, ER 4 Ha: (17.7 x 10.3)3 (19.3 x 11.2)ER Cranes: 4x25t	**1 oil engine** driving 1 FP propeller Total Power: 5,553kW (7,550hp) 14.0kn B&W 6L55GBE 1 x 2 Stroke 6 Cy. 550 x 1380 5553kW (7550bhp) Mitsui Engineering & Shipbuilding CLtd-Japan AuxGen: 2 x 400kW
9195418 *PBDE* -	**THEA MARIEKE** *ex* Nordic Bianca *-2007* *ex* Korsar *-2005* *ex* Athos *-2005* **Thea M Shipping BV** W & R Shipping BV *Rotterdam* *Netherlands* MMSI: 246064000 Official number: 39590	**2,311** 1,305 3,149	Class: GL	**2001-09 Daewoo-Mangalia Heavy Industries S.A. — Mangalia** (Hull) Yd No: 1022 **2001-09 Scheepswerf Pattje B.V. — Waterhuizen** Yd No: 421 Loa 82.50 Br ex - Dght 5.300 Lbp 78.90 Br md 12.40 Dpth 6.70 Welded, 1 dk	**(A31A2GX) General Cargo Ship** Grain: 4,782; Bale: 4,782 TEU 132 C.Ho 96/20' (40') C. Dk 36/20' (40') incl. 12 ref C. Compartments: 1 Ho, ER 1 Ha: (56.3 x 10.2)ER Ice Capable	**1 oil engine** with flexible couplings & sr gearedto sc. shaft driving 1 CP propeller Total Power: 1,800kW (2,447hp) 11.5kn MaK 6M25 1 x 4 Stroke 6 Cy. 255 x 400 1800kW (2447bhp) MaK Motoren GmbH & Co. KG-Kiel AuxGen: 1 x 240kW 220/380V a.c, 3 x 90kW 220/380V a.c Thrusters: 1 Thwart. FP thruster (f) Fuel: 184.0 (d.f.) (Heating Coils) 6.0pd
9232412 *V2AF4* -	**THEA S** *ex* Niledutch Shanghai *-2013* *ex* Thea S *-2010* *ex* CSAV Rio Petrohue *-2009* *completed as* Safmarine Kei *-2004* *ex* Thea S *-2002* **ms 'Thea S' Rudolf Schepers Schiffahrts GmbH & Co KG** Reederei Rudolf Schepers GmbH & Co KG (Reederei Schepers) SatCom: Inmarsat C 430444910 *Saint John's* *Antigua & Barbuda* MMSI: 304449000 Official number: 2414	**25,630** 12,591 33,501 T/cm 45.0	Class: GL	**2002-10 Volkswerft Stralsund GmbH — Stralsund** Yd No: 441 Loa 207.40 (BB) Br ex - Dght 11.400 Lbp 195.40 Br md 29.80 Dpth 16.40 Welded, 1 dk	**(A33A2CC) Container Ship (Fully Cellular)** Double Bottom Entire Compartment Length TEU 2474 C Ho 992 TEU C Dk 1482 TEU incl 420 ref C. Compartments: 5 Cell Ho, ER Cranes: 3x45t	**1 oil engine** driving 1 FP propeller Total Power: 20,930kW (28,456hp) 21.0kn B&W 7L70MC 1 x 2 Stroke 7 Cy. 700 x 2268 20930kW (28456bhp) Doosan Engine Co Ltd-South Korea AuxGen: 3 x 1500kW 220/440V a.c Thrusters: 1 Thwart. FP thruster (f)
9162916 *SZTD* -	**THEANO** *completed as* Alam Bintang *-1997* **Golden Seagull Maritime Inc** Super-Eco Tankers Management Inc SatCom: Inmarsat B 330910810 *Chios* *Greece* MMSI: 239884000 Official number: 398	**28,400** 12,385 47,198 T/cm 50.3	Class: LR (NV) (AB) **100A1** SS 10/2012 oil & chemical tanker, Ship Type 3 ESP **LMC** **UMS IGS** Eq.Ltr: H†; Cable: 577.5/73.0 U3	**1997-10 Onomichi Dockyard Co Ltd — Onomichi HS** Yd No: 425 Converted From: Oil Tanker-2007 Converted From: Chemical/Products Tanker-2007 Loa 182.50 (BB) Br ex - Dght 12.650 Lbp 172.00 Br md 32.20 Dpth 19.10 Welded, 1 dk	**(A12B2TR) Chemical/Products Tanker** Double Hull (13F) Liq: 49,436; Liq (Oil): 49,436 Compartments: 2 Ta, 12 Wing Ta, 2 Wing Slop Ta, ER 4 Cargo Pump (s): 4x1000m^3/hr	**1 oil engine** driving 1 FP propeller Total Power: 8,561kW (11,640hp) 14.8kn MAN-B&W 6S50MC 1 x 2 Stroke 6 Cy. 500 x 1910 8561kW (11640bhp) Mitsui Engineering & Shipbuilding CLtd-Japan AuxGen: 3 x 420kW 220/440V 60Hz a.c Boilers: AuxB (ex.g.) 14.3kgf/cm^2 (14.0bar), WTAuxB (o.f.) 18.0kgf/cm^2 (17.7bar) Fuel: 1364.0 (r.f.) 33.0pd
9219410 *8PSM* -	**THEBAUD SEA** **McDermott Gulf Operating Co Inc** J Ray McDermott Canada Ltd *Bridgetown* *Barbados* MMSI: 314204000 Official number: 733457	**2,594** 778 3,406	Class: NV	**1999-09 Moss Point Marine, Inc. — Escatawpa, Ms** Yd No: 146 Loa 81.38 Br ex - Dght 5.810 Lbp 73.53 Br md 16.46 Dpth 7.01 Welded, 1 dk	**(B21A20S) Platform Supply Ship**	**6 diesel electric oil engines** driving 6 gen. each 1825kW 600V a.c Connecting to 2 elec. motors driving 2 Azimuth electric drive units Total Power: 11,172kW (15,192hp) 13.0kn Caterpillar 3516TA 6 x Vee 4 Stroke 16 Cy. 170 x 190 each-1862kW (2532bhp) Caterpillar Inc-USA AuxGen: 1 x 590kW 60Hz a.c Thrusters: 2 Thwart. FP thruster (f)
9199696 *V2OS* -	**THEBE** **Sunship Schiffahrtskontor KG Reederei M Lauterjung MLB Manfred Lauterjung Befrachtung GmbH** Sunship Schiffahrtskontor KG *Saint John's* *Antigua & Barbuda* MMSI: 304011026	**1,846** 1,081 2,500	Class: BV	**2000-06 SC Santierul Naval Tulcea SA — Tulcea** Yd No: 305 Loa 89.71 Br ex - Dght 4.480 Lbp 84.94 Br md 11.65 Dpth 5.80 Welded, 1 dk	**(A31A2GX) General Cargo Ship** Grain: 3,900; Bale: 3,750 TEU 126 C.Ho 72/20' C.Dk 54/20' incl.16 ref C. Compartments: 1 Ho, ER 1 Ha: (57.8 x 9.3)ER Ice Capable	**1 oil engine** reduction geared to sc. shaft driving 1 FP propeller Total Power: 1,500kW (2,039hp) 13.0kn Deutz SBV8M628 1 x 4 Stroke 8 Cy. 240 x 280 1500kW (2039bhp) Motoren Werke Mannheim AG (MWM)-Mannheim AuxGen: 2 x 134kW 220/380V 50Hz a.c Thrusters: 1 Thwart. FP thruster (f) Fuel: 126.9 (d.f.) 6.8pd
9261023 *V7UJ8* -	**THEBES** *ex* Parat *-2010* **Thebes LLC** Maritime Equity Management LLC *Majuro* *Marshall Islands* MMSI: 538002179	**19,795** 11,034 31,829 T/cm 45.4	Class: NV (NK)	**2003-02 The Hakodate Dock Co Ltd — Hakodate HK** Yd No: 786 Loa 176.82 (BB) Br ex - Dght 9.560 Lbp 168.00 Br md 29.40 Dpth 13.50 Welded, 1 dk	**(A21A2BC) Bulk Carrier** Double Hull Grain: 42,620; Bale: 39,680 Compartments: 5 Ho, ER 5 Ha: 4 (20.0 x 19.6)ER (13.6 x 15.0) Cranes: 4x30t	**1 oil engine** driving 1 FP propeller Total Power: 6,620kW (9,001hp) 14.0kn Mitsubishi 6UEC52LA 1 x 2 Stroke 6 Cy. 520 x 1600 6620kW (9001bhp) Akasaka Tekkosho KK (Akasaka DieselLtd)-Japan Fuel: 1430.0
5304114 - - -	**THEEQAR** *ex* Saad *-1971* - -	*112* - 220	Class: (GL)	**1960 F Schichau GmbH — Bremerhaven** Yd No: 1704 L reg 26.74 Br ex 6.94 Dght - Lbp - Br md - Dpth - Welded, 1 dk	**(B32A2ST) Tug**	**1 oil engine** driving 1 FP propeller Deutz RBV8M545 1 x 4 Stroke 8 Cy. 320 x 450 Kloeckner Humboldt Deutz AG-West Germany
7112084 *5IM509* -	**THEKKADY** *ex* Hormar *-2005* *ex* Juto *-1993* *ex* Scot *-1987* *ex* Sirius *-1986* *ex* Tyr *-1986* *ex* Nina Chris *-1984* *ex* Romeo *-1984* *ex* Liselil *-1976* **Golden Coast Shipping Inc** - *Zanzibar* *Tanzania (Zanzibar)* MMSI: 677040900 Official number: 300249	**483** 244 710	Class: (BV)	**1971-03 A/S Nordsovaerftet — Ringkobing** Yd No: 58 Loa 49.76 Br ex 8.34 Dght 3.480 Lbp 44.43 Br md 8.30 Dpth 5.50 Welded, 2 dks	**(A31A2GX) General Cargo Ship** Grain: 1,312; Bale: 1,159 Compartments: 1 Ho, ER 1 Ha: (24.5 x 5.0)ER Derricks: 2x5t; Winches: 2 Ice Capable	**1 oil engine** driving 1 CP propeller Total Power: 441kW (600hp) 11.0kn Alpha 406-26VO 1 x 2 Stroke 6 Cy. 260 x 400 441kW (600bhp) Alpha Diesel A/S-Denmark AuxGen: 2 x 48kW 380V 50Hz a.c Fuel: 100.5 (d.f.)

9215919 *9VPY3* -	**THEKLA SCHULTE** *ex* P&O Nedlloyd Antisana *-2005* *ex* Thekla Schulte *-2001* **Pesak Island Shipping Co Pte Ltd** Bernhard Schulte Shipmanagement (Hellas) SPLLC SatCom: Inmarsat C 456547310 *Singapore* *Singapore* MMSI: 565473000 Official number: 393109	**26,718** 12,715 34,677 T/cm 51.1	Class: NV (LR) ✠	**2001-10 Hyundai Heavy Industries Co Ltd — Ulsan** Yd No: 1301 Loa 210.00 (BB) Br ex - Dght 11.500 Lbp 199.00 Br md 30.20 Dpth 16.70 Welded, 1 dk	**(A33A2CC) Container Ship (Fully Cellular)** TEU 2556 C Ho 944 TEU C Dk 1612 TEU incl 600 ref C. Compartments: 5 Cell Ho, ER 10 Ha: (12.6 x 15.4)Tappered (12.6 x 20.4)Tappered (12.6 x 25.7)Tappered 7 (12.6 x 25.7)ER Cranes: 4x45t	**1 oil engine** driving 1 FP propeller Total Power: 21,560kW (29,313hp) 22.0kn Sulzer 7RTA72U 1 x 2 Stroke 7 Cy. 720 x 2500 21560kW (29313bhp) Hyundai Heavy Industries Co Ltd-South Korea AuxGen: 4 x 1600kW 220/450V 60Hz a.c Thrusters: 1 Thwart. CP thruster (f) Fuel: 150.0 (d.f.) (Heating Coils) 4100.0 (r.f.) 102.0pd
9463592 *9HA2503* -	**THELISIS** *ex* SPP Sacheon H1039 *-2010* **Sandstone Shipping Co Ltd** Adelfia Shipping Enterprises SA SatCom: Inmarsat C 424876610 *Valletta* *Malta* MMSI: 248766000 Official number: 9463592	**34,374** 19,565 58,814 T/cm 59.1	Class: AB	**2010-11 SPP Plant & Shipbuilding Co Ltd — Sacheon** Yd No: H1039 Loa 196.00 (BB) Br ex - Dght 13.000 Lbp 189.00 Br md 32.26 Dpth 18.60 Welded, 1 dk	**(A21A2BC) Bulk Carrier** Grain: 75,531; Bale: 70,734 Compartments: 5 Ho, ER 5 Ha: ER Cranes: 4x36t	**1 oil engine** driving 1 FP propeller Total Power: 9,960kW (13,542hp) 14.5kn MAN-B&W 6S50MC-C 1 x 2 Stroke 6 Cy. 500 x 2000 9960kW (13542bhp) Doosan Engine Co Ltd-South Korea AuxGen: 3 x 600kW a.c Fuel: 145.0 (d.f.) 2200.0 (r.f.)
8034069 - -	**THELMA J** - **Joint Adventures Inc** - *Mobile, AL* *United States of America* Official number: 617735	*114* 78 -		**1980 Rodriguez Boat Builders, Inc. — Coden, Al** L reg 22.10 Br ex 6.76 Dght - Lbp - Br md - Dpth 3.38 Welded, 1 dk	**(B11B2FV) Fishing Vessel**	**1 oil engine** driving 1 FP propeller Total Power: 405kW (551hp) Caterpillar 1 x 4 Stroke 405kW (551bhp) Caterpillar Tractor Co-USA
8522406 *OZEL* -	**THEMIS** *ex* Sunnanoe *-2010* *ex* Mette Holm *-2008* **Partrederiet Themis** *Skagen* *Denmark* MMSI: 219340000	**735** 276 1,080	Class: NV	**1986-09 Marstal Staalskibsvaerft og Maskinfabrik A/S — Marstal** Yd No: 106 Loa 48.55 Br ex 9.69 Dght 6.600 Lbp - Br md 9.65 Dpth 7.24 Welded, 2 dks	**(B11A2FS) Stern Trawler** Ice Capable	**1 oil engine** driving 1 CP propeller Total Power: 1,599kW (2,174hp) MaK 8M332AK 1 x 4 Stroke 8 Cy. 240 x 330 1599kW (2174bhp) Krupp MaK Maschinenbau GmbH-Kiel AuxGen: 2 x 112kW 380V 50Hz a.c Thrusters: 1 Thwart. CP thruster (f); 1 Tunnel thruster (a)
8979922 *ZCSZ6* -	**THEMIS** *ex* Allegra *-2000* *ex* Victory Lane *-2000* **Crystal Marine Two Ltd** Romo Inc *George Town* *Cayman Islands (British)* MMSI: 319939000 Official number: 733361	**421** 126 -	Class: AB	**1998-10 Trinity Yachts LLC — New Orleans LA** Yd No: 006 Loa 42.28 Br ex 8.53 Dght 2.770 Lbp - Br md 8.17 Dpth 3.69 Welded, 1 dk	**(X11A2YP) Yacht** Hull Material: Aluminium Alloy Passengers: cabins: 5	**2 oil engines** reverse reduction geared to sc. shafts driving 2 FP propellers Total Power: 3,356kW (4,562hp) 20.0kn Caterpillar 3516B-TA 2 x Vee 4 Stroke 16 Cy. 170 x 190 each-1678kW (2281bhp) Caterpillar Inc-USA AuxGen: 2 x 99kW 208V 60Hz a.c Thrusters: 1 Tunnel thruster (f)
9452543 *V7VL7* -	**THEMIS** **Ithaca Shipping SA** Navina Maritime SA SatCom: Inmarsat C 453835340 *Majuro* *Marshall Islands* MMSI: 538004153 Official number: 4153	**34,378** 19,565 58,487 T/cm 59.1	Class: AB	**2011-03 SPP Shipbuilding Co Ltd — Tongyeong** Yd No: H1040 Loa 196.00 (BB) Br ex - Dght 12.980 Lbp 189.00 Br md 32.26 Dpth 18.60 Welded, 1 dk	**(A21A2BC) Bulk Carrier** Grain: 75,531; Bale: 70,734 Compartments: 5 Ho, ER 5 Ha: ER Cranes: 4x36t	**1 oil engine** driving 1 FP propeller Total Power: 9,960kW (13,542hp) 14.5kn MAN-B&W 6S50MC-C8 1 x 2 Stroke 6 Cy. 500 x 2000 9960kW (13542bhp) Doosan Engine Co Ltd-South Korea AuxGen: 3 x 600kW a.c
9553115 *3FCI5* -	**THEMIS LEADER** **FPG Shipholding Panama SA** Nippon Yusen Kabushiki Kaisha (NYK Line) SatCom: Inmarsat C 437196510 *Panama* *Panama* MMSI: 371965000 Official number: 4189010	**61,804** 18,542 20,037 T/cm 55.6	Class: NK	**2010-07 Imabari Shipbuilding Co Ltd — Marugame KG (Marugame Shipyard)** Yd No: 1522 Loa 199.94 (BB) Br ex 32.26 Dght 10.016 Lbp 190.00 Br md 32.26 Dpth 34.80 Welded, 12 dks	**(A35B2RV) Vehicles Carrier** Side door/ramp (s) Len: 20.00 Wid: 4.20 Swl: 15 Quarter stern door/ramp (s. a.) Len: 35.00 Wid: 8.00 Swl: 80 Cars: 5,415	**1 oil engine** driving 1 FP propeller Total Power: 15,540kW (21,128hp) 20.0kn Mitsubishi 8UEC60LSII 1 x 2 Stroke 8 Cy. 600 x 2300 15540kW (21128bhp) Kobe Hatsudoki KK-Japan Thrusters: 1 Tunnel thruster (f) Fuel: 3636.0 (r.f.)
9075539 *3FKK4* -	**THEMIS P** *ex* Royal Pilot *-2000* **Sealink Investment SA** Iolcos Hellenic Maritime Enterprises Co Ltd SatCom: Inmarsat A 1360421 *Panama* *Panama* MMSI: 353781000 Official number: 2183495E	**36,559** 23,279 70,165 T/cm 65.0	Class: NK	**1994-09 Sumitomo Heavy Industries Ltd. — Oppama Shipyard, Yokosuka** Yd No: 1196 Loa 225.00 (BB) Br ex - Dght 13.291 Lbp 217.00 Br md 32.26 Dpth 18.30 Welded, 1 dk	**(A21A2BC) Bulk Carrier** Grain: 81,839; Bale: 78,529 Compartments: 7 Ho, ER 7 Ha: ER	**1 oil engine** driving 1 FP propeller Total Power: 7,723kW (10,500hp) 14.0kn Sulzer 6RTA62 1 x 2 Stroke 6 Cy. 620 x 2150 7723kW (10500bhp) Diesel United Ltd.-Aioi AuxGen: 3 x 420kW 450V 60Hz a.c Fuel: 2320.0 (r.f.) 27.0pd
9682837 *9V2051* -	**THEMISTOCLES** **Themistocles Shipping Venture Pte Ltd** Western Shipping Pte Ltd *Singapore* *Singapore* MMSI: 563656000 Official number: 398548	**31,538** 18,720 55,793 T/cm 56.9	Class: NK	**2014-02 Japan Marine United Corp (JMU) — Yokohama KN (Isogo Shipyard)** Yd No: 3342 Loa 190.00 Br ex - Dght 12.735 Lbp 185.00 Br md 32.26 Dpth 18.10 Welded, 1 dk	**(A21A2BC) Bulk Carrier** Grain: 72,111; Bale: 67,062 Compartments: 5 Ho, ER 5 Ha: 4 (20.9 x 18.6)ER (14.6 x 18.6)	**1 oil engine** driving 1 FP propeller Total Power: 10,470kW (14,235hp) 14.5kn Wartsila 6RT-flex50 1 x 2 Stroke 6 Cy. 500 x 2050 10470kW (14235bhp) Diesel United Ltd.-Aioi
6814219 - - -	**THEMISTOKLES** - - -	*717* 196 -		**1968 Th. Zervas & Sons — Piraeus** Loa 62.11 Br ex 11.51 Dght 1.702 Lbp 56.01 Br md - Dpth - Welded, 1 dk	**(A36A2PR) Passenger/Ro-Ro Ship (Vehicles)**	**2 oil engines** driving 2 FP propellers Total Power: 1,030kW (1,400hp) Skoda 6L275A2 2 x 4 Stroke 6 Cy. 275 x 350 each-515kW (700bhp) CKD Praha-Praha
9183843 *CQLG* -	**THEMSESTERN** **mt 'Themsestern' Schifffahrtsgesellschaft mbH & Co KG** Nordic Tankers Trading A/S *Madeira* *Portugal (MAR)* MMSI: 255804940 Official number: TEMP149M	**14,400** 6,937 21,871 T/cm 38.9	Class: GL	**2000-06 Stocznia Gdynia SA — Gdynia** Yd No: 8189/4 Loa 162.16 Br ex - Dght 8.500 Lbp 155.00 Br md 27.18 Dpth 12.00 Welded, 1 dk	**(A12B2TR) Chemical/Products Tanker** Double Hull (13F) Liq: 23,970; Liq (Oil): 23,970 Compartments: 1 Ta, 12 Wing Ta, 1 Wing Slop Ta, ER 14 Cargo Pump (s): 6x550m³/hr, 8x350m³/hr Manifold: Bow/CM: 80.6m Ice Capable	**1 oil engine** driving 1 CP propeller Total Power: 7,878kW (10,711hp) 15.0kn MAN-B&W 6S46MC-C 1 x 2 Stroke 6 Cy. 460 x 1932 7878kW (10711bhp) H Cegielski Poznan SA-Poland AuxGen: 1 x 720kW 220/440V a.c, 3 x 665kW 220/440V a.c Thrusters: 1 Tunnel thruster (f) Fuel: 1276.0 (r.f.)
9262194 *C6SY5* -	**THEO T** **Afinity Maritime SA** Ionia Management SA *Nassau* *Bahamas* MMSI: 311538000 Official number: 8000646	**40,013** 20,903 73,021 T/cm 66.8	Class: AB	**2003-08 Samsung Heavy Industries Co Ltd — Geoje** Yd No: 1407 Loa 227.50 (BB) Br ex - Dght 14.018 Lbp 219.00 Br md 32.24 Dpth 20.20 Welded, 1 dk	**(A13A2TV) Crude Oil Tanker** Double Hull (13F) Liq: 75,754; Liq (Oil): 75,754 Cargo Heating Coils Compartments: 12 Wing Ta, 2 Wing Slop Ta, ER 3 Cargo Pump (s): 3x2000m³/hr Manifold: Bow/CM: 110m	**1 oil engine** driving 1 FP propeller Total Power: 10,371kW (14,100hp) 14.5kn B&W 6S60MC 1 x 2 Stroke 6 Cy. 600 x 2292 10371kW (14100bhp) Doosan Engine Co Ltd-South Korea AuxGen: 3 x 690kW 440/220V 60Hz a.c
9291406 *9HA3251* -	**THEODOR OLDENDORFF** *ex* Nord Mercury *-2013* **Oldendorff Carriers GmbH & Co KG** - *Valletta* *Malta* MMSI: 229343000 Official number: 9291406	**40,097** 25,703 77,171 T/cm 67.1	Class: AB	**2008-07 Oshima Shipbuilding Co Ltd — Saikai NS** Yd No: 10398 Loa 225.00 (BB) Br ex - Dght 14.100 Lbp 220.00 Br md 32.26 Dpth 19.39 Welded, 1 dk	**(A21A2BC) Bulk Carrier** Double Hull Grain: 90,200; Bale: 88,984 Compartments: 7 Ho, ER 7 Ha: ER	**1 oil engine** driving 1 FP propeller Total Power: 9,326kW (12,680hp) 14.5kn MAN-B&W 6S60MC 1 x 2 Stroke 6 Cy. 600 x 2292 9326kW (12680bhp) Mitsui Engineering & Shipbuilding CLtd-Japan Fuel: 230.0 (d.f.) 2175.0 (r.f.)
9248679 *D5EJ7* -	**THEODOR STORM** *ex* TS Nagoya *-2012* *ex* Theodor Storm *-2010* **ms 'Theodor Storm' Schiffahrtsges Schluter KG** Norddeutsche Reederei H Schuldt GmbH & Co KG *Monrovia* *Liberia* MMSI: 636092499 Official number: 92499	**28,270** 13,327 33,297	Class: GL (AB)	**2004-12 Jurong Shipyard Pte Ltd — Singapore** Yd No: 1066 Loa 213.00 (BB) Br ex - Dght 11.500 Lbp 202.10 Br md 32.20 Dpth 16.50 Welded, 1 dk	**(A33A2CC) Container Ship (Fully Cellular)** TEU 2586 incl 400 ref C.	**1 oil engine** driving 1 FP propeller Total Power: 25,228kW (34,300hp) 22.7kn B&W 7K80MC-C 1 x 2 Stroke 7 Cy. 800 x 2300 25228kW (34300bhp) Hitachi Zosen Corp-Japan AuxGen: 4 x 1360kW 440/220V 60Hz a.c Thrusters: 1 Tunnel thruster (f) Fuel: 435.0 (d.f.) 3735.0 (r.f.) 103.0pd

9005338 *PHYG* -	**THEODORA** **Bulgersteyn BV** Tarbit Tankers BV SatCom: Inmarsat C 424436710 *Rotterdam* *Netherlands* MMSI: 244367000 Official number: 5838	**4,098** 1,460 6,616 T/cm 15.4	Class: BV	**1991-04 BV Scheepswerf & Mfbk 'De Merwede' v/h van Vliet & Co — Hardinxveld** Yd No: 658 Converted From: Products Tanker Loa 110.60 (BB) Br ex - Dght 7.050 Lbp 104.29 Br md 17.00 Dpth 9.36 Welded, 1 dk	**(A12B2TR) Chemical/Products Tanker** Double Hull (13F) Liq: 5,138; Liq (Oil): 5,138; Asphalt: 5,138 Cargo Heating Coils Compartments: 6 Wing Ta, 3 Ta, ER 3 Cargo Pump (s): 3x310m³/hr Manifold: Bow/CM: 52m Ice Capable	**1 oil engine** sr geared to sc. shaft driving 1 CP propeller Total Power: 3,000kW (4,079hp) 14.5kn Wartsila 8R32E 1 x 4 Stroke 8 Cy. 320 x 350 3000kW (4079bhp) Wartsila Diesel Oy-Finland AuxGen: 4 x 200kW 380V 50Hz a.c Thrusters: 1 Thwart. FP thruster (f) Fuel: 380.0 (d.f.) 13.2pd
8663078 *SV7254* -	**THEODORA** *ex* Ileana **Mediterranean Cruises Co Ltd** - *Piraeus* *Greece* MMSI: 239718000 Official number: 7664	**223** 66 -		**1980-01 D. C. Anastassiades & A. Ch. Tsortanides — Perama** Loa 33.08 Br ex - Dght - Lbp - Br md 6.30 Dpth 3.45 Welded, 1 dk	**(X11A2YP) Yacht**	**2 oil engines** reduction geared to sc. shafts driving 2 Propellers Total Power: 736kW (1,000hp) Caterpillar 2 x each-368kW (500bhp) Caterpillar Inc-USA
7042203 *SV2091* -	**THEODORA** *ex* Archangelos *-2002* **Vassilios Arzoglou** - *Kavala* *Greece* MMSI: 237044700 Official number: 305	*118* 56 59		**1971 Th. Zervas & Sons — Piraeus** Yd No: 94 Loa 27.51 Br ex 6.30 Dght 2.350 Lbp 23.50 Br md 6.20 Dpth 3.20 Welded, 1 dk	**(B11A2FT) Trawler**	**1 oil engine** driving 1 FP propeller Total Power: 294kW (400hp) Alpha 404-26VO 1 x 2 Stroke 4 Cy. 260 x 400 294kW (400bhp) Alpha Diesel A/S-Denmark
7350313 - -	**THEODORA** *ex* Theodora R *-2010* *ex* Nikolaos K *-2008* *ex* Parthenon *-1988* **Coastal Resources SA**	*583* 304 224		**1975-01 General Shipyards of Greece — Eleusis** Yd No: 65 Loa - Br ex 11.82 Dght 1.499 Lbp 61.50 Br md - Dpth 3.20 Welded, 1 dk	**(A36A2PR) Passenger/Ro-Ro Ship (Vehicles)**	**2 oil engines** driving 2 FP propellers Total Power: 824kW (1,120hp) Blackstone 2 x 4 Stroke each-412kW (560bhp) Mirrlees Blackstone (Stamford)Ltd.-Stamford
9027441 - -	**THEODORE I** - **PT Surya Maritim Shippindo** - *Samarinda* *Indonesia*	**149** 89 -	Class: KI	**2003-06 P.T. Suryanusa Permatabahari — Samarinda** Loa 25.25 Br ex - Dght 2.700 Lbp 23.80 Br md 7.00 Dpth 3.50 Welded, 1 dk	**(B32A2ST) Tug**	**2 oil engines** geared to sc. shafts driving 2 Propellers Total Power: 882kW (1,200hp) 9.0kn Caterpillar 3412TA 2 x Vee 4 Stroke 12 Cy. 137 x 152 each-441kW (600bhp) Caterpillar Inc-USA AuxGen: 2 x 60kW 380/220V a.c
9029774 - -	**THEODORE II** - **PT Rukuy Jaya Abadi** - *Samarinda* *Indonesia*	**154** 92 -	Class: KI	**2004-01 P.T. Suryanusa Permatabahari — Samarinda** Loa 25.00 Br ex - Dght - Lbp 23.32 Br md 7.50 Dpth 3.10 Welded, 1 dk	**(B32A2ST) Tug**	**2 oil engines** geared to sc. shafts driving 2 Propellers Total Power: 904kW (1,230hp) Caterpillar 3412E 2 x Vee 4 Stroke 12 Cy. 137 x 152 each-452kW (615bhp) Caterpillar Inc-USA AuxGen: 2 x 118kW 400/230V a.c
9068847 - -	**THEODORE III** - **PT Surya Maritim Shippindo** - *Samarinda* *Indonesia*	**154** 92 -	Class: KI	**2004-07 P.T. Suryanusa Permatabahari — Samarinda** Loa 25.00 Br ex - Dght - Lbp 23.32 Br md 7.50 Dpth 3.10 Welded, 1 dk	**(B32A2ST) Tug**	**2 oil engines** geared to sc. shafts driving 2 Propellers Total Power: 904kW (1,230hp) Caterpillar 3412E 2 x Vee 4 Stroke 12 Cy. 137 x 152 each-452kW (615bhp) Caterpillar Inc-USA
6807333 - -	**THEODOROS** *ex* Zoe *-2003* *ex* Aragon *-1998* **Ivoire Shipping Corp** Eurotec Srl	**634** 286 980	Class: (RI) (BV)	**1967-01 Ateliers & Chantiers de La Rochelle-Pallice — La Rochelle** Yd No: 5155 Loa 62.79 Br ex 9.91 Dght 3.739 Lbp 57.00 Br md 9.89 Dpth 4.09 Welded, 1 dk	**(A12C2LW) Wine Tanker** Liq: 1,080 Compartments: 20 Ta, ER 2 Cargo Pump (s): 2x80m³/hr Manifold: Bow/CM: 18m	**1 oil engine** driving 1 FP propeller Total Power: 1,092kW (1,485hp) 12.0kn MAN G7V30/45ATL 1 x 4 Stroke 7 Cy. 300 x 450 1092kW (1485bhp) Maschinenbau Augsburg Nuernberg (MAN)-Augsburg Fuel: 90.0 (d.f.) 4.0pd
6421660 - -	**THEODOROS** *ex* Basbosa *-2013* *ex* Blue Sea *-2012* *ex* Petroil Vergina *-2011* *ex* Olga T *-2006* *ex* Giokamoy *-2002* *ex* Mopa Kjear *-1993* *ex* Bellan Tre *-1984* *ex* Margrethe Hoyer *-1977* **ADJ Shipping Co**	**543** 237 619	Class: (BV)	**1964-03 Heinrich Brand KG Schiffswerft — Oldenburg** Yd No: 165 Loa 55.35 Br ex 8.72 Dght 3.201 Lbp 48.29 Br md 8.68 Dpth 3.43 Welded, 1 dk	**(A13B2TU) Tanker (unspecified)** Liq: 885; Liq (Oil): 885 Cargo Heating Coils Compartments: 8 Ta, ER Ice Capable	**1 oil engine** driving 1 FP propeller Total Power: 367kW (499hp) 10.8kn MaK 6MU451 1 x 4 Stroke 6 Cy. 320 x 450 367kW (499bhp) Maschinenbau Kiel AG (MaK)-Kiel Fuel: 26.5 (d.f.) 1.5pd
8853843 *HP6142* -	**THEODOROS DINOS** *ex* Skylark No. 1 *-1991* *ex* Timco No. 1 *-1985* *ex* Sanyo Maru No. 18 *-1985* **Bahamas Maritime Inc** - *Panama* *Panama* Official number: 20651PEXT	*141* 98 -		**1974 Otsuchi Zosen Kogyo K.K. — Otsuchi** L reg 26.88 Br ex - Dght - Lbp - Br md 5.64 Dpth 2.19 Welded, 1 dk	**(B11B2FV) Fishing Vessel**	**1 oil engine** driving 1 FP propeller Total Power: 662kW (900hp) 9.5kn Yanmar 1 x 4 Stroke 662kW (900bhp) Yanmar Diesel Engine Co Ltd-Japan
9103831 *SXJQ* -	**THEODOROS I. V.** *launched as* Diamond *-1999* **Vamos Shipping Co** Avin International SA SatCom: Inmarsat C 423959710 *Piraeus* *Greece* MMSI: 239597000 Official number: 10620	**31,183** 11,862 44,500 T/cm 55.0	Class: LR (RS) ✠ **100A1** SS 03/2009 oil & chemical tanker (Double Hull), Ship Type 3 SG 1.55 in cargo tanks 1, 3, 5 & 7 ESP LI ✠ **LMC** **UMS IGS** Eq.Ltr: O†; Cable: 675.0/81.0 U3	**1999-03 DAHK Chernomorskyi Sudnobudivnyi Zavod — Mykolayiv** Yd No: 205 Loa 182.90 Br ex 32.23 Dght 12.110 Lbp 178.48 Br md 32.20 Dpth 18.60 Welded, 1 dk	**(A12B2TR) Chemical/Products Tanker** Double Hull (13F) Liq: 49,220; Liq (Oil): 49,220 Compartments: 7 Ta, 2 Slop Ta, ER 7 Cargo Pump (s): 7x975m³/hr Manifold: Bow/CM: 90.2m	**1 oil engine** driving 1 CP propeller Total Power: 10,400kW (14,140hp) 14.5kn B&W 6S60MC 1 x 2 Stroke 6 Cy. 600 x 2292 10400kW (14140bhp) AO Bryanskiy MashinostroitelnyyZavod (BMZ)-Bryansk AuxGen: 3 x 785kW 400/380V 50Hz a.c Boilers: e (ex.g.) 10.7kgf/cm² (10.5bar), AuxB (o.f.) 8.4kgf/cm² (8.2bar) Thrusters: 1 Thwart. FP thruster (f) Fuel: 195.0 (d.f.) (Heating Coils) 2213.2 (r.f.) 45.3pd
8969082 *V3PF9* -	**THEODOROS MARIA Z** - - *Belize City* *Belize* MMSI: 312671000 Official number: 751310002	*479* 144 -		**1976 Th. Zervas & Sons — Piraeus** Loa 61.50 Br ex - Dght 1.950 Lbp 61.50 Br md 15.10 Dpth 2.60 Welded, 1 dk	**(A37B2PS) Passenger Ship**	**2 oil engines** reduction geared to sc. shafts driving 2 FP propellers Total Power: 1,060kW (1,442hp) 12.5kn Baudouin 12P15.2SR 2 x Vee 4 Stroke 12 Cy. 150 x 150 each-530kW (721bhp) Societe des Moteurs Baudouin SA-France
8612160 *SV5739* -	**THEODOROS VASSILIKI** **K Hatzopoulos** - *Piraeus* *Greece* MMSI: 237498000 Official number: 4462	**128** 38 91		**1988-01 Homatas Brothers Shipyard — Thessaloniki** Yd No: 88 Loa 28.00 Br ex 6.90 Dght 3.141 Lbp - Br md 6.88 Dpth 3.25 Welded, 1 dk	**(B11A2FS) Stern Trawler** Ins: 70 Compartments: 1 Ta, ER	**1 oil engine** with clutches & sr geared to sc. shaft driving 1 FP propeller Total Power: 368kW (500hp) Kelvin TGSC8 1 x 4 Stroke 8 Cy. 165 x 184 368kW (500bhp) Kelvin Diesels Ltd., GECDiesels-Glasgow
9275751 *V7H02* -	**THEODOSIA** *ex* LR Regulus *-2013* *ex* FR8 Reginamar *-2013* *ex* Overseas Reginamar *-2009* *ex* Reginamar *-2005* **Canary Pacific Ltd** Halkidon Shipping Corp SatCom: Inmarsat Mini-M 764444171 *Majuro* *Marshall Islands* MMSI: 538002272 Official number: 2272	**42,307** 19,834 70,312 T/cm 67.5	Class: AB	**2004-06 Daewoo Shipbuilding & Marine Engineering Co Ltd — Geoje** Yd No: 5242 Loa 228.00 (BB) Br ex 32.22 Dght 13.771 Lbp 219.00 Br md 32.20 Dpth 20.90 Welded, 1 dk	**(A13B2TP) Products Tanker** Double Hull (13F) Liq: 80,987; Liq (Oil): 78,400 Compartments: 12 Wing Ta, ER, 2 Wing Slop Ta 12 Cargo Pump (s): 12x900m³/hr Manifold: Bow/CM: 111.5m	**1 oil engine** driving 1 FP propeller Total Power: 11,451kW (15,569hp) 14.6kn MAN-B&W 5S60MC-C 1 x 2 Stroke 5 Cy. 600 x 2400 11451kW (15569bhp) Doosan Engine Co Ltd-South Korea AuxGen: 3 x 900kW a.c Fuel: 270.0 (d.f.) 2164.0 (r.f.)
9224025 *D5FG4* -	**THEOFANO** *ex* Volumnia *-2013* *ex* Lietta *-2007* *ex* Kanaris *-2007* **Present Shipping Co SA** Rainbow Shipmanagement SA *Monrovia* *Liberia* MMSI: 636016257 Official number: 16257	**40,002** 26,101 76,015 T/cm 67.7	Class: LR ✠ **100A1** SS 03/2012 bulk carrier strengthened for heavy cargoes, Nos. 2, 4 & 6 holds may b e empty ESP *IWS LI ESN **ShipRight** (SDA, FDA, CM) ✠ **LMC** **UMS** Eq.Ltr: O†; Cable: 660.0/78.0 U3 (a)	**2002-03 Tsuneishi Shipbuilding Co Ltd — Fukuyama HS** Yd No: 1207 Loa 225.00 (BB) Br ex 32.30 Dght 14.035 Lbp 217.00 Br md 32.20 Dpth 19.15 Welded, 1 dk	**(A21A2BC) Bulk Carrier** Grain: 91,356 Compartments: 7 Ho, ER 7 Ha: (15.6 x 12.8) (17.3 x 15.5)5 (17.3 x 15.4)ER	**1 oil engine** driving 1 FP propeller Total Power: 8,550kW (11,625hp) 14.5kn B&W 6S60MC 1 x 2 Stroke 6 Cy. 600 x 2292 8550kW (11625bhp) Mitsui Engineering & Shipbuilding CLtd-Japan AuxGen: 3 x 600kW 450V 60Hz a.c Boilers: WTAuxB (Comp) 7.1kgf/cm² (7.0bar) Fuel: 164.0 (d.f.) 2642.0 (r.f.) 33.0pd

9177997 *V7C07* -	**THEOFANO STAR** *ex* Oriental Sun *-2013* **Anixis Maritime SA** Seamax Marine Inc *Majuro* *Marshall Islands* MMSI: 538005297 Official number: 5297	**37,773** 23,948 72,651 T/cm 66.9	Class: KR (NK)	**1998**-03 **Sasebo Heavy Industries Co. Ltd. — Sasebo Yard, Sasebo** Yd No: 442 Loa 225.00 (BB) Br ex - Dght 13.521 Lbp 218.00 Br md 32.20 Dpth 18.70 Welded, 1 dk	**(A21A2BC) Bulk Carrier** Grain: 84,790 Compartments: 7 Ho, ER 7 Ha: (15.3 x 12.8)6 (17.0 x 14.4)ER	**1 oil engine** driving 1 FP propeller Total Power: 8,827kW (12,001hp) 14.5kn B&W 6S60MC 1 x 2 Stroke 6 Cy. 600 x 2292 8827kW (12001bhp) Mitsui Engineering & Shipbuilding CLtd-Japan
7362108 *SWJC* -	**THEOFILOS** *ex* Pollux *-1995* *ex* Abel Tasman *-1994* *ex* Nils Holgersson *-1985* **Maritime Company of Lesvos SA** NEL Lines (Maritime Co of Lesvos SA) *Mytilene* *Greece* MMSI: 239369000 Official number: 35	**13,572** 7,718 3,472	Class: RS (HR) (GL)	**1975**-04 **Werft Nobiskrug GmbH — Rendsburg** Yd No: 682 Loa 148.88 (BB) Br ex 23.98 Dght 6.100 Lbp 135.82 Br md 23.50 Dpth 16.59 Welded, 5 dks	**(A36A2PR) Passenger/Ro-Ro Ship (Vehicles)** Passengers: unberthed: 701; cabins: 280; berths: 860 Bow door & ramp Len: 9.25 Wid: 6.65 Swl: - Stern door/ramp (p) Len: 5.58 Wid: 5.96 Swl: - Stern door/ramp (s) Len: 5.58 Wid: 5.96 Swl: - Lane-Len: 1430 Lane-Wid: 5.95 Lane-clr ht: 4.55 Cars: 210, Trailers: 34	**2 oil engines** reduction geared to sc. shafts driving 2 CP propellers Total Power: 15,510kW (21,088hp) 19.5kn Pielstick 16PC2-5V-400 2 x Vee 4 Stroke 16 Cy. 400 x 460 each-7755kW (10544bhp) Blohm + Voss AG-West Germany AuxGen: 4 x 800kW 440V 60Hz a.c Thrusters: 2 Thwart. FP thruster (f) Fuel: 191.5 (d.f.) 820.0 (r.f.) 60.0pd
7637618 *SY2723* -	**THEOFILOS SEA** *ex* Mary C *-2002* *ex* Fiducia *-1989* *ex* Ligato *-1988* **Charalampos Maritime Co** - *Piraeus* *Greece* MMSI: 239987000 Official number: 11046	*963* - 2,440	Class: (LR) (BV) Classed LR until 25/5/05	**1977**-10 **Scheepswerf "Voorwaarts" B.V. — Hoogezand** Yd No: 222 Loa 66.10 Br ex 13.09 Dght 5.092 Lbp 59.97 Br md 13.00 Dpth 6.23 Welded, 1 dk	**(A31A2GX) General Cargo Ship** Grain: 2,935; Bale: 2,878 Compartments: 1 Ho, ER 1 Ha: (38.7 x 10.2)ER	**1 oil engine** sr geared to sc. shaft driving 1 CP propeller Total Power: 739kW (1,005hp) 12.8kn Nohab F28V 1 x Vee 4 Stroke 8 Cy. 250 x 300 739kW (1005bhp) AB Bofors NOHAB-Sweden AuxGen: 2 x 80kW 380V 50Hz a.c, 1 x 40kW 380V 50Hz a.c Thrusters: 1 Thwart. FP thruster (f) Fuel: 149.5 (d.f.)
9081112 *9HRC8* -	**THEOFYLAKTOS** *ex* Nordmoritz *-2006* **Kingsley Shipping Co Ltd** General Maritime Enterprises Corp *Valletta* *Malta* MMSI: 256321000 Official number: 9081112	**39,027** 24,110 74,523 T/cm 66.4	Class: LR (GL) **100A1** SS 02/2010 bulk carrier strengthened for heavy cargoes, Nos. 2, 4 & 6 holds may be empty ESN-Hold 1 ESP **LMC** **UMS** Cable: 660.0/78.0 U3 (a)	**1995**-02 **Daewoo Heavy Industries Ltd — Geoje** Yd No: 1084 Loa 224.80 (BB) Br ex - Dght 13.820 Lbp 216.00 Br md 32.20 Dpth 19.10 Welded, 1 dk	**(A21A2BC) Bulk Carrier** Grain: 85,704 Compartments: 7 Ho, ER 7 Ha: ER	**1 oil engine** driving 1 FP propeller Total Power: 9,213kW (12,526hp) 14.5kn B&W 6S60MC 1 x 2 Stroke 6 Cy. 600 x 2292 9213kW (12526bhp) Hyundai Heavy Industries Co Ltd-South Korea AuxGen: 2 x 500kW 220/440V a.c Boilers: AuxB (Comp) 8.0kgf/cm² (7.8bar) Fuel: 2505.0
8989549 - -	**THEOKHARIS L** - -	**982** 497 -		**2001 in Greece** Loa - Br ex - Dght - Lbp - Br md - Dpth - Welded, 1 dk	**(A37B2PS) Passenger Ship**	**1 oil engine** driving 1 Propeller Total Power: 1,383kW (1,880hp)
8989537 *SY2437* -	**THEOLOGOS-ELENI** **Michalakis II Naftiki Eteria** - *Piraeus* *Greece* MMSI: 237545900 Official number: 10858	**843** 190 -		**2002 in Greece** Loa - Br ex - Dght - Lbp - Br md - Dpth - Welded, 1 dk	**(A37B2PS) Passenger Ship**	**1 oil engine** driving 1 Propeller Total Power: 1,324kW (1,800hp)
9223150 *SZNB* -	**THEOLOGOS P** *ex* Ferry Kochi *-2006* **Cyclades Fast Ferries Maritime Co** Panagiotis Panagiotakis *Piraeus* *Greece* MMSI: 240521000 Official number: 11479	*4,140* 2,122 3,227	Class: BV	**2000**-07 **Yamanishi Corp — Ishinomaki MG** Yd No: 1018 Loa 118.14 (BB) Br ex - Dght 5.200 Lbp 109.00 Br md 21.00 Dpth 6.80 Welded	**(A36A2PR) Passenger/Ro-Ro Ship (Vehicles)** Passengers: unberthed: 475 Bow door/ramp Len: 11.70 Wid: 4.85 Swl: - Quarter stern door/ramp (s) Len: 12.90 Wid: 6.20 Swl: - Lorries: 10, Cars: 73	**2 oil engines** driving 2 CP propellers Total Power: 9,930kW (13,500hp) 19.4kn Pielstick 9PC2-6L-400 2 x 4 Stroke 9 Cy. 400 x 460 each-4965kW (6750bhp) Niigata Engineering Co Ltd-Japan AuxGen: 3 x 600kW a.c Thrusters: 1 Thwart. FP thruster (f) Fuel: 370.0 (d.f.) 38.0pd
9568354 - -	**THEOLOGOS V** **Theologos Shipping Co** Agios Nikolaos - Salamina Shipping Co *Panama* *Panama* Official number: 45332PEXT	**997** 647 -	Class: (HR)	**2009**-07 **Sithironaftiki Ltd. — Greece** Yd No: 198 Loa 105.40 Br ex - Dght 2.400 Lbp 83.90 Br md 18.08 Dpth - Welded, 1 dk	**(A36A2PR) Passenger/Ro-Ro Ship (Vehicles)** Passengers: unberthed: 500 Bow ramp (centre) Cars: 146	**4 oil engines** reduction geared to sc. shafts driving 4 Propellers Total Power: 3,880kW (5,276hp) 13.0kn Caterpillar C32 4 x Vee 4 Stroke 12 Cy. 145 x 162 each-970kW (1319bhp) Caterpillar Inc-USA
9595759 *J8B4532* -	**THEOMETOR** **Latona Maritime Co** Vamvaship Maritime SA SatCom: Inmarsat C 437527110 *Kingstown* *St Vincent & The Grenadines* MMSI: 375271000 Official number: 11005	**32,543** 18,519 55,695 T/cm 57.0	Class: KR	**2011**-07 **Hyundai Mipo Dockyard Co Ltd — Ulsan** Yd No: 6099 Loa 187.88 (BB) Br ex - Dght 12.868 Lbp 182.50 Br md 32.26 Dpth 18.30 Welded, 1 dk	**(A21A2BC) Bulk Carrier** Grain: 71,000 Compartments: 5 Ho, ER 5 Ha: 4 (21.3 x 18.4)ER (16.4 x 18.4) Cranes: 4x30t	**1 oil engine** driving 1 FP propeller Total Power: 8,820kW (11,992hp) 14.5kn MAN-B&W 6S50MC-C 1 x 2 Stroke 6 Cy. 500 x 2000 8820kW (11992bhp) Hyundai Heavy Industries Co Ltd-South Korea AuxGen: 3 x 600kW 450V a.c
9078335 *V7ED9* -	**THEOMITOR** *ex* Dion *-2010* *ex* Scarlet Success *-2002* **Mount Kadisto Shipping Ltd** Anbros Maritime SA SatCom: Inmarsat C 453832082 *Majuro* *Marshall Islands* MMSI: 538001780 Official number: 1780	**17,428** 9,829 28,510 T/cm 39.3	Class: NK	**1994**-03 **Kanda Zosensho K.K. — Kawajiri** Yd No: 356 Loa 170.00 (BB) Br ex 27.04 Dght 9.766 Lbp 162.00 Br md 27.00 Dpth 13.80 Welded, 1 dk	**(A21A2BC) Bulk Carrier** Grain: 37,500; Bale: 35,600 Compartments: 5 Ho, ER 5 Ha: (14.1 x 15.0)4 (19.2 x 18.0)ER Cranes: 4x30t	**1 oil engine** driving 1 FP propeller Total Power: 5,884kW (8,000hp) 14.0kn Mitsubishi 5UEC52LA 1 x 2 Stroke 5 Cy. 520 x 1600 5884kW (8000bhp) Akasaka Tekkosho KK (Akasaka DieselLtd)-Japan AuxGen: 3 x 367kW a.c Fuel: 1240.0 (r.f.)
8647816 *SY4317* -	**THEOMITOR** **European Shipping Co** Koinopraxia Epivatochimatagogon Salaminos *Piraeus* *Greece* MMSI: 237746400 Official number: 11078	**992** 561 -		**2004 in Greece** Loa 83.56 Br ex - Dght - Lbp - Br md 19.40 Dpth - Welded, 1 dk	**(A36A2PR) Passenger/Ro-Ro Ship (Vehicles)**	**4 oil engines** reduction geared to sc. shafts driving 4 Propellers
8902759 *SW5406* -	**THEOSKEPASTI** **Saint Argangels Maritime Co** - *Piraeus* *Greece* MMSI: 237020600 Official number: 4896	*137* 31 75		**1990**-06 **Kanellos Bros. — Piraeus** Yd No: 173 Loa 31.10 Br ex 10.52 Dght 1.600 Lbp 26.50 Br md 10.50 Dpth 2.50 Welded, 1 dk	**(A37B2PS) Passenger Ship**	**2 oil engines** reverse geared to sc. shafts driving 2 FP propellers Total Power: 368kW (500hp) MAN D2866LE 2 x 4 Stroke 6 Cy. 128 x 155 each-184kW (250bhp) MAN Nutzfahrzeuge AG-Nuernberg
9268978 *J8B3918* -	**THEOSKEPASTI** *ex* Nord Whale *-2009* **Charente Navigation SA** Vamvaship Maritime SA *Kingstown* *St Vincent & The Grenadines* MMSI: 377152000 Official number: 10391	**27,989** 17,077 50,354 T/cm 53.5	Class: NK (BV)	**2004**-03 **Kawasaki Shipbuilding Corp — Kobe HG** Yd No: 1550 Loa 189.80 (BB) Br ex - Dght 11.925 Lbp 181.00 Br md 32.26 Dpth 16.90 Welded, 1 dk	**(A21A2BC) Bulk Carrier** Grain: 63,198; Bale: 60,713 Compartments: 5 Ho, ER 5 Ha: 4 (20.2 x 18.0)ER (17.6 x 18.0) Cranes: 4x30.5t	**1 oil engine** driving 1 FP propeller Total Power: 8,090kW (10,999hp) 14.5kn MAN-B&W 6S50MC-C 1 x 2 Stroke 6 Cy. 500 x 2000 8090kW (10999bhp) Kawasaki Heavy Industries Ltd-Japan Fuel: 1767.0 (r.f.) 35.0pd
9595761 *J8B4535* -	**THEOTOKOS** **Kabira Navigation SA** Vamvaship Maritime SA *Kingstown* *St Vincent & The Grenadines* MMSI: 377531000 Official number: 11008	**32,543** 18,519 55,698 T/cm 57.0	Class: KR	**2011**-09 **Hyundai Mipo Dockyard Co Ltd — Ulsan** Yd No: 6100 Loa 187.88 (BB) Br ex - Dght 12.868 Lbp 182.50 Br md 32.26 Dpth 18.30 Welded, 1 dk	**(A21A2BC) Bulk Carrier** Grain: 71,000 Compartments: 5 Ho, ER 5 Ha: 4 (21.3 x 18.4)ER (16.4 x 18.4) Cranes: 4x30t	**1 oil engine** driving 1 FP propeller Total Power: 8,820kW (11,992hp) 14.5kn MAN-B&W 6S50MC-C 1 x 2 Stroke 6 Cy. 500 x 2000 8820kW (11992bhp) Hyundai Heavy Industries Co Ltd-South Korea AuxGen: 3 x 600kW 450V a.c

IMO / Call sign	Name / Owner / Manager / Port	Tonnage	Class	Builder / Dimensions	Type / Cargo	Machinery
8978007 *SY2775* -	**THEOTOKOS** - **Theotokos Naftiki Eteria** Koinopraxia Epivatochimatagogon Salaminos *Piraeus* Greece MMSI: 237622300 Official number: 10962	**761** 409 654		**2002 at Salamis** Loa 82.40 Br ex - Dght 2.200 Lbp 69.98 Br md 17.12 Dpth 3.20 Welded, 1 dk	**(A36A2PR) Passenger/Ro-Ro Ship (Vehicles)** Passengers: unberthed: 1110 Bow door/ramp (f) Stern door/ramp (a) Lane-clr ht: 4.60 Cars: 114	**4 oil engines** Reduction geared to sc. shafts driving 4 FP propellers Total Power: 1,412kW (1,920hp) 12.0kn GUASCOR F240TA-SP 4 x 4 Stroke 8 Cy. 152 x 165 each-353kW (480bhp) Gutierrez Ascunce Corp (GUASCOR)-Spain AuxGen: 3 x 85kW 60Hz a.c
9142980 *3FJD8* -	**THEOXENIA** *ex* Normannia *-2013 ex* Batu *-2007* **Theoxenia Shipping Co** - *Panama* Panama MMSI: 372099000 Official number: 4500313	**24,987** 13,532 42,648 T/cm 48.8	Class: GL (BV)	**1997-08 Ishikawajima-Harima Heavy Industries Co Ltd (IHI) — Tokyo** Yd No: 3075 Loa 181.50 (BB) Br ex - Dght 11.350 Lbp 172.00 Br md 30.50 Dpth 16.40 Welded, 1 dk	**(A21A2BC) Bulk Carrier** Double Bottom Entire Compartment Length Grain: 53,852; Bale: 52,379 Compartments: 5 Ho, ER 5 Ha: (15.2 x 12.8)4 (19.2 x 15.2)ER Cranes: 4x25t	**1 oil engine** driving 1 FP propeller Total Power: 6,990kW (9,504hp) 14.2kn Sulzer 6RTA48T 1 x 2 Stroke 6 Cy. 480 x 2000 6990kW (9504bhp) Diesel United Ltd.-Aioi AuxGen: 3 x 520kW a.c Fuel: 189.0 (d.f.) 1600.0 (r.f.) 26.5pd
8834029 - -	**THEPSIRINTA-1** - **Intertransport Co Ltd** -	**130** 39 16	Class: (RS)	**1989 in the U.S.S.R.** Loa 34.50 Br ex - Dght 1.100 Lbp 32.25 Br md 10.30 Dpth 1.80 Welded	**(A37B2PS) Passenger Ship** Hull Material: Aluminium Alloy Passengers: unberthed: 140	**2 oil engines** geared to sc. shafts driving 2 FP propellers Total Power: 1,920kW (2,610hp) 34.0kn M.T.U. 12V396 2 x Vee 4 Stroke 12 Cy. 165 x 185 each-960kW (1305bhp) MTU Friedrichshafen GmbH-Friedrichshafen
8834031 - -	**THEPSIRINTA-2** - **Intertransport Co Ltd** -	**130** 39 16	Class: (RS)	**1989 in the U.S.S.R.** Loa 34.50 Br ex - Dght 1.100 Lbp 32.25 Br md 10.30 Dpth 1.80 Welded	**(A37B2PS) Passenger Ship** Hull Material: Aluminium Alloy Passengers: unberthed: 140	**2 oil engines** geared to sc. shafts driving 2 FP propellers Total Power: 1,920kW (2,610hp) 34.0kn M.T.U. 12V396 2 x Vee 4 Stroke 12 Cy. 165 x 185 each-960kW (1305bhp) MTU Friedrichshafen GmbH-Friedrichshafen
8834043 - -	**THEPSIRINTA-3** - **Intertransport Co Ltd** -	**130** 39 16	Class: (RS)	**1989 in the U.S.S.R.** Loa 34.50 Br ex - Dght 1.100 Lbp 32.25 Br md 10.30 Dpth 1.80 Welded	**(A37B2PS) Passenger Ship** Hull Material: Aluminium Alloy Passengers: unberthed: 140	**2 oil engines** geared to sc. shafts driving 2 FP propellers Total Power: 1,920kW (2,610hp) 34.0kn M.T.U. 12V396 2 x Vee 4 Stroke 12 Cy. 165 x 185 each-960kW (1305bhp) MTU Friedrichshafen GmbH-Friedrichshafen
8834055 - -	**THEPSIRINTA-4** - **Intertransport Co Ltd** -	**130** 39 16	Class: (RS)	**1989 in the U.S.S.R.** Loa 34.50 Br ex - Dght 1.100 Lbp 32.25 Br md 10.30 Dpth 1.80 Welded	**(A37B2PS) Passenger Ship** Hull Material: Aluminium Alloy Passengers: unberthed: 140	**2 oil engines** geared to sc. shafts driving 2 FP propellers Total Power: 1,920kW (2,610hp) 34.0kn M.T.U. 12V396 2 x Vee 4 Stroke 12 Cy. 165 x 185 each-960kW (1305bhp) MTU Friedrichshafen GmbH-Friedrichshafen
7935058 *HSB2279* -	**THEPSUDA** *ex* Big Sea 3 *-2009 ex* Ryoan Maru No. 7 *-1994* **Major Chem Tanker Co Ltd** Smooth Sea Co Ltd *Bangkok* Thailand MMSI: 567027900 Official number: 371000084	*998* 776 2,395		**1979 Sasaki Shipbuilding Co Ltd — Osakikamijima HS** Yd No: 334 Loa 78.00 (BB) Br ex - Dght 4.984 Lbp 74.00 Br md 12.01 Dpth 5.31 Welded, 1 dk	**(A13B2TP) Products Tanker** Single Hull Liq: 2,685; Liq (Oil): 2,685 Compartments: 5 Ta, ER 2 Cargo Pump (s): 2x750m³/hr	**1 oil engine** driving 1 FP propeller Total Power: 1,618kW (2,200hp) Akasaka DM38A 1 x 4 Stroke 6 Cy. 380 x 600 1618kW (2200bhp) Akasaka Tekkosho KK (Akasaka DieselLtd)-Japan
8817162 *HSB2869* -	**THEPTARA 3** *ex* Wakashima Maru *-2002* **Trans Ocean Supply (1992) Co Ltd** - Thailand Official number: 451000340	**491** 216 751		**1988-10 Kurinoura Dockyard Co Ltd — Yawatahama EH** Yd No: 256 Loa 53.60 Br ex 8.82 Dght 3.716 Lbp 49.00 Br md 8.80 Dpth 4.10 Welded, 1 dk	**(A13B2TP) Products Tanker** Liq: 740; Liq (Oil): 740 Compartments: 6 Ta, ER	**1 oil engine** with clutches & reverse reduction geared to sc. shaft driving 1 FP propeller Total Power: 625kW (850hp) Hanshin 6LU26G 1 x 4 Stroke 6 Cy. 260 x 440 625kW (850bhp) The Hanshin Diesel Works Ltd-Japan
9215036 *SXEE* -	**THERA** - **Layhill Shipping Corp** Kyklades Maritime Corp (Kyklades Naftiki Eteria) SatCom: Inmarsat C 423982410 *Piraeus* Greece MMSI: 239824000 Official number: 10876	**78,845** 47,271 150,678 T/cm 118.0	Class: LR ✠ **100A1** SS 05/2011 Double Hull oil tanker ESP *IWS LI **ShipRight** (SDA, FDA, CM) ✠ **LMC** **UMS IGS** Eq.Ltr: X†; Cable: 742.5/97.0 U3 (a)	**2001-05 Nippon Kokan KK (NKK Corp) — Tsu ME** Yd No: 207 Loa 274.20 (BB) Br ex 48.04 Dght 16.022 Lbp 263.00 Br md 48.00 Dpth 22.40 Welded, 1 dk	**(A13A2TW) Crude/Oil Products Tanker** Double Hull (13F) Liq: 163,918; Liq (Oil): 166,710 Cargo Heating Coils Compartments: 12 Wing Ta, ER, 2 Wing Slop Ta 3 Cargo Pump (s): 3x3500m³/hr Manifold: Bow/CM: 134m	**1 oil engine** driving 1 FP propeller Total Power: 16,460kW (22,379hp) 15.4kn Sulzer 6RTA72 1 x 2 Stroke 6 Cy. 720 x 2500 16460kW (22379bhp) Diesel United Ltd.-Aioi AuxGen: 3 x 750kW 450V 60Hz a.c Boilers: 2 AuxB (o.f.) 18.1kgf/cm² (17.8bar), e (ex.g.) 23.0kgf/cm² (22.6bar) Fuel: 300.0 (d.f.) (Heating Coils) 3830.0 (r.f.)
9225952 - -	**THERAPUTHTHABHAYA** - **Government of The Democratic Socialist Republic of Sri Lanka (Ports Authority)** - *Colombo* Sri Lanka	**320** 96 181	Class: LR ✠ **100A1** SS 06/2011 tug Sri Lanka coastal service ✠ **LMC** Eq.Ltr: F; Cable: 275.0/19.0 U2 (a)	**2001-06 Colombo Dockyard Ltd. — Colombo** Yd No: 155 Loa 30.50 Br ex 9.84 Dght 3.800 Lbp 29.50 Br md 9.60 Dpth 4.48 Welded, 1 dk	**(B32A2ST) Tug**	**2 oil engines** reduction geared to sc. shafts driving 2 Directional propellers Total Power: 1,440kW (1,958hp) 12.0kn Wartsila 4L20 2 x 4 Stroke 4 Cy. 200 x 280 each-720kW (979bhp) Wartsila Finland Oy-Finland AuxGen: 2 x 120kW 440V 50Hz a.c
8333506 *JVUW4* -	**THERESA** *ex* Nasser *-2006* **Trinity Marine Services Inc** Midgulf Offshore Ship Chartering LLC *Ulaanbaatar* Mongolia MMSI: 457545000 Official number: 31031283	**495** 148 -	Class: BV (AB)	**1978 IMC — Tonnay-Charente** Yd No: 272 Loa 40.20 Br ex - Dght 3.663 Lbp 26.01 Br md 7.80 Dpth 3.92 Welded, 1 dk	**(B32A2ST) Tug**	**2 oil engines** reverse reduction geared to sc. shafts driving 2 FP propellers Total Power: 1,708kW (2,322hp) 10.0kn G.M. (Detroit Diesel) 16V-149-TI 2 x Vee 2 Stroke 16 Cy. 146 x 146 each-854kW (1161bhp) General Motors Detroit DieselAllison Divn-USA AuxGen: 2 x 131kW 415/240V 50Hz a.c Fuel: 200.0
7523348 - -	**THERESA** *ex* Sjurdarberg *-2007 ex* Patricia X *-2002* *ex* Sjurdarberg *-2002 ex* Gilston *-2002* *ex* Olympic Champion *-1994 ex* Karina *-1990* **Salvation Merchant Fishing Co Ltd** - *Takoradi* Ghana Official number: GSR 0041	**1,204** 533 619	Class: (NV)	**1976-12 Voldnes Skipsverft AS — Fosnavaag** Yd No: 16 Lengthened-1984 Loa 63.00 (BB) Br ex 10.04 Dght 4.800 Lbp 53.90 Br md 9.91 Dpth 6.78 Welded, 1 dk	**(B11A2FG) Factory Stern Trawler** Ins: 800 Ice Capable	**1 oil engine** driving 1 CP propeller Total Power: 1,324kW (1,800hp) 13.0kn Wichmann 6AXA 1 x 2 Stroke 6 Cy. 300 x 450 1324kW (1800bhp) Wichmann Motorfabrikk AS-Norway AuxGen: 1 x 236kW 380V 50Hz a.c, 2 x 112kW 380V 50Hz a.c Fuel: 264.0 (d.f.) 6.0pd
6910910 *5NGL* -	**THERESA** *ex* Marianne Wonsild *-1982 ex* Kis Skou *-1979* **Cocco Holdings Ltd** - *Lagos* Nigeria Official number: 375895	*500* 315 1,126	Class: (LR) ✠ Classed LR until 10/12/86	**1969-04 Aarhus Flydedok og Maskinkompagni A/S — Aarhus** Yd No: 138 Loa 59.92 Br ex 10.32 Dght 3.893 Lbp 55.00 Br md 10.20 Dpth 4.20 Welded, 1 dk	**(A12B2TR) Chemical/Products Tanker** Liq: 1,384; Liq (Oil): 1,384 Cargo Heating Coils Compartments: 10 Ta, ER Ice Capable	**1 oil engine** driving 1 FP propeller Total Power: 1,118kW (1,520hp) 11.0kn MaK 6Z451AK 1 x 4 Stroke 6 Cy. 320 x 450 1118kW (1520bhp) Atlas MaK Maschinenbau GmbH-Kiel AuxGen: 2 x 48kW 380V 50Hz a.c, 1 x 30kW 380V 50Hz a.c Fuel: 56.0 (d.f.) 4.0pd
8420608 *T2XH2* -	**THERESA ANTARCTIC** *ex* Sitakathrine *-2008 ex* Burwain Atlantic *-1996* *ex* Nordflex *-1991* **Sabrina Shipping Co Pte Ltd** Raffles Shipmanagement Services Pte Ltd *Funafuti* Tuvalu MMSI: 572536000	**43,733** 26,618 83,920 T/cm 67.6	Class: BV (NV)	**1986-12 B&W Skibsvaerft A/S — Copenhagen** Yd No: 919 Loa 228.61 (BB) Br ex 32.28 Dght 16.069 Lbp 218.70 Br md 32.24 Dpth 21.57 Welded, 1 dk	**(A12B2TR) Chemical/Products Tanker** Double Hull (13F) Liq: 86,783; Liq (Oil): 86,783 Compartments: 12 Wing Ta, 2 Wing Slop Ta, ER 12 Cargo Pump (s): 12x860m³/hr Manifold: Bow/CM: 115.6m	**1 oil engine** driving 1 FP propeller Total Power: 8,018kW (10,901hp) 14.3kn B&W 5L70MCE 1 x 2 Stroke 5 Cy. 700 x 2268 8018kW (10901bhp) MAN B&W Diesel A/S-Denmark AuxGen: 1 x 1200kW 440V 60Hz a.c, 2 x 600kW 440V 60Hz a.c Fuel: 374.5 (d.f.) 2679.5 (r.f.) 32.5pd
9435806 *9V9871* -	**THERESA AQUARIUS** *ex* Vasi *-2012* **Angelina Shipping Co Pte Ltd** Raffles Shipmanagement Services Pte Ltd *Singapore* Singapore MMSI: 566426000 Official number: 397686	**8,247** 3,725 12,923 T/cm 21.8	Class: BV (AB)	**2008-11 STX Shipbuilding Co Ltd — Busan** Yd No: 5028 Loa 120.00 (BB) Br ex 20.40 Dght 8.710 Lbp 113.00 Br md 20.40 Dpth 11.90 Welded, 1 dk	**(A12B2TR) Chemical/Products Tanker** Double Hull (13F) Liq: 13,674; Liq (Oil): 13,674 Cargo Heating Coils Compartments: 10 Wing Ta, 2 Wing Slop Ta, ER 10 Cargo Pump (s): 10x350m³/hr Manifold: Bow/CM: 58.4m	**1 oil engine** driving 1 FP propeller Total Power: 4,454kW (6,056hp) 13.6kn MAN-B&W 6S35MC 1 x 2 Stroke 6 Cy. 350 x 1400 4454kW (6056bhp) STX Engine Co Ltd-South Korea AuxGen: 3 x 450kW a.c Fuel: 65.0 (d.f.) 530.0 (r.f.)
8715508 *T2XJ2* -	**THERESA ARCTIC** *ex* Sitamia *-2008 ex* Petrobulk Mars *-1997* **Lydia Shipping Co Ltd Pte** Raffles Shipmanagement Services Pte Ltd *Funafuti* Tuvalu MMSI: 572537000	**43,414** 19,867 84,040 T/cm 67.5	Class: BV (NV)	**1988-11 B&W Skibsvaerft A/S — Copenhagen** Yd No: 922 Loa 228.60 (BB) Br ex 32.28 Dght 16.076 Lbp 218.70 Br md 32.24 Dpth 21.60 Welded, 1 dk	**(A12B2TR) Chemical/Products Tanker** Double Hull (13F) Liq: 86,783; Liq (Oil): 86,783 Compartments: 12 Wing Ta, 2 Wing Slop Ta, ER 12 Cargo Pump (s): 12x860m³/hr Manifold: Bow/CM: 115.6m	**1 oil engine** driving 1 FP propeller Total Power: 8,017kW (10,900hp) 12.9kn B&W 5L70MCE 1 x 2 Stroke 5 Cy. 700 x 2268 8017kW (10900bhp) Hyundai Engine & Machinery Co Ltd-South Korea AuxGen: 1 x 1200kW 440V 60Hz a.c, 2 x 600kW 440V 60Hz a.c Fuel: 359.8 (d.f.) 2623.5 (r.f.) 30.0pd

9348508 *9VDX9* -	**THERESA ARIES** **Naka Trans Ocean SA** Raffles Technical Services Pte Ltd *Singapore* *Singapore* MMSI: 565202000 Official number: 3378308A	**11,438** 5,037 17,112 T/cm 28.0	Class: BV	**2006-09 Jiujiang Yinxing Shipbuilding Co Ltd — Xingzi County JX** Yd No: YX001 Converted From: Chemical/Products Tanker-2010 Loa 144.30 (BB) Br ex 23.03 Dght 8.800 Lbp 134.50 Br md 23.00 Dpth 12.50 Welded, 1 dk	**(A12B2TR) Chemical/Products Tanker** Double Hull (13F) Liq: 19,588; Liq (Oil): 19,588 Compartments: 12 Wing Ta, 2 Wing Slop Ta, ER 4 Cargo Pump (s): 4x500m³/hr	**1 oil engine** driving 1 FP propeller Total Power: 4,440kW (6,037hp) 13.5kn MAN-B&W 6S35MC 1 x 2 Stroke 6 Cy. 350 x 1400 4440kW (6037bhp) STX Engine Co Ltd-South Korea AuxGen: 3 x 465kW 400/220V 60Hz a.c Thrusters: 1 Tunnel thruster (f)
9078103 *T2EB4* -	**THERESA BEGONIA** *ex* Sunrise Begonia *-2009* **Elena Shipping Co Pte Ltd** Raffles Shipmanagement Services Pte Ltd *Funafuti* *Tuvalu* MMSI: 572452210 Official number: 27189412	**4,893** 2,490 8,253 T/cm 16.8	Class: NK	**1994-04 Fukuoka Shipbuilding Co Ltd — Fukuoka FO** Yd No: 1178 Loa 110.50 (BB) Br ex 18.20 Dght 7.496 Lbp 102.00 Br md 18.20 Dpth 9.30 Welded, 1 dk	**(A12A2TC) Chemical Tanker** Double Bottom Entire Compartment Length Cargo Heating Coils Compartments: 6 Ta (s.stl), 10 Wing Ta, 1 Slop Ta, ER 14 Cargo Pump (s): 10x200m³/hr, 4x100m³/hr Manifold: Bow/CM: 52m	**1 oil engine** driving 1 FP propeller Total Power: 3,089kW (4,200hp) 14.0kn Mitsubishi 6UEC37LA 1 x 2 Stroke 6 Cy. 370 x 880 3089kW (4200bhp) Akasaka Tekkosho KK (Akasaka DieselLtd)-Japan AuxGen: 3 x a.c Thrusters: 1 Thwart. CP thruster (f) Fuel: 223.0 (d.f.) 337.0 (r.f.)
9124055 *9V9086* -	**THERESA DUA** *ex* Golden Georgia *-2010* **Halona Shipping Co Pte Ltd** Raffles Technical Services Pte Ltd *Singapore* *Singapore* MMSI: 565658000 Official number: 396612	**9,597** 5,132 16,337 T/cm 26.5	Class: BV (NK)	**1996-10 Kurinoura Dockyard Co Ltd — Yawatahama EH** Yd No: 305 Loa 149.00 (BB) Br ex 22.03 Dght 9.100 Lbp 138.00 Br md 22.00 Dpth 11.65 Welded, 1 dk	**(A12B2TR) Chemical/Products Tanker** Double Hull Liq: 17,863; Liq (Oil): 17,863 Cargo Heating Coils Compartments: 24 Wing Ta (s.stl), 2 Wing Slop Ta (s.stl), ER 24 Cargo Pump (s): 10x300m³/hr, 8x200m³/hr, 6x100m³/hr Manifold: Bow/CM: 70.2m	**1 oil engine** driving 1 FP propeller Total Power: 5,296kW (7,200hp) 13.5kn Mitsubishi 6UEC45LA 1 x 2 Stroke 6 Cy. 450 x 1350 5296kW (7200bhp) Kobe Hatsudoki KK-Japan AuxGen: 3 x 370kW a.c Thrusters: 1 Tunnel thruster (f) Fuel: 177.0 (d.f.) 1117.0 (r.f.)
8618889 *T2HH3* -	**THERESA DUMAI** *ex* Kvarven *-2009* *ex* Bunga Tanjung *-2006* **Liliana Shipping Co Pte Ltd** Raffles Shipmanagement Services Pte Ltd *Funafuti* *Tuvalu* MMSI: 572790000 Official number: 20629009	**18,453** 9,759 29,500 T/cm 39.0	Class: BV (LR) ✠ Classed LR until 2/11/09	**1991-01 Hanjin Heavy Industries Co Ltd — Busan** Yd No: 2019 Loa 172.21 (BB) Br ex 26.04 Dght 11.015 Lbp 163.68 Br md 26.00 Dpth 15.20 Welded, 1 dk	**(A12B2TR) Chemical/Products Tanker** Double Bottom Entire Compartment Length Liq: 34,963; Liq (Oil): 34,963 Cargo Heating Coils Compartments: 17 Ta, ER, 2 Wing Slop Ta, 16 Wing Ta 37 Cargo Pump (s): 2x500m³/hr, 3x450m³/hr, 3x350m³/hr, 13x250m³/hr, 16x190m³/hr Manifold: Bow/CM: 86m	**1 oil engine** driving 1 FP propeller Total Power: 7,274kW (9,890hp) 14.5kn Sulzer 5RTA62 1 x 2 Stroke 5 Cy. 620 x 2150 7274kW (9890bhp) Hyundai Heavy Industries Co Ltd-South Korea AuxGen: 3 x 835kW 450V 60Hz a.c, 1 x 700kW 450V 60Hz a.c Boilers: 2 AuxB (o.f.) 9.0kgf/cm² (8.8bar), e (ex.g.) 12.0kgf/cm² (11.8bar) Thrusters: 1 Thwart. CP thruster (f) Fuel: 195.8 (d.f.) 1518.3 (r.f.) 23.0pd
9317195 *9V9955* -	**THERESA GALAXY** *ex* Oak Galaxy *-2012* **Bernice Shipping Co Pte Ltd** Raffles Technical Services Pte Ltd *Singapore* *Singapore* MMSI: 566457000 Official number: 397787	**12,105** 6,378 19,997 T/cm 30.3	Class: BV (NK)	**2005-05 Shin Kurushima Dockyard Co. Ltd. — Akitsu** Yd No: 5336 Loa 147.83 (BB) Br ex 24.23 Dght 9.461 Lbp 141.00 Br md 24.20 Dpth 12.85 Welded, 1 dk	**(A12B2TR) Chemical/Products Tanker** Double Hull (13F) Liq: 20,864; Liq (Oil): 21,925 Compartments: 22 Wing Ta (s.stl), ER 22 Cargo Pump (s): 14x330m³/hr, 8x200m³/hr Manifold: Bow/CM: 76.6m	**1 oil engine** driving 1 FP propeller Total Power: 6,230kW (8,470hp) 15.0kn Mitsubishi 7UEC45LA 1 x 2 Stroke 7 Cy. 450 x 1350 6230kW (8470bhp) Kobe Hatsudoki KK-Japan AuxGen: 3 x 500kW 450V 60Hz a.c Thrusters: 1 Thwart. CP thruster (f) Fuel: 64.2 (d.f.) 1026.2 (r.f.)
9591818 *VRKE6* -	**THERESA GUANGDONG** **Monalisa Shipping Co Pte Ltd** Raffles Shipmanagement Services Pte Ltd SatCom: Inmarsat C 447703946 *Hong Kong* *Hong Kong* MMSI: 477700800 Official number: HK-3432	**44,686** 27,932 82,000 T/cm 71.9	Class: BV	**2012-05 Jiangsu Eastern Heavy Industry Co Ltd — Jingjiang JS** Yd No: 10C-019 Loa 229.00 Br ex - Dght 14.580 Lbp 225.15 Br md 32.26 Dpth 20.05 Welded, 1 dk	**(A21A2BC) Bulk Carrier** Grain: 98,740; Bale: 90,784 Compartments: 7 Ho, ER 7 Ha: ER	**1 oil engine** driving 1 FP propeller Total Power: 11,300kW (15,363hp) 14.1kn MAN-B&W 5S60MC-C 1 x 2 Stroke 5 Cy. 600 x 2400 11300kW (15363bhp) Doosan Engine Co Ltd-South Korea AuxGen: 3 x 615kW 60Hz a.c
9607124 *VRLJ9* -	**THERESA HAINAN** **Edna Shipping Co Pte Ltd** Raffles Technical Services Pte Ltd *Hong Kong* *Hong Kong* MMSI: 477444200 Official number: HK-3687	**43,974** 27,688 82,000	Class: BV	**2013-05 Sainty Shipbuilding (Yangzhou) Corp Ltd — Yizheng JS** Yd No: SAM 10017B Loa 229.00 (BB) Br ex 32.60 Dght 14.450 Lbp 225.50 Br md 32.26 Dpth 20.05 Welded, 1 dk	**(A21A2BC) Bulk Carrier** Grain: 97,000 Compartments: 7 Ho, ER 7 Ha: ER	**1 oil engine** driving 1 FP propeller Total Power: 11,300kW (15,363hp) 14.1kn MAN-B&W 5S60MC-C 1 x 2 Stroke 5 Cy. 600 x 2400 11300kW (15363bhp) Doosan Engine Co Ltd-South Korea
9591832 *VRKB4* -	**THERESA HEBEI** **Rayna Shipping Co Pte Ltd** Wilmar International Ltd *Hong Kong* *Hong Kong* MMSI: 477792400 Official number: HK-3406	**43,951** 27,703 81,707	Class: LR ✠**100A1** SS 03/2012 bulk carrier CSR BC-A GRAB (20) Nos. 2, 4 & 6 holds may be empty ESP **ShipRight** (CM,ACS (B)) *IWS LI ✠**LMC** **UMS** Cable: 687.5/81.0 U3 (a)	**2012-03 Sainty Shipbuilding (Yangzhou) Corp Ltd — Yizheng JS** Yd No: SAM 10007B Loa 229.00 (BB) Br ex 32.31 Dght 14.400 Lbp 225.50 Br md 32.26 Dpth 20.05 Welded, 1 dk	**(A21A2BC) Bulk Carrier** Grain: 97,000 Compartments: 7 Ho, ER 7 Ha: ER	**1 oil engine** driving 1 FP propeller Total Power: 11,300kW (15,363hp) 14.1kn MAN-B&W 5S60MC-C 1 x 2 Stroke 5 Cy. 600 x 2400 11300kW (15363bhp) Doosan Engine Co Ltd-South Korea AuxGen: 3 x 600kW 440V 60Hz a.c Boilers: AuxB (Comp) 8.6kgf/cm² (8.4bar)
9591844 *VRKB3* -	**THERESA JIANGSU** **Serena Shipping Co Pte Ltd** Wilmar International Ltd *Hong Kong* *Hong Kong* MMSI: 477792300 Official number: HK-3405	**43,951** 27,717 81,680	Class: LR ✠**100A1** SS 03/2012 bulk carrier CSR BC-A GRAB (20) Nos 2, 4 & 6 holds may be empty ESP **ShipRight** (CM, ACS (B)) *IWS LI ✠**LMC** **UMS** Cable: 687.5/81.0 U3 (a)	**2012-03 Sainty Shipbuilding (Yangzhou) Corp Ltd — Yizheng JS** Yd No: SAM 10008B Loa 228.97 (BB) Br ex 32.30 Dght 14.400 Lbp 225.50 Br md 32.26 Dpth 20.05 Welded, 1 dk	**(A21A2BC) Bulk Carrier** Grain: 97,000 Compartments: 7 Ho, ER 7 Ha: ER	**1 oil engine** driving 1 FP propeller Total Power: 11,300kW (15,363hp) 14.1kn MAN-B&W 5S60MC-C 1 x 2 Stroke 5 Cy. 600 x 2400 11300kW (15363bhp) Doosan Engine Co Ltd-South Korea AuxGen: 3 x 600kW 440V 60Hz a.c Boilers: AuxB (Comp) 9.2kgf/cm² (9.0bar)
9603972 *VRKM6* -	**THERESA JILIN** **Juliana Shipping Co Pte Ltd** Raffles Shipmanagement Services Pte Ltd SatCom: Inmarsat C 447704286 *Hong Kong* *Hong Kong* MMSI: 477311400 Official number: HK-3497	**43,974** 27,688 82,000	Class: BV	**2012-06 Sainty Shipbuilding (Yangzhou) Corp Ltd — Yizheng JS** Yd No: SAM 10014B Loa 229.00 (BB) Br ex 32.60 Dght 14.450 Lbp 225.50 Br md 32.26 Dpth 20.05 Welded, 1 dk	**(A21A2BC) Bulk Carrier** Grain: 98,091 Compartments: 7 Ho, ER 7 Ha: ER	**1 oil engine** driving 1 FP propeller Total Power: 9,800kW (13,324hp) 14.1kn MAN-B&W 5S60MC-C8 1 x 2 Stroke 5 Cy. 600 x 2400 9800kW (13324bhp) Doosan Engine Co Ltd-South Korea AuxGen: 3 x 600kW 60Hz a.c Fuel: 2750.0
9348534 *S6EN2* -	**THERESA LEO** **Patricia Shipping Co Pte Ltd** Raffles Technical Services Pte Ltd *Singapore* *Singapore* MMSI: 565205000 Official number: 391956	**11,254** 4,831 16,500 T/cm 28.0	Class: BV	**2007-09 Jiujiang Yinxing Shipbuilding Co Ltd — Xingzi County JX** Yd No: YX004 Loa 144.00 (BB) Br ex - Dght 8.800 Lbp 135.60 Br md 23.00 Dpth 12.50 Welded, 1 dk	**(A12B2TR) Chemical/Products Tanker** Double Hull (13F) Liq: 19,588; Liq (Oil): 19,588 Compartments: 12 Wing Ta, 2 Wing Slop Ta, ER 4 Cargo Pump (s): 4x500m³/hr	**1 oil engine** driving 1 FP propeller Total Power: 4,440kW (6,037hp) 13.5kn MAN-B&W 6S35MC 1 x 2 Stroke 6 Cy. 350 x 1400 4440kW (6037bhp) STX Engine Co Ltd-South Korea AuxGen: 3 x 465kW 400/220V 60Hz a.c Thrusters: 1 Tunnel thruster (f)
9348510 *9VCM2* -	**THERESA LIBRA** **Gold River Pte Ltd** Raffles Technical Services Pte Ltd *Singapore* *Singapore* MMSI: 565203000 Official number: 391663	**11,254** 4,831 17,112 T/cm 28.0	Class: BV	**2007-12 Jiujiang Yinxing Shipbuilding Co Ltd — Xingzi County JX** Yd No: YX002 Converted From: Chemical/Products Tanker-2010 Loa 144.30 (BB) Br ex - Dght 8.800 Lbp 134.83 Br md 23.00 Dpth 12.50 Welded, 1 dk	**(A12A2TC) Chemical Tanker** Double Hull (13F) Liq: 18,814; Liq (Oil): 19,196 Compartments: 12 Wing Ta, 2 Wing Slop Ta, ER 4 Cargo Pump (s): 4x500m³/hr	**1 oil engine** driving 1 FP propeller Total Power: 4,440kW (6,037hp) 13.5kn MAN-B&W 6S35MC 1 x 2 Stroke 6 Cy. 350 x 1400 4440kW (6037bhp) STX Engine Co Ltd-South Korea AuxGen: 3 x 465kW 400/220V 60Hz a.c Thrusters: 1 Tunnel thruster (f) Fuel: 548.0

IMO / Call sign	Name, former names, owner, manager, port, flag	Tonnage	Class	Build and dimensions	Type and cargo	Machinery
7613648 *WYX3941* -	**THERESA MARIE** **Marwin Inc** - *Petersburg, AK* *United States of America* Official number: 561428	**179** 53 -		**1974 Marine Power & Equipment Co. Ltd. — Seattle, Wa** L reg 22.35 Br ex 7.45 Dght - Lbp - Br md - Dpth 3.66 Welded, 1 dk	**(B11B2FV) Fishing Vessel**	**1 oil engine** driving 1 FP propeller Total Power: 500kW (680hp)
8603729 *T3RM* -	**THERESA MARS** *ex* Hedda *-2009* *ex* Rachel B *-2008* **Supertanker Ltd** Raffles Shipmanagement Services Pte Ltd *Tarawa* *Kiribati* MMSI: 529205000 Official number: K-11870974	**7,955** 4,711 13,749 T/cm 20.0	Class: IZ KI (AB)	**1987-03 Kyokuyo Shipyard Corp — Shimonoseki YC** Yd No: 2485 Loa 132.00 (BB) Br ex 20.43 Dght 8.821 Lbp 124.00 Br md 20.40 Dpth 11.20 Welded, 1 dk	**(A12A2TC) Chemical Tanker** Single Hull Liq: 16,458 Cargo Heating Coils Compartments: 24 Ta, ER 28 Cargo Pump (s) Manifold: Bow/CM: 61.8m	**1 oil engine** driving 1 FP propeller Total Power: 2,574kW (3,500hp) 14.0kn Mitsubishi 5UEC45LA 1 x 2 Stroke 5 Cy. 450 x 1350 2574kW (3500bhp) Kobe Hatsudoki KK-Japan AuxGen: 3 x 360kW 450V 60Hz a.c, 1 x 280kW 450V 60Hz a.c Thrusters: 1 Thwart. FP thruster (f); 1 Thwart. FP thruster (a) Fuel: 125.0 (d.f.) 690.0 (r.f.) 12.5pd
9317250 *VRKT2* -	**THERESA MICRONESIA** *ex* Golden Micronesia *-2012* **Mandy Shipping Co Pte Ltd** Raffles Technical Services Pte Ltd SatCom: Inmarsat C 447704291 *Hong Kong* *Hong Kong* MMSI: 477938600 Official number: HK-3549	**5,489** 2,749 9,091 T/cm 17.0	Class: BV (NK)	**2004-07 Kurinoura Dockyard Co Ltd — Yawatahama EH** Yd No: 378 Loa 120.00 Br ex - Dght 7.850 Lbp 112.40 Br md 17.80 Dpth 9.80 Welded, 1 dk	**(A12B2TR) Chemical/Products Tanker** Double Hull (13F) Liq: 9,790; Liq (Oil): 9,790 8 Cargo Pump (s) Manifold: Bow/CM: 54m	**1 oil engine** driving 1 FP propeller Total Power: 3,400kW (4,623hp) 13.0kn Mitsubishi 6UEC33LSII 1 x 2 Stroke 6 Cy. 330 x 1050 3400kW (4623bhp) Akasaka Tekkosho KK (Akasaka DieselLtd)-Japan Fuel: 799.0 (r.f.)
8009961 *5NJL9* -	**THERESA N** *ex* Theresa *-2010* *ex* High Quest *-2010* *ex* H. O. S. High Quest *-1997* *ex* John Adams *-1994* **Pheranzy Gas Ltd** *Lagos* *Nigeria* MMSI: 657524000 Official number: SR1429	**801** 240 1,200	Class: AB	**1980-11 Halter Marine, Inc. — Lockport, La** Yd No: 930 Loa 57.20 Br ex - Dght 3.937 Lbp 56.70 Br md 12.20 Dpth 4.58 Welded, 1 dk	**(B21A2OS) Platform Supply Ship**	**2 oil engines** reverse reduction geared to sc. shafts driving 2 FP propellers Total Power: 2,206kW (3,000hp) 11.0kn EMD (Electro-Motive) 12-645-E6 2 x Vee 2 Stroke 12 Cy. 230 x 254 each-1103kW (1500bhp) General Motors Corp.Electro-Motive Div.-La Grange AuxGen: 2 x 99kW 440V 60Hz a.c Thrusters: 1 Thwart. FP thruster (f)
9401386 *VRKL3* -	**THERESA ORION** *ex* Willing *-2012* *ex* Golden Willing *-2012* **Carolina Shipping Co Pte Ltd** Raffles Technical Services Pte Ltd *Hong Kong* *Hong Kong* MMSI: 477598900 Official number: HK-3486	**7,745** 3,992 12,999 T/cm 22.3	Class: BV (NK)	**2009-02 K.K. Miura Zosensho — Saiki** Yd No: 1325 Loa 128.72 (BB) Br ex 20.02 Dght 8.772 Lbp 120.04 Br md 20.00 Dpth 11.20 Welded, 1 dk	**(A12B2TR) Chemical/Products Tanker** Double Hull (13F) Liq: 13,188; Liq (Oil): 13,794 Cargo Heating Coils Compartments: 16 Wing Ta, 2 Wing Slop Ta, 1 Slop Ta, ER 16 Cargo Pump (s): 10x330m³/hr, 6x200m³/hr Manifold: Bow/CM: 64m	**1 oil engine** driving 1 FP propeller Total Power: 4,192kW (5,699hp) 13.6kn MAN-B&W 6S35MC 1 x 2 Stroke 6 Cy. 350 x 1400 4192kW (5699bhp) The Hanshin Diesel Works Ltd-Japan Thrusters: 1 Tunnel thruster (f) Fuel: 82.4 (d.f.) 831.7 (r.f.)
8618877 *T2JG3* -	**THERESA PADANG** *ex* Stolzen *-2009* *ex* Bunga Mawar *-2006* **Venus Bulk Shipping Ltd** Raffles Shipmanagement Services Pte Ltd *Funafuti* *Tuvalu* MMSI: 572813000 Official number: 20929009	**18,453** 9,759 29,974 T/cm 38.9	Class: BV (LR) ✠ Classed LR until 25/11/09	**1990-05 Korea Shipbuilding & Engineering Corp — Busan** Yd No: 2018 Loa 172.21 (BB) Br ex 26.04 Dght 11.015 Lbp 163.00 Br md 26.00 Dpth 15.20 Welded, 1 dk	**(A12B2TR) Chemical/Products Tanker** Single Hull Liq: 32,958; Liq (Oil): 34,963 Cargo Heating Coils Compartments: 17 Ta, ER, 2 Wing Slop Ta, 16 Wing Ta 51 Cargo Pump (s): 3x450m³/hr, 3x350m³/hr, 13x250m³/hr, 16x150m³/hr, 16x190m³/hr Manifold: Bow/CM: 88.8m	**1 oil engine** driving 1 FP propeller Total Power: 7,275kW (9,891hp) 14.5kn Sulzer 5RTA62 1 x 2 Stroke 5 Cy. 620 x 2150 7275kW (9891bhp) Hyundai Heavy Industries Co Ltd-South Korea AuxGen: 3 x 836kW 450V 60Hz a.c, 1 x 700kW 450V 60Hz a.c Boilers: 2 AuxB (o.f.) 9.0kgf/cm² (8.8bar), e (ex.g.) 12.0kgf/cm² (11.8bar) Thrusters: 1 Thwart. CP thruster (f) Fuel: 195.8 (d.f.) 1518.3 (r.f.)
8618231 *T2HV3* -	**THERESA PELINTUNG** *ex* Skarven *-2009* *ex* Bunga Cenderawasih *-2006* **Marianna Shipping Co Pte Ltd** Raffles Shipmanagement Services Pte Ltd *Funafuti* *Tuvalu* MMSI: 572802000 Official number: 20779009	**18,453** 9,759 29,928 T/cm 38.9	Class: BV (LR) ✠ Classed LR until 15/1/10	**1990-01 Korea Shipbuilding & Engineering Corp — Busan** Yd No: 2017 Converted From: Chemical Tanker-2006 Loa 172.21 (BB) Br ex 26.04 Dght 11.030 Lbp 163.00 Br md 26.00 Dpth 15.20 Welded, 1 dk	**(A12B2TR) Chemical/Products Tanker** Double Bottom Entire Compartment Length Liq: 34,963; Liq (Oil): 34,963 Cargo Heating Coils Compartments: 17 Ta, ER, 2 Wing Slop Ta, 16 Wing Ta 49 Cargo Pump (s): 14x190m³/hr, 3x450m³/hr, 3x350m³/hr, 13x250m³/hr, 16x190m³/hr Manifold: Bow/CM: 88.3m	**1 oil engine** driving 1 FP propeller Total Power: 7,275kW (9,891hp) 14.5kn Sulzer 5RTA62 1 x 2 Stroke 5 Cy. 620 x 2150 7275kW (9891bhp) Hyundai Heavy Industries Co Ltd-South Korea AuxGen: 3 x 836kW 450V 60Hz a.c, 1 x 700kW 450V 60Hz a.c Boilers: 2 AuxB (o.f.) 9.0kgf/cm² (8.8bar), e (ex.g.) 12.0kgf/cm² (11.8bar) Fuel: 195.8 (d.f.) 1518.3 (r.f.)
9169770 *T2JL4* -	**THERESA PISCES** *ex* Hartzi *-2012* *ex* Ilandag *-2007* *ex* Maikop *-2006* **Audrey Shipping Co Pte Ltd** Raffles Technical Services Pte Ltd *Funafuti* *Tuvalu* MMSI: 572556210 Official number: 28539913	**10,321** 5,054 15,441 T/cm 29.0	Class: BV (NV) (RS)	**1999-07 Aker MTW Werft GmbH — Wismar** Yd No: 276 Loa 144.53 Br ex - Dght 8.700 Lbp 135.94 Br md 22.50 Dpth 11.25 Welded, 1 dk	**(A12B2TR) Chemical/Products Tanker** Double Hull (13F) Liq: 16,947; Liq (Oil): 16,947 Compartments: 14 Wing Ta, ER 3 Cargo Pump (s): 1x684m³/hr, 2x472m³/hr Manifold: Bow/CM: 75m Ice Capable	**1 oil engine** driving 1 CP propeller Total Power: 5,300kW (7,206hp) 14.4kn B&W 8S35MC 1 x 2 Stroke 8 Cy. 350 x 1400 5300kW (7206bhp) MAN B&W Diesel A/S-Denmark Thrusters: 1 Thwart. CP thruster (f)
9591806 *VRKE7* -	**THERESA SHANDONG** **Lisa Shipping Co Pte Ltd** Raffles Shipmanagement Services Pte Ltd SatCom: Inmarsat C 447703948 *Hong Kong* *Hong Kong* MMSI: 477700700 Official number: HK-3433	**44,686** 27,932 82,000 T/cm 71.9	Class: BV	**2012-05 Jiangsu Eastern Heavy Industry Co Ltd — Jingjiang JS** Yd No: 10C-018 Loa 229.00 (BB) Br ex - Dght 14.580 Lbp 225.15 Br md 32.26 Dpth 20.05 Welded, 1 dk	**(A21A2BC) Bulk Carrier** Grain: 98,740; Bale: 90,784 Compartments: 7 Ho, ER 7 Ha: ER	**1 oil engine** driving 1 FP propeller Total Power: 11,300kW (15,363hp) 14.1kn MAN-B&W 5S60MC-C 1 x 2 Stroke 5 Cy. 600 x 2400 11300kW (15363bhp) Doosan Engine Co Ltd-South Korea AuxGen: 3 x 615kW 60Hz a.c Fuel: 3330.0
9112753 *T2CN4* -	**THERESA SUCCESS** *ex* Tambov *-2012* **Gloria Shipping Co Pte Ltd** Raffles Shipmanagement Services Pte Ltd *Funafuti* *Tuvalu* MMSI: 572415210	**26,218** 13,581 40,727 T/cm 50.8	Class: BV (LR) ✠ Classed LR until 27/4/12	**1996-07 Brodosplit - Brodogradiliste doo — Split** Yd No: 389 Converted From: Chemical/Products Tanker-2011 Loa 181.00 (BB) Br ex 32.03 Dght 12.060 Lbp 173.80 Br md 31.98 Dpth 16.99 Welded, 1 dk	**(A12B2TR) Chemical/Products Tanker** Double Hull (13F) Liq: 49,168; Liq (Oil): 49,168 Cargo Heating Coils Compartments: 10 Wing Ta, 2 Wing Slop Ta, ER 10 Cargo Pump (s): 10x550m³/hr Manifold: Bow/CM: 90m	**1 oil engine** driving 1 FP propeller Total Power: 8,313kW (11,302hp) 14.4kn B&W 6S50MC 1 x 2 Stroke 6 Cy. 500 x 1910 8313kW (11302bhp) Brodosplit Tvornica Dizel Motorадoo-Croatia AuxGen: 3 x 1080kW 450V 60Hz a.c Boilers: e (ex.g.) 10.2kgf/cm² (10.0bar), AuxB (o.f.) 10.2kgf/cm² (10.0bar) Fuel: 146.0 (d.f.) 1599.0 (r.f.)
9348522 *S6EN3* -	**THERESA TAURUS** **SK Transportation SA** Raffles Technical Services Pte Ltd *Singapore* *Singapore* MMSI: 565204000 Official number: 391957	**11,254** 4,831 16,500 T/cm 28.0	Class: BV	**2007-09 Jiujiang Yinxing Shipbuilding Co Ltd — Xingzi County JX** Yd No: YX003 Converted From: Chemical/Products Tanker-2010 Loa 144.00 (BB) Br ex - Dght 8.800 Lbp 134.50 Br md 23.00 Dpth 12.50 Welded, 1 dk	**(A12A2TC) Chemical Tanker** Double Hull (13F) Liq: 19,588; Liq (Oil): 19,588 Compartments: 12 Wing Ta, 2 Wing Slop Ta, ER 4 Cargo Pump (s): 4x500m³/hr	**1 oil engine** driving 1 FP propeller Total Power: 4,440kW (6,037hp) 13.5kn MAN-B&W 6S35MC 1 x 2 Stroke 6 Cy. 350 x 1400 4440kW (6037bhp) STX Engine Co Ltd-South Korea AuxGen: 3 x 465kW 450V 60Hz a.c Thrusters: 1 Tunnel thruster (f)
9146039 *9V9106* -	**THERESA TIGA** *ex* Shintoku *-2010* **Nelina Shipping Co Pte Ltd** Raffles Shipmanagement Services Pte Ltd SatCom: Inmarsat C 456500010 *Singapore* *Singapore* MMSI: 565000000 Official number: 396639	**12,148** 5,667 18,523 T/cm 30.6	Class: BV (NK)	**1996-11 Sasebo Heavy Industries Co. Ltd. — Sasebo Yard, Sasebo** Yd No: 702 Loa 149.50 (BB) Br ex 24.23 Dght 9.218 Lbp 141.00 Br md 24.20 Dpth 13.20 Welded, 1 dk	**(A12B2TR) Chemical/Products Tanker** Double Hull Liq: 21,793; Liq (Oil): 22,879 Cargo Heating Coils Compartments: 18 Wing Ta, 2 Wing Slop Ta, ER 20 Cargo Pump (s): 20x330m³/hr Manifold: Bow/CM: 70m	**1 oil engine** driving 1 FP propeller Total Power: 5,980kW (8,130hp) 14.5kn B&W 6L42MC 1 x 2 Stroke 6 Cy. 420 x 1360 5980kW (8130bhp) Mitsui Engineering & Shipbuilding CLtd-Japan Fuel: 171.0 (d.f.) 1204.0 (r.f.)
8819081 *T2WU3* -	**THERESA VENUS** *ex* Stolt Peak *-2011* *ex* Montana Blue *-2006* *ex* Blue Sapphire *-2002* **Isabel Shipping Co Pte Ltd** Raffles Shipmanagement Services Pte Ltd *Funafuti* *Tuvalu* MMSI: 572304210 Official number: 25379111	**22,650** 13,121 39,656 T/cm 49.0	Class: BV (LR) (NV) ✠ Classed LR until 1/7/91	**1991-06 Brodogradiliste 'Uljanik' — Pula** Yd No: 394 Conv to DH-2006 Loa 176.00 (BB) Br ex 32.03 Dght 11.247 Lbp 169.43 Br md 32.00 Dpth 15.10 Welded, 1 dk	**(A12B2TR) Chemical/Products Tanker** Double Hull (13F) Liq: 43,271; Liq (Oil): 43,270 Cargo Heating Coils Compartments: 6 Ta, 12 Wing Ta, 2 Wing Slop Ta, ER 18 Cargo Pump (s): 6x550m³/hr, 12x250m³/hr Manifold: Bow/CM: 90m	**1 oil engine** driving 1 FP propeller Total Power: 9,600kW (13,052hp) 14.3kn B&W 5L60MC 1 x 2 Stroke 5 Cy. 600 x 1944 9600kW (13052bhp) Tvornica Dizel Motora 'Uljanik'-Yugoslavia AuxGen: 1 x 1200kW 450V 60Hz a.c, 1 x 1000kW 450V 60Hz a.c, 1 x 850kW 450V 60Hz a.c Fuel: 295.0 (d.f.) (Heating Coils) 1525.0 (r.f.)

IMO / Call sign / Fishing No.	Name / Owner / Port	Tonnage	Class	Builder / Dimensions	Type / Cargo	Machinery
9331866 *V7KV7* -	**THERESE SELMER** **Wehr Bulkcarriers GmbH & Co KG** Oskar Wehr KG (GmbH & Co) *Majuro* *Marshall Islands* MMSI: 538090258 Official number: 90258	**31,222** 18,534 55,682 T/cm 55.8	Class: NV	**2006-12 Mitsui Eng. & SB. Co. Ltd. — Tamano** Yd No: 1632 Loa 189.99 (BB) Br ex 32.30 Dght 12.550 Lbp 182.00 Br md 32.26 Dpth 17.90 Welded, 1 dk	**(A21A2BC) Bulk Carrier** Grain: 70,811; Bale: 68,084 Compartments: 5 Ho, ER 5 Ha: 4 (21.1 x 18.9)ER (17.6 x 18.9) Cranes: 4x30.5t	**1 oil engine** driving 1 FP propeller Total Power: 9,480kW (12,889hp) 14.5kn MAN-B&W 6S50MC-C 1 x 2 Stroke 6 Cy. 500 x 2000 9480kW (12889bhp) Mitsui Engineering & Shipbuilding CLtd-Japan AuxGen: 3 x 475kW a.c
7321025 *DUHG8*	**THERESIAN STARS** *ex* Cagayan Princess *-2008* *ex* Cebu Princess *-1987* *ex* Uwakai *-1983* **Roble Shipping Lines Inc** *Cebu* *Philippines* Official number: CEB1000569	*925* 318 -	Class: (BV)	**1973 Usuki Iron Works Co Ltd — Usuki OT** Yd No: 856 Loa 69.70 Br ex 13.64 Dght 3.260 Lbp 63.94 Br md 13.62 Dpth 4.50 Welded, 1 dk	**(A36A2PR) Passenger/Ro-Ro Ship (Vehicles)** Passengers: unberthed: 662; berths: 180 Bow ramp (f) Stern ramp (a)	**2 oil engines** reduction geared to sc. shafts driving 2 FP propellers Total Power: 1,766kW (2,402hp) Daihatsu 6DSM-26 2 x 4 Stroke 6 Cy. 260 x 320 each-883kW (1201bhp) Daihatsu Diesel Manufacturing Co Lt-Japan
9099456 *FMBA* ST 925333	**THERESINA II** **Theresina Armement** - *Sete* *France* Official number: 925333	**156** - -		**2004-01 Chantiers Navals Bernard SA — Locmiquelic** Loa 24.90 (BB) Br ex - Dght - Lbp 23.74 Br md - Dpth - Welded, 1 dk	**(B11A2FS) Stern Trawler**	**1 oil engine** driving 1 Propeller Total Power: 316kW (430hp) Thrusters: 1 Thwart. FP thruster (f)
8034174 - -	**THEREZA** - -	*612* - 520	Class: (BV)	**1975 Estaleiros Amazonia S.A. (ESTANAVE) — Manaus** Loa 45.01 Br ex - Dght - Lbp - Br md 10.80 Dpth 3.61 Welded, 1 dk	**(A31A2GX) General Cargo Ship** Grain: 600 Compartments: 1 Ho, ER	**1 oil engine** driving 1 FP propeller Total Power: 313kW (426hp) 9.0kn Caterpillar D353SCAC 1 x 4 Stroke 6 Cy. 159 x 203 313kW (426bhp) Caterpillar Tractor Co-USA AuxGen: 1 x 40kW
9114189 *P3YU6* -	**THERMAIKOS** *ex* CMA CGM Colibri *-2012* *ex* Thermaikos *-2004* *ex* Norasia Punjab *-2004* *ex* Thermaikos *-2003* *ex* Puerto Cabello *-2003* *ex* Thermaikos *-2002* *ex* P&O Nedlloyd Santos *-2001* *ex* Zim Buenos Aires *-1998* *ex* Thermaikos *-1996* *launched as* Alvaro Diaz *-1996* **Nireus Navigation Co Ltd** Dioryx Maritime Corp SatCom: Inmarsat C 421211210 *Limassol* *Cyprus* MMSI: 212112000 Official number: 9114189	**19,147** 7,600 24,457	Class: AB	**1996-01 Hyundai Heavy Industries Co Ltd — Ulsan** Yd No: 934 Loa 171.09 (BB) Br ex 27.64 Dght 10.516 Lbp 160.00 Br md 27.60 Dpth 16.10 Welded, 1 dk	**(A33A2CC) Container Ship (Fully Cellular)** TEU 1561 incl 150 ref C. Compartments: 4 Cell Ho, ER 7 Ha: ER Cranes: 3x45t	**1 oil engine** driving 1 FP propeller Total Power: 14,314kW (19,461hp) 19.5kn B&W 7S60MC 1 x 2 Stroke 7 Cy. 600 x 2292 14314kW (19461bhp) Hyundai Heavy Industries Co Ltd-South Korea AuxGen: 3 x 1100kW a.c Thrusters: 1 Thwart. FP thruster (f) Fuel: 123.0 (d.f.) (Heating Coils) 1650.0 (r.f.) 57.0pd
8901511 *TFPC* RE 101	**THERNEY** *completed as* Mikhail Levashov *-1993* **HB Grandi hf** - SatCom: Inmarsat C 425112310 *Reykjavik* *Iceland* MMSI: 251123000 Official number: 2203	**1,901** 570 1,283	Class: NV	**1992-02 Sterkoder AS — Kristiansund** Yd No: 135 Loa 64.00 Br ex - Dght 6.435 Lbp 55.55 Br md 13.00 Dpth 8.85 Welded, 2 dks	**(B11A2FG) Factory Stern Trawler** Ins: 950 Ice Capable	**1 oil engine** reduction geared to sc. shaft driving 1 FP propeller Total Power: 2,458kW (3,342hp) Wartsila 6R32E 1 x 4 Stroke 6 Cy. 320 x 350 2458kW (3342bhp) Wartsila Diesel Oy-Finland AuxGen: 1 x 1304kW 380V 50Hz a.c, 2 x 336kW 380V 50Hz a.c Thrusters: 1 Thwart. FP thruster (f)
9025479 - -	**THESALONICA** *ex* Sejuk Jaya *-2005* **PT Sinar Bahari** *Manado* *Indonesia*	**219** 119 -	Class: (KI)	**1989-02 P.T. Industri Kapal Indonesia (IKI) — Bitung** L reg 40.26 Br ex - Dght 2.100 Lbp 33.10 Br md 7.10 Dpth 2.70 Welded, 1 dk	**(A31A2GX) General Cargo Ship**	**1 oil engine** geared to sc. shaft driving 1 Propeller Total Power: 420kW (571hp) 12.5kn MAN D2842LE 1 x Vee 4 Stroke 12 Cy. 128 x 142 420kW (571bhp) MAN Nutzfahrzeuge AG-Nuernberg
8718770 *SMIB* VG 106	**THESEUS** *ex* Tisnaren *-2000* *ex* Nordanland *-1990* **H/B VG 106 Theseus** - *Traslovslage* *Sweden* MMSI: 266062000	**139** 41 -		**1988-12 Scheepswerf Bijlsma BV — Wartena** Yd No: 643 Loa 22.31 Br ex - Dght 2.301 Lbp 18.80 Br md 6.51 Dpth 3.51 Welded, 1 dk	**(B11A2FS) Stern Trawler** Ins: 90	**1 oil engine** sr geared to sc. shaft driving 1 FP propeller Total Power: 370kW (503hp) Caterpillar 3412 1 x Vee 4 Stroke 12 Cy. 137 x 152 370kW (503bhp) Caterpillar Inc-USA Thrusters: 1 Thwart. FP thruster (f)
9390159 *V2FQ9* -	**THESEUS** **Argonauten Holding GmbH & Co KG** Wessels Reederei GmbH & Co KG *Saint John's* *Antigua & Barbuda* MMSI: 305761000 Official number: 4905	**2,452** 1,369 3,666	Class: GL	**2009-06 Slovenske Lodenice a.s. — Komarno** Yd No: 2978 Loa 87.83 (BB) Br ex - Dght 5.490 Lbp 81.32 Br md 12.80 Dpth 7.10 Welded, 1 dk	**(A31A2GX) General Cargo Ship** Grain: 4,585 TEU 176 Compartments: 1 Ho, ER 1 Ha: ER Ice Capable	**1 oil engine** reduction geared to sc. shaft driving 1 CP propeller Total Power: 1,520kW (2,067hp) 11.7kn MaK 8M20C 1 x 4 Stroke 8 Cy. 200 x 300 1520kW (2067bhp) Caterpillar Motoren GmbH & Co. KG-Germany AuxGen: 1 x 240kW 400/220V a.c, 2 x 184kW 400/220V a.c Thrusters: 1 Tunnel thruster (f)
9199256 *V2OU* -	**THESEUS** **Reederei M Lauterjung GmbH & Co KG Sunship Eurocoaster** Sunship Schiffahrtskontor KG *Saint John's* *Antigua & Barbuda* MMSI: 304011027	**1,846** 1,081 2,500	Class: BV	**2000-08 SC Santierul Naval Tulcea SA — Tulcea** Yd No: 307 Loa 89.75 Br ex 11.68 Dght 4.480 Lbp 84.60 Br md 11.65 Dpth 5.80 Welded, 1 dk	**(A31A2GX) General Cargo Ship** Grain: 3,900; Bale: 3,750 TEU 124 C Ho 52 TEU C Dk 72 TEU incl 16 ref C. Compartments: 1 Ho, ER 1 Ha: (57.8 x 9.3)ER Ice Capable	**1 oil engine** reduction geared to sc. shaft driving 1 FP propeller Total Power: 1,500kW (2,039hp) 11.0kn Deutz SBV8M628 1 x 4 Stroke 8 Cy. 240 x 280 1500kW (2039bhp) Motoren Werke Mannheim AG (MWM)-Mannheim AuxGen: 2 x 134kW 220/380V 50Hz a.c Thrusters: 1 Thwart. FP thruster (f) Fuel: 126.9 (d.f.) 6.8pd
9342841 *SVBV6* -	**THESSALONIKI** *ex* Yusho Regulus *-2013* **Thessaloniki Special Maritime Enterprise (ENE)** Chronos Shipping Co Ltd *Piraeus* *Greece* Official number: 12188	**39,736** 25,724 76,598 T/cm 66.6	Class: NK	**2006-06 Imabari Shipbuilding Co Ltd — Marugame KG (Marugame Shipyard)** Yd No: 1418 Loa 224.94 (BB) Br ex - Dght 14.139 Lbp 217.00 Br md 32.26 Dpth 19.50 Welded, 1 dk	**(A21A2BC) Bulk Carrier** Grain: 90,644 Compartments: 7 Ho, ER 7 Ha: 6 (17.1 x 15.6)ER (17.1 x 12.8)	**1 oil engine** driving 1 FP propeller Total Power: 10,320kW (14,031hp) 15.2kn MAN-B&W 6S60MC 1 x 2 Stroke 6 Cy. 600 x 2292 10320kW (14031bhp) Kawasaki Heavy Industries Ltd-Japan Fuel: 2770.0
9368792 *V2DD7* -	**THETAGAS** **Partenreederei mt 'Thetagas'** Sloman Neptun Schiffahrts-Aktiengesellschaft *Saint John's* *Antigua & Barbuda* MMSI: 305178000 Official number: 4409	**9,110** 2,734 10,309 T/cm 21.3	Class: NV	**2008-02 STX Shipbuilding Co Ltd — Busan** Yd No: 5020 Loa 119.00 (BB) Br ex 19.83 Dght 8.800 Lbp 112.40 Br md 19.80 Dpth 11.20 Welded, 1 dk	**(A11B2TG) LPG Tanker** Double Sides Entire Compartment Length Liq (Gas): 8,925 2 x Gas Tank (s); 2 independent (5% Ni.stl) cyl horizontal 2 Cargo Pump (s): 2x450m³/hr Manifold: Bow/CM: 55.2m	**1 oil engine** driving 1 FP propeller Total Power: 5,347kW (7,270hp) 16.0kn MAN-B&W 8S35MC 1 x 2 Stroke 8 Cy. 350 x 1400 5347kW (7270bhp) STX Engine Co Ltd-South Korea AuxGen: 3 x 1100kW 450V 60Hz a.c Thrusters: 1 Tunnel thruster (f) Fuel: 111.0 (d.f.) 1021.0 (r.f.)
9312315 *A8TT6* -	**THETIS** *ex* Ocean Lotus *-2009* **Doris Shipping Corp** Commercial Shipping & Trading Co Ltd *Monrovia* *Liberia* MMSI: 636014425 Official number: 14425	**16,960** 10,498 28,432 T/cm 39.7	Class: NK	**2004-07 Imabari Shipbuilding Co Ltd — Imabari EH (Imabari Shipyard)** Yd No: 594 Loa 169.26 (BB) Br ex - Dght 9.780 Lbp 160.40 Br md 27.20 Dpth 13.60 Welded, 1 dk	**(A21A2BC) Bulk Carrier** Grain: 37,523; Bale: 35,762 Compartments: 5 Ho, ER 5 Ha: 4 (19.2 x 17.6)ER (13.6 x 16.0) Cranes: 4x30.5t	**1 oil engine** driving 1 FP propeller Total Power: 5,850kW (7,954hp) 14.0kn B&W 6S42MC 1 x 2 Stroke 6 Cy. 420 x 1764 5850kW (7954bhp) Makita Corp-Japan Fuel: 1245.0
9252527 *PBKF* -	**THETIS** **Thetis BV** Svitzer Europe Holding BV *IJmuiden* *Netherlands* MMSI: 245354000 Official number: 39878	**331** 99 237	Class: GL	**2003-10 Brodogradiliste 'Dunav' AD — Bezdan** (Hull) Yd No: 285 **2003-10 IHC DeltaShipyard BV — Sliedrecht** Yd No: 989 Loa 29.08 Br ex 11.20 Dght 4.560 Lbp 26.64 Br md 10.00 Dpth 5.10 Welded, 1 dk	**(B32A2ST) Tug** Ice Capable	**2 oil engines** geared to sc. shafts driving 2 Directional propellers Total Power: 3,380kW (4,596hp) Wartsila 9L20 2 x 4 Stroke 9 Cy. 200 x 280 each-1690kW (2298bhp) Wartsila Finland Oy-Finland AuxGen: 2 x 104kW a.c Thrusters: 1 Tunnel thruster (f) Fuel: 160.0 (d.f.)

9283992 *C6VB8* -	**THETIS** *ex Bolina -2005* **Changame Compania Armadora SA** Diana Shipping Services SA *Nassau* *Bahamas* MMSI: 308632000 Official number: 8001119	**40,160** 25,869 73,624 T/cm 64.0	Class: BV (AB)	**2004-08 Jiangnan Shipyard (Group) Co Ltd — Shanghai** Yd No: H2298 Loa 225.00 (BB) Br ex 32.68 Dght 14.000 Lbp 217.00 Br md 32.26 Dpth 19.20 Welded, 1 dk	**(A21A2BC) Bulk Carrier** Grain: 90,624; Bale: 86,173 Compartments: 7 Ho, ER 7 Ha: 6 (15.5 x 15.0)ER (15.5 x 13.2)	**1 oil engine** driving 1 FP propeller Total Power: 10,223kW (13,899hp) 14.0kn B&W 5S60MC 1 x 2 Stroke 5 Cy. 600 x 2292 10223kW (13899bhp) Hudong Heavy Machinery Co Ltd-China
7811616 *J8B4579* -	**THETIS** *ex Vliet -2013* **Nobel Marine Ltd** Atlantic Dredging Corp *Kingstown* *St Vincent & The Grenadines* MMSI: 375827000 Official number: 11052	**463** 138 414	Class: BV	**1979-01 Scheepsbouwwerf Slob B.V. — Sliedrecht** Yd No: 335 Loa 52.78 Br ex - Dght 2.050 Lbp 50.71 Br md 9.00 Dpth 3.35 Welded, 1 dk	**(B34A2SH) Hopper, Motor** Hopper: 454	**2 oil engines** reverse reduction geared to sc. shafts driving 2 FP propellers Total Power: 536kW (728hp) Caterpillar 3408TA 2 x Vee 4 Stroke 8 Cy. 137 x 152 each-268kW (364bhp) Caterpillar Tractor Co-USA
9372274 *D5BV6* -	**THETIS D** *ex Thetis -2012* **ms 'Thetis' Schiffahrts GmbH & Co KG** Drevin Bereederungs GmbH & Co KG *Monrovia* *Liberia* MMSI: 636092412 Official number: 92412	**17,488** 8,125 17,882	Class: GL	**2009-03 J.J. Sietas KG Schiffswerft GmbH & Co. — Hamburg** Yd No: 1262 Loa 168.11 (BB) Br ex - Dght 9.620 Lbp 155.40 Br md 26.80 Dpth 14.00 Welded, 1 dk	**(A33A2CC) Container Ship (Fully Cellular)** TEU 1421 C Ho 1133 TEU C Dk 288 TEU incl 300 ref C Ice Capable	**1 oil engine** reduction geared to sc. shaft driving 1 CP propeller Total Power: 11,047kW (15,020hp) 19.5kn MAN-B&W 8L58/64 1 x 4 Stroke 8 Cy. 580 x 640 11047kW (15020bhp) MAN B&W Diesel AG-Augsburg AuxGen: 3 x 1040kW a.c, 1 x 2288kW a.c Thrusters: 1 Tunnel thruster (f); 1 Tunnel thruster (a) Fuel: 207.0 (d.f.) 1175.0 (r.f.)
9364394 *3EPU4* -	**THETIS GLORY** **Avance Gas 2 Inc** Northern Marine Management Ltd *Panama* *Panama* MMSI: 351704000 Official number: 3420308B	**48,425** 17,129 54,789 T/cm 70.8	Class: NV	**2008-04 Daewoo Shipbuilding & Marine Engineering Co Ltd — Geoje** Yd No: 2322 Loa 226.00 (BB) Br ex 36.64 Dght 11.822 Lbp 215.00 Br md 36.60 Dpth 22.20 Welded, 1 dk	**(A11B2TG) LPG Tanker** Double Bottom Entire Compartment Length Liq (Gas): 81,992 4 x Gas Tank (s); 4 independent (C.mn.stl) pri horizontal 8 Cargo Pump (s): 8x600m³/hr Manifold: Bow/CM: 114.2m	**1 oil engine** driving 1 FP propeller Total Power: 13,560kW (18,436hp) 15.0kn MAN-B&W 6S60MC-C 1 x 2 Stroke 6 Cy. 600 x 2400 13560kW (18436bhp) Doosan Engine Co Ltd-South Korea AuxGen: 3 x 1630kW a.c Fuel: 338.0 (d.f.) 3377.0 (r.f.)
9492919 *3EOZ5* -	**THETISIA** *launched as Xin Jin Tai -2008* **Thrinakie Maritima SA** Fuji Marine Ltd *Panama* *Panama* MMSI: 371994000 Official number: 3459209A	**10,219** 3,065 12,841	Class: BV (CC)	**2008-03 in the People's Republic of China** Yd No: 001-06 Converted From: Container Ship (Fully Cellular)-2008 Loa 138.80 Br ex 21.32 Dght 8.470 Lbp 130.70 Br md 21.00 Dpth 11.00 Welded, 1 dk	**(A12A2LP) Molten Sulphur Tanker** Double Hull (13F) Liq: 6,650 Compartments: 6 Ta, ER	**1 oil engine** reduction geared to sc. shaft driving 1 FP propeller Total Power: 4,400kW (5,982hp) 14.0kn Pielstick 8PC2-6 1 x 4 Stroke 8 Cy. 400 x 460 4400kW (5982bhp) Shaanxi Diesel Heavy Industry Co Lt-China AuxGen: 3 x 350kW 50Hz a.c Fuel: 869.0
9066007 *FGTO* -	**THETYS II** **CNRS** SatCom: Inmarsat C 422721210 *Marseille* *France* MMSI: 227212000 Official number: 860803F	*150* 35	Class: (BV)	**1993-08 Chantiers Piriou — Concarneau** Loa - Br ex 7.50 Dght 2.771 Lbp - Br md - Dpth - Welded	**(B31A2SR) Research Survey Vessel**	**1 oil engine** reduction geared to sc. shaft driving 1 FP propeller Total Power: 478kW (650hp) 10.0kn Poyaud UD25V12M4D 1 x Vee 4 Stroke 12 Cy. 150 x 180 478kW (650bhp) SACM Diesel SA-France AuxGen: 2 x 50kW 220/380V 50Hz a.c
8873104 *DSAL450* -	**THEZONEFERRY** *ex Seosan Ongjini -2009* *ex Shinhan Ferry 3 -2007* *ex Wonkwang Ferry -2005* *ex Wando Car Ferry No. 5 -2005* **Jungwoo Shipping Co Ltd** *Mokpo* *South Korea* MMSI: 440000279 Official number: MPR-934444	*163* - 82	Class: (KR)	**1993-07 Mokpo Shipbuilding & Engineering Co Ltd — Mokpo** Yd No: 93-92 Loa 48.10 Br ex - Dght 1.459 Lbp 39.00 Br md 9.00 Dpth 1.90 Welded, 1 dk	**(A36A2PR) Passenger/Ro-Ro Ship (Vehicles)**	**2 oil engines** reduction geared to sc. shafts driving 2 FP propellers Total Power: 412kW (560hp) 14.3kn M.T.U. 12V183AA61 2 x Vee 4 Stroke 12 Cy. 128 x 142 each-206kW (280bhp) Daewoo Heavy Industries Ltd-South Korea AuxGen: 1 x 70kW 225V a.c
8522236 *3XS3* -	**THIANGUI-701** *ex Oymur -2009* - - SatCom: Inmarsat C 463200016 *Guinea* MMSI: 632201100	**1,895** 568 690	Class: (RS)	**1985-10 VEB Volkswerft Stralsund — Stralsund** Yd No: 689 Loa 62.21 Br ex - Dght 5.220 Lbp 55.02 Br md 13.81 Dpth 9.22 Welded, 2 dks	**(B11A2FS) Stern Trawler** Ins: 580 Ice Capable	**2 oil engines** sr geared to sc. shaft driving 1 CP propeller Total Power: 1,764kW (2,398hp) 12.9kn S.K.L. 8VD26/20AL-2 2 x 4 Stroke 8 Cy. 200 x 260 each-882kW (1199bhp) VEB Schwermaschinenbau "KarlLiebknecht" (SKL)-Magdeburg AuxGen: 1 x 640kW a.c, 3 x 568kW a.c, 1 x 260kW d.c Fuel: 364.0 (d.f.)
5207744 *HQLU6* -	**THIELLA-S** *ex Aghis Trias -1993 ex Libra -1966* **National Shipping Co SA** *San Lorenzo* *Honduras* Official number: L-0324814	*391* 195 513	Class: (LR) *Classed BC until 7/72	**1938-08 Gebr. van Diepen — Waterhuizen** Yd No: 833 Loa 46.69 Br ex 7.95 Dght 3.087 Lbp 43.21 Br md 7.93 Dpth - Riveted, 1 dk	**(A31A2GX) General Cargo Ship**	**1 oil engine** driving 1 FP propeller Total Power: 221kW (300hp) Bolnes 6L50/430 1 x 2 Stroke 6 Cy. 190 x 350 221kW (300bhp) NV Machinefabriek 'Bolnes' v/h JHvan Cappellen-Netherlands
8833843 - -	**THIEN AN 02** **Tai Chinh Shipping Co Ltd (Cong Ty Tnhh Van Tai Bien Tai Chinh)** - *Da Nang* *Vietnam*	**382** 185 400	Class: (VR)	**1989 Hanoi Shipyard — Hanoi** Loa 48.50 Br ex - Dght 3.200 Lbp - Br md 8.20 Dpth 4.10 Welded, 1 dk	**(A31A2GX) General Cargo Ship** Grain: 656 Compartments: 2 Ho, ER 2 Ha: 2 (8.0 x 4.5)ER	**1 oil engine** driving 1 FP propeller Total Power: 300kW (408hp) 10.0kn S.K.L. 8NVD36-1U 1 x 4 Stroke 8 Cy. 240 x 360 300kW (408bhp) VEB Schwermaschinenbau "KarlLiebknecht" (SKL)-Magdeburg AuxGen: 2 x 50kW a.c
9023134 *3WFF* -	**THIEN ANH 07-ALCI** *ex Hai Tien 17-ALCI -2005* **Agriculture Leasing Co I** Thien Anh River Sea Transport JSC *Haiphong* *Vietnam* MMSI: 574012113 Official number: VN-1820-VT	**499** 337 971	Class: VR	**2004-05 Song Dao Shipyard — Nam Dinh** Yd No: TB-07E1 Loa 56.00 Br ex 9.27 Dght 3.280 Lbp 53.27 Br md 9.25 Dpth 3.97 Welded, 1 dk	**(A31A2GX) General Cargo Ship**	**1 oil engine** geared to sc. shaft driving 1 Propeller Total Power: 405kW (551hp) 10.0kn Yanmar 6LAAM-UTE 1 x 4 Stroke 6 Cy. 148 x 165 405kW (551bhp) Yanmar Diesel Engine Co Ltd-Japan
9026679 *XVRS* -	**THIEN ANH 08-ALCI** *ex Hai Duong 25-ALCI -2006* **Agriculture Leasing Co I** Hai Duong Commercial Service Co Ltd (Cong Ty Tnhh Dich Vu Thuong Mai Hai Duong) *Haiphong* *Vietnam*	**499** 285 940	Class: VR	**2004-08 Song Dao Shipyard — Nam Dinh** Yd No: HT-43 Loa 56.00 Br ex 9.02 Dght 3.330 Lbp 52.20 Br md 9.00 Dpth 3.97 Welded, 1 dk	**(A31A2GX) General Cargo Ship**	**1 oil engine** geared to sc. shaft driving 1 Propeller Total Power: 405kW (551hp) 10.7kn Yanmar 6LMM-UTE 1 x 4 Stroke 6 Cy. 148 x 165 405kW (551bhp) Yanmar Diesel Engine Co Ltd-Japan
9022908 *XVEU* -	**THIEN ANH 09-ALCI** *ex An Hai 18 -2007 ex Huu Nghi 18 -2003* **Agriculture Leasing Co I** Thien Anh River Sea Transport JSC *Haiphong* *Vietnam* MMSI: 574012114 Official number: VN-1388-VT	**825** 504 1,566	Class: VR	**2001-03 Vinacoal Shipbuilding Co — Ha Long** Yd No: HN-18 Loa 68.90 Br ex 9.32 Dght 4.150 Lbp 63.80 Br md 9.30 Dpth 4.95 Welded, 1 dk	**(A31A2GX) General Cargo Ship**	**1 oil engine** driving 1 FP propeller Total Power: 425kW (578hp) 10.0kn S.K.L. 8NVD36A-1U 1 x 4 Stroke 8 Cy. 240 x 360 425kW (578bhp) SKL Motoren u. Systemtechnik AG-Magdeburg
9022661 - -	**THIEN BINH** *ex Hoa Tieu 01 -2003* **Pilotage Corp of Third Zone** *Haiphong* *Vietnam*	**143** 43 -	Class: VR	**1976-01 Bach Dang Shipyard — Haiphong** Loa 29.45 Br ex 6.70 Dght 1.700 Lbp 26.60 Br md 6.40 Dpth 3.20 Welded, 1 dk	**(B34N2QP) Pilot Vessel**	**1 oil engine** driving 1 Propeller Total Power: 224kW (305hp) 10.0kn S.K.L. 8NVD36-1U 1 x 4 Stroke 8 Cy. 240 x 360 224kW (305bhp) VEB Schwermaschinenbau "KarlLiebknecht" (SKL)-Magdeburg
8602543 *XVXK* -	**THIEN QUANG 06** *ex Thien Quang -2009* *ex Continental Taiga -2000* **Anh Viet Trading & Shipping Investment JSC** SatCom: Inmarsat C 457410410 *Haiphong* *Vietnam* MMSI: 574104000 Official number: VN-23TT-VT	**4,096** 1,922 6,082	Class: VR (NK)	**1986-05 Nishi Shipbuilding Co Ltd — Imabari EH** Yd No: 341 Loa 97.21 (BB) Br ex 18.52 Dght 5.744 Lbp 89.97 Br md 18.51 Dpth 9.22 Welded, 2 dks	**(A31A2GX) General Cargo Ship** Grain: 9,314; Bale: 8,933 Compartments: 2 Ho, ER 2 Ha: ER Derricks: 3x25t	**1 oil engine** driving 1 FP propeller Total Power: 2,059kW (2,799hp) 11.0kn Akasaka A38 1 x 4 Stroke 6 Cy. 380 x 740 2059kW (2799bhp) Akasaka Tekkosho KK (Akasaka DieselLtd)-Japan

IMO / Call sign	Name / Owner / Port / Flag	Tonnage	Class	Build / Dimensions	Type	Machinery
8662402 - -	**THIEN TAI 68** - **Thien Tai Co Ltd** - *Haiphong* *Vietnam* Official number: VN-3510-TK	**207** 62 136	Class: VR	**2012-12 Nghe An Shipbuilding Mechanical JSC — Vinh** Loa 27.99 Br ex 8.00 Dght 2.900 Lbp 24.70 Br md 7.80 Dpth 3.80 Welded, 1 dk	**(B32A2ST) Tug**	**2 oil engines** reduction geared to sc. shafts driving 2 FP propellers Total Power: 1,200kW (1,632hp) Chinese Std. Type Z8170ZLC 2 x 4 Stroke 8 Cy. 170 x 200 each-600kW (816bhp) Weichai Power Co Ltd-China AuxGen: 1 x 50kW 400V a.c
8969434 *WDB2755* -	**THIEN THANH** *ex* Thunder III *-2002* **Thang Duc Tran** - *New Orleans, LA* *United States of America* MMSI: 366879430 Official number: 1111828	**168** 50 -		**2001** Yd No: 194 L reg 25.96 Br ex - Dght - Lbp - Br md 7.62 Dpth 3.81 Welded, 1 dk	**(B11B2FV) Fishing Vessel**	**1 oil engine** driving 1 FP propeller
8930299 - -	**THIEN THANH BINH 02** *ex* Da Nang 19 *-2006* *ex* Huu Nghi 19 *-2002* *ex* Huan Luyen 36 *-2000* **Thien Thanh Binh Transport Maritime Co Ltd (Cong Ty Tnhh Van Tai Bien Thien Thanh Binh)** - *Da Nang* *Vietnam* Official number: VNDN-189-VT	**229** 149 384	Class: (VR)	**1996-01 Technical & Prof. College ofTransport No. 2 — Haiphong** Loa 40.50 Br ex - Dght 2.450 Lbp - Br md 6.70 Dpth 2.70 Welded, 1 dk	**(A31A2GX) General Cargo Ship** Bale: 444 Compartments: 2 Ho 2 Ha: 2 (7.5 x 4.0)	**1 oil engine** driving 1 FP propeller Total Power: 140kW (190hp) 8.0kn Skoda 6L160PN 1 x 4 Stroke 6 Cy. 160 x 225 140kW (190bhp) CKD Praha-Praha AuxGen: 1 x 3kW a.c
9447615 *3WAA9* -	**THIEN UNG 01** *ex* Skandi Emerald *-2010* **Drilling & Workover Division VIETSOVPETRO Vietnam Soviet Joint Venture Corp (Xi Nghiep Lien Doanh Dau Khi Viet Xo)** - *Saigon* *Vietnam* MMSI: 574000540 Official number: VNSG - 2028 - DV	**3,172** 1,129 3,191	Class: NV VR	**2010-05 STX Vietnam Offshore Ltd — Vung Tau** Yd No: 001 Loa 74.70 (BB) Br ex 17.43 Dght 7.000 Lbp 68.15 Br md 17.40 Dpth 8.50 Welded, 1 dk	**(B21B20A) Anchor Handling Tug Supply**	**2 oil engines** reduction geared to sc. shafts driving 2 CP propellers Total Power: 12,000kW (16,316hp) 15.0kn Bergens B32: 40V12P 2 x Vee 4 Stroke 12 Cy. 320 x 400 each-6000kW (8158bhp) Rolls Royce Marine AS-Norway AuxGen: 2 x 405kW 450V a.c, 2 x 2400kW 450V a.c Thrusters: 2 Tunnel thruster (f); 2 Tunnel thruster (f)
6423175 - -	**THIERRY LA FRONDE** - - -	*147* 49 -	Class: (BV)	**1964 Ch. Nav. Franco-Belges — Villeneuve-la-Garenne** Yd No: 535 Loa 27.59 Br ex 6.92 Dght - Lbp - Br md 6.86 Dpth 3.66 Welded, 1 dk	**(B11A2FT) Trawler** 2 Ha: 2 (1.2 x 1.0) Derricks: 1	**1 oil engine** driving 1 FP propeller Total Power: 441kW (600hp) 11.3kn Baudouin DVX12 1 x Vee 4 Stroke 12 Cy. 185 x 200 441kW (600bhp) Societe des Moteurs Baudouin SA-France Fuel: 31.0 (d.f.)
8819990 *OXIF2* -	**THIES MAERSK** *ex* Cornelia Maersk *-2001* **A P Moller - Maersk A/S** A P Moller SatCom: Inmarsat C 421933610 *Thyboron* *Denmark (DIS)* MMSI: 219336000 Official number: D3315	**16,982** 7,449 21,825	Class: AB (LR) ✠ Classed LR until 10/11/96	**1992-04 Odense Staalskibsvaerft A/S — Munkebo (Lindo Shipyard)** Yd No: 137 Loa 162.26 (BB) Br ex 27.83 Dght 10.320 Lbp 151.90 Br md 27.80 Dpth 15.23 Welded, 1 dk	**(A33A2CC) Container Ship (Fully Cellular)** TEU 1446 C Ho 539 TEU C Dk 907 TEU incl 114 ref C. Compartments: 8 Cell Ho, ER 9 Ha: ER 12 Wing Ha: Gantry cranes: 1x35t	**1 oil engine** driving 1 FP propeller Total Power: 10,480kW (14,249hp) 18.5kn B&W 8S50MC 1 x 2 Stroke 8 Cy. 500 x 1910 10480kW (14249bhp) Mitsui Engineering & Shipbuilding CLtd-Japan AuxGen: 3 x 1250kW 440V 60Hz a.c Thrusters: 1 Thwart. CP thruster (f); 1 Tunnel thruster (a)
8106666 *HSB4311* -	**THIGAYU** *ex* Yi Zhan *-2009* *ex* Elite Leader *-2008* *ex* Elite Grace 1 *-1995* *ex* Elite Grace *-1994* *ex* Cambridge *-1988* *ex* Myran Star *-1982* **Krung Dhana Nava Co Ltd** - *Bangkok* *Thailand* MMSI: 567363000 Official number: 520081851	*5,629* 3,201 8,964	Class: (CR) (NK)	**1982-01 Towa Zosen K.K. — Shimonoseki** Yd No: 536 Loa 116.03 (BB) Br ex 18.65 Dght 7.630 Lbp 107.02 Br md 18.61 Dpth 9.50 Welded, 1 dk	**(A31A2GX) General Cargo Ship** Grain: 11,150; Bale: 10,789 Compartments: 3 Ho, ER 3 Ha: (11.3 x 9.8) (21.7 x 9.8) (22.4 x 9.8)ER Derricks: 4x20t,1x15t	**1 oil engine** driving 1 FP propeller Total Power: 3,347kW (4,551hp) 12.3kn Mitsubishi 7UEC37H-II 1 x 2 Stroke 7 Cy. 370 x 880 3347kW (4551bhp) Kobe Hatsudoki KK-Japan
5358921 *XYUB* -	**THIHA** - **Board of Management for The Port of Yangon** - *Yangon* *Myanmar* Official number: 1091	*768* 331 -	Class: (LR) ✠ Classed LR until 5/60	**1955-05 H C Stuelcken Sohn — Hamburg** Yd No: 836 Loa 57.84 Br ex 11.59 Dght 3.683 Lbp 49.38 Br md 11.28 Dpth 4.86 Riveted\Welded, 1 dk	**(B34Q2QB) Buoy Tender**	**2 oil engines** driving 2 FP propellers Deutz RV6M536 2 x 4 Stroke 6 Cy. 270 x 360 Kloeckner Humboldt Deutz AG-West Germany
9192143 - -	**THIHA-DIPA** - **Government of The Union of Myanmar (Myanmar Ports Corp)** - *Myanmar*	**1,669** 501 2,047	Class: (NK)	**1998-09 Mitsubishi Heavy Industries Ltd. — Kobe** Yd No: 1238 Loa 68.32 Br ex - Dght 4.019 Lbp 65.20 Br md 14.00 Dpth 5.15 Welded, 1 dk	**(B33A2DU) Dredger (unspecified)** Grain: 1,009; Hopper: 1,000	**2 oil engines** reduction geared to sc. shafts driving 2 FP propellers Total Power: 2,206kW (3,000hp) 10.0kn Mitsubishi S6U-MTK 2 x 4 Stroke 6 Cy. 240 x 260 each-1103kW (1500bhp) Mitsubishi Heavy Industries Ltd-Japan
8812033 *TFKY* SF 025	**THINGANES** - **Skinney-Thinganes hf** - *Hornafjordur* *Iceland* MMSI: 251323110 Official number: 2040	**262** 79 -	Class: NV	**1991-01 Estaleiros Navais S.A. (CARNAVE) — Aveiro** Yd No: 134 Loa 25.96 Br ex - Dght 3.750 Lbp 21.67 Br md 7.92 Dpth 6.20 Welded, 1 dk	**(B11A2FS) Stern Trawler** Ice Capable	**1 oil engine** with flexible couplings & sr geared to sc. shaft driving 1 CP propeller Total Power: 736kW (1,001hp) 9.0kn Deutz SBV6M628 1 x 4 Stroke 6 Cy. 240 x 280 736kW (1001bhp) Kloeckner Humboldt Deutz AG-Germany AuxGen: 1 x a.c, 1 x a.c Thrusters: 1 Thwart. FP thruster (f)
8510972 *OWLM* L 525	**THINGHOLT** *ex* Jean Enevoldsen *-2006* **Dan Hovgaard Schmidt, Palle Smedegard Christensen, Preben Thomsen Schmidt & Rene Hovgaard Schmidt** Preben Thomsen Schmidt *Thyboron* *Denmark* MMSI: 219446000 Official number: H933	**630** 344 495		**1986-06 A/S Nakskov Skibsvaerft — Nakskov** (Hull launched by) **1986-06 ApS Struer Skibsvaerft — Struer** (Hull completed by) Yd No: 459 Lengthened-1997 Loa 51.90 Br ex - Dght - Lbp - Br md 8.40 Dpth 5.80 Welded, 1 dk	**(B11A2FT) Trawler**	**1 oil engine** geared to sc. shaft driving 1 FP propeller Alpha 1 x 4 Stroke 6 Cy. MAN B&W Diesel A/S-Denmark
9026083 - -	**THINH AN 09-ALCI** *ex* Hoang Anh 09-Alci *-2010* **Agriculture Leasing Co I** Thinh An Trading & Service Co Ltd *Haiphong* *Vietnam* Official number: VN-1742-VT	**499** 335 997	Class: VR	**2003-12 Haiphong Mechanical & Trading Co. — Haiphong** Yd No: HP-0309 Loa 58.16 Br ex 9.22 Dght 3.400 Lbp 53.90 Br md 9.20 Dpth 4.05 Welded, 1 dk	**(A31A2GX) General Cargo Ship**	**1 oil engine** geared to sc. shaft driving 1 FP propeller Total Power: 330kW (449hp) 10.0kn Weifang X6170ZC 1 x 4 Stroke 6 Cy. 170 x 200 330kW (449bhp) (new engine 2008) Weifang Diesel Engine Factory-China
8665002 - -	**THINH AN 36-ALCI** *ex* Phat Dat 36-ALCI *-2010* **Agriculture Leasing Co I** Thinh An Trading & Service Co Ltd *Haiphong* *Vietnam* Official number: VN-3051-VT	**1,599** 1,032 3,229	Class: VR	**2009-12 Nam Ha Shipyard — Nam Ha** Yd No: S07-002.24 Loa 78.63 Br ex 12.62 Dght 5.350 Lbp 73.60 Br md 12.60 Dpth 6.48 Welded, 1 dk	**(A31A2GX) General Cargo Ship** Grain: 3,798; Bale: 3,422 Compartments: 2 Ho, ER 2 Ha: ER 2 (19.8 x 8.4)	**1 oil engine** reduction geared to sc. shaft driving 1 FP propeller Total Power: 1,103kW (1,500hp) 10.0kn Chinese Std. Type 8300ZLC 1 x 4 Stroke 8 Cy. 300 x 380 1103kW (1500bhp) Zibo Diesel Engine Factory-China AuxGen: 1 x 33kW 400V a.c
9155212 - -	**THINH CUONG 01** *ex* Hong Hoa 01 *-2010* **Thinh Cuong Co Ltd (Cong Ty Tnhh Thinh Cuong)** - *Haiphong* *Vietnam* MMSI: 574999581 Official number: VN-1285-VT	**366** 196 664	Class: (VR)	**1996 at Haiphong** Loa 48.05 Br ex 8.42 Dght 3.300 Lbp 44.42 Br md 8.20 Dpth 3.95 Welded, 1 dk	**(A31A2GX) General Cargo Ship** Grain: 714 Compartments: 2 Ho, ER 2 Ha: 2 (9.0 x 4.8)ER	**1 oil engine** driving 1 FP propeller Total Power: 224kW (305hp) 10.0kn S.K.L. 6NVD36-1U 1 x 4 Stroke 6 Cy. 240 x 360 224kW (305bhp) SKL Motoren u. Systemtechnik AG-Magdeburg AuxGen: 1 x 3kW a.c
8843135 *3WER* -	**THINH HUNG 36** *ex* An Giang 25 *-2012* *ex* Thap Muoi 01 *-1989* *ex* Cuu Long Giang 01 *-1989* **Trung Kien Co Ltd (Cong Ty Tnhh Trung Kien)** - *Saigon* *Vietnam* MMSI: 574143133 Official number: VNSG-1509-TH	**1,306** 725 2,425	Class: VR	**1986 Ho Chi Minh City Shipyard — Ho Chi Minh City** Loa 81.86 Br ex 10.52 Dght 4.800 Lbp 76.20 Br md 10.50 Dpth 6.00 Welded, 1 dk	**(A31A2GX) General Cargo Ship** Grain: 1,532	**1 oil engine** driving 1 FP propeller Total Power: 662kW (900hp) 10.0kn Dvigatel Revolyutsii 6CHRN36/45 1 x 4 Stroke 6 Cy. 360 x 450 662kW (900bhp) Zavod "Dvigatel Revolyutsii"-Gorkiy AuxGen: 2 x 60kW a.c

9023615
-
-
THINH LONG 02
-
Thanh Chung River-Sea Co Ltd
-
Haiphong *Vietnam*
Official number: VN-1746-VT
280
184
464
Class: VR
1994-01 Nam Ha Shipyard — Nam Ha
Loa 44.50 Br ex 7.27 Dght 2.940
Lbp 42.12 Br md 7.05 Dpth 3.60
Welded, 1 dk
(A31A2GX) General Cargo Ship
1 oil engine driving 1 Propeller
Total Power: 140kW (190hp) 8.0kn
S.K.L. 6NVD26-2
1 x 4 Stroke 6 Cy. 180 x 260 140kW (190bhp)
SKL Motoren u. Systemtechnik AG-Magdeburg

9105853
VTZY
-
THINNAKARA
-
Government of The Republic of India (Administration of Union Territory of Lakshadweep)
Lakshadweep Development Corp Ltd
Mumbai *India*
MMSI: 419290000
Official number: 2509
738
297
960
Class: IR
1993-08 Alcock, Ashdown & Co. Ltd. — Bhavnagar
Loa 57.50 Br ex 11.02 Dght 2.700
Lbp 55.50 Br md 11.00 Dpth 3.50
Welded, 1 dk
(A31A2GX) General Cargo Ship
Grain: 1,100; Bale: 900
Compartments: 2 Ho, ER
2 Ha: 2 (7.0 x 9.0)ER
Derricks: 4x3t; Winches: 4
2 oil engines with clutches, flexible couplings & sr reverse geared to sc. shafts driving 2 FP propellers
Total Power: 776kW (1,056hp) 10.0kn
Cummins VTA-1710-M
2 x Vee 4 Stroke 12 Cy. 140 x 152 each-388kW (528bhp)
Kirloskar Cummins Ltd-India
AuxGen: 3 x 60kW 415V 50Hz a.c

9134490
9HA3305
-
THIRA
ex Conti Seattle *-2013*
ex Delmas Libreville *-2012* *ex* Tiger Bay *-2007*
ex APL Melbourne *-2006* *ex* Vancouver *-2004*
ex Ivory Star 1 *-2003* *ex* Conti Seattle *-2002*
ex CCNI Antartico *-2002* *ex* Sea Lynx *-2000*
ex Conti Seattle *-1997*
Venetian Corp
Goldenport Shipmanagement Ltd
Valletta *Malta*
MMSI: 229403000
Official number: 9134490
24,053
12,958
28,370
T/cm
48.8
Class: BV (GL)
1997-06 Daewoo Heavy Industries Ltd — Geoje
Yd No: 4047
Loa 205.72 (BB) Br ex - Dght 10.117
Lbp 195.78 Br md 27.40 Dpth 15.80
Welded, 1 dk
(A33A2CC) Container Ship (Fully Cellular)
TEU 2113 C Ho 870 TEU C Dk 1243 TEU incl 240 ref C.
Compartments: 6 Cell Ho, ER
10 Ha: 10 (12.6 x 23.4)ER
Cranes: 4x40t
1 oil engine driving 1 FP propeller
Total Power: 13,386kW (18,200hp) 20.0kn
B&W 7L60MC
1 x 2 Stroke 7 Cy. 600 x 1944 13386kW (18200bhp)
Korea Heavy Industries & ConstrCo Ltd (HANJUNG)-South Korea
AuxGen: 3 x 850kW 220/380V 60Hz a.c
Thrusters: 1 Thwart. CP thruster (f)

9108520
ATKI
-
THIRUVALLUVAR
-
V O Chidambaranar Port Trust
-
Chennai *India*
MMSI: 419074300
Official number: 2583
377
113
156
Class: IR
1995-02 Cochin Shipyard Ltd — Ernakulam
Yd No: BY-18
Loa 32.48 Br ex 10.00 Dght 4.700
Lbp 32.23 Br md 9.90 Dpth 4.25
Welded, 1 dk
(B32A2ST) Tug
2 oil engines gearing integral to driving 2 Directional propellers
Total Power: 2,540kW (3,454hp) 11.0kn
Nohab 6R25
2 x 4 Stroke 6 Cy. 250 x 300 each-1270kW (1727bhp)
Wartsila Diesel AB-Sweden
AuxGen: 2 x 100kW 415V 50Hz a.c
Fuel: 50.0 (d.f.)

1008669
ONGN
-
THIS IS US
ex Skylge *-2010*
ex Holland Jachtbouw 061 *-2005*
Parfinim NV-SA
Exmar Shipmanagement NV
Antwerpen *Belgium*
MMSI: 205573000
Official number: 01 00755 2010
110
33
-
Class: LR
✠ **100A1** SS 12/2010
SSC
Yacht, mono, G6
LMC Cable: 137.5/16.0 U2 (a)
2005-12 Scheepswerf Made B.V. — Made (Hull)
Yd No: (061)
2005-12 Holland Jachtbouw B.V. — Zaandam
Yd No: 061
Loa 41.83 Br ex 7.58 Dght 1.750
Lbp 26.88 Br md 7.45 Dpth 3.37
Welded, 1 dk
(X11A2YP) Yacht
1 oil engine with clutches, flexible couplings & sr geared to sc. shaft driving 1 CP propeller
Total Power: 312kW (424hp) 13.6kn
Lugger L6125A
1 x 4 Stroke 6 Cy. 125 x 150 312kW (424bhp)
Alaska Diesel Electric Inc-USA
AuxGen: 2 x 33kW 400V 50Hz a.c
Thrusters: 1 Thwart. FP thruster (f)

7206342
SX7015
-
THISSEAS
ex Taxiarchis II *-2002* *ex* Gefo Baltic *-1998*
ex Tarpenbek *-1980*
Thissefs Shipping Co
-
SatCom: Inmarsat C 423957810
Piraeus *Greece*
MMSI: 239578000
Official number: 10583
1,198
625
1,757
T/cm
6.2
Class: (GL)
1972-05 JG Hitzler Schiffswerft und Masch GmbH & Co KG — Lauenburg Yd No: 728
Loa 74.00 (BB) Br ex 10.75 Dght 4.642
Lbp 68.81 Br md 10.72 Dpth 6.00
Welded, 1 dk.
(A12A2TC) Chemical Tanker
Liq: 2,286
Cargo Heating Coils
Compartments: 8 Ta, ER
2 Cargo Pump (s): 2x220m³/hr
Manifold: Bow/CM: 23m
Ice Capable
1 oil engine driving 1 FP propeller
Total Power: 846kW (1,150hp) 11.5kn
MWM TBD484-8
1 x 4 Stroke 8 Cy. 320 x 480 846kW (1150bhp)
Motoren Werke Mannheim AG (MWM)-West Germany

9493896
A8YE2
-
THISSEAS
-
Eesome Development Corp
Lavinia Corp
SatCom: Inmarsat C 463711630
Monrovia *Liberia*
MMSI: 636015033
Official number: 15033
41,101
25,643
75,200
T/cm
68.3
Class: BV
2012-04 Penglai Zhongbai Jinglu Ship Industry Co Ltd — Penglai SD Yd No: JL0007 (B)
Loa 225.00 Br ex - Dght 14.200
Lbp 217.92 Br md 32.26 Dpth 19.60
Welded, 1 dk
(A21A2BC) Bulk Carrier
Grain: 89,728
Compartments: 7 Ho, ER
7 Ha: ER
1 oil engine driving 1 FP propeller
Total Power: 8,833kW (12,009hp) 14.5kn
MAN-B&W 5S60MC-C
1 x 2 Stroke 5 Cy. 600 x 2400 8833kW (12009bhp)
Hyundai Heavy Industries Co Ltd-South Korea
AuxGen: 3 x 560kW 60Hz a.c
Fuel: 3040.0

8943870
9YEP
-
THISTLE
ex Waterfowl *-1999*
Coloured Fin Ltd (CFL)
-
Port of Spain *Trinidad & Tobago*
288
86
300
1974 Drypool Group Ltd. (Cochrane Shipyard) — Selby Yd No: 1546
Loa 40.10 Br ex 7.85 Dght 2.630
Lbp 37.50 Br md 7.55 Dpth 3.50
Welded, 1 dk
(A14A2LO) Water Tanker
3 Cargo Pump (s)
1 oil engine geared to sc. shaft driving 1 FP propeller
Total Power: 441kW (600hp) 11.0kn
Blackstone ERS8M
1 x 4 Stroke 8 Cy. 222 x 292 441kW (600bhp)
Mirrlees Blackstone (Stamford)Ltd.-Stamford
Fuel: 16.0

7811604
J8B4580
-
THOE
ex Mark *-2013*
Nobel Marine Ltd
Atlantic Dredging Corp
Kingstown *St Vincent & The Grenadines*
MMSI: 375828000
Official number: 11053
463
138
250
Class: BV
1978-12 Scheepsbouwwerf Slob B.V. — Sliedrecht Yd No: 334
Loa 52.71 Br ex - Dght 2.050
Lbp 50.91 Br md 9.00 Dpth 3.38
Welded, 1 dk
(B34A2SH) Hopper, Motor
Hopper: 454
Compartments: 1 Ho, ER
2 oil engines reverse reduction geared to sc. shafts driving 2 FP propellers
Total Power: 536kW (728hp) 16.5kn
Caterpillar 3408TA
2 x Vee 4 Stroke 8 Cy. 137 x 152 each-268kW (364bhp)
Caterpillar Tractor Co-USA
AuxGen: 2 x 68kW 380V 50Hz a.c

7512026
WDD5678
-
THOMAS
ex Ocean Voyager *-1986*
Weeks Marine Inc
-
New York, NY *United States of America*
MMSI: 367161960
Official number: 573482
404
121
-
Class: (AB)
1976-06 McDermott Shipyards Inc — New Iberia LA Yd No: 103
Loa - Br ex - Dght 4.172
Lbp 36.66 Br md 10.37 Dpth 4.88
Welded, 1 dk
(B32A2ST) Tug
2 oil engines reverse reduction geared to sc. shafts driving 2 FP propellers
Total Power: 2,868kW (3,900hp) 13.0kn
EMD (Electro-Motive) 16-645-E5
2 x Vee 2 Stroke 16 Cy. 230 x 254 each-1434kW (1950bhp)
General Motors Corp.Electro-Motive Div.-La Grange
AuxGen: 2 x 75kW
Fuel: 448.0 (d.f.)

8645246
WCS2783
-
THOMAS A. BAUM
-
State of North Carolina (Ferry Division)
-
Manns Harbor, NC *United States of America*
Official number: 1025834
248
81
-
1995 Steiner Shipyard, Inc. — Bayou La Batre, Al
Yd No: 333
Loa 45.64 Br ex 12.80 Dght -
Lbp - Br md 10.35 Dpth 8.43
Welded, 1 dk
(A36A2PR) Passenger/Ro-Ro Ship (Vehicles)
Passengers: unberthed: 149
Vehicles: 30
1 oil engine geared to sc. shaft driving 1 Propeller
Total Power: 390kW (530hp)
G.M. (Detroit Diesel) 12V-71
1 x Vee 2 Stroke 12 Cy. 108 x 127 390kW (530bhp)
Detroit Diesel Corporation-Detroit, Mi

9099597
FRAG
ST 900290
THOMAS ANTOINE II
-
SNC Thomas Antoine II
-
Sete *France*
Official number: 900290
148
-
-
2003-01 in France
Loa 24.90 (BB) Br ex - Dght -
Lbp 22.00 Br md - Dpth -
Bonded, 1 dk
(B11A2FS) Stern Trawler
Hull Material: Reinforced Plastic
1 oil engine driving 1 Propeller
Total Power: 316kW (430hp)

6601698
ZR4475
-
THOMAS B. DAVIE
-
Offshore & Ship Supplies Pty Ltd
-
Cape Town *South Africa*
Official number: 350482
190
57
-
Class: (LR)
✠ Classed LR until 27/4/94
1966-10 Globe Engineering Works Ltd. — Cape Town Yd No: 142
Loa 29.42 Br ex 7.04 Dght 2.744
Lbp 25.61 Br md 7.01 Dpth 3.36
Welded
(B11A2FT) Trawler
1 oil engine driving 1 CP propeller
Total Power: 375kW (510hp) 10.8kn
Alpha 406-24VO
1 x 2 Stroke 6 Cy. 240 x 400 375kW (510bhp)
Alpha Diesel A/S-Denmark
AuxGen: 1 x 26kW 380V 50Hz a.c, 1 x 12kW 380V 50Hz a.c
Fuel: 40.5 (d.f.)

8331833
DMIZ
SH-4
THOMAS BACH
ex Heidi Sanne *-1993*
Thomas-Bach-Fishing GmbH
E O Muller Schiffsausrustungen GmbH
Heiligenhafen *Germany*
MMSI: 211410690
Official number: 2756
374
155
-
Class: (NV)
1983 Strandby Skibsvaerft I/S — Strandby
Yd No: 78
Lengthened-1997
Loa 37.08 Br ex 7.50 Dght -
Lbp - Br md - Dpth 3.61
Welded, 2 dks
(B11B2FV) Fishing Vessel
Ice Capable
1 oil engine driving 1 FP propeller
Total Power: 690kW (938hp)
Alpha 6T23L-VO
1 x 4 Stroke 6 Cy. 225 x 300 690kW (938bhp)
B&W Alpha Diesel A/S-Denmark
AuxGen: 1 x 66kW 380V 50Hz a.c
Thrusters: 1 Thwart. FP thruster (f)

IMO / Call sign	Name / Owner	Tonnage	Class	Builder / Dimensions	Type	Machinery
9450820 *V7SN7* -	**THOMAS C** **Four Navigation Co LLC** Apex Bulk Carriers LLC SatCom: Inmarsat C 453835772 *Majuro* *Marshall Islands* MMSI: 538003688 Official number: 3688	**23,456** 11,522 34,372	Class: NK (AB)	**2011-01 SPP Shipbuilding Co Ltd — Tongyeong** Yd No: H4012 Loa 180.00 (BB) Br ex - Dght 9.920 Lbp 172.00 Br md 30.00 Dpth 14.70 Welded, 1 dk	**(A21A2BC) Bulk Carrier** Single Hull Grain: 48,766; Bale: 46,815 Compartments: 5 Ho, ER 5 Ha: ER Cranes: 4x35t	**1 oil engine** driving 1 FP propeller Total Power: 7,900kW (10,741hp) 14.0kn MAN-B&W 5S50MC-C 1 x 2 Stroke 5 Cy. 500 x 2000 7900kW (10741bhp) Doosan Engine Co Ltd-South Korea AuxGen: 3 x 600kW a.c Fuel: 185.0 (d.f.) 1560.0 (r.f.)
8841905 *WDD8916* -	**THOMAS D WITTE** *ex* Kendall P Brake *-2007* *ex* Reliance *-2005* *ex* Tammy *-2005* *ex* Matty J *-1999* *ex* June C *-1990* *ex* Valoil *-1990* **Donjon Marine Co Inc** - *New York, NY* *United States of America* MMSI: 367304530 Official number: 287149	*168* 114 -		**1961 American Marine Corp. — New Orleans, La** Yd No: 791 Loa 25.91 Br ex - Dght 3.181 Lbp 24.61 Br md 8.53 Dpth 3.51 Welded, 1 dk	**(B32A2ST) Tug**	**1 oil engine** driving 1 FP propeller Total Power: 1,552kW (2,110hp)
7621786 *WDC6084* -	**THOMAS DANN** *ex* Yabucoa Service *-2005* *ex* Yabucoa *-1999* *ex* Yabucoa Sun *-1997* *ex* Danielle *-1986* *ex* Captain Martin *-1985* **Thomas Dann Inc** Dann Ocean Towing Inc *Tampa, FL* *United States of America* MMSI: 367051030 Official number: 566365	**317** 95 186		**1975-06 Bollinger Machine Shop & Shipyard, Inc. — Lockport, La** Yd No: 94 Loa - Br ex - Dght 3.901 Lbp 30.61 Br md 9.15 Dpth 4.47 Welded, 1 dk	**(B32A2ST) Tug**	**2 oil engines** reduction geared to sc. shafts driving 2 FP propellers Total Power: 2,206kW (3,000hp) EMD (Electro-Motive) 12-645-E6 2 x Vee 2 Stroke 12 Cy. 230 x 254 each-1103kW (1500bhp) General Motors Corp.Electro-Motive Div.-La Grange AuxGen: 2 x 75kW a.c
7052961 *D6E03* -	**THOMAS DE GAUWDIEF** *ex* Pauliturm *-1985* **Synergy Maritime Inc** Mubarak Marine LLC *Moroni* *Union of Comoros* MMSI: 616686000	**555** 192 734	Class: GL	**1971 JG Hitzler Schiffswerft und Masch GmbH & Co KG — Lauenburg** Yd No: 723 Loa 54.51 Br ex 11.33 Dght 3.431 Lbp 49.43 Br md 11.02 Dpth 3.97 Welded, 1 dk	**(B21B20A) Anchor Handling Tug Supply** Derricks: 1x5t Ice Capable	**2 oil engines** reverse reduction geared to sc. shafts driving 2 FP propellers Total Power: 2,206kW (3,000hp) 12.5kn MAN V6V22/30ATL 2 x Vee 4 Stroke 12 Cy. 220 x 300 each-1103kW (1500bhp) Maschinenbau Augsburg Nuernberg (MAN)-Augsburg AuxGen: 3 x 140kW 400/200V 50Hz a.c Thrusters: 1 Tunnel thruster (f) Fuel: 429.0 (r.f.)
8642971 *CXYD* -	**THOMAS EDISON** **Los Cipreses SA (BUQUEBUS)** - *Montevideo* *Uruguay* MMSI: 770576237	**575** 181 36	Class: RI (NV)	**2000-03 Pequot River Shipworks Inc — New London CT** Yd No: PRS3 Loa 45.00 Br ex - Dght 1.570 Lbp 40.00 Br md 11.80 Dpth 4.78 Welded, 1 dk	**(A37B2PS) Passenger Ship** Hull Material: Aluminium Alloy Passengers: unberthed: 302	**2 Gas Turbs** 2 Gas Turbines geared to sc. shafts driving 2 Water jets Total Power: 10,298kW (14,002hp) 47.0kn Solar Turbines TAURUS 60 2 x Gas Turb each-5149kW (7001shp) Solar Turbines Inc.-San Diego, Ca AuxGen: 2 x 174kW 110/440V 60Hz a.c
8983636 *WDA9165* -	**THOMAS G** **Thomas G Inc** - *Port Lavaca, TX* *United States of America* MMSI: 366862150 Official number: 1127433	**139** 41 -		**2002 T.M. Jemison Construction Co., Inc. — Bayou La Batre, Al** Yd No: 179 L reg 24.14 Br ex - Dght - Lbp - Br md 7.31 Dpth 3.65 Welded, 1 dk	**(B11B2FV) Fishing Vessel**	**1 oil engine** driving 1 Propeller
8814419 *KTDQ* -	**THOMAS G. THOMPSON** **Government of The United States of America (Department of The Navy)** University of Washington SatCom: Inmarsat C 430311610 *Seattle, WA* *United States of America* MMSI: 366345000 Official number: 976826	**3,095** 928 -	Class: AB	**1991-06 Halter Marine, Inc. — Moss Point, Ms** Yd No: 1148 Loa 83.50 Br ex - Dght 5.600 Lbp 75.38 Br md 16.00 Dpth 8.08 Welded	**(B31A2SR) Research Survey Vessel**	**5 diesel electric oil engines** driving 3 gen. each 1500kW 3 gen. each 715kW Connecting to 2 elec. motors driving 2 Directional propellers Total Power: 3,631kW (4,938hp) 15.0kn Caterpillar 3508TA 3 x Vee 4 Stroke 8 Cy. 170 x 190 each-519kW (706bhp) Caterpillar Inc-USA Caterpillar 3516TA 2 x Vee 4 Stroke 16 Cy. 170 x 190 each-1037kW (1410bhp) Caterpillar Inc-USA
8611324 *ZMTH* -	**THOMAS HARRISON** *ex* Isak Lyberth *-1993* *ex* Bronnoybas *-1992* **Sealord Group Ltd** - SatCom: Inmarsat C 451200453 *Nelson* *New Zealand* MMSI: 512000015 Official number: 876102	**1,048** 314 425	Class: LR (NV) **100A1** SS 08/2013 stern trawler Ice Class 1B **LMC** Cable: 385.0/32.0 U2	**1989-11 Estaleiros Sao Jacinto S.A. — Aveiro** Yd No: 167 Loa 42.50 (BB) Br ex 12.02 Dght 5.457 Lbp 36.50 Br md 12.00 Dpth 7.40 Welded, 1 dk	**(B11A2FS) Stern Trawler** Ice Capable	**1 oil engine** with flexible couplings & sr geared to sc. shaft driving 1 CP propeller Total Power: 1,759kW (2,392hp) 11.0kn Alpha 12V23/30 1 x Vee 4 Stroke 12 Cy. 225 x 300 1759kW (2392bhp) MAN B&W Diesel A/S-Denmark AuxGen: 1 x 1170kW 440V 60Hz a.c, 2 x 412kW 440V 60Hz a.c Thrusters: 1 Thwart. CP thruster (f)
8892033 *WTEA* -	**THOMAS JEFFERSON** *ex* Littlehales *-2003* **Government of The United States of America (Department of Commerce)** Government of The United States of America (National Oceanic & Atmospheric Administration - Marine & Aviation Operations) (NOAA) *Norfolk, VA* *United States of America* MMSI: 369958000 Official number: CG 034222	*1,767* 530 -	Class: AB	**1991-12 Halter Marine, Inc. — Moss Point, Ms** Yd No: 1169 Loa 57.91 Br ex 13.72 Dght 3.990 Lbp 53.34 Br md 13.72 Dpth 6.93 Welded, 1 dk	**(B31A2SR) Research Survey Vessel**	**1 oil engine** reverse reduction geared to sc. shaft driving 1 FP propeller Total Power: 1,876kW (2,551hp) 12.7kn EMD (Electro-Motive) 12-645-F7B 1 x Vee 2 Stroke 12 Cy. 230 x 254 1876kW (2551bhp) General Motors Detroit DieselAllison Divn-USA AuxGen: 3 x 350kW a.c Fuel: 694.0 (d.f.)
9064267 *OUVB2* -	**THOMAS MAERSK** *ex* Maersk Tennessee *-2002* *ex* Thomas Maersk *-1997* **A P Moller** - SatCom: Inmarsat A 1555103 *Copenhagen* *Denmark (DIS)* MMSI: 220158000 Official number: D4009	**18,859** 8,468 25,431 T/cm 41.7	Class: AB (LR) ✠ Classed LR until 13/11/96	**1994-01 Tsuneishi Shipbuilding Co Ltd — Fukuyama HS** Yd No: 1025 Loa 176.40 (BB) Br ex 27.83 Dght 10.300 Lbp 166.53 Br md 27.80 Dpth 15.23 Welded, 1 dk	**(A33A2CC) Container Ship (Fully Cellular)** TEU 1325 C Ho 629 TEU C Dk 696 TEU incl 114 ref C. Compartments: 9 Cell Ho, ER 9 Ha: ER Gantry cranes: 1x40t	**1 oil engine** driving 1 FP propeller Total Power: 11,418kW (15,524hp) 18.5kn B&W 8S50MC 1 x 2 Stroke 8 Cy. 500 x 1910 11418kW (15524bhp) Mitsui Engineering & Shipbuilding CLtd-Japan AuxGen: 3 x 1250kW 450V 60Hz a.c Thrusters: 2 Directional thruster (f); 1 Tunnel thruster (a)
9248667 *9HA3135* -	**THOMAS MANN** *ex* TS Tokyo *-2012* *ex* Thomas Mann *-2003* **KG ms ' Thomas Mann' Schiffahrtsgesellschaft mbH & Co** Norddeutsche Reederei H Schuldt GmbH & Co KG SatCom: Inmarsat C 422918910 *Valletta* *Malta* MMSI: 229189000	**28,270** 13,327 33,297	Class: GL (AB)	**2003-11 Jurong Shipyard Pte Ltd — Singapore** Yd No: 1065 Loa 213.00 (BB) Br ex - Dght 11.500 Lbp 202.10 Br md 32.20 Dpth 16.50 Welded, 1 dk	**(A33A2CC) Container Ship (Fully Cellular)** Double Hull TEU 2586 incl. 400 ref C.	**1 oil engine** driving 1 FP propeller Total Power: 25,270kW (34,357hp) 22.7kn B&W 7K80MC-C 1 x 2 Stroke 7 Cy. 800 x 2300 25270kW (34357bhp) Hitachi Zosen Corp-Japan AuxGen: 4 x 1360kW 60Hz a.c Thrusters: 1 Tunnel thruster (f) Fuel: 435.0 (d.f.) 3735.0 (r.f.) 103.0pd
7309429 *WDA4004* -	**THOMAS MICHAEL** **Carlos A Luna** - *Westport, WA* *United States of America* MMSI: 366804710 Official number: 512140	*130* 88 -		**1967 Master Marine, Inc. — Bayou La Batre, Al** L reg 22.19 Br ex 6.81 Dght - Lbp - Br md - Dpth 3.56 Welded	**(B11B2FV) Fishing Vessel**	**1 oil engine** driving 1 FP propeller Total Power: 279kW (379hp)
8957352 *XCQR* -	**THOMAS TIDE** *ex* Toni Lynn II *-2003* **Operaciones Tecnicas Marinas Ltda (OTM)** - *Ciudad del Carmen* *Mexico* MMSI: 345070076	**108** 33 -	Class: (GL)	**1975 Camcraft, Inc. — Crown Point, La** Yd No: 124 L reg 28.21 Br ex - Dght 1.700 Lbp - Br md 6.45 Dpth 2.94 Welded, 1 dk	**(B21A20C) Crew/Supply Vessel** Hull Material: Aluminium Alloy	**3 oil engines** reduction geared to sc. shafts driving 3 FP propellers Total Power: 1,125kW (1,530hp) 20.0kn G.M. (Detroit Diesel) 12V-71-TI 3 x Vee 2 Stroke 12 Cy. 108 x 127 each-375kW (510bhp) General Motors Detroit DieselAllison Divn-USA AuxGen: 2 x 30kW 220V a.c

9579925 *KRTF* -	**THOMAS WAINWRIGHT** *ex* Southern Cross *-2012* **GulfMark Americas Inc** - *New Orleans, LA* *United States of America* MMSI: 338228000 Official number: 1223869	**1,656** 612 2,448	Class: AB	2010-06 **Thoma-Sea Marine Constructors LLC — Lockport LA** Yd No: 117 Loa 73.78 Br ex - Dght 4.260 Lbp 71.34 Br md 16.46 Dpth 5.18 Welded, 1 dk	**(B21A2OS) Platform Supply Ship**	**2 oil engines** reduction geared to sc. shafts driving 2 Directional propellers Total Power: 5,050kW (6,866hp) 12.0kn Caterpillar 3516C 2 x Vee 4 Stroke 16 Cy. 170 x 215 each-2525kW (3433bhp) Caterpillar Inc-USA AuxGen: 2 x 425kW a.c Thrusters: 2 Tunnel thruster (f)
9389459 *YJVB6* -	**THOMPSON TIDE** - **Tidewater Properties Ltd** Tidewater Marine International Inc *Port Vila* *Vanuatu* MMSI: 576181000 Official number: 1722	**2,256** 676 2,113	Class: AB	**2007-09 Stocznia Polnocna SA (Northern Shipyard) — Gdansk (Hull)** Yd No: B844/03 **2007-09 Gdanska Stocznia 'Remontowa' SA — Gdansk** Yd No: 1674/03 Loa 70.00 (BB) Br ex - Dght 5.100 Lbp 63.60 Br md 15.50 Dpth 6.60 Welded, 1 dk	**(B21B20A) Anchor Handling Tug Supply**	**2 oil engines** reduction geared to sc. shafts driving 2 CP propellers Total Power: 5,970kW (8,116hp) 13.0kn EMD (Electro-Motive) 20-710-G7B 2 x Vee 2 Stroke 20 Cy. 230 x 279 each-2985kW (4058bhp) General Motors Corp.Electro-Motive Div.-La Grange AuxGen: 2 x 250kW a.c, 2 x 1500kW a.c Thrusters: 2 Tunnel thruster (f) Fuel: 830.0
8027298 *9HUI9* -	**THOMSON CELEBRATION** *ex* Noordam *-2004* **TUI UK Ltd** Columbia Shipmanagement Ltd *Valletta* *Malta* MMSI: 249544000 Official number: 8027298	**33,933** 16,050 4,243	Class: GL (LR) ✠ Classed LR until 16/3/11	**1984-04 Chantiers de l'Atlantique — St-Nazaire** Yd No: X27 Loa 214.66 (BB) Br ex 27.26 Dght 7.700 Lbp 181.62 Br md 27.22 Dpth 18.83 Welded, 4 dks, 5th dk (clear of eng.room), 6th dk (fwd of eng. room)	**(A37A2PC) Passenger/Cruise** Passengers: cabins: 627; berths: 1378	**2 oil engines** driving 2 CP propellers Total Power: 21,600kW (29,368hp) 21.0kn Sulzer 7RLB66 2 x 2 Stroke 7 Cy. 660 x 1400 each-10800kW (14684bhp) Cie de Constructions Mecaniques (CCM), procede Sulzer-France AuxGen: 2 x 2400kW 440V 60Hz a.c, 2 x 2000kW 440V 60Hz a.c, 2 x 900kW 440V 60Hz a.c Thrusters: 1 Thwart. CP thruster (f); 1 Tunnel thruster (a) Fuel: 216.5 (d.f.) 1974.5 (r.f.)
8407735 *9HA2381* -	**THOMSON DREAM** *ex* Costa Europa *-2010* *ex* Westerdam *-2002* *ex* Homeric *-1988* **Grand Cruise Investments Unipessoal Lda** Columbia Shipmanagement Ltd *Valletta* *Malta* MMSI: 248481000 Official number: 8407735	**54,763** 28,505 5,340	Class: GL (LR) (RI) (AB) Classed LR until 27/11/02	**1986-05 Jos L Meyer GmbH & Co — Papenburg** Yd No: 610 Lengthened-1990 Loa 243.20 (BB) Br ex 29.73 Dght 7.219 Lbp 219.25 Br md 29.00 Dpth 14.50 Welded, 12 dks	**(A37A2PC) Passenger/Cruise** Passengers: cabins: 747; berths: 1744	**2 oil engines** driving 2 CP propellers Total Power: 23,796kW (32,354hp) 19.0kn B&W 10L55GB 2 x 2 Stroke 10 Cy. 550 x 1380 each-11898kW (16177bhp) MAN B&W Diesel A/S-Denmark AuxGen: 4 x 2250kW 450V 60Hz a.c, 1 x 1700kW 450V 60Hz a.c Boilers: 4 AuxB (ex.g.) 10.2kgf/cm² (10.0bar), 2 e (ex.g.) 9.2kgf/cm² (9.0bar), 2 AuxB (o.f.) 10.2kgf/cm² (10.0bar) Thrusters: 2 Thwart. CP thruster (f); 1 Tunnel thruster (a) Fuel: 103.0 (d.f.) 3018.0 (r.f.) 85.0pd
8814744 *9HA2188* -	**THOMSON MAJESTY** *ex* Louis Majesty *-2012* *ex* Norwegian Majesty *-2009* *ex* Royal Majesty *-1997* **Majesty Trading Opco LLC** Core Marine Ltd *Valletta* *Malta* MMSI: 248124000 Official number: 8814744	**40,876** 21,984 2,700	Class: NV (LR) Classed LR until 12/1/98	**1992-07 Kvaerner Masa-Yards Inc — Turku** Yd No: 1312 Lengthened-1999 Loa 207.10 (BB) Br ex 33.20 Dght 6.200 Lbp 185.80 Br md 27.60 Dpth 16.70 Welded, 8 dks	**(A37A2PC) Passenger/Cruise** Passengers: cabins: 731; berths: 1850 Ice Capable	**4 oil engines** with clutches, flexible couplings & sr geared to sc. shafts driving 2 CP propellers Total Power: 21,108kW (28,700hp) 19.0kn Wartsila 6R46 4 x 4 Stroke 6 Cy. 460 x 580 each-5277kW (7175bhp) Wartsila Diesel Oy-Finland AuxGen: 4 x 593kW 660V 50Hz a.c Thrusters: 2 Thwart. CP thruster (f) Fuel: 341.0 (d.f.) 1650.0 (r.f.) 115.0pd
8024014 *9HA2336* -	**THOMSON SPIRIT** *ex* Spirit *-2003* *ex* Nieuw Amsterdam *-2002* *ex* Patriot *-2002* *ex* Nieuw Amsterdam *-2000* **Spirit Trading Opco LLC** Core Marine Ltd *Valletta* *Malta* MMSI: 248368000 Official number: 8024014	**33,930** 16,027 4,217	Class: LR ✠ **100A1** SS 05/2013 ✠ **LMC** Eq.Ltr: K†; Cable: 660.0/78.0 U3 (a)	**1983-05 Chantiers de l'Atlantique — St-Nazaire** Yd No: V27 Loa 214.66 (BB) Br ex 27.26 Dght 7.516 Lbp 181.62 Br md 27.21 Dpth 18.83 Welded, 4 dks, 5th dk (clear of engine room), 6th dk (fwd of engine room)	**(A37A2PC) Passenger/Cruise** Passengers: cabins: 627; berths: 1374	**2 oil engines** driving 2 CP propellers Total Power: 22,706kW (30,872hp) 21.0kn Sulzer 7RLB66 2 x 2 Stroke 7 Cy. 660 x 1400 each-11353kW (15436bhp) Cie de Constructions Mecaniques (CCM), procede Sulzer-France AuxGen: 2 x 2400kW 440V 60Hz a.c, 2 x 2000kW 440V 60Hz a.c, 2 x 900kW 440V 60Hz a.c Thrusters: 1 Thwart. CP thruster (f); 1 Tunnel thruster (a) Fuel: 216.5 (d.f.) 1974.5 (r.f.)
8973784 - -	**THONG EK** - **Suprom Sorathanasak** - *Bangkok* *Thailand* Official number: 450900050	**441** 203 -		**2001-12 Mahachai Dockyard Co., Ltd. — Samut Sakhon** Loa 45.00 Br ex 8.00 Dght - Lbp - Br md - Dpth 4.80 Welded, 1 dk	**(A13B2TU) Tanker (unspecified)** Double Hull (13F)	**1 oil engine** geared to sc. shaft driving 1 FP propeller Total Power: 746kW (1,014hp) Cummins 1 x 4 Stroke 746kW (1014bhp) Cummins Engine Co Inc-USA
7821544 *HSB2594* -	**THONGDEE 9** *ex* Matsuyama Maru No. 12 *-1994* **Effective Management Co Ltd** - *Thailand* Official number: 371004054	**495** 233 698		**1978-11 Kochi Jyuko K.K. — Kochi** Yd No: 1285 Loa 49.70 Br ex - Dght 3.601 Lbp 45.01 Br md 9.52 Dpth 4.63 Riveted\Welded, 1 dk	**(A13B2TU) Tanker (unspecified)**	**1 oil engine** driving 1 FP propeller Total Power: 736kW (1,001hp) Niigata 6L28X 1 x 4 Stroke 6 Cy. 280 x 440 736kW (1001bhp) Niigata Engineering Co Ltd-Japan
9286310 - -	**THONGWATANA 1** - **Sudchai Dechvilaisri** - *Bangkok* *Thailand* Official number: 450900018	**362** 171 -		**2002-01 Mits Decisions Co., Ltd. — Samut Sakhon** Loa 38.00 Br ex 8.00 Dght - Lbp - Br md - Dpth 4.80 Welded, 1 dk	**(B12B2FC) Fish Carrier**	**1 oil engine** geared to sc. shaft driving 1 FP propeller Total Power: 783kW (1,065hp) Cummins KT-2300-M 1 x Vee 4 Stroke 12 Cy. 159 x 159 783kW (1065bhp) Cummins Engine Co Inc-USA
8707094 - -	**THOORI** *ex* Taihei Maru *-2006* **State Trading Organization Plc** - *Male* *Maldives* Official number: 129484	*128* 89 330		**1987-07 K.K. Taihei Kogyo — Akitsu** Yd No: 1975 Loa 45.00 (BB) Br ex 8.89 Dght 2.710 Lbp 40.00 Br md 8.80 Dpth 4.80 Welded, 1 dk	**(A31A2GX) General Cargo Ship** Grain: 927; Bale: 661 Compartments: 1 Ho, ER 1 Ha: ER	**1 oil engine** with clutches & reverse reduction geared to sc. shaft driving 1 FP propeller Total Power: 316kW (430hp) Hanshin 6L24GSH 1 x 4 Stroke 6 Cy. 240 x 400 316kW (430bhp) Hanshin Nainenki Kogyo-Japan
8855839 *WSR4656* -	**THOR** - **Thor Fishing Corp** - *Fairhaven, MA* *United States of America* MMSI: 366988020 Official number: 671986	*173* 117 -		**1984 Tarpon Springs Boat Yard — Tarpon Springs, Fl** Yd No: 401 Loa - Br ex - Dght - Lbp 25.91 Br md 7.32 Dpth 3.35 Welded, 1 dk	**(B11B2FV) Fishing Vessel**	**1 oil engine** driving 1 FP propeller
8023890 *HQWY8* -	**THOR** *ex* April Moran *-2002* *ex* April *-1998* *ex* Richmond Bay *-1997* *ex* Amoco Richmond *-1989* **Beracah Lubricants Nigeria Ltd** - *San Lorenzo* *Honduras* Official number: L-1728230	**562** 168 419	Class: (AB)	**1982-01 McDermott Shipyards Inc — Morgan City LA** Yd No: 261 Loa - Br ex - Dght 5.372 Lbp 39.02 Br md 10.98 Dpth 6.86 Welded, 1 dk	**(B32B2SP) Pusher Tug**	**2 oil engines** sr geared to sc. shaft driving 1 CP propeller Total Power: 4,266kW (5,800hp) 15.0kn EMD (Electro-Motive) 16-645-E7B 2 x Vee 2 Stroke 16 Cy. 230 x 254 each-2133kW (2900bhp) General Motors Corp.Electro-Motive Div.-La Grange AuxGen: 2 x 210kW
8016914 *DLIC* -	**THOR** - **Government of The Federal Republic of Germany (Land Niedersachsen Bezirksregierung Weser-Ems Dez 307)** - *Wilhelmshaven* *Germany* MMSI: 211261100 Official number: 245	**172** 87 318	Class: GL	**1981-10 C. Luehring Schiffswerft GmbH & Co. KG — Brake** Yd No: 8006 Loa 34.50 Br ex 8.23 Dght 2.723 Lbp 31.09 Br md 8.01 Dpth 3.13 Welded, 1 dk	**(B34G2SE) Pollution Control Vessel** Ice Capable	**2 oil engines** reduction geared to sc. shafts driving 2 FP propellers Total Power: 358kW (486hp) 9.0kn Deutz SBA6M816 2 x 4 Stroke 6 Cy. 142 x 160 each-179kW (243bhp) Kloeckner Humboldt Deutz AG-West Germany Thrusters: 2 Thwart. FP thruster (f)
8650411 - -	**THOR** *ex* Solthorn *-2009* - -	*111* 32 -		**1967 Yacht- u. Bootswerft Abeking & Rasmussen — Lemwerder** Loa - Br ex - Dght - Lbp - Br md - Dpth - Welded, 1 dk	**(B34Q2QX) Lighthouse Tender**	**1 oil engine** driving 1 Propeller

7363750 *V5TH* -	**THOR** *ex* Thorn *-2002* *ex* Jose Dolores *-1995* **Venesba Fishing Pty Ltd** - SatCom: Inmarsat C 465918610 *Walvis Bay* *Namibia* MMSI: 659186000 Official number: 2001WB003	*194* 86 -	Class: (GL)	**1974-10 Ast. Ojeda y Aniceto S.A. — Aviles** Yd No: 10 Loa 31.93 Br ex 7.17 Dght 3.175 Lbp 27.03 Br md 7.14 Dpth 3.69 Welded, 1 dk	**(B11A2FT) Trawler** Ins: 170	**1 oil engine** reduction geared to sc. shaft driving 1 FP propeller Total Power: 589kW (801hp) Deutz SBA8M528 1 x 4 Stroke 8 Cy. 220 x 280 589kW (801bhp) (new engine 2000) Deutz AG-Koeln
6901660 *MYEN4* -	**THOR** *ex* Jadi *-2011* *ex* Butjadingen *-1996* **R J Harvey** Marine Services (Grimsby) Ltd *Grimsby* *United Kingdom* MMSI: 235090244	**143** 43 77	Class: (GL)	**1968 Jadewerft Wilhelmshaven GmbH — Wilhelmshaven** Yd No: 119 Loa 25.56 Br ex 7.88 Dght 3.601 Lbp 24.01 Br md 7.50 Dpth 3.03 Welded, 1 dk	**(B32A2ST) Tug** Ice Capable	**1 oil engine** sr geared to sc. shaft driving 1 Directional propeller Total Power: 736kW (1,001hp) 10.0kn Deutz SBV8M545 1 x 4 Stroke 8 Cy. 320 x 450 736kW (1001bhp) Kloeckner Humboldt Deutz AG-West Germany AuxGen: 2 x 220V d.c
6717239 *5NWO* -	**THOR** *ex* Dolphin V *-2001* *ex* Dudley *-2000* *ex* Ejisu *-1999* *ex* Aloni *-1997* *ex* Dolphin V *-1997* *ex* Servol *-1993* *ex* Campogenil *-1992* - - SatCom: Inmarsat A 1341562 *Nigeria*	**4,380** 2,420 6,291	Class: (LR) ✠ Classed LR until 4/1/95	**1967-11 Sociedad Espanola de Construccion Naval SA — Puerto Real** Yd No: 140 Loa 123.88 (BB) Br ex 16.54 Dght 5.931 Lbp 115.80 Br md 16.50 Dpth 7.42 Riveted\Welded, 1 dk	**(A13B2TP) Products Tanker** Single Hull Liq: 8,523; Liq (Oil): 8,523 Compartments: 12 Ta, ER 2 Cargo Pump (s): 2x200m³/hr	**1 oil engine** driving 1 FP propeller Total Power: 2,832kW (3,850hp) 14.0kn B&W 5-50VT2BF-110 1 x 2 Stroke 5 Cy. 500 x 1100 2832kW (3850bhp) Sociedad Espanola de ConstruccionNaval-Spain AuxGen: 3 x 240kW 380V 50Hz a.c
5428817 *XPMB* TG 788	**THOR** *ex* Anita *-2011* *ex* Klippstein *-1999* *ex* Robert Senior *-1978* **P/F Thor** - *Trongisvagur* *Faeroe Islands (Danish)* MMSI: 231100000	**292** 87 -	Class: NV	**1963-10 Bolsones Verft AS — Molde** Yd No: 194 Lengthened-1965 Loa 34.88 Br ex 6.86 Dght 4.150 Lbp 32.31 Br md 6.84 Dpth 5.71 Welded, 1 dk	**(B11B2FV) Fishing Vessel** Compartments: 2 Ho, ER 2 Ha: (0.9 x 0.9) (3.5 x 1.6)ER Derricks: 1x2.5t; Winches: 1 Ice Capable	**1 oil engine** driving 1 FP propeller Total Power: 460kW (625hp) 10.0kn Wichmann 5ACA 1 x 2 Stroke 5 Cy. 280 x 420 460kW (625bhp) Wichmann Motorfabrikk AS-Norway AuxGen: 1 x 18kW 220V d.c, 1 x 15kW 220V d.c, 1 x Thrusters: 1 Thwart. FP thruster (f)
9288198 *CA4651* -	**THOR** *ex* Starnav Thor *-2013* *ex* Thor *-2010* **Detroit Chile SA** - *Chile* MMSI: 725001165	**498** 149 663		**2003-02 Detroit Chile SA — Puerto Montt** Yd No: 70 Loa 45.56 (BB) Br ex 12.75 Dght 3.113 Lbp 40.15 Br md 12.00 Dpth 4.00 Welded, 1 dk	**(A31C2GD) Deck Cargo Ship**	**2 oil engines** reduction geared to sc. shafts driving 2 FP propellers Total Power: 1,204kW (1,636hp) 12.0kn M.T.U. 12V183TE72 2 x Vee 4 Stroke 12 Cy. 128 x 142 each-602kW (818bhp) MTU Friedrichshafen GmbH-Friedrichshafen Thrusters: 1 Tunnel thruster (f)
9291418 *V7PI9* -	**THOR** *ex* CMB Florentina *-2008* **Spartacus Navigation Corp** Primerose Shipping Co Ltd *Majuro* *Marshall Islands* MMSI: 538003238 Official number: 3238	**40,060** 25,440 76,838	Class: BV	**2005-01 Oshima Shipbuilding Co Ltd — Saikai NS** Yd No: 10428 Loa 225.00 (BB) Br ex - Dght 14.120 Lbp 215.00 Br md 32.26 Dpth 19.39 Welded, 1 dk	**(A21A2BC) Bulk Carrier** Double Hull Grain: 90,200; Bale: 88,871 Compartments: 7 Ho, ER 7 Ha: 5 (17.0 x 15.9)ER 2 (16.0 x 14.1)	**1 oil engine** driving 1 FP propeller Total Power: 9,385kW (12,760hp) 14.5kn MAN-B&W 5S60MC-C 1 x 2 Stroke 5 Cy. 600 x 2400 9385kW (12760bhp) Mitsui Engineering & Shipbuilding CLtd-Japan AuxGen: 3 x 380kW 440/100V 60Hz a.c
9350551 *WDD8608* -	**THOR** - **Suderman & Young Towing Co LP** - *Houston, TX* *United States of America* MMSI: 367300350 Official number: 1199475	**399** 119 427	Class: AB	**2007-07 Main Iron Works, Inc. — Houma, La** Yd No: 422 Loa 30.05 Br ex - Dght - Lbp 28.04 Br md 12.01 Dpth 5.03 Welded, 1 dk	**(B32A2ST) Tug**	**2 oil engines** gearing integral to driving 2 Z propellers Total Power: 5,050kW (6,866hp) Caterpillar 3516C 2 x Vee 4 Stroke 16 Cy. 170 x 215 each-2525kW (3433bhp) Caterpillar Inc-USA
9577147 *DIAV2* -	**THOR** - **Streif Baulogistik GmbH** HOCHTIEF Solutions AG *Hamburg* *Germany* MMSI: 218389000 Official number: 22542	**6,831** 2,030 1,649	Class: GL	**2010-05 'Crist' Sp z oo — Gdansk** Yd No: 1110 Loa 92.77 Br ex 40.30 Dght 4.600 Lbp 66.70 Br md 40.00 Dpth 6.00 Welded, 1 dk	**(Z11C4ZM) Support Platform, jack up** Cranes: 1x400t	**4 diesel electric oil engines** driving 4 gen. Connecting to 4 elec. motors each (750kW) driving 4 Azimuth electric drive units Total Power: 4,610kW (6,267hp) 6.5kn
9426893 *TFIA* -	**THOR** - **Government of The Republic of Iceland (Landhelgisgaesla - Coast Guard)** - *Reykjavik* *Iceland* MMSI: 251604000 Official number: 2769	**4,052** 1,214 2,089	Class: LR ✠ **100A1** SS 09/2011 fire-fighting Ship 1 (2400m3/h) with water spray, occasional oil recovery duties EP Ice Class 1B FS at a draught of 5.814m Max/min draughts fwd 5.214/3.414m Max/min draughts aft 6.363/4.586m Power required 1246kw, power installed 9000kw ✠ **LMC** **UMS** Eq.Ltr: V; Cable: 495.0/44.0 U3 (a)	**2011-09 Ast. y Maestranzas de la Armada (ASMAR Chile) — Talcahuano** Yd No: 106 Loa 93.80 (BB) Br ex 16.06 Dght 5.800 Lbp 82.45 Br md 16.00 Dpth 7.20 Welded, 1 dk	**(B34H2SQ) Patrol Vessel** Ice Capable	**2 oil engines** with clutches, flexible couplings & sr geared to sc. shafts driving 2 CP propellers Total Power: 9,000kW (12,236hp) 19.0kn Bergens B32: 40L9P 2 x 4 Stroke 9 Cy. 320 x 400 each-4500kW (6118bhp) Rolls Royce Marine AS-Norway AuxGen: 2 x 601kW 440V 60Hz a.c, 2 x 1600kW 440V 60Hz a.c Boilers: AuxB (o.f.) 7.1kgf/cm² (7.0bar) Thrusters: 2 Tunnel thruster (f); 1 Retract. directional thruster (f); 1 Tunnel thruster (a)
9424857 *9V8781* -	**THOR ACHIEVER** *ex* Teo *-2010* **Thoresen Shipping Singapore Pte Ltd** - *Singapore* *Singapore* MMSI: 565929000 Official number: 396239	**32,957** 19,231 57,015 T/cm 58.8	Class: BV	**2010-01 Qingshan Shipyard — Wuhan HB** Yd No: 20060350 Loa 189.99 (BB) Br ex - Dght 12.800 Lbp 185.00 Br md 32.26 Dpth 18.00 Welded, 1 dk	**(A21A2BC) Bulk Carrier** Grain: 71,634; Bale: 68,200 Compartments: 5 Ho, ER 5 Ha: ER Cranes: 4x30t	**1 oil engine** driving 1 FP propeller Total Power: 9,480kW (12,889hp) 14.2kn MAN-B&W 6S50MC-C 1 x 2 Stroke 6 Cy. 500 x 2000 9480kW (12889bhp) STX Engine Co Ltd-South Korea AuxGen: 2 x 720kW 60Hz a.c, 1 x 600kW 60Hz a.c
9458559 *OZ2070* -	**THOR ALPHA** - **P/F Thor** - *Hosvik* *Faeroe Islands (Danish)* MMSI: 231074000	**1,051** 315 1,575	Class: NV	**2008-02 p/f Torshavnar Skipasmidja — Torshavn** Yd No: 56 Loa 55.10 (BB) Br ex - Dght 5.250 Lbp 50.56 Br md 12.50 Dpth 5.50 Welded, 1 dk	**(B21B20T) Offshore Tug/Supply Ship** Passengers: 34; berths: 16 Cranes: 1x5t	**4 diesel electric oil engines** driving 4 gen. each 440kW a.c Connecting to 2 elec. motors each (650kW) driving 2 Azimuth electric drive units Total Power: 1,876kW (2,552hp) Scania DI16 M 4 x Vee 4 Stroke 8 Cy. 127 x 154 each-469kW (638bhp) Scania AB-Sweden Thrusters: 1 Water jet (f) Fuel: 470.0 (d.f.) 880.0 (r.f.)
9358618 *OZ2061* -	**THOR ASSISTER** *ex* Jaya Puffin 5 *-2006* **P/F Thor** - *Hosvik* *Faeroe Islands (Danish)* MMSI: 231013000	**675** 202 589	Class: NV (AB)	**2006-01 Yuexin Shipbuilding Co Ltd — Guangzhou GD** Yd No: 3050 Loa 45.00 Br ex 11.83 Dght 3.812 Lbp 39.40 Br md 11.80 Dpth 4.60 Welded, 1 dk	**(B21B20T) Offshore Tug/Supply Ship** Passengers: 12; berths: 16	**2 oil engines** driving 3 gen. each 245kW a.c reduction geared to sc. shafts driving 2 FP propellers Total Power: 2,984kW (4,058hp) 10.0kn Caterpillar 3516B 2 x Vee 4 Stroke 16 Cy. 170 x 190 each-1492kW (2029bhp) Caterpillar Inc-USA AuxGen: 3 x 245kW 415V 50Hz a.c Thrusters: 1 Tunnel thruster (f) Fuel: 550.0 (d.f.) 14.0pd
8884737 *SGVZ* -	**THOR AV GRUMS** *ex* Thor *-1996* *ex* Garpen *-1996* **Bloms Bogsertjanst HB** - *Grums* *Sweden* MMSI: 265563780	**130** 39 -		**1954 AB Hammarbyverken — Stockholm** Yd No: 37 Loa - Br ex - Dght - Lbp 22.76 Br md 6.87 Dpth 3.64 Welded, 1 dk	**(B32A2ST) Tug**	**1 oil engine** driving 1 FP propeller Total Power: 794kW (1,080hp)

IMO / Call sign	Ship / Owner	Tonnage	Class	Built / Dimensions	Type / Capacity	Machinery
8700589 *0Z2058* -	**THOR BEAMER** *ex* Katharina K *-2006* *ex* Broedertrouw *-2002* **P/F Thor** - *Hosvik* *Faeroe Islands (Danish)* MMSI: 231429000 Official number: DF4030	494 148 -	Class: NV (GL)	**1988-05 Scheepswerf Visser B.V. — Den Helder** Yd No: 118 Converted From: Trawler-2002 Loa 42.83 (BB) Br ex 9.17 Dght 4.497 Lbp 38.49 Br md 9.01 Dpth 5.31 Welded, 1 dk	**(B22G20Y) Standby Safety Vessel** Passengers: berths: 4	**1 oil engine** with clutches, flexible couplings & dr reverse geared to sc. shaft driving 1 FP propeller Total Power: 2,171kW (2,952hp) 9.0kn Stork-Werkspoor 9SW280 1 x 4 Stroke 9 Cy. 280 x 300 2171kW (2952bhp) Stork Werkspoor Diesel BV-Netherlands AuxGen: 2 x 100kW 380/220V 50Hz a.c Thrusters: 1 Thwart. FP thruster (f) Fuel: 125.0 (d.f.) 3.5pd
9474797 *9V6451* -	**THOR BRAVE** - **Thoresen Shipping Singapore Pte Ltd** - *Singapore* *Singapore* MMSI: 566716000 Official number: 398007	32,637 18,070 53,506 T/cm 65.0	Class: NV	**2012-11 Ha Long Shipbuilding Co Ltd — Ha Long** Yd No: HR-53-HL15 Loa 190.00 (BB) Br ex - Dght 12.620 Lbp 183.05 Br md 32.26 Dpth 17.50 Welded, 1 dk	**(A21A2BC) Bulk Carrier** Grain: 65,945; Bale: 64,626 Compartments: 5 Ho, ER 5 Ha: 4 (21.6 x 22.4)ER (19.2 x 20.8) Cranes: 4x36t	**1 oil engine** driving 1 FP propeller Total Power: 9,480kW (12,889hp) 14.2kn MAN-B&W 6S50MC-C 1 x 2 Stroke 6 Cy. 500 x 2000 9480kW (12889bhp) Doosan Engine Co Ltd-South Korea AuxGen: 3 x 700kW a.c
9474802 *9V6895* -	**THOR BREEZE** - **Thoresen Shipping Singapore Pte Ltd** Thoresen & Co (Bangkok) Ltd *Singapore* *Singapore* MMSI: 566985000 Official number: 398476	32,637 18,070 53,464 T/cm 57.3	Class: NV	**2013-08 Ha Long Shipbuilding Co Ltd — Ha Long** Yd No: HR-53-HL16 Loa 190.00 (BB) Br ex 32.30 Dght 12.600 Lbp 180.05 Br md 32.26 Dpth 17.50 Welded, 1 dk	**(A21A2BC) Bulk Carrier** Grain: 65,945; Bale: 64,626 Compartments: 5 Ho, ER 5 Ha: 4 (21.6 x 22.4)ER (19.2 x 20.8) Cranes: 4x36t	**1 oil engine** driving 1 FP propeller Total Power: 9,480kW (12,889hp) 14.2kn MAN-B&W 6S50MC-C 1 x 2 Stroke 6 Cy. 500 x 2000 9480kW (12889bhp) Doosan Engine Co Ltd-South Korea AuxGen: 3 x 700kW a.c
9488633 *V2DG5* -	**THOR BRONCO** *ex* BBC Tasmania *-2010* *ex* FCC Pioneer *-2008* **ms 'Pioneer' GmbH & Co KG** Internaut Shipping Ltd *Saint John's* *Antigua & Barbuda* MMSI: 305206000 Official number: 4431	6,569 2,847 8,090	Class: GL (CC)	**2008-01 Chongqing Dongfeng Ship Industry Co — Chongqing** Yd No: K06-1008 Loa 116.23 (BB) Br ex - Dght 7.000 Lbp 110.00 Br md 18.00 Dpth 10.40 Welded, 1 dk	**(A31A2GX) General Cargo Ship** Grain: 11,705; Bale: 11,681 TEU 275 Compartments: 2 Ho, 2 Tw Dk, ER 2 Ha: (44.8 x 15.0)ER (25.9 x 15.0) Cranes: 2x45t Ice Capable	**1 oil engine** reverse reduction geared to sc. shaft driving 1 FP propeller Total Power: 2,574kW (3,500hp) 12.5kn Yanmar 6N330-EN 1 x 4 Stroke 6 Cy. 330 x 440 2574kW (3500bhp) Qingdao Zichai Boyang Diesel EngineCo Ltd-China AuxGen: 3 x 256kW 400V a.c
6710358 *J8B2384* -	**THOR CHASER** *ex* Mars Chaser *-2012* *ex* Arni Fridriksson *-2001* **P/F Thor** - SatCom: Inmarsat C 425150510 *Kingstown* *St Vincent & The Grenadines* MMSI: 376139000 Official number: 8856	523 156 117	Class: IV NV (LR) ✠ Classed LR until 25/6/08	**1967-09 Brooke Marine Ltd. — Lowestoft** Yd No: 357 Converted From: Stern Trawler-1990 Loa 41.38 Br ex 9.86 Dght 3.671 Lbp 36.51 Br md 9.76 Dpth 4.73 Welded, 1 dk, 2nd dk fwd of mchy. space	**(B22G20Y) Standby Safety Vessel** Passengers: berths: 30 Derricks: 1x3t,1x1t Ice Capable	**2 oil engines** sr geared to sc. shaft driving 1 CP propeller Total Power: 758kW (1,030hp) 9.5kn MAN G6V235/330ATL 2 x 4 Stroke 6 Cy. 235 x 330 each-379kW (515bhp) (, added 1990) in Germany AuxGen: 1 x 230kW 380V 50Hz a.c, 1 x 373kW 380V 50Hz a.c Fuel: 74.0 (d.f.)
9559872 *V2FP5* -	**THOR COMMANDER** *launched as* Sinus Aestuum *-2011* **MarShip GmbH & Co KG ms 'Sinus Aestuum'** MarShip GmbH *Saint John's* *Antigua & Barbuda* MMSI: 305749000	6,351 3,617 9,739	Class: BV	**2011-10 Jiangsu Yangzi Changbo Shipbuilding Co Ltd — Jingjiang JS** (Hull) Yd No: 07-017 **2011-10 Volharding Shipyards B.V. — Foxhol** Yd No: 699 Loa 132.20 (BB) Br ex 15.90 Dght 7.780 Lbp 124.56 Br md 15.87 Dpth 9.65 Welded, 1 dk	**(A31A2GX) General Cargo Ship** Grain: 12,822 Compartments: 2 Ho, ER 2 Ha: ER Cranes: 2x60t Ice Capable	**1 oil engine** reduction geared to sc. shaft driving 1 CP propeller Total Power: 4,000kW (5,438hp) 14.8kn Bergens B32: 40L8P 1 x 4 Stroke 8 Cy. 320 x 400 4000kW (5438bhp) Rolls Royce Marine AS-Norway AuxGen: 1 x 555kW 440V 60Hz a.c, 2 x 324kW 440V 60Hz a.c Fuel: 610.0
8913526 *9V9625* -	**THOR DYNAMIC** *ex* Asante *-2004* *ex* Great Lake *-1999* **Thoresen Shipping Singapore Pte Ltd** - SatCom: Inmarsat C 456629610 *Singapore* *Singapore* MMSI: 566296000 Official number: 397377	25,905 13,656 43,497 T/cm 49.0	Class: BV (NK) (NV)	**1991-04 Tsuneishi Shipbuilding Co Ltd — Fukuyama HS** Yd No: 647 Loa 185.84 (BB) Br ex - Dght 11.323 Lbp 177.00 Br md 30.40 Dpth 16.20 Welded, 1 dk	**(A21A2BC) Bulk Carrier** Grain: 53,594; Bale: 52,270 Compartments: 5 Ho, ER 5 Ha: (19.2 x 15.3)4 (20.8 x 15.3)ER Cranes: 4x30t Ice Capable	**1 oil engine** driving 1 FP propeller Total Power: 7,120kW (9,680hp) 14.0kn B&W 6L60MCE 1 x 2 Stroke 6 Cy. 600 x 1944 7120kW (9680bhp) Mitsui Engineering & Shipbuilding CLtd-Japan AuxGen: 3 x 330kW 440V 60Hz a.c Fuel: 276.0 (d.f.) 1574.0 (r.f.) 27.0pd
9074793 *9V9629* -	**THOR ENDEAVOUR** *ex* Royal Sea *-2005* *ex* Sanko Resource *-2000* **Thoresen Shipping Singapore Pte Ltd** - *Singapore* *Singapore* MMSI: 566295000 Official number: 397387	25,676 13,991 42,529 T/cm 49.1	Class: NK	**1995-04 Namura Shipbuilding Co Ltd — Imari SG** Yd No: 935 Loa 184.93 (BB) Br ex - Dght 11.535 Lbp 177.00 Br md 30.50 Dpth 16.20 Welded, 1 dk	**(A21A2BC) Bulk Carrier** Grain: 47,753; Bale: 46,536 Compartments: 8 Ho, ER 8 Ha: (8.8 x 13.0) (13.6 x 25.9)2 (12.8 x 25.9)3 (14.4 x 25.9) (8.8 x 16.2)ER Cranes: 4x30t	**1 oil engine** driving 1 FP propeller Total Power: 8,091kW (11,001hp) 14.5kn B&W 6S50MC 1 x 2 Stroke 6 Cy. 500 x 1910 8091kW (11001bhp) Hitachi Zosen Corp-Japan AuxGen: 3 x 560kW a.c Fuel: 1581.0 (r.f.) 27.8pd
9074781 *9V9630* -	**THOR ENERGY** *ex* Athena Sea *-2005* *ex* Sanko Request *-2000* **Thoresen Shipping Singapore Pte Ltd** - *Singapore* *Singapore* MMSI: 566298000 Official number: 397388	25,676 13,991 42,529 T/cm 49.1	Class: NK	**1994-11 Namura Shipbuilding Co Ltd — Imari SG** Yd No: 934 Loa 184.93 (BB) Br ex - Dght 11.535 Lbp 177.00 Br md 30.50 Dpth 16.20 Welded, 1 dk	**(A21A2BC) Bulk Carrier** Grain: 47,753; Bale: 46,536 Compartments: 8 Ho, ER 8 Ha: (8.8 x 13.0) (13.6 x 25.9)2 (12.8 x 25.9)3 (14.4 x 25.9) (8.8 x 16.2)ER Cranes: 4x30t	**1 oil engine** driving 1 FP propeller Total Power: 8,091kW (11,001hp) 14.5kn B&W 6S50MC 1 x 2 Stroke 6 Cy. 500 x 1910 8091kW (11001bhp) Hitachi Zosen Corp-Japan AuxGen: 4 x a.c Fuel: 1735.0 (r.f.)
9074822 *9V9624* -	**THOR ENTERPRISE** *ex* Sanko Ranger *-2004* **Thoresen Shipping Singapore Pte Ltd** - SatCom: Inmarsat C 456626610 *Singapore* *Singapore* MMSI: 566266000 Official number: 397376	25,676 13,991 42,529 T/cm 49.1	Class: NV (LR) (BV) (NK) Classed LR until 12/6/09	**1995-07 Namura Shipbuilding Co Ltd — Imari SG** Yd No: 938 Loa 184.93 (BB) Br ex 30.55 Dght 11.535 Lbp 177.00 Br md 30.50 Dpth 16.20 Welded, 1 dk	**(A21A2BC) Bulk Carrier** Grain: 51,035; Bale: 49,818 Compartments: 8 Ho, ER 8 Ha: (8.8 x 13.0) (13.6 x 25.9)2 (12.8 x 25.9)3 (14.4 x 25.9) (8.8 x 16.2)ER Cranes: 4x30t	**1 oil engine** driving 1 FP propeller Total Power: 8,562kW (11,641hp) 14.5kn B&W 6S50MC 1 x 2 Stroke 6 Cy. 500 x 1910 8562kW (11641bhp) Hitachi Zosen Corp-Japan AuxGen: 3 x 560kW 440V 60Hz a.c Boilers: AuxB (Comp) 7.0kgf/cm² (6.9bar)
9317341 *9V2183* -	**THOR FEARLESS** *ex* Simurgh *-2013* **Thoresen Shipping Singapore Pte Ltd** - *Singapore* *Singapore* MMSI: 566969000 Official number: 398714	31,385 17,161 54,881	Class: NK	**2005-11 Oshima Shipbuilding Co Ltd — Saikai NS** Yd No: 10400 Loa 189.99 (BB) Br ex - Dght 12.515 Lbp 185.79 Br md 32.26 Dpth 17.62 Welded, 1 dk	**(A21A2BC) Bulk Carrier** Double Hull Grain: 64,824; Bale: 64,391 Compartments: 5 Ho, ER 5 Ha: 3 (25.5 x 25.8) (19.1 x 25.8)ER (13.3 x 19.0) Cranes: 4x30t	**1 oil engine** driving 1 FP propeller Total Power: 8,208kW (11,160hp) 14.0kn B&W 6S50MC-C 1 x 2 Stroke 6 Cy. 500 x 2000 8208kW (11160bhp) Kawasaki Heavy Industries Ltd-Japan Fuel: 2488.0 (r.f.)
9424613 *9V9284* -	**THOR FORTUNE** - **Thor Fortune Shipping Pte Ltd** Thoresen & Co (Bangkok) Ltd *Singapore* *Singapore* MMSI: 564853000 Official number: 396873	31,487 16,730 54,123	Class: NK	**2011-06 Oshima Shipbuilding Co Ltd — Saikai NS** Yd No: 10608 Loa 189.99 (BB) Br ex - Dght 12.444 Lbp 185.79 Br md 32.26 Dpth 17.62 Welded, 1 dk	**(A21A2BC) Bulk Carrier** Double Hull Grain: 63,847; Bale: 63,358 Compartments: 5 Ho, ER 5 Ha: ER Cranes: 4x36t	**1 oil engine** driving 1 FP propeller Total Power: 8,208kW (11,160hp) 14.5kn MAN-B&W 6S50MC-C 1 x 2 Stroke 6 Cy. 500 x 2000 8208kW (11160bhp) Kawasaki Heavy Industries Ltd-Japan
9499967 *VREV4* -	**THOR FRIEND** - **Ocean Friend Corp Ltd** Pacific Ship Management Co Ltd *Hong Kong* *Hong Kong* MMSI: 477185300 Official number: HK-2321	8,545 3,848 11,878 T/cm 20.0	Class: NK	**2008-12 Higaki Zosen K.K. — Imabari** Yd No: 628 Loa 116.90 (BB) Br ex - Dght 8.864 Lbp 109.01 Br md 19.60 Dpth 14.00 Welded, 1 dk	**(A31A2GX) General Cargo Ship** Grain: 17,666; Bale: 17,023 Compartments: 2 Ho, 2 Tw Dk, ER 2 Ha: ER 2 (29.3 x 15.0) Cranes: 2x30.7t; Derricks: 1x30t	**1 oil engine** driving 1 FP propeller Total Power: 3,900kW (5,302hp) 13.5kn MAN-B&W 6L35MC 1 x 2 Stroke 6 Cy. 350 x 1050 3900kW (5302bhp) The Hanshin Diesel Works Ltd-Japan Fuel: 785.0
9424601 *9V8438* -	**THOR FRIENDSHIP** - **Thor Friendship Shipping Pte Ltd** Thoresen & Co (Bangkok) Ltd *Singapore* *Singapore* MMSI: 565155000 Official number: 395784	31,487 16,730 54,123	Class: NK	**2010-01 Oshima Shipbuilding Co Ltd — Saikai NS** Yd No: 10607 Loa 189.99 (BB) Br ex - Dght 12.444 Lbp 185.79 Br md 32.26 Dpth 17.62 Welded, 1 dk	**(A21A2BC) Bulk Carrier** Double Hull Grain: 63,847; Bale: 63,358 Compartments: 5 Ho, ER 5 Ha: ER Cranes: 4x36t	**1 oil engine** driving 1 FP propeller Total Power: 8,208kW (11,160hp) 14.5kn MAN-B&W 6S50MC-C 1 x 2 Stroke 6 Cy. 500 x 2000 8208kW (11160bhp) Kawasaki Heavy Industries Ltd-Japan AuxGen: 3 x 560kW a.c Fuel: 1920.0
9543897 *3EYV5* -	**THOR GLORY** - **Eastern Comet Maritime SA** P&F Marine Co Ltd *Panama* *Panama* MMSI: 354280000 Official number: 40507PEXT1	10,021 4,520 13,802	Class: NK	**2010-04 Honda Zosen — Saiki** Yd No: 1065 Loa 124.56 (BB) Br ex - Dght 9.166 Lbp 116.00 Br md 21.20 Dpth 14.00 Welded, 1 dk	**(A31A2GX) General Cargo Ship** Grain: 20,683; Bale: 19,621 TEU 538 Compartments: 2 Ho, 2 Tw Dk, ER 2 Ha: (41.3 x 15.0)ER (25.3 x 15.0) Cranes: 2x50t	**1 oil engine** driving 1 FP propeller Total Power: 4,200kW (5,710hp) 13.0kn MAN-B&W 6S35MC 1 x 2 Stroke 6 Cy. 350 x 1400 4200kW (5710bhp) Makita Corp-Japan AuxGen: 3 x 338kW a.c Thrusters: 1 Tunnel thruster (f) Fuel: 767.0 (r.f.)

IMO / Call sign	Name / Owner / Flag	Tonnage	Class	Builder / Dimensions	Type / Capacity	Machinery
7122699 *OWNT2* -	**THOR GUARDIAN** *ex* Gorm *-2006* *ex* Naleraq *-1996* *ex* Putford Dart *-1988* *ex* Boston Sea Dart *-1985* **P/F Thor** - *Hanstholm* *Denmark (DIS)* MMSI: 219587000 Official number: D3206	**334** 100 168	Class: NV (LR) ✠ Classed LR until 18/4/07	**1972-04 Hugh McLean & Sons Ltd. — Renfrew** Yd No: 5008 Converted From: Stern Trawler-1998 Converted From: Standby Safety Vessel-1988 Converted From: Stern Trawler-1984 Loa 35.97 Br ex 8.21 Dght 3.840 Lbp 30.79 Br md 8.18 Dpth 4.58 Welded, 1 dk	**(B22G20Y) Standby Safety Vessel** Passengers: berths: 15 Compartments: 1 Ho, ER 1 Ha: (1.8 x 1.2) Derricks: 1x2t	**1 oil engine** with clutches, flexible couplings & sr reverse geared to sc. shaft driving 1 CP propeller Total Power: 625kW (850hp) 8.0kn Alpha 5L23/30 1 x 4 Stroke 5 Cy. 225 x 300 625kW (850bhp) (new engine 1991) MAN B&W Diesel A/S-Denmark AuxGen: 1 x 144kW 415V 50Hz a.c, 1 x 116kW 415V 50Hz a.c, 1 x a.c Thrusters: 1 Tunnel thruster (f) Fuel: 38.0 (d.f.)
9137105 *9V9623* -	**THOR HARMONY** *ex* Ramin *-2004* *ex* Birte Oldendorff *-2002* **Thoresen Shipping Singapore Pte Ltd** - SatCom: Inmarsat C 456626510 *Singapore* *Singapore* MMSI: 566265000 Official number: 397375	**32,491** 13,221 47,111	Class: NV (BV)	**2001-03 P.T. PAL Indonesia — Surabaya** Yd No: 140 Converted From: General Cargo Ship-2009 Converted From: Open Hatch Cargo Ship-2007 Loa 195.00 (BB) Br ex 30.53 Dght 12.820 Lbp 185.00 Br md 30.50 Dpth 19.00 Welded, 1 dk	**(A21A2BC) Bulk Carrier** Grain: 60,836 TEU 1988 Compartments: 7 Ho, ER 7 Ha: (13.6 x 15.5) (12.8 x 20.5)3 (12.8 x 27.1) (19.2 x 27.1) (20.2 x 20.5)ER Cranes: 4x40t Ice Capable	**1 oil engine** driving 1 FP propeller Total Power: 12,269kW (16,681hp) 16.0kn B&W 6S60MC 1 x 2 Stroke 6 Cy. 600 x 2292 12269kW (16681bhp) Hyundai Heavy Industries Co Ltd-South Korea AuxGen: 3 x 1000kW a.c Thrusters: 1 Thwart. FP thruster (f)
5221491 *DKQH* -	**THOR HEYERDAHL** *ex* Minnow *-1982* *ex* Silke *-1977* *ex* Marga Henning *-1965* *ex* Tinka *-1959* **Segelschiff 'Thor Heyerdahl' eV** - *Kiel* *Germany* MMSI: 211232340	*211* 118 315	Class: (GL)	**1931 E.J. Smit & Zoon's Scheepswerven N.V. — Westerbroek** Converted From: General Cargo Ship Rebuilt-2009 Lengthened-1951 Loa 49.80 Br ex 6.53 Dght 2.210 Lbp - Br md 6.48 Dpth 2.80 Riveted, 1 dk	**(A37B2PS) Passenger Ship** Passengers: berths: 28	**1 oil engine** driving 1 FP propeller Total Power: 294kW (400hp) 8.0kn Deutz RV6M436 1 x 4 Stroke 6 Cy. 240 x 360 294kW (400bhp) (new engine 1952) Kloeckner Humboldt Deutz AG-West Germany AuxGen: 2 x a.c
9137117 *9VNV8* -	**THOR HORIZON** *ex* Beautiful Queen *-2007* *ex* Eboni *-2005* *launched as* Tete Oldendorff *-2002* **Thor Horizon Shipping Pte Ltd** Thoresen & Co (Bangkok) Ltd *Singapore* *Singapore* MMSI: 565364000 Official number: 392598	**32,491** 14,955 47,119	Class: BV (LR) (NV) (GL) Classed LR until 27/5/09	**2002-10 P.T. PAL Indonesia — Surabaya** Yd No: 141 Converted From: General Cargo Ship-2009 Converted From: Open Hatch Cargo Ship-2007 Loa 195.00 (BB) Br ex - Dght 12.840 Lbp 185.05 Br md 30.49 Dpth 19.00 Welded, 1 dk	**(A21A2BC) Bulk Carrier** Grain: 59,905; Bale: 58,581 TEU 1988 Compartments: 7 Ho, ER 7 Ha: ER Cranes: 4x40t Ice Capable	**1 oil engine** driving 1 FP propeller Total Power: 12,240kW (16,642hp) 16.0kn B&W 6S60MC 1 x 2 Stroke 6 Cy. 600 x 2292 12240kW (16642bhp) Hyundai Heavy Industries Co Ltd-South Korea AuxGen: 3 x 960kW 440V 60Hz a.c Boilers: e (ex.g.) 10.0kgf/cm² (9.8bar), AuxB (o.f.) 10.0kgf/cm² (9.8bar) Thrusters: 1 Tunnel thruster (f)
8876481 *LDUF* -	**THOR III** - **Drammen Port Authority** Bukser og Berging AS *Drammen* *Norway* MMSI: 257062600 Official number: 15404	**292** 87 -	Class: NV	**1960-11 A.M. Liaaen Skipsverft & Mek. Verksted — Aalesund** Yd No: 98 Loa 35.07 Br ex - Dght 4.550 Lbp 30.84 Br md 9.32 Dpth 4.50 Welded, 1 dk	**(B32A2ST) Tug** Ice Capable	**1 oil engine** driving 1 FP propeller Total Power: 1,052kW (1,430hp) Sulzer 1 x 1052kW (1430bhp) Sulzer Bros Ltd-Switzerland
9222510 *9V9088* -	**THOR INDEPENDENCE** *ex* Yasa H. Mehmet *-2010* **Thoresen Shipping Singapore Pte Ltd** - *Singapore* *Singapore* MMSI: 564731000 Official number: 396614	**30,303** 17,734 52,407 T/cm 55.5	Class: NK	**2001-10 Tsuneishi Heavy Industries (Cebu) Inc — Balamban** Yd No: SC-029 Loa 189.99 (BB) Br ex - Dght 12.024 Lbp 182.00 Br md 32.26 Dpth 17.00 Welded, 1 dk	**(A21A2BC) Bulk Carrier** Grain: 67,756; Bale: 65,601 Compartments: 5 Ho, ER 5 Ha: (20.4 x 18.4)4 (21.3 x 18.4)ER Cranes: 4x30t	**1 oil engine** driving 1 FP propeller Total Power: 7,800kW (10,605hp) 14.5kn B&W 6S50MC 1 x 2 Stroke 6 Cy. 500 x 1910 7800kW (10605bhp) Mitsui Engineering & Shipbuilding CLtd-Japan Fuel: 2170.0
9238466 *9V9071* -	**THOR INFINITY** *ex* Yasa H. Mulla *-2010* **Thoresen Shipping Singapore Pte Ltd** - *Singapore* *Singapore* MMSI: 564724000 Official number: 396594	**30,303** 17,734 52,383 T/cm 55.5	Class: NK	**2002-02 Tsuneishi Heavy Industries (Cebu) Inc — Balamban** Yd No: SC-027 Loa 189.99 (BB) Br ex - Dght 12.024 Lbp 182.00 Br md 32.26 Dpth 17.00 Welded, 1 dk	**(A21A2BC) Bulk Carrier** Grain: 67,756; Bale: 65,601 Compartments: 5 Ho, ER 5 Ha: (20.4 x 18.4)4 (21.3 x 18.4)ER Cranes: 4x30t	**1 oil engine** driving 1 FP propeller Total Power: 7,800kW (10,605hp) 14.3kn B&W 6S50MC 1 x 2 Stroke 6 Cy. 500 x 1910 7800kW (10605bhp) Mitsui Engineering & Shipbuilding CLtd-Japan Fuel: 2170.0
9298533 *9V7082* -	**THOR INSUVI** *ex* Treasure Island *-2012* **Thoresen Shipping Singapore Pte Ltd** Thoresen & Co (Bangkok) Ltd *Singapore* *Singapore* MMSI: 566636000 Official number: 398096	**30,051** 17,738 52,489 T/cm 55.5	Class: NK	**2005-11 Tsuneishi Heavy Industries (Cebu) Inc — Balamban** Yd No: SC-053 Loa 189.99 Br ex - Dght 12.022 Lbp 182.00 Br md 32.26 Dpth 17.00 Welded, 1 dk	**(A21A2BC) Bulk Carrier** Grain: 67,756; Bale: 65,601 Compartments: 5 Ho, ER 5 Ha: 4 (21.3 x 18.4)ER (20.4 x 18.4) Cranes: 4x30t	**1 oil engine** driving 1 FP propeller Total Power: 7,800kW (10,605hp) 14.5kn B&W 6S50MC 1 x 2 Stroke 6 Cy. 500 x 1910 7800kW (10605bhp) Mitsui Engineering & Shipbuilding CLtd-Japan Fuel: 2150.0
9222493 *9V9627* -	**THOR INTEGRITY** *ex* Century Sea *-2004* **Thoresen Shipping Singapore Pte Ltd** - *Singapore* *Singapore* MMSI: 566274000 Official number: 397385	**30,008** 17,843 52,375 T/cm 55.5	Class: BV	**2001-04 Tsuneishi Heavy Industries (Cebu) Inc — Balamban** Yd No: SC-019 Loa 190.00 Br ex - Dght 12.000 Lbp 182.00 Br md 32.26 Dpth 17.00 Welded, 1 dk	**(A21A2BC) Bulk Carrier** Grain: 67,500; Bale: 65,601 Compartments: 5 Ho, ER 5 Ha: 4 (21.2 x 18.4)ER (20.4 x 18.4) Cranes: 4x33t	**1 oil engine** driving 1 FP propeller Total Power: 8,562kW (11,641hp) 14.5kn B&W 6S50MC 1 x 2 Stroke 6 Cy. 500 x 1910 8562kW (11641bhp) Mitsui Engineering & Shipbuilding CLtd-Japan
9303041 *9V2628* -	**THOR MAGNHILD** *ex* Ikan Serong *-2014* **Thoresen Shipping Singapore Pte Ltd** Thoresen & Co (Bangkok) Ltd *Singapore* *Singapore* MMSI: 564415000 Official number: 399241	**31,247** 18,504 56,023 T/cm 55.8	Class: NK	**2006-06 Mitsui Eng. & SB. Co. Ltd. — Tamano** Yd No: 1614 Loa 189.99 (BB) Br ex - Dght 12.575 Lbp 182.00 Br md 32.26 Dpth 17.90 Welded, 1 dk	**(A21A2BC) Bulk Carrier** Grain: 70,811; Bale: 68,084 Compartments: 5 Ho, ER 5 Ha: 4 (21.1 x 18.9)ER (17.6 x 18.9) Cranes: 4x30.5t	**1 oil engine** driving 1 FP propeller Total Power: 9,480kW (12,889hp) 14.5kn MAN-B&W 6S50MC-C 1 x 2 Stroke 6 Cy. 500 x 2000 9480kW (12889bhp) Mitsui Engineering & Shipbuilding CLtd-Japan AuxGen: 3 x 475kW a.c Fuel: 2510.0
9300221 *9V2557* -	**THOR MERCURY** *ex* Medi Chennai *-2014* **Thoresen Shipping Singapore Pte Ltd** - *Singapore* *Singapore* MMSI: 564220000	**30,822** 18,103 55,862 T/cm 56.1	Class: AB (Class contemplated) RI (NK)	**2005-10 Kawasaki Shipbuilding Corp — Kobe HG** Yd No: 1560 Loa 189.90 (BB) Br ex - Dght 12.522 Lbp 185.00 Br md 32.26 Dpth 17.80 Welded, 1 dk	**(A21A2BC) Bulk Carrier** Grain: 69,450; Bale: 66,368 Compartments: 5 Ho, ER 5 Ha: 4 (20.5 x 18.6)ER (17.8 x 18.6) Cranes: 4x30.5t	**1 oil engine** driving 1 FP propeller Total Power: 8,201kW (11,150hp) 14.6kn MAN-B&W 6S50MC-C 1 x 2 Stroke 6 Cy. 500 x 2000 8201kW (11150bhp) Kawasaki Heavy Industries Ltd-Japan Fuel: 1790.0
9487823 *OZ2065* -	**THOR OMEGA** - **P/F Thor** - *Hosvik* *Faeroe Islands (Danish)* MMSI: 231085000	**1,061** 318 1,575	Class: NV	**2008-09 p/f Torshavnar Skipasmidja — Torshavn** Yd No: 57 Loa 55.10 (BB) Br ex - Dght 5.000 Lbp 50.56 Br md 12.50 Dpth 5.50 Welded, 1 dk	**(B21B20T) Offshore Tug/Supply Ship** Passengers: 34; berths: 16 Cranes: 1x5t	**4 diesel electric oil engines** driving 4 gen. each 440kW 440V a.c Connecting to 2 elec. motors each (650kW) driving 2 Azimuth electric drive units Total Power: 1,876kW (2,552hp) 9.0kn Scania DI16 M 4 x Vee 4 Stroke 8 Cy. 127 x 154 each-469kW (638bhp) Scania AB-Sweden Thrusters: 1 Water jet (centre) Fuel: 550.0 (d.f.) 990.0 (r.f.) 8.0pd
7816862 *J8B2998* -	**THOR PIONEER** *ex* Skude Pioneer *-2004* *ex* Leifur Eiriksson *-1995* *ex* Britannia Champion *-1994* *ex* Suffolk Champion *-1989* **P/F Thor** - *Kingstown* *St Vincent & The Grenadines* MMSI: 377697000 Official number: 9470	**362** 108 282	Class: NV (LR) ✠ Classed LR until 20/3/10	**1980-02 Richards (Shipbuilders) Ltd — Great Yarmouth** Yd No: 546 Converted From: Stern Trawler-1984 Loa 33.23 Br ex 9.22 Dght 4.041 Lbp 29.01 Br md 9.16 Dpth 4.78 Welded, 1 dk	**(B22G20Y) Standby Safety Vessel** Passengers: berths: 19	**1 oil engine** reduction geared to sc. shaft driving 1 CP propeller Total Power: 1,000kW (1,360hp) 10.0kn Caterpillar 3512B-TA 1 x Vee 4 Stroke 12 Cy. 170 x 190 1000kW (1360bhp) (new engine 1999) Caterpillar Inc-USA AuxGen: 2 x 64kW 440V 50Hz a.c, 1 x 180kW 440V 50Hz a.c Thrusters: 1 Thwart. CP thruster (f) Fuel: 220.0 (d.f.)
8971633 *V3MZ8* -	**THOR PROVIDER** *ex* Isa Reis *-2005* *ex* Frigo *-2000* **P/F Thor** - *Belize City* *Belize* MMSI: 312641000 Official number: 100510017	**386** 116 533	Class: BV (Class contemplated)	**2000 Torgem Gemi Insaat Sanayii ve Ticaret a.s. — Tuzla, Istanbul** Converted From: Refrigerated Cargo Ship-2005 Loa 46.00 Br ex - Dght 4.300 Lbp 41.20 Br md 9.00 Dpth 4.73 Welded, 1 dk	**(B31A2SR) Research Survey Vessel** Passengers: cabins: 13; berths: 14 Bale: 329 Compartments: 2 Ho, ER 1 Ha: ER Cranes: 1x3t	**2 oil engines** reduction geared to sc. shafts driving 2 FP propellers Total Power: 956kW (1,300hp) 8.0kn GUASCOR 2 x 4 Stroke each-478kW (650bhp) Gutierrez Ascunce Corp (GUASCOR)-Spain AuxGen: 2 x 140kW a.c Fuel: 370.0 (d.f.) 5.0pd

8325262 *OZDW2* -	**THOR R** *ex* Whale *-1990* **RN Shipping A/S** Rohde Nielsen A/S *Esbjerg* *Denmark (DIS)* MMSI: 219573000 Official number: D3576	**2,147** 644 2,087	Class: GL (BV)	**1984-09 IHC Sliedrecht BV — Sliedrecht** Yd No: C01170 Loa 78.95 Br ex 14.10 Dght 3.820 Lbp 74.99 Br md 14.01 Dpth 4.91 Welded, 1 dk	**(B33B2DT) Trailing Suction Hopper Dredger** Hopper: 2,507	**2 oil engines** sr geared to sc. shafts driving 2 CP propellers Total Power: 2,880kW (3,916hp) 11.4kn Wartsila 8L20 2 x 4 Stroke 8 Cy. 200 x 280 each-1440kW (1958bhp) (new engine 2005) AuxGen: 2 x 75kW 220/380V a.c Thrusters: 1 Tunnel thruster (f)
7710549 *V3UQ4* -	**THOR SERVER** *ex* Hamour *-2003* *ex* Ara *-1998* *ex* Al-Mojil XVIII *-1997* *ex* Al-Jubail VIII *-1985* **P/F Thor** - *Belize City* *Belize* MMSI: 312952000 Official number: 130110562	**278** 83 247	Class: AB	**1978-03 Marine Builders Pte Ltd — Singapore** Yd No: 1016 Converted From: Tug-2003 Loa 34.00 Br ex - Dght 3.500 Lbp 32.52 Br md 8.51 Dpth 3.51 Welded, 1 dk	**(B22A20R) Offshore Support Vessel**	**2 oil engines** reverse reduction geared to sc. shafts driving 2 FP propellers Total Power: 1,074kW (1,460hp) 9.5kn Mitsubishi S6R2-MPTK 2 x 4 Stroke 6 Cy. 170 x 220 each-537kW (730bhp) (new engine 2002) Mitsubishi Heavy Industries Ltd-Japan AuxGen: 2 x 62kW 415V 50Hz a.c Fuel: 210.0 (d.f.) 2.5pd
7700594 *V3NV5* -	**THOR SKANDIA** *ex* Crystal Ice *-2012* *ex* Ocean Therese *-2009* *ex* Skandia *-2003* *ex* Green Skandia *-1999* *ex* Skandia *-1996* *ex* Star Skandia *-1992* *ex* Skandia *-1991* *ex* Star Skandia *-1987* *ex* Coaster Conny *-1981* **P/F Thor** - *Belize City* *Belize* MMSI: 312930000 Official number: 700920001	**1,290** 473 1,150	Class: IV NV	**1978-06 Gravdal Skipsbyggeri — Sunde i Sunnhordland** Yd No: 369 Converted From: General Cargo Ship (with Ro-Ro Facility)-1997 Lengthened-1978 Loa 63.28 Br ex 11.03 Dght 4.112 Lbp 58.30 Br md 11.00 Dpth 8.02 Welded, 1 dk & S dk	**(A34A2GR) Refrigerated Cargo Ship** Ins: 2,076 TEU 32 C. 32/20' Compartments: 1 Ho, ER, 1 Tw Dk 1 Ha: (13.0 x 6.3)ER Cranes: 1x5t Ice Capable	**1 oil engine** reduction geared to sc. shaft driving 1 CP propeller Total Power: 828kW (1,126hp) 8.0kn Caterpillar 3512TA 1 x Vee 4 Stroke 12 Cy. 170 x 190 828kW (1126bhp) (new engine 1997) Caterpillar Inc-USA AuxGen: 2 x 82kW 220V 50Hz a.c Thrusters: 1 Thwart. FP thruster (f) Fuel: 100.0 (d.f.) 4.0pd
9530060 *PPXP* -	**THOR SUPPLIER** **Bram Offshore Transportes Maritimos Ltda** Opmar Servicos Maritimos Ltda *Itajai* *Brazil* MMSI: 710001520 Official number: 4430473897	**2,999** 1,434 4,725	Class: AB	**2009-09 Estaleiro Navship Ltda — Navegantes** Yd No: 112 Loa 84.73 Br ex - Dght 6.240 Lbp 81.69 Br md 18.29 Dpth 7.32 Welded, 1 dk	**(B21B20T) Offshore Tug/Supply Ship**	**2 oil engines** geared to sc. shafts driving 2 Directional propellers Total Power: 4,920kW (6,690hp) Caterpillar C280-8 2 x 4 Stroke 8 Cy. 280 x 300 each-2460kW (3345bhp) Caterpillar Inc-USA AuxGen: 2 x 2050kW a.c, 2 x 910kW a.c Thrusters: 1 Retract. directional thruster (f); 1 Tunnel thruster (f)
9369136 *VRCT2* -	**THOR THUNDER** *ex* Mishima *-2010* **Full Virtue Ltd** P&F Marine Co Ltd *Hong Kong* *Hong Kong* MMSI: 477791100 Official number: HK-1887	**9,881** 4,711 14,451 T/cm 22.0	Class: NK	**2007-04 Higaki Zosen K.K. — Imabari** Yd No: 601 Loa 127.66 (BB) Br ex 19.60 Dght 9.446 Lbp 119.50 Br md 19.60 Dpth 14.50 Welded, 1 dk	**(A31A2GX) General Cargo Ship** Grain: 20,145; Bale: 19,176 Compartments: 2 Ho, 2 Tw Dk, ER 2 Ha: (30.8 x 14.9)ER (31.5 x 14.9) Cranes: 2x30.8t; Derricks: 2x30t	**1 oil engine** driving 1 FP propeller Total Power: 4,200kW (5,710hp) 13.5kn MAN-B&W 6S35MC 1 x 2 Stroke 6 Cy. 350 x 1400 4200kW (5710bhp) The Hanshin Diesel Works Ltd-Japan AuxGen: 3 x 940kW a.c Fuel: 820.0
9139775 *9V9628* -	**THOR WAVE** *ex* Great Rainbow *-2004* **Thoresen Shipping Singapore Pte Ltd** - *Singapore* *Singapore* MMSI: 566289000 Official number: 397386	**25,889** 12,179 39,042	Class: AB BV (Class contemplated)	**1998-07 Jurong Shipyard Ltd — Singapore** Yd No: 1054 Loa 187.00 (BB) Br ex - Dght 10.900 Lbp 177.00 Br md 29.00 Dpth 16.00 Welded, 1 dk	**(A21A2BC) Bulk Carrier** Double Hull Grain: 45,067; Bale: 43,801 TEU 1581 C Ho 940 TEU C Dk 641 TEU Compartments: 5 Ho, ER 5 Ha: ER Cranes: 4x30t	**1 oil engine** driving 1 FP propeller Total Power: 8,562kW (11,641hp) 15.0kn B&W 6S50MC 1 x 2 Stroke 6 Cy. 500 x 1910 8562kW (11641bhp) Kawasaki Heavy Industries Ltd-Japan AuxGen: 3 x 840kW a.c Thrusters: 1 Thwart. FP thruster (f)
9146388 *9V9626* -	**THOR WIND** *ex* Great Fortune *-2004* **Thoresen Shipping Singapore Pte Ltd** Thoresen & Co (Bangkok) Ltd *Singapore* *Singapore* MMSI: 566275000 Official number: 397378	**25,889** 12,179 39,087	Class: BV (AB)	**1998-11 Jurong Shipyard Ltd — Singapore** Yd No: 1055 Loa 187.00 (BB) Br ex - Dght 11.420 Lbp 177.00 Br md 29.00 Dpth 16.00 Welded, 1 dk	**(A21A2BC) Bulk Carrier** Double Hull Grain: 45,067; Bale: 43,801 TEU 1581 C Ho 940 TEU C Dk 641 TEU Compartments: 5 Ho, ER 5 Ha: ER Cranes: 4x30t	**1 oil engine** driving 1 FP propeller Total Power: 8,562kW (11,641hp) 15.0kn B&W 6S50MC 1 x 2 Stroke 6 Cy. 500 x 1910 8562kW (11641bhp) Kawasaki Heavy Industries Ltd-Japan AuxGen: 3 x 840kW a.c Thrusters: 1 Thwart. FP thruster (f)
7347354 *GUVV* -	**THORA** **Government of The United Kingdom (Shetland Islands Council Ferry Services)** - *Lerwick* *United Kingdom* MMSI: 232003599 Official number: 361283	*147* 76 54	Class: (LR) ✠	**1975-09 p/f Torshavnar Skipasmidja — Torshavn** Yd No: 21 Loa 25.23 Br ex 7.88 Dght 2.083 Lbp 22.64 Br md 7.85 Dpth 3.20 Welded, 1 dk	**(A36A2PR) Passenger/Ro-Ro Ship (Vehicles)** Passengers: unberthed: 93 Bow door/ramp Len: 1.40 Wid: 4.50 Swl: - Stern door/ramp Len: 1.40 Wid: 4.50 Swl: - Lane-Len: 46 Lane-Wid: 4.50 Lane-clr ht: 4.50 Cars: 10	**2 oil engines** sr geared to sc. shafts driving 2 CP propellers Total Power: 264kW (358hp) 8.5kn Kelvin TA6 2 x 4 Stroke 6 Cy. 165 x 184 each-132kW (179bhp) GEC Diesels Ltd.Kelvin Marine Div.-Glasgow AuxGen: 2 x 29kW 240V 50Hz a.c Thrusters: 1 Thwart. FP thruster (f) Fuel: 6.0 (d.f.)
8136831 - -	**THORA 51** **Scancey Trading Co Ltd** - *Colombo* *Sri Lanka* Official number: 1012	*202* 111 -		**1978 San Yang Shipbuilding Co., Ltd. — Kaohsiung** Loa - Br ex 6.51 Dght 3.301 Lbp 31.50 Br md - Dpth - Welded, 1 dk	**(B11B2FV) Fishing Vessel**	**1 oil engine** driving 1 FP propeller Total Power: 441kW (600hp) 10.0kn Matsui MU623BHS 1 x 4 Stroke 6 Cy. 230 x 380 441kW (600bhp) Matsui Iron Works Co Ltd-Japan
8136843 - -	**THORA 52** **Scancey Trading Co Ltd** - *Colombo* *Sri Lanka*	*202* 111 -		**1978 San Yang Shipbuilding Co., Ltd. — Kaohsiung** Loa - Br ex 6.51 Dght 3.301 Lbp 31.50 Br md - Dpth - Welded, 1 dk	**(B11B2FV) Fishing Vessel**	**1 oil engine** driving 1 FP propeller Total Power: 441kW (600hp) 10.0kn Matsui MU623BHS 1 x 4 Stroke 6 Cy. 230 x 380 441kW (600bhp) Matsui Iron Works Co Ltd-Japan
9056789 *LMHU* -	**THORAX** **Bugsertjeneste II AS KS** Ostensjo Rederi AS *Haugesund* *Norway* MMSI: 258313000	**1,229** 368 733	Class: NV	**1993-04 SIMEK AS — Flekkefjord** Yd No: 83 Loa 45.48 Br ex 15.00 Dght 6.180 Lbp 40.07 Br md 13.80 Dpth 7.60 Welded, 1 dk	**(B32A2ST) Tug** Passengers: cabins: 10	**2 oil engines** with clutches, flexible couplings & sr geared to sc. shafts driving 2 Directional propellers Total Power: 5,280kW (7,178hp) 11.0kn Wichmann 8V28B 2 x Vee 4 Stroke 8 Cy. 280 x 360 each-2640kW (3589bhp) Wartsila Wichmann Diesel AS-Norway AuxGen: 1 x 750kW 380V 50Hz a.c, 2 x 232kW 380V 50Hz a.c Thrusters: 1 Thwart. CP thruster (f) Fuel: 382.0 (d.f.) 16.0pd
9392614 *VRCM6* -	**THORCO ACE** *ex* Thor Ace *-2012* **Thorco Ace K/S** Thorco Shipping A/S *Hong Kong* *Hong Kong* MMSI: 477656400 Official number: HK-1835	**9,684** 3,810 12,121	Class: NK	**2007-01 Honda Zosen — Saiki** Yd No: 1050 Loa 120.00 (BB) Br ex - Dght 8.510 Lbp 111.50 Br md 21.20 Dpth 14.30 Welded, 1 dk	**(A31A2GX) General Cargo Ship** Grain: 20,576; Bale: 19,888 Compartments: 2 Ho, 2 Tw Dk, ER 2 Ha: ER 2 (29.3 x 15.0) Cranes: 2x30.5t; Derricks: 2x25t	**1 oil engine** driving 1 FP propeller Total Power: 3,900kW (5,302hp) 12.5kn MAN-B&W 6L35MC 1 x 2 Stroke 6 Cy. 350 x 1050 3900kW (5302bhp) Makita Corp-Japan Fuel: 890.0
9448451 *V2DM6* -	**THORCO ADVENTURE** *ex* Nina Scan *-2013* *ex* BBC New York *-2011* *ex* Beluga Nation *-2009* *launched as* Dutch Carina *-2009* **Bremer Lloyd Schiffahrtsgesellschaft mbH & Co KG ms 'Johann von Bremen'** Bremer Lloyd Reederei GmbH & Co KG *Saint John's* *Antigua & Barbuda* MMSI: 305266000 Official number: 4480	**6,351** 3,617 9,851	Class: GL (BV)	**2009-03 Qingdao Heshun Shipyard Co Ltd — Qingdao SD** (Hull) Yd No: HS-8501 **2009-03 Volharding Shipyards B.V. — Foxhol** Yd No: 634 Loa 132.20 (BB) Br ex 15.90 Dght 7.780 Lbp 124.56 Br md 15.87 Dpth 9.65 Welded, 1 dk	**(A31A2GX) General Cargo Ship** Grain: 11,831 TEU 474 C Ho 264 TEU C Dk 210 TEU Compartments: 2 Ho, ER 2 Ha: (52.5 x 13.2)ER (40.0 x 13.2) Cranes: 2x60t Ice Capable	**1 oil engine** geared to sc. shaft driving 1 CP propeller Total Power: 3,840kW (5,221hp) 14.8kn MaK 8M32C 1 x 4 Stroke 8 Cy. 320 x 480 3840kW (5221bhp) Caterpillar Motoren GmbH & Co. KG-Germany AuxGen: 1 x 555kW 440/230V 60Hz a.c, 2 x 324kW 440/230V 60Hz a.c Thrusters: 1 Tunnel thruster (f) Fuel: 53.0 (d.f.) 620.0 (r.f.) 16.0pd
9543926 *VRHP6* -	**THORCO AFRICA** **Thor Ship II K/S** Thorco Shipping A/S *Hong Kong* *Hong Kong* MMSI: 477962800 Official number: HK-2902	**9,721** 3,733 12,022	Class: NK	**2010-10 Honda Zosen — Saiki** Yd No: 1067 Loa 120.00 (BB) Br ex - Dght 8.614 Lbp 111.50 Br md 21.19 Dpth 14.30 Welded, 1 dk	**(A31A2GX) General Cargo Ship** Grain: 19,957; Bale: 18,738 TEU 84 Compartments: 2 Ho, 2 Tw Dk, ER 2 Ha: ER 2 (29.3 x 15.0) Cranes: 2x78t	**1 oil engine** driving 1 FP propeller Total Power: 3,900kW (5,302hp) 12.5kn MAN-B&W 6L35MC 1 x 2 Stroke 6 Cy. 350 x 1050 3900kW (5302bhp) Makita Corp-Japan

9559884 **THORCO ALLIANCE**
V2FW3 *ex* Velocity Scan *-2012*
\- *launched as* Sinus Iridium *-2012*
MarShip GmbH & Co KG ms 'Sinus Iridium'
MarShip GmbH
Saint John's *Antigua & Barbuda*
MMSI: 305822000

6,351 Class: BV
3,617
9,677

2012-03 Jiangsu Yangzi Changbo Shipbuilding Co Ltd — Jingjiang JS (Hull) Yd No: 07-018
2012-03 Volharding Shipyards B.V. — Foxhol
Yd No: 700
Loa 132.20 (BB) Br ex 15.90 Dght 7.780
Lbp 124.56 Br md 15.87 Dpth 9.65
Welded, 1 dk

(A31A2GX) General Cargo Ship
Grain: 12,822
TEU 468 C Ho 258 TEU C Dk 210 TEU incl 20 ref C
Compartments: 2 Ho, ER
2 Ha: ER
Cranes: 2x60t
Ice Capable

1 oil engine reduction geared to sc. shaft driving 1 CP propeller
Total Power: 4,000kW (5,438hp) 14.8kn
Bergens B32: 40L8P
1 x 4 Stroke 8 Cy. 320 x 400 4000kW (5438bhp)
Rolls Royce Marine AS-Norway
AuxGen: 2 x 324kW 60Hz a.c, 1 x 555kW 60Hz a.c
Thrusters: 1 Tunnel thruster (f)
Fuel: 60.0 (d.f.) 541.0 (r.f.)

9484247 **THORCO AMBER**
V2QL8 *ex* Enya *-2012*
\- **TS Thorco Amber Ltd**
Reedereiverwaltung Heino Winter GmbH & Co KG
Saint John's *Antigua & Barbuda*
MMSI: 305703000

6,351 Class: BV
3,617
9,862

2011-08 Qingdao Heshun Shipyard Co Ltd — Qingdao SD (Hull) Yd No: HS-8506
2011-08 Volharding Shipyards B.V. — Foxhol
Yd No: 660
Loa 132.20 (BB) Br ex 15.90 Dght 7.780
Lbp 124.56 Br md 15.87 Dpth 11.16
Welded, 1 dk

(A31A2GX) General Cargo Ship
Grain: 12,822
TEU 474 C HO 264 TEU C dk 210 TEU
Compartments: 2 Tw Dk, ER, 2 Ho
2 Ha: (52.9 x 13.6)ER (40.4 x 13.6)
Cranes: 2x40t
Ice Capable

1 oil engine geared to sc. shaft driving 1 CP propeller
Total Power: 3,840kW (5,221hp) 14.8kn
MaK 8M32C
1 x 4 Stroke 8 Cy. 320 x 480 3840kW (5221bhp)
Caterpillar Motoren GmbH & Co. KG-Germany
AuxGen: 1 x 555kW 400V 60Hz a.c, 2 x 324kW 400V 60Hz a.c
Thrusters: 1 Tunnel thruster (f)
Fuel: 50.0 (d.f.) 589.0 (r.f.) 16.0pd

9356414 **THORCO AMBITION**
V2BS2 *ex* Beluga Navigation *-2011*
\- *ex* BBC Trinidad *-2009*
launched as Beluga Navigation *-2006*
ms 'Marie' Shipping Gmbh & Co KG
Thorco Shipping A/S
Saint John's *Antigua & Barbuda*
MMSI: 304909000

6,296 Class: BV
3,617
9,775

2006-08 Volharding Shipyards B.V. — Foxhol
Yd No: 626
Loa 132.20 (BB) Br ex - Dght 7.730
Lbp 123.84 Br md 15.87 Dpth 9.65
Welded, 1 dk

(A31A2GX) General Cargo Ship
Grain: 12,813
TEU 474 C Ho 264 TEU C Dk 210 TEU incl 20 ref C
Compartments: 2 Ho, ER
2 Ha: (52.5 x 13.2)ER (40.0 x 13.2)
Cranes: 2x40t

1 oil engine reduction geared to sc. shaft driving 1 CP propeller
Total Power: 3,840kW (5,221hp) 14.8kn
MaK 8M32
1 x 4 Stroke 8 Cy. 320 x 480 3840kW (5221bhp)
Caterpillar Motoren GmbH & Co. KG-Germany
AuxGen: 2 x 315kW 60Hz a.c, 1 x 312kW 440/230V 60Hz a.c
Thrusters: 1 Tunnel thruster (f)
Fuel: 50.1 (d.f.) 590.6 (r.f.) 18.0pd

9484209 **THORCO ARCTIC**
V2DX6 *ex* BBC Newcastle *-2011*
\- *ex* Beluga Notion *-2011*
launched as Dutch Regina *-2009*
ms 'Dutch Regina' Shipping GmbH & Co KG
MarShip Bereederungs GmbH & Co KG
Saint John's *Antigua & Barbuda*
MMSI: 305367000

6,351 Class: BV
3,617
9,775

2009-12 Qingdao Heshun Shipyard Co Ltd — Qingdao SD (Hull) Yd No: HS-8503
2009-12 Volharding Shipyards B.V. — Foxhol
Yd No: 657
Loa 132.20 (BB) Br ex 15.90 Dght 7.780
Lbp 124.56 Br md 15.87 Dpth 9.65
Welded, 1 dk

(A31A2GX) General Cargo Ship
Grain: 12,822
TEU 474 C Ho 264 TEU C Dk 210 TEU
Compartments: 2 Ho, ER
2 Ha: ER 2 (40.0 x 13.2)
Cranes: 2x40t
Ice Capable

1 oil engine geared to sc. shaft driving 1 CP propeller
Total Power: 3,840kW (5,221hp) 14.8kn
MaK 8M32C
1 x 4 Stroke 8 Cy. 320 x 480 3840kW (5221bhp)
Caterpillar Motoren GmbH & Co. KG-Germany
AuxGen: 1 x 648kW 440/230V 60Hz a.c, 2 x 315kW 440/230V 60Hz a.c
Thrusters: 1 Tunnel thruster (f)
Fuel: 50.0 (d.f.) 590.6 (r.f.) 16.0pd

9484235 **THORCO ATLANTIC**
V2QL7 *ex* Rocco *-2011* *ex* Beluga Notification *-2011*
\- *launched as* Dutch Katja *-2010*
ex Volharding 659 *-2009*
KG Schifffahrtsgesellschaft ms Rocco mbH & Co
Reedereiverwaltung Heino Winter GmbH & Co KG
SatCom: Inmarsat C 430566911
Saint John's *Antigua & Barbuda*
MMSI: 305669000
Official number: 3128

6,351 Class: BV
3,617
9,700

2010-12 Qingdao Heshun Shipyard Co Ltd — Qingdao SD (Hull) Yd No: HS-8505
2010-12 Volharding Shipyards B.V. — Foxhol
Yd No: 659
Loa 132.20 (BB) Br ex 15.90 Dght 7.780
Lbp 124.56 Br md 15.87 Dpth 9.65
Welded, 1 dk

(A31A2GX) General Cargo Ship
Grain: 12,822
TEU 474 C HO 264 TEU C Dk 210 TEU
Compartments: 2 Ho, ER, 2 Tw Dk
2 Ha: (52.9 x 13.6)ER (40.4 x 13.6)
Cranes: 2x40t
Ice Capable

1 oil engine reduction geared to sc. shaft driving 1 CP propeller
Total Power: 3,840kW (5,221hp) 14.8kn
MaK 8M32C
1 x 4 Stroke 8 Cy. 320 x 480 3840kW (5221bhp)
Caterpillar Motoren GmbH & Co. KG-Germany
AuxGen: 1 x 650kW 440/230V 60Hz a.c, 2 x 315kW 440/230V 60Hz a.c
Thrusters: 1 Tunnel thruster (f)
Fuel: 50.0 (d.f.) 589.0 (r.f.) 16.0pd

9484194 **THORCO ATLAS**
V2DX5 *ex* Nikita Scan *-2013* *ex* BBC Niteroi *-2011*
\- *completed as* Beluga Negotiation *-2009*
ex Dutch Maren *-2009*
Johann Philipp Specht Schiffahrtsgesellschaft mbH & Co KG
Bremer Lloyd Reederei GmbH & Co KG
SatCom: Inmarsat C 430536610
Saint John's *Antigua & Barbuda*
MMSI: 305366000

6,351 Class: GL (BV)
3,617
9,813

2009-07 Qingdao Heshun Shipyard Co Ltd — Qingdao SD (Hull) Yd No: HS-8502
2009-07 Volharding Shipyards B.V. — Foxhol
Yd No: 656
Loa 132.20 (BB) Br ex 15.90 Dght 7.780
Lbp 124.56 Br md 15.87 Dpth 9.65
Welded, 1 dk

(A31A2GX) General Cargo Ship
Grain: 11,831
TEU 474 C Ho 264 TEU C Dk 210 TEU
Compartments: ER, 1 Tw Dk, 3 Ho
2 Ha: (52.9 x 13.6)ER (40.4 x 13.6)
Cranes: 2x60t
Ice Capable

1 oil engine geared to sc. shaft driving 1 CP propeller
Total Power: 3,840kW (5,221hp) 14.8kn
MaK 8M32C
1 x 4 Stroke 8 Cy. 320 x 480 3840kW (5221bhp)
Caterpillar Motoren GmbH & Co. KG-Germany
AuxGen: 1 x 648kW 440/230V 60Hz a.c, 2 x 315kW 440/230V 60Hz a.c
Thrusters: 1 Tunnel thruster (f)
Fuel: 53.0 (d.f.) 620.0 (r.f.) 16.0pd

9356402 **THORCO ATTRACTION**
V2BS1 *ex* Nomination *-2011*
\- *ex* Beluga Nomination *-2011*
ex BBC Ireland *-2009*
launched as Beluga Nomination *-2006*
ms 'Dutch Neele' Shipping GmbH & Co KG
MarShip Bereederungs GmbH & Co KG
Saint John's *Antigua & Barbuda*
MMSI: 304908000

6,296 Class: BV
3,617
9,775

2006-03 Volharding Shipyards B.V. — Foxhol
Yd No: 625
Loa 132.20 (BB) Br ex - Dght 7.730
Lbp 123.84 Br md 15.87 Dpth 9.65
Welded, 1 dk

(A31A2GX) General Cargo Ship
Grain: 12,822
TEU 474 C Ho 264 TEU C Dk 210 TEU
Compartments: 2 Ho, ER
2 Ha: (52.5 x 13.2)ER (40.0 x 13.2)
Cranes: 2x40t

1 oil engine reduction geared to sc. shaft driving 1 CP propeller
Total Power: 3,840kW (5,221hp) 15.5kn
MaK 8M32
1 x 4 Stroke 8 Cy. 320 x 480 3840kW (5221bhp)
Caterpillar Motoren GmbH & Co. KG-Germany
AuxGen: 1 x 312kW 440/230V 60Hz a.c, 2 x 315kW 440/230V 60Hz a.c
Thrusters: 1 Tunnel thruster (f)
Fuel: 53.0 (d.f.) 620.0 (r.f.) 16.0pd

9559901 **THORCO AURORA**
V2FW7 *ex* Sinus Roris *-2012*
\- **MarShip GmbH & Co KG ms 'Sinus Roris'**
MarShip GmbH
Saint John's *Antigua & Barbuda*
MMSI: 305826000

6,351 Class: BV
3,617
9,688

2012-06 Jiangsu Yangzi Changbo Shipbuilding Co Ltd — Jingjiang JS (Hull) Yd No: 07-020
2012-06 Volharding Shipyards B.V. — Foxhol
Yd No: 702
Loa 132.20 Br ex 15.90 Dght 7.780
Lbp 124.56 Br md 15.87 Dpth 9.65
Welded, 1 dk

(A31A2GX) General Cargo Ship
Grain: 12,822
Compartments: 2 Ho, ER
2 Ha: ER
Cranes: 2x60t
Ice Capable

1 oil engine reduction geared to sc. shaft driving 1 CP propeller
Total Power: 4,000kW (5,438hp) 14.8kn
Bergens B32: 40L8P
1 x 4 Stroke 8 Cy. 320 x 400 4000kW (5438bhp)
Rolls Royce Marine AS-Norway
AuxGen: 1 x 555kW 60Hz a.c, 2 x 324kW 60Hz a.c
Fuel: 590.0

9484223 **THORCO AVANTGARDE**
V2ET5 *ex* BBC Naples *-2013* *ex* Beluga Novation *-2011*
\- *launched as* Dutch Verena *-2010*
ms 'Dutch Verena' Shipping GmbH & Co KG
Thorco Shipping A/S
Saint John's *Antigua & Barbuda*
MMSI: 305546000

6,351 Class: BV
3,617
9,755

2010-06 Qingdao Heshun Shipyard Co Ltd — Qingdao SD (Hull) Yd No: HS-8504
2010-06 Volharding Shipyards B.V. — Foxhol
Yd No: 658
Loa 132.20 (BB) Br ex 15.90 Dght 7.780
Lbp 124.56 Br md 15.87 Dpth 9.65
Welded, 1 dk

(A31A2GX) General Cargo Ship
Grain: 12,822
TEU 474 C Ho 264 TEU C Dk 210 TEU
Compartments: 2 Tw Dk, ER, 2 Ho
2 Ha: (52.9 x 13.6)ER (40.4 x 13.6)
Cranes: 2x40t
Ice Capable

1 oil engine reduction geared to sc. shaft driving 1 CP propeller
Total Power: 3,840kW (5,221hp) 14.8kn
MaK 8M32C
1 x 4 Stroke 8 Cy. 320 x 480 3840kW (5221bhp)
Caterpillar Motoren GmbH & Co. KG-Germany
AuxGen: 1 x 555kW 400/230V 60Hz a.c, 2 x 324kW 400/230V 60Hz a.c
Thrusters: 1 Tunnel thruster (f)
Fuel: 50.0 (d.f.) 570.0 (r.f.) 16.0pd

9258997 **THORCO CELEBRATION**
V2FU4 *ex* BBC Brazil *-2011* *ex* Ursula *-2005*
\- *completed as* Ile de Re *-2002*
ms 'Ile de Reunion' GmbH & Co KG
Reederei Eckhoff GmbH & Co KG
Saint John's *Antigua & Barbuda*
MMSI: 305798000
Official number: 4932

7,576 Class: GL
3,855
10,300
T/cm
21.0

2002-09 B.V. Scheepswerf Damen Hoogezand — Foxhol Yd No: 832
2003 Santierul Naval Damen Galati S.A. — Galati (Hull) Yd No: 1000
Loa 142.69 (BB) Br ex - Dght 7.330
Lbp 136.74 Br md 18.25 Dpth 10.15
Welded, 1 dk

(A31A2GX) General Cargo Ship
Grain: 14,695
TEU 668 C Ho 291 TEU C Dk 377 TEU incl 60 ref C.
Compartments: 2 Ho, ER
Cranes: 2x80t
Ice Capable

1 oil engine geared to sc. shaft driving 1 CP propeller
Total Power: 4,320kW (5,873hp) 14.7kn
MaK 9M32
1 x 4 Stroke 9 Cy. 320 x 480 4320kW (5873bhp)
Caterpillar Motoren GmbH & Co. KG-Germany
AuxGen: 3 x 350kW 380V a.c, 1 x 680kW 380V a.c
Thrusters: 1 Tunnel thruster (f)

9369095 **THORCO CHALLENGER**
V2FB8 *ex* Marina 1 *-2010* *ex* Clipper Marina *-2009*
\- *ex* Marina 1 *-2008*
MarShip GmbH & Co KG ms 'Sinus Fidei'
Thorco Shipping A/S
Saint John's *Antigua & Barbuda*
MMSI: 305315000
Official number: 3010

7,878 Class: LR
3,909 ✠ **100A1** SS 07/2013
11,200 strengthened for heavy cargoes, container cargoes in holds and on upper deck hatch covers
LI
Ice Class 1A FS at a draught of 7.574m
Max/min draught fwd 7.574/3.60m
Max/min draught aft 7.574/4.80m
Required power 3558kw, installed power 4320kw
✠ **LMC** **UMS**
Eq.Ltr: A†;
Cable: 522.0/50.0 U3 (a)

2008-07 Damen Shipyards Yichang Co Ltd — Yichang HB (Hull)
2008-07 B.V. Scheepswerf Damen — Gorinchem
Yd No: 567304
Loa 145.63 (BB) Br ex 18.29 Dght 7.450
Lbp 138.62 Br md 18.25 Dpth 10.30
Welded, 1 dk

(A31A2GX) General Cargo Ship
Grain: 14,878
TEU 671 C Ho 302 TEU C Dk 369 TEU incl 60 ref C.
Compartments: 2 Ho, ER
2 Ha: ER
Cranes: 2x80t
Ice Capable

1 oil engine with flexible couplings & sr reverse geared to sc. shaft driving 1 CP propeller
Total Power: 4,320kW (5,873hp) 14.2kn
MaK 9M32C
1 x 4 Stroke 9 Cy. 320 x 480 4320kW (5873bhp)
Caterpillar Motoren GmbH & Co. KG-Germany
AuxGen: 3 x 350kW 380V 50Hz a.c, 1 x 680kW 400V 50Hz a.c
Boilers: e (ex.g.) 10.2kgf/cm² (10.0bar), TOH (o.f.) 10.2kgf/cm² (10.0bar)
Thrusters: 1 Thwart. FP thruster (f)

IMO / Call sign	Name / Owner	Tonnage	Class	Builder / Dimensions	Type / Cargo	Machinery
9549592 *V2QM5* -	**THORCO CHILE** *ex* BBC Peru *-2013* **mv 'Tinnum' BV** Reederei Eckhoff GmbH & Co KG *Saint John's* *Antigua & Barbuda* MMSI: 305933000 Official number: 3134	**9,963** 4,937 13,524 T/cm 27.0	Class: LR ✠ **100A1** SS 12/2012 strengthened for heavy cargoes, container cargoes in holds and on upper deck hatch covers LI Ice Class 1A FS at draught of 8.450m Max/min draught fwd 8.450/3.82m Max/min draught aft 8.490/5.12m Required power 4488kw, installed power 6000kw ✠ **LMC** **UMS** Eq.Ltr: D†; Cable: 550.0/54.0 U3 (a)	**2012-12 Damen Shipyards Yichang Co Ltd — Yichang HB** (Hull) Yd No: 567504 **2012-12 B.V. Scheepswerf Damen — Gorinchem** Yd No: 567504 Loa 146.25 (BB) Br ex 20.20 Dght 8.250 Lbp 136.99 Br md 20.10 Dpth 11.45 Welded, 1 dk	**(A31A2GX) General Cargo Ship** Grain: 17,260; Bale: 17,260 TEU 712 C Ho 312 TEU C Dk 400 TEU incl 80 ref C Compartments: 2 Ho, ER 2 Ha: ER Cranes: 2x80t Ice Capable	**1 oil engine** with flexible couplings & sr geared to sc. shaft driving 1 CP propeller Total Power: 6,000kW (8,158hp) 15.5kn MaK 6M43C 1 x 4 Stroke 6 Cy. 430 x 610 6000kW (8158bhp) Caterpillar Motoren GmbH & Co. KG-Germany AuxGen: 3 x 460kW 400V 50Hz a.c, 1 x 1148kW 400V 50Hz a.c Boilers: TOH (ex.g.) 10.2kgf/cm² (10.0bar), TOH (o.f.) 10.2kgf/cm² (10.0bar) Thrusters: 1 Thwart. FP thruster (f)
9535591 *V2EY4* -	**THORCO CLAIRVAUX** *ex* STX Alpha *-2013* *ex* Rotes Kliff *-2010* **ms 'Rotes Kliff' GmbH & Co KG** Reederei Eckhoff GmbH & Co KG *Saint John's* *Antigua & Barbuda* MMSI: 305598000 Official number: 4763	**8,059** 3,909 10,872	Class: LR ✠ **100A1** SS 07/2010 strengthened for heavy cargoes, container cargoes in holds and on upper deck hatch covers LI Ice Class 1A FS at a draught of 7.574m Max/min draught fwd 7.574/3.60m Max/min draught aft 7.574/4.80m Required power 3558kw, installed power 4320kw ✠ **LMC** **UMS** Eq.Ltr: A†; Cable: 522.5/50.0 U3 (a)	**2010-07 Damen Shipyards Yichang Co Ltd — Yichang HB** (Hull) Yd No: 567309 **2010-07 B.V. Scheepswerf Damen — Gorinchem** Yd No: 567309 Loa 145.63 (BB) Br ex 18.33 Dght 7.400 Lbp 136.80 Br md 18.25 Dpth 10.30 Welded, 1 dk	**(A31A2GX) General Cargo Ship** Grain: 14,878 TEU 671 C Ho 302 TEU C Dk 369 TEU Compartments: 2 Ho, ER 2 Ha: ER Cranes: 2x80t Ice Capable	**1 oil engine** with flexible couplings & sr reverse geared to sc. shaft driving 1 CP propeller Total Power: 4,320kW (5,873hp) 14.2kn MaK 9M32C 1 x 4 Stroke 9 Cy. 320 x 480 4320kW (5873bhp) Caterpillar Motoren GmbH & Co. KG-Germany AuxGen: 3 x 350kW 400V 50Hz a.c, 1 x 760kW 400V 50Hz a.c Boilers: e (ex.g.) 10.2kgf/cm² (10.0bar), TOH (o.f.) 10.2kgf/cm² (10.0bar) Thrusters: 1 Thwart. FP thruster (f)
9290050 *V2FU6* -	**THORCO CLOUD** *ex* BBC Brazil *-2013* *ex* Molene *-2012* *ex* S. Partner *-2010* *ex* UAL Gabon *-2008* *ex* S. Partner *-2006* **ms 'Ile de Molene' GmbH & Co KG** Reederei Eckhoff GmbH & Co KG *Saint John's* *Antigua & Barbuda* MMSI: 305800000 Official number: 4934	**7,813** 3,856 10,385 T/cm 23.2	Class: GL (LR) ✠ 8/7/04	**2004-07 B.V. Scheepswerf Damen Hoogezand — Foxhol** Yd No: 828 **2004-07 Santierul Naval Damen Galati S.A. — Galati** (Hull) Yd No: 1014 Loa 145.63 (BB) Br ex 18.36 Dght 7.347 Lbp 139.38 Br md 18.25 Dpth 10.30 Welded, 2 dks	**(A31A2GX) General Cargo Ship** Grain: 14,695; Bale: 13,975 TEU 679 C Ho 302 TEU C Dk 377 TEU incl 60 ref C. Compartments: 2 Ho, ER Cranes: 2x60t Ice Capable	**1 oil engine** with flexible couplings & sr geared to sc. shaft driving 1 CP propeller Total Power: 4,320kW (5,873hp) 14.8kn MaK 9M32C 1 x 4 Stroke 9 Cy. 320 x 480 4320kW (5873bhp) Caterpillar Motoren GmbH & Co. KG-Germany AuxGen: 1 x 440kW 400V 50Hz a.c, 3 x 350kW 400V 50Hz a.c Boilers: TOH (o.f.) 10.2kgf/cm² (10.0bar), TOH (ex.g.) 10.2kgf/cm² (10.0bar) Thrusters: 1 Thwart. CP thruster (f)
9535618 *V2QF8* -	**THORCO COPENHAGEN** *ex* Wenningstedt *-2011* **mv 'Wenningstedt' BV** Reederei Hans-Peter Eckhoff GmbH & Co KG *Saint John's* *Antigua & Barbuda* MMSI: 305700000 Official number: 3082	**8,059** 3,909 10,872	Class: LR ✠ **100A1** SS 04/2011 strengthened for heavy cargoes, container cargoes in holds and on upper deck hatch covers LI Ice Class 1A FS at a draught of 7.574m Max/min draught fwd 7.574/3.60m Max/min draught aft 7.574/4.80m Required power 3558kw, installed power 4320kw ✠ **LMC** **UMS** Eq.Ltr: A†; Cable: 522.5/50.0 U3 (a)	**2011-04 Damen Shipyards Yichang Co Ltd — Yichang HB** (Hull) Yd No: 567311 **2011-04 B.V. Scheepswerf Damen — Gorinchem** Yd No: 567311 Loa 145.63 (BB) Br ex 18.33 Dght 7.400 Lbp 136.80 Br md 18.25 Dpth 10.30 Welded, 1 dk	**(A31A2GX) General Cargo Ship** Grain: 14,878 TEU 671 C Ho 302 TEU C Dk 369 TEU Compartments: 2 Ho, ER 2 Ha: (65.4 x 13.2)ER (39.0 x 13.2) Cranes: 2x80t Ice Capable	**1 oil engine** with flexible couplings & sr reverse geared to sc. shaft driving 1 CP propeller Total Power: 4,320kW (5,873hp) 14.2kn MaK 9M32C 1 x 4 Stroke 9 Cy. 320 x 480 4320kW (5873bhp) Caterpillar Motoren GmbH & Co. KG-Germany AuxGen: 1 x 760kW 400V 50Hz a.c, 3 x 350kW 400V 50Hz a.c Boilers: TOH (o.f.) 10.2kgf/cm² (10.0bar), TOH (ex.g.) 10.2kgf/cm² (10.0bar) Thrusters: 1 Thwart. FP thruster (f) Fuel: 60.0 (d.f.) 650.0 (r.f.)
9267285 *V2GK6* -	**THORCO COURAGE** *ex* Natacha C *-2013* **MarShip GmbH & Co KG ms 'Sinus Honoris'** MarShip GmbH *Saint John's* *Antigua & Barbuda* MMSI: 305975000 Official number: 5049	**7,752** 3,856 10,621 T/cm 22.5	Class: LR ✠ **100A1** SS 01/2013 containers in holds and on upper deck hatch covers, strengthened for heavy cargoes, LI *IWS Ice Class 1A (Finnish-Swedish Ice Class Rules 1985) Max draught midship 7.52m Max/min draught aft 7.627/4.8m Max/min draught fwd 7.627/3.2m Power required 3658kw, installed 4320kw ✠ **LMC** **UMS** Eq.Ltr: A†; Cable: 632.5/46.0 U3 (a)	**2003-01 B.V. Scheepswerf Damen Hoogezand — Foxhol** Yd No: 834 **2003-01 Santierul Naval Damen Galati S.A. — Galati** (Hull) Yd No: 1003 Loa 145.63 (BB) Br ex 18.35 Dght 7.361 Lbp 139.38 Br md 18.25 Dpth 10.30 Welded, 1 dk	**(A31A2GX) General Cargo Ship** Grain: 14,695; Bale: 13,975 TEU 673 C Ho 302 TEU C Dk 371 TEU incl 60 ref C. Compartments: 2 Ho, ER 2 Ha: (65.4 x 13.2)ER (39.0 x 13.2) Cranes: 2x60t Ice Capable	**1 oil engine** with flexible couplings & sr geared to sc. shaft driving 1 CP propeller Total Power: 4,320kW (5,873hp) 14.0kn MaK 9M32 1 x 4 Stroke 9 Cy. 320 x 480 4320kW (5873bhp) Caterpillar Motoren GmbH & Co. KG-Germany AuxGen: 1 x 440kW 400V 50Hz a.c, 3 x 259kW 400V 50Hz a.c Boilers: TOH (ex.g.) 10.2kgf/cm² (10.0bar), TOH (o.f.) 10.2kgf/cm² (10.0bar) Thrusters: 1 Thwart. CP thruster (f) Fuel: 50.0 (d.f.) 555.0 (r.f.) 18.0pd
9349291 *V2BM3* -	**THORCO DENMARK** *ex* Freya Scan *-2013* *ex* Opal Gallant *-2011* *ex* Beluga Foundation *-2011* *launched as* Amber *-2006* **ms 'Amber' Kai Freese GmbH & Co KG** Freese Shipping GmbH & Co KG *Saint John's* *Antigua & Barbuda* MMSI: 304868000 Official number: 4051	**9,611** 4,260 12,730	Class: GL	**2006-10 Qingshan Shipyard — Wuhan HB** Yd No: 20040304 Loa 138.02 (BB) Br ex 21.37 Dght 8.000 Lbp 130.00 Br md 21.00 Dpth 11.00 Welded, 1 dk	**(A31A2GX) General Cargo Ship** Double Bottom Partial Compartment Length Grain: 15,952; Bale: 14,856 TEU 669 C.Ho 334 TEU C.Dk 331 TEU incl 25 ref C. Compartments: 3 Ho, ER 2 Ha: (42.0 x 17.5)ER ER (18.8 x 15.0) Cranes: 2x120t Ice Capable	**1 oil engine** reduction geared to sc. shaft driving 1 CP propeller Total Power: 5,400kW (7,342hp) 15.5kn MaK 6M43 1 x 4 Stroke 6 Cy. 430 x 610 5400kW (7342bhp) Caterpillar Motoren GmbH & Co. KG-Germany AuxGen: 3 x 395kW 400/230V a.c, 1 x 750kW 400/230V a.c Thrusters: 1 Thwart. FP thruster (f) Fuel: 127.5 (d.f.) 900.6 (r.f.) 23.0pd
9384320 *A8TD6* -	**THORCO DIAMOND** *ex* Formation *-2014* *ex* Beluga Formation *-2011* **Beluga Shipping GmbH & Co KG ms 'Beluga Formation'** Hermann Buss GmbH & Cie KG *Monrovia* *Liberia* MMSI: 636091817 Official number: 91817	**9,611** 4,260 12,705	Class: GL	**2007-04 Jiangdong Shipyard — Wuhu AH** Yd No: 12000-5 Loa 138.07 (BB) Br ex - Dght 8.000 Lbp 130.00 Br md 21.00 Dpth 11.00 Welded, 1 dk	**(A31A2GX) General Cargo Ship** Double Bottom Entire Compartment Length Grain: 15,952; Bale: 14,856 TEU 665 C.Ho 334 TEU C.Dk 331 TEU incl 25 ref C. Compartments: 3 Ho, ER 3 Ha: (42.0 x 17.5) (25.5 x 17.5)ER (18.8 x 15.0) Cranes: 2x120t Ice Capable	**1 oil engine** reduction geared to sc. shaft driving 1 CP propeller Total Power: 5,400kW (7,342hp) 14.0kn MaK 6M43C 1 x 4 Stroke 6 Cy. 430 x 610 5400kW (7342bhp) Caterpillar Motoren GmbH & Co. KG-Germany AuxGen: 3 x 395kW 400/230V a.c, 1 x 700kW 400/230V 50Hz a.c Thrusters: 1 Tunnel thruster (f) Fuel: 127.5 (d.f.) 900.6 (r.f.) 27.0pd
9283966 *V2OV7* -	**THORCO DISCOVERY** *ex* Jette *-2013* *ex* BBC Wisconsin *-2013* *ex* Jette *-2012* *ex* Beluga Windward *-2011* *ex* Beluga Eternity *-2010* *ex* Asian Voyage *-2005* **ms 'Eternity' Schiffahrts GmbH & Co KG** BD-Shipsnavo GmbH & Co Reederei KG *Saint John's* *Antigua & Barbuda* MMSI: 304726000 Official number: 3910	**9,611** 4,260 12,806	Class: GL RI	**2004-11 Jiangdong Shipyard — Wuhu AH** Yd No: 12000-4 Loa 138.07 (BB) Br ex - Dght 8.000 Lbp 130.00 Br md 21.00 Dpth 11.00 Welded, 1 dk	**(A31A2GX) General Cargo Ship** Double Bottom Entire Compartment Length Grain: 15,952; Bale: 14,856 TEU 673 C Ho 334TEU C Dk 331 TEU Compartments: 3 Ho, ER 3 Ha: (42.0 x 17.5) (25.5 x 17.5)ER (18.8 x 15.0) Cranes: 2x120t Ice Capable	**1 oil engine** reduction geared to sc. shaft driving 1 CP propeller Total Power: 5,400kW (7,342hp) 14.0kn MaK 6M43 1 x 4 Stroke 6 Cy. 430 x 610 5400kW (7342bhp) Caterpillar Motoren GmbH & Co. KG-Germany AuxGen: 3 x 395kW 400/230V 50Hz a.c, 1 x 700kW 440/230V 50Hz a.c Thrusters: 1 Tunnel thruster (f) Fuel: 127.5 (d.f.) 900.6 (r.f.) 23.0pd

IMO / Call sign	Name / Owner / Flag	Tonnage	Class	Builder / Dimensions	Type / Capacity	Machinery
9349289 *V2BM4* -	**THORCO DIVA** *ex* Frida Scan *-2013* *ex* Jasper *-2011* *ex* Beluga Federation *-2011* *completed as* Jasper *-2006* **ms 'Jasper' Kai Freese GmbH & Co KG** Freese Shipping GmbH & Co KG *Saint John's* *Antigua & Barbuda* MMSI: 304869000 Official number: 4052	**9,611** 4,260 12,737	Class: GL	**2006**-06 **Qingshan Shipyard — Wuhan HB** Yd No: 20040303 Loa 138.11 (BB) Br ex 21.37 Dght 8.000 Lbp 130.00 Br md 21.00 Dpth 11.00 Welded, 1 dk	**(A31A2GX) General Cargo Ship** Double Bottom Partial Compartment Length Grain: 15,952; Bale: 14,856 TEU 669 C.Ho 334 TEU C.Dk 331 TEU incl 25 ref C. Compartments: 3 Ho, ER 3 Ha: (42.0 x 17.5) (25.5 x 17.5)ER (18.8 x 15.0) Cranes: 2x120t Ice Capable	**1 oil engine** reduction geared to sc. shaft driving 1 CP propeller Total Power: 5,400kW (7,342hp) 15.5kn MaK 6M43 1 x 4 Stroke 6 Cy. 430 x 610 5400kW (7342bhp) Caterpillar Motoren GmbH & Co. KG-Germany AuxGen: 3 x 395kW 400/230V a.c, 1 x 750kW 400/230V a.c Thrusters: 1 Thwart. FP thruster (f) Fuel: 127.5 (d.f.) 900.6 (r.f.) 23.0pd
9357999 *V2BK3* -	**THORCO DOLPHIN** *ex* Clipper Anita *-2013* *ex* OXL Avatar *-2013* *ex* Jule *-2011* *ex* Beluga Expectation *-2011* **KG Schifffahrtsgesellschaft ms 'Jule' mbH & Co** Reedereiverwaltung Heino Winter GmbH & Co KG SatCom: Inmarsat C 430484410 *Saint John's* *Antigua & Barbuda* MMSI: 304844000	**9,611** 4,260 12,760	Class: BV (GL)	**2005**-12 **Qingshan Shipyard — Wuhan HB** Yd No: 20040301 Loa 138.06 (BB) Br ex 21.37 Dght 8.000 Lbp 130.00 Br md 21.00 Dpth 11.00 Welded, 1 dk	**(A31A2GX) General Cargo Ship** Double Bottom Entire Compartment Length Grain: 15,952; Bale: 14,856 TEU 665 C Ho 334 TEU C Dk 331 TEU. Compartments: 3 Ho, ER 3 Ha: (42.0 x 17.5) (25.5 x 17.5)ER (18.8 x 15.0) Cranes: 2x120t Ice Capable	**1 oil engine** reduction geared to sc. shaft driving 1 CP propeller Total Power: 5,400kW (7,342hp) 14.0kn MaK 6M43 1 x 4 Stroke 6 Cy. 430 x 610 5400kW (7342bhp) Caterpillar Motoren GmbH & Co. KG-Germany AuxGen: 3 x 395kW a.c, 1 x 700kW a.c Thrusters: 1 Thwart. FP thruster (f) Fuel: 127.5 (d.f.) 900.6 (r.f.) 23.0pd
9543938 *VRIA5* -	**THORCO EMPIRE** **M Exocoetidae SA** Thorco Shipping A/S SatCom: Inmarsat C 447703358 *Hong Kong* *Hong Kong* MMSI: 477550400 Official number: HK-2990	**9,721** 4,069 12,876	Class: NK	**2011**-02 **Honda Zosen — Saiki** Yd No: 1068 Loa 120.00 (BB) Br ex - Dght 8.994 Lbp 111.50 Br md 21.20 Dpth 14.30 Welded, 1 dk	**(A31A2GX) General Cargo Ship** Grain: 19,957; Bale: 18,738 TEU 84 Compartments: 2 Ho, 2 Tw Dk, ER 2 Ha: ER Cranes: 2x78t	**1 oil engine** driving 1 FP propeller Total Power: 3,900kW (5,302hp) 12.5kn MAN-B&W 6L35MC 1 x 2 Stroke 6 Cy. 350 x 1050 3900kW (5302bhp) Makita Corp-Japan Fuel: 955.0 (r.f.)
9449352 *VREO3* -	**THORCO GALAXY** *ex* Thor Galaxy *-2011* **Thor Shipinvest II K/S** Thorco Shipping A/S *Hong Kong* *Hong Kong* MMSI: 477144200 Official number: HK-2265	**10,021** 4,520 13,802	Class: NK	**2008**-09 **Honda Zosen — Saiki** Yd No: 1056 Loa 124.56 (BB) Br ex - Dght 9.166 Lbp 116.00 Br md 21.20 Dpth 14.00 Welded, 1 dk	**(A31A2GX) General Cargo Ship** Grain: 20,683; Bale: 19,621 TEU 538 Compartments: 2 Ho, ER 2 Ha: ER Cranes: 2x50t	**1 oil engine** driving 1 FP propeller Total Power: 4,200kW (5,710hp) 13.0kn MAN-B&W 6S35MC 1 x 2 Stroke 6 Cy. 350 x 1400 4200kW (5710bhp) Makita Corp-Japan Thrusters: 1 Tunnel thruster (f) Fuel: 770.0
9469780 *V7DX5* -	**THORCO ISABELLA** *ex* Maersk Texas *-2014* **Maersk Line Ltd** Thorco Shipping A/S *Majuro* *Marshall Islands* MMSI: 538005481 Official number: 5481	**13,816** 5,359 19,638	Class: LR (GL) **100A1** SS 09/2011 strengthened for heavy cargoes any hold may be empty, container cargoes in all holds and on all hatch covers *IWS LI Ice Class 1A FS at a draught of 10.01/5.87m Max/min draughts fwd 10.01/4.94m Max/min draughts aft 10.77/6.80m Power required 6950kw, power installed 8730kw **LMC** **UMS**	**2011**-09 **Tongfang Jiangxin Shipbuilding Co Ltd — Hukou County JX** (Hull launched by) Yd No: JX626 **2011**-09 **Jiangsu Newyangzi Shipbuilding Co Ltd — Jingjiang JS** (Hull completed by) Loa 148.00 (BB) Br ex 23.43 Dght 9.814 Lbp 140.30 Br md 23.40 Dpth 13.50 Welded, 1 dk	**(A31A2GX) General Cargo Ship** Grain: 21,600 TEU 964 C Ho 440 TEU C Dk 524 TEU incl 40 ref C Compartments: 3 Ho, ER 3 Ha: (25.9 x 18.0) (52.5 x 18.0)ER (6.3 x 12.8) Cranes: 2x240t Ice Capable	**1 oil engine** driving 1 FP propeller Total Power: 8,730kW (11,869hp) 16.0kn Wartsila 6RTA48T 1 x 2 Stroke 6 Cy. 480 x 2000 8730kW (11869bhp) Wartsila Finland Oy-Finland Thrusters: 1 Tunnel thruster (f)
9469778 *V7FB6* -	**THORCO ISADORA** *ex* Maersk Illinois *-2014* **Maersk Line Ltd** Thorco Shipping A/S *Majuro* *Marshall Islands* MMSI: 538005564 Official number: 5564	**13,816** 5,359 19,592	Class: LR (GL) **100A1** SS 09/2011 strengthened for heavy cargoes any hold may be empty, container cargoes in all holds and on all hatch covers *IWS LI Ice Class 1A FS at draught of 10.01/5.87m Max/min draught fwd 10.01/4.94m Max/min draught aft 10.77/6.80m Power required 6950kw, power installed 8730kw **LMC** **UMS**	**2011**-09 **Tongfang Jiangxin Shipbuilding Co Ltd — Hukou County JX** Yd No: JX625 **2011**-09 **Jiangsu Newyangzi Shipbuilding Co Ltd — Jingjiang JS** (Hull completed by) Loa 148.00 (BB) Br ex - Dght 9.800 Lbp 140.30 Br md 23.40 Dpth 13.50 Welded, 1 dk	**(A31A2GX) General Cargo Ship** Grain: 21,600 TEU 964 C Ho 440 TEU C Dk 524 TEU incl 40 ref C Cranes: 2x240t Ice Capable	**1 oil engine** driving 1 FP propeller Total Power: 8,730kW (11,869hp) 16.0kn Wartsila 6RTA48T 1 x 2 Stroke 6 Cy. 480 x 2000 8730kW (11869bhp) Wartsila Finland Oy-Finland Thrusters: 1 Tunnel thruster (f)
9673173 *3FCN4* -	**THORCO LEGACY** **Garnet Tree Shipping SA** P&F Marine Co Ltd *Panama* *Panama* MMSI: 371046000 Official number: 45471TJ	**13,110** 5,042 16,954	Class: NK	**2014**-01 **Honda Zosen — Saiki** Yd No: 1080 Loa 131.66 (BB) Br ex - Dght 9.616 Lbp 122.00 Br md 23.00 Dpth 16.00 Welded, 1 dk	**(A31A2GX) General Cargo Ship** Grain: 26,066; Bale: 24,669 TEU 200 Compartments: 2 Ho, ER 2 Ha: ER Cranes: 2x50t	**1 oil engine** driving 1 FP propeller Total Power: 5,180kW (7,043hp) 14.8kn MAN-B&W 7S35MC 1 x 2 Stroke 7 Cy. 350 x 1400 5180kW (7043bhp) Makita Corp-Japan AuxGen: 2 x 380kW a.c Fuel: 1003.0
9660152 *VRMB5* -	**THORCO LEGEND** **A Reefer Line SA** Thorco Shipping A/S *Hong Kong* *Hong Kong* MMSI: 477608700 Official number: HK-3827	**13,110** 5,042 16,956	Class: NK	**2013**-04 **Honda Zosen — Saiki** Yd No: 1078 Loa 131.66 (BB) Br ex - Dght 9.620 Lbp 122.00 Br md 23.00 Dpth 16.00 Welded, 1 dk	**(A31A2GX) General Cargo Ship** Grain: 26,066; Bale: 24,669 TEU 212 Compartments: 2 Ho, ER 2 Ha: ER Cranes: 2x50t	**1 oil engine** driving 1 FP propeller Total Power: 5,180kW (7,043hp) 14.8kn MAN-B&W 7S35MC 1 x 2 Stroke 7 Cy. 350 x 1400 5180kW (7043bhp) Makita Corp-Japan AuxGen: 2 x 400kW a.c Fuel: 1000.0
9643623 *VRLM5* -	**THORCO LIVA** **M Exocoetidae SA** Thorco Shipping A/S *Hong Kong* *Hong Kong* MMSI: 477017300 Official number: HK-3707	**13,110** 5,042 16,901	Class: NK	**2012**-11 **Honda Zosen — Saiki** Yd No: 1077 Loa 131.66 (BB) Br ex - Dght 9.616 Lbp 122.00 Br md 23.00 Dpth 16.00 Welded, 1 dk	**(A31A2GX) General Cargo Ship** Grain: 26,066; Bale: 24,669 TEU 212 Compartments: 2 Ho, ER 2 Ha: ER Cranes: 2x50t	**1 oil engine** driving 1 FP propeller Total Power: 5,180kW (7,043hp) 14.8kn MAN-B&W 7S35MC 1 x 2 Stroke 7 Cy. 350 x 1400 5180kW (7043bhp) Makita Corp-Japan AuxGen: 3 x 852kW a.c Fuel: 1003.0
9310783 *VRZU2* -	**THORCO SAPPHIRE** *ex* First Bright *-2011* **Sansha Shipping SA** Thorco Shipping A/S *Hong Kong* *Hong Kong* MMSI: 477837000 Official number: HK-1270	**8,987** 3,111 10,037	Class: NK	**2004**-03 **Kegoya Dock K.K. — Kure** Yd No: 1085 Loa 119.11 (BB) Br ex - Dght 7.881 Lbp 110.02 Br md 19.60 Dpth 8.60 Welded	**(A31A2GA) General Cargo Ship (with Ro-Ro facility)** Angled stern door & ramp (a) Grain: 19,501; Bale: 18,350 2 Ha: (32.9 x 14.0)ER (25.2 x 14.0) Cranes: 1x60t,2x30t; Derricks: 1x30t	**1 oil engine** driving 1 FP propeller Total Power: 4,192kW (5,699hp) 13.8kn B&W 6S35MC 1 x 2 Stroke 6 Cy. 350 x 1400 4192kW (5699bhp) Hitachi Zosen Corp-Japan AuxGen: 2 x 285kW a.c Fuel: 600.0
9303405 *VRZL7* -	**THORCO SERENITY** *ex* Venture Ace *-2011* **Venture Ace SA** Thorco Shipping A/S *Hong Kong* *Hong Kong* MMSI: 477530000 Official number: HK-1204	**8,987** 3,111 10,037	Class: NK	**2004**-01 **Kegoya Dock K.K. — Kure** Yd No: 1083 Loa 119.11 (BB) Br ex - Dght 7.880 Lbp 110.02 Br md 19.60 Dpth 14.30 Welded	**(A31A2GA) General Cargo Ship (with Ro-Ro facility)** Angled stern door & ramp (a) Grain: 19,501; Bale: 18,350 2 Ha: (32.9 x 14.0)ER (25.2 x 14.0) Cranes: 2x30t; Derricks: 1x30t	**1 oil engine** driving 1 FP propeller Total Power: 4,192kW (5,699hp) 13.9kn MAN-B&W 6S35MC 1 x 2 Stroke 6 Cy. 350 x 1400 4192kW (5699bhp) The Hanshin Diesel Works Ltd-Japan AuxGen: 2 x 300kW a.c Fuel: 600.0
9426570 *VREH9* -	**THORCO SVENDBORG** *ex* Thor Svendborg *-2011* **Thor Shipinvest I K/S** Thorco Shipping A/S *Hong Kong* *Hong Kong* MMSI: 477111500 Official number: HK-2215	**10,021** 4,520 13,802	Class: NK	**2008**-06 **Honda Zosen — Saiki** Yd No: 1055 Loa 124.56 (BB) Br ex - Dght 9.166 Lbp 116.00 Br md 21.20 Dpth 14.00 Welded, 1 dk	**(A31A2GX) General Cargo Ship** Grain: 20,683; Bale: 19,621 TEU 538 Compartments: 2 Ho, 2 Tw Dk, ER 2 Ha: ER Cranes: 2x50t	**1 oil engine** driving 1 FP propeller Total Power: 4,200kW (5,710hp) 13.5kn MAN-B&W 6S35MC 1 x 2 Stroke 6 Cy. 350 x 1400 4200kW (5710bhp) Imex Co Ltd-Japan AuxGen: 3 x a.c Thrusters: 1 Retract. directional thruster (f)

Identity	Name / Owner	Tonnage	Class	Builder / Dimensions	Type / Capacity	Machinery
9456719 *PBRT* -	**THORCO TRIBUTE** *ex* Clipper Avalon *-2014* *ex* Helga *-2013* *ex* Kent Atlas *-2012* *ex* Helga *-2010* **Rederij van Dijk** Thorco Shipping A/S *Westerbork* *Netherlands* MMSI: 246435000 Official number: 52478	**8,999** 4,585 12,044	Class: BV (LR) ✠ Classed LR until 2/5/10	**2009-04 Damen Shipyards Yichang Co Ltd — Yichang HB** (Hull) Yd No: 567404 **2009-04 B.V. Scheepswerf Damen — Gorinchem** Yd No: 567404 Loa 142.95 (BB) Br ex 19.00 Dght 7.930 Lbp 134.96 Br md 18.90 Dpth 10.95 Welded, 1 dk	**(A31A2GX) General Cargo Ship** Grain: 17,273 TEU 684 C Ho 312 TEU C Dk 372 TEU Compartments: 2 Ho, 2 Tw Dk, ER 2 Ha: (56.0 x 15.8)ER (28.0 x 15.8) Cranes: 2x80t Ice Capable	**1 oil engine** with flexible couplings & sr reverse geared to sc. shaft driving 1 CP propeller Total Power: 6,000kW (8,158hp) 15.5kn MaK 6M43C 1 x 4 Stroke 6 Cy. 430 x 610 6000kW (8158bhp) Caterpillar Motoren GmbH & Co. KG-Germany AuxGen: 3 x 430kW 400V 50Hz a.c, 1 x 1000kW 400V 50Hz a.c Boilers: e (ex.g.) 10.2kgf/cm² (10.0bar), TOH (o.f.) 10.2kgf/cm² (10.0bar) Thrusters: 1 Thwart. CP thruster (f)
9625437 *3FBT2* -	**THORCO TRIUMPH** **Corebright Maritime SA** Shih Wei Navigation Co Ltd *Panama* *Panama* MMSI: 373875000 Official number: 4360412	**9,963** 4,544 14,226 T/cm 22.0	Class: NK	**2012-02 Higaki Zosen K.K. — Imabari** Yd No: 662 Loa 127.67 (BB) Br ex - Dght 9.446 Lbp 119.50 Br md 19.60 Dpth 14.50 Welded, 1 dk	**(A31A2GX) General Cargo Ship** Grain: 19,930; Bale: 18,598 Compartments: 2 Tw Dk, 3 Ho 2 Ha: ER Cranes: 2x30.7t; Derricks: 2x30t	**1 oil engine** driving 1 FP propeller Total Power: 4,200kW (5,710hp) 13.5kn MAN-B&W 6S35MC 1 x 2 Stroke 6 Cy. 350 x 1400 4200kW (5710bhp) Makita Corp-Japan Fuel: 970.0
9254757 *VRHN4* -	**THORCO WINNER** *ex* Thor Winner *-2010* *ex* Winning Run *-2009* **Shine Aspire Inc** Thorco Shipping A/S *Hong Kong* *Hong Kong* MMSI: 477959700 Official number: HK-2884	**6,381** 3,658 10,114	Class: NK	**2002-05 Shin Kochi Jyuko K.K. — Kochi** Yd No: 7148 Loa 100.60 (BB) Br ex - Dght 9.219 Lbp 93.50 Br md 18.80 Dpth 13.00 Welded, 2 dks	**(A31A2GX) General Cargo Ship** Grain: 13,999; Bale: 12,858 Compartments: 2 Ho, ER 2 Ha: (28.5 x 12.6)ER (19.5 x 12.6) Cranes: 2x30.7t; Derricks: 1x30t	**1 oil engine** driving 1 FP propeller Total Power: 3,250kW (4,419hp) 12.5kn B&W 5L35MC 1 x 2 Stroke 5 Cy. 350 x 1050 3250kW (4419bhp) Makita Corp-Japan AuxGen: 2 x 400kW 450V 60Hz a.c Thrusters: 1 Thwart. CP thruster (f) Fuel: 99.0 (d.f.) (Heating Coils) 557.0 (r.f.) 13.0pd
9467146 *A8XF7* -	**THORCO WINTER** *ex* BBC Winter *-2014* *ex* Atlantic Winter *-2012* *launched as* Beluga Prediction *-2011* **KG Schiffahrtsgesellschaft ms Atlantic Winter mbH & Co** Reedereiverwaltung Heino Winter GmbH & Co KG *Monrovia* *Liberia* MMSI: 636092132 Official number: 92132	**15,549** 6,089 19,306	Class: GL	**2011-11 Qingshan Shipyard — Wuhan HB** Yd No: 20060324 Loa 166.15 (BB) Br ex - Dght 9.800 Lbp 156.00 Br md 22.90 Dpth 13.90 Welded, 1 dk	**(A31A2GX) General Cargo Ship** Grain: 23,960; Bale: 23,960 TEU 1011 C Ho 507 TEU C Dk 504 TEU incl 124 ref C Compartments: 2 Ho, ER 2 Ha: ER Cranes: 2x400t,1x120t Ice Capable	**1 oil engine** reduction geared to sc. shafts driving 1 CP propeller Total Power: 9,800kW (13,324hp) 16.3kn MAN-B&W 7L58/64CD 1 x 4 Stroke 7 Cy. 580 x 640 9800kW (13324bhp) MAN B&W Diesel AG-Augsburg AuxGen: 3 x 500kW 450V 60Hz a.c, 1 x 1500kW 450V a.c Thrusters: 1 Tunnel thruster (f)
5359901 *V6CC* -	**THORFINN** *ex* Chester *-1978* *ex* Thorfinn *-1966* **Seaward Holdings Micronesia Inc** - SatCom: Inmarsat C 451000410 *Weno, Chuuk* *Micronesia* Official number: 326061	*599* 249 864	Class: (NV)	**1952-08 AS Stord Verft — Stord** Yd No: 19 Converted From: Whale-catcher-1977 Loa 51.62 Br ex 9.05 Dght 4.877 Lbp - Br md 9.00 Dpth - Welded, 2 dks	**(A37B2PS) Passenger Ship** Passengers: cabins: 13; berths: 26	**1 Steam Recip** driving 1 FP propeller Total Power: 1,471kW (2,000hp) 15.0kn Fredrikstad 1 x Steam Recip. 1471kW (2000ihp) AS Fredriksstad Mek Verksted-Norway AuxGen: 2 x 20kW 110V d.c Fuel: 254.0 (r.f.)
9395903 *TFAK* SF 77	**THORIR** **Skinney-Thinganes hf** - SatCom: Inmarsat C 425105710 *Hornafjordur* *Iceland* MMSI: 251057000 Official number: 2731	**383** 115 82	Class: NV	**2009-04 Ching Fu Shipbuilding Co Ltd — Kaohsiung** Yd No: 062 Loa 28.90 (BB) Br ex 9.21 Dght 4.100 Lbp 27.20 Br md 9.20 Dpth 4.30 Welded, 1 dk	**(B11A2FS) Stern Trawler** Ice Capable	**1 oil engine** reduction geared to sc. shaft driving 1 CP propeller Total Power: 1,103kW (1,500hp) Mitsubishi S6U-MPTK 1 x 4 Stroke 6 Cy. 240 x 260 1103kW (1500bhp) (made 2009) Mitsubishi Heavy Industries Ltd-Japan AuxGen: 1 x a.c, 1 x a.c Thrusters: 1 Tunnel thruster (f)
7530042 - -	**THORLAK** *ex* Sergent Decrocq *-2005* - -	*131* 62 -	Class: (BV)	**1975-11 Ziegler Freres — Dunkerque** Yd No: 189 Loa 26.50 Br ex 7.45 Dght 2.299 Lbp 24.01 Br md 6.99 Dpth 3.18 Welded, 1 dk	**(B34F2SF) Fire Fighting Vessel**	**2 oil engines** driving 2 FP propellers Total Power: 632kW (860hp) 12.0kn Baudouin DNP12M 2 x Vee 4 Stroke 12 Cy. 150 x 150 each-316kW (430bhp) Societe des Moteurs Baudouin SA-France
9240366 *TFQK* IS 015	**THORLAKUR** **Jakob Valgeir Ehf** - *Bolungarvik* *Iceland* MMSI: 251447110 Official number: 2446	**251** 75 -		**2000-08 Velasalan Nauta Shipyard Sp z oo — Gdynia** Yd No: NB1-99/2975 Loa 28.90 Br ex - Dght 2.900 Lbp 26.50 Br md 7.50 Dpth 5.55 Welded, 1 dk	**(B11A2FS) Stern Trawler**	**1 oil engine** geared to sc. shaft driving 1 CP propeller Total Power: 364kW (495hp) Cummins KTA-19-M2 1 x 4 Stroke 6 Cy. 159 x 159 364kW (495bhp) Cummins Engine Co Ltd-United Kingdom
9226970 *C6RS7* -	**THORNBURY** **Lundqvist Shipping Co Ltd** Lundqvist Rederierna AB *Nassau* *Bahamas* MMSI: 311168000 Official number: 8000292	**56,115** 28,647 98,893 T/cm 96.0	Class: NV	**2001-04 Daewoo Shipbuilding & Marine Engineering Co Ltd — Geoje** Yd No: 5177 Loa 248.00 (BB) Br ex - Dght 13.500 Lbp 238.30 Br md 43.00 Dpth 19.80 Welded, 1 dk	**(A13A2TV) Crude Oil Tanker** Double Hull (13F) Liq: 112,095; Liq (Oil): 112,095 Cargo Heating Coils Compartments: 12 Wing Ta, ER 3 Cargo Pump (s): 3x2500m³/hr Manifold: Bow/CM: 126m	**1 oil engine** driving 1 FP propeller Total Power: 14,049kW (19,101hp) 15.2kn B&W 5S70MC 1 x 2 Stroke 5 Cy. 700 x 2674 14049kW (19101bhp) Hyundai Heavy Industries Co Ltd-South Korea AuxGen: 3 x 650kW 440V 60Hz a.c Fuel: 159.7 (d.f.) (Heating Coils) 3809.0 (r.f.) 37.0pd
8311998 *MPHP5* -	**THORNGARTH** *ex* Tenzan *-1991* **Svitzer Marine Ltd** - *Milford Haven* *United Kingdom* MMSI: 232004165 Official number: 712596	**365** 109 89	Class: LR **100A1** SS 09/2011 tug for service within the near continental trading area *IWS **LMC** Eq.Ltr: F; Cable: 300.0/28.0 U1	**1983-09 Hanasaki Zosensho K.K. — Yokosuka** Yd No: 191 Loa 36.28 Br ex 10.52 Dght 3.150 Lbp 30.80 Br md 10.00 Dpth 4.40 Welded, 1 dk	**(B32A2ST) Tug**	**2 oil engines** dr geared to sc. shafts driving 2 Directional propellers Total Power: 2,500kW (3,400hp) Niigata 6L28BXE 2 x 4 Stroke 6 Cy. 280 x 320 each-1250kW (1700bhp) Niigata Engineering Co Ltd-Japan AuxGen: 2 x 88kW 220V 60Hz a.c
8992297 *WDD6171* -	**THORNTON BROS** *ex* Mischief *-2011* *ex* Thornton Bros *-2009* *ex* Cissi *-2007* *ex* Cissi Reinauer *-2005* *ex* Morania No. 12 *-2005* *ex* John E. Matton *-2005* **Marine Steel Marine Transport Line** - *New York, NY* *United States of America* Official number: 276627	*151* 103 -		**1958-01 Matton Shipyard Co., Inc. — Cohoes, NY** Yd No: 325 L reg 25.51 Br ex - Dght - Lbp - Br md 7.62 Dpth 3.35 Welded, 1 dk	**(B32A2ST) Tug**	**1 oil engine** driving 1 Propeller
9111723 *LHNG* -	**THOROLF KVELDULFSON** **Boreal Transport Nord AS** - *Sandnessjoen* *Norway* MMSI: 257165600	**207** 64 100	Class: (NV)	**1995-03 Rosendal Verft AS — Rosendal** Yd No: 265 Loa 28.75 Br ex 8.20 Dght 1.400 Lbp 27.44 Br md 8.00 Dpth 3.10 Welded, 1 dk	**(A37B2PS) Passenger Ship** Hull Material: Aluminium Alloy Passengers: unberthed: 100	**4 oil engines** reduction geared to sc. shafts driving 2 FP propellers Total Power: 2,200kW (2,992hp) 32.0kn M.T.U. 12V183TE72 4 x Vee 4 Stroke 12 Cy. 128 x 142 each-550kW (748bhp) MTU Friedrichshafen GmbH-Friedrichshafen
7947831 - -	**THORPE'S PRIDE** *ex* Master Brad *-2001* **Paul Arthur McLaughlin** - *Honduras* Official number: G-0328225	*170* 116 -		**1979 at Bayou La Batre, Al** L reg 26.89 Br ex 7.47 Dght - Lbp - Br md - Dpth 3.51 Welded, 1 dk	**(B11B2FV) Fishing Vessel**	**1 oil engine** driving 1 FP propeller Total Power: 515kW (700hp)
6403175 *LCMV* -	**THORSLAND** *ex* Stafnes *-1990* *ex* Asthor *-1981* **North-West Management AS** - *Aalesund* *Norway* MMSI: 257122000	**189** 56 -	Class: (NV)	**1964 Flekkefjord Slipp & Maskinfabrikk AS AS — Flekkefjord** Yd No: 73 Loa 33.47 Br ex 6.74 Dght 3.423 Lbp 27.30 Br md 6.71 Dpth 3.56 Welded, 1 dk	**(B11B2FV) Fishing Vessel** Compartments: 1 Ho, ER 2 Ha: (0.9 x 1.3) (2.2 x 1.6)ER Derricks: 1x3t; Winches: 1	**1 oil engine** geared to sc. shaft driving 1 FP propeller Total Power: 364kW (495hp) Blackstone ERS6 1 x 4 Stroke 6 Cy. 222 x 292 364kW (495bhp) Lister Blackstone Marine Ltd.-Dursley

6607379 *TFFE* GK 014	**THORSNES** *ex* Marta Agustsdottir *-2012* *ex* Bergur Vigfus *-2012* *ex* Keflvikingur *-1995* **Utgerdarfelagid Eldhamar Ehf** - SatCom: Inmarsat C 425125410 *Stykkisholmur* *Iceland* MMSI: 251254000 Official number: 0967	*362* 108 -	Class: (NV)	**1964 VEB Elbewerft — Boizenburg** Lengthened-1978 Loa 40.52 Br ex 7.22 Dght - Lbp 38.21 Br md 7.19 Dpth 5.85 Welded, 1 dk	**(B11B2FV) Fishing Vessel**	**1 oil engine** driving 1 FP propeller Total Power: 507kW (689hp) Callesen 6-427-FOT 1 x 4 Stroke 6 Cy. 270 x 400 507kW (689bhp) (new engine 1975) Aabenraa Motorfabrik, HeinrichCallesen A/S-Denmark AuxGen: 1 x 50kW 220V d.c, 1 x 40kW 220V d.c, 1 x 33kW 220V d.c
7406356 *TFKJ* SH 109	**THORSNES II** - **Thorsnes hf** - *Stykkisholmur* *Iceland* MMSI: 251251110 Official number: 1424	**233** 69 -		**1975 Slippstodin h/f — Akureyri** Yd No: 56 Loa 31.07 Br ex 6.71 Dght 3.277 Lbp 27.69 Br md 6.68 Dpth 3.33 Welded, 1 dk	**(B11A2FS) Stern Trawler**	**1 oil engine** geared to sc. shaft driving 1 CP propeller Total Power: 563kW (765hp) MWM TBD440-6 1 x 4 Stroke 6 Cy. 230 x 270 563kW (765bhp) Motoren Werke Mannheim AG (MWM)-West Germany
6821004 - -	**THORSTEINN** *ex* Sveinborg *-1987* *ex* Gudmundur I Tungu *-1981* *ex* Trausti *-1978* *ex* Nord-Rollnes *-1975* - -	*318* 101 -	Class: (NV)	**1968 Sterkoder Mek. Verksted AS — Kristiansund** Yd No: 8 Loa 44.40 Br ex 9.20 Dght 4.153 Lbp 38.00 Br md 9.17 Dpth 6.51 Welded, 2 dks	**(B11A2FS) Stern Trawler** Compartments: 1 Ho, ER 2 Ha: 2 (1.7 x 2.0)ER Cranes: 1x2t Ice Capable	**1 oil engine** driving 1 FP propeller Total Power: 1,103kW (1,500hp) Deutz RBV8M545 1 x 4 Stroke 8 Cy. 320 x 450 1103kW (1500bhp) Kloeckner Humboldt Deutz AG-West Germany AuxGen: 2 x 100kW 380V 50Hz a.c
8709860 *TFSR* TH 360	**THORSTEINN** *ex* Helga II *-1995* **Isfelag Vestmannaeyja hf** - SatCom: Inmarsat C 425117910 *Thorshofn* *Iceland* MMSI: 251179000 Official number: 1903	**1,835** 621 1,397	Class: NV	**1988-10 Ulstein Hatlo AS — Ulsteinvik** Yd No: 209 Lengthened-2001 Loa 70.15 Br ex 12.55 Dght 6.501 Lbp 64.80 Br md 12.51 Dpth 9.74 Welded, 2 dks	**(B11A2FS) Stern Trawler** Grain: 1,831 Ice Capable	**1 oil engine** with clutches, flexible couplings & sr geared to sc. shaft driving 1 CP propeller Total Power: 2,205kW (2,998hp) Normo BRM-6 1 x 4 Stroke 6 Cy. 320 x 360 2205kW (2998bhp) AS Bergens Mek Verksteder-Norway AuxGen: 1 x 1200kW 380V 50Hz a.c, 2 x 320kW 380V 50Hz a.c, 1 x 64kW 380V 50Hz a.c Thrusters: 1 Thwart. CP thruster (f); 1 Thwart. CP thruster (a)
5272127 *PHYN* HA 5	**THORSTEN J** *ex* Eldor *-1979* *ex* Paul Scheu *-1973* - - *Harlingen* *Netherlands* MMSI: 244185000 Official number: 31432	**216** 112 365	Class: (GL)	**1962-07 Heinrich Brand KG Schiffswerft — Oldenburg** Yd No: 161 Converted From: General Cargo Ship-1996 Loa 41.58 Br ex 7.37 Dght 1.990 Lbp 38.03 Br md 7.24 Dpth 2.65 Welded, 1 dk	**(B11B2FV) Fishing Vessel** Ice Capable	**1 oil engine** reverse reduction geared to sc. shaft driving 1 FP propeller Total Power: 195kW (265hp) 8.5kn MaK MV423 1 x 4 Stroke 4 Cy. 290 x 420 195kW (265bhp) Maschinenbau Kiel AG (MaK)-Kiel
9149873 *P3XS7* -	**THORSTREAM** *ex* Nordstar *-2011* *ex* P&O Nedlloyd Pampas *-2002* *ex* Nordstar *-2001* *ex* Niver Austral *-2000* *ex* Nordstar *-1999* *ex* CSAV Rio Uruguay *-1999* **TDSC Opportunity AS** Thor Dahl Management AS (TDM) SatCom: Inmarsat B 321258110 *Limassol* *Cyprus* MMSI: 212581000 Official number: P537	**16,803** 8,648 23,007 T/cm 37.1	Class: NV (GL)	**1998-04 Stocznia Szczecinska SA — Szczecin** Yd No: B170/1/15 Loa 184.70 (BB) Br ex - Dght 9.889 Lbp 171.94 Br md 25.30 Dpth 13.50 Welded, 1 dk	**(A33A2CC) Container Ship (Fully Cellular)** TEU 1730 C Ho 634 TEU C Dk 1096 TEU incl 200 ref C. Compartments: 4 Cell Ho, ER 9 Ha: (12.5 x 13.0)8 (12.5 x 20.6)ER Cranes: 3x45t	**1 oil engine** driving 1 FP propeller Total Power: 13,320kW (18,110hp) 19.6kn Sulzer 6RTA62U 1 x 2 Stroke 6 Cy. 620 x 2150 13320kW (18110bhp) H Cegielski Poznan SA-Poland AuxGen: 3 x 1090kW 440/220V 60Hz a.c Thrusters: 1 Tunnel thruster (f) Fuel: 120.0 (r.f.) 1987.0 (r.f.) 55.0pd
9014743 *MNLY8* -	**THORSVOE** - **Orkney Islands Council** Orkney Ferries Ltd *Kirkwall* *United Kingdom* MMSI: 235018907 Official number: 719645	**385** 115 140		**1991-08 Campbeltown Shipyard Ltd. — Campbeltown** Yd No: 089 Loa 35.00 Br ex 10.00 Dght 1.800 Lbp 31.20 Br md 9.50 Dpth 3.40 Welded, 1 dk	**(A36B2PL) Passenger/Landing Craft** Passengers: unberthed: 122 Vehicles: 16	**2 oil engines** with clutches, flexible couplings & sr geared to sc. shafts driving 2 Directional propellers Total Power: 690kW (938hp) 10.6kn Volvo Penta TAMD162 2 x 4 Stroke 6 Cy. 144 x 165 each-345kW (469bhp) AB Volvo Penta-Sweden Thrusters: 1 Directional thruster (f)
9463360 *TFMU* VE 401	**THORUNN SVEINSDOTTIR** - **Os hf** - *Vestmannaeyjar* *Iceland* MMSI: 251427000 Official number: 2401	**779** 234 350	Class: NV	**2010-12 'Odys' Stocznia Sp z oo — Gdansk** (Hull) Yd No: (409) **2010-12 Karstensens Skibsvaerft A/S — Skagen** Yd No: 409 Loa 39.95 (BB) Br ex - Dght 5.500 Lbp 35.80 Br md 11.20 Dpth 7.10 Welded, 1 dk	**(B11A2FS) Stern Trawler** Ice Capable	**1 oil engine** reduction geared to sc. shaft driving 1 CP propeller Total Power: 1,520kW (2,067hp) MaK 8M20C 1 x 4 Stroke 8 Cy. 200 x 300 1520kW (2067bhp) Caterpillar Motoren GmbH & Co. KG-Germany AuxGen: 2 x a.c, 1 x a.c Thrusters: 1 Tunnel thruster (f)
7227346 *VC7402* -	**THOUSAND ISLANDER** - **Gananoque Boat Line Ltd** - *Kingston, ON* *Canada* Official number: 345071	*200* 154 -		**1972 Marlin Yachts Co Ltd — Gananoque ON** L reg 29.54 Br ex 6.74 Dght 1.651 Lbp - Br md - Dpth - Welded	**(A37B2PS) Passenger Ship** Hull Material: Aluminium Alloy	**3 oil engines** driving 3 FP propellers Total Power: 804kW (1,092hp) 20.0kn Caterpillar 3406PCTA 3 x 4 Stroke 6 Cy. 137 x 165 each-268kW (364bhp) Caterpillar Tractor Co-USA
7329936 *VA3476* -	**THOUSAND ISLANDER II** - **Gananoque Boat Line Ltd** - *Kingston, ON* *Canada* Official number: 345075	*200* 153 -		**1973 Marlin Yachts Co Ltd — Gananoque ON** Loa - Br ex - Dght - Lbp 30.18 Br md 6.74 Dpth - Welded	**(A37B2PS) Passenger Ship** Hull Material: Aluminium Alloy	**3 oil engines** driving 3 FP propellers Total Power: 738kW (1,002hp) 18.0kn Caterpillar 3306SCAC 3 x 4 Stroke 6 Cy. 121 x 152 each-246kW (334bhp) Caterpillar Tractor Co-USA
8744963 - -	**THOUSAND ISLANDER III** - **Gananoque Boat Line Ltd** - *Kingston, ON* *Canada* Official number: 348015	**376** 290 -		**1975-01 Gananoque Boat Line Ltd — Gananoque ON** L reg 33.74 Br ex - Dght - Lbp - Br md 8.53 Dpth 2.59 Welded, 1 dk	**(A37B2PS) Passenger Ship** Hull Material: Aluminium Alloy	**3 oil engines** reduction geared to sc. shafts driving 3 Propellers Total Power: 738kW (1,002hp) 18.0kn
7947984 *VA3436* -	**THOUSAND ISLANDER IV** - **Gananoque Boat Line Ltd** - *Kingston, ON* *Canada* Official number: 348020	*347* 256 -		**1976 Gananoque Boat Line Ltd — Gananoque ON** Loa - Br ex 8.64 Dght - Lbp 33.76 Br md - Dpth 3.26 Welded, 1 dk	**(A37B2PS) Passenger Ship** Hull Material: Aluminium Alloy	**2 oil engines** driving 2 FP propellers Total Power: 492kW (668hp) 14.0kn Caterpillar D353TA 2 x 4 Stroke 6 Cy. 159 x 203 each-246kW (334bhp) Caterpillar Tractor Co-USA
8745187 - -	**THOUSAND ISLANDER V** - **Gananoque Boat Line Ltd** - *Kingston, ON* *Canada* Official number: 391696	**189** 84 -		**1979 Algan Shipyards Ltd — Gananoque ON** Loa 26.48 Br ex - Dght - Lbp - Br md 7.49 Dpth 2.22 Welded, 1 dk	**(A37B2PS) Passenger Ship** Hull Material: Aluminium Alloy	**2 oil engines** reduction geared to sc. shafts driving 2 Propellers Total Power: 866kW (1,178hp) Caterpillar 2 x 4 Stroke each-433kW (589bhp) Caterpillar Tractor Co-USA
9115121 *JM6388* -	**THOUSAND SUNNY GO** *ex* Jelly Fish *-2011* - - *Sasebo, Nagasaki* *Japan* Official number: 134485	*351* - -		**1994-09 K.K. Izutsu Zosensho — Nagasaki** Yd No: 1037 L reg 28.50 Br ex - Dght - Lbp - Br md 9.00 Dpth 3.00 Welded, 1 dk	**(A37B2PS) Passenger Ship**	**2 oil engines** driving 2 FP propellers Total Power: 536kW (728hp) 6.9kn G.M. (Detroit Diesel) 6V-92-TA 2 x Vee 2 Stroke 6 Cy. 123 x 127 each-268kW (364bhp) General Motors Corp-USA
9347932 *V7TE3* -	**THRASHER** - **Thrasher Shipping LLC** Eagle Shipping International (USA) LLC *Majuro* *Marshall Islands* MMSI: 538003788 Official number: 3788	**31,135** 18,571 53,360 T/cm 56.4	Class: NK	**2010-02 Yangzhou Dayang Shipbuilding Co Ltd — Yangzhou JS** Yd No: DY118 Loa 189.99 (BB) Br ex - Dght 12.508 Lbp 182.00 Br md 32.26 Dpth 17.20 Welded, 1 dk	**(A21A2BC) Bulk Carrier** Double Hull Grain: 65,045; Bale: 63,654 Compartments: 5 Ho, ER 5 Ha: 4 (21.3 x 18.3)ER (18.9 x 18.3) Cranes: 4x35t	**1 oil engine** driving 1 FP propeller Total Power: 9,480kW (12,889hp) 14.7kn MAN-B&W 6S50MC-C 1 x 2 Stroke 6 Cy. 500 x 2000 9480kW (12889bhp) Doosan Engine Co Ltd-South Korea AuxGen: 3 x a.c Fuel: 2050.0

IMO / Call sign	Name / Owner / Manager / Port	Tonnage	Class	Builder / Dimensions	Type	Machinery
9085209 *MSLM8* -	**THRAX** - **Torksey Ltd** Ostensjo Rederi AS *Peel* *Isle of Man (British)* MMSI: 232002070 Official number: 719662	**543** 163 430	Class: NV	**1994-09 SIMEK AS — Flekkefjord** Yd No: 80 Loa 35.11 Br ex 11.45 Dght 5.020 Lbp 32.50 Br md 10.80 Dpth 5.70 Welded, 1 dk	**(B32A2ST) Tug** Passengers: cabins: 7	**2 oil engines** geared to sc. shafts driving 2 Directional propellers Total Power: 3,600kW (4,894hp) 11.0kn Wichmann 6L28B 2 x 2 Stroke 6 Cy. 280 x 360 each-1800kW (2447bhp) Wartsila Wichmann Diesel AS-Norway AuxGen: 2 x 207kW 400V 50Hz a.c Thrusters: 1 Thwart. FP thruster (f) Fuel: 120.8 (d.f.)
8855293 - -	**THREE BROTHERS** *ex* St. Vincent Maria *-2007* *ex* Lost Angel *-2005* **Le Vincent** - *Gretna, LA* *United States of America* Official number: 679281	*130* 104 -		**1984 Quality Trawlers, Inc. — Montegut, La** Yd No: 3 Loa - Br ex - Dght - Lbp 23.47 Br md 6.71 Dpth 3.35 Welded, 1 dk	**(B11B2FV) Fishing Vessel**	**1 oil engine** driving 1 FP propeller
8962967 - -	**THREE BROTHERS** - **Carl Olsen McNab Jr** - *Roatan* *Honduras* Official number: U-1821805	*105* 69 -		**1986-06 Steiner Shipyard, Inc. — Bayou La Batre, Al** L reg 24.39 Br ex - Dght 2.010 Lbp - Br md 6.70 Dpth 3.50 Welded, 1 dk	**(B11A2FT) Trawler**	**1 oil engine** driving 1 FP propeller Total Power: 257kW (349hp) 10.0kn Caterpillar 3408TA 1 x Vee 4 Stroke 8 Cy. 137 x 152 257kW (349bhp) Caterpillar Tractor Co-USA
8306084 - -	**THREE BROTHERS** *ex* Butterfish *-2005* **Ferouz Amin** - *Georgetown* *Guyana* Official number: 708705	*108* 49 -		**1983-06 Bender Shipbuilding & Repair Co Inc — Mobile AL** Yd No: 181 Loa - Br ex - Dght - Lbp 21.95 Br md - Dpth - Welded, 1 dk	**(B11A2FT) Trawler**	**1 oil engine** sr geared to sc. shaft driving 1 FP propeller Total Power: 268kW (364hp) 9.3kn Caterpillar 3408TA 1 x Vee 4 Stroke 8 Cy. 137 x 152 268kW (364bhp) Caterpillar Tractor Co-USA AuxGen: 2 x 3kW 32V d.c Fuel: 43.5 (d.f.) 1.0pd
7530561 *HP5815* -	**THREE MOUNTAIN** *ex* Mizushima Maru No. 5 *-1990* **Three Mountain SA** - *Panama* *Panama* Official number: 1941391	*195* 122 699	Class: (CC)	**1976-05 Oka Zosen Tekko K.K. — Ushimado** Yd No: 235 Loa - Br ex - Dght 3.222 Lbp 50.02 Br md 9.01 Dpth 5.01 Welded, 1 dk	**(A31A2GX) General Cargo Ship**	**1 oil engine** driving 1 FP propeller Total Power: 809kW (1,100hp) Hanshin 6LU28G 1 x 4 Stroke 6 Cy. 280 x 440 809kW (1100bhp) Hanshin Nainenki Kogyo-Japan
9546784 *V2ES3* -	**THREE RIVERS** - **ms 'Three Rivers' Kai Freese GmbH & Co KG** Freese Shipping GmbH & Co KG SatCom: Inmarsat C 430553410 *Saint John's* *Antigua & Barbuda* MMSI: 305534000	**20,535** 9,704 29,975	Class: GL NV	**2010-01 Yangzhou Guoyu Shipbuilding Co Ltd — Yangzhou JS** Yd No: GY101 Loa 190.00 (BB) Br ex 23.74 Dght 10.100 Lbp 182.60 Br md 23.60 Dpth 14.60 Welded, 1 dk	**(A21A2BC) Bulk Carrier** Grain: 39,074; Bale: 38,879 Compartments: 6 Ho, ER 6 Ha: ER Cranes: 3x30t Ice Capable	**1 oil engine** driving 1 CP propeller Total Power: 7,800kW (10,605hp) 14.0kn Wartsila 6RTA48T 1 x 2 Stroke 6 Cy. 480 x 2000 7800kW (10605bhp) Yichang Marine Diesel Engine Co Ltd-China AuxGen: 2 x 680kW 60Hz a.c, 1 x 1000kW 60Hz a.c Thrusters: 1 Tunnel thruster (f)
9689811 *3EWU4* -	**THREE SASKIAS** *launched as* Saskia I *-2014* **Leo Ocean SA & Tokei Kaiun Ltd** Mitsui Co Ltd *Panama* *Panama* MMSI: 370367000 Official number: 45608TJ	**43,291** 27,379 80,800	Class: NK (Class contemplated)	**2014-03 Japan Marine United Corp (JMU) — Tsu ME** Yd No: 192 Loa 229.00 (BB) Br ex - Dght 14.450 Lbp - Br md 32.26 Dpth 20.00 Welded, 1 dk	**(A21A2BC) Bulk Carrier** Single Hull Grain: 97,500; Bale: 96,201 Compartments: 7 Ho, ER 7 Ha: ER	**1 oil engine** driving 1 FP propeller Total Power: 14,280kW (19,415hp) 14.5kn MAN-B&W 6S60ME-C 1 x 2 Stroke 6 Cy. 600 x 2400 14280kW (19415bhp)
8885640 *WDA3979* -	**THREE SISTERS** - **V T & L Inc** - *Intracoastal City, LA* *United States of America* MMSI: 366804430 Official number: 927885	*128* 87 -		**1988 Quang Van Nguyen — Chauvin, La** L reg 23.00 Br ex - Dght - Lbp - Br md 7.74 Dpth 3.07 Welded, 1 dk	**(B11B2FV) Fishing Vessel**	**1 oil engine** driving 1 FP propeller
9283655 *3ELI2* -	**THREE STARS** *ex* Golden Dena *-2007* **Three Stars Maritime SA** Irika Shipping SA *Panama* *Panama* MMSI: 372950000 Official number: 3328007A	**40,524** 26,145 74,759 T/cm 67.0	Class: LR ✠ **100A1** SS 06/2010 bulk carrier strengthened for heavy cargoes, Nos. 2, 4 & 6 holds may be empty ESP ESN *IWS LI **ShipRight** (SDA, FDA, CM) ✠ **LMC** **UMS** Eq.Ltr: Pt; Cable: 660.0/78.0 U3 (a)	**2005-06 Hudong-Zhonghua Shipbuilding (Group) Co Ltd — Shanghai** Yd No: H1335A Loa 225.00 (BB) Br ex 32.30 Dght 14.250 Lbp 217.00 Br md 32.26 Dpth 19.60 Welded, 1 dk	**(A21A2BC) Bulk Carrier** Grain: 91,717; Bale: 89,882 Compartments: 7 Ho, ER 7 Ha: 6 (14.6 x 15.0)ER (14.6 x 13.2)	**1 oil engine** driving 1 FP propeller Total Power: 10,200kW (13,868hp) 13.8kn MAN-B&W 5S60MC 1 x 2 Stroke 5 Cy. 600 x 2292 10200kW (13868bhp) Hudong Heavy Machinery Co Ltd-China AuxGen: 3 x 530kW 450V 60Hz a.c Boilers: AuxB (Comp) 7.9kgf/cm² (7.7bar)
8920971 *VTND* -	**THREEWIN SPLENDOUR** *ex* Maratha Clipper *-2002* **Shreeji Shipping Services (India) Ltd** Orion Ship Management SatCom: Inmarsat C 441959710 *Mumbai* *India* MMSI: 419425000 Official number: 2390	**1,446** 458 1,883	Class: IR (AB)	**1989-12 Sing Koon Seng Shipbuilding & Engineering Ltd — Singapore** Yd No: 686 Loa 75.00 Br ex - Dght 3.000 Lbp 71.60 Br md 15.20 Dpth 4.00 Welded, 1 dk	**(A31A2GX) General Cargo Ship** Grain: 1,729 Compartments: 2 Ho, ER 2 Ha: ER	**2 oil engines** reverse reduction geared to sc. shaft driving 2 FP propellers Total Power: 840kW (1,142hp) 9.0kn MAN D2842LE 2 x Vee 4 Stroke 12 Cy. 128 x 142 each-420kW (571bhp) MAN Nutzfahrzeuge AG-Nuernberg AuxGen: 3 x 64kW 415V 50Hz a.c Fuel: 283.0 (d.f.) 3.5pd
9008287 *VTNF* -	**THREEWIN SUCCESS** *ex* Maratha Cruiser *-2003* **Shreeji Shipping Services (India) Ltd** Orion Ship Management SatCom: Inmarsat C 441959410 *Mumbai* *India* MMSI: 419426000 Official number: 2391	*1,446* 458 1,884	Class: IR (AB)	**1991-03 Sing Koon Seng Shipbuilding & Engineering Ltd — Singapore** Yd No: 687 Loa 75.00 Br ex - Dght 3.000 Lbp 71.60 Br md 15.20 Dpth 4.00 Welded	**(A31A2GX) General Cargo Ship** Grain: 1,729 Compartments: 2 Ho, ER 2 Ha: ER	**2 oil engines** reverse reduction geared to sc. shaft driving 2 FP propellers Total Power: 840kW (1,142hp) 10.0kn MAN D2842LE 2 x Vee 4 Stroke 12 Cy. 128 x 142 each-420kW (571bhp) MAN Nutzfahrzeuge AG-Nuernberg AuxGen: 3 x 64kW a.c
9377951 *PHGW* -	**THRESHER** - **Chemgas Shipping BV** - *Rotterdam* *Netherlands* MMSI: 246295000 Official number: 44463	**2,294** 688 1,814 T/cm 10.0	Class: BV	**2007-10 Societatea Comerciala Severnav S.A. — Drobeta-Turnu Severin** (Hull) Yd No: 4650002 **2007-10 Machinefabriek Breko B.V. — Papendrecht** Yd No: 0574 Loa 99.90 Br ex 11.45 Dght 3.660 Lbp 96.79 Br md 11.40 Dpth 6.52 Welded, 1 dk	**(A11B2TG) LPG Tanker** Double Hull (13F) Liq (Gas): 2,646 3 x Gas Tank (s); 3 membrane (stl) 5 Cargo Pump (s): 5x200m³/hr Manifold: Bow/CM: 50m	**2 oil engines** reduction geared to sc. shafts driving 2 FP propellers Total Power: 2,110kW (2,869hp) 12.5kn Mitsubishi S6U-MPTK 2 x 4 Stroke 6 Cy. 240 x 260 each-1007kW (1369bhp) Mitsubishi Heavy Industries Ltd-Japan AuxGen: 2 x 168kW 400/230V a.c, 1 x 350kW 400/230V a.c Thrusters: 1 Tunnel thruster (f) Fuel: 202.0 (d.f.)
9628594 - -	**THRIVING-1** - **Thanh Thoi Co Ltd** - *Saigon* *Vietnam*	**474** 142 125	Class: VR	**2011-01 Saigon Shipbuilding Industry Co Ltd — Ho Chi Minh City** Loa 45.37 Br ex 14.00 Dght 1.400 Lbp 40.90 Br md 13.70 Dpth 2.55 Welded, 1 dk	**(A36A2PR) Passenger/Ro-Ro Ship (Vehicles)** Passengers: unberthed: 396	**2 oil engines** reduction geared to sc. shafts driving 2 FP propellers Total Power: 1,268kW (1,724hp) 12.0kn Cummins KTA-38-M0 2 x Vee 4 Stroke 12 Cy. 159 x 159 each-634kW (862bhp) Cummins Engine Co Inc-USA AuxGen: 2 x 75kW 380V a.c
9714434 *XVLE9* -	**THRIVING-2** - **Thanh Thoi Co Ltd** - *Saigon* *Vietnam* Official number: VNSG-2141-TKH	**497** 173 349	Class: VR	**2013-06 Saigon Shipbuilding Industry Co Ltd — Ho Chi Minh City** Loa 49.90 Br ex 13.99 Dght 1.700 Lbp 43.71 Br md 13.70 Dpth 3.10 Welded, 1 dk	**(A36A2PR) Passenger/Ro-Ro Ship (Vehicles)** Passengers: unberthed: 389	**2 oil engines** reduction geared to sc. shafts driving 2 FP propellers Total Power: 2,728kW (3,708hp) 10.0kn Cummins KTA-50-M2 2 x Vee 4 Stroke 16 Cy. 159 x 159 each-1364kW (1854bhp) Cummins Engine Co Ltd-United Kingdom AuxGen: 2 x 136kW 380V a.c

Ship	Tonnage	Class	Build / Dimensions	Type	Machinery
9347920 **THRUSH** *V7VF2* - **Thrush Shipping LLC** Navig8 Bulk Asia Pte Ltd SatCom: Inmarsat C 453836134 *Majuro* *Marshall Islands* MMSI: 538004106 Official number: 4106	**31,241** 18,571 53,297 T/cm 56.4	Class: NK	**2011-01 Yangzhou Dayang Shipbuilding Co Ltd — Yangzhou JS** Yd No: DY117 Loa 189.99 (BB) Br ex - Dght 12.510 Lbp 182.00 Br md 32.26 Dpth 17.20 Welded, 1 dk	**(A21A2BC) Bulk Carrier** Grain: 65,045; Bale: 63,654 Compartments: 5 Ho, ER 5 Ha: 4 (21.3 x 18.3)ER (18.9 x 18.3) Cranes: 4x35t	**1 oil engine** driving 1 FP propeller Total Power: 9,480kW (12,889hp) 14.7kn MAN-B&W 6S50MC-C 1 x 2 Stroke 6 Cy. 500 x 2000 9480kW (12889bhp) Doosan Engine Co Ltd-South Korea AuxGen: 3 x a.c
9003536 **THRUSTER** *E5U2631* - *ex* Wilson Horn *-2012* *ex* Thruster *-2005* *ex* Arklow Venture *-2000* **Deep Seas Shipping Corp** Gant Trading Shipping Corp *Avatiu* *Cook Islands* MMSI: 518684000 Official number: 1720	**2,827** 1,595 4,257 T/cm 10.9	Class: GL NK	**1990-05 Schiffs. Hugo Peters Wewelsfleth Peters & Co. GmbH — Wewelsfleth** Yd No: 628 Loa 88.20 Br ex - Dght 5.790 Lbp 84.90 Br md 13.60 Dpth 7.70 Welded, 1 dk	**(A31A2GX) General Cargo Ship** Double Hull Grain: 5,665; Bale: 5,665 TEU 173 C.Ho 105/20' C.Dk 68/20' Compartments: 1 Ho, ER 1 Ha: (56.4 x 11.0)ER Ice Capable	**1 oil engine** with clutches, flexible couplings & sr reverse geared to sc. shaft driving 1 FP propeller Total Power: 1,300kW (1,767hp) 11.0kn MaK 8M332AK 1 x 4 Stroke 8 Cy. 240 x 330 1300kW (1767bhp) Krupp MaK Maschinenbau GmbH-Kiel AuxGen: 3 x 88kW 380V 50Hz a.c, 1 x 25kW 380V 50Hz a.c Thrusters: 1 Thwart. FP thruster (f) Fuel: 75.7 (d.f.) 5.3pd
8200955 **THT 2** - - **Borneo Jaya (S) Pte Ltd** *San Lorenzo* *Honduras* Official number: L-1726405	**130** 39 -	Class: (AB)	**1982-07 Thai Hong Shipbuilding Pte Ltd — Singapore** Yd No: THT2 Loa - Br ex - Dght 2.261 Lbp 22.31 Br md 7.41 Dpth 2.87 Welded, 1 dk	**(B32A2ST) Tug**	**2 oil engines** reverse reduction geared to sc. shafts driving 2 FP propellers Total Power: 764kW (1,038hp) 11.0kn Caterpillar 3412TA 2 x Vee 4 Stroke 12 Cy. 137 x 152 each-382kW (519bhp) Caterpillar Tractor Co-USA AuxGen: 2 x 40kW
8807674 **THU BON 01** *XVKD* - *ex* Dong Du *-2005* *ex* Ocean Berani *-2003* *ex* Flora *-2002* *ex* Spica *-1995* **Thu Bon Transport Trading JSC** - *Saigon* *Vietnam* MMSI: 574320000 Official number: VNSG-1752-TH	**6,935** 2,739 8,229	Class: VR (NK)	**1989-03 Donghae Shipbuilding Co Ltd — Ulsan** Yd No: 8857 Loa 114.50 Br ex - Dght 7.214 Lbp 107.00 Br md 18.50 Dpth 13.00 Welded, 2 dks	**(A31A2GX) General Cargo Ship** Grain: 16,850; Bale: 15,447 Compartments: 2 Ho, ER 2 Ha: ER	**1 oil engine** driving 1 FP propeller Total Power: 2,427kW (3,300hp) 13.5kn B&W 6L35MCE 1 x 2 Stroke 6 Cy. 350 x 1050 2427kW (3300bhp) Mitsui Engineering & Shipbuilding CLtd-Japan
9334454 **THUAN AN 02** *3WLY* - **Lien Thanh River Sea Transport Co Ltd** *Haiphong* *Vietnam* Official number: VN-1955-VT	**499** 285 882	Class: VR	**2005-05 Marine Engineering Service JSC — Vietnam** Loa 56.00 Br ex 9.22 Dght 3.270 Lbp 52.20 Br md 9.00 Dpth 3.97 Welded, 1 dk	**(A31A2GX) General Cargo Ship**	**1 oil engine** geared to sc. shaft driving 1 FP propeller Total Power: 425kW (578hp) 12.0kn S.K.L. 8NVD36A-1U 1 x 4 Stroke 8 Cy. 240 x 360 425kW (578bhp) SKL Motoren u. Systemtechnik AG-Magdeburg
8667220 **THUAN HAI 36** *3WCF* - **Thuan Hai Service Trading JSC** - *Haiphong* *Vietnam* Official number: VN-2903-VT	**1,599** 1,090 3,177	Class: VR	**2009-06 Haiphong Mechanical & Trading Co. — Haiphong** Yd No: THB-30-66 Loa 79.80 Br ex 12.82 Dght 5.060 Lbp 74.80 Br md 12.80 Dpth 6.20 Welded, 1 dk	**(A31A2GX) General Cargo Ship** Grain: 3,653 Compartments: 2 Ho, ER 2 Ha: (19.8 x 8.0)ER (20.4 x 8.0)	**1 oil engine** driving 1 FP propeller 10.0kn Chinese Std. Type CW8200ZC 1 x 4 Stroke 8 Cy. 200 x 270 Weichai Power Co Ltd-China
9016181 **THUAN MY** *XVDY* - *ex* Dong Ho *-2010* *ex* Largo *-2001* *ex* Glorystar *-1993* **Hai Minh Trading Production Service Ocean Shipping Co Ltd** - SatCom: Inmarsat C 457418110 *Saigon* *Vietnam* MMSI: 574181000 Official number: VN-1448-VT	**5,518** 2,277 6,868	Class: VR (NK)	**1990-12 Iwagi Zosen Co Ltd — Kamijima EH** Yd No: 140 Loa 97.13 (BB) Br ex 18.03 Dght 7.493 Lbp 89.95 Br md 18.00 Dpth 13.00 Welded, 2 dks	**(A31A2GX) General Cargo Ship** Grain: 12,839; Bale: 11,915 TEU 202 C. 202/20' (40') incl. 6 ref C. Compartments: 2 Ho, ER 2 Ha: (21.0 x 10.5) (26.0 x 10.1)ER Derricks: 4x25t	**1 oil engine** driving 1 FP propeller Total Power: 2,427kW (3,300hp) 12.0kn Hanshin 6EL40 1 x 4 Stroke 6 Cy. 400 x 800 2427kW (3300bhp) The Hanshin Diesel Works Ltd-Japan AuxGen: 2 x 200kW a.c
8312485 **THUAN NGHIA STAR** *JVWC3* - *ex* Xitona *-2012* *ex* S1 Star *-2008* *ex* Bumyoung Lotus *-2007* *ex* Sookwang *-2006* *ex* Indriani *-2002* *ex* Andriana *-1987* **Thuan Nghia Maritime Co Ltd** - *Ulaanbaatar* *Mongolia* MMSI: 457121000 Official number: 23660883	**5,433** 2,104 6,539	Class: VR (KR) (KI) (NK)	**1983-10 Kochi Jyuko K.K. — Kochi** Yd No: 2328 Loa 100.44 (BB) Br ex - Dght 7.300 Lbp 89.82 Br md 18.01 Dpth 12.65 Welded, 2 dks	**(A31A2GX) General Cargo Ship** Grain: 12,321; Bale: 11,455 Compartments: 2 Ho, ER 2 Ha: 2 (20.3 x 10.2)ER Derricks: 4x25t	**1 oil engine** driving 1 FP propeller Total Power: 2,795kW (3,800hp) 12.8kn B&W 5L35MC 1 x 2 Stroke 5 Cy. 350 x 1050 2795kW (3800bhp) Makita Diesel Co Ltd-Japan AuxGen: 2 x 240kW 450V 60Hz a.c Fuel: 120.5 (d.f.) 540.5 (r.f.)
9023108 **THUAN PHAT 07** - - *ex* Hoang Phat 07 *-2004* **Thuan Phat Shipping & Trading JSC** - *Haiphong* *Vietnam* Official number: VN-1848-VT	**499** 332 959	Class: VR	**2003-12 Thanh Long Co Ltd — Haiphong** Yd No: HT-37 Loa 57.27 Br ex 9.22 Dght 3.500 Lbp 52.90 Br md 9.20 Dpth 4.20 Welded, 1 dk	**(A31A2GX) General Cargo Ship**	**1 oil engine** reduction geared to sc. shaft driving 1 Propeller Total Power: 425kW (578hp) Weifang 8170ZC 1 x 4 Stroke 8 Cy. 170 x 200 425kW (578bhp) Weifang Diesel Engine Factory-China
8667024 **THUAN PHAT 08** *XVRI* - **Thuan Phat Shipping JSC** - *Haiphong* *Vietnam* Official number: VN-2765-VT	**1,599** 1,051 3,252	Class: VR	**2008-12 Hang Giang Co Ltd — Haiphong** Yd No: S07-002-28 Loa 78.63 Br ex 12.62 Dght 5.350 Lbp 73.60 Br md 12.60 Dpth 6.48 Welded, 1 dk	**(A31A2GX) General Cargo Ship** Bale: 3,313 Compartments: 2 Ho, ER 2 Ha: ER 2 (19.8 x 8.4)	**1 oil engine** driving 1 FP propeller 10.0kn Chinese Std. Type G6300ZCA 1 x 4 Stroke 6 Cy. 300 x 380 Ningbo CSI Power & Machinery GroupCo Ltd-China
8667036 **THUAN PHAT 09** - - **Thuan Phat Shipping JSC** - *Haiphong* *Vietnam* MMSI: 574012521 Official number: VN-2989-VT	**1,599** 1,024 3,252	Class: VR	**2009-09 Hang Giang Co Ltd — Haiphong** Yd No: S07-002-29 Loa 78.70 Br ex 12.62 Dght 5.350 Lbp 73.60 Br md 12.60 Dpth 6.48 Welded, 1 dk	**(A31A2GX) General Cargo Ship** Bale: 3,381 Compartments: 2 Ho, ER 2 Ha: (19.2 x 8.4)ER (19.8 x 8.4)	**1 oil engine** driving 1 FP propeller Total Power: 441kW (600hp) 10.0kn Chinese Std. Type 6300ZC 1 x 4 Stroke 6 Cy. 300 x 380 441kW (600bhp) Ningbo CSI Power & Machinery GroupCo Ltd-China
9544786 **THUAN PHAT 17** *XVVP* - **Thuan Phat Shipping & Trading JSC** - *Haiphong* *Vietnam* MMSI: 574814000	**1,599** 1,069 3,009	Class: VR	**2009-03 in Vietnam** Yd No: HT-147B Loa 79.14 Br ex 12.62 Dght 5.300 Lbp 74.80 Br md 12.60 Dpth 6.48 Welded, 1 dk	**(A31A2GX) General Cargo Ship** Compartments: 2 Ho, ER 2 Ha: ER 2 (18.6 x 7.6)	**1 oil engine** reduction geared to sc. shaft driving 1 FP propeller Total Power: 736kW (1,001hp) 11.0kn Chinese Std. Type 8300ZLC 1 x 4 Stroke 8 Cy. 300 x 380 736kW (1001bhp) (made 2008) Zibo Diesel Engine Factory-China
9565259 **THUAN PHAT 18** *XVFH* - *ex* Cat Tuong 107 *-2010* **Thuan Phat Trading & Transportation JSC** - *Haiphong* *Vietnam* MMSI: 574972000	**1,599** 1,069 3,007	Class: VR	**2010-07 Cat Tuong Shipyard — Truc Ninh** Yd No: HT-147C Loa 79.14 Br ex 12.62 Dght 5.300 Lbp 74.80 Br md 12.60 Dpth 6.48 Welded, 1 dk	**(A21A2BC) Bulk Carrier** Grain: 3,932; Bale: 3,543 Compartments: 2 Ho, ER 2 Ha: ER 2 (18.6 x 7.6)	**1 oil engine** reduction geared to sc. shafts driving 1 FP propeller Total Power: 735kW (999hp) 11.0kn Chinese Std. Type 8300ZLC 1 x 4 Stroke 8 Cy. 300 x 380 735kW (999bhp) Zibo Diesel Engine Factory-China AuxGen: 2 x 75kW 400V 50Hz a.c Fuel: 75.0 (d.f.)
9311555 **THUAN PHUOC** *3WGF* - **Danang Shipping JSC (DANANGSHIP)** - SatCom: Inmarsat C 457423910 *Da Nang* *Vietnam* MMSI: 574239000 Official number: VNDN-202-VT	**4,039** 2,360 6,507	Class: VR	**2004-04 Ha Long Shipbuilding Co Ltd — Ha Long** Yd No: 141 Loa 102.79 Br ex 17.03 Dght 6.900 Lbp 94.50 Br md 17.00 Dpth 8.80 Welded, 1 dk	**(A31A2GX) General Cargo Ship** Grain: 8,610; Bale: 8,159 Derricks: 4	**1 oil engine** driving 1 FP propeller Total Power: 2,648kW (3,600hp) 12.0kn Hanshin LH41LA 1 x 4 Stroke 6 Cy. 410 x 800 2648kW (3600bhp) The Hanshin Diesel Works Ltd-Japan
8855841 **THUAN THANH** - - *ex* Thuan An No. II *-1994* **Ba Minh Ha** - *Abbeville, LA* *United States of America* Official number: 913566	*146* 99 -		**1987 Gulf Coast Marine — Chauvin, La** Yd No: 1150 Loa - Br ex - Dght - Lbp 25.97 Br md 7.01 Dpth 3.81 Welded, 1 dk	**(B11B2FV) Fishing Vessel**	**1 oil engine** driving 1 FP propeller

Number / Call sign	Name / Owner	Tonnage	Class	Build / Dimensions	Type	Machinery
9129134 *DQUG* -	**THULE** **ms 'Thule' Schiffahrtsgesellschaft mbH & Co KG** Schoening Schiffahrtsverwaltungs GmbH *Haren/Ems* *Germany* MMSI: 211245180 Official number: 4621	**2,842** 1,538 4,123	Class: BV	**1996-12 Bodewes Scheepswerf "Volharding" Foxhol B.V. — Foxhol** Yd No: 329 Loa 89.40 (BB) Br ex - Dght 5.720 Lbp 84.98 Br md 13.60 Dpth 7.20 Welded, 1 dk	**(A31A2GX) General Cargo Ship** Bale: 5,628 TEU 261 C. 246/20' incl. 20 ref C. Compartments: 1 Ho, ER 1 Ha: (62.9 x 11.0)ER Ice Capable	**1 oil engine** reduction geared to sc. shaft driving 1 CP propeller Total Power: 2,200kW (2,991hp) 13.0kn MaK 6M453C 1 x 4 Stroke 6 Cy. 320 x 420 2200kW (2991bhp) MaK Motoren GmbH & Co. KG-Kiel AuxGen: 1 x 648kW 380/220V 50Hz a.c, 3 x 111kW 380/220V 50Hz a.c Thrusters: 1 Tunnel thruster (f) Fuel: 400.0 (d.f.)
7939303 *WYC8396* -	**THUMPER** **Thumper Enterprises Inc** - *Astoria, OR* *United States of America* Official number: 600522	*128* 87 -		**1978 Desco Marine — Saint Augustine, Fl** L reg 20.85 Br ex 6.74 Dght - Lbp - Br md - Dpth 3.74 Bonded, 1 dk	**(B11A2FT) Trawler** Hull Material: Reinforced Plastic	**1 oil engine** driving 1 FP propeller Total Power: 268kW (364hp) Caterpillar 3408TA 1 x Vee 4 Stroke 8 Cy. 137 x 152 268kW (364bhp) Caterpillar Tractor Co-USA
9229063 *PBDK* -	**THUN GALAXY** *ex* BRO Galaxy *-2013* **Rederij Thun Galaxy** Erik Thun AB (Thunship Management Holland) *Delfzijl* *Netherlands* MMSI: 244089000 Official number: 38448	**4,107** 2,136 7,559 T/cm 15.8	Class: BV	**2001-10 Scheepswerf Ferus Smit BV — Westerbroek** Yd No: 334 Loa 114.66 (BB) Br ex - Dght 6.750 Lbp 109.50 Br md 15.00 Dpth 9.30 Welded, 1 dk	**(A12B2TR) Chemical/Products Tanker** Double Hull (13F) Liq: 8,034; Liq (Oil): 8,034 Compartments: 1 Ta, 8 Wing Ta, ER 9 Cargo Pump (s): 9x300m³/hr Manifold: Bow/CM: 67.5m Ice Capable	**1 oil engine** reduction geared to sc. shaft driving 1 CP propeller Total Power: 2,460kW (3,345hp) 12.0kn Wartsila 6R32LNE 1 x 4 Stroke 6 Cy. 320 x 350 2460kW (3345bhp) Wartsila Finland Oy-Finland AuxGen: 1 x 360kW 440/230V 60Hz a.c, 3 x 212kW 440/230V 60Hz a.c Thrusters: 1 Thwart. CP thruster (f) Fuel: 60.0 (d.f.) (Heating Coils) 248.0 (r.f.) 10.0pd
9393345 *PBLW* -	**THUN GARLAND** *ex* BRO Garland *-2013* **Thun Tankers BV** Erik Thun AB (Thunship Management Holland) SatCom: Inmarsat C 424467810 *Delfzijl* *Netherlands* MMSI: 244678000 Official number: 53008	**4,212** 1,911 7,559 T/cm 15.8	Class: BV	**2009-05 Scheepswerf Ferus Smit BV — Westerbroek** Yd No: 387 Loa 116.35 (BB) Br ex - Dght 6.760 Lbp 110.90 Br md 15.00 Dpth 9.30 Welded, 1 dk	**(A12B2TR) Chemical/Products Tanker** Double Hull (13F) Liq: 8,034; Liq (Oil): 8,034 Compartments: 1 Ta, 8 Wing Ta, ER 9 Cargo Pump (s): 9x300m³/hr Manifold: Bow/CM: 67.5m Ice Capable	**1 oil engine** reduction geared to sc. shaft driving 1 CP propeller Total Power: 2,430kW (3,304hp) 12.0kn Wartsila 6R32LNE 1 x 4 Stroke 6 Cy. 320 x 350 2430kW (3304bhp) Wartsila Finland Oy-Finland AuxGen: 3 x 62kW a.c, 1 x 360kW a.c Thrusters: 1 Thwart. CP thruster (f)
9393333 *PBQH* -	**THUN GAZELLE** *ex* BRO Gazelle *-2013* **Thun Tankers BV** Erik Thun AB (Thunship Management Holland) SatCom: Inmarsat C 424654110 *Delfzijl* *Netherlands* MMSI: 246541000 Official number: 52816	**4,212** 2,150 7,515 T/cm 15.8	Class: BV	**2009-02 Scheepswerf Ferus Smit BV — Westerbroek** Yd No: 386 Loa 116.35 (BB) Br ex - Dght 6.760 Lbp 109.50 Br md 15.00 Dpth 9.30 Welded, 1 dk	**(A12B2TR) Chemical/Products Tanker** Double Hull (13F) Liq: 8,047; Liq (Oil): 8,034 Compartments: 1 Ta, 8 Wing Ta, ER 9 Cargo Pump (s): 9x300m³/hr Manifold: Bow/CM: 67.5m Ice Capable	**1 oil engine** reduction geared to sc. shaft driving 1 CP propeller Total Power: 2,430kW (3,304hp) 12.0kn Wartsila 6R32LNE 1 x 4 Stroke 6 Cy. 320 x 350 2430kW (3304bhp) Wartsila Finland Oy-Finland AuxGen: 3 x 262kW a.c, 1 x 360kW a.c Thrusters: 1 Thwart. CP thruster (f) Fuel: 30.0 (d.f.) 200.0 (r.f.)
9263590 *PBJW* -	**THUN GEMINI** *ex* BRO Gemini *-2013* **Thun Tankers BV** Erik Thun AB (Thunship Management Holland) *Delfzijl* *Netherlands* MMSI: 245610000 Official number: 40558	**4,107** 2,136 7,559 T/cm 15.8	Class: BV	**2003-04 Scheepswerf Ferus Smit BV — Westerbroek** Yd No: 340 Loa 114.66 (BB) Br ex - Dght 6.750 Lbp 109.50 Br md 15.00 Dpth 9.30 Welded, 1 dk	**(A12B2TR) Chemical/Products Tanker** Double Hull (13F) Liq: 8,034; Liq (Oil): 8,064 Compartments: 1 Ta, 8 Wing Ta, ER 9 Cargo Pump (s): 9x300m³/hr Manifold: Bow/CM: 67.5m Ice Capable	**1 oil engine** reduction geared to sc. shaft driving 1 CP propeller Total Power: 2,430kW (3,304hp) 12.0kn Wartsila 6R32LNE 1 x 4 Stroke 6 Cy. 320 x 350 2430kW (3304bhp) Wartsila Finland Oy-Finland AuxGen: 3 x 262kW 440/230V 60Hz a.c, 1 x 360kW 440/230V 60Hz a.c Thrusters: 1 Thwart. CP thruster (f) Fuel: 45.0 (d.f.) 230.0 (r.f.) 10.0pd
9263605 *PBKM* -	**THUN GENIUS** *ex* BRO Genius *-2013* **Thun Tankers BV** Erik Thun AB (Thunship Management Holland) *Delfzijl* *Netherlands* MMSI: 245934000 Official number: 40559	**4,107** 2,136 7,559 T/cm 15.8	Class: BV	**2003-07 Scheepswerf Ferus Smit BV — Westerbroek** Yd No: 341 Loa 114.66 (BB) Br ex - Dght 6.760 Lbp 109.00 Br md 15.00 Dpth 9.30 Welded, 1 dk	**(A12B2TR) Chemical/Products Tanker** Double Hull (13F) Liq: 8,034; Liq (Oil): 8,032 Compartments: 1 Ta, 8 Wing Ta, ER 9 Cargo Pump (s): 9x300m³/hr Manifold: Bow/CM: 67.5m Ice Capable	**1 oil engine** reduction geared to sc. shaft driving 1 CP propeller Total Power: 2,430kW (3,304hp) 12.0kn Wartsila 6R32LNE 1 x 4 Stroke 6 Cy. 320 x 350 2430kW (3304bhp) Wartsila Finland Oy-Finland AuxGen: 3 x 265kW 440/230V 60Hz a.c, 1 x 360kW 440/230V 60Hz a.c Thrusters: 1 Thwart. FP thruster (f) Fuel: 49.3 (d.f.) 219.5 (r.f.) 10.0pd
9229051 *PBCA* -	**THUN GLOBE** *ex* BRO Globe *-2013* **Thun Tankers BV** Erik Thun AB (Thunship Management Holland) *Delfzijl* *Netherlands* MMSI: 245573000 Official number: 38447	**4,107** 2,136 7,559 T/cm 15.8	Class: BV	**2001-06 Scheepswerf Ferus Smit BV — Westerbroek** Yd No: 333 Loa 114.66 (BB) Br ex - Dght 6.750 Lbp 109.50 Br md 15.00 Dpth 9.30 Welded, 1 dk	**(A12B2TR) Chemical/Products Tanker** Double Hull (13F) Liq: 8,034; Liq (Oil): 8,034 Compartments: 1 Ta, 8 Wing Ta, ER 9 Cargo Pump (s): 9x300m³/hr Manifold: Bow/CM: 67m Ice Capable	**1 oil engine** reduction geared to sc. shaft driving 1 CP propeller Total Power: 2,430kW (3,304hp) 12.0kn Wartsila 6R32LNE 1 x 4 Stroke 6 Cy. 320 x 350 2430kW (3304bhp) Wartsila Finland Oy-Finland AuxGen: 3 x 262kW 440/230V 60Hz a.c, 1 x 360kW 440/230V 60Hz a.c Thrusters: 1 Tunnel thruster (f) Fuel: 50.0 (d.f.) (Heating Coils) 220.0 (r.f.)
9190200 *PCEH* -	**THUN GLORY** *ex* BRO Glory *-2012* *ex* United Glory *-2000* **Thun Tankers BV** Erik Thun AB (Thunship Management Holland) *Delfzijl* *Netherlands* MMSI: 245902000 Official number: 37611	**3,653** 1,825 6,535 T/cm 14.2	Class: BV	**2000-01 Scheepswerf Ferus Smit BV — Westerbroek** Yd No: 322 Loa 103.46 (BB) Br ex - Dght 7.100 Lbp 98.35 Br md 15.00 Dpth 9.30 Welded, 1 dk	**(A12B2TR) Chemical/Products Tanker** Double Hull (13F) Liq: 6,893; Liq (Oil): 6,893 Compartments: 1 Ta, 8 Wing Ta, ER 9 Cargo Pump (s): 9x300m³/hr Manifold: Bow/CM: 58m Ice Capable	**1 oil engine** geared to sc. shaft driving 1 CP propeller Total Power: 2,430kW (3,304hp) 13.0kn Wartsila 6R32E 1 x 4 Stroke 6 Cy. 320 x 350 2430kW (3304bhp) Wartsila NSD Finland Oy-Finland AuxGen: 1 x 360kW 440/230V 60Hz a.c, 3 x 224kW 440/230V 60Hz a.c Thrusters: 1 Thwart. FP thruster (f) Fuel: 51.4 (d.f.) (Heating Coils) 205.6 (r.f.) 12.5pd
9297204 *PBJV* -	**THUN GOLIATH** *ex* BRO Goliath *-2012* *ex* Mareld *-2007* **Thun Tankers BV** Erik Thun AB (Thunship Management Holland) SatCom: Inmarsat C 424487813 *Delfzijl* *Netherlands* MMSI: 244878000 Official number: 51064	**4,745** 2,245 7,108	Class: LR (BV) **100A1** SS 11/2009 Double Hull oil and chemical tanker, Ship Type 2 SG 1.54 ESP LI EP (bar above) **LMC** **UMS IGS**	**2004-12 Selah Makina Sanayi ve Ticaret A.S. — Tuzla, Istanbul** Yd No: 38 Loa 119.10 (BB) Br ex - Dght 6.750 Lbp 110.97 Br md 16.90 Dpth 8.40 Welded, 1 dk	**(A12B2TR) Chemical/Products Tanker** Double Hull (13F) Liq: 8,048; Liq (Oil): 8,048 Cargo Heating Coils Compartments: 12 Wing Ta, 2 Wing Slop Ta, ER 12 Cargo Pump (s): 12x200m³/hr Manifold: Bow/CM: 59m	**1 oil engine** with clutches & reduction geared to sc. shaft driving 1 CP propeller Total Power: 3,840kW (5,221hp) 14.5kn MAN-B&W 8L32/40 1 x 4 Stroke 8 Cy. 320 x 400 3840kW (5221bhp) MAN B&W Diesel AG-Augsburg AuxGen: 1 x 1250kW 440/220V 60Hz a.c, 3 x 500kW 440/220V 50Hz a.c Thrusters: 1 Thwart. CP thruster (f) Fuel: 87.0 (d.f.) 415.0 (r.f.) 15.7pd
9362140 *PCRW* -	**THUN GOTHENBURG** *ex* BRO Gothenburg *-2012* *ex* Red Teal *-2011* **Thun Tankers BV** Erik Thun AB (Thunship Management Holland) *Delfzijl* *Netherlands* MMSI: 246257000	**4,859** 2,289 6,844	Class: BV	**2007-01 Tuzla Gemi Endustrisi A.S. — Tuzla** Yd No: 31 Loa 119.10 (BB) Br ex - Dght 6.760 Lbp 111.60 Br md 16.90 Dpth 8.40 Welded, 1 dk	**(A12B2TR) Chemical/Products Tanker** Double Hull (13F) Liq: 7,831; Liq (Oil): 7,831 Cargo Heating Coils Compartments: 12 Wing Ta, 2 Wing Slop Ta, ER 12 Cargo Pump (s): 12x350m³/hr Manifold: Bow/CM: 57.1m Ice Capable	**1 oil engine** reduction geared to sc. shaft (s) driving 1 CP propeller Total Power: 3,840kW (5,221hp) 14.0kn MaK 8M32C 1 x 4 Stroke 8 Cy. 320 x 480 3840kW (5221bhp) Caterpillar Motoren GmbH & Co. KG-Germany AuxGen: 3 x 400kW 440/220V 60Hz a.c Thrusters: 1 Thwart. CP thruster (f) Fuel: 55.0 (d.f.) 385.0 (r.f.) 15.0pd
9260380 *PBJU* -	**THUN GOTHIA** *ex* BRO Gothia *-2012* *ex* Marisp *-2007* **Thun Tankers BV** Erik Thun AB (Thunship Management Holland) SatCom: Inmarsat C 424484314 *Delfzijl* *Netherlands* MMSI: 244843000 Official number: 43981	**4,814** 2,238 7,157 T/cm 16.8	Class: LR (GL) (NV) (BV) **100A1** SS 03/2013 Double Hull oil and chemical tanker, Ship Type 2 SG 1.54 ESP LI **LMC** **UMS**	**2003-04 Marmara Tersanesi — Yarimca** Yd No: 61 Loa 119.10 (BB) Br ex - Dght 6.775 Lbp 111.60 Br md 16.90 Dpth 8.40 Welded, 1 dk	**(A12B2TR) Chemical/Products Tanker** Double Hull (13F) Liq: 7,726; Liq (Oil): 7,722 Cargo Heating Coils Compartments: 16 Wing Ta, 1 Slop Ta, ER 16 Cargo Pump (s): 12x200m³/hr, 4x120m³/hr Manifold: Bow/CM: 59m Ice Capable	**1 oil engine** geared to sc. shaft driving 1 CP propeller Total Power: 3,840kW (5,221hp) 14.0kn MaK 8M32C 1 x 4 Stroke 8 Cy. 320 x 480 3840kW (5221bhp) MaK Motoren GmbH & Co. KG-Kiel AuxGen: 3 x 500kW 400/230V 50Hz a.c, 1 x 950kW 400/230V 50Hz a.c Thrusters: 1 Tunnel thruster (f) Fuel: 74.0 (d.f.) 394.3 (r.f.) 14.2pd

IMO / Call sign	Name / Owner	Tonnage	Class	Builder / Dimensions	Type	Machinery
9190195 *PCGF* -	**THUN GRACE** *ex* BRO Grace *-2012* *ex* United Grace *-2000* **Thun Tankers BV** Erik Thun AB (Thunship Management Holland) *Delfzijl* *Netherlands* MMSI: 245461000 Official number: 36471	**3,653** 1,825 6,535 T/cm 14.2	Class: BV	**1999-10 Scheepswerf Ferus Smit BV — Westerbroek** Yd No: 321 Loa 103.46 (BB) Br ex - Dght 6.761 Lbp 98.35 Br md 15.00 Dpth 9.30 Welded, 1 dk	**(A12B2TR) Chemical/Products Tanker** Double Hull (13F) Liq: 6,893; Liq (Oil): 6,893 Compartments: 1 Ta, 8 Wing Ta, ER 9 Cargo Pump (s): 9x300m³/hr Manifold: Bow/CM: 58m Ice Capable	**1 oil engine** with clutches, flexible couplings & sr geared to sc. shaft driving 1 CP propeller Total Power: 2,430kW (3,304hp) 13.5kn Wartsila 6R32E 1 x 4 Stroke 6 Cy. 320 x 350 2430kW (3304bhp) Wartsila NSD Finland Oy-Finland AuxGen: 1 x 360kW 440/230V 60Hz a.c, 3 x 224kW 440/230V 60Hz a.c Thrusters: 1 Thwart. CP thruster (f) Fuel: 51.4 (d.f.) (Heating Coils) 205.6 (r.f.) 12.5pd
9266425 *PBCH* -	**THUN GRANITE** *ex* BRO Granite *-2013* **Thun Tankers BV** Erik Thun AB (Thunship Management Holland) *Delfzijl* *Netherlands* MMSI: 244734000 Official number: 41063	**4,107** 2,136 7,559 T/cm 15.8	Class: BV	**2004-04 Scheepswerf Ferus Smit BV — Westerbroek** Yd No: 343 Loa 114.66 (BB) Br ex - Dght 6.750 Lbp 109.45 Br md 15.00 Dpth 9.30 Welded, 1 dk	**(A12B2TR) Chemical/Products Tanker** Double Hull (13F) Liq: 8,034; Liq (Oil): 8,032 Compartments: 1 Ta, 8 Wing Ta, ER 9 Cargo Pump (s): 9x300m³/hr Manifold: Bow/CM: 67.5m Ice Capable	**1 oil engine** reduction geared to sc. shaft driving 1 CP propeller Total Power: 2,430kW (3,304hp) 12.0kn Wartsila 6R32LNE 1 x 4 Stroke 6 Cy. 320 x 350 2430kW (3304bhp) Wartsila Finland Oy-Finland AuxGen: 3 x 262kW 440/230V 60Hz a.c, 1 x 360kW 440/230V 60Hz a.c Thrusters: 1 Thwart. CP thruster (f) Fuel: 60.0 (d.f.) (Heating Coils) 248.0 (r.f.) 10.0pd
9266413 *PBLL* -	**THUN GRATITUDE** *ex* BRO Gratitude *-2013* **Thun Tankers BV** Erik Thun AB (Thunship Management Holland) *Delfzijl* *Netherlands* MMSI: 245689000 Official number: 41062	**4,107** 2,136 7,559 T/cm 15.8	Class: BV	**2003-11 Scheepswerf Ferus Smit BV — Westerbroek** Yd No: 342 Loa 114.66 (BB) Br ex - Dght 6.760 Lbp 109.51 Br md 15.00 Dpth 9.30 Welded, 1 dk	**(A12B2TR) Chemical/Products Tanker** Double Hull (13F) Liq: 8,034; Liq (Oil): 7,164 Compartments: 1 Ta, 8 Wing Ta, ER 9 Cargo Pump (s): 9x300m³/hr Manifold: Bow/CM: 67.5m Ice Capable	**1 oil engine** reduction geared to sc. shaft driving 1 CP propeller Total Power: 2,460kW (3,345hp) 12.0kn Wartsila 6R32LNE 1 x 4 Stroke 6 Cy. 320 x 350 2460kW (3345bhp) Wartsila Finland Oy-Finland AuxGen: 3 x 262kW 440/220V 60Hz a.c, 1 x 360kW 440/220V 60Hz a.c Thrusters: 1 Thwart. CP thruster (f) Fuel: 60.0 (d.f.) (Heating Coils) 248.0 (r.f.) 10.0pd
8846151 *WDD9331* -	**THUNDER** - **Foss International Inc** - *Houston, TX* *United States of America* MMSI: 338618000 Official number: 977014	**1,213** 364 -	Class: (AB)	**1992-08 Upper Peninsular Shipbuilding Corp. — Ontonagon, Mi** (Hull launched by) Yd No: 101 **1992-08 Marine Specialty Co. — Friendswood, Tx** (Hull completed by) Yd No: 001 Loa 37.41 Br ex - Dght 6.840 Lbp 34.13 Br md 13.41 Dpth 8.99 Welded, 1 dk	**(B32B2SA) Articulated Pusher Tug**	**2 oil engines** sr geared to sc. shafts driving 2 CP propellers Total Power: 5,884kW (8,000hp) 14.0kn MaK 6M551AK 2 x 4 Stroke 6 Cy. 450 x 550 each-2942kW (4000bhp) Krupp MaK Maschinenbau GmbH-Kiel AuxGen: 2 x 400kW a.c
8422010 *ERRG* -	**THUNDER** *ex* Sandfeld *-2004* *ex* Paloma I *-1997* *ex* Paloma *-1996* *ex* Landkirchen *-1993* **Nergis Enterprises Inc** Success M&S Maritime SA *Giurgiulesti* *Moldova* MMSI: 214181807	**1,559** 784 1,735	Class: MB (GL)	**1984-12 Schiffs. Hugo Peters Wewelsfleth Peters & Co. GmbH — Wewelsfleth** Yd No: 603 Loa 82.45 Br ex 11.31 Dght 3.517 Lbp 77.35 Br md 11.30 Dpth 5.41 Welded, 2 dks	**(A31A2GX) General Cargo Ship** Grain: 2,915; Bale: 2,910 TEU 48 C. 48/20' (40') Compartments: 1 Ho, ER 1 Ha: (49.8 x 9.0)ER Ice Capable	**1 oil engine** with flexible couplings & sr reverse geared to sc. shaft driving 1 FP propeller Total Power: 441kW (600hp) 10.5kn Deutz SBA8M528 1 x 4 Stroke 8 Cy. 220 x 280 441kW (600bhp) Kloeckner Humboldt Deutz AG-West Germany AuxGen: 1 x 168kW 380V 50Hz a.c, 1 x 60kW 380V 50Hz a.c Thrusters: 1 Thwart. FP thruster (f)
8635203 *NNTB* -	**THUNDER BAY** - **Government of The United States of America (US Coast Guard)** - *United States of America* MMSI: 366999983	*500* - -		**1985-11 Bay City Marine, Inc. — San Diego, Ca** Loa 42.67 Br ex - Dght 3.658 Lbp 39.62 Br md 11.28 Dpth - Welded, 1 dk	**(B32A2ST) Tug** Ice Capable	**2 diesel electric oil engines** driving 2 gen. each 1200kW Connecting to 1 elec. Motor of (1839kW) driving 1 FP propeller Total Power: 1,838kW (2,498hp) 12.0kn Fairbanks, Morse 10-38D8-1/8 2 x 2 Stroke 10 Cy. 207 x 254 each-919kW (1249bhp) Colt Industries Fairbanks MorseEngine Div.-U.S.A. AuxGen: 1 x 125kW a.c Fuel: 71.0
5115886 - -	**THUNDER BAY** *ex* Primadona *-2011* *ex* Temeteron *-2009* *ex* Hesa *-2003* *ex* Biotoff *-1992* *ex* Vevosa *-1988* *ex* Godfjord *-1977* *ex* Kirsten *-1968* *ex* Fjordskar *-1965* *ex* Trysfjord *-1958* **Mid-Atlantic Shipping Co SA** -	**189** 107 295	Class: (BV) (NV)	**1956 Hollen Skipsverft — Sogne** Yd No: 125 Loa 32.06 Br ex 6.74 Dght 3.201 Lbp 29.57 Br md 6.74 Dpth 3.36 Welded, 1 dk	**(A31A2GX) General Cargo Ship** Grain: 382 Compartments: 1 Ho, ER 1 Ha: (12.7 x 3.9)ER Derricks: 1x2t; Winches: 1	**1 oil engine** driving 1 FP propeller Total Power: 441kW (600hp) 9.5kn Deutz SBF12M716 1 x Vee 4 Stroke 12 Cy. 135 x 160 441kW (600bhp) (new engine 1975) Kloeckner Humboldt Deutz AG-West Germany AuxGen: 1 x 6kW 24V d.c, 1 x 2kW 24V d.c Fuel: 8.0 (d.f.) 2.0pd
8855657 *WDF2257* -	**THUNDER BAY** *ex* Briana Nicole *-2009* *ex* Thunder Bay *-2006* **FV Thunder Bay LLC** - *Cape May, NJ* *United States of America* MMSI: 367426660 Official number: 687824	*158* 107 -		**1985 La Force Shipyard Inc — Coden AL** Yd No: 24 Loa 25.91 Br ex - Dght - Lbp 23.28 Br md 7.32 Dpth 3.60 Welded, 1 dk	**(B11B2FV) Fishing Vessel**	**1 oil engine** driving 1 FP propeller Total Power: 530kW (721hp) Caterpillar 3412TA 1 x Vee 4 Stroke 12 Cy. 137 x 152 530kW (721bhp) Caterpillar Tractor Co-USA
9601039 *CFN6288* -	**THUNDER BAY** *ex* Chengxi 9302 *-2013* **The CSL Group Inc (Canada Steamship Lines)** - *Montreal, QC* *Canada* MMSI: 316023339 Official number: 836913	**24,430** 8,112 34,433	Class: LR ✠ **100A1** Lake SS 05/2013 Great Lakes Bulk Carrier for service on the Great Lakes and River St. Lawrence **ShipRight** ACS (B) LI ECO ✠ **LMC** **UMS** Cable: 330.0/52.0 U3 (a)	**2013-05 Chengxi Shipyard Co Ltd — Jiangyin JS** Yd No: CX9302 Loa 225.46 (BB) Br ex 23.79 Dght 10.100 Lbp 222.60 Br md 23.76 Dpth 14.75 Welded, 1 dk	**(A23A2BK) Bulk Carrier, Self-discharging, Laker** Grain: 39,000 Compartments: 5 Ho, ER 5 Ha: ER	**1 oil engine** driving 1 CP propeller Total Power: 8,750kW (11,897hp) 13.0kn MAN-B&W 6S50ME-B9 1 x 2 Stroke 6 Cy. 500 x 2214 8750kW (11897bhp) Hudong Heavy Machinery Co Ltd-China AuxGen: 2 x 1250kW 450V 60Hz a.c, 1 x 938kW 450V 60Hz a.c, 1 x 2640kW 590V 60Hz a.c Boilers: TOH (ex.g.) 10.2kgf/cm² (10.0bar), TOH (o.f.) 10.2kgf/cm² (10.0bar), TOH (ex.g.) 10.2kgf/cm² (10.0bar) Thrusters: 1 Thwart. FP thruster (f); 1 Thwart. FP thruster (a)
7609489 - -	**THUNDER RIDGE** *ex* Morning Sun *-1997* *ex* Mi Dumplin *-1997* **Clifford E Mejia & M AA** - *Roatan* *Honduras* Official number: U-1822123	*113* 79 -		**1974 Quality Marine, Inc. — Theodore, Al** L reg 21.71 Br ex - Dght 1.830 Lbp - Br md 6.71 Dpth 3.26 Welded, 1 dk	**(B11B2FV) Fishing Vessel**	**1 oil engine** driving 1 FP propeller Total Power: 268kW (364hp)
8216447 *5VCB9* -	**THUNDER RIVER** *ex* Agnes Candies *-1997* *ex* Pacific Sentry *-1994* *ex* Agnes Candies *-1987* **Harmony Seas Inc** Artemiz Marine Services JLT *Lome* *Togo* MMSI: 671360000	**1,095** 328 1,200	Class: BV (AB)	**1983-07 Halter Marine, Inc. — Lockport, La** Yd No: 1097 Converted From: Offshore Supply Ship-1988 Loa 57.91 Br ex - Dght 3.963 Lbp 56.39 Br md 13.41 Dpth 4.57 Welded, 1 dk	**(B22A20R) Offshore Support Vessel**	**2 oil engines** reverse reduction geared to sc. shafts driving 2 FP propellers Total Power: 2,206kW (3,000hp) 12.0kn EMD (Electro-Motive) 12-645-E7A 2 x Vee 2 Stroke 12 Cy. 230 x 254 each-1103kW (1500bhp) (Reconditioned , Reconditioned & fitted 1983) General Motors Corp.Electro-Motive Div.-La Grange AuxGen: 3 x 150kW Thrusters: 1 Thwart. FP thruster (f)
8660090 *WDD5310* -	**THUNDERAMERICA** - **Abe's Boat Rentals Inc** - *Venice, LA* *United States of America* Official number: 970048	**199** - -		**1990-01 Breaux Brothers Enterprises, Inc. — Loreauville, La** Yd No: 168 L reg 35.53 Br ex - Dght - Lbp - Br md 7.62 Dpth 3.50 Welded, 1 dk	**(B21A20C) Crew/Supply Vessel** Hull Material: Aluminium Alloy	**2 oil engines** reduction geared to sc. shafts driving 2 Propellers
8841802 *WB3276* -	**THUNDERBIRD** *ex* Port Vincent *-1996* *ex* Standard No. 3 *-1993* *ex* Port Vincent *-1946* **Tyee Maritime Inc** - *Sitka, AK* *United States of America* Official number: 243309	*199* 87 -	Class: (AB)	**1943-05 Canulette Shipbuilding Co. — Slidell, La** Yd No: 4 Loa - Br ex - Dght 3.686 Lbp 28.73 Br md 7.62 Dpth 4.08 Welded, 1 dk	**(B32A2ST) Tug**	**1 oil engine** driving 1 FP propeller Total Power: 736kW (1,001hp) Enterprise 1 x 4 Stroke 8 Cy. 406 x 508 736kW (1001bhp) Enterprise Engine & Foundry Co-USA
8302478 - -	**THUNDERBIRD** - **Delmar M & Dave McNab** - *Roatan* *Honduras* Official number: RH-U25302	*105* 71 -		**1980 Steiner Shipyard, Inc. — Bayou La Batre, Al** Loa 22.86 Br ex - Dght - Lbp - Br md 6.72 Dpth 3.38 Welded, 1 dk	**(B11A2FT) Trawler**	**1 oil engine** driving 1 FP propeller Caterpillar 1 x 4 Stroke Caterpillar Tractor Co-USA

IMO / Call sign	Name / Owner	Tonnage	Class	Built	Type	Machinery
7700386 *J8PX8* -	**THUNDERER** *ex* Marmex VII *-2004* *ex* Drive Mar *-1998* *ex* Keverne *-1996* *ex* Groenland *-1990* **Prime Vertical Ltd** Coloured Fin Ltd (CFL) *Kingstown* *St Vincent & The Grenadines* MMSI: 377946000	**544** 163 -	Class: (BV)	**1977-12 B.V. Scheepswerf Jonker & Stans — Hendrik-Ido-Ambacht** Yd No: 341 Loa 41.41 Br ex 10.85 Dght 4.222 Lbp 39.68 Br md 10.51 Dpth 5.31 Welded, 1 dk	**(B32A2ST) Tug**	**2 oil engines** reduction geared to sc. shafts driving 2 CP propellers Total Power: 3,280kW (4,460hp) Alco 12V251F 2 x Vee 4 Stroke 12 Cy. 229 x 267 each-1640kW (2230bhp) White Industrial Power Inc-USA AuxGen: 2 x 230kW 220/440V 60Hz a.c Thrusters: 1 Thwart. FP thruster (f) Fuel: 499.0 (d.f.)
8741002 *XCMR6* -	**THUNDERSTAR** **Compania de Apoyo Maritimo Del Golfo SA de CV** - SatCom: Inmarsat C 434500024 *Ciudad del Carmen* *Mexico* MMSI: 345070243 Official number: 0401196521-5	**110** 35 -	Class: RI	**1978-03 Dynamic Shipbuilders Inc. — Jean Lafitte, La** Yd No: 08 Loa 30.78 Br ex - Dght - Lbp - Br md 7.13 Dpth 3.00 Welded, 1 dk	**(B21A2OC) Crew/Supply Vessel** Hull Material: Aluminium Alloy	**3 oil engines** reduction geared to sc. shafts driving 3 Propellers Total Power: 1,791kW (2,436hp) 16.0kn Cummins QSK19-M 3 x 4 Stroke 6 Cy. 159 x 159 each-597kW (812bhp) Cummins Engine Co Inc-USA
7912472 *YEPK* -	**THUNNUS No. 2** *ex* Hokai Maru No. 3 *-1989* *ex* Taihei Maru No. 38 *-1982* **PT Marine Sukses Gemilang** Shine Year Fishing Co Ltd *Jakarta* *Indonesia* Official number: 1990 BA NO.8611/N	*401* 139 269	Class: (KI) (NK)	**1979-08 Goriki Zosensho — Ise** Yd No: 821 Loa 45.00 Br ex - Dght 2.901 Lbp 38.90 Br md 7.80 Dpth 3.25 Welded, 1 dk	**(B11B2FV) Fishing Vessel**	**1 oil engine** driving 1 FP propeller Total Power: 588kW (799hp) Hanshin 6LU26G 1 x 4 Stroke 6 Cy. 260 x 440 588kW (799bhp) The Hanshin Diesel Works Ltd-Japan AuxGen: 2 x 176kW a.c
9208538 - -	**THURAYA** **Mohamed Bin Masaood & Sons** Masaood Marine Services *Abu Dhabi* *United Arab Emirates*	**137** - 60	Class: (LR) ✠ Classed LR until 27/5/03	**2000-02 Albwardy Marine Engineering LLC — Dubai** Yd No: 003 Loa 26.70 Br ex - Dght 1.250 Lbp 23.27 Br md 7.00 Dpth 2.45 Welded, 1 dk	**(B34T2QR) Work/Repair Vessel**	**2 oil engines** with clutches, flexible couplings & sr reverse geared to sc. shafts driving 2 Water jets Total Power: 588kW (800hp) 11.0kn Volvo Penta TAMD122A 2 x 4 Stroke 6 Cy. 130 x 150 each-294kW (400bhp) AB Volvo Penta-Sweden AuxGen: 2 x 47kW 380V 50Hz a.c
7927685 *VNW4617* -	**THURBURN BLUFF** **Tidal Corp Pty Ltd** - *Fremantle, WA* *Australia* Official number: 375288	*149* 93 -		**1979-10 Ocean Shipyards (WA) Pty Ltd — Fremantle WA** Loa 23.78 Br ex 6.86 Dght 3.850 Lbp 22.53 Br md 6.76 Dpth 2.49 Welded, 1 dk	**(B11B2FV) Fishing Vessel**	**1 oil engine** reverse reduction geared to sc. shaft driving 1 FP propeller Total Power: 268kW (364hp) 9.0kn Caterpillar 3408PCTA 1 x Vee 4 Stroke 8 Cy. 137 x 152 268kW (364bhp) Caterpillar Tractor Co-USA
9611618 *HBLF* -	**THURGAU** *ex* Universe 11 *-2011* **Massmariner SA** Massoel Ltd *Basel* *Switzerland* MMSI: 269217000	**20,924** 11,786 32,790	Class: BV	**2011-09 Universe Shipbuilding (Yangzhou) Co Ltd — Yizheng JS** Yd No: H07-006 Loa 179.90 (BB) Br ex - Dght 10.150 Lbp 171.50 Br md 28.40 Dpth 14.10 Welded, 1 dk	**(A21A2BC) Bulk Carrier** Grain: 43,128 Compartments: 5 Ho, ER 5 Ha: ER Cranes: 4x30.5t	**1 oil engine** driving 1 FP propeller Total Power: 6,480kW (8,810hp) 13.7kn MAN-B&W 6S42MC 1 x 2 Stroke 6 Cy. 420 x 1764 6480kW (8810bhp) STX Engine Co Ltd-South Korea AuxGen: 3 x 440kW 60Hz a.c Fuel: 1820.0
9238765 - -	**THURINGIA** *ex* Thuringia Express *-2012* *ex* CP Tamarind *-2006* *ex* Contship Tamarind *-2005* *ex* APL Honduras *-2004* *launched as* Lykes Adventurer *-2003* **Pacific Leasing Ltd** Eastern Pacific Shipping Pte Ltd *Monrovia* *Liberia*	**39,941** 24,458 50,790 T/cm 70.4	Class: LR ✠ **100A1** SS 04/2008 container ship *IWS LI **ShipRight** (SDA, FDA, CM) ✠ **LMC** **UMS** Eq.Ltr: St; Cable: 687.5/87.0 U3 (a)	**2003-04 Samsung Heavy Industries Co Ltd — Geoje** Yd No: 1394 Loa 260.05 (BB) Br ex 32.30 Dght 12.600 Lbp 244.80 Br md 32.25 Dpth 19.30 Welded, 1 dk	**(A33A2CC) Container Ship (Fully Cellular)** TEU 4253 C Ho 1584 TEU C Dk 2669 TEU incl 400 ref C. Compartments: ER, 7 Cell Ho 7 Ha: ER	**1 oil engine** driving 1 FP propeller Total Power: 36,515kW (49,646hp) 23.3kn B&W 8K90MC-C 1 x 2 Stroke 8 Cy. 900 x 2300 36515kW (49646bhp) Doosan Engine Co Ltd-South Korea AuxGen: 4 x 1700kW 450V 60Hz a.c Boilers: AuxB (Comp) 8.2kgf/cm² (8.0bar) Thrusters: 1 Thwart. CP thruster (f)
8915744 *5BZJ2* -	**THURKUS** *ex* Marie Christine *-2008* **Bluether Shipping Co Ltd** Unibaltic Sp z oo *Limassol* *Cyprus* MMSI: 209588000 Official number: IMO 8915744	**2,561** 1,289 3,284	Class: LR ✠ **100A1** SS 01/2011 *IWS Ice Class 1A FS at a draught of 5.311m Max/min draught fwd 5.311/2.783m Max/min draught aft 5.311/3.196m Power required 1803kw, power installed 1840kw ✠ **LMC** **UMS** Eq.Ltr: P; Cable: 440.0/32.0 U3	**1991-01 Niestern Sander B.V. — Delfzijl** Yd No: 801 Loa 87.96 Br ex 12.58 Dght 5.300 Lbp 84.93 Br md 12.50 Dpth 7.70 Welded, 2 dks	**(A31A2GX) General Cargo Ship** Grain: 5,548 TEU 129 C.Ho 102/20' C.Dk 27/20' Compartments: 1 Ho, ER, 1 Tw Dk 1 Ha: ER Gantry cranes: 1x15t Ice Capable	**1 oil engine** with clutches, flexible couplings & sr reverse geared to sc. shaft driving 1 FP propeller Total Power: 1,845kW (2,508hp) Caterpillar 3606TA 1 x 4 Stroke 6 Cy. 280 x 300 1845kW (2508bhp) Caterpillar Inc-USA AuxGen: 2 x 64kW 380V 50Hz a.c Thrusters: 1 Thwart. FP thruster (f) Fuel: 179.0 (d.f.)
5418018 *ECAR* -	**THURO** *ex* Uno *-1991* *ex* Stevnsklint *-1981* **Maritima Calypso SL** *Santa Cruz de Tenerife* *Spain (CSR)* Official number: 16/2002	**451** 221 670	Class: (BV)	**1963-07 Husumer Schiffswerft — Husum** Yd No: 1214 Loa 51.82 Br ex 8.69 Dght 3.290 Lbp 46.56 Br md 8.67 Dpth 3.71 Riveted\Welded, 1 dk	**(A31A2GX) General Cargo Ship** 2 Ha: 2 (12.1 x 5.0)ER Ice Capable	**1 oil engine** driving 1 CP propeller Total Power: 441kW (600hp) 10.0kn Alpha 406-26VO 1 x 2 Stroke 6 Cy. 260 x 400 441kW (600bhp) (new engine 1975) Alpha Diesel A/S-Denmark AuxGen: 2 x 7kW 115V d.c, 1 x 6kW 115V d.c
8819976 *OWNJ2* -	**THURO MAERSK** *ex* Chastine Maersk *-2001* **A P Moller - Maersk A/S** A P Moller SatCom: Inmarsat C 421930010 *Hellerup* *Denmark (DIS)* MMSI: 219300000 Official number: D3313	**16,982** 7,449 21,825	Class: AB (LR) ✠ Classed LR until 5/12/96	**1991-12 Odense Staalskibsvaerft A/S — Munkebo (Lindo Shipyard)** Yd No: 135 Loa 162.26 (BB) Br ex 27.83 Dght 10.320 Lbp 151.90 Br md 27.80 Dpth 15.23 Welded, 1 dk	**(A33A2CC) Container Ship (Fully Cellular)** TEU 1446 C Ho 539 TEU C Dk 907 TEU incl 114 ref C. Compartments: 8 Cell Ho, ER 9 Ha: ER 12 Wing Ha: Gantry cranes: 1x35t	**1 oil engine** driving 1 FP propeller Total Power: 10,480kW (14,249hp) 18.5kn B&W 8S50MC 1 x 2 Stroke 8 Cy. 500 x 1910 10480kW (14249bhp) Mitsui Engineering & Shipbuilding CLtd-Japan AuxGen: 3 x 1250kW 440V 60Hz a.c Thrusters: 1 Thwart. CP thruster (f); 1 Tunnel thruster (a)
9154737 - -	**THUY AN** **Hang Hai Co Ltd** - *Haiphong* *Vietnam* MMSI: 574855000	**421** 279 786	Class: VR	**1996-01 189 Company — Haiphong** Rebuilt-2000 Loa 51.55 Br ex 7.92 Dght 3.420 Lbp 48.30 Br md 7.75 Dpth 4.20 Welded, 1 dk	**(A31A2GX) General Cargo Ship** Bale: 434	**2 oil engines** reduction geared to sc. shafts driving 2 FP propellers Total Power: 198kW (270hp) 9.0kn Skoda 6L160 2 x 4 Stroke 6 Cy. 160 x 225 each-99kW (135bhp) CKD Praha-Praha AuxGen: 1 x 4kW a.c
9026332 *XVOH* -	**THUY AN 06** **Thuy An Transport Co Ltd** - *Haiphong* *Vietnam* MMSI: 574596000 Official number: VN-1771-VT	**999** 654 1,862	Class: VR	**2004-02 Thanh Long Co Ltd — Haiphong** Yd No: HT-29 Loa 69.75 Br ex 10.90 Dght 4.600 Lbp 66.30 Br md 10.80 Dpth 5.50 Welded, 1 dk	**(A31A2GX) General Cargo Ship**	**1 oil engine** driving 1 Propeller Total Power: 721kW (980hp) 10.0kn Skoda 6L350PN 1 x 4 Stroke 6 Cy. 350 x 500 721kW (980bhp) CKD Praha-Praha
8667232 *3WYB* -	**THUY AN 16** **Thuy An Transport Co Ltd** - *Haiphong* *Vietnam* Official number: VN-2574-VT	**1,432** 949 2,671	Class: VR	**2008-05 Haiphong Mechanical & Trading Co. — Haiphong** Yd No: THB-22 Loa 79.80 Br ex 12.02 Dght 4.700 Lbp 75.40 Br md 12.00 Dpth 5.70 Welded, 1 dk	**(A31A2GX) General Cargo Ship** Grain: 3,007 Compartments: 2 Ho, ER 2 Ha: ER 2 (21.0 x 8.0)	**1 oil engine** driving 1 FP propeller Total Power: 1,100kW (1,496hp) 10.0kn Chinese Std. Type 8300ZLCZA 1 x 4 Stroke 8 Cy. 300 x 380 1100kW (1496bhp) Zibo Diesel Engine Factory-China
8894249 *3WAR* -	**THUY BAC 01** *ex* TP-90 *-2001* **Northern Shipping JSC** - *Haiphong* *Vietnam*	**190** 85 70	Class: (VR)	**1989 Tam Bac Shipyard — Haiphong** Loa 31.50 Br ex - Dght 1.600 Lbp 28.00 Br md 7.25 Dpth 2.70 Welded, 1 dk	**(A31A2GX) General Cargo Ship**	**1 oil engine** reduction geared to sc. shaft driving 1 FP propeller Total Power: 147kW (200hp) 11.0kn S.K.L. 6NVD26-2 1 x 4 Stroke 6 Cy. 180 x 260 147kW (200bhp) (made 1984) VEB Schwermaschinenbau "KarlLiebknecht" (SKL)-Magdeburg AuxGen: 1 x 30kW a.c

8847399 - -	**THUY HAI 09** *ex* Phuong Mai 09 *ex* Tay Son *-1994* **Thuy Hai Co Ltd (Cong Ty TNHH Thuy Hai)** - *Haiphong* *Vietnam*	**385** 169 500	Class: (VR)	**1983 at Haiphong** Loa 48.50 Br ex - Dght 3.420 Lbp - Br md 8.20 Dpth 4.10 Welded, 1 dk	**(A31A2GX) General Cargo Ship** Grain: 698 Compartments: 2 Ho, ER 2 Ha: 2 (8.0 x 4.5)ER	**1 oil engine** reduction geared to sc. shaft driving 1 FP propeller Total Power: 294kW (400hp) 9.0kn S.K.L. 8NVD26A-2 1 x 4 Stroke 8 Cy. 180 x 260 294kW (400bhp) VEB Schwermaschinenbau "KarlLiebknecht" (SKL)-Magdeburg AuxGen: 1 x 50kW a.c, 1 x 30kW a.c
9024487 *3WFS* -	**THUY LONG 16** **Thuy Long River-Sea Transport Co Ltd** - *Haiphong* *Vietnam*	**499** 327 911	Class: VR	**2002-10 in Vietnam** Loa 56.75 Br ex 8.70 Dght 3.350 Lbp 52.00 Br md 8.47 Dpth 4.10 Welded, 1 dk	**(A31A2GX) General Cargo Ship**	**1 oil engine** driving 1 FP propeller Total Power: 300kW (408hp) 10.0kn S.K.L. 8NVD36-1U 1 x 4 Stroke 8 Cy. 240 x 360 300kW (408bhp) (made 1974) SKL Motoren u. Systemtechnik AG-Magdeburg
8869012 - -	**THUY NGUYEN 02** **Haiphong Sea Products Trading & Service Co (Cong Ty Kinh Doanh & Va Dich Vu Thuy San Hai Phong)** - *Haiphong* *Vietnam*	*118* 41 -	Class: (VR)	**1990 in the People's Republic of China** Loa 31.00 Br ex - Dght 2.300 Lbp - Br md 5.80 Dpth 2.90 Welded, 1 dk	**(B11B2FV) Fishing Vessel**	**1 oil engine** reduction geared to sc. shaft driving 1 FP propeller Total Power: 199kW (271hp) 10.0kn Chinese Std. Type 8E150C 1 x 4 Stroke 8 Cy. 150 x 225 199kW (271bhp) in China
8869000 - -	**THUY NGUYEN 04** **Haiphong Sea Products Trading & Service Co (Cong Ty Kinh Doanh & Va Dich Vu Thuy San Hai Phong)** - *Haiphong* *Vietnam*	*118* 41 -	Class: (VR)	**1990 in the People's Republic of China** Loa 31.00 Br ex - Dght 2.300 Lbp - Br md 5.80 Dpth 2.90 Welded, 1 dk	**(B11B2FV) Fishing Vessel**	**1 oil engine** reduction geared to sc. shaft driving 1 FP propeller Total Power: 199kW (271hp) 10.0kn Chinese Std. Type 8E150C 1 x 4 Stroke 8 Cy. 150 x 225 199kW (271bhp) in China
5012292 *SV7152* -	**THYELLA** *ex* Alnmouth *-1987* **Igoumenitsa Naftiki Eteria** *Piraeus* *Greece* MMSI: 237106200 Official number: 4422	*173* - -	Class: (LR) ✠ Classed LR until 6/89	**1962-05 R. Dunston (Hessle) Ltd. — Hessle** Yd No: S784 Loa 30.33 Br ex 7.70 Dght 3.029 Lbp 27.13 Br md 7.17 Dpth 3.66 Riveted\Welded, 1 dk	**(B32A2ST) Tug**	**1 oil engine** reverse reduction geared to sc. shaft driving 1 FP propeller Total Power: 699kW (950hp) Ruston 6ATCM 1 x 4 Stroke 6 Cy. 318 x 368 699kW (950bhp) Ruston & Hornsby Ltd.-Lincoln AuxGen: 2 x 28kW 220V d.c
9235268 *ONCP* -	**TI EUROPE** *ex* Hellespont Tara *-2004* **Euronav NV** Tankers (UK) Agencies Ltd SatCom: Inmarsat C 420540810 *Antwerpen* *Belgium* MMSI: 205408000 Official number: 01 00543 2004	**234,006** 162,477 441,561 T/cm 230.0	Class: LR ✠ **100A1** SS 11/2012 Double Hull oil tanker ESP **ShipRight** (SDA, FDA, CM) *IWS LI ✠ **LMC** **UMS IGS** Eq.Ltr: I*; Cable: 770.0/132.0 U3 (a)	**2002-11 Daewoo Shipbuilding & Marine Engineering Co Ltd — Geoje** Yd No: 5202 Converted From: Oil Storage Vessel-2013 Converted From: Crude Oil Tanker-2012 Loa 380.00 (BB) Br ex 68.05 Dght 24.525 Lbp 366.00 Br md 68.00 Dpth 34.00 Welded, 1 dk	**(A13A2TV) Crude Oil Tanker** Double Hull (13F) Liq: 490,505; Liq (Oil): 513,743 Compartments: 5 Ta, 14 Wing Ta, 2 Wing Slop Ta, ER 3 Cargo Pump (s): 3x5000m³/hr Manifold: Bow/CM: 185.6m	**1 oil engine** driving 1 FP propeller Total Power: 36,900kW (50,169hp) 16.0kn Sulzer 9RTA84T-D 1 x 2 Stroke 9 Cy. 840 x 3150 36900kW (50169bhp) Doosan Engine Co Ltd-South Korea AuxGen: 3 x 1450kW 450V 60Hz a.c Boilers: e (ex.g.) 27.0kgf/cm² (26.5bar), AuxB (o.f.) 22.5kgf/cm² (22.1bar) Fuel: 475.0 (d.f.) 12750.0 (r.f.)
9290086 *ONDQ* -	**TI HELLAS** *launched as* Chrysanthemum *-2005* **Euronav NV** Tankers (UK) Agencies Ltd SatCom: Inmarsat C 420544010 *Antwerpen* *Belgium* MMSI: 205440000 Official number: 01 00586 2005	**161,127** 110,526 319,254 T/cm 180.0	Class: LR ✠ **100A1** SS 05/2010 Double Hull oil tanker ESP **ShipRight** (SDA, FDA plus, CM) *IWS LI SPM ✠ **LMC** **UMS IGS** Eq.Ltr: D†; Cable: 770.0/114.0 U3 (a)	**2005-05 Hyundai Samho Heavy Industries Co Ltd — Samho** Yd No: S214 Loa 332.90 (BB) Br ex 60.04 Dght 22.500 Lbp 319.00 Br md 60.00 Dpth 30.40 Welded, 1 dk	**(A13A2TV) Crude Oil Tanker** Double Hull (13F) Liq: 339,070; Liq (Oil): 339,070 Compartments: 5 Ta, 10 Wing Ta, 2 Wing Slop Ta, ER	**1 oil engine** driving 1 FP propeller Total Power: 27,165kW (36,934hp) 15.6kn MAN-B&W 7S80MC-C 1 x 2 Stroke 7 Cy. 800 x 3200 27165kW (36934bhp) Hyundai Heavy Industries Co Ltd-South Korea AuxGen: 3 x 1180kW 450V 60Hz a.c Boilers: e (ex.g.) 22.2kgf/cm² (21.8bar), WTAuxB (o.f.) 18.3kgf/cm² (17.9bar) Fuel: 430.2 (d.f.) 6670.5 (r.f.)
9246633 *V7IG4* -	**TI OCEANIA** *ex* Hellespont Fairfax *-2004* **Oceania Tanker Corp** Tankers (UK) Agencies Ltd SatCom: Inmarsat C 453833728 *Majuro* *Marshall Islands* MMSI: 538002371 Official number: 2371	**234,006** 162,477 441,585 T/cm 230.2	Class: LR ✠ **100A1** SS 04/2008 Double Hull oil tanker ESP *IWS LI **ShipRight** (SDA, FDA, CM) ✠ **LMC** **UMS IGS** Eq.Ltr: I*; Cable: 770.0/132.0 U3 (a)	**2003-04 Daewoo Shipbuilding & Marine Engineering Co Ltd — Geoje** Yd No: 5204 Loa 380.00 (BB) Br ex 68.05 Dght 24.525 Lbp 366.00 Br md 68.00 Dpth 34.00 Welded, 1 dk	**(A13A2TV) Crude Oil Tanker** Double Hull (13F) Liq: 490,505; Liq (Oil): 513,743 Compartments: 5 Ta, 14 Wing Ta, 2 Wing Slop Ta, ER 3 Cargo Pump (s): 3x5000m³/hr Manifold: Bow/CM: 185.6m	**1 oil engine** driving 1 FP propeller Total Power: 35,090kW (47,708hp) 16.0kn Sulzer 9RTA84T-D 1 x 2 Stroke 9 Cy. 840 x 3150 35090kW (47708bhp) Doosan Engine Co Ltd-South Korea AuxGen: 3 x 1450kW 450V 60Hz a.c Boilers: e (ex.g.) 27.5kgf/cm² (27.0bar), WTAuxB (o.f.) 22.4kgf/cm² (22.0bar) Fuel: 475.8 (d.f.) 12755.9 (r.f.)
9230907 *ONDI* -	**TI TOPAZ** *ex* Crude Topaz *-2005* *ex* Oriental Topaz *-2005* **Euronav NV** Euronav Ship Management (Hellas) Ltd SatCom: Inmarsat C 420543810 *Antwerpen* *Belgium* MMSI: 205438000 Official number: 01 00582 2005	**161,135** 110,526 319,430 T/cm 180.7	Class: LR (KR) ✠ **100A1** SS 10/2012 Double Hull oil tanker ESP **ShipRight** (SDA, FDA, CM) *IWS LI SPM ✠ **LMC** **UMS IGS** Eq.Ltr: A†; Cable: 770.0/114.0 U3 (a)	**2002-10 Samho Heavy Industries Co Ltd — Samho** Yd No: 135 Loa 332.99 (BB) Br ex 60.05 Dght 22.500 Lbp 319.00 Br md 60.00 Dpth 30.40 Welded, 1 dk	**(A13A2TV) Crude Oil Tanker** Double Hull (13F) Liq: 339,055; Liq (Oil): 345,975 Compartments: Wing ER, 6 Ta, 9 Wing Ta, 2 Wing Slop Ta, ER 3 Cargo Pump (s)	**1 oil engine** driving 1 FP propeller Total Power: 29,340kW (39,891hp) 16.1kn B&W 6S90MC-C 1 x 2 Stroke 6 Cy. 900 x 3188 29340kW (39891bhp) Hyundai Heavy Industries Co Ltd-South Korea AuxGen: 3 x 1100kW 450V 60Hz a.c Boilers: e (ex.g.) 22.9kgf/cm² (22.5bar), WTAuxB (o.f.) 18.0kgf/cm² (17.7bar) Fuel: 363.0 (d.f.) (Heating Coils) 7850.0 (r.f.)
9386342 *V7QE5* -	**TI VOGLIO TANTO BENE** **Jeva Investment Ltd** - *Bikini* *Marshall Islands* MMSI: 538080053 Official number: 80053	**319** 95 -	Class: RI	**2007-03 ISA Produzione Srl — Ancona** Yd No: 133.04 Loa 41.40 Br ex - Dght 1.400 Lbp 34.35 Br md 7.80 Dpth 3.90 Bonded, 1 dk	**(X11A2YP) Yacht** Hull Material: Reinforced Plastic	**2 oil engines** reduction geared to sc. shafts driving 2 FP propellers Total Power: 5,370kW (7,302hp) M.T.U. 16V4000M90 2 x Vee 4 Stroke 16 Cy. 165 x 190 each-2685kW (3651bhp) MTU Friedrichshafen GmbH-Friedrichshafen
7919872 - -	**TIA-V** *ex* 1997-13 *-2000* *ex* James Sinclair *-1997* **ASL Technics Ltd** -	*315* 95 -		**1981-05 John Manly Shipyard Ltd — Vancouver BC** Yd No: 550 Converted From: Fishery Patrol Vessel-2000 Loa 37.80 Br ex - Dght 2.434 Lbp 36.61 Br md 8.39 Dpth 3.69 Welded, 1 dk	**(X11A2YP) Yacht** Hull Material: Aluminium Alloy	**2 oil engines** geared to sc. shafts driving 2 CP propellers Total Power: 3,384kW (4,600hp) 12.0kn M.T.U. 12V538TB91 2 x Vee 4 Stroke 12 Cy. 185 x 200 each-1692kW (2300bhp) MTU Friedrichshafen GmbH-Friedrichshafen
9411898 *ZMT2686* -	**TIAKI** **CentrePort Ltd** - *Wellington* *New Zealand* MMSI: 512000322 Official number: 876425	**250** 75 118	Class: LR ✠ **100A1** SS 12/2012 tug **LMC** **UMS** Eq.Ltr: F; Cable: 275.0/19.0 U2 (a)	**2007-12 Song Cam Shipyard — Haiphong** (Hull) **2007-12 B.V. Scheepswerf Damen — Gorinchem** Yd No: 512214 Loa 24.47 Br ex 11.33 Dght 3.650 Lbp 22.16 Br md 10.70 Dpth 4.60 Welded, 1 dk	**(B32A2ST) Tug**	**2 oil engines** gearing integral to driving 2 Z propellers Total Power: 4,200kW (5,710hp) Caterpillar 3516B-HD 2 x Vee 4 Stroke 16 Cy. 170 x 215 each-2100kW (2855bhp) Caterpillar Inc-USA AuxGen: 2 x 56kW 400V 50Hz a.c
9461348 *2BOW5* -	**TIAN** **Ammolite Holdings Ltd** - *Jersey* *Jersey* MMSI: 235068033	**213** 63 21	Class: RI	**2008-08 C.R.N. Cant. Nav. Ancona S.r.l. — Ancona** Yd No: 112/18 Loa 34.16 Br ex - Dght 1.400 Lbp 29.20 Br md 7.10 Dpth 3.50 Welded, 1 dk	**(X11A2YP) Yacht**	**2 oil engines** reduction geared to sc. shafts driving 2 FP propellers Total Power: 4,080kW (5,548hp) 28.0kn M.T.U. 12V4000M90 2 x Vee 4 Stroke 12 Cy. 165 x 190 each-2040kW (2774bhp) MTU Friedrichshafen GmbH-Friedrichshafen
9400564 *BOMQ* -	**TIAN AN HE** **COSCO Container Lines Co Ltd (COSCON)** - *Shanghai* *China* MMSI: 412714000 Official number: 0010000107	**54,005** 32,333 63,165	Class: CC (GL)	**2010-06 Shanghai Jiangnan Changxing Heavy Industry Co Ltd — Shanghai** Yd No: H2405 Loa 294.00 (BB) Br ex 32.25 Dght 12.000 Lbp 284.16 Br md 32.20 Dpth 21.80 Welded, 1 dk	**(A33A2CC) Container Ship (Fully Cellular)** TEU 5089 C Ho 2274 TEU C Dk 2815 TEU incl 385 ref C Compartments: 6 Cell Ho, ER Ice Capable	**1 oil engine** driving 1 FP propeller Total Power: 45,760kW (62,215hp) 25.2kn MAN-B&W 8K98MC 1 x 2 Stroke 8 Cy. 980 x 2660 45760kW (62215bhp) CSSC MES Diesel Co Ltd-China AuxGen: 4 x 1800kW 450V a.c Thrusters: 1 Tunnel thruster (f)

9218167 **TIAN BAI FENG** **39,042** Class: CC (BV)
VRWP5 25,025
- **Jin Yan Navigation Inc** 74,269
China Shipping (Hong Kong) Holdings Co Ltd T/cm
Hong Kong *Hong Kong* 66.3
MMSI: 477801000

2000-08 Namura Shipbuilding Co Ltd — Imari SG
Yd No: 983
Loa 224.89 (BB) Br ex - Dght 13.930
Lbp 215.00 Br md 32.20 Dpth 19.30
Welded, 1 dk

(A21A2BC) Bulk Carrier
Grain: 89,000
Compartments: 7 Ho, ER
7 Ha: (16.8 x 13.2)5 (16.8 x 14.9) (16.9 x 14.9)ER

1 oil engine driving 1 FP propeller
Total Power: 8,827kW (12,001hp) 14.5kn
B&W 7S50MC
1 x 2 Stroke 7 Cy. 500 x 1910 8827kW (12001bhp)
Hitachi Zosen Corp-Japan
AuxGen: 3 x 380kW 450V 60Hz a.c
Fuel: 85.1 (d.f.) (Heating Coils) 1943.3 (r.f.) 35.0pd

8979752 **TIAN BAO** **496**
- *ex* Ju Chun 277
- **Fujian Shishi Shipping Co** 1,000
-

1979 Jiaojiang No 1 Shipping Co — Taizhou ZJ
Loa 59.50 Br ex - Dght 2.700
Lbp 54.71 Br md 10.00 Dpth 4.31
Welded, 1 dk

(A31A2GX) General Cargo Ship

1 oil engine geared to sc. shaft driving 1 Propeller
Total Power: 441kW (600hp)
Chinese Std. Type 6300ZC
1 x 4 Stroke 6 Cy. 300 x 380 441kW (600bhp)
in China

9309019 **TIAN BAO HAI** **88,856** Class: CC
BOIA 58,333
- **Qingdao Ocean Shipping Co Ltd (COSCO QINGDAO)** 174,766
T/cm
119.0
SatCom: Inmarsat C 441309510
Qingdao, Shandong *China*
MMSI: 413095000

2004-12 Shanghai Waigaoqiao Shipbuilding Co Ltd — Shanghai Yd No: 1015
Loa 289.00 (BB) Br ex 45.05 Dght 18.200
Lbp 279.00 Br md 45.00 Dpth 24.50
Welded, 1 dk

(A21A2BC) Bulk Carrier
Grain: 193,134; Bale: 183,425
Compartments: 9 Ho, ER
9 Ha: 7 (15.5 x 20.0)ER 2 (15.5 x 16.5)

1 oil engine driving 1 FP propeller
Total Power: 16,858kW (22,920hp) 14.5kn
MAN-B&W 6S70MC
1 x 2 Stroke 6 Cy. 700 x 2674 16858kW (22920bhp)
Hudong Heavy Machinery Co Ltd-China
AuxGen: 3 x 750kW 450V a.c

9390616 **TIAN BAO HE** **54,005** Class: CC GL
BQBG 32,333
- **COSCO Container Lines Co Ltd (COSCON)** 62,997
-
Shanghai *China*
MMSI: 413760000
Official number: 0009000162

2009-10 Shanghai Jiangnan Changxing Heavy Industry Co Ltd — Shanghai
Yd No: H2390
Loa 294.00 (BB) Br ex 32.25 Dght 12.000
Lbp 284.16 Br md 32.20 Dpth 21.80
Welded, 1 dk

(A33A2CC) Container Ship (Fully Cellular)
Grain: 112,495
TEU 5089 C Ho 2274 TEU C Dk 2815 TEU incl 385 ref C
Compartments: 6 Cell Ho, ER
6 Ha: ER

1 oil engine driving 1 FP propeller
Total Power: 45,760kW (62,215hp) 25.2kn
MAN-B&W 8K98MC
1 x 2 Stroke 8 Cy. 980 x 2660 45760kW (62215bhp)
AuxGen: 4 x 1800kW 450V a.c
Thrusters: 1 Tunnel thruster (f)

8519514 **TIAN CHEN 8** **1,195** Class: UM
XURS7 *ex* Sakurakawa *-2008* *ex* Jin Ze No. 1 *-2002* 614
- *ex* Wen Deng *-1998* *ex* Hakuzan *-1998* 1,574
Yin Zhou Shipping Co Ltd
Tian Chen Int'l Shipping Management Co Ltd
SatCom: Inmarsat C 451415810
Phnom Penh *Cambodia*
MMSI: 514158000
Official number: 0285279

1985-12 Yamanaka Zosen K.K. — Imabari
Yd No: 318
Loa 72.73 Br ex - Dght 4.231
Lbp 68.03 Br md 11.51 Dpth 6.71
Welded, 2 dks

(A31A2GX) General Cargo Ship
Grain: 2,713; Bale: 2,629
Compartments: 1 Ho, ER
1 Ha: ER

1 oil engine with clutches, flexible couplings & sr reverse geared to sc. shaft driving 1 FP propeller
Total Power: 883kW (1,201hp)
Akasaka DM28AKFD
1 x 4 Stroke 6 Cy. 280 x 460 883kW (1201bhp)
Akasaka Tekkosho KK (Akasaka DieselLtd)-Japan

8805262 **TIAN CHEN 9** **1,395**
V3PM2 *ex* Sansha Maru No. 25 *-2008* 986
- **Tian Yuan Shipping Co Ltd** 1,176
Tian Chen Int'l Shipping Management Co Ltd
Belize City *Belize*
MMSI: 312243000
Official number: 741120004

1988-07 Shitanoe Shipbuilding Co Ltd — Usuki OT
Yd No: 1083
Loa 59.11 (BB) Br ex 12.02 Dght 3.323
Lbp 54.01 Br md 12.01 Dpth 6.10
Welded, 1 dk

(B33A2DG) Grab Dredger
Compartments: 1 Ho, ER
1 Ha: ER

1 oil engine with clutches & reduction geared to sc. shaft driving 1 FP propeller
Total Power: 552kW (750hp) 10.0kn
Daihatsu 6DLM-28FS
1 x 4 Stroke 6 Cy. 280 x 360 552kW (750bhp)
Daihatsu Diesel Manufacturing Co Lt-Japan

8746789 **TIAN CHENG 7** **2,911** Class: PD
V3RW7 *ex* Tian He 19 *-2013* 1,723
- **Lin Jianying** 5,000
Shanghai Chengan Ship Management Co Ltd
Belize City *Belize*
Official number: 281320188

2008-12 Zhoushan Xintai Shipbuilding & Repair Co Ltd — Zhoushan ZJ Yd No: 03
Loa 96.90 Br ex - Dght 5.850
Lbp 89.80 Br md 15.80 Dpth 7.40
Welded, 1 dk

(A31A2GX) General Cargo Ship
Grain: 6,800; Bale: 6,500

1 oil engine reduction geared to sc. shaft driving 1 Propeller
Total Power: 1,765kW (2,400hp) 11.0kn
Chinese Std. Type G8300ZC
1 x 4 Stroke 8 Cy. 300 x 380 1765kW (2400bhp)
Ningbo CSI Power & Machinery GroupCo Ltd-China

9363326 **TIAN CONG** **1,972** Class: CC
BBHD 1,395
- **Shandong Oumei Marine Shipping Co Ltd** 3,417
-
Yantai, Shandong *China*
MMSI: 412328030

2005-09 Rongcheng Xixiakou Shipyard Co Ltd — Rongcheng SD Yd No: 007
Loa 81.00 (BB) Br ex - Dght 5.500
Lbp 76.00 Br md 13.60 Dpth 6.80
Welded, 1 dk

(A31A2GX) General Cargo Ship
Grain: 2,268
Compartments: 2 Ho, ER
2 Ha: ER 2 (18.6 x 9.0)
Ice Capable

1 oil engine reduction geared to sc. shaft driving 1 FP propeller
Total Power: 1,618kW (2,200hp) 12.3kn
Daihatsu 6DKM-26
1 x 4 Stroke 6 Cy. 260 x 380 1618kW (2200bhp)
Anqing Marine Diesel Engine Works-China
AuxGen: 2 x 120kW 400V a.c

9338979 **TIAN DA** **2,358** Class: IZ
T3PM 1,367
- **Tian Da Co Ltd** 3,800
Hunchun Sino Unity Shipping (HongKong) Co Ltd
Tarawa *Kiribati*
MMSI: 529157000
Official number: K-11040821

2004-06 Zhejiang Dongfang Shipbuilding Co Ltd — Yueqing ZJ
Loa 82.50 (BB) Br ex - Dght 5.800
Lbp 76.50 Br md 14.20 Dpth 7.60
Welded, 1 dk

(A31A2GX) General Cargo Ship
Double Bottom Entire Compartment Length
Grain: 5,603
Compartments: 2 Ho, ER
2 Ha: ER 2 (22.8 x 9.0)
Ice Capable

1 oil engine geared to sc. shaft driving 1 FP propeller
Total Power: 1,471kW (2,000hp) 11.0kn
MAN-B&W 6L28/32A
1 x 4 Stroke 6 Cy. 280 x 320 1471kW (2000bhp)
Zhenjiang Marine Diesel Works-China
AuxGen: 2 x 240kW 380/220V 50Hz a.c
Fuel: 134.0 (d.f.)

9203497 **TIAN DU FENG** **38,767** Class: CC (NV)
VRXB6 25,807
- **Jin Lu Navigation Inc** 74,201
China Shipping International Shipmanagement Co Ltd
SatCom: Inmarsat C 447789410
Hong Kong *Hong Kong*
MMSI: 477894000
Official number: HK-0705

2001-06 Oshima Shipbuilding Co Ltd — Saikai NS
Yd No: 10279
Loa 225.00 (BB) Br ex - Dght 13.900
Lbp 216.00 Br md 32.26 Dpth 18.90
Welded, 1 dk

(A21A2BC) Bulk Carrier
Grain: 89,344; Bale: 87,774
Compartments: 7 Ho, ER
7 Ha: ER

1 oil engine driving 1 FP propeller
Total Power: 9,989kW (13,581hp) 14.0kn
B&W 7S50MC
1 x 2 Stroke 7 Cy. 500 x 1910 9989kW (13581bhp)
Kawasaki Heavy Industries Ltd-Japan

9538476 **TIAN E ZUO** **43,718** Class: CC
VRJW9 21,966
- **Tianezuo Shipping SA** 75,583
China Shipping Tanker Co Ltd T/cm
SatCom: Inmarsat C 447703790 68.0
Hong Kong *Hong Kong*
MMSI: 477340400
Official number: HK-3371

2012-02 Dalian Shipbuilding Industry Co Ltd — Dalian LN (No 1 Yard) Yd No: PC760-27
Loa 228.60 (BB) Br ex 32.30 Dght 14.700
Lbp 220.00 Br md 32.26 Dpth 21.20
Welded, 1 dk

(A13B2TP) Products Tanker
Double Hull (13F)
Liq: 80,740; Liq (Oil): 80,740
Cargo Heating Coils
Compartments: 12 Wing Ta, 2 Wing Slop Ta, ER
3 Cargo Pump (s): 3x2000m³/hr
Manifold: Bow/CM: 117.4m
Ice Capable

1 oil engine driving 1 FP propeller
Total Power: 13,560kW (18,436hp) 15.4kn
MAN-B&W 6S60MC-C
1 x 2 Stroke 6 Cy. 600 x 2400 13560kW (18436bhp)
Dalian Marine Diesel Co Ltd-China
AuxGen: 3 x 740kW 450V a.c
Fuel: 175.0 (d.f.) 2530.0 (r.f.)

9516521 **TIAN FA HAI** **107,000** Class: AB
3FSY4 67,880
- **Tianfahai Shipping Inc** 207,891
COSCO (HK) Shipping Co Ltd T/cm
Panama *Panama* 140.5
MMSI: 371112000
Official number: 45369PEXT

2014-02 Dalian COSCO KHI Ship Engineering Co Ltd (DACKS) — Dalian LN Yd No: DE002
Loa 300.00 Br ex 50.06 Dght 18.200
Lbp 295.00 Br md 50.00 Dpth 24.70
Welded, 1 dk

(A21A2BC) Bulk Carrier
Double Hull
Grain: 224,873

1 oil engine driving 1 FP propeller
Total Power: 17,696kW (24,059hp) 14.8kn
MAN-B&W 6S70MC-C
1 x 2 Stroke 6 Cy. 700 x 2800 17696kW (24059bhp)
CSSC MES Diesel Co Ltd-China

9158800 **TIAN FU HAI** **79,480** Class: CC
BOHX 49,261
- **COSCO Bulk Carrier Co Ltd (COSCO BULK)** 149,135
- T/cm
SatCom: Inmarsat B 341224210 108.2
Tianjin *China*
MMSI: 412242000

1998-01 Dalian New Shipbuilding Heavy Industries Co Ltd — Dalian LN
Yd No: BC1500-6
Loa 270.00 (BB) Br ex - Dght 17.500
Lbp 260.00 Br md 44.00 Dpth 24.00
Welded, 1 dk

(A21A2BC) Bulk Carrier
Grain: 167,400; Bale: 157,568
Compartments: 9 Ho, ER
9 Ha: (12.0 x 16.2)8 (14.4 x 19.8)ER

1 oil engine driving 1 FP propeller
Total Power: 14,300kW (19,442hp) 14.0kn
B&W 6S70MC
1 x 2 Stroke 6 Cy. 700 x 2674 14300kW (19442bhp)
Dalian Marine Diesel Works-China
AuxGen: 3 x 800kW 450V a.c

9437567 **TIAN FU HE** **54,005** Class: CC (GL)
BOMV 32,333
- **COSCO Container Lines Co Ltd (COSCON)** 63,143
-
Shanghai *China*
MMSI: 412746000
Official number: 0010000146

2010-07 Shanghai Jiangnan Changxing Heavy Industry Co Ltd — Shanghai
Yd No: H2445
Loa 294.00 (BB) Br ex - Dght 12.000
Lbp 284.16 Br md 32.26 Dpth 21.80
Welded, 1 dk

(A33A2CC) Container Ship (Fully Cellular)
TEU 5089 C Ho 2274 TEU C Dk 2815 TEU incl 385 ref C
Compartments: 6 Cell Ho, ER
Ice Capable

1 oil engine driving 1 FP propeller
Total Power: 45,760kW (62,215hp) 25.2kn
MAN-B&W 8K98MC
1 x 2 Stroke 8 Cy. 980 x 2660 45760kW (62215bhp)
CSSC MES Diesel Co Ltd-China
AuxGen: 4 x 1800kW 450V a.c
Thrusters: 1 Tunnel thruster (f)

9142265 **TIAN FU TIANJIN** **5,070** Class: CC (NK)
BFAD3 *ex* Liberty Spirit *-2009* 2,801
- **Tianjin International Marine Shipping Co** 6,602
-
Tianjin *China*
MMSI: 413301510

1996-09 Shin Kochi Jyuko K.K. — Kochi
Yd No: 7087
Loa 97.97 (BB) Br ex - Dght 6.768
Lbp 89.95 Br md 18.40 Dpth 10.60
Welded, 1 dk

(A33A2CC) Container Ship (Fully Cellular)
TEU 349 C Ho 160 TEU C Dk 189 TEU incl 136 ref C
Compartments: 2 Cell Ho, ER
4 Ha: ER

1 oil engine driving 1 FP propeller
Total Power: 3,236kW (4,400hp) 13.2kn
Mitsubishi 6UEC33LSII
1 x 2 Stroke 6 Cy. 330 x 1050 3236kW (4400bhp)
Akasaka Tekkosho KK (Akasaka DieselLtd)-Japan
Fuel: 230.0 (r.f.)

8311857 **TIAN HE** *5,492*
- 2,855
- **China Shipping Passenger Liner Co Ltd** 2,096
Dalian, Liaoning *China*

1983-11 Tianjin Xingang Shipyard — Tianjin
Yd No: 239
Loa 120.00 Br ex - Dght 5.801
Lbp 108.00 Br md 17.00 Dpth 7.80
Welded, 3 dks

(A32A2GF) General Cargo/Passenger Ship

2 oil engines driving 2 FP propellers
Total Power: 4,414kW (6,002hp)
Sulzer 6RD44
2 x 2 Stroke 6 Cy. 440 x 760 each-2207kW (3001bhp)
Shanghai Diesel Engine Co Ltd-China

IMO / Call sign	Name, former names, owner, registry	Tonnage	Class	Build	Type	Machinery
8631453 *HOYT* -	**TIAN HONG** *ex* Ji Hang 7 *-2011* *ex* Jiu Jiang 188 *-2008* *ex* Hutoshi Akria Maru No. 83 *-2003* *ex* Tai Zheng Wan No. 83 *-2003* *ex* Taisho Maru No. 83 *-2003* **Shantou Shunhai Shipping Co Ltd** - *Panama* *Panama* Official number: 41630PEXTF1	**2,812** 1,575 4,260	Class: OM	**1988 Nagashima Zosen KK — Kihoku ME** Converted From: Grab Dredger-1988 Lengthened-2003 Loa 96.41 Br ex 13.52 Dght 5.500 Lbp 89.50 Br md 13.50 Dpth 7.20 Welded, 1 dk	**(A31A2GX) General Cargo Ship**	**1 oil engine** geared to sc. shaft driving 1 FP propeller Total Power: 736kW (1,001hp) 11.5kn Hanshin 6LU35G 1 x 4 Stroke 6 Cy. 350 x 550 736kW (1001bhp) The Hanshin Diesel Works Ltd-Japan
8966212 *BP2014* -	**TIAN HOU NO. 1** *ex* Lien Chiang No. 1 *-2012* **Darong Shipping Co Ltd** - *Kaohsiung* *Chinese Taipei* MMSI: 416900050 Official number: 013259	**198** 71 52	Class: CR	**1996-07 Fong Kuo Shipbuilding Co Ltd — Kaohsiung** Loa 32.13 Br ex 7.05 Dght 1.800 Lbp 26.50 Br md 6.90 Dpth 3.60 Welded, 1 dk	**(A37B2PS) Passenger Ship**	**2 oil engines** driving 2 FP propellers Total Power: 2,060kW (2,800hp) 24.0kn Caterpillar 3516TA 2 x Vee 4 Stroke 16 Cy. 170 x 190 each-1030kW (1400bhp) Caterpillar Inc-USA AuxGen: 2 x 105kW a.c
7929401 - -	**TIAN HSIANG No. 137** *ex* Johnny No. 137 *-2012* *ex* Peter 2 *-2012* *ex* Koho No. 72 *-2012* *ex* Hoko Maru No. 72 *-1993* *ex* Sachi Maru No. 58 *-1993* - -	**546** 213 -		**1980-03 KK Kanasashi Zosen — Shizuoka SZ** Yd No: 2040 Loa 48.93 Br ex - Dght 3.536 Lbp 42.96 Br md 8.51 Dpth 3.64 Welded, 1 dk	**(B11B2FV) Fishing Vessel**	**1 oil engine** driving 1 FP propeller Total Power: 956kW (1,300hp) Niigata 6M28AGT 1 x 4 Stroke 6 Cy. 280 x 480 956kW (1300bhp) Niigata Engineering Co Ltd-Japan
8426602 - -	**TIAN HU** - **Dalian Steam Shipping Co** - SatCom: Inmarsat C 441300675 *Dalian, Liaoning* *China*	*5,002* 2,601 2,070		**1981 Tianjin Xingang Shipyard — Tianjin** Loa 120.00 Br ex - Dght 5.800 Lbp 108.00 Br md 17.00 Dpth 9.80 Welded, 3 dks	**(A32A2GF) General Cargo/Passenger Ship** Grain: 1,522; Bale: 1,340 Compartments: 2 Ho, ER 2 Ha: 2 (4.2 x 7.5) Derricks: 4x3t; Winches: 4	**2 oil engines** driving 1 FP propeller Total Power: 3,310kW (4,500hp) 14.8kn Shanghai 12V300 2 x Vee 2 Stroke 12 Cy. 300 x 550 each-1655kW (2250bhp) Shanghai Diesel Engine Co Ltd-China AuxGen: 3 x 250kW 390V 50Hz a.c
8831807 *BWBH* -	**TIAN HU SHAN** - **Fujian Shipping Co (FUSCO)** - *Fuzhou, Fujian* *China* MMSI: 412845000	**2,741** 1,471 3,881	Class: (CC)	**1981-07 Zhonghua Shipyard — Shanghai** Loa 101.15 Br ex - Dght 6.150 Lbp 92.30 Br md 13.80 Dpth 7.70 Welded, 1 dk	**(A31A2GX) General Cargo Ship**	**1 oil engine** driving 1 FP propeller Total Power: 2,207kW (3,001hp) 15.0kn Hudong 6ESDZ43/82B 1 x 2 Stroke 6 Cy. 430 x 820 2207kW (3001bhp) Hudong Shipyard-China AuxGen: 2 x 250kW 400V a.c
9270414 - -	**TIAN HUA** - **Hangton Pacific Co Ltd** - *Suva* *Fiji* Official number: 041020121	**300** 72 370		**2002-02 Huanghai Shipbuilding Co Ltd — Rongcheng SD** Loa 33.25 Br ex - Dght 2.700 Lbp 29.30 Br md 7.00 Dpth 3.20 Welded	**(B11B2FV) Fishing Vessel** Ins: 152	**1 oil engine** reduction geared to sc. shaft driving 1 Propeller Total Power: 400kW (544hp) 9.7kn Chinese Std. Type 6190ZLC 1 x 4 Stroke 6 Cy. 190 x 210 400kW (544bhp) Jinan Diesel Engine Co Ltd-China Fuel: 72.8 (r.f.)
9227687 *VRWX2* -	**TIAN HUA FENG** - **Jin Guan Navigation Inc** China Shipping International Shipmanagement Co Ltd *Hong Kong* *Hong Kong* MMSI: 477862000 Official number: HK0668	**38,860** 25,448 73,996 T/cm 66.0	Class: CC (AB)	**2001-02 Imabari Shipbuilding Co Ltd — Marugame KG (Marugame Shipyard)** Yd No: 1332 Loa 224.97 (BB) Br ex - Dght 14.013 Lbp 215.00 Br md 32.20 Dpth 19.30 Welded, 1 dk	**(A21A2BC) Bulk Carrier** Grain: 89,281 Compartments: 7 Ho, ER 7 Ha: 6 (17.9 x 15.6)ER (13.0 x 12.8)	**1 oil engine** driving 1 FP propeller Total Power: 8,826kW (12,000hp) 14.5kn B&W 7S50MC 1 x 2 Stroke 7 Cy. 500 x 1910 8826kW (12000bhp) Mitsui Engineering & Shipbuilding CLtd-Japan
9037109 - -	**TIAN JI No. 1** *ex* Solombala *-1995* **Tian Ji Shipping Co Ltd** - *Taichung* *Chinese Taipei* Official number: 12891	**1,527** 555 1,246	Class: CR (RS)	**1995-07 Santierul Naval Galati S.A. — Galati** Yd No: 823 Loa 72.50 Br ex - Dght 3.200 Lbp 65.60 Br md 13.00 Dpth 4.40 Welded	**(A35A2RR) Ro-Ro Cargo Ship** TEU 65 C. 65/20' Cranes: 1x12.5t	**2 oil engines** driving 2 FP propellers Total Power: 1,280kW (1,740hp) 10.5kn S.K.L. 6NVD48A-2U 2 x 4 Stroke 6 Cy. 320 x 480 each-640kW (870bhp) SKL Motoren u. Systemtechnik AG-Magdeburg AuxGen: 3 x 100kW 380V 50Hz a.c Fuel: 95.0 (d.f.) 123.0 (r.f.)
9437531 *BOPG* -	**TIAN JIN HE** - **COSCO Container Lines Co Ltd (COSCON)** - *Shanghai* *China* MMSI: 412633000 Official number: 0010000095	**54,005** 32,333 63,187	Class: CC (GL)	**2010-05 Shanghai Jiangnan Changxing Heavy Industry Co Ltd — Shanghai** Yd No: H2442 Loa 294.00 (BB) Br ex - Dght 12.000 Lbp 284.16 Br md 32.26 Dpth 21.80 Welded, 1 dk	**(A33A2CC) Container Ship (Fully Cellular)** TEU 5089 C Ho 2274 TEU C Dk 2815 TEU incl 385 ref C Compartments: 6 Cell Ho, ER Ice Capable	**1 oil engine** driving 1 FP propeller Total Power: 45,760kW (62,215hp) 25.2kn MAN-B&W 8K98MC 1 x 2 Stroke 8 Cy. 980 x 2660 45760kW (62215bhp) CSSC MES Diesel Co Ltd-China AuxGen: 4 x 1800kW 450V a.c Thrusters: 1 Tunnel thruster (f)
9549073 *BSSZ* -	**TIAN JING HAO** - **CCCC Tianjin Dredging Co Ltd** - SatCom: Inmarsat C 441219230 *Tianjin* *China* MMSI: 412018470	**6,017** 1,805 2,406	Class: CC	**2010-01 China Merchants Heavy Industry (Shenzhen) Co Ltd — Shenzhen GD** Yd No: 027 Loa 127.50 Br ex - Dght 6.000 Lbp 97.50 Br md 23.00 Dpth 8.30 Welded, 1 dk	**(B33A2DC) Cutter Suction Dredger** Ice Capable	**2 oil engines** geared to sc. shafts driving 2 Propellers Total Power: 8,826kW (12,000hp) 12.0kn Daihatsu 8DKM-36 2 x 4 Stroke 8 Cy. 360 x 480 each-4413kW (6000bhp) Daihatsu Diesel Manufacturing Co Lt-Japan AuxGen: 2 x 800kW 400V a.c, 1 x 600kW 400V a.c Thrusters: 1 Tunnel thruster (f) Fuel: 212.0 (d.f.) 1465.0 (r.f.)
9400576 *BOMR* -	**TIAN KANG HE** - **COSCO Container Lines Co Ltd (COSCON)** - *Shanghai* *China* MMSI: 412713000 Official number: 0010000115	**54,005** 32,333 63,296	Class: CC (GL)	**2010-06 Shanghai Jiangnan Changxing Heavy Industry Co Ltd — Shanghai** Yd No: H2406 Loa 294.00 (BB) Br ex 32.25 Dght 12.000 Lbp 284.16 Br md 32.20 Dpth 21.80 Welded, 1 dk	**(A33A2CC) Container Ship (Fully Cellular)** TEU 5089 C Ho 2274 TEU C Dk 2815 TEU incl 385 ref C Compartments: 6 Cell Ho, ER 6 Ha: ER Ice Capable	**1 oil engine** driving 1 FP propeller Total Power: 45,760kW (62,215hp) 25.2kn MAN-B&W 8K98MC 1 x 2 Stroke 8 Cy. 980 x 2660 45760kW (62215bhp) CSSC MES Diesel Co Ltd-China AuxGen: 4 x 1800kW 450V a.c Thrusters: 1 Tunnel thruster (f)
9515814 *BIKY* -	**TIAN LAN** - **CMB Financial Leasing Co Ltd** Xinao Marine Shipping Co Ltd *Shanghai* *China* MMSI: 412501340	**3,790** 1,137 2,736	Class: CC	**2008-05 Bohai Shipbuilding Heavy Industry Co Ltd — Huludao LN** Yd No: 513-4 Loa 99.00 Br ex 16.45 Dght 4.400 Lbp 92.00 Br md 16.40 Dpth 7.20 Welded, 1 dk	**(A11B2TG) LPG Tanker** Liq (Gas): 3,500 3 x Gas Tank (s); 2 independent (stl) cyl , ER Ice Capable	**1 oil engine** geared to sc. shaft driving 1 Propeller Total Power: 2,500kW (3,399hp) 13.6kn Daihatsu 8DKM-28 1 x 4 Stroke 8 Cy. 280 x 390 2500kW (3399bhp) Shaanxi Diesel Heavy Industry Co Lt-China AuxGen: 2 x 300kW 400V a.c
9551064 *V3MD* -	**TIAN LI 26** - **Hubei Jingzhou Tianli River & Sea Transportation Co Ltd** Fujian Hengfeng Shipping Co Ltd *Belize City* *Belize* MMSI: 312766000 Official number: 130920791	**4,049** 2,267 7,045	Class: IB (MT)	**2008-10 Fujian Southern Ship Industry Co Ltd — Fu'an FJ** Loa 115.02 Br ex - Dght 6.350 Lbp - Br md 16.80 Dpth 8.20 Welded, 1 dk	**(A31A2GX) General Cargo Ship**	**1 oil engine** reduction geared to sc. shaft driving 1 FP propeller Total Power: 2,206kW (2,999hp) 11.0kn Guangzhou 8320ZC 1 x 4 Stroke 8 Cy. 320 x 440 2206kW (2999bhp) Guangzhou Diesel Engine Factory CoLtd-China
8651465 - -	**TIAN LI GONG 368** - **Hubei Jingzhou Tianli River & Sea Transportation Co Ltd** - *Yichang, Hubei* *China* Official number: 120507000022	**740** 222 -	Class: ZC	**2001-07 Jinglun Yunye Shipyard — Jingzhou HB** Yd No: 2001K4300181 Loa 44.60 Br ex - Dght 1.800 Lbp - Br md 16.00 Dpth 3.60 Welded, 1 dk	**(B34B2SC) Crane Vessel**	**2 oil engines** driving 2 Propellers
9158812 *BOHY* -	**TIAN LI HAI** - **COSCO Bulk Carrier Co Ltd (COSCO BULK)** - SatCom: Inmarsat B 341224910 *Tianjin* *China* MMSI: 412249000 Official number: 98V4005	**79,480** 49,261 148,726 T/cm 108.2	Class: CC	**1999-01 Dalian New Shipbuilding Heavy Industries Co Ltd — Dalian LN** Yd No: BC1500-7 Loa 270.00 (BB) Br ex - Dght 17.520 Lbp 260.00 Br md 44.00 Dpth 24.00 Welded, 1 dk	**(A21A2BC) Bulk Carrier** Grain: 167,400; Bale: 157,568 Compartments: 9 Ho, ER 9 Ha: 2 (12.0 x 16.2)7 (14.4 x 19.8)ER	**1 oil engine** driving 1 FP propeller Total Power: 14,300kW (19,442hp) 14.0kn B&W 6S70MC 1 x 2 Stroke 6 Cy. 700 x 2674 14300kW (19442bhp) Dalian Marine Diesel Works-China AuxGen: 3 x 800kW 450V a.c

9400552 *BQBC* -
TIAN LI HE
COSCO Container Lines Co Ltd (COSCON)
-
Shanghai *China*
MMSI: 413965000
54,005 32,333 63,253
Class: CC (GL)
2010-04 Shanghai Jiangnan Changxing Heavy Industry Co Ltd — Shanghai
Yd No: H2404
Loa 294.00 (BB) Br ex 32.25 Dght 12.000
Lbp 284.16 Br md 32.20 Dpth 21.80
Welded, 1 dk
(A33A2CC) Container Ship (Fully Cellular)
TEU 5089 C Ho 2274 TEU C Dk 2815 TEU incl 385 ref C
Compartments: 6 Cell Ho, ER
Ice Capable
1 oil engine driving 1 FP propeller
Total Power: 45,760kW (62,215hp) 25.2kn
MAN-B&W 8K98MC
1 x 2 Stroke 8 Cy. 980 x 2660 45760kW (62215bhp)
CSSC MES Diesel Co Ltd-China
AuxGen: 4 x 1800kW 450V a.c
Thrusters: 1 Tunnel thruster (f)

9400538 *BQBH* -
TIAN LONG HE
COSCO Container Lines Co Ltd (COSCON)
-
Shanghai *China*
MMSI: 413761000
Official number: 0010000017
54,005 32,333 63,195
Class: CC (GL)
2010-01 Shanghai Jiangnan Changxing Heavy Industry Co Ltd — Shanghai
Yd No: H2393
Loa 294.00 (BB) Br ex 32.25 Dght 12.000
Lbp 284.16 Br md 32.20 Dpth 21.80
Welded, 1 dk
(A33A2CC) Container Ship (Fully Cellular)
TEU 5089 C Ho 2274 TEU C Dk 2815 TEU incl 385 ref C
Compartments: 6 Cell Ho, ER
Ice Capable
1 oil engine driving 1 FP propeller
Total Power: 45,760kW (62,215hp) 25.2kn
MAN-B&W 8K98MC
1 x 2 Stroke 8 Cy. 980 x 2660 45760kW (62215bhp)
CSSC MES Diesel Co Ltd-China
AuxGen: 4 x 1800kW 450V a.c
Thrusters: 1 Tunnel thruster (f)

9086849 *BPYY* -
TIAN LONG XING
Shanghai Time Shipping Co Ltd
-
SatCom: Inmarsat C 441219710
Shanghai *China*
MMSI: 412466000
Official number: 0101000
24,964 10,568 37,532
Class: (CC) (GL)
1995-09 Bremer Vulkan AG Schiffbau u. Maschinenfabrik — Bremen Yd No: 99
Loa 186.58 (BB) Br ex - Dght 10.800
Lbp 178.80 Br md 29.00 Dpth 15.20
Welded, 1 dk
(A23A2BD) Bulk Carrier, Self-discharging
Double Sides Entire Compartment Length
Grain: 39,563
Compartments: 5 Ho, ER
5 Ha: (18.0 x 10.0) (23.0 x 10.0)3 (25.0 x 10.0)ER
Cranes: 1x19.4t
Ice Capable
1 oil engine driving 1 FP propeller
Total Power: 6,130kW (8,334hp) 14.7kn
B&W 6L50MC
1 x 2 Stroke 6 Cy. 500 x 1620 6130kW (8334bhp)
Bremer Vulkan AG Schiffbau u.Maschinenfabrik-Bremen
AuxGen: 3 x 1010kW 400V 50Hz a.c
Thrusters: 1 Thwart. FP thruster (f)

9312602 *BPFS* -
TIAN LONG ZUO
China Shipping Tanker Co Ltd
-
Shanghai *China*
MMSI: 413152000
43,153 22,236 75,484 T/cm 66.5
Class: CC
2006-04 Dalian Shipbuilding Industry Co Ltd — Dalian LN (No 1 Yard) Yd No: OT750-3
Loa 228.60 Br ex 32.26 Dght 14.690
Lbp 217.00 Br md 32.00 Dpth 21.10
Welded, 1 dk
(A13B2TP) Products Tanker
Double Hull (13F)
Liq: 85,912; Liq (Oil): 85,912
Cargo Heating Coils
Compartments: 12 Wing Ta, 2 Wing Slop Ta, ER
3 Cargo Pump (s)
Manifold: Bow/CM: 114m
Ice Capable
1 oil engine driving 1 FP propeller
Total Power: 12,240kW (16,642hp) 14.0kn
MAN-B&W 6S60MC
1 x 2 Stroke 6 Cy. 600 x 2292 12240kW (16642bhp)
Dalian Marine Diesel Works-China

9298480 *BOIG* -
TIAN LU HAI
Qingdao Ocean Shipping Co Ltd (COSCO QINGDAO)
-
SatCom: Inmarsat C 441309910
Qingdao, Shandong *China*
MMSI: 413099000
88,856 58,333 174,398 T/cm 119.0
Class: CC
2005-03 Shanghai Waigaoqiao Shipbuilding Co Ltd — Shanghai Yd No: 1016
Loa 289.00 (BB) Br ex 45.05 Dght 18.200
Lbp 279.00 Br md 45.00 Dpth 24.50
Welded, 1 dk
(A21A2BC) Bulk Carrier
Grain: 193,134; Bale: 183,425
Compartments: 9 Ho, ER
9 Ha: 7 (15.0 x 20.0)ER 2 (15.0 x 16.5)
1 oil engine driving 1 FP propeller
Total Power: 16,858kW (22,920hp) 14.5kn
MAN-B&W 6S70MC
1 x 2 Stroke 6 Cy. 700 x 2674 16858kW (22920bhp)
Hudong Heavy Machinery Co Ltd-China
AuxGen: 3 x 750kW a.c

8422151 - -
TIAN LU HU
Chu Kong Shipping Enterprises (Holdings) Co Ltd
-
Guangzhou, Guangdong *China*
350 - 125
Class: (NV)
1985-09 Fjellstrand AS — Omastrand Yd No: 1567
Loa 38.82 Br ex 9.40 Dght -
Lbp 36.50 Br md - Dpth 3.51
Welded, 1 dk
(A37B2PS) Passenger Ship
Hull Material: Aluminium Alloy
Passengers: unberthed: 330
2 oil engines geared to sc. shafts driving 2 FP propellers
Total Power: 2,942kW (4,000hp) 28.0kn
M.T.U. 16V396TB83
2 x Vee 4 Stroke 16 Cy. 165 x 185 each-1471kW (2000bhp)
MTU Friedrichshafen GmbH-Friedrichshafen
AuxGen: 2 x 20kW 230V 50Hz a.c

7525401 - -
TIAN MU SHAN
ex Aegis Agent *-1979*
-
SatCom: Inmarsat C 441238110
Tianjin *China*
MMSI: 412252000
9,513 6,402 15,958 T/cm 25.0
Class: (CC) (AB)
1978-09 Astilleros Espanoles SA (AESA) — Bilbao
Yd No: 304
Loa 144.00 Br ex 21.47 Dght 8.900
Lbp 134.00 Br md 21.40 Dpth 12.20
Welded, 2 dks
(A31A2GX) General Cargo Ship
Grain: 22,011; Bale: 20,290
Compartments: 4 Ho, ER
4 Ha: (13.4 x 8.0) (7.3 x 12.5)2 (20.1 x 12.5)ER
Cranes: 3x12.5t
1 oil engine driving 1 FP propeller
Total Power: 4,523kW (6,149hp) 14.0kn
B&W 7K45GF
1 x 2 Stroke 7 Cy. 450 x 900 4523kW (6149bhp)
Astilleros Espanoles SA (AESA)-Spain
AuxGen: 3 x 252kW a.c

9546265 *XUDC6* -
TIAN PENG
ex Xin An *-2011* *ex* Trawind Angel *-2010*
ex Xin An *-2008*
launched as Chang Xin 16 *-2008*
Wang Mianli
Harmony Growing Ship Management Co Ltd
SatCom: Inmarsat C 451472511
Phnom Penh *Cambodia*
MMSI: 514725000
Official number: 1108788
2,956 1,872 5,500
Class: UB (MG) (IC)
2008-06 Wenling Xingyuan Shipbuilding & Repair Co Ltd — Wenling ZJ
Loa 99.56 Br ex - Dght 6.100
Lbp 92.56 Br md 15.60 Dpth 7.70
Welded, 1 dk
(A31A2GX) General Cargo Ship
1 oil engine reduction geared to sc. shaft driving 1 FP propeller
Total Power: 1,765kW (2,400hp) 11.0kn
Chinese Std. Type 8320ZC
1 x 4 Stroke 8 Cy. 320 x 440 1765kW (2400bhp)
Guangzhou Diesel Engine Factory CoLtd-China

9437555 *BOMY* -
TIAN QING HE
COSCO Container Lines Co Ltd (COSCON)
-
Shanghai *China*
MMSI: 412750000
Official number: 0010000142
54,005 32,333 63,259
Class: CC (GL)
2010-07 Shanghai Jiangnan Changxing Heavy Industry Co Ltd — Shanghai
Yd No: H2444
Loa 294.00 (BB) Br ex 32.25 Dght 12.000
Lbp 284.16 Br md 32.20 Dpth 21.80
Welded, 1 dk
(A33A2CC) Container Ship (Fully Cellular)
TEU 5089 C Ho 2274 TEU C Dk 2815 TEU incl 385 ref C
Compartments: 6 Cell Ho, ER
Ice Capable
1 oil engine driving 1 FP propeller
Total Power: 45,760kW (62,215hp) 25.2kn
MAN-B&W 8K98MC
1 x 2 Stroke 8 Cy. 980 x 2660 45760kW (62215bhp)
CSSC MES Diesel Co Ltd-China
AuxGen: 4 x 1800kW 450V a.c
Thrusters: 1 Tunnel thruster (f)

9340271 *T3QZ* -
TIAN REN
Royal Armadas International Co Ltd
Hunchun Sino Unity Shipping (HongKong) Co Ltd
Tarawa *Kiribati*
MMSI: 529193000
Official number: K16041304
2,358 1,320 3,800
Class: IZ
2004-11 Zhejiang Dongfang Shipbuilding Co Ltd — Yueqing ZJ
Loa 82.50 Br ex - Dght 5.800
Lbp 76.50 Br md 14.20 Dpth 7.60
Welded, 1 dk
(A31A2GX) General Cargo Ship
Grain: 5,603
Compartments: 2 Ho, ER
2 Ha: ER 2 (22.8 x 9.0)
1 oil engine geared to sc. shaft driving 1 FP propeller
Total Power: 1,470kW (1,999hp) 11.0kn
MAN-B&W 6L28/32A
1 x 4 Stroke 6 Cy. 280 x 320 1470kW (1999bhp) (made 2004)
Zhenjiang Marine Diesel Works-China

8902357 *3FWL9* -
TIAN REN
ex Blue Zephyr *-1999*
Marine Asia Shipping Inc
Tianjin-Inchon International Passenger & Cargo Shipping Co Ltd
SatCom: Inmarsat C 443185810
Panama *Panama*
MMSI: 357911000
Official number: 2700900D
26,463 14,194 5,989
Class: CC KR
1990-07 Kanda Zosensho K.K. — Kawajiri
Yd No: 331
Loa 186.50 (BB) Br ex 24.98 Dght 6.873
Lbp 171.00 Br md 24.40 Dpth 14.80
Welded, 2 dks
(A36A2PR) Passenger/Ro-Ro Ship (Vehicles)
Passengers: unberthed: 630; cabins: 32; berths: 64
Stern door/ramp
Len: - Wid: 7.02 Swl: -
Side door/ramp (s. a.)
Quarter bow door/ramp (s)
Len: - Wid: 7.25 Swl: -
Lane-Len: 1700
Lane-clr ht: 4.70
Lorries: 170, Cars: 140
2 oil engines sr geared to sc. shaft driving 2 CP propellers
Total Power: 23,830kW (32,400hp) 23.2kn
Pielstick 9PC40L570
2 x 4 Stroke 9 Cy. 570 x 750 each-11915kW (16200bhp)
Diesel United Ltd.-Aioi
AuxGen: 2 x 1000kW 450V a.c
Thrusters: 1 Thwart. CP thruster (f)

9032044 *BFAI* -
TIAN RONG
Tianjin Marine Shipping Co Ltd
-
Tianjin *China*
MMSI: 412800000
6,144 3,076 7,240
Class: CC
1992-11 Qiuxin Shipyard — Shanghai Yd No: 1212
Loa 120.90 (BB) Br ex - Dght 6.380
Lbp 110.00 Br md 20.20 Dpth 8.50
Welded, 1 dk
(A33A2CC) Container Ship (Fully Cellular)
TEU 412 C Ho 176 TEU C Dk 236 TEU
Compartments: 3 Cell Ho, ER
9 Ha: (6.7 x 10.8)8 (12.6 x 8.0)ER
1 oil engine driving 1 FP propeller
Total Power: 5,119kW (6,960hp) 14.4kn
B&W 6L42MC
1 x 2 Stroke 6 Cy. 420 x 1360 5119kW (6960bhp)
Hudong Shipyard-China

9270402 *BZSJ3* -
TIAN RONG
-
-
China
300 - 370
2002-03 Huanghai Shipbuilding Co Ltd — Rongcheng SD
Loa 33.25 Br ex - Dght 2.700
Lbp - Br md 7.00 Dpth 3.20
Welded
(B11B2FV) Fishing Vessel
Ins: 152
1 oil engine reduction geared to sc. shaft driving 1 Propeller
Total Power: 400kW (544hp) 9.7kn
Chinese Std. Type 6190ZLC
1 x 4 Stroke 6 Cy. 190 x 210 400kW (544bhp)
Jinan Diesel Engine Co Ltd-China
Fuel: 72.8 (r.f.)

8739413 *BFAP* -
TIAN RUI
Tianjin Harbor Dragon International Ocean Shipping Co Ltd
Zhejiang Liao Shipping Co Ltd
Tianjin *China*
MMSI: 412301530
Official number: 020003000081
2,838 1,589 4,334
2003-12 Wenling Songmen Xianfeng Shipyard Co Ltd — Wenling ZJ Yd No: 021
Loa 97.60 Br ex - Dght 5.650
Lbp 92.00 Br md 13.80 Dpth 7.20
Welded, 1 dk
(A31A2GX) General Cargo Ship
1 oil engine driving 1 Propeller

8924226 **TIAN SAN CARRIER V** 339 Class: BV (GL)
9V5381 102
\- **Tian San Shipping (Pte) Ltd** 271
\-
Singapore *Singapore*
Official number: 387497

1992-07 President Marine Pte Ltd — Singapore
Yd No: 118
Loa - Br ex - Dght 1.458
Lbp 40.32 Br md 14.00 Dpth 2.60
Welded, 1 dk

(A35D2RL) Landing Craft
Bow ramp (centre)

2 oil engines reduction geared to sc. shafts driving 2 Z propellers
Total Power: 556kW (756hp) 8.5kn
Caterpillar 3406B
2 x 4 Stroke 6 Cy. 137 x 165 each-278kW (378bhp)
Caterpillar Inc-USA

8924642 **TIAN SAN CARRIER VI** 369 Class: BV
9V5231 110
ex Seraya Cergas *-2000*
\- **Tian San Shipping (Pte) Ltd** -
\-
Singapore *Singapore*
Official number: 386297

1996-11 Cheoy Lee Shipyards Ltd — Hong Kong
Yd No: 4672
Loa 42.00 Br ex - Dght 2.240
Lbp 40.32 Br md 14.00 Dpth 2.60
Welded, 1 dk

(A36A2PR) Passenger/Ro-Ro Ship (Vehicles)

2 oil engines reduction geared to sc. shafts driving 2 FP propellers
Total Power: 600kW (816hp) 9.0kn
Caterpillar 3408TA
2 x Vee 4 Stroke 8 Cy. 137 x 152 each-300kW (408bhp)
Caterpillar Inc-USA
AuxGen: 2 x 80kW 220/415V 50Hz a.c
Fuel: 15.5 (d.f.)

9161857 **TIAN SHAN** 7,760 Class: KR (NK)
VRMG2 3,896
ex Wakasa *-2013* *ex* Kadar *-2002*
\- **Grand Mountain Shipping Ltd** 11,560
Dalian Changtian Shipping Ltd
Hong Kong *Hong Kong*
MMSI: 477220700
Official number: HK-3864

1997-11 Shin Kurushima Dockyard Co. Ltd. — Akitsu Yd No: 2952
Loa 113.22 (BB) Br ex - Dght 8.519
Lbp 105.40 Br md 19.60 Dpth 13.20
Welded, 2 dks

(A31A2GX) General Cargo Ship
Grain: 16,781; Bale: 15,193
TEU 48
Compartments: 2 Ho, 2 Tw Dk, ER
2 Ha: (20.3 x 14.8) (33.6 x 14.8)ER
Cranes: 2x65t; Derricks: 1x21t

1 oil engine driving 1 FP propeller
Total Power: 3,884kW (5,281hp) 13.3kn
B&W 6L35MC
1 x 2 Stroke 6 Cy. 350 x 1050 3884kW (5281bhp)
Makita Corp-Japan
Fuel: 650.0

8406444 **TIAN SHAN HAI** 26,703 Class: CC
BONO 14,713
\- **Xiamen Ocean Shipping Co (COSCO XIAMEN)** 45,884
\-
SatCom: Inmarsat A 1570563
Xiamen, Fujian *China*
MMSI: 412325000

1985-12 Osaka Shipbuilding Co Ltd — Osaka OS
Yd No: 435
Loa 194.50 (BB) Br ex - Dght 11.390
Lbp 185.00 Br md 30.50 Dpth 16.27
Welded, 1 dk

(A21A2BC) Bulk Carrier
Grain: 55,913; Bale: 55,096
Compartments: 5 Ho, ER
5 Ha: 2 (16.8 x 15.0)3 (17.6 x 15.0)ER
Cranes: 4
Ice Capable

1 oil engine driving 1 FP propeller
Total Power: 7,561kW (10,280hp) 14.5kn
B&W 6L60MCE
1 x 2 Stroke 6 Cy. 600 x 1944 7561kW (10280bhp)
Hitachi Zosen Corp-Japan

8203593 **TIAN SHENG** 10,544 Class: (CC) (AB) (GL)
BXGO 5,643
ex Shalamar *-2003* *ex* Ora Bhum *-1996*
\- *ex* Westertal *-1993* *ex* Ville d'Oman *-1991* 14,208
ex Westertal *-1988* *ex* Zim Australia *-1988*
ex Zim Sydney *-1986*
launched as Westertal *-1983*
Zhuhai Beiyang Shipping Co
\-
Zhuhai, Guangdong *China*
MMSI: 413005000

1983-12 Werft Nobiskrug GmbH — Rendsburg
Yd No: 715
Loa 151.11 (BB) Br ex 22.94 Dght 8.340
Lbp 138.03 Br md 22.92 Dpth 11.26
Welded, 1 dk

(A33A2CC) Container Ship (Fully Cellular)
TEU 1033 C Ho 362 TEU C Dk 671 TEU incl 75 ref C.
Compartments: 3 Cell Ho, ER
3 Ha: (12.6 x 12.8)2 (37.8 x 17.9)ER
Cranes: 2x40t
Ice Capable

1 oil engine with flexible couplings & sr gearedto sc. shaft driving 1 CP propeller
Total Power: 8,000kW (10,877hp) 16.3kn
MaK 8M601AK
1 x 4 Stroke 8 Cy. 580 x 600 8000kW (10877bhp)
Krupp MaK Maschinenbau GmbH-Kiel
AuxGen: 1 x 1000kW 440V 60Hz a.c, 2 x 448kW 440V 60Hz a.c
Thrusters: 1 Thwart. FP thruster (f)
Fuel: 247.5 (d.f.) 1177.0 (r.f.) 30.5pd

9002518 **TIAN SHENG 15** 57,450 Class: CC (NK)
BLAH8 29,654
ex Tian Sheng 5 *-2009* *ex* Spirit II *-2008*
\- *ex* Teekay Spirit *-2005* 100,336
Ningbo Tiansheng Shipping Co Ltd T/cm
\- 88.2
Ningbo, Zhejiang *China*
MMSI: 413494000
Official number: 070009000006

1991-11 Onomichi Dockyard Co Ltd — Onomichi HS Yd No: 351
Converted From: Crude Oil/Products Tanker-2008
Loa 244.80 (BB) Br ex 41.23 Dght 14.418
Lbp 234.00 Br md 41.20 Dpth 21.60
Welded, 1 dk

(A21A2BC) Bulk Carrier
Double Hull
Grain: 92,948
Compartments: 5 Ho, ER
5 Ha: ER

1 oil engine driving 1 FP propeller
Total Power: 13,130kW (17,852hp) 14.8kn
B&W 7S60MC
1 x 2 Stroke 7 Cy. 600 x 2292 13130kW (17852bhp)
Mitsui Engineering & Shipbuilding CLtd-Japan
AuxGen: 3 x 640kW 220/440V 50Hz a.c
Fuel: 238.0 (d.f.) 2942.0 (r.f.) 43.0pd

8908222 **TIAN SHENG 16** 53,892 Class: (CC) (NV) (NK)
BLAG8 25,530
ex Sea Lion *-2008* *ex* Genmar Leonidas *-2005*
\- *ex* Anella *-2001* *ex* Almanama *-2000* 97,002
ex Planier *-1992* T/cm
Ningbo Tiansheng Shipping Co Ltd 90.0
TOSCO KEYMAX International Ship Management Co Ltd
SatCom: Inmarsat C 441339810
Ningbo, Zhejiang *China*
MMSI: 413398000

1991-01 Koyo Dockyard Co Ltd — Mihara HS
Yd No: 2020
Converted From: Crude Oil Tanker-2008
Loa 246.80 (BB) Br ex - Dght 13.419
Lbp 235.00 Br md 42.00 Dpth 19.50
Welded, 1 dk

(A21A2BC) Bulk Carrier
Grain: 99,569
Compartments: 8 Ho, ER
8 Ha: (13.6 x 13.5) (18.0 x 13.5)ER 6 (13.5 x 13.5)

1 oil engine driving 1 FP propeller
Total Power: 10,151kW (13,801hp) 14.8kn
Sulzer 6RTA72
1 x 2 Stroke 6 Cy. 720 x 2500 10151kW (13801bhp)
Mitsubishi Heavy Industries Ltd-Japan
AuxGen: 3 x 680kW 440V 60Hz a.c
Fuel: 189.9 (d.f.) 2847.9 (r.f.)

9002506 **TIAN SHENG 17** 60,139 Class: CC (NK)
BLBB 20,326
ex Tian Sheng 7 *-2009* *ex* Lotus *-2008*
\- *ex* Palmstar Lotus *-2005* 97,728
Ningbo Tiansheng Shipping Co Ltd T/cm
\- 88.2
SatCom: Inmarsat C 441220511
Ningbo, Zhejiang *China*
MMSI: 412205000
Official number: 070009000019

1991-08 Onomichi Dockyard Co Ltd — Onomichi HS Yd No: 350
Converted From: Crude Oil/Products Tanker-2008
Loa 244.80 (BB) Br ex 41.23 Dght 14.418
Lbp 234.00 Br md 41.20 Dpth 21.60
Welded, 1 dk

(A21A2BC) Bulk Carrier
Double Sides Entire Compartment Length
Grain: 84,168
Compartments: 5 Ho, ER
5 Ha: 4 (13.7 x 17.8)ER (11.2 x 17.8)

1 oil engine driving 1 FP propeller
Total Power: 13,130kW (17,852hp) 14.8kn
B&W 7S60MC
1 x 2 Stroke 7 Cy. 600 x 2292 13130kW (17852bhp)
Mitsui Engineering & Shipbuilding CLtd-Japan
AuxGen: 3 x 680kW 450/220V 50Hz a.c
Fuel: 238.0 (d.f.) 2932.0 (r.f.) 43.0pd

9437543 **TIAN SHENG HE** 54,005 Class: CC (GL)
BOPH 32,333
\- **COSCO Container Lines Co Ltd (COSCON)** 63,292
\-
Shanghai *China*
MMSI: 412658000
Official number: 0010000088

2010-05 Shanghai Jiangnan Changxing Heavy Industry Co Ltd — Shanghai
Yd No: H2443
Loa 294.00 (BB) Br ex 32.25 Dght 12.000
Lbp 284.16 Br md 32.20 Dpth 21.80
Welded, 1 dk

(A33A2CC) Container Ship (Fully Cellular)
TEU 5089 C Ho 2274 TEU C Dk 2815 TEU incl 385 ref C
Compartments: 6 Cell Ho, ER
Ice Capable

1 oil engine driving 1 FP propeller
Total Power: 45,760kW (62,215hp) 25.2kn
MAN-B&W 8K98MC
1 x 2 Stroke 8 Cy. 980 x 2660 45760kW (62215bhp)
CSSC MES Diesel Co Ltd-China
AuxGen: 4 x 1800kW 450V a.c
Thrusters: 1 Tunnel thruster (f)

9635585 **TIAN SHENG YOU 2** 7,647 Class: CC
BLAN2 3,649
\- **Zhejiang Longhua Shipping Co Ltd** 11,984
\-
Ningbo, Zhejiang *China*
MMSI: 413444880

2012-06 Ningbo Dongfang Shipyard Co Ltd — Ningbo ZJ Yd No: DFC11-120
Loa 119.90 Br ex - Dght 8.430
Lbp 112.80 Br md 20.00 Dpth 11.50
Welded, 1 dk

(A13B2TP) Products Tanker
Double Hull (13F)
Liq: 12,628; Liq (Oil): 12,628
Compartments: 5 Wing Ta, 5 Wing Ta, 1 Wing Slop Ta, 1 Wing Slop Ta, ER
Ice Capable

1 oil engine reduction geared to sc. shaft driving 1 FP propeller
Total Power: 3,310kW (4,500hp) 12.0kn
Yanmar 8N330-EN
1 x 4 Stroke 8 Cy. 330 x 440 3310kW (4500bhp)
Qingdao Zichai Boyang Diesel EngineCo Ltd-China
AuxGen: 3 x 600kW 400V a.c

9214070 **TIAN SONG FENG** 39,042 Class: CC (BV)
VRYG5 25,025
\- **Jin Ying Navigation Inc** 74,271
China Shipping International Shipmanagement Co Ltd T/cm 66.3
Hong Kong *Hong Kong*
MMSI: 477084000

2000-03 Namura Shipbuilding Co Ltd — Imari SG
Yd No: 982
Loa 224.89 (BB) Br ex - Dght 13.950
Lbp 212.28 Br md 32.20 Dpth 19.30
Welded, 1 dk

(A21A2BC) Bulk Carrier
Double Bottom Entire Compartment Length
Grain: 89,236
Compartments: 7 Ho, ER
7 Ha: (16.8 x 13.2)5 (16.8 x 14.9) (16.9 x 14.9)ER

1 oil engine driving 1 FP propeller
Total Power: 8,826kW (12,000hp) 14.5kn
B&W 7S50MC
1 x 2 Stroke 7 Cy. 500 x 1910 8826kW (12000bhp)
Hitachi Zosen Corp-Japan
AuxGen: 3 x 380kW 450V 60Hz a.c
Fuel: 85.1 (d.f.) (Heating Coils) 1943.3 (r.f.) 35.0pd

8426896 **TIAN TAN** *5,002*
\- 2,601
\- **China Shipping Passenger Liner Co Ltd** 2,070
\-
Dalian, Liaoning *China*

1982 Tianjin Xingang Shipyard — Tianjin
Loa 120.00 Br ex - Dght 5.800
Lbp 108.00 Br md 17.00 Dpth 9.80
Welded, 3 dks

(A31A2GX) General Cargo Ship

2 oil engines driving 1 FP propeller
Total Power: 4,414kW (6,002hp) 15.0kn
Sulzer 6RD44
2 x 2 Stroke 6 Cy. 440 x 760 each-2207kW (3001bhp)
Shanghai Shipyard-China
AuxGen: 3 x 250kW 390V 50Hz a.c

8406432 **TIAN TAN HAI** 26,703 Class: CC
BONN 14,713
\- **Xiamen Ocean Shipping Co (COSCO XIAMEN)** 45,884
\-
SatCom: Inmarsat C 441294910
Xiamen, Fujian *China*
MMSI: 412329000

1985-09 Osaka Shipbuilding Co Ltd — Osaka OS
Yd No: 434
Loa 194.50 (BB) Br ex - Dght 11.390
Lbp 185.00 Br md 30.50 Dpth 16.27
Welded, 1 dk

(A21A2BC) Bulk Carrier
Grain: 55,913; Bale: 55,096
Compartments: 5 Ho, ER
5 Ha: 2 (16.8 x 15.0)3 (17.6 x 15.0)ER
Cranes: 4
Ice Capable

1 oil engine driving 1 FP propeller
Total Power: 7,561kW (10,280hp) 14.0kn
B&W 6L60MCE
1 x 2 Stroke 6 Cy. 600 x 1944 7561kW (10280bhp)
Hitachi Zosen Corp-Japan

8712348 **TIAN TONG** *2,266* Class: UB
XUCV2 1,328
ex Trawind Honor *-2011* 3,954
\- *ex* Tamayoshi Maru No. 15 *-2005*
Huiyang Ship Management Ltd
Harmony Growing Ship Management Co Ltd
Phnom Penh *Cambodia*
MMSI: 515528000
Official number: 1187679

1987-10 Kochi Jyuko K.K. — Kochi Yd No: 1986
Converted From: Suction Dredger-2006
Lengthened-2006
Loa 89.54 (BB) Br ex - Dght 5.600
Lbp 83.80 Br md 13.21 Dpth 7.27
Welded, 2 dks

(A31A2GX) General Cargo Ship
Grain: 5,025; Bale: 4,903
Compartments: 2 Ho, ER
2 Ha: ER 2 (20.3 x 9.2)

1 oil engine geared to sc. shaft driving 1 FP propeller
Total Power: 736kW (1,001hp) 11.0kn
Hanshin 6LU35G
1 x 4 Stroke 6 Cy. 350 x 550 736kW (1001bhp)
The Hanshin Diesel Works Ltd-Japan

8831792 **TIAN TONG** *685*
\- 356
\- *ex* Zhe Jiang 605 *-1989* -
Ningbo Marine (Group) Co Ltd (NMGC)
\-
Ningbo, Zhejiang *China*

1983-01 Wenzhou Shipyard — Wenzhou ZJ
Loa 45.11 Br ex - Dght 2.950
Lbp - Br md 12.60 Dpth 4.40
Welded, 2 dks

(A37B2PS) Passenger Ship

2 oil engines geared to sc. shafts driving 2 FP propellers
Total Power: 514kW (698hp) 10.0kn
Chinese Std. Type 6160A
2 x 4 Stroke 6 Cy. 160 x 225 each-257kW (349bhp)
Weifang Diesel Engine Factory-China
AuxGen: 2 x 50kW 400V a.c

9233363 *VRXA2* -	**TIAN TONG FENG** **Jin Peng Navigation Inc** China Shipping International Shipmanagement Co Ltd SatCom: Inmarsat C 447788210 *Hong Kong* *Hong Kong* MMSI: 477882000 Official number: HK0692	**39,042** 25,025 74,275 T/cm 66.3	Class: CC (BV)	**2001-04 Namura Shipbuilding Co Ltd — Imari SG** Yd No: 991 Loa 224.89 (BB) Br ex - Dght 13.930 Lbp 212.28 Br md 32.20 Dpth 19.30 Welded, 1 dk	**(A21A2BC) Bulk Carrier** Grain: 89,000 Compartments: 7 Ho, ER 7 Ha: (16.8 x 13.2)6 (16.8 x 14.8)ER	**1 oil engine** driving 1 FP propeller Total Power: 8,821kW (11,993hp) 14.5kn B&W 7S50MC 1 x 2 Stroke 7 Cy. 500 x 1910 8821kW (11993bhp) Hitachi Zosen Corp-Japan AuxGen: 3 x 1140kW 110/440V 60Hz a.c Fuel: 1987.6 (r.f.)
9464223 *3EOW4* -	**TIAN WANG XING** *ex* Top Glory *-2008* **Tianwangxing Maritime SA** COSCO Shipping Co Ltd (COSCOL) *Panama* *Panama* MMSI: 356475000 Official number: 3390008A	**7,460** 3,295 9,106	Class: CC	**2008-02 Yichang Shipyard — Yichang HB** Yd No: 2006-B011 Loa 122.20 (BB) Br ex - Dght 7.200 Lbp 116.00 Br md 19.80 Dpth 10.70 Welded, 1 dk	**(A31A2GX) General Cargo Ship** Grain: 13,350; Bale: 12,554 TEU 630 C Ho 264 TEU C Dk 366 TEU. Compartments: 2 Ho, ER 2 Ha: (50.4 x 15.3)ER (32.2 x 15.3) Cranes: 2x40t Ice Capable	**1 oil engine** reduction geared to sc. shaft driving 1 Propeller Total Power: 3,300kW (4,487hp) 13.5kn Pielstick 6PC2-6 1 x 4 Stroke 6 Cy. 400 x 460 3300kW (4487bhp) Shaanxi Diesel Heavy Industry Co Lt-China
8430562 *BZYI8* 004757	**TIAN XIANG 8** *ex* Daniel No. 2 *-2006* **Tianjin Mu Yang Fishing Co Ltd** - *Tianjin* *China* MMSI: 412695760 Official number: 041040102	*621* 190 -		**1989-12 Lien Ho Shipbuilding Co, Ltd — Kaohsiung** L reg 49.15 Br ex - Dght - Lbp - Br md 8.90 Dpth 3.75 Welded, 1 dk	**(B11B2FV) Fishing Vessel**	**1 oil engine** driving 1 FP propeller Total Power: 1,030kW (1,400hp) 12.0kn
8624876 *BVEA5* -	**TIAN XIANG 13** *ex* Bin Dong Shan 102 *-2009* *ex* Sansha Maru No. 35 *-2003* *ex* Yoshishige Maru No. 15 *-1994* **Fujian Nan'an Yanping Shipping Ltd** - *Quanzhou, Fujian* *China* Official number: 06D00114961	**2,898** 1,622 4,400	Class: ZC	**1985-01 Nagashima Zosen KK — Kihoku ME** Converted From: Grab Dredger-2004 Lengthened-2004 Loa 95.86 Br ex - Dght 5.500 Lbp 89.00 Br md 13.50 Dpth 7.20 Welded, 1 dk	**(A31A2GX) General Cargo Ship**	**1 oil engine** driving 1 FP propeller Total Power: 735kW (999hp) 12.0kn
8947553 *BZY16* 004758	**TIAN XIANG 16** *ex* Jeffrey No. 168 *-2006* **Tianjin Mu Yang Fishing Co Ltd** - *Tianjin* *China* MMSI: 413300480 Official number: 041040103	**573** 199 -		**1997-08 Jong Shyn Shipbuilding Co., Ltd. — Kaohsiung** L reg 47.30 Br ex - Dght - Lbp - Br md 8.60 Dpth 3.70 Welded, 1 dk	**(B11B2FV) Fishing Vessel**	**1 oil engine** driving 1 FP propeller Total Power: 883kW (1,201hp) 12.0kn Sumiyoshi 1 x 4 Stroke 883kW (1201bhp) Sumiyoshi Marine Diesel Co Ltd-Japan
8603690 *BZY19* 004838	**TIAN XIANG 18** *ex* Andrew No. 708 *-2006* *ex* Blue Top 101 *-2006* *ex* Fukutoku Maru No. 38 *-2006* **Tianjin Mu Yang Fishing Co Ltd** - *Tianjin* *China* MMSI: 412695770 Official number: 041040104	**619** 270 -		**1986-03 KK Kanasashi Zosen — Shizuoka SZ** Yd No: 3103 Loa 56.80 (BB) Br ex 8.84 Dght 3.450 Lbp 49.61 Br md 8.81 Dpth 3.84 Welded, 1 dk	**(B11B2FV) Fishing Vessel**	**1 oil engine** with clutches, flexible couplings & sr reverse geared to sc. shaft driving 1 FP propeller Total Power: 736kW (1,001hp) Niigata 6M28AFTE 1 x 4 Stroke 6 Cy. 280 x 480 736kW (1001bhp) Niigata Engineering Co Ltd-Japan
9674751 *BZSH9* -	**TIAN XIANG NO. 168** **Tianjin Mu Yang Fishing Co Ltd** *Tianjin* *China* Official number: FT-200016	**255** 103 -		**2012-03 Rongcheng Yandunjiao Shipbuilding Aquatic Co Ltd — Rongcheng SD** Loa 35.16 Br ex - Dght - Lbp - Br md 7.00 Dpth 3.70 Welded, 1 dk	**(B11B2FV) Fishing Vessel**	**1 oil engine** driving 1 Propeller
8905957 *BFA06* -	**TIAN XIN** *ex* Da Xin Hua Ying Kou *-2013* *ex* Ville De Mars *-2009* *ex* Australian Endurance *-2000* *ex* Lykes Challenger *-1999* *ex* CGM Pasteur *-1998* *ex* Nedlloyd Pasteur *-1998* *ex* CGM Pasteur *-1995* *ex* Ville de Virgo *-1991* *ex* CGM Pasteur *-1990* **Tianjin Jinhai Marine Shipping Co Ltd** Tianjin Marine Shipping Co Ltd *Tianjin* *China* MMSI: 413903000	**37,235** 15,486 43,714 T/cm 64.1	Class: CC (BV)	**1990-09 Samsung Shipbuilding & Heavy Industries Co Ltd — Geoje** Yd No: 1073 Loa 242.25 (BB) Br ex - Dght 11.717 Lbp 226.70 Br md 32.20 Dpth 14.78 Welded, 1 dk	**(A33A2CC) Container Ship (Fully Cellular)** TEU 2954 C Ho 1350 TEU C Dk 1604 TEU incl 125 ref C. Compartments: ER, 7 Cell Ho 14 Ha: 2 (13.0 x 8.1)2 (13.0 x 10.5)ER 10 (12.6 x 10.5) 24 Wing Ha: 2 (12.6 x 5.4)5 (13.0 x 8.0)17 (12.6 x 8.0)	**1 oil engine** driving 1 FP propeller Total Power: 24,509kW (33,322hp) 22.0kn Sulzer 7RTA84 1 x 2 Stroke 7 Cy. 840 x 2400 24509kW (33322bhp) Korea Heavy Industries & ConstrCo Ltd (HANJUNG)-South Korea AuxGen: 3 x 1000kW 220/440V 60Hz a.c Thrusters: 1 Thwart. FP thruster (f)
8731930 *V3PG2* -	**TIAN XING** *ex* Zhe Tai Yu Leng 339 *-2014* *ex* Qiong Hua *-2007* **Fengmiao Shipping Co Ltd** - *Belize City* *Belize* Official number: 741420008	**798** 444 -		**1990-10 Jiangsu Jiangyang Shipyard Group Co Ltd — Yangzhou JS** Converted From: General Cargo Ship-2007 Loa 64.20 Br ex - Dght 3.600 Lbp 58.93 Br md 10.50 Dpth 4.40 Welded, 1 dk	**(A34A2GR) Refrigerated Cargo Ship** Compartments: 2 Ho, ER 2 Ha: ER	**1 oil engine** geared to sc. shaft driving 1 Propeller Total Power: 661kW (899hp) 10.0kn Chinese Std. Type 8300 1 x 4 Stroke 8 Cy. 300 x 380 661kW (899bhp) Zibo Diesel Engine Factory-China
9400526 *BQBI* -	**TIAN XING HE** **COSCO Container Lines Co Ltd (COSCON)** - *Shanghai* *China* MMSI: 413762000	**54,005** 32,333 63,001	Class: CC (GL)	**2009-10 Shanghai Jiangnan Changxing Heavy Industry Co Ltd — Shanghai** Yd No: H2392 Loa 294.00 (BB) Br ex 32.25 Dght 12.000 Lbp 284.16 Br md 32.20 Dpth 21.80 Welded, 1 dk	**(A33A2CC) Container Ship (Fully Cellular)** Grain: 112,495 TEU 5089 C Ho 2274 TEU C Dk 2815 TEU incl 385 ref C Compartments: 6 Cell Ho, ER 6 Ha: ER Ice Capable	**1 oil engine** driving 1 FP propeller Total Power: 45,760kW (62,215hp) 25.2kn MAN-B&W 8K98MC 1 x 2 Stroke 8 Cy. 980 x 2660 45760kW (62215bhp) AuxGen: 4 x 1800kW 450V a.c Thrusters: 1 Tunnel thruster (f)
9340269 *T3RC* -	**TIAN XIU** **Centrans Shipping Co Ltd** Hunchun Sino Unity Shipping (HongKong) Co Ltd *Tarawa* *Kiribati* MMSI: 529196000 Official number: K-11040865	**2,358** 1,320 3,800	Class: IZ	**2004-09 Zhejiang Dongfang Shipbuilding Co Ltd — Yueqing ZJ** Loa 82.50 Br ex - Dght 5.800 Lbp 76.50 Br md 14.20 Dpth 7.60 Welded, 1 dk	**(A31A2GX) General Cargo Ship** Grain: 5,603 Compartments: 2 Ho, ER 2 Ha: ER 2 (22.8 x 9.0)	**1 oil engine** geared to sc. shaft driving 1 FP propeller Total Power: 1,470kW (1,999hp) 11.0kn MAN-B&W 6L28/32A 1 x 4 Stroke 6 Cy. 280 x 320 1470kW (1999bhp) Zhenjiang Marine Diesel Works-China
9400540 *BQBD* -	**TIAN XIU HE** **COSCO Container Lines Co Ltd (COSCON)** - *Shanghai* *China* MMSI: 413966000	**54,005** 32,333 63,188	Class: CC (GL)	**2010-03 Shanghai Jiangnan Changxing Heavy Industry Co Ltd — Shanghai** Yd No: H2403 Loa 294.00 (BB) Br ex 32.25 Dght 12.000 Lbp 284.16 Br md 32.20 Dpth 21.80 Welded, 1 dk	**(A33A2CC) Container Ship (Fully Cellular)** TEU 5089 C Ho 2274 TEU C Dk 2815 TEU incl 385 ref C Compartments: 6 Cell Ho, ER Ice Capable	**1 oil engine** driving 1 FP propeller Total Power: 45,760kW (62,215hp) 25.2kn MAN-B&W 8K98MC 1 x 2 Stroke 8 Cy. 980 x 2660 45760kW (62215bhp) CSSC MES Diesel Co Ltd-China AuxGen: 4 x 1800kW 450V a.c Thrusters: 1 Tunnel thruster (f)
8831780 *BXIT* -	**TIAN YA** **China National Cereals, Oils & Foodstuffs Import & Export Corp** *Sanya, Hainan* *China*	*499* 196 607	Class: (CC)	**1988 Wang Tak Engineering & Shipbuilding Co Ltd — Hong Kong** Loa 53.56 Br ex - Dght 3.400 Lbp 48.00 Br md 8.80 Dpth 4.20 Welded, 1 dk	**(A31A2GX) General Cargo Ship** Grain: 734; Bale: 720 Compartments: 2 Ho, ER 2 Ha: 2 (7.0 x 5.2)ER Cranes: 2x1.5t	**1 oil engine** geared to sc. shaft driving 1 FP propeller Total Power: 800kW (1,088hp) 12.0kn MAN 8L20/27 1 x 4 Stroke 8 Cy. 200 x 270 800kW (1088bhp) Shanghai Xinzhong Power MachinePlant-China AuxGen: 2 x 90kW 380V a.c, 1 x 40kW 380V a.c
9227699 *VRWU2* -	**TIAN YANG FENG** **Jin He Navigation Inc** China Shipping International Shipmanagement Co Ltd *Hong Kong* *Hong Kong* MMSI: 477839000 Official number: HK0644	**38,860** 25,448 74,027 T/cm 66.0	Class: CC (AB)	**2000-12 Imabari Shipbuilding Co Ltd — Marugame KG (Marugame Shipyard)** Yd No: 1333 Loa 225.00 (BB) Br ex - Dght 14.013 Lbp 215.00 Br md 32.20 Dpth 19.30 Welded, 1 dk	**(A21A2BC) Bulk Carrier** Double Bottom Entire Compartment Length Grain: 89,281 Compartments: 7 Ho, ER 7 Ha: (13.0 x 12.8) (16.3 x 15.6)5 (17.9 x 15.6)ER	**1 oil engine** driving 1 FP propeller Total Power: 8,827kW (12,001hp) 14.5kn B&W 7S50MC 1 x 2 Stroke 7 Cy. 500 x 1910 8827kW (12001bhp) Mitsui Engineering & Shipbuilding CLtd-Japan AuxGen: 3 x 360kW 110/450V 60Hz a.c Fuel: 154.1 (d.f.) (Heating Coils) 2783.8 (r.f.) 36.0pd

9155016 *3FHK4* -	**TIAN YI** *ex* X-Press Karnaphuli *-2014* *ex* Hansa Commodore *-2013* *ex* Delmas Tanzania *-2009* *ex* Hansa Commodore *-2008* **Boon Tat Inc** ASP Ship Management (India) Pvt Ltd *Panama* *Panama* MMSI: 370440000 Official number: 45562PEXT	**16,915** 7,595 21,470 T/cm 38.4	Class: GL	1997-09 **Hanjin Heavy Industries Co Ltd — Busan** Yd No: 048 Loa 168.03 (BB) Br ex - Dght 9.215 Lbp 158.00 Br md 27.20 Dpth 13.80 Welded, 1 dk	**(A33A2CC) Container Ship (Fully Cellular)** TEU 1645 C Ho 606 TEU C Dk 1039 TEU incl 128 ref C. Cranes: 2x40t,1x10t	**1 oil engine** driving 1 FP propeller Total Power: 11,950kW (16,247hp) 19.0kn B&W 6S60MC 1 x 2 Stroke 6 Cy. 600 x 2292 11950kW (16247bhp) Hyundai Heavy Industries Co Ltd-South Korea AuxGen: 3 x 600kW a.c Thrusters: 1 Thwart. CP thruster (f)
7927049 - -	**TIAN YI** *ex* Fei Da 802 *-2006* *ex* Kompak 802 *-2005* *ex* San Hsieh 306 *-2004* *ex* Green Gold No. 1 *-1998* *ex* Pan Viet No. 1 *-1995* *ex* Sanuki Maru *-1993* - -	**1,572** 442 1,208	Class: (CC) (RI) (NK)	1980-06 **Kochi Jyuko (Kaisei Zosen) K.K. — Kochi** Yd No: 1390 Loa 65.87 Br ex - Dght 4.340 Lbp 60.48 Br md 12.21 Dpth 4.40 Welded, 2 dks	**(A34A2GR) Refrigerated Cargo Ship** Ins: 1,418 2 Ha: 2 (4 x 4.5)ER Derricks: 4x5t	**1 oil engine** reverse geared to sc. shaft driving 1 FP propeller Total Power: 1,324kW (1,800hp) 12.3kn Akasaka DM36R 1 x 4 Stroke 6 Cy. 360 x 540 1324kW (1800bhp) Akasaka Tekkosho KK (Akasaka DieselLtd)-Japan AuxGen: 2 x 240kW
9653783 *BKOQ6* -	**TIAN YI ZHI CHEN** **Zhejiang Tianji Construction of the Sea Co Ltd** - *Zhoushan, Zhejiang* *China* MMSI: 413446820	**3,479** 1,043 3,115	Class: CC	2012-06 **Ningbo Zhenhe Shipbuilding Co Ltd — Xiangshan County ZJ** Yd No: ZHCCS0904 Loa 77.52 Br ex - Dght 6.200 Lbp 68.68 Br md 18.00 Dpth 7.50 Welded, 1 dk	**(B21B20T) Offshore Tug/Supply Ship**	**2 oil engines** reduction geared to sc. shafts driving 2 Propellers Total Power: 8,000kW (10,876hp) 16.0kn MAN-B&W 8L32/40 2 x 4 Stroke 8 Cy. 320 x 400 each-4000kW (5438bhp) STX Engine Co Ltd-South Korea AuxGen: 2 x 824kW 400V a.c, 2 x 1600kW 400V a.c
8651283 *BZSJ5* 004322	**TIAN YU 7** **Tian Jin Tian Xiang Fishing Co Ltd** - *Tianjin* *China* MMSI: 412694830 Official number: 041090002	**579** 223 -		**2004-04 Huanghai Shipbuilding Co Ltd — Rongcheng SD** Loa 46.75 Br ex 8.50 Dght - Lbp - Br md - Dpth 3.65 Welded, 1 dk	**(B11B2FV) Fishing Vessel**	**1 oil engine** driving 1 Propeller Total Power: 883kW (1,201hp)
8651295 *BZSJ6* 004321	**TIAN YU 8** **Tian Jin Tian Xiang Fishing Co Ltd** - *Tianjin* *China* MMSI: 412694840 Official number: 041050007	**579** 223 -		**2004-04 Huanghai Shipbuilding Co Ltd — Rongcheng SD** Loa 46.75 Br ex 8.50 Dght - Lbp - Br md - Dpth 3.65 Welded, 1 dk	**(B11B2FV) Fishing Vessel**	**1 oil engine** driving 1 Propeller Total Power: 883kW (1,201hp)
9233351 *VRWY4* -	**TIAN YU FENG** **Jin Peng Navigation Inc** China Shipping International Shipmanagement Co Ltd *Hong Kong* *Hong Kong* MMSI: 477873000 Official number: HK-0678	**39,042** 25,025 74,272 T/cm 66.3	Class: CC (BV)	2001-04 **Namura Shipbuilding Co Ltd — Imari SG** Yd No: 990 Loa 224.89 (BB) Br ex - Dght 13.950 Lbp 215.00 Br md 32.20 Dpth 19.30 Welded, 1 dk	**(A21A2BC) Bulk Carrier** Grain: 89,236 Compartments: 7 Ho, ER 7 Ha: (16.8 x 13.2)6 (16.8 x 14.8)ER	**1 oil engine** driving 1 FP propeller Total Power: 8,827kW (12,001hp) 14.1kn B&W 7S50MC 1 x 2 Stroke 7 Cy. 500 x 1910 8827kW (12001bhp) Hitachi Zosen Corp-Japan Fuel: 1988.0 (r.f.)
8614895 - -	**TIAN YUAN** *ex* Dae Hyun No. 501 *-2000* *ex* Melilla No. 501 *-2000* *ex* Chokyu Maru No. 38 *-1999* **China Tianjun Deepsea Fishing Co** *Argentina* Official number: 02173	*846* 310 926	Class: (KR)	1986-12 **Kitanihon Zosen K.K. — Hachinohe** Yd No: 215 Loa 67.75 (BB) Br ex - Dght 4.350 Lbp 57.00 Br md 10.20 Dpth 6.66 Welded, 2 dks	**(B11B2FV) Fishing Vessel** Ins: 924	**1 oil engine** driving 1 FP propeller Total Power: 1,177kW (1,600hp) 12.5kn Niigata 6M31AFTE 1 x 4 Stroke 6 Cy. 310 x 530 1177kW (1600bhp) Niigata Engineering Co Ltd-Japan
8747616 *3FOP9* -	**TIAN YUAN 1** **Zhejiang Jiade Shipping Co Ltd** Shanghai Haizheng Ship Management Co Ltd SatCom: Inmarsat C 435108710 *Panama* *Panama* MMSI: 351087000 Official number: 43128PEXTF	**2,983** 1,882 5,300	Class: PD	2005-03 **Zhoushan Zhaobao Shipbuilding & Repair Co Ltd — Zhoushan ZJ** Yd No: 04 Loa 98.00 Br ex - Dght 5.900 Lbp 93.39 Br md 15.80 Dpth 7.40 Welded, 1 dk	**(A31A2GX) General Cargo Ship** Grain: 6,825; Bale: 6,279	**1 oil engine** reduction geared to sc. shaft driving 1 FP propeller Total Power: 2,000kW (2,719hp) 11.0kn Chinese Std. Type G8300ZC 1 x 4 Stroke 8 Cy. 300 x 380 2000kW (2719bhp) Wuxi Antai Power Machinery Co Ltd-China
7375026 - -	**TIAN YUAN 3** *ex* Min Wai Leng 3 *-2007* *ex* Hai Xiang No. 702 *-1997* **Zhejiang Liao Yuan Shipping Co Ltd**	**1,194** 606 1,409	Class: (CC) (NK)	1974-12 **Nishii Dock Co. Ltd. — Ise** Yd No: 271 Loa 71.40 Br ex 11.03 Dght 4.814 Lbp 64.78 Br md 11.00 Dpth 5.52 Welded, 1 dk	**(A34A2GR) Refrigerated Cargo Ship** Ins: 1,490 Compartments: 3 Ho, ER 3 Ha: 3 (3.9 x 3.3)ER Derricks: 6x3t	**1 oil engine** driving 1 FP propeller Total Power: 1,692kW (2,300hp) 12.5kn Hanshin 6LUS38 1 x 4 Stroke 6 Cy. 380 x 580 1692kW (2300bhp) The Hanshin Diesel Works Ltd-Japan AuxGen: 3 x 450kW 380V 50Hz a.c Fuel: 355.5 (d.f.) 8.0pd
8747446 *3FGY2* -	**TIAN YUAN 6** **Zhejiang Jiade Shipping Co Ltd** Shanghai Haizheng Ship Management Co Ltd SatCom: Inmarsat C 437019410 *Panama* *Panama* MMSI: 370194000 Official number: 43470PEXTF	**2,994** 1,723 6,100	Class: PD	**2009-08 Wuhu Hongyu Shipbuilding & Repair Co Ltd — Wuhu AH** Loa 96.90 Br ex - Dght 5.900 Lbp 89.80 Br md 15.80 Dpth 7.40 Welded, 1 dk	**(A31A2GX) General Cargo Ship**	**1 oil engine** reduction geared to sc. shafts driving 1 FP propeller Total Power: 2,000kW (2,719hp) 11.0kn Chinese Std. Type G8300ZC 1 x 4 Stroke 8 Cy. 300 x 380 2000kW (2719bhp) Wuxi Antai Power Machinery Co Ltd-China
8311871 - -	**TIAN YUN** **China Shipping (Group) Co** - SatCom: Inmarsat C 441255715 *Dalian, Liaoning* *China*	*5,500* 2,800 2,000		1984-11 **Tianjin Xingang Shipyard — Tianjin** Yd No: 248 Loa 120.02 Br ex - Dght 5.801 Lbp 108.01 Br md 17.01 Dpth 7.83 Welded, 3 dks	**(A32A2GF) General Cargo/Passenger Ship** Passengers: 948	**2 oil engines** driving 2 FP propellers Total Power: 4,414kW (6,002hp) Sulzer 6RD44 2 x 2 Stroke 6 Cy. 440 x 760 each-2207kW (3001bhp) Shanghai Diesel Engine Co Ltd-China
9400514 *BQBJ* -	**TIAN YUN HE** **COSCO Container Lines Co Ltd (COSCON)** - *Shanghai* *China* MMSI: 413763000 Official number: 0009000168	**54,005** 32,333 63,142	Class: CC GL	**2009-11 Shanghai Jiangnan Changxing Heavy Industry Co Ltd — Shanghai** Yd No: H2391 Loa 294.00 (BB) Br ex 32.25 Dght 12.000 Lbp 284.16 Br md 32.20 Dpth 21.80 Welded, 1 dk	**(A33A2CC) Container Ship (Fully Cellular)** TEU 5089 C Ho 2274 TEU C Dk 2815 TEU incl 385 ref C Compartments: 6 Cell Ho, ER	**1 oil engine** driving 1 FP propeller Total Power: 45,760kW (62,215hp) 25.2kn MAN-B&W 8K98MC 1 x 2 Stroke 8 Cy. 980 x 2660 45760kW (62215bhp) CSSC MES Diesel Co Ltd-China AuxGen: 4 x 1800kW a.c Thrusters: 1 Tunnel thruster (f)
9578311 *BKQA5* -	**TIAN ZE 806** **Zhejiang Zhoushan Tianze Maritime Operation Co Ltd** Yangpu Zhenye Offshore Engineering Service Co Ltd *Zhoushan, Zhejiang* *China* MMSI: 413438190	**2,108** 632 1,896	Class: CC	**2010-08 Taizhou Hongda Shipbuilding Co Ltd — Linhai ZJ** Yd No: 2008-05 Loa 67.00 Br ex 16.35 Dght 4.200 Lbp 60.62 Br md 16.00 Dpth 6.50 Welded, 1 dk	**(B21B20T) Offshore Tug/Supply Ship** Ice Capable	**2 oil engines** reduction geared to sc. shafts driving 2 Propellers Total Power: 4,412kW (5,998hp) Chinese Std. Type G8300ZC 2 x 4 Stroke 8 Cy. 300 x 380 each-2206kW (2999bhp) Ningbo CSI Power & Machinery GroupCo Ltd-China AuxGen: 2 x 1272kW 400V a.c, 2 x 372kW 400V a.c
9340257 *T3RN* -	**TIAN ZHI** **Royal Armadas International Co Ltd** Hunchun Sino Unity Shipping (HongKong) Co Ltd *Tarawa* *Kiribati* MMSI: 529206000 Official number: K1541297	**2,358** 1,320 3,800	Class: IZ	**2004-09 Zhejiang Dongfang Shipbuilding Co Ltd — Yueqing ZJ** Loa 82.50 Br ex - Dght 5.800 Lbp 76.50 Br md 14.20 Dpth 7.60 Welded, 1 dk	**(A31A2GX) General Cargo Ship** Grain: 5,603 Compartments: 2 Ho, ER 2 Ha: ER 2 (22.8 x 9.0)	**1 oil engine** reduction geared to sc. shaft driving 1 Propeller Total Power: 1,471kW (2,000hp) 11.0kn MAN-B&W 6L28/32A 1 x 4 Stroke 6 Cy. 280 x 320 1471kW (2000bhp) Zhenjiang Marine Diesel Works-China
8655411 *BH2916*	**TIAN ZHI XIANG** *ex* Fu Chang No. 6 *-2010* **Tian Zhi Xiang Oceanic Enterprise Co Ltd** - *Kaohsiung* *Chinese Taipei*	**478** 182 -		1983-07 **San Yang Shipbuilding Co., Ltd. — Kaohsiung** Loa 43.95 Br ex - Dght - Lbp - Br md 8.20 Dpth 3.60 Welded, 1 dk	**(B11B2FV) Fishing Vessel**	**1 oil engine** driving 1 Propeller

8114869 *BAIA* -	**TIAN ZHOU** *ex* Zhou Shui Yu 3 *-2001* *ex* Hinode Maru No. 5 *-1984* **Dalian Tianzhou Haitong Import & Export Co Ltd** Dalian Hualong Group Aquatic Product Co Ltd *Dalian, Liaoning* *China* MMSI: 412206330 Official number: 030006000084	**470** 141 557	Class: CC	**1981-10 Sasaki Shipbuilding Co Ltd — Osakikamijima HS** Yd No: 278 Converted From: Chemical/Products Tanker-2008 Loa 52.51 Br ex 8.21 Dght 3.200 Lbp 48.11 Br md 8.20 Dpth 3.81 Welded, 1 dk	**(B12B2FC) Fish Carrier**	**1 oil engine** geared to sc. shaft driving 1 FP propeller Total Power: 588kW (799hp) 10.8kn Yanmar MF24-UT 1 x 4 Stroke 6 Cy. 240 x 420 588kW (799bhp) Yanmar Diesel Engine Co Ltd-Japan
9338981 *T3PN* -	**TIAN ZHU** **Tian Zhu Co Ltd** Hunchun Sino Unity Shipping (HongKong) Co Ltd *Tarawa* *Kiribati* MMSI: 529158000 Official number: K-11040822	**2,358** 1,320 3,800	Class: IZ	**2004-06 Zhejiang Dongfang Shipbuilding Co Ltd — Yueqing ZJ** Loa 82.50 Br ex - Dght 5.800 Lbp 76.50 Br md 14.20 Dpth 7.60 Welded, 1 dk	**(A31A2GX) General Cargo Ship** Double Bottom Entire, Double Sides Partial Grain: 5,603 Compartments: 2 Ho, ER 2 Ha: ER 2 (22.8 x 9.0)	**1 oil engine** geared to sc. shaft driving 1 FP propeller Total Power: 1,471kW (2,000hp) 11.0kn MAN-B&W 6L28/32A 1 x 4 Stroke 6 Cy. 280 x 320 1471kW (2000bhp) Zhenjiang Marine Diesel Works-China
9203485 *VRWR8* -	**TIAN ZHU FENG** **Jin Que Navigation Inc** China International Ship Management Co Ltd (CISM) *Hong Kong* *Hong Kong* MMSI: 477816000 Official number: HK-0626	**38,767** 25,807 74,200	Class: CC (NV)	**2000-10 Oshima Shipbuilding Co Ltd — Saikai NS** Yd No: 10278 Loa 225.00 (BB) Br ex - Dght 13.900 Lbp 216.00 Br md 32.26 Dpth 18.90 Welded, 1 dk	**(A21A2BC) Bulk Carrier** Grain: 89,344; Bale: 87,774 Compartments: 7 Ho, ER 7 Ha: ER	**1 oil engine** driving 1 FP propeller Total Power: 9,989kW (13,581hp) 14.0kn B&W 7S50MC 1 x 2 Stroke 7 Cy. 500 x 1910 9989kW (13581bhp) Kawasaki Heavy Industries Ltd-Japan
8888927 *BUOZ* -	**TIAN ZHU SHAN** **China Yangtze River Shipping Co Ltd** Shanghai Changjiang Shipping Corp *Shanghai* *China* MMSI: 412076010	**4,061** 1,827 4,944	Class: CC	**1995 Wuhu Shipyard — Wuhu AH** Loa 98.50 (BB) Br ex - Dght 5.800 Lbp 92.00 Br md 16.80 Dpth 7.80 Welded, 1 dk	**(A31A2GX) General Cargo Ship** Grain: 6,165; Bale: 6,080 Compartments: 1 Tw Dk, 2 Ho, ER 2 Ha: (37.7 x 12.6)ER (19.5 x 12.6) Ice Capable	**2 oil engines** geared to sc. shafts driving 2 FP propellers Total Power: 2,828kW (3,844hp) 12.4kn Alpha 8L23/30 2 x 4 Stroke 8 Cy. 225 x 300 each-1414kW (1922bhp) Zhenjiang Marine Diesel Works-China AuxGen: 3 x 90kW 400V a.c Fuel: 240.0
8747862 *XUDA6* -	**TIAN ZHUI** **Haitai Shipping Co Ltd** Yuan Da Shipping Co Ltd *Phnom Penh* *Cambodia* MMSI: 514139000 Official number: 1309178	**8,574** 4,801 13,226	Class: UB ZC	**2009-09 Yueqing Jianghai Shipbuilding Co Ltd — Yueqing ZJ** Loa 141.36 (BB) Br ex - Dght 7.800 Lbp 132.50 Br md 20.00 Dpth 10.80 Welded, 1 dk	**(A21A2BC) Bulk Carrier** Grain: 18,500 Cranes: 3x30t	**1 oil engine** driving 1 FP propeller Total Power: 2,941kW (3,999hp) 11.0kn
8664400 *T3LE2* -	**TIANJI18139-1** *ex* Yue She Yu Gong 18139 *-2013* - - *Tarawa* *Kiribati* MMSI: 529679000 Official number: K-17091342	*988* 554 -		**2009-09 Fujian Jianli Shipbuilding Co Ltd — Fu'an FJ** Yd No: FZ-200001 Loa 56.00 Br ex - Dght 3.000 Lbp 52.00 Br md 14.00 Dpth 7.00 Welded, 1 dk	**(B11A2FG) Factory Stern Trawler**	**2 oil engines** reduction geared to sc. shafts driving 2 Propellers Total Power: 1,320kW (1,794hp) Weifang 2 x each-660kW (897bhp) Weifang Diesel Engine Factory-China
9398462 *A8SJ2* -	**TIANJIN** *ex* Zim Tianjin *-2011* **Pelican Maritime (S348) Co Ltd** Zim Integrated Shipping Services Ltd SatCom: Inmarsat C 463706750 *Monrovia* *Liberia* MMSI: 636014224 Official number: 14224	**114,044** 58,784 116,440	Class: LR ✠ **100A1** SS 07/2010 container ship **ShipRight** (SDA, FDA, CM) *IWS LI EP (B) ✠ **LMC** **UMS** Eq.Ltr: D*; Cable: 770.0/114.0 U3 (a)	**2010-07 Hyundai Samho Heavy Industries Co Ltd — Samho** Yd No: S348 Loa 349.00 (BB) Br ex 45.73 Dght 15.000 Lbp 334.00 Br md 45.60 Dpth 27.30 Welded, 1 dk	**(A33A2CC) Container Ship (Fully Cellular)** TEU 10062 C Ho 4878 TEU C Dk 5184 TEU incl 800 ref C Compartments: 10 Cell Ho, ER	**1 oil engine** driving 1 FP propeller Total Power: 68,640kW (93,323hp) 24.8kn MAN-B&W 12K98MC 1 x 2 Stroke 12 Cy. 980 x 2660 68640kW (93323bhp) Hyundai Heavy Industries Co Ltd-South Korea AuxGen: 2 x 2800kW 6600V 60Hz a.c, 3 x 2195kW 6600V 60Hz a.c Boilers: e (ex.g.) 10.7kgf/cm² (10.5bar), WTAuxB (o.f.) 8.3kgf/cm² (8.1bar) Thrusters: 1 Thwart. CP thruster (f)
9294355 *3EDE7* -	**TIANJIN HIGHWAY** **Bullet Navigation SA** Taiyo Nippon Kisen Co Ltd *Panama* *Panama* MMSI: 371559000 Official number: 3135306A	**48,927** 14,679 15,461	Class: NK	**2005-11 Nantong COSCO KHI Ship Engineering Co Ltd (NACKS) — Nantong JS** Yd No: 035 Loa 179.99 (BB) Br ex - Dght 9.417 Lbp 167.00 Br md 32.20 Dpth 32.21 Welded, 12 dks. incl. 3 movable dks.	**(A35B2RV) Vehicles Carrier** Side door/ramp (s) Quarter stern door/ramp (s. a.) Cars: 5,036	**1 oil engine** driving 1 FP propeller Total Power: 12,500kW (16,995hp) 20.0kn MAN-B&W 7S60ME-C 1 x 2 Stroke 7 Cy. 600 x 2400 12500kW (16995bhp) Kawasaki Heavy Industries Ltd-Japan AuxGen: 3 x 760kW 450/220V 60Hz a.c Thrusters: 1 Thwart. CP thruster (f) Fuel: 2660.0 (r.f.)
9291092 *VRAZ9* -	**TIANJIN PIONEER** **Continent Maritime SA** Kotoku Kaiun Co Ltd (Kotoku Kaiun KK) *Hong Kong* *Hong Kong* MMSI: 477994800 Official number: HK-1525	**38,871** 25,194 75,744 T/cm 66.5	Class: NK	**2005-05 Sanoyas Hishino Meisho Corp — Kurashiki OY** Yd No: 1226 Loa 225.00 (BB) Br ex - Dght 13.994 Lbp 217.00 Br md 32.26 Dpth 19.30 Welded, 1 dk	**(A21A2BC) Bulk Carrier** Grain: 89,201 Compartments: 7 Ho, ER 7 Ha: 6 (17.1 x 15.0)ER (16.3 x 13.4)	**1 oil engine** driving 1 FP propeller Total Power: 8,973kW (12,200hp) 14.5kn B&W 7S50MC-C 1 x 2 Stroke 7 Cy. 500 x 2000 8973kW (12200bhp) Mitsui Engineering & Shipbuilding CLtd-Japan Fuel: 2810.0
9457294 *VRFM4* -	**TIANJIN VENTURE** **Clear Mountain Shipping Ltd** Wah Kwong Ship Management (Hong Kong) Ltd *Hong Kong* *Hong Kong* MMSI: 477559900	**32,505** 17,674 53,600 T/cm 57.3	Class: BV	**2009-09 Chengxi Shipyard Co Ltd — Jiangyin JS** Yd No: CX4247 Loa 189.89 (BB) Br ex - Dght 12.540 Lbp 181.50 Br md 32.26 Dpth 17.50 Welded, 1 dk	**(A21A2BC) Bulk Carrier** Grain: 65,900; Bale: 64,000 Compartments: 5 Ho, ER 5 Ha: 4 (21.6 x 22.4)ER (19.2 x 20.8) Cranes: 4x36t	**1 oil engine** driving 1 FP propeller Total Power: 9,480kW (12,889hp) 14.2kn MAN-B&W 6S50MC-C 1 x 2 Stroke 6 Cy. 500 x 2000 9480kW (12889bhp) Hudong Heavy Machinery Co Ltd-China AuxGen: 3 x 680kW 60Hz a.c Fuel: 215.0 (d.f.) 2000.0 (r.f.) 34.5pd
9378369 *C6WZ8* -	**TIANLONG SPIRIT** **Tianlong Spirit LLC** Teekay Marine (Singapore) Pte Ltd SatCom: Inmarsat C 430968610 *Nassau* *Bahamas* MMSI: 309686000 Official number: 9000267	**85,037** 52,155 159,021 T/cm 119.1	Class: LR (CC) ✠ **100A1** SS 01/2014 Double Hull oil tanker ESP **ShipRight** (SDA, FDA, CM) *IWS LI SPM ✠ **LMC** **UMS IGS** Eq.Ltr: Y†; Cable: 742.5/97.0 U3 (a)	**2009-01 Bohai Shipbuilding Heavy Industry Co Ltd — Huludao LN** Yd No: 508-4 Loa 274.64 (BB) Br ex 48.03 Dght 17.300 Lbp 264.00 Br md 48.00 Dpth 24.00 Welded, 1 dk	**(A13A2TV) Crude Oil Tanker** Double Hull (13F) Liq: 176,816; Liq (Oil): 180,588 Cargo Heating Coils Compartments: 12 Wing Ta, 2 Wing Slop Ta, ER 3 Cargo Pump (s): 3x3500m³/hr Manifold: Bow/CM: 139.3m	**1 oil engine** driving 1 FP propeller Total Power: 16,860kW (22,923hp) 14.8kn MAN-B&W 6S70MC 1 x 2 Stroke 6 Cy. 700 x 2674 16860kW (22923bhp) Dalian Marine Diesel Co Ltd-China AuxGen: 3 x 900kW 450V 60Hz a.c Boilers: e (ex.g.) 19.1kgf/cm² (18.7bar), WTAuxB (o.f.) 17.8kgf/cm² (17.5bar) Fuel: 186.0 (d.f.) 3184.0 (r.f.)
9203112 *H3GD* -	**TIANRONGHAI** **Sea Landa SA** Qingdao Ocean Shipping Co Ltd (COSCO QINGDAO) SatCom: Inmarsat C 435324610 *Panama* *Panama* MMSI: 353246000 Official number: 2717700C	**87,625** 56,865 171,861 T/cm 120.0	Class: CC (AB)	**2000-06 Hyundai Heavy Industries Co Ltd — Ulsan** Yd No: 1186 Loa 288.97 (BB) Br ex - Dght 17.700 Lbp 279.00 Br md 45.00 Dpth 24.10 Welded, 1 dk	**(A21A2BC) Bulk Carrier** Grain: 191,597 Cargo Heating Coils Compartments: 9 Ho, ER 9 Ha: 9 (15.5 x 20.8)ER	**1 oil engine** driving 1 FP propeller Total Power: 14,329kW (19,482hp) 15.0kn MAN-B&W 6S70MC 1 x 2 Stroke 6 Cy. 700 x 2674 14329kW (19482bhp) Hyundai Heavy Industries Co Ltd-South Korea AuxGen: 3 x 650kW 450V a.c Fuel: 781.5 (d.f.) (Heating Coils) 1950.1 (r.f.)
9137600 *3FAJ7* -	**TIANSHENGHAI** **Tianshenghai Maritime Inc** Qingdao Ocean Shipping Co Ltd (COSCO QINGDAO) SatCom: Inmarsat B 335538510 *Panama* *Panama* MMSI: 355385000 Official number: 2368597CH	**85,676** 55,142 170,401 T/cm 118.2	Class: CC (LR) ✠ Classed LR until 27/8/01	**1997-03 Daewoo Heavy Industries Ltd — Geoje** Yd No: 1113 Loa 289.08 (BB) Br ex 45.06 Dght 17.580 Lbp 278.00 Br md 45.00 Dpth 23.90 Welded, 1 dk	**(A21A2BC) Bulk Carrier** Grain: 185,086 Compartments: 9 Ho, ER 9 Ha: 7 (14.6 x 20.4)2 (14.6 x 15.3)ER	**1 oil engine** driving 1 FP propeller Total Power: 16,870kW (22,936hp) 15.0kn B&W 6S70MC 1 x 2 Stroke 6 Cy. 700 x 2674 16870kW (22936bhp) Korea Heavy Industries & ConstrCo Ltd (HANJUNG)-South Korea AuxGen: 3 x 600kW 450V 60Hz a.c
9203124 *H3KQ* -	**TIANSHUNHAI** **Sea Lansa SA** Qingdao Ocean Shipping Co Ltd (COSCO QINGDAO) SatCom: Inmarsat C 435476510 *Panama* *Panama* MMSI: 354765000 Official number: 2720900C	**87,625** 56,865 171,877 T/cm 120.0	Class: CC	**2000-08 Hyundai Heavy Industries Co Ltd — Ulsan** Yd No: 1187 Loa 289.00 (BB) Br ex - Dght 17.700 Lbp 279.00 Br md 45.00 Dpth 24.10 Welded, 1 dk	**(A21A2BC) Bulk Carrier** Grain: 182,127 Cargo Heating Coils Compartments: 9 Ho, ER 9 Ha: 2 (15.5 x 20.6)7 (15.5 x 17.2)ER	**1 oil engine** driving 1 FP propeller Total Power: 16,858kW (22,920hp) 15.0kn B&W 6S70MC 1 x 2 Stroke 6 Cy. 700 x 2674 16858kW (22920bhp) Hyundai Heavy Industries Co Ltd-South Korea AuxGen: 3 x 650kW a.c Fuel: 781.5 (d.f.) (Heating Coils) 1950.1 (r.f.)

IMO / Call sign	Name / Owner	Tonnage	Class	Builder / Dimensions	Type / Capacity	Machinery
9137612 *3FFW7* -	**TIANYANGHAI** *ex* Tian Yang Hai *-2010* **Tianyanghai Maritime Inc** Qingdao Ocean Shipping Co Ltd (COSCO QINGDAO) SatCom: Inmarsat B 335106310 *Panama* *Panama* MMSI: 351063000 Official number: 2381697CH	**85,676** 55,142 169,999 T/cm 118.2	Class: CC	**1997-05 Daewoo Heavy Industries Ltd — Geoje** Yd No: 1114 Loa 289.08 (BB) Br ex - Dght 17.580 Lbp 278.00 Br md 45.00 Dpth 23.90 Welded, 1 dk	**(A21A2BC) Bulk Carrier** Grain: 185,086 Compartments: 9 Ho, ER 9 Ha: 7 (14.6 x 20.4)2 (14.6 x 15.3)ER	**1 oil engine** driving 1 FP propeller Total Power: 16,844kW (22,901hp) 15.0kn B&W 6S70MC 1 x 2 Stroke 6 Cy. 700 x 2674 16844kW (22901bhp) Korea Heavy Industries & ConstrCo Ltd (HANJUNG)-South Korea AuxGen: 3 x 600kW
9105530 *BFHH* -	**TIANZUO** *ex* Paiute *-2012* **Beikun Shipping Tianjin Co Ltd** - SatCom: Inmarsat C 441411310 *Tianjin* *China* MMSI: 414113000	**36,615** 23,344 70,293 T/cm 65.0	Class: CC (NV) (AB)	**1995-05 Sanoyas Hishino Meisho Corp — Kurashiki OY** Yd No: 1128 Loa 225.00 (BB) Br ex 32.30 Dght 13.271 Lbp 217.00 Br md 32.26 Dpth 18.30 Welded, 1 dk	**(A21A2BC) Bulk Carrier** Grain: 81,839; Bale: 78,529 Compartments: 7 Ho, ER 7 Ha: (16.7 x 13.4)Tappered 6 (16.7 x 15.3)ER	**1 oil engine** driving 1 FP propeller Total Power: 7,834kW (10,651hp) 14.0kn Sulzer 7RTA52U 1 x 2 Stroke 7 Cy. 520 x 1800 7834kW (10651bhp) Diesel United Ltd.-Aioi AuxGen: 3 x 420kW 440/220V 60Hz a.c Fuel: 239.0 (d.f.) (Part Heating Coils) 2498.0 (r.f.) 30.7pd
8713304 *DSNQ3* -	**TIARA** *ex* S & B No. 9 *-2011* *ex* Fukujin Maru *-2004* **Daeyoo Merchant Marine Co Ltd** Seok Chang Maritime Co Ltd *Jeju* *South Korea* MMSI: 440067000 Official number: JJR-040636	**1,212** 767 1,600	Class: KR	**1987-11 Kochi Jyuko K.K. — Kochi** Yd No: 2541 Loa 70.34 (BB) Br ex - Dght 4.422 Lbp 60.00 Br md 11.51 Dpth 6.51 Welded, 2 dks	**(A31A2GX) General Cargo Ship** Grain: 2,503; Bale: 2,388 Compartments: 1 Ho, ER 1 Ha: ER	**1 oil engine** sr reverse geared to sc. shaft driving 1 FP propeller Total Power: 1,030kW (1,400hp) 13.3kn Hanshin 6LUN28ARG 1 x 4 Stroke 6 Cy. 280 x 480 1030kW (1400bhp) The Hanshin Diesel Works Ltd-Japan
1007835 *ZCNB7* -	**TIARA** - **CAP-10 LP** YCO SAM *George Town* *Cayman Islands (British)* MMSI: 319346000 Official number: 736892	**428** - 70	Class: LR ✠ **100A1** SS 01/2009 SSC Yacht, mono, G6 **LMC** **CCS** Cable: 275.0/17.5 U2 (a)	**2004-05 Alloy Yachts — Auckland** Yd No: 30 Loa 55.23 Br ex 11.01 Dght 5.250 Lbp 44.60 Br md 10.89 Dpth 4.55 Welded, 1 dk	**(X11A2YP) Yacht** Hull Material: Aluminium Alloy	**1 oil engine** with clutches, flexible couplings & sr geared to sc. shaft driving 1 CP propeller Total Power: 1,044kW (1,419hp) 15.6kn Caterpillar 3412E 1 x Vee 4 Stroke 12 Cy. 137 x 152 1044kW (1419bhp) Caterpillar Inc-USA AuxGen: 2 x 104kW 400V 50Hz a.c Thrusters: 1 Thwart. FP thruster (f); 1 Thwart. FP thruster (a)
8420763 *3FQH9* -	**TIARA 108** *ex* Nova Terra *-2010* *ex* Adriatic Universal *-1990* **Tiara Marine SA** Hua Fu International Group SA SatCom: Inmarsat C 435702010 *Panama* *Panama* MMSI: 357020000 Official number: 4192710	**4,361** 2,627 5,475	Class: CR (BV) (NK)	**1985-04 Kitanihon Zosen K.K. — Hachinohe** Yd No: 201 Loa 109.00 (BB) Br ex - Dght 7.665 Lbp 100.80 Br md 16.40 Dpth 10.00 Welded	**(A34A2GR) Refrigerated Cargo Ship** Ins: 6,526 Compartments: 3 Ho, ER 3 Ha: ER Derricks: 6x5t	**1 oil engine** driving 1 FP propeller Total Power: 4,781kW (6,500hp) 16.0kn Mitsubishi 6UEC45LA 1 x 2 Stroke 6 Cy. 450 x 1350 4781kW (6500bhp) Akasaka Tekkosho KK (Akasaka DieselLtd)-Japan AuxGen: 4 x 306kW a.c
9145530 *V7NR8* -	**TIARA GLOBE** *ex* Selendang Tiara *-2007* **Elysium Maritime Ltd** Globus Shipmanagement Corp *Majuro* *Marshall Islands* MMSI: 538003007 Official number: 3007	**39,755** 25,379 72,928 T/cm 66.0	Class: BV (AB)	**1998-04 Hudong Shipbuilding Group — Shanghai** Yd No: H1241A Loa 225.00 (BB) Br ex - Dght 14.018 Lbp 217.00 Br md 32.26 Dpth 19.20 Welded, 1 dk	**(A21A2BC) Bulk Carrier** Double Bottom Entire Compartment Length Grain: 89,430; Bale: 78,698 Compartments: 7 Ho, ER 7 Ha: ER Cranes: 4x30t	**1 oil engine** driving 1 FP propeller Total Power: 9,415kW (12,801hp) 14.6kn B&W 6S60MC 1 x 2 Stroke 6 Cy. 600 x 2292 9415kW (12801bhp) Hudong Shipyard-China AuxGen: 3 x 530kW 450V 60Hz a.c Fuel: 210.0 (d.f.) (Heating Coils) 2600.0 (r.f.) 34.5pd
9391971 *A8SA8* -	**TIARE** - **Max Navigation BV** Marwave Shipmanagement BV *Monrovia* *Liberia* MMSI: 636014190 Official number: 14190	**44,213** 27,095 83,688 T/cm 71.0	Class: AB	**2009-04 Sanoyas Hishino Meisho Corp — Kurashiki OY** Yd No: 1275 Loa 229.00 (BB) Br ex 33.00 Dght 14.520 Lbp 223.00 Br md 32.24 Dpth 20.20 Welded, 1 dk	**(A21A2BC) Bulk Carrier** Grain: 96,080 Compartments: 7 Ho, ER 7 Ha: ER	**1 oil engine** driving 1 FP propeller Total Power: 13,560kW (18,436hp) 14.0kn MAN-B&W 6S60MC-C 1 x 2 Stroke 6 Cy. 600 x 2400 13560kW (18436bhp) Kawasaki Heavy Industries Ltd-Japan AuxGen: 3 x 470kW a.c Fuel: 222.0 (d.f.) 2750.0 (r.f.)
8912871 *J7CG4* -	**TIARE MOANA** *ex* Antung *-2012* *ex* Scarlett Lucy *-2012* *ex* Tristein *-2008* *ex* Kestutis *-2006* *ex* Sider Trader *-2000* *ex* Poyarkovo *-1998* **Neptune Pacific Line Pte Ltd** Elliott Associates Pte Ltd *Portsmouth* *Dominica* MMSI: 325569000	**3,972** 1,617 4,152	Class: NV (LR) (KR) (BV) (RS) Classed LR until 16/6/08	**1993-04 Sedef Gemi Endustrisi A.S. — Gebze** Yd No: 92 Loa 97.80 Br ex 17.34 Dght 5.976 Lbp 90.22 Br md 17.30 Dpth 7.00 Welded, 1 dk	**(A31A2GX) General Cargo Ship** Grain: 5,242; Bale: 5,227 TEU 221 C.Ho 111/20' C.Dk 110/20' incl. 12 ref C. Compartments: 2 Ho, ER 2 Ha: 2 (25.7 x 12.5)ER Cranes: 2x25t Ice Capable	**1 oil engine** driving 1 CP propeller Total Power: 3,360kW (4,568hp) 12.5kn B&W 6L35MC 1 x 2 Stroke 6 Cy. 350 x 1050 3360kW (4568bhp) H Cegielski Poznan SA-Poland AuxGen: 1 x 300kW 220/380V 50Hz a.c, 2 x 264kW 220/380V 50Hz a.c Boilers: e (ex.g.) 6.1kgf/cm² (6.0bar), WTAuxB (o.f.) 6.1kgf/cm² (6.0bar) Thrusters: 1 Tunnel thruster (f) Fuel: 90.0 (d.f.) 275.0 (r.f.) 12.7pd
6401232 - -	**TIARE TAPORO** *ex* Zebroid *-2011* *ex* Rupert Brand VII *-1977* **Pacific Schooners Ltd**	*297* 103 203	Class: (LR) ✠ Classed LR until 12/66	**1963-12 Geo T Davie & Sons Ltd — Levis QC** Yd No: 87 Converted From: Trawler-2013 Loa 39.32 Br ex 8.03 Dght - Lbp 35.06 Br md 7.93 Dpth 4.35 Welded	**(A32A2GF) General Cargo/Passenger Ship** Passengers: berths: 30 Compartments: 1 Ho, ER 2 Ha: 2 (1.3 x 1.2)	**1 oil engine** driving 1 FP propeller Total Power: 563kW (765hp) Deutz RBV6M545 1 x 4 Stroke 6 Cy. 320 x 450 563kW (765bhp) Kloeckner Humboldt Deutz AG-West Germany AuxGen: 2 x 30kW 220V 60Hz a.c
8879275 *EPBS9* -	**TIBA** *ex* Samur 15 *-2012* *ex* Boris Kornilov *-2004* *ex* ST-1307 *-1995* - - *Bandar Anzali* *Iran* MMSI: 422033200	**1,846** 639 1,776	Class: (RS)	**1984-06 Volgogradskiy Sudostroitelnyy Zavod — Volgograd** Yd No: 124 Loa 86.70 Br ex 12.30 Dght 3.000 Lbp 83.10 Br md 12.00 Dpth 3.50 Welded, 1 dk	**(A31A2GX) General Cargo Ship** Grain: 2,230 Compartments: 1 Ho, ER 2 Ha: 2 (19.8 x 9.0)ER	**2 oil engines** driving 2 FP propellers Total Power: 1,030kW (1,400hp) 10.0kn S.K.L. 6NVDS48A-2U 2 x 4 Stroke 6 Cy. 320 x 480 each-515kW (700bhp) VEB Schwermaschinenbau "KarlLiebknecht" (SKL)-Magdeburg AuxGen: 3 x 100kW a.c Fuel: 93.0 (d.f.)
7403017 *A6E3129* -	**TIBA FOLK** *ex* Asso Undici *-2008* *ex* Augustea Undici *-1998* *ex* Adler Supplier *-1990* *ex* Forest Stream *-1980* *ex* Skaustream *-1977* **Folk Shipping LLC** - *Dubai* *United Arab Emirates* MMSI: 470981000	*1,338* 436 1,978	Class: RI (NV)	**1975-05 Oy Laivateollisuus Ab — Turku** Yd No: 306 Loa 64.65 Br ex 13.87 Dght 4.719 Lbp 58.15 Br md 13.82 Dpth 6.91 Welded, 1 dk	**(B21B20A) Anchor Handling Tug Supply**	**2 oil engines** sr geared to sc. shafts driving 2 CP propellers Total Power: 5,178kW (7,040hp) 8.5kn Nohab F216V 2 x Vee 4 Stroke 16 Cy. 250 x 300 each-2589kW (3520bhp) AB NOHAB-Sweden AuxGen: 3 x 160kW 450V 60Hz a.c Thrusters: 1 Thwart. FP thruster (f) Fuel: 914.5 (r.f.) 27.5pd
7856068 - -	**TIBAY** *ex* Tensha Maru *-1981* *ex* Nikko Maru *-1981* **Subic Shipyard & Engineering Inc** - *Manila* *Philippines* Official number: 00-0001269	*228* 103 -		**1969 Kanagawa Zosen — Kobe** Loa 30.46 Br ex - Dght 3.001 Lbp 27.01 Br md 8.60 Dpth 4.02 Welded, 1 dk	**(B32A2ST) Tug**	**2 oil engines** driving 2 FP propellers Total Power: 2,206kW (3,000hp) 13.0kn Hanshin 2 x 4 Stroke each-1103kW (1500bhp) The Hanshin Diesel Works Ltd-Japan
8907747 - -	**TIBER** *launched as* Diana *-1989* **Pesquera La Totorita SA** - *Chimbote* *Peru* Official number: CE-012514-PM	**274** 118 381	Class: (LR) ✠ Classed LR until 21/2/96	**1989-12 Fujian Shangyou Ship Steel Structure Co Ltd — Fuqing FJ** Yd No: 806-1 Loa 38.50 Br ex - Dght 3.600 Lbp 34.00 Br md 8.20 Dpth 4.20 Welded, 1 dk	**(B11B2FV) Fishing Vessel**	**1 oil engine** with clutches, flexible couplings & sr reverse geared to sc. shaft driving 1 FP propeller Total Power: 600kW (816hp) 11.0kn MAN 6L20/27 1 x 4 Stroke 6 Cy. 200 x 270 600kW (816bhp) Sichuan Diesel Engine Factory-China AuxGen: 2 x 40kW 400V 50Hz a.c

IMO / Call sign	Ship / Owner / Manager	Tonnages	Class	Builder / Dimensions	Type	Machinery
9546473 *PCUC* -	**TIBERBORG** **Tiberborg Beheer BV** Wagenborg Shipping BV *Delfzijl* *Netherlands* MMSI: 244750715	**14,695** 6,695 21,301	Class: LR ✠ **100A1** SS 07/2013 strengthened for heavy cargoes and any holds may be empty, container cargoes in all holds and on upper deck and on all hatch covers **ShipRight** ACS (B) *IWS LI Ice Class 1A FS at draught of 9.535m Max/min draught fwd 9.535/4.015m Max/min draught aft 9.535/5.715m required power 7500kw, installed power 7500kw ✠ **LMC** **UMS** Eq.Ltr: H†; Cable: 576.9/60.0 U3 (a)	**2013-07 Hudong-Zhonghua Shipbuilding (Group) Co Ltd — Shanghai** Yd No: H1597A Loa 172.28 (BB) Br ex 21.74 Dght 9.380 Lbp 161.29 Br md 21.49 Dpth 13.31 Welded, 1 dk	**(A31A2GX) General Cargo Ship** Grain: 23,000; Bale: 23,000 TEU 1228 C Ho 586 TEU C Dk 642 TEU incl 72 ref C Compartments: 2 Ho, ER 2 Ha: (58.7 x 17.8)ER (55.4 x 17.8) Cranes: 4x60t Ice Capable	**1 oil engine** with clutches, flexible couplings & sr geared to sc. shafts driving 1 CP propeller Total Power: 7,500kW (10,197hp) 14.5kn Wartsila 6L46F 1 x 4 Stroke 6 Cy. 460 x 580 7500kW (10197bhp) Wartsila Italia SpA-Italy AuxGen: 1 x 800kW 450V 60Hz a.c, 3 x 450kW 450V 60Hz a.c Boilers: TOH (o.f.) 10.2kgf/cm² (10.0bar), TOH (ex.g.) 10.2kgf/cm² (10.0bar) Thrusters: 1 Thwart. CP thruster (f)
9049700 - -	**TIBERHYAS V** **PT Samudra Intim Jaya Shipping** - *Samarinda* *Indonesia*	**119** 61 -	Class: (KI)	**2001-01 C.V. Karya Lestari Industri — Samarinda** L reg 30.00 Br ex - Dght 1.590 Lbp 28.90 Br md 6.60 Dpth 2.00 Welded, 1 dk	**(A35D2RL) Landing Craft** Bow ramp (centre)	**2 oil engines** geared to sc. shafts driving 2 Propellers Total Power: 398kW (542hp) Mitsubishi 6D22 2 x 4 Stroke 6 Cy. 130 x 140 each-199kW (271bhp) Mitsubishi Heavy Industries Ltd-Japan
8823707 *XUMU3* -	**TIBOR** *ex* Hong Xiang *-2011* *ex* Tatsumi Maru No. 10 *-2006* **Rich Mine Co Ltd** Dalian Xinsheng Shipping Agency Co Ltd *Phnom Penh* *Cambodia* MMSI: 514786000 Official number: 0688347	**2,333** 1,434 1,180	Class: UB	**1988 Azumi Zosen Kensetsu K.K. — Himeji** Loa 60.00 Br ex - Dght 4.120 Lbp 55.00 Br md 13.00 Dpth 6.00 Welded, 1 dk	**(B33A2DG) Grab Dredger**	**1 oil engine** driving 1 FP propeller Total Power: 736kW (1,001hp) Hanshin 6LU32G 1 x 4 Stroke 6 Cy. 320 x 510 736kW (1001bhp) The Hanshin Diesel Works Ltd-Japan
8136336 - -	**TIBRIKU** - -	**358** 107 138	Class: (RS)	**1983-05 Sudostroitelnyy Zavod "Avangard" — Petrozavodsk** Yd No: 409 Loa 35.72 Br ex 8.92 Dght 3.429 Lbp 31.00 Br md - Dpth 5.95 Welded, 1 dk	**(B11A2FS) Stern Trawler** Ins: 110 Compartments: 1 Ho, ER 1 Ha: (1.3 x 1.3) Derricks: 2x1.5t Ice Capable	**1 oil engine** geared to sc. shaft driving 1 FP propeller Total Power: 250kW (340hp) 10.5kn S.K.L. 8VD36/24-1 1 x 4 Stroke 8 Cy. 240 x 360 250kW (340bhp) VEB Schwermaschinenbau "KarlLiebknecht" (SKL)-Magdeburg Fuel: 81.0 (d.f.)
8823135 - -	**TIBURON** - -	**130** 39 16	Class: (RS)	**1987-06 Zavod im. "Ordzhonikidze" — Poti** Yd No: 117 Loa 34.50 Br ex 10.30 Dght 1.110 Lbp 32.25 Br md - Dpth 1.80 Welded, 1 dk	**(A37B2PS) Passenger Ship** Hull Material: Aluminium Alloy	**2 oil engines** geared to sc. shafts driving 2 FP propellers Total Power: 1,920kW (2,610hp) 34.0kn M.T.U. 12V396 2 x Vee 4 Stroke 12 Cy. 165 x 185 each-960kW (1305bhp) MTU Friedrichshafen GmbH-Friedrichshafen
9055242 *UFMY* -	**TIBURON** **Akros Fishing Co Ltd (A/O Akros)** - SatCom: Inmarsat A 1406416 *Petropavlovsk-Kamchatskiy* *Russia* MMSI: 273840900 Official number: 931933	**1,315** 395 820	Class: RS (NV)	**1994-04 Elbewerft Boizenburg GmbH — Boizenburg** Yd No: 106 Loa 52.50 Br ex 11.59 Dght 5.060 Lbp 45.00 Br md 11.50 Dpth 8.05 Welded, 2 dks	**(B11B2FV) Fishing Vessel** Ins: 850 Ice Capable	**1 oil engine** with flexible couplings & sr geared to sc. shaft driving 1 CP propeller Total Power: 1,060kW (1,441hp) MAN-B&W 8L23/30A 1 x 4 Stroke 8 Cy. 225 x 300 1060kW (1441bhp) MAN B&W Diesel AG-Augsburg AuxGen: 1 x 560kW a.c, 2 x 291kW a.c Thrusters: 1 Thwart. FP thruster (f)
9133616 - -	**TIBURON 3** **Pesquera Luciana SAC** - *Chimbote* *Peru* Official number: CE-12972-PM	**458** 178 470	Class: (GL)	**1995-09 Andina de Desarrollo S.A. — Callao** Yd No: 138 Loa - Br ex - Dght 3.840 Lbp 41.60 Br md 8.89 Dpth 4.32 Welded, 1 dk	**(B11B2FV) Fishing Vessel**	**1 oil engine** reduction geared to sc. shaft driving 1 FP propeller Total Power: 791kW (1,075hp) 13.5kn Caterpillar 3512TA 1 x Vee 4 Stroke 12 Cy. 170 x 190 791kW (1075bhp) Caterpillar Inc-USA
9156292 - -	**TIBURON 7** **PEEA Luciana SCR Ltda** - *Chimbote* *Peru* Official number: CO-16854-PM	**339** 107 465	Class: (GL)	**1997-08 Andina de Desarrollo S.A. — Callao** Yd No: 162 Loa - Br ex - Dght - Lbp 39.40 Br md 8.80 Dpth 4.32 Welded, 1 dk	**(B11B2FV) Fishing Vessel**	**1 oil engine** reduction geared to sc. shaft driving 1 FP propeller Total Power: 791kW (1,075hp) 13.0kn Caterpillar 3512TA 1 x Vee 4 Stroke 12 Cy. 170 x 190 791kW (1075bhp) Caterpillar Inc-USA AuxGen: 1 x 40kW 220V a.c
7322184 *DUA2506* -	**TIBURON I** *ex* Howa *-1990* **Malayan Towage & Salvage Corp (SALVTUG)** - *Manila* *Philippines* Official number: MNLD000605	**270** 81 101	Class: (LR) ✠ Classed LR until 26/8/91	**1973-06 Hibikinada Dock Co. Ltd. — Kitakyushu** Yd No: 127 Loa 32.31 Br ex 8.74 Dght 3.010 Lbp 29.01 Br md 8.50 Dpth 3.81 Welded, 1 dk	**(B32A2ST) Tug**	**2 oil engines** dr geared to sc. shafts driving 2 CP propellers Total Power: 2,354kW (3,200hp) Daihatsu 8DSM-26 2 x 4 Stroke 8 Cy. 260 x 320 each-1177kW (1600bhp) Daihatsu Diesel Manufacturing Co Lt-Japan AuxGen: 2 x 40kW 225V 60Hz a.c
9394911 *YYV5017* -	**TIBURON II** *ex* Tiburon *-2011* *ex* Axebow 101 *-2007* **Inversiones Setin 2010 CA** Global Shipmanagement SA *Puerto la Cruz* *Venezuela* Official number: AGSP-3271	**169** 57 40	Class: (BV)	**2006-09 Damen Shipyards Singapore Pte Ltd — Singapore** (Hull) Yd No: 83 **2006-09 B.V. Scheepswerf Damen — Gorinchem** Yd No: 544801 Loa 33.57 Br ex - Dght 1.950 Lbp - Br md 7.36 Dpth 3.30 Welded, 1 dk	**(B21A20C) Crew/Supply Vessel** Hull Material: Aluminium Alloy Passengers: unberthed: 75	**3 oil engines** reduction geared to sc. shafts driving 3 FP propellers Total Power: 3,000kW (4,080hp) 18.0kn Caterpillar C32 3 x Vee 4 Stroke 12 Cy. 145 x 162 each-1000kW (1360bhp) Caterpillar Inc-USA AuxGen: 2 x 60kW 230/415V 50Hz a.c Thrusters: 1 Tunnel thruster (f)
5353244 - -	**TIBURON LISTO** *ex* Resolute *-1991* *ex* Resolve *-1985* *ex* Torten *-1985* *ex* Voila *-1983* *ex* Karob *-1980* *ex* Afon Wen *-1978* *ex* Tasman Zee *-1977* **Ready Shark Investments** - *San Lorenzo* *Honduras* Official number: L-1724025	*490* 23 -	Class: (LR) ✠ Classed LR until 2/5/84	**1958-07 L Smit & Zoon's Scheeps- & Werktuigbouw NV — Kinderdijk** Yd No: 945 Loa 46.18 Br ex 9.61 Dght 4.312 Lbp 41.00 Br md 9.20 Dpth 4.81 Welded, 1 dk	**(B32A2ST) Tug**	**2 oil engines** with fluid couplings & sr reverse geared to sc. shaft driving 1 FP propeller Total Power: 1,250kW (1,700hp) 20.0kn Kromhout 8FHD240 2 x 4 Stroke 8 Cy. 240 x 260 each-625kW (850bhp) (new engine 1967) Kromhout Motorenfabriek D. GoedkoopJr. N.V.-Amsterdam AuxGen: 2 x 80kW 220V d.c, 1 x 70kW 220V d.c, 1 x 20kW 220V d.c
8615916 *EGKV* -	**TIBURON TERCERO** **Punta Delgada SL** - *Vigo* *Spain* MMSI: 224132670 Official number: 3-9988/	**197** 58 162	Class: (BV)	**1988-06 Construcciones Navales Santodomingo SA — Vigo** Yd No: 634 Loa 31.00 (BB) Br ex - Dght 3.480 Lbp 27.20 Br md 6.50 Dpth 5.40 Welded, 1 dk	**(B11A2FT) Trawler**	**1 oil engine** with flexible couplings & sr gearedto sc. shaft driving 1 FP propeller Total Power: 397kW (540hp) 10.3kn Caterpillar D353SCAC 1 x 4 Stroke 6 Cy. 159 x 203 397kW (540bhp) Caterpillar Inc-USA AuxGen: 2 x 48kW 220/380V a.c
8130198 *XCKH* -	**TIBURON V** **Productos Pesqueros Mexicanos SA de CV** - *La Paz* *Mexico*	*299* 83 269	Class: (NK)	**1982-04 Miho Zosensho K.K. — Shimizu** Yd No: 1207 Loa 44.46 Br ex 8.21 Dght 3.095 Lbp 38.31 Br md 8.01 Dpth 3.20 Welded, 1 dk	**(B11B2FV) Fishing Vessel** Ins: 299	**1 oil engine** with clutches, flexible couplings & sr geared to sc. shaft driving 1 CP propeller Total Power: 662kW (900hp) 10.5kn Niigata 6MG25BX 1 x 4 Stroke 6 Cy. 250 x 320 662kW (900bhp) Niigata Engineering Co Ltd-Japan AuxGen: 2 x 122kW
7114252 *WYZ4076* -	**TICA** **Robert R & Everett A Reahard** - *Tampa, Fl* *United States of America* Official number: 532662	*127* 87 -		**1971-05 Desco Marine — Saint Augustine, Fl** Yd No: 101-F L reg 20.97 Br ex - Dght 2.744 Lbp - Br md 6.75 Dpth 3.81 Bonded, 1 dk	**(B11B2FV) Fishing Vessel** Hull Material: Reinforced Plastic	**1 oil engine** driving 1 FP propeller Total Power: 268kW (364hp) Caterpillar 3408PCTA 1 x Vee 4 Stroke 8 Cy. 137 x 152 268kW (364bhp) Caterpillar Tractor Co-USA

7336628 - -	**TICHITT 2** *ex Habbaba -1988 ex Nuevo Barbate -1982* **Cherif Hamahallah** Inter-Arika SA *Nouadhibou* *Mauritania*	*238* 81 203	Class: (BV)	**1974 Sociedad Metalurgica Duro Felguera — Gijon** Yd No: 103 Loa 37.34 Br ex 7.47 Dght 3.849 Lbp 35.41 Br md 7.40 Dpth 4.02 Welded, 1 dk	**(B11A2FT) Trawler**	**1 oil engine** driving 1 FP propeller Total Power: 736kW (1,001hp) 11.5kn Krupps 1 x 4 Stroke 8 Cy. 295 x 420 736kW (1001bhp) La Maquinista Terrestre y Mar (MTM)-Spain AuxGen: 2 x 128kW 220V 50Hz a.c Fuel: 125.0 (d.f.)
8701143 - -	**TICHITT I** *ex Yamana -1988* **Cherif Hamahallah** Inter-Arika SA *Nouadhibou* *Mauritania* Official number: 634	**222** 70 138	Class: (BV) (RI)	**1987-04 Astilleros Armon SA — Navia** Yd No: 129 Loa 29.49 Br ex - Dght 3.152 Lbp 25.56 Br md 7.76 Dpth 4.22 Welded, 1 dk	**(B11A2FS) Stern Trawler**	**1 oil engine** with clutches, flexible couplings & reverse reduction geared to sc. shaft driving 1 FP propeller Total Power: 570kW (775hp) 11.2kn Caterpillar 3508TA 1 x Vee 4 Stroke 8 Cy. 170 x 190 570kW (775bhp) Caterpillar Inc-USA AuxGen: 2 x 160kW 220/380V 50Hz a.c
8812136 - -	**TICHITT V** *ex El Hodh -1992 ex Map DW1 -1992* **Cherif Hamahallah** Inter-Arika SA *Nouadhibou* *Mauritania*	**220** 70 146	Class: (RI)	**1988-08 Astilleros Armon SA — Navia** Yd No: 196 Loa 29.50 Br ex - Dght 3.240 Lbp 25.55 Br md 7.76 Dpth 4.22 Welded, 1 dk	**(B11A2FS) Stern Trawler** Ins: 187	**1 oil engine** with clutches, flexible couplings & reverse reduction geared to sc. shaft driving 1 FP propeller Total Power: 570kW (775hp) Caterpillar 3508TA 1 x Vee 4 Stroke 8 Cy. 170 x 190 570kW (775bhp) Caterpillar Inc-USA
8710792 - -	**TICHITT VI** *ex Dolphin 1 -1992* **Cherif Hamahallah** Inter-Arika SA *Nouadhibou* *Mauritania*	**222** 70 138	Class: (BV)	**1987-07 Astilleros Armon SA — Navia** Yd No: 167 Loa 29.49 Br ex - Dght 3.241 Lbp 25.56 Br md 7.76 Dpth 4.22 Welded, 1 dk	**(B11B2FV) Fishing Vessel** Ins: 187	**1 oil engine** with clutches, flexible couplings & reverse reduction geared to sc. shaft driving 1 FP propeller Total Power: 570kW (775hp) 11.2kn Caterpillar 3508TA 1 x Vee 4 Stroke 8 Cy. 170 x 190 570kW (775bhp) Caterpillar Inc-USA AuxGen: 2 x 80kW 380V a.c
7614563 *VHS3179* -	**TICKERA** *ex Tapir -2011 ex Wyong -1988* **Svitzer Australia Pty Ltd & Stannard Marine Pty Ltd** Svitzer Australia Pty Ltd (Svitzer Australasia) *Port Lincoln, SA* *Australia* MMSI: 503184800 Official number: 374395	*266* 52 -	Class: AB	**1976-12 Carrington Slipways Pty Ltd — Newcastle NSW** Yd No: 122 Loa 29.01 Br ex 9.96 Dght 4.001 Lbp 26.22 Br md 9.54 Dpth 4.73 Welded, 1 dk	**(B32A2ST) Tug**	**2 oil engines** reverse reduction geared to sc. shafts driving 2 FP propellers Total Power: 1,838kW (2,498hp) 12.0kn Blackstone EZSL8 2 x 4 Stroke 8 Cy. 222 x 292 each-919kW (1249bhp) Mirrlees Blackstone (Stamford)Ltd.-Stamford AuxGen: 2 x 68kW a.c
7386063 *IIFU2* -	**TICO** *ex Marbella -2009* **Societa Italiana Lavori Edili Marittimi Srl (SILEM)** - *Reggio Calabria* *Italy* MMSI: 247219500 Official number: 74	*139* 48 94	Class: (LR) (RI) ✠ Classed LR until 22/6/07	**1975-01 Astilleros de Santander SA (ASTANDER) — El Astillero** Yd No: 97 Loa 29.44 Br ex 7.60 Dght 2.915 Lbp 26.40 Br md 7.41 Dpth 3.41 Welded, 1 dk	**(B32A2ST) Tug**	**2 oil engines** with clutches, flexible couplings & sr geared to sc. shaft driving 1 CP propeller Total Power: 1,104kW (1,500hp) 12.0kn GUASCOR E318 2 x Vee 4 Stroke 12 Cy. 150 x 150 each-552kW (750bhp) Internacional Diesel S.A.-Zumaya AuxGen: 2 x 60kW 220V 50Hz a.c
8212269 *D3R2332* -	**TICO-TICO** **Empresa Nacional de Abastecimiento Tecnico Material a Industria de Pesca (ENATIP)** - *Luanda* *Angola* Official number: C-790	*135* 60 107	Class: (BV)	**1984-07 Astilleros y Talleres Ferrolanos S.A. (ASTAFERSA) — Ferrol** Yd No: 235 Loa 26.01 Br ex - Dght 2.701 Lbp 22.51 Br md 6.51 Dpth 3.26 Welded, 1 dk	**(B11B2FV) Fishing Vessel** Ins: 146	**1 oil engine** with clutches, flexible couplings & sr reverse geared to sc. shaft driving 1 FP propeller Total Power: 368kW (500hp) 10.3kn GUASCOR E318T-SP 1 x Vee 4 Stroke 12 Cy. 150 x 150 368kW (500bhp) Gutierrez Ascunce Corp (GUASCOR)-Spain AuxGen: 2 x 32kW 380V 50Hz a.c
5238016 *WDC4509* -	**TICONDEROGA** *ex Mobil 9 -1991 ex Socony 9 -1960* **Charles G Gural** - *New York, NY* *United States of America* MMSI: 367025790 Official number: 268843	*185* 71 -	Class: (AB)	**1954-01 Baltimore Marine Repair Shops Inc. — Baltimore, Md** Yd No: 53 Loa 27.36 Br ex 7.73 Dght 3.493 Lbp 26.12 Br md 7.70 Dpth 3.76 Riveted\Welded, 1 dk	**(B32A2ST) Tug**	**1 oil engine** sr & reverse geared to sc. shaft driving 1 FP propeller Total Power: 883kW (1,201hp) General Motors 12-278A 1 x Vee 2 Stroke 12 Cy. 222 x 267 883kW (1201bhp) General Motors Corp-USA AuxGen: 2 x 30kW 110V d.c Fuel: 62.0 (d.f.)
8428648 - -	**TIDAL TRADER** *ex Irwell Trader -1989* **Bullas Tankcraft Co Ltd** - *Liverpool* *United Kingdom* Official number: 364443	*492* 356 800		**1977-01 Yorkshire D.D. Co. Ltd. — Hull** Loa 42.47 Br ex 9.99 Dght 3.620 Lbp 39.60 Br md 9.50 Dpth 4.75 Welded, 1 dk	**(A31A2GX) General Cargo Ship**	**2 oil engines** geared to sc. shafts driving 2 FP propellers Total Power: 552kW (750hp) 9.0kn Caterpillar 3406TA 2 x 4 Stroke 6 Cy. 137 x 165 each-276kW (375bhp) Caterpillar Tractor Co-USA
8855669 - -	**TIDAL WAVE '84** - **Noble House Seafoods Co Ltd** - *Georgetown* *Guyana* Official number: 0000416	*101* 69 -		**1984 Steiner Shipyard, Inc. — Bayou La Batre, Al** Loa 22.86 Br ex - Dght - Lbp 20.33 Br md 6.71 Dpth 3.32 Welded, 1 dk	**(B11A2FT) Trawler**	**1 oil engine** geared to sc. shaft driving 1 FP propeller Total Power: 268kW (364hp) Cummins KT-1150-M 1 x 4 Stroke 6 Cy. 159 x 159 268kW (364bhp) Cummins Engine Co Inc-USA
7408031 *WYT6624* -	**TIDAL WAVE II** - - *Seattle, WA* *United States of America* Official number: 556222	*127* 87 -		**1974-05 Desco Marine — Saint Augustine, Fl** Yd No: 171-F Loa 22.86 Br ex - Dght 2.744 Lbp 20.99 Br md 6.74 Dpth 3.81 Bonded, 1 dk	**(B11A2FT) Trawler** Hull Material: Reinforced Plastic	**1 oil engine** driving 1 FP propeller Total Power: 268kW (364hp) 10.0kn Caterpillar D343SCAC 1 x 4 Stroke 6 Cy. 137 x 165 268kW (364bhp) Caterpillar Tractor Co-USA Fuel: 51.0 (d.f.)
8902589 *OZ2126* -	**TIDAN** **Erik Thun AB (Thunship Management Holland)** *Torshavn* *Faeroe Islands (Danish)* MMSI: 231840000	**2,250** 1,327 4,250 T/cm 10.6	Class: LR ✠ **100A1** SS 03/2010 Ice Class 1B at draught 5.582m Max/min draught fwd 5.582/2.60m Max/min draught aft 5.582/4.00m Power required 1516kw, installed 1690kw ✠ **LMC** **UMS** Eq.Ltr: P; Cable: 440.0/32.0 U3	**1990-03 Scheepswerf Bijlsma BV — Wartena** (Hull) Yd No: 650 **1990-03 Scheepswerf Ferus Smit BV — Westerbroek** Yd No: 277 Loa 88.29 (BB) Br ex 13.21 Dght 5.459 Lbp 84.90 Br md 13.17 Dpth 7.00 Welded, 1 dk	**(A31A2GX) General Cargo Ship** Grain: 4,827 Compartments: 1 Ho, ER 2 Ha: 2 (26.0 x 10.2)ER Ice Capable	**1 oil engine** with flexible couplings & sr geared to sc. shaft driving 1 CP propeller Total Power: 1,690kW (2,298hp) 12.0kn Nohab 8V25 1 x Vee 4 Stroke 8 Cy. 250 x 300 1690kW (2298bhp) Wartsila Diesel AB-Sweden AuxGen: 1 x 220kW 380V 50Hz a.c, 1 x 140kW 380V 50Hz a.c Thrusters: 1 Water jet (f) Fuel: 23.0 (d.f.) 139.0 (r.f.)
8700292 *YECN* -	**TIDAR** **Government of The Republic of Indonesia (Direktorat Jenderal Perhubungan Laut - Ministry of Sea Communications)** PT Pelayaran Nasional Indonesia (PELNI) SatCom: Inmarsat A 1525104 *Semarang* *Indonesia* MMSI: 525005015	*14,501* 5,354 3,200	Class: KI (GL)	**1988-09 Jos L Meyer GmbH & Co — Papenburg** Yd No: 617 Loa 146.50 (BB) Br ex 23.70 Dght 5.900 Lbp 130.00 Br md 23.40 Dpth 13.42 Welded, 4 dks	**(A37B2PS) Passenger Ship** Passengers: unberthed: 1488; cabins: 90; berths: 416 Grain: 1,250; Bale: 1,000 Compartments: 1 Ho, ER, 2 Tw Dk 1 Ha: (8.0 x 6.0)ER Cranes: 2x7t	**2 oil engines** with flexible couplings & dr geared to sc. shafts driving 2 FP propellers Total Power: 12,798kW (17,400hp) 20.0kn MaK 6M601AK 2 x 4 Stroke 6 Cy. 580 x 600 each-6399kW (8700bhp) Krupp MaK Maschinenbau GmbH-Kiel AuxGen: 4 x 800kW 220/380V a.c Thrusters: 1 Thwart. FP thruster (f)
9031208 *DBMN* -	**TIDE** **Government of The Federal Republic of Germany (Bundesminister fuer Verkehr-WSV)** - *Bremerhaven* *Germany* MMSI: 211225940	**227** 68 226	Class: GL	**1990-04 Deutsche Industrie-Werke GmbH — West Berlin** Yd No: 147 Loa 31.60 Br ex 8.03 Dght 2.000 Lbp 29.56 Br md 7.50 Dpth 3.50 Welded, 1dk	**(B31A2SR) Research Survey Vessel** Cranes: 1x2.5t Ice Capable	**1 oil engine** geared to sc. shaft driving 1 FP propeller Total Power: 513kW (697hp) 11.3kn MWM TBD604BL6 1 x 4 Stroke 6 Cy. 170 x 195 513kW (697bhp) Motoren Werke Mannheim AG (MWM)-West Germany
7923421 *HQXJ5* -	**TIDE** *ex Apollo Tide -2012 ex Sallis Tide -1984* **Del Mar SA** - *Honduras* MMSI: 334042000	**684** 205 1,000	Class: (AB) (RI)	**1980-08 McDermott Shipyards Inc — New Iberia LA** Yd No: 128 Loa 54.87 Br ex - Dght 3.718 Lbp 50.65 Br md 12.20 Dpth 4.27 Welded, 1 dk	**(B21A20S) Platform Supply Ship**	**2 oil engines** reverse reduction geared to sc. shafts driving 2 FP propellers Total Power: 1,654kW (2,248hp) 12.0kn Caterpillar D399SCAC 2 x Vee 4 Stroke 16 Cy. 159 x 203 each-827kW (1124bhp) Caterpillar Tractor Co-USA AuxGen: 2 x 125kW a.c

IMO / Call sign	Name / Owner	Tonnage / Class	Builder / Dimensions	Type	Machinery
9438963 *LARN* -	**TIDE CRUISE** **Norled AS** Tide ASA *Stavanger* *Norway* MMSI: 258088000	**179** 71 19	**2008-06 Brodrene Aa AS — Hyen** Yd No: 253 Loa 24.50 Br ex - Dght 0.950 Lbp 22.60 Br md 8.00 Dpth 2.60 Bonded, 1 dk	**(A37B2PS) Passenger Ship** Hull Material: Carbon Fibre Sandwich Passengers: unberthed: 147	**2 oil engines** reduction geared to sc. shafts driving 2 CP propellers Total Power: 1,498kW (2,036hp) 28.0kn MAN D2842LE 2 x Vee 4 Stroke 12 Cy. 128 x 142 each-749kW (1018bhp) MAN Nutzfahrzeuge AG-Nuernberg
9264489 *LLVG* -	**TIDEBRIS** *ex* Vindafjord *-2008* **Norled AS** - *Bergen* *Norway* MMSI: 258108000	**224** 79 30	**2002-04 Batservice Mandal AS — Mandal** Yd No: 26 Loa 27.25 Br ex - Dght - Lbp - Br md 9.00 Dpth 3.65 Welded, 1 dk	**(A37B2PS) Passenger Ship** Hull Material: Aluminium Alloy Passengers: unberthed: 180	**2 oil engines** geared to sc. shafts driving 2 FP propellers Total Power: 2,000kW (2,720hp) Mitsubishi S12R-MPTK 2 x Vee 4 Stroke 12 Cy. 170 x 180 each-1000kW (1360bhp) Mitsubishi Heavy Industries Ltd-Japan
9481829 *LCBK* -	**TIDEEKSPRESS** **Norled AS** - *Bergen* *Norway* MMSI: 258416000	**416** 142 50	**2008-08 Oma Baatbyggeri AS — Stord** Yd No: 525 Loa 32.50 (BB) Br ex - Dght - Lbp 32.00 Br md 10.60 Dpth 3.64 Welded, 1 dk	**(A37B2PS) Passenger Ship** Hull Material: Aluminium Alloy Passengers: unberthed: 296	**4 oil engines** geared to sc. shafts driving 4 Water jets Total Power: 3,236kW (4,400hp) 34.0kn MAN D2842LE 4 x Vee 4 Stroke 12 Cy. 128 x 142 each-809kW (1100bhp) MAN Nutzfahrzeuge AG-Nuernberg AuxGen: 2 x 46kW a.c
9419204 *LAVB* -	**TIDEFJORD** **Norled AS** - *Aalesund* *Norway* MMSI: 258220500	**2,979** Class: (NV) 893 1,050	**2008-04 UAB Vakaru Laivu Remontas (JSC Western Shiprepair) — Klaipeda** (Hull) Yd No: (59) **2008-04 Fiskerstrand Verft AS — Fiskarstrand** Yd No: 59 Loa 113.90 Br ex - Dght 3.100 Lbp 105.00 Br md 16.80 Dpth 5.50 Welded, 1 dk	**(A36A2PR) Passenger/Ro-Ro Ship (Vehicles)** Passengers: unberthed: 350 Bow ramp (centre) Stern ramp (centre) Cars: 120	**4 diesel electric oil engines** driving 2 gen. 2 gen. Connecting to 2 elec. motors driving 2 Azimuth electric drive units Total Power: 3,640kW (4,948hp) Mitsubishi S12R-MPTK 2 x Vee 4 Stroke 12 Cy. 170 x 180 each-1210kW (1645bhp) Mitsubishi Heavy Industries Ltd-Japan Mitsubishi S6R2-MPTK 2 x 4 Stroke 6 Cy. 170 x 220 each-610kW (829bhp) Mitsubishi Heavy Industries Ltd-Japan
7309443 *WX5026* -	**TIDELANDS** **Omega Protein Inc** - *Reedville, VA* *United States of America* MMSI: 367108820 Official number: 501955	*572* 304 -	**1965 Atlantic Marine — Jacksonville, Fl** Loa - Br ex - Dght - Lbp 61.04 Br md 9.73 Dpth 3.28 Welded, 1 dk	**(B11B2FV) Fishing Vessel**	**1 oil engine** driving 1 FP propeller Total Power: 1,250kW (1,700hp) G.M. (Detroit Diesel) 16V-149 1 x Vee 2 Stroke 16 Cy. 146 x 146 1250kW (1700bhp) General Motors Corp-USA
9517185 *LCJF* -	**TIDELYN** **Norled AS** - *Bergen* *Norway* MMSI: 259276000	**192** 76 20	**2009-03 Oma Baatbyggeri AS — Stord** Yd No: 527 Loa 24.46 (BB) Br ex - Dght 1.400 Lbp 23.95 Br md 9.00 Dpth 3.41 Welded, 1 dk	**(A37B2PS) Passenger Ship** Hull Material: Aluminium Alloy Passengers: unberthed: 125	**2 oil engines** reduction geared to sc. shafts driving 2 Water jets Total Power: 1,498kW (2,036hp) 30.0kn MAN D2842LE 2 x Vee 4 Stroke 12 Cy. 128 x 142 each-749kW (1018bhp) MAN Nutzfahrzeuge AG-Nuernberg AuxGen: 2 x 28kW a.c
9510242 *LEGL* -	**TIDEROSE** **Norled AS** - *Bergen* *Norway* MMSI: 258289500	**179** 71 19	**2009-04 Brodrene Aa AS — Hyen** Yd No: 257 Loa 24.50 Br ex - Dght 0.950 Lbp 22.60 Br md 8.00 Dpth 2.60 Bonded, 1 dk	**(A37B2PS) Passenger Ship** Hull Material: Carbon Fibre Sandwich Passengers: unberthed: 147	**2 oil engines** reduction geared to sc. shafts driving 2 CP propellers Total Power: 1,618kW (2,200hp) 30.0kn MAN D2842LE 2 x Vee 4 Stroke 12 Cy. 128 x 142 each-809kW (1100bhp) MAN Nutzfahrzeuge AG-Nuernberg AuxGen: 2 x 26kW a.c Thrusters: 1 Tunnel thruster (f)
9419216 *LAOA* -	**TIDESUND** **Norled AS** - *Aalesund* *Norway* MMSI: 258221500	**2,979** Class: (NV) 893 1,050	**2008-06 UAB Vakaru Laivu Remontas (JSC Western Shiprepair) — Klaipeda** (Hull) Yd No: 32 **2008-06 Fiskerstrand Verft AS — Fiskarstrand** Yd No: 60 Loa 113.90 Br ex - Dght 3.100 Lbp 104.90 Br md 16.80 Dpth 5.50 Welded, 1 dk	**(A36A2PR) Passenger/Ro-Ro Ship (Vehicles)** Passengers: unberthed: 350 Bow ramp (centre) Stern ramp (centre) Cars: 120	**4 diesel electric oil engines** driving 2 gen. 2 gen. Connecting to 2 elec. motors driving 2 Azimuth electric drive units Total Power: 3,640kW (4,948hp) Mitsubishi S12R-MPTA 1 x Vee 4 Stroke 12 Cy. 170 x 180 1210kW (1645bhp) Mitsubishi Heavy Industries Ltd-Japan Mitsubishi S12R-MPTK 1 x Vee 4 Stroke 12 Cy. 170 x 180 1210kW (1645bhp) Mitsubishi Heavy Industries Ltd-Japan Mitsubishi S6R2-MPTK 2 x 4 Stroke 6 Cy. 170 x 220 each-610kW (829bhp) Mitsubishi Heavy Industries Ltd-Japan
9473494 *LDHI* -	**TIDEVIND** **Norled AS** - *Bergen* *Norway* MMSI: 258266500	**176** 70 19	**2008-11 Brodrene Aa AS — Hyen** Yd No: 256 Loa 24.50 Br ex - Dght 0.950 Lbp 22.60 Br md 8.00 Dpth 2.60 Bonded, 1 dk	**(A37B2PS) Passenger Ship** Hull Material: Carbon Fibre Sandwich Passengers: unberthed: 147	**2 oil engines** reduction geared to sc. shafts driving 2 CP propellers Total Power: 1,618kW (2,200hp) 30.0kn MAN D2842LE 2 x Vee 4 Stroke 12 Cy. 128 x 142 each-809kW (1100bhp) MAN Nutzfahrzeuge AG-Nuernberg AuxGen: 2 x 26kW a.c Thrusters: 1 Tunnel thruster (s. f.) Fuel: 4.0
8855671 - -	**TIDEWATER** **Curby Kirk Warren Bodden** - *Roatan* *Honduras* Official number: U-1826618	*101* 69 -	**1983 Steiner Shipyard, Inc. — Bayou La Batre, Al** Loa 22.80 Br ex - Dght - Lbp 20.33 Br md 6.71 Dpth 3.32 Welded, 1 dk	**(B11A2FT) Trawler**	**1 oil engine** geared to sc. shaft driving 1 FP propeller Total Power: 268kW (364hp) Cummins KT-1150-M 1 x 4 Stroke 6 Cy. 159 x 159 268kW (364bhp) Cummins Engine Co Inc-USA
9440203 *XCUL9* -	**TIDEWATER ENABLER** *launched as* Enabler *-2010* **Crimson Fleet Ltd** Tidewater de Mexico S de RL de CV *Isla del Carmen* *Mexico* MMSI: 345070303 Official number: 04013632324	**4,769** Class: AB (NV) 1,676 4,660	**2010-01 STX RO Offshore Braila SA — Braila** (Hull) Yd No: 1124 **2010-01 STX Norway Offshore AS Brevik — Brevik** Yd No: 67 Loa 96.25 (BB) Br ex - Dght 6.670 Lbp 84.99 Br md 20.00 Dpth 8.00 Welded, 1 dk	**(B22A2OR) Offshore Support Vessel** Double Hull (13F) Cranes: 1x100t	**4 diesel electric oil engines** driving 4 gen. each 2100kW 690V a.c Connecting to 2 elec. motors each (2200kW) driving 2 Azimuth electric drive units Total Power: 10,100kW (13,732hp) 14.0kn Caterpillar 3516C 4 x Vee 4 Stroke 16 Cy. 170 x 215 each-2525kW (3433bhp) Caterpillar Inc-USA Thrusters: 2 Thwart. FP thruster (f); 1 Retract. directional thruster (f)
7814101 *PHYR* -	**TIDEWAY ROLLINGSTONE** *ex* Super Servant 1 *-1994* **Dredging International Luxembourg SA** Tideway BV SatCom: Inmarsat A 1302564 *Vlissingen* *Netherlands* MMSI: 245746000 Official number: 692	**13,489** Class: AB 4,046 14,310	**1979-06 Oshima Shipbuilding Co Ltd — Saikai NS** Yd No: 10040 Converted From: Heavy Load Carrier, Semi-submersible-1994 Loa 139.02 Br ex 32.03 Dght 6.181 Lbp 130.03 Br md 32.02 Dpth 8.51 Welded, 1 dk	**(B22K20B) Pipe Burying Vessel**	**2 oil engines** with flexible couplings & sr gearedto sc. shafts driving 2 CP propellers Total Power: 6,252kW (8,500hp) 13.0kn Werkspoor 6TM410 2 x 4 Stroke 6 Cy. 410 x 470 each-3126kW (4250bhp) Stork Werkspoor Diesel BV-Netherlands AuxGen: 2 x 400kW 450V 60Hz a.c, 4 x 190kW 450V 60Hz a.c Thrusters: 2 Thwart. CP thruster (f); 2 Directional thruster (a) Fuel: 201.0 (d.f.) 1439.5 (r.f.) 30.0pd
7623447 *YBZJ* -	**TIDORE** **PT East Indonesian Fishery** - *Jakarta* *Indonesia*	*111* - -	**1962 Nichiro Zosen — Japan** Loa - Br ex - Dght - Lbp 26.80 Br md 5.67 Dpth 2.70 Welded, 1 dk	**(B11B2FV) Fishing Vessel**	**1 oil engine** driving 1 FP propeller Total Power: 456kW (620hp) Akasaka MA6SS 1 x 4 Stroke 6 Cy. 270 x 400 456kW (620bhp) Akasaka Tekkosho KK (Akasaka DieselLtd)-Japan
9096284 - -	**TIE BA** *ex* Feng Yu Jun 9 *-2008* **Government of The Republic of Iraq (State Organisation of Iraqi Ports)** -	**4,275** 1,282 5,574	**2006-04 Zhoushan Dinghai Cezi Shipyard — Zhoushan ZJ** Loa 99.60 Br ex - Dght 6.450 Lbp 94.60 Br md 17.00 Dpth 8.20 Welded, 1 dk	**(B33A2DS) Suction Dredger**	**2 oil engines** geared to sc. shafts driving 2 Propellers Total Power: 2,940kW (3,998hp) 11.0kn Chinese Std. Type G8300ZC 2 x 4 Stroke 8 Cy. 300 x 380 each-1470kW (1999bhp) Wuxi Antai Power Machinery Co Ltd-China
9690377 *BXSI* -	**TIE JIAN TUO 01** **CRCC Harbour & Channel Engineering Bureau Group Co Ltd** - *Zhuhai, Guangdong* *China* MMSI: 412477490	**618** Class: CC 185 776	**2014-02 Taizhou Kouan Shipbuilding Co Ltd — Taizhou JS** Yd No: TKG005 Loa 39.20 Br ex 13.60 Dght 4.000 Lbp 33.06 Br md 11.60 Dpth 5.00 Welded, 1 dk	**(B32A2ST) Tug**	**2 oil engines** reduction geared to sc. shafts driving 2 Propellers Total Power: 2,940kW (3,998hp) MAN-B&W 6L28/32A 2 x 4 Stroke 6 Cy. 280 x 320 each-1470kW (1999bhp) Zhenjiang Marine Diesel Works-China

9023029 *XVZO* -	**TIEN DAT 09-ALCI** *ex* Dai Phat 09 *-2003* **Agriculture Leasing Co I** Donghung Co Ltd *Haiphong* *Vietnam* MMSI: 574000490	**493** 357 960	Class: VR	**2002-10 Nam Ha Shipyard — Nam Ha** Yd No: TB-05 Loa 56.00 Br ex - Dght 3.200 Lbp 53.27 Br md 9.25 Dpth 3.97 Welded, 1 dk	**(A31A2GX) General Cargo Ship** Compartments: 2 Ho, ER 2 Ha: ER 2 (13.0 x 5.6)	**1 oil engine** reduction geared to sc. shaft driving 1 Propeller Total Power: 434kW (590hp) 9.0kn Weifang X6170ZC 1 x 4 Stroke 6 Cy. 170 x 200 434kW (590bhp) Weifang Diesel Engine Factory-China
8978538 - -	**TIEN DAT 25-ALCI** *ex* Quang Phuong 25 *-2003* *ex* Long Thanh 25 *-2003* **Agriculture Leasing Co I** - *Haiphong* *Vietnam*	**456** 306 842	Class: VR	**2001-11 Nam Ha Shipyard — Nam Ha** Yd No: ND-08B-01 Loa 55.50 Br ex 8.72 Dght 3.000 Lbp 53.00 Br md 8.50 Dpth 3.70 Welded, 1 dk	**(A31A2GX) General Cargo Ship**	**2 oil engines** reduction geared to sc. shafts driving 2 Propellers Total Power: 564kW (766hp) Chinese Std. Type 6160A 2 x 4 Stroke 6 Cy. 160 x 225 each-282kW (383bhp) Weifang Diesel Engine Factory-China
8666240 *3WYO* -	**TIEN DAT 89** *ex* Pjt-17 *-2011* *ex* Song Kim 17 *-2008* **Tien Dat Commercial Investment & Service Co** - *Haiphong* *Vietnam* Official number: VN-3277-VT	**1,599** 696 3,206	Class: VR	**2008-10 Cat Tuong Shipyard — Truc Ninh** Yd No: S07-008.01 Loa 78.63 Br ex 12.62 Dght 5.350 Lbp 73.60 Br md 12.60 Dpth 6.48 Welded, 1 dk	**(A31A2GX) General Cargo Ship** Grain: 2,595; Bale: 2,337 Compartments: 2 Ho, ER 2 Ha: (19.2 x 8.4)ER (19.8 x 8.4)	**1 oil engine** driving 1 FP propeller Total Power: 1,324kW (1,800hp) 11.0kn Chinese Std. Type G6300ZC 1 x 4 Stroke 6 Cy. 300 x 380 1324kW (1800bhp) Ningbo CSI Power & Machinery GroupCo Ltd-China
9611321 *VRKH7* -	**TIEN FEI** **Aquarius Ltd** Fenwick Shipping Services Ltd *Hong Kong* *Hong Kong* MMSI: 477914900 Official number: HK-3457	**16,835** 7,499 24,377	Class: LR ✠ **100A1** SS 09/2012 bulk carrier CSR (holds Nos. 2 & 4 may be empty) GRAB (20) ESP **ShipRight** (CM,ACS (B,D)) LI *IWS ✠ **LMC** **UMS** Eq.Ltr: H†; Cable: 609.0/62.0 U3 (a)	**2012-09 Shanhaiguan Shipbuilding Industry Co Ltd — Qinhuangdao HE** Yd No: BC240-01 Loa 158.60 (BB) Br ex 25.03 Dght 9.800 Lbp 150.00 Br md 25.00 Dpth 14.20 Welded, 1 dk	**(A21A2BC) Bulk Carrier** Grain: 30,000 Compartments: 5 Ho, ER 5 Ha: ER Cranes: 4x36t	**1 oil engine** driving 1 FP propeller Total Power: 5,220kW (7,097hp) 13.6kn MAN-B&W 6S35ME-B9 1 x 2 Stroke 6 Cy. 350 x 1550 5220kW (7097bhp) Yichang Marine Diesel Engine Co Ltd-China AuxGen: 3 x 500kW 450V 60Hz a.c Boilers: AuxB (Comp) 9.2kgf/cm² (9.0bar)
9634763 *3WDM9* -	**TIEN GIANG 36** **Tien Giang Sea Transport JSC** - *Haiphong* *Vietnam* MMSI: 574012229	**999** 642 1,970	Class: VR	**2011-05 Song Ninh Co-operative — Vietnam** Yd No: TKT129M Loa 69.86 Br ex 10.82 Dght 4.550 Lbp 65.60 Br md 10.80 Dpth 5.40 Welded, 1 dk	**(A31A2GX) General Cargo Ship** Grain: 2,195; Bale: 1,980 Compartments: 2 Ho, ER 2 Ha: ER 2 (17.1 x 7.2)	**1 oil engine** reduction geared to sc. shaft driving 1 FP propeller Total Power: 551kW (749hp) 11.0kn Chinese Std. Type 6210ZLC 1 x 4 Stroke 6 Cy. 210 x 290 551kW (749bhp) Zibo Diesel Engine Factory-China Fuel: 26.0
8134089 *BDAP* -	**TIEN HUO No. 1** - - *Kaohsiung* *Chinese Taipei* MMSI: 416000127 Official number: 8374	*354* 99 297	Class: (CR)	**1982-04 Kambara Marine Development & Shipbuilding Co Ltd — Fukuyama HS** Loa 30.99 Br ex 11.31 Dght 3.550 Lbp 28.00 Br md 9.30 Dpth 3.92 Welded, 1 dk	**(B32B2SP) Pusher Tug**	**2 oil engines** geared to sc. shafts driving 2 FP propellers Total Power: 2,648kW (3,600hp) 12.3kn Daihatsu 6DSM-28 2 x 4 Stroke 6 Cy. 280 x 340 each-1324kW (1800bhp) Daihatsu Diesel Manufacturing Co Lt-Japan
8134091 *BDAQ* -	**TIEN HUO No. 2** - - *Kaohsiung* *Chinese Taipei* MMSI: 416000128 Official number: 8375	*354* 99 298	Class: (CR)	**1982-04 Kambara Marine Development & Shipbuilding Co Ltd — Fukuyama HS** Loa 30.99 Br ex 11.31 Dght 3.550 Lbp 28.00 Br md 9.30 Dpth 3.92 Welded, 1 dk	**(B32B2SP) Pusher Tug**	**2 oil engines** geared to sc. shafts driving 2 FP propellers Total Power: 2,648kW (3,600hp) 12.3kn Daihatsu 6DSM-28 2 x 4 Stroke 6 Cy. 280 x 340 each-1324kW (1800bhp) Daihatsu Diesel Manufacturing Co Lt-Japan
9015917 *BDGA* -	**TIEN KUANG No. 1** **Taiwan Power Co** - SatCom: Inmarsat A 1350736 *Keelung* *Chinese Taipei* Official number: 12072	**834** 250 738	Class: CR	**1991-08 China Shipbuilding Corp — Keelung** Yd No: 512 Loa 53.00 Br ex 10.74 Dght 3.600 Lbp 48.00 Br md 10.50 Dpth 5.00 Welded, 1 dk	**(A38D2GN) Nuclear Fuel Carrier** Compartments: 3 Ho, ER 3 Ha: ER	**2 oil engines** with clutches, flexible couplings & sr geared to sc. shafts driving 2 FP propellers Total Power: 956kW (1,300hp) Yanmar T240-ET 2 x 4 Stroke 6 Cy. 240 x 310 each-478kW (650bhp) Yanmar Diesel Engine Co Ltd-Japan Thrusters: 1 Thwart. CP thruster (f)
6522127 *BNIQ* -	**TIEN MING No. 1** *ex* Ta Ming No. 1 *-1976* *ex* Kaiken Maru No. 1 *-1975* **Tien Ming Steamship Co Ltd** - *Kaohsiung* *Chinese Taipei* Official number: 5567	*432* 212 683	Class: (CR)	**1965 Ishikawajima Ship & Chemical Plant Co Ltd — Tokyo** Yd No: 328 Loa 49.46 Br ex 8.03 Dght 3.480 Lbp 45.01 Br md 8.01 Dpth 4.02 Welded, 1 dk	**(A24D2BA) Aggregates Carrier** Grain: 666; Bale: 634 Compartments: 1 Ho, ER 1 Ha: (20.9 x 5.0)ER Derricks: 1x3t,1x2t; Winches: 2	**1 oil engine** driving 1 FP propeller Total Power: 397kW (540hp) 9.0kn Kanegafuchi 1 x 4 Stroke 6 Cy. 270 x 400 397kW (540bhp) Kanegafuchi Diesel-Japan AuxGen: 1 x 5kW 110V d.c
6522139 *BNIW* -	**TIEN MING No. 2** *ex* Ta Ming No. 2 *-1976* *ex* Kaiken Maru No. 2 *-1975* **Tien Ming Steamship Co Ltd** - *Kaohsiung* *Chinese Taipei* Official number: 5568	*432* 212 683	Class: (CR)	**1965 Ishikawajima Ship & Chemical Plant Co Ltd — Tokyo** Yd No: 329 Loa 45.12 Br ex 8.03 Dght 2.961 Lbp 45.01 Br md 8.01 Dpth 4.02 Welded, 1 dk	**(A24D2BA) Aggregates Carrier** Grain: 666; Bale: 634 Compartments: 1 Ho, ER 1 Ha: (20.9 x 5.0)ER Derricks: 1x3t,1x2t; Winches: 2	**1 oil engine** driving 1 FP propeller Total Power: 397kW (540hp) 9.0kn Kanegafuchi 1 x 4 Stroke 6 Cy. 270 x 400 397kW (540bhp) Kanegafuchi Diesel-Japan AuxGen: 1 x 5kW 110V d.c
8869024 - -	**TIEN PHONG 08** **Tien Phuong Co-operative (Hop Tac Xa Tien Phong Ha Tinh)** - *Vietnam*	*171* - -	Class: (VR)	**1988 at Nghe An** Loa 36.55 Br ex - Dght 1.710 Lbp - Br md 7.00 Dpth 2.50 Welded, 1 dk	**(A31A2GX) General Cargo Ship** Grain: 264 Compartments: 2 Ho, ER 2 Ha: 2 (6.5 x 4.0)ER	**1 oil engine** reduction geared to sc. shaft driving 1 FP propeller Total Power: 103kW (140hp) 9.0kn Yanmar 5KDGGE 1 x 4 Stroke 5 Cy. 145 x 170 103kW (140bhp) Yanmar Diesel Engine Co Ltd-Japan
7649350 *HQLQ3* -	**TIEN SOON** *ex* Soon Huat *-1994* *ex* Odomi *-1994* *ex* Kiyokaze Maru *-1993* *ex* Taisho Maru No. 1 *-1993* **Kam Fap Shipping Trading Co SA** - *San Lorenzo* *Honduras* Official number: L-0324769	**1,076** 552 1,600		**1975-05 Yaizu Dock — Yaizu** Loa 63.94 Br ex - Dght 4.401 Lbp 58.50 Br md 11.00 Dpth 6.10 Welded, 2dks	**(A31A2GX) General Cargo Ship** Grain: 2,234; Bale: 1,800 1 Ha: (32.3 x 8.0)ER	**1 oil engine** driving 1 FP propeller Total Power: 1,324kW (1,800hp) 12.0kn Hanshin 6LU35 1 x 4 Stroke 6 Cy. 350 x 550 1324kW (1800bhp) The Hanshin Diesel Works Ltd-Japan
7908342 *WDA9213* -	**TIEN THANH** *ex* Maria *-2001* *ex* Royal Prince *-1991* *ex* Lisa Lee *-1991* **Tien Van Nguyen** - *Port Arthur, TX* *United States of America* MMSI: 366862720 Official number: 599384	*116* 79 -		**1978-10 Quality Marine, Inc. — Bayou La Batre, Al** Yd No: 84 L reg 23.47 Br ex 6.71 Dght 2.440 Lbp 20.76 Br md - Dpth 3.28 Welded, 1 dk	**(B11A2FS) Stern Trawler**	**1 oil engine** driving 1 FP propeller Total Power: 441kW (600hp) 12.0kn G.M. (Detroit Diesel) 12V-92-T 1 x Vee 2 Stroke 12 Cy. 123 x 127 441kW (600bhp) General Motors Detroit DieselAllison Divn-USA
8893465 - -	**TIEN THANH 09** *ex* Hoa Binh 09 *-2005* **Tien Thanh Transport & Trading Co Ltd (Cong Ty Tnhh Van Tai Thuong Mai Tien Thanh)** - *Haiphong* *Vietnam*	**305** 186 575	Class: (VR)	**1994 Kien An Shipbuilding Works — Haiphong** Lengthened-2002 Loa 47.90 Br ex 7.02 Dght 3.050 Lbp 43.80 Br md 6.98 Dpth 3.75 Welded, 1 dk	**(A31A2GX) General Cargo Ship**	**1 oil engine** reduction geared to sc. shaft driving 1 FP propeller Total Power: 147kW (200hp) S.K.L. 6NVD26-2 1 x 4 Stroke 6 Cy. 180 x 260 147kW (200bhp) CKD Praha-Praha AuxGen: 2 x a.c
9663087 *3WGI9* -	**TIEN THANH 09** **Tien Thanh Co Ltd** - *Haiphong* *Vietnam*	**1,599** 940 3,040	Class: VR	**2012-02 Dai Nguyen Duong Co Ltd — Xuan Truong** Yd No: TKT140M Loa 79.57 Br ex 12.62 Dght 5.270 Lbp 75.37 Br md 12.60 Dpth 6.20 Welded, 1 dk	**(A31A2GX) General Cargo Ship** Grain: 3,472; Bale: 3,128 Compartments: 2 Ho, ER 2 Ha: (18.2 x 8.0)ER (19.3 x 8.0)	**1 oil engine** reduction geared to sc. shaft driving 1 FP propeller Total Power: 882kW (1,199hp) 10.0kn Chinese Std. Type 8300ZLC 1 x 4 Stroke 8 Cy. 300 x 380 882kW (1199bhp) Zibo Diesel Engine Factory-China AuxGen: 1 x 84kW 400V a.c

IMO / Call sign	Name / Owner / Port	Tonnage	Class	Built / Dimensions	Type	Machinery
9627071 *3WDU9* -	**TIEN THANH 26** **Tien Thanh JSC** - *Haiphong* *Vietnam* MMSI: 574001120 Official number: VN-3360-TD	**1,700** 924 2,952	Class: VR	**2011-11 Phu Hung Shipbuilding Industry JSC — Y Yen** Yd No: DKTB-02-20 Loa 79.60 Br ex 12.82 Dght 5.100 Lbp 74.80 Br md 12.80 Dpth 6.10 Welded, 1 dk	**(A13B2TP) Products Tanker** Double Hull (13F) Liq: 3,320; Liq (Oil): 3,320 Compartments: 5 Wing Ta, 5 Wing Ta, ER	**1 oil engine** reduction geared to sc. shaft driving 1 FP propeller Total Power: 1,100kW (1,496hp) 10.0kn Chinese Std. Type 8300ZLC 1 x 4 Stroke 8 Cy. 300 x 380 1100kW (1496bhp) Zibo Diesel Engine Factory-China AuxGen: 2 x 199kW 400V a.c Fuel: 60.8
8655174 *3WQS* -	**TIEN THANH 45** **Tien Thanh Shipping Co Ltd** - *Haiphong* *Vietnam*	**999** 621 1,926	Class: VR	**2007-10 Song Chanh Shipbuilding JSC — Yen Hung** Yd No: TKT 31-06-01 Loa 67.50 Br ex 11.02 Dght 4.500 Lbp 63.70 Br md 11.00 Dpth 5.30 Welded, 1 dk	**(A31A2GX) General Cargo Ship** Grain: 2,012 Compartments: 2 Ho, ER 2 Ha: (14.6 x 7.3)ER (15.4 x 7.3)	**1 oil engine** reduction geared to sc. shaft driving 1 FP propeller Total Power: 600kW (816hp) 11.0kn Chinese Std. Type 8170ZLC 1 x 4 Stroke 8 Cy. 170 x 200 600kW (816bhp) Zibo Diesel Engine Factory-China AuxGen: 2 x 49kW 390V a.c Fuel: 38.0
8655198 *3WXO* -	**TIEN THANH 68** *completed as* Hai Phuong 36 *-2009* **Tien Thanh JSC** - *Haiphong* *Vietnam* Official number: VN-2621-VT	**1,599** 1,004 3,075	Class: VR	**2008-06 Fishipco — Vietnam** Loa 74.36 Br ex 12.62 Dght 5.340 Lbp 70.90 Br md 12.60 Dpth 6.30 Welded, 1 dk	**(A31A2GX) General Cargo Ship** Bale: 3,341 Compartments: 2 Ho, ER 2 Ha: (17.0 x 8.0)ER (19.3 x 8.0)	**1 oil engine** driving 1 FP propeller Total Power: 736kW (1,001hp) 9.5kn S.K.L. 8NVD48A-1U 1 x 4 Stroke 8 Cy. 320 x 480 736kW (1001bhp) (, fitted 1989) VEB Schwermaschinenbau "KarlLiebknecht" (SKL)-Magdeburg AuxGen: 2 x 32kW 400V a.c Fuel: 80.0
8655186 *XVRX* -	**TIEN THANH 126** *completed as* Hai Phuong 125 *-2008* **Tien Thanh JSC** - *Haiphong* *Vietnam* Official number: VN-2445-VT	**999** 591 1,927	Class: VR	**2008-01 Technical & Prof. College ofTransport No. 2 — Haiphong** Loa 67.50 Br ex 11.02 Dght 4.500 Lbp 63.70 Br md 11.00 Dpth 5.30 Welded, 1 dk	**(A31A2GX) General Cargo Ship** Grain: 2,012 Compartments: 2 Ho, ER 2 Ha: (14.1 x 7.3)ER (16.0 x 7.3)	**1 oil engine** driving 1 FP propeller Total Power: 721kW (980hp) 11.0kn Skoda 6L350PN 1 x 4 Stroke 6 Cy. 350 x 500 721kW (980bhp) (made 1985, fitted 2008) CKD Praha-Praha AuxGen: 2 x 30kW 400V a.c Fuel: 21.0
8909434 *XVFI* -	**TIEN YEN** *ex* Sinar Pahlawan *-2002* *ex* Eastern Parrot *-1992* *ex* Echo Fighter *-1992* *ex* Prosper Star *-1991* **Vietnam Ocean Shipping JSC (VOSCO) (Cong Ty Co Phan Van Tai Bien Viet Nam)** - *Haiphong* *Vietnam* MMSI: 574202000 Official number: VN-1515-VT	**4,565** 2,829 7,060	Class: VR (NK)	**1989-07 Higaki Zosen K.K. — Imabari** Yd No: 372 Loa 112.70 (BB) Br ex - Dght 6.391 Lbp 105.00 Br md 18.60 Dpth 8.20 Welded, 1 dk	**(A31A2GX) General Cargo Ship** Grain: 10,023; Bale: 9,564 Compartments: 2 Ho, ER 2 Ha: 2 (32.2 x 9.5)ER Cranes: 4x25t	**1 oil engine** driving 1 FP propeller Total Power: 2,427kW (3,300hp) 12.1kn Hanshin 6EL40 1 x 4 Stroke 6 Cy. 400 x 800 2427kW (3300bhp) The Hanshin Diesel Works Ltd-Japan AuxGen: 3 x 201kW a.c Fuel: 460.0 (r.f.)
7236799 *CB5999* -	**TIERRA DEL FUEGO** *ex* Angelina *-1997* *ex* Zensei Maru No. 11 *-1997* **Pesca Chile SA** - *Valparaiso* *Chile* MMSI: 725000770 Official number: 2905	**636** 173 -	Class: (BV)	**1972 Niigata Engineering Co Ltd — Niigata NI** Yd No: 1122 Loa 53.68 Br ex 8.72 Dght 3.353 Lbp 47.22 Br md 8.69 Dpth 3.71 Welded, 1 dk	**(B11B2FV) Fishing Vessel**	**1 oil engine** driving 1 FP propeller Total Power: 625kW (850hp) Niigata 6M28KHS 1 x 4 Stroke 6 Cy. 280 x 440 625kW (850bhp) Niigata Engineering Co Ltd-Japan
7713553 - -	**TIERRA DEL FUEGO 150-C** **Government of The Argentine Republic (Direccion Nacional de Construcciones Portuarias y Vias Navegables)** -	**935** 327 1,416	Class: (LR) ✠ Classed LR until 22/12/82	**1978-09 Astilleros Espanoles SA (AESA) — Sestao** Yd No: 215 Loa 70.52 Br ex 13.31 Dght 4.001 Lbp 66.02 Br md 13.01 Dpth 5.01 Welded, 1 dk	**(B33B2DG) Grab Hopper Dredger**	**1 diesel electric oil engine** driving 2 gen. each 260kW 400V a.c Connecting to 2 elec. motors driving 2 FP propellers Total Power: 2,383kW (3,240hp) 12.8kn Sulzer 12ASV25/30 1 x Vee 4 Stroke 12 Cy. 250 x 300 2383kW (3240bhp) Astilleros Espanoles SA (AESA)-Spain
8017475 *WDB2065* -	**TIFAIMOANA** *ex* Blue Sea *-2005* *ex* Lady Linda *-2001* *ex* Commander *-1998* *ex* Lisa Maria *-1998* *ex* Elizabeth Ashley *-1998* **Longline Services Inc** - *Utulei, AS* *United States of America* MMSI: 369189000 Official number: 611929	*183* 124 -		**1980 St Augustine Trawlers, Inc. — Saint Augustine, Fl** Yd No: S-35 L reg 23.50 Br ex 7.50 Dght - Lbp - Br md - Dpth 3.10 Welded, 1 dk	**(B11A2FS) Stern Trawler**	**2 oil engines** driving 2 FP propellers Total Power: 496kW (674hp) G.M. (Detroit Diesel) 12V-149 2 x Vee 2 Stroke 12 Cy. 146 x 146 each-248kW (337bhp) General Motors Detroit DieselAllison Divn-USA
8011419 *YFOC* -	**TIFELIN K** *ex* Manpo *-2005* *ex* Manpo Maru *-1996* **PT Citra Baru Adinusantara** - *Surabaya* *Indonesia*	**484** 205 450	Class: KI	**1980-12 Nakatani Shipyard Co. Ltd. — Etajima** Yd No: 463 Loa 43.52 Br ex - Dght 3.317 Lbp 41.03 Br md 8.01 Dpth 5.21 Welded, 1 dk	**(A31A2GX) General Cargo Ship**	**1 oil engine** geared to sc. shaft driving 1 FP propeller Total Power: 405kW (551hp) Matsui 6M26KGHS 1 x 4 Stroke 6 Cy. 260 x 400 405kW (551bhp) (made 1980) Matsui Iron Works Co Ltd-Japan
8207501 *5N123* -	**TIFFANY** *ex* Explorer Seahorse *-2008* **Lenimar Ocean Trawlers Ltd** - *Lagos* *Nigeria* Official number: SR1098	**867** 260 1,132	Class: IS RS (AB)	**1982-12 Eastern Marine, Inc. — Panama City, Fl** Yd No: 57 Loa 59.13 Br ex - Dght 3.909 Lbp 54.70 Br md 12.20 Dpth 4.58 Welded, 1 dk	**(B21B20A) Anchor Handling Tug Supply**	**2 oil engines** reverse reduction geared to sc. shafts driving 2 FP propellers Total Power: 3,310kW (4,500hp) 11.4kn EMD (Electro-Motive) 16-645-E3 2 x Vee 2 Stroke 16 Cy. 230 x 254 each-1655kW (2250bhp) (Re-engined ,made 1974, Reconditioned & fitted 1982) General Motors Corp.Electro-Motive Div.-La Grange AuxGen: 2 x 99kW Thrusters: 1 Thwart. FP thruster (f)
7309455 *WDC7857* -	**TIFFANY** *ex* Bluebonnet (WAGL-257) *-1966* **Ronald D Carnagey** - SatCom: Inmarsat C 436740810 *Newport, OR* *United States of America* MMSI: 367077970 Official number: 504543	*144* 98 -		**1939-11 Dubuque Boat & Boiler Works — Dubuque, Ia** L reg 26.19 Br ex 7.04 Dght - Lbp 24.99 Br md - Dpth 2.32 Welded	**(B11B2FV) Fishing Vessel**	**2 oil engines** driving 2 FP propellers Total Power: 206kW (280hp) General Motors 2 x 2 Stroke each-103kW (140bhp) General Motors Corp-USA
8938930 *WDC5541* -	**TIFFANY LADY** **Thanh Van Dang** - *Garland, TX* *United States of America* MMSI: 367042670 Official number: 1033241	**133** 42 -		**1995 J & J Marine, Inc. — Bayou La Batre, Al** Yd No: 106 L reg 23.35 Br ex - Dght - Lbp - Br md 7.32 Dpth 3.81 Welded, 1 dk	**(B11B2FV) Fishing Vessel**	**1 oil engine** driving 1 FP propeller
7513226 *WYP8339* -	**TIFFANY-LYNN** *ex* Hilary Kennedy *-1966* **Tuan Any Nguyen** - *New Orleans, LA* *United States of America* Official number: 550061	*133* 98 -		**1973 A.W. Covacevich Shipyard, Inc. — Biloxi, Ms** L reg 21.22 Br ex 7.07 Dght - Lbp - Br md - Dpth 3.43 Welded, 1 dk	**(B11A2FT) Trawler**	**1 oil engine** driving 1 FP propeller Total Power: 257kW (349hp)
8880236 - -	**TIFFANY ROSE** *ex* Hatsuhiro *-1995* *ex* Bisan *-1995* **Santo Rosario Navegacion SA** -	*140* 51 -		**1968 K.K. Saidaiji Zosensho — Okayama** Loa 34.30 Br ex - Dght 2.200 Lbp 29.95 Br md 8.00 Dpth 2.80 Welded, 1 dk	**(A37B2PS) Passenger Ship**	**1 oil engine** driving 1 FP propeller Total Power: 478kW (650hp) Yanmar 1 x 4 Stroke 478kW (650bhp) Yanmar Diesel Engine Co Ltd-Japan

IMO / Call sign	Name / Owner	Tonnage	Class	Built	Type	Machinery
7209253 *3FHJ8* -	**TIFFANY S** *ex* Yehya *-1996* *ex* Bandon *-1987* *ex* Gerda Maria *-1986* *ex* Bamse *-1978* **Daz Maritime SA** UAB 'Sea First International' SatCom: Inmarsat C 435425110 *Panama* *Panama* MMSI: 354251000 Official number: 3065205A	**1,729** 670 2,499	Class: HR (PR) (NV)	1972-05 **AS Storviks Mek. Verksted — Kristiansund** Yd No: 48 Loa 70.11 Br ex 13.14 Dght 5.462 Lbp 61.78 Br md 13.11 Dpth 7.75 Welded, 1 dk	**(A34A2GR) Refrigerated Cargo Ship** Grain: 1,178; Bale: 611; Ins: 2,815 Compartments: 1 Ho, ER 1 Ha: (37.4 x 10.2)ER Cranes: 1x5t Ice Capable	**1 oil engine** driving 1 CP propeller Total Power: 971kW (1,320hp) 10.5kn Wichmann WX28L4 1 x 4 Stroke 4 Cy. 280 x 420 971kW (1320bhp) Wichmann Motorfabrikk AS-Norway AuxGen: 2 x 180kW 220V 50Hz a.c, 2 x 68kW 220V 50Hz a.c Fuel: 86.5 (d.f.) 4.5pd
8410316 *J8B4776* -	**TIFJORD** *ex* Molo Sun *-2012* *ex* Myrtun *-2007* *ex* Anja *-1999* *ex* Anna *-1990* *ex* Butjadingen *-1988* **Berge Rederi AS** Transmar AS *Kingstown* *St Vincent & The Grenadines* MMSI: 375103000 Official number: 11249	**1,477** 623 1,770	Class: BV (GL)	1985-06 **C. Luehring Schiffswerft GmbH & Co. KG — Brake** Yd No: 8402 Lengthened-1992 Loa 77.36 Br ex 11.41 Dght 3.812 Lbp 70.81 Br md 11.31 Dpth 5.90 Welded, 2 dks	**(A31A2GX) General Cargo Ship** Grain: 2,730; Bale: 2,700 TEU 60 C. 60/20' (40') Compartments: 1 Ho, ER 1 Ha: (37.2 x 9.0)ER Ice Capable	**1 oil engine** driving 1 FP propeller Total Power: 600kW (816hp) 11.0kn MaK 6M452AK 1 x 4 Stroke 6 Cy. 320 x 450 600kW (816bhp) Krupp MaK Maschinenbau GmbH-Kiel AuxGen: 2 x 48kW 220/380V 50Hz a.c, 1 x 24kW 220/380V 50Hz a.c Thrusters: 1 Water jet (f)
8100026 *LW3433* -	**TIFON** - **Rio Lujan Navegacion SA de Transportes Fluviales y Remolques (Rio Lujan Navegacion SA Towage & Salvage)** - *Argentina* MMSI: 701006104 Official number: 02510	*267* 54 337	Class: (AB)	1982-07 **Astilleros Mestrina S.A. — Tigre** Yd No: 57 Loa 33.51 Br ex 9.81 Dght 3.201 Lbp - Br md 9.42 Dpth 4.32 Welded, 1 dk	**(B32A2ST) Tug**	**1 oil engine** with clutches, flexible couplings & dr geared to sc. shaft driving 1 CP propeller Total Power: 2,059kW (2,799hp) 13.0kn Alpha 12U28L-VO 1 x Vee 4 Stroke 12 Cy. 280 x 320 2059kW (2799bhp) B&W Alpha Diesel A/S-Denmark AuxGen: 2 x 110kW
7206512 *CL2059* -	**TIFON** *ex* San Blas I *-1986* *ex* Masuei Maru No. 22 *-1980* **Empresa de Navegacion Caribe** - *Cuba*	**164** 49 -	Class: RC (GL) (NK)	1971 **Kanagawa Zosen — Kobe** Yd No: 115 Loa 27.82 Br ex 8.64 Dght 2.598 Lbp 23.50 Br md 8.62 Dpth 3.81 Riveted\Welded, 1 dk	**(B32A2ST) Tug**	**2 oil engines** geared to sc. shafts driving 2 Directional propellers Total Power: 1,766kW (2,402hp) 11.5kn Niigata 6L25BX 2 x 4 Stroke 6 Cy. 250 x 320 each-883kW (1201bhp) Niigata Engineering Co Ltd-Japan AuxGen: 1 x 64kW, 1 x 40kW
8715780 - -	**TIFON** - **Isla de Los Estados SA** -	**107** 65 80	Class: (AB)	1989-06 **SANYM S.A. — Buenos Aires** Yd No: 107 Loa 23.50 Br ex - Dght 3.001 Lbp 20.91 Br md 6.51 Dpth 3.31 Welded	**(B11A2FS) Stern Trawler** Ins: 115	**1 oil engine** reverse reduction geared to sc. shaft driving 1 FP propeller Total Power: 325kW (442hp) Caterpillar 3408T 1 x Vee 4 Stroke 8 Cy. 137 x 152 325kW (442bhp) Caterpillar Inc-USA
9027453 *YD6258* -	**TIGA BERLIAN** - **PT Suryanusa Permata Bahari** - *Samarinda* *Indonesia*	**150** 90 -	Class: KI	1997-11 **P.T. Suryanusa Permatabahari — Samarinda** L reg 21.00 Br ex - Dght - Lbp 18.75 Br md 6.50 Dpth 2.75 Welded, 1 dk	**(B32A2ST) Tug**	**2 oil engines** geared to sc. shafts driving 2 Propellers Total Power: 786kW (1,068hp) 13.0kn Caterpillar D353 2 x 4 Stroke 6 Cy. 159 x 203 each-393kW (534bhp) Caterpillar Inc-USA
9142394 - -	**TIGA DAM** - **Nigerian Ports Authority (NPA)** - *Lagos* *Nigeria*	**250** - -		1996-12 **Ceske Lodenice a.s. — Usti nad Labem** (Hull) Yd No: 708 1996-12 **Rijnwaal Shipyards B.V. — Hardinxveld-Giessendam** Yd No: 708 Loa 44.00 Br ex - Dght 2.200 Lbp - Br md 7.50 Dpth 2.90 Welded, 1 dk	**(B34A2SH) Hopper, Motor**	**1 oil engine** driving 1 Directional propeller Total Power: 220kW (299hp) Deutz BF6M1015MC 1 x Vee 4 Stroke 6 Cy. 132 x 145 220kW (299bhp) KHD Industriemotoren GmbH-Koeln
9027465 - -	**TIGA PERMATA** - **PT Suryanusa Permata Bahari** - *Samarinda* *Indonesia*	**189** 56 -	Class: KI	1998-12 **P.T. Suryanusa Permatabahari — Samarinda** L reg 19.00 Br ex - Dght 1.980 Lbp 16.65 Br md 8.00 Dpth 2.50 Welded, 1 dk	**(B32A2ST) Tug**	**2 oil engines** geared to sc. shafts driving 2 Propellers Total Power: 786kW (1,068hp) 12.0kn Caterpillar D353 2 x 4 Stroke 6 Cy. 159 x 203 each-393kW (534bhp) Caterpillar Inc-USA
7810753 *YGEU*	**TIGA RODA** *ex* Flag Rolaco *-1991* *ex* Baikyang *-1982* **PT Bahana Indonor** PT Samudera Sukses Makmur *Jakarta* *Indonesia* MMSI: 525017048	**6,870** 2,631 10,351	Class: KI (NV) (KR)	1978-12 **Tsuneishi Shipbuilding Co Ltd — Fukuyama HS** Yd No: 438 Loa 129.50 (BB) Br ex - Dght 7.980 Lbp 122.50 Br md 20.62 Dpth 9.61 Welded, 1 dk	**(A24A2BT) Cement Carrier** Grain: 8,536	**1 oil engine** driving 1 FP propeller Total Power: 4,413kW (6,000hp) 13.3kn Mitsubishi 6UET52/90D 1 x 2 Stroke 6 Cy. 520 x 900 4413kW (6000bhp) Kobe Hatsudoki KK-Japan AuxGen: 3 x 240kW 445V a.c
9027477 - -	**TIGA TERATAI** - **PT Suryanusa Permata Bahari** - *Samarinda* *Indonesia*	**121** 72 -	Class: KI	2001-07 **P.T. Suryanusa Permatabahari — Samarinda** L reg 19.00 Br ex - Dght 1.980 Lbp 16.65 Br md 8.00 Dpth 2.50 Welded, 1 dk	**(B32A2ST) Tug**	**2 oil engines** geared to sc. shafts driving 2 Propellers Total Power: 786kW (1,068hp) 9.0kn Caterpillar D353 2 x 4 Stroke 6 Cy. 159 x 203 each-393kW (534bhp) Caterpillar Inc-USA
8971035 *WDD9276* -	**TIGER** *ex* Siegfried Tiger *-2001* *ex* Demarco 10 *-1979* *ex* Gulf Tiger *-1976* **Kirby Offshore Marine Pacific LLC** - *Seattle, WA* *United States of America* MMSI: 367309310 Official number: 502116	**191** 57 -	Class: (AB)	1966-01 **Bollinger Machine Shop & Shipyard, Inc. — Lockport, La** Yd No: 55 L reg 27.55 Br ex - Dght 3.050 Lbp - Br md 8.22 Dpth 3.65 Welded, 1 dk	**(B32A2ST) Tug**	**1 oil engine** driving 1 FP propeller Total Power: 1,618kW (2,200hp)
7821465 *5IM261* -	**TIGER** *ex* Naft-1 *-2009* *ex* Zuiyo Maru *-1988* **Harmoush Shipping Co** - *Zanzibar* *Tanzania (Zanzibar)* MMSI: 677016100 Official number: 300025	*1,818* 901 3,261	Class: (NK)	1979-01 **Higaki Zosen K.K. — Imabari** Yd No: 213 Loa 84.20 (BB) Br ex - Dght 5.695 Lbp 78.50 Br md 13.00 Dpth 6.40 Riveted\Welded, 1 dk	**(A13B2TP) Products Tanker** Double Bottom Entire Compartment Length Liq: 3,252; Liq (Oil): 3,252	**1 oil engine** driving 1 FP propeller Total Power: 2,059kW (2,799hp) 12.3kn Makita GSLH641 1 x 4 Stroke 6 Cy. 410 x 650 2059kW (2799bhp) Makita Diesel Co Ltd-Japan AuxGen: 1 x 176kW 445V 60Hz a.c, 1 x 160kW 445V 60Hz a.c Fuel: 22.0 (d.f.) 136.5 (r.f.) 9.0pd
8117990 - -	**TIGER** *ex* Asso Quindici *-2012* *ex* Augustea Quindici *-1998* *ex* Tender Gela *-1993* *ex* Castalia Azzurra *-1991* *ex* Tender Gela *-1989* *ex* Tender Bounty *-1984* **Logistica Inc**	**753** 226 881	Class: (RI) (AB)	1982-09 **Mangone Swiftships, Inc. — Houston, Tx** Yd No: 135 Loa 55.89 Br ex 11.59 Dght 4.174 Lbp 51.03 Br md 11.56 Dpth 4.88 Welded, 1 dk	**(B21B20A) Anchor Handling Tug Supply**	**2 oil engines** sr geared to sc. shafts driving 2 CP propellers Total Power: 2,952kW (4,014hp) 12.0kn EMD (Electro-Motive) 16-645-E6 2 x Vee 2 Stroke 16 Cy. 230 x 254 each-1476kW (2007bhp) General Motors Corp.Electro-Motive Div.-La Grange AuxGen: 1 x 150kW 440V 60Hz a.c, 2 x 125kW 440V 60Hz a.c Thrusters: 1 Thwart. FP thruster (f) Fuel: 305.0 (d.f.) 10.0pd
5424926 *WG7036* -	**TIGER** *ex* Jodee Lee *-2010* *ex* Aurous *-2006* *ex* Silver Ice *-1999* *ex* Dolphin *-1999* *ex* New Tide *-1970* *ex* Tiger *-1963* **Ted Morehouse** - *Homer, AK* *United States of America* Official number: 270744	*188* 128 -		1955-12 **Equitable Equipment Co. — Madisonville, La** Yd No: 870 Converted From: Offshore Supply Ship-1970 L reg 35.79 Br ex 9.66 Dght 2.417 Lbp 35.36 Br md 9.61 Dpth 2.82 Welded, 1 dk	**(B11B2FV) Fishing Vessel**	**2 oil engines** geared to sc. shafts driving 2 FP propellers Total Power: 434kW (590hp) G.M. (Detroit Diesel) 12V-71 2 x Vee 2 Stroke 12 Cy. 108 x 127 each-217kW (295bhp) General Motors Corp-USA Fuel: 48.0
7518044 - -	**TIGER** *ex* Blazer *-2011* *ex* Tiger *-2010* *ex* Duma *-2007* *ex* Al Farhan *-2006* *ex* Nanak *-2003* *ex* Papa *-1994* **Nader Saadollah Azadeh**	*224* 68 97	Class: IS (RI) (NK)	1974-07 **Robin Shipyard Pte Ltd — Singapore** Loa 30.48 Br ex - Dght 3.015 Lbp 26.98 Br md 8.77 Dpth 3.79 Welded, 1 dk	**(B32A2ST) Tug**	**2 oil engines** driving 2 CP propellers Total Power: 3,018kW (4,104hp) 12.3kn Fuji 8S32F 2 x 4 Stroke 8 Cy. 320 x 500 each-1509kW (2052bhp) Fuji Diesel Co Ltd-Japan AuxGen: 2 x 36kW a.c Fuel: 38.5 (d.f.) 13.5pd

IMO / Call sign	Name / Owner / Manager	Tonnage	Class	Builder / Dimensions	Type / Capacity	Machinery
9591416 *LXKX* -	**TIGER** **Vasco SA** Jan De Nul Luxembourg SA *Luxembourg* *Luxembourg* MMSI: 253447000	**3,843** 1,164 6,200	Class: BV	**2012-06 Tianjin Xinhe Shipbuilding Heavy Industry Co Ltd — Tianjin** Yd No: SB814 Loa 98.00 (BB) Br ex - Dght 5.850 Lbp 92.00 Br md 19.40 Dpth 6.30 Welded, 1 dk	**(B34A2SH) Hopper, Motor** Hopper: 3,700	**2 oil engines** reduction geared to sc. shaft (s) driving 2 Z propellers Total Power: 3,536kW (4,808hp) 12.4kn A.B.C. 8DZC 2 x 4 Stroke 8 Cy. 256 x 310 each-1768kW (2404bhp) Anglo Belgian Corp NV (ABC)-Belgium AuxGen: 2 x 500kW 50Hz a.c Thrusters: 1 Tunnel thruster (f)
9452751 *3WQK* -	**TIGER** *ex* Ocean Spirit *-2013* *ex* Thai An *-2009* **Hoang Gia Ocean Shipping Co Ltd (Cong Ty TNHH VTB Hoang Gia)** - *Haiphong* *Vietnam* MMSI: 574476000 Official number: VN-3566-VT	**1,999** 1,186 3,484	Class: VR	**2007-07 Dai Duong Shipbuilding Co Ltd — Haiphong** Yd No: HP-610 Loa 88.31 Br ex 12.62 Dght 5.280 Lbp 82.00 Br md 12.60 Dpth 6.48 Welded, 1 dk	**(A31A2GX) General Cargo Ship** Grain: 4,451 Compartments: 2 Ho, ER 2 Ha: ER 2 (21.6 x 7.8) Cranes: 2x10t	**1 oil engine** reduction geared to sc. shaft driving 1 FP propeller Total Power: 1,200kW (1,632hp) 12.8kn Chinese Std. Type CW12V200ZC 1 x Vee 4 Stroke 12 Cy. 200 x 270 1200kW (1632bhp) (made 2006) Weichai Power Co Ltd-China AuxGen: 2 x 170kW 400V 50Hz a.c
9415442 *WDE3479* -	**TIGER** **GulfMark Americas Inc** - SatCom: Inmarsat C 436901565 *New Orleans, LA* *United States of America* MMSI: 367339650 Official number: 1207719	**498** 149 552	Class: AB	**2009-07** Yd No: 98 Loa 55.00 Br ex - Dght 3.750 Lbp 50.00 Br md 10.37 Dpth 4.23 Welded, 1 dk	**(B21A2OC) Crew/Supply Vessel** Hull Material: Aluminium Alloy Passengers: unberthed: 36	**4 oil engines** reduction geared to sc. shafts driving 4 FP propellers Total Power: 5,296kW (7,200hp) 15.0kn Cummins KTA-50-M2 4 x Vee 4 Stroke 16 Cy. 159 x 159 each-1324kW (1800bhp) Cummins Engine Co Inc-USA AuxGen: 2 x 160kW a.c Thrusters: 1 Retract. directional thruster (f) Fuel: 110.0 (d.f.)
9505039 *9HA2271* -	**TIGER** **Wilhelmsen Lines Car Carrier Ltd** Wilhelmsen Ship Management Sdn Bhd SatCom: Inmarsat C 424822310 *Valletta* *Malta* MMSI: 248223000 Official number: 9505039	**74,255** 26,747 30,140	Class: LR ✠ **100A1** SS 06/2011 vehicle carrier moveable decks, deck No. 1, 3, 5 & 8 strengthened for the carriage of roll on/roll off cargoes *IWS LI ✠ **LMC** **UMS** Eq.Ltr: St†; Cable: 687.5/87.0 U3 (a)	**2011-06 Daewoo Shipbuilding & Marine Engineering Co Ltd — Geoje** Yd No: 4458 Loa 231.60 (BB) Br ex - Dght 11.300 Lbp 219.30 Br md 32.26 Dpth 34.70 Welded, 12 dks incl 4 hoistable decks	**(A35B2RV) Vehicles Carrier** Side door/ramp (s) Len: 25.00 Wid: 6.50 Swl: 22 Quarter bow door/ramp (s. a.) Len: 39.00 Wid: 7.00 Swl: 150 Cars: 7,800	**1 oil engine** driving 1 FP propeller Total Power: 19,040kW (25,887hp) 20.1kn MAN-B&W 8S60ME-C 1 x 2 Stroke 8 Cy. 600 x 2400 19040kW (25887bhp) Doosan Engine Co Ltd-South Korea AuxGen: 1 x 1256kW 430V 60Hz a.c, 2 x 1700kW 450V 60Hz a.c Boilers: AuxB (ex.g.) 9.2kgf/cm² (9.0bar), WTAuxB (o.f.) 9.2kgf/cm² (9.0bar) Thrusters: 1 Thwart. FP thruster (f)
9527879 *UBAG7* -	**TIGER** **LLC Transneft-Service** - *Novorossiysk* *Russia* MMSI: 273343030	**284** 85 151	Class: RS	**2009-03 DP Craneship — Kerch** Yd No: 402 Loa 27.19 Br ex 10.00 Dght 3.700 Lbp 25.00 Br md 9.80 Dpth 4.99 Welded, 1 dk	**(B32A2ST) Tug**	**2 oil engines** reduction geared to sc. shafts driving 2 Directional propellers Total Power: 2,460kW (3,344hp) Caterpillar 3512B-TA 2 x Vee 4 Stroke 12 Cy. 170 x 190 each-1230kW (1672bhp) Caterpillar Inc-USA AuxGen: 2 x 52kW a.c Fuel: 65.0 (d.f.)
9307841 *A8XH8* -	**TIGER** *ex* Maersk Naha *-2010* **Renta Reederei GmbH** Johann M K Blumenthal GmbH & Co KG SatCom: Inmarsat C 463708862 *Monrovia* *Liberia* MMSI: 636092140 Official number: 92140	**25,756** 12,591 33,082 T/cm 45.0	Class: GL NK	**2005-11 Volkswerft Stralsund GmbH — Stralsund** Yd No: 458 Loa 207.46 (BB) Br ex - Dght 11.400 Lbp 196.84 Br md 29.80 Dpth 16.40 Welded, 1 dk	**(A33A2CC) Container Ship (Fully Cellular)** TEU 2524 C Ho 992 TEU C Dk 1532 incl 550 ref C. Cranes: 3x45t	**1 oil engine** driving 1 FP propeller Total Power: 24,533kW (33,355hp) 22.6kn MAN-B&W 8L70MC-C 1 x 2 Stroke 8 Cy. 700 x 2360 24533kW (33355bhp) Doosan Engine Co Ltd-South Korea AuxGen: 3 x 1850kW 450/230V 60Hz a.c, 1 x 1300kW 450/230V 60Hz a.c Thrusters: 1 Tunnel thruster (f) Fuel: 3060.0
9063342 - -	**TIGER 2** *ex* Artemis *-1998* - -	*167* - 22		**1993-11 Hitachi Zosen Corp — Kawasaki KN** Yd No: 117307 Loa 31.00 Br ex - Dght 1.892 Lbp 27.00 Br md 9.00 Dpth 3.00 Welded, 1 dk	**(A37B2PS) Passenger Ship** Hull Material: Aluminium Alloy Passengers: unberthed: 200	**2 oil engines** with clutches, flexible couplings & sr reverse geared to sc. shafts driving 2 Water jets Total Power: 3,678kW (5,000hp) 34.0kn Niigata 16V16FX 2 x Vee 4 Stroke 16 Cy. 165 x 185 each-1839kW (2500bhp) Niigata Engineering Co Ltd-Japan AuxGen: 2 x 60kW 225V 60Hz a.c
9097587 *WDC3998* -	**TIGER 5** **Tuger Tug 5 LLC** P & R Water Taxi Ltd *Honolulu, HI* *United States of America* MMSI: 367017630 Official number: 1166594	**180** 54 -		**2005-01 Honolulu Marine LLC — Honolulu HI** Yd No: 04012 L reg 26.21 Br ex - Dght - Lbp - Br md 10.36 Dpth 3.50 Welded, 1 dk	**(B32A2ST) Tug**	**2 oil engines** geared to sc. shafts driving 2 Propellers Total Power: 3,282kW (4,462hp) Caterpillar 3516B-TA 2 x Vee 4 Stroke 16 Cy. 170 x 190 each-1641kW (2231bhp) Caterpillar Inc-USA
9097599 *WDD9482* -	**TIGER 6** **Tiger Tug 6 & 7 LLC** P & R Water Taxi Ltd *Honolulu, HI* *United States of America* MMSI: 367312090 Official number: 1201934	**180** 54 -		**2007-07 Honolulu Marine LLC — Honolulu HI** Yd No: 06014 L reg 26.21 Br ex - Dght - Lbp - Br md 10.36 Dpth 3.50 Welded, 1 dk	**(B32A2ST) Tug**	**2 oil engines** geared to sc. shafts driving 2 Propellers Total Power: 3,282kW (4,462hp) Caterpillar 3516B-TA 2 x Vee 4 Stroke 16 Cy. 170 x 190 each-1641kW (2231bhp) Caterpillar Inc-USA AuxGen: 2 x 75kW a.c
9097604 *WDD8628* -	**TIGER 7** **Tiger Tug 6 & 7 LLC** P & R Water Taxi Ltd *Honolulu, HI* *United States of America* MMSI: 367300660 Official number: 1201935	**180** 54 -	Class: AB	**2007-07 Honolulu Marine LLC — Honolulu HI** Yd No: 06015 Loa 27.66 Br ex - Dght 2.130 Lbp 26.21 Br md 10.36 Dpth 3.50 Welded, 1 dk	**(B32A2ST) Tug**	**2 oil engines** geared to sc. shafts driving 2 Propellers Total Power: 3,282kW (4,462hp) Caterpillar 3516B-TA 2 x Vee 4 Stroke 16 Cy. 170 x 190 each-1641kW (2231bhp) Caterpillar Inc-USA AuxGen: 2 x 90kW a.c
8666501 *WDE9353* -	**TIGER 8** **Tiger Tug 8 LLC** P & R Water Taxi Ltd *Honolulu, HI* *United States of America* Official number: 1221071	**180** 54 -		**2009 Honolulu Marine LLC — Honolulu HI** Yd No: 08017 Loa 26.21 Br ex - Dght - Lbp - Br md 10.36 Dpth 3.50 Welded, 1 dk	**(B32A2ST) Tug**	**2 oil engines** reduction geared to sc. shafts driving 2 Propellers Total Power: 3,840kW (5,220hp) 12.0kn Caterpillar 3516B-HD 2 x Vee 4 Stroke 16 Cy. 170 x 215 each-1920kW (2610bhp) Caterpillar Inc-USA
8666513 *WDF3003* -	**TIGER 9** **Tiger Tug 9 LLC** P & R Water Taxi Ltd *Honolulu, HI* *United States of America* Official number: 1221072	**180** 54 -		**2009 Honolulu Marine LLC — Honolulu HI** Yd No: 08018 Loa 26.21 Br ex - Dght - Lbp - Br md 10.36 Dpth 3.50 Welded, 1 dk	**(B32A2ST) Tug**	**2 oil engines** reduction geared to sc. shafts driving 2 Propellers Total Power: 3,840kW (5,220hp) 12.0kn Caterpillar 3516B-HD 2 x Vee 4 Stroke 16 Cy. 170 x 215 each-1920kW (2610bhp) Caterpillar Inc-USA
9289881 *VRNB7* -	**TIGER AUTUMN** *ex* Eastern Knight *-2014* **Tiger Ship No 3 Ltd** Greathorse International Ship Management Co Ltd *Hong Kong* *Hong Kong* MMSI: 477407800	**5,453** 2,639 8,924 T/cm 17.7	Class: AB	**2003-12 Shin Kurushima Dockyard Co. Ltd. — Hashihama, Imabari** Yd No: 5277 Loa 113.98 (BB) Br ex 18.23 Dght 7.578 Lbp 108.50 Br md 18.20 Dpth 9.75 Welded, 1 dk	**(A12A2TC) Chemical Tanker** Double Hull (13F) Liq: 8,614 Cargo Heating Coils Compartments: 16 Wing Ta (s.stl), 2 Wing Slop Ta (s.stl), ER 18 Cargo Pump (s): 18x200m³/hr Manifold: Bow/CM: 57.1m	**1 oil engine** driving 1 FP propeller Total Power: 3,900kW (5,302hp) 14.2kn MAN-B&W 6L35MC 1 x 2 Stroke 6 Cy. 350 x 1050 3900kW (5302bhp) Makita Corp-Japan AuxGen: 2 x 450kW a.c Thrusters: 1 Tunnel thruster (f) Fuel: 50.0 (d.f.) 584.0 (r.f.)
8901884 *V7NO7* -	**TIGER BRIDGE** *ex* City of Hamburg *-2007* *ex* Astrid Schulte *-2003* *ex* Ibn al Kadi *-1998* *ex* Choyang Green *-1997* *ex* American Senator *-1994* *launched as* Astrid Schulte *-1990* **Tiger Navigation Corp** Eurobulk Ltd *Majuro* *Marshall Islands* MMSI: 538002988 Official number: 2988	**24,495** 10,304 31,628 T/cm 47.5	Class: GL (LR) ✠ Classed LR until 15/1/91	**1990-11 Hyundai Heavy Industries Co Ltd — Ulsan** Yd No: 676 Loa 181.62 (BB) Br ex 31.41 Dght 10.300 Lbp 172.00 Br md 31.40 Dpth 16.00 Welded, 1 dk	**(A33A2CC) Container Ship (Fully Cellular)** Passengers: cabins: 2; berths: 4 TEU 2228 C Ho 928 TEU C Dk 1300 TEU incl 100 ref C. Compartments: 4 Cell Ho, ER 18 Ha: 2 (12.8 x 5.3)Tappered 2 (12.8 x 10.4)Tappered 14 (12.8 x 13.1)ER	**1 oil engine** driving 1 FP propeller Total Power: 13,120kW (17,838hp) 18.0kn B&W 7S60MC 1 x 2 Stroke 7 Cy. 600 x 2292 13120kW (17838bhp) Hyundai Heavy Industries Co Ltd-South Korea AuxGen: 2 x 720kW 220/440V 60Hz a.c, 1 x 500kW 220/440V 60Hz a.c Fuel: 298.0 (d.f.) 2284.0 (r.f.) 53.0pd

8034435 - -	**TIGER CAT** - -	*105* 71 -		1981-04 **Steiner Shipyard, Inc. — Bayou La Batre, Al** Loa 23.80 Br ex - Dght 3.661 Lbp - Br md 6.72 Dpth - Welded, 1 dk	**(B11A2FT) Trawler** Ins: 65	**1 oil engine** geared to sc. shaft driving 1 FP propeller Total Power: 268kW (364hp) Caterpillar 3408TA 1 x Vee 4 Stroke 8 Cy. 137 x 152 268kW (364bhp) Caterpillar Tractor Co-USA
9630743 *VRLT5* -	**TIGER DI** **Tiger Pisces Ltd** Navig8 Bulk Asia Pte Ltd *Hong Kong* *Hong Kong* MMSI: 477427100 Official number: HK-3763	32,839 19,559 58,000 T/cm 59.2	Class: BV	2013-02 **Zhejiang Shipbuilding Co Ltd — Fenghua ZJ** Yd No: ZJB10-196 Loa 189.99 (BB) Br ex - Dght 12.950 Lbp 185.00 Br md 32.26 Dpth 18.00 Welded, 1 dk	**(A21A2BC) Bulk Carrier** Grain: 71,549; Bale: 69,760 Compartments: 5 Ho, ER 5 Ha: ER Cranes: 4x35t	**1 oil engine** driving 1 FP propeller Total Power: 8,700kW (11,829hp) 14.3kn MAN-B&W 6S50MC-C 1 x 2 Stroke 6 Cy. 500 x 2000 8700kW (11829bhp) Doosan Engine Co Ltd-South Korea AuxGen: 3 x 610kW 60Hz a.c Fuel: 2370.0
9619842 *VRKE2* -	**TIGER EAST** **Bless Industrial Ltd** Greathorse International Ship Management Co Ltd *Hong Kong* *Hong Kong* MMSI: 477427300 Official number: HK-3428	42,114 25,817 76,000	Class: NV	2013-03 **Shanhaiguan Shipbuilding Industry Co Ltd — Qinhuangdao HE** Yd No: BC760-01 Loa 225.00 (BB) Br ex 32.30 Dght 14.200 Lbp 219.00 Br md 32.26 Dpth 19.60 Welded, 1 dk	**(A21A2BC) Bulk Carrier** Grain: 90,100 Compartments: 7 Ho, ER 7 Ha: ER	**1 oil engine** driving 1 FP propeller Total Power: 9,108kW (12,383hp) 14.5kn Wartsila 5RT-flex58T 1 x 2 Stroke 5 Cy. 580 x 2416 9108kW (12383bhp) Yichang Marine Diesel Engine Co Ltd-China AuxGen: 3 x a.c
8102658 *D6D05* -	**TIGER FISH II** *ex* Tiger Fish *-2008* *ex* Tiger Fish II *-1993* *ex* Tiger Fish *-1985* *ex* Tiger Fish II *-1983* **SEACOR Smit Offshore Ltd** SEACOR Marine (West Africa) SAS *Moroni* *Union of Comoros* MMSI: 616521000	1,693 507 1,418	Class: (LR) (BV) ✠ Classed LR until 3/93	**1982-11 Gul Engineering Pte Ltd — Singapore** Yd No: 6011 Loa 59.64 Br ex 15.70 Dght 5.314 Lbp 51.97 Br md 15.00 Dpth 6.51 Welded, 1 dk	**(B21B20A) Anchor Handling Tug Supply** Passengers: berths: 12 Ice Capable	**4 oil engines** with clutches, flexible couplings & sr geared to sc. shafts driving 2 CP propellers Total Power: 5,880kW (7,996hp) 12.0kn Wichmann 5AXAG 4 x 2 Stroke 5 Cy. 300 x 450 each-1470kW (1999bhp) Wichmann Motorfabrikk AS-Norway AuxGen: 2 x 752kW 400V 50Hz a.c, 1 x 370kW 400V 50Hz a.c Thrusters: 1 Thwart. CP thruster (f); 1 Tunnel thruster (a) Fuel: 563.0 (d.f.)
8614144 - -	**TIGER IV** *ex* Taupo Cat *-1995* **Fullers Cruises Northland Ltd** - *Fiji*	*194* 145 52 T/cm 2.1	Class: (NV)	1987-06 **North Queensland Engineers & Agents Pty Ltd — Cairns QLD** Yd No: 148 Loa 25.16 Br ex 8.94 Dght 1.890 Lbp 21.50 Br md 8.72 Dpth 2.56 Welded, 1 dk	**(A37B2PS) Passenger Ship** Hull Material: Aluminium Alloy Passengers: unberthed: 205	**2 oil engines** with clutches, flexible couplings & sr reverse geared to sc. shafts driving 2 FP propellers Total Power: 1,510kW (2,052hp) 27.0kn MWM TBD234V16 2 x Vee 4 Stroke 16 Cy. 128 x 140 each-755kW (1026bhp) Motoren Werke Mannheim AG (MWM)-West Germany AuxGen: 2 x 60kW 440V 50Hz a.c Fuel: 11.0 (d.f.) 1.0pd
9229609 *S6AR8* -	**TIGER MANGO** *ex* New Dynamic *-2012* **New Dynamic Shipping Pte Ltd** Wilhelmsen Ship Management Singapore Pte Ltd SatCom: Inmarsat C 456418110 *Singapore* *Singapore* MMSI: 564181000 Official number: 390725	13,764 5,157 16,400	Class: AB	2001-05 **Jurong Shipyard Pte Ltd — Singapore** Yd No: 1059 Loa 154.00 (BB) Br ex 25.04 Dght 9.500 Lbp 145.00 Br md 25.00 Dpth 13.60 Welded, 1 dk	**(A33A2CC) Container Ship (Fully Cellular)** TEU 1078 incl 150 ref C. Cranes: 2x40t	**1 oil engine** driving 1 FP propeller Total Power: 13,387kW (18,201hp) 19.5kn B&W 7L60MC 1 x 2 Stroke 7 Cy. 600 x 1944 13387kW (18201bhp) Hudong Heavy Machinery Co Ltd-China AuxGen: 3 x 830kW a.c Thrusters: 1 Tunnel thruster (f)
9619878 *VRKE5* -	**TIGER NORTH** *ex* Bei Fang Hu *-2013* **Loyal Easy Industrial Ltd** Greathorse International Ship Management Co Ltd *Hong Kong* *Hong Kong* MMSI: 477631300 Official number: HK-3431	42,114 25,821 76,000	Class: NV	2013-07 **Shanhaiguan Shipbuilding Industry Co Ltd — Qinhuangdao HE** Yd No: BC760-04 Loa 225.00 (BB) Br ex 32.30 Dght 14.200 Lbp 219.00 Br md 32.26 Dpth 19.60 Welded, 1 dk	**(A21A2BC) Bulk Carrier** Grain: 90,100 Compartments: 7 Ho, ER 7 Ha: ER	**1 oil engine** driving 1 FP propeller Total Power: 9,108kW (12,383hp) 14.5kn Wartsila 5RT-flex58T 1 x 2 Stroke 5 Cy. 580 x 2416 9108kW (12383bhp) Yichang Marine Diesel Engine Co Ltd-China AuxGen: 3 x a.c
9071210 *9VMJ3* -	**TIGER PEARL** *ex* Cebu Trader *-2012* *ex* Tiger Pearl *-2011* *ex* Prosperity Container *-2003* **II Open Waters Tiger Pearl Pte Ltd** Hanse Bereederungs GmbH *Singapore* *Singapore* MMSI: 565912000 Official number: 394274	17,125 6,816 24,136	Class: GL (AB) (CR)	1994-07 **Shin Kurushima Dockyard Co. Ltd. — Onishi** Yd No: 2793 Loa 182.83 (BB) Br ex - Dght 9.530 Lbp 170.00 Br md 28.00 Dpth 14.00 Welded, 1 dk	**(A33A2CC) Container Ship (Fully Cellular)** TEU 1510 C Ho 558 TEU C Dk 952 TEU incl 100 ref C.	**1 oil engine** driving 1 FP propeller Total Power: 11,680kW (15,880hp) 19.0kn B&W 6S60MC 1 x 2 Stroke 6 Cy. 600 x 2292 11680kW (15880bhp) Mitsui Engineering & Shipbuilding CLtd-Japan AuxGen: 3 x 560kW 440/220V a.c
7309467 *WX9273* -	**TIGER POINT** **Omega Protein Inc** *Cameron, LA* *United States of America* MMSI: 367002630 Official number: 508606	*537* 366 -		1967 **Burton Shipyard Co., Inc. — Port Arthur, Tx** Yd No: 425 L reg 49.57 Br ex 10.09 Dght - Lbp - Br md - Dpth 3.61 Welded	**(B11B2FV) Fishing Vessel**	**1 oil engine** driving 1 FP propeller Total Power: 1,125kW (1,530hp)
8992936 *WDC6782* -	**TIGER PRIDE** *ex* Durdy Dudley *-2005* **Tiger Tugz LLC** *Morgan City, LA* *United States of America* MMSI: 367061250 Official number: 629534	*118* 80 -		1980-01 **in the United States of America** Yd No: 12 L reg 17.98 Br ex - Dght - Lbp - Br md 7.35 Dpth 2.74 Welded, 1 dk	**(B32B2SP) Pusher Tug**	**2 oil engines** reduction geared to sc. shafts driving 2 FP propellers Total Power: 882kW (1,200hp) Cummins KTA-19-M3 2 x 4 Stroke 6 Cy. 159 x 159 each-441kW (600bhp) (new engine 1980) Cummins Engine Co Inc-USA
9301108 *A8ZB6* -	**TIGER RIVER** *ex* Tiger Spring *-2011* *ex* Beluga Motivation *-2009* *ex* Zealand *-2008* *ex* OOCL Sweden *-2007* *completed as* Beluga Motivation *-2006* **HCI Capital AG** Drevin Bereederungs GmbH & Co KG *Monrovia* *Liberia* MMSI: 636092241 Official number: 92241	8,971 4,776 10,700 T/cm 27.3	Class: GL	2006-08 **OAO Damen Shipyards Okean — Nikolayev** (Hull) Yd No: 9120 2006-08 **Volharding Shipyards B.V. — Foxhol** Yd No: 568 Loa 154.85 (BB) Br ex - Dght 6.974 Lbp 144.80 Br md 21.50 Dpth 9.30 Welded, 1 dk	**(A33A2CC) Container Ship (Fully Cellular)** Double Bottom Entire Compartment Length TEU 917 C Ho 267 TEU C Dk 650 TEU incl 200 ref C. Compartments: 4 Cell Ho, ER 4 Ha: (12.7 x 18.5)ER 3 (25.5 x 18.5) Ice Capable	**1 oil engine** reduction geared to sc. shaft driving 1 CP propeller Total Power: 7,999kW (10,875hp) 14.0kn MaK 8M43 1 x 4 Stroke 8 Cy. 430 x 610 7999kW (10875bhp) Caterpillar Motoren GmbH & Co. KG-Germany AuxGen: 2 x 416kW a.c, 1 x 1150kW a.c Thrusters: 1 Thwart. CP thruster (f) Fuel: 93.5 (d.f.) 703.0 (r.f.)
8764963 *3FZX* -	**TIGER SHARK** *ex* Ana *-2005* **Hercules Liftboat Co LLC** - *Panama* *Panama* Official number: 45013PEXT	1,403 420 -		2001 **Conrad Industries, Inc. — Morgan City, La** Yd No: 692 Loa 41.75 Br ex - Dght - Lbp 36.57 Br md 23.77 Dpth 4.26 Welded, 1 dk	**(B22A2ZM) Offshore Construction Vessel, jack up**	**2 oil engines** reduction geared to sc. shafts driving 2 Propellers Total Power: 1,544kW (2,100hp) 7.5kn Caterpillar 3508 2 x Vee 4 Stroke 8 Cy. 170 x 190 each-772kW (1050bhp) Caterpillar Inc-USA
7604049 *WYT9707* -	**TIGER SHARK** *ex* Sandy Marie *-2005* *ex* Capt. Thao *-2001* *ex* Sandy Marie *-1999* **Rocky Lee Curtis** *Biloxi, MS* *United States of America* Official number: 554127	*114* 77 -		1974 **S & R Boat Builders, Inc. — Bayou La Batre, Al** Yd No: 6 L reg 21.98 Br ex - Dght - Lbp - Br md 6.77 Dpth 3.38 Welded, 1 dk	**(B11A2FT) Trawler**	**1 oil engine** driving 1 FP propeller Total Power: 257kW (349hp)
7212420 *WUY5990* -	**TIGER SHOAL** *ex* Arabian Seahorse *-1986* **Omega Protein Inc** *Cameron, LA* *United States of America* Official number: 538363	*384* 261 610	Class: (AB)	1972-03 **Burton Shipyard Co., Inc. — Port Arthur, Tx** Yd No: 483 Converted From: Offshore Tug/Supply Ship-1986 Loa 53.65 Br ex 11.69 Dght 3.372 Lbp 50.88 Br md 11.59 Dpth 3.97 Welded, 1 dk	**(B11B2FV) Fishing Vessel**	**2 oil engines** driving 2 FP propellers Total Power: 1,654kW (2,248hp) 10.0kn Caterpillar D399SCAC 2 x Vee 4 Stroke 16 Cy. 159 x 203 each-827kW (1124bhp) (Re-engined ,made 1972, Reconditioned & fitted 1986) Caterpillar Tractor Co-USA AuxGen: 2 x 75kW Fuel: 253.0 (d.f.)
9619854 *VRKE3* -	**TIGER SOUTH** *launched as* Nan Fang Hu *-2013* **Great Star Industrial Ltd** Greathorse International Ship Management Co Ltd *Hong Kong* *Hong Kong* MMSI: 477832600 Official number: HK-3429	42,114 25,821 76,000	Class: NV	2013-04 **Shanhaiguan Shipbuilding Industry Co Ltd — Qinhuangdao HE** Yd No: BC760-02 Loa 225.00 (BB) Br ex 32.68 Dght 14.200 Lbp 219.00 Br md 32.26 Dpth 19.60 Welded, 1 dk	**(A21A2BC) Bulk Carrier** Grain: 90,100 Compartments: 7 Ho, ER 7 Ha: ER	**1 oil engine** driving 1 FP propeller Total Power: 9,108kW (12,383hp) 14.5kn Wartsila 5RT-flex58T 1 x 2 Stroke 5 Cy. 580 x 2416 9108kW (12383bhp) Yichang Marine Diesel Engine Co Ltd-China AuxGen: 3 x a.c

IMO / Call sign	Name / Owner / Manager / Flag	Tonnage	Class	Builder / Dimensions	Type / Cargo	Machinery
9353747 *V2EQ5* -	**TIGER SPIRIT** *ex* Tiger Cliff *-2013* *ex* SITC Melody *-2011* *launched as* Unisky *-2009* **Unitas Schiffahrtsges mbH & Co ms 'Unisky' KG** Unitas Shipmanagement GmbH & Co KG *Saint John's* *Antigua & Barbuda* MMSI: 305510000 Official number: 4700	**9,056** 4,776 10,600	Class: BV	**2009-12 Sainty Shipbuilding (Yangzhou) Corp Ltd — Yizheng JS** (Hull) Yd No: 07STIG222 **2009-12 Volharding Shipyards B.V. — Foxhol** Yd No: 590 Loa 154.85 (BB) Br ex - Dght 6.970 Lbp 144.90 Br md 21.50 Dpth 9.30 Welded, 1 dk	**(A33A2CC) Container Ship (Fully Cellular)** TEU 1012 incl 200 ref C. Compartments: 5 Cell Ho, ER Ice Capable	**1 oil engine** reduction geared to sc. shaft driving 1 CP propeller Total Power: 8,000kW (10,877hp) 18.0kn MaK 8M43C 1 x 4 Stroke 8 Cy. 430 x 610 8000kW (10877bhp) Caterpillar Motoren GmbH & Co. KG-Germany AuxGen: 1 x 1200kW 440/230V 60Hz a.c, 2 x 416kW 440/230V 60Hz a.c Thrusters: 1 Thwart. CP thruster (f)
9489120 *VRLF2* -	**TIGER SPRING** *ex* New Wealth *-2012* *ex* Ubt Sea *-2009* **Tiger Ship No 1 Ltd** Greathorse International Ship Management Co Ltd *Hong Kong* *Hong Kong* MMSI: 477335100	**6,152** 2,883 9,380 T/cm 17.8	Class: BV	**2009-11 Dongfang Shipbuilding Group Co Ltd — Yueqing ZJ** Yd No: DF92-1 Loa 117.60 (BB) Br ex - Dght 7.588 Lbp 109.60 Br md 19.00 Dpth 10.00 Welded, 1 dk	**(A12B2TR) Chemical/Products Tanker** Double Hull (13F) Liq: 10,084; Liq (Oil): 10,084 Compartments: 10 Wing Ta, 2 Wing Slop Ta, ER 10 Cargo Pump (s): 6x100m³/hr, 4x300m³/hr Manifold: Bow/CM: 56.5m	**1 oil engine** reduction geared to sc. shaft driving 1 FP propeller Total Power: 2,970kW (4,038hp) 13.5kn MaK 9M25C 1 x 4 Stroke 9 Cy. 255 x 400 2970kW (4038bhp) Caterpillar Motoren GmbH & Co. KG-Germany AuxGen: 3 x 445kW 60Hz a.c Thrusters: 1 Tunnel thruster (f) Fuel: 100.0 (d.f.) 400.0 (r.f.)
8115588 *9WCQ8* -	**TIGER SPRING** *ex* Confidence *-2001* *ex* Tiger Spring *-2000* *ex* Tiger Star *-1999* *ex* Builder Pioneer *-1998* *ex* Alkaid *-1997* *ex* Pul Aman *-1991* *ex* Alkaid *-1990* *ex* ScanDutch Orient *-1990* *ex* Alkaid *-1989* *ex* Schwabenland *-1988* *ex* Bumi Pertiwi *-1987* *ex* Ganges Pioneer *-1986* *ex* Schwabenland *-1985* **Chong Fui Shipping & Forwarding Sdn Bhd** - *Kota Kinabalu* *Malaysia* MMSI: 533022700 Official number: 328018	**4,455** 2,409 6,154	Class: (GL)	**1983-12 Zhonghua Shipyard — Shanghai** Yd No: 8106 Loa 105.82 (BB) Br ex 17.56 Dght 6.901 Lbp 96.02 Br md 17.51 Dpth 9.02 Welded, 2 dks	**(A31A2GX) General Cargo Ship** Grain: 7,930 TEU 343 C. 343/20' (40') Compartments: 2 Ho, ER 2 Ha: (25.8 x 13.9) (38.4 x 13.9)ER Cranes: 2x36t Ice Capable	**1 oil engine** driving 1 CP propeller Total Power: 2,868kW (3,899hp) 13.5kn Mitsubishi 6UEC37/88H 1 x 2 Stroke 6 Cy. 370 x 880 2868kW (3899bhp) Akasaka Tekkosho KK (Akasaka DieselLtd)-Japan Thrusters: 1 Thwart. FP thruster (f)
9084891 *9MLV2* -	**TIGER STAR** *ex* Nissho Maru *-2011* **Trans Ocean Environment Sdn Bhd** Chancellor Maritime & Offshore Sdn Bhd *Port Klang* *Malaysia* MMSI: 533062300 Official number: 334358	*453* - 905		**1994-04 K.K. Miura Zosensho — Saiki** Yd No: 1088 Loa 60.50 Br ex 9.80 Dght 3.359 Lbp 54.00 Br md 9.50 Dpth 4.00 Welded\, 1 dk	**(A13B2TP) Products Tanker**	**1 oil engine** geared to sc. shaft driving 1 FP propeller Total Power: 1,030kW (1,400hp) Hanshin LH28G 1 x 4 Stroke 6 Cy. 280 x 460 1030kW (1400bhp) The Hanshin Diesel Works Ltd-Japan
9360520 *V2EQ6* -	**TIGER STREAM** *ex* Unisea *-2013* *ex* SITC Miracle *-2011* *launched as* Unisea *-2010* **Unitas Schiffahrtsges mbH & Co ms 'Unisea' KG** Unitas Shipmanagement GmbH & Co KG *Saint John's* *Antigua & Barbuda* MMSI: 305517000	**9,056** 4,776 10,600	Class: BV	**2010-01 Sainty Shipbuilding (Yangzhou) Corp Ltd — Yizheng JS** (Hull) Yd No: 07STIG223 **2010-01 Volharding Shipyards B.V. — Foxhol** Yd No: 621 Loa 154.85 (BB) Br ex - Dght 6.980 Lbp 144.90 Br md 21.50 Dpth 9.30 Welded, 1 dk	**(A33A2CC) Container Ship (Fully Cellular)** TEU 1012 incl 200 ref C. Compartments: 4 Cell Ho, ER Ice Capable	**1 oil engine** reduction geared to sc. shaft driving 1 CP propeller Total Power: 8,000kW (10,877hp) 18.0kn MaK 8M43C 1 x 4 Stroke 8 Cy. 430 x 610 8000kW (10877bhp) Caterpillar Motoren GmbH & Co. KG-Germany AuxGen: 1 x 1200kW 440V 60Hz a.c, 2 x 416kW 440V 60Hz a.c Thrusters: 1 Thwart. CP thruster (f)
9510553 *VRLF5* -	**TIGER SUMMER** *ex* New Success *-2012* **Tiger Ship No 2 Ltd** Greathorse International Ship Management Co Ltd *Hong Kong* *Hong Kong* MMSI: 477305300 Official number: HK-3651	**6,153** 2,915 9,118 T/cm 18.0	Class: BV	**2009-11 Dongfang Shipbuilding Group Co Ltd — Yueqing ZJ** Yd No: DF90-8 Loa 117.60 (BB) Br ex - Dght 7.500 Lbp 109.60 Br md 19.00 Dpth 10.00 Welded, 1 dk	**(A12B2TR) Chemical/Products Tanker** Double Hull (13F) Liq: 9,402; Liq (Oil): 9,402 Compartments: 10 Wing Ta, 2 Wing Slop Ta, ER 10 Cargo Pump (s): 10x300m³/hr Manifold: Bow/CM: 56.3m Ice Capable	**1 oil engine** reduction geared to sc. shaft driving 1 FP propeller Total Power: 2,970kW (4,038hp) 13.0kn MaK 9M25C 1 x 4 Stroke 9 Cy. 255 x 400 2970kW (4038bhp) Caterpillar Motoren GmbH & Co. KG-Germany AuxGen: 3 x 520kW 60Hz a.c Thrusters: 1 Tunnel thruster (f) Fuel: 40.0 (d.f.) 325.0 (r.f.)
9630731 *VRLT4* -	**TIGER TIAN** **Tiger Gemini Ltd** Navig8 Bulk Asia Pte Ltd *Hong Kong* *Hong Kong* MMSI: 477224900 Official number: HK-3762	**32,839** 19,559 58,000 T/cm 59.2	Class: BV	**2013-01 Zhejiang Shipbuilding Co Ltd — Fenghua ZJ** Yd No: ZJB10-195 Loa 189.99 (BB) Br ex - Dght 12.950 Lbp 185.00 Br md 32.26 Dpth 18.00 Welded, 1 dk	**(A21A2BC) Bulk Carrier** Grain: 71,549; Bale: 69,760 Compartments: 5 Ho, ER 5 Ha: ER Cranes: 4x35t	**1 oil engine** driving 1 FP propeller Total Power: 8,700kW (11,829hp) 14.3kn MAN-B&W 6S50MC-C 1 x 2 Stroke 6 Cy. 500 x 2000 8700kW (11829bhp) Doosan Engine Co Ltd-South Korea AuxGen: 3 x 610kW 60Hz a.c Fuel: 2370.0
9279135 - -	**TIGER V** *ex* Stewart Islander *-2005* - -	**129** 58 -	Class: (LR) ✠ Classed LR until 28/11/05	**2004-08 Sabre Catamarans Pty Ltd — Fremantle WA** Yd No: 145 Loa 22.50 Br ex 5.00 Dght 1.290 Lbp 19.60 Br md 4.80 Dpth 2.85 Welded, 1 dk	**(A37B2PS) Passenger Ship** Hull Material: Aluminium Alloy	**2 oil engines** with clutches & sr reverse geared to sc. shafts driving 2 FP propellers Total Power: 1,576kW (2,142hp) M.T.U. 12V2000M70 2 x Vee 4 Stroke 12 Cy. 130 x 150 each-788kW (1071bhp) MTU Friedrichshafen GmbH-Friedrichshafen AuxGen: 2 x 35kW 415V 50Hz a.c
9619866 *VRKE4* -	**TIGER WEST** **Most Famous Industrial Ltd** Greathorse International Ship Management Co Ltd *Hong Kong* *Hong Kong* MMSI: 477631200 Official number: HK-3430	**42,114** 25,821 76,000	Class: NV	**2013-06 Shanhaiguan Shipbuilding Industry Co Ltd — Qinhuangdao HE** Yd No: BC760-03 Loa 225.00 (BB) Br ex 32.68 Dght 14.200 Lbp 219.00 Br md 32.26 Dpth 19.60 Welded, 1 dk	**(A21A2BC) Bulk Carrier** Grain: 90,100 Compartments: 7 Ho, ER 7 Ha: ER	**1 oil engine** driving 1 FP propeller Total Power: 9,108kW (12,383hp) 14.5kn Wartsila 5RT-flex58T 1 x 2 Stroke 5 Cy. 580 x 2416 9108kW (12383bhp) Yichang Marine Diesel Engine Co Ltd-China AuxGen: 3 x a.c
9542910 *VRLF4* -	**TIGER WINTER** *ex* Mount Tianzhu *-2012* *ex* Ievoli Summer *-2011* **Tiger Ship No 4 Ltd** Greathorse International Ship Management Co Ltd *Hong Kong* *Hong Kong* MMSI: 477334800	**6,445** 2,914 9,055 T/cm 18.7	Class: BV	**2011-01 Dongfang Shipbuilding Group Co Ltd — Yueqing ZJ** Yd No: DF90-5 Loa 117.60 (BB) Br ex - Dght 7.500 Lbp 109.60 Br md 19.00 Dpth 10.00 Welded, 1 dk	**(A12B2TR) Chemical/Products Tanker** Double Hull (13F) Liq: 10,088; Liq (Oil): 10,088 Cargo Heating Coils Compartments: 5 Wing Ta, 5 Wing Ta, 1 Wing Slop Ta, 1 Wing Slop Ta, ER 10 Cargo Pump (s): 10x300m³/hr Manifold: Bow/CM: 60m	**1 oil engine** reduction geared to sc. shaft driving 1 FP propeller Total Power: 2,970kW (4,038hp) 13.0kn MaK 9M25C 1 x 4 Stroke 9 Cy. 255 x 400 2970kW (4038bhp) Caterpillar Motoren GmbH & Co. KG-Germany AuxGen: 3 x 520kW 450V 60Hz a.c Thrusters: 1 Tunnel thruster (f) Fuel: 50.0 (d.f.) 406.0 (r.f.)
8965024 *HO6242* -	**TIGERFISH** *ex* Glenn K. Craig *-2006* **Hercules Oilfield Services Ltd** Hercules Liftboat Co LLC *Panama* *Panama* Official number: 1169082I	*209* 106 -		**1980 Sun Contractors, Inc. — Harvey, La** L reg 22.56 Br ex - Dght - Lbp - Br md 11.58 Dpth 2.13 Welded, 1 dk	**(B22A2ZM) Offshore Construction Vessel, jack up**	**2 oil engines** driving 2 FP propellers Total Power: 706kW (960hp) 8.0kn General Motors 2 x each-353kW (480bhp) General Motors Corp-USA
8705137 *FIAV* DP 651429	**TIGER'S 2** **Tigers'II JPS** - *Dieppe* *France* MMSI: 227559000 Official number: 651429	**193** - -		**1986-12 Forges Caloin — Etaples** Yd No: 47 Loa 24.97 Br ex 7.27 Dght 3.201 Lbp 22.08 Br md 7.21 Dpth 4.02 Welded, 1 dk	**(B11A2FS) Stern Trawler** Ins: 120	**1 oil engine** with clutches, flexible couplings & sr geared to sc. shaft driving 1 CP propeller Total Power: 441kW (600hp) Kromhout 6FHD240 1 x 4 Stroke 6 Cy. 240 x 260 441kW (600bhp) Stork Werkspoor Diesel BV-Netherlands
5225904 *ERPA* -	**TIGHNABRUAICH** *ex* Brake *-2012* *ex* Marlies *-1990* **Melbar Trading SA** Moon Stone Shipping Co SA *Giurgiulesti* *Moldova* MMSI: 214181601	**603** 351 817	Class: MB (GL)	**1957-06 C. Luehring — Brake** Yd No: 5604 Lengthened-1978 Loa 57.50 Br ex 8.54 Dght 3.410 Lbp 52.25 Br md 8.49 Dpth 3.46 Riveted\Welded, 1 dk	**(A31A2GX) General Cargo Ship** Grain: 850; Bale: 770 Compartments: 1 Ho, ER 1 Ha: (28.8 x 5.0)ER Ice Capable	**1 oil engine** driving 1 FP propeller Total Power: 265kW (360hp) 9.5kn MaK MSU423 1 x 4 Stroke 6 Cy. 290 x 420 265kW (360bhp) Maschinenbau Kiel AG (MaK)-Kiel
8108066 *UHWG* -	**TIGIL** *ex* Fierce Sea *-2000* *ex* Meghan Hope *-1996* *ex* PBR/360 *-1989* **Government of The Russian Federation** Aleut Ltd *Petropavlovsk-Kamchatskiy* *Russia* MMSI: 273847020 Official number: 814299	**833** 320 1,181	Class: RS (AB)	**1981-01 Zigler Shipyards Inc — Jennings LA** Yd No: 279 Converted From: Offshore Tug/Supply Ship-1989 Loa 50.30 Br ex 11.61 Dght 3.555 Lbp 47.10 Br md 11.59 Dpth 3.97 Welded, 1 dk	**(B11B2FV) Fishing Vessel**	**2 oil engines** reverse reduction geared to sc. shafts driving 2 FP propellers Total Power: 1,368kW (1,860hp) 12.0kn G.M. (Detroit Diesel) 16V-149 2 x Vee 2 Stroke 16 Cy. 146 x 146 each-684kW (930bhp) General Motors Detroit DieselAllison Divn-USA AuxGen: 2 x 99kW 440V 60Hz a.c Thrusters: 1 Thwart. FP thruster (f) Fuel: 400.0 (d.f.)

IMO / Call sign / Flag	Name / Owner / Port	Tonnage	Class	Builder / Dimensions	Type	Machinery
7341130 - -	**TIGRAN** *ex* Kapitan Volodin *-1999* *ex* Erland *-1988* **Justmore Trading Ltd** -	**298** 89 103	Class: RS (LR) ✠ Classed LR until 14/1/97	**1974**-05 **Richards (Shipbuilders) Ltd — Lowestoft** Yd No: 514 Loa 33.02 Br ex 10.06 Dght 4.300 Lbp 29.37 Br md 9.50 Dpth 5.31 Welded, 1 dk	**(B32A2ST) Tug** Ice Capable	**1 oil engine** sr geared to sc. shaft driving 1 CP propeller Total Power: 2,471kW (3,360hp) 13.5kn Ruston 12ATCM 1 x Vee 4 Stroke 12 Cy. 318 x 368 2471kW (3360bhp) Ruston Paxman Diesels Ltd.-Colchester AuxGen: 2 x 100kW 380V 50Hz a.c Thrusters: 1 Thwart. FP thruster (f) Fuel: 65.0 (d.f.)
8728880 *UCUX* -	**TIGRAN MARTIROSYAN** *ex* Staratelnyy *-2008* **PJSC 'Fleet of Novorossiysk Commercial Sea Port'** - *Novorossiysk* *Russia* MMSI: 273152100 Official number: 885580	**165** 49 27	Class: RS	**1989**-06 **RO Brodogradiliste Novi Sad — Novi Sad** Yd No: 271 Loa 23.50 Br ex 9.00 Dght 3.250 Lbp 21.01 Br md - Dpth 3.50 Welded, 1 dk	**(B32B2SP) Pusher Tug**	**2 oil engines** geared to sc. shafts driving 2 Directional propellers Total Power: 600kW (816hp) 10.0kn MAN D2840LE 2 x Vee 4 Stroke 10 Cy. 128 x 142 each-300kW (408bhp) MAN Nutzfahrzeuge AG-Nuernberg AuxGen: 2 x 50kW a.c
9394480 *UBGF7*	**TIGRAN MARTIROSYAN** **Elv Shipping Group Ltd** Era Ltd *Novorossiysk* *Russia* MMSI: 273332610	**2,985** 1,363 4,807	Class: RS (CC)	**2006**-09 **Wenling Xingyuan Shipbuilding & Repair Co Ltd — Wenling ZJ** Yd No: 0501 Loa 99.86 Br ex 15.20 Dght 6.250 Lbp 93.00 Br md 15.20 Dpth 7.60 Welded, 1 dk	**(A13B2TP) Products Tanker** Double Hull (13F) Liq: 4,819; Liq (Oil): 4,819 Compartments: 10 Wing Ta, ER Ice Capable	**1 oil engine** reduction geared to sc. shaft driving 1 FP propeller Total Power: 1,765kW (2,400hp) 11.0kn Chinese Std. Type G8300ZC 1 x 4 Stroke 8 Cy. 300 x 380 1765kW (2400bhp) Wuxi Antai Power Machinery Co Ltd-China AuxGen: 2 x 256kW a.c Fuel: 178.0 (d.f.)
6617673 - TM84	**TIGRE 1** *ex* Leslie *-1979* **Alfonso Medina Rojas** - *Supe* *Peru* Official number: SE-004298-PM	*164* 63 -	Class: (LR) ✠ Classed LR until 31/10/75	**1966**-12 **Fabricaciones Metallicas E.P.S. (FABRIMET) — Callao** Yd No: 325 Loa 25.20 Br ex 7.14 Dght 3.175 Lbp 21.49 Br md 7.01 Dpth 3.46 Welded, 1 dk	**(B11B2FV) Fishing Vessel**	**1 oil engine** reverse reduction geared to sc. shaft driving 1 FP propeller Total Power: 386kW (525hp) G.M. (Detroit Diesel) 12V-71-N 1 x Vee 2 Stroke 12 Cy. 108 x 127 386kW (525bhp) General Motors Corp-USA
6617697 - -	**TIGRE 2** *ex* Mily *-1979* - -	*120* - -	Class: (LR) ✠ Classed LR until 14/5/76	**1966**-12 **Fabricaciones Metallicas E.P.S. (FABRIMET) — Callao** Yd No: 327 Loa 25.20 Br ex 7.14 Dght 2.693 Lbp 21.49 Br md 7.01 Dpth 3.46 Welded, 1 dk	**(B11B2FV) Fishing Vessel**	**1 oil engine** reverse reduction geared to sc. shaft driving 1 FP propeller Total Power: 386kW (525hp) G.M. (Detroit Diesel) 12V-71-N 1 x Vee 2 Stroke 12 Cy. 108 x 127 386kW (525bhp) General Motors Corp-USA
6704880 - -	**TIGRE 4** *ex* Milagro I *-1979* - -	*120* - -	Class: (LR) ✠ Classed LR until 3/68	**1967**-01 **Fabricaciones Metallicas E.P.S. (FABRIMET) — Callao** Yd No: 342 Loa 25.20 Br ex 7.14 Dght 3.175 Lbp 21.49 Br md 7.01 Dpth 3.46 Welded, 1 dk	**(B11B2FV) Fishing Vessel**	**1 oil engine** reverse reduction geared to sc. shaft driving 1 FP propeller Total Power: 386kW (525hp) G.M. (Detroit Diesel) 12V-71-N 1 x Vee 2 Stroke 12 Cy. 108 x 127 386kW (525bhp) General Motors Corp-USA
6705078 - -	**TIGRE 5** *ex* Milagro II *-1979* **Pesquera San Antonio-Pisco SA** - *Mollendo* *Peru* Official number: MO-005475-PM	*164* 62 -	Class: (LR) ✠ Classed LR until 3/68	**1967**-01 **Fabricaciones Metallicas E.P.S. (FABRIMET) — Callao** Yd No: 343 Loa 25.20 Br ex 7.14 Dght 3.175 Lbp 21.49 Br md 7.01 Dpth 3.46 Welded, 1 dk	**(B11B2FV) Fishing Vessel**	**1 oil engine** reverse reduction geared to sc. shaft driving 1 FP propeller Total Power: 386kW (525hp) G.M. (Detroit Diesel) 12V-71-N 1 x Vee 2 Stroke 12 Cy. 108 x 127 386kW (525bhp) General Motors Corp-USA
6705341 - -	**TIGRE 6** *ex* Milagro III *-1979* - -	*120* - -	Class: (LR) ✠ Classed LR until 3/68	**1967**-01 **Fabricaciones Metallicas E.P.S. (FABRIMET) — Callao** Yd No: 346 Loa 25.20 Br ex 7.14 Dght 3.175 Lbp 21.49 Br md 7.01 Dpth 3.46 Welded, 1 dk	**(B11B2FV) Fishing Vessel**	**1 oil engine** reverse reduction geared to sc. shaft driving 1 FP propeller Total Power: 386kW (525hp) G.M. (Detroit Diesel) 12V-71-N 1 x Vee 2 Stroke 12 Cy. 108 x 127 386kW (525bhp) General Motors Corp-USA
6712485 - -	**TIGRE 7** *ex* Milagro IV *-1979* - -	*120* - -	Class: (LR) ✠ Classed LR until 8/68	**1967**-04 **Fabricaciones Metallicas E.P.S. (FABRIMET) — Callao** Yd No: 351 Loa 25.20 Br ex 7.14 Dght 3.175 Lbp 21.49 Br md 7.01 Dpth 3.46 Welded, 1 dk	**(B11B2FV) Fishing Vessel**	**1 oil engine** reverse reduction geared to sc. shaft driving 1 FP propeller Total Power: 386kW (525hp) G.M. (Detroit Diesel) 12V-71-N 1 x Vee 2 Stroke 12 Cy. 108 x 127 386kW (525bhp) General Motors Corp-USA
6713829 - -	**TIGRE 8** *ex* Milagro V *-1979* **Pesquera San Martin de Porres SCR Ltda** - *Ilo* *Peru* Official number: IO-000963-PM	*164* 66 -	Class: (LR) ✠ Classed LR until 8/68	**1967**-05 **Fabricaciones Metallicas E.P.S. (FABRIMET) — Callao** Yd No: 353 Loa 25.15 Br ex 7.14 Dght 3.175 Lbp 21.49 Br md 7.01 Dpth 3.46 Welded, 1 dk	**(B11B2FV) Fishing Vessel**	**1 oil engine** reverse reduction geared to sc. shaft driving 1 FP propeller Total Power: 386kW (525hp) G.M. (Detroit Diesel) 12V-71-N 1 x Vee 2 Stroke 12 Cy. 108 x 127 386kW (525bhp) General Motors Corp-USA
1007809 - -	**TIGRE D'OR** **Tigre D'Or**	**107** 32 -	Class: (LR) ✠ Classed LR until 6/5/11	**2004**-07 **Scheepswerf Made B.V. — Made** (Hull) Yd No: 1012 **2004**-07 **Scheepsbouw en Machinefabriek Hakvoort B.V. — Monnickendam** Yd No: 237 Loa 29.88 Br ex 4.90 Dght 1.250 Lbp 28.40 Br md 4.68 Dpth 1.60 Welded, 1 dk	**(X11A2YP) Yacht**	**2 diesel electric oil engines** driving 2 gen. each 55kW 400V a.c Connecting to 2 elec. motors each (55kW) driving 1 FP propeller Total Power: 110kW (150hp) 8.0kn Lugger MP 455H 2 x 4 Stroke 4 Cy. 106 x 127 each-55kW (75bhp) Alaska Diesel Electric Inc-USA Thrusters: 1 Thwart. FP thruster (f)
9130042 - -	**TIGRE III** - -	**290** - 300		**1995**-09 **Remesa Astilleros S.A. — Callao** Yd No: 78 Loa - Br ex - Dght - Lbp - Br md - Dpth - Welded, 1 dk	**(B11B2FV) Fishing Vessel**	**1 oil engine** driving 1 FP propeller
7208596 *VQPY2* -	**TIGRILLO** *ex* Marseillais 15 *-1979* **Purple Water Ltd** Navigest Trust Services & Ship Management SA *London* *United Kingdom* MMSI: 235009958 Official number: 907080	**264** 79	Class: BV	**1972 Ziegler Freres — Dunkerque** Yd No: 184 Loa 31.63 Br ex 9.25 Dght - Lbp 29.37 Br md 8.79 Dpth 3.66 Welded, 1 dk	**(B32A2ST) Tug**	**2 oil engines** geared to sc. shaft driving 1 FP propeller Total Power: 1,838kW (2,498hp) 11.5kn Crepelle 8SN1 2 x 4 Stroke 8 Cy. 260 x 280 each-919kW (1249bhp) Crepelle et Cie-France Fuel: 90.0 (d.f.)
8727032 - -	**TIGRIS** **PJSC 'Fleet of Novorossiysk Commercial Sea Port'** - *Novorossiysk* *Russia* MMSI: 273459330	**270** 81 89	Class: RS	**1987**-07 **Brodogradiliste 'Tito' — Belgrade** Yd No: 1118 Loa 35.78 Br ex 9.49 Dght 3.280 Lbp 30.10 Br md 9.00 Dpth 4.50 Welded, 1 dk	**(B32A2ST) Tug** Ice Capable	**2 oil engines** driving 1 CP propeller Total Power: 1,854kW (2,520hp) 13.5kn Sulzer 6ASL25/30 2 x 4 Stroke 6 Cy. 250 x 300 each-927kW (1260bhp) in Yugoslavia AuxGen: 1 x 150kW a.c
8931750 - -	**TIGRIS** **Port of Yuzhnyy** - *Yuzhnyy* *Ukraine* Official number: 782793	*264* - 76	Class: (RS)	**1979**-09 **Brodogradiliste 'Tito' — Belgrade** Yd No: 1035 Loa 35.83 Br ex 9.30 Dght 3.040 Lbp 32.07 Br md - Dpth 4.50 Welded, 1 dk	**(B32A2ST) Tug** Ice Capable	**2 oil engines** geared to sc. shaft driving 1 CP propeller Total Power: 1,854kW (2,520hp) 13.2kn Sulzer 6ASL25/30 2 x 4 Stroke 6 Cy. 250 x 300 each-927kW (1260bhp) in Yugoslavia AuxGen: 2 x 100kW a.c Fuel: 42.0 (d.f.)
9263112 *SXQG* -	**TIGRIS** **Falmouth Maritime Special Maritime Enterprise (ENE)** Niovis Shipping Co SA *Piraeus* *Greece* MMSI: 240138000 Official number: 11235	**30,057** 18,207 52,454 T/cm 55.5	Class: NK	**2003**-11 **Tsuneishi Corp — Fukuyama HS** Yd No: 1251 Loa 189.99 (BB) Br ex - Dght 12.022 Lbp 182.00 Br md 32.26 Dpth 17.00 Welded, 1 dk	**(A21A2BC) Bulk Carrier** Double Bottom Entire Compartment Length Grain: 67,756; Bale: 65,601 Compartments: 5 Ho (s.stl), ER (s.stl) 5 Ha: 4 (21.5 x 18.4)ER (20.4 x 18.4) Cranes: 4x30t	**1 oil engine** driving 1 FP propeller Total Power: 7,800kW (10,605hp) 14.0kn B&W 6S50MC 1 x 2 Stroke 6 Cy. 500 x 1910 7800kW (10605bhp) Mitsui Engineering & Shipbuilding CLtd-Japan AuxGen: 3 x 480kW 440/110V 60Hz a.c Fuel: 150.0 (d.f.) 2000.0 (r.f.) 34.0pd

9443841 *V7SB4* -	**TIGRIS** *ex* Navig8 Tigris *-2011* *ex* Tigris *-2010* **Tigris Trading SA** Benetech Surveys SA SatCom: Inmarsat C 453834420 *Majuro* *Marshall Islands* MMSI: 538003615 Official number: 3615	**8,247** 3,725 12,920 T/cm 21.7	Class: AB	**2009**-07 **STX Offshore & Shipbuilding Co Ltd — Busan** Yd No: 5034 Loa 120.00 (BB) Br ex 20.43 Dght 8.664 Lbp 113.00 Br md 20.40 Dpth 11.90 Welded, 1 dk	**(A12B2TR) Chemical/Products Tanker** Double Hull (13F) Liq: 13,687; Liq (Oil): 13,685 Cargo Heating Coils Compartments: 10 Wing Ta, 2 Wing Slop Ta, ER 10 Cargo Pump (s): 10x300m^3/hr Manifold: Bow/CM: 61.4m	**1 oil engine** driving 1 FP propeller Total Power: 4,454kW (6,056hp) 13.6kn MAN-B&W 6S35MC 1 x 2 Stroke 6 Cy. 350 x 1400 4454kW (6056bhp) STX Engine Co Ltd-South Korea AuxGen: 3 x 450kW a.c Thrusters: 1 Tunnel thruster (f) Fuel: 70.0 (d.f.) 538.0 (r.f.)
9660401 *ZGCV4* -	**TIGRIS** *ex* Okko *-2013* - - *George Town* *Cayman Islands (British)* MMSI: 319311000 Official number: 743814	**366** 109 59	Class: AB	**2013**-04 **Mondo Marine SpA — Savona** Yd No: 18/7 Loa 40.45 Br ex 8.20 Dght 2.260 Lbp 40.45 Br md 8.10 Dpth 4.10 Welded, 1 dk	**(X11A2YP) Yacht** Hull Material: Aluminium Alloy	**2 oil engines** reduction geared to sc. shafts driving 2 Propellers Total Power: 2,206kW (3,000hp) 14.0kn M.T.U. 12V2000M91 2 x Vee 4 Stroke 12 Cy. 130 x 150 each-1103kW (1500bhp) MTU Friedrichshafen GmbH-Friedrichshafen AuxGen: 2 x 70kW a.c
8305315 - -	**TIGUA** - **Compania Pesquera Vikingos de Colombia SA** -	*132* 24 -		**1982**-01 **Desco Marine — Saint Augustine, Fl** Loa 22.86 Br ex 6.71 Dght 4.271 Lbp 19.99 Br md 6.51 Dpth 4.09 Bonded, 1 dk	**(B11A2FT) Trawler** Hull Material: Reinforced Plastic Ins: 67 Compartments: 1 Ho, ER 1 Ha:	**1 oil engine** with clutches & sr geared to sc. shaft driving 1 FP propeller Total Power: 331kW (450hp) Caterpillar 3412T 1 x Vee 4 Stroke 12 Cy. 137 x 152 331kW (450bhp) Caterpillar Tractor Co-USA
5261350 *9A2167* -	**TIJAT** *ex* Ohrid *-1997* **Jadrolinija** - *Rijeka* *Croatia* MMSI: 238115540 Official number: 2T-19	*191* 79 15	Class: CS (LR) (JR) ✠ Classed LR until 5/56	**1955**-05 **Brodogradiliste Split (Brodosplit) — Split** Yd No: 128 Loa 37.47 Br ex 7.07 Dght 2.413 Lbp 34.52 Br md 7.01 Dpth 3.31 Riveted\Welded, 1 dk	**(A32A2GF) General Cargo/Passenger Ship** Compartments: 1 Ho, ER 1 Ha: (2.2 x 1.6) Derricks: 1x1t; Winches: 1	**1 oil engine** driving 1 FP propeller Total Power: 335kW (455hp) 12.5kn Sulzer 6TD24 1 x 2 Stroke 6 Cy. 240 x 400 335kW (455bhp) Sulzer Bros Ltd-Switzerland AuxGen: 2 x 20kW 220V d.c Fuel: 14.0
8115708 *YYFM* -	**TIJERETO** *ex* Pacific Horizon *-1989* *ex* State Spirit *-1987* **Servicios Picardi SA (SERVIPICA)** - *Puerto la Cruz* *Venezuela* MMSI: 775305000 Official number: AGSP-3074	**1,255** 1,011 820	Class: AB	**1982**-06 **Bender Shipbuilding & Repair Co Inc — Mobile AL** Yd No: 1001 Converted From: Offshore Supply Ship-1989 Loa 58.53 Br ex 12.20 Dght 3.658 Lbp 53.62 Br md 12.04 Dpth 4.27 Welded, 1 dk	**(A31C2GD) Deck Cargo Ship** TEU 48 C.48/20' (40') incl. 4 ref C. Compartments: 4 Ta, ER	**2 oil engines** reverse reduction geared to sc. shafts driving 2 FP propellers Total Power: 1,654kW (2,248hp) 12.0kn Caterpillar D399SCAC 2 x Vee 4 Stroke 16 Cy. 159 x 203 each-827kW (1124bhp) Caterpillar Tractor Co-USA AuxGen: 2 x 75kW 208V 60Hz a.c Thrusters: 1 Thwart. FP thruster (f)
9377511 *LAFV7* -	**TIJUCA** - **Wilhelmsen Lines Shipowning Malta Ltd** Wilhelmsen Ship Management (Norway) AS SatCom: Inmarsat C 425980510 *Tonsberg* *Norway (NIS)* MMSI: 259805000	**71,673** 33,513 30,089	Class: LR ✠ **100A1** SS 12/2013 vehicle carrier, movable decks, deck Nos. 1, 3, 5 and 8 strengthened for the carriage of roll on-roll off cargoes *IWS LI ✠ **LMC** **UMS** Eq.Ltr: S†; Cable: 687.5/87.0 U3 (a)	**2008**-12 **Daewoo Shipbuilding & Marine Engineering Co Ltd — Geoje** Yd No: 4451 Loa 231.60 (BB) Br ex 32.58 Dght 11.300 Lbp 219.30 Br md 32.26 Dpth 34.70 Welded, 13 dks	**(A35B2RV) Vehicles Carrier** Stern door/ramp (centre) Len: 7.04 Wid: 15.40 Swl: 237 Side door/ramp (s) Len: 6.01 Wid: 5.80 Swl: 30 Cars: 8,000	**1 oil engine** driving 1 FP propeller Total Power: 18,080kW (24,582hp) 20.8kn MAN-B&W 8S60ME-C 1 x 2 Stroke 8 Cy. 600 x 2400 18080kW (24582bhp) Doosan Engine Co Ltd-South Korea AuxGen: 2 x 1700kW 450V 60Hz a.c, 1 x 1132kW 420V 60Hz a.c Boilers: e (ex.g.) 9.2kgf/cm^2 (9.0bar), WTAuxB (o.f.) 9.2kgf/cm^2 (9.0bar) Thrusters: 1 Thwart. CP thruster (f) Fuel: 4590.0 57.0pd
7738113 *P24325* -	**TIKANA** *ex* Koris *-1984* **Rakaman Shipping Pty Ltd** - *Rabaul* *Papua New Guinea* Official number: 000417	*203* 100 136	Class: (BV)	**1975** **Wang Tak Engineering & Shipbuilding Co Ltd — Hong Kong** Yd No: 751 Loa 29.70 Br ex - Dght - Lbp 26.01 Br md 7.00 Dpth 3.26 Welded, 1 dk	**(A35D2RL) Landing Craft** Bow door/ramp Grain: 225; Bale: 191 Compartments: 1 Ho, ER 1 Ha: (10.9 x 4.5)ER Derricks: 1x2.5t	**2 oil engines** geared to sc. shafts driving 2 FP propellers Total Power: 558kW (758hp) Caterpillar 3306SCAC 2 x 4 Stroke 6 Cy. 121 x 152 each-279kW (379bhp) Caterpillar Tractor Co-USA
9101883 *UDUL* -	**TIKHIY** *ex* Ursdon *-1999* **Trans-Marin Co Ltd** - *Petropavlovsk-Kamchatskiy* *Russia*	**190** 57 70	Class: RS	**1993**-06 **OAO Astrakhanskaya Sudoverf — Astrakhan** Yd No: 109 Loa 31.85 Br ex 7.08 Dght 2.100 Lbp 27.80 Br md 6.90 Dpth 3.15 Welded, 1 dk	**(B12B2FC) Fish Carrier** Ins: 100 Compartments: 2 Ho 2 Ha: 2 (2.1 x 2.4) Derricks: 2x1t Ice Capable	**1 oil engine** geared to sc. shaft driving 1 FP propeller Total Power: 232kW (315hp) 10.2kn Daldizel 6CHSPN2A18-315 1 x 4 Stroke 6 Cy. 180 x 220 232kW (315bhp) Daldizel-Khabarovsk AuxGen: 2 x 25kW Fuel: 14.0 (d.f.)
8722161 *UGGQ* -	**TIKHIY OKEAN** *ex* Balashikhinskiy *-1999* **Insof Marine Co Ltd (OOO 'Insof Marin')** - *Nakhodka* *Russia* MMSI: 273565500 Official number: 861482	**813** 243 283	Class: RS	**1987**-04 **Volgogradskiy Sudostroitelnyy Zavod — Volgograd** Yd No: 237 Loa 53.74 Br ex 10.71 Dght 4.400 Lbp 47.92 Br md 10.50 Dpth 6.00 Welded, 1 dk	**(B11A2FS) Stern Trawler** Ice Capable	**1 oil engine** driving 1 CP propeller Total Power: 970kW (1,319hp) 12.6kn S.K.L. 8NVD48A-2U 1 x 4 Stroke 8 Cy. 320 x 480 970kW (1319bhp) VEB Schwermaschinenbau "KarlLiebknecht" (SKL)-Magdeburg AuxGen: 1 x 300kW a.c, 3 x 160kW a.c, 2 x 135kW a.c
8138578 *UDFX* -	**TIKHMENEVO** - **JSC 'Fishery Kolkhoz Primorets'** - *Nakhodka* *Russia* MMSI: 273895700 Official number: 821659	**778** 233 332	Class: RS	**1983**-08 **Volgogradskiy Sudostroitelnyy Zavod — Volgograd** Yd No: 211 Loa 53.75 Br ex 10.72 Dght 4.290 Lbp 47.92 Br md - Dpth 6.74 Welded, 1 dk	**(B11A2FS) Stern Trawler** Ins: 218 Compartments: 1 Ho, ER 1 Ha: (1.6 x 1.6) Derricks: 2x1.5t Ice Capable	**1 oil engine** driving 1 FP propeller Total Power: 971kW (1,320hp) 12.8kn S.K.L. 8NVD48A-2U 1 x 4 Stroke 8 Cy. 320 x 480 971kW (1320bhp) VEB Schwermaschinenbau "KarlLiebknecht" (SKL)-Magdeburg Fuel: 182.0 (d.f.)
8038273 *UGKR* -	**TIKHON SYOMUSHKIN** - **Flot-4 Co Ltd** JSC Kamchatmorflot *Petropavlovsk-Kamchatskiy* *Russia* MMSI: 273176100	**4,598** 1,855 5,485	Class: (RS)	**1982**-09 **Navashinskiy Sudostroitelnyy Zavod 'Oka' — Navashino** Yd No: 1210 Loa 124.42 Br ex 16.41 Dght 5.501 Lbp 117.02 Br md 15.82 Dpth 7.52 Welded, 1 dk	**(A31A2GX) General Cargo Ship** Bale: 5,800 TEU 165 Compartments: 4 Ho, ER 4 Ha: (13.2 x 10.5)3 (13.2 x 12.8)ER Cranes: 4x8t Ice Capable	**2 oil engines** driving 2 FP propellers Total Power: 2,206kW (3,000hp) 13.0kn Dvigatel Revolyutsii 6CHRNP36/45 2 x 4 Stroke 6 Cy. 360 x 450 each-1103kW (1500bhp) Zavod "Dvigatel Revolyutsii"-Gorkiy AuxGen: 3 x 160kW Fuel: 436.0 (r.f.)
9105073 *ELTH8* -	**TIKHORETSK** - **Tikhoretsk Shipping Inc** SCF Novoship JSC (Novorossiysk Shipping Co) SatCom: Inmarsat A 1260566 *Monrovia* *Liberia* MMSI: 636010513 Official number: 10513	**26,218** 11,286 40,791 T/cm 51.2	Class: LR ✠ **100A1** SS 07/2011 oil & chemical tanker (Double Hull), Ship Type 3 caustic soda only ESP SPM LI Maximum filling height with Caustic Soda 67% depth , SG 1.53 ✠ **LMC** **UMS IGS** Eq.Ltr: L†; Cable: 638.5/70.0 U3	**1996**-07 **'Uljanik' Brodogradiliste dd — Pula** Yd No: 415 Loa 181.00 (BB) Br ex 32.03 Dght 11.017 Lbp 173.80 Br md 32.00 Dpth 17.00 Welded, 1 dk	**(A12B2TR) Chemical/Products Tanker** Double Hull (13F) Liq: 49,168; Liq (Oil): 49,168 Cargo Heating Coils Compartments: 10 Wing Ta, 2 Wing Slop Ta, ER 10 Cargo Pump (s): 10x550m^3/hr Manifold: Bow/CM: 90m	**1 oil engine** driving 1 FP propeller Total Power: 8,313kW (11,302hp) 14.4kn B&W 6S50MC 1 x 2 Stroke 6 Cy. 500 x 1910 8313kW (11302bhp) 'Uljanik' Strojogradnja dd-Croatia AuxGen: 3 x 1080kW 450V 60Hz a.c Boilers: e (ex.g.) 10.2kgf/cm^2 (10.0bar), AuxB (o.f.) 10.2kgf/cm^2 (10.0bar) Fuel: 150.0 (d.f.) (Heating Coils) 1561.0 (r.f.) 32.5pd
7050078 *WDB4940* -	**TIKI XIV** *ex* Sea Bird *-1999* **Tiki XIV Inc** - *Ocean City, MD* *United States of America* Official number: 512432	*123* 83 -		**1968** **Master Marine, Inc. — Bayou La Batre, Al** L reg 21.86 Br ex 6.71 Dght - Lbp - Br md - Dpth 3.61 Welded	**(B11B2FV) Fishing Vessel**	**1 oil engine** driving 1 FP propeller Total Power: 246kW (334hp)
5218456 *TJCI* -	**TIKO** *ex* Malika *-1973* **L'Office National des Ports du Cameroon (ONPC)** - *Douala* *Cameroon*	*157* - -	Class: (BV)	**1960** **Niehuis & van den Berg's Scheepsrep.bed. N.V. — Rotterdam** Yd No: 9 Loa 28.78 Br ex 8.26 Dght 3.864 Lbp 25.00 Br md - Dpth 3.97 Welded, 1 dk	**(B32A2ST) Tug**	**1 oil engine** driving 1 FP propeller Total Power: 552kW (750hp) 11.5kn Deutz RBV6M545 1 x 4 Stroke 6 Cy. 320 x 450 552kW (750bhp) Kloeckner Humboldt Deutz AG-West Germany Fuel: 44.5 (d.f.)

LR No. / Call sign	Name / Owners / Port / Flag	Tonnage	Class	Builder / Dimensions	Type / Cargo	Machinery
8966042 *CB3396* -	**TIL-TIL** - **Sociedad Pesquera Coloso SA** - *Valparaiso* *Chile* MMSI: 725000044 Official number: 2197	*208* - -		**1979 Astilleros Marco Chilena Ltda. — Iquique** L reg 23.60 Br ex - Dght - Lbp - Br md 7.96 Dpth 4.27 Welded, 1 dk	**(B11B2FV) Fishing Vessel**	**1 oil engine** driving 1 FP propeller
8739798 *XCMC9* -	**TILA** *ex* Sarena B *-2009* *ex* Marsha G *-2009* *ex* Saba Queen *-2009* *ex* Keith Tide *-2009* *ex* C/Violator *-2009* *ex* Dawn Star *-2009* **Marinsa de Mexico SA de CV** - *Ciudad del Carmen* *Mexico* MMSI: 345070235 Official number: 0401196027-1	**135** 40 49	Class: RI	**1981 Swiftships-Lafitte Inc — Marrero LA** Yd No: 258 Loa 30.78 Br ex - Dght 2.810 Lbp 27.80 Br md 6.70 Dpth 3.15 Welded, 1 dk	**(B21A20C) Crew/Supply Vessel** Hull Material: Aluminium Alloy	**3 oil engines** reduction geared to sc. shafts driving 3 Propellers 16.0kn G.M. (Detroit Diesel) 12V-71-TI 3 x Vee 2 Stroke 12 Cy. 108 x 127 General Motors Detroit DieselAllison Divn-USA
9174359 *ZIQT4* -	**TILDA KOSAN** *ex* Tarquin Dell *-2002* **Lauritzen Kosan A/S** - *Douglas* *Isle of Man (British)* MMSI: 235508000 Official number: 734746	**4,693** 1,754 5,992 T/cm 15.0	Class: BV	**1999-02 Hyundai Heavy Industries Co Ltd — Ulsan** Yd No: 1123 Loa 106.30 (BB) Br ex 15.72 Dght 7.250 Lbp 99.07 Br md 15.70 Dpth 8.25 Welded, 1 dk	**(A11B2TG) LPG Tanker** Double Bottom Entire Compartment Length Liq (Gas): 6,387 2 x Gas Tank (s); 2 independent (stl) cyl 2 Cargo Pump (s): 2x350m³/hr Manifold: Bow/CM: 54m Ice Capable	**1 oil engine** driving 1 CP propeller Total Power: 3,500kW (4,759hp) 15.0kn B&W 5S35MC 1 x 2 Stroke 5 Cy. 350 x 1400 3500kW (4759bhp) Hyundai Heavy Industries Co Ltd-South Korea AuxGen: 3 x 378kW 440/220V 60Hz a.c, 1 x 400kW 440/220V 60Hz a.c Thrusters: 1 Thwart. FP thruster (f) Fuel: 150.0 (d.f.) 582.0 (r.f.)
8901339 *5ARQ* -	**TILEEL** - **Bohoor Al Kairat Fishing Co** - *Benghazi* *Libya* Official number: SB 340	**227** 173 -	Class: (LR) ✠ Classed LR until 11/9/96	**1991-11 Chungmu Shipbuilding Co Inc — Tongyeong** Yd No: 227 Loa 31.15 (BB) Br ex 7.72 Dght - Lbp 25.25 Br md 7.70 Dpth 3.50 Welded, 1 dk	**(B11A2FS) Stern Trawler** Ins: 100	**1 oil engine** with clutches, flexible couplings & sr geared to sc. shaft driving 1 CP propeller Total Power: 704kW (957hp) Blackstone ESL6MK2 1 x 4 Stroke 6 Cy. 222 x 292 704kW (957bhp) Mirrlees Blackstone (Stamford)Ltd.-Stamford AuxGen: 2 x 72kW 380V 50Hz a.c
7831135 *UARO* AI-1472	**TILIGUL** - **Belomor Fishing Collective (Rybolovetskiy Kolkhoz 'Belomor')** - *Murmansk* *Russia* MMSI: 273292100	**737** 221 395	Class: (RS)	**1980-01 Zavod "Leninskaya Kuznitsa" — Kiyev** Yd No: 1472 Loa 54.82 Br ex 9.96 Dght 4.139 Lbp 50.29 Br md 9.80 Dpth 5.01 Welded, 1 dk	**(B11A2FS) Stern Trawler** Bale: 414 Compartments: 2 Ho, ER 3 Ha: 3 (1.5 x 1.6) Derricks: 2x1.3t Ice Capable	**1 oil engine** driving 1 FP propeller Total Power: 852kW (1,158hp) 12.0kn S.K.L. 8NVD48A-2U 1 x 4 Stroke 8 Cy. 320 x 480 852kW (1158bhp) (new engine ,made 1985) VEB Schwermaschinenbau "KarlLiebknecht" (SKL)-Magdeburg Fuel: 154.0 (d.f.)
8305779 *UZUW* -	**TILIGULSKIY** - **Black Sea & Azov Sea Dredging Co (Upravleniye Morskikh Putey) (CHERAZMORPUT)** - *Odessa* *Ukraine* MMSI: 272214000 Official number: 842424	*2,628* 788 2,044	Class: (RS)	**1985-10 Brodogradiliste Split (Brodosplit) — Split** Yd No: 334 Loa 80.02 Br ex 15.12 Dght 4.101 Lbp 75.42 Br md 15.10 Dpth 5.62 Welded, 1 dk	**(B33A2DS) Suction Dredger** Hopper: 1,300 Ice Capable	**2 oil engines** sr geared to sc. shafts driving 2 CP propellers Total Power: 2,220kW (3,018hp) Alpha 6SL28L-VO 2 x 4 Stroke 6 Cy. 280 x 320 each-1110kW (1509bhp) Titovi Zavodi 'Litostroj'-Yugoslavia Thrusters: 1 Thwart. CP thruster (f)
9390381 *V2FF7* -	**TILL** *ex* Stella Maris *-2010* **ms 'Till' Boehe Schiffahrt GmbH & Co KG** Lubeca Marine (Germany) GmbH & Co KG SatCom: Inmarsat C 430522510 *Saint John's* *Antigua & Barbuda* MMSI: 305225000 Official number: 4814	**1,867** 810 2,639	Class: GL	**2008-09 Ananda Shipyard & Slipways Ltd — Sonargaon** Yd No: 226/23 Loa 81.35 (BB) Br ex 13.39 Dght 4.650 Lbp 77.25 Br md 13.15 Dpth 6.20 Welded, 1 dk	**(A31A2GX) General Cargo Ship** Grain: 3,000; Bale: 3,000 TEU 136 C Ho 64 TEU C Ha 72 TEU Compartments: 1 Ho, ER 1 Ha: ER (49.2 x 10.2) Ice Capable	**1 oil engine** reduction geared to sc. shaft driving 1 CP propeller Total Power: 1,720kW (2,339hp) 11.5kn MAN-B&W 8L21/31 1 x 4 Stroke 8 Cy. 210 x 310 1720kW (2339bhp) MAN Diesel A/S-Denmark AuxGen: 2 x 168kW 400V a.c, 1 x 350kW 400V a.c Thrusters: 1 Tunnel thruster (f) Fuel: 180.0 (d.f.)
9482861 *A8XG6* -	**TILL JACOB** - **Jacob Tank Dritte Beteiligungsgesellschaft mbH & Co KG** Ernst Jacob GmbH & Co KG *Monrovia* *Liberia* MMSI: 636092137 Official number: 92137	**43,980** 21,958 75,564 T/cm 68.0	Class: AB NV	**2012-02 Dalian Shipbuilding Industry Co Ltd — Dalian LN (No 1 Yard)** Yd No: PC760-21 Loa 228.60 (BB) Br ex 32.30 Dght 14.700 Lbp 219.98 Br md 32.26 Dpth 21.20 Welded, 1 dk	**(A13B2TP) Products Tanker** Double Hull (13F) Liq: 80,740; Liq (Oil): 80,740 Cargo Heating Coils Compartments: 12 Wing Ta, 2 Wing Slop Ta, ER 3 Cargo Pump (s): 3x2000m³/hr Manifold: Bow/CM: 117.4m	**1 oil engine** driving 1 FP propeller Total Power: 12,240kW (16,642hp) 15.4kn MAN-B&W 6S60MC 1 x 2 Stroke 6 Cy. 600 x 2292 12240kW (16642bhp) Dalian Marine Diesel Co Ltd-China AuxGen: 3 x 600kW a.c Fuel: 175.0 (d.f.) 2530.0 (r.f.)
8836120 *WL3377* -	**TILLIKUM** - **State of Washington (Department of Transportation)** Washington State Department of Transportation (Washington State Ferries) *Seattle, WA* *United States of America* MMSI: 366773090 Official number: 278437	*1,334* 907 -		**1959 Puget Sound Bridge & Drydock Co. — Seattle, Wa** Yd No: 104 Loa - Br ex - Dght - Lbp 90.43 Br md 22.28 Dpth 7.07 Welded	**(A36A2PR) Passenger/Ro-Ro Ship (Vehicles)** Passengers: unberthed: 1140 Bow door/ramp (centre) Stern door/ramp (centre) Cars: 87	**2 diesel electric oil engines** driving 1 FP propeller Total Power: 3,678kW (5,000hp) 13.0kn
9470894 *V2ER9* -	**TILLY RUSS** *ex* MCC Davao *-2013* *ex* TILLY RUSS *-2010* **ms 'Tilly Russ' Schiffahrtsgesellschaft mbH & Co KG** Ernst Russ GmbH & Co KG SatCom: Inmarsat C 430556810 *Saint John's* *Antigua & Barbuda* MMSI: 305568000 Official number: 4712	**16,137** 6,128 17,142	Class: GL	**2010-11 Jiangsu Yangzijiang Shipbuilding Co Ltd — Jiangyin JS** Yd No: 2007-796C Loa 161.27 (BB) Br ex - Dght 9.500 Lbp 149.60 Br md 25.00 Dpth 14.90 Welded, 1 dk	**(A33A2CC) Container Ship (Fully Cellular)** TEU 1341 incl 449 ref C. Cranes: 2x45t	**1 oil engine** driving 1 FP propeller Total Power: 12,640kW (17,185hp) 19.3kn MAN-B&W 8S50ME-C 1 x 2 Stroke 8 Cy. 500 x 2000 12640kW (17185bhp) STX Engine Co Ltd-South Korea AuxGen: 2 x 1520kW 450V a.c, 2 x 1140kW 450V a.c Thrusters: 1 Tunnel thruster (f)
9102760 *YFCD* -	**TILONGKABILA** - **Government of The Republic of Indonesia (Direktorat Jenderal Perhubungan Laut - Ministry of Sea Communications)** PT Pelayaran Nasional Indonesia (PELNI) *Gorontalo* *Indonesia* MMSI: 525005016	**6,022** 1,806 1,438	Class: KI (GL)	**1995-06 Jos L Meyer GmbH & Co — Papenburg** Yd No: 641 Loa 99.80 (BB) Br ex 18.30 Dght 4.200 Lbp 91.50 Br md 18.00 Dpth 6.90 Welded, 1 dk	**(A37B2PS) Passenger Ship** Passengers: unberthed: 916; cabins: 17; berths: 54	**2 oil engines** with clutches, flexible couplings & sr geared to sc. shafts driving 2 FP propellers Total Power: 3,200kW (4,350hp) 14.0kn MaK 6M453C 2 x 4 Stroke 6 Cy. 320 x 420 each-1600kW (2175bhp) Krupp MaK Maschinenbau GmbH-Kiel
9417945 *9V9298* -	**TILOS** - **Tilos Shipping Pte Ltd** Aegean Bunkering (Singapore) Pte Ltd SatCom: Inmarsat C 456476910 *Singapore* *Singapore* MMSI: 564769000 Official number: 396898	**4,580** 1,967 6,262 T/cm 15.5	Class: GL (NV)	**2011-03 Qingdao Hyundai Shipbuilding Co Ltd — Jiaonan SD** Yd No: 226 Loa 102.50 Br ex 17.82 Dght 6.600 Lbp 95.00 Br md 17.80 Dpth 8.80 Welded, 1 dk	**(A13B2TP) Products Tanker** Double Hull (13F) Liq: 6,639; Liq (Oil): 6,639 Cargo Heating Coils Compartments: 5 Wing Ta, 5 Wing Ta, 1 Wing Slop Ta, 1 Wing Slop Ta, ER 3 Cargo Pump (s): 2x750m³/hr, 1x300m³/hr	**1 oil engine** reduction geared to sc. shaft driving 1 FP propeller Total Power: 2,218kW (3,016hp) 11.7kn Hyundai Himsen 9H25/33P 1 x 4 Stroke 9 Cy. 250 x 330 2218kW (3016bhp) Hyundai Heavy Industries Co Ltd-South Korea AuxGen: 3 x 400kW 450V a.c Thrusters: 1 Tunnel thruster (f)

IMO / Call sign	Name / Owner	Tonnages	Class	Builder / Dimensions	Type / Capacity	Machinery
9412074 *SVAP2* -	**TILOS** **Tilos Special Maritime Enterprise (ENE)** Eletson Corp SatCom: Inmarsat C 424090110 *Piraeus* *Greece* MMSI: 240901000 Official number: 11913	**22,971** 6,891 26,587 T/cm 41.5	Class: LR ✠ **100A1** SS 08/2009 liquefied gas carrier, Ship Type 2G Anhydrous ammonia, butane, butane and propane mixtures, butadiene, butylene, propane and propylene in independent tanks Type A, maximum SG 0.70, partial loading VCM with maximum SG 0.97, maximum vapour pressure 0.25 bar (0.45 bar in harbour), minimum cargo temperature minus 50 degree C LI *IWS **ShipRight** (SDA, FDA, CM) EP ✠ **LMC UMS +Lloyd's RMC (LG)** Eq.Ltr: K†; Cable: 632.5/68.0 U3 (a)	**2009-08 Hyundai Mipo Dockyard Co Ltd — Ulsan** Yd No: 8013 Loa 173.70 (BB) Br ex 28.03 Dght 10.400 Lbp 165.00 Br md 28.00 Dpth 17.80 Welded, 1 dk	**(A11B2TG) LPG Tanker** Double Bottom Entire Compartment Length Liq (Gas): 34,300 3 x Gas Tank (s); 3 independent (C.mn.stl) pri horizontal 8 Cargo Pump (s): 8x400m³/hr Manifold: Bow/CM: 88.7m	**1 oil engine** driving 1 FP propeller Total Power: 9,480kW (12,889hp) 16.4kn MAN-B&W 6S50MC-C 1 x 2 Stroke 6 Cy. 500 x 2000 9480kW (12889bhp) Hyundai Heavy Industries Co Ltd-South Korea AuxGen: 2 x 900kW 450V 60Hz a.c, 1 x 760kW 450V 60Hz a.c Boilers: AuxB (Comp) 9.2kgf/cm² (9.0bar) Fuel: 131.0 (d.f.) 1497.0 (r.f.)
9434151 *5BLC2* -	**TIM** **ms 'Tim' Interscan Shipmanagement GmbH & Co KG** Interscan Schiffahrtsgesellschaft mbH *Limassol* *Cyprus* MMSI: 212571000	**2,474** 1,412 3,450	Class: BV (LR) ✠ Classed LR until 8/7/08	**2008-09 Marine Projects Ltd Sp z oo — Gdansk** Yd No: (701) **2008-09 Bodewes' Scheepswerven B.V. — Hoogezand** Yd No: 701 Loa 82.50 (BB) Br ex 12.60 Dght 5.300 Lbp 79.54 Br md 12.50 Dpth 6.80 Welded, 1 dk	**(A31A2GX) General Cargo Ship** Grain: 5,014 TEU 34 Compartments: 1 Ho, ER 1 Ha: ER (55.0 x 10.3) Ice Capable	**1 oil engine** with flexible couplings & sr geared to sc. shaft driving 1 CP propeller Total Power: 1,850kW (2,515hp) 12.5kn MaK 6M25 1 x 4 Stroke 6 Cy. 255 x 400 1850kW (2515bhp) Caterpillar Motoren GmbH & Co. KG-Germany AuxGen: 1 x 264kW 400V 50Hz a.c, 1 x 150kW 400V 50Hz a.c Thrusters: 1 Water jet (f)
9508641 *9HA2493* -	**TIM B** **Dritte MLB Bulktransport Gmbh & Co KG** MarLink Schiffahrtskontor GmbH & Co KG *Valletta* *Malta* MMSI: 248743000 Official number: 9508641	**3,556** 1,535 4,757	Class: GL	**2010-10 Weihai Donghai Shipyard Co Ltd — Weihai SD** Yd No: DHZ-07-16 Loa 89.98 (BB) Br ex 15.40 Dght 5.800 Lbp 84.99 Br md 15.39 Dpth 7.60 Welded, 1 dk	**(A31A2GX) General Cargo Ship** Compartments: 1 Ho, ER 1 Ha: ER Ice Capable	**1 oil engine** reverse reduction geared to sc. shaft driving 1 FP propeller Total Power: 1,960kW (2,665hp) 11.5kn MAN-B&W 8L28/32A 1 x 4 Stroke 8 Cy. 280 x 320 1960kW (2665bhp) Zhenjiang Marine Diesel Works-China AuxGen: 2 x 350kW 400V a.c Thrusters: 1 Tunnel thruster (f)
8994441 - -	**TIM B.** **Inland & Offshore Contractors Ltd** *Port of Spain* *Trinidad & Tobago* Official number: TT030039	**118** 35 -		**1982-02 DH & D Ironworks Inc — Larose, La** Yd No: 9 L reg 25.29 Br ex - Dght - Lbp - Br md 7.83 Dpth 2.43 Welded, 1 dk	**(B34L2QU) Utility Vessel**	**1 oil engine** driving 1 Propeller
8127177 *5NRH1* -	**TIM BEGELE** *ex* Atlantic *-2010* *ex* Atlantic Moon *-2007* **Tim Afrique Services Ltd** *Lagos* *Nigeria* Official number: SR1328	**731** 219 810	Class: AB	**1982-09 Asia-Pacific Shipyard Pte Ltd — Singapore** Yd No: 366 Loa - Br ex - Dght 4.220 Lbp 54.89 Br md 12.20 Dpth 4.88 Welded, 1 dk	**(B21B20A) Anchor Handling Tug Supply**	**2 oil engines** reverse reduction geared to sc. shafts driving 2 FP propellers Total Power: 3,016kW (4,100hp) 12.0kn Alco 12V251C 2 x Vee 4 Stroke 12 Cy. 229 x 267 each-1508kW (2050bhp) (Reconditioned , Reconditioned & fitted 1982) Alco Power Inc-USA AuxGen: 2 x 125kW a.c Thrusters: 1 Thwart. FP thruster (f)
8206832 *SSAU* -	**TIM HOPE** **Timsah Shipbuilding Co** *Alexandria* *Egypt* MMSI: 622120113 Official number: 2676	**776** 232 610	Class: AB	**1984 Leevac Shipyards Inc — Jennings LA** Yd No: 283 Loa 56.39 Br ex 12.50 Dght 3.885 Lbp 53.80 Br md 12.20 Dpth 4.58 Welded, 1 dk	**(B21A20S) Platform Supply Ship**	**2 oil engines** with clutches, flexible couplings & sr reverse geared to sc. shafts driving 2 FP propellers Total Power: 2,442kW (3,320hp) 12.0kn EMD (Electro-Motive) 16-645-E6 2 x Vee 2 Stroke 16 Cy. 230 x 254 each-1221kW (1660bhp) General Motors Corp.Electro-Motive Div.-La Grange AuxGen: 2 x 150kW 440V 60Hz a.c Thrusters: 1 Thwart. FP thruster (f)
8987917 *WDB6570* -	**TIM QUIGG** **Majestic Lion LLC** Millennium Maritime Inc *Portland, OR* *United States of America* MMSI: 366926740 Official number: 1150866	**257** 77 4		**2004-04 Diversified Marine, Inc. — Portland, Or** Yd No: 16 Loa 24.37 Br ex - Dght 3.960 Lbp - Br md 9.75 Dpth 5.10 Welded, 1 dk	**(B32A2ST) Tug**	**2 oil engines** geared to sc. shafts driving 2 Z propellers Total Power: 2,648kW (3,600hp) Caterpillar 3512B 2 x Vee 4 Stroke 12 Cy. 170 x 190 each-1324kW (1800bhp) Caterpillar Inc-USA AuxGen: 2 x 99kW 60Hz a.c
9303742 *V2BK2* -	**TIM-S.** *ex* Emirates Excellence *-2011* *ex* CMA CGM Excellence *-2009* **ms 'Tim S' GmbH & Co KG** Reederei Rudolf Schepers GmbH & Co KG (Reederei Schepers) *Saint John's* *Antigua & Barbuda* MMSI: 304843000 Official number: 4032	**35,581** 19,407 44,135	Class: GL	**2005-10 Hanjin Heavy Industries & Construction Co Ltd — Busan** Yd No: 148 Loa 222.50 (BB) Br ex - Dght 12.000 Lbp 212.00 Br md 32.20 Dpth 19.30 Welded, 1 dk	**(A33A2CC) Container Ship (Fully Cellular)** TEU 3398 C Ho 1399 TEU C Dk 1999 TEU incl 300 ref C	**1 oil engine** driving 1 FP propeller Total Power: 28,880kW (39,265hp) 22.4kn MAN-B&W 8K80MC-C 1 x 2 Stroke 8 Cy. 800 x 2300 28880kW (39265bhp) Doosan Engine Co Ltd-South Korea AuxGen: 4 x 1200kW 450/230V a.c Thrusters: 1 Thwart. CP thruster (f)
6800919 *VGPY* -	**TIM S. DOOL** *ex* Algoville *-2008* *ex* Senneville *-1994* **Algoma Central Corp (ACC)** *St Catharines, ON* *Canada* MMSI: 316001696 Official number: 328536	*18,700* 10,067 28,471	Class: LR (AB) ✠ **100A1** Lake SS 06/2013 Great Lakes and River St. Lawrence service ✠ **LMC** Eq.Ltr: (o†) ; Cable: U2	**1967-11 Saint John Shipbuilding & Dry Dock Co Ltd — Saint John NB** Yd No: 1084 Widened-1996 Loa 222.51 Br ex 23.76 Dght 8.230 Lbp 216.57 Br md 23.74 Dpth 12.10 Welded, 1 dk	**(A21A2BG) Bulk Carrier, Laker Only** Grain: 39,465 Compartments: 6 Ho, ER 18 Ha: 18 (6.1 x 15.8)ER	**1 oil engine** with clutches, flexible couplings & sr geared to sc. shaft driving 1 CP propeller Total Power: 8,000kW (10,877hp) 15.5kn MaK 8M43C 1 x 4 Stroke 8 Cy. 430 x 610 8000kW (10877bhp) (new engine 2007) Caterpillar Motoren GmbH & Co. KG-Germany AuxGen: 2 x 600kW 450V 60Hz a.c, 1 x 750kW 450V 60Hz a.c Boilers: 2 AuxB 10.5kgf/cm² (10.3bar) Thrusters: 1 Thwart. CP thruster (f) Fuel: 591.5 (r.f.)
7396719 *SUBK* -	**TIM SHINE** *ex* Normand Flipper *-1981* **Timsah Shipbuilding Co** - *Alexandria* *Egypt* MMSI: 622120111	*1,130* 339 782	Class: LR (NV) **100A1** SS 01/2010 **LMC** Eq.Ltr: N; Cable: 412.5/34.0 U2	**1975-09 B.V. Scheepswerf "Waterhuizen" J. Pattje — Waterhuizen** Yd No: 312 Loa 58.98 Br ex 12.62 Dght 4.122 Lbp 50.60 Br md 12.00 Dpth 5.90 Welded, 2 dks	**(B21B20T) Offshore Tug/Supply Ship** Passengers: berths: 12	**2 oil engines** geared to sc. shafts driving 2 CP propellers Total Power: 2,280kW (3,100hp) 12.0kn Alpha 10V23LU 2 x Vee 4 Stroke 10 Cy. 225 x 300 each-1140kW (1550bhp) Alpha Diesel A/S-Denmark AuxGen: 2 x 170kW 440V 60Hz a.c Thrusters: 1 Thwart. FP thruster (f) Fuel: 484.5 (r.f.) 12.5pd
6609171 *SUVG* -	**TIM SUMED** *ex* Wimbrown Three *-1977* **Timsah Shipbuilding Co** - *Alexandria* *Egypt* MMSI: 622120115	*696* 246 691	Class: LR ✠ **100A1** SS 03/2008 ✠ **LMC** Eq.Ltr: J; Cable: 357.5/26.0 U2 (a)	**1966-04 Clelands Shipbuilding Co. Ltd. — Wallsend** Yd No: 290 Loa 49.43 Br ex 11.41 Dght 3.366 Lbp 45.42 Br md 10.98 Dpth 4.73 Welded, 1 dk	**(B21A20S) Platform Supply Ship**	**2 oil engines** with clutches, flexible couplings & sr reverse geared to sc. shafts driving 2 FP propellers Total Power: 1,310kW (1,782hp) M.T.U. 8V396TE74 2 x Vee 4 Stroke 8 Cy. 165 x 185 each-655kW (891bhp) (new engine 1993) MTU Friedrichshafen GmbH-Friedrichshafen AuxGen: 2 x 120kW 415V 50Hz a.c Thrusters: 1 Thwart. CP thruster (f)
8423648 - -	**TIM TIMONDI** *ex* Marine Endeavour *-2003* *ex* Cleveland Explorer *-1993* *ex* Caledonian Explorer *-1990* *ex* Norland Queen *-1986* *ex* Cleddau Queen *-1986* **Tim Afrique Services Ltd** *Lagos* *Nigeria*	**205** 61 292	Class: IS (LR) ✠ Classed LR until 1/11/02	**1956-01 Hancocks SB. Co. Ltd. — Pembroke Dock** Yd No: 20 Converted From: Fishery Support Vessel-1990 Converted From: Research Vessel-1988 Loa 30.79 Br ex 7.60 Dght 2.134 Lbp 29.42 Br md 7.32 Dpth 2.75 Welded, 1 dk	**(B22A20R) Offshore Support Vessel**	**2 oil engines** reverse reduction geared to sc. shafts driving 2 FP propellers Total Power: 492kW (668hp) 9.0kn Caterpillar D343TA 2 x 4 Stroke 6 Cy. 137 x 165 each-246kW (334bhp) (new engine 1968) Caterpillar Tractor Co-USA AuxGen: 2 x 225kW 450V 50Hz a.c

9267077 *VRAA7* -	**TIMARU STAR** **Pacific Basin Chartering (No 6) Ltd** Pacific Basin Shipping (HK) Ltd *Hong Kong* *Hong Kong* MMSI: 477280800 Official number: HK-1323	**19,779** 10,800 31,893 T/cm 45.1	Class: NK	**2004-05 The Hakodate Dock Co Ltd — Hakodate HK** Yd No: 794 Loa 175.53 (BB) Br ex - Dght 9.569 Lbp 167.00 Br md 29.40 Dpth 13.70 Welded, 1 dk	**(A21A2BC) Bulk Carrier** Grain: 42,657; Bale: 41,095 Compartments: 5 Ho, ER 5 Ha: 4 (19.6 x 19.6)ER (12.8 x 15.0) Cranes: 4x30.5t	**1 oil engine** driving 1 FP propeller Total Power: 6,840kW (9,300hp) 14.3kn Mitsubishi 6UEC52LA 1 x 2 Stroke 6 Cy. 520 x 1600 6840kW (9300bhp) Akasaka Tekkosho KK (Akasaka DieselLtd)-Japan AuxGen: 3 x 390kW a.c Fuel: 160.0 (d.f.) 1440.0 (r.f.)
9068275 - -	**TIMAU** **PD Kelautan Kabupaten Kubang** - *Jakarta* *Indonesia*	**253** 75 -	Class: KI	**2004-03 PT Karya Teknik Utama — Batam** Loa 38.50 Br ex - Dght 0.930 Lbp 32.25 Br md 8.00 Dpth 2.50 Welded, 1 dk	**(A35D2RL) Landing Craft** Bow ramp (centre)	**2 oil engines** geared to sc. shafts driving 2 Propellers Total Power: 470kW (640hp) 9.0kn Yanmar 6HA-DTE 2 x 4 Stroke 6 Cy. 130 x 150 each-235kW (320bhp) (made 2003) Yanmar Diesel Engine Co Ltd-Japan
7237195 *WYZ7099* -	**TIMBALIER BAY** *ex* Zapata Timbalier Bay *-1979* **Omega Protein Inc** - *Abbeville, LA* *United States of America* MMSI: 366986130 Official number: 539206	*533* 370 -		**1972 Zigler Shipyards Inc — Jennings LA** Yd No: 226 L reg 49.69 Br ex 10.22 Dght - Lbp - Br md - Dpth 3.64 Welded, 1 dk	**(B11B2FV) Fishing Vessel**	**1 oil engine** geared to sc. shaft driving 1 FP propeller Total Power: 1,125kW (1,530hp) Caterpillar 1 x 4 Stroke 1125kW (1530bhp) Caterpillar Tractor Co-USA
5299474 - -	**TIMBER CASTLE** *ex* Stacy S *-2003* *ex* Duane *-1999* *ex* Willig *-1977* *ex* Rondal *-1970* *ex* Rordal *-1965* **Jainarine Singh & Dhanmattie Singh** - *Georgetown* *Guyana* Official number: 356990	*188* 111 187	Class: (BV)	**1938 A/S Svendborg Skibsvaerft — Svendborg** Yd No: 46 Loa 40.19 Br ex 6.35 Dght 2.591 Lbp - Br md 6.30 Dpth - Riveted, 1 dk	**(A31A2GX) General Cargo Ship** Compartments: 1 Ho, ER 1 Ha: (11.8 x 3.5)ER Derricks: 1x1.5t; Winches: 1	**1 oil engine** driving 1 FP propeller Total Power: 250kW (340hp) 9.0kn Alpha 404-24VO 1 x 2 Stroke 4 Cy. 240 x 400 250kW (340bhp) (new engine 1966) Alpha Diesel A/S-Denmark Fuel: 5.0 (d.f.)
9124201 *9VHP5* -	**TIMBER DYNASTY** **Glory-Pacific Shipping (S) Pte Ltd** Glory Navigation Co Ltd *Singapore* *Singapore* MMSI: 565910000 Official number: 394022	**5,543** 2,393 6,965	Class: NK	**1995-04 Nishi Shipbuilding Co Ltd — Imabari EH** Yd No: 387 Loa 97.55 (BB) Br ex - Dght 7.422 Lbp 89.95 Br md 18.80 Dpth 12.90 Welded, 1 dk	**(A31A2GX) General Cargo Ship** Grain: 13,516; Bale: 12,296 Compartments: 2 Ho, ER 2 Ha: (22.4 x 10.2) (25.2 x 10.2)ER Cranes: 4x25t	**1 oil engine** driving 1 FP propeller Total Power: 3,236kW (4,400hp) 10.5kn Mitsubishi 6UEC33LSII 1 x 2 Stroke 6 Cy. 330 x 1050 3236kW (4400bhp) Akasaka Tekkosho KK (Akasaka DieselLtd)-Japan AuxGen: 2 x 220kW 440V 60Hz a.c Fuel: 67.2 (d.f.) 308.0 (r.f.) 13.0pd
9124885 *9VHP6* -	**TIMBER MAJESTY** *ex* Timber Majestic *-2008* **Glory-Pacific Shipping (S) Pte Ltd** Glory Navigation Co Ltd *Singapore* *Singapore* MMSI: 565883000 Official number: 394023	**5,543** 2,393 6,960	Class: NK	**1995-08 Nishi Shipbuilding Co Ltd — Imabari EH** Yd No: 388 Loa 97.55 Br ex - Dght 7.422 Lbp 89.95 Br md 18.80 Dpth 12.90 Welded, 2 dks	**(A31A2GX) General Cargo Ship** Grain: 13,516; Bale: 12,296 Compartments: 2 Ho, ER 2 Ha: (22.4 x 10.2) (25.2 x 10.2)ER Derricks: 4x25t	**1 oil engine** driving 1 FP propeller Total Power: 3,236kW (4,400hp) 13.0kn Mitsubishi 6UEC33LSII 1 x 2 Stroke 6 Cy. 330 x 1050 3236kW (4400bhp) Akasaka Tekkosho KK (Akasaka DieselLtd)-Japan Fuel: 430.0 (r.f.)
9071167 *3FTW3* -	**TIMBER TRADER XI** **Glory Asia Shipping Corp** Glory Navigation Co Ltd *Panama* *Panama* MMSI: 352638000 Official number: 2123194D	**5,542** 2,393 6,984	Class: NK	**1993-11 Iwagi Zosen Co Ltd — Kamijima EH** (Hull) Yd No: 153 **1993-11 Imabari Shipbuilding Co Ltd — Imabari EH (Imabari Shipyard)** Loa 97.55 Br ex - Dght 7.422 Lbp 89.95 Br md 18.80 Dpth 7.95 Welded, 1 dk	**(A31A2GX) General Cargo Ship** Grain: 13,539; Bale: 12,319 Compartments: 2 Ho, ER 2 Ha: (22.4 x 10.2) (25.2 x 10.2)ER Derricks: 2x25t,2x15t	**1 oil engine** driving 1 FP propeller Total Power: 3,236kW (4,400hp) 13.0kn Mitsubishi 6UEC33LSII 1 x 2 Stroke 6 Cy. 330 x 1050 3236kW (4400bhp) Akasaka Tekkosho KK (Akasaka DieselLtd)-Japan AuxGen: 2 x 220kW 440V 60Hz a.c Fuel: 75.8 (d.f.) 329.1 (r.f.) 10.5pd
9119062 *3FRA5* -	**TIMBER WEALTHY** **Wealthy Shipping Corp** Glory Navigation Co Ltd SatCom: Inmarsat C 435573510 *Panama* *Panama* MMSI: 355735000 Official number: 2263396CH	**5,543** 2,393 6,952	Class: NK	**1995-12 Nishi Shipbuilding Co Ltd — Imabari EH** Yd No: 389 Loa 97.55 Br ex - Dght 7.422 Lbp 89.95 Br md 18.30 Dpth 12.90 Welded, 1 dk	**(A31A2GX) General Cargo Ship** Grain: 13,516; Bale: 12,296 Compartments: 2 Ho, ER 2 Ha: (22.4 x 10.2) (25.2 x 10.2)ER Derricks: 4x25t	**1 oil engine** driving 1 FP propeller Total Power: 3,236kW (4,400hp) 13.0kn Mitsubishi 6UEC33LSII 1 x 2 Stroke 6 Cy. 330 x 1050 3236kW (4400bhp) Akasaka Tekkosho KK (Akasaka DieselLtd)-Japan Fuel: 425.0 (r.f.)
8842791 *WDA5151* -	**TIMBER WOLF** *ex* Fishermen XI *-1986* **Jason & Danielle Inc** - *Point Judith, RI* *United States of America* MMSI: 367105430 Official number: 905305	*118* 80 -		**1986 Rodriguez Boat Builders, Inc. — Coden, Al** Yd No: 51 Loa - Br ex - Dght - Lbp 21.98 Br md 6.77 Dpth 3.38 Welded, 1 dk	**(B11B2FV) Fishing Vessel**	**1 oil engine** driving 1 FP propeller
9204790 *2FEI7* -	**TIMBERLAND** *ex* Aquila Companion *-2011* *ex* MSC Java *-2007* *ex* Julia Oldendorff *-2004* **Midlife Shipping Ltd** Imperial Ship Management AB SatCom: Inmarsat C 423593031 *London* *United Kingdom* MMSI: 235090537 Official number: 918036	**13,066** 6,901 20,406	Class: GL	**2000-04 Flensburger Schiffbau-Ges. mbH & Co. KG — Flensburg** Yd No: 706 Loa 153.22 Br ex - Dght 9.720 Lbp 145.75 Br md 23.60 Dpth 13.50 Welded, 1 dk	**(A31A2GX) General Cargo Ship** Grain: 24,425; Bale: 24,365 TEU 1300 C Ho 556 TEU C Dk 744 TEU incl 63 ref C. Compartments: 5 Ho, ER 5 Ha: (14.0 x 8.0) (12.5 x 15.6)3 (25.0 x 20.6)ER Cranes: 2x60t Ice Capable	**1 oil engine** driving 1 FP propeller Total Power: 8,250kW (11,217hp) 15.5kn Mitsubishi 6UEC50LSII 1 x 2 Stroke 6 Cy. 500 x 1950 8250kW (11217bhp) Mitsubishi Heavy Industries Ltd-Japan AuxGen: 2 x 612kW 220/440V a.c Thrusters: 1 Thwart. CP thruster (f) Fuel: 1056.0 (r.f.) 32.5pd
8036665 *WDC7442* -	**TIMBERLINE I** **Let Vessels LLC** - *Atlantic City, NJ* *United States of America* MMSI: 366214160 Official number: 622203	*191* 57 -		**1980 Eastern Marine, Inc. — Panama City, Fl** Yd No: 22 L reg 25.03 Br ex 7.14 Dght - Lbp - Br md - Dpth 3.71 Welded, 1 dk	**(B11B2FV) Fishing Vessel**	**1 oil engine** driving 1 FP propeller Total Power: 335kW (455hp) G.M. (Detroit Diesel) 16V-71-N 1 x Vee 2 Stroke 16 Cy. 108 x 127 335kW (455bhp) General Motors Detroit DieselAllison Divn-USA
9555979 *PPZY* -	**TIMBOPEBA** - **Vale SA** - *Sao Luis* *Brazil* MMSI: 710006240	**482** 144 366		**2010-11 Detroit Brasil Ltda — Itajai** Yd No: 351 Loa 32.00 Br ex - Dght 4.280 Lbp 29.70 Br md 11.60 Dpth 5.36 Welded, 1 dk	**(B32A2ST) Tug**	**2 oil engines** reduction geared to sc. shafts driving 2 Z propellers Total Power: 3,372kW (4,584hp) 11.0kn Caterpillar 3516B-HD 2 x Vee 4 Stroke 16 Cy. 170 x 215 each-1686kW (2292bhp) Caterpillar Inc-USA
9198680 *DIBC* -	**TIMBUS** *ex* Brar Braren *-1999* **ms 'Brar Braren' GmbH & Co KG** Roerd Braren Bereederungs GmbH & Co KG *Hamburg* *Germany* MMSI: 211317180 Official number: 18791	**4,230** 2,150 6,389 T/cm 14.4	Class: GL	**1999-12 Peterswerft Wewelsfleth GmbH & Co. — Wewelsfleth** Yd No: 656 Loa 99.98 (BB) Br ex 17.20 Dght 7.285 Lbp 92.40 Br md 17.00 Dpth 9.25 Welded, 1 dk	**(A31A2GX) General Cargo Ship** Grain: 7,137; Bale: 6,779 TEU 314 C. 314/20' Compartments: 1 Ho, ER 1 Ha: ER Cranes: 2x40t Ice Capable	**1 oil engine** with clutches, flexible couplings & sr reverse geared to sc. shaft driving 1 CP propeller Total Power: 3,780kW (5,139hp) 15.5kn MaK 8M32 1 x 4 Stroke 8 Cy. 320 x 480 3780kW (5139bhp) MaK Motoren GmbH & Co. KG-Kiel AuxGen: 1 x 540kW 400V 50Hz a.c, 1 x 512kW 400V 50Hz a.c Thrusters: 1 Thwart. FP thruster (f) Fuel: 300.0 (d.f.) 13.5pd
9307358 *PHFL* -	**TIMCA** **CV Scheepvaartonderneming Timca** Spliethoff's Bevrachtingskantoor BV SatCom: Inmarsat C 424652110 *Amsterdam* *Netherlands* MMSI: 246521000 Official number: 42575	**28,301** 8,486 18,250	Class: LR ✠**100A1** SS 07/2011 roll on-roll off cargo ship, container cargoes in hold on trailer deck and weather deck *IWS LI Ice Class 1A FS at draught 8.67m Max/min draught fwd 8.67/4.0m Max/min draught aft 8.67/6.50m Required power 6602kw, installed power 25200kw ✠**LMC** **UMS** Eq.Ltr: A†; Cable: 632.5/70.0 U3 (a)	**2006-07 Stocznia Szczecinska Nowa Sp z oo — Szczecin** Yd No: B201/II/01 Loa 205.00 (BB) Br ex 25.80 Dght 8.500 Lbp 190.00 Br md 25.50 Dpth 15.65 Welded, 3 dks	**(A35A2RR) Ro-Ro Cargo Ship** Passengers: driver berths: 12 Stern door/ramp (centre) Len: 17.50 Wid: 25.00 Swl: 85 Lane-Len: 2963 TEU 643 C Ho 346 TEU C Dk 297 TEU incl 20 ref C Compartments: 1 Ho, ER Ice Capable	**2 oil engines** with flexible couplings & sr geared to sc. shafts driving 2 CP propellers Total Power: 25,200kW (34,262hp) 22.0kn Wartsila 12V46 2 x Vee 4 Stroke 12 Cy. 460 x 580 each-12600kW (17131bhp) Wartsila Finland Oy-Finland AuxGen: 2 x 1700kW 450V a.c, 2 x 1292kW 450V 60Hz a.c Boilers: e (ex.g.) 10.2kgf/cm² (10.0bar), TOH (o.f.) 10.2kgf/cm² (10.0bar), TOH (o.f.) (fitted: 2006) 13.3kgf/cm² (13.0bar) Thrusters: 2 Tunnel thruster (f) Fuel: 475.0 (d.f.) 1900.0 (r.f.)

IMO / Call sign	Name / Owner	Tonnage	Class	Build / Dimensions	Type	Machinery
8137770 *PFXD* -	**TIME** *ex* Time Is Money *-2011* *ex* Meander *-2000* *ex* Latona *-1995* **Lutana Watertransport BV** Jogo Short Sea Shipping BV *Terschelling* *Netherlands* MMSI: 245549000 Official number: 1049	*804* 378 1,130		**1973-07 Scheepswerf G Bijlsma & Zoon BV — Wartena** Yd No: 591 Loa 76.41 Br ex 8.13 Dght 3.020 Lbp 74.88 Br md - Dpth 4.30 Welded, 1 dk	**(A31A2GX) General Cargo Ship** Grain: 1,642	**1 oil engine** driving 1 FP propeller Total Power: 625kW (850hp) 9.0kn Caterpillar 1 x 4 Stroke 8 Cy. 625kW (850bhp) Caterpillar Tractor Co-USA
9152571 *DSNQ6* -	**TIME ACE** *ex* World Leader *-2009* *ex* Yusung *-2004* *ex* Hae Wang *-2004* **Time Shipping Co Ltd** - *Jeju* *South Korea* MMSI: 440072000 Official number: JJR-961781	**2,140** 1,173 3,225	Class: KR	**1996-11 Banguhjin Engineering & Shipbuilding Co Ltd — Ulsan** Yd No: 102 Loa 81.00 Br ex - Dght 5.391 Lbp 73.60 Br md 15.00 Dpth 6.30 Welded, 1 dk	**(A31A2GX) General Cargo Ship** Grain: 2,007 Compartments: 1 Ho 1 Ha: (25.8 x 12.0) Cranes: 1x15t	**1 oil engine** geared to sc. shaft driving 1 FP propeller Total Power: 1,851kW (2,517hp) 12.5kn Caterpillar 3606TA 1 x 4 Stroke 6 Cy. 280 x 300 1851kW (2517bhp) Caterpillar Inc-USA AuxGen: 2 x 190kW 445V a.c Fuel: 128.0 (d.f.)
8852356 *WCX2255* -	**TIME BANDIT** - **Time Bandit LLC** - *Juneau, AK* *United States of America* MMSI: 338564000 Official number: 973238	**278** 83 -		**1991 Giddings Boat Works, Inc. — Charleston, Or** Yd No: 18 Loa - Br ex - Dght - Lbp 30.48 Br md 8.53 Dpth 2.44 Welded, 1 dk	**(B11B2FV) Fishing Vessel**	**2 oil engines** reduction geared to sc. shafts driving 2 FP propellers Total Power: 1,194kW (1,624hp) Cummins QSK19-M 2 x 4 Stroke 6 Cy. 159 x 159 each-597kW (812bhp) (new engine 2012) Cummins Engine Co Inc-USA
9291303 *D8CG* -	**TIME HOPE** *ex* Crystal Heart *-2014* **Time Merchant Marine Co Ltd** Time Shipping Co Ltd *South Korea* MMSI: 441979000	**7,443** 3,353 9,999	Class: KR (NK)	**2004-01 Nishi Shipbuilding Co Ltd — Imabari EH** Yd No: 437 Loa 110.67 Br ex - Dght 8.479 Lbp 102.00 Br md 19.20 Dpth 13.50 Welded, 1 dk	**(A31A2GX) General Cargo Ship** Grain: 15,504; Bale: 14,333 2 Ha: (33.6 x 14.0)ER (20.3 x 14.0) Cranes: 2x36t; Derricks: 1x30t	**1 oil engine** driving 1 FP propeller Total Power: 3,900kW (5,302hp) 13.2kn B&W 6L35MC 1 x 2 Stroke 6 Cy. 350 x 1050 3900kW (5302bhp) The Hanshin Diesel Works Ltd-Japan Fuel: 710.0
9680231 *9MQN3* -	**TIME RINA** *ex* Intrepid Sentinel *-2013* **Nam Cheong International Ltd** - *Port Klang* *Malaysia* MMSI: 533180019 Official number: 334592	**1,683** 504 1,319	Class: AB	**2013-10 Fujian Southeast Shipyard — Fuzhou FJ** Yd No: SK81 Loa 59.24 Br ex - Dght 4.964 Lbp 52.21 Br md 14.95 Dpth 6.10 Welded, 1 dk	**(B21B20A) Anchor Handling Tug Supply**	**2 oil engines** reduction geared to sc. shafts driving 2 CP propellers Total Power: 3,840kW (5,220hp) 11.0kn Caterpillar 3516C-HD 2 x Vee 4 Stroke 16 Cy. 170 x 215 each-1920kW (2610bhp) Caterpillar Inc-USA AuxGen: 2 x 800kW a.c, 2 x 350kW a.c Thrusters: 1 Tunnel thruster (f); 1 Tunnel thruster (a) Fuel: 520.0
9029592 *VVDN* -	**TIME SKIPPER** - **Dolphin Offshore Shipping Ltd** - *Mumbai* *India* MMSI: 419028300 Official number: 2706	**101** 30 27	Class: IR	**2002-03 Alang Marine Ltd — Bhavnagar** Yd No: 501 Loa 23.50 Br ex 6.62 Dght 2.210 Lbp 20.45 Br md 6.60 Dpth 3.00 Welded, 1 dk	**(B32A2ST) Tug**	**2 oil engines** geared to sc. shafts driving 2 Directional propellers Total Power: 744kW (1,012hp) 12.0kn Cummins KTA-1150-M 2 x 4 Stroke 6 Cy. 159 x 159 each-372kW (506bhp) Cummins India Ltd-India AuxGen: 2 x 12kW 415V 50Hz a.c
9029607 *AUAL* -	**TIME TRADER** - **Time Shipping Ltd** - *Mumbai* *India* MMSI: 419058500 Official number: 2980	**101** 34 27	Class: (IR)	**2004-05 Alang Marine Ltd — Bhavnagar** Yd No: 502 Loa 23.50 Br ex 6.61 Dght 2.000 Lbp 21.40 Br md 6.60 Dpth 3.00 Welded, 1 dk	**(B32A2ST) Tug**	**2 oil engines** geared to sc. shafts driving 2 Directional propellers Total Power: 700kW (952hp) Cummins KTA-1150-M 2 x 4 Stroke 6 Cy. 159 x 159 each-350kW (476bhp) Kirloskar Oil Engines Ltd-India Fuel: 6.0 (d.f.)
6409636 *HO5365* -	**TIMI** *ex* Old Wine *-2013* *ex* Lady Raffaella *-1997* *ex* Heinrich Essberger *-1975* **Matco Trading LLC** Veesham Shipping Inc *Panama* *Panama* MMSI: 370321000 Official number: 37559PEXT2	*1,212* 583 1,628	Class: (RI) (GL)	**1964-03 Elsflether Werft AG — Elsfleth** Yd No: 340 Converted From: Chemical/Products Tanker-1997 Lengthened-1997 Loa 73.60 Br ex 10.44 Dght 5.188 Lbp 59.85 Br md 10.41 Dpth 6.00 Welded, 1 dk	**(A12C2LW) Wine Tanker** Compartments: 12 Wing Ta, ER	**1 oil engine** driving 1 FP propeller Total Power: 971kW (1,320hp) 12.3kn Deutz RBV8M545 1 x 4 Stroke 8 Cy. 320 x 450 971kW (1320bhp) Kloeckner Humboldt Deutz AG-West Germany AuxGen: 3 x 87kW 400V 50Hz a.c Fuel: 96.5 (d.f.) 5.0pd
9027489 - -	**TIMIKA** - **PT Budhi Segara Lines** - *Surabaya* *Indonesia*	**397** 120 400	Class: KI	**1991-07 P.T. Gresik Jaya Dockyard — Gresik** L reg 46.20 Br ex - Dght 2.480 Lbp 41.70 Br md 10.00 Dpth 2.95 Welded, 1 dk	**(A35D2RL) Landing Craft** Bow ramp (centre)	**2 oil engines** geared to sc. shafts driving 2 Propellers Total Power: 536kW (728hp) 9.0kn Cummins KT-19-M 2 x 4 Stroke 6 Cy. 159 x 159 each-268kW (364bhp) Cummins Engine Co Ltd-United Kingdom
8714619 *OWOE* GR 612	**TIMMIARMIUT** *ex* Atlantic Viking *-2013* *ex* Saeviking *-2006* *ex* Regina C *-2001* **Timmiarmiut Shipping A/S** - *Nuuk* *Denmark* MMSI: 331070000	**1,772** 531 788	Class: NV	**1988-08 Orskov Christensens Staalskibsvaerft A/S — Frederikshavn** (Aft section) Yd No: 175 **1988-08 Bruces Verkstad AB — Landskrona** (Fwd section) Yd No: 14 Loa 55.22 (BB) Br ex 13.06 Dght 5.680 Lbp 47.60 Br md 13.01 Dpth 8.20 Welded, 2 dks	**(B11A2FS) Stern Trawler** Ice Capable	**1 oil engine** with clutches, flexible couplings & sr geared to sc. shaft driving 1 CP propeller Total Power: 2,722kW (3,701hp) Wartsila 8R32BC 1 x 4 Stroke 8 Cy. 320 x 350 2722kW (3701bhp) Wartsila Diesel Oy-Finland AuxGen: 1 x 1440kW 440V 60Hz a.c, 2 x 495kW 440V 60Hz a.c
9372561 *UBQF5* -	**TIMOFEY GUZHENKO** - **Lorama Shipping Co Ltd** Unicom Management Services (St Petersburg) Ltd *St Petersburg* *Russia* MMSI: 273330620 Official number: 080202	**49,597** 21,075 72,722 T/cm 80.4	Class: AB RS	**2009-02 Samsung Heavy Industries Co Ltd — Geoje** Yd No: 1662 Loa 257.00 Br ex 34.06 Dght 14.200 Lbp 234.70 Br md 34.00 Dpth 21.00 Welded, 1 dk	**(A13A2TS) Shuttle Tanker** Double Hull (13F) Liq: 84,641; Liq (Oil): 84,641 Cargo Heating Coils Compartments: 10 Wing Ta, 2 Wing Slop Ta 10 Cargo Pump (s): 10x800m³/hr Manifold: Bow/CM: 119.9m Ice Capable	**3 diesel electric oil engines** driving 2 gen. Connecting to 2 elec. motors each (10000kW) driving 2 Azimuth electric drive units Total Power: 27,550kW (37,456hp) 16.0kn Wartsila 16V38 2 x Vee 4 Stroke 16 Cy. 380 x 475 each-11600kW (15771bhp) Wartsila France SA-France Wartsila 6L38 1 x 4 Stroke 6 Cy. 380 x 475 4350kW (5914bhp) Wartsila France SA-France Thrusters: 1 Thwart. CP thruster (f) Fuel: 296.0 (d.f.) 3401.2 (r.f.)
8727135 *UFWN* TE-1240	**TIMOFEY KOVALYOV** - **Far East Fishing Industry LLC** - *Petropavlovsk-Kamchatskiy* *Russia* Official number: 850543	**448** 134 207	Class: RS	**1986-06 Zavod 'Nikolayevsk-na-Amure' — Nikolayevsk-na-Amure** Yd No: 1240 Loa 44.88 Br ex 9.47 Dght 3.770 Lbp 39.37 Br md 9.30 Dpth 5.13 Welded, 1 dk	**(B11A2FS) Stern Trawler** Ice Capable	**1 oil engine** driving 1 CP propeller Total Power: 588kW (799hp) 11.5kn S.K.L. 6NVD48A-2U 1 x 4 Stroke 6 Cy. 320 x 480 588kW (799bhp) VEB Schwermaschinenbau "KarlLiebknecht" (SKL)-Magdeburg AuxGen: 3 x 150kW a.c
7519816 *CB2637* -	**TIMOR** - **South Pacific Korp SA (SPK)** - *Valparaiso* *Chile* MMSI: 725000078 Official number: 2366	*566* 182 639	Class: (NV)	**1974-12 FEAB-Karlstadverken — Karlstad** Yd No: 106 Loa 49.00 Br ex 10.37 Dght 4.877 Lbp 42.98 Br md 9.50 Dpth 7.32 Welded, 1 dk & S dk	**(B11A2FT) Trawler** Ice Capable	**1 oil engine** driving 1 CP propeller Total Power: 1,416kW (1,925hp) 13.0kn Wichmann 7AXA 1 x 2 Stroke 7 Cy. 300 x 450 1416kW (1925bhp) Wichmann Motorfabrikk AS-Norway AuxGen: 2 x 132kW 220V 50Hz a.c, 1 x 52kW 220V 50Hz a.c Thrusters: 1 Thwart. FP thruster (f); 1 Tunnel thruster (a)
7505047 *HO2123* -	**TIMOR** *ex* Telco Timor *-2003* *ex* Poolster *-1991* **Carina Offshore Ltd** - *Panama* *Panama* MMSI: 372265000 Official number: 3494009A	**236** 71 -	Class: (BV)	**1975-02 Havenbedrijf "Vlaardingen-Oost" B.V. (HVO) — Vlaardingen** Yd No: 790023 Converted From: Trawler-1993 Loa 32.01 Br ex - Dght 3.200 Lbp - Br md 7.54 Dpth 3.41 Welded, 1 dk	**(B22G2OY) Standby Safety Vessel**	**1 oil engine** geared to sc. shaft driving 1 FP propeller Total Power: 736kW (1,001hp) 10.5kn De Industrie 6D7HD 1 x 4 Stroke 6 Cy. 305 x 460 736kW (1001bhp) B.V. Motorenfabriek "De Industrie"-Alphen a/d Rijn AuxGen: 3 x 81kW 220V 50Hz a.c Fuel: 50.0

8009404 *YCUA* -	**TIMOR** **Government of The Republic of Indonesia (Direktorat Jenderal Perhubungan Laut - Ministry of Sea Communications)** PT (Persero) Pengerukan Indonesia *Jakarta* *Indonesia* MMSI: 525019032	*3,801* 1,141 4,002	Class: KI (NK)	**1981**-03 **Ishikawajima Ship & Chemical Plant Co Ltd — Tokyo** Yd No: 516 Loa 95.03 Br ex 18.45 Dght 5.022 Lbp 89.01 Br md 18.41 Dpth 7.01 Welded, 1 dk	**(B33B2DT) Trailing Suction Hopper Dredger** Hopper: 2,000	**2 oil engines** sr geared to sc. shafts driving 2 FP propellers Total Power: 3,090kW (4,202hp) 12.0kn Niigata 6MG31EZ 2 x 4 Stroke 6 Cy. 310 x 380 each-1545kW (2101bhp) Niigata Engineering Co Ltd-Japan AuxGen: 3 x 480kW Thrusters: 1 Tunnel thruster (f)
6402901 *HO4822* -	**TIMOR CHALLENGER** *ex* Viking Challenger *-2007* *ex* Britannia Challenger *-1998* *ex* Britannia de Hoop *-1990* *ex* De Hoop *-1989* **Wexford Shipping & Trading Inc** Hakvoort Transport Shipping BV *Panama* *Panama* MMSI: 372174000 Official number: 37242PEXT2	**999** 299 287	Class: (LR) ✠ Classed LR until 1/7/06	**1964**-04 **N.V. Scheepswerf Gebr. Pot — Bolnes** Yd No: 950 Converted From: Hospital Vessel-1990 Loa 64.45 Br ex 10.32 Dght 4.700 Lbp 54.00 Br md 10.22 Dpth 6.70 Welded, 2 dks	**(B22G20Y) Standby Safety Vessel** Derricks: 1x1.5t Ice Capable	**1 oil engine** sr reverse geared to sc. shaft driving 1 FP propeller Total Power: 662kW (900hp) 12.0kn Bolnes 12DL75/475 1 x Vee 2 Stroke 12 Cy. 190 x 350 662kW (900bhp) NV Machinefabriek 'Bolnes' v/h JHvan Cappellen-Netherlands AuxGen: 2 x 76kW 380V 50Hz a.c Thrusters: 1 Thwart. FP thruster (f)
7618210 - -	**TIMOR SEA** *ex* Little Curtis *-1989* - -	*152* 103 -	Class: (AB)	**1960 Equitable Equipment Co. — Madisonville, La** Yd No: 1193 Loa - Br ex 7.32 Dght - Lbp 23.78 Br md 7.27 Dpth 3.15 Welded, 1 dk	**(B32A2ST) Tug**	**2 oil engines** sr reverse geared to sc. shafts driving 2 FP propellers Total Power: 882kW (1,200hp) Caterpillar D398TA 2 x Vee 4 Stroke 12 Cy. 159 x 203 each-441kW (600bhp) Caterpillar Tractor Co-USA Fuel: 69.0 (d.f.)
8202434 *YCVT* -	**TIMOR SPIRIT** *ex* Nissen Maru No. 5 *-2003* **PT Indobaruna Bulk Transport** - *Jakarta* *Indonesia*	**498** 164 683	Class: (KI)	**1982**-10 **K.K. Miura Zosensho — Saiki** Yd No: 661 Loa 48.01 Br ex - Dght 3.701 Lbp 44.58 Br md 9.01 Dpth 4.02 Welded, 1 dk	**(A24A2BT) Cement Carrier** Grain: 574	**1 oil engine** with flexible couplings & sr gearedto sc. shaft driving 1 FP propeller Total Power: 588kW (799hp) Daihatsu 6PSHTCM-26H 1 x 4 Stroke 6 Cy. 260 x 320 588kW (799bhp) Daihatsu Diesel Manufacturing Co Lt-Japan
9172947 *A8IN9* -	**TIMOR STREAM** *ex* Stream Express *-2005* **'Timor Stream' Schifffahrtsgesellschaft mbH & Co KG** Triton Schiffahrts GmbH *Monrovia* *Liberia* MMSI: 636091006 Official number: 91006	**9,307** 4,983 11,013	Class: BV (NK)	**1998**-09 **Kitanihon Zosen K.K. — Hachinohe** Yd No: 318 Loa 150.00 (BB) Br ex - Dght 9.268 Lbp 138.50 Br md 22.00 Dpth 13.30 Welded, 2 dks	**(A34A2GR) Refrigerated Cargo Ship** Ins: 15,152 TEU 343 C Ho 42 TEU C Dk 301 TEU incl 126 ref C Compartments: 4 Ho, ER 4 Ha: 4 (7.0 x 8.0)ER Cranes: 2x40t,2x8t	**1 oil engine** driving 1 FP propeller Total Power: 12,622kW (17,161hp) 20.2kn B&W 8S50MC-C 1 x 2 Stroke 8 Cy. 500 x 2000 12622kW (17161bhp) Hitachi Zosen Corp-Japan AuxGen: 4 x 800kW 440/110V 60Hz a.c Thrusters: 1 Tunnel thruster (f) Fuel: 100.0 (d.f.) 1250.0 (r.f.) 45.0pd
7902049 *WDB4634* -	**TIMOTHY L. REINAUER** *ex* Bridget McAllister *-2009* *ex* Ocean Star *-2003* **Reinauer Transportation Companies LLC** - *New York, NY* *United States of America* MMSI: 366900580 Official number: 609835	**451** 135 -	Class: (AB)	**1979**-08 **McDermott Shipyards Inc — Morgan City LA** Yd No: 245 Loa 38.41 Br ex 10.37 Dght 4.182 Lbp 36.38 Br md 10.36 Dpth 4.88 Welded, 1 dk	**(B32A2ST) Tug**	**2 oil engines** reverse reduction geared to sc. shafts driving 2 FP propellers Total Power: 2,868kW (3,900hp) 11.8kn EMD (Electro-Motive) 16-645-E6 2 x Vee 2 Stroke 16 Cy. 230 x 254 each-1434kW (1950bhp) General Motors Corp.Electro-Motive Div.-La Grange AuxGen: 2 x 125kW a.c
8997895 *WDC8133* -	**TIMOTHY MCALLISTER** *ex* Osprey *-2005* *ex* Barbara McAllister *-2005* *ex* Wapato (YTB-788) *-2002* **McAllister Maritime Tugs Inc** McAllister Towing of New York LLC *New York, NY* *United States of America* MMSI: 367082130 Official number: 1138958	*240* 72 -		**1966**-06 **Marinette Marine Corp — Marinette WI** Loa 33.22 Br ex 9.44 Dght 4.260 Lbp - Br md - Dpth 4.87 Welded, 1 dk	**(B32A2ST) Tug**	**1 oil engine** driving 1 Propeller Total Power: 1,471kW (2,000hp)
8855750 *WDD5541* -	**TIMOTHY MICHAEL** **Palombo Fisheries Ltd** - *Newport, RI* *United States of America* MMSI: 367159840 Official number: 673582	*106* 85 -		**1984 Newport Offshore Ltd. — Newport, RI** Loa - Br ex - Dght - Lbp 23.47 Br md 6.71 Dpth 2.74 Welded, 1 dk	**(B11B2FV) Fishing Vessel**	**1 oil engine** driving 1 FP propeller
8945701 *DUA2603* -	**TIMOTHY T. L.** *ex* Mary Anne *-2002* *ex* Cheryl-T *-2002* **Goldmark Sea Carriers Inc** - *Manila* *Philippines* Official number: MNLD002327	*476* 314 -		**1995 at Manila** L reg 47.01 Br ex - Dght - Lbp - Br md 10.36 Dpth 3.35 Welded, 1 dk	**(A13B2TU) Tanker (unspecified)**	**1 oil engine** geared to sc. shaft driving 1 FP propeller Total Power: 294kW (400hp) Caterpillar 1 x 4 Stroke 6 Cy. 294kW (400bhp) Caterpillar Inc-USA
9400629 - -	**TIMRAR** **P&O Maritime FZE** - *Dubai* *United Arab Emirates* Official number: 6280	**250** 75 150	Class: LR ✠ **100A1** SS 03/2009 tug **LMC** **UMS** Eq.Ltr: F; Cable: 275.0/19.0 U2 (a)	**2009**-03 **Song Thu Co. — Da Nang** (Hull) Yd No: (512217) **2009**-03 **B.V. Scheepswerf Damen — Gorinchem** Yd No: 512217 Loa 24.47 Br ex 11.33 Dght 3.650 Lbp 22.16 Br md 10.70 Dpth 4.60 Welded, 1 dk	**(B32A2ST) Tug**	**2 oil engines** gearing integral to driving 2 Directional propellers Total Power: 4,200kW (5,710hp) Caterpillar 3516B 2 x Vee 4 Stroke 16 Cy. 170 x 190 each-2100kW (2855bhp) Caterpillar Inc-USA AuxGen: 2 x 60kW 400V 50Hz a.c
7435228 - -	**TIMSAH 1** **Suez Canal Authority** - *Ismailia* *Egypt*	*200* - 350	Class: (LR) ✠ Classed LR until 3/86	**1980**-07 **Canal Naval Construction Co. — Port Said (Port Fuad)** (Hull) **1980**-07 **Timsah SB. Co. — Ismailia** Yd No: 107 Loa 38.51 Br ex 7.32 Dght 2.501 Lbp 36.00 Br md 7.00 Dpth 3.00 Welded, 1 dk	**(A14A2LO) Water Tanker** Liq: 300 Compartments: 6 Ta, ER	**1 oil engine** with clutches, flexible couplings & sr reverse geared to sc. shaft driving 1 FP propeller Total Power: 282kW (383hp) Blackstone E6 1 x 4 Stroke 6 Cy. 222 x 292 282kW (383bhp) Mirrlees Blackstone (Stamford)Ltd.-Stamford AuxGen: 1 x 75kW 120V d.c
7435242 - -	**TIMSAH 2** **Suez Canal Authority** - *Ismailia* *Egypt*	*200* - 350	Class: (LR) ✠ Classed LR until 28/2/86	**1980**-07 **Canal Naval Construction Co. — Port Said (Port Fuad)** (Hull) **1980**-07 **Timsah SB. Co. — Ismailia** Yd No: 108 Loa 38.51 Br ex 7.32 Dght 2.501 Lbp 36.00 Br md 7.00 Dpth 3.00 Welded, 1 dk	**(A14A2LO) Water Tanker** Liq: 300 Compartments: 6 Ta, ER	**1 oil engine** with clutches, flexible couplings & sr reverse geared to sc. shaft driving 1 FP propeller Total Power: 282kW (383hp) Blackstone E6 1 x 4 Stroke 6 Cy. 222 x 292 282kW (383bhp) Mirrlees Blackstone (Stamford)Ltd.-Stamford AuxGen: 1 x 75kW 120V d.c
7928316 - -	**TIMSAH 3** **Suez Canal Authority** - *Port Said* *Egypt*	*260* - 300	Class: (GL)	**1982**-08 **Canal Naval Construction Co. — Port Said (Port Fuad)** Yd No: 216 Loa 43.36 Br ex 8.16 Dght 2.661 Lbp 42.22 Br md 7.75 Dpth 3.00 Welded, 1 dk	**(A13B2TP) Products Tanker** Compartments: 6 Ta, ER	**2 oil engines** reverse reduction geared to sc. shafts driving 2 FP propellers Total Power: 970kW (1,318hp) 10.0kn G.M. (Detroit Diesel) 12V-71-TI 2 x Vee 2 Stroke 12 Cy. 108 x 127 each-485kW (659bhp) General Motors Detroit DieselAllison Divn-USA
5395917 - -	**TIMSAH II** *ex* Faye B. *-1977* *ex* Yoko Maru *-1969* **Timsah Shipbuilding Co** - *Alexandria* *Egypt* Official number: 1341	*366* 11 -	Class: (AB) (BV)	**1962 Iino Jukogyo KK — Maizuru KY** Yd No: 64 Loa - Br ex 8.97 Dght 3.169 Lbp 34.90 Br md 8.95 Dpth 4.20 Riveted\Welded, 1 dk	**(B32A2ST) Tug**	**2 oil engines** dr geared to sc. shafts driving 2 CP propellers Total Power: 1,324kW (1,800hp) 12.5kn Fuji 6SD34 2 x 4 Stroke 6 Cy. 340 x 470 each-662kW (900bhp) Fuji Diesel Co Ltd-Japan AuxGen: 1 x 60kW a.c, 2 x 25kW a.c, 1 x 12kW a.c Fuel: 168.5 (d.f.)
8823329 *YGSX* -	**TIMUR CEPAT** *ex* Koshi Maru *-2004* **PT Dharma Ichtiar Indo Lines** - *Surabaya* *Indonesia* Official number: 00899246	**520** 340 543	Class: KI	**1989**-01 **YK Furumoto Tekko Zosensho — Osakikamijima** Loa 48.92 Br ex - Dght 3.270 Lbp 45.70 Br md 8.30 Dpth 5.10 Welded, 1 dk	**(A31A2GX) General Cargo Ship**	**1 oil engine** driving 1 FP propeller Total Power: 515kW (700hp) Matsui 6M26KGHS 1 x 4 Stroke 6 Cy. 260 x 400 515kW (700bhp) Matsui Iron Works Co Ltd-Japan AuxGen: 1 x 50kW 220V a.c

IMO / Call sign	Name / Owner	Tonnage	Class	Built / Dimensions	Type / Capacity	Machinery
8318594 *PNFF* -	**TIMUR LAUT MAS** *ex* ILIS Virgo *-2010* *ex* Sun Royal *-1999* **Baruna Lintas Samudra Shipping PT** - *Tanjung Priok* *Indonesia* MMSI: 525016600	**1,522** 700 2,352	Class: KI (NV) (NK)	**1983**-12 **Hakata Zosen K.K. — Imabari** Yd No: 283 Loa 81.01 Br ex 12.04 Dght 4.950 Lbp 75.01 Br md 12.00 Dpth 5.70 Welded, 1 dk	**(A12B2TR) Chemical/Products Tanker** Liq: 2,453; Liq (Oil): 2,453	**1 oil engine** with clutches, flexible couplings & sr geared to sc. shaft driving 1 CP propeller Total Power: 1,471kW (2,000hp) 12.0kn Hanshin 6EL32 1 x 4 Stroke 6 Cy. 320 x 640 1471kW (2000bhp) The Hanshin Diesel Works Ltd-Japan AuxGen: 3 x 112kW
9064217 *JZAF* -	**TIMUR LAUT MAS 2** *ex* Rengganis *-2013* **Dildar Shipping Inc** Calmsea Ship Management Ltd *Jakarta* *Indonesia* MMSI: 525019634	**2,543** 1,074 3,667 T/cm 10.8	Class: BV NK	**1993**-03 **Hayashikane Dockyard Co Ltd — Nagasaki NS** Yd No: 998 Loa 89.95 (BB) Br ex 14.72 Dght 5.612 Lbp 82.50 Br md 14.60 Dpth 7.40 Welded, 1 dk	**(A12B2TR) Chemical/Products Tanker** Double Hull (13F) Liq: 3,856; Liq (Oil): 3,856 Cargo Heating Coils Compartments: 1 Ta, 8 Wing Ta, ER 9 Cargo Pump (s): 8x150m³/hr, 1x100m³/hr Manifold: Bow/CM: 44.3m	**1 oil engine** driving 1 FP propeller Total Power: 2,185kW (2,971hp) 12.6kn B&W 6S26MC 1 x 2 Stroke 6 Cy. 260 x 980 2185kW (2971bhp) Makita Corp-Japan AuxGen: 2 x 220kW a.c Fuel: 80.0 (d.f.) 185.0 (r.f.)
8122476 *YFWO* -	**TIMUR MANDIRI** *ex* Duyiung-101 *-2006* *ex* Kyoriki Maru *-2000* *ex* Chiyo Maru No. 5 *-1989* **Lefinus Tunggal Tual** - *Ambon* *Indonesia*	**391** 225 350	Class: KI	**1981**-09 **Maeno Zosen KK — Sanyoonoda YC** Yd No: 68 Loa 42.50 Br ex - Dght 3.120 Lbp 41.00 Br md 7.50 Dpth 4.90 Welded, 1 dk	**(A31A2GX) General Cargo Ship**	**1 oil engine** driving 1 FP propeller Total Power: 294kW (400hp) 9.0kn Matsui 6M26KGS 1 x 4 Stroke 6 Cy. 260 x 400 294kW (400bhp) Matsui Iron Works Co Ltd-Japan
8877461 *HP5211* -	**TIN TIN** *ex* Wing Sang *-1995* **Multiwise Development Ltd** - *Panama* *Panama* Official number: 1828189C	**109** 33 -		**1976 Miyama Zosen Kogyo — Japan** L reg 25.25 Br ex - Dght - Lbp - Br md 5.37 Dpth 2.30 Welded, 1 dk	**(A31A2GX) General Cargo Ship**	**1 oil engine** driving 1 FP propeller
8974207 *9A8941* -	**TIN UJEVIC** *ex* Ano Chora Express *-2003* **Jadrolinija** - *Rijeka* *Croatia* MMSI: 238078000	*4,103* 2,044 -	Class: CS	**2001 in Greece** Loa 98.39 Br ex - Dght 2.700 Lbp 81.20 Br md 17.00 Dpth 3.80 Welded, 1 dk	**(A36A2PR) Passenger/Ro-Ro Ship (Vehicles)** Passengers: unberthed: 1300 Bow ramp (f) Stern ramp (a)	**4 oil engines** geared to sc. shafts driving 4 FP propellers Total Power: 3,280kW (4,460hp) 14.0kn Caterpillar 3508B 4 x Vee 4 Stroke 8 Cy. 170 x 190 each-820kW (1115bhp) Caterpillar Inc-USA
7827952 - -	**TIN YI** *ex* Yuan Feng No. 1 *-2005* *ex* Global 6 *-2004* *ex* Universal 8 *-2002* *ex* Global 8 *-2002* *ex* Daisen *-2001* *ex* Kowa Maru *-1993* *ex* Tenryu Maru No. 15 *-1984* - -	**1,371** 789 2,060	Class: (BV)	**1978**-01 **Kochi Jyuko K.K. — Kochi** Yd No: 1271 Loa 72.63 Br ex - Dght 5.010 Lbp 68.00 Br md 11.51 Dpth 6.81 Welded, 1 dk	**(A31A2GX) General Cargo Ship** Grain: 3,050 Compartments: 1 Ho, ER 1 Ha: (37.2 x 8.0)ER	**1 oil engine** driving 1 FP propeller Total Power: 1,618kW (2,200hp) 14.0kn Hanshin 6LU35 1 x 4 Stroke 6 Cy. 350 x 550 1618kW (2200bhp) Hanshin Nainenki Kogyo-Japan
8405074 *9WFD4* -	**TINA** *ex* Glory Selatan V *-2001* **Kusin Jaya Sdn Bhd** Apollo Agencies (1980) Sdn Bhd *Kuching* *Malaysia* MMSI: 533519000 Official number: 329404	**1,673** 1,009 2,871	Class: (NK)	**1984**-05 **Iwagi Zosen Co Ltd — Kamijima EH** Yd No: 102 Loa 74.66 (BB) Br ex 13.03 Dght 5.812 Lbp 68.00 Br md 13.01 Dpth 7.01 Welded, 1 dk	**(A31A2GX) General Cargo Ship** Grain: 3,533; Bale: 3,137 Compartments: 2 Ho, ER 2 Ha: (16.9 x 6.5) (14.3 x 6.5)ER Derricks: 2x12t	**1 oil engine** driving 1 FP propeller Total Power: 1,103kW (1,500hp) 11.0kn Hanshin 6LU32 1 x 4 Stroke 6 Cy. 320 x 510 1103kW (1500bhp) The Hanshin Diesel Works Ltd-Japan AuxGen: 2 x 96kW a.c
5410315 *HP6047* -	**TINA** *ex* Ernestine *-1991* *ex* Atlantis IV *-1984* *ex* Atlandtis IV *-1982* *ex* Atlantis IV *-1981* *ex* Atlantis *-1980* **Chrismar Marine Co** - *Panama* *Panama* Official number: 20469PEXT2	**422** 399 740	Class: (GL)	**1963 Jadewerft Wilhelmshaven GmbH — Wilhelmshaven** Yd No: 89 Loa 53.62 Br ex 9.33 Dght 3.210 Lbp 49.00 Br md 9.30 Dpth 5.39 Welded, 1 dk & S dk	**(A31A2GX) General Cargo Ship** Grain: 1,517; Bale: 1,430 Compartments: 1 Ho, ER 1 Ha: (26.6 x 5.4)ER Derricks: 2x2t Ice Capable	**1 oil engine** sr geared to sc. shaft driving 1 FP propeller Total Power: 221kW (300hp) 9.0kn MWM RHS435SU 1 x 4 Stroke 6 Cy. 250 x 350 221kW (300bhp) Motoren Werke Mannheim AG (MWM)-West Germany
5120908 - -	**TINA** *ex* Timo *-1994* *ex* Freiheit *-1978* **BV Shallow Shipping** -	**328** 199 518	Class: GL	**1960**-08 **J.J. Sietas Schiffswerft — Hamburg** Yd No: 465 Lengthened & Deepened-1982 Lengthened-1969 Loa 47.15 Br ex 7.27 Dght 2.558 Lbp 43.79 Br md 7.26 Dpth 3.71 Welded, 1 dk	**(A31A2GX) General Cargo Ship** Grain: 781 Compartments: 1 Ho, ER 1 Ha: (26.0 x 4.9)ER Derricks: 1x1.5t	**1 oil engine** reduction geared to sc. shaft driving 1 Directional propeller Total Power: 146kW (199hp) 8.0kn Deutz RA6M528 1 x 4 Stroke 6 Cy. 220 x 280 146kW (199bhp) Kloeckner Humboldt Deutz AG-West Germany
7634953 *WAI2196* -	**TINA** *ex* Diane Karen III *-1989* *ex* Tina *-1989* **Nascimento Ruela** - *Perth Amboy, NJ* *United States of America* MMSI: 367013530 Official number: 563878	*135* 92 -		**1975 Marine Builders, Inc. — Mobile, Al** Yd No: 85 L reg 23.47 Br ex 6.84 Dght - Lbp - Br md - Dpth 3.38 Welded, 1 dk	**(B11B2FV) Fishing Vessel**	**1 oil engine** driving 1 FP propeller Total Power: 313kW (426hp) Caterpillar D353SCAC 1 x 4 Stroke 6 Cy. 159 x 203 313kW (426bhp) Caterpillar Tractor Co-USA
8973007 *WDC3702* -	**TINA** **Wilmington Tug Inc** - *New Castle, DE* *United States of America* MMSI: 367012670 Official number: 580169	*109* 86 -		**1977**-02 **Gladding-Hearn SB. Duclos Corp. — Somerset, Ma** Yd No: F-180 Loa 19.80 Br ex - Dght - Lbp - Br md 7.90 Dpth 2.86 Welded, 1 dk	**(B32A2ST) Tug**	**2 oil engines** gearing integral to driving 2 Z propellers Total Power: 1,060kW (1,442hp) G.M. (Detroit Diesel) 16V-71 2 x Vee 2 Stroke 16 Cy. 108 x 127 each-530kW (721bhp) General Motors Detroit DieselAllison Divn-USA
8733316 *ZR4854* CTA 186	**TINA** **Joenardo Fishing CC** - *Cape Town* *South Africa* MMSI: 601620000 Official number: 10722	*137* 41 -		**2007**-01 **Tallie Marine Pty Ltd — St Helena Bay** Loa 21.10 (BB) Br ex - Dght 2.400 Lbp - Br md 7.20 Dpth 3.60 Bonded, 1 dk	**(B11B2FV) Fishing Vessel** Hull Material: Reinforced Plastic	**1 oil engine** driving 1 Propeller 9.0kn
9277383 *PBKA* -	**TINA** *ex* Gotland *-2011* *completed as* Tina *-2003* **Scheepvaartonderneming Tina II CV** Holwerda Shipmanagement BV *Heerenveen* *Netherlands* MMSI: 244198000 Official number: 41651	**7,519** 3,570 8,634	Class: GL	**2003**-04 **J.J. Sietas KG Schiffswerft GmbH & Co. — Hamburg** Yd No: 1159 Loa 137.50 (BB) Br ex - Dght 7.470 Lbp 126.42 Br md 21.30 Dpth 9.36 Welded	**(A33A2CC) Container Ship (Fully Cellular)** Double Bottom Entire Compartment Length TEU 822 C Ho 226 TEU C Dk 596 TEU incl 150 ref C. Compartments: 4 Cell Ho, ER 4 Ha: ER Ice Capable	**1 oil engine** geared to sc. shaft driving 1 CP propeller Total Power: 8,400kW (11,421hp) 19.0kn MaK 9M43 1 x 4 Stroke 9 Cy. 430 x 610 8400kW (11421bhp) Caterpillar Motoren GmbH & Co. KG-Germany AuxGen: 2 x 535kW 380V a.c Thrusters: 1 Thwart. CP thruster (f) Fuel: 168.0 (d.f.) 803.0 (r.f.)
9215749 *A8OV8* -	**TINA** *ex* Astrale *-2011* *ex* Bergen Trader *-2008* **Oceanfront Maritime Co Ltd** Athenian Ship Management Inc *Monrovia* *Liberia* MMSI: 636013718 Official number: 13718	**39,126** 25,373 75,933	Class: BV (NK)	**2000**-10 **Kanasashi Heavy Industries Co Ltd — Toyohashi AI** Yd No: 3525 Loa 224.99 (BB) Br ex - Dght 14.029 Lbp 217.00 Br md 32.26 Dpth 19.30 Welded, 1 dk	**(A21A2BC) Bulk Carrier** Grain: 90,165; Bale: 86,467 Compartments: 7 Ho, ER 7 Ha: (16.2 x 12.8)6 (18.7 x 14.0)ER	**1 oil engine** driving 1 FP propeller Total Power: 9,342kW (12,701hp) 14.5kn B&W 7S50MC-C 1 x 2 Stroke 7 Cy. 500 x 2000 9342kW (12701bhp) Kawasaki Heavy Industries Ltd-Japan
9466221 *PBYP* -	**TINA** **Tina Shipping BV** W & R Shipping BV SatCom: Inmarsat C 424457210 *Rotterdam* *Netherlands* MMSI: 245301000 Official number: 52529	**2,622** 1,421 3,500	Class: BV	**2010**-11 **Anqing Zhouyang Shipbuilding Co Ltd — Zongyang County AH** Yd No: 3500-06-02 Loa 88.30 (BB) Br ex 12.95 Dght 5.400 Lbp 83.44 Br md 12.90 Dpth 7.00 Welded, 1 dk	**(A31A2GX) General Cargo Ship** Double Hull Grain: 5,178 TEU 163 Compartments: 1 Ho, 1 Tw Dk, ER 1 Ha: ER Ice Capable	**1 oil engine** reduction geared to sc. shafts driving 1 FP propeller Total Power: 2,206kW (2,999hp) 12.5kn A.B.C. 12VDZC 1 x Vee 4 Stroke 12 Cy. 256 x 310 2206kW (2999bhp) Anglo Belgian Corp NV (ABC)-Belgium AuxGen: 1 x 360kW 400V a.c, 2 x 230kW 400V a.c Thrusters: 1 Tunnel thruster (f) Fuel: 48.0 (d.f.) 240.0 (r.f.)

IMO / Call sign	Name / Owner	Tonnage	Class	Builder / Dimensions	Type	Machinery
9416331 *2APY2* -	**TINA C** **Carisbrooke Shipping 638 Ltd** Carisbrooke Shipping Ltd *Cowes* *United Kingdom* MMSI: 235061987 Official number: 914829	**3,391** 1,963 5,664 T/cm 13.0	Class: BV	**2008-09 Construcciones Navales P Freire SA — Vigo** Yd No: 638 Loa 99.60 (BB) Br ex - Dght 6.200 Lbp - Br md 14.50 Dpth 7.35 Welded, 1 dk	**(A31A2GX) General Cargo Ship** Grain: 6,982 Compartments: 2 Ho, ER 2 Ha: ER	**1 oil engine** reduction geared to sc. shaft driving 1 CP propeller Total Power: 1,980kW (2,692hp) 11.0kn MaK 6M25 1 x 4 Stroke 6 Cy. 255 x 400 1980kW (2692bhp) Caterpillar Motoren GmbH & Co. KG-Germany AuxGen: 1 x 312kW 400V 50Hz a.c, 2 x 168kW 400V 50Hz a.c Thrusters: 1 Tunnel thruster (f)
8108626 - -	**TINA CHRISTINA** *ex* Anders Nees *-1999* - -	*217* 64 200		**1982-03 Johs Kristensen Skibsbyggeri A/S — Hvide Sande** Yd No: 158 Loa 26.22 Br ex 7.45 Dght 3.841 Lbp 23.02 Br md 7.36 Dpth 3.92 Welded, 1 dk	**(B11B2FV) Fishing Vessel** Grain: 165 Compartments: 1 Ho, ER 1 Ha:	**1 oil engine** driving 1 CP propeller Total Power: 423kW (575hp) Callesen 5-427-EOT 1 x 4 Stroke 5 Cy. 270 x 400 423kW (575bhp) Aabenraa Motorfabrik, HeinrichCallesen A/S-Denmark
9465772 *3EYG* -	**TINA IV** **Virgilia Shipmanagement Ltd** First Lines Co SA *Panama* *Panama* MMSI: 371699000 Official number: 4043309A	**40,170** 25,603 75,187	Class: AB	**2009-04 Hudong-Zhonghua Shipbuilding (Group) Co Ltd — Shanghai** Yd No: H1503A Loa 225.00 (BB) Br ex 32.30 Dght 14.250 Lbp 217.00 Br md 32.26 Dpth 19.60 Welded, 1 dk	**(A21A2BC) Bulk Carrier** Grain: 91,717; Bale: 89,882 Compartments: 7 Ho, ER 7 Ha: 6 (14.6 x 15.0)ER (14.6 x 13.2)	**1 oil engine** driving 1 FP propeller Total Power: 11,300kW (15,363hp) 14.0kn MAN-B&W 5S60MC-C 1 x 2 Stroke 5 Cy. 600 x 2400 11300kW (15363bhp) Hudong Heavy Machinery Co Ltd-China AuxGen: 3 x 570kW a.c Fuel: 135.0 (d.f.) 2627.0 (r.f.)
8416449 *OWWM* E 689	**TINA-JEANETTE** *ex* Darwin *-2011* *ex* Cattleya S. *-2007* *ex* Cattleya *-2006* **P/R Jens Peter Langer** - *Esbjerg* *Denmark* MMSI: 219138000 Official number: H896	**498** 288 724		**1984-11 Carl B Hoffmanns Maskinfabrik A/S — Esbjerg** (Hull) Yd No: 52 **1984-11 Grumsens Maskinfabrik A/S — Esbjerg** Yd No: 1 Loa 42.30 Br ex 8.41 Dght - Lbp - Br md - Dpth 5.80 Welded, 1 dk	**(B11A2FT) Trawler**	**1 oil engine** geared to sc. shaft driving 1 FP propeller Total Power: 809kW (1,100hp) Alpha 6T23L-KVO 1 x 4 Stroke 6 Cy. 225 x 300 809kW (1100bhp) MAN B&W Diesel A/S-Denmark
7612010 *WDC3947* - -	**TINA LYNN** *ex* Kathy Ann *-1990* *ex* Eleanor Eileen XV *-1990* *ex* Quiet Waters *-1980* **Hill Enterprises Inc** - *Cape May, NJ* *United States of America* MMSI: 367016870 Official number: 559595	*166* 114 -		**1974 Toche Enterprises, Inc. — Ocean Springs, Ms** L reg 24.27 Br ex 7.47 Dght - Lbp - Br md - Dpth 3.76 Welded, 1 dk	**(B11B2FV) Fishing Vessel**	**1 oil engine** driving 1 FP propeller Total Power: 338kW (460hp)
7629116 *WYT9854* -	**TINA MARIA** **Jason E Meyers** - *Atlantic City, NJ* *United States of America* Official number: 562034	*127* 95 -		**1974 Master Marine, Inc. — Bayou La Batre, Al** Yd No: 170 L reg 22.59 Br ex 6.71 Dght - Lbp - Br md - Dpth 3.41 Welded, 1 dk	**(B11B2FV) Fishing Vessel**	**1 oil engine** driving 1 FP propeller Total Power: 268kW (364hp) General Motors 1 x Vee 2 Stroke 12 Cy. 268kW (364bhp) General Motors Detroit DieselAllison Divn-USA
5144318 *OZPP* GR 62 98	**TINA ROSENGREN** *ex* Midvingur *-1998* *ex* Havornin *-1996* **Polar Scallop AS** - *Nuuk* *Denmark* Official number: H1360	**241** 81 200	Class: (BV)	**1961 Ateliers et Chantiers de La Manche — Dieppe** Yd No: 1162 Loa 36.17 Br ex 7.27 Dght 3.302 Lbp 31.20 Br md 7.22 Dpth 3.76 Welded, 1 dk	**(B11A2FT) Trawler**	**1 oil engine** driving 1 CP propeller Total Power: 368kW (500hp) 11.0kn Alpha 405-26VO 1 x 2 Stroke 5 Cy. 260 x 400 368kW (500bhp) (new engine 1969) Alpha Diesel A/S-Denmark AuxGen: 2 x 64kW 220V 50Hz a.c
9478298 *OWEU2* -	**TINA THERESA** **Herning Shipping A/S** - SatCom: Inmarsat Mini-M 764917852 *Herning* *Denmark (DIS)* MMSI: 219057000 Official number: D4453	**5,706** 2,406 7,963 T/cm 17.0	Class: BV	**2009-09 Nantong Mingde Heavy Industry Co Ltd — Tongzhou JS** Yd No: 44-8000CT-06 Loa 101.39 (BB) Br ex 19.05 Dght 7.610 Lbp 94.96 Br md 19.05 Dpth 10.53 Welded, 1 dk	**(A12B2TR) Chemical/Products Tanker** Double Hull (13F) Liq: 8,963; Liq (Oil): 8,963 Cargo Heating Coils Compartments: 8 Wing Ta, 2 Wing Slop Ta, ER 8 Cargo Pump (s): 8x200m³/hr Manifold: Bow/CM: 48.6m	**1 oil engine** reduction geared to sc. shaft driving 1 CP propeller Total Power: 2,943kW (4,001hp) 12.6kn Bergens B32: 40L8P 1 x 4 Stroke 8 Cy. 320 x 400 2943kW (4001bhp) Rolls Royce Marine AS-Norway AuxGen: 3 x 420kW 50Hz a.c, 1 x 1080kW 50Hz a.c Thrusters: 1 Tunnel thruster (f) Fuel: 101.0 (d.f.) 504.0 (r.f.)
8512944 *C6QD3* -	**TINAMOU ARROW** *ex* Westwood Marianne *-2007* **Gearbulk Shipowning Ltd** Gearbulk Ltd SatCom: Inmarsat A 1320306 *Nassau* *Bahamas* MMSI: 308987000 Official number: 731065	**28,805** 13,964 45,252	Class: NV (NK)	**1986-10 Ishikawajima-Harima Heavy Industries Co Ltd (IHI) — Aioi HG** Yd No: 2951 Loa 199.90 (BB) Br ex - Dght 11.720 Lbp 188.70 Br md 30.51 Dpth 16.21 Welded, 1 dk	**(A31A2GO) Open Hatch Cargo Ship** Grain: 51,006; Bale: 50,000 TEU 2029 C. 2029/20' (40') Compartments: 11 Ho, ER 11 Ha: (6.5 x 13.0)10 (13.1 x 25.3)ER Gantry cranes: 2x40t	**1 oil engine** driving 1 FP propeller Total Power: 8,076kW (10,980hp) 14.6kn Sulzer 6RTA62 1 x 2 Stroke 6 Cy. 620 x 2150 8076kW (10980bhp) Ishikawajima Harima Heavy IndustrieCo Ltd (IHI)-Japan AuxGen: 4 x 520kW 450V 60Hz a.c, 1 x 80kW 450V 60Hz a.c
7505798 *TCRV* -	**TINAZTEPE S** *ex* Nurettin Kalkavan *-2005* *ex* Nazim Kalkavan *-1997* **Batu Denizcilik Ltd Sti** - SatCom: Inmarsat C 427112290 *Istanbul* *Turkey* MMSI: 271002039 Official number: 4631	**1,900** 1,201 3,201	Class: BR (LR) (TL) ✠ Classed LR until 5/5/00	**1979-03 Degas Izmir Tersanesi Gemi Insaat ve Demir Imalat — Izmir** Yd No: 4 Loa 81.62 Br ex 13.80 Dght 5.571 Lbp 74.50 Br md 13.76 Dpth 6.61 Welded, 1 dk	**(A31A2GX) General Cargo Ship** Grain: 4,140; Bale: 3,800 TEU 96 C.Ho 72/20' C.Dk 24/20' Compartments: 2 Ho, ER 2 Ha: (18.5 x 10.1) (19.2 x 10.1)ER Derricks: 1x10t,1x5t,2x3t; Winches: 4	**1 oil engine** dr geared to sc. shaft driving 1 FP propeller Total Power: 1,228kW (1,670hp) Skoda 9L350IIPS 1 x 4 Stroke 9 Cy. 350 x 500 1228kW (1670bhp) CKD Praha-Praha AuxGen: 2 x 99kW 380V 50Hz a.c, 1 x 58kW 380V 50Hz a.c, 1 x 36kW 380V 50Hz a.c
9152040 *IFOJ* -	**TINDARI JET** **Bluferries Srl** Rete Ferroviaria Italiana (RFI) *Catania* *Italy* MMSI: 247042500 Official number: 273	**493** 325 56	Class: RI	**1999-08 Rodriquez Cantieri Navali SpA — Messina** Yd No: 273 Loa 50.46 Br ex - Dght 1.470 Lbp 43.00 Br md 8.78 Dpth 4.20 Welded, 1 dk	**(A37B2PS) Passenger Ship** Hull Material: Aluminium Alloy Passengers: unberthed: 500	**2 oil engines** with clutches, flexible couplings & sr geared to sc. shafts driving 2 Water jets Total Power: 4,000kW (5,438hp) M.T.U. 16V396TE74L 2 x Vee 4 Stroke 16 Cy. 165 x 185 each-2000kW (2719bhp) MTU Friedrichshafen GmbH-Friedrichshafen AuxGen: 2 x 100kW 220/380V 50Hz a.c Thrusters: 1 Thwart. FP thruster (f)
8505800 - -	**TINDEWJA I** *ex* Ennasr II *-1994* **ETS CPA Consignation Peche Armement** - *Nouadhibou* *Mauritania* Official number: 588	**190** 57 127	Class: (RI) (BV)	**1986-03 Astilleros Armon SA — Navia** Yd No: 112 Loa 28.22 Br ex - Dght 3.082 Lbp 25.56 Br md 7.76 Dpth 3.76 Welded, 1 dk	**(B11B2FV) Fishing Vessel** Ins: 160	**1 oil engine** with clutches, flexible couplings & sr reverse geared to sc. shaft driving 1 FP propeller Total Power: 570kW (775hp) 11.8kn Caterpillar 3508TA 1 x Vee 4 Stroke 8 Cy. 170 x 190 570kW (775bhp) Caterpillar Tractor Co-USA AuxGen: 2 x 80kW 220/380V 50Hz a.c
8101379 *LKYK* -	**TINDSOY** *ex* Aqua-Boy *-2011* *ex* Konkurs 1 *-1988* *ex* Antonsen Senior *-1987* *ex* Peer Gynt *-1985* **Oytrans AS** - *Myre* *Norway* MMSI: 258192000	**312** 97 320		**1982-05 Moen Slip og Mekanisk Verksted AS — Kolvereid** Yd No: 16 Loa 33.20 Br ex 7.83 Dght 3.250 Lbp 28.71 Br md 7.80 Dpth 3.61 Welded, 1 dk	**(B12C2FL) Live Fish Carrier (Well Boat)** Grain: 180 Compartments: 1 Ho, ER 1 Ha: (13.0 x 5.2)ER	**1 oil engine** driving 1 FP propeller Total Power: 206kW (280hp) 10.0kn Wichmann 4ACA 1 x 2 Stroke 4 Cy. 280 x 420 206kW (280bhp) (made 1966, fitted 1982) Wichmann Motorfabrikk AS-Norway Thrusters: 1 Thwart. FP thruster (f)
9498107 *EAUU* -	**TINERFE** *ex* Samho Freedom *-2009* **Distribuidora Maritima Petrogas SLU** - SatCom: Inmarsat C 422402510 *Santa Cruz de Tenerife* *Spain (CSR)* MMSI: 224025000 Official number: 16/2009	**11,290** 5,263 17,540 T/cm 28.5	Class: GL (KR)	**2009-11 Samho Shipbuilding Co Ltd — Tongyeong** Yd No: 1106 Loa 144.06 (BB) Br ex - Dght 9.200 Lbp 135.00 Br md 22.60 Dpth 12.50 Welded, 1 dk	**(A12B2TR) Chemical/Products Tanker** Double Hull (13F) Liq: 19,020; Liq (Oil): 19,020 Compartments: 14 Wing Ta, 2 Wing Slop Ta, ER	**1 oil engine** driving 1 FP propeller Total Power: 5,349kW (7,273hp) 15.0kn MAN-B&W 8S35MC 1 x 2 Stroke 8 Cy. 350 x 1400 5349kW (7273bhp) STX Engine Co Ltd-South Korea AuxGen: 3 x 750kW 450V a.c Thrusters: 1 Tunnel thruster (f)
9323742 *VRAP3* -	**TING KAU** **Hongkong United Dockyards Ltd** The Hongkong Salvage & Towage Co Ltd SatCom: Inmarsat C 477991600 *Hong Kong* *Hong Kong* MMSI: 477991600 Official number: HK-1439	**297** 89 40	Class: LR ✠ **100A1** SS 07/2010 tug ✠ **LMC** Eq.Ltr: F; Cable: 302.5/22.0 U2 (a)	**2005-07 Hin Lee (Zhuhai) Shipyard Co Ltd — Zhuhai GD** (Hull) Yd No: 080 **2005-07 Cheoy Lee Shipyards Ltd — Hong Kong** Yd No: 4848 Loa 29.07 Br ex 11.12 Dght 3.900 Lbp 23.50 Br md 9.50 Dpth 4.70 Welded, 1 dk	**(B32A2ST) Tug**	**2 oil engines** gearing integral to driving 2 Z propellers Total Power: 2,942kW (4,000hp) 11.5kn Yanmar 6N260L-EN 2 x 4 Stroke 6 Cy. 260 x 360 each-1471kW (2000bhp) Yanmar Diesel Engine Co Ltd-Japan AuxGen: 2 x 80kW 385V 50Hz a.c

6824575 **TINGANES** *OZ2045* *ex* Havsand *-2008* *ex* Rheia *-2004* - **Sekstant Sp/f** - *Runavik* *Faeroe Islands (Danish)* MMSI: 231336000	**458** 128 -		**1967-03 Limfjords-Vaerftet A/S — Aalborg** Yd No: 23 Loa 49.94 Br ex 9.25 Dght 3.800 Lbp - Br md 9.20 Dpth - Welded, 1 dk	**(B33B2DU) Hopper/Dredger (unspecified)** Compartments: 1 Ho, ER	**1 oil engine** driving 1 FP propeller Total Power: 368kW (500hp) Alpha 406-26VO 1 x 2 Stroke 6 Cy. 260 x 400 368kW (500bhp) Alpha Diesel A/S-Denmark AuxGen: 2 x 27kW 380V 50Hz a.c Fuel: 20.5 (d.f.)
9185619 **TINGARI** *VZBW* - **Svitzer Australia Pty Ltd (Svitzer Australasia)** - *Port Adelaide, SA* *Australia* MMSI: 503341000 Official number: 856160	**395** 118 336	Class: AB	**2000-04 PT Nanindah Mutiara Shipyard — Batam** Yd No: T57 Loa 31.88 Br ex 11.24 Dght 5.700 Lbp 29.43 Br md - Dpth 5.56 Welded, 1 dk	**(B32A2ST) Tug**	**2 oil engines** with clutches & dr geared to sc. shafts driving 2 Directional propellers Total Power: 3,600kW (4,894hp) 12.3kn Daihatsu 6DKM-28 2 x 4 Stroke 6 Cy. 280 x 390 each-1800kW (2447bhp) Daihatsu Diesel Manufacturing Co Lt-Japan AuxGen: 2 x 85kW 415V 50Hz a.c Fuel: 101.3 (d.f.) 8.0pd
9347803 **TINGHIR** *CNA4376* *ex* Medbaltic *-2007* - **International Maritime Transport Corp SA** International Maritime Transport Corp (IMTC) *Tangier* *Morocco* MMSI: 242961000 Official number: 3-350/MM-CM	**9,981** 4,900 11,808	Class: LR (GL) **100A1** SS 01/2012 container ship *IWS LI **LMC** **UMS**	**2006-12 Yangfan Group Co Ltd — Zhoushan ZJ** Yd No: 2033 Loa 139.14 (BB) Br ex - Dght 8.800 Lbp 129.00 Br md 22.60 Dpth 11.80 Welded, 1 dk	**(A33A2CC) Container Ship (Fully Cellular)** Double Bottom Partial Compartment Length TEU 957 incl 240 ref C. Cranes: 2x45t Ice Capable	**1 oil engine** reduction geared to sc. shaft driving 1 CP propeller Total Power: 9,600kW (13,052hp) 18.8kn MAN-B&W 8L48/60B 1 x 4 Stroke 8 Cy. 480 x 600 9600kW (13052bhp) MAN B&W Diesel AG-Augsburg AuxGen: 2 x 960kW 450/230V a.c, 1 x 2000kW 450/230V a.c Thrusters: 1 Tunnel thruster (f); 1 Tunnel thruster (f)
9310197 **TINGIS** *CNA4486* *ex* Plevne *-2010* - **Societe de Cabotage Petrolier SA (PETROCAB)** - *Casablanca* *Morocco* MMSI: 242924000	**4,471** 2,240 6,937 T/cm 16.8	Class: LR (AB) **100A1** SS 07/2010 Double Hull oil and chemical tanker, Ship Type 2 ESP LI **LMC** **UMS**	**2005-07 Celiktekne Sanayii ve Ticaret A.S. — Tuzla, Istanbul** Yd No: 55 Loa 119.10 (BB) Br ex 16.93 Dght 6.800 Lbp 111.60 Br md 16.90 Dpth 8.40 Welded, 1 dk	**(A12B2TR) Chemical/Products Tanker** Double Hull (13F) Liq: 7,735; Liq (Oil): 7,735 Compartments: 12 Wing Ta, 1 Slop Ta, ER 12 Cargo Pump (s): 12x200m³/hr Manifold: Bow/CM: 58.8m	**1 oil engine** driving 1 FP propeller Total Power: 3,250kW (4,419hp) 14.4kn B&W 5L35MC 1 x 2 Stroke 5 Cy. 350 x 1050 3250kW (4419bhp) AuxGen: 3 x 500kW 50Hz a.c, 1 x 440kW 50Hz a.c Thrusters: 1 Tunnel thruster (f) Fuel: 51.3 (d.f.) 322.7 (r.f.) 12.0pd
9064279 **TINGLEV MAERSK** *OUSW2* *ex* Maersk Texas *-2002* - *ex* Tinglev Maersk *-1997* **A P Moller - Maersk A/S** A P Moller *Aabenraa* *Denmark (DIS)* MMSI: 220159000 Official number: D4010	**18,859** 8,468 25,431 T/cm 41.7	Class: AB (LR) ✠ Classed LR until 30/10/96	**1994-03 Tsuneishi Shipbuilding Co Ltd — Fukuyama HS** Yd No: 1026 Loa 176.40 (BB) Br ex 27.83 Dght 10.300 Lbp 166.53 Br md 27.80 Dpth 15.23 Welded, 1 dk	**(A33A2CC) Container Ship (Fully Cellular)** TEU 1325 C Ho 629 TEU C Dk 696 TEU incl 114 ref C. Compartments: 9 Cell Ho, ER 9 Ha: ER Gantry cranes: 1x40t	**1 oil engine** driving 1 FP propeller Total Power: 11,414kW (15,518hp) 18.6kn B&W 8S50MC 1 x 2 Stroke 8 Cy. 500 x 1910 11414kW (15518bhp) Mitsui Engineering & Shipbuilding CLtd-Japan AuxGen: 3 x 1250kW a.c Thrusters: 2 Thwart. FP thruster (f); 1 Tunnel thruster (a) Fuel: 1375.0 (r.f.)
7220180 **TINGVOLL** *LGIL* - **Fjord1 AS** - *Kristiansund* *Norway* MMSI: 257397400	**743** 255 -	Class: (NV)	**1972-07 AS Haugesunds Slip — Haugesund** Yd No: 15 Loa 64.47 Br ex 11.13 Dght 3.036 Lbp 58.98 Br md 11.10 Dpth 4.22 Welded, 1 dk	**(A36A2PR) Passenger/Ro-Ro Ship (Vehicles)** Passengers: 300 Bow door & ramp Stern ramp Cars: 50	**1 oil engine** driving 2 Propellers aft, 1 fwd Total Power: 919kW (1,249hp) Wichmann 5AXA 1 x 2 Stroke 5 Cy. 300 x 450 919kW (1249bhp) Wichmann Motorfabrikk AS-Norway AuxGen: 2 x 72kW 220V 50Hz a.c
8957508 **TINJU** *YDA4582* *ex* Jaya Hercules *-2005* - **PT Mawar Hitam Shipping** - *Jakarta* *Indonesia* MMSI: 525016602	**296** 88 -	Class: BV	**2000-07 Guangzhou Fishing Vessel Shipyard — Guangzhou GD** Yd No: XY-2101 Loa 31.80 Br ex 9.62 Dght 3.200 Lbp 29.34 Br md 9.60 Dpth 4.15 Welded, 1 dk	**(B32A2ST) Tug**	**2 oil engines** geared to sc. shafts driving 2 FP propellers Total Power: 1,884kW (2,562hp) 12.0kn Caterpillar 3512B 2 x Vee 4 Stroke 12 Cy. 170 x 190 each-942kW (1281bhp) Caterpillar Inc-USA
9045077 **TINKA** *V2WC* *ex* Inka Dede *-2006* *ex* Judith Borchard *-2003* - *ex* Gracechurch Comet *-2002* *ex* Inka Dede *-2001* *ex* Armada Sprinter *-1996* *ex* Inka Dede *-1995* *ex* Rhein Liffey *-1994* *ex* Inka Dede *-1993* **Admiral Tinka Shipping Co Ltd** Midocean (IOM) Ltd SatCom: Inmarsat C 430401246 *Saint John's* *Antigua & Barbuda* MMSI: 304010534	**5,006** 2,522 6,580	Class: GL	**1992-04 J.J. Sietas KG Schiffswerft GmbH & Co. — Hamburg** Yd No: 1055 Loa 116.77 (BB) Br ex 18.15 Dght 6.858 Lbp 108.00 Br md 17.90 Dpth 8.80 Welded, 1 dk	**(A33A2CC) Container Ship (Fully Cellular)** TEU 510 C Ho 162 TEU C Dk 348 TEU incl 50 ref C. Compartments: 3 Cell Ho, ER 3 Ha: ER	**1 oil engine** with flexible couplings & sr geared to sc. shaft driving 1 CP propeller Total Power: 4,750kW (6,458hp) 16.0kn MAN 6L48/60 1 x 4 Stroke 6 Cy. 480 x 600 4750kW (6458bhp) MAN B&W Diesel AG-Augsburg AuxGen: 1 x 800kW 220/380V 50Hz a.c, 2 x 200kW 220/380V 50Hz a.c Thrusters: 1 Thwart. FP thruster (f) Fuel: 513.0 (d.f.)
8614273 **TINKERBELL MAR** *9HBA9* *ex* Ariake Maru No. 12 *-2007* - **Triton Shipping SA** Neptune Lines Shipping & Managing Enterprises SA *Valletta* *Malta* MMSI: 256707000 Official number: 8614273	**4,968** 3,408 2,012	Class: NK	**1987-02 Honda Zosen — Saiki** Yd No: 756 Loa 102.01 (BB) Br ex - Dght 4.885 Lbp 94.00 Br md 15.51 Dpth 5.90 Welded	**(A35B2RV) Vehicles Carrier** Quarter stern door/ramp (p) Len: 17.20 Wid: 4.30 Swl: 40 Lane-Len: 400 Lane-clr ht: 4.20 Cars: 501	**1 oil engine** driving 1 FP propeller Total Power: 3,604kW (4,900hp) 16.0kn Mitsubishi 7UEC37LA 1 x 2 Stroke 7 Cy. 370 x 880 3604kW (4900bhp) Akasaka Tekkosho KK (Akasaka DieselLtd)-Japan Fuel: 300.0 (r.f.)
8908806 **TINNO** *8PAK2* - **Wilson Shipowning AS** Wilson EuroCarriers AS *Bridgetown* *Barbados* MMSI: 314418000	**1,986** 1,246 3,504 T/cm 10.4	Class: BV (LR) ✠ Classed LR until 23/11/10	**1991-05 Bodewes' Scheepswerven B.V. — Hoogezand** Yd No: 562 Loa 88.15 (BB) Br ex 14.18 Dght 5.001 Lbp 83.20 Br md 14.00 Dpth 6.35 Welded, 1 dk	**(A31A2GX) General Cargo Ship** Grain: 4,262; Bale: 4,237 TEU 103 C.Ho 64/20' C.Dk 39/20' Compartments: 1 Ho, ER 2 Ha: 2 (25.4 x 10.2)ER Cranes: 1x35t Ice Capable	**1 oil engine** with flexible couplings & sr geared to sc. shaft driving 1 FP propeller Total Power: 1,176kW (1,599hp) 12.0kn MaK 6MU452AK 1 x 4 Stroke 6 Cy. 320 x 450 1176kW (1599bhp) Krupp MaK Maschinenbau GmbH-Kiel AuxGen: 2 x 52kW 380V 50Hz a.c Thrusters: 1 Thwart. FP thruster (f) Fuel: 176.8 (d.f.) 5.6pd
9428786 **TINOS** *V2CR6* *ex* Thor Bright *-2014* *ex* BBC Togo *-2010* - *ex* FCC Wealthy *-2008* **ms 'Wealthy' GmbH & Co KG** Candler Schiffahrt GmbH *Saint John's* *Antigua & Barbuda* MMSI: 305087000 Official number: 10130	**6,569** 2,872 8,280	Class: GL (CC)	**2007-07 Yichang Shipyard — Yichang HB** Yd No: 2006-B004 Loa 116.23 (BB) Br ex - Dght 7.000 Lbp 110.00 Br md 18.00 Dpth 10.40 Welded, 1 dk	**(A31A2GX) General Cargo Ship** Grain: 11,705; Bale: 11,681 Compartments: 2 Ho, ER 2 Ha: (44.8 x 15.0)ER (25.9 x 15.0) Cranes: 2x45t Ice Capable	**1 oil engine** reverse reduction geared to sc. shaft driving 1 FP propeller Total Power: 2,500kW (3,399hp) 12.5kn Daihatsu 8DKM-28 1 x 4 Stroke 8 Cy. 280 x 390 2500kW (3399bhp) Shaanxi Diesel Heavy Industry Co Lt-China AuxGen: 3 x 250kW 400V a.c
9162007 **TINOS WARRIOR** *3FRR9* *ex* Esteem Grandeur *-2012* - *ex* River Dream *-2007* **Legendary Carrier Co** Polembros Shipping Ltd SatCom: Inmarsat C 435703610 *Panama* *Panama* MMSI: 357036000 Official number: 4179010C	**56,854** 31,716 105,426 T/cm 88.3	Class: BV (NK)	**1997-09 Namura Shipbuilding Co Ltd — Imari SG** Yd No: 955 Loa 240.99 (BB) Br ex 42.03 Dght 14.970 Lbp 232.00 Br md 42.00 Dpth 21.20 Welded, 1 dk	**(A13B2TP) Products Tanker** Double Hull (13F) Liq: 117,209; Liq (Oil): 117,209 Cargo Heating Coils Compartments: 14 Wing Ta, ER 3 Cargo Pump (s): 3x2600m³/hr Manifold: Bow/CM: 118m	**1 oil engine** driving 1 FP propeller Total Power: 12,791kW (17,391hp) 14.0kn Sulzer 7RTA62 1 x 2 Stroke 7 Cy. 620 x 2150 12791kW (17391bhp) Mitsubishi Heavy Industries Ltd-Japan AuxGen: 3 x 520kW 450V 60Hz a.c Fuel: 92.1 (d.f.) (Heating Coils) 2497.6 (r.f.) 48.3pd
8607086 **TINRO** *UDDL* - **TINRO Centre - Pacific Research Fisheries Centre** - SatCom: Inmarsat A 1401752 *Vladivostok* *Russia* MMSI: 273813300 Official number: 872561	**2,062** 618 617	Class: RS	**1987-07 VEB Volkswerft Stralsund — Stralsund** Yd No: 780 Loa 62.22 Br ex 13.81 Dght 5.130 Lbp 55.00 Br md 13.80 Dpth 9.20 Welded, 2 dks	**(B11A2FS) Stern Trawler** Ice Capable	**2 oil engines** geared to sc. shaft driving 1 CP propeller Total Power: 1,766kW (2,402hp) 12.9kn S.K.L. 8VD26/20AL-2 2 x 4 Stroke 8 Cy. 200 x 260 each-883kW (1201bhp) VEB Schwermaschinenbau "KarlLiebknecht" (SKL)-Magdeburg AuxGen: 1 x 640kW 380V 50Hz a.c, 2 x 568kW 380V 50Hz a.c, 1 x 325kW 380V 50Hz a.c Thrusters: 1 Thwart. FP thruster (f); 1 Tunnel thruster (a)
9119567 **TINSDAL** *V2AJ2* - **ms 'Tinsdal' Schiffahrts GmbH & Co KG** Wessels Reederei GmbH & Co KG *Saint John's* *Antigua & Barbuda* MMSI: 305573000 Official number: 4717	**2,981** 1,505 4,310	Class: GL	**1998-10 Rousse Shipyard Ltd — Rousse** Yd No: 390 Loa 89.95 (BB) Br ex - Dght 5.641 Lbp 84.80 Br md 15.20 Dpth 7.10 Welded, 1 dk	**(A31A2GX) General Cargo Ship** Grain: 5,519; Bale: 5,250 TEU 114 C 1 Ha: ER Ice Capable	**1 oil engine** reduction geared to sc. shaft driving 1 CP propeller Total Power: 2,080kW (2,828hp) 12.3kn MaK 6M453C 1 x 4 Stroke 6 Cy. 320 x 420 2080kW (2828bhp) MaK Motoren GmbH & Co. KG-Kiel AuxGen: 1 x 440kW 380V a.c, 2 x 224kW 380/220V a.c Thrusters: 1 Tunnel thruster (f) Fuel: 234.0

LR/IMO No. / Call sign / Flag	Ship name / Former names / Owner / Port	Tonnage	Class	Builder / Dimensions	Type / Capacities	Machinery
8862533 *SDCO* -	**TINTIN** *ex* Director Louise Gutjahr Vi *-2011* *ex* Karl-Alfred *-2009* *ex* Karl-Manfred af Gryt *-1996* *ex* Doggen *-1991* *ex* Ellwe *-1956* *ex* Doggen *-1919* *ex* Director Louis Gutjahr VI *-1917* **Linus Lars Hook** - *Malmo* *Sweden*	**150** 45 -		**1902 in the Netherlands** Loa 31.34 Br ex - Dght 3.200 Lbp - Br md 6.03 Dpth - Welded, 1 dk	**(B32A2ST) Tug**	**4 oil engines** driving 1 FP propeller Total Power: 824kW (1,120hp) Volvo Penta 4 x 4 Stroke 6 Cy. each-206kW (280bhp) (new engine 1976) AB Volvo Penta-Sweden
7369168 *E5U2301* -	**TINTO** *ex* Tello *-2011* *ex* Zafeiri *-2006* *ex* Harlan *-2004* *ex* Tello *-2001* *ex* Nornanborg *-1985* *ex* Lysholmen *-1980* **Norwegian Ship Assistance Consulting AS (NSAC AS)** - SatCom: Inmarsat C 451835110 *Avatiu* *Cook Islands* MMSI: 518351000 Official number: 1385	**1,739** 851 1,175	Class: IV (NV)	**1974-05 Orens Mek. Verksted — Trondheim** Yd No: 59 Lengthened-1986 Loa 82.47 (BB) Br ex 12.70 Dght 3.690 Lbp 75.40 Br md 12.68 Dpth 6.51 Welded, 2 dks	**(A31A2GX) General Cargo Ship** Grain: 3,127; Bale: 2,852 Compartments: 2 Ho, ER 2 Ha: (9.0 x 9.7) (16.8 x 9.7)ER Cranes: 2x25t; Derricks: 1x5t; Winches: 1 Ice Capable	**1 oil engine** geared to sc. shaft driving 1 FP propeller Total Power: 1,640kW (2,230hp) 12.5kn Caterpillar 3606TA 1 x 4 Stroke 6 Cy. 280 x 300 1640kW (2230bhp) (new engine 1990) Caterpillar Inc-USA AuxGen: 2 x 116kW 220V 50Hz a.c, 1 x 50kW 220V 50Hz a.c Thrusters: 1 Thwart. FP thruster (f)
5301265 *OJKP* -	**TINTO** *ex* Stor-Joel *-2003* *ex* Grissly *-1996* *ex* Snik *-1991* *ex* Grissly *-1990* *ex* Hinna *-1986* *ex* Stor-Viking *-1985* *ex* Royal *-1967* *ex* Assi *-1957* **Rauma Cata Oy** - *Rauma* *Finland* Official number: 12262	**107** 33 -	Class: (BV)	**1953 J. Vos & Zoon — Groningen** Yd No: 101 Loa 23.80 Br ex - Dght 3.277 Lbp 22.15 Br md 7.05 Dpth 3.46 Riveted\Welded, 1 dk	**(B32A2ST) Tug** Ice Capable	**1 oil engine** driving 1 FP propeller Total Power: 736kW (1,001hp) MaK 6M451AK 1 x 4 Stroke 6 Cy. 320 x 450 736kW (1001bhp) (new engine 1967) Atlas MaK Maschinenbau GmbH-Kiel Thrusters: 1 Tunnel thruster (f)
9234599 *A8AR7* -	**TINTOMARA** - **Rederi AB Gnisvard & Whitefin Shipping Co Ltd** Laurin Maritime (America) Inc SatCom: Inmarsat C 463694614 *Monrovia* *Liberia* MMSI: 636011659 Official number: 11659	**26,914** 14,288 46,733 T/cm 52.8	Class: NV	**2003-02 Brodotrogir dd - Shipyard Trogir — Trogir** Yd No: 303 Loa 182.90 (BB) Br ex 32.22 Dght 12.196 Lbp 176.00 Br md 32.20 Dpth 17.20 Welded, 1 dk	**(A12B2TR) Chemical/Products Tanker** Double Hull (13F) Liq: 51,910; Liq (Oil): 51,910 Compartments: 14 Wing Ta, 2 Wing Slop Ta, ER 14 Cargo Pump (s): 6x400m³/hr, 8x250m³/hr Manifold: Bow/CM: 91.5m	**2 oil engines** with clutches, hydraulic couplings & dr geared to sc. shaft driving 1 CP propeller Total Power: 7,680kW (10,442hp) 14.5kn MaK 8M32C 2 x 4 Stroke 8 Cy. 320 x 480 each-3840kW (5221bhp) Caterpillar Motoren GmbH & Co. KG-Germany AuxGen: 2 x a.c, 1 x a.c Fuel: 113.9 (d.f.) 1425.6 (r.f.) 32.8pd
8733988 *EAXZ* 3-TA-31-00	**TIO GEL SEGON** - - *L'Ametlla de Mar* *Spain* Official number: 3-1/2000	**225** 67 -		**1999 Chantier Naval Martinez — Saint-Cyprien** Loa 35.95 Br ex - Dght 2.370 Lbp 33.46 Br md 8.20 Dpth 3.44 Bonded, 1 dk	**(B11B2FV) Fishing Vessel** Hull Material: Reinforced Plastic	**1 oil engine** driving 1 Propeller Total Power: 899kW (1,222hp)
9120580 - -	**TIO JOSE** **Austral Group SAA** - *Callao* *Peru* Official number: IO-012185-PM	**422** 182 567	Class: (GL)	**1995-06 Remesa Astilleros S.A. — Callao** Yd No: 63 Loa 40.00 Br ex - Dght 3.937 Lbp 33.50 Br md 8.80 Dpth 4.40 Welded, 1 dk	**(B11B2FV) Fishing Vessel** Ins: 490	**1 oil engine** reduction geared to sc. shaft driving 1 FP propeller Total Power: 790kW (1,074hp) 12.0kn Caterpillar 3512TA 1 x Vee 4 Stroke 12 Cy. 170 x 190 790kW (1074bhp) Caterpillar Inc-USA AuxGen: 2 x 55kW 220V a.c
9120554 - -	**TIO LUCAS** *launched as* Juancho *-1995* **Austral Group SAA** - *Callao* *Peru* Official number: CO-12233-PM	**422** 182 567	Class: (GL)	**1995-06 Remesa Astilleros S.A. — Callao** Yd No: 60 Loa 40.00 Br ex - Dght 3.940 Lbp 33.50 Br md 8.80 Dpth 4.40 Welded, 1 dk	**(B11B2FV) Fishing Vessel** Ins: 490	**1 oil engine** reduction geared to sc. shaft driving 1 FP propeller Total Power: 790kW (1,074hp) 12.0kn Caterpillar 3512TA 1 x Vee 4 Stroke 12 Cy. 170 x 190 790kW (1074bhp) Caterpillar Inc-USA AuxGen: 2 x 55kW 220V a.c
8511160 *S9B31* -	**TIO PEDRO** *ex* Jinyang No. 1 *-2008* *ex* Saehwa No. 3 *-2005* *ex* Sanzen Maru *-1996* - - *Sao Tome & Principe* MMSI: 668134414	**510** - 1,191	Class: (KR)	**1985-09 Hakata Zosen K.K. — Imabari** Yd No: 325 Loa 65.00 Br ex 10.04 Dght 4.146 Lbp 60.00 Br md 10.00 Dpth 4.45 Welded, 1 dk	**(A12A2TC) Chemical Tanker** Liq: 1,199 Compartments: 8 Ta, ER	**1 oil engine** driving 1 FP propeller Total Power: 956kW (1,300hp) Hanshin 6LU32G 1 x 4 Stroke 6 Cy. 320 x 510 956kW (1300bhp) The Hanshin Diesel Works Ltd-Japan
5102827 - -	**TIO TAVO** *ex* Aida Luz *-2002* *ex* Venere *-1994* *ex* Samios *-1980* *ex* Elster *-1968* - -	*413* 154 983	Class: (BV) (GL)	**1958 Adler Werft GmbH — Bremen** Yd No: 14 Loa 59.54 Br ex 9.05 Dght 2.699 Lbp 54.03 Br md 9.00 Dpth 4.91 Welded, 1 dk & S dk	**(A31A2GX) General Cargo Ship** Grain: 1,214; Bale: 1,172; Ins: 41 Compartments: 1 Ho, ER 1 Ha: (25.1 x 5.1)ER Derricks: 1x10t,4x5t; Winches: 4	**1 oil engine** driving 1 FP propeller Total Power: 552kW (750hp) 11.3kn Deutz RBV6M545 1 x 4 Stroke 6 Cy. 320 x 450 552kW (750bhp) Kloeckner Humboldt Deutz AG-West Germany AuxGen: 1 x 55kW 220V d.c, 1 x 33kW 220V d.c Fuel: 43.5 (d.f.)
9122734 *WDE7327* -	**TIOGA** **Vessel Management Services Inc** - *San Francisco, CA* *United States of America* MMSI: 366888880 Official number: 1021169	*223* 66 -		**1994 Tri-Star Marine, Inc. — Seattle, Wa** Yd No: G-0106 Loa 25.60 Br ex - Dght - Lbp - Br md 9.14 Dpth 4.66 Welded, 1 dk	**(B32A2ST) Tug** Ice Capable	**2 oil engines** gearing integral to driving 2 Z propellers Total Power: 2,942kW (4,000hp) 13.0kn Caterpillar 3516TA 2 x Vee 4 Stroke 16 Cy. 170 x 190 each-1471kW (2000bhp) Caterpillar Inc-USA AuxGen: 2 x 60kW
9072484 *9MLJ6* -	**TIOMAN SATU** *ex* Eastern Star *-2010* *ex* Sankei Maru *-2009* **Zone Arctic Sdn Bhd** - *Port Klang* *Malaysia* MMSI: 533045400 Official number: 334245	**998** 681 1,900		**1993-04 Hakata Zosen K.K. — Imabari** Yd No: 553 Loa - Br ex - Dght 4.750 Lbp 68.00 Br md 11.20 Dpth 5.25 Welded, 1 dk	**(A13B2TP) Products Tanker**	**1 oil engine** reverse geared to sc. shaft driving 1 FP propeller Total Power: 1,765kW (2,400hp) Hanshin 6EL35G 1 x 4 Stroke 6 Cy. 350 x 700 1765kW (2400bhp) The Hanshin Diesel Works Ltd-Japan
9117947 *9V5077* -	**TIONG WOON OCEAN 6** *ex* Tiong Woon VI *-1994* **TW (Sabah) Pte Ltd** Tiong Woon Marine Pte Ltd *Singapore* *Singapore* MMSI: 563679000 Official number: 386367	**110** 33 113	Class: NK	**1994-09 Huten Marine Sdn Bhd — Kuching** Yd No: 01/93 Loa 23.17 Br ex - Dght 2.385 Lbp 21.76 Br md 7.00 Dpth 2.90 Welded, 1 dk	**(B32A2ST) Tug**	**2 oil engines** reduction geared to sc. shafts driving 2 FP propellers Total Power: 794kW (1,080hp) Cummins KTA-19-M 2 x 4 Stroke 6 Cy. 159 x 159 each-397kW (540bhp) Cummins Engine Co Inc-USA AuxGen: 2 x 25kW a.c Fuel: 74.0 (d.f.)
9188702 *9V5531* -	**TIONG WOON OCEAN 11** **TW (Sabah) Pte Ltd** Tiong Woon Marine Pte Ltd *Singapore* *Singapore* MMSI: 563683000 Official number: 387964	**123** 37 -	Class: BV	**1998-02 Tuong Aik (Sarawak) Sdn Bhd — Sibu** Yd No: 9705 Loa 23.26 Br ex - Dght 2.220 Lbp 21.03 Br md 7.00 Dpth 2.90 Welded, 1 dk	**(B32A2ST) Tug**	**2 oil engines** geared to sc. shafts driving 2 FP propellers Total Power: 784kW (1,066hp) 10.8kn Yanmar 6LAAL-DT 2 x 4 Stroke 6 Cy. 148 x 165 each-392kW (533bhp) Yanmar Diesel Engine Co Ltd-Japan AuxGen: 2 x 20kW 415V 50Hz a.c Fuel: 73.0 (d.f.)
7718981 *HQSO4* -	**TIONG WOON OCEAN 12** *ex* Sumpile Mariner *-2003* *ex* Haruna *-1982* **Tiong Woon Offshore Pte Ltd** - *San Lorenzo* *Honduras* MMSI: 334918000 Official number: L-1726559	**368** 111 326	Class: (NK)	**1977-12 Yoshiura Zosen — Kure** Yd No: 265 Loa 37.50 Br ex - Dght 3.911 Lbp 32.01 Br md 9.01 Dpth 4.22 Welded, 1 dk	**(B32A2ST) Tug**	**2 oil engines** driving 2 FP propellers Total Power: 2,206kW (3,000hp) 12.0kn Fuji 6S30B 2 x 4 Stroke 6 Cy. 300 x 450 each-1103kW (1500bhp) Fuji Diesel Co Ltd-Japan AuxGen: 3 x 48kW

IMO / Call sign	Name / Owner / Manager / Flag	Tonnage	Class	Builder / Dimensions	Type	Machinery
9327877 *9V6641* -	**TIONG WOON OCEAN 16** *ex* Uni Haul Ina *-2005* *ex* Uni-Haul Ina *-2005* **TW (Sabah) Pte Ltd** Tiong Woon Marine Pte Ltd *Singapore* *Singapore* MMSI: 565068000 Official number: 391069	**278** 83 245	Class: LR **✠100A1** SS 02/2010 tug **✠LMC** Eq.Ltr: f; Cable: 275.0/19.0 U2 (a)	**2005-02 PT Nanindah Mutiara Shipyard — Batam** Yd No: T131 Loa 31.00 Br ex 9.02 Dght 4.100 Lbp 28.36 Br md 9.00 Dpth 4.52 Welded, 1 dk	**(B32A2ST) Tug**	**2 oil engines** with clutches, flexible couplings & sr reverse geared to sc. shafts driving 2 Propellers Total Power: 2,238kW (3,042hp) 11.0kn Caterpillar 3512B-TA 2 x Vee 4 Stroke 12 Cy. 170 x 190 each-1119kW (1521bhp) Caterpillar Inc-USA AuxGen: 2 x 80kW 415V 50Hz a.c
9529542 *9V7404* -	**TIONG WOON OCEAN 18** **Tiong Woon Marine Pte Ltd** - *Singapore* *Singapore* MMSI: 563721000 Official number: 394080	**454** 136 -	Class: BV	**2008-12 Guangzhou Panyu Yuefeng Shiprepair & Building Yard — Guangzhou GD** Yd No: GMG0631 Loa 36.50 Br ex - Dght 4.200 Lbp 31.50 Br md 10.40 Dpth 5.00 Welded, 1 dk	**(B21B20A) Anchor Handling Tug Supply**	**2 oil engines** reduction geared to sc. shafts driving 2 FP propellers Total Power: 2,378kW (3,234hp) 12.0kn Cummins KTA-50-M2 2 x Vee 4 Stroke 16 Cy. 159 x 159 each-1189kW (1617bhp) Cummins Engine Co Inc-USA AuxGen: 2 x 240kW a.c Thrusters: 1 Tunnel thruster (f)
9554999 *9V8000* -	**TIONG WOON OCEAN 19** **Tiong Woon Marine Pte Ltd** Tiong Woon Offshore Pte Ltd *Singapore* *Singapore* MMSI: 563983000 Official number: 395149	**453** 135 500	Class: BV	**2010-01 Guangzhou Panyu Yuefeng Shiprepair & Building Yard — Guangzhou GD** Yd No: GMG0782 Loa 36.50 Br ex - Dght 4.200 Lbp 31.50 Br md 10.40 Dpth 5.00 Welded, 1 dk	**(B21B20A) Anchor Handling Tug Supply**	**2 oil engines** reduction geared to sc. shafts driving 2 FP propellers Total Power: 2,392kW (3,252hp) 12.0kn Cummins KTA-50-M2 2 x Vee 4 Stroke 16 Cy. 159 x 159 each-1196kW (1626bhp) Cummins Engine Co Ltd-United Kingdom AuxGen: 2 x 240kW 50Hz a.c
9629859 *9WLH6* -	**TIP TOP 1** **Top Intergroup Sdn Bhd** - *Kuching* *Malaysia* Official number: 333371	**147** 45 90	Class: NK	**2011-06 Nga Chai Shipyard Sdn Bhd — Sibu** Yd No: 3312 Loa 23.50 Br ex - Dght 2.510 Lbp 21.08 Br md 7.32 Dpth 3.10 Welded, 1 dk	**(B32B2SP) Pusher Tug**	**2 oil engines** geared to sc. shafts driving 2 Propellers Total Power: 970kW (1,318hp) Yanmar 6AYM-WST 2 x 4 Stroke 6 Cy. 155 x 180 each-485kW (659bhp) Yanmar Diesel Engine Co Ltd-Japan Fuel: 90.0 (d.f.)
8979087 *HC2058* -	**TIP TOP II** **Rolf Wittmer Turismo Galapagos Compania Ltda** - *Puerto Ayora* *Ecuador* Official number: TN-01-0039	**130** 39 -		**1998 Nestor Huayamabe S. — Ecuador** L reg 25.90 Br ex - Dght 1.500 Lbp - Br md 6.10 Dpth - Welded, 1 dk	**(A37A2PC) Passenger/Cruise** Passengers: cabins: 9; berths: 16	**2 oil engines** driving 2 Propellers Total Power: 258kW (350hp) 9.0kn G.M. (Detroit Diesel) 6V-71-T 2 x Vee 2 Stroke 6 Cy. 108 x 127 each-129kW (175bhp) (made 1980, fitted 1998) Detroit Diesel Corporation-Detroit, Mi AuxGen: 2 x 40kW 220/110V a.c
8979099 *HC2103* -	**TIP TOP III** **Rolf Wittmer Turismo Galapagos Compania Ltda** - *Puerto Ayora* *Ecuador* Official number: TN-01-0108	**175** - -		**2001-01 Jacht- en Scheepswerf C. van Lent & Zonen B.V. — Kaag** L reg 29.87 Br ex - Dght 1.500 Lbp - Br md 6.70 Dpth - Welded, 1 dk	**(A37A2PC) Passenger/Cruise** Passengers: cabins: 10; berths: 16	**2 oil engines** geared to sc. shafts driving 2 Propellers Total Power: 588kW (800hp) 12.0kn Cummins N14-M 2 x 4 Stroke 6 Cy. 140 x 152 each-294kW (400bhp) Cummins Engine Co Inc-USA AuxGen: 2 x 55kW 220/110V a.c
9092874 *HC4757* -	**TIP TOP IV** **Rolf Wittmer Turismo Galapagos Compania Ltda** - *Puerto Ayora* *Ecuador* MMSI: 735057700 Official number: TN-01-0212	**252** 75 -		**2006-03 Pesca Polaris SA — Guayaquil** Loa 38.26 Br ex - Dght - Lbp - Br md 7.70 Dpth 3.35 Welded, 1 dk	**(A37A2PC) Passenger/Cruise** Passengers: cabins: 10; berths: 18	**2 oil engines** reduction geared to sc. shafts driving 2 Propellers Total Power: 650kW (884hp) Deutz 2 x 4 Stroke each-325kW (442bhp) Deutz AG-Koeln
8102191 - -	**TIR** **Government of The Republic of India (Navy Department)** - *India*	*2,941* 882 3,900	Class: (IR) (AB)	**1986-02 Mazagon Dock Ltd. — Mumbai** Yd No: 579 Loa - Br ex - Dght - Lbp 100.51 Br md 13.21 Dpth 6.20 Welded, 2 dks	**(B34K2QT) Training Ship**	**2 oil engines** geared to sc. shafts driving 2 FP propellers Total Power: 5,104kW (6,940hp) 18.0kn Pielstick 8PC2-5L-400 2 x 4 Stroke 8 Cy. 400 x 460 each-2552kW (3470bhp) NEI A.P.E. Ltd. W. H. Allen-Bedford AuxGen: 4 x 248kW a.c
8972962 *WCZ5237* -	**TIRA LANI** **Sause Bros Inc** Sause Bros Ocean Towing Co Inc *Honolulu, HI* *United States of America* Official number: 1077568	**208** 62 -		**1999 Southern Oregon Marine Inc (SOMAR) — Coos Bay, Or** L reg 22.92 Br ex - Dght - Lbp - Br md 9.84 Dpth 4.05 Welded, 1 dk	**(B32A2ST) Tug**	**2 oil engines** gearing integral to driving 2 Z propellers Total Power: 2,942kW (4,000hp) 12.0kn Caterpillar 3516B 2 x Vee 4 Stroke 16 Cy. 170 x 190 each-1471kW (2000bhp) Caterpillar Inc-USA
9219109 *VWYO* -	**TIRACOL II** **Mormugao Port Trust** - *Visakhapatnam* *India* MMSI: 419041400 Official number: 2941	**437** 131 150	Class: (IR)	**2003-04 Hindustan Shipyard Ltd — Visakhapatnam** Yd No: 1172 Loa 31.75 Br ex 11.25 Dght 4.940 Lbp 29.93 Br md 11.24 Dpth 4.38 Welded, 1 dk	**(B32A2ST) Tug**	**2 oil engines** gearing integral to driving 2 Voith-Schneider propellers Total Power: 3,820kW (5,194hp) 12.0kn Wartsila 6L26 2 x 4 Stroke 6 Cy. 260 x 320 each-1910kW (2597bhp) Wartsila Finland Oy-Finland AuxGen: 2 x 140kW 415V 50Hz a.c
7618038 - -	**TIRAD PASS** **Philippine Coast Guard** - *Manila* *Philippines*	*282* 86 -	Class: (AB)	**1976-04 Sumidagawa Zosen K.K. — Tokyo** Yd No: N50-04 Loa 44.00 Br ex 7.32 Dght - Lbp 40.80 Br md 7.28 Dpth 3.51 Welded, 1 dk	**(B34M2QS) Search & Rescue Vessel**	**4 oil engines** reverse reduction geared to sc. shafts driving 4 FP propellers Total Power: 3,236kW (4,400hp) 27.0kn M.T.U. 12V493TY70 4 x Vee 4 Stroke 12 Cy. 175 x 205 each-809kW (1100bhp) Ikegai Tekkosho-Japan AuxGen: 2 x 80kW Fuel: 34.0
8746076 - -	**TIRAMANA 002** *ex* Bosowa X *-2009* **PT Tiramana** - *Makassar* *Indonesia*	**198** 60 -	Class: KI	**1990-01 PT Bahtera Bahari Shipyard — Batam** Loa 26.80 Br ex - Dght 2.600 Lbp 24.91 Br md 8.20 Dpth 4.20 Welded, 1 dk	**(B32A2ST) Tug**	**2 oil engines** reduction geared to sc. shafts driving 2 Propellers
7640275 *YCGA* -	**TIRAMINA 01** **PT Tirta Raya Mina (Java Fisheries Development Project)** Soeyadi Stswohardjojo *Semarang* *Indonesia* Official number: 0015/PHB	*165* 38 102	Class: (KI) (NK)	**1976-12 Daedong Shipbuilding Co Ltd — Busan** Yd No: 163 Loa 33.43 Br ex 6.23 Dght 2.147 Lbp 29.55 Br md 6.20 Dpth 2.70 Welded, 1 dk	**(B12B2FC) Fish Carrier** Ins: 108 1 Ha: (1.3 x 1.3)ER	**1 oil engine** with hydraulic couplings & geared to sc. shaft driving 1 FP propeller Total Power: 272kW (370hp) 10.0kn Yanmar 6ML-HT 1 x 4 Stroke 6 Cy. 200 x 240 272kW (370bhp) Yanmar Diesel Engine Co Ltd-Japan
7640299 *YCGC* -	**TIRAMINA 03** **PT Tirta Raya Mina (Java Fisheries Development Project)** Soeyadi Stswohardjojo *Semarang* *Indonesia* Official number: 0033/PHB	*165* 38 102	Class: (KI) (NK)	**1976-12 Daedong Shipbuilding Co Ltd — Busan** Yd No: 165 Loa 33.43 Br ex 6.23 Dght 2.147 Lbp 29.55 Br md 6.20 Dpth 2.70 Welded, 1 dk	**(B12B2FC) Fish Carrier** Ins: 108	**1 oil engine** with hydraulic couplings & geared to sc. shaft driving 1 FP propeller Total Power: 272kW (370hp) 10.0kn Yanmar 6ML-HT 1 x 4 Stroke 6 Cy. 200 x 240 272kW (370bhp) Yanmar Diesel Engine Co Ltd-Japan
8889440 *ERVK* -	**TIRAS** *ex* Danapris 3 *-2014* *ex* Biysk *-2007* **Volga-Dnieper Shipping Co** LLC 'Capital Shipping Co' *Moldova* MMSI: 214182211	**2,360** 870 3,183	Class: UA (RS)	**1986-07 Santierul Naval Oltenita S.A. — Oltenita** Yd No: 259 Loa 108.40 Br ex 15.00 Dght 3.190 Lbp 105.00 Br md 14.80 Dpth 5.00 Welded, 1 dk	**(A31A2GX) General Cargo Ship**	**2 oil engines** driving 2 FP propellers Total Power: 1,030kW (1,400hp) 10.0kn S.K.L. 6NVD48A-2U 2 x 4 Stroke 6 Cy. 320 x 480 each-515kW (700bhp) VEB Schwermaschinenbau "KarlLiebknecht" (SKL)-Magdeburg AuxGen: 3 x 50kW a.c Fuel: 84.0 (d.f.)
9087178 *ZM2279* -	**TIRI CAT** *ex* Quickcat Ii *-2011* **360 Discovery Ltd** - *Auckland* *New Zealand* Official number: 876062	**232** 176 50	Class: (BV)	**1993-12 Sabre Catamarans Pty Ltd — Fremantle WA** Yd No: 129 Loa 22.00 Br ex - Dght 1.200 Lbp 19.99 Br md 8.50 Dpth 4.90 Welded, 2 dks	**(A37B2PS) Passenger Ship** Hull Material: Aluminium Alloy Passengers: unberthed: 195	**2 oil engines** sr geared to sc. shafts driving 2 FP propellers Total Power: 1,220kW (1,658hp) 24.0kn M.T.U. 12V183TE72 2 x Vee 4 Stroke 12 Cy. 128 x 142 each-610kW (829bhp) MTU Friedrichshafen GmbH-Friedrichshafen

7210111 - NDB 512	**TIRIS** *ex* Shintoku Maru No. 26 - - *Nouadhibou* *Mauritania*	*499* 180 517	Class: (RI)	**1972 Usuki Iron Works Co Ltd — Usuki OT** Yd No: 822 Loa 60.76 Br ex 9.73 Dght 3.798 Lbp 54.01 Br md 9.71 Dpth 6.56 Welded, 2 dks	**(B11A2FT) Trawler**	**1 oil engine** driving 1 FP propeller Total Power: 1,545kW (2,101hp) Akasaka AH38 1 x 4 Stroke 6 Cy. 380 x 560 1545kW (2101bhp) Akasaka Tekkosho KK (Akasaka DieselLtd)-Japan
7350222 *5TAD*	**TIRIS II** *ex* Ouadane I *-1990* *ex* Delfini *-1980* **Feten Ould Moulaye** - *Nouadhibou* *Mauritania* Official number: 43	*399* 155 -	Class: (LR) ✠ Classed LR until 19/8/92	**1975-07 D. C. Anastassiades & A. Ch. Tsortanides — Perama** Yd No: 74 Loa 42.91 Br ex 8.64 Dght 4.877 Lbp 37.01 Br md 8.60 Dpth 4.91 Welded, 2 dks	**(B11A2FS) Stern Trawler** Ins: 340 Compartments: 1 Ho, ER 2 Ha: (1.1 x 1.1) (1.6 x 1.6)ER	**1 oil engine** driving 1 CP propeller Total Power: 662kW (900hp) Alpha 409-26VO 1 x 2 Stroke 9 Cy. 260 x 400 662kW (900bhp) Alpha Diesel A/S-Denmark AuxGen: 2 x 154kW 380V 50Hz a.c
9377523 *LAFU7* -	**TIRRANNA** - **Wilhelmsen Lines Shipowning Malta Ltd** Wilhelmsen Ship Management (Norway) AS SatCom: Inmarsat C 425989510 *Tonsberg* *Norway (NIS)* MMSI: 259895000	**71,673** 33,513 29,936	Class: LR ✠ **100A1** SS 06/2009 vehicle carrier movable decks deck Nos. 1, 3, 5 and 8 strengthened for the carraige of roll on-roll off cargoes *IWS LI ✠ **LMC** **UMS** Eq.Ltr: S†; Cable: 687.5/87.0 U3 (a)	**2009-06 Daewoo Shipbuilding & Marine Engineering Co Ltd — Geoje** Yd No: 4452 Loa 231.60 (BB) Br ex 32.58 Dght 11.300 Lbp 219.30 Br md 32.26 Dpth 34.70 Welded, 13 dks	**(A35B2RV) Vehicles Carrier** Stern door/ramp (centre) Len: 7.04 Wid: 15.40 Swl: 237 Side door/ramp (s) Len: 6.01 Wid: 5.80 Swl: 30 Cars: 7,887	**1 oil engine** driving 1 FP propeller Total Power: 18,080kW (24,582hp) 20.8kn MAN-B&W 8S60ME-C 1 x 2 Stroke 8 Cy. 600 x 2400 18080kW (24582bhp) Doosan Engine Co Ltd-South Korea AuxGen: 2 x 1700kW 450V 60Hz a.c Boilers: e (ex.g.) 9.2kgf/cm² (9.0bar), WTAuxB (o.f.) 9.2kgf/cm² (9.0bar) Thrusters: 1 Thwart. CP thruster (f) Fuel: 355.0 (d.f.) 4625.0 (r.f.)
9359181 *IFPS2* -	**TIRRENO** *completed as* Sanmar Eskort IV *-2006* **Everblacks Towage Servicos Maritimos Unipessoal Lda** - *Genoa* *Italy* MMSI: 247176600 Official number: 3841	**466** 139 175	Class: RI (AB)	**2006-08 Sahin Celik Sanayi A.S. — Tuzla** Yd No: 42 Loa 32.20 Br ex 12.20 Dght 4.790 Lbp 26.21 Br md 11.60 Dpth 5.36 Welded, 1 dk	**(B32A2ST) Tug**	**2 oil engines** gearing integral to driving 2 Z propellers Total Power: 4,046kW (5,500hp) 13.0kn Wartsila 6L26A 2 x 4 Stroke 6 Cy. 260 x 320 each-2023kW (2750bhp) Wartsila France SA-France AuxGen: 2 x 140kW a.c Fuel: 166.6 (d.f.)
8127919 *GDBP* -	**TIRRICK** - **Shetland Islands Council Towage Operations** - *Lerwick* *United Kingdom* MMSI: 232003478 Official number: 399392	**538** 161 226	Class: LR ✠ **100A1** CS 06/2008 tug ✠ **LMC** **UMS** Eq.Ltr: I; Cable: 330.0/30.0 U2 (a)	**1983-06 Ferguson-Ailsa Ltd — Port Glasgow** Yd No: 489 Loa 37.44 Br ex 11.82 Dght 5.360 Lbp 35.01 Br md 11.31 Dpth 4.20 Welded, 1 dk	**(B32A2ST) Tug**	**2 oil engines** with flexible couplings & sr gearedto sc. shafts driving 2 Voith-Schneider propellers Total Power: 2,942kW (4,000hp) Ruston 12RKCM 2 x Vee 4 Stroke 12 Cy. 254 x 305 each-1471kW (2000bhp) Ruston Diesels Ltd.-Newton-le-Willows AuxGen: 3 x 80kW 440V 50Hz a.c Fuel: 141.0 (d.f.) 14.5pd
8892564 - -	**TIRTA** - **PT Mitratirta Lokalestari** - *Semarang* *Indonesia*	**151** 90 -	Class: KI	**1990 P.T. Karta Putra — Tegal** Loa 22.04 Br ex - Dght 2.660 Lbp 20.53 Br md 6.53 Dpth 3.34 Welded, 1 dk	**(B32A2ST) Tug**	**2 oil engines** geared to sc. shafts driving 2 FP propellers Total Power: 552kW (750hp) Caterpillar D353C 2 x 4 Stroke 6 Cy. 159 x 203 each-276kW (375bhp) Caterpillar Inc-USA
8125791 *YD4634* -	**TIRTA 88** *ex* Itsukushima *-1999* **PT Mitratirta Lokalestari** - *Jambi* *Indonesia*	*258* 78 100	Class: KI	**1981-12 Kyoei Zosen KK — Mihara HS** Yd No: 118 Loa 28.10 Br ex 8.03 Dght 3.200 Lbp 26.01 Br md 8.01 Dpth 3.81 Welded, 1 dk	**(B32A2ST) Tug**	**2 oil engines** driving 2 FP propellers Total Power: 956kW (1,300hp) Hanshin 6LU28 2 x 4 Stroke 6 Cy. 280 x 440 each-478kW (650bhp) The Hanshin Diesel Works Ltd-Japan
8518728 *YB5233* -	**TIRTA ABADI** *ex* Nisshin Maru *-2005* **PT Pelayaran Prima Tirta Jaya** - *Surabaya* *Indonesia*	**624** 236 700	Class: KI	**1985-10 Kishigami Zosen K.K. — Akitsu** Yd No: 1855 Loa 53.40 (BB) Br ex 9.00 Dght 3.370 Lbp 49.50 Br md - Dpth 5.50 Welded, 1 dk	**(A31A2GX) General Cargo Ship** Compartments: 1 Ho, ER 1 Ha: ER	**1 oil engine** geared to sc. shaft driving 1 FP propeller Total Power: 405kW (551hp) Matsui MS25GSC 1 x 4 Stroke 6 Cy. 250 x 470 405kW (551bhp) Matsui Iron Works Co Ltd-Japan
9027491 - -	**TIRTA ALAM** - **PT Tirta Alam** - *Balikpapan* *Indonesia*	**277** 84 -	Class: KI	**1998-07 C.V. Karya Lestari Industri — Samarinda** L reg 41.75 Br ex - Dght - Lbp 39.80 Br md 9.00 Dpth 2.80 Welded, 1 dk	**(A35D2RL) Landing Craft** Bow ramp (centre)	**2 oil engines** geared to sc. shafts driving 2 Propellers Total Power: 736kW (1,000hp) 12.0kn Yanmar 6LAA-DT 2 x 4 Stroke 6 Cy. 148 x 165 each-368kW (500bhp) Yanmar Diesel Engine Co Ltd-Japan
8999415 - -	**TIRTA ALAM I** - **PT Tirta Alam** - *Balikpapan* *Indonesia*	**170** 52 -	Class: KI	**2004-11 C.V. Karya Lestari Industri — Samarinda** Loa 37.50 Br ex - Dght 2.070 Lbp 35.62 Br md 8.00 Dpth 2.40 Welded, 1 dk	**(A35D2RL) Landing Craft** Bow ramp (centre)	**2 oil engines** reduction geared to sc. shafts driving 2 Propellers Total Power: 486kW (660hp) Yanmar 6HA2M-HTE 2 x 4 Stroke 6 Cy. 130 x 165 each-243kW (330bhp) Yanmar Diesel Engine Co Ltd-Japan AuxGen: 2 x 88kW 400V a.c
8631166 *YCZW* -	**TIRTA AMARTA** *ex* Dwi No. 2 *-2009* *ex* Eiju Maru *-2006* **PT Karya Cemerlang** - *Tanjung Priok* *Indonesia*	**764** 252 893	Class: KI	**1987-10 Y.K. Takasago Zosensho — Naruto** Yd No: 160 Converted From: Suction Dredger-2009 Loa 49.10 Br ex 11.62 Dght 4.250 Lbp 44.41 Br md 11.60 Dpth 5.10 Welded, 1 dk	**(A31A2GX) General Cargo Ship**	**1 oil engine** driving 1 FP propeller Total Power: 736kW (1,001hp) Niigata 6M28BGT 1 x 4 Stroke 6 Cy. 280 x 480 736kW (1001bhp) Niigata Engineering Co Ltd-Japan AuxGen: 2 x 74kW 225/130V
9027506 - -	**TIRTA III** - **PT Mitratirta Lokalestari** - *Jambi* *Indonesia*	**149** 45 -	Class: KI	**1998-09 PT Mitratirta Lokalestari — Jambi** L reg 26.00 Br ex - Dght 2.990 Lbp 23.65 Br md 7.50 Dpth 3.50 Welded, 1 dk	**(B32A2ST) Tug**	**2 oil engines** geared to sc. shafts driving 2 Propellers Total Power: 956kW (1,300hp) 11.0kn Caterpillar 3412 2 x Vee 4 Stroke 12 Cy. 137 x 152 each-478kW (650bhp) Caterpillar Inc-USA
7733888 *YCNM* -	**TIRTA IV** *ex* Disetco Pisces *-1992* *ex* Golden Ocean *-1977* **PT Tirta Alam** - *Jakarta* *Indonesia* Official number: 3826+LLA	*117* 117 -	Class: KI (AB)	**1977-06 Hip Hing Cheung Shipyard Ltd. — Hong Kong** Yd No: 548 L reg 22.25 Br ex 6.88 Dght 2.261 Lbp 21.34 Br md 6.86 Dpth 3.13 Welded, 1 dk	**(B32A2ST) Tug**	**2 oil engines** reverse reduction geared to sc. shafts driving 2 FP propellers Total Power: 720kW (978hp) 10.0kn Yanmar 6LA-ST 2 x 4 Stroke 6 Cy. 150 x 165 each-360kW (489bhp) (, fitted 2005) Yanmar Diesel Engine Co Ltd-Japan AuxGen: 2 x 20kW
9068471 - -	**TIRTA IX** - **PT Samudra Kencana Jaya** - *Jambi* *Indonesia*	**180** 54 -	Class: KI	**2000-01 PT Mitratirta Lokalestari — Jambi** Loa - Br ex - Dght - Lbp 25.00 Br md 7.50 Dpth 3.75 Welded, 1 dk	**(B32A2ST) Tug**	**2 oil engines** geared to sc. shafts driving 2 Propellers Total Power: 1,060kW (1,442hp) 6.0kn Caterpillar 3412 2 x Vee 4 Stroke 12 Cy. 137 x 152 each-530kW (721bhp) (made 1974, fitted 2000) Caterpillar Tractor Co-USA
5122750 *YEWO* -	**TIRTA KARSA** *ex* Pan Glory *-1997* *ex* Fujihisa Maru *-1976* **PT Taruna Cipta Kencana** - *Jakarta* *Indonesia* MMSI: 525021004 Official number: 1993BA9664/L	**1,241** 758 1,862	Class: KI	**1962-03 Imabari Shipbuilding Co Ltd — Imabari EH (Imabari Shipyard)** Yd No: 96 Loa 71.10 Br ex 10.47 Dght 5.073 Lbp 64.98 Br md 10.39 Dpth 5.44 Riveted\Welded, 1 dk	**(A13B2TP) Products Tanker** Liq: 2,207; Liq (Oil): 2,207 Compartments: 4 Ta, ER	**1 oil engine** driving 1 FP propeller Total Power: 1,545kW (2,101hp) 10.5kn Hanshin 6LU38 1 x 4 Stroke 6 Cy. 380 x 580 1545kW (2101bhp) (new engine 1980) The Hanshin Diesel Works Ltd-Japan AuxGen: 2 x 15kW 115V d.c Fuel: 77.0 4.5pd
8340030 - -	**TIRTA LAMANDAU I** - **PT Sinar Bahtera Maju** - *Pangkalanbuun* *Indonesia*	*147* 78 -	Class: KI	**1975 P.T. Bina Kapal Ikan — Tegal** Loa 30.00 Br ex - Dght - Lbp 27.61 Br md 7.00 Dpth 2.42 Welded, 1 dk	**(A13B2TU) Tanker (unspecified)**	**1 oil engine** driving 1 FP propeller Total Power: 190kW (258hp) Deutz SBF6M716 1 x 4 Stroke 6 Cy. 135 x 160 190kW (258bhp) Kloeckner Humboldt Deutz AG-West Germany
8922979 *YD4672* -	**TIRTA MAS** *ex* Mitra Kencana III *-2008* *ex* Taisei Maru *-1999* *ex* Zenei Maru No. 77 *-1999* *ex* Kaio Maru No. 3 *-1999* **PT Patria Nusasegara** - *Jakarta* *Indonesia*	*129* 39 -	Class: KI	**1969-08 Nishi Nippon Zosen Tekko K.K. — Shimonoseki** Loa 29.50 Br ex - Dght 3.000 Lbp 24.50 Br md 6.50 Dpth 3.20 Welded, 1 dk	**(B32A2ST) Tug**	**1 oil engine** driving 1 FP propeller Total Power: 736kW (1,001hp) 11.0kn Hanshin 6LU28 1 x 4 Stroke 6 Cy. 280 x 440 736kW (1001bhp) The Hanshin Diesel Works Ltd-Japan

8011031 *YGVV* -	**TIRTA NIAGA III** *ex* Elsa *-2001* *ex* Yeon Byeon No. 2 *-1997* *ex* Bei Hai I *-1997* *ex* Yeon Byeon No. 2 *-1996* *ex* Takachiho Maru No. 3 *-1993* *ex* Kintai Maru *-1985* - - *Palembang* *Indonesia*	**1,936** 934 3,405	Class: (CC) (KI) (NK)	**1980-08 Kochi Jyuko K.K. — Kochi** Yd No: 2156 Loa 84.13 Br ex - Dght 6.154 Lbp 78.01 Br md 13.01 Dpth 6.81 Welded, 1 dk	**(A13B2TP) Products Tanker** Liq: 3,248; Liq (Oil): 3,248	**1 oil engine** driving 1 FP propeller Total Power: 1,687kW (2,294hp) 12.5kn Hanshin 6LU40 1 x 4 Stroke 6 Cy. 400 x 640 1687kW (2294bhp) The Hanshin Diesel Works Ltd-Japan AuxGen: 2 x 250kW 450V 60Hz a.c Fuel: 32.0 (d.f.) 123.5 (r.f.) 9.0pd
9183051 *YD4775* -	**TIRTA NIAGA V** *ex* Tenaga Perkasa *-2001* **PT Tirta Arung Inti Niaga** - *Palembang* *Indonesia* MMSI: 525015462	**104** 62 -	Class: KI (BV)	**1997-01 Nga Chai Shipyard Sdn Bhd — Sibu** (Hull) Yd No: 9711 **1997-01 Kiong Nguong Shipbuilding Contractor Co — Sibu** Yd No: (9711) Loa 24.25 Br ex - Dght 2.500 Lbp 21.69 Br md 7.30 Dpth 3.00	**(B32A2ST) Tug**	**2 oil engines** geared to sc. shafts driving 2 FP propellers Total Power: 942kW (1,280hp) Yanmar 6LAH-ST 2 x 4 Stroke 6 Cy. 150 x 165 each-471kW (640bhp) Yanmar Diesel Engine Co Ltd-Japan AuxGen: 2 x 20kW 380V a.c Fuel: 73.0 (d.f.)
8734188 *YD3377* -	**TIRTA NIAGA X** *ex* Sindo Ocean II *-2007* **PT Sinar Alam Permai** - *Dumai* *Indonesia*	**227** 69 -	Class: KI	**2007 PT Usda Seroja Jaya — Rengat** Loa 30.00 Br ex - Dght 2.790 Lbp 28.00 Br md 9.00 Dpth 3.40 Welded, 1 dk	**(B32A2ST) Tug**	**2 oil engines** driving 2 Propellers Total Power: 1,766kW (2,402hp) 10.0kn Niigata 6M28AGT 2 x 4 Stroke 6 Cy. 280 x 480 each-883kW (1201bhp) (made 1991, fitted 2007) Niigata Engineering Co Ltd-Japan AuxGen: 2 x 49kW 220V a.c
7326984 *YCXS* -	**TIRTA SAMUDERA I** *ex* Intan 12 *-2002* *ex* Olympic 88 *-1996* *ex* Putra Indah X *-1996* *ex* Seiryu Maru No. 5 *-1981* - - *Jakarta* *Indonesia* MMSI: 525015428	*832* 500 1,434	Class: (KI)	**1973-06 Asakawa Zosen K.K. — Imabari** Yd No: 226 Loa 62.57 Br ex 9.83 Dght - Lbp 58.07 Br md 9.81 Dpth 4.86 Riveted\Welded, 1 dk	**(A13B2TP) Products Tanker**	**1 oil engine** driving 1 FP propeller Total Power: 1,177kW (1,600hp) Hanshin 6LU35 1 x 4 Stroke 6 Cy. 350 x 550 1177kW (1600bhp) Hanshin Nainenki Kogyo-Japan
8864385 *YD3206* -	**TIRTA SAMUDERA VI** *ex* Yoshi Maru No. 11 *-2003* **PT Naga Bahtera Lines** - *Dumai* *Indonesia*	**145** 44 -	Class: KI	**1981-07 Shunkei Abe — Nandan, Hyogo Pref.** Yd No: 115 Loa 29.50 Br ex - Dght 2.550 Lbp 26.00 Br md 6.70 Dpth 2.99 Welded, 1 dk	**(B32A2ST) Tug**	**1 oil engine** driving 1 FP propeller Total Power: 662kW (900hp) Yanmar MF28-UT 1 x 4 Stroke 6 Cy. 280 x 450 662kW (900bhp) Yanmar Diesel Engine Co Ltd-Japan AuxGen: 1 x 60kW 225/130V a.c
8323288 *YD4755* -	**TIRTA SAMUDRA II** *ex* Masuei Maru No. 27 *-2005* *ex* Kitano Maru *-1992* **PT Tirtacipta Mulyapersada** - *Palembang* *Indonesia*	*222* 67 -	Class: KI	**1984-03 Kanagawa Zosen — Kobe** Yd No: 257 Loa 30.82 Br ex 8.62 Dght 2.701 Lbp 25.51 Br md 8.60 Dpth 3.79 Welded, 1 dk	**(B32A2ST) Tug**	**2 oil engines** sr geared to sc. shafts driving 2 Directional propellers Total Power: 1,912kW (2,600hp) 10.0kn Niigata 6L25BX 2 x 4 Stroke 6 Cy. 250 x 320 each-956kW (1300bhp) Niigata Engineering Co Ltd-Japan AuxGen: 2 x 68kW 225V 60Hz a.c Fuel: 43.0 (d.f.) 10.0pd
9549748 *PMSG* -	**TIRTA SAMUDRA IX** **PT Tirtacipta Mulyapersada** - *Belawan* *Indonesia* MMSI: 525015427	**1,934** 1,054 -	Class: KI	**2008-12 Yichang Shipyard — Yichang HB** Yd No: 200801 Loa 87.26 Br ex - Dght 3.700 Lbp 83.16 Br md 15.60 Dpth 4.40 Welded, 1 dk	**(B35E2TF) Bunkering Tanker** Double Hull (13F)	**2 oil engines** reduction geared to sc. shafts driving 2 Propellers Total Power: 794kW (1,080hp) Weifang X6170ZC 2 x 4 Stroke 6 Cy. 170 x 200 each-397kW (540bhp) Weifang Diesel Engine Factory-China
7503611 *YDA4010* -	**TIRTA SAMUDRA VII** *ex* Salvalet *-2004* **PT Tirtacipta Mulyapersada** - *Jakarta* *Indonesia*	**168** 51 108	Class: KI (LR) ✠ Classed LR until 29/9/04	**1976-03 Selco Shipyard Pte Ltd — Singapore** Yd No: 205 Loa 26.50 Br ex 8.16 Dght 3.017 Lbp 23.27 Br md 7.62 Dpth 3.51 Welded, 1 dk	**(B32A2ST) Tug**	**1 oil engine** with clutches, flexible couplings & sr reverse geared to sc. shaft driving 1 FP propeller Total Power: 662kW (900hp) 11.5kn MWM TBD440-6 1 x 4 Stroke 6 Cy. 230 x 270 662kW (900bhp) Motoren Werke Mannheim AG (MWM)-West Germany AuxGen: 2 x 64kW 400V 50Hz a.c Fuel: 77.0 (d.f.)
8804804 *PMEL* -	**TIRTA SAMUDRA VIII** *ex* Yufukujin Maru *-2007* **PT Tirtacipta Mulyapersada** - *Dumai* *Indonesia* MMSI: 525016338	*995* 602 2,106	Class: KI	**1988-05 Hakata Zosen K.K. — Imabari** Yd No: 373 L reg 72.10 Br ex - Dght 4.801 Lbp 72.01 Br md 11.50 Dpth 5.00 Welded, 1 dk	**(A13B2TP) Products Tanker** Double Bottom Entire Compartment Length Liq: 2,190; Liq (Oil): 2,190 Compartments: 10 Ta, ER 2 Cargo Pump (s): 2x750m³/hr	**1 oil engine** driving 1 CP propeller Total Power: 1,324kW (1,800hp) Hanshin 6EL30 1 x 4 Stroke 6 Cy. 300 x 600 1324kW (1800bhp) The Hanshin Diesel Works Ltd-Japan AuxGen: 1 x 160kW 445V a.c, 1 x 60kW 445V a.c
8910366 *PMJJ* -	**TIRTA SAMUDRA X** *ex* Toei Maru *-2008* **PT Tirtacipta Mulyapersada** - *Pontianak* *Indonesia* MMSI: 525015482	*1,013* 626 2,103	Class: KI	**1989-12 Hakata Zosen K.K. — Imabari** Yd No: 506 Loa 75.83 (BB) Br ex - Dght 4.789 Lbp 72.00 Br md 11.50 Dpth 5.33 Welded, 1 dk	**(A13A2TV) Crude Oil Tanker** Liq: 2,190; Liq (Oil): 2,190 Compartments: 10 Ta, ER	**1 oil engine** reverse geared to sc. shaft driving 1 FP propeller Total Power: 1,177kW (1,600hp) 11.2kn Yanmar MF33-DT 1 x 4 Stroke 6 Cy. 330 x 620 1177kW (1600bhp) Matsue Diesel KK-Japan AuxGen: 2 x 130kW 445V a.c, 1 x 40kW 445V a.c
9033799 *PMKS* -	**TIRTA SAMUDRA XI** *ex* Kwang Yang Pioneer *-2009* **PT Tirtacipta Mulyapersada** - *Pontianak* *Indonesia* MMSI: 525015485	**2,269** 1,088 3,498	Class: KI (KR)	**1991-12 Daedong Shipbuilding Co Ltd — Busan** Yd No: 367 Loa 86.34 Br ex - Dght 5.521 Lbp 79.80 Br md 14.60 Dpth 7.00 Welded, 1 dk	**(A12B2TR) Chemical/Products Tanker** Liq: 3,942; Liq (Oil): 3,942 Compartments: 8 Ta, ER	**1 oil engine** driving 1 FP propeller Total Power: 2,189kW (2,976hp) 13.1kn B&W 6S26MC 1 x 2 Stroke 6 Cy. 260 x 980 2189kW (2976bhp) Ssangyong Heavy Industries Co Ltd-South Korea AuxGen: 2 x 266kW 445V a.c
8829490 *PMMO* -	**TIRTA SAMUDRA XII** *ex* Jian She 7 *-2008* **PT Tirtacipta Mulyapersada** - *Dumai* *Indonesia* MMSI: 525015484	**3,336** 1,698 5,288	Class: KI (CC)	**1986 Jiangxi Jiangzhou Shipyard — Ruichang JX** Loa 107.42 Br ex - Dght 6.400 Lbp 98.00 Br md 15.00 Dpth 7.49 Welded, 1 dk	**(A13B2TP) Products Tanker** Single Hull Liq: 6,620; Liq (Oil): 6,620 Compartments: 5 Ta, ER	**1 oil engine** driving 1 FP propeller Total Power: 2,795kW (3,800hp) 13.2kn B&W 5L35MC 1 x 2 Stroke 5 Cy. 350 x 1050 2795kW (3800bhp) Hudong Shipyard-China AuxGen: 2 x 250kW 400V a.c, 1 x 64kW 400V a.c
9577903 *PNLW* -	**TIRTA SAMUDRA XIX** **PT Tirtacipta Mulyapersada** - *Belawan* *Indonesia* MMSI: 525015671	**2,007** 1,156 3,000	Class: KI	**2010-06 Yichang Shipyard — Yichang HB** Yd No: 002 Loa 87.26 Br ex - Dght 3.600 Lbp 83.16 Br md 15.00 Dpth 4.60 Welded, 1 dk	**(A13B2TP) Products Tanker** Double Hull (13F)	**2 oil engines** reduction geared to sc. shafts driving 2 Propellers Total Power: 764kW (1,038hp) Weifang X6170ZC 2 x 4 Stroke 6 Cy. 170 x 200 each-382kW (519bhp) Weifang Diesel Engine Factory-China
9577496 *PNJS* -	**TIRTA SAMUDRA XVIII** **PT Tirtacipta Mulyapersada** - *Belawan* *Indonesia* MMSI: 525015670	**1,825** 1,001 3,000	Class: KI	**2010-03 Yichang Shipyard — Yichang HB** Yd No: 001 Loa 87.26 Br ex - Dght 3.700 Lbp 83.16 Br md 15.00 Dpth 4.60 Welded, 1 dk	**(A13B2TP) Products Tanker** Double Hull (13F)	**2 oil engines** reduction geared to sc. shafts driving 2 Propellers Total Power: 764kW (1,038hp) Weifang X6170ZC 2 x 4 Stroke 6 Cy. 170 x 200 each-382kW (519bhp) Weifang Diesel Engine Factory-China AuxGen: 2 x 132kW 400V a.c
9577915 *PLNX* -	**TIRTA SAMUDRA XX** **PT Tirtacipta Mulyapersada** - *Belawan* *Indonesia* MMSI: 525015648	**2,007** 1,156 3,000	Class: KI	**2010-06 Yichang Shipyard — Yichang HB** Yd No: 003 Loa 87.26 Br ex - Dght 3.600 Lbp 85.12 Br md 15.00 Dpth 4.60 Welded, 1 dk	**(A13B2TP) Products Tanker** Double Hull (13F)	**2 oil engines** reduction geared to sc. shafts driving 2 Propellers Total Power: 764kW (1,038hp) 10.0kn Weifang X6170ZC 2 x 4 Stroke 6 Cy. 170 x 200 each-382kW (519bhp) Weichai Power Co Ltd-China
9577939 *PNUH* -	**TIRTA SAMUDRA XXII** **PT Tirtacipta Mulyapersada** - *Belawan* *Indonesia* MMSI: 525015756	**2,261** 1,266 3,000	Class: KI	**2011-01 Shandong Huahai Shipbuilding Co Ltd — Rizhao SD** Yd No: 2 Loa 87.26 Br ex - Dght 3.700 Lbp 85.12 Br md 15.60 Dpth 4.60 Welded, 1 dk	**(A13B2TP) Products Tanker** Double Hull	**2 oil engines** reduction geared to sc. shafts driving 2 Propellers Total Power: 764kW (1,038hp) 10.0kn Weifang X6170ZC 2 x 4 Stroke 6 Cy. 170 x 200 each-382kW (519bhp) Weifang Diesel Engine Factory-China AuxGen: 2 x 120kW 400V a.c

IMO / Call sign	Name / Owner / Port	Tonnage	Class	Builder / Dimensions	Type	Machinery
9577941 *PNWA* -	**TIRTA SAMUDRA XXIII** **PT Tirtacipta Mulyapersada** - *Belawan* *Indonesia* MMSI: 525015757	**2,007** 1,156 3,000	Class: KI	**2011-01 Shandong Huahai Shipbuilding Co Ltd — Rizhao SD** Yd No: 3 Loa 87.26 Br ex - Dght 3.600 Lbp 85.00 Br md 15.60 Dpth 4.60 Welded, 1 dk	**(A13B2TP) Products Tanker** Double Hull (13F)	**2 oil engines** reduction geared to sc. shafts driving 2 Propellers Total Power: 764kW (1,038hp) 10.0kn Weifang X6170ZC 2 x 4 Stroke 6 Cy. 170 x 200 each-382kW (519bhp) Weifang Diesel Engine Factory-China
9664158 *POWC* -	**TIRTA SAMUDRA XXIX** **PT Tirtacipta Mulyapersada** - *Batam* *Indonesia* MMSI: 525020107	**2,217** 1,394 3,400	Class: KI (Class contemplated)	**2012-09 PT Usda Seroja Jaya — Rengat** Yd No: 011 Loa 87.26 Br ex - Dght 4.200 Lbp 83.16 Br md 15.60 Dpth 5.60 Welded, 1 dk	**(A38B2GB) Barge Carrier**	**2 oil engines** reduction geared to sc. shafts driving 2 Propellers Total Power: 764kW (1,038hp) Chinese Std. Type 6170ZC 2 x 4 Stroke 6 Cy. 170 x 200 each-382kW (519bhp) Weichai Power Co Ltd-China
9577953 *YGQQ* -	**TIRTA SAMUDRA XXV** **PT Tirtacipta Mulyapersada** - *Belawan* *Indonesia* MMSI: 525015758	**2,007** 1,156 3,000	Class: KI	**2011-03 Shandong Huahai Shipbuilding Co Ltd — Rizhao SD** Yd No: 4 Loa 87.26 Br ex - Dght 3.600 Lbp 85.00 Br md 15.60 Dpth 4.60 Welded, 1 dk	**(A13B2TP) Products Tanker** Double Hull (13F)	**2 oil engines** reduction geared to sc. shafts driving 2 FP propellers Total Power: 764kW (1,038hp) 10.0kn Weifang X6170ZC 2 x 4 Stroke 6 Cy. 170 x 200 each-382kW (519bhp) Weifang Diesel Engine Factory-China
9642655 *POJH* -	**TIRTA SAMUDRA XXVI** *ex* Wadiman *-2011* **PT Tirtacipta Mulyapersada** - *Batam* *Indonesia* MMSI: 525022013 Official number: 2011 PPMNO.1969/L	**2,217** 1,394 3,000	Class: KI	**2011-09 PT Usda Seroja Jaya — Rengat** Yd No: 04 Loa 87.26 Br ex 15.60 Dght - Lbp 83.16 Br md - Dpth 5.60 Welded, 1 dk	**(A21A2BC) Bulk Carrier**	**1 oil engine** driving 1 Propeller 11.0kn
8313740 *YD3813* -	**TIRTA SAMUDRA XXVII** *ex* Marlin *-2011* **PT Tirtacipta Mulyapersada** - *Dumai* *Indonesia*	**251** 75 -	Class: KI (LR) ✠ Classed LR until 18/11/05	**1984-07 Sabah Shipyard Sdn Bhd — Labuan** (Assembled by) Yd No: 124 **1984-07 Muetzelfeldtwerft GmbH — Cuxhaven** (Parts for assembly by) Yd No: C-124 Loa 28.76 Br ex 9.15 Dght 3.101 Lbp 25.90 Br md 9.11 Dpth 3.66 Welded, 1 dk	**(B32A2ST) Tug**	**2 oil engines** with clutches, flexible couplings & sr geared to sc. shafts driving 2 Directional propellers Total Power: 2,000kW (2,720hp) 9.0kn Deutz SBV6M628 2 x 4 Stroke 6 Cy. 240 x 280 each-1000kW (1360bhp) Kloeckner Humboldt Deutz AG-West Germany AuxGen: 2 x 54kW 415V 50Hz a.c Fuel: 91.5 (d.f.) 21.5pd
9664146 *POWB* -	**TIRTA SAMUDRA XXVIII** **PT Tirtacipta Mulyapersada** - *Batam* *Indonesia* MMSI: 525020106	**2,217** 1,394 3,400	Class: KI	**2012-08 PT Usda Seroja Jaya — Rengat** Yd No: 010 Loa 87.26 Br ex - Dght 4.200 Lbp 83.16 Br md 15.60 Dpth 5.60 Welded, 1 dk	**(A38B2GB) Barge Carrier**	**2 oil engines** reduction geared to sc. shafts driving 2 Propellers Total Power: 764kW (1,038hp) Chinese Std. Type 6170ZC 2 x 4 Stroke 6 Cy. 170 x 200 each-382kW (519bhp) Weichai Power Co Ltd-China
9678836 *POYN* -	**TIRTA SAMUDRA XXX** **PT Tirtacipta Mulyapersada** - *Batam* *Indonesia* MMSI: 525021088	**2,217** 1,394 3,400	Class: KI	**2012-11 PT Usda Seroja Jaya — Rengat** Yd No: 012 Loa 87.26 Br ex - Dght 4.300 Lbp 83.16 Br md 15.60 Dpth 5.60 Welded, 1 dk	**(A38B2GB) Barge Carrier**	**2 oil engines** reduction geared to sc. shafts driving 2 Propellers Total Power: 970kW (1,318hp) Yanmar 6AYM-WST 2 x 4 Stroke 6 Cy. 155 x 180 each-485kW (659bhp) Yanmar Diesel Engine Co Ltd-Japan
9678848 *POYO* -	**TIRTA SAMUDRA XXXI** **PT Tirtacipta Mulyapersada** - *Batam* *Indonesia* MMSI: 525021105	**2,217** 1,394 3,400	Class: KI (Class contemplated)	**2012-11 PT Usda Seroja Jaya — Rengat** Yd No: 013 Loa 87.26 Br ex - Dght 4.300 Lbp 83.16 Br md 15.60 Dpth 5.60 Welded, 1 dk	**(A38B2GB) Barge Carrier**	**2 oil engines** reduction geared to sc. shafts driving 2 Propellers Total Power: 970kW (1,318hp) Yanmar 6AYM-WST 2 x 4 Stroke 6 Cy. 155 x 180 each-485kW (659bhp) Yanmar Diesel Engine Co Ltd-Japan
9688958 *JZFM* -	**TIRTA SAMUDRA XXXII** **PT Tirtacipta Mulyapersada** - *Batam* *Indonesia* MMSI: 525023147	**2,223** 1,402 3,400	Class: KI (Class contemplated)	**2013-03 PT Usda Seroja Jaya — Rengat** Yd No: 014 Loa 87.26 Br ex - Dght 4.300 Lbp 83.16 Br md 15.60 Dpth 5.60 Welded, 1 dk	**(A38B2GB) Barge Carrier**	**2 oil engines** reduction geared to sc. shafts driving 2 Propellers Total Power: 970kW (1,318hp) Yanmar 6AYM-WST 2 x 4 Stroke 6 Cy. 155 x 180 each-485kW (659bhp) Yanmar Diesel Engine Co Ltd-Japan AuxGen: 2 x 60kW 400V a.c
8655332 - -	**TIRTA VII** **PT Tirta Alam** - *Balikpapan* *Indonesia*	**101** 31 -	Class: KI	**2008-01 PT Sarana Daya Hutama — Balikpapan** Loa 24.00 Br ex - Dght 2.050 Lbp 22.27 Br md 6.55 Dpth 2.75 Welded, 1 dk	**(B32A2ST) Tug**	**2 oil engines** reduction geared to sc. shafts driving 2 FP propellers AuxGen: 2 x 40kW 400V a.c
9027518 - -	**TIRTA VII** **PT Anugrah Surya Sentosa** - *Jambi* *Indonesia*	**163** 49 -	Class: KI	**2001-09 PT Mitratirta Lokalestari — Jambi** L reg 26.00 Br ex - Dght 2.750 Lbp 23.25 Br md 7.50 Dpth 3.50 Welded, 1 dk	**(B32A2ST) Tug**	**2 oil engines** geared to sc. shafts driving 2 Propellers Total Power: 1,332kW (1,810hp) 10.0kn Caterpillar 3508TA 2 x Vee 4 Stroke 8 Cy. 170 x 190 each-666kW (905bhp) Caterpillar Inc-USA
9068354 - -	**TIRTA XI** **PT Samudra Kencana Jaya** - *Jambi* *Indonesia*	**146** 87 -	Class: KI	**1999-01 PT Mitratirta Lokalestari — Jambi** Loa - Br ex - Dght - Lbp 21.60 Br md 7.60 Dpth 3.70 Welded, 1 dk	**(B32A2ST) Tug**	**2 oil engines** geared to sc. shafts driving 2 Propellers Total Power: 1,302kW (1,770hp) 6.0kn Caterpillar 3412D 2 x Vee 4 Stroke 12 Cy. 145 x 162 each-651kW (885bhp) Caterpillar Inc-USA
9151125 *PMVH* -	**TIRTASARI** **PT Banyu Laju Shipping** Gold Bridge Shipping Ltd *Jakarta* *Indonesia* MMSI: 525007028 Official number: 2009 PST NO. 5701/L	**3,752** 1,744 5,878 T/cm 13.8	Class: NK	**1997-05 Fukuoka Shipbuilding Co Ltd — Fukuoka FO** Yd No: 1195 Loa 99.90 (BB) Br ex - Dght 6.664 Lbp 93.90 Br md 16.50 Dpth 8.50 Welded, 1 dk	**(A12B2TR) Chemical/Products Tanker** Double Hull (13F) Liq: 5,010; Liq (Oil): 6,247 Cargo Heating Coils Compartments: 8 Wing Ta, 2 Wing Slop Ta, ER 10 Cargo Pump (s): 8x200m³/hr, 2x100m³/hr Manifold: Bow/CM: 44m	**1 oil engine** driving 1 FP propeller Total Power: 2,795kW (3,800hp) 13.1kn B&W 6L35MC 1 x 2 Stroke 6 Cy. 350 x 1050 2795kW (3800bhp) Makita Corp-Japan AuxGen: 3 x 360kW 450V 60Hz a.c Fuel: 488.0 (r.f.)
9617832 *YDA4801* -	**TIRTAYASA I - 212** **PT Pelabuhan Indonesia II (Persero) (Indonesia Port Corp II) (PELINDO II)** - *Tanjung Priok* *Indonesia*	**296** 89 121	Class: KI	**2011-03 P.T. Daya Radar Utama — Jakarta** Yd No: 140 Loa 30.20 Br ex - Dght 3.800 Lbp 27.93 Br md 9.50 Dpth 3.80 Welded, 1 dk	**(B32A2ST) Tug**	**2 oil engines** reduction geared to sc. shafts driving 2 Propellers Total Power: 1,766kW (2,402hp) Yanmar 6N21A-SV 2 x 4 Stroke 6 Cy. 210 x 290 each-883kW (1201bhp) Yanmar Diesel Engine Co Ltd-Japan AuxGen: 2 x 180kW 380V a.c
9617844 *YDA4849* -	**TIRTAYASA II - 212** **PT Pelabuhan Indonesia II (Persero) Cabang Pelabuhan Tanjung Priok (Indonesia Port Corp II, Tanjung Priok)** - *Banten* *Indonesia* MMSI: 525016698	**269** 81 121	Class: KI	**2011-06 P.T. Daya Radar Utama — Jakarta** Yd No: 141 Loa 30.20 Br ex - Dght 3.800 Lbp 27.93 Br md 9.50 Dpth 3.80 Welded, 1 dk	**(B32A2ST) Tug**	**2 oil engines** reduction geared to sc. shafts driving 2 Propellers Total Power: 1,766kW (2,402hp) Yanmar 6N21A-SV 2 x 4 Stroke 6 Cy. 210 x 290 each-883kW (1201bhp) Yanmar Diesel Engine Co Ltd-Japan AuxGen: 2 x 180kW 380V a.c
9617856 *YDA4827* -	**TIRTAYASA III - 216** **PT Pelabuhan Indonesia II (Persero) (Indonesia Port Corp II) (PELINDO II)** - *Tanjung Priok* *Indonesia* MMSI: 525016696	**296** 89 126	Class: KI	**2011-07 P.T. Daya Radar Utama — Jakarta** Yd No: 142 Loa 30.20 Br ex - Dght 2.840 Lbp 27.93 Br md 9.50 Dpth 3.80 Welded, 1 dk	**(B32A2ST) Tug**	**2 oil engines** reduction geared to sc. shafts driving 2 Propellers Total Power: 2,354kW (3,200hp) Yanmar 8N21A-SN 2 x 4 Stroke 8 Cy. 210 x 290 each-1177kW (1600bhp) Yanmar Diesel Engine Co Ltd-Japan AuxGen: 2 x 180kW 380V a.c
9617882 *YDA4867* -	**TIRTAYASA IV - 216** **PT Pelabuhan Indonesia II (Persero) (Indonesia Port Corp II) (PELINDO II)** - *Tanjung Priok* *Indonesia* MMSI: 525016699	**296** 89 126	Class: KI	**2011-04 P.T. Daya Radar Utama — Jakarta** Yd No: 152 Loa 30.20 Br ex - Dght 2.840 Lbp 27.93 Br md 9.50 Dpth 3.80 Welded, 1 dk	**(B32A2ST) Tug**	**2 oil engines** reduction geared to sc. shafts driving 2 Propellers Total Power: 2,942kW (4,000hp) Niigata 6L26HLX 2 x 4 Stroke 6 Cy. 260 x 350 each-1471kW (2000bhp) Niigata Engineering Co Ltd-Japan AuxGen: 2 x 186kW 380V a.c

8660014 *YDB4008* -	**TIRTAYASA V-208** **PT Pelabuhan Indonesia II (Persero) Cabang Pelabuhan Banten (Indonesia Port Corp II, Banten)** - *Jakarta* *Indonesia* Official number: 7088	**128** 39 -	Class: KI	**2011-09 PT Meranti Nusa Bahari — Balkpapan** Yd No: 1 Loa 23.00 Br ex - Dght - Lbp - Br md 7.00 Dpth - Welded, 1 dk	**(B32A2ST) Tug**	**1 oil engine** driving 1 Propeller
8660026 - -	**TIRTAYASA VI-208** **PT Pelabuhan Indonesia II (Persero) Cabang Pelabuhan Banten (Indonesia Port Corp II, Banten)** - *Jakarta* *Indonesia* Official number: 7089	**128** 39 -	Class: KI	**2011-09 PT Meranti Nusa Bahari — Balkpapan** Yd No: 2 Loa 23.00 Br ex - Dght - Lbp - Br md 7.00 Dpth - Welded, 1 dk	**(B32A2ST) Tug**	**1 oil engine** driving 1 Propeller
9612882 *D5AD8* -	**TIRUA** **Hull 1976 Co Ltd** Compania SudAmericana de Vapores SA (CSAV) SatCom: Inmarsat C 463712398 *Monrovia* *Liberia* MMSI: 636015356 Official number: 15356	**88,586** 42,897 94,374	Class: GL	**2012-07 Samsung Heavy Industries Co Ltd — Geoje** Yd No: 1976 Loa 299.97 (BB) Br ex - Dght 13.500 Lbp 285.00 Br md 45.60 Dpth 24.60 Welded, 1 dk	**(A33A2CC) Container Ship (Fully Cellular)** TEU 8004 C Ho 3574 TEU C Dk 4430 TEU incl 1500 ref C.	**1 oil engine** driving 1 FP propeller Total Power: 43,610kW (59,292hp) 23.0kn MAN-B&W 7K98ME7 1 x 2 Stroke 7 Cy. 980 x 2660 43610kW (59292bhp) Doosan Engine Co Ltd-South Korea AuxGen: 2 x 2880kW a.c, 3 x 3360kW a.c Thrusters: 1 Tunnel thruster (f) Fuel: 290.0 (d.f.) 8600.0 (r.f.)
8808991 - -	**TIRUCHI** **Government of The Republic of India (Central Inland Water Transport Corp Ltd)** - *India*	**200** - 53	Class: (IR)	**1994-06 Central Inland Water Transport Corp. Ltd. — Kolkata** Yd No: 400 Loa 29.55 Br ex 8.41 Dght - Lbp 27.50 Br md 8.00 Dpth 2.60 Welded, 1 dk	**(B32B2SP) Pusher Tug**	**2 oil engines** geared to sc. shafts driving 2 FP propellers Total Power: 698kW (950hp) Cummins KTA-1150-M 2 x 4 Stroke 6 Cy. 159 x 159 each-349kW (475bhp) Kirloskar Cummins Ltd-India
9034705 *3FGC5* -	**TIRUMALA GAS** *ex Arctic Gas -2013 ex Helene Maersk -2006* **Green Spanker Shipping SA** Nissen Kaiun Co Ltd (Nissen Kaiun KK) *Panama* *Panama* MMSI: 352843000 Official number: 45481KJ	**18,360** 5,508 23,256 T/cm 35.0	Class: BV (LR) **IGS** ✠ Classed LR until 26/9/06	**1993-03 Hyundai Heavy Industries Co Ltd — Ulsan** Yd No: 776 Loa 159.98 (BB) Br ex 25.63 Dght 10.920 Lbp 152.20 Br md 25.60 Dpth 16.40 Welded, 1 dk	**(A11B2TG) LPG Tanker** Double Bottom Entire Compartment Length Liq (Gas): 20,268 8 x Gas Tank (s); 8 independent (stl) dcy horizontal 8 Cargo Pump (s): 8x225m³/hr Manifold: Bow/CM: 81.1m	**1 oil engine** driving 1 FP propeller Total Power: 13,395kW (18,212hp) 18.0kn MAN-B&W 7L60MC 1 x 2 Stroke 7 Cy. 600 x 1944 13395kW (18212bhp) (made 1992) Hyundai Heavy Industries Co Ltd-South Korea AuxGen: 3 x 980kW 440/220V 60Hz a.c Boilers: AuxB (o.f.) 8.2kgf/cm² (8.0bar), AuxB (Comp) 8.2kgf/cm² (8.0bar) Fuel: 269.5 (d.f.) 2784.0 (r.f.)
6525739 - -	**TIRZA** - -	*188* 56 -	Class: (LR) ✠ Classed LR until 24/9/97	**1965-09 Atlas Werke AG — Bremen** Yd No: 432 Loa 30.51 Br ex 8.03 Dght 3.163 Lbp 26.01 Br md 7.82 Dpth 4.02 Welded, 1 dk	**(B32A2ST) Tug**	**2 oil engines** with flexible couplings & sr reverse geared to sc. shaft driving 1 FP propeller Total Power: 1,192kW (1,620hp) 11.0kn Deutz RA8M528 2 x 4 Stroke 8 Cy. 220 x 280 each-596kW (810bhp) Kloeckner Humboldt Deutz AG-West Germany AuxGen: 2 x 380kW
8206650 *CNHW* -	**TISIRENE** **Omnium Marocaine de Peche** - SatCom: Inmarsat C 424238310 *Agadir* *Morocco* Official number: 8-643	*324* 143 405	Class: (BV)	**1983-05 Construcciones Navales Santodomingo SA — Vigo** Yd No: 485 Loa 38.31 Br ex 8.59 Dght 4.050 Lbp 34.78 Br md 8.51 Dpth 6.15 Welded, 1 dk	**(B11A2FS) Stern Trawler** Grain: 402	**1 oil engine** with clutches, flexible couplings & sr geared to sc. shaft driving 1 FP propeller Total Power: 853kW (1,160hp) 12.3kn Deutz SBA8M528 1 x 4 Stroke 8 Cy. 220 x 280 853kW (1160bhp) Hijos de J Barreras SA-Spain AuxGen: 2 x 140kW 380V 50Hz a.c
6602692 - -	**TITA** - -	*105* - -	Class: (LR) ✠ Classed LR until 8/3/74	**1965-12 Fabricaciones Metallicas E.P.S. (FABRIMET) — Callao** Yd No: 303 Loa 22.36 Br ex 6.76 Dght - Lbp 19.13 Br md 6.63 Dpth 3.18 Welded	**(B11B2FV) Fishing Vessel**	**1 oil engine** reverse reduction geared to sc. shaft driving 1 FP propeller Total Power: 386kW (525hp) G.M. (Detroit Diesel) 12V-71-N 1 x Vee 2 Stroke 12 Cy. 108 x 127 386kW (525bhp) General Motors Corp-USA
6711936 *HQPA9* -	**TITA** *ex Santa Cristina -2006 ex Bull -1988* *ex Age -1987 ex Hartwig Buss -1986* **Tita Owner Compania** - *San Lorenzo* *Honduras* Official number: L-0326508	*499* 324 1,168	Class: (GL)	**1967 J.J. Sietas Schiffswerft — Hamburg** Yd No: 594 Loa 68.36 Br ex 10.55 Dght 3.960 Lbp 62.11 Br md 10.51 Dpth 6.25 Welded, 2 dks	**(A31A2GX) General Cargo Ship** Grain: 2,452; Bale: 2,248 Compartments: 2 Ho, ER 2 Ha: (12.5 x 6.4) (21.6 x 7.6)ER Derricks: 3x3t Ice Capable	**1 oil engine** driving 1 FP propeller Total Power: 599kW (814hp) 11.5kn Deutz RBV6M545 1 x 4 Stroke 6 Cy. 320 x 450 599kW (814bhp) Kloeckner Humboldt Deutz AG-West Germany
5362295 *SV2381* -	**TITAN** *ex Titanus -2012* **Hellenic Shipyards SA** - *Piraeus* *Greece* MMSI: 237194800 Official number: 1677	*259* - -	Class: (LR) (HR) ✠ Classed LR until 15/11/85	**1962-07 N.V. Nieuwe Noord Nederlandse Scheepswerven — Groningen** Yd No: 324 Loa 31.93 Br ex 8.72 Dght 3.741 Lbp 29.01 Br md 8.21 Dpth 4.50 Welded, 1 dk	**(B32A2ST) Tug**	**1 oil engine** sr reverse geared to sc. shaft driving 1 FP propeller Total Power: 883kW (1,201hp) MAN G9V30/45ATL 1 x 4 Stroke 9 Cy. 300 x 450 883kW (1201bhp) Maschinenbau Augsburg Nuernberg (MAN)-Augsburg
4902921 *IIJY2* -	**TITAN** *ex Beagle -2002* **Titan Srl** Norbulk Enterprise Ship Management Srl *Genoa* *Italy* MMSI: 247244300 Official number: R.I. SEZ. I N.119	**1,140** 342 309	Class: RI (LR) ✠ Classed LR until 17/5/08	**1968-05 Brooke Marine Ltd. — Lowestoft** Yd No: 359 Converted From: Research Vessel-2005 Loa 60.38 Br ex - Dght 4.215 Lbp 51.36 Br md 11.43 Dpth 6.02 Welded, 1 dk	**(A37B2PS) Passenger Ship**	**4 oil engines** with clutches, flexible couplings & sr geared to sc. shafts driving 2 CP propellers Total Power: 1,968kW (2,676hp) 12.0kn Blackstone ERS8M 4 x 4 Stroke 8 Cy. 222 x 292 each-492kW (669bhp) Lister Blackstone Marine Ltd.-Dursley AuxGen: 2 x 325kW 440V 60Hz a.c
1010478 *ZCED2* -	**TITAN** **Nadder Enterprises Ltd** Atlantic-Med Marine Ltd *Hamilton* *Bermuda (British)* MMSI: 310598000 Official number: 740501	**2,116** 634 220	Class: LR ✠ **100A1** SS 10/2010 SSC Yacht (P), mono G6 ✠ **LMC** **UMS** Cable: 385.0/30.0 U2 (a)	**2010-09 Rosslauer Schiffswerft GmbH — Rosslau** (Hull) Yd No: (6483) **2010-09 Schiffs- u. Yachtwerft Abeking & Rasmussen GmbH & Co. — Lemwerder** Yd No: 6483 Loa 78.43 Br ex 12.60 Dght 3.350 Lbp 65.63 Br md 12.40 Dpth 6.45 Welded, 1 dk	**(X11A2YP) Yacht**	**2 oil engines** with clutches, flexible couplings & sr reverse geared to sc. shafts driving 2 FP propellers Total Power: 2,984kW (4,058hp) 14.0kn Caterpillar 3516B-TA 2 x Vee 4 Stroke 16 Cy. 170 x 190 each-1492kW (2029bhp) Caterpillar Inc-USA AuxGen: 3 x 412kW 400V 50Hz a.c Thrusters: 1 Thwart. FP thruster (f); 1 Water jet (a)
5151749 *V4CG* -	**TITAN** *ex Tristan -1994 ex Nim -1992* *ex Hjalnafossur -1965* **Blue Again Ltd Inc** - *Port Zante* *St Kitts & Nevis* MMSI: 341058000 Official number: SKN 1001058	**319** 95 -	Class: LR (NV) **100A1** SS 12/2009 fishing vessel **LMC** Cable: 275.0/19.0 U1	**1961-12 Hatlo Verksted AS — Ulsteinvik** Yd No: 14 Loa 39.60 Br ex 7.26 Dght 3.474 Lbp 35.02 Br md 7.16 Dpth 3.66 Welded, 1 dk	**(B11B2FV) Fishing Vessel** Compartments: 2 Ho, ER 3 Ha: (0.9 x 0.9)2 (1.6 x 1.3)ER Derricks: 1x1.5t; Winches: 1	**1 oil engine** driving 1 CP propeller Total Power: 507kW (689hp) 12.0kn Callesen 6-427-FOT 1 x 4 Stroke 6 Cy. 270 x 400 507kW (689bhp) (new engine 1975) Aabenraa Motorfabrik, HeinrichCallesen A/S-Denmark AuxGen: 3 x 80kW 380V 50Hz a.c
7368619 *ENLW* -	**TITAN** *ex Hans Oskar -1979* **SE Sea Commercial Port of Illichivsk** - SatCom: Inmarsat C 427230710 *Illichevsk* *Ukraine* MMSI: 272307000 Official number: 721959	*450* - 268	Class: (RS) (NV)	**1974-03 Georg Eides Sonner AS — Hoylandsbygd** Yd No: 97 Loa 36.35 Br ex 10.04 Dght 5.460 Lbp 31.91 Br md 10.00 Dpth 7.90 Welded, 1 dk	**(B32A2ST) Tug** Ice Capable	**1 oil engine** driving 1 FP propeller Total Power: 2,501kW (3,400hp) MaK 8M551AK 1 x 4 Stroke 8 Cy. 450 x 550 2501kW (3400bhp) MaK Maschinenbau GmbH-Kiel AuxGen: 2 x 130kW 380V 50Hz a.c, 1 x 64kW 380V 50Hz a.c Thrusters: 1 Thwart. FP thruster (f) Fuel: 190.0 (d.f.)
8126410 *PP9138* -	**TITAN** **Saveiros Camuyrano - Servicos Maritimos SA** - *Santos* *Brazil*	*209* 63 -	Class: (LR) ✠ Classed LR until 23/12/13	**1984-03 Maclaren IC Estaleiros e Servicos S.A. — Niteroi** Yd No: 267 Loa 28.20 Br ex 9.35 Dght - Lbp 26.50 Br md 9.11 Dpth 3.66 Welded, 1 dk	**(B32A2ST) Tug**	**2 oil engines** dr geared to sc. shafts driving 2 Directional propellers Total Power: 1,596kW (2,170hp) Alpha 7T23L-VO 2 x 4 Stroke 7 Cy. 225 x 300 each-798kW (1085bhp) Equipamentos Villares SA-Brazil AuxGen: 2 x 66kW 440V 60Hz a.c Fuel: 57.5 (d.f.)

IMO / Call sign	Name / Owner	Tonnage	Class	Builder / Dimensions	Type	Machinery
7819589 *WYA3059* -	**TITAN** **Suderman & Young Towing Co LP** *Galveston, TX* *United States of America* MMSI: 366921850 Official number: 603677	*172* 117 -	Class: (AB)	**1979-04 Diamond Manufacturing Co. Ltd. — Savannah, Ga** Yd No: M-469 Loa 29.16 Br ex 9.78 Dght 4.890 Lbp 26.12 Br md 9.76 Dpth 5.74 Welded, 1 dk	**(B32A2ST) Tug**	**1 oil engine** reverse reduction geared to sc. shaft driving 1 FP propeller Total Power: 2,115kW (2,876hp) 9.0kn EMD (Electro-Motive) 16-645-E7 1 x Vee 2 Stroke 16 Cy. 230 x 254 2115kW (2876bhp) General Motors Corp.Electro-Motive Div.-La Grange AuxGen: 2 x 100kW
8227537 *WDD7142* -	**TITAN** - **Seabulk Towing Inc** *Houston, TX* *United States of America* MMSI: 366268050 Official number: 587625	*182* 124 -		**1977 Delta Shipyard — Houma, La** Yd No: 113 Loa - Br ex - Dght 3.906 Lbp 29.80 Br md 9.11 Dpth 4.50 Welded, 1 dk	**(B32A2ST) Tug**	**2 oil engines** reduction geared to sc. shafts driving 2 FP propellers Total Power: 2,868kW (3,900hp) EMD (Electro-Motive) 16-645-E2 2 x Vee 2 Stroke 16 Cy. 230 x 254 each-1434kW (1950bhp) in the United States of America AuxGen: 2 x 60kW 60Hz a.c
8424123 *WAW9232*	**TITAN** *ex* Marine Crusader *-1990* *ex* Harris Bay *-1988* *ex* Marine Crusader *-1985* *ex* John R. Hayden *-1983* *ex* LT-830 *-1947* **Sause Bros Ocean Towing Co Inc** - *Portland, OR* *United States of America* MMSI: 367008790 Official number: 253495	*199* 135 -		**1945-08 Tampa Marine Corp — Tampa FL** Yd No: 40 Loa - Br ex - Dght 4.871 Lbp 42.98 Br md 10.06 Dpth 5.74 Welded, 1 dk	**(B32A2ST) Tug**	**1 oil engine** driving 1 FP propeller
9126998 *V2HZ* -	**TITAN** *ex* Cala Pacuare *-2006* *ex* Hispaniola *-2002* *completed as* Titan *-1996* **Reederei Heinz Corleis ms 'Titan' GmbH & Co KG** Reederei Heinz Corleis KG SatCom: Inmarsat C 430449610 *Saint John's* *Antigua & Barbuda* MMSI: 304496000	**12,029** 6,171 14,587 T/cm 28.6	Class: GL	**1996-08 Volkswerft Stralsund GmbH — Stralsund** Yd No: 409 Loa 157.12 (BB) Br ex - Dght 9.300 Lbp 147.00 Br md 23.50 Dpth 12.80 Welded, 1dk	**(A33A2CC) Container Ship (Fully Cellular)** TEU 1122 C Ho 454 TEU C Dk 668 TEU incl 150 ref C. Compartments: 4 Cell Ho, ER 7 Ha: (12.5 x 15.4)Tappered 6 (12.5 x 20.4)ER Cranes: 2x45t	**1 oil engine** driving 1 CP propeller Total Power: 10,920kW (14,847hp) 19.6kn Sulzer 7RTA52U 1 x 2 Stroke 7 Cy. 520 x 1800 10920kW (14847bhp) Dieselmotorenwerk Vulkan GmbH-Rostock AuxGen: 1 x 1000kW 450V 60Hz a.c, 2 x 950kW 450V 60Hz a.c Thrusters: 1 Thwart. CP thruster (f) Fuel: 174.0 (d.f.) 1582.0 (r.f.) 50.0pd
8727628 *CL3010* -	**TITAN** *ex* 0230 *-1996* **Empresa de Navegacion Caribe** *Havana* *Cuba*	**182** 54 57	Class: (RS)	**1988-07 Gorokhovetskiy Sudostroitelnyy Zavod — Gorokhovets** Yd No: 230 Loa 29.30 Br ex 8.60 Dght 3.400 Lbp 27.00 Br md - Dpth 4.30 Welded, 1 dk	**(B32A2ST) Tug** Ice Capable	**2 oil engines** driving 2 CP propellers Total Power: 1,180kW (1,604hp) 11.5kn Pervomaysk 8CHNSP25/34 2 x 4 Stroke 8 Cy. 250 x 340 each-590kW (802bhp) Pervomaydizelmash (PDM)-Pervomaysk
8949549 - -	**TITAN** *ex* Viking 1 *-2011* *ex* Harward I *-2008* *ex* Harward *-2006* *ex* Slavutich *-2006* *ex* Vega *-2004* *ex* Kopachevo *-1994* **Greenway Maritime Ltd** Grace Ship Management Co Ltd	**185** 59 141	Class: (RS)	**1973-05 Sudoremontnyy Zavod "Krasnaya Kuznitsa" — Arkhangelsk** Yd No: 12 Loa 35.75 Br ex - Dght 1.710 Lbp 33.50 Br md 7.50 Dpth 2.40 Welded, 1 dk	**(A31A2GX) General Cargo Ship** Grain: 261 Compartments: 3 Ho 3 Ha: 3 (2.0 x 2.0)	**1 oil engine** geared to sc. shaft driving 1 FP propeller Total Power: 165kW (224hp) 8.5kn Daldizel 6CHNSP18/22 1 x 4 Stroke 6 Cy. 180 x 220 165kW (224bhp) Daldizel-Khabarovsk AuxGen: 1 x 37kW, 1 x 20kW Fuel: 19.0 (d.f.)
8855308 *WTJ8548* -	**TITAN** *ex* Luke & Sarah *-2010* **Titan Fisheries Inc** *New Bedford, MA* *United States of America* MMSI: 366164060 Official number: 906149	**246** 103 -		**1986 La Force Shipyard Inc — Coden AL** Yd No: 30 Loa - Br ex - Dght - Lbp 26.12 Br md 7.32 Dpth 4.15 Welded, 1 dk	**(B11B2FV) Fishing Vessel**	**1 oil engine** driving 1 FP propeller
8848068 *WDF7565* -	**TITAN** *ex* Decisive *-2013* *ex* Alice Amanda *-2007* **HD Fisheries LLC** *Warrenton, OR* *United States of America* MMSI: 367485780 Official number: 943737	*171* 137 -		**1989 Deep Sea Boat Builders, Inc. — Bayou La Batre, Al** Yd No: 144 Loa - Br ex - Dght - Lbp 25.66 Br md 7.86 Dpth 3.93 Welded, 1 dk	**(B11B2FV) Fishing Vessel**	**1 oil engine** driving 1 FP propeller
8882947 *WDD9601* -	**TITAN** *ex* Grimrock Titan *-2000* *ex* Pacific Titan *-1998* **Global International Marine Inc** - *Houma, LA* *United States of America* MMSI: 367313650 Official number: 580952	**232** 69 -		**1977 Pacific Tow Boat & Salvage Co. — Long Beach, Ca** Yd No: 27 Loa - Br ex - Dght - Lbp - Br md - Dpth - Welded, 1 dk	**(B32A2ST) Tug**	**2 oil engines** geared to sc. shafts driving 2 FP propellers Total Power: 1,626kW (2,210hp) Caterpillar D399 2 x Vee 4 Stroke 16 Cy. 159 x 203 each-813kW (1105bhp) Caterpillar Tractor Co-USA
9625750 *UBXI9* -	**TITAN** **LLC Transneft-Service** *Vostochnyy* *Russia* MMSI: 273354870	**865** 259 941	Class: RS	**2012-05 DP Craneship — Kerch** Yd No: 801 Loa 52.35 Br ex 11.10 Dght 4.000 Lbp 48.36 Br md 10.50 Dpth 5.50 Welded, 1 dk	**(B34E2SW) Waste Disposal Vessel** Liq: 833 Compartments: 4 Wing Ta, 4 Wing Ta, ER	**1 oil engine** driving 1 Directional propeller Total Power: 1,081kW (1,470hp) 8.0kn Caterpillar C32 ACERT 1 x Vee 4 Stroke 12 Cy. 145 x 162 1081kW (1470bhp) Caterpillar Inc-USA Fuel: 59.0 (d.f.)
9558907 *3FPN2* -	**TITAN** *ex* Prisco Udokan *-2012* **Titan Maritime Enterprises SA** First Lines Co SA *Panama* *Panama* MMSI: 373781000 Official number: 4441312	**33,218** 18,886 57,337 T/cm 57.3	Class: NK	**2009-09 STX Offshore & Shipbuilding Co Ltd — Changwon (Jinhae Shipyard)** Yd No: 1405 Loa 190.00 (BB) Br ex - Dght 13.020 Lbp 183.30 Br md 32.26 Dpth 18.50 Welded, 1 dk	**(A21A2BC) Bulk Carrier** Grain: 71,903; Bale: 70,111 Compartments: 5 Ho, ER 5 Ha: ER Cranes: 4x30t	**1 oil engine** driving 1 FP propeller Total Power: 9,480kW (12,889hp) 14.5kn MAN-B&W 6S50MC-C 1 x 2 Stroke 6 Cy. 500 x 2000 9480kW (12889bhp) STX Engine Co Ltd-South Korea Fuel: 2000.0
9517070 *UBDG4* -	**TITAN** **Titan Cargo Ltd** Prime Shipping LLC SatCom: Inmarsat C 427303083 *Taganrog* *Russia* MMSI: 273344330	**4,378** 1,313 5,526 T/cm 22.0	Class: RS	**2009-10 Sudostroitelnyy Zavod "Krasnoye Sormovo" — Nizhniy Novgorod** Yd No: 19614/14 Loa 141.00 Br ex 16.90 Dght 3.740 Lbp 134.88 Br md 16.80 Dpth 6.10 Welded, 1 dk	**(A13B2TP) Products Tanker** Double Hull (13F) Liq: 6,587; Liq (Oil): 6,721 Cargo Heating Coils Compartments: 12 Wing Ta, 1 Slop Ta, ER 2 Cargo Pump (s): 2x250m³/hr Manifold: Bow/CM: 70m Ice Capable	**2 oil engines** reduction geared to sc. shafts driving 2 FP propellers Total Power: 1,860kW (2,528hp) 10.0kn Wartsila 6L20 2 x 4 Stroke 6 Cy. 200 x 280 each-930kW (1264bhp) Wartsila Finland Oy-Finland AuxGen: 3 x 160kW a.c Thrusters: 1 Tunnel thruster (f) Fuel: 174.0 (d.f.)
9326627 *XCFI4* -	**TITAN** *ex* H 278 *-2005* **GulfMark de Mexico S de RL de CV** GulfMark Offshore Inc *Dos Bocas* *Mexico* MMSI: 345050013 Official number: 2701332635-8	**1,674** 502 1,645	Class: AB	**2005-03 Keppel Singmarine Pte Ltd — Singapore** Yd No: 278 Loa 60.70 Br ex 16.00 Dght 4.850 Lbp 54.00 Br md 15.75 Dpth 6.00 Welded, 1 dk	**(B21B20A) Anchor Handling Tug Supply**	**2 oil engines** geared to sc. shafts driving 2 CP propellers Total Power: 4,412kW (5,998hp) 11.0kn Yanmar 8N280-SN 2 x 4 Stroke 8 Cy. 280 x 380 each-2206kW (2999bhp) Yanmar Diesel Engine Co Ltd-Japan AuxGen: 2 x 370kW 440V 60Hz a.c Thrusters: 1 Thwart. CP thruster (f) Fuel: 585.4 (r.f.)
9254094 *C9F4584* -	**TITAN** **Companhia de Sena Sarl** *Beira* *Mozambique* Official number: B-1520-R	**144** 44 121	Class: (NK)	**2001-06 Forward Shipbuilding Enterprise Sdn Bhd — Sibu** Yd No: 80 Loa 23.50 Br ex - Dght 2.712 Lbp 21.79 Br md 7.32 Dpth 3.20 Welded, 1 dk	**(B32A2ST) Tug**	**2 oil engines** driving 2 FP propellers Total Power: 1,074kW (1,460hp) Caterpillar 3412E 2 x Vee 4 Stroke 12 Cy. 137 x 152 each-537kW (730bhp) Caterpillar Inc-USA Fuel: 100.0 (d.f.)
9602954 *YD3782* -	**TITAN 01** **PT Nusantara Teminal Terpadu Graha BIP** - *Batam* *Indonesia* Official number: GT 254 NO.2682/PPM	**254** 77 -	Class: KI	**2010-09 PT Bandar Abadi — Batam** Yd No: 061 Loa 28.05 Br ex - Dght 3.350 Lbp 25.13 Br md 8.60 Dpth 4.30 Welded, 1 dk	**(B32A2ST) Tug**	**2 oil engines** driving 1 Propeller Total Power: 824kW (1,120hp) Mitsubishi 2 x 4 Stroke each-412kW (560bhp) Mitsubishi Heavy Industries Ltd-Japan

8129656 *ENKU* -	**TITAN-2** **National JSC 'Chernomorneftegaz'** Oceanografia SA de CV SatCom: Inmarsat A 1405565 *Chernomorskiy* *Ukraine* MMSI: 272013000	**19,813** 5,944 3,343	Class: RS (AB) (NV)	**1985-01 Oy Wartsila Ab — Turku** Yd No: 1278 Loa 141.40 Br ex 54.00 Dght 4.001 Lbp 121.00 Br md - Dpth 13.00 Welded, 1 dk	**(B34B2SC) Crane Vessel** Cranes: 1x600t Ice Capable	**3 diesel electric oil engines** driving 3 gen. each 1880kW 660V a.c Connecting to 2 elec. motors driving 2 Directional propellers Total Power: 5,553kW (7,551hp) 11.0kn Wartsila 6R32 3 x 4 Stroke 6 Cy. 320 x 350 each-1851kW (2517bhp) Oy Wartsila Ab-Finland AuxGen: 3 x 180kW 380V 50Hz a.c Thrusters: 2 Thwart. CP thruster (f) Fuel: 772.0 (r.f.)
9625578 - -	**TITAN 03** **PT Nusantara Teminal Terpadu Graha BIP** - *Batam* *Indonesia* Official number: 3080/PPM	**255** 77 -	Class: KI	**2011-07 PT Bandar Abadi — Batam** Yd No: 067 Loa 28.05 Br ex - Dght 3.350 Lbp 25.13 Br md 8.60 Dpth 4.30 Welded, 1 dk	**(B32A2ST) Tug**	**2 oil engines** reduction geared to sc. shafts driving 2 Propellers Total Power: 1,500kW (2,040hp) Mitsubishi S6R2-MTK3L 2 x 4 Stroke 6 Cy. 170 x 220 each-750kW (1020bhp) Mitsubishi Heavy Industries Ltd-Japan AuxGen: 2 x 56kW 380V a.c
9613484 - -	**TITAN 05** **PT Nusantara Teminal Terpadu Graha BIP** - *Batam* *Indonesia* Official number: 2853/PPM	**254** 77 -	Class: KI	**2011-02 PT Bandar Abadi — Batam** Yd No: 068 Loa 28.05 Br ex - Dght 3.350 Lbp 26.20 Br md 8.60 Dpth 4.30 Welded, 1 dk	**(B32A2ST) Tug**	**2 oil engines** reduction geared to sc. shafts driving 2 Propellers Total Power: 1,518kW (2,064hp) Mitsubishi S6R2-MTK3L 2 x 4 Stroke 6 Cy. 170 x 220 each-759kW (1032bhp) Mitsubishi Heavy Industries Ltd-Japan AuxGen: 2 x 56kW 380V a.c
7419432 - -	**TITAN 7** *ex* Bounty 7 *-2007* *ex* Fong Yin *-2006* *ex* Hung Yun *-1999* *ex* Hannah Lu *-1986* *ex* Regent Leo *-1979* - -	**6,263** 3,767 10,029	Class: (NK) (CR)	**1975-12 Kochiken Zosen — Kochi** Yd No: 588 Loa 127.97 Br ex 18.34 Dght 7.765 Lbp 119.00 Br md 18.31 Dpth 9.91 Welded, 1 dk	**(A31A2GX) General Cargo Ship** Grain: 13,036; Bale: 12,450 Compartments: 4 Ho, ER 4 Ha: (16.0 x 8.9) (16.4 x 8.9)2 (15.7 x 8.9)ER Derricks: 2x20t,2x15t	**1 oil engine** driving 1 FP propeller Total Power: 4,560kW (6,200hp) 13.5kn Mitsubishi 6UEC52/105E 1 x 2 Stroke 6 Cy. 520 x 1050 4560kW (6200bhp) Akasaka Tekkosho KK (Akasaka DieselLtd)-Japan AuxGen: 2 x 240kW 445V 60Hz a.c Fuel: 829.0 (r.f.)
8664474 - -	**TITAN 42** *ex* Yuejianghang 02 *-2013* **PT Nusantara Teminal Terpadu Graha BIP** - *Jakarta* *Indonesia*	**1,401** 785 -		**2007-10 Guangdong Qingyuan Baimiao Shipyard — Qingyuan GD** Loa 67.80 Br ex 14.85 Dght - Lbp - Br md 14.60 Dpth 3.98 Welded, 1 dk	**(B34W2QJ) Trans Shipment Vessel**	**2 oil engines** reduction geared to sc. shafts driving 2 Propellers Total Power: 894kW (1,216hp) Cummins KTA-19-M 2 x 4 Stroke 6 Cy. 159 x 159 each-447kW (608bhp) Chongqing Cummins Engine Co Ltd-China
9629342 *JZHC* -	**TITAN 70** **PT Nusantara Teminal Terpadu Graha BIP** - *Jakarta* *Indonesia* MMSI: 525018102	**5,770** 1,731 10,000	Class: BV	**2013-06 Nanjing Hathaway Runqi Marine Engineering Co Ltd — Nanjing JS** Yd No: HR2008020 Loa 106.02 Br ex - Dght 5.900 Lbp 101.60 Br md 25.00 Dpth 8.00 Welded, 1 dk	**(A31C2GD) Deck Cargo Ship**	**2 oil engines** reduction geared to sc. shaft (s) driving 2 FP propellers Total Power: 2,940kW (3,998hp) 10.0kn Chinese Std. Type LB8250ZLC 2 x 4 Stroke 8 Cy. 250 x 320 each-1470kW (1999bhp) Zibo Diesel Engine Factory-China AuxGen: 2 x 200kW 50Hz a.c
5362192 - -	**TITAN A** *ex* Titan *-1983* **Levine Shipping Ltd** -	*245* 13 -	Class: (BV)	**1956 C.V. Schpsw. en Ghbw. Jonker & Stans — Hendrik-Ido-Ambacht** Yd No: 276 Loa 31.98 Br ex 8.23 Dght 3.563 Lbp 29.60 Br md 8.21 Dpth 4.20 Riveted\Welded, 1 dk	**(B32A2ST) Tug** Derricks: 1x2t; Winches: 1	**2 oil engines** geared to sc. shaft driving 1 FP propeller Total Power: 882kW (1,200hp) 11.8kn Bolnes 8DL75/475 2 x 2 Stroke 8 Cy. 190 x 350 each-441kW (600bhp) NV Machinefabriek 'Bolnes' v/h JHvan Cappellen-Netherlands Fuel: 81.5 (d.f.)
9438200 *9VCA6* -	**TITAN BRAVE** **Alco Shipping Services LLC** - SatCom: Inmarsat C 456588110 *Singapore* *Singapore* MMSI: 565881000 Official number: 393239	**5,034** 1,958 7,008 T/cm 15.6	Class: LR ✠ **100A1** SS 06/2008 Double Hull oil tanker carriage of oils with an FP exceeding 60 degree C not exceeding 30 nautical miles Singapore coastal service ESP LI *IWS ✠ **LMC** Eq.Ltr: X; Cable: 495.0/50.0 U2 (a)	**2008-06 Titan Quanzhou Shipyard Co Ltd — Hui'an County FJ** Yd No: H0004 Loa 99.36 (BB) Br ex 18.07 Dght 7.000 Lbp 94.00 Br md 18.00 Dpth 10.00 Welded, 1 dk	**(A13B2TP) Products Tanker** Double Hull (13F) Liq: 7,272; Liq (Oil): 7,272 Compartments: 10 Wing Ta, 2 Wing Slop Ta, ER 2 Cargo Pump (s): 2x1000m³/hr Manifold: Bow/CM: 52.2m	**2 oil engines** with clutches, flexible couplings & dr reverse geared to sc. shafts driving 2 FP propellers Total Power: 2,940kW (3,998hp) 11.0kn MAN-B&W 6L28/32A 2 x 4 Stroke 6 Cy. 280 x 320 each-1470kW (1999bhp) Zhenjiang Marine Diesel Works-China AuxGen: 2 x 360kW 400V 50Hz a.c Boilers: AuxB (o.f.) 7.9kgf/cm² (7.7bar) Thrusters: 1 Thwart. FP thruster (f) Fuel: 97.3 (d.f.) 300.8 (r.f.)
9012513 *3ESA9* -	**TITAN EXPRESS** - **Florida Star Corp** Americas Marine Management Services Inc *Panama* *Panama* MMSI: 355983000 Official number: 2119494D	**2,602** 1,217 3,359	Class: (LR) (BV) ✠ Classed LR until 11/8/00	**1992-12 Sing Koon Seng Shipbuilding & Engineering Ltd — Singapore** Yd No: 695 Loa 84.40 (BB) Br ex 15.07 Dght 5.307 Lbp 77.90 Br md 15.00 Dpth 6.55 Welded, 1 dk	**(A31A2GX) General Cargo Ship** Bale: 4,233 TEU 161 C.Ho 68/20' incl 25 ref C. C.Dk 93/20' Compartments: 1 Ho, ER 2 Ha: ER Ice Capable	**1 oil engine** driving 1 FP propeller Total Power: 2,691kW (3,659hp) 13.0kn B&W 6L35MCE 1 x 2 Stroke 6 Cy. 350 x 1050 2691kW (3659bhp) Ssangyong Heavy Industries Co Ltd-South Korea AuxGen: 1 x 500kW 440V 60Hz a.c, 2 x 290kW 440V 60Hz a.c Thrusters: 1 Thwart. CP thruster (f); 1 Tunnel thruster (a) Fuel: 64.9 (d.f.) 362.4 (r.f.) 10.5pd
9438195 *9VCA5* -	**TITAN FAITH** *ex* Taishan Zhencheng *-2009* *completed as* Titan Faith *-2008* **Sun Jazz Marine Pte Ltd** Oceanic Shipping Pte Ltd SatCom: Inmarsat C 456588010 *Singapore* *Singapore* MMSI: 565880000 Official number: 393238	**5,034** 1,958 6,981 T/cm 15.6	Class: CC (LR) ✠ Classed LR until 30/7/08	**2008-06 Titan Quanzhou Shipyard Co Ltd — Hui'an County FJ** Yd No: H0003 Loa 99.36 (BB) Br ex 18.07 Dght 7.200 Lbp 94.00 Br md 18.00 Dpth 10.00 Welded, 1 dk	**(A13B2TP) Products Tanker** Double Hull (13F) Liq: 7,196; Liq (Oil): 7,196 Compartments: 10 Wing Ta, 2 Wing Slop Ta, ER	**2 oil engines** with clutches, flexible couplings & dr reverse geared to sc. shafts driving 2 FP propellers Total Power: 2,940kW (3,998hp) 11.5kn MAN-B&W 6L28/32A 2 x 4 Stroke 6 Cy. 280 x 320 each-1470kW (1999bhp) Zhenjiang Marine Diesel Works-China AuxGen: 2 x 360kW 400V 50Hz a.c Boilers: AuxB (o.f.) 7.9kgf/cm² (7.7bar) Thrusters: 1 Thwart. FP thruster (f)
9438262 *9VDP4* -	**TITAN GLORY** **Singapore Tankers Pte Ltd** Oceanic Shipping Pte Ltd *Singapore* *Singapore* MMSI: 563275000 Official number: 393245	**6,190** 2,900 9,027 T/cm 18.9	Class: LR ✠ **100A1** SS 04/2010 Double Hull oil and chemical tanker, Ship Type 2 ESP *IWS LI ✠ **LMC** Eq.Ltr: Z; Cable: 519.5/48.0 U3 (a)	**2010-04 Titan Quanzhou Shipyard Co Ltd — Hui'an County FJ** Yd No: H0010 Loa 117.60 (BB) Br ex 19.02 Dght 7.500 Lbp 109.90 Br md 19.00 Dpth 9.99 Welded, 1 dk	**(A12B2TR) Chemical/Products Tanker** Double Hull (13F) Compartments: 10 Wing Ta, 2 Wing Slop Ta, ER 10 Cargo Pump (s): 10x300m³/hr Manifold: Bow/CM: 56.5m	**1 oil engine** sr geared to sc. shaft driving 1 FP propeller Total Power: 3,310kW (4,500hp) 13.0kn MAN-B&W 7L32/40 1 x 4 Stroke 7 Cy. 320 x 400 3310kW (4500bhp) Shanghai Diesel Engine Co Ltd-China AuxGen: 3 x 465kW 450V 60Hz a.c Boilers: e (ex.g.) 8.0kgf/cm² (7.8bar), AuxB (o.f.) 8.0kgf/cm² (7.8bar) Thrusters: 1 Thwart. FP thruster (f) Fuel: 175.0 (d.f.) 252.0 (r.f.)
9205079 *H8XE* -	**TITAN GLORY** *ex* Millennium Maersk *-2004* **DS-Rendite-Fonds Nr 106 mt 'Titan Glory' GmbH & Co Tankshiff KG** Gulf Marine Management (Deutschland) GmbH & Co KG SatCom: Inmarsat C 435658510 *Panama* *Panama* MMSI: 356585000 Official number: 33485PEXTF4	**159,187** 104,027 308,491 T/cm 169.0	Class: NV (LR) ✠ Classed LR until 27/7/04	**2000-09 Hyundai Heavy Industries Co Ltd — Ulsan** Yd No: 1238 Loa 332.95 Br ex 58.05 Dght 22.700 Lbp 316.85 Br md 58.00 Dpth 31.00 Welded, 1 dk	**(A13A2TV) Crude Oil Tanker** Double Hull (13F) Liq: 334,897; Liq (Oil): 334,897 Compartments: 5 Ta, 10 Wing Ta, ER, 2 Wing Slop Ta 3 Cargo Pump (s): 3x5500m³/hr	**1 oil engine** driving 1 FP propeller Total Power: 27,165kW (36,934hp) 16.4kn Sulzer 7RTA84T 1 x 2 Stroke 7 Cy. 840 x 3150 27165kW (36934bhp) Hyundai Heavy Industries Co Ltd-South Korea AuxGen: 3 x 980kW 450V 60Hz a.c Boilers: 2 AuxB (o.f.) 20.4kgf/cm² (20.0bar), e (ex.g.) 24.5kgf/cm² (24.0bar)
9245108 *J8B2788* -	**TITAN I** *ex* Bintang Bahagia *-2003* **Archirodon Construction Overseas Co SA** Saudi Archirodon Ltd *Kingstown* *St Vincent & The Grenadines* MMSI: 377524000 Official number: 9260	**138** 42 90	Class: NK	**2001-01 Lingco Marine Sdn Bhd — Sibu** Yd No: 1800 Loa 22.40 Br ex - Dght 2.412 Lbp - Br md 7.32 Dpth 3.00 Welded, 1 dk	**(B32B2SP) Pusher Tug**	**2 oil engines** reduction geared to sc. shafts driving 2 FP propellers Total Power: 746kW (1,014hp) 10.0kn Cummins KTA-19-M 2 x 4 Stroke 6 Cy. 159 x 159 each-373kW (507bhp) Cummins Engine Co Inc-USA Fuel: 60.0 (d.f.)
7046687 *DUA2670* -	**TITAN I** *ex* Kakuho Maru *-1996* **Malayan Towage & Salvage Corp (SALVTUG)** - *Manila* *Philippines* Official number: 00-0001238	*238* 145 -		**1969-12 Towa Zosen K.K. — Shimonoseki** Yd No: 385 Loa 30.26 Br ex 9.02 Dght 3.607 Lbp 29.11 Br md 9.00 Dpth 3.81 Welded, 1 dk	**(B32A2ST) Tug**	**2 oil engines** gearing integral to driving 2 Z propellers Total Power: 2,574kW (3,500hp) Fuji 6SD37BH 2 x 4 Stroke 6 Cy. 370 x 550 each-1287kW (1750bhp) Fuji Diesel Co Ltd-Japan

IMO / Call sign	Name / Owner	Tonnage	Class	Builder / Dimensions	Type	Machinery
9246853 *J8B2789* -	**TITAN II** *ex* Bintang Sejahtera *-2003* **Archirodon Construction Overseas Co SA** Saudi Archirodon Ltd *Kingstown* *St Vincent & The Grenadines* MMSI: 377525000 Official number: 9261	**138** 42 90	Class: NK	**2001-02 Lingco Marine Sdn Bhd — Sibu** Yd No: 2100 Loa 22.40 Br ex - Dght 2.412 Lbp 20.52 Br md 7.32 Dpth 3.00 Welded, 1 dk	**(B32B2SP) Pusher Tug**	**2 oil engines** reduction geared to sc. shafts driving 2 FP propellers Total Power: 746kW (1,014hp) 10.0kn Cummins KTA-19-M 2 x 4 Stroke 6 Cy. 159 x 159 each-373kW (507bhp) Cummins Engine Co Inc-USA Fuel: 60.0 (d.f.)
9438327 *3ENX7* -	**TITAN LOYALTY** **Sameer Ships Pte Ltd** Flair Shipping Trading FZE *Panama* *Panama* MMSI: 352477000 Official number: 44778PEXTF1	**4,996** 1,959 6,989 T/cm 15.6	Class: LR ✠ **100A1** SS 03/2012 Double Hull oil tanker carriage of oils with a FP exceeding 60 degree C ESP *IWS LI ✠ **LMC** Eq.Ltr: X; Cable: 495.0/50.0 U2 (a)	**2012-03 Titan Quanzhou Shipyard Co Ltd — Hui'an County FJ** Yd No: H0016 Loa 99.36 (BB) Br ex 18.07 Dght 7.000 Lbp 94.00 Br md 18.00 Dpth 10.00 Welded, 1 dk	**(A13B2TP) Products Tanker** Double Hull (13F) Liq: 7,600; Liq (Oil): 7,600 Compartments: 5 Wing Ta, 5 Wing Ta, 1 Wing Slop Ta, 1 Wing Slop Ta, ER 2 Cargo Pump (s): 2x1000m³/hr	**2 oil engines** with clutches, flexible couplings & sr reverse geared to sc. shafts driving 2 FP propellers Total Power: 2,940kW (3,998hp) 11.5kn MAN-B&W 6L28/32A 2 x 4 Stroke 6 Cy. 280 x 320 each-1470kW (1999bhp) Zhenjiang Marine Diesel Works-China AuxGen: 2 x 288kW 400V 50Hz a.c Boilers: WTAuxB (o.f.) 7.7kgf/cm² (7.6bar) Thrusters: 1 Tunnel thruster (f)
9438250 *9VCA8* -	**TITAN PEACE** **Singapore Tankers Pte Ltd** Oceanic Shipping Pte Ltd *Singapore* *Singapore* MMSI: 564548000 Official number: 393241	**6,190** 2,898 9,057 T/cm 18.9	Class: LR ✠ **100A1** SS 03/2010 Double Hull oil and chemical tanker, Ship Type 2 ESP *IWS LI ✠ **LMC** Eq.Ltr: Z; Cable: 519.5/48.0 U3 (a)	**2010-03 Titan Quanzhou Shipyard Co Ltd — Hui'an County FJ** Yd No: H0009 Loa 117.50 (BB) Br ex 19.02 Dght 7.513 Lbp 109.90 Br md 19.00 Dpth 9.99 Welded, 1 dk	**(A12B2TR) Chemical/Products Tanker** Double Hull (13F) Compartments: 10 Wing Ta, 2 Wing Slop Ta, ER Manifold: Bow/CM: 56.5m	**1 oil engine** sr geared to sc. shaft driving 1 FP propeller Total Power: 3,310kW (4,500hp) 13.0kn MAN-B&W 7L32/40 1 x 4 Stroke 7 Cy. 320 x 400 3310kW (4500bhp) Shanghai Diesel Engine Co Ltd-China AuxGen: 3 x 465kW 450V 60Hz a.c Boilers: e (ex.g.) 8.0kgf/cm² (7.8bar), AuxB (o.f.) 8.0kgf/cm² (7.8bar) Thrusters: 1 Thwart. FP thruster (f) Fuel: 60.0 (d.f.) 370.0 (r.f.)
7427673 *WDB3674* -	**TITAN TIDE** *ex* Ensco Titan *-2003* *ex* Golden Shell *-1988* *ex* Big Pro *-1988* *ex* A. W. Martin *-1980* **DeWayle International Ltd** *New Orleans, LA* *United States of America* MMSI: 366188000 Official number: 569686	**1,200** 360 1,305	Class: (AB)	**1975-10 Halter Marine, Inc. — Moss Point, Ms** Yd No: 497 Lengthened-1987 Loa - Br ex - Dght 4.992 Lbp 64.39 Br md 13.11 Dpth 5.80 Welded, 1 dk	**(B21A20S) Platform Supply Ship** Ice Capable	**2 oil engines** reverse reduction geared to sc. shafts driving 2 FP propellers Total Power: 5,884kW (8,000hp) 12.0kn Werkspoor 6TM410 2 x 4 Stroke 6 Cy. 410 x 470 each-2942kW (4000bhp) Stork Werkspoor Diesel BV-Netherlands AuxGen: 2 x 300kW 60Hz a.c Thrusters: 1 Thwart. FP thruster (f) Fuel: 485.5 (d.f.)
9438274 *9VCA9* -	**TITAN UNITY** **Singapore Tankers Pte Ltd** Oceanic Shipping Pte Ltd *Singapore* *Singapore* MMSI: 564915000 Official number: 393242	**5,034** 1,958 7,022 T/cm 15.6	Class: LR ✠ **100A1** SS 01/2009 Double Hull oil tanker not exceeding 30 nautical miles Singapore coastal service carriage of oils with a FP exceeding 60 degree C ESP LI *IWS ✠ **LMC** Eq.Ltr: X; Cable: 495.0/50.0 U2 (a)	**2009-01 Titan Quanzhou Shipyard Co Ltd — Hui'an County FJ** Yd No: H0011 Loa 99.36 (BB) Br ex 18.08 Dght 7.000 Lbp 94.00 Br md 18.00 Dpth 10.00 Welded, 1 dk	**(A13B2TP) Products Tanker** Double Hull (13F) Compartments: 10 Wing Ta, 2 Wing Slop Ta, ER	**2 oil engines** with clutches, flexible couplings & dr reverse geared to sc. shafts driving 2 FP propellers Total Power: 2,940kW (3,998hp) 11.0kn MAN-B&W 6L28/32A 2 x 4 Stroke 6 Cy. 280 x 320 each-1470kW (1999bhp) Zhenjiang Marine Diesel Works-China AuxGen: 2 x 360kW 400V 50Hz a.c Boilers: AuxB (o.f.) 7.7kgf/cm² (7.6bar) Thrusters: 1 Thwart. CP thruster (f)
9438286 *9VDP2* -	**TITAN VALOR** **Alco Shipping Services LLC** - *Singapore* *Singapore* MMSI: 564913000 Official number: 393243	**5,034** 1,958 7,005 T/cm 15.6	✠ **100A1** SS 01/2009 Double Hull oil tanker, carriage of oils with a FP exceeding 60 degree C ESP LI *IWS Singapore up to 30 nautical miles coastal service ✠ **LMC** Eq.Ltr: X; Cable: 495.0/50.0 U2 (a)	**2009-01 Titan Quanzhou Shipyard Co Ltd — Hui'an County FJ** Yd No: H0012 Loa 99.36 (BB) Br ex 18.08 Dght 7.000 Lbp 94.00 Br md 18.00 Dpth 10.00 Welded, 1 dk	**(A13B2TP) Products Tanker** Double Hull (13F) Compartments: 10 Wing Ta, 2 Wing Slop Ta, ER	**2 oil engines** with clutches, flexible couplings & dr reverse geared to sc. shafts driving 2 FP propellers Total Power: 2,940kW (3,998hp) 11.0kn MAN-B&W 6L28/32A 2 x 4 Stroke 6 Cy. 280 x 320 each-1470kW (1999bhp) Zhenjiang Marine Diesel Works-China AuxGen: 2 x 360kW 400V 50Hz a.c Boilers: AuxB (o.f.) 7.7kgf/cm² (7.6bar) Thrusters: 1 Thwart. CP thruster (centre)
9438248 *9VCA7* -	**TITAN VISION** **Singapore Tankers Pte Ltd** Oceanic Shipping Pte Ltd *Singapore* *Singapore* MMSI: 565654000 Official number: 393240	**6,190** 2,901 9,016 T/cm 18.9	Class: LR ✠ **100A1** SS 02/2010 Double Hull oil and chemical tanker, Ship Type 2 ESP LI *IWS ✠ **LMC** Eq.Ltr: Z†; Cable: 522.5/48.0 U3 (a)	**2010-02 Titan Quanzhou Shipyard Co Ltd — Hui'an County FJ** Yd No: H0008 Loa 117.60 (BB) Br ex 19.03 Dght 7.513 Lbp 109.60 Br md 19.00 Dpth 9.99 Welded, 1 dk	**(A12B2TR) Chemical/Products Tanker** Double Hull (13F) Liq: 9,439; Liq (Oil): 9,439 Compartments: 12 Wing Ta, ER Manifold: Bow/CM: 56.5m	**1 oil engine** with clutches, flexible couplings & sr reverse geared to sc. shaft driving 1 FP propeller Total Power: 3,310kW (4,500hp) 13.0kn MAN-B&W 7L32/40 1 x 4 Stroke 7 Cy. 320 x 400 3310kW (4500bhp) Shaanxi Diesel Heavy Industry Co Lt-China AuxGen: 3 x 465kW 450V 60Hz a.c Boilers: e (ex.g.) 7.3kgf/cm² (7.2bar), WTAuxB (o.f.) 7.5kgf/cm² (7.4bar) Thrusters: 1 Thwart. FP thruster (f) Fuel: 175.0 (d.f.) 252.0 (r.f.)
9505053 *9HA2272* -	**TITANIA** **Wilhelmsen Lines Shipowning Malta Ltd** Wilhelmsen Ship Management Sdn Bhd *Valletta* *Malta* MMSI: 248225000 Official number: 9505053	**74,255** 26,747 30,907	Class: LR ✠ **100A1** SS 12/2011 vehicle carrier movable decks, deck Nos. 1, 3 5 & 8 strengthened for the carriage of roll on/roll off cargoes *IWS LI ✠ **LMC** **UMS** Eq.Ltr: S†; Cable: 687.5/87.0 U3 (a)	**2011-12 Daewoo Shipbuilding & Marine Engineering Co Ltd — Geoje** Yd No: 4460 Loa 231.60 (BB) Br ex - Dght 11.300 Lbp 219.30 Br md 32.26 Dpth 34.70 Welded, 12 dks incl 4 hoistable decks	**(A35B2RV) Vehicles Carrier** Side door/ramp (s) Len: 25.00 Wid: 6.50 Swl: 22 Quarter stern door/ramp (s. a.) Len: 39.00 Wid: 7.00 Swl: 150 Cars: 7,800	**1 oil engine** driving 1 FP propeller Total Power: 19,040kW (25,887hp) 20.1kn MAN-B&W 8S60ME-C 1 x 2 Stroke 8 Cy. 600 x 2400 19040kW (25887bhp) Doosan Engine Co Ltd-South Korea AuxGen: 1 x 1256kW 430V 60Hz a.c, 2 x 1700kW 450V 60Hz a.c Boilers: AuxB (ex.g.) 9.2kgf/cm² (9.0bar), WTAuxB (o.f.) 9.2kgf/cm² (9.0bar) Thrusters: 1 Thwart. FP thruster (f)
7359204 *3EMI7* -	**TITANIA** *ex* Aastun *-2012* *ex* Talisman *-1996* **Coolmore Shipping Inc** Arabella Enterprises Corp *Panama* *Panama* MMSI: 356032000 Official number: 36069PEXT1	**3,136** 1,496 4,743	Class: GL (BV) (NV)	**1975-11 A/S Svendborg Skibsvaerft — Svendborg** Yd No: 148 Loa 94.42 (BB) Br ex 15.42 Dght 6.546 Lbp 84.99 Br md 15.40 Dpth 8.31 Welded, 2 dks	**(A31A2GX) General Cargo Ship** Grain: 5,490 Compartments: 1 Ho, ER 1 Ha: (52.7 x 11.2)ER Cranes: 1; Winches: 2 Ice Capable	**1 oil engine** reduction geared to sc. shaft driving 1 CP propeller Total Power: 1,470kW (1,999hp) 13.0kn Alpha 18V23L-VO 1 x Vee 4 Stroke 18 Cy. 225 x 300 1470kW (1999bhp) Alpha Diesel A/S-Denmark AuxGen: 2 x 144kW 380V 50Hz a.c Fuel: 316.0 (d.f.) 9.0pd
1008695 *2DPT8* -	**TITANIA** *ex* Apoise *-2012* *launched as* Marlin *-2006* **Titania 2012 Ltd** Yacht Management Consultants Sarl (Hill Robinson Yacht Management Consultants) *Douglas* *Isle of Man (British)* MMSI: 235081036 Official number: 739102	**1,894** 568 316	Class: LR ✠ **100A1** SS 05/2011 SSC Yacht (P), mono, G6 ✠ **LMC** **UMS** Cable: 400.0/28.0 U3 (a)	**2006-05 Kroeger Werft GmbH & Co. KG — Schacht-Audorf** Yd No: 13640 Lengthened-2012 Loa 71.00 (BB) Br ex 13.11 Dght 3.650 Lbp - Br md 12.80 Dpth 6.75 Welded, 1 dk	**(X11A2YP) Yacht**	**2 oil engines** with clutches, flexible couplings & reverse reduction geared to sc. shafts driving 2 FP propellers Total Power: 3,000kW (4,078hp) 12.0kn Caterpillar 3512B-TA 2 x Vee 4 Stroke 12 Cy. 170 x 190 each-1500kW (2039bhp) Caterpillar Inc-USA AuxGen: 3 x 240kW 400V 50Hz a.c Thrusters: 1 Thwart. CP thruster (f)
7338561 *V4LE* -	**TITANIC** *ex* Kelso *-2009* *ex* Toko Maru *-1996* **White Star Ltd** - *Basseterre* *St Kitts & Nevis* MMSI: 341832000 Official number: SKN 1001832	**1,678** 504 890	Class: IS	**1971-02 Hayashikane Shipbuilding & Engineering Co Ltd — Nagasaki NS** Yd No: 800 Converted From: Fishing Vessel-2009 Loa 78.64 Br ex 11.00 Dght 5.481 Lbp 68.00 Br md 10.98 Dpth 8.01 Welded, 1 dk	**(X11A2YP) Yacht**	**4 oil engines** sr geared to sc. shaft driving 1 CP propeller Total Power: 5,884kW (8,000hp) 14.0kn Niigata 6MQG31EZ 4 x 4 Stroke 6 Cy. 310 x 380 each-1471kW (2000bhp) Niigata Engineering Co Ltd-Japan AuxGen: 1 x 176kW 450V 60Hz a.c Fuel: 584.0 (d.f.) 21.0pd
9709300 *JZOH* -	**TITANIUM** *launched as* Bo Yuan Chang *-2013* **PT Salam Pacific Indonesia Lines** - *Surabaya* *Indonesia* MMSI: 525018199	**5,569** 3,118 8,000	Class: KI (Class contemplated)	**2013-09 Linhai Jianghai Shipbuilding Co Ltd — Linhai ZJ** Yd No: JH1205 Loa 118.10 Br ex - Dght 6.150 Lbp 110.90 Br md 18.20 Dpth 8.20 Welded, 1 dk	**(A31A2GX) General Cargo Ship**	**1 oil engine** driving 1 Propeller Total Power: 2,574kW (3,500hp) Yanmar 6N330-EN 1 x 4 Stroke 6 Cy. 330 x 440 2574kW (3500bhp) Yanmar Diesel Engine Co Ltd-Japan

IMO / Call sign	Name / Owner / Port	Tonnage	Class	Builder / Dimensions	Type	Machinery
9506590 *C6XT4* -	**TITANIUM EXPLORER** **Vantage Drilling Poland Sp zoo (Vantage Drilling Poland-Luxembourg Branch)** **TMT Co Ltd** SatCom: Inmarsat C 431101220 *Nassau* *Bahamas* MMSI: 311000110 Official number: 9000306	**67,825** 20,347 75,307	Class: AB	**2012-04 Daewoo Shipbuilding & Marine Engineering Co Ltd — Geoje** Yd No: 3602 Loa 238.04 Br ex 42.00 Dght 11.880 Lbp 230.00 Br md 41.75 Dpth 18.89 Welded, 1 dk	**(B22B2OD) Drilling Ship** Cranes: 4x85t	**6 diesel electric oil engines** driving 6 gen. Connecting to 2 elec. motors each (5500kW) driving 2 Azimuth electric drive units Total Power: 41,484kW (56,400hp) 13.5kn MAN-B&W 14V32/40 6 x Vee 4 Stroke 14 Cy. 320 x 400 each-6914kW (9400bhp) STX Engine Co Ltd-South Korea AuxGen: 1 x 2250kW a.c Thrusters: 4 Directional thruster Fuel: 10441.0 (d.f.) 193.8 (r.f.)
8905048 - -	**TITANIUM OXIDE DREDGER** - - -	*600* - -		**1989-08 Promet Pte Ltd — Singapore** Yd No: 1113 Loa 59.44 Br ex 15.86 Dght - Lbp - Br md - Dpth 2.90 Welded, 1 dk	**(B33A2DU) Dredger (unspecified)**	**1 oil engine** driving 1 FP propeller
8727147 *UFBO* -	**TITANIYA** **Preobrazheniye Trawler Fleet Base (Preobrazhenskaya Baza Tralovogo Flota)** *Nakhodka* *Russia* MMSI: 273827710 Official number: 872275	**683** 233 474	Class: RS	**1988-07 Khabarovskiy Sudostroitelnyy Zavod im Kirova — Khabarovsk** Yd No: 868 Loa 55.00 Br ex 9.52 Dght 4.340 Lbp 50.04 Br md 9.30 Dpth 5.16 Welded, 1 dk	**(B12B2FC) Fish Carrier** Ice Capable	**1 oil engine** driving 1 FP propeller Total Power: 589kW (801hp) 11.3kn S.K.L. 6NVD48A-2U 1 x 4 Stroke 6 Cy. 320 x 480 589kW (801bhp) VEB Schwermaschinenbau "KarlLiebknecht" (SKL)-Magdeburg AuxGen: 3 x 150kW a.c
8427668 *DUA2367* -	**TITANO** *ex* Patrick G *ex* Sinta **White Gold Marine Services** - *Manila* *Philippines* Official number: 00-0001257	*260* 152 -		**1967 at Manila** Lengthened L reg 41.62 Br ex 7.35 Dght - Lbp - Br md 7.32 Dpth 2.44 Welded, 1 dk	**(A13B2TU) Tanker (unspecified)**	**1 oil engine** driving 1 FP propeller Total Power: 231kW (314hp)
7712547 *ILTB* -	**TITANUS** **Rimorchiatori Riuniti Panfido e Compagnia Srl** *Venice* *Italy* MMSI: 247004800 Official number: 689	*197* 28 236	Class: RI	**1978-06 Cantieri Navali Campanella SpA — Savona** Yd No: 84 Loa 30.71 Br ex 8.82 Dght 4.401 Lbp 26.52 Br md 8.41 Dpth 4.65 Welded, 1 dk	**(B32A2ST) Tug**	**1 oil engine** reduction geared to sc. shaft driving 1 CP propeller Total Power: 1,839kW (2,500hp) Nohab F212V 1 x Vee 4 Stroke 12 Cy. 250 x 300 1839kW (2500bhp) AB Bofors NOHAB-Sweden
7333987 - -	**TITANYIA** **Port Fleet (Bourgas) Ltd** *Bourgas* *Bulgaria* Official number: 168	**150** 44 44	Class: (BR)	**1969 "Petrozavod" — Leningrad** Loa 29.32 Br ex 8.49 Dght 3.090 Lbp 25.20 Br md 8.31 Dpth 4.35 Welded, 1 dk	**(B32A2ST) Tug** Ice Capable	**2 oil engines** driving 2 CP propellers Total Power: 882kW (1,200hp) 11.0kn Russkiy 6DR30/50-4-2 2 x 2 Stroke 6 Cy. 300 x 500 each-441kW (600bhp) Mashinostroitelnyy Zavod"Russkiy-Dizel"-Leningrad AuxGen: 2 x 24kW 230V a.c
8896986 *S2YK* -	**TITAS** *ex* Hong Qi 083 **Bangladesh Inland Water Transport Corp** - *Chittagong* *Bangladesh*	*874* 395 1,202		**1969 Guangzhou Shipyard — Guangzhou GD** Loa 64.64 Br ex - Dght 4.200 Lbp 59.00 Br md 10.80 Dpth 5.10 Welded, 1 dk	**(A31A2GX) General Cargo Ship** Grain: 1,549; Bale: 1,420 Compartments: 2 Ho, ER 2 Ha: 2 (10.8 x -)ER	**1 oil engine** driving 1 FP propeller Total Power: 950kW (1,292hp) 13.0kn Fiat A300.6S 1 x 4 Stroke 6 Cy. 300 x 450 950kW (1292bhp) SA Fiat SGM-Torino AuxGen: 3 x 48kW 230V a.c
9610145 *PMIM* -	**TITIAN KALTIM** **PT Titian Mahakam Line** - *Samarinda* *Indonesia*	**628** 244 1,002	Class: KI (RI)	**2011-01 PT Titian Mahakam Line — Samarinda** Yd No: TML-05 Loa 60.00 Br ex - Dght 3.220 Lbp 53.20 Br md 10.88 Dpth 4.00 Welded, 1 dk	**(A13B2TP) Products Tanker** Double Hull (13F)	**2 oil engines** reduction geared to sc. shafts driving 2 FP propellers Total Power: 1,766kW (2,402hp) 9.0kn Mitsubishi S6A3-MPTK 2 x 4 Stroke 6 Cy. 150 x 175 each-883kW (1201bhp) Mitsubishi Heavy Industries Ltd-Japan
6725523 *YFAB* -	**TITIAN MURNI** *ex* Crusader I *-2001* *ex* Awa Maru *-1993* **PT Jembatan Nusantara** - *Jakarta* *Indonesia* MMSI: 525002061	*3,614* 1,085 1,101	Class: KI	**1967-09 Mitsubishi Heavy Industries Ltd. — Shimonoseki** Yd No: 645 Loa 93.50 Br ex 15.80 Dght 3.683 Lbp 84.00 Br md 15.78 Dpth 5.44 Welded, 1 dk	**(A36A2PT) Passenger/Ro-Ro Ship (Vehicles/Rail)** Passengers: unberthed: 1800 Bow door/ramp Stern door/ramp Lane-Len: 175	**2 oil engines** driving 2 CP propellers Total Power: 3,398kW (4,620hp) 14.5kn B&W 14-26MTBF-40V 2 x Vee 4 Stroke 14 Cy. 260 x 400 each-1699kW (2310bhp) Mitsui Shipbuilding & Engineering CLtd-Japan AuxGen: 2 x 560kW 445V 60Hz a.c Fuel: 106.0 (d.f.) 13.0pd
7125952 *YGDS* -	**TITIAN NUSANTARA** *ex* Bridge Island I *-1999* *ex* Otome Maru *-1998* **PT Prima Vista** - *Semarang* *Indonesia* MMSI: 525002084	**5,532** 1,659 871	Class: KI	**1971-09 Fukuoka Shipbuilding Co Ltd — Fukuoka FO** Yd No: 987 Loa 101.58 Br ex 19.26 Dght 5.004 Lbp 94.01 Br md 19.21 Dpth 6.15 Welded, 2 dks	**(A36A2PR) Passenger/Ro-Ro Ship (Vehicles)** Passengers: unberthed: 850	**4 oil engines** reduction geared to sc. shafts driving 2 FP propellers Total Power: 5,884kW (8,000hp) 18.8kn Niigata 6MG31EZ 4 x 4 Stroke 6 Cy. 310 x 380 each-1471kW (2000bhp) Niigata Engineering Co Ltd-Japan AuxGen: 3 x 600kW 450V 60Hz a.c Fuel: 31.0 (d.f.) 115.0 (r.f.) 30.0pd
7026065 *SYVX* -	**TITIKA** *ex* Vacha *-1990* *ex* Belatrix *-1970* **Leti Shipping Co** Evangelos Malkogiorgos *Piraeus* *Greece* Official number: 9626	*1,756* 553 1,618 T/cm 7.7	Class: (BR) (HR)	**1968 Sudostroitelnyy Zavod "Zaliv" — Kerch** Loa 83.57 Br ex 12.04 Dght 4.649 Lbp 74.00 Br md 11.97 Dpth 5.34 Welded, 1 dk	**(A13B2TP) Products Tanker** Liq: 3,029; Liq (Oil): 3,029 Cargo Heating Coils Compartments: 12 Ta, ER 4 Cargo Pump (s): 4x125m³/hr Manifold: Bow/CM: 40m Ice Capable	**1 oil engine** driving 1 FP propeller Total Power: 1,471kW (2,000hp) 10.5kn Skoda 8DR43/61-V1 1 x 2 Stroke 8 Cy. 430 x 610 1471kW (2000bhp) CKD Praha-Praha AuxGen: 3 x 100kW 380V a.c, 1 x 20kW 380V a.c Fuel: 142.0 (d.f.) (Heating Coils) 7.0pd
8214542 *ZM3584* -	**TITIRANGI** *ex* Fukuoka Maru *-1998* *ex* Kyoto Maru No. 2 *-1993* **Eastland Port Ltd** *Auckland* *New Zealand* Official number: 876304	*137* - -		**1982-09 Kanagawa Zosen — Kobe** Yd No: 241 Loa 26.01 Br ex - Dght 2.401 Lbp 23.12 Br md 7.61 Dpth 3.20 Welded, 1 dk	**(B32A2ST) Tug**	**2 oil engines** sr geared to sc. shafts driving 2 FP propellers Total Power: 1,324kW (1,800hp) Niigata 6MG22LX 2 x 4 Stroke 6 Cy. 220 x 290 each-662kW (900bhp) Niigata Engineering Co Ltd-Japan
7711672 *IZMG* -	**TITO** *ex* Barra de Leixoes *-2002* *ex* Punta Service *-1999* *ex* Remolcanosa Diez *-1981* **Fratelli Neri SpA (Neri Group)** SatCom: Inmarsat C 424707550 *Livorno* *Italy* MMSI: 247075500 Official number: 917	*1,171* 361 1,243	Class: RI (BV)	**1981-07 Ast. de Huelva S.A. — Huelva** Yd No: 105 Loa 63.10 Br ex 13.21 Dght 5.001 Lbp 55.02 Br md 13.01 Dpth 6.02 Welded, 1 dk	**(B21B20T) Offshore Tug/Supply Ship**	**2 oil engines** geared to sc. shafts driving 2 CP propellers Total Power: 6,472kW (8,800hp) 14.5kn Deutz SBV8M540 2 x 4 Stroke 8 Cy. 370 x 400 each-3236kW (4400bhp) Hijos de J Barreras SA-Spain
9319167 *IQRH* -	**TITO NERI** **Fratelli Neri SpA (Neri Group)** SatCom: Inmarsat C 424747720 *Genoa* *Italy* MMSI: 247131200 Official number: 3839	**398** 117 280	Class: RI	**2004-11 Cant. Nav. Rosetti — Ravenna** Yd No: 76 Loa 31.27 Br ex - Dght 3.460 Lbp 28.94 Br md 11.50 Dpth 4.00 Welded, 1 dk	**(B32A2ST) Tug**	**2 oil engines** gearing integral to driving 2 Z propellers Total Power: 4,104kW (5,580hp) 10.0kn Deutz SBV9M628 2 x 4 Stroke 9 Cy. 240 x 280 each-2052kW (2790bhp) Deutz AG-Koeln AuxGen: 3 x 130kW 50Hz a.c
8900464 *IVCC* -	**TITO NERI DECIMO** *ex* Algerina Neri *-1981* **Fratelli Neri SpA (Neri Group)** - *Livorno* *Italy* Official number: 877	*197* 41 -	Class: (RI)	**1989-12 Cooperativa Metallurgica Ing G Tommasi Srl — Ancona** Yd No: 59 Loa 32.10 Br ex 8.52 Dght 3.680 Lbp 28.01 Br md 8.50 Dpth 4.25 Welded, 1 dk	**(B32A2ST) Tug**	**1 oil engine** with flexible couplings & sr geared to sc. shaft driving 1 FP propeller Total Power: 1,520kW (2,067hp) 13.5kn Nohab F38V 1 x Vee 4 Stroke 8 Cy. 250 x 300 1520kW (2067bhp) Wartsila Diesel AB-Sweden
8715974 *IXVV* -	**TITO NERI NONO** **Fratelli Neri SpA (Neri Group)** - *Livorno* *Italy* Official number: 873	*197* 41 -	Class: RI	**1988-11 Cooperativa Metallurgica Ing G Tommasi Srl — Ancona** Yd No: 56 Loa 32.10 Br ex 8.52 Dght 3.750 Lbp 28.01 Br md 8.50 Dpth 4.25 Welded, 1 dk	**(B32A2ST) Tug**	**1 oil engine** with flexible couplings & sr geared to sc. shaft driving 1 FP propeller Total Power: 1,520kW (2,067hp) Nohab F38V 1 x Vee 4 Stroke 8 Cy. 250 x 300 1520kW (2067bhp) Wartsila Diesel AB-Sweden

IMO / Call sign	Name / Owner	Tonnage	Class	Builder / Dimensions	Type	Machinery
8715962 *IXVW* -	**TITO NERI OTTAVO** **Fratelli Neri SpA (Neri Group)** - *Livorno* *Italy* Official number: 863	*197* 41 -	Class: RI	**1988**-01 **Cooperativa Metallurgica Ing G Tommasi Srl — Ancona** Yd No: 55 Loa 31.27 Br ex - Dght 3.680 Lbp - Br md 8.51 Dpth 4.27 Welded, 1 dk	**(B32A2ST) Tug**	**1 oil engine** with clutches & sr reverse geared to sc. shaft driving 1 FP propeller Total Power: 1,520kW (2,067hp) 14.0kn Nohab F38V 1 x Vee 4 Stroke 8 Cy. 250 x 300 1520kW (2067bhp) Wartsila Diesel AB-Sweden AuxGen: 2 x 75kW 380V 50Hz a.c Fuel: 83.0 (d.f.) 6.8pd
8303575 *IRNY* -	**TITO NERI SESTO** **Fratelli Neri SpA (Neri Group)** - *Livorno* *Italy* Official number: 818	**200** 73 160	Class: RI	**1984**-01 **Cooperativa Metallurgica Ing G Tommasi Srl — Ancona** Yd No: 46 Loa 32.11 Br ex 8.51 Dght 3.800 Lbp 28.02 Br md 8.49 Dpth 4.27 Welded, 1 dk	**(B32A2ST) Tug**	**1 oil engine** sr geared to sc. shaft driving 1 CP propeller Total Power: 1,618kW (2,200hp) MAN G9V30/45ATL 1 x 4 Stroke 9 Cy. 300 x 450 1618kW (2200bhp) Maschinenbau Augsburg Nuernberg (MAN)-Augsburg
7817139 *IWCX* -	**TITO NERI TERZO** - - - *Livorno* *Italy* Official number: 827	*199* 58 -	Class: (RI)	**1979 Cooperativa Metallurgica Ing G Tommasi Srl — Ancona** Yd No: 34 Loa 32.11 Br ex 9.17 Dght 3.655 Lbp 28.02 Br md 8.30 Dpth 4.25 Welded, 1 dk	**(B32A2ST) Tug**	**1 oil engine** reverse reduction geared to sc. shaft driving 1 FP propeller Total Power: 1,261kW (1,714hp) MAN G7V30/45ATL 1 x 4 Stroke 7 Cy. 300 x 450 1261kW (1714bhp) Maschinenbau Augsburg Nuernberg (MAN)-Augsburg
9100865 *UIXR* -	**TITOVKA** **Hermes Co Ltd-Murmansk (OOO 'Germes')** - *Murmansk* *Russia*	**117** 35 30	Class: (RS)	**1993**-06 **Sosnovskiy Sudostroitelnyy Zavod — Sosnovka** Yd No: 836 Loa 25.50 Br ex 7.00 Dght 2.390 Lbp 22.00 Br md 6.80 Dpth 3.30 Welded, 1 dk	**(B11A2FS) Stern Trawler** Grain: 64 Compartments: 1 Ho 1 Ha: (1.4 x 1.5) Ice Capable	**1 oil engine** driving 1 FP propeller Total Power: 220kW (299hp) 9.5kn S.K.L. 6NVD26A-2 1 x 4 Stroke 6 Cy. 180 x 260 220kW (299bhp) SKL Motoren u. Systemtechnik AG-Magdeburg
9100188 *C6SE9* -	**TITRAN** *ex* Leistein *-2010* *ex* Lukas *-2006* *ex* Emily-C *-2004* **Berge Rederi AS** Transmar AS *Nassau* *Bahamas* MMSI: 311874000 Official number: 8001283	**2,744** 1,590 4,775 T/cm 10.7	Class: NV (LR) (GL) ✠ Classed LR until 19/11/06	**1996**-10 **PO SevMash Predpriyatiye — Severodvinsk** (Hull) Yd No: 93058 **1996**-10 **B.V. Scheepswerf Damen Hoogezand — Foxhol** Yd No: 708 Loa 89.00 (BB) Br ex 13.22 Dght 6.095 Lbp 84.99 Br md 13.17 Dpth 7.15 Welded, 1 dk	**(A31A2GX) General Cargo Ship** Grain: 5,763 TEU 197 C.Ho 117 TEU C.Dk 80 TEU Compartments: 1 Ho, ER 1 Ha: (62.5 x 11.0)ER Gantry cranes: 1 Ice Capable	**1 oil engine** reduction geared to sc. shaft driving 1 CP propeller Total Power: 1,800kW (2,447hp) 11.5kn MaK 6M453C 1 x 4 Stroke 6 Cy. 320 x 420 1800kW (2447bhp) Krupp MaK Maschinenbau GmbH-Kiel AuxGen: 2 x 83kW 380/220V 50Hz a.c, 1 x 216kW 380/220V 50Hz a.c Thrusters: 1 Tunnel thruster (f)
6912633 - -	**TITU MEER** **Bangladesh Railways Board** - *Dhaka* *Bangladesh*	*360* - -	Class: (LR) ✠ Classed LR until 1/71	**1969**-07 **Friedr. Krupp GmbH Ruhrorter Schiffswerft — Duisburg** Yd No: 455 Loa 45.90 Br ex 9.53 Dght - Lbp 42.68 Br md 9.15 Dpth 2.67 Welded, 1 dk	**(B32A2ST) Tug** 2 Ha: 2 (0.8 x 0.8)	**2 oil engines** driving 2 FP propellers Total Power: 1,200kW (1,632hp) 14.3kn MaK 6MU451A 2 x 4 Stroke 6 Cy. 320 x 450 each-600kW (816bhp) Atlas MaK Maschinenbau GmbH-Kiel AuxGen: 2 x 20kW 110V d.c Fuel: 29.5 (d.f.)
8727329 *UIGG* -	**TITUVENAY** *ex* Tytuvenai *-2001* *ex* Tituvenay *-1992* **Sevros Ltd** - *Murmansk* *Russia* MMSI: 273420840 Official number: 853255	**356** 107 146	Class: RS	**1985**-09 **Sudostroitelnyy Zavod "Avangard" — Petrozavodsk** Yd No: 420 Converted From: Deck Cargo Vessel-2001 Converted From: Stern Trawler-1995 Loa 35.72 Br ex 8.92 Dght 3.430 Lbp 31.00 Br md - Dpth 5.95 Welded, 2 dks	**(B11A2FS) Stern Trawler** Ice Capable	**1 oil engine** driving 1 FP propeller Total Power: 589kW (801hp) 10.9kn S.K.L. 6NVD48A-2U 1 x 4 Stroke 6 Cy. 320 x 480 589kW (801bhp) VEB Schwermaschinenbau "KarlLiebknecht" (SKL)-Magdeburg AuxGen: 2 x 160kW a.c
7517650 *9LE2101* -	**TIUBODA** *ex* Janat *-2013* *ex* Allaguia *-2012* *ex* Irfan Akansu *-2012* *ex* Allaguia *-2011* *ex* Irfan Akansu *-2010* *ex* Erim Kaptan *-2007* *ex* Mustafa Bey *-2004* *ex* Haci Arif Kaptan *-1995* **Murad Ismail Ghaly Al Tweny** - *Freetown* *Sierra Leone* Official number: SL100602	**1,823** 1,045 3,442	Class: (TL) (AB)	**1977**-03 **Gaye Ltd. Sirketi Fener — Istanbul** Yd No: 5 Loa 80.25 Br ex 12.27 Dght 6.310 Lbp 76.75 Br md 12.26 Dpth 7.30 Welded, 1 dk	**(A31A2GX) General Cargo Ship** Grain: 3,900; Bale: 3,800 Compartments: 3 Ho, ER 3 Ha: (11.9 x 7.3) (10.3 x 7.0) (9.7 x 7.5)ER	**1 oil engine** driving 1 FP propeller Total Power: 1,228kW (1,670hp) 10.0kn Skoda 9L350IIPS 1 x 4 Stroke 9 Cy. 350 x 500 1228kW (1670bhp) CKD Praha-Praha AuxGen: 2 x 120kW 220/380V 50Hz a.c, 1 x 36kW 220/380V 50Hz a.c
7642405 *LZQG* -	**TIULENOVO** **Marine Antipollution Enterprise** - *Varna* *Bulgaria* MMSI: 207231000 Official number: 237	**209** 123 299	Class: (BR)	**1955 'Georgi Dimitrov' Shipyard — Varna** Loa 40.42 Br ex 6.41 Dght 2.761 Lbp - Br md - Dpth 3.00 Welded, 1 dk	**(B35E2TF) Bunkering Tanker** Liq: 171; Liq (Oil): 171 Compartments: 2 Ta, ER	**1 oil engine** driving 1 FP propeller Total Power: 147kW (200hp) MWM RHS526S 1 x 4 Stroke 6 Cy. 180 x 260 147kW (200bhp) Motoren Werke Mannheim AG (MWM)-West Germany AuxGen: 1 x 12kW 230V d.c
8102892 *HO2865* -	**TIUNA** *ex* Tunamar *-1990* **Augusta Fishery Corp (Tiuna) Ltd** - *Panama* *Panama* MMSI: 352419000 Official number: 30473PEXTF5	*1,329* 598 1,550	Class: (RI) (RP)	**1981**-06 **Campbell Industries — San Diego, Ca** Yd No: 131 Loa 67.52 Br ex 12.65 Dght 5.792 Lbp 59.70 Br md 12.26 Dpth 8.26 Welded, 2 dks	**(B11B2FV) Fishing Vessel**	**1 oil engine** reverse reduction geared to sc. shaft driving 1 FP propeller Total Power: 2,648kW (3,600hp) 12.0kn EMD (Electro-Motive) 20-645-E7 1 x Vee 2 Stroke 20 Cy. 230 x 254 2648kW (3600bhp) General Motors Corp.Electro-Motive Div.-La Grange AuxGen: 3 x 300kW 400V a.c
9349992 *V7XK6* -	**TIVERTON** *ex* Global Hera *-2011* *ex* Geestedijk *-2007* *ex* Sky *-2007* *ex* Sider Sky *-2006* **Tiverton Shipping Co Ltd** Briese Schiffahrts GmbH & Co KG *Majuro* *Marshall Islands* MMSI: 538004502 Official number: 4502	**5,164** 2,913 7,448 T/cm 17.5	Class: BV	**2006**-09 **Ningbo Xinle Shipbuilding Co Ltd — Ningbo ZJ** Yd No: 2005-3 Loa 119.95 (BB) Br ex - Dght 6.265 Lbp 112.80 Br md 16.80 Dpth 8.20 Welded, 1 dk	**(A21A2BC) Bulk Carrier** Grain: 10,106; Bale: 9,904 Compartments: 2 Ho, ER 2 Ha: ER 2 (29.9 x 12.6)	**1 oil engine** reduction geared to sc.shaft driving 1 FP propeller Total Power: 2,500kW (3,399hp) 12.0kn Daihatsu 8DKM-28 1 x 4 Stroke 8 Cy. 280 x 390 2500kW (3399bhp) Shaanxi Diesel Heavy Industry Co Lt-China AuxGen: 2 x 200kW 400/220V 50Hz a.c Fuel: 200.0
9443384 *VRFS8* -	**TIWAI POINT** **Francesca Shipping (BVI) Ltd** Pacific Basin Shipping (HK) Ltd *Hong Kong* *Hong Kong* MMSI: 477612900 Official number: HK-2507	**20,987** 11,734 32,919 T/cm 46.1	Class: LR ✠ **100A1** SS 11/2009 bulk carrier CSR BC-A Nos. 2 & 4 holds may be empty GRAB (20) **ShipRight** (CM) timber deck cargoes ESP LI *IWS EP ✠ **LMC** **CCS** Eq.Ltr: It; Cable: 605.0/64.0 U3 (a)	**2009**-11 **Jiangmen Nanyang Ship Engineering Co Ltd — Jiangmen GD** Yd No: 113 Loa 179.90 (BB) Br ex 28.45 Dght 10.200 Lbp 171.50 Br md 28.40 Dpth 14.10 Welded, 1 dk	**(A21A2BC) Bulk Carrier** Grain: 43,124; Bale: 41,101 Compartments: 5 Ho, ER 5 Ha: 3 (20.0 x 19.2) (18.4 x 19.2)ER (14.4 x 17.6) Cranes: 4x30.5t	**1 oil engine** driving 1 FP propeller Total Power: 6,480kW (8,810hp) 13.7kn MAN-B&W 6S42MC 1 x 2 Stroke 6 Cy. 420 x 1764 6480kW (8810bhp) STX Engine Co Ltd-South Korea AuxGen: 3 x 440kW 450V 60Hz a.c Boilers: WTAuxB (Comp) 7.9kgf/cm² (7.7bar) Fuel: 105.0 (d.f.) 1400.0 (r.f.)
9376775 *V2DX3* -	**TIWALA** *launched as* Emstransporter *-2008* **ms 'Tiwala' GmbH & Co KG** Reederei Eicke GmbH & Co KG *Saint John's* *Antigua & Barbuda* MMSI: 305364000 Official number: 4566	**4,102** 1,851 5,484	Class: GL	**2008**-11 **Societatea Comerciala Severnav S.A. — Drobeta-Turnu Severin** (Hull) Yd No: (692) **2008**-11 **Bodewes' Scheepswerven B.V. — Hoogezand** Yd No: 692 Loa 106.78 Br ex - Dght 5.250 Lbp 100.62 Br md 15.20 Dpth 6.60 Welded, 1 dk	**(A31A2GX) General Cargo Ship** Grain: 8,353 TEU 279 C Ho 168 TEU C Dk 111 TEU Compartments: 2 Ho, ER 2 Ha: ER 2 (37.5 x 12.7) Ice Capable	**1 oil engine** reduction geared to sc. shaft driving 1 CP propeller Total Power: 2,010kW (2,733hp) 12.5kn MaK 6M25 1 x 4 Stroke 6 Cy. 255 x 400 2010kW (2733bhp) Caterpillar Motoren GmbH & Co. KG-Germany AuxGen: 1 x 350kW 400V a.c, 1 x 140kW 400V a.c Thrusters: 1 Tunnel thruster (f) Fuel: 68.0 (d.f.) 210.0 (r.f.)
7419999 *VNCW* -	**TIWI ISLANDER** *ex* Hyland Bay *-2008* *ex* Glenda Lee *-2000* **Tiwi Barge Services Pty Ltd** - *Darwin, NT* *Australia* MMSI: 503056000 Official number: 355444	*182* 49 204 T/cm 2.6	Class: (AB)	**1975**-05 **Barge Builders Pty Ltd — Ballina NSW** Yd No: 1 Loa 33.51 Br ex 9.00 Dght 1.772 Lbp 32.28 Br md 8.48 Dpth 2.09 Welded, 1 dk	**(A35D2RL) Landing Craft** Bow door/ramp Len: - Wid: 5.15 Swl: - Liq: 146 8 TEU C. 8/20' incl.6 ref C. Compartments: 15 Ta, ER	**2 oil engines** with clutches, flexible couplings & sr reverse geared to sc. shafts driving 2 FP propellers Total Power: 340kW (462hp) 10.0kn Cummins KTA-19-M 2 x 4 Stroke 6 Cy. 159 x 159 each-170kW (231bhp) (new engine 1975) Cummins Engine Co Inc-USA AuxGen: 2 x 40kW Fuel: 21.0 (d.f.) 2.5pd

IMO / Call sign	Name / Owner / Port	Tonnage	Class	Build	Type	Machinery
8326369 - -	**TIWI TRADER** *ex* Banksia *-1992* **Tiwi Barge Services Pty Ltd** - *Fremantle, WA* *Australia* Official number: 385833	*133* 80 90		**1979 Elder Prince Marine Services Pty Ltd — Fremantle WA** Converted From: Research Vessel-1992 Converted From: Landing Craft-1982 Loa 29.88 Br ex 7.73 Dght 1.820 Lbp - Br md 7.28 Dpth 2.27 Welded, 1 dk	**(A35D2RL) Landing Craft**	**4 oil engines** sr geared to sc. shafts driving 4 FP propellers Total Power: 472kW (640hp) 8.0kn Rolls Royce C6M-210 4 x 4 Stroke 6 Cy. 130 x 152 each-118kW (160bhp) Rolls Royce Motors of Australia PtyLtd-Australia Fuel: 42.0 (d.f.) 2.0pd
8023369 - -	**TIXMUCUY** *ex* Escama XXI *-1992* **Naviera Puerto Progreso SA de CV** - *Guaymas* *Mexico*	*208* 98 280	Class: (KR) (AB)	**1982-02 Astilleros Gondan SA — Castropol** Yd No: 204 Loa 37.83 Br ex - Dght 3.652 Lbp 32.01 Br md 8.31 Dpth 3.81 Welded, 1 dk	**(B11A2FS) Stern Trawler** Ins: 225 Compartments: 1 Ho, ER 2 Ha: ER	**1 oil engine** with clutches, flexible couplings & sr geared to sc. shaft driving 1 CP propeller Total Power: 827kW (1,124hp) 11.0kn Caterpillar D399SCAC 1 x Vee 4 Stroke 16 Cy. 159 x 203 827kW (1124bhp) Caterpillar Tractor Co-USA AuxGen: 2 x 90kW 440V 60Hz a.c Fuel: 94.0 (d.f.) 5.0pd
1000576 *9H7873* -	**TIZIANA** *ex* Aspasia Alpha *-2005* *ex* Tiziana *-2000* *ex* Tiziana Prima *-2000* *ex* Tiziana *-2000* **Navegador Ltd** S & D Yachts Ltd *Valletta* *Malta* Official number: 9611	*153* 104 -	Class: LR ✠ **100A1** SS 11/2010 Yacht **LMC**	**1963-06 Yacht- u. Bootswerft Abeking & Rasmussen — Lemwerder** Yd No: 5847 Loa 35.59 Br ex 7.41 Dght 3.170 Lbp 24.40 Br md - Dpth 3.41 Welded, 1 dk	**(X11A2YS) Yacht (Sailing)**	**1 oil engine** reduction geared to sc. shaft driving 1 CP propeller Total Power: 331kW (450hp) M.T.U. 12V2000M60 1 x Vee 4 Stroke 12 Cy. 130 x 150 331kW (450bhp) (new engine 2006) MTU Friedrichshafen GmbH-Friedrichshafen AuxGen: 1 x 55kW a.c
9111321 *INYX* -	**TIZIANO** - **Compagnia delle Isole SpA** - *Palermo* *Italy* MMSI: 247192500 Official number: 1212	*259* 171 21	Class: RI	**1994 Rodriquez Cantieri Navali SpA — Messina** Yd No: 246 Loa 31.20 Br ex 13.27 Dght 1.570 Lbp 26.40 Br md 6.78 Dpth 3.89 Welded, 1 dk	**(A37B2PS) Passenger Ship** Passengers: unberthed: 242	**2 oil engines** with clutches, flexible couplings & sr geared to sc. shafts driving 2 FP propellers Total Power: 3,100kW (4,214hp) 38.0kn M.T.U. 16V396TE74 2 x Vee 4 Stroke 16 Cy. 165 x 185 each-1550kW (2107bhp) MTU Friedrichshafen GmbH-Friedrichshafen
8030142 - -	**TIZOC** *ex* Escama XIII *-2000* **Compania Atunera del Pacifico SA de CV** - *Mazatlan* *Mexico*	*208* 97 266	Class: (AB)	**1982-03 Construcciones Navales P Freire SA — Vigo** Yd No: 165 Loa 37.80 (BB) Br ex 8.34 Dght 3.510 Lbp 32.01 Br md 8.31 Dpth 3.81 Welded, 1 dk	**(B11A2FS) Stern Trawler** Ins: 229 Compartments: 1 Ho, ER 2 Ha: ER	**1 oil engine** with clutches, flexible couplings & sr geared to sc. shaft driving 1 CP propeller Total Power: 827kW (1,124hp) 11.0kn Caterpillar D399SCAC 1 x Vee 4 Stroke 16 Cy. 159 x 203 827kW (1124bhp) Caterpillar Tractor Co-USA AuxGen: 2 x 90kW 440V 60Hz a.c Fuel: 94.0 (d.f.) 5.0pd
1006221 *ZCPZ9*	**TJ ESPERANZA** *ex* Thunder Gulch *-2007* **Al Monte Yachting Ltd** Camper & Nicholsons France SARL *George Town* *Cayman Islands (British)* MMSI: 319603000 Official number: 902146	**603** 180 -	Class: LR ✠ **100A1** SS 06/2009 Yacht ✠ **LMC** **UMS** Cable: 151.0/22.0 U2 (a)	**1999-06 Damen Shipyards Gdynia SA — Gdynia** (Hull) **1999-06 Amels Holland BV — Makkum** Yd No: 432 Loa 49.99 Br ex - Dght 3.200 Lbp 43.83 Br md 9.00 Dpth 4.90 Welded, 1 dk	**(X11A2YP) Yacht**	**2 oil engines** with clutches, flexible couplings & sr reverse geared to sc. shafts driving 2 FP propellers Total Power: 1,790kW (2,434hp) 15.0kn Cummins KTA-38-M 2 x Vee 4 Stroke 12 Cy. 159 x 159 each-895kW (1217bhp) Cummins Engine Co Inc-USA AuxGen: 2 x 150kW 380V 50Hz a.c Thrusters: 1 Thwart. FP thruster (f)
8960579 *JVZB4*	**TJ99** *ex* Daito Maru No. 5 *-2013* *ex* Akebono Maru No. 3 *-2013* **Haka Maritime** - *Ulaanbaatar* *Mongolia*	*116* - 230		**1978-02 Kanbara Zosen K.K. — Onomichi** Loa 31.40 Br ex - Dght 2.600 Lbp 29.00 Br md 6.00 Dpth 2.70 Welded, 1 dk	**(A13B2TU) Tanker (unspecified)**	**1 oil engine** driving 1 FP propeller Total Power: 250kW (340hp) 7.5kn
9220732 *YDA6144* -	**TJA 281** - **PT Batuah Abadi Lines** - *Banjarmasin* *Indonesia*	**258** 77 -	Class: AB KI	**1999-11 President Marine Pte Ltd — Singapore** Yd No: 251 Loa 29.40 Br ex - Dght 3.530 Lbp 26.60 Br md 8.70 Dpth 4.10 Welded, 1 dk	**(B32A2ST) Tug**	**2 oil engines** reverse reduction geared to sc. shafts driving 2 FP propellers Total Power: 2,060kW (2,800hp) 11.2kn Yanmar T240A-ET 2 x 4 Stroke 6 Cy. 240 x 310 each-1030kW (1400bhp) Yanmar Diesel Engine Co Ltd-Japan AuxGen: 2 x 135kW a.c
9229714 *YDA4217* -	**TJA 282** - **PT Rig Tenders Indonesia Tbk** - *Jakarta* *Indonesia* Official number: 388635	**253** 76 158	Class: AB KI	**2002-06 President Marine Pte Ltd — Singapore** Yd No: 304 Loa 29.00 Br ex - Dght 3.500 Lbp 26.50 Br md 9.00 Dpth 4.25 Welded, 1 dk	**(B32A2ST) Tug**	**2 oil engines** with clutches, flexible couplings & reverse reduction geared to sc. shafts driving 2 FP propellers Total Power: 2,060kW (2,800hp) 11.0kn Yanmar T240A-ET 2 x 4 Stroke 6 Cy. 240 x 310 each-1030kW (1400bhp) Yanmar Diesel Engine Co Ltd-Japan AuxGen: 2 x 161kW 415/220V 50Hz a.c Fuel: 147.0 (d.f.)
9350812 *YDA6145* -	**TJA 283** - **PT Batuah Abadi Lines** - *Banjarmasin* *Indonesia* Official number: 2008 IIA NO.2759/L	**255** 75 135	Class: AB KI	**2005-04 Jiangsu Wuxi Shipyard Co Ltd — Wuxi JS** (Hull) Yd No: (1179) **2005-04 Pacific Ocean Engineering & Trading Pte Ltd (POET) — Singapore** Yd No: 1179 Loa 29.50 Br ex - Dght 3.500 Lbp 27.49 Br md 9.00 Dpth 4.16 Welded, 1 dk	**(B32A2ST) Tug**	**2 oil engines** reduction geared to sc. shafts driving 2 CP propellers Total Power: 2,060kW (2,800hp) Yanmar 8N21A-UN 2 x 4 Stroke 8 Cy. 210 x 290 each-1030kW (1400bhp) Yanmar Diesel Engine Co Ltd-Japan AuxGen: 2 x 135kW 415V a.c
9350824 *YDA6210* -	**TJA 285** - **PT Batuah Abadi Lines** - *Banjarmasin* *Indonesia* Official number: 2009IIA NO 2789/L	**252** 75 133	Class: AB KI	**2005-04 Jiangsu Wuxi Shipyard Co Ltd — Wuxi JS** (Hull) Yd No: (1180) **2005-04 Pacific Ocean Engineering & Trading Pte Ltd (POET) — Singapore** Yd No: 1180 Loa 29.50 Br ex - Dght 3.500 Lbp 28.32 Br md 9.00 Dpth 4.16 Welded, 1 dk	**(B32A2ST) Tug**	**2 oil engines** reduction geared to sc. shafts driving 2 CP propellers Total Power: 2,060kW (2,800hp) Yanmar 8N21A-UN 2 x 4 Stroke 8 Cy. 210 x 290 each-1030kW (1400bhp) Yanmar Diesel Engine Co Ltd-Japan AuxGen: 2 x 135kW 415V a.c
9351646 *YDA6211* -	**TJA 286** - **PT Batuah Abadi Lines** - *Banjarmasin* *Indonesia* Official number: 390789	**252** 75 131	Class: AB KI	**2005-07 Jiangsu Wuxi Shipyard Co Ltd — Wuxi JS** (Hull) Yd No: (1181) **2005-07 Pacific Ocean Engineering & Trading Pte Ltd (POET) — Singapore** Yd No: 1181 Loa 29.50 Br ex - Dght 3.500 Lbp - Br md 9.00 Dpth 4.16 Welded, 1 dk	**(B32A2ST) Tug**	**2 oil engines** reduction geared to sc. shafts driving 2 Propellers Total Power: 2,060kW (2,800hp) Yanmar 8N21A-UN 2 x 4 Stroke 8 Cy. 210 x 290 each-1030kW (1400bhp) Yanmar Diesel Engine Co Ltd-Japan AuxGen: 2 x 135kW a.c
9351658 *YDA6212* -	**TJA 288** - **PT Batuah Abadi Lines** - *Banjarmasin* *Indonesia* Official number: 3080/IIA	**252** 75 132	Class: AB KI	**2005-07 Jiangsu Wuxi Shipyard Co Ltd — Wuxi JS** (Hull) Yd No: (1182) **2005-07 Pacific Ocean Engineering & Trading Pte Ltd (POET) — Singapore** Yd No: 1182 Loa 29.50 Br ex - Dght 3.500 Lbp - Br md 9.00 Dpth 4.16 Welded, 1 dk	**(B32A2ST) Tug**	**2 oil engines** reduction geared to sc. shafts driving 2 Propellers Total Power: 2,060kW (2,800hp) Yanmar 8N21A-UN 2 x 4 Stroke 8 Cy. 210 x 290 each-1030kW (1400bhp) Yanmar Diesel Engine Co Ltd-Japan AuxGen: 2 x 145kW 415V a.c
9351660 *YDA6304* -	**TJA 289** - **PT Batuah Abadi Lines** - *Banjarmasin* *Indonesia*	**252** 75 137	Class: AB KI	**2005-12 Bengbu Shenzhou Machinery Co Ltd — Bengbu AH** (Hull) Yd No: (1187) **2005-12 Pacific Ocean Engineering & Trading Pte Ltd (POET) — Singapore** Yd No: 1187 Loa 29.50 Br ex - Dght 3.500 Lbp 27.00 Br md 9.00 Dpth 4.16 Welded, 1 dk	**(B32A2ST) Tug**	**2 oil engines** reduction geared to sc. shafts driving 2 Propellers Total Power: 2,060kW (2,800hp) Yanmar 8N21A-UN 2 x 4 Stroke 8 Cy. 210 x 290 each-1030kW (1400bhp) Yanmar Diesel Engine Co Ltd-Japan AuxGen: 2 x 160kW 415V a.c
9351672 *YDA6305* -	**TJA 2810** - **PT Batuah Abadi Lines** - *Banjarmasin* *Indonesia*	**252** 75 137	Class: AB KI	**2006-03 Bengbu Shenzhou Machinery Co Ltd — Bengbu AH** (Hull) Yd No: (1188) **2006-03 Pacific Ocean Engineering & Trading Pte Ltd (POET) — Singapore** Yd No: 1188 Loa 29.50 Br ex - Dght 3.500 Lbp 27.00 Br md 9.00 Dpth 4.16 Welded, 1 dk	**(B32A2ST) Tug**	**2 oil engines** reduction geared to sc. shafts driving 2 Propellers Total Power: 2,060kW (2,800hp) Yanmar 8N21A-UN 2 x 4 Stroke 8 Cy. 210 x 290 each-1030kW (1400bhp) Yanmar Diesel Engine Co Ltd-Japan AuxGen: 2 x 145kW 415V a.c

9351684 - -	**TJA 2811** - **CH Logistics Pte Ltd** CH Ship Management Pte Ltd	**252** 75 142	Class: (AB)	**2006-04 Bengbu Shenzhou Machinery Co Ltd — Bengbu AH** (Hull) Yd No: (1189) **2006-04 Pacific Ocean Engineering & Trading Pte Ltd (POET) — Singapore** Yd No: 1189 Loa 27.48 Br ex - Dght 3.500 Lbp 27.00 Br md 9.00 Dpth 4.22 Welded, 1 dk	**(B32A2ST) Tug**	**2 oil engines** reduction geared to sc. shafts driving 2 Propellers Total Power: 2,060kW (2,800hp) Yanmar 8N21A-UN 2 x 4 Stroke 8 Cy. 210 x 290 each-1030kW (1400bhp) Yanmar Diesel Engine Co Ltd-Japan
9351696 *YDA6306* -	**TJA 2812** - **PT Batuah Abadi Lines** - *Banjarmasin* *Indonesia*	**252** 75 141	Class: AB KI	**2006-07 Bengbu Shenzhou Machinery Co Ltd — Bengbu AH** (Hull) Yd No: (1190) **2006-07 Pacific Ocean Engineering & Trading Pte Ltd (POET) — Singapore** Yd No: 1190 Loa 27.48 Br ex - Dght 3.500 Lbp - Br md 9.00 Dpth 4.22 Welded, 1 dk	**(B32A2ST) Tug**	**2 oil engines** reduction geared to sc. shafts driving 2 Propellers Total Power: 2,060kW (2,800hp) Yanmar 8N21A-UN 2 x 4 Stroke 8 Cy. 210 x 290 each-1030kW (1400bhp) Yanmar Diesel Engine Co Ltd-Japan AuxGen: 2 x 145kW 415V a.c
6410128 *TFCC* HF 177	**TJALDANES** *ex* Kristbjorg *-2013* *ex* Orvar II *-2009* *ex* Orvar *-2008* *ex* Vestri *-1995* *ex* Drangey *-1972* *ex* Frodaklettur *-1968* **Svartibakki Ehf** - *Hafnarfjordur* *Iceland* MMSI: 251383110 Official number: 0239	**290** 87 -	Class: (NV)	**1964 Ankerlokken Verft Floro AS — Floro** Yd No: 57 Loa 33.84 Br ex 7.22 Dght 3.709 Lbp 30.13 Br md 7.19 Dpth 3.81 Welded, 1 dk	**(B11B2FV) Fishing Vessel** Compartments: 1 Ho, ER 2 Ha: 2 (1.9 x 1.6)ER Derricks: 1x2.5t; Winches: 1 Ice Capable	**1 oil engine** geared to sc. shaft driving 1 FP propeller Total Power: 485kW (659hp) Blackstone ERS8M 1 x 4 Stroke 8 Cy. 222 x 292 485kW (659bhp) (new engine 1979) Mirrlees Blackstone (Stamford)Ltd.-Stamford AuxGen: 1 x 40kW 220V d.c, 1 x 33kW 220V d.c, 1 x 30kW 220V d.c
7617747 *XPRT* -	**TJALDRID** - **Foroyar Landsstyri** Fiskiveidieftirlitid (The Faeroe Islands Fisheries Inspection) SatCom: Inmarsat C 423100620 *Torshavn* *Faeroe Islands (Danish)* MMSI: 231006000 Official number: D2413	**453** 136 -	Class: NV	**1976-07 Svolvaer Mek. Verksted — Svolvaer** Yd No: 5 Loa 44.51 Br ex - Dght 4.026 Lbp 38.49 Br md 10.11 Dpth 4.20 Welded, 1 dk	**(B32A2ST) Tug**	**2 oil engines** geared to sc. shaft driving 1 CP propeller Total Power: 1,766kW (2,402hp) 15.0kn MWM TBD484-6 2 x 4 Stroke 8 Cy. 320 x 480 each-883kW (1201bhp) Motoren Werke Mannheim AG (MWM)-West Germany AuxGen: 3 x 78kW 380V 50Hz a.c Thrusters: 1 Thwart. FP thruster (f) Fuel: 122.0 (d.f.) 8.0pd
9050709 *TFKH* SH 270	**TJALDUR** - **KG Fiskverkun Ehf** - SatCom: Inmarsat C 425103910 *Rif* *Iceland* MMSI: 251039110 Official number: 2158	**689** 206 280	Class: NV	**1992-08 Solstrand Slip & Baatbyggeri AS — Tomrefjord** Yd No: 58 Loa 43.21 (BB) Br ex 9.00 Dght 5.000 Lbp 39.00 Br md - Dpth 6.80 Welded, 2 dks	**(B11B2FV) Fishing Vessel** Grain: 250; Ins: 223 Ice Capable	**1 oil engine** reduction geared to sc. shaft driving 1 FP propeller Total Power: 780kW (1,060hp) Caterpillar 3512TA 1 x Vee 4 Stroke 12 Cy. 170 x 190 780kW (1060bhp) Caterpillar Inc-USA AuxGen: 2 x 240kW 380V 50Hz a.c Thrusters: 1 Thwart. FP thruster (f)
6500193 - -	**TJALVE** *ex* Orcades Warrior *-1989* *ex* Pegwell Dawn *-1983* *ex* Kvalsund Senior *-1980* **Solfrid Ramfjord** Ramfjord Smr AS	*196* 101 -		**1965-01 Hjelmaas Slip & Mek. Verksted — Hjelmaas** Yd No: 7 Lengthened-1966 Loa 35.67 Br ex 6.76 Dght - Lbp - Br md 6.71 Dpth 3.66 Welded, 1 dk	**(B11B2FV) Fishing Vessel**	**1 oil engine** driving 1 FP propeller Total Power: 441kW (600hp) 11.0kn Alpha 406-26VO 1 x 2 Stroke 6 Cy. 260 x 400 441kW (600bhp) (new engine 1970) Alpha Diesel A/S-Denmark
8958801 - -	**TJANDRA II** - **PT Multi Agung Sarana Ananda** - *Balikpapan* *Indonesia*	**152** 91 -	Class: KI	**1999-11 C.V. Teknik Jaya Industri — Samarinda** Loa 23.20 Br ex - Dght - Lbp 21.80 Br md 7.00 Dpth 3.00 Welded, 1 dk	**(B32A2ST) Tug**	**2 oil engines** reduction geared to sc. shafts driving 2 FP propellers Total Power: 794kW (1,080hp) Caterpillar 3412TA 2 x Vee 4 Stroke 12 Cy. 137 x 152 each-397kW (540bhp) Caterpillar Inc-USA
9027520 - -	**TJANDRA III** - **PT Multi Agung Sarana Ananda** - *Samarinda* *Indonesia*	**220** 66 -	Class: KI	**1999-06 C.V. Teknik Jaya Industri — Samarinda** L reg 29.25 Br ex - Dght - Lbp 26.45 Br md 8.00 Dpth 3.75 Welded, 1 dk	**(B32A2ST) Tug**	**2 oil engines** geared to sc. shafts driving 2 Propellers Total Power: 1,382kW (1,878hp) 8.0kn Cummins KTA-38-M0 2 x Vee 4 Stroke 12 Cy. 159 x 159 each-691kW (939bhp) Cummins Engine Co Ltd-United Kingdom
6810952 *GCVA* BS 186	**TJEERD JACOBA** - **Scott Trawlers Ltd** - *Beaumaris* *United Kingdom* MMSI: 235002165 Official number: A15179	**133** 78 -		**1968-03 Holland Launch N.V. — Zaandam** Yd No: 418 Loa 26.29 Br ex 6.61 Dght - Lbp 23.27 Br md 6.58 Dpth 3.10 Welded, 1 dk	**(B11A2FS) Stern Trawler** Compartments: 1 Ho, ER	**1 oil engine** driving 1 FP propeller Total Power: 478kW (650hp) 10.0kn Stork 1 x 478kW (650bhp) (new engine 1977) Stork Werkspoor Diesel BV-Netherlands AuxGen: 1 x 19kW 110V, 1 x 18kW 110V Fuel: 20.5 (d.f.)
9684859 *LFNL* -	**TJELDEN** - **Norled AS** - *Stavanger* *Norway* MMSI: 258998000	**135** 40 8		**2013-12 Brodrene Aa AS — Hyen** Yd No: 270 Loa 25.70 Br ex - Dght 0.950 Lbp - Br md 8.00 Dpth - Bonded, 1 dk	**(A36A2PR) Passenger/Ro-Ro Ship (Vehicles)** Hull Material: Carbon Fibre Sandwich Passengers: unberthed: 47 Stern door (centre) Cars: 2	**2 oil engines** reduction geared to sc. shafts driving 2 Propellers Total Power: 1,026kW (1,394hp) 25.0kn Volvo Penta D13 2 x 4 Stroke 6 Cy. 131 x 158 each-513kW (697bhp) AB Volvo Penta-Sweden
8976803 *LMKI* -	**TJELDSUND** *ex* Borgsund *-1995* **Seaworks AS** - *Harstad* *Norway* MMSI: 258119000	**907** 347 -		**1973 AS Mjellem & Karlsen — Bergen** Yd No: 110 Converted From: Logistics Vessel (Naval Ro-Ro Cargo)-1995 Lengthened-1995 Loa 60.58 Br ex 10.50 Dght 2.100 Lbp - Br md - Dpth 3.50 Welded, 1 dk	**(A35D2RL) Landing Craft** Bow ramp (centre) Len: - Wid: 4.00 Swl: - Stern ramp (centre) Len: - Wid: 4.30 Swl: -	**2 oil engines** geared to sc. shafts driving 2 FP propellers Total Power: 900kW (1,224hp) 11.7kn MWM TBD234V12 2 x Vee 4 Stroke 12 Cy. 128 x 140 each-450kW (612bhp) (new engine 1995) Motoren Werke Mannheim AG (MWM)-Mannheim Thrusters: 2 Water jet (f) Fuel: 135.0 (d.f.)
9517240 *PCOX* -	**TJONGER** - **Stobbehoek BV** Drenth Ship Consult *Delfzijl* *Netherlands* MMSI: 246869000	**2,597** 1,460 3,741	Class: LR ✠ **100A1** SS 10/2012 strengthened for heavy cargoes, container cargoes in all holds and on all hatch covers Ice Class 1E at a maximum draught of 5.264m Min draught 3.20m ✠ **LMC** **UMS** Eq.Ltr: Q; Cable: 440.0/34.0 U3 (a)	**2012-10 DAHK Chernomorskyi Sudnobudivnyi Zavod — Mykolayiv** (Hull) Yd No: (9410) **2012-10 B.V. Scheepswerf Damen Bergum — Bergum** Yd No: 9410 Loa 88.60 Br ex 12.69 Dght 5.420 Lbp 84.99 Br md 12.50 Dpth 7.00 Welded, 1 dk	**(A31A2GX) General Cargo Ship** Double Bottom Entire Compartment Length Grain: 5,250 TEU 188 C Ho 108 TEU C Dk 80 TEU. Compartments: 1 Ho, ER 1 Ha: ER (62.5 x 10.1)	**1 oil engine** with clutches, flexible couplings & sr reverse geared to sc. shaft driving 1 CP propeller Total Power: 1,520kW (2,067hp) 11.5kn MaK 8M20 1 x 4 Stroke 8 Cy. 200 x 300 1520kW (2067bhp) Caterpillar Motoren GmbH & Co. KG-Germany AuxGen: 1 x 140kW 400V 50Hz a.c, 1 x 272kW 400V 50Hz a.c Thrusters: 1 Thwart. FP thruster (f) Fuel: 1.6 (d.f.) 179.0 (d.f.)
8811209 *LAUI* -	**TJOTTA** - **Boreal Transport Nord AS** - *Sandnessjoen* *Norway* MMSI: 257399400	**717** 231 100	Class: (NV)	**1989-06 FEAB-Marstrandverken — Marstrand** Yd No: 187 Loa 56.00 Br ex 11.25 Dght - Lbp - Br md - Dpth 4.00 Welded	**(A36A2PR) Passenger/Ro-Ro Ship (Vehicles)** Passengers: unberthed: 299 Ice Capable	**1 oil engine** geared to sc. shaft driving 1 FP propeller Total Power: 809kW (1,100hp) Alpha 6L23/30 1 x 4 Stroke 6 Cy. 225 x 300 809kW (1100bhp) MAN B&W Diesel A/S-Denmark AuxGen: 2 x 88kW 220V 50Hz a.c
9023263 - -	**TK 01** - **No 86 Construction Co** - *Saigon* *Vietnam*	**166** 50 70	Class: VR	**1972-01 Guangzhou Shipyard — Guangzhou GD** Loa 31.05 Br ex 8.04 Dght 1.800 Lbp 30.00 Br md 7.80 Dpth 2.60 Welded, 1 dk	**(B32A2ST) Tug**	**2 oil engines** geared to sc. shafts driving 2 FP propellers Total Power: 442kW (600hp) 7.0kn Chinese Std. Type D6-250 2 x 4 Stroke 6 Cy. 165 x 144 each-221kW (300bhp) in China
8137108 *DNBH* -	**TK 8** - **Taucher Knoth (Nachf) GmbH & Co KG** - *Hamburg* *Germany* Official number: 10429	*137* 43 -	Class: (GL)	**1962 R. Harmstorf Wasserbau u. Travewerft GmbH — Travemuende** Yd No: 7168 Loa 22.46 Br ex 9.66 Dght 1.401 Lbp 21.04 Br md 9.63 Dpth 2.01 Welded, 1 dk	**(B22A20V) Diving Support Vessel**	**2 oil engines** reverse geared to sc. shafts driving 2 FP propellers Total Power: 330kW (448hp) Daf DKT1160M 2 x 4 Stroke 6 Cy. 130 x 146 each-165kW (224bhp) (new engine 1981, fitted 1981) DAF Nederland Bedrijfswagen B.V.-Eindhoven AuxGen: 1 x 44kW 220/380V a.c

IMO / Call sign	Name / Owner	Tonnage	Class	Builder / Dimensions	Type	Machinery
8136960 *DGJX* -	**TK 12** *ex* Friedrich Matthias Harmstorf *-2010* *ex* F. M. Harmstorf *-2010* **Vibro-Einspueltech Duker & Wasserbau GmbH** - *Hamburg* *Germany* Official number: 8649	*121* 48 -		**1938 Werft Nobiskrug GmbH — Rendsburg** Converted From: General Cargo Barge, Non-propelled-1959 Widened-1959 Loa 27.41 Br ex 7.73 Dght 1.540 Lbp 27.36 Br md 7.70 Dpth 2.01 Welded, 1 dk	**(B34D2SL) Cable Layer**	**1 oil engine** reverse geared to sc. shaft driving 1 FP propeller Total Power: 228kW (310hp) Deutz SBA8M428 1 x 4 Stroke 8 Cy. 220 x 280 228kW (310bhp) (, fitted 1959) Kloeckner Humboldt Deutz AG-West Germany AuxGen: 1 x 12kW 220V a.c, 1 x 7kW 24V d.c
9025467 - -	**TK-61** - **Thai An Pte** - *Saigon* *Vietnam* Official number: VSNG-1666-TH	**107** 32 -	Class: VR	**2003-04 An Phu Works — Ho Chi Minh City** Loa 20.97 Br ex 7.22 Dght 2.400 Lbp 18.60 Br md 7.00 Dpth 3.20 Welded, 1 dk	**(B32A2ST) Tug**	**2 oil engines** geared to sc. shafts driving 2 FP propellers Total Power: 956kW (1,300hp) 8.0kn Cummins KTA-19-M3 2 x 4 Stroke 6 Cy. 159 x 159 each-478kW (650bhp) Cummins Engine Co Inc-USA
9025431 - -	**TK-62** - **Thai An Pte** - *Saigon* *Vietnam*	**107** 32 -	Class: VR	**2003-04 An Phu Works — Ho Chi Minh City** Yd No: 0203-TK2 Loa 20.97 Br ex 7.22 Dght 2.400 Lbp 18.60 Br md 7.00 Dpth 3.20 Welded, 1 dk	**(B32A2ST) Tug**	**2 oil engines** geared to sc. shafts driving 2 FP propellers Total Power: 956kW (1,300hp) 8.0kn Cummins KTA-19-M 2 x 4 Stroke 6 Cy. 159 x 159 each-478kW (650bhp) Cummins Engine Co Inc-USA
8897784 - -	**TK 151** - **Vietnam Union Salvage Corp (Xi Nghiep Lien Hiep Truc Vot Cuu Ho)** - *Saigon* *Vietnam*	*144* - -	Class: (VR)	**1986 Bach Dang Shipyard — Haiphong** Loa - Br ex - Dght - Lbp 27.00 Br md 7.30 Dpth 3.46 Welded, 1 dk	**(B32A2ST) Tug**	**1 oil engine** driving 1 FP propeller Total Power: 540kW (734hp) S.K.L. 6NVD48-1U 1 x 4 Stroke 6 Cy. 320 x 480 540kW (734bhp) (made 1978) VEB Schwermaschinenbau "KarlLiebknecht" (SKL)-Magdeburg
9023524 *XVBI* -	**TK 980** - **Quy Nhon Port** - *Da Nang* *Vietnam* Official number: VNDN-142-LD	**185** 55 -	Class: VR	**1983-01 Bach Dang Shipyard — Haiphong** Loa 29.70 Br ex 8.32 Dght 3.000 Lbp 27.07 Br md 8.00 Dpth 4.00 Welded, 1 dk	**(B32A2ST) Tug**	**1 oil engine** driving 1 FP propeller Total Power: 721kW (980hp) 8.0kn Skoda 6L350PN 1 x 4 Stroke 6 Cy. 350 x 500 721kW (980bhp) CKD Praha-Praha
9344459 *UPJ* -	**TK AKTAU** *ex* Aktau *-2009* **Raiffeisen Leasing Kazakhstan LLP** Kazmortransflot JSC (A/O 'Natsionalnaya Morskaya Sudokhodnaya Kompaniya Kazmortransflot') *Aqtau* *Kazakhstan* MMSI: 436000062	**7,224** 3,517 12,365 T/cm 24.3	Class: RS	**2006-08 OAO Vyborgskiy Sudostroitelnyy Zavod — Vyborg** Yd No: 215 Loa 149.35 (BB) Br ex 17.33 Dght 7.000 Lbp 143.15 Br md 17.30 Dpth 10.10 Welded, 1 dk	**(A13B2TP) Products Tanker** Double Hull (13F) Liq: 13,994; Liq (Oil): 14,280 Compartments: 12 Wing Ta, 2 Wing Slop Ta, ER 12 Cargo Pump (s): 12x125m³/hr Manifold: Bow/CM: 76m	**1 oil engine** driving 1 FP propeller Total Power: 2,600kW (3,535hp) 10.6kn Wartsila 8L26A 1 x 4 Stroke 8 Cy. 260 x 320 2600kW (3535bhp) Wartsila NSD Nederland BV-Netherlands AuxGen: 3 x 380kW a.c Fuel: 132.0 (d.f.)
9045613 *A8RG8* -	**TK ROTTERDAM** *ex* Aras *-2012* *ex* TK Rotterdam *-2005* *ex* Gaiesti *-2001* **Atlanta Oceanways Ltd** Pasifik Gemi Isletmeciligi ve Ticaret AS *Monrovia* *Liberia* MMSI: 636014098 Official number: 14098	**6,036** 3,522 8,861 T/cm 17.9	Class: RS (LR) (BV) (GL) (RN) Classed LR until 16/8/07	**2001-05 SC Santierul Naval SA Braila — Braila** Yd No: 1300 Loa 130.86 (BB) Br ex - Dght 8.100 Lbp 121.04 Br md 17.70 Dpth 10.20 Welded, 2 dks	**(A31A2GX) General Cargo Ship** Grain: 11,837; Bale: 11,094 TEU 106 C.Ho 78/20' (40') C.Dk 28/20' (40') Compartments: 4 Ho, ER 4 Ha: (11.8 x 6.2) (13.8 x 10.6) (13.5 x 10.6) (13.2 x 10.6)ER Cranes: 4x3.2t Ice Capable	**1 oil engine** driving 1 FP propeller Total Power: 4,524kW (6,151hp) 15.0kn MAN K6SZ52/105CL 1 x 2 Stroke 6 Cy. 520 x 1050 4524kW (6151bhp) U.C.M. Resita S.A.-Resita AuxGen: 3 x 264kW 380V 50Hz a.c Boilers: e (ex.g.) 7.1kgf/cm² (7.0bar), AuxB (o.f.) 7.1kgf/cm² (7.0bar) Fuel: 138.0 (d.f.) 948.0 (r.f.)
9023536 - -	**TK SONG CON** - **Quy Nhon Port** - *Da Nang* *Vietnam* Official number: VNDN-142-LD	**185** 55 -	Class: VR	**1984-08 Bach Dang Shipyard — Haiphong** Yd No: 601 Loa 29.00 Br ex 8.32 Dght 3.000 Lbp 26.88 Br md 8.00 Dpth 4.00 Welded, 1 dk	**(B32A2ST) Tug**	**1 oil engine** driving 1 FP propeller Total Power: 588kW (799hp) 7.0kn S.K.L. 8NVD48 1 x 4 Stroke 8 Cy. 320 x 480 588kW (799bhp) (Re-engined 1967, refitted 1967) SKL Motoren u. Systemtechnik AG-Magdeburg
8414312 - -	**TKB EMERALD** *ex* Cocoon *-2007* *ex* Crystal Moon *-2006* *ex* Ever Spring *-1998* *ex* Osei Maru *-1997* *ex* Tenryu Maru No. 55 *-1989* **Toyama Kaigai Boeki Shipping Co Ltd**	**1,935** 580 528	Class: IS (BV) (KR)	**1984-11 Kochi Jyuko (Kaisei Zosen) K.K. — Kochi** Yd No: 1727 Loa 71.81 Br ex - Dght 3.522 Lbp 68.03 Br md 13.61 Dpth 7.68 Welded, 2 dks	**(A36A2PR) Passenger/Ro-Ro Ship (Vehicles)** Stern door/ramp	**1 oil engine** driving 1 CP propeller Total Power: 1,030kW (1,400hp) 11.5kn Hanshin 6LUN28AG 1 x 4 Stroke 6 Cy. 280 x 480 1030kW (1400bhp) The Hanshin Diesel Works Ltd-Japan
9612260 - -	**TKSI 7** - **PT Trikarya Samudera Indonesia** - *Jakarta* *Indonesia*	**260** 78 -	Class: KI	**2010-02 PT Pahala Harapan Lestari — Pangkalpinang** Loa 30.00 Br ex - Dght 3.500 Lbp 28.80 Br md 8.60 Dpth 4.11 Welded, 1 dk	**(B32A2ST) Tug**	**2 oil engines** reduction geared to sc. shafts driving 2 Propellers Total Power: 1,472kW (2,002hp) Yanmar 6RY17P-GV 2 x 4 Stroke 6 Cy. 165 x 219 each-736kW (1001bhp) Yanmar Diesel Engine Co Ltd-Japan AuxGen: 2 x 53kW 380V a.c
9029437 *YD3253* -	**TKSI II** *ex* Kaiko Maru No. 25 *-2006* **PT Trikarya Samudera Indonesia** - *Dumai* *Indonesia*	**132** 40 -	Class: KI	**1983-11 Kumamoto Dock K.K. — Yatsushiro** Loa 26.07 Br ex - Dght 2.290 Lbp 23.59 Br md 7.00 Dpth 3.04 Welded, 1 dk	**(B32A2ST) Tug**	**1 oil engine** reverse geared to sc. shaft driving 1 FP propeller Total Power: 662kW (900hp) Akasaka AH25 1 x 4 Stroke 6 Cy. 250 x 410 662kW (900bhp) Akasaka Tekkosho KK (Akasaka DieselLtd)-Japan AuxGen: 1 x 92kW 225V a.c, 1 x 12kW 225V a.c
8925787 *3WAD* -	**TKV 03** *ex* Tien Sa *-2006* *ex* KS-02 *-1996* **Vietnam Maritime Safety Co No 1 (Cong Ty Bao Dam An Toan Hang Hai 1)** - *Haiphong* *Vietnam* Official number: VN-512-VT	**112** 34 50	Class: VR	**1975 Bach Dang Shipyard — Haiphong** Loa 29.46 Br ex 6.42 Dght 2.300 Lbp 26.60 Br md 6.40 Dpth 3.20 Welded, 1 dk	**(B34N2QP) Pilot Vessel**	**1 oil engine** driving 1 FP propeller Total Power: 224kW (305hp) 11.0kn S.K.L. 8NVD36-1U 1 x 4 Stroke 8 Cy. 240 x 360 224kW (305bhp) (made 1966) VEB Schwermaschinenbau "KarlLiebknecht" (SKL)-Magdeburg
7375375 *YGOE* -	**TL IX** *ex* Tonasa Marindo *-2010* *ex* Aso Maru *-2001* **PT Perusahaan Pelayaran Tonasa Lines** - *Makassar* *Indonesia* MMSI: 525105080	*2,294* 1,249 3,970	Class: KI (NK)	**1974-03 Oshima Dock KK — Imabari EH** Yd No: 550 Loa 83.37 Br ex 14.46 Dght 6.133 Lbp 78.21 Br md 14.41 Dpth 7.12 Riveted\Welded, 1 dk	**(A24A2BT) Cement Carrier** Grain: 3,293	**1 oil engine** geared to sc. shaft driving 1 FP propeller Total Power: 2,059kW (2,799hp) 12.8kn Daihatsu 8DSM-32 1 x 4 Stroke 8 Cy. 320 x 380 2059kW (2799bhp) Daihatsu Diesel Manufacturing Co Lt-Japan AuxGen: 2 x 160kW 445V 60Hz a.c Fuel: 20.5 (d.f.) 127.0 (r.f.) 10.0pd
7353846 *YGYH* -	**TL X** *ex* Tonasa Baru *-2010* *ex* HirAozan *-2001* *ex* Hiraozan Maru *-2000* **PT Perusahaan Pelayaran Tonasa Lines** - *Makassar* *Indonesia* MMSI: 525384612	*2,266* 1,211 3,994	Class: KI	**1973-10 Fukuoka Shipbuilding Co Ltd — Fukuoka FO** Yd No: 1022 Loa 92.00 Br ex 13.85 Dght 6.020 Lbp 85.50 Br md 13.80 Dpth 6.96 Welded, 1 dk	**(A24A2BT) Cement Carrier**	**1 oil engine** driving 1 FP propeller Total Power: 1,986kW (2,700hp) 12.0kn Akasaka AH40 1 x 4 Stroke 6 Cy. 400 x 600 1986kW (2700bhp) Akasaka Tekkosho KK (Akasaka DieselLtd)-Japan AuxGen: 2 x 160kW 445V 60Hz a.c Fuel: 19.0 (d.f.) 82.5 (r.f.) 7.5pd
6420094 *XC2151* -	**TLACOTALPAN** - **Banco Nacional de Fomento Cooperativo SA de CV (BANFOCO)** - *Alvarado* *Mexico*	*121* 57 -		**1964-08 Scheepswerf Haak N.V. — Zaandam** Yd No: 897 Loa 26.09 Br ex 7.22 Dght - Lbp 22.99 Br md 7.21 Dpth 2.70 Welded	**(B11A2FS) Stern Trawler**	**2 oil engines** geared to sc. shaft driving 1 FP propeller Total Power: 672kW (914hp) Caterpillar D343SCAC 2 x 4 Stroke 6 Cy. 137 x 165 each-336kW (457bhp) Caterpillar Tractor Co-USA
8033546 - -	**TLP SPARTAN** *ex* Spartan *-2012* *ex* K. C. Smith *-2012* **Transporte Y Logistica Portuaria SA** - *Cartagena de Indias* *Colombia* Official number: MC-05-674	*182* 124 -		**1979 Delta Shipyard — Houma, La** Yd No: 125 L reg 29.17 Br ex 9.17 Dght 3.647 Lbp 31.40 Br md 9.15 Dpth 4.27 Welded, 1 dk	**(B32A2ST) Tug**	**1 oil engine** driving 1 FP propeller Total Power: 2,868kW (3,899hp) 12.0kn

IMO / Call sign	Ship / Owner / Port	Tonnage	Class	Builder / Dimensions	Type	Machinery
8415201 *9HUB9* -	**TM AIBGA** *ex* Koralle *-2008* *ex* RMS Hollandia *-1994* *ex* Koralle *-1992* **Transmarine Projects Ltd** SL Transmarine BSS *Valletta* *Malta* MMSI: 249514000 Official number: 8415201	**1,851** 945 2,259	Class: (RS) (GL)	**1985-06 Krupp Ruhrorter Schiffswerft GmbH — Duisburg** Yd No: 721 Loa 80.02 Br ex 12.70 Dght 4.180 Lbp 75.21 Br md 12.60 Dpth 4.65 Welded, 2 dks	**(A31A2GX) General Cargo Ship** Grain: 3,177 TEU 142 C. 142/20' (40') Compartments: 1 Ho, ER 1 Ha: (51.3 x 10.2)ER	**1 oil engine** with flexible couplings & sr reverse geared to sc. shaft driving 1 FP propeller Total Power: 1,000kW (1,360hp) 10.5kn MaK 6M332AK 1 x 4 Stroke 6 Cy. 240 x 330 1000kW (1360bhp) Krupp MaK Maschinenbau GmbH-Kiel AuxGen: 2 x 85kW 380/220V 50Hz a.c, 1 x 34kW 380/220V 50Hz a.c Thrusters: 1 Directional thruster (f) Fuel: 125.0 (d.f.)
9689407 *5NXJ* -	**TMC EAGLE** **Damen Shipyards Group NV** - *Lagos* *Nigeria* MMSI: 657100100	**168** 50 61	Class: BV	**2013-07 Alumare Sp Zoo — Swinoujscie** (Hull) Yd No: (544822) **2013-08 B.V. Scheepswerf Damen — Gorinchem** Yd No: 544822 Converted From: Crewboat-2013 Loa 33.25 Br ex 7.35 Dght 1.940 Lbp 32.00 Br md 6.50 Dpth 3.30 Welded, 1 dk	**(B34H2SQ) Patrol Vessel** Hull Material: Aluminium Alloy	**3 oil engines** reduction geared to sc. shaft (s) driving 3 FP propellers Total Power: 2,460kW (3,345hp) 26.5kn Caterpillar C32 3 x Vee 4 Stroke 12 Cy. 145 x 162 each-820kW (1115bhp) Caterpillar Inc-USA AuxGen: 2 x 65kW 50Hz a.c Thrusters: 1 Tunnel thruster (f) Fuel: 46.0 (d.f.)
9035979 *HSB3661* -	**TMC KRABI 1** *ex* Seatran Line 2 *-2012* *ex* SS Masan *-2007* *ex* Han Bu *-2003* **Bomuang Wharf Commercial Co Ltd** *Bangkok* *Thailand* MMSI: 567328000 Official number: 500055018	**1,912** 1,070 2,913	Class: (KR)	**1991-01 Hanjin Heavy Industries Co Ltd — Ulsan** Yd No: 9063 Loa 82.80 (BB) Br ex - Dght 4.811 Lbp 77.30 Br md 14.80 Dpth 5.90 Welded, 1 dk	**(A33A2CC) Container Ship (Fully Cellular)** TEU 144 Compartments: 2 Cell Ho, ER 4 Ha: ER	**1 oil engine** driving 1 FP propeller Total Power: 2,220kW (3,018hp) B&W 6S26MC 1 x 2 Stroke 6 Cy. 260 x 980 2220kW (3018bhp) Ssangyong Heavy Industries Co Ltd-South Korea
9592147 *5NTZ* -	**TMC PRIMUS** *ex* Forsa *-2010* **Tamrose Ventures Ltd** - *Lagos* *Nigeria* MMSI: 657615000	**215** 64 64	Class: RI	**2010-05 Ergun Gemi Sanayi ve Ticaret Ltd Sti — Surmene** Yd No: 42 Loa 29.50 (BB) Br ex - Dght 3.100 Lbp - Br md 9.30 Dpth 3.40 Welded, 1 dk	**(B21A20S) Platform Supply Ship** A-frames: 1x20t; Cranes: 1x20t	**2 oil engines** reduction geared to sc. shafts driving 2 FP propellers Total Power: 1,640kW (2,230hp) 11.0kn Cummins KTA-38-M1 2 x Vee 4 Stroke 12 Cy. 159 x 159 each-820kW (1115bhp) Cummins Diesel International Ltd-USA Thrusters: 1 Tunnel thruster (f)
8746703 *YDA6357* -	**TMH 01** **PT Tanjung Mas Harapan** - *Samarinda* *Indonesia*	**159** 48 -	Class: KI	**2009 CV Sunjaya Abadi — Samarinda** Loa - Br ex - Dght 2.590 Lbp 22.32 Br md 7.20 Dpth 3.40 Welded, 1 dk	**(B32A2ST) Tug**	**2 oil engines** reduction geared to sc. shafts driving 2 Propellers Total Power: 1,302kW (1,770hp) Caterpillar 3412D 2 x Vee 4 Stroke 12 Cy. 145 x 162 each-651kW (885bhp) Caterpillar Inc-USA AuxGen: 2 x 29kW 400V a.c
9410703 *XCIT3* -	**TMM CUYUTLAN** **Transportacion Maritima Mexicana SA de CV** - *Manzanillo* *Mexico* MMSI: 345140006	**490** 147 225	Class: GL (BV)	**2007-12 Medyilmaz Gemi Sanayi ve Ticaret AS — Karadeniz Eregli** Yd No: 03 Loa 32.00 Br ex - Dght 4.300 Lbp 30.46 Br md 11.60 Dpth 5.36 Welded, 1 dk	**(B32A2ST) Tug**	**2 oil engines** reduction geared to sc. shafts driving 2 Z propellers Total Power: 3,840kW (5,220hp) Caterpillar 3516B 2 x Vee 4 Stroke 16 Cy. 170 x 190 each-1920kW (2610bhp) Caterpillar Inc-USA
9410698 *XCIS2* -	**TMM TEPALCATES** **Transportacion Maritima Mexicana SA de CV** - *Manzanillo* *Mexico* MMSI: 345140005 Official number: 0601133129-8	**490** 147 225	Class: GL (BV)	**2007-12 Medyilmaz Gemi Sanayi ve Ticaret AS — Karadeniz Eregli** Yd No: 02 Loa 32.00 Br ex - Dght 4.190 Lbp 30.46 Br md 11.60 Dpth 5.36 Welded, 1 dk	**(B32A2ST) Tug**	**2 oil engines** reduction geared to sc. shafts driving 2 Z propellers Total Power: 3,840kW (5,220hp) Caterpillar 3516B-HD 2 x Vee 4 Stroke 16 Cy. 170 x 215 each-1920kW (2610bhp) Caterpillar Inc-USA
9529944 *HSB4293* -	**TMN PIONEER** **Thai Maritime Navigation Co Ltd (TMN)** Kanchana Marine Co Ltd SatCom: Inmarsat C 456700220 *Bangkok* *Thailand* MMSI: 567361000 Official number: 520083853	**5,683** 2,032 7,124 T/cm 16.7	Class: BV	**2009-08 Nanjing East Star Shipbuilding Co Ltd — Nanjing JS** Yd No: TK2006-7002 Loa 101.39 (BB) Br ex - Dght 7.000 Lbp 94.96 Br md 19.05 Dpth 10.50 Welded, 1 dk	**(A12B2TR) Chemical/Products Tanker** Double Hull (13F) Liq: 8,712; Liq (Oil): 8,712 Cargo Heating Coils Compartments: 10 Wing Ta, ER 3 Cargo Pump (s): 3x500m³/hr Manifold: Bow/CM: 53m	**1 oil engine** reduction geared to sc. shaft driving 1 FP propeller Total Power: 3,030kW (4,120hp) 13.0kn Niigata 8MG28HX 1 x 4 Stroke 8 Cy. 280 x 370 3030kW (4120bhp) Niigata Engineering Co Ltd-Japan AuxGen: 3 x 450kW 60Hz a.c Thrusters: 1 Tunnel thruster (f) Fuel: 197.0 (d.f.) 400.0 (r.f.)
9333254 *HSB4614* -	**TMN PRIDE** *ex* High Century *-2011* **Thai Maritime Navigation Co Ltd (TMN)** - *Bangkok* *Thailand* MMSI: 567439000 Official number: 550000233	**28,799** 13,234 48,676 T/cm 51.8	Class: LR (NK) **100A1** SS 07/2011 Double Hull oil tanker ESP LI **LMC** **UMS IGS** Cable: 632.5/73.0 U3 (a)	**2006-07 Iwagi Zosen Co Ltd — Kamijima EH** Yd No: 240 Loa 179.99 (BB) Br ex 32.23 Dght 12.616 Lbp 172.00 Br md 32.20 Dpth 19.05 Welded, 1 dk	**(A13B2TP) Products Tanker** Double Hull (13F) Liq: 56,275; Liq (Oil): 56,275 Cargo Heating Coils Compartments: 16 Wing Ta, 2 Wing Slop Ta, ER 4 Cargo Pump (s): 4x1250m³/hr Manifold: Bow/CM: 92.4m	**1 oil engine** driving 1 FP propeller Total Power: 9,480kW (12,889hp) 15.1kn MAN-B&W 6S50MC-C 1 x 2 Stroke 6 Cy. 500 x 2000 9480kW (12889bhp) Mitsui Engineering & Shipbuilding CLtd-Japan AuxGen: 3 x 440kW 450V 60Hz a.c Boilers: e (ex.g.) 23.0kgf/cm² (22.6bar), WTAuxB (o.f.) 17.9kgf/cm² (17.6bar) Fuel: 2200.0
9161845 *HSB3727* -	**TMN PROGRESS** *ex* Wakato *-2007* *ex* Sakti *-2003* **Thai Maritime Navigation Co Ltd (TMN)** - *Bangkok* *Thailand* MMSI: 567336000 Official number: 5000 54931	**7,760** 2,595 8,739	Class: NK	**1997-08 Shin Kurushima Dockyard Co. Ltd. — Akitsu** Yd No: 2951 Loa 113.22 (BB) Br ex - Dght 7.309 Lbp 105.40 Br md 19.60 Dpth 13.20 Welded, 2 dks	**(A31A2GX) General Cargo Ship** Grain: 16,781; Bale: 15,193 TEU 48 Compartments: 2 Ho, ER, 2 Tw Dk 2 Ha: (20.3 x 14.8) (33.6 x 14.8)ER Cranes: 2x65t; Derricks: 1x25t	**1 oil engine** driving 1 FP propeller Total Power: 3,884kW (5,281hp) 13.3kn B&W 6L35MC 1 x 2 Stroke 6 Cy. 350 x 1050 3884kW (5281bhp) Makita Corp-Japan AuxGen: 2 x 320kW 450V 60Hz a.c Fuel: 662.0 (r.f.) 14.6pd
9610042 *HSB4605* -	**TMS 1** **Top Maritime Service Co Ltd** Marsun Logistics Co Ltd SatCom: Inmarsat C 456700457 *Bangkok* *Thailand* MMSI: 567436000	**205** 63 50	Class: BV	**2011-08 Marsun Co Ltd — Samut Prakan** Yd No: 229 Loa 36.00 Br ex 8.65 Dght 1.700 Lbp 32.00 Br md 7.60 Dpth 3.30 Welded, 1 dk	**(B21A20C) Crew/Supply Vessel** Hull Material: Aluminium Alloy Passengers: unberthed: 90	**3 oil engines** reduction geared to sc. shafts driving 3 FP propellers Total Power: 2,979kW (4,050hp) 21.0kn Cummins KTA-38-M2 3 x Vee 4 Stroke 12 Cy. 159 x 159 each-993kW (1350bhp) Cummins Engine Co Ltd-United Kingdom AuxGen: 2 x 80kW 50Hz a.c Thrusters: 1 Tunnel thruster (f) Fuel: 53.0 (d.f.)
9615236 *HSB4643* -	**TMS 2** *ex* Marsun 2 *-2012* **Top Maritime Service Co Ltd** Marsun Logistics Co Ltd *Bangkok* *Thailand* MMSI: 567448000	**205** 63 50	Class: BV	**2012-02 Marsun Co Ltd — Samut Prakan** Yd No: 233 Loa 36.00 Br ex - Dght 1.700 Lbp 32.00 Br md 7.60 Dpth 3.30 Welded, 1 dk	**(B21A20C) Crew/Supply Vessel** Hull Material: Aluminium Alloy Passengers: unberthed: 90	**3 oil engines** reduction geared to sc. shafts driving 3 FP propellers Total Power: 3,357kW (4,563hp) 21.0kn Cummins KTA-38-M2 3 x Vee 4 Stroke 12 Cy. 159 x 159 each-1119kW (1521bhp) Cummins Engine Co Ltd-United Kingdom AuxGen: 2 x 80kW 50Hz a.c Fuel: 53.0 (d.f.)
9615248 *HSB4644* -	**TMS 3** *ex* Marsun 3 *-2012* **Top Maritime Service Co Ltd** Marsun Logistics Co Ltd *Bangkok* *Thailand* MMSI: 567449000	**205** 63 50	Class: BV	**2012-02 Marsun Co Ltd — Samut Prakan** Yd No: 234 Loa 36.00 Br ex - Dght 1.700 Lbp 32.00 Br md 7.60 Dpth 3.30 Welded, 1 dk	**(B21A20C) Crew/Supply Vessel**	**3 oil engines** reduction geared to sc. shafts driving 3 FP propellers Total Power: 3,357kW (4,563hp) 21.0kn Cummins KTA-38-M2 3 x Vee 4 Stroke 12 Cy. 159 x 159 each-1119kW (1521bhp) Cummins Engine Co Ltd-United Kingdom AuxGen: 2 x 80kW 50Hz a.c
9658707 *HSB4752* -	**TMS 4** **Top Maritime Service Co Ltd** Nathalin Management Co Ltd *Bangkok* *Thailand* MMSI: 567000000	**229** 69 116	Class: BV	**2012-11 Marsun Co Ltd — Samut Prakan** Yd No: 246 Loa 36.00 Br ex - Dght 1.700 Lbp 33.50 Br md 7.60 Dpth 3.60 Welded, 1 dk	**(B21A20C) Crew/Supply Vessel** Hull Material: Aluminium Alloy	**3 oil engines** reduction geared to sc. shafts driving 3 FP propellers Total Power: 3,357kW (4,563hp) 24.0kn Cummins KTA-38-M2 3 x Vee 4 Stroke 12 Cy. 159 x 159 each-1119kW (1521bhp) Cummins Engine Co Ltd-United Kingdom AuxGen: 2 x 80kW 50Hz a.c Fuel: 60.0 (d.f.)

9658719 **TMS 5**
HSB4753
-
Top Maritime Service Co Ltd
Nathalin Management Co Ltd
Bangkok *Thailand*
MMSI: 567475000

229 Class: BV
69
116

2012-12 Marsun Co Ltd — Samut Prakan
Yd No: 247
Loa 36.00 Br ex - Dght 1.700
Lbp 33.50 Br md 7.60 Dpth 3.60
Welded, 1 dk

(B21A2OC) Crew/Supply Vessel
Hull Material: Aluminium Alloy

3 oil engines reduction geared to sc. shafts driving 3 FP propellers
Total Power: 3,357kW (4,563hp) 24.0kn
Cummins KTA-38-M2
3 x Vee 4 Stroke 12 Cy. 159 x 159 each-1119kW (1521bhp)
Cummins Engine Co Ltd-United Kingdom
AuxGen: 2 x 80kW 50Hz a.c
Fuel: 60.0 (d.f.)

9694268 **TMS 6**
HSB4903
-
Top Maritime Service Co Ltd
Nathalin Management Co Ltd
Bangkok *Thailand*
MMSI: 567063200
Official number: 560003908

229 Class: BV
69
116

2013-11 Marsun Co Ltd — Samut Prakan
Yd No: 252
Loa 36.00 Br ex - Dght 1.700
Lbp 33.50 Br md 7.60 Dpth 3.60
Welded, 1 dk

(B21A2OC) Crew/Supply Vessel
Hull Material: Aluminium Alloy

3 oil engines reduction geared to sc. shafts driving 3 FP propellers
Total Power: 2,982kW (4,053hp) 24.0kn
Cummins KTA-38-M2
3 x Vee 4 Stroke 12 Cy. 159 x 159 each-994kW (1351bhp)
Cummins Engine Co Ltd-United Kingdom
AuxGen: 2 x 80kW 50Hz a.c

9694282 **TMS 7**
HSB4928 *launched as* Tms 8 *-2014*
-
Top Maritime Service Co Ltd
Nathalin Management Co Ltd
Bangkok *Thailand*
MMSI: 567063600
Official number: 22848M

229 Class: BV
69
116

2014-02 Marsun Co Ltd — Samut Prakan
Yd No: 254
Loa 36.00 Br ex - Dght 1.700
Lbp 32.00 Br md 7.60 Dpth 3.60
Welded, 1 dk

(B21A2OC) Crew/Supply Vessel
Hull Material: Aluminium Alloy
Single Hull

3 oil engines reduction geared to sc.shafts driving 3 FP propellers
Total Power: 3,357kW (4,563hp)
Cummins KTA-38-M2
3 x Vee 4 Stroke 12 Cy. 159 x 159 each-1119kW (1521bhp)

9694270 **TMS 8**
HSB4917 *ex* Tms 7 *-2014*
-
Top Maritime Service Co Ltd
Nathalin Management Co Ltd
Bangkok *Thailand*
Official number: 570000122

229 Class: BV
69
116

2014-01 Marsun Co Ltd — Samut Prakan
Yd No: 253
Loa 36.00 Br ex - Dght 1.700
Lbp 32.00 Br md 7.60 Dpth 3.60
Welded, 1 dk

(B21A2OC) Crew/Supply Vessel
Hull Material: Aluminium Alloy
Single Hull

3 oil engines reduction geared to sc. shafts driving 3 FP propellers
Total Power: 3,357kW (4,563hp)
Cummins KTA-38-M2
3 x Vee 4 Stroke 12 Cy. 159 x 159 each-1119kW (1521bhp)

9065431 **TMS GLORY**
JZMV *ex* Asian Glory *-2013*
-
PT Tresnamuda Sejati
-
Indonesia
MMSI: 525018171

4,811 Class: (CC) (AB)
2,410
6,744
T/cm
16.5

1994-01 Dae Sun Shipbuilding & Engineering Co Ltd — Busan Yd No: 400
Loa 113.00 (BB) Br ex - Dght 6.470
Lbp 103.00 Br md 19.00 Dpth 8.50
Welded, 1 dk

(A33A2CC) Container Ship (Fully Cellular)
TEU 357 incl 40 ref C
Compartments: 5 Cell Ho, ER
6 Ha: ER

1 oil engine driving 1 FP propeller
Total Power: 3,354kW (4,560hp) 14.0kn
B&W 6L35MC
1 x 2 Stroke 6 Cy. 350 x 1050 3354kW (4560bhp)
Ssangyong Heavy Industries Co Ltd-South Korea
Thrusters: 1 Thwart. FP thruster (f)

9216963 **TMS MARIA**
9HGW9 *ex* CMB Talent *-2008* *ex* United Talent *-2004*
-
Maria Navigation Ltd
Third Millenium Shipping Ltd
Valletta *Malta*
MMSI: 256970000
Official number: 9216963

30,053 Class: LR (BV) (NK)
18,207 **100A1** SS 03/2011
52,403 bulk carrier
T/cm ESP
55.5 strengthened for heavy cargoes, Nos 2 & 4 holds may be empty
LI
ESN
LMC **UMS**

2001-03 Tsuneishi Shipbuilding Co Ltd — Tadotsu KG Yd No: 1190
Loa 190.00 (BB) Br ex - Dght 12.024
Lbp 182.00 Br md 32.26 Dpth 17.00
Welded, 1 dk

(A21A2BC) Bulk Carrier
Double Bottom Entire Compartment Length
Grain: 67,756; Bale: 65,601
Compartments: 5 Ho, ER
5 Ha: (20.4 x 18.4)4 (21.3 x 18.4)ER
Cranes: 4x30t

1 oil engine driving 1 FP propeller
Total Power: 7,797kW (10,601hp) 14.5kn
B&W 6S50MC
1 x 2 Stroke 6 Cy. 500 x 1910 7797kW (10601bhp)
Mitsui Engineering & Shipbuilding CLtd-Japan
AuxGen: 3 x 420kW a.c
Fuel: 159.0 (d.f.) (Heating Coils) 2359.0 (r.f.) 29.0pd

8894184 **TN-352**
-
-
South-West Fishery Service Corp (Cong Ty Thuong Mai Va Dich Vu Thuy San Tay Nam)
-
Saigon *Vietnam*

101 Class: (VR)
-
-

1988 in Thailand
Loa - Br ex - Dght 3.050
Lbp 21.30 Br md 6.30 Dpth 3.55
Welded, 1 dk

(B11B2FV) Fishing Vessel

1 oil engine driving 1 FP propeller
Total Power: 257kW (349hp) 8.0kn
Nissan RD8TA
1 x Vee 4 Stroke 8 Cy. 135 x 125 257kW (349bhp)
Nissan Diesel Motor Co. Ltd.-Ageo

8894158 **TN-452**
-
-
South-West Fishery Service Corp (Cong Ty Thuong Mai Va Dich Vu Thuy San Tay Nam)
-
Saigon *Vietnam*

107 Class: (VR)
-
-

1988 in Thailand
Loa - Br ex - Dght 2.800
Lbp 24.20 Br md 6.56 Dpth 3.20
Welded, 1 dk

(B11B2FV) Fishing Vessel

1 oil engine driving 1 FP propeller
Total Power: 331kW (450hp) 8.0kn

8869098 **TN-455**
-
-
South-West Fishery Service Corp (Cong Ty Thuong Mai Va Dich Vu Thuy San Tay Nam)
-
Saigon *Vietnam*

104 Class: (VR)
-
-

1988 in Thailand
Loa - Br ex - Dght 2.950
Lbp 22.00 Br md 6.50 Dpth 3.45
Welded, 1 dk

(B11B2FV) Fishing Vessel
Ins: 9

1 oil engine reduction geared to sc. shaft driving 1 FP propeller
Total Power: 331kW (450hp) 10.0kn
Nissan RD10TA
1 x Vee 4 Stroke 10 Cy. 135 x 125 331kW (450bhp)
Nissan Diesel Motor Co. Ltd.-Ageo
AuxGen: 2 x a.c

9373993 **TN DAWN**
V7XR8 *ex* Sanko King *-2011*
-
Dawn Maritime Inc
AM Nomikos Transworld Maritime Agencies SA
Majuro *Marshall Islands*
MMSI: 538004555
Official number: 4555

31,532 Class: NK
18,767
56,678
T/cm
56.9

2008-01 IHI Marine United Inc — Yokohama KN
Yd No: 3235
Loa 190.00 (BB) Br ex - Dght 12.735
Lbp 185.00 Br md 32.26 Dpth 18.10
Welded, 1 dk

(A21A2BC) Bulk Carrier
Grain: 72,111; Bale: 67,110
Compartments: 5 Ho, ER
5 Ha: 4 (20.9 x 18.6)ER (14.6 x 18.6)
Cranes: 4x30t

1 oil engine driving 1 FP propeller
Total Power: 8,890kW (12,087hp) 14.5kn
Wartsila 6RT-flex50
1 x 2 Stroke 6 Cy. 500 x 2050 8890kW (12087bhp)
Diesel United Ltd.-Aioi
AuxGen: 3 x a.c
Fuel: 2275.0

9415533 **TNL 1201**
YDA3140 *ex* Bina Ocean 19 *-2012*
-
PT Trans Nusantara Line
-
Batam *Indonesia*

161 Class: GL (NK)
49
144

2006-12 Far East Shipyard Co Sdn Bhd — Sibu
Yd No: 28/05
Loa 23.90 Br ex 7.30 Dght 2.912
Lbp 21.86 Br md 7.30 Dpth 3.50
Welded, 1 dk

(B32A2ST) Tug

2 oil engines reduction geared to sc. shafts driving 2 Propellers
Total Power: 940kW (1,278hp)
Yanmar 6LAH-STE3
2 x 4 Stroke 6 Cy. 150 x 165 each-470kW (639bhp)
Yanmar Diesel Engine Co Ltd-Japan
AuxGen: 2 x 25kW a.c

5416553 **TO CALLISTO**
SV3536 *ex* Illyria II *-2000* *ex* Marina *-1985*
-
Blue Sea Line Shipping Co
FleetPro Ocean Inc
SatCom: Inmarsat C 423974912
Piraeus *Greece*
MMSI: 239749000
Official number: 2971

499 Class: RS (HR) (GL)
169

1963 D.W. Kremer Sohn — Elmshorn Yd No: 1104
Loa 46.82 Br ex 8.03 Dght 2.299
Lbp 42.52 Br md 8.01 Dpth 3.51
Riveted\Welded, 1 dk

(A37B2PS) Passenger Ship
Passengers: berths: 34

2 oil engines driving 2 FP propellers
Total Power: 1,236kW (1,680hp)
MWM TRHS435A
2 x 4 Stroke 8 Cy. 250 x 350 each-618kW (840bhp)
Motoren Werke Mannheim AG (MWM)-West Germany

8976205 **TO CHAN NO. 2**
YJSZ7 *ex* Yuan Shin No. 16 *-2003*
-
Sun Rise Fishery Co Ltd
-
Port Vila *Vanuatu*
MMSI: 576877000
Official number: 1513

492
148
-

2002 Fuzhou Zhongyi Shipbuilding Co Ltd — Fuzhou FJ
Loa - Br ex - Dght -
Lbp - Br md - Dpth -
Welded, 1 dk

(B11B2FV) Fishing Vessel

1 oil engine driving 1 FP propeller

7643655 **TO INDEPENDENCE**
HP6923 *ex* Independence *-1992*
-
Shipping Logistic Inc
Smit International (Gabon) SA
SatCom: Inmarsat A 1337221
Panama *Panama*
MMSI: 354723000
Official number: 2077993C

690 Class: BV (AB)
207
-

1976-11 Halter Marine, Inc. — Moss Point, Ms
Yd No: 565
Loa 56.39 Br ex - Dght 3.671
Lbp 51.49 Br md 12.20 Dpth 4.27
Welded, 1 dk

(B21B20T) Offshore Tug/Supply Ship
Ice Capable

2 oil engines reverse reduction geared to sc. shafts driving 2 FP propellers
Total Power: 2,354kW (3,200hp) 13.0kn
EMD (Electro-Motive) 16-567-C
2 x Vee 2 Stroke 16 Cy. 216 x 254 each-1177kW (1600bhp)
(Re-engined ,made 1950, Reconditioned & fitted 1976)
General Motors Corp.Electro-Motive Div.-La Grange
AuxGen: 2 x 98kW
Thrusters: 1 Thwart. FP thruster (f)
Fuel: 286.5 (d.f.)

8839548 **TOA**
JG4873 *ex* Kimitsu Maru *-2006*
-
-
-
Muroran, Hokkaido *Japan*
Official number: 131116

243
-
-

1989-12 Keihin Dock Co Ltd — Yokohama
Yd No: 216
Loa 36.20 Br ex - Dght 3.200
Lbp 31.50 Br md 9.80 Dpth 4.38
Welded, 1 dk

(B32A2ST) Tug

2 oil engines gearing integral to driving 2 Z propellers
Total Power: 2,648kW (3,600hp)
Niigata 6L28HX
2 x 4 Stroke 6 Cy. 280 x 370 each-1324kW (1800bhp)
Niigata Engineering Co Ltd-Japan

IMO / Call sign	Name / Owner	Tonnage	Class	Build	Type	Machinery
9560443 *JD3038* -	**TOA MARU** **Japan Railway Construction, Transport & Technology Agency & Toa Kisen KK** Ikous Co Ltd *Kaminoseki, Yamaguchi* *Japan* MMSI: 431001288 Official number: 141206	*749* - 1,903	Class: NK	**2010-04 Maebata Zosen Tekko K.K. — Sasebo** Yd No: 295 Loa 74.31 Br ex - Dght 4.762 Lbp 69.95 Br md 11.50 Dpth 5.25 Welded, 1 dk	**(A13B2TP) Products Tanker** Double Hull (13F) Liq: 2,156; Liq (Oil): 2,156	**2 diesel electric oil engines** driving 2 gen. each 600kW a.c Connecting to 2 elec. motors each (500kW) driving 2 FP propellers Total Power: 980kW (1,332hp) Yanmar 2 x 4 Stroke each-490kW (666bhp) Yanmar Diesel Engine Co Ltd-Japan Fuel: 60.0 (d.f.)
9179139 - -	**TOA MARU NO. 1** *ex* Tama Maru *-2008* - -	*174* - -		**1997-10 Kanagawa Zosen — Kobe** Yd No: 453 Loa 33.20 Br ex - Dght - Lbp 29.00 Br md 8.80 Dpth 3.78 Welded, 1 dk	**(B32A2ST) Tug**	**2 oil engines** Geared Integral to driving 2 Z propellers Total Power: 2,280kW (3,100hp) 14.0kn Niigata 6L25HX 2 x 4 Stroke 6 Cy. 250 x 350 each-1140kW (1550bhp) Niigata Engineering Co Ltd-Japan
9072537 *JG5156* -	**TOA MARU NO. 3** *ex* Noshiro Maru *-2011* **Tokyo Kisen KK & Toho Senpaku KK** Tokyo Kisen KK *Yokohama, Kanagawa* *Japan* Official number: 133728	*164* - -		**1993-04 Kanagawa Zosen — Kobe** Yd No: 390 Loa 38.00 Br ex - Dght - Lbp 33.50 Br md 8.40 Dpth 3.40 Welded, 1 dk	**(B32A2ST) Tug**	**2 oil engines** geared integral to driving 2 Z propellers Total Power: 2,280kW (3,100hp) 12.5kn Niigata 6L25HX 2 x 4 Stroke 6 Cy. 250 x 350 each-1140kW (1550bhp) Niigata Engineering Co Ltd-Japan
9652313 *JD3405* -	**TOA MARU NO. 5** **Japan Railway Construction, Transport & Technology Agency & Toa Kisen KK** Toa Kisen KK *Kaminoseki, Yamaguchi* *Japan* MMSI: 431003911 Official number: 141752	*749* - 1,959	Class: NK	**2012-09 Kurinoura Dockyard Co Ltd — Yawatahama EH** Yd No: 426 Loa 72.67 Br ex - Dght 4.710 Lbp 68.00 Br md 11.80 Dpth 5.20 Welded, 1 dk	**(A13B2TP) Products Tanker** Double Hull (13F) Liq: 2,156; Liq (Oil): 2,200	**1 oil engine** reduction geared to sc. shaft driving 1 FP propeller Total Power: 1,471kW (2,000hp) 12.0kn Akasaka AX33BR 1 x 4 Stroke 6 Cy. 330 x 620 1471kW (2000bhp) Akasaka Tekkosho KK (Akasaka DieselLtd)-Japan Fuel: 90.0 (d.f.)
9054004 *JG5123* -	**TOA MARU NO. 6** *ex* Suruga Maru *-2009* **Tokyo Kisen KK** - *Yokohama, Kanagawa* *Japan* Official number: 133453	*166* - -		**1992-06 Kanagawa Zosen — Kobe** Yd No: 374 Loa 38.00 Br ex - Dght - Lbp 33.50 Br md 8.40 Dpth 3.30 Welded, 1 dk	**(B32A2ST) Tug**	**2 oil engines** Geared Integral to driving 2 Z propellers Total Power: 2,280kW (3,100hp) 13.5kn Niigata 6L25HX 2 x 4 Stroke 6 Cy. 250 x 350 each-1140kW (1550bhp) Niigata Engineering Co Ltd-Japan
8419386 - -	**TOA MARU No. 7** *ex* Uraga Maru *-2001* - -	*162* - -		**1985-02 Kanagawa Zosen — Kobe** Yd No: 270 Loa 37.75 Br ex - Dght 2.601 Lbp 33.51 Br md 8.41 Dpth 3.41 Welded, 1 dk	**(B32A2ST) Tug**	**2 oil engines** Geared Integral to driving 2 Z propellers Total Power: 2,206kW (3,000hp) 12.5kn Niigata 6L25CXE 2 x 4 Stroke 6 Cy. 250 x 320 each-1103kW (1500bhp) Niigata Engineering Co Ltd-Japan
8815396 *JG4773* -	**TOA MARU NO. 8** *ex* Azuma Maru *-2003* **Tokyo Kisen KK** - *Yokohama, Kanagawa* *Japan* Official number: 130302	*167* - -		**1988-09 Kanagawa Zosen — Kobe** Yd No: 315 Loa 38.00 Br ex - Dght 2.650 Lbp 33.50 Br md 8.40 Dpth 3.41 Welded, 1 dk	**(B32A2ST) Tug**	**2 oil engines** Geared Integral to driving 2 Z propellers Total Power: 2,280kW (3,100hp) Pielstick 6PA5L255 2 x 4 Stroke 6 Cy. 255 x 270 each-1140kW (1550bhp) Niigata Engineering Co Ltd-Japan
8916762 - -	**TOA MARU No. 8** -	*498* - 1,215	Class: (NK)	**1990-04 Shitanoe Shipbuilding Co Ltd — Usuki OT** Yd No: 1108 Loa 63.88 Br ex - Dght 4.111 Lbp 60.06 Br md 10.30 Dpth 4.50 Welded, 1 dk	**(A12A2TC) Chemical Tanker** Liq: 1,230 Compartments: 8 Ta, ER	**1 oil engine** with clutches & reverse geared to sc. shaft driving 1 FP propeller Total Power: 736kW (1,001hp) 11.1kn Hanshin 6LUN30AG 1 x 4 Stroke 6 Cy. 300 x 480 736kW (1001bhp) The Hanshin Diesel Works Ltd-Japan Fuel: 45.0 (d.f.)
8994350 *E5U2746* -	**TOAMOANA NO. 88** *ex* Teraka No. 1 *-2013* *ex* Katoa No. 6 *-2010* *ex* Philip No. 1 *-2005* **Toamoana Fishery Co Ltd** - *Avatiu* *Cook Islands* MMSI: 518799000 Official number: 1833	**142** 43 -		**2004-01 Shing Sheng Fa Boat Building Co — Kaohsiung** Yd No: TN2004-1421 L reg 23.79 Br ex - Dght 2.000 Lbp - Br md 5.79 Dpth 2.35 Bonded, 1 dk	**(B11B2FV) Fishing Vessel** Hull Material: Reinforced Plastic	**1 oil engine** reduction geared to sc. shaft driving 1 Propeller Total Power: 809kW (1,100hp) 11.0kn Yanmar 12LAK (M)-STE2 1 x Vee 4 Stroke 12 Cy. 150 x 165 809kW (1100bhp) Yanmar Diesel Engine Co Ltd-Japan
8430457 *E5U2717* -	**TOAMOANA NO. 168** *ex* Yu Chan No. 201 *-2013* **Toamoana Fishery Co Ltd** - *Avatiu* *Cook Islands* MMSI: 518770000 Official number: 1806	*705* 252 -		**1987-12 Fong Kuo Shipbuilding Co Ltd — Kaohsiung** Yd No: 255 Loa 56.50 Br ex - Dght - Lbp - Br md 8.90 Dpth 3.85 Welded, 1 dk	**(B11B2FV) Fishing Vessel**	**1 oil engine** driving 1 FP propeller Total Power: 883kW (1,201hp) 12.0kn Sumiyoshi S26RG 1 x 4 Stroke 6 Cy. 260 x 470 883kW (1201bhp) Sumiyoshi Marine Diesel Co Ltd-Japan
8978368 - -	**TOAN THANG 05** - **Phuong Linh Co Ltd** - *Haiphong* *Vietnam* Official number: VN-1426-VT	**499** 308 939	Class: VR	**2001 Sea Product Technical Service & Development Co. — Vietnam** Lengthened & Deepened-2004 Loa 56.48 Br ex 8.45 Dght 3.450 Lbp 53.01 Br md 8.28 Dpth 4.25 Welded, 1 dk	**(A31A2GX) General Cargo Ship**	**1 oil engine** driving 1 Propeller Total Power: 294kW (400hp) S.K.L. 8NVD26A-2 1 x 4 Stroke 8 Cy. 180 x 260 294kW (400bhp) SKL Motoren u. Systemtechnik AG-Magdeburg
8893972 - -	**TOAN THANG 08** *ex* Quang Minh 05 *-2001* **Toan Thang Shipping Co Ltd** - *Haiphong* *Vietnam* Official number: VN-2663-VT	**280** 171 504	Class: VR	**1985-01 Ben Thuy Shipyard — Nghi Xuan** Lengthened & Deepened-2003 Loa 43.18 Br ex 7.57 Dght 2.740 Lbp 42.11 Br md 7.40 Dpth 3.40 Welded, 1 dk	**(A31A2GX) General Cargo Ship**	**1 oil engine** driving 1 FP propeller Total Power: 103kW (140hp) Yanmar 1 x 4 Stroke 103kW (140bhp) (made 1977) Yanmar Diesel Engine Co Ltd-Japan AuxGen: 1 x 3kW a.c
8986793 *3WCJ* -	**TOAN THANG 27** *ex* Hai Yen 09 *-2004* *ex* Bao Van 09 *-2004* **Thanh Hoa Victory Trade Co** - SatCom: Inmarsat C 457499969 *Haiphong* *Vietnam* MMSI: 574000170	**493** 348 900	Class: VR	**2002-09 Ben Thuy Shipyard — Nghi Xuan** Yd No: 14 Loa 53.27 Br ex 9.02 Dght 3.500 Lbp 49.50 Br md 9.00 Dpth 4.20 Welded, 1 dk	**(A31A2GX) General Cargo Ship**	**1 oil engine** geared to sc. shaft driving 1 FP propeller Total Power: 300kW (408hp) Chinese Std. Type Z6170ZL 1 x 4 Stroke 6 Cy. 170 x 200 300kW (408bhp) (new engine 2007) Zibo Diesel Engine Factory-China
9022570 - -	**TOAN THINH 01** *ex* Hoang Gia 01 *-2004* *ex* Quang Huy 04 *-2004* **Toan Thinh Co Ltd** - *Haiphong* *Vietnam*	**291** 153 456	Class: VR	**1994-01 LISEMCO — Haiphong** Loa 43.50 Br ex 7.64 Dght 2.850 Lbp 40.50 Br md 7.32 Dpth 3.45 Welded, 1 dk	**(A31A2GX) General Cargo Ship** Grain: 564; Bale: 512 Compartments: 2 Ho, ER 2 Ha: (7.5 x 4.6)ER (7.0 x 4.6)	**1 oil engine** reduction geared to sc. shaft driving 1 FP propeller Total Power: 147kW (200hp) 9.0kn S.K.L. 6NVD26-2 1 x 4 Stroke 6 Cy. 180 x 260 147kW (200bhp) (made 1969, fitted 1994) VEB Schwermaschinenbau "KarlLiebknecht" (SKL)-Magdeburg
9023043 - -	**TOAN THINH 27** *ex* Truong An 27 *-2009* *ex* Minh Khai 27 *-2003* **Toan Thinh Co Ltd** - *Haiphong* *Vietnam*	**499** 338 944	Class: VR	**2003-06 Hoang Anh Shipbuilding Industry Joint Stock Co. — Vietnam** Yd No: THB-05 Loa 54.87 Br ex 9.22 Dght 3.350 Lbp 52.20 Br md 9.00 Dpth 4.05 Welded, 1 dk	**(A31A2GX) General Cargo Ship** Compartments: 2 Ho, ER 2 Ha: (12.0 x 5.4)ER (13.0 x 5.4)	**1 oil engine** driving 1 FP propeller Total Power: 315kW (428hp) 10.0kn S.K.L. 6VD36/24A-1 1 x 4 Stroke 6 Cy. 240 x 360 315kW (428bhp) (made 1990, fitted 2003) VEB Schwermaschinenbau "KarlLiebknecht" (SKL)-Magdeburg
8509674 *YYV2158* -	**TOAS** - **PDV Marina SA** - *Maracaibo* *Venezuela* Official number: AJZL-13929	**224** 67 -	Class: (LR) ✠ Classed LR until 16/3/05	**1988-06 Diques y Ast. Nac. C.A. (DIANCA) — Puerto Cabello** Yd No: 169 Loa 32.95 Br ex - Dght 4.401 Lbp 28.86 Br md 9.52 Dpth 4.91 Welded, 1 dk	**(B32A2ST) Tug**	**2 oil engines** with clutches, flexible couplings & sr geared to sc. shafts driving 2 CP propellers Total Power: 3,088kW (4,198hp) 12.0kn Kromhout 9FHD240 2 x 4 Stroke 9 Cy. 240 x 260 each-1544kW (2099bhp) Stork Werkspoor Diesel BV-Netherlands AuxGen: 2 x 90kW 440V 60Hz a.c Fuel: 182.0 (d.f.)

8738445 **TOB 01** **192** Class: KI
YDA6124 58
- **PT Manna Line International** -
-
Samarinda *Indonesia*
MMSI: 525015856

2008-05 PT Syukur Bersaudara — Samarinda **(B32A2ST) Tug**
Loa 29.50 Br ex - Dght 3.060
Lbp 27.37 Br md 8.15 Dpth 3.60
Welded, 1 dk

2 oil engines reduction geared to sc. shafts driving 2 FP propellers
Total Power: 1,220kW (1,658hp)
Yanmar 6AYM-ETE
2 x 4 Stroke 6 Cy. 155 x 180 each-610kW (829bhp)
Yanmar Diesel Engine Co Ltd-Japan
AuxGen: 2 x 88kW 380/220V a.c

8742836 **TOB 02** **219** Class: KI
YDA6215 66
- **PT Manna Line International** -
-
Samarinda *Indonesia*
MMSI: 525015857

2008-12 PT Syukur Bersaudara — Samarinda **(B32A2ST) Tug**
Loa 29.50 Br ex - Dght 3.000
Lbp 27.60 Br md 8.10 Dpth 3.60
Welded, 1 dk

2 oil engines reduction geared to sc. shafts driving 2 FP propellers
Total Power: 1,220kW (1,658hp)
Yanmar 6AYM-ETE
2 x 4 Stroke 6 Cy. 155 x 180 each-610kW (829bhp)
Yanmar Diesel Engine Co Ltd-Japan
AuxGen: 2 x 88kW 380V a.c

8738811 **TOB 03** **183** Class: KI
YDA6228 55
- **PT Manna Line International** -
-
Samarinda *Indonesia*
MMSI: 525015858

2009-04 C.V. Karya Lestari Industri — Samarinda **(B32A2ST) Tug**
Loa 27.50 Br ex - Dght -
Lbp 25.92 Br md 7.50 Dpth 3.05
Welded, 1 dk

2 oil engines reduction geared to sc. shafts driving 2 FP propellers
Total Power: 1,654kW (2,248hp)
Cummins QST30-G10
2 x Vee 4 Stroke 12 Cy. 140 x 165 each-827kW (1124bhp)
Cummins Engine Co Inc-USA
AuxGen: 2 x 88kW 400V a.c

8743646 **TOB 05** **236** Class: KI
YDA6234 71
- **PT Manna Line International** -
-
Samarinda *Indonesia*
MMSI: 525015859
Official number: 2009IIK NO.4640/L

2009-10 P.T. Rejeki Abadi Sakti — Samarinda **(B32A2ST) Tug**
Loa 30.10 Br ex - Dght -
Lbp 28.51 Br md 8.60 Dpth 3.75
Welded, 1 dk

2 oil engines reduction geared to sc. shafts driving 2 Propellers
Total Power: 1,716kW (2,334hp)
Mitsubishi S12A2-MPTK
2 x Vee 4 Stroke 12 Cy. 150 x 160 each-858kW (1167bhp)
Mitsubishi Heavy Industries Ltd-Japan
AuxGen: 2 x 35kW 415V a.c

8740759 **TOB 07** **216** Class: KI
YDA6251 65
- **PT Manna Line International** -
-
Samarinda *Indonesia*
MMSI: 525015860

2009-01 P.T. Rejeki Abadi Sakti — Samarinda **(B32A2ST) Tug**
Loa 28.40 Br ex - Dght -
Lbp 27.26 Br md 8.10 Dpth 3.60
Welded, 1 dk

2 oil engines reduction geared to sc. shafts driving 2 FP propellers
Total Power: 1,220kW (1,658hp)
Yanmar 6AYM-ETE
2 x 4 Stroke 6 Cy. 155 x 180 each-610kW (829bhp)
Yanmar Diesel Engine Co Ltd-Japan
AuxGen: 2 x 35kW 415V a.c

8629163 **TOB 08** **234** Class: KI
YDA6604 71
- **PT Manna Line International** -
-
Samarinda *Indonesia*
MMSI: 525015861
Official number: 2010IIKNo.5151/L

2010-03 PT Mangkupalas Mitra Makmur — Samarinda **(B32A2ST) Tug**
Loa 30.16 Br ex - Dght 2.810
Lbp 28.67 Br md 8.50 Dpth 3.75
Welded, 1 dk

2 oil engines reduction geared to sc. shafts driving 2 FP propellers
Total Power: 1,220kW (1,658hp)
Mitsubishi S6R2-MPTK
2 x 4 Stroke 6 Cy. 170 x 220 each-610kW (829bhp)
Mitsubishi Heavy Industries Ltd-Japan
AuxGen: 2 x 85kW 380V a.c

8749810 **TOB 09** **273** Class: KI
YDA6505 82
- **PT Manna Line International** -
-
Samarinda *Indonesia*
MMSI: 525015862

2010-01 PT Syukur Bersaudara — Samarinda **(B32A2ST) Tug**
Loa 31.49 Br ex - Dght 2.830
Lbp 29.61 Br md 8.50 Dpth 3.80
Welded, 1 dk

2 oil engines reduction geared to sc. shafts driving 2 Propellers
Total Power: 2,206kW (3,000hp)
Yanmar 16LAK (M)-STE1
2 x Vee 4 Stroke 16 Cy. 150 x 165 each-1103kW (1500bhp)
Yanmar Diesel Engine Co Ltd-Japan
AuxGen: 2 x 50kW 400V a.c

8749183 **TOB 10** **234** Class: KI
YDA6589 71
- **PT Manna Line International** -
-
Samarinda *Indonesia*
MMSI: 525015863
Official number: 2010IIKNo.5188/L

2010-12 PT Mangkupalas Mitra Makmur — Samarinda **(B32A2ST) Tug**
Loa 29.00 Br ex - Dght 2.890
Lbp 26.58 Br md 8.60 Dpth 3.75
Welded, 1 dk

2 oil engines reduction geared to sc. shafts driving 2 Propellers
Total Power: 1,220kW (1,658hp)
Mitsubishi S6R2-MPTK
2 x 4 Stroke 6 Cy. 170 x 220 each-610kW (829bhp)
Mitsubishi Heavy Industries Ltd-Japan
AuxGen: 2 x 60kW 280V a.c

8629175 **TOB 11** **215** Class: (KI)
YDA6640 65
- **PT Manna Line International** -
-
Samarinda *Indonesia*
MMSI: 525015864
Official number: 2010IIKNo.5428/L

2010-12 CV KBS Marine — Tenggarong **(B32A2ST) Tug**
Loa 28.80 Br ex - Dght 2.810
Lbp 27.46 Br md 8.00 Dpth 3.75
Welded, 1 dk

2 oil engines reduction geared to sc. shafts driving 2 Propellers
Total Power: 1,686kW (2,292hp)
Yanmar 12LAA-UTE1
2 x Vee 4 Stroke 12 Cy. 148 x 165 each-843kW (1146bhp)
Yanmar Diesel Engine Co Ltd-Japan

8629187 **TOB 12** **217** Class: (KI)
YDA6682 66
- **PT Manna Line International** -
-
Samarinda *Indonesia*
MMSI: 525015865
Official number: 2010IIKNO.5448/L

2010-12 CV KBS Marine — Tenggarong **(B32A2ST) Tug**
Loa 28.88 Br ex - Dght 2.700
Lbp 27.12 Br md 8.00 Dpth 3.60
Welded, 1 dk

2 oil engines reduction geared to sc. shafts driving 2 Propellers
Total Power: 1,686kW (2,292hp)
Yanmar 12LAA-UTE1
2 x Vee 4 Stroke 12 Cy. 148 x 165 each-843kW (1146bhp)
Yanmar Diesel Engine Co Ltd-Japan

9675286 **TOB 20** **165** Class: KI (Class contemplated)
- 50
- **PT Manna Line International** -
-
Batam *Indonesia*
MMSI: 525005159
Official number: 2012 PPm No. 2408/L

2012-07 PT Manna Shipyard — Batam **(B32A2ST) Tug**
Yd No: H-0001-MS
Loa 26.60 Br ex 7.60 Dght 2.400
Lbp 24.82 Br md 7.00 Dpth 3.20
Welded, 1 dk

2 oil engines reduction geared to sc. shafts driving 2 FP propellers
Total Power: 1,220kW (1,658hp)
Mitsubishi S6R2-MPTK
2 x 4 Stroke 6 Cy. 170 x 220 each-610kW (829bhp)
Mitsubishi Heavy Industries Ltd-Japan

9675298 **TOB 21** **165** Class: KI (Class contemplated)
- 50
- **PT Manna Line International** -
-
Batam *Indonesia*
MMSI: 525005160
Official number: 2012 PPm No. 2413/L

2012-07 PT Manna Shipyard — Batam **(B32A2ST) Tug**
Yd No: H-0003-MS
Loa 26.60 Br ex 7.60 Dght 2.400
Lbp 24.82 Br md 7.00 Dpth 3.20
Welded, 1 dk

2 oil engines reduction geared to sc. shafts driving 2 FP propellers
Total Power: 1,220kW (1,658hp)
Mitsubishi S6R2-MPTK
2 x 4 Stroke 6 Cy. 170 x 220 each-610kW (829bhp)
Mitsubishi Heavy Industries Ltd-Japan

8662579 **TOB 22** **165** Class: KI
YDA3271 50
- **PT Manna Line International** -
-
Batam *Indonesia*
MMSI: 525007203
Official number: 2012PPM NO. 2636/L

2012-10 PT Manna Shipyard — Batam **(B32A2ST) Tug**
Yd No: H-0008-MS
Loa 26.60 Br ex 8.00 Dght 2.000
Lbp 24.76 Br md 7.60 Dpth 3.20
Welded, 1 dk

2 oil engines reduction geared to sc. shafts driving 2 Directional propellers
Total Power: 1,220kW (1,658hp)
Mitsubishi S6R2-MPTK
2 x 4 Stroke 6 Cy. 170 x 220 each-610kW (829bhp)
Mitsubishi Heavy Industries Ltd-Japan

8662581 **TOB 23** **165** Class: KI
- 50
- **PT Manna Line International** -
-
Batam *Indonesia*

2012-11 PT Manna Shipyard — Batam **(B32A2ST) Tug**
Yd No: H-0009-MS
Loa 26.60 Br ex 8.00 Dght 2.000
Lbp 24.76 Br md 7.60 Dpth 3.20
Welded, 1 dk

2 oil engines reduction geared to sc. shafts driving 2 Directional propellers
Total Power: 1,220kW (1,658hp)
Mitsubishi S6R2-MPTK
2 x 4 Stroke 6 Cy. 170 x 220 each-610kW (829bhp)
Mitsubishi Heavy Industries Ltd-Japan

9677624 **TOB 25** **165** Class: KI
YDA3238 50
- **PT Manna Line International** -
-
Batam *Indonesia*
MMSI: 525007114
Official number: 2012 PPm No. 2553/L

2012-09 PT Manna Shipyard — Batam **(B32A2ST) Tug**
Yd No: H-0004-MS
Loa 26.60 Br ex - Dght 2.400
Lbp - Br md 7.60 Dpth 3.70
Welded, 1 dk

2 oil engines reduction geared to sc. shafts driving 2 FP propellers
Total Power: 1,220kW (1,658hp)
Mitsubishi S6R2-MPTK
2 x 4 Stroke 6 Cy. 170 x 220 each-610kW (829bhp)
Mitsubishi Heavy Industries Ltd-Japan

9677636 **TOB 26** **165** Class: KI
YDA3239 50
- **PT Manna Line International** -
-
Batam *Indonesia*
Official number: 2012 PPM NO. 2558/L

2012-09 PT Manna Shipyard — Batam **(B32A2ST) Tug**
Yd No: H-0006-MS
Loa 26.60 Br ex - Dght 2.400
Lbp - Br md 7.60 Dpth 3.70
Welded, 1 dk

2 oil engines reduction geared to sc. shafts driving 2 FP propellers
Total Power: 1,220kW (1,658hp)
Mitsubishi S6R2-MPTK
2 x 4 Stroke 6 Cy. 170 x 220 each-610kW (829bhp)
Mitsubishi Heavy Industries Ltd-Japan

9304655 *H9DW* -	**TOBA** **Toba Shipholding SA** Nippon Yusen Kabushiki Kaisha (NYK Line) SatCom: Inmarsat C 435235710 *Panama* *Panama* MMSI: 352357000 Official number: 3037105B	**160,068** 97,584 299,980 T/cm 183.2	Class: NK	**2004-10 Imabari Shipbuilding Co Ltd — Saijo EH (Saijo Shipyard)** Yd No: 8022 Loa 332.99 (BB) Br ex 60.04 Dght 20.556 Lbp 324.00 Br md 60.00 Dpth 29.00 Welded, 1 dk	**(A13A2TV) Crude Oil Tanker** Double Hull (13F) Liq: 335,109; Liq (Oil): 335,423 Compartments: 5 Ta, 10 Wing Ta, 2 Wing Slop Ta, ER 3 Cargo Pump (s): 3x5500m^3/hr Manifold: Bow/CM: 164.2m	**1 oil engine** driving 1 FP propeller Total Power: 27,960kW (38,014hp) 15.5kn MAN-B&W 8S80MC-C 1 x 2 Stroke 8 Cy. 800 x 3200 27960kW (38014bhp) Mitsui Engineering & Shipbuilding CLtd-Japan AuxGen: 2 x 1324kW 440/100V 60Hz a.c, 1 x 1200kW 440/100V 60Hz a.c Fuel: 640.5 (d.f.) 8369.0 (r.f.) 100.0pd
9140308 *JH3408* -	**TOBA MARU** **Isewan Ferry KK (Isewan Ferry Co Ltd)** - *Toba, Mie* *Japan* MMSI: 431200708 Official number: 134408	*2,399* - 574		**1996-06 Naikai Zosen Corp — Onomichi HS (Setoda Shipyard)** Yd No: 610 Loa 77.37 Br ex 14.02 Dght 3.750 Lbp 72.00 Br md 14.00 Dpth 4.90 Welded, 1 dk	**(A36A2PR) Passenger/Ro-Ro Ship (Vehicles)** Passengers: unberthed: 684 Bow door/ramp Stern door/ramp	**2 oil engines** driving 2 FP propellers Total Power: 2,942kW (4,000hp) 16.3kn Niigata 6M34AFT 2 x 4 Stroke 6 Cy. 340 x 620 each-1471kW (2000bhp) Niigata Engineering Co Ltd-Japan AuxGen: 2 x 440kW 445V a.c Fuel: 87.0 (d.f.) 10.5pd
9087960 *JH3304* -	**TOBA MARU** **Toba Shosen Koutosenmon Gakko** - SatCom: Inmarsat C 443158410 *Toba, Mie* *Japan* Official number: 134371	*244* - -		**1994-08 Mitsui Eng. & SB. Co. Ltd. — Tamano** Yd No: 1409 Loa 40.00 Br ex - Dght 2.800 Lbp 35.00 Br md 8.00 Dpth 3.30 Welded, 1 dk	**(B34K2QT) Training Ship**	**1 oil engine** driving 1 CP propeller Total Power: 956kW (1,300hp) 13.8kn Yanmar MF29-UT 1 x 4 Stroke 6 Cy. 290 x 520 956kW (1300bhp) Yanmar Diesel Engine Co Ltd-Japan AuxGen: 2 x 180kW a.c Thrusters: 1 Thwart. FP thruster (f)
7018800 *LW8174* -	**TOBA MARU** *ex* Sanko Maru No. 18 *-1989* *ex* Koei Maru No. 18 *-1979* **Perla Marina SA** Continental Armadores de Pesca SA (CONARPESA) SatCom: Inmarsat A 1540212 *Quequen* *Argentina* MMSI: 701000917 Official number: 0241	**391** 205 533	Class: (BV)	**1969 Miho Zosensho K.K. — Shimizu** Yd No: 720 Loa 54.79 Br ex 8.72 Dght 3.302 Lbp 49.00 Br md 8.69 Dpth 3.87 Welded, 1 dk	**(B11B2FV) Fishing Vessel**	**1 oil engine** driving 1 FP propeller Total Power: 919kW (1,249hp) Niigata 6M33HS 1 x 4 Stroke 6 Cy. 330 x 520 919kW (1249bhp) Niigata Engineering Co Ltd-Japan
8000018 *LW4562* -	**TOBA PEGASO** **Toba SAMCFI** Compania Naviera Horamar SA SatCom: Inmarsat C 470181552 *Buenos Aires* *Argentina* MMSI: 701000568 Official number: 02388	*3,757* - 9,010 T/cm 22.0	Class: (NV) (RI) (BV)	**1982-03 Astilleros Principe y Menghi S.A. — Avellaneda** Yd No: 151 Loa 119.82 Br ex 20.02 Dght 5.792 Lbp 114.51 Br md 20.01 Dpth 8.01 Welded, 1 dk	**(A13B2TP) Products Tanker** Single Hull Liq: 10,200; Liq (Oil): 10,200 Part Cargo Heating Coils Compartments: 12 Ta, ER	**2 oil engines** reduction geared to sc. shafts driving 2 FP propellers Total Power: 3,118kW (4,240hp) 12.0kn Alpha 8SL28L-VO 2 x 4 Stroke 8 Cy. 280 x 320 each-1559kW (2120bhp) Hitachi Zosen Corp-Japan
7619800 *WF7742* -	**TOBACCO POINTE** *ex* Bay Prince *-2004* *ex* Heron *-2004* *ex* Sharon Lee *-1972* **Blaha Towing Co LLC** - *Norfolk, VA* *United States of America* Official number: 268390	*167* 74 -	Class: (AB)	**1954 Calumet Shipyard & Dry Dock Co. — Chicago, Il** Yd No: 220 Loa - Br ex 7.93 Dght 3.201 Lbp 27.06 Br md 7.88 Dpth 3.54 Welded, 1 dk	**(B32A2ST) Tug**	**1 diesel electric oil engine** Connecting to 1 elec. Motor driving 1 FP propeller Total Power: 870kW (1,183hp) General Motors 12-278A 1 x Vee 2 Stroke 12 Cy. 222 x 267 870kW (1183bhp) General Motors Corp-USA Fuel: 83.5 (d.f.)
7814618 - -	**TOBAGO TRANSPORT** *ex* Transport Tide *-2008* *ex* Ensco Transport *-2003* *ex* Gulfstream II *-1989* *ex* Clipper Acapulco *-1989* **Tobago Marine Transport Co Ltd** - *Port of Spain* *Trinidad & Tobago*	**649** 194	Class: AB	**1979-03 Houma Welders Inc — Houma LA** Yd No: 61 Lengthened-1989 Loa - Br ex - Dght 3.752 Lbp 52.28 Br md 11.60 Dpth 4.35 Welded, 1 dk	**(B21A20S) Platform Supply Ship**	**2 oil engines** reverse reduction geared to sc. shafts driving 2 FP propellers Total Power: 1,368kW (1,860hp) 12.0kn G.M. (Detroit Diesel) 16V-149 2 x Vee 2 Stroke 16 Cy. 146 x 146 each-684kW (930bhp) General Motors Detroit DieselAllison Divn-USA AuxGen: 2 x 75kW Thrusters: 1 Thwart. FP thruster (f)
8819421 *EA8838* -	**TOBALINA** **Julio Pernas Otero & Juan Jose Pernas Pedreira** - *Gijon* *Spain* Official number: 3-2176/	**147** 44 88		**1989-02 Astilleros Armon SA — Navia** Yd No: 187 Loa 26.30 Br ex 7.01 Dght - Lbp 22.26 Br md 7.01 Dpth 5.31 Welded	**(B11B2FV) Fishing Vessel** Ins: 110	**1 oil engine** with clutches, flexible couplings & reduction geared to sc. shaft driving 1 FP propeller Total Power: 459kW (624hp) 10.0kn Caterpillar 3412TA 1 x Vee 4 Stroke 12 Cy. 137 x 152 459kW (624bhp) Caterpillar Inc-USA
8945232 *DYXM* -	**TOBI** *ex* Manuel D. Remo *-1991* **DMC Construction Equipment Resources Inc** - *Batangas* *Philippines* Official number: ZAM200116	*352* 220 -		**1978-01 at Zamboanga** L reg 45.12 Br ex - Dght - Lbp - Br md 10.98 Dpth 1.09 Welded, 1 dk	**(A35D2RL) Landing Craft**	**1 oil engine** geared to sc. shaft driving 1 FP propeller Total Power: 500kW (680hp) Caterpillar 1 x 4 Stroke 500kW (680bhp) Caterpillar Tractor Co-USA
7813341 *V5TO* -	**TOBIAS HAINYEKO** *ex* Havornen *-1993* **Government of The Republic of Namibia (Ministry of Fisheries & Marine Resources)** - SatCom: Inmarsat M 665911524 *Luderitz* *Namibia* Official number: 93LE042	**652** 195 160	Class: (NV)	**1979-06 Frederikshavn Vaerft A/S — Frederikshavn** Yd No: 384 Loa 49.99 Br ex - Dght 3.239 Lbp 45.83 Br md 10.51 Dpth 8.11 Welded, 1 dk	**(B12D2FP) Fishery Patrol Vessel**	**2 oil engines** driving 2 FP propellers Total Power: 3,648kW (4,960hp) 18.0kn Alpha 16V23L-VO 2 x Vee 4 Stroke 16 Cy. 225 x 300 each-1824kW (2480bhp) Alpha Diesel A/S-Denmark AuxGen: 2 x 134kW 440V 60Hz a.c
8210508 *DUA2635* -	**TOBIAS REYNALD** *ex* Kaio Maru No. 88 *-1996* **Trans-Pacific Journey Fishing Corp** - SatCom: Inmarsat C 454899040 *Manila* *Philippines* MMSI: 548004100 Official number: MNLD007561	*470* 240 661		**1982-08 Miho Zosensho K.K. — Shimizu** Yd No: 1225 Loa 56.01 (BB) Br ex - Dght 4.495 Lbp 50.02 Br md 11.41 Dpth 6.86 Welded, 1 dk	**(B11B2FV) Fishing Vessel** Ins: 805	**1 oil engine** driving 1 CP propeller Total Power: 1,618kW (2,200hp) 15.3kn Akasaka A34 1 x 4 Stroke 6 Cy. 340 x 660 1618kW (2200bhp) Akasaka Tekkosho KK (Akasaka DieselLtd)-Japan AuxGen: 3 x 300kW 445V a.c
9667904 *WDG8104* -	**TOBIE EYMARD** **Glencoe Inc** Offshore Marine Contractors Inc *New Orleans, LA* *United States of America* MMSI: 367574050 Official number: 1246620	**743** 222 -		**2013-07 Halimar Shipyard LLC — Morgan City, La** Yd No: 172 Loa 41.80 Br ex 20.70 Dght 2.290 Lbp - Br md - Dpth 3.05 Welded, 1 dk	**(B22A2ZM) Offshore Construction Vessel, jack up** Cranes: 1x175t,1x50t	**2 oil engines** reduction geared to sc. shaft driving 2 Propellers Total Power: 1,640kW (2,230hp) 6.0kn Caterpillar C32 1 x Vee 4 Stroke 12 Cy. 145 x 162 820kW (1115bhp) Caterpillar Inc-USA AuxGen: 2 x 199kW 60Hz a.c
9429364 *OUPS* HG 306	**TOBIS** **Kjaersgaard Hirtshals A/S** - *Hirtshals* *Denmark* MMSI: 219013001 Official number: H1623	**574** - 300		**2009-05 Safe Co Ltd Sp z oo — Gdynia** (Hull) **2009-05 Karstensens Skibsvaerft A/S — Skagen** Yd No: 406 Loa 39.95 (BB) Br ex - Dght 5.000 Lbp 34.50 Br md 10.00 Dpth 6.70 Welded, 1 dk	**(B11A2FS) Stern Trawler**	**1 oil engine** reduction geared to sc. shaft driving 1 CP propeller Total Power: 1,200kW (1,632hp) A.B.C. 6DZC 1 x 4 Stroke 6 Cy. 256 x 310 1200kW (1632bhp) Anglo Belgian Corp NV (ABC)-Belgium AuxGen: 2 x 220kW a.c Thrusters: 1 Tunnel thruster (f)
9641998 *JD3098* -	**TOBISHIMA** **Sakata Teiki Koro Jigyosho** - *Sakata, Yamagata* *Japan* MMSI: 431001583 Official number: 141291	*253* - -		**2010-06 Setouchi Craft Co Ltd — Onomichi** Yd No: 282 Loa 39.41 Br ex - Dght - Lbp 36.00 Br md 10.00 Dpth 3.80 Welded, 1 dk	**(A37B2PS) Passenger Ship** Hull Material: Aluminium Alloy Passengers: unberthed: 230	**2 oil engines** reduction geared to sc. shafts driving 2 Propellers Total Power: 3,480kW (4,732hp) 25.0kn M.T.U. 12V4000M70 2 x Vee 4 Stroke 12 Cy. 165 x 190 each-1740kW (2366bhp) MTU Friedrichshafen GmbH-Friedrichshafen
9145736 *JM6524* -	**TOBIUME MARU** **Dokai Marine Systems Ltd** - *Fukuoka, Fukuoka* *Japan* MMSI: 431600485 Official number: 134647	*194* - -		**1996-03 Kanagawa Zosen — Kobe** Yd No: 429 Loa 33.30 (BB) Br ex - Dght - Lbp 29.00 Br md 9.20 Dpth 4.20 Welded, 1 dk	**(B32A2ST) Tug**	**2 oil engines** reduction geared to sc. shafts driving 2 FP propellers Total Power: 2,648kW (3,600hp) Niigata 6L28HX 2 x 4 Stroke 6 Cy. 280 x 370 each-1324kW (1800bhp) Niigata Engineering Co Ltd-Japan

IMO / Call sign	Name / Owner	Tonnage	Class	Builder / Dimensions	Type	Machinery
7330868 - -	**TOBIUO No. 2** **Adachi Shipping** - *Chinese Taipei*	*134* 71 13	Class: (CR)	**1973**-09 **Hitachi Zosen Corp — Kawasaki KN** Yd No: 117053 Loa 27.54 Br ex 10.67 Dght 1.347 Lbp 26.34 Br md 5.80 Dpth 3.76 Riveted\Welded, 1 dk	**(A37B2PS) Passenger Ship** Passengers: unberthed: 133	**2 oil engines** driving 2 FP propellers Total Power: 1,618kW (2,200hp) 34.0kn M.T.U. 12V493TY70 2 x Vee 4 Stroke 12 Cy. 175 x 205 each-809kW (1100bhp) Ikegai Tekkosho-Japan
8603391 *UBZG2* -	**TOBOL** *ex* Solombala *-2011* *ex* Nord *-2008* *ex* Olma *-2002* *ex* Kapitan Ponomarev *-1999* *ex* Kapitan Ponomaryov *-1997* **Sakhalin Shipping Co (SASCO)** - *Kholmsk* *Russia* MMSI: 273351910	**6,395** 2,864 7,850	Class: RS (BV)	**1990**-02 **Stocznia Gdanska SA — Gdansk** Yd No: B352/06 Loa 131.60 Br ex 19.30 Dght 7.000 Lbp 122.00 Br md 19.30 Dpth 8.80 Welded, 1 dk	**(A31A2GX) General Cargo Ship** Grain: 10,076; Bale: 9,570 TEU 302 C. 302/20' Compartments: 4 Ho, ER 4 Ha: (12.6 x 10.3) (12.6 x 15.3)2 (18.9 x 15.3)ER Cranes: 4x12.5t Ice Capable	**1 oil engine** driving 1 FP propeller Total Power: 4,690kW (6,377hp) 14.6kn B&W 7L45GBE 1 x 2 Stroke 7 Cy. 450 x 1200 4690kW (6377bhp) Stocznia Gdanska SA-Poland AuxGen: 3 x 428kW 500V 50Hz a.c Fuel: 100.0 (d.f.) 710.0 (r.f.)
8407632 *EROW* -	**TOBOL** *ex* Mithat Vardal *-2011* **Toshkent Shipping Corp** AzovTransTerminal Ltd *Giurgiulesti* *Moldova* MMSI: 214181523	**1,581** 660 2,393	Class: RS (AB) (BV)	**1986**-08 **Hidrodinamik A.S. — Tuzla** Yd No: 21 Loa 77.32 Br ex - Dght 4.893 Lbp 70.01 Br md 12.22 Dpth 5.80 Welded, 1 dk	**(A12D2LV) Vegetable Oil Tanker** Liq: 2,510 Compartments: 10 Ta, ER	**1 oil engine** driving 1 FP propeller Total Power: 809kW (1,100hp) 11.5kn S.K.L. 8NVD48A-2U 1 x 4 Stroke 8 Cy. 320 x 480 809kW (1100bhp) VEB Schwermaschinenbau "KarlLiebknecht" (SKL)-Magdeburg AuxGen: 2 x 120kW a.c, 1 x 32kW a.c, 1 x 28kW a.c
9384631 *UPM* -	**TOBOL** **Raiffeisen Leasing Kazakhstan LLP** JSC NMSC Kazmortransflot *Aqtau* *Kazakhstan* MMSI: 436000065	**149** 44 123	Class: RS	**2006**-04 **Song Cam Shipyard — Haiphong** Yd No: 7704 Loa 24.50 Br ex - Dght 2.500 Lbp 23.50 Br md 7.60 Dpth 3.20 Welded, 1 dk	**(B32A2ST) Tug**	**2 oil engines** reduction geared to sc. shafts driving 2 FP propellers Total Power: 882kW (1,200hp) 11.0kn Daewoo V180TIH 2 x Vee 4 Stroke 10 Cy. 128 x 142 each-441kW (600bhp) Doosan Infracore Co Ltd-South Korea AuxGen: 2 x 68kW Fuel: 59.0 (d.f.)
9402407 *UBUE9* -	**TOBOY** - **LUKoil-Trans Co Ltd** - *Kaliningrad* *Russia* MMSI: 273348020	**4,406** 1,321 1,930	Class: RS	**2008**-08 **Keppel Singmarine Pte Ltd — Singapore** Yd No: 327 Loa 81.60 Br ex - Dght 9.300 Lbp 73.30 Br md 18.50 Dpth 11.20 Welded, 1 dk	**(B21B20A) Anchor Handling Tug Supply** Cranes: 1x10t Ice Capable	**3 diesel electric oil engines** driving 3 gen. each 4150kW a.c Connecting to 2 elec. motors each (5200kW) driving 2 Azimuth electric drive units Total Power: 12,960kW (17,619hp) 14.0kn Wartsila 9L32 3 x 4 Stroke 9 Cy. 320 x 400 each-4320kW (5873bhp) Wartsila Finland Oy-Finland AuxGen: 1 x 791kW a.c, 1 x 320kW a.c Thrusters: 2 Tunnel thruster (f) Fuel: 1648.0
8956671 *MYXY7* TN 2	**TOBRACH N** *ex* Solway Ranger *-2005* **TN Trawlers Ltd** - *Troon* *United Kingdom* MMSI: 232003852 Official number: C16633	*146* 83 -		**1999 Hepworth Shipyard Ltd — Hull** Loa 23.07 Br ex - Dght 3.200 Lbp - Br md 7.00 Dpth 3.50 Welded, 1 dk	**(B11B2FV) Fishing Vessel**	**1 oil engine** reduction geared to sc. shaft driving 1 FP propeller Total Power: 493kW (670hp) Caterpillar 3412TA 1 x Vee 4 Stroke 12 Cy. 137 x 152 493kW (670bhp) Caterpillar Inc-USA AuxGen: 1 x 80kW 415V a.c Fuel: 17.5 (d.f.)
9239989 *A8DH4* -	**TOCCATA** **Thisbe Maritime Co Ltd** Laurin Maritime (America) Inc *Monrovia* *Liberia* MMSI: 636012069 Official number: 12069	**26,914** 14,288 46,764 T/cm 52.8	Class: NV	**2004**-02 **Brodotrogir dd - Shipyard Trogir — Trogir** Yd No: 305 Loa 182.90 (BB) Br ex 32.21 Dght 12.180 Lbp 176.75 Br md 32.20 Dpth 17.10 Welded, 1 dk	**(A12B2TR) Chemical/Products Tanker** Double Hull (13F) Liq: 53,900; Liq (Oil): 53,900 Compartments: 14 Wing Ta, 2 Wing Slop Ta, ER 14 Cargo Pump (s): 6x400m³/hr, 8x250m³/hr Manifold: Bow/CM: 91.5m	**2 oil engines** geared to sc. shaft driving 1 CP propeller Total Power: 7,700kW (10,468hp) 14.5kn MaK 8M32C 2 x 4 Stroke 8 Cy. 320 x 480 each-3850kW (5234bhp) Caterpillar Motoren GmbH & Co. KG-Germany AuxGen: 2 x a.c, 1 x a.c
9477725 *9V8400* -	**TOCHO** **FT Logistics Pte Ltd** Fujitrans Corp *Singapore* *Singapore* MMSI: 564352000 Official number: 395727	**28,755** 8,627 6,220	Class: NK	**2010**-10 **Mitsubishi Heavy Industries Ltd. — Shimonoseki** Yd No: 1140 Loa 165.00 (BB) Br ex - Dght 6.522 Lbp 157.00 Br md 27.60 Dpth 24.15 Welded, 1 dk	**(A35B2RV) Vehicles Carrier** Quarter stern door/ramp (p. a.) Len: 25.00 Wid: 6.00 Swl: 45 Quarter stern door/ramp (s. a.) Len: 25.00 Wid: 6.00 Swl: 45 Cars: 2,021	**1 oil engine** driving 1 FP propeller Total Power: 11,935kW (16,227hp) 21.0kn Mitsubishi 7UEC52LSE 1 x 2 Stroke 7 Cy. 520 x 2000 11935kW (16227bhp) Mitsubishi Heavy Industries Ltd-Japan AuxGen: 2 x 1150kW a.c Thrusters: 1 Tunnel thruster (f) Fuel: 1543.0 (r.f.)
9373292 *CB9283* -	**TOCONAO** **CPT Empresas Maritimas SA** *Valparaiso* *Chile* MMSI: 725003760 Official number: 3159	**315** 93 162	Class: LR ✠ **100A1** SS 08/2011 tug ✠ **LMC** Eq.Ltr: F; Cable: 275.0/19.0 U2 (a)	**2006**-08 **Guangdong Hope Yue Shipbuilding Industry Ltd — Guangzhou GD** Yd No: 2138 Loa 30.50 Br ex 10.30 Dght 3.500 Lbp 27.20 Br md 9.80 Dpth 4.50 Welded, 1 dk	**(B32A2ST) Tug**	**2 oil engines** gearing integral to driving 2 Z propellers Total Power: 2,984kW (4,058hp) 12.8kn Caterpillar 3516B 2 x Vee 4 Stroke 16 Cy. 170 x 190 each-1492kW (2029bhp) Caterpillar Inc-USA AuxGen: 2 x 84kW 416V 50Hz a.c Fuel: 112.0
8965696 *CB3342* -	**TOCONAO II** **Pesquera Indo SA** - *Valparaiso* *Chile* MMSI: 725000018 Official number: 2482	*201* - -		**1986 Astilleros Arica S.A. — Arica** L reg 27.09 Br ex - Dght - Lbp - Br md 8.53 Dpth 3.56 Welded, 1 dk	**(B11B2FV) Fishing Vessel**	**1 oil engine** driving 1 FP propeller
6828674 - -	**TOCOPILLANO** *ex* Ultramar VII *-2005* *ex* Correct *-1979* **Naviera Ultranav Ltda** -	*147* - -	Class: (GL)	**1968 D.W. Kremer Sohn — Elmshorn** Yd No: 1137 Loa 29.39 Br ex 7.90 Dght 3.210 Lbp 26.01 Br md 7.59 Dpth 3.69 Welded, 1 dk	**(B32A2ST) Tug**	**1 oil engine** driving 1 FP propeller Total Power: 883kW (1,201hp) 12.0kn Deutz SBV8M545 1 x 4 Stroke 8 Cy. 320 x 450 883kW (1201bhp) Kloeckner Humboldt Deutz AG-West Germany AuxGen: 1 x 74kW 440V a.c
9209752 *CA3583* -	**TOCOPILLANO** *ex* Vladimir Kolotnev *-2010* **Remolcadores Ultratug Ltda** Administradora de Naves Humboldt Ltda *Valparaiso* *Chile* MMSI: 725000866 Official number: 3270	**180** 48 118	Class: LR (RS) ✠ **100A1** SS 11/2011 tug **LMC** Eq.Ltr: D; Cable: 24.7/17.5 U2 (a)	**2001**-11 **FGUP Mashinostroitelnoye Predp 'Zvyozdochka' — Severodvinsk** (Hull) **2001**-11 **B.V. Scheepswerf Damen — Gorinchem** Yd No: 507003 Loa 26.09 Br ex 7.99 Dght 3.443 Lbp 23.98 Br md 7.95 Dpth 4.05 Welded, 1 dk	**(B32A2ST) Tug** Ice Capable	**2 oil engines** with clutches, flexible couplings & sr reverse geared to sc. shafts driving 2 FP propellers Total Power: 2,350kW (3,196hp) 11.3kn Caterpillar 3512TA 2 x Vee 4 Stroke 12 Cy. 170 x 190 each-1175kW (1598bhp) Caterpillar Inc-USA AuxGen: 2 x 85kW 400V 50Hz a.c
9442823 *FIAP* -	**TOCQUEVILLE** **Compagnie Corsaire Sarl** - *Cherbourg* *France* MMSI: 228268800 Official number: 925074	**269** 115 35	Class: (BV)	**2007**-06 **Chantiers Navals Gamelin — La Rochelle** Yd No: BP 37/01 Loa 37.20 Br ex - Dght 1.190 Lbp 31.54 Br md 8.60 Dpth 3.09 Welded, 1 dk	**(A37B2PS) Passenger Ship** Hull Material: Aluminium Alloy Passengers: unberthed: 260	**2 oil engines** geared to sc. shafts driving 2 Water jets Total Power: 3,696kW (5,026hp) M.T.U. 16V4000M61 2 x Vee 4 Stroke 16 Cy. 165 x 190 each-1848kW (2513bhp) MTU Friedrichshafen GmbH-Friedrichshafen Thrusters: 1 Thwart. FP thruster (f)
7302988 - -	**TOCRA** *ex* Antonios K *-1979* **National Fishing & Marketing Co (NAFIMCO)** - *Benghazi* *Libya* Official number: 231	*149* 65 -	Class: (HR)	**1973 Th. Zervas & Sons — Ambelaki** Loa 33.53 Br ex - Dght 2.617 Lbp 28.00 Br md 6.80 Dpth 3.66 Welded, 1 dk	**(B11A2FT) Trawler**	**1 oil engine** driving 1 CP propeller Total Power: 441kW (600hp) 12.0kn Alpha 406-26VO 1 x 2 Stroke 6 Cy. 260 x 400 441kW (600bhp) Alpha Diesel A/S-Denmark Fuel: 49.0 (d.f.)
8023785 *WDB8070* -	**TODD DANOS** **Cashman Equipment Corp** *Houma, LA* *United States of America* MMSI: 338030000 Official number: 637906	**292** 87 -	Class: AB	**1981**-06 **Bollinger Machine Shop & Shipyard, Inc. — Lockport, La** Yd No: 135 Loa - Br ex - Dght 3.874 Lbp 32.01 Br md 9.15 Dpth 4.45 Welded, 1 dk	**(B32A2ST) Tug**	**2 oil engines** reverse reduction geared to sc. shafts driving 2 FP propellers Total Power: 2,074kW (2,820hp) 12.0kn Caterpillar 3516TA 2 x Vee 4 Stroke 16 Cy. 170 x 190 each-1037kW (1410bhp) Caterpillar Tractor Co-USA AuxGen: 2 x 75kW

IMO / Call sign	Name / Owner	Tonnage	Class	Builder / Dimensions	Type	Machinery
9202340 *WDF8454* -	**TODD G** *ex* Gulf Pride *-2011* *ex* Emelie Ann *-2007* **Guilbeau Marine Inc** - *New Orleans, LA* *United States of America* MMSI: 367495030 Official number: 1077092	**423** 136 750		**1999**-03 **Bollinger Machine Shop & Shipyard, Inc. — Lockport, La** Yd No: 338 Loa 44.35 Br ex - Dght - Lbp 39.87 Br md 10.97 Dpth 3.51 Welded, 1 dk	**(B21A20S) Platform Supply Ship**	**2 oil engines** reduction geared to sc. shafts driving 2 FP propellers Total Power: 1,118kW (1,520hp) 10.0kn G.M. (Detroit Diesel) 8V-149-TI 2 x Vee 2 Stroke 8 Cy. 146 x 146 each-559kW (760bhp) Detroit Diesel Corporation-Detroit, Mi Thrusters: 1 Tunnel thruster (f)
9243356 *CNA2352* -	**TODRA** *launched as* Cabicastro *-2001* **Kalid Fisheries SA** - *Agadir* *Morocco* MMSI: 242551000	**440** 132 -	Class: (BV)	**2001**-08 **Ast. de Huelva S.A. — Huelva** Yd No: 631 Loa 37.60 Br ex - Dght 3.600 Lbp 32.64 Br md 8.40 Dpth 5.75 Welded, 1 dk	**(B11A2FS) Stern Trawler** Ins: 272	**1 oil engine** reduction geared to sc. shaft driving 1 CP propeller Total Power: 1,007kW (1,369hp) Caterpillar 3512B 1 x Vee 4 Stroke 12 Cy. 170 x 190 1007kW (1369bhp) Caterpillar Inc-USA
9365051 *JD2161* -	**TOEI MARU** - **Atlas Marine Co Ltd** - *Yokohama, Kanagawa* *Japan* MMSI: 431402028 Official number: 140227	*749* - 1,211	Class: NK	**2005**-09 **Kegoya Dock K.K. — Kure** Yd No: 1101 Loa 67.90 (BB) Br ex - Dght 4.111 Lbp 63.00 Br md 11.50 Dpth 4.80 Welded, 1 dk	**(A11B2TG) LPG Tanker** Liq (Gas): 1,458	**1 oil engine** reduction geared to sc. shaft driving 1 CP propeller Total Power: 1,471kW (2,000hp) 12.5kn Akasaka AX33 1 x 4 Stroke 6 Cy. 330 x 620 1471kW (2000bhp) Akasaka Tekkosho KK (Akasaka DieselLtd)-Japan Fuel: 100.0
9494979 *JD2691* -	**TOEI MARU** - **ME Kaiun KK** - *Higashi-izu, Shizuoka* *Japan* MMSI: 431200379 Official number: 140776	*747* - 1,950		**2008**-06 **Maebata Zosen Tekko K.K. — Sasebo** Yd No: 287 Loa 72.25 Br ex - Dght 4.890 Lbp 68.00 Br md 11.50 Dpth 5.35 Welded, 1 dk	**(A13B2TP) Products Tanker** Double Hull (13F) Liq: 2,250; Liq (Oil): 2,250	**1 oil engine** driving 1 FP propeller Total Power: 1,471kW (2,000hp) 12.5kn Hanshin LH34LG 1 x 4 Stroke 6 Cy. 340 x 640 1471kW (2000bhp) The Hanshin Diesel Works Ltd-Japan
8214774 - -	**TOEI MARU** *ex* Tosho Maru *-1998* *ex* Fukuseki No. 17 *-1997* *ex* Kyoshin Maru No. 28 *-1993* **Yoshitake Kaneko**	*314* - 416		**1982**-11 **Niigata Engineering Co Ltd — Niigata NI** Yd No: 1765 Loa 51.57 (BB) Br ex - Dght 3.471 Lbp 45.78 Br md 8.62 Dpth 3.66 Welded, 1 dk	**(B11B2FV) Fishing Vessel** Ins: 459 Compartments: 4 Ho, ER 4 Ha: ER	**1 oil engine** with clutches, flexible couplings & sr reverse geared to sc. shaft driving 1 CP propeller Total Power: 883kW (1,201hp) Niigata 6M28AFT 1 x 4 Stroke 6 Cy. 280 x 480 883kW (1201bhp) Niigata Engineering Co Ltd-Japan
8505331 *JG4554* -	**TOEI MARU** - **Maizuru Eisen KK** - *Maizuru, Kyoto* *Japan* Official number: 128828	*170* - -		**1985**-08 **Sanyo Zosen K.K. — Onomichi** Yd No: 1008 Loa 31.30 Br ex 9.45 Dght 3.001 Lbp 27.01 Br md 8.81 Dpth 3.81 Welded, 1 dk	**(B32A2ST) Tug**	**2 oil engines** Geared Integral to driving 2 Z propellers Total Power: 2,206kW (3,000hp) 12.5kn Niigata 6L25CXE 2 x 4 Stroke 6 Cy. 250 x 320 each-1103kW (1500bhp) Niigata Engineering Co Ltd-Japan
8743323 *JD2913* -	**TOEI MARU** - **Shibuta Tug Boat KK** - *Wakkanai, Hokkaido* *Japan* Official number: 141005	*170* - -		**2009**-02 **Kanto Kogyo K.K. — Hakodate** Yd No: 181 Loa 32.30 Br ex - Dght - Lbp 28.00 Br md 9.00 Dpth 3.62 Welded, 1 dk	**(B32A2ST) Tug**	**2 oil engines** reduction geared to sc. shafts driving 2 Z propellers Total Power: 2,648kW (3,600hp) 13.0kn Niigata 6L26HLX 2 x 4 Stroke 6 Cy. 260 x 350 each-1324kW (1800bhp) Niigata Engineering Co Ltd-Japan AuxGen: 2 x 100kW a.c Fuel: 62.0 (d.f.)
8748294 *JD3028* -	**TOEI MARU NO. 2** - **Shibuta Tug Boat KK** - *Hiroo, Hokkaido* *Japan* Official number: 141193	*234* - -		**2010**-01 **Kanto Kogyo K.K. — Hakodate** Loa 36.25 Br ex - Dght - Lbp 31.00 Br md 9.60 Dpth 4.18 Welded, 1 dk	**(B32A2ST) Tug**	**2 oil engines** reduction geared to sc. shafts driving 2 Propellers Total Power: 3,676kW (4,998hp) Niigata 6L28HX 2 x 4 Stroke 6 Cy. 280 x 370 each-1838kW (2499bhp) Niigata Engineering Co Ltd-Japan
8909745 *JFZQ* KN1-702	**TOEI MARU No. 6** - **Sumiyoshi Gyogyo KK** - SatCom: Inmarsat B 343192410 *Miura, Kanagawa* *Japan* MMSI: 431924000 Official number: 131101	*439* - 531		**1989**-07 **Miho Zosensho K.K. — Shimizu** Yd No: 1365 Loa 65.30 (BB) Br ex 8.92 Dght 3.611 Lbp 49.80 Br md 8.90 Dpth 3.97 Welded	**(B11B2FV) Fishing Vessel** Ins: 817	**1 oil engine** with clutches & sr reverse geared to sc. shaft driving 1 FP propeller Total Power: 1,103kW (1,500hp) Niigata 6M31AFTE 1 x 4 Stroke 6 Cy. 310 x 530 1103kW (1500bhp) Niigata Engineering Co Ltd-Japan
9004437 *JRSG* KN1-713	**TOEI MARU No. 8** *launched as* Sumiyoshi Maru *-1990* **Nanyo Suisan KK** - SatCom: Inmarsat B 343189310 *Miura, Kanagawa* *Japan* MMSI: 431893000 Official number: 131903	*439* - 522		**1990**-08 **Miho Zosensho K.K. — Shimizu** Yd No: 1372 Loa 58.29 (BB) Br ex 9.12 Dght 3.603 Lbp 51.30 Br md 9.10 Dpth 3.96 Welded	**(B11B2FV) Fishing Vessel** Ins: 836	**1 oil engine** with clutches, flexible couplings & sr geared to sc. shaft driving 1 FP propeller Total Power: 1,103kW (1,500hp) Niigata 6M31AFTE 1 x 4 Stroke 6 Cy. 310 x 530 1103kW (1500bhp) Niigata Engineering Co Ltd-Japan
8815059 *JCSI* KN1-696	**TOEI MARU No. 15** - **Sumiyoshi Gyogyo KK** - SatCom: Inmarsat A 1204345 *Miura, Kanagawa* *Japan* MMSI: 432605000 Official number: 130306	*439* - 534		**1988**-12 **Miho Zosensho K.K. — Shimizu** Yd No: 1342 Loa 56.49 (BB) Br ex 8.92 Dght 3.611 Lbp 49.80 Br md 8.90 Dpth 3.97 Welded, 1 dk	**(B11B2FV) Fishing Vessel** Ins: 715	**1 oil engine** with clutches, flexible couplings & sr geared to sc. shaft driving 1 FP propeller Total Power: 1,103kW (1,500hp) Niigata 6M31AFTE 1 x 4 Stroke 6 Cy. 310 x 530 1103kW (1500bhp) Niigata Engineering Co Ltd-Japan
7505463 *CB4214* -	**TOEKAN** *ex* Westereems *-1989* *ex* Edith M *-1981* **Pesquera Bio Bio SA** - *Valparaiso* *Chile* MMSI: 725001050 Official number: 2638	*334* 156 400	Class: (BV)	**1975**-12 **Boot-Lemmer B.V. — Lemmer** Yd No: 1353 Loa 38.77 Br ex 8.03 Dght 4.100 Lbp 36.10 Br md 7.98 Dpth 4.35 Welded, 1 dk	**(B11A2FT) Trawler**	**1 oil engine** driving 1 FP propeller Total Power: 1,655kW (2,250hp) 14.0kn Deutz 1 x 4 Stroke 1655kW (2250bhp) (new engine 1982) Kloeckner Humboldt Deutz AG-West Germany Fuel: 80.5 (d.f.)
8865810 *FKFK* PY 1523	**TOERAU MOANA** - **Fishing Co-operative of Piareare de Rurutu** - *Papeete* *France* MMSI: 227111900	**154** - -	Class: (BV)	**1992** **Chantier Naval du Pacifique Sud (CNPS) — Papeete** Yd No: 164 Loa 24.80 Br ex - Dght 3.335 Lbp 21.79 Br md 7.40 Dpth 3.96 Welded, 1 dk	**(B11B2FV) Fishing Vessel** Ins: 70	**1 oil engine** reduction geared to sc. shaft driving 1 FP propeller Total Power: 323kW (439hp) 10.0kn Unidiesel UD150V12M1 1 x Vee 4 Stroke 12 Cy. 150 x 180 323kW (439bhp) Poyaud S.S.C.M.-Surgeres
5372408 *9BJE* -	**TOFIGH** *ex* Mubarak *-1992* *ex* Franka Bell *-1976* *ex* Ulla Mac *-1970* *ex* Ulla Rask *-1968* **Morid Salamat** Zarogheh Bandar Shipping Services *Bandar Abbas* *Iran* MMSI: 422548000 Official number: 10970	*472* 248 635	Class: AS (BV)	**1957**-07 **Buesumer Schiffswerft W. & E. Sielaff — Buesum** Yd No: 181 Lengthened-1964 Loa 55.40 Br ex 8.32 Dght 2.896 Lbp 49.94 Br md 8.30 Dpth 3.86 Riveted\Welded, 1 dk	**(A31A2GX) General Cargo Ship** Grain: 821; Bale: 765 Compartments: 1 Ho, ER 1 Ha: (29.9 x 5.0)ER Derricks: 2x2t; Winches: 2	**1 oil engine** geared to sc. shaft driving 1 FP propeller Total Power: 1,480kW (2,012hp) 9.5kn Caterpillar 3512B-HD 1 x Vee 4 Stroke 12 Cy. 170 x 215 1480kW (2012bhp) (new engine 1992) Caterpillar Inc-USA Fuel: 26.5 (d.f.) 1.5pd
7413440 *ZAPF* -	**TOFIK SKILJA** - **Arben Buzi** - *Durres* *Albania* Official number: 404-404	**112** 79 120		**1973** **Kantieri Detar "Durres" — Durres** Yd No: 404 Loa 22.00 Br ex 6.20 Dght 2.040 Lbp - Br md 6.00 Dpth 2.50 Welded, 1 dk	**(B11B2FV) Fishing Vessel**	**1 oil engine** driving 1 FP propeller Total Power: 294kW (400hp) 11.0kn S.K.L. 8NVD36A-1U 1 x 4 Stroke 8 Cy. 240 x 360 294kW (400bhp) VEB Schwermaschinenbau "KarlLiebknecht" (SKL)-Magdeburg
9111589 *HSB4848* -	**TOFTE 1** *ex* Prince Of Nature *-2013* **Tofte 1 Co Ltd** Highland Maritime Co Ltd *Bangkok* *Thailand* MMSI: 567488000 Official number: 560003487	**36,690** 18,305 43,924	Class: NK	**1995**-09 **Sanoyas Hishino Meisho Corp — Kurashiki OY** Yd No: 1132 Loa 195.00 (BB) Br ex - Dght 10.550 Lbp 188.00 Br md 32.20 Dpth 17.30 Welded, 1 dk	**(A24B2BW) Wood Chips Carrier** Grain: 91,140 Compartments: 6 Ho, ER 6 Ha: (13.4 x 12.3) (12.6 x 17.2)3 (15.0 x 17.2) (11.1 x 17.2)ER Cranes: 3x17.5t	**1 oil engine** driving 1 FP propeller Total Power: 9,268kW (12,601hp) 15.5kn Sulzer 7RTA52 1 x 2 Stroke 7 Cy. 520 x 1800 9268kW (12601bhp) Mitsubishi Heavy Industries Ltd-Japan

IMO / Call sign	Name / Owner / Port	Tonnage	Class	Builder / Dimensions	Type	Machinery
8026361 *LJIV* -	**TOFTE II** **Sodra Cell Tofte AS** Bukser og Berging AS *Drammen* *Norway* MMSI: 257080600 Official number: 19493	*177* - -	Class: NV	**1980 Mandals Slip & Mekaniske Verksted AS — Mandal** Yd No: 73 Loa 24.21 Br ex - Dght 3.647 Lbp 22.74 Br md 8.51 Dpth 4.32 Welded, 1 dk	**(B32B2SA) Articulated Pusher Tug** Ice Capable	**2 oil engines** driving 2 CP propellers Total Power: 1,762kW (2,396hp) 11.5kn Normo LDMB-6 2 x 4 Stroke 6 Cy. 250 x 300 each-881kW (1198bhp) (new engine 1983) AS Bergens Mek Verksteder-Norway AuxGen: 2 x 80kW 220V 50Hz a.c Fuel: 54.0 (d.f.)
9285847 *C6ZO5* -	**TOFTEVIKEN** *ex* Torinia *-2011 completed as* Gansky *-2005* **Tofteviken LLC** Taurus Tankers Ltd *Nassau* *Bahamas* MMSI: 311061400 Official number: 8001963	**62,806** 34,551 115,340 T/cm 99.8	Class: AB (NV)	**2005-07 Samsung Heavy Industries Co Ltd — Geoje** Yd No: 1474 Loa 249.87 (BB) Br ex 43.83 Dght 14.926 Lbp 239.00 Br md 43.80 Dpth 21.30 Welded, 1 dk	**(A13B2TP) Products Tanker** Double Hull (13F) Liq: 124,259; Liq (Oil): 124,259 Cargo Heating Coils Compartments: 12 Wing Ta, 2 Wing Slop Ta, ER 3 Cargo Pump (s): 3x3000m³/hr Manifold: Bow/CM: 124.5m	**1 oil engine** driving 1 FP propeller Total Power: 13,560kW (18,436hp) 15.3kn MAN-B&W 6S60MC-C 1 x 2 Stroke 6 Cy. 600 x 2400 13560kW (18436bhp) Doosan Engine Co Ltd-South Korea AuxGen: 3 x 740kW a.c Fuel: 139.0 (d.f.) 3258.0 (r.f.)
9134218 *JK5482* -	**TOFUKU MARU** - - *Shunan, Yamaguchi* *Japan* Official number: 134797	*199* - 510		**1996-10 Koa Sangyo KK — Takamatsu KG** Yd No: 588 Loa 49.06 Br ex - Dght - Lbp 45.00 Br md 7.80 Dpth 3.40 Welded, 1 dk	**(A12A2TC) Chemical Tanker**	**1 oil engine** driving 1 FP propeller Total Power: 736kW (1,001hp) 10.5kn Hanshin LH26G 1 x 4 Stroke 6 Cy. 260 x 440 736kW (1001bhp) The Hanshin Diesel Works Ltd-Japan
8864945 *JM6126* -	**TOFUKU MARU** **Toyo Kaiun KK** *Sasebo, Nagasaki* *Japan* Official number: 132692	*202* - 640		**1992-09 Y.K. Okajima Zosensho — Matsuyama** Yd No: 238 L reg 53.80 Br ex - Dght 3.200 Lbp - Br md 9.50 Dpth 5.40 Welded, 1 dk	**(A31A2GX) General Cargo Ship**	**1 oil engine** driving 1 FP propeller Total Power: 588kW (799hp) Matsui ML627GSC 1 x 4 Stroke 6 Cy. 270 x 480 588kW (799bhp) Matsui Iron Works Co Ltd-Japan
6514132 *HP7402* -	**TOGO** *ex* Bob Read II *-1985 ex* Boston Viking *-1983* **Barnum Trading Ltd** *Panama* *Panama* MMSI: 351716000 Official number: 40771PEXT2	*187* 56 -	Class: (LR) ✠ Classed LR until 2/93	**1965-10 R. Dunston (Hessle) Ltd. — Hessle** Yd No: S821 Converted From: Trawler-1985 L reg 28.69 Br ex 7.12 Dght 2.744 Lbp 27.08 Br md 7.01 Dpth 3.36 Welded	**(B22G2OY) Standby Safety Vessel**	**1 oil engine** sr reverse geared to sc. shaft driving 1 FP propeller Total Power: 388kW (528hp) 10.0kn Blackstone EVS8M 1 x 4 Stroke 8 Cy. 222 x 292 388kW (528bhp) Lister Blackstone Marine Ltd.-Dursley
6403149 - -	**TOGO PEIX TRES** *ex* Laxeiras *-1998* *ex* Almirante Nieto Antunez *-1987* **Togo Peix Sarl** - *Togo*	*187* 97 -	Class: (BV)	**1964 Astilleros Santodomingo — Vigo** Yd No: 320 Loa 33.48 Br ex 6.56 Dght 3.379 Lbp 29.49 Br md 6.50 Dpth 3.76 Riveted\Welded, 1 dk	**(B11A2FT) Trawler** 3 Ha: 3 (1.0 x 1.0)	**1 oil engine** driving 1 FP propeller Total Power: 552kW (750hp) 12.5kn Deutz RBV6M545 1 x 4 Stroke 6 Cy. 320 x 450 552kW (750bhp) Kloeckner Humboldt Deutz AG-West Germany AuxGen: 2 x 120kW Fuel: 76.0
8328812 - -	**TOGO YANMAR** **Tuong Aik Shipyard Sdn Bhd**	*130* 2 -	Class: (NK)	**1982 Ocean Shipyard Co Sdn Bhd — Sibu** Loa 24.69 Br ex - Dght - Lbp 22.81 Br md 7.01 Dpth 2.90 Welded, 1 dk	**(B32A2ST) Tug**	**2 oil engines** geared to sc. shafts driving 2 FP propellers Total Power: 530kW (720hp) 8.0kn Yanmar 6ML-T 2 x 4 Stroke 6 Cy. 200 x 240 each-265kW (360bhp) Yanmar Diesel Engine Co Ltd-Japan
7628605 *HC2916* -	**TOHALLI** **Government of The Republic of Ecuador (Instituto Nacional de Pesca)** *Guayaquil* *Ecuador* Official number: P-00-0555	*202* 73 163	Class: (NV)	**1977-10 Sigbjorn Iversen — Flekkefjord** Yd No: 43 Loa 32.62 Br ex 7.42 Dght 3.201 Lbp 28.05 Br md 7.40 Dpth 3.69 Welded, 1 dk	**(B12D2FR) Fishery Research Vessel** Compartments: 1 Ho, ER 1 Ha:	**1 oil engine** geared to sc. shaft driving 1 CP propeller Total Power: 625kW (850hp) 12.0kn Caterpillar D398SCAC 1 x Vee 4 Stroke 12 Cy. 159 x 203 625kW (850bhp) Caterpillar Tractor Co-USA AuxGen: 2 x 90kW 220V 50Hz a.c Thrusters: 1 Thwart. FP thruster (a)
9062427 *JK5166* -	**TOHEI MARU** **KK Nanyo Marine** *Shunan, Yamaguchi* *Japan* Official number: 133029	*496* - 1,344	Class: NK	**1993-05 Kyoei Zosen KK — Mihara HS** Yd No: 255 Loa 66.52 Br ex 10.02 Dght 4.265 Lbp 62.00 Br md 10.00 Dpth 4.50 Welded, 1 dk	**(A12A2TC) Chemical Tanker** Liq: 1,220	**1 oil engine** driving 1 FP propeller Total Power: 736kW (1,001hp) 10.5kn Yanmar MF29-UT 1 x 4 Stroke 6 Cy. 290 x 520 736kW (1001bhp) Yanmar Diesel Engine Co Ltd-Japan Fuel: 65.0 (d.f.)
8859354 *JK5031* -	**TOHO** **Toho Aen KK** *Osakikamijima, Hiroshima* *Japan* Official number: 131824	*244* - -		**1991-09 K.K. Kawamoto Zosensho — Osakikamijima** Loa 49.80 Br ex - Dght 2.500 Lbp 34.10 Br md 10.00 Dpth 3.50 Welded, 1 dk	**(A37B2PS) Passenger Ship** Passengers: unberthed: 200	**1 oil engine** driving 1 FP propeller Total Power: 883kW (1,201hp) 10.0kn Yanmar 1 x 4 Stroke 883kW (1201bhp) Yanmar Diesel Engine Co Ltd-Japan
9646431 *7JMC* -	**TOHO** **Higashi Nippon Senpaku KK** *Kesennuma, Miyagi* *Japan* Official number: 141689	**499** - -		**2012-09 Nagasaki Zosen K.K. — Nagasaki** Yd No: 1233 Loa 66.21 Br ex - Dght 4.000 Lbp - Br md 9.40 Dpth - Welded, 1 dk	**(B12D2FP) Fishery Patrol Vessel**	**1 oil engine** reduction geared to sc. shaft driving 1 Propeller Total Power: 1,914kW (2,602hp) Daihatsu 6DKM-28 1 x 4 Stroke 6 Cy. 280 x 390 1914kW (2602bhp) Daihatsu Diesel Manufacturing Co Lt-Japan
9561514 *JD2970* -	**TOHO MARU** **Nitto Tugboat KK** *Kurashiki, Okayama* *Japan* Official number: 141102	**194** - -		**2009-08 Kanagawa Zosen — Kobe** Yd No: 597 Loa 38.20 Br ex - Dght 3.000 Lbp 33.60 Br md 9.00 Dpth 3.79 Welded, 1 dk	**(B32A2ST) Tug**	**2 oil engines** reduction geared to sc. shafts driving 2 Propellers Total Power: 3,680kW (5,004hp) Yanmar 6EY26 2 x 4 Stroke 6 Cy. 260 x 385 each-1840kW (2502bhp) Yanmar Diesel Engine Co Ltd-Japan
9512874 *JD2888* -	**TOHO MARU** **Iino Gas Transport Co Ltd** *Kobe, Hyogo* *Japan* MMSI: 431000887 Official number: 140982	*749* - 1,024	Class: NK	**2009-03 K.K. Miura Zosensho — Saiki** Yd No: 1357 Loa 67.39 Br ex - Dght 3.880 Lbp 63.00 Br md 11.80 Dpth 4.70 Welded, 1 dk	**(A11B2TG) LPG Tanker** Liq (Gas): 1,440	**1 oil engine** driving 1 FP propeller Total Power: 1,471kW (2,000hp) 12.5kn Akasaka A34C 1 x 4 Stroke 6 Cy. 340 x 620 1471kW (2000bhp) Akasaka Tekkosho KK (Akasaka DieselLtd)-Japan Fuel: 135.0
8824440 *JM5774* -	**TOHO MARU No. 8** **YK Toko Kisen** *Kamiamakusa, Kumamoto* *Japan* Official number: 130429	*173* - 340		**1989-03 Hongawara Zosen K.K. — Fukuyama** Loa 40.00 Br ex - Dght 2.910 Lbp 37.00 Br md 7.50 Dpth 3.20 Welded, 1 dk	**(A12A2TC) Chemical Tanker** 1 Cargo Pump (s): 1x80m³/hr	**1 oil engine** driving 1 FP propeller Total Power: 441kW (600hp) Yanmar M200L-DT 1 x 4 Stroke 6 Cy. 200 x 260 441kW (600bhp) Yanmar Diesel Engine Co Ltd-Japan
9152533 *JM6560* -	**TOHO MARU No. 8** **Toho Kogyo KK** *Ibusuki, Kagoshima* *Japan* Official number: 135421	*499* - 1,541		**1996-08 Yamakawa Zosen Tekko K.K. — Kagoshima** Yd No: 738 Loa 67.75 (BB) Br ex - Dght 4.310 Lbp 62.00 Br md 13.30 Dpth 7.00 Welded, 1 dk	**(B33A2DS) Suction Dredger** Compartments: 1 Ho, ER 1 Ha: (18.6 x 8.9)ER	**1 oil engine** driving 1 FP propeller Total Power: 1,471kW (2,000hp) 11.8kn Niigata 6M34BGT 1 x 4 Stroke 6 Cy. 340 x 620 1471kW (2000bhp) Niigata Engineering Co Ltd-Japan Thrusters: 1 Tunnel thruster (f)
9085003 *JG5002* -	**TOHO MARU No. 12** *ex* Shinyo Maru No. 11 *-2000* **Toho Kairiku Unyu KK** *Tokyo* *Japan* Official number: 132772	*215* - 540		**1993-12 K.K. Tago Zosensho — Nishi-Izu** Yd No: 255 Loa 42.52 Br ex - Dght - Lbp 39.50 Br md 8.50 Dpth 3.60 Welded, 1 dk	**(A13B2TP) Products Tanker**	**1 oil engine** driving 1 FP propeller Total Power: 441kW (600hp) 9.1kn Sumiyoshi S23G 1 x 4 Stroke 6 Cy. 230 x 400 441kW (600bhp) Sumiyoshi Tekkosho-Japan
8843408 - -	**TOHOH MARU** **Southern Communication System** *Panama* *Panama* Official number: D3371789PEXT	*134* 39 -		**1974 Fukui Zosen K.K. — Japan** Loa 35.30 Br ex - Dght 2.550 Lbp 29.50 Br md 6.50 Dpth 2.85 Welded, 1 dk	**(B11A2FS) Stern Trawler**	**1 oil engine** driving 1 FP propeller Total Power: 736kW (1,001hp) Niigata 1 x 4 Stroke 736kW (1001bhp) Niigata Engineering Co Ltd-Japan

IMO / Call sign	Name / Owner / Manager / Port / Flag	Tonnage	Class	Builder / Dimensions	Type	Machinery
9477816 *3FUH8* -	**TOHOKU MARU** **Wealth Line Inc** Fukujin Kisen KK (Fukujin Kisen Co Ltd) *Panama* Panama MMSI: 370130000 Official number: 4023109	**48,026** 26,714 88,159 T/cm 79.7	Class: NK	**2009-02 Imabari Shipbuilding Co Ltd — Marugame KG (Marugame Shipyard)** Yd No: 1491 Loa 229.93 (BB) Br ex - Dght 13.819 Lbp 220.00 Br md 38.00 Dpth 19.90 Welded, 1 dk	**(A21A2BC) Bulk Carrier** Double Hull Grain: 101,695 Compartments: 5 Ho, ER 5 Ha: ER	**1 oil engine** driving 1 FP propeller Total Power: 12,240kW (16,642hp) 14.7kn MAN-B&W 6S60MC 1 x 2 Stroke 6 Cy. 600 x 2292 12240kW (16642bhp) Hitachi Zosen Corp-Japan Fuel: 2880.0
9227742 *JE3139* -	**TOHOKU MARU No. 2** - **Miyagi Marine Service KK** - *Ishinomaki, Miyagi* Japan Official number: 133379	*247* - -		**2000-06 Kanagawa Zosen — Kobe** Yd No: 485 Loa 37.20 Br ex - Dght - Lbp 32.70 Br md 9.80 Dpth 4.21 Welded, 1 dk	**(B32A2ST) Tug**	**2 oil engines** gearing integral to driving 2 Z propellers Total Power: 2,648kW (3,600hp) 14.4kn Niigata 6L28HX 2 x 4 Stroke 6 Cy. 280 x 370 each-1324kW (1800bhp) Niigata Engineering Co Ltd-Japan AuxGen: 2 x 80kW 225V 60Hz a.c Fuel: 53.0 (d.f.)
8213988 - -	**TOHOTMOS** - **Government of The Arab Republic of Egypt** - *Alexandria* Egypt	*103* - -	Class: (BV)	**1982-07 B.V. Scheepswerf Damen — Gorinchem** Yd No: 2714 Loa 22.46 Br ex - Dght - Lbp 20.22 Br md 6.63 Dpth 3.03 Welded, 1 dk	**(B32A2ST) Tug**	**2 oil engines** sr reverse geared to sc. shafts driving 2 FP propellers Total Power: 1,044kW (1,420hp) 11.5kn Deutz SBA12M816 2 x Vee 4 Stroke 12 Cy. 142 x 160 each-522kW (710bhp) Kloeckner Humboldt Deutz AG-West Germany
8923466 *JM6533* -	**TOHOZAN MARU No. 5** - **Maruho Kisen YK** - *Reihoku, Kumamoto* Japan Official number: 134648	*199* - 649		**1996-06 YK Furumoto Tekko Zosensho — Osakikamijima** Yd No: 622 Loa 59.32 Br ex - Dght 3.190 Lbp 53.00 Br md 9.50 Dpth 5.40 Welded, 1 dk	**(A31A2GX) General Cargo Ship**	**1 oil engine** driving 1 FP propeller Total Power: 736kW (1,001hp) 11.0kn Niigata 6M28BGT 1 x 4 Stroke 6 Cy. 280 x 480 736kW (1001bhp) Niigata Engineering Co Ltd-Japan
9320843 *3EJO5* -	**TOHSHI** - **Allegiance Maritime SA** Kyoei Tanker Co Ltd SatCom: Inmarsat Mini-M 761119995 *Panama* Panama MMSI: 372582000 Official number: 3257607A	**159,939** 97,016 300,363 T/cm 182.5	Class: NK	**2007-03 IHI Marine United Inc — Kure HS** Yd No: 3216 Loa 333.00 (BB) Br ex 60.04 Dght 20.535 Lbp 324.00 Br md 60.00 Dpth 29.00 Welded, 1 dk	**(A13A2TV) Crude Oil Tanker** Double Hull (13F) Liq: 330,419; Liq (Oil): 330,419 Compartments: 5 Ta, 10 Wing Ta, 2 Wing Slop Ta, ER 3 Cargo Pump (s): 3x5500m³/hr Manifold: Bow/CM: 163.5m	**1 oil engine** driving 1 FP propeller Total Power: 27,160kW (36,927hp) 15.5kn Wartsila 7RTA84T 1 x 2 Stroke 7 Cy. 840 x 3150 27160kW (36927bhp) Diesel United Ltd.-Aioi AuxGen: 3 x 1150kW 440V 50Hz a.c Fuel: 620.7 (d.f.) 7272.8 (r.f.)
7127417 *ZMLG* -	**TOIA** - **CentrePort Ltd** - *Wellington* New Zealand Official number: 332398	**302** 90 -	Class: LR ✠ **100A1** CS 10/2011 tug ✠ **LMC** Eq.Ltr: (d) ; Cable: U1	**1972-02 Whangarei Eng. & Construction Co. Ltd. — Whangarei** Yd No: 122 Loa 32.24 Br ex 9.68 Dght 3.302 Lbp 30.79 Br md 9.19 Dpth 4.04 Welded, 1 dk	**(B32A2ST) Tug**	**2 oil engines** gearing integral to driving 2 Voith-Schneider propellers Total Power: 992kW (1,348hp) 11.8kn Ruston 6RKCM 2 x 4 Stroke 6 Cy. 254 x 305 each-496kW (674bhp) Ruston Paxman Diesels Ltd.-Colchester AuxGen: 2 x 125kW 400V 50Hz a.c
9237694 *A8TM8* -	**TOISA CONQUEROR** - **Toisa Ltd** Sealion Shipping Ltd *Monrovia* Liberia MMSI: 636014383 Official number: 14383	**2,401** 966 3,248	Class: LR ✠ **100A1** SS 07/2011 offshore supply ship *IWS ✠ **LMC** **UMS** Eq.Ltr: (T) ; Cable: 660.0/42.0 U3	**2001-07 Appledore Shipbuilders Ltd — Bideford** Yd No: A.S.186 Loa 73.80 (BB) Br ex 16.05 Dght 6.280 Lbp 65.00 Br md 16.00 Dpth 7.40 Welded, 1 dk	**(B21A20S) Platform Supply Ship** Cranes: 1x3t	**2 oil engines** with clutches, flexible couplings & sr geared to sc. shafts driving 2 CP propellers Total Power: 3,900kW (5,302hp) 12.0kn Wartsila 6L26 2 x 4 Stroke 6 Cy. 260 x 320 each-1950kW (2651bhp) Wartsila Finland Oy-Finland AuxGen: 2 x 1270kW 440V 60Hz a.c, 2 x 276kW 440V 60Hz a.c Thrusters: 2 Thwart. FP thruster (f); 2 Tunnel thruster (a) Fuel: 856.0 (d.f.) 8.5pd
9182057 *MYMY6* -	**TOISA CORAL** - **Toisa Ltd** Sealion Shipping Ltd SatCom: Inmarsat B 323298710 *London* United Kingdom MMSI: 232987000 Official number: 901763	**2,401** 966 1,336	Class: LR ✠ **100A1** SS 02/2014 offshore supply ship *IWS ✠ **LMC** **UMS** Eq.Ltr: (T) ; Cable: 1045.0/42.0 U3	**1999-02 Appledore Shipbuilders Ltd — Bideford** Yd No: A.S.175 Loa 73.80 (BB) Br ex 16.05 Dght 6.330 Lbp 65.00 Br md 16.00 Dpth 7.40 Welded, 1 dk	**(B21A20S) Platform Supply Ship** Cranes: 1x3t	**2 oil engines** with clutches, flexible couplings & sr geared to sc. shafts driving 2 CP propellers Total Power: 3,900kW (5,302hp) 14.0kn Wartsila 6L26 2 x 4 Stroke 6 Cy. 260 x 320 each-1950kW (2651bhp) Wartsila NSD Nederland BV-Netherlands AuxGen: 2 x 1500kW 440V 60Hz a.c, 2 x 276kW 440V 60Hz a.c Boilers: HWH (o.f.) 3.0kgf/cm² (2.9bar) Thrusters: 2 Thwart. CP thruster (f); 2 Tunnel thruster (a) Fuel: 869.0 (d.f.)
9182215 *MYTA7* -	**TOISA CREST** - **Toisa Ltd** Sealion Shipping Ltd SatCom: Inmarsat C 423226510 *London* United Kingdom MMSI: 232265000 Official number: 901940	**2,401** 966 1,336	Class: LR ✠ **100A1** SS 05/2009 offshore supply ship *IWS ✠ **LMC** **UMS** Eq.Ltr: (T) ; Cable: 1045.0/42.0 U3	**1999-05 Appledore Shipbuilders Ltd — Bideford** Yd No: A.S.176 Loa 73.80 (BB) Br ex 16.05 Dght 6.290 Lbp 65.00 Br md 16.00 Dpth 7.40 Welded, 1 dk	**(B21A20S) Platform Supply Ship** Liq: 2,982; Liq (Oil): 2,982	**2 oil engines** with clutches, flexible couplings & sr geared to sc. shafts driving 2 CP propellers Total Power: 3,900kW (5,302hp) 12.0kn Wartsila 6L26 2 x 4 Stroke 6 Cy. 260 x 320 each-1950kW (2651bhp) Wartsila NSD Nederland BV-Netherlands AuxGen: 2 x 1500kW 440V 60Hz a.c, 2 x 276kW 440V 60Hz a.c Boilers: HWH (o.f.) 4.1kgf/cm² (4.0bar) Thrusters: 2 Thwart. CP thruster (f); 2 Tunnel thruster (a) Fuel: 869.0 (d.f.)
9307310 *C6VD3* -	**TOISA DARING** - **Toisa Ltd** Sealion Shipping Ltd *Nassau* Bahamas MMSI: 308623000 Official number: 8001135	**2,765** 897 2,298	Class: NV	**2007-01 Wuchang Shipyard — Wuhan HB** Yd No: A122M Loa 69.60 (BB) Br ex 17.02 Dght 6.200 Lbp 61.07 Br md 16.98 Dpth 7.30 Welded, 1 dk	**(B21B20A) Anchor Handling Tug Supply** Cranes: 1x5t	**2 oil engines** reduction geared to sc. shafts driving 2 CP propellers Total Power: 9,000kW (12,236hp) 13.0kn Wartsila 9L32 2 x 4 Stroke 9 Cy. 320 x 400 each-4500kW (6118bhp) Wartsila Finland Oy-Finland AuxGen: 2 x 320kW a.c, 2 x 1440kW a.c Thrusters: 2 Tunnel thruster (f); 1 Tunnel thruster (a)
9307322 *C6VD4* -	**TOISA DAUNTLESS** - **Toisa Ltd** Sealion Shipping Ltd *Nassau* Bahamas MMSI: 308335000 Official number: 8001136	**2,765** 897 2,298	Class: NV	**2007-03 Wuchang Shipyard — Wuhan HB** Yd No: A123M Loa 69.60 (BB) Br ex 17.02 Dght 6.200 Lbp 61.07 Br md 16.98 Dpth 7.30 Welded, 1 dk	**(B21B20A) Anchor Handling Tug Supply** Cranes: 1x5t	**2 diesel electric oil engines** reduction geared to sc. shafts driving 2 CP propellers Total Power: 9,000kW (12,236hp) 13.0kn Wartsila 9L32 2 x 4 Stroke 9 Cy. 320 x 400 each-4500kW (6118bhp) Wartsila Finland Oy-Finland AuxGen: 2 x 320kW a.c, 2 x 1440kW a.c Thrusters: 2 Tunnel thruster (f); 1 Tunnel thruster (a)
9307308 *C6VD2* -	**TOISA DEFIANT** - **Toisa Ltd** Sealion Shipping Ltd *Nassau* Bahamas MMSI: 308282000 Official number: 8001134	**2,765** 897 2,298	Class: NV	**2006-08 Wuchang Shipyard — Wuhan HB** Yd No: A121M Loa 69.60 (BB) Br ex 17.02 Dght 6.200 Lbp 61.07 Br md 16.98 Dpth 7.30 Welded, 1 dk	**(B21B20A) Anchor Handling Tug Supply** Cranes: 1x5t	**2 diesel electric oil engines** reduction geared to sc. shafts driving 2 CP propellers Total Power: 9,000kW (12,236hp) 13.0kn Wartsila 9L32 2 x 4 Stroke 9 Cy. 320 x 400 each-4500kW (6118bhp) Wartsila Finland Oy-Finland AuxGen: 2 x 1440kW a.c, 2 x 320kW a.c Thrusters: 2 Tunnel thruster (f); 1 Tunnel thruster (a)
9427043 *C6YX6* -	**TOISA ELAN** - **Toisa Ltd** Sealion Shipping Ltd *Nassau* Bahamas MMSI: 311048500 Official number: 8001854	**5,418** 1,626 4,427	Class: NV	**2013-03 Wuchang Shipbuilding Industry Co Ltd — Wuhan HB** Yd No: A171M Loa 83.02 Br ex 22.03 Dght 7.500 Lbp 72.94 Br md 21.99 Dpth 9.02 Welded, 1 dk	**(B21B20A) Anchor Handling Tug Supply** Cranes: 2x5t	**4 oil engines** reduction geared to sc. shafts driving 2 CP propellers Total Power: 18,000kW (24,472hp) 15.0kn Wartsila 9L32 4 x 4 Stroke 9 Cy. 320 x 400 each-4500kW (6118bhp) Wartsila Finland Oy-Finland AuxGen: 2 x 320kW 440V 60Hz a.c, 2 x 2500kW 440V 60Hz a.c Thrusters: 2 Tunnel thruster (f); 2 Tunnel thruster (a)

Ship	Tonnage	Class	Builder / Dimensions	Type	Machinery
9427055 **TOISA ENVOY** *C6YX7* - **Toisa Ltd** Sealion Shipping Ltd *Nassau* *Bahamas* MMSI: 311048600 Official number: 8001855	**5,418** 1,626 3,600	Class: NV	**2013**-09 **Wuchang Shipbuilding Industry Co Ltd — Wuhan HB** Yd No: A172M Loa 83.18 (BB) Br ex 22.02 Dght 7.500 Lbp 72.98 Br md 21.98 Dpth 9.00 Welded, 1 dk	**(B21B20A) Anchor Handling Tug Supply**	**4 oil engines** reduction geared to sc. shafts driving 2 CP propellers Total Power: 18,000kW (24,472hp) 15.0kn Wartsila 9L32 1 x 4 Stroke 9 Cy. 320 x 400 4500kW (6118bhp) Wartsila Finland Oy-Finland Wartsila 9L32 3 x 4 Stroke 9 Cy. 320 x 400 each-4500kW (6118bhp) Wartsila Finland Oy-Finland AuxGen: 2 x a.c, 2 x a.c Thrusters: 2 Tunnel thruster (f); 2 Tunnel thruster (f)
9427067 **TOISA EXPLORER** *C6YX8* - **Toisa Ltd** Sealion Shipping Ltd *Nassau* *Bahamas* MMSI: 311048700 Official number: 8001856	**5,418** 1,626 3,600	Class: NV	**2013**-11 **Wuchang Shipbuilding Industry Co Ltd — Wuhan HB** Yd No: A173M Loa 83.24 Br ex 22.04 Dght 7.300 Lbp 72.98 Br md 22.00 Dpth 9.00 Welded, 1 dk	**(B21B20A) Anchor Handling Tug Supply** Cranes: 2x5t	**4 oil engines** reduction geared to sc. shafts driving 2 CP propellers Total Power: 18,000kW (24,472hp) 13.0kn Wartsila 9L32 1 x 4 Stroke 9 Cy. 320 x 400 4500kW (6118bhp) Wartsila Finland Oy-Finland Wartsila 9L32 3 x 4 Stroke 9 Cy. 320 x 400 each-4500kW (6118bhp) Wartsila Finland Oy-Finland AuxGen: 2 x 2500kW 440V 60Hz a.c, 2 x 320kW 440V 60Hz a.c Thrusters: 2 Tunnel thruster (f); 2 Tunnel thruster (a)
9255957 **TOISA INDEPENDENT** *VQHR9* - **Edgewater Offshore Shipping Ltd** Sealion Shipping Ltd *London* *United Kingdom* MMSI: 235631000 Official number: 906827	**3,100** 1,268 3,830	Class: LR ✠ **100A1** SS 03/2013 offshore supply ship *IWS ✠ **LMC** **UMS** Eq.Ltr: W; Cable: 660.0/46.0 U3 (a)	**2003**-03 **Appledore Shipbuilders Ltd — Bideford** Yd No: A.S.188 Loa 83.20 (BB) Br ex 19.05 Dght 5.920 Lbp 74.10 Br md 19.00 Dpth 7.30 Welded, 2 dks	**(B21A20S) Platform Supply Ship**	**3 diesel electric oil engines** driving 3 gen. each 1720kW 690V a.c Connecting to 2 elec. motors each (2200kW) driving 2 Directional propellers Total Power: 5,400kW (7,341hp) 11.0kn MaK 6M25 3 x 4 Stroke 6 Cy. 255 x 400 each-1800kW (2447bhp) Caterpillar Motoren GmbH & Co. KG-Germany Thrusters: 2 Thwart. CP thruster (f)
9169744 **TOISA INTREPID** *C6PW6* - **Toisa Ltd** Sealion Shipping Ltd SatCom: Inmarsat B 330862110 *Nassau* *Bahamas* MMSI: 308621000 Official number: 731012	**2,990** 1,573 4,693	Class: LR ✠ **100A1** SS 06/2013 offshore supply ship *IWS ✠ **LMC** **UMS** Eq.Ltr: (V) ; Cable: 1210.0/46.0 U3	**1998**-06 **Kvaerner Govan Ltd — Glasgow** Yd No: 315 Loa 82.88 (BB) Br ex 19.05 Dght 6.343 Lbp 75.80 Br md 19.00 Dpth 7.60 Welded, 1 dk	**(B21A20S) Platform Supply Ship**	**2 oil engines** with clutches, flexible couplings & sr geared to sc. shafts driving 2 CP propellers Total Power: 4,920kW (6,690hp) 14.3kn Wartsila 6R32E 2 x 4 Stroke 6 Cy. 320 x 350 each-2460kW (3345bhp) Wartsila NSD Finland Oy-Finland AuxGen: 2 x 1760kW 440V 60Hz a.c, 2 x 335kW 440V 60Hz a.c Thrusters: 2 Thwart. CP thruster (f); 2 Tunnel thruster (a) Fuel: 279.0 (d.f.)
9169756 **TOISA INVINCIBLE** *C6PW7* - **Toisa Ltd** Sealion Shipping Ltd SatCom: Inmarsat B 330861910 *Nassau* *Bahamas* MMSI: 308619000 Official number: 731013	**2,990** 1,573 4,689	Class: LR ✠ **100A1** SS 03/2012 offshore supply ship *IWS ✠ **LMC** **UMS** Eq.Ltr: (V) ; Cable: 1210.0/46.0 U3	**1998**-07 **Kvaerner Govan Ltd — Glasgow** Yd No: 316 Loa 82.85 (BB) Br ex 19.05 Dght 6.320 Lbp 75.80 Br md 19.00 Dpth 7.61 Welded, 1 dk	**(B21A20S) Platform Supply Ship**	**2 oil engines** with clutches, flexible couplings & sr geared to sc. shafts driving 2 CP propellers Total Power: 4,920kW (6,690hp) 13.0kn Wartsila 6R32E 2 x 4 Stroke 6 Cy. 320 x 350 each-2460kW (3345bhp) Wartsila NSD Finland Oy-Finland AuxGen: 2 x 1760kW 440V 60Hz a.c, 2 x 335kW 440V 60Hz a.c Thrusters: 2 Thwart. CP thruster (f); 2 Tunnel thruster (a) Fuel: 279.0 (d.f.)
9388091 **TOISA PALADIN** *2AFQ8* - **Toisa Ltd** Sealion Shipping Ltd *London* *United Kingdom* MMSI: 235059213 Official number: 914043	**5,648** 1,695 4,600	Class: NV	**2008**-03 **Kleven Verft AS — Ulsteinvik** Yd No: 318 Loa 103.70 (BB) Br ex 19.74 Dght 6.135 Lbp 94.80 Br md 19.70 Dpth 7.70 Welded, 1 dk	**(B22A20V) Diving Support Vessel** Passengers: berths: 100 Cranes: 1x140t Ice Capable	**5 diesel electric oil engines** driving 4 gen. each 2100kW a.c 1 gen. Connecting to 2 elec. motors each (2200kW) driving 2 Azimuth electric drive units Total Power: 9,378kW (12,750hp) 11.0kn Caterpillar 3508 1 x Vee 4 Stroke 8 Cy. 170 x 190 746kW (1014bhp) Caterpillar Inc-USA Caterpillar 3516C 4 x Vee 4 Stroke 16 Cy. 170 x 215 each-2158kW (2934bhp) Caterpillar Inc-USA Thrusters: 2 Tunnel thruster (f); 1 Retract. directional thruster (f) Fuel: 1200.0
9392509 **TOISA PEGASUS** *A8SH2* - **Toisa Ltd** Sealion Shipping Ltd *Monrovia* *Liberia* MMSI: 636014212 Official number: 14212	**9,494** 2,849 7,800	Class: NV	**2009**-04 **Merwede Shipyard BV — Hardinxveld** Yd No: 712 Loa 131.70 (BB) Br ex - Dght 6.750 Lbp 117.70 Br md 22.00 Dpth 9.50 Welded, 1 dk	**(B22A20V) Diving Support Vessel** Passengers: 199 Cranes: 1x400t	**4 diesel electric oil engines** driving 4 gen. each 2680kW 690V a.c Connecting to 2 elec. motors driving 2 Directional propellers Total Power: 12,240kW (16,640hp) 12.0kn MAN-B&W 9L27/38 4 x 4 Stroke 9 Cy. 270 x 380 each-3060kW (4160bhp) MAN B&W Diesel AG-Augsburg AuxGen: 4 x 2820kW 60Hz a.c Thrusters: 1 Retract. directional thruster (f); 2 Tunnel thruster (f) Fuel: 1092.0
9171852 **TOISA PERSEUS** *A8VG4* - **Toisa Ltd** Sealion Shipping Ltd *Monrovia* *Liberia* MMSI: 636014604 Official number: 14604	**6,948** 2,085 6,340	Class: NV	**1998**-09 **van der Giessen-de Noord BV — Krimpen a/d IJssel** Yd No: 972 Loa 113.57 Br ex - Dght 6.750 Lbp 104.04 Br md 22.00 Dpth 9.50 Welded, 1 dk	**(B22A20R) Offshore Support Vessel** Cranes: 1x150t,1x30t	**4 diesel electric oil engines** driving 4 gen. each 2660kW 660V a.c Connecting to 2 elec. motors each (2200kW) driving 2 Directional propellers Total Power: 10,720kW (14,576hp) 13.5kn Wartsila 9L26 4 x 4 Stroke 9 Cy. 260 x 320 each-2680kW (3644bhp) Wartsila NSD Nederland BV-Netherlands Thrusters: 3 Thwart. CP thruster (f) Fuel: 1101.0 (d.f.)
9139074 **TOISA PISCES** *A8BV3* - *ex Fresnel -2003* **Toisa Horizon Inc** Sealion Shipping Ltd *Monrovia* *Liberia* MMSI: 636011860 Official number: 11860	**6,651** 1,996 7,200 T/cm 24.2	Class: NV	**1997**-03 **Ulstein Verft AS — Ulsteinvik** Yd No: 248 Converted From: Cable-layer-2003 Loa 103.65 (BB) Br ex 23.20 Dght 7.065 Lbp 96.65 Br md 22.76 Dpth 9.00 Welded, 1 dk	**(B22D20Z) Production Testing Vessel** Cranes: 2x15t Ice Capable	**3 diesel electric oil engines** driving 3 gen. each 3700kW 6600V a.c Connecting to 2 elec. motors each (3300kW) driving 2 Z propellers Total Power: 11,325kW (15,396hp) 12.0kn Normo BRM-9 3 x 4 Stroke 9 Cy. 320 x 360 each-3775kW (5132bhp) Ulstein Bergen AS-Norway Thrusters: 1 Retract. directional thruster (f); 2 Thwart. CP thruster (f) Fuel: 385.5 (d.f.) (Part Heating Coils) 2118.9 (r.f.) 37.0pd
9247522 **TOISA PROTEUS** *ELZQ4* - **Toisa Ltd** Sealion Shipping Ltd *Monrovia* *Liberia* MMSI: 636011499 Official number: 11499	**8,402** 2,521 8,710	Class: NV	**2002**-07 **YVC Ysselwerf B.V. — Capelle a/d IJssel** Yd No: 987 Converted From: Well-stimulation Vessel-2007 Loa 131.70 (BB) Br ex 22.60 Dght 6.250 Lbp 117.70 Br md 22.00 Dpth 9.50 Welded, 1 dk	**(B22A20R) Offshore Support Vessel** Passengers: berths: 100 Cranes: 1x342t,1x25t	**4 diesel electric oil engines** driving 4 gen. each 2680kW 660V a.c Connecting to 2 elec. motors each (3000kW) driving 2 Directional propellers Total Power: 11,700kW (15,908hp) 14.0kn Wartsila 9L26 4 x 4 Stroke 9 Cy. 260 x 320 each-2925kW (3977bhp) Wartsila Finland Oy-Finland AuxGen: 1 x 750kW 60Hz a.c Thrusters: 3 Thwart. CP thruster (f) Fuel: 1155.0 (r.f.)
8002626 **TOISA SENTINEL** *A8ES6* - *ex TNT Sentinel -1989 ex Seagair -1988* **Toisa Ltd** Sealion Shipping Ltd *Monrovia* *Liberia* MMSI: 636012326 Official number: 12326	**4,208** 1,262 2,996	Class: LR NV ✠ **100A1** CS 10/2006 ✠ **LMC** Eq.Ltr: V; Cable: 495.0/50.0 U2	**1982**-07 **Richards (Shipbuilders) Ltd — Lowestoft** Yd No: 550 Converted From: Standby Safety Vessel-1994 Loa 94.32 Br ex 19.82 Dght 4.674 Lbp 86.21 Br md 19.50 Dpth 7.29 Welded, 2 dks, 2nd dk clear of generator room	**(B22A20V) Diving Support Vessel** A-frames: 1x15t	**4 diesel electric oil engines** driving 4 gen. each 2280kW 3300V a.c Connecting to 2 elec. motors each (1865kW) driving 2 CP propellers Total Power: 9,416kW (12,800hp) 11.0kn Nohab F216V 4 x Vee 4 Stroke 16 Cy. 250 x 300 each-2354kW (3200bhp) British Polar Engines Ltd.-Glasgow AuxGen: 1 x 450kW 415V 50Hz a.c, 1 x 250kW 415V 50Hz a.c Thrusters: 2 Thwart. CP thruster (f); 1 Tunnel thruster (f); 2 Thwart. CP thruster (a) Fuel: 1693.0

9366641 *C6W03* -	**TOISA SERENADE** **Toisa Ltd** Sealion Shipping Ltd *Nassau* *Bahamas* MMSI: 309407000 Official number: 8001422	**3,665** 1,582 4,900	Class: NV	**2008-09 Wuchang Shipyard — Wuhan HB** Yd No: A159M Loa 87.40 (BB) Br ex 19.04 Dght 6.650 Lbp 80.41 Br md 18.98 Dpth 8.00 Welded, 1 dk	**(B21A2OS) Platform Supply Ship**	**2 oil engines** reduction geared to sc. shafts driving 2 CP propellers Total Power: 6,000kW (8,158hp) 12.0kn Wartsila 6L32 2 x 4 Stroke 6 Cy. 320 x 400 each-3000kW (4079bhp) Wartsila Finland Oy-Finland AuxGen: 2 x 2000kW a.c, 2 x 320kW a.c Thrusters: 2 Tunnel thruster (f); 2 Tunnel thruster (a) Fuel: 255.0 (d.f.)
9366653 *C6W04* -	**TOISA SOLITAIRE** **Toisa Ltd** Sealion Shipping Ltd *Nassau* *Bahamas* MMSI: 308201000 Official number: 8001423	**3,665** 1,582 4,900	Class: NV	**2009-02 Wuchang Shipyard — Wuhan HB** Yd No: A160M Loa 87.40 Br ex 19.04 Dght 6.650 Lbp 80.41 Br md 19.00 Dpth 8.00 Welded, 1 dk	**(B21A2OS) Platform Supply Ship**	**2 oil engines** reduction geared to sc. shafts driving 2 CP propellers Total Power: 6,000kW (8,158hp) 11.0kn Wartsila 6L32 2 x 4 Stroke 6 Cy. 320 x 400 each-3000kW (4079bhp) Wartsila Finland Oy-Finland AuxGen: 2 x 320kW a.c, 2 x a.c Thrusters: 2 Tunnel thruster (f); 2 Tunnel thruster (a)
9366665 *C6W02* -	**TOISA SONATA** **Toisa Ltd** Sealion Shipping Ltd *Nassau* *Bahamas* MMSI: 308421000 Official number: 8001421	**3,665** 1,582 4,900	Class: NV	**2009-03 Wuchang Shipyard — Wuhan HB** Yd No: A161M Loa 87.40 (BB) Br ex 19.04 Dght 6.650 Lbp 80.42 Br md 18.99 Dpth 8.00 Welded, 1 dk	**(B21A2OS) Platform Supply Ship** Passengers: cabins: 16	**2 oil engines** reduction geared to sc. shafts driving 2 CP propellers Total Power: 6,000kW (8,158hp) 12.0kn Wartsila 6L32 2 x 4 Stroke 6 Cy. 320 x 400 each-3000kW (4079bhp) Wartsila Finland Oy-Finland AuxGen: 2 x 250kW 440V 60Hz a.c, 2 x 2000kW 440V 60Hz a.c Thrusters: 2 Tunnel thruster (f); 2 Tunnel thruster (a)
8124448 - -	**TOISA TIGER** *ex TNT Tiger -1990* - -	**846** 328 1,500	Class: (LR) ✠ Classed LR until 10/6/13	**1983-04 R. Dunston (Hessle) Ltd. — Hessle** Yd No: H934 Loa 61.73 Br ex 11.84 Dght 4.001 Lbp 57.21 Br md 11.60 Dpth 4.65 Welded, 1 dk	**(B21A2OS) Platform Supply Ship** Grain: 232 Compartments: 2 Wing Ho, 1 Ho, ER	**2 oil engines** with clutches, flexible couplings & dr (ahead) tr (astern) geared to sc. shafts driving 2 FP propellers Total Power: 2,354kW (3,200hp) 12.0kn Yanmar 6ZL-ST 2 x 4 Stroke 6 Cy. 280 x 340 each-1177kW (1600bhp) Yanmar Diesel Engine Co Ltd-Japan AuxGen: 3 x 200kW 440/220V 60Hz a.c Thrusters: 1 Water jet (f) Fuel: 287.0 (d.f.) 5.5pd
9274410 *C6UM7* -	**TOISA VALIANT** **Toisa Ltd** Sealion Shipping Ltd *Nassau* *Bahamas* MMSI: 311962000 Official number: 8000998	**3,406** 1,131 3,500	Class: NV	**2005-12 Wuhu Shipyard — Wuhu AH** Yd No: W0211 Loa 80.50 Br ex 17.99 Dght 6.100 Lbp 70.20 Br md 17.96 Dpth 7.40 Welded, 1 dk	**(B21A2OS) Platform Supply Ship** Cranes: 1x20t	**2 oil engines** reduction geared to sc. shafts driving 2 CP propellers Total Power: 5,280kW (7,178hp) 11.0kn MaK 8M25 2 x 4 Stroke 8 Cy. 255 x 400 each-2640kW (3589bhp) Caterpillar Motoren GmbH & Co. KG-Germany AuxGen: 2 x 1600kW a.c, 2 x 350kW a.c Thrusters: 2 Tunnel thruster (f); 2 Tunnel thruster (a)
9282132 *C6UM8* -	**TOISA VIGILANT** **Toisa Ltd** Sealion Shipping Ltd *Nassau* *Bahamas* MMSI: 311963000 Official number: 8000999	**3,404** 1,131 3,500	Class: NV	**2005-12 Wuhu Shipyard — Wuhu AH** Yd No: W0212 Loa 80.50 Br ex - Dght 6.100 Lbp 70.22 Br md 17.96 Dpth 7.42 Welded, 1 dk	**(B21A2OS) Platform Supply Ship** Cranes: 1x35t	**2 oil engines** reduction geared to sc. shafts driving 2 CP propellers Total Power: 5,280kW (7,178hp) 11.0kn MaK 8M25 2 x 4 Stroke 8 Cy. 255 x 400 each-2640kW (3589bhp) Caterpillar Motoren GmbH & Co. KG-Germany AuxGen: 2 x 1600kW a.c, 2 x 350kW a.c Thrusters: 2 Tunnel thruster (f); 2 Tunnel thruster (a)
9282144 *C6UM9* -	**TOISA VOYAGER** **Toisa Ltd** Sealion Shipping Ltd SatCom: Inmarsat C 431196410 *Nassau* *Bahamas* MMSI: 311964000 Official number: 8001000	**3,404** 1,131 3,500	Class: NV	**2006-05 Wuhu Shipyard — Wuhu AH** Yd No: W0213 Loa 80.50 Br ex 17.99 Dght 6.100 Lbp 72.41 Br md 17.96 Dpth 7.40 Welded, 1 dk	**(B21A2OS) Platform Supply Ship** Cranes: 1x20t	**2 oil engines** reduction geared to sc. shafts driving 2 CP propellers Total Power: 5,280kW (7,178hp) 11.0kn MaK 8M25 2 x 4 Stroke 8 Cy. 255 x 400 each-2640kW (3589bhp) Caterpillar Motoren GmbH & Co. KG-Germany AuxGen: 2 x 1600kW a.c, 2 x 350kW a.c Thrusters: 2 Tunnel thruster (f); 2 Tunnel thruster (a)
9427108 *C6XY7* -	**TOISA WARRIOR** **Toisa Ltd** Sealion Shipping Ltd SatCom: Inmarsat C 431101118 *Nassau* *Bahamas* MMSI: 311026200 Official number: 8001678	**4,801** 1,441 4,860	Class: NV	**2011-05 Wuchang Shipbuilding Industry Co Ltd — Wuhan HB** Yd No: A169M Loa 87.40 (BB) Br ex - Dght 6.650 Lbp 80.40 Br md 19.00 Dpth 8.00 Welded, 1 dk	**(B21A2OS) Platform Supply Ship** Cranes: 1x5t	**2 oil engines** reduction geared to sc. shafts driving 2 CP propellers Total Power: 6,000kW (8,158hp) 12.0kn Wartsila 6L32 2 x 4 Stroke 6 Cy. 320 x 400 each-3000kW (4079bhp) Wartsila Finland Oy-Finland AuxGen: 2 x 2000kW 440V 60Hz a.c, 2 x 320kW 440V 60Hz a.c Thrusters: 2 Tunnel thruster (f); 2 Tunnel thruster (a) Fuel: 336.0 (d.f.)
9427110 *C6XY6* -	**TOISA WAVE** **Toisa Ltd** Sealion Shipping Ltd SatCom: Inmarsat C 431101128 *Nassau* *Bahamas* MMSI: 311026100 Official number: 8001677	**4,801** 1,441 4,860	Class: NV	**2011-08 Wuchang Shipbuilding Industry Co Ltd — Wuhan HB** Yd No: A170M Loa 87.40 (BB) Br ex - Dght 6.650 Lbp 80.40 Br md 19.00 Dpth 8.00 Welded, 1 dk	**(B21A2OS) Platform Supply Ship** Cranes: 1x70t,1x5t	**2 oil engines** reduction geared to sc. shafts driving 2 CP propellers Total Power: 6,000kW (8,158hp) 12.0kn Wartsila 6L32 2 x 4 Stroke 6 Cy. 320 x 400 each-3000kW (4079bhp) Wartsila Finland Oy-Finland AuxGen: 2 x 2000kW 440V 60Hz a.c, 2 x 320kW 440V 60Hz a.c Thrusters: 2 Tunnel thruster (f); 2 Tunnel thruster (a) Fuel: 336.0 (d.f.)
8805937 *LIYG* M-70-AV	**TOJAKO** *ex Sette Mari -2005* **Kare Garden og Sonner AS** *Kristiansund* *Norway* MMSI: 259476000	**315** 94 -		**1987 Gotaverken Arendal AB — Goteborg** Yd No: 656-065 Loa 28.48 Br ex - Dght - Lbp 25.81 Br md 7.68 Dpth 6.30 Welded, 1 dk	**(B11A2FS) Stern Trawler** Grain: 193; Ins: 160	**1 oil engine** reduction geared to sc. shaft driving 1 FP propeller Total Power: 750kW (1,020hp) Caterpillar 3512TA 1 x Vee 4 Stroke 12 Cy. 170 x 190 750kW (1020bhp) Caterpillar Inc-USA Thrusters: 1 Thwart. FP thruster (f)
8824414 - -	**TOKA MARU No. 18** - **Tai Chin Shipping** - *Chinese Taipei*	*496* - 1,237		**1989-04 Muneta Zosen K.K. — Akashi** Loa 51.00 Br ex - Dght 3.480 Lbp 49.31 Br md 16.00 Dpth 4.90 Welded, 1 dk	**(B33A2DG) Grab Dredger**	**2 oil engines** driving 2 FP propellers Total Power: 1,398kW (1,900hp) Yanmar MF24-ST 2 x 4 Stroke 6 Cy. 240 x 420 each-699kW (950bhp) Yanmar Diesel Engine Co Ltd-Japan
8014605 *JLPQ* -	**TOKACHI** **Government of Japan (Cabinet Office)** *Tokyo* *Japan* MMSI: 431800014 Official number: 123721	*527* - -		**1981-03 Narasaki Zosen KK — Muroran HK** Yd No: 996 Loa 67.80 Br ex 7.92 Dght 2.770 Lbp 63.00 Br md 7.90 Dpth 4.40 Welded, 2 dks	**(B34H2SQ) Patrol Vessel**	**2 oil engines** driving 2 FP propellers Total Power: 2,206kW (3,000hp) 18.0kn Niigata 6M31EX 2 x 4 Stroke 6 Cy. 310 x 460 each-1103kW (1500bhp) Niigata Engineering Co Ltd-Japan
9601390 *JD2996* -	**TOKACHI** **Shibuta Tug Boat KK** - *Hiroo, Hokkaido* *Japan* Official number: 141111	*169* - -		**2009-08 Kanto Kogyo K.K. — Hakodate** Yd No: 182 Loa 32.30 Br ex - Dght 2.800 Lbp 28.00 Br md 9.00 Dpth 3.62 Welded, 1 dk	**(B32A2ST) Tug**	**2 oil engines** reduction geared to sc. shafts driving 2 Propellers Total Power: 2,942kW (4,000hp) Niigata 6L26HLX 2 x 4 Stroke 6 Cy. 260 x 350 each-1471kW (2000bhp) Niigata Engineering Co Ltd-Japan
9280550 *JG5689* -	**TOKACHI** **Kinkai Yusen Butsuryu KK** Kinyu Ship Management Co Ltd *Tokyo* *Japan* MMSI: 431101024 Official number: 137147	*9,858* - 6,205	Class: NK	**2002-11 Imabari Shipbuilding Co Ltd — Imabari EH (Imabari Shipyard)** Yd No: 586 Loa 167.72 Br ex - Dght 7.215 Lbp 156.00 Br md 24.00 Dpth 10.70 Welded	**(A35A2RR) Ro-Ro Cargo Ship** Lane-Len: 1900 Cars: 103, Trailers: 128	**1 oil engine** reduction geared to sc. shaft driving 1 Propeller Total Power: 23,850kW (32,426hp) 21.0kn Pielstick 18PC4-2BV570 1 x Vee 4 Stroke 18 Cy. 570 x 660 23850kW (32426bhp) Diesel United Ltd.-Aioi AuxGen: 3 x 1250kW a.c Fuel: 890.0

Number / Call sign	Name, former names, owner, flag	Tonnage	Class	Built / Dimensions	Type	Machinery
8503242 *V3RS6* -	**TOKACHI FROST** *ex* Tokachi Star *-2007* *ex* Tokachi *-1996* *ex* Tokachi Maru *-1991* **Marenga Holdings Corp** Ship Service Agency JSC *Belize City* *Belize* MMSI: 312845000	**3,936** 2,110 3,621	Class: (RS) (BV) (NK)	**1985-08 Shimoda Dockyard Co. Ltd. — Shimoda** Yd No: 344 Loa 111.97 (BB) Br ex 16.44 Dght 7.314 Lbp 104.02 Br md 16.40 Dpth 9.61 Welded, 2 dks	**(A34A2GR) Refrigerated Cargo Ship** Ins: 5,172 Compartments: 3 Ho, ER 3 Ha: 3 (6.5 x 5.0)ER Derricks: 6x3t	**1 oil engine** driving 1 FP propeller Total Power: 3,273kW (4,450hp) 15.0kn Mitsubishi 6UEC45LA 1 x 2 Stroke 6 Cy. 450 x 1350 3273kW (4450bhp) Kobe Hatsudoki KK-Japan AuxGen: 2 x 560kW a.c
8633279 - -	**TOKACHI MARU** *ex* Watakabe Maru No. 5 *-1995* **PT Karya Cemerlang** - *Indonesia*	*100* - -		**1974-03 Kanayama Zosen K.K. — Japan** Loa 27.00 Br ex - Dght 2.500 Lbp 24.00 Br md 6.50 Dpth 3.20 Welded, 1 dk	**(B32A2ST) Tug**	**1 oil engine** driving 1 FP propeller Total Power: 883kW (1,201hp) 12.0kn Fuji 1 x 4 Stroke 883kW (1201bhp) Fuji Diesel Co Ltd-Japan
9472517 *JD2581* -	**TOKACHI MARU** **Tokyo Kisen KK** *Yokohama, Kanagawa* *Japan* Official number: 140703	*226* - -		**2008-02 Kanagawa Zosen — Kobe** Yd No: 576 Loa 37.20 Br ex - Dght 3.100 Lbp 32.70 Br md 9.80 Dpth 4.17 Welded, 1 dk	**(B32A2ST) Tug**	**2 oil engines** reduction geared to sc. shafts driving 2 Propellers Total Power: 2,942kW (4,000hp) 14.6kn Niigata 6l28HX 2 x 4 Stroke 6 Cy. 280 x 370 each-1471kW (2000bhp) Niigata Engineering Co Ltd-Japan
8005604 - -	**TOKACHI MARU No. 25** - -	*259* - -		**1980-07 Sanuki Shipbuilding & Iron Works Co Ltd — Mitoyo KG** Yd No: 1063 Loa - Br ex - Dght - Lbp 37.80 Br md 7.41 Dpth 3.05 Welded, 1 dk	**(B11B2FV) Fishing Vessel**	**1 oil engine** driving 1 FP propeller Total Power: 588kW (799hp) Matsui 6M26KGHS 1 x 4 Stroke 6 Cy. 260 x 400 588kW (799bhp) Matsui Iron Works Co Ltd-Japan
6825359 - -	**TOKAI 25** *ex* Tokai Maru No. 25 *-1994* -	*193* 72 -		**1968 Hayashikane Shipbuilding & Engineering Co Ltd — Nagasaki NS** Yd No: 673 Loa 38.94 Br ex 7.32 Dght 3.175 Lbp 33.99 Br md 7.29 Dpth 3.41 Welded, 1 dk	**(B11B2FV) Fishing Vessel**	**1 oil engine** driving 1 FP propeller Total Power: 515kW (700hp) Daihatsu 6PSTCM-26D 1 x 4 Stroke 6 Cy. 260 x 320 515kW (700bhp) Daihatsu Kogyo-Japan
7936375 - -	**TOKAI MARU No. 1** **Rainbow Marine Corp S de RL** -	*451* - 650		**1979-12 K.K. Yoshida Zosen Kogyo — Arida** Yd No: 327 Loa - Br ex - Dght - Lbp 39.91 Br md 10.00 Dpth 4.91 Welded, 1 dk	**(A31A2GX) General Cargo Ship**	**1 oil engine** driving 1 FP propeller Total Power: 625kW (850hp) Niigata 6MG25BXB 1 x 4 Stroke 6 Cy. 250 x 320 625kW (850bhp) Niigata Engineering Co Ltd-Japan
9180413 *JG4988* -	**TOKAI MARU No. 1** **Boshu Butsuryu KK** - *Tateyama, Chiba* *Japan* Official number: 132040	*495* - 531		**1997-02 Amakusa Zosen K.K. — Amakusa** Yd No: 118 Loa 50.00 Br ex - Dght 2.970 Lbp 43.00 Br md 12.00 Dpth 5.30 Welded, 1 dk	**(A24D2BA) Aggregates Carrier**	**1 oil engine** driving 1 FP propeller Total Power: 736kW (1,001hp) 10.0kn Niigata 6M26AGTE 1 x 4 Stroke 6 Cy. 260 x 460 736kW (1001bhp) Niigata Engineering Co Ltd-Japan
8840937 *JG4981* -	**TOKAI MARU No. 6** **Sanritsu Shori Kogyo KK** - *Kawasaki, Kanagawa* *Japan* Official number: 132034	*123* - 344		**1990-03 Takao Zosen Kogyo K.K. — Tateyama** Yd No: 106 Loa 35.30 Br ex - Dght 2.800 Lbp 30.00 Br md 8.00 Dpth 3.00 Welded, 1 dk	**(B34E2SW) Waste Disposal Vessel**	**1 oil engine** driving 1 FP propeller Total Power: 294kW (400hp) Niigata 6M22EGT 1 x 4 Stroke 6 Cy. 220 x 380 294kW (400bhp) Niigata Engineering Co Ltd-Japan
8627945 - -	**TOKAI MARU No. 7** **Dong Won Marine Bunkering Co Ltd** - *South Korea*	*495* - 1,179		**1986 Takao Zosen Kogyo K.K. — Tateyama** Yd No: 82 Loa 64.27 Br ex - Dght 4.060 Lbp 58.50 Br md 10.00 Dpth 4.60 Welded, 1 dk	**(A31A2GX) General Cargo Ship**	**1 oil engine** driving 1 FP propeller Total Power: 956kW (1,300hp) 12.5kn Niigata 1 x 4 Stroke 956kW (1300bhp) Niigata Engineering Co Ltd-Japan
8869854 *JK5038* -	**TOKAI MARU NO. 8** *ex* Wakayoshi Maru *-2007* **Boshu Butsuryu KK** - *Tateyama, Chiba* *Japan* Official number: 133659	*279* - 754		**1993-02 Shinwa Sangyo K.K. — Osakikamijima** Yd No: 506 Loa 53.00 Br ex - Dght 3.650 Lbp 48.00 Br md 11.50 Dpth 5.80 Welded, 1 dk	**(A31A2GX) General Cargo Ship**	**1 oil engine** driving 1 FP propeller Total Power: 736kW (1,001hp) 11.5kn Niigata 6M28BGT 1 x 4 Stroke 6 Cy. 280 x 480 736kW (1001bhp) Niigata Engineering Co Ltd-Japan
8627751 - -	**TOKAI MARU No. 10** - - *South Korea*	*175* - 511		**1985-06 Takao Zosen Kogyo K.K. — Tateyama** Yd No: 81 Loa 37.50 Br ex - Dght 3.501 Lbp 34.50 Br md 8.50 Dpth 3.71 Welded, 1 dk	**(B34X2QA) Anchor Handling Vessel**	**1 oil engine** driving 1 FP propeller Total Power: 441kW (600hp) 10.0kn Niigata 1 x 4 Stroke 441kW (600bhp) Niigata Engineering Co Ltd-Japan
6821468 - -	**TOKAI MARU No. 15** **Sammy Dee Sea Foods Ltd** - *Nigeria*	*193* - -		**1968 Hayashikane Shipbuilding & Engineering Co Ltd — Nagasaki NS** Yd No: 667 Loa 38.89 Br ex 7.32 Dght 2.947 Lbp 33.58 Br md 7.29 Dpth 3.41 Welded, 1 dk	**(B11B2FV) Fishing Vessel**	**1 oil engine** driving 1 FP propeller Total Power: 515kW (700hp) Daihatsu 6PSTCM-26D 1 x 4 Stroke 6 Cy. 260 x 320 515kW (700bhp) Daihatsu Kogyo-Japan
7912616 - -	**TOKAI MARU No. 57** **Government of The People's Republic of China** - *China*	*149* 54 -		**1979-11 Hayashikane Shipbuilding & Engineering Co Ltd — Nagasaki NS** Yd No: 880 Loa 37.72 Br ex 7.32 Dght 2.810 Lbp 31.50 Br md 6.90 Dpth 3.00 Welded, 1 dk	**(B11B2FV) Fishing Vessel**	**1 oil engine** reduction geared to sc. shaft driving 1 FP propeller Total Power: 647kW (880hp) 10.3kn Daihatsu 6DSM-26 1 x 4 Stroke 6 Cy. 260 x 320 647kW (880bhp) Daihatsu Diesel Manufacturing Co Lt-Japan
6918601 - -	**TOKAI MARU No. 58** *ex* Sayo Maru No. 65 *-1987* - -	*174* 64 -		**1969 Hayashikane Shipbuilding & Engineering Co Ltd — Nagasaki NS** Yd No: 685 Loa 36.56 Br ex 6.84 Dght 2.896 Lbp 31.81 Br md 6.81 Dpth 3.33 Welded, 1 dk	**(B11A2FT) Trawler**	**1 oil engine** driving 1 FP propeller Total Power: 515kW (700hp) Daihatsu 6PSHT6M-26DF 1 x 4 Stroke 6 Cy. 260 x 320 515kW (700bhp) Daihatsu Kogyo-Japan
6728202 - -	**TOKAI No. 3** *ex* Ryuo Maru No. 1 *-1979*	*261* 136 -		**1967 KK Kanasashi Zosen — Shizuoka SZ** Yd No: 785 Loa 45.70 Br ex 7.62 Dght 2.998 Lbp 40.49 Br md 7.60 Dpth 3.41 Welded, 1 dk	**(B11B2FV) Fishing Vessel**	**1 oil engine** driving 1 FP propeller Total Power: 552kW (750hp) Niigata 1 x 4 Stroke 6 Cy. 280 x 440 552kW (750bhp) Niigata Engineering Co Ltd-Japan
6915403 - -	**TOKAR** **Government of The Democratic Republic of The Sudan (Railways Department)** *Port Sudan* *Sudan*	*220* 70 -	Class: (LR) ✠ Classed LR until 1/71	**1969-11 Martin Jansen GmbH & Co. KG Schiffsw. u. Masch. — Leer** Yd No: 82 Loa 34.32 Br ex 8.36 Dght 3.887 Lbp 31.02 Br md 8.23 Dpth 3.97 Welded, 1 dk	**(B32A2ST) Tug**	**1 oil engine** reverse reduction geared to sc. shaft driving 1 FP propeller MAN G9V30/45ATL 1 x 4 Stroke 9 Cy. 300 x 450 Maschinenbau Augsburg Nuernberg (MAN)-Augsburg AuxGen: 2 x 22kW 45V d.c, 1 x 10kW 45V d.c
8980517 *JPRL* -	**TOKARA** **Government of Japan (Ministry of Land, Infrastructure & Transport) (The Coastguard)** - *Tokyo* *Japan* Official number: 137163	*362* - -		**2003-03 Universal Shipbuilding Corp — Yokohama KN (Keihin Shipyard)** Loa 56.00 Br ex - Dght - Lbp - Br md 8.50 Dpth 4.40 Welded, 1 dk	**(B34H2SQ) Patrol Vessel** Hull Material: Aluminium Alloy	**3 oil engines** reduction geared to sc. shafts driving 3 Water jets
9347970 *LYSX* -	**TOKATA** *ex* EWL West Indies *-2008* *ex* El Pionero *-2006* **Limarko Shipping Co AB (LSCo)** - *Klaipeda* *Lithuania* MMSI: 277387000 Official number: 801	**9,948** 5,020 13,729 T/cm 28.0	Class: BV (GL)	**2006-12 Yangzhou Dayang Shipbuilding Co Ltd — Yangzhou JS** Yd No: DY203 Loa 147.84 (BB) Br ex 23.45 Dght 8.500 Lbp 140.30 Br md 23.25 Dpth 11.50 Welded, 1 dk	**(A33A2CC) Container Ship (Fully Cellular)** Grain: 16,000; Bale: 16,000 TEU 1080 C Ho 334 TEU C Dk 746 incl 220 ref C Compartments: 5 Cell Ho, ER 7 Ha: 6 (12.6 x 18.0)ER (14.0 x 10.4) Cranes: 2x45t Ice Capable	**1 oil engine** reduction geared to sc. shaft driving 1 CP propeller Total Power: 9,730kW (13,229hp) 19.6kn MAN-B&W 7L58/64 1 x 4 Stroke 7 Cy. 580 x 640 9730kW (13229bhp) MAN B&W Diesel AG-Augsburg AuxGen: 1 x 1400kW 450V 60Hz a.c, 3 x 570kW 450V 60Hz a.c Thrusters: 1 Tunnel thruster (f) Fuel: 220.0 (d.f.) 1400.0 (r.f.)

7408885 *TCUL* -	**TOKAY AKAR** *ex* Kaptan Murat *-2007* *ex* Ufuk *-1995* *ex* Pep Altair *-1983* *ex* Mercandian Sun *-1981* **Akar Denizcilik ve Ticaret Ltd Sti** Darya Denizcilik Uluslararasi Nakliyat ve Ticaret Ltd Sti *Istanbul* Turkey MMSI: 271000422 Official number: 6767	**2,725** 1,828 4,040	Class: (TL) (BV) (NV)	**1976-04 Buesumer Werft GmbH — Buesum** Yd No: 257 Loa 89.77 (BB) Br ex 13.62 Dght 6.039 Lbp 83.34 Br md 13.61 Dpth 8.51 Welded, 2 dks	**(A31A2GX) General Cargo Ship** Grain: 6,262; Bale: 5,723 TEU 122 C.Ho 90/20' (40') C.Dk 32/20' (40') Compartments: 2 Ho, ER 2 Ha: 2 (25.2 x 10.2)ER Cranes: 1; Derricks: 2x5t Ice Capable	**1 oil engine** reduction geared to sc. shaft driving 1 CP propeller Total Power: 1,354kW (1,841hp) 14.0kn MaK 6M25 1 x 4 Stroke 6 Cy. 255 x 400 1354kW (1841bhp) (new engine ,made 1999) MaK Motoren GmbH & Co. KG-Kiel AuxGen: 2 x 104kW 380V 50Hz a.c, 1 x 72kW 380V 50Hz a.c Fuel: 309.0 (r.f.) 10.5pd
8717611 *JK4729* -	**TOKEI MARU** **Toyu Kaiun YK** - *Shunan, Yamaguchi* Japan Official number: 129652	*238* - -		**1988-06 Koa Sangyo KK — Takamatsu KG** Yd No: 532 Lengthened-2001 L reg 50.73 Br ex - Dght - Lbp - Br md 7.80 Dpth 3.40 Welded, 1 dk	**(A12A2TC) Chemical Tanker** Compartments: 7 Ta, ER 6 Cargo Pump (s)	**1 oil engine** driving 1 FP propeller Total Power: 588kW (799hp) Niigata 6M26AGTE 1 x 4 Stroke 6 Cy. 260 x 460 588kW (799bhp) Niigata Engineering Co Ltd-Japan
9050694 - -	**TOKELAU** *ex* Tutolu *-2000* **Samoa Shipping Corp Ltd** -	*182* 85 21	Class: LR **100A1** SS 01/2010 SSC work boat mono, G4 Inter Island service - Tokelau, Samoa, American Samoa and Cook Islands **LMC** Cable: U2 (a)	**1991-11 McMullen & Wing Ltd — Auckland** Converted From: Ferry (Passenger only)-2000 Lengthened Loa 31.05 Br ex 8.25 Dght 1.200 Lbp 28.86 Br md 8.00 Dpth 2.77 Welded, 1 dk	**(B34L2QU) Utility Vessel** Hull Material: Aluminium Alloy	**2 oil engines** with clutches, flexible couplings & sr reverse geared to sc. shafts driving 2 FP propellers Total Power: 596kW (810hp) 7.0kn Cummins NTA-855-M 2 x 4 Stroke 6 Cy. 140 x 152 each-298kW (405bhp) Cummins Brasil Ltda-Brazil AuxGen: 2 x 25kW 380V 50Hz a.c Thrusters: 1 Thwart. FP thruster (f) Fuel: 20.0 (d.f.)
9178123 *EASQ* 3-BI-41-98	**TOKI ALAI BERRIA** **Pesquerias Veiga SL** - SatCom: Inmarsat C 422418510 *Ondarroa* Spain MMSI: 224185000 Official number: 3-1/1998	**331** 99 -	Class: (BV)	**1999-02 Astilleros Zamakona SA — Santurtzi** Yd No: 426 Loa - Br ex - Dght 3.550 Lbp 27.70 Br md 8.10 Dpth 5.70 Welded, 1 dk	**(B11B2FV) Fishing Vessel**	**1 oil engine** driving 1 FP propeller Total Power: 552kW (750hp) 10.0kn Wartsila 6R20 1 x 4 Stroke 6 Cy. 200 x 280 552kW (750bhp) AuxGen: 2 x 112kW 380V 50Hz a.c
9434539 *3FYU5* -	**TOKI ARROW** **Million Comets SA** KK Kyowa Sansho *Panama* Panama MMSI: 353325000 Official number: 4210910	**36,925** 18,303 62,942	Class: NK	**2010-10 Oshima Shipbuilding Co Ltd — Saikai NS** Yd No: 10572 Loa 199.98 (BB) Br ex - Dght 13.507 Lbp 196.00 Br md 32.26 Dpth 19.22 Welded, 1 dk	**(A31A2GO) Open Hatch Cargo Ship** Double Hull Grain: 70,354; Bale: 70,283 TEU 270 on Dk Compartments: 8 Ho, ER 8 Ha: 6 (18.3 x 27.4) (18.3 x 13.8)ER (16.8 x 14.8) Cranes: 4x40t	**1 oil engine** driving 1 FP propeller Total Power: 8,605kW (11,699hp) 14.5kn MAN-B&W 6S50MC-C 1 x 2 Stroke 6 Cy. 500 x 2000 8605kW (11699bhp) Kawasaki Heavy Industries Ltd-Japan Thrusters: 1 Tunnel thruster (f)
9457701 *JD2543* -	**TOKI MARU** **Toyo Kaiun KK** - *Shizuoka, Shizuoka* Japan Official number: 140675	*499* - 1,750		**2008-01 K.K. Watanabe Zosensho — Nagasaki** Yd No: 147 Loa 74.70 Br ex - Dght 4.300 Lbp 69.00 Br md 12.00 Dpth 7.38 Welded, 1 dk	**(A31A2GX) General Cargo Ship**	**1 oil engine** driving 1 FP propeller Total Power: 1,618kW (2,200hp) 12.0kn Niigata 6M34BGT 1 x 4 Stroke 6 Cy. 340 x 620 1618kW (2200bhp) Niigata Engineering Co Ltd-Japan
9159165 *JL6526* -	**TOKI MARU** **Tadataka Odawara** - *Imabari, Ehime* Japan MMSI: 431400632 Official number: 135565	*186* - 614		**1997-01 Koa Sangyo KK — Takamatsu KG** Yd No: 596 L reg 50.55 Br ex - Dght 3.200 Lbp 49.00 Br md 9.40 Dpth 5.35 Welded, 1 dk	**(A31A2GX) General Cargo Ship**	**1 oil engine** driving 1 FP propeller Total Power: 736kW (1,001hp) 10.0kn Niigata 6M26AGTE 1 x 4 Stroke 6 Cy. 260 x 460 736kW (1001bhp) Niigata Engineering Co Ltd-Japan
8922797 *JG5434* -	**TOKINAMI** **Government of Japan (Ministry of Land, Infrastructure & Transport) (The Coastguard)** *Tokyo* Japan MMSI: 431400533 Official number: 135218	*113* - -		**1996-03 Yokohama Yacht Co Ltd — Yokohama KN** Loa 35.00 Br ex - Dght 1.250 Lbp 32.00 Br md 6.30 Dpth 3.43 Welded, 1 dk	**(B34H2SQ) Patrol Vessel**	**2 oil engines** geared to sc. shafts driving 2 FP propellers Total Power: 2,942kW (4,000hp) 25.0kn M.T.U. 12V396TB94 2 x Vee 4 Stroke 12 Cy. 165 x 185 each-1471kW (2000bhp) MTU Friedrichshafen GmbH-Friedrichshafen
9311270 *H8RL* -	**TOKIO** **Esteem Maritime** MMS Co Ltd SatCom: Inmarsat C 435422110 *Panama* Panama MMSI: 354221000 Official number: 3056605B	**159,953** 99,410 306,206 T/cm 181.8	Class: NK	**2005-02 Mitsubishi Heavy Industries Ltd. — Nagasaki** Yd No: 2201 Loa 333.00 (BB) Br ex - Dght 20.825 Lbp 324.00 Br md 60.00 Dpth 29.10 Welded, 1 dk	**(A13A2TV) Crude Oil Tanker** Double Hull (13F) Liq: 335,035; Liq (Oil): 350,042 Compartments: 5 Ta, 10 Wing Ta, 2 Wing Slop Ta, ER 3 Cargo Pump (s): 3x5500m³/hr Manifold: Bow/CM: 166.5m	**1 oil engine** driving 1 FP propeller Total Power: 27,022kW (36,739hp) 15.5kn Mitsubishi 7UEC85LSII 1 x 2 Stroke 7 Cy. 850 x 3150 27022kW (36739bhp) Mitsubishi Heavy Industries Ltd-Japan AuxGen: 2 x 1100kW a.c, 1 x 1200kW a.c Fuel: 475.0 (d.f.) 8260.0 (r.f.)
9568809 *7JIV* -	**TOKITSU MARU** **Nippon Yusen Kabushiki Kaisha (NYK Line)** JX Ocean Co Ltd 773178708 *Tokyo* Japan MMSI: 432805000 Official number: 141385	**159,963** 100,799 305,484 T/cm 182.1	Class: NK	**2011-04 Mitsubishi Heavy Industries Ltd. — Nagasaki** Yd No: 2273 Loa 333.00 (BB) Br ex 60.03 Dght 20.835 Lbp 324.00 Br md 60.00 Dpth 29.10 Welded, 1 dk	**(A13A2TV) Crude Oil Tanker** Double Hull (13F) Liq: 338,852; Liq (Oil): 340,102 Compartments: 5 Ta, 10 Wing Ta, ER, 2 Wing Slop Ta 3 Cargo Pump (s): 3x5000m³/hr Manifold: Bow/CM: 165.2m	**1 oil engine** driving 1 FP propeller Total Power: 27,020kW (36,736hp) 15.5kn Mitsubishi 7UEC85LSII 1 x 2 Stroke 7 Cy. 850 x 3150 27020kW (36736bhp) Mitsubishi Heavy Industries Ltd-Japan AuxGen: 2 x 1100kW a.c, 1 x 1200kW a.c Fuel: 360.0 (d.f.) 7510.0 (r.f.)
9114995 *JG5330* -	**TOKIWA** *ex* Yamato *-2006* **KK Daito Corp** *Tokyo* Japan Official number: 134970	*175* - -		**1994-08 Hanasaki Zosensho K.K. — Yokosuka** Yd No: 241 Loa 32.25 Br ex - Dght 2.900 Lbp 27.80 Br md 8.80 Dpth 3.89 Welded, 1 dk	**(B32A2ST) Tug**	**2 oil engines** with clutches, flexible couplings & reduction geared to sc. shafts driving 2 FP propellers Total Power: 2,280kW (3,100hp) Niigata 6L25HX 2 x 4 Stroke 6 Cy. 250 x 350 each-1140kW (1550bhp) Niigata Engineering Co Ltd-Japan
9146857 *JG5358* -	**TOKIWA MARU** **Shurin Tanker KK** - *Shimonoseki, Yamaguchi* Japan MMSI: 431100272 Official number: 134957	*1,735* - 3,322	Class: NK	**1996-11 Nishi Shipbuilding Co Ltd — Imabari EH** Yd No: 398 Loa 89.98 Br ex - Dght 5.857 Lbp 85.00 Br md 13.00 Dpth 6.35 Welded, 1 dk	**(A13B2TP) Products Tanker** Liq: 3,327; Liq (Oil): 3,395	**1 oil engine** reverse geared to sc. shaft driving 1 FP propeller Total Power: 2,427kW (3,300hp) 13.0kn Akasaka A41 1 x 4 Stroke 6 Cy. 410 x 800 2427kW (3300bhp) Akasaka Tekkosho KK (Akasaka DieselLtd)-Japan Fuel: 205.0 (r.f.)
9666699 *JD3579* -	**TOKIWA MARU** - - *Sado, Niigata* Japan MMSI: 431005219	*5,300* - 1,500	Class: FA	**2014-03 Kanda Zosensho K.K. — Kawajiri** Yd No: 540 Loa 125.00 Br ex - Dght 7.200 Lbp - Br md 21.80 Dpth - Welded, 1 dk	**(A36A2PR) Passenger/Ro-Ro Ship (Vehicles)** Single Hull	**2 oil engines** reduction geared to sc. shafts driving 2 Propellers Total Power: 8,826kW (12,000hp) Niigata 6MG41HX 2 x 4 Stroke 6 Cy. 410 x 560 each-4413kW (6000bhp) Niigata Engineering Co Ltd-Japan
7128203 - -	**TOKIWA MARU No. 2** *ex* Seisho Maru No. 8 *-1978* **Kotaro Koshino** -	*344* 179 236		**1971 KK Kanasashi Zosen — Shizuoka SZ** Yd No: 1049 Loa 54.31 Br ex 8.36 Dght 3.499 Lbp 45.50 Br md 8.31 Dpth 3.87 Welded, 1 dk	**(B11B2FV) Fishing Vessel**	**1 oil engine** driving 1 FP propeller Total Power: 1,214kW (1,651hp) Hanshin 6LU35 1 x 4 Stroke 6 Cy. 350 x 550 1214kW (1651bhp) Hanshin Nainenki Kogyo-Japan
8324153 *JJFE* NG1-85	**TOKIWA MARU No. 3** **Okura Gyogyo KK** - SatCom: Inmarsat B 343151110 *Niigata, Niigata* Japan MMSI: 431511000 Official number: 120046	*349* - 845		**1984-03 Niigata Engineering Co Ltd — Niigata NI** Yd No: 1803 Loa 61.45 (BB) Br ex - Dght 4.560 Lbp 53.93 Br md 11.82 Dpth 7.12 Welded, 2 dks	**(B11B2FV) Fishing Vessel** Ins: 1,036	**1 oil engine** with clutches, flexible couplings & sr reverse geared to sc. shaft driving 1 FP propeller Total Power: 1,912kW (2,600hp) Niigata 8MG31FZE 1 x 4 Stroke 8 Cy. 310 x 380 1912kW (2600bhp) Niigata Engineering Co Ltd-Japan

IMO / Call sign	Name / Owner	Tonnage	Class	Builder / Dimensions	Type	Machinery
8519992 - -	**TOKIWA MARU NO. 5** *ex* Kaiun Maru No. 15 *-1997* *ex* Shintoku Maru *-1990* - -	*141* - 465		**1985-12 Iisaku Zosen K.K. — Nishi-Izu** Yd No: 85125 Loa 40.21 Br ex 8.46 Dght 2.580 Lbp 38.00 Br md 8.36 Dpth 2.60 Welded, 1 dk	**(A13B2TP) Products Tanker** Compartments: 4 Ta, ER	**1 oil engine** with clutches & reverse reduction geared to sc. shaft driving 1 FP propeller Total Power: 331kW (450hp) Matsui ML624GS 1 x 4 Stroke 6 Cy. 240 x 400 331kW (450bhp) Matsui Iron Works Co Ltd-Japan
9031923 *JJHJ* -	**TOKIWA MARU No. 18** - **Okura Gyogyo KK** - SatCom: Inmarsat B 343131010 *Niigata, Niigata* *Japan* MMSI: 431310000 Official number: 120092	*349* - -		**1991-06 Niigata Engineering Co Ltd — Niigata NI** Yd No: 2213 Loa 63.24 (BB) Br ex - Dght - Lbp 55.00 Br md 12.00 Dpth 7.27 Welded	**(B11A2FS) Stern Trawler** Ins: 1,132	**1 oil engine** with clutches, flexible couplings & dr tandem geared to sc. shaft driving 1 FP propeller Total Power: 1,986kW (2,700hp) Niigata 6MG32CLX 1 x 4 Stroke 6 Cy. 320 x 420 1986kW (2700bhp) Niigata Engineering Co Ltd-Japan
9195028 *JKRN* -	**TOKIWA MARU No. 28** - **Okura Gyogyo KK** - SatCom: Inmarsat B 343139910 *Niigata, Niigata* *Japan* MMSI: 431399000 Official number: 120134	*349* - -		**1998-09 Niigata Engineering Co Ltd — Niigata NI** Yd No: 2351 Loa 63.00 (BB) Br ex - Dght - Lbp 55.00 Br md 12.00 Dpth 7.00 Welded, 1 dk	**(B11B2FV) Fishing Vessel** Ins: 1,077	**1 oil engine** with clutches, flexible couplings & sr geared to sc. shaft driving 1 FP propeller Total Power: 2,353kW (3,199hp) 15.8kn Niigata 6MG34HX 1 x 4 Stroke 6 Cy. 340 x 450 2353kW (3199bhp) Niigata Engineering Co Ltd-Japan AuxGen: 2 x 800kW a.c Thrusters: 1 Thwart. FP thruster (f)
7937161 *YD4669* -	**TOKO MAJU No. 10** *ex* Kotobuki Maru No. 1 *-2000* *ex* Kotobuki Maru No. 23 *-1987* **PT Aneka Atlanticindo Nidyatama** - *Palembang* *Indonesia*	*163* 49 -	Class: KI	**1977-08 Nichiro Zosen K.K. — Ishinomaki** Yd No: 383 Converted From: Fishing Vessel-2000 Loa 37.22 Br ex - Dght - Lbp 30.84 Br md 7.00 Dpth 2.80 Welded, 1 dk	**(B32A2ST) Tug**	**1 oil engine** geared to sc. shaft driving 1 FP propeller Total Power: 1,471kW (2,000hp) Yanmar 6ZL-DT 1 x 4 Stroke 6 Cy. 280 x 340 1471kW (2000bhp) Yanmar Diesel Engine Co Ltd-Japan
8520604 - -	**TOKO MARU** - - - *South Korea*	*182* - 390		**1986-01 K.K. Odo Zosen Tekko — Shimonoseki** Yd No: 317 Loa 39.91 Br ex 7.22 Dght 3.082 Lbp 36.00 Br md 7.21 Dpth 3.31 Welded, 1 dk	**(A12A2TC) Chemical Tanker** Liq: 174	**1 oil engine** with clutches, flexible couplings & sr geared to sc. shaft driving 1 FP propeller Total Power: 294kW (400hp) Yanmar 6ML-HTS 1 x 4 Stroke 6 Cy. 200 x 240 294kW (400bhp) Yanmar Diesel Engine Co Ltd-Japan
8613138 *JL5547* -	**TOKO MARU** - **Takamatsu Seiso KK** - *Takamatsu, Kagawa* *Japan* Official number: 129053	*160* - 370		**1986-12 Tokushima Zosen Sangyo K.K. — Komatsushima** Yd No: 1940 Loa 42.02 Br ex - Dght 2.601 Lbp 37.01 Br md 7.82 Dpth 2.90 Welded, 1 dk	**(B34E2SW) Waste Disposal Vessel** Liq: 407	**1 oil engine** geared to sc. shaft driving 1 FP propeller Total Power: 331kW (450hp) Yanmar S165L-UT 1 x 4 Stroke 6 Cy. 165 x 210 331kW (450bhp) Yanmar Diesel Engine Co Ltd-Japan
9046722 *JK5153* -	**TOKO MARU** - **Toa Kaiun YK** Tosoh Logistics Corp (Tosoh Butsuryu KK) *Shunan, Yamaguchi* *Japan* Official number: 132563	*199* - 503		**1992-04 Koa Sangyo KK — Takamatsu KG** Yd No: 565 Loa 55.00 Br ex - Dght 3.100 Lbp - Br md 7.80 Dpth 3.30 Welded, 1 dk	**(A12A2TC) Chemical Tanker** Liq: 393 Compartments: 6 Ta, ER 1 Cargo Pump (s): 1x150m³/hr	**1 oil engine** driving 1 FP propeller Total Power: 588kW (799hp) Niigata 6M26AGTE 1 x 4 Stroke 6 Cy. 260 x 460 588kW (799bhp) Niigata Engineering Co Ltd-Japan
8980567 *JK5639* -	**TOKO MARU** - **Japan Railway Construction, Transport & Technology Agency & KK Kyodo Kaiun** KK Kyodo Kaiun *Kure, Hiroshima* *Japan* Official number: 136204	*440* - 1,103		**2003-06 KK Ura Kyodo Zosensho — Awaji HG** Yd No: 318 Loa 61.61 Br ex - Dght 3.940 Lbp 57.00 Br md 10.00 Dpth 4.10 Welded, 1 dk	**(A12A2TC) Chemical Tanker** Double Hull (13F) Liq: 800 Compartments: 4 Wing Ta 2 Cargo Pump (s): 2x200m³/hr	**1 oil engine** reverse geared to sc. shaft driving 1 FP propeller Total Power: 1,029kW (1,399hp) 11.9kn Akasaka A28S 1 x 4 Stroke 6 Cy. 280 x 550 1029kW (1399bhp) Akasaka Tekkosho KK (Akasaka DieselLtd)-Japan
9011117 *JG4957* -	**TOKO MARU** - **Tokyo Kinkai Yuso KK & Nippon Marine Service & Engineering Co Ltd (Nippon Kaiji Kogyo KK)** Nippon Marine Service & Engineering Co Ltd (Nippon Kaiji Kogyo KK) *Tokyo* *Japan* Official number: 132006	*195* - -		**1990-10 Kanagawa Zosen — Kobe** Yd No: 350 Loa 34.70 Br ex - Dght - Lbp 30.00 Br md 9.00 Dpth 4.00 Welded	**(B32A2ST) Tug**	**2 oil engines** Geared Integral to driving 2 Z propellers Total Power: 2,500kW (3,400hp) 14.5kn Pielstick 6PA5 2 x 4 Stroke 6 Cy. 255 x 270 each-1250kW (1700bhp) Niigata Engineering Co Ltd-Japan
9138484 *JHEL* -	**TOKO MARU** - **Government of Japan (Ministry of Agriculture & Forestry - Fisheries Agency)** - SatCom: Inmarsat B 343185610 *Tokyo* *Japan* MMSI: 431856000 Official number: 135231	*2,071* - 1,109		**1996-05 Sumitomo Heavy Industries Ltd. — Oppama Shipyard, Yokosuka** Yd No: 1212 Loa 86.90 (BB) Br ex 14.03 Dght 6.000 Lbp 76.00 Br md 14.00 Dpth 9.10 Welded, 1 dk	**(B12D2FP) Fishery Patrol Vessel**	**2 oil engines** with clutches & dr geared to sc. shaft driving 1 CP propeller Total Power: 5,884kW (8,000hp) 17.0kn Yanmar 8N330-UN 2 x 4 Stroke 8 Cy. 330 x 440 each-2942kW (4000bhp) Yanmar Diesel Engine Co Ltd-Japan Thrusters: 1 Thwart. CP thruster (f)
9234965 *JG5599* -	**TOKO MARU** - **Fuel Tepco Ltd** - *Tokyo* *Japan* Official number: 136911	*754* - -		**2000-03 Murakami Hide Zosen K.K. — Imabari** Yd No: 507 Loa 74.92 Br ex - Dght - Lbp 70.00 Br md 12.00 Dpth 5.25 Welded, 1 dk	**(A13B2TU) Tanker (unspecified)**	**1 oil engine** driving 1 FP propeller Total Power: 1,471kW (2,000hp) 12.2kn Niigata 6M34BGT 1 x 4 Stroke 6 Cy. 340 x 620 1471kW (2000bhp) Niigata Engineering Co Ltd-Japan
9380439 *7JBO* -	**TOKO MARU** - **Nikko Sangyo KK** - *Hiroshima, Hiroshima* *Japan* MMSI: 432557000 Official number: 140328	*288* - 210		**2006-06 K.K. Izutsu Zosensho — Nagasaki** Yd No: 1123 Loa 39.70 Br ex - Dght 3.200 Lbp 33.50 Br md 9.60 Dpth 4.38 Welded, 1 dk	**(B32A2ST) Tug**	**2 oil engines** reduction geared to sc. shafts driving 2 Propellers Total Power: 3,236kW (4,400hp) 12.5kn Daihatsu 6DKM-26 2 x 4 Stroke 6 Cy. 260 x 380 each-1618kW (2200bhp) Daihatsu Diesel Manufacturing Co Lt-Japan
9578402 *JD2912* -	**TOKO MARU** - **Toko Kaiun KK** - *Hiroshima, Hiroshima* *Japan* Official number: 141013	*499* - 1,820		**2009-04 K.K. Matsuura Zosensho — Osakikamijima** Yd No: 568 L reg 70.06 (BB) Br ex - Dght 4.390 Lbp 68.00 Br md 12.00 Dpth 7.35 Welded, 1 dk	**(A31A2GX) General Cargo Ship**	**1 oil engine** reduction geared to sc. shaft driving 1 Propeller Total Power: 1,618kW (2,200hp) 13.7kn Hanshin LA32G 1 x 4 Stroke 6 Cy. 320 x 680 1618kW (2200bhp) The Hanshin Diesel Works Ltd-Japan
9172519 *JM6585* -	**TOKO MARU No. 5** - **Matsumura Kaiun YK** - *Kamiamakusa, Kumamoto* *Japan* Official number: 135445	*498* - 1,500		**1997-08 K.K. Yoshida Zosen Kogyo — Arida** Yd No: 507 Loa 76.32 Br ex - Dght - Lbp 70.00 Br md 12.00 Dpth 7.00 Welded, 1 dk	**(A31A2GX) General Cargo Ship** Compartments: 1 Ho, ER 1 Ha: (40.2 x 9.5)ER	**1 oil engine** driving 1 FP propeller Total Power: 736kW (1,001hp) 10.0kn Hanshin LH34LAG 1 x 4 Stroke 6 Cy. 340 x 640 736kW (1001bhp) The Hanshin Diesel Works Ltd-Japan
8310279 *JG4260* -	**TOKO MARU NO. 5** *ex* Toa Maru No. 5 *-2011* *ex* Nagato Maru *-1999* **Tokyo Kisen KK** - *Hiroshima, Hiroshima* *Japan* Official number: 126699	*162* - -		**1983-07 Kanagawa Zosen — Kobe** Yd No: 250 Loa 37.75 Br ex - Dght 2.601 Lbp 33.51 Br md 8.41 Dpth 3.41 Welded, 1 dk	**(B32A2ST) Tug**	**2 oil engines** Geared Integral to driving 2 Z propellers Total Power: 2,206kW (3,000hp) 15.5kn Niigata 6L25CXE 2 x 4 Stroke 6 Cy. 250 x 320 each-1103kW (1500bhp) Niigata Engineering Co Ltd-Japan AuxGen: 2 x 128kW 440V 60Hz a.c Fuel: 31.5 (d.f.) 8.0pd
7937018 - -	**TOKO MARU No. 7** - **Syarikat Eminent Co** -	*154* - -		**1976 Nichiro Zosen K.K. — Ishinomaki** Yd No: 361 Loa 38.87 Br ex - Dght - Lbp 33.00 Br md 6.71 Dpth 2.75 Welded, 1 dk	**(B11B2FV) Fishing Vessel**	**1 oil engine** driving 1 FP propeller Total Power: 736kW (1,001hp) Hanshin 6LUD26 1 x 4 Stroke 6 Cy. 260 x 440 736kW (1001bhp) The Hanshin Diesel Works Ltd-Japan

9123984 *JM6414* -	**TOKO MARU No. 8** - **Kowa Kaiun KK** - *Shimonoseki, Yamaguchi* *Japan* Official number: 134503	*198* - 542	**1995-06 Kanmon Zosen K.K. — Shimonoseki** Yd No: 567 Loa 47.61 (BB) Br ex 8.02 Dght 3.200 Lbp 44.00 Br md 8.00 Dpth 3.45 Welded, 1 dk	**(A13B2TP) Products Tanker** Liq: 581; Liq (Oil): 581 Compartments: 6 Ta, ER	**1 oil engine** with clutches & reverse geared to sc. shaft driving 1 FP propeller Total Power: 736kW (1,001hp) Hanshin LH26G 1 x 4 Stroke 6 Cy. 260 x 440 736kW (1001bhp) The Hanshin Diesel Works Ltd-Japan
9036777 *JQEC* MG1-1835	**TOKO MARU NO. 8** *ex* Tokuju Maru No. 7 *-2007* **KK Toko Gyogyo** - SatCom: Inmarsat A 1204544 *Kesennuma, Miyagi* *Japan* MMSI: 431702660 Official number: 132199	*379* - -	**1991-09 Niigata Engineering Co Ltd — Niigata NI** Yd No: 2220 Loa 54.55 (BB) Br ex - Dght 3.440 Lbp 47.90 Br md 8.70 Dpth 3.80 Welded	**(B11B2FV) Fishing Vessel** Ins: 503	**1 oil engine** with clutches, flexible couplings & sr geared to sc. shaft driving 1 CP propeller Total Power: 699kW (950hp) Niigata 6M28BFT 1 x 4 Stroke 6 Cy. 280 x 480 699kW (950bhp) Niigata Engineering Co Ltd-Japan
9159206 - -	**TOKO MARU No. 10** - **Ulleung-gun Suhyup** - *South Korea*	*199* - 450	**1996-12 Kyoei Zosen KK — Mihara HS** Yd No: 280 Loa 49.00 Br ex - Dght 3.150 Lbp 45.00 Br md 7.80 Dpth 3.30 Welded, 1 dk	**(A12A2LP) Molten Sulphur Tanker** Single Hull Liq: 404 2 Cargo Pump (s): 2x150m³/hr	**1 oil engine** reduction geared to sc. shaft driving 1 FP propeller Total Power: 736kW (1,001hp) 11.0kn Hanshin LH26G 1 x 4 Stroke 6 Cy. 260 x 440 736kW (1001bhp) The Hanshin Diesel Works Ltd-Japan AuxGen: 2 x 356kW a.c, 1 x 100kW a.c Thrusters: 1 Thwart. FP thruster (f)
9165061 *JK5486* -	**TOKO MARU No. 21** - **Kyodo Kaiun KK** - *Kudamatsu, Yamaguchi* *Japan* MMSI: 431400727 Official number: 135332	*730* - 1,957	**1997-07 K.K. Miura Zosensho — Saiki** Yd No: 1188 L reg 80.81 Br ex - Dght - Lbp 78.50 Br md 12.80 Dpth 7.70 Welded, 1 dk	**(A31A2GX) General Cargo Ship** Grain: 3,423	**1 oil engine** driving 1 FP propeller Total Power: 1,912kW (2,600hp) 12.5kn Hanshin LH36LAG 1 x 4 Stroke 6 Cy. 360 x 670 1912kW (2600bhp) The Hanshin Diesel Works Ltd-Japan
9031935 *JQDM* MG1-1831	**TOKO MARU NO. 68** *ex* Tenyu Maru No. 7 *-2007* **KK Toko Gyogyo** - SatCom: Inmarsat A 1204526 *Kesennuma, Miyagi* *Japan* MMSI: 431701870 Official number: 132195	*379* - 470	**1991-06 Niigata Engineering Co Ltd — Niigata NI** Yd No: 2216 Loa 54.56 (BB) Br ex - Dght 3.440 Lbp 47.90 Br md 8.70 Dpth 3.80 Welded	**(B11B2FV) Fishing Vessel** Ins: 491	**1 oil engine** with clutches, flexible couplings & sr geared to sc. shaft driving 1 CP propeller Total Power: 699kW (950hp) 13.1kn Niigata 6M28BFT 1 x 4 Stroke 6 Cy. 280 x 480 699kW (950bhp) Niigata Engineering Co Ltd-Japan AuxGen: 2 x 308kW 225V a.c Fuel: 264.0 (d.f.) 3.0pd
9016258 *JFBJ* K01-770	**TOKO MARU NO. 78** *ex* Daian Maru No. 1 *-2007* *ex* Hiro Maru No. 8 *-1993* **KK Toko Gyogyo** - SatCom: Inmarsat A 1204172 *Kesennuma, Miyagi* *Japan* MMSI: 431500790 Official number: 131496	*379* - -	**1991-02 KK Kanasashi Zosen — Shizuoka SZ** Yd No: 3243 Loa 55.16 (BB) Br ex 8.73 Dght 3.401 Lbp 48.10 Br md 8.70 Dpth 3.75 Welded	**(B11B2FV) Fishing Vessel** Ins: 573	**1 oil engine** with clutches, flexible couplings & sr reverse geared to sc. shaft driving 1 FP propeller Total Power: 736kW (1,001hp) Niigata 6M28HFT 1 x 4 Stroke 6 Cy. 280 x 480 736kW (1001bhp) Niigata Engineering Co Ltd-Japan
9016246 *JFBX* K01-730	**TOKO MARU NO. 88** *ex* Shinei Maru No. 85 *-2007* **KK Toko Gyogyo** - SatCom: Inmarsat A 1204225 *Kesennuma, Miyagi* *Japan* MMSI: 431500590 Official number: 131497	*379* - -	**1991-04 KK Kanasashi — Shizuoka SZ** Yd No: 3241 Loa 55.16 (BB) Br ex 8.73 Dght 3.401 Lbp 48.10 Br md 8.70 Dpth 3.75 Welded	**(B11B2FV) Fishing Vessel** Ins: 572	**1 oil engine** with clutches, flexible couplings & sr reverse geared to sc. shaft driving 1 FP propeller Total Power: 736kW (1,001hp) Niigata 6M28HFT 1 x 4 Stroke 6 Cy. 280 x 480 736kW (1001bhp) Niigata Engineering Co Ltd-Japan
9604782 *3FVU9* -	**TOKOMARU BAY** - **San Lorenzo Shipping SA** Pacific Basin Shipping (HK) Ltd *Panama* *Panama* MMSI: 370128000 Official number: 4321011	**17,027** Class: NK 10,108 28,258 T/cm 39.7	**2011-11 Imabari Shipbuilding Co Ltd — Imabari EH (Imabari Shipyard)** Yd No: 754 Loa 169.37 (BB) Br ex - Dght 9.820 Lbp 160.40 Br md 27.20 Dpth 13.60 Welded, 1 dk	**(A21A2BC) Bulk Carrier** Grain: 37,320; Bale: 35,742 Compartments: 5 Ho, ER 5 Ha: ER Cranes: 4x30.7t	**1 oil engine** driving 1 FP propeller Total Power: 5,850kW (7,954hp) 14.5kn MAN-B&W 6S42MC 1 x 2 Stroke 6 Cy. 420 x 1764 5850kW (7954bhp) Makita Corp-Japan Fuel: 1530.0
7518630 - -	**TOKU MARU NO. 18** *ex* Kotoku Maru No. 18 *-2006* *ex* Myojin Maru No. 12 *-1988* **Seong Shin Fisheries Co Ltd** - *South Korea*	*187* 71 199	**1975-07 K.K. Murakami Zosensho — Ishinomaki** Yd No: 968 Loa 38.44 Br ex 6.81 Dght 2.585 Lbp 32.85 Br md 6.51 Dpth 2.90 Welded, 1 dk	**(B11B2FV) Fishing Vessel**	**1 oil engine** driving 1 FP propeller Total Power: 736kW (1,001hp) Yanmar 6GL-UT 1 x 4 Stroke 6 Cy. 240 x 290 736kW (1001bhp) Yanmar Diesel Engine Co Ltd-Japan
9197272 *JL6619* -	**TOKU MARU No. 25** - **Matsuoka Senpaku KK** - *Higashikagawa, Kagawa* *Japan* Official number: 136478	*498* - 1,600	**1998-08 Yamanaka Zosen K.K. — Imabari** Yd No: 626 Loa 76.23 Br ex - Dght 4.080 Lbp 70.00 Br md 12.00 Dpth 7.01 Welded, 2 dks	**(A31A2GX) General Cargo Ship** Grain: 2,278 Compartments: 1 Ho, ER, 1 Tw Dk 1 Ha: (40.0 x 9.5)ER	**1 oil engine** driving 1 FP propeller Total Power: 1,324kW (1,800hp) 12.0kn Niigata 6M31BLGT 1 x 4 Stroke 6 Cy. 310 x 600 1324kW (1800bhp) Niigata Engineering Co Ltd-Japan
9715165 *JD3512* -	**TOKU MARU NO. 27** - **Japan Railway Construction, Transport & Technology Agency & Matsuoka Senpaku KK** Matsuoka Senpaku KK *Higashikagawa, Kagawa* *Japan* MMSI: 431004515 Official number: 141918	*499* - 1,700	**2013-05 Tokuoka Zosen K.K. — Naruto** Loa 75.00 (BB) Br ex - Dght - Lbp - Br md 12.00 Dpth - Welded, 1 dk	**(A31A2GX) General Cargo Ship**	**1 oil engine** reverse geared to sc. shaft driving 1 Propeller Total Power: 1,323kW (1,799hp) Akasaka AX31R 1 x 4 Stroke 6 Cy. 310 x 620 1323kW (1799bhp) Akasaka Tekkosho KK (Akasaka DieselLtd)-Japan
8823692 *JL5798* -	**TOKUEI MARU** - **Marushige Shoji KK** - *Niihama, Ehime* *Japan* Official number: 130674	*199* - 450	**1988-12 Hongawara Zosen K.K. — Fukuyama** Loa 45.25 Br ex - Dght 3.100 Lbp 41.00 Br md 7.60 Dpth 3.40 Welded, 1 dk	**(A12A2TC) Chemical Tanker** 1 Cargo Pump (s): 1x150m³/hr	**1 oil engine** driving 1 FP propeller Total Power: 478kW (650hp) Yanmar MF24-UT 1 x 4 Stroke 6 Cy. 240 x 420 478kW (650bhp) Yanmar Diesel Engine Co Ltd-Japan
9041801 *JH3238* -	**TOKUEI MARU No. 17** - **Tokuei Kaiun KK** - *Minami-ise, Mie* *Japan* Official number: 131590	*486* - 1,230	**1991-12 Sasaki Shipbuilding Co Ltd — Osakikamijima HS** Yd No: 562 Loa 64.42 Br ex 10.02 Dght 4.187 Lbp 60.00 Br md 10.00 Dpth 4.50 Welded, 1 dk	**(A13B2TP) Products Tanker** Compartments: 8 Ta, ER	**1 oil engine** driving 1 FP propeller Total Power: 736kW (1,001hp) Hanshin LH28G 1 x 4 Stroke 6 Cy. 280 x 460 736kW (1001bhp) The Hanshin Diesel Works Ltd-Japan
9105164 *JILY* -	**TOKUEI MARU No. 17** - **Hiroki Okinaka** - SatCom: Inmarsat B 343168010 *Owase, Mie* *Japan* MMSI: 431680000 Official number: 134375	*498* - 664	**1994-11 Goriki Zosensho — Ise** Yd No: 1053 Loa 56.12 (BB) Br ex - Dght 3.918 Lbp 56.00 Br md 9.50 Dpth 4.40 Welded, 1 dk	**(B11B2FV) Fishing Vessel** Ins: 730	**1 oil engine** reduction geared to sc. shaft driving 1 CP propeller Total Power: 1,471kW (2,000hp) 14.2kn Hanshin 6LU35G 1 x 4 Stroke 6 Cy. 350 x 550 1471kW (2000bhp) The Hanshin Diesel Works Ltd-Japan AuxGen: 2 x 308kW 445V a.c Fuel: 360.0 (d.f.) 5.0pd
9105279 *JM6398* -	**TOKUEI MARU NO. 23** *ex* Tobamaru *-2011* *ex* Tokuei Maru No. 23 *-2008* *ex* Daiju Maru No. 8 *-2006* **Tokuei Kaiun KK** - *Minami-ise, Mie* *Japan* MMSI: 431400378 Official number: 134471	*998* Class: NK - 2,425	**1994-10 Kambara Marine Development & Shipbuilding Co Ltd — Fukuyama HS** Yd No: OE-185 Loa 83.95 (BB) Br ex 12.32 Dght 5.166 Lbp 77.60 Br md 12.30 Dpth 5.80 Welded, 1 dk	**(A13B2TP) Products Tanker** Liq: 2,725; Liq (Oil): 2,725 Compartments: 10 Ta, ER	**1 oil engine** driving 1 CP propeller Total Power: 1,912kW (2,600hp) 13.5kn Akasaka A37 1 x 4 Stroke 6 Cy. 370 x 720 1912kW (2600bhp) Akasaka Tekkosho KK (Akasaka DieselLtd)-Japan AuxGen: 2 x 240kW 445V 60Hz a.c Thrusters: 1 Thwart. CP thruster (f) Fuel: 91.4 (d.f.) 7.4pd

IMO / Call sign / Flag	Name / Owner / Port	Tonnage	Class	Builder / Dimensions	Type / Cargo	Machinery
9154024 *JH3409* -	**TOKUEI MARU No. 25** **Tokuei Kaiun KK** - *Minami-ise, Mie* Japan MMSI: 431200143 Official number: 134410	*748* - 1,965	Class: NK	**1996-07 Mukaishima Zoki Co. Ltd. — Onomichi** Yd No: 307 Loa 74.99 Br ex - Dght 4.680 Lbp 69.95 Br md 11.50 Dpth 5.20 Welded, 1 dk	**(A12A2TC) Chemical Tanker** Liq: 2,072	**1 oil engine** driving 1 FP propeller Total Power: 1,618kW (2,200hp) 12.0kn Hanshin LH34LG 1 x 4 Stroke 6 Cy. 340 x 640 1618kW (2200bhp) The Hanshin Diesel Works Ltd-Japan Fuel: 76.0
9313539 *JH3487* -	**TOKUEI MARU NO. 28** - **Japan Railway Construction, Transport & Technology Agency & Tokuei Kaiun Co Ltd** Tokuei Kaiun KK *Minami-ise, Mie* Japan MMSI: 431200655 Official number: 135674	*2,985* - 4,999	Class: NK	**2004-03 Kanrei Zosen K.K. — Naruto** Yd No: 395 Loa 104.95 Br ex - Dght 6.266 Lbp 98.00 Br md 15.38 Dpth 7.50 Welded, 1 dk	**(A13B2TP) Products Tanker** Double Hull (13F) Liq: 5,390; Liq (Oil): 5,390	**1 oil engine** driving 1 FP propeller Total Power: 2,950kW (4,011hp) 13.5kn MAN-B&W 5L35MC 1 x 2 Stroke 5 Cy. 350 x 1050 2950kW (4011bhp) The Hanshin Diesel Works Ltd-Japan Fuel: 223.0
8808214 *JK4852* -	**TOKUHIRO** - **YK Fuji Kisen** - *Shunan, Yamaguchi* Japan Official number: 129659	*499* - 1,140		**1988-10 Kanmon Zosen K.K. — Shimonoseki** Yd No: 505 Loa 59.99 (BB) Br ex 10.52 Dght 4.100 Lbp 56.00 Br md 10.50 Dpth 4.50 Welded, 1 dk	**(A24A2BT) Cement Carrier** Grain: 940 Compartments: 4 Ho	**1 oil engine** with clutches & sr geared to sc. shaft driving 1 FP propeller Total Power: 1,030kW (1,400hp) Niigata 6M28BGT 1 x 4 Stroke 6 Cy. 280 x 480 1030kW (1400bhp) Niigata Engineering Co Ltd-Japan Thrusters: 1 Thwart. CP thruster (f)
8942383 - -	**TOKUHIRO MARU** *ex Sanei Maru No. 8* **Akihiko Suzuki**	*199* - -		**1970-07 K.K. Takagi — Matsuzaki** L reg 34.22 Br ex - Dght - Lbp - Br md 7.20 Dpth 2.80 Welded, 1 dk	**(B11B2FV) Fishing Vessel**	**1 oil engine** driving 1 FP propeller
8106549 - -	**TOKUHIRO MARU No. 31** - -	*143* 53 145		**1981-06 Tokushima Zosen K.K. — Fukuoka** Yd No: 1363 Loa 39.50 Br ex 6.63 Dght 2.590 Lbp 32.59 Br md 6.61 Dpth 2.95 Welded, 1 dk	**(B11A2FS) Stern Trawler**	**1 oil engine** reduction geared to sc. shaft driving 1 FP propeller Total Power: 699kW (950hp) 11.0kn Niigata 6M28AET 1 x 4 Stroke 6 Cy. 280 x 480 699kW (950bhp) Niigata Engineering Co Ltd-Japan
8824191 *PORU* -	**TOKUHISA** *ex Tokuhisa Maru -2012* - - Indonesia	*471* - 594		**1989-06 KK Ouchi Zosensho — Matsuyama EH** Loa 51.00 Br ex - Dght 3.320 Lbp 46.00 Br md 11.00 Dpth 5.47 Welded, 1 dk	**(B33A2DG) Grab Dredger**	**1 oil engine** driving 1 FP propeller Total Power: 552kW (750hp) Hanshin 6LUN28AG 1 x 4 Stroke 6 Cy. 280 x 480 552kW (750bhp) The Hanshin Diesel Works Ltd-Japan
9146168 *JK5478* -	**TOKUHO MARU** **Tokuyama Kairiku Unso KK** - *Shunan, Yamaguchi* Japan Official number: 134791	*498* - 1,120		**1996-05 Shitanoe Shipbuilding Co Ltd — Usuki OT** Yd No: 1177 Loa - Br ex - Dght 4.100 Lbp 62.00 Br md 10.00 Dpth 4.50 Welded, 1 dk	**(A12A2TC) Chemical Tanker** 2 Cargo Pump (s): 2x150m³/hr	**1 oil engine** driving 1 FP propeller Total Power: 736kW (1,001hp) Hanshin LH30LG 1 x 4 Stroke 6 Cy. 300 x 600 736kW (1001bhp) The Hanshin Diesel Works Ltd-Japan
9682215 *7JPZ* -	**TOKUHO MARU** **Iino Gas Transport Co Ltd** - *Kobe, Hyogo* Japan MMSI: 432945000 Official number: 142009	*1,356* 484 1,449	Class: NK	**2013-09 Shitanoe Shipbuilding Co Ltd — Usuki OT** Yd No: 1322 Loa 71.50 (BB) Br ex - Dght 4.518 Lbp 67.00 Br md 12.50 Dpth 5.55 Welded, 1 dk	**(A11B2TG) LPG Tanker** Liq (Gas): 1,820	**1 oil engine** driving 1 Propeller Total Power: 1,471kW (2,000hp) Akasaka AX33B 1 x 4 Stroke 6 Cy. 330 x 620 1471kW (2000bhp) Akasaka Tekkosho KK (Akasaka DieselLtd)-Japan Thrusters: 1 Thwart. FP thruster (f) Fuel: 200.0
9033268 - -	**TOKUJIN MARU No. 1** - - Philippines	*499* - 1,550		**1991-11 K.K. Matsuura Zosensho — Osakikamijima** Yd No: 381 Loa 75.87 (BB) Br ex 12.24 Dght 4.210 Lbp 70.00 Br md 12.00 Dpth 7.20 Welded	**(A31A2GX) General Cargo Ship** Compartments: 1 Ho, ER	**1 oil engine** geared to sc. shaft driving 1 FP propeller Total Power: 1,324kW (1,800hp) Hanshin 6EL30G 1 x 4 Stroke 6 Cy. 300 x 600 1324kW (1800bhp) The Hanshin Diesel Works Ltd-Japan
8839328 *JG4705* -	**TOKUJIN MARU No. 28** *ex Yusei Maru No. 28 -1998* **Kazumi Okada** - *Hazu, Aichi* Japan Official number: 130264	*242* - 350		**1987-12 Takao Zosen Kogyo K.K. — Tateyama** Yd No: 85 Loa 41.15 Br ex - Dght 2.800 Lbp 37.50 Br md 8.50 Dpth 3.00 Welded, 1 dk	**(A31A2GX) General Cargo Ship** 1 Ha: (21.5 x 6.0)ER	**1 oil engine** driving 1 FP propeller Total Power: 602kW (818hp) Mitsubishi S6R2-MTK 1 x 4 Stroke 6 Cy. 170 x 220 602kW (818bhp) Mitsubishi Heavy Industries Ltd-Japan
9195274 *JM6558* -	**TOKUMORI MARU NO. 2** *ex Tokuyo Maru No. 2 -2007* **Chintai Joho Matsuyama Co Ltd & Ohnishi Kaiun KK** Ohnishi Kaiun KK *Matsuyama, Ehime* Japan MMSI: 431601677 Official number: 136363	*699* - 977 T/cm 5.8	Class: NK	**1998-11 K.K. Miura Zosensho — Saiki** Yd No: 1213 Loa 65.04 (BB) Br ex - Dght 4.188 Lbp 60.00 Br md 11.00 Dpth 5.10 Welded, 1 dk	**(A11B2TG) LPG Tanker** Double Bottom Entire Compartment Length Liq (Gas): 1,247 2 x Gas Tank (s); 2 independent (C.mn.stl) cyl horizontal 2 Cargo Pump (s): 2x350m³/hr Manifold: Bow/CM: 30m	**1 oil engine** driving 1 FP propeller Total Power: 1,618kW (2,200hp) 12.5kn Akasaka A34C 1 x 4 Stroke 6 Cy. 340 x 620 1618kW (2200bhp) Akasaka Tekkosho KK (Akasaka DieselLtd)-Japan AuxGen: 2 x 240kW 445V 50Hz a.c Fuel: 44.0 (d.f.) (Heating Coils) 100.0 (r.f.) 4.9pd
9682162 *JD3549* -	**TOKUSAN MARU** **Tokuyama Kairiku Unso KK** - - Japan MMSI: 431004653	*455* - 1,534		**2013-07 Yamanaka Zosen K.K. — Imabari** Yd No: 837 Loa 59.99 Br ex - Dght 4.500 Lbp - Br md 12.10 Dpth - Welded, 1 dk	**(A24A2BT) Cement Carrier**	**1 oil engine** reduction geared to sc. shaft driving 1 FP propeller Total Power: 1,200kW (1,632hp) Daihatsu 6DEM-23 1 x 4 Stroke 6 Cy. 230 x 320 1200kW (1632bhp) Daihatsu Diesel Manufacturing Co Lt-Japan
8971229 *JH3499* -	**TOKUSEI MARU** - - *Isshiki, Aichi* Japan MMSI: 431401907 Official number: 135680	*125* - -		**2001-12 Hongawara Zosen K.K. — Fukuyama** Yd No: 538 L reg 21.86 Br ex - Dght - Lbp - Br md 8.20 Dpth 3.20 Welded, 1 dk	**(B32A2ST) Tug**	**2 oil engines** driving 2 FP propellers Total Power: 1,472kW (2,002hp) Matsui ML626GSC-4 1 x 4 Stroke 6 Cy. 260 x 480 736kW (1001bhp) Matsui Iron Works Co Ltd-Japan Matsui ML626GSC-4 1 x 4 Stroke 6 Cy. 260 x 480 736kW (1001bhp) (made 2001) Matsui Iron Works Co Ltd-Japan
7623655 - -	**TOKUSEN MARU** *ex Akebono -1987 ex Akebono Maru -1986* *ex Tokuei Maru No. 25 -1980* - - South Korea	*355* - 220	Class: (NK)	**1969 Sanyo Zosen K.K. — Onomichi** Yd No: 566 Loa 31.53 Br ex 9.50 Dght 3.912 Lbp 30.20 Br md 9.48 Dpth 4.20 Welded, 1 dk	**(B32B2SP) Pusher Tug**	**2 oil engines** driving 2 FP propellers Total Power: 2,206kW (3,000hp) 11.5kn Nippon Hatsudoki HS6NVA38 2 x 4 Stroke 6 Cy. 380 x 540 each-1103kW (1500bhp) Nippon Hatsudoki-Japan AuxGen: 2 x 80kW 230V a.c Fuel: 109.5 11.0pd
6720315 - -	**TOKUSEN MARU No. 2** *ex Meiko Maru -1988* - - South Korea	*193* - -		**1967 Shin Yamamoto Shipbuilding & Engineering Co Ltd — Kochi KC** Yd No: 93 Loa 29.95 Br ex 8.39 Dght 2.769 Lbp 27.74 Br md 8.34 Dpth 3.79 Riveted\Welded, 1 dk	**(B32A2ST) Tug**	**2 oil engines** geared to sc. shafts driving 2 FP propellers Total Power: 1,544kW (2,100hp) Fuji 6MD32H 2 x 4 Stroke 6 Cy. 320 x 380 each-772kW (1050bhp) Fuji Diesel Co Ltd-Japan AuxGen: 2 x 20kW 225V a.c Fuel: 52.0 5.0pd
8503321 *JG4553* -	**TOKUSHIN MARU** *ex Toshin Maru -2011* *ex Yoshu Maru No. 18 -2010* **Sonoda Kisen KK** - *Kobe, Hyogo* Japan MMSI: 431301121 Official number: 128827	*1,651* - 2,778		**1985-09 Ube Dockyard Co. Ltd. — Ube** Yd No: 192 Loa 82.02 Br ex 13.82 Dght 5.001 Lbp 76.00 Br md 13.81 Dpth 6.30 Welded, 1 dk	**(A24A2BT) Cement Carrier** Grain: 2,400 Compartments: 4 Ho, ER	**1 oil engine** with clutches, flexible couplings & sr geared to sc. shaft driving 1 FP propeller Total Power: 1,324kW (1,800hp) Hanshin 6EL30 1 x 4 Stroke 6 Cy. 300 x 600 1324kW (1800bhp) The Hanshin Diesel Works Ltd-Japan
8810542 *JJ3612* -	**TOKUSHIN MARU No. 5** **Teruo Nakagami** - *Himeji, Hyogo* Japan Official number: 130827	*487* - 626		**1988-10 Shitanoe Shipbuilding Co Ltd — Usuki OT** Yd No: 1087 Loa 49.92 (BB) Br ex 10.52 Dght 3.570 Lbp 46.00 Br md 10.50 Dpth 5.82 Welded, 1 dk	**(B33A2DG) Grab Dredger** Compartments: 1 Ho, ER 1 Ha: ER	**1 oil engine** driving 1 FP propeller Total Power: 588kW (799hp) Daihatsu 6DLM-24S 1 x 4 Stroke 6 Cy. 240 x 320 588kW (799bhp) Daihatsu Diesel Manufacturing Co Lt-Japan

IMO / Call sign	Name / Owner / Manager	GT / DWT	Class	Builder / Dimensions	Type / Cargo	Machinery
8923545 - -	TOKUSHO - -	499 - 1,499		1996-06 Mategata Zosen K.K. — Namikata Yd No: 1061 Loa 75.67 Br ex - Dght 3.990 Lbp 70.50 Br md 12.00 Dpth 7.00 Welded, 1 dk	(A31A2GX) General Cargo Ship Grain: 2,743; Bale: 2,490 Compartments: 1 Ho, ER 1 Ha: (40.2 x 9.5)ER	1 oil engine driving 1 FP propeller Total Power: 736kW (1,001hp) 12.0kn Niigata 6M31BLGT 1 x 4 Stroke 6 Cy. 310 x 600 736kW (1001bhp) Niigata Engineering Co Ltd-Japan
8702587 JK4721 -	TOKUTSUGI MARU - Tokuyama Kairiku Unso KK - Shunan, Yamaguchi Japan MMSI: 431401318 Official number: 129539	699 - 1,620		1987-07 Kanmon Zosen K.K. — Shimonoseki Yd No: 392 Loa - Br ex - Dght 4.301 Lbp 64.01 Br md 11.51 Dpth 4.73 Welded, 1 dk	(A24A2BT) Cement Carrier	1 oil engine driving 1 FP propeller Total Power: 1,103kW (1,500hp) Hanshin 1 x 4 Stroke 1103kW (1500bhp) The Hanshin Diesel Works Ltd-Japan
9054028 JK5158 -	TOKUYAMA 21ST CENTURY - Tokuyama Kairiku Unso KK - Shunan, Yamaguchi Japan MMSI: 431400048 Official number: 132567	1,877 - 3,273	Class: NK	1992-11 Kanmon Zosen K.K. — Shimonoseki Yd No: 535 Loa 75.00 (BB) Br ex 15.03 Dght 5.857 Lbp 72.00 Br md 15.00 Dpth 6.45 Welded, 1 dk	(A24A2BT) Cement Carrier Grain: 2,854 Compartments: 6 Ho, ER 6 Ha: ER	1 oil engine driving 1 CP propeller Total Power: 2,185kW (2,971hp) 11.8kn B&W 6S26MC 1 x 2 Stroke 6 Cy. 260 x 980 2185kW (2971bhp) The Hanshin Diesel Works Ltd-Japan AuxGen: 3 x 301kW a.c Thrusters: 1 Thwart. CP thruster (a) Fuel: 75.0 (r.f.)
9523627 JD2886 -	TOKUYAMA MARU - Seagate Corp - Shunan, Yamaguchi Japan Official number: 140974	223 - -		2009-02 Kanagawa Zosen — Kobe Yd No: 590 Loa 35.00 Br ex - Dght 3.100 Lbp 30.50 Br md 9.60 Dpth 4.17 Welded, 1 dk	(B32A2ST) Tug	2 oil engines reduction geared to sc. shafts driving 2 Propellers Total Power: 2,942kW (4,000hp) Niigata 6L28HX 2 x 4 Stroke 6 Cy. 280 x 370 each-1471kW (2000bhp) Niigata Engineering Co Ltd-Japan
9124770 JK5318 -	TOKUYAMA No. 1 - Tokuyama Logistics Corp & Tsukiboshi Kaiun Co Ltd Tokuyama Logistics Corp Shunan, Yamaguchi Japan MMSI: 431400487 Official number: 134781	4,381 - 6,530	Class: NK	1995-10 Kanda Zosensho K.K. — Kawajiri Yd No: 367 Loa 110.00 (BB) Br ex - Dght 6.714 Lbp 105.00 Br md 16.80 Dpth 8.50 Welded, 1 dk	(A24A2BT) Cement Carrier Grain: 5,588 Compartments: 3 Ho, ER	1 oil engine driving 1 CP propeller Total Power: 3,604kW (4,900hp) 13.3kn Mitsubishi 7UEC37LA 1 x 2 Stroke 7 Cy. 370 x 880 3604kW (4900bhp) Akasaka Tekkosho KK (Akasaka DieselLtd)-Japan AuxGen: 2 x 450kW a.c, 1 x 220kW a.c Thrusters: 1 Thwart. CP thruster (f) Fuel: 173.0 (d.f.) 12.7pd
9235921 JK5577 -	TOKUYAMA No. 2 - Corporation for Advanced Transport & Technology & Tokuyama Logistics Corp Tokuyama Logistics Corp Shunan, Yamaguchi Japan MMSI: 431401857 Official number: 136117	4,387 - 6,502	Class: NK	2000-12 Kanda Zosensho K.K. — Kawajiri Yd No: 414 Loa 110.00 (BB) Br ex - Dght 6.714 Lbp 105.00 Br md 16.80 Dpth 8.50 Welded, 1 dk	(A24A2BT) Cement Carrier Grain: 5,582	1 oil engine driving 1 CP propeller Total Power: 3,604kW (4,900hp) 13.3kn Mitsubishi 7UEC37LA 1 x 2 Stroke 7 Cy. 370 x 880 3604kW (4900bhp) Akasaka Tekkosho KK (Akasaka DieselLtd)-Japan AuxGen: 1 x 450kW 450V a.c, 1 x 265kW 450V a.c Fuel: 211.0 (d.f.)
9494931 JD2632 -	TOKUYAMA NO. 3 - Tokuyama Logistics Corp - Shunan, Yamaguchi Japan MMSI: 431000535 Official number: 140736	720 - 1,999		2008-03 K.K. Watanabe Zosensho — Nagasaki Yd No: 148 Loa 74.97 Br ex - Dght 4.570 Lbp 70.00 Br md 13.60 Dpth 7.05 Welded, 1 dk	(A24A2BT) Cement Carrier Bale: 1,991	1 oil engine driving 1 FP propeller Total Power: 1,765kW (2,400hp) 14.2kn Akasaka A34S 1 x 4 Stroke 6 Cy. 340 x 660 1765kW (2400bhp) Akasaka Tekkosho KK (Akasaka DieselLtd)-Japan
9152337 JH3379 -	TOKUYO MARU - YK Sasaki Kaiun Kumazawa Kaiun Co Ltd Higashi-izu, Shizuoka Japan MMSI: 431100271 Official number: 134427	699 - 922	Class: NK	1996-09 K.K. Miura Zosensho — Saiki Yd No: 1168 Loa 64.90 Br ex - Dght 4.050 Lbp 60.00 Br md 11.00 Dpth 5.10 Welded, 1 dk	(A11B2TG) LPG Tanker Liq (Gas): 1,247 2 x Gas Tank (s); 2 Worms/Gaz de France	1 oil engine driving 1 FP propeller Total Power: 1,471kW (2,000hp) 12.5kn Akasaka A34C 1 x 4 Stroke 6 Cy. 340 x 620 1471kW (2000bhp) Akasaka Tekkosho KK (Akasaka DieselLtd)-Japan Fuel: 150.0
9597458 JD3132 -	TOKUYO MARU NO. 3 - Japan Railway Construction, Transport & Technology Agency & Masunaga Kaiun Co Ltd Masunaga Kaiun KK Saiki, Oita Japan MMSI: 431002151 Official number: 141352	749 - 1,011	Class: NK	2010-12 K.K. Watanabe Zosensho — Nagasaki Yd No: 173 Loa 67.00 Br ex - Dght 4.100 Lbp 62.00 Br md 11.50 Dpth 4.85 Welded, 1 dk	(A11B2TG) LPG Tanker Liq (Gas): 1,511	1 oil engine reverse reduction geared to sc. shaft driving 1 Propeller Total Power: 1,325kW (1,801hp) Akasaka A31R 1 x 4 Stroke 6 Cy. 310 x 600 1325kW (1801bhp) Akasaka Tekkosho KK (Akasaka DieselLtd)-Japan Fuel: 141.0 (d.f.)
9132648 JL6426 -	TOKUYO MARU No. 7 - Shinomiya Tanker KK (Shinomiya Tanker Co Ltd) - Anan, Tokushima Japan MMSI: 431300334 Official number: 135080	996 - 1,289	Class: NK	1995-12 Hitachi Zosen Mukaishima Marine Co Ltd — Onomichi HS Yd No: 101 Loa 71.47 Br ex - Dght 4.412 Lbp 66.50 Br md 12.00 Dpth 5.50 Welded, 1 dk	(A11B2TG) LPG Tanker Liq (Gas): 1,777 2 x Gas Tank (s); independent	1 oil engine driving 1 FP propeller Total Power: 1,765kW (2,400hp) 13.0kn Akasaka A34S 1 x 4 Stroke 6 Cy. 340 x 660 1765kW (2400bhp) Akasaka Tekkosho KK (Akasaka DieselLtd)-Japan Fuel: 135.0 (d.f.)
9380946 JD2184 -	TOKUYO MARU NO. 15 - Iwasaki Kisen KK (Iwasaki Kisen Co Ltd) - Bizen, Okayama Japan MMSI: 431402034 Official number: 140255	749 - 993	Class: NK	2006-02 Fukushima Zosen Ltd. — Matsue Yd No: 351 Loa 67.00 Br ex - Dght 4.162 Lbp 62.00 Br md 11.40 Dpth 5.05 Welded, 1 dk	(A11B2TG) LPG Tanker Double Hull Liq (Gas): 1,400	1 oil engine driving 1 FP propeller Total Power: 1,471kW (2,000hp) Akasaka A34C 1 x 4 Stroke 6 Cy. 340 x 620 1471kW (2000bhp) Akasaka Tekkosho KK (Akasaka DieselLtd)-Japan Fuel: 210.0
9124768 JH3386 -	TOKUYO MARU No. 18 - YK Tokuyo Suisan - Noto, Ishikawa Japan MMSI: 431761000 Official number: 134383	174 - 175		1995-05 K.K. Izutsu Zosensho — Nagasaki Yd No: 1046 Loa 41.80 (BB) Br ex 7.35 Dght 2.857 Lbp 33.00 Br md 6.80 Dpth 3.05 Welded, 1 dk	(B11B2FV) Fishing Vessel Ins: 189	1 oil engine with clutches, flexible couplings & sr reverse geared to sc. shaft driving 1 FP propeller Total Power: 673kW (915hp) Pielstick 6PA5LX 1 x 4 Stroke 6 Cy. 255 x 270 673kW (915bhp) Niigata Engineering Co Ltd-Japan
9009994 JK4768 -	TOKUYO MARU No. 18 - Kyoei Line Co Ltd Kumazawa Kaiun Co Ltd Yokohama, Kanagawa Japan MMSI: 431401436 Official number: 131821	698 - 1,076	Class: NK	1990-09 Sasaki Shipbuilding Co Ltd — Osakikamijima HS Yd No: 548 Loa 64.80 (BB) Br ex - Dght 4.081 Lbp 60.00 Br md 11.00 Dpth 5.10 Welded, 1 dk	(A11B2TG) LPG Tanker Liq (Gas): 1,248 2 x Gas Tank (s);	1 oil engine driving 1 CP propeller Total Power: 1,324kW (1,800hp) 12.0kn Akasaka A31 1 x 4 Stroke 6 Cy. 310 x 600 1324kW (1800bhp) Akasaka Tekkosho KK (Akasaka DieselLtd)-Japan AuxGen: 3 x 217kW a.c Fuel: 100.0 (d.f.)
9228631 JK5540 -	TOKUYO MARU No. 21 - Corporation for Advanced Transport & Technology & Iwasaki Kisen KK (Unyu Shisetsu Seibi Jigyodan & Iwasaki Kisen KK) Iwasaki Kisen KK (Iwasaki Kisen Co Ltd) Bizen, Okayama Japan MMSI: 431401849 Official number: 136157	749 - 981	Class: NK	2000-09 Usuki Shipyard Co Ltd — Usuki OT Yd No: 1667 Loa 67.00 (BB) Br ex - Dght 4.162 Lbp 62.00 Br md 11.40 Dpth 5.05 Welded, 1 dk	(A11B2TG) LPG Tanker Double Hull Liq (Gas): 1,432 2 x Gas Tank (s); 2 independent (stl) vertical 2 Cargo Pump (s): 2x750m³/hr Manifold: Bow/CM: 22.2m	1 oil engine driving 1 FP propeller Total Power: 1,471kW (2,000hp) 13.0kn Akasaka A34C 1 x 4 Stroke 6 Cy. 340 x 620 1471kW (2000bhp) Akasaka Tekkosho KK (Akasaka DieselLtd)-Japan Thrusters: 1 Tunnel thruster (f) Fuel: 210.0
9109990 JH3308 -	TOKUYO MARU No. 38 - YK Tokuyo Suisan - Noto, Ishikawa Japan Official number: 133215	177 - -		1994-06 K.K. Izutsu Zosensho — Nagasaki Yd No: 1036 Loa - Br ex - Dght 2.800 Lbp 34.25 Br md 7.00 Dpth 3.12 Welded, 1 dk	(B11B2FV) Fishing Vessel	1 oil engine driving 1 FP propeller Total Power: 736kW (1,001hp) Niigata 1 x 4 Stroke 736kW (1001bhp) Niigata Engineering Co Ltd-Japan

9209269 *JH3448* - **TOKUYO MARU No. 68** *181* - -
YK Tokuyo Suisan
-
Noto, Ishikawa *Japan*
Official number: 135631
1999-05 K.K. Izutsu Zosensho — Nagasaki Yd No: 1085
Loa - Br ex - Dght -
Lbp 34.30 Br md 6.80 Dpth 3.00
Welded, 1 dk
(B11B2FV) Fishing Vessel
1 oil engine driving 1 FP propeller
Total Power: 1,029kW (1,399hp)
Niigata 6MG22HX
1 x 4 Stroke 6 Cy. 220 x 280 1029kW (1399bhp)
Niigata Engineering Co Ltd-Japan

9079482 *JI3537* - **TOKUYOSHI MARU** *199* - 533
Tokuyoshi Kaiun KK
-
Osaka, Osaka *Japan*
Official number: 134136
1993-08 Goriki Zosensho — Ise Yd No: 1031
Loa 48.14 Br ex - Dght 3.226
Lbp 44.00 Br md 8.00 Dpth 3.45
Welded, 1 dk
(A13B2TP) Products Tanker
Liq: 680; Liq (Oil): 680
1 oil engine driving 1 FP propeller
Total Power: 588kW (799hp)
Yanmar MF26-SD
1 x 4 Stroke 6 Cy. 260 x 500 588kW (799bhp)
Yanmar Diesel Engine Co Ltd-Japan

8863264 *HP7361* - **TOKUYOSHI MARU** *199* 112 500
Asahi Line SA
-
Panama *Panama*
Official number: D7291789YJ
1969-03 Imura Zosen K.K. — Komatsushima
Loa 42.00 Br ex - Dght 3.100
Lbp 37.00 Br md 7.30 Dpth 3.35
Welded, 1 dk
(A13B2TU) Tanker (unspecified)
Liq: 548; Liq (Oil): 548
Cargo Heating Coils
1 Cargo Pump (s): 1x400m³/hr
1 oil engine driving 1 FP propeller
Total Power: 405kW (551hp) 10.0kn

7933153 - - **TOKUYOSHI MARU No. 5** *413* - 854
ex Kinko Maru No. 5 *-1984*
Tae Shin Engineering Co Ltd
-
South Korea
1979 Yoshiura Zosen — Kure Yd No: 272
Loa 52.25 Br ex - Dght 4.026
Lbp 48.01 Br md 8.81 Dpth 4.20
Welded, 1 dk
(A13B2TU) Tanker (unspecified)
1 oil engine driving 1 FP propeller
Total Power: 588kW (799hp)
Niigata 6M26KEHS
1 x 4 Stroke 6 Cy. 260 x 400 588kW (799bhp)
Niigata Engineering Co Ltd-Japan

9605023 *HOID* - **TOKYO BULKER** **34,795** 20,209 61,439 T/cm 61.4 Class: NK
Toshin Kisen Co Ltd & East Bulk Shipping SA
Toshin Kisen Co Ltd
Panama *Panama*
MMSI: 373999000
Official number: 4345912
2012-01 Iwagi Zosen Co Ltd — Kamijima EH Yd No: 331
Loa 199.98 (BB) Br ex - Dght 13.010
Lbp 195.00 Br md 32.24 Dpth 18.60
Welded, 1 dk
(A21A2BC) Bulk Carrier
Grain: 77,674; Bale: 73,552
Compartments: 5 Ho, ER
5 Ha: 4 (23.5 x 19.0)ER (18.7 x 19.0)
Cranes: 4x30.7t
1 oil engine driving 1 FP propeller
Total Power: 8,450kW (11,489hp) 14.5kn
MAN-B&W 6S50MC-C8
1 x 2 Stroke 6 Cy. 500 x 2000 8450kW (11489bhp)
Mitsui Engineering & Shipbuilding CLtd-Japan
Fuel: 2560.0 32.0pd

9432907 *D5FF4* - **TOKYO CAR** **46,800** 14,217 12,352 T/cm 45.6 Class: NV
Roptin Shipping Inc
Zodiac Maritime Agencies Ltd
Monrovia *Liberia*
MMSI: 636016248
Official number: 16248
2008-11 Xiamen Shipbuilding Industry Co Ltd — Xiamen FJ Yd No: XSI404E
Loa 182.80 (BB) Br ex 31.53 Dght 9.000
Lbp 170.68 Br md 31.50 Dpth 12.80
Welded, 12 dks incl. 3 liftable dks.
(A35B2RV) Vehicles Carrier
Side door/ramp (s)
Len: 20.00 Wid: 4.70 Swl: 10
Quarter stern door/ramp (s. a.)
Len: 32.50 Wid: 7.50 Swl: 120
Cars: 4,943
1 oil engine driving 1 FP propeller
Total Power: 14,220kW (19,334hp) 20.0kn
MAN-B&W 9S50MC-C
1 x 2 Stroke 9 Cy. 500 x 2000 14220kW (19334bhp)
MAN Diesel A/S-Denmark
AuxGen: 2 x 1050kW 450V a.c, 1 x 750kW 450V a.c
Thrusters: 1 Thwart. FP thruster (f)
Fuel: 170.0 (d.f.) 3500.0 (r.f.) 57.0pd

9193290 *DGTX* - **TOKYO EXPRESS** **54,465** 23,876 67,145 T/cm 83.0 Class: GL
Hapag-Lloyd AG
Hamburg *Germany*
MMSI: 211327410
Official number: 18790
2000-05 Hyundai Heavy Industries Co Ltd — Ulsan Yd No: 1191
Loa 294.04 (BB) Br ex - Dght 13.550
Lbp 283.20 Br md 32.20 Dpth 21.80
Welded, 1 dk
(A33A2CC) Container Ship (Fully Cellular)
TEU 4890 C Ho 2326 TEU C Dk 2564 TEU incl 370 ref C
Compartments: 6 Cell Ho
17 Ha:
1 oil engine driving 1 FP propeller
Total Power: 40,040kW (54,438hp) 24.0kn
MAN-B&W 7K98MC
1 x 2 Stroke 7 Cy. 980 x 2660 40040kW (54438bhp)
Hyundai Heavy Industries Co Ltd-South Korea
AuxGen: 1 x 3000kW a.c, 2 x 2300kW a.c, 1 x 1750kW a.c
Thrusters: 1 Thwart. FP thruster (f)
Fuel: 335.0 (d.f.) 6612.0 (r.f.) 140.7pd

9261944 *JG5666* - **TOKYO MARU** *241* - -
Toko Service KK
-
Tokyo *Japan*
Official number: 137121
2002-04 Kanagawa Zosen — Kobe Yd No: 504
Loa 37.20 Br ex - Dght -
Lbp - Br md 9.80 Dpth 4.21
Welded, 1 dk
(B32A2ST) Tug
2 oil engines gearing integral to driving 2 Z propellers
Total Power: 2,648kW (3,600hp)
Yanmar 6N280-UN
2 x 4 Stroke 6 Cy. 280 x 380 each-1324kW (1800bhp)
Yanmar Diesel Engine Co Ltd-Japan
AuxGen: 2 x 104kW 225V 60Hz a.c
Fuel: 46.3 (d.f.) 55.0 (r.f.)

9617038 *7JOR* - **TOKYO MARU** **66,071** 37,726 120,158 Class: NK
JX Ocean Co Ltd
-
Yokohama, Kanagawa *Japan*
MMSI: 432916000
Official number: 141896
2013-05 Japan Marine United Corp (JMU) — Kure HS Yd No: 3332
Loa 246.80 (BB) Br ex - Dght 15.439
Lbp 238.40 Br md 44.40 Dpth 22.00
Welded, 1 dk
(A13A2TW) Crude/Oil Products Tanker
Double Hull (13F)
Liq: 142,126; Liq (Oil): 142,223
1 oil engine driving 1 FP propeller
Total Power: 12,210kW (16,601hp) 15.0kn
Wartsila 6RTA58T-B
1 x 2 Stroke 6 Cy. 580 x 2416 12210kW (16601bhp)
Diesel United Ltd.-Aioi
AuxGen: 3 x 760kW a.c
Fuel: 3370.0

8998265 *JD2076* - **TOKYO MARU** *241* - -
Wing Maritime Service Corp
-
Yokohama, Kanagawa *Japan*
Official number: 140125
2005-03 Keihin Dock Co Ltd — Yokohama Yd No: 269
Loa 35.50 Br ex - Dght -
Lbp - Br md 9.80 Dpth 4.38
Welded, 1 dk
(B32A2ST) Tug
2 oil engines reduction geared to sc. shafts driving 2 Propellers
Total Power: 2,942kW (4,000hp) 14.5kn
Yanmar 6N280-UV
2 x 4 Stroke 6 Cy. 280 x 380 each-1471kW (2000bhp)
Yanmar Diesel Engine Co Ltd-Japan

9669627 *VRMY4* - **TOKYO SPIRIT** **23,405** 11,922 36,000 Class: BV (Class contemplated)
Tokyo Spirit Shipping Ltd
Asia Maritime Pacific (Hong Kong) Ltd
Hong Kong *Hong Kong*
MMSI: 477407200
2014-04 Qingshan Shipyard — Wuhan HB Yd No: QS36000-8
Loa 179.90 (BB) Br ex - Dght 10.000
Lbp 175.00 Br md 30.00 Dpth 14.60
Welded, 1 dk
(A21A2BC) Bulk Carrier
Grain: 48,500; Bale: 46,500
Compartments: 5 Ho, ER
5 Ha: ER
Cranes: 4x30t
1 oil engine driving 1 FP propeller
Total Power: 8,280kW (11,257hp) 14.0kn
MAN-B&W 6S46ME-B8
1 x 2 Stroke 6 Cy. 460 x 1932 8280kW (11257bhp)

9384875 *MAQJ* - **TOKYO TOWER** **17,229** 7,875 21,981 Class: NK
Los Halillos Shipping Co SA
Zodiac Maritime Agencies Ltd
London *United Kingdom*
MMSI: 235050802
Official number: 912703
2007-03 Imabari Shipbuilding Co Ltd — Imabari EH (Imabari Shipyard) Yd No: 666
Loa 171.99 (BB) Br ex - Dght 9.516
Lbp 160.00 Br md 27.60 Dpth 14.00
Welded, 1 dk
(A33A2CC) Container Ship (Fully Cellular)
TEU 1708 C Ho 610 TEU C Dk 1098 incl 145 ref C
Compartments: ER, 8 Cell Ho
8 Ha: ER 7 (12.6 x 23.4) (12.6 x 13.2)
1 oil engine driving 1 FP propeller
Total Power: 15,820kW (21,509hp) 19.7kn
MAN-B&W 7S60MC-C
1 x 2 Stroke 7 Cy. 600 x 2400 15820kW (21509bhp)
Mitsui Engineering & Shipbuilding CLtd-Japan
AuxGen: 3 x a.c
Thrusters: 1 Tunnel thruster (f)
Fuel: 2180.0

9138343 *D5BW4* - **TOLAGA** **6,362** 3,998 7,225 T/cm 15.0 Class: GL
ex Inga Lena *-2012* *ex* Charlotte Borchard *-2001*
ex Inga Lena *-1998* *launched as* Hoheriff *-1997*
ms 'Tolaga' Schiffahrts GmbH & Co KG
Coral Shipmanagement GmbH & Co KG
Monrovia *Liberia*
MMSI: 636092530
Official number: 92530
1997-04 J.J. Sietas KG Schiffswerft GmbH & Co. — Hamburg Yd No: 1133
Loa 121.92 (BB) Br ex 18.45 Dght 6.690
Lbp 114.90 Br md 18.20 Dpth 8.30
Welded, 1 dk
(A33A2CC) Container Ship (Fully Cellular)
TEU 700 C Ho 108 TEU Open/Ho 324 TEU C Dk 268 TEU incl 70 ref.
Compartments: 4 Cell Ho, ER
3 Ha: (12.4 x 12.9) (12.4 x 15.6) (12.6 x 15.6)ER
1 oil engine with flexible couplings & sr gearedto sc. shaft driving 1 CP propeller
Total Power: 5,300kW (7,206hp) 16.5kn
MAN 8L40/54
1 x 4 Stroke 8 Cy. 400 x 540 5300kW (7206bhp)
MAN B&W Diesel AG-Augsburg
AuxGen: 1 x 556kW 220/380V 50Hz a.c, 2 x 320kW 400V 50Hz a.c
Thrusters: 1 Thwart. FP thruster (f)
Fuel: 130.0 (d.f.) (Heating Coils) 580.0 (r.f.) 31.0pd

9180073 *YD3276* - **TOLAK** **198** 60 157 Class: KI (NK)
PT Segara Adhiguna Hokindo
-
Tanjungpinang *Indonesia*
1997-09 Dalian Shipyard Co Ltd — Dalian LN Yd No: ST-2
Loa 26.54 Br ex - Dght 3.194
Lbp 25.08 Br md 8.00 Dpth 3.48
Welded, 1 dk
(B32B2SP) Pusher Tug
2 oil engines reduction geared to sc. shafts driving 2 FP propellers
Total Power: 912kW (1,240hp) 9.5kn
Yanmar 6LAHK-ST1
2 x 4 Stroke 6 Cy. 150 x 165 each-456kW (620bhp)
Yanmar Diesel Engine Co Ltd-Japan
AuxGen: 2 x 101kW a.c
Fuel: 70.0 (d.f.)

6907896 - - **TOLAK DUA** **230** 70 - Class: (GL)
ex Koei Maru No. 12 *-2000* *ex* Chitose *-2000*
ex Hakuho Maru *-1988* *ex* Eiho Maru *-1984*
-
-
1968 Osaka Shipbuilding Co Ltd — Osaka OS Yd No: 300
Loa 28.00 Br ex 8.23 Dght 2.794
Lbp 26.47 Br md 8.21 Dpth 3.89
Riveted\Welded, 1 dk
(B32A2ST) Tug
2 oil engines gearing integral to driving 2 Voith-Schneider propellers
Total Power: 1,692kW (2,300hp) 12.5kn
Fuji 6MD32H
2 x 4 Stroke 6 Cy. 320 x 380 each-846kW (1150bhp)
Fuji Diesel Co Ltd-Japan
AuxGen: 1 x 24kW 225V a.c

8839720 *9V7224* - **TOLAK EMPAT** **280** 84 - Class: BV
ex Oki Maru No. 3 *-2007*
East Marine Pte Ltd
-
Singapore *Singapore*
MMSI: 565638000
Official number: 393341
1989-10 Maekawa Zosensho — Japan
Loa 31.00 Br ex - Dght 3.400
Lbp 27.00 Br md 8.50 Dpth 4.00
Welded, 1 dk
(B32A2ST) Tug
1 oil engine driving 1 FP propeller
Total Power: 883kW (1,201hp) 10.3kn
Niigata 6M26AGTE
1 x 4 Stroke 6 Cy. 260 x 460 883kW (1201bhp)
Niigata Engineering Co Ltd-Japan

IMO / Call sign	Name / Owner	Tonnage	Class	Builder / Dimensions	Type	Machinery
9180578 *9V7549* -	**TOLAK ENAM** *ex* Meisei Maru No. 3 *-2008* **East Marine Pte Ltd** - *Singapore* *Singapore* Official number: 394427	*180* 54 -	Class: BV	**1997-04 Y.K. Yoshida Zosensho — Iyo-Mishima** Yd No: 135 Loa 24.50 Br ex - Dght - Lbp - Br md 8.00 Dpth 3.00 Welded, 1 dk	**(B32B2SP) Pusher Tug**	**2 oil engines** driving 2 FP propellers Total Power: 1,472kW (2,002hp) 10.0kn Niigata 6MG22HX 2 x 4 Stroke 6 Cy. 220 x 280 each-736kW (1001bhp) Niigata Engineering Co Ltd-Japan
9406570 *9V6983* -	**TOLAK LAPAN** *ex* Barlian 1 *-2007* **East Marine Pte Ltd** - *Singapore* *Singapore* MMSI: 563008360 Official number: 392417	**179** 54 343	Class: GL	**2006-09 Forward Marine Enterprise Sdn Bhd — Sibu** Yd No: FM-5 Loa 25.00 Br ex 8.12 Dght 3.000 Lbp 22.70 Br md 8.10 Dpth 3.60 Welded, 1 dk	**(B32A2ST) Tug**	**2 oil engines** reverse reduction geared to sc. shafts driving 2 FP propellers Total Power: 1,204kW (1,636hp) Mitsubishi S6R2-MPTK2 2 x 4 Stroke 6 Cy. 170 x 220 each-602kW (818bhp) (made 2005) Mitsubishi Heavy Industries Ltd-Japan AuxGen: 2 x 50kW 415/230V a.c
7312921 *9V6229* -	**TOLAK LIMA** *ex* Seiwa Maru No. 7 *-2003* *ex* Shinsei Maru No. 7 *-2002* *ex* Genkai Maru No. 2 *-1979* **East Marine Pte Ltd** - *Singapore* *Singapore* Official number: 389823	**198** 60 385	Class: GL (NK)	**1973 K.K. Odo Zosen Tekko — Shimonoseki** Yd No: 196 Loa 25.51 Br ex 8.51 Dght 2.769 Lbp 22.99 Br md 8.49 Dpth 3.61 Welded, 1 dk	**(B32B2SP) Pusher Tug**	**2 oil engines** driving 2 FP propellers Total Power: 1,104kW (1,500hp) 9.5kn Daihatsu 6PSHTC-26D 2 x 4 Stroke 6 Cy. 260 x 320 each-552kW (750bhp) Daihatsu Diesel Manufacturing Co Lt-Japan
6813825 - -	**TOLAK SATU** *ex* Taiho Maru No. 33 *-2006* *ex* Take Maru No. 33 *-1997* *ex* Sozan Maru *-1982* **East Marine Pte Ltd** -	*198* 69 -		**1968-03 Shin Yamamoto Shipbuilding & Engineering Co Ltd — Kochi KC** Yd No: 98 Loa 29.01 Br ex 8.23 Dght 2.744 Lbp 26.30 Br md 8.21 Dpth 3.81 Riveted\Welded, 1 dk	**(B32A2ST) Tug**	**2 oil engines** Geared Integral to driving 2 Z propellers Total Power: 1,220kW (1,658hp) 12.0kn Hanshin 6L32 2 x 4 Stroke 6 Cy. 320 x 390 each-610kW (829bhp) Hanshin Nainenki Kogyo-Japan AuxGen: 1 x 40kW 220V a.c, 1 x 28kW 220V a.c Fuel: 61.0 8.0pd
8350384 *HP6175* -	**TOLAK SAYANG** *ex* Kozan Maru *-1991* **Marina Del Este Inc** East Marine Pte Ltd *Panama* *Panama* Official number: 2027892B	**132** 39 -	Class: (KR)	**1964 Takuma Zosen K.K. — Mitoyo** Loa 23.50 Br ex - Dght 1.700 Lbp 22.00 Br md 9.00 Dpth 2.70 Welded, 1 dk	**(B34B2SC) Crane Vessel**	**2 oil engines** driving 2 FP propellers Total Power: 588kW (800hp) 8.0kn Yanmar 6MA-HT 2 x 4 Stroke 6 Cy. 200 x 240 each-294kW (400bhp) Yanmar Diesel Engine Co Ltd-Japan
9360001 *9V6767* -	**TOLAK SEMBILAN** *ex* Oriental Bay 3 *-2008* **East Marine Pte Ltd** - *Singapore* *Singapore* MMSI: 565649000 Official number: 391581	**196** 58 204	Class: GL (NK)	**2005-06 Forward Shipbuilding Enterprise Sdn Bhd — Sibu** Yd No: 93 Loa 26.00 Br ex - Dght 3.062 Lbp 24.23 Br md 8.00 Dpth 3.65 Welded, 1 dk	**(B32A2ST) Tug**	**2 oil engines** reduction geared to sc. shafts driving 2 Propellers Total Power: 1,516kW (2,062hp) Mitsubishi S6R2-MPTK2 2 x 4 Stroke 6 Cy. 170 x 220 each-758kW (1031bhp) Mitsubishi Heavy Industries Ltd-Japan Fuel: 130.0 (r.f.)
9277216 *9V6162* -	**TOLAK SEPULUH** *ex* Profit Legend *-2013* *ex* Profit Legend Two *-2010* *ex* Pacific Ocean *-2004* **East Marine Pte Ltd** - *Singapore* *Singapore* MMSI: 563002990 Official number: 389628	*361* 109 331	Class: NK	**2001-11 Dalian Shipyard Co Ltd — Dalian LN** Yd No: TU33-1 Loa 33.80 Br ex - Dght 3.872 Lbp 31.34 Br md 10.00 Dpth 4.55 Welded, 1 Dk.	**(B32B2SP) Pusher Tug**	**2 oil engines** driving 2 FP propellers Total Power: 1,472kW (2,002hp) 11.0kn Matsui ML626GSC-4 2 x 4 Stroke 6 Cy. 260 x 480 each-736kW (1001bhp) Matsui Iron Works Co Ltd-Japan AuxGen: 1 x 100kW a.c Fuel: 230.0
7238319 *9V3954* -	**TOLAK TIGA** *ex* Fujita *-2004* *ex* Fujita Maru *-1993* **East Marine Pte Ltd** - *Singapore* *Singapore* MMSI: 563798000 Official number: 385968	**312** 94 609	Class: NK	**1972 Kegoya Dock K.K. — Kure** Yd No: 603 Loa 25.00 Br ex - Dght 3.034 Lbp 22.00 Br md 11.00 Dpth 4.00 Welded, 1 dk	**(B32B2SP) Pusher Tug**	**2 oil engines** reduction geared to sc. shafts driving 2 FP propellers Total Power: 882kW (1,200hp) 11.3kn Niigata 6MG25BX 2 x 4 Stroke 6 Cy. 250 x 320 each-441kW (600bhp) Niigata Engineering Co Ltd-Japan Fuel: 90.0 (d.f.)
8942424 *9V9372* -	**TOLAK TUJUH** *ex* Shinyu Maru *-2011* **East Marine Pte Ltd** - *Singapore* *Singapore* MMSI: 563000000	**159** 47 174	Class: BV	**1984-07 Namikata Shipbuilding Co Ltd — Imabari EH** Yd No: 118 Loa 23.95 Br ex - Dght 2.470 Lbp 21.90 Br md 7.50 Dpth 2.89 Welded, 1 dk	**(B32B2SP) Pusher Tug**	**2 oil engines** driving 2 FP propellers Total Power: 1,104kW (1,500hp) 10.0kn Hanshin 6LU26G 2 x 4 Stroke 6 Cy. 260 x 440 each-552kW (750bhp) The Hanshin Diesel Works Ltd-Japan
7420649 - -	**TOLBACHIK** - **OOO 'Roll'** -	**172** 51 88	Class: (RS)	**1973-07 Zavod 'Nikolayevsk-na-Amure' — Nikolayevsk-na-Amure** Yd No: 77 Loa 33.96 Br ex 7.09 Dght 2.901 Lbp 29.97 Br md - Dpth 3.69 Welded, 1 dk	**(B11B2FV) Fishing Vessel** Bale: 115 Compartments: 1 Ho, ER 1 Ha: (1.6 x 1.3) Derricks: 2x2t Ice Capable	**1 oil engine** driving 1 FP propeller Total Power: 224kW (305hp) 9.5kn S.K.L. 8NVD36-1U 1 x 4 Stroke 8 Cy. 240 x 360 224kW (305bhp) VEB Schwermaschinenbau "KarlLiebknecht" (SKL)-Magdeburg
9611761 *ZGBE* -	**TOLD U SO** **Molori Yachting Ltd** - *George Town* *Cayman Islands (British)* MMSI: 319023700 Official number: 742966	**456** 136 90	Class: AB	**2011-05 Azimut-Benetti SpA — Viareggio** Yd No: BV016 Loa 43.60 Br ex 9.72 Dght 2.760 Lbp 37.00 Br md 8.96 Dpth 6.64 Bonded, 1 dk	**(X11A2YP) Yacht** Hull Material: Reinforced Plastic	**2 oil engines** reduction geared to sc. shaft (s) driving 2 Propellers Total Power: 1,940kW (2,638hp) 12.0kn Caterpillar C32 ACERT 2 x Vee 4 Stroke 12 Cy. 145 x 162 each-970kW (1319bhp) Caterpillar Inc-USA AuxGen: 2 x 125kW a.c Thrusters: 1 Tunnel thruster (f) Fuel: 63.0 (d.f.)
7900912 - -	**TOLEDA** *ex* Hua Sheng *-1997* *ex* Niihama Maru No. 23 *-1995* **Hua Sheng Ocean Shipping Corp** Dalian Hua Wei Ocean Shipping Corp	**1,193** 555 1,027	Class: (CC)	**1979-04 Shirahama Zosen K.K. — Honai** Yd No: 91 Loa 70.01 Br ex - Dght 3.380 Lbp 65.03 Br md 11.21 Dpth 6.28 Welded, 2 dks	**(A31A2GX) General Cargo Ship**	**1 oil engine** driving 1 FP propeller Total Power: 1,177kW (1,600hp) Hanshin 6LU32G 1 x 4 Stroke 6 Cy. 320 x 510 1177kW (1600bhp) The Hanshin Diesel Works Ltd-Japan
7638557 *V3SU2* -	**TOLEDO** *ex* Rosana *-2005* **Toledo Shipping & Trading Co Ltd** International Shipping Group & Trading Ltd SatCom: Inmarsat C 431299010 *Belize City* *Belize* MMSI: 312990000 Official number: 340530019	**12,355** 7,408 19,509 T/cm 29.1	Class: RS (AB)	**1978-03 Onomichi Dockyard Co Ltd — Onomichi HS** Yd No: 278 Loa 156.24 Br ex - Dght 9.502 Lbp 146.01 Br md 22.61 Dpth 12.91 Welded, 1 dk	**(A21A2BC) Bulk Carrier** Grain: 25,306; Bale: 24,200 TEU 181 C Ho 129 TEU C Dk 52 TEU Compartments: 4 Ho, ER 4 Ha: (17.2 x 10.4)3 (19.8 x 10.4)ER Derricks: 4x25t	**1 oil engine** driving 1 FP propeller Total Power: 6,105kW (8,300hp) 15.5kn B&W 6K62EF 1 x 2 Stroke 6 Cy. 620 x 1400 6105kW (8300bhp) Hitachi Zosen Corp-Japan AuxGen: 3 x 330kW 440V 60Hz a.c Fuel: 1159.0 (r.f.) 28.0pd
9293624 *MHBD7* -	**TOLEDO** **Lloyds TSB Maritime Leasing (No 16) Ltd** Wilhelmsen Lines Car Carrier Ltd SatCom: Inmarsat C 423224010 *Southampton* *United Kingdom* MMSI: 232240000 Official number: 909818	**61,321** 22,650 19,628 T/cm 52.5	Class: NV	**2005-01 Mitsubishi Heavy Industries Ltd. — Nagasaki** Yd No: 2197 Loa 199.99 (BB) Br ex 32.28 Dght 10.500 Lbp 192.00 Br md 32.26 Dpth 36.02 Welded, 12 dks including 4 liftable dks	**(A35B2RV) Vehicles Carrier** Side door/ramp (s) Len: 25.00 Wid: 6.50 Swl: 35 Quarter stern door/ramp (s. a.) Len: 38.00 Wid: 7.00 Swl: 237 Cars: 6,400	**1 oil engine** driving 1 FP propeller Total Power: 13,895kW (18,892hp) 19.5kn Mitsubishi 7UEC60LS 1 x 2 Stroke 7 Cy. 600 x 2200 13895kW (18892bhp) Mitsubishi Heavy Industries Ltd-Japan AuxGen: 3 x 1300kW 440/220V 60Hz a.c Thrusters: 1 Thwart. CP thruster (f) Fuel: 139.0 (d.f.) 3322.6 (r.f.)
9717539 *JVHD5* -	**TOLEDO** **Firstmark Timber International Pte Ltd** - *Ulaanbaatar* *Mongolia* MMSI: 457888000 Official number: 34331313	**472** 142 -	Class: SC (Class contemplated)	**2013-10 Borneo Shipping & Timber Agencies Sdn Ltd — Bintulu** Yd No: 181 Loa 46.82 Br ex - Dght 2.338 Lbp 45.45 Br md 12.19 Dpth 3.05 Welded, 1 dk	**(A31C2GD) Deck Cargo Ship**	**2 oil engines** reduction geared to sc. shafts driving 2 Propellers Total Power: 736kW (1,000hp) Cummins 2 x each-368kW (500bhp) Chongqing Cummins Engine Co Ltd-China

Ship	Tonnages / Class	Builder / Dimensions	Type / Cargo	Machinery
9078476 **TOLEDO CARRIER** *A8VE9* - **Toledo Shipping Corp** Norbulk Shipping UK Ltd *Monrovia* *Liberia* MMSI: 636014596 Official number: 14596	**5,994** Class: NK 3,362 7,255	**1994-02 Kyokuyo Shipyard Corp — Shimonoseki YC** Yd No: 386 Loa 134.01 (BB) Br ex 20.23 Dght 7.116 Lbp 127.00 Br md 20.20 Dpth 9.93 Welded, 1 dk	**(A34A2GR) Refrigerated Cargo Ship** Bale: 8,727; Ins: 8,727 TEU 98 incl 98 ref C Compartments: 4 Ho, ER, 4 Tw Dk 4 Ha: 4 (7.3 x 7.0)ER Derricks: 8x7t	**1 oil engine** driving 1 FP propeller Total Power: 8,250kW (11,217hp) 18.5kn Mitsubishi 6UEC50LSII 1 x 2 Stroke 6 Cy. 500 x 1950 8250kW (11217bhp) Kobe Hatsudoki KK-Japan Fuel: 1150.0 (r.f.)
9288899 **TOLEDO SPIRIT** *ECJA* - **Teekay Shipping Spain SL** Teekay Shipping Ltd SatCom: Inmarsat C 422430420 *Santa Cruz de Tenerife* *Spain (CSR)* MMSI: 224304000 Official number: 9/2004	**83,594** Class: NV 48,940 159,342 T/cm 118.0	**2005-07 Daewoo Shipbuilding & Marine Engineering Co Ltd — Geoje** Yd No: 5271 Loa 274.00 (BB) Br ex 48.04 Dght 16.951 Lbp 264.00 Br md 48.00 Dpth 23.70 Welded, 1 dk	**(A13A2TV) Crude Oil Tanker** Double Hull (13F) Liq: 167,809; Liq (Oil): 167,809 Cargo Heating Coils Compartments: 12 Wing Ta, 2 Wing Slop Ta, ER 3 Cargo Pump (s): 3x3500m³/hr Manifold: Bow/CM: 134m	**1 oil engine** driving 1 FP propeller Total Power: 16,858kW (22,920hp) 15.2kn B&W 6S70MC-C 1 x 2 Stroke 6 Cy. 700 x 2800 16858kW (22920bhp) AuxGen: 3 x a.c Fuel: 308.0 (d.f.) 3625.0 (r.f.)
7405974 **TOLEMA 1** - *ex* Tolema *-1994* - -	*633* Class: (LR) 622 ✠ Classed LR until 29/9/94 1,064	**1976-07 The Hornibrook Group — Brisbane QLD** Yd No: 19 Loa 49.76 Br ex 10.98 Dght 3.315 Lbp 47.60 Br md 10.61 Dpth 4.30 Welded, 1 dk	**(B35E2TF) Bunkering Tanker** Liq: 1,000; Liq (Oil): 1,000 Compartments: 8 Ta, ER 4 Cargo Pump (s)	**2 oil engines** reduction geared to sc. shafts driving 2 Directional propellers Total Power: 544kW (740hp) 7.5kn Cummins V12-500-M 2 x Vee 4 Stroke 12 Cy. 140 x 152 each-272kW (370bhp) Cummins Engine Co Inc-USA AuxGen: 1 x 20kW 415V 50Hz a.c
7721885 **TOLGA GENC** *TCEG* *ex* Salih Uzunoglu *-1996* **Genc Denizcilik Yatirim ve Ticaret Ltd Sti** GNC Denizcilik Hizmetleri ve Ticaret Ltd Sti (GNC Shipping) *Istanbul* *Turkey* MMSI: 271000082 Official number: 4673	**2,163** Class: (TL) (AB) 1,359 3,534	**1979-04 Gemi-is Kollektif Sirketi — Fener, Istanbul** Yd No: 24 Lengthened & Deepened-1989 Loa 89.95 Br ex 13.03 Dght 5.930 Lbp 80.25 Br md 13.01 Dpth 7.10 Welded, 1 dk	**(A31A2GX) General Cargo Ship** Grain: 4,849; Bale: 4,358 Compartments: 2 Ho, ER 2 Ha: (18.8 x 8.0) (25.4 x 8.0)ER Derricks: 4x5t	**1 oil engine** reduction geared to sc. shaft driving 1 FP propeller Total Power: 1,324kW (1,800hp) 12.0kn MaK 6M452AK 1 x 4 Stroke 6 Cy. 320 x 450 1324kW (1800bhp) MaK Maschinenbau GmbH-Kiel AuxGen: 2 x 144kW a.c, 1 x 36kW a.c, 1 x 32kW a.c
9424259 **TOLGA TOMBA** *TCTL4* - **Oktav Denizcilik ve Ticaret AS** Butoni Denizcilik ve Ticaret AS *Istanbul* *Turkey* MMSI: 271002656 Official number: 9729	**2,962** Class: AB 1,527 4,300	**2008-11 Niyazi Tomba Tersanesi — Tuzla** Yd No: 04 Loa 93.62 (BB) Br ex - Dght 6.060 Lbp 84.73 Br md 14.55 Dpth 7.60 Welded, 1 dk	**(A31A2GX) General Cargo Ship** Grain: 3,894 Compartments: 2 Ho, ER 2 Ha: ER	**1 oil engine** reduction geared to sc. shaft driving 1 FP propeller Total Power: 1,960kW (2,665hp) MAN-B&W 8L28/32A 1 x 4 Stroke 8 Cy. 280 x 320 1960kW (2665bhp) STX Engine Co Ltd-South Korea AuxGen: 2 x 288kW a.c, 1 x 425kW a.c Fuel: 40.0 (d.f.) 180.0 (r.f.)
9479670 **TOLI** *9HA2299* - **Toli Maritime Ltd** K Tankering & Shipmanagement Co (K Tankercilik ve Gemi Isletmeciligi AS) *Valletta* *Malta* MMSI: 248282000 Official number: 9479670	**2,637** Class: BV 1,129 3,442 T/cm 10.8	**2009-04 Desan Tersanesi — Tuzla, Istanbul** Yd No: 21 Loa 92.86 (BB) Br ex - Dght 5.690 Lbp 86.60 Br md 14.10 Dpth 7.20 Welded, 1 dk	**(A12B2TR) Chemical/Products Tanker** Double Hull (13F) Liq: 4,062; Liq (Oil): 4,073 Cargo Heating Coils Compartments: 1 Slop Ta, ER, 10 Wing Ta 10 Cargo Pump (s): 10x200m³/hr Manifold: Bow/CM: 42.4m Ice Capable	**1 oil engine** reduction geared to sc. shaft driving 1 CP propeller Total Power: 1,980kW (2,692hp) 13.5kn MaK 6M25 1 x 4 Stroke 6 Cy. 255 x 400 1980kW (2692bhp) Caterpillar Motoren GmbH & Co. KG-Germany AuxGen: 3 x 420kW 400V 50Hz a.c, 1 x 800kW 400V 50Hz a.c Thrusters: 1 Tunnel thruster (f) Fuel: 23.0 (d.f.) 149.0 (r.f.)
6916768 **TOLIKO** *ZR6381* *ex* Gerhard Bjornstein *-1983* **Terrasan Pelagies Visserye Eiendoms Bpk** *Cape Town* *South Africa* MMSI: 601531000 Official number: 78901	*300* 100 -	**1968 Rolf Rekdal AS — Tomrefjord** Yd No: 68 Lengthened-1972 Loa 34.96 Br ex 7.35 Dght - Lbp - Br md 7.32 Dpth 3.66 Welded, 1 dk	**(B11B2FV) Fishing Vessel**	**1 oil engine** driving 1 FP propeller Total Power: 883kW (1,201hp) Wichmann 4AX 1 x 2 Stroke 4 Cy. 300 x 450 883kW (1201bhp) (new engine 1985) Wichmann Motorfabrikk AS-Norway
9280500 **TOLKOVYY** *UBYB* - **PJSC 'Fleet of Novorossiysk Commercial Sea Port'** Novorossiysk Port Fleet JSC (ZAO 'Flot Novorossiyskogo Torgovogo Porta') *Novorossiysk* *Russia* MMSI: 273443140 Official number: 020269	**364** Class: RS 109 287	**2003-06 Astilleros Armon SA — Navia** Yd No: 566 Loa 30.00 Br ex 10.35 Dght 4.540 Lbp 21.50 Br md 9.85 Dpth 5.40 Welded	**(B32A2ST) Tug**	**2 oil engines** geared to sc. shafts driving 2 Propellers Total Power: 2,942kW (4,000hp) Caterpillar 3516 2 x Vee 4 Stroke 16 Cy. 170 x 190 each-1471kW (2000bhp) Caterpillar Inc-USA
9463061 **TOLL 1818** *PMCH* *ex* Kimtrans 1818 *-2010* **PT SK Pelayaran Indonesia** *Jakarta* *Indonesia*	**1,117** Class: KI 336 1,237	**2007-07 P.T. Tunas Karya Bahari Indonesia — Indonesia** Yd No: 125 Loa 54.86 Br ex - Dght - Lbp 52.67 Br md 18.29 Dpth 3.66 Welded, 1 dk	**(B34T2QR) Work/Repair Vessel**	**2 oil engines** reduction geared to sc. shafts driving 2 FP propellers Total Power: 760kW (1,034hp) Cummins KT-19-M 2 x 4 Stroke 6 Cy. 159 x 159 each-380kW (517bhp) Cummins Engine Co Ltd-United Kingdom
9569437 **TOLL ALPHA** *9WHX8* - **Toll Logistics (Asia) Ltd** *Kuching* *Malaysia* MMSI: 533046300 Official number: 333011	**136** 40 -	**2009-05 Kiong Nguong Shipbuilding Contractor Co — Sibu** Yd No: 2062 Loa 23.17 Br ex - Dght 2.262 Lbp 21.60 Br md 7.30 Dpth 2.90 Welded, 1 dk	**(B32A2ST) Tug**	**2 oil engines** reduction geared to sc. shafts driving 2 FP propellers Total Power: 882kW (1,200hp) Cummins KTA-19-M3 2 x 4 Stroke 6 Cy. 159 x 159 each-441kW (600bhp) Chongqing Cummins Engine Co Ltd-China
9343053 **TOLL CYCLONE** *YDA4228* *ex* Kimtrans Cyclone *-2010* **PT SK Pelayaran Indonesia** Toll Logistics (Asia) Ltd *Cirebon* *Indonesia* MMSI: 525015123	**280** Class: KI (GL) 84 -	**2005-02 Kiong Nguong Shipbuilding Contractor Co — Sibu** Yd No: 2024 Loa 29.00 Br ex - Dght 3.505 Lbp 26.06 Br md 8.53 Dpth 4.26 Welded, 1 dk	**(B32A2ST) Tug**	**2 oil engines** reverse reduction geared to sc. shafts driving 2 FP propellers Total Power: 2,080kW (2,828hp) Mitsubishi S12R-MPTK 2 x Vee 4 Stroke 12 Cy. 170 x 180 each-1040kW (1414bhp) Mitsubishi Heavy Industries Ltd-Japan AuxGen: 2 x 30kW 220/24V 50Hz a.c Fuel: 100.0 (d.f.) 6.0pd
9507269 **TOLL DIAMOND** - *ex* Rubia *-2009* **Toll Logistics (Asia) Ltd** *Philippines* Official number: 01-0000506	**297** Class: GL 90 236	**2009-06 SL Shipbuilding Contractor Sdn Bhd — Sibu** Yd No: 24 Loa 32.00 Br ex 9.16 Dght 3.500 Lbp 29.23 Br md 9.14 Dpth 4.20 Welded, 1 dk	**(B32A2ST) Tug**	**2 oil engines** reverse reduction geared to sc. shafts driving 2 FP propellers Total Power: 2,386kW (3,244hp) Cummins KTA-50-M2 2 x Vee 4 Stroke 16 Cy. 159 x 159 each-1193kW (1622bhp) Cummins Engine Co Inc-USA AuxGen: 2 x 80kW 415V a.c
9550656 **TOLL DRAGONFLY** *VJD3679* - **Perkins Shipping Pty Ltd** *Gladstone, Qld* *Australia* MMSI: 503692000 Official number: 860061	**1,120** Class: LR (AB) 336 **100A1** SS 08/2013 1,327 TOC contemplated	**2009-12 P.T. Tunas Karya Bahari Indonesia — Indonesia** Yd No: 209 Loa 54.38 Br ex - Dght 2.800 Lbp 52.46 Br md 18.00 Dpth 4.20 Welded, 1 dk	**(A35D2RL) Landing Craft** Bow ramp (centre)	**2 oil engines** reduction geared to sc. shafts driving 2 FP propellers Total Power: 956kW (1,300hp) 10.0kn Cummins KTA-19-M3 2 x 4 Stroke 6 Cy. 159 x 159 each-478kW (650bhp) Cummins Engine Co Inc-USA AuxGen: 2 x a.c Thrusters: 1 Retract. directional thruster (f)
9356347 **TOLL EAGLE** *9V6656* *ex* Kimtrans Eagle *-2008* **Toll Logistics (Asia) Ltd** *Singapore* *Singapore* MMSI: 564844000 Official number: 391120	**949** Class: AB 284 1,264	**2005-07 PT Karimun Sembawang Shipyard — Tanjungbalai Karimun** Yd No: 7046 Loa 58.60 Br ex 14.49 Dght 2.800 Lbp 55.10 Br md 14.20 Dpth 4.25 Welded, 1 dk	**(A35D2RL) Landing Craft** Bow ramp (f)	**2 oil engines** reduction geared to sc. shafts driving 2 Directional propellers Total Power: 942kW (1,280hp) Cummins KTA-19-M3 2 x 4 Stroke 6 Cy. 159 x 159 each-471kW (640bhp) Cummins Engine Co Inc-USA
9311397 **TOLL ECHO** *YDA4720* *ex* Kimtrans Echo *-2009* **PT SK Pelayaran Indonesia** *Jakarta* *Indonesia*	**267** Class: GL 81 -	**2003-11 Kiong Nguong Shipbuilding Contractor Co — Sibu** Yd No: 2013 Loa 29.00 Br ex - Dght 3.505 Lbp 27.02 Br md 8.53 Dpth 4.27 Welded, 1 dk	**(B32A2ST) Tug**	**2 oil engines** reverse reduction geared to sc. shafts driving 2 FP propellers Total Power: 1,516kW (2,062hp) Mitsubishi S6R2-MPTK2 2 x 4 Stroke 6 Cy. 170 x 220 each-758kW (1031bhp) Mitsubishi Heavy Industries Ltd-Japan

IMO / Call sign / Flag	Name / Owner / Port	GT / NT / DWT	Class	Built / Builder / Dimensions	Type	Machinery
9355927 *9V6673* -	**TOLL EMPEROR** *ex* Kimtrans Emperor *-2010* **Toll Logistics (Asia) Ltd** - *Singapore* *Singapore* MMSI: 564855000 Official number: 391237	**835** 250 855	Class: AB	**2006**-01 **P.T. Tunas Karya Bahari Indonesia — Indonesia** Yd No: 69 Loa 54.00 Br ex - Dght 2.200 Lbp 52.00 Br md 18.00 Dpth 3.60 Welded, 1 dk	**(A35D2RL) Landing Craft** Bow ramp (f) Len: 8.00 Wid: 10.00 Swl: 8 Lane-Len: 200 Lane-Wid: 3.00 Lane-clr ht: 6.30 Trailers: 18 Containers on Deck 60 , No. of Trailers 18	**2 oil engines** with clutches, flex coup & sr geared to sc. shaft (s) driving 2 Directional propellers Total Power: 942kW (1,280hp) Cummins KTA-19-M3 2 x 4 Stroke 6 Cy. 159 x 159 each-471kW (640bhp) Cummins Engine Co Inc-USA AuxGen: 2 x 80kW 415/230V 50Hz a.c
9404106 *9VJS5* -	**TOLL EMPRESS** *ex* Kimtrans Empress *-2010* **Sembawang Kimtrans Marine Pte Ltd** Toll Logistics (Asia) Ltd *Singapore* *Singapore* MMSI: 565211000 Official number: 391866	**3,781** 1,135 7,299	Class: GL	**2006**-12 **P.T. Tunas Karya Bahari Indonesia — Indonesia** Yd No: 94 Loa 97.54 Br ex 24.41 Dght 4.440 Lbp - Br md 24.38 Dpth 6.10 Welded, 1 dk	**(A31C2GD) Deck Cargo Ship**	**2 oil engines** reduction geared to sc. shafts driving 2 Directional propellers Total Power: 1,790kW (2,434hp) 9.0kn Cummins KTA-38-M2 2 x Vee 4 Stroke 12 Cy. 159 x 159 each-895kW (1217bhp) Cummins Engine Co Inc-USA AuxGen: 2 x 80kW 415/220V a.c Thrusters: 1 Retract. directional thruster (f)
9123544 *9V5090* -	**TOLL ENERGY** *ex* Kimtrans Energy *-2010* *ex* Jel Energy *-2000* **Toll Logistics (Asia) Ltd** - *Singapore* *Singapore* MMSI: 563001070 Official number: 386430	*358* 108 -	Class: GL	**1995**-01 **ASL Shipyard Pte Ltd — Singapore** Yd No: 084 Loa 40.00 Br ex - Dght 1.800 Lbp - Br md 14.00 Dpth 2.60 Welded, 1 dk	**(A36B2PL) Passenger/Landing Craft**	**2 oil engines** reduction geared to sc. shafts driving 2 Directional propellers 1 fwd and 1 aft Total Power: 578kW (786hp) 10.0kn Caterpillar 3406TA 2 x 4 Stroke 6 Cy. 137 x 165 each-289kW (393bhp) Caterpillar Inc-USA AuxGen: 2 x 42kW 50Hz a.c Fuel: 14.0 (d.f.) 0.5pd
9550723 *VJN3664* -	**TOLL FIREFLY** - **Perkins Shipping Pty Ltd** - *Gladstone, Qld* *Australia* MMSI: 503698000 Official number: 860123	**1,120** 336 1,320	Class: LR (AB) **100A1** SS 02/2010 TOC contemplated	**2010**-02 **P.T. Tunas Karya Bahari Indonesia — Indonesia** Yd No: 210 Loa 54.38 Br ex - Dght 2.800 Lbp - Br md 18.00 Dpth 4.20 Welded, 1 dk	**(A35D2RL) Landing Craft** Bow ramp (f)	**2 oil engines** reduction geared to sc. shafts driving 2 FP propellers Total Power: 956kW (1,300hp) 10.0kn Cummins KTA-19-M3 2 x 4 Stroke 6 Cy. 159 x 159 each-478kW (650bhp) Cummins Engine Co Inc-USA AuxGen: 2 x a.c Fuel: 80.0 (d.f.)
9367047 - -	**TOLL GALAXY** *ex* Kimtrans Galaxy *-2006* **PT Perusahaan Pelayaran Gebari Medan Segara** -	**268** 81 -	Class: GL	**2006**-04 **Kiong Nguong Shipbuilding Contractor Co — Sibu** Yd No: 2031 Loa 29.00 Br ex - Dght 3.505 Lbp 26.06 Br md 8.53 Dpth 4.27 Welded, 1 dk	**(B32A2ST) Tug**	**2 oil engines** reverse reduction geared to sc. shafts driving 2 FP propellers Total Power: 1,800kW (2,448hp) 11.0kn Chinese Std. Type 12V190 2 x Vee 4 Stroke 12 Cy. 190 x 210 each-900kW (1224bhp) Jinan Diesel Engine Co Ltd-China AuxGen: 2 x 48kW 415/230V a.c
9361043 *YDA4388* -	**TOLL HURRICANE** *ex* Kimtrans Hurricane *-2010* **PT SK Pelayaran Indonesia** - *Jakarta* *Indonesia*	**268** 81 -	Class: KI (GL)	**2005**-07 **Kiong Nguong Shipbuilding Contractor Co — Sibu** Yd No: 2030 Loa 29.00 Br ex - Dght 3.505 Lbp 26.06 Br md 8.53 Dpth 4.27 Welded, 1 dk	**(B32A2ST) Tug**	**2 oil engines** reverse reduction geared to sc. shafts driving 2 FP propellers Total Power: 1,790kW (2,434hp) 11.0kn Cummins KTA-38-M2 2 x Vee 4 Stroke 12 Cy. 159 x 159 each-895kW (1217bhp) Cummins Engine Co Inc-USA AuxGen: 2 x 48kW 415/230V a.c
9355915 *9V6672* -	**TOLL JADE** *ex* Kimtrans Jade *-2009* **Toll Logistics (Asia) Ltd** - *Singapore* *Singapore* MMSI: 564852000 Official number: 391236	**835** 250 859	Class: AB	**2005**-12 **P.T. Tunas Karya Bahari Indonesia — Indonesia** Yd No: 68 Loa 54.00 Br ex - Dght 2.200 Lbp 52.00 Br md 18.00 Dpth 3.60 Welded, 1 dk	**(A35D2RL) Landing Craft**	**2 oil engines** reduction geared to sc. shafts driving 2 Directional propellers Total Power: 942kW (1,280hp) Cummins KTA-19-M3 2 x 4 Stroke 6 Cy. 159 x 159 each-471kW (640bhp) Cummins Engine Co Inc-USA
8968571 *YDA4185* -	**TOLL JULIET** *ex* Kimtrans Juliet *-2012* **PT SK Pelayaran Indonesia** Toll Logistics (Asia) Ltd *Tanjung Priok* *Indonesia* MMSI: 525015122	**247** 75 -	Class: KI (GL) (NV)	**2001**-07 **Kiong Nguong Shipbuilding Contractor Co — Sibu** Yd No: 2005 Loa 29.00 Br ex - Dght 3.912 Lbp 26.50 Br md 8.60 Dpth 4.55 Welded, 1 dk	**(B32A2ST) Tug**	**2 oil engines** reverse reduction geared to sc. shafts driving 2 FP propellers Total Power: 1,192kW (1,620hp) Cummins KT-38-M 2 x Vee 4 Stroke 12 Cy. 159 x 159 each-596kW (810bhp) Cummins Engine Co Inc-USA AuxGen: 2 x 166kW 380/220V a.c
9143910 - -	**TOLL JUPITER** *ex* Kimtrans Jupiter *-2009* *ex* Aria Citra II *-1999* *ex* Goldcrest *-1997* - -	**177** 53 -	Class: (GL) (AB)	**1995**-12 **Fuchunjiang Shipyard — Fuyang ZJ** Yd No: SMT25/001/93 Loa 25.20 Br ex - Dght 2.409 Lbp 23.50 Br md 7.99 Dpth 2.99 Welded, 1 dk	**(B32A2ST) Tug**	**2 oil engines** reverse reduction geared to sc. shafts driving 2 FP propellers Total Power: 1,080kW (1,468hp) Chinese Std. Type G6190ZLC 2 x 4 Stroke 6 Cy. 190 x 210 each-540kW (734bhp) (new engine 2004) Jinan Diesel Engine Co Ltd-China
9656060 *VJN4054* -	**TOLL KESTREL** - **Perkins Shipping (Singapore) Pte Ltd** - *Gladstone, Qld* *Australia* MMSI: 503761000 Official number: 860486	**2,045** 613 1,815	Class: LR (AB) **100A1** SS 11/2012 TOC contemplated	**2012**-11 **Tianjin Xinhe Shipbuilding Heavy Industry Co Ltd — Tianjin** Yd No: NB124 Loa 84.67 Br ex - Dght 2.400 Lbp 80.60 Br md 16.50 Dpth 4.80 Welded, 1 dk	**(A35D2RL) Landing Craft** Bow ramp (centre)	**2 oil engines** reduction geared to sc. shafts driving 2 Propellers Total Power: 1,790kW (2,434hp) Cummins KTA-38-M2 2 x Vee 4 Stroke 12 Cy. 159 x 159 each-895kW (1217bhp) Cummins Engine Co Inc-USA AuxGen: 2 x 160kW a.c
8982606 - -	**TOLL KILO** *ex* Kimtrans Kilo *-2010* **PT SK Pelayaran Indonesia** Toll Logistics (Asia) Ltd *Indonesia*	**144** 44 -	Class: GL KI	**2003**-03 **Kiong Nguong Shipbuilding Contractor Co — Sibu** Yd No: 2016 Loa 23.10 Br ex - Dght 2.357 Lbp 20.90 Br md 7.32 Dpth 3.12 Welded, 1 dk	**(B32A2ST) Tug**	**2 oil engines** reverse reduction geared to sc. shafts driving 2 FP propellers Total Power: 940kW (1,278hp) 10.0kn Yanmar 6LAHM-STE 2 x 4 Stroke 6 Cy. 150 x 165 each-470kW (639bhp) Yanmar Diesel Engine Co Ltd-Japan
9403401 *YDA4661* -	**TOLL KOALA** *ex* Kimtrans Koala *-2009* *launched as* Isa I *-2007* **PT SK Pelayaran Indonesia** Toll Logistics (Asia) Ltd *Jakarta* *Indonesia*	**280** 84 107	Class: BV	**2007**-03 **Yizheng Jianghai Shiprepair & Building Co Ltd — Yizheng JS** Yd No: 0518 Loa 29.00 Br ex - Dght 3.900 Lbp 26.94 Br md 9.00 Dpth 4.25 Welded, 1 dk	**(B32A2ST) Tug**	**2 oil engines** reduction geared to sc. shafts driving 2 Propellers Total Power: 1,200kW (1,632hp) 11.0kn Cummins KTA-38-M2 2 x Vee 4 Stroke 12 Cy. 159 x 159 each-600kW (816bhp) Cummins Engine Co Inc-USA
9205500 *YDA4721* -	**TOLL LEO** *ex* Kimtrans Leo *-2011* **PT SK Pelayaran Indonesia** - *Jakarta* *Indonesia*	**125** 38 100	Class: KI (GL) (BV)	**1998**-05 **Nga Chai Shipyard Sdn Bhd — Sibu** (Hull) Yd No: 9720 Loa 23.15 Br ex - Dght 2.500 Lbp 21.69 Br md 7.30 Dpth 3.00 Welded, 1 dk	**(B32A2ST) Tug**	**2 oil engines** reverse reduction geared to sc. shafts driving 2 FP propellers Total Power: 892kW (1,212hp) Cummins KTA-19-M3 2 x 4 Stroke 6 Cy. 159 x 159 each-446kW (606bhp) Cummins Engine Co Inc-USA Fuel: 73.0 (d.f.)
9230555 *YDA4659* -	**TOLL LILY** *ex* Kimtrans Lily *-2008* *ex* RDC Lily *-2002* **PT SK Pelayaran Indonesia** Toll Logistics (Asia) Ltd *Jakarta* *Indonesia*	**152** 46 148	Class: GL KI (NK)	**2000**-04 **Tuong Aik (Sarawak) Sdn Bhd — Sibu** Yd No: 9801 Loa 25.30 Br ex - Dght 2.862 Lbp 23.29 Br md 7.30 Dpth 3.50 Welded, 1 dk	**(B32B2SP) Pusher Tug**	**2 oil engines** reduction geared to sc. shafts driving 2 FP propellers Total Power: 1,000kW (1,360hp) 12.0kn Caterpillar 3412C-TA 2 x Vee 4 Stroke 12 Cy. 137 x 152 each-500kW (680bhp) Caterpillar Inc-USA Fuel: 109.0 (d.f.)
9276494 *YDA4390* -	**TOLL LIMA** *ex* Kimtrans Lima *-2002* **PT SK Pelayaran Indonesia** Toll Logistics (Asia) Ltd *Jakarta* *Indonesia*	**237** 71 -	Class: GL KI (BV)	**2002**-06 **Fujian Fu'an Shuangfu Shipping Co Ltd — Fu'an FJ** Yd No: 2033 Loa 29.00 Br ex - Dght 3.180 Lbp 26.47 Br md 8.40 Dpth 3.80 Welded, 1 dk	**(B32A2ST) Tug**	**2 oil engines** geared to sc. shafts driving 2 FP propellers Total Power: 1,492kW (2,028hp) Cummins KTA-38-M 2 x Vee 4 Stroke 12 Cy. 159 x 159 each-746kW (1014bhp) Cummins Engine Co Ltd-United Kingdom
9306586 *YDA4660* -	**TOLL MIKE** *ex* Kimtrans Mike *-2008* **PT SK Pelayaran Indonesia** - *Jakarta* *Indonesia*	**267** 81 -	Class: KI (GL)	**2003**-10 **Kiong Nguong Shipbuilding Contractor Co — Sibu** Yd No: 2012 Loa - Br ex - Dght - Lbp 27.02 Br md 8.53 Dpth 4.26 Welded, 1 dk	**(B32A2ST) Tug**	**2 oil engines** reverse reduction geared to sc. shafts driving 2 FP propellers Total Power: 1,516kW (2,062hp) 10.0kn Mitsubishi S6R2-MPTK 2 x 4 Stroke 6 Cy. 170 x 220 each-758kW (1031bhp) Mitsubishi Heavy Industries Ltd-Japan AuxGen: 2 x 50kW 415V a.c

9570175 *9V9103* -	**TOLL OSBORNE** - **Toll Logistics (Asia) Ltd** - SatCom: Inmarsat C 456534811 *Singapore* *Singapore* MMSI: 565348000	**452** 135 -	Class: BV	**2010-12 Celtug Service Shipyard Sdn Bhd — Sibu** Yd No: 0803 Loa 36.00 Br ex - Dght 3.800 Lbp 31.50 Br md 10.40 Dpth 5.00 Welded, 1 dk	**(B32A2ST) Tug**	**2 oil engines** reduction geared to sc. shafts driving 2 FP propellers Total Power: 2,984kW (4,058hp) Cummins KTA-50-M2 2 x Vee 4 Stroke 16 Cy. 159 x 159 each-1492kW (2029bhp) Cummins Engine Co Ltd-United Kingdom AuxGen: 2 x 150kW 50Hz a.c
9656072 *VHCG* -	**TOLL OSPREY** - **Toll Logistics (Asia) Ltd** Perkins Shipping Pty Ltd *Gladstone, Qld* *Australia* MMSI: 503767000 Official number: 860540	**2,045** 613 1,797	Class: LR (AB) **100A1** SS 01/2013 TOC contemplated	**2013-01 Tianjin Xinhe Shipbuilding Heavy Industry Co Ltd — Tianjin** Yd No: NB125 Loa 84.67 Br ex - Dght 2.400 Lbp 80.60 Br md 16.50 Dpth 4.80 Welded, 1 dk	**(A35D2RL) Landing Craft** Bow ramp (centre)	**2 oil engines** reduction geared to sc. shafts driving 2 Propellers Total Power: 1,790kW (2,434hp) Cummins KTA-38-M2 2 x Vee 4 Stroke 12 Cy. 159 x 159 each-895kW (1217bhp) Cummins Engine Co Inc-USA AuxGen: 1 x 160kW a.c Fuel: 840.0
9578335 *VJN3683* -	**TOLL SANDFLY** - **Toll Logistics (Asia) Ltd** Mermaid Marine Australia Ltd *Dampier, WA* *Australia* MMSI: 503702000 Official number: 860095	**1,273** 414 1,650	Class: AB	**2010-12 Nanjing Yonghua Ship Co Ltd — Nanjing JS** Yd No: P205 Loa 54.47 Br ex - Dght 3.000 Lbp 51.78 Br md 18.00 Dpth 4.50 Welded, 1 dk	**(A35D2RL) Landing Craft** Bow ramp (centre)	**2 oil engines** reduction geared to sc. shafts driving 2 FP propellers Total Power: 954kW (1,298hp) Cummins KTA-19-M3 2 x 4 Stroke 6 Cy. 159 x 159 each-477kW (649bhp) Cummins Engine Co Inc-USA AuxGen: 3 x 80kW a.c
9391696 *YDA4389* -	**TOLL SOLARS** *ex* Kimtrans Solars **PT SK Pelayaran Indonesia** - *Jakarta* *Indonesia*	**271** 82 -	Class: KI (GL)	**2006-04 Kiong Nguong Shipbuilding Contractor Co — Sibu** Yd No: 2037 Loa 29.00 Br ex - Dght 3.500 Lbp 27.02 Br md 8.53 Dpth 4.27 Welded, 1 dk	**(B32A2ST) Tug** Double Bottom Partial Compartment Length	**2 oil engines** reduction geared to sc. shafts driving 2 FP propellers Total Power: 1,790kW (2,434hp) 10.0kn Cummins KTA-38-M2 2 x Vee 4 Stroke 12 Cy. 159 x 159 each-895kW (1217bhp) Cummins Engine Co Ltd-United Kingdom AuxGen: 2 x 50kW 415V a.c Fuel: 200.0
9341861 *YDCF* -	**TOLL SPB 3208** *ex* Kimtrans Spb 3208 *-2012* **PT SK Pelayaran Indonesia** - *Jakarta* *Indonesia* MMSI: 525015126	**3,695** 1,109 7,449	Class: KI (AB)	**2005-01 Lian Yi Shipbuilding & Construction Pte Ltd — Singapore** (Hull launched by) Yd No: 45 **2005-01 Galangan Kapal Tunas Harapan — Samarinda** (Hull completed by) Loa 97.53 Br ex - Dght 6.100 Lbp 94.80 Br md 24.38 Dpth 6.10 Welded, 1 dk	**(A31C2GD) Deck Cargo Ship**	**2 oil engines** reduction geared to sc. shafts driving 2 Z propellers Total Power: 1,792kW (2,436hp) Cummins KTA-38-M2 2 x Vee 4 Stroke 12 Cy. 159 x 159 each-896kW (1218bhp) Chongqing Cummins Engine Co Ltd-China
9404120 *YCMN* -	**TOLL SPB 3210** *ex* Kimtrans Spb 3210 *-2006* **PT SK Pelayaran Indonesia** - *Jakarta* *Indonesia* MMSI: 525015125	**3,695** 1,109 7,675	Class: KI (GL)	**2006-12 P.T. Tunas Karya Bahari Indonesia — Indonesia** Yd No: 96 Loa 97.54 Br ex 24.41 Dght 4.600 Lbp - Br md 24.38 Dpth 6.10 Welded, 1 dk	**(A31C2GD) Deck Cargo Ship**	**2 oil engines** reduction geared to sc. shafts driving 2 Z propellers Total Power: 2,238kW (3,042hp) Cummins KTA-38-M2 2 x Vee 4 Stroke 12 Cy. 159 x 159 each-1119kW (1521bhp) Cummins Engine Co Inc-USA AuxGen: 2 x 350kW 415V a.c
9415090 *PMAZ* -	**TOLL SPB 3211** *ex* Kimtrans Spb 3211 *-2007* **PT SK Pelayaran Indonesia** - *Jakarta* *Indonesia* MMSI: 525015448	**3,708** 1,113 7,675	Class: KI	**2007-06 PT Sentek Indonesia — Batam** Yd No: 06N12 Loa 97.54 Br ex 24.41 Dght 4.600 Lbp - Br md 24.38 Dpth 6.10 Welded, 1 dk	**(A31C2GD) Deck Cargo Ship**	**2 oil engines** reduction geared to sc. shafts driving 2 Propellers Total Power: 2,238kW (3,042hp) Cummins KTA-38-M2 2 x Vee 4 Stroke 12 Cy. 159 x 159 each-1119kW (1521bhp) Cummins Engine Co Inc-USA AuxGen: 2 x 90kW 415V a.c
9415105 *YECM* -	**TOLL SPB 3212** *ex* Kimtrans Spb 3212 *-2013* **PT SK Pelayaran Indonesia** - *Jakarta* *Indonesia* MMSI: 525015447	**3,708** 1,113 7,675	Class: KI	**2007-05 P.T. Tunas Karya Bahari Indonesia — Indonesia** Yd No: 103 Loa 97.54 Br ex 24.41 Dght 4.600 Lbp 95.34 Br md 24.38 Dpth 6.10 Welded, 1 dk	**(A31C2GD) Deck Cargo Ship**	**2 oil engines** reduction geared to sc. shafts driving 2 Propellers Total Power: 2,238kW (3,042hp) Cummins KTA-38-M2 2 x Vee 4 Stroke 12 Cy. 159 x 159 each-1119kW (1521bhp) Cummins Engine Co Inc-USA AuxGen: 2 x 90kW 415V a.c
9415129 *PMHC* -	**TOLL SPB 3218** *ex* Kimtrans Spb 3218 *-2013* **PT SK Pelayaran Indonesia** - *Jakarta* *Indonesia* MMSI: 525015305	**3,708** 1,113 7,675	Class: KI	**2007-12 P.T. Tunas Karya Bahari Indonesia — Indonesia** Yd No: 122 Loa 97.54 Br ex 24.41 Dght 4.600 Lbp 95.34 Br md 24.38 Dpth 6.10 Welded, 1 dk	**(A31C2GD) Deck Cargo Ship**	**2 oil engines** reduction geared to sc. shafts driving 2 Propellers Total Power: 1,766kW (2,402hp) 9.6kn Cummins KTA-38-M2 2 x Vee 4 Stroke 12 Cy. 159 x 159 each-883kW (1201bhp) Cummins Engine Co Inc-USA AuxGen: 2 x 65kW 415V a.c
9464170 *PMJL* -	**TOLL SPD 3308** *ex* Kimtrans Spd 3308 *-2008* **PT SK Pelayaran Indonesia** - *Jakarta* *Indonesia* MMSI: 525015315	**4,489** 1,347 8,903	Class: KI (GL)	**2008-04 P.T. Tunas Karya Bahari Indonesia — Indonesia** Yd No: 115 Loa 100.58 Br ex - Dght - Lbp 96.00 Br md 25.60 Dpth 6.71 Welded, 1 dk	**(A31A2GX) General Cargo Ship**	**2 oil engines** reduction geared to sc. shafts driving 2 FP propellers Total Power: 1,766kW (2,402hp) 9.0kn Cummins KTA-38-M2 2 x Vee 4 Stroke 12 Cy. 159 x 159 each-883kW (1201bhp) Cummins Engine Co Ltd-United Kingdom AuxGen: 2 x 80kW 415V a.c
9607942 *VJN4261* -	**TOLL TERRITORIAN** - **Australian Offshore Solutions Pty Ltd** - *Darwin, NT* *Australia* MMSI: 503779000 Official number: 860748	**1,107** 334 1,000	Class: BV	**2013-06 Vitawani Shipbuilding Sdn Bhd — Sibu** Yd No: VT9 Loa 68.00 Br ex 14.60 Dght 3.655 Lbp 62.86 Br md 14.00 Dpth 4.30 Welded, 1 dk	**(A35D2RL) Landing Craft** Bow ramp (centre)	**2 oil engines** reduction geared to sc. shafts driving 2 FP propellers Total Power: 1,472kW (2,002hp) 11.0kn Yanmar 6RY17P-GV 2 x 4 Stroke 6 Cy. 165 x 219 each-736kW (1001bhp) Yanmar Diesel Engine Co Ltd-Japan AuxGen: 2 x 80kW 50Hz a.c Thrusters: 1 Tunnel thruster (f) Fuel: 590.0
9541112 *YDA4549* -	**TOLL TORNADO** - **PT SK Pelayaran Indonesia** - *Jakarta* *Indonesia* Official number: 2010 PST NO.6326/L	**262** 79 308	Class: KI (NK)	**2008-12 Nga Chai Shipyard Sdn Bhd — Sibu** Yd No: 33/06 Loa 30.00 Br ex - Dght 3.512 Lbp 28.06 Br md 8.60 Dpth 4.11 Welded, 1 dk	**(B32A2ST) Tug**	**2 oil engines** reduction geared to sc. shafts driving 2 Propellers Total Power: 2,080kW (2,828hp) Mitsubishi S12R-MPTK 2 x Vee 4 Stroke 12 Cy. 170 x 180 each-1040kW (1414bhp) Mitsubishi Heavy Industries Ltd-Japan AuxGen: 2 x 99kW a.c Fuel: 200.0
9351074 *YDA4982* -	**TOLL TYPHOON** *ex* Kimtrans Typhoon *-2010* **PT SK Pelayaran Indonesia** - *Jakarta* *Indonesia*	**268** 81 -	Class: GL	**2005-05 Kiong Nguong Shipbuilding Contractor Co — Sibu** Yd No: 2029 Loa 29.00 Br ex - Dght 3.500 Lbp 26.06 Br md 8.53 Dpth 4.27 Welded, 1 dk	**(B32A2ST) Tug**	**2 oil engines** reduction geared to sc. shafts driving 2 FP propellers Total Power: 2,238kW (3,042hp) 11.0kn Cummins KTA-38-M2 2 x Vee 4 Stroke 12 Cy. 159 x 159 each-1119kW (1521bhp) Cummins Engine Co Inc-USA
9467378 *YDA4984* -	**TOLL WALLA** *launched as* Kimtrans Walla *-2008* **PT SK Pelayaran Indonesia** - *Jakarta* *Indonesia* Official number: 3813/PST	**191** 58 145	Class: KI (NK)	**2008-01 Tuong Aik Shipyard Sdn Bhd — Sibu** Yd No: 2712 Loa 26.00 Br ex - Dght 1.980 Lbp 24.35 Br md 8.00 Dpth 3.65 Welded, 1 dk	**(B32A2ST) Tug**	**2 oil engines** reduction geared to sc. shafts driving 2 Propellers Total Power: 1,518kW (2,064hp) Mitsubishi S6R2-MPTK3 2 x 4 Stroke 6 Cy. 170 x 220 each-759kW (1032bhp) Mitsubishi Heavy Industries Ltd-Japan Fuel: 148.0 (d.f.)
9518945 - -	**TOLL ZIRCON** - **Toll Logistics (Asia) Ltd** - *La Union* *Philippines* Official number: 01-0000492	**295** 89 243	Class: GL	**2010-02 Rajang Maju Shipbuilding Sdn Bhd — Sibu** Yd No: RMM0002 Loa 32.00 Br ex - Dght 3.500 Lbp 29.23 Br md 9.14 Dpth 4.20 Welded, 1 dk	**(B32A2ST) Tug**	**2 oil engines** reverse reduction geared to sc. shafts driving 2 FP propellers Total Power: 2,386kW (3,244hp) Cummins KTA-50-M2 2 x Vee 4 Stroke 16 Cy. 159 x 159 each-1193kW (1622bhp) Cummins Engine Co Inc-USA AuxGen: 2 x 80kW 400V a.c

Ship	Tonnage	Class	Build / Dimensions	Type	Machinery
9287388 **TOLL ZULU** *YDA4657* ex Kimtrans Zulu *-2010* - **PT SK Pelayaran Indonesia** Toll Logistics (Asia) Ltd *Jakarta* *Indonesia*	**254** 77 269	Class: GL KI (NV)	**2002**-12 **Jana Seribu Shipbuilding (M) Sdn Bhd — Sibu** Yd No: 0201 Loa 28.00 Br ex 8.53 Dght 3.416 Lbp 24.93 Br md 8.53 Dpth 4.27 Welded, 1 dk	**(B32A2ST) Tug**	**2 oil engines** reduction geared to sc. shafts driving 2 FP propellers Total Power: 1,060kW (1,442hp) Volvo Penta MD30A-MT 2 x 4 Stroke 6 Cy. 170 x 220 each-530kW (721bhp) AB Volvo Penta-Sweden AuxGen: 2 x 52kW a.c
8117615 **TOLMI** *SYXL* ex Pisces Venturer *-2002* ex Finnwood *-1997* - ex Lanka Abhaya *-1991* ex Finnwood *-1990* **Westdene Maritime Ltd** Doil Steamship Ltd SatCom: Inmarsat M 623490910 *Piraeus* *Greece* MMSI: 239929000 Official number: 10994	**21,305** 10,412 29,094 T/cm 44.0	Class: NV	**1989**-12 **Stocznia Gdanska im Lenina — Gdansk** Yd No: B539/02 Loa 184.51 (BB) Br ex - Dght 10.348 Lbp 175.40 Br md 27.50 Dpth 14.30 Welded, 1 dk	**(A21A2BC) Bulk Carrier** Grain: 36,847; Bale: 35,929 TEU 1100 Compartments: 5 Ho, ER 5 Ha: (17.8 x 19.6)4 (22.8 x 19.2)ER Cranes: 5x25t Ice Capable	**1 oil engine** driving 1 CP propeller Total Power: 7,080kW (9,626hp) 14.4kn Sulzer 6RTA58 1 x 2 Stroke 6 Cy. 580 x 1700 7080kW (9626bhp) Zaklady Przemyslu Metalowego 'HCegielski' SA-Poznan AuxGen: 3 x 832kW 380V 50Hz a.c Thrusters: 1 Thwart. FP thruster (f) Fuel: 236.0 (d.f.) 2038.0 (r.f.) 31.0pd
9147863 **TOLMIN** *V2QD8* ex Aurelia *-2010* - **Genshipping Corp** Splosna Plovba doo (Splosna plovba International Shipping & Chartering Ltd) *Saint John's* *Antigua & Barbuda* MMSI: 305597000 Official number: 3066	**5,381** 2,626 6,790 T/cm 17.2	Class: GL	**1998**-01 **Turkiye Gemi Sanayii A.S. — Camialti, Istanbul** Yd No: 240 Loa 107.57 (BB) Br ex - Dght 6.630 Lbp 103.12 Br md 18.20 Dpth 9.00 Welded, 1 dk	**(A21A2BC) Bulk Carrier** Double Hull Grain: 9,729 Compartments: 3 Ho, ER 3 Ha: (24.5 x 15.2) (28.4 x 15.2) (20.3 x 15.2)ER Ice Capable	**1 oil engine** driving 1 CP propeller Total Power: 2,400kW (3,263hp) 12.0kn B&W 6S26MC 1 x 2 Stroke 6 Cy. 260 x 980 2400kW (3263bhp) MAN B&W Diesel A/S-Denmark Thrusters: 1 Thwart. FP thruster (f)
5411149 **TOLOGI** *VM4270* ex Flinders Trader *-1995* - ex Milford Crouch *-1963* launched as Leillateah *-1957* **Progress Pty Ltd** - *Launceston, Tas* *Australia* Official number: 178474	*166* 94 177		**1957 R M Crouch & Co — Port Adelaide SA** Lengthened-1961 L reg 31.58 Br ex 5.85 Dght - Lbp - Br md 5.80 Dpth - Welded, 1 dk	**(A31A2GX) General Cargo Ship**	**1 oil engine** driving 1 FP propeller Daimler MB846A 1 x 4 Stroke 6 Cy. 150 x 190 Daimler Benz AG-West Germany
7513472 **TOLONG** *9WBA* - **Government of Malaysia (Director of Marine - Sabah)** - *Malaysia*	*220* - 100		**1977**-08 **Sabah Shipbuilding, Repairing & Engineering Sdn Bhd — Labuan** Yd No: 101 Loa - Br ex - Dght 2.593 Lbp 22.10 Br md 6.72 Dpth 3.05 Welded, 1 dk	**(B32A2ST) Tug**	**2 oil engines** driving 2 FP propellers Caterpillar 2 x 4 Stroke Caterpillar Tractor Co-USA
8318178 **TOLOU** *EQOD* ex Shafagh *-1985* - **NITC** - *Bushehr* *Iran* Official number: 16554	**178** 57 250	Class: AS (LR) ✠ Classed LR until 28/2/98	**1984**-03 **Scheepswerf Jac. den Breejen & Zoon B.V. — Hardinxveld-G.** (Hull) **1984**-03 **B.V. Scheepswerf Damen — Gorinchem** Yd No: 5102 Loa 34.14 Br ex 6.68 Dght 2.000 Lbp 31.75 Br md 6.56 Dpth 3.59 Welded, 1 dk	**(B21A20C) Crew/Supply Vessel**	**2 oil engines** with clutches, flexible couplings & sr reverse geared to sc. shafts driving 2 FP propellers Total Power: 2,500kW (3,400hp) MWM TBD603V16 2 x Vee 4 Stroke 16 Cy. 160 x 185 each-1250kW (1700bhp) Motoren Werke Mannheim AG (MWM)-West Germany AuxGen: 2 x 64kW 380V 50Hz a.c, 1 x 27kW 380V 50Hz a.c
8316120 **TOLOU SHARGH 6** *EPBU6* ex Cross East 6 *-2012* ex Marsea 6 *-2012* - ex Khandagh *-2006* **Hossein Rezaei** Cross East Shipping & Cargo Co LLC *Bushehr* *Iran* Official number: 1097	**472** 141 481	Class: AS (LR) (CC) ✠ Classed LR until 6/2/99	**1984**-08 **K.K. Imai Seisakusho — Kamijima** (Hull) Yd No: 242 **1984**-08 **Mitsui Ocean Development & Eng. Co. Ltd. — Japan** Yd No: S-181 Loa 38.54 Br ex 10.24 Dght 3.700 Lbp 35.39 Br md 10.00 Dpth 4.40 Welded, 1 dk	**(B21B20T) Offshore Tug/Supply Ship**	**2 oil engines** with clutches, flexible couplings & sr reverse geared to sc. shafts driving 2 FP propellers Total Power: 3,734kW (5,076hp) 12.0kn Deutz SBV6M628 1 x 4 Stroke 6 Cy. 240 x 280 1867kW (2538bhp) (new engine 1984) Kloeckner Humboldt Deutz-Netherlands Deutz SBV6M628 1 x 4 Stroke 6 Cy. 240 x 280 1867kW (2538bhp) (new engine 1988) Kloeckner Humboldt Deutz-Netherlands AuxGen: 2 x 128kW 380V 50Hz a.c Thrusters: 1 Thwart. CP thruster (f) Fuel: 90.5 (d.f.)
8316132 **TOLOU SHARGH 7** *EPBU5* ex Cross East 7 *-2012* ex Marsea 7 *-2012* - ex Kheibar *-2006* **Hossein Rezaei** Cross East Shipping & Cargo Co LLC *Bushehr* *Iran* Official number: 1096	**472** 141 481	Class: (LR) (CC) (AS) ✠ Classed LR until 1/6/98	**1984**-09 **K.K. Imai Seisakusho — Kamijima** (Hull) Yd No: 243 **1984**-09 **Mitsui Ocean Development & Eng. Co. Ltd. — Japan** Yd No: S-182 Loa 38.54 Br ex 10.24 Dght 3.700 Lbp 35.39 Br md 10.00 Dpth 4.40 Welded, 1 dk	**(B21B20T) Offshore Tug/Supply Ship**	**2 oil engines** with clutches, flexible couplings & sr reverse geared to sc. shafts driving 2 FP propellers Total Power: 3,734kW (5,076hp) 12.0kn Deutz SBV6M628 2 x 4 Stroke 6 Cy. 240 x 280 each-1867kW (2538bhp) Kloeckner Humboldt Deutz AG-West Germany AuxGen: 2 x 128kW 380V 50Hz a.c Thrusters: 1 Thwart. CP thruster (f) Fuel: 90.5 (d.f.)
5320522 **TOLTECA** *XCTR* ex Blue Whale *-1979* ex Sept Iles *-1974* - **Constructora y Arrendadora Mexico SA de CV (CAMSA)** - *Ciudad del Carmen* *Mexico* MMSI: 345070011	*16,378* 7,525 31,497	Class: LR ✠ **100A1** SS 02/2010 Gulf of Mexico and Caribbean Sea service ✠ **LMC** Eq.Ltr: p†; Cable: SQ	**1955**-12 **Furness S.B. Co. Ltd. — Middlesbrough** Yd No: 471 Converted From: Ore/Oil Carrier-1975 Loa 201.66 Br ex - Dght 9.970 Lbp 192.34 Br md 26.52 Dpth 13.87 Riveted\Welded, 1 dk	**(B22C2OQ) Pipe Layer Crane Vessel** 1 Ha: (21.1 x -)ER Cranes: 1x2000t	**1 Steam Turb** dr geared to sc. shaft driving 1 FP propeller Total Power: 10,113kW (13,750hp) Richardsons, Westgarth 1 x steam Turb 10113kW (13750shp) Richardsons, Westgarth & Co.Ltd.-Hartlepool AuxGen: 2 x 500kW 450V 50Hz a.c Boilers: 2 WTB 47.6kgf/cm² (46.7bar)180°C , sg 6.9kgf/cm² (6.8bar), sg (New boiler: 1955) 13.8kgf/cm² (13.5bar)
9612870 **TOLTEN** *D5AD7* - **Hull 1975 Co Ltd** Compania SudAmericana de Vapores SA (CSAV) SatCom: Inmarsat C 463712075 *Monrovia* *Liberia* MMSI: 636015355 Official number: 15355	**88,586** 42,897 94,600	Class: GL	**2012**-06 **Samsung Heavy Industries Co Ltd — Geoje** Yd No: 1975 Loa 299.94 (BB) Br ex - Dght 13.500 Lbp 285.00 Br md 45.60 Dpth 24.60 Welded, 1 dk	**(A33A2CC) Container Ship (Fully Cellular)** TEU 8004 C Ho 3574 TEU C Dk 4430 TEU incl 1500 ref C.	**1 oil engine** driving 1 FP propeller Total Power: 43,610kW (59,292hp) 23.0kn MAN-B&W 7K98ME7 1 x 2 Stroke 7 Cy. 980 x 2660 43610kW (59292bhp) Doosan Engine Co Ltd-South Korea AuxGen: 2 x 2880kW a.c, 3 x 3360kW a.c Thrusters: 1 Tunnel thruster (f) Fuel: 290.0 (d.f.) 8600.0 (r.f.) 162.0pd
8305377 **TOLU** - - **Compania Pesquera Vikingos de Colombia SA** - *Cartagena de Indias* *Colombia* Official number: MC-05-392	*132* 24 22		**1982 Desco Marine — Saint Augustine, Fl** Loa 22.86 Br ex 6.71 Dght 4.271 Lbp 19.99 Br md 6.51 Dpth 4.09 Bonded, 1 dk	**(B11A2FT) Trawler** Hull Material: Reinforced Plastic Ins: 67 Compartments: 1 Ho, ER 1 Ha:	**1 oil engine** with clutches & sr geared to sc. shaft driving 1 FP propeller Total Power: 331kW (450hp) Caterpillar 3412T 1 x Vee 4 Stroke 12 Cy. 137 x 152 331kW (450bhp) Caterpillar Tractor Co-USA
9085675 **TOLUNAY** *E5U2754* ex VTC Light *-2013* ex Bolivar Light *-2005* - ex Royal Highness *-2000* **Tolunay Shipping Ltd** Steffi Kohler (Tolunay Ship Management) *Avatiu* *Cook Islands* MMSI: 518807000 Official number: 1841	**13,865** 7,738 21,964	Class: NK VR	**1995**-02 **Saiki Heavy Industries Co Ltd — Saiki OT** (Hull) Yd No: 1038 **1995**-02 **Onomichi Dockyard Co Ltd — Onomichi HS** Yd No: 384 Loa 157.70 (BB) Br ex - Dght 9.115 Lbp 148.00 Br md 25.00 Dpth 12.70 Welded, 1 dk	**(A21A2BC) Bulk Carrier** Grain: 29,254; Bale: 28,299 Compartments: 4 Ho, ER 4 Ha: (20.0 x 11.7)3 (20.8 x 17.5)ER Cranes: 4x30t	**1 oil engine** driving 1 FP propeller Total Power: 5,296kW (7,200hp) 14.0kn Mitsubishi 6UEC45LA 1 x 2 Stroke 6 Cy. 450 x 1350 5296kW (7200bhp) Kobe Hatsudoki KK-Japan AuxGen: 2 x 400kW a.c Fuel: 1210.0 (r.f.) 22.2pd
9329746 **TOLYATTI** - - **OAO 'Tolyattiazot'** - *Novorossiysk* *Russia*	**187** 56 59	Class: (RS)	**2004**-07 **OOO Opytnyy Sudostroitelnyy Zavod 'Nordstroy' — Shlisselburg** Yd No: 274 Loa 29.30 Br ex 8.30 Dght 3.410 Lbp 27.00 Br md - Dpth 4.30 Welded, 1 dk	**(B32A2ST) Tug**	**2 oil engines** reduction geared to sc. shafts driving 2 CP propellers Total Power: 1,180kW (1,604hp) 11.0kn Pervomaysk 8CHNP25/34 2 x 4 Stroke 8 Cy. 250 x 340 each-590kW (802bhp) (made 1999) in Ukraine AuxGen: 2 x 65kW a.c Fuel: 52.0 (d.f.)
9325879 **TOLYATTIAZOT** - - **OAO 'Tolyattiazot'** - *Novorossiysk* *Russia* Official number: 030190	**188** 56 119	Class: (RS)	**2004**-06 **OAO Leningradskiy Sudostroitelnyy Zavod 'Pella' — Otradnoye** Yd No: 902 Loa 25.86 Br ex 9.25 Dght 3.390 Lbp 23.00 Br md 8.90 Dpth 4.30 Welded, 1 dk	**(B32A2ST) Tug**	**2 oil engines** driving 2 Directional propellers Total Power: 1,492kW (2,028hp) 12.0kn Cummins KTA-38-M1 2 x Vee 4 Stroke 12 Cy. 159 x 159 each-746kW (1014bhp) Cummins Engine Co Inc-USA Fuel: 80.0 (d.f.)

IMO / Call sign	Name / Owner / Port	Tonnage	Class	Builder / Dimensions	Type / Cargo	Machinery
8847167 *YL2494* -	**TOM** *ex Tom T -2002 ex Tom -1995* **AS PKL Flote** - *Riga* *Latvia* MMSI: 275165000 Official number: 0128	**182** 54 57	Class: RS	**1991-07 Gorokhovetskiy Sudostroitelnyy Zavod — Gorokhovets** Yd No: 248 Loa 29.30 Br ex 8.60 Dght 3.400 Lbp 27.00 Br md 8.24 Dpth 4.30 Welded, 1 dk	**(B32A2ST) Tug**	**2 oil engines** driving 2 CP propellers Total Power: 1,180kW (1,604hp) 11.5kn Pervomaysk 8CHNP25/34 2 x 4 Stroke 8 Cy. 250 x 340 each-590kW (802bhp) Pervomaydizelmash (PDM)-Pervomaysk AuxGen: 2 x 50kW a.c
7354773 *E5U2299* -	**TOM** *ex Daniel Solander -2009* *ex Kyowa Maru No. 32 -1982* *ex Bocho Maru No. 12 -1979* **Reef Fishing (Cook Islands) Ltd** - *Rarotonga* *Cook Islands* MMSI: 518349000 Official number: 1383	**508** 152 420		**1973 Miho Zosensho K.K. — Shimizu** Yd No: 942 Loa 53.60 Br ex 8.51 Dght 3.353 Lbp 47.02 Br md 8.50 Dpth 3.76 Welded, 1 dk	**(B11B2FV) Fishing Vessel**	**1 oil engine** reduction geared to sc. shaft driving 1 FP propeller Total Power: 956kW (1,300hp) Daihatsu 6DS-26 1 x 4 Stroke 6 Cy. 260 x 320 956kW (1300bhp) Daihatsu Diesel Manufacturing Co Lt-Japan
8941183 - -	**TOM CAT** - **Mara-M doo** - *Croatia*	**118** 35 -		**1997 Ocean Marine, Inc. — Bayou La Batre, Al** Yd No: 334 L reg 22.68 Br ex - Dght - Lbp - Br md 7.01 Dpth 3.72 Welded, 1 dk	**(B11B2FV) Fishing Vessel**	**1 oil engine** driving 1 FP propeller
9441946 *7JLR* -	**TOM PRICE** - **Birdland Shipping Inc** Mitsui OSK Lines Ltd (MOL) *Tokyo* *Japan* MMSI: 432849000 Official number: 141638	**119,446** 42,557 226,381	Class: NK	**2012-03 Namura Shipbuilding Co Ltd — Imari SG** Yd No: 328 Loa 319.58 (BB) Br ex - Dght 18.122 Lbp 308.00 Br md 54.00 Dpth 25.10 Welded, 1 dk	**(A21B2BO) Ore Carrier** Grain: 151,175 Compartments: 5 Ho, ER 9 Ha: ER	**1 oil engine** driving 1 FP propeller Total Power: 20,445kW (27,797hp) 15.1kn Mitsubishi 6UEC85LSII 1 x 2 Stroke 6 Cy. 850 x 3150 20445kW (27797bhp) Mitsubishi Heavy Industries Ltd-Japan AuxGen: 3 x 750kW a.c Fuel: 7410.0
8860793 *WSD9178* -	**TOM ROGERS** *ex Andre'R -2010 ex Adrienne L -1992* **James Marine Inc** - *Paducah, KY* *United States of America* Official number: 635081	*103* 57 -		**1981 Superior Boat Works Inc — Greenville MS** L reg 18.44 Br ex - Dght - Lbp - Br md 7.31 Dpth 2.62 Welded, 1 dk	**(B32A2ST) Tug**	**1 oil engine** driving 1 FP propeller
8703232 *DGRH*	**TOM SAWYER** *ex Nils Holgersson -2001 ex Robin Hood -1993* **Partenreederei ms Tom Sawyer** TT-Line GmbH & Co KG *Rostock* *Germany* MMSI: 211149000 Official number: 4026	**26,478** 8,139 6,080	Class: GL	**1989-01 Schichau Seebeckwerft AG — Bremerhaven** Yd No: 1064 Converted From: Ferry (Passenger/Vehicle/Train)-1993 Loa 177.20 (BB) Br ex 31.00 Dght 5.780 Lbp 165.00 Br md 26.00 Dpth 18.90 Welded, 3 dks	**(A36A2PR) Passenger/Ro-Ro Ship (Vehicles)** Passengers: unberthed: 76; cabins: 134; berths: 324 Bow door & ramp Len: 15.20 Wid: 4.30 Swl: - Stern door/ramp Len: 15.00 Wid: 11.40 Swl: - Lane-Len: 2258 Lane-Wid: 3.45 Lane-clr ht: 4.45 Trailers: 160 Ice Capable	**4 oil engines** with clutches & dr geared to sc. shafts driving 2 CP propellers Total Power: 14,800kW (20,122hp) 20.0kn MAN 6L40/45 2 x 4 Stroke 6 Cy. 400 x 450 each-3170kW (4310bhp) MAN B&W Diesel GmbH-Augsburg MAN 8L40/45 2 x 4 Stroke 8 Cy. 400 x 450 each-4230kW (5751bhp) MAN B&W Diesel GmbH-Augsburg AuxGen: 2 x 1300kW 220/440V a.c, 3 x 820kW 220/440V a.c, 1 x 500kW 220/440V a.c Thrusters: 2 Thwart. CP thruster (f)
9476630 *V7XB2* -	**TOM SELMER** - **ms 'Tom Selmer' Schifffahrtsgesellschaft mbH & Co KG** Oskar Wehr KG (GmbH & Co) *Majuro* *Marshall Islands* MMSI: 538090442 Official number: 90442	**92,079** 58,596 175,154 T/cm 120.8	Class: NV	**2011-10 New Times Shipbuilding Co Ltd — Jingjiang JS** Yd No: 0117617 Loa 291.86 (BB) Br ex 45.04 Dght 18.250 Lbp 282.21 Br md 45.00 Dpth 24.75 Welded, 1 dk	**(A21A2BC) Bulk Carrier** Grain: 198,122 Compartments: 9 Ho, ER 9 Ha: ER	**1 oil engine** driving 1 FP propeller Total Power: 16,860kW (22,923hp) 14.5kn MAN-B&W 6S70MC 1 x 2 Stroke 6 Cy. 700 x 2674 16860kW (22923bhp) AuxGen: 3 x a.c
9543495 *9WKB9* -	**TOM STAR** - **Tegas Offshore Marine Sdn Bhd** - *Kuching* *Malaysia* MMSI: 533000821 Official number: 333125	**498** 149 -	Class: BV	**2009-09 Sarawak Slipways Sdn Bhd — Miri** Yd No: 243 Loa 40.00 Br ex - Dght 4.000 Lbp 35.60 Br md 11.40 Dpth 4.95 Welded, 1 dk	**(B21B20A) Anchor Handling Tug Supply**	**2 oil engines** reduction geared to sc. shaft (s driving 2 FP propellers Total Power: 2,984kW (4,058hp) 12.0kn Cummins KTA-50-M2 2 x Vee 4 Stroke 16 Cy. 159 x 159 each-1492kW (2029bhp) Cummins Engine Co Ltd-United Kingdom AuxGen: 2 x 245kW 50Hz a.c Thrusters: 1 Tunnel thruster (f) Fuel: 170.0 (d.f.)
8112419 *VJTF* -	**TOM TOUGH** *launched as Heron -1983* **Svitzer Australia Pty Ltd (Svitzer Australasia)** - *Gladstone, Qld* *Australia* MMSI: 503033000 Official number: 850342	*396* 117 368	Class: AB	**1983-02 Carrington Slipways Pty Ltd — Newcastle NSW** Yd No: 154 Loa 33.91 Br ex 11.10 Dght 4.942 Lbp 29.67 Br md 10.83 Dpth 5.41 Welded, 1 dk	**(B32A2ST) Tug**	**2 oil engines** with clutches, flexible couplings & dr geared to sc. shafts driving 2 Directional propellers Total Power: 2,648kW (3,600hp) 12.0kn Daihatsu 6DSM-28 2 x 4 Stroke 6 Cy. 280 x 340 each-1324kW (1800bhp) Daihatsu Diesel Manufacturing Co Lt-Japan AuxGen: 2 x 125kW
9125774 *YDA6413* -	**TOM YAM** *ex Han Yum No. 50 -2002* **PT Maritim Barito Perkasa** - *Banjarmasin* *Indonesia* MMSI: 525002019	**203** 60 67	Class: LR (KR) **100A1** SS 12/2009 tug coastal service **LMC**	**1995-04 Seohae Shipbuilding & Engineering Co Ltd — Incheon** Yd No: 94-04 Loa 32.80 Br ex - Dght - Lbp 30.62 Br md 8.40 Dpth 3.20 Welded, 1 dk	**(B32A2ST) Tug**	**2 oil engines** with clutches & sr geared to sc. shafts driving 2 FP propellers Total Power: 2,236kW (3,040hp) 13.6kn Caterpillar 3512TA 2 x Vee 4 Stroke 12 Cy. 170 x 190 each-1118kW (1520bhp) Caterpillar Inc-USA AuxGen: 2 x 55kW 225V a.c
7733450 - -	**TOMA** *ex Amigo -2001 ex Granulit -1996* **Firm 'Neptun-1'** -	*163* 39 88	Class: (RS)	**1978 Astrakhanskaya Sudoverf im. "Kirova" — Astrakhan** Yd No: 104 Loa 34.02 Br ex 7.12 Dght 2.899 Lbp 29.98 Br md - Dpth 3.66 Welded, 1 dk	**(B11B2FV) Fishing Vessel** Bale: 78 Compartments: 1 Ho, ER 1 Ha: (1.6 x 1.3) Derricks: 2x2t; Winches: 2 Ice Capable	**1 oil engine** driving 1 FP propeller Total Power: 224kW (305hp) 9.0kn S.K.L. 8NVD36-1U 1 x 4 Stroke 8 Cy. 240 x 360 224kW (305bhp) VEB Schwermaschinenbau "KarlLiebknecht" (SKL)-Magdeburg
9552238 *YDA4460* -	**TOMA 01** - **PT Arumbae Maritime Services** - *Tanjung Priok* *Indonesia*	**251** 76 -	Class: KI	**2009-02 PT Karya Teknik Utama — Batam** Yd No: 238 Loa 28.05 Br ex - Dght 3.290 Lbp 25.92 Br md 8.60 Dpth 4.30 Welded, 1 dk	**(B32A2ST) Tug**	**2 oil engines** reduction geared to sc. shafts driving 2 Propellers Total Power: 1,618kW (2,200hp) Yanmar 12LAK (M)-STE2 2 x Vee 4 Stroke 12 Cy. 150 x 165 each-809kW (1100bhp) Yanmar Diesel Engine Co Ltd-Japan AuxGen: 2 x 56kW 380V a.c
8936322 *JD2738* -	**TOMAKOMAI MARU** - **Tomako Service KK** - *Tomakomai, Hokkaido* *Japan* MMSI: 431800186 Official number: 128519	*199* - -		**1997-11 Kanto Kogyo K.K. — Hakodate** Yd No: 165 Loa 36.12 Br ex - Dght - Lbp 30.00 Br md 9.20 Dpth 3.83 Welded, 1 dk	**(B32A2ST) Tug**	**2 oil engines** geared integral to driving 2 Z propellers Total Power: 2,648kW (3,600hp) 13.0kn Niigata 6L28HX 2 x 4 Stroke 6 Cy. 280 x 370 each-1324kW (1800bhp) Niigata Engineering Co Ltd-Japan
9458731 - -	**TOMALAH** - **Sea Ports Corp** - *Port Sudan* *Sudan*	**269** 80 202	Class: (LR) Eq.Ltr: F; ✠ Classed LR until 17/2/10	**2008-11 Santierul Naval Damen Galati S.A. — Galati** (Hull) Yd No: 1142 **2008-11 B.V. Scheepswerf Damen — Gorinchem** Yd No: 511618 Loa 29.24 Br ex 8.85 Dght 3.630 Lbp 26.63 Br md 8.80 Dpth 4.60 Welded, 1 dk	**(B32A2ST) Tug**	**2 oil engines** with flexible couplings & reduction geared to sc. shafts driving 2 FP propellers Total Power: 1,920kW (2,610hp) MAN-B&W 6L23/30A 2 x 4 Stroke 6 Cy. 225 x 300 each-960kW (1305bhp) MAN Diesel A/S-Denmark AuxGen: 2 x 80kW 400V 50Hz a.c Thrusters: 1 Thwart. FP thruster (f)

IMO / Call sign	Name / Owner / Port	Tonnage	Class	Builder / Dimensions	Type	Machinery
6416392 *9GUE* -	**TOMAN No. 2** *ex* Asubone *-1985* **Obuorwe & Co Ltd** Spaghan Fishing Co Ltd *Takoradi* *Ghana* Official number: 316525	*1,513* 670 -	Class: (LR) ✠ Classed LR until 20/2/85	**1965**-06 **Tangen Verft AS — Kragero** (Hull) Yd No: 21 **1965**-06 **AS Stord Verft — Stord** (Hull completed by) **1965**-06 **AS Akers Mekaniske Verksted — Oslo** Yd No: 569 Loa 70.59 Br ex 11.43 Dght 4.801 Lbp 61.30 Br md 11.41 Dpth 7.80 Welded, 2 dks	**(B11A2FS) Stern Trawler** Ins: 976	**1 oil engine** driving 1 CP propeller Total Power: 1,728kW (2,349hp) B&W 7-35VBF-62 1 x 2 Stroke 7 Cy. 350 x 620 1728kW (2349bhp) A/S Burmeister & Wain's Maskin ogSkibsbyggeri-Denmark
6417889 *9GUD* -	**TOMAN No. 3** *ex* Shama *-1985* **Spaghan Fishing Co Ltd** - *Takoradi* *Ghana* Official number: 316524	*1,513* 670 -	Class: (LR) ✠ Classed LR until 16/5/84	**1964**-11 **Tangen Verft AS — Kragero** (Hull) Yd No: 19 **1964**-12 **AS Stord Verft — Stord** (Hull completed by) **1964**-12 **AS Akers Mekaniske Verksted — Oslo** Yd No: 568 Loa 70.59 Br ex 11.49 Dght 4.801 Lbp 61.30 Br md 11.43 Dpth 5.49 Welded, 2 dks	**(B11A2FS) Stern Trawler** Ins: 976	**1 oil engine** driving 1 CP propeller Total Power: 1,728kW (2,349hp) B&W 7-35VBF-62 1 x 2 Stroke 7 Cy. 350 x 620 1728kW (2349bhp) A/S Burmeister & Wain's Maskin ogSkibsbyggeri-Denmark
9137301 *V2GF6* -	**TOMAR** *ex* Antares *-2005* *ex* RMS Antares *-1999* *ex* Antares *-1995* **Naveiro Transportes Maritimos (Madeira) Lda** NAVEIRO-Transportes Maritimos SA *Saint John's* *Antigua & Barbuda* MMSI: 305922000	**1,864** 938 2,499	Class: GL (LR) Classed LR until 28/5/12	**1996**-02 **Slovenske Lodenice a.s. — Komarno** Yd No: 1503 Loa 82.38 (BB) Br ex 11.46 Dght 4.798 Lbp 79.20 Br md 11.35 Dpth 6.10 Welded, 1 dk	**(A31A2GX) General Cargo Ship** Double Hull Grain: 3,485 TEU 82 C.Ho 46/20' (40') C.Dk 36/20' (40') incl. 10 ref C. Compartments: 1 Ho, ER 1 Ha: (53.5 x 9.0)ER Ice Capable	**1 oil engine** with clutches & sr reverse geared to sc. shaft driving 1 FP propeller Total Power: 1,350kW (1,835hp) 12.0kn Deutz SBV8M628 1 x 4 Stroke 8 Cy. 240 x 280 1350kW (1835bhp) Motoren Werke Mannheim AG (MWM)-Mannheim AuxGen: 3 x 75kW 220/380V 50Hz a.c Boilers: db (o.f.) Thrusters: 1 Water jet (f) Fuel: 120.0 (d.f.)
9375264 *2BPB3* -	**TOMAR** - **Wilhelmsen Lines Car Carrier Ltd** - SatCom: Inmarsat C 423591287 *Southampton* *United Kingdom* MMSI: 235068085 Official number: 915316	**61,328** 23,559 22,144 T/cm 52.5	Class: NV	**2008**-10 **Mitsubishi Heavy Industries Ltd. — Nagasaki** Yd No: 2237 Loa 199.99 (BB) Br ex - Dght 11.000 Lbp 192.00 Br md 32.26 Dpth 36.02 Welded, 12 dks including 4 liftable dks	**(A35B2RV) Vehicles Carrier** Side door/ramp (s) Len: 25.00 Wid: 6.50 Swl: 35 Quarter stern door/ramp (s. a.) Len: 38.00 Wid: 7.00 Swl: 237 Cars: 6,550	**1 oil engine** driving 1 gen. 2 gen. driving 1 FP propeller Total Power: 12,390kW (16,845hp) 19.5kn Mitsubishi 7UEC60LS 1 x 2 Stroke 7 Cy. 600 x 2200 12390kW (16845bhp) Mitsubishi Heavy Industries Ltd-Japan AuxGen: 3 x 1250kW a.c Thrusters: 1 Tunnel thruster (f)
8000680 - -	**TOMAS I** *ex* Nurymar 1 *-2010* **Fishing World SA** - *Argentina* Official number: 02279	*198* 97 300	Class: (LR) (NV) Classed LR until 11/11/92	**1981**-01 **B&W Skibsvaerft A/S — Copenhagen** Yd No: 903 Loa 31.65 (BB) Br ex 8.13 Dght 3.868 Lbp 27.21 Br md 7.90 Dpth 4.12 Welded, 1 dk	**(B11A2FS) Stern Trawler** Ins: 270; Liq: 55	**1 oil engine** driving 1 CP propeller Total Power: 566kW (770hp) 10.5kn Alpha 407-26VO 1 x 2 Stroke 7 Cy. 260 x 400 566kW (770bhp) B&W Alpha Diesel A/S-Denmark AuxGen: 2 x 50kW 220V 50Hz a.c
6611631 *TFSP* GK 010	**TOMAS THORVALDSSON** *ex* Thorbjorn *-2008* *ex* Haberg *-2008* *ex* Hrafn *-1988* *ex* Hedinn *-1975* **Thorbjorn Fiskanes hf** - *Grindavik* *Iceland* MMSI: 251136110 Official number: 1006	**504** 150 -	Class: (BV) (NV)	**1966**-05 **Ulstein Mek. Verksted AS — Ulsteinvik** Yd No: 40 Lengthened-1971 Loa 46.18 Br ex 8.23 Dght 3.709 Lbp 34.65 Br md 8.20 Dpth 5.67 Welded, 2 dks	**(B11B2FV) Fishing Vessel** Compartments: 6 Ho, ER 5 Ha: 3 (1.9 x 1.5) (2.2 x 1.9) (1.5 x 2.9)ER Derricks: 1x4t; Winches: 1 Ice Capable	**1 oil engine** geared to sc. shaft driving 1 CP propeller Total Power: 827kW (1,124hp) Caterpillar D399SCAC 1 x Vee 4 Stroke 16 Cy. 159 x 203 827kW (1124bhp) (new engine 1980) Caterpillar Tractor Co-USA AuxGen: 2 x 42kW 220V 50Hz a.c Thrusters: 1 Thwart. FP thruster (f); 1 Tunnel thruster (a)
9319753 *MPRD6* -	**TOMBARRA** - **Wilhelmsen Lines Car Carrier Ltd** - SatCom: Inmarsat C 423297113 *Southampton* *United Kingdom* MMSI: 232971000 Official number: 912354	**61,321** 22,650 19,628 T/cm 52.5	Class: NV	**2006**-09 **Mitsubishi Heavy Industries Ltd. — Nagasaki** Yd No: 2217 Loa 199.90 (BB) Br ex - Dght 10.700 Lbp 192.00 Br md 32.26 Dpth 36.02 Welded, 12 dks including 4 liftable dks	**(A35B2RV) Vehicles Carrier** Side door/ramp (s) Len: 25.00 Wid: 6.50 Swl: 35 Quarter stern door/ramp (s. a.) Len: 38.00 Wid: 7.00 Swl: 237 Cars: 6,400	**1 oil engine** driving 1 FP propeller Total Power: 12,390kW (16,845hp) 19.5kn Mitsubishi 7UEC60LS 1 x 2 Stroke 7 Cy. 600 x 2200 12390kW (16845bhp) Mitsubishi Heavy Industries Ltd-Japan AuxGen: 3 x a.c Thrusters: 1 Tunnel thruster (f)
7946485 *TC4799* -	**TOMBIK KAPTAN** *ex* Isik-I *-1999* *ex* N. Sukru Deniz IV *-1995* *ex* Akcakil *-1984* *ex* Baba Kaptan *-1984* - - *Istanbul* *Turkey* Official number: 3531	*298* 194 540		**1910 Deniz Insaat Kizaklari — Fener** Loa 43.21 Br ex - Dght 2.301 Lbp 38.66 Br md 7.05 Dpth 2.75 Welded, 1 dk	**(A31A2GX) General Cargo Ship**	**1 oil engine** driving 1 FP propeller Total Power: 147kW (200hp) S.K.L. 6NVD36 1 x 4 Stroke 6 Cy. 240 x 360 147kW (200bhp) (new engine 1970) VEB Schwermaschinenbau "KarlLiebknecht" (SKL)-Magdeburg
9290036 *D2U52* -	**TOMBWA** - **Government of The People's Republic of Angola (Missao de Estudos Bioceanologicos e de Pesca de Angola)** - *Luanda* *Angola* Official number: 01068	**321** 96 -	Class: (KR)	**2003**-04 **Yongsung Shipbuilding Co Ltd — Geoje** Yd No: 174 Loa 45.50 Br ex - Dght - Lbp - Br md 7.50 Dpth 3.60 Welded, 1 dk	**(B12D2FR) Fishery Research Vessel**	**1 oil engine** geared to sc. shaft driving 1 CP propeller Total Power: 883kW (1,201hp) 12.0kn Yanmar M220-EN 1 x 4 Stroke 6 Cy. 220 x 300 883kW (1201bhp) Yanmar Diesel Engine Co Ltd-Japan
7522291 *HC5183* -	**TOMEBAMBA** *ex* Aguila II *-2002* *ex* Dutch Pearl *-1980* **Ecuaestibas SA** - *Guayaquil* *Ecuador* MMSI: 735058845 Official number: R-00-00515	**159** 91	Class: (LR) ✠ Classed LR until 10/89	**1977**-03 **Scheepsbouwwerf en Machinefabriek H de Haas BV — Maassluis** Yd No: 168 Loa 24.01 Br ex 6.66 Dght 2.229 Lbp 23.75 Br md 6.25 Dpth 3.00 Welded, 1 dk	**(B32A2ST) Tug**	**2 oil engines** reverse reduction geared to sc. shafts driving 2 FP propellers Total Power: 514kW (698hp) 10.0kn G.M. (Detroit Diesel) 16V-71-N 2 x Vee 2 Stroke 16 Cy. 108 x 127 each-257kW (349bhp) (new engine 1980) General Motors Detroit DieselAllison Divn-USA AuxGen: 2 x 32kW 380V 50Hz a.c Fuel: 42.5 (d.f.)
7238864 - -	**TOMEI MARU** *ex* Iwate Maru *-1979* **Eguchi Reito Kanzume KK**	*242* 77 -		**1972 Yamanishi Shipbuilding Co Ltd — Ishinomaki MG** Yd No: 717 Loa - Br ex 7.35 Dght - Lbp 35.56 Br md 7.32 Dpth 3.31 Welded, 1 dk	**(B11B2FV) Fishing Vessel**	**1 oil engine** driving 1 FP propeller Total Power: 736kW (1,001hp) Niigata 6L25BX 1 x 4 Stroke 6 Cy. 250 x 320 736kW (1001bhp) Niigata Engineering Co Ltd-Japan
8419441 - -	**TOMEI MARU** - - -	*499* - 742	Class: (NK)	**1984**-12 **Kishigami Zosen K.K. — Akitsu** Yd No: 1756 Loa 58.51 (BB) Br ex - Dght 3.611 Lbp 54.01 Br md 9.91 Dpth 4.63 Welded, 1 dk	**(A11B2TG) LPG Tanker** Liq (Gas): 654 2 x Gas Tank (s);	**1 oil engine** driving 1 FP propeller Total Power: 1,030kW (1,400hp) 11.5kn Niigata 6M28AGTE 1 x 4 Stroke 6 Cy. 280 x 480 1030kW (1400bhp) Niigata Engineering Co Ltd-Japan AuxGen: 2 x 144kW a.c Fuel: 90.0 (d.f.)
9392597 *JD2403* -	**TOMEI MARU NO. 3** - **Tomei Kisen YK** - *Bizen, Okayama* *Japan* Official number: 140526	*498* - 1,278		**2007**-04 **KK Ura Kyodo Zosensho — Awaji HG** Yd No: 328 Loa 64.46 Br ex - Dght 4.210 Lbp 60.00 Br md 10.00 Dpth 4.50 Welded, 1 dk	**(A12A2TC) Chemical Tanker** Double Hull (13F) Liq: 1,230 Compartments: 8 Wing Ta, ER 2 Cargo Pump (s): 2x300m³/hr	**1 oil engine** reduction geared to sc. shaft driving 1 FP propeller Total Power: 736kW (1,001hp) 11.0kn Niigata 6M28BGT 1 x 4 Stroke 6 Cy. 280 x 480 736kW (1001bhp) Niigata Engineering Co Ltd-Japan
7856733 - -	**TOMI** - **Jeffrey Rogers (S) Pte Ltd**	*125* - -		**1968 Usuki Iron Works Co Ltd — Usuki OT** Loa 33.80 Br ex 6.22 Dght 1.800 Lbp 30.50 Br md 6.20 Dpth 2.29 Welded, 1 dk	**(B34H2SQ) Patrol Vessel**	**1 oil engine** driving 1 FP propeller Total Power: 662kW (900hp) 13.0kn Fuji 6MSB31HS 1 x 4 Stroke 6 Cy. 310 x 360 662kW (900bhp) Fuji Diesel Co Ltd-Japan
9128647 *JM6394* -	**TOMI MARU** - **JPEC Co Ltd** - *Saikai, Nagasaki* *Japan* Official number: 134493	*196* - -		**1995**-09 **Kanagawa Zosen — Kobe** Yd No: 425 Loa 32.30 Br ex - Dght 3.100 Lbp 28.00 Br md 9.20 Dpth 4.20 Welded, 1 dk	**(B32A2ST) Tug**	**2 oil engines** driving 2 FP propellers Total Power: 2,648kW (3,600hp) 14.0kn Niigata 6L28HX 2 x 4 Stroke 6 Cy. 280 x 370 each-1324kW (1800bhp) Niigata Engineering Co Ltd-Japan

IMO / Call sign / Reg.	Name / Owner / Port / Flag	GT / NT / DWT	Built / Dimensions	Type	Machinery
9104380 *JRFZ* HK1-128	**TOMI MARU NO. 5** *ex* Kaiun Maru No. 78 *-2012* *ex* Hokko Maru No. 87 *-1996* **Otaru Kisen Gyogyo GK** *Kushiro, Hokkaido* *Japan* Official number: 132868	*160* - -	**1994-04 Narasaki Zosen KK — Muroran HK** Yd No: 1145 Loa 38.00 (BB) Br ex - Dght 3.336 Lbp 31.50 Br md 7.60 Dpth 4.63 Welded, 2 dks	**(B11B2FV) Fishing Vessel** Ins: 114	**1 oil engine** with clutches, flexible couplings & sr geared to sc. shaft driving 1 CP propeller Total Power: 956kW (1,300hp) 13.3kn Hanshin 6MUH28A 1 x 4 Stroke 6 Cy. 280 x 340 956kW (1300bhp) The Hanshin Diesel Works Ltd-Japan AuxGen: 2 x 128kW 225V 60Hz a.c Fuel: 82.9 (d.f.)
8021476 *JD2512* HK1-771	**TOMI MARU No. 5** - - *Nemuro, Hokkaido* *Japan* MMSI: 432238000 Official number: 124457	*166* - -	**1980-12 Niigata Engineering Co Ltd — Niigata NI** Yd No: 1710 Loa 36.35 (BB) Br ex - Dght 2.452 Lbp 30.82 Br md 7.41 Dpth 4.68 Welded, 2 dks	**(B11A2FT) Trawler**	**1 oil engine** reduction geared to sc. shaft driving 1 FP propeller Total Power: 625kW (850hp) Niigata 6MG28BX 1 x 4 Stroke 6 Cy. 280 x 320 625kW (850bhp) Niigata Engineering Co Ltd-Japan
9067037 *JE3088* AM1-670	**TOMI MARU No. 8** **Akira Akiyama** *Hachinohe, Aomori* *Japan* Official number: 132236	*138* - -	**1993-07 Narasaki Zosen KK — Muroran HK** Yd No: 1136 Loa 35.00 (BB) Br ex - Dght 2.520 Lbp 28.00 Br md 7.20 Dpth 4.62 Welded, 1 dk	**(B11A2FS) Stern Trawler** Ins: 102	**1 oil engine** with clutches, flexible couplings & sr geared to sc. shaft driving 1 CP propeller Total Power: 736kW (1,001hp) 13.1kn Hanshin LH28L 1 x 4 Stroke 6 Cy. 280 x 530 736kW (1001bhp) The Hanshin Diesel Works Ltd-Japan AuxGen: 1 x 120kW 225V 60Hz a.c, 1 x 80kW 225V 60Hz a.c Fuel: 58.0 (d.f.)
9574872 *7JHD* -	**TOMI MARU NO. 15** **Kanai Gyogyo KK** *Kushiro, Hokkaido* *Japan* Official number: 141240	*160* - -	**2010-08 Niigata Shipbuilding & Repair Inc — Niigata NI** Yd No: 0050 Loa 38.39 Br ex - Dght 3.350 Lbp - Br md 7.80 Dpth 4.61 Welded, 1 dk	**(B11B2FV) Fishing Vessel**	**1 oil engine** reduction geared to sc. shaft driving 1 FP propeller Total Power: 1,838kW (2,499hp) Niigata 6MG28HX 1 x 4 Stroke 6 Cy. 280 x 370 1838kW (2499bhp) Niigata Engineering Co Ltd-Japan
7238395 - -	**TOMI MARU No. 17** *ex* Nisshin Maru No. 17 *-1990* *ex* Yakushi Maru No. 21 *-1987* *ex* Sumiyoshi Maru No. 8 *-1981* - -	*290* 129 -	**1972 Mie Shipyard Co. Ltd. — Yokkaichi** Yd No: 71 Loa - Br ex 7.80 Dght - Lbp 43.39 Br md 7.78 Dpth 3.64 Riveted\Welded, 1 dk	**(B11B2FV) Fishing Vessel**	**1 oil engine** driving 1 FP propeller Total Power: 993kW (1,350hp) Hanshin 6LU32 1 x 4 Stroke 6 Cy. 320 x 510 993kW (1350bhp) Hanshin Nainenki Kogyo-Japan
8005381 - -	**TOMI MARU No. 21** - -	*346* 164 438	**1980-06 Niigata Engineering Co Ltd — Niigata NI** Yd No: 1686 Loa 54.28 Br ex - Dght 3.615 Lbp 47.50 Br md 8.91 Dpth 3.76 Welded, 1 dk	**(B11B2FV) Fishing Vessel**	**1 oil engine** reduction geared to sc. shaft driving 1 FP propeller Total Power: 883kW (1,201hp) Niigata 6M31AFT 1 x 4 Stroke 6 Cy. 310 x 530 883kW (1201bhp) Niigata Engineering Co Ltd-Japan
8403820 - -	**TOMI MARU No. 33** *ex* Eisho Maru No. 31 *-1990* - - *China*	*238* - 293	**1984-06 K.K. Murakami Zosensho — Ishinomaki** Yd No: 1171 Loa 44.00 (BB) Br ex - Dght - Lbp 37.22 Br md 7.41 Dpth 3.26 Welded, 1 dk	**(B11B2FV) Fishing Vessel** Ins: 249 Compartments: 6 Ho, ER 6 Ha: ER	**1 oil engine** geared to sc. shaft driving 1 FP propeller Total Power: 1,008kW (1,370hp) Yanmar T260-ET 1 x 4 Stroke 6 Cy. 260 x 330 1008kW (1370bhp) Yanmar Diesel Engine Co Ltd-Japan
7815466 - -	**TOMI MARU No. 36** *ex* Marufuku Maru No. 51 *-1990* **GL Verunardo Marine Enterprise Inc** - *Philippines*	*124* 58 -	**1978-09 K.K. Murakami Zosensho — Ishinomaki** Yd No: 1017 Loa 31.98 (BB) Br ex - Dght - Lbp 31.02 Br md 6.46 Dpth 2.60 Welded, 1 dk	**(B11B2FV) Fishing Vessel**	**1 oil engine** driving 1 FP propeller Total Power: 515kW (700hp) Niigata 1 x 4 Stroke 6 Cy. 515kW (700bhp) Niigata Engineering Co Ltd-Japan
8614962 - -	**TOMI MARU No. 38** *ex* Eisho Maru No. 11 *-1990* **Transport Maritime ET Telesta** - *Myanmar*	*135* - 153	**1987-01 K.K. Murakami Zosensho — Ishinomaki** Yd No: 1202 Loa 43.69 (BB) Br ex - Dght 3.050 Lbp 34.98 Br md 7.60 Dpth 3.13 Welded, 1 dk	**(B11B2FV) Fishing Vessel**	**1 oil engine** with clutches, flexible couplings & sr geared to sc. shaft driving 1 FP propeller Total Power: 861kW (1,171hp) Yanmar 6Z280-ET 1 x 4 Stroke 6 Cy. 280 x 360 861kW (1171bhp) Yanmar Diesel Engine Co Ltd-Japan
8613621 *7LGH* -	**TOMI MARU No. 58** **Kanai Gyogyo KK** - SatCom: Inmarsat A 1200376 *Kushiro, Hokkaido* *Japan* MMSI: 432300000 Official number: 127153	*401* - 689	**1986-11 Niigata Engineering Co Ltd — Niigata NI** Yd No: 2025 Loa 67.95 (BB) Br ex - Dght 4.060 Lbp 58.60 Br md 11.02 Dpth 6.66 Welded, 1 dk	**(B11A2FG) Factory Stern Trawler** Ins: 727	**1 oil engine** with clutches, flexible couplings & sr geared to sc. shaft driving 1 CP propeller Total Power: 2,133kW (2,900hp) Niigata 8M40CFX 1 x 4 Stroke 8 Cy. 400 x 600 2133kW (2900bhp) Niigata Engineering Co Ltd-Japan
8921406 *JRXI* HK1-1175	**TOMI MARU No. 63** **Kanai Gyogyo KK** - SatCom: Inmarsat B 343150310 *Kushiro, Hokkaido* *Japan* MMSI: 431503000 Official number: 128542	*349* - -	**1990-05 Niigata Engineering Co Ltd — Niigata NI** Yd No: 2171 Loa 63.24 (BB) Br ex - Dght 4.460 Lbp 50.00 Br md 12.00 Dpth 7.27 Welded	**(B11B2FV) Fishing Vessel** Ins: 1,132	**1 oil engine** with clutches, flexible couplings & sr reverse geared to sc. shaft driving 1 FP propeller Total Power: 1,986kW (2,700hp) Niigata 6M40CFX 1 x 4 Stroke 6 Cy. 400 x 600 1986kW (2700bhp) Niigata Engineering Co Ltd-Japan Thrusters: 1 Thwart. FP thruster (f)
8324062 - -	**TOMI MARU No. 73** *ex* Eisho Maru No. 32 *-1990* - - *China*	*238* - 292	**1984-05 K.K. Murakami Zosensho — Ishinomaki** Yd No: 1155 Loa 44.00 (BB) Br ex - Dght 3.104 Lbp 37.22 Br md 7.41 Dpth 3.26 Welded, 1 dk	**(B11B2FV) Fishing Vessel** Ins: 254 Compartments: 6 Ho, ER 6 Ha: ER	**1 oil engine** geared to sc. shaft driving 1 FP propeller Total Power: 1,008kW (1,370hp) Yanmar T260-ET 1 x 4 Stroke 6 Cy. 260 x 330 1008kW (1370bhp) Yanmar Diesel Engine Co Ltd-Japan
8130370 - -	**TOMI MARU No. 77** *ex* Eisho Maru No. 35 *-1990* **Victory Venture Fishing Corp** - *Philippines*	*282* 105 299	**1982-01 K.K. Murakami Zosensho — Ishinomaki** Yd No: 1088 Loa 45.47 Br ex 7.78 Dght 2.925 Lbp 38.36 Br md 7.46 Dpth 3.08 Welded, 1 dk	**(B11B2FV) Fishing Vessel** Bale: 273	**1 oil engine** geared to sc. shaft driving 1 FP propeller Total Power: 809kW (1,100hp) Yanmar T260-ST 1 x 4 Stroke 6 Cy. 260 x 330 809kW (1100bhp) Yanmar Diesel Engine Co Ltd-Japan
8713419 *7LNQ* -	**TOMI MARU No. 87** **Kanai Gyogyo KK** - SatCom: Inmarsat A 1201503 *Kushiro, Hokkaido* *Japan* MMSI: 431800190 Official number: 127160	*411* - -	**1987-11 Niigata Engineering Co Ltd — Niigata NI** Yd No: 2058 Loa 67.98 (BB) Br ex - Dght 4.060 Lbp 58.60 Br md 11.00 Dpth 6.61 Welded, 1 dk	**(B11A2FG) Factory Stern Trawler** Ins: 639	**1 oil engine** with clutches, flexible couplings & sr geared to sc. shaft driving 1 CP propeller Total Power: 2,133kW (2,900hp) Niigata 8M40CFX 1 x 4 Stroke 8 Cy. 400 x 600 2133kW (2900bhp) Niigata Engineering Co Ltd-Japan
8864165 - -	**TOMIEI MARU** **PT Armada Contener Nusantara**	*331* - 999	**1992-01 K.K. Kamishima Zosensho — Osakikamijima** Yd No: 523 Loa 65.84 Br ex - Dght 3.750 Lbp 58.00 Br md 10.50 Dpth 6.20 Welded, 1 dk	**(A31A2GX) General Cargo Ship**	**1 oil engine** reverse geared to sc. shaft driving 1 FP propeller Total Power: 736kW (1,001hp) 10.5kn Hanshin LH28LG 1 x 4 Stroke 6 Cy. 280 x 530 736kW (1001bhp) The Hanshin Diesel Works Ltd-Japan
9180619 *JL6523* -	**TOMIEI MARU** - - *Imabari, Ehime* *Japan* Official number: 135561	*196* - -	**1997-01 Katsuura Dockyard Co. Ltd. — Nachi-Katsuura** Yd No: 352 Loa 56.00 Br ex - Dght - Lbp 51.00 Br md 9.40 Dpth 5.50 Welded, 1 dk	**(A31A2GX) General Cargo Ship** Compartments: 1 Ho, ER 1 Ha: (28.1 x 7.2)ER	**1 oil engine** reverse geared to sc. shaft driving 1 FP propeller Total Power: 736kW (1,001hp) 11.0kn Akasaka T26SKR 1 x 4 Stroke 6 Cy. 260 x 440 736kW (1001bhp) Akasaka Tekkosho KK (Akasaka DieselLtd)-Japan
9181235 *JJ4002* -	**TOMIEI MARU** **YK Nakajima Kaiun** *Awaji, Hyogo* *Japan* MMSI: 431300582 Official number: 134264	*699* - 1,650	**1997-06 Yamanaka Zosen K.K. — Imabari** Yd No: 612 Loa 76.44 Br ex - Dght 4.220 Lbp 70.00 Br md 14.00 Dpth 7.85 Welded, 1 dk	**(A24D2BA) Aggregates Carrier**	**1 oil engine** driving 1 FP propeller Total Power: 1,471kW (2,000hp) 12.0kn Niigata 6M38GT 1 x 4 Stroke 6 Cy. 380 x 720 1471kW (2000bhp) Niigata Engineering Co Ltd-Japan

9673771 *JD3429* -	**TOMIEI MARU** - **Tomiei Kaiun YK** - *Iki, Nagasaki* *Japan* Official number: 141789	*499* - 800		**2012-11 Yano Zosen K.K. — Imabari** Yd No: 270 Loa 74.93 Br ex - Dght 4.346 Lbp - Br md 12.00 Dpth - Welded, 1 dk	**(A31A2GX) General Cargo Ship** Double Hull Grain: 2,517; Bale: 2,428	**1 oil engine** reduction geared to sc. shaft driving 1 Propeller Total Power: 1,618kW (2,200hp) Hanshin LA32G 1 x 4 Stroke 6 Cy. 320 x 680 1618kW (2200bhp) The Hanshin Diesel Works Ltd-Japan
8877655 *JK4850* -	**TOMIEI MARU No. 3** - - - *Okinoshima, Shimane* *Japan* Official number: 133673	*131* - 338		**1994-06 Hongawara Zosen K.K. — Fukuyama** Loa 43.00 Br ex - Dght 2.900 Lbp 39.00 Br md 8.60 Dpth 4.45 Welded, 1 dk	**(A31A2GX) General Cargo Ship**	**1 oil engine** driving 1 FP propeller Total Power: 736kW (1,001hp) 11.0kn Niigata 6M26AGTE 1 x 4 Stroke 6 Cy. 260 x 460 736kW (1001bhp) Niigata Engineering Co Ltd-Japan
9115119 *JH3399* ME1-900	**TOMIEI MARU No. 17** - **Tomiei Suisan KK** - *Minami-ise, Mie* *Japan* MMSI: 431200120 Official number: 134394	*323* - 556		**1995-09 Ishii Zosen K.K. — Futtsu** Yd No: 330 Loa 58.20 (BB) Br ex 8.77 Dght 3.710 Lbp 51.00 Br md 8.70 Dpth 4.20 Welded, 1 dk	**(B12B2FC) Fish Carrier**	**1 oil engine** with clutches & sr reverse geared to sc. shaft driving 1 FP propeller Total Power: 1,471kW (2,000hp) Yanmar 6N260-EN 1 x 4 Stroke 6 Cy. 260 x 360 1471kW (2000bhp) Yanmar Diesel Engine Co Ltd-Japan Thrusters: 1 Thwart. FP thruster (f)
7209057 - -	**TOMIEI MARU No. 37** *ex* Kannon Maru No. 8 *-1980* *ex* Seisho Maru No. 1 *-1980* - -	*300* - 339		**1971 Miho Zosensho K.K. — Shimizu** Yd No: 793 Loa 50.07 Br ex 7.83 Dght 3.277 Lbp 42.02 Br md 7.80 Dpth 3.66 Welded, 1 dk	**(B11B2FV) Fishing Vessel**	**1 oil engine** driving 1 FP propeller Total Power: 1,103kW (1,500hp) Niigata 6M31X 1 x 4 Stroke 6 Cy. 310 x 460 1103kW (1500bhp) Niigata Engineering Co Ltd-Japan
7313975 - -	**TOMIEI MARU No. 76** *ex* Seiyu Maru No. 2 *-1986* - -	*482* 249 552		**1973 Mie Shipyard Co. Ltd. — Yokkaichi** Yd No: 85 Loa 59.52 Br ex 9.86 Dght 3.633 Lbp 50.60 Br md 8.62 Dpth 3.89 Riveted\Welded, 1 dk	**(B11B2FV) Fishing Vessel**	**1 oil engine** driving 1 FP propeller Total Power: 1,545kW (2,101hp) Niigata 6L37X 1 x 4 Stroke 6 Cy. 370 x 540 1545kW (2101bhp) Niigata Engineering Co Ltd-Japan
7727578 - -	**TOMIEI MARU No. 81** *ex* Chofuku Maru No. 1 *-1992* - -	*464* - -		**1978-02 K.K. Ichikawa Zosensho — Ise** Yd No: 1343 Loa - Br ex - Dght - Lbp 53.01 Br md 9.11 Dpth 4.20 Riveted\Welded, 1 dk	**(B11B2FV) Fishing Vessel**	**1 oil engine** driving 1 FP propeller Total Power: 1,471kW (2,000hp) Hanshin 6LU38G 1 x 4 Stroke 6 Cy. 380 x 580 1471kW (2000bhp) Hanshin Nainenki Kogyo-Japan
9057824 - -	**TOMIFUKU MARU** *ex* Fukutomi Maru *-1998* **Dong Chon Co Ltd** - *South Korea*	*199* - 550		**1994-01 Imura Zosen K.K. — Komatsushima** Yd No: 267 Loa 48.40 (BB) Br ex - Dght 3.210 Lbp 44.00 Br md 8.00 Dpth 3.45 Welded, 1 dk	**(A12A2TC) Chemical Tanker** Liq: 600 Compartments: 6 Ta, ER	**1 oil engine** driving 1 FP propeller Total Power: 625kW (850hp) Niigata 6M26BGT 1 x 4 Stroke 6 Cy. 260 x 460 625kW (850bhp) Niigata Engineering Co Ltd-Japan
8704341 *DSNN7* -	**TOMIKA** *ex* S. S. 2 *-2000* *ex* Shoei Maru No. 52 *-2000* **Yu Jin Shipping Co Ltd** - *Jeju* *South Korea* MMSI: 441407000 Official number: JJR-049324	**1,945** 1,116 3,313	Class: KR	**1987-06 Kasado Dockyard Co Ltd — Kudamatsu YC** Yd No: 368 Loa 73.80 (BB) Br ex 14.64 Dght 5.466 Lbp 69.00 Br md 14.61 Dpth 7.40 Welded, 2 dks	**(B33A2DG) Grab Dredger** Grain: 1,545 Compartments: 1 Ho, ER 1 Ha: (37.9 x 10.2)ER	**1 oil engine** with clutches, flexible couplings & sr geared to sc. shaft driving 1 CP propeller Total Power: 1,471kW (2,000hp) 12.9kn Fuji 6H32 1 x 4 Stroke 6 Cy. 320 x 470 1471kW (2000bhp) Fuji Diesel Co Ltd-Japan AuxGen: 1 x 180kW 445V a.c Thrusters: 1 Thwart. CP thruster (f)
9056442 *JL6078* -	**TOMISU** *ex* Toshin *-2010* **Morimoto Kaiun KK** - *Ozu, Ehime* *Japan* Official number: 132967	*499* - 1,600		**1992-09 K.K. Matsuura Zosensho — Osakikamijima** Yd No: 386 Loa 75.88 (BB) Br ex 12.02 Dght 4.210 Lbp 70.00 Br md 12.00 Dpth 7.20 Welded, 2 dks	**(A31A2GX) General Cargo Ship** Grain: 2,518 Compartments: 1 Ho, ER 1 Ha: ER	**1 oil engine** driving 1 FP propeller Total Power: 736kW (1,001hp) Akasaka A31 1 x 4 Stroke 6 Cy. 310 x 600 736kW (1001bhp) Akasaka Tekkosho KK (Akasaka DieselLtd)-Japan Thrusters: 1 Thwart. FP thruster (f)
7638923 - -	**TOMITAKA MARU** - **Seapower Shipping & Trading Pte Ltd** -	*565* 359 1,281		**1977-05 Higaki Zosen K.K. — Imabari** Yd No: 187 Loa - Br ex - Dght - Lbp 55.33 Br md 9.61 Dpth 4.53 Welded, 1 dk	**(A13B2TP) Products Tanker**	**1 oil engine** geared to sc. shaft driving 1 FP propeller Total Power: 1,103kW (1,500hp) Hanshin 6LU32G 1 x 4 Stroke 6 Cy. 320 x 510 1103kW (1500bhp) Hanshin Nainenki Kogyo-Japan
9197806 *ZDEC9* -	**TOMKE** - **Ventura Schiffahrts GmbH & Co KG ms 'Tomke'** Reederei Eilbrecht GmbH & Co KG SatCom: Inmarsat C 423611110 *Gibraltar* *Gibraltar (British)* MMSI: 236111000 Official number: 733607	**2,301** 1,289 3,171	Class: BV (LR) (GL) Classed LR until 25/5/13	**2000-06 Daewoo-Mangalia Heavy Industries S.A. — Mangalia** (Hull) Yd No: 1007 **2000-06 Scheepswerf Pattje B.V. — Waterhuizen** Yd No: 416 Loa 82.50 (BB) Br ex 12.60 Dght 5.300 Lbp 78.90 Br md 12.40 Dpth 6.70 Welded, 1 dk	**(A31A2GX) General Cargo Ship** Double Hull Grain: 4,782 TEU 132 C.Ho 96/20' (40') C. Dk 36/20' (40') Compartments: 1 Ho, ER 1 Ha: (56.3 x 10.2)ER	**1 oil engine** reduction geared to sc. shaft driving 1 CP propeller Total Power: 1,800kW (2,447hp) 12.0kn MaK 6M25 1 x 4 Stroke 6 Cy. 255 x 400 1800kW (2447bhp) MaK Motoren GmbH & Co. KG-Kiel AuxGen: 1 x 240kW 220/380V 50Hz a.c, 2 x 92kW 220/380V 50Hz a.c Thrusters: 1 Thwart. FP thruster (f) Fuel: 217.0 (r.f.)
9055307 *UADW* -	**TOMKOD** - **Kamchatka-Vostok Fishing Co Ltd** - SatCom: Inmarsat A 1407264 *Petropavlovsk-Kamchatskiy* *Russia* MMSI: 273843700	**1,315** 395 851	Class: RS (NV)	**1994-11 Elbewerft Boizenburg GmbH — Boizenburg** Yd No: 112 Loa 52.50 Br ex 11.59 Dght 5.426 Lbp 45.54 Br md 11.50 Dpth 8.05 Welded, 2 dks	**(B11B2FV) Fishing Vessel** Ins: 850 Ice Capable	**1 oil engine** with clutches & sr geared to sc. shaft driving 1 CP propeller Total Power: 1,060kW (1,441hp) MAN-B&W 8L23/30A 1 x 4 Stroke 8 Cy. 225 x 300 1060kW (1441bhp) MAN B&W Diesel AG-Augsburg AuxGen: 2 x 291kW a.c, 1 x 560kW a.c Thrusters: 1 Thwart. CP thruster (f)
7393638 *LNRA* -	**TOMMA** *ex* Haus *-1999* **Boreal Transport Nord AS** - *Sandnessjoen* *Norway* MMSI: 257275400	**560** 187 203	Class: (NV)	**1974-04 Loland Verft AS — Leirvik i Sogn** Yd No: 36 Loa 48.98 Br ex 11.28 Dght 2.998 Lbp 45.29 Br md 11.26 Dpth 4.22 Welded, 1 dk	**(A36A2PR) Passenger/Ro-Ro Ship (Vehicles)** Passengers: unberthed: 360 Lane-Len: 47 Lane-Wid: 5.35	**1 oil engine** driving 2 Propellers aft, 1 fwd Total Power: 607kW (825hp) Wichmann 5ACA 1 x 2 Stroke 5 Cy. 280 x 420 607kW (825bhp) Wichmann Motorfabrikk AS-Norway
9402172 *IIXX2* -	**TOMMASO ONORATO** *ex* Ilan Uno *-2010* *completed as* Ilan *-2009* **Moby SpA** - *Cagliari* *Italy* MMSI: 247288600	**395** 119 228	Class: RI (AB)	**2009-03 Union Naval Valencia SA (UNV) — Valencia** Yd No: 376 Loa 29.50 Br ex - Dght 3.500 Lbp 28.00 Br md 11.00 Dpth 4.00 Welded, 1 dk	**(B32A2ST) Tug**	**2 oil engines** reduction geared to sc. shafts driving 2 Voith-Schneider propellers Total Power: 3,996kW (5,432hp) Caterpillar 3516B-HD 2 x Vee 4 Stroke 16 Cy. 170 x 215 each-1998kW (2716bhp) Caterpillar Inc-USA AuxGen: 2 x 160kW 400V 50Hz a.c
6720913 - -	**TOMMERVIKODDEN** *ex* Willassen Senior *-2000* *ex* Alftafell *-1977* *ex* Gideon *-1970* - -	**303** 90 224	Class: (NV)	**1967 VEB Elbewerft — Boizenburg** Yd No: 444 Loa 33.79 Br ex 7.22 Dght 2.699 Lbp 29.60 Br md 7.19 Dpth 3.81 Welded, 1 dk	**(B11B2FV) Fishing Vessel**	**1 oil engine** geared to sc. shaft driving 1 FP propeller Total Power: 485kW (659hp) Blackstone ERS8M 1 x 4 Stroke 8 Cy. 222 x 292 485kW (659bhp) Lister Blackstone Marine Ltd.-Dursley AuxGen: 1 x 40kW 220V d.c, 1 x 33kW 220V d.c, 1 x 30kW 220V d.c Thrusters: 1 Thwart. FP thruster (f)
8734449 *CRXW7* -	**TOMMY** - **North Latitude Cruises SA** Sea Metria Srl *Madeira* *Portugal (MAR)* MMSI: 255909750 Official number: IC-024	**474** 142 -	Class: AB	**1995-07 Azimut SpA, Divisione Produttiva Fratelli Benetti — Viareggio** Yd No: FB216 Loa 52.00 Br ex - Dght 3.000 Lbp 42.41 Br md 8.90 Dpth 4.40 Welded, 1 dk	**(X11A2YP) Yacht**	**2 oil engines** reduction geared to sc. shafts driving 2 Propellers Total Power: 3,580kW (4,868hp) MWM TBD604BV16 2 x Vee 4 Stroke 16 Cy. 170 x 195 each-1790kW (2434bhp) Kloeckner Humboldt Deutz AG-Germany
5144899 - -	**TOMMY DEV** *ex* Shaula *-1994* *ex* Mister Cornishman *-1990* *ex* Hazelgarth *-1989* - -	*230* - 406	Class: (LR) ✠ Classed LR until 27/9/95	**1959-05 P K Harris & Sons Ltd — Bideford** Yd No: 111 Loa 32.01 Br ex 8.67 Dght 4.268 Lbp 29.57 Br md 8.23 Dpth 4.27 Welded, 1 dk	**(B32A2ST) Tug**	**2 oil engines** with fluid couplings & sr reverse geared to sc. shaft driving 1 FP propeller Total Power: 1,236kW (1,680hp) Ruston 7VGBXM 2 x 4 Stroke 7 Cy. 318 x 381 each-618kW (840bhp) Ruston & Hornsby Ltd.-Lincoln Fuel: 40.5

IMO / Call sign	Name / Owner	Tonnage	Class	Build	Type	Machinery
8941078 *WDF6487* -	**TOMMY GUN** *ex* Kevin Rico II *-2010* *ex* Black Sheep *-2001* **Tommy Gun LLC** - *Port Arthur, TX* *United States of America* MMSI: 366902820 Official number: 1055544	**147** 44 -		**1997 La Force Shipyard Inc — Coden AL** Yd No: 82 L reg 24.90 Br ex - Dght - Lbp - Br md 7.32 Dpth 3.75 Welded, 1 dk	**(B11B2FV) Fishing Vessel**	**1 oil engine** driving 1 FP propeller
8201088 *WDE4584* -	**TOMMY MUNRO** - **Gulf Coast Research Laboratory** - *Biloxi, MS* *United States of America* MMSI: 366940670 Official number: 634430	*158* 108 -		**1981 Bender Shipbuilding & Repair Co Inc — Mobile AL** Yd No: 1085 Loa 29.72 Br ex - Dght 2.539 Lbp 25.61 Br md 7.62 Dpth 3.66 Welded, 1 dk	**(B12D2FR) Fishery Research Vessel**	**1 oil engine** driving 1 FP propeller
9439668 *YJVU5* -	**TOMMY SHERIDAN TIDE** - **Silver Fleet Ltd** Sonatide Marine Services Ltd SatCom: Inmarsat C 457622310 *Port Vila* *Vanuatu* MMSI: 576223000 Official number: 1855	**2,301** 690 1,965	Class: AB	**2009-06 Stocznia Polnocna SA (Northern Shipyard) — Gdansk** (Hull) Yd No: B844/12 **2009-06 Gdanska Stocznia 'Remontowa' SA — Gdansk** Yd No: 1674/12 Loa 70.00 Br ex - Dght 5.290 Lbp 63.60 Br md 15.50 Dpth 6.60 Welded, 1 dk	**(B21B20A) Anchor Handling Tug Supply** Passengers: cabins: 13	**2 oil engines** reduction geared to sc. shafts driving 2 CP propellers Total Power: 10,120kW (13,760hp) 14.0kn Caterpillar C280-16 2 x Vee 4 Stroke 16 Cy. 280 x 300 each-5060kW (6880bhp) Caterpillar Inc-USA AuxGen: 2 x 1724kW a.c, 1 x 250kW a.c Thrusters: 2 Thwart. FP thruster (f); 1 Thwart. FP thruster (a) Fuel: 810.0
8323408 - -	**TOMO MARU No. 8** *ex* Miyaura Maru No. 28 *-1992* **Lubmain Shipping Services Sdn Bhd** -	*191* - -		**1983-12 Katsuura Dockyard Co. Ltd. — Nachi-Katsuura** Yd No: 275 Loa - Br ex - Dght 2.571 Lbp 32.01 Br md 6.91 Dpth 2.87 Welded, 1 dk	**(B11B2FV) Fishing Vessel** Ins: 164 Compartments: 4 Ho, ER 4 Ha: ER	**1 oil engine** driving 1 FP propeller Total Power: 493kW (670hp) Akasaka A24R 1 x 4 Stroke 6 Cy. 240 x 450 493kW (670bhp) Akasaka Tekkosho KK (Akasaka DieselLtd)-Japan
8910586 - -	**TOMO MARU No. 38** *ex* Ryuho Maru No. 78 *-1999* **Fresca Atun SA De CV** - *Mexico*	*241* - -		**1989-07 KK Kanasashi Zosen — Shizuoka SZ** Yd No: 3198 Loa 45.52 (BB) Br ex 7.52 Dght 2.890 Lbp 39.30 Br md 7.50 Dpth 3.15 Welded	**(B11B2FV) Fishing Vessel** Ins: 336	**1 oil engine** with clutches, flexible couplings & sr reverse geared to sc. shaft driving 1 FP propeller Total Power: 662kW (900hp) Akasaka K26SFD 1 x 4 Stroke 6 Cy. 260 x 480 662kW (900bhp) Akasaka Tekkosho KK (Akasaka DieselLtd)-Japan
8934049 *JD2752* -	**TOMOE** - **Hakodate Port Service KK** - *Hakodate, Hokkaido* *Japan* Official number: 132894	*166* - -		**1997-09 Kanto Kogyo K.K. — Hakodate** Yd No: 162 Loa 31.30 Br ex - Dght - Lbp 27.00 Br md 9.00 Dpth 3.63 Welded, 1 dk	**(B32A2ST) Tug**	**2 oil engines** geared integral to driving 2 Z propellers Total Power: 2,354kW (3,200hp) 12.5kn Niigata 6L25HX 2 x 4 Stroke 6 Cy. 250 x 350 each-1177kW (1600bhp) Niigata Engineering Co Ltd-Japan
9526863 *JD2926* -	**TOMOE MARU** - **YK Sewaki Kaiun** - *Kamiamakusa, Kumamoto* *Japan* MMSI: 431000951 Official number: 141036	*398* - 817		**2009-05 Taiyo Shipbuilding Co Ltd — Sanyoonoda YC** Yd No: 320 Loa 59.30 Br ex - Dght 3.610 Lbp 54.00 Br md 9.20 Dpth 4.20 Welded, 1 dk	**(A12A2TC) Chemical Tanker** Double Hull (13F) Liq: 501 1 Cargo Pump (s): 1x250m³/hr	**1 oil engine** driving 1 FP propeller Total Power: 736kW (1,001hp) Niigata 6M26AGT 1 x 4 Stroke 6 Cy. 260 x 460 736kW (1001bhp) Niigata Engineering Co Ltd-Japan
8804050 - -	**TOMOE MARU No. 3** *ex* Fuki Maru No. 3 *-2001* -	*198* - 520		**1988-10 Koa Sangyo KK — Takamatsu KG** Yd No: 535 Loa 49.59 Br ex - Dght 3.201 Lbp 45.00 Br md 7.80 Dpth 3.30 Welded, 1 dk	**(A12A2TC) Chemical Tanker** Liq: 393 Compartments: 6 Ta, ER	**1 oil engine** driving 1 FP propeller Total Power: 588kW (799hp) Yanmar MF26-HT 1 x 4 Stroke 6 Cy. 260 x 500 588kW (799bhp) Yanmar Diesel Engine Co Ltd-Japan
7805708 - -	**TOMOE MARU No. 8** *ex* Kyotoku Maru No. 18 *-1990* **Bashi Marine S de RL** - *San Lorenzo* *Honduras* Official number: L-0324155	*124* 50 220		**1978-05 Tokushima Zosen K.K. — Fukuoka** Yd No: 1302 Loa 36.76 (BB) Br ex 6.53 Dght 2.601 Lbp 30.82 Br md 6.51 Dpth 2.90 Welded, 1 dk	**(B12B2FC) Fish Carrier**	**1 oil engine** reduction geared to sc. shaft driving 1 FP propeller Total Power: 662kW (900hp) 11.5kn Niigata 6L25BX 1 x 4 Stroke 6 Cy. 250 x 320 662kW (900bhp) Niigata Engineering Co Ltd-Japan
5364138 - -	**TOMOE MARU No. 8** *ex* Tomakomai Maru *-1990* - -	*115* - -		**1963 Osaka Shipbuilding Co Ltd — Osaka OS** Yd No: 208 Loa 25.70 Br ex 7.02 Dght 2.200 Lbp 24.85 Br md 7.00 Dpth 3.00 Riveted\Welded, 1 dk	**(B32A2ST) Tug**	**2 oil engines** driving 2 FP propellers Total Power: 810kW (1,102hp) Fuji 2 x 4 Stroke 6 Cy. 275 x 320 each-405kW (551bhp) Fuji Diesel Co Ltd-Japan Fuel: 15.0
9275880 *JL6701* -	**TOMOFUJI MARU** - **Tomoshio Kisen YK** - *Imabari, Ehime* *Japan* MMSI: 431501737 Official number: 137037	*3,773* - 5,583	Class: NK	**2002-09 Hakata Zosen K.K. — Imabari** Yd No: 638 Loa 103.95 Br ex - Dght 6.614 Lbp 98.00 Br md 16.00 Dpth 8.50 Welded, 1 dk	**(A13B2TP) Products Tanker** Double Hull (13F) Liq: 6,370; Liq (Oil): 6,370	**1 oil engine** driving 1 FP propeller Total Power: 2,942kW (4,000hp) 13.5kn Hanshin LH46L 1 x 4 Stroke 6 Cy. 460 x 880 2942kW (4000bhp) The Hanshin Diesel Works Ltd-Japan Fuel: 275.0
9679282 *V7BI7* -	**TOMORROW** - **Hawk Marine Corp SA** Marine Ace Co Ltd (YK Marine Ace) *Majuro* *Marshall Islands* MMSI: 538005148 Official number: 5148	**31,753** 18,647 56,025	Class: NK	**2013-07 Minaminippon Shipbuilding Co Ltd — Usuki OT** Yd No: 740 Loa 189.99 (BB) Br ex 32.29 Dght 12.715 Lbp 182.00 Br md 32.25 Dpth 18.10 Welded, 1 dk	**(A21A2BC) Bulk Carrier** Grain: 71,345; Bale: 68,733 Compartments: 5 Ho, ER 5 Ha: ER Cranes: 4x30t	**1 oil engine** driving 1 FP propeller Total Power: 9,480kW (12,889hp) 14.5kn MAN-B&W 6S50MC-C 1 x 2 Stroke 6 Cy. 500 x 2000 9480kW (12889bhp) Mitsui Engineering & Shipbuilding CLtd-Japan AuxGen: 3 x 470kW a.c Fuel: 2313.0
9606405 *JD3268* -	**TOMOZURU MARU** - **Kowa Tugboat & Floating Crane** - *Nagasaki, Nagasaki* *Japan* Official number: 141555	*224* - -		**2011-11 Kanagawa Zosen — Kobe** Yd No: 633 Loa 33.80 Br ex - Dght 3.600 Lbp 29.50 Br md 9.30 Dpth 4.18 Welded, 1 dk	**(B32A2ST) Tug**	**2 oil engines** reduction geared to sc. shafts driving 2 Propellers Total Power: 3,676kW (4,998hp) Niigata 6L28HX 2 x 4 Stroke 6 Cy. 280 x 370 each-1838kW (2499bhp) Niigata Engineering Co Ltd-Japan
9126754 *TCRB8* -	**TOMRIZ A** *ex* YM Union *-2007* *ex* Ming Union *-2004* **Limar Liman ve Gemi Isletmeleri AS (Limar Port & Ship Operators SA)** Arkas Denizcilik ve Nakliyat AS (Arkas Shipping & Transport AS) *Izmir* *Turkey* MMSI: 271001058	**15,120** 6,764 19,338 T/cm 35.9	Class: AB	**1997-03 China Shipbuilding Corp (CSBC) — Kaohsiung** Yd No: 631 Loa 168.78 (BB) Br ex 27.34 Dght 8.615 Lbp 158.00 Br md 27.30 Dpth 13.50 Welded, 1 dk	**(A33A2CC) Container Ship (Fully Cellular)** TEU 1445 C Ho 881 TEU C Dk 564 TEU incl 120 ref C. Compartments: 4 Cell Ho, ER 16 Ha: 2 (12.6 x 8.5)14 (12.6 x 10.7)ER	**1 oil engine** driving 1 FP propeller Total Power: 9,526kW (12,952hp) 18.0kn B&W 7S50MC 1 x 2 Stroke 7 Cy. 500 x 1910 9526kW (12952bhp) Mitsui Engineering & Shipbuilding CLtd-Japan AuxGen: 3 x 560kW 440V 60Hz a.c Thrusters: 1 Tunnel thruster (f) Fuel: 95.2 (d.f.) (Heating Coils) 1857.2 (r.f.) 40.2pd
8811766 *3FCX5* -	**TOMSON GAS** *ex* Monsoon *-2013* *ex* Ben Nevis *-2004* **David Maritime Inc** Marine Shipping Line FZE *Panama* *Panama* MMSI: 357026000 Official number: 45502PEXT	**3,219** 966 3,814 T/cm 12.0	Class: NK	**1989-03 Higaki Zosen K.K. — Imabari** Yd No: 367 Loa 99.13 (BB) Br ex 16.03 Dght 5.349 Lbp 92.00 Br md 16.00 Dpth 7.20 Welded, 1 dk	**(A11B2TG) LPG Tanker** Double Bottom Entire Compartment Length Liq (Gas): 3,139 2 x Gas Tank (s); 2 independent (C.mn.stl) sph horizontal 2 Cargo Pump (s): 2x300m³/hr Manifold: Bow/CM: 48.3m	**1 oil engine** driving 1 FP propeller Total Power: 2,427kW (3,300hp) 12.7kn Mitsubishi 6UEC37LA 1 x 2 Stroke 6 Cy. 370 x 880 2427kW (3300bhp) Akasaka Tekkosho KK (Akasaka DieselLtd)-Japan AuxGen: 2 x 160kW a.c Fuel: 94.0 (d.f.) 301.0 (r.f.)
9345673 *XCGH2* -	**TOMY** *ex* Vevey *-2009* **Remolque y Lanchaje del Puerto de Veracruz SA de CV (Reylaver)** - *Veracruz* *Mexico* MMSI: 345030061 Official number: 30021272357	**267** 80 -	Class: LR ✠ **100A1** SS 12/2010 tug ✠ **LMC** Eq.Ltr: F; Cable: 275.0/19.0 U2 (a)	**2005-12 Guangdong Hope Yue Shipbuilding Industry Ltd — Guangzhou GD** Yd No: 2135 Loa 26.00 Br ex 9.85 Dght 3.500 Lbp 23.35 Br md 9.80 Dpth 4.50 Welded, 1 dk	**(B32A2ST) Tug**	**2 oil engines** gearing integral to driving 2 Z propellers Total Power: 3,132kW (4,258hp) 12.0kn Caterpillar 3516B-TA 2 x Vee 4 Stroke 16 Cy. 170 x 190 each-1566kW (2129bhp) Caterpillar Inc-USA AuxGen: 2 x 99kW 440V 60Hz a.c

IMO / Call sign	Name / Owners	Tonnage	Class	Builder / Dimensions	Type	Machinery
9643180 *ZGDN5* -	**TON HIL II** **Ton Hil Shipping SA** Equinox Maritime Ltd *George Town* *Cayman Islands (British)* MMSI: 319057600 Official number: 745171	**31,756** 18,653 56,047 T/cm 55.8	Class: NK	**2014-02 Mitsui Eng. & SB. Co. Ltd., Chiba Works — Ichihara** Yd No: 1852 Loa 189.99 (BB) Br ex - Dght 12.715 Lbp 182.00 Br md 32.25 Dpth 18.10 Welded, 1 dk	**(A21A2BC) Bulk Carrier** Grain: 70,811; Bale: 68,000	**1 oil engine** driving 1 FP propeller Total Power: 9,480kW (12,889hp) 14.5kn MAN-B&W 6S50MC-C 1 x 2 Stroke 6 Cy. 500 x 2000 9480kW (12889bhp) Mitsui Engineering & Shipbuilding CLtd-Japan
9109110 *7MGB* -	**TONAN MARU** **Okinawa Prefecture Suisan-Shikenjo** *Naha, Okinawa* *Japan* MMSI: 431645000 Official number: 133747	*176* - 136		**1995-02 Goriki Zosensho — Ise** Yd No: 1056 Loa 35.80 (BB) Br ex - Dght 2.726 Lbp 35.50 Br md 7.00 Dpth 3.00 Welded, 1 dk	**(B12D2FR) Fishery Research Vessel** Ins: 17	**1 oil engine** reduction geared to sc. shaft driving 1 FP propeller Total Power: 883kW (1,201hp) Niigata 6MG22HX 1 x 4 Stroke 6 Cy. 220 x 280 883kW (1201bhp) Niigata Engineering Co Ltd-Japan
8132029 *YCZB* -	**TONASA LINE** *ex* Andhika Pradipta **PT Perusahaan Pelayaran Tonasa Lines** *Jakarta* *Indonesia*	**115** 35 115	Class: (KI) (NK)	**1981 Mipe Shipbuilding Pte Ltd — Singapore** Yd No: ME-49 Loa 23.19 Br ex 7.42 Dght 2.401 Lbp 22.51 Br md 7.41 Dpth 2.80 Welded, 1 dk	**(B32A2ST) Tug**	**2 oil engines** geared to sc. shafts driving 2 FP propellers Total Power: 912kW (1,240hp) 11.0kn Deutz SBA8M816 2 x 4 Stroke 8 Cy. 142 x 160 each-456kW (620bhp) Kloeckner Humboldt Deutz AG-West Germany
7112606 *YFJL* -	**TONASA LINE V** *ex* Lucky Ocean No. 2 *-1995* *ex* Halliburton 601 *-1989* *ex* Hetland Courier *-1978* *ex* Dawn Justice *-1975* **PT Perusahaan Pelayaran Tonasa Lines** *Makassar* *Indonesia* MMSI: 525007098	**4,882** 1,465 7,169	Class: KI (NK) (AB) (BV)	**1971-07 Ujina Zosensho — Hiroshima** Yd No: 514 Converted From: General Cargo Ship-1978 Loa 118.01 Br ex 16.92 Dght 7.103 Lbp 110.01 Br md 16.81 Dpth 8.79 Welded, 1 dk	**(A24A2BT) Cement Carrier** Grain: 5,250	**1 oil engine** driving 1 FP propeller Total Power: 3,678kW (5,001hp) 14.0kn B&W 8K42EF 1 x 2 Stroke 8 Cy. 420 x 900 3678kW (5001bhp) Hitachi Zosen Corp-Japan AuxGen: 2 x 225kW 445V 60Hz a.c Fuel: 642.0 (r.f.)
7354199 *YFLK* -	**TONASA LINE VI** *ex* Duta Marindo No. 11 *-1997* *ex* Yoshu Maru No. 11 *-1996* **PT Perusahaan Pelayaran Tonasa Lines** - *Makassar* *Indonesia*	*2,485* 1,198 4,399	Class: KI	**1974-05 Usuki Iron Works Co Ltd — Usuki OT** Yd No: 897 Loa 84.99 Br ex 14.81 Dght 6.732 Lbp 79.69 Br md 14.79 Dpth 7.80 Welded, 1 dk	**(A24A2BT) Cement Carrier**	**1 oil engine** driving 1 FP propeller Total Power: 1,912kW (2,600hp) 12.5kn Hanshin 6LUS40 1 x 4 Stroke 6 Cy. 400 x 640 1912kW (2600bhp) Hanshin Nainenki Kogyo-Japan AuxGen: 2 x 120kW 225V a.c Fuel: 21.5 (d.f.) 118.0 (r.f.) 8.5pd
7377672 *YFRX* -	**TONASA LINE XI** *ex* Valerine *-1996* *ex* Genkai Maru *-1996* **PT Perusahaan Pelayaran Tonasa Lines** - *Jakarta* *Indonesia* MMSI: 525015088	*2,135* 1,028 3,745	Class: KI	**1974-06 Honda Zosen — Saiki** Yd No: 620 Loa 91.74 Br ex 14.53 Dght 5.470 Lbp 85.16 Br md 14.48 Dpth 6.23 Welded, 1 dk	**(A24A2BT) Cement Carrier**	**1 oil engine** driving 1 FP propeller Total Power: 1,839kW (2,500hp) 11.0kn Akasaka AH40 1 x 4 Stroke 6 Cy. 400 x 600 1839kW (2500bhp) Akasaka Tekkosho KK (Akasaka DieselLtd)-Japan AuxGen: 2 x 144kW 445V 60Hz a.c Fuel: 15.0 (d.f.) 77.5 (r.f.) 8.0pd
7334345 *YGVK* -	**TONASA LINE - XII** *ex* Tifany *-2010* *ex* Tonasa Glory *-2002* *ex* Leader Glory *-1999* *ex* Taiyu Maru *-1993* **PT Perusahaan Pelayaran Tonasa Lines** - *Jakarta* *Indonesia* MMSI: 525015017	**2,637** 1,344 4,486	Class: CR KI (NK)	**1973-11 Hashihama Shipbuilding Co Ltd — Imabari EH** Yd No: 519 Loa 84.99 Br ex 14.43 Dght 6.895 Lbp 78.52 Br md 14.40 Dpth 8.10 Riveted\Welded, 1 dk	**(A24A2BT) Cement Carrier** Grain: 3,605	**1 oil engine** driving 1 FP propeller Total Power: 3,310kW (4,500hp) 12.4kn Hanshin 6LU54 1 x 4 Stroke 6 Cy. 540 x 860 3310kW (4500bhp) Hanshin Nainenki Kogyo-Japan AuxGen: 2 x 200kW 445V 60Hz a.c Fuel: 22.0 (d.f.) 120.0 (r.f.) 15.0pd
7903964 *PNPB* -	**TONASA LINE XVI** *ex* Heritage *-2011* *ex* Chitose Maru *-2002* **PT Perusahaan Pelayaran Tonasa Lines** Nghison Cement Corp *Makassar* *Indonesia*	**4,676** 1,683 7,325	Class: KI (NK)	**1979-10 Nippon Kokan KK (NKK Corp) — Yokohama KN (Tsurumi Shipyard)** Yd No: 974 Loa 111.00 Br ex 17.43 Dght 7.250 Lbp 104.02 Br md 17.42 Dpth 8.97 Welded, 1 dk	**(A24A2BT) Cement Carrier** Grain: 5,482	**1 oil engine** driving 1 FP propeller Total Power: 3,310kW (4,500hp) 13.0kn Hanshin 6LU54 1 x 4 Stroke 6 Cy. 540 x 860 3310kW (4500bhp) The Hanshin Diesel Works Ltd-Japan AuxGen: 3 x 280kW 445V 60Hz a.c Fuel: 26.0 (d.f.) 164.0 (r.f.) 13.5pd
8408052 *YHUM* -	**TONASA LINE XVII** *ex* Lazarus *-2009* *ex* Nissen Maru No. 6 *-2004* **PT Indobaruna Bulk Transport** - *Jakarta* *Indonesia* MMSI: 525019256	**678** 247 980	Class: KI	**1984-11 K.K. Miura Zosensho — Saiki** Yd No: 710 Loa 52.00 Br ex - Dght 4.061 Lbp 48.52 Br md 10.71 Dpth 4.40 Welded, 1 dk	**(A24A2BT) Cement Carrier**	**1 oil engine** driving 1 FP propeller Total Power: 736kW (1,001hp) 10.0kn Yanmar 6T240-UT 1 x 4 Stroke 6 Cy. 240 x 310 736kW (1001bhp) Yanmar Diesel Engine Co Ltd-Japan
8210998 *PMLN* -	**TONASA LINES VIII** *ex* Perdana *-2008* *ex* Rissho Maru *-2007* **PT Perusahaan Pelayaran Tonasa Lines** - *Surabaya* *Indonesia*	*962* 489 1,370	Class: KI (NK)	**1982-07 Ube Dockyard Co. Ltd. — Ube** Yd No: 173 Loa 65.38 Br ex 10.55 Dght 4.226 Lbp 60.25 Br md 10.51 Dpth 4.70 Welded, 1 dk	**(A24A2BT) Cement Carrier** Grain: 1,235 Compartments: 4 Ho, ER	**1 oil engine** dr reverse geared to sc. shaft driving 1 FP propeller Total Power: 956kW (1,300hp) 10.6kn Daihatsu 6DSM-26A 1 x 4 Stroke 6 Cy. 260 x 300 956kW (1300bhp) Daihatsu Diesel Manufacturing Co Lt-Japan
7401411 *YGXY* -	**TONASA LINES - XIV** *ex* Sri Cibinong *-2010* *ex* Andalas IV *-2002* *ex* Semen Dua *-2000* *ex* Kanda Maru No. 7 *-1997* **PT Kunangan Citra Bahari** - *Jakarta* *Indonesia*	**922** 353 1,399	Class: KI	**1974-09 K.K. Miura Zosensho — Saiki** Yd No: 503 Loa 65.51 Br ex 10.52 Dght 4.242 Lbp 60.00 Br md 10.49 Dpth 4.65 Welded, 1 dk	**(A24A2BT) Cement Carrier**	**1 oil engine** geared to sc. shaft driving 1 FP propeller Total Power: 956kW (1,300hp) 10.5kn Daihatsu 6DSM-26 1 x 4 Stroke 6 Cy. 260 x 320 956kW (1300bhp) Daihatsu Diesel Manufacturing Co Lt-Japan
7376604 *YHBD* -	**TONASA LINES - XV** *ex* Tonasa Maru *-2010* *ex* Ryoyo Maru No. 2 *-2001* **PT Indo Batam Terminal** - *Padang* *Indonesia* MMSI: 525019186	*3,828* 1,716 6,706	Class: KI (NK)	**1974-09 Kagoshima Dock & I.W. Co. Ltd. — Kagoshima** Yd No: 74 Loa 113.06 Br ex 16.03 Dght 6.909 Lbp 104.15 Br md 16.01 Dpth 8.21 Welded, 1 dk	**(A24A2BT) Cement Carrier** Grain: 5,777	**1 oil engine** driving 1 FP propeller Total Power: 2,795kW (3,800hp) 13.0kn Mitsubishi 6UET45/75C 1 x 2 Stroke 6 Cy. 450 x 750 2795kW (3800bhp) Kobe Hatsudoki KK-Japan AuxGen: 3 x 150kW 450V 60Hz a.c Fuel: 16.5 (d.f.) 114.5 (r.f.) 12.0pd
9498834 *A8YF8* -	**TONDA SEA** **Ostranios Transport Services Co** NSC Shipping GmbH & Cie KG *Monrovia* *Liberia* MMSI: 636015043 Official number: 15043	**50,729** 30,722 93,246 T/cm 80.8	Class: GL (NV) (BV)	**2011-04 Yangfan Group Co Ltd — Zhoushan ZJ** Yd No: 2099 Loa 229.20 (BB) Br ex - Dght 14.900 Lbp 222.00 Br md 38.00 Dpth 20.70 Welded, 1 dk	**(A21A2BC) Bulk Carrier** Grain: 110,300 Compartments: 7 Ho, ER 7 Ha: 5 (17.9 x 17.0)ER 2 (15.3 x 14.6)	**1 oil engine** driving 1 FP propeller Total Power: 12,240kW (16,642hp) 14.1kn MAN-B&W 6S60MC 1 x 2 Stroke 6 Cy. 600 x 2292 12240kW (16642bhp) Hyundai Heavy Industries Co Ltd-South Korea AuxGen: 3 x a.c Fuel: 190.0 (d.f.) 3100.0 (r.f.) 40.5pd
7306051 *EPBR7* -	**TONDAR4** *ex* Tondar *-2012* *ex* Seabulk Power *-2001* *ex* GMMOS Power *-1997* *ex* Gulf Pride *-1990* **Oscar Shipping & Trading Co Ltd** Echo Cargo & Shipping LLC *Iran* MMSI: 422032100	**350** 105 -	Class: (GL) (AB)	**1973 Quality Equipment Inc — Houma LA** Yd No: 116 Loa 32.00 Br ex - Dght 3.963 Lbp 30.58 Br md 9.45 Dpth 4.27 Welded, 1 dk	**(B32A2ST) Tug**	**2 oil engines** dr reverse geared to sc. shafts driving 2 FP propellers Total Power: 1,434kW (1,950hp) 9.0kn EMD (Electro-Motive) 8-645-E2 2 x Vee 2 Stroke 8 Cy. 230 x 254 each-717kW (975bhp) General Motors Corp.Electro-Motive Div.-La Grange AuxGen: 2 x 75kW 220/440V 60Hz a.c Fuel: 408.0 (d.f.) 6.4pd
7824601 - -	**TONE** *ex* Dania-Carina *-2007* *ex* Katherine Borchard *-2000* *ex* Concordia *-1986* *ex* Katherine Borchard *-1986* *ex* Concordia *-1985* *ex* Zim Australia *-1982* *launched as* Concordia *-1979* **Patras AS** *St Kitts & Nevis*	**5,378** 3,018 7,283	Class: IS (GL)	**1979-07 J.J. Sietas KG Schiffswerft GmbH & Co. — Hamburg** Yd No: 798 Loa 126.27 (BB) Br ex 18.06 Dght 6.511 Lbp 115.55 Br md 18.01 Dpth 8.72 Welded, 2 dks	**(A31A2GX) General Cargo Ship** Grain: 10,215; Bale: 9,640 TEU 504 C Ho 172 TEU C Dk 332 TEU incl 40 ref C. Compartments: 2 Ho, ER, 2 Tw Dk 2 Ha: 2 (37.8 x 12.7)ER Ice Capable	**1 oil engine** reduction geared to sc. shaft driving 1 CP propeller Total Power: 2,942kW (4,000hp) 15.0kn MaK 8M551AK 1 x 4 Stroke 8 Cy. 450 x 550 2942kW (4000bhp) MaK Maschinenbau GmbH-Kiel AuxGen: 2 x 328kW 380V 50Hz a.c, 1 x 280kW 380V 50Hz a.c Thrusters: 1 Thwart. FP thruster
8890669 *JM6489* -	**TONE MARU** **Tone Kaiun YK** - *Iki, Nagasaki* *Japan* Official number: 134568	*199* - -		**1995-10 KK Yanase Dock — Onomichi HS** Yd No: 326 L reg 55.60 Br ex - Dght - Lbp - Br md 9.40 Dpth 5.50 Welded, 1 dk	**(A31A2GX) General Cargo Ship**	**1 oil engine** driving 1 FP propeller Total Power: 736kW (1,001hp) 11.3kn Niigata 6M28BGT 1 x 4 Stroke 6 Cy. 280 x 480 736kW (1001bhp) Niigata Engineering Co Ltd-Japan

LR/IMO No. Call sign	Name, owner, manager, port, flag	Tonnages	Class	Builder, dimensions	Type, capacity	Machinery
8735352 *JD2490* -	**TONE MARU NO. 8** **Tonemaru Kisen YK** - *Uwajima, Ehime* *Japan* Official number: 140619	*499* - 1,800		**2007-09 YK Nakanoshima Zosensho — Kochi KC** Yd No: 251 Loa 74.71 Br ex - Dght 4.320 Lbp 69.00 Br md 12.00 Dpth 7.35 Welded, 1 dk	**(A31A2GX) General Cargo Ship** Bale: 2,466 1 Ha: ER	**1 oil engine** driving 1 Propeller Total Power: 1,618kW (2,200hp) 12.5kn Niigata 6M34BGT 1 x 4 Stroke 6 Cy. 340 x 620 1618kW (2200bhp) Niigata Engineering Co Ltd-Japan
9079602 *JG5255* -	**TONEN No. 3** **Tonen General Kaiun YK** - *Tokyo* *Japan* Official number: 134002	*108* - -		**1993-06 Kanagawa Zosen — Kobe** Yd No: 393 Loa 27.00 Br ex - Dght - Lbp 23.50 Br md 8.00 Dpth 3.40 Welded, 1 dk	**(B34G2SE) Pollution Control Vessel**	**2 oil engines** reduction geared to sc. shafts driving 2 CP propellers Total Power: 662kW (900hp) 10.0kn Niigata 6NSE-Z 2 x 4 Stroke 6 Cy. 150 x 165 each-331kW (450bhp) Niigata Engineering Co Ltd-Japan AuxGen: 1 x 80kW 225V 60Hz a.c
7633404 *BVQZ*	**TONG AN** *ex* Fareast Victor *-1989* *ex* Lady Juliane *-1988* *ex* Juliane *-1987* *ex* Victory *-1986* *ex* Akak Victory *-1985* *ex* Juliane *-1984* *ex* Niedermehnen *-1983* *ex* Ibesca Portugal *-1982* *launched as* Niedermehnen *-1977* **Xiamen Special Economic Zone Shipping Co Ltd** - *Xiamen, Fujian* *China*	**1,670** 713 1,964	Class: (CC) (GL)	**1977-07 J.J. Sietas Schiffswerft — Hamburg** Yd No: 812 Loa 72.24 Br ex 12.83 Dght 4.460 Lbp 65.50 Br md 12.80 Dpth 6.80 Welded, 2 dks	**(A31A2GX) General Cargo Ship** Grain: 3,215; Bale: 3,140 TEU 127 C.Ho 53/20' (40') C.Dk 74/20' (40') Compartments: 1 Ho, ER 1 Ha: (43.8 x 10.2)ER Ice Capable	**1 oil engine** driving 1 FP propeller Total Power: 736kW (1,001hp) 12.0kn MaK 6M452AK 1 x 4 Stroke 6 Cy. 320 x 450 736kW (1001bhp) MaK Maschinenbau GmbH-Kiel
9593658 *9V9602*	**TONG AN CHENG** **PST Management Pte Ltd** Pacific International Lines (Pte) Ltd *Singapore* *Singapore* MMSI: 566689000 Official number: 397341	**18,189** 8,430 24,976	Class: LR ✠ **100A1** SS 10/2012 container cargoes in all holds and on upper deck and on all hatch covers **ShipRight** ACS (B) LI EP (B,I) ✠ **LMC** **UMS** Eq.Ltr: K†; Cable: 623.3/68.0 U3 (a)	**2012-10 Dalian Shipbuilding Industry Co Ltd — Dalian LN (No 1 Yard)** Yd No: MC240-5 Loa 161.37 (BB) Br ex 27.43 Dght 9.800 Lbp 151.98 Br md 27.40 Dpth 13.50 Welded, 1 dk	**(A31A2GX) General Cargo Ship** Grain: 30,240 TEU 1497 C Ho 675 TEU C Dk 822 TEU incl 60 ref C Compartments: 4 Ho, ER 4 Ha: ER Cranes: 2x100t,1x60t	**1 oil engine** driving 1 FP propeller Total Power: 9,960kW (13,542hp) 14.5kn MAN-B&W 6S50MC-C8 1 x 2 Stroke 6 Cy. 500 x 2000 9960kW (13542bhp) Dalian Marine Diesel Co Ltd-China AuxGen: 3 x 620kW 450V 60Hz a.c Boilers: e (ex.g.) 9.5kgf/cm² (9.3bar), WTAuxB (o.f.) 7.6kgf/cm² (7.5bar) Thrusters: 1 Thwart. FP thruster (f)
8708828 *V3VZ* -	**TONG AN HAI** *ex* Tong Xing Quan *-2005* *ex* Yu Ming *-2004* *ex* Sumiwaka Maru No. 28 *-2002* **An Hai Shipping Co Ltd** Xing Yuan Shipping Ltd *Belize City* *Belize* MMSI: 312931000 Official number: 060420688	**1,546** 936 1,266	Class: PD	**1987-08 Kurinoura Dockyard Co Ltd — Yawatahama EH** Yd No: 240 Converted From: Grab Dredger-2002 Loa 60.46 Br ex 12.53 Dght 4.720 Lbp 56.95 Br md 12.51 Dpth 6.51 Welded, 1 dk	**(A31A2GX) General Cargo Ship** Grain: 772 Compartments: 1 Ho, ER 1 Ha: ER	**1 oil engine** with clutches, flexible couplings & reverse reduction geared to sc. shaft driving 1 FP propeller Total Power: 1,295kW (1,761hp) 11.0kn Akasaka DM30R 1 x 4 Stroke 6 Cy. 300 x 480 1295kW (1761bhp) Akasaka Tekkosho KK (Akasaka DieselLtd)-Japan
9535747 *BSTO* -	**TONG CHENG** **CHEC Tianjin Dredging Corp** *Tianjin* *China* MMSI: 412018530	**19,432** 5,829 22,961	Class: CC	**2010-07 Guangzhou Wenchong Shipyard Co Ltd — Guangzhou GD** Yd No: 372 Loa 162.30 (BB) Br ex - Dght 9.500 Lbp 149.80 Br md 28.50 Dpth 15.00 Welded, 1 dk	**(B33B2DT) Trailing Suction Hopper Dredger** Hopper: 18,343 Compartments: 1 Ho, ER 1 Ha: ER (72.1 x 21.3)	**2 oil engines** reduction geared to sc. shafts driving 2 CP propellers Total Power: 17,400kW (23,658hp) 14.5kn Wartsila 12V38 2 x Vee 4 Stroke 12 Cy. 380 x 475 each-8700kW (11829bhp) Wartsila Italia SpA-Italy AuxGen: 2 x 7500kW 6600V a.c, 3 x 750kW 400V a.c Thrusters: 1 Tunnel thruster (f)
9603855 *3FTX5* -	**TONG CHENG 601** **Guangdong Tongcheng Shipping Co Ltd** Bao Xin Marine Ltd SatCom: Inmarsat C 435412611 *Panama* *Panama* MMSI: 354126000 Official number: 41745PEXTF1	**2,981** 894 5,821	Class: PD	**2010-06 Zhejiang Hongxin Shipbuilding Co Ltd — Taizhou ZJ** Yd No: 0918 Loa 89.80 (BB) Br ex - Dght 4.550 Lbp 84.70 Br md 21.80 Dpth 5.96 Welded, 1 dk	**(A31C2GD) Deck Cargo Ship**	**2 oil engines** reduction geared to sc. shafts driving 2 Propellers Total Power: 2,206kW (3,000hp) 12.0kn Chinese Std. Type G6300ZC 2 x 4 Stroke 6 Cy. 300 x 380 each-1103kW (1500bhp) Ningbo CSI Power & Machinery GroupCo Ltd-China
9603867 *3FJC3* -	**TONG CHENG 602** **Guangdong Tongcheng Shipping Co Ltd** Bao Xin Marine Ltd *Panama* *Panama* MMSI: 352600000 Official number: 41166PEXTF2	**2,981** 894 5,821	Class: PD	**2010-06 Zhejiang Hongxin Shipbuilding Co Ltd — Taizhou ZJ** Yd No: 0919 Loa 89.80 (BB) Br ex - Dght 4.550 Lbp 84.70 Br md 21.80 Dpth 5.96 Welded, 1 dk	**(A31C2GD) Deck Cargo Ship**	**2 oil engines** reduction geared to sc. shafts driving 2 Propellers Total Power: 2,206kW (3,000hp) 12.0kn Chinese Std. Type G6300ZC 2 x 4 Stroke 6 Cy. 300 x 380 each-1103kW (1500bhp) Ningbo CSI Power & Machinery GroupCo Ltd-China
9622564 *BYFQ* -	**TONG CHENG 603** **Guangdong Tongcheng Shipping Co Ltd** - *Shantou, Guangdong* *China* MMSI: 413467290 Official number: 110510000029	**2,981** 1,669 5,821		**2010-11 Zhejiang Hexing Shipyard — Wenling ZJ** Yd No: HX1004 Loa 89.80 Br ex - Dght 4.550 Lbp 84.70 Br md 21.80 Dpth 5.96 Welded, 1 dk	**(A31A2GX) General Cargo Ship**	**2 oil engines** reduction gaared to sc. shafts driving 2 FP propellers Total Power: 2,206kW (3,000hp) 11.8kn Chinese Std. Type G6300ZC 2 x 4 Stroke 6 Cy. 300 x 380 each-1103kW (1500bhp) in China
9550113 *BYCN* -	**TONG CHENG 701** **Guangdong Tongcheng Shipping Co Ltd** SatCom: Inmarsat C 441384510 *Shantou, Guangdong* *China* MMSI: 413845000	**5,092** 2,777 7,174	Class: CC	**2009-07 Zhejiang Hongxin Shipbuilding Co Ltd — Taizhou ZJ** Yd No: 2006-03 Loa 112.80 Br ex 17.24 Dght 6.900 Lbp 106.00 Br md 17.20 Dpth 9.10 Welded, 1 dk	**(A21A2BC) Bulk Carrier** Grain: 9,394 Compartments: 3 Ho, ER 3 Ha: ER 3 (17.7 x 11.2) Cranes: 2x25t	**1 oil engine** reduction geared to sc. shaft driving 1 Propeller Total Power: 2,574kW (3,500hp) 12.0kn Yanmar 6N330-EN 1 x 4 Stroke 6 Cy. 330 x 440 2574kW (3500bhp) Qingdao Zichai Boyang Diesel EngineCo Ltd-China AuxGen: 3 x 250kW 400V a.c
9621728 *BYGG* -	**TONG CHENG 702** **Guangdong Tongcheng Shipping Co Ltd** - *Shantou, Guangdong* *China* MMSI: 413470010	**5,092** 2,777 7,229	Class: CC	**2011-09 Zhejiang Hongxin Shipbuilding Co Ltd — Taizhou ZJ** Yd No: 2006-04 Loa 112.80 Br ex 17.24 Dght 6.900 Lbp 106.00 Br md 17.20 Dpth 9.10 Welded, 1 dk	**(A21A2BC) Bulk Carrier** Grain: 9,394 Compartments: 3 Ho, ER 3 Ha: ER Cranes: 2x25t Ice Capable	**1 oil engine** reduction geared to sc. shaft driving 1 FP propeller Total Power: 2,574kW (3,500hp) 12.0kn Yanmar 6N330-EN 1 x 4 Stroke 6 Cy. 330 x 440 2574kW (3500bhp) Qingdao Zichai Boyang Diesel EngineCo Ltd-China
7903811 - -	**TONG CHENG 818** *ex* Zhong An 818 *-2003* *ex* Propane Maru No. 18 *-1998* **Guangdong Tongcheng Shipping Co Ltd** - *Shantou, Guangdong* *China* MMSI: 412468860	**1,214** 680 1,135	Class: CC (NK)	**1979-10 Naikai Shipbuilding & Engineering Co Ltd — Onomichi HS (Taguma Shipyard)** Yd No: 446 Loa 65.28 Br ex 11.43 Dght 4.565 Lbp 60.03 Br md 11.41 Dpth 5.16 Welded, 1 dk	**(A11B2TG) LPG Tanker** Liq (Gas): 1,509 2 x Gas Tank (s); 2 independent cyl horizontal	**1 oil engine** driving 1 FP propeller Total Power: 1,545kW (2,101hp) 12.3kn Akasaka DM38AR 1 x 4 Stroke 6 Cy. 380 x 600 1545kW (2101bhp) Akasaka Tekkosho KK (Akasaka DieselLtd)-Japan AuxGen: 2 x 580kW
8829579 *P5CU* -	**TONG CHON** *ex* Son Gun Ho *-2013* *ex* Chol San Bong Chong Nyon Ho *-2011* **Sinpo Fishery Co** - *Wonsan* *North Korea* MMSI: 445015000 Official number: 3509200	*6,099* 3,778 9,760 T/cm 18.5	Class: KC	**1985 Chongjin Shipyard — Huichon** Loa 130.80 (BB) Br ex - Dght 7.900 Lbp - Br md 18.40 Dpth 10.40 Welded, 2 dks	**(A31A2GX) General Cargo Ship** Grain: 12,832; Bale: 12,191 Compartments: 4 Ho, ER 4 Ha: 2 (11.0 x 8.0)2 (6.0 x 9.0)ER Cranes: 1x5t; Derricks: 8x5t	**1 oil engine** driving 1 FP propeller 12.0kn
9363261 *V3CH* -	**TONG DA** **Tong Da Shipping Co Ltd** Yantai Guangtong International Ship Management Co Ltd *Belize City* *Belize* MMSI: 312958000 Official number: 060520722	**1,970** 1,068 2,803	Class: BV (CC)	**2006-02 Rongcheng Haida Shipbuilding Co Ltd — Rongcheng SD** Yd No: HDBC007 Loa 79.99 Br ex - Dght 5.200 Lbp 74.00 Br md 13.60 Dpth 7.00 Welded, 1 dk	**(A21A2BC) Bulk Carrier** Grain: 4,127; Bale: 3,893 Compartments: 1 Ho, ER 1 Ha: ER (38.4 x 9.0) Ice Capable	**1 oil engine** reduction geared to sc. shaft driving 1 FP propeller Total Power: 1,080kW (1,468hp) 11.7kn MAN-B&W 8L23/30 1 x 4 Stroke 8 Cy. 225 x 300 1080kW (1468bhp) Zhenjiang Marine Diesel Works-China AuxGen: 2 x 100kW 400V a.c

9069085 *BKST3* -	**TONG DA 2** **Zhoushan Tongda Shipping Co Ltd** - *Zhoushan, Zhejiang* *China* MMSI: 412438660	**3,099** 1,611 645	Class: (CC)	2006-04 **Zhoushan Haichen Marine Service & Engineering Co Ltd — Zhoushan ZJ** Loa 77.60 Br ex - Dght - Lbp 70.20 Br md 15.00 Dpth 5.50 Welded, 1 dk	**(A36A2PR) Passenger/Ro-Ro Ship (Vehicles)**	**2 oil engines** geared to sc. shafts driving 2 Propellers Total Power: 3,765kW (5,119hp) 11.0kn Chinese Std. Type G8300ZC 2 x 4 Stroke 8 Cy. 300 x 380 each-1765kW (2400bhp) Ningbo CSI Power & Machinery GroupCo Ltd-China AuxGen: 2 x 252kW 400V a.c
9350472 - -	**TONG DA 58** - - *China* MMSI: 412453980	**2,997** 1,678 5,500		2005-01 **Zhejiang Yueqing Qiligang Ship Industry Co Ltd — Yueqing ZJ** Loa 102.80 (BB) Br ex - Dght 5.500 Lbp 95.80 Br md 15.80 Dpth 7.20 Welded, 1 dk	**(A31A2GX) General Cargo Ship**	**1 oil engine** reduction geared to sc. shaft driving 1 FP propeller Total Power: 1,765kW (2,400hp) 10.5kn Chinese Std. Type G8300ZC 1 x 4 Stroke 8 Cy. 300 x 380 1765kW (2400bhp) Wuxi Antai Power Machinery Co Ltd-China AuxGen: 2 x 119kW 400V a.c Fuel: 30.0 (d.f.) 57.0 (r.f.)
9365350 *BYKY2* -	**TONG DA 568** **Fuqing Tongda Shipping Co Ltd** Guangzhou Eagle Ocean International Shipmanagement Co Ltd *Fuzhou, Fujian* *China* MMSI: 412454030	**2,880** 1,963 5,000	Class: ZC	2005-07 **Zhejiang Yueqing Qiligang Ship Industry Co Ltd — Yueqing ZJ** Loa 98.00 (BB) Br ex - Dght 5.900 Lbp 95.16 Br md 15.80 Dpth 7.40 Welded, 1 dk	**(A31A2GX) General Cargo Ship** Grain: 6,825; Bale: 6,279 Compartments: 2 Ho, ER 2 Ha: (27.1 x 12.9)ER (25.8 x 12.9)	**1 oil engine** reduction geared to sc. shaft driving 1 FP propeller Total Power: 1,765kW (2,400hp) 11.0kn Chinese Std. Type G8300ZC 1 x 4 Stroke 8 Cy. 300 x 380 1765kW (2400bhp) Wuxi Antai Power Machinery Co Ltd-China AuxGen: 2 x 130kW a.c Fuel: 130.0 (d.f.)
9366964 *BVKZ2* -	**TONG DA 618** **Fuqing Tongda Shipping Co Ltd** Sea Star Global Shipping Co Ltd *Fuzhou, Fujian* *China* MMSI: 412454040 Official number: 080105000158	**2,978** 1,667 5,176		2005-06 **Zhejiang Yueqing Qiligang Ship Industry Co Ltd — Yueqing ZJ** Loa 99.50 Br ex - Dght 5.950 Lbp 93.00 Br md 14.60 Dpth 7.40 Welded, 1 dk	**(A31A2GX) General Cargo Ship**	**1 oil engine** reduction geared to sc. shaft driving 1 FP propeller Total Power: 1,325kW (1,801hp) 11.0kn Guangzhou 6320ZCD 1 x 4 Stroke 6 Cy. 320 x 440 1325kW (1801bhp) Guangzhou Diesel Engine Factory CoLtd-China
9686675 *BJRE* -	**TONG GU LING** **Hainan Strait Shipping Co Ltd** - *China* MMSI: 413523220	**2,500** - 500	Class: ZC (Class contemplated)	2014-03 **Guangzhou Shipyard International Co Ltd — Guangzhou GD** Loa - Br ex - Dght - Lbp - Br md - Dpth - Welded, 1 dk	**(A36A2PR) Passenger/Ro-Ro Ship (Vehicles)** Passengers: unberthed: 999 Vehicles: 46	**1 oil engine** driving 1 Propeller
8132005 *BOFD* -	**TONG HAI** **Shenzhen Ocean Shipping Co (COSCO SHENZHEN)** - SatCom: Inmarsat A 1570502 *Shenzhen, Guangdong* *China* MMSI: 412403000	**17,119** 8,190 25,567	Class: (CC)	1981-10 **Hudong Shipyard — Shanghai** Loa 184.72 (BB) Br ex - Dght 10.091 Lbp 172.20 Br md 23.22 Dpth 14.20 Welded, 1 dk	**(A21A2BC) Bulk Carrier** Grain: 31,050; Bale: 29,783 Compartments: 6 Ho, ER 6 Ha: 4 (10.2 x 11.6)2 (11.9 x 11.6)ER Cranes: 4x8t Ice Capable	**1 oil engine** driving 1 FP propeller Total Power: 8,826kW (12,000hp) 15.5kn Sulzer 6RND76 1 x 2 Stroke 6 Cy. 760 x 1550 8826kW (12000bhp) Tvornica Dizel Motora '3 Maj'-Yugoslavia
8833570 *BSHE* -	**TONG HAI TUO 5** *ex* Yan Jiu 5 *-1990* **Tonghai Shipping Co Ltd** - *Shekou, Guangdong* *China*	*190* - -		**1975 Shanghai Shipyard — Shanghai** Loa 29.50 Br ex - Dght 2.800 Lbp 27.00 Br md 8.00 Dpth 3.80 Welded, 1 dk	**(B32A2ST) Tug**	**1 oil engine** driving 1 FP propeller Total Power: 721kW (980hp) 11.0kn Skoda 6L350IIPN 1 x 4 Stroke 6 Cy. 350 x 500 721kW (980bhp) Skoda-Praha AuxGen: 2 x 48kW 220V a.c
9609316 *BQEB* -	**TONG HENG** **CCCC Tianjin Dredging Co Ltd** - *Tianjin* *China* MMSI: 412303150	**12,105** 3,631 10,929	Class: CC	2012-08 **China Merchants Heavy Industry (Shenzhen) Co Ltd — Shenzhen GD** Yd No: CMHI-097 Loa 131.20 (BB) Br ex - Dght 7.000 Lbp 121.00 Br md 26.20 Dpth 9.65 Welded, 1 dk	**(B33B2DT) Trailing Suction Hopper Dredger** Hopper: 11,000 Ice Capable	**2 oil engines** reduction geared to sc. shafts driving 2 Propellers Total Power: 12,650kW (17,198hp) 15.0kn Daihatsu 12DKM-36 2 x Vee 4 Stroke 12 Cy. 360 x 480 each-6325kW (8599bhp) Daihatsu Diesel Manufacturing Co Lt-Japan AuxGen: 2 x 2500kW 690V a.c, 2 x 900kW 400V a.c Thrusters: 2 Tunnel thruster (f)
7213759 *BVWV* -	**TONG HONG No. 2** **Tong Hong Fishery Co Ltd** - SatCom: Inmarsat C 441653410 *Kaohsiung* *Chinese Taipei*	*377* 258 275	Class: (CR)	**1969 Korea Shipbuilding & Engineering Corp — Busan** Loa 43.59 Br ex 7.52 Dght 2.896 Lbp 38.61 Br md 7.50 Dpth 3.36 Welded, 1 dk	**(B11B2FV) Fishing Vessel** Compartments: 3 Ho, ER 4 Ha: 2 (1.0 x 1.0)2 (1.5 x 1.5)ER Derricks: 4x1t; Winches: 4	**1 oil engine** driving 1 FP propeller Total Power: 552kW (750hp) 11.5kn Niigata 1 x 4 Stroke 6 Cy. 280 x 440 552kW (750bhp) Niigata Engineering Co Ltd-Japan AuxGen: 2 x 80kW 230V 60Hz a.c
7738060 *BYPF* -	**TONG HONG No. 3** **Tong Hong Fishery Co Ltd** - *Kaohsiung* *Chinese Taipei* Official number: 5504	*582* 393 -	Class: (CR)	**1975 Chou Mao Shipbuilding Co., Ltd. — Kaohsiung** Loa 46.59 Br ex 8.01 Dght 3.201 Lbp 40.64 Br md - Dpth 3.46 Welded, 2 dks	**(B11B2FV) Fishing Vessel** Ins: 379 Compartments: 4 Ho, ER 6 Ha: 2 (1.0 x 1.0)2 (1.3 x 1.0) (1.6 x 1.6) (0.9 x 1.0)ER	**1 oil engine** driving 1 FP propeller Total Power: 809kW (1,100hp) 11.0kn Niigata 6L28X 1 x 4 Stroke 6 Cy. 280 x 440 809kW (1100bhp) Niigata Engineering Co Ltd-Japan AuxGen: 1 x 176kW 220V a.c, 1 x 144kW 220V a.c
8942266 - -	**TONG HUI** - -	**995** 636 -		**1996 Zhanjiang Haibin Shipyard — Zhanjiang GD** Loa 67.10 Br ex - Dght - Lbp 62.30 Br md 13.00 Dpth 5.30 Welded, 1 dk	**(A13B2TU) Tanker (unspecified)**	**1 oil engine** driving 1 FP propeller Total Power: 735kW (999hp) Chinese Std. Type 1 x 4 Stroke 735kW (999bhp) Zibo Diesel Engine Factory-China
8661575 *HMYI* -	**TONG HUNG 1** *ex* Bao Jiang 19 *-2013* **Tonghung Shipping & Trading Co Ltd** - *North Korea* MMSI: 445141000	**2,667** 1,493 -		2005-09 **Jiangdu Jierui Shipping Co Ltd — Yangzhou JS** Loa - Br ex - Dght - Lbp - Br md - Dpth - Welded, 1 dk	**(A31A2GX) General Cargo Ship**	**1 oil engine** driving 1 Propeller Total Power: 1,324kW (1,800hp) Chinese Std. Type G6300ZC 1 x 4 Stroke 6 Cy. 300 x 380 1324kW (1800bhp) Ningbo CSI Power & Machinery GroupCo Ltd-China
8882179 - -	**TONG IL** - -	*379* 114 190	Class: KC	**1964 Nampo Shipyard — Nampo** Loa 48.00 Br ex - Dght - Lbp - Br md - Dpth - Welded, 1 dk	**(A31A2GX) General Cargo Ship**	**2 oil engines** driving 2 FP propellers S.K.L. 6NVD36 2 x 4 Stroke 6 Cy. 240 x 360
8124931 *J8B2672* -	**TONG JI MEN** *ex* Harmen Oldendorff *-2003* *ex* Cape Nelson *-2002* *ex* Harmen Oldendorff *-2000* *ex* Cape Nelson *-2000* *ex* Harmen Oldendorff *-1997* *ex* Captain Kermadec *-1989* *ex* Hyundai Con Six *-1989* **YBM Shipping Co Ltd** Nanjing Ocean Shipping Co Ltd (NASCO) *Kingstown* *St Vincent & The Grenadines* MMSI: 377308000 Official number: 9144	**15,158** 9,108 23,476	Class: LR (KR) ✠**100A1** SS 08/2009 strengthened for heavy cargoes ✠**LMC** Eq.Ltr: G†; Cable: U3 (a)	1982-10 **Hyundai Heavy Industries Co Ltd — Ulsan** Yd No: 206 Loa 157.94 (BB) Br ex 26.34 Dght 10.018 Lbp 150.02 Br md 26.01 Dpth 14.03 Welded, 1 dk	**(A31A2GX) General Cargo Ship** Grain: 33,542; Bale: 31,866 TEU 598 C Ho 394 TEU C Dk 204 TEU Compartments: 4 Ho, ER, 4 Tw Dk 4 Ha: (19.2 x 15.3)ER Cranes: 4x25t	**1 oil engine** driving 1 FP propeller Total Power: 8,018kW (10,901bhp) 15.4kn B&W 5L67GFCA 1 x 2 Stroke 5 Cy. 670 x 1700 8018kW (10901bhp) Hyundai Engine & Machinery Co Ltd-South Korea AuxGen: 2 x 460kW 450V 60Hz a.c Fuel: 243.5 (d.f.) 1341.0 (r.f.)
8988038 - -	**TONG JIE** *ex* Shun Hang 126 *-2005* *ex* Yuan Da *-2004* **Dalian Xunjie Shipping Co Ltd** Dalian Jack Shipping Management Co Ltd	**947** 536 1,700		1983-01 **Weihai Shipyard — Weihai SD** Yd No: 9305K Loa 69.54 Br ex - Dght 4.500 Lbp 68.57 Br md 9.80 Dpth 5.70 Welded, 1 dk	**(A31A2GX) General Cargo Ship**	**1 oil engine** driving 1 Propeller Total Power: 736kW (1,001hp) Fiat 1 x 736kW (1001bhp) Fiat OM Applicazioni Industriali-Milano
9044231 *DSQO4* -	**TONG JIN** *ex* Cyber II *-2009* *ex* Tong Jin *-1999* **Tong Yang Cement Corp** - *Busan* *South Korea* MMSI: 441642000 Official number: BSR-090954	**4,794** 2,032 8,059	Class: KR	1992-05 **ShinA Shipbuilding Co Ltd — Tongyeong** Yd No: 356 Loa 112.50 (BB) Br ex 17.83 Dght 7.056 Lbp 106.00 Br md 17.80 Dpth 9.10 Welded, 1 dk	**(A24A2BT) Cement Carrier** Grain: 7,208 Compartments: 2 Ho, ER	**1 oil engine** driving 1 FP propeller Total Power: 3,354kW (4,560hp) 13.0kn B&W 6L35MC 1 x 2 Stroke 6 Cy. 350 x 1050 3354kW (4560bhp) Ssangyong Heavy Industries Co Ltd-South Korea Thrusters: 1 Thwart. CP thruster (f)

IMO / Call sign	Name / Owner	Tonnage	Class	Builder / Dimensions	Type	Machinery
7333729 *XUDZ7* -	**TONG LEONG** *ex* Nusa Abadi *-1989* *ex* Jaramac 35 *-1984* *ex* Eileen B. Ingram *-1972* **Eastern Navigation Pte Ltd** *Phnom Penh* *Cambodia* MMSI: 514035000 Official number: 9767001	**163** 48 -	Class: (KI) (AB)	**1967-09 Main Iron Works, Inc. — Houma, La** Yd No: 187 Loa 26.06 Br ex 8.23 Dght 2.590 Lbp 24.87 Br md - Dpth 3.66 Welded, 1 dk	**(B32A2ST) Tug**	**2 oil engines** reverse reduction geared to sc. shafts driving 2 FP propellers Total Power: 832kW (1,132hp) Caterpillar D379TA 2 x Vee 4 Stroke 8 Cy. 159 x 203 each-416kW (566bhp) Caterpillar Tractor Co-USA AuxGen: 2 x 30kW Fuel: 80.0 (d.f.)
9056832 *BSRB* -	**TONG LI** **CHEC Tianjin Dredging Corp** - SatCom: Inmarsat C 441248412 *Tianjin* *China* MMSI: 412620000	**6,296** 2,273 9,551	Class: CC	**1994-06 Merwede Shipyard BV — Hardinxveld** (Hull) Yd No: 664 **1994-06 IHC Holland NV Dredgers — Kinderdijk** Yd No: C01204 Loa 111.40 Br ex 21.00 Dght 8.200 Lbp 105.50 Br md 17.95 Dpth - Welded	**(B33B2DT) Trailing Suction Hopper Dredger** Hopper: 5,400	**2 oil engines** geared to sc. shafts driving 2 FP propellers Total Power: 6,600kW (8,974hp) 13.5kn Stork-Werkspoor 12SW280 2 x Vee 4 Stroke 12 Cy. 280 x 300 each-3300kW (4487bhp) Stork Wartsila Diesel BV-Netherlands AuxGen: 3 x 280kW 380V a.c Thrusters: 1 Tunnel thruster (f)
8408791 *T3MB2* -	**TONG MAO 1** *ex* Daejoo Ace *-2014* *ex* Hee Young Sun *-2002* *ex* Merry Stella *-2000* *ex* Sun Coral *-1991* **Qianhui Resources Ltd** Hongkong Renaissance Shipping Ltd *Tarawa* *Kiribati* MMSI: 529700000 Official number: K-17841471	**2,818** 1,771 5,164	Class: KR (NK)	**1984-09 Tokushima Zosen Sangyo K.K. — Komatsushima** Yd No: 1711 Loa 94.42 (BB) Br ex - Dght 6.040 Lbp 88.02 Br md 16.01 Dpth 7.35 Welded, 1 dk	**(A31A2GX) General Cargo Ship** Grain: 6,301; Bale: 5,450 TEU 74 C. 74/20' Compartments: 2 Ho, ER 6 Ha: ER Derricks: 1x30t,2x20t	**1 oil engine** driving 1 FP propeller Total Power: 2,060kW (2,801hp) 11.7kn Hanshin 6EL38 1 x 4 Stroke 6 Cy. 380 x 760 2060kW (2801bhp) The Hanshin Diesel Works Ltd-Japan AuxGen: 2 x 160kW a.c
9397561 *V3HR3* -	**TONG MAO 1** **Hong Kong Tomao International Marine Ltd** Tongmao Ship Management Inc *Belize City* *Belize* MMSI: 312111000 Official number: 130620720	**2,565** 1,436 3,815	Class: IB	**2006-05 Zhoushan Longtai Shipbuilding Co Ltd — Zhoushan ZJ** Loa 87.80 Br ex - Dght 5.900 Lbp 79.95 Br md 13.80 Dpth 7.45 Welded, 1 dk	**(A31A2GX) General Cargo Ship** Grain: 5,016; Bale: 5,016	**1 oil engine** reduction geared to sc. shaft driving 1 FP propeller Total Power: 1,325kW (1,801hp) 11.0kn Guangzhou 6320ZCD 1 x 4 Stroke 6 Cy. 320 x 440 1325kW (1801bhp) Guangzhou Diesel Engine Factory CoLtd-China
8991205 *V3HV* -	**TONG MAO 2** *ex* Bao Hong 2 *-2006* **Zhejiang Yonghang Shipping Co Ltd** Tongmao Ship Management Inc *Belize City* *Belize* MMSI: 312415000 Official number: 130620736-D	**2,268** 1,426 3,808	Class: IB	**2004-02 Zhoushan Zhengpei Shipbuilding & Repair Co Ltd — Zhoushan ZJ** Loa 87.00 Br ex - Dght 5.800 Lbp 79.95 Br md 13.80 Dpth 7.10 Welded, 1 dk	**(A31A2GX) General Cargo Ship** Grain: 4,787	**1 oil engine** reduction geared to sc. shaft driving 1 Propeller Total Power: 1,765kW (2,400hp) 11.5kn Chinese Std. Type 8320ZC 1 x 4 Stroke 8 Cy. 320 x 440 1765kW (2400bhp) Guangzhou Diesel Engine Factory CoLtd-China
9532422 *BKTB4* -	**TONG MAO 5** **Zhejiang Yonghang Shipping Co Ltd** *Zhoushan, Zhejiang* *China* MMSI: 413425610	**3,770** 1,960 5,716	Class: CC	**2008-09 Ningbo Beilun Lantian Shipbuilding Co Ltd — Ningbo ZJ** Yd No: LT0701 Loa 99.92 Br ex 16.52 Dght 6.280 Lbp 92.50 Br md 16.20 Dpth 8.00 Welded, 1 dk	**(A31A2GX) General Cargo Ship** Grain: 6,937; Bale: 6,937 Compartments: 2 Ho, ER 2 Ha: (27.5 x 10.4)ER (24.3 x 10.4) Ice Capable	**1 oil engine** reduction geared to sc. shaft driving 1 FP propeller Total Power: 2,060kW (2,801hp) 11.5kn Guangzhou 8320ZC 1 x 4 Stroke 8 Cy. 320 x 440 2060kW (2801bhp) Guangzhou Diesel Engine Factory CoLtd-China AuxGen: 3 x 150kW 400V a.c
9548196 *BKVQ4* -	**TONG MAO 7** **Zhejiang Yonghang Shipping Co Ltd** New Unite Marine Co Ltd *Zhoushan, Zhejiang* *China* MMSI: 413592000	**3,770** 1,960 5,758	Class: CC	**2009-02 Ningbo Beilun Lantian Shipbuilding Co Ltd — Ningbo ZJ** Yd No: LT0704 Loa 99.92 Br ex 16.52 Dght 6.280 Lbp 92.50 Br md 16.20 Dpth 8.00 Welded, 1 dk	**(A31A2GX) General Cargo Ship** Grain: 6,937; Bale: 6,937 Compartments: 2 Ho, ER 2 Ha: (27.5 x 10.4)ER (24.3 x 10.4) Ice Capable	**1 oil engine** reduction geared to sc. shaft driving 1 FP propeller Total Power: 2,060kW (2,801hp) 11.5kn Guangzhou 8320ZC 1 x 4 Stroke 8 Cy. 320 x 440 2060kW (2801bhp) Guangzhou Diesel Engine Factory CoLtd-China AuxGen: 3 x 150kW 400V a.c
9593189 *BKRU5* -	**TONG MAO 9** **Zhejiang Yonghang Shipping Co Ltd** - SatCom: Inmarsat C 441301627 *Zhoushan, Zhejiang* *China* MMSI: 413440260	**4,695** 2,320 6,632	Class: CC	**2010-12 Ningbo Beilun Lantian Shipbuilding Co Ltd — Ningbo ZJ** Yd No: LT0904 Loa 112.22 Br ex - Dght 6.350 Lbp 104.62 Br md 16.80 Dpth 8.50 Welded, 1 dk	**(A31A2GX) General Cargo Ship** Grain: 7,972 Compartments: 1 Ho, ER 1 Ha: ER (56.3 x 13.0) Ice Capable	**1 oil engine** reduction geared to sc. shaft driving 1 FP propeller Total Power: 2,206kW (2,999hp) 12.0kn Guangzhou 8320ZCD 1 x 4 Stroke 8 Cy. 320 x 440 2206kW (2999bhp) Guangzhou Diesel Engine Factory CoLtd-China AuxGen: 2 x 160kW 400V a.c
8736576 *V3NH* -	**TONG MAO 11** *ex* Quan Yuan 2 *-2009* **Zhoushan Quan Yuan Shipping Co Ltd** Tongmao Ship Management Inc SatCom: Inmarsat C 431235110 *Belize City* *Belize* MMSI: 312351000 Official number: 130920813	**2,996** 1,677 4,649	Class: IB	**2008-06 Zhoushan Honglisheng Ship Engineering Co Ltd — Zhoushan ZJ** Yd No: LJX4312 Loa 98.00 (BB) Br ex 16.12 Dght 5.900 Lbp 89.95 Br md 15.80 Dpth 7.35 Welded, 1 dk	**(A31A2GX) General Cargo Ship** Grain: 6,825; Bale: 6,279 Compartments: 2 Ho, ER 2 Ha: (27.1 x 12.9)ER (25.8 x 12.9)	**1 oil engine** reduction geared to sc. shaft driving 1 FP propeller Total Power: 2,000kW (2,719hp) 11.0kn Chinese Std. Type G8300ZC 1 x 4 Stroke 8 Cy. 300 x 380 2000kW (2719bhp) Ningbo CSI Power & Machinery GroupCo Ltd-China AuxGen: 2 x 130kW a.c Fuel: 139.0 (d.f.)
8992106 *XUCS5* -	**TONG MAO 12** *ex* Zhen Wei 1 *-2009* *ex* Xin Ming Zhou 1 *-2005* **Hearty Sun International Ltd** Hong Kong Tomao International Marine Ltd *Phnom Penh* *Cambodia* MMSI: 514452000 Official number: 1304232	**2,997** 1,678 4,980	Class: UM	**2004-02 Yueqing Donggang Shipbuilding Co Ltd — Yueqing ZJ** Loa 98.00 (BB) Br ex - Dght 5.900 Lbp 91.50 Br md 15.80 Dpth 7.40 Welded, 1 dk	**(A31A2GX) General Cargo Ship** Grain: 6,825; Bale: 6,279 Compartments: 2 Ho, ER 2 Ha: (27.1 x 12.9)ER (25.8 x 12.9)	**1 oil engine** driving 1 FP propeller Total Power: 1,765kW (2,400hp) 10.0kn Chinese Std. Type G8300ZC 1 x 4 Stroke 8 Cy. 300 x 380 1765kW (2400bhp) Ningbo CSI Power & Machinery GroupCo Ltd-China AuxGen: 2 x 130kW a.c Fuel: 139.0 (d.f.)
9528677 *V3QG8* -	**TONG MAO 16** *ex* Bing Ye *-2012* **Zhejiang Yonghang Shipping Co Ltd** Tong Mao Ship Management Ltd *Belize City* *Belize* MMSI: 312428000 Official number: 611220028	**2,930** 1,783 5,200	Class: IB PD	**2008-12 in the People's Republic of China** Loa 96.90 Br ex 15.82 Dght 5.850 Lbp 89.80 Br md 15.80 Dpth 7.40 Welded, 1 dk	**(A31A2GX) General Cargo Ship** Grain: 6,398; Bale: 6,398	**1 oil engine** reduction geared to sc. shaft driving 1 Propeller Total Power: 1,765kW (2,400hp) 12.0kn Chinese Std. Type 8300ZC 1 x 4 Stroke 8 Cy. 300 x 380 1765kW (2400bhp) Ningbo CSI Power & Machinery GroupCo Ltd-China
9563756 *BKPN4* -	**TONG MAO 101** **Zhejiang Yonghang Shipping Co Ltd** *Zhoushan, Zhejiang* *China* MMSI: 413435950	**8,934** 5,455 13,694	Class: CC	**2009-12 Ningbo Beilun Lantian Shipbuilding Co Ltd — Ningbo ZJ** Yd No: LT0804 Loa 140.70 Br ex 20.03 Dght 7.950 Lbp 131.80 Br md 20.00 Dpth 10.80 Welded, 1 dk	**(A31A2GX) General Cargo Ship** Grain: 18,786 Cranes: 3x30t Ice Capable	**1 oil engine** reduction geared to sc. shaft driving 1 FP propeller Total Power: 3,310kW (4,500hp) 12.5kn Yanmar 8N330-EN 1 x 4 Stroke 8 Cy. 330 x 440 3310kW (4500bhp) Qingdao Zichai Boyang Diesel EngineCo Ltd-China AuxGen: 3 x 350kW 400V a.c
7122235 *P6PI* -	**TONG MYONG SAN** *ex* Dong Myong San *-2011* *ex* Koryo Maru No. 7 *-1985* *ex* Takatori Maru No. 18 *-1982* **Wonsan Seafoods Export Co** *Wonsan* *North Korea* MMSI: 445324000 Official number: 2000914	*483* 145 475	Class: KC	**1970 KK Kanasashi Zosen — Shizuoka SZ** Yd No: 999 Loa 51.08 Br ex 8.34 Dght 3.460 Lbp 44.35 Br md 8.31 Dpth 5.85 Welded, 2 dks	**(B11B2FV) Fishing Vessel**	**1 oil engine** driving 1 FP propeller Total Power: 736kW (1,001hp) Hanshin 6LU28 1 x 4 Stroke 6 Cy. 280 x 440 736kW (1001bhp) Hanshin Nainenki Kogyo-Japan
6825361 *BVET* -	**TONG NAN No. 11** **Tong Nan Hwa Fishing Enterprises Co Ltd** - *Kaohsiung* *Chinese Taipei* Official number: CT5-0479	*192* 100 91		**1968 Chou Mao Shipbuilding Co., Ltd. — Kaohsiung** Loa 33.13 Br ex 6.23 Dght 2.363 Lbp 28.86 Br md 6.20 Dpth 2.77 Welded, 1 dk	**(B11B2FV) Fishing Vessel**	**1 oil engine** driving 1 FP propeller Total Power: 368kW (500hp) Hanshin 6L26AMSH 1 x 4 Stroke 6 Cy. 260 x 400 368kW (500bhp) Hanshin Nainenki Kogyo-Japan
7213814 *BVEH* -	**TONG PAO No. 11** **Tong Pao Marine Products Co Ltd** *Kaohsiung* *Chinese Taipei*	*211* 127 -	Class: (CR)	**1971 Chung Yi Shipbuilding Corp. — Kaohsiung** Loa 33.91 Br ex 6.38 Dght 2.388 Lbp 29.62 Br md 6.35 Dpth 2.80 Welded, 1 dk	**(B11B2FV) Fishing Vessel** Compartments: 3 Ho, ER 4 Ha: 2 (0.9 x 0.9)2 (1.1 x 1.1)ER	**1 oil engine** driving 1 FP propeller Total Power: 405kW (551hp) 9.0kn Alpha 405-26VO 1 x 2 Stroke 5 Cy. 260 x 400 405kW (551bhp) Taiwan Machinery ManufacturingCorp.-Kaohsiung AuxGen: 1 x 64kW 220V a.c, 1 x 40kW 220V a.c

IMO / Call sign	Name / Owner / Manager	Tonnage	Class	Built / Dimensions	Type	Machinery
9673563 *XUFN5* -	**TONG RUN 7** **Mr Xu Fatao** Weihai Hongfeng Shipping Co Ltd *Phnom Penh* *Cambodia* MMSI: 515666000	**2,997** 1,678 5,376	Class: UB	**2012-09 Wenling Yuanyang Shiprepair & Building Co Ltd — Wenling ZJ** Yd No: YY-2011-16 Loa 98.00 (BB) Br ex - Dght 5.900 Lbp 91.50 Br md 15.80 Dpth 7.40 Welded, 1 dk	**(A21A2BC) Bulk Carrier** Grain: 6,700	**1 oil engine** reduction geared to sc. shaft driving 1 FP propeller Total Power: 1,765kW (2,400hp) 14.0kn Chinese Std. Type 8320ZC 1 x 4 Stroke 8 Cy. 320 x 440 1765kW (2400bhp) Guangzhou Diesel Engine Factory CoLtd-China
7506792 *9WOU* -	**TONG SENG 8** *ex* Shapadu Salveda *-1988* *ex* Salveda *-1984* *ex* Asiatic Harmony *-1982* **Mee Lee Shipping Sdn Bhd** - *Kuching* *Malaysia* Official number: 325899	*124* 31 -	Class: (AB)	**1974 Sea Services Pte Ltd — Singapore** Yd No: Y39 L reg 23.50 Br ex 7.25 Dght 2.667 Lbp 22.92 Br md 7.21 Dpth 3.45 Welded, 1 dk	**(B32A2ST) Tug**	**2 oil engines** reverse reduction geared to sc. shafts driving 2 FP propellers Total Power: 536kW (728hp) 10.0kn Caterpillar 3406TA 2 x 4 Stroke 6 Cy. 137 x 165 each-268kW (364bhp) Caterpillar Tractor Co-USA AuxGen: 2 x 30kW a.c
7220087 *BVYW* -	**TONG SHENG No. 11** **Tong Chou Fishery Co Ltd** - *Kaohsiung* *Chinese Taipei*	*204* 100 -	Class: (CR)	**1970 Sen Koh Shipbuilding Corp — Kaohsiung** Loa 37.62 Br ex 6.35 Dght 2.363 Lbp 29.70 Br md 6.33 Dpth 2.75 Welded, 1 dk	**(B11B2FV) Fishing Vessel** Compartments: 3 Ho, ER 4 Ha: 2 (0.9 x 1.2)2 (1.2 x 1.2)ER	**1 oil engine** driving 1 FP propeller Total Power: 405kW (551hp) 9.0kn Alpha 405-26VO 1 x 2 Stroke 5 Cy. 260 x 400 405kW (551bhp) Taiwan Machinery ManufacturingCorp.-Kaohsiung AuxGen: 1 x 64kW a.c, 1 x 40kW a.c
9180530 - -	**TONG SHUN** *ex* Moroki Maru No. 5 *-2005* - -	**752** 229 -		**1997-03 K.K. Saidaiji Zosensho — Okayama** Loa 47.52 Br ex - Dght - Lbp - Br md 11.50 Dpth 3.50 Welded, 1 dk	**(A24D2BA) Aggregates Carrier**	**1 oil engine** driving 1 FP propeller Total Power: 736kW (1,001hp) 11.0kn Niigata 6M26AGTE 1 x 4 Stroke 6 Cy. 260 x 460 736kW (1001bhp) Niigata Engineering Co Ltd-Japan
8888654 *BABU* -	**TONG SHUN** *ex* Tong Bin *-2009* **Heilongjiang Province Longhang Heavy Equipment River & Sea Transport Co Ltd** Liaoning Foreign Trade Foodstuffs Shipping Co Ltd *Harbin, Heilongjiang* *China* MMSI: 412085030	**2,938** 958 3,001	Class: CC	**1995-01 Harbin Shipyard — Harbin HL** Loa 96.23 Br ex - Dght 4.200 Lbp 89.00 Br md 15.80 Dpth 6.80 Welded, 1 dk	**(A21A2BC) Bulk Carrier** Grain: 5,170; Bale: 5,015 Compartments: 2 Ho, ER 2 Ha: ER 2 (19.1 x 10.5) Cranes: 1x10t Ice Capable	**2 oil engines** reduction geared to sc. shafts driving 2 FP propellers Total Power: 1,104kW (1,500hp) 10.5kn Chinese Std. Type 6300ZC 2 x 4 Stroke 6 Cy. 300 x 380 each-552kW (750bhp) Guangzhou Diesel Engine Factory CoLtd-China AuxGen: 3 x 120kW 400V a.c
7642443 - -	**TONG SIONG** *ex* Nego Duke *-1980* *ex* William B. *-1976* *ex* Sanpuku Maru No. 1 *-1971* - - *Indonesia*	*203* 58 -	Class: (NK) (BV)	**1966 Sanyo Zosen K.K. — Onomichi** Loa 29.49 Br ex - Dght 3.001 Lbp 26.70 Br md 7.50 Dpth 3.81 Welded, 1 dk	**(B32A2ST) Tug**	**2 oil engines** driving 2 FP propellers Total Power: 1,250kW (1,700hp) 10.0kn Nippon Hatsudoki HS6NV325 2 x 4 Stroke 6 Cy. 325 x 460 each-625kW (850bhp) Nippon Hatsudoki-Japan AuxGen: 2 x 16kW Fuel: 91.5
9259678 *BSTF* -	**TONG TAN** **CCCC Tianjin Dredging Co Ltd** - *Tianjin* *China* MMSI: 412017370	**4,482** 1,345 5,785	Class: CC	**2003-02 IHC Holland NV Dredgers — Kinderdijk** Yd No: C01233 Loa 93.71 Br ex - Dght 6.500 Lbp 84.80 Br md 19.10 Dpth 7.20 Welded, 1 dk	**(B33B2DT) Trailing Suction Hopper Dredger** Hopper: 3,500	**2 oil engines** geared to sc. shafts driving 2 CP propellers Total Power: 5,200kW (7,070hp) 13.5kn Wartsila 8L26 2 x 4 Stroke 8 Cy. 260 x 320 each-2600kW (3535bhp) Wartsila Nederland BV-Netherlands Thrusters: 1 Tunnel thruster (f)
9606651 *BSEC* -	**TONG TU** **CCCC Tianjin Dredging Co Ltd** - *Tianjin* *China* MMSI: 414056000	**20,281** 6,084 22,929	Class: CC	**2011-12 Guangzhou Wenchong Shipyard Co Ltd — Guangzhou GD** Yd No: 410 Loa 160.30 Br ex - Dght 9.500 Lbp 146.40 Br md 30.00 Dpth 15.00 Welded, 1 dk	**(B33B2DT) Trailing Suction Hopper Dredger** Liq (Gas): 19,913 Compartments: 1 Ho, ER 1 Ha: ER (71.4 x 22.2)	**2 oil engines** reduction geared to sc. shafts driving 2 CP propellers Total Power: 17,400kW (23,658hp) 15.0kn Wartsila 12V38 2 x Vee 4 Stroke 12 Cy. 380 x 475 each-8700kW (11829bhp) Wartsila Italia SpA-Italy
6813887 - -	**TONG UN 1001** **Government of The Republic of South Korea** Hanjin Shipping Co Ltd *Busan* *South Korea*	*145* - 203		**1968 Sodeno Zosensho — Nagoya** Yd No: 202 Loa - Br ex 7.32 Dght 2.185 Lbp 28.00 Br md 7.29 Dpth 2.60 Riveted\Welded, 1 dk	**(A31A2GX) General Cargo Ship**	**1 oil engine** driving 1 FP propeller Total Power: 154kW (209hp) Usuki 1 x 4 Stroke 5 Cy. 240 x 370 154kW (209bhp) Usuki Tekkosho-Usuki
6813899 - -	**TONG UN 1002** **Government of The Republic of South Korea** Hanjin Shipping Co Ltd *Busan* *South Korea*	*145* - 203		**1968 Sodeno Zosensho — Nagoya** Yd No: 203 Loa - Br ex 7.32 Dght 2.185 Lbp 28.00 Br md 7.29 Dpth 2.60 Riveted\Welded, 1 dk	**(A31A2GX) General Cargo Ship**	**1 oil engine** driving 1 FP propeller Total Power: 154kW (209hp) Usuki 1 x 4 Stroke 5 Cy. 240 x 370 154kW (209bhp) Usuki Tekkosho-Usuki
6813904 - -	**TONG UN 1003** **Government of The Republic of South Korea** Hanjin Shipping Co Ltd *Busan* *South Korea*	*145* - 203		**1968 Sodeno Zosensho — Nagoya** Yd No: 204 Loa - Br ex 7.32 Dght 2.185 Lbp 28.00 Br md 7.29 Dpth 2.60 Riveted\Welded, 1 dk	**(A31A2GX) General Cargo Ship**	**1 oil engine** driving 1 FP propeller Total Power: 154kW (209hp) Usuki 1 x 4 Stroke 5 Cy. 240 x 370 154kW (209bhp) Usuki Tekkosho-Usuki
6813928 - -	**TONG UN 1006** **Government of The Republic of South Korea** Hanjin Shipping Co Ltd *Busan* *South Korea*	*145* - 203		**1968 Sodeno Zosensho — Nagoya** Yd No: 206 Loa - Br ex 7.32 Dght 2.185 Lbp 28.00 Br md 7.29 Dpth 2.60 Riveted\Welded, 1 dk	**(A31A2GX) General Cargo Ship**	**1 oil engine** driving 1 FP propeller Total Power: 154kW (209hp) Usuki 1 x 4 Stroke 5 Cy. 240 x 370 154kW (209bhp) Usuki Tekkosho-Usuki
6821884 - -	**TONG UN 1007** **Government of The Republic of South Korea** Hanjin Shipping Co Ltd *Busan* *South Korea*	*145* - 203		**1968 Sodeno Zosensho — Nagoya** Yd No: 207 Loa - Br ex 7.32 Dght 2.185 Lbp 28.00 Br md 7.29 Dpth 2.60 Riveted\Welded, 1 dk	**(A31A2GX) General Cargo Ship**	**1 oil engine** driving 1 FP propeller Total Power: 154kW (209hp) Usuki 1 x 4 Stroke 5 Cy. 240 x 370 154kW (209bhp) Usuki Tekkosho-Usuki
6821896 - -	**TONG UN 1008** **Government of The Republic of South Korea** Hanjin Shipping Co Ltd *Busan* *South Korea*	*145* - 203		**1968 Sodeno Zosensho — Nagoya** Yd No: 208 Loa - Br ex 7.32 Dght 2.185 Lbp 28.00 Br md 7.29 Dpth 2.60 Riveted\Welded, 1 dk	**(A31A2GX) General Cargo Ship**	**1 oil engine** driving 1 FP propeller Total Power: 154kW (209hp) Usuki 1 x 4 Stroke 5 Cy. 240 x 370 154kW (209bhp) Usuki Tekkosho-Usuki
6821901 - -	**TONG UN 1009** **Government of The Republic of South Korea** Hanjin Shipping Co Ltd *Busan* *South Korea*	*145* - 203		**1968 Sodeno Zosensho — Nagoya** Yd No: 209 Loa - Br ex 7.32 Dght 2.185 Lbp 28.00 Br md 7.29 Dpth 2.60 Riveted\Welded, 1 dk	**(A31A2GX) General Cargo Ship**	**1 oil engine** driving 1 FP propeller Total Power: 154kW (209hp) Usuki 1 x 4 Stroke 5 Cy. 240 x 370 154kW (209bhp) Usuki Tekkosho-Usuki
6827773 - -	**TONG UN 1010** **Government of The Republic of South Korea** Hanjin Shipping Co Ltd *Busan* *South Korea*	*145* - 203		**1968 Sodeno Zosensho — Nagoya** Yd No: 210 Loa - Br ex 7.32 Dght 2.185 Lbp 28.00 Br md 7.29 Dpth 2.60 Riveted\Welded, 1 dk	**(A31A2GX) General Cargo Ship**	**1 oil engine** driving 1 FP propeller Total Power: 154kW (209hp) Usuki 1 x 4 Stroke 5 Cy. 240 x 370 154kW (209bhp) Usuki Tekkosho-Usuki
6829018 - -	**TONG UN 1011** **Government of The Republic of South Korea** Hanjin Shipping Co Ltd *Busan* *South Korea*	*145* - 203		**1968 Sodeno Zosensho — Nagoya** Yd No: 211 Loa - Br ex 7.32 Dght 2.185 Lbp 28.00 Br md 7.29 Dpth 2.60 Riveted\Welded, 1 dk	**(A31A2GX) General Cargo Ship**	**1 oil engine** driving 1 FP propeller Total Power: 154kW (209hp) Usuki 1 x 4 Stroke 5 Cy. 240 x 370 154kW (209bhp) Usuki Tekkosho-Usuki
6827785 - -	**TONG UN 1012** **Government of The Republic of South Korea** Hanjin Shipping Co Ltd *Busan* *South Korea*	*145* - 203		**1968 Sodeno Zosensho — Nagoya** Yd No: 212 Loa - Br ex 7.32 Dght 2.185 Lbp 28.00 Br md 7.29 Dpth 2.60 Riveted\Welded, 1 dk	**(A31A2GX) General Cargo Ship**	**1 oil engine** driving 1 FP propeller Total Power: 154kW (209hp) Usuki 1 x 4 Stroke 5 Cy. 240 x 370 154kW (209bhp) Usuki Tekkosho-Usuki
6827797 - -	**TONG UN 1013** **Government of The Republic of South Korea** Hanjin Shipping Co Ltd *Busan* *South Korea*	*145* - 203		**1968 Sodeno Zosensho — Nagoya** Yd No: 213 Loa - Br ex 7.32 Dght 2.185 Lbp 28.00 Br md 7.29 Dpth 2.60 Riveted\Welded, 1 dk	**(A31A2GX) General Cargo Ship**	**1 oil engine** driving 1 FP propeller Total Power: 154kW (209hp) Usuki 1 x 4 Stroke 5 Cy. 240 x 370 154kW (209bhp) Usuki Tekkosho-Usuki
6827802 - -	**TONG UN 1014** **Government of The Republic of South Korea** Hanjin Shipping Co Ltd *Busan* *South Korea*	*145* - 203		**1968 Sodeno Zosensho — Nagoya** Yd No: 214 Loa - Br ex 7.32 Dght 2.185 Lbp 28.00 Br md 7.29 Dpth 2.60 Riveted\Welded, 1 dk	**(A31A2GX) General Cargo Ship**	**1 oil engine** driving 1 FP propeller Total Power: 154kW (209hp) Usuki 1 x 4 Stroke 5 Cy. 240 x 370 154kW (209bhp) Usuki Tekkosho-Usuki

7930606 *D7PI* -
TONG UN No. 301
CJ Korea Express Corp
-
Busan *South Korea*
Official number: BSR-806083
276 113 400
Class: (KR)
1980-10 Donghae Shipbuilding Co Ltd — Ulsan
Yd No: 7923
Loa 43.21 Br ex 7.83 Dght 2.691
Lbp 38.00 Br md 7.80 Dpth 3.13
Welded, 1 dk
(A31A2GX) General Cargo Ship
Grain: 446; Bale: 405
Compartments: 1 Ho, ER
1 Ha: (16.9 x 3.9)ER
Derricks: 3x2t
1 oil engine driving 1 FP propeller
Total Power: 368kW (500hp) 10.0kn
Matsui
1 x 4 Stroke 6 Cy. 160 x 200 368kW (500bhp)
Matsui Iron Works Co Ltd-Japan
AuxGen: 2 x 14kW 220V a.c

7930618 *D7TF* -
TONG UN No. 302
CJ Korea Express Corp
-
Busan *South Korea*
Official number: BSR-806091
276 113 400
Class: (KR)
1980-10 Donghae Shipbuilding Co Ltd — Ulsan
Yd No: 7924
Loa 43.21 Br ex 7.83 Dght 2.694
Lbp 38.00 Br md 7.80 Dpth 3.10
Welded, 1 dk
(A31A2GX) General Cargo Ship
Grain: 446; Bale: 405
Compartments: 1 Ho, ER
1 Ha: (16.9 x 3.9)ER
1 oil engine driving 1 FP propeller
Total Power: 368kW (500hp) 10.8kn
Matsui
1 x 4 Stroke 6 Cy. 160 x 200 368kW (500bhp)
Matsui Iron Works Co Ltd-Japan
AuxGen: 2 x 14kW 220V a.c

7930644 *D7TU* -
TONG UN No. 306
CJ Korea Express Corp
-
Busan *South Korea*
Official number: BSR-806267
276 113 400
Class: (KR)
1980-12 Donghae Shipbuilding Co Ltd — Ulsan
Yd No: 7927
Loa 43.21 Br ex 7.83 Dght 2.691
Lbp 38.00 Br md 7.80 Dpth 3.10
Welded, 1 dk
(A31A2GX) General Cargo Ship
Grain: 446; Bale: 405
1 Ha: (16.9 x 3.9)ER
Derricks: 3x2t
1 oil engine driving 1 FP propeller
Total Power: 368kW (500hp) 10.0kn
Matsui MU623CGHS
1 x 4 Stroke 6 Cy. 230 x 380 368kW (500bhp)
Matsui Iron Works Co Ltd-Japan
AuxGen: 2 x 14kW 220V a.c

8510661 *D7OT* -
TONG UN No. 307
CJ Korea Express Corp
-
Busan *South Korea*
Official number: BSR-855681
159 137 327
Class: (KR)
1985-08 ShinA Shipbuilding Co Ltd — Tongyeong
Yd No: 282
Loa 37.22 Br ex 7.50 Dght 2.899
Lbp 34.02 Br md - Dpth 3.31
Welded, 1 dk
(A31A2GX) General Cargo Ship
Grain: 463; Bale: 406
Compartments: 1 Ho, ER
1 Ha: ER
1 oil engine driving 1 FP propeller
Total Power: 368kW (500hp) 10.0kn
Hanshin 6L26BGSH
1 x 4 Stroke 6 Cy. 260 x 400 368kW (500bhp)
Ssangyong Heavy Industries Co Ltd-South Korea
AuxGen: 1 x 20kW 225V a.c

9031026 *D7UM* -
TONG UN No. 501
CJ Korea Express Corp
-
Busan *South Korea*
Official number: BSR-900081
325 - 579
Class: (KR)
1990-03 Kwangyang Shipbuilding & Engineering Co Ltd — Janghang
Loa 50.90 (BB) Br ex - Dght 3.010
Lbp 45.50 Br md 9.10 Dpth 3.60
Welded, 1 dk
(A31A2GX) General Cargo Ship
Bale: 835
Compartments: 1 Ho, ER
1 Ha: ER
1 oil engine with clutches & reverse reduction geared to sc. shaft driving 1 FP propeller
Total Power: 478kW (650hp) 11.5kn
Niigata 6NSD-M
1 x 4 Stroke 6 Cy. 160 x 210 478kW (650bhp)
Ssangyong Heavy Industries Co Ltd-South Korea

9031038 *6KJP* -
TONG UN No. 502
CJ Korea Express Corp
-
Busan *South Korea*
Official number: BSR-900098
325 - 579
Class: (KR)
1990-04 Kwangyang Shipbuilding & Engineering Co Ltd — Janghang
Loa 50.90 (BB) Br ex - Dght 3.010
Lbp 45.50 Br md 9.10 Dpth 3.60
Welded, 1 dk
(A31A2GX) General Cargo Ship
Bale: 835
Compartments: 1 Ho, ER
1 Ha: ER
1 oil engine with clutches & reverse reduction geared to sc. shaft driving 1 FP propeller
Total Power: 478kW (650hp) 11.5kn
Niigata 6NSD-M
1 x 4 Stroke 6 Cy. 160 x 210 478kW (650bhp)
Ssangyong Heavy Industries Co Ltd-South Korea

6400757 *6MBC* -
TONG WHA No. 71
ex Tenyu Maru No. 28 -1971
ex Sumi Maru No. 7 -1969
Tong Wha Co Ltd
-
Busan *South Korea*
Official number: BS-A-489
221 115 -
Class: (KR)
1963 Uchida Zosen — Ise Yd No: 589
L reg 37.80 Br ex 7.45 Dght 2.947
Lbp 37.50 Br md 7.40 Dpth 3.46
Riveted\Welded, 1 dk
(B11B2FV) Fishing Vessel
1 oil engine driving 1 FP propeller
Total Power: 515kW (700hp) 11.3kn
Hanshin V6
1 x 4 Stroke 6 Cy. 320 x 450 515kW (700bhp)
Hanshin Nainenki Kogyo-Japan
AuxGen: 2 x 50kW 230V a.c

9162966 *3FLL8* -
TONG XIANG
ex Jag Riddhi -2009 ex Halo Friends -2007
ex Harmonic Halo -2006
Xin He Shipping SA
Qingdao Da Tong International Shipping Management Co Ltd
SatCom: Inmarsat C 435460713
Panama *Panama*
MMSI: 354607000
Official number: 4226811
25,977 16,173 47,240 T/cm 50.7
Class: CC (NV) (IR) (NK)
1997-12 Oshima Shipbuilding Co Ltd — Saikai NS
Yd No: 10217
Loa 185.73 (BB) Br ex 30.98 Dght 11.778
Lbp 177.00 Br md 30.95 Dpth 16.40
Welded, 1 dk
(A21A2BC) Bulk Carrier
Grain: 59,387; Bale: 58,239
Compartments: 5 Ho, ER
5 Ha: (17.1 x 15.6)4 (19.8 x 15.6)ER
Cranes: 4x30t
1 oil engine driving 1 FP propeller
Total Power: 7,392kW (10,050hp) 14.5kn
Mitsubishi 6UEC50LSII
1 x 2 Stroke 6 Cy. 500 x 1950 7392kW (10050bhp)
Mitsubishi Heavy Industries Ltd-Japan
AuxGen: 3 x 529kW 440V 60Hz a.c
Fuel: 147.0 (d.f.) 1731.0 (r.f.)

8510142 *XUCV7* -
TONG XING
ex Shunsei Maru -2002
Tong Xing Shipping Co Ltd
Yun Xing Shipping Co Ltd
Phnom Penh *Cambodia*
MMSI: 515563000
Official number: 0485051
1,416 496 1,559
Class: UB
1985-10 Kochi Jyuko (Kaisei Zosen) K.K. — Kochi
Yd No: 1853
Loa 73.03 Br ex 12.40 Dght 4.031
Lbp 68.72 Br md 12.40 Dpth 7.00
Welded, 2 dks
(A31A2GX) General Cargo Ship
Grain: 3,081; Bale: 3,025
TEU 70 C. 70/20'
Compartments: 1 Ho, ER
1 Ha: ER
1 oil engine sr geared to sc. shaft driving 1 FP propeller
Total Power: 883kW (1,201hp)
Niigata 6M28AFTE
1 x 4 Stroke 6 Cy. 280 x 480 883kW (1201bhp)
Niigata Engineering Co Ltd-Japan

9403712 - -
TONG XU
CCCC Tianjin Dredging Co Ltd
-
SatCom: Inmarsat C 441300190
Tianjin *China*
MMSI: 413017070
14,801 4,440 19,900
Class: CC
2008-05 Guangzhou Wenchong Shipyard Co Ltd — Guangzhou GD Yd No: 348
Loa 155.00 (BB) Br ex - Dght 7.500
Lbp 140.80 Br md 27.00 Dpth 10.50
Welded, 1 dk
(B33B2DT) Trailing Suction Hopper Dredger
Hopper: 13,000
Gantry cranes: 1x30t
2 oil engines reduction geared to sc. shafts driving 2 CP propellers
Total Power: 17,400kW (23,658hp) 15.5kn
Wartsila 12V38
2 x Vee 4 Stroke 12 Cy. 380 x 475 each-8700kW (11829bhp)
Wartsila Italia SpA-Italy
AuxGen: 2 x 736kW 400V a.c, 2 x 2300kW 690V a.c
Thrusters: 2 Tunnel thruster (f)

9387968 *XULZ9* -
TONG YANG
Tong Yang Shipping Co Ltd
Yantai Pingyang Shipping Co Ltd
SatCom: Inmarsat C 451442210
Phnom Penh *Cambodia*
MMSI: 514422000
Official number: 0905066
2,978 1,667 5,176
Class: UM
2005-08 Zhejiang Yueqing Qiligang Ship Industry Co Ltd — Yueqing ZJ
Loa 99.50 Br ex - Dght 5.950
Lbp 93.00 Br md 14.60 Dpth 7.40
Welded, 1 dk
(A31A2GX) General Cargo Ship
1 oil engine reduction geared to sc. shaft driving 1 FP propeller
Total Power: 1,325kW (1,801hp) 11.0kn
Guangzhou 6320ZCD
1 x 4 Stroke 6 Cy. 320 x 440 1325kW (1801bhp)
Guangzhou Diesel Engine Factory CoLtd-China

8426743 *BRYT* -
TONG YANG HAI 1 HAO
ex Tong Yang Hai No. 1 -2009
ex Lian He Tian Shan -2008
ex Gang Shun -2006 ex Ting Jiang -2004
Beijing Tongyang Shipping Co Ltd
-
Guangzhou, Guangdong *China*
MMSI: 413328000
2,871 1,124 3,881
Class: (CC)
1981 Zhonghua Shipyard — Shanghai
Loa 101.15 Br ex - Dght 6.150
Lbp 92.30 Br md 13.80 Dpth 7.70
Welded, 2 dks
(A31A2GX) General Cargo Ship
Grain: 5,386; Bale: 4,848
Compartments: 3 Ho, ER
6 Ha: (9.6 x 7.0)3 (11.1 x 7.0)2 (13.7 x 7.0)
Derricks: 6x5t
1 oil engine driving 1 FP propeller
Total Power: 1,912kW (2,600hp) 14.0kn
Hudong 6ESDZ43/82B
1 x 2 Stroke 6 Cy. 430 x 820 1912kW (2600bhp)
Hudong Shipyard-China
AuxGen: 2 x 250kW 400V 50Hz a.c

8910639 *BNCB* -
TONG YEA NO. 3
ex Kaiei Maru No. 21 -2008
-
-
Chinese Taipei
MMSI: 416124900
699 - 1,950
1989-10 Matsuura Tekko Zosen K.K. — Osakikamijima Yd No: 354
Loa - Br ex - Dght 4.652
Lbp 68.51 Br md 12.01 Dpth 5.21
Welded, 1 dk
(A13B2TP) Products Tanker
1 oil engine driving 1 FP propeller
Total Power: 1,324kW (1,800hp)
Hanshin 6LU32G
1 x 4 Stroke 6 Cy. 320 x 510 1324kW (1800bhp)
The Hanshin Diesel Works Ltd-Japan

9153719 *BNCS* -
TONG YEA NO. 5
ex Ning Hua 416 -2010 ex Woo Choon -2004
Tong Yea Enterprise Co Ltd
Fu Sheng Shipping Safety Management Consultant Co Ltd
SatCom: Inmarsat C 441644610
Chinese Taipei
MMSI: 416446000
1,982 1,076 3,328 T/cm 9.8
Class: CR (CC) (KR)
1996-08 Shinyoung Shipbuilding Industry Co Ltd — Yeosu Yd No: 187
Loa 85.30 (BB) Br ex - Dght 5.490
Lbp 78.61 Br md 14.00 Dpth 6.60
Welded, 1 dk
(A12B2TR) Chemical/Products Tanker
Liq: 3,924; Liq (Oil): 3,924
Cargo Heating Coils
Compartments: 10 Wing Ta, 2 Wing Slop Ta, ER
3 Cargo Pump (s)
1 oil engine geared to sc. shaft driving 1 FP propeller
Total Power: 1,681kW (2,285hp) 12.0kn
Alpha 8L28/32
1 x 4 Stroke 8 Cy. 280 x 320 1681kW (2285bhp)
Ssangyong Heavy Industries Co Ltd-South Korea
AuxGen: 3 x 250kW 445V a.c
Fuel: 145.0 (d.f.)

7813822 *BFHE* -
TONG YI
ex Tong Yun -2007 ex Mild Tran -1994
ex New Zealand Trader -1987 ex Atlantic -1983
Centrans Shipping Co Ltd
Tianjin Centrans Shipping Management Co Ltd
Tianjin *China*
MMSI: 412915000
6,256 3,296 6,539
Class: (CC) (GL)
1980-11 China Shipbuilding Corp — Keelung
Yd No: 102
Loa 118.01 (BB) Br ex 18.24 Dght 8.002
Lbp 106.51 Br md 18.22 Dpth 10.32
Welded, 2 dks
(A31A2GX) General Cargo Ship
Grain: 11,162; Bale: 10,700
TEU 443 C Ho 190 TEU C Dk 253 incl 50 ref C
Compartments: 2 Ho, ER
2 Ha: (25.1 x 13.1) (37.8 x 13.1)ER
Ice Capable
1 oil engine driving 1 CP propeller
Total Power: 5,432kW (7,385hp) 15.8kn
MAN 7L52/55A
1 x 4 Stroke 7 Cy. 520 x 550 5432kW (7385bhp)
Kawasaki Heavy Industries Ltd-Japan
Thrusters: 1 Tunnel thruster (f)

8712477 **TONG YING**
3EEP *ex* Cemtex Hunter *-2006*
- **Sheng Da Shipping SA**
Da Tong Shipping SA
SatCom: Inmarsat C 435378410
Panama *Panama*
MMSI: 353784000
Official number: 3199006A

36,131 Class: (CC) (AB) (CR)
21,973
66,758

1989-01 China Shipbuilding Corp (CSBC) — Kaohsiung Yd No: 358
Loa 229.75 (BB) Br ex - Dght 12.601
Lbp 217.02 Br md 32.21 Dpth 18.20
Welded, 1 dk

(A21A2BC) Bulk Carrier
Grain: 77,362
Compartments: 7 Ho, ER
7 Ha: 7 (14.4 x 14.4)ER
Cranes: 4

1 oil engine driving 1 FP propeller
Total Power: 8,649kW (11,759hp) 14.0kn
B&W 6S60MC
1 x 2 Stroke 6 Cy. 600 x 2292 8649kW (11759bhp)
Hitachi Zosen Corp-Japan
AuxGen: 3 x 520kW a.c

9421661 **TONG YING**
BDXV -
- **Tangshan Jinhang Dredging Engineering Co Ltd**
-
Tangshan, Hebei *China*
MMSI: 413331000

6,070 Class: CC
1,821
5,595

2008-01 Guangzhou Wenchong Shipyard Co Ltd — Guangzhou GD Yd No: 357
Loa 113.00 Br ex - Dght 7.100
Lbp 106.40 Br md 18.80 Dpth 8.10
Welded, 1 dk

(B33B2DT) Trailing Suction Hopper Dredger
Hopper: 3,500

2 oil engines reduction geared to sc. shafts driving 2 Propellers
Total Power: 5,000kW (6,798hp) 11.5kn
Daihatsu 8DKM-28
2 x 4 Stroke 8 Cy. 280 x 390 each-2500kW (3399bhp)
Daihatsu Diesel Manufacturing Co Lt-Japan
AuxGen: 3 x 500kW 400V a.c
Thrusters: 1 Tunnel thruster (f)

8610485 **TONG YONG NO. 803**
DTBY2 *ex* Tomiei Maru No. 88 *-2011*
- *ex* Kotoshiro Maru No. 18 *-2005*
Tong Young Industries Co Ltd
-
Busan *South Korea*
MMSI: 441713000
Official number: 1006001-6261401

662
-
-

1986-08 KK Kanasashi Zosen — Shizuoka SZ Yd No: 3112
Loa 56.52 (BB) Br ex 8.92 Dght 3.552
Lbp 49.92 Br md 8.91 Dpth 3.97
Welded, 1 dk

(B11B2FV) Fishing Vessel

1 oil engine with clutches, flexible couplings & sr reverse geared to sc. shaft driving 1 FP propeller
Total Power: 1,177kW (1,600hp)
Akasaka DM30FD
1 x 4 Stroke 6 Cy. 300 x 480 1177kW (1600bhp)
Akasaka Tekkosho KK (Akasaka DieselLtd)-Japan

7331642 **TONG YOUNG NO. 301**
6KXU *ex* Dong Baeg No. 301 *-2011*
- *ex* Tae Chang No. 78 *-1993*
ex Cipsa No. 5 *-1983*
Tong Young Industries Co Ltd
-
Busan *South Korea*
MMSI: 440793000
Official number: 9512272-6260002

447 Class: (KR)
211
429

1973-09 Uchida Zosen — Ise Yd No: 732
Loa 55.48 Br ex 9.05 Dght 3.854
Lbp 48.98 Br md 9.00 Dpth 3.97
Welded, 1 dk

(B11B2FV) Fishing Vessel
Grain: 1,118; Bale: 629; Ins: 201

1 oil engine driving 1 FP propeller
Total Power: 1,030kW (1,400hp) 12.6kn
Hanshin 6LUN28
1 x 4 Stroke 6 Cy. 280 x 480 1030kW (1400bhp)
Hanshin Nainenki Kogyo-Japan
AuxGen: 3 x 300kW 225V a.c

7831367 **TONG YOUNG NO. 303**
HLLD *ex* Dong Baeg No. 303 *-2010*
- *ex* Dong Won No. 308 *-2010*
Tong Young Industries Co Ltd
-
Busan *South Korea*
MMSI: 440683000
Official number: 9510054-6260000

497 Class: (KR)
284
520

1979-09 Daedong Shipbuilding Co Ltd — Busan Yd No: 22
Loa 55.17 Br ex - Dght 3.745
Lbp 49.00 Br md 8.60 Dpth 4.02
Welded, 1 dk

(B11B2FV) Fishing Vessel
Ins: 643
3 Ha: 2 (1.2 x 0.9) (1.7 x 1.7)

1 oil engine reverse geared to sc. shaft driving 1 FP propeller
Total Power: 993kW (1,350hp) 13.0kn
Akasaka AH28R
1 x 4 Stroke 6 Cy. 280 x 440 993kW (1350bhp)
Akasaka Tekkosho KK (Akasaka DieselLtd)-Japan
AuxGen: 2 x 200kW 225V a.c

8614352 **TONG YOUNG NO. 808**
DTBS9 *ex* Ryoei Maru No. 68 *-1986*
- **Tong Young Industries Co Ltd**
-
Busan *South Korea*
MMSI: 440652000
Official number: 0701001-6263808

303
-
663

1986-11 Sanuki Shipbuilding & Iron Works Co Ltd — Mitoyo KG Yd No: 1166
Loa 66.38 (BB) Br ex - Dght 3.950
Lbp 57.30 Br md 10.20 Dpth 4.00
Welded, 2 dks

(B11B2FV) Fishing Vessel
Ins: 1,024

1 oil engine geared to sc. shaft driving 1 FP propeller
Total Power: 1,177kW (1,600hp)
Akasaka DM33FD
1 x 4 Stroke 6 Cy. 330 x 500 1177kW (1600bhp)
Akasaka Tekkosho KK (Akasaka DieselLtd)-Japan

8718378 **TONG YU**
BIIO *ex* Eiwa Maru No. 7 *-2000*
- **Shanghai Ya Tong Ocean Shipping Co Ltd**
-
Shanghai *China*
MMSI: 412370680

757 Class: (CC)
423
1,153

1988-03 Higaki Zosen K.K. — Imabari Yd No: 353
Loa 64.57 (BB) Br ex - Dght 4.012
Lbp 60.00 Br md 10.01 Dpth 4.50
Welded, 1 dk

(A12A2TC) Chemical Tanker
Liq: 1,285
Compartments: 8 Ta, ER

1 oil engine with clutches & reduction geared to sc. shaft driving 1 FP propeller
Total Power: 1,030kW (1,400hp) 11.0kn
Hanshin LH28G
1 x 4 Stroke 6 Cy. 280 x 460 1030kW (1400bhp)
The Hanshin Diesel Works Ltd-Japan

8430445 **TONG YU No. 6**
-
-
-
SatCom: Inmarsat A 1355627

715
292
-

1987 Fong Kuo Shipbuilding Co Ltd — Kaohsiung
L reg 50.50 Br ex - Dght 3.500
Lbp - Br md 8.90 Dpth 3.85
Welded, 1 dk

(B11B2FV) Fishing Vessel

1 oil engine driving 1 FP propeller
Total Power: 883kW (1,201hp) 12.0kn
Sumiyoshi
1 x 4 Stroke 883kW (1201bhp)
Sumiyoshi Marine Diesel Co Ltd-Japan

9638197 **TONG YUAN**
BQEC -
- **CCCC Tianjin Dredging Co Ltd**
-
Tianjin *China*
MMSI: 412303160
Official number: CN20119783762

12,105 Class: CC
3,631
10,898

2012-08 CCCC BOMESC Marine Industry Co Ltd — Tianjin Yd No: ZPMC-1035
Loa 131.20 Br ex - Dght 7.000
Lbp 121.00 Br md 26.20 Dpth 9.65
Welded, 1 dk

(B33B2DT) Trailing Suction Hopper Dredger
Hopper: 8,500
Compartments: 1 Ho, ER
1 Ha: ER (54.6 x 18.0)
Ice Capable

2 oil engines reduction geared to sc. shafts driving 2 Propellers
Total Power: 13,200kW (17,946hp) 15.0kn
Daihatsu 12DKM-36
2 x Vee 4 Stroke 12 Cy. 360 x 480 each-6600kW (8973bhp)
Daihatsu Diesel Manufacturing Co Lt-Japan
AuxGen: 2 x 2500kW 690V a.c, 2 x 900kW 400V a.c

8657847 **TONG YUAN HAI**
XUGW6 *ex* Zhe Xing 3 *-2012*
- **Dalian Xinpeng Shipping Co Ltd**
Liberty Shipping Co Ltd
Phnom Penh *Cambodia*
MMSI: 514127000
Official number: 1305137

2,958 Class: IT
1,861
-

2005-07 Viva Vessel Group Co Ltd — Yueqing ZJ Yd No: WH-0409
Loa 106.20 Br ex - Dght -
Lbp - Br md 16.20 Dpth 6.80
Welded, 1 dk

(A31A2GX) General Cargo Ship

1 oil engine reduction geared to sc. shaft driving 1 Propeller
Total Power: 1,765kW (2,400hp) 11.0kn
Guangzhou 8320ZCD
1 x 4 Stroke 8 Cy. 320 x 440 1765kW (2400bhp)
Guangzhou Diesel Engine Factory CoLtd-China

9566356 **TONG YUN**
BHFC -
- **CPC Corp Taiwan**
-
Kaohsiung *Chinese Taipei*
MMSI: 416450000

28,410 Class: BV CR
9,810
40,522

2011-07 CSBC Corp, Taiwan — Keelung (Main cargo section) Yd No: 982
Loa 182.00 (BB) Br ex - Dght 11.019
Lbp 174.00 Br md 32.20 Dpth 17.30
Welded, 1 dk

(A13B2TP) Products Tanker
Double Hull (13F)
Liq: 43,968; Liq (Oil): 43,968
Compartments: 6 Wing Ta, 6 Wing Ta, ER

1 oil engine driving 1 FP propeller
Total Power: 9,960kW (13,542hp) 14.6kn
Wartsila 6RT-flex50
1 x 2 Stroke 6 Cy. 500 x 2050 9960kW (13542bhp)
Hyundai Heavy Industries Co Ltd-South Korea
AuxGen: 4 x 720kW 60Hz a.c
Fuel: 1527.0

9569580 **TONG ZHOU 6**
BLAK6 -
- **Ningbo Lionteam Shipping Co Ltd**
-
Ningbo, Zhejiang *China*
MMSI: 413434150

2,798 Class: CC
976
3,034

2010-01 Zhejiang Tenglong Shipyard — Wenling ZJ Yd No: 0701
Loa 99.80 Br ex 14.85 Dght 5.000
Lbp 93.00 Br md 14.80 Dpth 7.20
Welded, 1 dk

(A11B2TG) LPG Tanker
Liq (Gas): 3,603
2 x Gas Tank (s); 2 independent horizontal
Manifold: Bow/CM: 45.1m
Ice Capable

1 oil engine reduction geared to sc. shaft driving 1 FP propeller
Total Power: 2,574kW (3,500hp) 13.0kn
Yanmar 6N330-EN
1 x 4 Stroke 6 Cy. 330 x 440 2574kW (3500bhp)
Qingdao Zichai Boyang Diesel EngineCo Ltd-China
AuxGen: 3 x 200kW 400V a.c

9655949 **TONG ZHOU 27**
BLAT7 -
- **Ningbo Lionteam Shipping Co Ltd**
-
Ningbo, Zhejiang *China*
MMSI: 413447510

2,993 Class: CC
1,004
3,048

2013-01 Ningbo Dacheng Shengli Shipyard — Ninghai County ZJ Yd No: NDC2010-08
Loa 99.96 Br ex 14.85 Dght 5.400
Lbp 93.00 Br md 14.80 Dpth 7.20
Welded, 1 dk

(A11B2TG) LPG Tanker
Liq (Gas): 3,700
3 x Gas Tank (s); independent, ER

1 oil engine reduction geared to sc. shaft driving 1 Propeller
Total Power: 2,574kW (3,500hp) 13.2kn
Yanmar 6N330-EN
1 x 4 Stroke 6 Cy. 330 x 440 2574kW (3500bhp)
Qingdao Zichai Boyang Diesel EngineCo Ltd-China
AuxGen: 3 x 150kW 400V a.c

9655937 **TONG ZHOU 29**
BLAT9 -
- **Ningbo Lionteam Shipping Co Ltd**
-
SatCom: Inmarsat C 441301820
Ningbo, Zhejiang *China*
MMSI: 413447490

2,993 Class: CC
1,004
3,071

2012-06 Ningbo Dacheng Shengli Shipyard — Ninghai County ZJ Yd No: NDC2010-07
Loa 99.96 Br ex 14.85 Dght 5.400
Lbp 93.00 Br md 14.80 Dpth 7.20
Welded, 1 dk

(A11B2TG) LPG Tanker
Liq (Gas): 3,700
3 x Gas Tank (s); 2 independent cyl horizontal, ER
Ice Capable

1 oil engine reduction geared to sc. shaft driving 1 Propeller
Total Power: 2,574kW (3,500hp) 13.2kn
Yanmar 6N330-EN
1 x 4 Stroke 6 Cy. 330 x 440 2574kW (3500bhp)
Qingdao Zichai Boyang Diesel EngineCo Ltd-China
AuxGen: 3 x 150kW 400V a.c

9051466 **TONGA**
-
- **Government of The Democratic Republic of Congo (Regie des Voies Maritime de Congo)**
-
Boma *Congo (Democratic Republic)*

300
-
500

1992-12 Stocznia 'Odra' — Szczecin (Hull)
1992-12 B.V. Scheepswerf Damen — Gorinchem Yd No: 6735
Loa - Br ex - Dght -
Lbp - Br md - Dpth -
Welded, 1 dk

(B34A2SH) Hopper, Motor

2 oil engines reduction geared to sc. shafts driving 2 FP propellers
Total Power: 446kW (606hp)
Caterpillar 3306TA
2 x 4 Stroke 6 Cy. 121 x 152 each-223kW (303bhp)
Caterpillar Inc-USA

9605786 **TONGALA**
9HA2776 -
- **Wilhelmsen Lines Shipowning Malta Ltd**
-
Valletta *Malta*
MMSI: 215654000
Official number: 9605786

61,106 Class: NV
23,696
22,585
T/cm
52.5

2012-09 Mitsubishi Heavy Industries Ltd. — Nagasaki Yd No: 2284
Loa 199.99 (BB) Br ex - Dght 14.450
Lbp 192.00 Br md 32.26 Dpth 36.02
Welded, 12 dks including 4 liftable dks

(A35B2RV) Vehicles Carrier
Side door/ramp (s)
Len: 25.00 Wid: 6.50 Swl: 35
Quarter stern door/ramp (s. a.)
Len: 38.00 Wid: 7.00 Swl: 237
Cars: 6,459

1 oil engine driving 1 FP propeller
Total Power: 14,315kW (19,463hp) 19.5kn
Mitsubishi 7UEC60LSII
1 x 2 Stroke 7 Cy. 600 x 2300 14315kW (19463bhp)
Mitsubishi Heavy Industries Ltd-Japan
AuxGen: 3 x a.c
Thrusters: 1 Tunnel thruster (f)

IMO / Call sign	Name / Owner	Tonnage	Class	Built / Dimensions	Type	Machinery
9371402 *D5CO5* -	**TONGAN** *ex* Wec Vermeer *-2009* *ex* Tongan *-2008* **ms 'Tongan' Schiffahrtsgesellschaft mbH & Co KG** Amazsa Hamburg GmbH *Monrovia* *Liberia* MMSI: 636092436 Official number: 92436	**10,965** 4,714 12,612 T/cm 28.4	Class: GL	**2007-10 Naval Gijon S.A. (NAGISA) — Gijon** Yd No: 701 Loa 140.42 (BB) Br ex - Dght 8.700 Lbp 131.00 Br md 22.80 Dpth 11.90 Welded, 1 dk	**(A33A2CC) Container Ship (Fully Cellular)** Double Bottom Entire Compartment Length TEU 925 C Ho 294 TEU C Dk 631 TEU incL 200 ref C. Compartments: 6 Cell Ho, ER 6 Ha: 5 (12.7 x 20.1)ER (12.7 x 12.7) Ice Capable	**1 oil engine** reduction geard to sc. shaft driving 1 CP propeller Total Power: 9,603kW (13,056hp) 18.3kn MAN-B&W 8L48/60B 1 x 4 Stroke 8 Cy. 480 x 600 9603kW (13056bhp) MAN B&W Diesel AG-Augsburg AuxGen: 1 x 1000kW 440V 60Hz a.c, 2 x 750kW 440V 60Hz a.c, 1 x 500kW 440V 60Hz a.c Thrusters: 1 Tunnel thruster (f) Fuel: 65.0 (d.f.) 950.0 (r.f.)
7398640 *5ROK* -	**TONGATSARA** - **Total Ocean Indien** - *Mahajanga* *Madagascar* MMSI: 647661201	*100* 39 183	Class: (BV)	**1973 Direction des Constr. et Armes Navales (DCAN) — Antsiranana** Loa - Br ex 5.80 Dght 2.134 Lbp 23.78 Br md - Dpth - Welded, 1 dk	**(A13B2TU) Tanker (unspecified)**	**1 oil engine** driving 1 FP propeller Total Power: 104kW (141hp) 6.0kn Baudouin 1 x 4 Stroke 4 Cy. 150 x 150 104kW (141bhp) Societe des Moteurs Baudouin SA-France
9669017 *9VCF9* -	**TONGBAO ODESSEY** - **Tongbao (Singapore) Shipping Pte Ltd** - *Singapore* *Singapore* MMSI: 563762000 Official number: 398117	**1,743** 522 1,200	Class: BV	**2014-01 Nanjing East Star Shipbuilding Co Ltd — Nanjing JS** Yd No: ESS100105 Loa 50.95 Br ex - Dght 5.500 Lbp 48.30 Br md 15.00 Dpth 7.00 Welded, 1 dk	**(B32A2ST) Tug**	**2 oil engines** reduction geared to sc. shafts driving 2 Propellers Yanmar 2 x 4 Stroke 6 Cy. 260 x 385 Yanmar Diesel Engine Co Ltd-Japan
9570967 *9V8347* -	**TONGBAO WORLD** *ex* Tongbao Earth *-2010* **Tongbao (Singapore) Shipping Pte Ltd** - SatCom: Inmarsat C 456408510 *Singapore* *Singapore* MMSI: 564085000 Official number: 395638	**3,096** 928 4,289	Class: BV (AB)	**2010-07 ES Offshore & Marine Eng (Thailand) Co Ltd — Prachuap Khiri Khan** Yd No: P901 Loa 85.60 (BB) Br ex - Dght 4.200 Lbp 79.30 Br md 28.50 Dpth 6.00 Welded, 1 dk	**(A31C2GD) Deck Cargo Ship**	**2 oil engines** reduction geared to sc. shafts driving 2 Propellers Total Power: 1,912kW (2,600hp) 10.0kn Yanmar 6N21A-EV 2 x 4 Stroke 6 Cy. 210 x 290 each-956kW (1300bhp) Yanmar Diesel Engine Co Ltd-Japan AuxGen: 2 x 265kW 380V 50Hz a.c Fuel: 750.0 (r.f.)
8017566 - -	**TONGDA** *ex* Asakaze No. 3 *-2010* *ex* Asaka Maru No. 10 *-1986* - - -	*1,932* 1,154 933		**1981-04 The Hakodate Dock Co Ltd — Hakodate HK** Yd No: 708 Loa 87.36 Br ex 15.22 Dght 3.764 Lbp 76.26 Br md 15.02 Dpth 4.81 Welded, 1 dk	**(A36A2PR) Passenger/Ro-Ro Ship (Vehicles)**	**2 oil engines** geared to sc. shafts driving 2 FP propellers Total Power: 4,414kW (6,002hp) Daihatsu 8DSM-32 2 x 4 Stroke 8 Cy. 320 x 380 each-2207kW (3001bhp) Daihatsu Diesel Manufacturing Co Lt-Japan
9166302 *BQAT* -	**TONGHAI** - **Tonghai Maritime Inc** COSCO Bulk Carrier Co Ltd (COSCO BULK) SatCom: Inmarsat C 441242610 *Tianjin* *China* MMSI: 413785000	**27,176** 15,533 47,980 T/cm 52.2	Class: CC (AB)	**1999-01 Kawasaki Heavy Industries Ltd — Sakaide KG** (Hull) Yd No: 1484 **1999-01 Nantong COSCO KHI Ship Engineering Co Ltd (NACKS) — Nantong JS** Loa 187.50 (BB) Br ex - Dght 11.771 Lbp 179.00 Br md 31.00 Dpth 16.75 Welded, 1 dk	**(A21A2BC) Bulk Carrier** Double Bottom Entire Compartment Length Grain: 59,444; Bale: 58,260 Compartments: 5 Ho, ER 5 Ha: (17.0 x 16.0)4 (20.3 x 16.0)ER Cranes: 4x25t	**1 oil engine** driving 1 FP propeller Total Power: 6,877kW (9,350hp) 14.5kn B&W 6S50MC 1 x 2 Stroke 6 Cy. 500 x 1910 6877kW (9350bhp) Kawasaki Heavy Industries Ltd-Japan AuxGen: 3 x 400kW 450V 60Hz a.c Fuel: 93.0 (d.f.) (Heating Coils) 1614.0 (r.f.) 30.0pd
7907116 *PNAY* -	**TONGHO 8** *ex* ABB *-2011* *ex* Tong Ho *-2009* *ex* Ta Ho *-2003* **PT Pelayaran Andalas Bahtera Baruna** - *Jakarta* *Indonesia* MMSI: 525015555	*5,890* 1,912 8,210	Class: KI (CR) (AB)	**1980-08 China Shipbuilding Corp — Keelung** Yd No: 170 Loa 119.77 Br ex 18.55 Dght 7.130 Lbp 112.00 Br md 18.51 Dpth 9.53 Welded, 1 dk	**(A24A2BT) Cement Carrier** Grain: 7,047 Compartments: 4 Ho, ER	**1 oil engine** driving 1 FP propeller Total Power: 3,236kW (4,400hp) 13.3kn B&W 5L45GFCA 1 x 2 Stroke 5 Cy. 450 x 1200 3236kW (4400bhp) Mitsui Engineering & Shipbuilding CLtd-Japan AuxGen: 3 x 280kW 450V 60Hz a.c Fuel: 395.0 (r.f.)
7036125 - -	**TONGKOL** *ex* Ferry Brug *-1980* **Government of The Republic of Indonesia (Direktorat Jenderal Perhubungan Darat - Ministry of Land Communications)** PT ASDP Indonesia Ferry (Persero) - Angkutan Sungai Danau & Penyeberangan *Jakarta* *Indonesia*	*259* 122 110	Class: KI	**1970-07 Matsuura Tekko Zosen K.K. — Osakikamijima** Yd No: 206 Loa 40.90 Br ex 8.92 Dght 2.172 Lbp 36.00 Br md 8.89 Dpth 3.00 Welded, 1 dk	**(A37B2PS) Passenger Ship** Passengers: unberthed: 350 Bow ramp (centre) Stern ramp (centre)	**2 oil engines** geared to sc. shafts driving 2 Propellers fwd and 2 aft Total Power: 442kW (600hp) Yanmar 6M-T 2 x 4 Stroke 6 Cy. 200 x 240 each-221kW (300bhp) Yanmar Diesel Engine Co Ltd-Japan
8965892 *CB3490* -	**TONGOY** - **Sociedad Pesquera Coloso SA** - *Valparaiso* *Chile* MMSI: 725000100 Official number: 2122	*194* - -		**1971 Astilleros Marco Chilena Ltda. — Iquique** L reg 30.05 Br ex - Lbp - Br md 7.85 Dpth 3.68 Welded, 1 dk	**(B11B2FV) Fishing Vessel**	**1 oil engine** driving 1 FP propeller
8741301 - -	**TONGYEONG 9 HO** - **Tongyeong Tug Co Ltd** - *Tongyeong* *South Korea* Official number: CMR-088206	**251** - 124	Class: KR	**2008-10 Yeunsoo Shipbuilding Co Ltd — Janghang** Yd No: 132 Loa 37.40 Br ex - Dght 3.450 Lbp 32.00 Br md 9.80 Dpth 4.40 Welded, 1 dk	**(B32A2ST) Tug**	**2 oil engines** reduction geared to sc. shafts driving 2 Propellers Total Power: 3,308kW (4,498hp) 13.0kn Niigata 6L28HX 2 x 4 Stroke 6 Cy. 280 x 370 each-1654kW (2249bhp) Niigata Engineering Co Ltd-Japan
8741313 - -	**TONGYEONG 11 HO** - **Tongyeong Tug Co Ltd** - *Tongyeong* *South Korea* Official number: CMR-084449	**251** - 124	Class: KR	**2008-12 Yeunsoo Shipbuilding Co Ltd — Janghang** Yd No: 133 Loa 37.40 Br ex - Dght 3.450 Lbp 32.00 Br md 9.80 Dpth 4.40 Welded, 1 dk	**(B32A2ST) Tug**	**2 oil engines** reduction geared to sc. shafts driving 2 Propellers Total Power: 3,308kW (4,498hp) 13.1kn Niigata 6L28HX 2 x 4 Stroke 6 Cy. 280 x 370 each-1654kW (2249bhp) Niigata Engineering Co Ltd-Japan
9639323 - -	**TONGYEONG NO. 1** - **Tongyeong Tug Co Ltd** - *Tongyeong* *South Korea* MMSI: 440148720 Official number: CMR-114424	**287** - 240	Class: KR	**2011-08 Geumgang Shipbuilding Co Ltd — Janghang** Yd No: GGS-07 Loa 38.00 Br ex - Dght 3.627 Lbp 32.50 Br md 10.00 Dpth 4.50 Welded, 1 dk	**(B32A2ST) Tug**	**2 oil engines** reduction geared to sc. shafts driving 2 Propellers Total Power: 3,840kW (5,220hp) 14.7kn Yanmar 6EY26 2 x 4 Stroke 6 Cy. 260 x 385 each-1920kW (2610bhp) Yanmar Diesel Engine Co Ltd-Japan
8425359 *DUA2434* -	**TONI DOMINIQUE** *ex* Nassa *-2000* **Sea Bass Carriers Inc** - *Batangas* *Philippines* Official number: 04-0000846	**490** 305 700		**1974 Philippine Iron Construction & Marine Works Inc. — Jasaan** Converted From: General Cargo Ship-1981 Lengthened Loa - Br ex 8.55 Dght - Lbp 57.55 Br md 8.40 Dpth 3.82 Welded, 1 dk	**(A12A2TC) Chemical Tanker** Liq: 613 Compartments: 9 Ta, ER	**2 oil engines** with clutches & sr reverse geared to sc. shafts driving 2 FP propellers Total Power: 398kW (542hp) 8.0kn Cummins KT-38-M 2 x Vee 4 Stroke 12 Cy. 159 x 159 each-199kW (271bhp) Cummins Engine Co Inc-USA AuxGen: 1 x 20kW 220V a.c, 1 x 16kW 220V a.c
8945543 *DUA2479* -	**TONI DOMINIQUE II** *ex* Southern Queen *-2000* **Sea Bass Carriers Inc** - *Batangas* *Philippines* Official number: 00-0000096	*478* 294 -		**1976 at Manila** L reg 48.76 Br ex - Dght - Lbp - Br md 10.51 Dpth - Welded, 1 dk	**(A13B2TU) Tanker (unspecified)**	**1 oil engine** driving 1 FP propeller Total Power: 515kW (700hp) Cummins 1 x 4 Stroke 515kW (700bhp) Cummins Engine Co Inc-USA
9280031 *CUPT7* PM-1244-C	**TONI PIRES** - **Antonio Pires Coelho** - *Portimao* *Portugal*	*255* - -		**2003-07 Navalfoz - Com. E Desenvolvimento de Proj. Navais Lda. — Figueira da Foz** Yd No: 43 Loa 28.70 Br ex - Dght - Lbp 24.06 Br md 7.60 Dpth 3.60 Welded, 1 dk	**(B11A2FS) Stern Trawler**	**1 oil engine** geared to sc. shaft driving 1 FP propeller Total Power: 368kW (500hp) GUASCOR F360-SP 1 x Vee 4 Stroke 12 Cy. 152 x 165 368kW (500bhp) Gutierrez Ascunce Corp (GUASCOR)-Spain
9622916 *D5AZ8* -	**TONIC SEA** - **Ost Two Shipping Co Ltd** NSC Shipping GmbH & Cie KG *Monrovia* *Liberia* MMSI: 636015479 Official number: 15479	**51,253** 31,173 93,005 T/cm 80.8	Class: GL (AB)	**2012-02 Taizhou CATIC Shipbuilding Heavy Industry Ltd — Taizhou JS** Yd No: TK0207 Loa 229.20 (BB) Br ex - Dght 14.900 Lbp 222.00 Br md 38.00 Dpth 20.70 Welded, 1 dk	**(A21A2BC) Bulk Carrier** Grain: 110,330 Compartments: 7 Ho, ER 7 Ha: 5 (17.9 x 17.0)ER 2 (15.3 x 14.6)	**1 oil engine** driving 1 FP propeller Total Power: 13,560kW (18,436hp) 15.5kn MAN-B&W 6S60MC-C 1 x 2 Stroke 6 Cy. 600 x 2400 13560kW (18436bhp) Hyundai Heavy Industries Co Ltd-South Korea AuxGen: 3 x 700kW a.c Fuel: 233.0 (d.f.) 3567.0 (r.f.) 48.0pd

IMO / Call sign	Name / Owner / Port of registry	Tonnage	Class	Build / Dimensions	Type / Capacity	Machinery
7505358 *YJTL3* -	**TONIJN** *ex* Schillig *-2013* **Tonijn Shipping Ltd** Van Laar Maritime BV *Port Vila* *Vanuatu* MMSI: 577179000 Official number: 2242	*183* 37 205	Class: GL	**1976-05 Julius Diedrich Schiffswerft GmbH & Co KG — Moormerland** Yd No: 131 Loa 34.29 Br ex 7.04 Dght 1.601 Lbp 30.03 Br md 7.01 Dpth 3.03 Welded, 1 dk	**(B34Q2QB) Buoy Tender** Cranes: 1x30t Ice Capable	**2 oil engines** geared to sc. shafts driving 2 FP propellers Total Power: 442kW (600hp) 10.5kn Deutz SF12M716 2 x Vee 4 Stroke 12 Cy. 120 x 160 each-221kW (300bhp) Kloeckner Humboldt Deutz AG-West Germany
8821565 *6NKJ* -	**TONINA No. 3** *ex* Tonina III *-1995* **Dongwon Industries Co Ltd** - *Busan* *South Korea* MMSI: 440648000 Official number: 9411015-6210007	**408** 256 450	Class: KR	**1989-08 Dae Sun Shipbuilding & Engineering Co Ltd — Busan** Yd No: 353 Loa 56.07 (BB) Br ex 8.82 Dght 3.733 Lbp 49.60 Br md 8.80 Dpth 3.84 Welded	**(B11B2FV) Fishing Vessel** Grain: 662; Bale: 555	**1 oil engine** with flexible couplings & reduction geared to sc. shaft driving 1 FP propeller Total Power: 883kW (1,201hp) 11.4kn Niigata 6M28AFTE 1 x 4 Stroke 6 Cy. 280 x 480 883kW (1201bhp) Ssangyong Heavy Industries Co Ltd-South Korea AuxGen: 2 x 304kW 225V a.c
9001423 *6NKA* -	**TONINA No. 5** *ex* Tonina V *-1994* **Dongwon Industries Co Ltd** - SatCom: Inmarsat A 1660731 *Busan* *South Korea* MMSI: 440645000 Official number: 9409001-6210008	**408** 256 455	Class: KR	**1989-08 Dae Sun Shipbuilding & Engineering Co Ltd — Busan** Yd No: 354 Loa 56.07 (BB) Br ex 8.82 Dght 3.733 Lbp 49.60 Br md 8.80 Dpth 3.84 Welded	**(B11B2FV) Fishing Vessel** Grain: 662; Bale: 555	**1 oil engine** with flexible couplings & reduction geared to sc. shaft driving 1 FP propeller Total Power: 883kW (1,201hp) Niigata 6M28AFTE 1 x 4 Stroke 6 Cy. 280 x 480 883kW (1201bhp) Ssangyong Heavy Industries Co Ltd-South Korea
9448152 *A8RE5* -	**TONNA** *ex* Fpmc P Fortune *-2013* **FPMC Fortune Marine Corp** Shell International Trading & Shipping Co Ltd (STASCO) *Monrovia* *Liberia* MMSI: 636014083 Official number: 14083	**42,340** 21,747 74,862 T/cm 68.0	Class: AB	**2009-09 STX Offshore & Shipbuilding Co Ltd — Changwon (Jinhae Shipyard)** Yd No: 4003 Loa 228.00 (BB) Br ex 32.26 Dght 14.300 Lbp 219.00 Br md 32.24 Dpth 20.65 Welded, 1 dk	**(A13B2TP) Products Tanker** Double Hull (13F) Liq: 80,392; Liq (Oil): 81,828 Compartments: 12 Wing Ta, 2 Wing Slop Ta, ER 3 Cargo Pump (s): 3x2000m³/hr Manifold: Bow/CM: 113.1m	**1 oil engine** driving 1 FP propeller Total Power: 11,060kW (15,037hp) 15.0kn MAN-B&W 7S50MC-C 1 x 2 Stroke 7 Cy. 500 x 2000 11060kW (15037bhp) STX Engine Co Ltd-South Korea AuxGen: 3 x 900kW a.c Fuel: 152.0 (d.f.) 2520.0 (r.f.)
7414690 *J8PX7* -	**TONNANT** *ex* Samand *-2004* **Coloured Fin Ltd (CFL)** - *Kingstown* *St Vincent & The Grenadines* Official number: 400663	**295** 88 -	Class: LR ✠ **100A1** SS 06/2006 tug ✠ **LMC** **UMS** Eq.Ltr: H; Cable: U2	**1976-01 Beliard-Murdoch S.A. — Oostende** Yd No: 225 Loa 29.98 Br ex 10.16 Dght 4.261 Lbp 27.11 Br md 10.01 Dpth 4.81 Welded, 1 dk	**(B32A2ST) Tug**	**2 oil engines** reverse reduction geared to sc. shafts driving 2 FP propellers Total Power: 3,162kW (4,300hp) EMD (Electro-Motive) 12-645-E5 2 x Vee 2 Stroke 12 Cy. 230 x 254 each-1581kW (2150bhp) General Motors Corp.Electro-Motive Div.-La Grange AuxGen: 2 x 76kW 440V 60Hz a.c, 1 x 32kW 440V 60Hz a.c Fuel: 159.5 (d.f.)
8813013 *OUIH* -	**TONNE** *ex* Tonne II *-1991* **Government of The Kingdom of Denmark (Kystinspektoratet)** - *Thorsminde* *Denmark* MMSI: 219798000 Official number: D3230	**473** 141 758	Class: BV	**1989-06 Esbjerg Oilfield Services A/S — Esbjerg** Yd No: 58 Loa 45.00 Br ex - Dght 3.201 Lbp 44.00 Br md 10.00 Dpth 3.50 Welded, 1 dk	**(B33B2DT) Trailing Suction Hopper Dredger** Hopper: 390	**2 oil engines** driving 2 FP propellers Total Power: 412kW (560hp) 8.5kn Deutz BF10L513 2 x Vee 4 Stroke 10 Cy. 125 x 130 each-206kW (280bhp) Kloeckner Humboldt Deutz AG-West Germany AuxGen: 2 x 28kW 380V a.c
5262263 *LLKH* -	**TONNY** *ex* Andrea *-2007* *ex* Senior *-2001* *ex* Roaldsen Senior *-1999* *ex* Ole Torressen *-1990* *ex* Suderoy X *-1962* *ex* Krebs *-1948* **Tonny AS** - *Aakrehamn* *Norway* MMSI: 258043000	**499** 149 -	Class: (NV)	**1942-12 AS Moss Vaerft & Dokk — Moss** Yd No: 104 Converted From: Fishing Vessel-2000 Converted From: Whale-catcher-1962 Lengthened & Deepened-1968 Loa 47.45 Br ex 7.73 Dght - Lbp 43.97 Br md 7.68 Dpth 5.50 Welded, 1 dk	**(A14A2LO) Water Tanker**	**1 oil engine** driving 1 FP propeller Total Power: 515kW (700hp) 11.0kn Wichmann 7ACA 1 x 2 Stroke 7 Cy. 280 x 420 515kW (700bhp) (new engine 1962) Wichmann Motorfabrikk AS-Norway Fuel: 163.5 (d.f.)
9551492 *HO7950* -	**TONOSI** - **Panama Canal Authority** - *Panama* *Panama* MMSI: 373591000 Official number: 019922326HK	**359** 107 136	Class: (LR) ✠ Classed LR until 15/3/13	**2011-12 Hin Lee (Zhuhai) Shipyard Co Ltd — Zhuhai GD** (Hull) Yd No: 215 **2011-12 Cheoy Lee Shipyards Ltd — Hong Kong** Yd No: 4999 Loa 27.40 Br ex - Dght 3.700 Lbp 25.20 Br md 12.20 Dpth 5.05 Welded, 1 dk	**(B32A2ST) Tug**	**2 oil engines** gearing integral to driving 2 Z propellers Total Power: 3,924kW (5,336hp) 12.0kn GE Marine 12V228 2 x Vee 4 Stroke 12 Cy. 229 x 267 each-1962kW (2668bhp) General Electric Co.-Lynn, Ma AuxGen: 2 x 103kW 208V 60Hz a.c Fuel: 110.0 (d.f.)
8961092 - -	**TONSAMUT 11** - **Boo Wanawivit** - *Bangkok* *Thailand* Official number: 432200062	**127** 86 -		**2000-12 Bunsith Khamprasert — Samut Sakhon** Loa 22.00 Br ex - Dght - Lbp - Br md 6.60 Dpth 3.50 Welded, 1 dk	**(A34A2GR) Refrigerated Cargo Ship**	**1 oil engine** driving 1 FP propeller Total Power: 373kW (507hp) Cummins 1 x 4 Stroke 373kW (507bhp) Cummins Engine Co Inc-USA
9515383 *9HA2066* -	**TONSBERG** - **Wilhelmsen Lines Shipowning Malta Ltd** Wilhelmsen Ship Management (Norway) AS SatCom: Inmarsat C 424990410 *Valletta* *Malta* MMSI: 249904000 Official number: 9515383	**75,251** 27,215 41,820	Class: NV	**2011-03 Mitsubishi Heavy Industries Ltd. — Nagasaki** Yd No: 2262 Loa 265.00 (BB) Br ex 32.27 Dght 12.300 Lbp 250.00 Br md 32.26 Dpth 33.22 Welded, 9 dks incl. 6 hoistable dks.	**(A35B2RV) Vehicles Carrier** Angled stern door/ramp (s. a.) Len: 44.30 Wid: 12.50 Swl: 505 Cars: 5,990 Bale: 138,000	**1 oil engine** driving 1 FP propeller Total Power: 20,100kW (27,328hp) 20.3kn MAN-B&W 7L70ME-C8 1 x 2 Stroke 7 Cy. 700 x 2360 20100kW (27328bhp) Kawasaki Heavy Industries Ltd-Japan AuxGen: 3 x 2360kW a.c, 1 x 1100kW a.c Thrusters: 1 Tunnel thruster (f); 1 Tunnel thruster (a) Fuel: 637.0 (d.f.) 5390.0 (r.f.)
9207819 *LLAD* T-2-H	**TONSNES** - **Nergard Havfiske AS** - *Tromso* *Norway* MMSI: 259666000	**1,194** 420 753	Class: NV	**2000-01 SC Santierul Naval SA Braila — Braila** (Hull) Yd No: 1397 **2000-01 Solstrand AS — Tomrefjord** Yd No: 68 Loa 51.20 (BB) Br ex - Dght 7.382 Lbp 43.20 Br md 12.60 Dpth 7.70 Welded, 1 dk	**(B11A2FG) Factory Stern Trawler** Ins: 480 Ice Capable	**1 oil engine** reduction geared to sc. shaft driving 1 CP propeller Total Power: 2,880kW (3,916hp) 14.0kn Wartsila 6L32 1 x 4 Stroke 6 Cy. 320 x 400 2880kW (3916bhp) Wartsila NSD Finland Oy-Finland AuxGen: 1 x 1130kW 440V 60Hz a.c Thrusters: 1 Thwart. CP thruster (f) Fuel: 320.0 (d.f.)
6912516 - -	**TONTINI PESCA CUARTO** - **Pesquera Roberto Bruno**	**1,082** 480 1,219	Class: (RI)	**1970-01 Cant. Nav. Giuliano — Trieste** Yd No: 83 Loa 74.99 Br ex 12.53 Dght 5.004 Lbp 65.99 Br md 12.50 Dpth 8.21 Welded, 2 dks	**(B11A2FS) Stern Trawler** Compartments: 2 Ho, ER	**1 oil engine** driving 1 FP propeller Total Power: 2,133kW (2,900hp) Werkspoor 1 x 4 Stroke 6 Cy. 450 x 700 2133kW (2900bhp) Stork Werkspoor Diesel BV-Netherlands
7046651 - -	**TONY** *ex* Tokuju Maru No. 6 *-1981* **AFC Fishing Corp** - *Manila* *Philippines*	*111* 35 62		**1970 Usuki Iron Works Co Ltd — Usuki OT** Yd No: 776 Loa 34.65 Br ex 6.81 Dght 2.363 Lbp 29.34 Br md 6.79 Dpth 2.80 Welded, 1 dk	**(B11B2FV) Fishing Vessel**	**1 oil engine** driving 1 FP propeller Total Power: 662kW (900hp) Niigata 6MG25BX 1 x 4 Stroke 6 Cy. 250 x 320 662kW (900bhp) Niigata Engineering Co Ltd-Japan
9432036 *A8UI4* -	**TONY** - **Fidelity Credit Ltd** Dynacom Tankers Management Ltd SatCom: Inmarsat C 463708473 *Monrovia* *Liberia* MMSI: 636014499 Official number: 14499	**85,496** 47,238 149,995 T/cm 122.3	Class: BV	**2010-09 New Times Shipbuilding Co Ltd — Jingjiang JS** Yd No: 0316309 Loa 274.20 (BB) Br ex 50.04 Dght 16.000 Lbp 264.00 Br md 50.00 Dpth 23.22 Welded, 1 dk	**(A13A2TV) Crude Oil Tanker** Double Hull (13F) Liq: 173,900; Liq (Oil): 173,900 Cargo Heating Coils Compartments: 12 Wing Ta, 2 Wing Slop Ta, ER 3 Cargo Pump (s): 3x4000m³/hr Manifold: Bow/CM: 139m	**1 oil engine** driving 1 FP propeller Total Power: 18,660kW (25,370hp) 15.3kn MAN-B&W 6S70MC-C 1 x 2 Stroke 6 Cy. 700 x 2800 18660kW (25370bhp) Hyundai Heavy Industries Co Ltd-South Korea AuxGen: 3 x 950kW 60Hz a.c Fuel: 210.0 (d.f.) 3965.0 (r.f.)
9022441 *YYV2670* -	**TONY B** - **-** - *Maracaibo* *Venezuela* Official number: AJZL-26211	*101* 30 -		**1966-01 Bender Welding & Machine Co Inc — Mobile AL** Yd No: 124 L reg 32.00 Br ex - Dght 2.220 Lbp - Br md 7.31 Dpth 3.71 Welded, 1 dk	**(B11B2FV) Fishing Vessel**	**1 oil engine** driving 1 Propeller

IMO / Call sign	Name / Owner / Registry	Tonnage	Class	Build / Dimensions	Type	Machinery
8968820 *H03472* -	**TONY I** *ex* Tony *ex* Maria I *ex* Escort Provider *-2002* *ex* John F. Wallace *-1997* **Nekavish Overseas Inc** World Shipping Management Corp SA *Panama* *Panama* Official number: 31886PEXT	*230* 126 -		**1960-10 Diamond Manufacturing Co. Ltd. — Savannah, Ga** Yd No: M-201 L reg 32.16 Br ex - Dght - Lbp - Br md 8.78 Dpth 4.34 Welded, 1 dk	**(B32A2ST) Tug**	**1 oil engine** driving 1 FP propeller Total Power: 1,765kW (2,400hp) 15.0kn Fairbanks, Morse 12-38D8-1/8 1 x 2 Stroke 12 Cy. 207 x 254 1765kW (2400bhp) Fairbanks Morse (Canada) Ltd-Canada
7227786 *VCMZ* -	**TONY MACKAY** *ex* Point Carroll *-2001* **McKeil Work Boats Ltd** McKeil Marine Ltd *Halifax, NS* *Canada* MMSI: 316003340 Official number: 358840	**373** 111 -	Class: (LR) ✠ Classed LR until 26/1/12	**1973-03 R. Dunston (Hessle) Ltd. — Hessle** Yd No: S889 Loa 39.40 Br ex 9.61 Dght 3.877 Lbp 35.51 Br md 9.16 Dpth 4.42 Welded, 1 dk	**(B32A2ST) Tug**	**1 oil engine** sr geared to sc. shaft driving 1 CP propeller Total Power: 1,942kW (2,640hp) English Electric 12RK3CM 1 x Vee 4 Stroke 12 Cy. 254 x 305 1942kW (2640bhp) Ruston Paxman Diesels Ltd.-Colchester AuxGen: 3 x 84kW 440V 60Hz a.c
7733333 *WYB6025* -	**TONY & RAB** - **Gary Bruce** - *Houma, LA* *United States of America* Official number: 586485	*127* 87 -		**1977 Desco Marine — Saint Augustine, Fl** Yd No: 226-F L reg 20.97 Br ex - Dght - Lbp - Br md 6.74 Dpth 3.79 Bonded, 1 dk	**(B11B2FV) Fishing Vessel** Hull Material: Reinforced Plastic	**1 oil engine** driving 1 FP propeller Total Power: 268kW (364hp) Caterpillar 1 x 4 Stroke 268kW (364bhp) Caterpillar Tractor Co-USA
9242912 *WDC8130* -	**TONY TWO** *ex* Miss Christine III *-2007* **f/v Tony One Inc** - *Hampton, VA* *United States of America* MMSI: 367082090 Official number: 1098003	**143** 42 -		**2000** Yd No: 174 Loa 23.95 Br ex - Dght - Lbp - Br md 7.31 Dpth 3.84 Welded, 1 dk	**(B11B2FV) Fishing Vessel**	**1 oil engine** driving 1 FP propeller
8212520 - -	**TONYA-J** - **Lady Kimberley Inc** - *Mobile, AL* *United States of America*	*150* - -		**1982 Quality Marine, Inc. — Bayou La Batre, Al** Yd No: 157 Loa 27.82 Br ex 6.71 Dght - Lbp - Br md - Dpth 3.36 Welded, 1 dk	**(B11B2FV) Fishing Vessel**	**1 oil engine** driving 1 FP propeller Total Power: 382kW (519hp) Caterpillar 3412TA 1 x Vee 4 Stroke 12 Cy. 137 x 152 382kW (519bhp) Caterpillar Tractor Co-USA
7940405 - -	**TONYA JANE** *ex* Miss Han *-2007* **North Coast Fish & Meats** - *Montego Bay* *Jamaica* Official number: JMF09005	*126* 85 -		**1978 Master Marine, Inc. — Bayou La Batre, Al** Yd No: 207 L reg 22.38 Br ex 6.74 Dght - Lbp - Br md - Dpth 3.18 Welded, 1 dk	**(B11B2FV) Fishing Vessel**	**1 oil engine** driving 1 FP propeller Total Power: 279kW (379hp) Caterpillar 3408TA 1 x Vee 4 Stroke 8 Cy. 137 x 152 279kW (379bhp) Caterpillar Tractor Co-USA
5427693 *CB4209* -	**TONYN** *ex* Marja Netty *-1989* *ex* Johanna Cornelia *-1969* **Pesquera Santa Lucia SA** - *Valparaiso* *Chile* MMSI: 725002990 Official number: 2646	*152* 62 -		**1963 Bijker's Aannemingsbedrijf — Gorinchem** Yd No: 170 Lengthened-1973 Loa 34.37 Br ex 6.61 Dght - Lbp - Br md 6.51 Dpth 3.28 Welded	**(B11A2FT) Trawler**	**1 oil engine** driving 1 FP propeller Total Power: 706kW (960hp) Deutz 1 x 4 Stroke 706kW (960bhp) (new engine 1973)
9018452 - -	**TOO MARU** - - - *South Korea*	*140* - -		**1990-02 KK Kitahama Zosen Tekko — Aomori AO** Yd No: 102 Loa 39.95 (BB) Br ex 7.90 Dght 2.591 Lbp 32.00 Br md 6.80 Dpth 2.90 Welded	**(B11A2FS) Stern Trawler**	**1 oil engine** with clutches, flexible couplings & sr geared to sc. shaft driving 1 CP propeller Total Power: 900kW (1,224hp) Niigata 6MG22HX 1 x 4 Stroke 6 Cy. 220 x 280 900kW (1224bhp) Niigata Engineering Co Ltd-Japan
9140152 *JK5479* -	**TOO MARU** - **Too Kaiun KK** - *Shunan, Yamaguchi* *Japan* Official number: 134793	*481* - 935		**1996-04 Kyoei Zosen KK — Mihara HS** Yd No: 273 Loa - Br ex - Dght 4.150 Lbp 56.50 Br md 9.50 Dpth 4.40 Welded, 1 dk	**(A12A2TC) Chemical Tanker** 2 Cargo Pump (s): 2x200m³/hr	**1 oil engine** driving 1 FP propeller Total Power: 736kW (1,001hp) Hanshin LH30LG 1 x 4 Stroke 6 Cy. 300 x 600 736kW (1001bhp) The Hanshin Diesel Works Ltd-Japan
8915067 *JK4976* -	**TOO MARU NO. 2** *ex* Toei Maru No. 2 *-1996* *ex* Toei Maru *-1990* **Too Kaiun KK** - *Shunan, Yamaguchi* *Japan* MMSI: 431400888 Official number: 131026	*370* - 780		**1989-10 Hitachi Zosen Mukaishima Marine Co Ltd — Onomichi HS** Yd No: 22 Loa 57.82 Br ex 9.28 Dght 3.500 Lbp 53.00 Br md 9.20 Dpth 4.00 Welded, 1 dk	**(A12A2TC) Chemical Tanker** Liq: 462 Compartments: 8 Ta, ER	**1 oil engine** with clutches, flexible couplings & reverse geared to sc. shaft driving 1 FP propeller Total Power: 736kW (1,001hp) Niigata 6M28BGT 1 x 4 Stroke 6 Cy. 280 x 480 736kW (1001bhp) Niigata Engineering Co Ltd-Japan
8621329 - -	**TOO MARU No. 33** *ex* Oigawa Maru *-1996* *ex* Kasuga Maru No. 8 *-1991* - -	*499* - 1,493		**1983 K.K. Yoshida Zosen Kogyo — Arida** Yd No: 381 Loa - Br ex - Dght 4.320 Lbp 63.81 Br md 11.80 Dpth 6.20 Welded, 1 dk	**(A31A2GX) General Cargo Ship**	**1 oil engine** driving 1 FP propeller Total Power: 1,177kW (1,600hp) Makita KGS31B 1 x 4 Stroke 6 Cy. 310 x 480 1177kW (1600bhp) Makita Corp-Japan
7410096 *HLOB* -	**TOOLEES NO. 79** *ex* Doo An No. 7 *-2005* *ex* Jaiwon No. 7 *-2000* *ex* Puk Yang No. 1 *-1995* *ex* Sirena No. 1 *-1983* **Toolees Co Ltd** - SatCom: Inmarsat A 1705137 *Busan* *South Korea* MMSI: 440679000 Official number: 9506119-6210001	**911** 184 755	Class: (KR)	**1974-09 Usuki Iron Works Co Ltd — Usuki OT** Yd No: 902 Loa 60.30 Br ex - Dght 4.412 Lbp 53.80 Br md 9.99 Dpth 6.20 Welded, 1 dk	**(B11A2FS) Stern Trawler** Ins: 570 2 Ha: (2.2 x 1.9) (2.2 x 2.4)ER	**1 oil engine** driving 1 FP propeller Total Power: 1,618kW (2,200hp) 13.0kn Akasaka AH38 1 x 4 Stroke 6 Cy. 380 x 560 1618kW (2200bhp) Akasaka Tekkosho KK (Akasaka DieselLtd)-Japan AuxGen: 2 x 216kW 225V a.c
8928181 *ESBR* EK 3231	**TOOLSE** *ex* MRTK-3231 *-1983* **OU Morobell** - *Tallinn* *Estonia* MMSI: 276262000 Official number: 1F00G56	**117** 35 30	Class: (RS)	**1975-07 Sosnovskiy Sudostroitelnyy Zavod — Sosnovka** Yd No: 3231 Loa 25.50 Br ex 7.00 Dght 2.390 Lbp 22.00 Br md 6.80 Dpth 3.30 Welded, 1 dk	**(B11A2FS) Stern Trawler** Compartments: 1 Ho 1 Ha: (1.4 x 1.5) Ice Capable	**1 oil engine** driving 1 FP propeller Total Power: 221kW (300hp) 9.5kn S.K.L. 6NVD26A-2 1 x 4 Stroke 6 Cy. 180 x 260 221kW (300bhp) VEB Schwermaschinenbau "KarlLiebknecht" (SKL)-Magdeburg AuxGen: 2 x 12kW a.c Fuel: 12.0 (d.f.)
8654338 *9BIJ* -	**TOORAN** *ex* Monavvar *-1995* **Khazeer Naslayeh** - *Bushehr* *Iran* MMSI: 422536000 Official number: 16776	*490* 325 -	Class: AS	**1972 in India** Loa 44.90 Br ex - Dght - Lbp - Br md 8.75 Dpth 4.30 Welded, 1 dk	**(A31A2GX) General Cargo Ship**	**2 oil engines** reduction geared to sc. shafts driving 2 Propellers Total Power: 1,104kW (1,500hp) Cummins VTA-28-M 2 x Vee 4 Stroke 12 Cy. 140 x 152 each-552kW (750bhp) (new engine 1972) Kirloskar Cummins Ltd-India
8915964 *EPPB5* -	**TOOSAN 110** *ex* Ilia *-2012* *ex* Benten Maru *-2010* **A Maymani** - *Bushehr* *Iran* MMSI: 422017600 Official number: 889	*494* - 458	Class: AS	**1990-05 Ishii Zosen K.K. — Futtsu** Yd No: 262 Loa 48.00 Br ex - Dght 3.473 Lbp 41.00 Br md 11.00 Dpth 3.50 Welded, 1 dk	**(A24D2BA) Aggregates Carrier** Grain: 283 Compartments: 1 Ho, ER 1 Ha: ER	**1 oil engine** with clutches & reverse geared to sc. shaft driving 1 FP propeller Total Power: 736kW (1,001hp) Yanmar MF28-ST 1 x 4 Stroke 6 Cy. 280 x 450 736kW (1001bhp) Matsue Diesel KK-Japan Thrusters: 1 Thwart. FP thruster (f)
8886668 - -	**TOOTUR** - **Russo Bros Inc** - *Los Angeles, CA* *United States of America* Official number: 659647	*116* 93 -		**1983 Slater Boat Works — Moss Landing, Ca** Yd No: 11 L reg 21.95 Br ex - Dght - Lbp - Br md 6.70 Dpth 3.35 Welded, 1 dk	**(B11B2FV) Fishing Vessel**	**1 oil engine** driving 1 FP propeller

9182162 *3FHR8* -	**TOP BRILLIANCE** *ex* Global Glory *-2013* *ex* Big Glory *-2004* **Kong Step Shipping Ltd** Top Wisdom Shipping Management Co Ltd SatCom: Inmarsat B 335433810 *Panama* *Panama* MMSI: 354338000 Official number: 2550298E	**26,003** 14,872 45,769 T/cm 49.8	Class: LR (NK) (AB) **100A1** SS 03/2013 bulk carrier ESP ESN Hold-1 LI **LMC**	**1998-03 Tsuneishi Shipbuilding Co Ltd — Fukuyama HS** Yd No: 1137 Loa 186.00 (BB) Br ex - Dght 11.620 Lbp 177.00 Br md 30.40 Dpth 16.50 Welded, 1 dk	**(A21A2BC) Bulk Carrier** Grain: 57,208; Bale: 55,564 Compartments: 5 Ho, ER 5 Ha: (20.0 x 15.3)4 (20.8 x 15.3)ER Cranes: 4x25t	**1 oil engine** driving 1 FP propeller Total Power: 8,312kW (11,301hp) 14.0kn B&W 6S50MC 1 x 2 Stroke 6 Cy. 500 x 1910 8312kW (11301bhp) Mitsui Engineering & Shipbuilding CLtd-Japan Fuel: 1540.0
9288526 *VRZY4* -	**TOP COURAGE** *ex* POS Courage *-2013* **White Willow Shipping SA** Cido Shipping (HK) Co Ltd *Hong Kong* *Hong Kong* MMSI: 477240400 Official number: HK-1304	**40,014** 25,301 76,801 T/cm 67.3	Class: KR	**2004-04 Sasebo Heavy Industries Co. Ltd. — Sasebo Yard, Sasebo** Yd No: 496 Loa 225.00 Br ex - Dght 14.221 Lbp 218.00 Br md 32.20 Dpth 19.80 Welded, 1 dk	**(A21A2BC) Bulk Carrier** Grain: 90,911; Bale: 88,950 Compartments: 7 Ho, ER 7 Ha: 6 (17.0 x 14.4)ER (15.3 x 12.8)	**1 oil engine** driving 1 FP propeller Total Power: 9,230kW (12,549hp) 14.5kn B&W 7S50MC-C 1 x 2 Stroke 7 Cy. 500 x 2000 9230kW (12549bhp) Mitsui Engineering & Shipbuilding CLtd-Japan
9288461 *VRBA4* -	**TOP ETERNITY** *ex* POS Eternity *-2013* **White Plum Shipping SA** Cido Shipping (HK) Co Ltd *Hong Kong* *Hong Kong* MMSI: 477994900 Official number: HK-1528	**39,964** 26,025 76,295 T/cm 67.8	Class: KR	**2005-05 Tsuneishi Corp — Tadotsu KG** Yd No: 1286 Loa 225.00 (BB) Br ex - Dght 14.038 Lbp 217.00 Br md 32.26 Dpth 19.30 Welded, 1 dk	**(A21A2BC) Bulk Carrier** Grain: 91,357 Compartments: 7 Ho, ER 7 Ha: 6 (17.3 x 15.4)ER (15.6 x 12.8)	**1 oil engine** driving 1 FP propeller Total Power: 8,830kW (12,005hp) 14.5kn MAN-B&W 7S50MC-C 1 x 2 Stroke 7 Cy. 500 x 2000 8830kW (12005bhp) Mitsui Engineering & Shipbuilding CLtd-Japan
9574846 *3EYF3* -	**TOP FAIR** **Top Fair Navigation SA** Fairweather Steamship Co Ltd *Panama* *Panama* MMSI: 352202000 Official number: 4174510	**30,974** 18,171 55,256 T/cm 56.3	Class: CC (NK)	**2010-07 Nantong COSCO KHI Ship Engineering Co Ltd (NACKS) — Nantong JS** Yd No: 119 Loa 189.90 (BB) Br ex 32.31 Dght 12.522 Lbp 185.00 Br md 32.26 Dpth 17.80 Welded, 1 dk	**(A21A2BC) Bulk Carrier** Grain: 69,452; Bale: 66,966 Compartments: 5 Ho, ER 5 Ha: 4 (20.5 x 18.6)ER (17.8 x 18.6) Cranes: 4x30.5t	**1 oil engine** driving 1 FP propeller Total Power: 8,200kW (11,149hp) 14.0kn MAN-B&W 6S50MC-C 1 x 2 Stroke 6 Cy. 500 x 2000 8200kW (11149bhp) Hudong Heavy Machinery Co Ltd-China AuxGen: 3 x 550kW 450V a.c
8105686 *HP7112* -	**TOP FENDERS 2** *ex* Pacific Scimitar *-2011* **Top Fenders 2 Ltd** Top Fenders Ltd *Panama* *Panama* MMSI: 354130000 Official number: 41720PEXT	**950** 332 1,120	Class: AB	**1981-11 Imamura Zosen — Kure** Yd No: 277 Loa 57.71 Br ex 12.22 Dght 3.893 Lbp 52.51 Br md 12.21 Dpth 4.50 Welded	**(B21B20A) Anchor Handling Tug Supply** Passengers: berths: 23	**2 oil engines** sr reverse geared to sc. shafts driving 2 FP propellers Total Power: 2,088kW (2,838hp) 12.0kn Yanmar T260-ST 2 x 4 Stroke 6 Cy. 260 x 330 each-1044kW (1419bhp) Yanmar Diesel Engine Co Ltd-Japan AuxGen: 3 x 160kW 440V 60Hz a.c Thrusters: 1 Thwart. CP thruster (f) Fuel: 291.0 (d.f.) 7.2pd
9334478 *ZCOR3* -	**TOP FIVE** *ex* Nice N Easy *-2010* *ex* Liquidity *-2005* **Top Five Ltd** - *George Town* *Cayman Islands (British)* MMSI: 319619000 Official number: 738489	**499** 149 63	Class: AB	**2005-01 Christensen Shipyards Ltd — Vancouver, Wa** Yd No: 27 Loa 47.90 Br ex 9.00 Dght 2.310 Lbp 41.70 Br md 8.84 Dpth 3.71 Bonded, 1 dk	**(X11A2YP) Yacht** Hull Material: Reinforced Plastic	**2 oil engines** reduction geared to sc. shafts driving 2 Propellers Total Power: 2,684kW (3,650hp) M.T.U. 16V4000M 2 x Vee 4 Stroke 16 Cy. 165 x 190 each-1342kW (1825bhp) MTU Friedrichshafen GmbH-Friedrichshafen
9291389 *VRBE9* -	**TOP FREEDOM** *ex* POS Freedom *-2013* **White Linden Shipping SA** Pan Ocean Co Ltd *Hong Kong* *Hong Kong* MMSI: 477998500 Official number: HK-1565	**30,743** 18,539 55,695 T/cm 55.9	Class: KR	**2005-07 Oshima Shipbuilding Co Ltd — Saikai NS** Yd No: 10394 Loa 190.00 (BB) Br ex - Dght 12.502 Lbp 185.79 Br md 32.26 Dpth 17.62 Welded, 1 dk	**(A21A2BC) Bulk Carrier** Double Hull Grain: 69,872; Bale: 68,798 Compartments: 5 Ho, ER 5 Ha: (18.6 x 18.6) (21.4 x 18.6)2 (22.3 x 18.6)ER (16.7 x 18.6) Cranes: 4x30t	**1 oil engine** driving 1 FP propeller Total Power: 8,208kW (11,160hp) 14.5kn B&W 6S50MC-C 1 x 2 Stroke 6 Cy. 500 x 2000 8208kW (11160bhp) Mitsui Engineering & Shipbuilding CLtd-Japan
9291391 *VRBI5* -	**TOP HARMONY** *ex* POS Harmony *-2013* **White Camellia Shipping SA** Cido Shipping (Korea) Co Ltd *Hong Kong* *Hong Kong* MMSI: 477020800 Official number: HK-1593	**30,743** 18,539 55,695 T/cm 55.9	Class: KR	**2005-10 Oshima Shipbuilding Co Ltd — Saikai NS** Yd No: 10395 Loa 190.00 (BB) Br ex - Dght 12.502 Lbp 181.79 Br md 32.26 Dpth 17.62 Welded, 1 dk	**(A21A2BC) Bulk Carrier** Double Hull Grain: 69,872; Bale: 68,798 Compartments: 5 Ho, ER 5 Ha: (18.6 x 18.6) (21.4 x 18.6)2 (22.3 x 18.6)ER (16.7 x 18.6) Cranes: 4x30t	**1 oil engine** driving 1 FP propeller Total Power: 8,208kW (11,160hp) 14.5kn B&W 6S50MC-C 1 x 2 Stroke 6 Cy. 500 x 2000 8208kW (11160bhp) Mitsui Engineering & Shipbuilding CLtd-Japan
9303924 *VRBZ5* -	**TOP ISLAND** *ex* POS Island *-2013* **White Persimmon Maritime SA** Pan Ocean Co Ltd *Hong Kong* *Hong Kong* MMSI: 477265200 Official number: HK-1730	**30,743** 18,539 55,710 T/cm 55.9	Class: KR	**2006-08 Oshima Shipbuilding Co Ltd — Saikai NS** Yd No: 10410 Loa 190.00 (BB) Br ex 32.26 Dght 12.502 Lbp 181.79 Br md 32.26 Dpth 17.62 Welded, 1 dk	**(A21A2BC) Bulk Carrier** Double Hull Grain: 69,872; Bale: 68,798 Compartments: 5 Ho, ER 5 Ha: (18.6 x 18.6) (21.4 x 18.6)2 (22.3 x 18.6)ER (16.7 x 18.6) Cranes: 4x30t	**1 oil engine** driving 1 FP propeller Total Power: 8,208kW (11,160hp) 14.5kn MAN-B&W 6S50MC-C 1 x 2 Stroke 6 Cy. 500 x 2000 8208kW (11160bhp) Mitsui Engineering & Shipbuilding CLtd-Japan AuxGen: 4 x 460kW 450V a.c
8031160 *WCZ6446* -	**TOP OCEAN** *ex* Punta Baltica *-1999* *ex* Baltiyskaya Kosa *-1994* **Top Ocean Inc** - *Kodiak, AK* *United States of America* MMSI: 338727000 Official number: 1072649	**4,059** 1,561 2,117	Class: (NV) (RS)	**1980-12 VEB Volkswerft Stralsund — Stralsund** Yd No: 253 Loa 101.45 Br ex 15.22 Dght 5.710 Lbp 91.83 Br md 15.20 Dpth 9.71 Welded, 2 dks	**(B11A2FG) Factory Stern Trawler** Bale: 380; Ins: 1,858 Compartments: 3 Ho, ER 3 Ha: (1.6 x 1.6) (2.3 x 2.3) (2.2 x 2.2) Derricks: 2x5t,4x3t Ice Capable	**1 oil engine** driving 1 FP propeller Total Power: 2,854kW (3,880hp) 16.3kn DMR 8ZD72/48AL-1 1 x 2 Stroke 8 Cy. 480 x 720 2854kW (3880bhp) VEB Dieselmotorenwerk Rostock-Rostock
9156785 *3FEK8* -	**TOP RICH** **Columba Marine Navigation Inc** Fairweather Steamship Co Ltd SatCom: Inmarsat B 335233710 *Panama* *Panama* MMSI: 352337000 Official number: 2549198C	**26,801** 16,005 46,027 T/cm 53.5	Class: AB	**1998-02 Sanoyas Hishino Meisho Corp — Kurashiki OY** Yd No: 1151 Loa 187.30 (BB) Br ex - Dght 11.300 Lbp 180.00 Br md 32.20 Dpth 16.10 Welded, 1 dk	**(A21A2BC) Bulk Carrier** Grain: 59,762; Bale: 58,068 Compartments: 5 Ho, ER 5 Ha: (20.0 x 15.0)4 (20.8 x 18.3)ER Cranes: 4x25t	**1 oil engine** driving 1 FP propeller Total Power: 7,208kW (9,800hp) 14.5kn Sulzer 6RTA48T 1 x 2 Stroke 6 Cy. 480 x 2000 7208kW (9800bhp) Diesel United Ltd.-Aioi AuxGen: 2 x 480kW a.c, 1 x 400kW a.c Fuel: 1759.0 (r.f.) 26.0pd
9631462 *3FMM8* -	**TOP WEATHER** **Top Weather Navigation SA** Fairweather Steamship Co Ltd SatCom: Inmarsat C 437318010 *Panama* *Panama* MMSI: 373180000 Official number: 4398712	**33,125** 19,130 58,689 T/cm 59.5	Class: CC (LR) ✠ Classed LR until 14/12/13	**2012-06 Nantong COSCO KHI Ship Engineering Co Ltd (NACKS) — Nantong JS** Yd No: 127 Loa 197.00 (BB) Br ex 32.30 Dght 12.650 Lbp 194.00 Br md 32.26 Dpth 18.10 Welded, 1 dk	**(A21A2BC) Bulk Carrier** Grain: 73,614; Bale: 70,963 Compartments: 5 Ho, ER 5 Ha: ER Cranes: 4x30.5t	**1 oil engine** driving 1 FP propeller Total Power: 8,630kW (11,733hp) 14.5kn MAN-B&W 6S50MC-C8 1 x 2 Stroke 6 Cy. 500 x 2000 8630kW (11733bhp) Hudong Heavy Machinery Co Ltd-China AuxGen: 3 x 500kW 440V 60Hz a.c Boilers: AuxB (Comp) 8.2kgf/cm² (8.0bar)
9156773 *3FBQ8* -	**TOP WING** **Wing Tai Marine Navigation Inc** Fairweather Steamship Co Ltd SatCom: Inmarsat B 335191310 *Panama* *Panama* MMSI: 351913000 Official number: 2539298C	**26,801** 16,005 46,013 T/cm 53.5	Class: AB	**1998-01 Sanoyas Hishino Meisho Corp — Kurashiki OY** Yd No: 1150 Loa 187.30 (BB) Br ex - Dght 11.300 Lbp 180.00 Br md 32.20 Dpth 16.10 Welded, 1 dk	**(A21A2BC) Bulk Carrier** Grain: 59,764; Bale: 58,068 Compartments: 5 Ho, ER 5 Ha: (20.0 x 15.0)4 (20.8 x 18.3)ER Cranes: 4x25t	**1 oil engine** driving 1 FP propeller Total Power: 7,208kW (9,800hp) 14.5kn Sulzer 6RTA48T 1 x 2 Stroke 6 Cy. 480 x 2000 7208kW (9800bhp) Diesel United Ltd.-Aioi AuxGen: 2 x 480kW a.c, 1 x 400kW a.c Fuel: 1759.0 (r.f.) 26.0pd
5409500 - -	**TOPADOR** **Government of The Argentine Republic (Empresa Flota Fluvial del Estado Argentino) (EFFDEA)** -	*196* 50 -	Class: (LR) ✠ Classed LR until 31/10/75	**1968-06 Astilleros Alianza S.A. — Avellaneda** Yd No: 10 Loa 30.61 Br ex 8.44 Dght - Lbp 28.00 Br md 8.01 Dpth 3.76 Welded, 1 dk	**(B32A2ST) Tug**	**2 diesel electric oil engines** driving 2 gen. each 340kW 440V d.c Connecting to 2 elec. motors driving 1 FP propeller Total Power: 882kW (1,200hp) MAN G7V235/330ATL 2 x 4 Stroke 7 Cy. 235 x 330 each-441kW (600bhp) (Re-engined ,made 1962, refitted 1968) Maschinenbau Augsburg Nuernberg (MAN)-Augsburg AuxGen: 2 x 36kW 220V d.c
7804663 *YFDH* -	**TOPAN JAYA** *ex* Osaka Maru *-1993* *ex* Nishi Maru *-1993* *ex* Libre *-1993* *ex* Otowa Maru No. 8 *-1993* **PT Pelayaran Internusa Bahari Persada** - *Jakarta* *Indonesia*	**898** 430 1,049	Class: (KI)	**1978-04 K.K. Matsuura Zosensho — Osakikamijima** Yd No: 258 Loa 62.64 Br ex 9.83 Dght 3.752 Lbp 57.03 Br md 9.80 Dpth 5.21 Welded, 2 dks	**(A31A2GX) General Cargo Ship**	**1 oil engine** driving 1 FP propeller Total Power: 699kW (950hp) Hanshin 6LU28 1 x 4 Stroke 6 Cy. 280 x 440 699kW (950bhp) Hanshin Nainenki Kogyo-Japan

8000135 **TOPAS** *OW2298* *ex* Nonhamar *-2013* *ex* Akranes *-2013* VA 261 *ex* Topas *-2001* *ex* Leivur I Hesti *-1987* **Var P/F** - *Sorvagur* *Faeroe Islands (Danish)* MMSI: 231027000	**215** 73 130	Class: (BV)	**1980-06 Forges Caloin — Etaples** Yd No: 24 Loa 31.00 Br ex - Dght 3.500 Lbp 27.50 Br md 6.80 Dpth 5.80 Welded, 1 dk	**(B11A2FS) Stern Trawler**	**1 oil engine** reduction geared to sc. shaft driving 1 CP propeller Total Power: 625kW (850hp) 11.5kn Caterpillar D398SCAC 1 x Vee 4 Stroke 12 Cy. 159 x 203 625kW (850bhp) Caterpillar Tractor Co-USA AuxGen: 2 x 52kW 220/380V a.c Fuel: 41.0 (d.f.)
8850425 **TOPAS** *JWLD* *ex* Gularoy *-2011* *ex* Radek *-2004* - *ex* Vestrefisk *-2002* *ex* Sjoglans *-1997* *ex* Tom Ivar *-1994* *ex* Campella/Maroy *-1991* *ex* Campella *-1988* **Topas Kystfiske AS** - *Aalesund* *Norway* MMSI: 257445509	**108** 43 -		**1985-05 Herfjord Slip & Verksted AS — Revsnes i Fosna** (Hull) **1985-05 Sletta Baatbyggeri AS — Mjosundet** Yd No: 60 Loa 20.34 Br ex - Dght - Lbp - Br md 6.10 Dpth 3.54 Welded, 1 dk	**(B11B2FV) Fishing Vessel** Grain: 45; Ins: 18	**1 oil engine** driving 1 FP propeller Total Power: 331kW (450hp) 9.0kn Nissan RD10TA 1 x Vee 4 Stroke 10 Cy. 135 x 125 331kW (450bhp) Nissan Diesel Motor Co. Ltd.-Ageo
9474632 **TOPAS** *9HA3493* *ex* POS Topas *-2013* - **Conti 179 Schiffahrts-GmbH & Co KG Nr 1** BBG-Bremer Bereederungsgesellschaft mbH & Co KG *Valletta* *Malta* MMSI: 229658000 Official number: 9474632	**51,195** 31,136 92,655 T/cm 80.9	Class: AB	**2011-11 COSCO (Zhoushan) Shipyard Co Ltd — Zhoushan ZJ** Yd No: N305 Loa 229.20 (BB) Br ex - Dght 14.900 Lbp 222.00 Br md 38.00 Dpth 20.70 Welded, 1 dk	**(A21A2BC) Bulk Carrier** Grain: 110,330 Compartments: 7 Ho, ER 7 Ha: ER	**1 oil engine** driving 1 FP propeller Total Power: 12,240kW (16,642hp) 14.1kn MAN-B&W 6S60MC 1 x 2 Stroke 6 Cy. 600 x 2292 12240kW (16642bhp) Doosan Engine Co Ltd-South Korea AuxGen: 3 x 730kW a.c Fuel: 233.0 (d.f.) 3597.0 (r.f.)
9215517 **TOPAS** *V2QH6* - **Torino Shipping Co Ltd** MarConsult Schiffahrt (GmbH & Co) KG *Saint John's* *Antigua & Barbuda* MMSI: 305783000 Official number: 3096	**4,028** 2,218 5,094	Class: GL (BV)	**1999-03 Jinling Shipyard — Nanjing JS** Yd No: 98-0101 Loa 100.51 (BB) Br ex - Dght 6.473 Lbp 95.40 Br md 18.50 Dpth 8.25 Welded, 1 dk	**(A31A2GX) General Cargo Ship** Grain: 7,646 TEU 502 C Ho 143 TEU C Dk 359 incl 60 ref C Compartments: 3 Cell Ho, ER, 3 Tw Dk 3 Ha: ER Cranes: 2x40t Ice Capable	**1 oil engine** reduction geared to sc. shaft driving 1 CP propeller Total Power: 3,960kW (5,384hp) 15.5kn MaK 9M32 1 x 4 Stroke 9 Cy. 320 x 480 3960kW (5384bhp) MaK Motoren GmbH & Co. KG-Kiel AuxGen: 1 x 624kW 400V 50Hz a.c, 3 x 340kW 400V 50Hz a.c Thrusters: 1 Thwart. FP thruster (f)
9279537 **TOPAZ** *V7WF3* *ex* Kavo Topaz *-2011* - **United Ventures SA** AM Nomikos Transworld Maritime Agencies SA *Majuro* *Marshall Islands* MMSI: 538004284 Official number: 4284	**38,845** 25,444 75,499 T/cm 66.5	Class: AB	**2004-06 Sanoyas Hishino Meisho Corp — Kurashiki OY** Yd No: 1218 Loa 225.00 (BB) Br ex - Dght 13.997 Lbp 217.00 Br md 32.26 Dpth 19.30 Welded, 1 Dk.	**(A21A2BC) Bulk Carrier** Grain: 89,250 Compartments: 7 Ho, ER 7 Ha: 6 (17.1 x 15.0)ER (16.3 x 13.4)	**1 oil engine** driving 1 FP propeller Total Power: 8,973kW (12,200hp) 14.5kn B&W 7S50MC-C 1 x 2 Stroke 7 Cy. 500 x 2000 8973kW (12200bhp) Mitsui Engineering & Shipbuilding CLtd-Japan AuxGen: 3 x 400kW a.c
9339882 **TOPAZ** *9V6608* - **Pembrooke Marine Pte Ltd** Chuan Hup Agencies Pte Ltd *Singapore* *Singapore* MMSI: 563813000 Official number: 390762	**1,585** 475 1,610	Class: AB	**2005-10 Piasau Slipways Sdn Bhd — Miri** Yd No: 197 Loa 60.00 Br ex - Dght 4.200 Lbp 58.74 Br md 16.00 Dpth 5.50 Welded, 1 dk	**(B21B20A) Anchor Handling Tug Supply**	**2 oil engines** geared to sc. shafts driving 2 Propellers Total Power: 4,046kW (5,500hp) 13.0kn Wartsila 6L26A 2 x 4 Stroke 6 Cy. 260 x 320 each-2023kW (2750bhp) Wartsila Italia SpA-Italy Thrusters: 2 Tunnel thruster (f)
9494199 **TOPAZ** *TCTP3* - **Topaz Denizcilik Petrol Urunleri Pazarlama Nakliyat ve Ticaret AS** Kaman Gemi Isletmeciligi AS *Istanbul* *Turkey* MMSI: 271002718	**1,803** 820 2,655 T/cm 8.4	Class: BV (RI)	**2009-09 Yildirim Gemi Insaat Sanayii A.S. — Tuzla** Yd No: 112 Loa 82.05 (BB) Br ex - Dght 5.200 Lbp 75.97 Br md 12.20 Dpth 6.10 Welded, 1 dk	**(A12B2TR) Chemical/Products Tanker** Double Hull (13F) Liq: 2,981; Liq (Oil): 2,981 Cargo Heating Coils Compartments: 12 Wing Ta, ER 4 Cargo Pump (s): 3x350m³/hr, 1x200m³/hr Manifold: Bow/CM: 42m	**1 oil engine** driving 1 CP propeller Total Power: 1,297kW (1,763hp) 12.0kn Hanshin LH31G 1 x 4 Stroke 6 Cy. 310 x 530 1297kW (1763bhp) The Hanshin Diesel Works Ltd-Japan AuxGen: 3 x 240kW 50Hz a.c Thrusters: 1 Tunnel thruster (f) Fuel: 27.0 (d.f.) 80.0 (r.f.)
9551454 **TOPAZ** *ZGBL4* - **Oceanus Maritime Ltd** Pearl Ships LLC *George Town* *Cayman Islands (British)* MMSI: 319054000 Official number: 743532	**12,532** 3,759 900	Class: LR ✠ **100A1** SS 08/2012 passenger ship **ShipRight** (SDA) ✠ **LMC** **UMS** Eq.Ltr: D†; Cable: 555.2/54.0 U3 (a)	**2012-08 Fr. Luerssen Werft GmbH & Co. — Bremen** Yd No: 13677 Loa 147.25 (BB) Br ex - Dght 5.700 Lbp 117.14 Br md 21.50 Dpth 12.50 Welded, 1 dk	**(X11A2YP) Yacht** Hull Material: Aluminium Alloy Passengers: 64	**6 diesel electric oil engines** driving 6 gen. each 2880kW 660V a.c Connecting to 2 elec. motors each (6000kW) driving 2 CP propellers Total Power: 18,000kW (24,474hp) 19.5kn Wartsila 6L32 6 x 4 Stroke 6 Cy. 320 x 400 each-3000kW (4079bhp) Wartsila Finland Oy-Finland Thrusters: 2 Thwart. CP thruster (f)
7740752 **TOPAZ** - *ex* Tasman *-2009* *ex* Star-4 *-2008* - *ex* Yelan *-2007* **Marine Service V&A Pte Ltd** -	**650** 195 304	Class: (RS)	**1978 Khabarovskiy Sudostroitelnyy Zavod im Kirova — Khabarovsk** Yd No: 268 Loa 54.84 Br ex 9.38 Dght 3.810 Lbp 49.99 Br md - Dpth 4.73 Welded, 1 dk	**(B11A2FT) Trawler** Ins: 284 Compartments: 2 Ho, ER 2 Ha: 2 (1.5 x 1.6) Derricks: 1x3t; Winches: 1 Ice Capable	**1 oil engine** driving 1 CP propeller Total Power: 588kW (799hp) 11.5kn S.K.L. 8NVD48-2U 1 x 4 Stroke 8 Cy. 320 x 480 588kW (799bhp) VEB Schwermaschinenbau "KarlLiebknecht" (SKL)-Magdeburg AuxGen: 3 x 88kW
8520953 **TOPAZ** *UIKQ* *ex* Lira *-1998* *ex* MPK-473 *-1989* - **OOO Gazflot** - *Kaliningrad* *Russia* MMSI: 273433510	**493** 31 40	Class: RS	**1988-06 Brodogradiliste 'Titovo' — Kraljevica** Yd No: 473 Loa 44.60 Br ex 8.80 Dght 2.800 Lbp 40.00 Br md 7.51 Dpth 4.60 Welded, 1 dk	**(B21A20C) Crew/Supply Vessel** Ice Capable	**2 oil engines** with clutches, flexible couplings & sr reverse geared to sc. shafts driving 2 FP propellers Total Power: 1,250kW (1,700hp) 13.5kn Pielstick 6PA4L185VG 2 x 4 Stroke 6 Cy. 185 x 210 each-625kW (850bhp) Tvornica Dizel Motora 'Uljanik'-Yugoslavia AuxGen: 2 x 125kW a.c
8228165 **TOPAZ** *UGDS* - **State Unitary Enterprise Baltic Basin Emergency-Rescue Management (FGUP Baltiyskoye Basseynoye Avariyno-Spasatelnoye Upravleniye) (Baltic BASU)** - *St Petersburg* *Russia* MMSI: 273149000	**1,160** 348 404	Class: (RS)	**1984-07 Yaroslavskiy Sudostroitelnyy Zavod — Yaroslavl** Yd No: 225 Loa 58.58 Br ex 12.68 Dght 4.671 Lbp 51.62 Br md 12.23 Dpth 5.92 Welded, 1 dk	**(B32A2ST) Tug** Derricks: 1x5t	**2 diesel electric oil engines** driving 2 gen. each 1000kW Connecting to 2 elec. motors each (1100kW) driving 1 FP propeller Total Power: 2,000kW (2,720hp) 13.2kn Kolomna 6CHN30/38 2 x 4 Stroke 6 Cy. 300 x 380 each-1000kW (1360bhp) Kolomenskiy Zavod-Kolomna AuxGen: 2 x 300kW, 2 x 160kW Fuel: 346.0 (d.f.)
6905915 **TOPAZ** *EOBF* - **Morstroy JSC (A/O 'Morstroy')** - *Sevastopol* *Ukraine* Official number: 680547	*236* 70 91	Class: (RS)	**1968 VEB Schiffswerft "Edgar Andre" — Magdeburg** Yd No: 7013 Loa 34.78 Br ex 8.51 Dght 2.744 Lbp 30.41 Br md 8.21 Dpth 3.70 Welded, 1 dk	**(B32A2ST) Tug** Ice Capable	**1 oil engine** driving 1 CP propeller Total Power: 551kW (749hp) 11.5kn S.K.L. 6NVD48A-2U 1 x 4 Stroke 6 Cy. 320 x 480 551kW (749bhp) VEB Schwermaschinenbau "KarlLiebknecht" (SKL)-Magdeburg AuxGen: 2 x 44kW Fuel: 48.0 (d.f.)
6818239 **TOPAZ** - *ex* Al Shaker *-1988* *ex* Ryuko Maru *-1980* - **Sam Suj Din Shipping** Jaisu Shipping Co Pvt Ltd	**224** 67 -	Class: (CS) (BV) (AB)	**1968 Sanyo Zosen K.K. — Onomichi** Yd No: 362 Loa 31.70 Br ex 9.33 Dght 3.277 Lbp 28.00 Br md 9.20 Dpth 4.20 Welded, 1 dk	**(B32A2ST) Tug**	**2 oil engines** driving 2 FP propellers Total Power: 1,692kW (2,300hp) 9.0kn Fuji 6SD37BH 2 x 4 Stroke 6 Cy. 370 x 550 each-846kW (1150bhp) Fuji Diesel Co Ltd-Japan AuxGen: 2 x 40kW 225V a.c Fuel: 40.5 6.0pd
7644348 **TOPAZ** *WSM6239* *ex* Jason *-1980* - **Chandler Fisheries Inc** - *Kodiak, AK* *United States of America* MMSI: 366444090 Official number: 575428	**151** 45 -		**1976 A.W. Covacevich Shipyard, Inc. — Biloxi, Ms** L reg 21.65 Br ex 6.43 Dght - Lbp - Br md - Dpth 3.64 Welded, 1 dk	**(B11B2FV) Fishing Vessel**	**1 oil engine** driving 1 FP propeller Total Power: 261kW (355hp)

Number / Call sign	Name / Owner / Manager	Tonnage	Class	Builder / Dimensions	Type	Machinery
7524392 - -	**TOPAZ** **Black Sea State Regional Geological & Exploration Ent (Geologo-Razvedyvatelnoye Predpriyatiye Prichemomorskoye Gasudarstvennoye Regionalnoye)** - *Illichevsk* *Ukraine* Official number: 743534	*166* 18 36	Class: (RS)	**1975 Sretenskiy Sudostroitelnyy Zavod — Sretensk** Yd No: 75 Loa 33.96 Br ex 7.09 Dght 2.590 Lbp 30.00 Br md - Dpth 3.69 Welded, 1 dk	**(B31A2SR) Research Survey Vessel** Derricks: 2x2t Ice Capable	**1 oil engine** driving 1 FP propeller Total Power: 224kW (305hp) 9.0kn S.K.L. 8NVD36-1U 1 x 4 Stroke 8 Cy. 240 x 360 224kW (305bhp) VEB Schwermaschinenbau "KarlLiebknecht" (SKL)-Magdeburg
9077836 *3FUE4* -	**TOPAZ ACE** **Back-Boned Maritime SA** Cido Shipping (HK) Co Ltd SatCom: Inmarsat C 435464610 *Panama* *Panama* MMSI: 354646000 Official number: 2199495CH	**48,210** 14,463 14,696 T/cm 44.2	Class: KR (LR) ✠ Classed LR until 4/2/00	**1995-02 Daewoo Heavy Industries Ltd — Geoje** Yd No: 4414 Loa 179.90 (BB) Br ex - Dght 9.118 Lbp 171.76 Br md 32.23 Dpth 14.40 Welded, 5 dks to freeboard dk plus 5 superstructure dks and 2 movable dks	**(A35B2RV) Vehicles Carrier** Side door/ramp (p) Len: 16.98 Wid: 4.50 Swl: 20 Side door/ramp (s) Len: 16.98 Wid: 4.50 Swl: 20 Quarter stern door/ramp (s. a.) Len: 34.00 Wid: 5.50 Swl: 70 Cars: 5,317	**1 oil engine** driving 1 FP propeller Total Power: 12,269kW (16,681hp) 18.5kn B&W 6S60MC 1 x 2 Stroke 6 Cy. 600 x 2292 12269kW (16681bhp) Korea Heavy Industries & ConstrCo Ltd (HANJUNG)-South Korea AuxGen: 3 x 820kW 450V 60Hz a.c Thrusters: 1 Thwart. CP thruster (f)
9671395 *V7CM7* -	**TOPAZ AMANI** *ex* SK Line 705 *-2013* **Team XXX Ltd** Nico Middle East Ltd (Topaz Marine) *Majuro* *Marshall Islands* MMSI: 538005285 Official number: 5285	**2,948** 913 3,130	Class: AB	**2013-10 Fujian Southeast Shipyard — Fuzhou FJ** Yd No: SK705 Loa 75.98 (BB) Br ex - Dght 6.500 Lbp 67.85 Br md 17.25 Dpth 8.00 Welded, 1 dk	**(B21A20S) Platform Supply Ship**	**2 oil engines** reduction geared to sc. shafts driving 2 Z propellers Total Power: 4,412kW (5,998hp) 14.5kn Niigata 8L28HX 2 x 4 Stroke 8 Cy. 280 x 370 each-2206kW (2999bhp) Niigata Engineering Co Ltd-Japan AuxGen: 2 x 1000kW a.c, 3 x 450kW a.c Thrusters: 2 Thwart. CP thruster (f) Fuel: 400.0 (d.f.) 350.0 (r.f.)
9207015 *4JOI* -	**TOPAZ ARROW** *ex* Adams Arrow *-2011* *ex* Midnight Arrow *-2005* **Team XXII Ltd** Nico Middle East Ltd (Topaz Marine) *Baku* *Azerbaijan* MMSI: 423357100 Official number: 4205	**1,383** 414 800	Class: AB	**1999-12 S.A. Balenciaga — Zumaya** Yd No: 388 Loa 60.00 Br ex - Dght 4.100 Lbp 55.39 Br md 13.30 Dpth 5.00 Welded, 1 dk	**(B22A20R) Offshore Support Vessel** Cranes: 1x45t	**2 oil engines** with clutches, flexible couplings & sr geared to sc. shafts driving 2 Directional propellers Total Power: 1,766kW (2,402hp) 11.0kn Caterpillar 3512TA 2 x Vee 4 Stroke 12 Cy. 170 x 190 each-883kW (1201bhp) Caterpillar Inc-USA AuxGen: 3 x 425kW 440/110V 60Hz a.c Thrusters: 2 Thwart. FP thruster (f) Fuel: 462.0 (d.f.)
9255115 *ZCPY5* -	**TOPAZ CAPTAIN** *ex* BOA Rover *-2011* *ex* Rover *-2007* *ex* Normand Rover *-2007* **Team XVI Ltd** Nico Middle East Ltd (Topaz Marine) *George Town* *Cayman Islands (British)* MMSI: 319613000 Official number: 739782	**3,992** 1,308 3,848	Class: NV	**2001-11 SC Aker Tulcea SA — Tulcea** (Hull) Yd No: 272 **2001-11 Soviknes Verft AS — Sovik** Yd No: 131 Loa 84.00 Br ex 18.83 Dght 6.350 Lbp 76.70 Br md 18.80 Dpth 7.60 Welded, 1 dk	**(B21B20A) Anchor Handling Tug Supply** Passengers: berths: 146	**4 diesel electric oil engines** driving 4 gen. each 1990kW 690V Connecting to 2 elec. motors each (2300kW) driving 2 Azimuth electric drive units Total Power: 10,440kW (14,196hp) 15.0kn Normo KRGB-9 4 x 4 Stroke 9 Cy. 250 x 300 each-2610kW (3549bhp) Rolls Royce Marine AS-Norway Thrusters: 2 Tunnel thruster (f); 1 Retract. directional thruster (f)
9194294 *J8B4336* -	**TOPAZ COMMANDER** *ex* Ocean Commander *-2010* *launched as* Ocean Lady *-1999* **Team XXI Ltd** Nico Middle East Ltd (Topaz Marine) *Kingstown* *St Vincent & The Grenadines* MMSI: 377521000 Official number: 10809	**3,465** 1,464 4,268	Class: AB (NV)	**1999-06 Societatea Comerciala Severnav S.A. — Drobeta-Turnu Severin** (Hull) Yd No: 300006 **1999-06 Myklebust Mek. Verksted AS — Gursken** Yd No: 20 Loa 84.00 Br ex - Dght 6.200 Lbp 76.20 Br md 18.80 Dpth 7.60 Welded, 1 dk	**(B21A20S) Platform Supply Ship** Cranes: 1	**2 oil engines** reduction geared to sc. shafts driving 2 FP propellers Total Power: 7,060kW (9,598hp) 16.4kn Normo BRM-8 2 x 4 Stroke 8 Cy. 320 x 360 each-3530kW (4799bhp) Ulstein Bergen AS-Norway AuxGen: 2 x 1920kW 220/440V 60Hz a.c, 3 x 590kW 220/440V 60Hz a.c Thrusters: 2 Thwart. FP thruster (f); 2 Tunnel thruster (a)
9654983 - -	**TOPAZ DIGNITY** *ex* Suc 25/11 *-2012* **BUE Caspian Ltd** - *Baku* *Azerbaijan* MMSI: 423378100 Official number: BR-055	**2,148** 644 2,163	Class: AB (Class contemplated)	**2012-09 Nico Craft LLC — Fujairah** Yd No: 121 Loa 67.40 Br ex - Dght 5.700 Lbp 60.30 Br md 16.00 Dpth 6.80 Welded, 1 dk	**(B21B20A) Anchor Handling Tug Supply** Cranes: 1x15.8t	**2 oil engines** reduction geared to sc. shafts driving 2 CP propellers Total Power: 5,440kW (7,396hp) 10.0kn MAN-B&W 8L27/38 2 x 4 Stroke 8 Cy. 270 x 380 each-2720kW (3698bhp) MAN B&W Diesel AG-Augsburg AuxGen: 2 x 1250kW 440V 60Hz a.c, 2 x 515kW 440V 60Hz a.c Thrusters: 2 Thwart. CP thruster (f); 1 Thwart. CP thruster (a) Fuel: 630.0
9552800 *3FWU9* -	**TOPAZ EXPRESS** **Diamond Camellia SA** Mitsui OSK Lines Ltd (MOL) *Panama* *Panama* MMSI: 371442000 Official number: 4085709	**27,976** 12,193 45,650 T/cm 49.9	Class: NK	**2009-09 Minaminippon Shipbuilding Co Ltd — Usuki OT** Yd No: 707 Loa 179.80 (BB) Br ex 32.49 Dght 12.123 Lbp 171.00 Br md 32.20 Dpth 18.80 Welded, 1 dk	**(A13B2TP) Products Tanker** Double Hull (13F) Liq: 54,806; Liq (Oil): 55,000 Cargo Heating Coils Compartments: 12 Wing Ta, 2 Wing Slop Ta, ER 4 Cargo Pump (s): 4x1000m³/hr Manifold: Bow/CM: 91.9m	**1 oil engine** driving 1 FP propeller Total Power: 8,580kW (11,665hp) 14.5kn MAN-B&W 6S50MC 1 x 2 Stroke 6 Cy. 500 x 1910 8580kW (11665bhp) Mitsui Engineering & Shipbuilding CLtd-Japan Fuel: 152.0 (d.f.) 2326.0 (r.f.)
9694115 *V7DL3* -	**TOPAZ FAYE** *ex* Sk Line 709 *-2014* **Team XXXII Ltd** Nico Middle East Ltd (Topaz Marine) *Majuro* *Marshall Islands* MMSI: 538005379 Official number: 5379	**2,955** 916 3,255	Class: AB	**2014-01 Xiamen Shipbuilding Industry Co Ltd — Xiamen FJ** Yd No: SK709 Loa 75.00 (BB) Br ex 17.27 Dght 6.600 Lbp 67.47 Br md 17.25 Dpth 8.00 Welded, 1 dk	**(B21A20S) Platform Supply Ship**	**2 oil engines** reduction geared to sc. shaft (s) driving 2 Z propellers Total Power: 4,412kW (5,998hp) 14.5kn Niigata 8L28HX 2 x 4 Stroke 8 Cy. 280 x 370 each-2206kW (2999bhp) Niigata Engineering Co Ltd-Japan Thrusters: 2 Thwart. CP thruster (f)
9518854 *V7SC7* -	**TOPAZ FUJAIRAH** **Team XX Ltd** Nico Middle East Ltd (Topaz Marine) *Majuro* *Marshall Islands* MMSI: 538003619 Official number: 3619	**215** 171 55	Class: NV (GL)	**2009-10 Nico Craft LLC — Fujairah** Yd No: 103 Loa 30.20 Br ex 10.30 Dght 1.200 Lbp 27.40 Br md 10.00 Dpth 2.82 Welded, 1 dk	**(B21A20C) Crew/Supply Vessel** Hull Material: Aluminium Alloy Passengers: 49	**2 oil engines** reverse reduction geared to sc. shafts driving 2 FP propellers Total Power: 2,088kW (2,838hp) 20.0kn Caterpillar C32 2 x Vee 4 Stroke 12 Cy. 145 x 162 each-1044kW (1419bhp) Caterpillar Inc-USA AuxGen: 2 x a.c
9560297 *UNCD* -	**TOPAZ GLORY** **Bovey Offshore V Ltd** BUE Marine Turkmenistan Ltd *Kazakhstan* MMSI: 436000198	**1,678** 503 1,360	Class: AB	**2010-04 Fujian Funing Shipyard Industry Co Ltd — Fu'an FJ** Yd No: 601-01 Loa 59.25 Br ex - Dght 4.950 Lbp 52.20 Br md 14.95 Dpth 6.10 Welded, 1 dk	**(B21B20A) Anchor Handling Tug Supply**	**2 oil engines** reduction geared to sc. shafts driving 2 Propellers Total Power: 3,282kW (4,462hp) 11.0kn Caterpillar 3516B-HD 2 x Vee 4 Stroke 16 Cy. 170 x 215 each-1641kW (2231bhp) Caterpillar Inc-USA AuxGen: 3 x 315kW a.c
9478858 *3FJH3* -	**TOPAZ HALO** **Sun Lanes Shipping SA** Nissen Kaiun Co Ltd (Nissen Kaiun KK) SatCom: Inmarsat C 435569712 *Panama* *Panama* MMSI: 355697000 Official number: 4290711	**31,218** 18,516 55,612 T/cm 55.8	Class: NK	**2011-08 Mitsui Eng. & SB. Co. Ltd. — Tamano** Yd No: 1708 Loa 189.99 (BB) Br ex - Dght 12.570 Lbp 182.00 Br md 32.26 Dpth 17.90 Welded, 1 dk	**(A21A2BC) Bulk Carrier** Grain: 70,868; Bale: 68,116 Compartments: 5 Ho, ER 5 Ha: ER Cranes: 4x30t	**1 oil engine** driving 1 FP propeller Total Power: 9,480kW (12,889hp) 14.5kn MAN-B&W 6S50MC-C 1 x 2 Stroke 6 Cy. 500 x 2000 9480kW (12889bhp) Mitsui Engineering & Shipbuilding CLtd-Japan Fuel: 2290.0
7924839 - -	**TOPAZ II** *ex* Pirgos *-2010* *ex* Sea Patron *-2004* *ex* Alam Teguh *-2002* *ex* Aran *-1989* **Moonlight Shipping & Trading Inc** Gulf of Aden Shipping LLC *Zanzibar* *Tanzania (Zanzibar)* Official number: 300440	**10,230** 6,259 17,169	Class: (LR) (RS) ✠ Classed LR until 22/5/08	**1980-09 Ishikawajima-Harima Heavy Industries Co Ltd (IHI) — Chita AI** Yd No: 2730 Loa 145.55 (BB) Br ex 21.04 Dght 9.486 Lbp 137.04 Br md 21.01 Dpth 13.11 Welded, 1 dk, 2nd dk portable	**(A31A2GX) General Cargo Ship** Grain: 21,173; Bale: 21,069 TEU 367 C Ho 311 TEU C Dk 56 TEU Compartments: 5 Ho, ER, 5 Tw Dk 5 Ha: (15.0 x 9.9) (12.7 x 15.6)3 (15.0 x 15.6)ER Cranes: 2x25t,2x22t,1x10t	**1 oil engine** sr geared to sc. shaft driving 1 CP propeller 14.5kn Total Power: 4,413kW (6,000hp) Pielstick 12PC2-2V-400 1 x Vee 4 Stroke 12 Cy. 400 x 460 4413kW (6000bhp) Ishikawajima Harima Heavy IndustrieCo Ltd (IHI)-Japan AuxGen: 1 x 500kW 450V 60Hz a.c, 1 x 160kW 450V 60Hz a.c Boilers: AuxB (Comp) 9.0kgf/cm² (8.8bar) Fuel: 146.5 (d.f.) 1049.5 (r.f.)

IMO / Call sign	Name / Owner	Tonnage	Class	Build / Dimensions	Type	Machinery
9199854 *J8B2641* -	**TOPAZ INSTALLER** *ex* Team Oman *-2013* *ex* Team Sea Spider *-2003* *ex* Sea Spider *-2002* **Team IV Ltd** Nico Middle East Ltd (Topaz Marine) *Kingstown* *St Vincent & The Grenadines* MMSI: 377265000 Official number: 9113	**4,904** 1,472 4,800	Class: NV (BV)	**1999-03 Scheepswerf De Hoop Lobith B.V. — Lobith** Yd No: 373 Loa 86.10 Br ex - Dght 4.500 Lbp 82.32 Br md 24.00 Dpth 5.50 Welded, 1 dk	**(B34D2SL) Cable Layer** Passengers: berths: 50 A-frames: 1x24t; Cranes: 1x15t	**4 diesel electric oil engines** driving 4 gen. Connecting to 2 elec. motors driving 2 Propellers FP Azimuthing Drive unit. Total Power: 5,680kW (7,722hp) 10.0kn Cummins Wartsila 16V170 2 x Vee 4 Stroke 16 Cy. 170 x 200 each-2060kW (2801bhp) Cummins Engine Co Ltd-United Kingdom Cummins Wartsila 6L170 2 x 4 Stroke 6 Cy. 170 x 200 each-780kW (1060bhp) Cummins Engine Co Ltd-United Kingdom Thrusters: 2 Thwart. FP thruster (f); 1 Retract. directional thruster (f) Fuel: 500.0 (d.f.) 20.0pd
9523847 *ZCXQ7* -	**TOPAZ JADDAF** *launched as* SK Line 21 *-2008* **Team XII Ltd** Nico Middle East Ltd (Topaz Marine) *George Town* *Cayman Islands (British)* MMSI: 319317000 Official number: 740749	**1,678** 503 1,360	Class: AB	**2008-09 Fujian Southeast Shipyard — Fuzhou FJ** Yd No: SK46 Loa 59.25 Br ex - Dght 4.950 Lbp 52.20 Br md 14.95 Dpth 6.10 Welded, 1 dk	**(B21B20A) Anchor Handling Tug Supply** Cranes: 1x3t	**2 oil engines** reduction geared to sc. shafts driving 2 CP propellers Total Power: 3,840kW (5,220hp) 10.0kn Caterpillar 3516B-HD 2 x Vee 4 Stroke 16 Cy. 170 x 215 each-1920kW (2610bhp) Caterpillar Inc-USA AuxGen: 3 x 315kW 415V 50Hz a.c Thrusters: 1 Tunnel thruster (f) Fuel: 530.0
9529073 *ZCXQ6* -	**TOPAZ JAFILIYA** *completed as* SK Line 40 *-2008* **Team XIII Ltd** Nico Middle East Ltd (Topaz Marine) *George Town* *Cayman Islands (British)* MMSI: 319002400 Official number: 740748	**1,678** 503 1,407	Class: AB	**2008-12 Fujian Southeast Shipyard — Fuzhou FJ** Yd No: SK40 Loa 59.25 Br ex - Dght 4.950 Lbp 52.20 Br md 14.95 Dpth 6.10 Welded, 1 dk	**(B21B20A) Anchor Handling Tug Supply** Cranes: 1x3t	**2 oil engines** reduction geared to sc. shafts driving 2 CP propellers Total Power: 3,840kW (5,220hp) 10.0kn Caterpillar 3516B-HD 2 x Vee 4 Stroke 16 Cy. 170 x 215 each-1920kW (2610bhp) Caterpillar Inc-USA AuxGen: 3 x 350kW 415V 50Hz a.c Thrusters: 1 Tunnel thruster (f) Fuel: 530.0
9504671 *ZCTX6* -	**TOPAZ JEBEL ALI** **Team V Ltd** Nico Middle East Ltd (Topaz Marine) *George Town* *Cayman Islands (British)* MMSI: 319325000 Official number: 740593	**1,678** 503 1,381	Class: AB	**2008-06 Fujian Southeast Shipyard — Fuzhou FJ** Yd No: SK37 Loa 59.25 Br ex - Dght 4.950 Lbp 52.20 Br md 14.95 Dpth 6.10 Welded, 1 dk	**(B21B20A) Anchor Handling Tug Supply** Cranes: 1x3t	**2 oil engines** reduction geared to sc. shafts driving 2 CP propellers Total Power: 3,840kW (5,220hp) 10.0kn Caterpillar 3516B-HD 2 x Vee 4 Stroke 16 Cy. 170 x 215 each-1920kW (2610bhp) Caterpillar Inc-USA AuxGen: 3 x 315kW 415V 50Hz a.c Thrusters: 1 Tunnel thruster (f) Fuel: 530.0
9564451 *V7TN5* -	**TOPAZ JOHOR** *ex* Bovey VIII *-2010* **Bovey Offshore VIII Ltd** Nico Middle East Ltd (Topaz Marine) *Majuro* *Marshall Islands* MMSI: 538003839 Official number: 3839	**1,678** 503 1,374	Class: AB	**2010-08 Fujian Funing Shipyard Industry Co Ltd — Fu'an FJ** Yd No: 601-04 Loa 59.25 Br ex - Dght 4.950 Lbp 52.20 Br md 14.95 Dpth 6.10 Welded, 1 dk	**(B21B20A) Anchor Handling Tug Supply**	**2 oil engines** reduction geared to sc. shafts driving 2 Propellers Total Power: 3,282kW (4,462hp) Caterpillar 3516B-HD 2 x Vee 4 Stroke 16 Cy. 170 x 215 each-1641kW (2231bhp) Caterpillar Inc-USA AuxGen: 3 x 350kW a.c
9463530 *ZCTX7* -	**TOPAZ JUMEIRAH** **Team V Ltd** Nico Middle East Ltd (Topaz Marine) *George Town* *Cayman Islands (British)* MMSI: 319064000 Official number: 740594	**1,678** 503 1,372	Class: AB	**2007-12 Fujian Southeast Shipyard — Fuzhou FJ** Yd No: SK36 Loa 59.25 Br ex - Dght 4.950 Lbp 52.20 Br md 14.95 Dpth 6.10 Welded, 1 dk	**(B21B20A) Anchor Handling Tug Supply** Cranes: 1x3t	**2 oil engines** reduction geared to sc. shafts driving 2 CP propellers Total Power: 3,840kW (5,220hp) 10.0kn Caterpillar 3516B-HD 2 x Vee 4 Stroke 16 Cy. 170 x 215 each-1920kW (2610bhp) Caterpillar Inc-USA AuxGen: 3 x 315kW 415V 50Hz a.c Thrusters: 1 Tunnel thruster (f) Fuel: 530.0
9563811 *V7TN4* -	**TOPAZ JURONG** *ex* Bovey Vii *-2010* *ex* Fujian Funing 601-03 *-2009* **Bovey Offshore VII Ltd** Nico Middle East Ltd (Topaz Marine) *Majuro* *Marshall Islands* MMSI: 538003838 Official number: 3838	**1,678** 503 1,366	Class: AB	**2010-07 Fujian Funing Shipyard Industry Co Ltd — Fu'an FJ** Yd No: 601-03 Loa 59.25 Br ex - Dght 4.950 Lbp 52.20 Br md 14.95 Dpth 6.10 Welded, 1 dk	**(B21B20A) Anchor Handling Tug Supply**	**2 oil engines** reduction geared to sc. shafts driving 2 Propellers Total Power: 3,840kW (5,220hp) Caterpillar 3516B 2 x Vee 4 Stroke 16 Cy. 170 x 190 each-1920kW (2610bhp) Caterpillar Inc-USA AuxGen: 3 x 350kW a.c Fuel: 530.0
9591260 *V7TA5* -	**TOPAZ KARAMA** **Topaz Karama Ltd** Nico Middle East Ltd (Topaz Marine) SatCom: Inmarsat C 453835730 *Majuro* *Marshall Islands* MMSI: 538003764 Official number: 3764	**1,678** 503 1,346	Class: AB	**2010-12 Fujian Southeast Shipyard — Fuzhou FJ** Yd No: DN59M-65 Loa 59.25 Br ex 14.97 Dght 4.950 Lbp 52.20 Br md 14.95 Dpth 6.10 Welded, 1 dk	**(B21B20A) Anchor Handling Tug Supply** Cranes: 1x3t	**2 oil engines** reduction geared to sc. shafts driving 2 CP propellers Total Power: 3,788kW (5,150hp) 11.0kn Caterpillar 3516B-HD 2 x Vee 4 Stroke 16 Cy. 170 x 215 each-1894kW (2575bhp) Caterpillar Inc-USA AuxGen: 2 x 800kW 415V 50Hz a.c, 2 x 350kW 415V 50Hz a.c Thrusters: 2 Tunnel thruster (f); 1 Tunnel thruster (a) Fuel: 520.0
9620463 *V7WE2* -	**TOPAZ KARZAKKAN** **Topaz Karzakkan Ltd** Nico Middle East Ltd (Topaz Marine) *Majuro* *Marshall Islands* MMSI: 538004276 Official number: 4276	**1,678** 503 1,311	Class: AB	**2011-10 Fujian Southeast Shipyard — Fuzhou FJ** Yd No: DN59M-68 Loa 59.25 Br ex - Dght 4.950 Lbp 52.20 Br md 14.95 Dpth 6.10 Welded, 1 dk	**(B21B20A) Anchor Handling Tug Supply** Cranes: 1x3t	**2 oil engines** reduction geared to sc. shafts driving 2 CP propellers Total Power: 3,840kW (5,220hp) 11.0kn Caterpillar 3516B-HD 2 x Vee 4 Stroke 16 Cy. 170 x 215 each-1920kW (2610bhp) Caterpillar Inc-USA AuxGen: 2 x 800kW 415V 50Hz a.c, 2 x 350kW 415V 50Hz a.c Thrusters: 2 Tunnel thruster (f) Fuel: 520.0
9591258 *V7TA4* -	**TOPAZ KHALIDIYA** **Topaz Khalidiya Ltd** Nico Middle East Ltd (Topaz Marine) *Majuro* *Marshall Islands* MMSI: 538003763 Official number: 3763	**1,678** 503 1,339	Class: AB	**2010-10 Fujian Southeast Shipyard — Fuzhou FJ** Yd No: DN59M-63 Loa 59.25 Br ex 14.97 Dght 4.950 Lbp 52.20 Br md 14.95 Dpth 6.10 Welded, 1 dk	**(B21B20A) Anchor Handling Tug Supply** Cranes: 1x3t	**2 oil engines** reduction geared to sc. shafts driving 2 CP propellers Total Power: 3,840kW (5,220hp) 11.0kn Caterpillar 3516B-HD 2 x Vee 4 Stroke 16 Cy. 170 x 215 each-1920kW (2610bhp) Caterpillar Inc-USA AuxGen: 2 x 800kW 415V 50Hz a.c, 2 x 350kW 415V 50Hz a.c Thrusters: 2 Tunnel thruster (f); 1 Tunnel thruster (a) Fuel: 520.0
9588940 *V7TA2* -	**TOPAZ KHOBAR** **Topaz Khobar Ltd** Nico Middle East Ltd (Topaz Marine) *Majuro* *Marshall Islands* MMSI: 538003761 Official number: 3761	**1,678** 503 1,339	Class: AB	**2010-07 Fujian Southeast Shipyard — Fuzhou FJ** Yd No: DN59M-55 Loa 59.25 Br ex - Dght 4.950 Lbp 52.20 Br md 14.95 Dpth 6.10 Welded, 1 dk	**(B21B20A) Anchor Handling Tug Supply** Cranes: 1x3t	**2 oil engines** reduction geared to sc. shafts driving 2 CP propellers Total Power: 3,840kW (5,220hp) 11.0kn Caterpillar 3516B-HD 2 x Vee 4 Stroke 16 Cy. 170 x 215 each-1920kW (2610bhp) Caterpillar Inc-USA AuxGen: 2 x 350kW 415V 50Hz a.c, 2 x 800kW 415V 50Hz a.c Thrusters: 2 Tunnel thruster (f); 1 Tunnel thruster (a) Fuel: 530.0 (d.f.)
9620451 *V7WE3* -	**TOPAZ KHUBAYB** **Topaz Khubayb Ltd** Nico Middle East Ltd (Topaz Marine) *Majuro* *Marshall Islands* MMSI: 538004277 Official number: 4277	**1,678** 503 1,340	Class: AB	**2011-06 Fujian Southeast Shipyard — Fuzhou FJ** Yd No: DN59M-67 Loa 59.25 Br ex - Dght 4.950 Lbp 52.20 Br md 14.95 Dpth 6.10 Welded, 1 dk	**(B21B20A) Anchor Handling Tug Supply** Cranes: 1x3t	**2 oil engines** reduction geared to sc. shafts driving 2 CP propellers Total Power: 3,840kW (5,220hp) 11.0kn Caterpillar 3516B-HD 2 x Vee 4 Stroke 16 Cy. 170 x 215 each-1920kW (2610bhp) Caterpillar Inc-USA AuxGen: 2 x 800kW 415V 50Hz a.c, 2 x 350kW 15V 50Hz a.c Thrusters: 2 Tunnel thruster (f) Fuel: 520.0

9588952 *V7TA3* -	**TOPAZ KHUWAIR** **Topaz Khuwair Ltd** Nico Middle East Ltd (Topaz Marine) *Majuro* *Marshall Islands* MMSI: 538003762 Official number: 3762	**1,678** 503 1,346	Class: AB	**2010**-08 **Fujian Southeast Shipyard — Fuzhou FJ** Yd No: DN59M-56 Loa 59.25 Br ex - Dght 4.950 Lbp 52.20 Br md 14.95 Dpth 6.10 Welded, 1 dk	**(B21B20A) Anchor Handling Tug Supply** Cranes: 1x3t	**2 oil engines** reduction geared to sc. shafts driving 2 CP propellers Total Power: 3,840kW (5,220hp) 11.0kn Caterpillar 3516B-HD 2 x Vee 4 Stroke 16 Cy. 170 x 215 each-1920kW (2610bhp) Caterpillar Inc-USA AuxGen: 2 x 800kW 415V 50Hz a.c, 2 x 350kW 415V 50Hz a.c Thrusters: 2 Tunnel thruster (f); 1 Tunnel thruster (a) Fuel: 520.0
9560302 *UNCC* -	**TOPAZ LEGEND** *ex* Bovey Vi *-2010* **Bovey Offshore VI Ltd** Topaz Energy & Marine Ltd (TEAM) *Aqtau* *Kazakhstan* MMSI: 436000197	**1,678** 503 1,386	Class: AB	**2010**-02 **Fujian Funing Shipyard Industry Co Ltd — Fu'an FJ** Yd No: 601-02 Loa 59.25 Br ex - Dght 4.950 Lbp 52.20 Br md 14.95 Dpth 6.10 Welded, 1 dk	**(B21B20A) Anchor Handling Tug Supply**	**2 oil engines** reduction geared to sc. shafts driving 2 CP propellers Total Power: 3,840kW (5,220hp) 11.0kn Caterpillar 3516B-HD 2 x Vee 4 Stroke 16 Cy. 170 x 215 each-1920kW (2610bhp) Caterpillar Inc-USA AuxGen: 3 x 315kW a.c Fuel: 485.0
9513074 *D6FJ4* -	**TOPAZ N** *ex* Popeye 1 *-2009* **Henford Logistics Ltd** - *Union of Comoros* MMSI: 616857000	**490** 147 -	Class: BV	**2009**-04 **Eregli Gemi Insa Sanayi ve Ticaret AS — Karadeniz Eregli** Yd No: 21 Loa 32.00 Br ex - Dght 4.560 Lbp 30.46 Br md 11.60 Dpth 5.36 Welded, 1 dk	**(B32A2ST) Tug**	**2 oil engines** reduction geared to sc. shafts driving 2 Directional propellers Total Power: 3,240kW (4,406hp) Wartsila 9L20 2 x 4 Stroke 9 Cy. 200 x 280 each-1620kW (2203bhp) Wartsila Finland Oy-Finland AuxGen: 2 x 175kW 50Hz a.c
9030383 *H09787* -	**TOPAZ PORT** *ex* Genius Port *-2012* *ex* Borcos 112 *-2009* **Topaz Tankers Shipping Inc** Topaz Tankers Shipmanagement Inc *Panama* *Panama* MMSI: 354178000 Official number: 4120710A	**117** 35 29	Class: LR ✠ **100A1** SS 08/2010 Persian Gulf coastal service ✠ **LMC** Cable: 190.0/12.5 U2	**1991**-06 **Aluminium Craft (88) Pte Ltd — Singapore** Yd No: 15 Loa 27.50 Br ex 6.35 Dght 1.650 Lbp 24.00 Br md 6.20 Dpth 2.80 Welded, 1 dk	**(B21A20C) Crew/Supply Vessel** Hull Material: Aluminium Alloy	**2 oil engines** with clutches & sr reverse geared to sc. shafts driving 2 FP propellers Total Power: 1,060kW (1,442hp) 16.0kn G.M. (Detroit Diesel) 12V-92-TA 2 x Vee 2 Stroke 12 Cy. 123 x 127 each-530kW (721bhp) General Motors Detroit DieselAllison Divn-USA AuxGen: 2 x 32kW 380V 50Hz a.c
8869529 *H09770* -	**TOPAZ POWER** *ex* Genius Power *-2012* *ex* Bahtera Jaya 2 *-2010* *ex* AKN Eagle *-2007* *ex* TSM 18 *-2005* *ex* TS 32-1 *-2001* **Topaz Tankers Shipping Inc** Topaz Tankers Shipmanagement Inc *Panama* *Panama* MMSI: 355353000 Official number: 4117910A	*259* 77 -	Class: LR (CC) (BV) **100A1** SS 03/2012 tug Arabian Gulf coastal service **LMC** Cable: 275.0/19.0 YY	**1993**-11 **Wenzhou Dongfang Shipyard — Yueqing ZJ** Yd No: 9107 Loa 32.00 Br ex - Dght 3.030 Lbp 29.10 Br md 8.60 Dpth 4.07 Welded, 1 dk	**(B32A2ST) Tug**	**2 oil engines** reduction geared to sc. shafts driving 2 FP propellers Total Power: 1,408kW (1,914hp) 11.0kn Cummins KTA-38-M 2 x Vee 4 Stroke 12 Cy. 159 x 159 each-704kW (957bhp) Cummins Engine Co Ltd-United Kingdom AuxGen: 2 x 64kW 400V 50Hz a.c Fuel: 122.0 (d.f.)
9349112 *V7ZF8* -	**TOPAZ RAYYAN** *ex* Sanko Dragon *-2012* *ex* Jaya Valiant 3 *-2007* **Team XXIII Ltd** Nico Middle East Ltd (Topaz Marine) *Majuro* *Marshall Islands* MMSI: 538004814 Official number: 4814	**2,679** 803 2,369	Class: AB	**2005**-12 **Fujian Southeast Shipyard — Fuzhou FJ** Yd No: 843 Loa 70.00 Br ex 16.82 Dght 6.100 Lbp 61.20 Br md 16.80 Dpth 7.50 Welded, 1 dk	**(B21B20A) Anchor Handling Tug Supply**	**2 oil engines** reduction geared to sc. shafts driving 1 CP propeller , 1 FP propeller Total Power: 5,918kW (8,046hp) 13.0kn Wartsila 6L32 2 x 4 Stroke 6 Cy. 320 x 400 each-2959kW (4023bhp) Wartsila Finland Oy-Finland AuxGen: 2 x 370kW a.c, 2 x 2875kW a.c Thrusters: 2 Tunnel thruster (f); 1 Tunnel thruster (a) Fuel: 1225.0 (r.f.)
9227106 *V7AV8* -	**TOPAZ SALALAH** *ex* Team Salalah *-2010* **Topaz Salalah Leasing Ltd** Nico Middle East Ltd (Topaz Marine) *Majuro* *Marshall Islands* MMSI: 538005078 Official number: 5078	**1,700** 510 1,725	Class: NV (AB)	**2000**-04 **Adyard Abu Dhabi LLC — Abu Dhabi** Yd No: 001 Loa 61.00 Br ex - Dght 4.800 Lbp 54.90 Br md 15.20 Dpth 6.40 Welded, 1 dk	**(B21B20A) Anchor Handling Tug Supply**	**2 oil engines** reduction geared to sc. shafts driving 2 CP propellers Total Power: 5,200kW (7,070hp) 15.0kn Wartsila 8L26 2 x 4 Stroke 8 Cy. 260 x 320 each-2600kW (3535bhp) Wartsila NSD Nederland BV-Netherlands AuxGen: 2 x 580kW 440V 60Hz a.c, 2 x 300kW 440V 60Hz a.c Thrusters: 1 Thwart. FP thruster (f); 1 Tunnel thruster (a)
9694127 *V7DL5* -	**TOPAZ SEEMA** *ex* Sk Line 710 *-2014* **Team XXXIII Ltd** Nico Middle East Ltd (Topaz Marine) *Majuro* *Marshall Islands* MMSI: 538005396 Official number: 5396	**2,955** 916 3,262	Class: AB	**2014**-01 **Xiamen Shipbuilding Industry Co Ltd — Xiamen FJ** Yd No: SK710 Loa 75.00 (BB) Br ex 17.27 Dght 6.600 Lbp 67.47 Br md 17.25 Dpth 8.00 Welded, 1 dk	**(B21A20S) Platform Supply Ship**	**2 oil engines** reduction geared to sc. shaft (s) driving 2 Z propellers Total Power: 4,412kW (5,998hp) 14.5kn Niigata 8L28HX 2 x 4 Stroke 8 Cy. 280 x 370 each-2206kW (2999bhp) Niigata Engineering Co Ltd-Japan Thrusters: 2 Thwart. CP thruster (f)
9541174 *V7ZC4* -	**TOPAZ SHAHEEN** *ex* SK Line 33 *-2009* **Team XXIV Ltd** Nico Middle East Ltd (Topaz Marine) *Majuro* *Marshall Islands* MMSI: 538004788 Official number: 4788	**1,706** 511 1,737	Class: AB	**2009**-07 **Fujian Crown Ocean Shipbuilding Industry Co Ltd — Lianjiang County FJ** Yd No: SK33 Loa 60.00 Br ex - Dght 5.100 Lbp 53.90 Br md 16.00 Dpth 6.00 Welded, 1 dk	**(B21B20A) Anchor Handling Tug Supply**	**2 oil engines** reduction geared to sc. shafts driving 2 CP propellers Total Power: 3,840kW (5,220hp) 11.0kn Yanmar 6EY26 2 x 4 Stroke 6 Cy. 260 x 385 each-1920kW (2610bhp) Yanmar Diesel Engine Co Ltd-Japan AuxGen: 2 x 1000kW a.c, 2 x 280kW a.c Fuel: 520.0
9680657 *V7CV9* -	**TOPAZ SOPHIE** *ex* Sk Line 707 *-2013* **Team XXXI Ltd** Nico Middle East Ltd (Topaz Marine) *Majuro* *Marshall Islands* MMSI: 538005335 Official number: 5335	**2,948** 913 3,130	Class: AB	**2013**-11 **Fujian Southeast Shipyard — Fuzhou FJ** Yd No: SK707 Loa 75.00 (BB) Br ex - Dght 6.500 Lbp 67.85 Br md 17.25 Dpth 8.00 Welded, 1 dk	**(B21A20S) Platform Supply Ship**	**2 oil engines** reduction geared to sc. shafts driving 2 Z propellers Total Power: 4,412kW (5,998hp) 14.5kn Niigata 8L28HX 2 x 4 Stroke 8 Cy. 280 x 370 each-2206kW (2999bhp) Niigata Engineering Co Ltd-Japan AuxGen: 2 x 1000kW a.c, 3 x 450kW a.c Thrusters: 2 Thwart. CP thruster (f)
9508940 *3FEI9* -	**TOPAZ-T** **Samfire Overseas Inc** Transal Denizcilik Ticaret AS SatCom: Inmarsat C 435322912 *Panama* *Panama* MMSI: 353229000 Official number: 4068009	**8,638** 4,498 13,966 T/cm 23.6	Class: NV (BV)	**2009**-06 **Selah Makina Sanayi ve Ticaret A.S. — Tuzla, Istanbul** Yd No: 53 Loa 136.59 (BB) Br ex - Dght 8.459 Lbp 130.00 Br md 20.00 Dpth 10.90 Welded, 1 dk	**(A12B2TR) Chemical/Products Tanker** Double Hull (13F) Liq: 15,056; Liq (Oil): 15,056 Cargo Heating Coils Compartments: 14 Wing Ta, 2 Wing Slop Ta, ER 14 Cargo Pump (s): 14x250m³/hr Manifold: Bow/CM: 67m	**2 oil engines** reduction geared to sc. shafts driving 2 CP propellers Total Power: 5,148kW (7,000hp) 14.0kn Yanmar 6N330-EN 2 x 4 Stroke 6 Cy. 330 x 440 each-2574kW (3500bhp) Yanmar Diesel Engine Co Ltd-Japan AuxGen: 3 x a.c, 2 x a.c Thrusters: 1 Tunnel thruster (f) Fuel: 80.0 (d.f.) 541.0 (r.f.)
9654995 *4JPH* -	**TOPAZ TRIUMPH** **Team XVIII Ltd** BUE Caspian Ltd *Baku* *Azerbaijan* MMSI: 423385100 Official number: BR-058	**2,148** 644 2,135	Class: AB	**2013**-01 **Nico Craft LLC — Fujairah** Yd No: 122 Loa 67.40 Br ex - Dght 5.700 Lbp 59.40 Br md 16.00 Dpth 6.80 Welded, 1 dk	**(B21B20A) Anchor Handling Tug Supply**	**2 oil engines** reduction geared to sc. shafts driving 2 CP propellers Total Power: 5,440kW (7,396hp) 10.0kn MAN-B&W 8L27/38 2 x 4 Stroke 8 Cy. 270 x 380 each-2720kW (3698bhp) MAN B&W Diesel AG-Augsburg AuxGen: 2 x 515kW 440V 60Hz a.c, 2 x 1250kW 440V 60Hz a.c Thrusters: 2 Thwart. CP thruster (f); 1 Thwart. CP thruster (a) Fuel: 630.0 (r.f.)
9680669 *V7EQ6* -	**TOPAZ XARA** *ex* Sk Line 708 *-2014* *ex* Fujian Southeast Sk708 *-2014* **Team XXXIV Ltd** Nico Middle East Ltd (Topaz Marine) *Majuro* *Marshall Islands* MMSI: 538005515 Official number: 5515	**2,948** 913 3,147	Class: AB	**2014**-03 **Fujian Southeast Shipyard — Fuzhou FJ** Yd No: SK708 Loa 75.00 (BB) Br ex - Dght 6.500 Lbp 67.85 Br md 17.25 Dpth 8.00 Welded, 1 dk	**(B21A20S) Platform Supply Ship**	**2 oil engines** reduction geared to sc. shafts driving 2 Z propellers 14.5kn Niigata 2 x 4 Stroke Niigata Engineering Co Ltd-Japan Thrusters: 2 Thwart. CP thruster (f)
9624990 *V7DS7* -	**TOPAZ ZENITH** **Team XXXV Ltd** Doha Marine Services WLL (DMS) *Majuro* *Marshall Islands* MMSI: 538005429 Official number: 5429	**134** 41 26	Class: NV	**2011**-06 **Nico Craft LLC — Fujairah** Yd No: 119 Loa 26.00 (BB) Br ex - Dght 1.350 Lbp 24.22 Br md 7.50 Dpth 3.20 Welded, 1 dk	**(B21A20C) Crew/Supply Vessel** Hull Material: Aluminium Alloy	**2 oil engines** reduction geared to sc. shafts driving 2 Water jets Total Power: 2,386kW (3,244hp) 28.0kn Caterpillar C32 ACERT 2 x Vee 4 Stroke 12 Cy. 145 x 162 each-1193kW (1622bhp) Caterpillar Inc-USA AuxGen: 2 x a.c

IMO / Call sign	Name / Owner	Tonnage	Class	Builder / Dimensions	Type	Machinery
9628477 *V7ZI8* -	**TOPAZ ZEPHYR** **Topaz Zephyr Leasing Ltd** Nico Middle East Ltd (Topaz Marine) *Majuro* *Marshall Islands* MMSI: 538004837 Official number: 4837	**145** 44 26	Class: NV	**2011-10 Nico Craft LLC — Fujairah** Yd No: 120 Loa 26.00 Br ex - Dght 1.350 Lbp 23.00 Br md 7.50 Dpth 3.20 Welded, 1 dk	**(B21A2OC) Crew/Supply Vessel** Hull Material: Aluminium Alloy	**2 oil engines** reduction geared to sc. shafts driving 2 Water jets Total Power: 1,640kW (2,230hp) 28.0kn Caterpillar C32 ACERT 2 x Vee 4 Stroke 12 Cy. 145 x 162 each-820kW (1115bhp) Caterpillar Inc-USA AuxGen: 2 x a.c
9015333 *3FTR3* -	**TOPAZIS** *ex* Fullam *-2011* *ex* Faithful *-2010* *ex* Norca *-2002* *ex* Nord-Gloria *-2000* *ex* Crystal River *-1997* **Yoshi Shipping Co Ltd** Oyster Cargo & Shipping LLC *Panama* *Panama* MMSI: 355441000 Official number: 41593PEXT3	**25,877** 12,610 45,720 T/cm 47.6	Class: (LR) (BV) (NK) Classed LR until 31/5/12	**1992-01 Tsuneishi Shipbuilding Co Ltd — Fukuyama HS** Yd No: 656 Loa 181.00 (BB) Br ex 30.03 Dght 12.500 Lbp 172.00 Br md 30.00 Dpth 18.20 Welded, 1 dk	**(A13A2TW) Crude/Oil Products Tanker** Double Hull (13F) Liq: 47,260; Liq (Oil): 47,260 Cargo Heating Coils Compartments: 7 Ta, 2 Wing Slop Ta, ER 4 Cargo Pump (s): 4x1250m³/hr	**1 oil engine** driving 1 FP propeller Total Power: 6,550kW (8,905hp) 14.0kn B&W 6L60MCE 1 x 2 Stroke 6 Cy. 600 x 1944 6550kW (8905bhp) Mitsui Engineering & Shipbuilding CLtd-Japan AuxGen: 3 x 440kW 440V 60Hz a.c Boilers: e (ex.g.) 22.0kgf/cm² (21.6bar), AuxB (o.f.) 18.0kgf/cm² (17.7bar) Fuel: 183.0 (d.f.) 1472.0 (r.f.) 24.5pd
8721882 *UDDS* -	**TOPAZOVYY** *ex* Angara *-2012* *ex* Mortransflotovets *-2009* **Parma Co Ltd** - *Kholmsk* *Russia* MMSI: 273899300	**737** 221 332	Class: RS	**1987-11 Volgogradskiy Sudostroitelnyy Zavod — Volgograd** Yd No: 243 Loa 53.74 (BB) Br ex 10.71 Dght 4.400 Lbp 47.92 Br md 10.50 Dpth 6.00 Welded, 1 dk	**(B11A2FS) Stern Trawler** Ice Capable	**1 oil engine** driving 1 CP propeller Total Power: 971kW (1,320hp) 12.7kn S.K.L. 8NVD48A-2U 1 x 4 Stroke 8 Cy. 320 x 480 971kW (1320bhp) VEB Schwermaschinenbau "KarlLiebknecht" (SKL)-Magdeburg AuxGen: 1 x 300kW a.c, 3 x 160kW a.c, 2 x 135kW a.c
7741421 - -	**TOPAZOVYY** *ex* Neptune *-2009* *ex* Topazovyy *-2006* - -	**677** 216 495	Class: (RS)	**1979-07 Khabarovskiy Sudostroitelnyy Zavod im Kirova — Khabarovsk** Yd No: 825 Loa 55.00 Br ex 9.53 Dght 4.341 Lbp 50.04 Br md 9.30 Dpth 5.19 Welded, 1 dk	**(B12B2FC) Fish Carrier** Ins: 632 Compartments: 2 Ho, ER 2 Ha: 2 (2.9 x 2.9) Derricks: 4x3.3t; Winches: 4 Ice Capable	**1 oil engine** driving 1 FP propeller 11.3kn S.K.L. 6NVD48-2U 1 x 4 Stroke 6 Cy. 320 x 480 VEB Schwermaschinenbau "KarlLiebknecht" (SKL)-Magdeburg Fuel: 109.0 (d.f.)
8421793 *TC4344* -	**TOPCULAR-I** *ex* Topcular I *-2012* **Istanbul Deniz Otobusleri Sanayi ve Ticaret AS (IDO)** - *Istanbul* *Turkey* MMSI: 271002494 Official number: 1072	*1,595* 630 608	Class: TL (AB)	**1986-03 Turkiye Gemi Sanayii A.S. — Pendik** Yd No: 005 Loa 80.71 Br ex - Dght 3.900 Lbp 78.78 Br md 22.00 Dpth 4.50 Welded	**(A36A2PR) Passenger/Ro-Ro Ship (Vehicles)** Passengers: unberthed: 1434 Cars: 112	**2 oil engines** with clutches, flexible couplings & sr geared to sc. shafts driving 2 CP propellers 1 fwd and 1 aft Total Power: 1,766kW (2,402hp) 11.0kn A.B.C. 8MDXC 2 x 4 Stroke 8 Cy. 242 x 320 each-883kW (1201bhp) Anglo Belgian Corp NV (ABC)-Belgium AuxGen: 2 x 120kW 220V 50Hz a.c Fuel: 82.0 (d.f.) 3.8pd
9211585 *9HZU8* -	**TOPEKA** *ex* Gianfranca d'Amato *-2007* **Oceantrade Owners Ltd** TMS Bulkers Ltd *Valletta* *Malta* MMSI: 256657000 Official number: 9211585	**40,562** 26,139 74,716 T/cm 67.0	Class: BV (RI) (AB)	**2000-05 Hudong Shipbuilding Group — Shanghai** Yd No: H1269A Loa 225.00 (BB) Br ex - Dght 14.250 Lbp 217.00 Br md 32.26 Dpth 19.60 Welded, 1 dk	**(A21A2BC) Bulk Carrier** Grain: 91,717; Bale: 89,882 Compartments: 7 Ho, ER 7 Ha: (14.6 x 13.2)2 (14.6 x 15.0)4 (14.6 x 15.0)ER	**1 oil engine** driving 1 FP propeller Total Power: 11,300kW (15,363hp) 14.0kn MAN-B&W 5S60MC-C 1 x 2 Stroke 5 Cy. 600 x 2400 11300kW (15363bhp) Hudong Heavy Machinery Co Ltd-China AuxGen: 2 x 530kW 220/440V a.c Fuel: 143.9 (d.f.) 2443.1 (r.f.)
9310109 *MPTP3* -	**TOPEKA** **Wilhelmsen Lines Car Carrier Ltd** - SatCom: Inmarsat C 423501141 *Southampton* *United Kingdom* MMSI: 232872000 Official number: 912017	**61,321** 22,650 19,628 T/cm 52.5	Class: NV	**2006-06 Mitsubishi Heavy Industries Ltd. — Nagasaki** Yd No: 2213 Loa 199.90 Br ex 32.29 Dght 10.500 Lbp 192.00 Br md 32.26 Dpth 36.02 Welded, 12 dks including 4 liftable dks	**(A35B2RV) Vehicles Carrier** Side door/ramp (s) Len: 25.00 Wid: 6.50 Swl: 35 Quarter stern door/ramp (s. a.) Len: 38.00 Wid: 7.00 Swl: 237 Cars: 6,400	**1 oil engine** driving 1 FP propeller Total Power: 14,315kW (19,463hp) 19.5kn Mitsubishi 7UEC60LSII 1 x 2 Stroke 7 Cy. 600 x 2300 14315kW (19463bhp) Mitsubishi Heavy Industries Ltd-Japan AuxGen: 3 x 1250kW a.c Thrusters: 1 Thwart. CP thruster (f) Fuel: 139.0 (d.f.) 3322.6 (r.f.)
9278882 *3ECD7* -	**TOPFLIGHT** **Azalea Shipping SA** Nitta Marine Service KK *Panama* *Panama* MMSI: 371316000 Official number: 3104005A	**30,051** 17,738 52,544 T/cm 55.5	Class: NK	**2005-08 Tsuneishi Heavy Industries (Cebu) Inc — Balamban** Yd No: SC-051 Loa 189.99 (BB) Br ex - Dght 12.020 Lbp 182.00 Br md 32.26 Dpth 17.00 Welded, 1 Dk.	**(A21A2BC) Bulk Carrier** Grain: 67,756; Bale: 65,601 Compartments: 5 Ho, ER 5 Ha: ER 5 (20.4 x 18.4) Cranes: 4x30t	**1 oil engine** driving 1 FP propeller Total Power: 8,561kW (11,640hp) 14.3kn B&W 6S50MC 1 x 2 Stroke 6 Cy. 500 x 1910 8561kW (11640bhp) Hitachi Zosen Corp-Japan AuxGen: 3 x 480kW 440V 60Hz a.c Fuel: 159.0 (d.f.) 2143.0 (r.f.)
8857124 *OJJJ* -	**TOPI** *ex* Volna 3 *-2004* **Sillanpaa Shipping Ltd Oy** OY Sillanpaa Trading Ltd *Naantali* *Finland* MMSI: 230997870 Official number: 12123	**473** 142 530	Class: BV (RS)	**1985-09 Deggendorfer Werft u. Eisenbau GmbH — Deggendorf** Yd No: 771 Converted From: Hopper-1992 Loa 51.15 Br ex 9.85 Dght 2.200 Lbp 50.00 Br md - Dpth 3.01 Welded, 1 dk	**(A31C2GD) Deck Cargo Ship** Ice Capable	**2 oil engines** driving 2 Directional propellers Total Power: 348kW (474hp) 7.5kn Deutz F12L413F 2 x Vee 4 Stroke 12 Cy. 125 x 130 each-174kW (237bhp) Kloeckner Humboldt Deutz AG-West Germany
7531620 *HP4968* -	**TOPIA PEARL** *ex* Rooster Ii *-2014* *ex* Medstar 3 *-2012* *ex* Bue Lewis *-2008* *ex* Sovereign Tide *-1999* *ex* Hornbeck Sovereign *-1998* *ex* Seaboard Sovereign *-1995* *ex* Salinas *-1990* **MMS Ship Invest Inc** ASE Shipping Inc *Panama* *Panama* MMSI: 351685000 Official number: 45470PEXT1	**844** 253 950	Class: IV (AB)	**1979-09 Maclaren Estaleiros e Servicos Maritimos S.A. — Rio de Janeiro** Yd No: 236 Converted From: Offshore Supply Ship-1990 Loa 55.66 Br ex 11.64 Dght 3.990 Lbp 52.00 Br md 11.60 Dpth 4.60 Welded, 1 dk	**(B21A20S) Platform Supply Ship**	**2 oil engines** reverse reduction geared to sc. shafts driving 2 FP propellers Total Power: 1,838kW (2,498hp) 10.0kn Alpha 8T23L-VO 2 x 4 Stroke 8 Cy. 225 x 300 each-919kW (1249bhp) Equipamentos Villares SA-Brazil AuxGen: 2 x 128kW Thrusters: 1 Thwart. FP thruster (f)
7022837 *TCBQ5* -	**TOPKAPI** **Istanbul Deniz Otobusleri Sanayi ve Ticaret AS (IDO)** - *Istanbul* *Turkey* MMSI: 271002500 Official number: 1073	**1,077** 391 -	Class: TL	**1970-12 Denizcilik Bankasi T.A.O. — Camialti, Istanbul** Yd No: 184 Loa 67.24 Br ex 20.50 Dght 3.100 Lbp 63.40 Br md 17.71 Dpth 4.10 Welded, 1 dk	**(A36A2PR) Passenger/Ro-Ro Ship (Vehicles)** Bow ramp (f) Stern ramp (a) Cars: 62	**2 oil engines** reduction geared to sc. shafts driving 2 FP propellers 1 fwd and 1 aft Total Power: 1,176kW (1,598hp) 11.0kn Sulzer 8AL20/24 2 x 4 Stroke 8 Cy. 200 x 240 each-588kW (799bhp) (, fitted 1970) Turkiye Gemi Sanayii AS-Turkey Fuel: 56.9 (d.f.)
9133757 *3FBW7* -	**TOPKAPI** *ex* Albinoni *-2012* *ex* Pioneer Star *-2007* *ex* Bunga Cempaka Dua *-2004* *completed as* Mary Red *-1997* **Topkapi Shipping Inc** Statu Gemi Kiralama ve Ticaret Ltd Sti (Statu Chartering & Shipping Agency Ltd) *Panama* *Panama* MMSI: 373251000 Official number: 4421812	**7,708** 3,514 9,387 T/cm 20.0	Class: BV (LR) ✠ Classed LR until 18/3/11	**1997-01 Varna Shipyard AD — Varna** Yd No: 284 Loa 125.96 (BB) Br ex 20.06 Dght 8.080 Lbp 114.87 Br md 20.00 Dpth 10.40 Welded, 1 dk	**(A31A2GX) General Cargo Ship** Grain: 11,960; Bale: 11,220 TEU 518 incl 30 ref C. Compartments: 3 Ho, ER 3 Ha: (12.8 x 9.0)2 (25.5 x 15.5)ER Cranes: 2x40t Ice Capable	**1 oil engine** driving 1 FP propeller Total Power: 4,481kW (6,092hp) 13.8kn B&W 8L35MC 1 x 2 Stroke 8 Cy. 350 x 1050 4481kW (6092bhp) H Cegielski Poznan SA-Poland AuxGen: 1 x 520kW 440V 50Hz a.c, 3 x 400kW 400V 50Hz a.c Boilers: e (ex.g.) 7.1kgf/cm² (7.0bar), AuxB (o.f.) 7.1kgf/cm² (7.0bar) Thrusters: 1 Thwart. CP thruster (f)
8732673 *TC5030* -	**TOPLU-3** - - *Bandirma* *Turkey* MMSI: 271062087 Official number: 880	**351** 54 258		**1987-01 in Turkey** Loa 28.45 Br ex - Dght - Lbp - Br md 8.40 Dpth - Welded, 1 dk	**(B11B2FV) Fishing Vessel**	**2 oil engines** driving 2 Propellers Total Power: 620kW (842hp) Volvo Penta 2 x 4 Stroke each-310kW (421bhp) AB Volvo Penta-Sweden
9221499 *9V5839* -	**TOPNICHE 2** **Tru-Resources Pte Ltd** Topniche Associates Pte Ltd *Singapore* *Singapore* MMSI: 563349000 Official number: 388712	**255** 76 -	Class: BV	**2000-06 Jiangsu Wuxi Shipyard Co Ltd — Wuxi JS** Yd No: 9929-02 Loa 29.20 Br ex - Dght 3.700 Lbp 27.00 Br md 9.00 Dpth 4.40 Welded, 1 dk	**(B32A2ST) Tug**	**2 oil engines** with clutches, flexible couplings & sr reverse geared to sc. shafts driving 2 FP propellers Total Power: 1,766kW (2,402hp) Yanmar M220-EN 2 x 4 Stroke 6 Cy. 220 x 300 each-883kW (1201bhp) Yanmar Diesel Engine Co Ltd-Japan AuxGen: 2 x 75kW 220/380V 50Hz a.c Fuel: 173.5 (d.f.) 8.6pd

IMO / Call sign	Name / Owner	Tonnage	Class	Builder / Dimensions	Type	Machinery
9253521 - -	**TOPNICHE 4** **Marine Logistics Pte Ltd** Topniche Associates Pte Ltd	**255** 76 107	Class: (BV)	**2001**-04 **Jiangsu Wuxi Shipyard Co Ltd — Wuxi JS** Yd No: 9929-04 Loa 29.20 Br ex - Dght 3.700 Lbp 27.39 Br md 9.00 Dpth 4.40 Welded, 1 dk	**(B32A2ST) Tug**	**2 oil engines** geared to sc. shafts driving 2 FP propellers Total Power: 1,766kW (2,402hp) 10.0kn Yanmar M220-EN 2 x 4 Stroke 6 Cy. 220 x 300 each-883kW (1201bhp) Yanmar Diesel Engine Co Ltd-Japan
9256547 *9V6055* -	**TOPNICHE 5** **Topniche Marine Pte Ltd** Topniche Associates Pte Ltd *Singapore* *Singapore* MMSI: 563075000 Official number: 389306	**255** 76 225	Class: BV	**2001**-08 **Nantong Gangzha Shipyard — Nantong JS** Yd No: J2000-5 Loa 29.20 Br ex - Dght 3.700 Lbp 27.39 Br md 9.00 Dpth 4.40 Welded, 1 dk	**(B32A2ST) Tug**	**2 oil engines** geared to sc. shafts driving 2 FP propellers Total Power: 1,766kW (2,402hp) Yanmar M220-EN 2 x 4 Stroke 6 Cy. 220 x 300 each-883kW (1201bhp) Yanmar Diesel Engine Co Ltd-Japan
8306694 *40AT* -	**TOPOLICA** **Luka Bar-Preduzece** *Bar* *Montenegro* MMSI: 262500070	*169* - -	Class: (JR)	**1984**-03 **Johann Oelkers KG — Hamburg** Yd No: 588 Loa 25.02 Br ex 8.79 Dght - Lbp 23.53 Br md 8.51 Dpth 3.61 Welded, 1 dk	**(B32A2ST) Tug**	**2 oil engines** with clutches, flexible couplings & sr geared to sc. shafts driving 2 Directional propellers Total Power: 1,188kW (1,616hp) 11.8kn Deutz SBA6M528 2 x 4 Stroke 6 Cy. 220 x 280 each-594kW (808bhp) Kloeckner Humboldt Deutz AG-West Germany AuxGen: 2 x 33kW 380V 50Hz a.c Fuel: 30.0 (d.f.)
5177846 - -	**TOPOS** *ex* Jutland *-1995* - -	**160** 48 -	Class: (DS)	**1957 Schiffbau u. Reparaturwerft Stralsund — Stralsund** Yd No: 2017 Converted From: Fishing Vessel-2011 Loa 26.45 Br ex 6.71 Dght 3.550 Lbp 23.40 Br md - Dpth 3.66 Welded, 1 dk	**(X11A2YP) Yacht** Compartments: 1 Ho, ER 1 Ha: ER Ice Capable	**1 oil engine** driving 1 FP propeller Total Power: 221kW (300hp) 9.0kn Halberstadt 6NVD36 1 x 4 Stroke 6 Cy. 240 x 360 221kW (300bhp) VEB Maschinenbau Halberstadt-Halberstadt AuxGen: 1 x 12kW 230V d.c, 1 x 11kW 230V d.c
9015113 *JD2335* -	**TOPPY 5** *ex* Princesa Teguise *-2006* **Iwasaki Corp KK** - *Okinoshima, Shimane* *Japan* Official number: 140426	*173* 169 100	Class: (AB)	**1991**-06 **Kawasaki Heavy Industries Ltd — Kobe HG** Yd No: F011 Loa 28.70 Br ex - Dght 1.530 Lbp 23.99 Br md 8.53 Dpth 2.59 Welded	**(A37B2PS) Passenger Ship** Hull Material: Aluminium Alloy Passengers: unberthed: 286	**2 Gas Turbs** geared to sc. shafts driving 2 Water jets Total Power: 5,590kW (7,600hp) 43.0kn Allison 501-KF 2 x Gas Turb each-2795kW (3800shp) General Motors Detroit DieselAllison Divn-USA AuxGen: 2 x 50kW 450V 60Hz a.c
7923172 *JF2054* -	**TOPPY 7** *ex* Toppy 4 *-2006* *ex* Mikado *-2003* **Iwasaki Corp KK** - *Kagoshima, Kagoshima* *Japan* Official number: 119990	*281* - -	Class: (AB)	**1979**-01 **Boeing Marine Systems — Seattle, Wa** Yd No: 0011 Loa 30.10 Br ex 9.50 Dght 5.301 Lbp 23.93 Br md 8.54 Dpth 2.60 Welded, 2 dks	**(A37B2PS) Passenger Ship** Hull Material: Aluminium Alloy Passengers: unberthed: 266	**2 Gas Turbs** dr geared to sc. shafts driving 2 Water jets Total Power: 5,442kW (7,398hp) 43.0kn Allison 501-K20B 2 x Gas Turb each-2721kW (3699shp) General Motors Detroit DieselAllison Divn-USA AuxGen: 2 x 50kW 440V 60Hz a.c Thrusters: 1 Thwart. FP thruster (f)
9051387 *JM6178* -	**TOPPY NO. 2** **Iwasaki Corp KK** *Nishinoomote, Kagoshima* *Japan* Official number: 132757	*163* - 100		**1992**-04 **Kawasaki Heavy Industries Ltd — Kobe HG** Yd No: F012 Loa 27.36 Br ex 9.14 Dght - Lbp 23.99 Br md 8.53 Dpth 2.59 Welded, 1 dk	**(A37B2PS) Passenger Ship** Hull Material: Aluminium Alloy Passengers: unberthed: 244	**2 Gas Turbs** geared to sc. shafts driving 2 Water jets Total Power: 5,590kW (7,600hp) 43.0kn Allison 501-KF 2 x Gas Turb each-2795kW (3800shp) General Motors Detroit DieselAllison Divn-USA AuxGen: 2 x 50kW 450V 60Hz a.c
9115169 *JM6440* -	**TOPPY No. 3** **Iwasaki Corp KK** *Kagoshima, Kagoshima* *Japan* Official number: 134535	*164* - 100		**1995**-03 **Kawasaki Heavy Industries Ltd — Kobe HG** Yd No: F013 Loa 30.33 Br ex - Dght 2.200 Lbp 24.00 Br md 8.53 Dpth 2.59 Welded, 1 dk	**(A37B2PS) Passenger Ship** Hull Material: Aluminium Alloy Passengers: unberthed: 244	**2 Gas Turbs** reduction geared to sc. shafts driving 2 Water jets Total Power: 5,590kW (7,600hp) Allison 501-KF 2 x Gas Turb each-2795kW (3800shp) General Motors Detroit DieselAllison Divn-USA
8228505 *ES2050* EK-9249	**TOPU** *ex* MRTK-0666 *-2003* **OU Abimerk** *Haapsalu* *Estonia* MMSI: 276181000 Official number: 1F00H62	**117** 35 30	Class: (RS)	**1984 Sosnovskiy Sudostroitelnyy Zavod — Sosnovka** Yd No: 666 Loa 25.50 Br ex 7.00 Dght 2.390 Lbp 22.00 Br md 6.80 Dpth 3.30 Welded, 1 dk	**(B11B2FV) Fishing Vessel** Ice Capable	**1 oil engine** driving 1 FP propeller Total Power: 221kW (300hp) 9.5kn S.K.L. 6NVD26A-2 1 x 4 Stroke 6 Cy. 180 x 260 221kW (300bhp) VEB Schwermaschinenbau "KarlLiebknecht" (SKL)-Magdeburg AuxGen: 2 x 12kW Fuel: 15.0 (d.f.)
9291042 *OA3467* -	**TOQUEPALA** **Trabajos Maritima SA (TRAMARSA)** - *Ilo* *Peru* Official number: IO-21303-EM	**248** 74 3	Class: AB (GL) (BV)	**2003**-04 **Yuexin Shipbuilding Co Ltd — Guangzhou GD** Yd No: XY-2119 Loa 26.00 Br ex 9.40 Dght - Lbp 23.30 Br md - Dpth 4.30 Welded, 1 dk	**(B32A2ST) Tug**	**2 oil engines** geared to sc. shafts driving 2 Propellers Total Power: 2,206kW (3,000hp) Caterpillar 3512B 2 x Vee 4 Stroke 12 Cy. 170 x 190 each-1103kW (1500bhp) Caterpillar Inc-USA
9353369 *LBHT* -	**TOR** **Fosvarets Logistikkorganisasjon** Government of The Kingdom of Norway (Kystvakt) SatCom: Inmarsat C 425925710 *Fosnavaag* *Norway* MMSI: 257083200	**761** 228 388	Class: (NV)	**2007**-12 **Szczecinska Stocznia Remontowa 'Gryfia' SA — Szczecin** Yd No: 301/V Loa 47.20 (BB) Br ex - Dght 3.250 Lbp 42.00 Br md 10.27 Dpth 5.00 Welded, 1 dk	**(B34H2SQ) Patrol Vessel** Ice Capable	**4 oil engines** driving 4 gen. Connecting to 2 elec. motors geared to sc. shafts driving 2 Directional propellers Total Power: 1,909kW (2,596hp) Cummins 6CT8.3-DM 1 x 4 Stroke 6 Cy. 114 x 135 261kW (355bhp) Cummins Engine Co Inc-USA Cummins KT-19-M 1 x 4 Stroke 6 Cy. 159 x 159 380kW (517bhp) Cummins Engine Co Inc-USA Cummins KT-38-M 2 x Vee 4 Stroke 12 Cy. 159 x 159 each-634kW (862bhp) Cummins Engine Co Inc-USA AuxGen: 2 x 830kW 440V 60Hz a.c Thrusters: 1 Tunnel thruster (f)
8514928 *UBRQ* -	**TOR** *ex* Seyo Maru *-2003* *ex* Shoyo Maru *-2002* *ex* Kaiyo Maru No. 18 *-1992* **JSC 'Kurilskiy Rybak'** - *Nevelsk* *Russia* MMSI: 273425070 Official number: 855424	**862** 292 360	Class: RS	**1985**-09 **Narasaki Zosen KK — Muroran HK** Yd No: 1076 Loa 58.96 (BB) Br ex 10.24 Dght 3.890 Lbp 51.23 Br md 10.20 Dpth 6.31 Welded, 2 dks	**(B11A2FS) Stern Trawler** Ins: 487	**1 oil engine** with flexible couplings & sr gearedto sc. shaft driving 1 CP propeller Total Power: 1,912kW (2,600hp) Akasaka AH40AK 1 x 4 Stroke 6 Cy. 400 x 640 1912kW (2600bhp) Akasaka Tekkosho KK (Akasaka DieselLtd)-Japan
5418197 *UBWX* -	**TOR** **Federal State Unitary Enterprise Rosmorport** - *St Petersburg* *Russia* MMSI: 273458860	**3,947** 1,184 -	Class: RS (NV)	**1964**-01 **Wartsila-Koncernen, AB Crichton-Vulcan — Turku** Yd No: 1107 Loa 84.49 Br ex 21.23 Dght 7.130 Lbp 77.53 Br md 21.20 Dpth 9.50 Welded, 3 dks	**(B34C2SI) Icebreaker** Cranes: 1x8t Ice Capable	**4 diesel electric oil engines** driving 4 gen. each 2400kW 800V d.c Connecting to 4 elec. motors driving 2 Propellers fwd and 2 aft Total Power: 10,120kW (13,760hp) Sulzer 9MH51 4 x 2 Stroke 9 Cy. 510 x 550 each-2530kW (3440bhp) Wartsila Koncernen, AbCrichton-Vulcan-Finland AuxGen: 4 x 340kW 450V 60Hz a.c Fuel: 880.0 (d.f.) 50.0pd
5364918 *OIJT* -	**TOR** **Sun Ferry Oy** - *Helsinki* *Finland* Official number: 11371	**148** 88 -	Class: (LR) ✠ Classed LR until 17/10/91	**1952**-03 **AB Hammarbyverken — Stockholm** Yd No: 32 Loa 24.44 Br ex - Dght 3.760 Lbp 22.26 Br md 6.85 Dpth 3.97 Riveted\Welded	**(B32A2ST) Tug** Ice Capable	**1 oil engine** driving 1 CP propeller Total Power: 706kW (960hp) 11.0kn MWM 1 x 4 Stroke 8 Cy. 320 x 480 706kW (960bhp) Motoren Werke Mannheim AG (MWM)-West Germany AuxGen: 1 x 30kW 110V d.c, 1 x 10kW 110V d.c Fuel: 14.0 (d.f.) 2.0pd
8862002 *UCSJ* -	**TOR** *ex* Yaroslavets *-2007* **Vega JSC** - SatCom: Inmarsat C 427300730 *Murmansk* *Russia* MMSI: 273555000 Official number: 910087	**823** 246 370	Class: RS	**1991**-12 **Yaroslavskiy Sudostroitelnyy Zavod — Yaroslavl** Yd No: 381 Loa 53.70 (BB) Br ex 10.71 Dght 4.600 Lbp 47.92 Br md 10.50 Dpth 6.00 Welded, 1 dk	**(B11A2FS) Stern Trawler** Ice Capable	**1 oil engine** driving 1 FP propeller Total Power: 852kW (1,158hp) 12.6kn S.K.L. 8NVD48A-2U 1 x 4 Stroke 8 Cy. 320 x 480 852kW (1158bhp) SKL Motoren u. Systemtechnik AG-Magdeburg

9217852 *SMIT* -	**TOR-ON** **Toronland H/B** - *Fiskeback* *Sweden* MMSI: 265816000	**846** 254 -	Class: (NV)	**2000-07 Flekkefjord Slipp & Maskinfabrikk AS AS — Flekkefjord** Yd No: 171 Loa 44.90 (BB) Br ex - Dght 4.950 Lbp 38.80 Br md 12.00 Dpth 7.35 Welded, 1 dk	**(B11B2FV) Fishing Vessel**	**1 oil engine** geared to sc. shaft driving 1 CP propeller Total Power: 3,680kW (5,003hp) Wartsila 8R32 1 x 4 Stroke 8 Cy. 320 x 350 3680kW (5003bhp) Wartsila NSD Finland Oy-Finland AuxGen: 1 x 1540kW a.c, 2 x 1168kW a.c Thrusters: 1 Thwart. FP thruster (f); 1 Tunnel thruster (a)
9199622 *SLJT* -	**TOR VIKING II** *ex Tor Viking -2003* **Viking Icebreaking & Offshore AS** Viking Supply Ships AS *Skarhamn* *Sweden* MMSI: 266004000	**3,382** 1,145 2,600	Class: NV	**2000-03 Havyard Leirvik AS — Leirvik i Sogn** Yd No: 282 Loa 83.70 Br ex - Dght 7.200 Lbp 75.20 Br md 18.00 Dpth 8.50 Welded, 1 dk	**(B21B20A) Anchor Handling Tug Supply** Passengers: berths: 23 Liq: 4,295 Cranes: 1x12t Ice Capable	**4 oil engines** reduction geared to sc. shafts driving 2 CP propellers Total Power: 13,440kW (18,274hp) 12.0kn MaK 6M32 2 x 4 Stroke 6 Cy. 320 x 480 each-2880kW (3916bhp) MaK Motoren GmbH & Co. KG-Kiel MaK 8M32 2 x 4 Stroke 8 Cy. 320 x 480 each-3840kW (5221bhp) MaK Motoren GmbH & Co. KG-Kiel AuxGen: 2 x 2640kW 690/400V 50Hz a.c, 2 x 400kW 690/400V 50Hz a.c Thrusters: 1 Retract. directional thruster (f); 1 Thwart. FP thruster (f); 1 Tunnel thruster (a) Fuel: 1020.0 (d.f.)
7721354 - -	**TORA EAGLE** *ex Tora -2007 ex Maria Theresa -1990* *ex Alice Langli -1980* **Fairwinds Maritime Services Ltd** -	**731** 327 1,163 T/cm 5.6	Class: (BV)	**1977-05 Carl B Hoffmanns Maskinfabrik A/S — Esbjerg** (Hull launched by) Yd No: 16 **1977-05 Soren Larsen & Sonners Skibsvaerft A/S — Nykobing Mors** (Hull completed by) Yd No: 135 Lengthened-1982 Loa 68.20 Br ex 9.91 Dght 3.250 Lbp 52.99 Br md - Dpth 3.89 Welded, 1 dk	**(A13B2TP) Products Tanker** Liq: 930; Liq (Oil): 930 Cargo Heating Coils Compartments: 12 Ta, ER 2 Cargo Pump (s): 2x160m³/hr Manifold: Bow/CM: 40m Ice Capable	**1 oil engine** driving 1 CP propeller Total Power: 515kW (700hp) 10.0kn Alpha 407-26VO 1 x 2 Stroke 7 Cy. 260 x 400 515kW (700bhp) Alpha Diesel A/S-Denmark Fuel: 95.5 (d.f.) 3.5pd
7425675 *9BSN* -	**TORAB** *ex Salam Ii -2011 ex Fadl Allah -2008* *ex Permina Supply No. 24 -2004* **Bahregan Marine Services Co Ltd** - *Iran* MMSI: 422796000	**1,209** 363 1,242	Class: (AB) (KI)	**1975-10 Shikoku Dockyard Co. Ltd. — Takamatsu** Yd No: 787 Loa 61.91 Br ex - Dght 4.901 Lbp 56.27 Br md 12.50 Dpth 5.25 Welded, 1 dk	**(B21B20A) Anchor Handling Tug Supply**	**2 oil engines** reverse reduction geared to sc. shafts driving 2 FP propellers Total Power: 4,414kW (6,002hp) 13.5kn Niigata 12MGV28BX 2 x Vee 4 Stroke 12 Cy. 280 x 320 each-2207kW (3001bhp) Niigata Engineering Co Ltd-Japan AuxGen: 3 x 160kW Thrusters: 1 Thwart. FP thruster (f) Fuel: 599.5 (d.f.)
9234886 *JL6586* -	**TORAFUKU MARU No. 5** **Oishi Shipping YK** - *Matsuyama, Ehime* *Japan* Official number: 135498	*199* - -		**2000-03 Taiyo Shipbuilding Co Ltd — Sanyoonoda YC** Yd No: 281 Loa 49.43 Br ex - Dght - Lbp 45.00 Br md 7.80 Dpth 3.30 Welded, 1 dk	**(A13B2TU) Tanker (unspecified)** Liq: 321; Liq (Oil): 321 2 Cargo Pump (s): 2x108m³/hr	**1 oil engine** driving 1 FP propeller Total Power: 736kW (1,001hp) 11.0kn Hanshin LH26G 1 x 4 Stroke 6 Cy. 260 x 440 736kW (1001bhp) The Hanshin Diesel Works Ltd-Japan Fuel: 18.0 (d.f.)
8815023 *DSRO9* -	**TORAH** **Boyang Ltd** Khana Marine Ltd *Jeju* *South Korea* MMSI: 440102000 Official number: JJR-131046	**4,212** 2,028 5,092	Class: KR (NK)	**1989-02 Kyokuyo Shipyard Corp — Shimonoseki YC** Yd No: 2623 Loa 115.80 (BB) Br ex 16.62 Dght 7.114 Lbp 108.00 Br md 16.60 Dpth 10.00 Welded, 1 dk	**(A34A2GR) Refrigerated Cargo Ship** Ins: 5,973 Compartments: 3 Ho, ER 3 Ha: ER Derricks: 6x5t	**1 oil engine** driving 1 FP propeller Total Power: 2,978kW (4,049hp) 15.0kn Mitsubishi 6UEC37LA 1 x 2 Stroke 6 Cy. 370 x 880 2978kW (4049bhp) Akasaka Tekkosho KK (Akasaka DieselLtd)-Japan AuxGen: 3 x 680kW 450V a.c Thrusters: 1 Tunnel thruster (f)
7230331 *ZR9382* -	**TORALLA** **Blue Continent Products Pty Ltd** - *Cape Town* *South Africa* Official number: 10304	**684** 183 -	Class: (RI) (BV)	**1973-03 Construcciones Navales P Freire SA — Vigo** Yd No: 75 Lengthened-1982 Loa 53.78 Br ex - Dght - Lbp 46.77 Br md 9.50 Dpth 6.63 Welded, 2 dks	**(B11A2FT) Trawler**	**1 oil engine** driving 1 CP propeller Total Power: 883kW (1,201hp) 12.0kn Duvant 8VNRS 1 x 4 Stroke 8 Cy. 315 x 480 883kW (1201bhp) Carmelo Unanue-Spain Fuel: 201.0 (d.f.)
6609016 - -	**TORANI** **Government of The Republic of Guyana (Transport & Harbours Department)** - *Georgetown* *Guyana* Official number: 315884	*560* 318 383	Class: (LR) ✠ Classed LR until 5/62	**1960-10 Sprostons Ltd. — Georgetown, Demerara** Yd No: 55 Loa 56.09 Br ex 11.89 Dght 2.210 Lbp 52.43 Br md 11.43 Dpth 3.43 Welded, 4 dks	**(A36A2PR) Passenger/Ro-Ro Ship (Vehicles)** Passengers: 1200 Side door (s) Len: 2.20 Wid: 3.50 Swl: - Lane-Wid: 4.50 Lane-clr ht: 4.70 Lorries: 15, Cars: 25	**2 oil engines** geared to sc. shafts driving 2 FP propellers Total Power: 706kW (960hp) 9.0kn Blackstone ERS6 2 x 4 Stroke 6 Cy. 222 x 292 each-353kW (480bhp) Lister Blackstone Marine Ltd.-Dursley AuxGen: 2 x 65kW 220V d.c Fuel: 11.0 (d.f.) 2.0pd
8918552 - -	**TORBAY** **M G Kailis Pty Ltd** - *Fremantle, WA* *Australia* Official number: 853269	*133* 39 -		**1989 Ocean Shipyards (WA) Pty Ltd — Fremantle WA** Loa 24.87 Br ex - Dght 2.801 Lbp - Br md 6.75 Dpth 3.79 Welded	**(B11A2FT) Trawler**	**1 oil engine** geared to sc. shaft driving 1 FP propeller Total Power: 237kW (322hp) 9.5kn Cummins KTA-19-M 1 x 4 Stroke 6 Cy. 159 x 159 237kW (322bhp) Cummins Engine Co Inc-USA
8332928 *IVQH* -	**TORCELLO** **Azienda del Consorzio Trasporti Veneziano (ACTV)** - *Venice* *Italy* MMSI: 247290400 Official number: 8049	*280* 169 107	Class: RI	**1983 Cant. Nav. M. Morini & C. — Ancona** Yd No: 208 Loa 38.38 Br ex - Dght 2.008 Lbp 34.02 Br md 7.75 Dpth 2.85 Welded, 1 dk	**(A37B2PS) Passenger Ship**	**2 oil engines** geared to sc. shaft driving 1 FP propeller Total Power: 618kW (840hp) Fiat 8291M 2 x Vee 4 Stroke 12 Cy. 145 x 130 each-309kW (420bhp) Fiat OM Applicazioni Industriali-Milano
8891041 *MQJA8* -	**TORCH** *ex Marineco Seeonee -2005* *ex MCS Nikki -2005 ex Diana -2005* **Clydeport Operations Ltd** - *Glasgow* *United Kingdom* MMSI: 235000379 Official number: 729250	*135* 75 -	Class: (BV)	**1994 Cosens & Co. — Portland** Yd No: 4970 Loa 20.00 Br ex - Dght 1.200 Lbp - Br md 9.00 Dpth 2.30 Welded, 1 dk	**(B34B2SC) Crane Vessel** Cranes: 1	**2 oil engines** reduction geared to sc. shafts driving 2 FP propellers Total Power: 560kW (762hp) 9.0kn Caterpillar 3406B 2 x 4 Stroke 6 Cy. 137 x 165 each-280kW (381bhp) Caterpillar Inc-USA AuxGen: 1 x 17kW 220V 50Hz a.c Fuel: 25.0 (d.f.)
9442067 *PQAH* -	**TORDA** **Magallanes Navegacao Brasileira SA** Wilson Sons Offshore SA SatCom: Inmarsat C 471011317 *Rio de Janeiro* *Brazil* MMSI: 710006540	**2,987** 1,023 4,394	Class: LR ✠ **100A1** SS 02/2011 offshore supply ship *IWS **LMC** **UMS** Eq.Ltr: U; Cable: 495.0/44.0 U3 (a)	**2011-02 Wilson, Sons SA — Guaruja** (Hull) Yd No: 107 **2011-02 B.V. Scheepswerf Damen — Gorinchem** Yd No: 552010 Loa 87.40 (BB) Br ex 16.04 Dght 6.200 Lbp 81.56 Br md 16.00 Dpth 7.50 Welded, 1 dk	**(B21A20S) Platform Supply Ship**	**4 diesel electric oil engines** driving 4 gen. each 1360kW 690V a.c Connecting to 2 elec. motors each (2000kW) driving 2 Directional propellers Total Power: 5,696kW (7,744hp) 12.2kn Caterpillar 3512B-TA 4 x Vee 4 Stroke 12 Cy. 170 x 190 each-1424kW (1936bhp) Caterpillar Inc-USA Thrusters: 2 Thwart. CP thruster (f)
7640213 *IRMT* -	**TORE** *ex Salvamar -1983* **Augustea Imprese Marittime e di Salvataggi SpA** Augustea Ship Management Srl SatCom: Inmarsat C 424725720 *Augusta* *Italy* MMSI: 247297000 Official number: 16	**457** 137 373	Class: (RI)	**1979-03 Cant. Nav. A. Giorgetti — Viareggio** Yd No: 26 Loa 40.11 Br ex 10.52 Dght 4.538 Lbp 36.02 Br md 10.51 Dpth 5.21 Welded, 1 dk	**(B32A2ST) Tug**	**2 oil engines** reduction geared to sc. shaft driving 1 CP propeller Total Power: 3,678kW (5,000hp) Nohab F212V 2 x Vee 4 Stroke 12 Cy. 250 x 300 each-1839kW (2500bhp) AB Bofors NOHAB-Sweden

IMO / Call sign	Ship / Owner	Tonnage	Class	Builder / Dimensions	Type / Cargo	Machinery
9274082 *ZMIQ* -	**TOREA** *ex* Nyathi *-2007* **Nyathi Ltd** Silver Fern Shipping Ltd *Wellington* *New Zealand* MMSI: 512175000 Official number: 876427	**25,400** 8,905 37,069 T/cm 49.1	Class: NV (LR) (AB) Classed LR until 28/8/11	**2004-06 ShinA Shipbuilding Co Ltd — Tongyeong** Yd No: 428 Loa 175.96 (BB) Br ex 31.03 Dght 10.500 Lbp 168.00 Br md 31.00 Dpth 17.20 Welded, 1 dk	**(A12B2TR) Chemical/Products Tanker** Double Hull (13F) Liq: 42,845; Liq (Oil): 42,845 Compartments: 12 Wing Ta, 2 Wing Slop Ta, ER 12 Cargo Pump (s): 12x500m^3/hr Manifold: Bow/CM: 88m	**1 oil engine** driving 1 FP propeller Total Power: 8,580kW (11,665hp) 15.0kn B&W 6S50MC 1 x 2 Stroke 6 Cy. 500 x 1910 8580kW (11665bhp) Doosan Engine Co Ltd-South Korea AuxGen: 4 x 740kW 450V 60Hz a.c Boilers: AuxB (Comp) 9.0kgf/cm^2 (8.8bar), AuxB (o.f.) 9.0kgf/cm^2 (8.8bar) Thrusters: 1 Tunnel thruster (f) Fuel: 200.0 (d.f.) 1400.0 (r.f.) 36.4pd
9515357 *V7QD8* -	**TOREACH PIONEER** *ex* Feng Hai 12 *-2008* **Dongguan Chemical Tankers AS** Toreach Marine Pte Ltd *Majuro* *Marshall Islands* MMSI: 538003338 Official number: 3338	**5,614** 2,538 8,126	Class: CC	**2008-09 Zhejiang Haifeng Shipbuilding Co Ltd — Linhai ZJ** Yd No: HF0618 Loa 120.11 Br ex 18.02 Dght 6.600 Lbp 112.00 Br md 18.00 Dpth 9.40 Welded, 1 dk	**(A12B2TR) Chemical/Products Tanker** Double Hull (13F) Liq: 9,031; Liq (Oil): 9,031 Compartments: 12 Wing Ta, 2 Wing Slop Ta, ER Ice Capable	**1 oil engine** reduction geared to sc. shaft driving 1 Propeller Total Power: 2,795kW (3,800hp) 12.0kn Chinese Std. Type GN8320ZC 1 x 4 Stroke 8 Cy. 320 x 380 2795kW (3800bhp) Ningbo CSI Power & Machinery GroupCo Ltd-China AuxGen: 2 x 372kW 400V a.c
9375288 *2BSG3* -	**TOREADOR** **Wilhelmsen Lines Car Carrier Ltd** - SatCom: Inmarsat C 423591470 *Southampton* *United Kingdom* MMSI: 235068882 Official number: 915413	**61,328** 23,559 22,098 T/cm 52.5	Class: NV	**2008-12 Mitsubishi Heavy Industries Ltd. — Nagasaki** Yd No: 2238 Loa 199.99 (BB) Br ex - Dght 11.000 Lbp 192.00 Br md 32.26 Dpth 36.02 Welded, 12 dks including 4 liftable dks	**(A35B2RV) Vehicles Carrier** Side door/ramp (s) Len: 25.00 Wid: 6.50 Swl: 35 Quarter stern door/ramp (s. a.) Len: 38.00 Wid: 7.00 Swl: 237 Cars: 6,556	**1 oil engine** driving 1 FP propeller Total Power: 14,315kW (19,463hp) 19.5kn Mitsubishi 7UEC60LSII 1 x 2 Stroke 7 Cy. 600 x 2300 14315kW (19463bhp) Mitsubishi Heavy Industries Ltd-Japan AuxGen: 3 x 1250kW a.c Thrusters: 1 Tunnel thruster (f)
5409512 - - -	**TOREADOR** **Government of The Argentine Republic (Empresa Flota Fluvial del Estado Argentino) (EFFDEA)** -	*325* - -	Class: (LR) ✠ Classed LR until 31/10/75	**1964-10 Astilleros Alianza S.A. — Avellaneda** Yd No: 11 Loa 30.48 Br ex 8.44 Dght - Lbp 28.02 Br md 8.01 Dpth 3.76 Riveted\Welded, 1 dk	**(B32A2ST) Tug**	**2 diesel electric oil engines** driving 2 gen. each 340kW 440V d.c Connecting to 2 elec. motors driving 1 FP propeller Total Power: 882kW (1,200hp) MAN G7V235/330ATL 2 x 4 Stroke 7 Cy. 235 x 330 each-441kW (600bhp) Maschinenbau Augsburg Nuernberg (MAN)-Augsburg AuxGen: 2 x 36kW 220V d.c
9331919 *3ELI5* -	**TORENIA** **YM Maritime Corp** Yamamaru Kisen KK (Yamamaru Kisen Co Ltd) *Panama* *Panama* MMSI: 372954000 Official number: 3288707A	**31,236** 18,504 56,049 T/cm 55.8	Class: NK	**2007-07 Mitsui Eng. & SB. Co. Ltd. — Tamano** Yd No: 1648 Loa 189.99 (BB) Br ex - Dght 12.573 Lbp 182.00 Br md 32.26 Dpth 17.90 Welded, 1 dk	**(A21A2BC) Bulk Carrier** Grain: 70,811; Bale: 68,084 Compartments: 5 Ho, ER 5 Ha: ER Cranes: 4x30t	**1 oil engine** driving 1 FP propeller Total Power: 9,480kW (12,889hp) 14.5kn MAN-B&W 6S50MC-C 1 x 2 Stroke 6 Cy. 500 x 2000 9480kW (12889bhp) Mitsui Engineering & Shipbuilding CLtd-Japan Fuel: 2380.0
9378773 *S6HE9* -	**TORERO** **Koyo Kaiun Asia Pte Ltd** Bernhard Schulte Shipmanagement (Singapore) Pte Ltd *Singapore* *Singapore* MMSI: 565214000 Official number: 392084	**5,518** 2,757 8,913 T/cm 18.3	Class: NK	**2006-09 Asakawa Zosen K.K. — Imabari** Yd No: 556 Loa 118.00 (BB) Br ex 18.66 Dght 7.413 Lbp 110.50 Br md 18.60 Dpth 9.50 Welded, 1 dk	**(A12B2TR) Chemical/Products Tanker** Double Hull (13F) Liq: 9,633; Liq (Oil): 9,633 Cargo Heating Coils Compartments: 18 Wing Ta (s.stl), 2 Wing Slop Ta (s.stl), ER 18 Cargo Pump (s): 18x200m^3/hr Manifold: Bow/CM: 56.1m	**1 oil engine** driving 1 FP propeller Total Power: 3,883kW (5,279hp) 14.0kn MAN-B&W 6L35MC 1 x 2 Stroke 6 Cy. 350 x 1050 3883kW (5279bhp) Makita Corp-Japan AuxGen: 2 x 450kW a.c Fuel: 89.0 (d.f.) 601.0 (r.f.)
7119264 *J8B2069* -	**TORGELOW** *ex* Gelo *-2000* *ex* Torgelow *-1992* **World Peace Navigation Inc** Motaku Shipping Agencies Ltd *Kingstown* *St Vincent & The Grenadines* MMSI: 375474000 Official number: 8541	**932** 401 918	Class: (BV) (DS) (GL)	**1972-07 VEB Elbewerften Boizenburg/Rosslau — Boizenburg** Yd No: 292 Loa 57.87 (BB) Br ex 10.37 Dght 4.100 Lbp 51.95 Br md 10.09 Dpth 5.80 Welded, 2 dks	**(A31A2GX) General Cargo Ship** Grain: 1,532; Bale: 1,400 Compartments: 2 Ho, ER 2 Ha: (8.9 x 7.7) (12.5 x 7.7)ER Cranes: 1x3t Ice Capable	**1 oil engine** driving 1 CP propeller Total Power: 853kW (1,160hp) 12.5kn S.K.L. 8NVD48A-2U 1 x 4 Stroke 8 Cy. 320 x 480 853kW (1160bhp) VEB Schwermaschinenbau "KarlLiebknecht" (SKL)-Magdeburg AuxGen: 1 x 128kW 390V 50Hz a.c, 1 x 116kW 390V 50Hz a.c, 1 x 77kW 390V 50Hz a.c Fuel: 65.0 (d.f.)
9327293 - -	**TORGEM 78** **ARPAS Ambarli Romorkaj Pilotaj Ticaret AS (Ambarli Tug-Boat & Pilotage Services Trading)** - *Turkey*	**232** 105 -		**2005-03 Torgem Gemi Insaat Sanayii ve Ticaret a.s. — Tuzla, Istanbul** Yd No: 78 Loa 24.40 Br ex - Dght - Lbp - Br md 10.50 Dpth 4.00 Welded, 1 dk	**(B32A2ST) Tug**	**2 oil engines** geared to sc. shafts driving 2 Propellers Total Power: 2,360kW (3,208hp) 13.0kn M.T.U. 16V4000M60 2 x Vee 4 Stroke 16 Cy. 165 x 190 each-1180kW (1604bhp) MTU Friedrichshafen GmbH-Friedrichshafen
9234707 *LLYB* -	**TORGHATTEN** **Torghatten Trafikkselskap AS** *Bronnoysund* *Norway* MMSI: 257279000	**1,327** 398 435	Class: (NV)	**2002-08 Szczecinska Stocznia Remontowa 'Gryfia' SA — Szczecin** Yd No: PN03 Loa 70.00 Br ex 14.70 Dght 3.500 Lbp - Br md 14.20 Dpth 4.80 Welded	**(A36A2PR) Passenger/Ro-Ro Ship (Vehicles)** Passengers: unberthed: 150 Lorries: 6, Cars: 50	**2 oil engines** geared to sc. shafts driving 2 Directional propellers 1 fwd and 1 aft Total Power: 1,400kW (1,904hp) Mitsubishi S12A2-MPTK 2 x Vee 4 Stroke 12 Cy. 150 x 160 each-700kW (952bhp) Mitsubishi Heavy Industries Ltd-Japan
9292046 *A8HA8* -	**TORGOVY BRIDGE** **Applewood Shipping Co Ltd** Sovcomflot (UK) Ltd *Monrovia* *Liberia* MMSI: 636012690 Official number: 12690	**27,725** 13,762 46,697 T/cm 52.3	Class: LR ✠ **100A1** SS 09/2010 Double Hull oil tanker ESP *IWS LI SPM **ShipRight** (SDA, FDA, CM) ✠ **LMC** **UMS IGS** Cable: 632.5/73.0 U3 (a)	**2005-09 Admiralteyskiy Sudostroitelnyy Zavod — Sankt-Peterburg** Yd No: 02743 Loa 182.32 (BB) Br ex 32.34 Dght 12.197 Lbp 174.69 Br md 32.20 Dpth 17.50 Welded, 1 dk	**(A13B2TP) Products Tanker** Double Hull (13F) Liq: 51,910; Liq (Oil): 51,910 Compartments: 10 Wing Ta, 2 Wing Slop Ta, ER 10 Cargo Pump (s): 10x550m^3/hr Manifold: Bow/CM: 90.9m	**1 oil engine** reverse geared to sc. shaft driving 1 FP propeller Total Power: 8,310kW (11,298hp) 14.0kn B&W 6S50MC-C 1 x 2 Stroke 6 Cy. 500 x 2000 8310kW (11298bhp) AO Bryanskiy MashinostroitelnyyZavod (BMZ)-Bryansk AuxGen: 1 x 680kW 440/220V 60Hz a.c, 2 x 1360kW 440/220V 60Hz a.c Boilers: e (ex.g.) 11.7kgf/cm^2 (11.5bar), AuxB (o.f.) 11.2kgf/cm^2 (11.0bar) Fuel: 122.9 (d.f.) 1556.0 (r.f.) 33.0pd
9189445 *LJMD* -	**TORGTIND** **Torghatten Trafikkselskap AS** - *Bronnoysund* *Norway* MMSI: 259546000	**2,384** 1,036 460	Class: (NV)	**1999-07 Szczecinska Stocznia Remontowa 'Gryfia' SA — Szczecin** Yd No: PN02 Loa 68.80 Br ex 13.70 Dght 3.700 Lbp 56.40 Br md 13.20 Dpth 5.00 Welded, 1 dk	**(A36A2PR) Passenger/Ro-Ro Ship (Vehicles)** Passengers: unberthed: 299 Lane-clr ht: 5.00 Lorries: 7, Cars: 50	**2 oil engines** dr geared to sc. shafts driving 2 Contra-rotating propellers 1 fwd and 1 aft Total Power: 1,760kW (2,392hp) 12.0kn Mitsubishi S12R-MPTA 2 x Vee 4 Stroke 12 Cy. 170 x 180 each-880kW (1196bhp) Mitsubishi Heavy Industries Ltd-Japan AuxGen: 2 x 140kW 220V 50Hz a.c
9082142 *UGUR* -	**TORIK** **Tyam Shipping Ltd** State Enterprise Makhachkala International Sea Commercial Port SatCom: Inmarsat C 427310229 *Taganrog* *Russia* MMSI: 273155400	**4,991** 1,781 5,828	Class: RS	**1993-05 Sudostroitelnyy Zavod "Krasnoye Sormovo" — Nizhniy Novgorod** Yd No: 19610/20 Loa 139.81 Br ex 16.56 Dght 4.900 Lbp 134.00 Br md 16.40 Dpth 6.70 Welded, 1 dk	**(A31A2GX) General Cargo Ship** Grain: 6,843; Bale: 6,785 TEU 140 C.Dk 140/20' Compartments: 4 Ho, ER 4 Ha: 4 (18.7 x 11.8)ER Ice Capable	**2 oil engines** driving 2 FP propellers Total Power: 1,940kW (2,638hp) 10.0kn S.K.L. 8NVD48A-3U 2 x 4 Stroke 8 Cy. 320 x 480 each-970kW (1319bhp) SKL Motoren u. Systemtechnik AG-Magdeburg AuxGen: 3 x 150kW a.c Thrusters: 1 Thwart. FP thruster (f) Fuel: 417.0 (d.f.) (Heating Coils)
9630030 *MRVZ8* -	**TORILL KNUTSEN** **Knutsen Shuttle Tankers 15 AS** Knutsen NYK Offshore Tankers AS *Aberdeen* *United Kingdom* MMSI: 235102583 Official number: 919703	**80,850** 36,065 123,166	Class: NV	**2013-11 Hyundai Heavy Industries Co Ltd — Ulsan** Yd No: 2532 Loa 275.70 (BB) Br ex - Dght 15.500 Lbp 256.00 Br md 46.00 Dpth 22.70 Welded, 1 dk	**(A13A2TS) Shuttle Tanker** Double Hull (13F) Ice Capable	**2 oil engines** driving 2 CP propellers Total Power: 19,920kW (27,084hp) 14.5kn MAN-B&W 6S50ME-C8 2 x 2 Stroke 6 Cy. 500 x 2000 each-9960kW (13542bhp) Thrusters: 2 Tunnel thruster (f); 1 Retract. directional thruster (p. a.); 1 Retract. directional thruster (s. a.)
8899744 *UFYO* -	**TORIN** *ex* Nubian Queen *-2005* *ex* Ingul *-2004* *ex* Dagon *-2003* **OOO 'Sem Ostrovov' (Seven Islands Ltd)** - *Murmansk* *Russia*	**359** 107 129	Class: RS	**1994-06 OAO Sudostroitelnyy Zavod "Avangard" — Petrozavodsk** Yd No: 646 Loa 35.72 Br ex 8.92 Dght 3.490 Lbp 31.00 Br md - Dpth 6.07 Welded, 1 dk	**(B11A2FS) Stern Trawler** Ins: 98 Ice Capable	**1 oil engine** driving 1 FP propeller Total Power: 589kW (801hp) 10.9kn S.K.L. 6NVD48A-2U 1 x 4 Stroke 6 Cy. 320 x 480 589kW (801bhp) SKL Motoren u. Systemtechnik AG-Magdeburg AuxGen: 2 x 200kW a.c Fuel: 82.0 (d.f.)

8820200 **TORINO**
9HA3248 *ex* Maersk Torino *-2013* *ex* Trein Maersk *-2007*
\- *ex* TRSL Arcturus *-1997* *ex* Trein Maersk *-1995*
Apollon Marine LLC
Technomar Shipping Inc
Valletta *Malta*
MMSI: 229340000
Official number: 8820200

17,700 / 7,244 / 21,229 / T/cm 38.7
Class: RI (LR)
✠ Classed LR until 24/3/11

1990-05 Tsuneishi Shipbuilding Co Ltd — Fukuyama HS Yd No: 627
Loa 161.02 (BB) Br ex 28.23 Dght 10.000
Lbp 152.00 Br md 28.20 Dpth 15.30
Welded, 1 dk

(A33A2CC) Container Ship (Fully Cellular)
TEU 1316 C Ho 554 TEU C Dk 762 TEU incl 118 ref C.
Compartments: 4 Cell Ho, ER
8 Ha: (6.5 x 12.9) (12.6 x 17.8)6 (14.2 x 22.8)ER
Gantry cranes: 1x40t

1 oil engine driving 1 FP propeller
Total Power: 10,480kW (14,249hp) 18.5kn
B&W 8S50MC
1 x 2 Stroke 8 Cy. 500 x 1910 10480kW (14249bhp)
Mitsui Engineering & Shipbuilding CLtd-Japan
AuxGen: 3 x 1160kW 450V 60Hz a.c
Boilers: AuxB (ex.g.), AuxB (o.f.) 7.0kgf/cm² (6.9bar)
Thrusters: 1 Thwart. CP thruster (f); 1 Thwart. CP thruster (a)

9398321 **TORINO**
2BZH7
\- **Wilhelmsen Lines Car Carrier Ltd**
\-
SatCom: Inmarsat C 423591620
Southampton *United Kingdom*
MMSI: 235070707
Official number: 915674

61,328 / 23,559 / 22,160 / T/cm 52.5
Class: NV

2009-03 Mitsubishi Heavy Industries Ltd. — Nagasaki Yd No: 2244
Loa 199.90 (BB) Br ex Dght 11.000
Lbp 192.00 Br md 32.26 Dpth 36.02
Welded, 12 dks including 4 liftable dks

(A35B2RV) Vehicles Carrier
Side door/ramp (s)
Len: 25.00 Wid: 6.50 Swl: 35
Quarter stern door/ramp (s. a.)
Len: 38.00 Wid: 7.00 Swl: 237
Cars: 6,542

1 oil engine driving 1 FP propeller
Total Power: 14,315kW (19,463hp) 19.5kn
Mitsubishi 7UEC60LSII
1 x 2 Stroke 7 Cy. 600 x 2300 14315kW (19463bhp)
Mitsubishi Heavy Industries Ltd-Japan
AuxGen: 3 x 1250kW a.c
Thrusters: 1 Tunnel thruster (f)
Fuel: 3580.0

7704746 **TORITA**
LHAH *ex* Torita I *-2001* *ex* Saetring I *-2001*
M-123-A *ex* Saetring *-2000* *ex* Geir Hans *-1993*
ex Geir *-1989*
Torita KS
\-
SatCom: Inmarsat C 425834810
Aalesund *Norway*
MMSI: 258348000

377 / 132 / 244

1978-07 Fiskerstrand Verft AS — Fiskarstrand Yd No: 33
Lengthened-1983
Loa 39.91 Br ex 7.35 Dght 3.801
Lbp 36.61 Br md 7.32 Dpth 3.92
Welded, 1 dk

(B11B2FV) Fishing Vessel

1 oil engine driving 1 CP propeller
Total Power: 294kW (400hp)
Alpha 404-26VO
1 x 2 Stroke 4 Cy. 260 x 400 294kW (400bhp)
Alpha Diesel A/S-Denmark

8117756 **TORIU**
P2V5455 *ex* Al Jaber III *-2011*
\- **East New Britain Port Services Pty Ltd**
\-
Port Moresby *Papua New Guinea*
MMSI: 553111628

1,000 / 319 / 1,253
Class: BV (AB)

1982-01 Santan Engineering Pte Ltd — Singapore Yd No: 8129
Loa 58.50 Br ex - Dght 3.177
Lbp 55.00 Br md 14.01 Dpth 4.22
Welded, 1 dk

(A35D2RL) Landing Craft
Bow door/ramp
Liq: 80; Asphalt: 80
Compartments: 4 Ta, ER

2 oil engines reverse reduction geared to sc. shafts driving 2 FP propellers
Total Power: 832kW (1,132hp) 8.8kn
Caterpillar D379SCAC
2 x Vee 4 Stroke 8 Cy. 159 x 203 each-416kW (566bhp)
Caterpillar Tractor Co-USA
AuxGen: 2 x 340kW 415V 50Hz a.c
Fuel: 210.0 (d.f.) 4.0pd

8732829 **TORLAKLAR-II**
TC5652
\- -
\-
Istanbul *Turkey*
Official number: 6023

196 / 59 / -

1990-01 in Turkey
Loa 36.42 Br ex - Dght 1.600
Lbp - Br md 9.52 Dpth 2.95
Welded, 1 dk

(B11B2FV) Fishing Vessel

2 oil engines geared to sc. shafts driving 2 Propellers
Total Power: 794kW (1,080hp) 14.0kn
Caterpillar 3406
2 x 4 Stroke 6 Cy. 137 x 165 each-397kW (540bhp)
Caterpillar Inc-USA

9217864 **TORLAND**
SMIW
GG 207 **Toronland H/B**
\-
Fiskeback *Sweden*
MMSI: 265817000

846 / 254 / -
Class: (NV)

2000-08 Flekkefjord Slipp & Maskinfabrikk AS AS — Flekkefjord Yd No: 172
Loa 44.90 (BB) Br ex - Dght 4.950
Lbp 38.80 Br md 12.00 Dpth 7.35
Welded, 1 dk

(B11B2FV) Fishing Vessel

1 oil engine geared to sc. shaft driving 1 CP propeller
Total Power: 3,680kW (5,003hp)
Wartsila 8R32
1 x 4 Stroke 8 Cy. 320 x 350 3680kW (5003bhp)
Wartsila NSD Finland Oy-Finland
AuxGen: 1 x 1540kW a.c, 2 x 1168kW a.c
Thrusters: 1 Thwart. FP thruster (f); 1 Tunnel thruster (a)

9465992 **TORM AGNES**
9V8553
\- **OCM Singapore Njord Holdings Agnes Pte Ltd**
TORM A/S
SatCom: Inmarsat C 456495810
Singapore *Singapore*
MMSI: 564958000
Official number: 395950

30,241 / 14,702 / 50,274 / T/cm 47.8
Class: NV

2011-01 Guangzhou Shipyard International Co Ltd — Guangzhou GD Yd No: 06131036
Loa 183.20 (BB) Br ex 32.23 Dght 13.500
Lbp 176.00 Br md 32.20 Dpth 18.20
Welded, 1 dk

(A12B2TR) Chemical/Products Tanker
Double Hull (13F)
Liq: 51,472; Liq (Oil): 50,370
Compartments: 12 Wing Ta, 2 Wing Slop Ta, ER
12 Cargo Pump (s): 12x550m³/hr
Manifold: Bow/CM: 89.8m

1 oil engine driving 1 CP propeller
Total Power: 9,960kW (13,542hp) 15.0kn
MAN-B&W 6S50ME-B8
1 x 2 Stroke 6 Cy. 500 x 2000 9960kW (13542bhp)
AuxGen: 3 x 910kW 440/220V 50Hz a.c
Fuel: 240.0 (d.f.) 1945.0 (r.f.)

9466013 **TORM AGNETE**
9V2615
\- **OCM Singapore Njord Holdings Agnete Pte Ltd**
TORM Singapore Pte Ltd
Singapore *Singapore*
MMSI: 564452000

30,241 / 14,702 / 50,247 / T/cm 55.5
Class: NV

2010-09 Guangzhou Shipyard International Co Ltd — Guangzhou GD Yd No: 06130042
Loa 183.30 (BB) Br ex 32.23 Dght 12.570
Lbp 176.00 Br md 32.20 Dpth 18.20
Welded, 1 dk

(A12B2TR) Chemical/Products Tanker
Double Hull (13F)
Liq: 51,472; Liq (Oil): 51,472
Compartments: 12 Wing Ta, 2 Wing Slop Ta, ER
12 Cargo Pump (s): 12x550m³/hr
Manifold: Bow/CM: 90m

1 oil engine driving 1 FP propeller
Total Power: 9,960kW (13,542hp) 15.0kn
MAN-B&W 6S50ME-B8
1 x 2 Stroke 6 Cy. 500 x 2000 9960kW (13542bhp)
Hitachi Zosen Corp-Japan
AuxGen: 3 x 910kW 60Hz a.c
Fuel: 205.0 (d.f.) 1770.0 (r.f.)

9466001 **TORM ALEXANDRA**
9V2614
\- **OCM Singapore Njord Holdings Alexandra Pte Ltd**
TORM Singapore Pte Ltd
Singapore *Singapore*
MMSI: 564458000
Official number: 399229

30,241 / 14,702 / 50,216 / T/cm 47.8
Class: NV

2010-05 Guangzhou Shipyard International Co Ltd — Guangzhou GD Yd No: 06130041
Loa 183.20 (BB) Br ex 32.23 Dght 12.580
Lbp 176.00 Br md 32.20 Dpth 18.20
Welded, 1 dk

(A12B2TR) Chemical/Products Tanker
Double Hull (13F)
Liq: 51,473; Liq (Oil): 51,473
Compartments: 12 Wing Ta, 2 Wing Slop Ta, ER
12 Cargo Pump (s): 12x550m³/hr
Manifold: Bow/CM: 90m

1 oil engine driving 1 FP propeller
Total Power: 9,960kW (13,542hp) 15.0kn
MAN-B&W 6S50ME-B8
1 x 2 Stroke 6 Cy. 500 x 2000 9960kW (13542bhp)
Hitachi Zosen Corp-Japan
AuxGen: 3 x 910kW 60Hz a.c
Fuel: 210.0 (d.f.) 1770.0 (r.f.)

9465966 **TORM ALICE**
9V2253
\- **OCM Singapore Njord Holdings Alice Pte Ltd**
TORM A/S
Singapore *Singapore*
MMSI: 563399000
Official number: 398804

30,241 / 14,702 / 50,216 / T/cm 47.8
Class: NV

2010-04 Guangzhou Shipyard International Co Ltd — Guangzhou GD Yd No: 06131033
Loa 183.20 (BB) Br ex 32.23 Dght 12.600
Lbp 176.00 Br md 32.20 Dpth 18.20
Welded, 1 dk

(A12B2TR) Chemical/Products Tanker
Double Hull (13F)
Liq: 51,473; Liq (Oil): 51,473
Compartments: 12 Wing Ta, 2 Wing Slop Ta, ER
12 Cargo Pump (s): 12x550m³/hr
Manifold: Bow/CM: 90m

1 oil engine driving 1 FP propeller
Total Power: 9,960kW (13,542hp) 15.0kn
MAN-B&W 6S50ME-B8
1 x 2 Stroke 6 Cy. 500 x 2000 9960kW (13542bhp)
AuxGen: 3 x 910kW 220/440V 60Hz a.c
Fuel: 205.0 (d.f.) 1770.0 (r.f.)

9465980 **TORM ALMENA**
9V8551
\- **OCM Singapore Njord Holdings Almena Pte Ltd**
TORM A/S
SatCom: Inmarsat Mini-M 764847851
Singapore *Singapore*
MMSI: 563450000
Official number: 395948

30,241 / 14,702 / 50,227 / T/cm 55.5
Class: NV

2010-10 Guangzhou Shipyard International Co Ltd — Guangzhou GD Yd No: 06131035
Loa 183.30 (BB) Br ex 32.23 Dght 12.620
Lbp 176.00 Br md 32.20 Dpth 18.20
Welded, 1 dk

(A12B2TR) Chemical/Products Tanker
Double Hull (13F)
Liq: 51,472; Liq (Oil): 51,472
Part Cargo Heating Coils
Compartments: 12 Wing Ta, 2 Wing Slop Ta, ER
12 Cargo Pump (s): 12x550m³/hr
Manifold: Bow/CM: 90m

1 oil engine driving 1 FP propeller
Total Power: 9,960kW (13,542hp) 15.0kn
MAN-B&W 6S50ME-B8
1 x 2 Stroke 6 Cy. 500 x 2000 9960kW (13542bhp)
AuxGen: 3 x 910kW a.c
Fuel: 205.0 (d.f.) 1770.0 (r.f.)

9466025 **TORM AMALIE**
9V8552
\- **OCM Singapore Njord Holdings Amalie Pte Ltd**
TORM A/S
SatCom: Inmarsat Mini-M 765068061
Singapore *Singapore*
MMSI: 564081000
Official number: 395949

30,241 / 14,702 / 50,246 / T/cm 55.4
Class: NV

2011-02 Guangzhou Shipyard International Co Ltd — Guangzhou GD Yd No: 06130043
Loa 183.20 (BB) Br ex 32.23 Dght 12.600
Lbp 176.00 Br md 32.20 Dpth 18.20
Welded, 1 dk

(A12B2TR) Chemical/Products Tanker
Double Hull (13F)
Liq: 51,472; Liq (Oil): 50,370
Compartments: 12 Wing Ta, 2 Wing Slop Ta, ER
12 Cargo Pump (s): 12x550m³/hr
Manifold: Bow/CM: 89.8m

1 oil engine driving 1 FP propeller
Total Power: 9,960kW (13,542hp) 15.0kn
MAN-B&W 6S50ME-B8
1 x 2 Stroke 6 Cy. 500 x 2000 9960kW (13542bhp)
Dalian Marine Diesel Co Ltd-China
AuxGen: 3 x 910kW 440/220V 50Hz a.c
Fuel: 237.0 (d.f.) 1945.0 (r.f.)

9251028 **TORM AMAZON**
3FRJ6 *ex* Amazon *-2007*
\- **T & T Marine SA**
TORM A/S
Panama *Panama*
MMSI: 372699000
Official number: 4098210A

28,539 / 12,385 / 47,275 / T/cm 51.0
Class: AB

2002-01 Onomichi Dockyard Co Ltd — Onomichi HS Yd No: 479
Loa 182.50 (BB) Br ex 32.23 Dght 12.636
Lbp 172.00 Br md 32.20 Dpth 19.10
Welded, 1 dk

(A13B2TP) Products Tanker
Double Hull (13F)
Liq: 52,536; Liq (Oil): 52,536
Cargo Heating Coils
Compartments: 2 Ta, 12 Wing Ta, 2 Wing Slop Ta, ER
4 Cargo Pump (s): 4x1000m³/hr
Manifold: Bow/CM: 92.9m

1 oil engine driving 1 FP propeller
Total Power: 8,562kW (11,641hp) 14.8kn
MAN-B&W 6S50MC
1 x 2 Stroke 6 Cy. 500 x 1910 8562kW (11641bhp)
Mitsui Engineering & Shipbuilding CLtd-Japan
Fuel: 111.8 (d.f.) (Heating Coils) 1506.6 (r.f.) 36.0pd

9543550 **TORM ANABEL**
9V9637
\- **OCM Singapore Njord Holdings Anabel Pte Ltd**
TORM Singapore Pte Ltd
Singapore *Singapore*
MMSI: 566254000
Official number: 397410

30,241 / 14,585 / 52,300 / T/cm 55.5
Class: NV

2012-03 Guangzhou Shipyard International Co Ltd — Guangzhou GD Yd No: 08130006
Loa 183.30 (BB) Br ex 32.33 Dght 12.600
Lbp 176.00 Br md 32.20 Dpth 18.20
Welded, 1 dk

(A12B2TR) Chemical/Products Tanker
Double Hull (13F)
Liq: 51,472; Liq (Oil): 51,470
Compartments: 12 Wing Ta, 2 Wing Slop Ta, ER
12 Cargo Pump (s): 12x550m³/hr
Manifold: Bow/CM: 90.9m

1 oil engine driving 1 FP propeller
Total Power: 9,960kW (13,542hp) 15.0kn
MAN-B&W 6S50ME-B8
1 x 2 Stroke 6 Cy. 500 x 2000 9960kW (13542bhp)
AuxGen: 3 x 910kW a.c
Fuel: 200.0 (d.f.) 1770.0 (r.f.)

9300556 **TORM ANHOLT** *S6AY5* - **VesselCo 7 Pte Ltd** TORM Singapore Pte Ltd *Singapore* *Singapore* MMSI: 565377000 Official number: 392815	**39,035** 24,735 74,195 T/cm 66.0	Class: NV (NK)	**2004**-02 **Namura Shipbuilding Co Ltd — Imari SG** Yd No: 235 Loa 224.93 (BB) Br ex - Dght 13.950 Lbp 215.00 Br md 32.20 Dpth 19.30 Welded, 1 dk	**(A21A2BC) Bulk Carrier** Grain: 89,267 Compartments: 7 Ho, ER 7 Ha: 6 (16.8 x 14.9)ER (16.8 x 13.2)	**1 oil engine** driving 1 FP propeller Total Power: 9,189kW (12,493hp) 14.5kn B&W 7S50MC-C 1 x 2 Stroke 7 Cy. 500 x 2000 9189kW (12493bhp) Hitachi Zosen Corp-Japan AuxGen: 3 x 560kW a.c
9180982 **TORM ANNE** *9VKJ* - **VesselCo 2 Pte Ltd** TORM Singapore Pte Ltd SatCom: Inmarsat C 456497610 *Singapore* *Singapore* MMSI: 564976000 Official number: 388590	**28,932** 11,802 45,507 T/cm 50.8	Class: LR ✠ **100A1** SS 06/2009 Double Hull oil tanker ESP *IWS LI ✠ **LMC** **UMS IGS** Eq.Ltr: N†; Cable: 660.0/76.0 U3	**1999**-06 **Halla Engineering & Heavy Industries, Ltd. — Samho** Yd No: 1037 Loa 180.50 (BB) Br ex 32.22 Dght 12.205 Lbp 171.00 Br md 32.20 Dpth 18.80 Welded, 1 dk	**(A13B2TP) Products Tanker** Double Hull (13F) Liq: 51,206; Liq (Oil): 51,206 Compartments: 12 Wing Ta, 2 Wing Slop Ta, ER 12 Cargo Pump (s): 12x550m^3/hr Manifold: Bow/CM: 92m	**1 oil engine** driving 1 FP propeller Total Power: 7,717kW (10,492hp) 14.5kn B&W 6S50MC 1 x 2 Stroke 6 Cy. 500 x 1910 7717kW (10492bhp) Hyundai Heavy Industries Co Ltd-South Korea AuxGen: 3 x 600kW 440V 60Hz a.c Boilers: e (ex.g.) 9.2kgf/cm^2 (9.0bar), AuxB (o.f.) 8.2kgf/cm^2 (8.0bar) Fuel: 191.0 (d.f.) (Heating Coils) 1616.0 (r.f.) 32.0pd
9543548 **TORM ARAWA** *9V9636* - **OCM Singapore Njord Holdings Arawa Pte Ltd** TORM Singapore Pte Ltd *Singapore* *Singapore* MMSI: 566253000 Official number: 397409	**30,241** 14,562 52,300	Class: NV	**2012**-01 **Guangzhou Shipyard International Co Ltd — Guangzhou GD** Yd No: 08130005 Loa 183.30 (BB) Br ex 32.23 Dght 12.540 Lbp 176.00 Br md 32.20 Dpth 18.20 Welded, 1 dk	**(A12B2TR) Chemical/Products Tanker** Double Hull (13F) Liq: 51,470; Liq (Oil): 51,470 Compartments: 12 Wing Ta, 2 Wing Slop Ta, ER 12 Cargo Pump (s): 12x550m^3/hr Manifold: Bow/CM: 90.9m	**1 oil engine** driving 1 FP propeller Total Power: 9,480kW (12,889hp) 15.0kn MAN-B&W 6S50ME-B8 1 x 2 Stroke 6 Cy. 500 x 2000 9480kW (12889bhp) AuxGen: 3 x 910kW a.c Fuel: 200.0 (d.f.) 1770.0 (r.f.)
9465978 **TORM ASLAUG** *9V2254* - **OCM Singapore Njord Holdings Aslaug Pte Ltd** TORM A/S *Singapore* *Singapore* MMSI: 563411000 Official number: 398805	**30,241** 14,702 50,263 T/cm 47.8	Class: NV	**2010**-07 **Guangzhou Shipyard International Co Ltd — Guangzhou GD** Yd No: 06131034 Loa 183.20 (BB) Br ex 32.23 Dght 12.600 Lbp 176.00 Br md 32.20 Dpth 18.20 Welded, 1 dk	**(A12B2TR) Chemical/Products Tanker** Double Hull (13F) Liq: 51,472; Liq (Oil): 51,472 Compartments: 12 Wing Ta, 2 Wing Slop Ta, ER 12 Cargo Pump (s): 12x550m^3/hr Manifold: Bow/CM: 90m	**1 oil engine** driving 1 FP propeller Total Power: 9,960kW (13,542hp) 15.0kn MAN-B&W 6S50ME-B8 1 x 2 Stroke 6 Cy. 500 x 2000 9960kW (13542bhp) Dalian Marine Diesel Co Ltd-China AuxGen: 3 x 910kW 60Hz a.c Fuel: 205.0 (d.f.) 1770.0 (r.f.)
9287132 **TORM BORNHOLM** *9VFQ9* - **VesselCo 7 Pte Ltd** TORM Singapore Pte Ltd *Singapore* *Singapore* MMSI: 565749000 Official number: 393406	**40,030** 25,920 75,912 T/cm 67.8	Class: LR (NK) **100A1** SS 11/2009 bulk carrier strengthened for heavy cargoes, Nos. 2, 4 & 6 holds may be empty ESP ESN LI **LMC** **UMS**	**2004**-11 **Tsuneishi Corp — Fukuyama HS** Yd No: 1271 Loa 225.00 (BB) Br ex 32.26 Dght 14.028 Lbp 217.00 Br md 32.26 Dpth 19.30 Welded, 1 dk	**(A21A2BC) Bulk Carrier** Grain: 91,311 Compartments: 7 Ho, ER 7 Ha: 6 (17.3 x 15.4)ER (15.6 x 12.8)	**1 oil engine** driving 1 FP propeller Total Power: 9,010kW (12,250hp) 14.0kn B&W 6S60MC 1 x 2 Stroke 6 Cy. 600 x 2292 9010kW (12250bhp) Mitsui Engineering & Shipbuilding CLtd-Japan AuxGen: 3 x 440kW 440/110V 60Hz a.c Fuel: 2960.0
9263693 **TORM CAMILLA** *OYZZ2* - *ex Gron Falk -2005* **VesselCo 3 K/S** TORM A/S *Copenhagen* *Denmark (DIS)* MMSI: 220402000 Official number: D4189	**30,024** 11,809 46,219 T/cm 51.6	Class: AB (RI)	**2003**-08 **STX Shipbuilding Co Ltd — Changwon (Jinhae Shipyard)** Yd No: 1103 Loa 183.00 (BB) Br ex 32.20 Dght 11.963 Lbp 173.90 Br md 32.17 Dpth 19.10 Welded, 1 dk	**(A12B2TR) Chemical/Products Tanker** Double Hull (13F) Liq: 52,165; Liq (Oil): 52,165 Compartments: 12 Wing Ta, ER, 2 Wing Slop Ta 12 Cargo Pump (s): 12x600m^3/hr Manifold: Bow/CM: 91.5m	**1 oil engine** driving 1 FP propeller Total Power: 8,185kW (11,128hp) 14.5kn MAN-B&W 6S50MC-C 1 x 2 Stroke 6 Cy. 500 x 2000 8185kW (11128bhp) STX Corp-South Korea AuxGen: 3 x 740kW 450V a.c Fuel: 214.9 (d.f.) 1563.2 (r.f.)
9263708 **TORM CARINA** *OYTD2* - *ex Guld Falk -2005* **TORM A/S** TORM Shipping India Pvt Ltd *Copenhagen* *Denmark (DIS)* MMSI: 220407000 Official number: D4190	**30,024** 11,809 46,219 T/cm 51.6	Class: AB (RI)	**2003**-09 **STX Shipbuilding Co Ltd — Changwon (Jinhae Shipyard)** Yd No: 1104 Loa 183.00 (BB) Br ex 32.20 Dght 12.200 Lbp 173.90 Br md 32.17 Dpth 19.10 Welded, 1 dk	**(A12B2TR) Chemical/Products Tanker** Double Hull (13F) Liq: 52,170; Liq (Oil): 52,165 Compartments: 12 Wing Ta, 2 Wing Slop Ta, ER 12 Cargo Pump (s): 12x600m^3/hr Manifold: Bow/CM: 90m	**1 oil engine** driving 1 FP propeller Total Power: 8,171kW (11,109hp) 14.5kn B&W 6S50MC-C 1 x 2 Stroke 6 Cy. 500 x 2000 8171kW (11109bhp) STX Corp-South Korea AuxGen: 3 x 740kW
9262091 **TORM CAROLINE** *OYEW2* - *ex Vit Falk -2005* **VesselCo 3 K/S** TORM A/S SatCom: Inmarsat B 322039620 *Copenhagen* *Denmark (DIS)* MMSI: 220396000 Official number: D4178	**28,381** 12,598 46,414 T/cm 51.9	Class: AB (RI)	**2002**-11 **STX Shipbuilding Co Ltd — Changwon (Jinhae Shipyard)** Yd No: 1084 Loa 183.00 (BB) Br ex 32.20 Dght 12.215 Lbp 174.50 Br md 32.20 Dpth 18.00 Welded, 1 dk	**(A12B2TR) Chemical/Products Tanker** Double Hull (13F) Liq: 49,510; Liq (Oil): 49,510 Cargo Heating Coils Compartments: 12 Wing Ta, ER, 2 Wing Slop Ta 12 Cargo Pump (s): 12x600m^3/hr Manifold: Bow/CM: 94m	**1 oil engine** driving 1 FP propeller Total Power: 9,480kW (12,889hp) 14.7kn MAN-B&W 6S50MC-C 1 x 2 Stroke 6 Cy. 500 x 2000 9480kW (12889bhp) Hyundai Heavy Industries Co Ltd-South Korea AuxGen: 3 x 740kW 440V 60Hz a.c Thrusters: 1 Thwart. FP thruster (f) Fuel: 203.0 (d.f.) (Heating Coils) 1410.0 (r.f.)
9215103 **TORM CECILIE** *OXTJ2* - *ex Rod Falk -2005 ex High Rod Falk -2003* **VesselCo 3 K/S** TORM A/S *Copenhagen* *Denmark (DIS)* MMSI: 220521000 Official number: D4289	**28,381** 12,598 46,414 T/cm 51.7	Class: AB (RI)	**2001**-02 **Daedong Shipbuilding Co Ltd — Changwon (Jinhae Shipyard)** Yd No: 1047 Loa 182.94 (BB) Br ex 32.23 Dght 12.185 Lbp 173.87 Br md 32.20 Dpth 19.10 Welded, 1 dk	**(A12B2TR) Chemical/Products Tanker** Double Hull (13F) Liq: 49,457; Liq (Oil): 49,457 Cargo Heating Coils Compartments: 12 Wing Ta, ER, 2 Wing Slop Ta 12 Cargo Pump (s): 12x600m^3/hr Manifold: Bow/CM: 91.6m	**1 oil engine** driving 1 FP propeller Total Power: 8,170kW (11,108hp) 14.8kn B&W 6S50MC-C 1 x 2 Stroke 6 Cy. 500 x 2000 8170kW (11108bhp) Hyundai Heavy Industries Co Ltd-South Korea AuxGen: 3 x 740kW 220/440V 60Hz a.c Fuel: 190.0 (d.f.) 1400.0 (r.f.)
9230854 **TORM CHARENTE** *OYNS2* - *ex Charente -2008* **VesselCo 3 K/S** TORM Shipping India Pvt Ltd *Copenhagen* *Denmark (DIS)* MMSI: 220569000 Official number: D4346	**23,784** 8,832 35,751 T/cm 44.6	Class: NV	**2001**-09 **Daedong Shipbuilding Co Ltd — Changwon (Jinhae Shipyard)** Yd No: 1052 Loa 183.00 (BB) Br ex - Dght 11.017 Lbp 174.50 Br md 27.40 Dpth 17.60 Welded, 1 dk	**(A12B2TR) Chemical/Products Tanker** Double Hull (13F) Liq: 41,339; Liq (Oil): 41,339 Cargo Heating Coils Compartments: 12 Wing Ta, 2 Wing Slop Ta, ER 12 Cargo Pump (s): 10x500m^3/hr, 2x300m^3/hr Manifold: Bow/CM: 90.1m	**1 oil engine** driving 1 FP propeller Total Power: 7,878kW (10,711hp) 14.0kn B&W 6S46MC-C 1 x 2 Stroke 6 Cy. 460 x 1932 7878kW (10711bhp) Hyundai Heavy Industries Co Ltd-South Korea AuxGen: 3 x a.c Thrusters: 1 Tunnel thruster (f)
9215098 **TORM CLARA** *OYET2* - *ex Svart Falk -2005 ex High Svart Falk -2003* **VesselCo 3 K/S** TORM A/S SatCom: Inmarsat Mini-M 762584475 *Copenhagen* *Denmark (DIS)* MMSI: 220406000 Official number: D4188	**28,381** 12,598 45,999 T/cm 51.9	Class: AB (RI)	**2000**-11 **Daedong Shipbuilding Co Ltd — Changwon (Jinhae Shipyard)** Yd No: 1046 Loa 182.94 (BB) Br ex 32.23 Dght 12.135 Lbp 173.90 Br md 32.20 Dpth 18.00 Welded, 1 dk	**(A12B2TR) Chemical/Products Tanker** Double Hull (13F) Liq: 49,447; Liq (Oil): 49,447 Cargo Heating Coils Compartments: 12 Wing Ta, ER, 2 Wing Slop Ta 12 Cargo Pump (s): 12x600m^3/hr Manifold: Bow/CM: 91.6m	**1 oil engine** driving 1 FP propeller Total Power: 8,170kW (11,108hp) 15.1kn B&W 6S50MC-C 1 x 2 Stroke 6 Cy. 500 x 2000 8170kW (11108bhp) Hyundai Heavy Industries Co Ltd-South Korea AuxGen: 3 x 740kW a.c Fuel: 155.0 (d.f.) (Heating Coils) 1246.2 (r.f.) 34.0pd
9277785 **TORM EMILIE** *OXTD2* - *ex Cenito -2005* **TORM A/S** - *Copenhagen* *Denmark (DIS)* MMSI: 220518000 Official number: D4282	**42,484** 21,828 74,999 T/cm 68.5	Class: LR (RI) ✠ **100A1** SS 06/2009 Double Hull oil tanker ESP *IWS LI SPM **ShipRight** (SDA, FDA plus, CM) ✠ **LMC** **UMS IGS** Eq.Ltr: Q†; Cable: 687.5/81.0 U3 (a)	**2004**-06 **Hyundai Heavy Industries Co Ltd — Ulsan** Yd No: 1515 Loa 228.19 (BB) Br ex 32.23 Dght 14.439 Lbp 219.00 Br md 32.20 Dpth 20.90 Welded, 1 dk	**(A13B2TP) Products Tanker** Double Hull (13F) Liq: 82,052; Liq (Oil): 82,052 Compartments: 12 Wing Ta, 2 Wing Slop Ta, ER 12 Cargo Pump (s): 12x900m^3/hr Manifold: Bow/CM: 111.5m	**1 oil engine** driving 1 FP propeller Total Power: 13,548kW (18,420hp) 16.0kn MAN-B&W 6S60MC-C 1 x 2 Stroke 6 Cy. 600 x 2400 13548kW (18420bhp) Hyundai Heavy Industries Co Ltd-South Korea AuxGen: 3 x 800kW 450V 60Hz a.c Boilers: e (ex.g.) 16.3kgf/cm^2 (16.0bar), WTAuxB (o.f.) 12.2kgf/cm^2 (12.0bar) Fuel: 248.1 (d.f.) 2386.7 (r.f.)
9277723 **TORM ESTRID** *OXMF2* - **TORM A/S** - *Copenhagen* *Denmark (DIS)* MMSI: 220237000 Official number: D4005	**42,432** 21,857 74,999 T/cm 68.5	Class: LR ✠ **100A1** SS 01/2014 Double Hull oil tanker ESP *IWS LI SPM **ShipRight** (SDA, FDA Plus, CM) ✠ **LMC** **UMS IGS** Eq.Ltr: Q†; Cable: 687.5/81.0 U3 (a)	**2004**-01 **Hyundai Heavy Industries Co Ltd — Ulsan** Yd No: 1509 Loa 228.19 (BB) Br ex 32.23 Dght 14.439 Lbp 219.00 Br md 32.20 Dpth 20.90 Welded, 1 dk	**(A13B2TP) Products Tanker** Double Hull (13F) Liq: 82,052; Liq (Oil): 82,052 Compartments: 12 Wing Ta, 2 Wing Slop Ta, ER 12 Cargo Pump (s): 12x900m^3/hr Manifold: Bow/CM: 111.5m	**1 oil engine** driving 1 FP propeller Total Power: 13,548kW (18,420hp) 16.0kn MAN-B&W 6S60MC-C 1 x 2 Stroke 6 Cy. 600 x 2400 13548kW (18420bhp) Hyundai Heavy Industries Co Ltd-South Korea AuxGen: 3 x 800kW 450V 60Hz a.c Boilers: e (ex.g.) 16.3kgf/cm^2 (16.0bar), WTAuxB (o.f.) 12.2kgf/cm^2 (12.0bar) Fuel: 276.0 (d.f.) 2411.0 (r.f.)

Identity	Name / Owner / Flag	Tonnage	Class	Builder / Dimensions	Type / Cargo	Machinery
9302114 *OYMH2* -	**TORM FOX** *ex* Fox *-2008* **VesselCo 1 K/S** TORM Shipping India Pvt Ltd *Copenhagen* *Denmark (DIS)* MMSI: 220568000 Official number: D4352	**23,246** 10,126 37,025 T/cm 46.1	Class: NV	**2005-05 Hyundai Mipo Dockyard Co Ltd — Ulsan** Yd No: 0367 Loa 182.55 (BB) Br ex 27.39 Dght 11.217 Lbp 175.00 Br md 27.34 Dpth 16.70 Welded, 1 dk	**(A12B2TR) Chemical/Products Tanker** Double Hull (13F) Liq: 41,078; Liq (Oil): 41,078 Cargo Heating Coils Compartments: 12 Wing Ta, 2 Wing Slop Ta, ER 10 Cargo Pump (s): 8x500m³/hr, 2x320m³/hr Manifold: Bow/CM: 92.2m Ice Capable	**1 oil engine** driving 1 FP propeller Total Power: 11,070kW (15,051hp) 14.5kn B&W 7S50MC-C 1 x 2 Stroke 7 Cy. 500 x 2000 11070kW (15051bhp) Hyundai Heavy Industries Co Ltd-South Korea AuxGen: 3 x 752kW 60Hz a.c Thrusters: 1 Thwart. FP thruster (f) Fuel: 156.1 (d.f.) 1172.5 (r.f.)
9250490 *OUWE2* -	**TORM FREYA** **VesselCo 2 K/S** TORM A/S SatCom: Inmarsat B 322017923 *Copenhagen* *Denmark (DIS)* MMSI: 220179000 Official number: D3962	**30,058** 11,742 46,350 T/cm 51.0	Class: NV	**2003-02 STX Shipbuilding Co Ltd — Changwon (Jinhae Shipyard)** Yd No: 1090 Loa 183.00 Br ex - Dght 12.200 Lbp 173.90 Br md 32.20 Dpth 19.10 Welded, 1 dk	**(A12B2TR) Chemical/Products Tanker** Double Hull (13F) Liq: 52,065; Liq (Oil): 52,070 Compartments: 12 Wing Ta, ER, 2 Wing Slop Ta 12 Cargo Pump (s): 12x600m³/hr Manifold: Bow/CM: 91.6m	**1 oil engine** driving 1 FP propeller Total Power: 9,480kW (12,889hp) 14.5kn MAN-B&W 6S50MC-C 1 x 2 Stroke 6 Cy. 500 x 2000 9480kW (12889bhp) Hyundai Heavy Industries Co Ltd-South Korea AuxGen: 3 x 740kW a.c Fuel: 175.0 (d.f.) 1500.0 (r.f.)
9288930 *OYMG2* -	**TORM GARONNE** *ex* Garonne *-2008* **VesselCo 1 K/S** TORM A/S *Copenhagen* *Denmark (DIS)* MMSI: 220567000 Official number: D4349	**23,246** 10,126 37,178 T/cm 46.2	Class: NV	**2004-04 Hyundai Mipo Dockyard Co Ltd — Ulsan** Yd No: 0255 Loa 182.55 Br ex 27.38 Dght 10.850 Lbp 175.00 Br md 27.34 Dpth 16.70 Welded, 1 dk	**(A12B2TR) Chemical/Products Tanker** Double Hull (13F) Liq: 41,078; Liq (Oil): 41,078 Cargo Heating Coils Compartments: 12 Wing Ta, 2 Wing Slop Ta, ER 12 Cargo Pump (s): 10x500m³/hr, 2x320m³/hr Manifold: Bow/CM: 92m Ice Capable	**1 oil engine** driving 1 FP propeller Total Power: 11,070kW (15,051hp) 14.5kn B&W 7S50MC-C 1 x 2 Stroke 7 Cy. 500 x 2000 11070kW (15051bhp) Hyundai Heavy Industries Co Ltd-South Korea AuxGen: 3 x 780kW 60Hz a.c Thrusters: 1 Thwart. FP thruster (f)
9240897 *OUOB2* -	**TORM GERD** **VesselCo 2 K/S** TORM A/S *Copenhagen* *Denmark (DIS)* MMSI: 220162000 Official number: D3960	**30,128** 11,742 46,350 T/cm 51.6	Class: NV	**2002-11 STX Shipbuilding Co Ltd — Changwon (Jinhae Shipyard)** Yd No: 1087 Loa 183.00 (BB) Br ex 32.23 Dght 12.200 Lbp 173.90 Br md 32.20 Dpth 19.10 Welded, 1 dk	**(A12B2TR) Chemical/Products Tanker** Double Hull (13F) Liq: 52,159; Liq (Oil): 52,159 Compartments: 12 Wing Ta, 2 Wing Slop Ta, ER 12 Cargo Pump (s): 12x600m³/hr Manifold: Bow/CM: 91.6m	**1 oil engine** driving 1 FP propeller Total Power: 8,185kW (11,128hp) 14.5kn B&W 6S50MC-C 1 x 2 Stroke 6 Cy. 500 x 2000 8185kW (11128bhp) Hyundai Heavy Industries Co Ltd-South Korea AuxGen: 3 x 740kW 450V a.c Fuel: 214.9 (d.f.) 1563.2 (r.f.)
9240885 *OUNL2* -	**TORM GERTRUD** **VesselCo 2 K/S** TORM A/S SatCom: Inmarsat B 322016321 *Copenhagen* *Denmark (DIS)* MMSI: 220163000 Official number: D3959	**30,128** 11,742 46,362 T/cm 51.7	Class: NV	**2002-11 STX Shipbuilding Co Ltd — Changwon (Jinhae Shipyard)** Yd No: 1086 Loa 183.00 (BB) Br ex 32.23 Dght 12.217 Lbp 173.90 Br md 32.20 Dpth 19.11 Welded, 1 dk	**(A12B2TR) Chemical/Products Tanker** Double Hull (13F) Liq: 52,157; Liq (Oil): 52,335 Compartments: 12 Wing Ta, 2 Wing Slop Ta, ER 12 Cargo Pump (s): 12x600m³/hr Manifold: Bow/CM: 92.7m	**1 oil engine** driving 1 FP propeller Total Power: 8,562kW (11,641hp) 14.5kn MAN-B&W 6S50MC-C 1 x 2 Stroke 6 Cy. 500 x 2000 8562kW (11641bhp) Hyundai Heavy Industries Co Ltd-South Korea AuxGen: 3 x 740kW a.c
9199127 *OWCY2* -	**TORM GUDRUN** **VesselCo 1 K/S** TORM Shipping India Pvt Ltd *Copenhagen* *Denmark (DIS)* MMSI: 220645000 Official number: D4432	**57,031** 29,612 101,155 T/cm 91.5	Class: NV	**2000-05 Hyundai Heavy Industries Co Ltd — Ulsan** Yd No: 1194 Loa 243.85 (BB) Br ex 42.04 Dght 14.190 Lbp 234.00 Br md 42.00 Dpth 21.02 Welded, 1 dk	**(A13B2TP) Products Tanker** Double Hull (13F) Liq: 115,410; Liq (Oil): 115,410 Cargo Heating Coils Compartments: 12 Wing Ta, 2 Wing Slop Ta, ER 4 Cargo Pump (s): 4x2000m³/hr Manifold: Bow/CM: 120.3m	**1 oil engine** driving 1 FP propeller Total Power: 12,269kW (16,681hp) 14.8kn B&W 6S60MC 1 x 2 Stroke 6 Cy. 600 x 2292 12269kW (16681bhp) Hyundai Heavy Industries Co Ltd-South Korea
9172193 *OYQA2* -	**TORM GUNHILD** **TORM A/S** - *Copenhagen* *Denmark (DIS)* MMSI: 219887000 Official number: D3832	**28,909** 11,775 45,457 T/cm 50.8	Class: LR (AB) **100A1** SS 05/2009 Double Hull oil tanker LI ESP *IWS **LMC** **UMS** Eq.Ltr: N†; Cable: 660.0/76.0 U3	**1999-05 Halla Engineering & Heavy Industries, Ltd. — Samho** Yd No: 1053 Loa 180.55 (BB) Br ex 32.23 Dght 12.200 Lbp 171.00 Br md 32.20 Dpth 18.80 Welded, 1 dk	**(A13B2TP) Products Tanker** Double Hull (13F) Liq: 51,205; Liq (Oil): 51,205 Compartments: 12 Wing Ta, 2 Wing Slop Ta, ER 12 Cargo Pump (s): 12x550m³/hr Manifold: Bow/CM: 92m	**1 oil engine** driving 1 FP propeller Total Power: 7,772kW (10,567hp) 14.5kn B&W 6S50MC 1 x 2 Stroke 6 Cy. 500 x 1910 7772kW (10567bhp) Hyundai Heavy Industries Co Ltd-South Korea AuxGen: 3 x 600kW 440V 60Hz a.c Boilers: e (ex.g.) 8.1kgf/cm² (7.9bar), AuxB (o.f.) 8.1kgf/cm² (7.9bar) Fuel: 191.0 (d.f.) (Heating Coils) 1616.0 (r.f.) 32.0pd
9425502 *OWDP2* -	**TORM GYDA** **VesselCo 1 K/S** TORM Shipping India Pvt Ltd *Copenhagen* *Denmark (DIS)* MMSI: 220638000 Official number: D4434	**23,332** 9,625 36,207 T/cm 44.8	Class: NV	**2009-01 Hyundai Mipo Dockyard Co Ltd — Ulsan** Yd No: 2112 Loa 184.32 (BB) Br ex 27.45 Dght 11.315 Lbp 176.02 Br md 27.39 Dpth 17.20 Welded, 1 dk	**(A12B2TR) Chemical/Products Tanker** Double Hull (13F) Liq: 40,759; Liq (Oil): 40,759 Compartments: 12 Wing Ta, 2 Wing Slop Ta, ER 12 Cargo Pump (s): 10x500m³/hr, 2x300m³/hr Manifold: Bow/CM: 92.6m Ice Capable	**1 oil engine** driving 1 FP propeller Total Power: 9,480kW (12,889hp) 15.0kn MAN-B&W 6S50MC-C 1 x 2 Stroke 6 Cy. 500 x 2000 9480kW (12889bhp) Hyundai Heavy Industries Co Ltd-South Korea AuxGen: 3 x a.c Thrusters: 1 Tunnel thruster (f) Fuel: 130.0 (d.f.) 1000.0 (r.f.)
9143532 *OZNO2* -	**TORM HELENE** **VesselCo 2 K/S** TORM Shipping India Pvt Ltd SatCom: Inmarsat B 321936620 *Copenhagen* *Denmark (DIS)* MMSI: 219366000 Official number: D3737	**57,031** 29,612 99,999 T/cm 91.4	Class: NV	**1997-08 Hyundai Heavy Industries Co Ltd — Ulsan** Yd No: 1018 Loa 243.74 Br ex 42.00 Dght 14.194 Lbp 234.00 Br md - Dpth 21.00 Welded, 1 dk	**(A13B2TP) Products Tanker** Double Hull (13F) Liq: 117,688; Liq (Oil): 117,688 Compartments: 12 Wing Ta, ER, 2 Wing Slop Ta 4 Cargo Pump (s): 4x2000m³/hr Manifold: Bow/CM: 120.3m	**1 oil engine** driving 1 FP propeller Total Power: 12,269kW (16,681hp) 14.0kn B&W 6S60MC 1 x 2 Stroke 6 Cy. 600 x 2292 12269kW (16681bhp) Hyundai Heavy Industries Co Ltd-South Korea AuxGen: 3 x 600kW 220/450V 60Hz a.c Fuel: 156.4 (d.f.) 2380.0 (r.f.)
9288021 *OYCM2* -	**TORM HELVIG** **TORM A/S** - SatCom: Inmarsat Mini-M 764146467 *Copenhagen* *Denmark (DIS)* MMSI: 220373000 Official number: D4166	**30,018** 11,781 46,187 T/cm 51.8	Class: LR ✠ **100A1** SS 04/2010 Double Hull oil & chemical tanker, Type 2 **ShipRight** (SDA, FDA Plus, CM) ESP LI *IWS ✠ **LMC** **UMS IGS** Eq.Ltr: M†; Cable: 632.5/73.0 U3 (a)	**2005-03 STX Shipbuilding Co Ltd — Changwon (Jinhae Shipyard)** Yd No: 1139 Loa 183.00 (BB) Br ex 32.23 Dght 12.210 Lbp 173.90 Br md 32.20 Dpth 19.10 Welded, 1 dk	**(A12B2TR) Chemical/Products Tanker** Double Hull (13F) Liq: 52,204; Liq (Oil): 52,204 Compartments: 12 Wing Ta, 2 Wing Slop Ta, ER 12 Cargo Pump (s): 12x600m³/hr Manifold: Bow/CM: 92m	**1 oil engine** driving 1 FP propeller Total Power: 9,480kW (12,889hp) 14.5kn B&W 6S50MC-C 1 x 2 Stroke 6 Cy. 500 x 2000 9480kW (12889bhp) STX Engine Co Ltd-South Korea AuxGen: 3 x 740kW 450V 60Hz a.c Boilers: WTAuxB (o.f.) 9.2kgf/cm² (9.0bar), WTAuxB (Comp) 9.2kgf/cm² (9.0bar)
9283710 *OYNM2* -	**TORM HORIZON** *ex* Horizon *-2008* *ex* Athenian Horizon *-2004* **VesselCo 1 K/S** TORM A/S *Copenhagen* *Denmark (DIS)* MMSI: 220566000 Official number: D4338	**29,242** 11,926 46,955 T/cm 52.3	Class: AB	**2004-06 Hyundai Mipo Dockyard Co Ltd — Ulsan** Yd No: 0234 Loa 183.20 (BB) Br ex - Dght 12.216 Lbp 174.00 Br md 32.20 Dpth 18.80 Welded, 1 dk	**(A12B2TR) Chemical/Products Tanker** Double Hull (13F) Liq: 51,593; Liq (Oil): 51,593 Cargo Heating Coils Compartments: 12 Wing Ta, 2 Wing Slop Ta, ER 14 Cargo Pump (s): 14x600m³/hr Manifold: Bow/CM: 91.5m	**1 oil engine** driving 1 FP propeller Total Power: 8,561kW (11,640hp) 14.5kn MAN-B&W 6S50MC 1 x 2 Stroke 6 Cy. 500 x 1910 8561kW (11640bhp) Hyundai Heavy Industries Co Ltd-South Korea AuxGen: 3 x 730kW a.c
9243320 *OWDC2* -	**TORM INGEBORG** **VesselCo 2 K/S** TORM Shipping India Pvt Ltd *Copenhagen* *Denmark (DIS)* MMSI: 220640000 Official number: D4430	**57,095** 29,836 99,999 T/cm 91.4	Class: NV	**2003-11 Hyundai Samho Heavy Industries Co Ltd — Samho** Yd No: S162 Loa 243.96 (BB) Br ex 42.03 Dght 14.217 Lbp 234.00 Br md 42.00 Dpth 21.02 Welded, 1 dk	**(A13A2TW) Crude/Oil Products Tanker** Double Hull (13F) Liq: 115,617; Liq (Oil): 115,617 Cargo Heating Coils Compartments: 12 Wing Ta, 2 Wing Slop Ta, ER 3 Cargo Pump (s): 3x2500m³/hr Manifold: Bow/CM: 121m	**1 oil engine** driving 1 FP propeller Total Power: 13,548kW (18,420hp) 14.0kn B&W 6S60MC-C 1 x 2 Stroke 6 Cy. 600 x 2400 13548kW (18420bhp) Hyundai Heavy Industries Co Ltd-South Korea AuxGen: 3 x 740kW 440/220V 60Hz a.c Fuel: 195.0 (d.f.) 2600.0 (r.f.)
9461130 *3ETU5* -	**TORM ISLAND** **Ambitious Line SA** Shikishima Kisen KK *Panama* *Panama* MMSI: 351040000 Official number: 4158110	**43,012** 27,239 82,194 T/cm 70.2	Class: NK	**2010-04 Tsuneishi Holdings Corp Tsuneishi Shipbuilding Co — Fukuyama HS** Yd No: 1439 Loa 228.99 Br ex - Dght 14.430 Lbp 222.00 Br md 32.26 Dpth 20.05 Welded, 1 dk	**(A21A2BC) Bulk Carrier** Grain: 97,381 Compartments: 7 Ho, ER 7 Ha: ER	**1 oil engine** driving 1 FP propeller Total Power: 9,710kW (13,202hp) 14.5kn MAN-B&W 6S60MC-C 1 x 2 Stroke 6 Cy. 600 x 2400 9710kW (13202bhp) Mitsui Engineering & Shipbuilding CLtd-Japan AuxGen: 3 x 400kW a.c Fuel: 2870.0 (r.f.)

9277797 **TORM ISMINI** *OUPT2* - **TORM A/S** - *Copenhagen* *Denmark (DIS)* MMSI: 220258000 Official number: D4008	**42,432** 21,857 74,999 T/cm 68.5	Class: LR ✠ **100A1** SS 06/2009 Double Hull oil tanker ESP *IWS LI SPM **ShipRight** (SDA, FDA plus, CM) ✠ **LMC** **UMS IGS** Eq.Ltr: Q†; Cable: 687.5/81.0 U3 (a)	**2004-06 Hyundai Heavy Industries Co Ltd — Ulsan** Yd No: 1516 Loa 228.19 (BB) Br ex 32.23 Dght 14.439 Lbp 219.00 Br md 32.20 Dpth 20.90 Welded, 1 dk	**(A13B2TP) Products Tanker** Double Hull (13F) Liq: 82,052; Liq (Oil): 82,052 Compartments: 12 Wing Ta, 2 Wing Slop Ta, ER 12 Cargo Pump (s): 12x900m^3/hr Manifold: Bow/CM: 111.5m	**1 oil engine** driving 1 FP propeller Total Power: 13,548kW (18,420hp) 16.0kn MAN-B&W 6S60MC-C 1 x 2 Stroke 6 Cy. 600 x 2400 13548kW (18420bhp) Hyundai Heavy Industries Co Ltd-South Korea AuxGen: 3 x 800kW 450V 60Hz a.c Boilers: e (ex.g.) 16.3kgf/cm^2 (16.0bar), WTAuxB (o.f.) 12.2kgf/cm^2 (12.0bar) Fuel: 276.0 (d.f.) 2411.0 (r.f.)
9290646 **TORM KANSAS** *OYNA2* *ex Kansas -2008* - **VesselCo 1 K/S** TORM A/S *Copenhagen* *Denmark (DIS)* MMSI: 220565000 Official number: D4340	**29,242** 11,926 46,922 T/cm 52.2	Class: AB	**2006-03 Hyundai Mipo Dockyard Co Ltd — Ulsan** Yd No: 0239 Loa 183.20 (BB) Br ex 32.47 Dght 12.216 Lbp 174.00 Br md 32.20 Dpth 18.80 Welded, 1 dk	**(A12B2TR) Chemical/Products Tanker** Double Hull (13F) Liq: 51,593; Liq (Oil): 51,593 Compartments: 12 Wing Ta, 2 Wing Slop Ta, ER 12 Cargo Pump (s): 12x600m^3/hr Manifold: Bow/CM: 91.5m	**1 oil engine** driving 1 FP propeller Total Power: 8,561kW (11,640hp) 14.5kn MAN-B&W 6S50MC-C 1 x 2 Stroke 6 Cy. 500 x 2000 8561kW (11640bhp) Hyundai Heavy Industries Co Ltd-South Korea
9169512 **TORM KRISTINA** *OWCW2* - **VesselCo 1 K/S** TORM Shipping India Pvt Ltd *Copenhagen* *Denmark (DIS)* MMSI: 220641000 Official number: D4431	**57,080** 32,280 105,002 T/cm 92.0	Class: NV	**1999-01 Halla Engineering & Heavy Industries, Ltd. — Samho** Yd No: 1040 Loa 244.00 (BB) Br ex - Dght 14.818 Lbp 235.77 Br md 42.00 Dpth 21.00 Welded, 1 dk	**(A13B2TP) Products Tanker** Double Hull (13F) Liq: 113,998; Liq (Oil): 113,998 Cargo Heating Coils Compartments: 12 Ta, ER, 2 Wing Slop Ta 3 Cargo Pump (s): 3x3000m^3/hr Manifold: Bow/CM: 121.5m	**1 oil engine** driving 1 FP propeller Total Power: 14,049kW (19,101hp) 15.8kn MAN-B&W 5S70MC 1 x 2 Stroke 5 Cy. 700 x 2674 14049kW (19101bhp) Hyundai Heavy Industries Co Ltd-South Korea AuxGen: 3 x 750kW 220/440V 60Hz a.c Fuel: 195.0 (d.f.) 3300.0 (r.f.) 54.0pd
9375616 **TORM LAURA** *OULU2* - **VesselCo 1 K/S** TORM A/S SatCom: Inmarsat Mini-M 764834529 *Copenhagen* *Denmark (DIS)* MMSI: 220603000 Official number: D4239	**29,283** 15,939 53,160 T/cm 54.0	Class: NV	**2008-05 Guangzhou Shipyard International Co Ltd — Guangzhou GD** Yd No: 05130013 Loa 183.20 (BB) Br ex 32.46 Dght 13.500 Lbp 174.50 Br md 32.20 Dpth 18.20 Welded, 1 dk	**(A12B2TR) Chemical/Products Tanker** Double Hull (13F) Liq: 50,369; Liq (Oil): 50,369 Compartments: 12 Wing Ta, 2 Wing Slop Ta, ER 12 Cargo Pump (s): 12x550m^3/hr Manifold: Bow/CM: 89.8m Ice Capable	**1 oil engine** driving 1 CP propeller Total Power: 11,340kW (15,418hp) 15.0kn Wartsila 7RT-flex50 1 x 2 Stroke 7 Cy. 500 x 2050 11340kW (15418bhp) Dalian Marine Diesel Works-China AuxGen: 4 x 1080kW 440/220V 50Hz a.c Thrusters: 1 Tunnel thruster (f) Fuel: 100.0 (d.f.) 1800.0 (r.f.)
9390769 **TORM LENE** *OUPE2* - **VesselCo 1 K/S** TORM A/S SatCom: Inmarsat Mini-M 76487818 *Copenhagen* *Denmark (DIS)* MMSI: 220620000 Official number: D4240	**29,283** 15,937 53,143 T/cm 54.0	Class: NV	**2008-10 Guangzhou Shipyard International Co Ltd — Guangzhou GD** Yd No: 05130015 Loa 183.20 (BB) Br ex 32.23 Dght 13.500 Lbp 174.40 Br md 32.20 Dpth 18.20 Welded, 1 dk	**(A12B2TR) Chemical/Products Tanker** Double Hull (13F) Liq: 50,369; Liq (Oil): 50,369 Compartments: 12 Wing Ta, 2 Wing Slop Ta, ER 12 Cargo Pump (s): 12x550m^3/hr Manifold: Bow/CM: 89.8m Ice Capable	**1 oil engine** driving 1 CP propeller Total Power: 11,636kW (15,820hp) 15.0kn Wartsila 7RT-flex50 1 x 2 Stroke 7 Cy. 500 x 2050 11636kW (15820bhp) Dalian Marine Diesel Works-China AuxGen: 4 x 1080kW 440/220V 50Hz a.c Thrusters: 1 Tunnel thruster (f) Fuel: 150.0 (d.f.) 1500.0 (r.f.)
9392470 **TORM LILLY** *OUPJ2* - **VesselCo 3 K/S** TORM A/S SatCom: Inmarsat C 422063410 *Copenhagen* *Denmark (DIS)* MMSI: 220634000 Official number: D4242	**29,283** 15,939 53,160 T/cm 54.0	Class: NV	**2009-08 Guangzhou Shipyard International Co Ltd — Guangzhou GD** Yd No: 05130017 Loa 183.20 (BB) Br ex 32.46 Dght 13.500 Lbp 174.50 Br md 32.20 Dpth 18.20 Welded, 1 dk	**(A12B2TR) Chemical/Products Tanker** Double Hull (13F) Liq: 50,369; Liq (Oil): 50,369 Compartments: 12 Wing Ta, 2 Wing Slop Ta, ER 12 Cargo Pump (s): 12x550m^3/hr Manifold: Bow/CM: 89.8m Ice Capable	**1 oil engine** driving 1 CP propeller Total Power: 11,620kW (15,799hp) 15.0kn Wartsila 7RT-flex50 1 x 2 Stroke 7 Cy. 500 x 2050 11620kW (15799bhp) Dalian Marine Diesel Co Ltd-China AuxGen: 4 x 1080kW 440/220V 50Hz a.c Thrusters: 1 Tunnel thruster (f) Fuel: 115.0 (d.f.) 1730.0 (r.f.)
9282986 **TORM LOIRE** *OYMI2* *ex Loire -2008* - **VesselCo 3 K/S** TORM A/S *Copenhagen* *Denmark (DIS)* MMSI: 220552000 Official number: D4350	**23,246** 10,126 37,106 T/cm 46.2	Class: NV	**2004-02 Hyundai Mipo Dockyard Co Ltd — Ulsan** Yd No: 0254 Loa 182.55 Br ex 27.38 Dght 11.220 Lbp 175.00 Br md 27.34 Dpth 16.70 Welded, 1 dk	**(A12B2TR) Chemical/Products Tanker** Double Hull (13F) Liq: 41,078; Liq (Oil): 41,078 Cargo Heating Coils Compartments: 12 Wing Ta, 2 Wing Slop Ta, ER 6 Cargo Pump (s): 6x500m^3/hr Manifold: Bow/CM: 92.2m Ice Capable	**1 oil engine** driving 1 FP propeller Total Power: 11,070kW (15,051hp) 14.5kn MAN-B&W 7S50MC-C 1 x 2 Stroke 7 Cy. 500 x 2000 11070kW (15051bhp) Hyundai Heavy Industries Co Ltd-South Korea AuxGen: 3 x a.c Thrusters: 1 Thwart. FP thruster (f)
9392468 **TORM LOTTE** *OUPG2* - **VesselCo 1 K/S** TORM A/S *Copenhagen* *Denmark (DIS)* MMSI: 220635000 Official number: D4241	**29,283** 15,937 53,160 T/cm 54.0	Class: NV	**2009-01 Guangzhou Shipyard International Co Ltd — Guangzhou GD** Yd No: 05130016 Loa 183.20 (BB) Br ex 32.46 Dght 13.500 Lbp 174.50 Br md 32.20 Dpth 18.20 Welded, 1 dk	**(A12B2TR) Chemical/Products Tanker** Double Hull (13F) Liq: 50,369; Liq (Oil): 50,369 Compartments: 12 Wing Ta, 2 Wing Slop Ta, ER 12 Cargo Pump (s): 12x550m^3/hr Manifold: Bow/CM: 89.8m Ice Capable	**1 oil engine** driving 1 CP propeller Total Power: 11,620kW (15,799hp) 15.0kn Wartsila 7RT-flex50 1 x 2 Stroke 7 Cy. 500 x 2050 11620kW (15799bhp) Wartsila Finland Oy-Finland AuxGen: 4 x 1080kW 440/220V 50Hz a.c Thrusters: 1 Tunnel thruster (f) Fuel: 116.0 (d.f.) 1732.0 (r.f.)
9392482 **TORM LOUISE** *OWEG2* - **VesselCo 1 K/S** TORM A/S SatCom: Inmarsat C 421901410 *Copenhagen* *Denmark (DIS)* MMSI: 219014000 Official number: D4439	**29,283** 15,937 53,160 T/cm 54.0	Class: NV	**2009-07 Guangzhou Shipyard International Co Ltd — Guangzhou GD** Yd No: 05130020 Loa 183.20 (BB) Br ex 32.46 Dght 13.500 Lbp 174.40 Br md 32.20 Dpth 18.20 Welded, 1 dk	**(A12B2TR) Chemical/Products Tanker** Double Hull (13F) Liq: 50,369; Liq (Oil): 50,369 Compartments: 12 Wing Ta, 2 Wing Slop Ta, ER 12 Cargo Pump (s): 12x550m^3/hr Manifold: Bow/CM: 89.8m Ice Capable	**1 oil engine** driving 1 CP propeller Total Power: 11,620kW (15,799hp) 15.0kn Wartsila 7RT-Flex50 1 x 2 Stroke 7 Cy. 500 x 2050 11620kW (15799bhp) Wartsila Finland Oy-Finland AuxGen: 4 x 1080kW 440/220V 50Hz a.c Thrusters: 1 Tunnel thruster (f) Fuel: 110.0 (d.f.) 1730.0 (r.f.)
9212383 **TORM MADISON** *OYNN2* *ex Madison -2008 ex Nina -2001* - **VesselCo 1 K/S** TORM A/S SatCom: Inmarsat C 422056410 *Copenhagen* *Denmark (DIS)* MMSI: 220564000 Official number: D4347	**23,842** 8,835 35,828 T/cm 44.6	Class: AB	**2000-06 Daedong Shipbuilding Co Ltd — Changwon (Jinhae Shipyard)** Yd No: 1041 Loa 183.07 (BB) Br ex 27.43 Dght 11.017 Lbp 174.50 Br md 27.40 Dpth 17.60 Welded, 1 dk	**(A12B2TR) Chemical/Products Tanker** Double Hull (13F) Liq: 41,326; Liq (Oil): 41,326 Cargo Heating Coils Compartments: 12 Wing Ta, ER, 2 Wing Slop Ta 12 Cargo Pump (s): 10x500m^3/hr, 2x300m^3/hr Manifold: Bow/CM: 90.1m	**1 oil engine** driving 1 FP propeller Total Power: 8,165kW (11,101hp) 14.0kn Sulzer 6RTA48T 1 x 2 Stroke 6 Cy. 480 x 2000 8165kW (11101bhp) Hyundai Heavy Industries Co Ltd-South Korea AuxGen: 3 x 500kW 440V 60Hz a.c Thrusters: 1 Thwart. FP thruster (f) Fuel: 106.0 (d.f.) (Heating Coils) 1315.0 (r.f.) 30.3pd
9358400 **TORM MAREN** *OULI2* - **TORM A/S** - SatCom: Inmarsat M 600933873 *Copenhagen* *Denmark (DIS)* MMSI: 220602000 Official number: D4384	**61,724** 32,744 109,672 T/cm 91.8	Class: LR ✠ **100A1** SS 08/2013 Double Hull oil tanker ESP **ShipRight** (SDA, FDA, CM) *IWS SPM LI ✠ **LMC** **UMS IGS** Eq.Ltr: U†; Cable: 715.0/92.0 U3 (a)	**2008-08 Dalian Shipbuilding Industry Co Ltd — Dalian LN (No 2 Yard)** Yd No: PC1100-31 Loa 244.60 (BB) Br ex 42.03 Dght 15.450 Lbp 233.00 Br md 42.00 Dpth 22.20 Welded, 1 dk	**(A13B2TP) Products Tanker** Double Hull (13F) Liq: 117,937; Liq (Oil): 117,937 Cargo Heating Coils Compartments: 12 Wing Ta, 2 Wing Slop Ta, ER 3 Cargo Pump (s): 3x3000m^3/hr Manifold: Bow/CM: 121.8m	**1 oil engine** driving 1 FP propeller Total Power: 15,260kW (20,747hp) 15.3kn Wartsila 7RT-flex58T 1 x 2 Stroke 7 Cy. 580 x 2416 15260kW (20747bhp) Dalian Marine Diesel Works-China AuxGen: 3 x 780kW 450V 60Hz a.c Boilers: AuxB (ex.g.) 8.2kgf/cm^2 (8.0bar), WTAuxB (o.f.) 18.4kgf/cm^2 (18.0bar) Fuel: 180.0 (d.f.) 3500.0 (r.f.)
9299343 **TORM MARGRETHE** *9V9491* **FSL-25 Pte Ltd** LR2 Management K/S *Singapore* *Singapore* MMSI: 566122000 Official number: 397188	**61,724** 32,726 109,672 T/cm 91.0	Class: LR ✠ **100A1** SS 06/2011 Double Hull oil tanker ESP *IWS SPM LI **ShipRight** (SDA, FDA, CM) ✠ **LMC** **UMS IGS** Eq.Ltr: U†; Cable: 715.0/92.0 U3 (a)	**2006-06 Dalian Shipbuilding Industry Co Ltd — Dalian LN (No 2 Yard)** Yd No: PC1100-21 Loa 244.60 (BB) Br ex 42.03 Dght 15.520 Lbp 233.00 Br md 42.00 Dpth 22.20 Welded, 1 dk	**(A13A2TW) Crude/Oil Products Tanker** Double Hull (13F) Liq: 117,815; Liq (Oil): 117,815 Compartments: 12 Wing Ta, 2 Wing Slop Ta, ER 3 Cargo Pump (s): 3x3000m^3/hr Manifold: Bow/CM: 122.7m	**1 oil engine** driving 1 FP propeller Total Power: 15,260kW (20,747hp) 15.3kn Wartsila 7RT-flex58T 1 x 2 Stroke 7 Cy. 580 x 2416 15260kW (20747bhp) Dalian Marine Diesel Works-China AuxGen: 3 x 780kW 450V 60Hz a.c Boilers: AuxB (ex.g.) 8.2kgf/cm^2 (8.0bar), WTAuxB (o.f.) 18.4kgf/cm^2 (18.0bar) Fuel: 96.0 (d.f.) 1781.0 (r.f.)

9299355 *9V9490* -	**TORM MARIE** **FSL-26 Pte Ltd** TORM Singapore Pte Ltd *Singapore* *Singapore* MMSI: 566123000 Official number: 397187	**61,724** 32,726 109,672 T/cm 91.0	Class: LR ✠ **100A1** SS 10/2011 Double Hull oil tanker ESP **ShipRight** (SDA, FDA, CM) *IWS SPM LI ✠ **LMC** **UMS IGS** Eq.Ltr: U†; Cable: 715.0/92.0 U3 (a)	**2006-10 Dalian Shipbuilding Industry Co Ltd — Dalian LN (No 2 Yard)** Yd No: PC1100-22 Loa 244.60 (BB) Br ex 42.03 Dght 15.520 Lbp 233.00 Br md 42.00 Dpth 22.20 Welded, 1 dk	**(A13A2TW) Crude/Oil Products Tanker** Double Hull (13F) Liq: 117,815; Liq (Oil): 117,815 Compartments: 12 Wing Ta, 2 Wing Slop Ta, ER 3 Cargo Pump (s): 3x3000m^3/hr Manifold: Bow/CM: 122.7m	**1 oil engine** driving 1 FP propeller Total Power: 15,260kW (20,747hp) 15.3kn Wartsila 7RT-flex58T 1 x 2 Stroke 7 Cy. 580 x 2416 15260kW (20747bhp) Dalian Marine Diesel Works-China AuxGen: 3 x 780kW 450V 60Hz a.c Boilers: AuxB (ex.g.) 8.2kgf/cm^2 (8.0bar), WTAuxB (o.f.) 18.4kgf/cm^2 (18.0bar) Fuel: 200.1 (d.f.) 3290.0 (r.f.)
9319698 *LADY7* -	**TORM MARINA** **VesselCo 3 K/S** TORM A/S SatCom: Inmarsat C 425898610 *Oslo* *Norway (NIS)* MMSI: 258986000	**61,724** 32,726 109,672 T/cm 89.9	Class: LR ✠ **100A1** SS 11/2012 Double Hull oil tanker ESP **ShipRight** (SDA, FDA, CM) *IWS SPM LI ✠ **LMC** **UMS IGS** Eq.Ltr: U†; Cable: 715.0/92.0 U3 (a)	**2007-11 Dalian Shipbuilding Industry Co Ltd — Dalian LN (No 2 Yard)** Yd No: PC1100-29 Loa 244.60 (BB) Br ex 42.03 Dght 15.450 Lbp 233.00 Br md 42.00 Dpth 22.20 Welded, 1 dk	**(A13A2TW) Crude/Oil Products Tanker** Double Hull (13F) Liq: 117,936; Liq (Oil): 117,936 Compartments: 12 Wing Ta, 2 Wing Slop Ta, ER 3 Cargo Pump (s): 3x3000m^3/hr Manifold: Bow/CM: 121.8m	**1 oil engine** driving 1 FP propeller Total Power: 15,260kW (20,747hp) 15.3kn Wartsila 7RT-flex58T 1 x 2 Stroke 7 Cy. 580 x 2416 15260kW (20747bhp) Dalian Marine Diesel Works-China AuxGen: 3 x 780kW 450V 60Hz a.c Boilers: AuxB (ex.g.) 8.2kgf/cm^2 (8.0bar), WTAuxB (o.f.) 18.4kgf/cm^2 (18.0bar) Fuel: 200.0 (d.f.) 3116.0 (r.f.)
9246798 *OUHU2* -	**TORM MARY** **VesselCo 2 K/S** TORM A/S SatCom: Inmarsat B 322011220 *Copenhagen* *Denmark (DIS)* MMSI: 220112000 Official number: D3957	**30,128** 11,742 46,348 T/cm 51.0	Class: NV	**2002-05 STX Shipbuilding Co Ltd — Changwon (Jinhae Shipyard)** Yd No: 1079 Loa 183.00 (BB) Br ex 32.23 Dght 12.148 Lbp 173.90 Br md 32.20 Dpth 19.10 Welded, 1 dk	**(A12B2TR) Chemical/Products Tanker** Double Hull (13F) Liq: 52,159; Liq (Oil): 52,065 Part Cargo Heating Coils Compartments: 12 Wing Ta, 2 Wing Slop Ta, ER 12 Cargo Pump (s): 12x600m^3/hr Manifold: Bow/CM: 91.6m	**1 oil engine** driving 1 FP propeller Total Power: 8,562kW (11,641hp) 14.5kn B&W 6S50MC-C 1 x 2 Stroke 6 Cy. 500 x 2000 8562kW (11641bhp) Hyundai Heavy Industries Co Ltd-South Korea AuxGen: 3 x 740kW a.c Fuel: 163.0 (d.f.) 1427.0 (r.f.)
9358412 *OULS2* -	**TORM MATHILDE** **TORM A/S** SatCom: Inmarsat Mini-M 764847820 *Copenhagen* *Denmark (DIS)* MMSI: 220629000 Official number: D4383	**61,724** 32,723 109,672 T/cm 91.8	Class: LR ✠ **100A1** SS 11/2013 Double Hull oil tanker ESP **ShipRight** (SDA, FDA, CM) *IWS SPM LI ✠ **LMC** **UMS IGS** Eq.Ltr: U†; Cable: 715.0/90.0 U3 (a)	**2008-11 Dalian Shipbuilding Industry Co Ltd — Dalian LN (No 2 Yard)** Yd No: PC1100-32 Loa 244.60 (BB) Br ex 42.03 Dght 15.450 Lbp 233.00 Br md 42.00 Dpth 22.20 Welded, 1 dk	**(A13B2TP) Products Tanker** Double Hull (13F) Liq: 117,937; Liq (Oil): 117,937 Cargo Heating Coils Compartments: 12 Wing Ta, 2 Wing Slop Ta, ER 3 Cargo Pump (s): 3x3000m^3/hr Manifold: Bow/CM: 121.8m	**1 oil engine** driving 1 FP propeller Total Power: 15,260kW (20,747hp) 15.3kn Wartsila 7RT-flex58T 1 x 2 Stroke 7 Cy. 580 x 2416 15260kW (20747bhp) Dalian Marine Diesel Works-China AuxGen: 3 x 780kW 450V 60Hz a.c Boilers: AuxB (ex.g.) 7.9kgf/cm^2 (7.7bar), WTAuxB (o.f.) 16.8kgf/cm^2 (16.5bar) Fuel: 170.0 (d.f.) 3100.0 (r.f.)
9254240 *OYNX2* -	**TORM MOSELLE** *ex* Moselle *-2008* **VesselCo 3 K/S** TORM A/S *Copenhagen* *Denmark (DIS)* MMSI: 220563000 Official number: D4355	**28,567** 12,385 47,024 T/cm 50.2	Class: AB	**2003-02 Onomichi Dockyard Co Ltd — Onomichi HS** Yd No: 484 Loa 182.50 (BB) Br ex 32.23 Dght 12.666 Lbp 172.00 Br md 32.20 Dpth 19.10 Welded, 1 dk	**(A13B2TP) Products Tanker** Double Hull (13F) Liq: 50,332; Liq (Oil): 50,332 Cargo Heating Coils Compartments: 2 Ta, 12 Wing Ta, 2 Wing Slop Ta, ER 4 Cargo Pump (s): 4x1000m^3/hr Manifold: Bow/CM: 92.9m	**1 oil engine** driving 1 FP propeller Total Power: 8,561kW (11,640hp) 15.3kn B&W 6S50MC 1 x 2 Stroke 6 Cy. 500 x 1910 8561kW (11640bhp) Mitsui Engineering & Shipbuilding CLtd-Japan AuxGen: 3 x 480kW a.c Fuel: 132.0 (d.f.) (Heating Coils) 1656.0 (r.f.) 36.0pd
9221671 *9VVK9* -	**TORM NECHES** *ex* Neches *-2007* *completed as* Alam Bayu *-2000* **VesselCo 7 Pte Ltd** TORM Singapore Pte Ltd *Singapore* *Singapore* MMSI: 565639000 Official number: 393579	**28,539** 12,385 47,052 T/cm 50.2	Class: AB	**2000-09 Onomichi Dockyard Co Ltd — Onomichi HS** Yd No: 454 Loa 182.50 (BB) Br ex 32.23 Dght 12.666 Lbp 172.00 Br md 32.20 Dpth 19.10 Welded, 1 dk	**(A13B2TP) Products Tanker** Double Hull (13F) Liq: 50,332; Liq (Oil): 50,332 Cargo Heating Coils Compartments: 2 Ta, 12 Wing Ta, 2 Wing Slop Ta, ER 4 Cargo Pump (s): 4x1000m^3/hr Manifold: Bow/CM: 92.9m	**1 oil engine** driving 1 FP propeller Total Power: 8,561kW (11,640hp) 14.8kn B&W 6S50MC 1 x 2 Stroke 6 Cy. 500 x 1910 8561kW (11640bhp) Mitsui Engineering & Shipbuilding CLtd-Japan AuxGen: 3 x 420kW 60Hz a.c Fuel: 111.8 (d.f.) (Heating Coils) 1506.6 (r.f.) 36.0pd
9234678 *OYMZ2* -	**TORM OHIO** *ex* Ohio *-2008* *launched as* Borak *-2001* **VesselCo 1 K/S** TORM Shipping India Pvt Ltd *Copenhagen* *Denmark (DIS)* MMSI: 220562000 Official number: D4348	**23,235** 10,129 37,278 T/cm 46.1	Class: NV	**2001-12 Hyundai Mipo Dockyard Co Ltd — Ulsan** Yd No: 0023 Loa 182.55 (BB) Br ex 27.38 Dght 11.217 Lbp 175.00 Br md 27.34 Dpth 16.70 Welded, 1 dk	**(A12B2TR) Chemical/Products Tanker** Double Hull (13F) Liq: 41,346; Liq (Oil): 41,346 Compartments: 12 Wing Ta, ER, 2 Wing Slop Ta 12 Cargo Pump (s): 12x500m^3/hr Manifold: Bow/CM: 91.9m Ice Capable	**1 oil engine** driving 1 FP propeller Total Power: 9,467kW (12,871hp) 14.5kn B&W 6S50MC-C 1 x 2 Stroke 6 Cy. 500 x 2000 9467kW (12871bhp) Hyundai Heavy Industries Co Ltd-South Korea AuxGen: 3 x a.c
9443009 *3EPC3* -	**TORM ORIENT** **Polestar Ship Line SA** Orient Line KK (Orient Line Co Ltd) *Panama* *Panama* MMSI: 354406000 Official number: 3356708A	**39,737** 25,754 76,636 T/cm 66.6	Class: NK	**2008-02 Imabari Shipbuilding Co Ltd — Marugame KG (Marugame Shipyard)** Yd No: 1483 Loa 224.94 (BB) Br ex 32.30 Dght 14.139 Lbp 217.00 Br md 32.26 Dpth 19.50 Welded, 1 dk	**(A21A2BC) Bulk Carrier** Grain: 90,740 Compartments: 7 Ho, ER 7 Ha: ER	**1 oil engine** driving 1 FP propeller Total Power: 10,320kW (14,031hp) 14.8kn MAN-B&W 6S60MC 1 x 2 Stroke 6 Cy. 600 x 2292 10320kW (14031bhp) Mitsui Engineering & Shipbuilding CLtd-Japan AuxGen: 4 x 313kW a.c Fuel: 5740.0
9290660 *OYNL2* -	**TORM PLATTE** *ex* Platte *-2008* **VesselCo 1 K/S** TORM A/S *Copenhagen* *Denmark (DIS)* MMSI: 220561000 Official number: D4342	**29,242** 11,926 46,955 T/cm 52.2	Class: AB	**2006-05 Hyundai Mipo Dockyard Co Ltd — Ulsan** Yd No: 0241 Loa 183.20 (BB) Br ex 32.47 Dght 12.216 Lbp 174.00 Br md 32.20 Dpth 18.80 Welded, 1 dk	**(A12B2TR) Chemical/Products Tanker** Double Hull (13F) Liq: 51,593; Liq (Oil): 51,593 Compartments: 12 Wing Ta, 2 Wing Slop Ta, ER 14 Cargo Pump (s): 12x600m^3/hr, 2x300m^3/hr Manifold: Bow/CM: 91.5m	**1 oil engine** driving 1 FP propeller Total Power: 8,561kW (11,640hp) 14.5kn MAN-B&W 6S50MC-C 1 x 2 Stroke 6 Cy. 500 x 2000 8561kW (11640bhp) Hyundai Heavy Industries Co Ltd-South Korea AuxGen: 3 x 730kW a.c Fuel: 204.4 (d.f.) 1429.2 (r.f.)
9290579 *OYCN2* -	**TORM RAGNHILD** **TORM A/S** *Copenhagen* *Denmark (DIS)* MMSI: 220374000 Official number: D4167	**30,018** 11,781 46,187 T/cm 51.3	Class: LR ✠ **100A1** SS 04/2010 Double Hull oil & chemical tanker, Ship Type 2 **ShipRight** (SDA, FDA plus, CM) ESP LI *IWS ✠ **LMC** **UMS IGS** Eq.Ltr: M†; Cable: 632.5/73.0 U3 (a)	**2005-04 STX Shipbuilding Co Ltd — Changwon (Jinhae Shipyard)** Yd No: 1140 Loa 183.00 (BB) Br ex 32.23 Dght 12.247 Lbp 173.90 Br md 32.20 Dpth 19.10 Welded, 1 dk	**(A12B2TR) Chemical/Products Tanker** Double Hull (13F) Liq: 52,218; Liq (Oil): 52,218 Compartments: 12 Wing Ta, 2 Wing Slop Ta, ER 12 Cargo Pump (s): 12x600m^3/hr Manifold: Bow/CM: 92.8m	**1 oil engine** driving 1 FP propeller Total Power: 9,480kW (12,889hp) 14.5kn MAN-B&W 6S50MC-C 1 x 2 Stroke 6 Cy. 500 x 2000 9480kW (12889bhp) STX Engine Co Ltd-South Korea AuxGen: 3 x 740kW 450V 60Hz a.c Boilers: AuxB (Comp) 9.2kgf/cm^2 (9.0bar), AuxB (o.f.) 9.2kgf/cm^2 (9.0bar)
9473834 *3FEZ2* -	**TORM REGINA** *ex* Jewel Of Bawshar *-2011* **Sun Cordia Marine SA** Nissho Odyssey Ship Management Pte Ltd *Panama* *Panama* MMSI: 372633000 Official number: 4275311	**31,572** 18,819 55,886 T/cm 56.9	Class: LR ✠ **100A1** SS 01/2011 bulk carrier CSR BC-A Nos. 2 & 4 holds may be empty GRAB (20) ESP LI ✠ **LMC** Cable: 632.5/73.0 U3 (a)	**2011-01 IHI Marine United Inc — Yokohama KN** Yd No: 3269 Loa 189.86 (BB) Br ex 32.30 Dght 12.700 Lbp 185.00 Br md 32.26 Dpth 18.10 Welded, 1 dk	**(A21A2BC) Bulk Carrier** Double Hull Grain: 72,111; Bale: 67,062 Compartments: 5 Ho, ER 5 Ha: ER Cranes: 4x30t	**1 oil engine** driving 1 FP propeller Total Power: 8,890kW (12,087hp) 14.5kn Wartsila 6RT-flex50 1 x 2 Stroke 6 Cy. 500 x 2050 8890kW (12087bhp) Diesel United Ltd.-Aioi AuxGen: 3 x 430kW 450V 60Hz a.c Boilers: WTAuxB (o.f.) 7.0kgf/cm^2 (6.9bar)
9290658 *OYNE2* -	**TORM REPUBLICAN** *ex* Republican *-2008* **VesselCo 1 K/S** TORM A/S SatCom: Inmarsat Mini-M 764834447 *Copenhagen* *Denmark (DIS)* MMSI: 220560000 Official number: D4341	**29,242** 11,926 46,955 T/cm 52.2	Class: AB	**2006-03 Hyundai Mipo Dockyard Co Ltd — Ulsan** Yd No: 0240 Loa 183.20 (BB) Br ex 32.47 Dght 12.216 Lbp 174.00 Br md 32.20 Dpth 18.80 Welded, 1 dk	**(A12B2TR) Chemical/Products Tanker** Double Hull (13F) Liq: 51,594; Liq (Oil): 51,594 Cargo Heating Coils Compartments: 12 Wing Ta, 2 Wing Slop Ta, ER 12 Cargo Pump (s): 12x600m^3/hr Manifold: Bow/CM: 91.5m	**1 oil engine** driving 1 FP propeller Total Power: 8,580kW (11,665hp) 14.5kn MAN-B&W 6S50MC 1 x 2 Stroke 6 Cy. 500 x 1910 8580kW (11665bhp) Hyundai Heavy Industries Co Ltd-South Korea AuxGen: 3 x 730kW a.c Fuel: 178.4 (d.f.) 1321.3 (r.f.)

Ship	Tonnage	Class	Builder / Dimensions	Type / Cargo	Machinery
9215086 **TORM RHONE** *OYNR2* *ex* Rhone *-2008* *ex* Prospero *-2001* - **VesselCo 1 K/S** TORM Shipping India Pvt Ltd *Copenhagen* *Denmark (DIS)* MMSI: 220559000 Official number: D4345	**23,740** 8,832 35,751 T/cm 44.6	Class: NV	**2000**-11 **Daedong Shipbuilding Co Ltd — Changwon (Jinhae Shipyard)** Yd No: 1045 Loa 183.00 (BB) Br ex - Dght 11.017 Lbp 174.50 Br md 27.40 Dpth 17.60 Welded, 1 dk	**(A12B2TR) Chemical/Products Tanker** Double Hull (13F) Liq: 41,305; Liq (Oil): 41,305 Cargo Heating Coils Compartments: 12 Wing Ta, ER 12 Cargo Pump (s): 10x500m³/hr, 2x300m³/hr Manifold: Bow/CM: 88.6m	**1 oil engine** driving 1 FP propeller Total Power: 7,878kW (10,711hp) 14.0kn B&W 6S46MC-C 1 x 2 Stroke 6 Cy. 460 x 1932 7878kW (10711bhp) Hyundai Heavy Industries Co Ltd-South Korea AuxGen: 3 x a.c Thrusters: 1 Tunnel thruster (f)
9254070 **TORM ROSETTA** *OYNV2* *ex* Rosetta *-2008* - **VesselCo 1 K/S** TORM A/S *Copenhagen* *Denmark (DIS)* MMSI: 220557000 Official number: D4356	**28,567** 12,385 47,038 T/cm 51.0	Class: AB	**2003**-03 **Onomichi Dockyard Co Ltd — Onomichi HS** Yd No: 490 Loa 182.50 (BB) Br ex - Dght 12.670 Lbp 172.00 Br md 32.20 Dpth 19.10 Welded, 1 dk	**(A13B2TP) Products Tanker** Double Hull (13F) Liq: 50,332; Liq (Oil): 50,332 Cargo Heating Coils Compartments: 1 Ta, 14 Wing Ta, ER, 2 Wing Slop Ta 4 Cargo Pump (s): 4x1000m³/hr Manifold: Bow/CM: 92.9m	**1 oil engine** driving 1 FP propeller Total Power: 8,561kW (11,640hp) 15.3kn B&W 6S50MC 1 x 2 Stroke 6 Cy. 500 x 1910 8561kW (11640bhp) Mitsui Engineering & Shipbuilding CLtd-Japan AuxGen: 3 x 480kW a.c Fuel: 111.8 (d.f.) (Heating Coils) 1506.6 (r.f.) 36.0pd
9247778 **TORM SAN JACINTO** *OYNU2* *ex* San Jacinto *-2008* - **VesselCo 1 K/S** TORM A/S *Copenhagen* *Denmark (DIS)* MMSI: 220558000 Official number: D4354	**28,539** 12,385 47,038 T/cm 50.6	Class: AB	**2002**-03 **Onomichi Dockyard Co Ltd — Onomichi HS** Yd No: 480 Loa 182.50 (BB) Br ex - Dght 12.670 Lbp 172.00 Br md 32.20 Dpth 19.10 Welded, 1 dk	**(A13A2TW) Crude/Oil Products Tanker** Double Hull (13F) Liq: 50,332; Liq (Oil): 50,332 Cargo Heating Coils Compartments: 2 Ta, 12 Wing Ta, 2 Wing Slop Ta, ER 4 Cargo Pump (s): 4x1000m³/hr Manifold: Bow/CM: 92m	**1 oil engine** driving 1 FP propeller Total Power: 8,561kW (11,640hp) 15.3kn B&W 6S50MC 1 x 2 Stroke 6 Cy. 500 x 1910 8561kW (11640bhp) Mitsui Engineering & Shipbuilding CLtd-Japan Fuel: 111.8 (d.f.) (Heating Coils) 1506.6 (r.f.) 36.0pd
9295323 **TORM SAONE** *OYMM2* *ex* Saone *-2007* - **VesselCo 3 K/S** TORM A/S *Copenhagen* *Denmark (DIS)* MMSI: 220570000 Official number: D4351	**23,246** 10,126 36,986 T/cm 46.1	Class: NV	**2004**-07 **Hyundai Mipo Dockyard Co Ltd — Ulsan** Yd No: 0258 Loa 182.55 Br ex 27.38 Dght 10.580 Lbp 175.00 Br md 27.34 Dpth 16.70 Welded, 1 dk	**(A12B2TR) Chemical/Products Tanker** Double Hull (13F) Liq: 41,078; Liq (Oil): 41,078 Cargo Heating Coils Compartments: 12 Wing Ta, 2 Wing Slop Ta, ER 12 Cargo Pump (s): 10x500m³/hr, 2x320m³/hr Manifold: Bow/CM: 92.2m Ice Capable	**1 oil engine** driving 1 FP propeller Total Power: 11,069kW (15,049hp) 14.5kn B&W 7S50MC-C 1 x 2 Stroke 7 Cy. 500 x 2000 11069kW (15049bhp) Hyundai Heavy Industries Co Ltd-South Korea AuxGen: 3 x 780kW 60Hz a.c Thrusters: 1 Thwart. FP thruster (f) Fuel: 100.0 (d.f.) 1100.0 (r.f.)
9273260 **TORM SARA** *S6AA9* *ex* Penyu Agar *-2005* - **VesselCo 6 Pte Ltd** TORM Singapore Pte Ltd *Singapore* *Singapore* MMSI: 564111000 Official number: 390309	**41,503** 20,972 72,718 T/cm 66.8	Class: LR (AB) **100A1** SS 11/2013 Double Hull oil tanker ESP *IWS LI EP (V) (bar above) **LMC** **UMS IGS** Cable: 660.0/78.0 U3 (a)	**2003**-11 **Samsung Heavy Industries Co Ltd — Geoje** Yd No: 1449 Loa 227.83 (BB) Br ex 32.28 Dght 14.022 Lbp 219.00 Br md 32.24 Dpth 20.60 Welded, 1 dk	**(A13B2TP) Products Tanker** Double Hull (13F) Liq: 78,813; Liq (Oil): 78,813 Cargo Heating Coils Compartments: 12 Wing Ta, 2 Wing Slop Ta, ER 3 Cargo Pump (s): 3x2000m³/hr Manifold: Bow/CM: 113.1m	**1 oil engine** driving 1 FP propeller Total Power: 12,268kW (16,680hp) 15.0kn MAN-B&W 6S60MC 1 x 2 Stroke 6 Cy. 600 x 2292 12268kW (16680bhp) Doosan Engine Co Ltd-South Korea AuxGen: 3 x 688kW 450V 60Hz a.c Fuel: 199.0 (d.f.) 2829.0 (r.f.)
9290957 **TORM SIGNE** *9VDX5* *launched as* Penyu Sisik *-2005* - **VesselCo 6 Pte Ltd** TORM Singapore Pte Ltd *Singapore* *Singapore* MMSI: 563357000 Official number: 391228	**41,503** 20,972 72,670 T/cm 66.8	Class: LR (AB) **100A1** SS 03/2010 Double Hull oil tanker ESP *IWS LI EP (V) (bar above) **LMC** **UMS IGS**	**2005**-03 **Samsung Heavy Industries Co Ltd — Geoje** Yd No: 1479 Loa 227.50 (BB) Br ex 32.28 Dght 14.022 Lbp 219.00 Br md 32.24 Dpth 20.60 Welded, 1 dk	**(A13B2TP) Products Tanker** Double Hull (13F) Liq: 78,813; Liq (Oil): 78,813 Cargo Heating Coils Compartments: 12 Wing Ta, 1 Slop Ta, 2 Wing Slop Ta, ER 3 Cargo Pump (s): 3x2000m³/hr Manifold: Bow/CM: 113.1m	**1 oil engine** driving 1 FP propeller Total Power: 12,438kW (16,911hp) 15.7kn MAN-B&W 6S60MC 1 x 2 Stroke 6 Cy. 600 x 2292 12438kW (16911bhp) Doosan Engine Co Ltd-South Korea AuxGen: 3 x 670kW a.c Fuel: 199.0 (d.f.) 2829.0 (r.f.)
9295086 **TORM SOFIA** *9VDG9* - **VesselCo 6 Pte Ltd** TORM Singapore Pte Ltd *Singapore* *Singapore* MMSI: 563472000 Official number: 391246	**41,503** 20,972 72,660 T/cm 66.8	Class: LR (AB) **100A1** SS 08/2010 Double Hull oil tanker ESP LI EP (Vc) (bar above) *IWS **LMC** **UMS IGS** Eq.Ltr: P†; Cable: 660.0/78.0 U3 (a)	**2005**-08 **Samsung Heavy Industries Co Ltd — Geoje** Yd No: 1521 Loa 227.83 (BB) Br ex 32.28 Dght 14.000 Lbp 219.00 Br md 32.24 Dpth 20.60 Welded, 1 dk	**(A13B2TP) Products Tanker** Double Hull (13F) Liq: 78,813; Liq (Oil): 78,813 Cargo Heating Coils Compartments: 12 Wing Ta, 2 Wing Slop Ta, ER 3 Cargo Pump (s): 3x2000m³/hr Manifold: Bow/CM: 113.1m	**1 oil engine** driving 1 FP propeller Total Power: 12,438kW (16,911hp) 15.0kn MAN-B&W 6S60MC 1 x 2 Stroke 6 Cy. 600 x 2292 12438kW (16911bhp) Doosan Engine Co Ltd-South Korea AuxGen: 3 x 688kW 450V 60Hz a.c Boilers: e (ex.g.), WTAuxB (o.f.) 18.4kgf/cm² (18.0bar) Fuel: 199.0 (d.f.) 2829.2 (r.f.)
9302126 **TORM TEVERE** *OYMY2* *ex* Tevere *-2008* - **VesselCo 1 K/S** TORM Shipping India Pvt Ltd *Copenhagen* *Denmark (DIS)* MMSI: 220556000 Official number: D4353	**23,246** 10,126 36,990 T/cm 46.2	Class: NV	**2005**-07 **Hyundai Mipo Dockyard Co Ltd — Ulsan** Yd No: 0368 Loa 182.55 Br ex 27.39 Dght 11.217 Lbp 175.00 Br md 27.34 Dpth 16.70 Welded, 1 dk	**(A12B2TR) Chemical/Products Tanker** Double Hull (13F) Liq: 41,078; Liq (Oil): 41,078 Cargo Heating Coils Compartments: 12 Wing Ta, 2 Wing Slop Ta, ER 10 Cargo Pump (s): 8x500m³/hr, 2x320m³/hr Manifold: Bow/CM: 92.2m Ice Capable	**1 oil engine** driving 1 FP propeller Total Power: 10,010kW (13,610hp) 14.5kn MAN-B&W 7S50MC 1 x 2 Stroke 7 Cy. 500 x 1910 10010kW (13610bhp) Hyundai Heavy Industries Co Ltd-South Korea AuxGen: 3 x 752kW 60Hz a.c Thrusters: 1 Thwart. FP thruster (f) Fuel: 158.5 (d.f.) 1123.0 (r.f.)
9318333 **TORM THAMES** *OYNK2* *ex* Thames *-2008* - **VesselCo 1 K/S** TORM A/S *Copenhagen* *Denmark (DIS)* MMSI: 220555000 Official number: D4343	**29,214** 12,307 47,036 T/cm 52.1	Class: AB	**2005**-07 **Hyundai Mipo Dockyard Co Ltd — Ulsan** Yd No: 0430 Loa 183.88 (BB) Br ex 32.25 Dght 12.416 Lbp 174.00 Br md 32.20 Dpth 18.00 Welded, 1 dk	**(A12B2TR) Chemical/Products Tanker** Double Hull (13F) Liq: 51,593; Liq (Oil): 51,593 Compartments: 12 Wing Ta, 2 Wing Slop Ta, ER 12 Cargo Pump (s): 12x600m³/hr Manifold: Bow/CM: 92.6m Ice Capable	**1 oil engine** driving 1 FP propeller Total Power: 11,636kW (15,820hp) 15.2kn B&W 7S50MC-C 1 x 2 Stroke 7 Cy. 500 x 2000 11636kW (15820bhp) Hyundai Heavy Industries Co Ltd-South Korea AuxGen: 3 x 840kW a.c Fuel: 192.0 (d.f.) 1334.0 (r.f.)
9250488 **TORM THYRA** *OUVN2* - **VesselCo 2 K/S** TORM A/S *Copenhagen* *Denmark (DIS)* MMSI: 220178000 Official number: D3961	**30,058** 11,742 46,308 T/cm 51.7	Class: NV	**2003**-01 **STX Shipbuilding Co Ltd — Changwon (Jinhae Shipyard)** Yd No: 1089 Loa 183.00 (BB) Br ex 32.23 Dght 12.200 Lbp 173.90 Br md 32.20 Dpth 19.10 Welded, 1 dk	**(A12B2TR) Chemical/Products Tanker** Double Hull (13F) Liq: 52,201; Liq (Oil): 52,201 Compartments: 12 Wing Ta, 2 Wing Slop Ta, ER 12 Cargo Pump (s): 12x600m³/hr Manifold: Bow/CM: 92m	**1 oil engine** driving 1 FP propeller Total Power: 8,562kW (11,641hp) 14.5kn MAN-B&W 6S50MC-C 1 x 2 Stroke 6 Cy. 500 x 2000 8562kW (11641bhp) Hyundai Heavy Industries Co Ltd-South Korea AuxGen: 3 x 740kW 450V a.c Fuel: 150.0 (d.f.) 1400.0 (r.f.)
9461142 **TORM TRADER** *3EZU4* - **A-1 Shipholding SA** TOSCO KEYMAX International Ship Management Co Ltd *Panama* *Panama* MMSI: 356218000 Official number: 4168710	**43,012** 27,239 82,181 T/cm 70.2	Class: NK	**2010**-06 **Tsuneishi Holdings Corp Tsuneishi Shipbuilding Co — Fukuyama HS** Yd No: 1440 Loa 228.99 Br ex - Dght 14.429 Lbp 222.00 Br md 32.26 Dpth 20.05 Welded, 1 dk	**(A21A2BC) Bulk Carrier** Grain: 97,381 Compartments: 7 Ho, ER 7 Ha: ER	**1 oil engine** driving 1 FP propeller Total Power: 9,710kW (13,202hp) 14.5kn MAN-B&W 6S60MC-C 1 x 2 Stroke 6 Cy. 600 x 2400 9710kW (13202bhp) Mitsui Engineering & Shipbuilding CLtd-Japan Fuel: 3184.0 (r.f.)
9212395 **TORM TRINITY** *OYND2* *ex* Trinity *-2008* *ex* Snipe *-2001* - **VesselCo 1 K/S** TORM A/S *Copenhagen* *Denmark (DIS)* MMSI: 220554000 Official number: D4344	**23,842** 8,835 35,834 T/cm 44.6	Class: AB	**2000**-07 **Daedong Shipbuilding Co Ltd — Changwon (Jinhae Shipyard)** Yd No: 1042 Loa 183.00 (BB) Br ex 27.43 Dght 11.017 Lbp 174.50 Br md 27.40 Dpth 17.60 Welded, 1 dk	**(A12B2TR) Chemical/Products Tanker** Double Hull (13F) Liq: 41,329; Liq (Oil): 41,329 Cargo Heating Coils Compartments: 12 Wing Ta, ER, 2 Wing Slop Ta 12 Cargo Pump (s): 10x500m³/hr, 2x300m³/hr Manifold: Bow/CM: 93m	**1 oil engine** driving 1 FP propeller Total Power: 8,165kW (11,101hp) 14.0kn Sulzer 6RTA48T 1 x 2 Stroke 6 Cy. 480 x 2000 8165kW (11101bhp) Hyundai Heavy Industries Co Ltd-South Korea AuxGen: 3 x 500kW 440V a.c Thrusters: 1 Thwart. FP thruster (f) Fuel: 99.0 (d.f.) (Heating Coils) 1250.0 (r.f.) 30.0pd
9243318 **TORM VALBORG** *OWDA2* - **VesselCo 2 K/S** TORM Shipping India Pvt Ltd *Copenhagen* *Denmark (DIS)* MMSI: 220639000 Official number: D4429	**57,095** 29,836 99,999 T/cm 88.8	Class: NV	**2003**-09 **Hyundai Samho Heavy Industries Co Ltd — Samho** Yd No: S161 Loa 243.96 (BB) Br ex 42.03 Dght 14.233 Lbp 234.00 Br md 42.00 Dpth 21.00 Welded, 1 dk	**(A13A2TW) Crude/Oil Products Tanker** Double Hull (13F) Liq: 115,617; Liq (Oil): 115,617 Cargo Heating Coils Compartments: 12 Wing Ta, ER, 2 Wing Slop Ta 3 Cargo Pump (s): 3x2500m³/hr Manifold: Bow/CM: 121m	**1 oil engine** driving 1 FP propeller Total Power: 13,548kW (18,420hp) 14.0kn B&W 6S60MC-C 1 x 2 Stroke 6 Cy. 600 x 2400 13548kW (18420bhp) Hyundai Heavy Industries Co Ltd-South Korea AuxGen: 3 x 740kW 440/220V 60Hz a.c Fuel: 180.0 (d.f.) 2550.0 (r.f.)

9307798 *LADF7* -	**TORM VENTURE** **VesselCo 1 K/S** TORM A/S SatCom: Inmarsat Mini-M 764683274 *Oslo* *Norway (NIS)* MMSI: 258938000	**42,048** 22,309 73,701 T/cm 67.1	Class: LR (BV) **100A1** SS 03/2012 Double Hull oil tanker ESP *IWS LI EP (V) bar above **LMC** **UMS IGS** Eq.Ltr: P†; Cable: 660.0/78.0 U3 (a)	2007-06 **New Century Shipbuilding Co Ltd — Jingjiang JS** Yd No: 0307324 Loa 228.60 (BB) Br ex 32.30 Dght 14.518 Lbp 219.70 Br md 32.26 Dpth 20.80 Welded, 1 dk	**(A13B2TP) Products Tanker** Double Hull (13F) Liq: 81,006; Liq (Oil): 81,006 Compartments: 12 Wing Ta, 2 Wing Slop Ta, ER 3 Cargo Pump (s): 3x2300m³/hr Manifold: Bow/CM: 111.8m	**1 oil engine** driving 1 FP propeller Total Power: 11,299kW (15,362hp) 14.0kn MAN-B&W 5S60MC-C 1 x 2 Stroke 5 Cy. 600 x 2400 11299kW (15362bhp) Hudong Heavy Machinery Co Ltd-China AuxGen: 3 x 900kW 450V 60Hz a.c Boilers: AuxB (o.f.) 19.2kgf/cm² (18.8bar), AuxB (Comp) 10.2kgf/cm² (10.0bar) Fuel: 238.2 (d.f.) 1867.8 (r.f.)
9246803 *OUJJ2* -	**TORM VITA** **VesselCo 2 K/S** TORM A/S *Copenhagen* *Denmark (DIS)* MMSI: 220123000 Official number: D3958	**30,128** 11,742 46,308 T/cm 51.7	Class: NV	2002-06 **STX Shipbuilding Co Ltd — Changwon (Jinhae Shipyard)** Yd No: 1080 Loa 183.00 (BB) Br ex 32.23 Dght 12.200 Lbp 173.90 Br md 32.20 Dpth 19.10 Welded, 1 dk	**(A12B2TR) Chemical/Products Tanker** Double Hull (13F) Liq: 52,117; Liq (Oil): 52,117 Compartments: 2 Slop Ta, 12 Ta 12 Cargo Pump (s): 12x600m³/hr Manifold: Bow/CM: 91.6m	**1 oil engine** driving 1 FP propeller Total Power: 8,562kW (11,641hp) 14.5kn MAN-B&W 6S50MC-C 1 x 2 Stroke 6 Cy. 500 x 2000 8562kW (11641bhp) Hyundai Heavy Industries Co Ltd-South Korea AuxGen: 1 x 740kW 450V a.c, 2 x a.c
7035389 - -	**TORMIDERAND** **Zemland-Eksima Co Ltd (A/O 'Zemland-Eksima')** -	**820** 246 353	Class: (RS)	**1968-08 Zelenodolskiy Sudostroitelnyy Zavod im. "Gorkogo" — Zelenodolsk** Yd No: 933 Loa 55.12 Br ex 9.53 Dght 3.112 Lbp 48.40 Br md - Dpth 4.50 Welded, 1 dk	**(B12B2FC) Fish Carrier** Ins: 360 Compartments: 1 Ho, ER 1 Ha: (2.4 x 2.4)ER Derricks: 1x2.5t; Winches: 1 Ice Capable	**2 diesel electric oil engines** driving 2 gen. each 331kW Connecting to 1 elec. Motor of (475kW) driving 1 FP propeller Total Power: 662kW (900hp) 10.3kn Pervomaysk 6CHN25/34 2 x 4 Stroke 6 Cy. 250 x 340 each-331kW (450bhp) Pervomaydizelmash (PDM)-Pervomaysk AuxGen: 1 x 100kW Fuel: 112.0 (d.f.)
7121750 *9A2529* -	**TORNADO** *ex* P-10 *-1971* **Boris Bajlo** - *Zadar* *Croatia* Official number: 2T-636	**162** 62 132	Class: CS	**1954-01 Brodogradiliste Split (Brodosplit) — Split** Yd No: 114 Converted From: General Cargo Ship-2003 Loa 32.64 Br ex 5.49 Dght 2.801 Lbp 30.51 Br md - Dpth - Welded, 1 dk	**(A37B2PS) Passenger Ship**	**1 oil engine** driving 1 FP propeller Total Power: 132kW (179hp) 8.0kn Alpha 344-F 1 x 2 Stroke 4 Cy. 200 x 340 132kW (179bhp) A/S Burmeister & Wain's Maskin ogSkibsbyggeri-Denmark
7700192 *UBQK6* -	**TORNADO** *ex* Bugsier 11 *-2013* **OOO 'Balt-Shtok'** - *Kaliningrad* *Russia* MMSI: 273333290 Official number: RM-22-44	*180* - 60	Class: GL	**1977-06 Schiffswerft u. Maschinenfabrik Max Sieghold — Bremerhaven** Yd No: 177 Loa 26.67 Br ex 8.84 Dght 2.801 Lbp 23.80 Br md 8.81 Dpth 3.61 Welded, 1 dk	**(B32A2ST) Tug** Ice Capable	**2 oil engines** geared to sc. shafts driving 2 Directional propellers Total Power: 1,280kW (1,740hp) Deutz SBA6M528 2 x 4 Stroke 6 Cy. 220 x 280 each-640kW (870bhp) Kloeckner Humboldt Deutz AG-West Germany
7723845 *LW9950* -	**TORNADO** *ex* Ciclon *-1993* *ex* Chagres I *-1986* *ex* Okitsu Maru *-1980* **Remolques Costeros SA** - *Buenos Aires* *Argentina* MMSI: 701006150 Official number: 0327	*188* 71 62	Class: (GL) (RC) (NK)	**1977-08 Sagami Zosen Tekko K.K. — Yokosuka** Yd No: 187 Loa 30.51 Br ex 8.84 Dght 2.599 Lbp 27.01 Br md 8.81 Dpth 3.51 Welded, 1 dk	**(B32A2ST) Tug**	**2 oil engines** geared to sc. shafts driving 2 Directional propellers Total Power: 1,912kW (2,600hp) 13.3kn Niigata 6L25BX 2 x 4 Stroke 6 Cy. 250 x 320 each-956kW (1300bhp) Niigata Engineering Co Ltd-Japan
7346207 - -	**TORNADO** *ex* Pieterjan *-1992* *ex* Ter Streep *-1984* - -	**102** 30 -		**1974-01 Beliard-Murdoch S.A. — Oostende** Yd No: 220 Loa 25.58 Br ex 6.48 Dght 2.490 Lbp 22.80 Br md 6.38 Dpth 3.20 Welded, 1 dk	**(B11A2FT) Trawler**	**1 oil engine** geared to sc. shaft driving 1 FP propeller Total Power: 276kW (375hp) 10.5kn A.B.C. 6MDX 1 x 4 Stroke 6 Cy. 242 x 320 276kW (375bhp) Anglo Belgian Co NV (ABC)-Belgium AuxGen: 1 x 12kW 110V a.c, 1 x 6kW 110V a.c Fuel: 23.5
7390636 - -	**TORNADO** *ex* Veesea Tornado *-2002* *ex* Cayman Island *-1991* **C & I Leasing Plc & Tent Finance & Investments Ltd** West Coast Shipping Co Ltd	*877* 188 1,021	Class: (AB)	**1974-07 American Marine Corp. — New Orleans, La** Yd No: 1116 Converted From: Offshore Tug/Supply Ship-1991 Loa 55.58 Br ex 11.59 Dght 3.925 Lbp 51.87 Br md 11.56 Dpth 4.58 Welded, 1 dk	**(B21A20S) Platform Supply Ship**	**2 oil engines** reverse reduction geared to sc. shafts driving 2 FP propellers Total Power: 2,354kW (3,200hp) 12.5kn EMD (Electro-Motive) 16-645-E7B 2 x Vee 2 Stroke 16 Cy. 230 x 254 each-1177kW (1600bhp) (Re-engined ,made 1947, Reconditioned & fitted 1974) General Motors Corp.Electro-Motive Div.-La Grange AuxGen: 2 x 75kW Thrusters: 1 Thwart. FP thruster (f) Fuel: 394.0 (d.f.)
9141572 *CB5761* -	**TORNADO** **Sociedad Pesquera Coloso SA** - *Valparaiso* *Chile* MMSI: 725001850 Official number: 2888	**574** - 674		**1996-05 Astilleros Marco Chilena Ltda. — Iquique** Yd No: 212 Loa 46.90 (BB) Br ex - Dght - Lbp 42.80 Br md 10.20 Dpth 5.00 Welded, 1 dk	**(B11B2FV) Fishing Vessel** Ins: 670	**1 oil engine** with clutches, flexible couplings & sr geared to sc. shaft driving 1 CP propeller Total Power: 1,824kW (2,480hp) 15.0kn Caterpillar 3606TA 1 x 4 Stroke 6 Cy. 280 x 300 1824kW (2480bhp) Caterpillar Inc-USA
8728529 *UCIL* -	**TORNADO** *ex* Izyskatel-3 *-2002* **OAO Baza Tekhnicheskogo Obsluzhivaniya Flota (OAO 'BTOF')** - *Korsakov* *Russia* MMSI: 273422200 Official number: 863187	**566** 169 356	Class: (RS)	**1987-09 Zavod 'Nikolayevsk-na-Amure' — Nikolayevsk-na-Amure** Yd No: 03003 Lengthened-2002 Loa 51.10 Br ex 9.30 Dght 3.810 Lbp 44.85 Br md - Dpth 5.18 Welded, 1 dk	**(B31A2SR) Research Survey Vessel** Ice Capable	**1 oil engine** driving 1 FP propeller Total Power: 589kW (801hp) 11.9kn S.K.L. 6NVD48A-2U 1 x 4 Stroke 6 Cy. 320 x 480 589kW (801bhp) VEB Schwermaschinenbau "KarlLiebknecht" (SKL)-Magdeburg AuxGen: 3 x 150kW a.c
8897526 - -	**TORNADO** **PJSC 'Fleet of Novorossiysk Commercial Sea Port'** LLC Shipping & Towing Co Novofleet *Odessa* *Ukraine* MMSI: 272593000	**331** 99 118	Class: (RS)	**1995-08 Brodogradiliste Beograd — Belgrade** Yd No: 1168 Loa 33.70 Br ex 9.95 Dght 3.360 Lbp 30.14 Br md 9.50 Dpth 4.50 Welded, 1 dk	**(B32A2ST) Tug** Ice Capable	**2 oil engines** geared to sc. shafts driving 2 CP propellers Total Power: 1,920kW (2,610hp) 12.8kn Alpha 6L23/30A 2 x 4 Stroke 6 Cy. 225 x 300 each-960kW (1305bhp) MAN B&W Diesel A/S-Denmark AuxGen: 3 x 58kW a.c Fuel: 61.0 (d.f.)
9394193 *UEZB* -	**TORNADO** **Baltic Fleet LLC** - *St Petersburg* *Russia*	**294** 88 200	Class: RS (LR) ✠ Classed LR until 11/1/09	**2007-11 Song Cam Shipyard — Haiphong** (Hull) Yd No: (511528) **2007-11 B.V. Scheepswerf Damen — Gorinchem** Yd No: 511528 Loa 28.67 Br ex 10.42 Dght 4.000 Lbp 25.78 Br md 9.80 Dpth 4.60 Welded, 1 dk	**(B32A2ST) Tug** Ice Capable	**2 oil engines** reduction geared to sc. shafts driving 2 Directional propellers Total Power: 3,132kW (4,258hp) Caterpillar 3516B-TA 2 x Vee 4 Stroke 16 Cy. 170 x 190 each-1566kW (2129bhp) Caterpillar Inc-USA AuxGen: 2 x 85kW 400V 50Hz a.c
9190808 *ZQVN2* -	**TORNEDALEN** **ms 'Tornedalen' GmbH & Co KG** Schiffahrtskontor tom Worden GmbH & Co KG SatCom: Inmarsat C 421130765 *Douglas* *Isle of Man (British)* MMSI: 235000940 Official number: DR0059	**4,211** 2,358 5,572	Class: GL	**2000-01 Slovenske Lodenice a.s. — Komarno** Yd No: 5101 Loa 99.85 (BB) Br ex - Dght 6.100 Lbp 95.31 Br md 16.50 Dpth 8.00 Welded, 1 dk	**(A31A2GX) General Cargo Ship** Double Hull Grain: 5,908 TEU 357 C Ho 141 TEU C Dk 216 TEU Compartments: 1 Ho, ER 1 Ha: (64.0 x 13.8)ER Ice Capable	**1 oil engine** reduction geared to sc. shaft driving 1 CP propeller Total Power: 3,360kW (4,568hp) 13.0kn MAN 7L32/40 1 x 4 Stroke 7 Cy. 320 x 400 3360kW (4568bhp) MAN B&W Diesel AG-Augsburg AuxGen: 1 x 600kW a.c, 2 x 300kW a.c Thrusters: 1 Thwart. FP thruster (f)
8651154 *S7QV* -	**TORNG TAY NO. 1** **New Century Ocean Enterprise Co Ltd** - *Victoria* *Seychelles* Official number: 50041	**490** 253 -		**2002-01 Fong Kuo Shipbuilding Co Ltd — Kaohsiung** Yd No: 388 Loa 55.90 Br ex 8.50 Dght 3.300 Lbp 48.70 Br md - Dpth - Welded, 1 dk	**(B11B2FV) Fishing Vessel**	**1 oil engine** reduction geared to sc. shaft driving 1 FP propeller Total Power: 1,030kW (1,400hp) 13.0kn Hanshin LH28G 1 x 4 Stroke 6 Cy. 280 x 460 1030kW (1400bhp) The Hanshin Diesel Works Ltd-Japan

8651166 *BH3125* CT6-1125	**TORNG TAY NO. 3** *ex* Yu Chyang No. 121 *-1988* *ex* Yu Mao No. 121 *-1988* **Torng Tay Fishery Co Ltd** - *Kaohsiung* *Chinese Taipei* Official number: 010855	**400** 135 -		**1988**-04 **Sen Koh Shipbuilding Corp — Kaohsiung** Loa 48.80 Br ex 8.00 Dght 2.260 Lbp 41.80 Br md - Dpth - Welded, 1 dk	**(B11B2FV) Fishing Vessel**	**1 oil engine** driving 1 Propeller
8327260 *DYVV* -	**TORO** *ex* Oto Maru *-1983* **Pacific Offshore SA** Malayan Towage & Salvage Corp (SALVTUG) *Manila* *Philippines* Official number: MNLD000547	*172* 2 -		**1970 Kanto Kogyo K.K. — Hakodate** Yd No: 17 Loa 28.50 Br ex - Dght 2.601 Lbp 23.02 Br md 8.01 Dpth 3.81 Welded, 1 dk	**(B32A2ST) Tug**	**2 oil engines** sr geared to sc. shafts driving 2 FP propellers Total Power: 1,324kW (1,800hp) 12.0kn Fuji 6S27.5CH 2 x 4 Stroke 6 Cy. 275 x 410 each-662kW (900bhp) Fuji Diesel Co Ltd-Japan
7516254 *HO3859* -	**TORO** *ex* Lion No. 1 *-2006* *ex* Insung No. 102 *-2005* *ex* In Sung No. 505 *-2004* *ex* Acacia No. 6 *-1994* **Lion International Shipping Co Ltd** - *Panama* *Panama* MMSI: 353169000 Official number: 3087705A	**674** 262 524	Class: (KR)	**1975**-03 **Busan Shipbuilding Co Ltd — Busan** Yd No: 130 Loa 54.89 Br ex 9.15 Dght 3.742 Lbp 49.05 Br md 9.00 Dpth 3.95 Welded, 1 dk	**(B11B2FV) Fishing Vessel** Grain: 599; Bale: 531; Ins: 671 5 Ha: (1.8 x 1.8)3 (1.3 x 0.9) (1.3 x 1.0) Derricks: 2x1t,2x0.5t	**1 oil engine** driving 1 FP propeller Total Power: 956kW (1,300hp) 13.6kn Niigata 6L28X 1 x 4 Stroke 6 Cy. 280 x 440 956kW (1300bhp) Niigata Engineering Co Ltd-Japan AuxGen: 2 x 200kW 230V a.c
8730273 - -	**TOROLA** *ex* PTR-50 No. 69 *-1996* **JSC 'Torola'** -	**190** 57 70	Class: (RS)	**1989**-11 **Astrakhanskaya Sudoverf im. "Kirova" — Astrakhan** Yd No: 69 Loa 31.86 Br ex 7.08 Dght 2.101 Lbp 27.82 Br md - Dpth 3.18 Welded	**(B12B2FC) Fish Carrier** Ins: 100 Compartments: 2 Ho 2 Ha: 2 (2.1 x 2.4) Derricks: 2x1t	**1 oil engine** geared to sc. shaft driving 1 FP propeller Total Power: 232kW (315hp) 10.3kn Daldizel 6CHSPN2A18-315 1 x 4 Stroke 6 Cy. 180 x 220 232kW (315bhp) Daldizel-Khabarovsk AuxGen: 2 x 25kW a.c Fuel: 14.0 (d.f.)
8727094 - -	**TORON** - **OOO 'Yuzhnyy Rybopromyslovyy Flot'** Pionerskiy Ocean Fishing Marine Center (Pionerskaya Baza Okeanicheskogo Rybolovnogo Flota (BORF))	**739** 221 414	Class: (RS)	**1985 Zavod "Leninskaya Kuznitsa" — Kiyev** Yd No: 1557 Loa 54.82 Br ex 9.95 Dght 4.140 Lbp 50.30 Br md - Dpth 5.00 Welded, 1 dk	**(B11A2FS) Stern Trawler** Ice Capable	**1 oil engine** driving 1 CP propeller Total Power: 853kW (1,160hp) 12.0kn S.K.L. 8NVD48A-2U 1 x 4 Stroke 8 Cy. 320 x 480 853kW (1160bhp) VEB Schwermaschinenbau "KarlLiebknecht" (SKL)-Magdeburg AuxGen: 4 x 160kW a.c
9302205 *MKKE3* -	**TORONTO** - **Lloyds TSB Maritime Leasing (No 16) Ltd** Wilhelmsen Lines Car Carrier Ltd SatCom: Inmarsat C 423266410 *Southampton* *United Kingdom* MMSI: 232664000 Official number: 909819	**61,321** 22,650 19,628 T/cm 52.5	Class: NV	**2005**-07 **Mitsubishi Heavy Industries Ltd. — Nagasaki** Yd No: 2208 Loa 199.99 (BB) Br ex 32.29 Dght 10.500 Lbp 192.00 Br md 32.26 Dpth 36.02 Welded, 12 dks including 4 liftable dks	**(A35B2RV) Vehicles Carrier** Side door/ramp (s) Len: 25.00 Wid: 6.50 Swl: 35 Quarter stern door/ramp (s. a.) Len: 38.00 Wid: 7.00 Swl: 237 Cars: 6,564	**1 oil engine** driving 1 FP propeller Total Power: 13,240kW (18,001hp) 19.5kn Mitsubishi 7UEC60LS 1 x 2 Stroke 7 Cy. 600 x 2200 13240kW (18001bhp) Mitsubishi Heavy Industries Ltd-Japan AuxGen: 3 x 1300kW 440/220V 60Hz a.c Thrusters: 1 Thwart. CP thruster (f) Fuel: 139.0 (d.f.) 3322.6 (r.f.)
9253727 *VQLL5* -	**TORONTO EXPRESS** *ex* CP Venture *-2006* *ex* Canmar Venture *-2005* **Amosola Vermietungsgesellschaft mbH** Hapag-Lloyd AG *London* *United Kingdom* MMSI: 235666000 Official number: 906105	**55,994** 22,426 47,840 T/cm 78.4	Class: NV	**2003**-06 **Daewoo Shipbuilding & Marine Engineering Co Ltd — Geoje** Yd No: 4089 Loa 294.00 (BB) Br ex 32.31 Dght 10.780 Lbp 281.00 Br md 32.26 Dpth 21.50 Welded, 1 dk	**(A33A2CC) Container Ship (Fully Cellular)** TEU 4402 C Ho 2332 C Dk 2070 incl 330 ref C. Compartments: ER, 8 Cell Ho Ice Capable	**1 oil engine** driving 1 FP propeller Total Power: 37,275kW (50,679hp) 23.0kn B&W 8K90MC-C 1 x 2 Stroke 8 Cy. 900 x 2300 37275kW (50679bhp) Doosan Engine Co Ltd-South Korea AuxGen: 3 x 2200kW 440/220V 60Hz a.c Thrusters: 1 Thwart. CP thruster (f); 1 Thwart. CP thruster (a) Fuel: 300.0 (d.f.) (Heating Coils) 4300.0 (r.f.)
9280495 *UDZZ* -	**TOROPLIVYY** - **PJSC 'Fleet of Novorossiysk Commercial Sea Port'** Novorossiysk Port Fleet JSC (ZAO 'Flot Novorossiyskogo Torgovogo Porta') *Novorossiysk* *Russia* MMSI: 273446520 Official number: 020112	**364** 109 287	Class: RS	**2003**-04 **Astilleros Armon SA — Navia** Yd No: 565 Loa 30.00 Br ex 10.35 Dght 4.540 Lbp 26.80 Br md 9.80 Dpth 5.40 Welded	**(B32A2ST) Tug**	**2 oil engines** geared to sc. shafts driving 2 Propellers Total Power: 2,942kW (4,000hp) 12.0kn Caterpillar 3516 2 x Vee 4 Stroke 16 Cy. 170 x 190 each-1471kW (2000bhp) Caterpillar Inc-USA
7327964 *UCSP* -	**TOROS** - **MASCO JSC (ZAO 'Malaya Sudokhodnaya Kompaniya')** - *Murmansk* *Russia* MMSI: 273138500	*283* 85 83	Class: RS	**1973 Brodogradiliste 'Tito' Beograd - Brod 'Tito' — Belgrade** Yd No: 896 Loa 35.44 Br ex 9.30 Dght 3.140 Lbp 30.00 Br md 9.00 Dpth 4.50 Welded, 1 dk	**(B32A2ST) Tug** Ice Capable	**2 oil engines** geared to sc. shaft driving 1 FP propeller Total Power: 1,700kW (2,312hp) B&W 7-26MTBF-40 2 x 4 Stroke 7 Cy. 260 x 400 each-850kW (1156bhp) Titovi Zavodi 'Litostroj'-Yugoslavia Fuel: 55.0 (d.f.)
8908791 *8PAK3* -	**TORPO** - **Wilson Shipowning AS** Wilson EuroCarriers AS *Bridgetown* *Barbados* MMSI: 314419000	**1,986** 1,246 3,504 T/cm 10.4	Class: BV (LR) ✠ Classed LR until 11/6/10	**1990**-06 **Bodewes' Scheepswerven B.V. — Hoogezand** Yd No: 561 Loa 88.15 (BB) Br ex 14.18 Dght 4.898 Lbp 83.20 Br md 14.00 Dpth 6.35 Welded, 1 dk	**(A31A2GX) General Cargo Ship** Grain: 4,262; Bale: 4,237 TEU 103 C.Ho 64/20' C.Dk 39/20' Compartments: 1 Ho, ER 2 Ha: 2 (25.4 x 10.2)ER Cranes: 1x35t Ice Capable	**1 oil engine** with flexible couplings & sr geared to sc. shaft driving 1 FP propeller Total Power: 1,176kW (1,599hp) 12.0kn MaK 6M452AK 1 x 4 Stroke 6 Cy. 320 x 450 1176kW (1599bhp) Krupp MaK Maschinenbau GmbH-Kiel AuxGen: 3 x 52kW 380V 50Hz a.c Thrusters: 1 Thwart. FP thruster (f) Fuel: 176.8 (d.f.) 5.5pd
8604644 *V5CF* -	**TORRA BAY** *ex* Cotobad *-2003* **Torra Bay Fishing (Pty) Ltd** Merlus Fishing Pty Ltd *Walvis Bay* *Namibia* MMSI: 659276000 Official number: 2002WB009	**1,558** 467 1,336	Class: (BV)	**1989**-12 **Hijos de J. Barreras S.A. — Vigo** Yd No: 1497 Loa 68.03 (BB) Br ex 12.64 Dght 5.000 Lbp 58.50 Br md 12.50 Dpth 7.30 Welded, 2 dks	**(B11A2FS) Stern Trawler** Ins: 1,525 Ice Capable	**1 oil engine** with flexible couplings & dr geared to sc. shaft driving 1 CP propeller Total Power: 1,765kW (2,400hp) 13.0kn Deutz SBV8M358 1 x 4 Stroke 8 Cy. 400 x 580 1765kW (2400bhp) Hijos de J Barreras SA-Spain
9278466 *IKXO* -	**TORRE AVOLOS** - **Augustea Imprese Marittime e di Salvataggi SpA** - *Catania* *Italy* MMSI: 247101700 Official number: 256	**381** 114 381	Class: RI	**2004**-06 **Cant. Nav. Rosetti — Ravenna** Yd No: 65 Loa 31.30 Br ex - Dght 4.100 Lbp 29.80 Br md 10.00 Dpth 5.00 Welded	**(B32A2ST) Tug**	**2 oil engines** geared to sc. shafts driving 2 Directional propellers Total Power: 3,650kW (4,962hp) 12.5kn Wartsila 6L26 2 x 4 Stroke 6 Cy. 260 x 320 each-1650kW (2243bhp) Wartsila Finland Oy-Finland
9292424 *EAKA* 3-HU-312-0	**TORRE DEL ORO R** - **Mariscos Rodriguez SA** - *Huelva* *Spain* MMSI: 224087000 Official number: 3-12/2003	**292** 88 -	Class: BV	**2004**-02 **Astilleros La Parrilla S.A. — San Esteban de Pravia** Yd No: 192 Loa 33.50 Br ex - Dght 3.310 Lbp - Br md 7.80 Dpth 3.55 Welded, 1 dk	**(B11A2FT) Trawler** Grain: 216	**1 oil engine** geared to sc. shaft driving 1 Propeller Caterpillar 3512TA 1 x Vee 4 Stroke 12 Cy. 170 x 190 Caterpillar Inc-USA
9151084 *FLSI* -	**TORRE GIULIA** - **Compagnie Francaise Du Thon Oceanique** - *Concarneau* *France* MMSI: 226312000 Official number: 929276	**2,137** 641 2,328	Class: BV (RI)	**1997**-06 **Chantiers Piriou — Concarneau** (Hull) Yd No: 184 **1997**-06 **Leroux et Lotz Naval — Nantes** Loa 81.90 Br ex - Dght 6.570 Lbp 75.10 Br md 13.70 Dpth 6.70 Welded, 1 dk	**(B11B2FV) Fishing Vessel** Ins: 1,790	**1 oil engine** reduction geared to sc. shaft driving 1 CP propeller Total Power: 3,690kW (5,017hp) 16.5kn Wartsila 9R32 1 x 4 Stroke 9 Cy. 320 x 350 3690kW (5017bhp) Wartsila Propulsion AS-Norway AuxGen: 1 x 1750kW a.c, 1 x 1750kW a.c, 1 x 630kW a.c Thrusters: 1 Thwart. FP thruster (f); 1 Tunnel thruster (a) Fuel: 535.0 (d.f.)

IMO / Call sign	Name / Owner / Manager / Port / Flag	Tonnage	Class	Builder / Dimensions	Type / Cargo	Machinery
8012279 *EAKN* -	**TORRE VIGIA** **Remolques Unidos SL** - *Malaga* — *Spain* Official number: 1-2/1992	*196* 7 172	Class: (LR) ✠ Classed LR until 1/10/02	**1982-01 Maritima del Musel S.A. — Gijon** Yd No: 229 Loa 27.56 Br ex 8.06 Dght 3.679 Lbp 25.02 Br md 8.01 Dpth 4.12 Welded, 1 dk	**(B32A2ST) Tug**	**1 oil engine** driving 1 CP propeller Total Power: 1,324kW (1,800hp) 13.0kn MWM TBD500-8 1 x 4 Stroke 8 Cy. 360 x 450 1324kW (1800bhp) Motoren Werke Mannheim AG (MWM)-West Germany AuxGen: 2 x 76kW 380V 50Hz a.c, 1 x 14kW 380V 50Hz a.c Fuel: 106.0 (d.f.) 6.5pd
6727571 *EFDY* -	**TORREBERMEJA** **Remolcadores y Servicios SA** - *Malaga* — *Spain* Official number: 1-1/1995	*108* 8 -	Class: (LR) ✠ Classed LR until 8/7/87	**1968-01 Enrique Lorenzo y Cia SA — Vigo** Yd No: 337 Loa 26.95 Br ex 6.84 Dght 2.648 Lbp 22.00 Br md 6.41 Dpth 3.05 Welded, 1 dk	**(B32A2ST) Tug**	**1 oil engine** driving 1 FP propeller Total Power: 772kW (1,050hp) 11.0kn MWM TRH348AU 1 x 4 Stroke 8 Cy. 320 x 480 772kW (1050bhp) Motoren Werke Mannheim AG (MWM)-West Germany AuxGen: 1 x 32kW 380V 50Hz a.c, 1 x 19kW 380V 50Hz a.c Fuel: 40.5
7203663 *A3B03* -	**TORRENS** *ex* Farid F *-2006* *ex* Bolivar Trader *-1994* *ex* Sijilmassa *-1990* *ex* Kungshamn *-1978* *ex* Lapland *-1976* **Livestock Carrier 1 BV** Livestock Express BV SatCom: Inmarsat C 457016510 *Nuku'alofa* — *Tonga* MMSI: 570165000 Official number: 241	**8,508** 2,553 9,217	Class: NV (RI)	**1972-04 Drammen Slip & Verksted — Drammen** Yd No: 72 Converted From: Refrigerated Cargo Ship-1994 Loa 140.62 (BB) Br ex 18.04 Dght 9.035 Lbp 131.88 Br md 18.01 Dpth 11.64 Welded, 4 dks	**(A38A2GL) Livestock Carrier**	**1 oil engine** driving 1 FP propeller Total Power: 10,922kW (14,850hp) 23.3kn Sulzer 9RND68 1 x 2 Stroke 9 Cy. 680 x 1250 10922kW (14850bhp) Sulzer Bros Ltd-Switzerland AuxGen: 3 x 520kW 440V 60Hz a.c
9293612 *MHBK6* -	**TORRENS** **Lloyds TSB Maritime Leasing (No 16) Ltd** Wilhelmsen Lines Car Carrier Ltd SatCom: Inmarsat C 423224810 *Southampton* — *United Kingdom* MMSI: 232248000 Official number: 909817	**61,321** 22,650 19,628 T/cm 52.5	Class: NV	**2004-10 Mitsubishi Heavy Industries Ltd. — Nagasaki** Yd No: 2196 Loa 199.99 (BB) Br ex 32.29 Dght 10.500 Lbp 192.00 Br md 32.26 Dpth 36.02 Welded, 12 dks including 4 liftable dks	**(A35B2RV) Vehicles Carrier** Side door/ramp (s) Len: 25.00 Wid: 6.50 Swl: 35 Quarter stern door/ramp (s. a.) Len: 38.00 Wid: 7.00 Swl: 237 Cars: 6,400	**1 oil engine** driving 1 FP propeller Total Power: 12,390kW (16,845hp) 19.5kn Mitsubishi 7UEC60LS 1 x 2 Stroke 7 Cy. 600 x 2200 12390kW (16845bhp) Mitsubishi Heavy Industries Ltd-Japan AuxGen: 3 x 1300kW 440/220V 60Hz a.c Thrusters: 1 Thwart. CP thruster (f) Fuel: 139.0 (d.f.) 3322.6 (r.f.)
9415210 *5BWL2* -	**TORRENT** **Nadjani II BV** Navarone SA *Limassol* — *Cyprus* MMSI: 209016000 Official number: 9415210	**19,814** 10,208 30,890	Class: GL	**2010-02 Shandong Weihai Shipyard — Weihai SD** Yd No: SN318 Loa 184.99 (BB) Br ex - Dght 10.400 Lbp 178.00 Br md 23.70 Dpth 14.60 Welded, 1 dk	**(A21A2BC) Bulk Carrier** Grain: 38,635; Bale: 37,476 Compartments: 6 Ho, ER 6 Ha: (16.0 x 17.4)3 (19.2 x 17.4) (13.6 x 17.4)ER (10.4 x 13.2) Cranes: 3x30t Ice Capable	**1 oil engine** driving 1 FP propeller Total Power: 7,200kW (9,789hp) 13.5kn MAN-B&W 6S46MC-C 1 x 2 Stroke 6 Cy. 460 x 1932 7200kW (9789bhp) STX Engine Co Ltd-South Korea AuxGen: 3 x 680kW 450/230V 60Hz a.c Thrusters: 1 Tunnel thruster (f) Fuel: 350.0 (d.f.) 1300.0 (r.f.)
9447914 *A8VQ2* -	**TORRENTE** **Hull 1800 Co Ltd** Compania SudAmericana de Vapores SA (CSAV) *Monrovia* — *Liberia* MMSI: 636014649 Official number: 14649	**88,586** 42,897 94,661	Class: GL	**2011-11 Samsung Heavy Industries Co Ltd — Geoje** Yd No: 1800 Loa 299.92 (BB) Br ex - Dght 13.500 Lbp 285.00 Br md 45.60 Dpth 24.60 Welded, 1 dk	**(A33A2CC) Container Ship (Fully Cellular)** TEU 8004 C Ho 3574 TEU C Dk 4430 TEU incl 1500 ref C.	**1 oil engine** driving 1 FP propeller Total Power: 43,610kW (59,292hp) 23.0kn MAN-B&W 7K98ME7 1 x 2 Stroke 7 Cy. 980 x 2660 43610kW (59292bhp) Doosan Engine Co Ltd-South Korea AuxGen: 2 x 2880kW 6600/450V a.c, 3 x 3360kW 6600/450V a.c Thrusters: 1 Tunnel thruster (f) Fuel: 290.0 (d.f.) 8600.0 (r.f.) 162.0pd
9520534 *H08238* -	**TORRENTE 26** *ex* Tekun 12331 *-2011* **Brumby Shipholdings SA** Royal Marine Management Pte Ltd *Panama* — *Panama* Official number: 019922497P1	**140** 42 107	Class: (BV) (GL)	**2010-11 Jana Seribu Shipbuilding (M) Sdn Bhd — Sibu** (Hull) Yd No: (82/07) **2010-11 Bonafile Shipbuilders & Repairs Sdn Bhd — Sandakan** Yd No: 82/07 Loa 23.50 Br ex - Dght 2.700 Lbp 21.96 Br md 7.32 Dpth 3.20 Welded, 1 dk	**(B32A2ST) Tug**	**2 oil engines** reverse reduction geared to sc. shafts driving 2 FP propellers Total Power: 894kW (1,216hp) 10.0kn Cummins KTA-19-M3 2 x 4 Stroke 6 Cy. 159 x 159 each-447kW (608bhp) Cummins Engine Co Inc-USA AuxGen: 2 x 30kW 415V a.c
9513335 *HP2337* -	**TORRENTE 27** *ex* Tekun 24268 *-2011* **Brumby Shipholdings SA** Royal Marine Shipmanagement Pte Ltd *Panama* — *Panama* MMSI: 353016000 Official number: 019922527PE	**259** 77 -	Class: (BV) (GL)	**2011-04 Kian Juan Dockyard Sdn Bhd — Miri** Yd No: 131 Loa 30.00 Br ex - Dght 3.500 Lbp 28.05 Br md 8.59 Dpth 4.11 Welded, 1 dk	**(B32A2ST) Tug**	**2 oil engines** reverse reduction geared to sc. shafts driving 2 FP propellers Total Power: 2,238kW (3,042hp) Cummins KTA-38-M2 2 x Vee 4 Stroke 12 Cy. 159 x 159 each-1119kW (1521bhp) Cummins Engine Co Inc-USA AuxGen: 2 x 80kW 415V 50Hz a.c
9488358 *HP5777* -	**TORRENTE 36** *ex* Tekun 20268 *-2011* **Brumby Shipholdings SA** - *Panama* — *Panama* Official number: 019922520PE	**254** 77 267	Class: (BV) (NK)	**2008-04 Bonafile Shipbuilders & Repairs Sdn Bhd — Sandakan** Yd No: 09/07 Loa 30.00 Br ex 8.62 Dght 3.512 Lbp 28.06 Br md 8.60 Dpth 4.12 Welded, 1 dk	**(B32A2ST) Tug**	**2 oil engines** reduction geared to sc. shafts driving 2 Propellers Total Power: 1,518kW (2,064hp) 11.0kn Mitsubishi S6R2-MTK3L 2 x 4 Stroke 6 Cy. 170 x 220 each-759kW (1032bhp) Mitsubishi Heavy Industries Ltd-Japan Fuel: 195.0 (d.f.)
9577795 *H05957* -	**TORRENTE 54** *ex* Bestwin 168 *-2011* **Brumby Shipholdings SA** Royal Marine Management Pte Ltd *Panama* — *Panama* Official number: 019922534PE	**169** 51 -	Class: (BV) (NK)	**2009-11 Moxen Shipyard Sdn Bhd — Sibu** Yd No: 5607 Loa 25.00 Br ex - Dght 2.700 Lbp 23.37 Br md 7.62 Dpth 3.20 Welded, 1 dk	**(B32A2ST) Tug**	**2 oil engines** reduction geared to sc. shafts driving 2 FP propellers Total Power: 1,060kW (1,442hp) Caterpillar 3412 2 x Vee 4 Stroke 12 Cy. 137 x 152 each-530kW (721bhp) Caterpillar Inc-USA Fuel: 110.0 (d.f.)
9585704 *H05938* -	**TORRENTE 72** *ex* Teguh 16500 *-2011* **Brumby Shipholdings SA** Royal Marine Shipmanagement Pte Ltd *Panama* — *Panama* Official number: 019922510PE	**176** 53 -	Class: (BV) (NK)	**2011-03 Pleasant Engineering Sdn Bhd — Sandakan** Yd No: 40396 Loa 26.20 Br ex - Dght 2.900 Lbp 24.51 Br md 8.00 Dpth 3.83 Welded, 1 dk	**(B32A2ST) Tug**	**2 oil engines** reduction geared to sc. shafts driving 2 FP propellers Total Power: 1,220kW (1,658hp) Yanmar 6AYM-ETE 2 x 4 Stroke 6 Cy. 155 x 180 each-610kW (829bhp) Yanmar Diesel Engine Co Ltd-Japan Fuel: 130.0 (d.f.)
9555058 *H09518* -	**TORRENTE 84** *ex* Tekun 24328 *-2011* **Brumby Shipholdings SA** Royal Marine Shipmanagement Pte Ltd *Panama* — *Panama* Official number: 019922524PE	**274** 82 -	Class: (BV)	**2011-04 Pleasant Engineering Sdn Bhd — Sandakan** Yd No: 80/07 Loa 29.20 Br ex - Dght 3.840 Lbp 27.46 Br md 9.00 Dpth 4.85 Welded, 1 dk	**(B32A2ST) Tug**	**2 oil engines** geared to sc. shafts driving 2 FP propellers Total Power: 2,238kW (3,042hp) Cummins KTA-38-M2 2 x Vee 4 Stroke 12 Cy. 159 x 159 each-1119kW (1521bhp) Cummins Engine Co Ltd-United Kingdom AuxGen: 2 x 80kW 50Hz a.c
7000712 *ERRZ* -	**TORRES** **Sonic Star Navigation Co** - — *Moldova* MMSI: 214181826	**125** 37 -	Class: (BV)	**1970 Sociedad Metalurgica Duro Felguera — Gijon** Yd No: 47 Loa 23.53 Br ex 7.27 Dght 2.769 Lbp 22.00 Br md 7.24 Dpth 3.15 Welded, 1 dk	**(B32A2ST) Tug**	**1 oil engine** driving 1 FP propeller Total Power: 662kW (900hp) 13.0kn MaK 6M281AK 1 x 4 Stroke 6 Cy. 240 x 280 662kW (900bhp) Atlas MaK Maschinenbau GmbH-Kiel
8520848 *CXBI* -	**TORRES DEL PAINE** *ex* Imanol Toxu *-1989* **Pesquera Altamar SA** - *Montevideo* — *Uruguay* MMSI: 770576071 Official number: 8078	**275** 82 137	Class: (BV)	**1987-05 Astilleros Zamakona SA — Santurtzi** Yd No: 126 Loa 31.50 Br ex 7.75 Dght 3.152 Lbp 25.71 Br md 7.71 Dpth 5.21 Welded, 2 dks	**(B11A2FS) Stern Trawler**	**1 oil engine** with flexible couplings & sr gearedto sc. shaft driving 1 CP propeller Total Power: 294kW (400hp) 11.5kn Alpha 5T23L-VO 1 x 4 Stroke 5 Cy. 225 x 300 294kW (400bhp) Construcciones Echevarria SA-Spain
8023125 *VJN3417* -	**TORRES STAR** *ex* Malu Raider *-2012* *ex* Moale Chief *-2005* **Formigal Holdings Pty Ltd** - *Cairns, Qld* — *Australia* Official number: 857915	*262* 120 301	Class: (LR) ✠ Classed LR until 1/9/03	**1981-12 Land & Sea Construction Services Pte Ltd — Singapore** Yd No: 025 Loa 33.94 Br ex 9.28 Dght 2.601 Lbp 28.88 Br md 9.01 Dpth 3.00 Welded, 1 dk	**(A35D2RL) Landing Craft** Bow door/ramp Len: 4.50 Wid: 3.70 Swl: - Bale: 192 Compartments: 1 Ho, ER 1 Ha: (9.4 x 5.9)ER Cranes: 1x1t	**2 oil engines** sr reverse geared to sc. shafts driving 2 FP propellers Total Power: 410kW (558hp) 10.0kn Caterpillar 3406PCTA 2 x 4 Stroke 6 Cy. 137 x 165 each-205kW (279bhp) Caterpillar Tractor Co-USA AuxGen: 2 x 7660kW 415V 50Hz a.c Fuel: 120.0 (d.f.) 2.5pd

IMO / Call sign	Name / Owner	Tonnage	Class	Builder / Dimensions	Type	Machinery
9357523 *A8TY2* -	**TORRES STRAIT** *ex* Ocean Mermaid *-2013* **ms 'Torres Strait' GmbH & Co KG** Carsten Rehder Schiffsmakler und Reederei GmbH & Co KG *Monrovia* *Liberia* MMSI: 636091864 Official number: 91864	**18,123** 7,996 22,314	Class: GL (KR)	**2008**-07 **CSBC Corp, Taiwan — Keelung** Yd No: 883 Loa 175.10 (BB) Br ex - Dght 9.526 Lbp 164.90 Br md 27.90 Dpth 13.80 Welded, 1 dk	**(A33A2CC) Container Ship (Fully Cellular)** TEU 1713 C Ho 618 TEU C Dk 1095 TEU incl 377 ref C 5 Ha: 3 (25.2 x 25.5) (12.6 x 25.5)ER (12.6 x 10.3) Cranes: 2x40t	**1 oil engine** driving 1 FP propeller Total Power: 15,806kW (21,490hp) 19.0kn MAN-B&W 7S60MC-C 1 x 2 Stroke 7 Cy. 600 x 2400 15806kW (21490bhp) Kawasaki Heavy Industries Ltd-Japan AuxGen: 4 x 1500kW 450V a.c Thrusters: 1 Tunnel thruster (f)
8953813 *JWLX* -	**TORRISLAKS 1** *ex* Fjordgar *-2013* *ex* Sundferja *-2013* **Jon Anton Henrik Swensen** - *Bodo* *Norway* MMSI: 257166700	*101* 55 -		**1957 Ankerlokken Slipper & Mek Verksted — Floro** Yd No: 13 Converted From: Ferry (Passenger only) Loa 23.65 Br ex - Dght - Lbp 22.08 Br md 6.92 Dpth 2.90 Welded, 1 dk	**(A31A2GX) General Cargo Ship**	**1 oil engine** driving 1 FP propeller
8955067 - -	**TORSAM** - - *Morocco*	*149* 44 72		**1993**-07 **Astilleros Armon SA — Navia** Yd No: 325 L reg 25.70 Br ex - Dght - Lbp - Br md 6.75 Dpth 3.00 Welded, 1 dk	**(B11B2FV) Fishing Vessel**	**1 oil engine** geared to sc. shaft driving 1 FP propeller Total Power: 294kW (400hp) 9.5kn Cummins KT-38-M 1 x Vee 4 Stroke 12 Cy. 159 x 159 294kW (400bhp) Cummins Engine Co Inc-USA
9644445 *OZ2130* -	**TORSBORG** **P/F 6 September 2006** P/F Skansi Offshore *Torshavn* *Faeroes (FAS)* MMSI: 231851000	**3,309** 1,372 4,300	Class: NV	**2012**-06 **Cemre Muhendislik Gemi Insaat Sanayi ve Ticaret Ltd Sti — Altinova** (Hull) Yd No: (109) **2012**-06 **Havyard Leirvik AS — Leirvik i Sogn** Yd No: 109 Loa 86.00 (BB) Br ex 18.20 Dght 6.400 Lbp 74.40 Br md 17.60 Dpth 7.70 Welded, 1 dk	**(B21A20S) Platform Supply Ship**	**4 diesel electric oil engines** driving 4 gen. each 1560kW Connecting to 2 elec. motors each (1600kW) driving 2 Azimuth electric drive units Total Power: 6,240kW (8,484hp) 14.5kn M.T.U. 12V4000M33S 4 x Vee 4 Stroke 12 Cy. 170 x 210 each-1560kW (2121bhp) MTU Friedrichshafen GmbH-Friedrichshafen Thrusters: 3 Tunnel thruster (f) Fuel: 1015.0
9623142 *PCLE* -	**TORSTEN** **Tug Team Partnership GmbH** Schramm Group GmbH & Co KG *Rotterdam* *Netherlands* MMSI: 245439000	**364** - 295	Class: GL	**2012**-03 **Gemsan Gemi Insa ve Gemi Isletmeciligi San. Ltd. — Tuzla** Yd No: 55 Loa 31.30 Br ex - Dght 3.000 Lbp 27.35 Br md 11.50 Dpth 3.80 Welded, 1 dk	**(B32A2ST) Tug** Cranes: 1	**2 oil engines** reduction geared to sc. shafts driving 2 Propellers Total Power: 2,460kW (3,344hp) Caterpillar 3512B 2 x Vee 4 Stroke 12 Cy. 170 x 190 each-1230kW (1672bhp) Caterpillar Inc-USA Thrusters: 1 Tunnel thruster (f)
6524084 *V5TR* L11	**TORSVER** *ex* L. O. Mogster *-1980* **Gendev of Namibia (Pty) Ltd** - SatCom: Inmarsat C 465901121 *Luderitz* *Namibia* Official number: 91LB066	*564* 186 -	Class: (NV)	**1965**-12 **Ankerlokken Verft Floro AS — Floro** Yd No: 70 Lengthened-1969 Loa 49.43 Br ex 8.21 Dght 5.341 Lbp 44.91 Br md 8.16 Dpth 6.81 Welded, 2 dks	**(B11B2FV) Fishing Vessel** Compartments: 1 Ho, 3 Ta, ER 3 Ha: 3 (3.5 x 2.9)ER Derricks: 1x3t; Winches: 1	**1 oil engine** driving 1 FP propeller Total Power: 1,545kW (2,101hp) Wichmann 7AX 1 x 2 Stroke 7 Cy. 300 x 450 1545kW (2101bhp) (new engine 1978) Wichmann Motorfabrikk AS-Norway AuxGen: 1 x 95kW 220V 50Hz a.c, 1 x 80kW 220V 50Hz a.c, 1 x 38kW 220V 50Hz a.c Thrusters: 1 Thwart. FP thruster (f); 1 Tunnel thruster (a)
7807316 *OZ2029* -	**TORSVIK** *ex* Lars A. Kruse *-1997* **P/F Thor** - *Hosvik* *Faeroe Islands (Danish)* MMSI: 231069000 Official number: D2649	**370** 111	Class: NV	**1979**-09 **A/S Bogense Skibsvaerft — Bogense** Yd No: 227 Converted From: Fishing Vessel-2006 Loa 39.20 (BB) Br ex 8.52 Dght 3.750 Lbp 35.76 Br md 8.50 Dpth 3.76 Welded, 1 dk	**(B22G20Y) Standby Safety Vessel** Passengers: berths: 22	**1 oil engine** driving 1 Directional propeller Total Power: 647kW (880hp) Alpha 408-26VO 1 x 2 Stroke 8 Cy. 260 x 400 647kW (880bhp) Alpha Diesel A/S-Denmark AuxGen: 3 x 54kW 380/220V 50Hz a.c Thrusters: 1 Tunnel thruster (f) Fuel: 95.0 (d.f.)
9620372 *HP7794* -	**TORTEL** *ex* Turtel *-2011* **Inversiones Maritimas CPT SA (INMARSA)** CPT Empresas Maritimas SA *Panama* *Panama* Official number: 43300VC	**277** 83 142	Class: AB	**2011**-06 **Shunde Huaxing Shipyard — Foshan GD** (Hull) Yd No: (HY-2176) **2011**-06 **Bonny Fair Development Ltd — Hong Kong** Yd No: HY2176 Loa 26.00 Br ex 10.30 Dght 3.500 Lbp 25.13 Br md 9.80 Dpth 4.50 Welded, 1 dk	**(B32A2ST) Tug**	**2 oil engines** gearing integral to driving 2 Z propellers Total Power: 3,372kW (4,584hp) Caterpillar 3516B-HD 2 x Vee 4 Stroke 16 Cy. 170 x 215 each-1686kW (2292bhp) Caterpillar Inc-USA AuxGen: 2 x 86kW a.c Fuel: 110.0 (d.f.)
8305212 *WDC3389* -	**TORTOLA FAST FERRY** *ex* Lewis & Clark *-2004* *ex* Victoria Clipper II *-2001* *ex* Spirit of the Northwest *-1996* *ex* Sun Rose *-1994* *ex* Alize Express *-1991* *ex* Nettuno Jet *-1988* **Caribbean Maritime Excursions Inc** - *St Thomas, VI* *United States of America* MMSI: 367007140 Official number: 1051693	**216** 82 261	Class: (NV) (BV) (RI)	**1984**-04 **Marinteknik Verkstads AB — Oregrund** Yd No: B51 Loa 29.95 Br ex 9.40 Dght 2.461 Lbp 23.80 Br md 9.39 Dpth - Welded, 1 dk	**(A37B2PS) Passenger Ship** Hull Material: Aluminium Alloy Passengers: unberthed: 230	**2 oil engines** with clutches, flexible couplings & sr geared to sc. shafts driving 2 Water jets Total Power: 2,354kW (3,200hp) 31.0kn M.T.U. 12V396 2 x Vee 4 Stroke 12 Cy. 165 x 185 each-1177kW (1600bhp) MTU Friedrichshafen GmbH-Friedrichshafen AuxGen: 2 x 36kW 380V 50Hz a.c Fuel: 6.0 (d.f.)
7611913 *H03796* -	**TORTOLA'S PRIDE** *ex* Maranda Stout II *-1988* *ex* Commander *-1988* *ex* Fay Hebert *-1987* **Caribbean Transport Ltd** - *Panama* *Panama* MMSI: 355921000 Official number: 3081405A	*568* 170 910	Class: HR (AB)	**1977**-05 **Halter Marine, Inc. — Moss Point, Ms** Yd No: 550 Loa 49.00 Br ex - Dght 3.379 Lbp 47.33 Br md 11.59 Dpth 3.97 Welded, 1 dk	**(B21A20C) Crew/Supply Vessel**	**2 oil engines** reverse reduction geared to sc. shafts driving 2 FP propellers Total Power: 1,368kW (1,860hp) 9.5kn G.M. (Detroit Diesel) 16V-149-NA 2 x Vee 2 Stroke 16 Cy. 146 x 146 each-684kW (930bhp) General Motors Detroit DieselAllison Divn-USA AuxGen: 2 x 75kW Thrusters: 1 Thwart. FP thruster (f)
7015054 - -	**TORTUGA 4** *ex* Isla Tortuga 4 *-1979* *ex* Santa Elena XX *-1975* - -	*158* 72	Class: (AB) (GL)	**1970 Metal Empresa S.A. — Callao** Yd No: L-21 Loa 25.02 Br ex 6.74 Dght - Lbp 21.49 Br md 6.71 Dpth 3.81 Welded, 1 dk	**(B11A2FT) Trawler** Compartments: 1 Ho, ER 1 Ha: (1.9 x 3.3)	**1 oil engine** sr geared to sc. shaft driving 1 FP propeller Total Power: 313kW (426hp) 10.0kn Caterpillar D353SCAC 1 x 4 Stroke 6 Cy. 159 x 203 313kW (426bhp) Caterpillar Tractor Co-USA Fuel: 5.0 (d.f.)
6800115 - -	**TORTUGA 5** *ex* Atlanta 6 *-1976* - -	*200* 89 -	Class: (GL)	**1967 Ast. Picsa S.A. — Callao** Loa 26.80 Br ex 7.07 Dght - Lbp - Br md 7.04 Dpth 3.43 Welded, 1 dk	**(B11B2FV) Fishing Vessel**	**1 oil engine** reverse reduction geared to sc. shaft driving 1 FP propeller Total Power: 279kW (379hp) Caterpillar D353SCAC 1 x 4 Stroke 6 Cy. 159 x 203 279kW (379bhp) Caterpillar Tractor Co-USA AuxGen: 1 x 4kW 24V a.c
6801200 - -	**TORTUGA 8** *ex* Atlanta 10 *-1976* - -	*200* 89 -	Class: (GL)	**1967 Ast. Picsa S.A. — Callao** Loa 26.80 Br ex 7.07 Dght - Lbp - Br md 7.04 Dpth 3.43 Welded, 1 dk	**(B11B2FV) Fishing Vessel**	**1 oil engine** reverse reduction geared to sc. shaft driving 1 FP propeller Total Power: 279kW (379hp) Caterpillar D353SCAC 1 x 4 Stroke 6 Cy. 159 x 203 279kW (379bhp) Caterpillar Tractor Co-USA AuxGen: 1 x 4kW 24V a.c
6722088 - -	**TORTUGA 9** *ex* Golden Rose VI *-1975* - -	*200* 89 -	Class: (GL)	**1967 Ast. Picsa S.A. — Callao** Loa 26.80 Br ex 7.07 Dght - Lbp - Br md 7.04 Dpth 3.43 Welded, 1 dk	**(B11B2FV) Fishing Vessel**	**1 oil engine** reverse reduction geared to sc. shaft driving 1 FP propeller Total Power: 279kW (379hp) Caterpillar D353SCAC 1 x 4 Stroke 6 Cy. 159 x 203 279kW (379bhp) (made 1966, fitted 1980) Caterpillar Tractor Co-USA AuxGen: 1 x 4kW 24V a.c
8870970 *IPFJ* -	**TORTUGA V** **Mareventi Srl** - *Naples* *Italy* MMSI: 247062500 Official number: 10851	**196** 130 100	Class: RI	**1993 Cant. Nav. di Ortona — Ortona** Yd No: 20/90 Loa 36.50 Br ex - Dght 2.100 Lbp 27.05 Br md 7.66 Dpth 5.95 Welded, 1 dk	**(A32A2GF) General Cargo/Passenger Ship**	**2 oil engines** reduction geared to sc. shafts driving 2 FP propellers Total Power: 648kW (882hp) Fiat 8281SRM 2 x Vee 4 Stroke 8 Cy. 145 x 130 each-324kW (441bhp) IVECO AIFO S.p.A.-Pregnana Milanese

6800139 **TORTUGA VI**
- *ex* Atlanta 8 *-1975*
- **Industria Maritima Pesquera SA**
-
Guayaquil *Ecuador*
Official number: P-00-0628

200 Class: (GL)
89
-

1967 Ast. Picsa S.A. — Callao Yd No: 209
Loa 26.80 Br ex 7.07 Dght -
Lbp 24.31 Br md 7.04 Dpth 3.43
Welded, 1 dk

(B11B2FV) Fishing Vessel

1 oil engine reverse reduction geared to sc. shaft driving 1 FP propeller
Total Power: 279kW (379hp)
Caterpillar D353SCAC
1 x 4 Stroke 6 Cy. 159 x 203 279kW (379bhp)
Caterpillar Tractor Co-USA
AuxGen: 1 x 4kW 24V a.c

7520463 **TORTUGA VIEJO**
WYU8425 *ex* Ingamar *-1975*
- **Chico Boy Inc**
-
Port Isabel, TX *United States of America*
Official number: 553387

103
70
-

1973 Marine Mart, Inc. — Port Isabel, Tx
L reg 19.69 Br ex 6.13 Dght -
Lbp - Br md - Dpth 3.43
Welded, 1 dk

(B11B2FV) Fishing Vessel

1 oil engine driving 1 FP propeller
Total Power: 268kW (364hp)
Caterpillar D353SCAC
1 x 4 Stroke 6 Cy. 159 x 203 268kW (364bhp)
Caterpillar Tractor Co-USA

9319765 **TORTUGAS**
MVQH7
- **Assetfinance December (R) Ltd**
Wilhelmsen Lines Car Carrier Ltd
SatCom: Inmarsat C 423500028
Southampton *United Kingdom*
MMSI: 235050734
Official number: 912619

61,321 Class: NV
22,650
14,512
T/cm
52.5

2006-12 Mitsubishi Heavy Industries Ltd. — Nagasaki Yd No: 2218
Loa 199.90 (BB) Br ex - Dght 10.500
Lbp 192.00 Br md 32.26 Dpth 36.02
Welded, 12 dks including 4 liftable dks

(A35B2RV) Vehicles Carrier
Side door/ramp (s)
Len: 25.00 Wid: 6.50 Swl: 35
Quarter stern door/ramp (s. a.)
Len: 38.00 Wid: 7.00 Swl: 237
Cars: 6,564

1 oil engine driving 1 FP propeller
Total Power: 12,390kW (16,845hp) 19.5kn
Mitsubishi 7UEC60LS
1 x 2 Stroke 7 Cy. 600 x 2200 12390kW (16845bhp)
Mitsubishi Heavy Industries Ltd-Japan
AuxGen: 3 x 1250kW a.c
Thrusters: 1 Tunnel thruster (f)
Fuel: 3582.0

8986327 **TORUNLAR**
TC5253 *ex* Aytekin 1 *-1975* *ex* Sahinbe Kiroglu II *-1975*
- **Beysan Yakit & Dezizcilik Sanayi Ticaret Ltd Sti**
-
Istanbul *Turkey*
MMSI: 271010662
Official number: 3801

126
59
170

1988 in Turkey Yd No: 18687
Loa 30.50 Br ex 6.30 Dght 2.390
Lbp 26.95 Br md - Dpth 2.95
Welded, 1 dk

(A13B2TU) Tanker (unspecified)

1 oil engine driving 1 Propeller
Total Power: 118kW (160hp)
General Motors
1 x 118kW (160bhp)
General Motors Detroit DieselAllison Divn-USA

6904935 **TORVAAG**
LAJB *ex* Nyvag *-2010* *ex* Torvag *-2006*
- *ex* Tresnes *-1996* *ex* Ringfjell *-1995*
ex Solvind *-1991* *ex* Biala *-1972*
ex Naeroy *-1971*
Molde Sjotransport AS
-
Molde *Norway*
MMSI: 258446000

373
270
673

1968-03 AS Hommelvik Mek. Verksted — Hommelvik Yd No: 113
Lengthened-1985
Loa 48.84 Br ex 7.65 Dght 3.048
Lbp - Br md 7.62 Dpth -
Welded, 1 dk

(A31A2GX) General Cargo Ship
Grain: 650
Compartments: 1 Ho, ER
1 Ha: (25.0 x 5.0)ER
Cranes: 1; Derricks: 1x5t; Winches: 2

1 oil engine driving 1 FP propeller
Total Power: 259kW (352hp) 10.0kn
Deutz
1 x 4 Stroke 8 Cy. 135 x 160 259kW (352bhp)
Kloeckner Humboldt Deutz AG-West Germany
Fuel: 23.5 (d.f.) 2.0pd

6902808 **TORVANG**
LDYV *ex* Aastind *-2012* *ex* Vestbulk *-1991*
- *ex* Aasvaer *-1985* *ex* Torpo *-1983*
Molde Sjotransport AS
Torhus Shipping AS
Molde *Norway*
MMSI: 257971000

998 Class: (BV) (NV)
458
2,218

1968 Batservice Verft AS — Mandal Yd No: 543
Loa 68.08 Br ex 11.43 Dght 5.010
Lbp 60.00 Br md 10.80 Dpth 5.80
Welded, 1 dk & S dk

(A31A2GX) General Cargo Ship
Grain: 2,249; Bale: 1,876
Compartments: 1 Ho, ER
1 Ha: (33.6 x 6.0)ER
Gantry cranes: 1
Ice Capable

1 oil engine sr geared to sc. shaft driving 1 CP propeller
Total Power: 662kW (900hp) 11.0kn
MaK 6M281AK
1 x 4 Stroke 6 Cy. 240 x 280 662kW (900bhp)
Atlas MaK Maschinenbau GmbH-Kiel
AuxGen: 2 x 100kW 220V 50Hz a.c
Fuel: 50.0 (d.f.) 3.5pd

9524774 **TORVANGER**
LMAJ7
-
Westfal-Larsen & Co AS
Westfal-Larsen Management AS
Bergen *Norway (NIS)*
MMSI: 257326000

29,712 Class: NV
12,289
45,318
T/cm
52.3

2012-01 Hyundai Mipo Dockyard Co Ltd — Ulsan Yd No: 2278
Loa 183.15 (BB) Br ex 32.23 Dght 12.315
Lbp 174.00 Br md 32.20 Dpth 18.80
Welded, 1 dk

(A12B2TR) Chemical/Products Tanker
Double Hull (13F)
Liq: 51,612; Liq (Oil): 53,457
Compartments: 20 Wing Ta, 2 Wing Slop Ta, ER
20 Cargo Pump (s): 20x600m³/hr
Manifold: Bow/CM: 91m

1 oil engine driving 1 FP propeller
Total Power: 9,480kW (12,889hp) 14.5kn
MAN-B&W 6S50MC-C
1 x 2 Stroke 6 Cy. 500 x 2000 9480kW (12889bhp)
Hyundai Heavy Industries Co Ltd-South Korea
AuxGen: 3 x 800kW 450V 60Hz a.c
Thrusters: 1 Tunnel thruster (f)
Fuel: 256.6 (d.f.) 1471.0 (r.f.)

7332490 **TORVIND**
LHPT *ex* Panomar *-2012* *ex* Molo Vik *-2008*
- *ex* Morefjord *-2006* *ex* Grinna *-1995*
Molde Sjotransport AS
Torhus Shipping AS
Molde *Norway*
MMSI: 258864000

887 Class: (BV) (NV)
462
950

1973-10 Hjorungavaag Verksted AS — Hjorungavaag Yd No: 18
Loa 60.81 Br ex 9.53 Dght 4.250
Lbp 54.77 Br md 9.50 Dpth 5.26
Welded, 2 dks

(A31A2GX) General Cargo Ship
Grain: 1,394
Compartments: 1 Ho, ER
2 Ha: (17.9 x 7.3) (16.8 x 7.3)ER
Cranes: 1x6t; Derricks: 2x5t; Winches: 2
Ice Capable

1 oil engine reduction geared to sc. shaft driving 1 CP propeller
Total Power: 794kW (1,080hp) 10.0kn
MWM TBD440-8
1 x 4 Stroke 8 Cy. 230 x 270 794kW (1080bhp)
Motoren Werke Mannheim AG (MWM)-West Germany
AuxGen: 2 x 50kW 220V 50Hz a.c

9115107 **TORYO MARU**
JGPC
- **Corporation for Advanced Transport & Technology & Yamane Shipping Co Ltd**
Yamane Shipping Co Ltd (Yamane Kaiun KK)
Tokyo *Japan*
MMSI: 431697000
Official number: 134987

1,351 Class: NK
-
1,605

1995-01 Imamura Zosen — Kure Yd No: 377
Loa 69.95 (BB) Br ex - Dght 4.683
Lbp 65.00 Br md 12.00 Dpth 5.60
Welded, 1 dk

(A12A2LP) Molten Sulphur Tanker
Liq: 802
Compartments: 6 Ta, ER

1 oil engine driving 1 FP propeller
Total Power: 1,471kW (2,000hp) 11.7kn
Hanshin 6EL35
1 x 4 Stroke 6 Cy. 350 x 700 1471kW (2000bhp)
The Hanshin Diesel Works Ltd-Japan
AuxGen: 3 x a.c
Fuel: 155.0 (r.f.)

9605970 **TORYU MARU**
JD3195
- **Too Kaiun KK**
-
Shunan, Yamaguchi *Japan*
Official number: 141442

198
-
360

2011-04 Koa Sangyo KK — Marugame KG Yd No: 647
Loa 42.57 Br ex - Dght 3.190
Lbp 38.50 Br md 7.60 Dpth 3.30
Welded, 1 dk

(A12A2TC) Chemical Tanker
Double Hull (13F)

1 oil engine geared to sc. shaft driving 1 Propeller
Total Power: 736kW (1,001hp)
Yanmar 6RY17P-GV
1 x 4 Stroke 6 Cy. 165 x 219 736kW (1001bhp)
Yanmar Diesel Engine Co Ltd-Japan

9382231 **TORYU MARU**
JD2269
- **Toko Kisen YK**
-
Fukuyama, Hiroshima *Japan*
Official number: 140340

499
-
1,580

2006-06 Yamanaka Zosen K.K. — Imabari Yd No: 723
Loa 76.38 Br ex - Dght 3.970
Lbp 70.18 Br md 12.30 Dpth 6.85
Welded, 2 dks

(A31A2GX) General Cargo Ship
1 Ha: ER (40.1 x 10.0)

1 oil engine driving 1 FP propeller
Total Power: 1,471kW (2,000hp) 12.8kn
Hanshin LH34LAG
1 x 4 Stroke 6 Cy. 340 x 640 1471kW (2000bhp)
The Hanshin Diesel Works Ltd-Japan

9016806 **TORYU MARU NO. 18**
JK5030 *ex* Koho Maru No. 3 *-2007*
- **KK Fujii Sekiyu**
-
Tokyo *Japan*
Official number: 132514

198
-
570

1991-05 KK Ura Kyodo Zosensho — Awaji HG Yd No: 284
Loa - Br ex - Dght 3.201
Lbp 44.02 Br md 8.01 Dpth 3.46
Welded, 1 dk

(A13B2TP) Products Tanker

1 oil engine geared to sc. shaft driving 1 FP propeller
Total Power: 625kW (850hp)
Hanshin LH26G
1 x 4 Stroke 6 Cy. 260 x 440 625kW (850bhp)
The Hanshin Diesel Works Ltd-Japan

7367469 **TOS INTEGRITY**
V4JO2 *ex* Overseas Integrity *-2009* *ex* Integrity *-2007*
- *ex* Chevron Oregon *-1999* *ex* Integrity *-1999*
ex Chevron Oregon *-1997*
Cooper's Offshore Warehousing Ltd
Cooper's Mechanical Oilfield Services Pte Ltd (CMOS)
Basseterre *St Kitts & Nevis*
MMSI: 341082000
Official number: SKN 1002253

22,761 Class: AB
12,905
39,847

1975-12 FMC Corp — Portland OR Yd No: 1
Converted From: Products Tanker-2010
Conv to DH-2005
Loa 198.13 Br ex 29.29 Dght 11.307
Lbp 190.48 Br md 29.24 Dpth 15.27
Welded, 1 dk

(A31A2GX) General Cargo Ship
Double Hull

1 turbo electric Gas Turb driving 1 gen. of 7640kW a.c Connecting to 1 elec. Motor driving 1 CP propeller
Total Power: 9,194kW (12,500hp) 14.5kn
GEC MS3002
1 x Gas Turb 9194kW (12500shp)
General Electric Co.-Lynn, Ma
AuxGen: 1 x 2200kW a.c, 1 x 400kW a.c
Thrusters: 1 Thwart. FP thruster (f)
Fuel: 1519.0 (r.f.) 55.0pd

8965127 **TOSA**
JPBQ *ex* Motobu *-2009*
- **Government of Japan (Ministry of Land, Infrastructure & Transport) (The Coastguard)**
-
Tokyo *Japan*
MMSI: 432257000
Official number: 136968

1,364
-
-

2000-10 Sasebo Heavy Industries Co. Ltd. — Sasebo Yard, Sasebo Yd No: 605
L reg 87.61 Br ex - Dght -
Lbp - Br md 11.50 Dpth 6.40
Welded, 1 dk

(B34H2SQ) Patrol Vessel

2 oil engines driving 2 FP propellers
Total Power: 5,884kW (8,000hp)
Yanmar 8N330-UN
2 x 4 Stroke 8 Cy. 330 x 440 each-2942kW (4000bhp)
Yanmar Diesel Engine Co Ltd-Japan

9343388 **TOSA**
7JIK
- **Nippon Yusen Kabushiki Kaisha (NYK Line)**
NYK Shipmanagement Pte Ltd
SatCom: Inmarsat C 443278410
Tokyo *Japan*
MMSI: 432784000
Official number: 141341

159,930 Class: NK
98,108
302,159
T/cm
182.6

2008-03 IHI Marine United Inc — Kure HS Yd No: 3220
Loa 333.00 (BB) Br ex 60.04 Dght 20.635
Lbp 324.00 Br md 60.00 Dpth 29.00
Welded, 1 dk

(A13A2TV) Crude Oil Tanker
Double Hull (13F)
Liq: 330,208; Liq (Oil): 330,208
Compartments: 5 Ta, 10 Wing Ta, 2 Wing Slop Ta, ER
3 Cargo Pump (s): 3x5500m³/hr
Manifold: Bow/CM: 169.4m

1 oil engine driving 1 FP propeller
Total Power: 27,160kW (36,927hp) 15.5kn
Wartsila 7RT-flex84T
1 x 2 Stroke 7 Cy. 840 x 3150 27160kW (36927bhp)
Diesel United Ltd.-Aioi
AuxGen: 3 x 1150kW 440V 50Hz a.c
Fuel: 517.1 (d.f.) 7273.2 (r.f.)

8997326 *JD2037* -	**TOSA MARU** **Sanyo Kaiji Co Ltd** - *Amagasaki, Hyogo* *Japan* Official number: 140074	*197* - -		**2004-10 Hatayama Zosen KK — Yura WK** Yd No: 243 Loa 36.02 Br ex - Dght 3.200 Lbp 30.00 Br md 9.00 Dpth 4.14 Welded, 1 dk	**(B32A2ST) Tug**	**2 oil engines** geared integral to driving 2 Z propellers Total Power: 2,942kW (4,000hp) 15.3kn Yanmar 6N280M-UV 2 x 4 Stroke 6 Cy. 280 x 380 each-1471kW (2000bhp) Yanmar Diesel Engine Co Ltd-Japan
8322997 *JJ3365* -	**TOSA MARU** **Ehime Zosen Service KK** - *Imabari, Ehime* *Japan* Official number: 125298	*146* - 90		**1984-02 Hikari Kogyo K.K. — Yokosuka** Yd No: 332 Loa 30.64 Br ex 8.62 Dght 2.731 Lbp 26.50 Br md 8.59 Dpth 3.51 Welded, 1 dk	**(B32A2ST) Tug**	**2 oil engines** driving 2 Directional propellers Total Power: 1,912kW (2,600hp) 12.5kn Yanmar 6T260L-ST 2 x 4 Stroke 6 Cy. 260 x 330 each-956kW (1300bhp) Yanmar Diesel Engine Co Ltd-Japan AuxGen: 2 x 80kW 440V 60Hz a.c Fuel: 34.0 (d.f.) 9.5pd
9615547 *7JJQ* -	**TOSAKAIEN MARU** **Government of Japan (Ministry of Education - Kochi)** - *Kochi, Kochi* *Japan* MMSI: 431000650 Official number: 141486	*486* - 360		**2011-08 Miho Zosensho K.K. — Shimizu** Yd No: 1548 Loa 55.50 Br ex - Dght 3.900 Lbp 47.00 Br md 9.50 Dpth 6.20 Welded, 1 dk	**(B11B2FV) Fishing Vessel**	**1 oil engine** driving 1 Propeller Total Power: 1,323kW (1,799hp) Hanshin LA28G 1 x 4 Stroke 6 Cy. 280 x 590 1323kW (1799bhp) The Hanshin Diesel Works Ltd-Japan
8004765 - -	**TOSAWAN** *ex* Sea Lion *ex* RCL-A *-2001* *ex* Sitra 1 *-1997* *ex* Eiko Maru *-1994* *ex* Acoop No. 8 *-1989* -	**1,160** 623 1,600	Class: (BV) (NK)	**1980-07 Mategata Zosen K.K. — Namikata** Yd No: 187 Loa 69.55 Br ex - Dght 4.423 Lbp 64.01 Br md 11.02 Dpth 6.23 Welded, 2 dks	**(A31A2GX) General Cargo Ship** Grain: 2,459; Bale: 2,338 1 Ha: (36.5 x 8.0)ER	**1 oil engine** driving 1 FP propeller Total Power: 1,177kW (1,600hp) 11.5kn Akasaka DM33 1 x 4 Stroke 6 Cy. 330 x 500 1177kW (1600bhp) Akasaka Tekkosho KK (Akasaka DieselLtd)-Japan AuxGen: 2 x 144kW
9605798 *9V9459* -	**TOSCA** **Wallstraits Shipping Pte Ltd** Wallenius Marine Singapore Pte Ltd *Singapore* *Singapore* MMSI: 566087000 Official number: 397117	**61,106** 23,696 22,585 T/cm 52.5	Class: NV	**2013-01 Mitsubishi Heavy Industries Ltd. — Nagasaki** Yd No: 2285 Loa 199.99 (BB) Br ex - Dght 11.000 Lbp 192.00 Br md 32.26 Dpth 36.02 Welded, 12 dks including 4 liftable dks	**(A35B2RV) Vehicles Carrier** Side door/ramp (s) Len: 25.00 Wid: 6.50 Swl: 35 Quarter stern door/ramp (s. a.) Len: 38.00 Wid: 7.00 Swl: 237 Cars: 6,459	**1 oil engine** driving 1 FP propeller Total Power: 14,315kW (19,463hp) 19.5kn Mitsubishi 7UEC60LSII 1 x 2 Stroke 7 Cy. 600 x 2300 14315kW (19463bhp) AuxGen: 3 x a.c Thrusters: 1 Tunnel thruster (f)
9251884 *A8EF7* -	**TOSCA** **Afrodite Maritime Co Ltd** Laurin Maritime (America) Inc *Monrovia* *Liberia* MMSI: 636012244 Official number: 12244	**26,914** 14,288 46,764 T/cm 52.7	Class: NV	**2004-06 Brodotrogir dd - Shipyard Trogir — Trogir** Yd No: 306 Loa 182.74 (BB) Br ex 32.21 Dght 12.180 Lbp 176.75 Br md 32.18 Dpth 17.21 Welded, 1 dk	**(A12B2TR) Chemical/Products Tanker** Double Hull (13F) Liq: 51,911; Liq (Oil): 53,900 Compartments: 14 Wing Ta, 2 Wing Slop Ta, ER 14 Cargo Pump (s): 6x400m³/hr, 8x250m³/hr Manifold: Bow/CM: 91.5m	**2 oil engines** geared to sc. shaft driving 1 CP propeller Total Power: 7,700kW (10,468hp) 14.5kn MaK 8M32C 2 x 4 Stroke 8 Cy. 320 x 480 each-3850kW (5234bhp) Caterpillar Motoren GmbH & Co. KG-Germany AuxGen: 2 x 650kW 60Hz a.c, 1 x 3200kW 60Hz a.c
9233052 *EA4581* 3-VI-75-00	**TOSCA TERCERO** **Cadilla/Martinez** - *La Guardia* *Spain* MMSI: 224005790 Official number: 3-5/2000	**201** 60 -		**2000-06 Montajes Cies S.L. — Vigo** Yd No: 69 Loa 25.30 Br ex - Dght 3.700 Lbp 22.40 Br md 6.50 Dpth 3.30 Welded, 1 dk	**(B11B2FV) Fishing Vessel**	**1 oil engine** reduction geared to sc. shaft driving 1 FP propeller GUASCOR SF240 1 x 4 Stroke 8 Cy. 152 x 165 Gutierrez Ascunce Corp (GUASCOR)-Spain
9398333 *2CQX6* -	**TOSCANA** **Wilhelmsen Lines Car Carrier Ltd** - SatCom: Inmarsat C 423591893 *Southampton* *United Kingdom* MMSI: 235075024 Official number: 916179	**61,328** 23,559 22,250 T/cm 52.5	Class: NV	**2009-06 Mitsubishi Heavy Industries Ltd. — Nagasaki** Yd No: 2245 Loa 199.99 (BB) Br ex - Dght 11.000 Lbp 192.00 Br md 32.26 Dpth 36.02 Welded, 12 dks including 4 liftable dks	**(A35B2RV) Vehicles Carrier** Side door/ramp (s) Len: 25.00 Wid: 6.50 Swl: 35 Quarter stern door/ramp (s. a.) Len: 38.00 Wid: 7.00 Swl: 237 Cars: 6,556	**1 oil engine** driving 1 FP propeller Total Power: 13,240kW (18,001hp) 19.5kn Mitsubishi 7UEC60LSII 1 x 2 Stroke 7 Cy. 600 x 2300 13240kW (18001bhp) Mitsubishi Heavy Industries Ltd-Japan AuxGen: 3 x 1250kW a.c Thrusters: 1 Tunnel thruster (f)
9158410 *9HFA5* -	**TOSCANA** *ex* Star Toscana *-1999* *ex* Cielo di Monfalcone *-1997* *ex* Toscana *-1997* **ms 'Toscana' Schiffahrtsgesellschaft mbH & Co KG** FH Bertling Reederei GmbH SatCom: Inmarsat B 324976110 *Valletta* *Malta* MMSI: 249761000 Official number: 5247	**25,719** 13,406 36,120 T/cm 43.4	Class: NV	**1996-12 Bohai Shipyard — Huludao LN** Yd No: 406-1 Lengthened-2006 Loa 189.70 (BB) Br ex 27.70 Dght 11.516 Lbp 178.40 Br md 27.68 Dpth 15.50 Welded, 1dk	**(A31A2GO) Open Hatch Cargo Ship** Grain: 40,168 TEU 1540 C Ho 796 TEU C Dk 744 TEU incl 80 ref C. Compartments: 8 Ho, ER 8 Ha: ER Cranes: 4x35t	**1 oil engine** driving 1 FP propeller Total Power: 8,520kW (11,584hp) 16.0kn Sulzer 6RTA52 1 x 2 Stroke 6 Cy. 520 x 1800 8520kW (11584bhp) Yichang Marine Diesel Engine Co Ltd-China AuxGen: 3 x 500kW 220/440V 60Hz a.c Fuel: 179.0 (d.f.) (Heating Coils) 1373.0 (r.f.) 30.5pd
9016301 *JK5053* -	**TOSEI** **Tosoh Logistics Corp (Tosoh Butsuryu KK)** - *Shunan, Yamaguchi* *Japan* MMSI: 431400992 Official number: 132463	*696* - 1,365		**1991-03 Kegoya Dock K.K. — Kure** Yd No: 917 Loa 85.01 (BB) Br ex 14.03 Dght 3.891 Lbp 80.00 Br md 14.00 Dpth 6.70 Welded, 1 dk	**(A33A2CC) Container Ship (Fully Cellular)** Bale: 3,000 TEU 80 C Ho 52 TEU C Dk 28 TEU Compartments: 1 Cell Ho, ER 1 Ha: (44.9 x 10.5)ER Gantry cranes: 1x21t	**1 oil engine** with flexible couplings & sr gearedto sc. shafts driving 1 CP propeller Total Power: 2,207kW (3,001hp) 14.3kn Niigata 6M38HFT 1 x 4 Stroke 6 Cy. 380 x 700 2207kW (3001bhp) Niigata Engineering Co Ltd-Japan AuxGen: 2 x 200kW 445V 60Hz a.c Thrusters: 1 Thwart. CP thruster (f) Fuel: 150.0 (d.f.) 7.0pd
8911188 *JL5843* -	**TOSEI MARU** **YK Kato Unyu** - *Seiyo, Ehime* *Japan* Official number: 131429	*486* - 601	Class: NK	**1989-12 Shirahama Zosen K.K. — Honai** Yd No: 143 Loa 61.00 Br ex 9.82 Dght 3.280 Lbp 56.00 Br md 9.80 Dpth 4.40 Welded, 1 dk	**(A11B2TG) LPG Tanker** Liq (Gas): 703	**1 oil engine** reverse geared to sc. shaft driving 1 FP propeller Total Power: 956kW (1,300hp) Akasaka K28R 1 x 4 Stroke 6 Cy. 280 x 480 956kW (1300bhp) Akasaka Tekkosho KK (Akasaka DieselLtd)-Japan AuxGen: 3 x 117kW a.c Fuel: 50.0 (d.f.)
9137014 - -	**TOSHI MARU** -	*697* - 2,100		**1995-09 Yamanaka Zosen K.K. — Imabari** Yd No: 578 Loa 76.44 (BB) Br ex - Dght 4.722 Lbp 70.00 Br md 14.00 Dpth 7.85 Welded, 1 dk	**(A31A2GX) General Cargo Ship** Grain: 1,653 Compartments: 1 Ho, ER 1 Ha: ER	**1 oil engine** driving 1 FP propeller Total Power: 1,471kW (2,000hp) Hanshin LH36LA 1 x 4 Stroke 6 Cy. 360 x 670 1471kW (2000bhp) The Hanshin Diesel Works Ltd-Japan Thrusters: 1 Thwart. FP thruster (f)
8948739 *JM6366* -	**TOSHI MARU No. 11** **Wasa Kogyo YK** - *Shimonoseki, Yamaguchi* *Japan* Official number: 114796	*100* - -		**1972-10 Toyo Zosen Tekko KK — Kitakyushu FO** Loa 29.30 Br ex - Dght 2.000 Lbp 25.00 Br md 6.20 Dpth 3.10 Welded, 1 dk	**(B32A2ST) Tug**	**1 oil engine** driving 1 FP propeller Total Power: 1,177kW (1,600hp) 10.0kn
8032516 *JG4152* -	**TOSHI MARU No. 18** *ex* Showa Maru No. 11 *-1993* *ex* Shoho Maru No. 11 *-1987* **Wasa Kogyo YK** - *Shimonoseki, Yamaguchi* *Japan* Official number: 121846	*173* - -		**1980-12 Sanriku Zosen Tekko K.K. — Japan** Loa - Br ex - Dght - Lbp 27.21 Br md 7.21 Dpth 3.51 Welded, 1 dk	**(B32A2ST) Tug**	**1 oil engine** driving 1 FP propeller Total Power: 1,545kW (2,101hp) Akasaka AH38 1 x 4 Stroke 6 Cy. 380 x 560 1545kW (2101bhp) Akasaka Tekkosho KK (Akasaka DieselLtd)-Japan
9580340 *JD3100* -	**TOSHIEI MARU NO. 8** **Toshiharu Hiramoto** - *Sakaide, Kagawa* *Japan* Official number: 141301	*199* - 700		**2010-07 Taiyo Shipbuilding Co Ltd — Sanyoonoda YC** Yd No: 323 Loa 55.63 (BB) Br ex - Dght 3.200 Lbp - Br md 9.50 Dpth 5.40 Welded, 1 dk	**(A31A2GX) General Cargo Ship**	**1 oil engine** reduction geared to sc. shaft driving 1 FP propeller Total Power: 882kW (1,199hp) Hanshin LH26G 1 x 4 Stroke 6 Cy. 260 x 440 882kW (1199bhp) The Hanshin Diesel Works Ltd-Japan Thrusters: 1 Thwart. FP thruster (f)

IMO / Call sign	Name / Owner	Tonnage	Class	Construction	Type	Machinery
8889701 - -	**TOSHIN** - **Ta Shan Shipping Co Ltd**	393 - 795		**1995-03 Y.K. Takasago Zosensho — Naruto** Yd No: 206 Loa 60.90 Br ex - Dght 3.850 Lbp 52.00 Br md 12.50 Dpth 6.00 Welded, 1 dk	**(A31A2GX) General Cargo Ship**	**1 oil engine** driving 1 FP propeller Total Power: 736kW (1,001hp) 11.0kn Matsui MA32GSC-2 1 x 4 Stroke 6 Cy. 320 x 600 736kW (1001bhp) Matsui Iron Works Co Ltd-Japan
8980543 *JH3504* -	**TOSHIN MARU** - **Topy Kaiun KK (Topy Marine Transport Ltd)** - *Toyohashi, Aichi* Japan Official number: 135685	429 - 1,199		**2003-04 K.K. Murakami Zosensho — Naruto** Yd No: 237 Loa 70.38 Br ex - Dght 3.890 Lbp 66.00 Br md 11.00 Dpth 6.60 Welded, 1 dk	**(A31A2GX) General Cargo Ship** Grain: 1,995 Compartments: 1 Ho, ER 1 Ha: ER (36.0 x 8.5)	**1 oil engine** reverse geared to sc. shaft driving 1 FP propeller Total Power: 1,324kW (1,800hp) 12.0kn Akasaka A31R 1 x 4 Stroke 6 Cy. 310 x 600 1324kW (1800bhp) Akasaka Tekkosho KK (Akasaka DieselLtd)-Japan
9073517 *JG5163* -	**TOSHIN MARU** - **Kyoei Kisen KK** - *Kaminoseki, Yamaguchi* Japan Official number: 134009	497 - 1,545		**1993-09 Narasaki Zosen KK — Muroran HK** Yd No: 1138 Loa 75.00 Br ex - Dght 4.071 Lbp 70.00 Br md 12.00 Dpth 7.00 Welded, 2 dks	**(A31A2GX) General Cargo Ship** Bale: 2,195 Compartments: 1 Ho, ER 1 Ha: ER	**1 oil engine** with flexible couplings & reverse geared to sc. shaft driving 1 FP propeller Total Power: 736kW (1,001hp) Akasaka A31R 1 x 4 Stroke 6 Cy. 310 x 600 736kW (1001bhp) Akasaka Tekkosho KK (Akasaka DieselLtd)-Japan Thrusters: 1 Thwart. FP thruster (f)
8632548 - -	**TOSHIN MARU No. 1** - -	123 - -		**1973-03 in Japan** L reg 29.20 Br ex - Dght 2.100 Lbp - Br md 6.20 Dpth 2.60 Welded, 1 dk	**(B11B2FV) Fishing Vessel**	**1 oil engine** driving 1 FP propeller
7512636 *JG3582* -	**TOSHIN MARU No. 7** *ex* Toa Maru No. 7 *-2000* *ex* Shinano Maru *-1988* **Toko Kaiun KK** - *Hiroshima, Hiroshima* Japan Official number: 117795	167 75 -		**1975-08 Kanagawa Zosen — Kobe** Yd No: 157 Loa 36.00 Br ex 8.62 Dght 2.490 Lbp 32.00 Br md 8.59 Dpth 3.38 Riveted\Welded, 1 dk	**(B32A2ST) Tug**	**2 oil engines** geared integral to driving 2 Z propellers Total Power: 1,912kW (2,600hp) 12.5kn Niigata 6L25BX 2 x 4 Stroke 6 Cy. 250 x 320 each-956kW (1300bhp) Niigata Engineering Co Ltd-Japan
8712831 - -	**TOSHO MARU** - -	497 - 740	Class: (NK)	**1987-08 Sasaki Shipbuilding Co Ltd — Osakikamijima HS** Yd No: 512 Loa 60.16 Br ex - Dght 3.532 Lbp 56.01 Br md 10.01 Dpth 4.60 Welded, 1 dk	**(A11B2TG) LPG Tanker** Liq (Gas): 842	**1 oil engine** with clutches, flexible couplings & reverse reduction geared to sc. shaft driving 1 FP propeller Total Power: 736kW (1,001hp) Niigata 6M28BFT 1 x 4 Stroke 6 Cy. 280 x 480 736kW (1001bhp) Niigata Engineering Co Ltd-Japan AuxGen: 3 x 99kW a.c Fuel: 70.0 (d.f.)
9414541 *JD2399* -	**TOSHO MARU** - **Toei Kisen KK** - *Etajima, Hiroshima* Japan MMSI: 431000166 Official number: 140520	499 - 1,740		**2007-04 Yamanaka Zosen K.K. — Imabari** Yd No: 736 Loa 74.20 Br ex - Dght 4.360 Lbp 68.00 Br md 12.00 Dpth 7.37 Welded, 1 dk	**(A31A2GX) General Cargo Ship** Grain: 2,450; Bale: 2,450 1 Ha: ER (40.0 x 9.5)	**1 oil engine** driving 1 FP propeller Total Power: 1,471kW (2,000hp) 12.4kn Hanshin LH34LAG 1 x 4 Stroke 6 Cy. 340 x 640 1471kW (2000bhp) The Hanshin Diesel Works Ltd-Japan
9048536 - -	**TOSHUN MARU** - - - Bangladesh	493 - 1,100		**1992-05 Matsuura Tekko Zosen K.K. — Osakikamijima** Yd No: 370 Loa 60.00 (BB) Br ex 10.57 Dght 4.050 Lbp 56.00 Br md 10.50 Dpth 4.30 Welded, 1 dk	**(A13B2TP) Products Tanker** Compartments: 8 Ta, ER	**1 oil engine** reverse geared to sc. shaft driving 1 FP propeller Total Power: 736kW (1,001hp) Niigata 6M28BGT 1 x 4 Stroke 6 Cy. 280 x 480 736kW (1001bhp) Niigata Engineering Co Ltd-Japan Thrusters: 1 Thwart. FP thruster (f)
9408073 *SVAL4* -	**TOSKA** *launched as* Tosca *-2009* **Picado Shipping Corp** Heidmar Inc SatCom: Inmarsat Mini-M 764881555 *Piraeus* Greece MMSI: 240830000 Official number: 11853	**83,545** 49,022 156,929 T/cm 119.8	Class: AB	**2009-03 Jiangsu Rongsheng Shipbuilding Co Ltd — Rugao JS** Yd No: 1012 Loa 274.50 (BB) Br ex 48.04 Dght 17.019 Lbp 264.00 Br md 48.00 Dpth 23.70 Welded, 1 dk	**(A13A2TV) Crude Oil Tanker** Double Hull (13F) Liq: 167,552; Liq (Oil): 167,552 Cargo Heating Coils Compartments: 12 Wing Ta, 2 Wing Slop Ta, ER 3 Cargo Pump (s): 3x3500m³/hr Manifold: Bow/CM: 138.8m	**1 oil engine** driving 1 FP propeller Total Power: 18,660kW (25,370hp) 15.1kn MAN-B&W 6S70MC-C 1 x 2 Stroke 6 Cy. 700 x 2800 18660kW (25370bhp) Hudong Heavy Machinery Co Ltd-China AuxGen: 3 x 940kW a.c Fuel: 257.3 (d.f.) 4492.0 (r.f.)
9425239 *D5CQ2* -	**TOSNA STAR** - **mt 'Tosna Star' Schifffahrtsgesellschaft mbH & Co KG** NSC Tank GmbH & Cie KG *Monrovia* Liberia MMSI: 636092442 Official number: 92442	**8,621** 4,014 12,589	Class: GL	**2010-12 Dae Sun Shipbuilding & Engineering Co Ltd — Busan** Yd No: 485 Loa 129.03 (BB) Br ex - Dght 8.700 Lbp 120.50 Br md 20.40 Dpth 11.50 Welded, 1 dk	**(A12B2TR) Chemical/Products Tanker** Double Hull (13F) Liq: 14,219; Liq (Oil): 14,063 Compartments: 12 Wing Ta, 2 Wing Slop Ta, ER 12 Cargo Pump (s): 12x300m³/hr Ice Capable	**1 oil engine** driving 1 FP propeller Total Power: 5,920kW (8,049hp) 13.8kn MAN-B&W 8S35MC 1 x 2 Stroke 8 Cy. 350 x 1400 5920kW (8049bhp) STX Engine Co Ltd-South Korea AuxGen: 3 x 600kW 450V a.c Thrusters: 1 Tunnel thruster (f)
9042087 *OVPK* -	**TOSTE** *ex* Toste II *-1992* **Government of The Kingdom of Denmark (Statshavneadministrationen - Statens Uddybriingsmateriel)** - *Esbjerg* Denmark MMSI: 219000615 Official number: D3491	**556** 166 632	Class: BV	**1992-07 Scheepswerf Bijlholt B.V. — Foxhol** (Hull) **1992-07 B.V. Scheepswerf Damen — Gorinchem** Yd No: 2156 Loa 45.70 Br ex - Dght 2.900 Lbp 44.70 Br md 10.50 Dpth 3.50 Welded, 1 dk	**(B33B2DT) Trailing Suction Hopper Dredger** Hopper: 480	**2 oil engines** reduction geared to sc. shafts driving 2 Directional propellers Total Power: 560kW (762hp) 7.5kn Caterpillar 3406TA 2 x 4 Stroke 6 Cy. 137 x 165 each-280kW (381bhp) Caterpillar Inc-USA
8942345 *JG2611* -	**TOSUI MARU No. 15** - **Nagasaki Kyusui KK** - *Nagasaki, Nagasaki* Japan Official number: 105167	107 - 210		**1968-10 Daido Zosen K.K. — Tokyo** Loa 27.00 Br ex - Dght 2.400 Lbp 23.80 Br md 6.56 Dpth 2.50 Welded, 1 dk	**(A14A2LO) Water Tanker**	**1 oil engine** driving 1 FP propeller Total Power: 88kW (120hp) 8.0kn Mitsubishi 6G-2 1 x 4 Stroke 6 Cy. 145 x 200 88kW (120bhp) Mitsubishi Heavy Industries Ltd-Japan
9005637 *XUAQ8* -	**TOTAI MARU** *ex* Shun Tian *-2010* *ex* Totai Maru *-2007* **Sunny Ocean Enterprise Ltd** Dalian Heyang Shipping Agency Co Ltd *Phnom Penh* Cambodia MMSI: 515139000 Official number: 0990035	**1,495** 825 1,595	Class: UM	**1990-08 Nakatani Shipyard Co. Ltd. — Etajima** Yd No: 537 Loa - Br ex - Dght 4.000 Lbp 70.00 Br md 12.00 Dpth 7.20 Welded	**(A31A2GX) General Cargo Ship** Compartments: 1 Ho, ER 1 Ha: ER	**1 oil engine** reverse geared to sc. shaft driving 1 FP propeller Total Power: 1,383kW (1,880hp) Hanshin 6EL30G 1 x 4 Stroke 6 Cy. 300 x 600 1383kW (1880bhp) The Hanshin Diesel Works Ltd-Japan
5200253 *DUA2775* -	**TOTAL** *ex* PNOC Taclobo *-2000* *ex* LSCO Taclobo *-1978* **Total Bulk Corp** - *Manila* Philippines Official number: MNLD000639	*1,544* 799 1,812	Class: (AB)	**1962-07 Osaka Shipbuilding Co Ltd — Osaka OS** Yd No: 183 Loa 78.59 Br ex 11.66 Dght 5.501 Lbp 73.00 Br md 11.60 Dpth 6.10 Riveted\Welded, 1 dk	**(A13B2TP) Products Tanker** Liq: 2,516; Liq (Oil): 2,516 Cargo Heating Coils Compartments: 8 Ta, ER	**1 oil engine** driving 1 FP propeller Total Power: 1,015kW (1,380hp) 17.0kn B&W 8-28VBF-50 1 x 2 Stroke 8 Cy. 280 x 500 1015kW (1380bhp) Hitachi Zosen Corp-Japan Fuel: 146.5 5.0pd
9713088 - -	**TOTAL** - **Total Marchandising & Trim Ltd** - *Chittagong* Bangladesh Official number: C1854	**998** - 1,500	Class: RI	**2013-12 Narayangonj Engineering & Shipbuilding Ltd (NESL) — Bandar** Yd No: NESL 13 Loa 68.60 Br ex - Dght 3.900 Lbp 63.50 Br md 10.80 Dpth 5.30 Welded, 1 dk	**(A13B2TP) Products Tanker** Double Hull (13F)	**2 oil engines** reduction geared to sc. shafts driving 2 Propellers Total Power: 1,060kW (1,442hp) 10.0kn
9027570 *YB6233* -	**TOTAL FINAELF I** - - - *Samarinda* Indonesia Official number: 2003 IIK NO. 2985/L	**108** 64 -	Class: KI	**2003-03 PT Trimanunggal Nugraha — Samarinda** Loa 24.25 Br ex - Dght 1.590 Lbp 23.00 Br md 7.60 Dpth 2.05 Welded, 1 dk	**(B34L2QU) Utility Vessel**	**2 oil engines** geared to sc. shafts driving 2 Propellers Total Power: 286kW (388hp) 8.0kn Chinese Std. Type 6135CA 2 x 4 Stroke 6 Cy. 135 x 150 each-143kW (194bhp) Chongqing Dongfeng Shipyard-China AuxGen: 2 x 96kW 400/115V a.c
8999350 - -	**TOTAL I** - **PT Agus Suta Lines** - *Samarinda* Indonesia	**184** 56 -	Class: KI	**2002-12 C.V. Karya Lestari Industri — Samarinda** L reg 31.00 Br ex - Dght 1.840 Lbp 29.50 Br md 7.70 Dpth 2.36 Welded, 1 dk	**(A35D2RL) Landing Craft** Bow ramp (centre)	**2 oil engines** reduction geared to sc. shafts driving 2 Propellers Total Power: 442kW (600hp) 7.0kn Hyundai Himsen H6D2T 2 x 4 Stroke 6 Cy. 130 x 140 each-221kW (300bhp) Hyundai Heavy Industries Co Ltd-South Korea

IMO / Call sign / Fishing no.	Name / Owner / Port	Tonnage	Class	Built / Dimensions	Type	Machinery
8999362 - -	**TOTAL II** **PT Agus Suta Lines** - *Samarinda* *Indonesia*	**191** - -	Class: (KI)	**2002**-05 **C.V. Karya Lestari Industri — Samarinda** L reg 32.00 Br ex - Dght - Lbp 29.90 Br md 8.00 Dpth 2.78 Welded, 1 dk	**(A35D2RL) Landing Craft** Bow ramp (centre)	**2 oil engines** reduction geared to sc. shafts driving 2 Propellers Total Power: 442kW (600hp) 9.0kn Hyundai Himsen H6D2T 2 x 4 Stroke 6 Cy. 130 x 140 each-221kW (300bhp) (made 2001) Hyundai Heavy Industries Co Ltd-South Korea
8999374 - -	**TOTAL III** **PT Agus Suta Lines** - *Samarinda* *Indonesia*	**191** 58 -	Class: KI	**2002**-06 **C.V. Karya Lestari Industri — Samarinda** Loa - Br ex - Dght - Lbp 38.20 Br md 8.00 Dpth 2.40 Welded, 1 dk	**(A35D2RL) Landing Craft** Bow ramp (centre)	**2 oil engines** reduction geared to sc. shafts driving 2 Propellers Total Power: 442kW (600hp) 10.0kn Hyundai Himsen H6D2T 2 x 4 Stroke 6 Cy. 130 x 140 each-221kW (300bhp) (made 2001) Hyundai Heavy Industries Co Ltd-South Korea
9027582 - -	**TOTAL IV** **PT Karyamas Kaltim Prima** - *Samarinda* *Indonesia*	**260** 78 -	Class: (KI)	**2002**-10 **P.T. Victory — Samarinda** Loa 37.00 Br ex - Dght 1.540 Lbp 29.20 Br md 8.00 Dpth 3.00 Welded, 1 dk	**(A35D2RL) Landing Craft** Bow ramp (centre)	**2 oil engines** geared to sc. shafts driving 2 Propellers Total Power: 442kW (600hp) 15.0kn Hyundai Himsen H6D2T 2 x 4 Stroke 6 Cy. 130 x 140 each-221kW (300bhp) (made 2001) Hyundai Heavy Industries Co Ltd-South Korea
9170092 - -	**TOTAL PERMAI II** **Neptune Shipbuilding & Engineering Pte Ltd** -	**344** 101 -		**1997**-04 **P.T. Fajar Nusa Borneo — Samarinda** Yd No: LCT/01/97 Loa 42.26 Br ex - Dght 2.200 Lbp 39.50 Br md 10.48 Dpth - Welded, 1 dk	**(A35D2RL) Landing Craft** Bow ramp (centre)	**2 oil engines** geared to sc. shafts driving 2 FP propellers Total Power: 620kW (842hp) Yanmar 6LA-DTE 2 x 4 Stroke 6 Cy. 148 x 165 each-310kW (421bhp) Yanmar Diesel Engine Co Ltd-Japan
9030620 *V4XZ2* -	**TOTEEL** *ex* Kakuko Maru *-2010* **Adema Energy DMCC** Babil Marine Shipping Services LLC *St Kitts & Nevis* MMSI: 341185000 Official number: SKN 1002657	*2,997* 899 5,428 T/cm 13.1	Class: NK	**1991**-09 **Naikai Shipbuilding & Engineering Co Ltd — Onomichi HS (Setoda Shipyard)** Yd No: 567 Loa 105.24 (BB) Br ex 15.22 Dght 6.833 Lbp 97.60 Br md 15.20 Dpth 7.50 Welded, 1 dk	**(A13B2TP) Products Tanker** Single Hull Liq: 5,528; Liq (Oil): 5,528 Compartments: 9 Ta, ER	**1 oil engine** with clutches, flexible couplings & geared to sc. shaft driving 1 CP propeller Total Power: 2,942kW (4,000hp) 13.3kn Hanshin 6EL44 1 x 4 Stroke 6 Cy. 440 x 880 2942kW (4000bhp) Hanshin Nainenki Kogyo-Japan AuxGen: 2 x 400kW a.c, 1 x 120kW a.c Thrusters: 1 Thwart. CP thruster (f) Fuel: 250.0 (r.f.)
6508303 - -	**TOTO** *ex* Bugsier 30 *-2000* **AdorTerMar Srl** - *Italy*	*101* - 27	Class: (RI) (GL)	**1965 F Schichau GmbH — Bremerhaven** Yd No: 1732 Loa 22.99 Br ex 7.45 Dght 2.569 Lbp 20.02 Br md 7.00 Dpth 3.15 Welded, 1 dk	**(B32A2ST) Tug** Ice Capable	**1 oil engine** reverse geared to sc. shaft driving 1 FP propeller Total Power: 777kW (1,056hp) 10.8kn Deutz RBV6M545 1 x 4 Stroke 6 Cy. 320 x 450 777kW (1056bhp) Kloeckner Humboldt Deutz AG-West Germany AuxGen: 1 x 16kW 230V d.c
9504279 *ICFJ* -	**TOTO BR** *ex* Heng Yuan 8 *-2010* **Barone Shipping Co SpA** - *Naples* *Italy* MMSI: 247285400	**6,478** 2,721 7,967	Class: RI (BV)	**2010**-01 **in the People's Republic of China** Yd No: HY070601 Loa 116.23 Br ex - Dght 7.700 Lbp 110.00 Br md 18.00 Dpth 10.40 Welded, 1 dk	**(A31A2GX) General Cargo Ship** Grain: 11,309; Bale: 11,309 Compartments: 2 Ho, ER 2 Ha: ER Cranes: 2x35t Ice Capable	**1 oil engine** reduction geared to sc. shaft driving 1 Propeller Total Power: 2,970kW (4,038hp) 12.2kn MaK 9M25C 1 x 4 Stroke 9 Cy. 255 x 400 2970kW (4038bhp) Caterpillar Motoren GmbH & Co. KG-Germany AuxGen: 3 x 350kW 400V 50Hz a.c
8109591 *P24115* -	**TOTOL** **Kambang Holding Ltd** Lutheran Shipping (LUSHIP) *Madang* *Papua New Guinea* Official number: 000317	*207* - 300	Class: (AB)	**1981**-08 **Singmarine Shipyard Pte Ltd — Singapore** Yd No: 042 Loa 29.98 Br ex - Dght 2.687 Lbp 28.91 Br md 7.56 Dpth 3.20 Welded, 1 dk	**(A32A2GF) General Cargo/Passenger Ship** Bale: 320 Compartments: 1 Ho, ER 1 Ha: (11.8 x 4.2)ER Derricks: 2x4t	**2 oil engines** reverse reduction geared to sc. shafts driving 2 FP propellers Total Power: 250kW (340hp) 10.0kn Gardner 8LXB 2 x 4 Stroke 8 Cy. 121 x 152 each-125kW (170bhp) L. Gardner & Sons Ltd.-Manchester Fuel: 11.5 (d.f.) 1.5pd
9439400 *ICNT* -	**TOTONNO BOTTIGLIERI** **Rizzo Bottiglieri De Carlini Armatori SpA** - SatCom: Inmarsat C 424703173 *Naples* *Italy* MMSI: 247293500	**60,185** 33,762 108,870 T/cm 91.3	Class: AB RI	**2010**-08 **Hudong-Zhonghua Shipbuilding (Group) Co Ltd — Shanghai** Yd No: H1549A Loa 243.00 (BB) Br ex 42.03 Dght 15.350 Lbp 233.00 Br md 42.00 Dpth 22.00 Welded, 1 dk	**(A13B2TP) Products Tanker** Double Hull (13F) Liq: 123,030; Liq (Oil): 123,030 Cargo Heating Coils Compartments: 12 Wing Ta, 2 Wing Slop Ta, ER 3 Cargo Pump (s): 3x2500m³/hr Manifold: Bow/CM: 119.5m	**1 oil engine** driving 1 FP propeller Total Power: 14,280kW (19,415hp) 14.7kn MAN-B&W 7S60MC 1 x 2 Stroke 7 Cy. 600 x 2292 14280kW (19415bhp) (made 2010) Hudong Heavy Machinery Co Ltd-China AuxGen: 3 x 720kW a.c Fuel: 140.0 (d.f.) 2840.0 (r.f.)
8604656 *EHWX* VI-5-10078	**TOTOROTA** **Perez Maya SL** - SatCom: Inmarsat C 422455810 *Vigo* *Spain* MMSI: 224558000 Official number: 3-1078/	**553** 166 268	Class: (BV)	**1989**-12 **Hijos de J. Barreras S.A. — Vigo** Yd No: 1498 Loa 36.50 Br ex 8.43 Dght 3.607 Lbp 31.53 Br md 8.30 Dpth 5.82 Welded, 1 dk	**(B11B2FV) Fishing Vessel** Ins: 255	**1 oil engine** with flexible couplings & dr geared to sc. shaft driving 1 CP propeller Total Power: 640kW (870hp) 11.0kn Deutz SBA6M528 1 x 4 Stroke 6 Cy. 220 x 280 640kW (870bhp) Hijos de J Barreras SA-Spain Fuel: 145.0 (d.f.)
9156735 *JFCM* TT1-11	**TOTTORI MARU No. 1** **Tottori Prefecture** - *Tottori, Tottori* *Japan* MMSI: 431920000 Official number: 131797	*199* - 172		**1997**-02 **Niigata Engineering Co Ltd — Niigata NI** Yd No: 2318 Loa 43.00 (BB) Br ex - Dght 3.164 Lbp 35.00 Br md 7.60 Dpth 3.30 Welded, 1 dk	**(B11A2FS) Stern Trawler** Ins: 16	**1 oil engine** with clutches, flexible couplings & sr geared to sc. shaft driving 1 CP propeller Total Power: 1,103kW (1,500hp) 14.5kn Niigata 6MG25HX 1 x 4 Stroke 6 Cy. 250 x 350 1103kW (1500bhp) Niigata Engineering Co Ltd-Japan AuxGen: 2 x 200kW 225V 60Hz a.c Thrusters: 1 Thwart. CP thruster (f) Fuel: 73.0 (d.f.)
9667966 *JD3528* -	**TOU SHOU MARU** - - *Shunan, Yamaguchi* *Japan* Official number: 141937	*353* - 692	Class: FA	**2013**-06 **Shitanoe Shipbuilding Co Ltd — Usuki OT** Yd No: 1318 Loa 51.90 Br ex - Dght 3.600 Lbp - Br md 8.80 Dpth - Welded, 1 dk	**(A12A2TC) Chemical Tanker** Double Hull (13F) Liq: 460	**1 oil engine** reduction geared to sc. shaft driving 1 Propeller Total Power: 956kW (1,300hp) Yanmar 6N21A-UW 1 x 4 Stroke 6 Cy. 210 x 290 956kW (1300bhp) Yanmar Diesel Engine Co Ltd-Japan
7213979 *J7AJ3* -	**TOUAREG** *ex* Gard I *-2007* *ex* Bugsier 6 *-1972* **Societe Maritime de Remorquage et d'Assistance SARL (Somara)** - *Portsmouth* *Dominica* MMSI: 325268000 Official number: 50268	**246** 73 146	Class: (GL)	**1972**-11 **Schichau-Unterweser AG — Bremerhaven** Yd No: 1758 Loa 31.42 Br ex 9.22 Dght 3.731 Lbp 27.51 Br md 9.20 Dpth 4.32 Welded, 1 dk	**(B32A2ST) Tug** Ice Capable	**1 oil engine** driving 1 FP propeller Total Power: 1,471kW (2,000hp) 12.5kn Deutz SBV6M358 1 x 4 Stroke 6 Cy. 400 x 580 1471kW (2000bhp) Kloeckner Humboldt Deutz AG-West Germany
8818087 *6WCI* DAK 995	**TOUBA** *ex* Otlan *-1996* **Hispano Senegalaise de Peche SA (HISEPEC)** - *Dakar* *Senegal*	**139** 74 90	Class: BV	**1989**-10 **Astilleros y Talleres Ferrolanos S.A. (ASTAFERSA) — Ferrol** Yd No: 242 Loa 27.00 Br ex - Dght 3.520 Lbp 22.51 Br md 6.71 Dpth 3.61 Welded, 1 dk	**(B11B2FV) Fishing Vessel** Ins: 90	**1 oil engine** with clutches, flexible couplings & sr reverse geared to sc. shaft driving 1 FP propeller Total Power: 459kW (624hp) 10.9kn Caterpillar 3412TA 1 x Vee 4 Stroke 12 Cy. 137 x 152 459kW (624bhp) Caterpillar Inc-USA AuxGen: 1 x 72kW 380V d.c, 1 x 60kW 380V d.c
8901640 *CNA2292* -	**TOUBKAL** *ex* Flemming Sif *-2002* *ex* Sea-Land Honduras *-2001* *ex* Flemming Sif *-1994* **International Maritime Transport Corp (IMTC)** - *Casablanca* *Morocco* MMSI: 242505000	**8,908** 3,257 9,786	Class: NV	**1990**-12 **Orskov Christensens Staalskibsvaerft A/S — Frederikshavn** Yd No: 164 Loa 133.70 (BB) Br ex 22.98 Dght 7.613 Lbp 120.00 Br md 22.70 Dpth 11.30 Welded, 1 dk	**(A33A2CC) Container Ship (Fully Cellular)** TEU 976 C Ho 296 TEU C Dk 680 TEU incl 218 ref C. Compartments: 4 Cell Ho, ER 6 Ha: (12.6 x 12.9)Tappered (14.0 x 18.1)4 (12.6 x 18.1)ER Cranes: 2x40t Ice Capable	**1 oil engine** reduction geared to sc. shaft driving 1 CP propeller Total Power: 8,800kW (11,964hp) 17.2kn MaK 8M601AK 1 x 4 Stroke 8 Cy. 580 x 600 8800kW (11964bhp) Krupp MaK Maschinenbau GmbH-Kiel AuxGen: 1 x 1464kW a.c, 3 x 570kW a.c Thrusters: 1 Tunnel thruster (f); 1 Tunnel thruster (a)

IMO / Call sign	Ship / Owner	Tonnage	Class	Builder / Dimensions	Type	Machinery
7033757 - -	**TOUCAN** **Continental Cement Ltd** -	*175* - -	Class: (BV)	**1970 Soc Industrielle et Commerciale de Consts Navales (SICCNa) — St-Malo** Yd No: 116 Loa 26.62 Br ex 7.93 Dght 3.429 Lbp 23.17 Br md 7.50 Dpth 4.09 Welded, 1 dk	**(B32A2ST) Tug**	**1 oil engine** reverse reduction geared to sc. shaft driving 1 FP propeller Total Power: 1,030kW (1,400hp) 11.0kn MaK 6M452AK 1 x 4 Stroke 6 Cy. 320 x 450 1030kW (1400bhp) Atlas MaK Maschinenbau GmbH-Kiel
9531002 *V4DD*	**TOUCAN** *ex* Orion T1601 *-2008* **World Wide Equipment St Lucia Ltd** World Wide Equipment Sales & Rental Support BV *Basseterre* *St Kitts & Nevis* MMSI: 341736000 Official number: SKN 1001736	**205** 62 179	Class: GL (NK)	**2008-10 Far East Shipyard Co Sdn Bhd — Sibu** Yd No: 43 Loa 26.00 Br ex - Dght 3.000 Lbp 23.59 Br md 8.00 Dpth 3.65 Welded, 1 dk	**(B32A2ST) Tug**	**2 oil engines** reduction geared to sc. shafts driving 2 Propellers Total Power: 1,220kW (1,658hp) Yanmar 6AYM-ETE 2 x 4 Stroke 6 Cy. 155 x 180 each-610kW (829bhp) Yanmar Diesel Engine Co Ltd-Japan
9105023 *C6NR5* -	**TOUCAN ARROW** **Gearbulk Shipowning Ltd** Gearbulk Ltd SatCom: Inmarsat C 430949710 *Nassau* *Bahamas* MMSI: 309497000 Official number: 727496	**35,998** 15,797 55,918 T/cm 58.1	Class: NV	**1996-06 Dalian New Shipbuilding Heavy Industries Co Ltd — Dalian LN** Yd No: BC460-1 Loa 199.70 (BB) Br ex 32.20 Dght 13.518 Lbp 192.00 Br md 32.20 Dpth 19.30 Welded, 1 dk	**(A31A2GO) Open Hatch Cargo Ship** Double Sides Entire Compartment Length Grain: 61,337 TEU 1788 Compartments: 10 Ho, ER 10 Ha: (13.2 x 18.0)7 (13.2 x 27.4)2 (13.2 x 23.0)ER Gantry cranes: 2x40t	**1 oil engine** driving 1 FP propeller Total Power: 11,520kW (15,663hp) 14.2kn B&W 6L60MC 1 x 2 Stroke 6 Cy. 600 x 1944 11520kW (15663bhp) Dalian Marine Diesel Works-China AuxGen: 3 x 912kW 220/440V 60Hz a.c Thrusters: 1 Tunnel thruster (f)
8886125 - -	**TOUCAN ONE** *ex* Sligo Bay *-2001* **Foyle Cruise Line Ltd** -	*207* 74 -		**1989 in the U.S.S.R.** Loa - Br ex - Dght - Lbp 32.93 Br md 6.50 Dpth 2.60 Welded, 1 dk	**(A37B2PS) Passenger Ship**	**2 oil engines** driving 2 FP propellers Total Power: 440kW (598hp) 11.0kn Russkiy 2 x 4 Stroke each-220kW (299bhp) Mashinostroitelnyy Zavod"Russkiy-Dizel"-Leningrad
9091521 *V7HX9* -	**TOUCH** *ex* T. Bone *-2003* **2858-1965 Quebec Inc** *Bikini* *Marshall Islands* MMSI: 538080017 Official number: 80017	**260** 78 185		**1987-01 in the United States of America** Loa 36.50 Br ex - Dght 2.430 Lbp - Br md 7.62 Dpth 4.40 Welded, 1 dk	**(X11A2YP) Yacht** Hull Material: Aluminium Alloy Passengers: cabins: 4; berths: 8	**2 oil engines** driving 2 Propellers Total Power: 1,440kW (1,958hp) 11.0kn M.T.U. 2 x 4 Stroke each-720kW (979bhp) Detroit Diesel Corporation-Detroit, Mi
9382281 *WDE2561* -	**TOUCHDOWN** **GulfMark Americas Inc** - *New Orleans, LA* *United States of America* MMSI: 367326550 Official number: 1204682	**1,691** 507 1,686	Class: AB	**2008-02 Bollinger Machine Shop & Shipyard, Inc. — Lockport, La** Yd No: 526 Loa 68.23 Br ex - Dght 4.300 Lbp 65.27 Br md 14.02 Dpth 5.50 Welded, 1 dk	**(B21A2OS) Platform Supply Ship** Passengers: cabins: 6	**3 diesel electric oil engines** driving 2 gen. each 1235kW 480V a.c 1 gen. of 435kW 480V a.c Connecting to 3 elec. motors each (843kW) driving 3 Z propellers Fixed unit only Total Power: 3,364kW (4,575hp) 10.5kn Cummins KTA-19-M 1 x 4 Stroke 6 Cy. 159 x 159 380kW (517bhp) Cummins Engine Co Inc-USA Cummins KTA-50-M2 2 x Vee 4 Stroke 16 Cy. 159 x 159 each-1492kW (2029bhp) Cummins Engine Co Inc-USA Thrusters: 2 Tunnel thruster (f) Fuel: 461.0 (r.f.)
9300635 *YJUL8* -	**TOUCHET TIDE** **Gulf Fleet Middle East Ltd** Tidewater Marine International Inc *Port Vila* *Vanuatu* MMSI: 576970000 Official number: 1603	**1,868** 588 1,952	Class: AB	**2004-11 Pan-United Marine Ltd — Singapore** Yd No: 150 Loa 64.80 Br ex 16.05 Dght 4.900 Lbp 63.00 Br md 16.00 Dpth 5.80 Welded, 1 dk	**(B21B20A) Anchor Handling Tug Supply**	**2 oil engines** reduction geared to sc. shafts driving 2 CP propellers Total Power: 5,280kW (7,178hp) 13.0kn MaK 8M25 2 x 4 Stroke 8 Cy. 255 x 400 each-2640kW (3589bhp) Caterpillar Motoren GmbH & Co. KG-Germany AuxGen: 2 x 370kW a.c, 2 x 800kW a.c Thrusters: 1 Tunnel thruster (f) Fuel: 510.0
8662517 *E5U2733* -	**TOUCHSTONE** *ex* Lisa III *-2013* *ex* Spirit of Colleen *-2009* **Eagle Crown Holdings Ltd** KK Superyachts *Avatiu* *Cook Islands* MMSI: 518786000 Official number: 1822	**184** 55 108	Class: BV	**2006-08 Cantiere Navale Arno Srl — Pisa** Yd No: 34/06 Loa 34.11 Br ex - Dght 1.200 Lbp 28.10 Br md 7.35 Dpth 3.75 Bonded, 1 dk	**(X11A2YP) Yacht** Hull Material: Reinforced Plastic	**3 oil engines** reduction geared to sc. shafts driving 3 Water jets Total Power: 4,413kW (6,000hp) M.T.U. 16V2000M91 3 x Vee 4 Stroke 16 Cy. 130 x 150 each-1471kW (2000bhp) MTU Friedrichshafen GmbH-Friedrichshafen AuxGen: 2 x 45kW 50Hz a.c
8615760 *5VAO8* -	**TOUEI MARU** *ex* Tenjin Maru No. 23 *-2004* *ex* Shinriki Maru No. 18 *-1993* **Jin Zhi Ship-Repairing Co Ltd** Dalian Fengshun International Shipping Co Ltd *Lome* *Togo* MMSI: 671118000	**2,135** 1,230 3,628	Class: UM	**1987-01 K.K. Matsuura Zosensho — Osakikamijima** Yd No: 333 Converted From: Grab Dredger-2004 Loa 89.43 (BB) Br ex 13.00 Dght 5.200 Lbp 83.85 Br md 13.00 Dpth 6.95 Welded, 2 dks	**(A31A2GX) General Cargo Ship** Single Hull Grain: 4,526; Bale: 4,164 Compartments: 2 Ho, ER 2 Ha: 2 (19.8 x 9.7)ER	**1 oil engine** with clutches & reverse reduction geared to sc. shaft driving 1 FP propeller Total Power: 736kW (1,001hp) 10.0kn Makita LN31L 1 x 4 Stroke 6 Cy. 310 x 600 736kW (1001bhp) Makita Diesel Co Ltd-Japan Thrusters: 1 Thwart. FP thruster (f)
8402553 AL 38	**TOUFIK** **Government of The Democratic & Popular Republic of Algeria (Institut Technologique des Peches et Aquaculture)** - *Alger* *Algeria*	**264** - -	Class: (BV)	**1985-04 B.V. Scheepswerf Damen Bergum — Bergum** (Hull) **1985-04 B.V. Scheepswerf Damen — Gorinchem** Yd No: 3604 Loa 26.00 Br ex - Dght 2.552 Lbp 23.77 Br md 7.00 Dpth 3.40 Welded, 1 dk	**(B12D2FR) Fishery Research Vessel**	**1 oil engine** with clutches & sr reverse geared to sc. shaft driving 1 FP propeller Total Power: 588kW (799hp) MAN 5L20/27 1 x 4 Stroke 5 Cy. 200 x 270 588kW (799bhp) MAN B&W Diesel GmbH-Augsburg AuxGen: 1 x 32kW 380V a.c
6904296 - -	**TOUFIK MASSRY** *ex* Mopa Marstal *-1994* *ex* Jette Wonsild *-1987* - -	**880** 353 1,221	Class: (BV)	**1968-03 Frederikshavn Vaerft og Tordok A/S — Frederikshavn** Yd No: 284 Loa 60.58 Br ex 10.29 Dght 4.217 Lbp 55.28 Br md 10.19 Dpth 5.74 Welded, 2 dks	**(A13B2TP) Products Tanker** Liq: 1,446; Liq (Oil): 1,446 Cargo Heating Coils Compartments: 12 Ta, ER Ice Capable	**1 oil engine** driving 1 CP propeller Total Power: 588kW (799hp) 10.5kn MaK 6M451AK 1 x 4 Stroke 6 Cy. 320 x 450 588kW (799bhp) Atlas MaK Maschinenbau GmbH-Kiel AuxGen: 2 x 137kW 380V 50Hz a.c, 1 x 39kW 380V 50Hz a.c Fuel: 59.0 (d.f.) (Heating Coils) 3.5pd
9037563 *JIZT* S01-1095	**TOUHOU** *ex* Musashi *-2012* *ex* Showa Maru No. 11 *-2001* **YK Shoei** SatCom: Inmarsat A 1204652 *Kesennuma, Miyagi* *Japan* MMSI: 431602049 Official number: 131559	*488* - -		**1991-10 KK Kanasashi — Shizuoka SZ** Yd No: 3277 Loa 56.70 (BB) Br ex 8.83 Dght 3.450 Lbp 49.90 Br md 8.80 Dpth 3.84 Welded	**(B11B2FV) Fishing Vessel** Ins: 527	**1 oil engine** with clutches, flexible couplings & sr reverse geared to sc. shaft driving 1 FP propeller Total Power: 1,177kW (1,600hp) Akasaka K31FD 1 x 4 Stroke 6 Cy. 310 x 530 1177kW (1600bhp) Akasaka Tekkosho KK (Akasaka DieselLtd)-Japan
8801852 *XUBS8* -	**TOUJI MARU** *ex* Nichiju Maru *-2002* **Eastern Sunocean Shipping Co Ltd** Huawei Shipping Co Ltd *Phnom Penh* *Cambodia* MMSI: 515130000 Official number: 0289055	*1,461* 724 1,401	Class: UB	**1987-11 Yamanaka Zosen K.K. — Imabari** Yd No: 358 Loa 76.54 (BB) Br ex - Dght 3.774 Lbp 71.02 Br md 12.51 Dpth 6.61 Welded, 2 dks	**(A31A2GX) General Cargo Ship** Compartments: 1 Ho, ER 1 Ha: ER	**1 oil engine** with clutches, flexible couplings & reverse reduction geared to sc. shaft driving 1 FP propeller Total Power: 1,177kW (1,600hp) Hanshin 6LU32G 1 x 4 Stroke 6 Cy. 320 x 510 1177kW (1600bhp) The Hanshin Diesel Works Ltd-Japan
9687382 *JD3517* -	**TOUKOU MARU NO. 8** **KK Fujii Sekiyu** *Tokyo* *Japan* Official number: 141924	*237* - 591		**2013-05 Imura Zosen K.K. — Komatsushima** Yd No: 353 Loa 44.13 Br ex - Dght 3.400 Lbp - Br md 8.50 Dpth - Welded, 1 dk	**(A13B2TP) Products Tanker** Double Hull (13F)	**1 oil engine** reduction geared to sc. shafts driving 1 Propeller Total Power: 1,370kW (1,863hp) Yanmar 6EY22 1 x 4 Stroke 6 Cy. 220 x 320 1370kW (1863bhp) Yanmar Diesel Engine Co Ltd-Japan
7829326 *5VBO2* -	**TOULON** *ex* Robin I *-2005* *ex* Princess Roby *-2004* *ex* Sammarina 1 *-2001* *ex* Foisor *-1994* **Arcadia Shipping Ltd** Vernon Shipping Ltd SatCom: Inmarsat C 467126310 *Lome* *Togo* MMSI: 671263000	**5,983** 3,531 8,750	Class: UA (RS) (PR) (GL) (RN)	**1978-01 Santierul Naval Braila — Braila** Yd No: 1185 Loa 130.75 (BB) Br ex - Dght 8.102 Lbp 121.90 Br md 17.70 Dpth 10.20 Welded, 1 dk & S dk	**(A31A2GX) General Cargo Ship** Grain: 11,980; Bale: 11,067 Compartments: 4 Ho, ER 4 Ha: (11.9 x 5.9)3 (13.6 x 9.9)ER Cranes: 4x5t Ice Capable	**1 oil engine** driving 1 FP propeller Total Power: 4,487kW (6,101hp) 13.0kn Sulzer 5RD68 1 x 2 Stroke 5 Cy. 680 x 1250 4487kW (6101bhp) Tvornica Dizel Motora '3 Maj'-Yugoslavia AuxGen: 3 x 250kW 400V 50Hz a.c Fuel: 624.0

6729206 *TO2092* -	**TOULONNAIS XVI** *ex* Diligent *-1996* **Societe Nouvelle de Remorquage et de Travaux Maritime** - *Toulon* *France* MMSI: 227001780 Official number: 275620	*192* - -	Class: (BV)	**1967 Ziegler Freres — Dunkerque** Yd No: 160 Loa 29.01 Br ex 8.51 Dght 2.510 Lbp 27.01 Br md 8.01 Dpth 6.30 Welded, 1 dk	**(B32A2ST) Tug**	**1 oil engine** geared to sc. shaft driving 1 Directional propeller Total Power: 956kW (1,300hp) 12.5kn Crepelle 8SN1 1 x 4 Stroke 8 Cy. 260 x 280 956kW (1300bhp) (new engine 1970) Crepelle et Cie-France AuxGen: 1 x 48kW 125V d.c, 1 x 20kW 125V d.c Fuel: 34.5 (d.f.)
8521139 - -	**TOULONNAIS XVII** *ex* Danimarca *-2010* **Societe Nouvelle de Remorquage et de Travaux Maritime** - *Toulon* *France*	**245** 73 140	Class: BV (RI)	**1988-02 Cant. Navale "Ferrari" S.p.A. — La Spezia** Yd No: 55 Loa 26.85 Br ex 9.56 Dght 3.200 Lbp 26.02 Br md 9.10 Dpth - Welded, 1 dk	**(B32A2ST) Tug**	**2 oil engines** with clutches, flexible couplings & sr geared to sc. shaft driving 2 Directional propellers Total Power: 2,060kW (2,800hp) 10.8kn Deutz SBV6M628 2 x 4 Stroke 6 Cy. 240 x 280 each-1030kW (1400bhp) (made 1986) Kloeckner Humboldt Deutz AG-West Germany AuxGen: 2 x 38kW 220/380V 50Hz a.c Fuel: 37.5 (d.f.) 5.5pd
9285316 *WDD3647* -	**TOULOUSE** - **GulfMark Americas Inc** - *New Orleans, LA* *United States of America* MMSI: 367039840 Official number: 1169977	**2,045** 797 3,463	Class: AB	**2005-06 Bender Shipbuilding & Repair Co Inc — Mobile AL** Yd No: 7429 Lengthened-2013 Loa 76.81 Br ex - Dght 4.900 Lbp 74.42 Br md 16.50 Dpth 5.80 Welded, 1 dk	**(B21A2OS) Platform Supply Ship**	**3 diesel electric oil engines** driving 2 gen. each 1825kW 480V a.c 1 gen. of 910kW 480V a.c Connecting to 2 elec. motors each (1566kW) driving 2 Z propellers Total Power: 4,560kW (6,199hp) 12.5kn Cummins KTA-38-M 1 x Vee 4 Stroke 12 Cy. 159 x 159 910kW (1237bhp) Cummins Engine Co Inc-USA Cummins QSK60-M 2 x Vee 4 Stroke 16 Cy. 159 x 190 each-1825kW (2481bhp) Cummins Engine Co Inc-USA Thrusters: 2 Thwart. CP thruster (f) Fuel: 728.0 (d.f.)
7395179 - -	**TOUMZIT** *ex* Diana Rosal *-1987* **Societe Shrimps Fisheries** - *Morocco*	*286* 133 -	Class: (BV)	**1975-05 Ast. de Huelva S.A. — Huelva** Yd No: 61 Loa 38.49 Br ex 7.27 Dght - Lbp 33.28 Br md 7.24 Dpth 3.89 Welded, 1 dk	**(B11A2FT) Trawler**	**1 oil engine** driving 1 FP propeller Total Power: 861kW (1,171hp) 10.5kn S.K.L. 8NVD48A-2 1 x 4 Stroke 8 Cy. 320 x 480 861kW (1171bhp) VEB Schwermaschinenbau "KarlLiebknecht" (SKL)-Magdeburg Fuel: 125.0 (d.f.)
9554468 *JD3061* -	**TOUNAN MARU** - **Tonan Kaiun KK** - *Osaka, Osaka* *Japan* MMSI: 431001357 Official number: 141236	*741* - 1,725		**2010-04 Koa Sangyo KK — Marugame KG** Yd No: 642 Loa 71.95 Br ex - Dght 4.750 Lbp 67.00 Br md 11.30 Dpth 5.50 Welded, 1 dk	**(A12A2TC) Chemical Tanker** Double Hull (13F) Liq: 887 2 Cargo Pump (s): 2x250m³/hr	**1 oil engine** geared to sc. shaft driving 1 FP propeller Total Power: 1,323kW (1,799hp) Hanshin LA28G 1 x 4 Stroke 6 Cy. 280 x 590 1323kW (1799bhp) The Hanshin Diesel Works Ltd-Japan
9364112 *EPBY7* -	**TOUR 2** *ex* Tour *-2012* **Auris Marine Co Ltd** IranoHind Shipping Co Ltd *Iran* MMSI: 422038400	**81,295** 52,045 158,817 T/cm 118.2	Class: (RS) (BV) (NV)	**2007-11 Hyundai Heavy Industries Co Ltd — Ulsan** Yd No: 1878 Loa 274.47 (BB) Br ex 48.04 Dght 17.072 Lbp 264.00 Br md 48.00 Dpth 23.10 Welded, 1 dk	**(A13A2TV) Crude Oil Tanker** Double Hull (13F) Liq: 167,931; Liq (Oil): 167,931 Cargo Heating Coils Compartments: 12 Wing Ta, 2 Wing Slop Ta, ER 3 Cargo Pump (s): 3x4000m³/hr Manifold: Bow/CM: 138m	**1 oil engine** driving 1 FP propeller Total Power: 16,860kW (22,923hp) 15.7kn MAN-B&W 6S70ME-C 1 x 2 Stroke 6 Cy. 700 x 2800 16860kW (22923bhp) Hyundai Heavy Industries Co Ltd-South Korea AuxGen: 3 x a.c Fuel: 172.0 (d.f.) 3500.0 (r.f.)
9034731 *9HBW8* -	**TOUR MARGAUX** - **Eitzen Chemical (Singapore) Pte Ltd** Eitzen Chemical (Spain) SA *Valletta* *Malta* MMSI: 215819000 Official number: 92244771	**5,499** 2,053 8,674 T/cm 17.0	Class: AB (BV)	**1992-12 YVC Ysselwerf B.V. — Capelle a/d IJssel** Yd No: 257 Conv to DH-2006 Loa 113.64 (BB) Br ex 17.70 Dght 8.000 Lbp 107.44 Br md 17.50 Dpth 11.20 Welded, 1 dk	**(A12B2TR) Chemical/Products Tanker** Double Hull (13F) Liq: 7,947; Liq (Oil): 9,516 Cargo Heating Coils Compartments: 11 Ta, 20 Wing Ta, 1 Slop Ta, ER 15 Cargo Pump (s): 6x150m³/hr, 5x100m³/hr, 2x200m³/hr, 2x120m³/hr Manifold: Bow/CM: 59.9m	**1 oil engine** reduction geared to sc. shaft driving 1 CP propeller Total Power: 3,640kW (4,949hp) 13.3kn Normo BRM-9 1 x 4 Stroke 9 Cy. 320 x 360 3640kW (4949bhp) Bergen Diesel AS-Norway AuxGen: 3 x 370kW 380/220V 50Hz a.c Thrusters: 1 Tunnel thruster (f) Fuel: 80.0 (d.f.) 626.0 (r.f.)
9171474 *9V9183* -	**TOUR POMEROL** - **Eitzen Chemical Invest (Singapore) Pte Ltd** Eitzen Chemical (Spain) SA *Singapore* *Singapore* MMSI: 563385000 Official number: 396759	**7,274** 2,184 10,373 T/cm 19.9	Class: AB (BV)	**1998-09 YVC Ysselwerf B.V. — Capelle a/d IJssel** Yd No: 271 Loa 119.99 (BB) Br ex 19.50 Dght 8.310 Lbp 113.75 Br md 19.25 Dpth 13.00 Welded, 1 dk	**(A12B2TR) Chemical/Products Tanker** Double Hull (13F) Liq: 10,503; Liq (Oil): 10,503 Cargo Heating Coils Compartments: 7 Ta, 24 Wing Ta, ER 33 Cargo Pump (s): 8x200m³/hr, 23x120m³/hr, 1x200m³/hr, 1x150m³/hr Manifold: Bow/CM: 61.4m	**1 oil engine** with flexible couplings & sr gearedto sc. shaft driving 1 CP propeller Total Power: 5,280kW (7,179hp) 15.0kn Wartsila 8L38 1 x 4 Stroke 8 Cy. 380 x 475 5280kW (7179bhp) Wartsila NSD Nederland BV-Netherlands AuxGen: 2 x 570kW 440V 60Hz a.c Thrusters: 1 Thwart. CP thruster (f) Fuel: 951.4 (d.f.) (Heating Coils) 131.0 (r.f.) 25.0pd
9134165 *VRXV4* -	**TOURAINE** *ex* Antwerpen Venture *-1997* **EXMAR Gas Shipping Ltd** Exmar Shipmanagement NV *Hong Kong* *Hong Kong* MMSI: 477171000 Official number: HK-0865	**25,337** 7,602 30,309 T/cm 46.4	Class: BV (NV)	**1996-11 Hitachi Zosen Corp — Nagasu KM** Yd No: 4889 Loa 195.94 (BB) Br ex - Dght 10.070 Lbp 186.00 Br md 29.40 Dpth 17.00 Welded, 1 dk	**(A11B2TG) LPG Tanker** Double Bottom Entire Compartment Length Liq (Gas): 38,484 3 x Gas Tank (s); 3 independent pri horizontal 6 Cargo Pump (s): 6x500m³/hr Manifold: Bow/CM: 98m	**1 oil engine** driving 1 FP propeller Total Power: 10,525kW (14,310hp) 19.3kn B&W 6S60MC 1 x 2 Stroke 6 Cy. 600 x 2292 10525kW (14310bhp) Hitachi Zosen Corp-Japan AuxGen: 3 x 850kW 450/220V 50Hz a.c Thrusters: 1 Thwart. CP thruster (f) Fuel: 280.0 (d.f.) (Heating Coils) 2078.0 (r.f.) 44.0pd
9478327 *EPAH5* -	**TOURAJ** *ex* Azuma Maru *-2008* **Iranian Oil Terminals Co** - *Bushehr* *Iran* MMSI: 422888000 Official number: 2.7465	**499** 149 291	Class: AS (LR) (NK) ✠ Classed LR until 13/10/09	**2008-07 Kanagawa Zosen — Kobe** Yd No: 581 Loa 34.10 Br ex 12.02 Dght 3.800 Lbp 29.30 Br md 12.00 Dpth 4.90 Welded, 1 dk	**(B32A2ST) Tug** Passengers: 8	**2 oil engines** reduction geared to sc. shafts driving 2 FP propellers Total Power: 3,676kW (4,998hp) Niigata 6L28HX 2 x 4 Stroke 6 Cy. 280 x 370 each-1838kW (2499bhp) Niigata Engineering Co Ltd-Japan AuxGen: 3 x 160kW 445V 50Hz a.c Thrusters: 1 Thwart. CP thruster (f) Fuel: 185.0 (d.f.)
8841371 *ITFP* -	**TOURIST FERRY BOAT PRIMO** - **Pozzuoli Ferries Srl** Medmar Navi SpA *Naples* *Italy* MMSI: 247222800 Official number: 161	*820* 469 -	Class: RI	**1968-07 D. C. Anastassiades & A. Ch. Tsortanides — Perama** Yd No: 51 Loa 82.71 Br ex 12.47 Dght 2.315 Lbp 73.04 Br md 10.21 Dpth 3.47 Welded, 1 dk	**(A36A2PR) Passenger/Ro-Ro Ship (Vehicles)** Passengers: unberthed: 150	**2 oil engines** driving 2 FP propellers Total Power: 2,210kW (3,004hp) Nohab F26R 2 x 4 Stroke 6 Cy. 250 x 300 each-1105kW (1502bhp) Nydqvist & Holm AB-Sweden AuxGen: 3 x 96kW 380V 50Hz a.c
8841383 *ITFQ* -	**TOURIST FERRY BOAT SECONDO** - **Medmar Navi SpA** - *Naples* *Italy* MMSI: 247049100 Official number: 166	*496* 249 -	Class: RI	**1969-03 D. C. Anastassiades & A. Ch. Tsortanides — Perama** Yd No: 52 Loa 82.71 Br ex 12.47 Dght 2.315 Lbp 73.04 Br md 10.20 Dpth 3.47 Welded, 1 dk	**(A36A2PR) Passenger/Ro-Ro Ship (Vehicles)**	**2 oil engines** driving 2 FP propellers Total Power: 2,210kW (3,004hp) Nohab F26R 2 x 4 Stroke 6 Cy. 250 x 300 each-1105kW (1502bhp) AB NOHAB-Sweden
8841395 *IQAQ* -	**TOURIST FERRY BOAT TERZO** *ex* Agios Sostis II *-1986* **Tra Spe Mar Srl** - *Naples* *Italy* MMSI: 247048900 Official number: 1912	*438* 96 212	Class: RI	**1967-03 Bekris & Eleftheropoulos — Piareus** Loa 58.35 Br ex 9.02 Dght 1.471 Lbp 53.25 Br md 9.00 Dpth 1.99 Welded, 1 dk	**(A36A2PR) Passenger/Ro-Ro Ship (Vehicles)** Passengers: unberthed: 300 Cars: 45	**2 oil engines** geared to sc. shafts driving 2 FP propellers Total Power: 1,280kW (1,740hp) 12.8kn Deutz SBA6M528 2 x 4 Stroke 6 Cy. 220 x 280 each-640kW (870bhp) (new engine 1975) Kloeckner Humboldt Deutz AG-West Germany

IMO / Call sign	Name / Owner	Tonnage	Class	Build / Dimensions	Type	Machinery
8219499 *FIGZ* CC 545762	**TOURMALET** **Sarl Klipper** Tourmalet SatCom: Inmarsat C 422738410 *Concarneau* *France* MMSI: 227384000 Official number: 545762	*222* 79 300	Class: BV	**1983-12 Con. Mec. de Normandie — Cherbourg** Yd No: 34/10 Loa 34.02 Br ex 8.31 Dght 3.701 Lbp 30.99 Br md 7.90 Dpth 6.41 Welded, 1 dk	**(B11A2FS) Stern Trawler** Ins: 180 Compartments: 1 Ho, ER 2 Ha:	**1 oil engine** with clutches, flexible couplings & sr geared to sc. shaft driving 1 CP propeller Total Power: 588kW (799hp) Crepelle 6PSN3 1 x 4 Stroke 6 Cy. 260 x 280 588kW (799bhp) Crepelle et Cie-France AuxGen: 1 x 72kW 380V 50Hz a.c, 1 x 56kW 380V 50Hz a.c Fuel: 50.0 (d.f.) 3.0pd
7430527 *AUGH* -	**TOURMALINE** *ex* Mansal 41 *-2000* *ex* Osa Jaguar *-1988* **Samson Maritime Ltd** - *Mumbai* *India* MMSI: 419053400 Official number: 4014	**1,011** 304 1,135	Class: IR NV (LR) (GL) ✠ Classed LR until 22/1/82	**1976-12 Taiwan Shipbuilding Corp — Keelung** Yd No: N-075 Loa 56.70 Br ex 13.52 Dght 4.193 Lbp 51.49 Br md 13.11 Dpth 4.80 Welded, 1 dk	**(B21B20A) Anchor Handling Tug Supply** Compartments: 16 Ta, ER Derricks: 1x8t	**2 oil engines** reverse reduction geared to sc. shafts driving 2 FP propellers Total Power: 2,574kW (3,500hp) 13.3kn Deutz SBA12M528 2 x Vee 4 Stroke 12 Cy. 220 x 280 each-1287kW (1750bhp) Kloeckner Humboldt Deutz AG-West Germany AuxGen: 3 x 220kW 440V 60Hz a.c Thrusters: 1 Thwart. FP thruster (f) Fuel: 358.0 (d.f.)
9363742 *9VGK8* -	**TOURMALINE** - **CH Offshore Ltd** Chuan Hup Agencies Pte Ltd *Singapore* *Singapore* MMSI: 565185000 Official number: 391339	**2,442** 796 2,435	Class: AB	**2006-12 Universal Shipbuilding Corp — Yokohama KN (Keihin Shipyard)** Yd No: 0024 Loa 68.00 Br ex - Dght 6.000 Lbp 61.45 Br md 16.40 Dpth 7.20 Welded, 1 dk	**(B21B20A) Anchor Handling Tug Supply**	**2 oil engines** reduction geared to sc. shafts driving 2 CP propellers Total Power: 9,000kW (12,236hp) Wartsila 9L32 2 x 4 Stroke 9 Cy. 320 x 400 each-4500kW (6118bhp) Wartsila Finland Oy-Finland AuxGen: 2 x 320kW 440V 60Hz a.c, 2 x 1800kW 440V 60Hz a.c Thrusters: 2 Thwart. CP thruster (f); 1 Thwart. CP thruster (a) Fuel: 828.2 (r.f.)
9496848 *VRKU8* -	**TOURSHEN** - **Tourshen Shipping Co Ltd** Global Marine Ship Management Co Ltd *Hong Kong* *Hong Kong* MMSI: 477077200 Official number: HK-3563	**3,729** 1,722 4,627	Class: CC	**2012-06 Yangzhou Huamei Shipbuilding Co Ltd — Yizheng JS** Yd No: JHY4800-06 Loa 99.90 Br ex 15.83 Dght 5.580 Lbp 96.00 Br md 15.80 Dpth 7.30 Welded, 1 dk	**(A31A2GX) General Cargo Ship** Grain: 6,176 TEU 255 C Ho 129 TEU C Dk 126 TEU Compartments: 2 Ho, ER 2 Ha: (32.5 x 12.8)ER (31.5 x 12.8) Cranes: 1x22.5t Ice Capable	**1 oil engine** reduction geared to sc. shafts driving 1 Propeller Total Power: 2,320kW (3,154hp) 12.4kn Hyundai Himsen 8H25/33P 1 x 4 Stroke 8 Cy. 250 x 330 2320kW (3154bhp) Hyundai Heavy Industries Co Ltd-South Korea AuxGen: 2 x 220kW 440V a.c, 1 x 440kW 440V a.c
9496836 *VRKU7* -	**TOURXIN** *launched as* Sally *-2012* **Tourxin Shipping Co Ltd** Global Marine Ship Management Co Ltd *Hong Kong* *Hong Kong* MMSI: 477077300 Official number: HK-3562	**3,729** 1,722 4,621	Class: CC	**2012-06 Yangzhou Huamei Shipbuilding Co Ltd — Yizheng JS** Yd No: JHY4800-05 Loa 99.90 Br ex 15.83 Dght 5.580 Lbp 96.00 Br md 15.80 Dpth 7.30 Welded, 1 dk	**(A31A2GX) General Cargo Ship** Grain: 6,176 TEU 255 C Ho 129 TEU C Dk 126 TEU. Compartments: 2 Ho, ER 2 Ha: (32.5 x 12.8)ER (31.5 x 12.8) Cranes: 1x22.5t Ice Capable	**1 oil engine** reduction geared to sc. shafts driving 1 Propeller Total Power: 2,320kW (3,154hp) 12.4kn Hyundai Himsen 8H25/33P 1 x 4 Stroke 8 Cy. 250 x 330 2320kW (3154bhp) Hyundai Heavy Industries Co Ltd-South Korea AuxGen: 2 x 220kW 440V a.c, 1 x 400kW 440V a.c
9328900 *EPBS4* -	**TOUSKA** *ex* Adalia *-2012* *ex* Sahand *-2012* *launched as* Iran Sahand *-2008* **Mosakhar Darya Shipping Co PJS** Rahbaran Omid Darya Ship Management Co *Qeshm Island* *Iran* MMSI: 422032600	**54,851** 34,827 66,432	Class: (LR) (BV) ✠ Classed LR until 9/2/12	**2008-04 Hyundai Heavy Industries Co Ltd — Ulsan** Yd No: 1818 Loa 294.10 (BB) Br ex 32.25 Dght 13.500 Lbp 283.20 Br md 32.20 Dpth 21.80 Welded, 1 dk	**(A33A2CC) Container Ship (Fully Cellular)** TEU 4795 C Ho 2299 TEU C Dk 2496 incl 330 ref C. Compartments: ER, 6 Cell Ho 17 Ha: (12.6 x 23.0)ER 15 (12.6 x 28.2) (12.6 x 13.0)	**1 oil engine** driving 1 FP propeller Total Power: 41,040kW (55,798hp) 23.5kn MAN-B&W 9K90MC-C 1 x 2 Stroke 9 Cy. 900 x 2300 41040kW (55798bhp) Hyundai Heavy Industries Co Ltd-South Korea AuxGen: 4 x 1700kW 450V 60Hz a.c Boilers: e (ex.g.) 10.9kgf/cm² (10.7bar), WTAuxB (o.f.) 8.2kgf/cm² (8.0bar) Thrusters: 1 Thwart. CP thruster (f) Fuel: 489.0 (d.f.) 6415.9 (r.f.)
8817019 *V3RD2* -	**TOUSYOU MARU** *ex* Shokei Maru No. 3 *-2003* **Very Nice Ltd** Dalian Fengshun International Shipping Co Ltd *Belize City* *Belize* MMSI: 312635000 Official number: 060420677	**2,390** 1,257 3,999	Class: IT	**1988-09 Higaki Zosen K.K. — Imabari** Yd No: 361 Loa 89.13 Br ex 14.40 Dght 5.200 Lbp 68.00 Br md 14.40 Dpth 7.10 Welded, 1 dk	**(A24D2BA) Aggregates Carrier** Single Hull Grain: 1,274	**1 oil engine** driving 1 FP propeller Total Power: 1,471kW (2,000hp) 10.0kn Niigata 6M34AGT 1 x 4 Stroke 6 Cy. 340 x 620 1471kW (2000bhp) Niigata Engineering Co Ltd-Japan
9037484 *JG5096* -	**TOUWA MARU** - **KK Sky Shipping** - *Yokohama, Kanagawa* *Japan* Official number: 133129	*499* - 1,129	Class: NK	**1992-02 Fujishin Zosen K.K. — Kamo** Yd No: 573 Loa 65.52 (BB) Br ex - Dght 4.003 Lbp 60.30 Br md 10.00 Dpth 4.50 Welded, 1 dk	**(A12A2TC) Chemical Tanker** Liq: 1,230	**1 oil engine** with clutches & reverse geared to sc. shaft driving 1 FP propeller Total Power: 1,030kW (1,400hp) 12.2kn Akasaka K28R 1 x 4 Stroke 6 Cy. 280 x 480 1030kW (1400bhp) Akasaka Tekkosho KK (Akasaka DieselLtd)-Japan AuxGen: 2 x 120kW a.c Fuel: 60.0 (d.f.)
6910879 - -	**TOUYA** *ex* Fils De Grace *-2011* *ex* Sir Arthur- J *-2007* *ex* STM Vega *-2003* *ex* VSO Surveyor I *-1991* *ex* Directeur Generaal Bast *-1989* **Priceless Opportunities Ltd** - *London* *United Kingdom* Official number: 917112	**711** 213 1,075	Class: (GL) (BV)	**1969-03 E.J. Smit & Zoon's Scheepswerven N.V. — Westerbroek** Yd No: 790 Converted From: Cable-layer-2004 Loa 54.96 Br ex 9.48 Dght 3.000 Lbp 48.40 Br md 9.40 Dpth 4.47 Welded, 1 dk	**(X11A2YP) Yacht**	**2 oil engines** reduction geared to sc. shafts driving 2 FP propellers Total Power: 514kW (698hp) 10.6kn Bolnes 5DL75/475 2 x 2 Stroke 5 Cy. 190 x 350 each-257kW (349bhp) NV Machinefabriek 'Bolnes' v/h JHvan Cappellen-Netherlands AuxGen: 1 x 112kW 380V 50Hz a.c, 1 x 42kW 380V 50Hz a.c Thrusters: 1 Tunnel thruster (f) Fuel: 46.5
8871637 *LHTM* -	**TOVAK** *ex* Bunker Esso *-1979* **Henriksen Oljetransport AS** - *Stavanger* *Norway* MMSI: 257106400	**103** 53 -	Class: (BV)	**1958 D.W. Kremer Sohn — Elmshorn** Yd No: 1070 Lengthened-1985 Loa 32.67 Br ex 5.70 Dght 1.970 Lbp 30.95 Br md - Dpth 2.20 Welded, 1 dk	**(B35E2TF) Bunkering Tanker** Liq: 162; Liq (Oil): 162 Compartments: 3 Ta, ER	**1 oil engine** reduction geared to sc. shaft driving 1 FP propeller Total Power: 296kW (402hp) Scania DSI14 1 x Vee 4 Stroke 8 Cy. 127 x 140 296kW (402bhp) (new engine 1991) Saab Scania AB-Sweden AuxGen: 1 x 6kW 220V a.c
7027681 *UUVA* -	**TOVARISHCH** *ex* Gorch Fock *-1951* **Kherson State Marine Academy** - *Kherson* *Ukraine* Official number: 330013	*1,392* 230 292	Class: (RS)	**1933-06 Blohm & Voss KG auf Aktien — Hamburg** Yd No: 495 Loa 73.64 Br ex 12.02 Dght 5.230 Lbp 68.51 Br md - Dpth 7.55 Welded, 1 dk	**(X11B2QN) Sail Training Ship**	**1 oil engine** driving 1 FP propeller Total Power: 386kW (525hp) 7.0kn Skoda 6L275PN 1 x 4 Stroke 6 Cy. 275 x 360 386kW (525bhp) (made 1965, fitted 1968) CKD Praha-Praha
5362087 *LYSF* -	**TOVE** *ex* Leona *-2007* *ex* Lands-End *-2006* *ex* Kathrine Skjold *-1995* *ex* Dendit *-1990* *ex* Tistelon *-1982* **JSC 'Banginis' (UAB 'Banginis')** - SatCom: Inmarsat C 427734610 *Klaipeda* *Lithuania* MMSI: 277346000 Official number: 788	**296** 88 -	Class: PR (NV)	**1961 Bolsones Verft AS — Molde** Yd No: 179 Lengthened-1975 Loa 34.93 Br ex 6.71 Dght - Lbp 31.22 Br md 6.68 Dpth 5.55 Welded, 1 dk	**(B11B2FV) Fishing Vessel** 4 Ha: (0.9 x 0.9) (1.3 x 1.2)2 (0.7 x 1.1)ER Ice Capable	**1 oil engine** sr geared to sc. shaft driving 1 FP propeller Total Power: 485kW (659hp) Blackstone ERS8M 1 x 4 Stroke 8 Cy. 222 x 292 485kW (659bhp) Lister Blackstone Marine Ltd.-Dursley
9156175 *ZDHX3* -	**TOVE** *ex* Arcturus *-2007* *ex* HAV Arcturus *-2006* *ex* RMS Arcturus *-2004* *ex* Arcturus *-1996* **Vaagebulk II KS** Vaage Ship Management AS SatCom: Inmarsat C 423638710 *Gibraltar* *Gibraltar (British)* MMSI: 236387000	**1,864** 938 2,517	Class: GL	**1996-10 Slovenske Lodenice a.s. — Komarno** Yd No: 1504 Loa 82.35 (BB) Br ex 11.46 Dght 4.798 Lbp 79.82 Br md 11.35 Dpth 6.10 Welded, 1 dk	**(A31A2GX) General Cargo Ship** Double Hull Grain: 3,486 TEU 82 C.Ho 46/20' C.Dk 36/20' incl. 10 ref C. Compartments: 1 Ho, ER 1 Ha: (53.5 x 9.0)ER Ice Capable	**1 oil engine** with clutches, flexible couplings & sr reverse geared to sc. shaft driving 1 FP propeller Total Power: 1,350kW (1,835hp) 10.0kn Deutz SBV8M628 1 x 4 Stroke 8 Cy. 240 x 280 1350kW (1835bhp) Motoren Werke Mannheim AG (MWM)-Mannheim AuxGen: 3 x 75kW 220/380V 50Hz a.c Thrusters: 1 Thwart. FP thruster (f) Fuel: 120.0 (d.f.)

8648303 *OXIQ* S 350
TOVE HOLM
Peter Ole Holm
-
Skagen *Denmark*
Official number: H190

127
55
-

1958 I/S Mortensens Skibsbyggeri — Frederikshavn Yd No: UN 2
Loa 25.18 Br ex - Dght -
Lbp - Br md 5.80 Dpth 2.80
Welded, 1 dk

(B11B2FV) Fishing Vessel

1 oil engine driving 1 Propeller

9568342 *OZCA* FN 436
TOVE KAJGAARD
Lars Kajgaard
-
SatCom: Inmarsat C 422030715
Strandby *Denmark*
MMSI: 219013485
Official number: H1595

165
50
-

2009-06 **Vestvaerftet ApS — Hvide Sande**
Yd No: 279
Loa 22.00 (BB) Br ex - Dght -
Lbp - Br md 6.70 Dpth 5.96
Welded, 1 dk

(B11A2FS) Stern Trawler

1 oil engine geared to sc. shafts driving 1 CP propeller
Total Power: 299kW (407hp)
G.M. (Detroit Diesel) SERIES 60
1 x 4 Stroke 6 Cy. 106 x 168 299kW (407bhp)
Detroit Diesel Corporation-Detroit, Mi
AuxGen: 2 x 91kW a.c

8715546 *LEOT3* -
TOVE KNUTSEN
Knutsen Terminal Tanker AS
Knutsen OAS Shipping AS
SatCom: Inmarsat C 425790510
Haugesund *Norway (NIS)*
MMSI: 257905000

61,206
26,964
105,295
T/cm
96.0

Class: NV

1989-12 **Astilleros Espanoles SA (AESA) — Sestao** Yd No: 275
Converted From: Crude Oil Tanker-1992
Conv to DH-2004
Loa 245.62 (BB) Br ex 42.53 Dght 14.590
Lbp 233.00 Br md 42.50 Dpth 21.00
Welded, 1 dk

(A13A2TS) Shuttle Tanker
Double Hull (13F)
Liq: 117,849; Liq (Oil): 117,849
Cargo Heating Coils
Compartments: 5 Ta, 6 Wing Ta, ER
4 Cargo Pump (s): 4x3000m³/hr
Manifold: Bow/CM: 122.7m

1 oil engine driving 1 CP propeller
Total Power: 10,761kW (14,631hp) 14.2kn
B&W 5S70MC
1 x 2 Stroke 5 Cy. 700 x 2674 10761kW (14631bhp)
Astilleros Espanoles SA (AESA)-Spain
AuxGen: 2 x 1200kW 450V 60Hz a.c, 1 x 850kW 450V 60Hz a.c
Thrusters: 1 Thwart. CP thruster (f); 1 Directional thruster (f); 1 Thwart. CP thruster (a)

8819988 *OXCB2* -
TOVE MAERSK
ex Charlotte Maersk *-2001*
A P Moller - Maersk A/S
A P Moller
SatCom: Inmarsat C 421932610
Marstal *Denmark (DIS)*
MMSI: 219326000
Official number: D3314

16,982
7,449
21,825

Class: AB (LR)
✠ Classed LR until 3/11/96

1992-02 **Odense Staalskibsvaerft A/S — Munkebo (Lindo Shipyard)** Yd No: 136
Loa 162.26 (BB) Br ex 27.83 Dght 10.000
Lbp 151.90 Br md 27.80 Dpth 15.23
Welded, 1 dk

(A33A2CC) Container Ship (Fully Cellular)
TEU 1446 C Ho 539 TEU C Dk 907 TEU incl 114 ref C.
Compartments: 8 Cell Ho, ER
9 Ha: ER 12 Wing Ha:
Gantry cranes: 1x35t

1 oil engine driving 1 FP propeller
Total Power: 10,480kW (14,249hp) 18.5kn
B&W 8S50MC
1 x 2 Stroke 8 Cy. 500 x 1910 10480kW (14249bhp)
Mitsui Engineering & Shipbuilding CLtd-Japan
AuxGen: 3 x 1250kW 440V 60Hz a.c
Thrusters: 1 Thwart. CP thruster (f); 1 Tunnel thruster (a)

7719002 *UIFM* -
TOVRA
ex Annette-J *-2005* *ex* Denfield *-1996*
ex Almaty *-1995* *ex* Militence *-1993*
Joint Stock Northern Shipping Co (A/O 'Severnoye Morskoye Parokhodstvo') (NSC ARKHANGELSK)
-
Arkhangelsk *Russia*
MMSI: 273433290
Official number: 775094

1,037
358
1,188

Class: RR (LR) (RS) (BV)
✠ Classed LR until 13/3/85

1978-06 **Clelands Shipbuilding Co. Ltd — Wallsend** Yd No: 342
Converted From: General Cargo Ship-1999
Loa 72.34 Br ex 11.26 Dght 3.300
Lbp 68.08 Br md 11.21 Dpth 4.14
Welded, 1 dk

(A12D2LV) Vegetable Oil Tanker
Liq: 1,275
Cargo Heating Coils
Compartments: 6 Wing Ta (s.stl), ER
2 Cargo Pump (s): 2x200m³/hr
Manifold: Bow/CM: 26m

1 oil engine geared to sc. shaft driving 1 CP propeller
Total Power: 912kW (1,240hp) 11.0kn
Alpha 8V23L-VO
1 x Vee 4 Stroke 8 Cy. 225 x 300 912kW (1240bhp) (new engine 1978)
Alpha Diesel A/S-Denmark
AuxGen: 1 x 90kW 415V 50Hz a.c, 1 x 88kW 415V 50Hz a.c, 1 x 32kW 415V 50Hz a.c
Thrusters: 1 Thwart. FP thruster (f)

7124635 *3DSU* -
TOVUTO
ex Babale *-1990* *ex* Eugene McDermott II *-1987*
Government of The Republic of The Fiji Islands (FIMSA)
-
Suva *Fiji*
Official number: 715453

848
254
-

Class: (LR)
✠ Classed LR until 20/7/01

1972-01 **Carrington Slipways Pty Ltd — Newcastle NSW** Yd No: 67
Loa 52.20 Br ex 12.04 Dght 3.639
Lbp 46.21 Br md 11.59 Dpth 4.27
Welded, 1 dk

(B31A2SR) Research Survey Vessel

2 oil engines reverse reduction geared to sc. shafts driving 2 FP propellers
Total Power: 1,678kW (2,282hp) 12.0kn
Caterpillar D399SCAC
2 x Vee 4 Stroke 16 Cy. 159 x 203 each-839kW (1141bhp)
Caterpillar Tractor Co-USA
AuxGen: 2 x 200kW 415V 50Hz a.c

7740881 *4JEB* -
TOVUZ
ex Gazli *-1994*
Azerbaijan State Caspian Shipping Co (ASCSS)
Meridian Shipping & Management LLC
SatCom: Inmarsat C 442306410
Baku *Azerbaijan*
MMSI: 423064100
Official number: DGR-0024

2,434
994
3,135
T/cm
13.0

Class: (RS)

1979 Sudostroitelnyy Zavod im Volodarskogo — Rybinsk Yd No: 78
Loa 114.03 Br ex 13.21 Dght 3.670
Lbp 108.01 Br md 12.98 Dpth 5.50
Welded, 1 dk

(A31A2GX) General Cargo Ship
Bale: 4,297
Compartments: 4 Ho, ER
4 Ha: (17.6 x 9.3)3 (18.0 x 9.3)ER
Ice Capable

2 oil engines driving 2 FP propellers
Total Power: 970kW (1,318hp) 10.8kn
S.K.L. 6NVD48A-2U
2 x 4 Stroke 6 Cy. 320 x 480 each-485kW (659bhp)
VEB Schwermaschinenbau "KarlLiebknecht" (SKL)-Magdeburg
Fuel: 102.0 (d.f.)

9140487 *JL6310* -
TOWA MARU
YK Kato Unyu
-
Seiyo, Ehime *Japan*
Official number: 134887

498
-
1,200

1996-04 **Shirahama Zosen K.K. — Honai**
Yd No: 175
Loa 64.41 Br ex - Dght 4.226
Lbp 60.00 Br md 10.00 Dpth 4.50
Welded, 1 dk

(A13B2TP) Products Tanker
Liq: 1,250; Liq (Oil): 1,250
Compartments: 10 Ta, ER

1 oil engine reverse geared to sc. shaft driving 1 FP propeller
Total Power: 736kW (1,001hp)
Akasaka A28
1 x 4 Stroke 6 Cy. 280 x 550 736kW (1001bhp)
Akasaka Tekkosho KK (Akasaka DieselLtd)-Japan
Thrusters: 1 Thwart. FP thruster (f)

9244348 *JI3681* -
TOWA MARU NO. 8
Ajkku Co Ltd & Asahimaru Kensetsu Co Ltd
Nakanishi Kikai Kogyosho Co Ltd
Osaka, Osaka *Japan*
Official number: 136810

282
-
149

Class: NK

2001-01 **Hangzhou Dongfeng Shipbuilding Co Ltd — Hangzhou ZJ** Yd No: DFS9903
Loa 27.50 Br ex 16.25 Dght 5.000
Lbp 25.02 Br md 9.00 Dpth 7.17
Welded, 1 dk

(B32B2SA) Articulated Pusher Tug

1 oil engine reduction geared to sc. shaft driving 1 FP propeller
Total Power: 2,427kW (3,300hp) 11.9kn
Akasaka 8U28AK
1 x 4 Stroke 8 Cy. 280 x 380 2427kW (3300bhp)
Akasaka Tekkosho KK (Akasaka DieselLtd)-Japan
AuxGen: 1 x 170kW a.c
Fuel: 105.0 (d.f.)

9321213 *3ECB7* -
TOWADA
Graf Shipholding SA
Nippon Yusen Kabushiki Kaisha (NYK Line)
SatCom: Inmarsat C 435284110
Panama *Panama*
MMSI: 352841000
Official number: 3196406A

159,982
99,410
305,801
T/cm
182.0

Class: NK

2006-07 **Mitsubishi Heavy Industries Ltd. — Nagasaki** Yd No: 2216
Loa 333.00 (BB) Br ex 60.04 Dght 20.825
Lbp 324.00 Br md 60.00 Dpth 29.10
Welded, 1 dk

(A13A2TV) Crude Oil Tanker
Double Hull (13F)
Liq: 335,066; Liq (Oil): 350,013
Compartments: 5 Ta, 10 Wing Ta, 1 Slop Ta, ER
3 Cargo Pump (s): 3x5500m³/hr
Manifold: Bow/CM: 166.5m

1 oil engine driving 1 FP propeller
Total Power: 27,020kW (36,736hp) 15.5kn
Mitsubishi 7UEC85LSII
1 x 2 Stroke 7 Cy. 850 x 3150 27020kW (36736bhp)
Mitsubishi Heavy Industries Ltd-Japan
AuxGen: 2 x 1100kW a.c, 1 x 1200kW a.c
Fuel: 430.0 (d.f.) 6555.0 (r.f.)

6609547 - -
TOWARTIT
Government of The Democratic Republic of The Sudan (Railways Department)
-
Port Sudan *Sudan*

221
72
-

Class: (LR)
✠ Classed LR until 10/66

1966-05 **Martin Jansen GmbH & Co. KG Schiffsw. u. Masch. — Leer** Yd No: 57
Loa 34.32 Br ex 8.39 Dght 3.506
Lbp 31.02 Br md 8.23 Dpth 3.97
Welded

(B32A2ST) Tug

1 oil engine sr reverse geared to sc. shaft driving 1 FP propeller
Total Power: 905kW (1,230hp)
MAN G9V30/45ATL
1 x 4 Stroke 9 Cy. 300 x 450 905kW (1230bhp)
Maschinenbau Augsburg Nuernberg (MAN)-Augsburg
AuxGen: 2 x 22kW 115V d.c, 1 x 10kW 115V d.c

9044102 *DSFK7* -
TOWDAH HANA
ex Kobe Pioneer *-2009*
Hana Marine Co Ltd
-
SatCom: Inmarsat C 444010040
Jeju *South Korea*
MMSI: 440993000
Official number: JJR-000998

1,485
716
2,458
T/cm
7.6

Class: KR

1992-11 **Daedong Shipbuilding Co Ltd — Busan**
Yd No: 382
Loa 74.22 (BB) Br ex 12.20 Dght 5.400
Lbp 67.80 Br md 12.00 Dpth 6.20
Welded, 1 dk

(A12B2TR) Chemical/Products Tanker
Double Bottom Entire Compartment Length
Liq: 2,485; Liq (Oil): 2,484
Compartments: 4 Ta, 8 Wing Ta, 2 Slop Ta, ER
3 Cargo Pump (s): 3x300m³/hr
Manifold: Bow/CM: 37.4m

1 oil engine reverse geared to sc. shaft driving 1 FP propeller
Total Power: 1,324kW (1,800hp) 11.5kn
Akasaka A31R
1 x 4 Stroke 6 Cy. 310 x 600 1324kW (1800bhp)
Hyundai Heavy Industries Co Ltd-South Korea
AuxGen: 2 x 104kW 445V a.c
Fuel: 34.0 (d.f.) 116.0 (r.f.)

5058272 *HO8512* -
TOWELL POWER
ex Caltex Bintang *-1979* *ex* Grace Moran *-1954*
Yovatt Co Ltd
-
Panama *Panama*
Official number: 310PEXT2

238
15
-

Class: (AB)

1949 Levingston SB. Co. — Orange, Tx Yd No: 441
L reg 30.33 Br ex 8.28 Dght 4.026
Lbp 30.48 Br md 8.23 Dpth 4.47
Welded, 1 dk

(B32A2ST) Tug

1 diesel electric oil engine driving 1 gen. of 1210kW 525V d.c Connecting to 1 elec. Motor driving 1 FP propeller
Total Power: 1,256kW (1,708hp)
General Motors 12-278A
1 x Vee 2 Stroke 12 Cy. 222 x 267 1256kW (1708bhp) (made 1943, fitted 1949)
General Motors Corp-USA
Fuel: 122.0

9292034 *A8ER5* -
TOWER BRIDGE
Bridgeton Maritime Co
SCF Novoship JSC (Novorossiysk Shipping Co)
SatCom: Inmarsat C 463699965
Monrovia *Liberia*
MMSI: 636012318
Official number: 12318

27,725
13,762
47,199
T/cm
52.3

Class: LR
✠ **100A1** SS 12/2009
Double Hull oil tanker
ESP
*IWS
LI
SPM
✠ **LMC** **UMS IGS**
Eq.Ltr: M†;
Cable: 632.5/73.0 U3 (a)

2004-12 **Admiralteyskiy Sudostroitelnyy Zavod — Sankt-Peterburg** Yd No: 02742
Loa 182.50 (BB) Br ex 32.34 Dght 12.197
Lbp 174.80 Br md 32.20 Dpth 17.50
Welded, 1 dk

(A13A2TW) Crude/Oil Products Tanker
Double Hull (13F)
Liq: 53,146; Liq (Oil): 51,910
Compartments: 10 Wing Ta, 2 Wing Slop Ta, ER
10 Cargo Pump (s): 10x550m³/hr
Manifold: Bow/CM: 90.9m

1 oil engine driving 1 FP propeller
Total Power: 8,310kW (11,298hp) 14.3kn
B&W 6S50MC-C
1 x 2 Stroke 6 Cy. 500 x 2000 8310kW (11298bhp)
AO Bryanskiy MashinostroitelnyyZavod (BMZ)-Bryansk
AuxGen: 1 x 680kW 450V 60Hz a.c, 2 x 1280kW 450V 60Hz a.c
Boilers: e (ex.g.) 11.2kgf/cm² (11.0bar), WTAuxB (o.f.) 11.2kgf/cm² (11.0bar)
Thrusters: 1 Tunnel thruster (f)
Fuel: 126.0 (d.f.) 1428.0 (r.f.)

8026438 *DUK2026* -	**TOWER OF DAVID** *ex* Mindanao Cement 7 *-2000* **Trishia Shipping Lines Inc** *Cagayan de Oro* *Philippines* Official number: CD07003381	*352* 220 492	Class: (LR) ✠ Classed LR until 15/7/83	**1981-10 Mayon Docks Inc. — Tabaco** Yd No: 008 Loa 41.51 Br ex 8.51 Dght 2.901 Lbp 38.51 Br md 8.50 Dpth 3.66 Welded, 1 dk	**(A31A2GX) General Cargo Ship** Grain: 637 Compartments: 1 Dp Ta in Hold, 2 Ho, ER 2 Ha: ER	**2 oil engines** sr reverse geared to sc. shafts driving 2 FP propellers Total Power: 372kW (506hp) Caterpillar 3306SCAC 2 x 4 Stroke 6 Cy. 121 x 152 each-186kW (253bhp) Caterpillar Tractor Co-USA AuxGen: 2 x 19kW 220V 60Hz a.c Fuel: 20.0 (d.f.)
8115930 - -	**TOWER TIDE** - **Jeftex Marine Services Ltd** -	**696** 208 814	Class: (AB)	**1982-05 McDermott Shipyards Inc — New Iberia LA** Yd No: 146 Loa 54.87 Br ex 12.40 Dght 3.728 Lbp 51.82 Br md 12.20 Dpth 4.27 Welded, 1 dk	**(B21B20T) Offshore Tug/Supply Ship**	**2 oil engines** sr reverse geared to sc. shafts driving 2 FP propellers Total Power: 2,354kW (3,200hp) 12.0kn EMD (Electro-Motive) 16-645-C 2 x Vee 2 Stroke 16 Cy. 230 x 254 each-1177kW (1600bhp) (Re-engined ,made 1960, Reconditioned & fitted 1982) General Motors Corp.Electro-Motive Div.-La Grange AuxGen: 2 x 150kW 450V 60Hz a.c Thrusters: 1 Thwart. FP thruster (f) Fuel: 223.5 (d.f.) 13.5pd
7502095 *ZR2667* -	**TOWERKOP** **Ntabeni Fishing Pty** - *Cape Town* *South Africa* MMSI: 601818000 Official number: 19722	*272* 81 -		**1986-06 Andina de Desarrollo S.A. — Callao** Yd No: 064 Loa 35.72 (BB) Br ex - Dght - Lbp 30.59 Br md 8.28 Dpth 4.12 Welded, 1 dk	**(B11A2FT) Trawler** Ins: 338	**1 oil engine** with clutches & sr reverse geared to sc. shaft driving 1 FP propeller Total Power: 633kW (861hp) 11.2kn Caterpillar D398SCAC 1 x Vee 4 Stroke 12 Cy. 159 x 203 633kW (861bhp) Caterpillar Tractor Co-USA AuxGen: 2 x 49kW 220/380V d.c Thrusters: 1 Thwart. FP thruster (f)
5229730 *WDB9011* -	**TOWMASTER** *ex* Valiant *-1989* *ex* Maurania II *-1989* **Thames Towboat Co Inc** - *New York, NY* *United States of America* Official number: 263099	*181* 123 -		**1952 Ira S. Bushey & Son, Inc. — New York, NY** Yd No: 604 Loa - Br ex 7.65 Dght 3.506 Lbp 30.64 Br md 7.62 Dpth 3.74 Welded, 1 dk	**(B32A2ST) Tug**	**1 oil engine** driving 1 FP propeller Total Power: 883kW (1,201hp) Fairbanks, Morse 1 x 2 Stroke 6 Cy. 405 x 510 883kW (1201bhp) Fairbanks Morse & Co.-New Orleans, La AuxGen: 1 x 40kW 115V d.c, 1 x 24kW 115V d.c
7110854 *WBK3245* -	**TOWN POINT** **Moran Towing Corp** - *Wilmington, DE* *United States of America* MMSI: 367190250 Official number: 511619	*258* 175 -	Class: AB	**1967 Jakobson Shipyard, Inc. — Oyster Bay, NY** Yd No: 434 Loa - Br ex - Dght 4.496 Lbp 28.83 Br md 8.23 Dpth 4.96 Welded, 1 dk	**(B32A2ST) Tug**	**1 oil engine** reverse reduction geared to sc. shaft driving 1 FP propeller Total Power: 1,736kW (2,360hp) EMD (Electro-Motive) 12-645-E5 1 x Vee 2 Stroke 12 Cy. 230 x 254 1736kW (2360bhp) General Motors Corp-USA AuxGen: 1 x 30kW, 1 x 25kW Fuel: 102.5 (d.f.)
9578294 *D5EX7* -	**TOWNSVILLE MARU** **Mars Shipping Co SA** Daiichi Chuo Marine Co Ltd (DC Marine) *Monrovia* *Liberia* MMSI: 636016190 Official number: 16190	**32,309** 19,458 58,086 T/cm 57.4	Class: NK	**2013-11 Tsuneishi Heavy Industries (Cebu) Inc — Balamban** Yd No: SC-179 Loa 189.99 Br ex - Dght 12.826 Lbp 185.60 Br md 32.26 Dpth 18.00 Welded, 1 dk	**(A21A2BC) Bulk Carrier** Grain: 72,674; Bale: 70,107 Compartments: 5 Ho, ER 5 Ha: ER Cranes: 4x30t	**1 oil engine** driving 1 FP propeller Total Power: 8,400kW (11,421hp) 14.5kn MAN-B&W 6S50MC-C 1 x 2 Stroke 6 Cy. 500 x 2000 8400kW (11421bhp) Mitsui Engineering & Shipbuilding CLtd-Japan AuxGen: 3 x 500kW a.c Fuel: 2380.0
8974362 *YFFI* -	**TOWO ARYO** **PT Pelayaran Umum Indonesia (Pelumin)** - *Jakarta* *Indonesia* MMSI: 525017077 Official number: 3928	**1,387** 472 1,500	Class: KI	**1995-07 P.T. Inggom Shipyard — Jakarta** Yd No: 05773 Loa 65.00 Br ex - Dght 3.200 Lbp 60.00 Br md 15.00 Dpth 4.50 Welded, 1 dk	**(A13B2TP) Products Tanker**	**2 oil engines** driving 2 Propellers Total Power: 1,324kW (1,800hp) 10.0kn Niigata 6MG19HX 2 x 4 Stroke 6 Cy. 190 x 260 each-662kW (900bhp) Niigata Engineering Co Ltd-Japan AuxGen: 1 x 450kW 440/231V a.c
9563419 *9HA2301* -	**TOXOTIS** **Freehold Equity Ltd** Sea Traders SA *Valletta* *Malta* MMSI: 248296000 Official number: 9563419	**33,044** 19,231 56,713 T/cm 58.8	Class: BV	**2010-04 COSCO (Guangdong) Shipyard Co Ltd — Dongguan GD** Yd No: N226 Loa 189.99 (BB) Br ex - Dght 12.800 Lbp 185.00 Br md 32.26 Dpth 18.00 Welded, 1 dk	**(A21A2BC) Bulk Carrier** Grain: 71,634; Bale: 68,200 Compartments: 5 Ho, ER 5 Ha: 4 (21.3 x 18.3)ER (18.9 x 18.3) Cranes: 4x30t	**1 oil engine** driving 1 FP propeller Total Power: 9,480kW (12,889hp) 14.2kn MAN-B&W 6S50MC-C 1 x 2 Stroke 6 Cy. 500 x 2000 9480kW (12889bhp) Mitsui Engineering & Shipbuilding CLtd-Japan AuxGen: 3 x 600kW 60Hz a.c Fuel: 2165.0 (r.f.)
9496850 *9HA2558* -	**TOY-A** **Navmar Investments Ltd** - *Valletta* *Malta* MMSI: 248874000 Official number: 9496850	**498** 149 -	Class: (AB)	**2009-07 Mondo Marine SpA — Savona** Yd No: 22/1 Loa 49.20 Br ex - Dght - Lbp 40.20 Br md 9.00 Dpth 4.40 Welded, 1 dk	**(X11A2YP) Yacht** Hull Material: Aluminium Alloy	**2 oil engines** reduction geared to sc. shafts driving 2 Propellers Total Power: 4,080kW (5,548hp) 18.0kn M.T.U. 12V4000M90 2 x Vee 4 Stroke 12 Cy. 165 x 190 each-2040kW (2774bhp) MTU Friedrichshafen GmbH-Friedrichshafen AuxGen: 2 x 125kW a.c Fuel: 60.0 (d.f.)
8650239 *LK8222* R-344-K	**TOYA** **Nye Toya AS** - *Kopervik* *Norway*	**324** 129 -		**2003 Ceske Lodenice a.s. — Usti nad Labem** Yd No: 0130/1 Loa 23.90 Br ex - Dght - Lbp - Br md 9.10 Dpth 6.30 Welded, 1 dk	**(B11B2FV) Fishing Vessel**	**1 oil engine** reduction geared to sc. shaft driving 1 Propeller Total Power: 375kW (510hp) Volvo Penta TAMD165C 1 x 4 Stroke 6 Cy. 144 x 165 375kW (510bhp) AB Volvo Penta-Sweden
9368106 *J8B3293* -	**TOYAKO** **Tazawako Shipping Co Ltd** Qingdao Harmony Shipping Co Ltd *Kingstown* *St Vincent & The Grenadines* MMSI: 375237000 Official number: 9765	**1,972** 1,395 3,385 T/cm 5.7	Class: KR (CC)	**2005-11 Qingdao Shipyard — Qingdao SD** Yd No: QDZ426 Loa 81.00 Br ex - Dght 5.500 Lbp 76.00 Br md 13.60 Dpth 6.80 Welded, 1 dk	**(A31A2GX) General Cargo Ship** Compartments: 2 Ho, ER 2 Ha: ER 2 (18.6 x 9.0) Ice Capable	**1 oil engine** with clutches, flex coup & sr rev geared to sc. shaft driving 1 FP propeller Total Power: 1,324kW (1,800hp) 12.0kn Chinese Std. Type G6300ZC 1 x 4 Stroke 6 Cy. 300 x 380 1324kW (1800bhp) Ningbo CSI Power & Machinery GroupCo Ltd-China AuxGen: 2 x 150kW 400/220V 50Hz a.c Fuel: 26.8 (d.f.) (Heating Coils) 135.1 (r.f.) 6.8pd
7364534 *TCGW* -	**TOYCA 1** *ex* Merzifon *-2006* **OF Denizcilik Ticaret AS (OF Shipping & Trading Co)** SatCom: Inmarsat C 427100239 *Istanbul* *Turkey* MMSI: 271000001 Official number: 4245	**3,641** 1,925 5,790	Class: TL (AB)	**1974-03 Marmara Tersanesi — Yarimca** Yd No: 3 Converted From: Oil Tanker-2005 Loa 111.28 Br ex 15.85 Dght 6.019 Lbp 102.01 Br md 15.80 Dpth 7.29 Welded, 1 dk	**(A31A2GX) General Cargo Ship** Compartments: 6 Ho, ER	**2 oil engines** sr geared to sc. shaft driving 1 CP propeller Total Power: 1,700kW (2,312hp) 12.0kn Nohab F26R 2 x 4 Stroke 6 Cy. 250 x 300 each-850kW (1156bhp) AB NOHAB-Sweden AuxGen: 2 x 80kW a.c, 1 x 60kW a.c, 2 x 48kW a.c Fuel: 171.5
9108881 *CB5505* -	**TOYITA** **Pesquera Bahia Coronel SA** - *Valparaiso* *Chile* MMSI: 725000360 Official number: 2857	**1,334** 431 2,189	Class: (LR) ✠ Classed LR until 2/7/97	**1995-03 Ast. y Maestranzas de la Armada (ASMAR Chile) — Talcahuano** Yd No: 65 Loa 66.00 Br ex 12.02 Dght 6.361 Lbp 57.80 Br md 12.00 Dpth 8.00 Welded, 2 dks	**(B11B2FV) Fishing Vessel** Ins: 1,500	**1 oil engine** with flexible couplings & sr geared to sc. shaft driving 1 CP propeller Total Power: 1,980kW (2,692hp) 13.0kn MaK 6M453C 1 x 4 Stroke 6 Cy. 320 x 420 1980kW (2692bhp) Krupp MaK Maschinenbau GmbH-Kiel AuxGen: 1 x 288kW 400V 50Hz a.c, 2 x 160kW 400V 50Hz a.c Thrusters: 1 Thwart. CP thruster (f); 1 Tunnel thruster (a)
9304667 *H3ZA* -	**TOYO** **Toyo Maritima SA** NYK Shipmanagement Pte Ltd SatCom: Inmarsat C 435302410 *Panama* *Panama* MMSI: 353024000 Official number: 3051505B	**160,098** 103,298 310,309 T/cm 184.0	Class: AB	**2005-01 Imabari Shipbuilding Co Ltd — Saijo EH (Saijo Shipyard)** Yd No: 8024 Loa 333.00 (BB) Br ex - Dght 21.100 Lbp 324.00 Br md 60.00 Dpth 29.00 Welded, 1 dk	**(A13A2TV) Crude Oil Tanker** Double Hull (13F) Liq: 334,905; Liq (Oil): 334,905 3 Cargo Pump (s): 3x5500m³/hr Manifold: Bow/CM: 164m	**1 oil engine** driving 1 FP propeller Total Power: 27,960kW (38,014hp) 15.6kn MAN-B&W 8S80MC-C 1 x 2 Stroke 8 Cy. 800 x 3200 27960kW (38014bhp) Mitsui Engineering & Shipbuilding CLtd-Japan AuxGen: 3 x 1324kW a.c

IMO / Call sign	Name / Owner	Tonnage	Class	Build / Dimensions	Type / Capacity	Machinery
9276937 *HOZS* -	**TOYO ENERGY** *ex* Sun Explorer *-2013* **Eastern Marine Corp Ltd** Dalian Ningxing Shipping Co Ltd *Panama* *Panama* MMSI: 357921000 Official number: 31014PEXT1	**8,552** 3,617 11,530	Class: NK	**2003-04 Higaki Zosen K.K. — Imabari** Yd No: 552 Loa 116.99 Br ex - Dght 8.665 Lbp 109.00 Br md 19.60 Dpth 14.00 Welded, 1 dk	**(A31A2GX) General Cargo Ship** Grain: 18,497; Bale: 17,077 Compartments: 2 Ho, 2 Tw Dk, ER 2 Ha: (30.8 x 14.9)ER (29.4 x 14.9) Cranes: 2x30.7t,1x30t; Derricks: 1x30t	**1 oil engine** driving 1 FP propeller Total Power: 4,200kW (5,710hp) 13.8kn B&W 6S35MC 1 x 2 Stroke 6 Cy. 350 x 1400 4200kW (5710bhp) The Hanshin Diesel Works Ltd-Japan Fuel: 780.0
9330147 *3ECA7* -	**TOYO HOPE** *ex* Apollo Sari *-2013* **Toyo Hope Shipping Co Ltd** Dalian Ningxing Shipping Co Ltd *Panama* *Panama* MMSI: 371279000 Official number: 3090305C	**7,156** 3,131 10,262	Class: NK	**2005-07 Higaki Zosen K.K. — Imabari** Yd No: 583 Loa 108.22 (BB) Br ex - Dght 8.603 Lbp 99.80 Br md 19.60 Dpth 13.20 Welded, 1 dk	**(A31A2GX) General Cargo Ship** Grain: 14,587; Bale: 13,292 2 Ha: (27.3 x 14.0)ER (24.5 x 14.0) Cranes: 1x60t,2x30.7t	**1 oil engine** driving 1 FP propeller Total Power: 3,900kW (5,302hp) 13.1kn B&W 6L35MC 1 x 2 Stroke 6 Cy. 350 x 1050 3900kW (5302bhp) Makita Corp-Japan Fuel: 670.0
9279604 *JI3710* -	**TOYO MARU** **Santoku Senpaku Co Ltd** - *Osaka, Osaka* *Japan* MMSI: 431401953 Official number: 137235	*4,238* - 3,743	Class: NK	**2003-05 Kegoya Dock K.K. — Kure** Yd No: 1076 Loa 124.70 (BB) Br ex - Dght 6.015 Lbp 115.87 Br md 20.50 Dpth 14.80 Welded	**(A35B2RV) Vehicles Carrier** Quarter stern door/ramp (p. a.) Quarter stern door/ramp (s. a.) Cars: 550	**1 oil engine** driving 1 FP propeller Total Power: 6,230kW (8,470hp) 20.0kn Mitsubishi 7UEC45LA 1 x 2 Stroke 7 Cy. 450 x 1350 6230kW (8470bhp) Akasaka Tekkosho KK (Akasaka DieselLtd)-Japan AuxGen: 2 x 400kW a.c Thrusters: 1 Tunnel thruster (f) Fuel: 425.0 (r.f.)
9215062 *JH3439* -	**TOYO MARU** **Corporation for Advanced Transport & Technology & Toyo Line Co Ltd** Toyo Kaiun Co Ltd *Shizuoka, Shizuoka* *Japan* Official number: 135619	*499* - 1,600	Class: NK	**1999-08 Yamakawa Zosen Tekko K.K. — Kagoshima** Yd No: 762 Loa 75.81 Br ex - Dght 4.140 Lbp 70.00 Br md 12.00 Dpth 7.10 Welded, 1 dk	**(A31A2GX) General Cargo Ship** Bale: 2,277 Compartments: 1 Ho, ER 1 Ha: (40.2 x 9.3)ER	**1 oil engine** driving 1 FP propeller Total Power: 1,471kW (2,000hp) 11.6kn Niigata 6M34BGT 1 x 4 Stroke 6 Cy. 340 x 620 1471kW (2000bhp) Niigata Engineering Co Ltd-Japan Fuel: 80.0 (d.f.)
9067166 *JVBW5* -	**TOYO MARU** *ex* Toyo Maru No. 82 *-2013* - - *Ulaanbaatar* *Mongolia* MMSI: 457780000	*1,527* - 2,981	Class: (NK)	**1993-08 Shitanoe Shipbuilding Co Ltd — Usuki OT** Yd No: 1141 Loa 88.80 Br ex - Dght 5.463 Lbp 82.00 Br md 13.00 Dpth 6.45 Welded, 1 dk	**(A12A2TC) Chemical Tanker** Liq: 3,292	**1 oil engine** driving 1 FP propeller Total Power: 2,060kW (2,801hp) 12.7kn Hanshin 6EL38 1 x 4 Stroke 6 Cy. 380 x 760 2060kW (2801bhp) The Hanshin Diesel Works Ltd-Japan AuxGen: 3 x 213kW a.c Fuel: 120.0 (r.f.)
8742757 *JD2839* -	**TOYO MARU** **Toyo Kaiun KK** - *Sasebo, Nagasaki* *Japan* Official number: 140893	*273* - 900		**2009-03 Y.K. Okajima Zosensho — Matsuyama** Yd No: 265 Loa 63.71 Br ex - Dght 3.430 Lbp 56.50 Br md 10.20 Dpth 5.80 Welded, 1 dk	**(A31A2GX) General Cargo Ship** 1 Ha: ER (33.0 x 7.7)	**1 oil engine** reduction geared to sc. shaft driving 1 Propeller Total Power: 1,029kW (1,399hp) 12.0kn Niigata 6M28BGT 1 x 4 Stroke 6 Cy. 280 x 480 1029kW (1399bhp) Niigata Engineering Co Ltd-Japan
9015280 *JE2950* -	**TOYO MARU NO. 1** *ex* Meisho Maru No. 37 *-2002* **Tojiro Sato** - *Kesennuma, Miyagi* *Japan* Official number: 130775	*119* - -		**1989-09 Kesennuma Tekko — Kesennuma** Yd No: 272 Loa 38.00 (BB) Br ex - Dght 2.400 Lbp 31.50 Br md 6.40 Dpth 2.80 Welded	**(B11B2FV) Fishing Vessel**	**1 oil engine** with clutches & reduction geared to sc. shaft driving 1 CP propeller Total Power: 592kW (805hp) Niigata 6M26AFTE 1 x 4 Stroke 6 Cy. 260 x 460 592kW (805bhp) Niigata Engineering Co Ltd-Japan
9496393 *JD2874* -	**TOYO MARU NO. 2** **Malox Co Ltd & Santoku Senpaku Co Ltd** Malox Co Ltd *Osaka, Osaka* *Japan* MMSI: 431000859 Official number: 140938	*4,898* - 3,605	Class: NK	**2009-02 Kegoya Dock K.K. — Kure** Yd No: 1107 Loa 124.70 (BB) Br ex - Dght 6.165 Lbp 115.87 Br md 20.50 Dpth 14.80 Welded, 1 dk	**(A35B2RV) Vehicles Carrier** Quarter stern door/ramp (p. a.) Cars: 715	**1 oil engine** driving 1 FP propeller Total Power: 6,230kW (8,470hp) 20.0kn Mitsubishi 7UEC45LA 1 x 2 Stroke 7 Cy. 450 x 1350 6230kW (8470bhp) Akasaka Tekkosho KK (Akasaka DieselLtd)-Japan AuxGen: 3 x 580kW a.c Thrusters: 1 Tunnel thruster (f) Fuel: 450.0 (r.f.)
8915093 *JL5905* -	**TOYO MARU NO. 8** *ex* Kyoei Maru No. 18 *-2013* *ex* Sumiko Maru *-2005* - - *Osaka, Osaka* *Japan* MMSI: 431500885 Official number: 130659	*197* - 550		**1990-02 Murakami Hide Zosen K.K. — Imabari** Yd No: 308 Loa - Br ex - Dght 3.301 Lbp 44.02 Br md 8.01 Dpth 3.51 Welded, 1 dk	**(A13B2TP) Products Tanker**	**1 oil engine** driving 1 FP propeller Total Power: 625kW (850hp) Niigata 6M26BGT 1 x 4 Stroke 6 Cy. 260 x 460 625kW (850bhp) Niigata Engineering Co Ltd-Japan
8748165 *JD2994* -	**TOYO MARU NO. 17** **Yamamasu Kaiun KK** - *Anan, Tokushima* *Japan* Official number: 141144	*499* - 1,840		**2009-10 Tokuoka Zosen K.K. — Naruto** Yd No: 320 Loa 74.60 Br ex - Dght 4.450 Lbp 69.00 Br md 11.80 Dpth 7.52 Welded, 1 dk	**(A31A2GX) General Cargo Ship** 1 Ha: ER (40.0 x 9.5)	**1 oil engine** reduction geared to sc. shaft driving 1 Propeller Total Power: 1,618kW (2,200hp) 11.5kn Niigata 6M34BGT 1 x 4 Stroke 6 Cy. 340 x 620 1618kW (2200bhp) Niigata Engineering Co Ltd-Japan
9094303 *JD2164* -	**TOYO MARU NO. 18** **Yamamasu Kaiun KK** - *Anan, Tokushima* *Japan* Official number: 140229	*498* - 1,750		**2005-09 Tokuoka Zosen K.K. — Naruto** Yd No: 286 Loa 74.59 Br ex - Dght 4.380 Lbp 69.00 Br md 12.10 Dpth 7.42 Welded, 1 dk	**(A31A2GX) General Cargo Ship** 1 Ha: ER (40.0 x 10.0)	**1 oil engine** driving 1 Propeller Total Power: 1,618kW (2,200hp) 11.5kn Niigata 6M34BGT 1 x 4 Stroke 6 Cy. 340 x 620 1618kW (2200bhp) Niigata Engineering Co Ltd-Japan
8717001 *7KME* HK1-1337	**TOYO MARU NO. 28** *ex* Hokuryo Maru No. 8 *-2007* *ex* Jutoku Maru No. 18 *-2002* **Ocean Fisheries YK** - SatCom: Inmarsat A 1204507 *Tokyo* *Japan* MMSI: 431603110 Official number: 129497	*379* - 231		**1988-01 KK Kanasashi Zosen — Shizuoka SZ** Yd No: 3153 Loa 53.61 (BB) Br ex - Dght 3.401 Lbp 47.20 Br md 8.72 Dpth 3.76 Welded, 1 dk	**(B11B2FV) Fishing Vessel** Ins: 546	**1 oil engine** with clutches, flexible couplings & sr reverse geared to sc. shaft driving 1 FP propeller Total Power: 736kW (1,001hp) Hanshin LH28G 1 x 4 Stroke 6 Cy. 280 x 460 736kW (1001bhp) The Hanshin Diesel Works Ltd-Japan
7300485 - -	**TOYO MARU No. 53** - -	*199* 104 499		**1968 Nishihara Zosen — Omishima** Yd No: 146 Loa 35.41 Br ex 7.04 Dght 3.175 Lbp - Br md 7.01 Dpth 3.48 Welded, 1 dk	**(A13B2TU) Tanker (unspecified)** Compartments: 7 Ta, ER	**1 oil engine** driving 1 FP propeller Total Power: 331kW (450hp) 10.0kn Matsue 1 x 4 Stroke 6 Cy. 330 x 480 331kW (450bhp) Matsue Diesel KK-Japan Fuel: 13.0
9053995 *JL6119* -	**TOYO MARU No. 83** *ex* Shin Yahata Maru *-2001* **Hisato Ota** - *Shimonoseki, Yamaguchi* *Japan* Official number: 132992	*498* - 1,250		**1993-03 Imura Zosen K.K. — Komatsushima** Yd No: 263 Loa 65.00 (BB) Br ex - Dght 4.200 Lbp 60.00 Br md 10.00 Dpth 4.50 Welded, 1 dk	**(A13B2TP) Products Tanker** Liq: 1,211; Liq (Oil): 1,211 Compartments: 8 Wing Ta, ER	**1 oil engine** with clutches & reverse geared to sc. shaft driving 1 FP propeller Total Power: 736kW (1,001hp) Sumiyoshi S28G 1 x 4 Stroke 6 Cy. 280 x 500 736kW (1001bhp) Sumiyoshi Marine Diesel Co Ltd-Japan
9296664 *JM6606* -	**TOYO MARU NO. 87** **Japan Railway Construction, Transport & Technology Agency & Daiwa Kaiun KK** Daiwa Kaiun KK *Shimonoseki, Yamaguchi* *Japan* MMSI: 431401968 Official number: 136825	*3,699* - 4,998	Class: NK	**2003-12 K.K. Miura Zosensho — Saiki** Yd No: 1268 Loa 104.45 Br ex - Dght 6.264 Lbp 99.20 Br md 16.00 Dpth 8.10 Welded, 1 dk	**(A12B2TR) Chemical/Products Tanker** Double Hull (13F) Liq: 6,200; Liq (Oil): 6,200	**1 oil engine** driving 1 FP propeller Total Power: 2,942kW (4,000hp) 13.5kn Hanshin LH46L 1 x 4 Stroke 6 Cy. 460 x 880 2942kW (4000bhp) The Hanshin Diesel Works Ltd-Japan Fuel: 310.0
9665994 *JD3535* -	**TOYO MARU NO. 88** **Japan Railway Construction, Transport & Technology Agency & Daiwa Kaiun KK** Daiwa Kaiun KK *Shimonoseki, Yamaguchi* *Japan* MMSI: 431004611 Official number: 141946	*2,009* - 3,122	Class: NK	**2013-06 K.K. Miura Zosensho — Saiki** Yd No: 1360 Loa 91.70 (BB) Br ex - Dght 5.410 Lbp 86.00 Br md 14.50 Dpth 7.00 Welded, 1 dk	**(A13B2TP) Products Tanker** Double Hull (13F)	**1 oil engine** reduction geared to sc. shaft driving 1 Propeller Total Power: 2,427kW (3,300hp) 13.0kn Hanshin LH41LG 1 x 4 Stroke 6 Cy. 410 x 800 2427kW (3300bhp) The Hanshin Diesel Works Ltd-Japan Fuel: 125.0

IMO / Call sign	Name / Owner / Manager / Port / Flag	Tonnage	Class	Build / Dimensions	Type	Machinery
7424592 *YBVU* -	**TOYO No. 15** **PT Toyo Fishing Industry Co Indonesia ('PT TOFICO')** - *Jakarta* *Indonesia*	*152* 46 -	Class: (KI)	**1974-06 Minami-Nippon Zosen KK — Ichikikushikino KS** Yd No: 210 Loa 28.30 Br ex 6.53 Dght 2.896 Lbp 24.74 Br md 6.51 Dpth 3.10 Welded, 1 dk	**(B11B2FV) Fishing Vessel**	**1 oil engine** driving 1 FP propeller Total Power: 416kW (566hp) Caterpillar D379TA 1 x Vee 4 Stroke 8 Cy. 159 x 203 416kW (566bhp) Caterpillar Tractor Co-USA AuxGen: 2 x 55kW 225V
7424607 *YE4746* -	**TOYO No. 16** **PT Toyo Fishing Industry Co Indonesia ('PT TOFICO')** - *Jakarta* *Indonesia*	*152* 46 -	Class: (KI)	**1974-06 Minami-Nippon Zosen KK — Ichikikushikino KS** Yd No: 211 Loa 28.30 Br ex 6.53 Dght 2.896 Lbp 24.74 Br md 6.51 Dpth 3.10 Welded, 1 dk	**(B11B2FV) Fishing Vessel**	**1 oil engine** driving 1 FP propeller Total Power: 416kW (566hp) Caterpillar D379TA 1 x Vee 4 Stroke 8 Cy. 159 x 203 416kW (566bhp) Caterpillar Tractor Co-USA AuxGen: 2 x 55kW 225V
7424619 *YE4747* -	**TOYO No. 17** **PT Toyo Fishing Industry Co Indonesia ('PT TOFICO')** - *Jakarta* *Indonesia*	*152* 46 -	Class: (KI)	**1974-07 Minami-Nippon Zosen KK — Ichikikushikino KS** Yd No: 212 Loa 28.33 Br ex 6.53 Dght 2.896 Lbp 24.74 Br md 6.51 Dpth 3.10 Welded, 1 dk	**(B11A2FT) Trawler**	**1 oil engine** driving 1 FP propeller Total Power: 416kW (566hp) Caterpillar D379TA 1 x Vee 4 Stroke 8 Cy. 159 x 203 416kW (566bhp) Caterpillar Tractor Co-USA AuxGen: 2 x 55kW 225V
8864684 *YE9090* -	**TOYO NO. 21** *ex* Mina Nusa No. 1 *-2000* *ex* Nissho Maru No. 8 *-1997* **PT Toyo Fishing Industry Co Indonesia ('PT TOFICO')** - *Ambon* *Indonesia*	*177* 58 -	Class: (KI)	**1981-03 Yamakawa Zosen Tekko K.K. — Kagoshima** Loa 33.35 Br ex - Dght 2.000 Lbp 26.70 Br md 6.20 Dpth 2.44 Welded, 1 dk	**(B11B2FV) Fishing Vessel**	**1 oil engine** geared to sc. shaft driving 1 FP propeller Total Power: 478kW (650hp) 10.0kn Hanshin 6L24GSH 1 x 4 Stroke 6 Cy. 240 x 400 478kW (650bhp) The Hanshin Diesel Works Ltd-Japan
7828475 - -	**TOYO NO. 23** *ex* Daikannon Maru *-2000* *ex* Daikannon Maru No. 1 *-1996* *ex* Daikannon Maru *-1990* *ex* Taihei Maru No. 16 *-1988* **PT Toyo Fishing Industry Co Indonesia ('PT TOFICO')** KK Kobayashi Shoten *Jakarta* *Indonesia*	**306** 106 -	Class: (KI)	**1979-08 K.K. Yoshida Zosen Tekko — Kesennuma** Yd No: 272 Loa 40.06 (BB) Br ex - Dght 2.401 Lbp 32.59 Br md 6.80 Dpth 2.70 Welded, 1 dk	**(B11B2FV) Fishing Vessel**	**1 oil engine** driving 1 FP propeller Total Power: 515kW (700hp) Akasaka DM28AR 1 x 4 Stroke 6 Cy. 280 x 460 515kW (700bhp) Akasaka Tekkosho KK (Akasaka DieselLtd)-Japan
8837112 - -	**TOYO No. 51** *ex* Samodra 51 *-1988* **PT Toyo Fishing Industry Co Indonesia ('PT TOFICO')** - *Jakarta* *Indonesia*	*195* 89 -	Class: (KI)	**1968 Nichiro Zosen — Japan** Loa 43.00 Br ex - Dght - Lbp - Br md 7.22 Dpth 2.45 Welded, 1 dk	**(B11B2FV) Fishing Vessel**	**1 oil engine** driving 1 FP propeller Total Power: 478kW (650hp) 10.7kn Niigata 6M26KGHS 1 x 4 Stroke 6 Cy. 260 x 400 478kW (650bhp) Niigata Tekkosho-Japan
7126011 *YE2002* -	**TOYO No. 53** *ex* Samodra No. 23 *-1988* *ex* Star Port No. 38 *-1988* *ex* Katsuei Maru No. 23 *-1979* **PT Toyo Fishing Industry Co Indonesia ('PT TOFICO')** - *Jakarta* *Indonesia*	*206* 62 161	Class: (KI)	**1971-09 Usuki Iron Works Co Ltd — Usuki OT** Yd No: 812 Loa 35.11 Br ex 7.01 Dght 2.566 Lbp 30.89 Br md 6.99 Dpth 2.78 Welded, 1 dk	**(B11A2FT) Trawler**	**1 oil engine** driving 1 FP propeller Total Power: 441kW (600hp) Niigata 6M26KGHS 1 x 4 Stroke 6 Cy. 260 x 400 441kW (600bhp) Niigata Engineering Co Ltd-Japan
6909466 *YBZO* -	**TOYO No. 56** *ex* Kurnia No. 1 *-1988* *ex* Nisshin Maru No. 67 *-1974* **PT Alfa Kurnia Fish Enterprise** - *Jakarta* *Indonesia*	*232* 91 -	Class: (KI)	**1969-02 Nichiro Zosen K.K. — Hakodate** Yd No: 272 Loa 37.01 Br ex 6.94 Dght 2.794 Lbp 31.98 Br md 6.91 Dpth 3.20 Welded, 1 dk	**(B11A2FT) Trawler**	**1 oil engine** driving 1 FP propeller Total Power: 736kW (1,001hp) Akasaka UHS27 1 x 4 Stroke 6 Cy. 270 x 420 736kW (1001bhp) Akasaka Tekkosho KK (Akasaka DieselLtd)-Japan AuxGen: 1 x 96kW 225V a.c
7393963 *YDWJ* -	**TOYO NO. 57** *ex* Kofide No. 1 *-1986* *ex* Yahata Maru No. 71 *-1986* *ex* Koei Maru No. 61 *-1985* **PT Toyo Fishing Industry Co Indonesia ('PT TOFICO')** - *Jakarta* *Indonesia*	*490* 184 377	Class: (KI) (NK)	**1974-05 Goriki Zosensho — Ise** Yd No: 763 Loa 49.00 Br ex 8.23 Dght 3.399 Lbp 43.21 Br md 8.21 Dpth 3.56 Riveted\Welded, 1 dk	**(B11B2FV) Fishing Vessel**	**1 oil engine** driving 1 FP propeller Total Power: 736kW (1,001hp) 10.8kn Niigata 6M28KEHS 1 x 4 Stroke 6 Cy. 280 x 440 736kW (1001bhp) Niigata Engineering Co Ltd-Japan AuxGen: 2 x 200kW a.c
9232541 *H3QG* -	**TOYO PEARL** *ex* Eastern Spirit *-2013* **Eastern Spirit Shipping SA** Qingdao Harmony Shipping Co Ltd *Panama* *Panama* MMSI: 351060000 Official number: 2751201CH	**8,739** 3,066 10,810	Class: NK	**2000-11 Watanabe Zosen KK — Imabari EH** Yd No: 322 Loa 111.97 Br ex 20.52 Dght 8.326 Lbp 105.00 Br md 20.50 Dpth 9.15 Welded, 1 dk	**(A31A2GX) General Cargo Ship** Grain: 18,338; Bale: 17,715 Compartments: 2 Ho, ER 2 Ha: (33.6 x 13.0) (20.3 x 13.0)ER Cranes: 2x30.7t; Derricks: 1x30.5t	**1 oil engine** driving 1 FP propeller Total Power: 3,884kW (5,281hp) 13.0kn B&W 6L35MC 1 x 2 Stroke 6 Cy. 350 x 1050 3884kW (5281bhp) The Hanshin Diesel Works Ltd-Japan
8351338 - -	**TOYOEI MARU** - **Tan Shun Steamship Co Ltd** -	*226* - 270		**1983 Nagashima Zosen KK — Kihoku ME** Yd No: 158 Loa - Br ex - Dght 2.610 Lbp 36.10 Br md 8.01 Dpth 2.90 Welded, 1 dk	**(A31A2GX) General Cargo Ship**	**1 oil engine** driving 1 FP propeller
9336919 *JD2152* -	**TOYOFUJI MARU** **Toyofuji Shipping Co Ltd (Toyofuji Kaiun KK)** Kagoshima Senpaku Kaisha Ltd *Tokai, Aichi* *Japan* MMSI: 431200683 Official number: 140215	*12,687* - 5,490	Class: NK	**2005-11 Mitsubishi Heavy Industries Ltd. — Shimonoseki** Yd No: 1112 Loa 165.00 (BB) Br ex - Dght 6.222 Lbp 157.00 Br md 27.60 Dpth 24.15 Welded	**(A35B2RV) Vehicles Carrier** Side door/ramp (p) Len: 15.00 Wid: 4.50 Swl: - Quarter stern door/ramp (p. a.) Len: 25.00 Wid: 6.00 Swl: 45 Quarter stern door/ramp (s. a.) Len: 25.00 Wid: 6.00 Swl: 45 Cars: 2,005	**1 oil engine** driving 1 FP propeller Total Power: 11,900kW (16,179hp) 21.0kn Mitsubishi 7UEC52LSE 1 x 2 Stroke 7 Cy. 520 x 2000 11900kW (16179bhp) Mitsubishi Heavy Industries Ltd-Japan AuxGen: 2 x 1200kW 50Hz a.c, 1 x 1045kW a.c Thrusters: 1 Tunnel thruster (f); 2 Tunnel thruster (a) Fuel: 120.0 (d.f.) 1100.0 (r.f.)
9412579 *7JDI* -	**TOYOFUJI MARU NO. 2** **Toyofuji Shipping Co Ltd (Toyofuji Kaiun KK)** Kagoshima Senpaku Kaisha Ltd *Tokai, Aichi* *Japan* MMSI: 432667000 Official number: 140781	**28,448** 8,534 6,090	Class: NK	**2008-08 Mitsubishi Heavy Industries Ltd. — Shimonoseki** Yd No: 1128 Loa 165.00 (BB) Br ex - Dght 6.522 Lbp 157.00 Br md 27.60 Dpth 24.15 Welded	**(A35B2RV) Vehicles Carrier** Side door/ramp (p) Len: 15.00 Wid: 4.50 Swl: - Quarter stern door/ramp (p. a.) Len: 25.00 Wid: 6.00 Swl: 45 Quarter stern door/ramp (s. a.) Len: 25.00 Wid: 6.00 Swl: 45 Cars: 2,003	**1 oil engine** driving 1 FP propeller Total Power: 11,935kW (16,227hp) 21.0kn Mitsubishi 7UEC52LSE 1 x 2 Stroke 7 Cy. 520 x 2000 11935kW (16227bhp) Mitsubishi Heavy Industries Ltd-Japan AuxGen: 2 x 1200kW a.c, 1 x 1000kW a.c Thrusters: 1 Tunnel thruster (f); 2 Tunnel thruster (a) Fuel: 120.0 (d.f.) 1100.0 (r.f.)
8512229 - -	**TOYOFUJI MARU No. 11** **CSC RoRo Logistics Co Ltd** CSC Shenzhen Ship Management Co Ltd *China*	*4,010* - 3,514	Class: (NK)	**1986-01 Naikai Shipbuilding & Engineering Co Ltd — Onomichi HS (Setoda Shipyard)** Yd No: 507 Loa 124.64 (BB) Br ex 18.32 Dght 6.050 Lbp 112.02 Br md 18.31 Dpth 6.15 Welded, 6 dks	**(A35B2RV) Vehicles Carrier** Angled stern door/ramp (p. a.) Len: 16.50 Wid: 4.00 Swl: - Angled stern door/ramp (s. a.) Len: 16.50 Wid: 4.00 Swl: - Cars: 475	**1 oil engine** driving 1 FP propeller Total Power: 3,736kW (5,079hp) 16.0kn B&W 8L35MC 1 x 2 Stroke 8 Cy. 350 x 1050 3736kW (5079bhp) Hitachi Zosen Corp-Japan AuxGen: 2 x 440kW a.c Thrusters: 1 Thwart. FP thruster (a) Fuel: 47.0 (d.f.) 179.5 (r.f.) 15.0pd
9336921 *JD2177* -	**TOYOFUKU MARU** **Fukuju Kigyo KK & Toyofuji Kaiun KK** Fukuju Kigyo Co Ltd *Shizuoka, Shizuoka* *Japan* MMSI: 431200688 Official number: 140244	*12,687* - 5,490	Class: NK	**2005-12 Mitsubishi Heavy Industries Ltd. — Shimonoseki** Yd No: 1113 Loa 165.00 (BB) Br ex - Dght 6.222 Lbp 157.00 Br md 27.60 Dpth 24.15 Welded	**(A35B2RV) Vehicles Carrier** Side door/ramp (p) Len: 15.00 Wid: 4.50 Swl: - Quarter stern door/ramp (p. a.) Len: 25.00 Wid: 6.00 Swl: 45 Quarter stern door/ramp (s. a.) Len: 25.00 Wid: 6.00 Swl: 45 Cars: 2,005	**1 oil engine** driving 1 FP propeller Total Power: 11,935kW (16,227hp) 21.0kn Mitsubishi 7UEC52LSE 1 x 2 Stroke 7 Cy. 520 x 2000 11935kW (16227bhp) Mitsubishi Heavy Industries Ltd-Japan AuxGen: 3 x 1080kW a.c Thrusters: 1 Tunnel thruster (f); 2 Tunnel thruster (a) Fuel: 120.0 (d.f.) 1100.0 (r.f.)

8844505 *XUHF9* -	**TOYOKAWA** *ex* Horai Maru No. 65 *-2005* **He Xin Shipping Co Ltd** Yantai Jinze International Shipping Management Co Ltd *Phnom Penh* *Cambodia* MMSI: 515799000 Official number: 0590051	**1,800** 1,176 1,383	Class: UB	**1990-06 Tokuoka Zosen K.K. — Naruto** Yd No: 182 Loa 64.11 Br ex - Dght 4.520 Lbp 58.00 Br md 12.80 Dpth 6.80 Welded, 1 dk	**(A24D2BA) Aggregates Carrier** 1 Ha: (12.8 x 6.8)ER	**1 oil engine** geared to sc. shaft driving 1 FP propeller Total Power: 1,471kW (2,000hp) 11.0kn Hanshin 6LU35G 1 x 4 Stroke 6 Cy. 350 x 550 1471kW (2000bhp) The Hanshin Diesel Works Ltd-Japan
8713134 - -	**TOYOKAWA MARU** - -	*195* - 487		**1987-09 Iisaku Zosen K.K. — Nishi-Izu** Yd No: 87132 Loa 43.52 (BB) Br ex - Dght 3.250 Lbp 38.99 Br md 7.21 Dpth 3.51 Welded, 1 dk	**(A12E2LE) Edible Oil Tanker** Compartments: 6 Ta, ER	**1 oil engine** with clutches & reverse reduction geared to sc. shaft driving 1 FP propeller Total Power: 736kW (1,001hp) Sumiyoshi S26G 1 x 4 Stroke 6 Cy. 260 x 470 736kW (1001bhp) Sumiyoshi Marine Diesel Co Ltd-Japan Thrusters: 1 Thwart. FP thruster (a)
8313453 *5VBP8* -	**TOYOKICHI** *ex* Feng Shun 9 *-2003* *ex* Kanyo *-1999* *ex* Shokei Maru *-1998* **Grand Luck Enterprise (HK) Ltd** Dalian Tianmiao International Shipping Co Ltd *Lome* *Togo* MMSI: 671277000	**1,490** 621 1,332	Class: UM	**1984-01 K.K. Uno Zosensho — Imabari** Yd No: 171 Loa 73.18 Br ex - Dght 3.912 Lbp 68.00 Br md 12.01 Dpth 6.91 Welded, 2 dks	**(A31A2GX) General Cargo Ship** Grain: 3,581; Bale: 3,485 TEU 64 C. 64/20' (40') Compartments: 1 Ho, ER 1 Ha: ER	**1 oil engine** with clutches, flexible couplings & sr reverse geared to sc. shaft driving 1 FP propeller Total Power: 956kW (1,300hp) 11.7kn Hanshin 6LUN28AG 1 x 4 Stroke 6 Cy. 280 x 480 956kW (1300bhp) The Hanshin Diesel Works Ltd-Japan
9323572 *7JFC* -	**TOYOKUNI** **Kawasaki Kisen Kaisha Ltd (Kawasaki Kisen KK) ('K' Line)** Taiyo Nippon Kisen Co Ltd SatCom: Inmarsat C 443271410 *Kobe, Hyogo* *Japan* MMSI: 432714000 Official number: 141014	**150,834** 53,573 297,584	Class: NK	**2009-07 Universal Shipbuilding Corp — Nagasu KM (Ariake Shipyard)** Yd No: 076 Loa 327.00 (BB) Br ex - Dght 21.433 Lbp 318.00 Br md 55.00 Dpth 29.25 Welded, 1 dk	**(A21B2BO) Ore Carrier** Grain: 180,474 Compartments: 6 Ho, ER 6 Ha: ER	**1 oil engine** driving 1 FP propeller Total Power: 22,700kW (30,863hp) 14.3kn MAN-B&W 6S80MC-C 1 x 2 Stroke 6 Cy. 800 x 3200 22700kW (30863bhp) Hitachi Zosen Corp-Japan Fuel: 7280.0
9134414 *JL6432* -	**TOYOKUNI MARU No. 3** **Toyomasu Kaiso KK** - *Anan, Tokushima* *Japan* MMSI: 431500399 Official number: 135137	*749* - 1,000		**1995-11 K.K. Tachibana Senpaku Tekko — Anan** Yd No: 847 Loa 82.09 Br ex - Dght 4.600 Lbp 77.00 Br md 13.00 Dpth 8.05 Welded, 1 dk	**(A31A2GX) General Cargo Ship**	**1 oil engine** driving 1 FP propeller Total Power: 1,471kW (2,000hp) 12.7kn Hanshin LH36LG 1 x 4 Stroke 6 Cy. 360 x 670 1471kW (2000bhp) The Hanshin Diesel Works Ltd-Japan
9115250 *JEHR* -	**TOYOKUNI MARU No. 8** **Toyokunimaru Gyogyo Seisan Kumiai** - SatCom: Inmarsat A 1206276 *Yaizu, Shizuoka* *Japan* MMSI: 431722000 Official number: 133265	*483* - 565		**1995-03 Miho Zosensho K.K. — Shimizu** Yd No: 1433 Loa 62.78 (BB) Br ex - Dght 3.764 Lbp 53.00 Br md 8.00 Dpth 4.00 Welded, 1 dk	**(B11B2FV) Fishing Vessel** Ins: 688	**1 oil engine** with flexible couplings & sr geared to sc. shaft driving 1 FP propeller Total Power: 736kW (1,001hp) Akasaka E28 1 x 4 Stroke 6 Cy. 280 x 480 736kW (1001bhp) Akasaka Tekkosho KK (Akasaka DieselLtd)-Japan
8631001 *JVFP5* -	**TOYOKUNI MARU NO. 15** *ex* Sts No. 1 *-2013* *ex* Mgm No. 1 *-2007* *ex* Hope Star *-2003* *ex* Orient Star No. 18 *-2002* *ex* Fukuyoshi Maru No. 128 *-2000* **S&B Global SA** Soosung Corp Ltd *Ulaanbaatar* *Mongolia* MMSI: 457900080	**1,598** 599 2,720		**1987-07 Nagashima Zosen KK — Kihoku ME** Loa 63.00 Br ex 13.42 Dght 4.170 Lbp 57.10 Br md 13.40 Dpth 6.20 Welded, 1 dk	**(B33A2DG) Grab Dredger**	**1 oil engine** geared to sc. shaft driving 1 FP propeller Total Power: 736kW (1,001hp) 10.5kn Hanshin 6LU35G 1 x 4 Stroke 6 Cy. 350 x 550 736kW (1001bhp) The Hanshin Diesel Works Ltd-Japan
9146778 *JJ3927* -	**TOYOMASA MARU** **Corporation for Advanced Transport & Technology & Toko Kaiun Co Ltd** Toko Kaiun Co Ltd (Toko Kaiun KK) *Kobe, Hyogo* *Japan* MMSI: 431300401 Official number: 134243	*2,996* - 5,349	Class: NK	**1996-06 Murakami Hide Zosen K.K. — Imabari** Yd No: 360 Loa 101.15 Br ex - Dght 6.758 Lbp 95.00 Br md 14.60 Dpth 7.70 Welded, 1 dk	**(A13B2TP) Products Tanker** Single Hull Liq: 5,599; Liq (Oil): 5,599	**1 oil engine** driving 1 FP propeller Total Power: 2,942kW (4,000hp) 13.5kn Akasaka DM47M 1 x 4 Stroke 6 Cy. 470 x 760 2942kW (4000bhp) Akasaka Tekkosho KK (Akasaka DieselLtd)-Japan Fuel: 140.0 (d.f.)
9601405 *JD2975* -	**TOYORA MARU** **Green Shipping Ltd** - *Kitakyushu, Fukuoka* *Japan* MMSI: 431001057 Official number: 141112	*193* - -		**2009-09 Kotobuki Kogyo KK — Ichikikushikino KS** Yd No: 131 Loa 39.47 Br ex - Dght 3.420 Lbp 35.00 Br md 9.60 Dpth 4.48 Welded, 1 dk	**(B32A2ST) Tug**	**2 oil engines** reduction geared to sc. shafts driving 2 Propellers Total Power: 3,676kW (4,998hp) Niigata 6L28HX 2 x 4 Stroke 6 Cy. 280 x 370 each-1838kW (2499bhp) Niigata Engineering Co Ltd-Japan
8949068 *JH2408* -	**TOYOSHI MARU** *ex* Taigen Maru *-2011* *ex* Seiko Maru *-1999* *ex* Dainichi Maru *-1999* **Toshiro Yamashita** - *Handa, Aichi* *Japan* Official number: 110000	*199* - 367		**1970-12 Katahara Zosen K.K. — Gamagori** Loa 38.40 Br ex - Dght 2.800 Lbp 34.90 Br md 6.80 Dpth 3.00 Welded, 1 dk	**(A31A2GX) General Cargo Ship**	**1 oil engine** driving 1 FP propeller Total Power: 405kW (551hp) 8.0kn Yanmar 1 x 4 Stroke 405kW (551bhp) Yanmar Diesel Engine Co Ltd-Japan
9384423 *7JBU* -	**TOYOSHIO MARU** **Government of Japan (Ministry of Education, Culture, Sports, Science & Technology)** Hiroshima University (Hiroshima Daigaku Seibutsu Seisan Gakubu) *Kure, Hiroshima* *Japan* MMSI: 432575000 Official number: 140428	*256* - 130		**2006-11 Mitsui Eng. & SB. Co. Ltd. — Tamano** Yd No: 1699 Loa 40.50 Br ex 8.52 Dght 3.100 Lbp 35.50 Br md 8.50 Dpth 3.70 Welded, 1 dk	**(B12D2FR) Fishery Research Vessel**	**2 diesel electric oil engines** reduction geared to sc. shafts driving 2 CP propellers Total Power: 400kW (544hp)
9134294 *JHJM* -	**TOYOSU MARU** **Tokyo LNG Tanker Co Ltd & Iino Kaiun Kaisha Ltd** Iino Marine Service Co Ltd SatCom: Inmarsat B 343190410 *Tokyo* *Japan* MMSI: 431904000 Official number: 135850	**44,652** 13,395 49,651 T/cm 69.4	Class: NK	**1997-01 Mitsubishi Heavy Industries Ltd. — Nagasaki** Yd No: 2108 Loa 230.00 (BB) Br ex - Dght 10.836 Lbp 219.00 Br md 36.60 Dpth 20.40 Welded, 1 dk	**(A11B2TG) LPG Tanker** Double Bottom Entire Compartment Length Liq (Gas): 78,462 4 x Gas Tank (s); 4 independent (s.stl) pri vertical 8 Cargo Pump (s): 8x550m³/hr Manifold: Bow/CM: 113m	**1 oil engine** driving 1 FP propeller Total Power: 12,357kW (16,801hp) 16.7kn Mitsubishi 7UEC60LS 1 x 2 Stroke 7 Cy. 600 x 2200 12357kW (16801bhp) Mitsubishi Heavy Industries Ltd-Japan AuxGen: 3 x 880kW 450V 60Hz a.c Fuel: 250.0 (d.f.) 2313.0 (r.f.) 48.0pd
8414257 *YCGE* -	**TOYOTA** *ex* Dwi No. 1 *-2008* *ex* Kyoritsu Maru No. 18 *-2006* **PT Samudra Inti Perkasa** - *Tanjung Priok* *Indonesia*	**1,257** 378 1,599	Class: KI	**1984-08 Kishigami Zosen K.K. — Akitsu** Yd No: 1705 Converted From: Bulk Aggregates Carrier Loa 65.02 Br ex - Dght 4.320 Lbp 60.00 Br md 12.51 Dpth 6.23 Welded, 1 dk	**(A31A2GX) General Cargo Ship** Grain: 878 Compartments: 1 Ho, ER 1 Ha: ER	**1 oil engine** reverse geared to sc. shaft driving 1 FP propeller Total Power: 1,177kW (1,600hp) Akasaka DM33 1 x 4 Stroke 6 Cy. 330 x 500 1177kW (1600bhp) Akasaka Tekkosho KK (Akasaka DieselLtd)-Japan AuxGen: 2 x 136kW 450V a.c
9041693 *JL6054* -	**TOYOTAKA MARU** **Japan Railway Construction, Transport & Technology Agency & Maruyoshi KK & Toyomasu Kaisou KK** Toyomasu Kaiso KK *Anan, Tokushima* *Japan* Official number: 132143	*391* - 1,009	Class: NK	**1991-12 K.K. Miura Zosensho — Saiki** Yd No: 1027 Loa 68.50 Br ex - Dght 3.770 Lbp 63.00 Br md 11.00 Dpth 3.85 Welded, 2 dks	**(A31A2GX) General Cargo Ship** Grain: 2,181; Bale: 2,012 1 Ha: (36.6 x 8.4)ER	**1 oil engine** geared to sc. shaft driving 1 FP propeller Total Power: 736kW (1,001hp) 10.0kn Akasaka K28SFD 1 x 4 Stroke 6 Cy. 280 x 500 736kW (1001bhp) Akasaka Tekkosho KK (Akasaka DieselLtd)-Japan AuxGen: 2 x 108kW a.c Fuel: 58.0 (d.f.)

IMO / Call sign	Name / Owner / Port	Tonnage	Class	Builder / Dimensions	Type / Cargo	Machinery
9163518 JM6535 -	**TOYOTAMA MARU No. 25** - **KK Murase Kaiun** - *Uki, Kumamoto* *Japan* Official number: 134650	*499* - 1,450		**1996**-11 **K.K. Watanabe Zosensho — Nagasaki** Yd No: 053 Loa 70.30 Br ex - Dght 4.430 Lbp 63.50 Br md 13.00 Dpth 7.39 Welded, 1 dk	**(A31A2GX) General Cargo Ship** Compartments: 1 Ho, ER 1 Ha: (23.4 x 10.2)ER Cranes: 1x15t	**1 oil engine** driving 1 FP propeller Total Power: 736kW (1,001hp) 11.0kn Niigata 6M34BGT 1 x 4 Stroke 6 Cy. 340 x 620 736kW (1001bhp) Niigata Engineering Co Ltd-Japan
9426568 JD2431 -	**TOYOTSU MARU** - **GK Nakatsuru Gumi** - *Tsukumi, Oita* *Japan* Official number: 140556	*499* - 1,720		**2007**-05 **K.K. Miura Zosensho — Saiki** Yd No: 1318 Loa 75.80 Br ex - Dght 4.310 Lbp 68.80 Br md 12.30 Dpth 7.32 Welded, 1 dk	**(A31A2GX) General Cargo Ship** Bale: 2,484	**1 oil engine** reduction geared to sc. shaft driving 1 FP propeller Total Power: 1,471kW (2,000hp) 2.5kn Niigata 6M34BGT 1 x 4 Stroke 6 Cy. 340 x 620 1471kW (2000bhp) Niigata Engineering Co Ltd-Japan
9343601 JD2127 -	**TOYOTURU MARU** - **Toyotsuru Shipping Co Ltd** Tsurumaru Shipping Co Ltd *Kitakyushu, Fukuoka* *Japan* MMSI: 431602306 Official number: 140183	*3,118* - 4,307	Class: NK	**2005**-09 **Kanda Zosensho K.K. — Kawajiri** Yd No: 477 Loa 97.00 Br ex - Dght 5.527 Lbp 91.50 Br md 16.20 Dpth 7.00 Welded, 1 dk	**(A24A2BT) Cement Carrier** Grain: 3,583	**1 oil engine** driving 1 FP propeller Total Power: 2,647kW (3,599hp) 14.0kn Akasaka A41S 1 x 4 Stroke 6 Cy. 410 x 800 2647kW (3599bhp) Akasaka Tekkosho KK (Akasaka DieselLtd)-Japan Fuel: 135.0
9062398 JL5926 -	**TOYU** - **Yuo Kaiun KK** - *Imabari, Ehime* *Japan* MMSI: 431500004 Official number: 132947	*696* - 1,639		**1992**-08 **Kyoei Zosen KK — Mihara HS** Yd No: 251 Loa 70.20 Br ex - Dght 4.500 Lbp 69.95 Br md 11.20 Dpth 5.00 Welded, 1 dk	**(A12A2TC) Chemical Tanker** Liq: 1,177 Compartments: 8 Ta, ER 2 Cargo Pump (s): 2x300m³/hr	**1 oil engine** driving 1 CP propeller Total Power: 2,060kW (2,801hp) Hanshin 6EL38 1 x 4 Stroke 6 Cy. 380 x 760 2060kW (2801bhp) The Hanshin Diesel Works Ltd-Japan Thrusters: 1 Thwart. FP thruster (f)
8815425 JI3334 -	**TOZAI MARU No. 1** - **Tozai Kaiun KK** - *Kainan, Wakayama* *Japan* Official number: 128738	*156* - -		**1988**-11 **Kanagawa Zosen — Kobe** Yd No: 318 L reg 27.20 Br ex - Dght 3.500 Lbp - Br md 8.60 Dpth 3.70 Welded, 1 dk	**(B32A2ST) Tug**	**2 oil engines** driving 2 FP propellers Total Power: 2,294kW (3,118hp) Niigata 6L25CXE 2 x 4 Stroke 6 Cy. 250 x 320 each-1147kW (1559bhp) Niigata Engineering Co Ltd-Japan
9624732 JD3055 -	**TOZAN MARU NO. 2** - **Tozai Kaiun KK** - *Kainan, Tokushima* *Japan* Official number: 141228	*166* - -		**2010**-04 **Hatayama Zosen KK — Yura WK** Yd No: 260 L reg 28.23 Br ex - Dght - Lbp - Br md 8.80 Dpth 3.88 Welded, 1 dk	**(B32A2ST) Tug**	**2 oil engines** reduction geared to sc. shafts driving 2 Propellers Total Power: 2,942kW (4,000hp) Niigata 6L26HLX 2 x 4 Stroke 6 Cy. 260 x 350 each-1471kW (2000bhp) Niigata Engineering Co Ltd-Japan
9004865 LW9713 -	**TOZUDO** - **Cabo Verde SA** - *Buenos Aires* *Argentina* MMSI: 701000728 Official number: 01219	**112** 67 113	Class: (RI)	**1990**-03 **Ast. Naval Federico Contessi y Cia. S.A. — Mar del Plata** Yd No: 57 Loa 24.00 Br ex 7.00 Dght 3.150 Lbp 23.24 Br md - Dpth 3.45 Welded, 1 dk	**(B11B2FV) Fishing Vessel** Ins: 135	**1 oil engine** with clutches & sr geared to sc. shaft driving 1 FP propeller Total Power: 496kW (674hp) Cummins VTA-28-M 1 x Vee 4 Stroke 12 Cy. 140 x 152 496kW (674bhp) Cummins Engine Co Inc-USA
9155834 YD4660 -	**TP 73 NO. 5** *ex* QM Pioneer 988 *-1999* **PT Angsana Putra Sumatera** - *Palembang* *Indonesia*	**118** 70 104	Class: KI (NK)	**1996**-07 **C E Ling Shipbuilding Sdn Bhd — Miri** Yd No: 002 Loa 23.26 Br ex - Dght 2.388 Lbp 21.76 Br md 7.00 Dpth 2.90 Welded, 1 dk	**(B32A2ST) Tug**	**2 oil engines** reduction geared to sc. shafts driving 2 FP propellers Total Power: 794kW (1,080hp) 10.0kn Caterpillar 3412TA 2 x Vee 4 Stroke 12 Cy. 137 x 152 each-397kW (540bhp) Caterpillar Inc-USA Fuel: 76.8 (d.f.)
8732415 YBTA -	**TPS ALPHA** *ex* PW Alpha *-2007* **PT Pelayaran Trans Parau Sorat** - *Batam* *Indonesia* MMSI: 525016149	**329** 99 165	Class: KI NV	**2007**-03 **Bengbu Shenzhou Machinery Co Ltd — Bengbu AH** Yd No: 1200 Loa 28.00 Br ex - Dght 4.490 Lbp 22.94 Br md 9.80 Dpth 4.90 Welded, 1 dk	**(B32A2ST) Tug**	**2 oil engines** reduction geared to sc. shafts driving 2 Directional propellers Total Power: 2,648kW (3,600hp) Yanmar 8N21A-EN 2 x 4 Stroke 8 Cy. 210 x 290 each-1324kW (1800bhp) Yanmar Diesel Engine Co Ltd-Japan
9121235 PMBY -	**TPS BETA** *ex* Maju 4 *-2007* **PT Pelayaran Trans Parau Sorat** - *Jambi* *Indonesia*	**323** 97 -	Class: KI (NK)	**1994**-10 **Donghai Shipyard — Shanghai** Yd No: 93328 Loa 32.83 Br ex 9.50 Dght 3.404 Lbp 26.50 Br md 9.50 Dpth 4.30 Welded, 1 dk	**(B32A2ST) Tug**	**2 oil engines** reduction geared to sc. shafts driving 2 FP propellers Total Power: 2,354kW (3,200hp) 12.7kn Daihatsu 6DLM-26 2 x 4 Stroke 6 Cy. 260 x 340 each-1177kW (1600bhp) Daihatsu Diesel Manufacturing Co Lt-Japan AuxGen: 2 x 75kW 380V 50Hz a.c Fuel: 48.0
9322762 V7EE4 -	**TR CROWN** *ex* Maple Creek *-2014* **Grafton Shipping Ltd** AM Nomikos Transworld Maritime Agencies SA *Majuro* *Marshall Islands* MMSI: 538005461 Official number: 5461	**30,002** 18,486 53,474	Class: NK	**2005**-02 **Imabari Shipbuilding Co Ltd — Imabari EH (Imabari Shipyard)** Yd No: 607 Loa 189.94 (BB) Br ex - Dght 12.303 Lbp 182.00 Br md 32.26 Dpth 17.30 Welded, 1 dk	**(A21A2BC) Bulk Carrier** Grain: 68,927; Bale: 65,526 Compartments: 5 Ho, ER 5 Ha: ER 5 (21.1 x 17.6) Cranes: 4x30.5t	**1 oil engine** driving 1 FP propeller Total Power: 9,480kW (12,889hp) 15.0kn B&W 6S50MC-C 1 x 2 Stroke 6 Cy. 500 x 2000 9480kW (12889bhp) Mitsui Engineering & Shipbuilding CLtd-Japan Fuel: 2090.0
8873180 - -	**TRA LY 01** - **Song Diem-Thai Binh Maritrans Enterprise (Xi Nghiep Van Tai Song Diem- Thai Binh)** - *Thai Binh* *Vietnam*	*166* 86 200	Class: (VR)	**1985 at Thai Binh** Loa 36.15 Br ex - Dght 1.950 Lbp 33.75 Br md 7.00 Dpth 2.50 Welded, 1 dk	**(A31A2GX) General Cargo Ship**	**1 oil engine** reduction geared to sc. shaft driving 1 FP propeller Total Power: 99kW (135hp) 8.5kn Skoda 6L160 1 x 4 Stroke 6 Cy. 160 x 225 99kW (135bhp) CKD Praha-Praha
8869074 - -	**TRA LY 03** - **Song Hoa Thai Binh Maritrans Enterprise (Xi Nghiep Van Tai Song Hoa Thai Binh)** - *Haiphong* *Vietnam*	**166** 86 200	Class: (VR)	**1986 at Thai Binh** Loa 36.35 Br ex - Dght 1.950 Lbp - Br md 7.00 Dpth 2.50 Welded, 1 dk	**(A31A2GX) General Cargo Ship** Grain: 311 Compartments: 2 Ho, ER 2 Ha: 2 (7.0 x 4.0)ER	**1 oil engine** reduction geared to sc. shaft driving 1 FP propeller Total Power: 99kW (135hp) 8.5kn Skoda 6L160 1 x 4 Stroke 6 Cy. 160 x 225 99kW (135bhp) CKD Praha-Praha AuxGen: 1 x 4kW a.c
8869050 - -	**TRA LY 05** - **Thai Thuy - Thai Binh Maritrans Enterprise (Xi Nghiep Van Tai Thai Thuy - Thai Binh)** - *Thai Binh* *Vietnam*	**154** 88 200	Class: (VR)	**1987 at Thai Binh** Loa 36.35 Br ex - Dght 1.950 Lbp - Br md 7.00 Dpth 2.50 Welded, 1 dk	**(A31A2GX) General Cargo Ship** Grain: 311 Compartments: 2 Ho, ER 2 Ha: 2 (7.0 x 4.0)ER	**1 oil engine** reduction geared to sc. shaft driving 1 FP propeller Total Power: 99kW (135hp) 8.5kn Skoda 6L160 1 x 4 Stroke 6 Cy. 160 x 225 99kW (135bhp) CKD Praha-Praha AuxGen: 1 x 6kW a.c
8612794 JXML R-15-K	**TRAAL** *ex* Rav II *-2003* *ex* Rav *-2003* **Traal AS** Kjell T Eriksen SatCom: Inmarsat C 425805410 *Skudeneshavn* *Norway* MMSI: 258054000 Official number: 20375	**1,011** 381 1,181	Class: NV	**1987**-10 **Vaagland Baatbyggeri AS — Vaagland** Yd No: 112 Loa 53.01 Br ex - Dght 6.613 Lbp 46.00 Br md 11.21 Dpth 7.52 Welded	**(B11B2FV) Fishing Vessel** Ice Capable	**1 oil engine** geared to sc. shaft driving 1 FP propeller Total Power: 2,399kW (3,262hp) 14.5kn Wichmann WX28V8 1 x Vee 4 Stroke 8 Cy. 280 x 360 2399kW (3262bhp) Wartsila Wichmann Diesel AS-Norway AuxGen: 2 x 461kW 440V 60Hz a.c, 1 x 1456kW 440V 60Hz a.c Thrusters: 1 Thwart. CP thruster (f); 1 Tunnel thruster (a)
7817945 DUAA -	**TRABAJADOR 1** *ex* Seiha Maru No. 2 *-2009* *ex* Sun Arrow *-1983* **Malayan Towage & Salvage Corp (SALVTUG)** - SatCom: Inmarsat C 454880011 *Manila* *Philippines* MMSI: 548800000 Official number: 00-0000092	**1,449** 434 1,039	Class: RI (NK)	**1979**-04 **Kochi Jyuko (Eiho Zosen) K.K. — Kochi** Yd No: 1292 Converted From: Tug-1983 Loa 69.00 Br ex 12.60 Dght 4.762 Lbp 63.24 Br md - Dpth 5.52 Riveted\Welded, 1 dk	**(B32A2ST) Tug**	**2 oil engines** driving 2 FP propellers Total Power: 6,032kW (8,202hp) 13.5kn Makita KSLH647 2 x 4 Stroke 6 Cy. 470 x 760 each-3016kW (4101bhp) Makita Diesel Co Ltd-Japan AuxGen: 2 x 200kW 445V 60Hz a.c Thrusters: 1 Thwart. FP thruster (f) Fuel: 176.0 (d.f.) 760.0 (r.f.) 29.0pd

IMO / Call sign	Name / Owner	Tonnage	Class	Builder / Dimensions	Type / Cargo	Machinery
6915635 *H04200* -	**TRABUNKER** *ex* Melina *-2005* *ex* Valio *-2001* *ex* Macoil *-1991* *ex* Black *-1989* *ex* Blackfoot *-1989* *ex* Victoriasand *-1977* **Essco Pioneer SA** Tramarine Ltd *Panama* *Panama* MMSI: 371612000 Official number: 33845PEXT	**1,141** 579 1,306	Class: HR (GL)	**1969-03 Buesumer Werft GmbH — Buesum** Yd No: 229 Loa 73.74 (BB) Br ex 12.02 Dght 3.649 Lbp 68.31 Br md 11.90 Dpth 5.01 Welded, 2 dks	**(A12B2TR) Chemical/Products Tanker** Liq: 1,740; Liq (Oil): 1,740 Cargo Heating Coils Compartments: 8 Ta, ER Ice Capable	**1 oil engine** driving 1 FP propeller Total Power: 736kW (1,001hp) 11.5kn MaK 4ZU451AK 1 x 4 Stroke 4 Cy. 320 x 450 736kW (1001bhp) Atlas MaK Maschinenbau GmbH-Kiel AuxGen: 2 x 60kW 380V 50Hz a.c Fuel: 110.5 (d.f.) 4.0pd
9595046 *9HA2783* -	**TRABZON** **Trabzon Maritime Ltd** Ciner Gemi Acente Isletmeleri Sanayi ve Ticaret AS (Ciner Ship Management) SatCom: Inmarsat C 421567910 *Valletta* *Malta* MMSI: 215679000 Official number: 9595046	**44,635** 26,712 81,660 T/cm 71.0	Class: LR (NV) **100A1** SS 11/2011 bulk carrier ESP CSR BC-A (Holds 2,4 & 6 may be empty) GRAB (25) **ShipRight** (ACS (B)) *IWS LI **LMC** **UMS** Cable: 687.5/81.0 SL	**2011-11 Hyundai Mipo Dockyard Co Ltd — Ulsan** Yd No: 6066 Loa 229.00 (BB) Br ex 32.30 Dght 14.500 Lbp 222.50 Br md 32.26 Dpth 20.30 Welded, 1 dk	**(A21A2BC) Bulk Carrier** Grain: 95,700 Compartments: 7 Ho, ER 7 Ha: ER	**1 oil engine** driving 1 FP propeller Total Power: 14,280kW (19,415hp) 14.5kn MAN-B&W 6S60MC-C8 1 x 2 Stroke 6 Cy. 600 x 2400 14280kW (19415bhp) Hyundai Heavy Industries Co Ltd-South Korea AuxGen: 3 x 600kW 450V 60Hz a.c Boilers: WTAuxB (Comp) 9.2kgf/cm² (9.0bar)
9204702 *PHAC* -	**TRACER** **Rederij Tracer** BigLift Shipping BV *Amsterdam* *Netherlands* MMSI: 245949000 Official number: 38069	**6,714** 2,888 8,734 T/cm 18.6	Class: BV (NV)	**1999-08 Zhonghua Shipyard — Shanghai** Yd No: 406 Loa 100.70 (BB) Br ex 20.60 Dght 8.200 Lbp 95.00 Br md 20.40 Dpth 11.10 Welded, 2 dks	**(A31A2GX) General Cargo Ship** Grain: 10,530; Bale: 10,300 TEU 371 C Ho 195 C Dk 176 incl 24 ref C. Compartments: 1 Ho, ER, 1 Tw Dk 1 Ha: (64.2 x 15.3)ER Cranes: 2x275t Ice Capable	**1 oil engine** with flexible couplings & sr gearedto sc. shaft driving 1 CP propeller Total Power: 7,800kW (10,605hp) 16.5kn Wartsila 8L46B 1 x 4 Stroke 8 Cy. 460 x 580 7800kW (10605bhp) Wartsila NSD Finland Oy-Finland AuxGen: 1 x 900kW 220/440V 60Hz a.c, 3 x 530kW 440V 60Hz a.c Thrusters: 1 Thwart. CP thruster (f) Fuel: 131.5 (d.f.) (Heating Coils) 775.3 (r.f.) 28.0pd
8976994 *WDA6354* -	**TRACEY C** **Tracey C Fishing LLC** - *Pago Pago, AS* *United States of America* MMSI: 369059000 Official number: 1102666	**170** 51 -		**1990 in Australia** L reg 29.48 Br ex - Dght - Lbp - Br md 5.79 Dpth 2.74 Welded, 1 dk	**(B11B2FV) Fishing Vessel**	**1 oil engine** geared to sc. shaft driving 1 FP propeller Caterpillar 1 x 4 Stroke Caterpillar Inc-USA
9525211 *2EYB2* -	**TRACEY KOSAN** **Lauritzen Kosan A/S** - *Douglas* *Isle of Man (British)* MMSI: 235089094 Official number: 742855	**3,728** 1,119 3,791 T/cm 13.5	Class: BV (NK)	**2011-11 Yangzhou Kejin Shipyard Co Ltd — Jiangdu JS** Yd No: 07075 Loa 99.96 (BB) Br ex 16.64 Dght 5.714 Lbp 93.73 Br md 16.60 Dpth 7.83 Welded, 1 dk	**(A11B2TG) LPG Tanker** Double Bottom Entire Compartment Length Liq (Gas): 3,598 2 x Gas Tank (s); 2 independent (stl) cyl horizontal 2 Cargo Pump (s): 2x300m³/hr Manifold: Bow/CM: 46.1m	**1 oil engine** reduction geared to sc. shaft driving 1 CP propeller Total Power: 2,720kW (3,698hp) 12.5kn MAN-B&W 8L27/38 1 x 4 Stroke 8 Cy. 270 x 380 2720kW (3698bhp) Zhenjiang Marine Diesel Works-China AuxGen: 3 x 410kW 60Hz a.c Thrusters: 1 Tunnel thruster (f) Fuel: 186.0 (d.f.) 347.0 (r.f.)
6725432 *CGBX* -	**TRACY** **Government of Canada (Canadian Coast Guard)** - *Ottawa, ON* *Canada* MMSI: 316001510 Official number: 328087	*837* 251 419	Class: (LR) ✠ Classed LR until 23/6/78	**1968-04 Port Weller Dry Docks — St Catharines ON** Yd No: 42 Loa 55.33 Br ex 11.64 Dght 3.658 Lbp 50.30 Br md 11.59 Dpth 4.88 Welded, 1 dk	**(B34Q2QB) Buoy Tender** Compartments: 1 Ho, ER 2 Ha: (3.8 x 6.1) (3.7 x 6.1)ER Cranes: 1x10t; Derricks: 1x4t Ice Capable	**2 diesel electric oil engines** driving 4 gen. each 405kW 600V d.c Connecting to 2 elec. motors driving 2 FP propellers Total Power: 1,960kW (2,664hp) 10.0kn Fairbanks, Morse 8-38D8-1/8 2 x 2 Stroke 8 Cy. 207 x 254 each-980kW (1332bhp) Fairbanks Morse (Canada) Ltd-Canada AuxGen: 3 x 110kW 440V 60Hz a.c Fuel: 131.0 (d.f.)
8855762 *WDE6281* -	**TRACY ANNE** **HLTA LLC** - *Seattle, WA* *United States of America* Official number: 904859	*138* 93 -		**1986 Rodriguez Boat Builders, Inc. — Coden, Al** Yd No: 50 Loa - Br ex - Dght - Lbp 26.30 Br md 7.32 Dpth 3.87 Welded, 1 dk	**(B11B2FV) Fishing Vessel**	**1 oil engine** driving 1 FP propeller
6515203 - -	**TRACY I** *ex* Tracy *-1998* *ex* Estelle Stone *-1998* *ex* LT-1947 *-1965* - -	*226* 153 -	Class: (AB)	**1953-01 Avondale Marine Ways Inc. — Westwego, La** Yd No: 406 L reg 31.09 Br ex 8.13 Dght 4.055 Lbp 30.56 Br md 8.08 Dpth 4.53 Welded, 1 dk	**(B32A2ST) Tug**	**1 oil engine** driving 1 FP propeller Total Power: 1,030kW (1,400hp) Enterprise 1 x 2 Stroke 6 Cy. 406 x 508 1030kW (1400bhp) Fairbanks Morse & Co.-New Orleans, La AuxGen: 2 x 40kW 115V d.c Fuel: 65.0 (d.f.)
8806723 - -	**TRACY MARTINA** **Tracey Martina Ltd** - *St John's, NL* *Canada* Official number: 809074	*101* 50 -		**1987-12 Bay d'Espoir Enterprises Ltd — St Albans NL** Loa 18.78 Br ex 6.89 Dght - Lbp 18.01 Br md 6.74 Dpth 3.79 Welded, 1 dk	**(B11B2FV) Fishing Vessel**	**1 oil engine** with clutches & sr reverse geared to sc. shaft driving 1 FP propeller Total Power: 504kW (685hp) Rolls Royce CV12M800T 1 x Vee 4 Stroke 12 Cy. 135 x 152 504kW (685bhp) Rolls Royce Ltd.-Coventry
9232046 *WDA2094* -	**TRACY MORAN** **Moran Towing Corp** - *Wilmington, DE* *United States of America* Official number: 1097426	**232** 69 -	Class: AB	**2000-05 Washburn & Doughty Associates Inc — East Boothbay ME** Yd No: 69 Loa 28.04 Br ex - Dght 3.535 Lbp 27.50 Br md 9.75 Dpth 4.19 Welded, 1 dk	**(B32A2ST) Tug**	**2 oil engines** gearing integral to driving 2 Z propellers Total Power: 3,090kW (4,202hp) EMD (Electro-Motive) 16-645-E2 2 x Vee 2 Stroke 16 Cy. 230 x 254 each-1545kW (2101bhp) General Motors Corp.Electro-Motive Div.-La Grange AuxGen: 2 x 50kW a.c
9631371 *PCYA* -	**TRADE NAVIGATOR** **FWN Trade BV** ForestWave Navigation BV (FWN) *Heerenveen* *Netherlands* MMSI: 244650331	**5,667** 3,048 8,200	Class: LR ✠ **100A1** SS 12/2013 strengthened for heavy cargoes, container cargoes in holds and on upper deck hatch covers **ShipRight** ACS (B) LI Ice Class 1A FS at draught of 7.350m Max/min draught fwd 7.350/3.250m Max/min draught aft 7.350/4.650m Required power 2900kw, installed power 2995kw ✠ **LMC** **UMS** Eq.Ltr: X; Cable: 495.0/46.0 U3 (a)	**2013-12 Damen Shipyards Yichang Co Ltd — Yichang HB** (Hull) Yd No: (9445) **2013-12 B.V. Scheepswerf Damen Bergum — Bergum** Yd No: 9445 Loa 118.14 (BB) Br ex 16.14 Dght 7.200 Lbp 111.60 Br md 15.90 Dpth 8.80 Welded, 1 dk	**(A31A2GX) General Cargo Ship** Grain: 10,795; Bale: 10,795 TEU 366 C Ho 177 TEU C Dk 189 TEU incl 20 ref C Compartments: 2 Ho, ER 2 Ha: ER Cranes: 2x60t Ice Capable	**1 oil engine** with flexible couplings & sr geared to sc. shaft driving 1 CP propeller Total Power: 2,995kW (4,072hp) 13.4kn MaK 6M32C 1 x 4 Stroke 6 Cy. 320 x 480 2995kW (4072bhp) Caterpillar Motoren GmbH & Co. KG-Germany AuxGen: 3 x 360kW 400V 50Hz a.c, 1 x 468kW 400V 50Hz a.c Boilers: HWH (o.f.) 5.1kgf/cm² (5.0bar), HWH (ex.g.) 6.1kgf/cm² (6.0bar) Thrusters: 1 Thwart. FP thruster (f) Fuel: 65.0 (d.f.) 490.0 (r.f.)
9561825 *3EUU3* -	**TRADE STAR** **Nikko Kisen Co Ltd & Sun Lanes Shipping SA** Nissen Kaiun Co Ltd (Nissen Kaiun KK) *Panama* *Panama* MMSI: 372868000 Official number: 40874KJ	**17,986** 10,380 29,627 T/cm 40.5	Class: NK	**2010-08 Shikoku Dockyard Co. Ltd. — Takamatsu** Yd No: 1063 Loa 170.70 (BB) Br ex - Dght 9.716 Lbp 163.50 Br md 27.00 Dpth 13.80 Welded, 1 dk	**(A21A2BC) Bulk Carrier** Grain: 40,031; Bale: 38,422 Compartments: 5 Ho, ER 5 Ha: ER Cranes: 4x30.5t	**1 oil engine** driving 1 FP propeller Total Power: 6,480kW (8,810hp) 14.3kn MAN-B&W 6S42MC 1 x 2 Stroke 6 Cy. 420 x 1764 6480kW (8810bhp) Mitsui Engineering & Shipbuilding CLtd-Japan Fuel: 1804.0 (r.f.)
9526485 *V7ZY4* -	**TRADE VISION** *ex* Nord Aquarius *-2012* **Trade Vision Inc** Marine Management Services MC *Majuro* *Marshall Islands* MMSI: 538004941 Official number: 4941	**45,259** 26,966 81,838 T/cm 72.2	Class: AB (LR) Classed LR until 30/9/13	**2011-08 Guangzhou Longxue Shipbuilding Co Ltd — Guangzhou GD** Yd No: L0017 Loa 229.00 (BB) Br ex - Dght 14.580 Lbp 223.50 Br md 32.26 Dpth 20.20 Welded, 1 dk	**(A21A2BC) Bulk Carrier** Grain: 97,115 Compartments: 7 Ho, ER 7 Ha: ER	**1 oil engine** driving 1 FP propeller Total Power: 11,060kW (15,037hp) 14.5kn MAN-B&W 7S50MC-C 1 x 2 Stroke 7 Cy. 500 x 2000 11060kW (15037bhp) Dalian Marine Diesel Works-China AuxGen: 3 x 620kW a.c Fuel: 200.0 (d.f.) 2900.0 (r.f.)

ID / Name / Owner	Tonnage	Class	Builder / Dimensions	Type / Cargo	Machinery
9528562 *V7ZY2* - **TRADE WILL** *ex* Nord Aquila *-2012* **Trade Will Inc** Marine Management Services MC *Majuro* *Marshall Islands* MMSI: 538004940 Official number: 4940	**45,259** 26,966 81,712 T/cm 72.2	Class: AB (LR) **100A1** SS 01/2012 bulk carrier CSR BC-A GRAB (25) Nos. 2, 4 & 6 holds may be empty ESP **ShipRight** (ACS (B)) *IWS LI **LMC** **UMS** Classed LR until 19/11/13	**2012-01 Guangzhou Longxue Shipbuilding Co Ltd — Guangzhou GD** Yd No: L0018 Loa 229.00 (BB) Br ex - Dght 14.580 Lbp 223.50 Br md 32.26 Dpth 20.20 Welded, 1 dk	**(A21A2BC) Bulk Carrier** Grain: 97,115 Compartments: 7 Ho, ER 7 Ha: ER	**1 oil engine** driving 1 FP propeller Total Power: 11,060kW (15,037hp) 14.5kn MAN-B&W 7S50MC-C 1 x 2 Stroke 7 Cy. 500 x 2000 11060kW (15037bhp) Dalian Marine Diesel Co Ltd-China AuxGen: 3 x 620kW a.c Boilers: AuxB (o.f.) 9.2kgf/cm² (9.0bar) Fuel: 212.0 (d.f.) 2932.0 (r.f.)
9360374 - **TRADE WIND** *ex* Bestwin 118 *-2007* **Adams Brothers Corp** -	**143** 43 119	Class: (NK)	**2005-06 Lingco Shipbuilding Pte Ltd — Singapore** Yd No: 4504 Loa 23.50 Br ex - Dght 2.712 Lbp 21.77 Br md 7.32 Dpth 3.20 Welded, 1 dk	**(B32A2ST) Tug**	**2 oil engines** reduction geared to sc. shafts driving 2 FP propellers Total Power: 954kW (1,298hp) 10.0kn Cummins KTA-19-M3 2 x 4 Stroke 6 Cy. 159 x 159 each-477kW (649bhp) Cummins Engine Co Inc-USA Fuel: 85.0 (d.f.)
9057214 *E5U2536* - **TRADER** *ex* Yulia *-2011* *ex* Kapitan Kabardukov *-2005* *ex* Seacross *-2002* *ex* Kometa *-2000* *ex* Lieke *-1995* *ex* Alma Ata *-1995* **Pantheon Marine Ltd** Jay Management Corp *Avatiu* *Cook Islands* MMSI: 518589000 Official number: 1625	**2,575** 1,163 3,092	Class: RS (BV)	**1992-08 Societatea Comerciala Severnav S.A. — Drobeta-Turnu Severin** Yd No: 006 Loa 86.04 (BB) Br ex - Dght 5.550 Lbp 79.84 Br md 14.50 Dpth 6.70 Welded, 1 dk	**(A31A2GX) General Cargo Ship** Grain: 4,122; Bale: 4,038 TEU 96 C. 96/20' Compartments: 2 Ho, ER 2 Ha: 2 (19.0 x 10.2)ER Cranes: 2x5t	**1 oil engine** driving 1 FP propeller Total Power: 1,802kW (2,450hp) 13.7kn B&W 4L35MCE 1 x 2 Stroke 4 Cy. 350 x 1050 1802kW (2450bhp) (made 1990) Hudong Shipyard-China AuxGen: 2 x 264kW 220/380V 50Hz a.c Fuel: 220.0 (d.f.)
9132014 *OJHU* - **TRADER** *ex* Birka Trader *-2013* *ex* United Trader *-2002* **Eckero Shipping AB Ltd** SatCom: Inmarsat C 423036811 *Mariehamn* *Finland* MMSI: 230368000 Official number: 55138	**12,251** 3,676 8,853 T/cm 27.5	Class: NV	**1998-05 Santierul Naval Galati S.A. — Galati** (Hull) Yd No: 907 **1998-05 Fosen Mek. Verksteder AS — Rissa** Yd No: 63 Loa 154.50 (BB) Br ex - Dght 6.950 Lbp 142.60 Br md 22.70 Dpth 14.80 Welded, 3 dks	**(A35A2RR) Ro-Ro Cargo Ship** Passengers: cabins: 12; berths: 12 Stern door/ramp (p) Len: 15.00 Wid: 4.50 Swl: 70 Stern door/ramp (s) Len: 15.00 Wid: 14.50 Swl: 70 Lane-Len: 1775 Trailers: 125 TEU 336 incl 40 ref C Ice Capable	**1 oil engine** with flexible couplings & sr gearedto sc. shaft driving 1 CP propeller Total Power: 15,600kW (21,210hp) 20.0kn Wartsila 16V46B 1 x Vee 4 Stroke 16 Cy. 460 x 580 15600kW (21210bhp) Wartsila NSD Finland Oy-Finland AuxGen: 1 x 1000kW 220/380V 50Hz a.c, 2 x 800kW 220/380V 50Hz a.c Thrusters: 1 Thwart. CP thruster (f) Fuel: 69.9 (r.f.) (Heating Coils) 1612.4 (r.f.)
8003888 *HP8346* - **TRADER** *ex* Cranz II *-2001* *ex* Cranz *-1998* *ex* Matthias *-1993* *ex* Vouksi *-1991* *ex* Matthias *-1991* *ex* Echo Matthias *-1990* *ex* Elbe *-1989* **Iron Shipping Inc** - *Panama* *Panama* MMSI: 373363000 Official number: 4423112	**1,527** 781 2,290	Class: GS (GL)	**1980-11 Schiffs. Hugo Peters Wewelsfleth Peters & Co. GmbH — Wewelsfleth** Yd No: 578 Loa 82.48 Br ex 11.38 Dght 4.190 Lbp 76.82 Br md 11.30 Dpth 5.41 Welded, 2 dks	**(A31A2GX) General Cargo Ship** Grain: 2,902; Bale: 2,898 TEU 80 C. 80/20' Compartments: 1 Ho, ER 1 Ha: (49.8 x 8.9)ER Ice Capable	**1 oil engine** reverse reduction geared to sc. shaft driving 1 FP propeller Total Power: 441kW (600hp) 10.5kn Deutz SBA8M528 1 x 4 Stroke 8 Cy. 220 x 280 441kW (600bhp) Kloeckner Humboldt Deutz AG-West Germany AuxGen: 2 x 92kW 220/380V 50Hz a.c, 1 x 41kW 220/380V 50Hz a.c Thrusters: 1 Thwart. FP thruster (f)
8511603 *PHEX* - **TRADER** *ex* Kent Trader *-2009* *ex* Normed Antwerp *-2003* *ex* Weser-Importer *-2002* *ex* Abitibi Claiborne *-2001* *ex* Weser-Importer *-1988* *ex* Scol Enterprise *-1987* *ex* Weser-Importer *-1986* **Rederi AB Lillgaard** BV Kustvaartbedrijf Moerman *Rotterdam* *Netherlands* MMSI: 246341000 Official number: 48101	**7,580** 3,648 7,875	Class: GL	**1986-09 Bremer Vulkan AG Schiffbau u. Maschinenfabrik — Bremen** Yd No: 81 Loa 123.02 (BB) Br ex - Dght 7.392 Lbp 115.63 Br md 20.01 Dpth 10.52 Welded, 2 dks	**(A31A2GX) General Cargo Ship** Grain: 13,081; Bale: 11,988 TEU 604 C Ho 202 TEU C Dk 402 TEU incl 25 ref C. Compartments: 1 Ho, ER, 1 Tw Dk 2 Ha: (32.0 x 8.0)Tappered (32.0 x 15.6)ER Cranes: 2x40t Ice Capable	**1 oil engine** reduction geared to sc. shaft driving 1 CP propeller Total Power: 3,943kW (5,361hp) 14.5kn MAN 7L40/45 1 x 4 Stroke 7 Cy. 400 x 450 3943kW (5361bhp) MAN B&W Diesel GmbH-Augsburg AuxGen: 1 x 600kW a.c, 2 x 358kW a.c, 2 x 240kW a.c Thrusters: 1 Thwart. FP thruster (f); 1 Tunnel thruster (a)
7125964 *PNXD* - **TRADER ARROW** *ex* Cem Clip *-2004* *ex* Cem Clipper *-2004* *ex* Clipper As *-2002* *ex* CemClipper *-1999* *ex* Seacement II *-1997* *ex* Suho Maru *-1995* **PT Bosowa Lloyd** Sekur Holdings Inc *Makassar* *Indonesia* MMSI: 525003088	**1,465** 466 2,498	Class: KI (HR)	**1971-09 Honda Zosen — Saiki** Yd No: 591 Loa 77.97 Br ex 12.32 Dght 5.182 Lbp 71.96 Br md 12.30 Dpth 5.80 Welded, 1 dk	**(A24A2BT) Cement Carrier** Compartments: 1 Ho, ER	**2 oil engines** geared to sc. shaft driving 1 FP propeller Total Power: 1,472kW (2,002hp) 12.5kn Daihatsu 8PSHTCM-26D 2 x 4 Stroke 8 Cy. 260 x 320 each-736kW (1001bhp) Daihatsu Diesel Manufacturing Co Lt-Japan AuxGen: 2 x 160kW 445V 60Hz a.c Fuel: 76.0 (d.f.) 6.0pd
7233060 *OZ2094* - **TRADER BULK** *ex* Tri Frakt *-2010* *ex* Frakt *-1994* *ex* Kiri *-1994* *ex* Makiri *-1992* *ex* Makiri Smits *-1984* **Sp/f Trader Bulk** Norock Ship Management AS *Torshavn* *Faeroes (FAS)* MMSI: 231759000 Official number: 311079428	**2,677** 1,424 4,415	Class: LR ✠**100A1** SS 06/2010 ✠**LMC** **UMS** Eq.Ltr: R; Cable: U2	**1973-01 N.V. Scheepsbouwwerf v/h de Groot & van Vliet — Bolnes** Yd No: 383 Loa 84.31 (BB) Br ex 14.41 Dght 7.150 Lbp 74.43 Br md 14.30 Dpth 8.77 Welded, 1 dk	**(A31A2GX) General Cargo Ship** Grain: 4,652 Compartments: 1 Ho, ER 1 Ha: (45.1 x 10.9)ER Cranes: 1x8t	**1 oil engine** driving 1 CP propeller Total Power: 1,839kW (2,500hp) 14.0kn Smit-Bolnes 308HDK 1 x 2 Stroke 8 Cy. 300 x 550 1839kW (2500bhp) Motorenfabriek Smit & Bolnes NV-Netherlands AuxGen: 3 x 160kW 380V 50Hz a.c Thrusters: 1 Tunnel thruster (f) Fuel: 325.0 (d.f.)
8704274 *2BNO7* - **TRADESMAN** *ex* Waglan *-2003* **SMS Towage Ltd** Specialist Marine Services Ltd *Hull* *United Kingdom* Official number: 915004	*197* - 72	Class: LR (BV) **100A1** SS 10/2010 tug coastal service **LMC** Cable: 302.5/22.0 U2 (a)	**1987-07 Imamura Zosen — Kure** Yd No: 322 Loa 22.80 Br ex 9.15 Dght 3.501 Lbp 18.40 Br md 8.51 Dpth 4.73 Welded, 1 dk	**(B32A2ST) Tug**	**2 oil engines** with clutches, flexible couplings & dr geared to sc. shafts driving 2 Directional propellers Total Power: 1,910kW (2,596hp) 11.5kn Niigata 6L25CXE 2 x 4 Stroke 6 Cy. 250 x 320 each-955kW (1298bhp) Niigata Engineering Co Ltd-Japan AuxGen: 2 x 64kW 380V 50Hz a.c Fuel: 44.0 (d.f.) 6.5pd
7729497 *WDE6438* - **TRADEWIND** *ex* Inmar Knight *-1979* **J Brady Marine LLC** - *Lafayette, LA* *United States of America* MMSI: 368235000 Official number: 600068	*284* 193 700	Class: (AB)	**1978-12 Greenville SB. Corp. — Greenville, Ms** Yd No: 54 Loa 52.43 Br ex 11.61 Dght 3.725 Lbp 50.30 Br md 11.59 Dpth 4.35 Welded, 1 dk	**(B21A20S) Platform Supply Ship**	**2 oil engines** reverse reduction geared to sc. shafts driving 2 FP propellers Total Power: 1,722kW (2,342hp) 14.0kn Kromhout 8F/SW240 2 x 4 Stroke 8 Cy. 240 x 260 each-861kW (1171bhp) Stork Werkspoor Diesel BV-Netherlands AuxGen: 2 x 99kW Thrusters: 1 Thwart. FP thruster (f)
8504636 *3FWH7* - **TRADEWIND** *ex* Botany Tradewind *-2007* *ex* Tradewind Express *-1998* **Chemical Venture Inc** Pendulum Shipmanagement Inc *Panama* *Panama* MMSI: 353751000 Official number: 4366112	**7,171** 4,053 12,752 T/cm 21.0	Class: NK (LR) Classed LR until 1/8/01	**1986-12 K.K. Taihei Kogyo — Akitsu** Yd No: 1775 Converted From: Chemical/Products Tanker-2001 Loa 123.30 (BB) Br ex 20.03 Dght 8.791 Lbp 116.00 Br md 20.01 Dpth 11.21 Welded, 1 dk	**(A12A2TC) Chemical Tanker** Double Bottom Entire Compartment Length Liq: 13,442; Liq (Oil): 13,442 Cargo Heating Coils Compartments: Wing ER, 11 Wing Ta, 7 Ta, 2 Wing Slop Ta, ER 10 Cargo Pump (s): 2x150m³/hr, 4x100m³/hr, 2x300m³/hr, 2x200m³/hr Manifold: Bow/CM: 59.4m	**1 oil engine** driving 1 FP propeller Total Power: 3,089kW (4,200hp) 13.0kn Mitsubishi 6UEC45HA 1 x 2 Stroke 6 Cy. 450 x 1150 3089kW (4200bhp) Akasaka Tekkosho KK (Akasaka DieselLtd)-Japan AuxGen: 3 x 360kW 450V 60Hz a.c Fuel: 105.8 (d.f.) 753.8 (r.f.)
9485590 *3EOE6* - **TRADEWIND ADVENTURE** **Asmara Services S de RL** Tradewind Tankers SL *Panama* *Panama* MMSI: 355350000 Official number: 3453108A	**8,302** 4,201 13,000 T/cm 23.8	Class: BV	**2008-09 Yangzhou Kejin Shipyard Co Ltd — Jiangdu JS** Yd No: 06021 Loa 130.20 (BB) Br ex 20.83 Dght 8.500 Lbp 122.00 Br md 20.80 Dpth 11.20 Welded, 1 dk	**(A12B2TR) Chemical/Products Tanker** Double Hull (13F) Liq: 13,685; Liq (Oil): 13,964 Part Cargo Heating Coils Compartments: 10 Wing Ta, 2 Wing Slop Ta, ER 10 Cargo Pump (s): 10x300m³/hr Manifold: Bow/CM: 69.3m	**2 oil engines** reduction geared to sc. shafts driving 2 FP propellers Total Power: 4,014kW (5,458hp) 13.4kn Yanmar 6N330-UN 2 x 4 Stroke 6 Cy. 330 x 440 each-2007kW (2729bhp) Qingdao Zichai Boyang Diesel EngineCo Ltd-China Thrusters: 1 Tunnel thruster (f) Fuel: 201.0 (d.f.) 657.0 (r.f.)

9127710 *H9NT* -	**TRADEWIND FORCE** *ex* Bunga Melawis Dua *-2005* **Wildeinest S de RL** Tradewind Tankers SL SatCom: Inmarsat Mini-M 764357757 *Panama* *Panama* MMSI: 355455000 Official number: 3080705CH	**6,373** 2,550 8,622 T/cm 18.5	Class: AB	**1997-08 Cheunggu Marine Industry Co Ltd — Ulsan** Yd No: 1103 Loa 116.60 (BB) Br ex 18.60 Dght 7.614 Lbp 107.40 Br md 18.60 Dpth 10.55 Welded, 1 dk	**(A12B2TR) Chemical/Products Tanker** Double Hull (13F) Liq: 8,997; Liq (Oil): 8,997 Compartments: 10 Wing Ta, 2 Wing Slop Ta, ER 12 Cargo Pump (s): 4x200m³/hr, 4x150m³/hr, 4x100m³/hr Manifold: Bow/CM: 58.3m	**1 oil engine** driving 1 FP propeller Total Power: 3,401kW (4,624hp) 11.5kn B&W 6L35MC 1 x 2 Stroke 6 Cy. 350 x 1050 3401kW (4624bhp) Hyundai Heavy Industries Co Ltd-South Korea AuxGen: 3 x 500kW a.c Fuel: 103.0 (d.f.) 464.0 (r.f.)
9291638 *OA2226* -	**TRADEWIND HOPE** *ex* Zhe Yue You 139 *-2004* **Skydome S de RL** Tradewind Tankers SL *Callao* *Peru* MMSI: 760000700	**6,501** 3,362 9,999 T/cm 21.4	Class: RI (LR) (CC) Classed LR until 18/9/12	**2003-05 Haidong Shipyard — Taizhou ZJ** Yd No: HD2001-01 Loa 128.80 (BB) Br ex 18.84 Dght 7.152 Lbp 120.08 Br md 18.80 Dpth 9.58 Welded, 1 dk	**(A13B2TP) Products Tanker** Double Hull (13F) Liq: 11,662; Liq (Oil): 11,662 Cargo Heating Coils Compartments: 5 Ta, 12 Wing Ta, ER 6 Cargo Pump (s): 2x500m³/hr, 4x200m³/hr Manifold: Bow/CM: 58.9m	**2 oil engines** reduction geared to sc. shafts driving 2 FP propellers Total Power: 2,940kW (3,998hp) 12.0kn Chinese Std. Type G8300ZC 2 x 4 Stroke 8 Cy. 300 x 380 each-1470kW (1999bhp) Wuxi Antai Power Machinery Co Ltd-China AuxGen: 3 x 252kW 400V 50Hz a.c Boilers: e (ex.g.) 8.0kgf/cm² (7.8bar), AuxB (o.f.) 9.0kgf/cm² (8.8bar) Fuel: 86.0 (d.f.) 690.0 (r.f.)
9503940 *3ESC3* -	**TRADEWIND LEGEND** **Roneo Trading S de RL** Tradewind Tankers SL *Panama* *Panama* MMSI: 370257000 Official number: 3455909A	**5,001** 2,411 7,739	Class: BV	**2008-07 Ningbo Xinle Shipbuilding Co Ltd — Ningbo ZJ** Yd No: 8800-02 Loa 118.00 (BB) Br ex 17.73 Dght 6.800 Lbp 110.00 Br md 17.60 Dpth 9.00 Welded, 1 dk	**(A12B2TR) Chemical/Products Tanker** Double Hull (13F) Liq: 8,290; Liq (Oil): 8,290 Cargo Heating Coils Compartments: 12 Wing Ta, 2 Wing Slop Ta, ER 14 Cargo Pump (s): 10x150m³/hr, 4x120m³/hr	**1 oil engine** geared to sc. shaft driving 1 CP propeller Total Power: 2,970kW (4,038hp) 13.0kn MaK 9M25 1 x 4 Stroke 9 Cy. 255 x 400 2970kW (4038bhp) Caterpillar Motoren GmbH & Co. KG-Germany Thrusters: 1 Tunnel thruster (f) Fuel: 70.0 (d.f.) 390.0 (r.f.)
9427146 *3EJE3* -	**TRADEWIND PALM** *ex* Satwa *-2007* **Bayaka S de RL** Tradewind Tankers SL *Panama* *Panama* MMSI: 372489000 Official number: 3325407A	**8,482** 3,816 12,000 T/cm 25.1	Class: RI (CC)	**2007-04 No 4807 Shipyard of PLA — Fu'an FJ** Yd No: 11 Loa 134.85 (BB) Br ex - Dght 7.543 Lbp 126.00 Br md 22.00 Dpth 10.60 Welded, 1 dk	**(A13B2TP) Products Tanker** Double Hull (13F) Liq: 14,254; Liq (Oil): 14,254 Cargo Heating Coils Compartments: 10 Wing Ta, 2 Wing Slop Ta, ER 2 Cargo Pump (s): 2x1000m³/hr Manifold: Bow/CM: 62.1m	**1 oil engine** driving 1 FP propeller Total Power: 4,440kW (6,037hp) 13.5kn MAN-B&W 6S35MC 1 x 2 Stroke 6 Cy. 350 x 1400 4440kW (6037bhp) Yichang Marine Diesel Engine Co Ltd-China Fuel: 67.3 (d.f.) 504.0 (r.f.)
9483619 *3EPL5* -	**TRADEWIND PASSION** **Canama Trading S de RL** Tradewind Tankers SL *Panama* *Panama* MMSI: 355973000 Official number: 3387808A	**5,001** 2,411 7,739 T/cm 17.8	Class: BV	**2008-04 Ningbo Xinle Shipbuilding Co Ltd — Ningbo ZJ** Yd No: 8800-01 Loa 118.00 (BB) Br ex 17.62 Dght 6.800 Lbp 110.00 Br md 17.60 Dpth 9.00 Welded, 1 dk	**(A12B2TR) Chemical/Products Tanker** Double Hull (13F) Liq: 8,105; Liq (Oil): 8,032 Compartments: 12 Wing Ta, 2 Wing Slop Ta, ER 12 Cargo Pump (s): 6x160m³/hr, 6x120m³/hr Manifold: Bow/CM: 58.2m	**1 oil engine** reduction geared to sc. shaft driving 1 FP propeller Total Power: 2,970kW (4,038hp) 13.0kn MaK 9M25 1 x 4 Stroke 9 Cy. 255 x 400 2970kW (4038bhp) Caterpillar Motoren GmbH & Co. KG-Germany Thrusters: 1 Tunnel thruster (f) Fuel: 57.0 (d.f.) 354.0 (r.f.)
7612307 *WCX7013* -	**TRADEWIND SERVICE** *ex* New Jersey Sun *-1999* *ex* Mister M *-1999* **Hornbeck Offshore Transportation LLC** - *New Orleans, LA* *United States of America* MMSI: 366738040 Official number: 566364	**317** 95 186		**1975 Bollinger Machine Shop & Shipyard, Inc. — Lockport, La** Yd No: 92 Loa 32.01 Br ex 9.15 Dght 3.901 Lbp 30.61 Br md 9.10 Dpth 4.47 Welded, 1 dk	**(B32A2ST) Tug**	**2 oil engines** reduction geared to sc. shafts driving 2 FP propellers Total Power: 2,074kW (2,820hp) 8.5kn Caterpillar 3516 1 x Vee 4 Stroke 16 Cy. 170 x 190 1037kW (1410bhp) Caterpillar Inc-USA
9175729 *3FSK7* -	**TRADEWIND UNION** *ex* Southern Lion *-2003* **Puiner Investments S de RL** Tradewind Tankers SL SatCom: Inmarsat B 335158610 *Panama* *Panama* MMSI: 351586000 Official number: 2507397CH	**5,999** 3,306 10,600 T/cm 19.1	Class: NK	**1997-09 Asakawa Zosen K.K. — Imabari** Yd No: 398 Loa 118.00 (BB) Br ex 19.40 Dght 8.255 Lbp 110.00 Br md 19.20 Dpth 10.40 Welded, 1 dk	**(A12B2TR) Chemical/Products Tanker** Double Hull (13F) Liq: 11,423; Liq (Oil): 11,423 Cargo Heating Coils Compartments: 4 Ta, 16 Wing Ta, ER 20 Cargo Pump (s): 8x150m³/hr, 12x200m³/hr Manifold: Bow/CM: 53m	**1 oil engine** driving 1 FP propeller Total Power: 4,193kW (5,701hp) 13.8kn B&W 6S35MC 1 x 2 Stroke 6 Cy. 350 x 1400 4193kW (5701bhp) Hitachi Zosen Corp-Japan AuxGen: 3 x 441kW 450V 60Hz a.c Thrusters: 1 Thwart. CP thruster (f) Fuel: 78.0 (d.f.) (Heating Coils) 602.0 (r.f.) 15.2pd
8852291 - -	**TRADEWINDS '86** - **Noble House Seafoods Co Ltd** - *Georgetown* *Guyana* Official number: 0000371	*101* 69 -		**1986 Steiner Shipyard, Inc. — Bayou La Batre, Al** Loa 24.39 Br ex 6.71 Dght 1.520 Lbp 20.33 Br md 6.71 Dpth 3.35 Welded, 1 dk	**(B11A2FT) Trawler**	**1 oil engine** driving 1 FP propeller
9024566 - -	**TRADIMEXCO 01** - **Haiphong Tradimexco** - *Haiphong* *Vietnam* Official number: VN-1576-VT	**201** 97 234	Class: VR	**2002-12 in Vietnam** Loa 36.33 Br ex - Dght 2.500 Lbp 32.60 Br md 6.80 Dpth 3.40 Welded, 1 dk	**(B12D2FU) Fishery Support Vessel**	**1 oil engine** reduction geared to sc. shaft driving 1 Propeller Total Power: 237kW (322hp) 9.0kn Caterpillar 3406 1 x 4 Stroke 6 Cy. 137 x 165 237kW (322bhp) Caterpillar Inc-USA
9481960 *9HA2646* -	**TRADING FABRIZIA** - **Capitalease SpA** Gorgonia di Navigazione Srl SatCom: Inmarsat C 421512010 *Valletta* *Malta* MMSI: 215120000 Official number: 9481960	**22,988** 11,574 35,000	Class: RI	**2011-03 SPP Shipbuilding Co Ltd — Tongyeong** Yd No: H4031 Loa 180.00 (BB) Br ex - Dght 9.900 Lbp 172.00 Br md 30.00 Dpth 14.70 Welded, 1 dk	**(A21A2BC) Bulk Carrier** Double Hull Grain: 48,766; Bale: 46,815 Compartments: 5 Ho, ER 5 Ha: ER Cranes: 4x35t	**1 oil engine** driving 1 FP propeller Total Power: 7,900kW (10,741hp) 14.0kn MAN-B&W 5S50MC-C 1 x 2 Stroke 5 Cy. 500 x 2000 7900kW (10741bhp) Doosan Engine Co Ltd-South Korea AuxGen: 3 x 600kW 440V 60Hz a.c
8031641 *YGYU* -	**TRADISI 7** *ex* Chahaya Victory *-2001* *ex* Tramasco 02 *-1996* *ex* Chun Ku *-1994* *ex* Kee Ryong *-1986* *ex* Jang Yung No. 31 *-1982* **PT Tradisi Bintangreksa Line** - *Jakarta* *Indonesia* MMSI: 525002040	**759** 395 1,192	Class: KI (VR) (KR)	**1980-08 ShinA Shipbuilding Co Ltd — Tongyeong** Loa 63.71 Br ex - Dght 4.100 Lbp 59.01 Br md 9.30 Dpth 4.60 Welded, 1 dk	**(A31A2GX) General Cargo Ship** Grain: 1,379; Bale: 1,216 1 Ha: (29.5 x 5.8) Derricks: 1x10t,1x5t	**1 oil engine** driving 1 FP propeller Total Power: 883kW (1,201hp) 12.0kn Hanshin 6LU28 1 x 4 Stroke 6 Cy. 280 x 440 883kW (1201bhp) Ssangyong Heavy Industries Co Ltd-South Korea AuxGen: 2 x 64kW 445V a.c
8129826 *PMQO* -	**TRADISI 8** *ex* Hai Long 02 *-2010* *ex* Ha Tinh 06 *-2004* *ex* Hong Lam 06 *-1992* *ex* Heiyo Maru *-1983* **Sakareksa Pacific Lines PT** - *Semarang* *Indonesia* MMSI: 525019478	**1,312** 776 2,080	Class: KI (VR)	**1982-04 Fukushima Zosen Ltd. — Matsue** Yd No: 307 Loa 72.50 Br ex 11.22 Dght 5.230 Lbp 66.14 Br md 11.20 Dpth 6.27 Welded, 1 dk	**(A31A2GX) General Cargo Ship** Grain: 1,441; Bale: 2,603 Compartments: 1 Ho, ER 1 Ha: (38.5 x 8.0)ER	**1 oil engine** driving 1 FP propeller Total Power: 1,177kW (1,600hp) 12.0kn Hanshin 6LU32 1 x 4 Stroke 6 Cy. 320 x 510 1177kW (1600bhp) The Hanshin Diesel Works Ltd-Japan AuxGen: 2 x 80kW a.c
8855786 *WBI4174* -	**TRADITION** - **Snug Harbor Marine LLC** - *Kenai, AK* *United States of America* Official number: 919309	**109** 32 -		**1987 Saigon Shipbuilders Co. — Harvey, La** Yd No: 101 Loa - Br ex - Dght - Lbp 23.16 Br md 6.46 Dpth 2.74 Welded, 1 dk	**(B11B2FV) Fishing Vessel**	**1 oil engine** driving 1 FP propeller
8719542 *WCZ7432* -	**TRADITION** - **Nordic Fisheries Inc** - *New Bedford, MA* *United States of America* Official number: 921057	*188* 127 -		**1987-12 Goudy & Stevens — East Boothbay, Me** Yd No: 234 Loa 31.70 Br ex - Dght - Lbp 28.10 Br md 7.92 Dpth 4.11 Welded, 1 dk	**(B11B2FV) Fishing Vessel**	**1 oil engine** geared to sc. shaft driving 1 FP propeller Total Power: 1,432kW (1,947hp) Caterpillar 3516TA 1 x Vee 4 Stroke 16 Cy. 170 x 190 1432kW (1947bhp) Caterpillar Inc-USA
8930342 - -	**TRADOCO 01** - **Vung Tau Trading & Oil Co (Cong Ty Thuong Mai Va Dai Ly Dau Vung Tau)** - *Saigon* *Vietnam* Official number: VNSG-1381-TD	**106** 63 176	Class: VR	**1987 in Thailand** Loa 26.00 Br ex 6.66 Dght 3.100 Lbp 24.40 Br md 6.65 Dpth 3.80 Welded, 1 dk	**(A13B2TU) Tanker (unspecified)** Liq: 193; Liq (Oil): 193	**1 oil engine** geared to sc. shaft driving 1 FP propeller Total Power: 349kW (475hp) Cummins KT-19-M 1 x 4 Stroke 6 Cy. 159 x 159 349kW (475bhp) Cummins Engine Co Inc-USA

IMO / Call sign	Name / Owner / Port / Flag	Tonnage	Class	Builder / Dimensions	Type	Machinery
9022934 - -	**TRADOCO 18** *ex* Phu Binh 16 **Vung Tau Trading & Oil Co (Cong Ty Thuong Mai Va Dai Ly Dau Vung Tau)** - *Saigon* *Vietnam* Official number: VNSG-1661-TD	**196** 119 359	Class: VR	**2001-11 An Phu Works — Ho Chi Minh City** Yd No: SLD300-01 Loa 39.59 Br ex 7.37 Dght 2.410 Lbp 36.90 Br md 7.15 Dpth 2.90 Welded, 1 dk	**(A13B2TP) Products Tanker**	**1 oil engine** geared to sc. shaft driving 1 Propeller Total Power: 397kW (540hp) 10.0kn Yanmar 1 x 4 Stroke 6 Cy. 133 x 160 397kW (540bhp) Yanmar Diesel Engine Co Ltd-Japan
8813001 *OUIF* -	**TRAEL** *ex* Trael II *-1991* **Government of The Kingdom of Denmark (Kystinspektoratet)** - *Hvide Sande* *Denmark* MMSI: 219797000 Official number: D3229	**473** 141 758	Class: BV	**1989-04 Esbjerg Oilfield Services A/S — Esbjerg** Yd No: 57 Loa 45.00 Br ex - Dght 3.201 Lbp - Br md 10.00 Dpth 3.50 Welded, 1 dk	**(B33B2DT) Trailing Suction Hopper Dredger** Hopper: 390	**2 oil engines** driving 2 FP propellers Total Power: 412kW (560hp) 8.5kn Deutz BF10L513 2 x Vee 4 Stroke 10 Cy. 125 x 130 each-206kW (280bhp) Kloeckner Humboldt Deutz AG-West Germany AuxGen: 2 x 28kW 380V a.c
7112230 *LAPC* -	**TRAELEN** - **Birger Bech** - *Tromso* *Norway* MMSI: 257075700	**119** 35 -	Class: (NV)	**1971 Skaalurens Skipsbyggeri AS — Rosendal** Yd No: 218/31 Loa 27.56 Br ex 7.52 Dght - Lbp - Br md 7.50 Dpth 3.20 Welded, 1 dk	**(A36A2PR) Passenger/Ro-Ro Ship (Vehicles)** Passengers: unberthed: 82	**2 oil engines** driving 2 Directional propellers Total Power: 236kW (320hp) Deutz F10L714 2 x Vee 4 Stroke 10 Cy. 120 x 140 each-118kW (160bhp) Kloeckner Humboldt Deutz AG-West Germany AuxGen: 2 x 16kW 220V 50Hz a.c
7607106 *LEZR* -	**TRAENEN** - **Kystverket Rederi** - *Aalesund* *Norway* MMSI: 257371500	*187* 51 -		**1977-06 Sigbjorn Iversen — Flekkefjord** Yd No: 41 Loa 26.01 Br ex - Dght 3.052 Lbp 23.80 Br md 7.01 Dpth 3.48 Welded, 1 dk	**(B34Q2QL) Buoy & Lighthouse Tender** Cranes: 1x2.5t	**1 oil engine** geared to sc. shaft driving 1 FP propeller Total Power: 515kW (700hp) G.M. (Detroit Diesel) 12V-149 1 x Vee 2 Stroke 12 Cy. 146 x 146 515kW (700bhp) General Motors Detroit DieselAllison Divn-USA Thrusters: 1 Thwart. FP thruster (f)
5378866 - -	**TRAEZ GWEN** *ex* Vers l'Horizon *-1991* - -	*195* 83 -	Class: (BV)	**1958 Anciens Chantiers Mougin — St-Malo** Yd No: 31 L reg 28.96 Br ex 8.31 Dght - Lbp - Br md - Dpth - Welded, 1 dk	**(A31A2GX) General Cargo Ship** 1 Ha: (6.2 x 7.7) Derricks: 1x4t	**2 oil engines** geared to sc. shaft driving 1 FP propeller Total Power: 220kW (300hp) 8.5kn Baudouin DK6 2 x 4 Stroke 6 Cy. 140 x 180 each-110kW (150bhp) Societe des Moteurs Baudouin SA-France Fuel: 21.5 (d.f.)
6606868 *9YEG* -	**TRAFALGAR** *ex* Vanquisher *-1999* *ex* Lady Alma *-1997* **Coloured Fin Ltd (CFL)** - *Port of Spain* *Trinidad & Tobago*	**232** 69 -	Class: LR ✠ **100A1** SS 03/2011 tug ✠ **LMC** Eq.Ltr: (c) ;	**1966-05 Charles D. Holmes & Co. Ltd. — Beverley** Yd No: 999 Loa 32.52 Br ex 9.07 Dght 3.340 Lbp 28.96 Br md 8.54 Dpth 4.12 Welded	**(B32A2ST) Tug**	**2 oil engines** sr reverse geared to sc. shafts driving 2 FP propellers Total Power: 1,488kW (2,024hp) Ruston 7VEBCM 2 x 4 Stroke 7 Cy. 260 x 368 each-744kW (1012bhp) Ruston & Hornsby Ltd.-Lincoln AuxGen: 2 x 35kW 400V 50Hz a.c, 1 x 7kW 400V 50Hz a.c Fuel: 51.0 (d.f.)
8023905 *WRA9063* -	**TRAFALGAR** *ex* Blue Moon *-2010* *ex* Atlanta Bay *-2008* *ex* Amoco Atlanta *-1985* **Trafalgar Shipping LLC** - *Beaumont, TX* *United States of America* MMSI: 303554000 Official number: 646348	**559** 167 419	Class: AB	**1982-04 McDermott Shipyards Inc — Morgan City LA** Yd No: 262 Loa - Br ex - Dght 5.941 Lbp 39.02 Br md 10.98 Dpth 6.86 Welded, 1 dk	**(B32B2SA) Articulated Pusher Tug**	**2 oil engines** sr geared to sc. shafts driving 1 CP propeller Total Power: 4,266kW (5,800hp) 7.3kn EMD (Electro-Motive) 16-645-E7B 2 x Vee 2 Stroke 16 Cy. 230 x 254 each-2133kW (2900bhp) General Motors Corp.Electro-Motive Div.-La Grange AuxGen: 2 x 210kW
8213081 - -	**TRAFALGAR SERVICE** - **Zapata Gulf Marine International Ltd** Tidewater Marine International Inc	**722** 216 915	Class: (AB)	**1983-03 Halter Marine, Inc. — Moss Point, Ms** Yd No: 1068 Loa 56.40 Br ex - Dght 3.693 Lbp 51.85 Br md 12.20 Dpth 4.27 Welded, 1 dk	**(B21B20T) Offshore Tug/Supply Ship**	**2 oil engines** reverse reduction geared to sc. shafts driving 2 FP propellers Total Power: 2,868kW (3,900hp) 12.0kn EMD (Electro-Motive) 16-645-E7 2 x Vee 2 Stroke 16 Cy. 230 x 254 each-1434kW (1950bhp) (Re-engined ,made 1964, Reconditioned & fitted 1983) General Motors Corp.Electro-Motive Div.-La Grange AuxGen: 2 x 150kW Thrusters: 1 Thwart. FP thruster (f)
7343372 - -	**TRAFFORD ENTERPRISE** *ex* Calemax Enterprise *-1985* *ex* Elf *-2005* *ex* Sibir *-1999* *ex* Seacombe Trader *-1998* - -	**507** 338 711		**1974-09 Yorkshire D.D. Co. Ltd. — Hull** Yd No: 232 Loa 42.47 Br ex 9.99 Dght 4.242 Lbp 39.60 Br md 9.50 Dpth 4.75 Welded, 1 dk	**(A31A2GX) General Cargo Ship**	**2 oil engines** driving 2 FP propellers Total Power: 536kW (728hp) 9.0kn Caterpillar D343SCAC 2 x 4 Stroke 6 Cy. 137 x 165 each-268kW (364bhp) Caterpillar Tractor Co-USA
9431654 *3WWX* -	**TRAI THIEN 68** *launched as* Phu Hai 45 *-2007* **Agribank Leasing Co II** Trai Thien Co Ltd SatCom: Inmarsat C 457444010 *Haiphong* *Vietnam* MMSI: 574440000	**1,599** 1,042 3,012	Class: VR	**2007-12 Hoang Anh Shipbuilding Industry Joint Stock Co. — Vietnam** Yd No: THB-15-02 Loa 79.50 Br ex 12.32 Dght 5.120 Lbp 75.45 Br md 12.30 Dpth 6.30 Welded, 1 dk	**(A31A2GX) General Cargo Ship**	**1 oil engine** geared to sc. shaft driving 1 FP propeller Total Power: 1,103kW (1,500hp) Chinese Std. Type 8300ZLC 1 x 4 Stroke 8 Cy. 300 x 380 1103kW (1500bhp) Weifang Diesel Engine Factory-China
9444015 *3WQX* -	**TRAI THIEN 86** *ex* Hai Ha 45 *-2008* **Agriculture Leasing Co II** Khanh Ha Co Ltd SatCom: Inmarsat C 457447710 *Haiphong* *Vietnam* MMSI: 574477000	**1,598** 1,256 3,050	Class: VR	**2007-12 Thanh Long Co Ltd — Haiphong** Yd No: THB-03 Loa 79.90 Br ex - Dght 5.000 Lbp 74.80 Br md 12.80 Dpth 6.08 Welded, 1 dk	**(A31A2GX) General Cargo Ship** Grain: 3,867	**1 oil engine** reduction geared to sc. shaft driving 1 FP propeller Total Power: 1,103kW (1,500hp) Chinese Std. Type 8300ZLC 1 x 4 Stroke 8 Cy. 300 x 380 1103kW (1500bhp) Zibo Diesel Engine Factory-China
7950383 - -	**TRAIANA** *ex* Bentley *-2010* *ex* Rusk *-2008* *ex* Ocean Dragon *-2006* *ex* Gera *-2005* *ex* St. Peter *-2005* *ex* Sung Jin No. 808 *-2004* *ex* Woo Heung No. 1 *-1999* *ex* Seo Won No. 101 *-1994* *ex* Saraton No. 1 *-1990* *ex* Han Gil No. 75 *-1986* *ex* Asahi Maru No. 6 *-1983* - -	**429** 213 360	Class: (KR)	**1972 Kochi Jyuko K.K. — Kochi** Yd No: 1185 Loa 49.73 Br ex - Dght 3.444 Lbp 43.20 Br md 8.30 Dpth 3.60 Welded, 1 dk	**(B11B2FV) Fishing Vessel** 3 Ha: 3 (1.4 x 1.1)	**1 oil engine** reverse geared to sc. shaft driving 1 FP propeller Total Power: 736kW (1,001hp) 11.5kn Akasaka AH28R 1 x 4 Stroke 6 Cy. 280 x 440 736kW (1001bhp) Akasaka Tekkosho KK (Akasaka DieselLtd)-Japan AuxGen: 2 x 352kW 225V a.c
9187679 *IFSX* -	**TRAIANO SECONDO** - **Rimorchiatori Laziali Impresa di Salvataggio e Rimorchi SpA** - *Naples* *Italy* MMSI: 247365000 Official number: 2001	**322** 96 164	Class: RI	**1999-02 Cant. Nav. Rosetti — Ravenna** Yd No: 30 Loa 30.30 Br ex - Dght 4.440 Lbp 28.33 Br md 9.50 Dpth 5.00 Welded, 1 dk	**(B32A2ST) Tug**	**2 oil engines** geared to sc. shafts driving 2 FP propellers Total Power: 3,090kW (4,202hp) 13.5kn Nohab 6R25 2 x 4 Stroke 6 Cy. 250 x 300 each-1545kW (2101bhp) Wartsila NSD Finland Oy-Finland AuxGen: 2 x 136kW 220/380V 50Hz a.c Thrusters: 1 Thwart. FP thruster (f) Fuel: 127.0 (d.f.)
8310138 *WDF2338* -	**TRAILBLAZER** - **Offshore Service Vessels LLC** Edison Chouest Offshore LLC SatCom: Inmarsat A 1507511 *Galliano, LA* *United States of America* MMSI: 367427550 Official number: 659377	**586** 175 645	Class: (AB)	**1983-07 North American Shipbuilding Inc — Larose LA** Yd No: 127 Loa 44.20 Br ex - Dght 4.007 Lbp 42.68 Br md 10.37 Dpth 4.22 Welded, 1 dk	**(B31A2SR) Research Survey Vessel**	**2 oil engines** geared to sc. shafts driving 2 FP propellers Total Power: 1,552kW (2,110hp) 14.0kn Caterpillar 3512TA 2 x Vee 4 Stroke 12 Cy. 170 x 190 each-776kW (1055bhp) Caterpillar Tractor Co-USA AuxGen: 2 x 75kW a.c Thrusters: 1 Thwart. FP thruster (f)
7729069 *WDE6541* -	**TRAILBLAZER** - **Trailblazer LLC** Alaska Seafood Producers Inc SatCom: Inmarsat A 1507511 *Newport, OR* *United States of America* MMSI: 366082000 Official number: 596514	**398** 119 -		**1978-09 Bender Welding & Machine Co Inc — Mobile AL** Yd No: 309 Loa 32.62 Br ex 9.81 Dght 4.344 Lbp 30.48 Br md 9.05 Dpth 4.37 Welded, 1 dk	**(B11B2FV) Fishing Vessel**	**2 oil engines** driving 2 FP propellers Total Power: 764kW (1,038hp) Caterpillar 3412PCTA 2 x Vee 4 Stroke 12 Cy. 137 x 152 each-382kW (519bhp) Caterpillar Tractor Co-USA

7941825 - -	**TRALMEYSTER KOKOYEV** *ex* Vyuga *-1996* **Sevrybkomflot JSC (A/O 'Sevrybkomflot')** -	**786** 235 405	Class: (RS)	**1981-02 Zavod "Leninskaya Kuznitsa" — Kiyev** Yd No: 1488 Loa 54.82 Br ex 9.96 Dght 4.140 Lbp 50.29 Br md - Dpth 5.01 Welded, 1 dk	**(B11A2FS) Stern Trawler** Ins: 414 Compartments: 2 Ho, ER 3 Ha: 3 (1.5 x 1.6) Derricks: 2x1.5t; Winches: 2 Ice Capable	**1 oil engine** driving 1 CP propeller Total Power: 736kW (1,001hp) 12.0kn S.K.L. 8NVD48A-2U 1 x 4 Stroke 8 Cy. 320 x 480 736kW (1001bhp) VEB Schwermaschinenbau "KarlLiebknecht" (SKL)-Magdeburg
8124151 *OA2294* -	**TRAMARSA 1** *ex* Tramarsa *-1999* *ex* Saam *-1993* **Trabajos Maritima SA (TRAMARSA)** - *Callao* Peru Official number: CO-11961-EM	*132* 89 -	Class: (GL) (AB)	**1981-11 Bender Shipbuilding & Repair Co Inc — Mobile AL** Yd No: 160 Loa - Br ex - Dght - Lbp 22.41 Br md 7.94 Dpth 3.13 Welded, 1 dk	**(B32A2ST) Tug**	**2 oil engines** reverse reduction geared to sc. shafts driving 2 FP propellers Total Power: 920kW (1,250hp) 9.5kn G.M. (Detroit Diesel) 16V-92 2 x Vee 2 Stroke 16 Cy. 123 x 127 each-460kW (625bhp) General Motors Detroit DieselAllison Divn-USA AuxGen: 2 x 30kW
7939975 - - -	**TRAMARSA 2** *ex* C. A. Davis *-1999* *ex* Scorpio N *-1994* *ex* Yak *-1993* **Trabajos Maritima SA (TRAMARSA)** - *Callao* Peru Official number: CO-13379-EM	**182** 54 46	Class: (GL) (HR) (DS)	**1977 Gorokhovetskiy Sudostroitelnyy Zavod — Gorokhovets** Loa 29.32 Br ex - Dght 4.050 Lbp 27.01 Br md 8.31 Dpth 4.35 Welded, 1 dk	**(B32A2ST) Tug** Ice Capable	**2 oil engines** driving 2 FP propellers Total Power: 882kW (1,200hp) 11.0kn Russkiy 6DR30/50-4 2 x 2 Stroke 6 Cy. 300 x 500 each-441kW (600bhp) Mashinostroitelnyy Zavod"Russkiy-Dizel"-Leningrad
7939963 - - -	**TRAMARSA 3** *ex* Hurricane H *-1995* *ex* Taurus II *-1994* *ex* Arni *-1993* **Trabajos Maritima SA (TRAMARSA)** - *Callao* Peru	**182** 54 46	Class: (HR) (GL) (DS)	**1977 Gorokhovetskiy Sudostroitelnyy Zavod — Gorokhovets** Yd No: 355 Loa 29.32 Br ex - Dght 3.201 Lbp - Br md 8.31 Dpth 4.30 Welded, 1 dk	**(B32A2ST) Tug** Ice Capable	**2 oil engines** driving 2 CP propellers Total Power: 884kW (1,202hp) 11.0kn Russkiy 6DR30/50-4 2 x 2 Stroke 6 Cy. 300 x 500 each-442kW (601bhp) Mashinostroitelnyy Zavod"Russkiy-Dizel"-Leningrad AuxGen: 2 x 20kW 220/380V a.c
9256731 *OA3632* -	**TRAMAX** *ex* A Venture *-2010* *ex* Jet Express *-2008* *ex* Lin I *-2007* *ex* Lin *-2001* *ex* Yun Tai You 12 *-2001* **Trabajos Maritima SA (TRAMARSA)** - Peru MMSI: 760000660	**2,218** 1,294 4,004 T/cm 10.1	Class: IS	**2001-08 Chongqing Dongfeng Ship Industry Co — Chongqing** Yd No: VYQ 530 Conv to DH-2010 Loa 89.80 (BB) Br ex 13.60 Dght 5.898 Lbp 83.00 Br md - Dpth 6.70 Welded, 1 dk	**(A13B2TP) Products Tanker** Double Hull (13F) Liq: 4,749; Liq (Oil): 4,749 Compartments: 10 Wing Ta, ER 2 Cargo Pump (s): 2x500m³/hr Manifold: Bow/CM: 52m	**1 oil engine** with clutches, flexible couplings & sr reverse geared to sc. shaft driving 1 FP propeller Total Power: 1,500kW (2,039hp) 12.0kn Chinese Std. Type G8300ZC 1 x 4 Stroke 8 Cy. 300 x 380 1500kW (2039bhp) Wuxi Antai Power Machinery Co Ltd-China AuxGen: 2 x 240kW 380/220V 50Hz a.c Fuel: 158.0 (d.f.) (Part Heating Coils) 5.0pd
7224461 *TCCD8* -	**TRAMOLA-1** *ex* Lale Unaldi *-2005* *ex* Monte Rotondo *-2002* **Tramola Tasimacilik ve Ticaret AS** Tramola Gemi Isletmeciligi ve Ticaret AS *Istanbul* Turkey MMSI: 271000683 Official number: 6087	**5,127** 1,538 2,860	Class: TL (BV)	**1973-01 Soc Nouvelle des Ats et Chs de La Rochelle-Pallice — La Rochelle** (Hull) Yd No: 1208 **1973-01 Societe Nouvelle des Ateliers et Chantiers du Havre — Le Havre** Yd No: 211 Loa 109.51 (BB) Br ex 17.53 Dght 5.531 Lbp 99.00 Br md 17.50 Dpth 9.35 Welded, 1 dk	**(A36A2PR) Passenger/Ro-Ro Ship (Vehicles)** Passengers: driver berths: 32 Stern door/ramp Len: 9.00 Wid: 7.00 Swl: - Lane-Len: 660 Lane-Wid: 2.90 Lane-clr ht: 4.50 Cars: 333, Trailers: 55 Grain: 4,900; Liq: 2,000 Compartments: 4 Ta, 1 Ho, ER	**2 oil engines** driving 2 CP propellers Total Power: 6,252kW (8,500hp) 17.0kn Pielstick 8PC2V-400 2 x 4 Stroke 8 Cy. 400 x 460 each-3126kW (4250bhp) At. & Ch. de Nantes (Bretagne-Loire)-Nantes AuxGen: 3 x 490kW 380V 50Hz a.c Thrusters: 1 Thwart. FP thruster (f) Fuel: 256.0 (d.f.) 28.0pd
7517519 *TCCS8* -	**TRAMOLA-2** *ex* Aslihan I *-2004* *ex* Clipper Cayenne *-2004* *ex* Mejerda *-1998* **Tramola Nakliyat ve Ticaret AS** Tramola Gemi Isletmeciligi ve Ticaret AS *Istanbul* Turkey MMSI: 271000743	**5,080** 1,524 2,797	Class: TL (BV)	**1977-04 Schulte & Bruns Schiffswerft — Emden** Yd No: 281 Converted From: Ro-Ro Cargo Ship-2004 Loa 101.00 (BB) Br ex 17.84 Dght 5.601 Lbp 91.01 Br md 17.80 Dpth 5.67 Welded, 2 dks	**(A36A2PR) Passenger/Ro-Ro Ship (Vehicles)** Stern door & ramp Side door (p) Side door (s) Bale: 6,933	**2 oil engines** driving 2 CP propellers Total Power: 4,708kW (6,400hp) 16.8kn MaK 9M453AK 2 x 4 Stroke 9 Cy. 320 x 420 each-2354kW (3200bhp) MaK Maschinenbau GmbH-Kiel AuxGen: 3 x 420kW 320V 50Hz a.c Thrusters: 1 Tunnel thruster (f)
7211165 *MDWB9*	**TRAMONTANE** *ex* Marseillais 16 *-1989* **Green Sea Shipping Ltd** Catherine O'Hanlon *Falmouth* United Kingdom MMSI: 235015424 Official number: 909085	**263** 78 248	Class: BV	**1972 Ziegler Freres — Dunkerque** Yd No: 185 Loa 31.63 Br ex 9.25 Dght 2.990 Lbp 29.37 Br md 8.79 Dpth 3.66 Welded, 1 dk	**(B32A2ST) Tug**	**2 oil engines** gearing integral to driving 2 Voith-Schneider propellers Total Power: 1,838kW (2,498hp) 11.6kn Crepelle 8SN1 2 x 4 Stroke 8 Cy. 260 x 280 each-919kW (1249bhp) Crepelle et Cie-France
9204697 *PHAA* -	**TRAMPER** **Rederij Tramper** BigLift Shipping BV *Amsterdam* Netherlands MMSI: 245867000 Official number: 37858	**6,714** 2,888 8,734 T/cm 18.6	Class: BV (NV)	**1999-09 Zhonghua Shipyard — Shanghai** Yd No: 405 Loa 100.42 (BB) Br ex 20.60 Dght 8.200 Lbp 96.01 Br md 20.40 Dpth 11.10 Welded, 2 dks	**(A31A2GX) General Cargo Ship** Grain: 10,530; Bale: 9,720 TEU 371 C Ho 195 C Dk 176 incl 24 ref C. Compartments: 1 Ho, ER, 1 Tw Dk 1 Ha: (64.2 x 15.3)ER Cranes: 2x275t Ice Capable	**1 oil engine** with flexible couplings & sr gearedto sc. shaft driving 1 CP propeller Total Power: 7,800kW (10,605hp) 16.5kn Wartsila 8L46B 1 x 4 Stroke 8 Cy. 460 x 580 7800kW (10605bhp) Wartsila NSD Finland Oy-Finland AuxGen: 1 x 900kW 220/440V 60Hz a.c, 3 x 530kW 440V 60Hz a.c Thrusters: 1 Thwart. CP thruster (f) Fuel: 131.5 (d.f.) (Heating Coils) 775.3 (r.f.) 28.0pd
8925608 *XVVF* -	**TRAN DE 01** **Mekofood (Cong Ty Luong Thuc Can Tho)** - *Saigon* Vietnam	**341** - -	Class: (VR)	**1965 in Japan** Loa - Br ex - Dght 3.000 Lbp 41.46 Br md 7.70 Dpth 3.45 Welded, 1 dk	**(B11B2FV) Fishing Vessel**	**1 oil engine** driving 1 FP propeller Total Power: 552kW (750hp) Niigata 6M28DHS 1 x 4 Stroke 6 Cy. 280 x 440 552kW (750bhp) Niigata Engineering Co Ltd-Japan
6922339 *XVJW* -	**TRAN HUNG DAO** *ex* Beachway *-1989* *ex* Transmundum III *-1974* **Vietnam Waterway Construction Corp (VINAWACO)** - *Haiphong* Vietnam Official number: VN-996-HB	*2,970* 1,814 5,000	Class: VR (BV)	**1969-08 Norderwerft Johann Rathje Koeser — Hamburg** Yd No: 867 Loa 95.00 Br ex 16.37 Dght 4.600 Lbp 91.65 Br md 16.01 Dpth 6.00 Welded, 1 dk	**(B33B2DS) Suction Hopper Dredger** Hopper: 3,399 Compartments: 2 Ho, ER Derricks: 2x10t,2x3t	**3 oil engines** reduction geared to sc. shafts driving 3 FP propellers Total Power: 2,316kW (3,150hp) 9.5kn Bolnes 7DNL150/600 3 x 2 Stroke 7 Cy. 190 x 350 each-772kW (1050bhp) (new engine 1969, fitted 1969) 'Bolnes' Motorenfabriek BV-Netherlands AuxGen: 3 x 135kW 400V 50Hz a.c Thrusters: 2 Thwart. FP thruster Fuel: 233.5 (d.f.)
8976956 *SFYW* -	**TRANAN** *ex* Kongedybet *-1970* *ex* Kirsten Piil *-1948* **Angsholmen Rederi AB** - *Stockholm* Sweden MMSI: 265563580	**137** 61 -		**1935-01 A/S Helsingors Jernskibs- og Maskinbyggeri — Helsingor** Yd No: 222 Converted From: General Cargo/Passenger Ship-1970 Converted From: Ferry (Passenger only)-1949 L reg 33.86 Br ex - Dght - Lbp - Br md 6.00 Dpth 2.50 Welded, 1 dk	**(A37B2PS) Passenger Ship**	**1 oil engine** driving 1 FP propeller Total Power: 257kW (349hp) 12.0kn Volvo Penta TAMD120 1 x 4 Stroke 6 Cy. 130 x 150 257kW (349bhp) (new engine 2010) AB Volvo Penta-Sweden
9382449 *JWNP* -	**TRANEN** **Norled AS** Tide ASA *Bergen* Norway MMSI: 259299000	**278** 84 30		**2007-01 Fjellstrand AS — Omastrand** Yd No: 1676 Loa 33.00 Br ex - Dght - Lbp - Br md 10.06 Dpth 3.35 Welded, 1 dk	**(A37B2PS) Passenger Ship** Hull Material: Aluminium Alloy Passengers: unberthed: 120	**4 oil engines** reduction geared to sc. shafts driving 2 CP propellers Total Power: 3,600kW (4,896hp) 35.0kn M.T.U. 10V2000M72 4 x Vee 4 Stroke 10 Cy. 135 x 156 each-900kW (1224bhp) MTU Friedrichshafen GmbH-Friedrichshafen
7704966 *CB3254*	**TRANOI** *ex* Stronoy *-1988* **Pesquera Humboldt y Cia Ltda** - *Valparaiso* Chile MMSI: 725000710 Official number: 2543	*680* 314 914	Class: (NV)	**1978-03 Karmsund Verft & Mek. Verksted — Avaldsnes** Yd No: 21 Loa 49.38 Br ex 9.61 Dght 6.200 Lbp 41.81 Br md - Dpth 7.57 Welded, 2 dks	**(B11A2FT) Trawler** Ice Capable	**1 oil engine** geared to sc. shaft driving 1 FP propeller Total Power: 1,596kW (2,170hp) 13.5kn Alpha 14V23L-VO 1 x Vee 4 Stroke 14 Cy. 225 x 300 1596kW (2170bhp) Alpha Diesel A/S-Denmark AuxGen: 2 x 128kW 220V 50Hz a.c, 1 x 54kW 220V 50Hz a.c Thrusters: 1 Thwart. FP thruster (f); 1 Tunnel thruster (a) Fuel: 140.0 7.0pd
9561253 *ZGAA7* -	**TRANQUIL ACE** **Pisces Line Shipping SA** MOL Ship Management Singapore Pte Ltd SatCom: Inmarsat C 431901311 *George Town* Cayman Islands (British) MMSI: 319013600 Official number: 742345	**58,939** 18,159 18,840	Class: NK	**2009-10 Minaminippon Shipbuilding Co Ltd — Usuki OT** Yd No: 708 Loa 199.95 (BB) Br ex 32.65 Dght 9.816 Lbp 190.00 Br md 32.20 Dpth 14.70 Welded, 12 dks	**(A35B2RV) Vehicles Carrier** Quarter stern door/ramp (s. a.) Side door/ramps (s) Cars: 6,233	**1 oil engine** driving 1 FP propeller Total Power: 15,813kW (21,499hp) 20.0kn MAN-B&W 7S60MC-C 1 x 2 Stroke 7 Cy. 600 x 2400 15813kW (21499bhp) Mitsui Engineering & Shipbuilding CLtd-Japan AuxGen: 3 x 1000kW a.c Thrusters: 1 Tunnel thruster (f) Fuel: 2660.0

8604216 *GHQL* ME 50	**TRANQUILITY** *ex* Denebula *-2011* **Tranquility Fishing Co Ltd** - *Lerwick* *United Kingdom* MMSI: 233098000 Official number: A12756	**222** - 131		**1986-10 James N. Miller & Sons Ltd. — St. Monans** Yd No: 1026 Loa 25.63 Br ex 7.40 Dght 3.537 Lbp 23.40 Br md 7.36 Dpth 3.92 Welded, 1 dk	**(B11A2FS) Stern Trawler**	**1 oil engine** with clutches, flexible couplings & sr reverse geared to sc. shaft driving 1 FP propeller Total Power: 500kW (680hp) Blackstone ESL5MK2 1 x 4 Stroke 5 Cy. 222 x 292 500kW (680bhp) Mirrlees Blackstone (Stamford)Ltd.-Stamford
8965426 *ZQHW9* PD 35	**TRANQUILITY** **Summer Isles Fishing Co Ltd** - *Peterhead* *United Kingdom* MMSI: 235000250 Official number: C17006	*218* 83 -		**2000 Miller (Methil) Ltd. — Leven** Loa 23.99 (BB) Br ex - Dght - Lbp - Br md 7.50 Dpth 4.20 Welded, 1 dk	**(B11B2FV) Fishing Vessel**	**1 oil engine** with clutches, flexible couplings & sr geared to sc. shaft driving 1 FP propeller Total Power: 592kW (805hp) 11.4kn Caterpillar 3508TA 1 x Vee 4 Stroke 8 Cy. 170 x 190 592kW (805bhp) Caterpillar Inc-USA AuxGen: 2 x 108kW 415V 50Hz a.c Fuel: 26.0 (d.f.)
1002093 *ZCGY5* -	**TRANQUILLITY** *ex* Jamaica Bay *-1999* **Tranquillity Partners Sarl** Yachting Partners International (Monaco) SAM *George Town* *Cayman Islands (British)* MMSI: 319706000 Official number: 735529	**373** - -	Class: LR ✠ **100A1** SS 11/2010 Yacht ✠ **LMC**	**1984-08 Amels BV — Makkum** Yd No: 386 Loa 42.02 Br ex 8.29 Dght 2.500 Lbp 36.60 Br md - Dpth 4.57 Welded, 1 dk	**(X11A2YP) Yacht**	**2 oil engines** driving 2 FP propellers Total Power: 1,268kW (1,724hp) 12.0kn Caterpillar D398TA 2 x Vee 4 Stroke 12 Cy. 159 x 203 each-634kW (862bhp) Caterpillar Tractor Co-USA
8734152 - -	**TRANS 38** *ex* Multi Prima *-2012* **PT Daya Bahtera Sumatera** - *Pontianak* *Indonesia*	**132** 40 -	Class: KI	**2003 CV Bina Citra — Pontianak** Loa 24.00 Br ex - Dght 2.550 Lbp 22.08 Br md 7.00 Dpth 3.35 Welded, 1 dk	**(B32A2ST) Tug**	**2 oil engines** driving 2 Propellers Total Power: 1,302kW (1,770hp) Caterpillar 3412D 2 x Vee 4 Stroke 12 Cy. 145 x 162 each-651kW (885bhp) Caterpillar Inc-USA
9263928 *C6YQ3* -	**TRANS ADRIATIC** *ex* Bow West *-2010* **Kjemi Trans II AS** Seatrans Chemical Tankers AS *Nassau* *Bahamas* MMSI: 311041700 Official number: 8001787	**6,837** 3,851 12,503 T/cm 21.0	Class: NV (NK)	**2002-11 Fukuoka Shipbuilding Co Ltd — Fukuoka FO** Yd No: 1226 Loa 123.19 (BB) Br ex 20.02 Dght 8.753 Lbp 115.85 Br md 20.00 Dpth 11.20 Welded, 1 dk	**(A12B2TR) Chemical/Products Tanker** Double Hull (13F) Liq: 12,780; Liq (Oil): 12,780 Cargo Heating Coils Compartments: 22 Wing Ta (s.stl), 1 Wing Slop Ta, 1 Wing Slop Ta (s.stl), ER (s.stl) 22 Cargo Pump (s): 8x300m³/hr, 8x200m³/hr, 6x100m³/hr Manifold: Bow/CM: 61.6m	**1 oil engine** driving 1 FP propeller Total Power: 3,883kW (5,279hp) 13.4kn B&W 6L35MC 1 x 2 Stroke 6 Cy. 350 x 1050 3883kW (5279bhp) Mitsui Engineering & Shipbuilding CLtd-Japan AuxGen: 3 x 460kW a.c Thrusters: 1 Tunnel thruster (f) Fuel: 95.0 (d.f.) 688.0 (r.f.)
9330953 *V2BW4* -	**TRANS ALREK** - Reederei Speck Gbr *Saint John's* *Antigua & Barbuda* MMSI: 304944000 Official number: 4144	**2,978** 1,314 4,720	Class: GL	**2006-05 Shandong Weihai Shipyard — Weihai SD** Yd No: CZ058 Loa 99.58 (BB) Br ex - Dght 5.920 Lbp 91.45 Br md 16.90 Dpth 7.55 Welded, 1 dk	**(A31A2GX) General Cargo Ship** Grain: 4,456; Bale: 4,166 TEU 366 C Ho 80 TEU C Dk 286 incl 46 ref C. Ice Capable	**1 oil engine** geared to sc. shaft driving 1 CP propeller Total Power: 3,840kW (5,221hp) 15.6kn MaK 8M32C 1 x 4 Stroke 8 Cy. 320 x 480 3840kW (5221bhp) Caterpillar Motoren GmbH & Co. KG-Germany AuxGen: 2 x 280kW 450/230V 60Hz a.c, 1 x 450/230V a.c Thrusters: 1 Thwart. CP thruster (f)
9071466 *YD4510* -	**TRANS AQUARIA** *ex* Erika *-2010* **PT Duta Bahari Pratama** - *Jakarta* *Indonesia*	**124** 38 118	Class: KI (AB) (NK)	**1992-12 Far East Shipyard Co Sdn Bhd — Sibu** Loa 24.40 Br ex - Dght 2.459 Lbp 23.06 Br md 6.70 Dpth 3.05 Welded, 1 dk	**(B32A2ST) Tug**	**2 oil engines** with flexible couplings & sr reverse geared to sc. shafts driving 2 FP propellers Total Power: 592kW (804hp) 10.0kn Caterpillar 3408TA 1 x Vee 4 Stroke 8 Cy. 137 x 152 296kW (402bhp) Caterpillar Inc-USA Caterpillar 3408TA 1 x Vee 4 Stroke 8 Cy. 137 x 152 296kW (402bhp) (, fitted 1985) Caterpillar Tractor Co-USA AuxGen: 2 x 26kW 220V 50Hz a.c Fuel: 30.0 (r.f.) 3.0pd
7212652 *DUHK9* -	**TRANS-ASIA** *ex* Kogane Maru *-1993* **Trans-Asia Shipping Lines Inc** - *Cebu* *Philippines* Official number: CEB1000318	**3,797** 2,072 3,163	Class: (BV)	**1972-03 Kanda Zosensho K.K. — Kure** Yd No: 164 Loa 94.01 Br ex 17.73 Dght 4.363 Lbp 87.00 Br md 17.71 Dpth 5.62 Welded, 1 dk	**(A36A2PR) Passenger/Ro-Ro Ship (Vehicles)** Passengers: 1365 Cars: 92	**4 oil engines** reduction geared to sc. shafts driving 2 FP propellers Total Power: 7,648kW (10,400hp) 19.5kn Niigata 8MG31EZ 4 x 4 Stroke 8 Cy. 310 x 380 each-1912kW (2600bhp) Niigata Engineering Co Ltd-Japan AuxGen: 2 x 480kW 445V 60Hz a.c Fuel: 123.0 (d.f.) 30.0pd
9683453 *YDB4270* -	**TRANS ASIA 1** *ex* Tan 1 *-2012* **PT Trans Asia Nusantara** - *Tanjung Priok* *Indonesia*	**154** 47 103	Class: NK	**2012-12 YCK Shipbuilding Sdn Bhd — Sibu** Yd No: 29018 Loa 23.50 Br ex - Dght 2.710 Lbp 21.99 Br md 7.32 Dpth 3.20 Welded, 1 dk	**(B32A2ST) Tug**	**2 oil engines** reduction geared to sc. shafts driving 2 FP propellers Total Power: 970kW (1,318hp) Yanmar 6AYM-WST 2 x 4 Stroke 6 Cy. 155 x 180 each-485kW (659bhp) Yanmar Diesel Engine Co Ltd-Japan Fuel: 89.0 (d.f.)
7620744 *DUH2265* -	**TRANS-ASIA 2** *ex* Lite Ferry I *-1998* *ex* Hayabusa No. 8 *-1996* *ex* Hayabusa *-1995* **Trans-Asia Shipping Lines Inc** - *Cebu* *Philippines* Official number: CEB1001608	*1,389* 831 700	Class: (LR) Classed LR until 31/10/01	**1977-03 The Hakodate Dock Co Ltd — Hakodate HK** Yd No: 656 Loa 88.02 Br ex 15.33 Dght 3.880 Lbp 76.26 Br md 15.00 Dpth 4.81 Welded, 3 dks	**(A36A2PR) Passenger/Ro-Ro Ship (Vehicles)** Stern door	**2 oil engines** reduction geared to sc. shafts driving 2 FP propellers Total Power: 4,414kW (6,002hp) Daihatsu 8DSM-32 2 x 4 Stroke 8 Cy. 320 x 380 each-2207kW (3001bhp) Daihatsu Diesel Manufacturing Co Lt-Japan AuxGen: 2 x 144kW 440V 60Hz a.c
8807131 *DUHP6* -	**TRANS-ASIA 3** *ex* New Shikoku *-1995* **Trans-Asia Shipping Lines Inc** - *Cebu* *Philippines* Official number: CEB1008037	**2,908** 2,232 1,292		**1989-03 Usuki Shipyard Co Ltd — Usuki OT** Yd No: 1590 Loa 110.00 (BB) Br ex 16.02 Dght 4.500 Lbp 100.00 Br md 16.00 Dpth 10.62 Welded	**(A36A2PR) Passenger/Ro-Ro Ship (Vehicles)** Passengers: unberthed: 576; cabins: 12; berths: 24 Cars: 12, Trailers: 36	**2 oil engines** with flexible couplings & sr geared to sc. shafts driving 2 CP propellers Total Power: 6,620kW (9,000hp) 19.0kn Pielstick 6PC2-6L-400 2 x 4 Stroke 6 Cy. 400 x 460 each-3310kW (4500bhp) (made 1988) Ishikawajima Harima Heavy IndustrieCo Ltd (IHI)-Japan Thrusters: 1 Thwart. CP thruster (a)
8817083 *DYGH* -	**TRANS-ASIA 5** *ex* Butuan Bay 1 *-2010* *ex* Koyo *-2001* *ex* Koyo Maru *-2001* **Trans-Asia Shipping Lines Inc** - *Cebu* *Philippines* Official number: CEB1006053	*4,790* 3,257 3,376	Class: (NK)	**1989-02 Iwagi Zosen Co Ltd — Kamijima EH** Yd No: 126 Loa 114.82 Br ex - Dght 5.815 Lbp 108.00 Br md 19.00 Dpth 9.60 Welded, 2 dks	**(A35A2RR) Ro-Ro Cargo Ship** Derricks: 2x3t	**1 oil engine** driving 1 FP propeller Total Power: 7,061kW (9,600hp) 17.9kn Mitsubishi 8UEC45LA 1 x 2 Stroke 8 Cy. 450 x 1350 7061kW (9600bhp) Akasaka Tekkosho KK (Akasaka DieselLtd)-Japan AuxGen: 3 x 347kW a.c
8312980 *DUH2580* -	**TRANS-ASIA 8** *ex* Dona Rita Sr. *-2011* *ex* Hanil Carferry No. 1 *-2007* *ex* Soya Maru No. 10 *-1997* **Trans-Asia Shipping Lines Inc** - *Cebu* *Philippines* Official number: CEB1006786	**2,019** 1,347 567	Class: (KR)	**1984-04 Naikai Shipbuilding & Engineering Co Ltd — Onomichi HS (Taguma Shipyard)** Yd No: 489 Loa 70.21 (BB) Br ex - Dght 3.794 Lbp 64.01 Br md 14.51 Dpth 4.63 Welded, 1 dk	**(A36A2PR) Passenger/Ro-Ro Ship (Vehicles)** Passengers: unberthed: 650 Cars: 62, Trailers: 25	**2 oil engines** with clutches & dr geared to sc. shafts driving 2 FP propellers Total Power: 2,354kW (3,200hp) 16.4kn Daihatsu 6DSM-28 2 x 4 Stroke 6 Cy. 280 x 340 each-1177kW (1600bhp) Daihatsu Diesel Manufacturing Co Lt-Japan AuxGen: 2 x 260kW 225V a.c Thrusters: 1 Thwart. CP thruster (f) Fuel: 57.0 (d.f.)
7823528 *DUAX2* -	**TRANS-ASIA 9** *ex* Dona Conchita Sr *-2012* *ex* Our Lady Of Good Voyage *-2011* *ex* Wilines Mabuhay 6 *-1996* *ex* Ferry Kikai *-1995* **Trans-Asia Shipping Lines Inc** - *Manila* *Philippines* Official number: MNLD007268	**5,463** 3,595 1,517	Class: (AB)	**1979-07 Fukuoka Shipbuilding Co Ltd — Fukuoka FO** Yd No: 1073 Loa 109.15 (BB) Br ex 17.89 Dght 4.749 Lbp 98.61 Br md 17.81 Dpth 6.33 Welded, 2 dks	**(A36A2PR) Passenger/Ro-Ro Ship (Vehicles)** Passengers: 1076 Lane-Len: 170 Cars: 30	**2 oil engines** driving 2 FP propellers Total Power: 5,590kW (7,600hp) 18.5kn Mitsubishi 6UET45/75C 2 x 2 Stroke 6 Cy. 450 x 750 each-2795kW (3800bhp) Kobe Hatsudoki KK-Japan AuxGen: 2 x 432kW 445V 60Hz a.c Fuel: 46.5 (d.f.) 238.5 (r.f.) 20.5pd

IMO / Call sign	Name / Owner / Manager	Tonnage	Class	Build / Dimensions	Type / Capacity	Machinery
9615470 *VRKA7* -	**TRANS AUTUMN** **Autumn Maritime Ltd** Amoysailing Maritime Co Ltd *Hong Kong* *Hong Kong* MMSI: 477423300 Official number: HK-3401	**33,044** 19,231 56,838 T/cm 58.8	Class: CC (BV)	**2012-04 Xiamen Shipbuilding Industry Co Ltd — Xiamen FJ** Yd No: XSI407F Loa 189.99 (BB) Br ex - Dght 12.800 Lbp 185.00 Br md 32.26 Dpth 18.00 Welded, 1 dk	**(A21A2BC) Bulk Carrier** Grain: 71,634; Bale: 68,200 Compartments: 5 Ho, ER 5 Ha: 4 (21.3 x 18.3)ER (18.9 x 18.3) Cranes: 4x30t	**1 oil engine** driving 1 FP propeller Total Power: 9,480kW (12,889hp) 14.2kn MAN-B&W 6S50MC-C 1 x 2 Stroke 6 Cy. 500 x 2000 9480kW (12889bhp) Hyundai Heavy Industries Co Ltd-South Korea AuxGen: 3 x 600kW 60Hz a.c Fuel: 2400.0
9086071 *V7IL9* -	**TRANS BAY** *ex* Balsfjord *-2007* *ex* Sumava *-1998* **Bulk Transloading AS** Pioneer Ship Management Services LLC (Transloader Division) *Majuro* *Marshall Islands* MMSI: 538002404 Official number: 2404	**37,550** 23,072 70,120 T/cm 65.5	Class: NV (LR) ✠ Classed LR until 27/1/01	**1996-01 Daewoo Heavy Industries Ltd — Geoje** Yd No: 1096 Converted From: Bulk Carrier-2001 Loa 225.00 (BB) Br ex 32.24 Dght 13.318 Lbp 215.00 Br md 32.20 Dpth 18.50 Welded, 1 dk	**(A23A2BD) Bulk Carrier, Self-discharging** Grain: 82,210; Bale: 78,338 Compartments: 7 Ho, ER 7 Ha: 7 (16.6 x 14.9)ER Cranes: 4x32.5t Ice Capable	**1 oil engine** driving 1 FP propeller Total Power: 7,850kW (10,673hp) 13.5kn B&W 6S50MC 1 x 2 Stroke 6 Cy. 500 x 1910 7850kW (10673bhp) Korea Heavy Industries & ConstrCo Ltd (HANJUNG)-South Korea AuxGen: 3 x 1500kW 390V 50Hz a.c Fuel: 229.0 (d.f.) (Heating Coils) 1802.0 (r.f.) 31.5pd
9221669 *9HA3236* -	**TRANS BORG** *ex* Irene *-2012* **Kjemikalietank AS** Seatrans AS *Valletta* *Malta* MMSI: 229327000 Official number: 9221669	**7,373** 3,637 11,921 T/cm 21.2	Class: NV (NK)	**2000-01 Kurinoura Dockyard Co Ltd — Yawatahama EH** Yd No: 351 Loa 131.00 (BB) Br ex 19.63 Dght 8.651 Lbp 122.00 Br md 19.60 Dpth 11.00 Welded, 1 dk	**(A12B2TR) Chemical/Products Tanker** Double Hull (13F) Liq: 12,692; Liq (Oil): 12,692 Cargo Heating Coils Compartments: 22 Wing Ta, 2 Wing Slop Ta, ER 22 Cargo Pump (s): 22x200m³/hr Manifold: Bow/CM: 66.8m	**1 oil engine** driving 1 FP propeller Total Power: 4,891kW (6,650hp) 14.2kn B&W 7S35MC 1 x 2 Stroke 7 Cy. 350 x 1400 4891kW (6650bhp) Makita Corp-Japan AuxGen: 3 x 300kW 450V 60Hz a.c Thrusters: 1 Tunnel thruster (f) Fuel: 95.0 (d.f.) 829.0 (r.f.)
9582829 *A6E2590* -	**TRANS C** *ex* Dorsa *-2012* **Control Contracting & Trading Co (Pvt) LLC** *Abu Dhabi* *United Arab Emirates* MMSI: 470486000	**1,195** 368 1,800	Class: BV	**2010-05 in Iran** Yd No: 08292 Loa 70.90 Br ex - Dght 2.650 Lbp 66.36 Br md 15.00 Dpth 3.80 Welded, 1 dk	**(A35D2RL) Landing Craft** Liq: 1,496; Liq (Oil): 1,496	**2 oil engines** reduction geared to sc. shafts driving 2 FP propellers Total Power: 1,600kW (2,176hp) 12.0kn Yanmar 6N21AL-SV 2 x 4 Stroke 6 Cy. 210 x 290 each-800kW (1088bhp) Yanmar Diesel Engine Co Ltd-Japan AuxGen: 2 x 152kW 50Hz a.c
8943856 - -	**TRANS CARIBBEAN 66** *ex* Chung I No. 66 *-1995* - -	*703* 268 -		**1986 Chung Yi Shipbuilding Corp. — Kaohsiung** L reg 47.26 Br ex - Dght - Lbp - Br md 8.50 Dpth 4.08 Welded, 1 dk	**(B11B2FV) Fishing Vessel**	**1 oil engine** driving 1 FP propeller Total Power: 809kW (1,100hp) 12.0kn Niigata 1 x 4 Stroke 6 Cy. 809kW (1100bhp) Niigata Engineering Co Ltd-Japan
8943741 - -	**TRANS CARIBBEAN 111** *ex* Chung I No. 111 *-1995* - -	*703* 268 -		**1986 Chung Yi Shipbuilding Corp. — Kaohsiung** L reg 47.26 Br ex - Dght - Lbp - Br md 8.50 Dpth 4.08 Welded, 1 dk	**(B11B2FV) Fishing Vessel**	**1 oil engine** driving 1 FP propeller Total Power: 809kW (1,100hp) 12.0kn Niigata 1 x 4 Stroke 6 Cy. 809kW (1100bhp) Niigata Engineering Co Ltd-Japan
8430196 - -	**TRANS CARIBBEAN 126** *ex* Chung I No. 126 *-1995* - -	**705** 268 -		**1987 Chung Yi Shipbuilding Corp. — Kaohsiung** L reg 47.26 Br ex - Dght - Lbp - Br md 8.51 Dpth 4.08 Welded, 1 dk	**(B11B2FV) Fishing Vessel**	**1 oil engine** driving 1 FP propeller 13.0kn
8943765 - -	**TRANS CARIBBEAN 127** *ex* Chung I No. 127 *-1994* - -	*705* 268 -		**1987 Chung Yi Shipbuilding Corp. — Kaohsiung** L reg 47.26 Br ex - Dght - Lbp - Br md 8.51 Dpth 4.08 Welded, 1 dk	**(B11B2FV) Fishing Vessel**	**1 oil engine** driving 1 FP propeller Total Power: 809kW (1,100hp) 12.0kn Niigata 1 x 4 Stroke 6 Cy. 809kW (1100bhp) Niigata Engineering Co Ltd-Japan
8943777 - -	**TRANS CARIBBEAN 132** *ex* Chung I No. 132 *-1994* - -	*705* 268 -		**1987 Chung Yi Shipbuilding Corp. — Kaohsiung** L reg 47.26 Br ex - Dght - Lbp - Br md 8.51 Dpth 4.08 Welded, 1 dk	**(B11B2FV) Fishing Vessel**	**1 oil engine** driving 1 FP propeller Total Power: 809kW (1,100hp) 12.0kn Niigata 1 x 4 Stroke 6 Cy. 809kW (1100bhp) Niigata Engineering Co Ltd-Japan
8943791 - -	**TRANS CARIBBEAN 203** *ex* Chung I No. 203 *-1994* - -	*730* 308 -		**1989 Chung Yi Shipbuilding Corp. — Kaohsiung** L reg 48.36 Br ex - Dght - Lbp - Br md 8.70 Dpth 3.94 Welded, 1 dk	**(B11B2FV) Fishing Vessel**	**1 oil engine** driving 1 FP propeller Total Power: 883kW (1,201hp) 12.0kn Niigata 1 x 4 Stroke 6 Cy. 883kW (1201bhp) Niigata Engineering Co Ltd-Japan
8943818 - -	**TRANS CARIBBEAN 231** *ex* Chung I No. 231 *-1994* - -	*730* 308 -		**1988 Chung Yi Shipbuilding Corp. — Kaohsiung** L reg 48.36 Br ex - Dght - Lbp - Br md 8.70 Dpth 3.94 Welded, 1 dk	**(B11B2FV) Fishing Vessel**	**1 oil engine** driving 1 FP propeller Total Power: 1,030kW (1,400hp) 12.0kn Niigata 1 x 4 Stroke 6 Cy. 1030kW (1400bhp) Niigata Engineering Co Ltd-Japan
8943832 - -	**TRANS CARIBBEAN 301** *ex* Chung I No. 301 *-1995* - -	*778* 296 -		**1989 Chung Yi Shipbuilding Corp. — Kaohsiung** L reg 50.05 Br ex - Dght - Lbp - Br md 8.90 Dpth 3.85 Welded, 1 dk	**(B11B2FV) Fishing Vessel**	**1 oil engine** driving 1 FP propeller Total Power: 1,030kW (1,400hp) 13.0kn Niigata 1 x 4 Stroke 6 Cy. 1030kW (1400bhp) Niigata Engineering Co Ltd-Japan
8943844 - -	**TRANS CARIBBEAN 302** *ex* Chung I No. 302 *-1995* - -	*777* 296 -		**1990 Chung Yi Shipbuilding Corp. — Kaohsiung** L reg 50.05 Br ex - Dght - Lbp - Br md 8.90 Dpth 3.85 Welded, 1 dk	**(B11B2FV) Fishing Vessel**	**1 oil engine** driving 1 FP propeller Total Power: 1,030kW (1,400hp) 13.0kn Niigata 1 x 4 Stroke 6 Cy. 1030kW (1400bhp) Niigata Engineering Co Ltd-Japan
8943868 - -	**TRANS CARIBBEAN 701** *ex* Chung I No. 701 *-1994* - -	*778* 296 -		**1990 Chung Yi Shipbuilding Corp. — Kaohsiung** L reg 50.05 Br ex - Dght - Lbp - Br md 8.90 Dpth 3.85 Welded, 1 dk	**(B11B2FV) Fishing Vessel**	**1 oil engine** driving 1 FP propeller Total Power: 1,030kW (1,400hp) 12.0kn Niigata 1 x 4 Stroke 6 Cy. 1030kW (1400bhp) Niigata Engineering Co Ltd-Japan
9007879 *C6RM5* -	**TRANS CARRIER** *ex* Swan Hunter *-1999* *ex* Parchim *-1997* *ex* Swan Hunter *-1996* *ex* Korsnas Link *-1994* **Sea-Cargo Skips AS** Seatrans AS *Nassau* *Bahamas* MMSI: 311102000 Official number: 8000239	**9,953** 2,986 7,193 T/cm 20.0	Class: NV	**1992-07 '3 Maj' Brodogradiliste dd — Rijeka** (Hull) Yd No: 653 **1992-07 Brodogradiliste Kraljevica dd — Kraljevica** Yd No: 492 Loa 144.15 (BB) Br ex 19.73 Dght 5.864 Lbp 133.40 Br md 19.70 Dpth 6.94 Welded, 2 dks	**(A35A2RR) Ro-Ro Cargo Ship** Stern door/ramp (p) Len: 18.00 Wid: 3.60 Swl: 80 Stern door/ramp (s) Len: 18.00 Wid: 9.80 Swl: 80 Lane-Len: 1068 Lane-Wid: 3.00 Lane-clr ht: 6.20 Trailers: 94 Bale: 13,500 TEU 330 incl 20 ref C. Ice Capable	**1 oil engine** reduction geared to sc. shaft driving 1 CP propeller Total Power: 4,500kW (6,118hp) 14.5kn Wartsila 12V32D 1 x Vee 4 Stroke 12 Cy. 320 x 350 4500kW (6118bhp) Wartsila Diesel Oy-Finland AuxGen: 2 x 368kW 400V 50Hz a.c, 1 x 660kW 400V 50Hz a.c Thrusters: 1 Tunnel thruster (f) Fuel: 97.6 (d.f.) 511.0 (r.f.) 22.0pd
9176694 *9VBJ8* -	**TRANS CATALONIA** *ex* Mont Blanc *-2005* **Trans Fjord Pte Ltd** Seatrans AS *Singapore* *Singapore* MMSI: 564469000 Official number: 391123	**13,005** 5,941 19,733 T/cm 31.2	Class: NV (BV)	**2000-05 Union Naval Valencia SA (UNV) — Valencia** Yd No: 254 Loa 151.48 (BB) Br ex 23.53 Dght 10.075 Lbp 142.70 Br md 23.50 Dpth 13.00 Welded, 1 dk	**(A11B2TH) LPG/Chemical Tanker** Double Hull (13F) Liq: 20,338; Liq (Gas): 10,516 Cargo Heating Coils Compartments: 10 Ta, 18 Wing Ta, ER 29 Cargo Pump (s): 20x300m³/hr, 9x200m³/hr Manifold: Bow/CM: 72.8m	**1 oil engine** driving 1 CP propeller Total Power: 9,467kW (12,871hp) 15.8kn B&W 6S50MC-C 1 x 2 Stroke 6 Cy. 500 x 2000 9467kW (12871bhp) Manises Diesel Engine Co. S.A.-Valencia AuxGen: 3 x 910kW 440V 60Hz a.c Thrusters: 1 Tunnel thruster (f) Fuel: 174.0 (d.f.) 1265.0 (r.f.)
8808604 *9HA2571* -	**TRANS DANIA** **K/S Dania Trans** Seatrans AS *Valletta* *Malta* MMSI: 248907000 Official number: 8808604	**5,167** 1,941 5,353	Class: NV	**1989-10 Hermann Suerken GmbH & Co. KG — Papenburg** Yd No: 363 Loa 113.40 Br ex 17.75 Dght 6.713 Lbp 106.40 Br md 17.50 Dpth 11.00 Welded, 2 dks	**(A31B2GP) Palletised Cargo Ship** Grain: 9,048; Bale: 7,870 Compartments: 2 Ho, ER Ice Capable	**1 oil engine** with clutches, flexible couplings & sr geared to sc. shaft driving 1 CP propeller Total Power: 2,942kW (4,000hp) 15.0kn Normo BRM-8 1 x 4 Stroke 8 Cy. 320 x 360 2942kW (4000bhp) Bergen Diesel AS-Norway AuxGen: 1 x 450kW 380V 50Hz a.c, 2 x 450kW 380V 50Hz a.c, 1 x 66kW 380V 50Hz a.c Thrusters: 1 Thwart. CP thruster (f) Fuel: 50.9 (d.f.) 479.9 (r.f.) 14.0pd

IMO / Call sign	Name / Owner / Manager	Tonnage	Class	Build / Dimensions	Type / Cargo	Machinery
9295452 *9HA2565* -	**TRANS EMERALD** **KS Kjemikalietank** Seatrans AS *Valletta* *Malta* MMSI: 248888000 Official number: 9295452	**5,815** 2,541 8,650 T/cm 18.8	Class: NV	**2005-11 INP Heavy Industries Co Ltd — Ulsan** Yd No: 1136 Loa 115.00 (BB) Br ex 18.83 Dght 7.400 Lbp 108.00 Br md 18.80 Dpth 9.70 Welded, 1 dk	**(A12B2TR) Chemical/Products Tanker** Double Hull (13F) Liq: 8,956; Liq (Oil): 8,956 Compartments: 16 Wing Ta, 2 Wing Slop Ta, ER 16 Cargo Pump (s): 12x300m³/hr, 2x200m³/hr, 2x100m³/hr Manifold: Bow/CM: 52.6m	**1 oil engine** driving 1 FP propeller Total Power: 4,200kW (5,710hp) 14.0kn MAN-B&W 6S35MC 1 x 2 Stroke 6 Cy. 350 x 1400 4200kW (5710bhp) Hyundai Heavy Industries Co Ltd-South Korea AuxGen: 3 x 560kW a.c Thrusters: 1 Tunnel thruster (f); 1 Tunnel thruster (a) Fuel: 73.0 (d.f.) 583.0 (r.f.)
9059951 *V7IM2* -	**TRANS EMIRATES** *ex* Bakra *-2007* *ex* Bakar *-1999* *ex* Beskydy *-1998* **Bulk Transloading AS** Pioneer Ship Management Services LLC (Transloader Division) *Majuro* *Marshall Islands* MMSI: 538002405 Official number: 2405	**37,550** 23,072 70,456 T/cm 60.5	Class: NK (LR) (NV) ✠ Classed LR until 2/11/00	**1993-09 Daewoo Shipbuilding & Heavy Machinery Ltd — Geoje** Yd No: 1065 Converted From: Bulk Carrier-1999 Loa 225.00 (BB) Br ex 32.23 Dght 13.317 Lbp 215.00 Br md 32.20 Dpth 18.51 Welded, 1 dk	**(A23A2BD) Bulk Carrier, Self-discharging** Grain: 82,210; Bale: 78,338 Compartments: 7 Ho, ER 7 Ha: 7 (16.6 x 14.9)ER Cranes: 4x32.5t Ice Capable	**1 oil engine** driving 1 FP propeller Total Power: 7,964kW (10,828hp) 13.5kn B&W 6S50MC 1 x 2 Stroke 6 Cy. 500 x 1910 7964kW (10828bhp) Korea Heavy Industries & ConstrCo Ltd (HANJUNG)-South Korea AuxGen: 3 x 500kW 380V 50Hz a.c Fuel: 197.5 (d.f.) 1555.2 (r.f.) 31.5pd
9645815 *YDA4983* -	**TRANS ENERGY 1945** **PT Trans Energy Indonesia** *Tanjung Priok* *Indonesia* Official number: 2619/L	**199** 60 169	Class: NK	**2011-12 Sky-E Marine Sdn Bhd — Sibu** Yd No: SKY001 Loa 26.00 Br ex - Dght 3.012 Lbp 23.99 Br md 8.00 Dpth 3.65 Welded, 1 dk	**(B32A2ST) Tug**	**2 oil engines** reduction geared to sc. shafts driving 2 Propellers Total Power: 1,220kW (1,658hp) Yanmar 6AYM-WET 2 x 4 Stroke 6 Cy. 155 x 180 each-610kW (829bhp) Yanmar Diesel Engine Co Ltd-Japan Fuel: 140.0
8747161 *YDA4718* -	**TRANS ENERGY 2909** **PT Trans Energy Indonesia** *Tanjung Priok* *Indonesia*	**209** 63 -	Class: KI	**2010-06 PT Mangkupalas Mitra Makmur — Samarinda** Loa 28.59 Br ex - Dght - Lbp 26.69 Br md 8.10 Dpth 3.60 Welded, 1 dk	**(B32A2ST) Tug**	**2 oil engines** reduction geared to sc. shafts driving 2 Propellers Total Power: 1,220kW (1,658hp) Yanmar 6AYM-ETE 2 x 4 Stroke 6 Cy. 155 x 180 each-610kW (829bhp) Yanmar Diesel Engine Co Ltd-Japan AuxGen: 2 x 66kW 230V a.c
8660844 *YD3915* -	**TRANS ENTRADA 1** **PT Trans Entrada** - *Batam* *Indonesia*	**140** 42 113	Class: GL	**2011-05 PT Nongsa Jaya Buana — Batam** Yd No: 53 Loa 23.50 Br ex - Dght 2.712 Lbp 21.90 Br md 7.32 Dpth 3.20 Welded, 1 dk	**(B32A2ST) Tug**	**2 oil engines** reverse reduction geared to sc. shafts driving 2 FP propellers Total Power: 894kW (1,216hp) 10.0kn Cummins KTA-19-M3 2 x 4 Stroke 6 Cy. 159 x 159 each-447kW (608bhp) Cummins Engine Co Inc-USA
9314753 *9HA2572* -	**TRANS EXETER** *launched as* Cape Exeter *-2004* **Euro Trans Skips AS** Seatrans AS *Valletta* *Malta* MMSI: 248908000 Official number: 9314753	**5,955** 2,533 8,550 T/cm 19.2	Class: NV	**2004-09 Sasaki Shipbuilding Co Ltd — Osakikamijima HS** Yd No: 649 Loa 118.14 (BB) Br ex 18.82 Dght 7.350 Lbp 111.06 Br md 18.80 Dpth 9.70 Welded, 1 dk	**(A12B2TR) Chemical/Products Tanker** Double Hull (13F) Liq: 8,902; Liq (Oil): 9,441 Cargo Heating Coils Compartments: ER, 18 Wing Ta 18 Cargo Pump (s): 4x200m³/hr, 10x300m³/hr, 4x100m³/hr Manifold: Bow/CM: 56m	**1 oil engine** driving 1 FP propeller Total Power: 4,457kW (6,060hp) 14.0kn MAN-B&W 6S35MC 1 x 2 Stroke 6 Cy. 350 x 1400 4457kW (6060bhp) MAN B&W Diesel A/S-Denmark AuxGen: 3 x 1320kW 450/100V 60Hz a.c Thrusters: 1 Thwart. FP thruster (f) Fuel: 62.0 (d.f.) 612.0 (r.f.)
9329306 *9HA2563* -	**TRANS FJELL** **Euro Trans Skips AS** Seatrans AS *Valletta* *Malta* MMSI: 248886000 Official number: 9329306	**3,049** 1,018 3,453 T/cm 11.0	Class: NV	**2007-10 Tuzla Gemi Endustrisi A.S. — Tuzla** Yd No: 29 Loa 88.00 (BB) Br ex 13.37 Dght 6.000 Lbp 84.00 Br md 13.35 Dpth 8.10 Welded, 1 dk	**(A12B2TR) Chemical/Products Tanker** Double Hull (13F) Liq: 3,776; Liq (Oil): 3,776 Cargo Heating Coils Compartments: 3 Ta (s.stl), 8 Wing Ta (s.stl), ER 11 Cargo Pump (s): 11x100m³/hr Manifold: Bow/CM: 38.3m Ice Capable	**2 oil engines** reduction geared to sc. shafts driving 2 CP propellers Total Power: 2,400kW (3,264hp) 13.0kn Wartsila 6L20 2 x 4 Stroke 6 Cy. 200 x 280 each-1200kW (1632bhp) Wartsila Finland Oy-Finland AuxGen: 1 x 300kW 60Hz a.c, 2 x 600kW 60Hz a.c Thrusters: 1 Tunnel thruster (f) Fuel: 141.0 (d.f.)
9487043 *VRFY5* -	**TRANS FRIENDSHIP I** **Friendship One Shipping Ltd** Sinotrans Ship Management Ltd SatCom: Inmarsat C 447703095 *Hong Kong* *Hong Kong* MMSI: 477851700 Official number: HK-2552	**19,994** 11,046 31,807	Class: CC	**2010-08 Guangzhou Huangpu Shipbuilding Co Ltd — Guangzhou GD** Yd No: 2283 Loa 177.50 (BB) Br ex - Dght 9.500 Lbp 168.00 Br md 28.20 Dpth 14.20 Welded, 1 dk	**(A31A2GO) Open Hatch Cargo Ship** Grain: 41,909 Compartments: 5 Ho, ER 5 Ha: 4 (19.2 x 16.8)ER (14.4 x 15.2) Cranes: 4x30t Ice Capable	**1 oil engine** driving 1 FP propeller Total Power: 6,480kW (8,810hp) 13.9kn MAN-B&W 6S42MC 1 x 2 Stroke 6 Cy. 420 x 1764 6480kW (8810bhp) AuxGen: 3 x 500kW 450V a.c
9487055 *VRFY6* -	**TRANS FRIENDSHIP II** **Friendship Two Shipping Ltd** Sinotrans Ship Management Ltd SatCom: Inmarsat C 447703249 *Hong Kong* *Hong Kong* MMSI: 477982100 Official number: HK-2553	**19,994** 11,046 32,000	Class: CC	**2010-12 Guangzhou Huangpu Shipbuilding Co Ltd — Guangzhou GD** Yd No: 2284 Loa 177.50 (BB) Br ex - Dght 9.500 Lbp 168.00 Br md 28.20 Dpth 14.20 Welded, 1 dk	**(A31A2GO) Open Hatch Cargo Ship** Grain: 41,909 Cranes: 4x30t	**1 oil engine** driving 1 FP propeller Total Power: 6,480kW (8,810hp) 13.9kn MAN-B&W 6S42MC 1 x 2 Stroke 6 Cy. 420 x 1764 6480kW (8810bhp)
9176216 *3FGB8* -	**TRANS FUTURE 1** **Feng Li Maritime Corp** Kagoshima Senpaku Kaisha Ltd SatCom: Inmarsat B 335332910 *Panama* *Panama* MMSI: 353329000 Official number: 2545198D	**25,667** 7,701 10,347	Class: NK	**1998-03 Naikai Zosen Corp — Onomichi HS (Setoda Shipyard)** Yd No: 628 Loa 172.00 (BB) Br ex - Dght 7.718 Lbp 160.00 Br md 25.00 Dpth 18.70 Welded, 6 dks incl 1 hoistable	**(A35B2RV) Vehicles Carrier** Quarter stern door/ramp (s. a.) Len: 25.00 Wid: 5.50 Swl: 50 Cars: 1,080 TEU 384	**1 oil engine** driving 1 FP propeller Total Power: 11,982kW (16,291hp) 20.7kn B&W 9L50MC 1 x 2 Stroke 9 Cy. 500 x 1620 11982kW (16291bhp) Hitachi Zosen Corp-Japan AuxGen: 2 x 740kW a.c Fuel: 1395.0 (r.f.) 47.0pd
9196400 *3FDE9* -	**TRANS FUTURE 2** **Feng Li Maritime Corp** Kagoshima Senpaku Kaisha Ltd SatCom: Inmarsat C 435721710 *Panama* *Panama* MMSI: 357217000 Official number: 2620999D	**25,667** 7,701 10,298	Class: NK	**1999-02 Naikai Zosen Corp — Onomichi HS (Setoda Shipyard)** Yd No: 646 Loa 172.00 (BB) Br ex - Dght 7.718 Lbp 160.00 Br md 25.00 Dpth 9.20 Welded, 5 dks plus 1 hoistable	**(A35B2RV) Vehicles Carrier** Quarter stern door/ramp (s. a.) Len: 25.00 Wid: 5.50 Swl: 50 Cars: 1,080 TEU 384	**1 oil engine** driving 1 FP propeller Total Power: 11,982kW (16,291hp) 20.7kn B&W 9L50MC 1 x 2 Stroke 9 Cy. 500 x 1620 11982kW (16291bhp) Hitachi Zosen Corp-Japan AuxGen: 2 x 740kW a.c Fuel: 1395.0 (r.f.) 47.6pd
9227613 *H3XD* -	**TRANS FUTURE 3** **Feng Li Maritime Corp** Kagoshima Senpaku Kaisha Ltd *Panama* *Panama* MMSI: 356948000 Official number: 2789101C	**25,157** 7,548 9,491	Class: NK	**2001-03 Mitsubishi Heavy Industries Ltd. — Shimonoseki** Yd No: 1073 Loa 171.40 (BB) Br ex - Dght 8.021 Lbp 162.70 Br md 25.00 Dpth 18.85 Welded, 7 dks incl 1 hoistable	**(A35B2RV) Vehicles Carrier** Quarter stern door/ramp (p) Len: 25.00 Wid: 7.00 Swl: 50 Cars: 1,923	**1 oil engine** driving 1 FP propeller Total Power: 11,548kW (15,701hp) 21.1kn Mitsubishi 8UEC50LSII 1 x 2 Stroke 8 Cy. 500 x 1950 11548kW (15701bhp) Mitsubishi Heavy Industries Ltd-Japan AuxGen: 3 x 800kW a.c Thrusters: 1 Thwart. FP thruster (f) Fuel: 1736.0 (r.f.)
9326079 *3EDA4* -	**TRANS FUTURE 5** **Feng Li Maritime Corp** Kagoshima Senpaku Kaisha Ltd SatCom: Inmarsat C 437152210 *Panama* *Panama* MMSI: 371522000 Official number: 3128406A	**60,414** 18,125 14,906	Class: NK	**2005-10 Mitsubishi Heavy Industries Ltd. — Nagasaki** Yd No: 2205 Loa 199.99 (BB) Br ex - Dght 9.025 Lbp 192.00 Br md 32.26 Dpth 36.21 Welded	**(A35B2RV) Vehicles Carrier** Side door/ramp (s) Len: 17.00 Wid: 4.20 Swl: - Quarter stern door/ramp (s. a.) Len: 30.00 Wid: 8.00 Swl: - Cars: 6,393	**1 oil engine** driving 1 FP propeller Total Power: 14,315kW (19,463hp) 20.5kn Mitsubishi 7UEC60LSII 1 x 2 Stroke 7 Cy. 600 x 2300 14315kW (19463bhp) Mitsubishi Heavy Industries Ltd-Japan AuxGen: 3 x 1090kW a.c Thrusters: 1 Thwart. CP thruster (f) Fuel: 200.0 (d.f.) 3200.0 (r.f.)
9326081 *3EER6* -	**TRANS FUTURE 6** **Feng Li Maritime Corp & Norwich Shipping Corp** Kagoshima Senpaku Kaisha Ltd SatCom: Inmarsat C 437179710 *Panama* *Panama* MMSI: 371797000 Official number: 3151206B	**60,401** 18,121 14,906	Class: NK	**2006-02 Mitsubishi Heavy Industries Ltd. — Nagasaki** Yd No: 2206 Loa 199.99 (BB) Br ex - Dght 9.025 Lbp 192.00 Br md 32.26 Dpth 36.21 Welded	**(A35B2RV) Vehicles Carrier** Side door/ramp (s) Len: 17.00 Wid: 4.20 Swl: - Quarter stern door/ramp (s. a.) Len: 30.00 Wid: 8.00 Swl: - Cars: 6,393	**1 oil engine** driving 1 FP propeller Total Power: 14,315kW (19,463hp) 20.5kn Mitsubishi 7UEC60LSII 1 x 2 Stroke 7 Cy. 600 x 2300 14315kW (19463bhp) Mitsubishi Heavy Industries Ltd-Japan AuxGen: 3 x 1090kW a.c Thrusters: 1 Thwart. CP thruster (f) Fuel: 3150.0

IMO / Call sign	Name / Owner / Manager / Flag	Tonnage	Class	Builder / Dimensions	Type / Cargo	Machinery
9326093 *3EEW3* -	**TRANS FUTURE 7** **Norwich Shipping Corp** Kagoshima Senpaku Kaisha Ltd SatCom: Inmarsat C 437182710 *Panama* Panama MMSI: 371827000 Official number: 3153206A	**60,401** 18,121 14,906	Class: NK	**2006**-03 **Mitsubishi Heavy Industries Ltd. — Nagasaki** Yd No: 2207 Loa 199.99 (BB) Br ex - Dght 9.025 Lbp 192.00 Br md 32.26 Dpth 36.21 Welded	**(A35B2RV) Vehicles Carrier** Side door/ramp (s) Len: 17.00 Wid: 4.20 Swl: - Quarter stern door/ramp (s. a.) Len: 30.00 Wid: 8.00 Swl: - Cars: 6,393	**1 oil engine** driving 1 FP propeller Total Power: 14,315kW (19,463hp) 20.5kn Mitsubishi 7UEC60LSII 1 x 2 Stroke 7 Cy. 600 x 2300 14315kW (19463bhp) Mitsubishi Heavy Industries Ltd-Japan AuxGen: 3 x 1090kW a.c Thrusters: 1 Tunnel thruster (f) Fuel: 3150.0
9477701 *3EZG6* -	**TRANS FUTURE 8** **Feng Li Maritime Corp** Toyofuji Shipping Co Ltd (Toyofuji Kaiun KK) *Panama* Panama MMSI: 371320000 Official number: 4160510	**28,755** 8,627 6,220	Class: NK	**2010**-05 **Mitsubishi Heavy Industries Ltd. — Shimonoseki** Yd No: 1138 Loa 165.00 (BB) Br ex - Dght 6.522 Lbp 157.00 Br md 27.60 Dpth 24.15 Welded, 1 dk	**(A35B2RV) Vehicles Carrier** Quarter stern door/ramp (p. a.) Len: 25.00 Wid: 6.00 Swl: 45 Quarter stern door/ramp (s. a.) Len: 25.00 Wid: 6.00 Swl: 45 Cars: 2,021	**1 oil engine** driving 1 FP propeller Total Power: 11,900kW (16,179hp) 21.0kn Mitsubishi 7UEC52LSE 1 x 2 Stroke 7 Cy. 520 x 2000 11900kW (16179bhp) Mitsubishi Heavy Industries Ltd-Japan AuxGen: 2 x 1150kW a.c Thrusters: 1 Tunnel thruster (f) Fuel: 1390.0 (r.f.)
9477713 *3FEN2* -	**TRANS FUTURE 10** **Feng Li Maritime Corp** Toyofuji Shipping Co Ltd (Toyofuji Kaiun KK) *Panama* Panama MMSI: 356143000 Official number: 4192510	**28,755** 8,627 6,220	Class: NK	**2010**-09 **Mitsubishi Heavy Industries Ltd. — Shimonoseki** Yd No: 1139 Loa 165.00 (BB) Br ex - Dght 6.522 Lbp 157.00 Br md 27.60 Dpth 24.15 Welded, 1 dk	**(A35B2RV) Vehicles Carrier** Quarter stern door/ramp (p. a.) Len: 25.00 Wid: 6.00 Swl: 45 Quarter stern door/ramp (s. a.) Len: 25.00 Wid: 6.00 Swl: 45 Cars: 2,021	**1 oil engine** driving 1 FP propeller Total Power: 11,935kW (16,227hp) 21.0kn Mitsubishi 7UEC52LSE 1 x 2 Stroke 7 Cy. 520 x 2000 11935kW (16227bhp) Mitsubishi Heavy Industries Ltd-Japan AuxGen: 2 x 1150kW a.c Thrusters: 1 Tunnel thruster (f) Fuel: 1543.0 (r.f.)
9477737 *3FXC3* -	**TRANS FUTURE 11** **Feng Li Maritime Corp** Toyofuji Shipping Co Ltd (Toyofuji Kaiun KK) SatCom: Inmarsat C 435646810 *Panama* Panama MMSI: 356468000 Official number: 4260811	**28,755** 8,627 6,220	Class: NK	**2011**-04 **Mitsubishi Heavy Industries Ltd. — Shimonoseki** Yd No: 1141 Loa 165.00 (BB) Br ex - Dght 6.522 Lbp 157.00 Br md 27.60 Dpth 24.15 Welded, 1 dk	**(A35B2RV) Vehicles Carrier** Quarter stern door/ramp (p. a.) Len: 25.00 Wid: 6.00 Swl: 45 Quarter stern door/ramp (s. a.) Len: 25.00 Wid: 6.00 Swl: 45 Cars: 2,021	**1 oil engine** driving 1 FP propeller Total Power: 11,900kW (16,179hp) 21.0kn Mitsubishi 7UEC52LSE 1 x 2 Stroke 7 Cy. 520 x 2000 11900kW (16179bhp) Mitsubishi Heavy Industries Ltd-Japan AuxGen: 2 x 1150kW a.c Thrusters: 1 Tunnel thruster (f) Fuel: 1510.0
8221313 - -	**TRANS GOLDEN No. 28** *ex* King Da Chang No. 1 *-2002* *ex* Dar Chahng No. 1 *-2002* - -	*1,400* 420 2,073	Class: (CR)	**1982**-11 **Hamamoto Zosensho K.K. — Tokushima** Yd No: 635 Loa 72.60 Br ex 14.03 Dght 3.501 Lbp 68.03 Br md 14.01 Dpth 4.63 Welded, 1 dk	**(A31A2GX) General Cargo Ship** Grain: 1,561 Compartments: 3 Ho, ER 3 Ha: 3 (14.4 x 7.8)ER	**2 oil engines** driving 2 FP propellers Total Power: 956kW (1,300hp) 7.5kn Niigata 6L18CX 2 x 4 Stroke 6 Cy. 180 x 240 each-478kW (650bhp) Niigata Engineering Co Ltd-Japan AuxGen: 2 x 60kW 485V 60Hz a.c
8221325 - -	**TRANS GOLDEN No. 88** *ex* King Da Chang No. 2 *-2002* *ex* Dar Chahng No. 2 *-2002* **Lian Mao International Ltd** -	*1,400* 420 2,073	Class: (CR)	**1983**-03 **Hamamoto Zosensho K.K. — Tokushima** Yd No: 637 Loa 72.60 Br ex 14.03 Dght 3.501 Lbp 68.03 Br md 14.01 Dpth 4.63 Welded, 1 dk	**(A31A2GX) General Cargo Ship** Grain: 1,561 Compartments: 3 Ho, ER 3 Ha: 3 (14.4 x 7.8)ER	**2 oil engines** driving 2 FP propellers Total Power: 956kW (1,300hp) 7.5kn Niigata 6L18CX 2 x 4 Stroke 6 Cy. 180 x 240 each-478kW (650bhp) Niigata Engineering Co Ltd-Japan AuxGen: 2 x 60kW 485V 60Hz a.c
7361283 *3FDT3* -	**TRANS GULF** *ex* Pacific Ii *-2013* *ex* Trans Gulf *-2006* *ex* Nada *-2003* *ex* Transgulf *-1996* *ex* Strong Roc *-1987* *ex* Sea Fisher *-1981* *ex* Nornan Fjord *-1979* **Sloman Shipping Line Inc** World Shipping Management Corp SA *Panama* Panama MMSI: 356266000 Official number: 4482013	**2,777** 834 1,727	Class: (NV)	**1974**-10 **D.W. Kremer Sohn — Elmshorn** Yd No: 1161 Loa 79.61 Br ex 13.83 Dght 4.832 Lbp 70.31 Br md 13.80 Dpth 9.75 Welded, 2 dks	**(A35A2RR) Ro-Ro Cargo Ship** Stern door & ramp Lane-Len: 192 Bale: 4,980 TEU 102 Compartments: 1 Ho, ER 2 Ha: (13.1 x 10.3) (20.4 x 10.3)ER Cranes: 1x22t Ice Capable	**2 oil engines** geared to sc. shaft driving 1 CP propeller Total Power: 2,574kW (3,500hp) 14.0kn Wichmann 7AX 2 x 2 Stroke 7 Cy. 300 x 450 each-1287kW (1750bhp) Wichmann Motorfabrikk AS-Norway AuxGen: 1 x 270kW 380V 50Hz a.c, 1 x 100kW 380V 50Hz a.c, 1 x 30kW 380V 50Hz a.c Thrusters: 1 Thwart. FP thruster (f) Fuel: 176.0 (r.f.) 12.0pd
8305406 - -	**TRANS-GULF XII** **Deep Trawl Inc** - *Houma, LA* United States of America Official number: 647557	*130* 103 -		**1982**-05 **Desco Marine — Saint Augustine, Fl** Loa 22.00 Br ex 6.74 Dght - Lbp 19.99 Br md - Dpth 4.09 Bonded, 1 dk	**(B11A2FT) Trawler** Hull Material: Reinforced Plastic Ins: 67 Compartments: 1 Ho, ER 1 Ha:	**1 oil engine** with clutches & sr geared to sc. shaft driving 1 FP propeller Total Power: 268kW (364hp) Caterpillar 3408TA 1 x Vee 4 Stroke 8 Cy. 137 x 152 268kW (364bhp) Caterpillar Tractor Co-USA
8305418 - -	**TRANS-GULF XIV** **Enterprise Shrimp Co Inc** - *Houma, LA* United States of America Official number: 648828	*142* 113 -		**1982**-06 **Desco Marine — Saint Augustine, Fl** Loa 22.00 Br ex 6.74 Dght - Lbp 19.99 Br md - Dpth 4.09 Bonded, 1 dk	**(B11A2FT) Trawler** Hull Material: Reinforced Plastic Ins: 67 Compartments: 1 Ho, ER 1 Ha:	**1 oil engine** with clutches & sr geared to sc. shaft driving 1 FP propeller Total Power: 268kW (364hp) Caterpillar 3408TA 1 x Vee 4 Stroke 8 Cy. 137 x 152 268kW (364bhp) Caterpillar Tractor Co-USA
9170597 *9HA2566* -	**TRANS IBERIA** **Kjemi Trans I KS** Seatrans AS *Valletta* Malta MMSI: 248889000 Official number: 9170597	**13,015** 6,004 19,733 T/cm 31.2	Class: NV	**1999**-12 **Union Naval Valencia SA (UNV) — Valencia** Yd No: 253 Loa 151.48 (BB) Br ex 23.53 Dght 10.075 Lbp 142.70 Br md 23.50 Dpth 13.00 Welded, 1 dk	**(A11B2TH) LPG/Chemical Tanker** Double Hull (13F) Liq: 20,338; Liq (Gas): 10,516 Cargo Heating Coils Compartments: 10 Ta, 18 Wing Ta, ER 29 Cargo Pump (s): 20x300m³/hr, 9x200m³/hr Manifold: Bow/CM: 72.8m	**1 oil engine** driving 1 CP propeller Total Power: 9,480kW (12,889hp) 15.8kn MAN-B&W 6S50MC-C 1 x 2 Stroke 6 Cy. 500 x 2000 9480kW (12889bhp) Manises Diesel Engine Co. S.A.-Valencia AuxGen: 1 x 1100kW 440V 60Hz a.c, 3 x 910kW 440V 60Hz a.c Thrusters: 1 Thwart. CP thruster (f) Fuel: 175.3 (d.f.) (Heating Coils) 1275.7 (r.f.) 28.0pd
8420854 *V8XR* -	**TRANS ISLAND** **New Island Shipping & Trading Co** - *Bandar Seri Begawan* Brunei	*254* 134 400	Class: (GL)	**1984 Greenbay Marine Pte Ltd — Singapore** Yd No: 44 Loa 36.91 Br ex 9.17 Dght 1.996 Lbp 35.21 Br md 9.16 Dpth 2.75 Welded, 1 dk	**(A35D2RL) Landing Craft** Bow door/ramp	**2 oil engines** driving 2 FP propellers Total Power: 440kW (598hp) 9.5kn Volvo Penta TMD120 2 x 4 Stroke 6 Cy. 130 x 150 each-220kW (299bhp) AB Volvo Penta-Sweden
9403736 *YFJC* -	**TRANS JAWA 9** *ex* Niaga Jaya 9 *-2011* **Elsy Wahjuni Soegondo** - *Balikpapan* Indonesia	**873** 262 -	Class: KI	**2006**-06 **Galangan Kapal Tunas Harapan — Samarinda** Loa 69.20 Br ex - Dght 2.663 Lbp 66.69 Br md 13.98 Dpth 3.55 Welded, 1 dk	**(A35D2RL) Landing Craft**	**2 oil engines** reduction geared to sc. shafts driving 2 Propellers Total Power: 1,002kW (1,362hp) Yanmar 6LAH-STE3 2 x 4 Stroke 6 Cy. 150 x 165 each-501kW (681bhp) Yanmar Diesel Engine Co Ltd-Japan AuxGen: 2 x 75kW 400V a.c
8653102 *POLF* -	**TRANS JAYA** *ex* Xin Yong Qiang 1 *-2012* *ex* Xin Yong Qiang *-2009* *ex* Shi Tai 38 *-2009* **PT Pelayaran Internusa Bahari Persada** - *Pontianak* Indonesia	**1,364** 686 1,640	Class: KI (ZC)	**2003**-10 **Wenling Yongfa Shiprepair & Building Co Ltd — Wenling ZJ** Loa 57.28 Br ex - Dght 3.960 Lbp 56.00 Br md 13.00 Dpth 6.00 Welded, 1 dk	**(A31A2GX) General Cargo Ship**	**2 oil engines** reduction geared to sc. shafts driving 2 Propellers Total Power: 700kW (952hp) Chinese Std. Type Z8170ZLC 2 x 4 Stroke 8 Cy. 170 x 200 each-350kW (476bhp) Zibo Diesel Engine Factory-China
9412567 *3EPP4* -	**TRANS LEADER** **Lucretia Shipping SA** Santoku Senpaku Co Ltd *Panama* Panama MMSI: 372849000 Official number: 3390508A	**43,810** 13,143 15,154	Class: NK	**2008**-04 **Mitsubishi Heavy Industries Ltd. — Shimonoseki** Yd No: 1127 Loa 180.00 (BB) Br ex 30.03 Dght 9.200 Lbp 171.70 Br md 30.00 Dpth 33.52 Welded, 10 dks. incl. 2 liftable dks.	**(A35B2RV) Vehicles Carrier** Side door/ramp (s) Len: - Wid: - Swl: 25 Quarter stern door/ramp (s. a.) Len: - Wid: - Swl: 100 Cars: 3,205	**1 oil engine** driving 1 FP propeller Total Power: 11,560kW (15,717hp) 19.9kn Mitsubishi 8UEC50LSII 1 x 2 Stroke 8 Cy. 500 x 1950 11560kW (15717bhp) Mitsubishi Heavy Industries Ltd-Japan AuxGen: 3 x 875kW 450V 60Hz a.c Thrusters: 1 Thwart. CP thruster (f) Fuel: 2090.0 (r.f.)
7430072 *DUA6975* -	**TRANS MITRAMAS 2** *ex* Kotoshiro Maru No. 28 *-2009* *ex* Nansei Maru No. 28 *-1983* **Trans-Pacific Journey Fishing Corp** - *Manila* Philippines Official number: MNLD001686	*481* 264 -		**1975**-09 **Mie Shipyard Co. Ltd. — Yokkaichi** Yd No: 151 Loa - Br ex 9.22 Dght 3.683 Lbp 53.98 Br md 9.20 Dpth 4.30 Riveted\Welded, 1 dk	**(B11B2FV) Fishing Vessel**	**1 oil engine** driving 1 FP propeller Total Power: 1,545kW (2,101hp) Hanshin 6LU38G 1 x 4 Stroke 6 Cy. 380 x 580 1545kW (2101bhp) Hanshin Nainenki Kogyo-Japan

7950670 *DUA2590* -	**TRANS MITRAMAS 111** *ex* Luz Marcelo *ex* Taisen Maru No. 2 *-1993* *ex* Miyasho Maru *-1982* **Trans-Pacific Journey Fishing Corp** - *Manila* Philippines Official number: MNLD003092	*360* 203 -		**1977 K.K. Murakami Zosensho — Ishinomaki** Loa 54.08 Br ex - Dght - Lbp 45.47 Br md 8.11 Dpth 3.61 Welded, 1 dk	**(B11B2FV) Fishing Vessel**	**1 oil engine** reverse geared to sc. shaft driving 1 FP propeller Total Power: 1,177kW (1,600hp) Akasaka AH30R 1 x 4 Stroke 6 Cy. 300 x 480 1177kW (1600bhp) Akasaka Tekkosho KK (Akasaka DieselLtd)-Japan
7238292 *DUA6301* -	**TRANS MITRAMAS 222** *ex* Fuki Maru No. 55 *-1990* *ex* Chokyu Maru No. 11 *-1983* **Trans-Pacific Journey Fishing Corp** - *Manila* Philippines MMSI: 548190100 Official number: MNLD001753	*538* 301 539		**1972 KK Kanasashi Zosen — Shizuoka SZ** Yd No: 1091 Loa 55.30 Br ex 8.64 Dght 3.398 Lbp 49.00 Br md 8.62 Dpth 3.89 Welded, 1 dk	**(B11B2FV) Fishing Vessel**	**1 oil engine** driving 1 FP propeller Total Power: 1,103kW (1,500hp) Hanshin 6LU35 1 x 4 Stroke 6 Cy. 350 x 550 1103kW (1500bhp) Hanshin Nainenki Kogyo-Japan
7208912 *DUA6022* -	**TRANS MITRAMAS 555** *ex* Choko Maru No. 78 *-1990* *ex* Shinei Maru No. 5 *-1983* *ex* Nadayoshi Maru No. 5 *-1980* **Trans-Pacific Journey Fishing Corp** - *Manila* Philippines Official number: MNLD000658	*577* 123 402		**1971 Miho Zosensho K.K. — Shimizu** Yd No: 769 Loa 53.32 Br ex 8.54 Dght 3.372 Lbp 47.00 Br md 8.51 Dpth 3.76 Welded	**(B11B2FV) Fishing Vessel**	**1 oil engine** driving 1 FP propeller Total Power: 772kW (1,050hp) Hanshin 6LU28 1 x 4 Stroke 6 Cy. 280 x 440 772kW (1050bhp) Hanshin Nainenki Kogyo-Japan
9496680 *D5AO8* -	**TRANS NANJING** **MCE ms 'Andromeda' Schifffahrtsgesellschaft mbH & Co KG** Chemikalien Seetransport GmbH SatCom: Inmarsat C 463710421 *Monrovia* Liberia MMSI: 636092336 Official number: 92336	**51,255** 31,192 93,226 T/cm 80.9	Class: AB (CC)	**2011-10 Jiangsu Newyangzi Shipbuilding Co Ltd — Jingjiang JS** Yd No: YZJ2006-853 Loa 230.00 (BB) Br ex - Dght 14.900 Lbp 222.00 Br md 38.00 Dpth 20.70 Welded, 1 dk	**(A21A2BC) Bulk Carrier** Grain: 110,330 Compartments: 7 Ho, ER 7 Ha: ER	**1 oil engine** driving 1 FP propeller Total Power: 13,560kW (18,436hp) 14.1kn MAN-B&W 6S60MC-C 1 x 2 Stroke 6 Cy. 600 x 2400 13560kW (18436bhp) Doosan Engine Co Ltd-South Korea AuxGen: 3 x 730kW a.c Fuel: 280.0 (d.f.) 3490.0 (r.f.)
8323214 *S2AS* -	**TRANS OCEAN 1** *ex* Pamakaristos *-2010* *ex* Sea Front *-2007* *ex* Chettinad Princess *-2003* *ex* Andhika Fatima *-1998* *ex* Western Sun *-1995* *ex* Western Future *-1993* *launched as* Vully *-1986* **Trans Ocean Lines Ltd** Nobpac Shipping Pte Ltd SatCom: Inmarsat C 440500153 *Chittagong* Bangladesh MMSI: 405000100 Official number: 231	**21,941** 12,538 38,398 T/cm 47.2	Class: LR (IR) ✠ **100A1** SS 07/2011 bulk carrier strengthened for heavy cargoes, Nos. 2 & 4 holds may be empty ESP ESN-Hold 1 ✠ **LMC** **UMS** Eq.Ltr: J†; Cable: 605.0/66.0 U3 (a)	**1986-09 Ishikawajima-Harima Heavy Industries Co Ltd (IHI) — Aioi HG** Yd No: 2897 Loa 180.80 (BB) Br ex 30.54 Dght 10.929 Lbp 171.02 Br md 30.51 Dpth 15.32 Welded, 1 dk	**(A21A2BC) Bulk Carrier** Grain: 46,112; Bale: 44,492 Compartments: 5 Ho, ER 5 Ha: (15.2 x 12.8)4 (19.2 x 15.2)ER Cranes: 4x25t	**1 oil engine** driving 1 FP propeller Total Power: 9,540kW (12,971hp) 13.0kn Sulzer 6RTA58 1 x 2 Stroke 6 Cy. 580 x 1700 9540kW (12971bhp) Ishikawajima Harima Heavy IndustrieCo Ltd (IHI)-Japan AuxGen: 3 x 540kW 450V 60Hz a.c Boilers: e 11.5kgf/cm² (11.3bar), AuxB (o.f.) 7.9kgf/cm² (7.7bar)
8400983 *S2CH* -	**TRANS OCEAN PROGRESS** *ex* Solon *-2012* *ex* Argolikos *-2005* *ex* Kelvin Endeavour *-1995* *ex* Angelic Hope *-1992* **Trans Ocean Ship Management Ltd** - SatCom: Inmarsat C 440500193 *Chittagong* Bangladesh MMSI: 405000114 Official number: 245	**25,169** 15,080 42,183	Class: LR ✠ **100A1** SS 01/2012 bulk carrier strengthened for heavy cargoes, Nos. 2 & 4 holds may be empty container cargoes in all holds, on U dk & on all hatch covers ESP ESN-Hold No. 1 LI ✠ **LMC** **UMS** Eq.Ltr: L†; Cable: 632.5/70.0 U3	**1987-01 Sasebo Heavy Industries Co. Ltd. — Sasebo Yard, Sasebo** Yd No: 350 Loa 185.91 (BB) Br ex 30.43 Dght 11.469 Lbp 177.02 Br md 30.41 Dpth 16.21 Welded, 1 dk	**(A21A2BC) Bulk Carrier** Grain: 57,725; Bale: 50,305 TEU 1014 Compartments: 5 Ho, ER 5 Ha: (19.2 x 15.3)4 (20.8 x 15.3)ER Cranes: 5x25t	**1 oil engine** driving 1 FP propeller Total Power: 9,540kW (12,971hp) 14.0kn Sulzer 6RTA58 1 x 2 Stroke 6 Cy. 580 x 1700 9540kW (12971bhp) Mitsubishi Heavy Industries Ltd-Japan AuxGen: 3 x 550kW 450V 60Hz a.c Boilers: e 9.9kgf/cm² (9.7bar), AuxB (o.f.) 6.9kgf/cm² (6.8bar) Fuel: 310.0 (d.f.) 1679.5 (r.f.)
9500699 *3FOD2* -	**TRANS OCEANIC** **Tradewind Navigation SA** Reitaku Kaiun Co Ltd (Reitaku Kaiun KK) SatCom: Inmarsat C 437348910 *Panama* Panama MMSI: 373489000 Official number: 4390412	**32,309** 19,458 58,168 T/cm 57.4	Class: NK	**2012-06 Tsuneishi Shipbuilding Co Ltd — Fukuyama HS** Yd No: 1532 Loa 189.99 Br ex - Dght 12.826 Lbp 185.60 Br md 32.26 Dpth 18.00 Welded, 1 dk	**(A21A2BC) Bulk Carrier** Grain: 72,689; Bale: 70,122 Compartments: 5 Ho, ER 5 Ha: ER Cranes: 4x30t	**1 oil engine** driving 1 FP propeller Total Power: 8,450kW (11,489hp) 14.5kn MAN-B&W 6S50MC-C 1 x 2 Stroke 6 Cy. 500 x 2000 8450kW (11489bhp) Mitsui Engineering & Shipbuilding CLtd-Japan AuxGen: 3 x 680kW a.c Fuel: 2380.0
9283643 *A8FI9*	**TRANS PACIFIC** *ex* CMB Eline *-2004* **Bream Navigation Inc** Belchem Singapore Pte Ltd *Monrovia* Liberia MMSI: 636012422 Official number: 12422	**40,485** 25,884 74,403 T/cm 67.0	Class: AB	**2004-11 Hudong-Zhonghua Shipbuilding (Group) Co Ltd — Shanghai** Yd No: H1305A Loa 225.00 (BB) Br ex - Dght 14.268 Lbp 217.00 Br md 32.26 Dpth 19.60 Welded, 1 dk	**(A21A2BC) Bulk Carrier** Grain: 91,717; Bale: 89,882 Compartments: 7 Ho, ER 7 Ha: 6 (14.6 x 15.0)ER (14.6 x 13.2)	**1 oil engine** driving 1 FP propeller Total Power: 11,300kW (15,363hp) 13.8kn MAN-B&W 5S60MC-C 1 x 2 Stroke 5 Cy. 600 x 2400 11300kW (15363bhp) Hudong Heavy Machinery Co Ltd-China AuxGen: 3 x 530kW Fuel: 156.0 (d.f.) 2710.0 (r.f.)
9582788 *YDA6365*	**TRANS PACIFIC 02** **PT Trans Pacific Jaya** *Balikpapan* Indonesia Official number: 200911DNO808/2	**205** 62 -	Class: KI	**2009-08 P.T. Rejeki Abadi Sakti — Samarinda** Loa 27.50 Br ex - Dght 3.100 Lbp 25.80 Br md 8.00 Dpth 3.65 Welded, 1 dk	**(B32A2ST) Tug**	**2 oil engines** reduction geared to sc. shafts driving 2 Propellers Total Power: 1,516kW (2,062hp) Mitsubishi S6R2-MTK 2 x 4 Stroke 6 Cy. 170 x 220 each-758kW (1031bhp) Mitsubishi Heavy Industries Ltd-Japan
9576105 *YDA6441*	**TRANS PACIFIC 03** **PT Trans Pacific Jaya** *Balikpapan* Indonesia Official number: 2009 IID NO. 802/L	**205** 62 -	Class: KI	**2009-08 P.T. Rejeki Abadi Sakti — Samarinda** Loa 27.50 Br ex - Dght 3.100 Lbp 25.80 Br md 8.00 Dpth 3.65 Welded, 1 dk	**(B32A2ST) Tug**	**2 oil engines** reduction geared to sc. shafts driving 2 Propellers Total Power: 1,516kW (2,062hp) Mitsubishi 2 x 4 Stroke each-758kW (1031bhp) Mitsubishi Heavy Industries Ltd-Japan
9582790 *YDA6469* -	**TRANS PACIFIC 05** **PT Trans Pacific Jaya** *Balikpapan* Indonesia Official number: 200911DNO803/L	**204** 62 -	Class: KI	**2009-12 P.T. Rejeki Abadi Sakti — Samarinda** Loa 27.50 Br ex - Dght 3.100 Lbp 25.80 Br md 8.00 Dpth 3.65 Welded, 1 dk	**(B32A2ST) Tug**	**2 oil engines** reduction geared to sc. shafts driving 2 Propellers Total Power: 1,220kW (1,658hp) Yanmar 6AYM-ETE 2 x 4 Stroke 6 Cy. 155 x 180 each-610kW (829bhp) Yanmar Diesel Engine Co Ltd-Japan
9019664 *3ETR9* -	**TRANS PACIFIC 5** **Feng Li Maritime Corp & Norwich Shipping Corp** Kagoshima Senpaku Kaisha Ltd SatCom: Inmarsat A 1336632 *Panama* Panama MMSI: 352995000 Official number: 2035992E	**17,736** 5,321 10,729	Class: NK	**1992-07 Mitsubishi Heavy Industries Ltd. — Shimonoseki** Yd No: 960 Loa 163.45 (BB) Br ex 25.03 Dght 8.200 Lbp 152.00 Br md 25.00 Dpth 12.75 Welded, 3 dks	**(A35B2RV) Vehicles Carrier** Quarter stern door/ramp (s. a.) Len: 25.00 Wid: 5.50 Swl: 50 Cars: 1,080 Bale: 19,919	**1 oil engine** driving 1 FP propeller Total Power: 9,415kW (12,801hp) 18.5kn Mitsubishi 8UEC52LA 1 x 2 Stroke 8 Cy. 520 x 1600 9415kW (12801bhp) Mitsubishi Heavy Industries Ltd-Japan AuxGen: 3 x 680kW a.c Thrusters: 1 Thwart. CP thruster (f) Fuel: 1575.0 (r.f.)
9576117 - -	**TRANS PACIFIC 06** **PT Trans Pacific Jaya** *Balikpapan* Indonesia	**205** 62 -	Class: KI	**2009-08 P.T. Rejeki Abadi Sakti — Samarinda** Loa 27.50 Br ex - Dght 3.050 Lbp 25.80 Br md 8.00 Dpth 3.65 Welded, 1 dk	**(B32A2ST) Tug**	**2 oil engines** reduction geared to sc. shafts driving 2 Propellers Total Power: 1,516kW (2,062hp) Mitsubishi 2 x 4 Stroke each-758kW (1031bhp) Mitsubishi Heavy Industries Ltd-Japan
8734516 *YDA6169*	**TRANS PACIFIC 07** **PT Trans Pacific Jaya** *Balikpapan* Indonesia Official number: 2008 IID NO. 748/L	**218** 66 -	Class: KI	**2007-12 P.T. Rejeki Abadi Sakti — Samarinda** Loa 27.50 Br ex - Dght 2.990 Lbp 25.65 Br md 8.00 Dpth 3.65 Welded, 1 dk	**(B32A2ST) Tug**	**2 oil engines** driving 2 Propellers Total Power: 1,220kW (1,658hp) Yanmar 6AYM-ETE 2 x 4 Stroke 6 Cy. 155 x 180 each-610kW (829bhp) Yanmar Diesel Engine Co Ltd-Japan

IMO / Call sign / Flag	Name / Owner / Port	Tonnage	Class	Builder / Dimensions	Type	Machinery
8734011 *YDA6168* -	**TRANS PACIFIC 08** **PT Trans Pacific Jaya** - *Balikpapan* *Indonesia* Official number: 2008 IID NO. 749/L	**218** 66 -	Class: KI	**2007 P.T. Rejeki Abadi Sakti — Samarinda** Loa 27.50 Br ex - Dght 2.990 Lbp 25.65 Br md 8.00 Dpth 3.65 Welded, 1 dk	**(B32A2ST) Tug**	**2 oil engines** driving 2 Propellers Total Power: 1,220kW (1,658hp) Yanmar 6AYM-ETE 2 x 4 Stroke 6 Cy. 155 x 180 each-610kW (829bhp) Yanmar Diesel Engine Co Ltd-Japan
8737257 *YDA5138* -	**TRANS PACIFIC 09** **PT Trans Pacific Jaya** - *Balikpapan* *Indonesia* Official number: 2009 IID NO. 781/L	**208** 63 -	Class: KI	**2007 P.T. Rejeki Abadi Sakti — Samarinda** Loa 27.50 Br ex - Dght 2.990 Lbp 25.65 Br md 8.00 Dpth 3.65 Welded, 1 dk	**(B32A2ST) Tug**	**2 oil engines** driving 2 Propellers Total Power: 1,220kW (1,658hp) Yanmar 6AYM-ETE 2 x 4 Stroke 6 Cy. 155 x 180 each-610kW (829bhp) Yanmar Diesel Engine Co Ltd-Japan
8739152 *YDA6241* -	**TRANS PACIFIC 10** **PT Trans Pacific Jaya** - *Balikpapan* *Indonesia* Official number: 2008 IID NO. 763/L	**202** 61 -	Class: KI	**2007-12 P.T. Rejeki Abadi Sakti — Samarinda** Loa 27.50 Br ex - Dght 2.990 Lbp 25.80 Br md 8.00 Dpth 3.65 Welded, 1 dk	**(B32A2ST) Tug**	**2 oil engines** driving 2 Propellers Total Power: 1,220kW (1,658hp) Yanmar 6AYM-ETE 2 x 4 Stroke 6 Cy. 155 x 180 each-610kW (829bhp) Yanmar Diesel Engine Co Ltd-Japan
9608245 *YDA4706* -	**TRANS PACIFIC 201** **PT Trans Pacific Jaya** - *Tanjung Priok* *Indonesia*	**211** 64 -	Class: KI	**2010-06 C.V. Mercusuar Mandiri — Batam** Yd No: 103 Loa 29.00 Br ex - Dght 3.050 Lbp 27.36 Br md 8.00 Dpth 3.70 Welded, 1 dk	**(B32A2ST) Tug**	**2 oil engines** reduction geared to sc. shafts driving 2 Propellers Total Power: 1,472kW (2,002hp) Yanmar 2 x 4 Stroke each-736kW (1001bhp) Yanmar Diesel Engine Co Ltd-Japan
9608257 *YDA4707* -	**TRANS PACIFIC 202** **PT Trans Pacific Jaya** - *Tanjung Priok* *Indonesia*	**211** 64 -	Class: KI	**2010-06 C.V. Mercusuar Mandiri — Batam** Yd No: 105 Loa 29.00 Br ex - Dght 3.050 Lbp 27.36 Br md 8.00 Dpth 3.70 Welded, 1 dk	**(B32A2ST) Tug**	**2 oil engines** reduction geared to sc. shafts driving 2 Propellers Total Power: 1,472kW (2,002hp) Yanmar 2 x 4 Stroke each-736kW (1001bhp) Yanmar Diesel Engine Co Ltd-Japan
8659041 - -	**TRANS PACIFIC 203** **PT Trans Pacific Jaya** - *Batam* *Indonesia*	**211** 64 -	Class: KI	**2011-07 C.V. Mercusuar Mandiri — Batam** Loa 29.00 Br ex - Dght - Lbp 26.88 Br md 8.00 Dpth 3.70 Welded, 1 dk	**(B32A2ST) Tug**	**2 oil engines** reduction geared to sc. shafts driving 2 FP propellers AuxGen: 2 x 30kW 400V a.c
9503885 *YDA4440* -	**TRANS POWER 161** *ex* Tekun 16218 *-2009* **PT Trans Power Marine** - *Jakarta* *Indonesia* Official number: 2008 IIA NO 5472/L	**163** 49 137	Class: KI (NK)	**2008-08 Bonafile Shipbuilders & Repairs Sdn Bhd — Sandakan** Yd No: 23/06 Loa 26.10 Br ex - Dght 2.762 Lbp 24.29 Br md 7.32 Dpth 3.35 Welded, 1 dk	**(B32A2ST) Tug**	**2 oil engines** reduction geared to sc. shafts driving 2 FP propellers Total Power: 1,220kW (1,658hp) Yanmar 6AYM-ETE 2 x 4 Stroke 6 Cy. 155 x 180 each-610kW (829bhp) Yanmar Diesel Engine Co Ltd-Japan Fuel: 110.0 (d.f.)
9503897 *YDA4466* -	**TRANS POWER 162** *ex* Tekun 16219 *-2009* *ex* Bonafile 25/06 *-2008* **PT Trans Power Marine** - *Jakarta* *Indonesia*	**163** 49 135	Class: KI (NK)	**2008-10 Bonafile Shipbuilders & Repairs Sdn Bhd — Sandakan** Yd No: 25/06 Loa 26.10 Br ex - Dght 2.762 Lbp 24.29 Br md 7.32 Dpth 3.35 Welded, 1 dk	**(B32A2ST) Tug**	**2 oil engines** reduction geared to sc. shafts driving 2 FP propellers Total Power: 1,220kW (1,658hp) Yanmar 6AYM-ETE 2 x 4 Stroke 6 Cy. 155 x 180 each-610kW (829bhp) Yanmar Diesel Engine Co Ltd-Japan AuxGen: 2 x 40kW a.c Fuel: 110.0 (d.f.)
9603661 *YDA4710* -	**TRANS POWER 163** **PT Trans Power Marine** - *Jakarta* *Indonesia* Official number: 3152PST	**210** 79 205	Class: BV	**2010-09 Rantau Megajaya Shipbuilding Sdn Bhd — Sibu** Yd No: RMJ05/08 Loa 26.00 Br ex - Dght 3.012 Lbp 23.98 Br md 8.00 Dpth 3.65 Welded, 1 dk	**(B32A2ST) Tug**	**2 oil engines** reduction geared to sc. shafts driving 2 FP propellers Total Power: 1,220kW (1,658hp) Yanmar 6AYM-ETE 2 x 4 Stroke 6 Cy. 155 x 180 each-610kW (829bhp) Yanmar Diesel Engine Co Ltd-Japan
9606223 *YDA4723* -	**TRANS POWER 165** **PT Trans Power Marine** - *Jakarta* *Indonesia* Official number: 3167/SPT	**203** 61 166	Class: NK	**2010-11 SC Yii Brothers Shipyard Sdn Bhd — Sibu** Yd No: 129 Loa 26.00 Br ex 8.02 Dght 3.012 Lbp 23.99 Br md 8.00 Dpth 3.65 Welded, 1 dk	**(B32A2ST) Tug**	**2 oil engines** reduction geared to sc. shafts driving 2 Propellers Total Power: 1,220kW (1,658hp) Yanmar 6AYM-ETE 2 x 4 Stroke 6 Cy. 155 x 180 each-610kW (829bhp) Yanmar Diesel Engine Co Ltd-Japan
9604718 *YDA4724* -	**TRANS POWER 166** *ex* Sapor 2 *-2010* **PT Trans Power Marine** - *Jakarta* *Indonesia* Official number: 3168/PST	**203** 61 201	Class: NK	**2010-12 Sapor Shipbuilding Industries Sdn Bhd — Sibu** Yd No: SAPOR 43 Loa 26.00 Br ex - Dght 3.012 Lbp 23.68 Br md 8.00 Dpth 3.65 Welded, 1 dk	**(B32A2ST) Tug**	**2 oil engines** reduction geared to sc. shafts driving 2 FP propellers Total Power: 1,220kW (1,658hp) Yanmar 6AYM-ETE 2 x 4 Stroke 6 Cy. 155 x 180 each-610kW (829bhp) Yanmar Diesel Engine Co Ltd-Japan AuxGen: 2 x 50kW a.c
9093543 *YD6720* -	**TRANS POWER 181** *ex* Asmar 2 *-2010* **PT Trans Power Marine** - *Samarinda* *Indonesia* Official number: 2005 IIK NO 3549/L	**174** 53 -	Class: KI	**2005-05 C.V. Dok & Galangan Kapal Perlun — Samarinda** Loa 27.50 Br ex - Dght - Lbp 24.90 Br md 7.50 Dpth 3.30 Welded, 1 dk	**(B32A2ST) Tug**	**2 oil engines** geared to sc. shafts driving 2 Propellers Total Power: 1,324kW (1,800hp) Mitsubishi S6R2-MPTK 2 x 4 Stroke 6 Cy. 170 x 220 each-662kW (900bhp) Mitsubishi Heavy Industries Ltd-Japan
9350410 *YDA4188* -	**TRANS POWER 202** *ex* Modalwan 2090 *-2006* **PT Trans Power Ocean** PT Trans Power Marine *Jakarta* *Indonesia*	**275** 83 107	Class: KI (BV)	**2005-05 Nanjing Tongkah Shipbuilding Co Ltd — Nanjing JS** Yd No: 2004-2904 Loa 29.20 Br ex 9.50 Dght 3.700 Lbp 27.30 Br md 9.00 Dpth 4.84 Welded, 1 dk	**(B32A2ST) Tug**	**2 oil engines** reduction geared to sc. shafts driving 2 CP propellers Total Power: 1,472kW (2,002hp) 11.0kn Cummins KTA-38-M1 2 x Vee 4 Stroke 12 Cy. 159 x 159 each-736kW (1001bhp) Cummins Engine Co Inc-USA AuxGen: 2 x 68kW 415V a.c
8999312 *YD6494* -	**TRANS POWER 203** *ex* Nitya 1 *-2010* **PT Multitrans Raya** - *Balikpapan* *Indonesia*	**207** 63 -	Class: KI	**2002-11 P.T. Galangan Balikpapan Utama — Balikpapan** L reg 28.25 Br ex - Dght 3.170 Lbp 26.00 Br md 8.30 Dpth 3.98 Welded, 1 dk	**(B32A2ST) Tug**	**2 oil engines** reduction geared to sc. shafts driving 2 Propellers Total Power: 1,728kW (2,350hp) 10.0kn Caterpillar 3512TA 2 x Vee 4 Stroke 12 Cy. 170 x 190 each-864kW (1175bhp) (made 2000) Caterpillar Inc-USA
9556387 *YDA4362* -	**TRANS POWER 204** **PT Trans Power Marine** - *Jakarta* *Indonesia* Official number: 4051/BC	**223** 67 -	Class: AB	**2008-01 PT Bayu Bahari Sentosa — Jakarta** Yd No: XII Loa 29.00 Br ex - Dght - Lbp 28.00 Br md 8.60 Dpth 4.10 Welded, 1 dk	**(B32A2ST) Tug**	**2 oil engines** reduction geared to sc. shafts driving 2 Propellers Total Power: 1,518kW (2,064hp) Mitsubishi S6R2-MTK3L 2 x 4 Stroke 6 Cy. 170 x 220 each-759kW (1032bhp) Mitsubishi Heavy Industries Ltd-Japan AuxGen: 2 x a.c
9465916 *YDA4301* -	**TRANS POWER 205** **PT Trans Power Marine** - *Jakarta* *Indonesia* Official number: 4647/L	**254** 77 196	Class: KI (NK)	**2007-08 PT Palma Progress Shipyard — Batam** Yd No: 291 Loa 28.05 Br ex - Dght 3.312 Lbp 26.03 Br md 8.60 Dpth 4.30 Welded, 1 dk	**(B32A2ST) Tug**	**2 oil engines** reduction geared to sc. shafts driving 2 FP propellers Total Power: 1,516kW (2,062hp) Mitsubishi S6R2-MTK3L 2 x 4 Stroke 6 Cy. 170 x 220 each-758kW (1031bhp) Mitsubishi Heavy Industries Ltd-Japan AuxGen: 2 x 75kW a.c Fuel: 200.0 (d.f.)
9465928 *YDA4303* -	**TRANS POWER 206** **PT Trans Power Marine** - *Jakarta* *Indonesia* Official number: 1529/PPM	**254** 77 190	Class: KI (NK)	**2007-08 PT Palma Progress Shipyard — Batam** Yd No: 292 Loa 28.05 Br ex - Dght 3.310 Lbp 26.03 Br md 8.60 Dpth 4.30 Welded, 1 dk	**(B32A2ST) Tug**	**2 oil engines** geared to sc. shafts driving 2 FP propellers Total Power: 1,518kW (2,064hp) Mitsubishi S6R2-MPTK3 2 x 4 Stroke 6 Cy. 170 x 220 each-759kW (1032bhp) Mitsubishi Heavy Industries Ltd-Japan Fuel: 200.0 (d.f.)

9471575 *YDA4309* -
TRANS POWER 207
PT Trans Power Marine
-
Jakarta *Indonesia*
Official number: 1542/PPM
249 75 202
Class: KI (NK)
2007-09 PT Palma Progress Shipyard — Batam Yd No: 294
Loa 28.05 Br ex - Dght 3.310
Lbp 26.03 Br md 8.60 Dpth 4.30
Welded, 1 dk
(B32A2ST) Tug
2 oil engines reduction geared to sc. shafts driving 2 FP propellers
Total Power: 1,518kW (2,064hp)
Mitsubishi S6R2-MPTK3
2 x 4 Stroke 6 Cy. 170 x 220 each-759kW (1032bhp)
Mitsubishi Heavy Industries Ltd-Japan
Fuel: 160.0 (d.f.)

9471587 *YDA4310* -
TRANS POWER 208
PT Trans Power Marine
-
Jakarta *Indonesia*
Official number: 1552/PPM
249 75 203
Class: KI (NK)
2007-09 PT Palma Progress Shipyard — Batam Yd No: 295
Loa 28.05 Br ex - Dght 3.310
Lbp 26.03 Br md 8.60 Dpth 4.30
Welded, 1 dk
(B32A2ST) Tug
2 oil engines reduction geared to sc. shafts driving 2 FP propellers
Total Power: 1,518kW (2,064hp)
Mitsubishi S6R2-MPTK3
2 x 4 Stroke 6 Cy. 170 x 220 each-759kW (1032bhp)
Mitsubishi Heavy Industries Ltd-Japan
Fuel: 160.0 (d.f.)

9592381 *YDA4690* -
TRANS POWER 209
PT Trans Power Marine
-
Jakarta *Indonesia*
265 80 265
Class: NK
2010-07 Tuong Aik Shipyard Sdn Bhd — Sibu Yd No: 2820
Loa 29.00 Br ex - Dght 3.612
Lbp 26.28 Br md 8.60 Dpth 4.20
Welded, 1 dk
(B32A2ST) Tug
2 oil engines reduction geared to sc. shafts driving 2 Propellers
Total Power: 1,518kW (2,064hp)
Mitsubishi S6R2-MTK3L
2 x 4 Stroke 6 Cy. 170 x 220 each-759kW (1032bhp)
Mitsubishi Heavy Industries Ltd-Japan

9554860 *YDA4712* -
TRANS POWER 210
PT Trans Power Marine
-
Jakarta *Indonesia*
260 78 265
Class: NK
2010-11 Tuong Aik Shipyard Sdn Bhd — Sibu Yd No: 2923
Loa 29.00 Br ex - Dght 3.612
Lbp 26.28 Br md 8.60 Dpth 4.20
Welded, 1 dk
(B32A2ST) Tug
2 oil engines geared to sc. shafts driving 2 FP propellers
Total Power: 1,472kW (2,002hp)
Yanmar 6RY17P-GV
2 x 4 Stroke 6 Cy. 165 x 219 each-736kW (1001bhp)
Yanmar Diesel Engine Co Ltd-Japan

9523988 *YDA6099* -
TRANS POWER 211
PT Trans Power Marine
-
Samarinda *Indonesia*
Official number: 2008 Iik No. 4400/L
200 60 -
Class: KI
2008-03 C.V. Dok & Galangan Kapal Perlun — Samarinda
Loa 26.21 Br ex - Dght -
Lbp - Br md 8.10 Dpth 3.40
Welded, 1 dk
(B32A2ST) Tug
2 oil engines geared to sc. shafts driving 2 Propellers
Total Power: 1,472kW (2,002hp)
Mitsubishi
2 x 4 Stroke each-736kW (1001bhp)
Mitsubishi Heavy Industries Ltd-Japan

9645190 *YDA4988* -
TRANS POWER 212
PT Trans Power Marine
-
Jakarta *Indonesia*
276 83 264
Class: NK
2012-02 Tuong Aik Shipyard Sdn Bhd — Sibu Yd No: 21016
Loa 29.00 Br ex - Dght 3.610
Lbp 27.17 Br md 8.60 Dpth 4.20
Welded, 1 dk
(B32A2ST) Tug
2 oil engines reduction geared to sc. shafts driving 2 FP propellers
Total Power: 1,518kW (2,064hp)
Mitsubishi S6R2-MTK3L
2 x 4 Stroke 6 Cy. 170 x 220 each-759kW (1032bhp)
Mitsubishi Heavy Industries Ltd-Japan
Fuel: 200.0 (d.f.)

9645205 *YDA4989* -
TRANS POWER 213
PT Trans Power Marine
-
Jakarta *Indonesia*
276 83 264
Class: NK
2012-02 Tuong Aik Shipyard Sdn Bhd — Sibu Yd No: 21102
Loa 29.00 Br ex - Dght 3.610
Lbp 27.17 Br md 8.60 Dpth 4.20
Welded, 1 dk
(B32A2ST) Tug
2 oil engines reduction geared to sc. shafts driving 2 Propellers
Total Power: 1,518kW (2,064hp)
Mitsubishi S6R2-MTK3L
2 x 4 Stroke 6 Cy. 170 x 220 each-759kW (1032bhp)
Mitsubishi Heavy Industries Ltd-Japan
Fuel: 200.0 (d.f.)

9399519 *YD6919* -
TRANS POWER 241
ex Modalwan 24136 *-2007*
PT Trans Power Ocean
PT Trans Power Marine
Banjarmasin *Indonesia*
Official number: 330023
270 81 -
Class: KI (BV)
2006-12 Bonafile Shipbuilders & Repairs Sdn Bhd — Sandakan Yd No: 35/04
Loa 29.29 Br ex - Dght 3.840
Lbp 27.53 Br md 9.00 Dpth 4.85
Welded, 1 dk
(B32A2ST) Tug
2 oil engines reduction geared to sc. shafts driving 2 Propellers
Total Power: 1,766kW (2,402hp)
Cummins KTA-38-M2
2 x Vee 4 Stroke 12 Cy. 159 x 159 each-883kW (1201bhp)
Cummins Engine Co Inc-USA
AuxGen: 2 x 80kW 415V a.c

9651888 *YDA4991* -
TRANS POWER 243
PT Trans Power Ocean
-
Jakarta *Indonesia*
MMSI: 525012199
Official number: 3837/Pst
276 83 -
Class: BV
2012-02 Zhenjiang Asia Star Shipbuilding Co Ltd — Zhenjiang JS Yd No: YX0901
Loa 29.00 Br ex - Dght 4.250
Lbp 26.50 Br md 9.00 Dpth 4.50
Welded, 1 dk
(B32A2ST) Tug
2 oil engines reduction geared to sc. shafts driving 2 FP propellers
Total Power: 1,766kW (2,402hp)
Cummins KTA-38-M2
2 x Vee 4 Stroke 12 Cy. 159 x 159 each-883kW (1201bhp)
Chongqing Cummins Engine Co Ltd-China
Fuel: 50.0 (d.f.)

7913725 *HSB2793* -
TRANS RAYONG
ex Yuko Maru No. 2 *-2001*
Major Chem Tanker Co Ltd
Thailand
MMSI: 567034200
Official number: 441001093
782 317 1,200 T/cm 5.2
1980-07 Omishima Dock K.K. — Imabari Yd No: 1082
Loa 64.11 Br ex - Dght 4.201
Lbp 59.52 Br md 10.00 Dpth 4.45
Welded, 1 dk
(A12A2TC) Chemical Tanker
1 oil engine reverse geared to sc. shaft driving 1 CP propeller
Total Power: 1,324kW (1,800hp)
Akasaka DM36R
1 x 4 Stroke 6 Cy. 360 x 540 1324kW (1800bhp)
Akasaka Tekkosho KK (Akasaka DieselLtd)-Japan

9039755 *9HA2564* -
TRANS SEA
ex Geneve *-2002*
Kjemikalietank AS
Seatrans AS
Valletta *Malta*
MMSI: 248887000
Official number: 9039755
4,433 2,015 6,783 T/cm 15.4
Class: NV (GL)
1992-06 YVC Ysselwerf B.V. — Capelle a/d IJssel Yd No: 255
Loa 106.83 (BB) Br ex 17.74 Dght 6.670
Lbp 98.63 Br md 17.50 Dpth 9.25
Welded, 1 dk
(A12B2TR) Chemical/Products Tanker
Double Hull (13F)
Liq: 7,191; Liq (Oil): 7,191
Cargo Heating Coils
Compartments: 14 Ta, ER
14 Cargo Pump (s): 14x120m³/hr
Manifold: Bow/CM: 50.4m
1 oil engine reduction geared to sc. shaft driving 1 CP propeller
Total Power: 3,300kW (4,487hp) 13.6kn
MaK 9M453C
1 x 4 Stroke 9 Cy. 320 x 420 3300kW (4487bhp)
Krupp MaK Maschinenbau GmbH-Kiel
AuxGen: 2 x 409kW 220/440V a.c, 1 x a.c
Thrusters: 1 Thwart. CP thruster (f)
Fuel: 94.0 (d.f.) 492.0 (r.f.) 14.0pd

9496678 *A8UO7* -
TRANS SHANGHAI
ex RBD Shanghai *-2012*
Chemikalien Seetransport GmbH
-
Monrovia *Liberia*
MMSI: 636091924
Official number: 91924
51,255 31,192 93,260 T/cm 80.9
Class: AB (RI)
2010-03 Jiangsu Newyangzi Shipbuilding Co Ltd — Jingjiang JS Yd No: YZJ2006-852
Loa 229.20 (BB) Br ex - Dght 14.900
Lbp 222.00 Br md 38.00 Dpth 20.70
Welded, 1 dk
(A21A2BC) Bulk Carrier
Grain: 110,330
Compartments: 7 Ho, ER
7 Ha: ER
1 oil engine driving 1 FP propeller
Total Power: 13,560kW (18,436hp) 14.1kn
MAN-B&W 6S60MC-C
1 x 2 Stroke 6 Cy. 600 x 2400 13560kW (18436bhp)
Doosan Engine Co Ltd-South Korea
AuxGen: 3 x 730kW a.c
Fuel: 210.0 (d.f.) 3790.0 (r.f.)

9615482 *VRJF6* -
TRANS SPRING
Spring Maritime Ltd
Amoysailing Maritime Co Ltd
Hong Kong *Hong Kong*
MMSI: 477328800
Official number: HK-3234
33,044 19,231 56,854 T/cm 58.8
Class: CC (BV)
2011-11 Xiamen Shipbuilding Industry Co Ltd — Xiamen FJ Yd No: XSI407G
Loa 189.99 (BB) Br ex - Dght 12.800
Lbp 185.00 Br md 32.26 Dpth 18.00
Welded, 1 dk
(A21A2BC) Bulk Carrier
Grain: 71,634; Bale: 68,200
Compartments: 5 Ho, ER
5 Ha: 4 (21.3 x 18.3)ER (18.9 x 18.3)
Cranes: 4x30t
1 oil engine driving 1 FP propeller
Total Power: 9,480kW (12,889hp) 14.2kn
MAN-B&W 6S50MC-C
1 x 2 Stroke 6 Cy. 500 x 2000 9480kW (12889bhp)
Hyundai Heavy Industries Co Ltd-South Korea
AuxGen: 3 x 600kW 60Hz a.c
Fuel: 2400.0

5409586 *CYLY* -
TRANS-ST-LAURENT
La Traverse Riviere du Loup- St Simeon Ltee
Clarke Inc
Quebec, QC *Canada*
MMSI: 316005974
Official number: 313966
2,173 927 645
Class: BV (Class contemplated) (LR)
✠ Classed LR until 8/7/09
1963-06 Geo T Davie & Sons Ltd — Levis QC Yd No: 79
Loa 79.84 Br ex 19.00 Dght 4.270
Lbp 75.72 Br md 18.28 Dpth 5.49
Welded, 1 dk
(A36A2PR) Passenger/Ro-Ro Ship (Vehicles)
Passengers: unberthed: 361
Bow door
Stern door
Ice Capable
2 oil engines with clutches, flexible couplings & sr geared to sc. shafts driving 2 CP propellers
Total Power: 2,852kW (3,878hp)
Alpha 6L28/32
2 x 4 Stroke 6 Cy. 280 x 320 each-1426kW (1939bhp) (new engine 1991)
MAN Diesel A/S-Denmark
AuxGen: 2 x 350kW 240/480V 60Hz a.c
Boilers: 2 AuxB 3.6kgf/cm² (3.5bar)
Thrusters: 1 Thwart. FP thruster (f)
Fuel: 416.5 (d.f.)

8307545 *PNFO* -
TRANS TENANG
ex Xanadu *-2009* *ex* Maria *-2002*
ex Cedrela *-1989* *ex* Western Jade *-1988*
ex Dimitros Criticos *-1988* *ex* Kepbrave *-1986*
PT Bintang Trans Lintas
-
Jakarta *Indonesia*
MMSI: 525016577
24,844 13,116 42,312 T/cm 49.8
Class: KI (NV) (RS)
1984-08 Mitsui Eng. & SB. Co. Ltd., Chiba Works — Ichihara Yd No: 1283
Loa 182.81 (BB) Br ex 30.54 Dght 11.019
Lbp 174.70 Br md 30.51 Dpth 15.78
Welded, 1 dk
(A21A2BC) Bulk Carrier
Grain: 49,970; Bale: 48,863
Compartments: 5 Ho, ER
5 Ha: (13.6 x 15.6)4 (16.8 x 15.6)ER
Cranes: 4x25t
1 oil engine driving 1 FP propeller
Total Power: 8,091kW (11,001hp) 14.8kn
B&W 6L67GFCA
1 x 2 Stroke 6 Cy. 670 x 1700 8091kW (11001bhp)
Mitsui Engineering & Shipbuilding CLtd-Japan
AuxGen: 3 x 540kW 450V 60Hz a.c
Fuel: 2046.0 (r.f.) 33.5pd

9326213 *3EAK6* -	**TRANS TRADER** *ex* Chemical Trader *-2011* **KT Neo Marine SA** Seatrans AS *Panama* *Panama* MMSI: 352171000 Official number: 3072405B	**5,383** 2,695 8,801 T/cm 17.8	Class: NK	**2005-04 Shitanoe Shipbuilding Co Ltd — Usuki OT** Yd No: 1245 Loa 112.00 (BB) Br ex 18.73 Dght 7.763 Lbp 105.00 Br md 18.70 Dpth 10.00 Welded, 1 dk	**(A12B2TR) Chemical/Products Tanker** Double Hull (13F) Liq: 9,595; Liq (Oil): 9,595 Cargo Heating Coils Compartments: 16 Wing Ta (s.stl), 2 Wing Slop Ta, ER 16 Cargo Pump (s): 4x100m³/hr, 8x200m³/hr, 4x300m³/hr Manifold: Bow/CM: 50.6m	**1 oil engine** driving 1 FP propeller Total Power: 3,898kW (5,300hp) 13.6kn MAN-B&W 6L35MC 1 x 2 Stroke 6 Cy. 350 x 1050 3898kW (5300bhp) Makita Corp-Japan AuxGen: 2 x 450kW a.c Thrusters: 1 Thwart. CP thruster (f) Fuel: 133.0 (d.f.) 563.0 (r.f.)
9187916 *ZDNJ3* -	**TRANSANDROMEDA** *ex* Andromeda *-2009* **Transatlantic Shipping (4) Ltd** Rederi AB Transatlantic *Gibraltar* *Gibraltar (British)* MMSI: 236111944	**4,871** 2,600 6,663	Class: GL (Class contemplated) (BV)	**1999-10 Bodewes' Scheepswerven B.V. — Hoogezand** Yd No: 587 Loa 118.55 (BB) Br ex - Dght 6.300 Lbp 111.85 Br md 15.20 Dpth 8.45 Welded, 1 dk	**(A31A2GX) General Cargo Ship** Grain: 9,302 TEU 390 C Ho 174 TEU C Dk 216 TEU Compartments: 2 Ho, ER 2 Ha: (39.0 x 12.7) (42.8 x 12.7)ER Ice Capable	**1 oil engine** reduction geared to sc. shaft driving 1 CP propeller Total Power: 3,840kW (5,221hp) 14.0kn MaK 8M32 1 x 4 Stroke 8 Cy. 320 x 480 3840kW (5221bhp) MaK Motoren GmbH & Co. KG-Kiel AuxGen: 1 x 350kW 400V 50Hz a.c, 2 x 264kW 400V 50Hz a.c Thrusters: 1 Thwart. FP thruster (f) Fuel: 446.0 (d.f.)
9349215 *C4RJ2* -	**TRANSANUND** *launched as* Astrosprinter *-2007* **ms 'Astrosprinter' GmbH & Co KG** Astromare Bereederungs GmbH & Co KG *Limassol* *Cyprus* MMSI: 210167000	**7,720** 3,614 9,526	Class: BV GL	**2007-02 Sainty Shipbuilding (Yangzhou) Corp Ltd — Yizheng JS** (Hull) Yd No: 04STIG006 **2007-02 All Ships Outfitting & Repairs — Krimpen a/d Lek** Yd No: 223 Loa 141.58 (BB) Br ex 20.95 Dght 7.300 Lbp 132.42 Br md 20.60 Dpth 9.50 Welded, 1 dk	**(A33A2CC) Container Ship (Fully Cellular)** TEU 809 C Ho 238 TEU C Dk 571 TEU incl 150 ref C. Ice Capable	**1 oil engine** reduction geared to sc. shaft driving 1 CP propeller Total Power: 8,002kW (10,880hp) 18.5kn MaK 8M43 1 x 4 Stroke 8 Cy. 430 x 610 8002kW (10880bhp) Caterpillar Motoren GmbH & Co. KG-Germany AuxGen: 2 x 590kW 440/230V 60Hz a.c, 1 x 1000kW 440/230V 60Hz a.c Thrusters: 1 Thwart. CP thruster (f)
9597238 *9HA3088* -	**TRANSATLANTIC** **Canzone Marine Ltd** Alpha Tankers & Freighters International Ltd *Valletta* *Malta* MMSI: 229125000 Official number: 9597238	**43,721** 26,541 81,250 T/cm 71.0	Class: LR ✠ **100A1** SS 08/2012 bulk carrier CSR BC-A GRAB (25) Nos. 2, 4 & 6 holds may be empty ESP **ShipRight** (CM,ACS (B)) *IWS LI ✠ **LMC** **UMS** Eq.Ltr: Q†; Cable: 687.5/81.0 U3 (a)	**2012-08 Hyundai Samho Heavy Industries Co Ltd — Samho** Yd No: S555 Loa 229.02 (BB) Br ex 32.29 Dght 14.500 Lbp 223.00 Br md 32.25 Dpth 20.10 Welded, 1 dk	**(A21A2BC) Bulk Carrier** Grain: 95,700 Compartments: 7 Ho, ER 7 Ha: ER	**1 oil engine** driving 1 FP propeller Total Power: 11,620kW (15,799hp) 14.5kn MAN-B&W 7S50MC-C8 1 x 2 Stroke 7 Cy. 500 x 2000 11620kW (15799bhp) Hyundai Heavy Industries Co Ltd-South Korea AuxGen: 3 x 700kW 450V 60Hz a.c Boilers: WTAuxB (Comp) 9.0kgf/cm² (8.8bar)
9148520 *WDC2769* -	**TRANSATLANTIC** *ex* Baffin Strait *-2011* *ex* Steamers Future *-2004* *ex* STL Future *-2001* *ex* Steamers Future *-2000* *ex* Mekong Star *-2000* *ex* Steamers Future *-1998* *ex* Eagle Faith *-1998* *ex* Steamers Future *-1997* **TransAtlantic Lines Shipholding II** TransAtlantic Lines LLC *New York, NY* *United States of America* MMSI: 366997520 Official number: 1164643	**4,276** 2,129 5,055	Class: NV (GL)	**1997-02 Wuhu Shipyard — Wuhu AH** Yd No: W9519 Loa 100.59 (BB) Br ex 16.24 Dght 6.401 Lbp 94.82 Br md 16.21 Dpth 8.20 Welded, 1dk	**(A31A2GX) General Cargo Ship** TEU 384 C.Ho 138 TEU C.Dk 246 TEU incl. 50 ref C. Compartments: 1 Ho, ER 1 Ha: ER Cranes: 2x40t Ice Capable	**1 oil engine** reduction geared to sc. shaft driving 1 CP propeller Total Power: 3,693kW (5,021hp) 15.5kn Wartsila 9R32E 1 x 4 Stroke 9 Cy. 320 x 350 3693kW (5021bhp) Wartsila Diesel AB-Sweden AuxGen: 2 x 500kW 440V 60Hz a.c, 1 x a.c Thrusters: 1 Tunnel thruster (f) Fuel: 100.0 (d.f.) (Heating Coils) 500.0 (r.f.) 15.0pd
9142643 *ZDHH4* -	**TRANSBRILLIANTE** *ex* Brilliante *-2013* *ex* Baltic Prestige *-2006* *ex* AKN Prestige *-2005* *ex* Morgenstond II *-2005* **Industrial Shipping AS** Rederi AB Transatlantic SatCom: Inmarsat C 423631810 *Gibraltar* *Gibraltar (British)* MMSI: 236318000	**3,782** 2,129 5,557	Class: GL (BV)	**1997-04 Scheepswerf Ferus Smit BV — Westerbroek** Yd No: 309 Loa 100.85 (BB) Br ex - Dght 6.410 Lbp 95.00 Br md 14.50 Dpth 8.25 Welded, 1 dk	**(A31A2GX) General Cargo Ship** Grain: 7,706; Bale: 7,600 TEU 287 C.Ho 124/20' C.Dk 163/20' Compartments: 1 Ho, ER 2 Ha: (32.2 x 12.0) (37.8 x 12.0)ER Ice Capable	**1 oil engine** with flexible couplings & sr gearedto sc. shafts driving 1 CP propeller Total Power: 2,925kW (3,977hp) 14.0kn Wartsila 9R26 1 x 4 Stroke 9 Cy. 260 x 320 2925kW (3977bhp) Stork Wartsila Diesel BV-Netherlands AuxGen: 1 x 450kW 420V 50Hz a.c, 2 x 150kW 420V a.c Thrusters: 1 Thwart. CP thruster (f) Fuel: 420.0 (d.f.) 14.5pd
9037795 *UBJE5* -	**TRANSBUNKER** *ex* Sumola *-1993* **Aquamarine Services Ltd** Transbunker-Novo Co Ltd *Novorossiysk* *Russia* MMSI: 273317910 Official number: 902502	**1,908** 739 3,258	Class: RS	**1993-07 Rousse Shipyard Ltd — Rousse** Yd No: 480 Loa 77.53 Br ex 14.50 Dght 5.350 Lbp 73.20 Br md 14.00 Dpth 6.50 Welded, 1 dk	**(A13B2TP) Products Tanker** Ins: 61; Liq: 3,514; Liq (Oil): 3,514 Cargo Heating Coils Compartments: 12 Ta, ER Ice Capable	**1 oil engine** driving 1 FP propeller Total Power: 882kW (1,199hp) 10.0kn S.K.L. 8NVD48A-2U 1 x 4 Stroke 8 Cy. 320 x 480 882kW (1199bhp) SKL Motoren u. Systemtechnik AG-Magdeburg AuxGen: 2 x 150kW a.c, 1 x 50kW a.c Thrusters: 1 Thwart. CP thruster (f) Fuel: 123.0 (d.f.)
9187928 *ZDNJ4* -	**TRANSCAPRICORN** *ex* Capricorn *-2010* **Transatlantic Shipping (5) Ltd** Rederi AB Transatlantic *Gibraltar* *Gibraltar (British)* MMSI: 236111945	**4,871** 2,600 6,663	Class: GL (BV)	**2000-03 Bodewes' Scheepswerven B.V. — Hoogezand** Yd No: 588 Loa 118.55 Br ex - Dght 6.310 Lbp 111.85 Br md 15.20 Dpth 8.45 Welded, 1 dk	**(A31A2GX) General Cargo Ship** Grain: 9,414 TEU 390 C Ho 174 TEU C Dk 216 TEU Compartments: 2 Ho, ER 2 Ha: (39.0 x 12.6) (42.7 x 12.6)ER Ice Capable	**1 oil engine** geared to sc. shaft driving 1 CP propeller Total Power: 3,840kW (5,221hp) 14.0kn MaK 8M32 1 x 4 Stroke 8 Cy. 320 x 480 3840kW (5221bhp) MaK Motoren GmbH & Co. KG-Kiel AuxGen: 1 x 350kW 220/380V 50Hz a.c, 2 x 264kW 220/380V 50Hz a.c Thrusters: 1 Thwart. FP thruster (f)
8972699 *ZQWY7* BF 61	**TRANSCEND** *ex* Maranatha *-2012* **BF61 Ltd** - *Ullapool* *United Kingdom* MMSI: 235001170 Official number: C17259	**168** 65 -		**2001 Astilleros Armon SA — Navia** Yd No: 524 Loa 19.92 Br ex - Dght - Lbp - Br md 7.26 Dpth 4.10 Welded, 1 dk	**(B11A2FS) Stern Trawler** Ins: 100	**1 oil engine** reduction geared to sc. shaft driving 1 FP propeller Total Power: 446kW (606hp) 10.5kn Mitsubishi S12A2-MPTK 1 x Vee 4 Stroke 12 Cy. 150 x 160 446kW (606bhp) Mitsubishi Heavy Industries Ltd-Japan Fuel: 24.5 (d.f.)
9437505 *9V8748* -	**TRANSCENDEN TIME** *ex* Nord Hong Kong *-2010* **ABL Shipping Pte Ltd** COSCO Bulk Carrier Co Ltd (COSCO BULK) *Singapore* *Singapore* MMSI: 564364000 Official number: 396196	**20,924** 11,786 32,688 T/cm 46.0	Class: LR (BV) **100A1** SS 10/2010 bulk carrier CSR BC-A GRAB (25) Nos. 2 & 4 holds may be empty ESP *IWS LI **LMC** **UMS**	**2010-10 Jiangmen Nanyang Ship Engineering Co Ltd — Jiangmen GD** Yd No: 110 Loa 179.90 (BB) Br ex - Dght 10.150 Lbp 171.50 Br md 28.40 Dpth 14.10 Welded, 1 dk	**(A21A2BC) Bulk Carrier** Grain: 42,565; Bale: 40,558 Compartments: 5 Ho, ER 5 Ha: ER Cranes: 4x30.5t	**1 oil engine** driving 1 FP propeller Total Power: 6,150kW (8,362hp) 13.7kn MAN-B&W 6S42MC 1 x 2 Stroke 6 Cy. 420 x 1764 6150kW (8362bhp) STX Engine Co Ltd-South Korea AuxGen: 3 x a.c
9167693 *3WAG* -	**TRANSCO SKY** *ex* Hawaiian Eye *-2009* *ex* Oriente Endeavor *-2002* **Transportation & Trading Services JSC (TRANSCO)** SatCom: Inmarsat C 457494810 *Haiphong* *Vietnam* MMSI: 574948000 Official number: VN-08TT-VT	**4,737** 2,905 7,833	Class: NK VR	**1997-11 Shin Kurushima Dockyard Co. Ltd. — Hashihama, Imabari** Yd No: 2956 Loa 100.52 Br ex 19.23 Dght 7.228 Lbp 93.00 Br md 19.20 Dpth 8.90 Welded, 1 dk	**(A31A2GX) General Cargo Ship** Grain: 10,092; Bale: 9,430 Compartments: 2 Ho, ER 2 Ha: 2 (25.2 x 10.2)ER Derricks: 4x25t	**1 oil engine** driving 1 FP propeller Total Power: 3,089kW (4,200hp) 13.2kn Mitsubishi 6UEC37LA 1 x 2 Stroke 6 Cy. 370 x 880 3089kW (4200bhp) Akasaka Tekkosho KK (Akasaka DieselLtd)-Japan Fuel: 420.0

IMO / Name / Owner	Tonnage	Class	Builder / Dimensions	Type	Machinery
9164172 **TRANSCO STAR** *3WVH* *ex* New Lucky XI *-2008* *ex* ID Crusader *-2007* - *ex* Global Wisdom *-2001* *ex* Asian Future *-1999* *ex* Brother Future *-1997* **Transportation & Trading Services JSC (TRANSCO)** - SatCom: Inmarsat C 457400710 *Haiphong* *Vietnam* MMSI: 574007000 Official number: VN-2509-VT	**4,749** 2,339 6,607	Class: NK VR	**1997-02 Sanyo Zosen K.K. — Onomichi** Yd No: 1076 Loa 97.20 Br ex - Dght 7.593 Lbp 84.90 Br md 17.70 Dpth 12.00 Welded, 2 dks	**(A31A2GX) General Cargo Ship** Grain: 10,845; Bale: 9,941 Compartments: 2 Ho, ER, 2 Tw Dk 2 Ha: (17.5 x 10.5) (31.5 x 10.5)ER Derricks: 3x25t	**1 oil engine** driving 1 FP propeller Total Power: 2,427kW (3,300hp) 12.0kn Hanshin LH41L 1 x 4 Stroke 6 Cy. 410 x 800 2427kW (3300bhp) The Hanshin Diesel Works Ltd-Japan Fuel: 69.0 (d.f.) 456.0 (r.f.) 9.0pd
8028668 **TRANSCO SUN** *XVVH* *ex* Hung Vuong 02 *-2010* *ex* Diamondstar *-1995* - *ex* Kapuas *-1989* *ex* Siti Helen *-1988* *ex* Betara Dua *-1986* *ex* Mobility *-1984* **Transportation & Trading Services JSC (TRANSCO)** Vinaship JSC SatCom: Inmarsat C 457405410 *Haiphong* *Vietnam* MMSI: 574045044 Official number: VN-2151-VT	**4,393** 2,810 7,071	Class: VR (NK)	**1981-01 Imai Shipbuilding Co Ltd — Kochi KC** Yd No: 505 Loa 107.19 Br ex 17.65 Dght 6.879 Lbp 100.01 Br md 17.61 Dpth 8.72 Welded, 1 dk	**(A31A2GX) General Cargo Ship** Grain: 9,671; Bale: 8,939 Compartments: 2 Ho, ER 2 Ha: 2 (28.7 x 8.9)ER Derricks: 4x15t	**1 oil engine** driving 1 FP propeller Total Power: 2,376kW (3,230hp) 11.5kn Mitsubishi 6UET45/75C 1 x 2 Stroke 6 Cy. 450 x 750 2376kW (3230bhp) Kobe Hatsudoki KK-Japan AuxGen: 2 x 148kW Fuel: 98.5 (d.f.) 479.0 (r.f.) 11.5pd
9199414 **TRANSDISTINTO** *ZDEQ2* *ex* Distinto *-2013* *ex* Grachtdiep *-2007* - **Industrial Shipping AS** Rederi AB Transatlantic SatCom: Inmarsat C 423615310 *Gibraltar* *Gibraltar (British)* MMSI: 236153000 Official number: 734628	**3,244** 1,554 4,160	Class: GL (LR) Classed LR until 3/4/08	**2000-12 Societatea Comerciala Severnav S.A. — Drobeta-Turnu Severin** Yd No: 750001 Loa 99.95 (BB) Br ex 16.50 Dght 4.600 Lbp 96.00 Br md 16.30 Dpth 6.30 Welded, 1 dk	**(A31A2GX) General Cargo Ship** Grain: 5,350; Bale: 5,350 TEU 264 C. 264/20' Compartments: 2 Ho, ER 2 Ha: ER Ice Capable	**1 oil engine** reduction geared to sc. shaft driving 1 CP propeller Total Power: 2,880kW (3,916hp) 13.5kn MaK 6M32 1 x 4 Stroke 6 Cy. 320 x 480 2880kW (3916bhp) MaK Motoren GmbH & Co. KG-Kiel AuxGen: 1 x 256kW 440V a.c, 2 x 184kW 440V a.c Thrusters: 1 Thwart. FP thruster (f) Fuel: 350.0 (d.f.)
8631178 **TRANSEND I** *DUH2503* *ex* Shinei Maru No. 8 *-2002* - *ex* Hoshun Maru *-1991* **Batanes Marine Transport Corp** - *Manila* *Philippines* Official number: 00-0001156	*230* 148 473		**1987-09 YK Furumoto Tekko Zosensho — Osakikamijima** Loa 49.60 Br ex 8.52 Dght 3.000 Lbp 44.00 Br md 8.50 Dpth 4.90 Welded, 1 dk	**(A31A2GX) General Cargo Ship**	**1 oil engine** driving 1 FP propeller Total Power: 441kW (600hp) Matsui 6M26KGHS 1 x 4 Stroke 6 Cy. 260 x 400 441kW (600bhp) Matsui Iron Works Co Ltd-Japan
7627302 **TRANSFAIR** *HOPR* *ex* Captain Rashad *-2012* *ex* San Wai *-2007* - *ex* Unison Great *-1996* *ex* Maya No. 7 *-1993* *ex* Ho Ming No. 7 *-1986* *ex* Nusantara IV *-1982* **Shejar Maritime SA** Tempus Maritime Sarl SatCom: Inmarsat C 435632810 *Panama* *Panama* MMSI: 356328000 Official number: 0775477L	**5,985** 3,766 10,176	Class: IV (PR) (NK)	**1977-02 Hashihama Shipbuilding Co Ltd — Imabari EH** Yd No: 650 Loa 127.97 Br ex 18.34 Dght 7.765 Lbp 119.00 Br md 18.31 Dpth 9.91 Welded, 1 dk	**(A31A2GX) General Cargo Ship** Grain: 13,333; Bale: 12,857 Compartments: 3 Ho, ER 3 Ha: (16.0 x 8.9) (30.7 x 8.9) (19.5 x 8.9)ER Derricks: 4x15t	**1 oil engine** driving 1 FP propeller Total Power: 4,413kW (6,000hp) 13.1kn Mitsubishi 6UET52/90 1 x 2 Stroke 6 Cy. 520 x 900 4413kW (6000bhp) Akasaka Tekkosho KK (Akasaka DieselLtd)-Japan AuxGen: 2 x 200kW a.c
9216626 **TRANSFIGHTER** *ZDNH3* *ex* Finnfighter *-2009* - **Transatlantic Shipping AB** Rederi AB Transatlantic *Gibraltar* *Gibraltar (British)* MMSI: 236626000	**20,851** 6,255 18,972	Class: LR ✠ **100A1** SS 12/2011 roll on - roll off cargo ship *IWS LI Nos.1 & 4 hold TwD's & No.2 hold inner btm, strengthened for regular discharge by heavy grabs (10T) Ice Class 1AS at 9.177 draught Max/min draught fwd 9.177/5.41m Max/min draught aft 9.177/7.00m Power required 9033kw, installed 12600kw ✠ **LMC** **UMS** Eq.Ltr: J†; Cable: 619.3/64.0	**2001-12 Stocznia Gdynia SA — Gdynia** Yd No: 8222/1 Lengthened-2006 Loa 178.60 (BB) Br ex 28.70 Dght 9.000 Lbp 168.00 Br md 25.60 Dpth 16.30 Welded, 2 dks	**(A35A2RR) Ro-Ro Cargo Ship** Stern door/ramp (centre) Lane-Len: 900 Bale: 30,019 TEU 759 Compartments: 5 Ho, ER 3 Ha: (19.2 x 21.0)2 (24.8 x 21.0)ER Ice Capable	**2 oil engines** with clutches, flexible couplings & sr geared to sc. shaft driving 1 CP propeller Total Power: 12,600kW (17,130hp) 17.5kn Wartsila 6L46C 2 x 4 Stroke 6 Cy. 460 x 580 each-6300kW (8565bhp) Wartsila Finland Oy-Finland AuxGen: 3 x 1028kW 410V 50Hz a.c, 1 x 1400kW a.c Boilers: TOH (o.f.) 10.7kgf/cm² (10.5bar), TOH (ex.g.) 10.7kgf/cm² (10.5bar) Thrusters: 1 Thwart. FP thruster (f) Fuel: 125.0 (d.f.) (Heating Coils) 1622.0 (r.f.)
8878714 **TRANSFLOT** - - - -	**106** 31 14	Class: (RS)	**1993-01 AO "Moryak" — Rostov-na-Donu** Yd No: 46 Loa 23.15 Br ex 6.24 Dght 1.850 Lbp 20.00 Br md - Dpth 2.80 Welded, 1 dk	**(A37B2PS) Passenger Ship** Ice Capable	**1 oil engine** geared to sc. shaft driving 1 FP propeller Total Power: 232kW (315hp) 9.0kn Daldizel 6CHSPN2A18-315 1 x 4 Stroke 6 Cy. 180 x 220 232kW (315bhp) Daldizel-Khabarovsk AuxGen: 1 x 16kW Fuel: 6.0 (d.f.)
9550216 **TRANSFORMER OL** *3EZY5* - **Transformer Maritime SA Panama** Oceanlance Maritime Co Ltd *Panama* *Panama* MMSI: 372789000 Official number: 4110210	**17,018** 10,108 28,375 T/cm 39.6	Class: NK	**2009-11 Shimanami Shipyard Co Ltd — Imabari EH** Yd No: 549 Loa 169.37 (BB) Br ex 27.23 Dght 9.819 Lbp 160.40 Br md 27.20 Dpth 13.60 Welded, 1 dk	**(A21A2BC) Bulk Carrier** Grain: 37,320; Bale: 35,742 Compartments: 5 Ho, ER 5 Ha: 4 (19.2 x 17.6)ER (13.6 x 16.0) Cranes: 4x30.5t	**1 oil engine** driving 1 FP propeller Total Power: 5,850kW (7,954hp) 14.0kn MAN-B&W 6S42MC 1 x 2 Stroke 6 Cy. 420 x 1764 5850kW (7954bhp) Makita Corp-Japan AuxGen: 3 x 440kW 60Hz a.c Fuel: 1235.0 (r.f.)
9318955 **TRANSFORTE** *ZDGR3* *ex* Forte *-2013* *ex* Volna *-2005* - **Transatlantic Shipping (7) Ltd** Rederi AB Transatlantic *Gibraltar* *Gibraltar (British)* MMSI: 236270000	**5,232** 2,382 6,419	Class: GL	**2004-12 Tianjin Xingang Shipyard — Tianjin** Yd No: 350-1 Loa 115.50 (BB) Br ex - Dght 5.700 Lbp 111.63 Br md 16.50 Dpth 7.95 Welded, 1 dk	**(A31A2GX) General Cargo Ship** Grain: 9,467; Bale: 9,467 TEU 315 Compartments: 2 Ho, ER 2 Ha: ER Ice Capable	**1 oil engine** reduction geared to sc. shaft driving 1 CP propeller Total Power: 3,840kW (5,221hp) 13.0kn MaK 8M32C 1 x 4 Stroke 8 Cy. 320 x 480 3840kW (5221bhp) Caterpillar Motoren GmbH & Co. KG-Germany AuxGen: 2 x 260kW 400/230V 50Hz a.c, 1 x 400kW 400/230V 60Hz a.c Thrusters: 1 Thwart. FP thruster (f)
9199402 **TRANSFORZA** *ZDNJ2* *ex* Forza *-2013* *ex* Gouwediep *-2006* - **Industrial Shipping AS** Rederi AB Transatlantic *Gibraltar* *Gibraltar (British)* MMSI: 236111943	**3,244** 1,554 4,275	Class: GL	**2000-07 Societatea Comerciala Severnav S.A. — Drobeta-Turnu Severin** Yd No: 740006 Loa 99.95 Br ex - Dght 4.600 Lbp 96.00 Br md 16.30 Dpth 6.30 Welded, 1 dk	**(A31A2GX) General Cargo Ship** Grain: 5,500 TEU 264 C. 264/20' Compartments: 2 Ho, ER 2 Ha: ER Ice Capable	**1 oil engine** reduction geared to sc. shaft driving 1 CP propeller Total Power: 2,880kW (3,916hp) 13.5kn MaK 6M32 1 x 4 Stroke 6 Cy. 320 x 480 2880kW (3916bhp) MaK Motoren GmbH & Co. KG-Kiel AuxGen: 1 x 256kW 220/380V a.c, 2 x 184kW 220/380V a.c Fuel: 350.0 (d.f.)
8206624 **TRANSGAS 1** - *ex* Transcarib *-2013* *ex* Galp Lisboa *-2009* - **Transgas Shipping Lines SAC** - *Callao* *Peru* MMSI: 760001120	**2,680** 876 3,571 T/cm 10.6	Class: BV RP (NV)	**1983-07 T. Ruiz de Velasco S.A. — Bilbao** Yd No: 157 Loa 83.50 (BB) Br ex 14.53 Dght 6.350 Lbp 81.00 Br md 14.51 Dpth 7.90 Welded, 1 dk	**(A11B2TG) LPG Tanker** Double Hull Liq (Gas): 3,176 3 x Gas Tank (s); 1 independent (C.mn.stl) dcy horizontal, 1 independent (C.mn.stl) cyl transverse, 1 independent (C.mn.stl) dcy horizontal 5 Cargo Pump (s): 5x80m³/hr Manifold: Bow/CM: 38m Ice Capable	**1 oil engine** with flexible couplings & sr gearedto sc. shaft driving 1 CP propeller Total Power: 2,869kW (3,901hp) Pielstick 6PC2-5L-400 1 x 4 Stroke 6 Cy. 400 x 460 2869kW (3901bhp) Astilleros Espanoles SA (AESA)-Spain AuxGen: 1 x 360kW 440V 60Hz a.c, 2 x 280kW 440V 60Hz a.c Thrusters: 1 Thwart. FP thruster (f) Fuel: 93.5 (d.f.) 279.0 (r.f.)

IMO / Call sign	Name / Owner / Port	Tonnage	Class	Builder / Dimensions	Type	Machinery
9248552 ZDGR8 -	**TRANSHAWK** *ex* Sandon *-2008* **Longitude Shipping (UK) Ltd** Rederi AB Transatlantic SatCom: Inmarsat C 423627210 *Gibraltar* *Gibraltar (British)* MMSI: 236272000	**13,340** 5,238 16,558 T/cm 28.7	Class: LR ✠ **100A1** SS 01/2010 strengthened for heavy cargoes *IWS LI Ice Class 1AS at a draught of 9.615m Max/min draught fwd 9.615/4.515m Max/min draught aft 9.615/5.515m Power required 7255kw, installed 9480kw ✠ **LMC** **UMS** Eq.Ltr: F†; Cable: 577.5/58.0 U3 (a)	**2004-12 Fujian Mawei Shipbuilding Ltd — Fuzhou FJ** Yd No: 436-3 Loa 142.43 (BB) Br ex 22.10 Dght 9.374 Lbp 132.29 Br md 22.00 Dpth 12.00 Welded, 1 dk	**(A31A2GX) General Cargo Ship** Grain: 18,577; Bale: 18,577 TEU 658 C Ho 400 TEU C Dk 258 TEU Compartments: 3 Ho, ER 3 Ha: ER Cranes: 3x35t Ice Capable	**1 oil engine** driving 1 CP propeller Total Power: 9,480kW (12,889hp) 15.5kn MAN-B&W 6S50MC-C 1 x 2 Stroke 6 Cy. 500 x 2000 9480kW (12889bhp) Hudong Heavy Machinery Co Ltd-China AuxGen: 1 x 1600kW 400V 50Hz a.c, 3 x 680kW 400V 50Hz a.c Boilers: TOH (o.f.) 10.2kgf/cm² (10.0bar), TOH (ex.g.) 10.2kgf/cm² (10.0bar) Thrusters: 1 Thwart. CP thruster (f)
9672791 POVN -	**TRANSINDO 8** - **PT Pelayaran Taruna Kusan Jaya (Taruna Kusan Jaya Shipping Inc)** - *Samarinda* *Indonesia* MMSI: 525020184	**820** 246 -	Class: KI	**2012-07 C.V. Teknik Jaya Industri — Samarinda** Yd No: 48 Loa 71.83 Br ex - Dght - Lbp 65.02 Br md 12.72 Dpth 2.73 Welded, 1 dk	**(A35D2RL) Landing Craft** Bow ramp (centre)	**2 oil engines** reduction geared to sc. shafts driving 2 Propellers Total Power: 970kW (1,318hp) Yanmar 2 x each-485kW (659bhp) Yanmar Diesel Engine Co Ltd-Japan
8854110 - -	**TRANSINDO 8** *ex* Is No. 4 *-2009* *ex* Zuiei Maru *-2009* **PT Transindo Bahari Perkasa** - *Tanjung Priok* *Indonesia*	**1,419** 426 1,599	Class: KI	**1991-04 Mategata Zosen K.K. — Namikata** Yd No: 1030 Loa 75.45 Br ex - Dght 4.330 Lbp 70.80 Br md 11.50 Dpth 7.20 Welded, 1 dk	**(A31A2GX) General Cargo Ship**	**1 oil engine** reduction geared to sc. shaft driving 1 FP propeller Total Power: 1,324kW (1,800hp) Hanshin 6EL30G 1 x 4 Stroke 6 Cy. 300 x 600 1324kW (1800bhp) The Hanshin Diesel Works Ltd-Japan AuxGen: 2 x 85kW 225V a.c
8957900 - -	**TRANSINDO I** - **PT Pelayaran Taruna Kusan Jaya (Taruna Kusan Jaya Shipping Inc)** - *Semarang* *Indonesia*	**498** 149 1,000	Class: KI	**1998-12 P.T. Pantai Mulia Semesta — Tegal** Loa 54.00 Br ex - Dght 2.380 Lbp 48.00 Br md 13.00 Dpth 3.00 Welded, 1 dk	**(A35D2RL) Landing Craft** Bow ramp (centre)	**2 oil engines** reduction geared to sc. shafts driving 2 FP propellers Total Power: 706kW (960hp) 9.0kn Caterpillar 3406TA 2 x 4 Stroke 6 Cy. 137 x 165 each-353kW (480bhp) (made 1998) Caterpillar Inc-USA
9027609 YGXA -	**TRANSINDO II** - **PT Bandar Niaga Raya** - *Cirebon* *Indonesia*	**493** 143 1,000	Class: KI	**2001-07 PT Palma Progress Shipyard — Batam** Loa 59.70 Br ex - Dght 2.400 Lbp 52.70 Br md 13.50 Dpth 3.00 Welded, 1 dk	**(A35D2RL) Landing Craft** Bow ramp (centre)	**2 oil engines** geared to sc. shafts driving 2 FP propellers Total Power: 706kW (960hp) 9.0kn Caterpillar 3412TA 2 x Vee 4 Stroke 12 Cy. 137 x 152 each-353kW (480bhp) Caterpillar Inc-USA
9027611 - -	**TRANSINDO III** - **PT Bandar Niaga Raya** - *Cirebon* *Indonesia* MMSI: 525019463	**495** 149 1,000	Class: KI	**2002-10 PT Palma Progress Shipyard — Batam** Loa 54.70 Br ex - Dght 2.400 Lbp 47.00 Br md 13.50 Dpth 3.00 Welded, 1 dk	**(A35D2RL) Landing Craft** Bow ramp (centre)	**2 oil engines** geared to sc. shafts driving 2 FP propellers Total Power: 536kW (728hp) 8.2kn Caterpillar 3406 2 x 4 Stroke 6 Cy. 137 x 165 each-268kW (364bhp) Caterpillar Inc-USA
9644902 POPK -	**TRANSKO ANDALAS** **PT PERTAMINA Trans Kontinental** - *Jakarta* *Indonesia* MMSI: 525003166	**1,559** 468 1,350	Class: BV KI	**2012-07 Guangzhou Hangtong Shipbuilding & Shipping Co Ltd — Jiangmen GD** (Hull) Yd No: HT102106 **2012-07 Bonny Fair Development Ltd — Hong Kong** Yd No: (HT102106) Loa 60.50 Br ex - Dght 4.750 Lbp 55.00 Br md 14.60 Dpth 5.50 Welded, 1 dk	**(B21B20A) Anchor Handling Tug Supply**	**2 oil engines** reduction geared to sc. shafts driving 2 CP propellers Total Power: 3,840kW (5,220hp) 13.5kn Caterpillar 3516B-HD 2 x Vee 4 Stroke 16 Cy. 170 x 215 each-1920kW (2610bhp) Caterpillar Inc-USA AuxGen: 2 x 1012kW 50Hz a.c, 2 x 450kW 50Hz a.c Thrusters: 2 Tunnel thruster (f) Fuel: 515.0
9644914 POPL -	**TRANSKO CELEBES** **PT PERTAMINA Trans Kontinental** - *Jakarta* *Indonesia* MMSI: 525003167	**1,575** 472 1,350	Class: BV KI	**2012-09 Guangzhou Hangtong Shipbuilding & Shipping Co Ltd — Jiangmen GD** (Hull) Yd No: HT102107 **2012-09 Bonny Fair Development Ltd — Hong Kong** Yd No: (HT102107) Loa 60.50 Br ex - Dght 4.500 Lbp 55.00 Br md 14.60 Dpth 5.50 Welded, 1 dk	**(B21B20A) Anchor Handling Tug Supply**	**2 oil engines** reduction geared to sc. shafts driving 2 CP propellers Total Power: 3,840kW (5,220hp) 13.5kn Caterpillar 3516B-HD 2 x Vee 4 Stroke 16 Cy. 170 x 215 each-1920kW (2610bhp) Caterpillar Inc-USA AuxGen: 2 x 1012kW 50Hz a.c, 2 x 450kW 50Hz a.c Thrusters: 2 Tunnel thruster (f) Fuel: 510.0
7429229 D6HL1 -	**TRANSLANDIA** *ex* Transparaden *-2004* *ex* Rosebay *-2001* *ex* Eurocruiser *-1998* *ex* Eurostar *-1997* *ex* Rosebay *-1997* *ex* Transgermania *-1993* **Salem Al Makrani Cargo Co** - *Moroni* *Union of Comoros* MMSI: 616999287 Official number: 1201460	**13,867** 4,161 4,113	Class: BV (GL)	**1976-10 J.J. Sietas Schiffswerft — Hamburg** Yd No: 792 Loa 135.49 (BB) Br ex 21.75 Dght 5.700 Lbp 119.92 Br md 21.71 Dpth 14.76 Welded, 2 dks	**(A36A2PR) Passenger/Ro-Ro Ship (Vehicles)** Passengers: cabins: 21; berths: 63; driver berths: 63 Stern door/ramp (centre) Len: 12.00 Wid: 9.60 Swl: 100 Lane-Len: 1624 Lane-clr ht: 4.30 Bale: 23,701 TEU 248 incl 20 ref C Compartments: 1 Ho, ER Ice Capable	**2 oil engines** reduction geared to sc. shafts driving 2 CP propellers Total Power: 9,312kW (12,660hp) 17.0kn MAN 6L52/55A 2 x 4 Stroke 6 Cy. 520 x 550 each-4656kW (6330bhp) Maschinenbau Augsburg Nuernberg (MAN)-Augsburg AuxGen: 2 x 736kW 380V 50Hz a.c, 1 x 672kW 380V 50Hz a.c Thrusters: 1 Thwart. FP thruster (f) Fuel: 91.5 (d.f.) 369.0 (r.f.) 37.5pd
9199385 ZDEP9 -	**TRANSLONTANO** *ex* Lontano *-2013* *ex* Grootdiep *-2007* **Short Sea Bulkers AS** Rederi AB Transatlantic SatCom: Inmarsat C 423615010 *Gibraltar* *Gibraltar (British)* MMSI: 236150000 Official number: 734624	**3,244** 1,554 4,135	Class: GL (LR) Classed LR until 22/6/08	**2000-03 Societatea Comerciala Severnav S.A. — Drobeta-Turnu Severin** Yd No: 720007 Loa 99.98 (BB) Br ex 16.50 Dght 4.600 Lbp 96.35 Br md 16.30 Dpth 6.30 Welded, 1 dk	**(A31A2GX) General Cargo Ship** Grain: 5,550 TEU 264 C.264/20' Compartments: 2 Ho, ER 2 Ha: ER Ice Capable	**1 oil engine** reduction geared to sc. shaft driving 1 CP propeller Total Power: 2,880kW (3,916hp) 13.0kn MaK 6M32 1 x 4 Stroke 6 Cy. 320 x 480 2880kW (3916bhp) MaK Motoren GmbH & Co. KG-Kiel AuxGen: 1 x 256kW 440V 50Hz a.c, 2 x 184kW 400V 50Hz a.c Thrusters: 1 Thwart. FP thruster (f) Fuel: 350.0 (d.f.)
9658484 S6NT -	**TRANSLUB** **Translub Marine Pte Ltd** LHYK Marine Pte Ltd *Singapore* *Singapore* MMSI: 563021390 Official number: 397945	**178** 53 200	Class: BV	**2012-12 Eastern Marine Shipbuilding Sdn Bhd — Sibu** Yd No: 102 Loa 26.00 Br ex - Dght 2.800 Lbp 24.20 Br md 7.50 Dpth 3.80 Welded, 1 dk	**(B35E2TF) Bunkering Tanker** Double Hull (13F)	**2 oil engines** reduction geared to sc. shafts driving 2 FP propellers Total Power: 668kW (908hp) 9.0kn Caterpillar C18 2 x 4 Stroke 6 Cy. 145 x 183 each-334kW (454bhp) Caterpillar Inc-USA AuxGen: 2 x 50kW 450V 60Hz a.c Fuel: 20.0 (d.f.)
7427611 J8B3537 -	**TRANSMAR** *ex* Al Karim *-2012* *ex* Reda *-2002* *ex* Marathon *-1996* *ex* Chivas *-1988* *ex* Whitehall *-1985* *ex* Bloempoort *-1983* *ex* Flowergate *-1982* **Moonlight Navigation Ltd** Tempus Maritime Sarl *Kingstown* *St Vincent & The Grenadines* MMSI: 376566000 Official number: 10010	**1,949** 1,053 3,110	Class: RS (LR) (GL) ✠ Classed LR until 2/86	**1976-04 B.V. v/h Scheepswerven Gebr. van Diepen — Waterhuizen** Yd No: 1008 Loa 83.52 Br ex 14.13 Dght 5.600 Lbp 74.86 Br md 14.00 Dpth 6.28 Welded, 1 dk	**(A31A2GX) General Cargo Ship** Grain: 3,720; Bale: 3,470 TEU 72 C. 72/20' (40') Compartments: 2 Ho, ER 2 Ha: 2 (19.8 x 10.5)ER Ice Capable	**1 oil engine** geared to sc. shaft driving 1 FP propeller Total Power: 1,776kW (2,415hp) 12.0kn MaK 8M452AK 1 x 4 Stroke 8 Cy. 320 x 450 1776kW (2415bhp) MaK Maschinenbau GmbH-Kiel AuxGen: 3 x 80kW 220/380V 50Hz a.c Fuel: 209.0 (d.f.)
9167332 ZDKA6 -	**TRANSMAR** **H & H Schiffahrts GmbH & Co KG ms 'Allertal'** Held Bereederungs GmbH & Co KG *Gibraltar* *Gibraltar (British)* MMSI: 236582000 Official number: 4567	**2,820** 1,503 4,106	Class: GL (BV)	**1998-04 Bodewes' Scheepswerven B.V. — Hoogezand** Yd No: 582 Loa 89.72 Br ex - Dght 5.690 Lbp 84.98 Br md 13.60 Dpth 7.20 Welded, 1 dk	**(A31A2GX) General Cargo Ship** Grain: 5,628 TEU 246 C.Ho 111/20' C.Dk 135/20' Compartments: 1 Ho, ER 1 Ha: (62.9 x 11.0)ER Ice Capable	**1 oil engine** geared to sc. shaft driving 1 CP propeller Total Power: 2,400kW (3,263hp) 12.5kn MaK 8M25 1 x 4 Stroke 8 Cy. 255 x 400 2400kW (3263bhp) MaK Motoren GmbH & Co. KG-Kiel AuxGen: 1 x 292kW 230/400V 50Hz a.c, 2 x 252kW 230/400V 50Hz a.c Thrusters: 1 Thwart. FP thruster (f) Fuel: 38.8 (d.f.) (Heating Coils) 276.0 (r.f.) 10.5pd

IMO No. / Call sign	Ship / Owner	Tonnage	Class	Builder / Dimensions	Type	Machinery
8114912 *J8B4195* -	**TRANSOCEAN** *ex* Alerce N *-2009* *ex* Alerce *-2006* *ex* Shinshima *-1995* *ex* Shinshima Maru *-1988* **Transocean Maritime SA** Tempus Maritime Sarl *Kingstown St Vincent & The Grenadines* MMSI: 377683000 Official number: 10668	**12,874** 8,063 21,304 T/cm 31.0	Class: NK (AB)	**1982-02 Shin Yamamoto Shipbuilding & Engineering Co Ltd — Kochi KC** Yd No: 261 Loa 152.60 (BB) Br ex - Dght 9.707 Lbp 142.00 Br md 24.00 Dpth 13.20 Welded, 1 dk	**(A21A2BC) Bulk Carrier** Grain: 28,331; Bale: 27,022 Compartments: 4 Ho, ER 4 Ha: (17.6 x 12.7)3 (20.0 x 12.7)ER Cranes: 3x25t; Derricks: 1x25t	**1 oil engine** driving 1 FP propeller Total Power: 5,914kW (8,041hp) 13.5kn Sulzer 6RLA56 1 x 2 Stroke 6 Cy. 560 x 1150 5914kW (8041bhp) Mitsubishi Heavy Industries Ltd-Japan AuxGen: 2 x 360kW 450V 60Hz a.c Fuel: 170.0 (d.f.) 1091.5 (r.f.) 25.0pd
8754499 *V7DO6* -	**TRANSOCEAN ARCTIC** *ex* Ross Rig *-1996* **Transocean Offshore International Ventures Ltd** Transocean Offshore Deepwater Drilling Inc *Majuro Marshall Islands* MMSI: 538001679 Official number: 1679	**22,194** 6,658 -	Class: NV	**1986-06 Mitsubishi Heavy Industries Ltd. — Hiroshima** Yd No: 338 Loa 99.60 Br ex 78.54 Dght 12.000 Lbp - Br md - Dpth 42.94 Welded, 1 dk	**(Z11C3ZE) Drilling Rig, semi Submersible** Passengers: berths: 100 Cranes: 1x50t,1x30t Ice Capable	**4 diesel electric oil engines** driving 4 gen. Connecting to 4 elec. motors driving 4 Azimuth electric drive units Total Power: 8,648kW (11,756hp) Wartsila 12V32D 4 x Vee 4 Stroke 12 Cy. 320 x 350 each-2162kW (2939bhp) Wartsila Diesel Oy-Finland
8768854 *V7ZT2* -	**TRANSOCEAN BARENTS** *ex* Aker Barents *-2011* **Transocean Barents ASA** Transocean Offshore Deepwater Drilling Inc *Majuro Marshall Islands* MMSI: 538004907 Official number: 4907	**37,878** 11,364 64,000	Class: NV	**2009-06 Drydocks World - Dubai LLC — Dubai** (Lower part) **2009-06 Aker Stord AS — Stord** (Upper part) Yd No: 802100 Loa 120.00 Br ex 77.03 Dght 23.000 Lbp - Br md 77.00 Dpth 39.00 Welded, 1 dk	**(Z11C3ZE) Drilling Rig, semi Submersible**	**8 diesel electric oil engines** driving 8 gen. Connecting to 8 elec. motors driving 4 Azimuth electric drive units , 4 Directional propellers Total Power: 48,000kW (65,264hp) Bergens B32: 40V12P 8 x Vee 4 Stroke 12 Cy. 320 x 400 each-6000kW (8158bhp) Rolls Royce Marine AS-Norway
7936351 - -	**TRANSOCEAN ENERGY** *ex* Pegasus Ace *-2003* *ex* Seifuku Maru *-1999* **Tomiura Nippon Chartering Pte Ltd** Transocean Oil Pte Ltd	**336** 140 485	Class: GL	**1980-02 Kogushi Zosen K.K. — Okayama** Yd No: 221 Loa - Br ex - Dght 2.990 Lbp 42.91 Br md 7.70 Dpth 3.31 Welded, 1 dk	**(A13B2TP) Products Tanker** Liq: 550; Liq (Oil): 550	**1 oil engine** driving 1 FP propeller Total Power: 552kW (750hp) 10.0kn Hanshin 6L26BGSH 1 x 4 Stroke 6 Cy. 260 x 400 552kW (750bhp) Hanshin Nainenki Kogyo-Japan
8752025 *YJQD5* -	**TRANSOCEAN JOHN SHAW** *ex* John Shaw *-1996* **Transocean Offshore Deepwater Drilling Inc** Transocean Offshore (UK) Inc *Port Vila Vanuatu* Official number: 1919	**15,425** 4,627 -	Class: NV	**1982-09 Mitsui Eng. & SB. Co. Ltd., Chiba Works — Ichihara** Yd No: F556 Loa 85.60 Br ex 64.60 Dght 7.420 Lbp - Br md - Dpth 35.36 Welded, 1 dk	**(Z11C3ZE) Drilling Rig, semi Submersible** Passengers: berths: 99 Cranes: 1x65t,2x43t	**4 diesel electric oil engines** driving 4 gen. each 1400kW Connecting to 4 elec. motors driving 2 FP propellers Total Power: 6,400kW (8,700hp) EMD (Electro-Motive) 16-645-E8 4 x Vee 2 Stroke 16 Cy. 230 x 254 each-1600kW (2175bhp) General Motors Corp.Electro-Motive Div.-La Grange
8756186 *V7ST8* -	**TRANSOCEAN LEADER** *ex* Transocean No. 8 *-1987* **Transocean Offshore International Ventures Ltd** Transocean Offshore Deepwater Drilling Inc *Majuro Marshall Islands* MMSI: 538003720 Official number: 3720	**25,822** 7,747 -	Class: NV	**1987-03 Hyundai Heavy Industries Co Ltd — Ulsan** Yd No: 517 Loa 123.50 Br ex 77.50 Dght 7.500 Lbp - Br md - Dpth 36.50 Welded, 1 dk	**(Z11C3ZE) Drilling Rig, semi Submersible** Passengers: berths: 100 Cranes: 2x45t Ice Capable	**4 diesel electric oil engines** driving 4 gen. each 3100kW a.c Connecting to 4 elec. motors driving 4 Azimuth electric drive units Total Power: 14,160kW (19,252hp) Bergens KVGS-16G4 1 x Vee 4 Stroke 16 Cy. 250 x 300 3540kW (4813bhp) (new engine 1997) Ulstein Bergen AS-Norway Bergens KVGS-16G4 3 x Vee 4 Stroke 16 Cy. 250 x 300 each-3540kW (4813bhp) (new engine 1997) Ulstein Bergen AS-Norway AuxGen: 4 x 3100kW a.c
8757960 *V7HC5* -	**TRANSOCEAN MARIANAS** *ex* P. Portia *-1998* *ex* Polyportia *-1996* *ex* Tharos *-1994* **Triton Asset Leasing GmbH** Transocean Offshore Deepwater Drilling Inc *Majuro Marshall Islands* MMSI: 538002209 Official number: 2209	**20,461** 6,138 11,525	Class: AB	**1979-09 Mitsubishi Heavy Industries Ltd. — Hiroshima** Yd No: 241018 Converted From: Drilling Rig, Semi-submersible-1998 Loa 91.44 Br ex 75.90 Dght 24.400 Lbp - Br md - Dpth 34.75 Welded, 1 dk	**(Z11C3ZE) Drilling Rig, semi Submersible** Passengers: berths: 150 Cranes: 1x317t,2x44t	**7 oil engines** driving 1 gen. of 1400kW a.c 6 gen. each 2500kW a.c Connecting to 8 elec. motors driving 1 Propeller Total Power: 17,322kW (23,550hp) EMD (Electro-Motive) 16-645-E6 1 x Vee 2 Stroke 16 Cy. 230 x 254 1434kW (1950bhp) General Motors Corp.Electro-Motive Div.-La Grange EMD (Electro-Motive) 20-645-E5 6 x Vee 2 Stroke 20 Cy. 230 x 254 each-2648kW (3600bhp) General Motors Corp.Electro-Motive Div.-La Grange Thrusters: 4 Thwart. CP thruster
8754487 *V7DO3* -	**TRANSOCEAN SEARCHER** *ex* Ross Isle *-1996* **Transocean Offshore International Ventures Ltd** Transocean Offshore (North Sea) Ltd *Majuro Marshall Islands* MMSI: 538001676 Official number: 1676	**14,962** 4,489 -	Class: NV	**1983-02 Kaldnes AS — Tonsberg** Yd No: 219 Loa 100.84 Br ex - Dght 23.510 Lbp - Br md 66.00 Dpth 35.99 Welded, 1 dk	**(Z11C3ZE) Drilling Rig, semi Submersible** Passengers: berths: 100 Cranes: 2x50t	**5 diesel electric oil engines** driving 5 gen. each 1808kW 6000V a.c Connecting to 4 elec. motors each (1550kW) driving 4 Azimuth electric drive units Total Power: 9,495kW (12,910hp) 7.0kn Bergens KVGB-12 5 x Vee 4 Stroke 12 Cy. 250 x 300 each-1899kW (2582bhp) AS Bergens Mek Verksteder-Norway
8768517 *V7ZS8* -	**TRANSOCEAN SPITSBERGEN** *ex* Aker Spitsbergen *-2011* **Transocean Spitsbergen ASA** Transocean Offshore Deepwater Drilling Inc *Majuro Marshall Islands* MMSI: 538004905 Official number: 4905	**37,878** 11,364 64,000	Class: NV	**2009-02 Drydocks World - Dubai LLC — Dubai** (Lower part) **2009-02 Aker Stord AS — Stord** (Upper part) Yd No: 802000 Loa 120.00 Br ex 77.03 Dght 23.000 Lbp - Br md 77.00 Dpth 39.00 Welded, 1 dk	**(Z11C3ZE) Drilling Rig, semi Submersible** Passengers: cabins: 140 Cranes: 2x85t	**8 diesel electric oil engines** driving 8 gen. Connecting to 8 elec. motors each (4500kW) driving 8 Azimuth electric drive units Total Power: 48,000kW (65,264hp) Bergens B32: 40V12P 8 x Vee 4 Stroke 12 Cy. 320 x 400 each-6000kW (8158bhp) Rolls Royce Marine AS-Norway
7920209 *HC2909* -	**TRANSOCEANICO I** *ex* Matsusei Maru No. 3 *-1994* **Megaocean CA** - *Manta Ecuador* MMSI: 735057610 Official number: P-04-0386	**607** 182 369		**1980-02 Miho Zosensho K.K. — Shimizu** Yd No: 1153 Loa 51.52 Br ex 8.62 Dght 3.282 Lbp 44.81 Br md 8.60 Dpth 3.61 Welded, 1 dk	**(B11B2FV) Fishing Vessel** Ins: 371	**1 oil engine** driving 1 CP propeller Total Power: 1,214kW (1,651hp) 13.0kn Akasaka DM30 1 x 4 Stroke 6 Cy. 300 x 480 1214kW (1651bhp) Akasaka Tekkosho KK (Akasaka DieselLtd)-Japan AuxGen: 2 x 250kW 225V a.c
6876839 - -	**TRANSOIL-2** *ex* Ruslan *-2003* **OOO 'Balt Star'** - *St Petersburg Russia* Official number: 670140	**181** 54 49	Class: (RS)	**1967-09 "Petrozavod" — Leningrad** Yd No: 724 Loa 29.30 Br ex 8.30 Dght 3.090 Lbp 27.00 Br md - Dpth 4.34 Welded	**(B32A2ST) Tug** Ice Capable	**2 oil engines** driving 2 CP propellers Total Power: 882kW (1,200hp) 11.0kn Russkiy 6D30/50-4-3 2 x 2 Stroke 6 Cy. 300 x 500 each-441kW (600bhp) (new engine 1976) Mashinostroitelnyy Zavod"Russkiy-Dizel"-Leningrad AuxGen: 2 x 25kW a.c Fuel: 46.0 (d.f.)
9213090 *ZDKB4* -	**TRANSOSPREY** *ex* Prinsenborg *-2010* **Osprey Maritime Ltd** Regal Agencies Corp *Gibraltar Gibraltar (British)* MMSI: 236586000	**16,037** 6,830 20,396 T/cm 28.7	Class: LR ✠ **100A1** SS 04/2013 strengthened for heavy cargoes, *IWS LI Ice Class 1A FS at 9.315m Max./min. draught aft 9.315/5.515m Max./min. draught fwd 9.315/5.515m Power required 6060kw, power installed 7562kw ✠ **LMC** **UMS** Eq.Ltr: F; Cable: 632.5/58.0 U3 (a)	**2003-04 Fujian Mawei Shipbuilding Ltd — Fuzhou FJ** Yd No: 436-2 Lengthened-2008 Loa 174.10 (BB) Br ex 22.10 Dght 9.000 Lbp 164.00 Br md 22.00 Dpth 12.81 Welded, 1 dk	**(A31A2GX) General Cargo Ship** Grain: 18,577; Bale: 18,577 TEU 658 C Ho 400 TEU C Dk 258 TEU Compartments: 4 Ho, ER 8 Ha: ER Cranes: 3x35t Ice Capable	**1 oil engine** driving 1 CP propeller Total Power: 7,560kW (10,279hp) 15.5kn MAN-B&W 7S42MC 1 x 2 Stroke 7 Cy. 420 x 1764 7560kW (10279bhp) Hudong Heavy Machinery Co Ltd-China AuxGen: 1 x 1600kW 400V 50Hz a.c, 3 x 680kW 400V 50Hz a.c Boilers: TOH (o.f.) 10.2kgf/cm² (10.0bar), TOH (ex.g.) 10.2kgf/cm² (10.0bar) Thrusters: 1 Thwart. FP thruster (f) Fuel: 150.0 (d.f.) 1010.0 (r.f.)

9597226 *9HA3089* -	**TRANSPACIFIC** **Hallmar Navigation Co** Alpha Tankers & Freighters International Ltd *Valletta* *Malta* MMSI: 229126000 Official number: 9597226	**43,721** 26,541 82,000 T/cm 71.0	Class: LR **✠100A1** SS 08/2012 bulk carrier CSR BC-A GRAB (25) Nos. 2, 4 & 6 holds may be empty ESP **ShipRight** (CM,ACS (B)) *IWS LI **✠LMC** **UMS** Eq.Ltr: Q†; Cable: 687.5/81.0 U3 (a)	**2012-08 Hyundai Samho Heavy Industries Co Ltd — Samho** Yd No: S554 Loa 229.00 (BB) Br ex 32.29 Dght 14.500 Lbp 223.00 Br md 32.25 Dpth 20.10 Welded, 1 dk	**(A21A2BC) Bulk Carrier** Grain: 95,700 Compartments: 7 Ho, ER 7 Ha: ER	**1 oil engine** driving 1 FP propeller Total Power: 11,620kW (15,799hp) 14.5kn MAN-B&W 7S50MC-C8 1 x 2 Stroke 7 Cy. 500 x 2000 11620kW (15799bhp) Hyundai Heavy Industries Co Ltd-South Korea AuxGen: 3 x 700kW 450V 60Hz a.c Boilers: WTAuxB (Comp) 9.0kgf/cm² (8.8bar)
9334959 *SKEC* -	**TRANSPAPER** **Baltic Container Shipping (UK) Ltd** Rederi AB Transatlantic *Skarhamn* *Sweden* MMSI: 266232000	**23,128** 6,938 15,960	Class: NV	**2006-08 Aker MTW Werft GmbH — Wismar** (Hull) Yd No: 419 **2006-08 Aker Yards Oy — Rauma** Yd No: 448 Loa 190.50 (BB) Br ex 30.60 Dght 7.800 Lbp 178.70 Br md 26.00 Dpth 15.30 Welded, 3 dks	**(A35A2RR) Ro-Ro Cargo Ship** Passengers: berths: 12 Stern door/ramp (centre) Len: 16.00 Wid: 23.60 Swl: - Lane-Len: 2774 Lane-clr ht: 5.20 Trailers: 155 Ice Capable	**2 oil engines** geared to sc. shaft driving 1 CP propeller Total Power: 18,000kW (24,472hp) 16.0kn MAN-B&W 9L48/60B 2 x 4 Stroke 9 Cy. 480 x 600 each-9000kW (12236bhp) MAN B&W Diesel AG-Augsburg AuxGen: 2 x 1500kW a.c, 1 x 2560kW a.c Thrusters: 1 Tunnel thruster (a); 2 Tunnel thruster (f) Fuel: 260.1 (d.f.) 923.4 (r.f.)
8330114 *EAKL* -	**TRANSPEIXE I** *ex* Transfish I *-1993* *ex* Michiel *-1991* *ex* Jacob Zwann *-1984* **Transpeixe Importacao & Exportacao** Inter Ocean de Pesca SL *Las Palmas* *Spain (CSR)* Official number: 3/1993	**197** 59 -	Class: (GL)	**1967 N.V. Scheepswerf en Machinefabriek "Vahali" — Gendt** Yd No: 405 Converted From: Fishing Vessel Loa 30.21 Br ex 6.41 Dght 2.361 Lbp 26.85 Br md 6.40 Dpth 3.14 Welded, 1 dk	**(A34A2GR) Refrigerated Cargo Ship**	**1 oil engine** reverse reduction geared to sc. shaft driving 1 FP propeller Total Power: 699kW (950hp) 10.0kn Kromhout 6FCHD240 1 x 4 Stroke 6 Cy. 240 x 260 699kW (950bhp) (new engine 1979) Stork Werkspoor Diesel BV-Netherlands AuxGen: 1 x 108kW 220V a.c
9216638 *SFIR* -	**TRANSPINE** *ex* Finnpine *-2008* **Longitude Shipping (UK) Ltd** Rederi AB Transatlantic *Skarhamn* *Sweden* MMSI: 265862000	**20,851** 5,486 18,855	Class: LR **✠100A1** SS 02/2012 roll on - roll off cargo ship *IWS LI Nos.1 & 4 hold TwD and No.2 hold inner btm, strengthened for regular discharge by heavy grabs 10T Ice Class 1AS at 9.177m draught Max/min draught fwd 9.177/5.41m Max/min draught aft 9.177/7.00m Power required 9033kw, installed 12600kw **✠LMC** **UMS** Eq.Ltr: J†; Cable: 619.8/64.0 U3 (a)	**2002-02 Stocznia Gdynia SA — Gdynia** Yd No: 8222/2 Lengthened-2006 Loa 178.60 (BB) Br ex 28.70 Dght 9.000 Lbp 168.00 Br md 25.60 Dpth 16.30 Welded, 2 dks	**(A35A2RR) Ro-Ro Cargo Ship** Stern door & ramp (centre) Lane-Len: 900 Bale: 30,019 TEU 759 Compartments: 5 Ho, ER 3 Ha: 2 (24.8 x 21.0) (19.2 x 21.0)ER Ice Capable	**2 oil engines** with clutches, flexible couplings & sr geared to sc. shaft driving 1 CP propeller Total Power: 12,600kW (17,130hp) 17.5kn Wartsila 6L46C 2 x 4 Stroke 6 Cy. 460 x 580 each-6300kW (8565bhp) Wartsila Finland Oy-Finland AuxGen: 1 x 1400kW 400V 50Hz a.c, 3 x 1028kW 400V 50Hz a.c Boilers: TOH (o.f.) 10.7kgf/cm² (10.5bar), TOH (ex.g.) 10.7kgf/cm² (10.5bar) Thrusters: 1 Thwart. FP thruster (f); 1 Thwart. FP thruster (a) Fuel: 124.5 (d.f.) 1622.1 (r.f.)
7122572 *J8MK* -	**TRANSPORT** *ex* Crioula *-2000* *ex* Ariane *-1997* *ex* Ariane 1 *-1990* *ex* Slano *-1987* *ex* Scan Glen *-1986* *ex* Biscayne Sky *-1982* *ex* Sligo *-1978* **Ariane Shipping Corp Ltd** Morton & Co *Kingstown* *St Vincent & The Grenadines* MMSI: 377901012	**1,919** 814 1,750	Class: (GL) (JR) (BV)	**1971-03 Astilleros Luzuriaga SA — Pasaia** Yd No: 200 Loa 74.71 Br ex - Dght 4.255 Lbp 67.01 Br md 13.03 Dpth 6.81 Welded, 2 dks	**(A31A2GX) General Cargo Ship** Grain: 4,049; Bale: 3,893 TEU 102 C.Ho 74/20' C.Dk 28/20' (30') Compartments: 1 Ho, ER 1 Ha: (44.4 x 10.5)ER Cranes: 1x40t Ice Capable	**1 oil engine** driving 1 FP propeller Total Power: 1,140kW (1,550hp) 13.0kn Werkspoor TMABS396 1 x 4 Stroke 6 Cy. 390 x 680 1140kW (1550bhp) Naval Stork Werkspoor SA-Spain AuxGen: 2 x 112kW 380V a.c, 1 x 76kW 380V a.c Fuel: 114.0 (d.f.)
9261164 *HO8554* -	**TRANSPORT EXPRESS** *ex* Transporter *-2013* *ex* UAL Transporter *-2013* *ex* Jaya Transporter 3 *-2002* **Caribship LLC** G & G Marine Inc *Panama* *Panama* MMSI: 373819000 Official number: 45300PEXT1	**1,092** 327 1,296	Class: (BV)	**2001-11 Tuong Aik (Sarawak) Sdn Bhd — Sibu** Yd No: 2001 Loa 63.80 Br ex - Dght 2.650 Lbp 60.80 Br md 14.00 Dpth 4.30 Welded, 1 dk	**(A35D2RL) Landing Craft** Bow ramp (centre) Len: 6.00 Wid: 8.00 Swl: 100 TEU 86 incl 6 ref C	**2 oil engines** reduction geared to sc. shafts driving 2 FP propellers Total Power: 1,054kW (1,434hp) 10.0kn Caterpillar 3412TA 2 x Vee 4 Stroke 12 Cy. 137 x 152 each-527kW (717bhp) Caterpillar Inc-USA AuxGen: 2 x 80kW 415/240V 50Hz a.c
9204714 *PHAL* -	**TRANSPORTER** **Rederij Transporter** Spliethoff's Bevrachtingskantoor BV *Amsterdam* *Netherlands* MMSI: 245981000	**6,714** 2,888 8,469 T/cm 18.6	Class: BV	**1999-10 Zhonghua Shipyard — Shanghai** Yd No: 407 Loa 100.70 (BB) Br ex - Dght 8.200 Lbp 95.00 Br md 20.40 Dpth 11.10 Welded, 2 dks	**(A31A2GX) General Cargo Ship** Grain: 10,530; Bale: 10,300; Liq: 650 TEU 371 C Ho 195 C Dk 176 incl 24 ref C. Compartments: 1 Ho, ER, 1 Tw Dk 1 Ha: (64.4 x 15.3)ER Cranes: 2x275t Ice Capable	**1 oil engine** with flexible couplings & sr geared to sc. shaft driving 1 CP propeller Total Power: 7,800kW (10,605hp) 16.5kn Wartsila 8L46B 1 x 4 Stroke 8 Cy. 460 x 580 7800kW (10605bhp) Wartsila NSD Finland Oy-Finland AuxGen: 1 x 900kW 440V 60Hz a.c, 3 x 530kW 440V 60Hz a.c Thrusters: 1 Thwart. CP thruster (f) Fuel: 98.0 (d.f.) (Heating Coils) 775.3 (r.f.) 28.0pd
8820858 *OJCW* -	**TRANSPORTER** *ex* Birka Transporter *-2013* *ex* Hamno *-2002* **Eckero Shipping AB Ltd** SatCom: Inmarsat C 423000032 *Mariehamn* *Finland* MMSI: 230189000 Official number: 51164	**6,620** 1,986 5,387 T/cm 18.1	Class: NV	**1991-02 Brodogradiliste 'Sava' — Macvanska Mitrovica** (Hull) Yd No: 303 **1991-02 Fosen Mek. Verksteder AS — Rissa** Yd No: 41 Loa 122.00 (BB) Br ex 19.04 Dght 6.363 Lbp 112.00 Br md 19.00 Dpth 12.40 Welded, 2 dks	**(A35A2RR) Ro-Ro Cargo Ship** Stern door/ramp (centre) Len: 14.00 Wid: 13.00 Swl: 70 Lane-Len: 1278 Lane-clr ht: 5.00 Bale: 12,014 TEU 296 Ice Capable	**1 oil engine** with flexible couplings & sr geared to sc. shaft driving 1 CP propeller Total Power: 5,880kW (7,994hp) 16.5kn Wartsila 16V32D 1 x Vee 4 Stroke 16 Cy. 320 x 350 5880kW (7994bhp) Wartsila Diesel Oy-Finland AuxGen: 1 x 600kW 440V 60Hz a.c, 2 x 328kW 440V 60Hz a.c Thrusters: 1 Thwart. FP thruster (f) Fuel: 47.0 (d.f.) 600.0 (r.f.) 24.0pd
8701387 *3FFV9* -	**TRANSPORTER** *ex* Almhmoud Transporter *-2012* *ex* Trust Dubai *-2009* *ex* Sun Bird *-2004* *ex* Ariake Maru No. 3 *-2002* **Global Transport for Livestock Co SA** Unifleet Management Co SA *Panama* *Panama* MMSI: 353589000 Official number: 4208710B	**8,070** 2,421 3,725	Class: IV (KR) (NK)	**1987-04 Minaminippon Shipbuilding Co Ltd — Usuki OT** Yd No: 589 Converted From: Vehicles Carrier-2010 Loa 108.50 (BB) Br ex 20.02 Dght 5.812 Lbp 100.00 Br md 20.00 Dpth 10.70 Welded, 2 dks	**(A38A2GL) Livestock Carrier**	**1 oil engine** driving 1 FP propeller Total Power: 7,061kW (9,600hp) Mitsubishi 8UEC45LA 1 x 2 Stroke 8 Cy. 450 x 1350 7061kW (9600bhp) Akasaka Tekkosho KK (Akasaka DieselLtd)-Japan Thrusters: 1 Thwart. CP thruster (f)
8918930 *PJWP* -	**TRANSPORTER** *ex* Sealift Transporter *-2007* *ex* Front Sunda *-2007* *ex* Sunda *-1999* **Dockwise Transporter BV** Dockwise Shipping BV *Willemstad* *Curacao* MMSI: 306877000 Official number: 2007-C	**42,609** 12,783 53,806 T/cm 108.0	Class: LR (NV) **100A1** SS 05/2012 *IWS LI **LMC** **UMS**	**1992-12 Brodosplit - Brodogradiliste doo — Split** Yd No: 369 Converted From: Crude Oil Tanker-2007 Loa 216.86 (BB) Br ex - Dght 10.500 Lbp 207.93 Br md 44.44 Dpth 14.00 Welded, 1 dk	**(A38C3GH) Heavy Load Carrier, semi submersible**	**1 oil engine** driving 1 FP propeller Total Power: 13,369kW (18,176hp) 14.0kn B&W 6S70MC 1 x 2 Stroke 6 Cy. 700 x 2674 13369kW (18176bhp) Brodosplit Tvornica Dizel Motoradoo-Croatia AuxGen: 3 x 1200kW 440V 60Hz a.c Thrusters: 1 Thwart. CP thruster (f) Fuel: 264.0 (d.f.) (Heating Coils) 4256.0 (r.f.) 53.0pd
8615148 *DDBE* -	**TRANSPORTER II** **Jade-Dienst GmbH** - *Wilhelmshaven* *Germany* MMSI: 211226450 Official number: 470	**202** 80 296	Class: GL	**1987-02 Scheepswerf Bijlholt B.V. — Foxhol** (Hull) Yd No: 644 **1987-02 B.V. Scheepswerf Damen — Gorinchem** Yd No: 4475 Loa 37.52 Br ex - Dght 1.904 Lbp - Br md 7.71 Dpth 2.70 Welded, 1 dk	**(B34E2SW) Waste Disposal Vessel** Double Bottom Entire Compartment Length Liq: 359	**2 oil engines** reverse reduction geared to sc. shafts driving 2 FP propellers Total Power: 420kW (572hp) 8.0kn MAN D2566MLE 2 x 4 Stroke 6 Cy. 125 x 155 each-210kW (286bhp) MAN Nutzfahrzeuge AG-Nuernberg

IMO / Call sign	Name / Owner / Manager	Tonnage	Class	Builder / Dimensions	Type	Machinery
8522066 - -	**TRANSPORTER II** *ex* Eerika *-1995* *ex* Otar *-1992* -	**1,898** 569 690	Class: (RS)	**1985-04 VEB Volkswerft Stralsund — Stralsund** Yd No: 672 Loa 62.26 Br ex 13.82 Dght 5.220 Lbp 55.02 Br md 13.81 Dpth 9.22 Welded, 2 dks	**(B11A2FS) Stern Trawler** Ins: 580 Ice Capable	**2 oil engines** sr geared to sc. shaft driving 1 CP propeller Total Power: 1,766kW (2,402hp) 12.9kn S.K.L. 8VD26/20AL-2 2 x 4 Stroke 8 Cy. 200 x 260 each-883kW (1201bhp) VEB Schwermaschinenbau "KarlLiebknecht" (SKL)-Magdeburg AuxGen: 1 x 640kW a.c, 3 x 568kW a.c, 1 x 260kW d.c
8121422 *YJRP5* -	**TRANSPORTER TIDE** *ex* Oil Transporter *-2000* *ex* Martin Viking *-1995* **Twenty Grand Offshore LLC** Tidewater Marine LLC SatCom: Inmarsat C 423365610 *Port Vila* *Vanuatu* MMSI: 576602000 Official number: 1255	**2,707** 812 2,550	Class: AB (GL) (NV)	**1983-02 Ankerlokken Verft Glommen AS — Fredrikstad** (Hull) Yd No: 199 **1983-02 AS Framnaes Mek. Vaerksted — Sandefjord** Yd No: 197 Loa 81.06 Br ex - Dght 4.970 Lbp 76.21 Br md 18.01 Dpth 7.12 Welded, 2 dks	**(B21A20P) Pipe Carrier**	**2 oil engines** with clutches, flexible couplings & sr geared to sc. shafts driving 2 CP propellers Total Power: 3,898kW (5,300hp) 15.0kn Nohab F212V 2 x Vee 4 Stroke 12 Cy. 250 x 300 each-1949kW (2650bhp) Nohab Diesel AB-Sweden AuxGen: 2 x 1224kW 440V 60Hz a.c, 2 x 224kW 440V 60Hz a.c Thrusters: 2 Thwart. CP thruster (f); 2 Tunnel thruster (a) Fuel: 1500.0 (d.f.) 12.0pd
9419694 *YDA4239* -	**TRANSPOWER 242** *launched as* Modalwan 24137 *-2006* **PT Trans Power Marine** - *Jakarta* *Indonesia* Official number: 2007 PST NO 4454/L	**274** 83 -	Class: KI (BV)	**2006-11 Bonafile Shipbuilders & Repairs Sdn Bhd — Sandakan** Yd No: 36/04 Loa 29.20 Br ex - Dght 3.840 Lbp 27.53 Br md 9.00 Dpth 4.85 Welded, 1 dk	**(B32A2ST) Tug**	**2 oil engines** reduction geared to sc. shafts driving 2 Propellers Total Power: 2,238kW (3,042hp) 11.0kn Cummins KTA-38-M2 2 x Vee 4 Stroke 12 Cy. 159 x 159 each-1119kW (1521bhp) Cummins Engine Co Inc-USA AuxGen: 2 x 90kW 415V a.c
9343261 *SKEI* -	**TRANSPULP** **Baltic Container Shipping (UK) Ltd** Rederi AB Transatlantic *Skarhamn* *Sweden* MMSI: 266248000	**23,128** 6,938 15,960	Class: NV	**2006-12 Aker Yards Oy — Rauma** Yd No: 449 Loa 190.70 (BB) Br ex 30.60 Dght 7.800 Lbp 178.70 Br md 26.00 Dpth 15.30 Welded, 3 dks	**(A35A2RR) Ro-Ro Cargo Ship** Passengers: 12 Stern door/ramp (centre) Len: 16.00 Wid: 23.60 Swl: - Lane-Len: 2774 Lane-clr ht: 5.20 Trailers: 155 Ice Capable	**2 oil engines** sr geared to sc. shaft driving 1 CP propeller Total Power: 18,000kW (24,472hp) 16.0kn MAN-B&W 9L48/60B 2 x 4 Stroke 9 Cy. 480 x 600 each-9000kW (12236bhp) MAN B&W Diesel AG-Augsburg AuxGen: 2 x 1500kW a.c, 1 x 3125kW a.c Thrusters: 1 Tunnel thruster (a); 2 Tunnel thruster (f) Fuel: 260.1 (d.f.) 923.4 (r.f.)
7829651 *WCU2239* -	**TRANSQUEST** **Case Blazyk** - *Sausalito, CA* *United States of America* Official number: 512598	*199* 83 83		**1967-05 Albina Engine & Machine Works, Inc. — Portland, Or** Yd No: 396 Loa 32.11 Br ex - Dght 2.439 Lbp - Br md 11.89 Dpth 3.69 Welded, 1 dk	**(B22A20R) Offshore Support Vessel** Cranes: 1	**2 oil engines** driving 2 FP propellers Total Power: 514kW (698hp) G.M. (Detroit Diesel) 8V-71-N 2 x Vee 2 Stroke 8 Cy. 108 x 127 each-257kW (349bhp) General Motors Detroit DieselAllison Divn-USA AuxGen: 2 x 250kW Thrusters: 1 Thwart. FP thruster (f)
8515893 *SLRP* -	**TRANSREEL** *ex* Viola Gorthon *-2009* **Transatlantic Shipping AB** Transatlantic Fleet Services AB SatCom: Inmarsat B 326515010 *Skarhamn* *Sweden* MMSI: 265150000	**18,773** 6,392 11,396 T/cm 32.8	Class: LR ✠ **100A1** SS 08/2011 ro-ro cargo ship Ice Class 1A ✠ **LMC** **UMS** Eq.Ltr: G†; Cable: 577.5/60.0 U3 (a)	**1987-08 Korea Shipbuilding & Engineering Corp — Busan** Yd No: 1036 Loa 166.02 (BB) Br ex 23.07 Dght 7.230 Lbp 157.21 Br md 22.61 Dpth 13.16 Welded, 3 dks	**(A35A2RR) Ro-Ro Cargo Ship** Stern door/ramp (centre) Len: 18.00 Wid: 12.00 Swl: 66 Lane-Len: 2628 Lane-Wid: 2.94 Lane-clr ht: 4.70 Cars: 100, Trailers: 160 Bale: 33,100 TEU 169 Ice Capable	**2 oil engines** with clutches, flexible couplings & sr geared to sc. shaft driving 1 CP propeller Total Power: 7,774kW (10,569hp) 20.0kn Wartsila 12V32 1 x Vee 4 Stroke 12 Cy. 320 x 350 4442kW (6039bhp) Ssangyong Heavy Industries Co Ltd-South Korea Wartsila 9R32 1 x 4 Stroke 9 Cy. 320 x 350 3332kW (4530bhp) Ssangyong Heavy Industries Co Ltd-South Korea AuxGen: 1 x 1200kW 450V 60Hz a.c, 2 x 825kW 450V 60Hz a.c Boilers: 2 e 9.1kgf/cm² (8.9bar), AuxB (o.f.) 8.7kgf/cm² (8.5bar) Thrusters: 1 Thwart. CP thruster (f); 1 Tunnel thruster (a) Fuel: 150.0 (d.f.) 810.0 (r.f.)
9143788 *ZDHI4* -	**TRANSRISOLUTO** *ex* Risoluto *-2013* *ex* Thamesis *-2006* **Industrial Shipping AS** Rederi AB Transatlantic *Gibraltar* *Gibraltar (British)* MMSI: 236323000	**2,848** 1,528 4,148	Class: GL	**1997-03 Bodewes Scheepswerf "Volharding" Foxhol B.V. — Foxhol** Yd No: 328 Loa 89.78 (BB) Br ex - Dght 5.710 Lbp 84.98 Br md 13.60 Dpth 7.20 Welded, 1 dk	**(A31A2GX) General Cargo Ship** Grain: 5,628; Bale: 5,296 TEU 261 C.Ho 111/20' (40') C.Dk 150/20' (40') incl. 20 ref C Compartments: 1 Ho, ER 1 Ha: (62.9 x 11.0)ER Ice Capable	**1 oil engine** sr geared to sc. shaft driving 1 CP propeller Total Power: 2,200kW (2,991hp) 13.0kn MaK 6M453C 1 x 4 Stroke 6 Cy. 320 x 420 2200kW (2991bhp) Krupp MaK Maschinenbau GmbH-Kiel AuxGen: 1 x 650kW 220/380V a.c, 2 x 136kW 220/380V a.c Thrusters: 1 Thwart. FP thruster (f)
8512279 *PJRR* -	**TRANSSHELF** **Transshelf BV** Dockwise Shipping BV SatCom: Inmarsat C 430670410 *Willemstad* *Curacao* MMSI: 306704000 Official number: 2004-C-1794	**26,890** 8,067 34,030	Class: LR (RS) **100A1** SS 12/2012 Ice Class 1D **LMC** **CCS** Eq.Ltr: O†; Cable: 660.0/78.0 U3	**1987-03 Wartsila Marine Industries Inc — Turku** Yd No: 1293 Loa 173.00 Br ex 40.06 Dght 8.800 Lbp 162.00 Br md 40.00 Dpth 12.00 Welded, 1 dk	**(A38C3GH) Heavy Load Carrier, semi submersible** Ice Capable	**2 oil engines** with clutches & sr geared to sc. shafts driving 2 CP propellers Total Power: 13,500kW (18,354hp) 15.0kn Wartsila 18V32 2 x Vee 4 Stroke 18 Cy. 320 x 350 each-6750kW (9177bhp) Wartsila Diesel Oy-Finland AuxGen: 2 x 840kW 380V 50Hz a.c, 2 x 600kW 380V 50Hz a.c Boilers: 2 e (ex.g.) 7.1kgf/cm² (7.0bar), WTAuxB (o.f.) 7.1kgf/cm² (7.0bar) Thrusters: 2 Thwart. CP thruster (f)
9382798 *A8PB6* -	**TRANSSIB BRIDGE** **Hargate Marine Inc** Unicom Management Services (Cyprus) Ltd SatCom: Inmarsat C 463701846 *Monrovia* *Liberia* MMSI: 636013748 Official number: 13748	**27,725** 13,762 47,185 T/cm 52.3	Class: LR ✠ **100A1** SS 04/2013 Double Hull oil tanker ESP **ShipRight** (SDA, FDA, CM) *IWS LI SPM EP ✠ **LMC** **UMS IGS** Eq.Ltr: M†; Cable: 639.8/73.0 U3 (a)	**2008-04 Admiralteyskiy Sudostroitelnyy Zavod — Sankt-Peterburg** Yd No: 02747 Loa 182.32 (BB) Br ex 32.21 Dght 12.197 Lbp 174.69 Br md 32.20 Dpth 17.50 Welded, 1 dk	**(A13B2TP) Products Tanker** Double Hull (13F) Liq: 52,970; Liq (Oil): 52,970 Compartments: 10 Wing Ta, 2 Wing Slop Ta, ER 10 Cargo Pump (s): 10x550m³/hr Manifold: Bow/CM: 90.9m	**1 oil engine** driving 1 FP propeller Total Power: 8,310kW (11,298hp) 15.0kn MAN-B&W 6S50MC-C 1 x 2 Stroke 6 Cy. 500 x 2000 8310kW (11298bhp) AO Bryanskiy MashinostroitelnyyZavod (BMZ)-Bryansk AuxGen: 1 x 680kW 450V 60Hz a.c, 2 x 1280kW 450V 60Hz a.c Boilers: e (ex.g.) 11.7kgf/cm² (11.5bar), WTAuxB (o.f.) 11.2kgf/cm² (11.0bar) Fuel: 90.0 (d.f.) 1300.0 (r.f.)
9199397 *ZDEN9* -	**TRANSSONORO** *ex* Sonoro *-2013* *ex* Gaastdiep *-2006* **Industrial Shipping AS** Rederi AB Transatlantic SatCom: Inmarsat C 423614610 *Gibraltar* *Gibraltar (British)* MMSI: 236146000	**3,244** 1,554 4,077	Class: GL (LR) Classed LR until 26/7/07	**2000-05 Societatea Comerciala Severnav S.A. — Drobeta-Turnu Severin** Yd No: 730002 Loa 99.95 (BB) Br ex 16.50 Dght 4.600 Lbp 96.00 Br md 16.30 Dpth 6.30 Welded, 1 dk	**(A31A2GX) General Cargo Ship** Grain: 5,350 TEU 264 Compartments: 2 Ho, ER 2 Ha: ER Ice Capable	**1 oil engine** reduction geared to sc. shaft driving 1 CP propeller Total Power: 2,880kW (3,916hp) 13.0kn MaK 6M32 1 x 4 Stroke 6 Cy. 320 x 480 2880kW (3916bhp) MaK Motoren GmbH & Co. KG-Kiel AuxGen: 1 x 256kW 440V 50Hz a.c, 2 x 184kW 400V 50Hz a.c Thrusters: 1 Thwart. FP thruster (f) Fuel: 350.0 (d.f.)
8888563 *AUVX* -	**TRANSTAR** *ex* Transtar 1303 *-2008* *ex* TSM 256 *-2007* *ex* TSM 25 *-2005* *ex* Anita I *-2005* *ex* Obor I *-2003* *ex* Regal 4 *-1996* **Transtar Marine & Offshore Services** Amba Shipping & Logistics Pvt Ltd *Mumbai* *India* MMSI: 419076900 Official number: 3464	**177** 53 124	Class: IR (AB) (KI)	**1995-12 Zhenjiang Shipyard — Zhenjiang JS** Yd No: 92/9 Loa 25.20 Br ex 8.01 Dght 2.409 Lbp 23.50 Br md 7.99 Dpth 2.99 Welded, 1 dk	**(B32A2ST) Tug**	**2 oil engines** reverse reduction geared to sc. shaft (s) driving 2 FP propellers Total Power: 1,176kW (1,598hp) 12.0kn Yanmar 6N165-EN 2 x 4 Stroke 6 Cy. 165 x 232 each-588kW (799bhp) Yanmar Diesel Engine Co Ltd-Japan
9501942 - -	**TRANSTAR 18** **Transtar Marine Pte Ltd** - *Indonesia*	**294** 89 -	Class: GL	**2009-08 Eastern Marine Shipbuilding Sdn Bhd — Sibu** Yd No: 82 Loa 30.00 Br ex - Dght 3.500 Lbp 28.72 Br md 8.60 Dpth 4.20 Welded, 1 dk	**(B32A2ST) Tug**	**2 oil engines** reduction geared to sc. shafts driving 2 FP propellers Total Power: 2,354kW (3,200hp) 12.0kn Cummins KTA-50-M2 2 x Vee 4 Stroke 16 Cy. 159 x 159 each-1177kW (1600bhp) Cummins Engine Co Inc-USA

LR/IMO No. / Call sign / Flag	Name / Owner / Manager	GT / NT / DWT	Class	Builder / Dimensions	Type / Cargo	Machinery
9343273 *SKHZ* -	**TRANSTIMBER** **Baltic Container Shipping (UK) Ltd** Rederi AB Transatlantic *Skarhamn* *Sweden* MMSI: 266247000	23,128 6,938 14,200	Class: NV	2007-04 **Stocznia Gdansk SA — Gdansk** (Aft & pt cargo sections) 2007-04 **Aker Yards Oy — Rauma** (Fwd & pt cargo sections) Yd No: 450 Loa 190.50 (BB) Br ex - Dght 7.800 Lbp 178.70 Br md 26.00 Dpth 15.30 Welded, 3 dks	**(A35A2RR) Ro-Ro Cargo Ship** Passengers: driver berths: 12 Stern door/ramp (centre) Len: 16.00 Wid: 23.60 Swl: - Lane-Len: 2774 Lane-clr ht: 5.20 Trailers: 155 Ice Capable	**2 oil engines** geared to sc. shaft driving 1 CP propeller Total Power: 18,000kW (24,472hp) 16.0kn MAN-B&W 9L48/60B 2 x 4 Stroke 9 Cy. 480 x 600 each-9000kW (12236bhp) MAN B&W Diesel AG-Augsburg AuxGen: 2 x 1500kW a.c, 1 x 2500kW a.c Thrusters: 1 Tunnel thruster (a); 2 Tunnel thruster (f) Fuel: 300.0 (d.f.) 970.0 (r.f.)
9595929 *9V9496* -	**TRANSTIME** **Transtime Marine Pte Ltd** Golden Harvest Marine Transportation Ltd *Singapore* *Singapore* MMSI: 566342000 Official number: 397198	32,987 19,231 56,726 T/cm 58.8	Class: LR ✠ **100A1** SS 01/2012 bulk carrier CSR BC-A GRAB (20) Nos. 2 & 4 holds may be empty ESP **ShipRight** (CM, ACS (B)) *IWS LI EP ✠ **LMC** **UMS** Cable: 632.5/73.0 U3 (a)	2012-01 **Jinling Shipyard — Nanjing JS** Yd No: JLZ9100408 Loa 189.99 (BB) Br ex 32.30 Dght 12.800 Lbp 185.00 Br md 32.26 Dpth 18.00 Welded, 1 dk	**(A21A2BC) Bulk Carrier** Grain: 71,634; Bale: 68,200 Compartments: 5 Ho, ER 5 Ha: ER Cranes: 4x30t	**1 oil engine** driving 1 FP propeller Total Power: 9,480kW (12,889hp) 14.2kn MAN-B&W 6S50MC-C 1 x 2 Stroke 6 Cy. 500 x 2000 9480kW (12889bhp) STX Engine Co Ltd-South Korea AuxGen: 3 x 600kW 450V 60Hz a.c Boilers: AuxB (Comp) 8.7kgf/cm² (8.5bar)
8747082 *FGE3996* -	**TRANSUD** - **Sarl TMDD** - *Pointe-a-Pitre* *France* MMSI: 329002750 Official number: 919679	188 - -		2006 **Chantiers Piriou — Concarneau** Loa 39.20 Br ex - Dght 2.400 Lbp - Br md 9.80 Dpth - Welded, 1 dk	**(A35D2RL) Landing Craft**	**2 oil engines** reduction geared to sc. shafts driving 2 Propellers Total Power: 866kW (1,178hp) 10.0kn Caterpillar 3406C-TA 2 x 4 Stroke 6 Cy. 137 x 165 each-433kW (589bhp) Caterpillar Inc-USA
9213088 *YLIC* -	**TRANSUND** *ex* Transeagle *-2013* *ex* Nordon *-2009* **VP Shipping Ltd** SIA 'Rix Shipmanagement' *Riga* *Latvia* MMSI: 275436000 Official number: 0482	13,340 5,157 16,612 T/cm 28.7	Class: LR ✠ **100A1** SS 09/2012 strengthened for heavy cargoes *IWS LI strengthened for regular discharge by heavy grab with maximum unladen weight of 25T Ice Class 1 A Max draught midship 9.615m Max/min draught aft 9.615/5.515m Max/min draught fwd 9.615/4.515m ✠ **LMC** **UMS** Eq.Ltr: F†; Cable: 577.5/55.0 U3 (a)	2002-09 **Fujian Mawei Shipbuilding Ltd — Fuzhou FJ** Yd No: 436-1 Loa 142.45 (BB) Br ex 22.10 Dght 9.380 Lbp 132.40 Br md 22.00 Dpth 12.80 Welded, 1 dk	**(A31A2GX) General Cargo Ship** Grain: 18,577; Bale: 18,577 TEU 658 C Ho 400 TEU C Dk 258 TEU Compartments: 3 Ho, Wing ER Cranes: 3x35t Ice Capable	**1 oil engine** driving 1 CP propeller Total Power: 7,562kW (10,281hp) 15.5kn MAN-B&W 7S42MC 1 x 2 Stroke 7 Cy. 420 x 1764 7562kW (10281bhp) Doosan Engine Co Ltd-South Korea AuxGen: 1 x 1600kW 400V 50Hz a.c, 3 x 680kW 400V 50Hz a.c Boilers: TOH (o.f.) 10.2kgf/cm² (10.0bar), TOH (ex.g.) 10.1kgf/cm² (9.9bar) Thrusters: 1 Thwart. FP thruster (f) Fuel: 130.0 (d.f.) 877.0 (r.f.) 27.0pd
9219460 *ZDEO2* -	**TRANSVOLANTE** *ex* Volante *-2013* *ex* Geuldiep *-2006* **Industrial Shipping AS** Rederi AB Transatlantic SatCom: Inmarsat C 423614710 *Gibraltar* *Gibraltar (British)* MMSI: 236147000 Official number: 734611	3,244 1,554 4,257	Class: GL (LR) Classed LR until 25/4/07	1999-12 **Societatea Comerciala Severnav S.A. — Drobeta-Turnu Severin** Yd No: 710003 Loa 99.95 (BB) Br ex 16.50 Dght 4.600 Lbp 96.35 Br md 16.30 Dpth 6.30 Welded, 1 dk	**(A31A2GX) General Cargo Ship** Grain: 5,578; Bale: 5,465 TEU 264 C. 264/20' Incl. 10 ref C. Compartments: 2 Ho, ER 2 Ha: (26.1 x 13.6) (39.7 x 13.6)ER Ice Capable	**1 oil engine** reduction geared to sc. shaft driving 1 CP propeller Total Power: 2,880kW (3,916hp) 12.5kn MaK 6M32 1 x 4 Stroke 6 Cy. 320 x 480 2880kW (3916bhp) MaK Motoren GmbH & Co. KG-Kiel AuxGen: 1 x 256kW 400V 50Hz a.c, 2 x 184kW 400V 50Hz a.c Thrusters: 1 Thwart. FP thruster (f) Fuel: 350.0 (d.f.)
9232785 *SJEI* -	**TRANSWOOD** *ex* Finnwood *-2008* **Longitude Shipping (UK) Ltd** Rederi AB Transatlantic SatCom: Inmarsat C 426588510 *Skarhamn* *Sweden* MMSI: 265885000	20,851 5,486 18,855	Class: LR ✠ **100A1** SS 04/2012 roll on-roll off cargo ship *IWS LI Nos.1 & 4 hold TwD's & No.2 hold inner btm, strengthened for regular discharge by heavy grabs (10T) Ice Class 1AS at 9.177m draught Max/min draught aft 9.177/7.00m Max/min draught fwd 9.177/5.41m Power required 9033kw, installed 12600kw ✠ **LMC** **UMS** Eq.Ltr: J†; Cable: 618.8/64.0 U3 (a)	2002-04 **Stocznia Gdynia SA — Gdynia** 2006-02 **Blohm + Voss GmbH — Hamburg** (Additional cargo section) Lengthened-2006 Loa 178.60 (BB) Br ex 25.99 Dght 9.000 Lbp 168.00 Br md 25.60 Dpth 16.30 Welded, 2 dks	**(A35A2RR) Ro-Ro Cargo Ship** Stern door/ramp (centre) Lane-Len: 900 Lane-clr ht: 6.20 Bale: 30,019 TEU 759 Compartments: 5 Ho, ER 3 Ha: (19.2 x 21.0)ER 2 (24.8 x 21.0) Ice Capable	**2 oil engines** with clutches, flexible couplings & sr geared to sc. shaft driving 1 CP propeller Total Power: 12,600kW (17,130hp) 17.5kn Wartsila 6L46C 2 x 4 Stroke 6 Cy. 460 x 580 each-6300kW (8565bhp) Wartsila Finland Oy-Finland AuxGen: 1 x 1400kW 400V 50Hz a.c, 3 x 700kW 400V 50Hz a.c Boilers: TOH (o.f.) 10.7kgf/cm² (10.5bar), TOH (ex.g.) 10.7kgf/cm² (10.5bar) Thrusters: 1 Tunnel thruster (f) Fuel: 165.0 (d.f.) 2019.0 (r.f.)
7703778 *5VCJ7* -	**TRANSWOOD** *ex* Yasin *-2013* *ex* Waren *-2004* *ex* Triumph Hong Kong *-2003* *ex* Hai Chun *-1999* **Transwood Maritime SA** Tempus Maritime Sarl *Lome* *Togo* MMSI: 671412000 Official number: TG-00496L	3,900 2,364 6,330	Class: PR (CR)	1979-02 **China Shipbuilding Corp (CSBC) — Kaohsiung** Yd No: 17 Loa 108.51 Br ex 16.31 Dght 6.651 Lbp 100.01 Br md 16.21 Dpth 8.11 Welded, 1 dk	**(A31A2GX) General Cargo Ship** Grain: 8,501; Bale: 8,000 Compartments: 2 Ho, ER 2 Ha: (28.1 x 8.3) (27.2 x 8.3)ER Derricks: 4x15t; Winches: 4	**1 oil engine** driving 1 FP propeller Total Power: 4,413kW (6,000hp) 10.5kn Mitsubishi 6UET45/75C 1 x 2 Stroke 6 Cy. 450 x 750 4413kW (6000bhp) Akasaka Tekkosho KK (Akasaka DieselLtd)-Japan AuxGen: 2 x 200kW 450V a.c Fuel: 557.0 (r.f.)
8631477 *JL5565* -	**TRANSWORLD** *ex* Kaiwa Maru *-2007* **Aoki Marine Co Ltd** - *Osaka, Osaka* *Japan* MMSI: 431500641 Official number: 129081	*171* - -		1988-03 **Y.K. Kaneko Zosensho — Hojo** Yd No: 155 Loa 28.00 Br ex 9.52 Dght 2.500 Lbp 25.00 Br md 9.50 Dpth 3.50 Welded, 1 dk	**(B32A2ST) Tug**	**2 oil engines** geared to sc. shaft driving 1 FP propeller Total Power: 736kW (1,000hp) 11.0kn Hanshin 6LU26G 2 x 4 Stroke 6 Cy. 260 x 440 each-368kW (500bhp) The Hanshin Diesel Works Ltd-Japan
9329605 *9MIB5* -	**TRANSWORLDMARK 05** *ex* Thuan An 05 *-2008* **Transworldmark Freight (M) Sdn Bhd** - *Port Klang* *Malaysia* MMSI: 533020300 Official number: 333900	999 603 1,805	Class: (VR)	2004-10 **Vinacoal Shipbuilding Co — Ha Long** Yd No: TKC-44 Loa 69.27 Br ex 10.82 Dght 4.200 Lbp 64.90 Br md 10.80 Dpth 5.10 Welded, 1 dk	**(A31A2GX) General Cargo Ship**	**1 oil engine** geared to sc. shaft driving 1 FP propeller Total Power: 530kW (721hp) Weifang 8170ZC 1 x 4 Stroke 8 Cy. 170 x 200 530kW (721bhp) Weifang Diesel Engine Factory-China
7017090 *9A8497* -	**TRAPA** *ex* Rosenort *-2002* **Jadran Tuna doo** - *Zadar* *Croatia*	115 34 41	Class: CS (DS) (GL)	1967 **VEB Schiffswerft "Edgar Andre" — Magdeburg** Yd No: 2828 Loa 26.42 Br ex 8.04 Dght 3.001 Lbp - Br md 7.60 Dpth 3.50 Welded, 1 dk	**(B32A2ST) Tug** Ice Capable	**1 oil engine** driving 1 CP propeller Total Power: 552kW (750hp) 10.0kn S.K.L. 6NVD48A-2U 1 x 4 Stroke 6 Cy. 320 x 480 552kW (750bhp) VEB Schwermaschinenbau "KarlLiebknecht" (SKL)-Magdeburg AuxGen: 2 x 34kW 220/380V 50Hz a.c
7337995 - -	**TRAPESUS 2** *ex* Kometa-19 *-2004* **Trapesus Tourism & Trading Inc** Gurgen Turizm ve Ticaret AS	120 36 14	Class: (RS)	1973 **Zavod im. "Ordzhonikidze" — Poti** Yd No: 831 Loa 35.11 Br ex 11.00 Dght 1.110 Lbp 30.36 Br md 6.00 Dpth 1.81 Welded, 1 dk	**(A37B2PS) Passenger Ship** Hull Material: Aluminium Alloy Passengers: unberthed: 114	**2 oil engines** geared to sc. shafts driving 2 Contra-rotating propellers Total Power: 1,620kW (2,202hp) 30.0kn Zvezda M416 2 x Vee 4 Stroke 12 Cy. 180 x 200 each-810kW (1101bhp) (new engine 1980) "Zvezda"-Leningrad AuxGen: 2 x 3kW, 1 x 4kW Fuel: 4.0 (d.f.)

Ship	Tonnage	Class	Build & dimensions	Type	Machinery
9145231 **TRAPEZITZA** *9HAZ8* - **Trapezitza Maritime Ltd** Navigation Maritime Bulgare SatCom: Inmarsat C 424963710 *Valletta* *Malta* MMSI: 249637000 Official number: 9194	**13,965** 7,250 21,454	Class: GL (BR)	**2004-12 Bulyard Shipbuilding Industry AD — Varna** Yd No: 456 Loa 168.58 Br ex - Dght 8.516 Lbp 158.00 Br md 25.00 Dpth 11.50 Welded, 1 dk	**(A21A2BC) Bulk Carrier** Grain: 24,948 Compartments: 5 Ho, ER 5 Ha: ER Cranes: 3x16t Ice Capable	**1 oil engine** driving 1 FP propeller Total Power: 5,884kW (8,000hp) 14.0kn MAN-B&W 8L42MC 1 x 2 Stroke 8 Cy. 420 x 1360 5884kW (8000bhp) AO Bryanskiy MashinostroitelnyyZavod (BMZ)-Bryansk
8650253 **TRASAVIK** *LNTU* R-82-ES **Sigmund Larsen** - *Egersund* *Norway*	**164** 65 -		**2006-01 Stocznia Polnocna SA (Northern Shipyard) — Gdansk** Yd No: 334/1 Loa 19.92 Br ex - Dght - Lbp - Br md 7.52 Dpth 3.80 Welded, 1 dk	**(B11B2FV) Fishing Vessel**	**1 oil engine** reduction geared to sc. shaft driving 1 FP propeller
8960270 **TRATICA** *9AA5211* - *ex* Miss Gena *-2001* **Ribarski Obrt Hrvatski Uspjeh doo** - *Zadar* *Croatia*	**100** 30 -	Class: CS	**2000 Capt. Russ, Jr., Inc. — Chauvin, La** Yd No: 141 Loa 23.12 Br ex - Dght - Lbp 19.58 Br md 8.12 Dpth 2.54 Welded, 1 dk	**(B11B2FV) Fishing Vessel**	**1 oil engine** geared to sc. shaft driving 1 FP propeller Total Power: 224kW (305hp) Cummins NT-855-M 1 x 4 Stroke 6 Cy. 140 x 152 224kW (305bhp) Cummins Engine Co Inc-USA AuxGen: 1 x 127kW 220V 60Hz a.c
7522045 **TRATRINGA III** *HQWX9* - *ex* Cote des Isles *-2006* *ex* Brittania *-1997* *ex* Ternoy *-1991* *ex* Fjorddrott *-1990* **Societe Comorienne de Navigation** - SatCom: Inmarsat C 433455010 *San Lorenzo* *Honduras* MMSI: 334550000 Official number: L-0328209	*199* 116 30	Class: (BV) (NV)	**1976-06 Westermoen Hydrofoil AS — Mandal** Yd No: 48 Loa 26.65 Br ex 9.05 Dght 1.700 Lbp 26.12 Br md 9.00 Dpth 2.60 Welded, 1 dk	**(A37B2PS) Passenger Ship** Hull Material: Aluminium Alloy Passengers: unberthed: 140	**2 oil engines** sr geared to sc. shafts driving 2 FP propellers Total Power: 1,618kW (2,200hp) 28.0kn M.T.U. 12V493TY70 2 x Vee 4 Stroke 12 Cy. 175 x 205 each-809kW (1100bhp) MTU Friedrichshafen GmbH-Friedrichshafen AuxGen: 1 x 12kW 220V 50Hz a.c
7321946 **TRATRINGA IV** - - *ex* Kongsbussen *-2010* **Societe Comorienne de Navigation**	**183** 66 -	Class: (NV)	**1973-04 Westermoen Hydrofoil AS — Mandal** Yd No: 27 Loa 26.65 Br ex - Dght - Lbp 24.80 Br md 9.00 Dpth 2.60 Welded, 1 dk	**(A37B2PS) Passenger Ship** Hull Material: Aluminium Alloy Passengers: unberthed: 140	**2 oil engines** geared to sc. shafts driving 2 FP propellers Total Power: 1,766kW (2,402hp) M.T.U. 12V396 2 x Vee 4 Stroke 12 Cy. 165 x 185 each-883kW (1201bhp) (new engine 1993) MTU Friedrichshafen GmbH-Friedrichshafen AuxGen: 1 x 25kW 220V 50Hz a.c
8104541 **TRAVEBERG** *V2DQ8* - *ex* Vudi *-2010* *ex* Tafelberg *-2004* *ex* Helga *-1992* **m/s Traveberg Schiffahrts GmbH & Co KG** Reederei Lutz Jeske *Saint John's* *Antigua & Barbuda* MMSI: 305309000	**1,939** 885 2,890	Class: BV (GL)	**1981-12 J.J. Sietas KG Schiffswerft GmbH & Co. — Hamburg** Yd No: 874 Loa 87.97 (BB) Br ex 11.33 Dght 4.671 Lbp 85.30 Br md 11.30 Dpth 6.75 Welded, 2 dks	**(A31A2GX) General Cargo Ship** Grain: 3,806; Bale: 3,781 TEU 90 C.Ho 54/20' C.Dk 36/20' Compartments: 1 Ho, ER 1 Ha: (55.9 x 9.3)ER	**1 oil engine** reverse reduction geared to sc. shaft driving 1 FP propeller Total Power: 735kW (999hp) 11.5kn Deutz SBV8M628 1 x 4 Stroke 8 Cy. 240 x 280 735kW (999bhp) Kloeckner Humboldt Deutz AG-West Germany Thrusters: 1 Tunnel thruster (f)
7309572 **TRAVELER** *WYZ6883* - **Westbank Corp** Daybrook Fisheries Inc *Morgan City, LA* *United States of America* Official number: 507744	*386* 263 -		**1967 Patterson Shipyard Inc. — Patterson, La** Yd No: 21 L reg 48.04 Br ex 9.15 Dght - Lbp - Br md - Dpth 3.51 Welded	**(B11B2FV) Fishing Vessel**	**1 oil engine** driving 1 FP propeller Total Power: 971kW (1,320hp)
8855695 **TRAVELER** *WDD5082* - **Traveler Fisheries LLC** - *Seattle, WA* *United States of America* MMSI: 367153430 Official number: 929356	**388** 116 -		**1988 Johnson Shipbuilding & Repair — Bayou La Batre, Al** Yd No: 10 Loa - Br ex - Dght - Lbp 27.65 Br md 8.23 Dpth 3.51 Welded, 1 dk	**(B11B2FV) Fishing Vessel**	**1 oil engine** driving 1 FP propeller
9027623 **TRAVELIS PACIFIC VII** - - **PT Pelayaran Marindo Pacific** - *Samarinda* *Indonesia*	**273** 82 -	Class: KI	**2003-01 C.V. Teknik Jaya Industri — Samarinda** Loa 42.00 Br ex - Dght 2.350 Lbp 40.00 Br md 9.00 Dpth 3.00 Welded, 1 dk	**(A35D2RL) Landing Craft** Bow ramp (centre)	**2 oil engines** geared to sc. shafts driving 2 Propellers Total Power: 456kW (620hp) 7.0kn Mitsubishi 6D22 2 x 4 Stroke 6 Cy. 130 x 140 each-228kW (310bhp) (made 1997) Mitsubishi Heavy Industries Ltd-Japan AuxGen: 2 x 30kW 380/220V a.c
9204726 **TRAVELLER** *PHAM* - **Rederij Traveller** BigLift Shipping BV *Amsterdam* *Netherlands* MMSI: 246111000 Official number: 38068	**6,714** 2,888 8,729 T/cm 18.6	Class: BV	**2000-01 Zhonghua Shipyard — Shanghai** Yd No: 408 Loa 100.70 (BB) Br ex - Dght 8.200 Lbp 95.00 Br md 20.40 Dpth 11.10 Welded, 2 dks	**(A31A2GX) General Cargo Ship** Grain: 10,530; Bale: 10,300 TEU 371 C Ho 195 C.Dk 176 incl 24 ref C. Compartments: 1 Ho, ER, 1 Tw Dk 1 Ha: (64.4 x 15.3)ER Cranes: 2x275t Ice Capable	**1 oil engine** with flexible couplings & sr gearedto sc. shaft driving 1 CP propeller Total Power: 7,800kW (10,605hp) 16.5kn Wartsila 8L46B 1 x 4 Stroke 8 Cy. 460 x 580 7800kW (10605bhp) Wartsila NSD Finland Oy-Finland AuxGen: 1 x 900kW 440V 60Hz a.c, 3 x 530kW 440V 60Hz a.c Thrusters: 1 Thwart. CP thruster (f) Fuel: 98.0 (d.f.) (Heating Coils) 775.3 (r.f.) 28.0pd
9099755 **TRAVESAU** *ECEX* 3-GI-63-03 **Musisi SC** - *Aviles* *Spain* Official number: 3-3/2003	**243** - -		**2004-10 Andres Cajeao Alonso (Gestinaval S.L.) — Cudillero** Loa 28.50 Br ex - Dght 3.000 Lbp 22.60 Br md 8.00 Dpth - Welded, 1 dk	**(B11A2FS) Stern Trawler** Ins: 135	**1 oil engine** driving 1 Propeller Total Power: 294kW (400hp)
9193367 **TRAVESIA** *EARF* 3-GI-61-99 **El Musel SL** - *Aviles* *Spain* Official number: 3-1/1999	**183** - -		**1999-01 Andres Cajeao Alonso (Gestinaval S.L.) — Cudillero** Yd No: 298 Loa - Br ex - Dght - Lbp 26.58 Br md 7.20 Dpth 3.30 Welded, 1 dk	**(B11A2FS) Stern Trawler**	**1 oil engine** geared to sc. shaft driving 1 FP propeller Total Power: 309kW (420hp) GUASCOR F360TA-SF 1 x Vee 4 Stroke 12 Cy. 152 x 165 309kW (420bhp) Gutierrez Ascunce Corp (GUASCOR)-Spain
9053206 **TRAVESTERN** *XJBG* - **Coastal Shipping Ltd** - *St John's, NL* *Canada* MMSI: 316024245 Official number: 837268	**11,423** 5,611 17,088 T/cm 30.8	Class: GL	**1993-11 MTW Schiffswerft GmbH — Wismar** Yd No: 128 Loa 161.36 Br ex - Dght 8.599 Lbp 153.00 Br md 23.00 Dpth 11.70 Welded, 1 dk	**(A12B2TR) Chemical/Products Tanker** Double Hull Liq: 19,610; Liq (Oil): 19,610 Cargo Heating Coils Compartments: 2 Ta, 16 Wing Ta, 2 Wing Slop Ta, ER 13 Cargo Pump (s): 4x500m³/hr, 9x300m³/hr Manifold: Bow/CM: 78m Ice Capable	**1 oil engine** with flexible couplings & sr geared to sc. shaft driving 1 CP propeller Total Power: 6,600kW (8,973hp) 14.5kn MAN 7L48/60 1 x 4 Stroke 7 Cy. 480 x 600 6600kW (8973bhp) MAN B&W Diesel AG-Augsburg AuxGen: 3 x 512kW 220/440V a.c, 1 x 480kW 220/440V a.c Thrusters: 1 Thwart. FP thruster (f) Fuel: 193.0 (d.f.) (Heating Coils) 806.0 (r.f.)
5126512 **TRAVETANK** *DNJK* - *ex* Nordbunker VII *-1987* *ex* Gasoel IV *-1969* **Harry Stallzus GmbH** - *Kiel* *Germany* MMSI: 211262590 Official number: 2697	**153** 80 258	Class: GL	**1960-06 Norderwerft Koeser u. Meyer — Hamburg** Yd No: 842 Lengthened-1965 Loa 41.13 Br ex 6.33 Dght 2.080 Lbp 38.66 Br md 6.30 Dpth 2.44 Welded, 1 dk	**(A13B2TU) Tanker (unspecified)** Liq: 288; Liq (Oil): 288 Ice Capable	**1 oil engine** driving 1 FP propeller Total Power: 195kW (265hp) 9.0kn MWM RH330S 1 x 4 Stroke 6 Cy. 215 x 300 195kW (265bhp) Motoren Werke Mannheim AG (MWM)-West Germany
8855700 **TRAVIS & NATALIE** *WSP7281* - **Travis & Natalie Inc** - *Cape May, NJ* *United States of America* MMSI: 367130870 Official number: 666328	*130* 88 -		**1984 at Bayou La Batre, Al** Loa - Br ex - Dght - Lbp 23.47 Br md 6.77 Dpth 3.63 Welded, 1 dk	**(B11B2FV) Fishing Vessel**	**1 oil engine** driving 1 FP propeller

8718483 **TRAWIND GLORY**
9LC2141 *ex* Shinko Maru *-2004*
\- *ex* Shinko Maru No. 35 *-2004*
Matrix Base Holdings Ltd
\-
Freetown *Sierra Leone*
MMSI: 667006048
Official number: SL106048

1,421 Class: IS
762
2,150

1988-03 K.K. Miura Zosensho — Saiki Yd No: 810
Loa 65.00 Br ex - Dght -
Lbp - Br md 12.01 Dpth 6.81
Welded

(A31A2GX) General Cargo Ship

2 oil engines driving 2 FP propellers
Total Power: 2,354kW (3,200hp) 10.0kn
Akasaka A31
2 x 4 Stroke 6 Cy. 310 x 600 each-1177kW (1600bhp)
Akasaka Tekkosho KK (Akasaka DieselLtd)-Japan

9615652 **TRAYCE**
A6E2824 *ex* Newton 1 *-2012*
\- **Liwa Marine Services LLC**
\-
Abu Dhabi *United Arab Emirates*
MMSI: 470633000
Official number: 0006811

321 Class: NK
97
271

2011-10 Sarawak Land Shipyard Sdn Bhd — Miri
Yd No: 17
Loa 31.00 Br ex - Dght 3.510
Lbp 27.99 Br md 9.15 Dpth 4.30
Welded, 1 dk

(B32A2ST) Tug

2 oil engines reduction geared to sc. shafts driving 2 FP propellers
Total Power: 1,518kW (2,064hp)
Mitsubishi S6R2-MTK3L
2 x 4 Stroke 6 Cy. 170 x 220 each-759kW (1032bhp)
Mitsubishi Heavy Industries Ltd-Japan
Fuel: 260.0

7903782 **TREASURE**
XULX3 *ex* Ruby-3 *-2011* *ex* Tairyo *-2011*
\- *ex* Granit *-2006* *ex* Masu Maru No. 12 *-2001*
North Cargo Co Ltd
\-
Phnom Penh *Cambodia*
MMSI: 514046000
Official number: 0679309

196
58
200

1979-05 Nagasaki Zosen K.K. — Nagasaki
Yd No: 685
Loa 34.02 Br ex 6.33 Dght -
Lbp 30.03 Br md 6.30 Dpth 2.82
Welded, 1 dk

(B11B2FV) Fishing Vessel

1 oil engine driving 1 FP propeller
Total Power: 883kW (1,201hp)
Niigata 6MG25BX
1 x 4 Stroke 6 Cy. 250 x 320 883kW (1201bhp)
Niigata Engineering Co Ltd-Japan

8617940 **TREASURE**
PJNS *ex* Front Traveller *-2008*
\- *ex* Genmar Traveller *-2004*
ex Crude Traveller *-2003*
ex Nord-Jahre Traveller *-2000*
ex Jahre Traveller *-1993*
Treasure BV
Dockwise Shipping BV
Willemstad *Curacao*
MMSI: 306878000
Official number: 2008-C-

42,515 Class: NV
12,755
53,818
T/cm
108.2

1990-07 Brodogradiliste Split (Brodosplit) — Split
Yd No: 362
Converted From: Crude Oil/Products Tanker-2008
Loa 216.75 (BB) Br ex - Dght 10.440
Lbp 207.82 Br md 44.50 Dpth 14.00
Welded, 1 dk

(A38C3GH) Heavy Load Carrier, semi submersible

1 oil engine driving 1 FP propeller
Total Power: 13,356kW (18,159hp) 14.0kn
B&W 6S70MC
1 x 2 Stroke 6 Cy. 700 x 2674 13356kW (18159bhp)
Brodogradiliste Split (Brodosplit)-Yugoslavia
AuxGen: 3 x 900kW 440V 60Hz a.c, 1 x 160kW 440V 60Hz a.c
Thrusters: 1 Tunnel thruster (f)
Fuel: 264.0 (d.f.) 4256.0 (r.f.) 4.8pd

7322093 **TREASURE CHEST**
WYZ9409
\- **Ralbo Inc**
\-
Tampa, FL *United States of America*
Official number: 546753

125
85
\-

1973 Desco Marine — Saint Augustine, Fl
Yd No: 132-F
Loa 22.86 Br ex 6.74 Dght 2.744
Lbp - Br md - Dpth 3.81
Bonded

(B11A2FT) Trawler
Hull Material: Reinforced Plastic

1 oil engine driving 1 FP propeller
Total Power: 268kW (364hp) 9.0kn
Caterpillar D353TA
1 x 4 Stroke 6 Cy. 159 x 203 268kW (364bhp)
Caterpillar Tractor Co-USA

9448267 **TREASURE COAST**
WDD5896
\- **Treasure Coast LC**
Dann Marine Towing LC
Chesapeake City, MD *United States of America*
MMSI: 367165450
Official number: 1195693

341 Class: AB
102
309

2007-01 Rodriguez Boat Builders, Inc. — Coden, Al Yd No: 249
Loa 31.70 Br ex 10.40 Dght 3.660
Lbp 29.87 Br md 10.36 Dpth 4.34
Welded, 1 dk

(B32A2ST) Tug

2 oil engines reduction geared to sc. shafts driving 2 FP propellers
Total Power: 2,236kW (3,040hp)
Caterpillar 3512B-TA
2 x Vee 4 Stroke 12 Cy. 170 x 190 each-1118kW (1520bhp)
Caterpillar Inc-USA
AuxGen: 2 x 75kW a.c

8971360 **TREASURE LADY**
\- *ex* Tar Heel V *-1993*
\- -
\-

320
\-
\-

1981-01 Scully Bros. Boat Building, Inc. — Morgan City, La Yd No: 77
Loa - Br ex - Dght 2.560
Lbp 35.35 Br md 7.92 Dpth 3.20
Welded, 1 dk

(B21A20S) Platform Supply Ship

2 oil engines driving 2 FP propellers

7736426 **TREASURE LIVE No. 3**
\- *ex* Takojima Maru No. 82 *-1995*
\- **Marusho Shipping**
\-
San Lorenzo *Honduras*
Official number: L-1925361

153
74
\-

1978 Kitanihon Zosen K.K. — Hachinohe
Yd No: 138
Loa 38.00 Br ex - Dght 2.501
Lbp 34.12 Br md 6.80 Dpth 2.90
Welded, 1 dk

(B11B2FV) Fishing Vessel

1 oil engine driving 1 FP propeller
Total Power: 956kW (1,300hp)
Daihatsu 6DSM-26
1 x 4 Stroke 6 Cy. 260 x 320 956kW (1300bhp)
Daihatsu Diesel Manufacturing Co Lt-Japan

9578804 **TREASURE OF GALAPAGOS I**
HC5070
\- **Island Travel Cia Ltd**
\-
Puerto Ayora *Ecuador*
Official number: TN-01-00265

342
102
39

2009-11 Factoria Guido Moreno — Guayaquil
Yd No: 32.00/008/09
Loa 39.20 Br ex - Dght 3.520
Lbp 31.97 Br md 28.08 Dpth 11.20
Bonded, 1 dk

(A37A2PC) Passenger/Cruise
Hull Material: Reinforced Plastic

2 oil engines reduction geared to sc. shafts driving 2 Propellers
Total Power: 1,000kW (1,360hp)
Caterpillar
2 x 4 Stroke each-500kW (680bhp)
Caterpillar Inc-USA

9036789 **TREASURE PRINCESS**
HSB4750 *ex* Vietfracht 01 *-2012* *ex* Sea Pastrale *-2001*
\- *ex* Nan Shin *-1999* *ex* Nanshin I *-1991*
Ayudhya Development Leasing Co Ltd (ADLC)
Soopanava Intertrans Co Ltd
Thailand

4,852 Class: (NK) (CR) (VR)
3,110
8,049

1991-10 Nishi Shipbuilding Co Ltd — Imabari EH
Yd No: 368
Loa 109.58 (BB) Br ex - Dght 7.252
Lbp 102.00 Br md 18.30 Dpth 9.35
Welded, 2 dks

(A31A2GX) General Cargo Ship
Grain: 10,417; Bale: 9,692
TEU 214 C. 214/20'
Compartments: 2 Ho, ER
2 Ha: 2 (31.5 x 10.2)ER
Derricks: 2x25t,1x20t,1x18t

1 oil engine driving 1 FP propeller
Total Power: 3,354kW (4,560hp) 13.0kn
B&W 6L35MC
1 x 2 Stroke 6 Cy. 350 x 1050 3354kW (4560bhp)
The Hanshin Diesel Works Ltd-Japan
AuxGen: 2 x 308kW 440V a.c
Fuel: 50.0 (d.f.) 500.0 (r.f.) 13.5pd

9544865 **TREASURE SUNSHINE**
9V8020
\- **Ryoma Maritime Pte Ltd**
\-
SatCom: Inmarsat C 456405710
Singapore *Singapore*
MMSI: 564057000
Official number: 395184

6,522 Class: NK
3,516
9,934

2009-06 Kurinoura Dockyard Co Ltd — Yawatahama EH Yd No: 406
Loa 101.50 Br ex - Dght 8.608
Lbp 93.50 Br md 19.60 Dpth 13.00
Welded, 1 dk

(A31A2GX) General Cargo Ship
Grain: 15,462; Bale: 14,848
Derricks: 4x30t

1 oil engine driving 1 FP propeller
Total Power: 3,900kW (5,302hp) 12.0kn
MAN-B&W 6L35MC
1 x 2 Stroke 6 Cy. 350 x 1050 3900kW (5302bhp)
The Hanshin Diesel Works Ltd-Japan
AuxGen: 2 x 270kW a.c
Fuel: 520.0

6705755 **TREBBA**
IUYD *ex* Tornado *-1984*
\- **Italfish Srl**
\-
Naples *Italy*
Official number: 1885

466 Class: (RI)
157
385

1967 Cant. Nav. Mario Morini — Ancona Yd No: 89
Loa 50.42 Br ex 8.67 Dght 3.980
Lbp 41.99 Br md 8.54 Dpth 4.63
Welded, 1 dk

(B11A2FT) Trawler
Compartments: 1 Ho, ER

1 oil engine driving 1 FP propeller
Total Power: 971kW (1,320hp)
Deutz RBV8M545
1 x 4 Stroke 8 Cy. 320 x 450 971kW (1320bhp)
Kloeckner Humboldt Deutz AG-West Germany

6829927 **TREDAGH**
\- *ex* Bela *-1972* *ex* Tredagh *-1970*
\- **Nitrigin Eireann Teoranta**
\-
Dublin *Irish Republic*
Official number: 400037

192 Class: (BV)
110
\-

1958 Baan Hofman N.V. — Gorinchem
L reg 35.33 Br ex 6.74 Dght -
Lbp - Br md - Dpth -
Welded, 1 dk

(B33A2DS) Suction Dredger
1 Ha: (13.1 x 4.2)

1 oil engine driving 1 FP propeller
Total Power: 184kW (250hp) 8.0kn
Bohn & Kahler
1 x 4 Stroke 4 Cy. 280 x 400 184kW (250bhp)
Bohn & Kahler-Kiel

9358503 **TREFIN LEADER**
9HWS8
\- **Sea Leader Shipping Co Ltd**
Trefin Tankers Ltd
Valletta *Malta*
MMSI: 256535000
Official number: 9358503

4,811 Class: BV
2,294
7,000
T/cm
16.8

2007-03 Marmara Tersanesi — Yarimca Yd No: 72
Loa 119.10 (BB) Br ex - Dght 6.750
Lbp 111.60 Br md 16.90 Dpth 8.40
Welded, 1 dk

(A12B2TR) Chemical/Products Tanker
Double Hull (13F)
Liq: 8,025; Liq (Oil): 8,073
Compartments: 12 Wing Ta, ER
12 Cargo Pump (s): 12x335m³/hr
Manifold: Bow/CM: 57.6m
Ice Capable

1 oil engine reduction geared to sc. shaft driving 1 CP propeller
Total Power: 3,840kW (5,221hp) 14.0kn
MAN-B&W 6L32/44CR
1 x 4 Stroke 6 Cy. 320 x 440 3840kW (5221bhp)
AuxGen: 3 x 620kW 450V 60Hz a.c, 1 x 1100kW 450V 60Hz a.c
Thrusters: 1 Thwart. CP thruster (f)
Fuel: 45.1 (d.f.) 409.5 (r.f.) 15.2pd

6407327 **TREGEAGLE**
GMZH *ex* Forth *-1986* *ex* Flying Demon *-1984*
\- **McCormick Transport Ltd**
\-
Fowey *United Kingdom*
Official number: 304176

131 Class: (LR)
\- ✠ Classed LR until 15/8/86
30

1964-03 J. Lewis & Sons Ltd. — Aberdeen
Yd No: 344
Loa 28.20 Br ex 7.19 Dght -
Lbp 25.00 Br md 6.76 Dpth 3.36
Welded, 1 dk

(B32A2ST) Tug

1 oil engine driving 1 CP propeller
Total Power: 736kW (1,001hp)
Polar MN16
1 x 2 Stroke 6 Cy. 340 x 570 736kW (1001bhp)
British Polar Engines Ltd.-Glasgow
AuxGen: 2 x 30kW 220V d.c

9268382 **TREHUACO**
CB7380 *ex* Pionero *-2013*
\- -
\-
Valparaiso *Chile*
MMSI: 725001960
Official number: 3061

605
185
300

2002-12 Astilleros y Servicios Navales S.A. (ASENAV) — Valdivia Yd No: 137
Loa 68.00 Br ex - Dght -
Lbp - Br md 14.60 Dpth 2.80
Welded

(A36A2PR) Passenger/Ro-Ro Ship (Vehicles)
Passengers: unberthed: 192

4 oil engines reduction geared to sc. shafts driving 4 Directional propellers 2 fwd and 2 aft
Total Power: 1,412kW (1,920hp)
Caterpillar 3406C-TA
4 x 4 Stroke 6 Cy. 137 x 165 each-353kW (480bhp)
Caterpillar Inc-USA

7803308 *5IM438* -	**TREIZ RADJAB** *ex* Cinq Juin *-2012* **Oceaniss Co Ltd** - *Zanzibar* *Tanzania*	*857* 449 271	Class: (BV)	**1978-12 Chantiers et Ateliers de La Perriere — Lorient** Yd No: 314 Loa 58.20 Br ex 11.66 Dght 1.880 Lbp 52.91 Br md - Dpth 3.69 Welded, 1 dk	**(A35D2RL) Landing Craft** Bow door/ramp	**2 oil engines** reduction geared to sc. shafts driving 2 FP propellers Total Power: 882kW (1,200hp) 9.0kn Poyaud A12150SCRM 2 x Vee 4 Stroke 12 Cy. 150 x 180 each-441kW (600bhp) Societe Surgerienne de ConstructionMecaniques-France
7925297 *SIZM*	**TRELLEBORG** - **Stena Line Scandinavia AB** - *Trelleborg* *Sweden* MMSI: 265186000	**20,028** 6,471 3,800	Class: LR ✠ **100A1** SS 01/2012 train & vehicle ferry Baltic and Kattegat service, south of Gothenburg-Frederikshavn Ice Class 1A ✠ **LMC** **UMS** Eq.Ltr: F†; Cable: 577.5/58.0 U3	**1982-05 Oresundsvarvet AB — Landskrona** Yd No: 271 Loa 170.19 Br ex 23.80 Dght 5.817 Lbp 158.50 Br md 23.78 Dpth 8.16 Welded, 1 dk, 2nd dk except in way of machinery spaces	**(A36A2PT) Passenger/Ro-Ro Ship (Vehicles/Rail)** Passengers: unberthed: 900; cabins: 23; berths: 50 Stern door/ramp (centre) Len: - Wid: 10.00 Swl: - Side door Lane-Len: 680 Lane-Wid: 4.20 Lane-clr ht: 5.00 Lorries: 20, Cars: 15, Rail Wagons: 55 Ice Capable	**4 oil engines** with clutches, flexible couplings & sr geared to sc. shafts driving 2 CP propellers Total Power: 17,600kW (23,928hp) 17.0kn MAN 8L40/45 4 x 4 Stroke 8 Cy. 400 x 450 each-4400kW (5982bhp) Maschinenbau Augsburg Nuernberg (MAN)-Augsburg AuxGen: 1 x 2320kW 390V 50Hz a.c, 3 x 1776kW 390V 50Hz a.c, 1 x 400kW 390V 50Hz a.c Boilers: TOH (o.f.) 7.1kgf/cm² (7.0bar), TOH (ex.g.) 7.1kgf/cm² (7.0bar) Thrusters: 2 Thwart. CP thruster (f) Fuel: 78.5 (d.f.) 324.0 (r.f.)
9051442 *IBRD*	**TREMESTIERI** *ex* Koningin Beatrix *-2004* **MPS Leasing & Factoring SpA** Caronte & Tourist SpA *Reggio Calabria* *Italy* MMSI: 247107100	*5,042* 2,887 1,404	Class: RI (LR) ✠ Classed LR until 9/8/05	**1993-11 Koninklijke Schelde Groep B.V. — Vlissingen** Yd No: 375 Loa 113.60 Br ex 19.15 Dght 4.750 Lbp 110.00 Br md 18.70 Dpth 7.30 Welded, 1 dk	**(A36A2PR) Passenger/Ro-Ro Ship (Vehicles)** Passengers: unberthed: 1000 Bow door/ramp Len: - Wid: 7.50 Swl: - Stern door/ramp Len: - Wid: 7.50 Swl: - Lane-Len: 933 Cars: 210	**4 diesel electric oil engines** driving 4 gen. each 1600kW 6000V a.c Connecting to 4 elec. motors each (1500kW) driving 4 Directional propellers 2 fwd and 2 aft Total Power: 6,320kW (8,592hp) 17.0kn Kromhout 9FHD240 4 x 4 Stroke 9 Cy. 240 x 260 each-1580kW (2148bhp) Stork Wartsila Diesel BV-Netherlands AuxGen: 4 x 220kW 380V 50Hz a.c Fuel: 350.0 (d.f.)
5409615 *EI2626* WD 98	**TREMINOU** *ex* Orskov *-1963* *launched as* Copemar 1 *-1963* **Dunmore Marine Supply Co Ltd** - *Waterford* *Irish Republic* Official number: 401359	*115* 49 -	Class: (BV)	**1963 Orskovs Staalskibsvaerft A/S — Frederikshavn** Yd No: 15 Loa 25.61 Br ex 6.05 Dght 3.023 Lbp 23.58 Br md 6.00 Dpth 3.18 Welded, 1 dk	**(B11A2FT) Trawler** 3 Ha: (1.0 x 0.9)2 (1.5 x 0.9)	**1 oil engine** driving 1 FP propeller Total Power: 313kW (426hp) 11.5kn Alpha 405-24VO 1 x 2 Stroke 5 Cy. 240 x 400 313kW (426bhp) Alpha Diesel A/S-Denmark Fuel: 20.5 (d.f.)
9086772 *ILCK*	**TREMITI JET** *ex* Ono Ono *-2004* **Navigazione Libera del Golfo Srl** - *Naples* *Italy* MMSI: 247112500	**569** 170 64	Class: RI (BV)	**1994-06 Austal Ships Pty Ltd — Fremantle WA** Yd No: 35 Loa 48.00 Br ex 9.31 Dght 1.300 Lbp 44.30 Br md 9.00 Dpth 3.40 Welded, 1 dk	**(A37B2PS) Passenger Ship** Hull Material: Aluminium Alloy Passengers: unberthed: 450	**3 oil engines** with clutches, flexible couplings & sr geared to sc. shafts driving 3 Water jets Total Power: 5,880kW (7,995hp) 35.0kn M.T.U. 16V396TE74L 3 x Vee 4 Stroke 16 Cy. 165 x 185 each-1960kW (2665bhp) MTU Friedrichshafen GmbH-Friedrichshafen
9235969 *A8CG4*	**TREMONIA** *ex* Sag Bulk Canada *-2011* *ex* Swakop *-2010* **Asia Energy Inc** RBC Shipping Co Ltd *Monrovia* *Liberia* MMSI: 636016324 Official number: 16324	**17,784** 9,924 28,083 T/cm 39.5	Class: LR (AB) **100A1** SS 03/2011 bulk carrier strengthened for heavy cargoes Nos. 2 & 4 holds may be empty ESP ESN LI **LMC** **UMS**	**2001-06 Bohai Shipyard — Huludao LN** Yd No: 407-6 Loa 169.00 (BB) Br ex - Dght 9.700 Lbp 160.30 Br md 27.20 Dpth 13.60 Welded, 1 dk	**(A21A2BC) Bulk Carrier** Grain: 37,505; Bale: 35,836 Compartments: 5 Ho, ER 5 Ha: 4 (20.0 x 17.6)ER (16.0 x 13.6) Cranes: 4x40t	**1 oil engine** driving 1 FP propeller Total Power: 6,804kW (9,251hp) 14.3kn Sulzer 5RTA52 1 x 2 Stroke 5 Cy. 520 x 1800 6804kW (9251bhp) Yichang Marine Diesel Engine Co Ltd-China AuxGen: 3 x 500kW a.c
7037894 *WDE7314* -	**TREMONT** *ex* Alaskan Rose *-2010* *ex* Tremont *-1994* **Pacific Castle LLC** - SatCom: Inmarsat A 1536227 *Seattle, WA* *United States of America* MMSI: 367087370 Official number: 529154	**621** 248 -	Class: (AB)	**1970 Bay Shipbuilding Co — Sturgeon Bay WI** Yd No: 705 Loa 39.68 Br ex - Dght - Lbp 35.06 Br md 8.54 Dpth 4.88 Welded, 1 dk	**(B11A2FT) Trawler**	**1 oil engine** reverse reduction geared to sc. shaft driving 1 FP propeller Total Power: 956kW (1,300hp) EMD (Electro-Motive) 12-645-E5 1 x Vee 2 Stroke 12 Cy. 230 x 254 956kW (1300bhp) General Motors Corp-USA AuxGen: 2 x 45kW
8808783 *EACU* -	**TRENERU** - **Candiamar de Cedeira SL** - *Ondarroa* *Spain* MMSI: 224044980 Official number: 3-220/	**247** 74 110	Class: (BV)	**1989-03 Astilleros de Murueta S.A. — Gernika-Lumo** Yd No: 169 Loa 32.00 Br ex - Dght 3.352 Lbp 26.01 Br md 7.21 Dpth 3.41 Welded, 2 dks	**(B11A2FS) Stern Trawler**	**1 oil engine** with clutches, flexible couplings & sr geared to sc. shaft driving 1 CP propeller Total Power: 291kW (396hp) 10.5kn Wartsila 4R22 1 x 4 Stroke 4 Cy. 220 x 240 291kW (396bhp) Construcciones Echevarria SA-Spain AuxGen: 2 x 240kW 380V a.c
8820107 *9HA2729* -	**TRENLAND** *ex* Trenden *-2011* **Trenland Shipping Ltd** Klip Marine Shipmanagement Ltd (Klip Marine Shipmanagement OU) *Valletta* *Malta* MMSI: 215432000 Official number: 8820107	**3,826** 2,013 4,402	Class: NV (LR) (GL) Classed LR until 1/4/11	**1989-06 J.J. Sietas KG Schiffswerft GmbH & Co. — Hamburg** Yd No: 1040 Loa 104.80 (BB) Br ex 16.25 Dght 5.780 Lbp 97.90 Br md 16.00 Dpth 7.75 Welded, 1 dk	**(A31A2GX) General Cargo Ship** Grain: 6,461; Bale: 6,367 TEU 326 C.Ho 140 TEU C.Dk 186 TEU Compartments: 1 Ho, ER 1 Ha: (65.1 x 12.8)ER Ice Capable	**1 oil engine** with flexible couplings & sr reverse geared to sc. shaft driving 1 CP propeller Total Power: 2,960kW (4,024hp) 14.0kn Wartsila 8R32 1 x 4 Stroke 8 Cy. 320 x 350 2960kW (4024bhp) Wartsila Diesel Oy-Finland AuxGen: 1 x 540kW 220/380V a.c, 2 x 158kW 220/380V a.c Thrusters: 1 Thwart. FP thruster (f)
9456159 *V7SQ5* -	**TRENTA** - **Genshipping Corp** Splosna Plovba doo (Splosna plovba International Shipping & Chartering Ltd) *Majuro* *Marshall Islands* MMSI: 538003702 Official number: 3702	**32,987** 19,231 56,838 T/cm 58.8	Class: LR ✠ **100A1** SS 03/2010 bulk carrier CSR BC-A GRAB (20) Nos 2 & 4 holds may be empty ESP **ShipRight** (CM) *IWS LI ✠ **LMC** **UMS** Cable: 633.5/73.0 U3 (a)	**2010-03 Jiangsu Hantong Ship Heavy Industry Co Ltd — Tongzhou JS** Yd No: 021 Loa 189.99 (BB) Br ex 32.30 Dght 12.800 Lbp 185.00 Br md 32.26 Dpth 18.00 Welded, 1 dk	**(A21A2BC) Bulk Carrier** Grain: 71,634; Bale: 68,200 Compartments: 5 Ho, ER 5 Ha: ER Cranes: 4x35t	**1 oil engine** driving 1 FP propeller Total Power: 9,480kW (12,889hp) 14.2kn MAN-B&W 6S50MC-C 1 x 2 Stroke 6 Cy. 500 x 2000 9480kW (12889bhp) Doosan Engine Co Ltd-South Korea AuxGen: 3 x 600kW 450V 60Hz a.c Boilers: AuxB (Comp) 8.0kgf/cm² (7.8bar)
8313984 *UGDA*	**TREPANG** - **Rusryba Co Ltd** - *Murmansk* *Russia*	**257** 77 82	Class: RS	**1984-06 Stocznia Ustka SA — Ustka** Yd No: B275/03 Loa 28.80 Br ex - Dght 3.280 Lbp 26.37 Br md 8.01 Dpth 4.02 Welded, 1 dk	**(B11A2FS) Stern Trawler**	**1 oil engine** geared to sc. shaft driving 1 FP propeller Total Power: 552kW (750hp) Sulzer 6AL20/24 1 x 4 Stroke 6 Cy. 200 x 240 552kW (750bhp) Zaklady Przemyslu Metalowego 'HCegielski' SA-Poznan Fuel: 52.0 (d.f.)
9008794 *LDSU* -	**TRESFJORD** - **Fjord1 AS** - *Molde* *Norway* MMSI: 257013700	**3,423** 1,259 200	Class: (NV)	**1991-04 Eide Contracting AS — Hoylandsbygd** (Hull) **1991-04 Fiskerstrand Verft AS — Fiskarstrand** Yd No: 39 Loa 96.95 (BB) Br ex 15.50 Dght 4.250 Lbp 79.20 Br md 15.00 Dpth 7.50 Welded, 1 dk	**(A36A2PR) Passenger/Ro-Ro Ship (Vehicles)** Passengers: unberthed: 500 Bow door (centre) Stern door (centre) Cars: 155	**2 diesel electric oil engines** driving 2 Directional propellers 1 fwd and 1 aft Total Power: 4,759kW (6,471hp) 15.0kn Bergens C26: 33L9PG 1 x 4 Stroke 9 Cy. 260 x 330 2430kW (3304bhp) (new engine 2011) Rolls Royce Marine AS-Norway Normo BRM-6 1 x 4 Stroke 6 Cy. 320 x 360 2329kW (3167bhp) Bergen Diesel AS-Norway AuxGen: 2 x 2280kW a.c
7727920 *DUG9015* -	**TRESKA** *ex* Susana *-2011* *ex* Taikei Maru No. 51 *-1996* **Starcki Ventures Corp** - *Manila* *Philippines* Official number: IL03002638	*330* 162 682		**1978-05 Shimoda Dockyard Co. Ltd. — Shimoda** Yd No: 282 Loa 57.10 Br ex 11.82 Dght 4.152 Lbp - Br md 11.41 Dpth 6.86 Welded, 1 dk	**(B11B2FV) Fishing Vessel**	**1 oil engine** driving 1 FP propeller Total Power: 1,839kW (2,500hp) Akasaka AH38A 1 x 4 Stroke 6 Cy. 380 x 600 1839kW (2500bhp) Akasaka Tekkosho KK (Akasaka DieselLtd)-Japan
8214748 *PMZE* -	**TRESNAWATI** *ex* Dongjin Apollo *-2009* *ex* Jinwamaru *-1996* *ex* Jinwa Maru *-1987* **PT Mega Finadana** - *Jakarta* *Indonesia*	**2,872** 1,806 4,122	Class: KI (KR) (NK)	**1983-03 Namikata Shipbuilding Co Ltd — Imabari EH** Yd No: 111 Loa 84.31 (BB) Br ex 14.53 Dght 6.321 Lbp 78.01 Br md 14.51 Dpth 8.50 Welded, 2 dks	**(A31A2GX) General Cargo Ship** Grain: 6,254; Bale: 5,618 TEU 99 C. 99/20' (40') Compartments: 2 Ho, ER 2 Ha: (12.3 x 10.0) (28.5 x 10.0)ER Derricks: 1x22t,2x15t	**1 oil engine** driving 1 FP propeller Total Power: 1,692kW (2,300hp) 10.3kn Akasaka DM38AK 1 x 4 Stroke 6 Cy. 380 x 600 1692kW (2300bhp) Akasaka Tekkosho KK (Akasaka DieselLtd)-Japan AuxGen: 2 x 177kW 445V 60Hz a.c Fuel: 75.0 (d.f.) 206.0 (r.f.) 9.0pd

IMO / Call sign / Fishing no.	Name / Former names / Owner / Port / Flag	GT / NT / DWT	Class	Built / Dimensions	Type	Machinery
8136192 MGQN8 PZ 193	**TREVESSA IV** ex Jannetje -1999 ex Pieter -1982 ex Geertruida -1981 W Stevenson & Sons - Penzance United Kingdom MMSI: 232005890 Official number: A21657	135 86 -		1970 N.V. Jacht- en Scheepswerf M. Veldthuis — Groningen Yd No: 229 Loa 26.22 Br ex - Dght - Lbp - Br md 6.63 Dpth 2.80 Welded, 1 dk	(B11B2FV) Fishing Vessel	1 oil engine driving 1 FP propeller Total Power: 588kW (799hp) Deutz 1 x 4 Stroke 588kW (799bhp) (new engine 1980) Kloeckner Humboldt Deutz AG-West Germany
9359698 FMJQ DI 925754	**TREVIGNON** - Compagnie Francaise Du Thon Oceanique - Dzaoudzi France MMSI: 660001900	2,319 695 2,165	Class: BV	2006-07 Gdanska Stocznia 'Remontowa' SA — Gdansk (Hull) Yd No: B337/2 2006-07 Chantiers Piriou — Concarneau Yd No: 275 Loa 84.10 (BB) Br ex - Dght 6.680 Lbp 72.20 Br md 13.80 Dpth - Welded, 1 dk	(B11B2FV) Fishing Vessel	1 oil engine reduction geared to sc. shaft driving 1 Propeller Total Power: 4,000kW (5,438hp) Wartsila 8L32 1 x 4 Stroke 8 Cy. 320 x 400 4000kW (5438bhp) Wartsila Finland Oy-Finland
7939638 WCP6921 -	**TREVOR** ex H. A. Walker -1994 ex Itco XVI -1978 Weeks Marine Inc - New York, NY United States of America MMSI: 366643140 Official number: 597716	147 100 -		1978 Main Iron Works, Inc. — Houma, La L reg 21.04 Br ex 7.93 Dght - Lbp - Br md - Dpth 2.90 Welded, 1 dk	(B32A2ST) Tug	1 oil engine driving 1 FP propeller Total Power: 1,177kW (1,600hp)
7231050 WCX9769 -	**TREY B** - Earl Branch Jr - Houston, TX United States of America Official number: 536000	122 83 -		1971 Davis Shipbuilding Co. — Freeport, Tx Yd No: 5 L reg 20.76 Br ex 6.71 Dght - Lbp - Br md - Dpth 3.69 Welded	(B11B2FV) Fishing Vessel	1 oil engine driving 1 FP propeller Total Power: 294kW (400hp)
7048154 WDD9080 -	**TREY DELOACH** ex Robin Cenac -2001 ex Robin Rose -1992 Ingram Barge Co - St Louis, MO United States of America MMSI: 367306540 Official number: 517110	146 99 203		1968 Parker Bros. & Co., Inc. — Houston, Tx L reg 21.65 Br ex 8.08 Dght - Lbp - Br md - Dpth 2.72 Welded, 1 dk	(B32B2SP) Pusher Tug	1 oil engine driving 1 FP propeller Total Power: 449kW (610hp) Caterpillar 3412 1 x Vee 4 Stroke 12 Cy. 137 x 152 449kW (610bhp) Caterpillar Tractor Co-USA
9098359 FW8662 -	**TREZENCE** - Conseil General de la Charente Maritime - Marennes France MMSI: 227313860 Official number: 924046	104 54 -	Class: BV	1999-07 Societe des Etablissemnets Merre (SEEM) — Nort-sur-Erdre Yd No: 1900 Loa 28.00 Br ex - Dght 1.700 Lbp 25.80 Br md 6.85 Dpth 2.30 Welded, 1 dk	(B33B2DS) Suction Hopper Dredger Hopper: 60	2 oil engines geared to sc. shafts driving 2 Water jets Total Power: 396kW (538hp) 7.5kn Cummins 6CTA8.3-M 2 x 4 Stroke 6 Cy. 114 x 135 each-198kW (269bhp) Cummins Engine Co Inc-USA AuxGen: 1 x 68kW 380/220V 50Hz a.c
7529469 EHJZ -	**TRHES** - Remolques Unidos SL - Santander Spain Official number: 1-3/1992	166 82 146	Class: BV	1977-07 Astilleros de Santander SA (ASTANDER) — El Astillero Yd No: 129 Loa 25.30 Br ex 8.26 Dght 3.201 Lbp 23.12 Br md 8.01 Dpth 3.92 Welded, 1 dk	(B32A2ST) Tug	1 oil engine reduction geared to sc. shaft driving 1 FP propeller Total Power: 1,214kW (1,651hp) Caterpillar 3512B 1 x Vee 4 Stroke 12 Cy. 170 x 190 1214kW (1651bhp) (new engine 2000) Caterpillar Motoren GmbH & Co. KG-Germany Thrusters: 1 Tunnel thruster (f)
9107734 YDA4934 -	**TRI BAHAGIA** ex Profit Offshore 3 -2011 PT Tri Putri Masindo - Jakarta Indonesia	114 35 112	Class: KI (NK)	1994-03 Eastern Marine Shipbuilding Sdn Bhd — Sibu Yd No: 1 Loa 23.17 Br ex - Dght 2.388 Lbp 21.76 Br md 7.00 Dpth 2.90 Welded, 1 dk	(B32A2ST) Tug	2 oil engines driving 2 FP propellers Total Power: 692kW (940hp) Caterpillar 3408 2 x Vee 4 Stroke 8 Cy. 137 x 152 each-346kW (470bhp) Caterpillar Inc-USA Fuel: 85.0 (d.f.)
8924915 - -	**TRI BANTEN I** ex Oni VIII -2004 ex Zenei Maru No. 2 -2001 ex Nihonkai Maru -1996 PT Tri Bhakti Mandiri Lines - Indonesia	225 68 -		1969-06 Ando Shipbuilding Co. Ltd. — Tokyo Yd No: 204 Loa 29.50 Br ex - Dght 2.500 Lbp 26.00 Br md 8.00 Dpth 3.49 Welded, 1 dk	(B32A2ST) Tug	1 oil engine driving 1 FP propeller Total Power: 1,324kW (1,800hp) 10.0kn Niigata 6MG25AMG 1 x 4 Stroke 6 Cy. 250 x 320 1324kW (1800bhp) Niigata Engineering Co Ltd-Japan
9509114 3FEL4	**TRI FRIEND** - Ocean Friend Corp Ltd Temm Maritime Co Ltd Panama Panama MMSI: 357502000 Official number: 4282811	7,141 2,681 8,936	Class: NK	2011-07 Jong Shyn Shipbuilding Co., Ltd. — Kaohsiung Yd No: 175 Loa 110.00 (BB) Br ex 18.83 Dght 7.960 Lbp 102.00 Br md 18.80 Dpth 12.70 Welded, 1 dk	(A31A2GX) General Cargo Ship Grain: 13,449; Bale: 12,661 Compartments: 2 Ho, 2 Tw Dk, ER 2 Ha: ER 2 (25.5 x 13.5) Cranes: 2x30t	1 oil engine driving 1 FP propeller Total Power: 3,309kW (4,499hp) 13.0kn Hanshin LH46LA 1 x 4 Stroke 6 Cy. 460 x 880 3309kW (4499bhp) The Hanshin Diesel Works Ltd-Japan Fuel: 560.0
9721607 - -	**TRI KHARISMA 01** - PT Mitha Samudera Wijaya - Pangkalbalam Indonesia Official number: GT.167 NO. 494/EED	167 51 -	Class: KI (Class contemplated)	2013-10 PT Pahala Harapan Lestari — Pangkalpinang Yd No: PHL-066 L reg 23.52 Br ex - Dght - Lbp - Br md 7.80 Dpth 3.40 Welded, 1 dk	(B32A2ST) Tug	2 oil engines reduction geared to sc. shafts driving 2 Propellers Total Power: 1,220kW (1,658hp) Yanmar 6AYM-ETE 2 x 4 Stroke 6 Cy. 155 x 180 each-610kW (829bhp) Yanmar Diesel Engine Co Ltd-Japan
7409475 YCRY -	**TRI LESTARI I** ex Mata IE-IV -1992 ex Sadewa -1991 PT Hokari Limex Pratama - Jakarta Indonesia	217 66	Class: KI	1975-09 P.T. Adiguna Shipbuilding & Engineering — Jakarta Yd No: 45 Converted From: Landing Craft-2007 Loa 39.48 Br ex - Dght 1.474 Lbp 36.43 Br md 9.73 Dpth 3.26 Welded	(A13B2TP) Products Tanker Bow door/ramp	2 oil engines driving 2 FP propellers Total Power: 354kW (482hp) Caterpillar D334 2 x 4 Stroke 6 Cy. 121 x 152 each-177kW (241bhp) Caterpillar Tractor Co-USA AuxGen: 2 x 40kW 415V a.c
8825274 - - -	**TRI LESTARI II** ex Bhaita Rahmat -1992 ex Irk II -1989 PT Adiguna Tri Lestari - Banjarmasin Indonesia	125 72 -	Class: (KI)	1984-02 P.T. Sama Marga — Banjarmasin Loa 29.00 Br ex 6.50 Dght 1.500 Lbp 26.75 Br md - Dpth 2.00 Welded, 1 dk	(A35D2RL) Landing Craft Bow door/ramp	2 oil engines geared to sc. shaft driving 1 FP propeller Total Power: 242kW (330hp) 8.0kn Yanmar 6HAL-ET 2 x 4 Stroke 6 Cy. 130 x 150 each-121kW (165bhp) (made 1981) Yanmar Diesel Engine Co Ltd-Japan AuxGen: 1 x 8kW 220V a.c
9068768 YD3356 -	**TRI MUKTI 03** ex Sriracha 1 -2006 PT Longkelai Hijau Bersama - Batam Indonesia	255 77 -	Class: KI	1994-01 Marine Acme Thai Dockyard — Thailand Loa 29.30 Br ex - Dght 3.000 Lbp 26.00 Br md 8.80 Dpth 3.80 Welded, 1 dk	(B32A2ST) Tug	2 oil engines driving 2 Propellers Total Power: 2,428kW (3,302hp) Fuji 6S32FH 2 x 4 Stroke 6 Cy. 320 x 500 each-1214kW (1651bhp) Fuji Diesel Co Ltd-Japan
7919925 HSSB -	**TRI PAKEE 2** ex Faifah Khanom No. 2 -2005 Phuket Tripakee Co Ltd - Phuket Thailand Official number: 231113650	694 320 1,065	Class: (NK)	1980-07 Uchida Zosen — Ise Yd No: 804 Loa 55.81 Br ex 10.04 Dght 4.012 Lbp 52.00 Br md 10.00 Dpth 4.60 Welded, 1 dk	(A13B2TU) Tanker (unspecified) Single Hull Liq: 1,109; Liq (Oil): 1,109	1 oil engine sr geared to sc. shaft driving 1 FP propeller Total Power: 883kW (1,201hp) 11.0kn Daihatsu 6PSHTCM-26D 1 x 4 Stroke 6 Cy. 260 x 320 883kW (1201bhp) Daihatsu Diesel Manufacturing Co Lt-Japan AuxGen: 2 x 72kW
8736899 YDKF -	**TRI SAKTI ADINDA** ex Labitra Adinda -2010 ex Sonbak 202 -2006 PT Tri Sakti Lautan Mas (Trimas Shipping) - Surabaya Indonesia Official number: 11514	669 201 1,000	Class: KI	2005 Wonsan Shipyard — Wonsan Yd No: 202 Loa 59.00 Br ex - Dght 2.630 Lbp 51.20 Br md 13.50 Dpth 3.16 Welded, 1 dk	(A35D2RL) Landing Craft	2 oil engines reduction geared to sc. shafts driving 2 Propellers Total Power: 896kW (1,218hp) Yanmar 6LAA-UTE 2 x 4 Stroke 6 Cy. 148 x 165 each-448kW (609bhp) Yanmar Diesel Engine Co Ltd-Japan

9482328 *PMID* -	**TRI SAKTI ELFINA** *ex* Labitra Risa *-2012* *ex* Sonbak 205 *-2009* **PT Tri Sakti Lautan Mas (Trimas Shipping)** - *Tanjung Priok* *Indonesia* MMSI: 525010181	**721** 217 1,000	Class: KI	**2007-12 Wonsan Shipyard — Wonsan** Yd No: 205-07 Converted From: Landing Craft-2012 Loa 61.10 Br ex - Dght 2.630 Lbp 51.36 Br md 13.50 Dpth 3.16 Welded, 1 dk	**(A36A2PR) Passenger/Ro-Ro Ship (Vehicles)** Passengers: unberthed: 177 Bow ramp (centre)	**2 oil engines** reduction geared to sc. shafts driving 2 FP propellers Total Power: 942kW (1,280hp) 10.0kn Cummins KTA-19-M3 2 x 4 Stroke 6 Cy. 159 x 159 each-471kW (640bhp) (made 2007) Chongqing Cummins Engine Co Ltd-China AuxGen: 2 x 64kW 400V a.c Fuel: 55.0
8858829 *YEXP* -	**TRI TUNGGAL** *ex* Pahala Baru *-2001* *ex* Terbit *-1994* *ex* Shinei Maru No. 11 *-1992* **PT Spectra Samudra Line** - *Jakarta* *Indonesia*	**658** 362 678	Class: (KI)	**1976-05 Higo Zosen — Kumamoto** Loa 52.60 Br ex - Dght 4.100 Lbp 49.30 Br md 9.30 Dpth 5.30 Welded, 1 dk	**(A31A2GX) General Cargo Ship** 1 Ha: (27.0 x 7.0)ER	**1 oil engine** driving 1 FP propeller Total Power: 736kW (1,001hp) 9.3kn Makita GNLH6275 1 x 4 Stroke 6 Cy. 275 x 450 736kW (1001bhp) Makita Diesel Co Ltd-Japan
7105146 *SMRJ* -	**TRIAD** *ex* Stromstjarna *-1995* *ex* Jernoy *-1988* **MMT Group AB** - *Gothenburg* *Sweden* MMSI: 265831000	**147** 44 20		**1970 Flekkefjord Slipp & Maskinfabrikk AS AS — Flekkefjord** Yd No: 105 Converted From: Ferry (Passenger/Vehicle) Loa 26.04 Br ex 7.01 Dght 2.439 Lbp 24.26 Br md 6.99 Dpth - Welded, 1 dk	**(B31A2SR) Research Survey Vessel** A-frames: 1x5t; Cranes: 1x2t	**1 oil engine** with clutches & sr geared to sc. shaft driving 1 CP propeller Total Power: 294kW (400hp) 9.0kn Volvo Penta D12D 1 x 4 Stroke 6 Cy. 131 x 150 294kW (400bhp) (new engine 2008) AB Volvo Penta-Sweden AuxGen: 1 x 38kW 220/380V 50Hz a.c Thrusters: 1 Thwart. FP thruster (f) Fuel: 12.7 (d.f.) 1.0pd
8937106 - -	**TRIADA** *ex* Delfin IV *-2006* *ex* Tornado I *-2003* *ex* Kolkhida-1 *-2003* **Russobalt Co Ltd** Alien Ltd	**132** 39 13	Class: (RS) (PR) (RR)	**1986-01 Zavod im. "Ordzhonikidze" — Poti** Yd No: 116 Loa 34.50 Br ex 5.80 Dght 1.120 Lbp 31.90 Br md - Dpth 1.80 Welded, 1 dk	**(A37B2PS) Passenger Ship** Passengers: unberthed: 136	**2 oil engines** geared to sc. shafts driving 2 FP propellers Total Power: 1,920kW (2,610hp) 34.0kn M.T.U. 12V396 2 x Vee 4 Stroke 12 Cy. 165 x 185 each-960kW (1305bhp) MTU Friedrichshafen GmbH-Friedrichshafen AuxGen: 2 x 8kW Fuel: 4.0 (d.f.)
9101869 *UFKE* -	**TRIADA** *ex* Julia *-2009* *ex* Triada *-2009* **Marine Alliance Co Ltd** - *Nevelsk* *Russia* MMSI: 273812060	**683** 233 529	Class: RS	**1993-07 Khabarovskiy Sudostroitelnyy Zavod im Kirova — Khabarovsk** Yd No: 892 Loa 54.99 Br ex 9.49 Dght 4.460 Lbp 50.04 Br md 9.30 Dpth 5.16 Welded, 1 dk	**(B12B2FC) Fish Carrier** Ins: 632 Compartments: 2 Ho 2 Ha: 2 (3.0 x 3.0) Derricks: 4x3t Ice Capable	**1 oil engine** driving 1 FP propeller Total Power: 589kW (801hp) 11.3kn S.K.L. 6NVD48A-2U 1 x 4 Stroke 6 Cy. 320 x 480 589kW (801bhp) SKL Motoren u. Systemtechnik AG-Magdeburg
9086019 *YFEU* -	**TRIAKSA 15** **PT Tridharma Wahana** - SatCom: Inmarsat C 452503110 *Jakarta* *Indonesia* MMSI: 525019021	**1,374** 539 1,524 T/cm 8.3	Class: KI (AB)	**1995-04 P.T. Dok & Perkapalan Kodja Bahari (Unit I) — Jakarta** Yd No: 1167 Loa 65.00 Br ex - Dght 3.302 Lbp 61.15 Br md 15.00 Dpth 4.50 Welded, 1 dk	**(A13B2TP) Products Tanker** Single Hull Liq: 1,972; Liq (Oil): 1,972 Cargo Heating Coils Compartments: 8 Ta, ER 8 Cargo Pump (s): 8x75m³/hr	**1 oil engine** driving 1 FP propeller Total Power: 1,177kW (1,600hp) 10.7kn Hanshin LH28L 1 x 4 Stroke 6 Cy. 280 x 530 1177kW (1600bhp) The Hanshin Diesel Works Ltd-Japan AuxGen: 3 x 150kW 450V 60Hz a.c Fuel: 165.0 (d.f.) 5.3pd
7050133 *WP8558* -	**TRIANGLE I** *ex* Capt. Gould *-2009* *ex* State Line *-1977* **Fisherman's Wharf Filet Inc** - *United States of America* Official number: 514692	*149* 89 -		**1968 Atlantic Marine — Jacksonville, Fl** L reg 22.86 Br ex 7.32 Dght - Lbp - Br md - Dpth - Welded	**(B11B2FV) Fishing Vessel**	**1 oil engine** driving 1 FP propeller Total Power: 313kW (426hp)
8520680 *LAIZ4* -	**TRIANON** *ex* Nosac Star *-1996* **Wilhelmsen Lines Shipowning AS** Wilhelmsen Lines Car Carrier Ltd SatCom: Inmarsat C 425742910 *Tonsberg* *Norway (NIS)* MMSI: 257429000	**49,792** 15,050 15,536 T/cm 39.9	Class: NV	**1987-04 Tsuneishi Shipbuilding Co Ltd — Fukuyama HS** Yd No: 588 Loa 190.00 (BB) Br ex 32.24 Dght 9.121 Lbp 180.96 Br md 32.23 Dpth 13.92 Welded, 12 dks, incl. 4 dks hoistable	**(A35B2RV) Vehicles Carrier** Side door & ramp (s) Len: 25.00 Wid: 5.00 Swl: 25 Quarter stern door/ramp (s. a.) Len: 40.00 Wid: 7.00 Swl: 118 Cars: 5,828	**1 oil engine** driving 1 FP propeller Total Power: 9,003kW (12,240hp) 18.0kn B&W 6S60MCE 1 x 2 Stroke 6 Cy. 600 x 2292 9003kW (12240bhp) Mitsui Engineering & Shipbuilding CLtd-Japan AuxGen: 2 x 1200kW 450V 60Hz a.c, 1 x 700kW 450V 60Hz a.c, 1 x 128kW 450V 60Hz a.c Thrusters: 1 Thwart. CP thruster (f) Fuel: 205.0 (d.f.) 2858.0 (r.f.) 29.5pd
8402905 *UBNB* -	**TRIAS** **Pacific Engineering Co Ltd (PECO)** - SatCom: Inmarsat A 1400601 *Korsakov* *Russia* MMSI: 273420200 Official number: 841313	**2,559** 767 1,100	Class: RS	**1984-08 Fukushima Zosen Ltd. — Matsue** Yd No: 316 Loa 71.40 Br ex 16.00 Dght 4.500 Lbp 63.78 Br md - Dpth 7.00 Welded, 1 dk	**(B31A2SR) Research Survey Vessel**	**2 oil engines** geared to sc. shafts driving 2 CP propellers Total Power: 2,060kW (2,800hp) 12.0kn Fuji 6L27.5X 2 x 4 Stroke 6 Cy. 275 x 320 each-1030kW (1400bhp) Fuji Diesel Co Ltd-Japan AuxGen: 3 x 500kW a.c, 1 x 200kW a.c Fuel: 520.0 (r.f.)
9233222 *SYDF* -	**TRIATHLON** **Figaro Shipping Co Ltd** Tsakos Columbia Shipmanagement (TCM) SA SatCom: Inmarsat C 423782710 *Piraeus* *Greece* MMSI: 237827000 Official number: 11075	**84,586** 53,710 164,445 T/cm 123.1	Class: AB	**2002-12 Samho Heavy Industries Co Ltd — Samho** Yd No: 140 Loa 274.00 (BB) Br ex 50.30 Dght 17.022 Lbp 264.00 Br md 50.00 Dpth 23.10 Welded, 1 dk	**(A13A2TV) Crude Oil Tanker** Double Hull (13F) Liq: 173,947; Liq (Oil): 173,947 Cargo Heating Coils Compartments: 12 Wing Ta, 2 Wing Slop Ta, ER 3 Cargo Pump (s): 3x4000m³/hr Manifold: Bow/CM: 135.8m Ice Capable	**1 oil engine** driving 1 FP propeller Total Power: 18,624kW (25,321hp) 15.5kn B&W 6S70MC-C 1 x 2 Stroke 6 Cy. 700 x 2800 18624kW (25321bhp) Hyundai Heavy Industries Co Ltd-South Korea AuxGen: 3 x 850kW a.c Fuel: 152.0 (d.f.) 3780.0 (r.f.)
6512225 *VWYT* -	**TRIBENI** **Kolkata Port Trust** - *Kolkata* *India* Official number: 1184	*918* 216 204	Class: (LR) (IR) ✠ Classed LR until 27/10/78	**1965-06 Henry Robb Ltd. — Leith** Yd No: 493 Loa 61.12 (BB) Br ex 10.77 Dght 3.582 Lbp 53.35 Br md 10.67 Dpth 5.19 Riveted\Welded, 1 dk	**(B31A2SR) Research Survey Vessel**	**2 Steam Recips** driving 2 FP propellers 13.3kn Christiansen & Meyer Christiansen & Meyer-West Germany AuxGen: 3 x 85kW 220V d.c Fuel: 152.5 (r.f.)
9693240 *TCA3064* -	**TRIBILIN** *launched as* Bogazici 14 *-2014* **International Offshore Engineering & Development (IOED) Co CA** - *Istanbul* *Turkey* Official number: 1469	**463** 139 280	Class: BV	**2014-01 Dentas Gemi Insaat ve Onarim Sanayii A.S. — Istanbul** Yd No: 06-019 Loa 32.50 Br ex - Dght 4.300 Lbp 27.60 Br md 11.70 Dpth 5.60 Welded, 1 dk	**(B32A2ST) Tug**	**2 oil engines** reducation geared to sc.shafts driving 2 Directional propellers Total Power: 4,202kW (5,714hp) 13.0kn Caterpillar 3516C 2 x Vee 4 Stroke 16 Cy. 170 x 190 each-2101kW (2857bhp) Caterpillar Inc-USA
7315325 *YYV2862* -	**TRIBON** *ex* Renga *-2004* *ex* Tomma *-1997* **Galadriel SA** - *Venezuela* MMSI: 775312000	**514** 189 132	Class: (NV)	**1973-04 Sandnessjoen Slip & Mek. Verksted — Sandnessjoen** Yd No: 27 Loa 37.11 Br ex 9.68 Dght 2.769 Lbp 33.30 Br md 9.66 Dpth 4.12 Welded, 1 dk	**(A36A2PR) Passenger/Ro-Ro Ship (Vehicles)** Passengers: 200 Bow door & ramp Stern door & ramp Cranes: 1x4t Ice Capable	**1 oil engine** driving 1 CP propeller Total Power: 618kW (840hp) 11.0kn Normo LDMB-6 1 x 4 Stroke 6 Cy. 250 x 300 618kW (840bhp) AS Bergens Mek Verksteder-Norway AuxGen: 2 x 40kW 220V 50Hz a.c Thrusters: 1 Thwart. FP thruster (f) Fuel: 30.0 (d.f.)
9458664 *IN2440* -	**TRIBU** **Charter Ship Srl** Fraser Worldwide SAM *Genoa* *Italy* MMSI: 247215900	**783** - -	Class: RI	**2007-07 Mondo Marine SpA — Savona** Yd No: 21/1 Loa 50.50 Br ex 10.13 Dght 3.000 Lbp 46.00 Br md 9.80 Dpth 5.20 Welded, 1 dk	**(X11A2YP) Yacht**	**2 oil engines** reduction geared to sc. shafts driving 2 CP propellers Total Power: 1,840kW (2,502hp) 13.0kn Deutz TBD620V8 2 x Vee 4 Stroke 8 Cy. 170 x 195 each-920kW (1251bhp) Deutz AG-Koeln AuxGen: 2 x 180kW a.c Fuel: 100.0 (d.f.)
8405206 *YFOI* -	**TRIBUANA 1** *ex* Kawanoe No. 2 *-1997* **PT Tribuana Antar Nusa** - *Jakarta* *Indonesia*	**6,186** 1,856 2,658	Class: KI	**1984-05 Kochi Jyuko K.K. — Kochi** Yd No: 2326 Loa 115.63 (BB) Br ex - Dght 4.517 Lbp 107.02 Br md 21.01 Dpth 10.90 Welded, 2 dks	**(A36A2PR) Passenger/Ro-Ro Ship (Vehicles)** Passengers: unberthed: 400 Bow door/ramp Stern door/ramp Lane-Len: 580 Trailers: 62	**2 oil engines** sr geared to sc. shafts driving 2 FP propellers Total Power: 6,620kW (9,000hp) 17.5kn MaK 6M552AK 2 x 4 Stroke 6 Cy. 450 x 520 each-3310kW (4500bhp) Ube Industries Ltd-Japan AuxGen: 2 x 510kW 450V 60Hz a.c, 1 x 300kW 450V 60Hz a.c Fuel: 36.0 (d.f.) 220.0 (r.f.) 23.5pd

9307384 *PHLV* -	**TRICA** **CV Scheepvaartonderneming Trica II** Spliethoff's Bevrachtingskantoor BV SatCom: Inmarsat C 424491211 *Amsterdam* *Netherlands* MMSI: 244912000 Official number: 47393	**28,289** 8,486 18,250	Class: LR ✠ **100A1** SS 10/2012 roll on-roll off cargo ship container cargoes in hold, on trailer deck and weather deck *IWS LI Ice Class 1AS FS at a draught of 8.67m from bottom of keel Max/min draught fwd 8.67/4.00m from bottom of keel Max/min draught aft 8.67/6.50m from bottom of keel Power required 6602kw, power installed 25200kw ✠ **LMC** **UMS** Eq.Ltr: L†; Cable: 632.5/70.0 U3 (a)	**2007-09 Stocznia Szczecinska Nowa Sp z oo — Szczecin** Yd No: B201/II/04 Loa 205.00 (BB) Br ex 25.80 Dght 8.500 Lbp 190.00 Br md 25.50 Dpth 15.65 Welded, 3 dks	**(A35A2RR) Ro-Ro Cargo Ship** Passengers: driver berths: 12 Stern door/ramp (centre) Len: 17.50 Wid: 25.00 Swl: 85 Lane-Len: 2963 TEU 643 C Ho 346 TEU C Dk 297 TEU incl 20 ref C Compartments: 1 Ho, 1 RoRo Dk, ER Ice Capable	**2 oil engines** with clutches & sr geared to sc. shafts driving 2 CP propellers Total Power: 25,200kW (34,262hp) 22.7kn Wartsila 12V46 2 x Vee 4 Stroke 12 Cy. 460 x 580 each-12600kW (17131bhp) Wartsila Finland Oy-Finland AuxGen: 2 x 1700kW 450V 60Hz a.c, 2 x 1292kW 450V 60Hz a.c Boilers: e (ex.g.) 10.2kgf/cm² (10.0bar), TOH (o.f.) 10.2kgf/cm² (10.0bar) Thrusters: 2 Thwart. CP thruster (f) Fuel: 475.0 (d.f.) 1900.0 (r.f.)
9086514 *CB5224* -	**TRICAHUE** **Blumar Seafoods** - *Valparaiso* *Chile* MMSI: 725001500 Official number: 2834	**800** - 1,136	Class: (BV)	**1995-03 Ast. y Maestranzas de la Armada (ASMAR Chile) — Talcahuano** Yd No: 95 Loa 52.70 Br ex - Dght 5.950 Lbp 49.50 Br md 10.00 Dpth 6.90 Welded, 1 dk	**(B11B2FV) Fishing Vessel**	**1 oil engine** geared to sc. shaft driving 1 FP propeller Total Power: 1,765kW (2,400hp) 14.0kn Deutz SBV8M628 1 x 4 Stroke 8 Cy. 240 x 280 1765kW (2400bhp) Motoren Werke Mannheim AG (MWM)-Mannheim
9276987 *CA2705* -	**TRICAHUE I** *ex* Tongyeong No. 3 *-2008* **Sudamericana Agencias Aereas y Maritimas SA (SAAM)** - *Valparaiso* *Chile* MMSI: 725001793 Official number: 3226	**338** 101 -	Class: BV (KR)	**2002-07 Yeunsoo Shipbuilding Co Ltd — Janghang** Yd No: 8 Loa 34.10 Br ex - Dght 2.100 Lbp 28.60 Br md 9.50 Dpth 4.00 Welded, 1 dk	**(B32A2ST) Tug**	**2 oil engines** reduction geared to sc. shafts driving 2 FP propellers Total Power: 3,132kW (4,258hp) Caterpillar 3516 2 x Vee 4 Stroke 16 Cy. 170 x 190 each-1566kW (2129bhp) Caterpillar Inc-USA AuxGen: 2 x 100kW 225V a.c
8916906 *CUMB* -	**TRICANA DE AVEIRO** **Pescarias Beira Litoral Sarl** - SatCom: Inmarsat C 426344210 *Aveiro* *Portugal*	**172** 51 110	Class: RP	**1991-06 Estaleiros Sao Jacinto S.A. — Aveiro** Yd No: 181 Loa 24.00 Br ex 7.43 Dght 3.000 Lbp 20.97 Br md - Dpth 3.50 Welded, 1 dk	**(B11A2FS) Stern Trawler**	**1 oil engine** sr geared to sc. shaft driving 1 CP propeller Total Power: 441kW (600hp) 10.0kn Cummins KT-38-M 1 x Vee 4 Stroke 12 Cy. 159 x 159 441kW (600bhp) Cummins Engine Co Ltd-United Kingdom
9021459 *PMSL* -	**TRICHEM BONITA** *ex* Ratu Anggraini *-2010* *ex* Nickel Maru No. 8 *-2009* **PT Trichem International Shipping** - *Tanjung Priok* *Indonesia*	**736** 259 1,203	Class: KI	**1992-02 KK Ura Kyodo Zosensho — Awaji HG** Yd No: 286 Loa 64.73 (BB) Br ex - Dght - Lbp 60.00 Br md 10.00 Dpth 4.50 Welded, 1 dk	**(A13B2TP) Products Tanker** Liq: 1,350; Liq (Oil): 1,350 Compartments: 4 Ta, ER	**1 oil engine** geared to sc. shaft driving 1 FP propeller Total Power: 736kW (1,001hp) 12.0kn Hanshin LH28G 1 x 4 Stroke 6 Cy. 280 x 460 736kW (1001bhp) The Hanshin Diesel Works Ltd-Japan AuxGen: 1 x 133kW 225/130V a.c
8806333 *PNCW* -	**TRICHEM MARLIN** *ex* Ratu Paramitha *-2009* *ex* Sansen Maru *-2009* **PT Trichem International Shipping** - *Jakarta* *Indonesia* MMSI: 525019529	**744** 344 1,261 T/cm 5.3	Class: KI	**1988-04 Shin Kurushima Dockyard Co. Ltd. — Akitsu** Yd No: 2561 Loa 65.00 Br ex 10.03 Dght 4.161 Lbp 61.12 Br md 10.00 Dpth 4.50 Welded, 1 dk	**(A12A2TC) Chemical Tanker** Double Hull (13F) Liq: 1,229 Cargo Heating Coils Compartments: 8 Wing Ta, ER 2 Cargo Pump (s): 2x150m³/hr Manifold: Bow/CM: 24.6m	**1 oil engine** driving 1 FP propeller Total Power: 956kW (1,300hp) Hanshin 6LUN28 1 x 4 Stroke 6 Cy. 280 x 480 956kW (1300bhp) The Hanshin Diesel Works Ltd-Japan AuxGen: 2 x 107kW 225V a.c, 1 x 28kW 225V a.c Fuel: 7.0 (d.f.) 27.0 (r.f.)
9416484 *V7QV7* -	**TRICIA K** **Asian Offshore I AS** RK Offshore Management Pte Ltd *Majuro* *Marshall Islands* MMSI: 538003447 Official number: 3447	**1,763** 529 1,810	Class: AB	**2009-01** Yd No: 7033 Loa 60.00 Br ex - Dght 5.100 Lbp 54.10 Br md 16.00 Dpth 6.00 Welded, 1 dk	**(B21B20A) Anchor Handling Tug Supply**	**2 oil engines** reduction geared to sc. shafts driving 2 CP propellers Total Power: 4,412kW (5,998hp) 12.0kn Niigata 6MG28HLX 2 x 4 Stroke 6 Cy. 280 x 400 each-2206kW (2999bhp) Niigata Engineering Co Ltd-Japan AuxGen: 2 x 370kW a.c, 2 x 937kW a.c Fuel: 560.0
8134235 *YD4332* -	**TRIDAYA BARUNA 11** **PT Perusahaan Pelayaran Nasional Tasikmadu (Tasikmadu Shipping Co Ltd)** - *Jakarta* *Indonesia*	*112* 67 -	Class: (KI) (AB)	**1982-07 Greenbay Marine Pte Ltd — Singapore** Yd No: 27 Loa 21.60 Br ex - Dght 2.250 Lbp 20.55 Br md 6.89 Dpth 2.70 Welded, 1 dk	**(B32A2ST) Tug**	**2 oil engines** reverse reduction geared to sc. shafts driving 2 FP propellers Total Power: 764kW (1,038hp) 9.5kn Caterpillar 3412TA 2 x Vee 4 Stroke 12 Cy. 137 x 152 each-382kW (519bhp) Caterpillar Tractor Co-USA AuxGen: 2 x 30kW a.c
8134247 - -	**TRIDAYA BARUNA 12** **PT Tridaya Baruna** - *Jakarta* *Indonesia*	*112* 67 -	Class: KI (AB)	**1982-05 Greenbay Marine Pte Ltd — Singapore** Yd No: 28 Loa 21.60 Br ex - Dght 2.250 Lbp 20.55 Br md 6.89 Dpth 2.70 Welded, 1 dk	**(B32A2ST) Tug**	**2 oil engines** reverse reduction geared to sc. shafts driving 2 FP propellers Total Power: 764kW (1,038hp) 9.5kn Caterpillar 3412TA 2 x Vee 4 Stroke 12 Cy. 137 x 152 each-382kW (519bhp) Caterpillar Tractor Co-USA AuxGen: 2 x 30kW
8208490 - -	**TRIDAYA BARUNA 15** **PT Perusahaan Pelayaran Nasional Tasikmadu (Tasikmadu Shipping Co Ltd)** - *Jakarta* *Indonesia*	*144* 44 116	Class: (KI) (AB)	**1982-09 Heng Huat Shipbuilding & Construction Pte Ltd — Singapore** Yd No: T5 Loa - Br ex - Dght 2.700 Lbp 23.50 Br md 7.51 Dpth 3.13 Welded, 1 dk	**(B32A2ST) Tug**	**2 oil engines** reverse reduction geared to sc. shafts driving 2 FP propellers Total Power: 810kW (1,102hp) 9.0kn Yanmar S165L-ST 2 x 4 Stroke 6 Cy. 165 x 210 each-405kW (551bhp) Yanmar Diesel Engine Co Ltd-Japan AuxGen: 2 x 22kW
8322131 *YDHW* -	**TRIDAYA BARUNA 16** **PT Perusahaan Pelayaran Nasional Tasikmadu (Tasikmadu Shipping Co Ltd)** - *Jakarta* *Indonesia*	*123* 73 -	Class: KI (GL)	**1983 Greenbay Marine Pte Ltd — Singapore** Yd No: 30 Loa 23.90 Br ex 7.19 Dght 2.201 Lbp 22.41 Br md 7.17 Dpth 2.80 Welded, 1 dk	**(B32A2ST) Tug**	**2 oil engines** reverse reduction geared to sc. shafts driving 2 FP propellers Total Power: 764kW (1,038hp) 10.0kn Caterpillar 3412TA 2 x Vee 4 Stroke 12 Cy. 137 x 152 each-382kW (519bhp) Caterpillar Tractor Co-USA
8134259 - -	**TRIDAYA BARUNA 18** *ex* Tridaya Baruna 14 *-2012* **PT Tridaya Baruna** - *Jakarta* *Indonesia*	**113** 34 -	Class: KI (AB)	**1982-01 Greenbay Marine Pte Ltd — Singapore** Yd No: 29 Loa 21.60 Br ex - Dght 2.250 Lbp 20.55 Br md 6.86 Dpth 2.70 Welded, 1 dk	**(B32A2ST) Tug**	**2 oil engines** reverse reduction geared to sc. shafts driving 2 FP propellers Total Power: 764kW (1,038hp) 9.5kn Caterpillar 3412PCTA 2 x Vee 4 Stroke 12 Cy. 137 x 152 each-382kW (519bhp) Caterpillar Tractor Co-USA AuxGen: 2 x 30kW
8742991 - -	**TRIDAYA JAYA VI** **PT Pelayaran Prima Antar Bahari** - *Samarinda* *Indonesia*	**224** 134 161	Class: KI	**2009-10 in Indonesia** Loa 25.00 Br ex - Dght 2.730 Lbp 23.61 Br md 7.00 Dpth 3.25 Welded, 1 dk	**(B32A2ST) Tug**	**2 oil engines** reduction geared to sc. shafts driving 2 Propellers Total Power: 912kW (1,240hp) 10.0kn Yanmar 6LAH-STE3 2 x 4 Stroke 6 Cy. 150 x 165 each-456kW (620bhp) Yanmar Diesel Engine Co Ltd-Japan AuxGen: 2 x 35kW 415/380V a.c
8821852 *PBVO* -	**TRIDENS** **Government of The Kingdom of The Netherlands (Rijkswaterstaat Directie Noordzee)** - SatCom: Inmarsat A 1300345 *Rijswijk, Zuid Holland* *Netherlands* MMSI: 244033000 Official number: 2576	**2,199** 659 600	Class: BV (LR) ✠ Classed LR until 10/3/10	**1990-03 BV Scheepswerf & Mfbk 'De Merwede' v/h van Vliet & Co — Hardinxveld** Yd No: 653 Loa 73.54 (BB) Br ex 14.08 Dght 4.730 Lbp 64.02 Br md 13.86 Dpth 7.70 Welded, 2 dks	**(B12D2FR) Fishery Research Vessel** Ice Capable	**2 oil engines** with clutches, flexible couplings & sr geared to sc. shafts driving 2 CP propellers Total Power: 3,200kW (4,350hp) 14.0kn Deutz SBV8M628 2 x 4 Stroke 8 Cy. 240 x 280 each-1600kW (2175bhp) Kloeckner Humboldt Deutz AG-West Germany AuxGen: 1 x 625kW 380V 50Hz a.c, 2 x 530kW 380V 50Hz a.c Thrusters: 1 Thwart. CP thruster (f); 1 Thwart. CP thruster (a)

IMO / Call sign	Name / Owner	Tonnage	Class	Builder / Dimensions	Type	Machinery
1009986 *ZCYT9* -	**TRIDENT** **Kotero Marine Ltd** Megayacht Technical Services International Inc SatCom: Inmarsat C 431900185 *George Town* *Cayman Islands (British)* MMSI: 319764000 Official number: 742301	**1,226** 367 -	Class: LR ✠ **100A1** SS 07/2009 SSC Yacht (P), mono, G6 **LMC** **UMS** Cable: 385.0/28.0 U2 (a)	**2009-07 NMC Alblasserdam BV — Alblasserdam** (Hull) Yd No: (800) **2009-07 Jacht- en Scheepswerf C. van Lent & Zonen B.V. — Kaag** Yd No: (800) Loa 65.22 Br ex 11.43 Dght 3.520 Lbp 57.94 Br md 11.10 Dpth 5.75 Welded, 1 dk	**(X11A2YP) Yacht**	**2 oil engines** with clutches, flexible couplings & sr geared to sc. shafts driving 2 FP propellers Total Power: 2,800kW (3,806hp) M.T.U. 16V4000M60 2 x Vee 4 Stroke 16 Cy. 165 x 190 each-1400kW (1903bhp) MTU Friedrichshafen GmbH-Friedrichshafen AuxGen: 3 x 308kW 400V 50Hz a.c Thrusters: 1 Thwart. FP thruster (f); 1 Thwart. FP thruster (a)
9541693 *8PZA* -	**TRIDENT** **Barbados Coast Guard** *Bridgetown* *Barbados* MMSI: 314294000	**241** 72 60	Class: (BV)	**2009-01 Scheepswerf J Talsma BV — Franeker** (Hull) Yd No: (549867) **2009-01 B.V. Scheepswerf Damen — Gorinchem** Yd No: 549867 Loa 42.80 Br ex - Dght 2.520 Lbp 39.80 Br md 7.11 Dpth 3.77 Welded, 1 dk	**(B34H2SQ) Patrol Vessel**	**2 oil engines** with clutches, flexible couplings & sr geared to sc. shafts driving 2 FP propellers Total Power: 4,200kW (5,710hp) 24.0kn Caterpillar 3516B-HD 2 x Vee 4 Stroke 16 Cy. 170 x 215 each-2100kW (2855bhp) Caterpillar Inc-USA Thrusters: 1 Tunnel thruster (f)
9367970 *C6XI3* -	**TRIDENT** **Continent Maritime SA** Kotoku Kaiun Co Ltd (Kotoku Kaiun KK) *Nassau* *Bahamas* MMSI: 311010400 Official number: 8001563	**9,549** 5,672 12,561	Class: NK	**2008-09 Kyokuyo Shipyard Corp — Shimonoseki YC** Yd No: 483 Loa 145.12 (BB) Br ex - Dght 8.200 Lbp 134.00 Br md 22.40 Dpth 11.00 Welded, 1 dk	**(A33A2CC) Container Ship (Fully Cellular)** TEU 907 incl 120 ref C.	**1 oil engine** driving 1 FP propeller Total Power: 7,988kW (10,860hp) 17.3kn MAN-B&W 6L50MC 1 x 2 Stroke 6 Cy. 500 x 1620 7988kW (10860bhp) Hitachi Zosen Corp-Japan AuxGen: 3 x 540kW a.c Fuel: 1070.0
7356226 *VNW3522* -	**TRIDENT AURORA** **Clipper Holdings Pty Ltd** SatCom: Inmarsat C 450300287 *Fremantle, WA* *Australia* Official number: 355489	*169* 82 173	Class: (NV) (AB)	**1974-04 Carrington Slipways Pty Ltd — Newcastle NSW** Yd No: 95 Loa 29.88 Br ex 7.75 Dght 3.048 Lbp 26.22 Br md 7.73 Dpth 3.66 Welded, 1 dk	**(B11A2FT) Trawler**	**1 oil engine** driving 1 CP propeller Total Power: 423kW (575hp) 10.0kn Callesen 5-427-EOT 1 x 4 Stroke 5 Cy. 270 x 400 423kW (575bhp) Aabenraa Motorfabrik, HeinrichCallesen A/S-Denmark AuxGen: 1 x 114kW 415V 50Hz a.c, 1 x 72kW 415V 50Hz a.c Fuel: 74.0 (d.f.)
9555149 *V7TY7* -	**TRIDENT CHALLENGER** **Felicitae Investment Ltd** Marine Managers Ltd SatCom: Inmarsat C 453836176 *Majuro* *Marshall Islands* MMSI: 538003908 Official number: 3908	**33,044** 19,231 56,543 T/cm 58.8	Class: NK (BV)	**2010-11 Qingshan Shipyard — Wuhan HB** Yd No: 20060376 Loa 189.99 Br ex - Dght 12.820 Lbp 185.00 Br md 32.26 Dpth 18.00 Welded, 1 dk	**(A21A2BC) Bulk Carrier** Grain: 71,634; Bale: 68,200 Compartments: 5 Ho, ER 5 Ha: ER Cranes: 4x35t	**1 oil engine** driving 1 FP propeller Total Power: 9,480kW (12,889hp) 14.2kn MAN-B&W 6S50MC-C 1 x 2 Stroke 6 Cy. 500 x 2000 9480kW (12889bhp) Doosan Engine Co Ltd-South Korea AuxGen: 3 x a.c Fuel: 2400.0
9271377 *HOWJ* -	**TRIDENT HOPE** **Zahara Shipping Ltd** New Shipping Ltd *Panama* *Panama* MMSI: 357044000 Official number: 2901203C	**56,365** 32,506 105,985 T/cm 90.4	Class: AB	**2003-02 Namura Shipbuilding Co Ltd — Imari SG** Yd No: 233 Loa 241.03 (BB) Br ex - Dght 14.923 Lbp 232.00 Br md 42.00 Dpth 21.20 Welded, 1 dk	**(A13A2TV) Crude Oil Tanker** Double Hull (13F) Liq: 113,310; Liq (Oil): 119,674 Cargo Heating Coils Compartments: 12 Wing Ta, 2 Wing Slop Ta, ER 3 Cargo Pump (s): 3x2500m³/hr Manifold: Bow/CM: 119m	**1 oil engine** driving 1 FP propeller Total Power: 11,770kW (16,002hp) 15.0kn MAN-B&W 6S60MC 1 x 2 Stroke 6 Cy. 600 x 2292 11770kW (16002bhp) Mitsui Engineering & Shipbuilding CLtd-Japan AuxGen: 3 x 500kW a.c Fuel: 240.0 (d.f.) 2870.0 (r.f.)
9618513 *V7XA9* -	**TRIDENT LEGACY** **Kyraelma Shipping Ltd** Marine Managers Ltd SatCom: Inmarsat C 453837557 *Majuro* *Marshall Islands* MMSI: 538004437 Official number: 4437	**33,044** 19,231 57,000 T/cm 58.8	Class: NK (BV)	**2012-06 Qingshan Shipyard — Wuhan HB** Yd No: 20060386 Loa 189.99 (BB) Br ex - Dght 12.820 Lbp 185.00 Br md 32.26 Dpth 18.00 Welded, 1 dk	**(A21A2BC) Bulk Carrier** Grain: 71,634; Bale: 68,200 Compartments: 5 Ho, ER 5 Ha: 4 (21.3 x 18.3)ER (18.9 x 18.3) Cranes: 4x30t	**1 oil engine** driving 1 FP propeller Total Power: 9,480kW (12,889hp) 14.5kn MAN-B&W 6S50MC-C 1 x 2 Stroke 6 Cy. 500 x 2000 9480kW (12889bhp) STX Engine Co Ltd-South Korea AuxGen: 3 x 720kW 60Hz a.c Fuel: 2405.0
9206073 *V7WX3* -	**TRIDENT NAVIGATOR** *ex* Conquistador *-2011* *ex* Kookaburra *-2008* **Homeland Maritime Ltd** Marine Managers Ltd *Majuro* *Marshall Islands* MMSI: 538004414 Official number: 4414	**38,802** 25,378 75,607 T/cm 66.5	Class: NK (BV) (AB)	**2000-05 Sanoyas Hishino Meisho Corp — Kurashiki OY** Yd No: 1174 Loa 225.00 (BB) Br ex - Dght 13.997 Lbp 217.00 Br md 32.26 Dpth 19.30 Welded, 1 dk	**(A21A2BC) Bulk Carrier** Grain: 89,250 Compartments: 7 Ho, ER 7 Ha: (16.2 x 13.4)6 (17.1 x 15.0)ER	**1 oil engine** driving 1 FP propeller Total Power: 9,342kW (12,701hp) 14.5kn Sulzer 7RTA48T 1 x 2 Stroke 7 Cy. 480 x 2000 9342kW (12701bhp) Diesel United Ltd.-Aioi AuxGen: 3 x 400kW a.c Fuel: 3100.0 (r.f.) 34.0pd
8764511 *V7NP3* -	**TRIDENT ONE** *ex* Trident Bibby One *-2007* **Trident One LLC** Millennium Offshore Services Management Co FZE *Majuro* *Marshall Islands* MMSI: 538002991 Official number: 2991	**2,434** 730 1,451	Class: NV	**2001-03 Arab Heavy Industries PJSC — Ajman** Yd No: AS036 Converted From: Floating Crane-2008 Loa 50.29 Br ex 42.67 Dght 3.650 Lbp - Br md - Dpth 4.57 Welded, 1 dk	**(B22A2ZM) Offshore Construction Vessel, jack up** Passengers: berths: 60 Cranes: 2x50t	**3 diesel electric oil engines** driving 3 gen. each 1070kW a.c Connecting to 2 elec. motors driving 2 FP propellers Total Power: 4,500kW (6,117hp) 5.0kn Caterpillar 3512B-HD 3 x Vee 4 Stroke 12 Cy. 170 x 215 each-1500kW (2039bhp) Caterpillar Inc-USA Thrusters: 1 Tunnel thruster (f); 1 Tunnel thruster (a)
9343211 *9V7923* -	**TRIDENT STAR** **Trident Star Pte Ltd** Teekay Shipping (Singapore) Pte Ltd *Singapore* *Singapore* MMSI: 566763000 Official number: 398353	**56,365** 32,506 105,996 T/cm 90.4	Class: AB	**2005-11 Namura Shipbuilding Co Ltd — Imari SG** Yd No: 250 Loa 241.03 (BB) Br ex 42.03 Dght 14.923 Lbp 232.00 Br md 42.00 Dpth 21.20 Welded, 1 dk	**(A13A2TV) Crude Oil Tanker** Double Hull (13F) Liq: 113,310; Liq (Oil): 122,000 Cargo Heating Coils Compartments: 12 Wing Ta, 2 Wing Slop Ta, ER 3 Cargo Pump (s): 3x2500m³/hr Manifold: Bow/CM: 119m	**1 oil engine** driving 1 FP propeller Total Power: 11,770kW (16,002hp) 15.0kn MAN-B&W 6S60MC 1 x 2 Stroke 6 Cy. 600 x 2292 11770kW (16002bhp) Mitsui Engineering & Shipbuilding CLtd-Japan AuxGen: 3 x 500kW a.c Fuel: 220.0 (d.f.) 2700.0 (r.f.)
7805253 *FQHF* -	**TRIDENT VII** *ex* Siken *-1991* *ex* Tumleren *-1984* **Societe Sofinabail** Compagnie Generale Maritime et Financiere (CGMF) *St-Malo* *France* MMSI: 227006300 Official number: 785860	*234* 121 30	Class: (BV) (NV)	**1979-05 Westermoen Hydrofoil AS — Mandal** Yd No: 68 Loa 30.00 Br ex 9.05 Dght 1.420 Lbp 27.77 Br md - Dpth 3.13 Welded, 1 dk	**(A37B2PS) Passenger Ship** Hull Material: Aluminium Alloy Passengers: unberthed: 191	**2 oil engines** geared to sc. shafts driving 2 FP propellers Total Power: 2,648kW (3,600hp) 29.0kn AGO 195V12RVR 2 x Vee 4 Stroke 12 Cy. 195 x 180 each-1324kW (1800bhp) Societe Alsacienne de ConstructionsMecaniques (SACM)-France AuxGen: 2 x 36kW 220V 50Hz a.c
9086497 *CB5226* -	**TRIDENTE** **Blumar Seafoods** SatCom: Inmarsat C 472540023 *Valparaiso* *Chile* MMSI: 725001400 Official number: 2829	*777* 310 1,064		**1994-03 Astilleros y Servicios Navales S.A. (ASENAV) — Valdivia** Yd No: 093 Loa 52.70 (BB) Br ex 10.12 Dght 5.550 Lbp 49.50 Br md 10.00 Dpth 6.90 Welded, 1 dk	**(B11B2FV) Fishing Vessel** Ins: 997	**1 oil engine** with clutches, flexible couplings & sr geared to sc. shaft driving 1 CP propeller Total Power: 1,765kW (2,400hp) 14.0kn Deutz SBV8M628 1 x 4 Stroke 8 Cy. 240 x 280 1765kW (2400bhp) Motoren Werke Mannheim AG (MWM)-Mannheim Thrusters: 1 Thwart. FP thruster (f); 1 Tunnel thruster (a)
9464443 *AVAZ* -	**TRIDEVI PREM** *ex* Triloki Prem *-2009* *ex* Dong Hai Jun 2 *-2007* **Mercator Ltd** Ind-Aust Maritime Pvt Ltd *Mumbai* *India* MMSI: 419791000 Official number: 3595	**4,992** 1,497 7,058	Class: IR	**2006-12 Zhoushan Qifan Shiprepair & Building Co Ltd — Zhoushan ZJ** Yd No: 619 Loa 102.00 Br ex 18.82 Dght 6.610 Lbp 96.80 Br md 18.80 Dpth 8.60 Welded, 1 dk	**(B33B2DU) Hopper/Dredger (unspecified)**	**2 oil engines** geared to sc. shafts driving 2 FP propellers Total Power: 2,884kW (3,922hp) 12.0kn MAN G8V30/45ATL 2 x 4 Stroke 8 Cy. 300 x 450 each-1442kW (1961bhp) Ningbo CSI Power & Machinery GroupCo Ltd-China AuxGen: 3 x 300kW 400V 50Hz a.c Fuel: 235.0 (d.f.) 423.0 (r.f.)
8866278 *V4V02* -	**TRIFON** *ex* Solnes *-2013* *ex* Christina Bla *-2011* *ex* Skjervoyvaering *-2006* *ex* Arvikfisk *-2005* *ex* Alfredson *-1999* **Silver Haven SA** - *St Kitts & Nevis* MMSI: 341673000 Official number: SKN 1002588	*124* 49 -		**1971 Solstrand Slip & Baatbyggeri AS — Tomrefjord** Yd No: 19 Lengthened-1984 Loa 24.22 Br ex 6.36 Dght - Lbp - Br md - Dpth - Welded, 1 dk	**(B11B2FV) Fishing Vessel** Ins: 116	**1 oil engine** reduction geared to sc. shaft driving 1 FP propeller Total Power: 459kW (624hp) 10.5kn Caterpillar 3412TA 1 x Vee 4 Stroke 12 Cy. 137 x 152 459kW (624bhp) (new engine 1991) Caterpillar Inc-USA

IMO / Call sign / Flag	Name / Former names / Owner	Tonnage	Class	Builder / Dimensions	Type	Machinery
8217099 *YDHY* -	**TRIFOSA** *ex* Sinar Sejati 2 *-2012* *ex* Andhika Perdana *-2002* - - SatCom: Inmarsat C 452501410 *Jakarta* *Indonesia* MMSI: 525006001	**5,380** 2,242 6,774	Class: KI (NK)	**1983**-02 **Kochi Jyuko K.K. — Kochi** Yd No: 2271 Loa 100.17 Br ex - Dght 7.576 Lbp 89.79 Br md 18.80 Dpth 12.90 Welded, 1 dk	**(A31A2GX) General Cargo Ship** Grain: 12,600; Bale: 11,519 Compartments: 2 Ho, ER 2 Ha: ER Cranes: 4x20t	**1 oil engine** driving 1 FP propeller Total Power: 2,427kW (3,300hp) 14.0kn Hanshin 6EL40 1 x 4 Stroke 6 Cy. 400 x 800 2427kW (3300bhp) The Hanshin Diesel Works Ltd-Japan AuxGen: 3 x 470kW 420V a.c Fuel: 82.0 (d.f.) 431.5 (r.f.) 10.5pd
7436806 *WC8177* -	**TRIG LIND** *ex* Jerico Spirit *-2002* *ex* Universal Voyager *-2002* *ex* Annette Jones *-2002* *ex* Alice Ingram *-2002* **Lind Marine Inc** Jerico Products Inc *Petaluma, CA* *United States of America* MMSI: 366508420 Official number: 259926	*122* 83 -		**1950 Nashville Bridge Co. — Nashville, Tn** Yd No: 889 Loa - Br ex - Dght - Lbp 21.80 Br md 6.86 Dpth 2.67 Welded, 1 dk	**(B32A2ST) Tug**	**2 oil engines** geared to sc. shafts driving 2 FP propellers Total Power: 736kW (1,000hp) G.M. (Detroit Diesel) 12V-71 2 x Vee 2 Stroke 12 Cy. 108 x 127 each-368kW (500bhp) General Motors Detroit DieselAllison Divn-USA
7407324 *ODVX* -	**TRIGGER** *ex* Barcelona *-1992* *ex* Trigger *-1991* *ex* Nosac Trigger *-1988* *ex* Trigger *-1985* *ex* Hoegh Trigger *-1984* **Tia Shipping Sarl** Tamara Shipping *Beirut* *Lebanon* MMSI: 450553000 Official number: B-4353	**24,831** 7,938 8,405	Class: BV (KR) (NV)	**1976**-03 **B.V. Koninklijke Mij. "De Schelde" — Vlissingen** Yd No: 349 Converted From: Vehicles Carrier-2010 Loa 187.53 (BB) Br ex 22.94 Dght 8.010 Lbp 173.50 Br md 22.90 Dpth 16.79 Welded, 3 dks	**(A38A2GL) Livestock Carrier** Cargo Heating Coils Ice Capable	**1 oil engine** driving 1 FP propeller Total Power: 9,709kW (13,200hp) 18.0kn Sulzer 8RND68 1 x 2 Stroke 8 Cy. 680 x 1250 9709kW (13200bhp) BV Koninklijke Mij 'De Schelde'-Netherlands AuxGen: 3 x 550kW 440V 60Hz a.c Fuel: 2572.5 (r.f.) (Heating Coils) 44.5pd
8767537 *WDC8207* -	**TRIGGERFISH** *ex* Eric Danos *-2005* **All Coast LLC** - *New Orleans, LA* *United States of America* MMSI: 367083330 Official number: 902606	**273** 81 -		**1986 Blue Streak Industries, Inc. — Chalmette, La** Yd No: BLU JB 73 L reg 21.33 Br ex - Dght - Lbp - Br md 11.58 Dpth 2.43 Welded, 1 dk	**(B22A2ZM) Offshore Construction Vessel, jack up** Cranes: 1x40t	**2 oil engines** geared to sc. shafts driving 2 Propellers 8.0kn G.M. (Detroit Diesel) 12V-71-N 2 x Vee 2 Stroke 12 Cy. 108 x 127 Detroit Diesel Corporation-Detroit, Mi AuxGen: 2 x 50kW a.c
9144304 *A8NN8* -	**TRIGLAV** *ex* Andrea D *-2007* *ex* Western Island *-2004* **Genshipping Corp** Splosna Plovba doo (Splosna plovba International Shipping & Chartering Ltd) *Monrovia* *Liberia* MMSI: 636013529 Official number: 13529	**24,954** 13,530 42,527 T/cm 48.8	Class: BV (LR) (NV) ✠ Classed LR until 23/5/00	**1998**-02 **Ishikawajima-Harima Heavy Industries Co Ltd (IHI) — Kure** Yd No: 3084 Loa 181.50 (BB) Br ex 30.53 Dght 11.373 Lbp 172.00 Br md 30.50 Dpth 16.40 Welded, 1 dk	**(A21A2BC) Bulk Carrier** Grain: 53,853; Bale: 52,379 Compartments: 5 Ho, ER 5 Ha: (15.2 x 12.8)4 (19.2 x 15.2)ER Cranes: 4x30t	**1 oil engine** driving 1 FP propeller Total Power: 6,990kW (9,504hp) 14.3kn Sulzer 6RTA48T 1 x 2 Stroke 6 Cy. 480 x 2000 6990kW (9504bhp) Diesel United Ltd.-Aioi AuxGen: 3 x 490kW 450V 60Hz a.c Fuel: 197.9 (d.f.) 1551.6 (r.f.)
8827337 *YB6004* -	**TRIGUNA SEPULUH** - **PT Rejeki Abadi Sakti** - *Samarinda* *Indonesia*	*168* 107 -	Class: (KI)	**1981 P.T. Rejeki Abadi Sakti — Samarinda** Loa 33.52 Br ex 7.70 Dght 1.500 Lbp 32.96 Br md - Dpth 2.00 Welded, 1 dk	**(A35D2RL) Landing Craft** Bow door/ramp	**2 oil engines** driving 2 FP propellers Total Power: 514kW (698hp) Rolls Royce 2 x Vee 4 Stroke 12 Cy. each-257kW (349bhp) Rolls Royce Ltd.-Coventry AuxGen: 1 x 24kW 380V a.c
8615758 *YHLG* -	**TRIHANDAL 23** *ex* Tamayoshi Maru No. 12 *-2003* **PT Dharma Ichtiar Indo Lines** - *Surabaya* *Indonesia*	**786** 236 1,000	Class: KI	**1986**-10 **K.K. Matsuura Zosensho — Osakikamijima** Yd No: 332 Converted From: Grab Dredger-2006 Loa 51.06 (BB) Br ex 12.02 Dght 4.500 Lbp 46.00 Br md 12.00 Dpth 5.60 Welded, 1 dk	**(A31A2GX) General Cargo Ship** Grain: 523 Compartments: 1 Ho, ER 1 Ha: ER	**1 oil engine** with clutches, flexible couplings & reverse reduction geared to sc. shaft driving 1 FP propeller Total Power: 588kW (799hp) 8.3kn Niigata 6M28BGT 1 x 4 Stroke 6 Cy. 280 x 480 588kW (799bhp) Niigata Engineering Co Ltd-Japan AuxGen: 1 x 85kW 225V a.c Thrusters: 1 Thwart. FP thruster (f)
8318532 - -	**TRIHUT** - **Government of The Republic of India (Central Inland Water Transport Corp Ltd)** - *Kolkata* *India*	*219* - 62	Class: (LR) ✠ Classed LR until 15/12/87	**1987**-08 **Central Inland Water Transport Corp. Ltd. — Kolkata** Yd No: 396 Loa 29.70 Br ex 7.93 Dght 1.696 Lbp 27.41 Br md 7.61 Dpth 2.52 Welded, 1 dk	**(B32B2SP) Pusher Tug**	**2 oil engines** with clutches, flexible couplings & sr reverse geared to sc. shafts driving 2 FP propellers Total Power: 994kW (1,352hp) MAN R8V16/18TL 2 x 4 Stroke 8 Cy. 160 x 180 each-497kW (676bhp) Garden Reach Shipbuilders &Engineers Ltd-India AuxGen: 2 x 24kW 415V 50Hz a.c
8228098 - -	**TRIIN** *ex* Bester *-1992* *ex* RS-300 No. 172 *-1984* **Aleksandra Sazinova** -	**171** 51 88	Class: (RS)	**1984 Astrakhanskaya Sudoverf im. "Kirova" — Astrakhan** Yd No: 172 Converted From: Fishing Vessel-1992 Loa 33.97 Br ex 7.10 Dght 2.900 Lbp 29.98 Br md 7.00 Dpth 3.66 Welded, 1 dk	**(B12D2FP) Fishery Patrol Vessel** Ice Capable	**1 oil engine** driving 1 FP propeller Total Power: 224kW (305hp) 9.5kn S.K.L. 8NVD36-1U 1 x 4 Stroke 8 Cy. 240 x 360 224kW (305bhp) VEB Schwermaschinenbau "KarlLiebknecht" (SKL)-Magdeburg AuxGen: 2 x 75kW a.c, 1 x 28kW a.c Fuel: 7.0 (d.f.)
8207513 *PNVN* -	**TRIJAYA 1** *ex* Pioneer Tide *-2011* *ex* Asie Pioneer *-2001* *ex* Pioneer Seahorse *-1989* **PT Indoliziz Marine** - *Cirebon* *Indonesia* MMSI: 525016687	**867** 260 1,200	Class: AB KI	**1983 Eastern Marine, Inc. — Panama City, Fl** Yd No: 58 Loa - Br ex - Dght 3.911 Lbp 58.53 Br md 12.20 Dpth 4.58 Welded, 1 dk	**(B21B20A) Anchor Handling Tug Supply**	**2 oil engines** reverse reduction geared to sc. shafts driving 2 FP propellers Total Power: 3,310kW (4,500hp) 13.0kn EMD (Electro-Motive) 16-645-E7 2 x Vee 2 Stroke 16 Cy. 230 x 254 each-1655kW (2250bhp) (Re-engined ,made 1974, Reconditioned & fitted 1982) General Motors Corp.Electro-Motive Div.-La Grange AuxGen: 2 x 99kW Thrusters: 1 Thwart. FP thruster (f)
8207496 *PNXR* -	**TRIJAYA 2** *ex* Longbeach Tide *-2011* *ex* Asie Longbeach *-2001* *ex* Long Beach Seahorse *-1989* **PT Trijaya Global Marindo** - *Tanjung Priok* *Indonesia* Official number: 8768	**867** 260 1,115	Class: KI (AB)	**1982**-11 **Eastern Marine, Inc. — Panama City, Fl** Yd No: 56 Loa - Br ex - Dght 3.909 Lbp 58.53 Br md 12.20 Dpth 4.58 Welded, 1 dk	**(B21B20A) Anchor Handling Tug Supply**	**2 oil engines** reverse reduction geared to sc. shafts driving 2 FP propellers Total Power: 3,310kW (4,500hp) 13.0kn EMD (Electro-Motive) 16-645-E3 2 x Vee 2 Stroke 16 Cy. 230 x 254 each-1655kW (2250bhp) (Re-engined ,made 1974, Reconditioned & fitted 1982) General Motors Corp.Electro-Motive Div.-La Grange AuxGen: 2 x 99kW Thrusters: 1 Thwart. FP thruster (f)
8630801 *YGPG* -	**TRIJAYA ABADI** *ex* Seizan Maru No. 3 *-2004* **PT Pelayaran Mutiara Samudra Tirta Bahari** - *Surabaya* *Indonesia*	**1,108** 352 1,500	Class: KI	**1987**-02 **Katsumi Nakata — Japan** Converted From: Grab Dredger-2006 Loa 60.72 Br ex 12.52 Dght 4.750 Lbp 55.00 Br md 12.50 Dpth 6.30 Welded, 1 dk	**(A31A2GX) General Cargo Ship**	**1 oil engine** driving 1 FP propeller Total Power: 736kW (1,001hp) 10.0kn Niigata 6M28BGT 1 x 4 Stroke 6 Cy. 280 x 480 736kW (1001bhp) Niigata Engineering Co Ltd-Japan
8823410 *YHPB* -	**TRIJAYA LESTARI** *ex* Ryuzan Maru No. 15 *-2003* **PT Pelayaran Mutiara Samudra Tirta Bahari** - *Surabaya* *Indonesia*	*1,244* 439 1,500	Class: KI	**1988**-08 **Y.K. Takasago Zosensho — Naruto** Loa 71.44 Br ex - Dght 5.300 Lbp 65.00 Br md 11.00 Dpth 6.50 Welded, 1 dk	**(A31A2GX) General Cargo Ship**	**1 oil engine** driving 1 FP propeller Total Power: 736kW (1,001hp) Hanshin 6LU32G 1 x 4 Stroke 6 Cy. 320 x 510 736kW (1001bhp) The Hanshin Diesel Works Ltd-Japan AuxGen: 1 x 110kW 225V a.c
6705183 *YFVO* -	**TRIJAYA SAMUDRA** *ex* Samudra Jaya *-1998* *ex* Melaka Jaya III *-1997* *ex* Eastern Gold *-1986* *ex* Medway *-1982* *ex* Obrestad *-1978* *ex* Bore VIII *-1973* **PT Sinar Samudra Tripratama** - *Jakarta* *Indonesia* MMSI: 525013782	**1,307** 859 2,234	Class: KI (LR) ✠ Classed LR until 22/8/86	**1967**-04 **Oy Laivateollisuus Ab — Turku** Yd No: 256 Loa 71.91 Br ex 11.03 Dght 5.462 Lbp 66.88 Br md 11.00 Dpth 6.61 Welded, 2 dks	**(A31A2GX) General Cargo Ship** Grain: 3,248; Bale: 2,851 Compartments: 1 Ho, ER 2 Ha: (18.5 x 6.4) (13.1 x 6.4)ER Cranes: 1x5t,1x3t Ice Capable	**1 oil engine** driving 1 CP propeller Total Power: 1,030kW (1,400hp) 12.5kn Deutz RBV8M545 1 x 4 Stroke 8 Cy. 320 x 450 1030kW (1400bhp) Kloeckner Humboldt Deutz AG-West Germany AuxGen: 2 x 140kW 450V 60Hz a.c, 1 x 62kW 450V 60Hz a.c Fuel: 100.5 (d.f.) 4.5pd
8630370 *YGXZ* -	**TRIJAYA SENTOSA** *ex* Masuei Maru *-2001* **PT Pelayaran Mutiara Samudra Tirta Bahari** - *Surabaya* *Indonesia*	**664** 268 672	Class: KI	**1986**-09 **Katsumi Nakata — Japan** Loa 56.78 Br ex 9.42 Dght 3.290 Lbp 51.00 Br md 9.40 Dpth 5.50 Welded, 1 dk	**(A31A2GX) General Cargo Ship**	**1 oil engine** geared to sc. shaft driving 1 FP propeller Total Power: 625kW (850hp) 12.0kn Niigata 6M26AGTE 1 x 4 Stroke 6 Cy. 260 x 460 625kW (850bhp) Niigata Engineering Co Ltd-Japan

7816381 - -	**TRIJNTJE** - -	*146* 89 159		**1978**-07 **W. Visser & Zoon B.V. Werf "De Lastdrager" — Den Helder** Yd No: 89 Loa 36.20 Br ex 8.21 Dght 6.001 Lbp 33.61 Br md 7.01 Dpth 1.43 Welded, 1 dk	**(B11B2FV) Fishing Vessel**	**2 oil engines** geared to sc. shaft driving 1 FP propeller Total Power: 264kW (358hp) 7.0kn Scania DS8 2 x 4 Stroke 6 Cy. 115 x 125 each-132kW (179bhp) Saab Scania AB-Sweden
9179098 *DJEI* WYK 3	**TRIJNTJE** **Adriaan Leuschel Muschelfischereibetrieb** - *Wyk auf Foehr* *Germany* MMSI: 211282410 Official number: 2500	**377** 113 401	Class: (GL)	**1998**-07 **'Crist' Sp z oo — Gdansk** (Hull) **1998**-07 **B.V. Scheepswerf Maaskant — Bruinisse** Yd No: 525 Loa 42.90 Br ex 10.30 Dght 1.756 Lbp 39.30 Br md 10.00 Dpth 2.75 Welded, 1 dk	**(B11A2FT) Trawler**	**2 oil engines** reduction geared to sc. shafts driving 2 FP propellers Total Power: 588kW (800hp) 13.0kn Caterpillar 3412C-TA 2 x Vee 4 Stroke 12 Cy. 137 x 152 each-294kW (400bhp) Caterpillar Inc-USA
8870774 *YL2452* -	**TRIKS** *ex* Antey *-1992* **Tosmare Shipyard JSC** *Riga* *Latvia* Official number: 0113	**178** 53 46	Class: (RS)	**1971**-11 **"Petrozavod" — Leningrad** Yd No: 796 Loa 28.81 Br ex 7.10 Dght 3.650 Lbp 25.62 Br md - Dpth 3.66 Welded, 1 dk	**(B32A2ST) Tug** Ice Capable	**2 oil engines** driving 2 CP propellers Total Power: 882kW (1,200hp) 11.4kn Russkiy 6DR30/50-4-2 2 x 2 Stroke 6 Cy. 300 x 500 each-441kW (600bhp) Mashinostroitelnyy Zavod"Russkiy-Dizel"-Leningrad AuxGen: 2 x 25kW a.c
9534858 *VRIZ8* -	**TRIKWONG VENTURE** **Trikwong Maritime Inc** Dalian Ocean Shipping Co (COSCO DALIAN) SatCom: Inmarsat C 447703881 *Hong Kong* *Hong Kong* MMSI: 477274600 Official number: HK-3186	**157,225** 98,981 296,722 T/cm 177.9	Class: BV	**2012**-01 **Dalian Shipbuilding Industry Co Ltd — Dalian LN (No 2 Yard)** Yd No: T3000-43 Loa 330.00 (BB) Br ex 60.05 Dght 21.500 Lbp 316.00 Br md 60.00 Dpth 29.70 Welded, 1 dk	**(A13A2TV) Crude Oil Tanker** Double Hull (13F) Liq: 324,600; Liq (Oil): 335,000 Compartments: 5 Ta, 10 Wing Ta, ER, 2 Wing Slop Ta 3 Cargo Pump (s): 3x5500m³/hr	**1 oil engine** driving 1 FP propeller Total Power: 25,480kW (34,643hp) 15.8kn MAN-B&W 7S80MC 1 x 2 Stroke 7 Cy. 800 x 3056 25480kW (34643bhp) Doosan Engine Co Ltd-South Korea AuxGen: 3 x 975kW 60Hz a.c Fuel: 6830.0
7941552 *IUTA* -	**TRILONA** **Pietro Carponetti** - *Palermo* *Italy* Official number: 3201	*112* 51 -		**1970 Cant. Nav. A. Giorgetti — Viareggio** Loa 27.11 Br ex 6.23 Dght 2.690 Lbp 22.00 Br md 6.20 Dpth 2.90 Welded, 1 dk	**(B11B2FV) Fishing Vessel**	**1 oil engine** driving 1 FP propeller Total Power: 338kW (460hp) Caterpillar 3412TA 1 x Vee 4 Stroke 12 Cy. 137 x 152 338kW (460bhp) (new engine 1987) Caterpillar Inc-USA
7801219 *XUBU5* -	**TRIM** *ex* Adams *-2012* *ex* Priora *-2011* *ex* Koryo Maru No. 1 *-2010* *ex* Koryo Maru No. 11 *-2009* **Benefit Ltd** - *Phnom Penh* *Cambodia* MMSI: 515370000 Official number: 1078630	**493** 249 -		**1978**-04 **KK Kanasashi Zosen — Shizuoka SZ** Yd No: 1253 Converted From: Fishing Vessel-2010 Loa 55.89 Br ex - Dght 3.552 Lbp - Br md 8.91 Dpth 3.92 Welded	**(B12B2FC) Fish Carrier**	**1 oil engine** driving 1 FP propeller Total Power: 956kW (1,300hp) 10.0kn Hanshin 6LU32G 1 x 4 Stroke 6 Cy. 320 x 510 956kW (1300bhp) Hanshin Nainenki Kogyo-Japan
9003782 *JZEH* -	**TRIMA JAYA 9** *ex* Jaya *-2012* *ex* Princess Nomi *-2008* - - *Indonesia* MMSI: 525000090	*366* - 90		**1990**-03 **Matsuura Tekko Zosen K.K. — Osakikamijima** Yd No: 358 Loa 45.30 Br ex 9.82 Dght 2.700 Lbp 42.00 Br md 9.60 Dpth 3.70 Welded, 1 dk	**(A37B2PS) Passenger Ship**	**2 oil engines** sr reverse geared to sc. shafts driving 2 FP propellers Total Power: 2,060kW (2,800hp) Yanmar T260-ST 2 x 4 Stroke 6 Cy. 260 x 330 each-1030kW (1400bhp) Yanmar Diesel Engine Co Ltd-Japan Thrusters: 1 Thwart. FP thruster (f)
8666422 *XUHH2* -	**TRIMAS ELLISA II** *ex* Zi Jing Ba Hao *-1994* **PT Tri Sakti Lautan Mas (Trimas Shipping)** - *Phnom Penh* *Cambodia* MMSI: 515068000 Official number: 1494259	**2,977** 1,548 -		**1994**-06 **Zhoushan Shipyard — Zhoushan ZJ** Yd No: 0032 Loa 85.10 Br ex - Dght - Lbp - Br md 15.40 Dpth - Welded, 1 dk	**(A36A2PR) Passenger/Ro-Ro Ship (Vehicles)**	**2 oil engines** driving 2 Propellers Total Power: 2,648kW (3,600hp) 10.0kn Chinese Std. Type G6300ZC 2 x 4 Stroke 6 Cy. 300 x 380 each-1324kW (1800bhp) Ningbo Zhonghua Dongli PowerMachinery Co Ltd -China
8663092 *JZPU* -	**TRIMAS EXPRESS** *ex* Hu Hang 16 *-2013* **PT Tri Sakti Lautan Mas (Trimas Shipping)** - *Indonesia* MMSI: 525012283	**1,392** 835 -	Class: ZC	**1998**-12 **Shanghai Tonghua High Speed Ship Engineering Co Ltd — Shanghai** Loa 61.50 Br ex 13.20 Dght 2.800 Lbp 56.80 Br md 12.70 Dpth 4.40 Welded, 1 dk	**(A36A2PR) Passenger/Ro-Ro Ship (Vehicles)**	**2 oil engines** with clutches, flex coup & dr geared to sc. shafts driving 2 FP propellers Total Power: 1,200kW (1,632hp) MAN 6L20/27 1 x 4 Stroke 6 Cy. 200 x 20 600kW (816bhp) Shanghai Xinzhong Power MachinePlant-China MAN 6L20/27 1 x 4 Stroke 6 Cy. 200 x 270 600kW (816bhp) Shanghai Xinzhong Power MachinePlant-China
9376505 *V2FV8* -	**TRINA** **SAL Heavy Lift GmbH** - SatCom: Inmarsat C 430500491 *Saint John's* *Antigua & Barbuda* MMSI: 305816000 Official number: 4946	**13,058** 4,647 11,940	Class: GL	**2008**-11 **J.J. Sietas KG Schiffswerft GmbH & Co. — Hamburg** Yd No: 1277 Loa 159.80 (BB) Br ex - Dght 9.080 Lbp 148.31 Br md 24.00 Dpth 13.20 Welded	**(A31A2GX) General Cargo Ship** Grain: 19,299; Bale: 18,005 Compartments: 1 Ho, ER 1 Ha: ER Cranes: 2x700t,1x350t	**1 oil engine** reduction geared to sc. shaft driving 1 CP propeller Total Power: 12,600kW (17,131hp) 18.0kn MAN-B&W 9L58/64 1 x 4 Stroke 9 Cy. 580 x 640 12600kW (17131bhp) MAN B&W Diesel AG-Augsburg AuxGen: 3 x 1020kW a.c, 1 x 1500kW a.c Thrusters: 1 Tunnel thruster (f) Fuel: 200.0 (d.f.) 1400.0 (r.f.)
9642370 *D5DG7* -	**TRINA OLDENDORFF** **Oldendorff Carriers GmbH & Co KG** - *Monrovia* *Liberia* MMSI: 636092466 Official number: 92466	**41,091** 25,573 75,200 T/cm 68.3	Class: BV	**2013**-01 **Penglai Zhongbai Jinglu Ship Industry Co Ltd — Penglai SD** Yd No: JL0029 (B) Loa 225.00 (BB) Br ex - Dght 14.200 Lbp 217.00 Br md 32.26 Dpth 19.60 Welded, 1 dk	**(A21A2BC) Bulk Carrier** Grain: 89,728 Compartments: 7 Ho, ER 7 Ha: 6 (15.5 x 14.4)ER (14.6 x 13.2)	**1 oil engine** driving 1 FP propeller Total Power: 8,833kW (12,009hp) 14.5kn MAN-B&W 5S60MC-C 1 x 2 Stroke 5 Cy. 600 x 2400 8833kW (12009bhp) Hyundai Heavy Industries Co Ltd-South Korea AuxGen: 3 x 560kW 60Hz a.c Fuel: 2980.0
9261542 *ICBB* -	**TRINACRIA** **Tomasos Transport & Tourism** - *Naples* *Italy* MMSI: 247079100 Official number: 220	**24,409** 7,500 7,000	Class: RI	**2002**-11 **Cantiere Navale Visentini Srl — Porto Viro** Yd No: 194 Loa 186.25 (BB) Br ex - Dght 6.533 Lbp 169.50 Br md 25.60 Dpth 9.15 Welded	**(A36A2PR) Passenger/Ro-Ro Ship (Vehicles)** Passengers: 950 Lane-Len: 2100 Trailers: 156	**2 oil engines** geared to sc. shafts driving 2 CP propellers Total Power: 18,900kW (25,696hp) 24.0kn MAN 9L48/60 2 x 4 Stroke 9 Cy. 480 x 600 each-9450kW (12848bhp) MAN B&W Diesel AG-Augsburg
8519241 *V2EN5* -	**TRINE** *ex* Katrin *-2009* *launched as* Odin *-1986* **Trine Maritime OU** MPV Management Ltd SatCom: Inmarsat C 430548610 *Saint John's* *Antigua & Barbuda* MMSI: 305486000	**3,448** 1,851 4,139	Class: RS (GL)	**1986**-08 **Detlef Hegemann Rolandwerft GmbH & Co. KG — Berne** Yd No: 135 Loa 101.45 Br ex 15.24 Dght 5.148 Lbp 95.03 Br md 15.21 Dpth 7.50 Welded, 2 dks	**(A31A2GX) General Cargo Ship** Grain: 6,512 TEU 134 C. 134/20' (40') Compartments: 2 Ho, ER 2 Ha: ER Ice Capable	**1 oil engine** with flexible couplings & sr gearedto sc. shaft driving 1 CP propeller Total Power: 2,430kW (3,304hp) 12.5kn Deutz SBV6M640 1 x 4 Stroke 6 Cy. 370 x 400 2430kW (3304bhp) Kloeckner Humboldt Deutz AG-West Germany AuxGen: 1 x 480kW a.c, 2 x 320kW a.c Thrusters: 1 Thwart. FP thruster (f)
7636987 *LMRY* -	**TRINE CHARLOTTE** *ex* Stabben Junior *-2004* *ex* Margriet *-1997* *ex* Alecto *-1989* *ex* Marjan *-1986* **Seaworks AS** - *Trondheim* *Norway* MMSI: 257233000	**1,114** 586 1,570	Class: (LR) (BV) Classed LR until 30/9/10	**1977**-10 **van Goor's Scheepswerf en Mfbk B.V. — Monnickendam** Yd No: 663 Loa 65.84 Br ex - Dght 4.320 Lbp 59.97 Br md 10.74 Dpth 5.11 Welded, 1 dk	**(A31A2GX) General Cargo Ship** Grain: 2,009; Bale: 1,953 Compartments: 1 Ho, ER	**1 oil engine** with clutches, flexible couplings & sr reverse geared to sc. shaft driving 1 FP propeller Total Power: 575kW (782hp) 12.0kn Nohab F26R 1 x 4 Stroke 6 Cy. 250 x 300 575kW (782bhp) AB Bofors NOHAB-Sweden AuxGen: 3 x 40kW 380V 50Hz a.c Fuel: 54.0 (d.f.) 92.3 (r.f.)
9444120 *V7RV6* -	**TRINE K** **Asian Offshore III AS** RK Offshore Management Pte Ltd *Majuro* *Marshall Islands* MMSI: 538003585 Official number: 3585	**1,731** 519 1,300	Class: AB	**2010**-03 **PT ASL Shipyard Indonesia — Batam** (Hull) Yd No: (865) **2010**-02 **ASL Shipyard Pte Ltd — Singapore** Yd No: 865 Loa 60.00 Br ex - Dght 4.800 Lbp 53.90 Br md 16.00 Dpth 6.00 Welded, 1 dk	**(B21B20A) Anchor Handling Tug Supply**	**2 oil engines** reduction geared to sc. shafts driving 2 Propellers Total Power: 3,676kW (4,998hp) Niigata 6L28HX 2 x 4 Stroke 6 Cy. 280 x 370 each-1838kW (2499bhp) Niigata Engineering Co Ltd-Japan AuxGen: 3 x 317kW a.c Fuel: 491.0

Ship	Tonnage	Class	Build / Dimensions	Type	Machinery
9582130 **TRINI FLASH** *9YHS* - **National Infrastructure Development Co Ltd (NIDCO)** - *Port of Spain* *Trinidad & Tobago* MMSI: 362064000	**562** 193 40	Class: NV	**2010-07 Image Marine Pty Ltd — Fremantle WA** Yd No: 238 Loa 41.30 Br ex 11.20 Dght 1.490 Lbp 36.77 Br md 10.90 Dpth 4.30 Welded, 1 dk	**(A37B2PS) Passenger Ship** Hull Material: Aluminium Alloy	**4 oil engines** reduction geared to sc. shafts driving 4 Water jets Total Power: 5,760kW (7,832hp) M.T.U. 16V2000M72 4 x Vee 4 Stroke 16 Cy. 135 x 156 each-1440kW (1958bhp) MTU Friedrichshafen GmbH-Friedrichshafen AuxGen: 2 x a.c
9462653 **TRINIDAD** *LXNI* - **Trivisa SA** Jan De Nul Luxembourg SA *Luxembourg* *Luxembourg* MMSI: 253272000	**2,392** 717 3,400	Class: BV	**2010-05 Tianjin Xinhe Shipbuilding Heavy Industry Co Ltd — Tianjin** Yd No: SB709 Loa 80.00 (BB) Br ex - Dght 4.500 Lbp 76.40 Br md 17.20 Dpth 5.90 Welded, 1 dk	**(B34A2SH) Hopper, Motor** Hopper: 1,800	**2 oil engines** reduction geared to sc. shafts driving 2 Z propellers Total Power: 1,566kW (2,130hp) 11.0kn Caterpillar 3508B 2 x Vee 4 Stroke 8 Cy. 170 x 190 each-783kW (1065bhp) Caterpillar Inc-USA AuxGen: 2 x 245kW 50Hz a.c Thrusters: 1 Tunnel thruster (f)
8602579 **TRINIDAD** *LAIY4* *ex* Nosac Sky *-1996* - **Wilhelmsen Lines Shipowning AS** Wilhelmsen Lines Car Carrier Ltd SatCom: Inmarsat C 425744810 *Tonsberg* *Norway (NIS)* MMSI: 257448000	**49,750** 15,029 15,528 T/cm 39.9	Class: NV	**1987-09 Tsuneishi Shipbuilding Co Ltd — Fukuyama HS** Yd No: 593 Loa 190.00 (BB) Br ex 32.24 Dght 9.121 Lbp 180.96 Br md 32.23 Dpth 13.92 Welded, 12 dks, incl. 4 dks hoistable	**(A35B2RV) Vehicles Carrier** Side door & ramp (p) Len: 20.00 Wid: 5.00 Swl: 25 Side door & ramp (s) Len: 25.00 Wid: 5.00 Swl: 25 Quarter stern door/ramp (s. a.) Len: 40.00 Wid: 7.00 Swl: 118 Cars: 5,858	**1 oil engine** driving 1 FP propeller Total Power: 9,000kW (12,236hp) 18.0kn B&W 6S60MCE 1 x 2 Stroke 6 Cy. 600 x 2292 9000kW (12236bhp) Mitsui Engineering & Shipbuilding CLtd-Japan AuxGen: 2 x 1200kW 450V 60Hz a.c, 1 x 700kW 450V 60Hz a.c Thrusters: 1 Thwart. CP thruster (f) Fuel: 205.0 (d.f.) 2858.0 (r.f.) 29.5pd
8965866 **TRINIDAD** *CB3935* - **Leasing Andino SA** Blumar Seafoods *Valparaiso* *Chile* MMSI: 725001330 Official number: 2911	*464* - -		**1989 Astilleros y Servicios Navales S.A. (ASENAV) — Valdivia** L reg 40.22 Br ex - Dght - Lbp - Br md 8.60 Dpth 6.80 Welded, 1 dk	**(B11B2FV) Fishing Vessel**	**1 oil engine** driving 1 FP propeller
8943375 **TRINITY** *WDE5978* *ex* Bobby D *-2009* *ex* Luke David *-2003* - **The Grand Ltd** Laredo Offshore Services Inc *New Orleans, LA* *United States of America* MMSI: 367374140 Official number: 1070560	**871** 261 -		**1999-02 Conrad Industries, Inc. — Morgan City, La** Yd No: 664 Converted From: Deck-Cargo Pontoon, Non-propelled-2006 Converted From: Crane Vessel, Offshore-2003 Loa 29.87 Br ex - Dght 2.900 Lbp - Br md 23.77 Dpth 3.96 Welded, 1 dk	**(B22A2ZM) Offshore Construction Vessel, jack up** Cranes: 1x125t,1x70t	**2 oil engines** reduction geared to sc. shafts driving 2 Propellers Total Power: 898kW (1,220hp) 6.0kn Caterpillar 3412 1 x Vee 4 Stroke 12 Cy. 137 x 152 449kW (610bhp) (new engine 2006) Caterpillar Inc-USA AuxGen: 2 x 175kW 60Hz a.c Thrusters: 1 Tunnel thruster (f)
9367944 **TRINITY** *C6WB6* - **Legenda Maritime SA** Kotoku Kaiun Co Ltd (Kotoku Kaiun KK) *Nassau* *Bahamas* MMSI: 308759000 Official number: 8001344	**9,549** 5,672 12,582	Class: NK	**2007-04 Kyokuyo Shipyard Corp — Shimonoseki YC** Yd No: 477 Loa 145.12 (BB) Br ex - Dght 8.215 Lbp 134.00 Br md 22.40 Dpth 11.00 Welded, 1 dk	**(A33A2CC) Container Ship (Fully Cellular)** TEU 907 incl 120 ref C.	**1 oil engine** driving 1 FP propeller Total Power: 7,988kW (10,860hp) 18.0kn MAN-B&W 6L50MC 1 x 2 Stroke 6 Cy. 500 x 1620 7988kW (10860bhp) Hitachi Zosen Corp-Japan AuxGen: 3 x 560kW a.c Thrusters: 1 Tunnel thruster (f) Fuel: 106.2 (d.f.) 1049.5 (r.f.)
9476252 **TRINITY 1** *XUEW3* *ex* Jing Hing 99 *-2007* - **Brantas Sdn Bhd** *Phnom Penh* *Cambodia* MMSI: 514704000 Official number: 0799809	**469** 141 671	Class: IS	**1999-01 Kiong Nguong Shipbuilding Contractor Co — Sibu** Loa 47.91 Br ex - Dght 3.050 Lbp 45.73 Br md 15.24 Dpth 3.10 Welded, 1 dk	**(A35D2RL) Landing Craft**	**2 oil engines** geared to sc. shafts driving 2 Propellers Total Power: 536kW (728hp) 8.0kn Cummins NT-855-M 2 x 4 Stroke 6 Cy. 140 x 152 each-268kW (364bhp) Cummins Engine Co Inc-USA
6618885 **TRINITY 2** - *ex* Tambulan *-2008* *ex* Shinko Maru No. 8 *-1999* - **Trilliant Investment Pte Ltd** -	**206** 62 124		**1966 Kegoya Dock K.K. — Kure** Yd No: 285 Loa 33.05 Br ex 8.02 Dght 2.604 Lbp 30.00 Br md 8.00 Dpth 3.60 Welded, 1 dk	**(B32A2ST) Tug**	**2 oil engines** geared to sc. shaft driving 1 FP propeller Total Power: 1,080kW (1,468hp) 10.0kn Chinese Std. Type 6190ZLC 2 x 4 Stroke 6 Cy. 190 x 210 each-540kW (734bhp) (new engine 1999) Jinan Diesel Engine Co Ltd-China AuxGen: 1 x 24kW 230V a.c, 1 x 16kW 230V a.c Fuel: 127.0 5.0pd
8017982 **TRINITY AMAN** *V3LN* *ex* Tottori Maru No. 1 *-2007* - **Trinity Marine Ltd** Trinity Offshore Pte Ltd *Belize City* *Belize* MMSI: 312196000 Official number: 130710749	**174** 52 103		**1981-02 Wakamatsu Zosen K.K. — Kitakyushu** Yd No: 312 Loa 36.10 Br ex 6.84 Dght 2.901 Lbp 30.28 Br md 6.80 Dpth 5.82 Welded, 1 dk	**(B12D2FR) Fishery Research Vessel**	**1 oil engine** reduction geared to sc. shaft driving 1 FP propeller Total Power: 588kW (799hp) 8.5kn Niigata 6MG22LX 1 x 4 Stroke 6 Cy. 220 x 290 588kW (799bhp) Niigata Engineering Co Ltd-Japan
9319404 **TRINITY ARROW** *3EPD8* - **Cypress Maritime (Panama) SA, Luster Maritime SA & Los Halillos Shipping Co SA** 'K' Line LNG Shipping (UK) Ltd SatCom: Inmarsat C 435339212 *Panama* *Panama* MMSI: 353392000 Official number: 3383908C	**101,094** 30,328 79,556 T/cm 107.5	Class: LR ✠ **100A1** SS 03/2013 liquefied gas tanker, Ship Type 2G methane (LNG) in membrane tanks maximum vapour pressure 0.25 bar minimum temperature minus 163 degree C **ShipRight** (SDA, FDA plus, CM) *IWS LI ✠ **LMC** **UMS** Eq.Ltr: A†; Cable: 752.5/107.0 U3 (a)	**2008-03 Koyo Dockyard Co Ltd — Mihara HS** Yd No: 2258 Loa 289.93 (BB) Br ex 44.73 Dght 12.073 Lbp 276.00 Br md 44.70 Dpth 26.00 Welded, 1 dk	**(A11A2TN) LNG Tanker** Double Hull Liq (Gas): 152,655 5 x Gas Tank (s); 4 membrane (s.stl) pri horizontal, ER 8 Cargo Pump (s): 8x1700m³/hr Manifold: Bow/CM: 146m	**1 Steam Turb** with flexible couplings & dr reverse geared to sc. shaft driving 1 FP propeller Total Power: 29,420kW (39,999hp) 20.2kn Kawasaki UA-400 1 x steam Turb 29420kW (39999shp) Kawasaki Heavy Industries Ltd-Japan AuxGen: 1 x 3250kW 6600V 60Hz a.c, 2 x 3250kW 6600V 60Hz a.c Boilers: wtdb (o.f.) 77.0kgf/cm² (75.5bar) Superheater 525°C 65.0kgf/cm² (63.7bar) Thrusters: 1 Thwart. CP thruster (f) Fuel: 660.0 (d.f.) 5835.0 (r.f.) 163.4pd
9149990 **TRINITY BAY** *VJEQ* *ex* Faseco No. 103 *-1998* - **Sea Swift Pty Ltd** - SatCom: Inmarsat C 450300523 *Cairns, Qld* *Australia* MMSI: 503609000 Official number: 856091	**1,594** 988 3,158	Class: (NV) (KR)	**1996-05 Far East Shipbuilding Co Ltd — Geoje** Yd No: 374 Loa 80.95 (BB) Br ex - Dght 5.384 Lbp 74.08 Br md 15.00 Dpth 6.30 Welded, 1 dk	**(A32A2GF) General Cargo/Passenger Ship** Passengers: 38 TEU 125 Compartments: 1 Ho, ER 1 Ha: (25.8 x 12.0) Cranes: 1x15t	**1 oil engine** reduction geared to sc. shaft driving 1 FP propeller Total Power: 1,851kW (2,517hp) 13.5kn Caterpillar 3606TA 1 x 4 Stroke 6 Cy. 280 x 300 1851kW (2517bhp) Caterpillar Inc-USA AuxGen: 2 x 190kW 220/440V 60Hz a.c Fuel: 920.0
7908160 **TRINITY EXPLORER** *V3GN3* *ex* Fairfield Explorer *-2005* *ex* Digicon Explorer *-1995* - **Trinity Offshore Inc** Trinity Offshore Pte Ltd *Belize City* *Belize* MMSI: 312646000 Official number: 130520699	**1,466** 439 632	Class: AB	**1980-05 Modern Marine Power, Inc. — Houma, La** Yd No: 29 Loa 56.70 Br ex - Dght 4.170 Lbp 52.00 Br md 12.20 Dpth 4.58 Welded, 1 dk	**(B31A2SR) Research Survey Vessel** Cranes: 1x3t	**2 oil engines** sr geared to sc. shafts driving 2 CP propellers Total Power: 1,986kW (2,700hp) 9.0kn Wichmann 4AXA 2 x 2 Stroke 4 Cy. 300 x 450 each-993kW (1350bhp) Wichmann Motorfabrikk AS-Norway AuxGen: 3 x 150kW a.c, 1 x 175kW a.c Thrusters: 1 Thwart. FP thruster (f) Fuel: 418.0 (r.f.)

IMO / Call sign	Name / Owner	Tonnage	Class	Builder / Dimensions	Type	Machinery
9350927 *3FMV6* -	**TRINITY GLORY** **Cypress Maritime (Panama) SA, Luster Maritime SA & Los Halillos Shipping Co SA** 'K' Line LNG Shipping (UK) Ltd SatCom: Inmarsat C 437066810 *Panama* *Panama* MMSI: 370668000 Official number: 4020309A	**101,126** 30,337 79,605 T/cm 107.5	Class: LR ✠ **100A1** SS 03/2014 liquefied gas tanker, Ship Type 2G methane (LNG) in membrane tanks maximum vapour pressure 0.25 bar minimum temperature minus 163 degree C **ShipRight** (SDA, FDA plus, CM) *IWS LI ✠ **LMC** **UMS** Eq.Ltr: A*; Cable: 749.5/107.0 U3 (a)	**2009-03 Koyo Dockyard Co Ltd — Mihara HS** Yd No: 2260 Loa 289.93 (BB) Br ex 44.73 Dght 12.073 Lbp 276.00 Br md 44.70 Dpth 26.00 Welded, 1 dk.	**(A11A2TN) LNG Tanker** Double Hull Liq (Gas): 152,675 4 x Gas Tank (s); 4 membrane (s.stl) pri horizontal 8 Cargo Pump (s): 8x1700m³/hr Manifold: Bow/CM: 146m	**1 Steam Turb** with flexible couplings & dr reverse geared to sc. shaft driving 1 FP propeller Total Power: 29,420kW (39,999hp) 20.2kn Kawasaki UA-400 1 x steam Turb 29420kW (39999shp) Kawasaki Heavy Industries Ltd-Japan AuxGen: 1 x 3250kW 6600V 60Hz a.c, 2 x 3250kW 6600V 60Hz a.c Boilers: wtdb (o.f.) 76.8kgf/cm² (75.3bar) Superheater 525°C 65.0kgf/cm² (63.7bar) Thrusters: 1 Thwart. CP thruster (f) Fuel: 690.0 (d.f.) 5885.0 (r.f.)
8767408 *WDF3138* -	**TRINITY I** *ex* Superior Force *-2009* *ex* J. Scarboro *-2009* *ex* Blue Streak 12 *-2009* **Trinity Liftboat Services No 1 LLC** Trinity Liftboat Services LLC *New Orleans, LA* *United States of America* MMSI: 366817930 Official number: 629196	*191* 130 -		**1980 Blue Streak Industries, Inc. — Chalmette, La** Yd No: BLU JB 41 L reg 23.16 Br ex - Dght - Lbp - Br md 16.45 Dpth 2.43 Welded, 1 dk	**(B22A2ZM) Offshore Construction Vessel, jack up**	**2 oil engines** driving 2 Propellers
8767381 *WDF3141* -	**TRINITY II** *ex* Superior Focus *-2009* *ex* J. M. Mitchell *-2009* *ex* Southern Cross Three *-2009* **Trinity Liftboat Services No 2 LLC** Trinity Liftboat Services LLC *New Orleans, LA* *United States of America* MMSI: 367436390 Official number: 653353	*185* 125 -		**1982 Blue Streak Industries, Inc. — Chalmette, La** Yd No: BLU JB 62 L reg 24.07 Br ex - Dght - Lbp - Br md 11.58 Dpth 2.43 Welded, 1 dk	**(B22A2ZM) Offshore Construction Vessel, jack up**	**2 oil engines** driving 2 Propellers
8736447 *SY2740* -	**TRINITY II** *ex* Elenesse II *-2009* *ex* Antares *-2000* **Trinity Yachts Ltd** *Piraeus* *Greece* MMSI: 237843000 Official number: 11077	**303** 90 66	Class: HR (Class contemplated)	**1991-09 Azimut SpA, Divisione Produttiva Fratelli Benetti — Viareggio** Yd No: FB205 Loa 42.00 Br ex - Dght 3.110 Lbp 35.10 Br md 8.40 Dpth 4.15 Welded, 1 dk	**(X11A2YP) Yacht**	**2 oil engines** driving 2 FP propellers Total Power: 1,472kW (2,002hp) Caterpillar 2 x Vee 4 Stroke 12 Cy. each-736kW (1001bhp) Caterpillar Inc-USA
7535690 *HP5640* -	**TRINITY II** *ex* Teno Maru No. 1 *-1990* **Quan Well Co** *Panama* *Panama* Official number: D2671789PEXT	*116* - -		**1975-09 K.K. Izutsu Zosensho — Nagasaki** Yd No: 712 Loa 38.51 Br ex 7.70 Dght - Lbp 31.53 Br md 6.90 Dpth 2.77 Welded, 1 dk	**(B11B2FV) Fishing Vessel**	**1 oil engine** reduction geared to sc. shaft driving 1 FP propeller Total Power: 883kW (1,201hp) Yanmar 6ZL-DT 1 x 4 Stroke 6 Cy. 280 x 340 883kW (1201bhp) Yanmar Diesel Engine Co Ltd-Japan
8763098 *WDF3142* -	**TRINITY III** *ex* Superior Courage *-2009* *ex* Gulf Island VII *-2009* **Trinity Liftboat Services No 3 LLC** Trinity Liftboat Services LLC *New Orleans, LA* *United States of America* MMSI: 366817810 Official number: 693643	*195* 161 -		**1985 Crown Point Industries — Marrero, La** Yd No: 115 L reg 20.94 Br ex - Dght 1.830 Lbp - Br md 12.19 Dpth 2.13 Welded, 1 dk	**(B22A2ZM) Offshore Construction Vessel, jack up** Cranes: 1x50t	**2 oil engines** geared to sc. shafts driving 2 Propellers Total Power: 662kW (900hp) G.M. (Detroit Diesel) 12V-71 2 x Vee 2 Stroke 12 Cy. 108 x 127 each-331kW (450bhp) Detroit Diesel Corporation-Detroit, Mi
8767379 *WDA5230* -	**TRINITY IV** *ex* Superior Concept *-2009* *ex* H. G. Louviere *-2009* *ex* Southern Cross Five *-2009* **Trinity Liftboat Services No 4 LLC** Trinity Liftboat Services LLC *New Orleans, LA* *United States of America* MMSI: 367436420 Official number: 630849	*177* 120 -		**1980 Crown Point Industries — Marrero, La** Yd No: 101 L reg 22.21 Br ex - Dght - Lbp - Br md 10.97 Dpth 2.13 Welded, 1 dk	**(B22A2ZM) Offshore Construction Vessel, jack up**	**2 oil engines** driving 2 Propellers
7349443 *V3T08* -	**TRINITY LONDON** *ex* OSA London *-2008* *ex* Josephturm *-1984* **Trinity Discovery Inc** Trinity Offshore Pte Ltd *Belize City* *Belize* MMSI: 312557000	**1,321** 396 1,530	Class: AB (GL)	**1974-03 Gutehoffnungshuette Sterkrade AG Rheinwerft Walsum — Duisburg** Yd No: 1111 Converted From: Pipe Carrier-2008 Loa 56.14 Br ex 14.30 Dght 5.138 Lbp 51.01 Br md 14.28 Dpth 7.57 Welded, 2 dks	**(B21A20S) Platform Supply Ship** Grain: 140 Cranes: 1x5t	**2 oil engines** reduction geared to sc. shafts driving 2 FP propellers Total Power: 2,610kW (3,548hp) 10.0kn MWM TBD441V12 2 x Vee 4 Stroke 12 Cy. 230 x 270 each-1305kW (1774bhp) Motoren Werke Mannheim AG (MWM)-West Germany AuxGen: 3 x 112kW 380V 50Hz a.c Thrusters: 1 Thwart. FP thruster (f) Fuel: 336.0 (d.f.)
7527590 *V3LQ3* -	**TRINITY REVIVAL** *ex* Sarku Sipadan *-2008* *ex* Merlion *-2003* *ex* GSI Merlion *-1993* *ex* Kaiyo Maru *-1988* **Trinity Offshore (Labuan) Inc** Trinity Offshore Pte Ltd *Belize City* *Belize* MMSI: 312568000 Official number: 130820773	**1,575** 472 739	Class: BV (NK)	**1976-04 Mitsubishi Heavy Industries Ltd. — Shimonoseki** Yd No: 774 Loa 75.98 Br ex 12.02 Dght 4.573 Lbp 67.98 Br md 11.99 Dpth 4.60 Welded, 2 dks	**(B31A2SR) Research Survey Vessel** 1 Ha: (1.8 x 1.8)ER Cranes: 1x3t,1x2t Ice Capable	**2 oil engines** driving 2 CP propellers Total Power: 3,090kW (4,202hp) 10.0kn Daihatsu 6DSM-32 2 x 4 Stroke 6 Cy. 320 x 380 each-1545kW (2101bhp) Daihatsu Diesel Manufacturing Co Lt-Japan AuxGen: 3 x 450kW 60Hz a.c Thrusters: 1 Thwart. FP thruster (f) Fuel: 475.0 (d.f.)
8225486 *VCXJ* -	**TRINITY SEA** *ex* Neftegaz-2 *-1998* **3260818 Nova Scotia Ltd** Secunda Canada LP *St John's, NL* *Canada* MMSI: 316302000 Official number: 820678	**2,623** 821 2,860	Class: NV (RS)	**1983-06 Stocznia Szczecinska im A Warskiego — Szczecin** Yd No: B92/02 Loa 81.16 Br ex 16.30 Dght 6.090 Lbp 71.46 Br md 15.97 Dpth 7.22 Welded, 2 dks	**(B21B20A) Anchor Handling Tug Supply** Cranes: 1x12.5t Ice Capable	**2 oil engines** reduction geared to sc. shafts driving 2 CP propellers Total Power: 7,300kW (9,926hp) 15.0kn Nohab 16V25 2 x Vee 4 Stroke 16 Cy. 250 x 300 each-3650kW (4963bhp) (Re-engined 1983, refitted 1983) Wartsila NSD Sweden AB-Sweden AuxGen: 1 x 1170kW 400V 50Hz a.c, 2 x 1700kW 400V 50Hz a.c Thrusters: 1 Tunnel thruster (f); 1 Tunnel thruster (f); 1 Thwart. CP thruster (a) Fuel: 660.0
8204755 *V3GY3* -	**TRINITY SEEKER** *ex* Seeker I *-2006* *ex* Astro Curima *-2003* **Trinity Offshore Inc** Trinity Offshore Pte Ltd *Belize City* *Belize* MMSI: 312421000 Official number: 130610708	*296* 88 376	Class: AB	**1984-04 Maclaren IC Estaleiros e Servicos S.A. — Niteroi** Yd No: 271 Loa 40.16 Br ex 8.87 Dght 3.029 Lbp 34.70 Br md 8.63 Dpth 3.51 Welded, 1 dk	**(B21A20S) Platform Supply Ship** A-frames: 1x5t	**3 oil engines** sr reverse geared to sc. shafts driving 3 FP propellers Total Power: 798kW (1,086hp) 7.0kn Scania DSI1440M 3 x Vee 4 Stroke 8 Cy. 127 x 140 each-266kW (362bhp) Saab Scania do Brasil SA-Brazil AuxGen: 2 x 100kW 440V 60Hz a.c Thrusters: 1 Tunnel thruster (f) Fuel: 140.0 (d.f.) 3.0pd
7309596 *WSS2630* -	**TRINITY SHOAL** **Omega Protein Inc** *Abbeville, LA* *United States of America* Official number: 281152	*470* 320 -		**1960 Burton Shipyard Co., Inc. — Port Arthur, Tx** L reg 45.82 Br ex 9.78 Dght - Lbp - Br md - Dpth 3.26 Welded	**(B11B2FV) Fishing Vessel**	**1 oil engine** driving 1 FP propeller Total Power: 671kW (912hp) G.M. (Detroit Diesel) 12V-149 1 x Vee 2 Stroke 12 Cy. 146 x 146 671kW (912bhp) General Motors Corp-USA

IMO / Call sign	Name / Owner	Tonnage	Classification	Builder / Dimensions	Type / Capacity	Machinery
7370325 *5MVQ* -	**TRINITY SPIRIT** *ex* Independence *-2005* *ex* Venture Independence *-1988* *ex* Conoco Independence *-1978* **Allenne Ltd** Alliance Marine Services SatCom: Inmarsat A 1242225 *Monrovia* *Liberia* MMSI: 636005748 Official number: 5748	**132,995** 99,817 274,774 T/cm 161.3	Class: AB	**1976-06 Ishikawajima-Harima Heavy Industries Co Ltd (IHI) — Kure** Yd No: 2437 Converted From: Crude Oil Tanker-1997 Loa 337.05 (BB) Br ex - Dght 21.002 Lbp 319.99 Br md 54.49 Dpth 26.99 Welded, 1 dk	**(B22E2OF) FPSO, Oil** Liq: 313,000; Liq (Oil): 313,000 Compartments: 22 Ta, ER 4 Cargo Pump (s): 4x4500m³/hr Manifold: Bow/CM: 166m	**1 Steam Turb** dr geared to sc. shaft driving 1 FP propeller Total Power: 29,420kW (39,999hp) 16.0kn Ishikawajima 1 x steam Turb 29420kW (39999shp) Ishikawajima Harima Heavy IndustrieCo Ltd (IHI)-Japan AuxGen: 1 x 1600kW 450V 60Hz a.c, 2 x 800kW 450V 60Hz a.c Fuel: 8066.5 (r.f.) (Heating Coils) 328.0 (d.f.) 183.0pd
9500704 *3FHN2* -	**TRINITY STAR** **Green Spanker Shipping SA** Nissen Kaiun Co Ltd (Nissen Kaiun KK) *Panama* *Panama* MMSI: 371121000 Official number: 4261411	**92,379** 60,235 180,643	Class: NK	**2011-05 Tsuneishi Heavy Industries (Cebu) Inc — Balamban** Yd No: SC-156 Loa 291.90 (BB) Br ex - Dght 18.068 Lbp 286.90 Br md 45.00 Dpth 24.50 Welded, 1 dk	**(A21A2BC) Bulk Carrier** Grain: 200,998 Compartments: 9 Ho, ER 9 Ha: ER	**1 oil engine** driving 1 FP propeller Total Power: 17,690kW (24,051hp) 15.2kn MAN-B&W 7S65ME-C 1 x 2 Stroke 7 Cy. 650 x 2730 17690kW (24051bhp) Mitsui Engineering & Shipbuilding CLtd-Japan
8130095 - -	**TRINITY SUPPORTER** *ex* Sakura 2 *-2010* *ex* Sakura *-2009* **PT Trinity Offshore Services** Trinity Offshore Pte Ltd *Jakarta* *Indonesia*	**13,593** 4,078 20,627	Class: NK	**1982-11 K.K. Uwajima Zosensho — Uwajima** Yd No: 2192 Converted From: Chemical Tanker-2009 Loa 155.50 (BB) Br ex - Dght 9.670 Lbp 146.01 Br md 25.01 Dpth 13.01 Welded, 1 dk	**(B34T2QR) Work/Repair Vessel** Double Bottom Entire Compartment Length Cranes: 1x60t,1x25t,2x15t	**1 oil engine** driving 1 FP propeller Total Power: 5,884kW (8,000hp) 14.3kn Mitsubishi 7UEC52/125H 1 x 2 Stroke 7 Cy. 520 x 1250 5884kW (8000bhp) Akasaka Tekkosho KK (Akasaka DieselLtd)-Japan AuxGen: 3 x 450kW Fuel: 313.0 (d.f.) 1168.0 (r.f.) 24.0pd
8767422 *WDF7165* -	**TRINITY V** *ex* Superior Legacy *-2011* *ex* P. J. Richard *-2011* *ex* Southern Cross One *-2011* **Trinity Liftboat Services No 5 LLC** Trinity Liftboat Services LLC *New Orleans, LA* *United States of America* MMSI: 367481740 Official number: 634022	**282** 84 -		**1981 Bollinger Machine Shop & Shipyard, Inc. — Lockport, La** Yd No: 45 Loa 24.69 Br ex 11.58 Dght - Lbp - Br md - Dpth 2.43 Welded, 1 dk	**(B22A2ZM) Offshore Construction Vessel, jack up** Cranes: 1x45t,1x25t	**2 oil engines** reduction geared to sc. shafts driving 2 Propellers Total Power: 662kW (900hp) 4.0kn G.M. (Detroit Diesel) 12V-71 2 x Vee 2 Stroke 12 Cy. 108 x 127 each-331kW (450bhp) Detroit Diesel Corporation-Detroit, Mi AuxGen: 1 x 50kW 60Hz a.c, 1 x 99kW 60Hz a.c
9546485 *PCWU* -	**TRINITYBORG** **Trinityborg Beheer BV** Wagenborg Shipping BV *Delfzijl* *Netherlands* MMSI: 244810209	**14,695** 6,695 21,277	Class: LR ✠ **100A1** SS 11/2013 strengthened for heavy cargoes, any hold may be empty, container cargoes in all holds, on upper deck and on all hatch covers **ShipRight** ACS (B) *IWS LI Ice Class 1A at a draught of 9.535m Max/min draughts fwd 9.535/4.015m Max/min draughts aft 9.535/5.715m Power required 7500kw, power installed 7500kw ✠ **LMC** **UMS** Eq.Ltr: H†; Cable: 576.9/60.0 U3 (a)	**2013-11 Hudong-Zhonghua Shipbuilding (Group) Co Ltd — Shanghai** Yd No: H1598A Loa 172.34 (BB) Br ex 21.74 Dght 9.380 Lbp 161.34 Br md 21.50 Dpth 13.30 Welded, 1 dk	**(A31A2GX) General Cargo Ship** Grain: 23,000; Bale: 23,000 TEU 1228 C Ho 586 TEU C Dk 642 TEU incl 72 ref C Compartments: 2 Ho, ER 2 Ha: (58.7 x 17.8)ER (55.4 x 17.8) Cranes: 4x60t Ice Capable	**1 oil engine** with clutches, flexible couplings & sr geared to sc. shaft driving 1 CP propeller Total Power: 7,500kW (10,197hp) 14.5kn Wartsila 6L46F 1 x 4 Stroke 6 Cy. 460 x 580 7500kW (10197bhp) Wartsila Italia SpA-Italy AuxGen: 1 x 800kW 450V 60Hz a.c, 3 x 450kW 450V 60Hz a.c Boilers: TOH (o.f.) 10.2kgf/cm² (10.0bar), TOH (ex.g.) 10.2kgf/cm² (10.0bar) Thrusters: 1 Thwart. CP thruster (f)
7725776 *STRI* -	**TRINKITAT** **Sea Ports Corp** *Port Sudan* *Sudan* Official number: 151	*300* 58 273	Class: (LR) ✠ Classed LR until 15/4/92	**1980-03 Martin Jansen GmbH & Co. KG Schiffsw. u. Masch. — Leer** Yd No: 151 Loa 37.19 Br ex 9.89 Dght 3.961 Lbp 33.53 Br md 9.45 Dpth 4.27 Welded, 1 dk, 2nd dk f of mchy space	**(B32A2ST) Tug**	**1 oil engine** reverse reduction geared to sc. shaft driving 1 FP propeller Total Power: 1,341kW (1,823hp) 13.0kn MAN G9V30/45ATL 1 x 4 Stroke 9 Cy. 300 x 450 1341kW (1823bhp) Maschinenbau Augsburg Nuernberg (MAN)-Augsburg AuxGen: 2 x 42kW 400V 50Hz a.c
8615291 *JXPQ* N-212-V	**TRINTO** *ex* Andenesfisk *-2004* *ex* Bleiksoy *-1997* *ex* Sifjordvaering *-1996* **Age Siversten AS** *Svolvaer* *Norway* MMSI: 258247000	**657** 212 -		**1987-06 H. & E. Nordtveit Skipsbyggeri AS — Nordtveitgrend** Yd No: 77 Lengthened-2011 Loa 44.78 (BB) Br ex - Dght - Lbp - Br md 9.50 Dpth 5.60 Welded, 1 dk	**(B11B2FV) Fishing Vessel**	**1 oil engine** reduction geared to sc. shaft driving 1 FP propeller Total Power: 449kW (610hp) Mitsubishi S8N-MPTK 1 x 4 Stroke 8 Cy. 160 x 180 449kW (610bhp) Mitsubishi Heavy Industries Ltd-Japan Thrusters: 1 Tunnel thruster (f)
8706492 *LHYD* N-216-VR	**TRIO** *ex* Meloyfjell *-2012* *ex* Breistrand *-2007* *ex* Faroybuen *-2002* *ex* Fjelldur *-1997* *ex* Lovon *-1996* **Sorvik Fisk AS** *Myre* *Norway* MMSI: 257522600	**245** 83 -		**1988-01 Gotaverken Cityvarvet AB — Gothenburg** (Hull) Yd No: 656-066 **1988-01 Ronnangs Svets AB — Ronnang** Yd No: 115 Loa 23.70 Br ex - Dght - Lbp - Br md 7.00 Dpth 4.68 Welded, 1 dk	**(B11A2FS) Stern Trawler**	**1 oil engine** sr geared to sc. shaft driving 1 FP propeller Total Power: 662kW (900hp) Caterpillar 3412TA 1 x Vee 4 Stroke 12 Cy. 137 x 152 662kW (900bhp) Caterpillar Inc-USA
7116133 *9LD2278* -	**TRIO VEGA** *ex* Myrtind *-1999* *ex* Ina *-1993* *ex* Sanna *-1993* *ex* Inger *-1988* *ex* Sanna *-1987* *ex* Teka *-1985* **Coolmore Shipping Inc** Arabella Enterprises Corp *Freetown* *Sierra Leone* MMSI: 667977000 Official number: SL100977	**1,366** 659 1,808	Class: (BV) (GL)	**1971-03 N.V. Scheepswerf "Westerbroek" v/h J.G. Broerken — Westerbroek** Yd No: 194 Loa 70.80 Br ex 11.10 Dght 4.501 Lbp 64.00 Br md 11.00 Dpth 5.63 Welded, 2 dks	**(A31A2GX) General Cargo Ship** Grain: 3,030; Bale: 2,832 Compartments: 1 Ho, ER 1 Ha: (40.2 x 7.7)ER Ice Capable	**1 oil engine** driving 1 FP propeller Total Power: 736kW (1,001hp) 11.5kn MWM TBD484-8U 1 x 4 Stroke 8 Cy. 320 x 480 736kW (1001bhp) Motoren Werke Mannheim AG (MWM)-West Germany
9192533 *FW9137* -	**TRIOMPHANT** **Boluda France SAS** Boluda Dunkerque *Dunkirk* *France* MMSI: 227006730 Official number: 924427	**313** 93 335	Class: BV	**1999-08 Alstom Leroux Naval SA — St-Malo** (Hull launched by) Yd No: 636 **1999-08 Alstom Leroux Naval SA — Lanester** (Hull completed by) Loa 30.00 Br ex - Dght 5.100 Lbp 28.50 Br md 10.40 Dpth 3.80 Welded, 1 dk	**(B32A2ST) Tug**	**2 oil engines** reduction geared to sc. shafts driving 2 Z propellers Total Power: 2,600kW (3,534hp) 12.0kn A.B.C. 6MDZC 2 x 4 Stroke 6 Cy. 256 x 310 each-1300kW (1767bhp) Anglo Belgian Corp NV (ABC)-Belgium AuxGen: 2 x 76kW 400V 50Hz a.c Fuel: 56.0 (d.f.)
5119363 *PIAY* -	**TRIP JUNIOR** *ex* Hunter *-1982* *ex* Francina *-1977* **'Trip' Sportvisbedrijf** - *Scheveningen* *Netherlands* MMSI: 245351000 Official number: 797	**235** 70 -		**1957-01 A. de Jong N.V. Scheepswerf en Machinefabriek — Vlaardingen** Yd No: 103 Converted From: Trawler-1977 Loa 40.59 Br ex 7.29 Dght 2.850 Lbp 36.33 Br md 7.19 Dpth 3.79 Welded	**(X11A2YP) Yacht**	**1 oil engine** driving 1 FP propeller Deutz 1 x 4 Stroke 8 Cy. 270 x 500 Kloeckner Humboldt Deutz AG-West Germany
8433083 *PIBA* -	**TRIP SENIOR** **Rederij Trip** *Scheveningen* *Netherlands* MMSI: 245349000 Official number: 800	**105** 34 -		**1964 Holland Launch N.V. — Zaandam** Yd No: 328 Loa 29.16 Br ex - Dght 2.550 Lbp 26.25 Br md 6.00 Dpth 3.00 Welded, 1 dk	**(X11A2YP) Yacht**	**1 oil engine** driving 1 FP propeller
1008956 *2BHE7* -	**TRIPLE 8** *ex* Caneli *-2012* *ex* Aarhus Vaerft 247 *-2008* **Triple 8 Marine Inc** Triple 8 Marine Services Ltd *Douglas* *Isle of Man (British)* MMSI: 235065392 Official number: 740803	**498** 149 91	Class: LR ✠ **100A1** SS 10/2008 SSC Yacht, mono, G6 ✠ **LMC** Cable: 275.0/19.0 U2 (a)	**2008-10 UAB Vakaru Laivu Remontas (JSC Western Shiprepair) — Klaipeda** (Hull) **2008-10 Aarhus Vaerft A/S — Aarhus** Yd No: 247 Loa 43.40 Br ex 9.00 Dght 2.880 Lbp 36.50 Br md 8.75 Dpth 5.15 Welded, 1 dk	**(X11A2YP) Yacht**	**2 oil engines** gearing integral to driving 2 Directional propellers Total Power: 1,492kW (2,028hp) 13.0kn Caterpillar 3508B 2 x Vee 4 Stroke 8 Cy. 170 x 190 each-746kW (1014bhp) Caterpillar Inc-USA AuxGen: 3 x 93kW 380V 50Hz a.c Thrusters: 1 Thwart. FP thruster (f)

IMO / Call sign	Name / Owner / Manager / Port	Tonnage	Class	Built / Dimensions	Type / Cargo	Machinery
9322152 *V7JL6* -	**TRIPLE A** **Walworth Holding SA** NGM Energy SA *Majuro* *Marshall Islands* MMSI: 538002543 Official number: 2543	**8,539** 4,117 13,040 T/cm 23.2	Class: AB	**2006-04 21st Century Shipbuilding Co Ltd — Tongyeong** Yd No: 211 Loa 128.60 (BB) Br ex - Dght 8.714 Lbp 120.40 Br md 20.40 Dpth 11.50 Welded, 1 dk	**(A12B2TR) Chemical/Products Tanker** Double Hull (13F) Liq: 13,423; Liq (Oil): 13,423 Cargo Heating Coils Compartments: 12 Wing Ta, 2 Wing Slop Ta, ER 12 Cargo Pump (s): 12x300m³/hr Manifold: Bow/CM: 60.7m	**1 oil engine** driving 1 FP propeller Total Power: 4,440kW (6,037hp) 13.5kn MAN-B&W 6S35MC 1 x 2 Stroke 6 Cy. 350 x 1400 4440kW (6037bhp) STX Engine Co Ltd-South Korea AuxGen: 3 x 480kW a.c Thrusters: 1 Thwart. FP thruster (f) Fuel: 69.1 (d.f.) 678.3 (r.f.)
8937730 *WDG6494* - -	**TRIPLE DRAGON** *ex* Victoria *-2012* **Triple Dragon LLC** - *Honolulu, HI* *United States of America* Official number: 913733	*107* 85 -		**1987 Tu Du Huynh — Saint Mary parish, La** L reg 23.77 Br ex - Dght - Lbp - Br md 6.74 Dpth 2.83 Welded, 1 dk	**(B11B2FV) Fishing Vessel**	**1 oil engine** driving 1 FP propeller
9317121 *9V7518* -	**TRIPLE EVER** **Kambara Kisen Singapore Pte Ltd** Union Marine Management Services Pte Ltd *Singapore* *Singapore* MMSI: 566766000 Official number: 398231	**30,046** 18,207 52,454 T/cm 55.5	Class: NK	**2005-08 Tsuneishi Corp — Fukuyama HS** Yd No: 1336 Loa 189.99 Br ex - Dght 12.022 Lbp 182.00 Br md 32.26 Dpth 17.00 Welded, 1 dk	**(A21A2BC) Bulk Carrier** Grain: 67,756; Bale: 65,601 Compartments: 5 Ho, ER 5 Ha: 4 (21.3 x 18.4)ER (20.4 x 18.4) Cranes: 4x30t	**1 oil engine** driving 1 FP propeller Total Power: 7,800kW (10,605hp) 14.2kn B&W 6S50MC 1 x 2 Stroke 6 Cy. 500 x 1910 7800kW (10605bhp) Mitsui Engineering & Shipbuilding CLtd-Japan Fuel: 2150.0
8114493 - - - - - -	**TRIPLE GLORY** *ex* Tin Tin No. 8 *-1996* *ex* Hai Pai No. 3 *-1995* *ex* Kaiyo Maru No. 38 *-1993* *ex* Seiyo Maru No. 38 *-1991* *ex* Eisho Maru No. 38 *-1990* - -	*306* 107 -		**1981-08 K.K. Murakami Zosensho — Ishinomaki** Yd No: 1081 Loa 41.30 (BB) Br ex - Dght - Lbp 40.70 Br md 7.70 Dpth 3.26 Welded, 1 dk	**(B11B2FV) Fishing Vessel**	**1 oil engine** geared to sc. shaft driving 1 FP propeller Total Power: 809kW (1,100hp) Yanmar T260L-ST 1 x 4 Stroke 6 Cy. 260 x 330 809kW (1100bhp) Yanmar Diesel Engine Co Ltd-Japan
8921509 *9MFB7* -	**TRIPLE JOY** *ex* Eikoh Maru No. 10 *-2005* **Victory Supply Sdn Bhd** *Port Klang* *Malaysia* MMSI: 533014400 Official number: 332345	**3,098** 1,483 4,978	Class: NK (LR) Classed LR until 28/11/11	**1990-09 Shin Kurushima Dockyard Co. Ltd. — Hashihama, Imabari** Yd No: 2683 Loa 104.53 (BB) Br ex - Dght 6.450 Lbp 97.00 Br md 15.20 Dpth 7.59 Welded, 1 dk	**(A13B2TP) Products Tanker** Liq: 5,400; Liq (Oil): 5,400 Compartments: 10 Wing Ta, ER, 2 Wing Slop Ta	**1 oil engine** reverse geared to sc. shaft driving 1 CP propeller Total Power: 2,940kW (3,997hp) 13.3kn Akasaka A45 1 x 4 Stroke 6 Cy. 450 x 880 2940kW (3997bhp) Akasaka Tekkosho KK (Akasaka DieselLtd)-Japan AuxGen: 2 x 280kW 440V 60Hz a.c Boilers: AuxB (Comp) 7.0kgf/cm² (6.9bar) Thrusters: 1 Thwart. FP thruster (f) Fuel: 200.0
9382310 *WDD9837* -	**TRIPLE PLAY** **GulfMark Americas Inc** *New Orleans, LA* *United States of America* MMSI: 338425000 Official number: 1203989	**1,455** 436 1,686	Class: AB	**2007-11 Bollinger Machine Shop & Shipyard, Inc. — Lockport, La** Yd No: 523 Loa 57.91 Br ex - Dght 4.300 Lbp 54.90 Br md 14.02 Dpth 5.48 Welded, 1 dk	**(B21A2OS) Platform Supply Ship** Passengers: cabins: 6	**3 diesel electric oil engines** driving 2 gen. each 1235kW 480V a.c 1 gen. of 435kW 480V a.c Connecting to 3 elec. motors each (843kW) driving 3 Z propellers Fixed unit Total Power: 3,364kW (4,575hp) 10.5kn Cummins KTA-19-M 1 x 4 Stroke 6 Cy. 159 x 159 380kW (517bhp) Cummins Engine Co Inc-USA Cummins KTA-50-M2 2 x Vee 4 Stroke 16 Cy. 159 x 159 each-1492kW (2029bhp) Cummins Engine Co Inc-USA Thrusters: 2 Tunnel thruster (f) Fuel: 461.0 (r.f.)
9662382 *V2QN7* -	**TRIPLE S** **Triple S Ltd** Otto A Muller Schiffahrt GmbH *Saint John's* *Antigua & Barbuda* MMSI: 305948000	**3,845** 1,590 5,192	Class: GL	**2013-02 Israel Shipyards Ltd. — Haifa** Yd No: 2028 Loa 89.97 (BB) Br ex 15.58 Dght 6.130 Lbp 84.95 Br md 15.40 Dpth 7.60 Welded, 1 dk	**(A31A2GX) General Cargo Ship** Grain: 5,946 Compartments: 2 Ho 1 Ha: ER (54.6 x 12.6) Ice Capable	**1 oil engine** reduction geared to sc. shaft driving 1 CP propeller Total Power: 2,040kW (2,774hp) 11.8kn MAN-B&W 6L27/38 1 x 4 Stroke 6 Cy. 270 x 380 2040kW (2774bhp) MAN B&W Diesel AG-Augsburg Thrusters: 1 Tunnel thruster (f)
9374894 *ZGD07* -	**TRIPLE SEVEN** **Global Yacht Charters Pty Ltd** Nigel Burgess Ltd (BURGESS) *George Town* *Cayman Islands (British)* MMSI: 319058500	**1,393** 417 250	Class: LR (GL) **100A1** SS 11/2011 SSC Yacht mono G6 **LMC UMS** Cable: 385.0/26.0 U2	**2006-11 Nobiskrug GmbH — Rendsburg** Yd No: 777 Loa 67.40 (BB) Br ex 12.81 Dght 3.550 Lbp 55.10 Br md 12.00 Dpth 3.90 Welded, 2 dks	**(X11A2YP) Yacht** Passengers: berths: 12	**2 oil engines** reverse reduction geared to sc. shafts driving 2 FP propellers Total Power: 3,520kW (4,786hp) M.T.U. 16V4000M60 2 x Vee 4 Stroke 16 Cy. 165 x 190 each-1760kW (2393bhp) MTU Friedrichshafen GmbH-Friedrichshafen AuxGen: 2 x 252kW 400V 50Hz a.c, 1 x 156kW 400V 50Hz a.c
9317133 *3EDA5* -	**TRIPLE STAR** **Chijin Shipping SA** Kambara Kisen Co Ltd *Panama* *Panama* MMSI: 371523000 Official number: 3112705A	**30,046** 18,207 52,454 T/cm 55.5	Class: NV (NK)	**2005-10 Tsuneishi Corp — Fukuyama HS** Yd No: 1337 Loa 189.99 (BB) Br ex - Dght 12.022 Lbp 182.00 Br md 32.26 Dpth 17.00 Welded, 1 dk	**(A21A2BC) Bulk Carrier** Grain: 67,756; Bale: 65,601 Compartments: 5 Ho, ER 5 Ha: ER 5 (21.3 x 18.4) Cranes: 4x30t	**1 oil engine** driving 1 FP propeller Total Power: 7,800kW (10,605hp) 14.5kn MAN-B&W 6S50MC 1 x 2 Stroke 6 Cy. 500 x 1910 7800kW (10605bhp) Mitsui Engineering & Shipbuilding CLtd-Japan AuxGen: 3 x a.c Fuel: 2150.0
8940464 - - -	**TRIPLETS PRODUCTION** - **Triplets Production LLC** - *Delcambre, LA* *United States of America* Official number: 1042161	**131** 39 -		**1996 Rodriguez Boat Builders, Inc. — Coden, Al** Yd No: 145 L reg 24.63 Br ex - Dght - Lbp - Br md 7.32 Dpth 3.75 Welded, 1 dk	**(B11B2FV) Fishing Vessel**	**1 oil engine** driving 1 FP propeller
6814257 - -	**TRIPOLI STAR** *ex* Najmat Tarabolus *-1998* *ex* Tripoli Star *-1992* *ex* Haugland *-1991* *ex* Virna *-1984* *launched as* Bergum *-1968* **Alex Fuel & Trading Co (AFTC)** UNIMAS	**454** 211 508	Class: (NV) (HR)	**1968 Karmsund Verft & Mek. Verksted — Avaldsnes** Yd No: 8 Lengthened-1974 Loa 51.34 Br ex 8.54 Dght 3.296 Lbp 46.00 Br md 8.50 Dpth 3.48 Welded, 1 dk	**(A13B2TU) Tanker (unspecified)** Liq: 616; Liq (Oil): 616 Cargo Heating Coils Compartments: 8 Ta, ER	**1 oil engine** driving 1 FP propeller Total Power: 313kW (426hp) 10.0kn Caterpillar D353SCAC 1 x 4 Stroke 6 Cy. 159 x 203 313kW (426bhp) (new engine 1979) Caterpillar Tractor Co-USA AuxGen: 1 x 72kW 230V 50Hz a.c, 1 x 50kW 230V 50Hz a.c Fuel: 30.5 (d.f.) 1.5pd
8918899 *5ASA* -	**TRIPOLITANIA** *ex* Tagreft *-2013* **Gulf Fishing Co** *Tripoli* *Libya*	**276** 95 -	Class: (LR) ✠ Classed LR until 4/3/98	**1991-05 Scheepswerf Bijlholt B.V. — Foxhol** (Hull) Yd No: 679 **1991-05 B.V. Scheepswerf Damen — Gorinchem** Yd No: 3616 Loa 32.00 (BB) Br ex 8.22 Dght 3.301 Lbp 28.46 Br md 8.00 Dpth 4.25 Welded, 1 dk	**(B11B2FV) Fishing Vessel**	**1 oil engine** with clutches, flexible couplings & sr geared to sc. shaft driving 1 CP propeller Total Power: 743kW (1,010hp) Blackstone ESL6MK2 1 x 4 Stroke 6 Cy. 222 x 292 743kW (1010bhp) Mirrlees Blackstone (Stamford)Ltd.-Stamford AuxGen: 2 x 127kW 280V 50Hz a.c Thrusters: 1 Thwart. FP thruster (f)
8713835 *YEEI* -	**TRISAKTI** **PT Bahana Utama Line** *Jakarta* *Indonesia* MMSI: 525016037	**9,339** 3,818 11,140	Class: KI (GL)	**1988-11 J.J. Sietas KG Schiffswerft GmbH & Co. — Hamburg** Yd No: 954 Loa 120.00 (BB) Br ex 21.72 Dght 7.001 Lbp 116.90 Br md 21.70 Dpth 10.50 Welded, 1 dk	**(A24C2BU) Urea Carrier** Grain: 15,877 Compartments: 2 Ho, ER 6 Ha: ER	**1 oil engine** with flexible couplings & sr geared to sc. shaft driving 1 FP propeller Total Power: 3,000kW (4,079hp) 12.3kn MaK 9M453C 1 x 4 Stroke 9 Cy. 320 x 420 3000kW (4079bhp) Krupp MaK Maschinenbau GmbH-Kiel AuxGen: 3 x 400kW 220/380V a.c, 1 x 80kW 220/380V a.c Thrusters: 1 Thwart. FP thruster (f)
9089906 *YD6946* -	**TRISAKTI** **Herman Hadiyanto** - *Samarinda* *Indonesia*	**144** 44 -	Class: KI	**2006-09 PT Succes Ocean Shipping — Samarinda** Loa 22.90 Br ex - Dght - Lbp 21.26 Br md 7.33 Dpth 3.05 Welded, 1 dk	**(B32A2ST) Tug**	**2 oil engines** geared to sc. shafts driving 2 Propellers Total Power: 810kW (1,102hp) Volvo Penta TAMD165A 2 x 4 Stroke 6 Cy. 144 x 165 each-405kW (551bhp) AB Volvo Penta-Sweden
8651582 *YDA6648* -	**TRISAKTI II** **PT Pelayaran Indomaritim** - *Samarinda* *Indonesia* MMSI: 525024009 Official number: 2010 IIk No. 5305/L	**168** 51 -	Class: KI	**2010-11 C.V. Swadaya Utama — Samarinda** Yd No: 0155 Loa 25.87 Br ex - Dght 2.250 Lbp 23.92 Br md 7.30 Dpth 3.00 Welded, 1 dk	**(B32A2ST) Tug**	**2 oil engines** reduction geared to sc. shafts driving 2 FP propellers Total Power: 894kW (1,216hp) Cummins KTA-19-M3 2 x 4 Stroke 6 Cy. 159 x 159 each-447kW (608bhp) Cummins Engine Co Inc-USA

IMO / Call sign	Name / Owner	Tonnage	Class	Builder / Dimensions	Type	Machinery
7428354 - -	**TRISAKTI JAYA** *ex* Uco VIII *-1990* *ex* Olympic 3 *-1978* *ex* Kay Chuan III *-1975* **Trisakti Utama Shipping Pte Ltd** -	*103* 24 -	Class: (AB) (BV)	**1974-01 Sing Koon Seng Pte Ltd — Singapore** Yd No: 153 Loa 22.43 Br ex 6.41 Dght 2.896 Lbp 21.16 Br md 6.39 Dpth 3.74 Welded, 1 dk	**(B32A2ST) Tug**	**2 oil engines** geared to sc. shafts driving 2 FP propellers Total Power: 588kW (800hp) 9.5kn Deutz SBF8M716 2 x Vee 4 Stroke 8 Cy. 135 x 160 each-294kW (400bhp) Kloeckner Humboldt Deutz AG-West Germany AuxGen: 2 x 22kW Fuel: 60.0 (d.f.)
8849555 *YD5059* -	**TRISAKTI LANCAR** **PT Ersihan Satya Pratama** - *Surabaya* *Indonesia*	**180** 108 -	Class: (KI) (AB)	**1991-05 Jiangsu Wuxi Shipyard Co Ltd — Wuxi JS** Yd No: VEN1002 Loa 22.50 Br ex - Dght 2.400 Lbp 21.00 Br md 7.50 Dpth 3.20 Welded, 1 dk	**(B32A2ST) Tug**	**2 oil engines** sr geared to sc. shafts driving 2 FP propellers Total Power: 736kW (1,000hp) Cummins KTA-19-M 2 x 4 Stroke 6 Cy. 159 x 159 each-368kW (500bhp) Cummins Engine Co Inc-USA AuxGen: 2 x 24kW a.c
8849567 *YD6811* -	**TRISAKTI LANGGENG** **PT Kencana Gloria Marine** - *Balikpapan* *Indonesia* Official number: IID 892	*132* 39 -	Class: AB	**1991-05 Jiangsu Wuxi Shipyard Co Ltd — Wuxi JS** Yd No: VEN1001 Loa 22.50 Br ex - Dght 2.400 Lbp 21.00 Br md 7.50 Dpth 3.20 Welded, 1 dk	**(B32A2ST) Tug**	**2 oil engines** sr geared to sc. shafts driving 2 FP propellers Total Power: 736kW (1,000hp) Cummins KTA-19-M 2 x 4 Stroke 6 Cy. 159 x 159 each-368kW (500bhp) Cummins Engine Co Inc-USA AuxGen: 2 x 24kW a.c
9027635 - -	**TRISAKTI STAR** **PT Tri Astro Shipping** - *Surabaya* *Indonesia*	**108** 64 -	Class: (KI)	**1990-01 Zarah Sdn Bhd — Tawau** L reg 19.00 Br ex - Dght 2.000 Lbp 17.00 Br md 6.00 Dpth 2.85 Welded, 1 dk	**(B32A2ST) Tug**	**2 oil engines** geared to sc. shafts driving 2 Propellers Total Power: 514kW (698hp) 10.0kn Caterpillar 3406B 2 x 4 Stroke 6 Cy. 137 x 165 each-257kW (349bhp) Caterpillar Inc-USA
9071363 - -	**TRISAKTI SURYA** - -	**132** 40 123	Class: (AB) (GL)	**1992-12 Jiangsu Wuxi Shipyard Co Ltd — Wuxi JS** Yd No: 92-02 Loa 23.20 Br ex - Dght 2.000 Lbp 21.79 Br md 7.40 Dpth 2.80 Welded, 1 dk	**(B32A2ST) Tug**	**2 oil engines** with flexible couplings & sr reverse geared to sc. shafts driving 2 FP propellers Total Power: 866kW (1,178hp) Cummins KTA-19-M 2 x 4 Stroke 6 Cy. 159 x 159 each-433kW (589bhp) Cummins Engine Co Ltd-United Kingdom AuxGen: 2 x 28kW 240V 50Hz a.c Fuel: 70.0 (d.f.)
8608509 *DUJ2236* -	**TRISHA KERSTIN** *ex* Wakashio *-2006* **Aleson Shipping Lines Inc** - *Zamboanga* *Philippines* Official number: ZAM2D01325	*320* 72 133		**1986-07 Fujiwara Zosensho — Imabari** Yd No: 102 L reg 39.61 Br ex - Dght 2.401 Lbp 39.53 Br md 11.61 Dpth 3.31 Welded	**(A36A2PR) Passenger/Ro-Ro Ship (Vehicles)** Passengers: unberthed: 400 Cars: 3, Trailers: 4	**1 oil engine** geared to sc. shaft driving 1 FP propeller Total Power: 956kW (1,300hp) 12.5kn Yanmar T260-ST 1 x 4 Stroke 6 Cy. 260 x 330 956kW (1300bhp) Yanmar Diesel Engine Co Ltd-Japan
8824373 *DUJ2241* -	**TRISHA KERSTIN 2** *ex* Geiyo *-2003* **Aleson Shipping Lines Inc** - *Zamboanga* *Philippines* Official number: ZAM2D01384	*637* 241 290		**1989-05 Fujiwara Zosensho — Imabari** Yd No: 111 Loa 59.54 Br ex - Dght 2.830 Lbp 55.00 Br md 12.25 Dpth 3.09 Welded, 1 dk	**(A37B2PS) Passenger Ship**	**2 oil engines** driving 2 FP propellers Total Power: 2,206kW (3,000hp) 14.5kn Pielstick 6PA5 2 x 4 Stroke 6 Cy. 255 x 270 each-1103kW (1500bhp) Niigata Engineering Co Ltd-Japan
9125516 *DUJ2263* -	**TRISHA KERSTIN 3** *ex* Camellia 2 *-2010* **Aleson Shipping Lines Inc** - *Zamboanga* *Philippines* Official number: ZAM2D01800	*622* 412 250		**1995-07 Wakamatsu Zosen K.K. — Kitakyushu** Yd No: 513 Loa 47.90 Br ex 12.00 Dght 2.880 Lbp 44.00 Br md 11.20 Dpth 3.70 Welded, 1 dk	**(A36A2PR) Passenger/Ro-Ro Ship (Vehicles)**	**2 oil engines** with clutches, flexible couplings & dr reverse geared to sc. shafts driving 2 FP propellers Total Power: 1,912kW (2,600hp) Daihatsu 6DLM-24S 2 x 4 Stroke 6 Cy. 240 x 320 each-956kW (1300bhp) Daihatsu Diesel Manufacturing Co Lt-Japan Thrusters: 1 Thwart. CP thruster (f)
9288667 - -	**TRISHNA** **Port Authority of Mongla** - *Bangladesh*	**384** - 600		**2005-01 Karnafuly Ship Builders Ltd — Chittagong** Yd No: 010 Loa 45.00 Br ex - Dght 2.900 Lbp 42.90 Br md 8.00 Dpth 3.55 Welded, 1 dk	**(A14A2LO) Water Tanker**	**2 oil engines** geared to sc. shafts driving 2 Propellers Total Power: 882kW (1,200hp) Volvo Penta TAMD165A 2 x 4 Stroke 6 Cy. 144 x 165 each-441kW (600bhp) AB Volvo Penta-Sweden
8997493 *YFLQ* -	**TRISILA BHAKTI I** **PT Yala Bhakti Yasbhum** - *Jakarta* *Indonesia*	**585** 175 -	Class: KI	**1996-09 P.T. Najatim Dockyard — Surabaya** Loa 60.00 Br ex - Dght 2.090 Lbp 51.50 Br md 13.50 Dpth 3.00 Welded, 1 dk	**(A36A2PR) Passenger/Ro-Ro Ship (Vehicles)** Passengers: unberthed: 310	**2 oil engines** reduction geared to sc. shafts driving 2 Propellers Total Power: 986kW (1,340hp) 10.0kn Yanmar 8LAAM-UTE 2 x Vee 4 Stroke 8 Cy. 148 x 165 each-493kW (670bhp) Showa Precision Mchy. Co. Ltd.-Amagasaki
8741973 *PNBV* -	**TRISILA BHAKTI II** **PT Pelayaran Penyeberangan Trisila Laut** - *Surabaya* *Indonesia* MMSI: 525016532	**525** 158 336	Class: KI	**2009-08 PT Dumas — Surabaya** Loa 51.00 Br ex - Dght 2.000 Lbp 41.76 Br md 13.50 Dpth 3.00 Welded, 1 dk	**(A37B2PS) Passenger Ship**	**2 oil engines** reduction geared to sc. shafts driving 2 Propellers Total Power: 736kW (1,000hp) 8.0kn Yanmar 6HYM-ETE 2 x 4 Stroke 6 Cy. 133 x 165 each-368kW (500bhp) Yanmar Diesel Engine Co Ltd-Japan AuxGen: 2 x 75kW 380V a.c
7397294 *PLUT* -	**TRISNA DWITYA** *ex* Bhaita Dwitya *-2003* **PT Lintas Sarana Nusantara** - *Jakarta* *Indonesia* MMSI: 525000900 Official number: 6054+BA	*876* 326 1,899	Class: KI (AB) (NV)	**1975-06 Singapore Shipbuilding & Engineering Pte Ltd — Singapore** Yd No: 82 Loa 53.78 Br ex 14.43 Dght 2.507 Lbp 52.91 Br md 14.41 Dpth 3.51 Welded, 1 dk	**(A35D2RL) Landing Craft** Bow door/ramp	**2 oil engines** driving 2 FP propellers Total Power: 1,014kW (1,378hp) 10.0kn M.T.U. 8R362TB61 2 x 4 Stroke 8 Cy. 160 x 180 each-507kW (689bhp) MTU Friedrichshafen GmbH-Friedrichshafen AuxGen: 1 x 36kW 415V 50Hz a.c, 1 x 28kW 415V 50Hz a.c
7311068 *YFPF* -	**TRISNA I** *ex* United Spirit *-2000* *ex* Oglethorpe *-2000* *ex* Toyo Maru No. 2 *-2000* *ex* Harbour Star *-2000* *ex* Tung Ying *-1991* *ex* Ace *-1990* *ex* Kaiyo Maru No. 1 *-1990* **PT Trisna Samudra Perdana** - *Cirebon* *Indonesia*	**1,166** 391 1,200	Class: (KI)	**1971-06 Okayama Zosen K.K. — Hinase** Yd No: 216 Loa 65.75 Br ex 11.52 Dght 3.250 Lbp 60.02 Br md 11.49 Dpth 4.04 Welded, 2 dks	**(A31A2GX) General Cargo Ship** Grain: 1,950; Bale: 1,750 Compartments: 1 Ho, ER 1 Ha: (33.6 x 9.5)ER	**1 oil engine** driving 1 FP propeller Total Power: 1,177kW (1,600hp) 12.0kn Niigata 8MG25BX 1 x 4 Stroke 8 Cy. 250 x 320 1177kW (1600bhp) Niigata Engineering Co Ltd-Japan AuxGen: 2 x 40kW 220V a.c Fuel: 45.5 4.5pd
9482392 *YDA4336* -	**TRISNA POWER 1800-1** **PT Trisna Samudra Perdana** - *Jakarta* *Indonesia*	**140** 42 -	Class: KI (GL)	**2007-12 Tuong Aik Shipyard Sdn Bhd — Sibu** Yd No: 2710 Loa 23.50 Br ex - Dght 2.700 Lbp 21.79 Br md 7.32 Dpth 3.20 Welded, 1 dk	**(B32A2ST) Tug**	**2 oil engines** geared to sc. shafts driving 2 Propellers Total Power: 1,220kW (1,658hp) Yanmar 6AYM-ETE 2 x 4 Stroke 6 Cy. 155 x 180 each-610kW (829bhp) Yanmar Diesel Engine Co Ltd-Japan
9499620 *YDA4373* -	**TRISNA POWER 1800-3** **PT Trisna Samudra Perdana** - *Jakarta* *Indonesia*	**194** 59 180	Class: KI (GL)	**2007-12 Forward Marine Enterprise Sdn Bhd — Sibu** Yd No: FM-32 Loa 26.00 Br ex - Dght 3.000 Lbp 24.30 Br md 8.00 Dpth 3.65 Welded, 1 dk	**(B32A2ST) Tug**	**2 oil engines** reduction geared to sc. shafts driving 2 FP propellers Total Power: 1,220kW (1,658hp) Yanmar 6AYM-ETE 2 x 4 Stroke 6 Cy. 155 x 180 each-610kW (829bhp) Yanmar Diesel Engine Co Ltd-Japan
8321333 *SKWI* -	**TRISTAN** **Walleniusrederierna AB (Wallenius Lines AB)** Wallenius Marine AB SatCom: Inmarsat C 426501910 *Stockholm* *Sweden* MMSI: 265019000	**51,071** 20,650 28,070 T/cm 53.3	Class: LR ✠ **100A1** SS 03/2010 vehicle carrier CR movable decks LI Ice Class 3 ✠ **LMC** **UMS** Eq.Ltr: P†; Cable: 660.0/78.0 U3	**1985-02 Kockums AB — Malmo** Yd No: 598 Loa 198.00 (BB) Br ex 32.29 Dght 11.645 Lbp 190.74 Br md 32.25 Dpth 31.20 Welded, 2 dks, 1 dk fwd of Machy space - 6 intermediate fixed & 4 movable car decks,: dks Nos. 4, 6 & 9 str. for ro-ro cargoes	**(A35B2RV) Vehicles Carrier** Side door/ramp (s) Len: 24.70 Wid: 4.50 Swl: 15 Quarter stern door/ramp (s. a.) Len: 42.10 Wid: 7.00 Swl: 200 Lane-clr ht: 6.20 Cars: 5,293 Ice Capable	**1 oil engine** driving 1 FP propeller Total Power: 15,190kW (20,652hp) 20.0kn Sulzer 7RTA68 1 x 2 Stroke 7 Cy. 680 x 2000 15190kW (20652bhp) Mitsubishi Heavy Industries Ltd-Japan AuxGen: 3 x 1600kW 450V 60Hz a.c Boilers: e 18.3kgf/cm² (17.9bar), AuxB (o.f.) (New boiler: 1985) 12.2kgf/cm² (12.0bar) Thrusters: 1 Thwart. CP thruster (f) Fuel: 417.0 (d.f.) 3578.0 (r.f.) 58.0pd
9636773 *WDF7657* -	**TRISTAN K.** **Moran Towing of Lake Charles LLC** - *Wilmington, DE* *United States of America* MMSI: 367486750 Official number: 1232889	**399** 119 -	Class: AB	**2011-06 Washburn & Doughty Associates Inc — East Boothbay ME** Yd No: 100 Loa 30.02 Br ex - Dght 4.100 Lbp 28.04 Br md 11.99 Dpth 5.03 Welded, 1 dk	**(B32A2ST) Tug**	**2 oil engines** gearing integral to driving 2 Z propellers Total Power: 4,480kW (6,092hp) M.T.U. 16V4000M70 2 x Vee 4 Stroke 16 Cy. 165 x 190 each-2240kW (3046bhp) MTU Friedrichshafen GmbH-Friedrichshafen AuxGen: 2 x 179kW a.c

IMO / Call sign	Name / Owner / Port	Tonnage	Class	Builder / Dimensions	Type	Machinery
8659950 *POYS* -	**TRISTAN PERKASA** *ex* Heng Tong 68 *-2012* **Tristan Marine Services** - *Jakarta* *Indonesia* Official number: 801	**1,169** 669 1,738	Class: KI	**2009-11 Jiangyan Xingzhen Shipyard — Taizhou, Jiangsu** Yd No: 068 Loa 78.00 Br ex 16.00 Dght - Lbp 74.26 Br md 15.80 Dpth 3.60 Welded, 1 dk	**(A24D2BA) Aggregates Carrier**	**2 oil engines** reduction geared to sc. shafts driving 2 Propellers Chinese Std. Type Zibo Diesel Engine Factory-China
8210950 *YGZI* -	**TRISTAR 2** *ex* Olive Maru No. 3 *-2001* **PT Darma Bahari Utama** - *Jakarta* *Indonesia* MMSI: 525001069	**1,776** 834 75	Class: KI	**1983-04 Tokushima Zosen Sangyo K.K. — Komatsushima** Yd No: 1593 Loa 57.54 Br ex - Dght 3.101 Lbp 54.01 Br md 13.01 Dpth 9.00 Welded, 1 dk	**(A36A2PR) Passenger/Ro-Ro Ship (Vehicles)** Passengers: unberthed: 488 Bow door/ramp (centre)	**2 oil engines** driving 2 FP propellers Total Power: 2,354kW (3,200hp) 14.5kn Niigata 6M31AGT 2 x 4 Stroke 6 Cy. 310 x 530 each-1177kW (1600bhp) Niigata Engineering Co Ltd-Japan
8032798 *DUAB9* -	**TRISTAR A** *ex* Angel *-1981* **Oceanic Charters Corp** - *Manila* *Philippines* Official number: MNLD000566	*185* 71 -		**1964 Kanda Zosensho K.K. — Kure** Yd No: 92 L reg 30.00 Br ex 6.20 Dght - Lbp - Br md - Dpth 2.80 Welded, 1 dk	**(A37B2PS) Passenger Ship**	**1 oil engine** driving 1 FP propeller Total Power: 368kW (500hp) Daihatsu 6PSTBM-26D 1 x 4 Stroke 6 Cy. 260 x 320 368kW (500bhp) Daihatsu Diesel Manufacturing Co Lt-Japan
9540912 *A6E2568* -	**TRISTAR COURAGE** *ex* Courage *-2009* *ex* Gac Energy *-2009* **Tristar Transport LLC** - *Fujairah* *United Arab Emirates* MMSI: 470473000 Official number: 6246	**498** 162 660	Class: BV	**2008-04 El Etr Shipyard — Port Said** Yd No: 201 Loa 45.00 Br ex - Dght 3.300 Lbp 42.50 Br md 9.00 Dpth 4.50 Welded, 1 dk	**(B35E2TF) Bunkering Tanker** Double Hull (13F) Liq: 614; Liq (Oil): 614 Compartments: 8 Wing Ta, ER	**2 oil engines** reduction geared to sc. shaft driving 2 FP propellers Total Power: 1,176kW (1,598hp) 10.0kn MAN D2842LE 2 x Vee 4 Stroke 12 Cy. 128 x 142 each-588kW (799bhp) MAN Nutzfahrzeuge AG-Nuernberg AuxGen: 3 x 83kW 50Hz a.c
9632325 *3BRU*	**TRISTAR GLORY** - **Tristar Transport LLC** - *Port Louis* *Mauritius* MMSI: 645350000	**499** 201 813	Class: BV	**2011-12 Akdeniz Gemi Insa Sanayi ve Ticaret AS — Yumurtalik** Yd No: 05 Loa 49.94 Br ex - Dght 2.900 Lbp 48.68 Br md 9.50 Dpth 4.00 Welded, 1 dk	**(B35E2TF) Bunkering Tanker** Double Hull (13F) Liq: 818; Liq (Oil): 818 Compartments: 7 Ta, ER	**2 oil engines** reduction geared to sc. shafts driving 2 FP propellers Total Power: 956kW (1,300hp) 8.0kn Yanmar 6HYM-ETE 2 x 4 Stroke 6 Cy. 133 x 165 each-478kW (650bhp) Yanmar Diesel Engine Co Ltd-Japan AuxGen: 2 x 138kW 50Hz a.c Thrusters: 1 Tunnel thruster (f) Fuel: 42.3
9505479 *A6E2909* -	**TRISTAR LEGEND** *ex* FSL Legend *-2012* **Tristar Transport LLC** - *Sharjah* *United Arab Emirates* MMSI: 470714000 Official number: 6321	**481** 152 700	Class: BV (AB) (GL)	**2010-06 Mech Marine Engineers Pvt Ltd — Vasai** Yd No: 170 Loa 48.25 Br ex 10.80 Dght 2.500 Lbp 47.00 Br md 10.30 Dpth 3.50 Welded, 1 dk	**(A13B2TP) Products Tanker** Double Hull (13F) Liq: 650; Liq (Oil): 650 Compartments: 12 Wing Ta, 2 Wing Slop Ta, ER	**2 oil engines** reduction geared to sc. shafts driving 2 FP propellers Total Power: 648kW (882hp) Caterpillar 3406C 2 x 4 Stroke 6 Cy. 137 x 165 each-324kW (441bhp) Caterpillar Inc-USA AuxGen: 2 x a.c
9029994 *A6E2788* -	**TRISTAR PRIDE** *ex* F. S. L. Pride *-2012* *ex* Castrol Pride *-2002* *ex* Susan *-1997* **Tristar Transport LLC** - *Sharjah* *United Arab Emirates* MMSI: 470498000 Official number: UAE/SHJ/4424	**203** 79 300	Class: BV (Class contemplated) GL	**1997-01 Mech Marine Engineers Pvt Ltd — Vasai** Yd No: 125 Converted From: Water Tanker-1999 Loa 36.32 Br ex - Dght 1.807 Lbp 36.00 Br md 8.00 Dpth 2.50 Welded, 1 dk	**(A13B2TU) Tanker (unspecified)** Liq: 234; Liq (Oil): 234	**2 oil engines** reverse reduction geared to sc. shafts driving 2 FP propellers Total Power: 216kW (294hp) 8.0kn Volvo Penta TAMD41M 2 x 4 Stroke 6 Cy. 92 x 90 each-108kW (147bhp) AB Volvo Penta-Sweden
9541241 *A6E3078* -	**TRISTAR SPIRIT** - **Tristar Transport LLC** - *Fujairah* *United Arab Emirates* MMSI: 470917000 Official number: 6109	**490** 151 634	Class: BV (AB)	**2010-04 Mech Marine Engineers Pvt Ltd — Vasai** Yd No: 169 Loa 49.25 Br ex - Dght 2.500 Lbp 47.00 Br md 10.30 Dpth 3.50 Welded, 1 dk	**(B35E2TF) Bunkering Tanker** Double Hull (13F) Liq: 640; Liq (Oil): 640 Compartments: 16 Wing Ta, ER	**2 oil engines** reduction geared to sc. shafts driving 2 FP propellers Total Power: 954kW (1,298hp) Cummins KTA-19-M3 2 x 4 Stroke 6 Cy. 159 x 159 each-477kW (649bhp) Cummins Engine Co Inc-USA AuxGen: 2 x 86kW a.c Fuel: 50.0 (d.f.)
9104445 *H03179* -	**TRISTEN** *ex* Seongho Venus *-2003* *ex* Genei Maru *-2001* **Asia Indo Navigation SA** Superin Chemical (S) Pte Ltd *Panama* *Panama* MMSI: 353129000 Official number: 2927403C	**1,997** 919 2,952	Class: KR (NV) (NK)	**1995-04 Sasaki Shipbuilding Co Ltd — Osakikamijima HS** Yd No: 593 Converted From: Products Tanker-2005 Loa 89.73 Br ex 13.23 Dght 5.436 Lbp 85.00 Br md 13.20 Dpth 6.40 Welded, 1 dk	**(A12A2TC) Chemical Tanker** Liq: 3,349; Liq (Oil): 3,349	**1 oil engine** driving 1 FP propeller Total Power: 2,060kW (2,801hp) Akasaka A38 1 x 4 Stroke 6 Cy. 380 x 740 2060kW (2801bhp) Akasaka Tekkosho KK (Akasaka DieselLtd)-Japan
9049762 *YHRT* -	**TRISULA** - **Government of The Republic of Indonesia (Direktorat Jenderal Perhubungan Laut - Ministry of Sea Communications)** - *Jakarta* *Indonesia*	**878** 263 310	Class: (KI)	**2004-06 PT Dumas — Surabaya** Loa 61.80 Br ex - Dght 3.200 Lbp 55.82 Br md 9.70 Dpth 4.70 Welded, 1 dk	**(B34H2SQ) Patrol Vessel**	**2 oil engines** driving 2 Propellers Total Power: 4,640kW (6,308hp) 18.0kn M.T.U. 16V4000M70 2 x Vee 4 Stroke 16 Cy. 165 x 190 each-2320kW (3154bhp) (made 2003) MTU Friedrichshafen GmbH-Friedrichshafen
7813286 *CUUE* -	**TRITAO** - **Pescarias Euromar Lda** - *Leixoes* *Portugal* Official number: L-523-C	**236** 70 113	Class: (RP)	**1980-08 Estaleiros Navais do Mondego S.A. — Figueira da Foz** Yd No: 188 Loa 34.52 Br ex - Dght 2.598 Lbp 29.32 Br md 7.61 Dpth 3.64 Welded, 1 dk	**(B11A2FS) Stern Trawler**	**1 oil engine** geared to sc. shaft driving 1 FP propeller Total Power: 883kW (1,201hp) MaK 6M332AK 1 x 4 Stroke 6 Cy. 240 x 330 883kW (1201bhp) Krupp MaK Maschinenbau GmbH-Kiel
7711256 - -	**TRITAO** *ex* Sarandi *-1987* **Government of The Federative Republic of Brazil (Ministerio da Marinha do Brasil)** - *Rio de Janeiro* *Brazil*	*499* - 950	Class: (AB)	**1981-03 Estaleiros Amazonia S.A. (ESTANAVE) — Manaus** Yd No: 145 Converted From: Offshore Supply Ship-1987 Loa 53.52 Br ex - Dght 3.950 Lbp 50.02 Br md 11.61 Dpth 4.60 Welded, 1 dk	**(B32A2ST) Tug**	**2 oil engines** reverse reduction geared to sc. shafts driving 2 FP propellers Total Power: 1,824kW (2,480hp) 12.0kn Alpha 8V23LU 2 x Vee 4 Stroke 8 Cy. 225 x 300 each-912kW (1240bhp) Equipamentos Villares SA-Brazil AuxGen: 2 x 160kW 440V 60Hz a.c
8913772 *J8B4609* -	**TRITOINS** *ex* Alexandretta *-2013* *ex* Hamburg Express *-2009* *ex* Hamburg *-2005* *ex* Judith Borchard *-1997* *ex* Hamburg *-1991* **Aljazeera Maritime Co SA** Alfamarine Shipping Co Ltd SatCom: Inmarsat C 437620810 *Kingstown* *St Vincent & The Grenadines* MMSI: 376208000 Official number: 11082	**3,466** 1,910 5,020	Class: GL	**1991-08 Marmara Tersanesi — Yarimca** Yd No: 48A Loa 94.26 (BB) Br ex - Dght 6.250 Lbp 86.91 Br md 15.82 Dpth 7.90 Welded, 1 dk	**(A31A2GX) General Cargo Ship** Grain: 6,315; Bale: 5,380 TEU 343 C Ho 133 TEU C Dk 210 TEU incl 60 ref C. Compartments: 1 Ho, ER 1 Ha: (55.8 x 12.9)ER Cranes: 2x30t Ice Capable	**1 oil engine** with flexible couplings & sr geared to sc. shaft driving 1 CP propeller Total Power: 2,200kW (2,991hp) 14.0kn MaK 8M453C 1 x 4 Stroke 8 Cy. 320 x 420 2200kW (2991bhp) Krupp MaK Maschinenbau GmbH-Kiel AuxGen: 1 x 702kW 220/380V 50Hz a.c, 2 x 292kW 220/380V 50Hz a.c Thrusters: 1 Retract. directional thruster (f) Fuel: 62.2 (d.f.) 277.8 (r.f.) 11.2pd
8910770 *9MLG4* -	**TRITON** *ex* Ryoka Maru No. 2 *-2010* **Lannic Sdn Bhd** - *Port Klang* *Malaysia* MMSI: 533051100 Official number: 334174	**463** 138 668 T/cm 3.5		**1989-10 Mukaishima Zoki Co. Ltd. — Onomichi** Yd No: 260 Loa 50.70 Br ex 9.02 Dght 3.608 Lbp 46.00 Br md 9.00 Dpth 3.80 Welded, 1 dk	**(A12A2TC) Chemical Tanker** Liq: 457 Cargo Heating Coils Compartments: 6 Ta, ER 3 Cargo Pump (s): 3x80m³/hr Manifold: Bow/CM: 23m	**1 oil engine** reverse geared to sc. shaft driving 1 CP propeller Total Power: 736kW (1,001hp) 10.8kn Hanshin LH28G 1 x 4 Stroke 6 Cy. 280 x 460 736kW (1001bhp) The Hanshin Diesel Works Ltd-Japan AuxGen: 2 x 191kW 220V 60Hz a.c Fuel: 62.9 (d.f.) 3.0pd
8661410 - -	**TRITON** *ex* Soberano *-1980* **Autoridad Portuaria de Guayaquil** - *Guayaquil* *Ecuador* Official number: R-00-0079	**127** - -		**1962-01 Blount Marine Corp. — Warren, RI** Yd No: 78 Loa - Br ex - Dght - Lbp - Br md - Dpth - Welded, 1 dk	**(B32A2ST) Tug**	**1 oil engine** reduction geared to sc. shaft driving 1 Propeller

IMO / Call sign / Flag	Name / Owner / Port	Tonnage	Class	Builder / Dimensions	Type	Machinery
9110858 - -	**TRITON** **Inversiones Maritimas CPT Peru SAC (INMARSA)** *Callao* *Peru*	**145** 51 -	Class: LR ✠ **100A1** SS 10/2009 tug Peruvian, Equadorian, Columbian & Chilean coastal service, South to latitude 45 degrees, 45 minutes **LMC** Eq.Ltr: (A) ; Cable: 250.0/16.0 U2	**1995 Stocznia Tczew Sp z oo — Tczew** (Hull) **1994-12 B.V. Scheepswerf Damen — Gorinchem** Yd No: 6517 Loa 22.55 Br ex 7.45 Dght 2.750 Lbp 19.82 Br md 7.20 Dpth 3.74 Welded, 1 dk	**(B32A2ST) Tug**	**2 oil engines** with clutches, flexible couplings & sr reverse geared to sc. shafts driving 2 FP propellers Total Power: 1,560kW (2,120hp) 11.4kn Cummins KTA-38-M 2 x Vee 4 Stroke 12 Cy. 159 x 159 each-780kW (1060bhp) Cummins Engine Co Inc-USA AuxGen: 2 x 40kW 440V 60Hz a.c
9093799 *V7GF5* -	**TRITON** **Tropic Marine Ventures Ltd** *Bikini* *Marshall Islands* MMSI: 538070070 Official number: 70070	**527** 158 -	Class: (AB)	**2004-08 Delta Marine Industries, Inc. — Seattle, Wa** Yd No: 158001 Loa - Br ex - Dght - Lbp 39.80 Br md 9.34 Dpth 4.70 Bonded, 1 dk	**(X11A2YP) Yacht** Hull Material: Reinforced Plastic	**2 oil engines** reverse reduction geared to sc. shafts driving 2 Propellers Total Power: 1,492kW (2,028hp) Caterpillar 3508B 2 x Vee 4 Stroke 8 Cy. 170 x 190 each-746kW (1014bhp) Caterpillar Inc-USA
9123025 *DBHK* -	**TRITON** **Government of The Federal Republic of Germany (Bundesminister fuer Verkehr-WSV)** Government of The Federal Republic of Germany (Wasser- und Schiffahrtsamt Tonning) *Toenning* *Germany* MMSI: 211249300	**532** 159 98	Class: GL	**1997-06 Stocznia Polnocna SA (Northern Shipyard) — Gdansk** (Hull) Yd No: B100/1 **1997-06 B.V. Scheepswerf Maaskant — Stellendam** Yd No: 517 Loa 49.30 Br ex 9.20 Dght 2.100 Lbp 45.00 Br md 9.00 Dpth 3.60 Welded, 1 dk	**(B34Q2QB) Buoy Tender**	**1 oil engine** with clutches, flexible couplings & sr reverse geared to sc. shaft driving 1 FP propeller Total Power: 740kW (1,006hp) 12.0kn M.T.U. 8V396TE74 1 x Vee 4 Stroke 8 Cy. 165 x 185 740kW (1006bhp) MTU Friedrichshafen GmbH-Friedrichshafen AuxGen: 1 x 78kW 220/380V a.c Thrusters: 1 Water jet (f) Fuel: 35.6 (d.f.)
9159945 *UGJB* -	**TRITON** *ex* Vladimir Girenko *-2013* **OOO Dionysus** - *Nevelsk* *Russia* MMSI: 273898600	**749** 217 414	Class: RS	**1996-07 ATVT Zavod "Leninska Kuznya" — Kyyiv** Yd No: 1690 Loa 54.82 Br ex 10.15 Dght 4.140 Lbp 50.30 Br md 9.80 Dpth 5.00 Welded, 1 dk	**(B11A2FS) Stern Trawler**	**1 oil engine** driving 1 CP propeller Total Power: 852kW (1,158hp) 12.0kn S.K.L. 8NVD48A-2U 1 x 4 Stroke 8 Cy. 320 x 480 852kW (1158bhp) SKL Motoren u. Systemtechnik AG-Magdeburg AuxGen: 3 x 200kW a.c Fuel: 155.0 (d.f.)
9161302 - -	**TRITON** *ex* Triton I *-2011* **Dana Petroleum Plc, Shell UK Ltd, Esso Exploration & Production UK Ltd, Endeavour** Dana Petroleum (E&P) Ltd *Flag not required*	**59,081** 30,842 103,429		**1998-07 Samsung Heavy Industries Co Ltd — Geoje** Yd No: 1226 Converted From: Crude Oil Tanker-1999 Loa 243.80 Br ex - Dght 14.700 Lbp 233.00 Br md 42.00 Dpth 21.30 Welded, 1 dk	**(B22E2OF) FPSO, Oil** Double Hull (13F)	**1 oil engine** driving 1 FP propeller Total Power: 12,269kW (16,681hp) 14.5kn B&W 6S60MC 1 x 2 Stroke 6 Cy. 600 x 2292 12269kW (16681bhp) Samsung Heavy Industries Co Ltd-South Korea
7329819 *UEXE* -	**TRITON** *ex* Ilpyr *-2011* **Teploenergokompleks Ltd** - *Petropavlovsk-Kamchatskiy* *Russia*	**172** 51 94	Class: RS	**1973-06 Zavod 'Nikolayevsk-na-Amure' — Nikolayevsk-na-Amure** Yd No: 75 Loa 33.96 Br ex 7.09 Dght 2.900 Lbp 29.97 Br md 7.00 Dpth 3.69 Welded, 1 dk	**(B11B2FV) Fishing Vessel** Bale: 115 Compartments: 1 Ho, ER 1 Ha: (1.3 x 1.6) Derricks: 2x2t; Winches: 2 Ice Capable	**1 oil engine** driving 1 FP propeller Total Power: 224kW (305hp) 9.5kn S.K.L. 8NVD36-1U 1 x 4 Stroke 8 Cy. 240 x 360 224kW (305bhp) VEB Schwermaschinenbau "KarlLiebknecht" (SKL)-Magdeburg Fuel: 24.0 (d.f.)
7236141 *UISR* -	**TRITON** *ex* Remmar *-2005* *ex* Gwentgarth *-1997* *ex* Norderney *-1983* **Joint Stock Northern Shipping Co (A/O 'Severnoye Morskoye Parokhodstvo') (NSC ARKHANGELSK)** - *Arkhangelsk* *Russia* Official number: 724092	**161** 49 76	Class: RS (GL)	**1972-12 C Cassens Schiffswerft — Emden** Yd No: 109 Loa 28.50 Br ex 7.32 Dght 3.530 Lbp 25.02 Br md 7.29 Dpth 4.20 Welded, 1 dk	**(B32A2ST) Tug** Ice Capable	**1 oil engine** reverse reduction geared to sc. shaft driving 1 FP propeller Total Power: 956kW (1,300hp) 11.5kn MWM TD500-6 1 x 4 Stroke 6 Cy. 360 x 450 956kW (1300bhp) Motoren Werke Mannheim AG (MWM)-West Germany Fuel: 50.0 (d.f.)
7393999 *CXTL* -	**TRITON** *ex* Hangzhou *-1994* *ex* Z-Peller No. 1 *-1989* **Remolcadores y Lanchas SA** - *Montevideo* *Uruguay* MMSI: 770576126 Official number: 7860	**228** 69 149	Class: (GL) (KI) (NV)	**1974-06 Masui Zosensho K.K. — Nandan** Yd No: 118 Loa 28.22 Br ex - Dght 3.220 Lbp 25.00 Br md 8.62 Dpth 3.81 Riveted\Welded, 1 dk	**(B32A2ST) Tug**	**2 oil engines** reduction geared to sc. shafts driving 2 Z propellers Total Power: 1,912kW (2,600hp) Niigata 6L25BX 2 x 4 Stroke 6 Cy. 250 x 320 each-956kW (1300bhp) Niigata Engineering Co Ltd-Japan AuxGen: 2 x 48kW 220V 60Hz a.c Thrusters: 2 Thwart. FP thruster (f)
7435204 - -	**TRITON** *ex* Alex *-1989* **Ocean Fishing Maritime Co Hellas Sarl** - *Douala* *Cameroon*	*231* 98 -	Class: (BV)	**1975-06 Vassiliadis Bros — Salamina** Yd No: 22 Loa 30.89 Br ex 7.60 Dght 2.401 Lbp 25.30 Br md 6.99 Dpth 3.92 Welded, 1 dk	**(B11A2FT) Trawler**	**1 oil engine** reduction geared to sc. shaft driving 1 FP propeller Total Power: 416kW (566hp) 12.0kn Caterpillar D379SCAC 1 x Vee 4 Stroke 8 Cy. 159 x 203 416kW (566bhp) Caterpillar Tractor Co-USA
5056298 - -	**TRITON** *ex* C. F. O. Tontini *-1973* *ex* Ernst Groschel *-1960* **Pesqueria Dalia SRL** -	**374** 176 -	Class: (GL) (RI)	**1949 Rickmers Werft — Bremerhaven** Yd No: 208 Loa 48.06 Br ex 8.03 Dght 4.268 Lbp 43.31 Br md 8.01 Dpth 4.73 Riveted\Welded, 1 dk	**(B11A2FT) Trawler** Bale: 380 Compartments: 1 Ho, ER Winches: 1	**1 oil engine** driving 1 FP propeller Total Power: 662kW (900hp) 10.0kn Ansaldo 1 x 4 Stroke 6 Cy. 370 x 560 662kW (900bhp) (new engine 1960) SA Ansaldo Stabilimento Meccaniche-Italy
4906551 *VNPA* -	**TRITON** **Gardline Shipping Ltd** Gardline Australia Pty Ltd *Darwin, NT* *Australia* MMSI: 503532000 Official number: 858262	**2,291** 688 -	Class: NV	**2000-08 Vosper Thornycroft (UK) Ltd — Southampton** Yd No: 4292 Loa 98.70 Br ex 22.50 Dght 3.200 Lbp 90.00 Br md 21.50 Dpth 9.00 Welded, 1 dk	**(B31A2SR) Research Survey Vessel**	**2 diesel electric oil engines** driving 2 gen. Connecting to 3 elec. motors each (4000kW) driving 1 FP propeller ,fixed pitch Total Power: 4,170kW (5,670hp) 12.0kn Paxman 12VP185 2 x Vee 4 Stroke 12 Cy. 185 x 196 each-2085kW (2835bhp) Paxman Diesels Ltd.-Colchester Thrusters: 2 Directional thruster (a); 1 Thwart. CP thruster (f)
6605254 *WDC9955* -	**TRITON** *ex* Sea Lion *-2001* **Dahl Tug & Barge Inc** - SatCom: Inmarsat C 433854610 *Seattle, WA* *United States of America* MMSI: 367109120 Official number: 500707	**336** 100 -	Class: (AB)	**1965 Pacific Coast Eng. Co. — Alameda, Ca** Yd No: 210 Loa 37.04 Br ex 9.76 Dght 4.506 Lbp 35.16 Br md 9.45 Dpth 5.01 Welded, 1 dk	**(B32A2ST) Tug**	**1 oil engine** sr geared to sc. shaft driving 1 FP propeller Total Power: 1,765kW (2,400hp) 14.0kn EMD (Electro-Motive) 16-567-BC 1 x Vee 2 Stroke 16 Cy. 216 x 254 1765kW (2400bhp) General Motors Corp-USA AuxGen: 2 x 60kW 208V 60Hz a.c Fuel: 264.0
7943108 *EROF* -	**TRITON** *ex* Salvor I *-2005* *ex* M. S. C. Tarn *-1981* **Alkali Enterprises Corp** Target Marine SA *Giurgiulesti* *Moldova*	*118* 3	Class: BR (LR) (RI) ✠ Classed LR until 7/63	**1962-01 P K Harris & Sons Ltd — Bideford** Yd No: 150 Loa 28.50 Br ex 7.78 Dght 2.744 Lbp - Br md - Dpth - Welded, 1 dk	**(B32A2ST) Tug**	**2 oil engines** with flexible couplings & sr reverse geared to sc. shafts driving 2 FP propellers Total Power: 742kW (1,008hp) Ruston 6VEBWM 2 x 4 Stroke 6 Cy. 260 x 368 each-371kW (504bhp) Ruston & Hornsby Ltd.-Lincoln
8033613 *WDD3942* -	**TRITON** *ex* Tuscarora *-1981* *ex* ATA-245 *-1981* *ex* YT-77 *-1981* *ex* YT-341 *-1981* *ex* YTB-341 *-1981* **Puerto Rico Towing & Barge Co** - *Wilmington, DE* *United States of America* MMSI: 367138370 Official number: 607767	**485** 145 -		**1941-12 Levingston SB. Co. — Orange, Tx** Yd No: 185 L reg 38.01 Br ex 9.15 Dght 5.004 Lbp 37.72 Br md 9.14 Dpth 5.34 Welded, 1 dk	**(B32A2ST) Tug**	**2 oil engines** reduction geared to sc. shafts driving 2 FP propellers Total Power: 3,130kW (4,256hp) EMD (Electro-Motive) 16-645-E6 2 x Vee 2 Stroke 16 Cy. 230 x 254 each-1565kW (2128bhp) (new engine 2000) in the United States of America
8320028 *3YJW* -	**TRITON** *ex* Ivar Senior *-2011* *ex* Gunnar Junior *-1998* **Eli Star AS** - *Kristiansund* *Norway* MMSI: 257668000	**339** 107 260		**1983-08 Vaagland Baatbyggeri AS — Vaagland** Yd No: 107 Loa - Br ex - Dght 3.620 Lbp 32.01 Br md 7.50 Dpth 4.50 Welded, 1 dk	**(B12C2FL) Live Fish Carrier (Well Boat)**	**1 oil engine** geared to sc. shaft driving 1 FP propeller Total Power: 610kW (829hp) 12.0kn Grenaa 6FR24TK 1 x 4 Stroke 6 Cy. 240 x 300 610kW (829bhp) A/S Grenaa Motorfabrik-Denmark Thrusters: 1 Thwart. FP thruster (f) Fuel: 58.0 (d.f.) 3.0pd

IMO / Call sign	Name / Owner / Manager / Flag	Tonnage	Class	Builder / Dimensions	Type / Capacities	Machinery
8502860 *HP3957* -	**TRITON** *ex* Linsa *-2008* *ex* Rebun Maru No. 21 *-2001* **Top Vision Marine Co Ltd** SM Lito Shipmanagement Pte Ltd *Panama* *Panama* MMSI: 355631000 Official number: 44341PEXT	**999** 573 1,674	Class: IS (NK)	**1985-08 Matsuura Tekko Zosen K.K. — Osakikamijima** Yd No: 313 Loa 73.00 (BB) Br ex 11.43 Dght 4.336 Lbp 68.03 Br md 11.41 Dpth 5.29 Welded, 1 dk	**(A13B2TP) Products Tanker** Liq: 2,148; Liq (Oil): 2,148 Compartments: 10 Ta, ER	**1 oil engine** with clutches, flexible couplings & sr reverse geared to sc. shaft driving 1 FP propeller Total Power: 1,177kW (1,600hp) 11.3kn Akasaka A31R 1 x 4 Stroke 6 Cy. 310 x 600 1177kW (1600bhp) Akasaka Tekkosho KK (Akasaka DieselLtd)-Japan Fuel: 74.0
8333441 *ZPDH* -	**TRITON** - **Paranave SA** Navemar Srl *Asuncion* *Paraguay* Official number: 1862	*199* 96 -	Class: (NK)	**1946 Luders Marine Construction Co. — Stamford, Ct** Yd No: 532 Loa - Br ex - Dght - Lbp 28.73 Br md 7.62 Dpth 4.12 Welded, 1 dk	**(B32A2ST) Tug**	**2 oil engines** driving 1 FP propeller Total Power: 934kW (1,270hp) Enterprise DMG6 2 x 4 Stroke 6 Cy. 305 x 381 each-467kW (635bhp) Enterprise Engine & Foundry Co-USA
8639728 *PIAR* -	**TRITON** - **Ballast Nedam Bagger- en Exploitatiemaatschappij BV** - SatCom: Inmarsat C 424469110 *Zeist* *Netherlands* MMSI: 244039000 Official number: 805	*662* 198 -		**1968-01 Scheepswerf Lanser B.V. — Sliedrecht** Loa 81.50 Br ex 11.50 Dght 2.400 Lbp 49.00 Br md - Dpth 3.80 Welded, 1 dk	**(B33A2DC) Cutter Suction Dredger**	**1 oil engine** driving 1 Propeller
9642356 *D5CV9* -	**TRITON** - **Mila Navigation Corp** Lavinia Corp *Monrovia* *Liberia* MMSI: 636015790 Official number: 15790	**41,091** 25,573 75,009 T/cm 68.3	Class: BV	**2012-11 Penglai Zhongbai Jinglu Ship Industry Co Ltd — Penglai SD** Yd No: JL0027 (B) Loa 225.00 (BB) Br ex - Dght 14.200 Lbp 217.00 Br md 32.26 Dpth 19.60 Welded, 1 dk	**(A21A2BC) Bulk Carrier** Grain: 89,941 Compartments: 7 Ho, ER 7 Ha: ER	**1 oil engine** driving 1 FP propeller Total Power: 8,833kW (12,009hp) 14.5kn MAN-B&W 5S60MC-C 1 x 2 Stroke 5 Cy. 600 x 2400 8833kW (12009bhp) Hyundai Heavy Industries Co Ltd-South Korea AuxGen: 3 x 560kW 60Hz a.c Fuel: 2960.0
9511545 *JD2765* -	**TRITON** - **Nihon Tug-Boat Co Ltd** - *Sakaide, Kagawa* *Japan* Official number: 140804	*209* - -		**2008-07 Kanagawa Zosen — Kobe** Yd No: 580 Loa 42.00 Br ex - Dght 3.100 Lbp 36.50 Br md 9.00 Dpth 3.80 Welded, 1 dk	**(B32A2ST) Tug**	**2 oil engines** reduction geared to sc. shafts driving 2 Propellers Total Power: 3,236kW (4,400hp) Niigata 6L28HX 2 x 4 Stroke 6 Cy. 280 x 370 each-1618kW (2200bhp) Niigata Engineering Co Ltd-Japan
9451537 *PHOF* -	**TRITON** *launched as* Pinar *-2008* **Triton Tug BV** Sleepdienst B Iskes & Zoon BV *IJmuiden* *Netherlands* MMSI: 244469000 Official number: 51396	**476** 142 -	Class: GL (BV) (RI)	**2008-05 Dearsan Gemi Insaat ve Sanayii Koll. Sti. — Tuzla** Yd No: 2043 Loa 32.03 Br ex - Dght 4.300 Lbp 26.28 Br md 11.61 Dpth 5.37 Welded, 1 dk	**(B32A2ST) Tug**	**2 oil engines** reduction geared to sc. shafts driving 2 Directional propellers Total Power: 3,824kW (5,200hp) A.B.C. 8DZC 2 x 4 Stroke 8 Cy. 256 x 310 each-1912kW (2600bhp) Anglo Belgian Corp NV (ABC)-Belgium Thrusters: 1 Tunnel thruster (f)
9416745 *C4ZP2* -	**TRITON** - **Mandamar Maritime Co Ltd** Empresa de Navegacion Caribe *Limassol* *Cyprus* MMSI: 212704000	**133** 40 53	Class: LR ✠ **100A1** SS 11/2012 tug **LMC** Eq.Ltr: C; Cable: 275.0/16.0 U2 (a)	**2007-11 COTECMAR — Cartagena de Indias** (Hull) **2007-11 B.V. Scheepswerf Damen — Gorinchem** Yd No: 509632 Loa 22.57 Br ex - Dght 2.950 Lbp 22.00 Br md 7.84 Dpth 3.74 Welded, 1 dk	**(B32A2ST) Tug**	**2 oil engines** with flexible couplings & reverse reduction geared to sc. shafts driving 2 FP propellers Total Power: 2,028kW (2,758hp) 10.0kn Caterpillar 3512B-TA 2 x Vee 4 Stroke 12 Cy. 170 x 190 each-1014kW (1379bhp) Caterpillar Inc-USA AuxGen: 2 x 55kW 440V 60Hz a.c
9225043 *C6RT3* -	**TRITON** - **Husky Trading SA** Diana Shipping Services SA *Nassau* *Bahamas* MMSI: 311179000 Official number: 8000300	**40,570** 24,975 75,336 T/cm 67.9	Class: GL (LR) ✠ Classed LR until 9/12/10	**2001-03 Samho Heavy Industries Co Ltd — Samho** Yd No: 1118 Loa 225.00 (BB) Br ex 32.30 Dght 14.150 Lbp 217.68 Br md 32.25 Dpth 19.80 Welded, 1 dk	**(A21A2BC) Bulk Carrier** Grain: 89,000 Compartments: 7 Ho, ER 7 Ha: (15.1 x 12.0)6 (15.1 x 15.0)ER	**1 oil engine** driving 1 FP propeller Total Power: 11,169kW (15,185hp) 14.8kn B&W 6S60MC 1 x 2 Stroke 6 Cy. 600 x 2292 11169kW (15185bhp) Hyundai Heavy Industries Co Ltd-South Korea AuxGen: 3 x 600kW 440V 60Hz a.c, 1 x 142kW 440V 60Hz a.c Boilers: AuxB (Comp) 9.1kgf/cm² (8.9bar)
9691826 *JZRR* -	**TRITON 501** - **PT Triton Laut Biru** Marine Regent Pte Ltd *Jakarta* *Indonesia*	**1,495** 466 -	Class: BV	**2013-12 Tuong Aik Shipyard Sdn Bhd — Sibu** Yd No: 21116 Loa 58.70 Br ex - Dght 4.750 Lbp 56.35 Br md 14.60 Dpth 5.50 Welded, 1 dk	**(B21B20A) Anchor Handling Tug Supply**	**2 oil engines** geared to sc. shafts driving 2 CP propellers Total Power: 3,788kW (5,150hp) 13.5kn Caterpillar 3516C 2 x Vee 4 Stroke 16 Cy. 170 x 190 each-1894kW (2575bhp) Caterpillar Inc-USA
9519121 *3FFC7* -	**TRITON ACE** - **Arena Shipping SA** Mitsui OSK Lines Ltd (MOL) SatCom: Inmarsat C 437186211 *Panama* *Panama* MMSI: 371862000 Official number: 39632PEXT2	**60,876** 18,263 22,723	Class: NK	**2009-10 Imabari Shipbuilding Co Ltd — Marugame KG (Marugame Shipyard)** Yd No: 1504 Loa 199.94 (BB) Br ex - Dght 10.020 Lbp 190.00 Br md 32.26 Dpth 15.00 Welded, 12 dks incl 4 movable	**(A35B2RV) Vehicles Carrier** Side door/ramp (s) Len: 20.00 Wid: 4.20 Swl: 15 Quarter stern door/ramp (s. a.) Len: 35.00 Wid: 8.00 Swl: 80 Cars: 6,502	**1 oil engine** driving 1 FP propeller Total Power: 16,360kW (22,243hp) 19.5kn Mitsubishi 8UEC60LSII 1 x 2 Stroke 8 Cy. 600 x 2300 16360kW (22243bhp) Kobe Hatsudoki KK-Japan Thrusters: 1 Tunnel thruster (f) Fuel: 3310.0
7722009 *WDD8829* -	**TRITON ACHIEVER** *ex* Dover *-2007* *ex* H. O. S. Dover *-1996* *ex* Point Dover *-1991* **Triton Diving Services LLC** - *Belle Chasse, LA* *United States of America* MMSI: 367303260 Official number: 597269	*829* 248 1,200	Class: (AB)	**1978-03 Halter Marine, Inc. — Lockport, La** Yd No: 628 Loa 56.39 Br ex - Dght 3.709 Lbp 51.85 Br md 12.20 Dpth 4.27 Welded, 1 dk	**(B21B20A) Anchor Handling Tug Supply**	**2 oil engines** reverse reduction geared to sc. shafts driving 2 FP propellers Total Power: 2,206kW (3,000hp) 12.0kn EMD (Electro-Motive) 12-645-E6 2 x Vee 2 Stroke 12 Cy. 230 x 254 each-1103kW (1500bhp) (Re-engined , Reconditioned & fitted 1978) General Motors Corp.Electro-Motive Div.-La Grange AuxGen: 2 x 99kW a.c Thrusters: 1 Thwart. FP thruster (f)
7368073 *3EHF6* -	**TRITON BLUE** *ex* Ibrahim Junior *-2006* *ex* Abdul Razzaka *-2002* *ex* Arachovitika Bay *-2001* *ex* Evdokia Luck *-1995* *ex* Patricia Sky *-1991* *ex* Loira *-1985* *ex* Azores Star *-1981* *ex* Groesbeek *-1980* **Triton Navigation Co Inc** Blue Gulf Shipping Inc *Panama* *Panama* Official number: 3247407A	**1,690** 1,083 3,118	Class: (LR) (RI) ✠ Classed LR until 9/82	**1974-01 Scheepswerf Gebr. Suurmeijer B.V. — Foxhol** Yd No: 232 Loa 74.02 Br ex 12.73 Dght 5.817 Lbp 70.80 Br md 12.60 Dpth 6.99 Welded, 1 dk	**(A31A2GX) General Cargo Ship** Grain: 3,908; Bale: 3,684 Compartments: 1 Ho, ER 2 Ha: 2 (20.4 x 9.1)ER Cranes: 3x6t Ice Capable	**1 oil engine** sr geared to sc. shaft driving 1 FP propeller Total Power: 1,320kW (1,795hp) 12.5kn MaK 6M452AK 1 x 4 Stroke 6 Cy. 320 x 450 1320kW (1795bhp) MaK Maschinenbau GmbH-Kiel AuxGen: 3 x 68kW 380V 50Hz a.c
9409077 *3FGX6* -	**TRITON BULKER** - **Triton Navigation BV** Lauritzen Bulkers A/S SatCom: Inmarsat C 435682912 *Panama* *Panama* MMSI: 356829000 Official number: 4043809	**31,251** 18,506 55,651 T/cm 55.8	Class: NK	**2009-06 Mitsui Eng. & SB. Co. Ltd., Chiba Works — Ichihara** Yd No: 1704 Loa 189.99 (BB) Br ex - Dght 12.575 Lbp 182.00 Br md 32.26 Dpth 17.90 Welded, 1 dk	**(A21A2BC) Bulk Carrier** Grain: 70,815; Bale: 68,083 Compartments: 5 Ho, ER 5 Ha: ER Cranes: 4x30t	**1 oil engine** driving 1 FP propeller Total Power: 9,480kW (12,889hp) 14.5kn MAN-B&W 6S50MC-C 1 x 2 Stroke 6 Cy. 500 x 2000 9480kW (12889bhp) Mitsui Engineering & Shipbuilding CLtd-Japan Fuel: 2390.0
9545170 *3FHH6* -	**TRITON CONDOR** - **Triton Navigation BV** Daiichi Chuo Marine Co Ltd (DC Marine) SatCom: Inmarsat C 435347810 *Panama* *Panama* MMSI: 353478000 Official number: 4079509	**90,399** 59,281 180,274 T/cm 121.0	Class: BV	**2009-10 Koyo Dockyard Co Ltd — Mihara HS** Yd No: 2298 Loa 289.00 (BB) Br ex - Dght 18.190 Lbp 280.80 Br md 45.00 Dpth 24.70 Welded, 1 dk	**(A21A2BC) Bulk Carrier** Grain: 199,725 Compartments: 9 Ho, ER 9 Ha: ER	**1 oil engine** driving 1 FP propeller Total Power: 18,660kW (25,370hp) 14.5kn MAN-B&W 6S70MC-C 1 x 2 Stroke 6 Cy. 700 x 2800 18660kW (25370bhp) Mitsui Engineering & Shipbuilding CLtd-Japan AuxGen: 3 x 600kW 60Hz a.c
8023840 *WCE3923* -	**TRITON CRUSADER** *ex* Black Gold *-2007* *ex* H. O. S. Black Gold *-1996* *ex* Jonathan *-1994* **Triton Diving Services LLC** - *Belle Chasse, LA* *United States of America* MMSI: 367346050 Official number: 636322	**780** 234 1,200	Class: (AB)	**1981-05 Halter Marine, Inc. — Lockport, La** Yd No: 975 Loa - Br ex - Dght 3.944 Lbp 56.70 Br md 12.20 Dpth 4.58 Welded, 1 dk	**(B21A20S) Platform Supply Ship**	**2 oil engines** reverse reduction geared to sc. shafts driving 2 FP propellers Total Power: 2,206kW (3,000hp) 12.0kn EMD (Electro-Motive) 12-645-E6 2 x Vee 2 Stroke 12 Cy. 230 x 254 each-1103kW (1500bhp) General Motors Corp.Electro-Motive Div.-La Grange AuxGen: 2 x 99kW a.c Thrusters: 1 Thwart. FP thruster (f)

IMO / Call sign	Name / Owner / Manager / Flag	Tonnage	Class	Builder / Dimensions	Type / Cargo	Machinery
9641170 *AVOX* -	**TRITON ENERGY** **Triton Maritime Pvt Ltd** - *Mumbai* *India* MMSI: 419000392 Official number: 3900	373 111 568	Class: BV IR	2011-09 Yong Choo Kui Shipyard Sdn Bhd — Sibu Yd No: 27131 Loa 33.20 Br ex 9.78 Dght 3.500 Lbp 30.68 Br md 9.76 Dpth 4.30 Welded, 1 dk	(B32A2ST) Tug	**2 oil engines** reduction geared to sc. shafts driving 2 FP propellers Total Power: 2,984kW (4,058hp) Cummins KTA-50-M2 2 x Vee 4 Stroke 16 Cy. 159 x 159 each-1492kW (2029bhp) Cummins Engine Co Ltd-United Kingdom AuxGen: 2 x 78kW 50Hz a.c Fuel: 290.0 (d.f.)
7029043 *WDE2903* -	**TRITON EXPLORER** *ex* Premier Explorer *-2013* *ex* American Salvor *-2007* *ex* Arctic Salvor *-1993* *ex* Manati *-1980* **TVAC LLC** Triton Diving Services LLC SatCom: Inmarsat A 1511626 *Morgan City, LA* *United States of America* MMSI: 368059000 Official number: 527280	1,147 344 -	Class: AB	1970-06 Equitable Equipment Co. — Madisonville, La Yd No: 1558 Converted From: Ro-Ro Cargo Ship-1980 Loa 63.40 Br ex 16.21 Dght 3.652 Lbp 59.44 Br md 16.16 Dpth 4.42 Welded, 1 dk	(B34P2QV) Salvage Ship Cranes: 1x35t	**2 oil engines** geared to sc. shafts driving 2 FP propellers Total Power: 1,654kW (2,248hp) Caterpillar D399 2 x Vee 4 Stroke 16 Cy. 159 x 203 each-827kW (1124bhp) (Re-engined ,made 1970, Reconditioned & refitted 1980) Caterpillar Tractor Co-USA AuxGen: 2 x 210kW 450V 60Hz a.c, 2 x 50kW 450V 60Hz a.c Thrusters: 1 Thwart. FP thruster (f) Fuel: 332.0
7366893 *WDF2983* -	**TRITON FREEDOM** *ex* Gulf Diver V *-2009* *ex* Salem River *-2006* *ex* Lincoln *-2001* *ex* San Patricio *-1995* *ex* OMS San Patricio *-1994* *ex* Andie *-1990* *ex* Andrea Martin *-1989* **Triton Diving Services LLC** - *New Orleans, LA* *United States of America* MMSI: 367434140 Official number: 555837	729 218 784	Class: (AB)	1974-04 Halter Marine Fabricators, Inc. — Moss Point, Ms Yd No: 422 Loa - Br ex 11.59 Dght 3.645 Lbp 50.42 Br md 11.56 Dpth 4.27 Welded, 1 dk	(B21A20S) Platform Supply Ship	**2 oil engines** driving 2 FP propellers Total Power: 1,434kW (1,950hp) 12.0kn EMD (Electro-Motive) 8-645-E6 2 x Vee 2 Stroke 8 Cy. 230 x 254 each-717kW (975bhp) General Motors Corp.Electro-Motive Div.-La Grange AuxGen: 2 x 99kW Thrusters: 1 Thwart. FP thruster (f) Fuel: 240.0 (d.f.)
9414151 *3FOV7* -	**TRITON GANNET** **Triton Navigation BV** Mitsui OSK Lines Ltd (MOL) *Panama* *Panama* MMSI: 357654000 Official number: 4014409	41,662 25,647 78,821	Class: NK	2009-02 Sanoyas Hishino Meisho Corp — Kurashiki OY Yd No: 1278 Loa 225.00 (BB) Br ex - Dght 14.379 Lbp 219.00 Br md 32.24 Dpth 19.90 Welded, 1 dk	(A21A2BC) Bulk Carrier Grain: 91,188 Compartments: 7 Ho, ER 7 Ha: ER	**1 oil engine** driving 1 FP propeller Total Power: 9,560kW (12,998hp) 14.5kn MAN-B&W 7S50MC-C 1 x 2 Stroke 7 Cy. 500 x 2000 9560kW (12998bhp) Mitsui Engineering & Shipbuilding CLtd-Japan Fuel: 2480.0
9425679 *3FPP2* -	**TRITON HAWK** **Triton Navigation BV** Mitsui OSK Lines Ltd (MOL) *Panama* *Panama* MMSI: 355806000 Official number: 4126510	41,662 25,647 78,000	Class: NK	2010-02 Sanoyas Hishino Meisho Corp — Kurashiki OY Yd No: 1283 Loa 225.00 (BB) Br ex - Dght 14.350 Lbp 219.00 Br md 32.24 Dpth 19.90 Welded, 1 dk	(A21A2BC) Bulk Carrier Grain: 91,188 Compartments: 7 Ho, ER 7 Ha: ER	**1 oil engine** driving 1 FP propeller Total Power: 11,060kW (15,037hp) 14.5kn MAN-B&W 7S50MC-C 1 x 2 Stroke 7 Cy. 500 x 2000 11060kW (15037bhp) Fuel: 2480.0
8612263 *3FQA9* -	**TRITON HIGHWAY** **St Paul Maritime Corp** Taiyo Nippon Kisen Co Ltd *Panama* *Panama* MMSI: 370537000 Official number: 4152210	45,783 13,734 14,034	Class: NK	1987-06 Kawasaki Heavy Industries Ltd — Sakaide KG Yd No: 1408 Loa 179.99 (BB) Br ex 32.24 Dght 9.117 Lbp 167.01 Br md 32.20 Dpth 14.99 Welded, 2 dks	(A35B2RV) Vehicles Carrier Stern door/ramp (s. a.) Side door/ramp (p) Side door/ramp (s) Lane-Len: 5200 Cars: 4,857	**1 oil engine** driving 1 FP propeller Total Power: 10,298kW (14,001hp) 20.8kn B&W 8S60MCE 1 x 2 Stroke 8 Cy. 600 x 2292 10298kW (14001bhp) Kawasaki Heavy Industries Ltd-Japan AuxGen: 4 x 602kW Thrusters: 1 Thwart. CP thruster (f) Fuel: 2460.0 (r.f.)
9086502 *CB5225* -	**TRITON I** **Blumar Seafoods** - *Valparaiso* *Chile* MMSI: 725001300 Official number: 2825	*777* 310 1,064		1994-01 Astilleros y Servicios Navales S.A. (ASENAV) — Valdivia Yd No: 094 Loa 52.70 (BB) Br ex 10.12 Dght 5.550 Lbp 49.50 Br md 10.00 Dpth 6.90 Welded, 1 dk	(B11B2FV) Fishing Vessel Ins: 997	**1 oil engine** with clutches, flexible couplings & sr geared to sc. shaft driving 1 CP propeller Total Power: 1,765kW (2,400hp) 14.0kn Deutz SBV8M628 1 x 4 Stroke 8 Cy. 240 x 280 1765kW (2400bhp) Motoren Werke Mannheim AG (MWM)-Mannheim Thrusters: 1 Thwart. FP thruster (f); 1 Tunnel thruster (a)
9037537 - -	**TRITON-I** *ex* Kinsho Maru No. 18 *-2006* **Punta Brava Fishing SA** -	616 235 -		1991-08 KK Kanasashi — Shizuoka SZ Yd No: 3271 Loa 55.16 (BB) Br ex 8.73 Dght 3.400 Lbp 48.10 Br md 8.70 Dpth 3.75 Welded	(B11B2FV) Fishing Vessel Ins: 498	**1 oil engine** with clutches, flexible couplings & sr reverse geared to sc. shaft driving 1 FP propeller Total Power: 736kW (1,001hp) Niigata 6M28HFT 1 x 4 Stroke 6 Cy. 280 x 480 736kW (1001bhp) Niigata Engineering Co Ltd-Japan
7232602 *WCB5810* -	**TRITON II** **Triton II Fisheries Inc** - *St Augustine, FL* *United States of America* Official number: 539155	*125* 85 -		1972 Desco Marine — Saint Augustine, Fl Yd No: 106-F L reg 20.97 Br ex 6.74 Dght - Lbp - Br md - Dpth 3.81 Bonded	(B11A2FT) Trawler Hull Material: Reinforced Plastic Ins: 45	**1 oil engine** driving 1 FP propeller Total Power: 268kW (364hp) Caterpillar 1 x 4 Stroke 268kW (364bhp) Caterpillar Tractor Co-USA
9553103 *3FFE9* -	**TRITON LEADER** **Arena Shipping SA** Wilhelmsen Ship Management Sdn Bhd SatCom: Inmarsat C 435779512 *Panama* *Panama* MMSI: 357795000 Official number: 4142210	60,876 18,263 22,657	Class: NK	2010-03 Imabari Shipbuilding Co Ltd — Marugame KG (Marugame Shipyard) Yd No: 1506 Loa 199.94 (BB) Br ex - Dght 10.016 Lbp 190.00 Br md 32.26 Dpth 34.80 Welded, 12 dks incl 4 movable	(A35B2RV) Vehicles Carrier Side door/ramp (s) Len: 20.00 Wid: 4.20 Swl: 15 Quarter stern door/ramp (s. a.) Len: 35.00 Wid: 8.00 Swl: 80 Cars: 6,502	**1 oil engine** driving 1 FP propeller Total Power: 15,540kW (21,128hp) 19.5kn Mitsubishi 8UEC60LSII 1 x 2 Stroke 8 Cy. 600 x 2300 15540kW (21128bhp) Kobe Hatsudoki KK-Japan Thrusters: 1 Tunnel thruster (f) Fuel: 3310.0
7332050 *WDF4756* -	**TRITON PATRIOT** *ex* Sea Fox *-2011* *ex* Offshore Pacific *-2011* *ex* Tidal Seahorse *-1994* *ex* Red Beard *-1981* **Triton Diving Services LLC** - *Morgan City, LA* *United States of America* MMSI: 367455480 Official number: 551454	685 205 -	Class: (AB)	1973 Halter Marine Fabricators, Inc. — Moss Point, Ms Yd No: 391 Loa 53.60 Br ex - Dght 3.645 Lbp 50.45 Br md 11.59 Dpth 4.27 Welded, 1 dk	(B21A20S) Platform Supply Ship	**2 oil engines** reverse reduction geared to sc. shafts driving 2 FP propellers Total Power: 1,632kW (2,218hp) 12.0kn Kromhout 9F/SW240 2 x 4 Stroke 9 Cy. 240 x 260 each-816kW (1109bhp) Stork Werkspoor Diesel BV-Netherlands AuxGen: 2 x 100kW Fuel: 215.5 (d.f.)
8911102 *ELLM5* -	**TRITON REEFER** **NYK Reefers Ltd** NYKCool AB SatCom: Inmarsat A 1242665 *Monrovia* *Liberia* MMSI: 636008972 Official number: 8972	8,818 3,810 9,683 T/cm 22.0	Class: NK	1990-01 Shin Kurushima Dockyard Co. Ltd. — Onishi Yd No: 2656 Loa 144.03 (BB) Br ex - Dght 8.125 Lbp 136.02 Br md 21.61 Dpth 12.86 Welded	(A34A2GR) Refrigerated Cargo Ship Bale: 12,862; Ins: 12,863 TEU 76 incl 50 ref C Compartments: 4 Ho, ER 4 Ha: (7.4 x 6.0)3 (8.1 x 6.0)ER Cranes: 2x30t,2x5t	**1 oil engine** driving 1 FP propeller Total Power: 7,945kW (10,802hp) 18.3kn Mitsubishi 6UEC52LS 1 x 2 Stroke 6 Cy. 520 x 1850 7945kW (10802bhp) Kobe Hatsudoki KK-Japan AuxGen: 2 x 800kW 450V 60Hz a.c, 2 x 400kW 450V 60Hz a.c Fuel: 71.7 (d.f.) 1113.0 (r.f.) 28.5pd
9324150 *3EMN* -	**TRITON SEAGULL** **Triton Navigation BV** Fednav Ltd *Panama* *Panama* MMSI: 372220000 Official number: 3316507A	31,247 18,504 56,058 T/cm 55.8	Class: NK	2007-09 Mitsui Eng. & SB. Co. Ltd. — Tamano Yd No: 1653 Loa 189.99 (BB) Br ex - Dght 12.573 Lbp 182.00 Br md 32.26 Dpth 17.90 Welded, 1 dk	(A21A2BC) Bulk Carrier Grain: 70,811; Bale: 68,084 Compartments: 5 Ho, ER 5 Ha: ER Cranes: 4x30t	**1 oil engine** driving 1 FP propeller Total Power: 9,480kW (12,889hp) 14.5kn MAN-B&W 6S50MC-C 1 x 2 Stroke 6 Cy. 500 x 2000 9480kW (12889bhp) Mitsui Engineering & Shipbuilding CLtd-Japan Fuel: 2380.0
9574004 *3FPH9* -	**TRITON SEAHAWK** **Triton Navigation BV** Belships Management Singapore Pte Ltd SatCom: Inmarsat C 435602715 *Panama* *Panama* MMSI: 356027000 Official number: 4255111	30,653 15,707 51,201	Class: NK	2011-03 Imabari Shipbuilding Co Ltd — Imabari EH (Imabari Shipyard) Yd No: 700 Loa 182.98 (BB) Br ex - Dght 12.331 Lbp 178.00 Br md 32.26 Dpth 17.45 Welded, 1 dk	(A21A2BC) Bulk Carrier Double Hull Grain: 59,675; Bale: 57,478 Compartments: 5 Ho, ER 5 Ha: ER Cranes: 4x30.5t	**1 oil engine** driving 1 FP propeller Total Power: 9,480kW (12,889hp) 14.7kn MAN-B&W 6S50MC-C 1 x 2 Stroke 6 Cy. 500 x 2000 9480kW (12889bhp) Mitsui Engineering & Shipbuilding CLtd-Japan AuxGen: 3 x a.c Fuel: 2142.0

9328675 *H3WL* -	**TRITON STORK** **Triton Navigation BV** - *Panama* *Panama* MMSI: 352231000 Official number: 3051105B	**31,242** 18,504 56,024 T/cm 55.8	Class: NK	**2004-12 Mitsui Eng. & SB. Co. Ltd. — Tamano** Yd No: 1577 Loa 189.99 (BB) Br ex - Dght 12.575 Lbp 182.00 Br md 32.26 Dpth 17.90 Welded, 1 dk	**(A21A2BC) Bulk Carrier** Grain: 70,811; Bale: 68,044 Compartments: 5 Ho, ER 5 Ha: 4 (21.1 x 18.9)ER (17.6 x 18.9) Cranes: 4x30t	**1 oil engine** driving 1 FP propeller Total Power: 9,480kW (12,889hp) 14.5kn MAN-B&W 6S50MC-C 1 x 2 Stroke 6 Cy. 500 x 2000 9480kW (12889bhp) Mitsui Engineering & Shipbuilding CLtd-Japan Fuel: 2260.0
9479034 *3FSY* -	**TRITON SWALLOW** **Triton Navigation BV** Belships Management Singapore Pte Ltd SatCom: Inmarsat C 437062512 *Panama* *Panama* MMSI: 370625000 Official number: 4254511	**31,250** 18,516 55,580 T/cm 55.8	Class: NK	**2011-03 Mitsui Eng. & SB. Co. Ltd. — Tamano** Yd No: 1760 Loa 189.99 (BB) Br ex - Dght 12.572 Lbp 182.00 Br md 32.26 Dpth 17.90 Welded, 1 dk	**(A21A2BC) Bulk Carrier** Grain: 70,868; Bale: 68,116 Compartments: 5 Ho, ER 5 Ha: ER Cranes: 4x30t	**1 oil engine** driving 1 FP propeller Total Power: 9,480kW (12,889hp) 14.5kn MAN-B&W 6S50MC-C 1 x 2 Stroke 6 Cy. 500 x 2000 9480kW (12889bhp) Mitsui Engineering & Shipbuilding CLtd-Japan Fuel: 2290.0
9632985 *H9ZR* -	**TRITON SWAN** **Triton Navigation BV** - *Panama* *Panama* MMSI: 353506000 Official number: 4428212	**34,800** 20,209 61,457 T/cm 61.4	Class: NK	**2012-10 Iwagi Zosen Co Ltd — Kamijima EH** Yd No: 301 Loa 199.98 (BB) Br ex - Dght 13.010 Lbp 195.00 Br md 32.24 Dpth 18.60 Welded, 1 dk	**(A21A2BC) Bulk Carrier** Grain: 77,674; Bale: 73,552 Compartments: 5 Ho, ER 5 Ha: 4 (23.5 x 19.0)ER (18.7 x 19.0) Cranes: 4x30.5t	**1 oil engine** driving 1 FP propeller Total Power: 8,450kW (11,489hp) 14.5kn MAN-B&W 6S50MC-C8 1 x 2 Stroke 6 Cy. 500 x 2000 8450kW (11489bhp) Hitachi Zosen Corp-Japan Fuel: 2560.0
9621003 *H3AS* -	**TRITON WIND** **Red Coral Shipping SA** Hellenic Carriers Corp SA *Panama* *Panama* MMSI: 354569000 Official number: 44782PEXT2	**24,196** 12,211 37,113 T/cm 49.7	Class: LR ✠ **100A1** SS 07/2013 bulk carrier CSR BC-A GRAB (25) Nos. 2, 4 holds may be empty ESP **ShipRight** (CM, ACS (B,D))) *IWS LI EP Ice Class 1C FS at a draught of 10.518m Max/min draughts fwd 10.736/4.09m Max/min draughts aft 12.6/5.6m Power required 6075kw, power insatlled 7000kw ✠ **LMC** **UMS** Cable: 605.0/66.0 U3 (a)	**2013-07 Zhejiang Ouhua Shipbuilding Co Ltd — Zhoushan ZJ** Yd No: 636 Loa 189.90 (BB) Br ex 28.35 Dght 10.500 Lbp 183.00 Br md 28.30 Dpth 15.20 Welded, 1 dk	**(A21A2BC) Bulk Carrier** Grain: 48,500; Bale: 46,753 Compartments: 5 Ho, ER 5 Ha: ER Cranes: 4x30.5t Ice Capable	**1 oil engine** driving 1 FP propeller Total Power: 8,730kW (11,869hp) 14.0kn Wartsila 6RTA48T 1 x 2 Stroke 6 Cy. 480 x 2000 8730kW (11869bhp) Yichang Marine Diesel Engine Co Ltd-China AuxGen: 3 x 570kW 450V 60Hz a.c Boilers: WTAuxB (Comp) 8.1kgf/cm² (7.9bar)
6719964 *H03594* -	**TRITON X** *ex* Triton *-2004* **Remolcatuna SL** - *Panama* *Panama* Official number: 3156306A	**156** 46 66	Class: (GL)	**1967 Jadewerft Wilhelmshaven GmbH — Wilhelmshaven** Yd No: 110 Loa 30.16 Br ex 7.88 Dght 3.118 Lbp 27.26 Br md 7.51 Dpth 3.84 Welded, 1 dk	**(B32A2ST) Tug** Ice Capable	**1 oil engine** reverse reduction geared to sc. shaft driving 1 FP propeller Total Power: 883kW (1,201hp) 12.5kn Deutz SBV8M545 1 x 4 Stroke 8 Cy. 320 x 450 883kW (1201bhp) Kloeckner Humboldt Deutz AG-West Germany AuxGen: 2 x 28kW 220/380V 50Hz a.c Fuel: 33.5 (d.f.)
9363314 *VRCM2* -	**TRITONIA** **Ohka Shipping Corp Ltd** Blue Marine Management Corp *Hong Kong* *Hong Kong* MMSI: 477653500 Official number: HK-1831	**20,238** 10,947 32,285 T/cm 43.8	Class: NK	**2007-01 Kanda Zosensho K.K. — Kawajiri** Yd No: 489 Loa 177.13 (BB) Br ex - Dght 10.020 Lbp 168.50 Br md 28.40 Dpth 14.25 Welded, 1 dk	**(A31A2GO) Open Hatch Cargo Ship** Double Hull Grain: 42,595; Bale: 41,124 Compartments: 5 Ho, ER 5 Ha: 3 (20.8 x 24.0) (19.2 x 24.0)ER (13.6 x 15.8) Cranes: 4x30.5t	**1 oil engine** driving 1 FP propeller Total Power: 6,620kW (9,001hp) 14.3kn Mitsubishi 6UEC52LA 1 x 2 Stroke 6 Cy. 520 x 1600 6620kW (9001bhp) Kobe Hatsudoki KK-Japan AuxGen: 2 x 450kW a.c Fuel: 1740.0
7943122 - -	**TRIUMF** *ex* Stroyno *-2007* *ex* Blestyashchiy *-2002* **Ferromagnitniy Bezopasniy Poisk Ltd** SatCom: Inmarsat C 427302234 *Kaliningrad* *Russia*	**270** 137 198	Class: (RS)	**1981 Astrakhanskaya Sudoverf im. "Kirova" — Astrakhan** Yd No: 141 Converted From: Fishing Vessel Lengthened-1997 Loa 36.00 Br ex 7.10 Dght 2.899 Lbp 29.98 Br md - Dpth 3.66 Welded, 1 dk	**(A31A2GX) General Cargo Ship** Bale: 115 Compartments: 1 Ho, ER 1 Ha: (1.6 x 1.3) Derricks: 2x2t; Winches: 2 Ice Capable	**1 oil engine** driving 1 CP propeller Total Power: 224kW (305hp) 9.0kn S.K.L. 8NVD36-1U 1 x 4 Stroke 8 Cy. 240 x 360 224kW (305bhp) VEB Schwermaschinenbau "KarlLiebknecht" (SKL)-Magdeburg Fuel: 17.0 (d.f.)
8902967 *PJVQ* -	**TRIUMPH** *ex* Marble *-2008* **Triumph BV** Dockwise Shipping BV *Willemstad* *Curacao* MMSI: 306861000 Official number: 2008-C-	**42,515** 12,755 53,818 T/cm 107.7	Class: NV	**1992-01 Brodosplit - Brodogradiliste doo — Split** Yd No: 368 Converted From: Crude Oil Tanker-2008 Loa 216.75 (BB) Br ex 44.54 Dght 10.400 Lbp 209.69 Br md 44.50 Dpth 24.20 Welded, 1 dk	**(A38C3GH) Heavy Load Carrier, semi submersible** Compartments: ER	**1 oil engine** driving 1 FP propeller Total Power: 13,369kW (18,176hp) 14.0kn B&W 6S70MC 1 x 2 Stroke 6 Cy. 700 x 2674 13369kW (18176bhp) Brodogradiliste Split (Brodosplit)-Yugoslavia AuxGen: 3 x 900kW 440V 60Hz a.c, 1 x 160kW 440V 60Hz a.c Thrusters: 1 Tunnel thruster (f) Fuel: 280.0 (d.f.) 4209.0 (r.f.)
8985000 *V4YB* -	**TRIUMPH** *ex* Foxbay *-2004* *ex* Foxhound *-2004* *ex* Boxer *-1977* **Tortola Barge Services Ltd** *Basseterre* *St Kitts & Nevis* MMSI: 341625000 Official number: SKN 1001625	**151** 45 -	Class: IS	**1963-01 R. Dunston (Hessle) Ltd. — Hessle** Yd No: S795 Loa 28.35 Br ex 7.72 Dght 2.740 Lbp 25.84 Br md 7.39 Dpth 3.66 Welded, 1 dk	**(B32A2ST) Tug**	**2 oil engines** sr reverse geared to sc. shafts driving 2 Propellers Total Power: 970kW (1,318hp) 10.0kn Blackstone ERS8 2 x 4 Stroke 8 Cy. 222 x 292 each-485kW (659bhp) Blackstone & Co.-Stamford
9003940 *UBBJ5* -	**TRIUMPH** *ex* Daishin Maru *-2012* **Triumph Co Ltd** - *Nakhodka* *Russia* MMSI: 273352380	**449** 135 573	Class: RS	**1990-03 Mukaishima Zoki Co. Ltd. — Onomichi** Yd No: 266 Loa 50.11 Br ex - Dght 3.280 Lbp 46.00 Br md 8.60 Dpth 3.70 Welded, 1 dk	**(A12A2TC) Chemical Tanker** Liq: 475 Compartments: 6 Ta, ER	**1 oil engine** with clutches & reverse geared to sc. shaft driving 1 FP propeller Total Power: 588kW (799hp) 10.7kn Yanmar MF24-UT 1 x 4 Stroke 6 Cy. 240 x 420 588kW (799bhp) Matsue Diesel KK-Japan
9342798 *C6WN2* -	**TRIUMPH** **Continent Maritime SA** Kotoku Kaiun Co Ltd (Kotoku Kaiun KK) *Nassau* *Bahamas* MMSI: 309459000 Official number: 8001412	**9,549** 5,672 12,597	Class: NK	**2007-10 Kyokuyo Shipyard Corp — Shimonoseki YC** Yd No: 473 Loa 145.12 (BB) Br ex 22.40 Dght 8.215 Lbp 134.00 Br md 22.40 Dpth 11.00 Welded, 1 dk	**(A33A2CC) Container Ship (Fully Cellular)** TEU 907 incl 120 ref C.	**1 oil engine** driving 1 FP propeller Total Power: 7,988kW (10,860hp) 18.0kn MAN-B&W 6L50MC 1 x 2 Stroke 6 Cy. 500 x 1620 7988kW (10860bhp) Hitachi Zosen Corp-Japan AuxGen: 3 x 560kW a.c Thrusters: 1 Tunnel thruster (f) Fuel: 106.2 (d.f.) 1049.5 (r.f.)
9432892 *D5EZ8* -	**TRIUMPH** **Lombard Corporate Finance (December 3) Ltd** Eastern Pacific Shipping (UK) Ltd *Monrovia* *Liberia* MMSI: 636016206 Official number: 16206	**46,800** 14,217 12,272 T/cm 45.6	Class: AB (NV)	**2008-05 Xiamen Shipbuilding Industry Co Ltd — Xiamen FJ** Yd No: XSI404D Loa 182.80 (BB) Br ex 31.53 Dght 9.016 Lbp 170.68 Br md 31.50 Dpth 12.80 Welded, 12 dks incl. 3 liftable dks.	**(A35B2RV) Vehicles Carrier** Side door/ramp (s) Len: 20.00 Wid: 4.70 Swl: 10 Quarter stern door/ramp (s. a.) Len: 32.50 Wid: 7.50 Swl: 120 Cars: 4,943	**1 oil engine** driving 1 FP propeller Total Power: 14,220kW (19,334hp) 20.0kn MAN-B&W 9S50MC-C 1 x 2 Stroke 9 Cy. 500 x 2000 14220kW (19334bhp) MAN Diesel A/S-Denmark AuxGen: 2 x 1050kW 450V a.c, 1 x 750kW 450V a.c Thrusters: 1 Thwart. FP thruster (f) Fuel: 170.0 (d.f.) 3500.0 (r.f.) 57.0pd
9209506 *H3CB* -	**TRIUMPH ACE** **Aurora Car Maritime Transport SA** New Asian Shipping Co Ltd *Panama* *Panama* MMSI: 352062000 Official number: 2701100C	**55,880** 16,764 20,131 T/cm 51.2	Class: NK	**2000-03 Imabari Shipbuilding Co Ltd — Marugame KG (Marugame Shipyard)** Yd No: 1321 Loa 199.94 (BB) Br ex - Dght 10.016 Lbp 190.00 Br md 32.20 Dpth 14.69 Welded, 12 dks	**(A35B2RV) Vehicles Carrier** Side door/ramp1 (p) 1 (s) Len: 17.00 Wid: 4.50 Swl: 20 Quarter stern door/ramp (s. a.) Len: 32.55 Wid: 7.00 Swl: 100 Cars: 6,043	**1 oil engine** driving 1 FP propeller Total Power: 14,123kW (19,202hp) 20.0kn Mitsubishi 8UEC60LS 1 x 2 Stroke 8 Cy. 600 x 2200 14123kW (19202bhp) Kobe Hatsudoki KK-Japan Thrusters: 1 Tunnel thruster (f) Fuel: 2880.0

IMO / Call sign	Name / Owner	Tonnage	Class	Builder / Dimensions	Type	Machinery
8954350 *V4JA2* -	**TRIUMPH-R** *ex* Rufus Castle *-2012* *ex* Basset Hound *-2012* *ex* Basset *-1996* *ex* Beagle *-1996* **Tortola Barge Services Ltd** - *Basseterre* *St Kitts & Nevis* MMSI: 341061000 Official number: SKN 1002234	*151* 45 -		**1963 Appledore Shipbuilders Ltd — Bideford** Loa 28.35 Br ex 7.74 Dght 3.658 Lbp 25.84 Br md - Dpth 4.00 Welded, 1 dk	**(B32A2ST) Tug**	**2 oil engines** driving 2 FP propellers Total Power: 970kW (1,318hp) 10.0kn Blackstone ERS8 2 x 4 Stroke 8 Cy. 222 x 292 each-485kW (659bhp) Blackstone & Co. Ltd.-Stamford
8627672 *V7RS4* -	**TRIUMPHANT LADY** *ex* Bengal No. 1 *-2004* **Trilady Marine Ltd** Fairport Inc (Fairport Yacht Support) *Bikini* *Marshall Islands* MMSI: 538070630 Official number: 70630	**489** 146 -	Class: AB	**1985 Nishii Dock Co. Ltd. — Ise** Loa 40.87 Br ex - Dght - Lbp 38.92 Br md 8.01 Dpth 4.20 Bonded, 1 dk	**(X11A2YP) Yacht** Hull Material: Reinforced Plastic	**1 oil engine** driving 1 FP propeller
8120272 - -	**TRIUNFADOR** **Maruba SCA Empresa de Navegacion Maritima**	**213** 37 -		**1980-05 Quality Marine, Inc. — Theodore, Al** Yd No: 141 Loa 24.39 Br ex - Dght - Lbp - Br md 6.72 Dpth 3.38 Welded, 1 dk	**(B32A2ST) Tug**	**1 oil engine** driving 1 FP propeller Total Power: 382kW (519hp) Caterpillar 3412TA 1 x Vee 4 Stroke 12 Cy. 137 x 152 382kW (519bhp) Caterpillar Tractor Co-USA
7832050 *WDE4699* -	**TRIUNFO** *ex* Vila de Olhao *-2004* **Tyler Fishing LLC** - *New Bedford, MA* *United States of America* MMSI: 367356690 Official number: 596397	*128* 87 -		**1978 Bender Welding & Machine Co Inc — Mobile AL** L reg 20.85 Br ex 6.71 Dght - Lbp - Br md - Dpth 3.38 Welded, 1 dk	**(B11A2FS) Stern Trawler**	**1 oil engine** driving 1 FP propeller Total Power: 331kW (450hp) Caterpillar 3412T 1 x Vee 4 Stroke 12 Cy. 137 x 152 331kW (450bhp) Caterpillar Tractor Co-USA
5161304 - -	**TRIVA II** *ex* Tuskar Rock *-2011* *ex* Gribbin Head *-1996* *ex* Ingleby Cross *-1968* **Britannia Shipping International Ltd** -	*118* 35 24	Class: IS (LR) ✠ Classed LR until 12/1/94	**1955-10 Scott & Sons — Bowling** Yd No: 408 Loa 26.27 Br ex 7.29 Dght 3.144 Lbp 24.39 Br md 7.17 Dpth 3.36 Riveted, 1 dk	**(B32A2ST) Tug**	**1 oil engine** sr geared to sc. shaft driving 1 FP propeller Total Power: 883kW (1,201hp) MaK 8M282AK 1 x 4 Stroke 8 Cy. 240 x 280 883kW (1201bhp) (new engine 1969) MaK Maschinenbau GmbH-Kiel
8109345 *VTDW* -	**TRIYA** **Marshall Seafoods Pvt Ltd** - *Mumbai* *India* Official number: 1939	*115* 38 81	Class: IR (LR) ✠ Classed LR until 1/12/93	**1981-11 B.V. Scheepswerf "De Hoop" — Hardinxveld-Giessendam** Yd No: 761 Loa 23.68 Br ex 6.58 Dght 2.909 Lbp 21.24 Br md 6.51 Dpth 3.43 Welded, 1 dk	**(B11A2FT) Trawler** Ins: 70	**1 oil engine** with clutches, flexible couplings & sr reverse geared to sc. shaft driving 1 FP propeller Total Power: 405kW (551hp) Caterpillar 3408TA 1 x Vee 4 Stroke 8 Cy. 137 x 152 405kW (551bhp) Caterpillar Tractor Co-USA AuxGen: 2 x 12kW 380V 50Hz a.c
5368952 - -	**TROCHUS** **Boral Resources (QLD) Pty Ltd** - *Brisbane, Qld* *Australia* Official number: 332851	*535* 125 686	Class: (LR) ✠ Classed LR until 10/57	**1956-06 Brooke Marine Ltd. — Lowestoft** Yd No: 231 Loa 52.02 Br ex 10.29 Dght 3.379 Lbp 48.77 Br md 10.06 Dpth 3.97 Riveted, 1 dk	**(B34A2SH) Hopper, Motor**	**1 oil engine** driving 1 FP propeller Total Power: 618kW (840hp) 11.0kn Crossley 1 x 2 Stroke 5 Cy. 254 x 305 618kW (840bhp) Crossley Bros. Ltd.-Manchester AuxGen: 2 x 40kW 110V d.c, 1 x 5kW 110V d.c
8820004 *OUVE2* -	**TROENSE MAERSK** *ex* Maersk Colorado *-2003* *ex* Clifford Maersk *-1997* **A P Moller - Maersk A/S** A P Moller *Troense* *Denmark (DIS)* MMSI: 220156000 Official number: D4013	**16,982** 7,449 21,825	Class: AB (LR) ✠ Classed LR until 9/11/96	**1992-05 Odense Staalskibsvaerft A/S — Munkebo (Lindo Shipyard)** Yd No: 138 Loa 162.26 (BB) Br ex 27.83 Dght 10.320 Lbp 151.90 Br md 27.80 Dpth 15.23 Welded, 1 dk	**(A33A2CC) Container Ship (Fully Cellular)** TEU 1446 C Ho 539 TEU C Dk 907 TEU incl 114 ref C. Compartments: 8 Cell Ho, ER 9 Ha: ER 12 Wing Ha: Gantry cranes: 1x35t	**1 oil engine** driving 1 FP propeller Total Power: 10,480kW (14,249hp) 18.5kn B&W 8S50MC 1 x 2 Stroke 8 Cy. 500 x 1910 10480kW (14249bhp) Mitsui Engineering & Shipbuilding CLtd-Japan AuxGen: 3 x 1250kW 440V 60Hz a.c Thrusters: 1 Thwart. CP thruster (f); 1 Tunnel thruster (a)
6604573 - -	**TROFA** *ex* Boy Matthiesen *-1981* **Yugecoresurs Ltd** - *Sevastopol* *Ukraine* MMSI: 272576000	*999* 685 1,750	Class: (BV) (GL)	**1966 Schiffswerft Hugo Peters — Wewelsfleth** Yd No: 523 Converted From: General Cargo Ship-2008 Loa 71.61 Br ex 11.21 Dght 5.110 Lbp 64.42 Br md 11.18 Dpth 5.69 Riveted\Welded, 1 dk	**(B33A2DU) Dredger (unspecified)** Hopper: 1,000	**1 oil engine** driving 1 FP propeller Total Power: 883kW (1,201hp) 11.5kn MaK 6ZU451AK 1 x 4 Stroke 6 Cy. 320 x 450 883kW (1201bhp) Maschinenbau Kiel AG (MaK)-Kiel AuxGen: 2 x 25kW Fuel: 96.5 (d.f.)
9222572 *9A7311* -	**TROGIR** *ex* Arena *-2007* **Trogir Maritime Inc** Jadroplov International Maritime Transport Ltd (Jadroplov dd) *Split* *Croatia* MMSI: 238179000 Official number: 5T-958	**25,600** 14,558 44,314 T/cm 51.3	Class: BV CS (LR) ✠ Classed LR until 1/12/05	**2001-03 'Uljanik' Brodogradiliste dd — Pula** Yd No: 435 Loa 182.80 (BB) Br ex 32.66 Dght 11.000 Lbp 175.00 Br md 32.20 Dpth 16.10 Welded, 1 dk	**(A21A2BC) Bulk Carrier** Grain: 54,832 Compartments: 5 Ho, ER 5 Ha: 5 (16.0 x 15.6)ER Cranes: 4x30t	**1 oil engine** driving 1 FP propeller Total Power: 8,260kW (11,230hp) 14.4kn B&W 6S50MC 1 x 2 Stroke 6 Cy. 500 x 1910 8260kW (11230bhp) 'Uljanik' Strojogradnja dd-Croatia AuxGen: 3 x 540kW 440V 60Hz a.c Boilers: AuxB (Comp) 10.2kgf/cm² (10.0bar) Thrusters: 1 Thwart. CP thruster (f)
8652603 - -	**TROIS** *ex* TM 1 *-2011* **PT Trois Marine** *Pontianak* *Indonesia*	**217** 66 -	Class: KI	**2010-11 CV Bina Citra — Pontianak** Loa - Br ex - Dght - Lbp 24.62 Br md 7.60 Dpth 3.80 Welded, 1 dk	**(B32A2ST) Tug**	**2 oil engines** reduction geared to sc. shafts driving 2 Propellers AuxGen: 2 x 35kW a.c
7216737 - -	**TROIS ANGES** *ex* St. Pierre *-2000* *ex* Lady Evelyn *-1995* *ex* Trojan *-1986* -	**383** 123 700		**1965 Halter Marine Services, Inc. — New Orleans, La** Yd No: 106 L reg 45.72 Br ex 10.37 Dght 2.918 Lbp 42.68 Br md 10.36 Dpth 3.51 Welded	**(B21A20S) Platform Supply Ship**	**2 oil engines** geared to sc. shafts driving 2 FP propellers Total Power: 1,442kW (1,960hp) 12.0kn G.M. (Detroit Diesel) 12V-71 2 x Vee 2 Stroke 12 Cy. 108 x 127 each-721kW (980bhp) General Motors Corp-USA
8653994 - -	**TROISON** **PT Trois Marine** *Pontianak* *Indonesia*	**217** 66 -	Class: KI	**2011-02 CV Bina Citra — Pontianak** Loa - Br ex - Dght - Lbp 24.62 Br md 7.60 Dpth 3.80 Welded, 1 dk	**(B32A2ST) Tug**	**2 oil engines** reduction geared to sc. shafts driving 2 FP propellers Total Power: 1,220kW (1,658hp) Mitsubishi S6R2-MPTK 2 x 4 Stroke 6 Cy. 170 x 220 each-610kW (829bhp) Mitsubishi Heavy Industries Ltd-Japan AuxGen: 2 x 35kW 415V a.c
8226478 *UGFK* -	**TROITSKOYE** **OOO 'Vostok-Ryba'** *Petropavlovsk-Kamchatskiy* *Russia* MMSI: 273560500	**815** 221 335	Class: (RS)	**1983-11 Volgogradskiy Sudostroitelnyy Zavod — Volgograd** Yd No: 214 Converted From: Stern Trawler-2005 Loa 53.67 Br ex 10.71 Dght 4.290 Lbp 47.92 Br md 10.50 Dpth 6.00 Welded, 1 dk	**(B12A2FF) Fish Factory Ship** Ins: 218 Compartments: 1 Ho, ER 1 Ha: (1.6 x 1.6) Derricks: 2x1.5t Ice Capable	**1 oil engine** driving 1 CP propeller Total Power: 971kW (1,320hp) 12.8kn S.K.L. 8NVD48A-2U 1 x 4 Stroke 8 Cy. 320 x 480 971kW (1320bhp) VEB Schwermaschinenbau "KarlLiebknecht" (SKL)-Magdeburg AuxGen: 1 x 300kW a.c, 3 x 160kW a.c, 2 x 135kW a.c Fuel: 182.0 (d.f.)
9258167 *A8AP7* -	**TROITSKY BRIDGE** **Ramvik Shipping Co Ltd** Unicom Management Services (Cyprus) Ltd *Monrovia* *Liberia* MMSI: 636011643 Official number: 11643	**27,725** 13,762 47,199 T/cm 52.3	Class: LR ✠ **100A1** SS 11/2013 Double Hull oil tanker ESP *IWS LI SPM ✠ **LMC** **UMS IGS** Eq.Ltr: M†; Cable: 670.0/73.0 U3 (a)	**2003-11 Admiralteyskiy Sudostroitelnyy Zavod — Sankt-Peterburg** Yd No: 02740 Loa 182.28 (BB) Br ex 32.34 Dght 12.197 Lbp 175.79 Br md 32.20 Dpth 17.50 Welded, 1 dk	**(A13A2TW) Crude/Oil Products Tanker** Double Hull (13F) Liq: 51,910; Liq (Oil): 51,910 Compartments: 10 Wing Ta, 2 Wing Slop Ta, ER 10 Cargo Pump (s): 10x550m³/hr Manifold: Bow/CM: 90.9m	**1 oil engine** driving 1 FP propeller Total Power: 8,310kW (11,298hp) 14.3kn B&W 6S50MC-C 1 x 2 Stroke 6 Cy. 500 x 2000 8310kW (11298bhp) AO Bryanskiy MashinostroitelnyyZavod (BMZ)-Bryansk AuxGen: 2 x 1280kW 450V 60Hz a.c, 1 x 680kW 450V 60Hz a.c Boilers: e (ex.g.) 11.7kgf/cm² (11.5bar), WTAuxB (o.f.) 11.2kgf/cm² (11.0bar) Fuel: 99.0 (d.f.) 1419.0 (r.f.)
8945749 *DXIL* -	**TROJAN HORSE** *ex* Jojoy *-1986* - - *Manila* *Philippines* Official number: T0038	*567* 421 -		**1986 at Manila** L reg 53.66 Br ex - Dght - Lbp - Br md 10.98 Dpth 3.20 Welded, 1 dk	**(A13B2TU) Tanker (unspecified)**	**1 oil engine** driving 1 FP propeller Total Power: 552kW (750hp) Cummins 1 x 4 Stroke 552kW (750bhp) Cummins Engine Co Inc-USA

5369059 *H02335* -	**TROJAN II** *ex* Trojan *-2001* *ex* Ben B *-2001* *ex* I. B. Pevoto *-2001* **Millenium Holding Ltd** - *Panama* *Panama* Official number: 29468PEXT1	*143* 97 -		**1949 Harrisburg Machine Co Inc. — Houston, Tx** Loa 27.01 Br ex 7.12 Dght - Lbp - Br md - Dpth 2.92 Welded, 1 dk	**(B32A2ST) Tug**	**1 oil engine** driving 1 FP propeller Total Power: 736kW (1,001hp) 10.0kn EMD (Electro-Motive) 12-567-BC 1 x Vee 2 Stroke 12 Cy. 216 x 254 736kW (1001bhp) (made 1943, fitted 1949) General Motors Corp-USA AuxGen: 2 x 20kW 110/220V d.c
7408108 *WDB3675* -	**TROJAN TIDE** *ex* Ensco Trojan *-2004* *ex* Golden Shore *-1988* *ex* Mr. Eric II *-1988* *ex* Andy Martin *-1981* **Twenty Grand Marine Service LLC** Tidewater Marine LLC *New Orleans, LA* *United States of America* MMSI: 366128000 Official number: 561982	*999* 299 1,309	Class: AB	**1975-02 Halter Marine, Inc. — Moss Point, Ms** Yd No: 423 Lengthened-1987 Loa - Br ex 12.20 Dght 4.379 Lbp 63.84 Br md 12.18 Dpth 5.19 Welded, 1 dk	**(B21B20T) Offshore Tug/Supply Ship** Ice Capable	**2 oil engines** sr geared to sc. shafts driving 2 CP propellers Total Power: 5,296kW (7,200hp) 12.0kn EMD (Electro-Motive) 20-645-E5 2 x Vee 2 Stroke 20 Cy. 230 x 254 each-2648kW (3600bhp) General Motors Corp.Electro-Motive Div.-La Grange AuxGen: 2 x 150kW a.c Thrusters: 1 Thwart. FP thruster (f) Fuel: 457.0 (d.f.)
5340821 *J7AG5* -	**TROLL** *ex* Mega Mammut *-2003* *ex* Sterkodder *-1980* **Inter Carib AS** Saga Shipping & Trading Nevis Ltd *Portsmouth* *Dominica* Official number: 50053	**264** 79 -	Class: (NV)	**1957 Ankerlokken Slipper & Mek Verksted — Floro** Yd No: 12 Loa 38.31 Br ex 7.85 Dght 4.014 Lbp 32.49 Br md 7.80 Dpth 4.02 Welded, 1 dk	**(B34P2QV) Salvage Ship** 1 Ha: (2.7 x 2.1) Derricks: 1x10t; Winches: 1 Ice Capable	**1 oil engine** geared to sc. shaft driving 1 CP propeller Total Power: 1,747kW (2,375hp) 12.0kn Deutz SBV9M628 1 x 4 Stroke 9 Cy. 240 x 280 1747kW (2375bhp) (new engine 1983) Kloeckner Humboldt Deutz AG-West Germany AuxGen: 1 x 96kW 220V 50Hz a.c, 1 x 36kW 220V 50Hz a.c Thrusters: 1 Thwart. FP thruster (f); 1 Tunnel thruster (a) Fuel: 66.0 (d.f.)
8770338 *YJVJ5* -	**TROLL SOLUTION** *ex* Remedial Esv Solution *-2011* *ex* ESV Michael D. Brown *-2010* *ex* COSCO Nantong 112 *-2009* **Trollrig1 Ltd** North Sea Drilling Group AS *Port Vila* *Vanuatu* MMSI: 576368000 Official number: 1774	**7,530** 2,259 2,000	Class: AB	**2010-06 COSCO (Nantong) Shipyard Co Ltd — Nantong JS** Yd No: N112 Loa 73.15 Br ex 55.78 Dght - Lbp 70.23 Br md - Dpth 7.62 Welded, 1 dk	**(B22A2ZM) Offshore Construction Vessel, jack up** Cranes: 1x280t,2x45t	**4 diesel electric oil engines** driving 1 gen. of 1300kW 4160V a.c 3 gen. each 2500kW 4160V a.c Connecting to 3 elec. motors each (2500kW) driving 3 Azimuth electric drive units Total Power: 9,781kW (13,299hp) 6.0kn General Electric 7FDM16 3 x Vee 4 Stroke 16 Cy. 229 x 267 each-2819kW (3833bhp) General Electric Co.-Lynn, Ma General Electric 7FDM8 1 x Vee 4 Stroke 8 Cy. 229 x 267 1324kW (1800bhp) General Electric Co.-Lynn, Ma
9233258 *LLVT* -	**TROLLFJORD** - **Hurtigruten ASA** - *Tromso* *Norway* MMSI: 258465000	**16,140** 6,291 1,186	Class: NV	**2002-05 Bruces Verkstad AB — Landskrona** (Hull) Yd No: 246 **2002-05 Fosen Mek. Verksteder AS — Rissa** Yd No: 72 Loa 133.00 Br ex - Dght 5.100 Lbp 118.70 Br md 21.50 Dpth 7.50 Welded	**(A36A2PR) Passenger/Ro-Ro Ship (Vehicles)** Passengers: unberthed: 332; cabins: 313; berths: 650 Cars: 50 Bale: 1,100; Ins: 490 Ice Capable	**2 oil engines** reduction geared to sc. shafts driving 2 Directional propellers contra-rotating propellers Total Power: 8,282kW (11,260hp) 16.0kn Wartsila 9L32 2 x 4 Stroke 9 Cy. 320 x 400 each-4141kW (5630bhp) Wartsila France SA-France AuxGen: 2 x a.c Thrusters: 2 Thwart. FP thruster (f) Fuel: 60.0 (d.f.) 247.0 (r.f.)
9334301 *9HWC8* -	**TROMA** *launched as* Urartian *-2007* **Mowinckel Tankers AS** Mowinckel Ship Management AS SatCom: Inmarsat M 600641694 *Valletta* *Malta* MMSI: 249689000 Official number: 9334301	**3,981** 1,824 5,565 T/cm 15.0	Class: NV (BV)	**2007-03 Celiktekne Sanayii ve Ticaret A.S. — Tuzla, Istanbul** Yd No: 58 Loa 109.10 (BB) Br ex 16.03 Dght 5.740 Lbp 99.80 Br md 16.00 Dpth 8.00 Welded, 1 dk	**(A12B2TR) Chemical/Products Tanker** Double Hull (13F) Liq: 6,350; Liq (Oil): 6,359 Cargo Heating Coils Compartments: 12 Wing Ta, 1 Slop Ta, ER 12 Cargo Pump (s): 4x150m³/hr, 8x200m³/hr Manifold: Bow/CM: 51m Ice Capable	**1 oil engine** reduction geared to sc. shaft driving 1 CP propeller Total Power: 2,720kW (3,698hp) 14.0kn MAN-B&W 8L27/38 1 x 4 Stroke 8 Cy. 270 x 380 2720kW (3698bhp) MAN Diesel A/S-Denmark AuxGen: 1 x 850kW a.c, 3 x 438kW a.c Thrusters: 1 Thwart. FP thruster (f) Fuel: 51.0 (d.f.) 250.0 (r.f.)
9299410 *OA2056* -	**TROMPETEROS I** *ex* Meriom Wave *-2009* **Petrolera Transoceanica SA** - *Callao* *Peru* MMSI: 760000470 Official number: CO-37848-MM	**25,507** 11,043 38,847 T/cm 45.7	Class: AB (RI)	**2004-08 Guangzhou Shipyard International Co Ltd — Guangzhou GD** Yd No: 03130003 Loa 173.96 (BB) Br ex 29.03 Dght 12.320 Lbp 163.60 Br md 29.00 Dpth 18.40 Welded, 1 dk	**(A12B2TR) Chemical/Products Tanker** Double Hull Liq: 41,850; Liq (Oil): 45,000 Part Cargo Heating Coils Compartments: 10 Wing Ta, 2 Wing Slop Ta, ER 10 Cargo Pump (s): 10x600m³/hr Manifold: Bow/CM: 91m	**1 oil engine** driving 1 FP propeller Total Power: 7,877kW (10,710hp) 14.5kn B&W 6S46MC-C 1 x 2 Stroke 6 Cy. 460 x 1932 7877kW (10710bhp) (made 2004) Hudong Heavy Machinery Co Ltd-China Fuel: 153.0 (d.f.) 1484.0 (r.f.)
9694000 *LKNL* -	**TROMS ARCTURUS** **Troms Offshore Fleet 2 AS** Troms Offshore Management AS *Tromso* *Norway* MMSI: 257131000	**4,969** 1,861 5,580	Class: NV	**2014-01 Vard Braila SA — Braila** (Hull) Yd No: (817) **2014-01 Vard Aukra — Aukra** Yd No: 817 Loa 94.65 (BB) Br ex - Dght 6.950 Lbp 84.75 Br md 21.00 Dpth 8.50 Welded, 1 dk	**(B21A20S) Platform Supply Ship** Ice Capable	**3 diesel electric oil engines** driving 3 gen. Connecting to 2 elec. motors driving 2 Azimuth electric drive units Total Power: 6,960kW (9,462hp) Bergens C25: 33L8P 1 x 4 Stroke 8 Cy. 250 x 330 2320kW (3154bhp) Rolls Royce Marine AS-Norway Bergens C25: 33L8P 2 x 4 Stroke 8 Cy. 250 x 330 each-2320kW (3154bhp) Rolls Royce Marine AS-Norway Thrusters: 2 Tunnel thruster (f); 1 Retract. directional thruster (a)
9544516 *3YOV* -	**TROMS ARTEMIS** *ex* Vestland Insula *-2011* **GSE Shipping I KS** Troms Offshore AS *Tromso* *Norway* MMSI: 257055000	**4,344** 1,800 4,900	Class: NV	**2011-11 Stocznia Gdansk SA — Gdansk** (Hull) Yd No: 253/1 **2011-11 Hellesoy Verft AS — Lofallstrand** Yd No: 148 Loa 85.00 (BB) Br ex 20.03 Dght 7.160 Lbp 77.64 Br md 20.00 Dpth 8.60 Welded, 1 dk	**(B21A20S) Platform Supply Ship** Ice Capable	**4 diesel electric oil engines** driving 4 gen. each 1825kW 690V a.c Connecting to 2 elec. motors each (2300kW) driving 2 Azimuth electric drive units Total Power: 7,300kW (9,924hp) 12.5kn Caterpillar 3516B 4 x Vee 4 Stroke 16 Cy. 170 x 190 each-1825kW (2481bhp) Caterpillar Inc-USA Thrusters: 1 Tunnel thruster (f); 1 Retract. directional thruster (f)
9480722 *2HDJ5* -	**TROMS CAPELLA** *launched as* Skandi Kochi *-2011* **Troms Offshore Fleet 2 AS** Secunda Canada LP *Douglas* *Isle of Man (British)* MMSI: 235102712 Official number: 744972	**4,059** 1,627 4,800	Class: NV	**2011-07 Cochin Shipyard Ltd — Ernakulam** Yd No: BY-81 Loa 86.60 (BB) Br ex - Dght 6.600 Lbp 78.10 Br md 19.00 Dpth 8.00 Welded, 1 dk	**(B21A20S) Platform Supply Ship** Cranes: 1x5t	**4 diesel electric oil engines** driving 4 gen. each 1242kW a.c Connecting to 2 elec. motors each (2200kW) driving 2 Azimuth electric drive units Total Power: 6,480kW (8,812hp) 11.0kn Wartsila 9L20 4 x 4 Stroke 9 Cy. 200 x 280 each-1620kW (2203bhp) Wartsila Finland Oy-Finland Thrusters: 1 Tunnel thruster (f); 1 Retract. directional thruster (f) Fuel: 1070.0
9422213 *LALC* -	**TROMS CASTOR** **Troms Offshore Fleet 1 AS** Troms Offshore AS SatCom: Inmarsat C 425817010 *Tromso* *Norway* MMSI: 258170000	**4,366** 1,813 4,900	Class: NV	**2009-02 Istanbul Tersanecilik ve Denizcilik Sanayi Tic Ltd Sti — Istanbul (Tuzla)** (Hull) Yd No: 006 **2009-02 Hellesoy Verft AS — Lofallstrand** Yd No: 144 Loa 85.00 (BB) Br ex 20.02 Dght 7.163 Lbp 77.70 Br md 20.00 Dpth 8.60 Welded, 1 dk	**(B21A20S) Platform Supply Ship** Ice Capable	**4 diesel electric oil engines** driving 4 gen. each 1901kW a.c Connecting to 2 elec. motors each (2450kW) driving 2 Azimuth electric drive units Total Power: 7,680kW (10,440hp) 12.0kn Caterpillar 3516B 4 x Vee 4 Stroke 16 Cy. 170 x 215 each-1920kW (2610bhp) Caterpillar Inc-USA Thrusters: 2 Tunnel thruster (f); 1 Retract. directional thruster (f)
9348211 *2EB05* -	**TROMS FJORD** **Troms Fjord KS** Troms Offshore AS *Douglas* *Isle of Man (British)* MMSI: 235083745 Official number: 742815	**2,467** 906 3,597	Class: NV	**2005-12 Flekkefjord Slipp & Maskinfabrikk AS — Feda** Yd No: 183 Loa 73.40 (BB) Br ex 16.62 Dght 6.500 Lbp 64.00 Br md 16.60 Dpth 7.60 Welded, 1 dk	**(B21A20S) Platform Supply Ship** Double Bottom Entire Compartment Length	**2 oil engines** reduction geared to sc. shafts driving 2 CP propellers Total Power: 5,280kW (7,178hp) 14.5kn MaK 8M25 2 x 4 Stroke 8 Cy. 255 x 400 each-2640kW (3589bhp) Caterpillar Motoren GmbH & Co. KG-Germany AuxGen: 2 x a.c, 1 x a.c, 1 x a.c Thrusters: 2 Tunnel thruster (f); 2 Tunnel thruster (a)

No. / Call sign	Name / Owner / Flag	Tonnage	Class	Builder / Dimensions	Type	Machinery
9649184 *LFYG* -	**TROMS LYRA** **Troms Offshore Fleet 2 AS** Troms Offshore AS *Tromso* Norway MMSI: 258646000	**3,409** 1,418 3,650	Class: NV	**2013-06 Vard Braila SA — Braila** (Hull) **2013-05 Vard Brevik — Brevik** Yd No: 756 Loa 81.70 (BB) Br ex - Dght 6.500 Lbp 73.92 Br md 18.00 Dpth 7.80 Welded, 1 dk	**(B21A20S) Platform Supply Ship**	**4 diesel electric oil engines** driving 1 gen. of 500kW 690V a.c 3 gen. each 1700kW 690V a.c Connecting to 2 elec. motors each (1900kW) driving 2 Azimuth electric drive units Total Power: 5,828kW (7,925hp) 11.0kn Caterpillar 3512C 1 x Vee 4 Stroke 12 Cy. 170 x 215 1765kW (2400bhp) Caterpillar Inc-USA Caterpillar 3512C 2 x Vee 4 Stroke 12 Cy. 170 x 215 each-1765kW (2400bhp) Caterpillar Inc-USA Caterpillar C18 1 x 4 Stroke 6 Cy. 145 x 183 533kW (725bhp) Caterpillar Inc-USA Thrusters: 3 Tunnel thruster (f)
9439022 *LAZR* -	**TROMS POLLUX** **Troms Offshore Fleet 1 AS** Troms Offshore AS SatCom: Inmarsat C 425846710 *Tromso* Norway MMSI: 258467000	**4,366** 1,813 4,900	Class: NV	**2009-10 Istanbul Tersanecilik ve Denizcilik Sanayi Tic Ltd Sti — Istanbul (Tuzla)** (Hull) Yd No: 007 **2009-10 Hellesoy Verft AS — Lofallstrand** Yd No: 145 Loa 85.00 (BB) Br ex - Dght 6.800 Lbp 77.70 Br md 20.00 Dpth 8.60 Welded, 1 dk	**(B21A20S) Platform Supply Ship** Ice Capable	**4 diesel electric oil engines** driving 4 gen. Connecting to 2 elec. motors each (2450kW) driving 2 Azimuth electric drive units Total Power: 7,680kW (10,440hp) 12.5kn Caterpillar 3516B 4 x Vee 4 Stroke 16 Cy. 170 x 190 each-1920kW (2610bhp) Caterpillar Inc-USA Thrusters: 2 Tunnel thruster (f); 1 Retract. directional thruster (f)
9628386 *LDGG* -	**TROMS SIRIUS** **Troms Offshore Fleet 1 AS** Troms Offshore AS *Tromso* Norway MMSI: 257825000	**4,201** 1,799 4,868	Class: NV	**2012-05 STX OSV Tulcea SA — Tulcea** (Hull) **2012-05 STX OSV Soviknes — Sovik** Yd No: 773 Loa 93.50 (BB) Br ex - Dght 6.500 Lbp 84.54 Br md 19.00 Dpth 8.00 Welded, 1 dk	**(B21A20S) Platform Supply Ship**	**4 diesel electric oil engines** driving 4 gen. each 1980kW a.c Connecting to 2 elec. motors driving 2 Azimuth electric drive units Total Power: 8,380kW (11,392hp) 11.0kn Caterpillar 3516C 4 x Vee 4 Stroke 16 Cy. 170 x 190 each-2095kW (2848bhp) Caterpillar Inc-USA Thrusters: 1 Retract. directional thruster (f); 2 Tunnel thruster (f)
5338505 *LAWQ* -	**TROMSBAS** *ex Furen -2004 ex Tromsbas -1999* *ex Garpeskjaer -1997 ex Sun Tuna -1975* *ex Star I -1971* **Chrisma AS** - SatCom: Inmarsat C 425830610 *Tromso* Norway MMSI: 258306000 Official number: 14433	**1,535** 460 -	Class: (NV)	**1956-10 AS Pusnes Mek. Verksted — Arendal** (Hull) Yd No: 95 **1956-10 AS Fredriksstad Mek. Verksted — Fredrikstad** Converted From: Whale-catcher-1971 Loa 66.55 Br ex 10.09 Dght 6.640 Lbp 59.77 Br md 9.76 Dpth 7.17 Riveted\Welded, 1 dk	**(B11B2FV) Fishing Vessel** Compartments: 1 Ho, 9 Ta, ER 5 Ha: 5 (2.3 x 1.7)ER Derricks: 1x5t,2x2t; Winches: 3 Ice Capable	**1 oil engine** sr geared to sc. shaft driving 1 CP propeller Total Power: 3,119kW (4,241hp) 15.0kn Alpha 16U28L-VO 1 x Vee 4 Stroke 16 Cy. 280 x 320 3119kW (4241bhp) (new engine 1980) Alpha Diesel A/S-Denmark AuxGen: 3 x 152kW 380V 50Hz a.c Thrusters: 1 Tunnel thruster (f); 1 Tunnel thruster (a) Fuel: 215.0 (d.f.) 12.0pd
9435791 *C6XL5* -	**TROMSO** *ex M. Y. Arctic -2011 ex Gemi -2008* **Tromso Shipping Co Ltd** World Tankers Management Pte Ltd *Nassau* Bahamas MMSI: 311013300 Official number: 8001588	**8,247** 3,725 12,934 T/cm 21.8	Class: AB	**2008-07 STX Shipbuilding Co Ltd — Busan** Yd No: 5024 Loa 120.00 (BB) Br ex 20.43 Dght 8.650 Lbp 113.00 Br md 20.40 Dpth 11.90 Welded, 1 dk	**(A12B2TR) Chemical/Products Tanker** Double Hull (13F) Liq: 12,986; Liq (Oil): 13,693 Compartments: 10 Wing Ta, 2 Wing Slop Ta, ER 10 Cargo Pump (s): 10x300m³/hr Manifold: Bow/CM: 60m	**1 oil engine** driving 1 FP propeller Total Power: 4,454kW (6,056hp) 13.6kn MAN-B&W 6S35MC 1 x 2 Stroke 6 Cy. 350 x 1400 4454kW (6056bhp) STX Engine Co Ltd-South Korea AuxGen: 3 x 450kW a.c Thrusters: 1 Thwart. FP thruster (f) Fuel: 64.0 (d.f.) 530.0 (r.f.)
8811302 *3YHZ* T-115-T	**TROMSOY** *ex Stapin -2010 ex Gandi -2002* *ex Loran I -1999 ex Loran -1999* **Ostbas AS** - *Tromso* Norway MMSI: 258380500	**466** 184 244	Class: NV	**1989-12 N A Kyeds Maskinfabrik A/S — Norresundby** (Hull) **1989-12 Karstensens Skibsvaerft A/S — Skagen** Yd No: 359 Loa 34.00 Br ex - Dght - Lbp - Br md 8.20 Dpth 4.00 Welded	**(B11B2FV) Fishing Vessel** Ice Capable	**1 oil engine** geared to sc. shaft driving 1 FP propeller Total Power: 627kW (852hp) Caterpillar 3508TA 1 x Vee 4 Stroke 8 Cy. 170 x 190 627kW (852bhp) Caterpillar Inc-USA AuxGen: 2 x 200kW 380V 50Hz a.c
8717025 *XUCF4* -	**TRON** *ex Scorpion -2012 ex Fuji Maru -2010* **Greenway Maritime Ltd** Grace Ship Management Co Ltd *Phnom Penh* Cambodia MMSI: 514922000 Official number: 1187727	**485** 146 480		**1988-02 KK Kanasashi Zosen — Shizuoka SZ** Yd No: 3157 Loa 51.21 (BB) Br ex 8.34 Dght 3.301 Lbp 43.31 Br md 8.31 Dpth 3.61 Welded, 1 dk	**(A34A2GR) Refrigerated Cargo Ship** Ins: 100	**1 oil engine** with clutches, flexible couplings & sr reverse geared to sc. shaft driving 1 FP propeller Total Power: 1,177kW (1,600hp) Akasaka K28S 1 x 4 Stroke 6 Cy. 280 x 500 1177kW (1600bhp) Akasaka Tekkosho KK (Akasaka DieselLtd)-Japan Thrusters: 1 Thwart. FP thruster (f); 1 Tunnel thruster (a)
5425645 *LW4748* -	**TRONADOR** **Maruba SCA Empresa de Navegacion Maritima** - Argentina Official number: 02472	*196* 50 -	Class: (LR) ✠ Classed LR until 10/10/75	**1964-04 Ryan Astilleros Argentinos S.A. — Avellaneda** Yd No: C.2 Loa 30.79 Br ex 8.44 Dght - Lbp 28.02 Br md 8.01 Dpth 3.76 Riveted\Welded, 1 dk	**(B32A2ST) Tug**	**2 diesel electric oil engines** driving 2 gen. each 340kW 440V d.c Connecting to 2 elec. motors driving 1 FP propeller Total Power: 882kW (1,200hp) MAN G7V235/330ATL 2 x 4 Stroke 7 Cy. 235 x 330 each-441kW (600bhp) Maschinenbau Augsburg Nuernberg (MAN)-Augsburg AuxGen: 2 x 36kW 220V d.c
9184639 *LJVY* NT-500-V	**TRONDERBAS** **Tronderbas AS** Bernt I Ulsund *Rorvik* Norway MMSI: 259612000	**2,213** 663 -	Class: NV	**1999-06 Stocznia Polnocna SA (Northern Shipyard) — Gdansk** (Hull) Yd No: B305/01 **1999-06 West Contractors AS — Olensvaag** Yd No: 18 Loa 68.10 (BB) Br ex - Dght 6.500 Lbp 60.00 Br md 14.00 Dpth 9.65 Welded, 1 dk	**(B11A2FT) Trawler** Ice Capable	**1 oil engine** geared to sc. shaft driving 1 FP propeller Total Power: 5,517kW (7,501hp) 19.0kn Wartsila 12V32 1 x Vee 4 Stroke 12 Cy. 320 x 350 5517kW (7501bhp) Wartsila NSD Finland Oy-Finland AuxGen: 1 x 2000kW a.c, 2 x 590kW a.c Thrusters: 2 Thwart. FP thruster (f); 1 Tunnel thruster (a)
9029243 *LLJN* ST-30-RS	**TRONDERHAV** **Tronderhav AS** - *Trondheim* Norway MMSI: 257559600	**479** 203 -		**2001-03 Stocznia Ustka Sp z oo — Ustka** (Hull launched by) **2001-03 Trondheim Verft AS — Trondheim** (Hull completed by) Yd No: 6/78 Lengthened-2008 Loa 36.40 (BB) Br ex - Dght 5.500 Lbp - Br md 8.50 Dpth 7.00 Welded, 1 dk	**(B11B2FV) Fishing Vessel**	**1 oil engine** reduction geared to sc. shaft driving 1 Propeller Total Power: 750kW (1,020hp) Caterpillar 3512B 1 x Vee 4 Stroke 12 Cy. 170 x 190 750kW (1020bhp) Caterpillar Inc-USA Thrusters: 1 Tunnel thruster (f)
9277670 *LLVN* NT-200-V	**TRONDERKARI** **Tronderkari AS** - *Rorvik* Norway MMSI: 259208000	**442** 132 -		**2002-08 Voldnes Skipsverft AS — Fosnavaag** Yd No: 61 Loa 28.00 Br ex - Dght 5.800 Lbp - Br md 9.40 Dpth - Welded	**(B11B2FV) Fishing Vessel**	**1 oil engine** geared to sc. shaft driving 1 FP propeller
9018634 *LGEF* -	**TRONDHEIM** **FosenNamsos Sjo AS** - *Trondheim* Norway MMSI: 257015700	**3,418** 1,284 870	Class: (NV)	**1992-12 Brattvaag Skipsverft AS — Brattvaag** Yd No: 55 Loa 96.95 Br ex 15.50 Dght 4.600 Lbp 79.20 Br md 15.00 Dpth 7.50 Welded, 2 dks	**(A36A2PR) Passenger/Ro-Ro Ship (Vehicles)** Passengers: unberthed: 500 Cars: 155	**1 oil engine** sr geared to sc. shafts driving 2 CP propellers Total Power: 3,000kW (4,079hp) 15.0kn Wichmann 10V28B 1 x Vee 2 Stroke 10 Cy. 280 x 360 3000kW (4079bhp) Wartsila Wichmann Diesel AS-Norway AuxGen: 3 x 350kW 380V 50Hz a.c Fuel: 100.0 (d.f.)
9432177 *LAPA* -	**TRONDHEIMSFJORD I** **FosenNamsos Sjo AS** - *Trondheim* Norway MMSI: 257304900	**176** 70 19		**2008-03 Brodrene Aa AS — Hyen** Yd No: 251 Loa 24.50 Br ex - Dght 0.950 Lbp 22.60 Br md 8.00 Dpth 2.60 Bonded, 1 dk	**(A37B2PS) Passenger Ship** Hull Material: Carbon Fibre Sandwich Passengers: unberthed: 130	**2 oil engines** reduction geared to sc. shafts driving 2 CP propellers Servo gear 9P 805 Total Power: 1,498kW (2,036hp) 28.0kn MAN D2842LE 2 x Vee 4 Stroke 12 Cy. 128 x 142 each-749kW (1018bhp) MAN Nutzfahrzeuge AG-Nuernberg AuxGen: 2 x 26kW a.c Thrusters: 1 Tunnel thruster (s. f.) Fuel: 4.0

IMO / Call sign / Flag	Name / Owner / Port	Tonnage	Class	Builder / Dimensions	Type	Machinery
9432189 *LAPB* -	**TRONDHEIMSFJORD II** **FosenNamsos Sjo AS** - *Trondheim* *Norway* MMSI: 257114400	**176** 70 19		**2008-04 Brodrene Aa AS — Hyen** Yd No: 252 Loa 24.50 Br ex - Dght 0.950 Lbp 22.60 Br md 8.00 Dpth 2.60 Bonded, 1 dk	**(A37B2PS) Passenger Ship** Hull Material: Carbon Fibre Sandwich Passengers: unberthed: 130	**2 oil engines** reduction geared to sc. shafts driving 2 CP propellers Total Power: 1,498kW (2,036hp) 28.0kn MAN D2842LE 2 x Vee 4 Stroke 12 Cy. 128 x 142 each-749kW (1018bhp) MAN Nutzfahrzeuge AG-Nuernberg AuxGen: 2 x 26kW a.c Thrusters: 1 Tunnel thruster (s. f.) Fuel: 4.0
9463255 *XPXM* -	**TRONDUR I GOTU** **P/F Hvamm** - *Gota* *Faeroe Islands (Danish)* MMSI: 231036000 Official number: 28337	**3,527** 1,059 3,500	Class: NV	**2010-03 Stocznia Marynarki Wojennej SA (Naval Shipyard Gdynia) — Gdynia** (Hull) **2010-03 Karstensens Skibsvaerft A/S — Skagen** Yd No: 192 Loa 81.60 (BB) Br ex - Dght 8.200 Lbp 71.80 Br md 16.60 Dpth 10.00 Welded, 1 dk	**(B11B2FV) Fishing Vessel** Ice Capable	**1 oil engine** reduction geared to sc. shafts driving 1 CP propeller Total Power: 6,000kW (8,158hp) 17.5kn Wartsila 12V32 1 x Vee 4 Stroke 12 Cy. 320 x 400 6000kW (8158bhp) Wartsila Finland Oy-Finland AuxGen: 1 x 1450kW a.c, 1 x 1110kW a.c, 1 x 3000kW a.c Thrusters: 1 Tunnel thruster (f); 1 Tunnel thruster (a)
9571789 *3WZC* -	**TRONG ANH 09** *ex* Phat Dat 09 *-2012* **Quy Trong Anh Co Ltd** - *Haiphong* *Vietnam* MMSI: 574000060	**1,358** 875 2,523	Class: VR	**2010-02 Song Dao Shipyard — Nam Dinh** Yd No: THB-26-05 Loa 74.70 Br ex 11.22 Dght 4.950 Lbp 70.00 Br md 11.20 Dpth 6.00 Welded, 1 dk	**(A21A2BC) Bulk Carrier** Grain: 3,237; Bale: 2,916 Compartments: 2 Ho, ER 2 Ha: (18.7 x 7.6)ER (19.3 x 7.6)	**1 oil engine** reduction geared to sc. shaft driving 1 FP propeller Total Power: 721kW (980hp) 10.0kn Chinese Std. Type CW8200ZC 1 x 4 Stroke 8 Cy. 200 x 270 721kW (980bhp) Weifang Diesel Engine Factory-China AuxGen: 2 x 60kW a.c
8665014 - -	**TRONG ANH 27** *ex* Duy Phuong 45 *-2008* **Tan Trong Anh Shipping JSC** - *Haiphong* *Vietnam* Official number: VN-2479-VT	**499** 345 956	Class: VR	**2008-01 Nam Ha Shipyard — Nam Ha** Yd No: TKT-457E Loa 57.00 Br ex 9.22 Dght 3.500 Lbp 52.90 Br md 9.20 Dpth 4.20 Welded, 1 dk	**(A31A2GX) General Cargo Ship** Grain: 1,315; Bale: 1,184 Compartments: 2 Ho, ER 2 Ha: ER 2 (12.1 x 5.2)	**1 oil engine** reduction geared to sc. shaft driving 1 FP propeller Total Power: 382kW (519hp) 10.0kn Chinese Std. Type X6170ZCA 1 x 4 Stroke 6 Cy. 170 x 200 382kW (519bhp) Weifang Diesel Engine Factory-China AuxGen: 1 x 10kW 400V a.c
8656491 *XVSX* -	**TRONG ANH 45** **Nam Thanh Shipping JS Co** - *Haiphong* *Vietnam*	**999** 665 1,950	Class: VR	**2009-07 Nguyen Van Tuan Mechanical Shipbuilding IPE — Kien Xuong** Yd No: THB-12-17 Loa 69.85 Br ex 10.82 Dght 4.500 Lbp 65.95 Br md 10.80 Dpth 5.40 Welded, 1 dk	**(A31A2GX) General Cargo Ship** Grain: 2,638 Compartments: 2 Ho, ER 2 Ha: ER 2 (17.6 x 7.0)	**1 oil engine** reduction geared to sc. shaft driving 1 FP propeller Total Power: 530kW (721hp) 10.0kn Weifang 8170ZC 1 x 4 Stroke 8 Cy. 170 x 200 530kW (721bhp) Weifang Diesel Engine Factory-China AuxGen: 2 x 22kW 400V a.c
9361603 *ZDLS* -	**TRONIO** **Pesquerias Arnela SL** Georgia Seafood Ltd *Stanley* *Falkland Islands (British)* MMSI: 740382000	**1,058** 317 648	Class: (BV)	**2005-10 Astilleros Armon SA — Navia** Yd No: 628 Loa 57.85 Br ex 11.00 Dght 4.430 Lbp 46.00 Br md 10.20 Dpth 6.40 Welded, 1 dk	**(B11B2FV) Fishing Vessel** Ins: 632 Ice Capable	**1 oil engine** reduction geared to sc. shaft driving 1 FP propeller Total Power: 1,641kW (2,231hp) 14.0kn Caterpillar 3516B 1 x Vee 4 Stroke 16 Cy. 170 x 190 1641kW (2231bhp) Caterpillar Inc-USA AuxGen: 3 x 320kW 380/220V 50Hz a.c
7900522 - -	**TROODOS** *ex* Naranco *-2006* *ex* Leyla *-1997* *ex* Otaru 1 *-1996* *ex* Reina Navegante No. 8 *-1989* *ex* Reina Navegante *-1986* *ex* Hakko Minerva *-1985* **Naftaservice Trading (Cyprus) Ltd** Arkada PS Ltd	**3,890** 1,526 6,304 T/cm 14.9	Class: (NV) (NK)	**1979-05 Kochi Jyuko K.K. — Kochi** Yd No: 1306 Loa 113.77 (BB) Br ex - Dght 7.014 Lbp 105.01 Br md 17.43 Dpth 8.41 Welded, 1 dk	**(A12B2TR) Chemical/Products Tanker** Double Hull Liq: 5,507; Liq (Oil): 5,507 Cargo Heating Coils 12 Cargo Pump (s)	**1 oil engine** driving 1 FP propeller Total Power: 2,869kW (3,901hp) 14.5kn Pielstick 6PC2-5L-400 1 x 4 Stroke 6 Cy. 400 x 460 2869kW (3901bhp) Ishikawajima Harima Heavy IndustrieCo Ltd (IHI)-Japan AuxGen: 2 x 250kW 100/440V 60Hz a.c Thrusters: 1 Tunnel thruster (f)
8020812 *ITIH* -	**TROPESCA SECONDO** **Societa Cooperativa Tropesca Srl** - *Mazara del Vallo* *Italy* Official number: 242	*199* 73 -	Class: (RI)	**1982-05 Cant. Nav. F. Giacalone — Mazara del Vallo** Yd No: 45 Loa 33.51 Br ex 7.32 Dght 3.101 Lbp 27.28 Br md 7.31 Dpth 3.92 Welded, 1 dk	**(B11A2FS) Stern Trawler**	**1 oil engine** geared to sc. shaft driving 1 FP propeller Total Power: 1,048kW (1,425hp) Crepelle 6PSN3L 1 x 4 Stroke 6 Cy. 260 x 320 1048kW (1425bhp) Crepelle et Cie-France
8906315 *V3RP7* -	**TROPIC BREEZE** *ex* Tropicshell *-1996* **BTCI Tankers Ltd** Maritime Management LLC *Belize City* *Belize* MMSI: 312815000 Official number: 119510218	**348** 187 750	Class: NV (AB)	**1989-09 Tille Scheepsbouw B.V. — Kootstertille** (Hull) Yd No: 278 **1989-09 B.V. Scheepswerf Damen — Gorinchem** Yd No: 8689 Loa 58.00 Br ex - Dght 2.280 Lbp 46.76 Br md 8.00 Dpth 3.03 Welded, 1 dk	**(A13B2TP) Products Tanker** 2 Cargo Pump (s)	**2 oil engines** reduction geared to sc. shafts driving 2 FP propellers Total Power: 442kW (600hp) 8.2kn Caterpillar 3406TA 2 x 4 Stroke 6 Cy. 137 x 165 each-221kW (300bhp) Caterpillar Inc-USA AuxGen: 2 x 65kW 115/230V 60Hz a.c
9225263 *J8PE3* -	**TROPIC CARIB** **Tropical Shipping & Construction Co Ltd** Tropical Shipping Co Ltd *Kingstown* *St Vincent & The Grenadines* MMSI: 375939000 Official number: 400497	**10,851** 3,601 12,418	Class: BV	**2001-09 Shanghai Edward Shipbuilding Co Ltd — Shanghai** Yd No: 120 Loa 159.90 (BB) Br ex - Dght 8.250 Lbp 151.20 Br md 22.60 Dpth 12.00 Welded, 1 dk	**(A31A2GX) General Cargo Ship** Grain: 16,900 TEU 973 incl 187 ref C. Cranes: 2x45t	**2 oil engines** with clutches, flexible couplings & reduction geared to sc. shafts driving 1 CP propeller Total Power: 14,400kW (19,578hp) 20.0kn MaK 8M43 2 x 4 Stroke 8 Cy. 430 x 610 each-7200kW (9789bhp) Caterpillar Motoren GmbH & Co. KG-Germany AuxGen: 2 x 960kW 440V 60Hz a.c Thrusters: 1 Thwart. CP thruster (f); 1 Tunnel thruster (a)
9404132 *J8B4934* -	**TROPIC DAWN** *ex* Kimtrans Prince *-2006* **Satram Marine SA** - *Kingstown* *St Vincent & The Grenadines* MMSI: 375096000 Official number: 11407	**1,678** 503 1,886	Class: BV (AB)	**2006-08 PT Karimun Sembawang Shipyard — Tanjungbalai Karimun** Yd No: 7045 Loa 76.00 Br ex 17.39 Dght 3.000 Lbp 71.00 Br md 17.20 Dpth 4.80 Welded, 1 dk	**(A35D2RL) Landing Craft**	**2 oil engines** reduction geared to sc. shafts driving 2 Propellers Total Power: 1,766kW (2,402hp) Cummins KTA-38-M2 2 x Vee 4 Stroke 12 Cy. 159 x 159 each-883kW (1201bhp) Cummins Engine Co Inc-USA AuxGen: 2 x 80kW a.c Fuel: 558.1 (r.f.)
9510046 *J8QB8* -	**TROPIC EXPRESS** **Tropical Shipping Co Ltd** - *Kingstown* *St Vincent & The Grenadines* MMSI: 377901024	**3,744** 1,123 5,000	Class: BV	**2011-05 Chongqing Dongfeng Ship Industry Co — Chongqing** Yd No: K08-1015 Loa 106.68 Br ex - Dght 4.215 Lbp 99.10 Br md 20.60 Dpth 5.80 Welded, 1 dk	**(A31A2GX) General Cargo Ship** TEU 368 incl 80 ref C.	**2 oil engines** reduction geared to sc. shafts driving 2 FP propellers Total Power: 4,000kW (5,438hp) 12.5kn MaK 6M25C 2 x 4 Stroke 6 Cy. 255 x 400 each-2000kW (2719bhp) Caterpillar Motoren GmbH & Co. KG-Germany AuxGen: 2 x 550kW 60Hz a.c
7800265 *J8NY* -	**TROPIC JADE** **Tropical Shipping & Construction Co Ltd** - *Kingstown* *St Vincent & The Grenadines* MMSI: 377907000	**1,827** 548 2,536	Class: BV	**1978-10 Miho Zosensho K.K. — Shimizu** Yd No: 1096 Loa 90.05 (BB) Br ex - Dght 4.815 Lbp 82.91 Br md 17.07 Dpth 5.80 Welded, 1 dk	**(A35A2RR) Ro-Ro Cargo Ship** Stern door/ramp (centre) Len: 6.09 Wid: 14.62 Swl: 250 TEU 176 incl.50 ref C.	**2 oil engines** reduction geared to sc. shafts driving 2 FP propellers Total Power: 2,586kW (3,516hp) 14.5kn EMD (Electro-Motive) 16-645-E6 2 x Vee 2 Stroke 16 Cy. 230 x 254 each-1293kW (1758bhp) General Motors Corp.Electro-Motive Div.-La Grange AuxGen: 4 x 197kW 445/115V 60Hz a.c Thrusters: 1 Tunnel thruster (f) Fuel: 359.0 (d.f.) 12.0pd
8204171 *J8PD* -	**TROPIC LURE** **Birdsall Shipping SA** Tropical Shipping Co Ltd *Kingstown* *St Vincent & The Grenadines* MMSI: 377912000	**1,827** 548 2,563	Class: BV	**1983-02 Miho Zosensho K.K. — Shimizu** Yd No: 1215 Converted From: Ro-Ro Cargo Ship Loa 90.05 (BB) Br ex 17.10 Dght 4.801 Lbp 82.91 Br md 17.07 Dpth 5.80 Welded, 1 dk	**(A31A2GX) General Cargo Ship** Grain: 1,566; Bale: 1,355 TEU 135 C. 135/20' (40') Compartments: 1 Ho, ER 1 Ha: ER	**2 oil engines** with clutches, flexible couplings & dr reverse geared to sc. shafts driving 2 FP propellers Total Power: 2,868kW (3,900hp) EMD (Electro-Motive) 16-645-E6 2 x Vee 2 Stroke 16 Cy. 230 x 254 each-1434kW (1950bhp) General Motors Corp.Electro-Motive Div.-La Grange Thrusters: 1 Thwart. FP thruster (f)
8204183 *J8NZ* -	**TROPIC MIST** **Tropical Shipping & Construction Co Ltd** Tropical Shipping Co Ltd *Kingstown* *St Vincent & The Grenadines* MMSI: 377908000	**1,827** 548 2,563	Class: BV	**1983-04 Miho Zosensho K.K. — Shimizu** Yd No: 1216 Loa 90.05 (BB) Br ex 17.10 Dght 4.801 Lbp 82.91 Br md 17.07 Dpth 5.80 Welded, 1 dk	**(A35A2RR) Ro-Ro Cargo Ship** Stern door/ramp Len: 14.62 Wid: 4.57 Swl: - Grain: 1,566; Bale: 1,355 TEU 198 Compartments: 1 Ho, ER 1 Ha: ER	**2 oil engines** with clutches & sr geared to sc. shafts driving 2 FP propellers Total Power: 2,868kW (3,900hp) EMD (Electro-Motive) 16-645-E6 2 x Vee 2 Stroke 16 Cy. 230 x 254 each-1434kW (1950bhp) General Motors Corp.Electro-Motive Div.-La Grange Thrusters: 1 Thwart. FP thruster (f)

7523673 *J8NX* -	**TROPIC NIGHT** *ex* CMS Island Express *-1996* *ex* Tropic Night *-1994* *ex* Inagua Island *-1986* **Tropical Shipping & Construction Co Ltd** Tropical Shipping Co Ltd *Kingstown* *St Vincent & The Grenadines* MMSI: 377906000 Official number: 400205	**1,561** 468 2,333	Class: BV	1976-12 **Bellinger Shipyards, Inc. — Jacksonville, Fl** Yd No: 111 Loa 81.41 Br ex 18.52 Dght 3.641 Lbp 79.25 Br md 15.55 Dpth 4.91 Welded, 1 dk	**(A35D2RL) Landing Craft** Bow door/ramp	**3 oil engines** reverse reduction geared to sc. shafts driving 3 FP propellers Total Power: 1,689kW (2,295hp) 12.0kn Caterpillar D398TA 3 x Vee 4 Stroke 12 Cy. 159 x 203 each-563kW (765bhp) Caterpillar Tractor Co-USA AuxGen: 1 x 250kW 460V 60Hz a.c, 2 x 135kW 460V 60Hz a.c Fuel: 713.5 (d.f.) 9.0pd
8035269 *J8NW* -	**TROPIC OPAL** *ex* Inagua Shore *-1986* **Tropical Shipping & Construction Co Ltd** Tropical Shipping Co Ltd *Kingstown* *St Vincent & The Grenadines* MMSI: 377909000	**1,561** 468 2,334	Class: BV	1979-07 **Wiley Mfg. Co. — Port Deposit, Md** Yd No: 36 Converted From: Landing Craft-1979 Loa 81.60 Br ex 18.52 Dght 3.660 Lbp 76.63 Br md 18.28 Dpth 4.87 Welded, 1 dk	**(A31C2GD) Deck Cargo Ship** Bow door & ramp Len: 9.25 Wid: 5.50 Swl: - Stern door/ramp Len: 2.75 Wid: 15.00 Swl: - TEU 157 incl 36 ref C Cranes: 1	**3 oil engines** driving 3 FP propellers Total Power: 2,484kW (3,378hp) 13.0kn Caterpillar D399SCAC 3 x Vee 4 Stroke 16 Cy. 159 x 203 each-828kW (1126bhp) Caterpillar Tractor Co-USA AuxGen: 1 x 260kW 460V 60Hz a.c, 2 x 210kW 460V 60Hz a.c Thrusters: 1 Tunnel thruster (f) Fuel: 727.5 (d.f.) 9.0pd
8217752 *PMXS* -	**TROPIC ORION** *ex* Osam Cougar *-1983* **Geooffshore Pte Ltd** PT Bahtera Niaga Internasional *Jakarta* *Indonesia* MMSI: 525016521 Official number: 2009 PST NO. 5854/L	**957** 287 1,200	Class: AB KI	1982-12 **Tonoura Dock Co. Ltd. — Miyazaki** Yd No: 52 Loa 57.70 Br ex - Dght 4.323 Lbp 52.51 Br md 12.21 Dpth 5.01 Welded, 1 dk	**(B21A20S) Platform Supply Ship**	**2 oil engines** with clutches & dr reverse geared to sc. shafts driving 2 FP propellers Total Power: 3,530kW (4,800hp) 13.0kn Fuji 8L27.5G 2 x 4 Stroke 8 Cy. 275 x 320 each-1765kW (2400bhp) Fuji Diesel Co Ltd-Japan AuxGen: 2 x 200kW Thrusters: 1 Thwart. CP thruster (f)
7625964 *J8PB* -	**TROPIC PALM** *ex* Inagua Tide *-1986* **Tropical Shipping & Construction Co Ltd** Tropical Shipping Co Ltd *Kingstown* *St Vincent & The Grenadines* MMSI: 377911000	**3,048** 1,595 4,810	Class: BV	1978-09 **Bellinger Shipyards, Inc. — Jacksonville, Fl** Yd No: 114 Loa 100.69 Br ex 21.75 Dght 4.709 Lbp 97.54 Br md 21.34 Dpth 6.10 Welded, 1 dk	**(A35A2RR) Ro-Ro Cargo Ship** Stern ramp Lane-Len: 567 285 TEU C. Dk. 285	**3 oil engines** reverse reduction geared to sc. shafts driving 3 FP propellers Total Power: 2,481kW (3,372hp) 13.0kn Caterpillar D399SCAC 3 x Vee 4 Stroke 16 Cy. 159 x 203 each-827kW (1124bhp) Caterpillar Tractor Co-USA AuxGen: 3 x 210kW 460V 60Hz a.c, 1 x 100kW 460V 60Hz a.c Fuel: 986.5 (d.f.) 9.0pd
6726826 *HC2120* -	**TROPIC SUN** *ex* Humber Guardian *-1993* **Jorge Sotomayor Neira** - *Puerto Ayora* *Ecuador* Official number: TN-01-0000	*790* - 241	Class: (LR) ✠ Classed LR until 14/2/96	1967-12 **R. Dunston (Hessle) Ltd. — Hessle** Yd No: S850 Converted From: Buoy Tender Loa 51.82 Br ex 10.16 Dght 3.048 Lbp 45.80 Br md 10.06 Dpth 4.81 Riveted\Welded, 1 dk, 2nd dk fwd of mchy. space	**(X11A2YP) Yacht** Compartments: 2 Ho, ER 1 Ha: (4.2 x 4.0)ER	**2 oil engines** sr reverse geared to sc. shafts driving 2 FP propellers Total Power: 920kW (1,250hp) 12.5kn Polar SF15RS-C 2 x 4 Stroke 5 Cy. 250 x 300 each-460kW (625bhp) Nydqvist & Holm AB-Sweden AuxGen: 2 x 60kW 220V d.c Fuel: 91.5 (d.f.)
8957388 *9GSG* -	**TROPIC SUN** *ex* Mona III *-2001* *ex* Black Dragon *-2001* *ex* Marie G *-2000* *ex* Lana Jean *-1995* *ex* Fortuna *-1992* **Cotrima Shipping Ltd** - *Takoradi* *Ghana* Official number: 316976	**177** 53 -		**1978 Swiftships Inc — Morgan City LA** L reg 33.41 Br ex - Dght - Lbp - Br md 7.03 Dpth 3.10 Welded, 1 dk	**(B34J2SD) Crew Boat** Hull Material: Aluminium Alloy	**3 oil engines** driving 3 FP propellers Total Power: 1,491kW (2,028hp) 25.0kn Caterpillar 3 x 4 Stroke each-497kW (676bhp) Caterpillar Tractor Co-USA
9039016 *J8AZ2* -	**TROPIC SUN** - **Birdsall Shipping SA** Tropical Shipping & Construction Co Ltd SatCom: Inmarsat C 435218110 *Kingstown* *St Vincent & The Grenadines* MMSI: 375902000 Official number: 400447	**6,536** 1,961 7,450	Class: BV	1992-12 **Singapore Shipbuilding & Engineering Pte Ltd — Singapore** Yd No: 320 Converted From: Ro-Ro Cargo Ship Loa 121.20 (BB) Br ex 22.35 Dght 6.200 Lbp 109.94 Br md 22.00 Dpth 9.61 Welded	**(A31A2GX) General Cargo Ship** TEU 392 C. 392/20' (40') incl. 100 ref C. Compartments: 1 Ho, ER 1 Ha: ER Cranes: 2x40t	**2 oil engines** geared to sc. shafts driving 2 FP propellers Total Power: 6,620kW (9,000hp) 15.0kn MaK 9M453C 2 x 4 Stroke 9 Cy. 320 x 420 each-3310kW (4500bhp) Krupp MaK Maschinenbau GmbH-Kiel Thrusters: 1 Thwart. FP thruster (f)
8521373 *VZQ9125* -	**TROPIC SUNBIRD** - **Sunlover Reef Cruises Pty Ltd** - *Melbourne, Vic* *Australia* Official number: 852042	*444* 176 20		1986-09 **SBF Shipbuilders (1977) Pty Ltd — Fremantle WA** Yd No: QC34 Loa 33.38 (BB) Br ex 13.37 Dght - Lbp 32.59 Br md 13.01 Dpth 3.71 Welded, 1 dk	**(A37B2PS) Passenger Ship** Passengers: unberthed: 500	**2 oil engines** with clutches, flexible couplings & sr reverse geared to sc. shafts driving 2 FP propellers Total Power: 2,324kW (3,160hp) MWM TBD604BV12 2 x Vee 4 Stroke 12 Cy. 170 x 195 each-1162kW (1580bhp) Motoren Werke Mannheim AG (MWM)-West Germany
8614156 - -	**TROPIC SUNSEEKER** - **Sunlover Reef Cruises Pty Ltd** - *Melbourne, Vic* *Australia* Official number: 852408	*444* 176 50		1986-12 **Precision Marine Holding Pty Ltd — Fremantle WA** Yd No: 787 Loa 33.38 Br ex 13.37 Dght - Lbp 32.59 Br md 13.01 Dpth 3.71 Welded, 1 dk	**(A37B2PS) Passenger Ship** Hull Material: Aluminium Alloy Passengers: unberthed: 500	**2 oil engines** geared to sc. shafts driving 2 FP propellers Total Power: 2,000kW (2,720hp) MWM TBD604V12 2 x Vee 4 Stroke 12 Cy. 160 x 185 each-1000kW (1360bhp) Motoren Werke Mannheim AG (MWM)-West Germany
9039028 *J8AZ3* -	**TROPIC TIDE** - **Tropical Shipping & Construction Co Ltd** Tropical Shipping Co Ltd SatCom: Inmarsat A 1337611 *Kingstown* *St Vincent & The Grenadines* MMSI: 375903000	**6,536** 1,961 7,430	Class: BV	1993-04 **Singapore Shipbuilding & Engineering Pte Ltd — Singapore** Yd No: 321 Loa 121.20 (BB) Br ex 22.35 Dght 6.300 Lbp 109.94 Br md 22.00 Dpth 9.61 Welded, 1 dk	**(A35A2RR) Ro-Ro Cargo Ship** Stern door/ramp Len: 13.00 Wid: 7.62 Swl: - Lane-Len: 1080 TEU 392 incl 100 ref C. Cranes: 2x40t	**2 oil engines** with clutches, flexible couplings & sr geared to sc. shafts driving 2 FP propellers Total Power: 6,620kW (9,000hp) 15.0kn MaK 9M453C 2 x 4 Stroke 9 Cy. 320 x 420 each-3310kW (4500bhp) Krupp MaK Maschinenbau GmbH-Kiel AuxGen: 2 x 700kW 480V 60Hz a.c, 2 x 560kW 480V 60Hz a.c, 1 x 350kW 480V 60Hz a.c Thrusters: 1 Thwart. FP thruster (f) Fuel: 250.0 (d.f.) 1050.0 (r.f.) 22.0pd
9225275 *J8PE4* -	**TROPIC UNITY** - **Tropical Shipping & Construction Co Ltd** - *Kingstown* *St Vincent & The Grenadines* MMSI: 377913000	**10,851** 3,601 12,418	Class: BV	2002-01 **Shanghai Edward Shipbuilding Co Ltd — Shanghai** Yd No: 121 Loa 159.90 (BB) Br ex - Dght 8.250 Lbp 151.21 Br md 22.60 Dpth 12.00 Welded, 1 dk	**(A31A2GX) General Cargo Ship** Grain: 16,900 TEU 973 incl 187 ref C. Cranes: 2x45t	**2 oil engines** geared to sc. shaft driving 1 FP propeller Total Power: 14,400kW (19,578hp) 20.0kn MaK 8M43 2 x 4 Stroke 8 Cy. 430 x 610 each-7200kW (9789bhp) Caterpillar Motoren GmbH & Co. KG-Germany Thrusters: 1 Thwart. CP thruster (f); 1 Tunnel thruster (a)
9318280 *3CAE* -	**TROPICAL** - **Remolcadores del Muni SA** - *Bata* *Equatorial Guinea* MMSI: 631831000 Official number: 05069M	**489** 263 750	Class: (BV)	2005-04 **Sahin Celik Sanayi A.S. — Tuzla** Yd No: 35 Loa 64.90 Br ex - Dght 2.200 Lbp 60.00 Br md 17.00 Dpth 3.20 Welded, 1 dk	**(A35D2RL) Landing Craft** Bow ramp (f)	**2 oil engines** geared to sc. shafts driving 2 Propellers Total Power: 1,154kW (1,568hp) GUASCOR SF240 2 x 4 Stroke 8 Cy. 152 x 165 each-577kW (784bhp) Gutierrez Ascunce Corp (GUASCOR)-Spain
6406440 - -	**TROPICAL** - -	*245* 105 238	Class: (BV)	**1964 S.A. des Ancien Chantiers Dubigeon — Nantes-Chantenay** Yd No: 804 Loa 31.96 Br ex 7.60 Dght 3.731 Lbp 25.66 Br md 7.51 Dpth 4.07 Welded, 1 dk	**(B11B2FV) Fishing Vessel** Liq: 150 Derricks: 1x3t,2x0.5t	**1 oil engine** driving 1 FP propeller Total Power: 456kW (620hp) 10.5kn Deutz SBA8M528 1 x 4 Stroke 8 Cy. 220 x 280 456kW (620bhp) Kloeckner Humboldt Deutz AG-West Germany Fuel: 48.5 (d.f.)
9567348 *3FRW4* -	**TROPICAL BINTANG** - **Tropical Line SA** Kawasaki Kinkai Kisen KK (Kawasaki Kinkai Kisen Kaisha Ltd) SatCom: Inmarsat C 435798710 *Panama* *Panama* MMSI: 357987000 Official number: 4267111	**9,595** 3,660 12,913	Class: NK	2011-04 **Kanasashi Heavy Industries Co Ltd — Shizuoka SZ** Yd No: 8132 Loa 119.99 (BB) Br ex - Dght 8.820 Lbp 111.50 Br md 21.20 Dpth 14.30 Welded, 1 dk	**(A31A2GX) General Cargo Ship** Grain: 20,505; Bale: 19,520 Compartments: 2 Ho, ER 2 Ha: ER Cranes: 2x30.7t	**1 oil engine** driving 1 FP propeller Total Power: 3,900kW (5,302hp) 12.5kn MAN-B&W 6L35MC 1 x 2 Stroke 6 Cy. 350 x 1050 3900kW (5302bhp) The Hanshin Diesel Works Ltd-Japan
9256444 *H9NM* -	**TROPICAL BREEZE** - **Tropical Line SA** Blue Marine Management Corp *Panama* *Panama* MMSI: 351970000 Official number: 2821602B	**18,680** 7,934 21,624	Class: NK	2001-09 **Iwagi Zosen Co Ltd — Kamijima EH** Yd No: 198 Loa 154.94 Br ex - Dght 8.766 Lbp 145.00 Br md 26.00 Dpth 18.10 Welded, 1 dk	**(A24B2BW) Wood Chips Carrier** Grain: 44,439 Compartments: 4 Ho, ER 4 Ha: 4 (16.8 x 12.8)ER Cranes: 2x14.5t	**1 oil engine** driving 1 FP propeller Total Power: 4,200kW (5,710hp) 13.3kn B&W 6S35MC 1 x 2 Stroke 6 Cy. 350 x 1400 4200kW (5710bhp) The Hanshin Diesel Works Ltd-Japan Fuel: 1050.0

8022573 *9V6407* -	**TROPICAL EAGLE** *ex Lang Hindek -2003* **Ewan Marine Pte Ltd** Masindra Shipping (M) Sdn Bhd *Singapore* *Singapore* MMSI: 564801000 Official number: 390395	**209** 63 -	Class: BV (AB)	**1982-03 Penang Shipbuilding Corp Sdn Bhd — Penang** Yd No: 11054 Loa 28.53 Br ex 8.31 Dght 3.001 Lbp 25.51 Br md 8.11 Dpth 4.02 Welded, 1 dk	**(B32A2ST) Tug**	**2 oil engines** sr geared to sc. shafts driving 2 CP propellers Total Power: 1,694kW (2,304hp) 10.0kn Ruston 6AP230 2 x 4 Stroke 6 Cy. 230 x 273 each-847kW (1152bhp) Ruston Diesels Ltd.-Newton-le-Willows AuxGen: 2 x 64kW
9385219 *3FLZ* -	**TROPICAL ISLANDER** **Virgo Marine Ltd SA** Hachiuma Steamship Co Ltd (Hachiuma Kisen KK) *Panama* *Panama* MMSI: 370180000 Official number: 4013809	**18,174** 11,005 18,144	Class: NK	**2009-03 Shin Kochi Jyuko K.K. — Kochi** Yd No: 7222 Loa 160.70 (BB) Br ex - Dght 9.340 Lbp 151.20 Br md 25.00 Dpth 12.80 Welded, 1 dk	**(A31A2GA) General Cargo Ship (with Ro-Ro facility)** Angled stern door/ramp (centre) Bale: 15,218 TEU 970 incl 100 ref C. Cranes: 2x40t	**1 oil engine** driving 1 FP propeller Total Power: 9,625kW (13,086hp) 18.9kn Mitsubishi 7UEC50LSII 1 x 2 Stroke 7 Cy. 500 x 1950 9625kW (13086bhp) Kobe Hatsudoki KK-Japan AuxGen: 3 x 790kW a.c Thrusters: 1 Tunnel thruster (f) Fuel: 1640.0
8022999 *FHHO* -	**TROPICAL JET** *ex Spirit Ii -2010 ex Acajou -2008* *ex Trident 4 -1998 ex Celestina -1987* **Karu Lines** - SatCom: Inmarsat C 422606610 *St-Malo* *France* MMSI: 227006200	**220** 82 30	Class: (BV) (RI)	**1981-05 Westamarin AS — Alta** Yd No: 81 Loa 29.06 Br ex 9.02 Dght 1.490 Lbp 27.13 Br md 9.01 Dpth 3.10 Welded, 1 dk	**(A37B2PS) Passenger Ship** Hull Material: Aluminium Alloy Passengers: unberthed: 218	**2 oil engines** geared to sc. shafts driving 2 FP propellers Total Power: 2,648kW (3,600hp) 30.0kn AGO 195V12CSHR 2 x Vee 4 Stroke 12 Cy. 195 x 180 each-1324kW (1800bhp) Societe Alsacienne de ConstructionsMecaniques (SACM)-France
8408868 *C6FS2* -	**TROPICAL MIST** **Ventura Trading Ltd** Reefership Marine Services Ltd SatCom: Inmarsat C 431108910 *Nassau* *Bahamas* MMSI: 311089000 Official number: 8000372	**9,749** 5,841 11,998	Class: NV	**1986-02 Korea Shipbuilding & Engineering Corp — Busan** Yd No: 1029 Loa 149.41 (BB) Br ex 21.70 Dght 9.743 Lbp 137.62 Br md 21.51 Dpth 12.86 Welded, 4 dks	**(A34A2GR) Refrigerated Cargo Ship** Ins: 13,933 TEU 48 Compartments: 4 Ho, ER, 12 Tw Dk 4 Ha: 4 (9.0 x 7.0)ER Cranes: 2x30t,2x10t	**1 oil engine** driving 1 FP propeller Total Power: 7,149kW (9,720hp) 20.0kn B&W 6L60MCE 1 x 2 Stroke 6 Cy. 600 x 1944 7149kW (9720bhp) Hyundai Engine & Machinery Co Ltd-South Korea AuxGen: 2 x 860kW 440V 60Hz a.c, 1 x 680kW 440V 60Hz a.c, 1 x 440kW 440V 60Hz a.c Fuel: 98.5 (d.f.) 1048.0 (r.f.) 30.5pd
8927606 *9V5467* -	**TROPICAL OCEAN** **Tropical Shipping & Trading Co Pte Ltd** Masindra Shipping (M) Sdn Bhd *Singapore* *Singapore* MMSI: 563028000 Official number: 387738	**129** 38 -	Class: BV	**1997-10 Billion Zone — Malaysia** Yd No: 3 Loa 24.32 Br ex - Dght 2.400 Lbp 23.06 Br md 7.00 Dpth 2.90 Welded, 1 dk	**(B32A2ST) Tug**	**2 oil engines** geared to sc. shafts driving 2 FP propellers Total Power: 894kW (1,216hp) Cummins KTA-19-M3 2 x 4 Stroke 6 Cy. 159 x 159 each-447kW (608bhp) Cummins Engine Co Inc-USA
9223655 *H9AO* -	**TROPICAL PEGASUS** **Pegasus Shipholding SA** Pegasus Maritime Co Ltd *Panama* *Panama* MMSI: 355872000 Official number: 2778001B	**18,525** 8,366 22,332	Class: NK	**2001-03 Shin Kochi Jyuko K.K. — Kochi** Yd No: 7131 Loa 151.03 Br ex - Dght 9.130 Lbp 143.00 Br md 26.20 Dpth 15.01 Welded, 1 dk	**(A24B2BW) Wood Chips Carrier** Double Bottom Entire Compartment Length Grain: 43,610 Cargo Heating Coils Compartments: 4 Ho, ER 4 Ha: (12.8 x 12.8)3 (16.0 x 12.8)ER Cranes: 2x14.5t	**1 oil engine** driving 1 FP propeller Total Power: 4,457kW (6,060hp) 14.6kn B&W 6S35MC 1 x 2 Stroke 6 Cy. 350 x 1400 4457kW (6060bhp) Makita Corp-Japan AuxGen: 3 x 455kW a.c Thrusters: 1 Thwart. FP thruster (f) Fuel: 122.4 (d.f.) (Heating Coils) 873.7 (r.f.)
9298521 *3ECQ7* -	**TROPICAL QUEEN** **Primavera Montana SA** Misuga Kaiun Co Ltd *Panama* *Panama* MMSI: 371421000 Official number: 3110805A	**30,051** 17,738 52,498 T/cm 55.5	Class: NK	**2005-10 Tsuneishi Heavy Industries (Cebu) Inc — Balamban** Yd No: SC-052 Loa 189.99 Br ex - Dght 12.022 Lbp 182.00 Br md 32.26 Dpth 17.00 Welded, 1 dk	**(A21A2BC) Bulk Carrier** Grain: 67,756; Bale: 65,601 Compartments: 5 Ho, ER 5 Ha: 4 (21.3 x 18.4)ER (20.4 x 18.4) Cranes: 4x30t	**1 oil engine** driving 1 FP propeller Total Power: 7,800kW (10,605hp) 14.5kn B&W 6S50MC 1 x 2 Stroke 6 Cy. 500 x 1910 7800kW (10605bhp) Mitsui Engineering & Shipbuilding CLtd-Japan Fuel: 2150.0
8408870 *C6FR7* -	**TROPICAL REEFER** *ex Tropical Morn -2011* **Avgerinos Shipping Corp** Chartworld Shipping Corp SatCom: Inmarsat C 431108610 *Nassau* *Bahamas* MMSI: 311086000 Official number: 8000368	**9,749** 5,841 11,979	Class: BV (NV)	**1986-03 Korea Shipbuilding & Engineering Corp — Busan** Yd No: 1030 Loa 149.62 (BB) Br ex 21.70 Dght 9.743 Lbp 137.62 Br md 21.51 Dpth 12.97 Welded, 4 dks	**(A34A2GR) Refrigerated Cargo Ship** Ins: 13,944 TEU 48 Compartments: 4 Ho, ER, 12 Tw Dk 4 Ha: 4 (9.0 x 7.0)ER Cranes: 2x30t,2x10t	**1 oil engine** driving 1 FP propeller Total Power: 7,149kW (9,720hp) 20.0kn B&W 6L60MCE 1 x 2 Stroke 6 Cy. 600 x 1944 7149kW (9720bhp) Hyundai Engine & Machinery Co Ltd-South Korea AuxGen: 2 x 860kW 440V 60Hz a.c, 1 x 680kW 440V 60Hz a.c, 1 x 440kW 440V 60Hz a.c Fuel: 98.5 (d.f.) 1048.0 (r.f.) 30.5pd
8408882 *C6FR9* -	**TROPICAL SKY** **Ventura Trading Ltd** Reefership Marine Services Ltd SatCom: Inmarsat C 431108815 *Nassau* *Bahamas* MMSI: 311088000 Official number: 8000371	**9,749** 5,841 11,998	Class: NV	**1986-10 Korea Shipbuilding & Engineering Corp — Busan** Yd No: 1031 Loa 149.41 (BB) Br ex - Dght 9.753 Lbp 137.01 Br md 21.51 Dpth 12.98 Welded, 4 dks	**(A34A2GR) Refrigerated Cargo Ship** Ins: 13,934 TEU 48 Compartments: 4 Ho, ER, 12 Tw Dk 4 Ha: 4 (9.0 x 7.0)ER Cranes: 2x30t,2x10t	**1 oil engine** driving 1 FP propeller Total Power: 7,149kW (9,720hp) 20.0kn B&W 6L60MCE 1 x 2 Stroke 6 Cy. 600 x 1944 7149kW (9720bhp) Hyundai Engine & Machinery Co Ltd-South Korea AuxGen: 2 x 880kW 450V 60Hz a.c, 1 x 670kW 450V 60Hz a.c, 1 x 440kW 450V 60Hz a.c Fuel: 98.5 (d.f.) 1048.0 (r.f.) 30.5pd
8408894 *C6FR8* -	**TROPICAL STAR** **Ventura Trading Ltd** Reefership Marine Services Ltd SatCom: Inmarsat B 33108715 *Nassau* *Bahamas* MMSI: 311087000 Official number: 8000369	**9,749** 5,841 11,998	Class: NV	**1986-12 Korea Shipbuilding & Engineering Corp — Busan** Yd No: 1032 Loa 149.41 (BB) Br ex - Dght 9.757 Lbp 137.62 Br md 21.51 Dpth 12.98 Welded, 4 dks	**(A34A2GR) Refrigerated Cargo Ship** Side doors (p) Side doors (s) Ins: 13,936 TEU 48 Compartments: 4 Ho, ER, 12 Tw Dk 4 Ha: 4 (9.0 x 7.0)ER Cranes: 2x30t,2x10t	**1 oil engine** driving 1 FP propeller Total Power: 7,921kW (10,769hp) 20.0kn B&W 6L60MCE 1 x 2 Stroke 6 Cy. 600 x 1944 7921kW (10769bhp) Hyundai Engine & Machinery Co Ltd-South Korea AuxGen: 2 x 860kW 440V 60Hz a.c, 1 x 680kW 440V 60Hz a.c, 1 x 440kW 440V 60Hz a.c Fuel: 98.5 (d.f.) 1048.0 (r.f.) 30.5pd
8307181 *3FQH8* -	**TROPICAL STAR** *ex Grand Fortune -2009* *ex Fortune Queen -2007 ex Axon Queen -2004* *ex Nimet Pisak -2000 ex New Opal -1994* *ex Sanko Sapphire -1991* **Tropical Beauty Navigation SA** Mingtai Navigation Co Ltd *Panama* *Panama* MMSI: 371867000 Official number: 4083409	**22,361** 12,680 38,248 T/cm 45.6	Class: CR (NK)	**1984-04 Kawasaki Heavy Industries Ltd — Kobe HG** Yd No: 1358 Loa 179.40 (BB) Br ex - Dght 10.823 Lbp 172.00 Br md 29.00 Dpth 15.40 Welded, 1 dk	**(A21A2BC) Bulk Carrier** Grain: 47,871; Bale: 45,645 TEU 140 Compartments: 5 Ho, ER 5 Ha: (16.0 x 14.0)4 (19.2 x 14.0)ER Cranes: 4x25t	**1 oil engine** driving 1 FP propeller Total Power: 5,884kW (8,000hp) 14.0kn B&W 5L60MC 1 x 2 Stroke 5 Cy. 600 x 1944 5884kW (8000bhp) Kawasaki Heavy Industries Ltd-Japan AuxGen: 3 x 400kW 450V 60Hz a.c Fuel: 173.0 (d.f.) (Heating Coils) 1425.0 (r.f.) 24.0pd
7047590 *V3RF3* -	**TROPICAL STAR** *ex Recovery VI -1991 ex Mister Chip -1987* **Tropical Shipping & Trading Co Pte Ltd** Masindra Shipping (M) Sdn Bhd *Belize City* *Belize* MMSI: 312520000 Official number: 130310621	**290** 87 -	Class: BV (AB)	**1969-06 Halter Marine Services, Inc. — New Orleans, La** Yd No: 221 Loa 31.89 Br ex - Dght 4.293 Lbp 31.88 Br md 9.50 Dpth 5.01 Welded, 1 dk	**(B32A2ST) Tug**	**1 oil engine** driving 1 FP propeller Total Power: 1,655kW (2,250hp) 12.0kn Caterpillar D399SCAC 1 x Vee 4 Stroke 16 Cy. 159 x 203 1655kW (2250bhp) Caterpillar Tractor Co-USA
9153587 *9V5298* -	**TROPICAL SUCCESS** **Tropical Success & Trading Co Pte Ltd** Tropical Shipping & Trading Co Pte Ltd *Singapore* *Singapore* MMSI: 564662000 Official number: 387154	**123** 37 -	Class: BV	**1996-05 Tuong Aik (Sarawak) Sdn Bhd — Sibu** Yd No: 9504 Loa 23.26 Br ex - Dght 2.220 Lbp 21.96 Br md 7.00 Dpth 2.90 Welded, 1 dk	**(B32A2ST) Tug**	**2 oil engines** geared to sc. shafts driving 2 FP propellers Total Power: 810kW (1,102hp) 10.0kn Caterpillar 3412TA 2 x Vee 4 Stroke 12 Cy. 137 x 152 each-405kW (551bhp) Caterpillar Inc-USA
9430014 *3FPO7* -	**TROPICAL VENUS** **Tropical Line SA** Kawasaki Kinkai Kisen KK (Kawasaki Kinkai Kisen Kaisha Ltd) *Panama* *Panama* MMSI: 351794000 Official number: 38026TJ	**9,593** 3,732 12,970	Class: NK	**2009-02 Kanasashi Heavy Industries Co Ltd — Shizuoka SZ** Yd No: 8116 Loa 119.99 (BB) Br ex - Dght 8.800 Lbp 111.50 Br md 21.20 Dpth 14.30 Welded, 1 dk	**(A31A2GX) General Cargo Ship** Grain: 20,895; Bale: 19,874 Compartments: 2 Ho, ER 2 Ha: ER Cranes: 2x30.7t	**1 oil engine** driving 1 FP propeller Total Power: 3,900kW (5,302hp) 12.5kn MAN-B&W 6L35MC 1 x 2 Stroke 6 Cy. 350 x 1050 3900kW (5302bhp) The Hanshin Diesel Works Ltd-Japan Fuel: 890.0

9018830 - -	**TROPICAL WAVE** *ex* Sepideh *-2001* *ex* Westamaran *-1994* **Safeway Maritime Transportation** *La Ceiba* *Honduras*	**497** 152 33	Class: (NV) (NK)	**1991**-06 **Westamarin AS — Mandal** Yd No: 108 Lengthened-2011 Loa 44.81 Br ex 10.31 Dght 1.600 Lbp 40.00 Br md 10.00 Dpth 4.11 Welded, 1 dk	**(A37B2PS) Passenger Ship** Hull Material: Aluminium Alloy Passengers: unberthed: 300	**4 oil engines** reduction geared to sc. shafts driving 4 Water jets Total Power: 4,476kW (6,084hp) 35.0kn Cummins KTA-38-M2 4 x Vee 4 Stroke 12 Cy. 159 x 159 each-1119kW (1521bhp) Cummins Engine Co Inc-USA AuxGen: 3 x 45kW a.c
8522418 *PP9944* -	**TROPICALIENTE** *ex* Norsul Pindare *-1995* **Industrial Naval do Ceara SA (INACE)** - *Rio de Janeiro* *Brazil* Official number: 3810395731	*174* 52 31	Class: (NV)	**1986**-07 **Industria Naval do Ceara S.A. (INACE) — Fortaleza** Yd No: 203 Loa 32.57 Br ex 7.83 Dght 1.731 Lbp 30.94 Br md 7.80 Dpth 3.23 Welded, 1 dk	**(B34J2SD) Crew Boat**	**3 oil engines** with clutches & sr geared to sc. shafts driving 3 FP propellers Total Power: 939kW (1,278hp) Cummins NTA-855-M 3 x 4 Stroke 6 Cy. 140 x 152 each-313kW (426bhp) Cummins Brasil Ltda-Brazil AuxGen: 2 x 64kW 220V 60Hz a.c
8663987 *SVA5388* -	**TROPICANA** *ex* Se al Mar Cala la Luna *-2013* **Mira MCPY** - *Piraeus* *Greece* MMSI: 239800500 Official number: 10964	**182** 54 -		**2004**-01 **Cantieri Navali Lavagna Srl (CNL) — Lavagna** Yd No: 108 Loa 32.00 Br ex 7.10 Dght 2.300 Lbp - Br md 6.84 Dpth - Welded, 1 dk	**(X11A2YP) Yacht** Hull Material: Aluminium Alloy	**2 oil engines** reduction geared to sc. shafts driving 2 Propellers Total Power: 3,360kW (4,568hp) M.T.U. 12V396TE94 2 x Vee 4 Stroke 12 Cy. 165 x 185 each-1680kW (2284bhp) MTU Friedrichshafen GmbH-Friedrichshafen
8744547 *ZR8202* -	**TROPICO** - **Isocorp Investment (Pty) Ltd** - *Cape Town* *South Africa* Official number: 19406	**121** - -		**1994**-11 **in the Republic of South Africa** L reg 21.10 Br ex - Dght - Lbp - Br md - Dpth - Bonded, 1 dk	**(A37B2PS) Passenger Ship** Hull Material: Reinforced Plastic	**2 oil engines** geared to sc. shafts driving 2 Propellers Total Power: 92kW (126hp) 12.0kn
8325444 *CUZH* -	**TROPICO** - **Sociedade de Pesca do Miradouro Lda** - SatCom: Inmarsat C 426356310 *Aveiro* *Portugal* Official number: A-3194-A	*266* 102 225	Class: (LR) ✠ Classed LR until 8/3/93	**1985**-04 **Estaleiros Navais do Mondego S.A. — Figueira da Foz** Yd No: 204 Loa 35.01 Br ex 8.62 Dght 3.776 Lbp 30.03 Br md 8.40 Dpth 4.02 Welded, 1 dk	**(B11A2FS) Stern Trawler** Ins: 200	**1 oil engine** with flexible couplings & sr gearedto sc. shaft driving 1 CP propeller Total Power: 809kW (1,100hp) 12.0kn MaK 6MU451AK 1 x 4 Stroke 6 Cy. 320 x 450 809kW (1100bhp) (Re-engined ,made 1969, Reconditioned & fitted 1985) Atlas MaK Maschinenbau GmbH-Kiel AuxGen: 1 x 100kW 400V 50Hz a.c, 1 x 72kW 400V 50Hz a.c Fuel: 100.0 (d.f.) 4.0pd
7947673 *WQZ3775* -	**TROPICO** *ex* Madelyn V *-1991* *ex* Virginia Generals *-1991* **Tropico Fishing Inc** - *New Bedford, MA* *United States of America* Official number: 609937	*165* 112 -		**1979 Quality Marine, Inc. — Bayou La Batre, Al** Yd No: 108 L reg 24.88 Br ex 7.32 Dght - Lbp - Br md - Dpth 3.84 Welded, 1 dk	**(B11B2FV) Fishing Vessel**	**1 oil engine** geared to sc. shaft driving 1 FP propeller Total Power: 533kW (725hp) Caterpillar D348SCAC 1 x Vee 4 Stroke 12 Cy. 137 x 165 533kW (725bhp) Caterpillar Tractor Co-USA
7395478 *HQBD3* -	**TROPICS** - **Mandel R Borden** - *Roatan* *Honduras* Official number: U-1920717	*127* 85 -		**1974**-02 **Desco Marine — Saint Augustine, Fl** Yd No: 165-F Loa 22.86 Br ex - Dght 2.744 Lbp 20.99 Br md 6.74 Dpth 3.81 Bonded, 1 dk	**(B11A2FT) Trawler** Hull Material: Reinforced Plastic	**1 oil engine** driving 1 FP propeller Total Power: 268kW (364hp) Caterpillar D343SCAC 1 x 4 Stroke 6 Cy. 137 x 165 268kW (364bhp) Caterpillar Tractor Co-USA
8855724 - -	**TROPICS '84** - **Sahlman Seafoods Inc** - *Kingstown* *St Vincent & The Grenadines*	*101* 69 -		**1984 Steiner Shipyard, Inc. — Bayou La Batre, Al** Loa 22.86 Br ex - Dght - Lbp 20.33 Br md 6.71 Dpth 3.32 Welded, 1 dk	**(B11A2FT) Trawler**	**1 oil engine** geared to sc. shaft driving 1 FP propeller Total Power: 268kW (364hp) Cummins KT-1150-M 1 x 4 Stroke 6 Cy. 159 x 159 268kW (364bhp) Cummins Engine Co Inc-USA
7833248 *UGEP* -	**TROPIK-2** *ex* Salomatinsk *-2002* **Korsakov Ocean Fishing Fleet Base (Korsakovskaya Baza Okeanicheskogo Rybolovnogo Flota)** - *Vladivostok* *Russia* MMSI: 273816600	**829** 221 332	Class: (RS)	**1980**-10 **Zavod "Leninskaya Kuznitsa" — Kiyev** Yd No: 246 Loa 53.75 (BB) Br ex 10.72 Dght 4.290 Lbp 47.92 Br md 10.50 Dpth 6.00 Welded, 1 dk	**(B11A2FS) Stern Trawler** Ins: 218 Compartments: 1 Ho, ER 1 Ha: (1.6 x 1.6) Derricks: 2x1.5t Ice Capable	**1 oil engine** driving 1 FP propeller Total Power: 971kW (1,320hp) 12.8kn S.K.L. 8NVD48A-2U 1 x 4 Stroke 8 Cy. 320 x 480 971kW (1320bhp) VEB Schwermaschinenbau "KarlLiebknecht" (SKL)-Magdeburg Fuel: 185.0 (d.f.)
4902713 *9YEA* -	**TROUBADOR** *ex* Wyepress *-1998* *ex* Labrador *-1996* **Coloured Fin Ltd (CFL)** - *Port of Spain* *Trinidad & Tobago*	**151** 45 -	Class: LR ✠ **100A1** SS 06/2009 tug Trinidad coastal service ✠ **LMC** Cable: 137.0/22.3	**1966**-11 **Appledore Shipbuilders Ltd — Bideford** Yd No: A.S. 17 Loa 28.67 Br ex 7.72 Dght 2.740 Lbp 25.84 Br md 7.39 Dpth 3.66 Welded, 1 dk	**(B32A2ST) Tug**	**2 oil engines** sr reverse geared to sc. shafts driving 2 FP propellers Total Power: 970kW (1,318hp) 12.0kn Blackstone ERS8 2 x 4 Stroke 8 Cy. 222 x 292 each-485kW (659bhp) Blackstone & Co. Ltd.-Stamford AuxGen: 2 x 40kW 220V d.c Fuel: 55.0 (d.f.)
9048639 *J8B3723* -	**TROUBADOUR** - **Waterway Shipping Ltd** Baltnautic Shipping Ltd *Kingstown* *St Vincent & The Grenadines* MMSI: 375784000 Official number: 10196	**1,789** 958 2,450	Class: BV	**1992**-07 **Barkmeijer Stroobos B.V. — Stroobos** Yd No: 265 Loa 89.99 Br ex 11.44 Dght 3.900 Lbp 84.64 Br md 11.40 Dpth 5.30 Welded, 1 dk	**(A31A2GX) General Cargo Ship** Grain: 3,665 TEU 98 C. 98/20' Compartments: 2 Ho, ER 2 Ha: 2 (31.2 x 9.2)ER Gantry cranes: 1	**1 oil engine** with flexible couplings & sr reverse geared to sc. shaft driving 1 FP propeller Total Power: 1,135kW (1,543hp) 10.0kn Kromhout 8FHD240 1 x 4 Stroke 8 Cy. 240 x 260 1135kW (1543bhp) Stork Wartsila Diesel BV-Netherlands AuxGen: 1 x 69kW, 1 x 52kW Thrusters: 1 Thwart. FP thruster (f) Fuel: 104.4 (d.f.)
9511856 *YJVV3* -	**TROUNSON TIDE** - **Tidewater Marine International Inc** Tidewater Marine International Inc *Port Vila* *Vanuatu* MMSI: 576247000 Official number: 1861	**2,177** 1,044 3,250	Class: NV	**2010**-07 **Cochin Shipyard Ltd — Ernakulam** Yd No: BY-72 Loa 73.60 Br ex 16.04 Dght 5.830 Lbp 68.30 Br md 16.00 Dpth 7.00 Welded, 1 dk	**(B21A20S) Platform Supply Ship**	**2 oil engines** reduction geared to sc. shafts driving 2 CP propellers Total Power: 3,480kW (4,732hp) 13.0kn Bergens C25: 33L6P 2 x 4 Stroke 6 Cy. 250 x 330 each-1740kW (2366bhp) Rolls Royce Marine AS-Norway AuxGen: 2 x 260kW a.c Thrusters: 2 Tunnel thruster (f); 2 Tunnel thruster (a)
9003275 *5BHX2* -	**TROUT** - **Chemgas Intercoastal Shipping BV** Chemgas Shipping BV *Limassol* *Cyprus* MMSI: 210583000	**1,997** 599 1,520 T/cm 11.6	Class: BV	**1990**-11 **B.V. Scheepswerf De Kaap — Meppel** Yd No: 217 Loa 105.56 (BB) Br ex 11.98 Dght 3.020 Lbp 103.00 Br md 11.92 Dpth 6.05 Welded, 1dk	**(A11B2TG) LPG Tanker** Double Hull (13F) Liq (Gas): 2,560 7 x Gas Tank (s); 6 independent (stl) cyl horizontal, 1 independent (stl) dcy horizontal 7 Cargo Pump (s): 7x60m³/hr Manifold: Bow/CM: 59.2m	**2 oil engines** with flexible couplings & sr reverse geared to sc. shaft driving 2 FP propellers Total Power: 1,046kW (1,422hp) 11.0kn Stork DRO218K 2 x 4 Stroke 8 Cy. 210 x 300 each-523kW (711bhp) Stork Wartsila Diesel BV-Netherlands AuxGen: 3 x 235kW 220/380V 50Hz a.c Thrusters: 1 Thwart. FP thruster (f) Fuel: 143.0 (d.f.)
5369451 - -	**TROUZ AR MOOR** - **Armement Edouard Cotonnec** - *Pointe Noire* *Congo*	*103* 36 -		**1958 At. & Ch. de l'Adour — Anglet** L reg 23.11 Br ex 6.56 Dght - Lbp - Br md - Dpth - Welded, 1 dk	**(B11A2FT) Trawler** 2 Ha: 2 (0.9 x 0.9) Derricks: 1x5t	**2 oil engines** geared to sc. shaft driving 1 FP propeller Total Power: 242kW (330hp) 10.5kn Baudouin DK6 2 x 4 Stroke 6 Cy. 140 x 180 each-121kW (165bhp) Societe des Moteurs Baudouin SA-France Fuel: 27.5 (d.f.)
5409627 - -	**TROVADOR** - **Maruba SCA Empresa de Navegacion Maritima** - *Buenos Aires* *Argentina* Official number: 02479	*196* 50 -	Class: (LR) ✠ Classed LR until 29/4/77	**1963**-12 **Ryan Astilleros Argentinos S.A. — Avellaneda** Yd No: C.1 Loa 30.79 Br ex 8.44 Dght - Lbp 28.02 Br md 8.01 Dpth 3.76 Riveted\Welded, 1 dk	**(B32A2ST) Tug**	**2 diesel electric oil engines** driving 2 gen. each 340kW Connecting to 2 elec. motors driving 1 FP propeller Total Power: 882kW (1,200hp) MAN G7V235/330ATL 2 x 4 Stroke 7 Cy. 235 x 330 each-441kW (600bhp) Maschinenbau Augsburg Nuernberg (MAN)-Augsburg AuxGen: 2 x 36kW 220V d.c

IMO / Call sign	Name / Owner	Tonnage	Class	Builder / Dimensions	Type / Cargo	Machinery
9285859 *C6ZT9* -	**TROVIKEN** *ex* Trochus *-2012 launched as* Gansea *-2006* **Troviken LLC** Viken Shipping AS *Nassau* *Bahamas* MMSI: 311066200 Official number: 8002009	**62,806** 34,551 115,341 T/cm 99.8	Class: AB (NV)	**2006-01 Samsung Heavy Industries Co Ltd — Geoje** Yd No: 1504 Loa 249.87 (BB) Br ex 43.84 Dght 14.900 Lbp 239.00 Br md 43.80 Dpth 21.30 Welded, 1 dk	**(A13B2TP) Products Tanker** Double Hull (13F) Liq: 124,259; Liq (Oil): 130,000 Compartments: 12 Wing Ta, 2 Wing Slop Ta, ER 3 Cargo Pump (s): 3x3000m^3/hr Manifold: Bow/CM: 124.5m	**1 oil engine** driving 1 FP propeller Total Power: 13,560kW (18,436hp) 15.3kn MAN-B&W 6S60MC-C 1 x 2 Stroke 6 Cy. 600 x 2400 13560kW (18436bhp) Doosan Engine Co Ltd-South Korea AuxGen: 3 x 740kW Fuel: 139.0 (d.f.) 3258.0 (r.f.)
9327205 *9HGQ8* -	**TROY** **Gelibolu Shipping Ltd** ABC Maritime AG *Valletta* *Malta* MMSI: 215964000 Official number: 9774	**2,632** 1,137 3,577 T/cm 10.8	Class: BV	**2005-08 Gelibolu Gemi Insa Sanayi ve Ticaret AS — Gelibolu** Yd No: 26 Loa 92.86 (BB) Br ex - Dght 5.700 Lbp 86.65 Br md 14.10 Dpth 7.20 Welded, 1 dk	**(A12B2TR) Chemical/Products Tanker** Double Hull (13F) Liq: 4,092; Liq (Oil): 4,092 Cargo Heating Coils Compartments: 10 Wing Ta, 1 Ta, ER 11 Cargo Pump (s): 11x150m^3/hr Manifold: Bow/CM: 42m Ice Capable	**1 oil engine** geared to sc. shaft driving 1 CP propeller Total Power: 1,850kW (2,515hp) 11.5kn MaK 6M25 1 x 4 Stroke 6 Cy. 255 x 400 1850kW (2515bhp) Caterpillar Motoren GmbH & Co. KG-Germany AuxGen: 1 x 600kW 400V 50Hz a.c, 3 x 246kW 400V 50Hz a.c Thrusters: 1 Tunnel thruster (f) Fuel: 46.0 (d.f.) 182.0 (r.f.) 8.1pd
1007641 *MERX5* -	**TROYANDA** *ex* High Chaparral *-2010* **Oxinel International Inc** Camper & Nicholsons France SARL *Ramsey* *Isle of Man (British)* MMSI: 235007520 Official number: 737163	**684** 205 146	Class: LR ✠100A1 SS 06/2009 SSC Yacht mono G6 **LMC** **UMS** Cable: 361.0/22.0 U2 (a)	**2004-06 Scheepswerf Slob B.V. — Papendrecht** (Hull) **2004-06 de Vries Scheepsbouw B.V. — Aalsmeer** Yd No: 668 Loa 49.99 Br ex 9.70 Dght 3.350 Lbp 43.31 Br md 9.30 Dpth 5.00 Welded, 1 dk	**(X11A2YP) Yacht**	**2 oil engines** with clutches, flexible couplings & sr reverse geared to sc. shafts driving 2 FP propellers Total Power: 1,910kW (2,596hp) 13.5kn Caterpillar 3512B-TA 2 x Vee 4 Stroke 12 Cy. 170 x 190 each-955kW (1298bhp) Caterpillar Inc-USA AuxGen: 2 x 144kW 415V 50Hz a.c Thrusters: 1 Thwart. FP thruster (f)
7722035 *XCQU5* -	**TROYANO** *ex* Isla De Lobos *-2010* *ex* Bay Island *-1994* *ex* Blue Fish *-1988* *ex* Saturn *-1979* **Desarrollo Naviero Mexicano SA de CV** *Coatzacoalcos* *Mexico* Official number: 3003555632-1	*644* 193 450	Class: AB	**1978-05 Halter Marine, Inc. — Lockport, La** Yd No: 642 Loa 54.87 Br ex - Dght 3.658 Lbp 51.85 Br md 11.60 Dpth 4.27 Welded, 1 dk	**(B21A2OS) Platform Supply Ship**	**2 oil engines** reverse reduction geared to sc. shafts driving 2 FP propellers Total Power: 1,368kW (1,860hp) 11.0kn G.M. (Detroit Diesel) 16V-149 2 x Vee 2 Stroke 16 Cy. 146 x 146 each-684kW (930bhp) General Motors Detroit DieselAllison Divn-USA AuxGen: 3 x 99kW Thrusters: 1 Thwart. FP thruster (f)
6618811 *SIDL* -	**TRUBADUREN** *ex* Otilia II *-2005* *ex* Juliane *-1995* *ex* Pellworm *-1979* **Skargardslinjen in Goteborgs & Bohuslan AB** *Gothenburg* *Sweden* MMSI: 265579090	**298** 113 51	Class: (GL)	**1966 Husumer Schiffswerft — Husum** Yd No: 1241 Loa 32.16 Br ex 9.81 Dght 1.600 Lbp 30.71 Br md 9.61 Dpth 3.00 Welded, 1 dk	**(A37B2PS) Passenger Ship** Ice Capable	**2 oil engines** reverse reduction geared to sc. shafts driving 2 FP propellers Total Power: 288kW (392hp) 10.0kn MWM RHS518A 2 x 4 Stroke 8 Cy. 140 x 180 each-144kW (196bhp) Motoren Werke Mannheim AG (MWM)-West Germany
8879366 - -	**TRUCK LAGOON** *ex* Reisen Maru No. 58 *-2002* *ex* Mitsu Maru No. 58 *-2000* *ex* Kyotoku Maru No. 11 *-2000* **Blue Lagoon Trading** -	**149** 44 2		**1980-04 K.K. Kinan Zosensho — Nachi-Katsuura** L reg 26.75 Br ex - Dght 1.100 Lbp - Br md 5.80 Dpth 2.30 Welded, 1 dk	**(B11B2FV) Fishing Vessel**	**1 oil engine** driving 1 FP propeller Total Power: 484kW (658hp) Niigata 1 x 4 Stroke 484kW (658bhp) Ssangyong Heavy Industries Co Ltd-South Korea
8932572 *UZQA* -	**TRUD** **Sea Commercial Port of Odessa (Odesskiy Morskiy Port)** - *Odessa* *Ukraine* MMSI: 272873600 Official number: 703325	**177** 53 46	Class: (RS)	**1970-08 "Petrozavod" — Leningrad** Yd No: 772 Loa 29.30 Br ex 8.49 Dght 3.090 Lbp 27.00 Br md - Dpth 4.34 Welded, 1 dk	**(B32A2ST) Tug** Ice Capable	**2 oil engines** driving 2 CP propellers Total Power: 882kW (1,200hp) 11.4kn Russkiy 6DR30/50-4-2 2 x 2 Stroke 6 Cy. 300 x 500 each-441kW (600bhp) Mashinostroitelnyy Zavod"Russkiy-Dizel"-Leningrad AuxGen: 2 x 25kW a.c Fuel: 36.0 (d.f.)
8957156 *OWZP2* -	**TRUD R** *ex* V27 *-2001* **RN Shipping A/S** Rohde Nielsen A/S *Grenaa* *Denmark (DIS)* MMSI: 219964000 Official number: D3924	**1,414** 425 1,785	Class: GL (BV)	**1995-03 Jiangsu Jiangyang Shipyard Group Co Ltd — Yangzhou JS** Converted From: Hopper-2010 Lengthened-2009 Loa 75.49 Br ex - Dght 3.010 Lbp 74.40 Br md 12.80 Dpth 4.50 Welded, 1 dk	**(B33B2DT) Trailing Suction Hopper Dredger** Hopper: 1,230 1 Ha: ER (40.0 x 9.6)	**2 oil engines** geared to sc. shafts driving 2 FP propellers Total Power: 918kW (1,248hp) 9.0kn Chinese Std. Type 8V190C 2 x Vee 4 Stroke 8 Cy. 190 x 210 each-459kW (624bhp) Jinan Diesel Engine Co Ltd-China Thrusters: 1 Tunnel thruster (f)
9415246 *A8UE2* -	**TRUDY** *completed as* Cresty *-2009* **Reederei ms 'Trudy' GmbH & Co KG** MST Mineralien Schiffahrt Spedition und Transport GmbH *Monrovia* *Liberia* MMSI: 636091888 Official number: 91888	**19,814** 10,208 30,790	Class: LR (GL) **100A1** SS 11/2009 bulk carrier BC-A strengthened for havy cargoes, Nos. 2, 4 & 6 holds may be empty ESP ESN *IWS LI Ice Class 1C FS at a draught of 10.400m Max/min draughts fwd 10.400/3.100m Max/min draughts aft 11.000/6.00m Power required 4371kw, power installed 7200kw **LMC** **UMS**	**2009-11 Jiangsu Eastern Heavy Industry Co Ltd — Jingjiang JS** Yd No: 06C-012 Loa 184.99 Br ex - Dght 10.400 Lbp 178.00 Br md 23.70 Dpth 14.60 Welded, 1 dk	**(A21A2BC) Bulk Carrier** Grain: 38,635; Bale: 37,476 Compartments: 6 Ho, ER 6 Ha: ER Cranes: 3x30t Ice Capable	**1 oil engine** driving 1 FP propeller Total Power: 8,280kW (11,257hp) 13.5kn MAN-B&W 6S46MC-C 1 x 2 Stroke 6 Cy. 460 x 1932 8280kW (11257bhp) STX Engine Co Ltd-South Korea AuxGen: 3 x 680kW 450V a.c Thrusters: 1 Tunnel thruster (f)
9419450 *9HA2353* -	**TRUE** **True Shipping Ltd** Geden Operations Ltd *Valletta* *Malta* MMSI: 248412000 Official number: 9419450	**61,341** 35,396 115,800 T/cm 99.0	Class: NV	**2010-06 Samsung Heavy Industries Co Ltd — Geoje** Yd No: 1740 Loa 248.96 (BB) Br ex 43.84 Dght 14.900 Lbp 239.00 Br md 43.80 Dpth 21.00 Welded, 1 dk	**(A13A2TV) Crude Oil Tanker** Double Hull (13F) Liq: 123,640; Liq (Oil): 123,640 Cargo Heating Coils Compartments: 12 Wing Ta, 2 Wing Slop Ta, ER 3 Cargo Pump (s): 3x2800m^3/hr Manifold: Bow/CM: 125.2m	**1 oil engine** driving 1 FP propeller Total Power: 13,560kW (18,436hp) 15.3kn MAN-B&W 6S60MC-C 1 x 2 Stroke 6 Cy. 600 x 2400 13560kW (18436bhp) Doosan Engine Co Ltd-South Korea AuxGen: 3 x 800kW a.c Fuel: 240.0 (d.f.) 3200.0 (r.f.)
8513091 *9V5165* -	**TRUE BEARING** **Eastwind Organisation Pte Ltd** Everlast Marine Services Pte Ltd *Singapore* *Singapore* Official number: 383378	**150** 50 -	Class: (AB)	**1985-12 Maroil Engineers & Shipbuilders Pte Ltd — Singapore** Yd No: 1042 Loa - Br ex - Dght - Lbp 24.82 Br md 5.81 Dpth 3.03 Welded, 1 dk	**(A37B2PS) Passenger Ship**	**2 oil engines** geared to sc. shafts driving 2 FP propellers Total Power: 410kW (558hp) Caterpillar 3406T 2 x 4 Stroke 6 Cy. 137 x 165 each-205kW (279bhp) Caterpillar Tractor Co-USA
8316522 *V3VY4* -	**TRUE BROTHERS** *ex* Federal Agno *-2014* *ex* Federal Asahi *-1989* **January Marine Inc** Island-Star Maritime *Belize City* *Belize* MMSI: 312035000 Official number: 701430045	**17,821** 10,390 29,643	Class: NK	**1985-03 Nippon Kokan KK (NKK Corp) — Shizuoka SZ** Yd No: 418 Loa 182.80 Br ex - Dght 10.559 Lbp 174.00 Br md 23.10 Dpth 14.80 Welded, 1 dk	**(A21A2BC) Bulk Carrier** Grain: 34,627; Bale: 33,331 TEU 104 Compartments: 5 Ho, ER 5 Ha: (13.4 x 9.6)4 (20.1 x 11.2)ER Cranes: 4x25t Ice Capable	**1 oil engine** driving 1 FP propeller Total Power: 6,988kW (9,501hp) 14.5kn Sulzer 6RTA58 1 x 2 Stroke 6 Cy. 580 x 1700 6988kW (9501bhp) Sumitomo Heavy Industries Ltd-Japan AuxGen: 3 x 440kW 450V 60Hz a.c Fuel: 1675.0 (r.f.)
9050400 *D5AK3* -	**TRUE COLORS** *ex* Sichem Padua *-2011* *ex* Sichem Anne *-2002* *ex* Anne Sif *-2001* **True Colors Shipping Inc** Mare Shipmanagement SA *Monrovia* *Liberia* MMSI: 636015387 Official number: 15387	**6,544** 3,081 9,215 T/cm 19.2	Class: BV (NV)	**1993-09 Hyundai Heavy Industries Co Ltd — Ulsan** Yd No: P064 Loa 116.59 (BB) Br ex 19.00 Dght 7.813 Lbp 110.00 Br md 19.00 Dpth 10.13 Welded, 1 dk	**(A12B2TR) Chemical/Products Tanker** Double Hull Liq: 10,496; Liq (Oil): 10,721 Cargo Heating Coils Compartments: 8 Wing Ta, 2 Ta, ER 12 Cargo Pump (s): 10x200m^3/hr, 2x100m^3/hr Manifold: Bow/CM: 58m Ice Capable	**1 oil engine** dr geared to sc. shaft driving 1 CP propeller Total Power: 4,050kW (5,506hp) 14.1kn MaK 6M552C 1 x 4 Stroke 6 Cy. 450 x 520 4050kW (5506bhp) Krupp MaK Maschinenbau GmbH-Kiel AuxGen: 1 x 1600kW 440V 60Hz a.c, 1 x 1600kW 440V 60Hz a.c, 1 x 450kW 440V 60Hz a.c Thrusters: 1 Thwart. CP thruster (f); 1 Tunnel thruster (a) Fuel: 60.0 (d.f.) (Heating Coils) 477.0 (r.f.) 17.0pd

8513106 *9V5166* -	**TRUE COURSE** **Eastwind Organisation Pte Ltd** Everlast Marine Services Pte Ltd *Singapore* *Singapore* Official number: 383379	**150** 50 50	Class: (AB)	**1985-12 Maroil Engineers & Shipbuilders Pte Ltd — Singapore** Yd No: 1043 Loa - Br ex - Dght - Lbp 24.82 Br md 5.81 Dpth 3.00 Welded, 1 dk	**(A37B2PS) Passenger Ship**	**2 oil engines** geared to sc. shafts driving 2 FP propellers Total Power: 410kW (558hp) Caterpillar 3406T 2 x 4 Stroke 6 Cy. 137 x 165 each-205kW (279bhp) Caterpillar Tractor Co-USA
7048398 *HP8950* -	**TRUE GRIT** *ex* Al-Kumze *-1992* *ex* True Grit *-1990* **IMI Marine Operations Inc** Intermarine LLC *Panama* *Panama* MMSI: 353522000 Official number: 2902003B	**761** 228 757	Class: AB	**1971-03 Halter Marine Fabricators, Inc. — Moss Point, Ms** Yd No: 267 Loa 55.48 Br ex 12.25 Dght 4.490 Lbp 51.34 Br md 12.20 Dpth 5.19 Welded, 1 dk	**(B21B20T) Offshore Tug/Supply Ship**	**2 oil engines** reverse reduction geared to sc. shafts driving 2 FP propellers Total Power: 4,414kW (6,002hp) 14.0kn Alco 16V251F 2 x Vee 4 Stroke 16 Cy. 229 x 267 each-2207kW (3001bhp) White Industrial Power Inc-USA AuxGen: 2 x 98kW 450V 60Hz a.c Thrusters: 1 Tunnel thruster (f) Fuel: 570.0
9473523 *V7XG5* -	**TRUE LIGHT** *ex* Ocean Flavor *-2011* **Bright Eleven Inc** Nobuhara Kisen Co Ltd *Majuro* *Marshall Islands* MMSI: 538004474 Official number: 4474	**7,727** 2,819 9,046	Class: NK	**2008-06 Kanasashi Heavy Industries Co Ltd — Shizuoka SZ** Yd No: 8206 Loa 104.83 Br ex 20.02 Dght 8.216 Lbp 96.77 Br md 20.00 Dpth 13.80 Welded, 1 dk	**(A31A2GX) General Cargo Ship** Grain: 15,738; Bale: 14,865 Compartments: 2 Ho, ER 2 Ha: ER Cranes: 1x60t,2x30.7t	**1 oil engine** driving 1 FP propeller Total Power: 2,812kW (3,823hp) 13.5kn Hanshin LH46LA 1 x 4 Stroke 6 Cy. 460 x 880 2812kW (3823bhp) The Hanshin Diesel Works Ltd-Japan Fuel: 800.0
9308651 *VM3994* -	**TRUE NORTH** **North Star Cruises Australia Pty Ltd** - *Fremantle, WA* *Australia* MMSI: 503486000 Official number: 857707	**776** 242 80	Class: LR ✠ **100A1** SS 03/2013 SSC passenger, mono LDC G4 ✠ **LMC** Cable: 165.0/19.0 U2 (a)	**2005-01 Image Marine Pty Ltd — Fremantle WA** Yd No: 287 Loa 49.90 Br ex 10.30 Dght 2.200 Lbp 44.50 Br md 10.00 Dpth 4.05 Welded, 1 dk	**(A37A2PC) Passenger/Cruise** Hull Material: Aluminium Alloy Passengers: cabins: 18; berths: 36	**2 oil engines** with clutches, flexible couplings & sr reverse geared to sc. shafts driving 2 FP propellers Total Power: 1,566kW (2,130hp) 13.0kn Caterpillar 3508B 2 x Vee 4 Stroke 8 Cy. 170 x 190 each-783kW (1065bhp) Caterpillar Inc-USA AuxGen: 2 x 148kW 415V 50Hz a.c Thrusters: 1 Thwart. FP thruster (f)
8704286 *2BNP2* -	**TRUEMAN** *ex* Tai Tam *-2003* **SMS Towage Ltd** Specialist Marine Services Ltd *Hull* *United Kingdom* Official number: 914937	*197* 50 72	Class: LR (BV) **100A1** SS 11/2010 tug coastal service **LMC** Cable: 302.5/22.0 U2 (a)	**1987-07 Imamura Zosen — Kure** Yd No: 323 Loa 22.80 Br ex 9.15 Dght 3.700 Lbp 18.40 Br md 8.51 Dpth 4.73 Welded, 1 dk	**(B32A2ST) Tug**	**2 oil engines** with clutches, flexible couplings & dr geared to sc. shafts driving 2 Directional propellers Total Power: 1,910kW (2,596hp) 11.5kn Niigata 6L25CXE 2 x 4 Stroke 6 Cy. 250 x 320 each-955kW (1298bhp) Niigata Engineering Co Ltd-Japan AuxGen: 2 x 64kW 380V 50Hz a.c Fuel: 45.0 (d.f.) 6.5pd
5062431 *LW4229* -	**TRUENO DEL PLATA** *ex* Capitan Rey *-1995* *ex* Eugene F. Moran *-1947* **RM Maritima SA** *Argentina* Official number: 02515	**453** 138 -		**1944 Levingston SB. Co. — Orange, Tx** Yd No: 330 Loa 43.72 Br ex 10.09 Dght 3.887 Lbp - Br md 10.04 Dpth - Welded, 1 dk	**(B32A2ST) Tug**	**2 diesel electric oil engines** Connecting to 2 elec. motors driving 1 FP propeller Total Power: 1,324kW (1,800hp) 12.0kn General Motors 12-278A 2 x Vee 2 Stroke 12 Cy. 222 x 267 each-662kW (900bhp) General Motors Corp-USA
8917091 *CB4238* -	**TRUENO I** **Sociedad Pesquera Coloso SA** - *Valparaiso* *Chile* MMSI: 725000047 Official number: 2690	*463* 154 594	Class: (BV)	**1990-08 Astilleros Marco Chilena Ltda. — Iquique** Yd No: 195 Loa 44.70 (BB) Br ex 10.30 Dght 3.000 Lbp 40.70 Br md 10.10 Dpth 5.00 Welded	**(B11B2FV) Fishing Vessel** Ins: 580	**1 oil engine** with clutches, flexible couplings & sr geared to sc. shaft driving 1 FP propeller Total Power: 1,037kW (1,410hp) 13.5kn Caterpillar 3516TA 1 x Vee 4 Stroke 16 Cy. 170 x 190 1037kW (1410bhp) Caterpillar Inc-USA Thrusters: 1 Thwart. FP thruster (f); 1 Thwart. FP thruster (a)
8816120 *MFTX2* FD 283	**TRUI VAN HINTE** *ex* Avontuur *-2004* *ex* Zeldenrust *-1996* **North Sea Fisheries Ltd** Danbrit Ship Management Ltd *Fleetwood* *United Kingdom* MMSI: 235007860 Official number: C18304	**474** 142 -		**1989-12 Stocznia im Komuny Paryskiej — Gdynia** Yd No: B276/20 Loa 40.25 (BB) Br ex - Dght - Lbp - Br md 9.00 Dpth 5.10 Welded	**(B11A2FT) Trawler**	**1 oil engine** reverse reduction geared to sc. shaft driving 1 FP propeller Total Power: 883kW (1,201hp) 13.0kn Stork-Werkspoor 6SW280 1 x 4 Stroke 6 Cy. 280 x 300 883kW (1201bhp) Stork Wartsila Diesel BV-Netherlands AuxGen: 2 x 200kW 220/380V 50Hz a.c Thrusters: 1 Thwart. FP thruster (f)
9397250 *3FYD5* -	**TRUMP SW** **Trump Pescadores SA** Shih Wei Navigation Co Ltd *Panama* *Panama* MMSI: 370857000 Official number: 3458209A	**11,743** 6,457 18,978 T/cm 30.7	Class: NK (CR)	**2008-11 Yamanishi Corp — Ishinomaki MG** Yd No: 1055 Loa 139.92 (BB) Br ex - Dght 8.496 Lbp 132.00 Br md 25.00 Dpth 11.50 Welded, 1 dk	**(A21A2BC) Bulk Carrier** Grain: 23,161; Bale: 22,563 Compartments: 4 Ho, ER 4 Ha: ER Cranes: 3x30.5t	**1 oil engine** driving 1 FP propeller Total Power: 5,180kW (7,043hp) 13.0kn MAN-B&W 7S35MC 1 x 2 Stroke 7 Cy. 350 x 1400 5180kW (7043bhp) Makita Corp-Japan Fuel: 1070.0
9023196 - -	**TRUNG DONG 18** *ex* Nghia Hong 16 *-2007* **Dong Bac JSC (Cong Ty Co Phan Dong Bac)** - *Haiphong* *Vietnam* MMSI: 574694000 Official number: VN-1646-VT	**598** 308 1,227	Class: VR	**2002-12 in Vietnam** Yd No: TKT-068NC Lengthened & Deepened-2004 Loa 55.90 Br ex 9.02 Dght 4.100 Lbp 52.00 Br md 9.00 Dpth 4.80 Welded, 1 dk	**(A31A2GX) General Cargo Ship**	**1 oil engine** driving 1 Propeller Total Power: 441kW (600hp) 8.0kn Hanshin 1 x 4 Stroke 6 Cy. 300 x 420 441kW (600bhp) The Hanshin Diesel Works Ltd-Japan
8836895 *XVAE* -	**TRUNG DUC 10** *ex* Vu Long 24 *-2007* *ex* Dong A 02 *-2007* *ex* Bach Dang 14 *-2004* **Trung Duc Trading & Transportation JSC (Cong Ty Co Phan TM VTB Trung Duc)** - *Haiphong* *Vietnam* MMSI: 574012080 Official number: VN-1014-VT	**1,238** 608 2,087	Class: VR	**1986 Bach Dang Shipyard — Haiphong** Deepened-2003 Loa 81.20 Br ex 10.52 Dght 4.400 Lbp 75.76 Br md 10.50 Dpth 5.50 Welded, 1 dk	**(A31A2GX) General Cargo Ship** Grain: 1,302 Compartments: 2 Ho, Wing ER 2 Ha: 2 (16.1 x -)ER	**1 oil engine** driving 1 FP propeller Total Power: 721kW (980hp) 10.5kn Skoda 6L350IIPN 1 x 4 Stroke 6 Cy. 350 x 500 721kW (980bhp) Skoda-Praha AuxGen: 1 x 96kW 380V a.c, 1 x 80kW 380V a.c
9548689 *XVQT* -	**TRUNG DUNG 06** **Trung Dung Shipping Co Ltd** Viet Thuan Transport Co Ltd *Haiphong* *Vietnam* MMSI: 574429000	**1,599** 1,077 2,978	Class: VR	**2008-12 Dai Nguyen Duong Co Ltd — Xuan Truong** Yd No: THB-25-01 Loa 79.80 Br ex 12.82 Dght 4.900 Lbp 74.80 Br md 12.80 Dpth 6.08 Welded, 1 dk	**(A31A2GX) General Cargo Ship** Grain: 3,959; Bale: 3,566 Compartments: 2 Ho, ER 2 Ha: ER 2 (20.4 x 8.4)	**1 oil engine** reduction geared to sc. shaft driving 1 FP propeller Total Power: 720kW (979hp) 10.0kn Chinese Std. Type CW8200ZC 1 x 4 Stroke 8 Cy. 200 x 270 720kW (979bhp) Weichai Power Co Ltd-China
9557484 *3WHN9* -	**TRUNG DUNG 09** **Trung Dung Shipping Co Ltd** - *Haiphong* *Vietnam* MMSI: 574001580 Official number: VN-3426-VT	**1,616** 1,116 3,049	Class: VR	**2012-06 Khien Ha Trading Co Ltd — Haiphong** Yd No: THB-36-02 Loa 79.80 Br ex 12.82 Dght 4.940 Lbp 74.80 Br md 12.80 Dpth 6.20 Welded, 1 dk	**(A31A2GX) General Cargo Ship** Grain: 4,098 Compartments: 2 Ho, ER 2 Ha: ER 2 (20.4 x 8.0)	**1 oil engine** reduction geared to sc. shaft driving 1 FP propeller Total Power: 928kW (1,262hp) 10.0kn Chinese Std. Type XCW8200ZC 1 x 4 Stroke 8 Cy. 200 x 270 928kW (1262bhp) Weichai Power Co Ltd-China AuxGen: 2 x 84kW 400V a.c
9575979 *3WXL* -	**TRUNG DUNG 26** *ex* Dong Phong 06 *-2009* **Trung Dung Transport & Trading JSC** - *Haiphong* *Vietnam* Official number: VN-3227-VT	**499** 300 936	Class: VR	**2009-10 Kim Son Shipbuilding & Transport Co — Dong Trieu** Yd No: TKT457A Loa 56.95 Br ex 9.22 Dght 3.450 Lbp 52.68 Br md 9.20 Dpth 4.20 Welded, 1 dk	**(A31A2GX) General Cargo Ship** Grain: 1,066; Bale: 906 Compartments: 1 Ho, ER 1 Ha: ER (24.2 x 5.2)	**1 oil engine** reduction geared to sc. shaft driving 1 FP propeller Total Power: 400kW (544hp) 9.0kn Chinese Std. Type Z8170ZL 1 x 4 Stroke 8 Cy. 170 x 200 400kW (544bhp) Zibo Diesel Engine Factory-China AuxGen: 1 x 32kW 400V a.c Fuel: 15.0 (d.f.)
9026851 *3WIJ* -	**TRUNG HAI 07** **Trung Hai Transport Co-operative** - *Haiphong* *Vietnam*	**499** 260 877	Class: VR	**2004-12 Hoang Tho Duc Co. Ltd. — Nam Dinh** Yd No: TKT-155A Loa 55.00 Br ex 9.67 Dght 2.700 Lbp 52.69 Br md 9.50 Dpth 3.40 Welded, 1 dk	**(A31A2GX) General Cargo Ship**	**2 oil engines** geared to sc. shafts driving 2 FP propellers Total Power: 400kW (544hp) 10.5kn Weifang X6170ZC 2 x 4 Stroke 6 Cy. 170 x 200 each-200kW (272bhp) Weifang Diesel Engine Factory-China

IMO / Call sign	Name / Owners	Tonnage	Class	Construction	Type	Machinery
9581746 *3WAX9* -	**TRUNG HAI 15** **Trung Hai Co Ltd** - SatCom: Inmarsat C 457400024 *Haiphong* *Vietnam*	**1,599** 1,085 3,046	Class: VR	**2011-02 Viet Tien Co Ltd — Xuan Truong** Yd No: THB-30-06 Loa 79.80 Br ex 12.82 Dght 4.940 Lbp 74.80 Br md 12.80 Dpth 6.20 Welded, 1 dk	**(A21A2BC) Bulk Carrier** Grain: 3,988; Bale: 3,593 Compartments: 2 Ho, ER 2 Ha: (19.8 x 8.0)ER (20.4 x 8.0)	**1 oil engine** reduction geared to sc. shaft driving 1 FP propeller Total Power: 735kW (999hp) 11.5kn Chinese Std. Type G6300ZCA 1 x 4 Stroke 6 Cy. 300 x 380 735kW (999bhp) Zibo Diesel Engine Factory-China AuxGen: 2 x 100kW 400V a.c Fuel: 76.0
8667244 *3WUD* -	**TRUNG HAI 25** **Vietnam Bank for Industry & Trade (VietinBank)** Trung Hai Co Ltd *Haiphong* *Vietnam* Official number: VN-2462-VT	**998** 670 1,958	Class: VR	**2008-02 Haiphong Mechanical & Trading Co. — Haiphong** Yd No: THB-12-10 Loa 69.85 Br ex 10.82 Dght 4.500 Lbp 65.95 Br md 10.80 Dpth 5.40 Welded, 1 dk	**(A31A2GX) General Cargo Ship** Grain: 2,242 Compartments: 2 Ho, ER 2 Ha: ER 2 (18.2 x 7.0)	**1 oil engine** driving 1 FP propeller Total Power: 441kW (600hp) 10.0kn Chinese Std. Type 6300ZC 1 x 4 Stroke 6 Cy. 300 x 380 441kW (600bhp) in China
9568641 *3WCL* -	**TRUNG HIEU 17** **Trung Hieu Transport Co Ltd** - SatCom: Inmarsat C 457497010 *Haiphong* *Vietnam* MMSI: 574970000	**1,599** 1,026 3,117	Class: VR	**2011-09 Truong An Transport & Trading JSC — Truc Ninh** Yd No: A30-09 Loa 78.63 Br ex 12.62 Dght 5.220 Lbp 73.60 Br md 12.60 Dpth 6.48 Welded, 1 dk	**(A31A2GX) General Cargo Ship** Grain: 3,948; Bale: 3,589 Compartments: 2 Ho, ER 2 Ha: ER 2 (19.8 x 8.4)	**1 oil engine** reduction geared to sc. shaft driving 1 FP propeller Total Power: 720kW (979hp) 10.0kn Chinese Std. Type CW8200ZC 1 x 4 Stroke 8 Cy. 200 x 270 720kW (979bhp) Weichai Power Co Ltd-China AuxGen: 2 x 75kW 400V a.c Fuel: 51.0
8986963 - -	**TRUNG HUNG 01** *ex* Ngoc Phat 68 *-2008* *ex* Cong Thanh 25 *-2006* **Trung Hung Shipping & Trading JSC** - SatCom: Inmarsat C 457490710 *Haiphong* *Vietnam* MMSI: 574012077 Official number: VN-2091-VT	**488** 349 978	Class: VR	**2003-12 Hoang Anh Shipbuilding Industry Joint Stock Co. — Vietnam** Loa 54.40 Br ex 9.07 Dght 3.400 Lbp 50.50 Br md 8.80 Dpth 4.05 Welded, 1 dk	**(A31A2GX) General Cargo Ship**	**1 oil engine** geared to sc. shaft driving 1 Propeller Total Power: 425kW (578hp) Weifang 8170ZC 1 x 4 Stroke 8 Cy. 170 x 200 425kW (578bhp) Weifang Diesel Engine Factory-China
9527374 - -	**TRUNG HUNG 09** **Trung Hung Shipping & Trading JSC** - SatCom: Inmarsat C 457441510 *Da Nang* *Vietnam* MMSI: 574012292	**1,599** 1,010 3,068	Class: VR	**2008-08 in Vietnam** Yd No: HT-150NC Loa 79.99 Br ex 12.62 Dght 5.300 Lbp 74.80 Br md 12.60 Dpth 6.48 Welded, 1 dk	**(A31A2GX) General Cargo Ship** Compartments: 2 Ho, ER 2 Ha: ER 2 (18.6 x 7.6)	**1 oil engine** reduction geared to sc. shaft driving 1 FP propeller Total Power: 720kW (979hp) 11.0kn Chinese Std. Type CW8200ZC 1 x 4 Stroke 8 Cy. 200 x 270 720kW (979bhp) (made 2007) Weichai Power Co Ltd-China
8954178 *XVEV* -	**TRUNG NGHIA 02** *ex* Minh Tuan 02 *-2008* *ex* Nam Dinh *-1998* **Nam Trung Nghia Transport Co Ltd** - *Haiphong* *Vietnam* Official number: VN-2507-VT	**495** 313 1,002	Class: VR	**1998 Thanh Long Co Ltd — Haiphong** Rebuilt-2005 Loa 53.75 Br ex 8.59 Dght 3.800 Lbp 49.80 Br md 8.55 Dpth 4.50 Welded, 1 dk	**(A31A2GX) General Cargo Ship** Grain: 680 Compartments: 1 Ho, ER 2 Ha: (11.0 x 4.7) (11.5 x 4.7)ER	**1 oil engine** driving 1 FP propeller Total Power: 300kW (408hp) 9.2kn S.K.L. 8NVD36-1U 1 x 4 Stroke 8 Cy. 240 x 360 300kW (408bhp) (new engine 1985) VEB Schwermaschinenbau "KarlLiebknecht" (SKL)-Magdeburg AuxGen: 1 x 5kW 230V a.c Fuel: 33.0 (d.f.)
9025027 - -	**TRUNG NGHIA 07** *ex* Hoang Sang 09 *-2011* *ex* Thai Thinh 09 *-2009* **Nam Trung Nghia Transport Co Ltd** - *Haiphong* *Vietnam*	**499** 358 957	Class: VR	**2003-03 Hoang Anh Shipbuilding Industry Joint Stock Co. — Vietnam** Yd No: ND-09A-01 Loa 56.00 Br ex 9.00 Dght 3.550 Lbp 52.91 Br md 8.95 Dpth 4.30 Welded, 1 dk	**(A31A2GX) General Cargo Ship**	**1 oil engine** driving 1 FP propeller Total Power: 425kW (578hp) 12.0kn S.K.L. 8NVD36A-1U 1 x 4 Stroke 8 Cy. 240 x 360 425kW (578bhp) SKL Motoren u. Systemtechnik AG-Magdeburg
9555448 *3WCD* -	**TRUNG NGUYEN 01** *ex* Phu Hung 03 *-2013* **Hai Nguyen Shipping JSC** - *Haiphong* *Vietnam* MMSI: 574513000 Official number: VN-3525-VT	**1,599** 1,078 2,983	Class: VR	**2009-12 Truong An Transport & Trading JSC — Truc Ninh** Yd No: THB-11-41 Loa 79.80 Br ex 12.82 Dght 4.900 Lbp 74.80 Br md 12.80 Dpth 6.08 Welded, 1 dk	**(A21A2BC) Bulk Carrier** Grain: 3,964; Bale: 3,571 Compartments: 2 Ho, ER 2 Ha: ER 2 (20.4 x 8.4)	**1 oil engine** reduction geared to sc. shaft driving 1 FP propeller Total Power: 735kW (999hp) 11.0kn Chinese Std. Type 8300ZLC 1 x 4 Stroke 8 Cy. 300 x 380 735kW (999bhp) Zibo Diesel Engine Factory-China AuxGen: 2 x 60kW 400V a.c
9476197 *XVTZ* -	**TRUNG NGUYEN 05** **Dai Trung Nguyen Trading & Construction Co Ltd** - *Saigon* *Vietnam* MMSI: 574012451 Official number: VNSG-1941-TH	**1,599** 1,032 3,205	Class: VR	**2009-04 Da Nang Shipyard — Da Nang** Yd No: S07-002-01 Loa 78.63 Br ex 12.62 Dght 5.300 Lbp 73.60 Br md 12.60 Dpth 6.48 Welded, 1 dk	**(A31A2GX) General Cargo Ship** Grain: 3,340 Compartments: 2 Ho, ER 2 Ha: ER 2 (19.2 x 8.4)	**1 oil engine** driving 1 FP propeller Total Power: 956kW (1,300hp) Sumiyoshi S631SS 1 x 4 Stroke 6 Cy. 310 x 480 956kW (1300bhp) (made 2004, fitted 2009) Sumiyoshi Marine Diesel Co Ltd-Japan AuxGen: 2 x 54kW 380V a.c
8930354 - -	**TRUNG SON 08** *ex* NH 2633 *-1996* **Van Dung Nguyen** - *Haiphong* *Vietnam*	**143** 69 200	Class: (VR)	**1994 at Nam Ha** Loa 36.50 Br ex - Dght 2.000 Lbp - Br md 6.80 Dpth 2.40 Welded, 1 dk	**(A31A2GX) General Cargo Ship**	**1 oil engine** reduction geared to sc. shaft driving 1 FP propeller Total Power: 99kW (135hp) Skoda 6L160 1 x 4 Stroke 6 Cy. 160 x 225 99kW (135bhp) (made 1988) CKD Praha-Praha
8665052 *XVKT* -	**TRUNG THANH 18-ALCI** *ex* Vien Dong 28-ALCI *-2013* *ex* Anh Duong 68-ALCI *-2009* *ex* Minh Cong 45 *-2007* **Agriculture Leasing Co I** Trung Thanh Shipping Service JSC *Haiphong* *Vietnam* Official number: VN-2276-VT	**1,598** 1,062 3,145	Class: VR	**2007-08 Nam Ha Shipyard — Nam Ha** Yd No: THB-11-08 Loa 79.80 Br ex 12.82 Dght 5.100 Lbp 74.80 Br md 12.80 Dpth 6.08 Welded, 1 dk	**(A31A2GX) General Cargo Ship** Grain: 3,767; Bale: 3,425 Compartments: 2 Ho, ER 2 Ha: ER 2 (20.4 x 8.4)	**1 oil engine** reduction geared to sc. shaft driving 1 FP propeller Total Power: 970kW (1,319hp) 10.0kn S.K.L. 8NVD48A-2U 1 x 4 Stroke 8 Cy. 320 x 480 970kW (1319bhp) (made 1992, fitted 2007) SKL Motoren u. Systemtechnik AG-Magdeburg AuxGen: 2 x 30kW 400V a.c
8665026 *3WTE* -	**TRUNG THANH 36-ALCI** *ex* Bien Dong 09-ALCI *-2007* **Trung Thanh Shipping Service JSC** - *Haiphong* *Vietnam* Official number: VN-2343-VT	**1,598** 1,062 3,141	Class: VR	**2007-11 Nam Ha Shipyard — Nam Ha** Yd No: THB-11.05 Loa 79.80 Br ex 12.82 Dght 5.100 Lbp 74.80 Br md 12.80 Dpth 6.08 Welded, 1 dk	**(A31A2GX) General Cargo Ship** Grain: 5,806; Bale: 5,230 Compartments: 2 Ho, ER 2 Ha: ER 2 (20.4 x 8.4)	**1 oil engine** reduction geared to sc. shaft driving 1 FP propeller Total Power: 720kW (979hp) 10.0kn Chinese Std. Type CW8200ZC 1 x 4 Stroke 8 Cy. 200 x 270 720kW (979bhp) Weichai Power Co Ltd-China AuxGen: 2 x 30kW 400V a.c
9700598 *3WHH9* -	**TRUNG THAO 36-BLC** **Agribank Leasing Co II** Trung Thao Sea & Rivers Transport Co Ltd *Haiphong* *Vietnam* MMSI: 574012709 Official number: VN-73.TT-TD	**1,599** 954 3,037	Class: VR	**2012-09 Duong Xuan 1 Ltd** (Hull launched by) Yd No: VS30-TS **2012-09 Pacific Shipbuilding JSC — Haiphong** (Hull completed by) Loa 81.74 Br ex 13.22 Dght 4.750 Lbp 76.00 Br md 13.20 Dpth 6.25 Welded, 1 dk	**(A13B2TP) Products Tanker** Double Hull (13F) Liq: 3,451; Liq (Oil): 3,451 Compartments: 4 Wing Ta, 4 Wing Ta, ER	**1 oil engine** reduction geared to sc. shafts driving 1 FP propeller Total Power: 647kW (880hp) 6.0kn S.K.L. 8NVD48A-2U 1 x 4 Stroke 8 Cy. 320 x 480 647kW (880bhp) (made 1988, fitted 2012) SKL Dieselmotorenwerk LeipzigGmbH-Leipzig AuxGen: 2 x 147kW 380V a.c Fuel: 98.0
9616371 - -	**TRUNG THAO 1818-BLC** **Trung Thao Sea & Rivers Transport Co Ltd** - *Haiphong* *Vietnam*	**1,590** - 2,750		**2013-06 Vinashin Casting Industry** Yd No: S06-006.02 **2013-06 Bac Song Cam Mechanical JSC — Haiphong** (Hull completed by) Yd No: S06-006.02 Loa 75.70 Br ex - Dght 5.430 Lbp 71.20 Br md 12.60 Dpth 6.48 Welded, 1 dk	**(A13B2TP) Products Tanker** Double Hull (13F)	**1 oil engine** driving 1 Propeller

7638296 *YB5182* -	**TRUNOJOYO** **PT Dharma Lautan Utama** - *Jakarta* *Indonesia*	*178* 54 150	Class: KI	**1977-06 P.T. Pakin — Jakarta** Yd No: 647 Loa 31.50 Br ex - Dght 1.501 Lbp 29.80 Br md 9.01 Dpth 2.42 Welded, 2 dks	**(A37B2PS) Passenger Ship**	**4 oil engines** reduction geared to sc. shafts driving 4 FP propellers Total Power: 728kW (990hp) Yanmar 6GH-UTE 2 x 4 Stroke 6 Cy. 117 x 140 each-243kW (330bhp) Yanmar Diesel Engine Co Ltd-Japan Yanmar 6KDE 2 x 4 Stroke 6 Cy. 145 x 170 each-121kW (165bhp) Yanmar Diesel Engine Co Ltd-Japan
8838960 - -	**TRUONG AN 07** *ex* Trang An 01 *-2004* *ex* Phu Ninh *-1998* **Truong An Transport & Trading Co Ltd (Cong Ty Tnhh Van Tai Va Thuong Mai Truong An)** - *Haiphong* *Vietnam*	**497** 265 715	Class: (VR)	**1983 Bach Dang Shipyard — Haiphong** Lengthened-1998 Loa 58.50 Br ex 8.52 Dght 3.300 Lbp 54.00 Br md 8.20 Dpth 4.10 Welded, 1 dk	**(A31A2GX) General Cargo Ship** Compartments: 2 Ho, ER 2 Ha: 2 (7.9 x 4.5)ER	**1 oil engine** reduction geared to sc. shaft driving 1 FP propeller Total Power: 294kW (400hp) 10.0kn S.K.L. 8NVD26A-2 1 x 4 Stroke 8 Cy. 180 x 260 294kW (400bhp) VEB Schwermaschinenbau "KarlLiebknecht" (SKL)-Magdeburg AuxGen: 1 x 50kW a.c, 1 x 30kW a.c
9665188 *3WIC9* -	**TRUONG AN 16** **Truong An Sea Transport Co Ltd** - *Haiphong* *Vietnam*	**1,599** 940 3,040	Class: VR	**2012-04 Dai Nguyen Duong Co Ltd — Xuan Truong** Yd No: TKT140P Loa 79.57 Br ex 12.62 Dght 5.270 Lbp 75.37 Br md 12.60 Dpth 6.20 Welded, 1 dk	**(A31A2GX) General Cargo Ship** Grain: 3,472; Bale: 3,128 Compartments: 2 Ho, ER 2 Ha: (18.2 x 8.0)ER (19.3 x 8.0)	**1 oil engine** reduction geared to sc. shaft driving 1 FP propeller Total Power: 1,100kW (1,496hp) 10.0kn Chinese Std. Type 8300ZLC 1 x 4 Stroke 8 Cy. 300 x 380 1100kW (1496bhp) Zibo Diesel Engine Factory-China AuxGen: 1 x 90kW 400V a.c
9643441 *3WEK9* -	**TRUONG AN 17** **Truong An Sea Transport Co Ltd** - *Haiphong* *Vietnam*	**1,599** 940 3,040	Class: VR	**2011-08 Dai Nguyen Duong Co Ltd — Xuan Truong** Yd No: TKT140H Loa 79.57 Br ex 12.62 Dght 5.270 Lbp 75.37 Br md 12.60 Dpth 6.20 Welded, 1 dk	**(A31A2GX) General Cargo Ship** Grain: 3,472; Bale: 3,128 Compartments: 2 Ho, ER 2 Ha: (18.2 x 8.0)ER (19.3 x 8.0)	**1 oil engine** reduction geared to sc. shaft driving 1 FP propeller Total Power: 882kW (1,199hp) 10.0kn Chinese Std. Type 8300ZLC 1 x 4 Stroke 8 Cy. 300 x 380 882kW (1199bhp) Zibo Diesel Engine Factory-China Fuel: 77.0
8667919 *XVKU* -	**TRUONG AN 19** **Truong An Transport Co Ltd** *Haiphong* *Vietnam*	**1,173** 739 2,065	Class: VR	**2008-07 Thang Loi Enterprise — Kim Thanh** Yd No: HP705 Loa 72.85 Br ex 11.52 Dght 3.820 Lbp 69.55 Br md 11.50 Dpth 4.65 Welded, 1 dk	**(A31A2GX) General Cargo Ship** Grain: 2,325 Compartments: 2 Ho, ER 2 Ha: ER 2 (20.9 x 7.5)	**2 oil engines** driving 2 Propellers S.K.L. 6NVD36-1U 2 x 4 Stroke 6 Cy. 240 x 360 VEB Schwermaschinenbau "KarlLiebknecht" (SKL)-Magdeburg
8667921 *XVOR* -	**TRUONG AN 29** **Truong An Transport Co Ltd** *Haiphong* *Vietnam* Official number: VN-2676-VT	**1,599** 1,037 3,096	Class: VR	**2008-09 Thang Loi Enterprise — Kim Thanh** Yd No: HP707.02 Loa 79.86 Br ex 12.82 Dght 4.820 Lbp 74.56 Br md 12.80 Dpth 5.85 Welded, 1 dk	**(A31A2GX) General Cargo Ship** Grain: 3,337 Compartments: 2 Ho, ER 2 Ha: ER 2 (21.0 x 7.8)	**1 oil engine** driving 1 FP propeller Total Power: 970kW (1,319hp) 10.0kn S.K.L. 8NVD48A-2U 1 x 4 Stroke 8 Cy. 320 x 480 970kW (1319bhp) (made 1991) VEB Schwermaschinenbau "KarlLiebknecht" (SKL)-Magdeburg
8668042 *3WHX* -	**TRUONG AN 35** **Truong An Transport Co Ltd** *Haiphong* *Vietnam* Official number: VN-3001-VT	**1,599** 1,030 3,036	Class: VR	**2009-10 Hai Hao Co Ltd — Haiphong** Yd No: HP907-02 Loa 79.99 Br ex 14.22 Dght 4.420 Lbp 74.56 Br md 14.20 Dpth 5.27 Welded, 1 dk	**(A31A2GX) General Cargo Ship** Bale: 3,774 Compartments: 2 Ho, ER 2 Ha: ER 2 (21.0 x 8.2)	**1 oil engine** driving 1 FP propeller Total Power: 970kW (1,319hp) 10.0kn S.K.L. 8NVD48A-2U 1 x 4 Stroke 8 Cy. 320 x 480 970kW (1319bhp) (made 1991) SKL Motoren u. Systemtechnik AG-Magdeburg
8668054 *XVSV* -	**TRUONG AN 45** **Truong An Transport Co Ltd** *Haiphong* *Vietnam* Official number: VN-2875-VT	**1,599** 1,037 3,096	Class: VR	**2009-04 Hai Hao Co Ltd — Haiphong** Yd No: HP707-03 Loa 79.86 Br ex 12.82 Dght 4.820 Lbp 74.56 Br md 12.80 Dpth 5.85 Welded, 1 dk	**(A31A2GX) General Cargo Ship** Grain: 3,337 Compartments: 2 Ho, ER 2 Ha: ER 2 (21.0 x 7.8)	**1 oil engine** driving 1 FP propeller Total Power: 970kW (1,319hp) 10.0kn S.K.L. 8NVD48A-2U 1 x 4 Stroke 8 Cy. 320 x 480 970kW (1319bhp) SKL Motoren u. Systemtechnik AG-Magdeburg
9610858 *3WZV* -	**TRUONG AN 135** **Truong An Transport Co Ltd** - *Haiphong* *Vietnam*	**1,599** 1,025 3,036	Class: VR	**2010-01 Hai Hao Co Ltd — Haiphong** Yd No: HP907 Loa 79.99 Br ex 14.22 Dght 4.420 Lbp 74.56 Br md 14.20 Dpth 5.27 Welded, 1 dk	**(A31A2GX) General Cargo Ship** Bale: 3,774 Compartments: 2 Ho, ER 2 Ha: ER 2 (21.0 x 8.2)	**1 oil engine** driving 1 FP propeller Total Power: 736kW (1,001hp) 10.0kn S.K.L. 8NVD48A-2U 1 x 4 Stroke 8 Cy. 320 x 480 736kW (1001bhp) (Re-engined ,made 1991, refitted 2010) SKL Motoren u. Systemtechnik AG-Magdeburg AuxGen: 2 x 60kW 400V a.c
9643439 *3WDN9* -	**TRUONG AN 136** **Truong An Transport Co Ltd** - *Haiphong* *Vietnam*	**999** 652 1,970	Class: VR	**2011-09 Phu Hung Shipbuilding Industry JSC — Y Yen** Yd No: TKT129D9 Loa 69.86 Br ex 10.82 Dght 4.550 Lbp 65.85 Br md 10.80 Dpth 5.40 Welded, 1 dk	**(A31A2GX) General Cargo Ship** Grain: 2,219; Bale: 1,999 Compartments: 2 Ho, ER 2 Ha: ER 2 (17.1 x 7.2)	**1 oil engine** reduction geared to sc. shaft driving 1 FP propeller Total Power: 662kW (900hp) 10.0kn Chinese Std. Type 6210ZLC 1 x 4 Stroke 6 Cy. 210 x 290 662kW (900bhp) Zibo Diesel Engine Factory-China Fuel: 34.0
8668066 *3WRM* -	**TRUONG AN PHU 46** *ex* Hai Nam 27 *-2008* **Truong An Phu Trading & Transport Co Ltd (Cong Ty Tnhh Thuong Mai Va Van Tai Truong An Phu)** - *Haiphong* *Vietnam* Official number: vn-2374-vt	**1,232** 902 2,169	Class: VR	**2007-10 Hai Hao Co Ltd — Haiphong** Yd No: HP614 Loa 73.10 Br ex 11.82 Dght 4.200 Lbp 69.00 Br md 11.80 Dpth 5.05 Welded, 1 dk	**(A31A2GX) General Cargo Ship** Grain: 2,684; Bale: 2,684 Compartments: 2 Ho, ER 2 Ha: ER 2 (15.5 x 7.8)	**2 oil engines** driving 2 Propellers 11.0kn S.K.L. 6NVD36-1U 2 x 4 Stroke 6 Cy. 240 x 360 SKL Motoren u. Systemtechnik AG-Magdeburg
8656427 - -	**TRUONG DUNG 01** **Trung Dung Transport & Trading JSC** *Haiphong* *Vietnam*	**499** 256 951	Class: VR	**2009-06 Marine Service Co. No. 1 — Haiphong** Yd No: VL08-18 Loa 56.08 Br ex 9.52 Dght 3.000 Lbp 53.65 Br md 9.50 Dpth 3.74 Welded, 1 dk	**(A13B2TP) Products Tanker** Double Hull (13F) Liq: 972; Liq (Oil): 972 Compartments: 8 Wing Ta, ER	**1 oil engine** redcution geared to sc. shaft driving 1 FP propeller Total Power: 330kW (449hp) 9.0kn Chinese Std. Type X6170ZCA 1 x 4 Stroke 6 Cy. 170 x 200 330kW (449bhp) Weifang Diesel Engine Factory-China AuxGen: 1 x 90kW 400V a.c Fuel: 12.2
9026942 *3WLX* -	**TRUONG GIANG 09-ALCI** **Agriculture Leasing Co I** Truong Giang Shipping Co Ltd *Haiphong* *Vietnam* MMSI: 574570000	**990** 630 1,981	Class: VR	**2005-04 Hoang Anh Shipbuilding Industry Joint Stock Co. — Vietnam** Yd No: TKT-129 Loa 69.83 Br ex 10.82 Dght 4.500 Lbp 65.85 Br md 10.80 Dpth 5.40 Welded, 1 dk	**(A31A2GX) General Cargo Ship**	**1 oil engine** geared to sc. shaft driving 1 Propeller Total Power: 600kW (816hp) 10.0kn Chinese Std. Type CW6200ZC 1 x 4 Stroke 6 Cy. 200 x 270 600kW (816bhp) in China
9544803 *XVTT* -	**TRUONG GIANG 45** **Truong Giang Shipping Co Ltd** - *Haiphong* *Vietnam* MMSI: 574012429	**999** 639 1,908	Class: VR	**2009-02 Song Ninh Co-operative — Vietnam** Yd No: TKT-129M-SD Loa 69.86 Br ex 10.82 Dght 4.450 Lbp 65.85 Br md 10.80 Dpth 5.40 Welded, 1 dk	**(A31A2GX) General Cargo Ship** Grain: 2,387; Bale: 2,150 Compartments: 2 Ho, ER 2 Ha: ER 2 (17.1 x 7.2)	**1 oil engine** reduction geared to sc. shaft driving 1 FP propeller Total Power: 700kW (952hp) 11.0kn Chinese Std. Type CW6200ZC 1 x 4 Stroke 6 Cy. 200 x 270 700kW (952bhp) Weifang Diesel Engine Factory-China AuxGen: 2 x 60kW 400V a.c
9342437 *3WKX* -	**TRUONG HAI** **Agribank Leasing Co II** Truong Hai Co Ltd *Haiphong* *Vietnam* MMSI: 574549000	**499** 361 934	Class: VR	**2005-01 Trung Hai Private Enterprise — Haiphong** Loa 56.45 Br ex 9.17 Dght 3.310 Lbp 52.70 Br md 9.15 Dpth 4.05 Welded, 1 dk	**(A31A2GX) General Cargo Ship** 1 Ha: ER (13.2 x 5.2) 1 Wing Ha:	**1 oil engine** reduction geared to sc. shaft driving 1 FP propeller Total Power: 330kW (449hp) Weifang X6170ZC 1 x 4 Stroke 6 Cy. 170 x 200 330kW (449bhp) (new engine 2007) Weifang Diesel Engine Factory-China AuxGen: 2 x 40kW 400V a.c
8869141 - -	**TRUONG HAI 05** *ex* Song Ma 05 *-2008* **Truong Hai Gneral Business Co Ltd** - *Haiphong* *Vietnam*	**289** 173 483	Class: VR	**1986 Thanh Hoa Shipbuilding JSC — Thanh Hoa** Rebuilt-2003 Loa 44.35 Br ex 7.59 Dght 2.650 Lbp 41.98 Br md 7.43 Dpth 3.40 Welded, 1 dk	**(A31A2GX) General Cargo Ship** Grain: 277 Compartments: 2 Ho, ER 2 Ha: 2 (6.5 x 4.0)ER	**1 oil engine** reduction geared to sc. shaft driving 1 FP propeller Total Power: 103kW (140hp) 8.0kn Yanmar 5KDGGE 1 x 4 Stroke 5 Cy. 145 x 170 103kW (140bhp) (made 1977) Yanmar Diesel Engine Co Ltd-Japan

IMO / Call sign	Name / Owner	Tonnage	Class	Builder / Dimensions	Type / Capacity	Machinery
9419606 *3WPZ* -	**TRUONG HAI STAR 2** *ex* Sea Puma *-2007* **Chu Lai - Truong Hai Ship Co Ltd** Binh Minh Shipping Co Ltd SatCom: Inmarsat C 457446710 *Haiphong* *Vietnam* MMSI: 574467000 Official number: VN-2419-VT	**2,998** 1,678 4,463	Class: VR	**2007-05 Dai Duong Shipbuilding Co Ltd — Haiphong** Yd No: HP-504 Loa 99.90 Br ex - Dght 5.750 Lbp 84.80 Br md 15.40 Dpth 7.30 Welded, 1 dk	**(A31A2GX) General Cargo Ship** Grain: 4,818 TEU 228 Compartments: 2 Ho, ER 2 Ha: ER 2 (22.6 x 12.7)	**1 oil engine** reduction geared to sc. shaft (s) driving 1 FP propeller Total Power: 2,206kW (2,999hp) 12.0kn Chinese Std. Type G8300ZC 1 x 4 Stroke 8 Cy. 300 x 380 2206kW (2999bhp) Wuxi Antai Power Machinery Co Ltd-China AuxGen: 1 x 638kW 400V 50Hz a.c, 2 x 330kW 400V 50Hz a.c
8868795 - -	**TRUONG LAM** - **Haiphong Shipping Supply & Investment Co (Cong Ty Dau Tu Cung Ung Tau Bien Hai Phong)** *Haiphong* *Vietnam*	*171* - 150	Class: (VR)	**1986 Song Lam Shipbuilding Works — Nghi Xuan** Loa 36.55 Br ex - Dght 1.700 Lbp - Br md 7.00 Dpth 2.50 Welded, 1 dk	**(A31A2GX) General Cargo Ship** Grain: 264 Compartments: 2 Ho, ER 2 Ha: 2 (7.0 x 4.0)ER	**1 oil engine** reduction geared to sc. shaft driving 1 FP propeller Total Power: 103kW (140hp) 9.0kn Yanmar 5KDGGE 1 x 4 Stroke 5 Cy. 145 x 170 103kW (140bhp) (made 1977) Yanmar Diesel Engine Co Ltd-Japan
9587714 *XVWT* -	**TRUONG LOC 16** **Truong Loc Trading & Shipping JSC** SatCom: Inmarsat C 457499944 *Haiphong* *Vietnam* MMSI: 574000400	**2,998** 1,860 5,193	Class: VR	**2010-12 Nam Ha Shipyard — Nam Ha** Yd No: S52-06 Loa 91.94 Br ex 15.33 Dght 6.300 Lbp 84.97 Br md 15.30 Dpth 7.90 Welded, 1 dk	**(A21A2BC) Bulk Carrier** Grain: 6,724; Bale: 6,057 Compartments: 2 Ho, ER 2 Ha: (21.0 x 10.0)ER (20.3 x 10.0) Cranes: 2x10t	**1 oil engine** reduction geared to sc. shaft driving 1 FP propeller Total Power: 1,765kW (2,400hp) 11.0kn Chinese Std. Type 8320ZC 1 x 4 Stroke 8 Cy. 320 x 440 1765kW (2400bhp) Guangzhou Diesel Engine Factory CoLtd-China AuxGen: 2 x 170kW 400V a.c
9589425 *3WAP9* -	**TRUONG MINH 99** *ex* Ruby 01 *-2012* **Truong Minh International JSC** - SatCom: Inmarsat C 457499713 *Haiphong* *Vietnam* MMSI: 574000640 Official number: VN-3441-VT	**2,969** 1,858 5,143	Class: VR	**2010-12 Dong Bac Shipbuilding Industry JSC — Cam Pha** Yd No: DB-01 Loa 92.06 Br ex 15.33 Dght 6.400 Lbp 84.96 Br md 15.30 Dpth 8.00 Welded, 1 dk	**(A21A2BC) Bulk Carrier** Grain: 6,671 Compartments: 2 Ho, ER 2 Ha: (21.0 x 10.0)ER (19.7 x 10.0) Cranes: 1x15t	**1 oil engine** reduction geared to sc. shaft driving 1 FP propeller Total Power: 1,765kW (2,400hp) 12.0kn Chinese Std. Type LC8250ZLC 1 x 4 Stroke 8 Cy. 250 x 320 1765kW (2400bhp) Zibo Diesel Engine Factory-China AuxGen: 1 x 170kW 400V a.c Fuel: 230.0
9668128 *3EXS8* -	**TRUONG MINH OCEAN** **Truong Minh International JSC** *Panama* *Panama* MMSI: 352377000 Official number: 45432PEXT	**8,196** 5,295 12,500	Class: RI	**2014-03 Dong Bac Shipbuilding Industry JSC — Cam Pha** Yd No: DB-05 Loa 136.40 (BB) Br ex - Dght 8.200 Lbp 126.00 Br md 20.20 Dpth 11.30 Welded, 1 dk	**(A31A2GX) General Cargo Ship** Grain: 18,601; Bale: 17,744	**1 oil engine** driving 1 FP propeller Total Power: 3,964kW (5,389hp) 13.2kn Mitsubishi 7UEC33LSII 1 x 2 Stroke 7 Cy. 330 x 1050 3964kW (5389bhp) Akasaka Tekkosho KK (Akasaka DieselLtd)-Japan
9631723 *3FUR2* -	**TRUONG MINH STAR** **Truong Minh International JSC** - *Panama* *Panama* MMSI: 373772000 Official number: 4487213	**6,627** 3,852 10,156	Class: RI	**2012-12 Dong Bac Shipbuilding Industry JSC — Cam Pha** Yd No: DB-04 Loa 118.83 (BB) Br ex 19.93 Dght 7.600 Lbp 110.60 Br md 19.90 Dpth 9.85 Welded, 1 dk	**(A21A2BC) Bulk Carrier** Grain: 12,780 Compartments: 2 Ho, ER 2 Ha: ER Cranes: 1x30t,2x20t	**1 oil engine** driving 1 FP propeller Total Power: 3,311kW (4,502hp) 12.5kn Akasaka A45S 1 x 4 Stroke 6 Cy. 450 x 880 3311kW (4502bhp) Akasaka Tekkosho KK (Akasaka DieselLtd)-Japan AuxGen: 2 x 310kW 60Hz a.c
9637789 *3WGX9* -	**TRUONG MINH SUN** **Truong Minh International JSC** - *Haiphong* *Vietnam* MMSI: 574001440 Official number: VN-3415-VT	**2,979** 1,856 5,203	Class: VR	**2012-04 Dong Bac Shipbuilding Industry JSC — Cam Pha** Yd No: DB-03 Loa 92.06 Br ex 15.33 Dght 6.400 Lbp 84.96 Br md 15.30 Dpth 8.00 Welded, 1 dk	**(A21A2BC) Bulk Carrier** Grain: 6,710 Compartments: 2 Ho, ER 2 Ha: (21.0 x 10.0)ER (19.7 x 10.0) Cranes: 2x15t	**1 oil engine** reduction geared to sc. shaft driving 1 FP propeller Total Power: 1,765kW (2,400hp) 12.0kn Chinese Std. Type LC8250ZLC 1 x 4 Stroke 8 Cy. 250 x 320 1765kW (2400bhp) Zibo Diesel Engine Factory-China AuxGen: 2 x 160kW 380V a.c Fuel: 270.0
9490284 *3WVR* -	**TRUONG MINH VICTORY** *ex* Long Thinh Star *-2013* *ex* Thai An Ms *-2008* **Truong Minh Shipping JSC** *Saigon* *Vietnam* MMSI: 574265000	**2,551** 1,497 4,373	Class: VR	**2008-03 Dai Duong Shipbuilding Co Ltd — Haiphong** Yd No: HP703-03 Loa 90.72 Br ex 13.00 Dght 6.160 Lbp 84.90 Br md 12.98 Dpth 7.60 Welded, 1 dk	**(A31A2GX) General Cargo Ship** Grain: 4,850 Compartments: 2 Ho, ER 2 Ha: ER 2 (21.0 x 8.0) Cranes: 1x10t	**1 oil engine** reduction geared to sc. shaft driving 1 FP propeller Total Power: 1,500kW (2,039hp) 11.0kn Chinese Std. Type G8300ZC 1 x 4 Stroke 8 Cy. 300 x 380 1500kW (2039bhp) Wuxi Antai Power Machinery Co Ltd-China AuxGen: 2 x 162kW 400V a.c
9611967 *XVWK* -	**TRUONG NGUYEN 18** **Truong Nguyen Bus Transport Import - Export Co Ltd** - SatCom: Inmarsat C 457499940 *Haiphong* *Vietnam* MMSI: 574000420	**1,441** 949 2,499	Class: VR	**2010-11 at Haiphong** Yd No: THK-74-01 Loa 79.19 Br ex 12.82 Dght 4.230 Lbp 74.00 Br md 12.80 Dpth 5.10 Welded, 1 dk	**(A31A2GX) General Cargo Ship** Bale: 2,738 Compartments: 2 Ho, ER 2 Ha: ER 2 (19.8 x 8.8)	**1 oil engine** reduction geared to sc. shaft driving 1 FP propeller Total Power: 698kW (949hp) 10.5kn Chinese Std. Type CW6200ZC 1 x 4 Stroke 6 Cy. 200 x 270 698kW (949bhp) Weichai Power Co Ltd-China AuxGen: 2 x 60kW 400V a.c
9265859 *3WFA9* -	**TRUONG NGUYEN 26** *ex* Ho Tay 8 *-2011* *ex* Binh Minh 8 *-2006* **Truong Nguyen Bus Transport Import - Export Co Ltd** - SatCom: Inmarsat C 457424510 *Haiphong* *Vietnam* MMSI: 574999020	**998** 637 1,933	Class: VR	**2002-03 Ha Long Shipbuilding Co Ltd — Ha Long** Yd No: H143A Loa 69.98 Br ex 10.82 Dght 4.400 Lbp 66.50 Br md 10.80 Dpth 5.30 Welded, 1 dk	**(A31A2GX) General Cargo Ship**	**1 oil engine** geared to sc. shaft driving 1 FP propeller Total Power: 736kW (1,001hp) Chinese Std. Type 8300 1 x 4 Stroke 8 Cy. 300 x 380 736kW (1001bhp) Zibo Diesel Engine Factory-China
9601481 *XVWM* -	**TRUONG NGUYEN 36** **Truong Nguyen Bus Transport Import - Export Co Ltd** - SatCom: Inmarsat C 457499941 *Haiphong* *Vietnam* MMSI: 574000410	**1,430** 822 2,506	Class: VR	**2010-07 at Haiphong** Yd No: TQT-208 Loa 79.19 Br ex 12.82 Dght 4.230 Lbp 74.00 Br md 12.80 Dpth 5.10 Welded, 1 dk	**(A31A2GX) General Cargo Ship** Bale: 2,738 Compartments: 2 Ho, ER 2 Ha: ER 2 (19.8 x 8.8)	**1 oil engine** reduction geared to sc. shaft driving 1 FP propeller Total Power: 698kW (949hp) 10.5kn Chinese Std. Type CW6200ZC 1 x 4 Stroke 6 Cy. 200 x 270 698kW (949bhp) Weichai Power Co Ltd-China AuxGen: 2 x 60kW 400V a.c
8667256 *XVPG* -	**TRUONG NGUYEN 68** *ex* Hai Van 05 *-2009* **Truong Nguyen Bus Transport Import - Export Co Ltd** - *Haiphong* *Vietnam* Official number: VN-3025-VT	**999** 656 1,965	Class: VR	**2008-11 Haiphong Mechanical & Trading Co. — Haiphong** Yd No: TQT-01/01 Loa 70.10 Br ex 10.82 Dght 4.680 Lbp 65.80 Br md 10.80 Dpth 5.55 Welded, 1 dk	**(A31A2GX) General Cargo Ship** Grain: 2,329 Compartments: 2 Ho, ER 2 Ha: ER 2 (15.0 x 7.0)	**1 oil engine** driving 1 FP propeller Total Power: 441kW (600hp) 10.0kn Chinese Std. Type 6300ZC 1 x 4 Stroke 6 Cy. 300 x 380 441kW (600bhp) Ningbo CSI Power & Machinery GroupCo Ltd-China
9544774 *XVPR* -	**TRUONG PHAT 01-ALCI** *ex* Bac Son 126-Alci *-2009* **Agriculture Leasing Co I** Truong Phat Trading & International Shipping JSC SatCom: Inmarsat C 457441610 *Haiphong* *Vietnam* MMSI: 574416000	**1,599** 1,043 3,139	Class: VR	**2008-12 Nam Trieu Shipbuilding Industry Co. Ltd. — Haiphong** Yd No: S07-045 Loa 78.63 Br ex 12.62 Dght 5.220 Lbp 73.58 Br md 12.60 Dpth 6.48 Welded, 1 dk	**(A21A2BC) Bulk Carrier** Grain: 3,503 Compartments: 2 Ho, ER 2 Ha: ER 2 (19.8 x 8.4)	**1 oil engine** reduction geared to sc. shaft driving 1 FP propeller Total Power: 735kW (999hp) 9.0kn Chinese Std. Type LB6250ZLC 1 x 4 Stroke 6 Cy. 250 x 320 735kW (999bhp) Zibo Diesel Engine Factory-China AuxGen: 2 x 90kW 400V 50Hz a.c
9545778 *XVVG* -	**TRUONG PHAT 02-ALCI** *ex* Limco *-2011* **Agriculture Leasing Co I** Truong Phat Trading & International Shipping JSC SatCom: Inmarsat C 457441110 *Haiphong* *Vietnam* MMSI: 574411000	**999** 654 1,852	Class: VR	**2008-11 Haiphong PTS Shipbuilding Co Ltd — Haiphong** Yd No: S07-047.04 Loa 69.95 Br ex 10.82 Dght 4.470 Lbp 65.83 Br md 10.80 Dpth 5.50 Welded, 1 dk	**(A31A2GX) General Cargo Ship** Bale: 2,105 Compartments: 2 Ho, ER 2 Ha: (16.0 x 7.0)ER (15.4 x 7.0)	**1 oil engine** reduction geared to sc. shaft driving 1 FP propeller Total Power: 736kW (1,001hp) 10.0kn Chinese Std. Type 6210ZLC 1 x 4 Stroke 6 Cy. 210 x 290 736kW (1001bhp) Zibo Diesel Engine Factory-China AuxGen: 2 x 75kW 400V a.c Fuel: 55.0
9327619 *3WHJ* -	**TRUONG PHAT 36** **Truong Phat Waterway & Land Transport JSC** - SatCom: Inmarsat C 457425710 *Haiphong* *Vietnam* MMSI: 574257000 Official number: VN-1862-VT	**1,599** 1,097 3,065	Class: VR	**2004-09 Vinacoal Shipbuilding Co — Ha Long** Yd No: TKC-48.1 Loa 74.36 Br ex 12.64 Dght 5.270 Lbp 70.90 Br md 12.60 Dpth 6.30 Welded, 1 dk	**(A31A2GX) General Cargo Ship** Compartments: 2 Ho, ER 2 Ha: (16.4 x 8.0)ER (19.8 x 8.0)	**1 oil engine** driving 1 Propeller Total Power: 736kW (1,001hp) S.K.L. 8NVD48A-1U 1 x 4 Stroke 8 Cy. 320 x 480 736kW (1001bhp) AuxGen: 2 x 75kW 400V a.c

IMO / Call sign / Flag	Name / Owner	Tonnage	Class	Build / Dimensions	Type / Capacity	Machinery
9576002 *3WDA9* -	**TRUONG PHAT 45** **Truong Phat Waterway & Land Transport JSC** - *Haiphong* Vietnam	**2,484** 1,547 4,501	Class: VR	**2012-06 Marine Service Co. No. 1 — Haiphong** Yd No: TKC38.07SD Loa 86.63 Br ex - Dght 6.200 Lbp 81.46 Br md 13.28 Dpth 7.38 Welded, 1 dk	**(A31A2GX) General Cargo Ship** Bale: 5,625 Compartments: 2 Ho, ER 2 Ha: (25.5 x 8.4)ER (19.2 x 8.4) Cranes: 2x8t	**1 oil engine** reduction geared to sc. shaft driving 1 FP propeller Total Power: 1,471kW (2,000hp) 10.0kn Chinese Std. Type G6300ZC 1 x 4 Stroke 6 Cy. 300 x 380 1471kW (2000bhp) Ningbo CSI Power & Machinery GroupCo Ltd-China Fuel: 212.0
8665662 *3WYL* -	**TRUONG PHONG 27** *ex* Hai Phuong 69 *-2009* **Truong Phong Transport Co Ltd** - *Haiphong* Vietnam Official number: VN-2966-VT	**999** 588 1,927	Class: VR	**2008-10 Technical & Prof. College ofTransport No. 2 — Haiphong** Yd No: TKC31-06A4 Loa 67.50 Br ex 11.02 Dght 4.500 Lbp 63.70 Br md 11.00 Dpth 5.30 Welded, 1 dk	**(A31A2GX) General Cargo Ship** Grain: 2,013 Compartments: 2 Ho, ER 2 Ha: (14.1 x 7.3)ER (16.0 x 7.3)	**1 oil engine** reduction geared to sc. shaft driving 1 FP propeller Total Power: 600kW (816hp) Chinese Std. Type CW6200ZC 1 x 4 Stroke 6 Cy. 200 x 270 600kW (816bhp) Weichai Power Co Ltd-China AuxGen: 2 x 30kW 400V a.c
8129644 *3WJC*	**TRUONG SA** *ex* Titan-1 *-1990* **Joint Venture 'VIETSOVPETRO'** SatCom: Inmarsat C 457407510 *Saigon* Vietnam MMSI: 574075065 Official number: VNSG-1249N-TCC	**20,338** 6,101 3,343	Class: NV (VR) (RS)	**1984-09 Oy Wartsila Ab — Turku** Yd No: 1277 Loa 141.41 Br ex - Dght 7.992 Lbp 121.75 Br md 54.51 Dpth 13.01 Welded, 1 dk	**(B34B2SC) Crane Vessel** Passengers: berths: 100 Grain: 640 Compartments: 1 Ho, ER 1 Ha: (10.4 x 5.0)ER Cranes: 1x600t	**3 diesel electric oil engines** driving 3 gen. each 1880kW 660V a.c Connecting to 2 elec. motors driving 2 Azimuth electric drive units Total Power: 5,553kW (7,551hp) 11.0kn Wartsila 6R32 3 x 4 Stroke 6 Cy. 320 x 350 each-1851kW (2517bhp) Oy Wartsila Ab-Finland AuxGen: 3 x 180kW 380V 50Hz a.c Thrusters: 2 Tunnel thruster (f)
8868783 - -	**TRUONG SA 01** **Truong Sa Construction Management of Navy Command (Ban Quan Ly Cong Trinh Truong Sa)** - *Haiphong* Vietnam	**1,038** 513 1,364	Class: (VR)	**1989 Ha Long Shipbuilding Co Ltd — Ha Long** Loa 70.75 Br ex - Dght 3.700 Lbp - Br md 11.80 Dpth 4.82 Welded, 1 dk	**(A31A2GX) General Cargo Ship** Grain: 1,610 Compartments: 2 Ho, ER 2 Ha: 2 (10.8 x 6.6)ER	**2 oil engines** driving 2 FP propellers Total Power: 1,442kW (1,960hp) 12.0kn Skoda 6L350IIPN 2 x 4 Stroke 6 Cy. 350 x 500 each-721kW (980bhp) CKD Praha-Praha AuxGen: 2 x 150kW a.c
8868812 - -	**TRUONG SA 02** **Truong Sa Construction Management of Navy Command (Ban Quan Ly Cong Trinh Truong Sa)** - *Haiphong* Vietnam	**1,038** 513 1,120	Class: (VR)	**1990 Ha Long Shipbuilding Co Ltd — Ha Long** Loa 70.75 Br ex - Dght 3.700 Lbp - Br md 11.80 Dpth 4.82 Welded, 1 dk	**(A31A2GX) General Cargo Ship** Grain: 1,610 Compartments: 2 Ho, ER 2 Ha: 2 (10.8 x 6.6)ER	**2 oil engines** driving 2 FP propellers Total Power: 1,442kW (1,960hp) 12.0kn Skoda 6L350IIPN 2 x 4 Stroke 6 Cy. 350 x 500 each-721kW (980bhp) CKD Praha-Praha AuxGen: 2 x 150kW a.c
8868771 - -	**TRUONG SA 02** **Waterway Transport Enterprise of Nghe An Port (Xi Nghiep Van Tai Thuy-Cang Nghe An)** Vietnam	*185* 116 160	Class: (VR)	**1988 at Haiphong** L reg 27.62 Br ex - Dght 2.900 Lbp - Br md 6.70 Dpth 3.65 Welded, 1 dk	**(A31A2GX) General Cargo Ship** Grain: 239 Compartments: 2 Ho, ER 2 Ha: (5.0 x 4.0) (5.0 x 3.2)ER	**1 oil engine** reduction geared to sc. shaft driving 1 FP propeller Total Power: 147kW (200hp) 8.0kn S.K.L. 6NVD26-2 1 x 4 Stroke 6 Cy. 180 x 260 147kW (200bhp) (made 1985) VEB Schwermaschinenbau "KarlLiebknecht" (SKL)-Magdeburg
8868800 - -	**TRUONG SA 04** **Truong Sa Construction Management of Navy Command (Ban Quan Ly Cong Trinh Truong Sa)** - *Haiphong* Vietnam	**1,038** 513 1,364	Class: (VR)	**1991 Ha Long Shipbuilding Co Ltd — Ha Long** Loa 70.75 Br ex - Dght 3.700 Lbp - Br md 11.80 Dpth 4.82 Welded, 1 dk	**(A31A2GX) General Cargo Ship** Grain: 1,610 Compartments: 2 Ho, ER 2 Ha: 2 (10.8 x 6.6)ER	**2 oil engines** driving 2 FP propellers Total Power: 1,442kW (1,960hp) 12.0kn Skoda 6L350PN 2 x 4 Stroke 6 Cy. 350 x 500 each-721kW (980bhp) CKD Praha-Praha AuxGen: 2 x 100kW a.c
8893491 - -	**TRUONG SA 06** **Truong Sa Construction Management of Navy Command (Ban Quan Ly Cong Trinh Truong Sa)** - *Haiphong* Vietnam	**1,038** 513 1,364	Class: (VR)	**1993 Ha Long Shipbuilding Co Ltd — Ha Long** Loa 70.75 Br ex - Dght 3.700 Lbp 65.00 Br md 11.80 Dpth 4.82 Welded, 1 dk	**(A31A2GX) General Cargo Ship** Grain: 1,610 Compartments: 2 Ho, ER 2 Ha: 2 (10.8 x 6.6)ER	**2 oil engines** driving 2 FP propellers Total Power: 1,442kW (1,960hp) 12.0kn Skoda 6L350PN 2 x 4 Stroke 6 Cy. 350 x 500 each-721kW (980bhp) CKD Praha-Praha AuxGen: 2 x 100kW a.c
8893506 - -	**TRUONG SA 08** **Truong Sa Construction Management of Navy Command (Ban Quan Ly Cong Trinh Truong Sa)** - *Haiphong* Vietnam	**1,038** 513 1,364	Class: (VR)	**1994 Ha Long Shipbuilding Co Ltd — Ha Long** Loa 70.75 Br ex - Dght 3.700 Lbp 65.11 Br md 11.80 Dpth 4.82 Welded, 1 dk	**(A31A2GX) General Cargo Ship** Grain: 1,610 Compartments: 2 Ho, ER 2 Ha: 2 (10.8 x 6.6)ER	**2 oil engines** driving 2 FP propellers Total Power: 1,442kW (1,960hp) 12.0kn Skoda 6L350PN 2 x 4 Stroke 6 Cy. 350 x 500 each-721kW (980bhp) CKD Praha-Praha AuxGen: 2 x 100kW a.c
9112507 - -	**TRUONG SA 10** **Truong Sa Construction Management of Navy Command (Ban Quan Ly Cong Trinh Truong Sa)** - *Haiphong* Vietnam	**1,038** 513 1,364	Class: (VR)	**1994 Ha Long Shipbuilding Co Ltd — Ha Long** Loa 70.75 Br ex - Dght 3.700 Lbp 65.00 Br md 11.80 Dpth 4.82 Welded, 1 dk	**(A31A2GX) General Cargo Ship** Grain: 1,610 Compartments: 2 Ho, ER 2 Ha: 2 (10.8 x 6.6)ER	**2 oil engines** driving 2 FP propellers Total Power: 1,442kW (1,960hp) 12.0kn Skoda 6L350PN 2 x 4 Stroke 6 Cy. 350 x 500 each-721kW (980bhp) CKD Praha-Praha AuxGen: 2 x 140kW a.c
8665430 *3WRE* -	**TRUONG THANH 01** *ex* Trung Thao 17 *-2008* *ex* Anh Tu 450 *-2007* **Agribank Leasing Co II** Tuong Thanh Transport Corp *Haiphong* Vietnam Official number: VNSG-02008-TD	**1,597** 724 2,813	Class: VR	**2007-10 Ha Long Shipbuilding Engineering JSC — Haiphong** Yd No: TKC48A - 01 Loa 74.36 Br ex 12.62 Dght 5.340 Lbp 70.90 Br md 12.60 Dpth 6.30 Welded, 1 dk	**(A12B2TR) Chemical/Products Tanker** Double Hull (13F) Liq: 2,791; Liq (Oil): 2,791 Compartments: 4 Wing Ta, 4 Wing Ta, ER	**1 oil engine** driving 1 FP propeller Total Power: 736kW (1,001hp) 9.5kn S.K.L. 8NVD48A-2U 1 x 4 Stroke 8 Cy. 320 x 480 736kW (1001bhp) (made 1990, fitted 2007) VEB Schwermaschinenbau "KarlLiebknecht" (SKL)-Magdeburg Fuel: 80.0
8665820 *3WTJ* -	**TRUONG THANH 08** *ex* Trng Nghia 18 *-2011* *ex* Hai Long 18 *-2008* **Truong Thanh Private Co** - *Haiphong* Vietnam Official number: VN-3230-VT	**499** 371 912	Class: VR	**2007-12 Thanh Long Shipbuilding Industry Co Ltd — Haiphong** Yd No: HT-141-02 Loa 55.85 Br ex 9.52 Dght 3.200 Lbp 52.98 Br md 9.50 Dpth 3.85 Welded, 1 dk	**(A31A2GX) General Cargo Ship** Bale: 1,218 Compartments: 2 Ho, ER 2 Ha: (13.0 x 5.6)ER (12.5 x 5.6)	**1 oil engine** driving 1 FP propeller Total Power: 600kW (816hp) 10.0kn Chinese Std. Type Z8170ZLC 1 x 4 Stroke 8 Cy. 170 x 200 600kW (816bhp) Weifang Diesel Engine Factory-China
8953942 *XVXE* -	**TRUONG THANH 09** *ex* Hoang Long 09 *-2003* *ex* Duc Tho 10 *-2000* **Truong Thanh Private Co** - *Haiphong* Vietnam Official number: VN-1331-VT	**370** 222 721	Class: VR	**1994 Song Lo Shipyard — Vinh Phu** Lengthened Loa 50.16 Br ex 7.60 Dght 3.450 Lbp 46.54 Br md 7.38 Dpth 4.10 Welded, 1 dk	**(A31A2GX) General Cargo Ship** Compartments: 2 Ho, ER 2 Ha: (10.5 x 4.0) (13.0 x 4.0)ER	**1 oil engine** driving 1 FP propeller Total Power: 294kW (400hp) S.K.L. 8NVD26A-2 1 x 4 Stroke 8 Cy. 180 x 260 294kW (400bhp) VEB Schwermaschinenbau "KarlLiebknecht" (SKL)-Magdeburg AuxGen: 1 x 4kW a.c Fuel: 22.0 (d.f.)
9023770 - -	**TRUONG VINH 09** **Truong Vinh Co Ltd** - *Haiphong* Vietnam Official number: VN-1488-VT	**499** 339 1,012	Class: VR	**2001-01 Thanh Long Co Ltd — Haiphong** Loa 55.60 Br ex 9.22 Dght 3.800 Lbp 51.50 Br md 9.00 Dpth 4.50 Welded, 1 dk	**(A31A2GX) General Cargo Ship**	**1 oil engine** driving 1 Propeller Total Power: 294kW (400hp) 10.0kn S.K.L. 8NVD26A-2 1 x 4 Stroke 8 Cy. 180 x 260 294kW (400bhp) (Re-engined ,made 1973, refitted 2001) SKL Motoren u. Systemtechnik AG-Magdeburg
8985579 - -	**TRUONG VINH 16** *ex* Moico-Alci *-2011* *ex* Hoang Long 05-ALCI *-2006* *ex* Hoang Phat 16 *-2004* *ex* Phu An 16 *-2004* **Agriculture Leasing Co I** Giang Son Tradind Shipping JSC *Haiphong* Vietnam MMSI: 574012577 Official number: VN-1801-VT	**499** 339 949	Class: VR	**2002-11 Trung Hai Private Enterprise — Haiphong** Loa 55.66 Br ex 9.02 Dght 3.400 Lbp 51.50 Br md 9.00 Dpth 4.10 Welded, 1 dk	**(A31A2GX) General Cargo Ship** Grain: 1,230 Compartments: 2 Ho, ER 2 Ha: ER 2 (12.5 x 5.6)	**1 oil engine** driving 1 FP propeller Total Power: 299kW (407hp) 10.0kn S.K.L. 8NVD36 1 x 4 Stroke 8 Cy. 240 x 360 299kW (407bhp) (Re-engined ,made 1987, refitted 2002) SKL Motoren u. Systemtechnik AG-Magdeburg AuxGen: 2 x 278kW 220V a.c Fuel: 17.0 (d.f.)

IMO / Call sign	Name / Owner / Port	Tonnage	Class	Build / Dimensions	Type	Machinery
9354002 *3WMC* -	**TRUONG XUAN 06-ALCI** **Agriculture Leasing Co I** Truong Xuan Shipping JSC (Cong Ty Co Phan VTB Truong Xuan) SatCom: Inmarsat C 457461010 *Haiphong* *Vietnam* MMSI: 574610000	**999** 615 1,965	Class: VR	**2005-04 Nam Ha Shipyard — Nam Ha** Loa 69.40 Br ex - Dght 4.400 Lbp 65.79 Br md 10.80 Dpth 5.50 Welded, 1 dk	**(A31A2GX) General Cargo Ship** Compartments: 2 Ho, ER 2 Ha: (15.0 x 7.3)ER (16.8 x 7.3)	**1 oil engine** driving 1 FP propeller Total Power: 721kW (980hp) Skoda 6L350PN 1 x 4 Stroke 6 Cy. 350 x 500 721kW (980bhp) CKD Praha-Praha AuxGen: 2 x 60kW 400V a.c
8667268 *3WYV* -	**TRUONG XUAN 08** *ex* Thai Phat 18 *-2013* **Xuan Truong Shipping Co Ltd** - *Haiphong* *Vietnam* Official number: VN-2728-VT	**999** 663 1,947	Class: VR	**2008-10 Haiphong Mechanical & Trading Co. — Haiphong** Yd No: THB12-19 Loa 69.85 Br ex 10.82 Dght 4.500 Lbp 65.95 Br md 10.80 Dpth 5.40 Welded, 1 dk	**(A31A2GX) General Cargo Ship** Grain: 2,268 Compartments: 2 Ho, ER 2 Ha: ER 2 (17.6 x 7.0)	**1 oil engine** driving 1 FP propeller Total Power: 720kW (979hp) 10.0kn Chinese Std. Type XCW6200ZC 1 x 4 Stroke 6 Cy. 200 x 270 720kW (979bhp) Weichai Power Co Ltd-China
9026760 *3WHU* -	**TRUONG XUAN 09-ALCI** **Agriculture Leasing Co I** Truong Xuan Shipping JSC (Cong Ty Co Phan VTB Truong Xuan) *Haiphong* *Vietnam* MMSI: 574719000	**999** 615 2,028	Class: VR	**2004-10 Nam Ha Shipyard — Nam Ha** Yd No: HT-27 Loa 69.40 Br ex 10.82 Dght 4.500 Lbp 65.80 Br md 10.80 Dpth 5.50 Welded, 1 dk	**(A31A2GX) General Cargo Ship**	**1 oil engine** driving 1 FP propeller Total Power: 736kW (1,001hp) 10.0kn S.K.L. 8NVD48A-1U 1 x 4 Stroke 8 Cy. 320 x 480 736kW (1001bhp) (made 1980) SKL Motoren u. Systemtechnik AG-Magdeburg
8665038 *3WVI* -	**TRUONG XUAN 18** *ex* Ngoc Anh 18 *-2007* **Truong Xuan Shipping JSC (Cong Ty Co Phan VTB Truong Xuan)** - *Haiphong* *Vietnam* Official number: VN-2167-VT	**999** 609 1,974	Class: VR	**2005-10 Nam Ha Shipyard — Nam Ha** Yd No: HT63 Loa 69.40 Br ex 10.82 Dght 4.500 Lbp 65.80 Br md 10.80 Dpth 5.50 Welded, 1 dk	**(A31A2GX) General Cargo Ship** Grain: 2,280 Compartments: 2 Ho, ER 2 Ha: ER 2 (15.0 x 7.0)	**1 oil engine** reduction geared to sc. shaft driving 1 FP propeller Total Power: 566kW (770hp) 9.5kn S.K.L. 8NVD48A-2U 1 x 4 Stroke 8 Cy. 320 x 480 566kW (770bhp) (made 2000, fitted 2005) SKL Motoren u. Systemtechnik AG-Magdeburg AuxGen: 2 x 56kW 400V a.c
8226777 *UIGS* -	**TRUSOVSKIY** **Transvneshtrade Ltd** - *Astrakhan* *Russia* Official number: 833124	**2,399** 719 913	Class: (RS)	**1983-12 Sudostroitelnyy Zavod "Baltiya" — Klaypeda** Yd No: 503 Loa 85.10 Br ex 13.03 Dght 3.901 Lbp 76.80 Br md 13.00 Dpth 6.51 Welded	**(B11B2FV) Fishing Vessel** Ins: 1,313 Compartments: 2 Ho Ice Capable	**1 oil engine** driving 1 FP propeller Total Power: 853kW (1,160hp) 11.3kn S.K.L. 8NVD48A-2U 1 x 4 Stroke 8 Cy. 320 x 480 853kW (1160bhp) VEB Schwermaschinenbau "KarlLiebknecht" (SKL)-Magdeburg AuxGen: 2 x 320kW a.c, 1 x 150kW a.c Fuel: 213.0 (d.f.)
7602314 *9LD2408* -	**TRUST** *ex* Swift Trader *-1999* *ex* Swift *-1985* **Shipright Traders Co SA** Trust Marine *Freetown* *Sierra Leone* MMSI: 667005108 Official number: SL105108	*1,072* 724 2,621	Class: IM (GL) (BV)	**1977-05 Bodewes' Scheepswerven B.V. — Hoogezand** Yd No: 530 Loa 79.81 Br ex - Dght 5.173 Lbp 72.62 Br md 13.01 Dpth 7.52 Welded, 1 dk & S dk	**(A31A2GX) General Cargo Ship** Grain: 4,286; Bale: 3,856 2 Ha: (21.5 x 9.5) (14.4 x 9.5)ER Cranes: 2x15t,1x3t	**1 oil engine** reduction geared to sc. shaft driving 1 FP propeller Total Power: 1,324kW (1,800hp) 12.0kn MaK 6M452AK 1 x 4 Stroke 6 Cy. 320 x 450 1324kW (1800bhp) MaK Maschinenbau GmbH-Kiel
8901690 - -	**TRUST** *ex* Daitom *-2008* *ex* Vega II *-2008* *ex* Sakichi Maru No. 7 *-2004* *ex* Kaigata Maru No. 67 *-2001* - -	*149* 49 -		**1988 Kesennuma Tekko — Kesennuma** Yd No: 268 L reg 31.60 Br ex - Dght 2.500 Lbp - Br md 6.40 Dpth 2.80 Welded	**(B11B2FV) Fishing Vessel**	**1 oil engine** driving 1 FP propeller
6801080 - -	**TRUST 1** *ex* Geni II *-2009* *ex* Jinan *-2000* *ex* Irismed *-1996* *ex* Cattle Trail Two *-1995* *ex* Samir One *-1994* *ex* Samir I *-1993* *ex* Taibah V *-1992* *ex* Afros *-1985* *ex* Bore V *-1977* **Trust Shipping SA** -	**3,282** 2,058 3,485	Class: (LR) (GL) (NV) ✠ Classed LR until 22/3/89	**1968-04 Rauma-Repola Oy — Rauma** Yd No: 187 Converted From: Ro-Ro Cargo Ship-1992 Lengthened-1971 Loa 100.01 Br ex 14.56 Dght 6.217 Lbp 92.21 Br md 14.50 Dpth 8.01 Welded, 2 dks	**(A35A2RR) Ro-Ro Cargo Ship** Stern door & ramp Grain: 7,089; Bale: 6,051 Compartments: 1 Ho, ER, 1 Tw Dk 3 Ha: (14.3 x 8.6)2 (8.9 x 8.6)ER Cranes: 1x10t,2x5t Ice Capable	**2 oil engines** sr geared to sc. shaft driving 1 CP propeller Total Power: 2,428kW (3,302hp) 14.5kn MWM TBRHS345SU 2 x 4 Stroke 6 Cy. 360 x 450 each-1214kW (1651bhp) Motoren Werke Mannheim AG (MWM)-West Germany AuxGen: 2 x 164kW 450V 60Hz a.c, 1 x 137kW 450V 60Hz a.c Fuel: 334.5 (r.f.) 10.0pd
8102995 *HP5990* -	**TRUST 2** *ex* Lamnalco 22 *-2009* *ex* Lamnalco Merlin *-1982* **GT Oil DMCC** - *Panama* *Panama* Official number: 4254311	**226** 67 -	Class: (BV) (AB)	**1980-10 Hudson Shipbuilders, Inc. (HUDSHIP) — Pascagoula, Ms** Yd No: 73 Loa 34.14 Br ex 7.95 Dght 3.020 Lbp 32.85 Br md 7.92 Dpth 3.35 Welded, 1 dk	**(B34L2QU) Utility Vessel**	**2 oil engines** sr reverse geared to sc. shafts driving 2 FP propellers Total Power: 884kW (1,202hp) 10.0kn G.M. (Detroit Diesel) 16V-92 2 x Vee 2 Stroke 16 Cy. 123 x 127 each-442kW (601bhp) General Motors Detroit DieselAllison Divn-USA AuxGen: 2 x 50kW 440V 60Hz a.c Fuel: 67.0 (d.f.) 4.5pd
8657108 *YDA6886* -	**TRUST 17** **PT Trust Eadyra Line** - *Samarinda* *Indonesia* MMSI: 525015979 Official number: 2011 Ilk No.6031/L	**145** 44 -	Class: KI	**2012-03 PT Syukur Bersaudara — Samarinda** Yd No: 15349 Loa 24.03 Br ex - Dght 2.790 Lbp 24.01 Br md 7.00 Dpth 3.40 Welded, 1 dk	**(B32A2ST) Tug**	**2 oil engines** reduction geared to sc. shafts driving 2 Propellers Total Power: 970kW (1,318hp) Yanmar 6AYM-WST 2 x 4 Stroke 6 Cy. 155 x 180 each-485kW (659bhp) Yanmar Diesel Engine Co Ltd-Japan AuxGen: 2 x 44kW 400V a.c
8652067 - -	**TRUST-18** **PT Trust Line Marine** - *Samarinda* *Indonesia*	**173** 52 -	Class: KI	**2011-04 PT Mangkupalas Mitra Makmur — Samarinda** Loa 25.50 Br ex - Dght 2.690 Lbp 24.00 Br md 7.50 Dpth 3.30 Welded, 1 dk	**(B32A2ST) Tug**	**2 oil engines** reduction geared to sc. shafts driving 2 Propellers AuxGen: 2 x 30kW 400V a.c
8657081 *YDA4928* -	**TRUST 19** **PT Trust Eadyra Line** - *Tanjung Priok* *Indonesia* Official number: 2011 Ba No.2452/L	**183** 55 -	Class: KI	**2011-08 PT Mangkupalas Mitra Makmur — Samarinda** Yd No: 15043 Loa 26.00 Br ex - Dght 2.880 Lbp 24.72 Br md 8.00 Dpth 3.60 Welded, 1 dk	**(B32A2ST) Tug**	**2 oil engines** reduction geared to sc. shafts driving 2 Propellers Total Power: 1,104kW (1,500hp) Volvo Penta D16MH 2 x 4 Stroke 6 Cy. 144 x 165 each-552kW (750bhp) AB Volvo Penta-Sweden AuxGen: 2 x 65kW 400V a.c
8958813 *YD6376* -	**TRUST 27** *ex* Syukur 02 *-1998* **PT Trust Line Marine** - *Samarinda* *Indonesia* Official number: 1999 IIK NO. 2447/L	**145** 44 -	Class: KI	**1998-02 PT Syukur Bersaudara — Samarinda** Loa 26.00 Br ex - Dght - Lbp 23.25 Br md 7.00 Dpth 3.00 Welded, 1 dk	**(B32A2ST) Tug**	**2 oil engines** reduction geared to sc. shafts driving 2 FP propellers Total Power: 1,176kW (1,598hp) Yanmar 6N165-EN 2 x 4 Stroke 6 Cy. 165 x 232 each-588kW (799bhp) Yanmar Diesel Engine Co Ltd-Japan
9675157 *YDA6919* -	**TRUST 29** **PT Trust Line Marine** - *Samarinda* *Indonesia* Official number: 2012 IIK NO. 6087/L	**151** 46 -	Class: KI	**2012-06 PT Syukur Bersaudara — Samarinda** Yd No: 15630 Loa 23.98 Br ex 7.00 Dght 2.790 Lbp 22.60 Br md - Dpth 3.40 Welded, 1 dk	**(B32A2ST) Tug**	**2 oil engines** reduction geared to sc. shafts driving 2 Propellers Total Power: 980kW (1,332hp) Mitsubishi S6A3-MPTK 2 x 4 Stroke 6 Cy. 150 x 175 each-490kW (666bhp) Mitsubishi Heavy Industries Ltd-Japan AuxGen: 3 x 44kW 400V a.c
8652079 *YDA6694* -	**TRUST-33** **PT Trust Line Marine** - *Samarinda* *Indonesia* Official number: 2011 IIK NO. 5442/L	**229** 69 -	Class: KI	**2011-03 PT Mangkupalas Mitra Makmur — Samarinda** Yd No: 14430 Loa 29.50 Br ex 8.50 Dght 1.690 Lbp 27.84 Br md 7.50 Dpth 3.60 Welded, 1 dk	**(B32A2ST) Tug**	**2 oil engines** reduction geared to sc. shafts driving 2 Propellers Total Power: 1,716kW (2,334hp) Mitsubishi S12A2-MPTK 2 x Vee 4 Stroke 12 Cy. 150 x 160 each-858kW (1167bhp) Mitsubishi Heavy Industries Ltd-Japan AuxGen: 2 x 60kW 400V a.c
8657079 *YDB4035* -	**TRUST 38** **PT Trust Eadyra Line** - *Tanjung Priok* *Indonesia* MMSI: 525015980 Official number: 2012 Ba No.2720/L	**149** 45 -	Class: KI	**2012-01 PT Syukur Bersaudara — Samarinda** Yd No: 15105 Loa 23.97 Br ex - Dght 2.790 Lbp 22.60 Br md 7.00 Dpth 3.40 Welded, 1 dk	**(B32A2ST) Tug**	**2 oil engines** reduction geared to sc. shafts driving 2 FP propellers Total Power: 980kW (1,332hp) Mitsubishi S6A3-MPTK 2 x 4 Stroke 6 Cy. 150 x 175 each-490kW (666bhp) Mitsubishi Heavy Industries Ltd-Japan AuxGen: 2 x 44kW 400V a.c

8657093 *YDA6716* -	**TRUST 55** - **PT Trust Eadyra Line** - *Samarinda* *Indonesia* Official number: 2011 IIk No.5879/L	**217** 66 -	Class: KI	**2011-11 PT Mangkupalas Mitra Makmur — Samarinda** Yd No: 15106 Loa 28.97 Br ex - Dght 2.990 Lbp 26.83 Br md 8.00 Dpth 3.80 Welded, 1 dk	**(B32A2ST) Tug**	**2 oil engines** reduction geared to sc. shafts driving 2 Propellers Total Power: 1,766kW (2,402hp) Mitsubishi S12A3-MTK 2 x Vee 4 Stroke 12 Cy. each-883kW (1201bhp) Mitsubishi Heavy Industries Ltd-Japan AuxGen: 2 x 66kW 400V a.c
8662995 - -	**TRUST 72** - **PT Trust Eadyra Line** - *Batam* *Indonesia*	**222** 67 -	Class: KI	**2012-10 PT Batam Marina Shipyard — Batam** Loa 29.00 Br ex - Dght - Lbp 27.09 Br md 8.00 Dpth 3.70 Welded, 1 dk	**(B32A2ST) Tug**	**2 oil engines** reduction geared to sc. shafts driving 2 FP propellers Total Power: 1,766kW (2,402hp) Yanmar 12AYM-WST 2 x Vee 4 Stroke 12 Cy. 155 x 180 each-883kW (1201bhp) Yanmar Diesel Engine Co Ltd-Japan AuxGen: 2 x 47kW a.c
7410321 *9GEC* AFT 23	**TRUST 77** *ex* Gbese 9 *-2004* *ex* Baek Du San No. 9 *-1982* **Trust Allied Fishing Ventures Ltd** - *Takoradi* *Ghana* MMSI: 627679000 Official number: 316679	*416* 201 489	Class: (KR) (NK)	**1975-05 Miho Zosensho K.K. — Shimizu** Yd No: 1027 Loa 55.45 Br ex 8.51 Dght 3.549 Lbp 47.00 Br md 8.49 Dpth 3.94 Welded, 1 dk	**(B11B2FV) Fishing Vessel** Bale: 418 12 Ha: (1.6 x 1.6)10 (1.3 x 1.3) (0.9 x 0.9) Derricks: 1x0.5t	**1 oil engine** driving 1 FP propeller Total Power: 1,177kW (1,600hp) 12.0kn Niigata 6M31X 1 x 4 Stroke 6 Cy. 310 x 460 1177kW (1600bhp) Niigata Engineering Co Ltd-Japan AuxGen: 2 x 200kW Fuel: 227.5 6.0pd
9596416 *YDA4677* -	**TRUST-77** - **PT Trust Line Marine** - *Tanjung Priok* *Indonesia*	**233** 70 -	Class: KI	**2010-06 PT Timas Merak — Cilegon** Yd No: /TMS-MRK/GAL Loa 29.00 Br ex - Dght 2.930 Lbp 27.84 Br md 8.50 Dpth 3.75 Welded, 1 dk	**(B32A2ST) Tug**	**2 oil engines** reduction geared to sc. shafts driving 2 Propellers Total Power: 1,618kW (2,200hp) Mitsubishi S12A2-MPTK 2 x Vee 4 Stroke 12 Cy. 150 x 160 each-809kW (1100bhp) Mitsubishi Heavy Industries Ltd-Japan AuxGen: 2 x 50kW 400V a.c
7626956 *9GJP* AFT 51	**TRUST 79** *ex* Joe B *-2008* *ex* Taiyo Maru No. 8 *-1995* *ex* Waka Maru No. 25 *-1984* **Trust Allied Fishing Ventures Ltd** - *Takoradi* *Ghana* MMSI: 627850000 Official number: 316850	*499* 263 -		**1977-01 Uchida Zosen — Ise** Yd No: 772 Loa - Br ex - Dght 3.852 Lbp 54.56 Br md 9.31 Dpth 4.27 Welded, 1 dk	**(B11B2FV) Fishing Vessel**	**1 oil engine** driving 1 FP propeller Total Power: 1,545kW (2,101hp) Daihatsu 6DSM-32 1 x 4 Stroke 6 Cy. 320 x 380 1545kW (2101bhp) Daihatsu Diesel Manufacturing Co Lt-Japan
9602497 *YDA4688* -	**TRUST-88** - **PT Trust Line Marine** - *Tanjung Priok* *Indonesia* Official number: Ba No. 1930/L	**233** 70 -	Class: KI	**2010-07 PT Timas Merak — Cilegon** Yd No: TMS/VII/2010 Loa 29.00 Br ex - Dght 3.750 Lbp 27.84 Br md 8.50 Dpth 3.75 Welded, 1 dk	**(B32A2ST) Tug**	**2 oil engines** reduction geared to sc. shafts driving 2 Propellers Total Power: 1,716kW (2,334hp) Mitsubishi S12A2-MPTK 2 x Vee 4 Stroke 12 Cy. 150 x 160 each-858kW (1167bhp) Mitsubishi Heavy Industries Ltd-Japan
8652055 *YDA6629* -	**TRUST-99** - **PT Trust Line Marine** - *Samarinda* *Indonesia* Official number: 2010 IIK NO. 5376/L	**259** 78 -	Class: KI	**2010-12 PT Mangkupalas Mitra Makmur — Samarinda** Yd No: 13482 Loa 29.50 Br ex - Dght 2.800 Lbp 27.84 Br md 9.00 Dpth 3.75 Welded, 1 dk	**(B32A2ST) Tug**	**2 oil engines** reduction geared to sc. shafts driving 2 Propellers Total Power: 1,618kW (2,200hp) Yanmar 12LAK (M)-STE2 2 x Vee 4 Stroke 12 Cy. 150 x 165 each-809kW (1100bhp) Yanmar Diesel Engine Co Ltd-Japan
9460655 *9V9097* -	**TRUST AGILITY** - **Trust Energy Resources Pte Ltd** Bernhard Schulte Shipmanagement (Hong Kong) Ltd *Singapore* *Singapore* MMSI: 566064000 Official number: 396627	**94,817** 58,778 180,585 T/cm 124.0	Class: AB	**2011-05 STX Offshore & Shipbuilding Co Ltd — Changwon (Jinhae Shipyard)** Yd No: 3019 Loa 292.00 (BB) Br ex - Dght 18.200 Lbp 283.00 Br md 45.00 Dpth 24.80 Welded, 1 dk	**(A21A2BC) Bulk Carrier** Double Bottom Entire Compartment Length Grain: 199,536 Compartments: 9 Ho, ER 9 Ha: 6 (15.8 x 20.4)ER 3 (15.8 x 15.3)	**1 oil engine** driving 1 FP propeller Total Power: 18,660kW (25,370hp) 14.3kn MAN-B&W 6S70MC-C 1 x 2 Stroke 6 Cy. 700 x 2800 18660kW (25370bhp) STX Engine Co Ltd-South Korea AuxGen: 3 x 900kW a.c Fuel: 260.0 (d.f.) 4540.0 (r.f.)
7121695 *3ECZ* -	**TRUST GLORY** *ex* Chang Xin 101 *-2005* *ex* Ryoko Maru *-1995* **S Glory Shipping SA** Se Ha Co Ltd *Panama* *Panama* MMSI: 371497000 Official number: 3136506B	*5,396* 1,971 8,438	Class: UV (CC) (NK)	**1972-01 Mitsubishi Heavy Industries Ltd. — Shimonoseki** Yd No: 705 Loa 123.98 Br ex 17.73 Dght 7.200 Lbp 115.02 Br md 17.68 Dpth 9.20 Welded, 1 dk	**(A24A2BT) Cement Carrier** Grain: 7,117	**1 oil engine** driving 1 FP propeller Total Power: 3,236kW (4,400hp) 13.3kn Mitsubishi 7UET45/75C 1 x 2 Stroke 7 Cy. 450 x 750 3236kW (4400bhp) Kobe Hatsudoki Seizosho-Japan AuxGen: 3 x 200kW 450V 60Hz a.c Fuel: 21.0 (d.f.) 168.5 (r.f.) 14.0pd
8419362 *PMMT* -	**TRUST HONOR** *ex* Golden Craig *-2006* **PT Waruna Nusa Sentana** - *Belawan* *Indonesia* MMSI: 525015371	**4,409** 2,286 7,088 T/cm 15.7	Class: KI (NK)	**1985-01 Higaki Zosen K.K. — Imabari** Yd No: 322 Loa 107.78 (BB) Br ex 17.63 Dght 6.893 Lbp 100.01 Br md 17.61 Dpth 8.41 Welded, 1 dk	**(A12B2TR) Chemical/Products Tanker** Liq: 7,850; Liq (Oil): 7,850 Cargo Heating Coils Compartments: 12 Ta, ER 5 Cargo Pump (s) Manifold: Bow/CM: 53m	**1 oil engine** driving 1 FP propeller Total Power: 2,868kW (3,899hp) 12.3kn Mitsubishi 6UEC37L 1 x 2 Stroke 6 Cy. 370 x 880 2868kW (3899bhp) Kobe Hatsudoki KK-Japan AuxGen: 2 x 240kW a.c
9479888 *9V9098* -	**TRUST INTEGRITY** - **Trust Energy Resources Pte Ltd** Bernhard Schulte Shipmanagement (Singapore) Pte Ltd *Singapore* *Singapore* MMSI: 566121000 Official number: 396628	**94,817** 58,778 180,556 T/cm 124.0	Class: AB	**2011-06 STX Offshore & Shipbuilding Co Ltd — Changwon (Jinhae Shipyard)** Yd No: 3020 Loa 292.00 (BB) Br ex - Dght 18.200 Lbp 283.00 Br md 45.00 Dpth 24.80 Welded, 1 dk	**(A21A2BC) Bulk Carrier** Double Bottom Entire Compartment Length Grain: 199,536 Compartments: 9 Ho, ER 9 Ha: 7 (15.8 x 20.4)ER 2 (15.8 x 15.3)	**1 oil engine** driving 1 FP propeller Total Power: 18,660kW (25,370hp) 14.3kn MAN-B&W 6S70MC-C 1 x 2 Stroke 6 Cy. 700 x 2800 18660kW (25370bhp) STX Engine Co Ltd-South Korea AuxGen: 3 x 900kW a.c Fuel: 260.0 (d.f.) 4540.0 (r.f.)
9610236 *3FIV7* -	**TRUST STAR** - **Nissen Kaiun Co Ltd & Southern Route Maritime SA** Nissen Kaiun Co Ltd (Nissen Kaiun KK) *Panama* *Panama* MMSI: 371416000 Official number: 4436912	**21,699** 12,253 36,338	Class: NK	**2012-11 Shikoku Dockyard Co. Ltd. — Takamatsu** Yd No: 1080 Loa 176.50 (BB) Br ex - Dght 10.718 Lbp 168.50 Br md 28.80 Dpth 15.20 Welded, 1 dk	**(A21A2BC) Bulk Carrier** Grain: 47,089; Bale: 45,414 Compartments: 5 Ho, ER 5 Ha: ER Cranes: 4x30.5t	**1 oil engine** driving 1 FP propeller Total Power: 7,300kW (9,925hp) 14.3kn MAN-B&W 6S46MC-C 1 x 2 Stroke 6 Cy. 460 x 1932 7300kW (9925bhp) Mitsui Engineering & Shipbuilding CLtd-Japan AuxGen: 3 x 421kW a.c Fuel: 1950.0
8902955 *PJIZ* -	**TRUSTEE** *ex* Front Granite *-2008* *ex* Granite *-2001* **Trustee BV** Dockwise Shipping BV *Willemstad* *Curacao* MMSI: 306009000 Official number: 2008-C-1943	**42,515** 12,755 54,013 T/cm 108.0	Class: NV	**1991-03 Brodogradiliste Split (Brodosplit) — Split** Yd No: 367 Converted From: Crude Oil Tanker-2008 Shortened-2008 Loa 216.81 (BB) Br ex 44.54 Dght 10.432 Lbp 207.87 Br md 44.51 Dpth 14.01 Welded, 1 dk	**(A38C3GH) Heavy Load Carrier, semi submersible**	**1 oil engine** driving 1 FP propeller Total Power: 11,952kW (16,250hp) 14.0kn B&W 6S70MC 1 x 2 Stroke 6 Cy. 700 x 2674 11952kW (16250bhp) Brodogradiliste Split (Brodosplit)-Yugoslavia AuxGen: 3 x 1200kW 440V 60Hz a.c Thrusters: 1 Tunnel thruster (f) Fuel: 272.0 (d.f.) 4117.0 (r.f.) 45.0pd
7713876 *XUEW5* -	**TRUSTWORTHY** *ex* Irine M. *-2011* *ex* Perseus *-2004* *ex* Aghia Marina *-2000* *ex* Bright Skies *-1994* *ex* Bright Peak *-1984* **Realistic Stand Shipping SA** - SatCom: Inmarsat C 451571110 *Phnom Penh* *Cambodia* MMSI: 515711000 Official number: 1277914	**10,704** 6,461 17,720 T/cm 27.4	Class: BR (Class contemplated) PR (BV) (NK)	**1978-04 Imabari Shipbuilding Co Ltd — Imabari EH (Imabari Shipyard)** Yd No: 374 Loa 146.69 (BB) Br ex 22.92 Dght 9.056 Lbp 136.02 Br md 22.86 Dpth 12.22 Welded, 1 dk	**(A21A2BC) Bulk Carrier** Grain: 22,606; Bale: 21,684 Compartments: 4 Ho, ER 4 Ha: (14.4 x 9.6)3 (17.6 x 11.2)ER Derricks: 4x17.5t	**1 oil engine** driving 1 FP propeller Total Power: 5,884kW (8,000hp) 14.0kn Mitsubishi 6UEC52/105E 1 x 2 Stroke 6 Cy. 520 x 1050 5884kW (8000bhp) Akasaka Tekkosho KK (Akasaka DieselLtd)-Japan AuxGen: 2 x 320kW
8848678 - -	**TRUSTY** *ex* Cygnus *-2009* *ex* Fukuho Maru No. 23 *-2003* **Epsilon Co Ltd** Epsilon Co Ltd	**207** 63 -		**1976 Kitanihon Zosen K.K. — Hachinohe** L reg 28.80 Br ex - Dght - Lbp - Br md 6.20 Dpth 2.60 Welded, 1 dk	**(B11B2FV) Fishing Vessel**	**1 oil engine** driving 1 FP propeller Total Power: 353kW (480hp) Daihatsu 1 x 4 Stroke 353kW (480bhp) Daihatsu Diesel Manufacturing Co Lt-Japan

9238545 *9HA2867* -	**TRUVA 1** *ex Chiloe -2011* **Horizon Bulk SA** Horizon Gemi Isletmeciligi Sanayi ve Ticaret AS *Valletta* *Malta* MMSI: 256466000 Official number: 9238545	**26,234** 15,577 46,708 T/cm 50.2	Class: NK	**2001-01 Kanasashi Heavy Industries Co Ltd — Toyohashi AI** Yd No: 3537 Loa 183.04 (BB) Br ex - Dght 11.671 Lbp 174.30 Br md 31.00 Dpth 16.47 Welded, 1 dk	**(A21A2BC) Bulk Carrier** Grain: 59,077; Bale: 58,014 Compartments: 5 Ho, ER 5 Ha: (14.4 x 15.6)4 (20.0 x 15.6)ER Cranes: 4x30t	**1 oil engine** driving 1 FP propeller Total Power: 7,488kW (10,181hp) 14.3kn Mitsubishi 6UEC52LS 1 x 2 Stroke 6 Cy. 520 x 1850 7488kW (10181bhp) Kobe Hatsudoki KK-Japan AuxGen: 3 x 440kW 450V a.c Fuel: 1902.0
9311543 *UBEG6* -	**TRUVOR** *ex Eridan -2009* **JSC 'Sovfracht-Primorsk'** - *St Petersburg* *Russia* MMSI: 273348430	**468** 140 175 T/cm 3.3	Class: RS	**2004-11 UAB Vakaru Laivu Remontas (JSC Western Shiprepair) — Klaipeda** (Hull) Yd No: 17 **2004-11 BLRT Laevaehitus OU — Tallinn** Loa 34.20 Br ex 12.70 Dght 3.900 Lbp 30.46 Br md 12.10 Dpth 5.63 Welded, 1 dk	**(B32A2ST) Tug** Cranes: 1x5.3t Ice Capable	**2 oil engines** geared to sc. shafts driving 2 Z propellers Total Power: 3,730kW (5,072hp) 11.0kn Caterpillar 3516B 2 x Vee 4 Stroke 16 Cy. 170 x 190 each-1865kW (2536bhp) Caterpillar Inc-USA AuxGen: 2 x 150kW 380/220V 50Hz a.c Fuel: 120.0 (d.f.)
8932584 - -	**TRUZHENIK** *launched as* BK-903 *-1974* **SE Sea Commercial Port of Illichivsk** - *Illichevsk* *Ukraine* Official number: 731895	*111* - 24	Class: (RS)	**1974 "Petrozavod" — Leningrad** Yd No: 562 Loa 24.20 Br ex 7.25 Dght 2.260 Lbp 22.55 Br md - Dpth 2.96 Welded, 1 dk	**(B32A2ST) Tug**	**2 oil engines** gearing integral to driving 2 Voith-Schneider propellers Total Power: 662kW (900hp) 9.8kn Pervomaysk 6CHN25/34 2 x 4 Stroke 6 Cy. 250 x 340 each-331kW (450bhp) Pervomaydizelmash (PDM)-Pervomaysk AuxGen: 1 x 30kW, 1 x 25kW Fuel: 16.0 (d.f.)
9100451 *UBHK9* -	**TRUZHENIK** *ex Nichiyasu Maru -2013* **'Supplier' Co Ltd (OOO Snabzhenets)** - *Vostochnyy* *Russia* MMSI: 273332070	**732** 314 1,119	Class: RS (NK)	**1994-06 Narasaki Zosen KK — Muroran HK** Yd No: 1144 Loa 65.89 (BB) Br ex - Dght 3.952 Lbp 61.00 Br md 10.20 Dpth 4.55 Welded, 1 dk	**(A12A2TC) Chemical Tanker** Liq: 1,196	**1 oil engine** reverse geared to sc. shaft driving 1 FP propeller Total Power: 736kW (1,001hp) 10.5kn Akasaka A28S 1 x 4 Stroke 6 Cy. 280 x 550 736kW (1001bhp) Akasaka Tekkosho KK (Akasaka DieselLtd)-Japan AuxGen: 2 x 120kW a.c Fuel: 60.0 (d.f.)
7111523 - -	**TRUZHENIK** - **OOO 'Itaka'** -	**172** 51 100	Class: (RS)	**1971-05 Astrakhanskaya Sudoverf im. "Kirova" — Astrakhan** Yd No: 22 Loa 34.02 Br ex 7.12 Dght 2.890 Lbp 31.19 Br md - Dpth 3.66 Welded, 1 dk	**(B11B2FV) Fishing Vessel** Bale: 95 Compartments: 1 Ho, ER 1 Ha: (1.6 x 1.3) Derricks: 2x2t; Winches: 2 Ice Capable	**1 oil engine** driving 1 FP propeller Total Power: 224kW (305hp) 9.0kn S.K.L. 8NVD36-1U 1 x 4 Stroke 8 Cy. 240 x 360 224kW (305bhp) VEB Schwermaschinenbau "KarlLiebknecht" (SKL)-Magdeburg
9160322 *LNUN* H-718-B	**TRYGVASON** *ex Saevikson -2009 ex Western Viking -2005* **Trygvason AS** - *Haugesund* *Norway* MMSI: 259111000	**832** 249 1,000	Class: NV	**1997-09 Karstensens Skibsvaerft A/S — Skagen** Yd No: 374 Loa 48.30 (BB) Br ex - Dght - Lbp 42.48 Br md 10.50 Dpth 5.30 Welded, 2 dks	**(B11A2FT) Trawler** Liq: 870	**1 oil engine** reduction geared to sc. shaft driving 1 CP propeller Total Power: 2,641kW (3,591hp) 14.5kn MaK 6M32 1 x 4 Stroke 6 Cy. 320 x 480 2641kW (3591bhp) MaK Motoren GmbH & Co. KG-Kiel AuxGen: 1 x 1505kW 220/380V 50Hz a.c, 1 x 760kW 220/380V 50Hz a.c Thrusters: 1 Thwart. FP thruster (f); 1 Tunnel thruster (a)
9083419 *YD2036* -	**TS 24.5 1** - **Interbenua Medan Perkasa Pte Ltd** - *Belawan* *Indonesia*	**158** 94 102	Class: KI (BV)	**1993-06 Hangzhou Dongfeng Shipyard — Hangzhou ZJ** Yd No: 229 Loa 24.50 Br ex 7.60 Dght 3.220 Lbp 22.90 Br md - Dpth 3.86 Welded, 1 dk	**(B32A2ST) Tug**	**2 oil engines** geared to sc. shafts driving 2 FP propellers Total Power: 1,538kW (2,092hp) 10.0kn Caterpillar 3412TA 2 x Vee 4 Stroke 12 Cy. 137 x 152 each-769kW (1046bhp) Caterpillar Inc-USA Fuel: 78.0 (d.f.)
8861797 *YD2034* -	**TS 29-3** - **PT Raja Garuda Maskapai** - *Belawan* *Indonesia*	**209** 63 -	Class: KI (BV)	**1991 Jiangsu Xinhua Shipyard Co Ltd — Nanjing JS** Yd No: 189 Loa 29.90 Br ex 8.20 Dght 3.110 Lbp 24.04 Br md - Dpth 4.07 Welded, 1 dk	**(B32A2ST) Tug**	**2 oil engines** reduction geared to sc. shafts driving 2 FP propellers Total Power: 1,194kW (1,624hp) 11.0kn Cummins KTA-38-M 2 x Vee 4 Stroke 12 Cy. 159 x 159 each-597kW (812bhp) Cummins Engine Co Ltd-United Kingdom AuxGen: 2 x 128kW 220/400V 50Hz a.c
8884646 - -	**TS 802** *ex Unicast -1997* **UDL Marine Assets (Hong Kong) Ltd** -	*166* - -	Class: (BV)	**1989 Guangdong New China Shipyard Co Ltd — Dongguan GD** Loa 22.57 Br ex - Dght 2.450 Lbp 20.50 Br md 6.80 Dpth 3.41 Welded, 1 dk	**(B32A2ST) Tug**	**1 oil engine** geared to sc. shaft driving 1 FP propeller Total Power: 637kW (866hp) 11.0kn Caterpillar 3508TA 1 x Vee 4 Stroke 8 Cy. 170 x 190 637kW (866hp) Caterpillar Inc-USA Fuel: 19.0 (d.f.)
8845327 - -	**TS 803** *ex Unichamp -1996* - - -	*137* 91 -	Class: (BV)	**1990 Xiamen Shipyard — Xiamen FJ** Yd No: 431 Loa 23.65 Br ex - Dght - Lbp 21.60 Br md 6.80 Dpth 3.60 Welded, 1 dk	**(B32A2ST) Tug**	**1 oil engine** geared to sc. shaft driving 1 FP propeller Total Power: 637kW (866hp) 8.0kn Caterpillar 3508TA 1 x Vee 4 Stroke 8 Cy. 170 x 190 637kW (866bhp) Caterpillar Inc-USA
8890229 - -	**TS 804** *ex Uniwealth -1996* - - -	*137* 91 -	Class: (BV)	**1990 Xiamen Shipyard — Xiamen FJ** Yd No: 44 Loa 23.65 Br ex - Dght 2.720 Lbp 21.60 Br md 6.80 Dpth 3.60 Welded, 1 dk	**(B32A2ST) Tug**	**1 oil engine** geared to sc. shaft driving 1 FP propeller Total Power: 637kW (866hp) 8.0kn Caterpillar 3508TA 1 x Vee 4 Stroke 8 Cy. 170 x 190 637kW (866bhp) Caterpillar Inc-USA
8860987 - -	**TS 1201** *ex Unison -1995 ex Marine Lord No. 2 -1992* **UDL Offshore Pte Ltd** -	**142** 94 -	Class: (BV)	**1989-01 Guangdong Jiangmen Shipyard — Jiangmen GD** Yd No: 4 Loa 24.01 Br ex 6.80 Dght 2.550 Lbp 21.66 Br md - Dpth 3.60 Welded, 1 dk	**(B32A2ST) Tug**	**1 oil engine** driving 1 FP propeller Total Power: 953kW (1,296hp) Caterpillar 3512TA 1 x Vee 4 Stroke 12 Cy. 170 x 190 953kW (1296bhp) Caterpillar Inc-USA Fuel: 26.0 (d.f.)
8865705 - -	**TS 1202** *ex Unifame -1995 ex Marine Lord No. 1 -1993* **UDL Offshore Pte Ltd** -	*142* 94 -	Class: (BV)	**1989-01 Guangdong Jiangmen Shipyard — Jiangmen GD** Yd No: 3 Loa 23.65 Br ex 6.80 Dght 2.550 Lbp 21.60 Br md - Dpth 3.60 Welded, 1 dk	**(B32A2ST) Tug**	**1 oil engine** reduction geared to sc. shaft driving 1 FP propeller Total Power: 953kW (1,296hp) Caterpillar 3512TA 1 x Vee 4 Stroke 12 Cy. 170 x 190 953kW (1296bhp) Caterpillar Inc-USA Fuel: 26.0 (d.f.)
8872186 - -	**TS 1203** *ex Uniking -1995 ex Marine Lord No. 5 -1993* **UDL Offshore Pte Ltd** -	*141* 94 -	Class: (BV)	**1989-01 Guangdong Jiangmen Shipyard — Jiangmen GD** Loa 24.01 Br ex - Dght 2.550 Lbp 21.60 Br md 6.80 Dpth 3.60 Welded, 1 dk	**(B32A2ST) Tug**	**1 oil engine** reduction geared to sc. shaft driving 1 FP propeller Total Power: 942kW (1,281hp) Caterpillar 3512TA 1 x Vee 4 Stroke 12 Cy. 170 x 190 942kW (1281bhp) Caterpillar Inc-USA Fuel: 26.0 (d.f.)
8650526 *PR9959* -	**TS ABUSADO** - **Tranship Transportes Maritimos** - *Rio de Janeiro* *Brazil* Official number: 3810491284	**148** - -		**1999 in Brazil** Loa 23.00 Br ex - Dght 3.200 Lbp - Br md 8.40 Dpth 3.70 Welded, 1 dk	**(B32A2ST) Tug**	**3 oil engines** reduction geared to sc. shafts driving 3 Propellers Total Power: 1,347kW (1,830hp) Caterpillar 3412 3 x Vee 4 Stroke 12 Cy. 137 x 152 each-449kW (610bhp) Caterpillar Inc-USA
9613460 *YDA4870* -	**TS ADMIRA** - **PT Tirta Samudra Emas** - *Jakarta* *Indonesia*	**251** 75 -	Class: BV	**2011-07 Bengbu Shenzhou Machinery Co Ltd — Bengbu AH** (Hull) Yd No: (1443) **2011-07 Pacific Ocean Engineering & Trading Pte Ltd (POET) — Singapore** Yd No: 1443 Loa 29.00 Br ex 9.60 Dght 4.160 Lbp 27.44 Br md 9.00 Dpth 4.16 Welded, 1 dk	**(B32A2ST) Tug**	**2 oil engines** reduction geared to sc. shafts driving 2 FP propellers Total Power: 1,860kW (2,528hp) Chinese Std. Type XCW8200ZC 2 x 4 Stroke 8 Cy. 200 x 270 each-930kW (1264bhp) Weichai Power Co Ltd-China Fuel: 180.0 (d.f.)

9613458 *YDA4869* -	**TS ADORA** - **PT Tirta Samudra Emas** - *Tanjung Priok* *Indonesia*	**254** 77 -	Class: BV	**2011-06 Bengbu Shenzhou Machinery Co Ltd — Bengbu AH** (Hull) Yd No: (1442) **2011-06 Pacific Ocean Engineering & Trading Pte Ltd (POET) — Singapore** Yd No: 1442 Loa 29.00 Br ex 9.60 Dght 3.500 Lbp 27.44 Br md 9.00 Dpth 4.16 Welded, 1 dk	**(B32A2ST) Tug**	**2 oil engines** reduction geared to sc. shafts driving 2 FP propellers Total Power: 1,858kW (2,526hp) Chinese Std. Type CW8200ZC 2 x 4 Stroke 8 Cy. 200 x 270 each-929kW (1263bhp) Weichai Power Co Ltd-China AuxGen: 2 x 100kW 450V 60Hz a.c Fuel: 170.0 (d.f.)
8650148 *PPUL* -	**TS ARROJADO** - **Tranship Transportes Maritimos** - SatCom: Inmarsat Mini-M 761151710 *Brazil* MMSI: 710002440	**226** - -		**2006-04 Detroit Brasil Ltda — Itajai** Loa 26.00 Br ex - Dght 3.200 Lbp - Br md 9.60 Dpth 3.70 Welded, 1 dk	**(B34S2QM) Mooring Vessel**	**3 oil engines** reduction geared to sc. shafts driving 3 Propellers Total Power: 2,238kW (3,042hp) Caterpillar 3508B 3 x Vee 4 Stroke 8 Cy. 170 x 190 each-746kW (1014bhp) Caterpillar Inc-USA AuxGen: 2 x 55kW 220V a.c
8650538 *PR9960* -	**TS ASSANHADO** - **Tranship Transportes Maritimos** - *Rio de Janeiro* *Brazil* Official number: 3810485136	**184** - -		**1999 in Brazil** Loa 24.50 Br ex - Dght 3.200 Lbp - Br md 8.40 Dpth 3.70 Welded, 1 dk	**(B32A2ST) Tug**	**3 oil engines** reduction geared to sc. shafts driving 3 Propellers Total Power: 1,347kW (1,830hp) Caterpillar 3412 3 x Vee 4 Stroke 12 Cy. 137 x 152 each-449kW (610bhp) Caterpillar Inc-USA
8650540 - -	**TS ATIRADO** - **Tranship Transportes Maritimos** - *Rio de Janeiro* *Brazil* Official number: 3810499358	**108** - -		**2001 in Brazil** Loa 19.98 Br ex - Dght 2.400 Lbp - Br md 7.60 Dpth 3.35 Welded, 1 dk	**(B32A2ST) Tug**	**2 oil engines** reduction geared to sc. shafts driving 2 Propellers Total Power: 1,210kW (1,646hp) Volvo Penta D25A MT 2 x 4 Stroke 6 Cy. 170 x 180 each-605kW (823bhp) AB Volvo Penta-Sweden
9642954 - -	**TS FABULOSO** - **Tranship Transportes Maritimos** - *Brazil*	**242** - -		**2011-04 Detroit Brasil Ltda — Itajai** Loa 29.00 Br ex - Dght - Lbp - Br md 9.60 Dpth 3.70 Welded, 1 dk	**(B34S2QM) Mooring Vessel**	**3 oil engines** reduction geared to sc. shafts driving 3 Propellers Total Power: 2,277kW (3,096hp) Mitsubishi S6R2-MTK3L 3 x 4 Stroke 6 Cy. 170 x 220 each-759kW (1032bhp) Mitsubishi Heavy Industries Ltd-Japan AuxGen: 2 x 80kW 220V a.c
8650150 *PS7175* -	**TS FIEL** - **Tranship Transportes Maritimos** - *Brazil* MMSI: 710000850	**242** - -		**2005-01 Detroit Brasil Ltda — Itajai** Loa 29.00 Br ex - Dght - Lbp - Br md 9.60 Dpth 3.70 Welded, 1 dk	**(B34S2QM) Mooring Vessel**	**3 oil engines** reduction geared to sc. shafts driving 3 Propellers Total Power: 1,455kW (1,977hp) Volvo Penta D25AM 3 x 4 Stroke 6 Cy. 170 x 180 each-485kW (659bhp) AB Volvo Penta-Sweden AuxGen: 2 x 55kW 220V a.c
8650162 *PPVU* -	**TS FISSURADO** - **Tranship Transportes Maritimos** - *Brazil* MMSI: 710000286	**242** - -		**2008-04 Detroit Brasil Ltda — Itajai** Loa 29.00 Br ex - Dght - Lbp - Br md 9.60 Dpth 3.70 Welded, 1 dk	**(B34S2QM) Mooring Vessel**	**3 oil engines** reduction geared to sc. shafts driving 3 Propellers Total Power: 1,830kW (2,487hp) Mitsubishi S6R2-MPTK 3 x 4 Stroke 6 Cy. 170 x 220 each-610kW (829bhp) Mitsubishi Heavy Industries Ltd-Japan AuxGen: 2 x 80kW 220V a.c
9348493 *3EKS9* -	**TS HONGKONG** *launched as* Hammonia Xenia *-2006* **TS Hong Kong Shipping Corp** Peter Doehle Schiffahrts-KG *Panama* *Panama* MMSI: 372818000 Official number: 3314107A	**15,487** 7,838 20,643	Class: NK (GL)	**2006-12 Jiangsu Yangzijiang Shipbuilding Co Ltd — Jiangyin JS** Yd No: 2004-678C Loa 167.99 (BB) Br ex - Dght 10.220 Lbp 158.00 Br md 25.30 Dpth 13.50 Welded, 1 dk	**(A33A2CC) Container Ship (Fully Cellular)** Bale: 25,780 TEU 1574 incl 250 ref C. Ice Capable	**1 oil engine** driving 1 FP propeller Total Power: 16,520kW (22,461hp) 19.5kn Sulzer 7RT-flex60C 1 x 2 Stroke 7 Cy. 600 x 2250 16520kW (22461bhp) Hudong Heavy Machinery Co Ltd-China AuxGen: 2 x 1290kW 450V a.c, 1 x 1080kW 450V a.c, 1 x 960kW 450V a.c Thrusters: 1 Thwart. CP thruster (f); 1 Thwart. CP thruster (a) Fuel: 2170.0
9444948 *3ENP8* -	**TS JAPAN** - **Kyowa Kisen Co Ltd & Green Spanker Shipping SA** Synergy Maritime Pvt Ltd *Panama* *Panama* MMSI: 351388000 Official number: 3333507B	**17,515** 8,074 21,916	Class: NK	**2007-11 Imabari Shipbuilding Co Ltd — Imabari EH (Imabari Shipyard)** Yd No: 651 Loa 171.99 (BB) Br ex 27.60 Dght 9.517 Lbp 160.00 Br md 27.60 Dpth 14.00 Welded, 1 dk	**(A33A2CC) Container Ship (Fully Cellular)** TEU 1708 C Ho 610 TEU C Dk 1098 incl 344 ref C	**1 oil engine** driving 1 FP propeller Total Power: 15,820kW (21,509hp) 19.7kn MAN-B&W 7S60MC-C 1 x 2 Stroke 7 Cy. 600 x 2400 15820kW (21509bhp) Mitsui Engineering & Shipbuilding CLtd-Japan AuxGen: 3 x a.c Thrusters: 1 Tunnel thruster (f) Fuel: 2180.0
9339595 *A8OP7* -	**TS KOREA** *completed as* Artemis *-2008* **ms 'Artemis' Schiffahrtsgesellschaft mbH & Co KG** Peter Doehle Schiffahrts-KG *Monrovia* *Liberia* MMSI: 636091495 Official number: 91495	**26,358** 12,990 34,438	Class: GL	**2008-02 Jiangsu Yangzijiang Shipbuilding Co Ltd — Jiangyin JS** Yd No: 2004-689C Loa 209.01 (BB) Br ex - Dght 11.600 Lbp 196.90 Br md 29.80 Dpth 16.40 Welded, 1 dk	**(A33A2CC) Container Ship (Fully Cellular)** TEU 2554 incl 400 ref C. Ice Capable	**1 oil engine** driving 1 FP propeller Total Power: 21,660kW (29,449hp) 22.0kn MAN-B&W 6K80ME-C 1 x 2 Stroke 6 Cy. 800 x 2300 21660kW (29449bhp) Hudong Heavy Machinery Co Ltd-China AuxGen: 3 x 1808kW 450V 60Hz a.c, 1 x 960kW 450V 60Hz a.c Thrusters: 1 Tunnel thruster (f)
9555888 - -	**TS MARRENTO** - **Tranship Transportes Maritimos** - *Brazil*	**242** - -		**2011-04 Detroit Brasil Ltda — Itajai** Yd No: 334 Loa 29.00 Br ex - Dght 3.700 Lbp - Br md 9.60 Dpth 3.70 Welded, 1 dk	**(B34S2QM) Mooring Vessel**	**3 oil engines** reduction geared to sc. shafts driving 3 FP propellers Total Power: 1,932kW (2,628hp) 10.5kn Mitsubishi S6R2-MPTK 3 x 4 Stroke 6 Cy. 170 x 220 each-644kW (876bhp) Mitsubishi Heavy Industries Ltd-Japan AuxGen: 2 x 81kW 220V a.c Fuel: 160.0 (d.f.)
8650174 - -	**TS OURICADO** - **Tranship Transportes Maritimos** - *Brazil*	**242** - -		**2003-07 Detroit Brasil Ltda — Itajai** Loa 25.50 Br ex - Dght - Lbp - Br md 8.65 Dpth 4.29 Welded, 1 dk	**(B34S2QM) Mooring Vessel**	**2 oil engines** reduction geared to sc. shafts driving 2 Propellers Total Power: 970kW (1,318hp) Volvo Penta D25AM 2 x 4 Stroke 6 Cy. 170 x 180 each-485kW (659bhp) AB Volvo Penta-Sweden AuxGen: 2 x 50kW 220V a.c
8650198 *PPTN* -	**TS PEREGRINO** - **Tranship Transportes Maritimos** - SatCom: Inmarsat Mini-M 764614544 *Brazil* MMSI: 710078000	**204** - -		**2002-01 Detroit Brasil Ltda — Itajai** Loa 26.53 Br ex - Dght 3.200 Lbp - Br md 9.60 Dpth 3.70 Welded, 1 dk	**(B34S2QM) Mooring Vessel**	**3 oil engines** reduction geared to sc. shafts driving 3 Propellers Total Power: 2,910kW (3,957hp) Volvo Penta D49A MS 3 x Vee 4 Stroke 12 Cy. 170 x 180 each-970kW (1319bhp) AB Volvo Penta-Sweden AuxGen: 2 x 40kW 220V a.c
8650203 *PPVD* -	**TS PODEROSO** - **Tranship Transportes Maritimos** - SatCom: Inmarsat Mini-M 764847483 *Brazil* MMSI: 710000279	**242** - -		**2007-10 Detroit Brasil Ltda — Itajai** Loa 29.00 Br ex - Dght - Lbp - Br md 9.60 Dpth 3.70 Welded, 1 dk	**(B34S2QM) Mooring Vessel**	**3 oil engines** reduction geared to sc. shafts driving 3 Propellers Total Power: 1,830kW (2,487hp) Mitsubishi S6R2-MPTK 3 x 4 Stroke 6 Cy. 170 x 220 each-610kW (829bhp) Mitsubishi Heavy Industries Ltd-Japan AuxGen: 2 x 80kW 220V a.c
9376141 *V2CR9* -	**TS PUSAN** *completed as* Johannes - S *-2008* **Rudolf Schepers Schiffahrtsges mbH & Co KG ms 'Johannes S'** Reederei Rudolf Schepers GmbH & Co KG (Reederei Schepers) *Saint John's* *Antigua & Barbuda* MMSI: 305090000 Official number: 4320	**26,435** 12,990 34,330	Class: GL	**2008-02 Jiangsu Yangzijiang Shipbuilding Co Ltd — Jiangyin JS** Yd No: 2005-710C Loa 208.95 (BB) Br ex - Dght 11.600 Lbp 196.90 Br md 29.80 Dpth 16.40 Welded, 1 dk	**(A33A2CC) Container Ship (Fully Cellular)** TEU 2546 incl 536 ref C. Cranes: 3x45t	**1 oil engine** driving 1 FP propeller Total Power: 20,930kW (28,456hp) 22.0kn Wartsila 7RT-flex68 1 x 2 Stroke 7 Cy. 680 x 2720 20930kW (28456bhp) Hudong Heavy Machinery Co Ltd-China AuxGen: 2 x 1520kW 450V 60Hz a.c, 2 x 1711kW 450V 60Hz a.c Thrusters: 1 Tunnel thruster (f)

IMO / Call sign	Name / Owner	Tonnage	Class	Builder / Dimensions	Type	Machinery
9360697 *A8QD6* -	**TS SINGAPORE** *completed as* Apollon *-2008* **ms 'Apollon' Schiffahrtsgesellschaft mbH & Co KG** Peter Doehle Schiffahrts-KG *Monrovia* *Liberia* MMSI: 636091614 Official number: 91614	**26,358** 12,990 34,361	Class: GL	**2008-07 Jiangsu Yangzijiang Shipbuilding Co Ltd — Jiangyin JS** Yd No: 2004-690C Loa 208.96 (BB) Br ex - Dght 11.600 Lbp 196.90 Br md 29.79 Dpth 16.40 Welded, 1 dk	**(A33A2CC) Container Ship (Fully Cellular)** TEU 2554 incl 536 ref C.	**1 oil engine** driving 1 FP propeller Total Power: 21,660kW (29,449hp) 22.0kn MAN-B&W 6K80ME-C 1 x 2 Stroke 6 Cy. 800 x 2300 21660kW (29449bhp) Hudong Heavy Machinery Co Ltd-China AuxGen: 3 x 1800kW 450V a.c, 1 x 960kW 450V a.c Thrusters: 1 Tunnel thruster (f)
9553476 *PY2024* -	**TS SOBERANO** **Tranship Transportes Maritimos** - *Rio de Janeiro* *Brazil* Official number: 3813878694	**367** 110 560		**2011-01 TWB SA — Navegantes** Yd No: CN-147 Loa 32.00 Br ex 11.22 Dght 4.100 Lbp 28.89 Br md 11.20 Dpth 4.10 Welded, 1 dk	**(B21B20A) Anchor Handling Tug Supply** Cranes: 1x60t	**3 oil engines** reduction geared to sc. shafts driving 3 FP propellers Total Power: 4,044kW (5,499hp) 11.0kn Mitsubishi S16R-MPTK 3 x Vee 4 Stroke 16 Cy. 170 x 180 each-1348kW (1833bhp) Mitsubishi Heavy Industries Ltd-Japan AuxGen: 2 x 80kW 220V a.c Thrusters: 1 Tunnel thruster (f)
9348481 *BINS* -	**TS TAIPEI** *launched as* Hammonia Benita *-2006* **TS Lines Co Ltd** - *Keelung* *Chinese Taipei* MMSI: 416448000 Official number: 015104	**15,487** 7,838 20,615	Class: CR NK (GL)	**2006-10 Jiangsu Yangzijiang Shipbuilding Co Ltd — Jiangyin JS** Yd No: 2004-677C Loa 167.98 (BB) Br ex - Dght 10.200 Lbp 158.00 Br md 25.30 Dpth 13.50 Welded, 1 dk	**(A33A2CC) Container Ship (Fully Cellular)** Bale: 25,780 TEU 1574 incl 250 ref C.	**1 oil engine** driving 1 FP propeller Total Power: 16,520kW (22,461hp) 18.0kn Sulzer 7RT-flex60C 1 x 2 Stroke 7 Cy. 600 x 2250 16520kW (22461bhp) Hudong Heavy Machinery Co Ltd-China AuxGen: 3 x 1160kW 450V a.c, 2 x 1120kW 450V a.c Thrusters: 1 Thwart. CP thruster (f); 1 Thwart. CP thruster (a) Fuel: 2170.0
8650186 *PPTK* -	**TS VALENTE** **Tranship Transportes Maritimos** - SatCom: Inmarsat Mini-M 764614545 *Brazil* MMSI: 710000880	**242** - -		**2005-01 Detroit Brasil Ltda — Itajai** Loa 29.00 Br ex - Dght - Lbp - Br md 9.60 Dpth 3.70 Welded, 1 dk	**(B34S2QM) Mooring Vessel**	**3 oil engines** reduction geared to sc. shafts driving 3 Propellers Total Power: 1,455kW (1,977hp) Volvo Penta D25AM 3 x 4 Stroke 6 Cy. 170 x 180 each-485kW (659bhp) AB Volvo Penta-Sweden AuxGen: 2 x 55kW 220V a.c
8743919 - -	**TSARA 4** **SNP Boat Service SA** Navilux SA	**176** 52 -		**2008-10 Cantiere Navale Arno Srl — Pisa** Yd No: 32/08 Loa - Br ex - Dght - Lbp - Br md - Dpth - Welded, 1 dk	**(X11A2YP) Yacht**	**3 oil engines** reduction geared to sc. shafts driving 3 Propellers Total Power: 3,597kW (4,890hp) M.T.U. 3 x 4 Stroke each-1199kW (1630bhp) MTU Friedrichshafen GmbH-Friedrichshafen
8203218 *UEPW* -	**TSAREVSKIY** *ex* Valiant Fish *-1998* *ex* Oil Prowler *-1991* *ex* Bourgogne *-1987* *ex* Tender Bourgogne *-1987* **OOO 'Global-Flot'** - *Kaliningrad* *Russia* MMSI: 273418310 Official number: 825202	**943** 282 1,015	Class: RS (BV)	**1983-09 Ateliers et Chantiers du Sud-Ouest — Bordeaux** Yd No: 1199 Loa 53.57 Br ex 11.82 Dght 4.540 Lbp 47.86 Br md 11.51 Dpth 5.52 Welded, 1 dk	**(B21B20A) Anchor Handling Tug Supply**	**2 oil engines** driving 2 CP propellers Total Power: 2,942kW (4,000hp) 12.7kn Wichmann 7AXA 2 x 2 Stroke 7 Cy. 300 x 450 each-1471kW (2000bhp) Wichmann Motorfabrikk AS-Norway AuxGen: 1 x 330kW 380V 50Hz a.c, 2 x 200kW 380V 50Hz a.c Thrusters: 1 Thwart. CP thruster (f) Fuel: 387.0 (d.f.) 14.0pd
7518965 *HO3483* -	**TSAVLIRIS HELLAS** *ex* Zouros Hellas *-2007* *ex* Magdelan Sea *-2004* *ex* Salvor General *-1990* *ex* Abeille Normandie *-1987* **Newstart Maritime Enterprises SA** Tsavliris Salvage (International) Ltd *Panama* *Panama* MMSI: 353444000 Official number: 3085405B	**1,487** 448 2,646	Class: RI (NV) (BV)	**1977-09 Beliard-Murdoch S.A. — Oostende** Yd No: 229 Loa 66.76 Br ex - Dght 5.701 Lbp 61.02 Br md 13.01 Dpth 6.35 Welded, 1 dk	**(B32A2ST) Tug** Ice Capable	**2 oil engines** reduction geared to sc. shafts driving 2 CP propellers Total Power: 7,062kW (9,602hp) 15.5kn AGO 240V20ESHR 2 x Vee 4 Stroke 20 Cy. 240 x 220 each-3531kW (4801bhp) Societe Alsacienne de ConstructionsMecaniques (SACM)-France AuxGen: 2 x 480kW 220/380V 60Hz a.c, 1 x 160kW 220/380V 60Hz a.c Thrusters: 1 Thwart. FP thruster (f)
8119091 *3EQP5* -	**TSAVLIRIS UNITY** *ex* Seaways 5 *-2008* *ex* Deymos *-2002* **Unity Salvage & Towage Co** Tsavliris Salvage (International) Ltd SatCom: Inmarsat C 435449210 *Panama* *Panama* MMSI: 354492000 Official number: 3452108B	**3,112** 934 1,669	Class: RI (BV) (RS)	**1983-05 Oy Wartsila Ab — Helsinki** Yd No: 461 Loa 72.67 Br ex 18.32 Dght 6.700 Lbp 60.84 Br md 17.62 Dpth 9.02 Welded, 1 dk	**(B32A2ST) Tug** Ice Capable	**2 oil engines** sr geared to sc. shafts driving 2 CP propellers Total Power: 5,152kW (7,004hp) 13.0kn Russkiy 6CHN40/46 2 x 4 Stroke 6 Cy. 400 x 460 each-2576kW (3502bhp) Mashinostroitelnyy Zavod"Russkiy-Dizel"-Leningrad AuxGen: 3 x 508kW a.c Thrusters: 1 Thwart. FP thruster (f) Fuel: 1117.0 (r.f.) 21.0pd
9522049 *V4BH2* -	**TSC NARIMAN** *ex* Ruby Queen *-2011* **Damen Charter International 1 BV** Team Shipping Co LLC *Basseterre* *St Kitts & Nevis* MMSI: 341752000 Official number: SKN1002023	**135** 135 -	Class: LR ✠ **100A1** SS 06/2011 tug **LMC** Eq.Ltr: U; Cable: 247.5/17.5 U2 (a)	**2010-07 Abu Dhabi Ship Building PJSC — Abu Dhabi** (Hull) Yd No: (509835) **2010-07 B.V. Scheepswerf Damen — Gorinchem** Yd No: 509835 Loa 26.09 Br ex - Dght 3.443 Lbp 23.96 Br md 7.94 Dpth 4.05 Welded, 1 dk	**(B32A2ST) Tug**	**2 oil engines** with clutches, flexible couplings & sr reverse geared to sc. shafts driving 2 FP propellers Total Power: 2,574kW (3,500hp) Caterpillar 3512B 2 x Vee 4 Stroke 12 Cy. 170 x 215 each-1287kW (1750bhp) Caterpillar Inc-USA AuxGen: 2 x 52kW 380/220V 50Hz a.c Fuel: 80.0 (d.f.)
9528811 *J8B3938* -	**TSC ROSTAM** **Team Shipping Co LLC** - SatCom: Inmarsat C 437739511 *Kingstown* *St Vincent & The Grenadines* MMSI: 377395000 Official number: 10411	**316** 94 -	Class: BV	**2009-06 Albwardy Marine Engineering LLC — Dubai** Yd No: 016 Converted From: Tug-2009 Loa 30.00 Br ex - Dght 2.800 Lbp 29.00 Br md 12.00 Dpth 3.50 Welded, 1 dk	**(B34L2QU) Utility Vessel** Cranes: 1x9t	**2 oil engines** reduction geared to sc. shafts driving 2 FP propellers Total Power: 1,492kW (2,028hp) Caterpillar 3508B 2 x Vee 4 Stroke 8 Cy. 170 x 190 each-746kW (1014bhp) Caterpillar Inc-USA AuxGen: 2 x 86kW 380V 50Hz a.c
9528809 *J8B3939* -	**TSC SOHRAB** **Team Shipping Co LLC** - SatCom: Inmarsat C 437615810 *Kingstown* *St Vincent & The Grenadines* MMSI: 376158000 Official number: 10412	**316** 94 -	Class: BV	**2009-06 Albwardy Marine Engineering LLC — Dubai** Yd No: 015 Converted From: Tug-2009 Loa 30.00 Br ex - Dght 2.800 Lbp 29.00 Br md 12.00 Dpth 3.50 Welded, 1 dk	**(B34L2QU) Utility Vessel** Cranes: 1x22.5t	**2 oil engines** geared to sc. shafts driving 2 FP propellers Total Power: 806kW (1,096hp) Caterpillar 3412B 2 x Vee 4 Stroke 12 Cy. 137 x 152 each-403kW (548bhp) Caterpillar Inc-USA AuxGen: 2 x 86kW 380/220V 50Hz a.c Fuel: 120.0 (d.f.)
9522051 *V4OI2* -	**TSC VIRA** **Damen Charter International 3 BV** Team Shipping Co LLC *Basseterre* *St Kitts & Nevis* MMSI: 341289000 Official number: SKN 1002383	**135** - -	Class: LR ✠ **100A1** SS 09/2012 tug **LMC** Eq.Ltr: U; Cable: 247.5/17.5 U2 (a)	**2012-09 Albwardy Marine Engineering LLC — Dubai** (Hull) Yd No: 42 **2012-09 B.V. Scheepswerf Damen — Gorinchem** Yd No: 509836 Loa 26.16 (BB) Br ex 7.94 Dght 3.100 Lbp 23.96 Br md 7.90 Dpth 4.05 Welded, 1 dk	**(B32A2ST) Tug**	**2 oil engines** with clutches, flexible couplings & sr reverse geared to sc. shafts driving 2 FP propellers Total Power: 3,000kW (4,078hp) Caterpillar 3512B 2 x Vee 4 Stroke 12 Cy. 170 x 215 each-1500kW (2039bhp) Caterpillar Inc-USA AuxGen: 2 x 34kW 400V 50Hz a.c
8927321 - -	**TSEFEI** *ex* Polina *-2000* **El Sayed El Sayed Sobh & Emad El Said El Gelda** -	**117** 35 30	Class: (RS)	**1993 Sosnovskiy Sudostroitelnyy Zavod — Sosnovka** Yd No: 843 Loa 25.50 Br ex 7.00 Dght 2.390 Lbp 22.00 Br md - Dpth 3.30 Welded, 1 dk	**(B11A2FS) Stern Trawler** Ice Capable	**1 oil engine** driving 1 FP propeller Total Power: 220kW (299hp) 9.5kn S.K.L. 6NVD26A-3 1 x 4 Stroke 6 Cy. 180 x 260 220kW (299bhp) SKL Motoren u. Systemtechnik AG-Magdeburg AuxGen: 2 x 14kW a.c Fuel: 15.0 (d.f.)
9486752 *UBEJ3* -	**TSEMES** *ex* Carlis *-2012* **Trans Oil Service Co Ltd (OOO 'Trans Oyl Servis')** - *Novorossiysk* *Russia* MMSI: 273351580	**2,143** 989 3,797	Class: RS (LR) ✠ Classed LR until 27/12/12	**2012-08 Hangzhou Dongfeng Shipbuilding Co Ltd — Hangzhou ZJ** Yd No: FS2006-7/673 Loa 83.40 (BB) Br ex 13.00 Dght 5.650 Lbp 79.50 Br md 12.90 Dpth 7.45 Welded, 1 dk	**(A13B2TP) Products Tanker** Double Hull (13F) Compartments: 10 Wing Ta, 1 Slop Ta, ER	**1 oil engine** with clutches, flexible couplings & sr geared to sc. shaft driving 1 CP propeller Total Power: 1,560kW (2,121hp) 11.0kn Wartsila 8L20 1 x 4 Stroke 8 Cy. 200 x 280 1560kW (2121bhp) Wartsila Finland Oy-Finland AuxGen: 2 x 325kW 440V 60Hz a.c Boilers: TOH (o.f.) 10.2kgf/cm² (10.0bar), TOH (ex.g.) 10.2kgf/cm² (10.0bar)

Identity	Ship / Owner	Tonnage	Class	Construction	Type	Machinery
8836948 *UHQO* -	**TSENTAVR** *ex 82 -1997* **Oplot Mira JSC (A/O 'Oplot Mira')** *Nevelsk* *Russia*	**190** 57 70	Class: RS	**1990-12 Astrakhanskaya Sudoverf im. "Kirova" — Astrakhan** Yd No: 82 Loa 31.86 Br ex 7.09 Dght 2.101 Lbp 27.80 Br md 6.90 Dpth 3.18 Welded, 1 dk	**(B12B2FC) Fish Carrier** Ins: 100	**1 oil engine** geared to sc. shaft driving 1 FP propeller Total Power: 232kW (315hp) 10.3kn Daldizel 6CHSPN2A18-315 1 x 4 Stroke 6 Cy. 180 x 220 232kW (315bhp) Daldizel-Khabarovsk AuxGen: 2 x 25kW a.c Fuel: 14.0 (d.f.)
8033144 *EOWK* -	**TSENTAVR** **National JSC 'Chernomorneftegaz'** - SatCom: Inmarsat C 427300142 *Sevastopol* *Ukraine* MMSI: 272319000 Official number: 812679	**1,167** 350 404	Class: (RS)	**1981-09 Yaroslavskiy Sudostroitelnyy Zavod — Yaroslavl** Yd No: 218 Loa 58.55 Br ex 12.67 Dght 4.690 Lbp 51.62 Br md - Dpth 5.90 Welded, 1 dk	**(B32A2ST) Tug** Ice Capable	**2 diesel electric oil engines** driving 2 gen. each 1000kW 900V Connecting to 2 elec. motors each (950kW) driving 1 FP propeller Total Power: 2,208kW (3,002hp) 13.2kn Kolomna 6CHN30/38 2 x 4 Stroke 6 Cy. 300 x 380 each-1104kW (1501bhp) Kolomenskiy Zavod-Kolomna AuxGen: 2 x 300kW 400V a.c, 2 x 160kW 400V a.c Fuel: 77.0 (d.f.)
8921298 *UBEG9* -	**TSETAN** *ex Cosmo Ulsan -2009 ex Orient Glory 1 -2006* *ex Kotoku Maru No. 11 -2002* **Goodrich Fortune Co Ltd** OOO 'Tsetan' (Tsetan Co Ltd) SatCom: Inmarsat C 427303657 *Nakhodka* *Russia* MMSI: 273345530	**741** 314 1,125	Class: RS (KR) (BV)	**1990-01 Hitachi Zosen Mukaishima Marine Co Ltd — Onomichi HS** Yd No: 23 Loa 66.30 Br ex 10.02 Dght 3.910 Lbp 61.80 Br md 10.00 Dpth 4.50 Welded, 1 dk	**(A12B2TR) Chemical/Products Tanker** Double Hull Liq: 1,200; Liq (Oil): 1,200 Compartments: 8 Ta, ER	**1 oil engine** with clutches, flexible couplings & reverse geared to sc. shaft driving 1 FP propeller Total Power: 736kW (1,001hp) 10.7kn Akasaka K28R 1 x 4 Stroke 6 Cy. 280 x 480 736kW (1001bhp) Akasaka Tekkosho KK (Akasaka DieselLtd)-Japan Fuel: 36.0 (d.f.)
7922817 *UGOJ* -	**TSEZAR** *ex Alfa Marin -2005 ex Else -2000* *ex Arran Convoy -1999 ex Else -1999* *ex Saga Cob -1990 ex Sara Cob -1984* **Nakhodka-Portbunker Co Ltd** - SatCom: Inmarsat A 1406121 *Nakhodka* *Russia* MMSI: 273562010	**2,597** 1,030 3,029 T/cm 10.0	Class: RS (LR) ✠ Classed LR until 11/10/93	**1980-11 Gotaverken Solvesborg AB — Solvesborg** Yd No: 91 Converted From: General Cargo/Tanker (COB Ship)-1993 Loa 87.03 Br ex 13.16 Dght 5.590 Lbp 84.00 Br md 13.01 Dpth 6.81 Welded, 1 dk	**(A13B2TP) Products Tanker** Bale: 2,800; Liq: 3,525; Liq (Oil): 3,525 Cargo Heating Coils Compartments: 5 Ta, ER 3 Cargo Pump (s) Ice Capable	**1 oil engine** sr geared to sc. shaft driving 1 FP propeller Total Power: 1,765kW (2,400hp) 14.0kn Normo KVM-12 1 x Vee 4 Stroke 12 Cy. 250 x 300 1765kW (2400bhp) AS Bergens Mek Verksteder-Norway AuxGen: 1 x 700kW 450V 60Hz a.c, 1 x 197kW 450V 60Hz a.c Thrusters: 1 Thwart. FP thruster (f) Fuel: 155.0 (d.f.)
7504639 *WBHU* -	**TSGT JOHN A. CHAPMAN** *ex Merlin -2005 ex American Merlin -2001* *ex CGM Utrillo -1992 ex Utrillo -1987* **Sealift LLC** Sealift Inc SatCom: Inmarsat C 433833810 *Philadelphia, PA* *United States of America* MMSI: 338338000 Official number: 988732	**26,409** 9,364 26,763	Class: AB (BV)	**1978-05 Chantiers Navals de La Ciotat — La Ciotat** Yd No: 323 Lengthened-1987 Loa 204.15 (BB) Br ex 26.55 Dght 10.501 Lbp 195.11 Br md 26.51 Dpth 16.31 Welded, 3 dks	**(A31A2GA) General Cargo Ship (with Ro-Ro facility)** Stern door & ramp (centre) Len: 25.00 Wid: 5.14 Swl: - Lane-Len: 1400 Grain: 42,975 TEU 1063 incl 65 ref C. Compartments: 5 Ho, ER 7 Ha: 2 (6.4 x 8.0)5 (12.7 x 8.0) 10 Wing Ha: 2 (12.7 x 2.6)8 (12.7 x 5.4) Cranes: 3x40t,2x25t	**2 oil engines** reduction geared to sc. shaft driving 1 FP propeller Total Power: 17,212kW (23,402hp) 18.0kn Pielstick 18PC2-5V-400 2 x Vee 4 Stroke 18 Cy. 400 x 460 each-8606kW (11701bhp) Alsthom Atlantique-France AuxGen: 3 x 960kW 440V 60Hz a.c Thrusters: 1 Thwart. FP thruster (f) Fuel: 3008.5
9382360 - -	**TSHD ABUL** **Karachi Port Trust** - *Karachi* *Pakistan* MMSI: 463033101	**6,469** 1,940 9,200	Class: LR ✠ **100A1** SS 10/2012 hopper dredger ✠ **LMC** **UMS** Eq.Ltr: A†; Cable: 522.0/50.0 U3 (a)	**2007-10 IHC Holland Beaver Dredgers BV — Sliedrecht** Yd No: C01245 Loa 104.40 Br ex 20.02 Dght 6.800 Lbp 98.60 Br md 20.00 Dpth 8.80 Welded, 1 dk	**(B33B2DT) Trailing Suction Hopper Dredger** Hopper: 6,000 Compartments: 1 Ho, ER	**2 oil engines** with clutches, flexible couplings & sr reverse geared to sc. shafts driving 2 CP propellers Total Power: 6,200kW (8,430hp) 13.0kn Wartsila 9L32 2 x 4 Stroke 9 Cy. 320 x 400 each-3100kW (4215bhp) Wartsila Finland Oy-Finland AuxGen: 2 x 350kW 400V 50Hz a.c Thrusters: 2 Tunnel thruster (f)
8884971 *PNBP* -	**TSHD MEKAR 501** *ex Mailiao 501 -2012 ex SHB 2001S -2012* **PT Teratai Intan Sari** *Samarinda* *Indonesia*	**1,741** 523 3,487	Class: KI (CR) (BV)	**1993-07 Wusong Shipyard — Shanghai** Yd No: 287 Loa - Br ex - Dght 4.520 Lbp 65.20 Br md 16.00 Dpth 5.67 Welded, 1 dk	**(B34A2SH) Hopper, Motor** Hopper: 2,000 Compartments: 1 Ho, ER	**2 oil engines** geared to sc. shafts driving 2 FP propellers Total Power: 1,194kW (1,624hp) Cummins KT-38-M 2 x Vee 4 Stroke 12 Cy. 159 x 159 each-597kW (812bhp) Cummins Engine Co Ltd-United Kingdom AuxGen: 2 x 74kW 380V a.c
7905778 *3FYM2* -	**TSHD VERMONT 170** *ex Hang Jun 1007 -2011 ex Esprit V -2000* *ex Primorye -1998* **WCE Waterways Construction Equipments Inc** SDC Waterway Construction Co Ltd *Panama* *Panama* Official number: 42005PEXT1	**2,394** 718 1,964	Class: (CC) (BV) (RS)	**1981-03 Brodogradiliste Split (Brodosplit) — Split** Yd No: 305 Loa 80.00 Br ex 15.14 Dght 4.100 Lbp 75.42 Br md 15.10 Dpth 5.60 Welded, 1 dk	**(B33A2DS) Suction Dredger** Liq: 1,000; Hopper: 1,700 Ice Capable	**2 oil engines** geared to sc. shafts driving 2 FP propellers Total Power: 2,160kW (2,936hp) 10.5kn Sulzer 8ASL25/30 2 x 4 Stroke 8 Cy. 250 x 300 each-1080kW (1468bhp) Tvornica Dizel Motora 'Jugoturbina'-Yugoslavia
6804800 - -	**TSHELA** **Societe Congolaise des Industries de Raffinage (SOCIR)** - *Moanda* *Congo (Democratic Republic)*	*154* 35 -	Class: (BV)	**1968-01 INMA SpA — La Spezia** Yd No: 66 Loa 26.80 Br ex 7.01 Dght 1.936 Lbp 26.19 Br md 6.99 Dpth 2.75 Welded, 1 dk	**(B32B2SP) Pusher Tug**	**2 oil engines** geared to sc. shafts driving 2 FP propellers Total Power: 1,126kW (1,530hp) 11.0kn Caterpillar D398TA 2 x Vee 4 Stroke 12 Cy. 159 x 203 each-563kW (765bhp) Caterpillar Tractor Co-USA
7504512 - -	**TSHUAPA** **Government of The Democratic Republic of Congo (Ministere des Transports et Communications - Service des Voies Navigables)** - *Boma* *Congo (Democratic Republic)*	*2,011* 1,009 2,100	Class: (BV)	**1976-06 A. Vuijk & Zonen's Scheepswerven B.V. — Capelle a/d IJssel** Yd No: 873 Loa 82.81 Br ex - Dght 4.801 Lbp 77.02 Br md 14.00 Dpth 6.02 Welded, 1 dk	**(B33B2DU) Hopper/Dredger (unspecified)** Hopper: 1,500	**2 oil engines** geared to sc. shafts driving 2 FP propellers Total Power: 1,986kW (2,700hp) 11.8kn Bolnes 9DNL150/600 2 x 2 Stroke 9 Cy. 190 x 350 each-993kW (1350bhp) 'Bolnes' Motorenfabriek BV-Netherlands
8834859 - -	**TSIKLON** **Danube Hydrometeorological Observatory (Dunayskaya Gidrometeorologicheskaya Observatoriya)** *Izmail* *Ukraine* MMSI: 272653000 Official number: 892762	**115** 34 24	Class: (RS)	**1990-09 Azovskaya Sudoverf — Azov** Yd No: 1039 Loa 26.50 Br ex 6.60 Dght 2.061 Lbp 22.08 Br md 6.50 Dpth 3.08 Welded, 1 dk	**(B31A2SR) Research Survey Vessel**	**1 oil engine** geared to sc. shaft driving 1 FP propeller Total Power: 165kW (224hp) 9.5kn Daldizel 6CHNSP18/22 1 x 4 Stroke 6 Cy. 180 x 220 165kW (224bhp) Daldizel-Khabarovsk AuxGen: 2 x 30kW Fuel: 9.0 (d.f.)
8727458 - -	**TSIKLON** **Federal State Unitary Enterprise Rosmorport** - *Petropavlovsk-Kamchatskiy* *Russia* Official number: 873776	**182** 54 57	Class: RS	**1988-05 Gorokhovetskiy Sudostroitelnyy Zavod — Gorokhovets** Yd No: 232 Loa 29.30 Br ex 8.60 Dght 3.650 Lbp 27.00 Br md 8.24 Dpth 4.30 Welded, 1 dk	**(B32A2ST) Tug** Ice Capable	**2 oil engines** driving 2 CP propellers Total Power: 1,180kW (1,604hp) 11.5kn Pervomaysk 8CHNP25/34 2 x 4 Stroke 8 Cy. 250 x 340 each-590kW (802bhp) Pervomaydizelmash (PDM)-Pervomaysk
7014177 *UGRI* -	**TSIKONIYA** **DV Kurs Co Ltd** - *Okhotsk* *Russia* MMSI: 273445010	**2,545** 763 1,533	Class: (RS) (BR)	**1970-12 VEB Volkswerft Stralsund — Stralsund** Yd No: 290 Loa 82.04 Br ex 13.64 Dght 5.200 Lbp 73.00 Br md 13.62 Dpth 9.56 Welded, 2 dks	**(B11A2FG) Factory Stern Trawler** Ins: 1,211 Compartments: 3 Ho, ER 3 Ha: (1.8 x 1.2)2 (2.2 x 2.2) Derricks: 2x5t,2x3t; Winches: 4 Ice Capable	**2 oil engines** geared to sc. shaft driving 1 CP propeller Total Power: 1,708kW (2,322hp) 13.5kn S.K.L. 8NVD48A-2U 2 x 4 Stroke 8 Cy. 320 x 480 each-854kW (1161bhp) VEB Schwermaschinenbau "KarlLiebknecht" (SKL)-Magdeburg AuxGen: 2 x 336kW, 2 x 256kW Fuel: 612.0 (d.f.)
9027154 *UADI9* -	**TSIMLYANSK GES** **OOO 'Leasing Co Uralsib'** OOO 'PETROPROM' *St Petersburg* *Russia* MMSI: 273443840 Official number: 83041	*1,933* - 3,369	Class: RR	**1960-01 Sudostroitelnyy Zavod "Krasnoye Sormovo" — Gorkiy** Yd No: 20 Loa 110.12 Br ex 13.40 Dght 3.510 Lbp 106.80 Br md - Dpth 4.80 Welded, 1 dk	**(A13B2TP) Products Tanker**	**2 oil engines** driving 2 Propellers Total Power: 736kW (1,000hp) S.K.L. 6NVD48-1U 2 x 4 Stroke 6 Cy. 320 x 480 each-368kW (500bhp) VEB Schwermaschinenbau "KarlLiebknecht" (SKL)-Magdeburg

Ship	Tonnage	Class	Builder / Dimensions	Type	Machinery
9127100 *VRVE8* - **TSING CHAU** **SITA Waste Services Ltd** The Hongkong Salvage & Towage Co Ltd *Hong Kong* *Hong Kong* Official number: HK-0324	**1,897** 569 1,763 T/cm 11.0	Class: LR ✠**100A1** SS 10/2011 container ship hatch covers omitted Hong Kong waters service ✠**LMC** Eq.Ltr: P; Cable: 440.0/36.0 U2	**1996-10 Daedong Shipbuilding Co Ltd — Busan** Yd No: 406 Loa 69.20 Br ex 18.17 Dght 3.000 Lbp 66.74 Br md 18.00 Dpth 5.00 Welded, 1 dk	**(A33A2CC) Container Ship (Fully Cellular)** TEU 95 Compartments: 1 Cell Ho, ER 1 Ha: (32.2 x 13.2)ER Gantry cranes: 1x20t	**2 oil engines** with clutches, flexible couplings & sr reverse geared to sc. shafts driving 2 FP propellers Total Power: 1,324kW (1,800hp) 11.0kn Alpha 6L23/30 2 x 4 Stroke 6 Cy. 225 x 300 each-662kW (900bhp) Ssangyong Heavy Industries Co Ltd-South Korea AuxGen: 2 x 400kW 385V 50Hz a.c, 2 x 120kW 385V 50Hz a.c Thrusters: 1 Thwart. CP thruster (f)
7645811 - - **TSING HOI** *ex Man Lok -1978* - *Hong Kong* *Hong Kong* Official number: 196059	*387* 129 272		**1951-06 Hong Kong & Whampoa Dock Co Ltd — Hong Kong** Yd No: 900 Loa 39.63 Br ex 13.21 Dght 2.667 Lbp 39.17 Br md 12.76 Dpth 3.66 Welded, 1 dk	**(A36A2PR) Passenger/Ro-Ro Ship (Vehicles)**	**2 oil engines** with flexible couplings & sr reverse geared to sc. shafts driving 2 FP propellers Total Power: 736kW (1,000hp) 10.5kn Cummins KTA-19-M 2 x 4 Stroke 6 Cy. 159 x 159 each-368kW (500bhp) (new engine 1980) Cummins Engine Co Inc-USA AuxGen: 2 x 53kW d.c Fuel: 56.8 (d.f.) 2.0pd
9230309 *H9YF* - **TSING MA BRIDGE** **OA Navigation SA** Osaka Asahi Kaiun KK (Osaka Asahi Marine Transportation Co Ltd) SatCom: Inmarsat C 435159310 *Panama* *Panama* MMSI: 351593000 Official number: 2846202B	**68,687** 25,395 71,310	Class: NK	**2002-04 Hyundai Heavy Industries Co Ltd — Ulsan** Yd No: 1369 Loa 284.60 (BB) Br ex - Dght 14.022 Lbp 271.27 Br md 40.00 Dpth 24.40 Welded, 1 dk	**(A33A2CC) Container Ship (Fully Cellular)** TEU 5610 C Ho 2802 TEU C Dk 2808 TEU incl 500 ref C. Compartments: 16 Cell Ho, ER 16 Ha: ER	**1 oil engine** driving 1 FP propeller Total Power: 58,840kW (79,999hp) 25.1kn MAN-B&W 11K98MC 1 x 2 Stroke 11 Cy. 980 x 2660 58840kW (79999bhp) Hyundai Heavy Industries Co Ltd-South Korea AuxGen: 4 x 2600kW 440/220V 60Hz a.c Thrusters: 1 Thwart. CP thruster (f) Fuel: 10140.0
9615303 *V7VS3* - **TSINGSHAN** **Tsingshan Special Maritime Enterprise Co Ltd** Zhejiang Tsingshan Transportation Co Ltd *Majuro* *Marshall Islands* MMSI: 538004200 Official number: 4200	**33,042** 19,132 56,628 T/cm 58.8	Class: GL	**2011-09 Qingshan Shipyard — Wuhan HB** Yd No: 20100310 Loa 189.99 (BB) Br ex - Dght 12.800 Lbp 185.00 Br md 32.26 Dpth 18.00 Welded, 1 dk	**(A21A2BC) Bulk Carrier** Grain: 71,634; Bale: 68,200 Compartments: 5 Ho, ER 5 Ha: ER Cranes: 4x30t	**1 oil engine** driving 1 FP propeller Total Power: 9,480kW (12,889hp) 14.2kn MAN-B&W 6S50MC-C 1 x 2 Stroke 6 Cy. 500 x 2000 9480kW (12889bhp) STX Engine Co Ltd-South Korea
9320702 *DDYL2* - **TSINGTAO EXPRESS** **Hapag-Lloyd AG** SatCom: Inmarsat C 421806310 *Hamburg* *Germany* MMSI: 218063000 Official number: 21212	**93,750** 37,699 103,631 T/cm 122.0	Class: GL	**2007-04 Hyundai Heavy Industries Co Ltd — Ulsan** Yd No: 1741 Loa 335.47 (BB) Br ex - Dght 14.610 Lbp 319.00 Br md 42.80 Dpth 24.50 Welded, 1 dk	**(A33A2CC) Container Ship (Fully Cellular)** Double Bottom Entire Compartment Length TEU 8749 C Ho 3881 TEU C Dk 4868 TEU incl 730 ref C.	**1 oil engine** driving 1 FP propeller Total Power: 68,640kW (93,323hp) 25.2kn MAN-B&W 12K98ME 1 x 2 Stroke 12 Cy. 980 x 2660 68640kW (93323bhp) Hyundai Heavy Industries Co Ltd-South Korea AuxGen: 2 x 4267kW 6600V 60Hz a.c, 1 x 2454kW 6600V 60Hz a.c, 1 x 4000kW 6600V 60Hz a.c, 1 x 1867kW 6600V 60Hz a.c Thrusters: 1 Tunnel thruster (f)
7524380 - - **TSIRKON** **Satta Ltd** -	**177** 53 68	Class: (RS)	**1975-07 Sretenskiy Sudostroitelnyy Zavod — Sretensk** Yd No: 76 Converted From: Research Vessel Loa 33.96 Br ex 7.09 Dght 2.770 Lbp 29.86 Br md - Dpth 3.69 Welded, 1 dk	**(A31A2GX) General Cargo Ship** Derricks: 2x2t Ice Capable	**1 oil engine** driving 1 FP propeller Total Power: 224kW (305hp) 9.0kn S.K.L. 8NVD36-1U 1 x 4 Stroke 8 Cy. 240 x 360 224kW (305bhp) VEB Schwermaschinenbau "KarlLiebknecht" (SKL)-Magdeburg AuxGen: 1 x 86kW, 1 x 60kW, 1 x 28kW Fuel: 12.0 (d.f.)
8139106 - - **TSISKARA** **Adjarriba Ltd** -	*163* 39 88	Class: (RS)	**1983 Astrakhanskaya Sudoverf im. "Kirova" — Astrakhan** Yd No: 164 Loa 33.99 Br ex 7.12 Dght 2.901 Lbp 29.98 Br md - Dpth 3.66 Welded, 1 dk	**(B11B2FV) Fishing Vessel** Grain: 78 Compartments: 1 Ho, ER 1 Ha: (1.6 x 1.3) Derricks: 2x2t; Winches: 2 Ice Capable	**1 oil engine** driving 1 FP propeller Total Power: 224kW (305hp) 9.5kn S.K.L. 8NVD36-1U 1 x 4 Stroke 8 Cy. 240 x 360 224kW (305bhp) VEB Schwermaschinenbau "KarlLiebknecht" (SKL)-Magdeburg AuxGen: 2 x 75kW Fuel: 17.0 (d.f.)
9681936 *FAB2751* - **TSM ALBATRE** **Bleu Marine SAS** Thomas Services Maritime *Dieppe* *France* MMSI: 227186230	**122** 36 -	Class: (BV)	**2013-02 Machinefabriek Padmos Stellendam B.V. — Stellendam** Yd No: 187 Loa 19.60 Br ex - Dght 2.600 Lbp 17.55 Br md 8.20 Dpth 3.60 Welded, 1 dk	**(B32A2ST) Tug** A-frames: 1	**2 oil engines** reduction geared to sc. shaft (s) driving 2 Directional propellers Total Power: 2,088kW (2,838hp) Mitsubishi S12R-MPTA 2 x Vee 4 Stroke 12 Cy. 170 x 180 each-1044kW (1419bhp) Mitsubishi Heavy Industries Ltd-Japan AuxGen: 2 x 36kW 50Hz a.c Fuel: 33.0 (d.f.)
8012827 *A9D3218* - **TSM ANCORA** *ex Ancora -2013 ex Waterway -2007* *ex Union Venus -1994* **Two Seas Marine Services Ltd** - *Bahrain* MMSI: 408527000	**1,010** 547 1,395	Class: GL (LR) ✠ Classed LR until 18/12/81	**1981-04 A/S Nordsovaerftet — Ringkobing** Yd No: 147 Loa 69.88 Br ex 11.28 Dght 3.388 Lbp 66.15 Br md 11.21 Dpth 4.17 Welded, 1 dk	**(A31A2GX) General Cargo Ship** Grain: 1,874; Bale: 1,862 Compartments: 1 Ho, ER 1 Ha: (40.0 x 7.4)ER	**1 oil engine** with clutches, flexible couplings & sr geared to sc. shaft driving 1 CP propeller Total Power: 800kW (1,088hp) 11.0kn Alpha 7T23L-KVO 1 x 4 Stroke 7 Cy. 225 x 300 800kW (1088bhp) B&W Alpha Diesel A/S-Denmark AuxGen: 3 x 64kW 413V 50Hz a.c Fuel: 26.5 (d.f.) 4.0pd
9689067 *FAB7384* - **TSM BREHAT** *ex Padmos Stellandam -2013* **Thomas Services Maritime** - *Rouen* *France* MMSI: 227233030	**130** - -		**2013-09 Machinefabriek Padmos Stellendam B.V. — Stellendam** Loa 20.35 Br ex - Dght 4.200 Lbp - Br md 8.20 Dpth - Welded, 1 dk	**(B32A2ST) Tug**	**2 oil engines** reduction geared to sc. shaft (s) driving 2 Z propellers Total Power: 1,920kW (2,610hp) 11.4kn Mitsubishi S12R-MPTA 2 x Vee 4 Stroke 12 Cy. 170 x 180 each-960kW (1305bhp) Mitsubishi Heavy Industries Ltd-Japan
8012815 *A9D3219* - **TSM CLARITY** *ex Clarity -2013 ex Union Mars -2001* **Two Seas Marine Services Ltd** - *Bahrain* MMSI: 408528000	**986** 513 1,395	Class: GL (LR) ✠ Classed LR until 18/12/81	**1981-04 A/S Nordsovaerftet — Ringkobing** Yd No: 146 Loa 69.88 Br ex 11.28 Dght 3.388 Lbp 66.15 Br md 11.21 Dpth 4.17 Welded, 1 dk	**(A31A2GX) General Cargo Ship** Grain: 1,918; Bale: 1,862 Compartments: 1 Ho, ER 1 Ha: (40.0 x 7.4)ER	**1 oil engine** with clutches, flexible couplings & sr geared to sc. shaft driving 1 CP propeller Total Power: 800kW (1,088hp) 11.0kn Alpha 7T23L-KVO 1 x 4 Stroke 7 Cy. 225 x 300 800kW (1088bhp) B&W Alpha Diesel A/S-Denmark AuxGen: 3 x 64kW 415V 50Hz a.c Fuel: 26.5 (d.f.) 4.0pd
7528764 *A9D2437* - **TSM DOKHAN** *ex Dokhan -2013* **Two Seas Marine Services Ltd** - *Bahrain* *Bahrain* Official number: A1426	**207** 62 136	✠**100A1** SS 04/2010 tug Arabian Gulf service ✠**LMC** Eq.Ltr: (F) D; Cable: U2	**1977-06 Estaleiros Navais Lda. H. Parry & Son — Cacilhas** Yd No: 76 Loa 33.36 Br ex 9.00 Dght 3.825 Lbp 30.00 Br md 8.50 Dpth 4.30 Welded, 1 dk	**(B32A2ST) Tug**	**1 oil engine** reverse reduction geared to sc. shaft driving 1 FP propeller Total Power: 1,765kW (2,400hp) MWM TBD500-8 1 x 4 Stroke 8 Cy. 360 x 450 1765kW (2400bhp) Motoren Werke Mannheim AG (MWM)-West Germany AuxGen: 1 x 48kW 380/220V 50Hz a.c, 1 x 32kW 380/220V 50Hz a.c
9671670 *YDB4241* - **TSP 201** *launched as Tm 201 -2012* **PT Trans Samudera Perkasa** - *Tanjung Priok* *Indonesia*	**264** 80 262	Class: NK	**2012-11 Tuong Aik Shipyard Sdn Bhd — Sibu** Yd No: 21202 Loa 29.00 Br ex - Dght 3.612 Lbp 27.17 Br md 8.60 Dpth 4.20 Welded, 1 dk	**(B32A2ST) Tug**	**2 oil engines** reduction geared to sc. shafts driving 2 FP propellers Total Power: 1,518kW (2,064hp) Mitsubishi S6R2-MTK3L 2 x 4 Stroke 6 Cy. 170 x 220 each-759kW (1032bhp) Mitsubishi Heavy Industries Ltd-Japan Fuel: 200.0 (d.f.)
9671682 *YDB4242* - **TSP 202** *launched as Tm 202 -2012* **PT Trans Samudera Perkasa** - *Tanjung Priok* *Indonesia* Official number: 2012 BA NO.3239/L	**264** 80 261	Class: NK	**2012-11 Tuong Aik Shipyard Sdn Bhd — Sibu** Yd No: 21203 Loa 29.00 Br ex - Dght 3.612 Lbp 27.17 Br md 8.60 Dpth 4.20 Welded, 1 dk	**(B32A2ST) Tug**	**2 oil engines** reduction geared to sc. shafts driving 2 Propellers Total Power: 1,518kW (2,064hp) Mitsubishi S6R2-MTK3L 2 x 4 Stroke 6 Cy. 170 x 220 each-759kW (1032bhp) Mitsubishi Heavy Industries Ltd-Japan Fuel: 200.0 (d.f.)

8506919 *HQKT8* -	**TSS API** **CH Ship Management Pte Ltd** - *San Lorenzo* *Honduras* Official number: L-0323968	*126* 37 -	Class: (KI) (NV) (BV)	**1985-01 Asia-Pacific Shipyard Pte Ltd — Singapore** Yd No: 841 Loa 23.17 Br ex - Dght 1.680 Lbp 22.26 Br md 7.01 Dpth 2.16 Welded, 1 dk	**(B34G2SE) Pollution Control Vessel**	**2 oil engines** geared to sc. shafts driving 2 FP propellers Total Power: 480kW (652hp) Yanmar 6HAL-HTE 2 x 4 Stroke 6 Cy. 130 x 150 each-240kW (326bhp) Yanmar Diesel Engine Co Ltd-Japan AuxGen: 2 x 56kW 380V 50Hz a.c
8202862 *PMXP* -	**TSS BEATA** *ex* Pink Jaguar *-1984* **PT Bahtera Niaga Internasional** - *Jakarta* *Indonesia* MMSI: 525016522 Official number: 2009 PST NO.5855/L	**1,008** 302 1,924	Class: AB KI	**1982-12 Southern Ocean Shipbuilding Co Pte Ltd — Singapore** Yd No: 132 Loa 56.00 Br ex - Dght 4.301 Lbp 38.51 Br md 12.00 Dpth 5.00 Welded, 1 dk	**(B21A2OS) Platform Supply Ship**	**2 oil engines** sr reverse geared to sc. shafts driving 2 FP propellers Total Power: 3,530kW (4,800hp) 14.0kn Yanmar 8Z280L-ET 2 x 4 Stroke 8 Cy. 280 x 360 each-1765kW (2400bhp) Yanmar Diesel Engine Co Ltd-Japan AuxGen: 2 x 128kW Thrusters: 1 Thwart. FP thruster (f)
8300793 *PMXQ* -	**TSS PIONEER 4** *ex* TSS Bastian *-1985* *ex* Bastian *-1985* *ex* TSS Pioneer 4 *-1984* **PT Bahtera Niaga Internasional** - *Jakarta* *Indonesia* MMSI: 525016525	**983** 295 1,000	Class: AB KI	**1983-03 Tonoura Dock Co. Ltd. — Miyazaki** Yd No: 61 Loa 58.30 Br ex 12.22 Dght 4.323 Lbp 52.51 Br md 12.21 Dpth 5.01 Welded, 1 dk	**(B21A2OS) Platform Supply Ship**	**2 oil engines** with clutches & dr reverse geared to sc. shafts driving 2 FP propellers Total Power: 3,530kW (4,800hp) 13.0kn Fuji 8L27.5G 2 x 4 Stroke 8 Cy. 275 x 320 each-1765kW (2400bhp) Fuji Diesel Co Ltd-Japan AuxGen: 2 x 200kW Thrusters: 1 Thwart. CP thruster (f)
8300781 *PMXR* -	**TSS PIONEER 5** *ex* Tropic Orion 1 *-1983* **PT Bahtera Niaga Internasional** - *Jakarta* *Indonesia* MMSI: 525016502 Official number: 2717/PST	**991** 298 1,000	Class: AB KI	**1983-02 Tonoura Dock Co. Ltd. — Miyazaki** Yd No: 60 Loa 58.30 Br ex 12.22 Dght 4.323 Lbp 52.51 Br md 12.21 Dpth 5.21 Welded, 1 dk	**(B21A2OS) Platform Supply Ship**	**2 oil engines** with clutches & dr reverse geared to sc. shafts driving 2 FP propellers Total Power: 3,530kW (4,800hp) 13.0kn Fuji 8L27.5G 2 x 4 Stroke 8 Cy. 275 x 320 each-1765kW (2400bhp) Fuji Diesel Co Ltd-Japan AuxGen: 2 x 200kW Thrusters: 1 Thwart. CP thruster (f)
7396525 *HP8254* -	**TSU CHANG** *ex* Asia Star No. 3 *-1998* *ex* Victor King *-1996* *ex* Chung Yuan *-1995* *ex* Success II *-1995* *ex* Ying Ta *-1993* *ex* Taiyo *-1990* *ex* Taiyo Maru *-1987* **Yeuan Chang SA** - *Panama* *Panama* MMSI: 352831000 Official number: 2307796A	**1,125** 605 1,505	Class: (KR)	**1974-08 Sasaki Shipbuilding Co Ltd — Osakikamijima HS** Yd No: 192 Loa 63.10 Br ex 11.00 Dght 4.801 Lbp 61.30 Br md 10.98 Dpth 6.10 Welded	**(A31A2GX) General Cargo Ship** Compartments: 1 Ho, ER 1 Ha: (33.9 x 7.4)ER	**1 oil engine** driving 1 FP propeller Total Power: 1,324kW (1,800hp) Makita 1 x 4 Stroke 1324kW (1800bhp) Makita Tekkosho-Japan
7650581 *HP8301* -	**TSU LIH** *ex* Naikai Maru No. 15 *-1981* **Taksong Marine SA** - *Panama* *Panama* MMSI: 355414000 Official number: 2252396	**591** 292 1,032	Class: (CR)	**1969 Hakata Zosen K.K. — Imabari** Yd No: 68 Loa 54.11 Br ex - Dght 4.301 Lbp 49.51 Br md 9.30 Dpth 4.70 Welded, 1 dk	**(A31A2GX) General Cargo Ship** Grain: 1,119; Bale: 941 Compartments: 1 Ho, ER 1 Ha: (24.0 x 5.7)ER Derricks: 2x5t; Winches: 2	**1 oil engine** driving 1 FP propeller Total Power: 919kW (1,249hp) 11.0kn Makita ESLH633 1 x 4 Stroke 6 Cy. 330 x 500 919kW (1249bhp) Makita Diesel Co Ltd-Japan AuxGen: 1 x 28kW 225V a.c, 1 x 24kW 225V a.c
9646443 *JD3385* -	**TSUBAKI** **Kyushu Shosen Co Ltd** - *Nagasaki, Nagasaki* *Japan* MMSI: 431003967 Official number: 141715	*1,590* 670		**2012-12 Naikai Zosen Corp — Onomichi HS (Setoda Shipyard)** Yd No: 757 Loa 78.00 Br ex - Dght 4.300 Lbp - Br md 14.50 Dpth - Welded, 1 dk	**(A36A2PR) Passenger/Ro-Ro Ship (Vehicles)**	**2 oil engines** reduction geared to sc. shafts driving 2 CP propellers Total Power: 5,884kW (8,000hp) 20.0kn Daihatsu 6DCM-32 2 x 4 Stroke 6 Cy. 320 x 400 each-2942kW (4000bhp) Daihatsu Diesel Manufacturing Co Lt-Japan
9011258 *JK5048* -	**TSUBAKI 2** **Hagi Kaiun YK** - *Hagi, Yamaguchi* *Japan* Official number: 132458	*113* - 52		**1990-09 Mitsubishi Heavy Industries Ltd. — Shimonoseki** Yd No: 947 Loa 33.00 Br ex 6.72 Dght 2.011 Lbp 29.00 Br md 6.50 Dpth 2.80 Welded	**(A32A2GF) General Cargo/Passenger Ship** Bale: 90 Compartments: 1 Ho, ER 1 Ha: ER	**1 oil engine** with clutches & sr reverse geared to sc. shaft driving 1 FP propeller Total Power: 883kW (1,201hp) Daihatsu 6DLM-24S 1 x 4 Stroke 6 Cy. 240 x 320 883kW (1201bhp) Daihatsu Diesel Manufacturing Co Lt-Japan Thrusters: 1 Thwart. CP thruster (f)
9172375 *JH3467* -	**TSUBAKI MARU** **Cosmo Kaiun KK** - *Yokkaichi, Mie* *Japan* Official number: 134400	*127* - -		**1997-09 Kanagawa Zosen — Kobe** Yd No: 452 Loa 28.50 Br ex - Dght - Lbp 25.00 Br md 8.00 Dpth 3.50 Welded, 1 dk	**(B34G2SE) Pollution Control Vessel**	**2 oil engines** gearing integral to driving 2 Z propellers Total Power: 956kW (1,300hp) 11.5kn Niigata 6L19HX 2 x 4 Stroke 6 Cy. 190 x 260 each-478kW (650bhp) Niigata Engineering Co Ltd-Japan AuxGen: 2 x 104kW 225V 60Hz a.c Fuel: 16.0 (d.f.) 4.7pd
8715601 *JF2129* -	**TSUBASA** **Sado Kisen KK** - *Sado, Niigata* *Japan* Official number: 120078	*164* - 20		**1989-03 Kawasaki Heavy Industries Ltd — Kobe HG** Yd No: F001 Loa 30.33 Br ex - Dght 1.501 Lbp 23.99 Br md 8.53 Dpth 2.59 Welded, 1 dk	**(A37B2PS) Passenger Ship** Hull Material: Aluminium Alloy Passengers: unberthed: 266	**2 Gas Turbs** geared to sc. shafts driving 2 Water jets Total Power: 5,590kW (7,600hp) 43.0kn Allison 501-KF 2 x Gas Turb each-2795kW (3800shp) General Motors Detroit DieselAllison Divn-USA AuxGen: 2 x 50kW 450V 60Hz a.c
9213260 *JG5382* -	**TSUBASA** **Government of Japan (Ministry of Finance)** Government of Japan (Yokohama Customs Office) *Yokohama, Kanagawa* *Japan* Official number: 136754	*131* - -		**2000-03 Mitsubishi Heavy Industries Ltd. — Shimonoseki** Yd No: 1067 Loa 36.40 Br ex - Dght - Lbp 32.50 Br md 6.70 Dpth 3.33 Welded, 1 dk	**(B34H2SQ) Patrol Vessel** Hull Material: Aluminium Alloy	**2 oil engines** geared to sc. shafts driving 2 FP propellers Total Power: 4,076kW (5,542hp) 32.6kn M.T.U. 16V396TB94 2 x Vee 4 Stroke 16 Cy. 165 x 185 each-2038kW (2771bhp) MTU Friedrichshafen GmbH-Friedrichshafen
9672698 *JD3458* -	**TSUBASA** **Wing Maritime Service Corp** - *Yokohama, Kanagawa* *Japan* Official number: 141829	*257* - 100		**2013-03 Keihin Dock Co Ltd — Yokohama** Yd No: 305 Loa 37.20 Br ex - Dght 3.200 Lbp 33.00 Br md 9.80 Dpth 4.37 Welded, 1 dk	**(B32A2ST) Tug**	**2 oil engines** gearing integral to driving 2 Z propellers Total Power: 3,676kW (4,998hp) Niigata 6L28HX 2 x 4 Stroke 6 Cy. 280 x 370 each-1838kW (2499bhp) Niigata Engineering Co Ltd-Japan
9669952 *7JND* -	**TSUBASA** **Dokai Marine Systems Ltd** - *Kitakyushu, Fukuoka* *Japan* MMSI: 432889000 Official number: 141775	**496** 148 436	Class: NK	**2012-11 Kanagawa Zosen — Kobe** Yd No: 643 Loa 43.00 Br ex - Dght 4.340 Lbp 40.26 Br md 10.00 Dpth 5.00 Welded, 1 dk	**(B32A2ST) Tug**	**2 oil engines** reduction geared to sc. shafts driving 2 Propellers Total Power: 3,676kW (4,998hp) Niigata 6L28HX 2 x 4 Stroke 6 Cy. 280 x 370 each-1838kW (2499bhp) Niigata Engineering Co Ltd-Japan
9454498 *3FQN7* -	**TSUGARU** **Honos Shipping Pte Ltd** NYK Shipmanagement Pte Ltd *Panama* *Panama* MMSI: 357061000 Official number: 4484513	**160,145** 97,999 301,498 T/cm 170.1	Class: NK	**2010-09 IHI Marine United Inc — Kure HS** Yd No: 3252 Loa 333.00 (BB) Br ex 60.04 Dght 20.635 Lbp 324.00 Br md 60.00 Dpth 29.00 Welded, 1 dk	**(A13A2TV) Crude Oil Tanker** Double Hull (13F) Liq: 330,000; Liq (Oil): 330,000 Compartments: 5 Ta, 10 Wing Ta, 2 Wing Slop Ta, ER 3 Cargo Pump (s): 3x5500m³/hr Manifold: Bow/CM: 163.6m	**1 oil engine** driving 1 FP propeller Total Power: 27,160kW (36,927hp) 15.6kn Wartsila 7RT-flex84T 1 x 2 Stroke 7 Cy. 840 x 3150 27160kW (36927bhp) Diesel United Ltd.-Aioi AuxGen: 3 x 930kW a.c Fuel: 730.0 (d.f.) 6630.0 (r.f.)
7804405 *JQUI* -	**TSUGARU** **Government of Japan (Ministry of Land, Infrastructure & Transport) (The Coastguard)** - SatCom: Inmarsat C 431243000 *Tokyo* *Japan* MMSI: 431243000 Official number: 121644	*3,221* - -		**1979-04 Ishikawajima-Harima Heavy Industries Co Ltd (IHI) — Tokyo** Yd No: 2714 Loa 105.40 Br ex 14.64 Dght 5.100 Lbp 97.23 Br md 14.60 Dpth 8.00 Welded	**(B34H2SQ) Patrol Vessel**	**2 oil engines** geared to sc. shafts driving 2 CP propellers Total Power: 11,474kW (15,600hp) 22.8kn Pielstick 12PC2-5V-400 2 x Vee 4 Stroke 12 Cy. 400 x 460 each-5737kW (7800bhp) Ishikawajima Harima Heavy IndustrieCo Ltd (IHI)-Japan AuxGen: 2 x 520kW 450V 60Hz a.c, 2 x 120kW 450V 60Hz a.c Thrusters: 1 Thwart. FP thruster (f) Fuel: 730.0 (d.f.) 49.0pd

9151278 *JD2735* -	**TSUGARU MARU** **Eikichi Kaiun KK & Kitanihon Tug Boat Co Ltd** Eikichi Kaiun KK *Tomakomai, Hokkaido* *Japan* Official number: 128516	*192* - -		**1996-09 Kanagawa Zosen — Kobe** Yd No: 433 Loa 36.20 Br ex - Dght - Lbp 31.60 Br md 8.80 Dpth 3.79 Welded, 1 dk	**(B32A2ST) Tug**	**2 oil engines** Geared Integral to driving 2 Z propellers Total Power: 2,648kW (3,600hp) 14.4kn Niigata 6L28HX 2 x 4 Stroke 6 Cy. 280 x 370 each-1324kW (1800bhp) Niigata Engineering Co Ltd-Japan
7639898 - -	**TSUIKI MARU No. 10** *ex* Taisei Maru No. 85 *-1989* - -	*145* - 234		**1977-03 Tokushima Zosen K.K. — Fukuoka** Yd No: 1231 Loa 39.81 (BB) Br ex 6.84 Dght 2.337 Lbp 33.91 Br md 6.81 Dpth 3.13 Welded, 1 dk	**(B12B2FC) Fish Carrier**	**1 oil engine** driving 1 FP propeller Total Power: 736kW (1,001hp) Hanshin 6LU28G 1 x 4 Stroke 6 Cy. 280 x 440 736kW (1001bhp) Hanshin Nainenki Kogyo-Japan
7937070 - -	**TSUIKI MARU No. 11** *ex* Yama Maru No. 11 *-1991* **Netsan Enterprises Inc** *Philippines*	*149* - -		**1977 Nichiro Zosen K.K. — Ishinomaki** Yd No: 378 Loa 38.87 (BB) Br ex - Dght - Lbp 33.00 Br md 6.71 Dpth 2.75 Welded, 1 dk	**(B11B2FV) Fishing Vessel**	**1 oil engine** driving 1 FP propeller Total Power: 662kW (900hp) Niigata 6L25BX 1 x 4 Stroke 6 Cy. 250 x 320 662kW (900bhp) Niigata Engineering Co Ltd-Japan
8633372 - -	**TSUIKI MARU No. 28** *ex* Zuikei Maru No. 1 *-1988* - -	*198* 59 -		**1976-02 Kesennuma Tekko — Kesennuma** L reg 29.60 Br ex - Dght 2.100 Lbp - Br md 6.20 Dpth 2.60 Welded, 1 dk	**(B11B2FV) Fishing Vessel**	**1 oil engine** driving 1 FP propeller
9691242 *JD3561* -	**TSUKASA** **Matsuda Kaiun KK** - *Komatsushima, Tokushima* *Japan* MMSI: 431004957 Official number: 141987	*3,615* - 4,999	Class: NK	**2013-10 Kanrei Zosen K.K. — Naruto** Yd No: 431 Loa 104.95 (BB) Br ex - Dght 6.220 Lbp 98.80 Br md 16.00 Dpth 8.30 Welded, 1 dk	**(A13B2TP) Products Tanker** Double Hull (13F) Liq: 5,499; Liq (Oil): 5,499	**1 oil engine** driving 1 Propeller Total Power: 3,250kW (4,419hp) MAN-B&W 5L35MC 1 x 2 Stroke 5 Cy. 350 x 1050 3250kW (4419bhp) The Hanshin Diesel Works Ltd-Japan Fuel: 215.0
9100578 *JM6368* -	**TSUKI MARU No. 11** **Tsukimaru Kaiun KK** *Shimonoseki, Yamaguchi* *Japan* Official number: 133655	*496* - 1,082	Class: NK	**1994-06 Shitanoe Shipbuilding Co Ltd — Usuki OT** Yd No: 1151 Loa 64.00 Br ex - Dght 3.892 Lbp 60.00 Br md 10.00 Dpth 4.50 Welded, 1 dk	**(A13B2TP) Products Tanker** Liq: 1,249; Liq (Oil): 1,249	**1 oil engine** driving 1 FP propeller Total Power: 736kW (1,001hp) 10.5kn Hanshin LH28LG 1 x 4 Stroke 6 Cy. 280 x 530 736kW (1001bhp) The Hanshin Diesel Works Ltd-Japan Fuel: 60.0 (d.f.)
7920778 - -	**TSUKI No. 3** *ex* Tsuki Maru No. 3 *-1994* - -	*464* 276 700		**1979-09 K.K. Miura Zosensho — Saiki** Yd No: 581 Loa 54.21 Br ex - Dght - Lbp 50.02 Br md 8.40 Dpth 3.92 Welded, 1 dk	**(A13B2TU) Tanker (unspecified)**	**1 oil engine** driving 1 FP propeller Total Power: 736kW (1,001hp) Hanshin 1 x 4 Stroke 736kW (1001bhp) The Hanshin Diesel Works Ltd-Japan
9443217 *3ELY5* -	**TSUKIBOSHI** **Tsukiboshi Shipping Corp SA** Busan Shipping Co Ltd *Panama* *Panama* MMSI: 357693000 Official number: 3327907B	**3,675** 1,103 3,713	Class: NK	**2007-09 Tsuji Heavy Industries (Jiangsu) Co Ltd — Zhangjiagang JS** Yd No: S-1 Loa 80.00 (BB) Br ex - Dght 3.514 Lbp 75.00 Br md 26.00 Dpth 6.30 Welded, 1 dk	**(A31A2GX) General Cargo Ship** Bale: 1,645	**2 oil engines** reduction geared to sc. shafts driving 2 FP propellers Total Power: 2,058kW (2,798hp) 11.0kn Niigata 6M28BGT 2 x 4 Stroke 6 Cy. 280 x 480 each-1029kW (1399bhp) Niigata Engineering Co Ltd-Japan Fuel: 375.0
8971279 *JI3695* -	**TSUKIBOSHI MARU** **Tsukiboshi Kaiun KK** *Osaka, Osaka* *Japan* MMSI: 431301596 Official number: 137081	*150* - -		**2001-11 K.K. Watanabe Zosensho — Nagasaki** Yd No: 093 Loa 17.61 Br ex - Dght - Lbp - Br md 12.25 Dpth 6.30 Welded, 1 dk	**(B32A2ST) Tug**	**1 oil engine** driving 1 FP propeller Total Power: 2,206kW (2,999hp) Niigata 6MG28HLX 1 x 4 Stroke 6 Cy. 280 x 400 2206kW (2999bhp) Niigata Engineering Co Ltd-Japan
9542219 *HPSY* -	**TSUKIBOSHI NO. 3** **Tsukiboshi Shipping Corp SA** Busan Shipping Co Ltd *Panama* *Panama* MMSI: 370716000 Official number: 4011709	**2,081** 890 3,609	Class: KR	**2008-12 Yangzhou Nakanishi Shipbuilding Co Ltd — Yizheng JS** Yd No: LC-730 Loa 84.90 Br ex 13.02 Dght 5.700 Lbp 79.02 Br md 13.00 Dpth 7.50 Welded, 1 dk	**(A31A2GX) General Cargo Ship** Compartments: 1 Ho, ER 1 Ha: ER (45.0 x 10.0)	**1 oil engine** driving 1 Propeller Total Power: 1,618kW (2,200hp) Niigata 6M34BGT 1 x 4 Stroke 6 Cy. 340 x 620 1618kW (2200bhp) Niigata Engineering Co Ltd-Japan AuxGen: 2 x 72kW 445V a.c
9674593 *JD3547* -	**TSUKUBA** **Kashima Futo KK** *Japan* MMSI: 431004713	*192* - 78	Class: FA	**2013-07 Keihin Dock Co Ltd — Yokohama** Yd No: 307 Loa 33.30 Br ex - Dght 3.900 Lbp - Br md 9.20 Dpth - Welded, 1 dk	**(B32A2ST) Tug**	**2 oil engines** gearing integral to driving 2 Z propellers Total Power: 3,676kW (4,998hp) Niigata 6L28HX 2 x 4 Stroke 6 Cy. 280 x 370 each-1838kW (2499bhp) Niigata Engineering Co Ltd-Japan
8742410 *7JEA* -	**TSUKUBA** **Government of Japan (Ministry of Land, Infrastructure & Transport) (The Coastguard)** - *Tokyo* *Japan* Official number: 140834	*209* - 40		**2009-03 Mitsubishi Heavy Industries Ltd. — Shimonoseki** Loa 46.00 Br ex - Dght 1.500 Lbp - Br md 7.80 Dpth 4.13 Welded, 1 dk	**(B34H2SQ) Patrol Vessel** Hull Material: Aluminium Alloy	**3 oil engines** reduction geared to sc. shafts driving 3 Water jets Total Power: 6,912kW (9,399hp) 35.0kn
8503606 *JG4490* -	**TSUKUBA MARU** - - *Susaki, Kochi* *Japan* Official number: 127658	*166* - -		**1985-06 Kanagawa Zosen — Kobe** Yd No: 275 Loa 31.60 Br ex - Dght 2.701 Lbp 27.00 Br md 8.60 Dpth 3.77 Welded, 1 dk	**(B32A2ST) Tug**	**2 oil engines** Geared Integral to driving 2 Z propellers Total Power: 2,206kW (3,000hp) 12.5kn Niigata 6L25CXE 2 x 4 Stroke 6 Cy. 250 x 320 each-1103kW (1500bhp) Niigata Engineering Co Ltd-Japan
9524035 *3FUJ4* -	**TSUKUBA MARU** **Tsukuba Shipping SA** Daiichi Chuo Kisen Kaisha *Panama* *Panama* MMSI: 352300000 Official number: 4504213	**106,368** 64,032 206,542	Class: NK	**2013-07 Japan Marine United Corp (JMU) — Nagasu KM (Ariake Shipyard)** Yd No: 153 Loa 299.70 (BB) Br ex - Dght 18.230 Lbp 291.75 Br md 50.00 Dpth 25.00 Welded, 1 dk	**(A21A2BC) Bulk Carrier** Double Hull Grain: 218,684 Compartments: 9 Ho, ER 9 Ha: ER	**1 oil engine** driving 1 FP propeller Total Power: 16,810kW (22,855hp) 14.0kn MAN-B&W 7S65ME-C 1 x 2 Stroke 7 Cy. 650 x 2730 16810kW (22855bhp) Mitsui Engineering & Shipbuilding CLtd-Japan AuxGen: 3 x 550kW a.c Fuel: 5330.0
9263162 *JJ4050* -	**TSUKUSHI** **Hankyu Ferry Co Ltd** - *Kobe, Hyogo* *Japan* MMSI: 431301679 Official number: 135998	*13,353* - 5,560		**2003-06 Mitsubishi Heavy Industries Ltd. — Shimonoseki** Yd No: 1091 Loa 195.00 Br ex - Dght 6.700 Lbp 180.00 Br md 26.40 Dpth 9.90 Welded	**(A36A2PR) Passenger/Ro-Ro Ship (Vehicles)** Passengers: unberthed: 667 Lane-Len: 640 Cars: 128, Trailers: 229	**2 oil engines** geared to sc. shafts driving 2 FP propellers Total Power: 20,152kW (27,398hp) 23.5kn Wartsila 16V38B 2 x Vee 4 Stroke 16 Cy. 380 x 475 each-10076kW (13699bhp) Wartsila Finland Oy-Finland
8949848 *JG3138* -	**TSUKUSHI MARU** **Eirin Kensetsu KK** *Osaka, Osaka* *Japan* Official number: 112886	*126* - -		**1972-07 Shimoda Dockyard Co. Ltd. — Shimoda** Loa 25.70 Br ex - Dght 1.400 Lbp 24.00 Br md 8.00 Dpth 2.30 Welded, 1 dk	**(B34X2QA) Anchor Handling Vessel**	**2 oil engines** driving 2 FP propellers Total Power: 308kW (418hp) 6.0kn Mitsubishi 2 x each-154kW (209bhp) Mitsubishi Heavy Industries Ltd-Japan
7634886 *9GXH* -	**TSUKWEI** *ex* Pandion V *-1975* **Tema Cold Stores Ltd** - *Takoradi* *Ghana* Official number: 316608	*121* 84 -		**1974 Bender Welding & Machine Co Inc — Mobile AL** L reg 20.73 Br ex 6.71 Dght - Lbp - Br md - Dpth - Welded, 1 dk	**(B11A2FT) Trawler**	**2 oil engines** geared to sc. shaft driving 1 FP propeller Total Power: 1,030kW (1,400hp) 12.0kn G.M. (Detroit Diesel) 16V-71-N 2 x Vee 2 Stroke 16 Cy. 108 x 127 each-515kW (700bhp) General Motors Detroit DieselAllison Divn-USA
9095618 *9GAV* -	**TSUKWEI I** *ex* Fu Yuan Yu 302 *-2007* **Bossgie Ltd** - *Takoradi* *Ghana* MMSI: 627045000 Official number: GSR 0045	**146** 51 -		**1999-01 No. 4810 Factory of P.L.A. — Dalian** Loa 31.01 Br ex - Dght - Lbp - Br md 6.20 Dpth 2.95 Welded, 1 dk	**(B11B2FV) Fishing Vessel**	**1 oil engine** reduction geared to sc. shaft driving 1 Propeller Total Power: 330kW (449hp) 11.0kn Chinese Std. Type Z8170ZL 1 x 4 Stroke 8 Cy. 170 x 200 330kW (449bhp) Zibo Diesel Engine Factory-China

IMO / Call sign / Flag	Name / Owner	Tonnage	Class	Builder / Dimensions	Type	Machinery
9095620 *9GAW* -	**TSUKWEI II** *ex* Fu Yuan Yu 303 *-2007* **Bossgie Ltd** - *Takoradi* *Ghana* MMSI: 627046000 Official number: GSR 0046	**146** 51 -		**1999-01 No. 4810 Factory of P.L.A. — Dalian** Loa 31.01 Br ex - Dght - Lbp - Br md 6.20 Dpth 2.95 Welded, 1 dk	**(B11B2FV) Fishing Vessel**	**1 oil engine** reduction geared to sc. shaft driving 1 Propeller Total Power: 330kW (449hp) 11.0kn Chinese Std. Type Z8170ZL 1 x 4 Stroke 8 Cy. 170 x 200 330kW (449bhp) Zibo Diesel Engine Factory-China
9599676 *ZGCP8* -	**TSUMAT** - **New Winds Ltd Partnership** - *George Town* *Cayman Islands (British)* MMSI: 319937000 Official number: 743771	**499** 149 128		**2012-10 Trinity Yachts LLC — Gulfport MS** Yd No: 057 Loa 45.40 Br ex 8.53 Dght 2.600 Lbp 42.81 Br md 8.13 Dpth 4.10 Welded, 1 dk	**(X11A2YP) Yacht** Hull Material: Aluminium Alloy	**2 oil engines** reduction geared to sc. shafts driving 2 Propellers Total Power: 5,050kW (6,866hp) Caterpillar 3516C-HD 2 x Vee 4 Stroke 16 Cy. 170 x 215 each-2525kW (3433bhp) Caterpillar Inc-USA AuxGen: 2 x 130kW a.c
8990201 *JK2326* -	**TSUNAS 3** - **Okamoto Kaiun KK** - *Fukuyama, Hiroshima* *Japan* MMSI: 431401984 Official number: 140002	*140* - -		**2004-08 K.K. Watanabe Zosensho — Nagasaki** Loa 19.50 Br ex - Dght - Lbp 18.00 Br md 12.85 Dpth 5.50 Welded, 1 dk	**(B32B2SP) Pusher Tug**	**1 oil engine** geared to sc. shaft driving 1 Propeller Total Power: 736kW (1,001hp) 11.0kn Daihatsu 6DKM-26 1 x 4 Stroke 6 Cy. 260 x 380 736kW (1001bhp) Daihatsu Diesel Manufacturing Co Lt-Japan
7936349 - -	**TSUNEFUKU GO** *ex* Kaiun No. 2 *-1990* - - *Indonesia*	*499* - -		**1980-02 Ishikawajima-Harima Heavy Industries Co Ltd (IHI) — Aioi HG** Yd No: 17 Loa - Br ex - Dght - Lbp 45.22 Br md 17.01 Dpth 3.20 Welded, 1 dk	**(B34B2SC) Crane Vessel**	**2 oil engines** driving 2 FP propellers Total Power: 882kW (1,200hp) Niigata 6MG20CX 2 x 4 Stroke 6 Cy. 200 x 260 each-441kW (600bhp) Niigata Engineering Co Ltd-Japan
7214181 *BKIU* -	**TSUNG MAO** *ex* Chung Der No. 1 *-2003* *ex* Obako No. 36 *-1999* *ex* Obako Maru No. 36 *-1985* **Tsung Mao Enterprise Co Ltd** - *Kaohsiung* *Chinese Taipei* Official number: 8995	*447* 134 304	Class: CR (NK)	**1972-04 Kishimoto Zosen — Osakikamijima** Yd No: 427 Converted From: Tug-1980 Loa 50.02 Br ex 9.89 Dght 4.090 Lbp 45.01 Br md 9.50 Dpth 4.47 Welded, 1 dk	**(B32B2SP) Pusher Tug**	**2 oil engines** geared to sc. shafts driving 2 FP propellers Total Power: 2,354kW (3,200hp) 12.0kn Daihatsu 8DSM-26 2 x 4 Stroke 8 Cy. 260 x 320 each-1177kW (1600bhp) Daihatsu Diesel Manufacturing Co Lt-Japan AuxGen: 2 x 80kW
9205990 *H3OX* -	**TSUNOMINE** - **Citrus Shipping SA, Chijin Shipping SA & Em Carriers SA** Magsaysay MOL Ship Management Inc SatCom: Inmarsat C 435624210 *Panama* *Panama* MMSI: 356242000 Official number: 2737100C	**83,496** 49,636 156,818 T/cm 115.1	Class: NK	**2000-10 Tsuneishi Shipbuilding Co Ltd — Tadotsu KG** Yd No: 1165 Loa 275.00 (BB) Br ex - Dght 16.630 Lbp 265.00 Br md 46.80 Dpth 23.60 Welded, 1 dk	**(A21A2BC) Bulk Carrier** Double Bottom Entire Compartment Length Grain: 184,631 Cargo Heating Coils Compartments: 7 Ho, ER 7 Ha: (21.6 x 17.2)6 (21.6 x 22.4)ER	**1 oil engine** driving 1 FP propeller Total Power: 16,859kW (22,921hp) 15.2kn B&W 6S70MC 1 x 2 Stroke 6 Cy. 700 x 2674 16859kW (22921bhp) Mitsui Engineering & Shipbuilding CLtd-Japan AuxGen: 3 x 660kW 450V 60Hz a.c Fuel: 148.0 (d.f.) (Heating Coils) 4394.0 (r.f.)
8720591 *JJ3586* -	**TSUNOMINE MARU No. 2** - **YK Fukui Kaiun Kensetsu** - *Himeji, Hyogo* *Japan* Official number: 130801	*321* - 583		**1988-05 Tokuoka Zosen K.K. — Naruto** Loa 56.60 Br ex 11.02 Dght 3.300 Lbp 52.86 Br md 11.00 Dpth 5.44 Welded, 1 dk	**(B33A2DG) Grab Dredger** Grain: 530 Cranes: 1x1.8t	**1 oil engine** driving 1 FP propeller Total Power: 515kW (700hp) 10.3kn Matsui ML628GSC 1 x 4 Stroke 6 Cy. 280 x 520 515kW (700bhp) Matsui Iron Works Co Ltd-Japan
8351314 - -	**TSURU 20** *ex* Sumiriki Maru No. 28 *-2005* *ex* Sachi Maru No. 38 *-1992* **Marina Estrella S de RL** - *San Lorenzo* *Honduras* Official number: L-1728124	*274* 82 -		**1983 Kochi Jyuko (Eiho Zosen) K.K. — Kochi** Yd No: 1607 Loa 29.42 Br ex - Dght - Lbp 26.00 Br md 8.21 Dpth 3.71 Welded, 1 dk	**(B32B2SP) Pusher Tug**	**2 oil engines** driving 2 FP propellers Total Power: 1,472kW (2,002hp) 12.0kn Akasaka A245R 2 x 4 Stroke 6 Cy. 245 x 450 each-736kW (1001bhp) Akasaka Tekkosho KK (Akasaka DieselLtd)-Japan
8512968 *C6TL2* -	**TSURU ARROW** *ex* Norsul Vancouver *-2004* *ex* Westwood Cleo *-2002* **Tsuru Shipping Sarl** Gearbulk Ltd *Nassau* *Bahamas* MMSI: 311683000 Official number: 8000766	**28,805** 13,964 45,295	Class: NV	**1987-01 Ishikawajima-Harima Heavy Industries Co Ltd (IHI) — Aioi HG** Yd No: 2953 Loa 199.90 (BB) Br ex - Dght 11.720 Lbp 190.62 Br md 30.51 Dpth 16.21 Welded, 1 dk	**(A31A2GO) Open Hatch Cargo Ship** Grain: 51,006; Bale: 50,000 TEU 2029 Compartments: 11 Ho, ER 11 Ha: (6.5 x 13.0)10 (13.1 x 25.3)ER Gantry cranes: 2x40t	**1 oil engine** driving 1 FP propeller Total Power: 8,363kW (11,370hp) 14.6kn Sulzer 6RTA62 1 x 2 Stroke 6 Cy. 620 x 2150 8363kW (11370bhp) Ishikawajima Harima Heavy IndustrieCo Ltd (IHI)-Japan AuxGen: 4 x 520kW 450V 60Hz a.c, 1 x 80kW 450V 60Hz a.c
6825373 - -	**TSURU MARU** - -	*154* 40		**1968 Hayashikane Shipbuilding & Engineering Co Ltd — Nagasaki NS** Yd No: 686 Loa 30.61 Br ex 6.53 Dght 2.769 Lbp 26.60 Br md 6.51 Dpth 2.82 Welded, 1 dk	**(B11B2FV) Fishing Vessel**	**1 oil engine** driving 1 FP propeller Total Power: 368kW (500hp) Niigata 6MG20X 1 x 4 Stroke 6 Cy. 200 x 260 368kW (500bhp) Niigata Engineering Co Ltd-Japan
9089267 - -	**TSURU MARU NO. 3** - -	*111* - -		**1990-11 Amakusa Zosen K.K. — Amakusa** L reg 25.47 Br ex - Dght 1.800 Lbp - Br md 7.50 Dpth 2.60 Welded, 1 dk	**(A31A2GX) General Cargo Ship**	**1 oil engine** driving 1 Propeller Total Power: 294kW (400hp) 10.0kn Matsui 1 x 4 Stroke 294kW (400bhp) Matsui Iron Works Co Ltd-Japan
8998045 *JD2042* -	**TSURU MARU NO. 5** - **YK Higashiyama Kaiun** - *Kamiamakusa, Kumamoto* *Japan* Official number: 136435	*218* - -		**1999-11 Amakusa Zosen K.K. — Amakusa** Loa 32.05 Br ex - Dght 4.620 Lbp 28.80 Br md 9.00 Dpth 4.80 Welded, 1 dk	**(A24D2BA) Aggregates Carrier**	**1 oil engine** driving 1 FP propeller Total Power: 662kW (900hp) Matsui ML624GSC-5 1 x 4 Stroke 6 Cy. 240 x 400 662kW (900bhp) Matsui Iron Works Co Ltd-Japan
7123150 - -	**TSURU MARU No. 5** - - - *South Korea*	*252* - -		**1971-08 Shimoda Dockyard Co. Ltd. — Shimoda** Yd No: 192 Loa - Br ex 8.54 Dght - Lbp 26.50 Br md 8.51 Dpth 3.89 Welded, 2 dks	**(B32A2ST) Tug**	**2 oil engines** driving 2 FP propellers Total Power: 1,912kW (2,600hp) Daihatsu 6DSM-26 2 x 4 Stroke 6 Cy. 260 x 320 each-956kW (1300bhp) Daihatsu Diesel Manufacturing Co Lt-Japan
7322378 - -	**TSURU MARU No. 6** - **Marina Estrella S de RL** Toa Corp *Honduras* Official number: L-1728290	*289* - -		**1973-05 Hashimoto Zosensho — Kobe** Yd No: 362 Loa 31.02 Br ex - Dght 3.010 Lbp 28.00 Br md 9.00 Dpth 3.89 Riveted\Welded, 1 dk	**(B32B2SA) Articulated Pusher Tug**	**2 oil engines** driving 2 FP propellers Total Power: 2,354kW (3,200hp) 13.0kn Hanshin 6LUD32G 2 x 4 Stroke 6 Cy. 320 x 510 each-1177kW (1600bhp) Hanshin Nainenki Kogyo-Japan
7353638 *HOXH6* -	**TSURU MARU No. 7** - **Toa Harbor (S) Pte Ltd** - *San Lorenzo* *Honduras* MMSI: 334830000 Official number: L-3828388	*341* 102 -		**1973-11 Kagoshima Dock & I.W. Co. Ltd. — Kagoshima** Yd No: 62 Loa 30.48 Br ex 9.33 Dght 2.794 Lbp 28.00 Br md 9.30 Dpth 3.89 Welded, 1 dk	**(B32B2SA) Articulated Pusher Tug**	**2 oil engines** geared to sc. shafts driving 2 FP propellers Total Power: 2,354kW (3,200hp) Daihatsu 8DSM-26 2 x 4 Stroke 8 Cy. 260 x 320 each-1177kW (1600bhp) Daihatsu Diesel Manufacturing Co Lt-Japan
7854773 *HQT03* -	**TSURU MARU No. 10** *ex* Shinkai Maru No. 15 *-1997* *ex* Kumagai Maru No. 2 *-1982* **Marina Estrella S de RL** - *San Lorenzo* *Honduras* Official number: L-1726833	*285* 85 -		**1970-03 Taguma Zosen KK — Onomichi HS** (Hull) Yd No: 82 **1970-03 Hitachi Zosen Corp — Onomichi HS (Innoshima Shipyard)** Loa 30.99 Br ex - Dght 2.901 Lbp 28.50 Br md 9.00 Dpth 4.02 Welded, 1 dk	**(B32B2SP) Pusher Tug**	**2 oil engines** geared to sc. shafts driving 2 FP propellers Total Power: 2,354kW (3,200hp) 9.0kn Daihatsu 8DSM-26 2 x 4 Stroke 8 Cy. 260 x 320 each-1177kW (1600bhp) Daihatsu Diesel Manufacturing Co Lt-Japan

9266798 *JM6724* -	**TSURUFUJI MARU** - **Corporation for Advanced Transport & Technology & Hinode Kaiun KK** Hinode Kaiun KK *Fukuoka, Fukuoka* *Japan* MMSI: 431602142 Official number: 136855	*3,676* - 4,998	Class: NK	**2002-10 K.K. Miura Zosensho — Saiki** Yd No: 1257 Loa 104.98 Br ex - Dght 6.264 Lbp 99.20 Br md 16.00 Dpth 8.30 Welded, 1 dk	**(A13B2TP) Products Tanker** Double Hull (13F) Liq: 6,400; Liq (Oil): 6,400	**1 oil engine** driving 1 FP propeller Total Power: 3,309kW (4,499hp) Akasaka 1 x 4 Stroke 6 Cy. 450 x 880 3309kW (4499bhp) Akasaka Tekkosho KK (Akasaka DieselLtd)-Japan Fuel: 245.0	13.5kn A45S
9439058 *3EVP8* -	**TSURUGA** - **Cannon Dale Maritima SA** NYK Shipmanagement Pte Ltd SatCom: Inmarsat Mini-M 764937937 *Panama* *Panama* MMSI: 352091000 Official number: 4086309	**160,068** 103,103 309,960 T/cm 183.7	Class: NK	**2009-10 Imabari Shipbuilding Co Ltd — Saijo EH (Saijo Shipyard)** Yd No: 8063 Loa 332.99 (BB) Br ex - Dght 21.123 Lbp 324.00 Br md 60.00 Dpth 29.00 Welded, 1 dk	**(A13A2TV) Crude Oil Tanker** Double Hull (13F) Liq: 335,177; Liq (Oil): 335,177 Compartments: 5 Ta, 10 Wing Ta, 2 Wing Slop Ta, ER 3 Cargo Pump (s): 3x5500m³/hr Manifold: Bow/CM: 164m	**1 oil engine** driving 1 FP propeller Total Power: 31,040kW (42,202hp) MAN-B&W 1 x 2 Stroke 8 Cy. 800 x 3200 31040kW (42202bhp) Mitsui Engineering & Shipbuilding CLtd-Japan AuxGen: 4 x 960kW a.c Fuel: 7250.0 (r.f.)	15.5kn 8S80MC-C
9151254 *JG5486*	**TSURUGA** *ex Hokuto 3 -2002* **Izumi Kisen KK (Izumi Shipping Co Ltd)** - *Tokyo* *Japan* MMSI: 431100287 Official number: 135853	*8,608* - 5,952	Class: NK	**1997-01 Imabari Shipbuilding Co Ltd — Marugame KG (Marugame Shipyard)** Yd No: 1267 Loa 167.72 (BB) Br ex - Dght 7.015 Lbp 156.00 Br md 24.00 Dpth 9.30 Welded, 2 dks	**(A35A2RR) Ro-Ro Cargo Ship** Passengers: berths: 8 Quarter bow door/ramp (s) Len: - Wid: - Swl: 50 Quarter stern door/ramp (s) Len: - Wid: - Swl: 70 Lane-Len: 1440 Trailers: 120 TEU 40	**1 oil engine** reduction geared to sc. shaft driving 1 FP propeller Total Power: 19,662kW (26,732hp) Pielstick 1 x Vee 4 Stroke 18 Cy. 570 x 660 19662kW (26732bhp) Nippon Kokan KK (NKK Corp)-Japan AuxGen: 2 x 1270kW a.c, 2 x 635kW a.c Thrusters: 1 Thwart. FP thruster (f); 2 Tunnel thruster (a) Fuel: 911.0 (r.f.)	23.3kn 18PC4-2BV570
9203069 *JG5374* -	**TSURUGA MARU NO. 2** *ex Asama Maru -2009* **Nichido Kaiun KK** - *Tsuruga, Fukui* *Japan* MMSI: 431200084 Official number: 136613	*166* - -		**1998-01 Keihin Dock Co Ltd — Yokohama** Yd No: 247 Loa 30.80 Br ex - Dght 2.700 Lbp 27.00 Br md 8.80 Dpth 3.58 Welded, 1 dk	**(B32A2ST) Tug**	**2 oil engines** Geared Integral to driving 2 Z propellers Total Power: 2,280kW (3,100hp) Niigata 2 x 4 Stroke 6 Cy. 250 x 350 each-1140kW (1550bhp) Niigata Engineering Co Ltd-Japan	13.5kn 6L25HX
9227405 *JG5620* -	**TSURUGI** - **Government of Japan (Ministry of Land, Infrastructure & Transport) (The Coastguard)** - *Tokyo* *Japan* Official number: 136986	*230* - -		**2001-02 Hitachi Zosen Corp — Kawasaki KN** Yd No: 117107 Loa 48.50 Br ex - Dght - Lbp - Br md 7.80 Dpth 4.21 Welded, 1 dk	**(B34H2SQ) Patrol Vessel** Hull Material: Aluminium Alloy	**3 oil engines** geared to sc. shafts driving 3 Water jets Total Power: 12,960kW (17,619hp) M.T.U. 3 x Vee 4 Stroke 16 Cy. 190 x 210 each-4320kW (5873bhp) MTU Friedrichshafen GmbH-Friedrichshafen	40.0kn 16V595TE90
8738213 *JD2656*	**TSURUGI** - **Kansai Kowan Service KK** - *Sakai, Osaka* *Japan* Official number: 140759	*271* - -		**2008-05 Hatayama Zosen KK — Yura WK** Yd No: 253 Loa 38.00 Br ex - Dght 3.710 Lbp 32.00 Br md 9.60 Dpth 4.49 Welded, 1 dk	**(B32A2ST) Tug**	**2 oil engines** reduction geared to sc. shafts driving 2 Propellers Total Power: 3,676kW (4,998hp) Niigata 2 x 4 Stroke 6 Cy. 280 x 370 each-1838kW (2499bhp) Niigata Engineering Co Ltd-Japan	13.5kn 6L28HX
9100566 *JL6197* -	**TSURUHIRO MARU** - **Tsuruhiro Kaiun KK** Shinpo Kaiun KK *Matsuyama, Ehime* *Japan* MMSI: 431500239 Official number: 133974	*699* - 1,903	Class: NK	**1994-07 Shirahama Zosen K.K. — Honai** Yd No: 165 Loa 70.80 (BB) Br ex - Dght 4.700 Lbp 66.00 Br md 11.80 Dpth 5.30 Welded, 1 dk	**(A13B2TP) Products Tanker** Liq: 2,200; Liq (Oil): 2,200 Compartments: 10 Ta, ER	**1 oil engine** with clutches & reverse geared to sc. shaft driving 1 FP propeller Total Power: 736kW (1,001hp) Hanshin 1 x 4 Stroke 6 Cy. 300 x 600 736kW (1001bhp) The Hanshin Diesel Works Ltd-Japan AuxGen: 3 x 117kW a.c Fuel: 65.0 (d.f.)	10.5kn LH30LG
9275907 *JK5637* -	**TSURUHIRO MARU** - **Koan Kigyo KK** - *Kure, Hiroshima* *Japan* MMSI: 431401935 Official number: 136202	*749* - 1,907	Class: NK	**2002-12 Hakata Zosen K.K. — Imabari** Yd No: 652 Loa 69.93 Br ex - Dght 5.033 Lbp 66.00 Br md 11.50 Dpth 5.60 Welded, 1 dk	**(A12B2TR) Chemical/Products Tanker** Double Hull (13F) Liq: 2,200; Liq (Oil): 2,200	**1 oil engine** driving 1 FP propeller Total Power: 1,618kW (2,200hp) Akasaka 1 x 4 Stroke 6 Cy. 340 x 620 1618kW (2200bhp) Akasaka Tekkosho KK (Akasaka DieselLtd)-Japan Fuel: 85.0	12.5kn A34C
9303675 *JK5612* -	**TSURUKABUTO** - **Mori Kaiun YK** Toshin Yusosen Co Ltd (Toshin Yusosen KK) *Kasaoka, Okayama* *Japan* MMSI: 431401969 Official number: 136166	*749* - 1,830		**2004-01 K.K. Miura Zosensho — Saiki** Yd No: 1271 Loa 94.50 (BB) Br ex - Dght 3.684 Lbp 85.00 Br md 14.00 Dpth 6.85 Welded, 1 dk	**(A33A2CC) Container Ship (Fully Cellular)** TEU 239 incl 52 ref C.	**1 oil engine** driving 1 FP propeller Total Power: 2,059kW (2,799hp) Hanshin 1 x 4 Stroke 6 Cy. 380 x 760 2059kW (2799bhp) The Hanshin Diesel Works Ltd-Japan Thrusters: 1 Tunnel thruster (f)	12.5kn LH38L
9264893 *HPGH* -	**TSURUMI** - **Kei Enterprise Inc** NYK Shipmanagement Pte Ltd SatCom: Inmarsat C 435311210 *Panama* *Panama* MMSI: 353112000 Official number: 2933103B	**159,960** 97,016 300,610 T/cm 182.4	Class: NK	**2003-07 IHI Marine United Inc — Kure HS** Yd No: 3171 Loa 333.00 (BB) Br ex - Dght 20.529 Lbp 324.00 Br md 60.00 Dpth 29.00 Welded, 1 dk	**(A13A2TV) Crude Oil Tanker** Double Hull (13F) Liq: 330,175; Liq (Oil): 340,000 Compartments: 5 Ta, 10 Wing Ta, 2 Wing Slop Ta, ER 3 Cargo Pump (s): 3x5500m³/hr Manifold: Bow/CM: 163.6m	**1 oil engine** driving 1 FP propeller Total Power: 27,160kW (36,927hp) Sulzer 1 x 2 Stroke 7 Cy. 840 x 3150 27160kW (36927bhp) Diesel United Ltd.-Aioi AuxGen: 3 x 1200kW 440/110V 60Hz a.c Fuel: 500.0 (d.f.) (Heating Coils) 7832.0 (r.f.)	15.7kn 7RTA84T
8971255 *JK5617* -	**TSURUMI** - **Tetsuo Shigeeda** - *Hofu, Yamaguchi* *Japan* MMSI: 431401905 Official number: 136182	*499* - 1,360		**2001-10 K.K. Miura Zosensho — Saiki** Yd No: 1237 Loa 80.00 (BB) Br ex - Dght - Lbp - Br md 13.20 Dpth 6.60 Welded, 1 dk	**(A33A2CC) Container Ship (Fully Cellular)**	**1 oil engine** driving 1 FP propeller Total Power: 1,765kW (2,400hp) Hanshin 1 x 4 Stroke 6 Cy. 360 x 670 1765kW (2400bhp) The Hanshin Diesel Works Ltd-Japan	14.0kn LH36L
9246281 *HOMT* -	**TSURUSAKI** - **Kingfisher Shipholding SA & Stork Panama SA** NYK Shipmanagement Pte Ltd SatCom: Inmarsat C 435552310 *Panama* *Panama* MMSI: 355523000 Official number: 2881302B	**154,338** 99,476 300,838 T/cm 172.8	Class: NK	**2002-10 IHI Marine United Inc — Kure HS** Yd No: 3159 Loa 333.00 (BB) Br ex 60.04 Dght 21.428 Lbp 319.60 Br md 60.00 Dpth 29.50 Welded, 1 dk	**(A13A2TV) Crude Oil Tanker** Double Hull (13F) Liq: 333,700; Liq (Oil): 340,000 Compartments: 5 Ta, 10 Wing Ta, 2 Wing Slop Ta, ER 3 Cargo Pump (s): 3x5500m³/hr Manifold: Bow/CM: 163.6m	**1 oil engine** driving 1 FP propeller Total Power: 27,165kW (36,934hp) Sulzer 1 x 2 Stroke 7 Cy. 840 x 3150 27165kW (36934bhp) Diesel United Ltd.-Aioi AuxGen: 3 x 920kW 450V 60Hz a.c Fuel: 430.0 (d.f.) 6430.0 (r.f.)	16.0kn 7RTA84T-B
9186546 *JM6510* -	**TSURUSATO MARU** - **Tsurusato Unyu KK** - *Shimonoseki, Yamaguchi* *Japan* MMSI: 431401103 Official number: 135449	*749* - 1,950		**1998-05 Maebata Zosen Tekko K.K. — Sasebo** Yd No: 235 Loa 74.15 Br ex - Dght 4.850 Lbp 69.00 Br md 11.40 Dpth 5.35 Welded, 1 dk	**(A13A2TV) Crude Oil Tanker**	**1 oil engine** driving 1 FP propeller Total Power: 1,324kW (1,800hp) Hanshin 1 x 4 Stroke 6 Cy. 300 x 600 1324kW (1800bhp) The Hanshin Diesel Works Ltd-Japan	12.0kn LH30LG
8416097 - - -	**TSURUSHIMA MARU** - - - *South Korea*	*496* - 1,200		**1984-10 K.K. Odo Zosen Tekko — Shimonoseki** Yd No: 308 Loa 61.93 Br ex 9.73 Dght 4.201 Lbp 56.01 Br md 9.71 Dpth 4.47 Welded, 1 dk	**(A13B2TP) Products Tanker** Liq: 1,148; Liq (Oil): 1,148 Compartments: 8 Ta, ER	**1 oil engine** driving 1 FP propeller Total Power: 956kW (1,300hp) Hanshin 1 x 4 Stroke 6 Cy. 320 x 510 956kW (1300bhp) The Hanshin Diesel Works Ltd-Japan	6LU32
9046693 *JM6131* -	**TSURUSHIO MARU No. 2** - **Tsurushio Kaiun YK** - *Shimonoseki, Yamaguchi* *Japan* Official number: 132708	*355* - 749		**1992-05 Kanmon Zosen K.K. — Shimonoseki** Yd No: 536 Loa 55.51 (BB) Br ex 9.02 Dght 3.500 Lbp 51.50 Br md 9.00 Dpth 4.10 Welded, 1 dk	**(A13B2TP) Products Tanker** Liq: 733; Liq (Oil): 733 Compartments: 8 Ta, ER	**1 oil engine** reverse geared to sc. shaft driving 1 FP propeller Total Power: 736kW (1,001hp) Hanshin 1 x 4 Stroke 6 Cy. 280 x 460 736kW (1001bhp) The Hanshin Diesel Works Ltd-Japan	LH28G

9078347 *JM6261* -	**TSURUSHIO MARU No. 8** **Tsurushio Kaiun YK** - *Shimonoseki, Yamaguchi* *Japan* Official number: 133599	*370* - 776		**1993**-09 **Kanmon Zosen K.K. — Shimonoseki** Yd No: 556 Loa 56.99 (BB) Br ex 9.02 Dght 3.662 Lbp 52.60 Br md 9.00 Dpth 4.10 Welded, 1 dk	**(A13B2TP) Products Tanker** Liq: 758; Liq (Oil): 758 Compartments: 8 Ta, ER	**1 oil engine** with clutches & reverse geared to sc. shaft driving 1 FP propeller Total Power: 736kW (1,001hp) Hanshin LH28G 1 x 4 Stroke 6 Cy. 280 x 460 736kW (1001bhp) The Hanshin Diesel Works Ltd-Japan
9690341 *JD3586* -	**TSURUTAMA MARU NO. 2** **Tamai Steamship Co Ltd & Japan Railway Construction, Transport & Technology Agency** Tamai Steamship Co Ltd *Tokyo* *Japan* MMSI: 431004883 Official number: 142030	*3,767* - 5,600	Class: NK	**2013**-10 **Hakata Zosen K.K. — Imabari** Yd No: 763 Loa 104.99 Br ex - Dght 6.713 Lbp 98.00 Br md 16.00 Dpth 8.50 Welded, 1 dk	**(A13B2TP) Products Tanker** Double Hull (13F) Liq: 5,780; Liq (Oil): 5,999	**1 oil engine** driving 1 Propeller Total Power: 3,309kW (4,499hp) Hanshin LH46LA 1 x 4 Stroke 6 Cy. 460 x 880 3309kW (4499bhp) The Hanshin Diesel Works Ltd-Japan Fuel: 385.0
8919960 *JM5967* -	**TSURUWA MARU** **Kyowa Kisen KK (Kyowa Steamship Co Ltd)** Shinwa Naiko Kaiun Kaisha Ltd *Fukuoka, Fukuoka* *Japan* MMSI: 431600939 Official number: 131356	*4,884* - 7,900	Class: NK	**1990**-03 **Iwagi Zosen Co Ltd — Kamijima EH** Yd No: 132 Loa 106.00 Br ex - Dght 7.373 Lbp 99.99 Br md 18.70 Dpth 9.45 Welded, 1 dk	**(A24E2BL) Limestone Carrier** Grain: 6,004	**1 oil engine** driving 1 FP propeller Total Power: 3,347kW (4,551hp) 14.5kn Mitsubishi 7UEC37LA 1 x 2 Stroke 7 Cy. 370 x 880 3347kW (4551bhp) Akasaka Tekkosho KK (Akasaka DieselLtd)-Japan Fuel: 230.0 (r.f.)
8926353 *JK5507* -	**TSURUYOSHI MARU NO. 1** *ex* Koan Maru No. 7 *-2005* **Yamakawa Kaiun YK** - *Kasaoka, Okayama* *Japan* Official number: 135255	*199* - 699		**1996**-10 **Kimura Zosen K.K. — Kure** Loa 57.20 Br ex - Dght 3.200 Lbp 52.50 Br md 9.40 Dpth 5.50 Welded, 1 dk	**(A31A2GX) General Cargo Ship**	**1 oil engine** driving 1 FP propeller Total Power: 736kW (1,001hp) 11.7kn Hanshin LH28G 1 x 4 Stroke 6 Cy. 280 x 460 736kW (1001bhp) The Hanshin Diesel Works Ltd-Japan
8889854 *JL6388* -	**TSURUYOSHI MARU NO. 2** *ex* Hinode Maru *-2006* **Yamakawa Kaiun YK** - *Kasaoka, Okayama* *Japan* Official number: 135072	*274* - 688		**1995**-06 **Y.K. Takasago Zosensho — Naruto** Yd No: 207 Loa 57.40 Br ex - Dght 3.520 Lbp 53.00 Br md 9.50 Dpth 5.55 Welded, 1 dk	**(A31A2GX) General Cargo Ship** Bale: 1,405 Compartments: 1 Ho, ER 1 Ha: (30.3 x 7.5)ER	**1 oil engine** driving 1 FP propeller Total Power: 736kW (1,001hp) 10.0kn Hanshin LH28G 1 x 4 Stroke 6 Cy. 280 x 460 736kW (1001bhp) The Hanshin Diesel Works Ltd-Japan
9715177 *JD3519* -	**TSURUYOSHI MARU NO. 3** **Yamakawa Kaiun YK** - *Kasaoka, Okayama* *Japan* MMSI: 431004452 Official number: 141926	*269* - 900		**2013**-04 **K.K. Murakami Zosensho — Naruto** Loa 61.00 Br ex - Dght - Lbp 55.40 Br md 9.80 Dpth 6.00 Welded, 1 dk	**(A31A2GX) General Cargo Ship**	**1 oil engine** reduction geared to sc. shaft driving 1 Propeller Total Power: 735kW (999hp)
9677258 *JD3527* -	**TSURUYOSHI MARU NO. 5** **Yamakawa Kaiun YK** - *Kasaoka, Okayama* *Japan* Official number: 141935	*447* - 1,300		**2013**-05 **Yano Zosen K.K. — Imabari** Yd No: 278 Loa 72.31 Br ex - Dght 3.911 Lbp - Br md 11.00 Dpth 6.78 Welded, 1 dk	**(A31A2GX) General Cargo Ship** Double Hull Grain: 1,963; Bale: 1,963 Compartments: 1 Ho, ER 1 Ha: ER	**1 oil engine** reduction geared to sc. shaft driving 1 Propeller Total Power: 1,176kW (1,599hp) Niigata 6M28NTG 1 x 4 Stroke 6 Cy. 280 x 480 1176kW (1599bhp) Niigata Engineering Co Ltd-Japan
9608025 *JD3237* -	**TSURUYOSHI MARU NO. 8** **Yamakawa Kaiun YK** - *Kasaoka, Okayama* *Japan* MMSI: 431002815 Official number: 141506	*267* - 800		**2011**-08 **Yano Zosen K.K. — Imabari** Yd No: 232 Loa 61.00 Br ex - Dght 3.428 Lbp 55.40 Br md 9.80 Dpth 6.00 Welded, 1 dk	**(A31A2GX) General Cargo Ship** Double Hull Grain: 1,371; Bale: 1,328 1 Ha: (31.0 x 7.5)	**1 oil engine** reduction geared to sc. shaft driving 1 Propeller Total Power: 1,029kW (1,399hp) Niigata 6M28BGT 1 x 4 Stroke 6 Cy. 280 x 480 1029kW (1399bhp) Niigata Engineering Co Ltd-Japan
7932927 - -	**TSURUYOSHI MARU No. 18** *ex* Fukutoku Maru *-1984* **Asia Ship Trader Inc** -	*145* - 349		**1979 KK Ouchi Zosensho — Matsuyama EH** Yd No: 153 L reg 35.82 Br ex - Dght 2.910 Lbp - Br md 7.80 Dpth 4.81 Welded, 1 dk	**(A31A2GX) General Cargo Ship**	**1 oil engine** driving 1 FP propeller Matsui 1 x 4 Stroke Matsui Iron Works Co Ltd-Japan
9472804 *JD2541* -	**TSUSHIMA** **Soki Kisen KK** - *Imabari, Ehime* *Japan* Official number: 140672	*499* - 1,815		**2007**-11 **Yamanaka Zosen K.K. — Imabari** Yd No: 755 Loa 74.20 Br ex - Dght 4.360 Lbp 68.00 Br md 12.00 Dpth 7.37 Welded, 1 dk	**(A31A2GX) General Cargo Ship** Grain: 2,919; Bale: 2,836 1 Ha: (40.0 x 9.5)	**1 oil engine** driving 1 FP propeller Total Power: 1,618kW (2,200hp) 12.4kn Hanshin LH34LA 1 x 4 Stroke 6 Cy. 340 x 640 1618kW (2200bhp) The Hanshin Diesel Works Ltd-Japan
9387267 *9VHE8* -	**TSUSHIMA** **Maybaru Shipping & Trading Pte Ltd** MMS Co Ltd SatCom: Inmarsat C 456445411 *Singapore* *Singapore* MMSI: 564454000 Official number: 393938	**160,116** 103,527 310,391 T/cm 183.9	Class: NK	**2008**-12 **Mitsui Eng. & SB. Co. Ltd., Chiba Works — Ichihara** Yd No: 1697 Loa 333.00 (BB) Br ex 60.04 Dght 20.943 Lbp 324.00 Br md 60.00 Dpth 28.80 Welded, 1 dk	**(A13A2TV) Crude Oil Tanker** Double Hull (13F) Liq: 339,525; Liq (Oil): 347,597 Compartments: 5 Ta, 10 Wing Ta, 2 Wing Slop Ta, ER 4 Cargo Pump (s): 3x5500m³/hr, 1x2300m³/hr Manifold: Bow/CM: 167.3m	**1 oil engine** driving 1 FP propeller Total Power: 27,160kW (36,927hp) 15.9kn MAN-B&W 7S80MC-C 1 x 2 Stroke 7 Cy. 800 x 3200 27160kW (36927bhp) Mitsui Engineering & Shipbuilding CLtd-Japan AuxGen: 3 x 1050kW 440V 60Hz a.c Fuel: 420.0 (d.f.) 7900.0 (r.f.)
8737984 *9LY2508* -	**TT STAR** *ex* Xin Huang *-2012* **Zhejiang Xinyi Transportation Co Ltd** Hong Kong Tian Cheng International Ship Management Co Ltd *Freetown* *Sierra Leone* MMSI: 667003311 Official number: SL103311	**5,675** 3,240 8,310	Class: PD	**2008**-11 **Zhejiang Shunhang Ship Manufacturing Co Ltd — Yueqing ZJ** Loa 122.00 Br ex - Dght 6.900 Lbp 113.00 Br md 17.80 Dpth 9.10 Welded, 1 dk	**(A31A2GX) General Cargo Ship**	**1 oil engine** reduction geared to sc. shaft driving 1 Propeller Total Power: 2,206kW (2,999hp) 10.0kn Guangzhou 8320ZCD 1 x 4 Stroke 8 Cy. 320 x 440 2206kW (2999bhp) Guangzhou Diesel Engine Factory CoLtd-China
9068706 - -	**TTB 1601** *ex* Atk 2012 *-2010* **PT Trada Tug & Barge** PT Trada Maritime *Surabaya* *Indonesia*	**204** 62 -	Class: KI	**2005**-12 **PT Ben Santosa — Surabaya** Loa 28.00 Br ex - Dght 2.990 Lbp 26.11 Br md 8.00 Dpth 3.80 Welded, 1 dk	**(B32A2ST) Tug**	**2 oil engines** geared to sc. shafts driving 2 Propellers Total Power: 1,220kW (1,658hp) Yanmar 6AYM-ETE 2 x 4 Stroke 6 Cy. 155 x 180 each-610kW (829bhp) Yanmar Diesel Engine Co Ltd-Japan
9069554 *YD6900* -	**TTB 2001** *ex* ATK 2006 *-2008* **PT Trada Tug & Barge** PT Trada Maritime *Samarinda* *Indonesia*	**222** 67 -	Class: KI	**2004**-01 **PT Candi Pasifik — Samarinda** Loa - Br ex - Dght - Lbp 26.73 Br md 8.00 Dpth 3.70 Welded, 1 dk	**(B32A2ST) Tug**	**2 oil engines** geared to sc. shafts driving 2 Propellers Total Power: 1,618kW (2,200hp) Yanmar 12LAK (M)-STE2 2 x Vee 4 Stroke 12 Cy. 150 x 165 each-809kW (1100bhp) Yanmar Diesel Engine Co Ltd-Japan
9089853 *YD6861* -	**TTB 2002** *ex* Atk 2008 *-2013* **PT Trada Tug & Barge** PT Trada Maritime *Samarinda* *Indonesia*	**210** 63 -	Class: KI	**2005**-12 **PT Candi Pasifik — Samarinda** L reg 29.00 Br ex - Dght 2.890 Lbp 26.50 Br md 8.00 Dpth 3.70 Welded, 1 dk	**(B32A2ST) Tug**	**2 oil engines** geared to sc. shafts driving 2 Propellers Total Power: 1,618kW (2,200hp) Yanmar 12LAK (M)-STE2 2 x Vee 4 Stroke 12 Cy. 150 x 165 each-809kW (1100bhp) Yanmar Diesel Engine Co Ltd-Japan
9097848 *YD6862* -	**TTB 2003** *ex* Atk 2015 *-2013* **PT Trada Tug & Barge** PT Trada Maritime *Samarinda* *Indonesia*	**208** 63 -	Class: KI	**2005**-12 **PT Candi Pasifik — Samarinda** Loa 28.90 Br ex - Dght - Lbp 26.50 Br md 8.00 Dpth 3.75 Welded, 1 dk	**(B32A2ST) Tug**	**2 oil engines** reduction geared to sc. shafts driving 2 Propellers Total Power: 1,516kW (2,062hp) Mitsubishi S6R2-MPTK2 2 x 4 Stroke 6 Cy. 170 x 220 each-758kW (1031bhp) Mitsubishi Heavy Industries Ltd-Japan
9093361 *YD6860* -	**TTB 2004** *ex* Atk 2007 *-2010* **PT Trada Tug & Barge** PT Trada Maritime *Samarinda* *Indonesia*	**212** 64 -	Class: KI	**2005**-12 **PT Candi Pasifik — Samarinda** Loa 29.00 Br ex - Dght - Lbp 27.50 Br md 8.00 Dpth 3.70 Welded, 1 dk	**(B32A2ST) Tug**	**2 oil engines** geared to sc. shafts driving 2 Propellers Total Power: 1,618kW (2,200hp) Yanmar 12LAK (M)-STE2 2 x Vee 4 Stroke 12 Cy. 150 x 165 each-809kW (1100bhp) Yanmar Diesel Engine Co Ltd-Japan
9095761 *YD6858* -	**TTB 2005** *ex* Atk 2002 *-2010* **PT Trada Tug & Barge** PT Trada Maritime *Samarinda* *Indonesia*	**213** 64 -	Class: KI	**2005**-12 **PT Candi Pasifik — Samarinda** Loa - Br ex - Dght - Lbp 26.50 Br md 8.00 Dpth 3.70 Welded, 1 dk	**(B32A2ST) Tug**	**2 oil engines** geared to sc. shafts driving 2 Propellers Total Power: 1,472kW (2,002hp) Yanmar 6RY17P-GV 2 x 4 Stroke 6 Cy. 165 x 219 each-736kW (1001bhp) Yanmar Diesel Engine Co Ltd-Japan

9098098 *YD6863* -	**TTB 2006** *ex* Surya Iii **PT Trada Tug & Barge** PT Trada Maritime *Samarinda* *Indonesia*	**201** 61 -	Class: KI	**2005-12 PT Candi Pasifik — Samarinda** Loa 27.40 Br ex - Dght - Lbp 25.50 Br md 8.00 Dpth 3.70 Welded, 1 dk	**(B32A2ST) Tug**	**2 oil engines** reduction geared to sc. shafts driving 2 Propellers Total Power: 1,618kW (2,200hp) Yanmar 12LAK (M)-STE2 2 x Vee 4 Stroke 12 Cy. 150 x 165 each-809kW (1100bhp) Yanmar Diesel Engine Co Ltd-Japan AuxGen: 2 x 80kW a.c
9092276 *YD6857* -	**TTB 2007** *ex* Atk 2001 **PT Trada Tug & Barge** PT Trada Maritime *Samarinda* *Indonesia*	**211** 64 -	Class: KI	**2005-01 PT Candi Pasifik — Samarinda** Loa - Br ex - Dght - Lbp 26.73 Br md 8.00 Dpth 3.70 Welded, 1 dk	**(B32A2ST) Tug**	**2 oil engines** geared to sc. shafts driving 2 Propellers Total Power: 1,472kW (2,002hp) Yanmar 6RY17P-GV 1 x 4 Stroke 6 Cy. 165 x 219 736kW (1001bhp) Yanmar Diesel Engine Co Ltd-Japan
9097769 *YD6908* -	**TTB 2008** *ex* Surya I **PT Trada Tug & Barge** PT Trada Maritime *Samarinda* *Indonesia*	**206** 62 -	Class: KI	**2005-01 PT Candi Pasifik — Samarinda** Loa - Br ex - Dght - Lbp 26.40 Br md 8.00 Dpth 3.45 Welded, 1 dk	**(B32A2ST) Tug**	**2 oil engines** reduction geared to sc. shafts driving 2 Propellers Total Power: 1,618kW (2,200hp) Yanmar 12LAK (M)-STE2 2 x Vee 4 Stroke 12 Cy. 150 x 165 each-809kW (1100bhp) Yanmar Diesel Engine Co Ltd-Japan
9093359 *YD6899* -	**TTB 2009** *ex* Atk 2004 *-2010* **PT Trada Tug & Barge** PT Trada Maritime *Samarinda* *Indonesia*	**222** 67 -	Class: KI	**2005-12 PT Candi Pasifik — Samarinda** Loa 29.00 Br ex - Dght - Lbp 26.50 Br md 8.00 Dpth 3.70 Welded, 1 dk	**(B32A2ST) Tug**	**2 oil engines** geared to sc. shafts driving 2 Propellers Total Power: 1,472kW (2,002hp) Yanmar 6RY17P-GV 2 x 4 Stroke 6 Cy. 165 x 219 each-736kW (1001bhp) Yanmar Diesel Engine Co Ltd-Japan
8218251 *HP2965* -	**TTB SALVOR** *ex* Puma Tide *-2010* *ex* Ocean Puma *-1998* **T&T Bisso Salvage Asia Pte Ltd** - *Panama* *Panama* MMSI: 354763000 Official number: 4237911	**729** 218 953	Class: (AB)	**1983-05 Southern Ocean Shipbuilding Co Pte Ltd — Singapore** Yd No: 141 Loa 49.36 Br ex - Dght 4.395 Lbp 44.40 Br md 12.01 Dpth 5.01 Welded, 1 dk	**(B21A20S) Platform Supply Ship**	**2 oil engines** sr reverse geared to sc. shafts driving 2 FP propellers Total Power: 2,924kW (3,976hp) 12.0kn Yanmar 6Z280L-ET 2 x 4 Stroke 6 Cy. 280 x 360 each-1462kW (1988bhp) Yanmar Diesel Engine Co Ltd-Japan AuxGen: 2 x 128kW Thrusters: 1 Thwart. FP thruster (f)
9492490 *3FWK4* -	**TTM BRILLIANCE** *ex* Conti Sarder *-2011* **New Brilliance Maritime SA** Haeyoung Maritime Services Co Ltd *Panama* *Panama* MMSI: 370769000 Official number: 4331511	**41,074** 25,643 75,092 T/cm 68.3	Class: NK (BV)	**2011-07 Penglai Zhongbai Jinglu Ship Industry Co Ltd — Penglai SD** Yd No: JL0016 (B) Loa 225.00 (BB) Br ex - Dght 14.220 Lbp 217.00 Br md 32.26 Dpth 19.60 Welded, 1 dk	**(A21A2BC) Bulk Carrier** Grain: 90,136 Compartments: 7 Ho, ER 7 Ha: 6 (15.5 x 14.4)ER (14.6 x 13.2)	**1 oil engine** driving 1 FP propeller Total Power: 8,833kW (12,009hp) 14.5kn MAN-B&W 5S60MC-C 1 x 2 Stroke 5 Cy. 600 x 2400 8833kW (12009bhp) Hyundai Heavy Industries Co Ltd-South Korea AuxGen: 3 x 560kW 60Hz a.c Fuel: 3040.0
9478561 *3EWE6* -	**TTM DRAGON** **Ocean Dragon Maritime SA** Ta-Tong Marine Co Ltd *Panama* *Panama* MMSI: 351160000 Official number: 4159610	**31,532** 18,765 55,947 T/cm 56.9	Class: NK	**2010-05 IHI Marine United Inc — Yokohama KN** Yd No: 3263 Loa 189.96 (BB) Br ex - Dght 12.735 Lbp 185.00 Br md 32.26 Dpth 18.10 Welded, 1 dk	**(A21A2BC) Bulk Carrier** Grain: 72,062; Bale: 67,062 Compartments: 5 Ho, ER 5 Ha: 4 (20.9 x 18.6)ER (14.6 x 18.6) Cranes: 4x30t	**1 oil engine** driving 1 FP propeller Total Power: 9,720kW (13,215hp) 14.5kn Wartsila 6RT-flex50 1 x 2 Stroke 6 Cy. 500 x 2050 9720kW (13215bhp) Diesel United Ltd.-Aioi AuxGen: 3 x 430kW a.c Fuel: 2170.0 (r.f.)
9514016 *3FDH7* -	**TTM HARMONY** **New Harmony Maritime SA** Ta-Tong Marine Co Ltd *Panama* *Panama* MMSI: 371749000 Official number: 41850PEXT	**31,540** 18,765 55,873 T/cm 56.9	Class: NK	**2011-05 IHI Marine United Inc — Kure HS** Yd No: 3291 Loa 190.00 (BB) Br ex - Dght 12.735 Lbp 185.00 Br md 32.26 Dpth 18.10 Welded, 1 dk	**(A21A2BC) Bulk Carrier** Grain: 72,062; Bale: 67,062 Compartments: 5 Ho, ER 5 Ha: 4 (20.9 x 18.6)ER (14.6 x 18.6) Cranes: 4x30t	**1 oil engine** driving 1 FP propeller Total Power: 8,890kW (12,087hp) 14.5kn Wartsila 6RT-flex50 1 x 2 Stroke 6 Cy. 500 x 2050 8890kW (12087bhp) Diesel United Ltd.-Aioi Fuel: 2400.0
9514028 *3FKJ* -	**TTM HARVEST** **New Harvest Maritime SA** Ta-Tong Marine Co Ltd *Panama* *Panama* MMSI: 373190000 Official number: 4378712	**31,540** 18,765 55,873 T/cm 56.9	Class: NK	**2012-04 IHI Marine United Inc — Yokohama KN** Yd No: 3292 Loa 189.96 (BB) Br ex - Dght 12.735 Lbp 185.00 Br md 32.26 Dpth 18.10 Welded, 1 dk	**(A21A2BC) Bulk Carrier** Grain: 72,062; Bale: 67,062 Compartments: 5 Ho, ER 5 Ha: ER Cranes: 4x30t	**1 oil engine** driving 1 FP propeller Total Power: 8,890kW (12,087hp) 14.5kn Wartsila 6RT-flex50 1 x 2 Stroke 6 Cy. 500 x 2050 8890kW (12087bhp) Diesel United Ltd.-Aioi Fuel: 2470.0
9512044 *HOLU* -	**TTM HOPE** **New Hope Maritime SA** Ta-Tong Marine Co Ltd *Panama* *Panama* MMSI: 373805000 Official number: 4424412	**64,642** 37,594 119,496	Class: NK	**2012-09 Sanoyas Shipbuilding Corp — Kurashiki OY** Yd No: 1309 Loa 245.00 (BB) Br ex - Dght 15.404 Lbp 238.00 Br md 43.00 Dpth 21.65 Welded, 1 dk	**(A21A2BC) Bulk Carrier** Grain: 135,717 Compartments: 7 Ho, ER 7 Ha: ER	**1 oil engine** driving 1 FP propeller Total Power: 13,560kW (18,436hp) 14.5kn MAN-B&W 6S60MC-C 1 x 2 Stroke 6 Cy. 600 x 2400 13560kW (18436bhp) Mitsui Engineering & Shipbuilding CLtd-Japan Fuel: 3900.0
9478573 *3EUB2* -	**TTM PHOENIX** **Ocean Phoenix Maritime SA** Ta-Tong Marine Co Ltd *Panama* *Panama* MMSI: 354520000 Official number: 4169410	**31,532** 18,765 55,947 T/cm 56.9	Class: NK	**2010-06 IHI Marine United Inc — Yokohama KN** Yd No: 3264 Loa 190.00 (BB) Br ex - Dght 12.735 Lbp 185.00 Br md 32.26 Dpth 18.10 Welded, 1 dk	**(A21A2BC) Bulk Carrier** Grain: 72,062; Bale: 67,062 Compartments: 5 Ho, ER 5 Ha: 4 (20.9 x 18.6)ER (14.6 x 18.6) Cranes: 4x30t	**1 oil engine** driving 1 FP propeller Total Power: 8,890kW (12,087hp) 14.5kn Wartsila 6RT-flex50 1 x 2 Stroke 6 Cy. 500 x 2050 8890kW (12087bhp) Diesel United Ltd.-Aioi AuxGen: 3 x 430kW a.c Fuel: 2165.0 (r.f.)
9566655 *3ELM9* -	**TTM SUCCESS** **New Success Maritime SA** Ta-Tong Marine Co Ltd *Panama* *Panama* MMSI: 372390000 Official number: 45670TJ	**29,207** 15,556 50,428	Class: NK	**2014-03 Oshima Shipbuilding Co Ltd — Saikai NS** Yd No: 10647 Loa 182.98 Br ex - Dght 12.151 Lbp 179.30 Br md 32.26 Dpth 17.15 Welded, 1 dk	**(A21A2BC) Bulk Carrier** Grain: 59,117; Bale: 58,700 Cranes: 4x30t	**1 oil engine** driving 1 FP propeller Total Power: 7,760kW (10,550hp) 14.5kn MAN-B&W 6S50MC-C 1 x 2 Stroke 6 Cy. 500 x 2000 7760kW (10550bhp) Mitsui Engineering & Shipbuilding CLtd-Japan
9221425 *9YAP* -	**TTS CHACACHACARE** *ex* Andrew *-2008* *ex* Seabulk St Andrew *-2007* **Government of The Republic of Trinidad & Tobago** - *Chaguaramas* *Trinidad & Tobago* MMSI: 362035000	**309** 92 -	Class: (AB)	**1999-10 Breaux Bay Craft, Inc. — Loreauville, La** Yd No: 1709 Loa 45.72 Br ex - Dght 2.220 Lbp 42.37 Br md 9.14 Dpth 3.81 Welded, 1 dk	**(B21A20C) Crew/Supply Vessel**	**4 oil engines** reverse reduction geared to sc. shafts driving 4 FP propellers Total Power: 3,280kW (4,460hp) 24.0kn Cummins KTA-38-M1 4 x Vee 4 Stroke 12 Cy. 159 x 159 each-820kW (1115bhp) (new engine 2007) Cummins Engine Co Inc-USA AuxGen: 2 x 50kW a.c Fuel: 50.0 (d.f.)
9511478 *3WWU* -	**TU CUONG 09** **Tu Cuong Co Ltd** - SatCom: Inmarsat C 457441410 *Haiphong* *Vietnam* MMSI: 574012311	**999** 532 1,876	Class: VR	**2008-10 Hong Ha Shipbuilding Works — Giao Thuy** Yd No: TKT-532 Loa 68.86 Br ex 11.72 Dght 3.700 Lbp 65.95 Br md 11.50 Dpth 4.70 Welded, 1 dk	**(A31A2GX) General Cargo Ship** Grain: 1,999; Bale: 1,801 Compartments: 2 Ho, ER 2 Ha: (18.7 x 7.7)ER (19.3 x 7.7)	**2 oil engines** geared to sc. shafts driving 2 FP propellers Total Power: 600kW (816hp) Chinese Std. Type Z6170ZL 2 x 4 Stroke 6 Cy. 170 x 200 each-300kW (408bhp) Zibo Diesel Engine Factory-China AuxGen: 2 x 50kW 400V a.c
9582776 *XVDU* -	**TU CUONG 27** **Tu Cuong Co Ltd** - SatCom: Inmarsat C 457499977 *Haiphong* *Vietnam* MMSI: 574000110	**2,998** 1,848 5,219	Class: VR	**2010-11 Minh Khai Shipyard — Truc Ninh** Yd No: S52-49 Loa 91.94 Br ex 15.32 Dght 6.300 Lbp 84.97 Br md 15.30 Dpth 7.90 Welded, 1 dk	**(A21A2BC) Bulk Carrier** Grain: 6,683; Bale: 6,021 Compartments: 2 Ho, ER 2 Ha: (20.0 x 10.0)ER (21.0 x 10.0)	**1 oil engine** reduction geared to sc. shaft driving 1 FP propeller Total Power: 1,765kW (2,400hp) 11.0kn Chinese Std. Type LC8250ZLC 1 x 4 Stroke 8 Cy. 250 x 320 1765kW (2400bhp) Zibo Diesel Engine Factory-China AuxGen: 2 x 180kW 400V a.c Fuel: 270.0
8893532 - -	**TU LIEM 02** **Tu Liem Hanoi Transport Enterprise (Xi Nghiep Van Tai Tu Liem Hanoi)** - *Haiphong* *Vietnam*	**196** - 200	Class: (VR)	**1986 Ha Long Shipbuilding Engineering JSC — Haiphong** Loa - Br ex - Dght 2.100 Lbp 32.00 Br md 7.00 Dpth 2.60 Welded, 1 dk	**(A31A2GX) General Cargo Ship**	**1 oil engine** reduction geared to sc. shaft driving 1 FP propeller Total Power: 99kW (135hp) S.K.L. 4NVD26-2 1 x 4 Stroke 4 Cy. 180 x 260 99kW (135bhp) VEB Schwermaschinenbau "KarlLiebknecht" (SKL)-Magdeburg AuxGen: 1 x 3kW a.c

IMO / Call sign	Name / Owner	Tonnage	Class	Builder / Dimensions	Type	Machinery
9267510 *FQXN* -	**TU MOANA** **Bora Bora Cruises (Bora Bora Croisieres)** - *Papeete* *France* MMSI: 546003000	**1,697** 631 78	Class: (BV)	**2003**-04 **Austal Ships Pty Ltd — Fremantle WA** Yd No: 172 Loa 69.10 Br ex - Dght 2.100 Lbp 59.40 Br md 13.80 Dpth 4.80 Welded, 1 dk	**(A37A2PC) Passenger/Cruise** Hull Material: Aluminium Alloy Passengers: cabins: 37; berths: 40	**2 oil engines** geared to sc. shafts driving 2 FP propellers Total Power: 1,600kW (2,176hp) 14.0kn M.T.U. 16V2000M60 2 x Vee 4 Stroke 16 Cy. 130 x 150 each-800kW (1088bhp) MTU Friedrichshafen GmbH-Friedrichshafen Thrusters: 1 Tunnel thruster (f) Fuel: 41.0 (r.f.) 7.7pd
9154581 *3FNG8* -	**TU QIANG** **Strongfull Shipping Inc** COSCO (HK) Shipping Co Ltd SatCom: Inmarsat B 335138510 *Panama* *Panama* MMSI: 351385000 Official number: 2569598C	**26,078** 16,175 47,324 T/cm 50.7	Class: CC (AB)	**1998**-07 **Oshima Shipbuilding Co Ltd — Saikai NS** Yd No: 10224 Loa 185.73 (BB) Br ex - Dght 11.740 Lbp 177.00 Br md 30.95 Dpth 16.40 Welded, 1 dk	**(A21A2BC) Bulk Carrier** Grain: 59,100; Bale: 57,900 Compartments: 5 Ho, ER 5 Ha: (17.1 x 15.6)4 (19.8 x 15.6)ER Cranes: 4x25t	**1 oil engine** driving 1 FP propeller Total Power: 7,025kW (9,551hp) 14.3kn B&W 6S50MC 1 x 2 Stroke 6 Cy. 500 x 1910 7025kW (9551bhp) Kawasaki Heavy Industries Ltd-Japan
8882040 *HMYY* -	**TU RU BONG** **Korea Tumangang Shipping Co** - *Chongjin* *North Korea* MMSI: 445506000 Official number: 4001771	*2,736* 953 2,978	Class: KC	**1990 Chongjin Shipyard — Huichon** Loa 83.10 Br ex - Dght 6.460 Lbp - Br md 14.60 Dpth - Welded, 1 dk	**(A31A2GX) General Cargo Ship**	**1 oil engine** driving 1 FP propeller
8891869 *HMYQ* -	**TU RU BONG 1** *ex* Myong Gwang 2 *-2003* *ex* Tu Ru Bong 1 *-2001* *ex* Venus 325 *-2001* **Korea Tumangang Shipping Co** - *Chongjin* *North Korea* MMSI: 445372000 Official number: 1202770	*298* 132 405	Class: KC	**1962 KK Kanasashi Zosen — Shizuoka SZ** Loa 49.00 Br ex - Dght 3.230 Lbp 45.00 Br md 8.00 Dpth - Welded, 1 dk	**(A31A2GX) General Cargo Ship**	**1 oil engine** driving 1 FP propeller
7379618 *HMYX2* -	**TU RU BONG 2** *ex* Hai De *-2004* *ex* Pan Pacific 86 *-2004* *ex* Akita Maru No. 11 *-1986* **Korea Tumangang Shipping Co** - *Chongjin* *North Korea* MMSI: 445373000 Official number: 2404251	**255** 122 2,148	Class: (CC) (KR)	**1974**-02 **Miho Zosensho K.K. — Shimizu** Yd No: 965 Loa 46.82 (BB) Br ex 8.13 Dght 3.200 Lbp 40.62 Br md 8.11 Dpth 3.38 Welded, 1 dk	**(B11B2FV) Fishing Vessel** Ins: 110	**1 oil engine** driving 1 FP propeller Total Power: 736kW (1,001hp) 11.5kn Niigata 6M28KGHS 1 x 4 Stroke 6 Cy. 280 x 440 736kW (1001bhp) Niigata Engineering Co Ltd-Japan AuxGen: 2 x 176kW 225V 50Hz a.c
8891871 *HMYU* -	**TU RU BONG 3** *ex* Daiichi Harunichi Maru *-1986* **Korea Tumangang Shipping Co** - *Chongjin* *North Korea* MMSI: 445374000 Official number: 2004025	*299* 90 367	Class: KC	**1970 KK Kanasashi Zosen — Shizuoka SZ** Loa - Br ex - Dght 3.300 Lbp 41.28 Br md 8.10 Dpth - Welded, 1 dk	**(A31A2GX) General Cargo Ship**	**1 oil engine** driving 1 FP propeller Akasaka 1 x 4 Stroke Akasaka Tekkosho KK (Akasaka DieselLtd)-Japan
9379545 *3WOY* -	**TU SON** **Lam Kinh Shipping Co Ltd** - SatCom: Inmarsat C 457444210 *Haiphong* *Vietnam* MMSI: 574442000 Official number: VN-2144-VT	**4,022** 2,513 6,581	Class: VR	**2007**-05 **Nam Trieu Shipbuilding Industry Co. Ltd. — Haiphong** Loa 99.92 Br ex 16.82 Dght 6.900 Lbp 93.60 Br md 16.80 Dpth 8.80 Welded, 1 dk	**(A31A2GX) General Cargo Ship** Grain: 6,540	**1 oil engine** reduction geared to sc. shaft driving 1 FP propeller Total Power: 2,610kW (3,549hp) 10.0kn Hyundai Himsen 9H25/33P 1 x 4 Stroke 9 Cy. 250 x 330 2610kW (3549bhp) Hyundai Heavy Industries Co Ltd-South Korea
9628611 *3WCN9* -	**TU THANH 15 - BIDV** **BIDV Leasing Co** Tu Thanh Transport Service Co Ltd *Haiphong* *Vietnam*	**999** 640 1,985	Class: VR	**2011**-03 **Marine Service Co. No. 1 — Haiphong** Yd No: TKT 129D4 Loa 69.86 Br ex 10.82 Dght 4.550 Lbp 65.85 Br md 10.80 Dpth 5.40 Welded, 1 dk	**(A31A2GX) General Cargo Ship** Bale: 2,143 Compartments: 2 Ho, ER 2 Ha: ER 2 (17.1 x 7.2)	**1 oil engine** driving 1 FP propeller Total Power: 721kW (980hp) 10.0kn Skoda 6L350PN 1 x 4 Stroke 6 Cy. 350 x 500 721kW (980bhp) (made 1971, fitted 2011) CKD Praha-Praha
9526435 *9MGY5* -	**TUAH 1** **Penaga Timur (M) Sdn Bhd** - *Port Klang* *Malaysia* MMSI: 533019300 Official number: 332306	**150** 50 -		**2008**-09 **P.T. Palindo — Tanjungpinang** Yd No: T1423 Loa - Br ex - Dght - Lbp 33.00 Br md 6.20 Dpth 2.80 Welded, 1 dk	**(A37B2PS) Passenger Ship**	**3 oil engines** reduction geared to sc. shafts driving 3 Propellers Total Power: 2,238kW (3,042hp) MAN-B&W 3 x 4 Stroke each-746kW (1014bhp) MAN B&W Diesel AG-Augsburg
9526447 *9MGY6* -	**TUAH 2** **Penaga Timur (M) Sdn Bhd** - *Port Klang* *Malaysia* MMSI: 533019400 Official number: 332307	**168** 63 -		**2010**-08 **P.T. Palindo — Tanjungpinang** Yd No: T1424 Loa 33.00 Br ex - Dght 1.240 Lbp 33.00 Br md 6.20 Dpth 1.70 Welded, 1 dk	**(A37B2PS) Passenger Ship**	**3 oil engines** driving 3 Propellers Total Power: 2,238kW (3,042hp) MAN-B&W 3 x 4 Stroke each-746kW (1014bhp) MAN B&W Diesel AG-Augsburg
8619132 *9MGD4* -	**TUAH SEJAGAT** *ex* Eiho Maru *-2002* **Platinum Sector Sdn Bhd** Victory Supply Sdn Bhd *Port Klang* *Malaysia* MMSI: 533000093 Official number: 330363	**268** 155 520		**1987**-03 **Murakami Hide Zosen K.K. — Imabari** Yd No: 265 Loa - Br ex - Dght 3.301 Lbp 42.02 Br md 8.01 Dpth 3.51 Welded, 1 dk	**(A13B2TP) Products Tanker**	**1 oil engine** driving 1 FP propeller Total Power: 625kW (850hp) Niigata 6M26BGT 1 x 4 Stroke 6 Cy. 260 x 460 625kW (850bhp) Niigata Engineering Co Ltd-Japan
9134529 *ZM2000* -	**TUAKANA** **Port Taranaki Ltd** - *New Plymouth* *New Zealand* Official number: 876261	**347** 104	Class: LR ✠ **100A1** SS 12/2011 tug New Zealand coastal service ✠ **LMC** **UMS** Eq.Ltr: (E) ; Cable: 247.5/19.0 U2	**1996**-12 **Marine Steel (Northland) Ltd — Whangarei** Yd No: 120 Loa 29.43 Br ex - Dght 3.610 Lbp 29.15 Br md 11.00 Dpth 4.25 Welded, 1 dk	**(B32A2ST) Tug**	**2 oil engines** gearing integral to driving 2 Voith-Schneider propellers Total Power: 2,900kW (3,942hp) 12.5kn Wartsila 9R20 2 x 4 Stroke 9 Cy. 200 x 280 each-1450kW (1971bhp) Wartsila Diesel Oy-Finland AuxGen: 2 x 144kW 400V 50Hz a.c Fuel: 82.0 (d.f.) 6.0pd
8893817 *XVWU* -	**TUAN ANH 01** *ex* Phu Lam 02 *-2009* *ex* Hoang Minh 02 *-2003* **Tuan Anh Transport Co Ltd** - *Haiphong* *Vietnam* Official number: VN-1671-VT	**458** 267 910	Class: VR	**1994**-01 **Nam Trieu Shipbuilding Industry Co. Ltd. — Haiphong** Lengthened & Deepened-2004 Loa 52.32 Br ex 8.47 Dght 3.530 Lbp 48.89 Br md 8.25 Dpth 4.37 Welded, 1 dk	**(A31A2GX) General Cargo Ship** Grain: 1,026; Bale: 1,026 Compartments: 2 Ho, ER 2 Ha: 2 (11.0 x 4.3)ER	**2 oil engines** reduction geared to sc. shafts driving 2 FP propellers Total Power: 198kW (270hp) Skoda 6L160 2 x 4 Stroke 6 Cy. 160 x 225 each-99kW (135bhp) CKD Praha-Praha AuxGen: 1 x 5kW a.c Fuel: 10.0 (d.f.)
9024475 - -	**TUAN ANH 08** **Tu Tai Co Ltd** - *Haiphong* *Vietnam*	**475** 272 874	Class: VR	**2002**-10 **Vinacoal Shipbuilding Co — Ha Long** Loa 54.25 Br ex 9.25 Dght 3.200 Lbp 50.95 Br md 9.00 Dpth 3.90 Welded, 1 dk	**(A31A2GX) General Cargo Ship**	**1 oil engine** geared to sc. shaft driving 1 Propeller Total Power: 368kW (500hp) 10.0kn Chinese Std. Type Z8E160C 1 x 4 Stroke 8 Cy. 160 x 225 368kW (500bhp) Guangzhou Diesel Engine Factory CoLtd-China
8656439 *XVXB* -	**TUAN CHAU** **TKV - Cam Pha Port & Dock Warehouse Co** - *Haiphong* *Vietnam*	**249** 75 - T/cm 251.8	Class: VR	**2009**-06 **Ha Long Shipbuilding Engineering JSC — Haiphong** Loa 30.90 Br ex 8.40 Dght 2.900 Lbp 27.68 Br md 8.20 Dpth 4.00 Welded, 1 dk	**(B32A2ST) Tug**	**2 oil engines** reduction geared to sc. shafts driving 2 FP propellers Total Power: 1,440kW (1,958hp) Chinese Std. Type CW8200ZC 2 x 4 Stroke 8 Cy. 200 x 270 each-720kW (979bhp) Weichai Power Co Ltd-China AuxGen: 2 x 40kW 400V a.c

IMO / Call sign	Name / Owner	Tonnage	Class	Build	Type	Machinery
8893582 - -	**TUAN CUONG 05** *ex* Hoang Ngan 36 *-1996* *ex* Lach Tray 31 *-1995* **Tuanh Quynh Co Ltd (Cong Ty Trach Nhiem Huu Han Tuan Quynh)** - *Haiphong* *Vietnam* Official number: VN-1204-VT	**253** 141 446	Class: (VR)	**1994-01 Technical & Prof. College ofTransport No. 2 — Haiphong** Rebuilt-2000 Loa 47.13 Br ex 7.18 Dght 2.860 Lbp 43.00 Br md 7.00 Dpth 3.45 Welded, 1 dk	**(A31A2GX) General Cargo Ship** Grain: 435 Compartments: 2 Ho, ER 2 Ha: 2 (7.5 x 4.5)ER	**1 oil engine** reduction geared to sc. shaft driving 1 FP propeller Total Power: 147kW (200hp) Skoda 6L160PN 1 x 4 Stroke 6 Cy. 160 x 225 147kW (200bhp) CKD Praha-Praha AuxGen: 1 x 12kW a.c
8861553 3WSM -	**TUAN CUONG 25** *ex* Le Loi *-2002* **Tuanh Quynh Co Ltd (Cong Ty Trach Nhiem Huu Han Tuan Quynh)** - SatCom: Inmarsat C 457404210 *Haiphong* *Vietnam* MMSI: 574042032 Official number: VN-942-VT	**1,157** 708 1,895	Class: VR	**1992 Ben Kien Shipyard — Haiphong** Deepened-2002 Loa 71.87 Br ex 11.22 Dght 5.150 Lbp 65.81 Br md 11.20 Dpth 5.93 Welded, 1 dk	**(A31A2GX) General Cargo Ship** Grain: 1,541 Compartments: 2 Ho, ER 2 Ha: 2 (13.2 x 7.0)ER Cranes: 1x2t	**1 oil engine** driving 1 FP propeller Total Power: 721kW (980hp) Skoda 6L350IIPN 1 x 4 Stroke 6 Cy. 350 x 500 721kW (980bhp) CKD Praha-Praha
9543835 3FPL2 -	**TUAN DAO WAN** **Qingdao Shunhe Shipping Co Ltd** - *Panama* *Panama* MMSI: 355785000 Official number: 38475PEXTF1	**8,461** 5,356 15,000	Class: OM	**2008-05 Zhejiang Richland Shipbuilding Co Ltd — Zhoushan ZJ** Loa 140.19 Br ex - Dght 7.800 Lbp 131.80 Br md 20.00 Dpth 10.50 Welded, 1 dk	**(A21A2BC) Bulk Carrier** Grain: 17,964; Bale: 16,500 Cranes: 3x30t	**1 oil engine** geared to sc. shaft driving 1 FP propeller Total Power: 2,648kW (3,600hp) 10.0kn Chinese Std. Type 8320ZC 1 x 4 Stroke 8 Cy. 320 x 440 2648kW (3600bhp) Ningbo CSI Power & Machinery GroupCo Ltd-China
9547922 XVWZ -	**TUAN DUNG 25** *ex* Tuan Dung 02-Alci *-2012* **Agriculture Leasing Co I** Tuandung Co Ltd *Haiphong* *Vietnam* MMSI: 574012405	**1,599** 1,068 2,947	Class: VR	**2009-04 Minh Tuan Transport & Trading JSC — Truc Ninh** Yd No: HT-147.02 Loa 79.94 Br ex 12.64 Dght 5.300 Lbp 74.80 Br md 12.60 Dpth 6.48 Welded, 1 dk	**(A31A2GX) General Cargo Ship** Grain: 3,726; Bale: 3,357 Compartments: 2 Ho, ER 2 Ha: ER 2 (18.6 x 7.6)	**1 oil engine** reduction geared to sc. shaft driving 1 FP propeller Total Power: 1,103kW (1,500hp) 10.0kn Chinese Std. Type 8300ZLC 1 x 4 Stroke 8 Cy. 300 x 380 1103kW (1500bhp) Zibo Diesel Engine Factory-China AuxGen: 2 x 84kW 400V a.c Fuel: 70.0
9610860 - -	**TUAN DUNG 26** *ex* Nghiem Phat 01 *-2012* **Hinh Thinh General Trading Co** - *Haiphong* *Vietnam* MMSI: 574012568	**1,599** 1,026 3,222	Class: VR	**2010-01 Viet Tien Co Ltd — Xuan Truong** Yd No: S07-002.61 Loa 78.63 Br ex 12.62 Dght 5.350 Lbp 73.60 Br md 12.60 Dpth 6.48 Welded, 1 dk	**(A31A2GX) General Cargo Ship** Grain: 3,779; Bale: 3,405 Compartments: 2 Ho, ER 2 Ha: ER 2 (19.8 x 8.4)	**1 oil engine** reduction geared to sc. shaft driving 1 FP propeller Total Power: 735kW (999hp) 11.0kn Chinese Std. Type 8300ZLC 1 x 4 Stroke 8 Cy. 300 x 380 735kW (999bhp) Zibo Diesel Engine Factory-China
8892992 - -	**TUAN HUNG 05** *ex* Quang Minh 08 *-2002* **Tuan Hung Transport Co (Cong Ty Van Tai Tuan Hung)** - *Haiphong* *Vietnam* Official number: VN-1524-VT	**293** 171 526	Class: VR	**1991-01 Haiphong Shipyard — Haiphong** Lengthened & Deepened-2002 Loa 45.69 Br ex 7.57 Dght 2.830 Lbp 42.14 Br md 7.40 Dpth 3.40 Welded, 1 dk	**(A31A2GX) General Cargo Ship** Grain: 311 Compartments: 2 Ho, ER 2 Ha: 2 (7.0 x 4.0)ER	**1 oil engine** reduction geared to sc. shaft driving 1 FP propeller Total Power: 132kW (179hp) S.K.L. 6NVD26-2 1 x 4 Stroke 6 Cy. 180 x 260 132kW (179bhp) SKL Motoren u. Systemtechnik AG-Magdeburg
8665961 XVXZ -	**TUAN HUNG 06** *ex* Hai Chung 06 *-2013* *ex* Hai Chung 36 *-2013* **Tuan Hung Transport Co (Cong Ty Van Tai Tuan Hung)** - *Haiphong* *Vietnam* Official number: VN-2971-VT	**1,599** 1,043 3,130	Class: VR	**2009-08 Phu Hung Shipbuilding Industry JSC — Y Yen** Yd No: DKTB02-03 Loa 79.60 Br ex 12.82 Dght 5.150 Lbp 74.80 Br md 12.80 Dpth 6.10 Welded, 1 dk	**(A31A2GX) General Cargo Ship** Grain: 3,839; Bale: 3,459 Compartments: 2 Ho, ER 2 Ha: ER 2 (20.4 x 8.4)	**1 oil engine** driving 1 FP propeller Total Power: 1,100kW (1,496hp) 10.0kn Chinese Std. Type 8300ZLCZA 1 x 4 Stroke 8 Cy. 300 x 380 1100kW (1496bhp) Zibo Diesel Engine Factory-China
8665040 XVNJ -	**TUAN HUNG 16** *ex* Thao Linh 01 *-2010* *ex* Viet Thang 08 *-2008* **Tuan Hung Transport Co (Cong Ty Van Tai Tuan Hung)** - *Haiphong* *Vietnam* Official number: VN-3154-VT	**1,599** 1,002 3,066	Class: VR	**2008-01 Nam Ha Shipyard — Nam Ha** Yd No: TKC48A-03 Loa 74.36 Br ex 12.62 Dght 5.340 Lbp 70.90 Br md 12.60 Dpth 6.30 Welded, 1 dk	**(A31A2GX) General Cargo Ship** Grain: 3,691; Bale: 3,356 Compartments: 2 Ho, ER 2 Ha: (17.0 x 8.0)ER (19.3 x 8.0)	**1 oil engine** driving 1 FP propeller Total Power: 736kW (1,001hp) 9.0kn S.K.L. 8NVD48A-1U 1 x 4 Stroke 8 Cy. 320 x 480 736kW (1001bhp) (made 1991) SKL Motoren u. Systemtechnik AG-Magdeburg AuxGen: 2 x 32kW 400V a.c
8984185 - -	**TUAN KIET** *ex* Master Ricky III *-2005* **Hoang H Nguyen** - *Bayou La Batre, AL* *United States of America* Official number: 1122566	**162** 48 -		**2002 Master Boat Builders, Inc. — Coden, Al** Yd No: 319 L reg 25.96 Br ex - Dght - Lbp - Br md 7.62 Dpth 3.96 Welded, 1 dk	**(B11B2FV) Fishing Vessel**	**1 oil engine** driving 1 Propeller
8667270 - -	**TUAN THANH 02** **Tuan Thanh Transport Trading Co Ltd** - *Haiphong* *Vietnam* Official number: VN-2491-VT	**1,272** 845 2,401	Class: VR	**2008-02 Haiphong Mechanical & Trading Co. — Haiphong** Yd No: HP704 Loa 76.67 Br ex 11.87 Dght 4.240 Lbp 72.56 Br md 11.85 Dpth 5.10 Welded, 1 dk	**(A31A2GX) General Cargo Ship** Grain: 2,668 Compartments: 2 Ho, ER 2 Ha: ER 2 (20.4 x 7.8)	**1 oil engine** driving 1 FP propeller 10.0kn S.K.L. 8NVD48-2U 1 x 4 Stroke 8 Cy. 320 x 480 MaK Motoren GmbH & Co. KG-Kiel
8666886 3WUP -	**TUAN THANH 28-BIDV** *ex* Duc Hien 36-BIDV *-2009* *ex* Quy Duc 18-BIDV *-2009* **BIDV Financial Leasing Co Ltd** Tuan Thanh Transport Trading Co Ltd *Haiphong* *Vietnam* Official number: VN-2548-VT	**999** 631 1,948	Class: VR	**2008-04 Diem Dien Shipbuilding Industry Co — Thai Thuy** Yd No: TH-142.08 Loa 70.10 Br ex 10.82 Dght 4.570 Lbp 65.80 Br md 10.80 Dpth 5.55 Welded, 1 dk	**(A31A2GX) General Cargo Ship** Bale: 2,140 Compartments: 1 Ho, 1 Ho, ER 2 Ha: ER 2 (15.0 x 7.0)	**1 oil engine** driving 1 FP propeller Total Power: 530kW (721hp) 10.0kn Chinese Std. Type Z8170ZL 1 x 4 Stroke 8 Cy. 170 x 200 530kW (721bhp) Zibo Diesel Engine Factory-China AuxGen: 2 x 22kW 400V a.c Fuel: 38.0
8035922 9MEN7 -	**TUBA No. 5** *ex* Yusho Maru No. 5 *-2001* **Marine Teamwork Sdn Bhd** - *Port Klang* *Malaysia* Official number: 328476	**140** 93 232		**1981-07 Y.K. Akamatsu Zosen — Uwajima** Yd No: 88 L reg 29.57 Br ex - Dght 2.500 Lbp - Br md 6.51 Dpth 2.80 Welded, 1 dk	**(A13B2TU) Tanker (unspecified)**	**1 oil engine** driving 1 FP propeller Total Power: 250kW (340hp) 8.5kn Yanmar 1 x 4 Stroke 250kW (340bhp) Yanmar Diesel Engine Co Ltd-Japan
9355680 YDA4066 -	**TUBAN** **PT Buana Jaya Pratama** PT Arpeni Pratama Ocean Line Tbk *Jakarta* *Indonesia*	**263** 79 210	Class: RI (NK)	**2005-05 Far East Shipyard Co Sdn Bhd — Sibu** Yd No: 19/04 Loa 29.50 Br ex - Dght 3.578 Lbp 27.48 Br md 9.00 Dpth 4.16 Welded, 1 dk	**(B32A2ST) Tug**	**2 oil engines** reduction geared to sc. shafts driving 2 Propellers Total Power: 1,766kW (2,402hp) 12.0kn Yanmar 6N21A-S 2 x 4 Stroke 6 Cy. 210 x 290 each-883kW (1201bhp) Yanmar Diesel Engine Co Ltd-Japan Fuel: 180.0 (d.f.)
8313142 YHFW -	**TUBANAN INDAH** *ex* Shiomi Maru *-2007* *ex* Kanagawa Maru *-1990* **PT Buana Jaya Pratama** - *Jakarta* *Indonesia*	**379** 114 -	Class: KI	**1983-09 Sagami Zosen Tekko K.K. — Yokosuka** Yd No: 222 Loa 36.95 Br ex - Dght 3.360 Lbp 32.50 Br md 9.81 Dpth 4.40 Welded, 1 dk	**(B32A2ST) Tug**	**2 oil engines** Geared Integral to driving 2 Z propellers Total Power: 2,500kW (3,400hp) Niigata 6L28BX 2 x 4 Stroke 6 Cy. 280 x 320 each-1250kW (1700bhp) Niigata Engineering Co Ltd-Japan
9346160 C6YB8 -	**TUBARAO** *ex* City *-2009* **Jacamar Shipping Co Ltd** Sun Enterprises Ltd *Nassau* *Bahamas* MMSI: 311028800 Official number: 8001696	**32,474** 17,790 53,350 T/cm 57.3	Class: LR (NV) **100A1** SS 03/2012 bulk carrier BC-A Nos. 2 & 4 holds or No. 3 hold may be empty ESP ESN LI *IWS upper deck and hatch covers strengthened for a load of 4.5 and 2.5 tonnes/m2 **LMC** **UMS**	**2007-03 Shanghai Shipyard Co Ltd — Shanghai** Yd No: 1120 Loa 190.00 (BB) Br ex 32.29 Dght 12.540 Lbp 183.05 Br md 32.26 Dpth 17.50 Welded, 1 dk	**(A21A2BC) Bulk Carrier** Grain: 65,781; Bale: 64,000 Compartments: 5 Ho, ER 5 Ha: 4 (21.6 x 22.4)ER (19.2 x 20.8) Cranes: 4x36t	**1 oil engine** driving 1 FP propeller Total Power: 9,480kW (12,889hp) 14.2kn MAN-B&W 6S50MC- 1 x 2 Stroke 6 Cy. 500 x 2000 9480kW (12889bhp) Hudong Heavy Machinery Co Ltd-China AuxGen: 3 x 680kW 450V 60Hz a.c Fuel: 230.0 (d.f.) (Heating Coils) 2000.0 (r.f.) 34.5pd

IMO / Call sign	Name / Owner / Flag	Tonnage	Class	Builder / Dimensions	Type / Capacity	Machinery
9339961 *3ESH6* -	**TUBARAO MARU** **GOD Shipping SA** Doun Kisen KK (Doun Kisen Co Ltd) SatCom: Inmarsat C 437030310 *Panama* Panama MMSI: 370303000 Official number: 3419808A	**160,774** 62,589 327,127	Class: NK	**2008-08 Mitsui Eng. & SB. Co. Ltd., Chiba Works — Ichihara** Yd No: 1668 Loa 340.00 (BB) Br ex - Dght 21.173 Lbp 325.00 Br md 60.00 Dpth 28.15 Welded, 1 dk	**(A21B2BO) Ore Carrier** Grain: 200,867 Compartments: 9 Ho, ER 9 Ha: 8 (19.6 x 16.2)ER (24.5 x 16.2)	**1 oil engine** driving 1 FP propeller Total Power: 27,160kW (36,927hp) 15.0kn MAN-B&W 7S80MC-C 1 x 2 Stroke 7 Cy. 800 x 3200 27160kW (36927bhp) Mitsui Engineering & Shipbuilding CLtd-Japan Fuel: 7880.0
7225489 *DUTU8* -	**TUBBATAHA** *ex* Poya *-2009* *ex* Helios Maru *-2007* **Malayan Towage & Salvage Corp (SALVTUG)** - *Manila* Philippines MMSI: 548300100 Official number: 00-0000093	**200** 60 80		**1972-05 Towa Zosen K.K. — Shimonoseki** Yd No: 428 Loa 30.48 Br ex 8.84 Dght 2.598 Lbp 27.01 Br md 8.82 Dpth 3.51 Welded, 1 dk	**(B32A2ST) Tug**	**2 oil engines** Geared Integral to driving 2 Z propellers Total Power: 1,766kW (2,402hp) 12.0kn Niigata 6L25BX 2 x 4 Stroke 6 Cy. 250 x 320 each-883kW (1201bhp) Niigata Engineering Co Ltd-Japan AuxGen: 1 x 240kW 440V a.c Fuel: 61.0 10.0pd
7437965 *DUA2306* -	**TUBIGON FERRY** *ex* Jerome *-2007* *ex* Guillermo *-2007* *ex* Aioi Maru No. 18 *-1974* **Roly Shipping Lines Inc** - *Cebu* Philippines Official number: CEB1000628	*207* 46 -		**1957 Hashihama Shipbuilding Co Ltd — Imabari EH** Yd No: 55 Loa 39.43 Br ex 7.01 Dght - Lbp 38.64 Br md 6.99 Dpth 2.77 Welded	**(A37B2PS) Passenger Ship** Passengers: 467	**1 oil engine** driving 1 FP propeller Total Power: 478kW (650hp) Hanshin V6 1 x 4 Stroke 6 Cy. 320 x 450 478kW (650bhp) Hanshin Nainenki Kogyo-Japan
9633355 *TCVK2* -	**TUBITAK MARMARA** **Tubitak Marmara Arastirma Merkezi** - *Istanbul* Turkey MMSI: 271043343	**496** 148 -	Class: TL	**2013-06 Ceksan Tersanesi — Turkey** Yd No: 47 Loa 41.20 Br ex - Dght 3.150 Lbp - Br md 9.55 Dpth 4.50 Welded, 1 dk	**(B31A2SR) Research Survey Vessel** Ice Capable	**2 oil engines** reduction geared to sc. shafts driving 2 Propellers Total Power: 2,050kW (2,788hp) 13.0kn Mitsubishi S12R-MPTA 2 x Vee 4 Stroke 12 Cy. 170 x 180 each-1025kW (1394bhp) Mitsubishi Heavy Industries Ltd-Japan AuxGen: 2 x 310kW a.c
7819424 - -	**TUBROK** - **Government of Libya (Socialist Ports Co)** - *Tripoli* Libya	*1,453* 521 203	Class: (LR) (GL) Classed LR until 11/9/96	**1979-11 Osterreichische Schiffswerften AG Linz-Korneuburg — Linz** Yd No: 1266 Loa - Br ex - Dght 2.510 Lbp 50.25 Br md 23.64 Dpth 3.99 Welded, 1 dk	**(B34B2SC) Crane Vessel** Cranes: 1x200t	**2 diesel electric oil engines** driving 1 gen. of 300kW 400V a.c 1 gen. of 250kW 400V a.c Connecting to 2 elec. motors each (473kW) driving 2 Voith-Schneider propellers Total Power: 1,590kW (2,162hp) 6.0kn MWM TBD440-8 2 x 4 Stroke 8 Cy. 230 x 270 each-795kW (1081bhp) Motoren Werke Mannheim AG (MWM)-West Germany
7920780 *HSB3071* -	**TUBTIM** *ex* Nikko II *-2006* *ex* Nikko Maru *-1994* **Andaman Fisheries Supply Co Ltd** - *Bangkok* Thailand MMSI: 567040500 Official number: 460001858	**934** 570 2,190		**1979-12 K.K. Miura Zosensho — Saiki** Yd No: 586 Loa - Br ex - Dght 4.601 Lbp 66.02 Br md 10.81 Dpth 5.01 Welded, 1 dk	**(A13B2TP) Products Tanker**	**1 oil engine** driving 1 FP propeller Total Power: 1,324kW (1,800hp) Akasaka DM36 1 x 4 Stroke 6 Cy. 360 x 540 1324kW (1800bhp) Akasaka Tekkosho KK (Akasaka DieselLtd)-Japan
9294721 *FTCC* -	**TUBUAI RAVA'AI** **SEML Tahiti Nui Rava'ai** - *Papeete* France MMSI: 546002400	**163** 49 -	Class: (BV)	**2003-10 Fujian Southeast Shipyard — Fuzhou FJ** Yd No: 2002-07 Loa 23.90 Br ex - Dght 2.900 Lbp 21.33 Br md 7.40 Dpth 3.80 Welded, 1 dk	**(B11B2FV) Fishing Vessel**	**1 oil engine** geared to sc. shaft driving 1 FP propeller Total Power: 405kW (551hp) Wartsila UD25L6M5D 1 x 4 Stroke 6 Cy. 150 x 180 405kW (551bhp) Wartsila Finland Oy-Finland
9447873 *A8VP8* -	**TUBUL** **Hull 1796 Co Ltd** Compania SudAmericana de Vapores SA (CSAV) *Monrovia* Liberia MMSI: 636014647 Official number: 14647	**88,586** 42,897 94,665	Class: GL	**2011-09 Samsung Heavy Industries Co Ltd — Geoje** Yd No: 1796 Loa 299.96 (BB) Br ex - Dght 13.500 Lbp 285.00 Br md 45.60 Dpth 24.60 Welded, 1 dk	**(A33A2CC) Container Ship (Fully Cellular)** TEU 8004 C Ho 3574 TEU C Dk 4430 TEU incl 1500 ref C.	**1 oil engine** driving 1 FP propeller Total Power: 43,610kW (59,292hp) 23.0kn MAN-B&W 7K98ME7 1 x 2 Stroke 7 Cy. 980 x 2660 43610kW (59292bhp) Doosan Engine Co Ltd-South Korea AuxGen: 2 x 2880kW 6600/450V a.c, 3 x 3360kW 6600/450V a.c Thrusters: 1 Tunnel thruster (f) Fuel: 290.0 (d.f.) 8600.0 (r.f.) 162.0pd
6423199 - -	**TUCAN** - -	*221* 79 -	Class: (BV)	**1964 Hijos de J. Barreras S.A. — Vigo** Yd No: 1306 Loa 32.80 Br ex 7.85 Dght 3.633 Lbp 28.81 Br md 7.80 Dpth 3.92 Welded, 1 dk	**(B11A2FT) Trawler** 3 Ha: 3 (1.0 x 1.0)	**1 oil engine** driving 1 FP propeller Total Power: 618kW (840hp) 11.5kn A.B.C. 8MDXS 1 x 4 Stroke 8 Cy. 242 x 320 618kW (840bhp) Anglo Belgian Co NV (ABC)-Belgium Fuel: 49.5 (d.f.)
6502438 *HQBY6* -	**TUCAN** *ex* Ecopa *-2004* *ex* Hallelujah No. 21 *-1995* *ex* Heung Yang No. 9 *-1986* *ex* Sam Won No. 21 *-1979* *ex* Gonei Maru No. 25 *-1972* - - *San Lorenzo* Honduras Official number: L-1921702	*231* 115 305	Class: (KR)	**1964 Nishii Dock Co. Ltd. — Ise** Yd No: 101 Loa 42.70 Br ex 7.57 Dght 2.998 Lbp 38.21 Br md 7.50 Dpth 3.36 Riveted\Welded, 1 dk	**(B11B2FV) Fishing Vessel** Ins: 308	**1 oil engine** driving 1 FP propeller Total Power: 515kW (700hp) 10.8kn Hanshin V6 1 x 4 Stroke 6 Cy. 320 x 450 515kW (700bhp) Hanshin Nainenki Kogyo-Japan AuxGen: 2 x 72kW 230V a.c Fuel: 155.5
9455674 *PBAQ* -	**TUCANA** **CV Scheepvaartonderneming Tucana** Toucan Maritime *Heerhugowaard* Netherlands MMSI: 245050000 Official number: 52011	**2,545** 1,460 3,783	Class: BV (LR) ✠ Classed LR until 18/8/11	**2008-10 Nevskiy Sudostroitelnyy i Sudorem. Zavod — Shlisselburg** (Hull) Yd No: (9372) **2008-10 B.V. Scheepswerf Damen Bergum — Bergum** Yd No: 9372 Loa 88.60 Br ex - Dght 5.420 Lbp 84.99 Br md 12.50 Dpth 7.00 Welded, 1 dk	**(A31A2GX) General Cargo Ship** Double Bottom Entire Compartment Length Grain: 5,250 TEU 188 C Ho 108 TEU C Dk 80 TEU. Compartments: 1 Ho, ER 1 Ha: ER (62.7 x 10.1) Ice Capable	**1 oil engine** with clutches, flexible couplings & sr reverse geared to sc. shaft driving 1 FP propeller Total Power: 1,520kW (2,067hp) 10.5kn MaK 8M20C 1 x 4 Stroke 8 Cy. 200 x 300 1520kW (2067bhp) Caterpillar Motoren GmbH & Co. KG-Germany AuxGen: 1 x 140kW 400V 50Hz a.c, 1 x 348kW 400V 50Hz a.c Thrusters: 1 Water jet (f) Fuel: 1.6 (d.f.) 179.0 (d.f.)
9355472 *V2CX7* -	**TUCANA J** **ms 'Tucana J' Schiffahrtsgesellschaft UG (haftungsbeschrankt) & Co KG** Jungerhans Maritime Services GmbH & Co KG *Saint John's* Antigua & Barbuda MMSI: 305140000 Official number: 4368	**8,246** 4,002 11,152	Class: GL	**2007-08 Detlef Hegemann Rolandwerft GmbH & Co. KG — Berne** Yd No: 238 Loa 139.60 (BB) Br ex - Dght 7.360 Lbp 133.25 Br md 22.20 Dpth 9.50 Welded, 1 dk	**(A33A2CC) Container Ship (Fully Cellular)** TEU 962C Ho 218 TEU C Dk 744 TEU incl 170 ref C. Compartments: 3 Cell Ho, ER 3 Ha: ER	**1 oil engine** reduction geared to sc. shafts driving 1 CP propeller Total Power: 8,402kW (11,423hp) 17.9kn MaK 9M43 1 x 4 Stroke 9 Cy. 430 x 610 8402kW (11423bhp) Caterpillar Motoren GmbH & Co. KG-Germany AuxGen: 2 x 584kW 440/230V 60Hz a.c, 1 x 1200kW 440/230V 60Hz a.c Thrusters: 1 Thwart. CP thruster (f)
6816621 *CB2067* -	**TUCANO** *ex* Petur Jonsson *-1988* *ex* Haforn *-1980* *ex* Loftur Baldvinsson *-1980* **Blumar Seafoods** - *Valparaiso* Chile Official number: 2522	*400* 209 -	Class: (NV)	**1968 AS Hommelvik Mek. Verksted — Hommelvik** Yd No: 110 Lengthened-1973 Loa 49.92 Br ex 8.34 Dght 3.506 Lbp 44.81 Br md 8.22 Dpth 4.50 Welded, 1 dk	**(B11B2FV) Fishing Vessel** Compartments: 2 Ho, ER 4 Ha: 2 (2.5 x 1.6)2 (2.9 x 1.6)ER Derricks: 1x4.5t; Winches: 1 Ice Capable	**1 oil engine** driving 1 CP propeller Total Power: 1,030kW (1,400hp) MWM 1 x 4 Stroke 8 Cy. 320 x 480 1030kW (1400bhp) Motoren Werke Mannheim AG (MWM)-West Germany AuxGen: 1 x 75kW 380V 50Hz a.c, 1 x 60kW 380V 50Hz a.c, 1 x 28kW 380V 50Hz a.c Thrusters: 1 Thwart. FP thruster (f); 1 Tunnel thruster (a)
9569970 *A8VQ3* -	**TUCAPEL** **Hull 1906 Co Ltd** Compania SudAmericana de Vapores SA (CSAV) *Monrovia* Liberia MMSI: 636014650 Official number: 14650	**88,586** 42,897 94,707	Class: GL	**2012-01 Samsung Heavy Industries Co Ltd — Geoje** Yd No: 1906 Loa 299.92 (BB) Br ex - Dght 13.500 Lbp 285.00 Br md 45.60 Dpth 24.60 Welded, 1 dk	**(A33A2CC) Container Ship (Fully Cellular)** TEU 8004 C Ho 3574 TEU C Dk 4430 TEU incl 1500 ref C.	**1 oil engine** driving 1 FP propeller Total Power: 43,610kW (59,292hp) 23.0kn MAN-B&W 7K98ME7 1 x 2 Stroke 7 Cy. 980 x 2660 43610kW (59292bhp) Doosan Engine Co Ltd-South Korea AuxGen: 2 x 2880kW 6600/450V a.c, 3 x 3360kW 6600/450V a.c Thrusters: 1 Tunnel thruster (f) Fuel: 290.0 (d.f.) 8600.0 (r.f.) 162.0pd

9258179 *A8AP8* -	**TUCHKOV BRIDGE** **Seabrook Marine Ltd** Unicom Management Services (Cyprus) Ltd *Monrovia* *Liberia* MMSI: 636011644 Official number: 11644	**27,725** 13,762 47,199 T/cm 52.4	Class: LR ✠**100A1** SS 04/2009 Double Hull oil tanker ESP *IWS LI SPM ✠**LMC** **UMS IGS** Eq.Ltr: M†; Cable: 632.5/73.0 U3 (a)	**2004-04 Admiralteyskiy Sudostroitelnyy Zavod — Sankt-Peterburg** Yd No: 02741 Loa 182.40 (BB) Br ex 32.34 Dght 12.197 Lbp 174.80 Br md 32.20 Dpth 17.50 Welded, 1 dk	**(A13A2TW) Crude/Oil Products Tanker** Double Hull (13F) Liq: 53,146; Liq (Oil): 51,910 Compartments: 10 Wing Ta, 2 Wing Slop Ta, ER 10 Cargo Pump (s): 10x550m³/hr Manifold: Bow/CM: 90.9m	**1 oil engine** driving 1 FP propeller Total Power: 8,310kW (11,298hp) 14.0kn B&W 6S50MC-C 1 x 2 Stroke 6 Cy. 500 x 2000 8310kW (11298bhp) AO Bryanskiy MashinostroitelnyyZavod (BMZ)-Bryansk AuxGen: 2 x 1280kW 450/230V 60Hz a.c, 1 x 680kW 450/230V 60Hz a.c Boilers: e (ex.g.) 11.7kgf/cm² (11.5bar), WTAuxB (o.f.) 11.2kgf/cm² (11.0bar) Fuel: 126.0 (d.f.) 1428.0 (r.f.) 34.0pd
9452713 *WDD9657* -	**TUCKAHOE** **Vane Line Bunkering Inc** *Baltimore, MD* *United States of America* MMSI: 367314520 Official number: 1199143	**327** 98 404		**2007-06 Thoma-Sea Boatbuilders Inc — Houma LA** Yd No: 129 Loa - Br ex - Dght - Lbp 30.26 Br md 10.40 Dpth 4.60 Welded, 1 dk	**(B32B2SP) Pusher Tug**	**2 oil engines** reverse reduction geared to sc. shafts driving 2 FP propellers Total Power: 3,090kW (4,202hp) Caterpillar 3516B 2 x Vee 4 Stroke 16 Cy. 170 x 190 each-1545kW (2101bhp) Caterpillar Inc-USA
9577678 *WDG7253* -	**TUCKER CANDIES** **Otto Candies LLC** - *New Orleans, LA* *United States of America* MMSI: 338002000 Official number: 1242288	**3,365** 1,009 5,400	Class: LR ✠**100A1** SS 05/2013 *IWS ✠**LMC** Eq.Ltr: W; Cable: 495.0/44.0 U3 (a)	**2013-05 Candies Shipbuilders LLC — Houma LA** Yd No: 151 Loa 88.45 (BB) Br ex 18.71 Dght 5.900 Lbp 81.97 Br md 18.26 Dpth 7.32 Welded, 1 dk	**(B21A2OS) Platform Supply Ship**	**4 diesel electric oil engines** driving 4 gen. each 1700kW 480V a.c Connecting to 2 elec. motors each (1700kW) driving 2 Directional propellers Total Power: 7,160kW (9,736hp) 10.0kn Caterpillar 3512C-HD 4 x Vee 4 Stroke 12 Cy. 170 x 215 each-1790kW (2434bhp) Caterpillar Inc-USA Thrusters: 2 Thwart. FP thruster (f)
1007471 *ZCGQ4* -	**TUEQ** **Sete Triton Ltd** Sete Yacht Management SA *George Town* *Cayman Islands (British)* MMSI: 319784000 Official number: 735463	**2,282** 687 499	Class: LR ✠**100A1** SS 06/2012 SSC Yacht (P) Mono, G6 ✠**LMC** **UMS** Eq.Ltr: Y; Cable: 192.5/32.0 U3 (a)	**2002-06 van der Giessen-de Noord BV — Krimpen a/d IJssel** Yd No: 983 Lengthened-2007 Loa 78.47 Br ex 13.60 Dght 3.000 Lbp 71.45 Br md 13.50 Dpth 6.60 Welded, 1 dk	**(X11A2YP) Yacht**	**2 oil engines** with clutches, flexible couplings & sr geared to sc. shafts driving 2 CP propellers Total Power: 7,200kW (9,790hp) Wartsila 18V200 2 x Vee 4 Stroke 18 Cy. 200 x 240 each-3600kW (4895bhp) Wartsila France SA-France AuxGen: 3 x 480kW 400V 50Hz a.c Boilers: HWH Thrusters: 1 Thwart. FP thruster (f); 1 Thwart. FP thruster (a)
9474618 *9HA3505* -	**TUERKIS** *ex POS Tuerkis -2013* **Conti 180 Schifffahrts-GmbH & Co KG Nr 1** BBG-Bremer Bereederungsgesellschaft mbH & Co KG *Valletta* *Malta* MMSI: 229672000 Official number: 9474618	**51,195** 31,136 92,759 T/cm 80.9	Class: AB	**2012-01 COSCO (Zhoushan) Shipyard Co Ltd — Zhoushan ZJ** Yd No: N199 Loa 229.20 (BB) Br ex - Dght 14.900 Lbp 222.00 Br md 38.00 Dpth 20.70 Welded, 1 dk	**(A21A2BC) Bulk Carrier** Grain: 110,330 Compartments: 7 Ho, ER 7 Ha: ER	**1 oil engine** driving 1 FP propeller Total Power: 12,240kW (16,642hp) 14.1kn MAN-B&W 6S60MC 1 x 2 Stroke 6 Cy. 600 x 2292 12240kW (16642bhp) Doosan Engine Co Ltd-South Korea AuxGen: 3 x 730kW a.c Fuel: 233.0 (d.f.) 3597.0 (r.f.)
9393163 *5BMK2* -	**TUFTY** **Taboga Shipping Co Ltd** Navarone SA *Limassol* *Cyprus* MMSI: 212049000	**19,814** 10,208 30,802	Class: GL	**2009-03 Shanhaiguan Shipbuilding Industry Co Ltd — Qinhuangdao HE** Yd No: 020 Loa 185.14 (BB) Br ex - Dght 10.400 Lbp 178.00 Br md 23.70 Dpth 14.60 Welded, 1 dk	**(A21A2BC) Bulk Carrier** Grain: 38,635; Bale: 37,476 Compartments: 6 Ho, ER 6 Ha: (16.0 x 17.4)3 (19.2 x 17.4) (13.6 x 17.4)ER (10.4 x 13.2) Cranes: 3x30t Ice Capable	**1 oil engine** driving 1 FP propeller Total Power: 7,200kW (9,789hp) 13.5kn MAN-B&W 6S46MC-C 1 x 2 Stroke 6 Cy. 460 x 1932 7200kW (9789bhp) Yichang Marine Diesel Engine Co Ltd-China AuxGen: 3 x 680kW a.c Thrusters: 1 Tunnel thruster (f)
7349106 *SDIH* -	**TUG** *ex Merchantman -2001* *ex Nore Commander -2000 ex Balt-2 -1999* *ex Bugsier 5 -1999* **Marin & Hamnservice KA AB** Marin & Haverikonsult KA AB *Stockholm* *Sweden* MMSI: 265567430	**176** 52 107	Class: GL RI	**1974-07 Schiffswerft u. Maschinenfabrik Max Sieghold — Bremerhaven** Yd No: 165 Loa 26.05 Br ex 8.84 Dght 2.790 Lbp 23.80 Br md 8.80 Dpth 3.59 Welded, 1 dk	**(B32A2ST) Tug** Ice Capable	**2 oil engines** geared to sc. shafts driving 2 Directional propellers Total Power: 1,280kW (1,740hp) Deutz SBA6M528 2 x 4 Stroke 6 Cy. 220 x 280 each-640kW (870bhp) Kloeckner Humboldt Deutz AG-West Germany
7916155 *9LY2661* -	**TUG 8** *ex Hokusei Maru -2013 ex Sakura Maru -2007* *ex Kaisei Maru -1992* **Cebu Sea Charterers Inc** *Freetown* *Sierra Leone* MMSI: 667074000 Official number: SL103464	*194* - -		**1979-11 Kanagawa Zosen — Kobe** Yd No: 204 Loa 30.30 Br ex - Dght 2.601 Lbp 25.76 Br md 8.62 Dpth 3.81 Welded, 1 dk	**(B32A2ST) Tug**	**2 oil engines** Geared Integral to driving 2 Z propellers Total Power: 1,912kW (2,600hp) Niigata 6L25BX 2 x 4 Stroke 6 Cy. 250 x 320 each-956kW (1300bhp) Niigata Engineering Co Ltd-Japan
7314395 - -	**TUG 118** *ex Saga Maru No. 77 -2013* *ex Take Maru No. 36 -1995* *ex Katsura Maru No. 2 -1981* **Cebu Sea Charterers Inc**	*194* - -		**1973-05 Sagami Zosen Tekko K.K. — Yokosuka** Yd No: 161 Loa 30.61 Br ex 8.82 Dght 2.598 Lbp 27.00 Br md 8.79 Dpth 3.48 Welded	**(B32A2ST) Tug**	**2 oil engines** Geared Integral to driving 2 Z propellers Total Power: 1,912kW (2,600hp) Niigata 6L25BX 2 x 4 Stroke 6 Cy. 250 x 320 each-956kW (1300bhp) Niigata Engineering Co Ltd-Japan
5367922 - -	**TUG 180** *ex Mabco 180 -1983 ex G. W. 180 -1975* *ex Tregarth -1970 ex Neylandia -1961* **Swan Hunter (Trinidad) Ltd** - *Trinidad & Tobago*	*102* - -	Class: (LR) ✠ Classed LR until 20/2/85	**1958-09 N.V. Scheepswerf "Alphen" P. de Vries Lentsch — Alphen a/d Rijn** Yd No: 391 Loa 25.00 Br ex 6.79 Dght 2.775 Lbp 23.02 Br md 6.41 Dpth 3.10 Riveted\Welded, 1 dk	**(B32A2ST) Tug**	**1 oil engine** sr reverse geared to sc. shaft driving 1 FP propeller Total Power: 368kW (500hp) Deutz RBV6M545 1 x 4 Stroke 6 Cy. 320 x 450 368kW (500bhp) Kloeckner Humboldt Deutz AG-West Germany AuxGen: 2 x 15kW 220V d.c
5121500 *LCNV* -	**TUG FRIER** *ex Heros -2011 ex Leam -2008 ex Frier -2005* **Morland & Karlsen AS** - *Kragero* *Norway* MMSI: 259904000	**102** 40 -	Class: (NV)	**1959 Fa. G. de Vries Lentsch, Scheepsw. "Het Fort" — Amsterdam** Yd No: 1045 Loa 22.05 Br ex 6.58 Dght 2.871 Lbp 20.10 Br md 6.34 Dpth 4.04 Welded, 1 dk	**(B32A2ST) Tug** Ice Capable	**1 oil engine** driving 1 FP propeller Total Power: 883kW (1,201hp) 10.0kn Deutz SBV8M545 1 x 4 Stroke 8 Cy. 320 x 450 883kW (1201bhp) (new engine 1967) Kloeckner Humboldt Deutz AG-West Germany Fuel: 17.5 (d.f.)
7734143 *HP4751* -	**TUG MARLIN** *ex Marlin -2012 ex Gaucho -1992* **San Martin Group Ltd** *Panama* *Panama* Official number: 4466413	**568** 170 -	Class: (AB)	**1976 Bludco Barge & Towing, Inc. — Houston, Tx** Yd No: 100 Loa 29.27 Br ex - Dght 5.823 Lbp - Br md 10.66 Dpth 6.86 Welded, 1 dk	**(B32B2SA) Articulated Pusher Tug**	**2 oil engines** reverse reduction geared to sc. shafts driving 2 FP propellers Total Power: 3,530kW (4,800hp) 12.0kn Fairbanks, Morse 12-38D8-1/8 2 x 2 Stroke 12 Cy. 207 x 254 each-1765kW (2400bhp) Fairbanks Morse (Canada) Ltd-Canada AuxGen: 2 x 99kW
8976138 - -	**TUG TYSON** *ex Itco Xii -2003* **St Christopher Air & Sea Ports Authority (SCASPA)** - *St Kitts & Nevis* Official number: SKN 1001687	*153* 104 -		**1975 Master Marine, Inc. — Bayou La Batre, Al** L reg 21.21 Br ex - Dght - Lbp - Br md 7.92 Dpth 3.05 Welded, 1 dk	**(B32A2ST) Tug**	**3 oil engines** geared to sc. shaft driving 3 FP propellers G.M. (Detroit Diesel) 12V-71 3 x Vee 2 Stroke 12 Cy. 108 x 127 General Motors Detroit DieselAllison Divn-USA
1006867 *ZCOX4* -	**TUGATSU** *ex September Blue -2003* **Farr Horizons Marine Ltd** - *George Town* *Cayman Islands (British)* MMSI: 319790000 Official number: 717300	**432** - -	Class: LR **100A1** SS 12/2009 Yacht **LMC** Cable: 292.5/20.0	**1989 Jacht- en Scheepswerf C. van Lent & Zonen B.V. — Kaag** Loa 42.50 Br ex 8.48 Dght 2.600 Lbp 39.92 Br md 8.18 Dpth 4.30 Welded, 2 dks	**(X11A2YP) Yacht**	**2 oil engines** with flexible couplings & reverse reduction geared to sc. shafts driving 2 FP propellers Total Power: 1,132kW (1,540hp) 12.5kn G.M. (Detroit Diesel) 16V-92-TA 2 x Vee 2 Stroke 16 Cy. 123 x 127 each-566kW (770bhp) General Motors Corp-USA AuxGen: 2 x 90kW 380V 50Hz a.c Thrusters: 1 Thwart. FP thruster (f) Fuel: 43.3 (d.f.)

9505065 *9HA2292* -	**TUGELA** **Wilhelmsen Lines Shipowning Malta Ltd** Wilhelmsen Ship Management Sdn Bhd *Valletta* *Malta* MMSI: 248264000 Official number: 9505065	**72,295** 35,099 28,837	Class: NV	**2011-07 Hyundai Heavy Industries Co Ltd — Ulsan** Yd No: 2261 Loa 229.99 (BB) Br ex - Dght 11.300 Lbp 217.10 Br md 32.25 Dpth 34.70 Welded, 13 Dks. incl. 5 liftable Dks.	**(A35B2RV) Vehicles Carrier** Quarter stern door/ramp (s. a.) Len: - Wid: 12.00 Swl: 320 Cars: 7,880	**1 oil engine** driving 1 FP propeller Total Power: 18,080kW (24,582hp) 20.0kn MAN-B&W 8S60ME-C8 1 x 2 Stroke 8 Cy. 600 x 2400 18080kW (24582bhp) AuxGen: 3 x a.c, 1 x a.c Thrusters: 1 Tunnel thruster (f)
8922565 *V3SQ4* -	**TUGELITE** *ex* Dranske (Y 1658) *-2012* *ex* Kormoran (Y 1658) *-2000* **STT-Ships-Towing-Trading OU** - *Belize City* *Belize* MMSI: 312854000 Official number: 581210013	**205** 61 -	Class: (GL)	**1989-12 VEB Yachtwerft Berlin — East Berlin** Yd No: 02 Loa 31.00 Br ex - Dght 2.501 Lbp 27.21 Br md 8.50 Dpth 3.50 Welded	**(B32A2ST) Tug**	**1 oil engine** driving 1 FP propeller Total Power: 530kW (721hp) 11.0kn S.K.L. 6VDS26/20AL-1 1 x 4 Stroke 6 Cy. 200 x 260 530kW (721bhp) VEB Schwermaschinenbau "KarlLiebknecht" (SKL)-Magdeburg
9200861 *LXTU* -	**TUGEN** **Tugen Shipping SA** Intershipping SA *Luxembourg* *Luxembourg* MMSI: 253196000 Official number: 2807	**5,412** 2,026 7,450 T/cm 17.6	Class: BV (RI) (AB)	**1999-09 Atlantis Shipyard Pte Ltd — Singapore** Yd No: 1033 Loa 104.99 (BB) Br ex 19.07 Dght 6.700 Lbp 98.50 Br md 19.05 Dpth 9.90 Welded, 1 dk	**(A13B2TP) Products Tanker** Double Hull (13F) Liq: 8,343; Liq (Oil): 8,343 Cargo Heating Coils Compartments: 12 Wing Ta, ER, 2 Wing Slop Ta 3 Cargo Pump (s): 3x750m³/hr Manifold: Bow/CM: 52.7m	**1 oil engine** driving 1 CP propeller Total Power: 2,450kW (3,331hp) 11.0kn Wartsila 6R32 1 x 4 Stroke 6 Cy. 320 x 350 2450kW (3331bhp) Wartsila NSD Finland Oy-Finland AuxGen: 2 x 260kW 415/220V 50Hz a.c, 1 x 350kW 415/220V 50Hz a.c Thrusters: 1 Thwart. CP thruster (f) Fuel: 110.5 (d.f.) (Heating Coils) 299.7 (r.f.)
8832942 *ES2095* -	**TUGEV** *ex* Russo-Balt *-1993* **BLRT Grupp AS** MPV Management Ltd *Tallinn* *Estonia* MMSI: 276338000 Official number: 1T00C16	**182** 54 69	Class: RS	**1990-08 Pribaltiyskiy Sudostroitelnyy Zavod "Yantar" — Kaliningrad** Yd No: 809 Loa 29.30 Br ex 8.59 Dght 3.650 Lbp 27.00 Br md 8.24 Dpth 4.30 Welded, 1dk	**(B32A2ST) Tug**	**2 oil engines** driving 2 CP propellers Total Power: 1,180kW (1,604hp) 11.0kn Pervomaysk 8CHNP25/34 2 x 4 Stroke 8 Cy. 250 x 340 each-590kW (802bhp) Pervomaydizelmash (PDM)-Pervomaysk
9533983 *UBEF9* -	**TUGNUY** **Daltransugol Ltd (OOO 'Daltransugol')** - *Vanino* *Russia* MMSI: 273330410	**451** 347 162	Class: RS	**2008-07 OAO Leningradskiy Sudostroitelnyy Zavod 'Pella' — Otradnoye** Yd No: 608 Loa 28.50 Br ex 9.50 Dght 3.500 Lbp 26.50 Br md 9.28 Dpth 4.80 Welded, 1 dk	**(B32B2SP) Pusher Tug**	**2 oil engines** reduction geared to sc. shafts driving 2 Directional propellers Total Power: 2,982kW (4,054hp) Caterpillar 3516B 2 x Vee 4 Stroke 16 Cy. 170 x 190 each-1491kW (2027bhp) Caterpillar Inc-USA AuxGen: 2 x 84kW a.c Fuel: 82.0 (d.f.)
8932596 - -	**TUGUR** *launched as* BK-761 *-1969* **000 'Port-Market'** - *Nakhodka* *Russia* Official number: 691043	*225* 46	Class: RS	**1969 "Petrozavod" — Leningrad** Yd No: 761 Loa 29.30 Br ex 8.49 Dght 3.090 Lbp 27.00 Br md 8.30 Dpth 4.34 Welded, 1 dk	**(B32A2ST) Tug** Ice Capable	**2 oil engines** driving 2 CP propellers Total Power: 884kW (1,202hp) 11.4kn Russkiy 6D30/50-4-2 2 x 2 Stroke 6 Cy. 300 x 500 each-442kW (601bhp) Mashinostroitelnyy Zavod"Russkiy-Dizel"-Leningrad AuxGen: 2 x 25kW a.c Fuel: 36.0 (d.f.)
8323331 *UDQX* -	**TUGUR** *ex* Chiho Maru No. 8 *-2006* *ex* Kiryo Maru No. 38 *-2002* *ex* Kasuga Maru No. 38 *-1994* **JSC Dalryba (A/O 'Dalryba')** - *Vladivostok* *Russia* MMSI: 273444180 Official number: 836264	**626** 286 480	Class: RS	**1984-03 KK Kanasashi Zosen — Shizuoka SZ** Yd No: 3028 Loa 53.29 (BB) Br ex 8.70 Dght 3.610 Lbp 46.89 Br md 8.70 Dpth 3.76 Welded, 1 dk	**(B11B2FV) Fishing Vessel**	**1 oil engine** with clutches, flexible couplings & sr reverse geared to sc. shaft driving 1 FP propeller Total Power: 736kW (1,001hp) Akasaka DM28AFD 1 x 4 Stroke 6 Cy. 280 x 460 736kW (1001bhp) Akasaka Tekkosho KK (Akasaka DieselLtd)-Japan Fuel: 222.0 (d.f.)
9607473 *FFZF* -	**TUHAA PAE IV** **Societe de Navigation des Australes (SNA) 'Tuhaa Pae'** - *Papeete* *France*	**2,346** 704 1,489	Class: BV	**2012-02 Harwood Marine International Inc — Cebu** Yd No: 1 Loa 79.41 (BB) Br ex - Dght 3.800 Lbp 69.57 Br md 13.60 Dpth 6.01 Welded, 1 dk	**(A33B2CP) Passenger/Container Ship** Passengers: 98; berths: 50 Bale: 1,880 TEU 43 on dk Compartments: 3 Ho, ER 3 Ha: ER Cranes: 1x40t,1x5t	**2 oil engines** reduction geared to sc. shafts driving 2 FP propellers Total Power: 2,352kW (3,198hp) 12.0kn Daihatsu 6DLM-26 2 x 4 Stroke 6 Cy. 260 x 340 each-1176kW (1599bhp) Daihatsu Diesel Manufacturing Co Lt-Japan AuxGen: 2 x 400kW 380V 50Hz a.c Thrusters: 1 Thwart. FP thruster (f) Fuel: 360.0
8865808 *FKFJ* -	**TUHEIAVA** **Ronald Natua** - *Papeete* *France* MMSI: 227120600	**154** - -	Class: (BV)	**1992 Chantier Naval du Pacifique Sud (CNPS) — Papeete** Yd No: 163 Loa 24.80 Br ex - Dght 3.335 Lbp 21.79 Br md 7.40 Dpth 3.96 Welded, 1 dk	**(B11B2FV) Fishing Vessel** Ins: 70	**1 oil engine** reduction geared to sc. shaft driving 1 FP propeller Total Power: 331kW (450hp) 11.0kn Baudouin 12P15.2 1 x Vee 4 Stroke 12 Cy. 150 x 150 331kW (450bhp) Societe des Moteurs Baudouin SA-France
9177765 *AVGW* -	**TUHINA** *ex* Active *-2010* **Essar Shipping Ltd** - *Mumbai* *India* MMSI: 419000156 Official number: 3731	**7,918** 4,611 13,347	Class: IR (GL) (NK)	**1998-10 Honda Zosen — Saiki** Yd No: 1014 Loa 128.04 (BB) Br ex - Dght 8.467 Lbp 118.00 Br md 21.20 Dpth 11.30 Welded, 2 dks	**(A21A2BC) Bulk Carrier** Double Hull Grain: 15,645; Bale: 15,440 Compartments: 3 Ho, ER 3 Ha: (18.9 x 12.6)2 (23.1 x 15.0)ER Cranes: 2x30t	**1 oil engine** driving 1 FP propeller Total Power: 4,200kW (5,710hp) 13.3kn B&W 6S35MC 1 x 2 Stroke 6 Cy. 350 x 1400 4200kW (5710bhp) Makita Corp-Japan AuxGen: 2 x 320kW 450V a.c Fuel: 141.0 (d.f.) 604.0 (r.f.) 17.0pd
7910644 *3DQM* -	**TUI TAI** **Beachcomber Island Resort & Cruises Ltd (Beachcomber Cruises Ltd)** - *Suva* *Fiji* Official number: 373772	*540* 317 180		**1980 Carpenters Industrial — Suva** Yd No: 44 Loa 39.96 Br ex 9.25 Dght 2.701 Lbp 31.53 Br md 9.20 Dpth 3.92 Welded, 2 dks	**(A37B2PS) Passenger Ship**	**2 oil engines** reverse reduction geared to sc. shafts driving 2 FP propellers Total Power: 338kW (460hp) Gardner 8L3B 2 x 4 Stroke 8 Cy. 140 x 197 each-169kW (230bhp) L. Gardner & Sons Ltd.-Manchester
6809771 *V4KJ2* -	**TUIZIDI** *ex* Ofelia *-2012* **Roris Maritime Co Ltd** - *Basseterre* *St Kitts & Nevis* MMSI: 341052000 Official number: SKN 1002274	**3,638** 1,257 780	Class: IS (Class contemplated) (LR) (BV) ✠ Classed LR until 5/69	**1968-11 Kroegerwerft GmbH & Co. KG — Schacht-Audorf** Yd No: 1348 Loa 74.38 Br ex 16.52 Dght 3.817 Lbp 64.52 Br md 16.50 Dpth 5.10 Welded, 2 dks	**(A36A2PR) Passenger/Ro-Ro Ship (Vehicles)** Passengers: unberthed: 800 Bow door & ramp Stern door & ramp Ice Capable	**2 oil engines** driving 2 CP propellers Total Power: 2,556kW (3,476hp) 14.5kn MaK 8M452AK 2 x 4 Stroke 8 Cy. 320 x 450 each-1278kW (1738bhp) Atlas MaK Maschinenbau GmbH-Kiel AuxGen: 4 x 269kW 380/220V 50Hz a.c Thrusters: 1 Thwart. CP thruster (f)
9443920 *C6YL5* -	**TUJU ARROW** **East Blue Marlin SA** Gearbulk Ltd *Nassau* *Bahamas* MMSI: 311037400 Official number: 8001758	**44,684** 22,141 72,863	Class: NV	**2010-10 Oshima Shipbuilding Co Ltd — Saikai NS** Yd No: 10606 Loa 225.00 (BB) Br ex - Dght 14.340 Lbp 221.00 Br md 32.26 Dpth 20.56 Welded, 1 dk	**(A31A2GO) Open Hatch Cargo Ship** Grain: 85,028 TEU 445 C Dk Compartments: 8 Ho, ER 8 Ha: ER Gantry cranes: 2x70t	**1 oil engine** driving 1 FP propeller Total Power: 12,577kW (17,100hp) 15.5kn MAN-B&W 6S60ME-C8 1 x 2 Stroke 6 Cy. 600 x 2400 12577kW (17100bhp) Kawasaki Heavy Industries Ltd-Japan AuxGen: 2 x 1300kW a.c, 1 x 880kW a.c Thrusters: 1 Tunnel thruster (f)
9309772 *VMQ9957* -	**TUKANG** **Pacific Marine Group Pty Ltd (PMG)** - *Townsville, Qld* *Australia* MMSI: 503689000 Official number: 860037	**404** 121 700	Class: LR ✠ **100A1** SS 12/2010 tug ✠ **LMC** Eq.Ltr: 0; Cable: 144.0/24.0 U3 (a)	**2005-12 Jiangsu Wuxi Shipyard Co Ltd — Wuxi JS** (Hull) Yd No: (1163) **2005-12 Pacific Ocean Engineering & Trading Pte Ltd (POET) — Singapore** Yd No: 1163 Loa 31.95 Br ex 10.04 Dght 3.810 Lbp 28.40 Br md 9.80 Dpth 4.80 Welded, 1 dk	**(B32A2ST) Tug**	**2 oil engines** with clutches, flexible couplings & sr geared to sc. shafts driving 2 FP propellers Total Power: 2,354kW (3,200hp) Yanmar 8N21A-EN 2 x 4 Stroke 8 Cy. 210 x 290 each-1177kW (1600bhp) Yanmar Diesel Engine Co Ltd-Japan AuxGen: 2 x 150kW 415V 50Hz a.c
6405264 *D2U50* -	**TUKAS** *ex* Anja Funk *-2003* *ex* Theresia M *-1980* *ex* Ilona *-1973* **Comercio e Transportes Transgilas Lda** - *Angola*	**530** 199 560	Class: (GL)	**1963 Martin Jansen GmbH & Co. KG Schiffsw. u. Masch. — Leer** Yd No: 60 Loa 47.78 Br ex 8.79 Dght 3.060 Lbp 43.01 Br md 8.74 Dpth 5.31 Welded, 1 dk & S dk	**(A31A2GX) General Cargo Ship** Grain: 1,218; Bale: 1,161 Compartments: 1 Ho, ER 1 Ha: (27.9 x 4.9)ER Ice Capable	**1 oil engine** sr geared to sc. shaft driving 1 FP propeller Total Power: 320kW (435hp) 9.5kn Deutz RBA6M528 1 x 4 Stroke 6 Cy. 220 x 280 320kW (435bhp) Kloeckner Humboldt Deutz AG-West Germany AuxGen: 1 x 39kW 220V d.c Fuel: 30.5 (d.f.)

9248875 *EBXE* 3-SS-14-01	**TUKU TUKU** **Eugenio Elduayen Eizaguirre y otros CB** - *Pasaia* *Spain* Official number: 3-4/2001	**160** 48 173		**2002-03 Astilleros de Pasaia SA — Pasaia** Yd No: 316 Loa 32.00 Br ex - Dght 3.300 Lbp 27.00 Br md 7.10 Dpth 3.80 Welded, 1 dk	**(B11B2FV) Fishing Vessel**	**1 oil engine** geared to sc. shaft driving 1 FP propeller Total Power: 662kW (900hp) Mitsubishi 1 x 4 Stroke 662kW (900bhp) Mitsubishi Heavy Industries Ltd-Japan
9283734 *XCRC4* -	**TULA** *ex* Luit Spirit *-2008* *ex* Lauren *-2007* *launched as* Athenian Lady *-2005* **TMM Division Maritima SA de CV** - *Manzanillo* *Mexico* MMSI: 345140007	**29,242** 11,926 46,911 T/cm 52.3	Class: LR (AB) **100A1** SS 01/2010 Double Hull oil and chemical tanker, Ship Type 3 ESP *IWS LI (EP (barred) suspended) **LMC** **UMS IGS** Eq.Ltr: N†; Cable: 660.0/76.0 U3 (a)	**2005-01 Hyundai Mipo Dockyard Co Ltd — Ulsan** Yd No: 0236 Loa 183.20 (BB) Br ex 32.20 Dght 12.216 Lbp 174.00 Br md 32.20 Dpth 18.80 Welded, 1 dk	**(A12B2TR) Chemical/Products Tanker** Double Hull (13F) Liq: 52,732; Liq (Oil): 52,732 Cargo Heating Coils Compartments: 14 Wing Ta, ER 14 Cargo Pump (s) Manifold: Bow/CM: 91m	**1 oil engine** driving 1 FP propeller Total Power: 8,580kW (11,665hp) 14.5kn B&W 6S50MC-C 1 x 2 Stroke 6 Cy. 500 x 2000 8580kW (11665bhp) Hyundai Heavy Industries Co Ltd-South Korea AuxGen: 3 x 730kW 440V 60Hz a.c Boilers: e (ex.g.) 12.0kgf/cm^2 (11.8bar), AuxB (o.f.) 9.2kgf/cm^2 (9.0bar)
9505089 *9HA2293* -	**TULANE** - **Wilhelmsen Lines Shipowning Malta Ltd** Wilhelmsen Ship Management Sdn Bhd SatCom: Inmarsat C 424826512 *Valletta* *Malta* MMSI: 248265000 Official number: 9505089	**72,295** 35,099 28,818	Class: NV	**2012-06 Hyundai Heavy Industries Co Ltd — Ulsan** Yd No: 2263 Loa 229.99 (BB) Br ex - Dght 11.000 Lbp 217.10 Br md 32.26 Dpth 34.70 Welded, 13 Dks. incl. 5 liftable Dks.	**(A35B2RV) Vehicles Carrier** Quarter stern door/ramp (s. a.) Len: - Wid: 12.00 Swl: 320 Cars: 7,900	**1 oil engine** driving 1 FP propeller Total Power: 18,080kW (24,582hp) 20.0kn MAN-B&W 8S60ME-C8 1 x 2 Stroke 8 Cy. 600 x 2400 18080kW (24582bhp) Hyundai Heavy Industries Co Ltd-South Korea AuxGen: 3 x , 1 x a.c Thrusters: 1 Tunnel thruster (f)
9026198 *YB4307* -	**TULANG BAWANG JAYA** *ex* Sumber Bangka III *-1999* **Koperasi Peg Rep Indonesia Sai Bumi Nengah Nyappur** - *Palembang* *Indonesia*	**137** 42 -	Class: (KI)	**1999-09 P.T. Sumber Sumatera Raya — Palembang** L reg 35.00 Br ex - Dght 1.500 Lbp 31.00 Br md 4.70 Dpth 2.00 Welded, 1 dk	**(A37B2PS) Passenger Ship**	**2 oil engines** geared to sc. shafts driving 2 Propellers Total Power: 1,472kW (2,002hp) 25.0kn MAN D2842LE 2 x Vee 4 Stroke 12 Cy. 128 x 142 each-736kW (1001bhp) MAN Nutzfahrzeuge AG-Nuernberg
7516917 *LZH2238* -	**TULENOVO 2** *ex* Gastrader 2 *-2013* *ex* Claso *-2006* *ex* Szrenica *-1994* **Marine Antipollution Enterprise** - *Varna* *Bulgaria* MMSI: 207822380 Official number: 402	**341** 131 419	Class: (GL) (PR)	**1975-03 Wroclawska Stocznia Rzeczna — Wroclaw** Yd No: ZB400/C3 Loa 43.36 Br ex 8.13 Dght 3.000 Lbp 39.50 Br md 8.08 Dpth 3.41 Welded, 1 dk	**(A13B2TP) Products Tanker** Liq: 458; Liq (Oil): 458 Compartments: 10 Ta, ER Ice Capable	**1 oil engine** reduction geared to sc. shaft driving 1 FP propeller Total Power: 315kW (428hp) 10.0kn S.K.L. 6NVD36A-1U 1 x 4 Stroke 6 Cy. 240 x 360 315kW (428bhp) VEB Schwermaschinenbau "KarlLiebknecht" (SKL)-Magdeburg AuxGen: 2 x 38kW 400V a.c
8991542 - -	**TULIJA** *ex* Kingfish II *-2007* **Servicios Maritimos Dos Bocas SA de CV** - *Dos Bocas* *Mexico* MMSI: 345002601 Official number: 2701335231-5	**117** 37 -	Class: (RI)	**1971 Camcraft, Inc. — Crown Point, La** Converted From: Yacht-2007 Converted From: Supply Tender Loa 30.10 Br ex - Dght 1.960 Lbp 28.74 Br md 6.70 Dpth 2.90 Welded, 1 dk	**(B34N2QP) Pilot Vessel** Hull Material: Aluminium Alloy	**3 oil engines** reduction geared to sc. shafts driving 3 FP propellers G.M. (Detroit Diesel) 12V-71-TI 3 x Vee 2 Stroke 12 Cy. 108 x 127 Detroit Diesel Corporation-Detroit, Mi
7423328 - -	**TULIP** - **Bahrain Fishing Co (BAFCO)** - *Bahrain*	*105* - -		**1975-12 Ingenieria y Maq. Especializada S.A. (IMESA) — Salina Cruz** Yd No: 124 Loa 21.01 Br ex - Dght - Lbp - Br md 5.64 Dpth 2.72 Welded, 1 dk	**(B11A2FT) Trawler**	**1 oil engine** driving 1 FP propeller Total Power: 268kW (364hp) 9.5kn Caterpillar 1 x 4 Stroke 268kW (364bhp) Caterpillar Tractor Co-USA
9521447 *5BSP3*	**TULIP** *ex* Nordtulip *-2013* **Nordtulip Navigation Co Ltd** Reederei Nord Ltd *Limassol* *Cyprus* MMSI: 210224000 Official number: 9521447	**57,081** 31,074 104,280 T/cm 88.9	Class: LR ✠ **100A1** SS 01/2013 Double Hull oil tanker CSR ESP **ShipRight** (ACS (B),CM) *IWS LI DSPM4 ✠ **LMC** **UMS IGS** Eq.Ltr: S†; Cable: 522.0/87.0 U3 (a)	**2013-01 Sumitomo Heavy Industries Marine & Engineering Co., Ltd. — Yokosuka** Yd No: 1366 Loa 228.60 (BB) Br ex 42.04 Dght 14.800 Lbp 217.80 Br md 42.00 Dpth 21.50 Welded, 1 dk	**(A13A2TV) Crude Oil Tanker** Double Hull (13F) Liq: 98,700; Liq (Oil): 98,700 Cargo Heating Coils Compartments: 12 Wing Ta, 2 Wing Slop Ta, ER 3 Cargo Pump (s): 3x2500m^3/hr Manifold: Bow/CM: 116.6m	**1 oil engine** driving 1 FP propeller Total Power: 13,560kW (18,436hp) 14.8kn MAN-B&W 6S60MC-C 1 x 2 Stroke 6 Cy. 600 x 2400 13560kW (18436bhp) Mitsui Engineering & Shipbuilding CLtd-Japan AuxGen: 3 x 960kW 450V 60Hz a.c Boilers: e (ex.g.) 22.4kgf/cm^2 (22.0bar), WTAuxB (o.f.) 18.3kgf/cm^2 (17.9bar) Fuel: 250.0 (d.f.) 2170.0 (r.f.)
9198018 *VWYN* -	**TULIP-1** *ex* Tulip *-2006* *ex* Kimtrans Taurus *-2003* **Polestar Maritime Ltd** - *Mumbai* *India* MMSI: 419020900 Official number: 2940	**127** 38 111	Class: IR (BV)	**1998-06 Nga Chai Shipyard Sdn Bhd — Sibu** (Hull) Yd No: 9801 **1998-06 Kiong Nguong Shipbuilding Contractor Co — Sibu** Yd No: (9801) Loa 23.15 Br ex - Dght 2.500 Lbp 21.69 Br md 7.30 Dpth 3.00 Welded, 1 dk	**(B32A2ST) Tug**	**2 oil engines** geared to sc. shafts driving 2 FP propellers Total Power: 892kW (1,212hp) Cummins KTA-19-M3 2 x 4 Stroke 6 Cy. 159 x 159 each-446kW (606bhp) Cummins Engine Co Inc-USA AuxGen: 2 x 20kW 415V 50Hz a.c Fuel: 87.0 (d.f.)
8332514 *IVFL*	**TULIPANO N** **Cooperativa Mazarpesca** - *Mazara del Vallo* *Italy* Official number: 250	*317* 123 -	Class: (RI)	**1982 Cant. Nav. F. Giacalone — Mazara del Vallo** Yd No: 47 Loa 38.51 Br ex 8.03 Dght 3.301 Lbp 31.88 Br md 8.01 Dpth 4.09 Welded, 1 dk	**(B11B2FV) Fishing Vessel**	**1 oil engine** geared to sc. shaft driving 1 FP propeller Total Power: 900kW (1,224hp) MAN 9L20/27 1 x 4 Stroke 9 Cy. 200 x 270 900kW (1224bhp) Maschinenbau Augsburg Nuernberg (MAN)-Augsburg
8418057 - -	**TULIPE TWO** *ex* Comac Eclipse *-1995* - -	**143** 43 -	Class: (NV)	**1984 Australian Shipbuilding Industries (WA) Pty Ltd — Fremantle WA** Yd No: 220 Loa 24.92 Br ex - Dght - Lbp 21.16 Br md 7.43 Dpth 3.92 Welded, 1 dk	**(B11B2FV) Fishing Vessel**	**1 oil engine** sr geared to sc. shaft driving 1 FP propeller Total Power: 405kW (551hp) 10.0kn Yanmar S165L-ST 1 x 4 Stroke 6 Cy. 165 x 210 405kW (551bhp) Yanmar Diesel Engine Co Ltd-Japan AuxGen: 1 x 103kW 415V 50Hz a.c
9005261 *3EUL8* -	**TULJA** *ex* Al Samidoon *-2010* **Atlantic Bluewater Services Ltd** Sterling Oil Resources Ltd SatCom: Inmarsat C 437194110 *Panama* *Panama* MMSI: 371941000 Official number: 4226111	**149,719** 101,519 284,890 T/cm 162.7	Class: NV	**1992-08 Daewoo Shipbuilding & Heavy Machinery Ltd — Geoje** Yd No: 5057 Loa 322.00 (BB) Br ex 56.04 Dght 21.622 Lbp 310.00 Br md 56.00 Dpth 31.40 Welded, 1 dk	**(A13A2TV) Crude Oil Tanker** Single Hull Liq: 313,273; Liq (Oil): 313,273 Compartments: 6 Ta, 6 Wing Ta, 2 Wing Slop Ta, ER 3 Cargo Pump (s): 3x5000m^3/hr Manifold: Bow/CM: 164m	**1 oil engine** driving 1 FP propeller Total Power: 18,777kW (25,529hp) 14.4kn B&W 6S80MC 1 x 2 Stroke 6 Cy. 800 x 3056 18777kW (25529bhp) Hyundai Heavy Industries Co Ltd-South Korea AuxGen: 3 x 785kW 440V 60Hz a.c Fuel: 380.4 (d.f.) (Heating Coils) 5327.0 (r.f.) 72.0pd
8969848 - -	**TULJAN DVA** *ex* Tammy Lady *-2008* **mb 'Tuljan' Ribarstvo doo** - *Zadar* *Croatia*	**195** 58 -		**2001 Kennedy Ship & Repair, LP — Galveston, Tx** Yd No: H-101 Loa 32.00 Br ex - Dght - Lbp - Br md 8.22 Dpth 4.05 Welded, 1 dk	**(B11B2FV) Fishing Vessel**	**2 oil engines** reduction geared to sc. shaft driving 1 FP propeller Total Power: 794kW (1,080hp) Caterpillar 3412TA 2 x Vee 4 Stroke 12 Cy. 137 x 152 each-397kW (540bhp) Caterpillar Inc-USA AuxGen: 2 x 50kW a.c
8651386 *ZJL5389* -	**TULLY** - **Biltmore Management Ltd** - *Road Harbour* *British Virgin Islands* MMSI: 378019000 Official number: 729100	**324** 92 -	Class: AB	**1993-07 Azimut-Benetti SpA — Viareggio** Yd No: FB209 Loa 40.48 Br ex 8.46 Dght 2.000 Lbp 34.28 Br md 8.40 Dpth 5.03 Welded, 1 dk	**(X11A2YP) Yacht**	**2 oil engines** reduction geared to sc. shafts driving 2 Propellers Total Power: 2,000kW (2,720hp) M.T.U. 8V396TE74 2 x Vee 4 Stroke 8 Cy. 165 x 185 each-1000kW (1360bhp) MTU Friedrichshafen GmbH-Friedrichshafen
9113599 *UANJ* -	**TULOS** - **Baltasar Shipping SA** CJSC 'Onegoship' *St Petersburg* *Russia* MMSI: 273335000	**1,596** 831 2,300	Class: RS	**1995-01 Arminius Werke GmbH — Bodenwerder** Yd No: 10529 Loa 81.44 Br ex 11.46 Dght 4.220 Lbp 77.44 Br md 11.30 Dpth 5.40 Welded, 1 dk	**(A31A2GX) General Cargo Ship** Grain: 2,926 Compartments: 1 Ho, ER 1 Ha: ER	**1 oil engine** with clutches & sr reverse geared to sc. shaft driving 1 FP propeller Total Power: 1,100kW (1,496hp) 11.0kn MaK 6M332C 1 x 4 Stroke 6 Cy. 240 x 330 1100kW (1496bhp) Krupp MaK Maschinenbau GmbH-Kiel AuxGen: 2 x 161kW 400V 50Hz a.c Thrusters: 1 Thwart. FP thruster (f) Fuel: 90.0 (d.f.) 4.4pd

9263083 **TULPAR**
UNQ
\- **Roosalka Shipping Ltd**
BUE Marine Ltd
SatCom: Inmarsat C 443600428
Aqtau *Kazakhstan*
MMSI: 436000017

3,343 / 1,003 / 4,000
Class: BV (Class contemplated) NV

2002-09 Maritim Shipyard Sp z oo — Gdansk (Hull)
2002-09 Ulstein Verft AS — Ulsteinvik Yd No: 268
Loa 94.00 Br ex 21.03 Dght 3.969
Lbp 88.11 Br md 21.00 Dpth 5.00
Welded, 1 dk

(B21A2OS) Platform Supply Ship
Ice Capable

3 diesel electric oil engines driving 3 gen. Connecting to 2 elec. motors each (2000kW) driving 2 Azimuth electric drive units
Total Power: 6,060kW (8,238hp) 13.0kn
Cummins Wartsila 12V200
3 x Vee 4 Stroke 12 Cy. 200 x 240 each-2020kW (2746bhp)
Wartsila France SA-France
AuxGen: 3 x 2000kW 690/230V a.c
Thrusters: 2 Water jet (f)

9589011 **TULSI DAS**
\- *ex* Success Ii *-2011*
\- **Semirara Mining Corp**
\-
Zamboanga *Philippines*
Official number: ZAM2D01894

297 / 90 / 349
Class: (RI) (GL)

2010-06 Hung Seng Shipbuilding Sdn Bhd — Sibu Yd No: 16
Loa 31.10 Br ex - Dght 3.570
Lbp - Br md 9.50 Dpth 4.20
Welded, 1 dk

(B32A2ST) Tug

2 oil engines reverse reduction geared to sc. shafts driving 2 FP propellers
Total Power: 1,790kW (2,434hp)
Cummins KTA-38-M2
2 x Vee 4 Stroke 12 Cy. 159 x 159 each-895kW (1217bhp)
Cummins Engine Co Inc-USA
AuxGen: 2 x 78kW 415V a.c

9222560 **TULUM**
XCRB3 *ex* St. Clemens *-2008*
\- **TMM Division Maritima SA de CV**
\-
Manzanillo *Mexico*
MMSI: 345140008

28,534 / 12,369 / 47,131 / T/cm 50.3
Class: LR (NK)
100A1 SS 08/2010
Double Hull oil tanker
ESP
LI
LMC **UMS IGS**
Eq.Ltr: M†;
Cable: 632.5/73.0 U3 (a)

2000-08 Onomichi Dockyard Co Ltd — Onomichi HS Yd No: 453
Loa 182.50 (BB) Br ex 32.20 Dght 12.666
Lbp 172.00 Br md 32.20 Dpth 19.10
Welded, 1 dk

(A13B2TP) Products Tanker
Double Hull (13F)
Liq: 50,328; Liq (Oil): 50,328
Cargo Heating Coils
Compartments: 2 Ta, 12 Wing Ta, 2 Wing Slop Ta, ER
4 Cargo Pump (s): 4x1000m³/hr
Manifold: Bow/CM: 92.9m

1 oil engine driving 1 FP propeller
Total Power: 8,562kW (11,641hp) 15.3kn
B&W 6S50MC
1 x 2 Stroke 6 Cy. 500 x 1910 8562kW (11641bhp)
Mitsui Engineering & Shipbuilding CLtd-Japan
AuxGen: 3 x 420kW 450V 60Hz a.c
Boilers: e (ex.g.) 22.0kgf/cm² (21.6bar), AuxB (o.f.) 17.9kgf/cm² (17.6bar)
Fuel: 110.0 (d.f.) 1569.2 (r.f.)

8301096 **TULUM**
XCNT7 *ex* Cape Fear *-2010*
\- **Central de Desarrollos Marinos SA de CV**
Condux SA de CV
Ciudad del Carmen *Mexico*
MMSI: 345070261

700 / 210 / 1,200
Class: AB

1983-01 Moss Point Marine, Inc. — Escatawpa, Ms Yd No: 38
Loa - Br ex - Dght 3.666
Lbp 55.25 Br md 12.20 Dpth 4.27
Welded, 1 dk

(B21A2OS) Platform Supply Ship

2 oil engines reverse reduction geared to sc. shafts driving 2 FP propellers
Total Power: 2,206kW (3,000hp) 12.0kn
EMD (Electro-Motive) 12-645-E7A
2 x Vee 2 Stroke 12 Cy. 230 x 254 each-1103kW (1500bhp)
(Reconditioned , Reconditioned & fitted 1983)
General Motors Corp.Electro-Motive Div.-La Grange
AuxGen: 2 x 99kW
Thrusters: 1 Thwart. FP thruster (f)

9130860 **TULUN**
UCLJ *ex* Kapitan Prikhodko *-2002*
\- **OOO 'Region'**
\-
Kholmsk *Russia*
MMSI: 273814100
Official number: 930319

688 / 233 / 516
Class: (RS)

1995-06 AO Oston — Khabarovsk Yd No: 898
Loa 54.90 Br ex 9.49 Dght 4.460
Lbp 50.04 Br md - Dpth 5.16
Welded, 1 dk

(B12B2FC) Fish Carrier
Ins: 632
Compartments: 2 Ho, ER
2 Ha: 2 (3.0 x 3.0)ER
Cranes: 4x3t

1 oil engine reduction geared to sc. shaft driving 1 FP propeller
Total Power: 589kW (801hp) 11.3kn
S.K.L. 6NVD48A-2U
1 x 4 Stroke 6 Cy. 320 x 480 589kW (801bhp)
SKL Motoren u. Systemtechnik AG-Magdeburg
AuxGen: 3 x 160kW a.c
Fuel: 104.0 (d.f.)

9487366 **TULUS**
YDA6512
\- **PT Maritim Barito Perkasa**
\-
Banjarmasin *Indonesia*
MMSI: 525012050
Official number: 3257/IIA

249 / 74 / 167
Class: AB

2008-12 PT Perkasa Melati — Batam Yd No: PM022
Loa 29.50 Br ex 9.75 Dght 3.500
Lbp 28.36 Br md 9.00 Dpth 4.16
Welded, 1 dk

(B32A2ST) Tug

2 oil engines reverse reduction geared to sc. shafts driving 2 FP propellers
Total Power: 2,080kW (2,828hp)
Mitsubishi S12R-MPTK
2 x Vee 4 Stroke 12 Cy. 170 x 180 each-1040kW (1414bhp)
Mitsubishi Heavy Industries Ltd-Japan
AuxGen: 2 x 80kW a.c
Fuel: 72.0 (d.f.)

8822961 **TULUS BERSAMA 23**
\- *ex* Man Hua No. 7 *-2002*
\- **Li An Hwat Overseas Transport Pte Ltd**
Pacific Taiping Pte Ltd

101 / 31 / -
Class: (NK)

1983 Ocean Shipyard Co Sdn Bhd — Sibu
Loa 21.49 Br ex 6.50 Dght 2.083
Lbp 19.97 Br md 6.40 Dpth 2.60
Welded, 1 dk

(B32A2ST) Tug

2 oil engines reduction geared to sc. shafts driving 2 FP propellers
Total Power: 536kW (728hp) 9.0kn
Caterpillar 3408TA
2 x Vee 4 Stroke 8 Cy. 137 x 152 each-268kW (364bhp)
Caterpillar Tractor Co-USA
Fuel: 29.0 (d.f.)

8863941 **TULYA**
DXRT
\- **Batangas Bay Carriers Inc**
\-
Manila *Philippines*
Official number: 225805

472 / 310 / 700

1981 Mayon Docks Inc. — Tabaco
Loa 47.56 Br ex 9.38 Dght 2.280
Lbp 45.65 Br md 9.23 Dpth 3.65
Welded, 1 dk

(A13B2TP) Products Tanker
Liq: 789; Liq (Oil): 789
Compartments: 6 Ta, ER

3 oil engines with clutches & sr reverse geared to sc. shafts driving 3 FP propellers
Total Power: 339kW (462hp) 8.0kn
Isuzu E120-MF6R
3 x 4 Stroke 6 Cy. 135 x 140 each-113kW (154bhp)
Isuzu Marine Engine Inc-Japan
AuxGen: 1 x 28kW 220V a.c, 1 x 10kW 220V a.c

7388700 **TUMA**
5NIG *ex* Sea Breeze *-1985*
\- **Nigerian National Petroleum Corp (NNPC)**
\-
SatCom: Inmarsat C 465749118
Lagos *Nigeria*
MMSI: 657601000
Official number: 376156

68,442 / 52,046 / 136,100 / T/cm 102.0
Class: IS (AB) (GL) (NV)

1975-06 Eriksbergs Mekaniska Verkstads AB (Lindholmen Div.) — Goteborg (Aft section) Yd No: 673
1975-06 Lisnave - Estaleiros Navais de Lisboa SARL — Lisbon (Fwd section)
Converted From: Crude Oil Tanker-1985
Loa 280.04 (BB) Br ex 41.20 Dght 16.701
Lbp 268.00 Br md 41.15 Dpth 21.98
Welded, 1 dk

(B22H2OF) FSO, Oil
Single Hull
Liq: 167,697; Liq (Oil): 167,697
Cargo Heating Coils
Compartments: 12 Ta, ER
4 Cargo Pump (s): 4x3000m³/hr
Manifold: Bow/CM: 140m

1 oil engine driving 1 FP propeller
Total Power: 18,388kW (25,000hp) 15.0kn
B&W 10K84EF
1 x 2 Stroke 10 Cy. 840 x 1800 18388kW (25000bhp)
Eriksbergs Mekaniska Verkstads AB-Sweden
AuxGen: 3 x 900kW 440V 60Hz a.c
Fuel: 487.5 (d.f.) (Heating Coils) 5857.5 (r.f.) 69.0pd

8858178 **TUMAN**
\- *ex* BK-1277 *-1985*
\- **Real Estate Management Committee of St Petersburg City Executive Board**
JSC 'Port Fleet Ltd' (ZAO 'Portovyy Flot')
St Petersburg *Russia*
Official number: 733180

180 / 54 / 46
Class: RS

1973 "Petrozavod" — Leningrad Yd No: 831
Loa 29.30 Br ex 8.62 Dght 3.090
Lbp 25.20 Br md - Dpth 4.35
Welded, 1 dk

(B32A2ST) Tug
Ice Capable

2 oil engines driving 2 CP propellers
Total Power: 882kW (1,200hp) 11.4kn
Russkiy 6DR30/50-4-2
2 x 2 Stroke 6 Cy. 300 x 500 each-441kW (600bhp)
Mashinostroitelnyy Zavod"Russkiy-Dizel"-Leningrad
AuxGen: 2 x 25kW a.c

8932340 **TUMAN**
\-
\- **PJSC 'Fleet of Novorossiysk Commercial Sea Port'**
LLC Shipping & Towing Co Novofleet
Odessa *Ukraine*

331 / 99 / 118
Class: (RS)

1995-03 Brodogradiliste Beograd — Belgrade Yd No: 1167
Loa 33.70 Br ex 9.95 Dght 3.360
Lbp 30.14 Br md 9.50 Dpth 4.50
Welded, 1 dk

(B32A2ST) Tug
Ice Capable

2 oil engines geared to sc. shafts driving 2 CP propellers
Total Power: 1,920kW (2,610hp) 12.8kn
Alpha 6L23/30A
2 x 4 Stroke 6 Cy. 225 x 300 each-960kW (1305bhp)
MAN B&W Diesel A/S-Denmark
AuxGen: 3 x 58kW a.c
Fuel: 61.0 (d.f.)

8829232 **TUMANNYY**
UCDW *ex* Kootsaare *-2005* *ex* MRTK-0777 *-1992*
\- **Arcticpack Co Ltd (OOO 'Arktikpak')**
\-
Murmansk *Russia*
Official number: 894240

117 / 35 / 30
Class: RS

1990-05 Sosnovskiy Sudostroitelnyy Zavod — Sosnovka Yd No: 777
Loa 25.50 Br ex - Dght 2.391
Lbp 22.00 Br md 7.00 Dpth 3.30
Welded, 1 dk

(B11A2FS) Stern Trawler
Ice Capable

1 oil engine driving 1 FP propeller
Total Power: 220kW (299hp) 9.5kn
S.K.L. 6NVD26A-2
1 x 4 Stroke 6 Cy. 180 x 260 220kW (299bhp)
VEB Schwermaschinenbau "KarlLiebknecht" (SKL)-Magdeburg

7115763 **TUMANNYY**
\-
\- **ZAO 'F P M'**
\-

177 / 53 / 94
Class: (RS)

1971-05 Zavod 'Nikolayevsk-na-Amure' — Nikolayevsk-na-Amure Yd No: 42
Loa 33.96 Br ex 7.09 Dght 2.901
Lbp 29.97 Br md - Dpth 3.69
Welded, 1 dk

(B11B2FV) Fishing Vessel
Bale: 115
Compartments: 1 Ho, ER
1 Ha: (1.6 x 1.3)
Derricks: 2x2t; Winches: 2

1 oil engine driving 1 FP propeller
Total Power: 224kW (305hp) 9.5kn
S.K.L. 8NVD36-1U
1 x 4 Stroke 8 Cy. 240 x 360 224kW (305bhp)
VEB Schwermaschinenbau "KarlLiebknecht" (SKL)-Magdeburg
AuxGen: 1 x 75kW a.c, 1 x 50kW a.c
Fuel: 17.0 (d.f.)

7644829 **TUMANTE**
HO3182 *ex* Tarpon I *-2003* *ex* Tarpon *-2000*
\- *ex* YO-201 *-1976*
International North Baltic Marine Operation
\-
Panama *Panama*
MMSI: 353182000
Official number: 31212PEXT

499 / 339 / -

1945 Manitowoc Shipbuilding Co — Manitowoc Wi Yd No: 407
Converted From: Replenishment Tanker-1976
Loa 50.60 Br ex 9.78 Dght -
Lbp - Br md - Dpth 4.58
Welded, 1 dk

(B11B2FV) Fishing Vessel

1 oil engine driving 1 FP propeller
Total Power: 478kW (650hp)

IMO / Call sign	Name / Owner	Tonnage / Class	Builder / Dimensions	Type	Machinery
9242091 *CB6585* -	**TUMBES** **Santiago Leasing SA** CPT Empresas Maritimas SA *Valparaiso* *Chile* MMSI: 725010400 Official number: 3007	**247** Class: AB 74 -	**2000**-12 **President Marine Pte Ltd — Singapore** Yd No: 257 Loa 29.00 Br ex - Dght 3.500 Lbp 26.50 Br md 9.00 Dpth 4.25 Welded, 1 dk	**(B32A2ST) Tug**	**2 oil engines** reduction geared to sc. shafts driving 2 FP propellers Total Power: 2,318kW (3,152hp) Caterpillar 3512B 2 x Vee 4 Stroke 12 Cy. 170 x 190 each-1159kW (1576bhp) Caterpillar Inc-USA
7014907 - -	**TUMBES 1** *ex* Virgen de Begona 2 *-1975* - -	*258* Class: (BV) 132 146	**1970 Construcciones Navales SA (CONASA) — Callao** Loa 31.70 Br ex 7.65 Dght - Lbp - Br md 7.62 Dpth 3.92 Welded, 1 dk	**(B11B2FV) Fishing Vessel** Compartments: 2 Ho, ER 1 Ha: (2.9 x 3.8)	**1 oil engine** geared to sc. shaft driving 1 FP propeller Total Power: 416kW (566hp) 10.0kn Caterpillar D398SCAC 1 x Vee 4 Stroke 12 Cy. 159 x 203 416kW (566bhp) Caterpillar Tractor Co-USA
7008269 - -	**TUMBES 3** *ex* PA 21 *-1976* **Eliseo Pena Cayetano** - *Chimbote* *Peru* Official number: CE-005069-PM	*310* Class: (GL) 140 -	**1970 Ast. Picsa S.A. — Callao** Yd No: 299 L reg 35.09 Br ex 8.03 Dght - Lbp - Br md 8.01 Dpth 3.84 Welded, 1 dk	**(B11B2FV) Fishing Vessel**	**1 oil engine** reverse reduction geared to sc. shaft driving 1 FP propeller Total Power: 530kW (721hp) MAN G6V235/330ATL 1 x 4 Stroke 6 Cy. 235 x 330 530kW (721bhp) Maschinenbau Augsburg Nuernberg (MAN)-Augsburg
7008271 - -	**TUMBES 4** *ex* PA 22 *-1975* - -	*310* Class: (GL) 140 -	**1970 Ast. Picsa S.A. — Callao** Yd No: 300 L reg 35.09 Br ex 8.03 Dght - Lbp - Br md 8.01 Dpth - Welded, 1 dk	**(B11B2FV) Fishing Vessel**	**1 oil engine** driving 1 FP propeller Total Power: 530kW (721hp) MAN G6V235/330ATL 1 x 4 Stroke 6 Cy. 235 x 330 530kW (721bhp) Maschinenbau Augsburg Nuernberg (MAN)-Augsburg
7015066 - -	**TUMBES 7** *ex* PA 25 *-1976* - -	*310* Class: (GL) 140 -	**1969 Ast. Picsa S.A. — Callao** Yd No: 303 L reg 35.09 Br ex 8.03 Dght - Lbp - Br md 8.01 Dpth 3.84 Welded, 1 dk	**(B11B2FV) Fishing Vessel**	**1 oil engine** driving 1 FP propeller Total Power: 530kW (721hp) 12.0kn MAN G6V235/330ATL 1 x 4 Stroke 6 Cy. 235 x 330 530kW (721bhp) Maschinenbau Augsburg Nuernberg (MAN)-Augsburg
7015561 - -	**TUMBES 10** *ex* PA 28 *-1976* - -	*310* Class: (GL) 140 -	**1970 Ast. Picsa S.A. — Callao** Yd No: 306 L reg 35.09 Br ex 8.03 Dght - Lbp - Br md 8.01 Dpth 3.84 Welded, 1 dk	**(B11B2FV) Fishing Vessel**	**1 oil engine** reverse reduction geared to sc. shaft driving 1 FP propeller Total Power: 530kW (721hp) 12.0kn MAN G6V235/330ATL 1 x 4 Stroke 6 Cy. 235 x 330 530kW (721bhp) Maschinenbau Augsburg Nuernberg (MAN)-Augsburg
7734349 *WCB9098* -	**TUMBLEWEED** *ex* H. W. Zarling *-2009* *ex* Aja *-2004* *ex* Laguna Cruz *-2004* **Guy Derosa** - *Portland, OR* *United States of America* Official number: 587243	*121* 82 -	**1977 Marine Mart, Inc. — Port Isabel, Tx** Yd No: 161 L reg 19.39 Br ex - Dght - Lbp - Br md 6.13 Dpth 3.87 Welded, 1 dk	**(B11B2FV) Fishing Vessel**	**1 oil engine** driving 1 FP propeller Total Power: 268kW (364hp)
8418617 *UAXP* -	**TUMCHA** *ex* Neftegaz-71 *-2004* **'Arktikmorneftegazrazvedka' OJSC** - SatCom: Inmarsat C 427300722 *Murmansk* *Russia* MMSI: 273413100 Official number: 901069	**2,684** Class: (RS) 805 1,393	**1990**-12 **Stocznia Szczecinska im A Warskiego — Szczecin** Yd No: B92/221 Loa 81.37 Br ex 16.30 Dght 4.900 Lbp 71.45 Br md 15.96 Dpth 7.20 Welded, 1 dk	**(B21B20A) Anchor Handling Tug Supply** Cranes: 1x12.5t Ice Capable	**2 oil engines** reduction geared to sc. shafts driving 2 CP propellers Total Power: 5,298kW (7,204hp) 9.5kn Sulzer 6ZL40/48 2 x 4 Stroke 6 Cy. 400 x 480 each-2649kW (3602bhp) Zaklady Przemyslu Metalowego 'HCegielski' SA-Poznan AuxGen: 3 x 400kW 400V 50Hz a.c Thrusters: 2 Tunnel thruster (f) Fuel: 659.0 10.0pd
8914817 *5NQN* -	**TUMINI** *ex* Tradewind Sunrise *-2009* *ex* Ambroise *-2001* *ex* Kristina *-1995* **Petroleum Brokers Ltd** Tubal Cane Shipmanagement Nigeria Ltd SatCom: Inmarsat C 465741810 *Lagos* *Nigeria* MMSI: 657418000	**4,094** Class: (NV) 2,129 6,330 T/cm 15.4	**1991**-08 **Argos Engineering Co Pte Ltd — Singapore** Yd No: 8631 Loa 101.52 (BB) Br ex 17.50 Dght 6.096 Lbp 95.52 Br md - Dpth 8.00 Welded, 1 dk	**(A12B2TR) Chemical/Products Tanker** Double Bottom Entire Compartment Length Liq: 7,291; Liq (Oil): 7,291 Cargo Heating Coils Compartments: 10 Wing Ta, ER 10 Cargo Pump (s) Ice Capable	**1 oil engine** with flexible couplings & sr geared to sc. shaft driving 1 CP propeller Total Power: 2,942kW (4,000hp) 12.0kn Normo BRM-8 1 x 4 Stroke 8 Cy. 320 x 360 2942kW (4000bhp) Bergen Diesel AS-Norway AuxGen: 3 x 350kW 440V 60Hz a.c Thrusters: 1 Thwart. FP thruster (f)
9255232 *XPKF* -	**TUMMAS T** *ex* Norderveg *-2013* *ex* Brennholm *-2006* **Sp/F Gulenni** - *Faeroe Islands (Danish)* MMSI: 231049000	**1,514** Class: NV 454 -	**2002**-09 **Stocznia Polnocna SA (Northern Shipyard) — Gdansk** (Hull) Yd No: B312/3 **2002**-09 **Eidsvik Skipsbyggeri AS — Uskedalen** Yd No: 70 Loa 64.50 (BB) Br ex 13.30 Dght 6.080 Lbp 56.40 Br md 13.00 Dpth 8.60 Welded, 1 dk	**(B11B2FV) Fishing Vessel**	**1 oil engine** geared to sc. shaft driving 1 CP propeller Total Power: 3,460kW (4,704hp) 17.5kn Caterpillar 3612TA 1 x Vee 4 Stroke 12 Cy. 280 x 300 3460kW (4704bhp) Caterpillar Inc-USA Thrusters: 1 Tunnel thruster (f); 1 Tunnel thruster (a)
8116685 *2GAF7* -	**TUMMEL** *ex* VS Rotterdam *-2012* *ex* Adrett *-2002* *ex* Brake *-2000* **Forth Crossing Bridge Constructors JV** Briggs Marine Contractors Ltd *Leith* *United Kingdom* MMSI: 235095722 Official number: 918674	**218** Class: GL 65 101	**1982**-07 **Detlef Hegemann Rolandwerft GmbH — Bremen** Yd No: 116 Loa 28.17 Br ex 8.84 Dght 2.701 Lbp 26.52 Br md 8.81 Dpth 3.03 Welded, 1 dk	**(B32A2ST) Tug** Ice Capable	**2 oil engines** geared to sc. shafts driving 2 Directional propellers Total Power: 1,176kW (1,598hp) Deutz SBV6M628 2 x 4 Stroke 6 Cy. 240 x 280 each-588kW (799bhp) Kloeckner Humboldt Deutz AG-West Germany
8874445 *UHPV*	**TUMNIN** **50-letiya Oktyabrya Fishing Collective (Rybkolkhoz imeni 50-letiya Oktyabrya)** - SatCom: Inmarsat A 1406222 *Sovetskaya Gavan* *Russia* MMSI: 273873400 Official number: 911060	**4,407** Class: RS 1,322 1,810	**1993**-10 **DAHK Chernomorskyi Sudnobudivnyi Zavod — Mykolayiv** Yd No: 601 Loa 104.50 Br ex 16.03 Dght 5.900 Lbp 96.40 Br md 16.00 Dpth 10.20 Welded, 1 dk	**(B11A2FG) Factory Stern Trawler** Grain: 420 Ice Capable	**1 oil engine** driving 1 FP propeller Total Power: 2,576kW (3,502hp) Russkiy 6CHN40/46 1 x 4 Stroke 6 Cy. 400 x 460 2576kW (3502bhp) Mashinostroitelnyy Zavod"Russkiy-Dizel"-Leningrad
8860755 *UGCP* -	**TUMNINSKIY** **50-letiya Oktyabrya Fishing Collective (Rybkolkhoz imeni 50-letiya Oktyabrya)** - *Sovetskaya Gavan* *Russia* Official number: 912307	**448** Class: RS 134 207	**1992**-06 **AO Zavod 'Nikolayevsk-na-Amure' — Nikolayevsk-na-Amure** Yd No: 1286 Loa 44.88 Br ex 9.47 Dght 3.770 Lbp 39.37 Br md 9.30 Dpth 5.13 Welded, 1 dk	**(B11A2FS) Stern Trawler** Ice Capable	**1 oil engine** driving 1 FP propeller Total Power: 588kW (799hp) 11.5kn S.K.L. 6NVD48A-2U 1 x 4 Stroke 6 Cy. 320 x 480 588kW (799bhp) SKL Motoren u. Systemtechnik AG-Magdeburg
8846436 *9A3378* -	**TUNA** *ex* PO-52 *-2000* **Ranko Naranca** - *Split* *Croatia* MMSI: 238106540 Official number: 5T-861	**163** Class: CS (JR) 86 -	**1955**-01 **Brodogradiliste Split (Brodosplit) — Split** Converted From: Munitions Carrier Loa 32.63 Br ex 5.50 Dght 2.500 Lbp 30.50 Br md - Dpth 2.80 Welded, 1 dk	**(A31A2GX) General Cargo Ship** Derricks: 1x2t	**1 oil engine** driving 1 FP propeller Total Power: 147kW (200hp) Alpha 344-F 1 x 2 Stroke 4 Cy. 200 x 340 147kW (200bhp) (new engine 1961) A/S Burmeister & Wain's Maskin ogSkibsbyggeri-Denmark AuxGen: 1 x 12kW 24V d.c, 1 x 4kW 24V d.c
8992821 *YFPW* -	**TUNA** **Government of The Republic of Indonesia (Direktorat Jenderal Perhubungan Darat - Ministry of Land Communications)** PT ASDP Indonesia Ferry (Persero) - Angkutan Sungai Danau & Penyeberangan *Jakarta* *Indonesia*	**718** Class: KI 271 -	**1993**-04 **PT Dumas — Surabaya** Loa 45.40 Br ex - Dght 2.100 Lbp 38.50 Br md 14.00 Dpth 3.50 Welded, 2 dks	**(A36A2PR) Passenger/Ro-Ro Ship (Vehicles)**	**2 oil engines** driving 2 FP propellers Total Power: 1,324kW (1,800hp) 10.0kn Niigata 6NCS-M 2 x 4 Stroke 6 Cy. 190 x 260 each-662kW (900bhp) Niigata Engineering Co Ltd-Japan
8230041 *XUGC9* -	**TUNA** *ex* Alexino *-2007* *ex* Komsomol Karelii *-1998* *ex* Volgo-Balt 165 *-1998* **Mediterranean International Shipping Co Inc** Cevahir Denizcilik ve Ticaret AS *Phnom Penh* *Cambodia* MMSI: 514778000 Official number: 0272011	**2,457** Class: IS (RS) (RR) 1,134 2,877	**1972**-07 **Zavody Tazkeho Strojarstva (ZTS) — Komarno** Yd No: 1365 Loa 113.85 Br ex 13.19 Dght 3.530 Lbp 110.52 Br md 13.00 Dpth 6.50 Welded, 1 dk	**(A31A2GX) General Cargo Ship**	**2 oil engines** driving 2 FP propellers Total Power: 1,030kW (1,400hp) Skoda 6L275A2 2 x 4 Stroke 6 Cy. 275 x 350 each-515kW (700bhp) CKD Praha-Praha

IMO / Call sign / Flag	Name / Owner	Tonnage	Class	Builder / Dimensions	Type	Machinery
7725374 *ERIX* -	**TUNA** *ex* Gelendzhik Express *-2014* *ex* Silver Coral *-2010* *ex* Cimarron *-2007* *ex* Spirit of Freedom *-2000* *ex* Mercandian Exporter II *-1987* **Tuna Shipping SA** Akdeniz Roro Deniz Tasimaciligi Turizm Sanayi ve Ticaret Ltd Sti *Giurgiulesti* *Moldova* MMSI: 214180924	**4,998** 1,499 3,297	Class: TL (MG) (RS) (NV)	**1979-11 Frederikshavn Vaerft A/S — Frederikshavn** Yd No: 381 Loa 105.62 (BB) Br ex 18.83 Dght 4.971 Lbp 96.02 Br md 18.82 Dpth 8.91 Welded, 2 dks	**(A35A2RR) Ro-Ro Cargo Ship** Stern door/ramp Len: 15.40 Wid: 7.70 Swl: - Side door/ramp (s. a.) Len: 13.35 Wid: 4.30 Swl: - Lane-Len: 870 Lane-Wid: 7.70 Lane-clr ht: 4.70 Cars: 450, Trailers: 63 Grain: 10,320; Bale: 10,188 TEU 256 C RoRo Dk 58 TEU C Dk 198 TEU incl 50 ref C.	**1 oil engine** sr geared to sc. shaft driving 1 CP propeller Total Power: 3,310kW (4,500hp) 15.0kn MaK 12M453AK 1 x Vee 4 Stroke 12 Cy. 320 x 420 3310kW (4500bhp) MaK Maschinenbau GmbH-Kiel AuxGen: 3 x 280kW 440V 60Hz a.c Thrusters: 1 Thwart. FP thruster (f) Fuel: 482.0 (d.f.) 13.0pd
9306691 *PHBX* -	**TUNA** **Thunrederier AB** Marin Ship Management BV *Delfzijl* *Netherlands* MMSI: 244321000 Official number: 42473	**2,810** 1,652 4,775	Class: BV	**2004-10 Ferus Smit Leer GmbH — Leer** Yd No: 357 Loa 89.00 Br ex - Dght 5.850 Lbp 84.99 Br md 13.35 Dpth 7.50 Welded, 1 dk	**(A31A2GX) General Cargo Ship** Grain: 5,097 Ice Capable	**1 oil engine** geared to sc. shaft driving 1 CP propeller Total Power: 1,900kW (2,583hp) 11.8kn Wartsila 6L26 1 x 4 Stroke 6 Cy. 260 x 320 1900kW (2583bhp) Wartsila Finland Oy-Finland AuxGen: 1 x 284kW a.c, 1 x 175kW a.c Thrusters: 1 Tunnel thruster (f) Fuel: 35.0 (d.f.) 211.0 (r.f.)
9148491 *E5U2633* -	**TUNA 1** *ex* Neri *-2013* *ex* Bai Handelas *-2010* *ex* Ocean Bride *-2009* *ex* Mir Damad *-2008* *ex* Steamers Fervour *-1997* **Tuna Holding Inc** Bergen Denizcilik Ltd Sti *Avatiu* *Cook Islands* MMSI: 518686000 Official number: 1722	**4,276** 2,177 5,055	Class: NK (BV) (GL)	**1997-06 Jinling Shipyard — Nanjing JS** Yd No: 96-7007 Loa 100.59 (BB) Br ex 16.23 Dght 6.401 Lbp 94.80 Br md 16.20 Dpth 8.20 Welded, 1 dk	**(A31A2GX) General Cargo Ship** Grain: 7,267; Bale: 7,021 TEU 384 incl 50 ref C. Cranes: 2x40t Ice Capable	**1 oil engine** reduction geared to sc. shaft driving 1 CP propeller Total Power: 3,690kW (5,017hp) 15.0kn Wartsila 9R32E 1 x 4 Stroke 9 Cy. 320 x 350 3690kW (5017bhp) Wartsila Diesel AB-Sweden AuxGen: 1 x 440kW 440/220V a.c, 3 x 330kW 440/220V a.c Thrusters: 1 Thwart. FP thruster (f)
9205952 *TCXT3* -	**TUNA 7** *ex* Bright Ocean 2 *-2009* *ex* Mississippi Rainbow *-2001* **Yapi Kredi Finansal Kiralama AO (Yapi Kredi Leasing AO)** Horizon Gemi Isletmeciligi Sanayi ve Ticaret AS *Istanbul* *Turkey* MMSI: 271040352 Official number: TUGS1830	**19,707** 10,825 32,128 T/cm 41.0	Class: NK	**1999-08 Saiki Heavy Industries Co Ltd — Saiki OT** Yd No: 1087 Loa 171.59 (BB) Br ex - Dght 10.418 Lbp 163.60 Br md 27.00 Dpth 14.80 Welded, 1 dk	**(A31A2GO) Open Hatch Cargo Ship** Grain: 41,756; Bale: 41,138 Compartments: 5 Ho, ER 5 Ha: (13.4 x 15.0)3 (20.5 x 22.9) (19.8 x 18.0)ER Cranes: 4x30t	**1 oil engine** driving 1 FP propeller Total Power: 7,061kW (9,600hp) 14.0kn Mitsubishi 6UEC52LA 1 x 2 Stroke 6 Cy. 520 x 1600 7061kW (9600bhp) Kobe Hatsudoki KK-Japan AuxGen: 2 x 400kW a.c Fuel: 1670.0
7903548 *J8AP8* -	**TUNA BRAS NO. 11** *ex* Hsiang Jang 11 *-2005* *ex* Atlantic No. 78 *-1997* *ex* Tenyu Maru No. 78 *-1990* *ex* Shigetoku Maru No. 35 *-1987* **Sacrosanct International Co Ltd** - *Kingstown* *St Vincent & The Grenadines* MMSI: 375916000 Official number: 400370	*506* 151 353		**1979-07 Miho Zosensho K.K. — Shimizu** Yd No: 1129 Loa 50.14 Br ex - Dght 3.222 Lbp 43.63 Br md 8.50 Dpth 3.45 Welded, 1 dk	**(B11B2FV) Fishing Vessel**	**1 oil engine** driving 1 FP propeller Niigata Niigata Engineering Co Ltd-Japan
8002016 - -	**TUNA BRAS NO. 206** *ex* Crusader *-2011* *ex* Sachi Maru No. 108 *-1994* - -	**756** 226 -		**1980-02 Niigata Engineering Co Ltd — Niigata NI** Yd No: 1670 Loa 49.92 (BB) Br ex 8.62 Dght 3.291 Lbp 44.02 Br md 8.60 Dpth 3.66 Welded, 1 dk	**(B11B2FV) Fishing Vessel**	**1 oil engine** reduction geared to sc. shaft driving 1 FP propeller Total Power: 736kW (1,001hp) Niigata 6M28AFT 1 x 4 Stroke 6 Cy. 280 x 480 736kW (1001bhp) Niigata Engineering Co Ltd-Japan
9386469 *HSB3444* -	**TUNA HUNTER 1** **Five Star Tuna Line Co Ltd** - *Bangkok* *Thailand* Official number: 480001585	**151** 103 -		**2005-06 Mahachai Dockyard Co., Ltd. — Samut Sakhon** Loa 28.00 (BB) Br ex - Dght - Lbp 26.50 Br md 7.00 Dpth 3.00 Welded, 1 dk	**(B11B2FV) Fishing Vessel**	**1 oil engine** reduction geared to sc. shaft driving 1 FP propeller Total Power: 597kW (812hp) Yanmar 1 x 4 Stroke 597kW (812bhp) Yanmar Diesel Engine Co Ltd-Japan AuxGen: 2 x 261kW a.c
9422914 *HSB3554* -	**TUNA HUNTER 2** **Five Star Tuna Line Co Ltd** - *Bangkok* *Thailand* Official number: 480002670	**175** 119 -		**2005-12 Mahachai Dockyard Co., Ltd. — Samut Sakhon** Loa 30.50 Br ex - Dght - Lbp 29.00 Br md 7.00 Dpth 3.30 Welded, 1 dk	**(B11B2FV) Fishing Vessel**	**1 oil engine** reduction geared to sc. shaft driving 1 FP propeller Total Power: 455kW (619hp) Yanmar 1 x 4 Stroke 455kW (619bhp) Yanmar Diesel Engine Co Ltd-Japan
7050236 - -	**TUNA LADY** *ex* Hannah Lee *-2009* *ex* Hungry Dog *-2009* *ex* Captain Lee *-1993* *ex* Tiki VIII *-1993* **Banner Maritime Corp** - *Chaguaramas* *Trinidad & Tobago*	*128* 87 -		**1968 Graham Boats, Inc. — Pascagoula, Ms** Loa 26.33 Br ex 7.31 Dght - Lbp - Br md 6.46 Dpth 3.66 Welded	**(B11B2FV) Fishing Vessel**	**1 oil engine** driving 1 FP propeller Total Power: 338kW (460hp) 9.0kn Caterpillar 1 x 4 Stroke 338kW (460bhp) Caterpillar Tractor Co-USA
9314612 *YJQT4* -	**TUNA PRINCESS** **Star Navigation SA** Shinko Kaiun Co Ltd *Port Vila* *Vanuatu* MMSI: 576139000 Official number: 1996	**4,522** 2,131 4,909	Class: NK	**2005-09 Kyokuyo Shipyard Corp — Shimonoseki YC** Yd No: 461 Loa 120.75 (BB) Br ex - Dght 6.914 Lbp 112.90 Br md 16.60 Dpth 10.00 Welded, 3 dks	**(A34A2GR) Refrigerated Cargo Ship** Ins: 5,211 4 Ha: ER 4 (4.0 x 4.0) Derricks: 8x5t	**1 oil engine** driving 1 FP propeller Total Power: 2,993kW (4,069hp) 14.5kn B&W 6L35MC 1 x 2 Stroke 6 Cy. 350 x 1050 2993kW (4069bhp) Makita Corp-Japan Fuel: 1070.0
7729796 - -	**TUNA PRO NO. 1** *ex* Melilla No. 206 *-2007* *ex* Focus No. 101 *-2007* *ex* O Yang No. 101 *-1997* **Malta Fishfarming Ltd** - *Conakry* *Guinea*	*449* 246 470	Class: (KR)	**1978-09 Dae Sun Shipbuilding & Engineering Co Ltd — Busan** Yd No: 217 Loa 55.50 Br ex - Dght 3.742 Lbp 49.00 Br md 9.01 Dpth 3.97 Welded, 1 dk	**(B11B2FV) Fishing Vessel** Ins: 554 2 Ha: (1.3 x 0.9) (1.7 x 1.7)ER	**1 oil engine** driving 1 FP propeller Total Power: 956kW (1,300hp) 13.8kn Niigata 6L28X 1 x 4 Stroke 6 Cy. 280 x 440 956kW (1300bhp) Niigata Engineering Co Ltd-Japan AuxGen: 2 x 160kW 225V a.c
9278612 *HPFK* -	**TUNA QUEEN** **Star Navigation SA** Shinko Kaiun Co Ltd *Panama* *Panama* MMSI: 352894000 Official number: 2923303C	**4,499** 2,130 4,940	Class: NK	**2003-06 Kyokuyo Shipyard Corp — Shimonoseki YC** Yd No: 446 Loa 120.75 Br ex - Dght 6.914 Lbp 112.90 Br md 16.60 Dpth 10.00 Welded, 1 dk	**(A34A2GR) Refrigerated Cargo Ship** Ins: 5,090	**1 oil engine** driving 1 FP propeller Total Power: 2,993kW (4,069hp) 14.5kn B&W 6L35MC 1 x 2 Stroke 6 Cy. 350 x 1050 2993kW (4069bhp) Makita Corp-Japan Fuel: 1070.0
8740668 *PMGB* -	**TUNA TOMINI** **PT ASDP Indonesia Ferry (Persero) - Angkutan Sungai Danau & Penyeberangan** - *Jakarta* *Indonesia*	**546** 164 647	Class: KI	**2005-12 P.T. Palindo — Tanjungpinang** Loa 43.30 Br ex - Dght 1.950 Lbp 38.08 Br md 10.50 Dpth 2.80 Welded, 1 dk	**(A37B2PS) Passenger Ship**	**2 oil engines** driving 2 Propellers Total Power: 912kW (1,240hp) Yanmar 6LAH-STE3 2 x 4 Stroke 6 Cy. 150 x 165 each-456kW (620bhp) Yanmar Diesel Engine Co Ltd-Japan
8811314 *SGPB* -	**TUNAFJORD** *ex* Nissum *-2008* *ex* Aurora *-1999* *ex* Biscaya *-1993* **Roine Johansson** - *Glommen* *Sweden* MMSI: 266305000	**207** 62 -		**1988-06 Poul Ree A/S — Stokkemarke (Hull)** Yd No: 4800 **1988-06 Johs Kristensen Skibsbyggeri A/S — Hvide Sande** Loa 23.79 Br ex 7.27 Dght - Lbp - Br md 7.22 Dpth 5.08 Welded	**(B11A2FT) Trawler** Ins: 140	**1 oil engine** reduction geared to sc. shaft driving 1 FP propeller Total Power: 675kW (918hp) Caterpillar 3508TA 1 x Vee 4 Stroke 8 Cy. 170 x 190 675kW (918bhp) Caterpillar Inc-USA

9230581 *YJRL6* -	**TUNAGO No. 31** - **Tunago Fishery Co Ltd** - *Port Vila* *Vanuatu* MMSI: 576594000 Official number: 1232	**498** 160 -		**2000-05 Lien Cherng Shipbuilding Co, Ltd — Kaohsiung** Yd No: 088 Loa - Br ex - Dght - Lbp - Br md - Dpth - Welded, 1 dk	**(B11B2FV) Fishing Vessel** Bale: 321; Ins: 109	**1 oil engine** driving 1 FP propeller Total Power: 736kW (1,001hp) Yanmar DY26-SN 1 x 4 Stroke 6 Cy. 260 x 440 736kW (1001bhp) Yanmar Diesel Engine Co Ltd-Japan
9230593 *YJRL7* -	**TUNAGO No. 32** - **Tunago Fishery Co Ltd** - *Port Vila* *Vanuatu* MMSI: 576595000 Official number: 1233	**498** 160 -		**2000-06 Lien Cherng Shipbuilding Co, Ltd — Kaohsiung** Yd No: 089 Loa - Br ex - Dght - Lbp - Br md - Dpth - Welded, 1 dk	**(B11B2FV) Fishing Vessel** Bale: 321; Ins: 109	**1 oil engine** driving 1 FP propeller Total Power: 736kW (1,001hp) Yanmar DY26-SN 1 x 4 Stroke 6 Cy. 260 x 440 736kW (1001bhp) Yanmar Diesel Engine Co Ltd-Japan
9230608 *YJRP4* -	**TUNAGO No. 51** - **Tunago Fishery Co Ltd** - *Port Vila* *Vanuatu* MMSI: 576608000 Official number: 1254	**499** 161 -		**2000-09 Lien Cherng Shipbuilding Co, Ltd — Kaohsiung** Yd No: 093 Loa - Br ex - Dght - Lbp - Br md - Dpth - Welded, 1 dk	**(B11B2FV) Fishing Vessel** Bale: 321; Ins: 109	**1 oil engine** geared to sc. shaft driving 1 FP propeller Total Power: 883kW (1,201hp) Akasaka K26SFD 1 x 4 Stroke 6 Cy. 260 x 480 883kW (1201bhp) Akasaka Tekkosho KK (Akasaka DieselLtd)-Japan
9230610 *YJRQ3* -	**TUNAGO No. 52** - **Tunago Fishery Co Ltd** - *Port Vila* *Vanuatu* MMSI: 576609000 Official number: 1261	**499** 161 -		**2000-10 Lien Cherng Shipbuilding Co, Ltd — Kaohsiung** Yd No: 095 Loa - Br ex - Dght - Lbp - Br md - Dpth - Welded, 1 dk	**(B11B2FV) Fishing Vessel** Bale: 321; Ins: 109	**1 oil engine** geared to sc. shaft driving 1 FP propeller Total Power: 1,030kW (1,400hp) Akasaka K26SFD 1 x 4 Stroke 6 Cy. 260 x 480 1030kW (1400bhp) Akasaka Tekkosho KK (Akasaka DieselLtd)-Japan
8996061 *YJRX9* -	**TUNAGO NO. 61** - **Tunago Fishery Co Ltd** - *Port Vila* *Vanuatu* MMSI: 576678000 Official number: 1323	**498** 161 -		**2001-01 Lien Cherng Shipbuilding Co, Ltd — Kaohsiung** Yd No: LC-103 L reg 53.50 Br ex - Dght - Lbp - Br md - Dpth - Welded, 1 dk	**(B11B2FV) Fishing Vessel** Ins: 555	**1 oil engine** driving 1 Propeller
9260225 *YJSA2* -	**TUNAGO No. 62** - **Tunago Fishery Co Ltd** - *Port Vila* *Vanuatu* MMSI: 576679000 Official number: 1324	**498** 161 -		**2001 Lien Cherng Shipbuilding Co, Ltd — Kaohsiung** Yd No: 105 Loa - Br ex - Dght - Lbp - Br md - Dpth - Welded, 1 dk	**(B11B2FV) Fishing Vessel**	**1 oil engine** geared to sc. shaft driving 1 FP propeller Total Power: 1,030kW (1,400hp) Akasaka K26SFD 1 x 4 Stroke 6 Cy. 260 x 480 1030kW (1400bhp) Akasaka Tekkosho KK (Akasaka DieselLtd)-Japan
7409138 - -	**TUNAMAR** *ex Teguise -2009 ex Sea Witch -2003* *ex Haladeiro -1994* **America Tower I Corp** -	**1,098** 386 1,550	Class: (BV)	**1978-02 EN Bazan de Construcciones Navales Militares SA — Cartagena (Sp)** Yd No: 171 Loa 76.76 Br ex - Dght 6.090 Lbp 67.92 Br md 13.50 Dpth 8.72 Welded, 2 dks	**(B11A2FS) Stern Trawler**	**1 oil engine** geared to sc. shaft driving 1 FP propeller Total Power: 2,942kW (4,000hp) 14.0kn Pielstick 12PA6V280 1 x Vee 4 Stroke 12 Cy. 280 x 290 2942kW (4000bhp) Alsthom Atlantique-France Fuel: 488.5 (d.f.)
7383750 *YYP5157* -	**TUNANTAL** - **Flota Industrial Pesca Atunera Caribe CA (FIPACA)** - *Puerto Sucre* *Venezuela* Official number: APNN-6067	*630* 198 900		**1989-09 SIMA Serv. Ind. de la Marina Chimbote (SIMACH) — Chimbote** Yd No: 400 Loa 51.51 Br ex - Dght - Lbp 46.99 Br md 10.67 Dpth 5.66 Welded	**(B11B2FV) Fishing Vessel**	**1 oil engine** geared to sc. shaft driving 1 FP propeller Total Power: 1,405kW (1,910hp) MAN G9V30/45 1 x 4 Stroke 9 Cy. 300 x 450 1405kW (1910bhp) MAN B&W Diesel GmbH-Augsburg
7395375 - -	**TUNAPESCA** *ex Pescatun -2011 ex Roberto M -2004* *ex Pacifico C -1998 ex Top Wave -1991* **Pescatun Panama SA** Pescatun SA	**1,040** 312 1,294	Class: (GL)	**1973-11 Campbell Industries — San Diego, Ca** Yd No: 94 Loa 66.45 Br ex 12.20 Dght - Lbp - Br md 12.20 Dpth 5.01 Welded	**(B11B2FV) Fishing Vessel**	**1 oil engine** reduction geared to sc. shaft driving 1 FP propeller Total Power: 2,685kW (3,651hp) 14.0kn EMD (Electro-Motive) 20-645-E7 1 x Vee 2 Stroke 20 Cy. 230 x 254 2685kW (3651bhp) General Motors Detroit DieselAllison Divn-USA AuxGen: 3 x 300kW 220/440V a.c
7383748 *YYP5156* -	**TUNAPUY** - **Flota Industrial Pesca Atunera Caribe CA (FIPACA)** - *Puerto Sucre* *Venezuela* Official number: APNN-6063	*630* 198 900		**1989-09 SIMA Serv. Ind. de la Marina Chimbote (SIMACH) — Chimbote** Yd No: 399 Loa 51.51 Br ex - Dght - Lbp 46.99 Br md 10.67 Dpth 5.66 Welded	**(B11B2FV) Fishing Vessel**	**1 oil engine** geared to sc. shaft driving 1 FP propeller Total Power: 1,405kW (1,910hp) MAN G9V30/45 1 x 4 Stroke 9 Cy. 300 x 450 1405kW (1910bhp) MAN B&W Diesel GmbH-Augsburg
7853339 *YEME* -	**TUNAS** *ex Yoyada -1997 ex Bethany Syukur -1992* *ex Kosei Maru -1990* **PT Pelayaran Berkah Setanggi Timur** - *Jakarta* *Indonesia*	**950** 450 1,047	Class: (KI)	**1976-08 K.K. Yoshida Zosen Kogyo — Arida** Loa 56.51 Br ex - Dght 3.801 Lbp 55.00 Br md 10.41 Dpth 5.69 Welded, 1 dk	**(A31A2GX) General Cargo Ship**	**1 oil engine** driving 1 FP propeller Total Power: 956kW (1,300hp) 11.5kn Makita 1 x 4 Stroke 956kW (1300bhp) Makita Diesel Co Ltd-Japan
8974776 *JM6754* -	**TUNAS** - **Suehiro Kaiun KK** - *Kitakyushu, Fukuoka* *Japan* Official number: 136874	*153* - 270		**2002-03 K.K. Watanabe Zosensho — Nagasaki** Yd No: 095 Loa 19.51 Br ex - Dght 4.320 Lbp 18.00 Br md 12.02 Dpth 6.39 Welded, 1 dk	**(B32B2SP) Pusher Tug**	**1 oil engine** reduction geared to sc. shaft driving 1 Propeller Total Power: 1,618kW (2,200hp) Daihatsu 6DKM-26 1 x 4 Stroke 6 Cy. 260 x 380 1618kW (2200bhp) Daihatsu Diesel Manufacturing Co Lt-Japan
9094810 *PMDC* -	**TUNAS 5** *ex Fajarindo 7 -2010 ex Arung I -2009* *ex Bao Xin Cheng -2008 ex Xu Yun 203 -2001* **PT Pelayaran Satya Arung Samudra** - *Semarang* *Indonesia* MMSI: 525015503	**1,226** 823 2,155	Class: KI	**1991-02 Guangzhou Huangpu Shipyard — Guangzhou GD** Loa 75.31 Br ex - Dght - Lbp - Br md 10.00 Dpth 6.20 Welded, 1 dk	**(A31A2GX) General Cargo Ship**	**1 oil engine** driving 1 Propeller Total Power: 720kW (979hp) Skoda 6L350PN 1 x 4 Stroke 6 Cy. 350 x 500 720kW (979bhp) CKD Praha-Praha
8300872 *YDNJ* -	**TUNAS 6** *ex Fajarindo II -2010 ex Baharindo II -2009* *ex Adhiguna Purnamarga -2008* **PT Pelayaran Fajarindo** - *Jakarta* *Indonesia* MMSI: 525015286 Official number: PST 9475/L	**3,310** 1,660 5,837	Class: KI	**1984-03 Hyundai Mipo Dockyard Co Ltd — Ulsan** Yd No: 8291 Loa 93.00 Br ex 15.52 Dght - Lbp 87.03 Br md 15.51 Dpth 7.32 Welded, 1 dk	**(A31A2GX) General Cargo Ship** Asphalt: 5,253 Compartments: 2 Ho, ER 2 Ha: (17.5 x 10.0) (30.0 x 10.0)ER Derricks: 3x9t; Winches: 3	**2 oil engines** with clutches & sr reverse geared to sc. shafts driving 2 FP propellers Total Power: 2,354kW (3,200hp) 10.8kn Niigata 6MG28BXE 2 x 4 Stroke 6 Cy. 280 x 320 each-1177kW (1600bhp) Niigata Engineering Co Ltd-Japan AuxGen: 3 x 136kW 385V 50Hz a.c
8017877 *YFWQ* -	**TUNAS DUA** *ex Tropicana II -2000 ex Tsukuba -1998* *ex Gyokuzan -1984* **PT Pelayaran Royal Samudera Nasional Line (ROSANAS)** - *Jakarta* *Indonesia* MMSI: 525020882	**2,281** 1,261 3,209	Class: KI (NK)	**1980-11 Namikata Shipbuilding Co Ltd — Imabari EH** Yd No: 102 Loa 80.09 Br ex 13.57 Dght 5.569 Lbp 75.01 Br md 13.50 Dpth 5.67 Welded, 2 dks	**(A31A2GX) General Cargo Ship** Grain: 5,194; Bale: 4,851 2 Ha: (12.5 x 9.5) (23.7 x 9.5)ER Derricks: 1x15t,2x10t	**1 oil engine** driving 1 FP propeller Total Power: 1,692kW (2,300hp) 11.3kn Makita GSLH637 1 x 4 Stroke 6 Cy. 370 x 590 1692kW (2300bhp) Makita Diesel Co Ltd-Japan AuxGen: 2 x 120kW 445V 60Hz a.c Fuel: 52.5 (d.f.) 252.5 (r.f.) 8.5pd
8658750 - -	**TUNAS SATRIA** - **Pelayaran Josh Tirto PT** - *Pontianak* *Indonesia*	**104** 32 -	Class: KI	**2011-05 in Indonesia** Loa - Br ex - Dght - Lbp 19.45 Br md 6.50 Dpth 3.00 Welded, 1 dk	**(B32A2ST) Tug**	**2 oil engines** reduction geared to sc. shafts driving 2 FP propellers

9583811 *YDA4840* -	**TUNAS TERAFULK-I** - **PT Tunas Terafulk Lines** - *Jakarta* *Indonesia* MMSI: 525004094	**179** 54 50	Class: KI	**2011-06 PT Bintang Timur Samudera — Samudera** Loa 30.00 Br ex 7.16 Dght 1.500 Lbp 27.45 Br md 7.00 Dpth 3.20 Welded, 1 dk	**(B21A2OC) Crew/Supply Vessel** Hull Material: Aluminium Alloy	**3 oil engines** reduction geared to sc. shafts driving 3 Propellers Total Power: 1,566kW (2,130hp) 19.5kn Cummins KTA-19-M4 3 x 4 Stroke 6 Cy. 159 x 159 each-522kW (710bhp) Chongqing Cummins Engine Co Ltd-China AuxGen: 2 x 90kW 380V a.c
8607751 *PMKU* -	**TUNAS TIGA** *ex* Da Cheng *-2008* *ex* My Fortune *-2000* *ex* Brother Fortune *-1999* *ex* Radiance *-1995* *ex* Pixy May *-1993* *ex* Pioneer Lapan *-1990* **PT Pelayaran Korindo** - *Jakarta* *Indonesia* MMSI: 525015308	**2,825** 1,784 5,160	Class: KI (CC) (NK)	**1986-02 K.K. Imai Seisakusho — Kamijima** Yd No: 251 Loa 93.60 Br ex - Dght 6.135 Lbp 87.03 Br md 16.01 Dpth 7.62 Welded, 1 dk	**(A31A2GX) General Cargo Ship** Grain: 6,253; Bale: 5,573 Compartments: 2 Ho, ER 2 Ha: (17.4 x 8.5) (31.8 x 8.5)ER Derricks: 1x30t,2x15t	**1 oil engine** driving 1 FP propeller Total Power: 2,059kW (2,799hp) 11.5kn Hanshin 6EL38 1 x 4 Stroke 6 Cy. 380 x 760 2059kW (2799bhp) The Hanshin Diesel Works Ltd-Japan AuxGen: 2 x 160kW a.c
8210015 *YHWD* -	**TUNAS WISESA 03** *ex* Uwajima 2 *-2004* **PT Buana Putera Perkasa** - *Jakarta* *Indonesia*	**3,869** 1,677 1,054	Class: KI	**1983-03 Hayashikane Shipbuilding & Engineering Co Ltd — Nagasaki NS** Yd No: 910 Loa 91.67 (BB) Br ex 15.63 Dght 4.311 Lbp 84.40 Br md 15.61 Dpth 5.80 Welded, 1 dk	**(A36A2PR) Passenger/Ro-Ro Ship (Vehicles)** Passengers: unberthed: 600 Bow door & ramp Stern door/ramp Cars: 22, Trailers: 30	**4 oil engines** with clutches, flexible couplings & sr reverse geared to sc. shafts driving 2 FP propellers Total Power: 5,296kW (7,200hp) 17.8kn Daihatsu 6DSM-32 4 x 4 Stroke 6 Cy. 320 x 380 each-1324kW (1800bhp) Daihatsu Diesel Manufacturing Co Lt-Japan AuxGen: 3 x 320kW 440V 60Hz a.c Thrusters: 1 Thwart. CP thruster (f) Fuel: 29.0 (d.f.) 107.0 (r.f.) 21.0pd
9068433 *YB4311* -	**TUNAS WISESA 05** *ex* Sumber Mas V *-2003* **PT Batam Nusa Kirana** - *Jambi* *Indonesia*	**106** 63 -	Class: KI	**1975-01 Jurong Shipyard Ltd — Singapore** Loa 24.00 Br ex - Dght 1.190 Lbp 22.79 Br md 7.50 Dpth 2.00 Welded, 1 dk	**(A35D2RL) Landing Craft** Bow ramp (centre)	**2 oil engines** geared to sc. shafts driving 2 Propellers Total Power: 298kW (406hp) Deutz F10L413 2 x Vee 4 Stroke 10 Cy. 120 x 125 each-149kW (203bhp) Kloeckner Humboldt Deutz AG-Germany
8999491 - -	**TUNAS WISESA 06** *ex* Express Bahari 13 *-2008* **PT Sakti Inti Makmur** - *Palembang* *Indonesia*	**225** 68 -	Class: KI	**2002-12 PT Marinatama Gemanusa — Batam** Loa 36.00 Br ex - Dght - Lbp 30.00 Br md 6.80 Dpth 3.20 Bonded, 1 dk	**(A37B2PS) Passenger Ship** Hull Material: Reinforced Plastic	**3 oil engines** geared to sc. shafts driving 3 Propellers Total Power: 2,427kW (3,300hp) Caterpillar 3412E 3 x Vee 4 Stroke 12 Cy. 137 x 152 each-809kW (1100bhp) Caterpillar Inc-USA AuxGen: 2 x 88kW 380V a.c
5000201 *TCCN2* -	**TUNC** *ex* Anadolu Kavagi *-1988* **Tunc Denizcilik Tankercilik Donatma Istiraki** - *Istanbul* *Turkey* MMSI: 271002095 Official number: 2040	*693* 445 590	Class: (LR) (TL) ✠ Classed LR until 2/12/83	**1961-08 Fairfield Shipbuilding & Engineering Co Ltd — Glasgow** Yd No: 805 Converted From: Ferry (Passenger only)-1988 Loa 70.41 Br ex - Dght 3.850 Lbp 67.20 Br md 10.90 Dpth 4.50 Riveted\Welded, 1 dk	**(A13B2TU) Tanker (unspecified)** Compartments: 10 Ta, ER	**2 Steam Recips** driving 2 FP propellers Christiansen & Meyer Christiansen & Meyer-West Germany
9398369 *TCB2059* -	**TUNCAY SAGUN 6** *ex* Giritlioglu Suleyman Reis *-2009* - - *Istanbul* *Turkey* MMSI: 271002463 Official number: 9109	**670** 201 -		**2006-04 Basaran Gemi Sanayi — Trabzon** Yd No: 64 Loa 49.30 Br ex - Dght 2.150 Lbp 44.98 Br md 15.00 Dpth 4.00 Welded, 1 dk	**(B11B2FV) Fishing Vessel**	**3 oil engines** reduction geared to sc. shafts driving 3 Propellers Total Power: 2,061kW (2,802hp) Cummins 3 x 4 Stroke each-687kW (934bhp) Cummins Engine Co Inc-USA
8226624 - -	**TUNDA** - **PT Wahana Papua Lines** - *Indonesia*	*152* 69 -		**1956 Singapore Harbour Board — Singapore** Yd No: 1519 Loa 25.91 Br ex 7.78 Dght - Lbp - Br md - Dpth 3.66 Welded, 1 dk	**(B32A2ST) Tug**	**2 oil engines** geared to sc. shafts driving 2 FP propellers Total Power: 718kW (976hp)
7625639 *9MNA* -	**TUNDA SATU** - **Government of Malaysia (Royal Malaysian Navy)** - *Malaysia*	*150* - -		**1978-08 Ironwoods Shipyard Sdn Bhd — Kuching** Yd No: 023 Loa 26.01 Br ex 8.06 Dght - Lbp 24.39 Br md 7.62 Dpth 3.84 Welded, 1 dk	**(B32A2ST) Tug**	**2 oil engines** driving 2 FP propellers Total Power: 456kW (620hp) Cummins VTA-1710-M2 2 x Vee 4 Stroke 12 Cy. 140 x 152 each-228kW (310bhp) Cummins Engine Co Inc-USA
9415208 *5BVN2* -	**TUNDRA** - **Prehniet Beheer BV** Navarone SA *Limassol* *Cyprus* MMSI: 209015000 Official number: 9415208	**19,814** 10,208 30,892	Class: GL	**2009-12 Shandong Weihai Shipyard — Weihai SD** Yd No: SN317 Loa 185.01 (BB) Br ex - Dght 10.416 Lbp 178.00 Br md 23.70 Dpth 14.60 Welded, 1 dk	**(A21A2BC) Bulk Carrier** Grain: 38,635; Bale: 37,476 Compartments: 6 Ho, ER 6 Ha: (16.0 x 17.4)3 (19.2 x 17.4) (13.6 x 17.4)ER (10.4 x 13.2) Cranes: 3x30t Ice Capable	**1 oil engine** driving 1 FP propeller Total Power: 7,200kW (9,789hp) 13.5kn MAN-B&W 6S46MC-C 1 x 2 Stroke 6 Cy. 460 x 1932 7200kW (9789bhp) STX Engine Co Ltd-South Korea AuxGen: 3 x 680kW 450/230V 60Hz a.c Thrusters: 1 Tunnel thruster (f) Fuel: 350.0 (d.f.) 1300.0 (r.f.)
8505410 *JWWM* N-26-V	**TUNFISK** *ex* Myrebas *-2005* *ex* Brennboen *-1995* *ex* Bovaering *-1988* **Magne Sjo AS** - *Bergen* *Norway* MMSI: 257580500	**226** 99 -		**1985-12 Aas Skipsbyggeri AS — Vestnes** Yd No: 125 Loa - Br ex - Dght - Lbp 22.86 Br md - Dpth - Welded, 1 dk	**(B11B2FV) Fishing Vessel**	**1 oil engine** geared to sc. shaft driving 1 FP propeller Total Power: 382kW (519hp) 9.0kn Caterpillar 3412T 1 x Vee 4 Stroke 12 Cy. 137 x 152 382kW (519bhp) Caterpillar Tractor Co-USA Thrusters: 1 Thwart. FP thruster (f)
5153230 *BNGF* -	**TUNG CHIN** *ex* Hokushin Maru No. 3 *-1970* **Tung Long Transportation Co Ltd** - *Keelung* *Chinese Taipei*	*490* 271 702	Class: (CR)	**1961 Takehara Zosen — Takehara** Yd No: 162 Loa 52.51 Br ex 7.83 Dght 3.506 Lbp 47.02 Br md 7.78 Dpth 4.02 Welded, 1 dk	**(A31A2GX) General Cargo Ship** Compartments: 1 Ho, ER 1 Ha: (21.7 x 4.8)ER	**1 oil engine** driving 1 FP propeller Total Power: 441kW (600hp) 11.0kn Kinoshita 1 x 4 Stroke 6 Cy. 300 x 420 441kW (600bhp) Kinoshita Tekkosho-Japan AuxGen: 1 x 5kW 115V d.c
8656790 *BI2589* -	**TUNG CHOU NO. 6** - **Tung Ghuo Oceanic International Co Ltd** - *Kaohsiung* *Chinese Taipei* Official number: 014431	**630** 313 -		**2004-12 Jong Shyn Shipbuilding Co., Ltd. — Kaohsiung** Loa 59.20 Br ex 9.00 Dght - Lbp - Br md - Dpth 3.75 Welded, 1 dk	**(B11B2FV) Fishing Vessel**	**1 oil engine** driving 1 FP propeller Hanshin The Hanshin Diesel Works Ltd-Japan
7041766 - -	**TUNG CHOU No. 7** - **Tung Chou Fishing Co Ltd** - *Kaohsiung* *Chinese Taipei*	*151* 94 -		**1970 Sen Koh Shipbuilding Corp — Kaohsiung** Loa 30.10 Br ex - Dght - Lbp 26.01 Br md 6.00 Dpth 2.60 Welded, 1 dk	**(B11A2FT) Trawler**	**1 oil engine** driving 1 FP propeller Total Power: 257kW (349hp) Sumiyoshi 1 x 4 Stroke 5 Cy. 240 x 400 257kW (349bhp) Sumiyoshi Marine Diesel Co Ltd-Japan
9024542 - -	**TUNG DUONG 02** - **Hoang Tung Co Ltd** - *Haiphong* *Vietnam* Official number: VN-1594-VT	**432** 290 771	Class: VR	**2002-12 Haiphong Mechanical & Trading Co. — Haiphong** Loa 52.95 Br ex - Dght 2.700 Lbp 49.50 Br md 8.70 Dpth 3.35 Welded, 1 dk	**(A31A2GX) General Cargo Ship**	**2 oil engines** geared to sc. shafts driving 2 Propellers Total Power: 424kW (576hp) 9.0kn Chinese Std. Type 6160A 2 x 4 Stroke 6 Cy. 160 x 225 each-212kW (288bhp) Weifang Diesel Engine Factory-China
9561772 - -	**TUNG DUONG 55** - **Tung Duong Shipping Co** - *Vietnam*	**1,599** - 2,500	Class: (VR)	**2009-07 Thanh Long Shipbuilding Industry Co Ltd — Haiphong** Yd No: DKTB-09 Loa 84.68 Br ex - Dght 7.200 Lbp - Br md 12.60 Dpth - Welded, 1 dk	**(A31A2GX) General Cargo Ship**	**1 oil engine** driving 1 FP propeller
9561784 - -	**TUNG DUONG 56** - **Tung Duong Shipping Co** - *Vietnam*	**2,120** - 2,500	Class: (VR)	**2009-12 Thanh Long Shipbuilding Industry Co Ltd — Haiphong** Yd No: S35-02 Loa 81.42 Br ex - Dght 6.800 Lbp - Br md 13.60 Dpth - Welded, 1 dk	**(A31A2GX) General Cargo Ship**	**1 oil engine** driving 1 FP propeller

9072381 - -	**TUNG HSIN** **Tung Hsin Steamship Co Ltd** - *Kaohsiung* *Chinese Taipei* Official number: 12562	*117* Class: (CR) 35 24	**1993 SBF Shipbuilders (1977) Pty Ltd — Fremantle WA** Yd No: TW27 Loa 26.55 Br ex 6.40 Dght 0.900 Lbp - Br md - Dpth - Welded, 2 dks	**(A37B2PS) Passenger Ship** Hull Material: Aluminium Alloy Passengers: unberthed: 185	**3 oil engines** geared to sc. shafts driving 3 FP propellers Total Power: 1,830kW (2,487hp) M.T.U. 12V183TE72 3 x Vee 4 Stroke 12 Cy. 128 x 142 each-610kW (829bhp) MTU Friedrichshafen GmbH-Friedrichshafen
8431097 - -	**TUNG I No. 801** - - -	*711* 272 -	**1990 Sen Koh Shipbuilding Corp — Kaohsiung** L reg 48.90 Br ex - Dght 3.500 Lbp - Br md 8.90 Dpth 3.85 Welded, 1 dk	**(B11B2FV) Fishing Vessel**	**1 oil engine** driving 1 FP propeller Total Power: 1,030kW (1,400hp) 13.0kn
8430603 *HQGQ3* -	**TUNG LUNG No. 6** **Lu Fa Fishery Co Ltd** - *San Lorenzo* *Honduras* Official number: L-1923338	*362* 164 -	**1978 San Yang Shipbuilding Co., Ltd. — Kaohsiung** L reg 42.76 Br ex - Dght 3.060 Lbp - Br md 7.50 Dpth 3.55 Welded	**(B11B2FV) Fishing Vessel**	**1 oil engine** driving 1 FP propeller Total Power: 809kW (1,100hp) 11.0kn
8430598 - -	**TUNG LUNG No. 7** - -	*362* 164 -	**1973 San Yang Shipbuilding Co., Ltd. — Kaohsiung** L reg 42.76 Br ex - Dght - Lbp - Br md 7.50 Dpth 3.55 Welded, 1 dk	**(B11B2FV) Fishing Vessel**	**1 oil engine** driving 1 FP propeller Total Power: 809kW (1,100hp) 11.0kn
8026957 *BYVW* -	**TUNG MAU No. 2** **Tung Mau Ocean Fishery Co Ltd** - *Kaohsiung* *Chinese Taipei*	*491* Class: (CR) 358 -	**1980-07 Shin Tien Erh Shipbuilding Co, Ltd — Kaohsiung** Loa 50.96 Br ex 8.46 Dght 3.250 Lbp 44.96 Br md 8.31 Dpth 3.66 Welded, 1 dk	**(B11B2FV) Fishing Vessel** Ins: 732 Compartments: 3 Ho, ER 3 Ha: (1.9 x 1.3) (1.5 x 1.5) (1.3 x 1.1)ER	**1 oil engine** driving 1 FP propeller Total Power: 736kW (1,001hp) 12.0kn Akasaka DM28AR 1 x 4 Stroke 6 Cy. 280 x 460 736kW (1001bhp) Akasaka Tekkosho KK (Akasaka DieselLtd)-Japan AuxGen: 2 x 200kW 220V a.c
7738072 *BYQE* -	**TUNG MING No. 1** **Tung Ming Ocean Enterprise Co Ltd** - *Kaohsiung* *Chinese Taipei*	*387* Class: (CR) 251 -	**1977 San Yang Shipbuilding Co., Ltd. — Kaohsiung** Loa 45.12 Br ex 7.55 Dght 2.961 Lbp 38.59 Br md 7.50 Dpth 3.41 Welded, 1 dk	**(B11B2FV) Fishing Vessel** Ins: 369 Compartments: 4 Ho, ER 4 Ha: 4 (1.5 x 1.5)ER	**1 oil engine** driving 1 FP propeller Total Power: 809kW (1,100hp) 10.0kn Otsuka SOD6-29C 1 x 4 Stroke 6 Cy. 290 x 420 809kW (1100bhp) KK Otsuka Diesel-Japan AuxGen: 1 x 100kW 230/225V a.c, 1 x 80kW 230/225V a.c
7738084 *BYQF* -	**TUNG MING No. 2** **Tung Ming Ocean Enterprise Co Ltd** - *Kaohsiung* *Chinese Taipei*	*387* Class: (CR) 251 -	**1978 San Yang Shipbuilding Co., Ltd. — Kaohsiung** Loa 45.12 Br ex 7.52 Dght 2.961 Lbp 38.59 Br md 7.50 Dpth 3.41 Welded, 1 dk	**(B11B2FV) Fishing Vessel** Ins: 369 Compartments: 4 Ho, ER 4 Ha: 4 (1.5 x 1.5)ER	**1 oil engine** driving 1 FP propeller Total Power: 809kW (1,100hp) 10.0kn Niigata 6L28X 1 x 4 Stroke 6 Cy. 280 x 440 809kW (1100bhp) Niigata Engineering Co Ltd-Japan AuxGen: 1 x 100kW 230/225V a.c, 1 x 80kW 230/225V a.c
8823745 *H02767*	**TUNG SHUEN** *ex* Ocean Star 1 *-2002* *ex* Keisho Maru *-2000* **Hai Yang Shipping S de RL** - *Panama* *Panama* MMSI: 352741000 Official number: 30278TT	**860** 258 1,052	**1988-10 K.K. Kamishima Zosensho — Osakikamijima** Loa 56.00 Br ex - Dght 4.020 Lbp 49.00 Br md 11.00 Dpth 5.80 Welded, 1 dk	**(B33A2DG) Grab Dredger** Bale: 796 Compartments: 1 Ho, ER 1 Ha: (17.6 x 8.6)ER Cranes: 1	**1 oil engine** driving 1 FP propeller Total Power: 736kW (1,001hp) 11.0kn Hanshin LH28G 1 x 4 Stroke 6 Cy. 280 x 460 736kW (1001bhp) The Hanshin Diesel Works Ltd-Japan
8951877 - -	**TUNG YANG NO. 88** *ex* Jih Sheng No. 101 *-2003* **Tung Yang Fishery Co Ltd** -	**608** 291	**1989 San Yang Shipbuilding Co., Ltd. — Kaohsiung** Loa 56.53 Br ex - Dght 3.700 Lbp 49.20 Br md 8.80 Dpth 4.16 Welded, 1 dk	**(B11B2FV) Fishing Vessel**	**1 oil engine** driving 1 FP propeller Hanshin 1 x 4 Stroke The Hanshin Diesel Works Ltd-Japan
8663107 - -	**TUNG YUEN NO. 3** *ex* Ta Kang No. 7 *-2007* **Eastern Link Petroleum & Shipping Ltd** Bravo Marine Ltd *Hong Kong* *Hong Kong*	**415** 188 598	**1999-12 Zhuhai Xiangzhou Shipyard — Zhuhai GD** Yd No: SD/L7834 Loa 43.50 Br ex - Dght - Lbp 39.96 Br md 9.50 Dpth 3.60 Welded, 1 dk	**(A13B2TP) Products Tanker** Double Hull (13F)	**2 oil engines** reduction geared to sc. shafts driving 2 Propellers Total Power: 746kW (1,014hp) Cummins KTA-19-M500 2 x 4 Stroke 6 Cy. 159 x 159 each-373kW (507bhp) Cummins Engine Co Inc-USA
9233105 - -	**TUNGA** *ex* Nuevo Martorres *-2009* **Tunacor Fisheries Ltd** - *Walvis Bay* *Namibia*	**504** Class: BV 151 -	**2000-12 Factoria Naval de Marin S.A. — Marin** Yd No: 140 Loa 34.00 Br ex - Dght 3.500 Lbp 32.05 Br md 9.00 Dpth 4.05 Welded, 1 dk	**(B11A2FS) Stern Trawler**	**1 oil engine** reduction geared to sc. shaft driving 1 FP propeller Total Power: 1,103kW (1,500hp) 10.0kn A.B.C. 6DZC 1 x 4 Stroke 6 Cy. 256 x 310 1103kW (1500bhp) Anglo Belgian Corp NV (ABC)-Belgium AuxGen: 1 x 240kW 380/220V a.c, 1 x 240kW 380/220V a.c
7321831 - -	**TUNGASUCA** *ex* Jan Maria *-1987* **Grupo de Negocios SA** - *Callao* *Peru* Official number: CO-010650-PM	*555* 265 -	**1973 T. van Duijvendijk's Scheepswerf N.V. — Lekkerkerk** Yd No: Z98 Lengthened-1980 Loa 61.96 Br ex 10.29 Dght 4.458 Lbp - Br md 9.99 Dpth 6.76 Welded, 2 dks	**(B11A2FS) Stern Trawler**	**1 oil engine** driving 1 CP propeller Total Power: 1,692kW (2,300hp) 15.0kn De Industrie 8D8HD 1 x 4 Stroke 8 Cy. 400 x 600 1692kW (2300bhp) B.V. Motorenfabriek "De Industrie"-Alphen a/d Rijn
9027659 - -	**TUNGGAL JAYA 5** *ex* Supphermnavee 1 *-1996* **PT Tunggal Jaya Abadi** - *Jakarta* *Indonesia*	**673** Class: (KI) 202 -	**1992-07 Mits Decisions Co., Ltd. — Samut Sakhon** Loa 50.10 Br ex - Dght 3.000 Lbp 43.60 Br md 10.00 Dpth 6.00 Welded, 1 dk	**(B11B2FV) Fishing Vessel**	**1 oil engine** geared to sc. shaft driving 1 Propeller Total Power: 1,331kW (1,810hp) 10.0kn Caterpillar 3516TA 1 x Vee 4 Stroke 16 Cy. 170 x 190 1331kW (1810bhp) Caterpillar Inc-USA
9049712 *YHJN* -	**TUNGKAL SAMUDRA 01** *ex* Marina Express 5 *-2002* **Government of The Republic of Indonesia (Pemerintah Kabupaten Tanjung Barat Propinsi Jambi - Jambi Provincial Govt, Tanjung Barat)** PT Marinatama Gemanusa *Batam* *Indonesia*	**494** Class: (KI) 149 -	**2002-03 PT Marinatama Gemanusa — Batam** L reg 45.00 Br ex - Dght - Lbp 43.25 Br md 8.40 Dpth 3.75 Bonded, 1 dk	**(A37B2PS) Passenger Ship** Hull Material: Reinforced Plastic	**4 oil engines** geared to sc. shafts driving 4 Propellers Total Power: 3,236kW (4,400hp) MAN D2842LE 4 x Vee 4 Stroke 12 Cy. 128 x 142 each-809kW (1100bhp) (, fitted 2002) MAN Nutzfahrzeuge AG-Nuernberg
8862052 - -	**TUNGSTEN** *ex* Birobedjan *-1998* *ex* PTR-0094 *-1997* *ex* 94 *-1997* - -	**190** Class: (RS) 57 70	**1991-12 Astrakhanskaya Sudoverf im. "Kirova" — Astrakhan** Yd No: 94 Loa 31.85 Br ex 7.08 Dght 2.100 Lbp 27.80 Br md - Dpth 3.15 Welded	**(B12B2FC) Fish Carrier** Ins: 100	**1 oil engine** geared to sc. shaft driving 1 FP propeller Total Power: 232kW (315hp) 10.2kn Daldizel 6CHSPN2A18-315 1 x 4 Stroke 6 Cy. 180 x 220 232kW (315bhp) Daldizel-Khabarovsk AuxGen: 2 x 25kW a.c Fuel: 14.0 (d.f.)
9631735 *C6ZF4* -	**TUNGSTEN EXPLORER** **Vantage Driller VI Co** - *Nassau* *Bahamas* MMSI: 311069300 Official number: 8001930	**68,486** Class: AB 20,546 64,969	**2013-07 Daewoo Shipbuilding & Marine Engineering Co Ltd — Geoje** Yd No: 3615 Loa 238.00 Br ex - Dght 12.000 Lbp 230.00 Br md 42.00 Dpth 19.00 Welded, 1 dk	**(B22B20D) Drilling Ship** Cranes: 3x85t	**6 diesel electric oil engines** driving 6 gen. each 6500kW Connecting to 2 elec. motors each (5500kW) driving 2 Azimuth electric drive units Total Power: 42,000kW (57,102hp) 13.5kn MAN-B&W 14V32/40 6 x Vee 4 Stroke 14 Cy. 320 x 400 each-7000kW (9517bhp) STX Engine Co Ltd-South Korea Thrusters: 4 Directional thruster (wing)
8962230 *TFIL* GK 150	**TUNGUFELL** *ex* Hans Jakob *-2012* *ex* Dalarost *-2009* *ex* Jon E. Bjarnason *-1984* *ex* Rolant II *-1983* **Saerost Ehf** - *Talknafjordur* *Iceland* MMSI: 251130110 Official number: 1639	*154* Class: (NV) 56 -	**1978 Tronderverftet AS — Hommelvik** Yd No: 39 Lengthened-1982 Loa 25.98 Br ex - Dght - Lbp - Br md 6.00 Dpth 5.20 Welded, 1 dk	**(B11B2FV) Fishing Vessel**	**1 oil engine** driving 1 FP propeller Total Power: 515kW (700hp) Mitsubishi 1 x 515kW (700bhp) (new engine 1985) Mitsubishi Heavy Industries Ltd-Japan

7045047 - -	**TUNGUS** - -	**632** Class: (RS) 200 323	**1969**-07 **Khabarovskiy Sudostroitelnyy Zavod im Kirova — Khabarovsk** Yd No: 175 Loa 54.23 Br ex 9.38 Dght 3.810 Lbp 49.99 Br md 9.30 Dpth 4.73 Welded, 1 dk	**(B11A2FT) Trawler** Ins: 284 Compartments: 2 Ho, ER 2 Ha: 2 (1.5 x 1.6) Derricks: 1x2t; Winches: 1 Ice Capable	**1 oil engine** driving 1 FP propeller Total Power: 588kW (799hp) 11.8kn S.K.L. 8NVD48AU 1 x 4 Stroke 8 Cy. 320 x 480 588kW (799bhp) VEB Schwermaschinenbau "KarlLiebknecht" (SKL)-Magdeburg AuxGen: 3 x 100kW Fuel: 167.0 (d.f.)
9044786 *PGBK* UK 224	**TUNIS VAN LUUT** **Zeevisserijbedrijf T de Boer en Zn BV** - SatCom: Inmarsat C 424601510 *Urk* *Netherlands* MMSI: 246015000 Official number: 35071	**331** 99 -	**1998**-07 **Porta Odra Sp z oo — Szczecin** (Hull) Yd No: TB665/02 **1998**-07 **B.V. Scheepswerf Maaskant — Stellendam** Yd No: 521 Loa 33.55 (BB) Br ex - Dght 2.930 Lbp 28.88 Br md 7.50 Dpth 3.90 Welded, 1 dk	**(B11A2FT) Trawler**	**1 oil engine** sr geared to sc. shaft driving 1 CP propeller Total Power: 759kW (1,032hp) 12.0kn Cummins Wartsila 8L170 1 x 4 Stroke 8 Cy. 170 x 200 759kW (1032bhp) Cummins Engine Co Ltd-United Kingdom Thrusters: 1 Thwart. FP thruster (f) Fuel: 41.0 (d.f.)
7944786 *9WDO* -	**TUNKU LAUT** **ORIX Leasing Malaysia Bhd** *Labuan* *Malaysia* Official number: 324875	*146* 90 -	**1979 Sersia Shipbuilding Factory — Singapore** Loa - Br ex 6.61 Dght - Lbp 27.61 Br md 2.99 Dpth - Welded, 2 dks	**(B11B2FV) Fishing Vessel**	**1 oil engine** driving 1 FP propeller Total Power: 421kW (572hp) 10.0kn Baudouin 1 x Vee 4 Stroke 8 Cy. 150 x 150 421kW (572bhp) Societe des Moteurs Baudouin SA-France
8907838 *HP5512* -	**TUNO** *launched as* Beatrice *-1990* **High Fortune Development Ltd** *Panama* *Panama* Official number: 1888690A	**274** Class: (LR) 118 ✠ Classed LR until 21/2/96 381	**1989**-12 **Mawei Shipyard — Fuzhou FJ** Yd No: 806A-2 Loa 38.50 Br ex - Dght 3.600 Lbp 34.00 Br md 8.20 Dpth 4.20 Welded, 1 dk	**(B11B2FV) Fishing Vessel**	**1 oil engine** reverse reduction geared to sc. shaft driving 1 FP propeller Total Power: 1,118kW (1,520hp) Caterpillar 3512TA 1 x Vee 4 Stroke 12 Cy. 170 x 190 1118kW (1520bhp) Caterpillar Inc-USA AuxGen: 2 x 40kW 400V 50Hz a.c
9107875 *OWUS* -	**TUNOFAERGEN** **Odder Kommune** *Hov* *Denmark* MMSI: 219000762 Official number: B304	**441** 135 60	**1993**-08 **Johs Kristensen Skibsbyggeri A/S — Hvide Sande** Yd No: 203 Loa 30.50 Br ex - Dght - Lbp - Br md 9.00 Dpth 5.70 Welded, 1 dk	**(A37B2PS) Passenger Ship** Passengers: unberthed: 200	**2 oil engines** driving 2 FP propellers Total Power: 442kW (600hp) 9.5kn Scania DSI11 2 x 4 Stroke 6 Cy. 127 x 145 each-221kW (300bhp) Saab Scania AB-Sweden
9570163 *CA2993* -	**TUNQUEN** **CPT Empresas Maritimas SA** - SatCom: Inmarsat C 472500222 *Valparaiso* *Chile* MMSI: 725000736 Official number: 3250	**463** Class: AB 139 208	**2009**-10 **Guangzhou Panyu Lingnan Shipbuilding Co Ltd — Guangzhou GD** (Hull) **2009**-10 **Bonny Fair Development Ltd — Hong Kong** Yd No: HY2155 Loa 31.00 Br ex - Dght 4.600 Lbp 27.70 Br md 11.00 Dpth 5.60 Welded, 1 dk	**(B32A2ST) Tug**	**2 oil engines** reduction geared to sc. shafts driving 2 Propellers Total Power: 3,650kW (4,962hp) Caterpillar 3516B-HD 2 x Vee 4 Stroke 16 Cy. 170 x 215 each-1825kW (2481bhp) Caterpillar Inc-USA AuxGen: 2 x 85kW a.c Fuel: 175.0 (d.f.)
8892552 - -	**TUNU PRATAMA** **PT Tunu Primatama** *Balikpapan* *Indonesia*	*290* Class: KI 88 -	**1994**-01 **P.T. Galangan Kapal Mahakam Permai Bakungan — Tenggarong** Loa 44.00 Br ex - Dght 2.180 Lbp 41.54 Br md 10.39 Dpth 2.76 Welded, 1 dk	**(A35D2RL) Landing Craft** Bow ramp (centre)	**2 oil engines** geared to sc. shafts driving 2 FP propellers Total Power: 588kW (800hp) 8.0kn Cummins NTA-855-M 2 x 4 Stroke 6 Cy. 140 x 152 each-294kW (400bhp) Cummins Engine Co Inc-USA
8749432 *YCSR* -	**TUNU PRATAMA JAYA** **PT Raputra Jaya** - *Balikpapan* *Indonesia*	**734** Class: KI 221 955	**2010**-11 **PT Galangan Kalimas — Balikpapan** Yd No: 0198 Loa 60.00 Br ex - Dght - Lbp 56.52 Br md - Dpth 3.60 Welded, 1 dk	**(A31A2GX) General Cargo Ship**	**1 oil engine** reduction geared to sc. shaft driving 1 Propeller Total Power: 353kW (480hp) Mitsubishi S6N-MTK 1 x 4 Stroke 6 Cy. 160 x 180 353kW (480bhp) (made 2000, fitted 2010) Mitsubishi Heavy Industries Ltd-Japan
8029014 - -	**TUNUPA** *ex* Sea Quest *-2011* *ex* Viking No. 1 *-2007* *ex* Sunny No. 1 *-2007* *ex* Sunny *-2007* *ex* Otomi Maru *-2007* *ex* Jyutoku Maru No. 21 *-1996* *ex* Kokei Maru No. 18 *-1994* - - *Callao* *Peru* Official number: CO-29771-PM	**614** 249 423	**1981**-06 **Miho Zosensho K.K. — Shimizu** Yd No: 1194 Loa 52.41 Br ex 8.82 Dght 3.410 Lbp 46.00 Br md 8.81 Dpth 3.76 Welded, 1 dk	**(B11B2FV) Fishing Vessel**	**1 oil engine** driving 1 FP propeller Total Power: 1,177kW (1,600hp) Akasaka A31 1 x 4 Stroke 6 Cy. 310 x 600 1177kW (1600bhp) Akasaka Tekkosho KK (Akasaka DieselLtd)-Japan
9044451 *3FEA3* -	**TUO FU 1** *ex* Hong Yuan 1 *-2010* *ex* Frontier Express *-2009* **Tuofu Ocean Shipping Ltd** Tuofu Shipping Management Ltd SatCom: Inmarsat C 435222010 *Panama* *Panama* MMSI: 352220000 Official number: 2076593D	**41,889** Class: RI (NK) 18,056 66,504 T/cm 66.1	**1993**-03 **Namura Shipbuilding Co Ltd — Imari SG** Yd No: 920 Converted From: Products Tanker-2010 Loa 229.06 (BB) Br ex - Dght 13.300 Lbp 219.60 Br md 32.20 Dpth 20.20 Welded, 1 dk	**(A21A2BC) Bulk Carrier** Grain: 77,640 Compartments: 8 Ho, ER 8 Ha: (17.6 x 14.6) (7.0 x 14.6)ER 6 (13.2 x 14.6)	**1 oil engine** driving 1 FP propeller Total Power: 8,312kW (11,301hp) 13.0kn Mitsubishi 6UEC60LS 1 x 2 Stroke 6 Cy. 600 x 2200 8312kW (11301bhp) Mitsubishi Heavy Industries Ltd-Japan AuxGen: 4 x 427kW a.c Fuel: 2400.0 (r.f.) 29.0pd
9013414 *3FKW3* -	**TUO FU 3** *ex* Sun River *-2010* *ex* Yang He *-1996* **Most Luck (China) Ltd** Tuofu Shipping Management Ltd SatCom: Inmarsat C 435401312 *Panama* *Panama* MMSI: 354013000 Official number: 4221111	**39,666** Class: RI (BV) (CC) 20,042 63,920 T/cm 64.9	**1993**-01 **Dalian New Shipbuilding Heavy Industries Co Ltd — Dalian LN** Yd No: T600/4 Converted From: Crude Oil Tanker-2010 Loa 228.50 (BB) Br ex - Dght 13.290 Lbp 219.76 Br md 32.20 Dpth 19.00 Welded, 1 dk	**(A21A2BC) Bulk Carrier** Double Hull Grain: 73,093 Compartments: 7 Ho, ER 7 Ha: 5 (13.0 x 15.6) (15.6 x 10.9)ER (13.0 x 10.9) Ice Capable	**1 oil engine** driving 1 FP propeller Total Power: 8,826kW (12,000hp) 14.3kn B&W 6L60MC 1 x 2 Stroke 6 Cy. 600 x 1944 8826kW (12000bhp) Dalian Marine Diesel Works-China AuxGen: 3 x 560kW 400V a.c
9640671 *VRLB8* -	**TUO FU 6** **Hongfu Shipping Ltd** Tuofu Shipping Management Ltd *Hong Kong* *Hong Kong* MMSI: 477464200 Official number: HK-3622	**44,315** Class: RI 27,890 81,588	**2013**-05 **Taizhou CATIC Shipbuilding Heavy Industry Ltd — Taizhou JS** Yd No: TC0103 Loa 229.00 (BB) Br ex 32.59 Dght 14.450 Lbp 225.50 Br md 32.26 Dpth 20.05 Welded, 1 dk	**(A21A2BC) Bulk Carrier** Grain: 97,000 Compartments: 7 Ho, ER 7 Ha: ER	**1 oil engine** driving 1 FP propeller Total Power: 10,900kW (14,820hp) 14.1kn Wartsila 5RT-flex58T 1 x 2 Stroke 5 Cy. 580 x 2416 10900kW (14820bhp)
9649249 *VRLP9* -	**TUO FU 8** **Yifu Shipping Ltd** Tuofu Shipping Management Ltd *Hong Kong* *Hong Kong* MMSI: 477319700 Official number: HK-3735	**44,315** Class: RI 27,000 81,721	**2013**-09 **Taizhou CATIC Shipbuilding Heavy Industry Ltd — Taizhou JS** Yd No: TC0104 Loa 229.00 (BB) Br ex 32.59 Dght 14.450 Lbp 225.50 Br md 32.26 Dpth 20.05 Welded, 1 dk	**(A21A2BC) Bulk Carrier** Grain: 97,000 Compartments: 7 Ho, ER 7 Ha: ER	**1 oil engine** driving 1 FP propeller Total Power: 9,800kW (13,324hp) 14.1kn Wartsila 5RT-flex58T 1 x 2 Stroke 5 Cy. 580 x 2416 9800kW (13324bhp) Qingdao Qiyao Wartsila MHI LinshanMarine Diesel Co Ltd (QMD)-China AuxGen: 3 x 600kW a.c
8220216 *BOHF* -	**TUO HAI** **COSCO Bulk Carrier Co Ltd (COSCO BULK)** - SatCom: Inmarsat C 441209910 *Tianjin* *China* MMSI: 412222000	**26,959** Class: CC 15,092 46,455	**1984**-01 **Osaka Shipbuilding Co Ltd — Osaka OS** Yd No: 416 Loa 189.68 (BB) Br ex - Dght 11.440 Lbp 180.00 Br md 32.20 Dpth 16.25 Welded, 1 dk	**(A21A2BC) Bulk Carrier** Grain: 55,934; Bale: 55,282 Compartments: 5 Ho, ER 5 Ha: (16.0 x 15.0)4 (17.6 x 15.0)ER Cranes: 5x16t Ice Capable	**1 oil engine** driving 1 FP propeller Total Power: 7,561kW (10,280hp) 14.5kn B&W 6L67GBE 1 x 2 Stroke 6 Cy. 670 x 1700 7561kW (10280bhp) Hitachi Zosen Corp-Japan AuxGen: 3 x 560kW 450V 60Hz a.c
8517360 *BLDK* -	**TUO ZHAN 1** *ex* Oceanic Confidence *-2011* *ex* Celia Dan *-1993* *ex* Camara *-1991* **Ningbo Pacific Shipping Co Ltd** - *Ningbo, Zhejiang* *China* MMSI: 412419520	**11,031** Class: ZC (BV) (NK) 6,176 17,832	**1986**-07 **Osaka Shipbuilding Co Ltd — Osaka OS** Yd No: 437 Loa 144.25 (BB) Br ex - Dght 9.059 Lbp 136.02 Br md 23.00 Dpth 12.22 Welded, 1 dk	**(A21A2BC) Bulk Carrier** Grain: 21,630; Bale: 21,344 Compartments: 4 Ho, ER 4 Ha: (15.2 x 10.0)3 (19.2 x 12.5)ER Cranes: 4x25t	**1 oil engine** driving 1 FP propeller Total Power: 4,509kW (6,130hp) 14.0kn B&W 5L50MC 1 x 2 Stroke 5 Cy. 500 x 1620 4509kW (6130bhp) Hitachi Zosen Corp-Japan

8901822 *BKAC5* -	**TUO ZHAN 5** *ex* Tate J *-2007* *ex* Lucky Wealth *-2001* *ex* Libre *-1996* *ex* Casuarina *-1990* **Ningbo Pacific Shipping Co Ltd** - *Ningbo, Zhejiang* *China* MMSI: 413411710	**25,891** 13,673 43,685 T/cm 49.0	Class: (AB) (NK)	**1989-11 Tsuneishi Shipbuilding Co Ltd — Fukuyama HS** Yd No: 625 Loa 185.84 (BB) Br ex - Dght 11.319 Lbp 177.00 Br md 30.40 Dpth 16.20 Welded, 1 dk	**(A21A2BC) Bulk Carrier** Grain: 53,594; Bale: 52,280 TEU 1082 C Ho 516 TEU C Dk 566 TEU Compartments: 5 Ho, ER 5 Ha: (19.2 x 15.3)4 (20.8 x 15.3)ER Cranes: 4x30t	**1 oil engine** driving 1 FP propeller Total Power: 7,120kW (9,680hp) 14.0kn B&W 6L60MCE 1 x 2 Stroke 6 Cy. 600 x 1944 7120kW (9680bhp) Mitsui Engineering & Shipbuilding CLtd-Japan AuxGen: 3 x 330kW 440V 60Hz a.c Fuel: 276.0 (d.f.) 1574.0 (r.f.) 27.0pd
8912314 *BKAC6* -	**TUO ZHAN 6** *ex* Steven C *-2007* *ex* Lucky Fortune *-2000* *ex* Universal River *-1993* **Ningbo Pacific Shipping Co Ltd** - *Ningbo, Zhejiang* *China* MMSI: 413411690	**25,891** 13,673 43,665 T/cm 49.0	Class: (AB) (NK)	**1990-01 Tsuneishi Shipbuilding Co Ltd — Fukuyama HS** Yd No: 641 Loa 185.84 (BB) Br ex 30.44 Dght 11.319 Lbp 177.00 Br md 30.40 Dpth 16.20 Welded, 1 dk	**(A21A2BC) Bulk Carrier** Grain: 53,594; Bale: 52,280 TEU 1082 C Ho 516 TEU C Dk 566 TEU Compartments: 5 Ho, ER 5 Ha: (19.2 x 15.3)4 (20.8 x 15.3)ER Cranes: 4x30t	**1 oil engine** driving 1 FP propeller Total Power: 7,120kW (9,680hp) 14.0kn B&W 6L60MCE 1 x 2 Stroke 6 Cy. 600 x 1944 7120kW (9680bhp) Mitsui Engineering & Shipbuilding CLtd-Japan AuxGen: 3 x 330kW 440V 60Hz a.c Fuel: 276.0 (d.f.) 1574.0 (r.f.) 27.0pd
9000857 *BLAE2* -	**TUO ZHAN 7** *ex* Angele N *-2008* *ex* Sea Clipper *-2000* **Ningbo Pacific Shipping Co Ltd** - SatCom: Inmarsat C 441200837 *Ningbo, Zhejiang* *China* MMSI: 412750730	**35,890** 23,407 69,315 T/cm 64.4	Class: (CC) (NK)	**1990-05 Imabari Shipbuilding Co Ltd — Marugame KG (Marugame Shipyard)** Yd No: 1179 Loa 224.98 (BB) Br ex - Dght 13.295 Lbp 215.02 Br md 32.21 Dpth 18.32 Welded, 1 dk	**(A21A2BC) Bulk Carrier** Grain: 81,215 Compartments: 7 Ho, ER 7 Ha: (12.8 x 12.8)6 (17.6 x 14.4)ER	**1 oil engine** driving 1 FP propeller Total Power: 8,091kW (11,001hp) 13.5kn Sulzer 6RTA62 1 x 2 Stroke 6 Cy. 620 x 2150 8091kW (11001bhp) Mitsubishi Heavy Industries Ltd-Japan AuxGen: 2 x 480kW 440V 60Hz a.c, 1 x 400kW 440V 60Hz a.c Fuel: 250.1 (d.f.) 2556.7 (r.f.) 28.5pd
7929097 *IRLP* -	**TUONO** - **Rimorchiatori Riuniti Spezzini-Imprese Marittime e Salvataggi Srl** - *Naples* *Italy* MMSI: 247090000 Official number: 1363	**231** 69 -	Class: RI	**1980-11 Cooperativa Metallurgica Ing G Tommasi Srl — Ancona** Yd No: 39 Loa 32.11 Br ex 8.51 Dght 3.150 Lbp 28.02 Br md 8.49 Dpth 4.27 Welded, 1 dk	**(B32A2ST) Tug**	**1 oil engine** geared to sc. shaft driving 1 FP propeller Total Power: 1,839kW (2,500hp) Nohab F212V 1 x Vee 4 Stroke 12 Cy. 250 x 300 1839kW (2500bhp) Nohab Diesel AB-Sweden
8904214 *BKET* -	**TUOZHAN 2** *ex* Blu Mistral *-2007* *ex* Easy Rider *-2003* *ex* Ever Majesty *-2002* *ex* Ken Kon *-1996* **China Communications Import & Export Corp** - *China* MMSI: 413037000	**13,695** 7,738 22,271 T/cm 32.9	Class: CC (NV) (NK)	**1989-12 Saiki Heavy Industries Co Ltd — Saiki OT** Yd No: 1006 Loa 157.50 (BB) Br ex 25.04 Dght 9.115 Lbp 148.00 Br md 25.00 Dpth 12.70 Welded, 1 dk	**(A21A2BC) Bulk Carrier** Grain: 29,301; Bale: 28,299 Compartments: 4 Ho, ER 4 Ha: (20.0 x 11.7)Tappered 3 (20.8 x 17.5)ER Cranes: 4x30t	**1 oil engine** driving 1 FP propeller Total Power: 4,590kW (6,241hp) 13.5kn Mitsubishi 6UEC45LA 1 x 2 Stroke 6 Cy. 450 x 1350 4590kW (6241bhp) Akasaka Tekkosho KK (Akasaka DieselLtd)-Japan AuxGen: 2 x 400kW 445V 60Hz a.c Fuel: 80.6 (d.f.) 804.9 (r.f.) 16.0pd
6727076 - -	**TUPA** - - -	*390* 236 -	Class: (AB)	**1968 Ishikawajima do Brasil Est. S.A. (ISHIBRAS) — Rio de Janeiro** Yd No: 21 Loa 37.01 Br ex 9.45 Dght 4.407 Lbp 34.80 Br md 9.35 Dpth 5.01 Welded, 1 dk	**(B32A2ST) Tug**	**1 oil engine** reverse reduction geared to sc. shaft driving 1 FP propeller Total Power: 1,581kW (2,150hp) EMD (Electro-Motive) 12-645-E5 1 x Vee 2 Stroke 12 Cy. 230 x 254 1581kW (2150bhp) General Motors Corp.Electro-Motive Div.-La Grange AuxGen: 2 x 60kW
8938239 *HC5465* -	**TUPAHUE** - **Servicios Y Agenciamientos Maritimos SA (SAGEMAR)** - *Guayaquil* *Ecuador* Official number: R-00-0523	*216* 64 -	Class: AB	**1995-08 President Marine Pte Ltd — Singapore** Yd No: 172 Loa 29.00 Br ex - Dght 3.920 Lbp 28.40 Br md 8.60 Dpth 4.11 Welded, 1 dk	**(B32A2ST) Tug**	**2 oil engines** reverse reduction geared to sc. shafts driving 2 FP propellers Total Power: 2,060kW (2,800hp) Yanmar T240A-ET 2 x 4 Stroke 6 Cy. 240 x 310 each-1030kW (1400bhp) Yanmar Diesel Engine Co Ltd-Japan AuxGen: 2 x 60kW a.c
9375874 *V2BT7* -	**TUPERNA** *ex* Southern Phoenix *-2010* *ex* Tuperna *-2009* *ex* Anette Scan *-2009* *ex* Tuperna *-2007* **Erwin Strahlmann** Reederei Erwin Strahlmann eK *Saint John's* *Antigua & Barbuda* MMSI: 304924000 Official number: 4120	**2,588** 1,376 3,345	Class: GL	**2006-12 Slovenske Lodenice a.s. — Komarno** Yd No: 1910 Loa 86.53 Br ex - Dght 5.546 Lbp 81.00 Br md 12.80 Dpth 7.10 Welded, 1 dk	**(A31A2GX) General Cargo Ship** TEU 167 C. Cranes: 2x35t Ice Capable	**1 oil engine** reduction geared to sc. shaft driving 1 CP propeller Total Power: 1,980kW (2,692hp) 12.1kn MaK 6M25 1 x 4 Stroke 6 Cy. 255 x 400 1980kW (2692bhp) Caterpillar Motoren GmbH & Co. KG-Germany AuxGen: 1 x 376kW 400V a.c, 2 x 296kW 400V a.c Thrusters: 1 Tunnel thruster (f)
9038701 *DYUH* -	**TUPI MAIDEN** *ex* KEN Blossom *-2008* *ex* Blossom Forever *-2000* **Vedado Maritime Corp** Roymar Ship Management Inc SatCom: Inmarsat C 454879010 *Manila* *Philippines* MMSI: 548790000 Official number: MNLA000713	**22,147** 12,665 38,852 T/cm 47.2	Class: LR (NK) **100A1** SS 10/2010 bulk carrier ESP ESN Hold No. 1 LI **LMC** **UMS**	**1992-10 Ishikawajima-Harima Heavy Industries Co Ltd (IHI) — Tokyo** Yd No: 3027 Loa 180.80 (BB) Br ex - Dght 10.931 Lbp 171.00 Br md 30.50 Dpth 15.30 Welded, 1 dk	**(A21A2BC) Bulk Carrier** Grain: 46,112; Bale: 44,492 Compartments: 5 Ho, ER 5 Ha: (15.2 x 12.8)4 (19.2 x 15.2)ER Cranes: 4x25t	**1 oil engine** driving 1 FP propeller Total Power: 5,811kW (7,901hp) 14.5kn Sulzer 6RTA52 1 x 2 Stroke 6 Cy. 520 x 1800 5811kW (7901bhp) Diesel United Ltd.-Aioi AuxGen: 3 x 450kW 450V a.c Fuel: 1650.0 (r.f.)
9487005 *UHLQ* -	**TUR** - **Arzalk Shipping Ltd** Ark Shipping Co Ltd *Novorossiysk* *Russia* MMSI: 273346530	**712** 213 -	Class: BV	**2009-10 Gelibolu Gemi Insa Sanayi ve Ticaret AS — Gelibolu** Yd No: 44 Loa 42.00 Br ex - Dght 2.750 Lbp 39.00 Br md 12.50 Dpth 4.83 Welded, 1 dk	**(B21B20A) Anchor Handling Tug Supply** Ice Capable	**3 oil engines** reduction geared to sc. shafts driving 3 FP propellers Total Power: 3,642kW (4,953hp) 13.0kn Cummins KTA-50-M2 3 x Vee 4 Stroke 16 Cy. 159 x 159 each-1214kW (1651bhp) Cummins Engine Co Ltd-United Kingdom AuxGen: 3 x 173kW 50Hz a.c
7945704 *ERMX* -	**TURA** *ex* Nikolay L *-2013* *ex* Nikolay Limonov *-2011* **Target Shipping & Trading Corp** - SatCom: Inmarsat C 421400421 *Giurgiulesti* *Moldova* MMSI: 214181324 Official number: MD-M-11-544	**2,466** 1,065 3,353	Class: MG (RS)	**1981-09 Sudostroitelnyy Zavod im Volodarskogo — Rybinsk** Yd No: 85 Loa 114.03 Br ex 13.21 Dght 3.810 Lbp 108.03 Br md 13.00 Dpth 5.52 Welded, 1 dk	**(A31A2GX) General Cargo Ship** Grain: 5,906; Bale: 4,297 Compartments: 4 Ho, ER 4 Ha: (17.6 x 9.3)3 (17.9 x 9.3)ER Ice Capable	**2 oil engines** driving 2 FP propellers Total Power: 970kW (1,318hp) 10.8kn S.K.L. 6NVD48-2U 2 x 4 Stroke 6 Cy. 320 x 480 each-485kW (659bhp) VEB Schwermaschinenbau "KarlLiebknecht" (SKL)-Magdeburg
9395185 *TCSQ2* -	**TURABI EFENDI** - **May Elektronik ve Ticaret Pazarlama Ltd Sti** Kutup Denizcilik ve Ticaret Ltd Sti (Kutup Shipping & Trading Ltd) *Istanbul* *Turkey* MMSI: 271000957	**2,963** 1,642 4,983	Class: BV	**2007-05 Turkoglu Gemi Insaa Sanayi Ticaret Ltd Sti — Istanbul (Tuzla)** Yd No: 114 Loa 93.10 Br ex - Dght 5.800 Lbp 84.98 Br md 16.00 Dpth 7.00 Welded, 1 dk	**(A31A2GX) General Cargo Ship** Grain: 5,958; Bale: 5,958 Compartments: 2 Ho, ER 2 Ha: ER	**1 oil engine** reduction geared to sc. shaft driving 1 FP propeller Total Power: 1,850kW (2,515hp) 13.3kn MaK 6M25 1 x 4 Stroke 6 Cy. 255 x 400 1850kW (2515bhp) Caterpillar Motoren GmbH & Co. KG-Germany AuxGen: 1 x 342kW 400V 50Hz a.c, 2 x 230kW 400V 50Hz a.c Thrusters: 1 Tunnel thruster (f) Fuel: 179.0
9655688 *POZY* -	**TURACO** - **PT Baruna Raya Logistics** - *Jakarta* *Indonesia* Official number: NO.3525/BA	**1,727** 518 1,311	Class: AB	**2013-01 Fujian Southeast Shipyard — Fuzhou FJ** Yd No: DN59M-101 Loa 59.85 Br ex 15.15 Dght 4.950 Lbp 52.80 Br md 14.95 Dpth 6.10 Welded, 1 dk	**(B21B20A) Anchor Handling Tug Supply**	**2 oil engines** reduction geared to sc. shafts driving 2 CP propellers Total Power: 3,840kW (5,220hp) 11.0kn Caterpillar 3516C-HD 2 x Vee 4 Stroke 16 Cy. 170 x 215 each-1920kW (2610bhp) Caterpillar Inc-USA AuxGen: 2 x 800kW a.c, 2 x 444kW a.c Fuel: 560.0
8907216 *9HCG8* -	**TURAMA** *ex* Columbus Caravelle *-2004* *ex* Sally Caravelle *-1991* *ex* Delfin Caravelle *-1991* **Kenora Consolidated Investments SA** Sete Yacht Management SA *Valletta* *Malta* MMSI: 215837000 Official number: 9470	**8,343** 2,502 1,058	Class: LR ✠ **100A1** SS 05/2010 passenger ship Ice Class 1A ✠ **LMC** **UMS** Eq.Ltr: (V) ; Cable: 495.0/44.0 U3	**1990-05 Rauma Yards Oy — Rauma** Yd No: 305 Loa 116.41 (BB) Br ex 17.22 Dght 4.380 Lbp 104.43 Br md 17.01 Dpth 9.71 Welded, 3 dks	**(A37A2PC) Passenger/Cruise** Passengers: cabins: 43; berths: 70 Ice Capable	**2 oil engines** with clutches, flexible couplings & sr geared to sc. shafts driving 2 CP propellers Total Power: 6,000kW (8,158hp) 17.0kn Wartsila 8R32D 2 x 4 Stroke 8 Cy. 320 x 350 each-3000kW (4079bhp) Wartsila Diesel Oy-Finland AuxGen: 2 x 1120kW 440V 60Hz a.c, 2 x 1000kW 440V 60Hz a.c Boilers: 3 HWH (o.f.) 10.2kgf/cm² (10.0bar), 2 HWH (ex.g.) 10.2kgf/cm² (10.0bar) Thrusters: 1 Thwart. CP thruster (f)

8894744 - -	**TURAN** *ex* Hokutatsu Maru No. 5 *-2004* *ex* Hisayoshi Maru No. 38 *-2004* - -	*134* - -		**1986-04 Sanuki Shipbuilding & Iron Works Co Ltd — Mitoyo KG** L reg 28.60 Br ex - Dght - Lbp - Br md 6.10 Dpth 2.45 Welded, 1 dk	**(B11B2FV) Fishing Vessel**	**1 oil engine** driving 1 FP propeller Daihatsu 1 x 4 Stroke Daihatsu Diesel Manufacturing Co Lt-Japan
9070450 *9V9825* -	**TURANDOT** **Parsifal Shipping Pte Ltd** Wallenius Marine Singapore Pte Ltd *Singapore* *Singapore* MMSI: 566441000	**55,598** 23,033 15,199 T/cm 52.9	Class: LR ✠ **100A1** SS 01/2010 vehicle carrier moveable decks, deck Nos. 2, 4 & 8 strengthened for the carriage of roll on/roll off cargoes *I.W.S. LI ✠ **LMC** **UMS** Eq.Ltr: Q†; Cable: 687.5/81.0 U3	**1995-01 Daewoo Heavy Industries Ltd — Geoje** Yd No: 4412 Loa 199.11 (BB) Br ex 32.29 Dght 9.520 Lbp 190.50 Br md 32.26 Dpth 32.98 Welded, 12 dks, incl. Nos. 4, 6, & 8 dks hoistable	**(A35B2RV) Vehicles Carrier** Side door/ramp (s) Len: 25.00 Wid: 5.00 Swl: 30 Quarter stern door/ramp (s) Len: 45.00 Wid: 7.00 Swl: 105 Cars: 5,846	**1 oil engine** driving 1 FP propeller Total Power: 16,358kW (22,240hp) 20.3kn B&W 8S60MC 1 x 2 Stroke 8 Cy. 600 x 2292 16358kW (22240bhp) Korea Heavy Industries & ConstrCo Ltd (HANJUNG)-South Korea AuxGen: 2 x 1400kW 450V 60Hz a.c, 1 x 1087kW 410V 60Hz a.c Boilers: AuxB (Comp) 9.2kgf/cm² (9.0bar) Thrusters: 1 Thwart. CP thruster (f)
7227736 *P2V5131* -	**TURANGUNA** *ex* Mclarty *-2011* **Pacific Towing (PNG) Pty Ltd** *Port Moresby* *Papua New Guinea* MMSI: 553111333	*159* 2 143	Class: (LR) ✠ Classed LR until 25/10/06	**1972-12 Carrington Slipways Pty Ltd — Newcastle NSW** Yd No: 77 Loa 25.81 Br ex 8.11 Dght 3.455 Lbp 22.26 Br md 7.78 Dpth 4.07 Welded, 1 dk	**(B32A2ST) Tug**	**2 oil engines** reverse reduction geared to sc. shafts driving 2 FP propellers Total Power: 1,472kW (2,002hp) Blackstone ESL8MK2 2 x 4 Stroke 8 Cy. 222 x 292 each-736kW (1001bhp) Mirrlees Blackstone (Stamford)Ltd.-Stamford AuxGen: 2 x 36kW 415V 50Hz a.c
7364429 *TCAC6* -	**TURANLAR 2** *ex* Turanlar Ii *-2005* *ex* Asli Ayanoglu *-1990* *ex* Mehmet Guveli *-1980* **Turkol Deniz Ticaret AS** Buyuk Ana Denizcilik Ticaret Ltd Sti *Istanbul* *Turkey* MMSI: 271002187 Official number: 4333	**969** 581 1,975	Class: TL (AB)	**1975-06 Gultekin Dokerel Gemi Insaat — Izmir** Yd No: 31 Loa 71.00 Br ex - Dght 2.700 Lbp 67.40 Br md 10.70 Dpth 3.76 Welded, 1 dk	**(A31A2GX) General Cargo Ship**	**1 oil engine** geared to sc. shaft driving 1 FP propeller Total Power: 838kW (1,139hp) 11.0kn Caterpillar D399 1 x Vee 4 Stroke 16 Cy. 159 x 203 838kW (1139bhp) (new engine 1975) Caterpillar Tractor Co-USA
8726997 - -	**TURBINELLA** **Premache Fishing Co Ltd** -	**944** 283 533	Class: (RS)	**1986-03 Pribaltiyskiy Sudostroitelnyy Zavod "Yantar" — Kaliningrad** Yd No: 021 Loa 55.53 Br ex 11.09 Dght 5.010 Lbp 49.82 Br md - Dpth 7.50 Welded, 2 dks	**(B11B2FV) Fishing Vessel**	**1 oil engine** driving 1 CP propeller Total Power: 1,673kW (2,275hp) 14.4kn Kolomna 8CHNRP30/38 1 x 4 Stroke 8 Cy. 300 x 380 1673kW (2275bhp) Kolomenskiy Zavod-Kolomna AuxGen: 3 x 280kW a.c
9535280 *JYA202* -	**TURBO JET** **Al Saif International Transportation for Passengers** *Aqaba* *Jordan* Official number: 109	**105** - -		**2008-07 Zhuhai Jianglong Shipbuilding Co Ltd — Zhuhai GD** Yd No: JL27S-03 Loa 24.00 Br ex - Dght 1.100 Lbp - Br md 6.00 Dpth 2.60 Bonded, 1 dk	**(A37B2PS) Passenger Ship** Hull Material: Reinforced Plastic Passengers: unberthed: 110	**2 oil engines** reduction geared to sc. shafts driving 2 Propellers Total Power: 610kW (830hp) Cummins NTA-855-M 2 x 4 Stroke 6 Cy. 140 x 152 each-305kW (415bhp) Cummins Engine Co Inc-USA
8906482 *IZOE* -	**TURBOCEM** *ex* Sider Crusader *-2005* *ex* Celtic Crusader *-2002* *ex* Begona B *-1999* *ex* Celtic Crusader *-1999* *ex* Begona B *-1999* *ex* Nenufar Uno *-1998* *ex* Celtic Crusader *-1995* *ex* Euro Trader *-1995* *ex* Celtic Crusader *-1993* **Medcem Srl** Shipping Technical Management Srl *Naples* *Italy* MMSI: 247074400	**3,907** 1,731 5,745	Class: BV (LR) ✠ Classed LR until 10/10/02	**1992-09 Madenci Gemi Sanayii Ltd. Sti. — Karadeniz Eregli** Yd No: 5 Converted From: General Cargo Ship-2005 Loa 92.80 (BB) Br ex 17.10 Dght 6.689 Lbp 84.55 Br md 17.00 Dpth 8.20 Welded, 1 dk	**(A24A2BT) Cement Carrier** Compartments: 1 Ho, ER 1 Ha: ER	**1 oil engine** with clutches, flexible couplings & sr geared to sc. shaft driving 1 CP propeller Total Power: 2,650kW (3,603hp) 13.5kn MaK 8M453C 1 x 4 Stroke 8 Cy. 320 x 420 2650kW (3603bhp) Krupp MaK Maschinenbau GmbH-Kiel AuxGen: 1 x 828kW 380V 50Hz a.c, 3 x 270kW 380V 50Hz a.c Thrusters: 1 Thwart. CP thruster (f); 1 Tunnel thruster (a)
9032927 *FGZB* CY 784709	**TURBOT 2** **Andre Florus** - *Cayenne* *France* Official number: 784709	*100* - -		**1991 Steiner Shipyard, Inc. — Bayou La Batre, Al** Loa 22.86 Br ex - Dght 3.352 Lbp - Br md - Dpth 6.71 Welded	**(B11B2FV) Fishing Vessel** Ins: 93	**1 oil engine** geared to sc. shaft driving 1 FP propeller Total Power: 313kW (426hp) Cummins KT-19-M 1 x 4 Stroke 6 Cy. 159 x 159 313kW (426bhp) Cummins Engine Co Inc-USA
9220354 *IBLE* -	**TURCHESE** **Finbeta SpA** - SatCom: Inmarsat Mini-M 763705254 *Ancona* *Italy* MMSI: 247604000 Official number: 1	**8,428** 3,934 12,000 T/cm 24.5	Class: RI (BV)	**2000-01 Cant. Nav. Mario Morini S.p.A. — Ancona** Yd No: 264 Loa 136.07 (BB) Br ex 20.65 Dght 8.030 Lbp 126.50 Br md 20.42 Dpth 10.30 Welded, 1 dk	**(A12B2TR) Chemical/Products Tanker** Double Hull (13F) Liq: 13,543; Liq (Oil): 13,545 Cargo Heating Coils Compartments: 1 Wing Ta, 19 Wing Ta (s.stl), ER (s.stl) 20 Cargo Pump (s): 14x250m³/hr, 4x100m³/hr, 2x50m³/hr Manifold: Bow/CM: 68m Ice Capable	**3 diesel electric oil engines** driving 3 gen. each 2400kW 3300V a.c Connecting to 2 elec. motors each (3300kW) driving 1 FP propeller Total Power: 7,800kW (10,605hp) 14.0kn Wartsila 6L32 3 x 4 Stroke 6 Cy. 320 x 400 each-2600kW (3535bhp) Wartsila NSD Finland Oy-Finland Thrusters: 1 Thwart. FP thruster (f) Fuel: 93.5 (d.f.) (Heating Coils) 594.7 (r.f.)
7432135 *3FES7* -	**TURDUS** *ex* Hermann *-2009* *ex* Inaba *-2007* *ex* Hermann *-2005* *ex* Oakpark *-1990* *ex* Hermann *-1990* *ex* Hermann Sif *-1984* **Sevenhill Overseas SA** Nautilus Shipping Overseas Corp SatCom: Inmarsat C 435493711 *Panama* *Panama* MMSI: 354937000 Official number: 4216711	**1,263** 624 2,597	Class: PD (GL) (BV)	**1976-11 E.J. Smit & Zoon's Scheepswerven B.V. — Westerbroek** Yd No: 811 Loa 79.79 Br ex 13.03 Dght 5.157 Lbp 72.50 Br md 13.01 Dpth 7.50 Welded, 2 dks	**(A31A2GX) General Cargo Ship** Grain: 4,234; Bale: 3,802 Compartments: 1 Ho, ER 2 Ha: (21.5 x 9.5) (14.4 x 9.5)ER Derricks: 1x15t,2x3t; Winches: 3 Ice Capable	**1 oil engine** driving 1 FP propeller Total Power: 1,324kW (1,800hp) 12.3kn MaK 8M452AK 1 x 4 Stroke 8 Cy. 320 x 450 1324kW (1800bhp) MaK Maschinenbau GmbH-Kiel
7230630 *WDC6809* -	**TURECAMO BOYS** *ex* Atlantic Tide *-1989* *ex* Gulf Tide *-1988* *ex* Newpark Sunshine *-1982* *ex* Miss Mildred *-1978* **Moran Towing Corp** - *Wilmington, DE* *United States of America* MMSI: 367061620 Official number: 542550	*193* 131 -	Class: AB	**1972 Main Iron Works, Inc. — Houma, La** Yd No: 266 Loa - Br ex - Dght 3.836 Lbp 32.44 Br md 9.15 Dpth 4.42 Welded, 1 dk	**(B32A2ST) Tug**	**2 oil engines** reverse reduction geared to sc. shafts driving 2 FP propellers Total Power: 2,354kW (3,200hp) EMD (Electro-Motive) 16-567-C 2 x Vee 2 Stroke 16 Cy. 216 x 254 each-1177kW (1600bhp) (Re-engined ,made 1956, Reconditioned & fitted 1972) General Motors Corp.Electro-Motive Div.-La Grange AuxGen: 2 x 75kW Fuel: 214.5 (d.f.)
6604781 *WDC3464* -	**TURECAMO GIRLS** *ex* Capt. Jan Porel *-1966* **Moran Towing Corp** - *New York, NY* *United States of America* MMSI: 366946710 Official number: 500066	*195* 132 -	Class: AB	**1965 Diamond Manufacturing Co. Ltd. — Savannah, Ga** Yd No: M-250 Loa - Br ex 8.28 Dght 3.928 Lbp 29.14 Br md 8.23 Dpth 4.30 Welded, 1 dk	**(B32B2SA) Articulated Pusher Tug**	**2 oil engines** reverse reduction geared to sc. shafts driving 2 FP propellers Total Power: 1,434kW (1,950hp) EMD (Electro-Motive) 8-645-E5 2 x Vee 2 Stroke 8 Cy. 230 x 254 each-717kW (975bhp) (new engine 1972) General Motors Corp-USA AuxGen: 2 x 30kW Fuel: 150.5
9242857 *9AA6280* -	**TURETA** *ex* Baby Doll *-2009* **Ittimurter doo** - *Sibenik* *Croatia* MMSI: 238900840 Official number: 3R-92	**165** 49 -	Class: CS	**2000 Ocean Marine, Inc. — Bayou La Batre, Al** Yd No: 374 Loa 29.10 Br ex - Dght 3.120 Lbp 24.60 Br md 7.57 Dpth 4.03 Welded, 1 dk	**(B11B2FV) Fishing Vessel**	**1 oil engine** reduction geared to sc. shaft driving 1 FP propeller Total Power: 449kW (610hp) 8.5kn Caterpillar 3412 1 x Vee 4 Stroke 12 Cy. 137 x 152 449kW (610bhp) Caterpillar Inc-USA
9188867 *TCTO* -	**TURGUT OZAL** **Istanbul Deniz Otobusleri Sanayi ve Ticaret AS (IDO)** - *Istanbul* *Turkey* MMSI: 271000539 Official number: 603	**5,992** 1,798 400	Class: TL (GL)	**1998-11 Austal Ships Pty Ltd — Fremantle WA** Yd No: 71 Loa 86.60 (BB) Br ex - Dght 3.287 Lbp 75.36 Br md 24.00 Dpth 7.30 Welded, 1 dk	**(A36A2PR) Passenger/Ro-Ro Ship (Vehicles)** Hull Material: Aluminium Alloy Passengers: unberthed: 800 Stern ramp Len: 9.85 Wid: 7.00 Swl: - Cars: 200	**4 oil engines** with clutches & reduction geared to sc. shafts driving 4 Water jets Total Power: 26,000kW (35,348hp) 42.0kn M.T.U. 20V1163TB73 4 x Vee 4 Stroke 20 Cy. 230 x 280 each-6500kW (8837bhp) MTU Friedrichshafen GmbH-Friedrichshafen AuxGen: 4 x 296kW 380/220V 50Hz a.c Fuel: 140.0

8706478 3FES3 -
TURGUT REIS
ex Vera I *-2012* *ex* Eastwind Ruhr *-2009*
ex EW Horsham *-2008* *ex* Horsham *-2004*
ex Sininni *-1999* *ex* Burwain Pollux *-1996*
ex Sonja *-1992*
Turgut Reis Shipping Ltd
Rana Denizcilik Nakliyat Sanayi ve Ticaret Ltd Sti
Panama *Panama*
MMSI: 354906000
Official number: 4098510B

17,895 9,137 27,910 T/cm 37.3
Class: NK (LR) (BV)
✠ Classed LR until 12/10/05

1992-01 Stocznia Szczecinska SA — Szczecin
Yd No: B560/05
Converted From: Products Tanker-2008
Loa 170.10 (BB) Br ex 25.32 Dght 10.860
Lbp 162.00 Br md 25.29 Dpth 14.48
Welded, 1 dk

(A21A2BC) Bulk Carrier
Grain: 32,424
Compartments: 6 Ho, ER
6 Ha: ER
Cranes: 3x30t

1 oil engine driving 1 FP propeller
Total Power: 6,500kW (8,837hp) 14.0kn
B&W 6L50MC
1 x 2 Stroke 6 Cy. 500 x 1620 6500kW (8837bhp)
H Cegielski Poznan SA-Poland
AuxGen: 3 x 640kW 440V 50Hz a.c
Boilers: 2 AuxB (o.f.) 17.3kgf/cm² (17.0bar), AuxB (ex.g.)
Fuel: 273.5 (d.f.) 1415.2 (r.f.)

9150975 T2PG4 -
TURGUT REIS I
Servicios y Concesiones Maritimas Ibicencas SA
International Maritime Services Pty Ltd
Funafuti *Tuvalu*
MMSI: 572672210
Official number: 29999713

2,695 809 184
Class: IZ (NV)

1997-05 Austal Ships Pty Ltd — Fremantle WA
Yd No: 54
Loa 59.90 Br ex 17.80 Dght 3.219
Lbp 51.20 Br md 17.50 Dpth 6.65
Welded, 2 dks

(A36A2PR) Passenger/Ro-Ro Ship (Vehicles)
Hull Material: Aluminium Alloy
Passengers: unberthed: 450
Stern ramp
Cars: 94

2 oil engines with clutches & reduction geared to sc. shafts driving 2 Water jets
Total Power: 13,000kW (17,674hp) 34.0kn
M.T.U. 20V1163TB73
2 x Vee 4 Stroke 20 Cy. 230 x 280 each-6500kW (8837bhp)
MTU Friedrichshafen GmbH-Friedrichshafen
AuxGen: 4 x 296kW 380/220V 50Hz a.c
Fuel: 32.0 (d.f.)

9583110 HBLK -
TURICUM
Azimuth Shipping AG
Reederei Zurich AG
Basel *Switzerland*
MMSI: 269025000
Official number: 207

32,315 19,458 58,097 T/cm 57.4
Class: NK

2012-06 Tsuneishi Group (Zhoushan) Shipbuilding Inc — Daishan County ZJ Yd No: SS-095
Loa 190.00 Br ex 32.29 Dght 12.830
Lbp 185.60 Br md 32.26 Dpth 18.00
Welded, 1 dk

(A21A2BC) Bulk Carrier
Grain: 72,689; Bale: 70,122
Compartments: 5 Ho, ER
5 Ha: ER
Cranes: 4x30t

1 oil engine driving 1 FP propeller
Total Power: 8,400kW (11,421hp) 14.5kn
MAN-B&W 6S50MC-C
1 x 2 Stroke 6 Cy. 500 x 2000 8400kW (11421bhp)
Mitsui Engineering & Shipbuilding CLtd-Japan
Fuel: 2380.0

7532040 - -
TURIHAUA
Eastland Port Ltd
Whangarei *New Zealand*
Official number: 349396

104 - -

1977-07 Whangarei Eng. & Construction Co. Ltd. — Whangarei Yd No: 150
Loa 22.38 Br ex 7.17 Dght 2.215
Lbp 21.19 Br md 6.96 Dpth 2.22
Welded, 1 dk

(B32A2ST) Tug

2 oil engines reduction geared to sc. shafts driving 2 FP propellers
Total Power: 924kW (1,256hp)
Caterpillar 3412TA
2 x Vee 4 Stroke 12 Cy. 137 x 152 each-462kW (628bhp) (, fitted 1995)
Caterpillar Inc-USA

9018907 YYV2418 -
TURIMIQUIRE
PDV Marina SA
Maracaibo *Venezuela*
Official number: AJZL - 27.280

325 98 -
Class: (AB)

1993-11 Astilleros de Oriente — Oriente Yd No: 15
Loa - Br ex - Dght 3.740
Lbp 32.00 Br md 9.80 Dpth 5.10
Welded, 1 dk

(B32A2ST) Tug

2 oil engines driving 2 FP propellers
Total Power: 2,568kW (3,492hp) 12.0kn
Wartsila 8R22
2 x 4 Stroke 8 Cy. 220 x 240 each-1284kW (1746bhp)
Wartsila Diesel Oy-Finland
AuxGen: 2 x 110kW a.c

7945778 - -
TURIST
Trading House Mortrans Co Ltd
Mortrans Co Ltd
Vladivostok *Russia*
MMSI: 273444620

253 75 48
Class: RS

1981-06 Nakhodkinskiy Sudoremontnyy Zavod — Nakhodka Yd No: 1
Loa 38.42 Br ex 6.71 Dght 2.200
Lbp 34.50 Br md - Dpth 2.90
Welded, 1 dk

(A37B2PS) Passenger Ship
Passengers: unberthed: 160
Ice Capable

2 oil engines geared to sc. shafts driving 2 FP propellers
Total Power: 464kW (630hp) 12.8kn
Daldizel 6CHNSP18/22
2 x 4 Stroke 6 Cy. 180 x 220 each-232kW (315bhp)
Daldizel-Khabarovsk
AuxGen: 3 x 14kW
Fuel: 18.0 (d.f.)

8860767 UGXI -
TURIY
Arkhangelsk Sea Commercial Port (Arkhangelskiy Morskoy Torgovyy Port)
-
Arkhangelsk *Russia*
Official number: 903512

182 54 57
Class: RS

1991-10 Gorokhovetskiy Sudostroitelnyy Zavod — Gorokhovets Yd No: 255
Loa 29.30 Br ex 8.60 Dght 3.400
Lbp 27.00 Br md 8.24 Dpth 4.30
Welded, 1 dk

(B32A2ST) Tug
Ice Capable

2 oil engines driving 2 CP propellers
Total Power: 1,180kW (1,604hp) 11.5kn
Pervomaysk 8CHNP25/34
2 x 4 Stroke 8 Cy. 250 x 340 each-590kW (802bhp)
Pervomaydizelmash (PDM)-Pervomaysk
AuxGen: 2 x 50kW
Fuel: 49.0 (d.f.)

8817992 3FYW6 -
TURK GAZ
ex Fgas 09 *-2013* *ex* Cotswold *-2010*
ex Diamante *-1991* *ex* Pennine *-1991*
Shine Way Dayanikli Tuketim Mallari ve Ham Maddeleri Sanayi ve Ticaret Ltd Sti
Penta Ocean Ship Management & Operation LLC
SatCom: Inmarsat C 437074710
Panama *Panama*
MMSI: 370747000
Official number: 42037PEXT1

3,368 1,011 4,142 T/cm 12.5
Class: BV MC VR (NK)

1989-09 Kurinoura Dockyard Co Ltd — Yawatahama EH Yd No: 274
Loa 99.10 (BB) Br ex - Dght 5.678
Lbp 92.00 Br md 15.80 Dpth 7.30
Welded, 1 dk

(A11B2TG) LPG Tanker
Double Bottom Entire Compartment Length
Liq (Gas): 3,143
2 x Gas Tank (s); 2 independent (C.mn.stl) cyl horizontal
3 Cargo Pump (s): 3x300m³/hr
Manifold: Bow/CM: 46.8m

1 oil engine driving 1 FP propeller
Total Power: 2,427kW (3,300hp) 12.7kn
Mitsubishi 6UEC37LA
1 x 2 Stroke 6 Cy. 370 x 880 2427kW (3300bhp)
Akasaka Tekkosho KK (Akasaka DieselLtd)-Japan
AuxGen: 2 x 240kW a.c
Fuel: 81.0 (d.f.) 377.0 (r.f.)

9673082 TCNG7 -
TURK YILDIZI-1
ICDAS Celik Enerji Tersane ve Ulasim Sanayi AS
Istanbul *Turkey*
MMSI: 271043631
Official number: 10888

2,930 1,626 5,035
Class: NK

2013-09 Icdas Celik Enerji Tersane ve Ulasim Sanayi AS — Biga Yd No: 20
Loa 83.12 (BB) Br ex - Dght 6.599
Lbp 78.05 Br md 15.80 Dpth 7.65
Welded, 1 dk

(A31A2GX) General Cargo Ship
TEU 211

1 oil engine driving 1 Propeller
Total Power: 750kW (1,020hp)
Hyundai Himsen 6H21/32P
1 x 4 Stroke 6 Cy. 210 x 320 750kW (1020bhp)
Hyundai Heavy Industries Co Ltd-South Korea
Fuel: 135.0

9250945 9HA2590 -
TURKAN SAYLAN
ex Mining Star *-2011*
Butamarin Shipping Ltd
Statu Gemi Kiralama ve Ticaret Ltd Sti (Statu Chartering & Shipping Agency Ltd)
Valletta *Malta*
MMSI: 248961000
Official number: 9250945

11,403 6,277 18,721
Class: BV

2002-01 Hakata Zosen K.K. — Imabari Yd No: 636
Loa 137.90 (BB) Br ex - Dght 8.420
Lbp 131.00 Br md 25.00 Dpth 11.50
Welded, 1 dk

(A21A2BC) Bulk Carrier
Grain: 22,918
Compartments: 4 Ho, ER
4 Ha: ER 4 (18.2 x 15.0)
Cranes: 3x36t

1 oil engine driving 1 FP propeller
Total Power: 5,180kW (7,043hp) 13.0kn
B&W 6S35MC
1 x 2 Stroke 6 Cy. 350 x 1400 5180kW (7043bhp)
The Hanshin Diesel Works Ltd-Japan

9396646 UNDV -
TURKESTAN
ex Vasiliy Klimov *-2014*
'KTZ Express' JSC
-
Aqtau *Kazakhstan*
MMSI: 436000242

4,182 2,373 5,471
Class: RS

2007-05 Onega Shipyard Ltd. — Petrozavodsk
Yd No: 007
Loa 108.33 Br ex 16.74 Dght 4.792
Lbp 102.20 Br md 16.50 Dpth 5.50
Welded, 1 dk

(A31A2GX) General Cargo Ship
Grain: 7,831
Compartments: 3 Ho, ER
3 Ha: (27.3 x 12.7) (26.5 x 12.7)ER (21.4 x 12.7)

2 oil engines reduction geared to sc. shafts driving 2 Directional propellers
Total Power: 2,100kW (2,856hp) 10.5kn
Wartsila 6L20
2 x 4 Stroke 6 Cy. 200 x 280 each-1050kW (1428bhp)
Wartsila Finland Oy-Finland
AuxGen: 2 x 180kW a.c
Fuel: 213.0 (d.f.)

8891924 EZAT -
TURKMENISTAN
The Turkmen Marine Merchant Fleet Authority
-
SatCom: Inmarsat C 427310433
Turkmenbashy *Turkmenistan*
MMSI: 434111000
Official number: 922629

3,086 925 3,152
Class: RS

1992-11 Slovenske Lodenice a.s. — Komarno
Yd No: 2342
Loa 115.60 Br ex 13.60 Dght 4.000
Lbp 111.20 Br md 13.00 Dpth 6.00
Welded, 1 dk

(A31A2GX) General Cargo Ship

2 oil engines driving 2 FP propellers
Total Power: 1,030kW (1,400hp)
Skoda 6L275A2
2 x 4 Stroke 6 Cy. 275 x 350 each-515kW (700bhp)
CKD Praha-Praha

8227240 - -
TURKMENSKIY RYBAK
ex Bakharden *-2014*
GPO 'Balkanbalyk'
-
Turkmenbashy *Turkmenistan*
Official number: 832812

722 217 451
Class: (RS)

1984 Zavod "Leninskaya Kuznitsa" — Kiyev
Yd No: 1535
Loa 54.84 Br ex 9.96 Dght 4.140
Lbp 50.30 Br md - Dpth 5.01
Welded, 1 dk

(B11A2FS) Stern Trawler
Ins: 412
Compartments: 2 Ho
Ice Capable

1 oil engine driving 1 CP propeller
Total Power: 852kW (1,158hp) 12.0kn
S.K.L. 8NVD48A-2U
1 x 4 Stroke 8 Cy. 320 x 480 852kW (1158bhp)
VEB Schwermaschinenbau "KarlLiebknecht" (SKL)-Magdeburg
AuxGen: 4 x 160kW a.c
Fuel: 162.0 (d.f.)

9068964 ZHFH8 -
TURKS & CAICOS AGGRESSOR II
ex Cayman Aggressor II *-2003*
ex C/Dominator *-1987*
Venture Charters Ltd
Caicos Live Aboard Diving
George Town *Cayman Islands (British)*
Official number: 708680

131 53 -

1973-01 Swiftships Inc — Morgan City LA
Yd No: 74
Converted From: Supply Tender-1985
Loa 39.60 Br ex - Dght 2.180
Lbp - Br md 6.70 Dpth 2.90
Welded, 1 dk

(X11A2YP) Yacht
Hull Material: Aluminium Alloy
Passengers: cabins: 9

2 oil engines geared to sc. shafts driving 2 Propellers
Total Power: 588kW (800hp) 15.0kn
Caterpillar 3406
2 x 4 Stroke 6 Cy. 137 x 165 each-294kW (400bhp)
Caterpillar Tractor Co-USA
AuxGen: 2 x 30kW

8987278 - -	**TURKS & CAICOS EXPLORER II** *ex* Ballymena *-2004* *ex* Allison G *-2004* **Arm Cayman Ltd** - *Turks & Caicos Islands (British)*	**238** 71 -		**1977 Swiftships Inc — Morgan City LA** Converted From: Diving Support Vessel-2009 Loa 37.80 Br ex - Dght 2.440 Lbp 35.05 Br md 6.70 Dpth - Welded, 1 dk	**(A37A2PC) Passenger/Cruise** Hull Material: Aluminium Alloy Passengers: cabins: 10; berths: 20	**2 oil engines** geared to sc. shafts driving 2 Propellers Total Power: 662kW (900hp) 14.0kn G.M. (Detroit Diesel) 12V-71 2 x Vee 2 Stroke 12 Cy. 108 x 127 each-331kW (450bhp) General Motors Detroit DieselAllison Divn-USA AuxGen: 1 x 125kW 220/110V a.c, 1 x 75kW 220/110V a.c
8655576 *TCUP8* - -	**TURKUAZ 2** **Turkuaz Gemi Ins Sanayi ve Ticaret Ltd Sti** - *Istanbul* *Turkey* MMSI: 271073016	**123** 69 -		**2007-04 in Turkey** Loa 25.10 Br ex - Dght - Lbp 22.37 Br md 7.00 Dpth 2.70 Welded, 1 dk	**(B32A2ST) Tug**	**1 oil engine** reduction geared to sc. shaft driving 1 Propeller Total Power: 736kW (1,001hp) Baudouin 12M26SRP 1 x Vee 4 Stroke 12 Cy. 150 x 150 736kW (1001bhp) Societe des Moteurs Baudouin SA-France
9211212 *DEFQ* -	**TURM** **L&R Lutgens & Reimers Schleppschiffahrt GmbH & Co KG** Unterweser Reederei GmbH (URAG Unterweser Reederei GmbH) *Bremen* *Germany* MMSI: 211690000 Official number: 4888	**452** 135 282	Class: GL (RI)	**2001-03 Astilleros Armon SA — Navia** Yd No: 497 Loa 32.50 Br ex - Dght 2.650 Lbp 30.24 Br md 11.00 Dpth 4.50 Welded, 1 dk	**(B32A2ST) Tug**	**2 oil engines** gearing integral to driving 2 Voith-Schneider propellers Total Power: 3,742kW (5,088hp) 13.0kn A.B.C. 8DZC 2 x 4 Stroke 8 Cy. 256 x 310 each-1871kW (2544bhp) Anglo Belgian Corp NV (ABC)-Belgium AuxGen: 2 x 160kW 380/220V 50Hz a.c Fuel: 142.4 (d.f.) 15.0pd
9474644 *9HA3499* -	**TURMALIN** *ex* POS Turmalin *-2013* **Conti 181 Schifffahrts-GmbH & Co KG Nr 1** BBG-Bremer Bereederungsgesellschaft mbH & Co KG *Valletta* *Malta* MMSI: 229664000 Official number: 9474644	**51,195** 31,136 92,762 T/cm 80.9	Class: AB	**2012-03 COSCO (Zhoushan) Shipyard Co Ltd — Zhoushan ZJ** Yd No: N307 Loa 229.20 (BB) Br ex - Dght 14.900 Lbp 222.00 Br md 38.00 Dpth 20.70 Welded, 1 dk	**(A21A2BC) Bulk Carrier** Grain: 110,330 Compartments: 7 Ho, ER 7 Ha: ER	**1 oil engine** driving 1 FP propeller Total Power: 12,240kW (16,642hp) 14.1kn MAN-B&W 6S60MC 1 x 2 Stroke 6 Cy. 600 x 2292 12240kW (16642bhp) Doosan Engine Co Ltd-South Korea AuxGen: 3 x 730kW a.c Fuel: 230.0 (d.f.) 3590.0 (r.f.)
8724808 *UEML* -	**TURMALIN** *ex* Aleksandr Ulgin *-2014* **Dilmas Co Ltd** *Nakhodka* *Russia* MMSI: 273434770 Official number: 863331	**1,895** 907 3,389	Class: RS	**1986-09 Shipbuilding & Shiprepairing Yard 'Ivan Dimitrov' — Rousse** Yd No: 451 Loa 77.53 Br ex 14.34 Dght 5.400 Lbp 73.24 Br md 14.00 Dpth 6.50 Welded, 1dk	**(A13B2TP) Products Tanker** Liq: 3,513; Liq (Oil): 3,513 Compartments: 12 Ta, ER Ice Capable	**1 oil engine** driving 1 FP propeller Total Power: 883kW (1,201hp) 10.2kn S.K.L. 8NVD48A-2U 1 x 4 Stroke 8 Cy. 320 x 480 883kW (1201bhp) VEB Schwermaschinenbau "KarlLiebknecht" (SKL)-Magdeburg AuxGen: 2 x 150kW a.c
9129172 - -	**TURMALINA** **Damen Marine Services BV**	**102** 40 -	Class: (BV)	**1996-09 Stocznia Kozle Serwis Sp z oo — Kedzierzyn-Kozle** (Hull) **1996-09 B.V. Scheepswerf Damen — Gorinchem** Yd No: 3031 Loa 18.70 Br ex - Dght 1.750 Lbp 18.00 Br md 8.06 Dpth 2.75 Welded, 1 dk	**(B34L2QU) Utility Vessel**	**2 oil engines** reduction geared to sc. shafts driving 2 FP propellers Total Power: 448kW (610hp) 9.3kn Caterpillar 3406TA 2 x 4 Stroke 6 Cy. 137 x 165 each-224kW (305bhp) Caterpillar Inc-USA
1008920 *ZCPA2* -	**TURMOIL** **Turmoil Marine LLC** International Yacht Collection *George Town* *Cayman Islands (British)* MMSI: 319821000 Official number: 738568	**1,428** 416 -	Class: LR ✠ **100A1** SS 08/2011 SSC Yacht, mono, G6 ✠ **LMC** **UMS** Cable: 385.0/30.0 U2 (a)	**2006-08 AS Rigas Kugu Buvetava (Riga Shipyard) — Riga** (Hull) **2006-08 Assens Skibsvaerft A/S — Assens** Yd No: 327 Loa 60.09 Br ex 12.06 Dght 3.700 Lbp 53.30 Br md 11.80 Dpth 6.85 Welded, 1 dk	**(X11A2YP) Yacht**	**2 oil engines** with clutches, flexible couplings & sr reverse geared to sc. shafts driving 2 FP propellers Total Power: 3,372kW (4,584hp) 14.0kn Caterpillar 3516B-HD 2 x Vee 4 Stroke 16 Cy. 170 x 215 each-1686kW (2292bhp) Caterpillar Inc-USA AuxGen: 2 x 215kW 450V 60Hz a.c Thrusters: 1 Thwart. FP thruster (f); 1 Thwart. FP thruster (a)
9479838 *3FWB6* -	**TURMOIL** **Mercator Navigation SA** Transpetrol Maritime Services Ltd 23675566 *Panama* *Panama* MMSI: 356423000 Official number: 4319611	**29,419** 13,762 50,358 T/cm 52.3	Class: NK	**2011-10 Onomichi Dockyard Co Ltd — Onomichi HS** Yd No: 565 Loa 182.50 (BB) Br ex 32.23 Dght 13.117 Lbp 175.00 Br md 32.20 Dpth 19.05 Welded, 1 dk	**(A12B2TR) Chemical/Products Tanker** Double Hull (13F) Liq: 51,984; Liq (Oil): 55,000 Cargo Heating Coils Compartments: 12 Wing Ta, 2 Wing Slop Ta, 1 Slop Ta, ER 12 Cargo Pump (s): 12x600m³/hr Manifold: Bow/CM: 88m	**1 oil engine** driving 1 FP propeller Total Power: 8,580kW (11,665hp) 14.8kn MAN-B&W 6S50MC 1 x 2 Stroke 6 Cy. 500 x 1910 8580kW (11665bhp) Mitsui Engineering & Shipbuilding CLtd-Japan AuxGen: 3 x 800kW 450V 60Hz a.c Fuel: 141.0 (d.f.) 2249.0 (r.f.)
9631618 *YMA5619* -	**TURNA TUR** **Turnatur Turizm Reklam ve Organizasyon Hizmetleri Sanayi Ticaret Ltd** - *Istanbul* *Turkey* Official number: G-1876	**318** 191 150	Class: TL	**2011-06 Medyilmaz Gemi Sanayi ve Ticaret AS — Karadeniz Eregli** Yd No: 17 Loa 41.96 Br ex - Dght 1.600 Lbp 38.03 Br md 10.00 Dpth 3.00 Welded, 1 dk	**(A37B2PS) Passenger Ship**	**2 oil engines** reduction geared to sc. shafts driving 2 Propellers Total Power: 1,046kW (1,422hp) 14.0kn Daewoo V222TIH 2 x Vee 4 Stroke 12 Cy. 128 x 142 each-523kW (711bhp) Doosan Infracore Co Ltd-South Korea AuxGen: 2 x 115kW a.c, 1 x 450kW a.c
9018933 *VNW5259* -	**TURNER** **BHP Billiton Minerals Pty Ltd (BHP Minerals) (Payroll Cannington) (BHP Minerals Perth)** Teekay Shipping (Australia) Pty Ltd *Port Hedland, WA* *Australia* MMSI: 503419000 Official number: 854079	*365* 109 251	Class: AB	**1992-01 Ocean Shipyards (WA) Pty Ltd — Fremantle WA** Yd No: 174 Loa 32.00 Br ex - Dght 4.550 Lbp 30.63 Br md 10.52 Dpth 5.00 Welded	**(B32A2ST) Tug**	**2 oil engines** with clutches & sr geared to sc. shafts driving 2 Directional propellers Total Power: 2,648kW (3,600hp) 12.0kn Daihatsu 6DLM-28S 2 x 4 Stroke 6 Cy. 280 x 360 each-1324kW (1800bhp) Daihatsu Diesel Manufacturing Co Lt-Japan AuxGen: 1 x 120kW 415V 50Hz a.c, 1 x 80kW 415V 50Hz a.c Fuel: 78.7 (d.f.)
1011173 *2EEP7* -	**TURQUOISE** **Insignia Yachts Ltd** Nigel Burgess Ltd (BURGESS) *London* *United Kingdom* MMSI: 235084441 Official number: 917239	**755** 226 640	Class: LR ✠ **100A1** SS 04/2011 SSC Yacht, mono, G6 ✠ **LMC** **UMS** Cable: 165.0/22.0 U2 (a)	**2011-04 Celikyat Insaa Sanayi ve Ticaret AS — Basiskele** (Hull) Yd No: (52) **2011-04 Proteksan-Turquoise Yachts Inc — Istanbul (Pendik)** Yd No: 52 Loa 55.40 Br ex 9.70 Dght 3.100 Lbp 47.61 Br md 9.30 Dpth 4.79 Welded, 1 dk	**(X11A2YP) Yacht**	**2 oil engines** with clutches, flexible couplings & reverse reduction geared to sc shafts driving 2 FP propellers Total Power: 2,238kW (3,042hp) 16.0kn Caterpillar 3512B 2 x Vee 4 Stroke 12 Cy. 170 x 190 each-1119kW (1521bhp) Caterpillar Inc-USA AuxGen: 2 x 150kW 400V 50Hz a.c
9380221 *XCAD8* -	**TURQUOISE** **CH Offshore Ltd** Chuan Hup Agencies Pte Ltd *Isla del Carmen* *Mexico* Official number: 04013678324	**2,428** 799 2,448	Class: AB	**2008-05 Universal Shipbuilding Corp — Yokohama KN (Keihin Shipyard)** Yd No: 0028 Loa 68.00 Br ex - Dght 6.000 Lbp 61.45 Br md 16.40 Dpth 7.20 Welded, 1 dk	**(B21B20A) Anchor Handling Tug Supply**	**2 oil engines** reduction geared to sc. shafts driving 2 CP propellers Total Power: 9,000kW (12,236hp) Wartsila 9L32 2 x 4 Stroke 9 Cy. 320 x 400 each-4500kW (6118bhp) Wartsila Finland Oy-Finland AuxGen: 2 x 320kW a.c, 2 x 1800kW a.c Thrusters: 2 Thwart. CP thruster (f); 1 Thwart. CP thruster (a) Fuel: 139.0 (r.f.)
7235903 *HO7978* -	**TURQUOISE BAY** **Hess Oil Virgin Islands Corp** HOVENSA LLC SatCom: Inmarsat A 1330424 *Panama* *Panama* MMSI: 354055000 Official number: 0384573G	**1,348** 404 -	Class: AB	**1973-07 Yarrows Ltd — Victoria BC** Yd No: 354 Loa 45.09 Br ex 14.48 Dght 7.317 Lbp - Br md 13.72 Dpth 8.32 Welded, 1 dk	**(B32A2ST) Tug**	**2 oil engines** reverse reduction geared to sc. shafts driving 2 FP propellers Total Power: 5,296kW (7,200hp) EMD (Electro-Motive) 20-645-E7B 2 x Vee 2 Stroke 20 Cy. 230 x 254 each-2648kW (3600bhp) General Motors Corp-USA AuxGen: 2 x 225kW
9618501 *D5AC8* -	**TURQUOISE OCEAN** **Lucretia Shipping SA** Santoku Senpaku Co Ltd SatCom: Inmarsat C 463710697 *Monrovia* *Liberia* MMSI: 636015352 Official number: 15352	**24,020** 12,015 38,529	Class: NK	**2011-08 Minaminippon Shipbuilding Co Ltd — Usuki OT** Yd No: 726 Loa 183.00 (BB) Br ex 29.76 Dght 10.366 Lbp 175.00 Br md 29.50 Dpth 15.00 Welded, 1 dk	**(A21A2BC) Bulk Carrier** Double Hull Grain: 48,142; Bale: 47,183 Compartments: 5 Ho, ER 5 Ha: ER Cranes: 4x30t	**1 oil engine** driving 1 FP propeller Total Power: 7,900kW (10,741hp) 14.5kn MAN-B&W 6S50MC-C 1 x 2 Stroke 6 Cy. 500 x 2000 7900kW (10741bhp) Mitsui Engineering & Shipbuilding CLtd-Japan Fuel: 2000.0

Number / Call sign / Flag	Name / Owner / Manager / Port	Tonnage	Class	Builder / Dimensions	Type / Cargo	Machinery
9404388 3ETB7 -	**TURQUOISE-T** Sarles Overseas Corp Transal Denizcilik Ticaret AS *Panama* Panama MMSI: 370563000 Official number: 3474409	8,638 4,498 13,947 T/cm 23.7	Class: NV (BV)	2008-10 Gisan Gemi Ins. San — Istanbul Yd No: 42 Loa 136.77 (BB) Br ex - Dght 9.500 Lbp 130.00 Br md 20.00 Dpth 10.90 Welded, 1 dk	(A12B2TR) Chemical/Products Tanker Double Hull (13F) Liq: 15,524; Liq (Oil): 15,524 Cargo Heating Coils Compartments: 14 Wing Ta, 2 Wing Slop Ta, ER Manifold: Bow/CM: 67m Ice Capable	**2 oil engines** reduction geared to sc. shafts driving 2 CP propellers Total Power: 5,148kW (7,000hp) 14.0kn Yanmar 6N330-EN 2 x 4 Stroke 6 Cy. 330 x 440 each-2574kW (3500bhp) Yanmar Diesel Engine Co Ltd-Japan AuxGen: 3 x 500kW 60Hz a.c, 1 x 960kW 440V 60Hz a.c Thrusters: 1 Tunnel thruster (f) Fuel: 95.0 (d.f.) 541.0 (r.f.)
9266750 A8FF4 -	**TURRIS** *ex Formosaproduct Alpine -2012* Formosa Alpine Marine Corp Formosa Plastics Marine Corp (FPMC) *Monrovia* *Liberia* MMSI: 636012393 Official number: 12393	39,307 20,742 70,426 T/cm 67.2	Class: BV	2004-11 Universal Shipbuilding Corp — Maizuru KY Yd No: 4998 Loa 228.50 (BB) Br ex - Dght 13.620 Lbp 219.00 Br md 32.20 Dpth 19.60 Welded, 1 dk	(A13A2TW) Crude/Oil Products Tanker Double Hull (13F) Liq: 77,264; Liq (Oil): 77,264 Compartments: 12 Wing Ta, 2 Wing Slop Ta, ER Manifold: Bow/CM: 117.2m	**1 oil engine** driving 1 FP propeller Total Power: 10,010kW (13,610hp) 15.2kn B&W 7S50MC 1 x 2 Stroke 7 Cy. 500 x 1910 10010kW (13610bhp) Hitachi Zosen Corp-Japan AuxGen: 3 x 560kW 440/110V 60Hz a.c Fuel: 270.0 (d.f.) 2312.0 (r.f.)
8036158 - -	**TURRIS** Scientific Research Institute of Hydroapparatus -	931 279 357	Class: (RS)	1982 Zavod "Leninskaya Kuznitsa" — Kiyev Yd No: 13 Converted From: Fishing Vessel-1988 Loa 55.53 Br ex 11.09 Dght 4.740 Lbp 49.82 Br md - Dpth 7.50 Welded, 1 dk	(B12D2FR) Fishery Research Vessel Ice Capable	**1 oil engine** driving 1 FP propeller Total Power: 1,100kW (1,496hp) 12.5kn Kolomna 8CHNRP30/38 1 x 4 Stroke 8 Cy. 300 x 380 1100kW (1496bhp) Kolomenskiy Zavod-Kolomna AuxGen: 3 x 264kW a.c Fuel: 179.0 (d.f.)
7829857 OFPR -	**TURSO** Alfons Hakans Oy AB - *Turku* *Finland* Official number: 10301	294 89 -		1950 Wartsila-Koncernen, Ab Sandvikens Skeppsdocka & MV — Helsinki Loa 36.07 Br ex 9.35 Dght 3.658 Lbp 32.69 Br md - Dpth - Welded	(B32A2ST) Tug Ice Capable	**2 oil engines** driving 2 FP propellers Total Power: 536kW (728hp) 5.0kn Polar M45I 2 x 2 Stroke 5 Cy. 250 x 420 each-268kW (364bhp) Atlas Diesel AB-Sweden
7025865 - -	**TURTLE** *ex Hosei Maru No. 3 -1982* - -	*284* 145 -		1970 Kochiken Zosen — Kochi Yd No: 395 Loa - Br ex 8.11 Dght 3.150 Lbp 42.02 Br md 8.08 Dpth 3.48 Riveted\Welded, 1 dk	(B11B2FV) Fishing Vessel	**1 oil engine** driving 1 FP propeller Total Power: 699kW (950hp) Hanshin 6LU28 1 x 4 Stroke 6 Cy. 280 x 440 699kW (950bhp) Hanshin Nainenki Kogyo-Japan
1008645 ZCPF -	**TUSCAN SUN** Maritime Solutions Ltd International Yacht Collection SatCom: Inmarsat C 431948711 *George Town* *Cayman Islands (British)* MMSI: 319487000 Official number: 739117	493 147 89	Class: LR ✠100A1 SS 07/2011 SSC Yacht, mono G6 **LMC** **UMS** Cable: 275.0/17.0 U2 (a)	2006-07 Navantia SA — San Fernando (Sp) Yd No: 404 Loa 45.00 Br ex 9.00 Dght 2.500 Lbp 39.73 Br md 8.60 Dpth 4.55 Welded, 1 dk	(X11A2YP) Yacht	**2 oil engines** with clutches, flexible couplings & reverse reduction geared to sc. shafts driving 2 FP propellers Total Power: 2,462kW (3,348hp) Caterpillar 3512B 2 x Vee 4 Stroke 12 Cy. 170 x 215 each-1231kW (1674bhp) Caterpillar Inc-USA AuxGen: 2 x 130kW 440V 60Hz a.c Thrusters: 1 Thwart. FP thruster (f)
8307600 DYIE -	**TUSCARORA BELLE** *ex Anangel Dignity -2005 ex Sun Ray -1986* *ex Sanko Antares -1986* Bristol Maritime Corp Roymar Ship Management Inc *Manila* *Philippines* MMSI: 548712000 Official number: MNLA000642	24,643 13,377 44,189 T/cm 48.7	Class: NK (NV)	1984-08 Mitsui Eng. & SB. Co. Ltd. — Tamano Yd No: 1289 Loa 182.81 (BB) Br ex - Dght 11.560 Lbp 174.02 Br md 30.51 Dpth 15.78 Welded, 1 dk	(A21A2BC) Bulk Carrier Grain: 51,025; Bale: 50,025 Compartments: 5 Ho, ER 5 Ha: (16.7 x 15.6)3 (19.2 x 15.6) (18.4 x 15.6)ER Cranes: 4x25t	**1 oil engine** driving 1 FP propeller Total Power: 5,266kW (7,160hp) 14.0kn B&W 6L60MCE 1 x 2 Stroke 6 Cy. 600 x 1944 5266kW (7160bhp) Mitsui Engineering & Shipbuilding CLtd-Japan AuxGen: 3 x 400kW 450V 60Hz a.c Fuel: 167.5 (d.f.) (Heating Coils) 1695.0 (r.f.) 23.5pd
8940969 WDD8758 -	**TUSITALA** The Tusitala Inc - *Grand Bay, AL* *United States of America* MMSI: 367302420 Official number: 1053288	141 42 -		1997 J-Built, Inc. — Bayou La Batre, Al Yd No: 107 L reg 24.14 Br ex - Dght - Lbp - Br md 7.32 Dpth 3.81 Welded, 1 dk	(B11B2FV) Fishing Vessel	**1 oil engine** driving 1 FP propeller
8116453 VKET -	**TUSKER** Svitzer Australia Pty Ltd (Svitzer Australasia) - *Port Adelaide, SA* *Australia* MMSI: 503080000 Official number: 850473	*426* 34 -	Class: AB	1983-04 Tamar Shipbuilding Pty Ltd — Launceston TAS Yd No: 36 Loa 32.31 Br ex 10.90 Dght 4.809 Lbp 32.01 Br md 10.61 Dpth 5.36 Welded, 1 dk	(B32A2ST) Tug	**2 oil engines** with clutches & sr geared to sc. shafts driving 2 Directional propellers Total Power: 2,648kW (3,600hp) 13.0kn Daihatsu 6DSM-28 2 x 4 Stroke 6 Cy. 280 x 340 each-1324kW (1800bhp) Daihatsu Diesel Manufacturing Co Lt-Japan AuxGen: 2 x 125kW
7224708 - -	**TUSSOY** Companhia Nacional de Navegacao 'Arca Verde' -	*142* 45 -		1972 Sigbjorn Iversen — Flekkefjord Yd No: 20 Loa 25.38 Br ex 7.47 Dght - Lbp 23.75 Br md 7.17 Dpth 2.49 Welded, 1 dk	(A36A2PR) Passenger/Ro-Ro Ship (Vehicles) Passengers: 60 Compartments: 1 Ho, ER 1 Ha: (2.9 x 1.9)ER	**1 oil engine** driving 1 CP propeller Total Power: 265kW (360hp) 10.0kn Deutz BF8M716 1 x 4 Stroke 8 Cy. 135 x 160 265kW (360bhp) Kloeckner Humboldt Deutz AG-West Germany AuxGen: 2 x 24kW 220V 50Hz a.c
7607364 LFOE -	**TUSTNA** Fjord1 AS - *Kristiansand* *Norway* MMSI: 257017700	1,117 416 150	Class: (NV)	1977-06 Voldnes Skipsverft AS — Fosnavaag Yd No: 17 Loa 56.32 Br ex - Dght 2.998 Lbp 51.01 Br md 11.63 Dpth 4.20 Welded, 1 dk	(A36A2PR) Passenger/Ro-Ro Ship (Vehicles) Passengers: unberthed: 399 Cars: 45	**1 oil engine** driving 1 FP propeller Total Power: 1,324kW (1,800hp) 14.0kn MWM TBD500-6 1 x 4 Stroke 6 Cy. 360 x 450 1324kW (1800bhp) (made 1977, fitted 1983) Motoren Werke Mannheim AG (MWM)-West Germany AuxGen: 2 x 100kW 220V 50Hz a.c Thrusters: 1 Thwart. FP thruster (f)
6421086 WNGW -	**TUSTUMENA** State of Alaska (Department of Transportation & Public Facilities) (Alaska Marine Highways System) - SatCom: Inmarsat C 430326710 *Kodiak, AK* *United States of America* MMSI: 303267000 Official number: 295172	*4,593* 1,377 - T/cm 27.0	Class: AB	1964-06 Christy Corp — Sturgeon Bay WI Yd No: 418 Lengthened-1969 Loa 89.87 Br ex 18.50 Dght 4.382 Lbp 81.08 Br md 17.99 Dpth 6.56 Welded, 1 dk & S dk	(A36A2PR) Passenger/Ro-Ro Ship (Vehicles) Passengers: unberthed: 118; cabins: 26; berths: 66 Side doors1 (p) 1 (s) Len: 6.63 Wid: 3.33 Swl: 30 Lane-Len: 289 Lane-Wid: 2.40 Lane-clr ht: 4.20 Trailers: 36 Compartments: 1 Ho, ER 1 Ha: (4.4 x 6.7)	**2 oil engines** with clutches, flexible couplings & sr reverse geared to sc. shafts driving 2 FP propellers Total Power: 3,752kW (5,102hp) 13.8kn EMD (Electro-Motive) 12-645-F7B 2 x Vee 2 Stroke 12 Cy. 230 x 254 each-1876kW (2551bhp) (new engine 1995) General Motors Corp.Electro-Motive Div.-La Grange AuxGen: 2 x 560kW 440V 60Hz a.c Thrusters: 1 Thwart. FP thruster (f) Fuel: 255.0 (d.f.) 7.3pd
6874776 - -	**TUTI** *ex Doker -1992 ex BK-605 -1992* OU Okoloog -	*109* - 24	Class: (RS)	1966 "Petrozavod" — Leningrad Yd No: 507 Loa 24.25 Br ex 7.00 Dght 1.460 Lbp - Br md 6.90 Dpth 2.90 Welded, 1 dk	(B32A2ST) Tug	**2 oil engines** gearing integral to driving 2 Voith-Schneider propellers Total Power: 442kW (600hp) 9.7kn Pervomaysk 6CHN25/34 2 x 4 Stroke 6 Cy. 250 x 340 each-221kW (300bhp) Pervomaydizelmash (PDM)-Pervomaysk AuxGen: 1 x 19kW, 1 x 12kW Fuel: 15.0 (d.f.)
9381598 AUKH -	**TUTICORIN** V O Chidambaranar Port Trust - *Chennai* *India* MMSI: 419060500 Official number: 3171	425 128 122	Class: (IR)	2006-08 Tebma Shipyards Ltd — Chengalpattu Yd No: 106 Loa 32.00 Br ex 10.67 Dght 5.100 Lbp 29.80 Br md 10.65 Dpth 4.70 Welded, 1 dk	(B32A2ST) Tug	**2 oil engines** reduction geared to sc. shafts driving 2 Voith-Schneider propellers Total Power: 3,760kW (5,112hp) 12.0kn Wartsila 6L26 2 x 4 Stroke 6 Cy. 260 x 320 each-1880kW (2556bhp) Wartsila Finland Oy-Finland AuxGen: 2 x 100kW 415V 60Hz a.c
8890891 9WCF6 -	**TUTON** *ex Modalwan No. 1 -1998* Fast Meridian Sdn Bhd - *Penang* *Malaysia* MMSI: 533002900 Official number: 327143	*170* 51 -	Class: GL	1995-08 Seri Modalwan Sdn Bhd — Sandakan Yd No: 020 Loa 26.20 Br ex - Dght 2.910 Lbp - Br md 8.00 Dpth 3.80 Welded, 1 dk	(B32A2ST) Tug	**2 oil engines** reduction geared to sc. shafts driving 2 FP propellers Total Power: 1,276kW (1,734hp) 9.0kn Caterpillar 3508TA 2 x Vee 4 Stroke 8 Cy. 170 x 190 each-638kW (867bhp) Caterpillar Inc-USA AuxGen: 2 x 32kW a.c

9263291 *OWLT* -	**TUUGAALIK** *ex* Hopen *-2013* **Qaleralik AS** Royal Greenland AS *Nuuk* *Denmark* MMSI: 331428000	**2,652** 795 -	Class: NV	**2001-12 SC Santierul Naval SA Braila — Braila** (Hull) Yd No: 1037 **2001-12 Myklebust Mek. Verksted AS — Gursken** Yd No: 30 Loa 66.40 Br ex 14.63 Dght - Lbp 58.20 Br md 14.60 Dpth 6.06 Welded, 1 dk	**(B11A2FS) Stern Trawler** Ice Capable	**1 oil engine** Reduction geared to sc. shafts driving 1 CP propeller Total Power: 5,520kW (7,505hp) 14.5kn Wartsila 12V32 1 x Vee 4 Stroke 12 Cy. 320 x 400 5520kW (7505bhp) Wartsila Finland Oy-Finland AuxGen: 1 x 1500kW 440V 60Hz a.c, 1 x 1360kW 440V 60Hz a.c Thrusters: 1 Tunnel thruster (f) Fuel: 800.0
7039660 *OGYI* -	**TUURA** **Oulun Kaupunki** Oulun Kaupungin Satamalaitos *Oulu* *Finland* MMSI: 230343000 Official number: 11384	**364** 110 177	Class: (GL)	**1971 AB Asi-Verken — Amal** Yd No: 94 Loa 35.49 Br ex 9.83 Dght 5.301 Lbp 30.71 Br md 9.78 Dpth 5.62 Welded, 1 dk	**(B32A2ST) Tug** Ice Capable	**3 diesel electric oil engines** driving 4 gen. each 136kW 380V a.c Connecting to 2 elec. motors each (1190kW) driving 1 FP propeller Total Power: 2,646kW (3,597hp) 13.0kn Wartsila 824TS 3 x 4 Stroke 8 Cy. 240 x 310 each-882kW (1199bhp) Oy Wartsila Ab-Finland Fuel: 59.0 (d.f.) 10.5pd
7421966 *3FVN3* -	**TUVAQ** *ex* Tiira *-2002* **Tuvaq International Inc** - *Panama* *Panama* MMSI: 357402000 Official number: 44945PEXT1	**11,290** 4,937 15,955 T/cm 29.5	Class: (NV)	**1977-05 Werft Nobiskrug GmbH — Rendsburg** Yd No: 688 Loa 164.47 Br ex 22.20 Dght 9.502 Lbp 150.02 Br md 21.51 Dpth 12.02 Welded, 1 dk	**(A13A2TW) Crude/Oil Products Tanker** Double Hull Liq: 17,207; Liq (Oil): 17,207 Cargo Heating Coils Compartments: 8 Ta, ER 8 Cargo Pump (s): 8x320m³/hr Manifold: Bow/CM: 84m Ice Capable	**2 oil engines** dr geared to sc. shaft driving 1 CP propeller Total Power: 11,700kW (15,908hp) 14.0kn Wartsila 6L46B 2 x 4 Stroke 6 Cy. 460 x 580 each-5850kW (7954bhp) (new engine 1997) Wartsila Diesel Oy-Finland AuxGen: 2 x 2800kW 380V 50Hz a.c, 2 x 416kW 380V 50Hz a.c Thrusters: 1 Thwart. FP thruster (f)
7050195 *WDC8084* -	**TUXEDNI** **Trident Seafoods Corp** - *Seattle, WA* *United States of America* MMSI: 367081420 Official number: 513354	**205** 61 -		**1968 Pacific Fishermen, Inc. — Seattle, Wa** Yd No: 9 L reg 25.18 Br ex 7.93 Dght - Lbp - Br md - Dpth 3.08 Welded	**(B11B2FV) Fishing Vessel**	**1 oil engine** driving 1 FP propeller Total Power: 360kW (489hp)
6416524 *XCZD* -	**TUXPAN** *launched as* Cosamaloapan *-1964* **Banco Nacional de Fomento Cooperativo SA de CV (BANFOCO)** - *Alvarado* *Mexico*	*121* 58 -		**1964-11 N.V. Scheepsbouwbedrijf v/h Th.J. Fikkers — Foxhol** Yd No: 103 Loa 26.12 Br ex 7.22 Dght - Lbp 22.99 Br md - Dpth 2.95 Welded	**(B11A2FT) Trawler**	**2 oil engines** driving 2 FP propellers Total Power: 672kW (914hp) Caterpillar D343SCAC 2 x 4 Stroke 6 Cy. 137 x 165 each-336kW (457bhp) Caterpillar Tractor Co-USA
6601973 - -	**TUXPAN** *ex* Whiting *-2005* **Government of Mexico (Secretaria de Marina-Armada de Mexico)** - *Veracruz* *Mexico*	*696* 151 206	Class: (AB)	**1963 Marietta Manufacturing Co. — Point Pleasant, WV** Yd No: 903 Loa 49.69 Br ex 10.14 Dght 3.271 Lbp 44.81 Br md 10.06 Dpth 5.19 Welded, 2 dks	**(B31A2SR) Research Survey Vessel** Ice Capable	**2 oil engines** sr geared to sc. shafts driving 2 CP propellers Total Power: 1,206kW (1,640hp) 12.0kn EMD (Electro-Motive) 8-567 2 x Vee 2 Stroke 8 Cy. 216 x 254 each-603kW (820bhp) General Motors Corp-USA AuxGen: 2 x 220kW 225/450V 60Hz a.c Fuel: 140.0 (d.f.)
5371375 - -	**TUZBURNU** **Government of The Republic of Turkey (Turkiye Cumhuriyeti Devlet Demir Yollari - Mersin Liman Isletmesi) (Turkish Republic State Railways - Mersin Harbour Management)** - *Mersin* *Turkey*	*108* 29 -	Class: (TL) (GL)	**1961 D.W. Kremer Sohn — Elmshorn** Yd No: 1079 Loa 26.17 Br ex 7.12 Dght - Lbp 24.49 Br md 6.73 Dpth 2.59 Welded, 1 dk	**(B32A2ST) Tug**	**1 oil engine** reverse reduction geared to sc. shaft driving 1 FP propeller Total Power: 588kW (799hp) Deutz SBV8M536 1 x 4 Stroke 8 Cy. 270 x 360 588kW (799bhp) Kloeckner Humboldt Deutz AG-West Germany AuxGen: 1 x 60kW 220V d.c
7920364 *E5U2644* -	**TUZLA** *ex* Maria P *-2010* *ex* Lady Virginie *-2007* *ex* Vitorino Nemesio *-2004* *ex* Nicolette *-1990* *ex* Nicole *-1987* **Golden Stone Maritime Ltd** Albedo Raspa Boya San Ic ve Dis Ticaret Ltd Sti *Cook Islands* MMSI: 518697000	**2,485** 1,463 3,943	Class: BR (LR) (RS) (NV) (RP) (GL) Classed LR until 8/8/09	**1980-04 Heinrich Brand Schiffswerft GmbH & Co. KG — Oldenburg** Yd No: 211 Loa 86.20 (BB) Br ex 14.03 Dght 6.330 Lbp 75.00 Br md 14.00 Dpth 7.90 Welded, 2 dks	**(A31A2GX) General Cargo Ship** Grain: 5,140; Bale: 5,005 TEU 153 C.Ho 93/20' C.Dk 60/20' Compartments: 1 Ho, ER 1 Ha: (50.2 x 10.2)ER Cranes: 1x25t	**1 oil engine** with flexible couplings & sr reverse geared to sc. shaft driving 1 FP propeller Total Power: 1,765kW (2,400hp) 13.5kn MaK 6MU453AK 1 x 4 Stroke 6 Cy. 320 x 450 1765kW (2400bhp) Krupp MaK Maschinenbau GmbH-Kiel AuxGen: 1 x 235kW 400V 50Hz a.c, 2 x 68kW 400V 50Hz a.c Thrusters: 1 Thwart. FP thruster (f) Fuel: 311.0 (r.f.)
8615394 *TCAK7* -	**TUZLA** **Government of The Republic of Turkey (Adalet Bakanligi Imrali Cezaevi Mudurlugu) (Ministry of Justice - Prison Directorate of Imrali)** - *Istanbul* *Turkey* MMSI: 271010131 Official number: 5854	*307* 77 100	Class: TL	**1989-01 Turkiye Gemi Sanayii A.S. — Alaybey, Izmir** Yd No: 78 Loa 49.15 Br ex - Dght - Lbp 47.37 Br md 8.97 Dpth 2.53 Welded, 1 dk	**(A37B2PS) Passenger Ship**	**1 oil engine** driving 1 FP propeller Total Power: 468kW (636hp) Sulzer 6AL20/24 1 x 4 Stroke 6 Cy. 200 x 240 468kW (636bhp) Turkiye Gemi Sanayii AS-Turkey
8942230 - -	**TUZLA** **Kimmerikon Commercial Firm (Kommercheskaya Firma 'Kimmerikon')** -	*145* 56 158	Class: (RS)	**1976 Sudoremontnyy Zavod "Krasnaya Kuznitsa" — Arkhangelsk** Yd No: 4 Loa 35.75 Br ex 7.40 Dght 1.710 Lbp 33.50 Br md - Dpth 2.40 Welded, 1 dk	**(A31C2GD) Deck Cargo Ship** Ice Capable	**1 oil engine** geared to sc. shaft driving 1 FP propeller Total Power: 165kW (224hp) 7.8kn Daldizel 6CHNSP18/22 1 x 4 Stroke 6 Cy. 180 x 220 165kW (224bhp) Daldizel-Khabarovsk AuxGen: 1 x 13kW, 1 x 12kW Fuel: 5.0 (d.f.)
8932601 - -	**TUZLA** **State Enterprise Kerch Sea Fishing Port** - *Kerch* *Ukraine* Official number: 760604	*199* 78 285	Class: (RS)	**1978 Svetlovskiy Sudoremontnyy Zavod — Svetlyy** Yd No: 13 Loa 29.17 Br ex 8.15 Dght 2.930 Lbp 28.50 Br md - Dpth 3.60 Welded, 1 dk	**(B34G2SE) Pollution Control Vessel** Liq: 239; Liq (Oil): 239 Compartments: 7 Ta Ice Capable	**1 oil engine** geared to sc. shaft driving 1 FP propeller Total Power: 165kW (224hp) 7.5kn Daldizel 6CHNSP18/22 1 x 4 Stroke 6 Cy. 180 x 220 165kW (224bhp) Daldizel-Khabarovsk AuxGen: 1 x 50kW a.c, 1 x 25kW a.c Fuel: 15.0 (d.f.)
1009699 *ZCXD5* -	**TV** *ex* Madsummer *-2011* *launched as* Bermuda *-2008* **Panga Ltd** Waters Edge Consulting Ltd *Bloody Bay* *Cayman Islands (British)* MMSI: 319840000 Official number: 740642	**2,334** 700 314	Class: LR ✠ **100A1** SS 10/2013 SSC Yacht (P), mono, G6 ✠ **LMC** **UMS** Eq.Ltr: 0; Cable: 445.0/34.0 U2 (a)	**2008-10 Kroeger Werft GmbH & Co. KG — Schacht-Audorf** Yd No: 13650 Loa 78.50 (BB) Br ex 14.00 Dght 3.800 Lbp 63.06 Br md 13.50 Dpth 7.00 Welded, 7 dks	**(X11A2YP) Yacht** Passengers: cabins: 9; berths: 12	**2 oil engines** with clutches, flexible couplings & sr reverse geared to sc. shafts driving 2 FP propellers Total Power: 4,000kW (5,438hp) 17.5kn Caterpillar 3516B-HD 2 x Vee 4 Stroke 16 Cy. 170 x 215 each-2000kW (2719bhp) Caterpillar Inc-USA AuxGen: 2 x 298kW 400V 50Hz a.c, 1 x 456kW 400V 50Hz a.c Thrusters: 1 Thwart. CP thruster (f); 1 Water jet (a)
8897796 *XVNO* -	**TV-102** **Salvage Enterprise II (Xi Nghiep Truc Vot Cuu Ho No II)** - *Da Nang* *Vietnam*	**311** 93 -	Class: VR	**1966 in the United States of America** Loa 38.50 Br ex 10.22 Dght 2.000 Lbp 36.60 Br md 10.00 Dpth 3.20 Welded, 1 dk	**(B34R2QY) Supply Tender**	**2 oil engines** reduction geared to sc. shafts driving 2 FP propellers Total Power: 442kW (600hp) 7.5kn Barnaultransmash 3D12A 2 x Vee 4 Stroke 12 Cy. 150 x 180 each-221kW (300bhp) (new engine 1974) Barnaultransmash-Barnaul AuxGen: 1 x 50kW a.c

IMO / Call sign	Name / Owner	Tonnage	Class	Builder / Dimensions	Type	Machinery
9344033 *A8KM7* -	**TVERSKOY BRIDGE** **Rural Shipping Ltd** SCF Novoship JSC (Novorossiysk Shipping Co) SatCom: Inmarsat C 463700594 *Monrovia* *Liberia* MMSI: 636013087 Official number: 13087	**27,725** 13,762 46,564 T/cm 52.3	Class: LR ✠ **100A1** SS 08/2012 Double Hull oil tanker ESP **ShipRight** (SDA, FDA, CM) SPM LI *IWS EP ✠ **LMC** **UMS IGS** Eq.Ltr: M†; Cable: 639.8/73.0 U3 (a)	**2007-08 Admiralteyskiy Sudostroitelnyy Zavod — Sankt-Peterburg** Yd No: 02746 Loa 182.50 (BB) Br ex 32.34 Dght 12.180 Lbp 174.80 Br md 32.20 Dpth 17.50 Welded, 1 dk	**(A13B2TP) Products Tanker** Double Hull (13F) Liq: 53,146; Liq (Oil): 51,910 Compartments: 10 Wing Ta, 2 Wing Slop Ta, ER 10 Cargo Pump (s): 10x550m^3/hr Manifold: Bow/CM: 90.9m	**1 oil engine** driving 1 FP propeller Total Power: 8,310kW (11,298hp) 15.0kn MAN-B&W 6S50MC-C 1 x 2 Stroke 6 Cy. 500 x 2000 8310kW (11298bhp) AO Bryanskiy MashinostroitelnyyZavod (BMZ)-Bryansk AuxGen: 2 x 1280kW 450V 60Hz a.c, 1 x 680kW 450V 60Hz a.c Boilers: e (ex.g.) 11.7kgf/cm^2 (11.5bar), WTAuxB (o.f.) 11.2kgf/cm^2 (11.0bar) Fuel: 126.0 (d.f.) 1428.0 (r.f.)
9177791 *AVGX* -	**TVISHA** *ex* Accurate *-2010* **Essar Shipping Ltd** - *Mumbai* *India* MMSI: 419000157 Official number: 3732	**7,918** 4,438 12,974	Class: IR (GL) (NK)	**1999-07 Honda Zosen — Saiki** Yd No: 1017 Loa 128.04 Br ex - Dght 8.460 Lbp 118.00 Br md 21.20 Dpth 11.30 Welded, 1 dk	**(A21A2BC) Bulk Carrier** Double Hull Grain: 15,645; Bale: 15,440 Compartments: 3 Ho, ER 3 Ha: (18.9 x 12.6)2 (23.1 x 15.0)ER Cranes: 2x30t	**1 oil engine** driving 1 FP propeller Total Power: 4,193kW (5,701hp) 14.0kn B&W 6S35MC 1 x 2 Stroke 6 Cy. 350 x 1400 4193kW (5701bhp) Makita Corp-Japan
9603506 *D5BF4* -	**TW BEIJING** **MV TW Beijing Shipping Co Ltd** Shanghai Run Yuan Shipping Management Co Ltd *Monrovia* *Liberia* MMSI: 636015511 Official number: 15511	**51,265** 31,203 93,243 T/cm 80.9	Class: GL (AB)	**2012-04 Jiangsu Newyangzi Shipbuilding Co Ltd — Jingjiang JS** Yd No: YZJ2006-929 Loa 229.20 (BB) Br ex 38.04 Dght 14.900 Lbp 222.00 Br md 38.00 Dpth 20.70 Welded, 1 dk	**(A21A2BC) Bulk Carrier** Grain: 110,330 Compartments: 7 Ho, ER 7 Ha: ER	**1 oil engine** driving 1 FP propeller Total Power: 13,650kW (18,559hp) 14.0kn MAN-B&W 6S60MC-C 1 x 2 Stroke 6 Cy. 600 x 2400 13650kW (18559bhp) STX Engine Co Ltd-South Korea AuxGen: 3 x 730kW a.c Fuel: 229.0 (d.f.) 3598.0 (r.f.)
9603520 *D5BF5* -	**TW HAMBURG** **mv TW Hamburg Shipping Co Ltd** Shanghai Run Yuan Shipping Management Co Ltd SatCom: Inmarsat C 4637116686 *Monrovia* *Liberia* MMSI: 636015512 Official number: 15512	**51,265** 31,203 93,229 T/cm 80.9	Class: LR (GL) (AB) **100A1** SS 01/2012 TOC contemplated	**2012-01 Jiangsu Newyangzi Shipbuilding Co Ltd — Jingjiang JS** Yd No: YZJ2006-941 Loa 229.20 (BB) Br ex 38.40 Dght 14.900 Lbp 222.00 Br md 38.00 Dpth 20.70 Welded, 1 dk	**(A21A2BC) Bulk Carrier** Grain: 110,330 Compartments: 7 Ho, ER 7 Ha: ER	**1 oil engine** driving 1 FP propeller Total Power: 13,560kW (18,436hp) 14.0kn MAN-B&W 6S60MC-C 1 x 2 Stroke 6 Cy. 600 x 2400 13560kW (18436bhp) Doosan Engine Co Ltd-South Korea AuxGen: 3 x 730kW a.c
9603532 *D5BF6* -	**TW JIANGSU** **mv TW Jiangsu Shipping Co Ltd** Shanghai Run Yuan Shipping Management Co Ltd *Monrovia* *Liberia* MMSI: 636015513 Official number: 15513	**51,265** 31,203 93,225 T/cm 80.9	Class: LR (GL) (AB) **100A1** SS 01/2012 TOC contemplated	**2012-01 Jiangsu Newyangzi Shipbuilding Co Ltd — Jingjiang JS** Yd No: YZJ2006-942 Loa 229.20 (BB) Br ex 38.04 Dght 14.900 Lbp 222.00 Br md 38.00 Dpth 20.70 Welded, 1 dk	**(A21A2BC) Bulk Carrier** Grain: 110,330 Compartments: 7 Ho, ER 7 Ha: ER	**1 oil engine** driving 1 FP propeller Total Power: 13,560kW (18,436hp) 14.0kn MAN-B&W 6S60MC-C 1 x 2 Stroke 6 Cy. 600 x 2400 13560kW (18436bhp) STX Engine Co Ltd-South Korea AuxGen: 3 x 730kW a.c Fuel: 230.0 (d.f.) 3590.0 (r.f.)
9594121 *D5BF3* -	**TW MANILA** **MV TW Manila Shipping Co Ltd** Shanghai Run Yuan Shipping Management Co Ltd *Monrovia* *Liberia* MMSI: 636015510 Official number: 15510	**51,265** 31,203 93,250 T/cm 80.9	Class: LR (GL) (AB) **100A1** SS 04/2012 TOC contemplated	**2012-04 Jiangsu Newyangzi Shipbuilding Co Ltd — Jingjiang JS** Yd No: YZJ2006-919 Loa 229.20 (BB) Br ex 38.04 Dght 14.900 Lbp 222.00 Br md 38.00 Dpth 20.70 Welded, 1 dk	**(A21A2BC) Bulk Carrier** Grain: 110,330 Compartments: 7 Ho, ER 7 Ha: ER	**1 oil engine** driving 1 FP propeller Total Power: 13,560kW (18,436hp) 14.0kn MAN-B&W 6S60MC-C 1 x 2 Stroke 6 Cy. 600 x 2400 13560kW (18436bhp) STX Engine Co Ltd-South Korea AuxGen: 3 x 730kW a.c Fuel: 250.0 (d.f.) 3868.0 (r.f.)
9572939 *YDA4717* -	**TW MAPLE** **PT Poet Indonesia** - *Jakarta* *Indonesia*	**249** 74 139	Class: AB	**2010-01 Bengbu Shenzhou Machinery Co Ltd — Bengbu AH** (Hull) Yd No: (1320) **2010-01 Pacific Ocean Engineering & Trading Pte Ltd (POET) — Singapore** Yd No: 1320 Loa 29.50 Br ex - Dght 3.500 Lbp 27.00 Br md 9.00 Dpth 4.16 Welded, 1 dk	**(B32A2ST) Tug**	**2 oil engines** reduction geared to sc. shafts driving 2 FP propellers Total Power: 2,984kW (4,058hp) Cummins KTA-50-M2 2 x Vee 4 Stroke 16 Cy. 159 x 159 each-1492kW (2029bhp) Cummins Engine Co Inc-USA AuxGen: 2 x 139kW a.c
8024193 *YEDJ* -	**TWADIKA** *ex* Dasa Enam *-1992* *ex* Magdalena Mare *-1988* *ex* Global Express *-1987* *ex* Magdalena Mare *-1986* *ex* Boni *-1986* *ex* Mount Santa *-1985* **PT Pelayaran Mana Lagi** - *Jakarta* *Indonesia* MMSI: 525015211 Official number: 4432	**4,472** 2,682 6,974	Class: KI (BV) (NK)	**1981-04 Higaki Zosen K.K. — Imabari** Yd No: 256 Loa 107.15 Br ex 17.63 Dght 6.871 Lbp 100.41 Br md 17.60 Dpth 8.70 Welded, 1 dk	**(A31A2GX) General Cargo Ship** Grain: 9,629; Bale: 8,719 Compartments: 2 Ho, ER 2 Ha: 2 (25.9 x 10.5)ER Cranes: 2x20t; Derricks: 2x20t	**1 oil engine** driving 1 FP propeller Total Power: 3,310kW (4,500hp) 12.8kn Mitsubishi 6UET45/80D 1 x 2 Stroke 6 Cy. 450 x 800 3310kW (4500bhp) Kobe Hatsudoki KK-Japan AuxGen: 2 x 280kW 110V a.c
8808915 - WB008	**TWAFIKA** *ex* Asuncion *-2002* *ex* Awserd II *-2000* *ex* SIP 4 *-2000* **Twafika Fishing Enterprises Pty Ltd** Namsov Fishing Enterprises Pty Ltd *Walvis Bay* *Namibia* Official number: 2001WB008	**486** 146 330	Class: BV	**1990-06 IMC — Tonnay-Charente** Yd No: 320 Loa 39.71 Br ex 9.63 Dght 3.801 Lbp 34.42 Br md 9.52 Dpth 4.02 Welded, 1 dk	**(B11A2FS) Stern Trawler** Ins: 295	**1 oil engine** with clutches, flexible couplings & sr reverse geared to sc. shaft driving 1 FP propeller Total Power: 706kW (960hp) Deutz SBA16M816 1 x Vee 4 Stroke 16 Cy. 142 x 160 706kW (960bhp) Kloeckner Humboldt Deutz AG-West Germany
9003287 *PICD* -	**TWAITE** **Chemgas Shipping BV** SatCom: Inmarsat C 424492210 *Rotterdam* *Netherlands* MMSI: 244922000 Official number: 6055	**1,997** 599 1,720 T/cm 11.6	Class: BV	**1991-04 B.V. Scheepswerf De Kaap — Meppel** Yd No: 218 Loa 105.56 (BB) Br ex 11.98 Dght 3.040 Lbp 100.00 Br md 11.92 Dpth 6.05 Welded, 1 dk	**(A11B2TG) LPG Tanker** Double Hull Liq (Gas): 2,560 7 x Gas Tank (s); 6 independent (stl) cyl horizontal, 1 independent (stl) dcy horizontal 7 Cargo Pump (s): 7x60m^3/hr Manifold: Bow/CM: 59.2m	**2 oil engines** with flexible couplings & sr reverse geared to sc. shaft driving 2 FP propellers Total Power: 1,046kW (1,422hp) 11.0kn Stork DRO218K 2 x 4 Stroke 8 Cy. 210 x 300 each-523kW (711bhp) Stork Wartsila Diesel BV-Netherlands AuxGen: 3 x 235kW 220/380V 50Hz a.c Thrusters: 1 Thwart. FP thruster (f) Fuel: 156.0 (d.f.)
8605387 - -	**TWEE GEBROEDERS** **Prins & Dingemanse Mosselkweek BV** -	*134* - -		**1986-04 Scheepswerf Vooruit B.V. — Zaandam** Yd No: 374 Loa 31.05 Br ex - Dght 0.501 Lbp - Br md 8.01 Dpth 2.11 Welded, 1 dk	**(B11B2FV) Fishing Vessel**	**2 oil engines** with flexible couplings & sr reverse geared to sc. shafts driving 2 FP propellers Total Power: 404kW (550hp) Cummins NT-855-M 2 x 4 Stroke 6 Cy. 140 x 152 each-202kW (275bhp) Cummins Engine Co Inc-USA
8224341 - -	**TWEE GEBROEDERS** *ex* Dirk Senior *-1990* - -	**323** 97 -		**1983-07 Scheepswerf Haak B.V. — Zaandam** Yd No: 962 Loa 39.55 Br ex 8.21 Dght 3.390 Lbp - Br md - Dpth 4.53 Welded, 1 dk	**(B11B2FV) Fishing Vessel**	**1 oil engine** driving 1 FP propeller Total Power: 1,350kW (1,835hp) Kromhout 9FHD240 1 x 4 Stroke 9 Cy. 240 x 260 1350kW (1835bhp) Stork Werkspoor Diesel BV-Netherlands
5371416 *9YBU* -	**TWEED** **Coloured Fin Ltd (CFL)** *Port of Spain* *Trinidad & Tobago* Official number: 315788	**122** 76 299		**1959 Furness Eng. (Trinidad) Ltd. — Port of Spain** (Assembled by) **1959 Rowhedge Ironworks Co. Ltd. — Rowhedge** (Parts for assembly by) Yd No: 880 L reg 34.29 Br ex 6.86 Dght - Lbp - Br md - Dpth 2.74 Welded, 1 dk	**(A14A2LO) Water Tanker**	**1 oil engine** reduction geared to sc. shaft driving 1 FP propeller Total Power: 132kW (179hp) G.M. (Detroit Diesel) 6V-71 1 x Vee 2 Stroke 6 Cy. 108 x 127 132kW (179bhp) (, fitted 1990) Detroit Diesel Corporation-Detroit, Mi
8932144 - -	**TWEIZEGTT 902** - - *Nouadhibou* *Mauritania* Official number: 74888	**317** 95 -	Class: (RI)	**1994-11 Yantai Fishing Vessel Shipyard — Yantai SD** Loa - Br ex - Dght 3.053 Lbp 38.60 Br md 7.80 Dpth 3.90 Welded, 1 dk	**(B11B2FV) Fishing Vessel**	**1 oil engine** geared to sc. shaft driving 1 FP propeller Total Power: 662kW (900hp) Chinese Std. Type 8300 1 x 4 Stroke 8 Cy. 300 x 380 662kW (900bhp) Zibo Diesel Engine Factory-China AuxGen: 2 x 90kW 220/400V 50Hz a.c
8894598 - -	**TWEIZEGTT 903** **Etablissement Abdellani Ould Noueigued** - *Nouadhibou* *Mauritania*	**317** 95 -	Class: (RI)	**1995 Yantai Fishing Vessel Shipyard — Yantai SD** Loa - Br ex - Dght 3.053 Lbp 38.60 Br md 7.80 Dpth 3.90 Welded, 1 dk	**(B11B2FV) Fishing Vessel**	**1 oil engine** geared to sc. shaft driving 1 FP propeller Total Power: 662kW (900hp) Chinese Std. Type 8300 1 x 4 Stroke 8 Cy. 300 x 380 662kW (900bhp) Zibo Diesel Engine Factory-China AuxGen: 2 x 90kW 220/440V 50Hz a.c

No. / Call sign / Fishing No.	Name / Owner / Port	Tonnage	Class	Built / Dimensions	Type	Machinery
8924604 - -	**TWEIZEGTT 908** **Etablissement Abdellani Ould Noueigued** - *Nouadhibou* *Mauritania*	**317** 95 -	Class: (RI)	**1995 Yantai Fishing Vessel Shipyard — Yantai SD** Loa - Br ex - Dght 3.053 Lbp 38.68 Br md 7.80 Dpth 3.90 Welded, 1 dk	**(B11B2FV) Fishing Vessel**	**1 oil engine** geared to sc. shaft driving 1 FP propeller Total Power: 662kW (900hp) Chinese Std. Type 8300 1 x 4 Stroke 8 Cy. 300 x 380 662kW (900bhp) Zibo Diesel Engine Factory-China AuxGen: 2 x 90kW 220/440V 50Hz a.c
8924616 - -	**TWEIZEGTT 909** **Etablissement Abdellani Ould Noueigued** - *Nouadhibou* *Mauritania*	**317** 95 -	Class: (RI)	**1995 Yantai Fishing Vessel Shipyard — Yantai SD** Loa - Br ex - Dght 3.053 Lbp 38.68 Br md 7.80 Dpth 3.90 Welded, 1 dk	**(B11B2FV) Fishing Vessel**	**1 oil engine** geared to sc. shaft driving 1 FP propeller Total Power: 662kW (900hp) Chinese Std. Type 8300 1 x 4 Stroke 8 Cy. 300 x 380 662kW (900bhp) Zibo Diesel Engine Factory-China AuxGen: 2 x 90kW 220/440V 50Hz a.c
9255220 *IZHY* 00MV00345M	**TWENTY** **Matteo, Cosimo & Vincenzo Asaro SnC** - SatCom: Inmarsat C 424798965 *Palermo* *Italy*	**580** 230	Class: RI	**2002-03 Cant. Nav. Mario Morini S.p.A. — Ancona** Yd No: 257 Loa 45.30 Br ex - Dght - Lbp 36.25 Br md 9.70 Dpth 4.20 Welded, 1 dk	**(B11B2FV) Fishing Vessel**	**1 oil engine** reduction geared to sc. shaft driving 1 FP propeller Total Power: 1,140kW (1,550hp) MaK 6M20 1 x 4 Stroke 6 Cy. 200 x 300 1140kW (1550bhp) Caterpillar Motoren GmbH & Co. KG-Germany
8649448 *IFZG2* 00CA00611M	**TWENTY FOUR** - - *Cagliari* *Italy*	**239** - -		**2008-01 Cant. Nav. Coop. "Il Carpentiere" — Mazara del Vallo** Loa 33.55 Br ex - Dght 3.160 Lbp 25.50 Br md 7.55 Dpth 3.73 Welded, 1 dk	**(B11A2FS) Stern Trawler**	**1 oil engine** driving 1 Propeller Total Power: 838kW (1,139hp)
8649412 *IQLU* 00CA00603M	**TWENTY ONE** - - *Cagliari* *Italy*	**239** - -		**2005-01 Cant. Nav. Coop. "Il Carpentiere" — Mazara del Vallo** Loa 33.55 Br ex - Dght 3.160 Lbp 25.50 Br md 7.55 Dpth 3.73 Welded, 1 dk	**(B11A2FS) Stern Trawler**	**1 oil engine** driving 1 Propeller Total Power: 736kW (1,001hp)
8649436 *IFZF2* 00CA00610M	**TWENTY THREE** - - *Cagliari* *Italy*	**239** - -		**2008-01 Cant. Nav. Coop. "Il Carpentiere" — Mazara del Vallo** Loa 33.55 Br ex - Dght 3.160 Lbp 25.50 Br md 7.55 Dpth 3.73 Welded, 1 dk	**(B11A2FS) Stern Trawler**	**1 oil engine** driving 1 Propeller Total Power: 838kW (1,139hp)
8649424 *IQNU* 00CA00605M	**TWENTY TWO** - - *Cagliari* *Italy*	**239** - -		**2006-01 Cant. Nav. Coop. "Il Carpentiere" — Mazara del Vallo** Loa 33.55 Br ex - Dght 3.160 Lbp 25.50 Br md 7.55 Dpth 3.73 Welded, 1 dk	**(B11A2FS) Stern Trawler**	**1 oil engine** driving 1 Propeller Total Power: 736kW (1,001hp)
8971126 *V3TL* -	**TWICA II** **Sezai Turkes Feyzi Akkaya Insaat AS (STFA Construction Co)** - *Belize City* *Belize* Official number: 220610139	**429** 406 -		**1981-05 IHC Gusto BV — Ridderkerk** Yd No: C01142 Loa 59.60 Br ex 9.55 Dght 2.510 Lbp 57.89 Br md 9.02 Dpth 3.34 Welded, 1 dk	**(B34A2SH) Hopper, Motor**	**2 oil engines** driving 2 FP propellers Total Power: 426kW (580hp) 12.0kn Scania 2 x 4 Stroke each-213kW (290bhp) Saab Scania AB-Sweden
7120392 *DBJZ* -	**TWIELENFLETH** **Government of The Federal Republic of Germany (Wasser- und Schifffahrtsamt Hamburg)** - *Hamburg* *Germany*	*125* 77 175		**1971 Muetzelfeldtwerft GmbH — Cuxhaven** Yd No: 184 Loa 29.85 Br ex 7.60 Dght 2.001 Lbp 27.01 Br md 7.31 Dpth 2.60 Welded, 1 dk	**(B32A2ST) Tug**	**2 oil engines** driving 2 CP propellers Total Power: 426kW (580hp) 10.0kn Deutz SBF12M716 2 x Vee 4 Stroke 12 Cy. 135 x 160 each-213kW (290bhp) Kloeckner Humboldt Deutz AG-West Germany AuxGen: 2 x 24kW 400V 50Hz a.c Fuel: 20.5 (d.f.)
1011733 *2GGS4* -	**TWILIGHT** **Oyster Marine Ltd** - *Douglas* *Isle of Man (British)* Official number: 743970	**199** 59 -	Class: LR ✠ **100A1** SS 05/2013 SSC Yacht, mono, G6 Cable: 220.0/16.0 U2 (a)	**2013-05 R.M.K. Tersanesi — Tuzla** Yd No: 87 Loa 38.10 Br ex 8.94 Dght 4.030 Lbp 34.10 Br md 8.36 Dpth 3.74 Welded, 1 dk	**(X11A2YP) Yacht**	**1 oil engine** with clutches, flexible couplings & dr reverse geared to sc. shaft driving 1 CP propeller Total Power: 448kW (609hp) 10.0kn Caterpillar C18 1 x 4 Stroke 6 Cy. 145 x 183 448kW (609bhp) Caterpillar Inc-USA AuxGen: 2 x 50kW 380V 50Hz a.c Thrusters: 1 Thwart. FP thruster (f); 1 Thwart. FP thruster (a) Fuel: 15.0 (d.f.)
9131931 *5NLK8* -	**TWILIGHT EHCO** *ex* Zakher Princess *-2009* *ex* Laser III *-2006* **Consolidated Discounts Ltd** Ehco Ventures Ltd *Lagos* *Nigeria* Official number: SR 1422	**408** 122 394	Class: (LR) (GL) (AB) Classed LR until 31/1/11	**1995-08 Sasacom Sdn Bhd — Kuching** Yd No: 106 Loa 41.80 Br ex 10.10 Dght 2.750 Lbp 38.45 Br md 9.60 Dpth 4.23 Welded, 1 dk	**(B34J2SD) Crew Boat**	**2 oil engines** reverse reduction geared to sc. shafts driving 2 FP propellers Total Power: 2,238kW (3,042hp) 15.5kn Paxman VEGA12.OCM 2 x Vee 4 Stroke 12 Cy. 160 x 190 each-1119kW (1521bhp) Paxman Diesels Ltd.-Colchester AuxGen: 3 x 99kW 415V 50Hz a.c Thrusters: 1 Thwart. FP thruster (f)
7010353 *MHDS4* PZ 137	**TWILIGHT III** *ex* Hanny *-1986* *ex* Elisabeth *-1982* *ex* Deo Volente II *-1974* **W Stevenson & Sons** - SatCom: Inmarsat C 423200578 *Penzance* *United Kingdom* MMSI: 232005780 Official number: A21621	**141** 42 -		**1970-03 Holland Launch N.V. — Zaandam** Yd No: 439 Loa 29.24 Br ex - Dght - Lbp 26.55 Br md 6.81 Dpth 3.23 Welded, 1 dk	**(B11B2FV) Fishing Vessel**	**1 oil engine** driving 1 FP propeller Total Power: 519kW (706hp) Stork 1 x 519kW (706bhp) (new engine 1977) Stork Werkspoor Diesel BV-Netherlands
9087740 *DSQQ9* -	**TWIN DRAGON** *ex* Sejahte *-2010* *ex* Sejahtera *-2010* *ex* Harmony *-2002* **Ssangyong Shipping Co Ltd** - *Jeju* *South Korea* MMSI: 441674000 Official number: JJR-101813	**35,889** 23,321 69,073 T/cm 64.4	Class: KR (NK)	**1994-04 Imabari Shipbuilding Co Ltd — Marugame KG (Marugame Shipyard)** Yd No: 1220 Loa 224.98 (BB) Br ex - Dght 13.295 Lbp 215.00 Br md 32.20 Dpth 18.30 Welded, 1 dk	**(A21A2BC) Bulk Carrier** Grain: 81,770 Compartments: 7 Ho, ER 7 Ha: (13.0 x 12.8)4 (17.9 x 14.4) (16.3 x 14.4) (14.7 x 14.4)ER	**1 oil engine** driving 1 FP propeller Total Power: 10,246kW (13,930hp) 14.5kn Sulzer 6RTA62 1 x 2 Stroke 6 Cy. 620 x 2150 10246kW (13930bhp) Mitsubishi Heavy Industries Ltd-Japan Fuel: 2300.0 (r.f.)
6903230 *HO2483* -	**TWIN DRILL** *ex* Jaramac 57 *-1984* *ex* Duplus *-1980* **Twinstar Funding Corp** - *Panama* *Panama* Official number: 08536PEXT3	*750* 328 453	Class: (AB) (BV)	**1968 Boele's Scheepswerven en Machinefabriek N.V. — Bolnes** Yd No: 1033 Loa 41.00 (BB) Br ex 17.18 Dght 5.227 Lbp 40.01 Br md 17.06 Dpth 10.90 Welded, 2 dks	**(B34T2QR) Work/Repair Vessel** Cranes: 1x75t,1x20t	**2 diesel electric oil engines** driving 2 gen. each 880kW 440V a.c Connecting to 2 elec. motors driving 2 CP propellers Total Power: 1,704kW (2,316hp) 9.0kn G.M. (Detroit Diesel) 16V-149-TI 2 x Vee 2 Stroke 16 Cy. 146 x 146 each-852kW (1158bhp) (made 1972, fitted 1976) General Motors Detroit DieselAllison Divn-USA AuxGen: 1 x 120kW 440V 60Hz a.c Thrusters: 2 Directional thruster (f); 2 Tunnel thruster (a) Fuel: 160.0 (d.f.)
8731617 *T2CJ3* -	**TWIN POWER 3** *ex* Yinson Power 3 *-2014* *ex* Sun Hop No. 6 *-2008* **Twin Power Marine Sdn Bhd** - *Funafuti* *Tuvalu* MMSI: 572670000 Official number: 30249314	**138** 41 -		**1993-01 Zhuhai Shipyard — Zhuhai GD** Loa 25.55 Br ex - Dght - Lbp - Br md 6.82 Dpth 3.12 Welded, 1 dk	**(B32A2ST) Tug**	**1 oil engine** geared to sc. shaft driving 1 Propeller Total Power: 638kW (867hp) Caterpillar 3508 1 x Vee 4 Stroke 8 Cy. 170 x 190 638kW (867bhp) Caterpillar Inc-USA
9651228 - -	**TWIN SISTER 305** **PT Muji Rahayu Shipyard** Central Marine Pte Ltd *Samarinda* *Indonesia*	**311** 94 -	Class: KI (Class contemplated)	**2011-12 PT Muji Rahayu Shipyard — Tenggarong** Yd No: 11130 Loa 34.74 Br ex 9.20 Dght 3.300 Lbp 32.53 Br md 9.00 Dpth 4.00 Welded, 1 dk	**(B32A2ST) Tug**	**2 oil engines** reduction geared to sc. shafts driving 2 Propellers Total Power: 1,492kW (2,028hp) Caterpillar C32 ACERT 2 x Vee 4 Stroke 12 Cy. 145 x 162 each-746kW (1014bhp) Caterpillar Inc-USA

IMO / Call sign / Flag	Name / Owner / Manager / Port	Tonnage	Class	Built	Type	Machinery
9561162 *PNWZ* -	**TWIN SISTER 306** - **Cindara Pratama Lines PT** - *Samarinda* *Indonesia* MMSI: 525010074 Official number: 2010 IIK NO. 5275/L	**418** 126 -	Class: KI	**2010-02 PT Muji Rahayu Shipyard — Tenggarong** Yd No: 08102 Loa 37.42 Br ex - Dght 3.600 Lbp 34.02 Br md 10.10 Dpth 4.50 Welded, 1 dk	**(B21A2OS) Platform Supply Ship**	**2 oil engines** reduction geared to sc. shafts driving 2 Propellers Total Power: 2,238kW (3,042hp) Cummins KTA-38-M2 2 x Vee 4 Stroke 12 Cy. 159 x 159 each-1119kW (1521bhp) Cummins Engine Co Inc-USA
9688300 - -	**TWIN SISTER 307** - **PT Marina Rindang Perkasa** PT Muji Rahayu Shipyard *Samarinda* *Indonesia*	**320** 95 -	Class: KI (Class contemplated)	**2013-03 PT Muji Rahayu Shipyard — Tenggarong** Yd No: 12131 Loa 37.00 Br ex 9.20 Dght 3.300 Lbp 32.50 Br md 9.00 Dpth 4.00 Welded, 1 dk	**(B21A2OS) Platform Supply Ship**	**2 oil engines** reduction geared to sc. shafts driving 2 Propellers Total Power: 1,640kW (2,230hp) Caterpillar C32 2 x Vee 4 Stroke 12 Cy. 145 x 162 each-820kW (1115bhp) Caterpillar Inc-USA
9561150 *POLL* -	**TWIN SISTER 405** - **PT Muji Rahayu Shipyard** Central Marine Pte Ltd *Samarinda* *Indonesia*	**600** - -	Class: BV (Class contemplated)	**2012-02 PT Muji Rahayu Shipyard — Tenggarong** Yd No: 08100 Loa 45.00 Br ex 10.80 Dght 3.600 Lbp 40.92 Br md 10.50 Dpth 4.50 Welded, 1 dk	**(B21A2OS) Platform Supply Ship**	**2 oil engines** reduction geared to sc. shafts driving 2 Propellers Total Power: 3,432kW (4,666hp) Cummins QSK60-M 2 x Vee 4 Stroke 16 Cy. 159 x 190 each-1716kW (2333bhp) Cummins Engine Co Inc-USA
9183453 - -	**TWIN STAR NO. 1** *ex Topniche 7 -2010 ex Ocean Silver 9 -2003* **Hyunjin KS Corp** - *Busan* *South Korea* Official number: BSR-101159	**250** 75 195	Class: (KR) (BV) (AB)	**1997-11 Jiangdong Shipyard — Wuhu AH** Yd No: XT-04 Loa 29.00 Br ex - Dght 3.950 Lbp 26.50 Br md 9.00 Dpth 4.25 Welded, 1 dk	**(B32A2ST) Tug**	**2 oil engines** reduction geared to sc. shafts driving 2 FP propellers Total Power: 1,766kW (2,402hp) Yanmar M220-EN 2 x 4 Stroke 6 Cy. 220 x 300 each-883kW (1201bhp) Yanmar Diesel Engine Co Ltd-Japan AuxGen: 2 x 70kW a.c
9512367 *V7YG2* -	**TWINKLE ISLAND** - **Paulownia Shipping Inc** Funada Kaiun KK *Majuro* *Marshall Islands* MMSI: 538004652 Official number: 4652	**43,013** 27,239 82,265 T/cm 70.2	Class: NK	**2012-04 Tsuneishi Shipbuilding Co Ltd — Fukuyama HS** Yd No: 1476 Loa 228.99 (BB) Br ex - Dght 14.429 Lbp 222.00 Br md 32.26 Dpth 20.05 Welded, 1 dk	**(A21A2BC) Bulk Carrier** Grain: 97,381 Compartments: 7 Ho, ER 7 Ha: ER	**1 oil engine** driving 1 FP propeller Total Power: 9,710kW (13,202hp) 14.5kn MAN-B&W 6S60MC-C 1 x 2 Stroke 6 Cy. 600 x 2400 9710kW (13202bhp) Mitsui Engineering & Shipbuilding CLtd-Japan Fuel: 3180.0
9633082 *3FMH3* -	**TWINKLE SALUTE** - **Nextream Shipholdings SA** MC Shipping Ltd *Panama* *Panama* MMSI: 371477000 Official number: 4449413	**50,625** 31,470 95,750	Class: NK	**2013-01 Imabari Shipbuilding Co Ltd — Marugame KG (Marugame Shipyard)** Yd No: 1586 Loa 235.00 (BB) Br ex - Dght 14.468 Lbp 227.00 Br md 38.00 Dpth 19.90 Welded, 1 dk	**(A21A2BC) Bulk Carrier** Grain: 109,476 Compartments: 7 Ho, ER 7 Ha: ER	**1 oil engine** driving 1 FP propeller Total Power: 12,950kW (17,607hp) 15.0kn MAN-B&W 6S60MC-C 1 x 2 Stroke 6 Cy. 600 x 2400 12950kW (17607bhp) Hitachi Zosen Corp-Japan AuxGen: 3 x 532kW a.c Fuel: 3900.0
9363780 *V7CO4* -	**TWINKLE STAR** *ex Twinkle Express -2013* **Express Shipping LLC** Product Shipping & Trading SA *Majuro* *Marshall Islands* MMSI: 538005294 Official number: 5294	**27,969** 12,193 45,750 T/cm 49.9	Class: BV (NK)	**2006-03 Minaminippon Shipbuilding Co Ltd — Usuki OT** Yd No: 689 Loa 179.80 (BB) Br ex 32.49 Dght 12.116 Lbp 171.00 Br md 32.20 Dpth 18.80 Welded, 1 dk	**(A13B2TP) Products Tanker** Double Hull (13F) Liq: 54,773; Liq (Oil): 54,773 Cargo Heating Coils Compartments: 12 Wing Ta, 2 Wing Slop Ta, ER 4 Cargo Pump (s): 4x950m³/hr Manifold: Bow/CM: 91.9m	**1 oil engine** driving 1 FP propeller Total Power: 8,580kW (11,665hp) 14.5kn MAN-B&W 6S50MC 1 x 2 Stroke 6 Cy. 500 x 1910 8580kW (11665bhp) Mitsui Engineering & Shipbuilding CLtd-Japan AuxGen: 3 x 560kW 450V 60Hz a.c Fuel: 162.9 (d.f.) 2442.1 (r.f.)
8891132 - -	**TWINKLING STAR** - **The Star Ferry Co Ltd** - *Hong Kong* *Hong Kong* Official number: 317299	*164* 40 -		**1964 Hong Kong & Whampoa Dock Co Ltd — Hong Kong** Yd No: 1035 Loa 33.78 Br ex 9.22 Dght 2.430 Lbp - Br md 8.57 Dpth 2.61 Welded, 1 dk	**(A37B2PS) Passenger Ship** Passengers: unberthed: 555	**1 oil engine** driving 1 FP propeller Total Power: 352kW (479hp) Crossley HGN6 1 x 2 Stroke 6 Cy. 267 x 343 352kW (479bhp) Crossley Bros. Ltd.-Manchester
9473767 *3FCW3* -	**TWINLUCK SW** - **Fortunate Maritime SA** Shih Wei Navigation Co Ltd *Panama* *Panama* MMSI: 373558000 Official number: 4398612	**19,817** 10,395 31,877 T/cm 45.1	Class: NK	**2012-06 The Hakodate Dock Co Ltd — Hakodate HK** Yd No: 847 Loa 175.53 Br ex - Dght 9.640 Lbp 167.00 Br md 29.40 Dpth 13.70 Welded, 1 dk	**(A21A2BC) Bulk Carrier** Double Hull Grain: 40,493; Bale: 39,270 Compartments: 5 Ho, ER 5 Ha: ER Cranes: 4x30t	**1 oil engine** driving 1 FP propeller Total Power: 6,840kW (9,300hp) 14.4kn Mitsubishi 6UEC45LSE 1 x 2 Stroke 6 Cy. 450 x 1840 6840kW (9300bhp) Kobe Hatsudoki KK-Japan Fuel: 1380.0
8855621 - -	**TWINS** - **Ricardo N Inc** - *Houston, TX* *United States of America* Official number: 656074	*117* 94 -		**1983 Marine Mart, Inc. — Port Isabel, Tx** Yd No: 227 Loa - Br ex - Dght - Lbp 21.34 Br md 6.10 Dpth 3.66 Welded, 1 dk	**(B11B2FV) Fishing Vessel**	**1 oil engine** driving 1 FP propeller Total Power: 405kW (551hp) Caterpillar 3408TA 1 x Vee 4 Stroke 8 Cy. 137 x 152 405kW (551bhp) Caterpillar Tractor Co-USA
8616245 *DHQI* -	**TWISTER** *ex Fairplay XI -2013 ex Hillsider -2000* *ex Lady Theresa -1994* **LUHRS Schifffahrt oHG** - *Hamburg* *Germany* MMSI: 211592170 Official number: 23579	**173** 51 104	Class: LR (PR) ✠ **100A1** SS 03/2013 tug coastal service in European waters restricted to 150nm and excluding North Atlantic and ice regions ✠ **LMC** **UMS** Eq.Ltr: D; Cable: U2 (a)	**1988-01 Cochrane Shipbuilders Ltd. — Selby** Yd No: 136 Loa 24.70 Br ex 7.73 Dght 3.185 Lbp 22.08 Br md 7.30 Dpth 3.80 Welded, 1 dk	**(B32A2ST) Tug**	**2 oil engines** with clutches, flexible couplings & dr reverse geared to sc. shafts driving 2 FP propellers Total Power: 1,398kW (1,900hp) 10.5kn Ruston 6AP230M 2 x 4 Stroke 6 Cy. 230 x 273 each-699kW (950bhp) Ruston Diesels Ltd.-Newton-le-Willows AuxGen: 2 x 80kW 415V 50Hz a.c Fuel: 33.5 (d.f.)
9507594 *PHTW* -	**TWISTER** - **Chemgas Shipping BV** - SatCom: Inmarsat C 424588110 *Rotterdam* *Netherlands* MMSI: 245881000 Official number: 51824	**2,410** 723 2,161 T/cm 13.0	Class: BV	**2010-12 Groningen Shipyard BV — Waterhuizen** Yd No: 112 Loa 99.95 Br ex 14.00 Dght 3.380 Lbp 96.59 Br md 13.94 Dpth 6.20 Welded, 1 dk	**(A11B2TG) LPG Tanker** Double Bottom Entire Compartment Length Liq (Gas): 2,700 2 x Gas Tank (s); 2 independent (stl) cyl horizontal 2 Cargo Pump (s): 2x135m³/hr Manifold: Bow/CM: 49.9m	**2 oil engines** reduction geared to sc. shafts driving 2 FP propellers Total Power: 2,000kW (2,720hp) 12.5kn Mitsubishi S6U-MPTK 2 x 4 Stroke 6 Cy. 240 x 260 each-1000kW (1360bhp) Mitsubishi Heavy Industries Ltd-Japan AuxGen: 2 x 208kW 60Hz a.c, 1 x 406kW 450V 60Hz a.c Thrusters: 1 Tunnel thruster (f) Fuel: 97.0 (d.f.)
1010363 *2DKS5* -	**TWIZZLE** - **Twizzle Marine LP** Dohle Private Clients Ltd *Castletown* *Isle of Man (British)* MMSI: 235079813 Official number: 736437	**496** 148	Class: LR ✠ **100A1** SS 09/2010 SSC Yacht, mono, G6 **LMC** **UMS** Cable: 330.0/24.0 U2 (a)	**2010-09 Royal Huisman Shipyard B.V. — Vollenhove** Yd No: 386 Loa 57.49 Br ex 11.58 Dght 3.970 Lbp 48.96 Br md 11.58 Dpth 5.44 Welded, 1 dk	**(X11A2YS) Yacht (Sailing)** Hull Material: Aluminium Alloy	**1 oil engine** with clutches, flexible couplings & sr reverse geared to sc. shafts driving 1 CP propeller Total Power: 970kW (1,319hp) 17.0kn Caterpillar C32 1 x Vee 4 Stroke 12 Cy. 145 x 162 970kW (1319bhp) Caterpillar Inc-USA AuxGen: 3 x 155kW 400V 50Hz a.c Thrusters: 1 Thwart. FP thruster (f); 1 Thwart. FP thruster (a)
8310633 *VHQ9184* -	**TWO** *ex Fantasea Monarch -2008* *ex South Molle Capricorn -2008* *ex Telford Capricorn -1986* **Ansett Australia Ltd** - *Hamilton Island, Qld* *Australia* Official number: 851447	*294* 116 60		**1983-11 North Queensland Engineers & Agents Pty Ltd — Cairns QLD** Yd No: 111 Loa 29.21 Br ex 11.51 Dght 1.750 Lbp 25.51 Br md 11.21 Dpth 2.85 Welded, 1 dk	**(A37B2PS) Passenger Ship** Hull Material: Aluminium Alloy Passengers: unberthed: 300	**2 oil engines** with clutches & sr geared to sc. shafts driving 2 FP propellers Total Power: 1,766kW (2,402hp) G.M. (Detroit Diesel) 16V-92-TA 2 x Vee 2 Stroke 16 Cy. 123 x 127 each-883kW (1201bhp) General Motors Detroit DieselAllison Divn-USA
8977003 *ZR4512*	**TWO BOYS** *ex Matsuei Maru -2003* **Two Boys Fishing CC** KZN Fishing Pty Ltd *Richards Bay* *South Africa* Official number: 20644	**149** 65 -		**1980-03 Kobayashi Zosensho — Osakikamijima** Loa 32.00 Br ex - Dght - Lbp - Br md 5.63 Dpth 2.31 Welded, 1 dk	**(B11B2FV) Fishing Vessel**	**1 oil engine** driving 1 Propeller Yanmar 1 x 4 Stroke Yanmar Diesel Engine Co Ltd-Japan
9069736 *WBC3018* -	**TWO BROTHERS** - **Vaud J Inc** - *Cape May, NJ* *United States of America* Official number: 677160	**103** 82 -		**1984-01 Deep Sea Boat Builders, Inc. — Bayou La Batre, Al** L reg 22.25 Br ex - Dght - Lbp - Br md 6.19 Dpth 3.35 Welded, 1 dk	**(B11B2FV) Fishing Vessel**	**1 oil engine** driving 1 Propeller

IMO / Call sign	Name / Former names / Owner / Flag	Tonnage	Class	Built	Type	Machinery
8947802 *HP9951* -	**TWO BROTHERS** *ex* Capt. Munoz *-2010* *ex* Ansell G *-2001* - - *Panama* *Panama* Official number: 42756PEXT	**123** 37 -		**1992 Master Boat Builders, Inc. — Coden, Al** L reg 25.90 Br ex - Dght - Lbp - Br md 7.30 Dpth 3.80 Welded, 1 dk	**(B11B2FV) Fishing Vessel**	**1 oil engine** driving 1 FP propeller Total Power: 268kW (364hp) 10.0kn Caterpillar 3408T 1 x Vee 4 Stroke 8 Cy. 137 x 152 268kW (364bhp) Caterpillar Inc-USA
8744731 *J8Y3931* -	**TWO KAY** *ex* Rasha *-2001* *ex* Bo Veerle *-2001* **Como Yachting Sarl** - *Kingstown* *St Vincent & The Grenadines* MMSI: 376677000 Official number: 40401	**208** 62 -	Class: RI	**2001 C.R.N. Cant. Nav. Ancona S.r.l. — Ancona** Yd No: 112/01 Loa 34.00 Br ex - Dght - Lbp - Br md 7.10 Dpth 3.50 Welded, 1 dk	**(X11A2YP) Yacht**	**2 oil engines** reduction geared to sc. shafts driving 2 Propellers Total Power: 4,080kW (5,548hp) M.T.U. 12V4000M90 2 x Vee 4 Stroke 12 Cy. 165 x 190 each-2040kW (2774bhp) MTU Friedrichshafen GmbH-Friedrichshafen
8030518 - -	**TWO MEGS** *ex* Jamie Leigh *-2013* *ex* Surf King *-2001* *ex* Desco Mariner *-2001* **Sustainable Seafood LLC** - *Boston, MA* *United States of America* Official number: 626766	*138* 124 -		**1980 Desco Marine — Saint Augustine, Fl** Yd No: 303-F Loa - Br ex - Dght 3.231 Lbp 22.86 Br md 6.71 Dpth 3.76 Bonded, 1 dk	**(B11A2FS) Stern Trawler** Hull Material: Reinforced Plastic	**1 oil engine** driving 1 FP propeller Total Power: 331kW (450hp)
9334571 *5BHK3* -	**TWO MILLION WAYS** *ex* Eagle Hope *-2011* **Nagilo Shipping Co Ltd** Reederei Nord Ltd SatCom: Inmarsat C 420929410 *Limassol* *Cyprus* MMSI: 209294000 Official number: 9334571	**40,865** 22,274 73,965 T/cm 67.0	Class: NV (AB)	**2008-02 Onomichi Dockyard Co Ltd — Onomichi HS** Yd No: 528 Loa 228.49 (BB) Br ex 32.24 Dght 14.368 Lbp 219.95 Br md 32.20 Dpth 20.65 Welded, 1 dk	**(A13A2TW) Crude/Oil Products Tanker** Double Hull (13F) Liq: 82,138; Liq (Oil): 82,138 Cargo Heating Coils Compartments: 12 Wing Ta, 2 Wing Slop Ta, ER 3 Cargo Pump (s): 3x2000m³/hr Manifold: Bow/CM: 115.5m Ice Capable	**1 oil engine** driving 1 FP propeller Total Power: 13,560kW (18,436hp) 15.7kn MAN-B&W 6S60MC-C 1 x 2 Stroke 6 Cy. 600 x 2400 13560kW (18436bhp) Mitsui Engineering & Shipbuilding CLtd-Japan AuxGen: 3 x 680kW a.c Fuel: 159.9 (d.f.) 2569.9 (r.f.)
7908469 *HPNQ* -	**TWO RIVERS** *ex* Eliana *-2003* *ex* Sea Comet *-2003* *ex* Seaboard Comet *-2000* *ex* Haymo *-1999* *ex* Hakata Maru *-1998* **Penn-Edison Commercial Inc** Awan Shipping Services *Panama* *Panama* MMSI: 352298000 Official number: 31453PEXT	**4,800** 2,293 4,652	Class: (NK)	**1979-10 Fukuoka Shipbuilding Co Ltd — Fukuoka FO** Yd No: 1072 Loa 120.00 (BB) Br ex 17.66 Dght 7.069 Lbp 110.01 Br md 17.61 Dpth 8.41 Welded, 1 dk	**(A31A2GX) General Cargo Ship** Grain: 8,247; Bale: 7,829 Compartments: 6 Ho, ER 6 Ha: (7.7 x 7.9)5 (7.7 x 13.1)ER Cranes: 1x20t	**1 oil engine** driving 1 FP propeller Total Power: 6,620kW (9,001hp) 18.5kn Mitsubishi 9UET52/90D 1 x 2 Stroke 9 Cy. 520 x 900 6620kW (9001bhp) Kobe Hatsudoki KK-Japan AuxGen: 2 x 400kW 445V 60Hz a.c Fuel: 113.5 (d.f.) 271.5 (r.f.) 27.0pd
7223986 *WYZ4266* -	**TWO SONS** *ex* Lady Jennifer *-1990* *ex* S Sue *-1990* **J R Corp** - *Boston, MA* *United States of America* Official number: 533063	*135* 92 -		**1971 Marine Builders, Inc. — Mobile, Al** L reg 23.47 Br ex 6.84 Dght - Lbp - Br md - Dpth 3.38 Welded	**(B11B2FV) Fishing Vessel**	**1 oil engine** driving 1 FP propeller Total Power: 257kW (349hp)
6708288 - -	**TWOFOLD BAY** - **Northern Trawling Co Ltd** - *Wellington* *New Zealand* Official number: 317895	*155* 116 71		**1966 Stannard Bros Slipway & Engineering Pty Ltd — Sydney NSW** Yd No: 750 Loa 22.86 Br ex 6.18 Dght 2.617 Lbp 20.12 Br md 5.94 Dpth 2.97 Welded, 1 dk	**(B11A2FT) Trawler**	**1 oil engine** driving 1 FP propeller Total Power: 386kW (525hp) 10.0kn G.M. (Detroit Diesel) 12V-71-N 1 x Vee 2 Stroke 12 Cy. 108 x 127 386kW (525bhp) General Motors Corp-USA
6820244 *6NGA* -	**TWOSTAR** *ex* Noah No. 3 *-2009* *ex* Sam Young No. 303 *-1994* *ex* Ensanda No. 5 *-1994* *ex* Atlanta No. 5 *-1988* *ex* Sam Young No. 303 *-1988* *ex* Il Woo No. 3 *-1983* *ex* Kyowa Maru No. 5 *-1975* **Seokyung Corp** - *Busan* *South Korea* MMSI: 440779000 Official number: BS02-A2171	*370* 128 -	Class: (KR)	**1968 Narasaki Zosen KK — Muroran HK** Yd No: 636 Loa 50.35 Br ex 8.72 Dght 3.685 Lbp 43.69 Br md 8.69 Dpth 3.89 Welded, 2 dks	**(B11A2FS) Stern Trawler** Ins: 358	**1 oil engine** driving 1 FP propeller Total Power: 1,214kW (1,651hp) 11.0kn Fuji 6S37C 1 x 4 Stroke 6 Cy. 370 x 550 1214kW (1651bhp) Fuji Diesel Co Ltd-Japan AuxGen: 2 x 128kW 225V a.c
9257747 - -	**TXIKIYA** - -	**260** 78 145		**2001-04 Astilleros Ria de Aviles SL — Nieva** Yd No: 67 Loa 31.30 Br ex - Dght 2.870 Lbp - Br md 7.60 Dpth 3.37 Welded, 1 dk	**(B11A2FT) Trawler**	**1 oil engine** geared to sc. shaft driving 1 FP propeller Total Power: 299kW (407hp) GUASCOR F480TA-SP 1 x Vee 4 Stroke 16 Cy. 152 x 165 299kW (407bhp) Gutierrez Ascunce Corp (GUASCOR)-Spain
8700618 *EHIP* -	**TXINBITO** *ex* Ereso *-1975* **Servicios Generales Maritimos SA** - *Las Palmas* *Spain (CSR)* MMSI: 224193000 Official number: 5/1999	**130** 64 42		**1986-04 Ast. y Varaderos de Tarragona S.A. — Tarragona** Yd No: 256 Loa 25.56 Br ex 7.07 Dght 1.975 Lbp 21.62 Br md 7.01 Dpth 2.87 Welded, 1 dk	**(A37B2PS) Passenger Ship** Passengers: unberthed: 245	**2 oil engines** sr geared to sc. shaft driving 2 FP propellers Total Power: 1,000kW (1,360hp) GUASCOR E318TAO-SP 2 x Vee 4 Stroke 12 Cy. 150 x 150 each-500kW (680bhp) Gutierrez Ascunce Corp (GUASCOR)-Spain
9280237 *ECCF* 3-SS-11-03	**TXINGUDI** - **Miguel & Francisco Amunarriz Darceles & Lorenzo, Jose Antonio & Josepa Mikel Aguirre Oronoz** - *Fuenterrabia* *Spain* Official number: 3-1/2003	**160** 48 -		**2003-04 Astilleros Ria de Aviles SL — Nieva** (Hull) Yd No: (174) **2003-04 Astilleros La Parrilla S.A. — San Esteban de Pravia** Yd No: 174 Loa - Br ex - Dght - Lbp - Br md - Dpth - Welded	**(B11B2FV) Fishing Vessel**	**1 oil engine** geared to sc. shaft driving 1 Propeller Total Power: 348kW (473hp) Caterpillar 3512TA 1 x Vee 4 Stroke 12 Cy. 170 x 190 348kW (473bhp) Caterpillar Inc-USA
7043960 *EFWC* -	**TXIRRINE** *ex* Alcaravan *-1987* *launched as* Alano *-1971* **Atuneros Vascos SA** - SatCom: Inmarsat A 1351544 *Bilbao* *Spain* Official number: 2584	**855** 264 640	Class: BV	**1971 Maritima de Axpe S.A. — Bilbao** Yd No: 52 Loa 47.50 Br ex - Dght 4.700 Lbp 42.70 Br md 10.41 Dpth 5.21 Welded, 1 dk	**(B11A2FT) Trawler**	**1 oil engine** driving 1 FP propeller Total Power: 1,214kW (1,651hp) 11.5kn MWM RHS345SU 1 x 4 Stroke 6 Cy. 360 x 450 1214kW (1651bhp) Naval Stork Werkspoor SA-Spain Fuel: 213.0 (d.f.)
8719310 *3EYS* -	**TXOPITUNA** *ex* Intertuna Dos *-2010* **Txopituna SL** - *Panama* *Panama* MMSI: 353770000 Official number: 4186410	**2,058** 668 1,905	Class: BV	**1990-03 Hijos de J. Barreras S.A. — Vigo** Yd No: 1528 Loa 77.30 (BB) Br ex - Dght 6.600 Lbp 66.45 Br md 13.60 Dpth 9.05 Welded	**(B11B2FV) Fishing Vessel** Ins: 1,880	**1 oil engine** with flexible couplings & sr geared to sc. shaft driving 1 FP propeller Total Power: 3,236kW (4,400hp) 12.5kn Deutz RBV12M350 1 x Vee 4 Stroke 12 Cy. 400 x 500 3236kW (4400bhp) Hijos de J Barreras SA-Spain Thrusters: 1 Thwart. FP thruster (f); 1 Thwart. FP thruster (a)
7805966 *H8EE* -	**TXOPITUNA DOS** *ex* Intertuna Uno *-2014* *ex* Maratun *-1990* *launched as* Pescamar Uno *-1980* **Txopituna SL** - *Panama* *Panama* MMSI: 353490000 Official number: 45637PEXT	**2,167** 650 1,499	Class: BV	**1980-03 Hijos de J. Barreras S.A. — Vigo** Yd No: 1457 Loa 77.32 Br ex 13.62 Dght 6.690 Lbp 68.43 Br md 13.61 Dpth 9.07 Welded, 2 dks	**(B11A2FT) Trawler**	**1 oil engine** geared to sc. shaft driving 1 FP propeller Total Power: 3,236kW (4,400hp) 15.1kn Deutz SBV12M540 1 x Vee 4 Stroke 12 Cy. 370 x 400 3236kW (4400bhp) Hijos de J Barreras SA-Spain AuxGen: 4 x 332kW 380V a.c Fuel: 584.0 (d.f.)
7622510 *S7JS* -	**TXORI** *ex* La Couronnee II *-2000* **Inpesca Fishing Ltd** Compania Internacional de Pesca y Derivados SA (INPESCA) SatCom: Inmarsat Mini-M 763935030 *Victoria* *Seychelles* MMSI: 664272000 Official number: 50149	**315** 94 -	Class: BV	**1976-04 Chantier J Chauvet — Paimboeuf** Converted From: Pilot Vessel-1976 Loa 34.96 Br ex - Dght 2.952 Lbp 30.51 Br md 7.82 Dpth 3.81 Welded, 2 dks	**(B12D2FU) Fishery Support Vessel**	**1 oil engine** geared to sc. shaft driving 1 CP propeller Total Power: 588kW (799hp) 12.5kn Deutz SBA8M528 1 x 4 Stroke 8 Cy. 220 x 280 588kW (799bhp) Kloeckner Humboldt Deutz AG-West Germany

IMO / Call sign	Name / Owner	Tonnage / Class	Build	Type	Machinery
9286724 *ECEQ* BI-2-1-03	**TXORI ARGI** **Compania Internacional de Pesca y Derivados SA (INPESCA)** - *Bermeo* *Spain* MMSI: 224103000 Official number: 3-1/2003	**4,134** Class: BV 1,240 3,250	**2004-03 Astilleros de Murueta S.A. — Gernika-Lumo** Yd No: 240 Loa 106.50 Br ex Dght 7.200 Lbp 93.50 Br md 16.00 Dpth 10.40 Welded, 1 dk	**(B11B2FV) Fishing Vessel**	**1 oil engine** geared to sc. shaft driving 1 CP propeller Total Power: 4,303kW (5,850hp) Wartsila 6L46B 1 x 4 Stroke 6 Cy. 460 x 580 4303kW (5850bhp) Wartsila Diesel S.A.-Bermeo
8208531 *S7SZ* -	**TXORI AUNDI** **Inpesca Fishing Ltd** Compania Internacional de Pesca y Derivados SA (INPESCA) SatCom: Inmarsat C 466426810 *Victoria* *Seychelles*	**2,020** Class: BV 735 1,826	**1984-02 Maritima de Axpe S.A. — Bilbao** Yd No: 159 Loa 78.01 (BB) Br ex - Dght 5.901 Lbp 67.01 Br md 13.61 Dpth 8.77 Welded, 2 dks	**(B11B2FV) Fishing Vessel**	**1 oil engine** with flexible couplings & sr gearedto sc. shaft driving 1 FP propeller Total Power: 3,199kW (4,349hp) 15.6kn MaK 6MU551AK 1 x 4 Stroke 6 Cy. 450 x 550 3199kW (4349bhp) Krupp MaK Maschinenbau GmbH-Kiel Thrusters: 1 Directional thruster (f)
9324019 *S7TV* -	**TXORI BAT** **Inpesca Fishing Ltd** Compania Internacional de Pesca y Derivados SA (INPESCA) *Victoria* *Seychelles*	**421** Class: BV 126 -	**2005-01 Astilleros Ria de Aviles SL — Nieva** Yd No: 108 L reg 35.13 Br ex - Dght 3.700 Lbp - Br md - Dpth 6.30 Welded, 1 dk	**(B11B2FV) Fishing Vessel**	**1 oil engine** geared to sc. shaft driving 1 CP propeller Total Power: 1,030kW (1,400hp) 10.0kn GUASCOR F480TA-SP 1 x Vee 4 Stroke 16 Cy. 152 x 165 1030kW (1400bhp) Gutierrez Ascunce Corp (GUASCOR)-Spain
9006033 *V3U09* -	**TXORI BERRI** **Inpesca Fishing Belize Ltd** Compania Internacional de Pesca y Derivados SA (INPESCA) *Belize City* *Belize* MMSI: 312590000 Official number: 011321838	**2,400** Class: BV 720 2,100	**1991-02 S.A. Balenciaga — Zumaya** Yd No: 338 Loa 81.00 Br ex - Dght 6.601 Lbp 69.00 Br md 14.40 Dpth 9.40 Welded	**(B11B2FV) Fishing Vessel**	**1 oil engine** with clutches, flexible couplings & sr geared to sc. shaft driving 1 FP propeller Total Power: 3,310kW (4,500hp) 12.0kn MaK 6M552AK 1 x 4 Stroke 6 Cy. 450 x 520 3310kW (4500bhp) Krupp MaK Maschinenbau GmbH-Kiel Thrusters: 1 Tunnel thruster (f); 1 Tunnel thruster (a)
9319789 *ECEE* 3-LU-32-03	**TXORI BI** *ex* Pino Montero Dos *-2013* **Compania Internacional de Pesca y Derivados SA (INPESCA)** - *Bermeo* *Spain* MMSI: 224218000 Official number: 3-2/2003	**392** Class: BV 118 216	**2004-03 Astilleros Armon Burela SA — Burela** Yd No: 244 Loa 37.80 (BB) Br ex - Dght 3.910 Lbp 31.00 Br md 8.40 Dpth 3.85 Welded, 1 dk	**(B11B2FV) Fishing Vessel** Ins: 228	**1 oil engine** with clutches, flexible couplings & sr reverse geared to sc. shaft driving 1 FP propeller Total Power: 441kW (600hp) A.B.C. 6DZC 1 x 4 Stroke 6 Cy. 256 x 310 441kW (600bhp) Anglo Belgian Corp NV (ABC)-Belgium
9383156 *ECNP* BI-2-1-07	**TXORI GORRI** **Compania Internacional de Pesca y Derivados SA (INPESCA)** - *Bermeo* *Spain* MMSI: 225375000 Official number: 3-1/2007	**2,950** Class: BV 881 2,151	**2007-11 Astilleros de Murueta S.A. — Gernika-Lumo** Yd No: 213 Loa 95.80 Br ex - Dght 6.800 Lbp 82.30 Br md 14.70 Dpth 9.30 Welded, 1 dk	**(B11B2FV) Fishing Vessel** Ins: 2,250	**1 oil engine** reduction geared to sc. shaft driving 1 CP propeller Total Power: 4,784kW (6,504hp) 18.0kn Wartsila 6L46B 1 x 4 Stroke 6 Cy. 460 x 580 4784kW (6504bhp) Wartsila Diesel S.A.-Bermeo
9196682 *EAXE* BI-2-4-99	**TXORI TOKI** **Compania Internacional de Pesca y Derivados SA (INPESCA)** - *Bermeo* *Spain* MMSI: 224934000 Official number: 3-4/1999	**4,134** Class: BV 1,240 3,250	**2000-03 Astilleros de Murueta S.A. — Gernika-Lumo** Yd No: 204 Loa 106.50 Br ex - Dght 7.700 Lbp 91.50 Br md 16.00 Dpth 10.40 Welded, 1 dk	**(B11B2FV) Fishing Vessel**	**1 oil engine** geared to sc. shaft driving 1 CP propeller Total Power: 5,852kW (7,956hp) Wartsila 6L46B 1 x 4 Stroke 6 Cy. 460 x 580 5852kW (7956bhp) Wartsila Diesel S.A.-Bermeo
7410670 *V3UX9* -	**TXORI URDIN** **Inpesca Fishing Belize Ltd** Compania Internacional de Pesca y Derivados SA (INPESCA) *Belize City* *Belize* MMSI: 312620000 Official number: 011321839	**1,286** Class: BV 480 1,300	**1976-02 Maritima de Axpe S.A. — Bilbao** Yd No: 81 Loa 63.33 Br ex - Dght 5.450 Lbp 56.11 Br md 11.81 Dpth 8.01 Welded, 2 dks	**(B11B2FV) Fishing Vessel**	**1 oil engine** driving 1 FP propeller Total Power: 2,207kW (3,001hp) 12.0kn MWM TBD501-8 1 x 4 Stroke 8 Cy. 360 x 450 2207kW (3001bhp) Fabrica de San Carlos SA-Spain AuxGen: 3 x 1000kW 380V a.c Fuel: 413.5 (d.f.)
9071428 *DSON5* -	**TY ANGEL** *ex* Sun Angel *-2005* **Taiyoung Shipping Co Ltd** *Jeju* *South Korea* MMSI: 440961000 Official number: JJR-051637	**1,528** Class: KR 556 2,183	**1993-12 Kwangyang Shipbuilding & Engineering Co Ltd — Janghang** Yd No: 92 Loa 79.44 Br ex - Dght 5.012 Lbp 73.50 Br md 12.00 Dpth 6.20 Welded, 1 dk	**(A31A2GX) General Cargo Ship** Grain: 1,698; Bale: 1,303	**1 oil engine** reduction geared to sc. shaft driving 1 FP propeller Total Power: 1,261kW (1,714hp) 13.2kn Alpha 6L28/32 1 x 4 Stroke 6 Cy. 280 x 320 1261kW (1714bhp) Ssangyong Heavy Industries Co Ltd-South Korea AuxGen: 2 x 160kW 450V a.c
9403920 *DSPF4* -	**TY EVER** **Taiyoung Shipping Co Ltd** *Jeju* *South Korea* MMSI: 440904000 Official number: JJR-079440	**4,105** Class: KR 1,997 6,260	**2007-05 Nanjing Shenghua Shipbuilding Co Ltd — Nanjing JS** Yd No: 409 Loa 99.30 (BB) Br ex - Dght 6.700 Lbp 92.00 Br md 17.00 Dpth 8.50 Welded, 1 dk	**(A31A2GX) General Cargo Ship** Grain: 6,965; Bale: 6,595 Compartments: 2 Ho, ER 2 Ha: ER 2 (25.2 x 12.4)	**1 oil engine** driving 1 Propeller Total Power: 2,647kW (3,599hp) 12.1kn Hanshin LH41LA 1 x 4 Stroke 6 Cy. 410 x 800 2647kW (3599bhp) The Hanshin Diesel Works Ltd-Japan AuxGen: 2 x 320kW 450V a.c
9472050 *DSQJ2* -	**TY GLORIA** **Taiyoung Shipping Co Ltd** Taiyoung Maritime Co Ltd SatCom: Inmarsat C 444059610 *Jeju* *South Korea* MMSI: 441596000 Official number: JJR-092166	**4,105** Class: KR 1,997 6,225	**2009-05 Jiangsu Wuxi Shipyard Co Ltd — Wuxi JS** Yd No: WX907 Loa 99.30 (BB) Br ex - Dght 6.713 Lbp 92.01 Br md 17.00 Dpth 8.50 Welded, 1 dk	**(A31A2GX) General Cargo Ship** Compartments: 2 Ho, ER 2 Ha: ER 2 (25.5 x 12.7)	**1 oil engine** driving 1 FP propeller Total Power: 2,648kW (3,600hp) 12.1kn Hanshin LH41LA 1 x 4 Stroke 6 Cy. 410 x 800 2648kW (3600bhp) The Hanshin Diesel Works Ltd-Japan
9163049 *S6OS* -	**TY GREEN** **Taiyoung Shipping (Singapore) Pte Ltd** Taiyoung Shipping Co Ltd *Singapore* *Singapore* MMSI: 564263000 Official number: 387702	**2,646** Class: KR (NK) 1,556 3,803	**1997-04 Sanyo Zosen K.K. — Onomichi** Yd No: 1077 Loa 91.80 Br ex - Dght 5.518 Lbp 84.90 Br md 14.50 Dpth 6.80 Welded, 1 dk	**(A31A2GX) General Cargo Ship** Grain: 5,327; Bale: 5,206 Compartments: 2 Ho, ER 2 Ha: (15.6 x 10.0) (25.8 x 10.0)ER Derricks: 1x25t,2x20t	**1 oil engine** driving 1 FP propeller Total Power: 1,912kW (2,600hp) 12.0kn Hanshin LH36LA 1 x 4 Stroke 6 Cy. 360 x 670 1912kW (2600bhp) The Hanshin Diesel Works Ltd-Japan AuxGen: 1 x 220kW 445V a.c
9400435 *DSOY4* -	**TY IRIS** **Taiyoung Shipping Co Ltd** *Jeju* *South Korea* MMSI: 440629000 Official number: JJR-069871	**4,105** Class: KR 1,997 6,260	**2007-01 Nanjing Shenghua Shipbuilding Co Ltd — Nanjing JS** Yd No: H408 Loa 99.30 (BB) Br ex - Dght 6.713 Lbp - Br md 17.00 Dpth 8.50 Welded, 1 dk	**(A31A2GX) General Cargo Ship** Grain: 6,965; Bale: 6,595 Compartments: 2 Ho, ER 2 Ha: ER 2 (25.2 x 12.4)	**1 oil engine** driving 1 Propeller Total Power: 2,647kW (3,599hp) 12.1kn Hanshin LH41LA 1 x 4 Stroke 6 Cy. 410 x 800 2647kW (3599bhp) (made 2005) The Hanshin Diesel Works Ltd-Japan
9354155 *DSOK2* -	**TY JIN** *ex* Ardor *-2012* *ex* JI Ace *-2010* *ex* Far East Young *-2007* **Sean Shipping Co Ltd** Sung Kyung Maritime Co Ltd (SK Maritime) SatCom: Inmarsat C 444095553 *Jeju* *South Korea* MMSI: 440784000 Official number: JJR-059520	**1,972** Class: KR (CC) 1,395 3,302	**2005-07 Zhejiang Hongxin Shipbuilding Co Ltd — Taizhou ZJ** Yd No: 0402 Loa 81.20 Br ex - Dght 5.500 Lbp 76.00 Br md 13.60 Dpth 6.80 Welded, 1 dk	**(A31A2GX) General Cargo Ship** Grain: 4,450	**1 oil engine** reduction geared to sc. shaft driving 1 FP propeller Total Power: 1,323kW (1,799hp) 12.0kn Chinese Std. Type G6300ZC 1 x 4 Stroke 6 Cy. 300 x 380 1323kW (1799bhp) Wuxi Antai Power Machinery Co Ltd-China
9218698 *DSNU7* -	**TY LOTUS** *ex* Tanya *-2004* **Taiyoung Shipping Co Ltd** *Jeju* *South Korea* MMSI: 440324000 Official number: JJR-000216	**2,216** Class: KR 1,081 3,366	**2000-03 Haedong Shipbuilding Co Ltd — Tongyeong** Yd No: 1027 Loa 80.80 Br ex - Dght 5.712 Lbp 74.00 Br md 14.20 Dpth 7.00 Welded, 1 dk	**(A31A2GX) General Cargo Ship** Grain: 3,818; Bale: 3,638 Compartments: 2 Ho, ER 2 Ha: 2 (15.0 x 10.4)ER Derricks: 2x15t	**1 oil engine** reduction geared to sc. shaft driving 1 FP propeller Total Power: 1,714kW (2,330hp) 11.6kn Alpha 7L28/32A 1 x 4 Stroke 7 Cy. 280 x 320 1714kW (2330bhp) Ssangyong Heavy Industries Co Ltd-South Korea AuxGen: 2 x 340kW 445V a.c

Ship	Tonnage / Class	Builder / Dimensions	Type	Machinery
9565209 **TY NOBLE** *DSQM9* - **Taiyoung Shipping Co Ltd** Taiyoung Maritime Co Ltd *Jeju* *South Korea* MMSI: 441631000 Official number: JJR-094294	**4,105** Class: KR 1,997 6,238	**2009-11 Jiangsu Suyang Marine Co Ltd — Yangzhong JS** Yd No: WX908 Loa 99.30 Br ex - Dght 6.713 Lbp 92.01 Br md 17.00 Dpth 8.50 Welded, 1 dk	**(A31A2GX) General Cargo Ship**	**1 oil engine** driving 1 Propeller Total Power: 2,647kW (3,599hp) 13.8kn Hanshin LH41LA 1 x 4 Stroke 6 Cy. 410 x 800 2647kW (3599bhp) The Hanshin Diesel Works Ltd-Japan
9313230 **TY PLUM** *D7ME* - **Taiyoung Shipping Co Ltd** *Jeju* *South Korea* MMSI: 440098000 Official number: JJR-131061	**4,116** Class: KR 1,997 6,233	**2005-05 Nanjing Shenghua Shipbuilding Co Ltd — Nanjing JS** Yd No: H403 Loa 99.30 (BB) Br ex 32.30 Dght 6.713 Lbp 92.00 Br md 17.00 Dpth 8.50 Welded, 1 dk	**(A31A2GX) General Cargo Ship** Grain: 6,965; Bale: 6,595 Compartments: 2 Ho, ER 2 Ha: (25.2 x 12.4)ER (25.2 x 12.4)	**1 oil engine** driving 1 FP propeller Total Power: 2,648kW (3,600hp) 12.1kn Hanshin LH41LA 1 x 4 Stroke 6 Cy. 410 x 800 2648kW (3600bhp) The Hanshin Diesel Works Ltd-Japan
9541071 **TY SONG** *DSRK7* *ex* Sea Ace *-2012* - **Ever Marine Co Ltd** Sung Kyung Maritime Co Ltd (SK Maritime) *Jeju* *South Korea* MMSI: 441894000 Official number: JJR121066	**3,138** Class: KR (CC) 1,996 5,082	**2008-10 Yizheng Shierwei Shipbuilding Co Ltd — Yizheng JS** Yd No: 03 Loa 96.50 Br ex - Dght - Lbp 90.90 Br md 15.80 Dpth 7.40 Welded, 1 dk	**(A21A2BC) Bulk Carrier**	**1 oil engine** reduction geared to sc. shaft driving 1 Propeller Total Power: 1,765kW (2,400hp) 11.6kn Chinese Std. Type G8300ZC 1 x 4 Stroke 8 Cy. 300 x 380 1765kW (2400bhp) Wuxi Antai Power Machinery Co Ltd-China
9418468 **TYANA** *V7XC4* - **Tyana Navigation Ltd** Andriaki Shipping Co Ltd SatCom: Inmarsat C 453836919 *Majuro* *Marshall Islands* MMSI: 538004445 Official number: 4445	**42,929** Class: AB (LR) 26,848 ✠ Classed LR until 30/6/11 82,158 T/cm 70.2	**2010-07 Tsuneishi Holdings Corp Tsuneishi Shipbuilding Co — Fukuyama HS** Yd No: 1444 Loa 228.99 Br ex 32.30 Dght 14.430 Lbp 221.00 Br md 32.26 Dpth 20.05 Welded, 1 dk	**(A21A2BC) Bulk Carrier** Grain: 97,000 Compartments: 7 Ho, ER 7 Ha: ER	**1 oil engine** driving 1 FP propeller Total Power: 13,560kW (18,436hp) 14.5kn MAN-B&W 6S60MC-C 1 x 2 Stroke 6 Cy. 600 x 2400 13560kW (18436bhp) Mitsui Engineering & Shipbuilding CLtd-Japan AuxGen: 3 x 400kW 450V 60Hz a.c Boilers: AuxB (Comp) 7.1kgf/cm² (7.0bar)
9007116 **TYCHO BRAHE** *OVIC2* - **Scandlines Helsingor-Helsingborg A/S** Scandlines Oresund I/S *Helsingor* *Denmark (DIS)* MMSI: 219230000 Official number: A441	**11,148** Class: LR (NV) 3,344 **100A1** SS 09/2011 2,500 passenger, vehicle and train ferry Kattegat-Baltic service, limited by a line between Frederikshavn to Gothenburg and Ystad to Sassnitz movable car deck Ice Class 1C **LMC** **UMS** Eq.Ltr: C†; Cable: 275.0/52.0 U3 (a)	**1991-09 Tangen Verft AS — Kragero** (Hull) Yd No: 99 **1991-09 Langsten Slip & Baatbyggeri AS — Tomrefjord** Yd No: 156 Loa 111.20 Br ex 28.20 Dght 5.500 Lbp 94.83 Br md 27.60 Dpth 7.75 Welded, 1 dk	**(A36A2PT) Passenger/Ro-Ro Ship (Vehicles/Rail)** Passengers: unberthed: 1250 Bow door Stern door Lane-Len: 535 Lane-clr ht: 5.30 Cars: 238 Ice Capable	**4 diesel electric oil engines** driving 4 gen. each 2460kW 660V a.c Connecting to 4 elec. motors each (1500kW) driving 4 CP propellers 2 fwd and 2 aft Total Power: 9,832kW (13,368hp) 13.5kn Wartsila 6R32E 4 x 4 Stroke 6 Cy. 320 x 350 each-2458kW (3342bhp) Wartsila Diesel Oy-Finland Fuel: 172.6 (d.f.)
8302284 **TYCHY** *3EYL8* *ex* Ville de Lattaquie *-1993* *ex* Tychy *-1992* - **Maritime Operators Inc** Reefer & General Ship-Management Co Inc SatCom: Inmarsat C 437389710 *Panama* *Panama* MMSI: 373897000 Official number: 4402012	**15,652** Class: PR 4,695 8,044	**1988-01 Stocznia im Komuny Paryskiej — Gdynia** Yd No: B488/02 Loa 147.48 (BB) Br ex - Dght 7.050 Lbp 135.12 Br md 23.51 Dpth 14.91 Welded, 3 dks	**(A35A2RR) Ro-Ro Cargo Ship** Passengers: berths: 6 Stern door/ramp (a) Len: 16.00 Wid: 12.00 Swl: 200 Lane-Len: 1366 Lane-Wid: 7.30 Lane-clr ht: 6.50 TEU 505 incl 50 ref C.	**2 oil engines** with flexible couplings & dr geared to sc. shafts driving 2 CP propellers Total Power: 4,800kW (6,526hp) 14.5kn Sulzer 6ZL40/48 2 x 4 Stroke 6 Cy. 400 x 480 each-2400kW (3263bhp) Zaklady Urzadzen Technicznych'Zgoda' SA-Poland AuxGen: 2 x 1200kW 400V 50Hz a.c, 2 x 842kW 400V 50Hz a.c Thrusters: 1 Thwart. CP thruster (f) Fuel: 194.0 (d.f.) 1481.0 (r.f.) 24.0pd
9215543 **TYCOON** *D5BC9* *ex* Merian *-2012* *ex* Cinzia d'Amato *-2008* - **Tycoon Maritime SA** Delek Transport Agency Inc SatCom: Inmarsat C 463711675 *Monrovia* *Liberia* MMSI: 636015499 Official number: 15499	**40,562** Class: NV (RI) 26,139 74,717 T/cm 67.0	**2000-08 Hudong Shipbuilding Group — Shanghai** Yd No: H1279A Loa 225.00 (BB) Br ex 32.30 Dght 14.268 Lbp 217.00 Br md 32.26 Dpth 19.60 Welded, 1 dk	**(A21A2BC) Bulk Carrier** Grain: 91,717; Bale: 89,882 Compartments: 7 Ho, ER 7 Ha: (14.6 x 13.2)6 (14.6 x 15.0)ER	**1 oil engine** driving 1 FP propeller Total Power: 11,300kW (15,363hp) 14.0kn MAN-B&W 5S60MC-C 1 x 2 Stroke 5 Cy. 600 x 2400 11300kW (15363bhp) Hudong Heavy Machinery Co Ltd-China AuxGen: 2 x 530kW 220/440V 60Hz a.c, 1 x 650kW 220/440V 60Hz a.c Fuel: 147.0 (d.f.) (Heating Coils) 2578.0 (r.f.) 37.5pd
8640363 **TYEE PRINCESS** - *ex* YF-874 *-2008* - **Maritime Heritage Society of Vancouver** - *Vancouver, BC* *Canada* Official number: 391407	*339* 179 -	**1945-01 American Bridge Co. — Ambridge, Pa** Loa - Br ex 9.40 Dght - Lbp 38.10 Br md - Dpth 3.44 Welded, 1 dk	**(B35A2QE) Exhibition Vessel**	**2 oil engines** driving 2 Propellers Total Power: 736kW (1,000hp) 10.0kn
6925824 **TYGRYS** *SR2486* - **Szczecinska Stocznia Remontowa 'Gryfia'** *Szczecin* *Poland*	*119* Class: PR 29 -	**1966-12 Gdynska Stocznia Remontowa — Gdynia** Yd No: H800/247 Loa 25.51 Br ex 6.81 Dght 2.501 Lbp 23.53 Br md - Dpth 3.41 Welded, 1 dk	**(B32A2ST) Tug** Ice Capable	**1 oil engine** driving 1 FP propeller Total Power: 588kW (799hp) 10.5kn S.K.L. 8NVD48AU 1 x 4 Stroke 8 Cy. 320 x 480 588kW (799bhp) VEB Schwermaschinenbau "KarlLiebknecht" (SKL)-Magdeburg AuxGen: 3 x 10kW 230V d.c
8036287 **TYLER** *WDH2928* *ex* Jennifer & Emily *-2013* *ex* Capt. Joe *-2001* *ex* Alfa I *-2000* *ex* Capt. Joe *-1999* - **f/v Tyler Inc** *Gloucester, MA* *United States of America* MMSI: 367602610 Official number: 619778	*105* 72 -	**1980 Goudy & Stevens — East Boothbay, Me** Yd No: 4 Loa 22.20 Br ex 6.41 Dght - Lbp 19.51 Br md - Dpth 3.20 Welded, 1 dk	**(B11B2FV) Fishing Vessel**	**1 oil engine** with clutches & sr reverse geared to sc. shaft driving 1 FP propeller Total Power: 313kW (426hp) Caterpillar 3412TA 1 x Vee 4 Stroke 12 Cy. 137 x 152 313kW (426bhp) Caterpillar Tractor Co-USA
8812289 **TYLER N. NOAH** *WDE6410* *ex* Addy J *-2008* *ex* Rita Sophia *-2005* *ex* Megan Elizabeth *-2001* *ex* Integrity *-1993* - **Vila Nova Fishing Inc** - *New Bedford, MA* *United States of America* MMSI: 367379950 Official number: 930728	*172* 117 -	**1988-04 Rodriguez Boat Builders, Inc. — Coden, Al** Yd No: 73 Loa 26.22 Br ex - Dght - Lbp 22.43 Br md 7.32 Dpth 4.11 Welded, 1 dk	**(B11B2FV) Fishing Vessel**	**1 oil engine** geared to sc. shaft driving 1 FP propeller Total Power: 530kW (721hp) Caterpillar 3412PCTA 1 x Vee 4 Stroke 12 Cy. 137 x 152 530kW (721bhp) Caterpillar Inc-USA
9398785 **TYM MULIA** *YDA4173* - **PT Tonggak Yakin Mulia** *Jakarta* *Indonesia* Official number: 1809/PST	**122** Class: KI (NK) 37 111	**2006-06 SL Shipbuilding Contractor Sdn Bhd — Sibu** Yd No: 11 Loa 23.17 Br ex - Dght 2.412 Lbp 21.39 Br md 7.00 Dpth 2.90 Welded, 1 dk	**(B32A2ST) Tug**	**2 oil engines** reduction geared to sc. shafts driving 2 FP propellers Total Power: 954kW (1,298hp) Cummins KTA-19-M3 2 x 4 Stroke 6 Cy. 159 x 159 each-477kW (649bhp) Cummins Engine Co Inc-USA AuxGen: 2 x 35kW 400V a.c
9421946 **TYM UTAMA** *YDA4231* - **PT Mulia Borneo Mandiri** *Jakarta* *Indonesia*	**119** Class: KI (NK) 36 110	**2006-12 SL Shipbuilding Contractor Sdn Bhd — Sibu** Yd No: 18 Loa 23.17 Br ex 7.00 Dght 2.412 Lbp 21.39 Br md 7.00 Dpth 2.90 Welded, 1 dk	**(B32A2ST) Tug**	**2 oil engines** reduction geared to sc. shafts driving 2 FP propellers Total Power: 741kW (1,007hp) Cummins KTA-19-M 2 x 4 Stroke 6 Cy. 159 x 159 each-368kW (500bhp) Cummins India Ltd-India AuxGen: 2 x 31kW 415V a.c
1004429 **TYNDAREO** *GCRF* *ex* Varmar *-1993* - **Ballymoss Ltd** FAGE AE *Southampton* *United Kingdom* MMSI: 232460000 Official number: 700351	**227** Class: (LR) - ✠ Classed LR until 1/3/12 -	**1982-07 C.R.N. Cant. Nav. Ancona S.r.l. — Ancona** Loa 42.82 Br ex 7.74 Dght 1.310 Lbp 35.95 Br md - Dpth 4.35 Welded, 1 dk	**(X11A2YP) Yacht**	**2 oil engines** driving 2 FP propellers Total Power: 2,210kW (3,004hp) Deutz SBV6M628 2 x 4 Stroke 6 Cy. 240 x 280 each-1105kW (1502bhp) Motoren Werke Mannheim AG (MWM)-West Germany

IMO / Call sign	Name / Owner	Tonnage	Class	Builder / Dimensions	Type	Machinery
7329792 UGDH -	**TYOPLYY** **Blaf-West Co Ltd (OOO 'Blaf-Zapadnyy')** - Petropavlovsk-Kamchatskiy Russia	172 51 94	Class: RS	**1973-07 Sretenskiy Sudostroitelnyy Zavod — Sretensk** Yd No: 46 Loa 33.97 Br ex 7.09 Dght 2.900 Lbp 30.00 Br md 7.00 Dpth 3.65 Welded, 1 dk	**(B11B2FV) Fishing Vessel** Bale: 96 Compartments: 1 Ho, ER 1 Ha: (1.6 x 1.5) Derricks: 2x2t; Winches: 2 Ice Capable	**1 oil engine** driving 1 FP propeller Total Power: 224kW (305hp) 9.0kn S.K.L. 8NVD36-1U 1 x 4 Stroke 8 Cy. 240 x 360 224kW (305bhp) VEB Schwermaschinenbau "KarlLiebknecht" (SKL)-Magdeburg Fuel: 17.0 (d.f.)
9580302 JD3104 -	**TYOUKAI MARU** **Nippo Shosen YK & Hoei Shosen YK** Nippo Shosen YK Imabari, Ehime Japan MMSI: 431001715 Official number: 141304	748 - 1,717	Class: NK	**2010-08 Yamanaka Zosen K.K. — Imabari** Yd No: 802 Loa 69.98 Br ex - Dght 4.700 Lbp 65.50 Br md 11.50 Dpth 5.35 Welded, 1 dk	**(A12A2TC) Chemical Tanker** Double Hull (13F) Liq: 884	**1 oil engine** reverse reduction geared to sc. shaft driving 1 FP propeller Total Power: 1,323kW (1,799hp) Niigata 6M31BFT 1 x 4 Stroke 6 Cy. 310 x 530 1323kW (1799bhp) Niigata Engineering Co Ltd-Japan Fuel: 98.0
9507582 PHTY -	**TYPHOON** **Chemgas Shipping BV** SatCom: Inmarsat C 424588911 Rotterdam Netherlands MMSI: 245889000 Official number: 51823	2,410 723 2,161 T/cm 13.0	Class: BV	**2010-06 Groningen Shipyard BV — Waterhuizen** Yd No: 110 Loa 99.90 Br ex 14.00 Dght 3.383 Lbp 97.96 Br md 13.94 Dpth 6.20 Welded, 1 dk	**(A11B2TG) LPG Tanker** Double Hull Liq (Gas): 2,657 5 x Gas Tank (s); 4 independent (stl) cyl horizontal, ER 4 Cargo Pump (s): 4x135m³/hr Manifold: Bow/CM: 49.9m	**2 oil engines** reduction geared to sc. shafts driving 2 FP propellers Total Power: 2,014kW (2,738hp) 12.5kn Mitsubishi S6U-MPTK 2 x 4 Stroke 6 Cy. 240 x 260 each-1007kW (1369bhp) Mitsubishi Heavy Industries Ltd-Japan AuxGen: 2 x 208kW 60Hz a.c, 1 x 406kW 60Hz a.c Thrusters: 1 Tunnel thruster (f) Fuel: 200.0 (d.f.)
9394181 UDVO -	**TYPHOON** *ex Tayfun -2008* **Baltic Fleet LLC** - St Petersburg Russia	294 88 200	Class: RS (LR) ✠ Classed LR until 11/1/09	**2007-11 Song Cam Shipyard — Haiphong** (Hull) **2007-11 B.V. Scheepswerf Damen — Gorinchem** Yd No: 511527 Loa 28.67 Br ex 10.42 Dght 4.000 Lbp 25.78 Br md 9.80 Dpth 4.60 Welded, 1 dk	**(B32A2ST) Tug** Ice Capable	**2 oil engines** reduction geared to sc. shafts driving 2 Directional propellers Total Power: 3,132kW (4,258hp) Caterpillar 3516B-TA 2 x Vee 4 Stroke 16 Cy. 170 x 190 each-1566kW (2129bhp) Caterpillar Inc-USA AuxGen: 2 x 85kW 400V 50Hz a.c Fuel: 82.0 (d.f.)
7514830 ZHBB9 -	**TYPHOON** *ex Veesea Typhoon -2000 ex Java Seal -1991* **Gem Shipping Ltd** SEACOR Marine (International) Ltd George Town Cayman Islands (British) MMSI: 319413000 Official number: 715918	936 280 -	Class: AB	**1976-05 Rockport Yacht & Supply Co. (RYSCO) — Rockport, Tx** Yd No: 102 Converted From: Research Vessel-1990 Converted From: Offshore Supply Ship-1976 Loa 56.39 Br ex 11.61 Dght 3.810 Lbp 53.01 Br md 11.59 Dpth 4.58 Welded, 1 dk	**(B22G20Y) Standby Safety Vessel** Liq: 108; Liq (Oil): 108 Compartments: 4 Ta, ER	**2 oil engines** reverse reduction geared to sc. shafts driving 2 FP propellers Total Power: 1,654kW (2,248hp) 10.0kn Caterpillar D399SCAC 2 x Vee 4 Stroke 16 Cy. 159 x 203 each-827kW (1124bhp) Caterpillar Tractor Co-USA AuxGen: 2 x 210kW a.c Thrusters: 1 Thwart. FP thruster (f)
6905408 - -	**TYPHOON 1** *ex Rubin -2003 ex Arctic Ranger -1998* *ex Vesturvon -1986* **ESTELLARES SA** Vistasur Holding Inc	1,175 388 660	Class: (NV)	**1969-03 Hatlo Verksted AS — Ulsteinvik** Yd No: 36 Loa 61.75 Br ex 10.24 Dght 4.973 Lbp 54.36 Br md 10.22 Dpth 7.01 Welded, 2dks	**(B11A2FG) Factory Stern Trawler** Ins: 997 Compartments: 3 Ho, ER 2 Ha: (2.9 x 1.7) (3.5 x 2.9)ER Derricks: 7x3t Ice Capable	**1 oil engine** driving 1 CP propeller Total Power: 1,618kW (2,200hp) 14.3kn MWM 1 x 4 Stroke 8 Cy. 360 x 450 1618kW (2200bhp) Motoren Werke Mannheim AG (MWM)-West Germany AuxGen: 3 x 115kW 380V 50Hz a.c Fuel: 332.0 (d.f.)
8855619 - -	**TYPHOON '88** **BEV Processors Inc** Georgetown Guyana Official number: 0000255	*112* 50 -		**1988 Steiner Shipyard, Inc. — Bayou La Batre, Al** Loa - Br ex - Dght - Lbp 19.75 Br md 6.71 Dpth 3.32 Welded, 1 dk	**(B11B2FV) Fishing Vessel**	**1 oil engine** driving 1 FP propeller
5371791 OIKX -	**TYR** *ex Tyri -1989 ex Tyr -1980* **K Jousmaa KY** Turku Finland Official number: 11386	135 41 -	Class: (LR) ✠ Classed LR until 6/2/81	**1960-01 AB Asi-Verken — Amal** Yd No: 50 Loa 25.02 Br ex 7.88 Dght 3.801 Lbp 22.81 Br md 7.65 Dpth 4.22 Welded, 1 dk	**(B32A2ST) Tug** Ice Capable	**1 oil engine** driving 1 CP propeller Total Power: 588kW (799hp) 11.0kn MaK 6MU451AK 1 x 4 Stroke 6 Cy. 320 x 450 588kW (799bhp) (new engine 1984) Maschinenbau Kiel AG (MaK)-Kiel AuxGen: 1 x 110kW 220V d.c, 1 x 13kW 220V d.c Thrusters: 1 Tunnel thruster (f) Fuel: 33.0 (d.f.)
7358420 TFGA -	**TYR** **Government of The Republic of Iceland (Landhelgisgaesla - Coast Guard)** - SatCom: Inmarsat C 425114211 Reykjavik Iceland MMSI: 251001000 Official number: 1421	1,271 364 513	Class: LR ✠ **100A1** SS 07/2012 Ice Class 3 ✠ **LMC** Eq.Ltr: L; Cable: U2	**1975-03 Aarhus Flydedok A/S — Aarhus** Yd No: 159 Loa 70.90 Br ex 10.11 Dght 4.865 Lbp 62.01 Br md 10.01 Dpth 5.90 Welded, 1 dk, 2nd dk fwd of mchy. space	**(B34H2SQ) Patrol Vessel** Ice Capable	**2 oil engines** geared to sc. shafts driving 2 FP propellers Total Power: 6,546kW (8,900hp) 19.0kn MAN 8L40/54A 2 x 4 Stroke 8 Cy. 400 x 540 each-3273kW (4450bhp) Maschinenbau Augsburg Nuernberg (MAN)-Augsburg AuxGen: 3 x 196kW 380V 50Hz a.c Thrusters: 1 Thwart. FP thruster (f) Fuel: 228.5 (d.f.)
8019409 - -	**TYR** *ex Standby Master -1995* **Fosvarets Logistikkorganisasjon** - Aalesund Norway	499 149 325	Class: NV	**1981-08 Voldnes Skipsverft AS — Fosnavaag** Yd No: 31 Loa 42.25 Br ex - Dght 4.530 Lbp 36.02 Br md 10.01 Dpth 5.80 Welded, 2 dks	**(B22G20Y) Standby Safety Vessel** Cranes: 1x3t,1x2t Ice Capable	**2 oil engines** sr geared to sc. shaft driving 1 CP propeller Total Power: 1,008kW (1,370hp) 13.0kn Deutz SBA12M816 2 x Vee 4 Stroke 12 Cy. 142 x 160 each-504kW (685bhp) Kloeckner Humboldt Deutz AG-West Germany AuxGen: 2 x 320kW 380V 50Hz a.c, 1 x 44kW 380V 50Hz a.c Thrusters: 1 Thwart. FP thruster (f); 1 Tunnel thruster (a)
9598983 HKET9 -	**TYR** **Transportacion Maritima Mexicana SA de CV (TMM LINES)** - Cartagena de Indias Colombia MMSI: 730109000 Official number: MC-05-664	472 141 295	Class: LR ✠ **100A1** SS 01/2012 tug, fire fighting Ship 1 (2400m3/h) with water spray ✠ **LMC** Eq.Ltr: H; Cable: 302.5/22.0 U2 (a)	**2012-01 Yuexin Shipbuilding Co Ltd — Guangzhou GD** Yd No: 3132 Loa 33.15 Br ex 12.23 Dght 4.300 Lbp 25.87 Br md 11.60 Dpth 5.36 Welded, 1 dk	**(B32A2ST) Tug**	**2 oil engines** gearing integral to driving 2 Directional propellers Total Power: 4,000kW (5,438hp) Caterpillar 3516B 2 x Vee 4 Stroke 16 Cy. 170 x 215 each-2000kW (2719bhp) Caterpillar Inc-USA AuxGen: 2 x 136kW 415V 50Hz a.c
9673094 - -	**TYR** **Detroit Chile SA** Valparaiso Chile MMSI: 725001071	1,573 472 2,219	Class: BV (Class contemplated)	**2013-10 Detroit Chile SA — Puerto Montt** Yd No: 104 Loa 62.85 (BB) Br ex 13.77 Dght 4.700 Lbp 57.20 Br md 13.50 Dpth 5.80 Welded, 1 dk	**(B12C2FL) Live Fish Carrier (Well Boat)**	**2 oil engines** reduction geared to sc. shafts driving 2 Propellers Total Power: 2,400kW (3,264hp) Chinese Std. Type CW12V200ZC 2 x Vee 4 Stroke 12 Cy. 200 x 270 each-1200kW (1632bhp) Weichai Power Co Ltd-China
9290012 WDF8333 -	**TYRANT** *ex Tennessee River -2011* **Tyrant Marine Offshore LLC** Comar Marine LLC New Orleans, LA United States of America Official number: 1136531	349 104 316	Class: (AB)	**2003-03 Gulf Craft LLC — Patterson LA** Yd No: 449 Loa 47.24 Br ex - Dght - Lbp 42.85 Br md 8.50 Dpth 4.17 Welded, 1 dk	**(B21A20C) Crew/Supply Vessel** Hull Material: Aluminium Alloy Passengers: unberthed: 78	**5 oil engines** reduction geared to sc. shafts driving 5 FP propellers Total Power: 5,035kW (6,845hp) 24.5kn Cummins KTA-38-M2 5 x Vee 4 Stroke 12 Cy. 159 x 159 each-1007kW (1369bhp) Cummins Engine Co Inc-USA AuxGen: 2 x 75kW a.c Thrusters: 1 Tunnel thruster (f)
8983363 - -	**TYRANT** *ex M/V Jenni Lee -2004 ex Sea Cat -2004* **A R Singh Contractors Ltd** Port of Spain Trinidad & Tobago	*135* 40 -		**1978 Swiftships Inc — Morgan City LA** Yd No: 191 Loa 30.48 Br ex - Dght - Lbp - Br md 6.58 Dpth 2.93 Welded, 1 dk	**(B34J2SD) Crew Boat** Hull Material: Aluminium Alloy	**3 oil engines** geared to sc. shaft driving 3 FP propellers Total Power: 757kW (1,030hp) 18.0kn G.M. (Detroit Diesel) 12V-71-TI 3 x Vee 2 Stroke 12 Cy. 108 x 127 each-7kW (10bhp) General Motors Detroit DieselAllison Divn-USA AuxGen: 3 x 30kW

IMO / Call sign / Flag	Name / Owner / Manager	Tonnage	Class	Builder / Dimensions	Ship type	Machinery
7718503 *ZQVU5* -	**TYRUSLAND** *ex* Jolly Ocra *-1985* *ex* Tyrusland *-1984* **Tyrusland Ltd** Imperial Ship Management AB SatCom: Inmarsat C 423514010 *London* *United Kingdom* MMSI: 235140000 Official number: 903793	**20,882** 6,264 16,600	Class: LR ✠**100A1** SS 12/2011 roll on-roll off cargo ship vehicle carrier Ice Class 1A at 8.422m draught Max/min draught forward 8.422/4.8m Max/min draught aft 10.015/6.2m Power required 9849kw, installed 15593kw ✠**LMC** **UMS** Eq.Ltr: I†; Cable: 620.0/64.0 U3	**1978-11 Mitsui Eng. & SB. Co. Ltd., Chiba Works — Ichihara** Yd No: 1182 Lengthened-1995 Loa 190.36 (BB) Br ex 25.94 Dght 8.230 Lbp 180.20 Br md 25.52 Dpth 16.41 Welded, 2 dks	**(A35A2RR) Ro-Ro Cargo Ship** Quarter stern door/ramp (s. a.) Len: 33.00 Wid: 9.00 Swl: 181 Lane-Len: 2204 Lane-clr ht: 6.30 Bale: 29,000 TEU 1008 incl 60 ref C. Ice Capable	**2 oil engines** driving 2 FP propellers Total Power: 15,594kW (21,202hp) 18.5kn B&W 12L45GF 2 x 2 Stroke 12 Cy. 450 x 1200 each-7797kW (10601bhp) Mitsui Engineering & Shipbuilding CLtd-Japan AuxGen: 4 x 760kW 450V 60Hz a.c Boilers: TOH (o.f.), TOH (ex.g.) Thrusters: 2 Thwart. CP thruster (f) Fuel: 298.0 (d.f.) 2978.0 (r.f.) 58.0pd
9264491 *LLVH* -	**TYRVING** *ex* Strandafjord *-2007* **Norled AS** - *Bergen* *Norway* MMSI: 258130000	**224** 79 30		**2002-04 Oma Baatbyggeri AS — Stord** Yd No: 516 Loa 27.25 (BB) Br ex - Dght - Lbp - Br md 9.00 Dpth 3.65 Welded, 1 dk	**(A37B2PS) Passenger Ship** Hull Material: Aluminium Alloy Passengers: unberthed: 180	**2 oil engines** geared to sc. shafts driving 2 FP propellers Total Power: 970kW (1,318hp) Mitsubishi S12R-MPTA 2 x Vee 4 Stroke 12 Cy. 170 x 180 each-485kW (659bhp) Mitsubishi Heavy Industries Ltd-Japan
9056301 *LGOB* -	**TYSFJORD** **Torghatten Nord AS** *Narvik* *Norway* MMSI: 257363500	**3,695** 1,773 740	Class: (NV)	**1993-05 Fiskerstrand Verft AS — Fiskarstrand** Yd No: 40 Loa 84.00 Br ex 15.50 Dght 4.100 Lbp 70.80 Br md 15.00 Dpth 4.50 Welded	**(A36A2PR) Passenger/Ro-Ro Ship (Vehicles)** Passengers: unberthed: 399 Cars: 75	**2 oil engines** sr geared to sc. shafts driving 2 Propellers 1 fwd and 1 aft Total Power: 2,650kW (3,602hp) 14.0kn Normo BRM-6 2 x 4 Stroke 6 Cy. 320 x 360 each-1325kW (1801bhp) Ulstein Bergen AS-Norway AuxGen: 3 x 250kW 220V 50Hz a.c Fuel: 38.7 (d.f.) 98.1 (r.f.) 8.5pd
9515400 *9HA2067* -	**TYSLA** **Wilhelmsen Lines Shipowning Malta Ltd** Wilhelmsen Ship Management (Norway) AS *Valletta* *Malta* MMSI: 249909000 Official number: 9515400	**75,251** 27,215 43,878	Class: NV	**2012-01 Mitsubishi Heavy Industries Ltd. — Nagasaki** Yd No: 2264 Loa 265.00 (BB) Br ex 33.27 Dght 12.300 Lbp 250.00 Br md 32.26 Dpth 33.22 Welded, 9 dks incl. 6 hoistable dks.	**(A35B2RV) Vehicles Carrier** Angled stern door/ramp (s. a.) Len: 44.30 Wid: 12.50 Swl: 505 Cars: 5,990 Bale: 138,000	**1 oil engine** driving 1 FP propeller Total Power: 21,770kW (29,598hp) 20.3kn MAN-B&W 7L70ME-C8 1 x 2 Stroke 7 Cy. 700 x 2360 21770kW (29598bhp) Kawasaki Heavy Industries Ltd-Japan AuxGen: 1 x 1100kW a.c, 3 x 2360kW a.c Thrusters: 1 Tunnel thruster (f); 1 Tunnel thruster (a) Fuel: 637.0 (d.f.) 5390.0 (r.f.)
6619396 *DUA2498* -	**TYSON** *ex* Diplomat *-2007* *ex* Choyo Maru No. 62 *-2007* **Sea Gold Fishing Corp** - *Manila* *Philippines* Official number: MNLD001639	*172* 83 236		**1966 Hayashikane Shipbuilding & Engineering Co Ltd — Nagasaki NS** Yd No: 599 Loa 36.56 Br ex 6.84 Dght 2.896 Lbp 31.81 Br md 6.81 Dpth 3.33 Welded, 1 dk	**(B11B2FV) Fishing Vessel** Bale: 176 Compartments: 2 Ho, ER 3 Ha: (1.0 x 1.0)2 (1.5 x 1.5)ER	**1 oil engine** driving 1 FP propeller Total Power: 478kW (650hp) Kobe 6G26SS 1 x 4 Stroke 6 Cy. 260 x 320 478kW (650bhp) Kobe Hatsudoki KK-Japan AuxGen: 2 x 30kW 225V 60Hz a.c
9114945 *MVGH7* -	**TYSTIE** **Shetland Islands Council Towage Operations** - *Lerwick* *United Kingdom* MMSI: 232002143 Official number: 728605	**797** 239 322	Class: LR ✠**100A1** CS 07/2011 tug fire fighting ship 1 (2400 cubic metre/hr) with water spray ✠**LMC** **UMS** Eq.Ltr: K; Cable: 357.5/30.0 U2	**1996-07 Ferguson Shipbuilders Ltd — Port Glasgow** Yd No: 609 Loa 38.37 Br ex 13.92 Dght 3.530 Lbp 34.49 Br md 13.40 Dpth 5.50 Welded, 1 dk	**(B32A2ST) Tug**	**2 oil engines** gearing integral to driving 2 Voith-Schneider propellers Total Power: 4,000kW (5,438hp) 12.9kn Caterpillar 3606TA 2 x 4 Stroke 6 Cy. 280 x 300 each-2000kW (2719bhp) Caterpillar Inc-USA AuxGen: 3 x 90kW 415V 50Hz a.c Fuel: 210.0 (d.f.) 20.0pd
9101194 *SPG2541* -	**TYTAN** **'WUZ' Port & Maritime Services Co Ltd ('WUZ' Sp z oo Przedsiebiorstwo Uslug Portowych i Morskich)** - *Gdansk* *Poland* MMSI: 261000140 Official number: ROG2576	**308** 92 108	Class: PR	**1994-12 Stocznia Remontowa 'Nauta' SA — Gdynia** Yd No: H-3000 Loa 29.35 Br ex 9.30 Dght 3.850 Lbp 27.76 Br md 9.00 Dpth 4.50 Welded, 1 dk	**(B32A2ST) Tug**	**2 oil engines** dr geared to sc. shafts driving 2 FP propellers Total Power: 2,864kW (3,894hp) 12.7kn Caterpillar 3516TA 2 x Vee 4 Stroke 16 Cy. 170 x 190 each-1432kW (1947bhp) Caterpillar Inc-USA AuxGen: 2 x 140kW a.c Fuel: 70.0 (d.f.) 3.8pd
8038285 - -	**TYULEN-2** **A/O 'Kazakhrybflot'** - *Bautino* *Kazakhstan* Official number: 801956	**340** 102 145	Class: (RS)	**1982 Astrakhanskaya Sudoverf im. "Kirova" — Astrakhan** Yd No: 2 Loa 39.10 Br ex 8.28 Dght 2.850 Lbp 34.45 Br md - Dpth 3.61 Welded, 1 dk	**(B11B2FV) Fishing Vessel** Ice Capable	**1 oil engine** driving 1 FP propeller Total Power: 425kW (578hp) 10.0kn S.K.L. 8VD36/24A-1U 1 x 4 Stroke 8 Cy. 240 x 360 425kW (578bhp) VEB Schwermaschinenbau "KarlLiebknecht" (SKL)-Magdeburg AuxGen: 2 x 75kW Fuel: 53.0 (d.f.)
8133695 - -	**TYULEN-3** **A/O 'Kazakhrybflot'** - *Bautino* *Kazakhstan* Official number: 801960	**340** 102 145	Class: (RS)	**1982 Astrakhanskaya Sudoverf im. "Kirova" — Astrakhan** Yd No: 3 Loa 39.10 Br ex 8.28 Dght 2.850 Lbp 34.45 Br md - Dpth 3.61 Welded, 1 dk	**(B11B2FV) Fishing Vessel** Ice Capable	**1 oil engine** driving 1 FP propeller Total Power: 425kW (578hp) 10.0kn S.K.L. 8VD36/24A-1U 1 x 4 Stroke 8 Cy. 240 x 360 425kW (578bhp) VEB Schwermaschinenbau "KarlLiebknecht" (SKL)-Magdeburg AuxGen: 2 x 75kW Fuel: 53.0 (d.f.)
8227044 - -	**TYULEN-5** **A/O 'Kazakhrybflot'** - *Bautino* *Kazakhstan* Official number: 822331	**340** 102 145	Class: (RS)	**1983 Astrakhanskaya Sudoverf im. "Kirova" — Astrakhan** Yd No: 5 Loa 39.10 Br ex 8.28 Dght 2.850 Lbp 34.45 Br md - Dpth 3.61 Welded, 1 dk	**(B11B2FV) Fishing Vessel** Ice Capable	**1 oil engine** driving 1 FP propeller Total Power: 425kW (578hp) 10.0kn S.K.L. 8VD36/24A-1U 1 x 4 Stroke 8 Cy. 240 x 360 425kW (578bhp) VEB Schwermaschinenbau "KarlLiebknecht" (SKL)-Magdeburg AuxGen: 2 x 75kW Fuel: 53.0 (d.f.)
8228799 *UGAJ* -	**TYULEN-6** **Magomed Saadulayevich Magomeddibirov** - *Makhachkala* *Russia* MMSI: 273610100	**340** 102 145	Class: (RS)	**1984-09 Astrakhanskaya Sudoverf im. "Kirova" — Astrakhan** Yd No: 6 Loa 39.10 Br ex 8.28 Dght 2.850 Lbp 34.45 Br md 8.27 Dpth 3.61 Welded, 1 dk	**(B11B2FV) Fishing Vessel** Ice Capable	**1 oil engine** driving 1 FP propeller Total Power: 425kW (578hp) 10.0kn S.K.L. 8VD36/24A-1U 1 x 4 Stroke 8 Cy. 240 x 360 425kW (578bhp) VEB Schwermaschinenbau "KarlLiebknecht" (SKL)-Magdeburg AuxGen: 2 x 75kW Fuel: 53.0 (d.f.)
8727305 - -	**TYULEN-9** **A/O 'Kazakhrybflot'** - *Bautino* *Kazakhstan* Official number: 852772	**340** 102 145	Class: (RS)	**1986-12 Astrakhanskaya Sudoverf im. "Kirova" — Astrakhan** Yd No: 9 Loa 39.10 Br ex 8.27 Dght 2.850 Lbp 34.46 Br md - Dpth 3.60 Welded, 1 dk	**(B11B2FV) Fishing Vessel** Ice Capable	**1 oil engine** driving 1 FP propeller Total Power: 425kW (578hp) 10.0kn S.K.L. 8VD36/24A-1U 1 x 4 Stroke 8 Cy. 240 x 360 425kW (578bhp) VEB Schwermaschinenbau "KarlLiebknecht" (SKL)-Magdeburg AuxGen: 2 x 75kW Fuel: 53.0 (d.f.)
8727317 *UGAH* -	**TYULEN-10** **OOO 'Kaspiy'** - *Makhachkala* *Russia* MMSI: 273612100	**340** 102 145	Class: RS	**1988-06 Astrakhanskaya Sudoverf im. "Kirova" — Astrakhan** Yd No: 10 Loa 39.10 Br ex 8.27 Dght 2.850 Lbp 34.45 Br md 8.10 Dpth 3.60 Welded, 1 dk	**(B11B2FV) Fishing Vessel** Ice Capable	**1 oil engine** driving 1 FP propeller Total Power: 425kW (578hp) 10.0kn S.K.L. 8VD36/24A-1U 1 x 4 Stroke 8 Cy. 240 x 360 425kW (578bhp) VEB Schwermaschinenbau "KarlLiebknecht" (SKL)-Magdeburg AuxGen: 2 x 75kW Fuel: 53.0 (d.f.)
8943492 *UEPE* -	**TYUMEN** **Zale International Inc** Azia Shipping Holding Ltd *Vanino* *Russia* MMSI: 273444860 Official number: 814458	**2,592** 1,282 4,004	Class: RS	**1981 Santierul Naval Oltenita S.A. — Oltenita** Yd No: 130 Loa 108.40 Br ex 15.34 Dght 3.810 Lbp 102.23 Br md - Dpth 5.00 Welded, 1 dk	**(A31A2GX) General Cargo Ship**	**2 oil engines** driving 2 FP propellers Total Power: 1,320kW (1,794hp) S.K.L. 6NVD48A-2U 2 x 4 Stroke 6 Cy. 320 x 480 each-660kW (897bhp) VEB Schwermaschinenbau "KarlLiebknecht" (SKL)-Magdeburg

8721492 *UDPN* -
TYUMEN-1
ex Amur-2523 -2007
Reskom Tyumen Ltd
-
St Petersburg *Russia*
MMSI: 273375200
Official number: 875574

3,086 999 3,329 — Class: RR RS

1988-02 Zavody Tazkeho Strojarstva (ZTS) — Komarno Yd No: 2323
Loa 116.03 Br ex 13.43 Dght 4.130
Lbp 111.20 Br md 13.00 Dpth 6.00
Welded, 1 dk

(A31A2GX) General Cargo Ship
Grain: 4,064
TEU 102 C.Ho 62/20' (40') C.Dk 40/20' (40')
Compartments: 3 Ho, ER
3 Ha: (11.6 x 10.1) (23.0 x 10.1) (24.0 x 10.1)ER

2 oil engines reverse reduction geared to sc. shafts driving 2 FP propellers
Total Power: 1,030kW (1,400hp) 10.0kn
Skoda 6L275A2
2 x 4 Stroke 6 Cy. 275 x 350 each-515kW (700bhp)
CKD Praha-Praha
AuxGen: 3 x 138kW 220/380V a.c, 1 x 25kW 220/380V a.c
Thrusters: 1 Thwart. FP thruster (f)
Fuel: 157.0 (d.f.)

8727848 *UGSQ* -
TYUMEN-2
ex Amur-2529 -2007
Reskom Tyumen Ltd
-
Novorossiysk *Russia*
MMSI: 273398000
Official number: 886047

3,086 925 3,148 T/cm 12.0 — Class: RS (RR)

1989-03 Zavody Tazkeho Strojarstva (ZTS) — Komarno Yd No: 2329
Loa 116.06 Br ex 13.40 Dght 4.001
Lbp 109.11 Br md 13.01 Dpth 6.02
Welded, 1 dk

(A31A2GX) General Cargo Ship
Grain: 4,064
TEU 102 C.Ho 62/20' (40') C.Dk 40/20' (40')
Compartments: 3 Ho, ER
3 Ha: (11.6 x 10.1) (23.0 x 10.1) (24.0 x 10.1)ER

2 oil engines reverse reduction geared to sc. shafts driving 2 FP propellers
Total Power: 1,030kW (1,400hp) 10.0kn
Skoda 6L275A2
1 x 4 Stroke 6 Cy. 275 x 350 515kW (700bhp)
CKD Praha-Praha
Skoda 6L275IIIPN
1 x 4 Stroke 6 Cy. 275 x 350 515kW (700bhp)
CKD Praha-Praha
AuxGen: 3 x 138kW 220/380V a.c, 1 x 25kW 220/380V a.c
Thrusters: 1 Thwart. FP thruster (f)
Fuel: 157.0 (d.f.)

8832083 *UBPE4* -
TYUMEN-3
ex Midland 101 -2007 ex Kegums -2002
Fonika Ltd Joint Venture Co (OOO 'Sovmestnoye Predpriyatiye Fonika')
Reskom Tyumen Ltd
St Petersburg *Russia*
MMSI: 273317780

3,086 999 3,152 T/cm 12.0 — Class: RS (RR)

1990-06 Zavody Tazkeho Strojarstva (ZTS) — Komarno Yd No: 2335
Loa 116.06 Br ex 13.44 Dght 4.001
Lbp 111.21 Br md 13.00 Dpth 6.02
Welded, 1 dk

(A31A2GX) General Cargo Ship
Grain: 4,064
TEU 102 C.Ho 62/20' (40') C.Dk 40/20' (40')
Compartments: 3 Ho, ER
3 Ha: (11.6 x 10.1) (23.0 x 10.1) (24.0 x 10.1)ER
Ice Capable

2 oil engines sr geared to sc. shafts driving 2 FP propellers
Total Power: 1,030kW (1,400hp) 10.0kn
Skoda 6L275A2
2 x 4 Stroke 6 Cy. 275 x 350 each-515kW (700bhp)
CKD Praha-Praha
AuxGen: 3 x 138kW a.c
Thrusters: 1 Thwart. FP thruster (f)
Fuel: 160.0 (d.f.) 7.5pd

9611101 *XUCP4* -
TYUMEN I
Tanner Overseas Corp
GBB Mining Ltd
Phnom Penh *Cambodia*
MMSI: 515627000
Official number: 1111659

5,223 2,959 6,041 — Class: RR (Class contemplated) UA

2011-08 OAO Khersonskiy Sudostroitelnyy Zavod — Kherson Yd No: 08123
Loa 137.00 Br ex 16.50 Dght 3.950
Lbp 131.85 Br md 16.00 Dpth 5.50
Welded, 1 dk

(A31A2GX) General Cargo Ship
Grain: 9,956; Bale: 9,843

2 oil engines reduction geared to sc. shafts driving 2 Propellers
Total Power: 1,940kW (2,638hp) 9.0kn
S.K.L. 8NVD48A-2U
2 x 4 Stroke 8 Cy. 320 x 480 each-970kW (1319bhp)
SKL Motoren u. Systemtechnik AG-Magdeburg

9145229 *9HYM5* -
TZAREVETZ
Veliko Tirnovo Shipping Co Ltd
Navigation Maritime Bulgare
SatCom: Inmarsat C 424830610
Valletta *Malta*
MMSI: 248306000
Official number: 6158

13,965 7,250 21,470 T/cm 26.1 — Class: GL (BR)

1998-11 Varna Shipyard AD — Varna Yd No: 455
Loa 168.58 Br ex - Dght 8.510
Lbp 158.00 Br md 25.00 Dpth 11.50
Welded, 1 dk

(A21A2BC) Bulk Carrier
Grain: 24,948
Compartments: 5 Ho, ER
5 Ha: 5 (18.6 x 14.3)ER
Cranes: 3x16t
Ice Capable

1 oil engine driving 1 FP propeller
Total Power: 5,884kW (8,000hp) 13.5kn
B&W 8L42MC
1 x 2 Stroke 8 Cy. 420 x 1360 5884kW (8000bhp)
AO Bryanskiy MashinostroitelnyyZavod (BMZ)-Bryansk

1005796 *ZCSY2* -
TZARINA
ex Teddy -2000 ex Tigre Dos -2000
ex Tigre d'Or -1999
Elmwood Ventures Ltd
George Town *Cayman Islands (British)*
MMSI: 319495000
Official number: 900278

603 180 589 — Class: (LR) ✠ Classed LR until 11/11/09

1997-06 Amels Holland BV — Makkum Yd No: 430
Loa 48.50 Br ex 9.42 Dght 3.200
Lbp 45.75 Br md 9.00 Dpth 4.90
Welded, 1 dk

(X11A2YP) Yacht

2 oil engines with clutches, flexible couplings & sr reverse geared to sc. shafts driving 2 FP propellers
Total Power: 1,790kW (2,434hp) 15.0kn
Cummins KTA-38-M2
2 x Vee 4 Stroke 12 Cy. 159 x 159 each-895kW (1217bhp)
Cummins Engine Co Inc-USA
AuxGen: 2 x 136kW 380V 50Hz a.c
Thrusters: 1 Thwart. FP thruster (f)

9625906 *9HA3246* -
TZINI
Seashell Shipping Ltd
Eastern Mediterranean Maritime Ltd
Valletta *Malta*
MMSI: 229338000
Official number: 9625906

20,239 7,688 24,121 — Class: BV GL

2013-01 SPP Shipbuilding Co Ltd — Sacheon Yd No: H4076
Loa 170.06 (BB) Br ex - Dght 9.500
Lbp 160.00 Br md 29.80 Dpth 14.50
Welded, 1 dk

(A33A2CC) Container Ship (Fully Cellular)
TEU 1756 incl 350 ref C
Cranes: 3x40t

1 oil engine driving 1 FP propeller
Total Power: 14,280kW (19,415hp) 20.0kn
MAN-B&W 6S60ME-C8
1 x 2 Stroke 6 Cy. 600 x 2400 14280kW (19415bhp)
Hyundai Heavy Industries Co Ltd-South Korea
Thrusters: 1 Tunnel thruster (f)

6825311 *HP4995* -
TZU HANG
ex Wakasa Maru -1988
ex Tatsumi Maru No. 8 -1988
Giant Shipping Lines SA
-
Panama *Panama*
Official number: 14234PEXT2

389 190 706

1968 K.K. Taihei Kogyo — Akitsu Yd No: 220
Loa 48.85 Br ex 8.03 Dght 3.887
Lbp 46.11 Br md 8.01 Dpth 4.09
Welded, 1 dk

(A31A2GX) General Cargo Ship
Grain: 772; Bale: 688
Compartments: 1 Ho, ER
1 Ha: (23.3 x 4.8)ER

1 oil engine driving 1 FP propeller
Total Power: 2,207kW (3,001hp) 10.0kn
Akasaka 6DM51SS
1 x 4 Stroke 6 Cy. 510 x 840 2207kW (3001bhp)
Akasaka Tekkosho KK (Akasaka DieselLtd)-Japan
AuxGen: 1 x 32kW 225V a.c, 1 x 16kW 225V a.c

8961456 *WDA3091* -
U-BOYS
U Boys LLC
Wanchese, NC *United States of America*
MMSI: 366794530
Official number: 1104089

135 40 -

2000-01 Thoma-Sea Boatbuilders Inc — Houma LA Yd No: 115
L reg 23.50 Br ex - Dght -
Lbp - Br md 7.31 Dpth 3.65
Welded, 1 dk

(B11B2FV) Fishing Vessel

1 oil engine driving 1 FP propeller

9130626 *3FNW6* -
U HAPPY
ex Oji New Century -2012
Uhappy Shipping Pte Ltd
Brother Marine Co Ltd
SatCom: Inmarsat C 435683810
Panama *Panama*
MMSI: 356838000
Official number: 25483PEXT3

36,712 18,305 43,906 — Class: NK

1996-09 Sanoyas Hishino Meisho Corp — Kurashiki OY Yd No: 1140
Loa 195.00 (BB) Br ex 32.24 Dght 10.550
Lbp 188.00 Br md 32.20 Dpth 21.50
Welded, 1 dk

(A24B2BW) Wood Chips Carrier
Grain: 91,140
Compartments: 6 Ho, ER
6 Ha: (13.4 x 12.3)5 (15.0 x 17.2)ER
Cranes: 3x15t

1 oil engine driving 1 FP propeller
Total Power: 9,268kW (12,601hp) 15.3kn
Mitsubishi 7UEC52LS
1 x 2 Stroke 7 Cy. 520 x 1850 9268kW (12601bhp)
Mitsubishi Heavy Industries Ltd-Japan
Fuel: 1890.0 (r.f.)

9617478 *VRIW5* -
U LUCKY
Wise Shipping Ltd
-
Hong Kong *Hong Kong*
MMSI: 477095100
Official number: HK-3168

33,044 19,231 57,000 T/cm 58.8 — Class: BV

2011-08 Xiamen Shipbuilding Industry Co Ltd — Xiamen FJ Yd No: XSI409C
Loa 189.99 Br ex - Dght 12.800
Lbp 185.00 Br md 32.26 Dpth 18.00
Welded, 1 dk

(A21A2BC) Bulk Carrier
Grain: 71,634; Bale: 68,200
Compartments: 5 Ho, ER
5 Ha: 4 (21.3 x 18.3)ER (18.9 x 18.3)
Cranes: 4x30t

1 oil engine driving 1 FP propeller
Total Power: 9,480kW (12,889hp) 14.2kn
MAN-B&W 6S50MC-C
1 x 2 Stroke 6 Cy. 500 x 2000 9480kW (12889bhp)
AuxGen: 3 x 650kW 60Hz a.c
Fuel: 2405.0 (r.f.)

9617480 *VRIW4* -
U NOBLE
United Express Shipping Ltd
-
Hong Kong *Hong Kong*
MMSI: 477435300
Official number: HK-3167

33,044 19,231 57,000 T/cm 58.8 — Class: BV

2012-01 Xiamen Shipbuilding Industry Co Ltd — Xiamen FJ Yd No: XSI409D
Loa 189.99 (BB) Br ex - Dght 12.800
Lbp 185.00 Br md 32.26 Dpth 18.00
Welded, 1 dk

(A21A2BC) Bulk Carrier
Grain: 71,634; Bale: 68,200
Compartments: 5 Ho, ER
5 Ha: ER
Cranes: 4x30t

1 oil engine driving 1 FP propeller
Total Power: 9,480kW (12,889hp) 14.2kn
MAN-B&W 6S50MC-C
1 x 2 Stroke 6 Cy. 500 x 2000 9480kW (12889bhp)
Hyundai Heavy Industries Co Ltd-South Korea
AuxGen: 3 x 600kW 60Hz a.c
Fuel: 2405.0

8519174 - -
U. S. ENTERPRISE
ex Magadan -1998 ex U. S. Enterprise -1997
Trident Seafoods Corp
-
SatCom: Inmarsat A 1511612
Seattle, WA *United States of America*
Official number: 921112

1,579 473 1,095 — Class: AB

1987-10 Halter Marine, Inc. — Moss Point, Ms Yd No: 1122
Loa 68.31 Br ex - Dght 4.806
Lbp 59.25 Br md 12.81 Dpth 4.88
Welded, 1 dk

(B11A2FS) Stern Trawler
Ins: 1,359

2 oil engines reverse reduction geared to sc. shafts driving 2 FP propellers
Total Power: 2,868kW (3,900hp) 13.0kn
EMD (Electro-Motive) 16-645-E6
2 x Vee 2 Stroke 16 Cy. 230 x 254 each-1434kW (1950bhp)
General Motors Corp.Electro-Motive Div.-La Grange
AuxGen: 2 x 250kW 480V 60Hz a.c
Thrusters: 1 Directional thruster (f)
Fuel: 489.5 (d.f.)

7802536 *WDE2670* -
U. S. INTREPID
ex Bristol Enterprise -2001
ex Bristol Bounty -1987
ex Inmar Monarch -1987
U S Fishing LLC
Fishermen's Finest Inc
SatCom: Inmarsat A 1555171
Seattle, WA *United States of America*
MMSI: 366761830
Official number: 604439

1,264 410 - — Class: (AB)

1979-04 Bourg Dry Dock & Service Co., Inc. — Bourg, La Yd No: 48
Converted From: Offshore Tug/Supply Ship-1987
Lengthened-1987
Loa 56.39 Br ex 12.20 Dght 4.683
Lbp 52.73 Br md 12.18 Dpth 4.73
Welded, 1 dk

(B11A2FG) Factory Stern Trawler

2 oil engines reverse reduction geared to sc. shafts driving 2 FP propellers
Total Power: 2,908kW (3,954hp) 13.0kn
Brons 12TD200
2 x Vee 2 Stroke 12 Cy. 220 x 380 each-1454kW (1977bhp)
B.V. Motorenfabriek "De Industrie"-Alphen a/d Rijn
AuxGen: 2 x 99kW
Thrusters: 1 Thwart. FP thruster (f)

Ship	Tonnage	Class	Build	Type	Machinery
7926526 **U. S. LIBERATOR** *WDB4152* *ex Gulf Wind -1998 ex Pelagos -1990* - **Liberator Fisheries LLC** SatCom: Inmarsat A 1555342 *Seattle, WA* *United States of America* MMSI: 369283000 Official number: 611520	**868** 221 -		**1980-03 Flohr Metal Fabrications, Inc. — Seattle, Wa** Lengthened-1990 Loa 47.85 Br ex 10.39 Dght 4.067 Lbp 46.30 Br md - Dpth 4.90 Welded, 1 dk	**(B11A2FS) Stern Trawler** Ins: 420	**2 oil engines** reduction geared to sc. shafts driving 2 FP propellers Total Power: 1,250kW (1,700hp) Caterpillar D398SCAC 2 x Vee 4 Stroke 12 Cy. 159 x 203 each-625kW (850bhp) Caterpillar Tractor Co-USA
8940086 **U. S. SHRIMP** *WDE4659* *ex Little Angel II -2008 ex Dolphin I -2005* - *ex Lucky Dragon -2005 ex Capt. Scott III -2001* **Tina Ngo** *Port Arthur, TX* *United States of America* MMSI: 367356110 Official number: 1039486	**158** 47 -		**1996 Master Boat Builders, Inc. — Coden, Al** Yd No: 216 L reg 25.88 Br ex - Dght - Lbp - Br md 7.62 Dpth 3.81 Welded, 1 dk	**(B11B2FV) Fishing Vessel**	**1 oil engine** driving 1 FP propeller
8978227 **U. T. M. I** *5NJV* *ex Sylvia F -2007* - **UTM Dredging Ltd** - *Nigeria* Official number: SR643	**201** 60 166		**1990-10 Gulf Craft Inc — Patterson LA** Yd No: 4 Loa 39.62 Br ex - Dght 3.040 Lbp 36.57 Br md 7.92 Dpth 3.65 Welded, 1 dk	**(B21A20C) Crew/Supply Vessel** Passengers: 72; cabins: 4	**4 oil engines** with clutches, flexible couplings & sr reverse geared to sc. shafts driving 4 FP propellers Total Power: 2,060kW (2,800hp) 20.0kn Cummins KTA-19-M3 4 x 4 Stroke 6 Cy. 159 x 159 each-515kW (700bhp) Cummins Engine Co Inc-USA AuxGen: 2 x 50kW Fuel: 34.0 (d.f.) 8.4pd
9254939 **UACC AL MEDINA** *3FZX2* *ex Nord Sea -2008* - **United Arab Chemical Carriers Ltd** ST Shipping & Transport Pte Ltd SatCom: Inmarsat C 437094910 *Panama* *Panama* MMSI: 370949000 Official number: 4015709	**28,059** 11,645 45,987 T/cm 50.5	Class: NV (NK)	**2003-07 Shin Kurushima Dockyard Co. Ltd. — Onishi** Yd No: 5178 Loa 179.88 (BB) Br ex 32.23 Dght 12.022 Lbp 172.00 Br md 32.20 Dpth 18.70 Welded, 1 dk	**(A13B2TP) Products Tanker** Double Hull (13F) Liq: 50,754; Liq (Oil): 50,754 Compartments: 14 Wing Ta, ER, 2 Wing Slop Ta 4 Cargo Pump (s): 4x1000m³/hr Manifold: Bow/CM: 91.3m	**1 oil engine** driving 1 FP propeller Total Power: 9,480kW (12,889hp) 15.1kn MAN-B&W 6S50MC-C 1 x 2 Stroke 6 Cy. 500 x 2000 9480kW (12889bhp) Mitsui Engineering & Shipbuilding CLtd-Japan AuxGen: 3 x 720kW 450V a.c Fuel: 1840.0
9296585 **UACC CONSENSUS** *3FXQ5* *ex High Consensus -2009* - **Consensus Tankers Inc** United Arab Chemical Carriers Ltd SatCom: Inmarsat Mini-M 764914840 *Panama* *Panama* MMSI: 352591000 Official number: 4105110A	**28,059** 11,645 45,896 T/cm 50.6	Class: NV (NK)	**2005-02 Shin Kurushima Dockyard Co. Ltd. — Onishi** Yd No: 5255 Loa 179.88 (BB) Br ex 32.23 Dght 12.022 Lbp 172.00 Br md 32.20 Dpth 18.70 Welded, 1 dk	**(A13B2TP) Products Tanker** Double Hull (13F) Liq: 50,753; Liq (Oil): 52,499 Cargo Heating Coils Compartments: 14 Wing Ta, ER, 3 Wing Slop Ta 4 Cargo Pump (s): 4x1000m³/hr Manifold: Bow/CM: 92.5m	**1 oil engine** driving 1 FP propeller Total Power: 9,267kW (12,599hp) 14.5kn Mitsubishi 6UEC60LA 1 x 2 Stroke 6 Cy. 600 x 1900 9267kW (12599bhp) Kobe Hatsudoki KK-Japan AuxGen: 3 x 300kW 440/110V 60Hz a.c Fuel: 183.0 (d.f.) 1850.0 (r.f.) 31.0pd
9550694 **UACC EAGLE** *V7VN8* *ex Summit Asia -2011* - **UACC Bergshav Tanker AS** United Arab Chemical Carriers Ltd *Majuro* *Marshall Islands* MMSI: 538004168 Official number: 4168	**42,010** 22,361 73,410 T/cm 66.8	Class: LR (AB) **100A1** SS 08/2009 Double Hull oil tanker CSR ESP *IWS LI SPM4 **LMC** **UMS IGS**	**2009-08 New Times Shipbuilding Co Ltd — Jingjiang JS** Yd No: 0307365 Loa 228.60 (BB) Br ex 32.26 Dght 14.498 Lbp 219.70 Br md 32.20 Dpth 20.80 Welded, 1 dk	**(A13B2TP) Products Tanker** Double Hull (13F) Liq: 81,185; Liq (Oil): 81,311 Cargo Heating Coils Compartments: 12 Wing Ta, 2 Wing Slop Ta, ER 3 Cargo Pump (s): 3x2300m³/hr Manifold: Bow/CM: 114.1m	**1 oil engine** driving 1 FP propeller Total Power: 11,300kW (15,363hp) 14.5kn MAN-B&W 5S60MC-C 1 x 2 Stroke 5 Cy. 600 x 2400 11300kW (15363bhp) Hudong Heavy Machinery Co Ltd-China AuxGen: 3 x 900kW a.c Fuel: 210.0 (d.f.) 1928.0 (r.f.)
9550682 **UACC FALCON** *V7VO3* *ex Summit Australia -2010* - **UACC Ross Tanker AS** United Arab Chemical Carriers Ltd *Majuro* *Marshall Islands* MMSI: 538004170 Official number: 4170	**42,010** 22,361 73,427 T/cm 65.0	Class: LR (AB) **100A1** SS 05/2009 Double Hull oil tanker CSR ESP *IWS LI SPM4 **LMC** **UMS IGS**	**2009-05 New Times Shipbuilding Co Ltd — Jingjiang JS** Yd No: 0307364 Loa 228.60 (BB) Br ex 32.26 Dght 14.500 Lbp 219.70 Br md 32.20 Dpth 20.80 Welded, 1 dk	**(A13B2TP) Products Tanker** Double Hull (13F) Liq: 81,160; Liq (Oil): 81,177 Cargo Heating Coils Compartments: 12 Wing Ta, 2 Wing Slop Ta, 1 Slop Ta, ER 3 Cargo Pump (s): 3x2300m³/hr Manifold: Bow/CM: 114.1m	**1 oil engine** driving 1 FP propeller Total Power: 11,300kW (15,363hp) 14.7kn MAN-B&W 5S60MC-C 1 x 2 Stroke 5 Cy. 600 x 2400 11300kW (15363bhp) Hudong Heavy Machinery Co Ltd-China AuxGen: 3 x 900kW a.c Boilers: WTAuxB (o.f.) 18.4kgf/cm² (18.0bar) Fuel: 245.0 (d.f.) 2067.0 (r.f.)
9288289 **UACC HARMONY** *3FZK8* *ex High Harmony -2009* - **Harmony Tankers Inc** United Arab Chemical Carriers Ltd SatCom: Inmarsat Mini-M 764911720 *Panama* *Panama* MMSI: 355331000 Official number: 4108410A	**28,059** 11,645 45,913 T/cm 50.6	Class: NV (NK) (AB)	**2005-01 Shin Kurushima Dockyard Co. Ltd. — Onishi** Yd No: 5253 Loa 179.88 (BB) Br ex 32.23 Dght 12.022 Lbp 172.00 Br md 32.20 Dpth 18.70 Welded, 1 dk	**(A13B2TP) Products Tanker** Double Hull (13F) Liq: 50,754; Liq (Oil): 53,796 Cargo Heating Coils Compartments: 14 Wing Ta, ER, 2 Wing Slop Ta 4 Cargo Pump (s): 4x1000m³/hr Manifold: Bow/CM: 91.3m	**1 oil engine** driving 1 FP propeller Total Power: 9,267kW (12,599hp) 14.6kn Mitsubishi 6UEC60LA 1 x 2 Stroke 6 Cy. 600 x 1900 9267kW (12599bhp) Kobe Hatsudoki KK-Japan AuxGen: 3 x 300kW 440/110V 60Hz a.c Fuel: 158.0 (d.f.) 1683.0 (r.f.) 31.0pd
9254927 **UACC IBN AL ATHEER** *HPBI* *ex Pacific Sunshine -2008* - **Atheer Tankers Inc** United Arab Chemical Carriers Ltd *Panama* *Panama* MMSI: 351616000 Official number: 2917603C	**28,059** 11,645 45,994 T/cm 50.7	Class: NV (NK)	**2003-05 Shin Kurushima Dockyard Co. Ltd. — Onishi** Yd No: 5168 Loa 179.88 (BB) Br ex 32.23 Dght 12.022 Lbp 172.00 Br md 32.20 Dpth 18.70 Welded, 1 dk	**(A13B2TP) Products Tanker** Double Hull (13F) Liq: 50,754; Liq (Oil): 52,000 Cargo Heating Coils Compartments: 14 Wing Ta, ER, 2 Wing Slop Ta 4 Cargo Pump (s): 4x1000m³/hr Manifold: Bow/CM: 91.3m	**1 oil engine** driving 1 FP propeller Total Power: 9,480kW (12,889hp) 15.1kn MAN-B&W 6S50MC-C 1 x 2 Stroke 6 Cy. 500 x 2000 9480kW (12889bhp) Mitsui Engineering & Shipbuilding CLtd-Japan AuxGen: 3 x 720kW 450V a.c Fuel: 414.4 (d.f.) 3834.0 (r.f.)
9485631 **UACC IBN AL HAITHAM** *9HVB9* - **Haitham Tankers Inc** United Arab Chemical Carriers Ltd SatCom: Inmarsat Mini-M 764893891 *Valletta* *Malta* MMSI: 249580000 Official number: 9485631	**42,010** 22,361 73,338 T/cm 67.1	Class: LR (AB) **100A1** SS 01/2014 Double Hull oil tanker CSR ESP *IWS LI SPM4 **LMC** **UMS IGS**	**2009-01 New Times Shipbuilding Co Ltd — Jingjiang JS** Yd No: 0307349 Loa 228.60 (BB) Br ex - Dght 14.498 Lbp 219.70 Br md 32.26 Dpth 20.80 Welded, 1 dk	**(A13A2TW) Crude/Oil Products Tanker** Double Hull (13F) Liq: 81,285; Liq (Oil): 84,345 Cargo Heating Coils Compartments: 12 Wing Ta, 2 Wing Slop Ta, ER 3 Cargo Pump (s): 3x2300m³/hr Manifold: Bow/CM: 114.8m	**1 oil engine** driving 1 FP propeller Total Power: 11,300kW (15,363hp) 14.7kn MAN-B&W 5S60MC-C 1 x 2 Stroke 5 Cy. 600 x 2400 11300kW (15363bhp) Hudong Heavy Machinery Co Ltd-China AuxGen: 3 x 900kW a.c
9485629 **UACC IBN SINA** *9HTT9* - **Sina Tankers Inc** United Arab Chemical Carriers Ltd *Valletta* *Malta* MMSI: 249497000 Official number: 9485629	**42,010** 22,361 73,338 T/cm 67.1	Class: LR (AB) **100A1** SS 11/2013 Double Hull oil tanker CSR ESP *IWS LI SPM4 ✠**LMC** **UMS IGS** Cable: 687.5/81.0 U3 (a)	**2008-11 New Times Shipbuilding Co Ltd — Jingjiang JS** Yd No: 0307348 Loa 228.60 (BB) Br ex - Dght 14.498 Lbp 219.70 Br md 32.26 Dpth 20.80 Welded, 1 dk	**(A13A2TW) Crude/Oil Products Tanker** Double Hull (13F) Liq: 81,285; Liq (Oil): 84,345 Cargo Heating Coils Compartments: 12 Wing Ta, 2 Wing Slop Ta, ER 3 Cargo Pump (s): 3x2300m³/hr Manifold: Bow/CM: 114.7m	**1 oil engine** driving 1 FP propeller Total Power: 11,300kW (15,363hp) 14.7kn MAN-B&W 5S60MC-C 1 x 2 Stroke 5 Cy. 600 x 2400 11300kW (15363bhp) Hudong Heavy Machinery Co Ltd-China Boilers: e (ex.g.) 10.2kgf/cm² (10.0bar), AuxB (o.f.) 18.4kgf/cm² (18.0bar) Fuel: 220.0 (d.f.) 1880.0 (r.f.)
9489089 **UACC MANSOURIA** *V7TP2* - **Mansouria Tankers Inc** United Arab Shipping Co (UASC) *Majuro* *Marshall Islands* MMSI: 538003850 Official number: 3850	**29,279** 11,677 45,293 T/cm 51.1	Class: NV	**2013-05 ShinaSB Yard Co Ltd — Tongyeong** Yd No: 546 Loa 183.00 (BB) Br ex 32.32 Dght 12.150 Lbp 174.00 Br md 32.20 Dpth 18.90 Welded, 1 dk	**(A12B2TR) Chemical/Products Tanker** Double Hull (13F) Liq: 50,813; Liq (Oil): 50,840 Part Cargo Heating Coils Compartments: 10 Wing Ta, 10 Wing Ta, 1 Wing Slop Ta, 1 Wing Slop Ta, ER 20 Cargo Pump (s): 12x500m³/hr, 8x360m³/hr Manifold: Bow/CM: 94.9m	**1 oil engine** driving 1 FP propeller Total Power: 9,480kW (12,889hp) 15.0kn MAN-B&W 6S50MC-C 1 x 2 Stroke 6 Cy. 500 x 2000 9480kW (12889bhp) MAN Diesel A/S-Denmark AuxGen: 2 x 750kW a.c, 1 x a.c Thrusters: 1 Tunnel thruster (f) Fuel: 300.0 (d.f.) 1553.0 (r.f.)
9489091 **UACC MARAH** *V7TP3* - **Marah Tankers Inc** United Arab Chemical Carriers Ltd *Majuro* *Marshall Islands* MMSI: 538003851 Official number: 3851	**29,279** 11,677 45,293 T/cm 52.1	Class: NV	**2013-07 ShinaSB Yard Co Ltd — Tongyeong** Yd No: 547 Loa 183.00 (BB) Br ex 32.23 Dght 12.150 Lbp 174.00 Br md 32.20 Dpth 18.90 Welded, 1 dk	**(A12B2TR) Chemical/Products Tanker** Double Hull (13F) Liq: 50,813; Liq (Oil): 50,840 Part Cargo Heating Coils Compartments: 10 Wing Ta, 10 Wing Ta, 1 Wing Slop Ta, 1 Wing Slop Ta, ER 20 Cargo Pump (s): 20x600m³/hr Manifold: Bow/CM: 94.9m	**1 oil engine** driving 1 FP propeller Total Power: 9,480kW (12,889hp) 15.0kn MAN-B&W 6S50MC-C 1 x 2 Stroke 6 Cy. 500 x 2000 9480kW (12889bhp) MAN Diesel SA-France AuxGen: 2 x 750kW a.c, 1 x a.c Thrusters: 1 Tunnel thruster (f) Fuel: 300.0 (d.f.) 1553.0 (r.f.)

9489065 **UACC MASAFI**
V7T08
\-
Masafi Tankers Inc
NCC Odfjell Chemical Tankers JLT
SatCom: Inmarsat C 453836541
Majuro *Marshall Islands*
MMSI: 538003848
Official number: 3848

29,279 Class: NV
11,678
45,352
T/cm
52.1

2012-08 ShinaSB Yard Co Ltd — Tongyeong
Yd No: 544
Loa 183.00 (BB) Br ex 32.23 Dght 12.165
Lbp 174.00 Br md 32.20 Dpth 18.90
Welded, 1 dk

(A12B2TR) Chemical/Products Tanker
Double Hull (13F)
Liq: 50,813; Liq (Oil): 50,384
Part Cargo Heating Coils
Compartments: 20 Wing Ta, 2 Wing Slop Ta, ER
20 Cargo Pump (s): 8x360m³/hr, 12x500m³/hr
Manifold: Bow/CM: 94.9m

1 oil engine driving 1 FP propeller
Total Power: 9,960kW (13,542hp) 15.0kn
MAN-B&W 6S50MC-C8
1 x 2 Stroke 6 Cy. 500 x 2000 9960kW (13542bhp)
MAN Diesel A/S-Denmark
AuxGen: 2 x 750kW a.c, 1 x a.c
Thrusters: 1 Tunnel thruster (f)
Fuel: 300.0 (d.f.) 1553.0 (r.f.)

9489077 **UACC MESSILA**
V7T09
\-
Messila Tankers Inc
United Arab Shipping Co (UASC)
Majuro *Marshall Islands*
MMSI: 538003849
Official number: 3849

29,279 Class: NV
11,678
45,335
T/cm
51.1

2012-11 ShinaSB Yard Co Ltd — Tongyeong
Yd No: 545
Loa 183.00 (BB) Br ex 32.23 Dght 12.150
Lbp 174.00 Br md 32.20 Dpth 18.90
Welded, 1 dk

(A12B2TR) Chemical/Products Tanker
Double Hull (13F)
Liq: 50,802; Liq (Oil): 50,384
Part Cargo Heating Coils
Compartments: 20 Wing Ta, 2 Wing Slop Ta, ER
20 Cargo Pump (s): 12x500m³/hr, 8x360m³/hr
Manifold: Bow/CM: 94.9m

1 oil engine driving 1 FP propeller
Total Power: 9,480kW (12,889hp) 15.0kn
MAN-B&W 6S50MC-C
1 x 2 Stroke 6 Cy. 500 x 2000 9480kW (12889bhp)
MAN Diesel SA-France
AuxGen: 2 x 750kW a.c, 1 x a.c
Thrusters: 1 Tunnel thruster (f)
Fuel: 300.0 (d.f.) 1553.0 (r.f.)

9402794 **UACC MIRDIF**
V7FE5
ex Ocean Leo *-2014*
\-
Mirdif Tankers Inc
United Arab Chemical Carriers Ltd
SatCom: Inmarsat C 453839776
Majuro *Marshall Islands*
MMSI: 538005585
Official number: 5585

26,916 Class: NK (AB)
13,704
47,366
T/cm
50.3

2010-04 Onomichi Dockyard Co Ltd — Onomichi HS Yd No: 550
Loa 182.50 (BB) Br ex - Dght 12.620
Lbp 172.00 Br md 32.20 Dpth 18.10
Welded, 1 dk

(A13B2TP) Products Tanker
Double Hull (13F)
Liq: 52,500; Liq (Oil): 52,500

1 oil engine driving 1 FP propeller
Total Power: 8,580kW (11,665hp) 15.3kn
MAN-B&W 6S50MC
1 x 2 Stroke 6 Cy. 500 x 1910 8580kW (11665bhp)
Mitsui Engineering & Shipbuilding CLtd-Japan
Fuel: 1740.0

9428360 **UACC SHAMS**
A8SK5
ex Tyrrhenian Wave *-2011* *ex* Indiana *-2009*
\-
Indiana R Shipping Co Ltd
United Arab Chemical Carriers Ltd
Monrovia *Liberia*
MMSI: 636014235
Official number: 14235

30,006 Class: NV (AB)
13,435
49,999
T/cm
52.0

2009-03 SPP Plant & Shipbuilding Co Ltd — Sacheon Yd No: S1029
Loa 183.09 (BB) Br ex - Dght 13.049
Lbp 174.00 Br md 32.20 Dpth 19.10
Welded, 1 dk

(A12B2TR) Chemical/Products Tanker
Double Hull (13F)
Liq: 52,100; Liq (Oil): 52,100
Cargo Heating Coils
Compartments: 12 Wing Ta, 2 Wing Slop Ta, ER
12 Cargo Pump (s): 12x600m³/hr
Manifold: Bow/CM: 90.8m

1 oil engine driving 1 FP propeller
Total Power: 9,480kW (12,889hp) 14.9kn
MAN-B&W 6S50MC-C
1 x 2 Stroke 6 Cy. 500 x 2000 9480kW (12889bhp)
Doosan Engine Co Ltd-South Korea
AuxGen: 3 x 900kW a.c
Fuel: 170.0 (d.f.) 1323.0 (r.f.)

9428358 **UACC SILA**
V7BB2
ex Ionian Wave *-2011* *ex* Banksy *-2009*
\-
Sila Tankers Inc
Executive Ship Management Pte Ltd
Majuro *Marshall Islands*
MMSI: 538005107
Official number: 5107

30,006 Class: NV (AB)
13,435
49,999
T/cm
52.0

2009-03 SPP Plant & Shipbuilding Co Ltd — Sacheon Yd No: S1027
Loa 183.09 (BB) Br ex - Dght 13.057
Lbp 174.00 Br md 32.20 Dpth 19.10
Welded, 1 dk

(A12B2TR) Chemical/Products Tanker
Double Hull (13F)
Liq: 53,511; Liq (Oil): 53,511
Cargo Heating Coils
Compartments: 14 Wing Ta, 2 Wing Slop Ta, ER
12 Cargo Pump (s): 12x600m³/hr
Manifold: Bow/CM: 90.8m

1 oil engine driving 1 FP propeller
Total Power: 9,480kW (12,889hp) 14.9kn
MAN-B&W 6S50MC-C
1 x 2 Stroke 6 Cy. 500 x 2000 9480kW (12889bhp)
Doosan Engine Co Ltd-South Korea
AuxGen: 3 x 900kW a.c
Fuel: 170.0 (d.f.) 1323.0 (r.f.)

9272395 **UACC SOUND**
3FRE2
ex Nord Sound *-2009*
\-
United Arab Chemical Carriers Ltd
ST Shipping & Transport Pte Ltd
SatCom: Inmarsat C 435467810
Panama *Panama*
MMSI: 354678000
Official number: 4005909A

28,059 Class: NV (NK)
11,645
45,975
T/cm
50.6

2003-08 Shin Kurushima Dockyard Co. Ltd. — Onishi Yd No: 5187
Loa 179.88 (BB) Br ex 32.23 Dght 12.022
Lbp 172.00 Br md 32.20 Dpth 18.70
Welded

(A13B2TP) Products Tanker
Double Hull (13F)
Liq: 50,741; Liq (Oil): 50,741
Cargo Heating Coils
Compartments: 14 Wing Ta, 2 Wing Slop Ta, ER
4 Cargo Pump (s): 4x1000m³/hr
Manifold: Bow/CM: 91.3m

1 oil engine driving 1 FP propeller
Total Power: 9,480kW (12,889hp) 15.1kn
MAN-B&W 6S50MC-C
1 x 2 Stroke 6 Cy. 500 x 2000 9480kW (12889bhp)
Mitsui Engineering & Shipbuilding CLtd-Japan
AuxGen: 3 x 800kW 440/110V 60Hz a.c
Fuel: 148.0 (d.f.) 1726.0 (r.f.) 32.4pd

9272400 **UACC STRAIT**
H8NI
ex Nord Strait *-2009*
\-
United Arab Chemical Carriers Ltd
SatCom: Inmarsat B 335260510
Panama *Panama*
MMSI: 352605000
Official number: 3010404C

28,059 Class: NV (NK)
11,645
45,934
T/cm
50.6

2004-07 Shin Kurushima Dockyard Co. Ltd. — Onishi Yd No: 5213
Loa 179.88 (BB) Br ex 32.23 Dght 12.022
Lbp 172.00 Br md 32.20 Dpth 18.70
Welded, 1 Dk.

(A13B2TP) Products Tanker
Double Hull (13F)
Liq: 50,754; Liq (Oil): 50,754
Cargo Heating Coils
Compartments: 14 Wing Ta, 2 Wing Slop Ta, ER
4 Cargo Pump (s): 4x1000m³/hr
Manifold: Bow/CM: 91.3m

1 oil engine driving 1 FP propeller
Total Power: 9,481kW (12,890hp) 15.1kn
MAN-B&W 6S50MC-C
1 x 2 Stroke 6 Cy. 500 x 2000 9481kW (12890bhp)
Mitsui Engineering & Shipbuilding CLtd-Japan
AuxGen: 3 x 720kW 450V a.c
Fuel: 183.0 (d.f.) 1849.0 (r.f.)

9124392 **UAFL ZANZIBAR**
D5DC9
ex R. Sea *-2012* *ex* Nordsea *-2011*
ex CCNI Veracruz *-2008* *ex* CSAV Maya *-2008*
ex Nordsea *-2007* *ex* Nordseas *-2006*
ex MOL Sprinter *-2004* *ex* Malacca Star *-2003*
ex Nordsea *-2001* *ex* Pacific Voyager *-2001*
ex Nordsea *-2000* *ex* Panaustral *-1998*
ex Nordsea *-1997*
\-
KG Einunddreissigste OCEANIA Schiffahrtsgesellschaft mbH & Co
John T Essberger GmbH & Co KG
Monrovia *Liberia*
MMSI: 636092463
Official number: 92463

16,264 Class: GL
8,719
22,386

1996-12 Stocznia Szczecinska SA — Szczecin
Yd No: B186/3/8
Loa 179.30 (BB) Br ex - Dght 9.940
Lbp 167.26 Br md 25.30 Dpth 13.50
Welded, 1 dk

(A33A2CC) Container Ship (Fully Cellular)
Grain: 29,676
TEU 1684 C Ho 630 TEU C Dk 1054 TEU incl 120 ref C.
Compartments: 4 Cell Ho, ER
9 Ha: ER
Cranes: 3x45t

1 oil engine driving 1 FP propeller
Total Power: 13,320kW (18,110hp) 19.0kn
Sulzer 6RTA62U
1 x 2 Stroke 6 Cy. 620 x 2150 13320kW (18110bhp)
H Cegielski Poznan SA-Poland
AuxGen: 1 x 1000kW 440V 60Hz a.c, 3 x 540kW 440V 60Hz a.c
Thrusters: 1 Thwart. CP thruster (f)
Fuel: 171.0 (d.f.) (Heating Coils) 1937.0 (r.f.) 48.8pd

9529243 **UAL AFRICA**
PBCC
\-
UAL Africa CV
Nescos A BV (Nescos Shipping BV)
Hoogezand *Netherlands*
MMSI: 245890000
Official number: 54295

5,568 Class: LR
2,581 ✠ **100A1** SS 09/2011
8,327 strengthened for heavy cargoes, container cargoes in all holds and on upper deck and on all hatch covers
*IWS
✠ **LMC** **UMS**
Eq.Ltr: W;
Cable: 495.0/44.0 U3 (a)

2011-09 Bodewes' Scheepswerven B.V. — Hoogezand Yd No: 760
Loa 119.05 Br ex - Dght 6.963
Lbp 116.95 Br md 15.80 Dpth 10.05
Welded, 1 dk

(A31A2GX) General Cargo Ship
Grain: 10,774; Bale: 10,774
TEU 287 Ho 177 TEU C Dk 110 TEU incl 50 ref C
Compartments: 2 Ho, ER
2 Ha: (57.0 x 13.3)ER (25.5 x 13.3)
Cranes: 2x60t

1 oil engine with flexible couplings & sr geared to sc. shaft driving 1 CP propeller
Total Power: 2,999kW (4,077hp) 13.5kn
MaK 6M32
1 x 4 Stroke 6 Cy. 320 x 480 2999kW (4077bhp)
Caterpillar Motoren GmbH & Co. KG-Germany
AuxGen: 1 x 452kW 400V 50Hz a.c, 3 x 272kW 400V 50Hz a.c
Boilers: HWH (o.f.) 3.6kgf/cm² (3.5bar)
Thrusters: 1 Thwart. CP thruster (f)

9320520 **UAL AMERICA**
MHUN3
ex Emily-C *-2006*
\-
ms 'Emily C' UG (haftungsbeschrankt) & Co KG
Carisbrooke Shipping (Management) GmbH
Cowes *United Kingdom*
MMSI: 235008900
Official number: 20461

7,767 Class: LR
3,856 ✠ **100A1** SS 08/2010
10,609 strengthened for heavy cargoes,
T/cm container cargoes in holds and
23.2 on upper deck hatch covers, LI
*IWS
Ice Class 1A FS at draught of 7.627m
Max/min draughts fwd 7.627/3.6m
Max/min draughts aft 7.627/4.8m
Required power 4320kw, installed power 4320kw
✠ **LMC** **UMS**
Eq.Ltr: A†;
Cable: 522.5/50.0 U3 (a)

2005-08 B.V. Scheepswerf Damen Hoogezand — Foxhol Yd No: 841
2005-08 Damen Shipyards Yichang Co Ltd — Yichang HB (Hull)
Loa 145.63 (BB) Br ex 18.29 Dght 7.627
Lbp 139.38 Br md 18.25 Dpth 10.30
Welded, 1 dk

(A31A2GX) General Cargo Ship
Grain: 14,878; Bale: 13,975
TEU 665 C Ho 302 TEU C Dk 363 TEU incl 60 ref C.
Compartments: 2 Ho, ER
2 Ha: (59.5 x 13.2)ER (39.0 x 13.2)
Cranes: 2x80t
Ice Capable

1 oil engine with flexible couplings & sr geared to sc. shaft driving 1 CP propeller
Total Power: 4,320kW (5,873hp) 14.2kn
MaK 9M32C
1 x 4 Stroke 9 Cy. 320 x 480 4320kW (5873bhp)
Caterpillar Motoren GmbH & Co. KG-Germany
AuxGen: 1 x 680kW 400V 50Hz a.c, 3 x 245kW 400V 50Hz a.c
Boilers: TOH (ex.g.) 10.2kgf/cm² (10.0bar), TOH (o.f.) 10.2kgf/cm² (10.0bar)
Thrusters: 1 Thwart. CP thruster (f)
Fuel: 50.0 (d.f.) 555.0 (r.f.) 18.0pd

9258222 **UAL ANGOLA**
V5QG6
ex Geja C *-2013* *ex* Geja-C *-2009*
\-
York Shipping Ltd
Carisbrooke Shipping (Management) GmbH
Douglas *Isle of Man (British)*
MMSI: 235006360
Official number: 743899

7,511 Class: GL
3,870
10,618
T/cm
21.0

2002-01 B.V. Scheepswerf Damen Hoogezand — Foxhol Yd No: 814
2002-01 Santierul Naval Damen Galati S.A. — Galati (Hull) Yd No: 971
Loa 142.69 (BB) Br ex 18.35 Dght 7.330
Lbp - Br md 18.25 Dpth 10.15
Welded, 1 dk

(A31A2GX) General Cargo Ship
Double Bottom Entire Compartment Length
Grain: 14,695
TEU 668 C Ho 291 TEU C Dk 377 TEU incl 60 ref C.
Compartments: 2 Ho, ER
2 Ha: (65.4 x 13.2)ER (39.0 x 13.2)
Cranes: 2x60t

1 oil engine reduction geared to sc. shaft driving 1 CP propeller
Total Power: 4,320kW (5,873hp) 14.0kn
MaK 9M32
1 x 4 Stroke 9 Cy. 320 x 480 4320kW (5873bhp)
MaK Motoren GmbH & Co. KG-Kiel
AuxGen: 1 x 440kW 380V a.c, 3 x 264kW 380/220V a.c
Thrusters: 1 Thwart. CP thruster (f)
Fuel: 50.0 (d.f.) 505.0 (r.f.) 18.5pd

9542336 *PCLO* -	**UAL BODEWES** **Nescos B BV** Nescos A BV (Nescos Shipping BV) *Hoogezand* *Netherlands* MMSI: 246704000	**5,569** 2,592 8,327	Class: LR ✠ **100A1** SS 04/2012 strengthened for heavy cargoes container cargoes in all holds and on all hatch covers *IWS ✠ **LMC** **UMS** Eq.Ltr: W; Cable: 495.0/44.0 U3 (a)	**2012-04 Bodewes' Scheepswerven B.V. —** **Hoogezand** Yd No: 761 Loa 119.05 Br ex - Dght 6.963 Lbp 116.95 Br md 15.80 Dpth 10.05 Welded, 1 dk	**(A31A2GX) General Cargo Ship** Grain: 10,774; Bale: 10,774 TEU 287 Ho 177 TEU C Dk 110 TEU incl 50 ref C Compartments: 2 Ho, ER 2 Ha: ER Cranes: 2x60t	**1 oil engine** with flexible couplings & sr geared to sc. shaft driving 1 CP propeller Total Power: 2,999kW (4,077hp) 13.5kn MaK 6M32 1 x 4 Stroke 6 Cy. 320 x 480 2999kW (4077bhp) Caterpillar Motoren GmbH & Co. KG-Germany AuxGen: 3 x 272kW 400V 50Hz a.c, 1 x 452kW 400V 50Hz a.c Boilers: HWH (o.f.) 3.6kgf/cm² (3.5bar) Thrusters: 1 Thwart. CP thruster (f)
9430129 *2BZI7* -	**UAL CAPETOWN** **Carisbrooke Shipping (CV 14) BV** Carisbrooke Shipping Ltd SatCom: Inmarsat C 423591618 *Cowes* *United Kingdom* MMSI: 235070715 Official number: 915670	**9,530** 4,398 12,948	Class: BV GL	**2009-06 Jiangsu Yangzijiang Shipbuilding Co Ltd** **— Jiangyin JS** Yd No: 2006-734C Loa 138.04 (BB) Br ex 21.33 Dght 8.056 Lbp 130.00 Br md 21.00 Dpth 11.00 Welded, 1 dk	**(A31A2GX) General Cargo Ship** Grain: 16,230 TEU 771 C Ho 366 TEU C Dk 405 TEU incl 50 ref C Compartments: 2 Ho, 2 Tw Dk, ER 2 Ha: (50.3 x 17.5)ER (37.5 x 17.5) Cranes: 2x80t Ice Capable	**1 oil engine** reduction geared to sc. shafts driving 1 CP propeller Total Power: 5,400kW (7,342hp) 14.5kn MaK 6M43C 1 x 4 Stroke 6 Cy. 430 x 610 5400kW (7342bhp) Caterpillar Motoren GmbH & Co. KG-Germany AuxGen: 1 x 750kW 450V a.c, 3 x 450kW 450V a.c Thrusters: 1 Tunnel thruster (f) Fuel: 30.0 (d.f.) 810.0 (r.f.)
9210725 *P3CV9* -	**UAL COBURG** *ex* Capitaine Tasman *-2010* *ex* Fua Kavenga II *-2002* **Ocean (Pacific) Ltd** Intership Navigation Co Ltd (ISN) *Limassol* *Cyprus* MMSI: 209495000	**7,091** 3,492 8,115 T/cm 20.4	Class: GL	**2002-02 Chengxi Shipyard — Jiangyin JS** Yd No: 4325 Loa 126.40 (BB) Br ex - Dght 7.222 Lbp 116.60 Br md 19.40 Dpth 9.50 Welded, 1 dk	**(A31A2GX) General Cargo Ship** Grain: 10,300 TEU 660 C Ho 186 TEU C Dk 474 TEU incl 76 ref C. Compartments: 2 Dp Ta in Hold, 2 Ho, ER 2 Ha: ER Cranes: 2x60t	**1 oil engine** driving 1 CP propeller Total Power: 4,977kW (6,767hp) 16.1kn B&W 5L42MC 1 x 2 Stroke 5 Cy. 420 x 1360 4977kW (6767bhp) Hudong Heavy Machinery Co Ltd-China AuxGen: 1 x 625kW 450V 60Hz a.c, 2 x 615kW 450V 60Hz a.c Thrusters: 1 Tunnel thruster (f) Fuel: 151.0 (d.f.) 602.0 (r.f.)
9681534 *PBCK* -	**UAL COLOGNE** **Nescos E BV** Nescos A BV (Nescos Shipping BV) *Hoogezand* *Netherlands* MMSI: 244620675	**5,925** 2,710 8,703	Class: LR (Class contemplated) **100A1** 03/2014 Class contemplated	**2014-03 Bodewes' Scheepswerven B.V. —** **Hoogezand** Yd No: 764 Loa 127.03 Br ex - Dght 6.766 Lbp 125.20 Br md 15.80 Dpth 10.05 Welded, 1 dk	**(A31A2GX) General Cargo Ship** Grain: 10,774; Bale: 10,774 TEU 370 C Ho 198 TEU C Dk 172 TEU	**1 oil engine** reduction geared to sc. shaft driving 1 CP propeller Total Power: 3,000kW (4,079hp) 13.5kn MaK 6M32C 1 x 4 Stroke 6 Cy. 320 x 480 3000kW (4079bhp) Caterpillar Motoren GmbH & Co. KG-Germany Thrusters: 1 Tunnel thruster (f)
9321093 *MKVS6* -	**UAL EUROPE** *ex* Jill-C *-2006* **ms 'Jill C' UG (haftungsbeschrankt) & Co KG** Carisbrooke Shipping (Management) GmbH *Douglas* *Isle of Man (British)* MMSI: 235010190 Official number: DR169	**7,767** 3,856 10,574 T/cm 23.2	Class: LR ✠ **100A1** SS 03/2011 strengthened for heavy cargoes, container cargoes in holds and on upper deck hatch covers LI *IWS Ice Class 1A FS at draught of 7.627m Max/min draught fwd 7.627/3.600m Max/min draught aft 7.627/4.800m Required power 4320kw, installed power 4320kw ✠ **LMC** **UMS** Eq.Ltr: A†; Cable: 522.5/50.0 U3 (a)	**2006-03 B.V. Scheepswerf Damen Hoogezand —** **Foxhol** Yd No: 842 **2006-03 Damen Shipyards Yichang Co Ltd —** **Yichang HB** (Hull) Loa 145.63 (BB) Br ex 18.29 Dght 7.674 Lbp 139.38 Br md 18.25 Dpth 10.30 Welded, 1 dk	**(A31A2GX) General Cargo Ship** Double Hull Grain: 14,878; Bale: 13,975 TEU 673 C Ho 302 TEU C Dk 371 TEU incl 60 ref C. Compartments: 2 Ho, ER 2 Ha: (59.4 x 13.1)ER (38.9 x 13.2) Cranes: 2x60t Ice Capable	**1 oil engine** with flexible couplings & sr geared to sc. shaft driving 1 CP propeller Total Power: 4,320kW (5,873hp) 14.2kn MaK 9M32C 1 x 4 Stroke 9 Cy. 320 x 480 4320kW (5873bhp) Caterpillar Motoren GmbH & Co. KG-Germany AuxGen: 3 x 245kW 400V 50Hz a.c, 1 x 680kW 400V 50Hz a.c Boilers: TOH (ex.g.) 10.2kgf/cm² (10.0bar), TOH (o.f.) 10.2kgf/cm² (10.0bar) Thrusters: 1 Thwart. CP thruster (f) Fuel: 50.0 (d.f.) 555.0 (r.f.) 18.0pd
9429754 *2BON5* -	**UAL GABON** *completed as* Jacqueline C *-2009* **Carisbrooke Shipping (CV 14) BV** Carisbrooke Shipping Ltd *Cowes* *United Kingdom* MMSI: 235067944 Official number: 915459	**9,530** 4,398 12,914	Class: BV GL	**2009-03 Jiangsu Yangzijiang Shipbuilding Co Ltd** **— Jiangyin JS** Yd No: 2006-733C Loa 138.06 (BB) Br ex 21.33 Dght 8.050 Lbp 130.00 Br md 21.00 Dpth 11.00 Welded, 1 dk	**(A31A2GX) General Cargo Ship** Grain: 16,230 TEU 771 C Ho 366 TEU C Dk 405 TEU incl 50 ref C Compartments: 2 Ho, 2 Tw Dk, ER 2 Ha: (50.3 x 17.5)ER (37.5 x 17.5) Cranes: 2x80t Ice Capable	**1 oil engine** reduction geared to sc. shafts driving 1 CP propeller Total Power: 5,400kW (7,342hp) 14.5kn MaK 6M43C 1 x 4 Stroke 6 Cy. 430 x 610 5400kW (7342bhp) Caterpillar Motoren GmbH & Co. KG-Germany AuxGen: 1 x 750kW 450V a.c, 3 x 450kW 450V a.c Thrusters: 1 Tunnel thruster (f) Fuel: 30.0 (d.f.) 805.0 (r.f.) 20.0pd
9542348 *PBDY* -	**UAL HOUSTON** *launched as* UAL Cape Town *-2012* *ex* Ileno *-2012* **Nescos C BV** Nescos A BV (Nescos Shipping BV) *Hoogezand* *Netherlands* MMSI: 246117000 Official number: 55297	**5,925** 2,710 8,703	Class: LR ✠ **100A1** SS 12/2012 strengthened for heavy cargoes, container cargoes in all holds and on all hatch covers **ShipRight** (ACS (B)) *IWS LI ✠ **LMC** Eq.Ltr: W; Cable: 495.0/44.0 U3 (a)	**2012-12 Bodewes' Scheepswerven B.V. —** **Hoogezand** Yd No: 762 Loa 127.30 Br ex - Dght 6.766 Lbp 125.20 Br md 15.80 Dpth 10.05 Welded, 1 dk	**(A31A2GX) General Cargo Ship** Grain: 11,970; Bale: 11,970 TEU 370 C Ho 198 TEU C Dk 172 TEU Compartments: 2 Ho, ER 2 Ha: ER Cranes: 2x60t	**1 oil engine** with flexible couplings & sr geared to sc. shaft driving 1 CP propeller Total Power: 2,999kW (4,077hp) 13.5kn MaK 6M32 1 x 4 Stroke 6 Cy. 320 x 480 2999kW (4077bhp) Caterpillar Motoren GmbH & Co. KG-Germany AuxGen: 1 x 452kW 400V 50Hz a.c, 3 x 272kW 400V 50Hz a.c Boilers: HWH (o.f.) 3.1kgf/cm² (3.0bar) Thrusters: 1 Thwart. CP thruster (f)
9265653 *PBJZ* -	**UAL LOBITO** **Seabox Shipping Forwarding & Trading BV** - *Rotterdam* *Netherlands* MMSI: 244057000 Official number: 41250	**3,153** 1,789 4,371	Class: BV (LR) ✠ Classed LR until 9/7/08	**2003-06 Societatea Comerciala Severnav S.A. —** **Drobeta-Turnu Severin** (Hull) Yd No: (622) **2003-06 Bodewes' Scheepswerven B.V. —** **Hoogezand** Yd No: 622 Loa 89.98 (BB) Br ex 15.22 Dght 5.350 Lbp 84.98 Br md 15.20 Dpth 6.60 Welded, 1 dk	**(A31A2GX) General Cargo Ship** Double Hull Grain: 6,174 TEU 218 C Ho 126 TEU C Dk 92 TEU incl 20 ref C Compartments: 1 Ho, ER 1 Ha: ER (58.3 x 13.0) Cranes: 2x36t Ice Capable	**1 oil engine** with flexible couplings & sr geared to sc. shaft driving 1 CP propeller Total Power: 1,850kW (2,515hp) 12.0kn MaK 6M25 1 x 4 Stroke 6 Cy. 255 x 400 1850kW (2515bhp) Caterpillar Motoren GmbH & Co. KG-Germany AuxGen: 2 x 280kW 440V 60Hz a.c, 1 x 360kW 440V 60Hz a.c Thrusters: 1 Thwart. FP thruster (f) Fuel: 43.0 (d.f.) 181.0 (d.f.)
9321108 *MMEE2* -	**UAL NIGERIA** *ex* UAL Antwerp *-2012* *completed as* Anna C *-2006* **ms 'Anna C' UG (haftungsbeschrankt) & Co KG** Carisbrooke Shipping (Management) GmbH *Douglas* *Isle of Man (British)* MMSI: 232766000 Official number: DR175	**7,767** 3,856 10,567 T/cm 23.2	Class: LR ✠ **100A1** SS 08/2011 strengthened for heavy cargoes, container cargoes in holds and on upper deck hatch covers LI *IWS Ice Class 1A FS at draught of 7.627m Max/min draughts fwd 7.627/3.600m Max/min draughts aft 7.627/4.800m Required power 4320kw, installed power 4320kw ✠ **LMC** **UMS** Eq.Ltr: A†; Cable: 522.5/50.0 U3 (a)	**2006-08 B.V. Scheepswerf Damen Hoogezand —** **Foxhol** Yd No: 843 **2006-08 Damen Shipyards Yichang Co Ltd —** **Yichang HB** (Hull) Loa 145.63 (BB) Br ex 18.29 Dght 7.627 Lbp 139.38 Br md 18.25 Dpth 10.30 Welded, 2 dks	**(A31A2GX) General Cargo Ship** Double Hull Grain: 14,878 TEU 665 C Ho 302 TEU C Dk 363 TEU Compartments: 2 Ho, ER 2 Ha: (59.4 x 13.1)ER (39.0 x 13.1) Cranes: 2x80t Ice Capable	**1 oil engine** with flexible couplings & sr geared to sc. shaft driving 1 CP propeller Total Power: 4,320kW (5,873hp) 14.2kn MaK 9M32C 1 x 4 Stroke 9 Cy. 320 x 480 4320kW (5873bhp) Caterpillar Motoren GmbH & Co. KG-Germany AuxGen: 3 x 245kW 400V 50Hz a.c, 1 x 680kW 400V 50Hz a.c Boilers: TOH (ex.g.) 10.2kgf/cm² (10.0bar), TOH (o.f.) 10.2kgf/cm² (10.0bar) Thrusters: 1 Thwart. CP thruster (f) Fuel: 60.0 (d.f.) 627.0 (r.f.) 18.0pd
9320518 *MGNC6* -	**UAL RODACH** *ex* Jade C *-2013* *ex* Jade-C *-2009* **ms 'Jade C' (haftungsbeschrankt) & Co KG** Carisbrooke Shipping (Management) GmbH *Douglas* *Isle of Man (British)* MMSI: 235008310 Official number: DR131	**7,767** 3,856 10,585 T/cm 23.2	Class: LR ✠ **100A1** SS 02/2010 strengthened for heavy cargoes, container cargoes in holds and on upper deck hatch covers LI *IWS Ice Class 1AFS at a draught not exceeding of 7.627m Max/min draught fwd 7.627/3.6m Max/min draught aft 7.627/4.8m ✠ **LMC** **UMS** Eq.Ltr: A†; Cable: 522.5/50.0 U3 (a)	**2005-02 B.V. Scheepswerf Damen Hoogezand —** **Foxhol** Yd No: 840 **2005-02 Damen Shipyards Yichang Co Ltd —** **Yichang HB** (Hull) Loa 145.63 (BB) Br ex 18.29 Dght 7.674 Lbp 139.38 Br md 18.25 Dpth 10.30 Welded, 1 dk	**(A31A2GX) General Cargo Ship** Double Hull Grain: 14,878; Bale: 13,975 TEU 665 C Ho 302 TEU C Dk 363 TEU incl 60 ref C. Compartments: 2 Ho, ER 2 Ha: (59.5 x 13.2)ER (39.0 x 13.2) Cranes: 2x80t Ice Capable	**1 oil engine** with flexible couplings & sr geared to sc. shaft driving 1 CP propeller Total Power: 4,320kW (5,873hp) 14.2kn MaK 9M32C 1 x 4 Stroke 9 Cy. 320 x 480 4320kW (5873bhp) Caterpillar Motoren GmbH & Co. KG-Germany AuxGen: 3 x 245kW 400V 50Hz a.c, 1 x 680kW 400V 50Hz a.c Boilers: TOH (ex.g.) 10.2kgf/cm² (10.0bar), TOH (o.f.) 10.2kgf/cm² (10.0bar) Thrusters: 1 Thwart. CP thruster (f) Fuel: 50.0 (d.f.) 555.0 (r.f.) 18.0pd

IMO / Call sign	Name / Owner	GT / NT / DWT	Classification	Builder / Dimensions	Type / Capacity	Machinery
9542350 *PCPY* -	**UAL TEXAS** **Nescos D BV** Nescos A BV (Nescos Shipping BV) *Hoogezand* *Netherlands* MMSI: 246676000	**5,925** 2,710 8,600	Class: LR ✠ **100A1** SS 06/2013 strengthened for heavy cargoes, container cargoes in all holds and on all hatch covers **ShipRight** ACS (B) *IWS LI ✠ **LMC** **UMS** Eq.Ltr: W; Cable: 495.0/44.0 U3 (a)	**2013-06 Bodewes' Scheepswerven B.V. — Hoogezand** Yd No: 763 Loa 127.03 Br ex - Dght 6.766 Lbp 125.20 Br md 15.80 Dpth 10.05 Welded, 1 dk	**(A31A2GX) General Cargo Ship** Grain: 10,774; Bale: 10,774 TEU 370 C Ho 198 TEU C Dk 172 TEU Compartments: 2 Ho, ER 2 Ha: (57.0 x 13.3)ER (25.5 x 13.3) Cranes: 2x60t	**1 oil engine** with flexible couplings & sr geared to sc. shaft driving 1 CP propeller Total Power: 2,999kW (4,077hp) 13.5kn MaK 6M32C 1 x 4 Stroke 6 Cy. 320 x 480 2999kW (4077bhp) Caterpillar Motoren GmbH & Co. KG-Germany AuxGen: 3 x 272kW 400V 50Hz a.c, 1 x 452kW 400V 50Hz a.c Boilers: HWH (o.f.) 3.1kgf/cm² (3.0bar) Thrusters: 1 Thwart. CP thruster (f)
9404754 *PJTP* -	**UAL TRADER** *launched as* Danum 55 *-2006* **UAL Coastal Service NV** - *Willemstad* *Curacao* MMSI: 306805000 Official number: 2006-C-1881	**1,668** 500 2,346	Class: BV	**2006-09 Piasau Slipways Sdn Bhd — Miri** Yd No: 232 Loa 78.10 Br ex - Dght 3.500 Lbp 72.70 Br md 16.00 Dpth 4.80 Welded, 1 dk	**(A31C2GD) Deck Cargo Ship** Bow ramp (centre) Len: 8.00 Wid: 8.00 Swl: 70 TEU 144 incl 8 ref C	**2 oil engines** reduction geared to sc. shafts driving 2 FP propellers Total Power: 1,472kW (2,002hp) 10.0kn Caterpillar 3508B 2 x Vee 4 Stroke 8 Cy. 170 x 190 each-736kW (1001bhp) Caterpillar Inc-USA Thrusters: 1 Tunnel thruster (f)
9510606 *J8B4815* -	**UAL TYCOON** **Ual Tycoon Services NV** Flinter Management BV *Kingstown* *St Vincent & The Grenadines* MMSI: 375836000 Official number: 11288	**1,681** 504 2,310	Class: BV	**2008-12 Piasau Slipways Sdn Bhd — Miri** Yd No: 280 Loa 78.10 Br ex - Dght 3.500 Lbp 72.70 Br md 16.00 Dpth 4.80 Welded, 1 dk	**(A31C2GD) Deck Cargo Ship** Bow ramp (centre) Len: 8.00 Wid: 8.00 Swl: - TEU 144 incl 16 ref C	**2 oil engines** reduction geared to sc. shafts driving 2 FP propellers Total Power: 1,986kW (2,700hp) 10.0kn Cummins KTA-38-M2 2 x Vee 4 Stroke 12 Cy. 159 x 159 each-993kW (1350bhp) Cummins Engine Co Inc-USA AuxGen: 2 x 150kW 415V 50Hz a.c Thrusters: 1 Tunnel thruster (f) Fuel: 446.0
9400174 *CQIR* -	**UASC AJMAN** *ex* JPO Taurus *-2010* **ms 'JPO Taurus' Schiffahrtsgesellschaft mbH & Co KG** Schiffahrtsgesellschaft Oltmann mbH & Co KG *Madeira* *Portugal (MAR)* MMSI: 255805567 Official number: TEMP185M	**42,609** 19,338 52,300	Class: LR ✠ **100A1** SS 01/2010 container ship **ShipRight** (SDA, FDA, CM) *IWS LI ✠ **LMC** **UMS** Eq.Ltr: St; Cable: 660.0/87.0 U3 (a)	**2010-01 CSBC Corp, Taiwan — Kaohsiung** Yd No: 933 Loa 268.80 (BB) Br ex 32.30 Dght 12.500 Lbp 256.50 Br md 32.20 Dpth 19.10 Welded, 1 dk	**(A33A2CC) Container Ship (Fully Cellular)** TEU 4178 C Ho. 1575 TEU C Dk 2603 TEU incl 879 ref C. Compartments: 7 Cell Ho, ER	**1 oil engine** driving 1 FP propeller Total Power: 40,040kW (54,438hp) 24.6kn Wartsila 7RT-flex96C 1 x 2 Stroke 7 Cy. 960 x 2500 40040kW (54438bhp) Doosan Engine Co Ltd-South Korea AuxGen: 4 x 2648kW 450V 60Hz a.c Boilers: e (ex.g.) 12.2kgf/cm² (12.0bar), AuxB (o.f.) 8.2kgf/cm² (8.0bar) Thrusters: 1 Thwart. CP thruster (f)
9397585 *5BWS3* -	**UASC DOHA** *launched as* Beatrice Schulte *-2009* **ms 'Beatrice Schulte' Shipping GmbH & Co KG** Ocean Shipmanagement GmbH *Limassol* *Cyprus* MMSI: 210635000	**40,030** 24,450 50,700 T/cm 70.4	Class: GL (NV)	**2009-06 Samsung Heavy Industries Co Ltd — Geoje** Yd No: 1704 Loa 260.05 (BB) Br ex - Dght 12.600 Lbp 244.80 Br md 32.25 Dpth 19.30 Welded, 1 dk	**(A33A2CC) Container Ship (Fully Cellular)** TEU 4253 C Ho 1584 C Dk 2669 incl 400 ref C.	**1 oil engine** driving 1 FP propeller Total Power: 36,560kW (49,707hp) 23.3kn MAN-B&W 8K90MC-C 1 x 2 Stroke 8 Cy. 900 x 2300 36560kW (49707bhp) Doosan Engine Co Ltd-South Korea AuxGen: 4 x 1700kW 450V a.c Thrusters: 1 Tunnel thruster (f)
9445576 *A8UL5* -	**UASC JEDDAH** *ex* Jeddah *-2009* *ex* CPO Jacksonville *-2009* **KG ms 'CPO Jacksonville' Offen Reederei GmbH & Co** Reederei Claus-Peter Offen GmbH & Co KG *Monrovia* *Liberia* MMSI: 636091911 Official number: 91911	**41,358** 24,234 51,687	Class: GL	**2009-09 Hyundai Heavy Industries Co Ltd — Ulsan** Yd No: 2070 Loa 262.06 (BB) Br ex 32.25 Dght 12.500 Lbp 248.70 Br md 32.20 Dpth 19.30 Welded, 1 dk	**(A33A2CC) Container Ship (Fully Cellular)** TEU 4255 C Ho 1566 TEU C Dk 2689 TEU incl 560 ref C.	**1 oil engine** driving 1 FP propeller Total Power: 36,160kW (49,163hp) 24.1kn Wartsila 8RTA82C 1 x 2 Stroke 8 Cy. 820 x 2646 36160kW (49163bhp) Hyundai Heavy Industries Co Ltd-South Korea AuxGen: 2 x 2255kW 450V a.c, 2 x 1690kW 450V a.c Thrusters: 1 Tunnel thruster (f) Fuel: 170.0 (d.f.) 4940.0 (r.f.)
9401063 *5BYE3* -	**UASC JUBAIL** *launched as* Benedict Schulte *-2009* **ms 'Benedict Schulte' Shipping GmbH & Co KG** Reederei Thomas Schulte GmbH & Co KG *Limassol* *Cyprus* MMSI: 212150000 Official number: 9401063	**40,030** 24,450 50,700 T/cm 70.4	Class: GL (NV)	**2009-09 Samsung Heavy Industries Co Ltd — Geoje** Yd No: 1706 Loa 260.05 (BB) Br ex 32.25 Dght 12.600 Lbp 244.80 Br md 32.25 Dpth 19.30 Welded, 1 dk	**(A33A2CC) Container Ship (Fully Cellular)** TEU 4253 C Ho 1584 C Dk 2669 incl 400 ref C Compartments: 7 Cell Ho, ER	**1 oil engine** driving 1 FP propeller Total Power: 36,560kW (49,707hp) 23.3kn MAN-B&W 8K90MC-C 1 x 2 Stroke 8 Cy. 900 x 2300 36560kW (49707bhp) Doosan Engine Co Ltd-South Korea AuxGen: 4 x 1700kW 450V 60Hz a.c Thrusters: 1 Tunnel thruster (f)
9445588 *A8UL6* -	**UASC KHOR FAKKAN** *ex* Khor Fakkan *-2009* *ex* CPO Miami *-2009* **KG ms 'CPO Miami' Offen Reederei GmbH & Co** Reederei Claus-Peter Offen GmbH & Co KG *Monrovia* *Liberia* MMSI: 636091912 Official number: 91912	**41,358** 24,234 51,737	Class: GL	**2009-09 Hyundai Heavy Industries Co Ltd — Ulsan** Yd No: 2071 Loa 262.06 (BB) Br ex 32.25 Dght 12.500 Lbp 248.70 Br md 32.20 Dpth 19.30 Welded, 1 dk	**(A33A2CC) Container Ship (Fully Cellular)** TEU 4255 C Ho 1566 TEU C Dk 2689 TEU incl 560 ref C.	**1 oil engine** driving 1 FP propeller Total Power: 36,160kW (49,163hp) 24.1kn Wartsila 8RTA82C 1 x 2 Stroke 8 Cy. 820 x 2646 36160kW (49163bhp) Hyundai Heavy Industries Co Ltd-South Korea AuxGen: 2 x 2255kW 450V a.c, 2 x 1690kW 450V a.c Thrusters: 1 Tunnel thruster (f) Fuel: 170.0 (d.f.) 4940.0 (r.f.)
9440825 *A8UL3* -	**UASC RAMADI** *ex* Ramadi *-2009* *ex* CPO Charleston *-2009* **KG ms 'CPO Charleston' Offen Reederei GmbH & Co** Reederei Claus-Peter Offen GmbH & Co KG *Monrovia* *Liberia* MMSI: 636091909 Official number: 91909	**41,358** 24,234 51,671	Class: GL	**2009-08 Hyundai Heavy Industries Co Ltd — Ulsan** Yd No: 2063 Loa 262.09 (BB) Br ex 32.25 Dght 12.500 Lbp 248.70 Br md 32.20 Dpth 19.30 Welded, 1 dk	**(A33A2CC) Container Ship (Fully Cellular)** TEU 4255 C Ho 1566 TEU C Dk 2689 TEU incl 560 ref C.	**1 oil engine** driving 1 FP propeller Total Power: 36,160kW (49,163hp) 24.1kn Wartsila 8RTA82C 1 x 2 Stroke 8 Cy. 820 x 2646 36160kW (49163bhp) Hyundai Heavy Industries Co Ltd-South Korea AuxGen: 2 x 2255kW 450V a.c, 2 x 1690kW 450V a.c Thrusters: 1 Tunnel thruster (f) Fuel: 170.0 (d.f.) 4940.0 (r.f.)
9401075 *A8TB3* -	**UASC SAMARRA** *launched as* Benita Schulte *-2009* **ms 'Benita Schulte' Shipping GmbH & Co KG** Reederei Thomas Schulte GmbH & Co KG SatCom: Inmarsat C 463706394 *Monrovia* *Liberia* MMSI: 636091811 Official number: 91811	**40,030** 24,450 50,716 T/cm 70.4	Class: GL (NV)	**2009-10 Samsung Heavy Industries Co Ltd — Geoje** Yd No: 1707 Loa 260.05 (BB) Br ex - Dght 12.626 Lbp 244.80 Br md 32.25 Dpth 19.30 Welded, 1 dk	**(A33A2CC) Container Ship (Fully Cellular)** TEU 4253 C Ho 1584 TEU C Dk 2669 TEU incl 400 ref C	**1 oil engine** driving 1 FP propeller Total Power: 36,560kW (49,707hp) 23.3kn MAN-B&W 8K90MC-C 1 x 2 Stroke 8 Cy. 900 x 2300 36560kW (49707bhp) Doosan Engine Co Ltd-South Korea AuxGen: 4 x 1700kW a.c Thrusters: 1 Tunnel thruster (f)
9440837 *A8UL4* -	**UASC SHUAIBA** *ex* Shuaiba *-2009* **KG ms 'CPO Savannah' Offen Reederei GmbH & Co** Reederei Claus-Peter Offen GmbH & Co KG *Monrovia* *Liberia* MMSI: 636091910 Official number: 91910	**41,358** 24,234 51,701	Class: GL	**2009-08 Hyundai Heavy Industries Co Ltd — Ulsan** Yd No: 2064 Loa 262.07 (BB) Br ex 32.25 Dght 12.500 Lbp 248.70 Br md 32.20 Dpth 19.30 Welded, 1 dk	**(A33A2CC) Container Ship (Fully Cellular)** TEU 4255 C Ho 1566 TEU C Dk 2689 TEU incl 560 ref C.	**1 oil engine** driving 1 FP propeller Total Power: 36,160kW (49,163hp) 24.1kn Wartsila 8RTA82C 1 x 2 Stroke 8 Cy. 820 x 2646 36160kW (49163bhp) Hyundai Heavy Industries Co Ltd-South Korea AuxGen: 2 x 2255kW 450V a.c, 2 x 1690kW 450V a.c Thrusters: 1 Tunnel thruster (f) Fuel: 170.0 (d.f.) 4940.0 (r.f.)
9401051 *A8TA9* -	**UASC SHUWAIKH** *launched as* Benjamin Schulte *-2009* **ms 'Hammonia Pescara' Schiffahrts GmbH & Co KG** Hammonia Reederei GmbH & Co KG SatCom: Inmarsat C 463705638 *Monrovia* *Liberia* MMSI: 636091809 Official number: 91809	**40,030** 24,450 50,849 T/cm 70.4	Class: LR (GL) (NV) **100A1** SS 07/2009 container ship *IWS LI **LMC** **UMS** Cable: 687.5/87.0 U3 (a)	**2009-07 Samsung Heavy Industries Co Ltd — Geoje** Yd No: 1705 Loa 260.05 (BB) Br ex 32.30 Dght 12.600 Lbp 244.80 Br md 32.25 Dpth 19.30 Welded, 1 dk	**(A33A2CC) Container Ship (Fully Cellular)** TEU 4253 C Ho 1584 C Dk 2669 incl 400 ref C Compartments: 7 Cell Ho, ER	**1 oil engine** driving 1 FP propeller Total Power: 36,560kW (49,707hp) 24.5kn MAN-B&W 8K90MC-C 1 x 2 Stroke 8 Cy. 900 x 2300 36560kW (49707bhp) Doosan Engine Co Ltd-South Korea AuxGen: 4 x 1700kW a.c Boilers: AuxB (Comp) 8.0kgf/cm² (7.8bar) Thrusters: 1 Thwart. CP thruster (f)
9397913 *A8SE2* -	**UASC SITRAH** *completed as* Amalthea *-2009* **ms 'Sophia' Schiffahrtsgesellschaft mbH & Co KG** Peter Doehle Schiffahrts-KG *Monrovia* *Liberia* MMSI: 636091742 Official number: 91742	**42,609** 19,338 52,788	Class: LR ✠ **100A1** SS 10/2009 container ship **ShipRight** (SDA,FDA,CM) *IWS LI ✠ **LMC** **UMS** Eq.Ltr: St; Cable: 660.0/87.0 U3 (a)	**2009-10 CSBC Corp, Taiwan — Kaohsiung** Yd No: 932 Loa 268.80 (BB) Br ex 32.30 Dght 12.500 Lbp 256.50 Br md 32.20 Dpth 19.10 Welded, 1 dk	**(A33A2CC) Container Ship (Fully Cellular)** TEU 4178 C Ho. 1575 TEU C Dk 2603 TEU incl 879 ref C. Compartments: 7 Cell Ho, ER 7 Ha: ER	**1 oil engine** driving 1 FP propeller Total Power: 40,040kW (54,438hp) 24.6kn Wartsila 7RT-flex96C 1 x 2 Stroke 7 Cy. 960 x 2500 40040kW (54438bhp) Doosan Engine Co Ltd-South Korea AuxGen: 4 x 2400kW 450V 60Hz a.c Boilers: e (ex.g.) 12.2kgf/cm² (12.0bar), AuxB (o.f.) 8.2kgf/cm² (8.0bar) Thrusters: 1 Thwart. FP thruster (f)

Ship	Tonnage / Class	Build / Dimensions	Type	Machinery
7338690 **UAT 1 CIDIPORT** *XCAC8* *ex* Albatross Iv *-2013* - **Universidad Autonoma de Tamaulipas** *Mexico*	**890** Class: (AB) 267 231	**1962 Southern SB. Corp. — Slidell, La** Yd No: 46 Loa 57.08 Br ex 10.09 Dght 4.900 Lbp 52.15 Br md 10.06 Dpth 5.01 Welded, 2 dks	**(B31A2SR) Research Survey Vessel** Ice Capable	**2 oil engines** sr geared to sc. shaft driving 1 CP propeller Total Power: 832kW (1,132hp) 11.0kn Caterpillar D379TA 2 x Vee 4 Stroke 8 Cy. 159 x 203 each-416kW (566bhp) Caterpillar Tractor Co-USA AuxGen: 2 x 215kW 450V 60Hz a.c Thrusters: 1 Thwart. FP thruster (f) Fuel: 215.5 (d.f.)
9101716 **UB KANAKA PERKASA** - *ex* Borcos 23 *-2013* - **PT Pelayaran Kanaka Dwimitra Manunggal** *Indonesia*	**181** Class: AB 54 123	**1994-03 Sarawak Slipways Sdn Bhd — Miri** Yd No: 180 Loa 34.00 Br ex - Dght 1.850 Lbp 31.00 Br md 7.00 Dpth 3.30 Welded, 1 dk	**(B22G20Y) Standby Safety Vessel** Passengers: unberthed: 12	**2 oil engines** geared to sc. shafts driving 2 FP propellers Total Power: 1,030kW (1,400hp) 12.0kn MAN D2842LE 2 x Vee 4 Stroke 12 Cy. 128 x 142 each-515kW (700bhp) MAN Nutzfahrzeuge AG-Nuernberg AuxGen: 2 x 88kW 415V 50Hz a.c Thrusters: 1 Tunnel thruster (f)
8656740 **UB. P. PROPINDO** *YDA4225* *ex* Fire Boat 6 *-2009* - **PT Hacienda Offshore** - *Tanjung Priok* *Indonesia*	**278** Class: KI 84 -	**2000-01 Cheoy Lee Shipyards Ltd — Hong Kong** Loa 35.11 Br ex - Dght 2.890 Lbp 32.69 Br md 7.97 Dpth 3.58 Welded, 1 dk	**(B32A2ST) Tug**	**2 oil engines** reduction geared to sc. shafts driving 2 Propellers Total Power: 1,176kW (1,598hp) Cummins KTA-38-M1 2 x Vee 4 Stroke 12 Cy. 159 x 159 each-588kW (799bhp) Cummins Engine Co Ltd-United Kingdom AuxGen: 2 x 95kW 220V a.c
9089140 **UB. PROPINDO** *YD6891* *ex* Hutanindo V *-2006* - **PT Dayak Samudra Pacific** - *Banjarmasin* *Indonesia*	**124** Class: KI 74 -	**2002-01 P.T. Dok Rahmat — Banjarmasin** Loa 21.75 Br ex - Dght - Lbp 20.80 Br md 7.25 Dpth 3.10 Welded, 1 dk	**(B32A2ST) Tug**	**2 oil engines** driving 2 Propellers Total Power: 1,088kW (1,480hp) 10.0kn Caterpillar 3412E 2 x Vee 4 Stroke 12 Cy. 137 x 152 each-544kW (740bhp) Caterpillar Inc-USA AuxGen: 2 x 150kW a.c
9082661 **UBAIDULLA** *VVDB* - **Government of The Republic of India (Administration of Union Territory of Lakshadweep)** Lakshadweep Development Corp Ltd *Mumbai* *India* MMSI: 419333000 Official number: 2511	**738** Class: IR 297 960	**1992-11 Alcock, Ashdown & Co. Ltd. — Bhavnagar** Loa 57.00 Br ex 11.02 Dght 2.700 Lbp 55.50 Br md 11.00 Dpth 3.50 Welded, 1 dk	**(A31A2GX) General Cargo Ship** Grain: 1,100; Bale: 900 Compartments: 2 Ho, ER 2 Ha: ER	**2 oil engines** with clutches, flexible couplings & sr geared to sc. shafts driving 2 FP propellers Total Power: 776kW (1,056hp) 10.0kn Cummins VTA-1710-M 2 x Vee 4 Stroke 12 Cy. 140 x 152 each-388kW (528bhp) Kirloskar Cummins Ltd-India AuxGen: 3 x 60kW 415V 50Hz a.c
9277060 **UBALDO DICIOTTI** *IGSS* - **Government of The Republic of Italy (Comando Generale del Corpo della Capitaneria di Porto)** - *Italy* MMSI: 247061800	**550** Class: (RI) 302 -	**2002-07 Fincantieri-Cant. Nav. Italiani S.p.A. — La Spezia** Yd No: 6083 Loa 53.05 Br ex - Dght - Lbp 47.20 Br md 8.10 Dpth 5.40 Welded	**(B34H2SQ) Patrol Vessel**	**4 oil engines** geared to sc. shafts driving 4 CP propellers Total Power: 9,440kW (12,836hp) Isotta Fraschini V1716 4 x Vee 4 Stroke 16 Cy. 170 x 170 each-2360kW (3209bhp) (made 2002) Isotta Fraschini SpA-Italy AuxGen: 3 x 220V 50Hz a.c, 1 x 220V 50Hz a.c
9152466 **UBC BALBOA** *P3MG7* *ex* Bahia *-2014* *ex* UBC Balboa *-2013* - *ex* Brooknes *-2001* *ex* Ocean Giant *-1998* **O Giant Shipping Co Ltd** Athena Marine Co Ltd SatCom: Inmarsat A 1125563 *Limassol* *Cyprus* MMSI: 212363000 Official number: 9152466	**14,661** Class: GL 8,088 23,484 T/cm 34.2	**1997-05 Saiki Heavy Industries Co Ltd — Saiki OT** Yd No: 1068 Loa 154.35 (BB) Br ex - Dght 9.518 Lbp 146.00 Br md 26.00 Dpth 13.35 Welded, 1 dk	**(A21A2BC) Bulk Carrier** Double Bottom Entire Compartment Length Grain: 31,006; Bale: 30,253 Compartments: 4 Ho, ER 4 Ha: (19.2 x 12.7)2 (20.0 x 17.5) (20.8 x 17.5)ER Cranes: 4x30t	**1 oil engine** driving 1 FP propeller Total Power: 5,295kW (7,199hp) 14.3kn Mitsubishi 6UEC45LA 1 x 2 Stroke 6 Cy. 450 x 1350 5295kW (7199bhp) Akasaka Tekkosho KK (Akasaka DieselLtd)-Japan AuxGen: 2 x 480kW 220/440V a.c Fuel: 832.0 (r.f.)
9177973 **UBC BATON ROUGE** *P3BC8* *ex* Baynes *-2001* - **GSH Bilbao Baton Rouge Ltd** Intership Navigation Co Ltd (ISN) SatCom: Inmarsat C 421264310 *Limassol* *Cyprus* MMSI: 212643000 Official number: 9177973	**14,706** Class: GL 8,385 24,035 T/cm 34.2	**1998-06 Saiki Heavy Industries Co Ltd — Saiki OT** Yd No: 1078 Loa 154.35 (BB) Br ex - Dght 9.650 Lbp 146.00 Br md 26.00 Dpth 13.35 Welded, 1 dk	**(A21A2BC) Bulk Carrier** Double Bottom Entire Compartment Length Grain: 30,978; Bale: 30,225 Compartments: 4 Ho, ER 4 Ha: (19.2 x 12.7)2 (20.0 x 17.5) (20.8 x 17.5)ER Cranes: 4x30t	**1 oil engine** driving 1 FP propeller Total Power: 5,296kW (7,200hp) 14.3kn Mitsubishi 6UEC45LA 1 x 2 Stroke 6 Cy. 450 x 1350 5296kW (7200bhp) Akasaka Tekkosho KK (Akasaka DieselLtd)-Japan AuxGen: 2 x 480kW 220/440V a.c
9152478 **UBC BOSTON** *P3NE7* *ex* Brimnes *-2001* - **GSH Bilbao Boston Ltd** Intership Navigation Co Ltd (ISN) SatCom: Inmarsat A 1125576 *Limassol* *Cyprus* MMSI: 212389000 Official number: 9152478	**14,661** Class: GL 8,088 23,544 T/cm 34.2	**1997-06 Saiki Heavy Industries Co Ltd — Saiki OT** Yd No: 1070 Loa 154.35 (BB) Br ex 26.00 Dght 9.518 Lbp 146.00 Br md 25.00 Dpth 13.35 Welded, 1 dk	**(A21A2BC) Bulk Carrier** Double Bottom Entire Compartment Length Grain: 31,006; Bale: 30,253 Compartments: 4 Ho, ER 4 Ha: (19.2 x 12.7)2 (20.0 x 17.5) (20.8 x 17.5)ER Cranes: 4x30t	**1 oil engine** driving 1 FP propeller Total Power: 5,295kW (7,199hp) 15.0kn Mitsubishi 6UEC45LA 1 x 2 Stroke 6 Cy. 450 x 1350 5295kW (7199bhp) Akasaka Tekkosho KK (Akasaka DieselLtd)-Japan AuxGen: 2 x 480kW 450V 60Hz a.c, 1 x 250kW 220/440V 60Hz a.c Fuel: 236.0 (d.f.) 597.0 (r.f.) 21.3pd
9177961 **UBC BREMEN** *P3ZA7* *ex* Birknes *-2001* - **GSH Bilbao Bremen Ltd** Intership Navigation Co Ltd (ISN) SatCom: Inmarsat B 321260210 *Limassol* *Cyprus* MMSI: 212602000 Official number: 9177961	**14,706** Class: GL 8,385 24,073 T/cm 34.2	**1998-05 Saiki Heavy Industries Co Ltd — Saiki OT** Yd No: 1077 Loa 154.35 (BB) Br ex - Dght 9.650 Lbp 146.00 Br md 26.00 Dpth 13.35 Welded, 1 dk	**(A21A2BC) Bulk Carrier** Grain: 31,141; Bale: 30,387 Compartments: 4 Ho, ER 4 Ha: (19.2 x 12.7)2 (20.0 x 17.5) (20.8 x 17.5)ER Cranes: 4x30t	**1 oil engine** driving 1 FP propeller Total Power: 5,296kW (7,200hp) 15.0kn Mitsubishi 6UEC45LA 1 x 2 Stroke 6 Cy. 450 x 1350 5296kW (7200bhp) Akasaka Tekkosho KK (Akasaka DieselLtd)-Japan AuxGen: 2 x 385kW 220/440V a.c
9577264 **UBC CANADA** *5BYX2* - **Cumeria Shipping Co Ltd** Intership Navigation Co Ltd (ISN) *Limassol* *Cyprus* MMSI: 212297000	**8,559** Class: CC 3,606 15,053	**2010-10 Huanghai Shipbuilding Co Ltd — Rongcheng SD** Yd No: HCY-130 Loa 132.00 (BB) Br ex 22.70 Dght 7.800 Lbp 125.00 Br md 22.50 Dpth 11.00 Welded, 1 dk	**(A24A2BT) Cement Carrier** Compartments: 3 Ho, ER 3 Ha: 2 (28.0 x 19.5)ER (28.0 x 12.0) Ice Capable	**2 oil engines** geared to sc. shafts driving 2 FP propellers Total Power: 5,000kW (6,798hp) 12.0kn Daihatsu 8DKM-28 2 x 4 Stroke 8 Cy. 280 x 390 each-2500kW (3399bhp) Shaanxi Diesel Heavy Industry Co Lt-China AuxGen: 2 x 300kW 450V 60Hz a.c, 2 x 2264kW 450V 60Hz a.c Thrusters: 1 Tunnel thruster (f)
9448281 **UBC CARTAGENA** *5BUF2* - **Onore Shipping Co Ltd** Intership Navigation Co Ltd (ISN) *Limassol* *Cyprus* MMSI: 210032000	**5,794** Class: CC GL 1,866 8,380	**2009-10 Huanghai Shipbuilding Co Ltd — Rongcheng SD** Yd No: HCY-70 Loa 116.72 (BB) Br ex 19.72 Dght 6.800 Lbp 110.00 Br md 19.70 Dpth 9.70 Welded, 1 dk	**(A24A2BT) Cement Carrier** Grain: 7,654 TEU 52 Compartments: 3 Ho, ER 3 Ha: 2 (23.4 x 16.7)ER (22.1 x 16.7) Ice Capable	**2 oil engines** reduction geared to sc. shafts driving 2 Propellers Total Power: 5,000kW (6,798hp) 13.8kn Daihatsu 8DKM-28L 2 x 4 Stroke 8 Cy. 280 x 390 each-2500kW (3399bhp) Shaanxi Diesel Heavy Industry Co Lt-China AuxGen: 2 x 2264kW a.c, 2 x 315kW 450V a.c Thrusters: 1 Tunnel thruster (f)
9577288 **UBC CHILE** *5BEB3* - **Atlantic Hunter Shipping Co Ltd** Intership Navigation Co Ltd (ISN) *Limassol* *Cyprus* MMSI: 209568000	**8,559** Class: CC 3,606 15,053	**2011-05 Huanghai Shipbuilding Co Ltd — Rongcheng SD** Yd No: HCY-132 Loa 132.00 (BB) Br ex 22.70 Dght 7.800 Lbp 125.00 Br md 22.50 Dpth 11.00 Welded, 1 dk	**(A24A2BT) Cement Carrier** Grain: 12,935 TEU 42 Compartments: 3 Ho, ER 3 Ha: 2 (28.0 x 19.5)ER (28.0 x 12.0) Ice Capable	**2 oil engines** geraed to sc. shafts driving 2 FP propellers Total Power: 5,000kW (6,798hp) 12.0kn Daihatsu 8DKM-28 2 x 4 Stroke 8 Cy. 280 x 390 each-2500kW (3399bhp) Shaanxi Diesel Heavy Industry Co Lt-China AuxGen: 2 x 300kW 450V 60Hz a.c, 2 x 2264kW 450V 60Hz a.c Thrusters: 1 Tunnel thruster (f)
9448279 **UBC CORK** *5BSP2* - **Torelo Shipping Co Ltd** Intership Navigation Co Ltd (ISN) SatCom: Inmarsat C 421005510 *Limassol* *Cyprus* MMSI: 210055000 Official number: 9448279	**5,794** Class: GL (CC) 1,866 8,388	**2009-07 Huanghai Shipbuilding Co Ltd — Rongcheng SD** Yd No: HCY-69 Loa 116.72 (BB) Br ex - Dght 6.800 Lbp 110.00 Br md 19.70 Dpth 9.70 Welded, 1 dk	**(A24A2BT) Cement Carrier** Grain: 7,654 TEU 52 Compartments: 3 Ho, ER 3 Ha: 2 (23.4 x 16.7)ER (22.1 x 16.7) Ice Capable	**2 oil engines** reduction geared to sc. shafts driving 2 Propellers Total Power: 5,000kW (6,798hp) 13.8kn Daihatsu 8DKM-28L 2 x 4 Stroke 8 Cy. 280 x 390 each-2500kW (3399bhp) Shaanxi Diesel Heavy Industry Co Lt-China AuxGen: 3 x 315kW 450V 60Hz a.c, 2 x 2264kW 450V 60Hz a.c Thrusters: 1 Thwart. FP thruster (f) Fuel: 80.0 (d.f.) 750.0 (r.f.)

9577276 *5BBG3* -
UBC CYPRUS
Intership Navigation Co Ltd (ISN)
-
SatCom: Inmarsat C 420994710
Limassol *Cyprus*
MMSI: 209947000
Official number: 9577276
8,559 3,606 15,053 Class: CC
2010-12 Huanghai Shipbuilding Co Ltd — Rongcheng SD Yd No: HCY-131
Loa 132.00 (BB) Br ex 22.70 Dght 7.800
Lbp 125.00 Br md 22.50 Dpth 11.00
Welded, 1 dk
(A24A2BT) Cement Carrier
Grain: 12,935
TEU 42
Compartments: 3 Ho, ER
3 Ha: 2 (28.0 x 19.5)ER (28.0 x 12.0)
Ice Capable
2 oil engines geared to sc. shafts driving 2 FP propellers
Total Power: 5,000kW (6,798hp) 12.0kn
Daihatsu 8DKM-28
2 x 4 Stroke 8 Cy. 280 x 390 each-2500kW (3399bhp)
Shaanxi Diesel Heavy Industry Co Lt-China
AuxGen: 2 x 300kW 450V 60Hz a.c, 2 x 2264kW 450V 60Hz a.c
Thrusters: 1 Tunnel thruster (f)

9395238 *A8QK8* -
UBC LAGUNA
completed as Dessau *-2009*
Atlas Trampship Reederei GmbH & Co ms 'Dessau' KG
Hartmann Schiffahrts GmbH & Co KG (Hartmann Reederei)
Monrovia *Liberia*
MMSI: 636091618
Official number: 91618
31,094 18,067 53,477 Class: GL
2009-01 Zhejiang Shipbuilding Co Ltd — Ningbo ZJ Yd No: 06-151
Loa 189.94 (BB) Br ex - Dght 12.500
Lbp 182.00 Br md 32.26 Dpth 17.20
Welded, 1 dk
(A21A2BC) Bulk Carrier
Grain: 65,045; Bale: 63,654
Compartments: 5 Ho, ER
5 Ha: 4 (21.3 x 18.3)ER (18.9 x 18.3)
Cranes: 4x35t
1 oil engine driving 1 FP propeller
Total Power: 9,480kW (12,889hp) 14.5kn
MAN-B&W 6S50MC-C
1 x 2 Stroke 6 Cy. 500 x 2000 9480kW (12889bhp)
Doosan Engine Co Ltd-South Korea
AuxGen: 3 x 720kW 450V 60Hz a.c
Fuel: 113.0 (d.f.) 1850.0 (r.f.) 38.0pd

9395226 *A8PW6* -
UBC LEMESSOS
ex Daewoo Challenge *-2009*
completed as Cuxhaven *-2008*
Atlas Trampship Reederei GmbH & Co ms 'Cuxhaven' KG
Hartmann Schiffahrts GmbH & Co KG (Hartmann Reederei)
Monrovia *Liberia*
MMSI: 636091605
Official number: 91605
31,094 18,067 53,571 Class: GL
2008-05 Zhejiang Shipbuilding Co Ltd — Ningbo ZJ Yd No: 06-150
Loa 189.94 (BB) Br ex - Dght 12.490
Lbp 182.00 Br md 32.26 Dpth 17.20
Welded, 1 dk
(A21A2BC) Bulk Carrier
Grain: 65,045; Bale: 63,654
Compartments: 5 Ho, ER
5 Ha: 4 (21.3 x 18.3)ER (18.9 x 18.3)
Cranes: 4x35t
1 oil engine driving 1 FP propeller
Total Power: 9,480kW (12,889hp) 14.5kn
MAN-B&W 6S50MC-C
1 x 2 Stroke 6 Cy. 500 x 2000 9480kW (12889bhp)
Doosan Engine Co Ltd-South Korea
AuxGen: 3 x 720kW 450V 60Hz a.c
Fuel: 115.0 (d.f.) 1850.0 (r.f.) 38.0pd

9395252 *A8SH5* -
UBC LIMAS
ex Gerolstein *-2009*
Atlas Tramship Reederei GmbH & Co ms 'Koln' KG
Hartmann Schiffahrts GmbH & Co KG (Hartmann Reederei)
Monrovia *Liberia*
MMSI: 636091759
Official number: 91759
31,094 18,067 53,406 Class: GL
2009-08 Zhejiang Shipbuilding Co Ltd — Fenghua ZJ Yd No: 06-153
Loa 189.94 (BB) Br ex - Dght 12.490
Lbp 185.00 Br md 32.26 Dpth 17.20
Welded, 1 dk
(A21A2BC) Bulk Carrier
Double Bottom Entire Compartment Length
Grain: 65,045; Bale: 63,654
Compartments: 5 Ho, ER
5 Ha: 4 (21.3 x 18.3)ER (18.9 x 18.3)
Cranes: 4x35t
1 oil engine driving 1 FP propeller
Total Power: 9,480kW (12,889hp) 14.7kn
MAN-B&W 6S50MC-C
1 x 2 Stroke 6 Cy. 500 x 2000 9480kW (12889bhp)
Doosan Engine Co Ltd-South Korea
AuxGen: 3 x 720kW 450V 60Hz a.c
Fuel: 113.0 (d.f.) 1850.0 (r.f.) 38.0pd

9395264 *9HA3514* -
UBC LIVORNO
ex Husum *-2009*
Atlas Trampship Reederei GmbH & Co ms 'Husum' KG
Hartmann Schiffahrts GmbH & Co KG (Hartmann Reederei)
Valletta *Malta*
MMSI: 229680000
Official number: 9395264
31,094 18,067 53,428 Class: GL
2009-12 Zhejiang Shipbuilding Co Ltd — Fenghua ZJ Yd No: 06-154
Loa 190.01 (BB) Br ex - Dght 12.500
Lbp 182.00 Br md 32.26 Dpth 17.20
Welded, 1 dk
(A21A2BC) Bulk Carrier
Double Bottom Entire Compartment Length
Grain: 65,045; Bale: 63,654
Compartments: 5 Ho, ER
5 Ha: 4 (21.3 x 18.3)ER (18.9 x 18.3)
Cranes: 4x35t
Ice Capable
1 oil engine driving 1 FP propeller
Total Power: 9,480kW (12,889hp) 14.7kn
MAN-B&W 6S50MC-C
1 x 2 Stroke 6 Cy. 500 x 2000 9480kW (12889bhp)
Doosan Engine Co Ltd-South Korea
AuxGen: 3 x 720kW 450V 60Hz a.c
Fuel: 114.0 (d.f.) 1855.0 (r.f.) 38.0pd

9395214 *9HA3536* -
UBC LONGKOU
ex Daewoo Brave *-2009*
completed as Handorf *-2008*
Atlas Trampship Reederei GmbH & Co ms 'Handorf' KG
Hartmann Schiffahrts GmbH & Co KG (Hartmann Reederei)
Valletta *Malta*
MMSI: 229708000
Official number: 9395214
31,094 18,067 53,408 Class: GL
2008-03 Zhejiang Shipbuilding Co Ltd — Ningbo ZJ Yd No: 06-149
Loa 189.94 (BB) Br ex - Dght 12.490
Lbp 182.00 Br md 32.26 Dpth 17.20
Welded, 1 dk
(A21A2BC) Bulk Carrier
Grain: 65,045; Bale: 63,654
Compartments: 5 Ho, ER
5 Ha: 4 (21.3 x 18.3)ER (18.9 x 18.3)
Cranes: 4x35t
1 oil engine reduction geared to sc. shaft driving 1 FP propeller
Total Power: 9,466kW (12,870hp) 14.5kn
MAN-B&W 6S50MC-C
1 x 2 Stroke 6 Cy. 500 x 2000 9466kW (12870bhp)
Doosan Engine Co Ltd-South Korea
AuxGen: 3 x 730kW 450V 60Hz a.c
Fuel: 115.0 (d.f.) 1850.0 (r.f.) 38.0pd

9395240 *A8RF6* -
UBC LUZON
completed as Flensburg *-2009*
Atlas Trampship Reederei GmbH & Co ms 'Flensburg' KG
Hartmann Schiffahrts GmbH & Co KG (Hartmann Reederei)
Monrovia *Liberia*
MMSI: 636091653
Official number: 91653
31,094 18,067 53,507 Class: GL
2009-04 Zhejiang Shipbuilding Co Ltd — Ningbo ZJ Yd No: 06-152
Loa 189.97 (BB) Br ex - Dght 12.500
Lbp 182.00 Br md 32.26 Dpth 17.20
Welded, 1 dk
(A21A2BC) Bulk Carrier
Grain: 65,045; Bale: 63,654
Compartments: 5 Ho, ER
5 Ha: 4 (21.3 x 18.3)ER (18.9 x 18.3)
Cranes: 4x35t
1 oil engine driving 1 FP propeller
Total Power: 9,480kW (12,889hp) 14.5kn
MAN-B&W 6S50MC-C
1 x 2 Stroke 6 Cy. 500 x 2000 9480kW (12889bhp)
Doosan Engine Co Ltd-South Korea
AuxGen: 3 x 720kW 450V 60Hz a.c
Fuel: 113.0 (d.f.) 1850.0 (r.f.) 38.0pd

9583043 *PCNF* -
UBC MANZANILLO
Beheermaatschappij ms 'UBC Manzanillo' BV
Feederlines BV
Groningen *Netherlands*
MMSI: 246841000
Official number: 54743
5,630 2,883 7,805 T/cm 17.8 Class: GL
2011-11 Nanjing Huatai Shipyard Co Ltd — Nanjing JS Yd No: 07-4-13
Loa 108.17 (BB) Br ex 18.47 Dght 7.010
Lbp 103.90 Br md 18.20 Dpth 9.00
Welded, 1 dk
(A31A2GX) General Cargo Ship
Grain: 10,291; Bale: 10,291
Compartments: 3 Ho, ER
3 Ha: (25.9 x 15.2) (25.2 x 15.2)ER (17.5 x 15.2)
Cranes: 2x36t
Ice Capable
1 oil engine reduction geared to sc. shaft driving 1 Propeller
Total Power: 3,000kW (4,079hp) 11.5kn
MaK 6M32C
1 x 4 Stroke 6 Cy. 320 x 480 3000kW (4079bhp)
Caterpillar Motoren GmbH & Co. KG-Germany
AuxGen: 2 x 388kW a.c
Thrusters: 1 Tunnel thruster (f)
Fuel: 60.0 (d.f.) 410.0 (r.f.)

9583055 *PCNG* -
UBC MARACAIBO
Beheermaatschappij ms UBC Maracaibo BV
Hartmann Schiffahrts GmbH & Co KG (Hartmann Reederei)
Groningen *Netherlands*
MMSI: 246842000
5,630 2,883 7,814 T/cm 17.8 Class: GL
2012-02 Nanjing Huatai Shipyard Co Ltd — Nanjing JS Yd No: 07-4-14
Loa 108.18 (BB) Br ex 18.47 Dght 7.010
Lbp 103.90 Br md 18.20 Dpth 9.00
Welded, 1 dk
(A31A2GX) General Cargo Ship
Grain: 10,194; Bale: 10,194
Compartments: 3 Ho, ER
3 Ha: (25.9 x 15.2) (25.2 x 15.2)ER (17.5 x 15.2)
Cranes: 2x36t
Ice Capable
1 oil engine reduction geared to sc. shaft driving 1 Propeller
Total Power: 3,000kW (4,079hp) 11.5kn
MaK 6M32C
1 x 4 Stroke 6 Cy. 320 x 480 3000kW (4079bhp)
Caterpillar Motoren GmbH & Co. KG-Germany

9421128 *V2QA3* -
UBC MARIEL
launched as Moadiep *-2009*
UBC Mariel Shipping Co Ltd
Feederlines BV
SatCom: Inmarsat C 430539810
Saint John's *Antigua & Barbuda*
MMSI: 305398000
5,630 2,883 7,816 T/cm 17.8 Class: GL
2009-05 Nanjing Huatai Shipyard Co Ltd — Nanjing JS Yd No: 06-4-08
Loa 108.17 (BB) Br ex 18.47 Dght 7.010
Lbp 103.90 Br md 18.20 Dpth 9.00
Welded, 1 dk
(A31A2GX) General Cargo Ship
Grain: 10,194; Bale: 10,194
Compartments: 3 Ho, ER
3 Ha: (25.9 x 15.2) (25.2 x 15.2)ER (17.5 x 15.2)
Cranes: 2x36t
Ice Capable
1 oil engine reduction geared to sc. shaft driving 1 CP propeller
Total Power: 3,000kW (4,079hp) 11.5kn
MaK 6M32C
1 x 4 Stroke 6 Cy. 320 x 480 3000kW (4079bhp)
Caterpillar Motoren GmbH & Co. KG-Germany
AuxGen: 2 x 365kW 450V a.c, 1 x 360kW 450V a.c
Thrusters: 1 Tunnel thruster (f)

9421130 *5BBG4* -
UBC MIAMI
Quansea Shipping Co Ltd
Intership Navigation Co Ltd (ISN)
Cyprus
MMSI: 210798000
5,630 2,883 7,811 T/cm 17.8 Class: GL
2009-11 Nanjing Huatai Shipyard Co Ltd — Nanjing JS Yd No: 06-4-10
Loa 108.20 (BB) Br ex 18.47 Dght 7.010
Lbp 103.90 Br md 18.20 Dpth 9.00
Welded, 1 dk
(A31A2GX) General Cargo Ship
Grain: 10,194; Bale: 10,194
Compartments: 3 Ho, ER
3 Ha: (25.9 x 15.2) (25.2 x 15.2)ER (17.5 x 15.2)
Cranes: 2x36t
Ice Capable
1 oil engine reduction geared to sc. shaft driving 1 CP propeller
Total Power: 3,000kW (4,079hp) 11.5kn
MaK 6M32C
1 x 4 Stroke 6 Cy. 320 x 480 3000kW (4079bhp)
Caterpillar Motoren GmbH & Co. KG-Germany
AuxGen: 1 x 360kW 450V a.c, 2 x 365kW 450V a.c
Thrusters: 1 Tunnel thruster (f)

9421142 *PBFG* -
UBC MOBILE
Beheermaatschappij ms UBC Mobile BV
Feederlines BV
Groningen *Netherlands*
MMSI: 244822000
Official number: 53496
5,630 2,883 7,815 T/cm 17.8 Class: GL
2010-01 Nanjing Huatai Shipyard Co Ltd — Nanjing JS Yd No: 06-4-12
Loa 108.20 (BB) Br ex 18.47 Dght 7.010
Lbp 103.90 Br md 18.20 Dpth 9.00
Welded, 1 dk
(A31A2GX) General Cargo Ship
Grain: 10,194; Bale: 10,194
Compartments: 3 Ho, ER
3 Ha: (25.9 x 15.2) (25.2 x 15.2)ER (17.5 x 15.2)
Cranes: 2x36t
Ice Capable
1 oil engine reduction geared to sc. shaft driving 1 CP propeller
Total Power: 3,000kW (4,079hp) 11.5kn
MaK 6M32C
1 x 4 Stroke 6 Cy. 320 x 480 3000kW (4079bhp)
Caterpillar Motoren GmbH & Co. KG-Germany
AuxGen: 1 x 360kW 450V a.c, 2 x 365kW 450V a.c
Thrusters: 1 Tunnel thruster (f)

9421154 *V2QA2* -
UBC MOIN
launched as Mobilediep *-2009*
UBC Moin Shipping Co Ltd
Feederlines BV
SatCom: Inmarsat C 430539610
Saint John's *Antigua & Barbuda*
MMSI: 305396000
5,630 2,883 7,807 T/cm 17.8 Class: GL
2009-04 Nanjing Huatai Shipyard Co Ltd — Nanjing JS Yd No: 06-4-07
Loa 108.17 (BB) Br ex 18.47 Dght 7.010
Lbp 103.90 Br md 18.20 Dpth 9.00
Welded, 1 dk
(A31A2GX) General Cargo Ship
Grain: 10,194; Bale: 10,194
Compartments: 3 Ho, ER
3 Ha: (25.9 x 15.2) (25.2 x 15.2)ER (17.5 x 15.2)
Cranes: 2x36t
Ice Capable
1 oil engine reduction geared to sc. shaft driving 1 CP propeller
Total Power: 3,000kW (4,079hp) 12.0kn
MaK 6M32C
1 x 4 Stroke 6 Cy. 320 x 480 3000kW (4079bhp)
Caterpillar Motoren GmbH & Co. KG-Germany
Thrusters: 1 Tunnel thruster (f)

9421166 **UBC MONTEGO BAY** 5,630 Class: GL
PBUP *ex Miamidiep -2009* 2,883
\- **Beheermaatschappij ms UBC Montego Bay BV** 7,811
Feederlines BV T/cm
SatCom: Inmarsat C 424661610 17.8
Groningen *Netherlands*
MMSI: 246616000
Official number: 53328

2009-08 Nanjing Huatai Shipyard Co Ltd — Nanjing JS Yd No: 06-4-09
Loa 108.16 (BB) Br ex 18.47 Dght 7.010
Lbp 103.90 Br md 18.20 Dpth 9.00
Welded, 1 dk

(A31A2GX) General Cargo Ship
Grain: 10,194; Bale: 10,194
Compartments: 3 Ho, ER
3 Ha: (25.9 x 15.2) (25.2 x 15.2)ER (17.5 x 15.2)
Cranes: 2x36t
Ice Capable

1 oil engine reduction geared to sc. shaft driving 1 CP propeller
Total Power: 3,000kW (4,079hp) 11.5kn
MaK 6M32C
1 x 4 Stroke 6 Cy. 320 x 480 3000kW (4079bhp)
Caterpillar Motoren GmbH & Co. KG-Germany
AuxGen: 1 x 360kW 450V a.c, 3 x 365kW 450V a.c
Thrusters: 1 Tunnel thruster (f)

9421178 **UBC MONTREAL** 5,630 Class: GL
PBIU 2,883
\- **Beheermaatschappij ms UBC Montreal BV** 7,801
Feederlines BV T/cm
Groningen *Netherlands* 17.8
MMSI: 244937000
Official number: 53433

2009-11 Nanjing Huatai Shipyard Co Ltd — Nanjing JS Yd No: 06-4-11
Loa 108.21 (BB) Br ex 18.47 Dght 7.010
Lbp 103.90 Br md 18.20 Dpth 9.00
Welded, 1 dk

(A31A2GX) General Cargo Ship
Grain: 10,194; Bale: 10,194
Compartments: 3 Ho, ER
3 Ha: (25.9 x 15.2) (25.2 x 15.2)ER (17.5 x 15.2)
Cranes: 2x36t
Ice Capable

1 oil engine reduction geared to sc. shaft driving 1 CP propeller
Total Power: 3,000kW (4,079hp) 11.5kn
MaK 6M32C
1 x 4 Stroke 6 Cy. 320 x 480 3000kW (4079bhp)
Caterpillar Motoren GmbH & Co. KG-Germany
AuxGen: 2 x 365kW 450V a.c, 1 x 360kW 450V a.c
Thrusters: 1 Tunnel thruster (f)

9463671 **UBC ODESSA** 65,976 Class: GL (NK)
PCMZ 38,905
\- **Beheermaatschappij ms UBC Odessa BV** 118,585
Feederlines BV
Groningen *Netherlands*
MMSI: 244947000

2011-12 Yangzhou Dayang Shipbuilding Co Ltd — Yangzhou JS Yd No: DY5006
Loa 260.36 (BB) Br ex - Dght 14.500
Lbp 254.00 Br md 43.00 Dpth 20.25
Welded, 1 dk

(A21A2BC) Bulk Carrier
Grain: 139,005
Compartments: 7 Ho, ER
7 Ha: 2 (21.6 x 20.8)4 (18.9 x 20.8)ER (18.9 x 17.2)

1 oil engine driving 1 FP propeller
Total Power: 13,560kW (18,436hp) 14.5kn
MAN-B&W 6S60MC-C
1 x 2 Stroke 6 Cy. 600 x 2400 13560kW (18436bhp)
Doosan Engine Co Ltd-South Korea
AuxGen: 3 x 730kW 450V a.c
Fuel: 400.0 (d.f.) 3500.0 (r.f.)

9462366 **UBC OHIO** 65,976 Class: GL
PBYT 38,906
\- **Beheermaatschappij ms UBC Ohio BV** 118,532
Feederlines BV
SatCom: Inmarsat C 424539210
Groningen *Netherlands*
MMSI: 245392000
Official number: 54291

2011-04 Yangzhou Dayang Shipbuilding Co Ltd — Yangzhou JS Yd No: DY5001
Loa 260.41 (BB) Br ex - Dght 14.500
Lbp 254.00 Br md 43.00 Dpth 20.25
Welded, 1 dk

(A21A2BC) Bulk Carrier
Grain: 139,005
Compartments: 7 Ho, ER
7 Ha: 2 (21.6 x 20.8)4 (18.9 x 20.8)ER (18.9 x 17.2)

1 oil engine driving 1 FP propeller
Total Power: 13,560kW (18,436hp) 14.5kn
MAN-B&W 6S60MC-C
1 x 2 Stroke 6 Cy. 600 x 2400 13560kW (18436bhp)
Doosan Engine Co Ltd-South Korea
AuxGen: 3 x 730kW 450V a.c
Fuel: 400.0 (d.f.) 3500.0 (r.f.)

9463669 **UBC OLIMBUS** 65,976 Class: GL
ZDKR3 38,906
\- **Beheermaatschappij ms UBC Olimbus BV** 118,472
Feederlines BV
Gibraltar *Gibraltar (British)*
MMSI: 236111783
Official number: 9463669

2011-10 Yangzhou Dayang Shipbuilding Co Ltd — Yangzhou JS Yd No: DY5005
Loa 260.46 (BB) Br ex - Dght 14.500
Lbp 254.00 Br md 43.00 Dpth 20.25
Welded, 1 dk

(A21A2BC) Bulk Carrier
Grain: 139,005
Compartments: 7 Ho, ER
7 Ha: 2 (21.6 x 20.8)4 (18.9 x 20.8)ER (18.9 x 17.2)

1 oil engine driving 1 FP propeller
Total Power: 13,560kW (18,436hp) 14.5kn
MAN-B&W 6S60MC-C
1 x 2 Stroke 6 Cy. 600 x 2400 13560kW (18436bhp)
Doosan Engine Co Ltd-South Korea
AuxGen: 3 x 730kW 450V a.c
Fuel: 400.0 (d.f.) 3500.0 (r.f.)

9463645 **UBC ONSAN** 65,976 Class: GL
PBRP 38,906
\- **Beheermaatschappij ms UBC Onsan BV** 118,590
Feederlines BV
Groningen *Netherlands*
MMSI: 246325000
Official number: 54492

2011-07 Yangzhou Dayang Shipbuilding Co Ltd — Yangzhou JS Yd No: DY5003
Loa 260.50 (BB) Br ex - Dght 14.500
Lbp 254.00 Br md 43.00 Dpth 20.30
Welded, 1 dk

(A21A2BC) Bulk Carrier
Grain: 139,005
Compartments: 7 Ho, ER
7 Ha: 2 (21.6 x 20.8)4 (18.9 x 20.8)ER (18.9 x 17.2)

1 oil engine driving 1 FP propeller
Total Power: 13,560kW (18,436hp) 14.5kn
MAN-B&W 6S60MC-C
1 x 2 Stroke 6 Cy. 600 x 2400 13560kW (18436bhp)
Doosan Engine Co Ltd-South Korea
AuxGen: 3 x 730kW 450V a.c
Fuel: 400.0 (d.f.) 3500.0 (r.f.)

9463657 **UBC ORISTANO** 65,976 Class: GL (NK)
ZDKR2 38,906
\- **Beheermaatschappij ms 'UBC Oristano' BV** 118,467
Feederlines BV
Gibraltar *Gibraltar (British)*
MMSI: 236111782

2011-08 Yangzhou Dayang Shipbuilding Co Ltd — Yangzhou JS Yd No: DY5004
Loa 260.37 (BB) Br ex - Dght 14.500
Lbp 254.00 Br md 43.00 Dpth 20.25
Welded, 1 dk

(A21A2BC) Bulk Carrier
Grain: 139,005
Compartments: 7 Ho, ER
7 Ha: 2 (21.6 x 20.8)4 (18.9 x 20.8)ER (18.9 x 17.2)

1 oil engine driving 1 FP propeller
Total Power: 13,560kW (18,436hp) 14.5kn
MAN-B&W 6S60MC-C
1 x 2 Stroke 6 Cy. 600 x 2400 13560kW (18436bhp)
Doosan Engine Co Ltd-South Korea
AuxGen: 3 x 730kW 450V a.c
Fuel: 400.0 (d.f.) 3500.0 (r.f.)

9463633 **UBC OTTAWA** 65,976 Class: GL
PCLP 38,906
\- **Beheermaatschappij ms UBC Ottawa BV** 118,625
Feederlines BV
Groningen *Netherlands*
MMSI: 245295000
Official number: 54465

2011-06 Yangzhou Dayang Shipbuilding Co Ltd — Yangzhou JS Yd No: DY5002
Loa 260.37 (BB) Br ex - Dght 14.500
Lbp 254.00 Br md 43.00 Dpth 20.30
Welded, 1 dk

(A21A2BC) Bulk Carrier
Grain: 139,005
Compartments: 7 Ho, ER
7 Ha: 2 (21.6 x 20.8)4 (18.9 x 20.8)ER (18.9 x 17.2)

1 oil engine driving 1 FP propeller
Total Power: 13,560kW (18,436hp) 14.5kn
MAN-B&W 6S60MC-C
1 x 2 Stroke 6 Cy. 600 x 2400 13560kW (18436bhp)
Doosan Engine Co Ltd-South Korea
AuxGen: 3 x 730kW 450V a.c
Fuel: 400.0 (d.f.) 3500.0 (r.f.)

9236080 **UBC SACRAMENTO** 19,746 Class: GL
P3CH9 *launched as Stemnes -2001* 10,669
\- **Karlin Navigation Ltd** 31,773
Athena Marine Co Ltd T/cm
Limassol *Cyprus* 41.0
MMSI: 209393000
Official number: 9236080

2001-10 Saiki Heavy Industries Co Ltd — Saiki OT Yd No: 1112
Loa 171.60 (BB) Br ex - Dght 10.418
Lbp 164.33 Br md 27.00 Dpth 14.80
Welded, 1 dk

(A21A2BC) Bulk Carrier
Grain: 41,287; Bale: 40,925
Compartments: 5 Ho, ER
5 Ha: 3 (21.0 x 22.9) (20.0 x 18.0)ER (13.0 x 15.0)
Cranes: 4x30t

1 oil engine driving 1 FP propeller
Total Power: 7,061kW (9,600hp) 14.5kn
Mitsubishi 6UEC52LA
1 x 2 Stroke 6 Cy. 520 x 1600 7061kW (9600bhp)
Akasaka Tekkosho KK (Akasaka DieselLtd)-Japan

9426867 **UBC SAGUNTO** 21,018 Class: NK
5BBF3 10,927
\- **Soreta Shipping Co Ltd** 33,313
Athena Marine Co Ltd
Limassol *Cyprus*
MMSI: 209933000
Official number: 9426867

2010-08 Saiki Heavy Industries Co Ltd — Saiki OT Yd No: 1186
Loa 171.90 (BB) Br ex - Dght 10.620
Lbp 165.50 Br md 28.00 Dpth 14.80
Welded, 1 dk

(A21A2BC) Bulk Carrier
Double Hull
Grain: 41,973; Bale: 41,516
Compartments: 5 Ho, ER
5 Ha: ER
Cranes: 4x36t

1 oil engine driving 1 FP propeller
Total Power: 7,458kW (10,140hp) 14.5kn
Mitsubishi 6UEC45LSE
1 x 2 Stroke 6 Cy. 450 x 1840 7458kW (10140bhp)
Akasaka Tekkosho KK (Akasaka DieselLtd)-Japan
Fuel: 1627.0 (r.f.)

9255062 **UBC SAIKI** 19,746 Class: GL
P3GY9 10,669
\- **Southern Queen Shipping Co Ltd** 31,770
Athena Marine Co Ltd T/cm
Limassol *Cyprus* 41.0
MMSI: 210777000
Official number: 9255062

2002-08 Saiki Heavy Industries Co Ltd — Saiki OT Yd No: 1118
Loa 171.64 (BB) Br ex - Dght 10.400
Lbp 163.60 Br md 27.00 Dpth 14.80
Welded, 1 dk

(A21A2BC) Bulk Carrier
Double Hull
Grain: 41,287; Bale: 40,925
Compartments: 5 Ho, ER
5 Ha: 3 (21.0 x 22.9) (20.0 x 18.0)ER (13.0 x 15.0)
Cranes: 4x30t

1 oil engine driving 1 FP propeller
Total Power: 7,061kW (9,600hp) 14.5kn
Mitsubishi 6UEC52LA
1 x 2 Stroke 6 Cy. 520 x 1600 7061kW (9600bhp)
Akasaka Tekkosho KK (Akasaka DieselLtd)-Japan

9426881 **UBC SALAVERRY** 21,018 Class: NK
5BDP3 10,927
\- **Lemona Shipping Co Ltd** 33,305
Intership Navigation Co Ltd (ISN)
SatCom: Inmarsat C 420910912
Limassol *Cyprus*
MMSI: 209109000
Official number: 9426881

2010-12 Saiki Heavy Industries Co Ltd — Saiki OT Yd No: 1188
Loa 171.93 (BB) Br ex - Dght 10.624
Lbp 165.50 Br md 28.00 Dpth 15.00
Welded, 1 dk

(A21A2BC) Bulk Carrier
Double Hull
Grain: 41,973; Bale: 41,516
Compartments: 5 Ho, ER
5 Ha: ER
Cranes: 4x36t

1 oil engine driving 1 FP propeller
Total Power: 7,470kW (10,156hp) 14.5kn
Mitsubishi 6UEC45LSE
1 x 2 Stroke 6 Cy. 450 x 1840 7470kW (10156bhp)
Akasaka Tekkosho KK (Akasaka DieselLtd)-Japan

9380805 **UBC SANTA MARTA** 19,748 Class: GL
5BDK2 10,341
\- **Canada Star Shipping Co Ltd** 31,582
Athena Marine Co Ltd T/cm
Limassol *Cyprus* 41.0
MMSI: 210234000

2008-05 Saiki Heavy Industries Co Ltd — Saiki OT Yd No: 1168
Loa 171.59 (BB) Br ex - Dght 10.400
Lbp 163.60 Br md 27.00 Dpth 14.80
Welded, 1 dk

(A21A2BC) Bulk Carrier
Double Hull
Grain: 41,500; Bale: 39,900
TEU 363
Compartments: 5 Ho, ER
5 Ha: 3 (20.5 x 22.8) (19.8 x 18.0)ER (13.4 x 15.0)
Cranes: 4x30t
Ice Capable

1 oil engine driving 1 FP propeller
Total Power: 7,080kW (9,626hp) 14.5kn
Mitsubishi 6UEC52LA
1 x 2 Stroke 6 Cy. 520 x 1600 7080kW (9626bhp)
Akasaka Tekkosho KK (Akasaka DieselLtd)-Japan
AuxGen: 2 x 480kW 450V a.c
Fuel: 314.0 (d.f.) 1256.0 (r.f.) 26.0pd

9376000 **UBC SANTOS** 19,748 Class: GL
5BCS2 10,341
\- **Woolko Shipping Co Ltd** 31,568
Athena Marine Co Ltd T/cm
Limassol *Cyprus* 41.0
MMSI: 212125000

2008-03 Saiki Heavy Industries Co Ltd — Saiki OT Yd No: 1167
Loa 171.59 (BB) Br ex - Dght 10.418
Lbp 163.60 Br md 27.00 Dpth 14.80
Welded, 1 dk

(A21A2BC) Bulk Carrier
Double Hull
Grain: 44,324; Bale: 39,900
TEU 363
Compartments: 5 Ho, ER
5 Ha: 3 (20.5 x 22.8) (19.8 x 18.0)ER (13.4 x 15.0)
Cranes: 4x30t
Ice Capable

1 oil engine driving 1 FP propeller
Total Power: 7,080kW (9,626hp) 14.5kn
Mitsubishi 6UEC52LA
1 x 2 Stroke 6 Cy. 520 x 1600 7080kW (9626bhp)
Akasaka Tekkosho KK (Akasaka DieselLtd)-Japan
AuxGen: 2 x 480kW 450V a.c
Fuel: 314.0 (d.f.) 1256.0 (r.f.) 26.3pd

9220976 **UBC SAVANNAH** 19,743 Class: GL
P3UW8 *ex Sandnes -2001* 10,718
\- **Groupero Shipping Co Ltd** 31,923
Athena Marine Co Ltd T/cm
Limassol *Cyprus* 41.0
MMSI: 209289000
Official number: 9220976

2000-10 Saiki Heavy Industries Co Ltd — Saiki OT Yd No: 1107
Loa 171.60 (BB) Br ex - Dght 10.400
Lbp 163.60 Br md 27.00 Dpth 14.80
Welded, 1 dk

(A21A2BC) Bulk Carrier
Grain: 41,756; Bale: 41,138
Compartments: 5 Ho, ER
5 Ha: (13.4 x 15.0)3 (20.5 x 22.9) (19.8 x 18.0)ER
Cranes: 4x30t
Ice Capable

1 oil engine driving 1 FP propeller
Total Power: 7,061kW (9,600hp) 14.7kn
Mitsubishi 6UEC52LA
1 x 2 Stroke 6 Cy. 520 x 1600 7061kW (9600bhp)
Akasaka Tekkosho KK (Akasaka DieselLtd)-Japan
AuxGen: 2 x 480kW 220/440V a.c

IMO / Call sign	Name / Owner / Manager	Tonnage	Class	Builder / Dimensions	Type / Capacities	Machinery
9255050 *P3GK9* -	**UBC SINGAPORE** **Southern Princess Shipping Co Ltd** Athena Marine Co Ltd *Limassol* *Cyprus* MMSI: 210059000 Official number: 9255050	**19,746** 10,669 31,759 T/cm 41.0	Class: GL	**2002-06 Saiki Heavy Industries Co Ltd — Saiki OT** Yd No: 1117 Loa 171.67 (BB) Br ex 27.00 Dght 10.418 Lbp 163.60 Br md 27.00 Dpth 14.80 Welded, 1 dk	**(A21A2BC) Bulk Carrier** Grain: 41,287; Bale: 40,925 Compartments: 5 Ho, ER 5 Ha: 3 (21.0 x 22.9) (20.0 x 18.0)ER (13.0 x 15.0) Cranes: 4x30t	**1 oil engine** driving 1 FP propeller Total Power: 7,061kW (9,600hp) 14.5kn Mitsubishi 6UEC52LA 1 x 2 Stroke 6 Cy. 520 x 1600 7061kW (9600bhp) Akasaka Tekkosho KK (Akasaka DieselLtd)-Japan
9287340 *P3XJ9* -	**UBC STAVANGER** **Portview Shipping Co Ltd** Mastermind Shipmanagement Ltd *Limassol* *Cyprus* MMSI: 209156000 Official number: 9287340	**19,748** 10,594 31,751 T/cm 41.0	Class: GL	**2004-10 Saiki Heavy Industries Co Ltd — Saiki OT** Yd No: 1131 Loa 171.60 (BB) Br ex - Dght 10.400 Lbp 164.33 Br md 27.00 Dpth 14.80 Welded, 1 dk	**(A21A2BC) Bulk Carrier** Grain: 40,200; Bale: 39,837 Compartments: 5 Ho, ER 5 Ha: 3 (20.5 x 22.8) (19.8 x 18.0)ER (13.4 x 15.0) Cranes: 4x30t	**1 oil engine** driving 1 FP propeller Total Power: 7,061kW (9,600hp) 14.5kn Mitsubishi 6UEC52LA 1 x 2 Stroke 6 Cy. 520 x 1600 7061kW (9600bhp) Akasaka Tekkosho KK (Akasaka DieselLtd)-Japan AuxGen: 2 x 650kW 440/220V 60Hz a.c Fuel: 319.5 (d.f.) 1327.0 (r.f.) 23.0pd
9236078 *P3AF9* -	**UBC SYDNEY** *ex Spraynes -2001* **Southern King Shipping Co Ltd** Athena Marine Co Ltd *Limassol* *Cyprus* MMSI: 209218000 Official number: 9236078	**19,746** 10,669 31,759 T/cm 41.0	Class: GL	**2001-08 Saiki Heavy Industries Co Ltd — Saiki OT** Yd No: 1111 Loa 171.60 (BB) Br ex - Dght 10.418 Lbp 163.60 Br md 27.00 Dpth 14.80 Welded, 1 dk	**(A21A2BC) Bulk Carrier** Double Hull Grain: 41,287; Bale: 40,925 Compartments: 5 Ho, ER 5 Ha: (13.4 x 15.0)3 (20.5 x 22.8) (19.7 x 18.0)ER Cranes: 4x30t	**1 oil engine** driving 1 FP propeller Total Power: 7,061kW (9,600hp) 14.5kn Mitsubishi 6UEC52LA 1 x 2 Stroke 6 Cy. 520 x 1600 7061kW (9600bhp) Akasaka Tekkosho KK (Akasaka DieselLtd)-Japan AuxGen: 2 x 480kW 450V 60Hz a.c Fuel: 319.5 (d.f.) (Heating Coils) 1327.0 (r.f.) 27.1pd
9416707 *5BVM2* -	**UBC TAMPA** **Tandino Shipping Co Ltd** Athena Marine Co Ltd *Limassol* *Cyprus* MMSI: 209136000 Official number: 9416707	**24,140** 13,402 37,724	Class: GL	**2009-09 Saiki Heavy Industries Co Ltd — Saiki OT** Yd No: 1180 Loa 182.59 (BB) Br ex - Dght 10.850 Lbp 174.60 Br md 28.60 Dpth 15.00 Welded, 1 dk	**(A21A2BC) Bulk Carrier** Double Hull Grain: 48,820; Bale: 48,500 Compartments: 6 Ho, ER 6 Ha: 4 (21.6 x 24.0) (14.4 x 24.0)ER (11.2 x 20.0) Cranes: 3x36t Ice Capable	**1 oil engine** driving 1 FP propeller Total Power: 7,980kW (10,850hp) 15.7kn Mitsubishi 6UEC52LS 1 x 2 Stroke 6 Cy. 520 x 1850 7980kW (10850bhp) Akasaka Tekkosho KK (Akasaka DieselLtd)-Japan AuxGen: 2 x 480kW 450V 60Hz a.c Fuel: 300.0 (d.f.) 1500.0 (r.f.) 32.0pd
9285354 *P3YN9* -	**UBC TAMPICO** **Premant Shipping Co Ltd** Intership Navigation Co Ltd (ISN) *Limassol* *Cyprus* MMSI: 210347000 Official number: 9285354	**24,140** 13,402 37,821	Class: GL (AB)	**2004-12 Saiki Heavy Industries Co Ltd — Saiki OT** Yd No: 1132 Loa 182.59 (BB) Br ex - Dght 10.850 Lbp 174.60 Br md 28.60 Dpth 15.00 Welded, 1 dk	**(A31A2GX) General Cargo Ship** Double Hull Grain: 43,699; Bale: 43,461 TEU 1153 C Ho 659 TEU C Dk 494 TEU Compartments: 6 Ho, ER 6 Ha: 4 (21.6 x 24.0) (14.4 x 24.0)ER (11.2 x 20.0) Cranes: 3x36t	**1 oil engine** driving 1 FP propeller Total Power: 7,680kW (10,442hp) 14.5kn Mitsubishi 6UEC52LS 1 x 2 Stroke 6 Cy. 520 x 1850 7680kW (10442bhp) Akasaka Tekkosho KK (Akasaka DieselLtd)-Japan AuxGen: 2 x 480kW 450/225V 60Hz a.c Fuel: 357.0 (d.f.) 1602.0 (r.f.)
9416719 *5BWR2* -	**UBC TARRAGONA** **Internova Shipping Co Ltd** Intership Navigation Co Ltd (ISN) *Limassol* *Cyprus* MMSI: 209017000	**24,140** 13,402 37,706	Class: GL	**2009-11 Saiki Heavy Industries Co Ltd — Saiki OT** Yd No: 1181 Loa 182.59 (BB) Br ex - Dght 10.850 Lbp 174.60 Br md 28.60 Dpth 15.00 Welded, 1 dk	**(A21A2BC) Bulk Carrier** Double Hull Grain: 48,820; Bale: 48,500 Compartments: 6 Ho, ER 6 Ha: 4 (21.6 x 24.0) (14.4 x 24.0)ER (11.2 x 20.0) Cranes: 3x36t	**1 oil engine** driving 1 FP propeller Total Power: 7,980kW (10,850hp) 15.7kn Mitsubishi 6UEC52LS 1 x 2 Stroke 6 Cy. 520 x 1850 7980kW (10850bhp) Akasaka Tekkosho KK (Akasaka DieselLtd)-Japan AuxGen: 2 x 480kW 450V 60Hz a.c
9416721 *5BXL2* -	**UBC TILBURY** **Altermar Shipping Co Ltd** Athena Marine Co Ltd *Limassol* *Cyprus* MMSI: 212040000	**24,140** 13,402 37,702	Class: GL	**2010-01 Saiki Heavy Industries Co Ltd — Saiki OT** Yd No: 1182 Loa 182.59 (BB) Br ex - Dght 10.850 Lbp 174.60 Br md 28.60 Dpth 15.00 Welded, 1 dk	**(A21A2BC) Bulk Carrier** Double Hull Grain: 48,820; Bale: 48,500 Compartments: 6 Ho, ER 6 Ha: 4 (21.6 x 24.0) (14.4 x 24.0)ER (11.2 x 20.0) Cranes: 3x36t Ice Capable	**1 oil engine** driving 1 FP propeller Total Power: 7,943kW (10,799hp) 15.7kn Mitsubishi 6UEC52LS 1 x 2 Stroke 6 Cy. 520 x 1850 7943kW (10799bhp) Akasaka Tekkosho KK (Akasaka DieselLtd)-Japan AuxGen: 2 x 480kW 450V 60Hz a.c
9300752 *C4DT2* -	**UBC TOKYO** **Speedwave Shipping Co Ltd** Athena Marine Co Ltd *Limassol* *Cyprus* MMSI: 210786000 Official number: 9300752	**24,140** 13,402 37,865	Class: GL	**2005-10 Saiki Heavy Industries Co Ltd — Saiki OT** Yd No: 1150 Loa 182.59 (BB) Br ex - Dght 10.850 Lbp 174.60 Br md 28.60 Dpth 15.00 Welded, 1 dk	**(A31A2GX) General Cargo Ship** Double Hull Grain: 43,699; Bale: 43,461 TEU 1153 C Ho 659 TEU C Dk 494 TEU Compartments: 6 Ho, ER 6 Ha: 4 (21.6 x 24.0)ER 2 (14.4 x 24.0) Cranes: 3x36t	**1 oil engine** driving 1 FP propeller Total Power: 7,980kW (10,850hp) 14.5kn Mitsubishi 6UEC52LS 1 x 2 Stroke 6 Cy. 520 x 1850 7980kW (10850bhp) Akasaka Tekkosho KK (Akasaka DieselLtd)-Japan AuxGen: 2 x 550kW 440/220V 60Hz a.c Fuel: 298.6 (d.f.) 1494.5 (r.f.) 31.5pd
9300764 *C4FY2* -	**UBC TORONTO** **Boltonio Shipping Co Ltd** Athena Marine Co Ltd *Limassol* *Cyprus* MMSI: 212439000 Official number: 9300764	**24,140** 13,402 37,832	Class: GL	**2005-12 Saiki Heavy Industries Co Ltd — Saiki OT** Yd No: 1151 Loa 182.60 (BB) Br ex - Dght 10.850 Lbp 174.60 Br md 28.60 Dpth 15.00 Welded, 1 dk	**(A31A2GX) General Cargo Ship** Double Hull Grain: 43,699; Bale: 43,461 TEU 1153 C Ho 659 TEU C Dk 494 TEU Compartments: 6 Ho, ER 6 Ha: 4 (21.6 x 24.0) (14.4 x 24.0)ER (11.2 x 20.0) Cranes: 3x36t	**1 oil engine** driving 1 FP propeller Total Power: 7,680kW (10,442hp) 14.2kn Mitsubishi 6UEC52LS 1 x 2 Stroke 6 Cy. 520 x 1850 7680kW (10442bhp) Akasaka Tekkosho KK (Akasaka DieselLtd)-Japan AuxGen: 2 x 650kW 450/225V 60Hz a.c Fuel: 289.6 (d.f.) (Heating Coils) 1494.5 (r.f.)
7238242 - - -	**UBE MARU** *ex Awaji Maru -1981* - -	*198* - -		**1972-11 Kanagawa Zosen — Kobe** Yd No: 122 L reg 30.03 Br ex 8.23 Dght 2.299 Lbp 29.49 Br md 8.21 Dpth 3.41 Riveted\Welded, 1 dk	**(B32A2ST) Tug**	**2 oil engines** Geared Integral to driving 2 Z propellers Total Power: 1,766kW (2,402hp) Niigata 6L25BX 2 x 4 Stroke 6 Cy. 250 x 320 each-883kW (1201bhp) Niigata Engineering Co Ltd-Japan
9314040 *MGVE7* FR 50	**UBEROUS** **The Uberous Partnership LLP** - *Fraserburgh* *United Kingdom* MMSI: 235008490 Official number: C18340	**163** 55 -		**2005-03 Macduff Shipyards Ltd — Macduff** Yd No: 628 Loa 18.60 (BB) Br ex - Dght - Lbp - Br md 6.80 Dpth - Welded, 1 dk	**(B11B2FV) Fishing Vessel**	**1 oil engine** geared to sc. shaft driving 1 FP propeller Total Power: 372kW (506hp) Caterpillar 3176B 1 x 4 Stroke 6 Cy. 125 x 140 372kW (506bhp) Caterpillar Inc-USA
8007573 *J8PX5* -	**UBERTY** *ex Oryong No. 86 -2007* *ex Tae Chang No. 79 -1993* **Regalia International Seafood Ltd** National Fisheries Co Ltd *Kingstown* *St Vincent & The Grenadines* Official number: 400660	**542** 275 447	Class: (KR)	**1980-05 Daedong Shipbuilding Co Ltd — Busan** Yd No: 237 Loa 55.16 Br ex - Dght 3.565 Lbp 49.40 Br md 8.60 Dpth 4.00 Welded, 1 dk	**(B11B2FV) Fishing Vessel** Ins: 603	**1 oil engine** reverse geared to sc. shaft driving 1 FP propeller Total Power: 883kW (1,201hp) 13.3kn Akasaka DM28AR 1 x 4 Stroke 6 Cy. 280 x 460 883kW (1201bhp) Akasaka Tekkosho KK (Akasaka DieselLtd)-Japan AuxGen: 2 x 200kW 225V 60Hz a.c Fuel: 378.5 (d.f.)
7638105 *TCXN* -	**UBEYD FEYZA** *ex Cem Sener -2013 ex Kutup Yildizi -1998* *ex Bora Burak -1986* **Yapi Kredi Finansal Kiralama AO (Yapi Kredi Leasing AO)** Kamer Denizcilik Nakliyat ve Ticaret AS *Istanbul* *Turkey* MMSI: 271000276 Official number: 4773	**2,902** 1,916 5,110	Class: TL (AB)	**1980-03 Marmara Tersanesi — Yarimca** Yd No: 9A Loa 91.29 (BB) Br ex - Dght 6.730 Lbp 85.35 Br md 14.22 Dpth 8.51 Welded, 2 dks	**(A31A2GX) General Cargo Ship** Grain: 6,682; Bale: 6,456 Compartments: 2 Ho, ER 2 Ha: (- x 10.2) (25.2 x 10.2)ER Derricks: 4x5t; Winches: 4	**1 oil engine** sr geared to sc. shaft driving 1 CP propeller Total Power: 2,501kW (3,400hp) 14.0kn Nohab F216V 1 x Vee 4 Stroke 16 Cy. 250 x 300 2501kW (3400bhp) Nohab Diesel AB-Sweden AuxGen: 2 x 172kW a.c, 1 x 25kW a.c
8226789 *UDDG*	**UBEZHDENNYY** **TINRO Centre - Pacific Research Fisheries Centre** - SatCom: Inmarsat C 427320867 *Vladivostok* *Russia*	**195** 58 35	Class: RS	**1983-12 Sretenskiy Sudostroitelnyy Zavod — Sretensk** Yd No: 125 Loa 33.97 Br ex 7.09 Dght 2.900 Lbp 30.00 Br md 7.00 Dpth 3.66 Welded, 1 dk	**(B31A2SR) Research Survey Vessel** Ice Capable	**1 oil engine** driving 1 FP propeller Total Power: 224kW (305hp) 9.1kn S.K.L. 8NVD36-1U 1 x 4 Stroke 8 Cy. 240 x 360 224kW (305bhp) VEB Schwermaschinenbau "KarlLiebknecht" (SKL)-Magdeburg AuxGen: 2 x 86kW, 1 x 28kW Fuel: 22.0 (d.f.)
9417490 *V7TR3* -	**UBT FJORD** **Brovig UBT AS** Bergshav Management AS *Majuro* *Marshall Islands* MMSI: 538003864 Official number: 3864	**6,149** 2,896 9,285 T/cm 18.9	Class: BV	**2008-05 Dongfang Shipbuilding Group Co Ltd — Yueqing ZJ** Yd No: DF90-2 Loa 117.60 (BB) Br ex - Dght 7.500 Lbp 109.60 Br md 19.00 Dpth 10.00 Welded, 1 dk	**(A12B2TR) Chemical/Products Tanker** Double Hull (13F) Liq: 9,507; Liq (Oil): 9,507 Cargo Heating Coils Compartments: 10 Wing Ta, 2 Wing Slop Ta, ER 10 Cargo Pump (s): 10x300m³/hr Manifold: Bow/CM: 61.6m	**1 oil engine** reduction geared to sc. shafts driving 1 FP propeller Total Power: 2,970kW (4,038hp) 13.0kn MaK 9M25 1 x 4 Stroke 9 Cy. 255 x 400 2970kW (4038bhp) Caterpillar Motoren GmbH & Co. KG-Germany AuxGen: 3 x 445kW 60Hz a.c Thrusters: 1 Tunnel thruster (f) Fuel: 82.0 (d.f.) 403.0 (r.f.)

7385253 *ZR5918* -	**UBUNTU** *ex* Drifter Ii *-2012* *ex* S. A. Kuswag II *-2012* **Tresso Trading 626 (Pty) Ltd** - *Cape Town* *South Africa* MMSI: 601799000 Official number: 350706	*185* 55 -	Class: (AB)	**1974**-03 **Sandock-Austral Ltd. — Durban** Yd No: 58 Loa 28.96 Br ex 6.43 Dght 2.744 Lbp 26.67 Br md 6.41 Dpth 3.36 Welded, 1 dk	**(B34G2SE) Pollution Control Vessel**	**1 oil engine** driving 1 CP propeller Total Power: 588kW (799hp) 11.0kn Alpha 408-26VO 1 x 2 Stroke 8 Cy. 260 x 400 588kW (799bhp) Alpha Diesel A/S-Denmark AuxGen: 2 x 88kW Fuel: 44.5
8645014 *TC3291* -	**UCANAT** **Eta Petrol Akaryakit Ticaret ve Nakliyat AS** - *Istanbul* *Turkey* MMSI: 271010208 Official number: TUGS 1804	**110** 20 180 T/cm 1.3		**1984 Cicek Tersanesi — Tuzla** Loa - Br ex - Dght - Lbp 29.70 Br md 5.60 Dpth 3.00 Welded, 1 dk	**(A13B2TP) Products Tanker** 2 Cargo Pump (s) Manifold: Bow/CM: 9m	**2 oil engines** driving 1 Propeller 9.0kn MAN Maschinenbau Augsburg Nuernberg (MAN)-Augsburg AuxGen: 1 x a.c
9668817 -	**UCAR SU** **Hasan Altun** - *Istanbul* *Turkey*	**297** 110 -	Class: (TL)	**2012**-06 **Cakirlar Tersane Isletmeciligi Sanayi Ticaret Ltd Sti — Altinova** Yd No: 12 Loa 33.90 Br ex - Dght - Lbp - Br md 8.00 Dpth 2.80 Welded, 1 dk	**(A37B2PS) Passenger Ship**	**2 oil engines** reduction geared to sc. shafts driving 2 Propellers Total Power: 514kW (698hp) G.M. (Detroit Diesel) 2 x each-257kW (349bhp) General Motors Detroit DieselAllison Divn-USA
6714940 - -	**UCAYALI 1** *ex* Lia *-1979* - -	*158* 69 -		**1967 Ast. Picsa S.A. — Callao** L reg 24.51 Br ex 6.71 Dght - Lbp - Br md - Dpth 3.46 Welded, 1 dk	**(B11B2FV) Fishing Vessel**	**1 oil engine** driving 1 FP propeller Total Power: 279kW (379hp) Caterpillar D353SCAC 1 x 4 Stroke 6 Cy. 159 x 203 279kW (379bhp) Caterpillar Tractor Co-USA
6621519 - -	**UCAYALI 2** *ex* Pegaso III *-1979* - -	*158* 69 -		**1966 Ast. Picsa S.A. — Callao** L reg 24.48 Br ex 6.10 Dght - Lbp - Br md - Dpth 3.28 Welded, 1 dk	**(B11B2FV) Fishing Vessel**	**1 oil engine** driving 1 FP propeller Total Power: 243kW (330hp) Caterpillar D353SCAC 1 x 4 Stroke 6 Cy. 159 x 203 243kW (330bhp) Caterpillar Tractor Co-USA
6605709 - -	**UCAYALI 3** *ex* Fernandito *-1979* -	*120* - -	Class: (LR) ✠ Classed LR until 9/67	**1966**-01 **Fabricaciones Metallicas E.P.S. (FABRIMET) — Callao** Yd No: 308 Loa 25.20 Br ex 7.14 Dght - Lbp 21.49 Br md 7.01 Dpth 3.46 Welded, 1 dk	**(B11B2FV) Fishing Vessel**	**1 oil engine** reverse reduction geared to sc. shaft driving 1 FP propeller Total Power: 399kW (542hp) Caterpillar D353SCAC 1 x 4 Stroke 6 Cy. 159 x 203 399kW (542bhp) Caterpillar Tractor Co-USA
6619190 - -	**UCAYALI 4** *ex* Nicky T *-1979* - -	*120* - -	Class: (LR) ✠ Classed LR until 12/67	**1966**-09 **Fabricaciones Metallicas E.P.S. (FABRIMET) — Callao** Yd No: 319 Loa 25.20 Br ex 7.14 Dght 2.693 Lbp 21.49 Br md 7.01 Dpth 3.46 Welded, 1 dk	**(B11B2FV) Fishing Vessel**	**1 oil engine** reverse reduction geared to sc. shaft driving 1 FP propeller Total Power: 399kW (542hp) Caterpillar D353SCAC 1 x 4 Stroke 6 Cy. 159 x 203 399kW (542bhp) Caterpillar Tractor Co-USA
6619217 - -	**UCAYALI 5** *ex* Richard T *-1979* - -	*120* - -	Class: (LR) ✠ Classed LR until 12/67	**1966**-10 **Fabricaciones Metallicas E.P.S. (FABRIMET) — Callao** Yd No: 328 Loa 25.20 Br ex 7.14 Dght 2.693 Lbp 21.49 Br md 7.01 Dpth 3.46 Welded, 1 dk	**(B11B2FV) Fishing Vessel**	**1 oil engine** reverse reduction geared to sc. shaft driving 1 FP propeller Total Power: 399kW (542hp) Caterpillar D353SCAC 1 x 4 Stroke 6 Cy. 159 x 203 399kW (542bhp) Caterpillar Tractor Co-USA
6619188 - -	**UCAYALI 6** *ex* Michele T *-1979* - -	*120* - -	Class: (LR) ✠ Classed LR until 12/67	**1966**-11 **Fabricaciones Metallicas E.P.S. (FABRIMET) — Callao** Yd No: 326 Loa 25.20 Br ex 7.14 Dght 2.693 Lbp 21.49 Br md 7.01 Dpth 3.46 Welded, 1 dk	**(B11B2FV) Fishing Vessel**	**1 oil engine** reverse reduction geared to sc. shaft driving 1 FP propeller Total Power: 399kW (542hp) Caterpillar D353SCAC 1 x 4 Stroke 6 Cy. 159 x 203 399kW (542bhp) Caterpillar Tractor Co-USA
6611617 - -	**UCAYALI 7** *ex* Petsa 9 *-1979* - -	*158* 69 -		**1965 Ast. Picsa S.A. — Callao** L reg 24.60 Br ex 6.71 Dght - Lbp - Br md - Dpth 3.46 Welded, 1 dk	**(B11B2FV) Fishing Vessel**	**1 oil engine** driving 1 FP propeller Total Power: 243kW (330hp) Caterpillar D353SCAC 1 x 4 Stroke 6 Cy. 159 x 203 243kW (330bhp) Caterpillar Tractor Co-USA
6703862 - -	**UCAYALI 8** *ex* PH 18 *-1976* - -	*158* 69 -	Class: (GL)	**1966 Ast. Picsa S.A. — Callao** Yd No: 164 Loa - Br ex 6.71 Dght - Lbp 22.61 Br md - Dpth 3.28 Welded, 1 dk	**(B11B2FV) Fishing Vessel**	**1 oil engine** driving 1 FP propeller Total Power: 243kW (330hp) Caterpillar D353SCAC 1 x 4 Stroke 6 Cy. 159 x 203 243kW (330bhp) Caterpillar Tractor Co-USA
6714952 - -	**UCAYALI 9** *ex* PA 2 *-1976* - -	*158* 69 -	Class: (GL)	**1966 Ast. Picsa S.A. — Callao** L reg 24.51 Br ex 6.71 Dght - Lbp - Br md - Dpth 3.46 Welded, 1 dk	**(B11B2FV) Fishing Vessel**	**1 oil engine** driving 1 FP propeller Total Power: 279kW (379hp) Caterpillar D353SCAC 1 x 4 Stroke 6 Cy. 159 x 203 279kW (379bhp) Caterpillar Tractor Co-USA
6606909 - -	**UCAYALI 10** *ex* Petsa 7 *-1979* - -	*158* 69 -		**1965 Ast. Picsa S.A. — Callao** L reg 24.60 Br ex 6.71 Dght - Lbp - Br md - Dpth 3.46 Welded, 1 dk	**(B11B2FV) Fishing Vessel**	**1 oil engine** driving 1 FP propeller Total Power: 243kW (330hp) Caterpillar D353SCAC 1 x 4 Stroke 6 Cy. 159 x 203 243kW (330bhp) Caterpillar Tractor Co-USA
9011569 *HQX02* -	**UCC CAT 1** *ex* Puglia Queen L *-2010* *ex* Vingtor *-2010* *ex* Jet Cat *-1996* *ex* Pattaya Express *-1991* **UrbaCon Trading & Contracting LLC (UCC)** - *San Lorenzo* *Honduras* MMSI: 334610000 Official number: L-0128578	**478** 160 100	Class: RI (NV)	**1990**-12 **Kvaerner Fjellstrand AS — Omastrand** Yd No: 1603 Loa 40.00 Br ex - Dght - Lbp - Br md 10.00 Dpth 3.96 Welded, 1 dk	**(A37B2PS) Passenger Ship** Hull Material: Aluminium Alloy Passengers: unberthed: 272	**2 oil engines** geared to sc. shafts driving 2 Water jets Total Power: 3,578kW (4,864hp) 32.5kn M.T.U. 16V396TE74L 2 x Vee 4 Stroke 16 Cy. 165 x 185 each-1789kW (2432bhp) MTU Friedrichshafen GmbH-Friedrichshafen AuxGen: 2 x 230/380V 50Hz a.c
8747185 *HQX05* -	**UCC LC 21** *ex* Elafonisos *-2013* **UrbaCon Trading & Contracting LLC (UCC)** - *San Lorenzo* *Honduras* MMSI: 334713000 Official number: L1228594	**202** 60 -	Class: RI	**1999 in Greece** Loa 48.50 Br ex - Dght 1.050 Lbp - Br md 14.50 Dpth 1.70 Welded, 1 dk	**(A35D2RL) Landing Craft**	**2 oil engines** reduction geared to sc. shafts driving 2 Propellers Total Power: 580kW (788hp) 9.0kn Iveco Aifo 2 x 4 Stroke each-290kW (394bhp) Iveco Pegaso-Madrid
9506992 - -	**UCC TGB 21** *ex* Kim Heng 3208 *-2013* **UrbaCon Trading & Contracting LLC (UCC)** - *San Lorenzo* *Honduras* Official number: L-3828590	**317** 96 284	Class: GL	**2009**-10 **Sapor Shipbuilding Industries Sdn Bhd — Sibu** Yd No: SAPOR 41 Loa 31.00 Br ex - Dght 3.500 Lbp 28.59 Br md 9.50 Dpth 4.20 Welded, 1 dk	**(B32A2ST) Tug**	**2 oil engines** reverse reduction geared to sc. shafts driving 2 FP propellers Total Power: 2,388kW (3,246hp) Cummins KTA-50-M2 2 x Vee 4 Stroke 16 Cy. 159 x 159 each-1194kW (1623bhp) Cummins Engine Co Inc-USA AuxGen: 2 x 79kW 415V a.c
9519456 *A7D6725* -	**UCC TGB 22** *ex* Tekun 32351 *-2014* **UrbaCon Trading & Contracting LLC (UCC)** - *Doha* *Qatar* Official number: 347/13	**298** 90 244	Class: BV NK	**2011**-06 **Rajang Maju Shipbuilding Sdn Bhd — Sibu** Yd No: RMM0006 Loa 32.00 Br ex - Dght 3.512 Lbp 29.23 Br md 9.14 Dpth 4.20 Welded, 1 dk	**(B32A2ST) Tug**	**2 oil engines** geared to sc. shafts driving 2 FP propellers Total Power: 2,669kW (3,629hp) Cummins KTA-50-M2 2 x Vee 4 Stroke 16 Cy. 159 x 159 each-1177kW (1600bhp) Cummins Engine Co Inc-USA AuxGen: 2 x 78kW a.c Fuel: 210.0 (d.f.)
9142411 *8PAI5* -	**UCCL ALARA** *ex* Jin Man He *-2012* **Upper Canada Container Line Inc** Menpas Shipping & Trading Inc SatCom: Inmarsat C 431440610 *Bridgetown* *Barbados* MMSI: 314406000 Official number: 6960	**2,900** 1,313 4,906	Class: CC (GL) **100A1** SS 09/2011 **LMC** **UMS**	**1996**-09 **Kroeger Werft GmbH & Co. KG — Schacht-Audorf** Yd No: 1537 Loa 98.43 (BB) Br ex - Dght 5.930 Lbp 91.45 Br md 16.90 Dpth 7.55 Welded, 2 dks	**(A31A2GX) General Cargo Ship** Grain: 4,456; Bale: 4,166 TEU 366 C Ho 80 TEU C Dk 286 TEU incl 46 ref C. Compartments: 1 Ho, ER, 1 Tw Dk 3 Ha: (25.7 x 10.6)Tappered (25.7 x 13.2) (6.2 x 10.5)ER Ice Capable	**1 oil engine** with flexible couplings & sr gearedto sc. shaft driving 1 CP propeller Total Power: 2,940kW (3,997hp) 13.5kn MaK 8M453C 1 x 4 Stroke 8 Cy. 320 x 420 2940kW (3997bhp) Krupp MaK Maschinenbau GmbH-Kiel AuxGen: 1 x 590kW 220/440V a.c, 2 x 256kW 220/440V a.c Thrusters: 1 Thwart. FP thruster (f) Fuel: 45.0 (d.f.) 230.4 (r.f.) 12.5pd

IMO / Call sign	Name / Owner	Tonnage	Class	Build / Dimensions	Type	Machinery
8847466 *TCBI9* -	**UCEL** *ex* Sovremennyy *-1996* **Ucel Denizcilik ve Ticaret AS** - *Istanbul* *Turkey* MMSI: 271002286 Official number: 6954	**516** 155 212	Class: TL	**1959 Dalian Shipyard Co Ltd — Dalian LN** Yd No: 2 Loa 45.79 Br ex 9.81 Dght 3.920 Lbp 41.68 Br md 9.40 Dpth 5.00 Welded, 1 dk	**(B32A2ST) Tug**	**2 oil engines** driving 2 FP propellers Total Power: 882kW (1,200hp) Russkiy 6DPN30/50 2 x 6 Cy. 300 x 500 each-441kW (600bhp) Mashinostroitelnyy Zavod"Russkiy-Dizel"-Leningrad
9481881 *8PAH9* -	**UCF-1** - **UCF Shipping One Ltd** United Cargo Fleet Ltd SatCom: Inmarsat C 431440210 *Bridgetown* *Barbados* MMSI: 314402000	**4,878** 2,618 5,185	Class: RS	**2012-09 Wuhan Huaxia Shipping Business Co Ltd — Wuhan HB** Yd No: RU-WH01 Loa 123.17 Br ex 16.70 Dght 4.200 Lbp 117.45 Br md 16.50 Dpth 5.50 Welded, 1 dk	**(A31A2GX) General Cargo Ship** Grain: 8,595 TEU 240 C Ho 180 TEU C Dk 60 TEU Compartments: 3 Ho, ER 3 Ha: ER 3 (25.2 x 12.7) Ice Capable	**2 oil engines** reduction geared to sc. shafts driving 2 FP propellers Total Power: 1,912kW (2,600hp) 10.0kn MAN-B&W 2 x each-956kW (1300bhp) AuxGen: 3 x 160kW a.c Thrusters: 1 Tunnel thruster (f) Fuel: 290.0
9481910 *8PAF5* -	**UCF-4** - **UCF Shipping Ltd** United Cargo Fleet Ltd SatCom: Inmarsat C 431438310 *Bridgetown* *Barbados* MMSI: 314383000	**4,879** 2,618 5,185	Class: RS	**2011-09 Wuhan Huaxia Shipping Business Co Ltd — Wuhan HB** (Hull launched by) Yd No: RU-WH04 **2011-09 Zhejiang Hengyu Shipbuilding Co Ltd — Zhoushan ZJ** (Hull completed by) Loa 123.17 Br ex 16.70 Dght 4.200 Lbp 117.45 Br md 16.50 Dpth 5.50 Welded, 1 dk	**(A31A2GX) General Cargo Ship** Grain: 8,595 TEU 240 C Ho 180 TEU C Dk 60 TEU Compartments: 3 Ho, ER 3 Ha: ER 3 (25.2 x 12.7)	**2 oil engines** reduction geared to sc. shafts driving 2 FP propellers Total Power: 2,206kW (3,000hp) 10.5kn MAN-B&W 2 x each-1103kW (1500bhp) in China AuxGen: 3 x 160kW a.c Thrusters: 1 Tunnel thruster (f) Fuel: 234.0
9481922 - -	**UCF-5** - **International Business & Finance Services Ltd** United Cargo Fleet Ltd *St Petersburg* *Russia*	**4,879** 2,618 5,185	Class: RS	**2013-08 Zhejiang Hengyu Shipbuilding Co Ltd — Zhoushan ZJ** Yd No: 1 Loa 123.18 (BB) Br ex 16.70 Dght 4.200 Lbp 117.45 Br md 16.50 Dpth 5.50 Welded, 1 dk	**(A31A2GX) General Cargo Ship** Grain: 8,595 TEU 240 C Ho 180 TEU C Dk 60 TEU Compartments: 3 Ho, ER 3 Ha: ER 3 (25.2 x 12.7) Ice Capable	**2 oil engines** reduction geared to sc. shafts driving 2 FP propellers Total Power: 2,240kW (3,046hp) 10.5kn AuxGen: 3 x 160kW a.c Thrusters: 1 Tunnel thruster (f) Fuel: 234.0
6815988 *LW9499* -	**UCHI** *ex* Bueno Gonzalez *-1975* **Pesquera Mayorazgo SAMCI** - *Puerto Deseado* *Argentina* MMSI: 701000742 Official number: 01901	**805** 420 353	Class: (LR) ✠ Classed LR until 25/8/82	**1968-12 Astilleros Luzuriaga SA — Pasaia** Yd No: 107 Loa 53.80 Br ex 10.55 Dght 4.700 Lbp 46.00 Br md 10.41 Dpth 7.12 Welded, 2 dks	**(B11A2FS) Stern Trawler** Ins: 530	**1 oil engine** driving 1 FP propeller Total Power: 1,140kW (1,550hp) Werkspoor TMAB396 1 x 4 Stroke 6 Cy. 390 x 680 1140kW (1550bhp) Naval Stork Werkspoor SA-Spain AuxGen: 2 x 300kW 380V 50Hz a.c, 1 x 150kW 380V 50Hz a.c
7856408 *YD4776* -	**UCHIDA** *ex* Metico 128 *-2001* *ex* Tensho Maru No. 31 *-1995* **PT Bahtera Adhiguna** - *Jakarta* *Indonesia*	*194* 116 -	Class: (KI)	**1972-09 Y.K. Matsubara Koki Zosen — Onomichi** Loa 28.00 Br ex - Dght 2.650 Lbp 26.60 Br md 8.50 Dpth 3.80 Welded, 1 dk	**(B32B2SP) Pusher Tug**	**2 oil engines** driving 2 FP propellers Total Power: 1,472kW (2,002hp) 11.5kn Makita 2 x 4 Stroke each-736kW (1001bhp) Makita Diesel Co Ltd-Japan
7901356 - -	**UCHUMI** - - -	**385** 116 273	Class: (NK)	**1980-03 Donghae Shipbuilding Co Ltd — Ulsan** Yd No: 7922 Loa 44.51 Br ex 8.03 Dght 3.090 Lbp 38.51 Br md 8.01 Dpth 3.20 Welded, 1 dk	**(B11B2FV) Fishing Vessel** Ins: 262	**1 oil engine** driving 1 FP propeller Total Power: 552kW (750hp) 10.8kn Makita GNLH624 1 x 4 Stroke 6 Cy. 240 x 410 552kW (750bhp) Makita Diesel Co Ltd-Japan AuxGen: 2 x 80kW
7730874 *A9D2073* -	**UCO III** - **UCO Marine Contracting WLL** - *Bahrain* *Bahrain* Official number: A1252	*176* 31 -	Class: BV (AB)	**1976 Sing Koon Seng Pte Ltd — Singapore** Yd No: SKS361 Loa 25.91 Br ex - Dght 3.060 Lbp 24.39 Br md 7.62 Dpth 3.81 Welded, 1 dk	**(B32A2ST) Tug**	**2 oil engines** reverse reduction geared to sc. shafts driving 2 FP propellers Total Power: 1,544kW (2,100hp) 11.0kn Caterpillar D398TA 2 x Vee 4 Stroke 12 Cy. 159 x 203 each-772kW (1050bhp) Caterpillar Tractor Co-USA AuxGen: 2 x 40kW 440/110V
7217444 *A9D2572* -	**UCO VI** *ex* Wadi Mai *-1993* *ex* Subtec Horizon *-1984* *ex* Toko Maru *-1982* **UCO Marine Contracting WLL** - *Bahrain* *Bahrain* Official number: BN 2027	*225* 68 61	Class: BV (AB)	**1972 Sanyo Zosen K.K. — Onomichi** Yd No: 632 Loa 30.48 Br ex 9.10 Dght 3.295 Lbp 27.01 Br md 8.79 Dpth 3.79 Riveted\Welded, 1 dk	**(B32A2ST) Tug**	**2 oil engines** sr geared to sc. shafts driving 2 CP propellers Total Power: 2,428kW (3,302hp) 13.0kn Fuji 8S32F 2 x 4 Stroke 8 Cy. 320 x 500 each-1214kW (1651bhp) Fuji Diesel Co Ltd-Japan AuxGen: 2 x 36kW
8950093 *A9D2651* -	**UCO X** - **UCO Marine Contracting WLL** - *Bahrain* *Bahrain* Official number: BN 2060	**296** 88 -	Class: BV	**1997-05 Shanghai Fishing Vessel Shipyard — Shanghai** Yd No: 2068 Loa 31.80 Br ex - Dght 3.200 Lbp 29.34 Br md 9.60 Dpth 4.15 Welded, 1 dk	**(B32A2ST) Tug**	**2 oil engines** geared to sc. shafts driving 2 FP propellers Total Power: 1,766kW (2,402hp) 11.0kn Cummins KTA-38-M2 2 x Vee 4 Stroke 12 Cy. 159 x 159 each-883kW (1201bhp) Cummins Diesel International Ltd-USA AuxGen: 2 x 80kW 220/440V 50Hz a.c Fuel: 178.0 (d.f.)
8202850 *A9D2179* -	**UCO XIV** - **UCO Marine Contracting WLL** - *Bahrain* *Bahrain* MMSI: 408725000 Official number: A1865	**374** 23 -	Class: BV (AB)	**1982-11 Sing Koon Seng Pte Ltd — Singapore** Yd No: SKS598 Loa 33.00 Br ex - Dght 4.701 Lbp 31.81 Br md 10.01 Dpth 4.75 Welded, 1 dk	**(B32A2ST) Tug**	**2 oil engines** reverse reduction geared to sc. shafts driving 2 FP propellers Total Power: 2,354kW (3,200hp) 11.0kn Yanmar 6Z-ST 2 x 4 Stroke 6 Cy. 280 x 340 each-1177kW (1600bhp) Yanmar Diesel Engine Co Ltd-Japan AuxGen: 2 x 100kW a.c Thrusters: 1 Thwart. FP thruster (f)
6522579 *A9D2238* -	**UCO XIX** *ex* Moderator *-1983* **UCO Marine Contracting WLL** - *Bahrain* *Bahrain* MMSI: 408364000 Official number: BN 1017	*836* 416 -	Class: (LR) ✠ Classed LR until 18/3/83	**1965-10 Boele's Scheepswerven en Machinefabriek N.V. — Bolnes** Yd No: 1018 Loa 59.44 Br ex 11.38 Dght 4.033 Lbp 55.78 Br md 8.23 Dpth 4.65 Welded, 1 dk	**(B33A2DS) Suction Dredger** Liq: 593; Hopper: 577	**1 oil engine** geared to sc. shaft driving 1 FP propeller Total Power: 588kW (799hp) 10.0kn Blackstone ESS8 1 x 4 Stroke 8 Cy. 222 x 292 588kW (799bhp) Lister Blackstone Marine Ltd.-Dursley Fuel: 38.5 (d.f.)
6407717 *A9D2239* -	**UCO XVIII** *ex* Instow *-1983* **UCO Marine Contracting WLL** - *Bahrain* *Bahrain* Official number: BN 1018	*735* 308 930	Class: (LR) ✠ Classed LR until 18/3/83	**1964-05 Scheepswerf "Foxhol" N.V. v/h Gebr. Muller — Foxhol** Yd No: 119 Loa 56.80 Br ex 10.39 Dght 3.810 Lbp 52.00 Br md 10.25 Dpth 4.20 Riveted\Welded, 1 dk	**(B33A2DS) Suction Dredger** Hopper: 435 Compartments: 1 Ho, ER Derricks: 1x2t	**1 oil engine** with flexible couplings & sr reverse geared to sc. shaft driving 1 FP propeller Total Power: 588kW (799hp) 10.0kn Blackstone ESS8 1 x 4 Stroke 8 Cy. 222 x 292 588kW (799bhp) Lister Blackstone Marine Ltd.-Dursley AuxGen: 2 x 29kW 440V 50Hz a.c, 1 x 10kW 440V 50Hz a.c Fuel: 35.0 (d.f.)
7112759 *A9D2532* -	**UCO XX** *ex* Kimitetsu Maru *-1991* **UCO Marine Contracting WLL** - *Bahrain* *Bahrain* MMSI: 408708000 Official number: A2002	**7,524** 2,609 13,143 T/cm 23.2	Class: BV (NK)	**1971-07 Nipponkai Heavy Ind. Co. Ltd. — Toyama** Yd No: 156 Loa 136.18 Br ex 20.07 Dght 8.281 Lbp 128.00 Br md 20.00 Dpth 11.21 Welded, 1 dk	**(A24E2BL) Limestone Carrier** Bale: 9,840 Compartments: 3 Ho, ER 8 Ha: 2 (20.4 x 5.0)4 (19.5 x 5.0)2 (15.0 x 6.0)ER	**1 oil engine** driving 1 FP propeller Total Power: 4,104kW (5,580hp) 13.3kn Pielstick 12PC2V-400 1 x Vee 4 Stroke 12 Cy. 400 x 460 4104kW (5580bhp) Ishikawajima Harima Heavy IndustrieCo Ltd (IHI)-Japan AuxGen: 2 x 260kW 445V 60Hz a.c Fuel: 54.0 (d.f.) 227.0 (r.f.) 18.5pd
7052818 *UDYU* TS-1225	**UDACHLIVYY** *ex* Kondovyy *-2001* **Fishing Co 'Gessar' (Rybolovetskaya Kompaniya 'Gessar')** - *Nevelsk* *Russia*	**172** 51 91	Class: (RS)	**1970 Sretenskiy Sudostroitelnyy Zavod — Sretensk** Yd No: 18 Loa 33.91 Br ex 7.09 Dght 2.899 Lbp 30.00 Br md 7.00 Dpth 3.69 Welded, 1 dk	**(B11B2FV) Fishing Vessel** Bale: 114 Compartments: 1 Ho, ER 1 Ha: (1.3 x 1.6) Derricks: 2x2t; Winches: 2 Ice Capable	**1 oil engine** driving 1 FP propeller Total Power: 224kW (305hp) 9.0kn S.K.L. 8NVD36-1U 1 x 4 Stroke 8 Cy. 240 x 360 224kW (305bhp) (new engine 1972) VEB Schwermaschinenbau "KarlLiebknecht" (SKL)-Magdeburg AuxGen: 1 x 86kW, 1 x 60kW Fuel: 20.0 (d.f.)

9183685 *UIRD* -	**UDACHLIVYY** *ex* Dong Yih No. 688 *-2010* **Nearshore Fishing Centre Ostrovnoy LLC** - *Nevelsk* *Russia* MMSI: 273351040	**650** 279 293	Class: RS	**1997 San Yang Shipbuilding Co., Ltd. — Kaohsiung** Loa - Br ex - Dght - Lbp 48.80 Br md 8.80 Dpth 3.75 Welded, 1 dk	**(B11B2FV) Fishing Vessel**	**1 oil engine** driving 1 FP propeller 11.0kn Akasaka 1 x 4 Stroke Akasaka Tekkosho KK (Akasaka DieselLtd)-Japan Fuel: 185.0 (d.f.)
8729248 *URCH* -	**UDACHNYY** *ex* Shchek *-2003* *ex* Vega *-2000* *ex* Shevardeni *-1995* **KMK Ltd** - *Kerch* *Ukraine*	**104** 31 58	Class: (RS)	**1989**-07 **Rybinskaya Sudoverf — Rybinsk** Yd No: 9 Loa 26.52 Br ex 6.50 Dght 2.321 Lbp 23.63 Br md - Dpth 3.08 Welded, 1 dk	**(B11A2FS) Stern Trawler** Ins: 66	**1 oil engine** driving 1 FP propeller Total Power: 220kW (299hp) 9.5kn S.K.L. 6NVD26A-2 1 x 4 Stroke 6 Cy. 180 x 260 220kW (299bhp) VEB Schwermaschinenbau "KarlLiebknecht" (SKL)-Magdeburg AuxGen: 2 x 25kW a.c
8737673 *YEB4033* -	**UDANG NO. 1** *ex* Inspiration *-2008* **PT West Irian Fishing Industry Co Ltd** - *Jakarta* *Indonesia*	**127** 39 -	Class: KI	**1985 Ocean Shipyards (WA) Pty Ltd — Fremantle WA** Loa 24.86 Br ex - Dght - Lbp 21.57 Br md 6.74 Dpth 3.75 Welded, 1 dk	**(B11A2FS) Stern Trawler**	**1 oil engine** driving 1 Propeller Total Power: 540kW (734hp) Caterpillar 3412 1 x Vee 4 Stroke 12 Cy. 137 x 152 540kW (734bhp) Caterpillar Tractor Co-USA
8615942 *YEB4034* -	**UDANG NO. 2** *ex* Surefire *-1986* **PT West Irian Fishing Industry Co Ltd** - *Jakarta* *Indonesia*	*128* 39 -	Class: KI	**1986**-10 **Ocean Shipyards (WA) Pty Ltd — Fremantle WA** Yd No: 157 Loa 24.86 Br ex - Dght - Lbp 22.56 Br md 6.74 Dpth 3.78 Welded, 1 dk	**(B11A2FS) Stern Trawler**	**1 oil engine** geared to sc. shaft driving 1 FP propeller Total Power: 599kW (814hp) 9.5kn Cummins KTA-19-M3 1 x 4 Stroke 6 Cy. 159 x 159 599kW (814bhp) Cummins Engine Co Inc-USA
8329775 *YBVH* -	**UDANG No. 17** - **PT West Irian Fishing Industry Co Ltd** - *Jakarta* *Indonesia*	*215* 96 -	Class: (KI)	**1967 Wakamatsu Zosen K.K. — Kitakyushu** Loa 34.12 Br ex - Dght - Lbp - Br md 6.80 Dpth 3.20 Welded, 1 dk	**(B11B2FV) Fishing Vessel**	**1 oil engine** driving 1 FP propeller Total Power: 625kW (850hp) Niigata 6M28KHS 1 x 4 Stroke 6 Cy. 280 x 440 625kW (850bhp) Niigata Engineering Co Ltd-Japan
8020678 *YE4049* -	**UDANG No. 20** *ex* Fukuei Maru No. 18 *-1986* **PT West Irian Fishing Industry Co Ltd** - *Jakarta* *Indonesia*	**206** 104 -	Class: KI	**1981**-03 **Fujishin Zosen K.K. — Kamo** Yd No: 366 Loa 45.06 Br ex - Dght 2.750 Lbp 37.32 Br md 7.51 Dpth 3.00 Welded, 1 dk	**(B11B2FV) Fishing Vessel**	**1 oil engine** driving 1 FP propeller Total Power: 515kW (700hp) 11.9kn Akasaka DM26R 1 x 4 Stroke 6 Cy. 260 x 440 515kW (700bhp) Akasaka Tekkosho KK (Akasaka DieselLtd)-Japan
7416715 *YE4632* -	**UDANG No. 27** - **PT West Irian Fishing Industry Co Ltd** - *Jakarta* *Indonesia*	*169* 67 162	Class: (KI)	**1974**-07 **Wakamatsu Zosen K.K. — Kitakyushu** Yd No: 253 Loa 27.79 Br ex 6.94 Dght 2.718 Lbp 25.00 Br md 6.91 Dpth 2.95 Welded, 1 dk	**(B11B2FV) Fishing Vessel**	**1 oil engine** sr geared to sc. shaft driving 1 FP propeller Total Power: 421kW (572hp) Caterpillar D379TA 1 x Vee 4 Stroke 8 Cy. 159 x 203 421kW (572bhp) Caterpillar Tractor Co-USA
7416703 *YBVW* -	**UDANG No. 28** - **PT West Irian Fishing Industry Co Ltd** - *Jakarta* *Indonesia*	*170* 68 162	Class: (KI)	**1974**-07 **Wakamatsu Zosen K.K. — Kitakyushu** Yd No: 252 Loa 27.79 Br ex 6.94 Dght 2.718 Lbp 25.00 Br md 6.91 Dpth 2.95 Welded, 1 dk	**(B11B2FV) Fishing Vessel**	**1 oil engine** sr geared to sc. shaft driving 1 FP propeller Total Power: 421kW (572hp) Caterpillar D379TA 1 x Vee 4 Stroke 8 Cy. 159 x 203 421kW (572bhp) Caterpillar Tractor Co-USA
7416727 *YE4633* -	**UDANG No. 30** - **PT West Irian Fishing Industry Co Ltd** - *Jakarta* *Indonesia*	*169* 69 162	Class: (KI)	**1974**-07 **Wakamatsu Zosen K.K. — Kitakyushu** Yd No: 255 Loa 27.79 Br ex 6.94 Dght 2.718 Lbp 25.00 Br md 6.91 Dpth 2.95 Welded, 1 dk	**(B11B2FV) Fishing Vessel**	**1 oil engine** sr geared to sc. shaft driving 1 FP propeller Total Power: 421kW (572hp) Caterpillar D379TA 1 x Vee 4 Stroke 8 Cy. 159 x 203 421kW (572bhp) Caterpillar Tractor Co-USA
7416739 *YE4634* -	**UDANG No. 31** - **PT West Irian Fishing Industry Co Ltd** - *Jakarta* *Indonesia*	**169** 69 163	Class: (KI)	**1974**-07 **Wakamatsu Zosen K.K. — Kitakyushu** Yd No: 256 Loa 27.79 Br ex 6.94 Dght 2.718 Lbp 25.00 Br md 6.91 Dpth 2.95 Welded, 1 dk	**(B11B2FV) Fishing Vessel**	**1 oil engine** sr geared to sc. shaft driving 1 FP propeller Total Power: 421kW (572hp) Caterpillar D379TA 1 x Vee 4 Stroke 8 Cy. 159 x 203 421kW (572bhp) Caterpillar Tractor Co-USA
7633131 *YE4655* -	**UDANG No. 32** - **PT West Irian Fishing Industry Co Ltd** - *Jakarta* *Indonesia*	**193** 67 142	Class: (KI)	**1977**-02 **Wakamatsu Zosen K.K. — Kitakyushu** Yd No: 272 Loa 31.58 Br ex 6.91 Dght 2.601 Lbp 27.01 Br md 6.90 Dpth 2.98 Welded, 1 dk	**(B11A2FT) Trawler**	**1 oil engine** reduction geared to sc. shaft driving 1 FP propeller Total Power: 421kW (572hp) Caterpillar D379TA 1 x Vee 4 Stroke 8 Cy. 159 x 203 421kW (572bhp) Caterpillar Tractor Co-USA
7930450 *YE4636* -	**UDANG No. 33** - **PT West Irian Fishing Industry Co Ltd** - *Jakarta* *Indonesia*	*173* 52 142	Class: (KI)	**1980**-03 **Wakamatsu Zosen K.K. — Kitakyushu** Yd No: 306 Loa 31.55 Br ex 6.91 Dght 2.601 Lbp 26.73 Br md 6.90 Dpth 2.93 Welded, 1 dk	**(B11A2FT) Trawler**	**1 oil engine** geared to sc. shaft driving 1 FP propeller Total Power: 421kW (572hp) 9.8kn Caterpillar D379TA 1 x Vee 4 Stroke 8 Cy. 159 x 203 421kW (572bhp) Caterpillar Tractor Co-USA
8827246 *YE4639* -	**UDANG No. 37** *ex* N. R. Robinson *-1986* **PT West Irian Fishing Industry Co Ltd** - *Sorong* *Indonesia*	*147* 64 -	Class: (KI)	**1974 Australian Shipbuilding Industries (WA) Pty Ltd — Fremantle WA** Yd No: 136 Loa 25.90 Br ex 6.83 Dght - Lbp 24.84 Br md - Dpth 3.88 Welded, 1 dk	**(B11B2FV) Fishing Vessel**	**1 oil engine** driving 1 FP propeller Total Power: 313kW (426hp) Caterpillar D353TA 1 x 4 Stroke 6 Cy. 159 x 203 313kW (426bhp) Caterpillar Tractor Co-USA AuxGen: 1 x 200kW 440V a.c
9022178 *YE4510* -	**UDANG NO. 38** - **PT West Irian Fishing Industry Co Ltd** - *Jakarta* *Indonesia*	**178** 46 -	Class: KI	**1992**-06 **P.T. Dok & Perkapalan Kodja Bahari — Semarang** L reg 31.55 Br ex - Dght 2.600 Lbp 26.95 Br md 6.90 Dpth 2.95 Welded, 1 dk	**(B11B2FV) Fishing Vessel**	**1 oil engine** geared to sc. shaft driving 1 Propeller Total Power: 519kW (706hp) 10.7kn Caterpillar 3508TA 1 x Vee 4 Stroke 8 Cy. 170 x 190 519kW (706bhp) Caterpillar Inc-USA
8873635 - -	**UDANG PUTIH** - **Government of The Republic of Indonesia (Direktorat Jenderal Perikanan Departeman Pertanian - Dept of Agriculture)** Government of The Republic of Indonesia *Ambon* *Indonesia*	**151** 45 -	Class: (KI)	**1992**-08 **P.T. PAL Indonesia — Surabaya** Loa 28.10 Br ex - Dght 2.650 Lbp 25.30 Br md 7.20 Dpth 3.20 Welded, 1 dk	**(B11B2FV) Fishing Vessel**	**1 oil engine** reduction geared to sc. shaft driving 1 FP propeller Total Power: 405kW (551hp) 10.0kn Niigata 6NSD-M 1 x 4 Stroke 6 Cy. 160 x 210 405kW (551bhp) Niigata Engineering Co Ltd-Japan AuxGen: 1 x 144kW 220V a.c
8933112 - -	**UDARNIK** - **Sea Commercial Port of Odessa (Odesskiy Morskiy Port)** - *Odessa* *Ukraine* Official number: 673238	**274** 82 83	Class: (RS)	**1968 Brodogradiliste 'Tito' — Belgrade** Yd No: 233 Loa 35.43 Br ex 9.21 Dght 3.170 Lbp 30.00 Br md - Dpth 4.50 Welded, 1 dk	**(B32A2ST) Tug** Ice Capable	**2 oil engines** geared to sc. shaft driving 1 CP propeller Total Power: 1,704kW (2,316hp) 13.6kn B&W 7-26MTBF-40 2 x 4 Stroke 7 Cy. 260 x 400 each-852kW (1158bhp) Titovi Zavodi 'Litostroj'-Yugoslavia AuxGen: 2 x 100kW a.c, 1 x 25kW a.c Fuel: 52.0 (d.f.)
8134223 - -	**UDAWA II** - **PT PERTAMINA (PERSERO)** - *Jakarta* *Indonesia* Official number: 6972+BA	*133* 40 -	Class: KI (AB)	**1981**-03 **P.T. Adiguna Shipbuilding & Engineering — Jakarta** Yd No: 044 Loa 27.14 Br ex - Dght 2.280 Lbp 26.83 Br md 7.45 Dpth 2.89 Welded, 1 dk	**(B32A2ST) Tug**	**2 oil engines** sr geared to sc. shafts driving 2 FP propellers Total Power: 1,250kW (1,700hp) 12.0kn Niigata 6MG25BX 2 x 4 Stroke 6 Cy. 250 x 320 each-625kW (850bhp) Niigata Engineering Co Ltd-Japan AuxGen: 1 x 24kW d.c, 1 x 12kW d.c
8827105 - -	**UDAWA III** - **PT PERTAMINA (PERSERO)** - *Jakarta* *Indonesia*	*403* 121	Class: KI	**1984**-12 **P.T. Adiguna Shipbuilding & Engineering — Jakarta** Yd No: 101 Loa 40.50 Br ex - Dght 3.950 Lbp 36.00 Br md 9.00 Dpth 4.50 Welded, 1 dk	**(B32A2ST) Tug**	**2 oil engines** driving 2 FP propellers Total Power: 2,354kW (3,200hp) 12.0kn Niigata 8MG25BX 2 x 4 Stroke 8 Cy. 250 x 320 each-1177kW (1600bhp) (made 1978, fitted 1984) Niigata Engineering Co Ltd-Japan AuxGen: 1 x 160kW 450V a.c
8837679 *YDXE* -	**UDAWA IV** - **PT PERTAMINA (PERSERO)** - *Jakarta* *Indonesia*	**436** 131 -	Class: KI	**1989**-07 **P.T. Adiguna Shipbuilding & Engineering — Jakarta** Loa 40.50 Br ex - Dght 3.950 Lbp 36.00 Br md 9.00 Dpth 4.50 Welded, 1 dk	**(B32A2ST) Tug**	**2 oil engines** geared to sc. shafts driving 2 FP propellers Total Power: 2,354kW (3,200hp) Niigata 8MG25BX 2 x 4 Stroke 8 Cy. 250 x 320 each-1177kW (1600bhp) (made 1978, fitted 1989) Niigata Engineering Co Ltd-Japan AuxGen: 2 x 80kW 440V a.c

8329828 - -	**UDAWA VI** **PT PERTAMINA (PERSERO)** - *Jakarta* *Indonesia*	**436** 131 -	Class: (KI)	**1981 P.T. Intan Sengkunyit — Palembang** Yd No: 205 Loa 40.52 Br ex - Dght - Lbp 38.92 Br md 9.01 Dpth 4.50 Welded, 1 dk	**(B32A2ST) Tug**	**2 oil engines** driving 2 FP propellers Total Power: 2,354kW (3,200hp) Niigata 8MG25BX 2 x 4 Stroke 8 Cy. 250 x 320 each-1177kW (1600bhp) Niigata Engineering Co Ltd-Japan
7911002 *A9KI* -	**UDC AQUA** *ex* Kiva *-2012* *ex* Delta *-2008* *ex* Reimerswaal *-1993* **United Dredging Co WLL** - *Bahrain* *Bahrain* MMSI: 408850000	**781** 232 1,384	Class: BV	**1980-04 van Goor's Scheepswerf en Mfbk B.V. — Monnickendam** Yd No: 670 Loa 67.10 Br ex - Dght 3.170 Lbp 64.93 Br md 9.52 Dpth 3.87 Welded, 1 dk	**(B33B2DS) Suction Hopper Dredger** Hopper: 778	**1 oil engine** driving 1 FP propeller Total Power: 765kW (1,040hp) 10.0kn Mitsubishi S12N-TK 1 x Vee 4 Stroke 12 Cy. 160 x 180 765kW (1040bhp) Mitsubishi Heavy Industries Ltd-Japan Thrusters: 1 Tunnel thruster (f)
8308628 *A9JU* -	**UDC BLUE** *ex* C Blu Bravo *-2012* *ex* Northerly Island *-2012* **United Dredging Co WLL** - *Bahrain* *Bahrain* MMSI: 408836000 Official number: BN6045	**1,786** 535 1,120	Class: BV (AB)	**1983-12 Southern SB. Corp. — Slidell, La** Yd No: 126 Loa 62.49 Br ex 14.64 Dght 4.298 Lbp 60.96 Br md 14.63 Dpth 5.06 Welded, 1 dk	**(B33B2DT) Trailing Suction Hopper Dredger** Hopper: 1,651	**2 oil engines** sr geared to sc. shafts driving 2 Directional propellers Total Power: 1,552kW (2,110hp) 9.0kn Caterpillar 3512TA 2 x Vee 4 Stroke 12 Cy. 170 x 190 each-776kW (1055bhp) Caterpillar Tractor Co-USA AuxGen: 2 x 320kW 480V 60Hz a.c Fuel: 340.5 (d.f.) 13.0pd
9135200 *JM6522* -	**UDO MARU** **Shinwa Naiko Kaiun Kaisha Ltd** - *Fukuoka, Fukuoka* *Japan* MMSI: 431600499 Official number: 134645	*749* - 2,100		**1996-03 K.K. Matsuura Zosensho — Osakikamijima** Yd No: 516 Loa 86.55 (BB) Br ex 12.83 Dght 4.480 Lbp 80.00 Br md 12.80 Dpth 7.80 Welded, 1 dk	**(A31A2GX) General Cargo Ship** Grain: 3,951; Bale: 3,837 Compartments: 1 Ho, ER 1 Ha: ER	**1 oil engine** driving 1 FP propeller Total Power: 1,765kW (2,400hp) Akasaka A34S 1 x 4 Stroke 6 Cy. 340 x 660 1765kW (2400bhp) Akasaka Tekkosho KK (Akasaka DieselLtd)-Japan Thrusters: 1 Thwart. FP thruster (f)
8727123 *UIMV* -	**UDOBNOYE** **Preobrazheniye Trawler Fleet Base (Preobrazhenskaya Baza Tralovogo Flota)** - *Nakhodka* *Russia* MMSI: 273823810 Official number: 840753	**738** 221 332	Class: (RS)	**1986-05 Zavod "Leninskaya Kuznitsa" — Kiyev** Yd No: 261 Loa 53.74 (BB) Br ex 10.71 Dght 4.360 Lbp 47.92 Br md 10.50 Dpth 6.00 Welded, 1 dk	**(B11A2FS) Stern Trawler** Ice Capable	**1 oil engine** driving 1 CP propeller Total Power: 971kW (1,320hp) 12.6kn S.K.L. 8NVD48A-2U 1 x 4 Stroke 8 Cy. 320 x 480 971kW (1320bhp) VEB Schwermaschinenbau "KarlLiebknecht" (SKL)-Magdeburg AuxGen: 1 x 300kW a.c, 1 x 300kW a.c
6615649 - -	**UDORN** *ex* C. S. P. 5 *-1995* *ex* Veeraon *-1995* *ex* Intellect Energy *-1991* *ex* Hui Shan *-1975* *ex* Keizan Maru *-1974* **CCM Marine Co Ltd** Cosmo Oil Co Ltd (Thailand) *Bangkok* *Thailand* Official number: 342000015	*2,033* 992 3,489 T/cm 9.4	Class: (CR)	**1966-04 Ujina Zosensho — Hiroshima** Yd No: 448 Loa 88.32 Br ex 12.83 Dght 5.893 Lbp 82.00 Br md 12.81 Dpth 6.61 Riveted\Welded, 1 dk	**(A13B2TP) Products Tanker** Liq: 3,037; Liq (Oil): 3,037 Cargo Heating Coils Compartments: 8 Ta, ER 2 Cargo Pump (s): 2x350m³/hr Manifold: Bow/CM: 40m	**1 oil engine** driving 1 FP propeller Total Power: 2,059kW (2,799hp) 12.5kn Hanshin Z750SH 1 x 4 Stroke 7 Cy. 500 x 700 2059kW (2799bhp) Hanshin Nainenki Kogyo-Japan AuxGen: 2 x 88kW 440V 60Hz a.c Fuel: 294.5 (r.f.) 11.5pd
8615461 *MRXG9* FD 526	**UDRA** *ex* Mar Bermejo *-2007* **Euroscott Ltd** - *Fleetwood* *United Kingdom* Official number: C18989	**355** 124 254	Class: (RI) (BV)	**1988-08 Astilleros Gondan SA — Castropol** Yd No: 287 Loa 35.00 (BB) Br ex - Dght 3.601 Lbp 29.01 Br md 8.21 Dpth 3.69 Welded, 1 dk	**(B11A2FS) Stern Trawler** Ins: 273	**1 oil engine** with clutches, flexible couplings & sr reverse geared to sc. shaft driving 1 CP propeller Total Power: 640kW (870hp) Deutz SBA6M528 1 x 4 Stroke 6 Cy. 220 x 280 640kW (870bhp) Hijos de J Barreras SA-Spain
8722240 - -	**UDRIYA** *ex* Udria *-1999* *ex* MRTK-0749 *-1992* **JSC Fiord Trade** - *Kaliningrad* *Russia*	**117** 35 26	Class: RS	**1988-11 Sosnovskiy Sudostroitelnyy Zavod — Sosnovka** Yd No: 749 Loa 25.50 Br ex 7.00 Dght 2.390 Lbp 22.00 Br md - Dpth 3.30 Welded, 1 dk	**(B11A2FS) Stern Trawler** Ice Capable	**1 oil engine** driving 1 FP propeller Total Power: 221kW (300hp) 9.5kn S.K.L. 6NVD26A-2 1 x 4 Stroke 6 Cy. 180 x 260 221kW (300bhp) VEB Schwermaschinenbau "KarlLiebknecht" (SKL)-Magdeburg Fuel: 12.0 (d.f.)
9077678 - -	**UDYL** - -	**446** 133 207	Class: (RS)	**1992-08 AO Zavod 'Nikolayevsk-na-Amure' — Nikolayevsk-na-Amure** Yd No: 1289 Loa 44.88 Br ex 9.47 Dght 3.770 Lbp 39.37 Br md - Dpth 5.13 Welded, 1 dk	**(B11A2FS) Stern Trawler** Ice Capable	**1 oil engine** driving 1 FP propeller Total Power: 588kW (799hp) 11.5kn S.K.L. 6NVD48A-2U 1 x 4 Stroke 6 Cy. 320 x 480 588kW (799bhp) SKL Motoren u. Systemtechnik AG-Magdeburg
9596545 *9V8992* -	**UE RUBY** **Highland Commodities (S) Pte Ltd** Focus Maritime Services Pte Ltd SatCom: Inmarsat C 456479610 *Singapore* *Singapore* MMSI: 564796000 Official number: 396486	**2,990** 1,191 4,000	Class: BV	**2010-10 Zhejiang Nangang Shipyard Co Ltd — Rui'an ZJ** Yd No: NG010 Loa 94.40 Br ex - Dght 5.850 Lbp 88.00 Br md 15.40 Dpth 7.60 Welded, 1 dk	**(A13B2TP) Products Tanker** Double Hull (13F) Liq: 3,916; Liq (Oil): 3,916 Compartments: 8 Wing Ta, ER	**1 oil engine** reduction geared to sc. shaft driving 1 FP propeller Total Power: 2,207kW (3,001hp) 12.9kn Yanmar 6N330-UN 1 x 4 Stroke 6 Cy. 330 x 440 2207kW (3001bhp) Qingdao Zichai Boyang Diesel EngineCo Ltd-China AuxGen: 3 x 300kW 60Hz a.c
9438315 *9V9175* -	**UE SAPPHIRE** *ex* Titan Wisdom *-2012* **Universal Energy Pte Ltd** Focus Maritime Services Pte Ltd SatCom: Inmarsat C 456638510 *Singapore* *Singapore* MMSI: 566385000 Official number: 396733	**4,996** 1,959 7,014 T/cm 15.6	Class: BV (LR) ✠ Classed LR until 21/2/14	**2012-03 Titan Quanzhou Shipyard Co Ltd — Hui'an County FJ** Yd No: H0015 Loa 99.36 (BB) Br ex 18.07 Dght 7.200 Lbp 94.00 Br md 18.00 Dpth 10.00 Welded, 1 dk	**(A13B2TP) Products Tanker** Double Hull (13F) Liq: 7,600; Liq (Oil): 7,600 Compartments: 5 Wing Ta, 5 Wing Ta, 1 Wing Slop Ta, 1 Wing Slop Ta, ER 2 Cargo Pump (s): 2x1000m³/hr	**2 oil engines** with clutches, flexible couplings & sr reverse geared to sc. shafts driving 2 FP propellers Total Power: 2,940kW (3,998hp) 11.0kn MAN-B&W 6L28/32A 2 x 4 Stroke 6 Cy. 280 x 320 each-1470kW (1999bhp) Zhenjiang Marine Diesel Works-China AuxGen: 2 x 288kW 400V 50Hz a.c Boilers: WTAuxB (o.f.) 7.5kgf/cm² (7.4bar) Thrusters: 1 Tunnel thruster (f)
9143611 *9HKR5* -	**UFA** *ex* Nikolay Smelyakov *-2003* **Ufa Ltd** JSC Volga Shipping (OAO Sudokhodnaya Kompaniya 'Volzhskoye Parokhodstvo') SatCom: Inmarsat C 424996410 *Valletta* *Malta* MMSI: 249964000 Official number: 5531	**2,914** 1,311 4,337	Class: RS	**1997-08 Sudostroitelnyy Zavod "Krasnoye Sormovo" — Nizhniy Novgorod** Yd No: 17310/4 Loa 96.30 Br ex 13.60 Dght 5.560 Lbp 93.50 Br md 13.40 Dpth 6.70 Welded, 1 dk	**(A31A2GX) General Cargo Ship** Grain: 4,796 TEU 122 C. 122/20' Compartments: 2 Ho, ER 2 Ha: 2 (26.4 x 10.3)ER Ice Capable	**1 oil engine** geared to sc. shaft driving 1 FP propeller Total Power: 1,480kW (2,012hp) 11.5kn S.K.L. 8VDS29/24AL-2 1 x 4 Stroke 8 Cy. 240 x 290 1480kW (2012bhp) SKL Motoren u. Systemtechnik AG-Magdeburg Thrusters: 1 Thwart. FP thruster (f)
8959453 *IURI* -	**UFO** **MAI Costruzioni SAS** MultiService Group Srl *Santa Margherita Ligure* *Italy* MMSI: 247177900 Official number: 10759	*143* 57 100	Class: RI	**1990 Fincantieri-Cant. Nav. Italiani S.p.A. — Trieste** Yd No: MB02 Loa 28.13 Br ex - Dght 1.250 Lbp 23.05 Br md 7.04 Dpth 2.52 Bonded, 1 dk	**(A37B2PS) Passenger Ship** Hull Material: Reinforced Plastic Passengers: unberthed: 300	**2 oil engines** reduction geared to sc. shafts driving 2 FP propellers Total Power: 1,716kW (2,334hp) 17.0kn Baudouin V12BTI1200 2 x Vee 4 Stroke 12 Cy. 150 x 150 each-858kW (1167bhp) Societe des Moteurs Baudouin SA-France
9085259 - -	**UFOLO** - - *Nigeria*	**350** - -		**1993-09 Stocznia 'Wisla' — Gdansk** Yd No: TR-13/V Loa - Br ex - Dght - Lbp - Br md - Dpth - Welded	**(B11A2FS) Stern Trawler**	**1 oil engine** driving 1 FP propeller MAN D2866E 1 x 4 Stroke 6 Cy. 128 x 155 MAN Nutzfahrzeuge AG-Nuernberg
9473298 *9MFI8* -	**UFS DUA** **United Flagship Services Sdn Bhd** - *Port Klang* *Malaysia* MMSI: 533016500 Official number: 332430	**236** 71 117	Class: AB	**2008-01 Penguin Shipyard International Pte Ltd — Singapore** Yd No: 151 Loa 36.00 Br ex 7.90 Dght 1.900 Lbp 33.20 Br md 7.60 Dpth 3.65 Welded, 1 dk	**(B21A2OC) Crew/Supply Vessel** Hull Material: Aluminium Alloy	**3 oil engines** reduction geared to sc. shafts driving 3 FP propellers Total Power: 3,021kW (4,107hp) 20.0kn Cummins KTA-38-M2 3 x Vee 4 Stroke 12 Cy. 159 x 159 each-1007kW (1369bhp) Cummins Engine Co Inc-USA AuxGen: 2 x 99kW a.c Fuel: 64.0 (d.f.)

IMO / Call sign	Ship / Owner / Port	Tonnage	Class	Builder / Dimensions	Type	Machinery
9473286 *9MFI7* -	**UFS SATU** **United Flagship Services Sdn Bhd** - *Port Klang* *Malaysia* MMSI: 533015500 Official number: 332429	**236** 71 122	Class: AB	**2007-11 Penguin Shipyard International Pte Ltd — Singapore** Yd No: 150 Loa 36.00 Br ex 7.90 Dght 1.900 Lbp 33.20 Br md 7.60 Dpth 3.65 Welded, 1 dk	**(B21A20C) Crew/Supply Vessel** Hull Material: Aluminium Alloy	**3 oil engines** reduction geared to sc. shafts driving 3 CP propellers Total Power: 3,021kW (4,107hp) 20.0kn Cummins KTA-38-M2 3 x Vee 4 Stroke 12 Cy. 159 x 159 each-1007kW (1369bhp) Cummins Engine Co Inc-USA AuxGen: 2 x 99kW a.c Fuel: 64.0 (d.f.)
9017317 - -	**UFULI** **Government of The Republic of The Maldives (Minister of Public Works & Labour)** Maldives National Shipping Agencies (S) Pte Ltd *Male* *Maldives* Official number: 15467-10-T	**108** 32 350	Class: (LR) ✠ Classed LR until 30/9/91	**1991-09 North Shipyard Pte Ltd — Singapore** Yd No: 1012 Loa 26.00 Br ex 8.04 Dght 1.287 Lbp 25.25 Br md 8.00 Dpth 2.10 Welded, 1 dk	**(A35D2RL) Landing Craft** Bow door/ramp	**2 oil engines** with clutches, flexible couplings & sr geared to sc. shafts driving 2 FP propellers Total Power: 352kW (478hp) 8.0kn Cummins NT-855-M 2 x 4 Stroke 6 Cy. 140 x 152 each-176kW (239bhp) Cummins Engine Co Inc-USA AuxGen: 1 x 15kW 230V 50Hz a.c
9060584 - -	**UFULI-2** **Male Municipality** *Male* *Maldives* Official number: 239-10-T	**127** 53 100	Class: (LR) ✠ Classed LR until 1/2/95	**1993-11 Tebma Engineering Ltd — Chengalpattu** Yd No: 021 Loa 26.50 Br ex 7.38 Dght 1.786 Lbp 25.25 Br md 7.20 Dpth 2.50 Welded, 1 dk	**(A31A2GX) General Cargo Ship** Compartments: 2 Ho, ER 2 Ha: ER	**2 oil engines** with clutches & sr reverse geared to sc. shafts driving 2 FP propellers Total Power: 150kW (204hp) Cummins N-495-M 2 x 4 Stroke 4 Cy. 130 x 152 each-75kW (102bhp) Kirloskar Cummins Ltd-India AuxGen: 1 x 8kW 220V 60Hz a.c
9323352 *V7LO3* -	**UGALE** **Sabile Navigation Inc** Latvian Shipping Co (Latvijas Kugnieciba) *Majuro* *Marshall Islands* MMSI: 538002777 Official number: 2777	**30,641** 15,318 52,642 T/cm 56.8	Class: NV	**2007-06 '3 Maj' Brodogradiliste dd — Rijeka** Yd No: 699 Loa 195.23 (BB) Br ex 32.23 Dght 12.518 Lbp 187.30 Br md 32.20 Dpth 17.80 Welded, 1 dk	**(A12B2TR) Chemical/Products Tanker** Double Hull (13F) Liq: 56,190; Liq (Oil): 56,190 Compartments: 12 Wing Ta, 2 Wing Slop Ta, ER 12 Cargo Pump (s): 12x550m³/hr Manifold: Bow/CM: 97.1m Ice Capable	**1 oil engine** driving 1 FP propeller Total Power: 10,185kW (13,848hp) 14.0kn Wartsila 7RTA48T 1 x 2 Stroke 7 Cy. 480 x 2000 10185kW (13848bhp) '3 Maj' Motori i Dizalice dd-Croatia AuxGen: 3 x 960kW 450V 60Hz a.c Fuel: 194.0 (d.f.) 1590.0 (r.f.) 35.0pd
9328223 *YKQW* -	**UGARIT** **Tartous General Port Co** - *Lattakia* *Syria*	**184** 55 52	Class: (BV)	**2004-12 Bharati Shipyard Ltd — Ratnagiri** Yd No: 286 Loa - Br ex - Dght 2.900 Lbp 24.60 Br md 8.60 Dpth 3.85 Welded, 1 dk	**(B32A2ST) Tug**	**2 oil engines** geared to sc. shafts driving 2 Propellers 10.0kn
7910682 *HC4385* -	**UGAVI** *ex* Guadalquivir *-1994* *ex* Participacion *-1989* **Pesquera Ugavi SA** - SatCom: Inmarsat A 1576367 *Manta* *Ecuador* MMSI: 735057587 Official number: P-04-0700	**1,529** 458 1,610	Class: BV	**1981-07 Ateliers et Chantiers de La Manche — Dieppe** Yd No: 1286 Loa 81.00 Br ex - Dght 5.981 Lbp 73.02 Br md 12.81 Dpth 6.18 Welded, 2 dks	**(B11B2FV) Fishing Vessel** Ins: 1,875	**1 oil engine** geared to sc. shaft driving 1 FP propeller Total Power: 3,089kW (4,200hp) 18.3kn AGO 240V20ESHR 1 x Vee 4 Stroke 20 Cy. 240 x 220 3089kW (4200bhp) Societe Alsacienne de ConstructionsMecaniques (SACM)-France AuxGen: 3 x 272kW 220V a.c Fuel: 356.0 (d.f.)
8206301 *HC4593* -	**UGAVI DOS** *ex* Albacora Dieciseis *-2002* **Uniocean SA** - *Manta* *Ecuador* MMSI: 735057638 Official number: P-04-0749	**2,165** 533 2,025	Class: BV	**1983-07 Hijos de J. Barreras S.A. — Vigo** Yd No: 1476 Loa 77.32 (BB) Br ex 13.62 Dght 6.370 Lbp 66.02 Br md 13.20 Dpth 9.07 Welded, 2 dks	**(B11B2FV) Fishing Vessel** Ins: 1,864	**1 oil engine** with clutches, flexible couplings & reverse reduction geared to sc. shaft driving 1 FP propeller Total Power: 3,236kW (4,400hp) 15.0kn Deutz RBV12M350 1 x Vee 4 Stroke 12 Cy. 400 x 500 3236kW (4400bhp) Hijos de J Barreras SA-Spain Thrusters: 1 Thwart. FP thruster (f); 1 Tunnel thruster (a) Fuel: 584.0 (d.f.)
7629403 - -	**UGHELI KINGDOM** *ex* Eisho Maru *-1984* **Oboli Nigeria Ltd** - *Lagos* *Nigeria* Official number: 376030	*998* 655 2,490		**1971 Hakata Zosen K.K. — Imabari** Loa 72.01 Br ex 12.02 Dght 3.506 Lbp 71.51 Br md 11.99 Dpth 5.49 Welded, 1 dk	**(A13B2TP) Products Tanker** Liq: 2,678; Liq (Oil): 2,678 Compartments: 4 Ta, ER	**1 oil engine** driving 1 FP propeller Total Power: 1,324kW (1,800hp) 11.8kn Niigata 1 x 4 Stroke 1324kW (1800bhp) Niigata Engineering Co Ltd-Japan Fuel: 42.5 4.0pd
8974922 *UBNG2* -	**UGLEGORSK-1** *ex* Kenyo Maru *-2010* **Sea Transport Logistics Co Ltd** - *Korsakov* *Russia*	*272* 81 194	Class: RS	**2002-09 K.K. Watanabe Zosensho — Nagasaki** Yd No: 102 Loa 41.31 Br ex 9.40 Dght 2.510 Lbp 35.00 Br md 9.24 Dpth 3.40 Welded, 1 dk	**(A31A2GX) General Cargo Ship**	**1 oil engine** driving 1 FP propeller Total Power: 1,029kW (1,399hp) 13.4kn Niigata 6MG22HX 1 x 4 Stroke 6 Cy. 220 x 280 1029kW (1399bhp) Niigata Engineering Co Ltd-Japan Fuel: 36.0 (d.f.)
8134974 *UEJQ* -	**UGLEKAMENSK** **Magellan JSC (ZAO 'Magellan')** - *Vladivostok* *Russia* Official number: 821555	**722** 217 405	Class: (RS)	**1983 Zavod "Leninskaya Kuznitsa" — Kiyev** Yd No: 1519 Loa 54.82 Br ex 9.96 Dght 4.141 Lbp 50.29 Br md - Dpth 5.01 Welded, 1 dk	**(B11A2FS) Stern Trawler** Ins: 414 Compartments: 2 Ho, ER Ice Capable	**1 oil engine** driving 1 CP propeller Total Power: 736kW (1,001hp) 12.0kn S.K.L. 8NVD48AU 1 x 4 Stroke 8 Cy. 320 x 480 736kW (1001bhp) VEB Schwermaschinenbau "KarlLiebknecht" (SKL)-Magdeburg AuxGen: 4 x 160kW a.c Fuel: 180.0 (d.f.)
7721079 *LHIF* -	**UGLEN** **Ugland Shipping AS** Ugland Marine Services AS *Grimstad* *Norway* MMSI: 257231000 Official number: 19193	**3,977** 1,193 2,600	Class: NV	**1978-08 Nymo Mek. Verksted AS — Grimstad** Yd No: 2 Loa 78.55 Br ex 26.04 Dght 3.270 Lbp 73.92 Br md 20.01 Dpth 6.43 Welded, 2 dks	**(Y11B4WL) Sheerlegs Pontoon** Cranes: 1x600t; Winches: 6	**3 diesel electric oil engines** driving 3 gen. each 1070kW 440V a.c Connecting to 2 elec. motors driving 2 Directional propellers Total Power: 3,375kW (4,590hp) 10.0kn Normo LDM-8 3 x 4 Stroke 8 Cy. 250 x 300 each-1125kW (1530bhp) AS Bergens Mek Verksteder-Norway AuxGen: 1 x 150kW 440V 60Hz a.c Thrusters: 2 Thwart. CP thruster (a)
9587403 *UBZG6* -	**UGLICH** **Government of The Russian Federation (Ministry of Transport of the Russian Federation)** - *Novorossiysk* *Russia* MMSI: 273359910	**367** 110 45	Class: RS	**2011-08 AO Yaroslavskiy Sudostroitelnyy Zavod — Yaroslavl** Yd No: 203 Loa 38.35 Br ex 7.92 Dght 2.350 Lbp 36.27 Br md 7.70 Dpth 3.20 Welded, 1 dk	**(B22A20V) Diving Support Vessel** Cranes: 1x2t Ice Capable	**2 oil engines** reduction geared to sc. shafts driving 2 CP propellers Total Power: 882kW (1,200hp) 8.0kn Baudouin 8M26SR 2 x 4 Stroke 8 Cy. 150 x 150 each-441kW (600bhp) Societe des Moteurs Baudouin SA-France AuxGen: 2 x 136kW a.c Thrusters: 1 Tunnel thruster (f)
9412294 *9AA6961* -	**UGLJAN** **Diadora Shipping Co Ltd** Tankerska Plovidba dd SatCom: Inmarsat C 423826010 *Zadar* *Croatia* MMSI: 238260000 Official number: 3T834	**24,099** 12,174 37,729 T/cm 50.0	Class: CS LR (BV) ✠ **100A1** SS 02/2010 bulk carrier BC-A strengthened for heavy cargoes, Nos. 2 & 4 holds may be empty all holds strengthened for regular discharge by heavy grabs ESP **ShipRight** (SDA, FDA, CM) *IWS LI Ice Class 1C FS at a draught of 10.634m Max/min draughts fwd 10.634/4.19m Max/min draughts aft 10.634/6.24m Power required 6054kw, power installed 7368kw ✠ **LMC** **UMS** Eq.Ltr: J†; Cable: 598.0/66.0 U3 (a)	**2010-02 Jiangsu Eastern Heavy Industry Co Ltd — Jingjiang JS** Yd No: 06C-031 Loa 189.96 (BB) Br ex 28.56 Dght 10.448 Lbp 182.96 Br md 28.50 Dpth 15.10 Welded, 1 dk	**(A21A2BC) Bulk Carrier** Grain: 48,957; Bale: 47,872 Compartments: 5 Ho, ER 5 Ha: ER Cranes: 4x30t Ice Capable	**1 oil engine** driving 1 FP propeller Total Power: 7,368kW (10,018hp) 14.0kn Wartsila 6RTA48T 1 x 2 Stroke 6 Cy. 480 x 2000 7368kW (10018bhp) Yichang Marine Diesel Engine Co Ltd-China AuxGen: 3 x 600kW 450V 60Hz a.c Boilers: AuxB (Comp) 9.2kgf/cm² (9.0bar)

Ship	Tonnage / Class	Construction	Type / Capacity	Machinery
7645433 **UGLOVOY** *UEQN* - **Priz JSC (A/O 'Priz')** - *Khasanskiy* *Russia* Official number: 771233	**172** Class: (RS) 51 88	**1977 Zavod 'Nikolayevsk-na-Amure' — Nikolayevsk-na-Amure** Yd No: 157 Loa 33.96 Br ex 7.09 Dght 2.901 Lbp 29.97 Br md - Dpth 3.69 Welded, 1 dk	**(B11B2FV) Fishing Vessel** Bale: 115 Compartments: 1 Ho, ER 1 Ha: (1.6 x 1.3) Derricks: 2x2t; Winches: 2 Ice Capable	**1 oil engine** driving 1 CP propeller Total Power: 224kW (305hp) 9.5kn S.K.L. 8NVD36-1U 1 x 4 Stroke 8 Cy. 240 x 360 224kW (305bhp) VEB Schwermaschinenbau "KarlLiebknecht" (SKL)-Magdeburg
9511466 **UGO DE CARLINI** *ICMB* - **Rizzo Bottiglieri De Carlini Armatori SpA** - SatCom: Inmarsat C 424702955 *Naples* *Italy* MMSI: 247286500 Official number: 456	**91,971** Class: RI (AB) 59,546 176,189 T/cm 120.8	**2010-01 Jinhai Heavy Industry Co Ltd — Daishan County ZJ** Yd No: J0036 Loa 291.80 (BB) Br ex - Dght 18.250 Lbp 282.20 Br md 45.00 Dpth 24.75 Welded, 1 dk	**(A21A2BC) Bulk Carrier** Grain: 198,476 Compartments: 9 Ho, ER 9 Ha: ER	**1 oil engine** driving 1 FP propeller Total Power: 16,860kW (22,923hp) 14.5kn MAN-B&W 6S70MC 1 x 2 Stroke 6 Cy. 700 x 2674 16860kW (22923bhp) Hitachi Zosen Corp-Japan AuxGen: 3 x 900kW 60Hz a.c
9529011 **UGODIE** *5NFV7* - **Fymak Marine Oil Services (Nigeria) Ltd** - *Lagos* *Nigeria* MMSI: 657270000 Official number: SR1157	**413** Class: AB 123 283	**2009-03 Horizon Shipbuilding, Inc. — Bayou La Batre, Al** Yd No: 102 Loa 51.83 Br ex - Dght 3.120 Lbp 49.40 Br md 9.45 Dpth 3.96 Welded, 1 dk	**(B21A2OC) Crew/Supply Vessel** Hull Material: Aluminium Alloy	**4 oil engines** reduction geared to sc. shaft (s) driving 4 Water jets Total Power: 5,368kW (7,300hp) Cummins KTA-50-M2 4 x Vee 4 Stroke 16 Cy. 159 x 159 each-1342kW (1825bhp) Cummins Engine Co Inc-USA AuxGen: 2 x 109kW
7319060 **UGONWAAFOR 1** *5NJL7* - *ex* Baltic Sea *-2010* *ex* S/R Albany *-2001* *ex* Tahchee *-2000* *ex* Mobil 2 *-1992* **Pheranzy Gas Ltd** - *Lagos* *Nigeria* MMSI: 657639000 Official number: SR1628	**333** Class: AB 99 -	**1973-10 Southern SB. Corp. — Slidell, La** Yd No: 105 Loa 32.92 Br ex 9.15 Dght 3.912 Lbp 31.30 Br md 9.10 Dpth 4.58 Welded, 1 dk	**(B32A2ST) Tug**	**2 oil engines** reverse reduction geared to sc. shafts driving 2 Directional propellers Total Power: 2,206kW (3,000hp) EMD (Electro-Motive) 12-645-E6 2 x Vee 2 Stroke 12 Cy. 230 x 254 each-1103kW (1500bhp) General Motors Corp.Electro-Motive Div.-La Grange AuxGen: 2 x 75kW a.c Fuel: 161.5
7367237 **UGONWAAFOR 2** *5NJL4* - *ex* Coral Sea *-2010* *ex* Venturer *-2001* **Pheranzy Gas Ltd** - *Lagos* *Nigeria* MMSI: 657640000 Official number: SR1629	**321** Class: AB 96 -	**1973-10 Main Iron Works, Inc. — Houma, La** Yd No: 281 Loa 32.50 Br ex - Dght 3.874 Lbp 32.49 Br md 9.76 Dpth 4.40 Welded, 1 dk	**(B32A2ST) Tug**	**2 oil engines** reverse reduction geared to sc. shafts driving 2 FP propellers Total Power: 2,412kW (3,280hp) EMD (Electro-Motive) 16-567-BC 2 x Vee 2 Stroke 16 Cy. 216 x 254 each-1206kW (1640bhp) General Motors Corp-USA AuxGen: 2 x 60kW 450/225V 60Hz a.c Fuel: 183.0 (d.f.)
7614642 **UGRA** - *ex* Ladoga-15 *-2005* - **Primeboat Ltd SA** INOK NV	**1,639** Class: (RS) 742 2,155	**1979-05 Rauma-Repola Oy — Uusikaupunki** Yd No: 290 Loa 80.96 Br ex 11.94 Dght 4.320 Lbp 77.65 Br md 11.75 Dpth 5.59 Welded, 1 dk	**(A31A2GX) General Cargo Ship** Grain: 2,635; Bale: 2,623 TEU 62 C. 62/20' Compartments: 2 Ho, ER 2 Ha: (16.9 x 8.2) (24.6 x 8.2)ER Ice Capable	**2 oil engines** driving 2 FP propellers Total Power: 1,280kW (1,740hp) 12.3kn S.K.L. 6NVD48-2U 2 x 4 Stroke 6 Cy. 320 x 480 each-640kW (870bhp) VEB Schwermaschinenbau "KarlLiebknecht" (SKL)-Magdeburg Thrusters: 1 Thwart. FP thruster (f) Fuel: 229.0 (d.f.) 15.0pd
8804074 **UGULAN** *UDFE* - *ex* Gyokuho Maru No. 6 *-2005* *ex* Take Maru No. 35 *-1999* **Antey Co Ltd (TOO 'Antey')** - *Nevelsk* *Russia* MMSI: 273431690 Official number: 887213	**642** Class: RS 300 476	**1988-06 Miho Zosensho K.K. — Shimizu** Yd No: 1332 Loa 54.79 (BB) Br ex 8.62 Dght 3.640 Lbp 48.01 Br md 8.60 Dpth 3.80 Welded, 1 dk	**(B11B2FV) Fishing Vessel** Ins: 500	**1 oil engine** with clutches, flexible couplings & sr reverse geared to sc. shaft driving 1 FP propeller Total Power: 736kW (1,001hp) Hanshin LH28G 1 x 4 Stroke 6 Cy. 280 x 460 736kW (1001bhp) The Hanshin Diesel Works Ltd-Japan
9554145 **UGUR DADAYLI** *TCXF2* - *ex* Kocatepe 2 *-2010* **Ugur Denizcilik AS** Dadaylilar Deniz Nakliyati Ticaret Kollektif Sti *Istanbul* *Turkey* MMSI: 271040234 Official number: 14086N	**2,976** Class: BV 1,843 4,400	**2010-01 Kocatepe Gemi Cekek ve Insaat Sanayi Ltd Sti — Altinova** Yd No: 2 Loa 93.63 (BB) Br ex - Dght 6.080 Lbp 84.73 Br md 14.55 Dpth 7.60 Welded, 1 dk	**(A31A2GX) General Cargo Ship** Grain: 5,496 Compartments: 2 Ho, ER 2 Ha: ER 2 (28.7 x 11.8)	**1 oil engine** reduction geared to sc. shaft driving 1 CP propeller Total Power: 1,710kW (2,325hp) 13.0kn MaK 9M20C 1 x 4 Stroke 9 Cy. 200 x 300 1710kW (2325bhp) (made 2008) Caterpillar Motoren GmbH & Co. KG-Germany AuxGen: 2 x 215kW 440V 60Hz a.c, 1 x 340kW 440V 60Hz a.c Thrusters: 1 Tunnel thruster (f) Fuel: 270.0
9539793 **UGURS** *TCWW2* - **Ugur Denizcilik Sanayi ve Ticaret Ltd Sti (Ugur Shipping)** Sumer Denizcilik ve Ticaret Ltd Sti *Istanbul* *Turkey* MMSI: 271040150 Official number: 1261	**2,979** Class: BV 1,448 4,406	**2010-03 Kocatepe Gemi Cekek ve Insa Sanayi Ltd. Sti. — Tuzla** Yd No: 1 Loa 93.73 Br ex - Dght 6.070 Lbp 84.73 Br md 14.55 Dpth 7.60 Welded, 1 dk	**(A31A2GX) General Cargo Ship** Grain: 5,277 Compartments: 2 Ho, ER 2 Ha: ER	**1 oil engine** driving 1 CP propeller Total Power: 1,495kW (2,033hp) 14.0kn Hanshin LA34 1 x 4 Stroke 6 Cy. 340 x 720 1495kW (2033bhp) The Hanshin Diesel Works Ltd-Japan AuxGen: 1 x 400kW 400V 50Hz a.c, 2 x 245kW 400V 50Hz a.c Fuel: 270.0
7368358 **UHURU** *5ITF* - *ex* Leonidas 21 *-1978* **Zanzibar Shipping Corp** - *Zanzibar* *Tanzania* Official number: 100004	*758* Class: (LR) 485 ✠ Classed LR until 18/10/95 1,262	**1974-04 B.V. Scheepswerf Jonker & Stans — Hendrik-Ido-Ambacht** Yd No: 330 Loa 74.40 Br ex 9.50 Dght 3.233 Lbp 70.67 Br md 9.45 Dpth 4.40 Welded, 1 dk	**(A13B2TP) Products Tanker** Liq: 1,525; Liq (Oil): 1,525 Cargo Heating Coils Compartments: 10 Ta, ER	**1 oil engine** reverse reduction geared to sc. shaft driving 1 FP propeller Total Power: 552kW (750hp) 10.0kn Bolnes 6DNL150/600 1 x 2 Stroke 6 Cy. 190 x 350 552kW (750bhp) 'Bolnes' Motorenfabriek BV-Netherlands AuxGen: 2 x 60kW 380V 50Hz a.c
7370026 **UHUVA** *ZR2535* - *ex* W. Marshall Clark *-2001* **Transnet Ltd** Portnet Dredging Services *Durban* *South Africa* Official number: 351133	*373* Class: (LR) - ✠ Classed LR until 26/9/75 -	**1974-08 Dorman Long Vanderbijl Corp. Ltd. (DORBYL) — Durban** Yd No: 2000 Loa 35.97 Br ex 11.59 Dght 4.115 Lbp 33.51 Br md 11.00 Dpth 4.63 Welded, 1 dk	**(B32A2ST) Tug**	**2 oil engines** gearing integral to driving 2 Voith-Schneider propellers Total Power: 2,898kW (3,940hp) Blackstone ESL16MK2 2 x Vee 4 Stroke 16 Cy. 222 x 292 each-1449kW (1970bhp) Mirrlees Blackstone (Stamford)Ltd.-Stamford AuxGen: 2 x 110kW 380/220V 50Hz a.c
6809173 **UI TA** - - **Kwang Hwa Steamship Co Ltd** - *Kaohsiung* *Chinese Taipei*	*273* 137 427	**1967 Koike Zosen Kaiun KK — Osakikamijima** Yd No: 145 Loa 38.92 Br ex 7.01 Dght 2.896 Lbp 35.01 Br md 6.99 Dpth 3.31 Welded, 1 dk	**(A31A2GX) General Cargo Ship**	**1 oil engine** driving 1 FP propeller Total Power: 331kW (450hp) Matsue 1 x 4 Stroke 6 Cy. 270 x 400 331kW (450bhp) Matsue Diesel KK-Japan
9247467 **UILENSPIEGEL** *ORMZ* - **Dredging International Luxembourg SA** Dredging International NV *Antwerpen* *Belgium* MMSI: 205146000 Official number: 01 00478 2002	**12,979** Class: BV 3,893 21,968	**2002-10 Merwede Shipyard BV — Hardinxveld** (Hull) Yd No: 694 **2002-10 IHC Holland NV Dredgers — Kinderdijk** Yd No: C01231 Loa 134.00 (BB) Br ex - Dght 9.800 Lbp 126.50 Br md 26.80 Dpth 10.80 Welded, 1 dk	**(B33B2DT) Trailing Suction Hopper Dredger** Liq: 13,700; Hopper: 13,695	**2 oil engines** geared to sc. shafts driving 2 CP propellers Total Power: 11,520kW (15,662hp) 16.3kn MAN 12V32/40 2 x Vee 4 Stroke 12 Cy. 320 x 400 each-5760kW (7831bhp) MAN B&W Diesel AG-Augsburg Thrusters: 2 Tunnel thruster (f)
9115248 **UJIGAMI MARU** *JL6298* - **YK Takeda Kaiun** - *Sanyoonoda, Yamaguchi* *Japan* Official number: 134875	*199* - 700	**1994-09 Matsuura Tekko Zosen K.K. — Osakikamijima** Yd No: 385 Loa - Br ex - Dght 3.260 Lbp 53.00 Br md 9.50 Dpth 5.50 Welded, 1 dk	**(A31A2GX) General Cargo Ship**	**1 oil engine** driving 1 FP propeller Total Power: 736kW (1,001hp) Hanshin LH26G 1 x 4 Stroke 6 Cy. 260 x 440 736kW (1001bhp) The Hanshin Diesel Works Ltd-Japan
6704385 **UJUNG LERO** *PLRU* - *ex* Sirontalo VI *-2001* *ex* Kekal Abadi *-1981* *ex* Sylvia I *-1975* **PT Pelayaran Nusantara Sejati** - *Jakarta* *Indonesia*	*765* Class: (LR) (KI) 413 ✠ Classed LR until 18/9/81 1,067	**1967-03 N.V. Scheepsbouwbedrijf v/h Th.J. Fikkers — Foxhol** Yd No: 107 Loa 61.42 Br ex 10.04 Dght 3.709 Lbp 55.66 Br md 9.85 Dpth 6.07 Welded, 1 dk	**(A31A2GX) General Cargo Ship** Grain: 1,548; Bale: 1,380	**1 oil engine** driving 1 FP propeller Total Power: 662kW (900hp) 11.0kn Brons 12GV 1 x Vee 2 Stroke 12 Cy. 220 x 380 662kW (900bhp) NV Appingedammer Bronsmotorenfabrie-Netherlands AuxGen: 2 x 10kW 220V d.c

IMO / Call sign	Name / Owner / Port	Tonnage	Class	Builder / Dimensions	Type	Machinery
6904210 *5ZWC* -	**UJUZI** *ex Awefu -1979* **Southern Engineering Co Ltd** - *Mombasa* *Kenya* Official number: 10058	*119* 34 -	Class: (LR) ✠ Classed LR until 15/1/88	**1968-12 Scheepswerf & Machinefabriek Fa A van Bennekum NV — Sliedrecht** Yd No: 72 Loa 23.98 Br ex 6.58 Dght - Lbp 20.71 Br md 6.51 Dpth 3.41 Welded, 1 dk	**(B11A2FT) Trawler**	**1 oil engine** reverse reduction geared to sc. shaft driving 1 CP propeller Total Power: 400kW (544hp) Caterpillar D353TA 1 x 4 Stroke 6 Cy. 159 x 203 400kW (544bhp) Caterpillar Tractor Co-USA AuxGen: 1 x 20kW 380V 60Hz a.c, 1 x 10kW 380V 60Hz a.c
9143427 *MWZL7* -	**UKD BLUEFIN** **UK Dredging Management Ltd** UK Dredging (UKD) *Swansea* *United Kingdom* MMSI: 232002803 Official number: 730426	**4,171** 1,251 5,797	Class: BV	**1997-04 Ferguson Shipbuilders Ltd — Port Glasgow** Yd No: 703 Loa 97.96 Br ex 18.25 Dght 5.950 Lbp 90.00 Br md 18.00 Dpth 7.80 Welded, 1 dk	**(B33B2DT) Trailing Suction Hopper Dredger** Hopper: 3,900 Compartments: 1 Ho, ER 1 Ha: ER	**2 oil engines** with clutches, flexible couplings & sr geared to sc. shafts driving 2 CP propellers Total Power: 4,920kW (6,690hp) 12.0kn Wartsila 6R32E 2 x 4 Stroke 6 Cy. 320 x 350 each-2460kW (3345bhp) Wartsila Diesel Oy-Finland AuxGen: 2 x 1080kW 415V 50Hz a.c Thrusters: 1 Thwart. FP thruster (f) Fuel: 300.0 (d.f.)
9064176 *MSBK2* -	**UKD MARLIN** *ex Humber Marlin -1997* **UK Dredging Management Ltd** UK Dredging (UKD) *Hull* *United Kingdom* MMSI: 232001610 Official number: 723646	**2,692** 856 3,735 T/cm 8.1	Class: BV (LR) ✠ Classed LR until 29/1/99	**1993-10 Appledore Shipbuilders Ltd — Bideford** Yd No: A.S.156 Loa 84.65 Br ex 16.20 Dght 5.090 Lbp 81.00 Br md 16.00 Dpth 6.40 Welded, 1 dk	**(B33B2DT) Trailing Suction Hopper Dredger** Hopper: 2,968	**2 oil engines** with clutches, flexible couplings & sr geared to sc. shafts driving 2 CP propellers Total Power: 2,160kW (2,936hp) 11.5kn Kromhout 6FHD240 2 x 4 Stroke 6 Cy. 240 x 260 each-1080kW (1468bhp) Stork Wartsila Diesel BV-Netherlands AuxGen: 2 x 550kW 415V 50Hz a.c, 1 x 130kW 415V 50Hz a.c Thrusters: 1 Thwart. FP thruster (f) Fuel: 148.0 (d.f.)
9491355 *2DCC4* -	**UKD ORCA** **Associated British Ports Holdings Plc** UK Dredging (UKD) *Cardiff* *United Kingdom* MMSI: 235077712 Official number: 916812	**3,087** 926 3,775	Class: BV	**2010-07 Barkmeijer Stroobos B.V. — Stroobos** Yd No: 323 Loa 78.00 (BB) Br ex - Dght 5.700 Lbp 75.95 Br md 15.85 Dpth 6.35 Welded, 1 dk	**(B33B2DT) Trailing Suction Hopper Dredger** Hopper: 2,373	**3 diesel electric oil engines** driving 3 gen. each 1200kW a.c Connecting to 2 elec. motors each (1500kW) driving 2 Azimuth electric drive units Total Power: 3,240kW (4,404hp) 10.0kn Wartsila 6L20 3 x 4 Stroke 6 Cy. 200 x 280 each-1080kW (1468bhp) Wartsila Nederland BV-Netherlands Thrusters: 1 Tunnel thruster (f)
9066655 *MZCW6* -	**UKD SEAHORSE** **Associated British Ports Holdings Plc** UK Dredging (UKD) *Southampton* *United Kingdom* MMSI: 232004441 Official number: 902801	**204** 61 -	Class: BV	**2000-01 OOO Belogorodskaya Sudoverf — Belyy Gorodok** (Hull) **2000-01 B.V. Scheepswerf Damen — Gorinchem** Yd No: 4008 Loa 25.97 Br ex - Dght 2.450 Lbp 24.90 Br md 10.06 Dpth 3.35 Welded, 1 dk	**(B33A2DU) Dredger (unspecified)** Cranes: 1x6.4t	**2 oil engines** with clutches, flexible couplings & sr reverse geared to sc. shafts driving 2 FP propellers Total Power: 954kW (1,298hp) 9.6kn Cummins KTA-19-M3 2 x 4 Stroke 6 Cy. 159 x 159 each-477kW (649bhp) Cummins Engine Co Ltd-United Kingdom AuxGen: 2 x 55kW 415V 50Hz a.c Fuel: 40.0 (d.f.) 2.1pd
9267314 *VSUX2* -	**UKD SEALION** **Associated British Ports Holdings Plc** UK Dredging (UKD) *Southampton* *United Kingdom* MMSI: 235004829 Official number: 906615	**224** 67 350	Class: BV	**2003-01 Santierul Naval Damen Galati S.A. — Galati** (Hull) Yd No: 999 **2003-01 B.V. Scheepswerf Damen — Gorinchem** Yd No: 519301 Loa 25.97 Br ex 10.06 Dght 2.630 Lbp 24.00 Br md 10.00 Dpth 3.35 Welded, 1 dk	**(B33A2DU) Dredger (unspecified)** A-frames: 1x20t; Cranes: 1	**2 oil engines** geared to sc. shafts driving 2 FP propellers Total Power: 958kW (1,302hp) 9.6kn Cummins KTA-19-M3 2 x 4 Stroke 6 Cy. 159 x 159 each-479kW (651bhp) Cummins Engine Co Inc-USA AuxGen: 2 x 164kW 440V 50Hz a.c
8023400 - -	**UKHOZI** *ex Cupesca Uno -1997* **Overberg Fishing Co (Pty) Ltd** - *Walvis Bay* *Namibia*	**357** 122 -	Class: IS (LR) (BV) (GL) Classed LR until 12/4/97	**1981-03 Factoria Naval de Marin S.A. — Marin** Yd No: 4 Loa 33.00 Br ex 8.68 Dght 3.801 Lbp 23.00 Br md 8.60 Dpth 3.90 Welded, 2 dks	**(B11A2FS) Stern Trawler**	**1 oil engine** sr reverse geared to sc. shaft driving 1 FP propeller Total Power: 640kW (870hp) 10.0kn Deutz SBA6M528 1 x 4 Stroke 6 Cy. 220 x 280 640kW (870bhp) Hijos de J Barreras SA-Spain AuxGen: 2 x 99kW 380V 50Hz a.c
9067958 *JH3303* -	**UKIKI MARU No. 28** **Osawa Kaiun Kensetsu YK** *Toba, Mie* *Japan* Official number: 133209	*480* - 1,000		**1993-12 Nagashima Zosen KK — Kihoku ME** Loa 50.00 Br ex - Dght - Lbp 45.55 Br md 11.00 Dpth 4.60 Welded, 1 dk	**(A24D2BA) Aggregates Carrier**	**1 oil engine** geared to sc. shaft driving 1 FP propeller Total Power: 736kW (1,001hp) 11.0kn Akasaka DM30R 1 x 4 Stroke 6 Cy. 300 x 480 736kW (1001bhp) Akasaka Tekkosho KK (Akasaka DieselLtd)-Japan
9230244 *OJIJ* -	**UKKO** **Neste Shipping Oy** - *Porvoo* *Finland* MMSI: 230946000 Official number: 12235	**583** 175 260	Class: NV	**2002-07 Astilleros Armon SA — Navia** Yd No: 537 Loa 33.50 Br ex - Dght 5.500 Lbp 30.94 Br md 12.80 Dpth 6.30 Welded, 1 dk	**(B32A2ST) Tug** Ice Capable	**2 oil engines** geared to sc. shafts driving 2 Directional propellers Total Power: 4,928kW (6,700hp) 13.0kn Wartsila 6R32E 2 x 4 Stroke 6 Cy. 320 x 350 each-2464kW (3350bhp) Wartsila Diesel S.A.-Bermeo
6610132 *OIOU* -	**UKKOPEKKA** *ex Hamina -1986 ex Turku -1982* **Hoyrylaivaosakeyhtio ss Ukkopekka** - *Turku* *Finland* MMSI: 230938590 Official number: 10253	**287** 97 -		**1938 Ab Sandvikens Skeppsdocka & Mekaniska Verkstads — Helsinki** Yd No: 274 Converted From: Lighthouse Tender Loa 35.06 Br ex 7.35 Dght 3.607 Lbp 32.24 Br md - Dpth - Riveted, 1 dk	**(A37B2PS) Passenger Ship** Passengers: unberthed: 199	**1 oil engine** driving 1 FP propeller Total Power: 294kW (400hp) AuxGen: 1 x 5kW 110V d.c
7740702 - -	**UKMERGE** - -	*187* 48 80	Class: (RS)	**1978 Sudostroitelnyy Zavod "Avangard" — Petrozavodsk** Yd No: 320 Loa 31.63 Br ex 7.32 Dght 2.899 Lbp 29.15 Br md - Dpth 3.51 Welded, 1 dk	**(B11B2FV) Fishing Vessel** Ins: 100 Compartments: 1 Ho, ER 1 Ha: (1.4 x 1.1) Derricks: 1x1.5t; Winches: 1 Ice Capable	**1 oil engine** driving 1 FP propeller Total Power: 221kW (300hp) 9.5kn S.K.L. 8NVD36-1U 1 x 4 Stroke 8 Cy. 240 x 360 221kW (300bhp) VEB Schwermaschinenbau "KarlLiebknecht" (SKL)-Magdeburg
9655195 *3CABB* -	**UKOMBA** **Government of The Republic of Equatorial Guinea (Port Administration)** - *Bata* *Equatorial Guinea* MMSI: 631084258 Official number: CN20101109350	**383** 115 172	Class: (CC)	**2012-03 Penglai Bohai Shipyard Co Ltd — Penglai SD** Yd No: PBZ10-96 Loa 33.98 Br ex 11.60 Dght 3.400 Lbp 30.50 Br md 10.00 Dpth 4.50 Welded, 1 dk	**(B32A2ST) Tug**	**2 oil engines** reduction geared to sc. shafts driving 2 Propellers Total Power: 2,386kW (3,244hp) Cummins KTA-50-M2 2 x Vee 4 Stroke 16 Cy. 159 x 159 each-1193kW (1622bhp) Cummins Engine Co Ltd-United Kingdom AuxGen: 2 x 140kW 400V a.c
7900962 *5ITQ* -	**UKOMBOZI** **Zanzibar Shipping Corp** - *Zanzibar* *Tanzania* MMSI: 674010013 Official number: 100007	**1,403** 696 2,288	Class: (LR) ✠ Classed LR until 21/6/11	**1980-06 Tsuneishi Shipbuilding Co Ltd — Fukuyama HS** Yd No: OE-81 Loa 74.50 Br ex 12.02 Dght 5.130 Lbp 68.00 Br md 11.90 Dpth 5.80 Welded, 1 dk	**(A13B2TP) Products Tanker** Single Hull Liq: 2,614; Liq (Oil): 2,614 Compartments: 8 Ta, ER 2 Cargo Pump (s): 2x300m³/hr	**1 oil engine** with clutches, flexible couplings & dr reverse geared to sc. shaft driving 1 FP propeller Total Power: 1,912kW (2,600hp) 14.0kn Niigata 8MG31EZ 1 x 4 Stroke 8 Cy. 310 x 380 1912kW (2600bhp) Niigata Engineering Co Ltd-Japan AuxGen: 2 x 180kW 445V 50Hz a.c Fuel: 158.0 (r.f.)
8727252 - -	**UKRAINETS** **Nikolayev Commercial Sea Port** - *Nikolayev* *Ukraine* Official number: 870710	**270** 81 89	Class: (RS)	**1987-12 Brodogradiliste 'Tito' — Belgrade** Yd No: 1120 Loa 35.78 Br ex 9.49 Dght 3.280 Lbp 30.23 Br md - Dpth 4.50 Welded, 1 dk	**(B32A2ST) Tug** Ice Capable	**2 oil engines** driving 1 CP propeller Total Power: 1,854kW (2,520hp) 13.5kn Sulzer 6ASL25/30 2 x 4 Stroke 6 Cy. 250 x 300 each-927kW (1260bhp) in Yugoslavia AuxGen: 1 x 150kW a.c
9294460 *UAZV* -	**UKRAINETS** **Baltasar Shipping SA** CJSC 'Onegoship' *St Petersburg* *Russia* MMSI: 273448990	**4,182** 2,373 5,499	Class: RS	**2005-07 Onega Shipyard Ltd. — Petrozavodsk** Yd No: 002 Loa 108.33 Br ex 16.70 Dght 4.792 Lbp 102.20 Br md 16.50 Dpth 5.50 Welded, 1 dk	**(A31A2GX) General Cargo Ship** Grain: 7,833 TEU 225 C. 225/20' Ice Capable	**2 oil engines** geared to sc. shafts driving 2 Directional propellers Total Power: 2,040kW (2,774hp) 10.5kn MaK 6M20 2 x 4 Stroke 6 Cy. 200 x 300 each-1020kW (1387bhp) Caterpillar Motoren GmbH & Co. KG-Germany AuxGen: 2 x 160kW Thrusters: 1 Thwart. FP thruster (f) Fuel: 180.0 (d.f.)

8933124 - -	**UKRAYINO** *ex* Ukraina *-2004* *ex* Lodma *-1966* **Izmail Ship Repair Yard** - *Illichevsk* *Ukraine* Official number: 490068	*102* 29 30	Class: (RS)	**1949 VEB Peene-Werft — Wolgast** Yd No: 54 Loa 26.00 Br ex 6.44 Dght 2.150 Lbp 23.20 Br md - Dpth 3.00 Welded, 1 dk	**(B32A2ST) Tug**	**1 oil engine** driving 1 FP propeller Total Power: 221kW (300hp) 10.0kn S.K.L. 8NVD36 1 x 4 Stroke 8 Cy. 240 x 360 221kW (300bhp) (new engine 1952) VEB Schwermaschinenbau "KarlLiebknecht" (SKL)-Magdeburg AuxGen: 2 x 12kW Fuel: 16.0 (d.f.)
9287235 *URBG* -	**UKRTRANSNAFTA** - **JSC 'Ukrtransnafta' (VAT 'Ukrtransnafta')** - *Odessa* *Ukraine* MMSI: 272884100	**355** 106 170	Class: (RS)	**2002-07 DAHK Chernomorskyi Sudnobudivnyi Zavod — Mykolayiv** Yd No: 805 Loa 31.80 Br ex 10.20 Dght 3.380 Lbp 27.92 Br md 9.70 Dpth 4.80 Welded, 1 dk	**(B32A2ST) Tug**	**2 oil engines** geared to sc. shafts driving 2 FP propellers Total Power: 3,220kW (4,378hp) 12.3kn Volvo Penta D65A MT 2 x Vee 4 Stroke 16 Cy. 170 x 180 each-1610kW (2189bhp) AB Volvo Penta-Sweden
6856542 - -	**UKU** *ex* Lielirbe *-1966* *ex* MB-6072 *-1966* **Soru Liinid OU** -	**116** 34 42	Class: (RS)	**1960 VEB Schiffswerft "Edgar Andre" — Magdeburg** Yd No: 6072 Loa 28.80 Br ex 6.82 Dght 2.430 Lbp 25.62 Br md 6.50 Dpth 3.02 Welded, 1 dk	**(B32A2ST) Tug** Ice Capable	**1 oil engine** driving 1 FP propeller Total Power: 294kW (400hp) 10.0kn S.K.L. R6DV148 1 x 4 Stroke 6 Cy. 320 x 480 294kW (400bhp) VEB Schwermaschinenbau "KarlLiebknecht" (SKL)-Magdeburg AuxGen: 2 x 27kW Fuel: 27.0 (d.f.)
8214516 *HMYN7* -	**UL JI BONG** *ex* Dou An *-2006* *ex* Sailing No. 2 *-2003* *ex* Core No. 7 *-1998* *ex* Daifuku *-1993* *ex* Daifuku Maru No. 11 *-1993* **Korea Uljibong Shipping Co** - SatCom: Inmarsat C 444523110 *Nampho* *North Korea* MMSI: 445231000 Official number: 3300269	**1,301** 569 2,166	Class: KC (GM) (CC) (BV)	**1983-01 Honda Zosen — Saiki** Yd No: 707 Converted From: General Cargo Ship-2009 Loa 71.15 Br ex 11.82 Dght 4.319 Lbp 66.02 Br md 11.80 Dpth 6.71 Welded, 1 dk	**(A31A2GX) General Cargo Ship** Grain: 2,660; Bale: 2,473 Compartments: 1 Ho, ER 1 Ha: ER	**1 oil engine** with clutches & reverse reduction geared to sc. shaft driving 1 CP propeller Total Power: 956kW (1,300hp) Niigata 6M28AFTE 1 x 4 Stroke 6 Cy. 280 x 480 956kW (1300bhp) Niigata Engineering Co Ltd-Japan
8035788 *HMYG2* -	**UL JI BONG 2** *ex* Hua Jie 3 *-2008* *ex* Seiun Maru No. 18 *-2006* **Korea Uljibong Shipping Co** - SatCom: Inmarsat C 444525810 *Nampho* *North Korea* MMSI: 445258000 Official number: 3507268	**1,227** 831 1,830	Class: KC	**1981-06 Yamanaka Zosen K.K. — Imabari** Yd No: 251 Converted From: General Cargo Ship-2009 Loa 69.26 Br ex - Dght 4.230 Lbp 64.00 Br md 11.50 Dpth 6.00 Welded, 1 dk	**(A31A2GX) General Cargo Ship**	**1 oil engine** driving 1 FP propeller Total Power: 1,177kW (1,600hp) Hanshin 6LU32 1 x 4 Stroke 6 Cy. 320 x 510 1177kW (1600bhp) The Hanshin Diesel Works Ltd-Japan
7645445 - -	**ULA** - - -	*187* 48 80	Class: (RS)	**1977 Sudostroitelnyy Zavod "Avangard" — Petrozavodsk** Yd No: 310 Loa 31.63 Br ex 7.35 Dght 2.901 Lbp 29.15 Br md - Dpth 3.54 Welded, 1 dk	**(B11B2FV) Fishing Vessel** Bale: 100 Compartments: 1 Ho, ER 1 Ha: (1.5 x 1.2) Derricks: 1x1.5t; Winches: 1 Ice Capable	**1 oil engine** driving 1 FP propeller Total Power: 221kW (300hp) 9.5kn S.K.L. 8NVD36-1U 1 x 4 Stroke 8 Cy. 240 x 360 221kW (300bhp) VEB Schwermaschinenbau "KarlLiebknecht" (SKL)-Magdeburg
9180310 *LIZS* -	**ULABRAND** - **Redningsselskapet - Norsk Selskab Til Skibbrudnes Redning** - *Oslo* *Norway* MMSI: 259466000	**141** 56 -	Class: NV	**1998-01 Kvaerner Mandal AS — Mandal** Yd No: 14 Loa 25.25 Br ex 6.20 Dght 1.600 Lbp 23.75 Br md 5.70 Dpth 3.85 Bonded, 1 dk	**(B34H2SQ) Patrol Vessel** Hull Material: Reinforced Plastic	**4 oil engines** with clutches, flexible couplings & reduction geared to sc. shafts driving 2 CP propellers Total Power: 2,744kW (3,732hp) 25.0kn G.M. (Detroit Diesel) 16V-92-TA 4 x Vee 2 Stroke 16 Cy. 123 x 127 each-686kW (933bhp) Detroit Diesel Corporation-Detroit, Mi AuxGen: 2 x 47kW 230V 50Hz a.c Thrusters: 2 Thwart. FP thruster (f) Fuel: 26.4 (d.f.) 16.7pd
8727264 *UDAR* -	**ULAN** - **OOO 'Yuzhnyy Rybopromyslovyy Flot'** Pionerskiy Ocean Fishing Marine Center (Pionerskaya Baza Okeanicheskogo Rybolovnogo Flota (BORF)) *Kaliningrad* *Russia* MMSI: 273532300 Official number: 850717	**737** 221 414	Class: (RS)	**1986-03 Zavod "Leninskaya Kuznitsa" — Kiyev** Yd No: 1559 Loa 54.82 Br ex 9.95 Dght 4.140 Lbp 50.30 Br md - Dpth 5.00 Welded, 1 dk	**(B11A2FS) Stern Trawler** Ins: 414 Ice Capable	**1 oil engine** driving 1 CP propeller Total Power: 853kW (1,160hp) 12.0kn S.K.L. 8NVD48A-2U 1 x 4 Stroke 8 Cy. 320 x 480 853kW (1160bhp) VEB Schwermaschinenbau "KarlLiebknecht" (SKL)-Magdeburg AuxGen: 4 x 160kW a.c
8652562 - -	**ULAYUT** - **Muhammad Eliansyah** - *Samarinda* *Indonesia*	**242** 73 -	Class: (KI)	**2010-03 C.V. Karya Lestari Industri — Samarinda** Loa 39.40 Br ex - Dght - Lbp 36.35 Br md 8.00 Dpth 2.40 Welded, 1 dk	**(A35D2RL) Landing Craft**	**2 oil engines** reduction geared to sc. shafts driving 2 Propellers
8727238 *UEID* -	**ULBROKA** - **JSC 'Nord Vey' (A/O 'Nord Vey')** - *Arkhangelsk* *Russia*	**157** 47 77	Class: RS	**1986-10 Astrakhanskaya Sudoverf im. "Kirova" — Astrakhan** Yd No: 20 Loa 31.85 Br ex 7.08 Dght 2.100 Lbp 27.80 Br md 6.90 Dpth 3.15 Welded, 1 dk	**(B11A2FT) Trawler** Ins: 100	**1 oil engine** geared to sc. shaft driving 1 FP propeller Total Power: 221kW (300hp) 10.2kn Daldizel 6CHNSP18/22-300 1 x 4 Stroke 6 Cy. 180 x 220 221kW (300bhp) Daldizel-Khabarovsk AuxGen: 2 x 25kW a.c Fuel: 14.0 (d.f.)
8887600 - -	**ULDUZ** *ex* Polyus *-1994* **Azerbaijan State Caspian Shipping Co (ASCSS)** - *Baku* *Azerbaijan* MMSI: 423265100 Official number: DGR-0478	*193* 78 145	Class: RS	**1976-10 Kanonerskiy Sudoremontnyy Zavod — Leningrad** Yd No: 7 Converted From: General Cargo Ship Loa 36.12 Br ex 7.40 Dght 2.000 Lbp 32.50 Br md 7.00 Dpth 3.10 Welded, 1 dk	**(B34L2QU) Utility Vessel** Ins: 199	**1 oil engine** geared to sc. shaft driving 1 FP propeller Total Power: 165kW (224hp) 9.0kn Daldizel 6CHNSP18/22 1 x 4 Stroke 6 Cy. 180 x 220 165kW (224bhp) Daldizel-Khabarovsk AuxGen: 2 x 30kW a.c Fuel: 7.0 (d.f.)
9226413 *DGRR* -	**ULF RITSCHER** *ex* NYK Espirito *-2009* *ex* Sea Tiger *-2004* *launched as* Ulf Ritscher *-2001* **ms 'Ulf Ritscher' GmbH & Co Reederei KG** Transeste Schiffahrt GmbH *Hamburg* *Germany* MMSI: 211349370 Official number: 19110	**25,703** 12,028 33,715 T/cm 52.0	Class: GL	**2001-04 Kvaerner Warnow Werft GmbH — Rostock** Yd No: 22 Loa 208.31 (BB) Br ex - Dght 11.400 Lbp 195.00 Br md 29.80 Dpth 16.40 Welded, 1 dk	**(A33A2CC) Container Ship (Fully Cellular)** TEU 2526 C Ho 960 TEU C Dk 1564 TEU incl 394 ref C. Cranes: 3x45t	**1 oil engine** driving 1 FP propeller Total Power: 19,810kW (26,934hp) 21.0kn B&W 7L70MC 1 x 2 Stroke 7 Cy. 700 x 2268 19810kW (26934bhp) Manises Diesel Engine Co. S.A.-Valencia AuxGen: 4 x 1200kW 440/220V 60Hz a.c Thrusters: 1 Tunnel thruster (f)
7724253 *XUCA4* -	**ULFAT** *ex* Ulfet *-2012* *ex* West Express *-2010* *ex* Merchant Bravery *-2008* *ex* Jolly Giallo *-1993* *ex* Norwegian Crusader *-1982* *ex* Jolly Giallo *-1982* *ex* Norwegian Crusader *-1980* *launched as* Stevi *-1978* **Reserved Capital Enterprises Corp** Sudoservice Shipping Consultancy & Trading Ltd SatCom: Inmarsat C 451411110 *Phnom Penh* *Cambodia* MMSI: 514111000 Official number: 1078712	**5,309** 1,592 5,238	Class: RS (NV) (RI) (BV)	**1978-12 Nylands Verksted — Oslo** Yd No: 792 Converted From: Ro-Ro Cargo Ship-2012 Rebuilt-2012 Loa 133.00 Br ex 21.65 Dght 5.031 Lbp 122.74 Br md 21.55 Dpth 8.00 Welded, 1 dk	**(A35A2RT) Rail Vehicles Carrier** Rail Wagons: 38 Ice Capable	**2 oil engines** sr geared to sc. shafts driving 2 CP propellers Total Power: 6,620kW (9,000hp) 12.0kn MaK 12M453AK 2 x Vee 4 Stroke 12 Cy. 320 x 420 each-3310kW (4500bhp) MaK Maschinenbau GmbH-Kiel AuxGen: 1 x 514kW 440V 60Hz a.c, 3 x 220kW 440V 60Hz a.c Thrusters: 2 Thwart. CP thruster (f) Fuel: 123.0 (d.f.) 795.6 (r.f.) 30.5pd
8017334 - -	**ULIA** *ex* Petrel *-2000* *ex* Villa Eustasia *-1995* *ex* Sun Isabel *-1994* *ex* Cape Race *-1988* *ex* F. J. Garaygordobil *-1987* *ex* F. Javier Garaygordobil *-1982* - -	**1,835** 682 2,255	Class: IS (BV)	**1981-11 Ast. del Cadagua W. E. Gonzalez S.A. — Bilbao** Yd No: 117 Loa 83.70 Br ex - Dght 5.201 Lbp 76.16 Br md 12.40 Dpth 6.80 Welded, 2 dks	**(A34A2GR) Refrigerated Cargo Ship** Ins: 2,625 Compartments: 6 Ho, ER, 6 Tw Dk Derricks: 6x3t	**1 oil engine** reduction geared to sc. shaft driving 1 FP propeller Total Power: 1,545kW (2,101hp) 13.5kn Deutz RBV6M358 1 x 4 Stroke 6 Cy. 400 x 580 1545kW (2101bhp) Hijos de J Barreras SA-Spain AuxGen: 3 x 320kW 220/380V 50Hz a.c Fuel: 233.0 (d.f.) 338.0 (r.f.)

8728218 *UBHF2* -	**ULIKA** *ex* Nadir *-2007* *ex* Nafta-3 *-2004* *ex* Neftyanik-3 *-1991* **Dakota Shipping Ltd** Transbunker-Novo Co Ltd *Novorossiysk* *Russia* MMSI: 273336610	**2,019** 842 3,008	Class: RS	1987-05 **Shipbuilding & Shiprepairing Yard 'Ivan Dimitrov' — Rousse** Yd No: 455 Loa 77.53 Br ex 14.34 Dght 5.230 Lbp 73.20 Br md 14.00 Dpth 6.50 Welded, 1 dk	**(A13B2TP) Products Tanker** Liq: 3,513; Liq (Oil): 3,513 Compartments: 12 Ta, ER Ice Capable	**1 oil engine** driving 1 FP propeller Total Power: 882kW (1,199hp) 10.2kn S.K.L. 8NVD48-2U 1 x 4 Stroke 8 Cy. 320 x 480 882kW (1199bhp) VEB Schwermaschinenbau "KarlLiebknecht" (SKL)-Magdeburg AuxGen: 2 x 150kW a.c
8108327 - -	**ULIMA** *ex* Oil Partridge *-1988* - -	*168* 36 51	Class: (BV) (AB)	1981-12 **Mickon Marine Industries Pte Ltd — Singapore** Yd No: 221 Loa 31.91 Br ex 6.43 Dght 2.000 Lbp 28.43 Br md 6.41 Dpth 3.31 Welded, 1 dk	**(B34L2QU) Utility Vessel**	**2 oil engines** sr reverse geared to sc. shafts driving 2 FP propellers Total Power: 1,242kW (1,688hp) 15.0kn G.M. (Detroit Diesel) 16V-92-TA 2 x Vee 2 Stroke 16 Cy. 123 x 127 each-621kW (844bhp) General Motors Detroit DieselAllison Divn-USA AuxGen: 2 x 25kW 415V 50Hz a.c Fuel: 28.5 (d.f.) 5.0pd
9080261 *YB5183* -	**ULIN FERRY** **PT Dharma Lautan Utama** - *Surabaya* *Indonesia*	*244* 49 119	Class: KI	1991-12 **PT Dok dan Perkapalan Surabaya (Persero) — Surabaya** Yd No: 548 Loa 41.00 Br ex - Dght 1.800 Lbp 33.25 Br md 10.20 Dpth 2.90 Welded, 1 dk	**(A36A2PR) Passenger/Ro-Ro Ship (Vehicles)**	**4 oil engines** geared to sc. shafts driving 4 Propellers Total Power: 708kW (964hp) Yanmar 6HA-HTE 4 x 4 Stroke 6 Cy. 130 x 150 each-177kW (241bhp) Yanmar Diesel Engine Co Ltd-Japan
7356094 - -	**ULISES** - **Armadores Unidos SA** - *Las Piedras* *Venezuela* Official number: AMMT-1073	*180* 81 154		1974-03 **Astilleros Unidos del Pacifico S.A. (AUPSA) — Mazatlan** Yd No: 466 Loa 25.00 Br ex 7.14 Dght 2.439 Lbp 23.53 Br md 7.01 Dpth 3.64 Welded, 1 dk	**(B11B2FV) Fishing Vessel**	**1 oil engine** geared to sc. shaft driving 1 FP propeller Total Power: 736kW (1,001hp) Deutz SBA6M528 1 x 4 Stroke 6 Cy. 220 x 280 736kW (1001bhp) Kloeckner Humboldt Deutz AG-West Germany
7381415 *LW6430* -	**ULISES** *ex* Mar Pionero *-1997* *ex* Ryuho Maru No. 37 *-1986* **Laspez Argentina SA** - *Puerto Deseado* *Argentina* MMSI: 701000616 Official number: 0641	**559** 239 512	Class: (BV)	1974-06 **Yamanishi Shipbuilding Co Ltd — Ishinomaki MG** Yd No: 778 Loa 56.01 Br ex 9.12 Dght 3.480 Lbp 50.81 Br md 9.10 Dpth 5.59 Welded, 2 dks	**(B11B2FV) Fishing Vessel**	**1 oil engine** driving 1 FP propeller Total Power: 1,986kW (2,700hp) Akasaka AH40 1 x 4 Stroke 6 Cy. 400 x 600 1986kW (2700bhp) Akasaka Tekkosho KK (Akasaka DieselLtd)-Japan
6922432 *COMC* -	**ULISES** *ex* Golfo de Tonkin *-1986* **Government of The Republic of Cuba (Instituto Cubano de Pesca)** - SatCom: Inmarsat C 432304410 *Cuba* MMSI: 323044000	**1,590** 477 1,321	Class: RC (BV)	1969-11 **Astilleros Construcciones SA — Meira** Yd No: 78 Converted From: Stern Trawler-1987 Loa 72.65 Br ex 12.02 Dght 4.750 Lbp 67.01 Br md 11.51 Dpth 7.29 Welded, 2 dks	**(B11A2FS) Stern Trawler** Ins: 1,593 Compartments: 3 Ho, ER 3 Ha: (3.8 x 1.3)2 (3.5 x 1.9)	**1 oil engine** driving 1 FP propeller Total Power: 1,964kW (2,670hp) 13.0kn Deutz RBV8M358 1 x 4 Stroke 8 Cy. 400 x 580 1964kW (2670bhp) Hijos de J Barreras SA-Spain Fuel: 521.0 (d.f.)
9148893 *UBOI4* -	**ULISS** *ex* Ulysses *-2012* *ex* Euro Mora *-2012* *ex* Isola Mora *-2005* **Uliss Co Ltd** Niko Co Ltd SatCom: Inmarsat C 427305492 *Vostochnyy* *Russia* MMSI: 273355760	**2,657** 1,069 3,746 T/cm 11.0	Class: RS (RI) (BV)	1998-10 **A/S Nordsovaerftet — Ringkobing** Yd No: 230 Converted From: Chemical/Products Tanker-2012 Loa 91.15 (BB) Br ex 14.00 Dght 5.924 Lbp 84.98 Br md 13.98 Dpth 7.10 Welded, 1 dk	**(A13B2TP) Products Tanker** Double Hull (13F) Liq: 3,779; Liq (Oil): 3,822 Cargo Heating Coils Compartments: 14 Wing Ta, 1 Slop Ta, ER 14 Cargo Pump (s): 14x120m³/hr Manifold: Bow/CM: 43.3m Ice Capable	**1 oil engine** reduction geared to sc. shaft driving 1 CP propeller Total Power: 2,500kW (3,399hp) 14.0kn Wartsila 6R32E 1 x 4 Stroke 6 Cy. 320 x 350 2500kW (3399bhp) Wartsila NSD Finland Oy-Finland AuxGen: 1 x 640kW a.c, 3 x 445kW a.c Thrusters: 1 Thwart. FP thruster (f) Fuel: 41.0 (d.f.) 351.0 (r.f.)
8913045 *UBIH2* -	**ULISS** *ex* Rhein Carrier *-2011* *ex* Churruca *-1998* *ex* Cimbria *-1993* *ex* Lloyd Iberia *-1992* *ex* Dana Sirena *-1991* *launched as* Cimbria *-1991* **Odyssey-Shipping Co Ltd** Poseidon-Shipping Co Ltd *Vostochnyy* *Russia* MMSI: 273357920	**3,815** 2,029 4,654	Class: RS (GL)	1991-03 **J.J. Sietas KG Schiffswerft GmbH & Co. — Hamburg** Yd No: 1034 Loa 103.54 (BB) Br ex 16.24 Dght 6.074 Lbp 96.90 Br md 16.00 Dpth 8.00 Welded, 1 dk	**(A31A2GX) General Cargo Ship** Grain: 6,788; Bale: 6,615 TEU 372 C.Ho 134/20' (40') C.Dk 240/20' (40') incl. 50 ref C. Compartments: 2 Ho, ER 3 Ha: (12.4 x 10.3)2 (25.1 x 12.8)ER Ice Capable	**1 oil engine** with flexible couplings & sr geared to sc. shaft driving 1 CP propeller Total Power: 3,300kW (4,487hp) 15.0kn MaK 9M453C 1 x 4 Stroke 9 Cy. 320 x 420 3300kW (4487bhp) Krupp MaK Maschinenbau GmbH-Kiel AuxGen: 1 x 500kW 220/380V 50Hz a.c, 2 x 228kW 220/380V 50Hz a.c Thrusters: 1 Thwart. FP thruster (f) Fuel: 80.1 (d.f.) 399.5 (r.f.) 16.3pd
7817828 *ILTD* -	**ULISSE** - **Caronte & Tourist SpA** - *Reggio Calabria* *Italy* MMSI: 247054500 Official number: 219	*1,396* 399 1,452	Class: RI	1978-12 **Cantiere Navale Visentini di Visentini F e C SAS — Porto Viro** Yd No: 135 Loa 94.19 Br ex 17.00 Dght 3.806 Lbp 86.04 Br md 16.98 Dpth 5.03 Welded, 1 dk	**(A36A2PR) Passenger/Ro-Ro Ship (Vehicles)** Passengers: unberthed: 500 Bow door/ramp Len: - Wid: 7.80 Swl: - Stern door/ramp Len: - Wid: 7.80 Swl: - Lane-Len: 320 Lane-clr ht: 4.40 Lorries: 52, Cars: 120, Trailers: 18	**2 oil engines** driving 2 Directional propellers Total Power: 3,678kW (5,000hp) Nohab F212V 2 x Vee 4 Stroke 12 Cy. 250 x 300 each-1839kW (2500bhp) AB Bofors NOHAB-Sweden
8949056 *INLN* -	**ULISSE PRIMO** - **Nuova CoEdMar Srl** - SatCom: Inmarsat C 424703311 *Venice* *Italy* MMSI: 247033000 Official number: 49	**593** 178 100	Class: RI	1995-06 **Cantieri Navali Chioggia Srl — Chioggia** Yd No: 03 Loa 49.95 Br ex - Dght 2.761 Lbp 47.48 Br md 11.98 Dpth 3.48 Welded, 1 dk	**(B34T2QR) Work/Repair Vessel**	**2 oil engines** geared to sc. shafts driving 2 CP propellers Total Power: 1,044kW (1,420hp) 11.0kn Cummins KT-38-M 2 x Vee 4 Stroke 12 Cy. 159 x 159 each-522kW (710bhp) Cummins Engine Co Inc-USA
7707023 *9A9359* -	**ULJANIK TRITON** *ex* Triton *-2003* **'Uljanik' Brodogradiliste dd** - *Pula* *Croatia* Official number: 1-T-157	*199* 33 252	Class: CS (RI)	1977-11 **Cantieri Navali Campanella SpA — Savona** Yd No: 83 Loa 31.02 Br ex 8.82 Dght 3.947 Lbp 26.52 Br md 8.41 Dpth 4.42 Welded, 1 dk	**(B32A2ST) Tug**	**1 oil engine** reduction geared to sc. shaft driving 1 CP propeller Total Power: 1,103kW (1,500hp) Nohab F28V 1 x Vee 4 Stroke 8 Cy. 250 x 300 1103kW (1500bhp) AB Bofors NOHAB-Sweden AuxGen: 2 x 51kW 220/380V 50Hz a.c Fuel: 125.0 (d.f.) 5.5pd
6522684 *OIES* -	**ULLA** *ex* Brage *-1974* *ex* Storgrogg *-1969* **Kemin Kaupunki (City of Kemi)** - *Kemi* *Finland* Official number: 11385	**126** 38 -	Class: (LR) ✠ Classed LR until 12/2/93	1965-12 **AB Asi-Verken — Amal** Yd No: 73 Loa 24.06 Br ex 7.37 Dght 2.896 Lbp 21.14 Br md 7.15 Dpth 3.79 Welded, 1 dk	**(B32A2ST) Tug** Passengers: 30 Ice Capable	**1 oil engine** with flexible couplings & sr reverse geared to sc. shaft driving 1 CP propeller Total Power: 978kW (1,330hp) 11.5kn Wartsila 824TS 1 x 4 Stroke 8 Cy. 240 x 310 978kW (1330bhp) (new engine 1980) Oy Wartsila Ab-Finland Fuel: 20.5 (d.f.) 3.5pd
8952871 *OXAL* S 107	**ULLA LINDBLAD** - **Lars Pedersen Mose** - *Skagen* *Denmark* MMSI: 219754000 Official number: H195	**125** 48 -		1958 **Nordhavnsvaerftet A/S — Copenhagen** Loa - Br ex - Dght - Lbp 23.63 Br md 5.81 Dpth 2.45 Welded, 1 dk	**(B11B2FV) Fishing Vessel**	**1 oil engine** driving 1 FP propeller
8513596 *JXES* -	**ULLENSVANG** - **Norled AS** Tide ASA *Bergen* *Norway* MMSI: 257020700	**2,871** 861 790	Class: (NV)	1986-06 **Ankerlokken Verft Forde AS — Forde** Yd No: 23 Loa 87.00 Br ex 14.81 Dght - Lbp 76.82 Br md - Dpth 7.40 Welded	**(A36A2PR) Passenger/Ro-Ro Ship (Vehicles)** Passengers: unberthed: 500 Bow door & ramp Stern door & ramp Lane-Wid: 7.00 Lane-clr ht: 4.50 Lorries: 12, Cars: 49	**1 oil engine** geared to sc. shaft driving 2 CP propellers Total Power: 1,986kW (2,700hp) 15.0kn Wichmann WX28V8 1 x Vee 4 Stroke 8 Cy. 280 x 360 1986kW (2700bhp) Wichmann Motorfabrikk AS-Norway AuxGen: 2 x 175kW 220V 50Hz a.c, 2 x 64kW 220V 50Hz a.c Fuel: 34.5 (d.f.) 52.0 (r.f.)

9395800 *V7PV6* -	**ULLSWATER** **Ullswater Subsea AS** Hallin Marine Singapore Pte Ltd SatCom: Inmarsat C 453833691 *Majuro* *Marshall Islands* MMSI: 538003296 Official number: 3296	**4,469** 1,340 2,737	Class: AB	**2009-01 PT Drydocks World Pertama — Batam** Yd No: 181 Loa 78.00 Br ex - Dght 5.500 Lbp 75.20 Br md 20.40 Dpth 7.00 Welded, 1 dk	**(B22A20V) Diving Support Vessel** Cranes: 1x50t	**2 oil engines** reduction geared to sc. shafts driving 2 Directional propellers Total Power: 4,060kW (5,520hp) 10.0kn Caterpillar 3606TA 2 x 4 Stroke 6 Cy. 280 x 300 each-2030kW (2760bhp) Caterpillar Inc-USA AuxGen: 3 x 590kW a.c, 2 x 1600kW a.c Thrusters: 3 Tunnel thruster (f)
8884593 *4JKT* -	**ULLUCHAY** *ex* MSK-11 *-1979* **Specialized Sea Oil Fleet Organisation, Caspian Sea Oil Fleet, State Oil Co of the Republic of Azerbaijan** - *Baku* *Azerbaijan* MMSI: 423116100 Official number: DGR-0243	**946** 284 343	Class: RS	**1979-11 Sudostroitelnyy Zavod "Krasnyye Barrikady" — Krasnyye Barrikady** Yd No: 11 Loa 54.49 Br ex 14.78 Dght 2.160 Lbp 51.50 Br md - Dpth 3.70 Welded, 1 dk	**(B34B2SC) Crane Vessel** Cranes: 1x25t	**2 oil engines** driving 2 FP propellers Total Power: 1,030kW (1,400hp) 11.0kn Russkiy 6DR30/50-6-3 2 x 2 Stroke 6 Cy. 300 x 500 each-515kW (700bhp) Mashinostroitelnyy Zavod"Russkiy-Dizel"-Leningrad AuxGen: 3 x 100kW a.c Fuel: 118.0 (d.f.)
8806876 *5VCQ9* -	**ULMAR** *ex* Fulmar *-2014* *ex* Overseas Fulmar *-2009* *ex* Fulmar *-2005* *ex* Kobe Spirit *-1993* **Providence Management Services Inc** Tomini Ship Management (Pvt) Ltd *Lome* *Togo* MMSI: 671465000	**25,368** 10,927 39,521 T/cm 47.5	Class: AB	**1989-06 Onomichi Dockyard Co Ltd — Onomichi HS** Yd No: 329 Loa 182.30 (BB) Br ex - Dght 10.970 Lbp 172.00 Br md 31.40 Dpth 17.20 Welded, 1 dk	**(A13A2TW) Crude/Oil Products Tanker** Double Sides Entire Compartment Length Liq: 47,889; Liq (Oil): 47,889 Cargo Heating Coils Compartments: 7 Ta, 2 Wing Slop Ta, ER 3 Cargo Pump (s): 3x1300m³/hr Manifold: Bow/CM: 91.1m	**1 oil engine** driving 1 FP propeller Total Power: 7,850kW (10,673hp) 15.1kn B&W 6S50MC 1 x 2 Stroke 6 Cy. 500 x 1910 7850kW (10673bhp) Mitsui Engineering & Shipbuilding CLtd-Japan AuxGen: 3 x 420kW 450V 50Hz a.c Fuel: 172.0 (d.f.) 1426.0 (r.f.) 31.0pd
9213923 *UEIV* -	**ULOVISTYY** *ex* Dong Yih No. 1 *-2010* **OOO 'Tsentr Pribrezhnogo Rybolovstva Ostrovnoy' (LLC Center of Offshore Fisheries 'Ostrovnoy')** - *Nevelsk* *Russia* MMSI: 273359030	**708** 303 341	Class: RS	**1999-11 San Yang Shipbuilding Co., Ltd. — Kaohsiung** Loa 56.18 Br ex - Dght - Lbp 49.68 Br md 8.60 Dpth 3.75 Welded, 1 dk	**(B11B2FV) Fishing Vessel**	**1 oil engine** geared to sc. shaft driving 1 FP propeller Total Power: 1,030kW (1,400hp) 11.0kn Akasaka K28FD 1 x 4 Stroke 6 Cy. 280 x 480 1030kW (1400bhp) Akasaka Tekkosho KK (Akasaka DieselLtd)-Japan Fuel: 191.0 (d.f.)
9589451 *3YLR* -	**ULOYTIND** **Torghatten Nord AS** - *Tromso* *Norway* MMSI: 257129600	**396** 118 125	Class: NV	**2011-09 Remontowa Shipbuilding SA — Gdansk** (Hull) Yd No: B610/2 **2011-09 Gdanska Stocznia 'Remontowa' SA — Gdansk** Yd No: B2398/2 Loa 36.02 Br ex 10.06 Dght 2.750 Lbp 35.47 Br md 9.64 Dpth 4.20 Welded, 1 dk	**(A36A2PR) Passenger/Ro-Ro Ship (Vehicles)** Passengers: unberthed: 47 Bow door (centre) Stern door (centre) Vehicles: 16	**2 oil engines** driving 2 Directional propellers Total Power: 1,104kW (1,500hp) Volvo Penta D16… 2 x 4 Stroke 6 Cy. 144 x 165 each-552kW (750bhp) AB Volvo Penta-Sweden AuxGen: 2 x a.c
9572367 *HP7404* -	**ULRIKA** *ex* Swordfish 1 *-2013* **International World Shipping Agencies SA** GAC Marine LLC *Panama* *Panama* MMSI: 354242000 Official number: 44573PEXT	**499** 149 402	Class: AB	**2010-03 Guangxi Guijiang Shipyard — Wuzhou GX** Yd No: H7055 Loa 40.00 Br ex - Dght 4.400 Lbp 36.80 Br md 11.40 Dpth 4.95 Welded, 1 dk	**(B32A2ST) Tug**	**2 oil engines** reduction geared to sc. shafts driving 2 FP propellers Total Power: 2,984kW (4,058hp) 12.5kn Mitsubishi S8U-MPTK 2 x 4 Stroke 8 Cy. 240 x 260 each-1492kW (2029bhp) Mitsubishi Heavy Industries Ltd-Japan AuxGen: 3 x 300kW a.c Fuel: 350.0 (r.f.)
9076686 *YL2344* -	**ULRIKA** *ex* Rubin *-1997* **Vergi Ltd** - *Riga* *Latvia* MMSI: 275143000 Official number: 0814	**112** 33 30	Class: (RS)	**1992-09 Sosnovskiy Sudostroitelnyy Zavod — Sosnovka** Yd No: 808 Loa 25.45 Br ex 7.00 Dght 2.390 Lbp 22.00 Br md 6.80 Dpth 3.30 Welded, 1 dk	**(B11A2FS) Stern Trawler** Ice Capable	**1 oil engine** driving 1 FP propeller Total Power: 220kW (299hp) 9.5kn S.K.L. 6NVD26A-2 1 x 4 Stroke 6 Cy. 180 x 260 220kW (299bhp) SKL Motoren u. Systemtechnik AG-Magdeburg
7015951 - -	**ULRIKA** **Osadjere Fishing Co Ltd** - *Apapa* *Nigeria*	*164* 70 -	Class: (BV)	**1970 VEB Rosslauer Schiffswerft — Rosslau** Yd No: 3249 Loa 33.63 Br ex 6.61 Dght 2.699 Lbp 29.57 Br md 6.58 Dpth 3.31 Welded, 1 dk	**(B11A2FT) Trawler**	**1 oil engine** driving 1 FP propeller Total Power: 552kW (750hp) Polar SF16RS… 1 x 4 Stroke 6 Cy. 250 x 300 552kW (750bhp) AB NOHAB-Sweden
9156113 *V2BY9* -	**ULRIKE G.** *ex* Kathrin *-2003* **Gerems Schiffahrts GmbH & Co KG ms 'Ulrike G'** Gerdes Bereederungs und Verwaltungs GmbH *Saint John's* *Antigua & Barbuda* MMSI: 304407000 Official number: 4167	**2,994** 1,733 4,419	Class: GL	**2002-08 Brodogradiliste 'Sava' — Macvanska Mitrovica** Yd No: 320 Loa 99.80 (BB) Br ex 13.04 Dght 5.630 Lbp 95.80 Br md 12.80 Dpth 7.55 Welded, 1 dk	**(A31A2GX) General Cargo Ship** Grain: 5,841 TEU 297 Compartments: 1 Ho, ER 1 Ha: ER Ice Capable	**1 oil engine** reduction geared to sc. shaft driving 1 Contra-rotating propeller Total Power: 2,551kW (3,468hp) 13.0kn MWM TBD645L6 1 x 4 Stroke 6 Cy. 330 x 450 2551kW (3468bhp) Deutz AG-Koeln AuxGen: 1 x 640kW 380/220V a.c, 2 x 168kW 380/220V a.c Thrusters: 1 Tunnel thruster (f)
9164835 *C6PZ3* -	**ULRIKEN** *ex* Antares Voyager *-2011* *ex* Frank A. Shrontz *-2003* **Golden State Petro IOM 1-A Plc** Frontline Management AS SatCom: Inmarsat C 430837510 *Nassau* *Bahamas* MMSI: 308375000 Official number: 731033	**160,036** 109,604 309,996 T/cm 172.0	Class: AB	**1998-12 Samsung Heavy Industries Co Ltd — Geoje** Yd No: 1228 Loa 333.07 (BB) Br ex 58.04 Dght 22.525 Lbp 318.40 Br md 58.00 Dpth 31.25 Welded, 1 dk	**(A13A2TV) Crude Oil Tanker** Double Hull (13F) Liq: 333,701; Liq (Oil): 179,700 Compartments: 5 Ta, 10 Wing Ta, ER, 2 Wing Slop Ta 3 Cargo Pump (s): 3x5000m³/hr Manifold: Bow/CM: 169.3m	**1 oil engine** driving 1 FP propeller Total Power: 25,487kW (34,652hp) 15.3k… B&W 7S80MC 1 x 2 Stroke 7 Cy. 800 x 3056 25487kW (34652bhp) Samsung Heavy Industries Co Ltd-South Korea AuxGen: 3 x 980kW a.c Fuel: 372.0 (d.f.) 8670.0 (r.f.)
7369118 *3FGL3* -	**ULS FERRY 1** *ex* Kapella *-2012* *ex* Marine Evangeline *-1998* *ex* Spirit of Boulogne *-1995* *ex* Marine Evangeline *-1993* *ex* Duke of Yorkshire *-1978* **Kapella Shipping Ltd** AS Universal Logistic System *Panama* *Panama* MMSI: 373907000 Official number: 4471913	**7,564** 2,270 1,642	Class: PR (BV) (NV)	**1974-06 Kristiansands Mek. Verksted AS — Kristiansand** Yd No: 221 Loa 110.14 (BB) Br ex - Dght 4.546 Lbp 98.00 Br md 20.10 Dpth 12.32 Welded, 1 dk	**(A36A2PR) Passenger/Ro-Ro Ship (Vehicles)** Passengers: berths: 50; driver berths: 50 Bow door & ramp Quarter stern door & ramp Lane-Len: 672 Bale: 11,160 Ice Capable	**4 oil engines** geared to sc. shafts driving 2 CP propellers Total Power: 7,504kW (10,204hp) 18.5k… Normo KVM-1… 4 x Vee 4 Stroke 16 Cy. 250 x 300 each-1876kW (2551bhp) AS Bergens Mek Verksteder-Norway AuxGen: 4 x 600kW 380V 50Hz a.c Thrusters: 1 Thwart. FP thruster (f)
7736361 *D7LX* -	**ULSAN 701** *ex* Kumgang No. 1 *-2013* *ex* Bukyong No. 1 *-2010* *ex* Kumgang 1 *-2005* *ex* Fukue Maru No. 6 *-2001* *ex* Kyoei Maru No. 85 *-1989* **Ulsan Shipping Co Ltd** - *Ulsan* *South Korea* MMSI: 440104290 Official number: USR-010765	**191** - 110	Class: RI	**1978 K.K. Izutsu Zosensho — Nagasaki** Yd No: 782 Converted From: Fishing Vessel-2001 Loa 37.80 Br ex 7.60 Dght 2.420 Lbp 30.84 Br md 7.00 Dpth 3.05 Welded, 1 dk	**(B32A2ST) Tug**	**1 oil engine** reduction geared to sc. shaft driving 1 FP propeller Total Power: 883kW (1,201hp) Niigata 6L28B… 1 x 4 Stroke 6 Cy. 280 x 320 883kW (1201bhp) Niigata Engineering Co Ltd-Japan
8029686 *DSET7* -	**ULSAN GAS** *ex* Bay Star *-2008* *ex* Vigas *-1995* *launched as* Fuji Gas *-1981* **E Marine Co Ltd** Smart Marine Co Ltd *Busan* *South Korea* MMSI: 440428000 Official number: BSR-971658	**2,693** 807 2,607 T/cm 10.8	Class: KR (NK)	**1981-02 Tokushima Zosen Sangyo K.K. — Komatsushima** Yd No: 1431 Loa 94.44 Br ex 14.41 Dght 5.265 Lbp 87.12 Br md 14.40 Dpth 6.51 Welded, 1 dk	**(A11B2TG) LPG Tanker** Double Hull (13F) Liq (Gas): 2,511 2 x Gas Tank (s); 2 Cargo Pump (s): 2x150m³/hr Manifold: Bow/CM: 41.4m	**1 oil engine** driving 1 FP propeller Total Power: 2,354kW (3,200hp) 13.5k… Akasaka DM4… 1 x 4 Stroke 6 Cy. 460 x 720 2354kW (3200bhp) Akasaka Tekkosho KK (Akasaka DieselLtd)-Japan AuxGen: 2 x 176kW 450V 60Hz a.c Fuel: 68.0 (d.f.) 520.0 (r.f.)
9161235 - -	**ULSAN HO** - **Chokwang Shipping Co Ltd** - *Ulsan* *South Korea* MMSI: 440100819 Official number: USR-967974	**204** - 122	Class: (KR)	**1996-12 Kyeong-In Engineering & Shipbuilding Co Ltd — Incheon** Yd No: 157 Loa 33.80 Br ex - Dght - Lbp 28.50 Br md 9.30 Dpth 4.15 Welded, 1dk	**(B32A2ST) Tug**	**2 oil engines** with clutches, flexible couplings & reduction geared to sc. shafts driving 2 FP propellers Total Power: 2,700kW (3,670hp) Caterpillar 3516T… 2 x Vee 4 Stroke 16 Cy. 170 x 190 each-1350kW (1835bhp) Caterpillar Inc-USA

7831484 *D8PN* -	**ULSAN NO. 703** *ex* Hyunjung No. 123 *-2013* *ex* Hyundai No. 123 *-1997* **Ulsan Shipping Co Ltd** - *Ulsan* *South Korea* Official number: USR-798023	*197* 46 137	Class: KR	**1979-09 Hyundai Mipo Dockyard Co Ltd — Ulsan** Yd No: KC-36 Loa 28.81 Br ex - Dght 3.288 Lbp 27.51 Br md 8.60 Dpth 3.81 Welded, 1 dk	**(B32A2ST) Tug**	**2 oil engines** driving 2 FP propellers Total Power: 1,912kW (2,600hp) 11.5kn Niigata 6MG25BX 2 x 4 Stroke 6 Cy. 250 x 320 each-956kW (1300bhp) (made 1978) Niigata Engineering Co Ltd-Japan AuxGen: 2 x 48kW 225V a.c
7606530 - -	**ULSAN SOBANG** **Government of The Republic of South Korea (Ministry of Home Affairs)** - *Ulsan* *South Korea*	*118* 37 -	Class: (NK)	**1971 Sumidagawa Zosen K.K. — Tokyo** Loa 27.72 Br ex - Dght - Lbp 25.00 Br md 6.51 Dpth 2.80 Welded, 1 dk	**(B34F2SF) Fire Fighting Vessel**	**2 oil engines** driving 2 FP propellers Total Power: 838kW (1,140hp) 12.5kn Mitsubishi 12DH20T 2 x Vee 4 Stroke 12 Cy. 135 x 160 each-419kW (570bhp) Mitsubishi Heavy Industries Ltd-Japan Fuel: 4.0 1.5pd
9004255 *D5AH8* -	**ULSNIS** *ex* Cala Pantanal *-2009* *ex* MSC Cameroon *-2005* *ex* Ulsnis *-2004* *ex* Ankara *-2004* *ex* Armada Sprinter *-2003* *ex* Nordwoge *-2001* *ex* Cala Palamos *-2000* *ex* SCL Africa *-2000* *ex* Nordwoge *-1998* *ex* CCNI Antofagasta *-1997* *ex* Nordwoge *-1996* *ex* Contship le Havre *-1995* *ex* Nordwoge *-1993* **ms 'Atlantic Star' Schiffahrtsgesellschaft mbH & Co KG** Brise Schiffahrts GmbH *Monrovia* *Liberia* MMSI: 636092318 Official number: 92318	**14,865** 7,642 20,150 T/cm 35.2	Class: GL	**1993-06 Kvaerner Warnow Werft GmbH — Rostock** Yd No: 422 Loa 167.24 (BB) Br ex 25.24 Dght 9.840 Lbp 156.71 Br md 25.00 Dpth 13.40 Welded, 1 dk	**(A33A2CC) Container Ship (Fully Cellular)** Grain: 26,094 TEU 1388 C Ho 534 TEU C Dk 854 TEU incl 150 ref C. Compartments: 6 Cell Ho, ER 8 Ha: (12.5 x 10.7)Tappered (12.5 x 15.9)6 (12.5 x 21.1)ER Cranes: 3x40t	**1 oil engine** driving 1 FP propeller Total Power: 11,130kW (15,132hp) 17.0kn Sulzer 7RTA58 1 x 2 Stroke 7 Cy. 580 x 1700 11130kW (15132bhp) Dieselmotorenwerk Rostock GmbH-Rostock AuxGen: 1 x 800kW 450V a.c, 3 x 640kW 450V a.c Thrusters: 1 Thwart. CP thruster (f) Fuel: 176.0 (d.f.) 1296.8 (r.f.) 45.0pd
9674646 *C6AV9* -	**ULTIMA** **Legenda Maritime SA** Kotoku Kaiun Co Ltd (Kotoku Kaiun KK) *Nassau* *Bahamas* MMSI: 311000169 Official number: 7000592	**9,568** 4,529 11,855	Class: NK	**2013-11 Kyokuyo Shipyard Corp — Shimonoseki YC** Yd No: 511 Loa 141.00 (BB) Br ex - Dght 8.214 Lbp 133.00 Br md 22.50 Dpth 11.40 Welded, 1 dk	**(A33A2CC) Container Ship (Fully Cellular)** TEU 1103 incl 150 ref C	**1 oil engine** driving 1 FP propeller Total Power: 8,280kW (11,257hp) 18.0kn MAN-B&W 6S46MC-C8 1 x 2 Stroke 6 Cy. 460 x 1932 8280kW (11257bhp) Hitachi Zosen Corp-Japan Fuel: 900.0
8854732 - -	**ULTIMA CRUZ** *ex* Galewinds '84 *-1993* **Ultima Cruz LLC** - *Port Isabel, TX* *United States of America* Official number: 665210	*101* 69 -		**1984 Steiner Shipyard, Inc. — Bayou La Batre, Al** Loa 22.86 Br ex - Dght - Lbp 20.33 Br md 6.71 Dpth 3.32 Welded, 1 dk	**(B11A2FT) Trawler**	**1 oil engine** geared to sc. shaft driving 1 FP propeller Total Power: 268kW (364hp) Cummins KT-1150-M 1 x 4 Stroke 6 Cy. 159 x 159 268kW (364bhp) Cummins Engine Co Inc-USA
8657811 - -	**ULTIMATE LADY** **Ultimate Lady Ltd (Ultimate Lady Charters)** - *Cook Islands*	**172** 129 -		**1998 Tournament Boats Charters — Auckland** Loa 28.00 Br ex - Dght 2.000 Lbp - Br md 10.00 Dpth - Welded, 1 dk	**(X11A2YP) Yacht** Hull Material: Aluminium Alloy	**2 oil engines** reduction geared to sc. shafts driving 2 Propellers Total Power: 1,618kW (2,200hp) 20.0kn MAN D2842LE 2 x Vee 4 Stroke 12 Cy. 128 x 142 each-809kW (1100bhp) MAN Nutzfahrzeuge AG-Nuernberg
9343479 *YJUX5* -	**ULTIMAX** **Stevens Line Co Ltd** Sato Steamship Co Ltd (Sato Kisen KK) *Port Vila* *Vanuatu* MMSI: 576071000 Official number: 1689	**43,591** 19,125 54,347	Class: NK	**2006-06 Oshima Shipbuilding Co Ltd — Saikai NS** Yd No: 10466 Loa 210.00 (BB) Br ex 32.26 Dght 11.500 Lbp 203.57 Br md 32.26 Dpth 22.98 Welded, 1 dk	**(A24B2BW) Wood Chips Carrier** Double Hull Grain: 109,043 Compartments: 6 Ho, ER 6 Ha: ER Cranes: 3x14.7t	**1 oil engine** driving 1 FP propeller Total Power: 9,194kW (12,500hp) 14.2kn Mitsubishi 7UEC50LSII 1 x 2 Stroke 7 Cy. 500 x 1950 9194kW (12500bhp) Mitsubishi Heavy Industries Ltd-Japan AuxGen: 3 x a.c Fuel: 3050.0
9624641 *HONE* -	**ULTRA BELLAMBI** **Marugame Kisen Kaisha Ltd & La Darien Navegacion SA** Shoei Kisen Kaisha Ltd SatCom: Inmarsat C 437381010 *Panama* *Panama* MMSI: 373810000 Official number: 4415012	**34,777** 20,209 61,470 T/cm 61.4	Class: NK	**2012-08 Shin Kasado Dockyard Co Ltd — Kudamatsu YC** Yd No: K-033 Loa 199.98 (BB) Br ex - Dght 13.010 Lbp 195.00 Br md 32.24 Dpth 18.60 Welded, 1 dk	**(A21A2BC) Bulk Carrier** Grain: 77,674; Bale: 73,552 Compartments: 5 Ho, ER 5 Ha: 4 (23.5 x 19.0)ER (18.7 x 19.0) Cranes: 4x30.5t	**1 oil engine** driving 1 FP propeller Total Power: 8,450kW (11,489hp) 14.5kn MAN-B&W 6S50MC-C8 1 x 2 Stroke 6 Cy. 500 x 2000 8450kW (11489bhp) Mitsui Engineering & Shipbuilding CLtd-Japan Fuel: 2560.0
9448217 *3EVT8* -	**ULTRA COLONSAY** *ex* U-Sea Colonsay *-2012* **Pedregal Maritime SA** Ultrabulk Shipping A/S SatCom: Inmarsat C 437101110 *Panama* *Panama* MMSI: 371011000 Official number: 4318511A	**34,778** 20,209 61,470 T/cm 61.4	Class: NK	**2011-10 Shin Kasado Dockyard Co Ltd — Kudamatsu YC** Yd No: K-028 Loa 199.99 (BB) Br ex - Dght 13.010 Lbp 195.00 Br md 32.24 Dpth 18.60 Welded, 1 dk	**(A21A2BC) Bulk Carrier** Grain: 77,674; Bale: 73,552 Compartments: 5 Ho, ER 5 Ha: 4 (23.5 x 19.0)ER (18.7 x 19.0) Cranes: 4x30.5t	**1 oil engine** driving 1 FP propeller Total Power: 8,450kW (11,489hp) 14.5kn MAN-B&W 6S50MC-C8 1 x 2 Stroke 6 Cy. 500 x 2000 8450kW (11489bhp) Mitsui Engineering & Shipbuilding CLtd-Japan Fuel: 2560.0
9675743 *3EFQ8* -	**ULTRA CORY** **San Lorenzo Shipping SA** SMTECH Ship Management Co Ltd *Panama* *Panama* MMSI: 357330000 Official number: 4565614	**34,794** 20,209 61,442 T/cm 61.4	Class: NK	**2014-02 Shin Kasado Dockyard Co Ltd — Kudamatsu YC** Yd No: K-045 Loa 199.98 (BB) Br ex - Dght 13.010 Lbp 195.00 Br md 32.24 Dpth 18.60 Welded, 1 dk	**(A21A2BC) Bulk Carrier** Grain: 77,674; Bale: 73,552 Compartments: 5 Ho, ER 5 Ha: 4 (23.5 x 19.0)ER (18.7 x 19.0) Cranes: 4x30.7t	**1 oil engine** driving 1 FP propeller Total Power: 9,960kW (13,542hp) 14.5kn MAN-B&W 6S50MC-C8 1 x 2 Stroke 6 Cy. 500 x 2000 9960kW (13542bhp) Hitachi Zosen Corp-Japan Fuel: 2570.0
9615157 *3EXP4* -	**ULTRA DWARKA** **Shoei Kisen Kaisha Ltd & Paraiso Shipping SA** Shoei Kisen Kaisha Ltd SatCom: Inmarsat C 437340310 *Panama* *Panama* MMSI: 373403000 Official number: 4389012	**34,832** 20,209 61,395 T/cm 61.4	Class: NK	**2012-05 Shin Kasado Dockyard Co Ltd — Kudamatsu YC** Yd No: K-031 Loa 199.98 (BB) Br ex - Dght 13.010 Lbp 195.00 Br md 32.24 Dpth 18.60 Welded, 1 dk	**(A21A2BC) Bulk Carrier** Grain: 77,674; Bale: 73,552 Compartments: 5 Ho, ER 5 Ha: 4 (23.5 x 19.0)ER (18.7 x 19.0) Cranes: 4x30.7t	**1 oil engine** driving 1 FP propeller Total Power: 8,450kW (11,489hp) 14.5kn MAN-B&W 6S50MC-C8 1 x 2 Stroke 6 Cy. 500 x 2000 8450kW (11489bhp) Mitsui Engineering & Shipbuilding CLtd-Japan Fuel: 2560.0
9589798 *9V9499* -	**ULTRA DYNAMIC** *ex* U-Sea Dynamic *-2012* **Ultrabulk Shipholding (Singapore) Pte Ltd** Belships Management Singapore Pte Ltd *Singapore* *Singapore* MMSI: 566157000 Official number: 397202	**34,798** 20,209 61,412 T/cm 61.4	Class: NK	**2011-07 Shin Kasado Dockyard Co Ltd — Kudamatsu YC** Yd No: K-025 Loa 199.98 (BB) Br ex - Dght 13.010 Lbp 195.00 Br md 32.24 Dpth 18.60 Welded, 1 dk	**(A21A2BC) Bulk Carrier** Grain: 77,674; Bale: 73,552 Compartments: 5 Ho, ER 5 Ha: 4 (23.5 x 19.0)ER (18.7 x 19.0) Cranes: 4x30.5t	**1 oil engine** driving 1 FP propeller Total Power: 8,450kW (11,489hp) 14.5kn MAN-B&W 6S50MC-C8 1 x 2 Stroke 6 Cy. 500 x 2000 8450kW (11489bhp) Mitsui Engineering & Shipbuilding CLtd-Japan Fuel: 2560.0
9643946 *3FLE3* -	**ULTRA ESTERHAZY** **Los Halillos Shipping Co SA** Shoei Kisen Kaisha Ltd *Panama* *Panama* MMSI: 373821000 Official number: 4422512	**23,264** 12,134 38,228	Class: NK	**2012-09 Mitsubishi Heavy Industries Ltd. — Shimonoseki** Yd No: 1163 Loa 179.97 (BB) Br ex - Dght 10.540 Lbp 173.00 Br md 29.80 Dpth 15.00 Welded, 1 dk	**(A21A2BC) Bulk Carrier** Grain: 47,125; Bale: 45,369 Compartments: 5 Ho, ER 5 Ha: ER Cranes: 4x30.5t	**1 oil engine** driving 1 FP propeller Total Power: 7,860kW (10,686hp) 14.7kn MAN-B&W 6S46MC-C 1 x 2 Stroke 6 Cy. 460 x 1932 7860kW (10686bhp) Makita Corp-Japan Fuel: 1940.0
9476927 *D5BM6* -	**ULTRA GUJARAT** *launched as* U-Sea Gujarat *-2012* **Lucretia Shipping SA** Santoku Senpaku Co Ltd *Monrovia* *Liberia* MMSI: 636015559 Official number: 15559	**33,910** 19,965 61,671 T/cm 60.0	Class: NK	**2012-03 Oshima Shipbuilding Co Ltd — Saikai NS** Yd No: 10550 Loa 199.98 (BB) Br ex - Dght 12.850 Lbp 196.00 Br md 32.26 Dpth 18.33 Welded, 1 dk	**(A21A2BC) Bulk Carrier** Grain: 76,912; Bale: 75,311 Compartments: 5 Ho, ER 5 Ha: ER Cranes: 4x30t	**1 oil engine** driving 1 FP propeller Total Power: 8,201kW (11,150hp) 14.5kn MAN-B&W 6S50MC-C 1 x 2 Stroke 6 Cy. 500 x 2000 8201kW (11150bhp) Kawasaki Heavy Industries Ltd-Japan Fuel: 1960.0

IMO / Call sign	Name / Owners / Flag	Tonnage	Class	Builder / Dimensions	Type / Capacity	Machinery
9370044 3EK08 -	**ULTRA INITIATOR** *ex* U-Sea Initiator *-2012* *ex* Sibulk Initiator *-2011* **Primate Shipping SA** NEOM Maritime (Singapore) Pte Ltd *Panama* *Panama* MMSI: 372788000 Official number: 3280107B	**31,244** 18,504 56,017 T/cm 55.8	Class: NK	**2007-06 Mitsui Eng. & SB. Co. Ltd. — Tamano** Yd No: 1657 Loa 189.99 (BB) Br ex 32.26 Dght 12.573 Lbp 182.00 Br md 32.26 Dpth 17.90 Welded, 1 dk	**(A21A2BC) Bulk Carrier** Grain: 70,811; Bale: 68,084 Compartments: 5 Ho, ER 5 Ha: 4 (21.1 x 18.9)ER (17.6 x 18.9) Cranes: 4x30t	**1 oil engine** driving 1 FP propeller Total Power: 9,480kW (12,889hp) 14.5kn MAN-B&W 6S50MC-C 1 x 2 Stroke 6 Cy. 500 x 2000 9480kW (12889bhp) Mitsui Engineering & Shipbuilding CLtd-Japan AuxGen: 3 x a.c Fuel: 2380.0
9520596 3FDL2 -	**ULTRA LANIGAN** **Sun Leaf Shipping SA** Toko Kisen Co Ltd (Toko Kisen YK) *Panama* *Panama* MMSI: 373949000 Official number: 42785TJ	**32,309** 19,458 58,032 T/cm 57.4	Class: NK	**2012-01 Tsuneishi Heavy Industries (Cebu) Inc — Balamban** Yd No: SC-148 Loa 189.99 Br ex - Dght 12.826 Lbp 185.60 Br md 32.26 Dpth 18.00 Welded, 1 dk	**(A21A2BC) Bulk Carrier** Grain: 72,689; Bale: 70,122 Compartments: 5 Ho, ER 5 Ha: ER Cranes: 4x30t	**1 oil engine** driving 1 FP propeller Total Power: 8,400kW (11,421hp) 14.5kn MAN-B&W 6S50MC-C 1 x 2 Stroke 6 Cy. 500 x 2000 8400kW (11421bhp) Mitsui Engineering & Shipbuilding CLtd-Japan Fuel: 2380.0
9442469 9V9229	**ULTRA PANACHE** *ex* U-Sea Panache *-2012* **Ultra Summit (Singapore) Pte Ltd** Belships Management Singapore Pte Ltd SatCom: Inmarsat C 456360511 *Singapore* *Singapore* MMSI: 563605000 Official number: 396814	**41,799** 25,953 78,450	Class: NK	**2011-02 Sanoyas Hishino Meisho Corp — Kurashiki OY** Yd No: 1292 Loa 225.00 (BB) Br ex - Dght 14.440 Lbp 220.00 Br md 32.24 Dpth 19.90 Welded, 1 dk	**(A21A2BC) Bulk Carrier** Grain: 91,144 Compartments: 7 Ho, ER 7 Ha: ER	**1 oil engine** driving 1 FP propeller Total Power: 9,560kW (12,998hp) 14.0kn MAN-B&W 7S50MC-C 1 x 2 Stroke 7 Cy. 500 x 2000 9560kW (12998bhp) Mitsui Engineering & Shipbuilding CLtd-Japan Fuel: 2750.0 (r.f.)
9375939 3ESA3	**ULTRA PANTHER** *ex* Star Of Emirates *-2012* **Sun Cordia Marine SA** MK Shipmanagement Co Ltd *Panama* *Panama* MMSI: 370235000 Official number: 3404508A	**44,251** 27,095 83,610 T/cm 71.0	Class: NK (AB)	**2008-07 Sanoyas Hishino Meisho Corp — Kurashiki OY** Yd No: 1272 Loa 229.00 (BB) Br ex - Dght 14.551 Lbp 223.00 Br md 32.24 Dpth 20.20 Welded, 1 dk	**(A21A2BC) Bulk Carrier** Grain: 96,080 Compartments: 7 Ho, ER 7 Ha: ER	**1 oil engine** driving 1 FP propeller Total Power: 11,640kW (15,826hp) 14.0kn MAN-B&W 6S60MC-C 1 x 2 Stroke 6 Cy. 600 x 2400 11640kW (15826bhp) Kawasaki Heavy Industries Ltd-Japan AuxGen: 3 x 400kW a.c Fuel: 193.0 (d.f.) 2514.0 (r.f.)
9426702 3FEL7 -	**ULTRA PROSPERITY** *ex* U-Sea Prosperity *-2012* *ex* Sibulk Prosperity *-2011* **Moon Rise Shipping Co SA** Nagashiki Shipping Co Ltd (Nagashiki Kisen KK) *Panama* *Panama* MMSI: 371553000 Official number: 4179310B	**33,922** 19,947 61,645 T/cm 60.0	Class: NK	**2010-07 Oshima Shipbuilding Co Ltd — Saikai NS** Yd No: 10536 Loa 199.98 (BB) Br ex - Dght 12.845 Lbp 196.00 Br md 32.26 Dpth 18.33 Welded, 1 dk	**(A21A2BC) Bulk Carrier** Grain: 76,913; Bale: 75,312 Compartments: 5 Ho, ER 5 Ha: ER Cranes: 4x30t	**1 oil engine** driving 1 FP propeller Total Power: 8,208kW (11,160hp) 14.5kn MAN-B&W 6S50MC-C 1 x 2 Stroke 6 Cy. 500 x 2000 8208kW (11160bhp) Kawasaki Heavy Industries Ltd-Japan
9667435 HPHA -	**ULTRA REGINA** **San Clemente Shipping SA & Tokyo Sangyo Kaisha Ltd** - *Panama* *Panama* MMSI: 352057000 Official number: 4526913	**34,794** 20,209 61,424 T/cm 61.4	Class: NK	**2013-10 Shin Kasado Dockyard Co Ltd — Kudamatsu YC** Yd No: K-043 Loa 199.98 (BB) Br ex - Dght 13.010 Lbp 195.00 Br md 32.24 Dpth 18.60 Welded, 1 dk	**(A21A2BC) Bulk Carrier** Grain: 77,674; Bale: 73,552 Compartments: 5 Ho, ER 5 Ha: 4 (23.5 x 19.0)ER (18.7 x 19.0) Cranes: 4x30t	**1 oil engine** driving 1 FP propeller Total Power: 8,450kW (11,489hp) 14.5kn MAN-B&W 6S50MC-C8 1 x 2 Stroke 6 Cy. 500 x 2000 8450kW (11489bhp) Hitachi Zosen Corp-Japan Fuel: 2560.0
9476965 3FLF9 -	**ULTRA ROCANVILLE** *launched as* U-Sea Rocanville *-2012* **Youth Ship Holdings SA** Belships Management Singapore Pte Ltd *Panama* *Panama* MMSI: 373043000 Official number: 4368812	**33,900** 20,020 61,683 T/cm 60.0	Class: AB	**2012-03 Oshima Shipbuilding Co Ltd — Saikai NS** Yd No: 10575 Loa 199.98 (BB) Br ex - Dght 12.800 Lbp 196.00 Br md 32.26 Dpth 18.33 Welded, 1 dk	**(A21A2BC) Bulk Carrier** Grain: 76,913; Bale: 75,312 Compartments: 5 Ho, ER 5 Ha: ER Cranes: 4x30t	**1 oil engine** driving 1 FP propeller Total Power: 8,201kW (11,150hp) 14.0kn MAN-B&W 6S50MC-C 1 x 2 Stroke 6 Cy. 500 x 2000 8201kW (11150bhp) Kawasaki Heavy Industries Ltd-Japan AuxGen: 3 x 440kW a.c Fuel: 174.0 (d.f.) 1939.0 (r.f.)
9570486 3EWF7 -	**ULTRA SASKATCHEWAN** *ex* U-Sea Saskatchewan *-2012* **Pedregal Maritime SA & Takumi Senpaku Kaisha Ltd** Shoei Kisen Kaisha Ltd SatCom: Inmarsat C 435517810 *Panama* *Panama* MMSI: 355178000 Official number: 4214610A	**34,795** 20,209 61,484 T/cm 61.4	Class: NK	**2010-11 Shin Kasado Dockyard Co Ltd — Kudamatsu YC** Yd No: K-017 Loa 199.98 (BB) Br ex - Dght 13.010 Lbp 195.00 Br md 32.24 Dpth 18.60 Welded, 1 dk	**(A21A2BC) Bulk Carrier** Grain: 77,674; Bale: 73,552 Compartments: 5 Ho, ER 5 Ha: 4 (23.5 x 19.0)ER (18.7 x 19.0) Cranes: 4x30.7t	**1 oil engine** driving 1 FP propeller Total Power: 8,450kW (11,489hp) 14.5kn MAN-B&W 6S50MC-C8 1 x 2 Stroke 6 Cy. 500 x 2000 8450kW (11489bhp) Mitsui Engineering & Shipbuilding CLtd-Japan
9448229 3FFG -	**ULTRA SASKATOON** **Cypress Maritime (Panama) SA & Koyo Shosen Kaisha Ltd** Shoei Kisen Kaisha Ltd *Panama* *Panama* MMSI: 373483000 Official number: 4340312	**34,778** 20,209 61,470 T/cm 61.4	Class: NK	**2012-01 Shin Kasado Dockyard Co Ltd — Kudamatsu YC** Yd No: K-030 Loa 199.98 Br ex - Dght 13.010 Lbp 195.00 Br md 32.24 Dpth 18.60 Welded, 1 dk	**(A21A2BC) Bulk Carrier** Grain: 77,674; Bale: 73,552 Compartments: 5 Ho, ER 5 Ha: ER 4 (23.5 x 19.0) (18.7 x 19.0) Cranes: 4x30.5t	**1 oil engine** driving 1 FP propeller Total Power: 8,450kW (11,489hp) 14.5kn MAN-B&W 6S50MC-C8 1 x 2 Stroke 6 Cy. 500 x 2000 8450kW (11489bhp) Mitsui Engineering & Shipbuilding CLtd-Japan Fuel: 2560.0
9414149 3FVR8 -	**ULTRA TIGER** *ex* Star Of Dubai *-2012* **Sun Cordia Marine SA** MK Shipmanagement Co Ltd *Panama* *Panama* MMSI: 355410000 Official number: 38428PEXT1	**44,251** 27,095 83,611 T/cm 71.0	Class: AB	**2009-01 Sanoyas Hishino Meisho Corp — Kurashiki OY** Yd No: 1277 Loa 229.00 (BB) Br ex - Dght 14.520 Lbp 223.00 Br md 32.24 Dpth 20.20 Welded, 1 dk	**(A21A2BC) Bulk Carrier** Grain: 96,152 Compartments: 7 Ho, ER 7 Ha: ER	**1 oil engine** driving 1 FP propeller Total Power: 13,560kW (18,436hp) 14.0kn MAN-B&W 6S60MC-C 1 x 2 Stroke 6 Cy. 600 x 2400 13560kW (18436bhp) Kawasaki Heavy Industries Ltd-Japan AuxGen: 3 x 440kW a.c
9442902 3EQG9	**ULTRA TRADITION** *ex* U-Sea Tradition *-2012* *ex* Sibulk Tradition *-2010* **Pedregal Maritime SA** Misuga Kaiun Co Ltd *Panama* *Panama* MMSI: 353936000 Official number: 3386408C	**30,018** 18,486 53,206 T/cm 55.3	Class: NK	**2008-05 Iwagi Zosen Co Ltd — Kamijima EH** Yd No: 295 Loa 189.90 (BB) Br ex - Dght 12.300 Lbp 182.00 Br md 32.26 Dpth 17.30 Welded, 1 dk	**(A21A2BC) Bulk Carrier** Grain: 68,927; Bale: 65,526 Compartments: 5 Ho, ER 5 Ha: ER Cranes: 4x30.5t	**1 oil engine** driving 1 FP propeller Total Power: 9,480kW (12,889hp) 14.5kn MAN-B&W 6S50MC-C 1 x 2 Stroke 6 Cy. 500 x 2000 9480kW (12889bhp) Mitsui Engineering & Shipbuilding CLtd-Japan AuxGen: 3 x a.c Fuel: 2014.0
9205615 CBUT	**ULTRA TRONADOR** *ex* Tronador *-2012* *ex* C. S. Star *-2010* **Naviera Ultranav Ltda** Ultrabulk Shipping A/S *Valparaiso* *Chile* MMSI: 725001193	**19,920** 11,044 32,874 T/cm 43.8	Class: NK	**2000-01 Kanda Zosensho K.K. — Kawajiri** Yd No: 400 Loa 177.00 (BB) Br ex - Dght 10.018 Lbp 168.50 Br md 28.40 Dpth 14.25 Welded, 1 dk	**(A21A2BC) Bulk Carrier** Grain: 42,673; Bale: 40,713 Compartments: 5 Ho, ER 5 Ha: (14.4 x 15.8)4 (20.0 x 19.0)ER Cranes: 4x30.5t	**1 oil engine** driving 1 FP propeller Total Power: 6,620kW (9,001hp) 14.2kn B&W 6S46MC-C 1 x 2 Stroke 6 Cy. 460 x 1932 6620kW (9001bhp) Mitsui Engineering & Shipbuilding CLtd-Japan AuxGen: 2 x 400kW 480V 60Hz a.c Fuel: 62.0 (d.f.) (Heating Coils) 1382.0 (r.f.) 22.0pd
9643958 3FJD4 -	**ULTRA VANSCOY** **Los Halillos Shipping Co SA** Shoei Kisen Kaisha Ltd *Panama* *Panama* MMSI: 371410000 Official number: 4453213A	**23,264** 12,134 38,215	Class: NK	**2013-01 Mitsubishi Heavy Industries Ltd. — Shimonoseki** Yd No: 1164 Loa 179.97 (BB) Br ex - Dght 10.536 Lbp 173.00 Br md 29.80 Dpth 15.00 Welded, 1 dk	**(A21A2BC) Bulk Carrier** Double Hull Grain: 47,125; Bale: 45,369 Compartments: 5 Ho, ER 5 Ha: ER Cranes: 4x30.5t	**1 oil engine** driving 1 FP propeller Total Power: 7,860kW (10,686hp) 14.7kn MAN-B&W 6S46MC-C 1 x 2 Stroke 6 Cy. 460 x 1932 7860kW (10686bhp) Fuel: 1940.0
9566576 C6YW5 -	**ULTRA WOLLONGONG** *ex* U-Sea Wollongong *-2012* **Libero Panama SA** Kasuga Shipping Co Ltd SatCom: Inmarsat C 431101185 *Nassau* *Bahamas* MMSI: 311047500 Official number: 8001843	**33,894** 20,020 61,684 T/cm 60.0	Class: AB (NK)	**2011-06 Oshima Shipbuilding Co Ltd — Saikai NS** Yd No: 10549 Loa 199.98 (BB) Br ex - Dght 12.800 Lbp 196.00 Br md 32.26 Dpth 18.33 Welded, 1 dk	**(A21A2BC) Bulk Carrier** Grain: 76,895; Bale: 75,311 Compartments: 5 Ho, ER 5 Ha: ER Cranes: 4x30t	**1 oil engine** driving 1 FP propeller Total Power: 8,201kW (11,150hp) 14.5kn MAN-B&W 6S50MC-C 1 x 2 Stroke 6 Cy. 500 x 2000 8201kW (11150bhp) Kawasaki Heavy Industries Ltd-Japan AuxGen: 3 x 440kW a.c Fuel: 130.0 (d.f.) 1930.0 (r.f.)
9364590 - -	**ULTRAMAR** - -	**350** - 50		**2005-03 Midship Marine, Inc. — New Orleans, La** Loa 39.30 Br ex - Dght - Lbp 35.20 Br md 7.62 Dpth - Welded, 1 dk	**(A37B2PS) Passenger Ship** Hull Material: Aluminium Alloy Passengers: unberthed: 450	**4 oil engines** geared to sc. shafts driving 2 Water jets Total Power: 3,560kW (4,840hp) 25.0kn Caterpillar 3412 2 x Vee 4 Stroke 12 Cy. 137 x 152 each-890kW (1210bhp) Caterpillar Inc-USA

IMO / Call sign	Name / Owner	Tonnage	Class	Build	Type	Machinery
9167320 *P3WF9* -	**ULTRAMAR** *launched as* Papagena *-1997* **Nordica Schiffahrtsgesellschaft mbH & Co KG ms 'Ultramar'** Held Bereederungs GmbH & Co KG *Limassol* *Cyprus* MMSI: 209662000 Official number: P541	**2,820** 1,503 4,106	Class: GL (BV)	**1997-12 Bodewes' Scheepswerven B.V. — Hoogezand** Yd No: 581 Loa 89.72 (BB) Br ex - Dght 5.690 Lbp 84.98 Br md 13.60 Dpth 7.20 Welded, 1 dk	**(A31A2GX) General Cargo Ship** Double Hull Grain: 5,628 TEU 246 C.Ho 111/20' C.Dk 135/20' Compartments: 1 Ho, ER 1 Ha: (62.9 x 11.0)ER Ice Capable	**1 oil engine** reduction geared to sc. shaft driving 1 CP propeller Total Power: 2,400kW (3,263hp) 13.0kn MaK 8M25 1 x 4 Stroke 8 Cy. 255 x 400 2400kW (3263bhp) MaK Motoren GmbH & Co. KG-Kiel AuxGen: 1 x 292kW 230/400V 50Hz a.c, 2 x 252kW 230/400V 50Hz a.c Thrusters: 1 Thwart. FP thruster (f) Fuel: 38.8 (d.f.) (Heating Coils) 276.0 (r.f.) 10.5pd
8660480 *XCUI6* -	**ULTRAMAR IV** **Arrendadora Ve Por Mas SA de CV** Naviera Magna SA de CV *Puerto Juarez* *Mexico* MMSI: 345110012 Official number: 2301356031-5	**306** 92 -		**2004-06 Midship Marine, Inc. — New Orleans, La** Yd No: 304 Loa 38.00 Br ex 7.92 Dght 1.370 Lbp 35.20 Br md 7.62 Dpth 3.20 Welded, 1 dk	**(A37B2PS) Passenger Ship** Hull Material: Aluminium Alloy Passengers: unberthed: 450	**4 oil engines** reduction geared to sc. shafts driving 4 Propellers Total Power: 1,796kW (2,440hp) Caterpillar 3412 4 x Vee 4 Stroke 12 Cy. 137 x 152 each-449kW (610bhp) Caterpillar Inc-USA
7636171 - -	**ULTRAMAR VI** - -	*163* 74 144	Class: (AB) (GL)	**1978-04 Astilleros de Santander SA (ASTANDER) — El Astillero** Yd No: 133 Loa 25.40 Br ex 8.26 Dght 3.201 Lbp 23.12 Br md 8.01 Dpth 3.92 Welded, 1 dk	**(B32A2ST) Tug**	**1 oil engine** reverse reduction geared to sc. shaft driving 1 FP propeller Total Power: 1,044kW (1,419hp) 11.5kn Waukesha L5792DSIM 1 x Vee 4 Stroke 12 Cy. 216 x 216 1044kW (1419bhp) Waukesha Engine Div. DresserIndustries Inc.-Waukesha, Wi AuxGen: 2 x 60kW
8321618 *LW7104* -	**ULTRAMAR X** **Antares Naviera SA** - *Buenos Aires* *Argentina* MMSI: 701007051 Official number: 02222	*237* 29 238	Class: (AB) (GL)	**1984-05 Martin Jansen GmbH & Co. KG Schiffsw. u. Masch. — Leer** Yd No: 169 Loa 30.26 Br ex 9.35 Dght 4.079 Lbp 25.51 Br md 9.01 Dpth 4.65 Welded, 1 dk	**(B32A2ST) Tug**	**2 oil engines** sr reverse geared to sc. shafts driving 2 Z propellers Total Power: 2,206kW (3,000hp) MWM TBD440-8K 2 x 4 Stroke 8 Cy. 230 x 270 each-1103kW (1500bhp) Motoren Werke Mannheim AG (MWM)-West Germany AuxGen: 2 x 150kW 380V 50Hz a.c Fuel: 134.5 (d.f.)
8600789 *PQ6944* -	**ULTRATEC II** **Maritima Petroleo E Engenharia Ltda** Safe Supply Offshore Ltda *Rio de Janeiro* *Brazil* MMSI: 710986000 Official number: 3810423025	**883** 265 1,109	Class: (NV) (AB)	**1986-10 Maclaren BA Est. e Servicos Maritimos S.A. — Rio de Janeiro** Yd No: 304 Loa 57.00 Br ex - Dght 4.206 Lbp 52.00 Br md 12.01 Dpth 4.91 Welded, 1 dk	**(B22F20W) Well Stimulation Vessel**	**2 oil engines** reverse reduction geared to sc. shafts driving 2 FP propellers Total Power: 2,206kW (3,000hp) 12.0kn Daihatsu 6DSM-26A 2 x 4 Stroke 6 Cy. 260 x 300 each-1103kW (1500bhp) Ishikawajima Harima Heavy IndustrieCo Ltd (IHI)-Japan AuxGen: 2 x 220kW a.c Thrusters: 1 Thwart. FP thruster (f)
8607892 *TCAK4* -	**ULUBATLI HASAN** **Istanbul Deniz Otobusleri Sanayi ve Ticaret AS (IDO)** - *Istanbul* *Turkey* MMSI: 271002474 Official number: 5605	**431** 166 125	Class: TL (NV)	**1987-09 Skaalurens Skipsbyggeri AS — Rosendal** Yd No: 1582 Loa 38.82 Br ex 9.71 Dght 1.550 Lbp 36.41 Br md 9.47 Dpth 3.92 Welded, 1 dk	**(A37B2PS) Passenger Ship** Hull Material: Aluminium Alloy Passengers: unberthed: 449	**2 oil engines** geared to sc. shafts driving 2 FP propellers Total Power: 2,000kW (2,720hp) M.T.U. 12V396TC82 2 x Vee 4 Stroke 12 Cy. 165 x 185 each-1000kW (1360bhp) MTU Friedrichshafen GmbH-Friedrichshafen AuxGen: 2 x 56kW 380V 50Hz a.c Fuel: 9.0 (d.f.)
8607907 *TCAX6* -	**ULUC ALI REIS** **Istanbul Deniz Otobusleri Sanayi ve Ticaret AS (IDO)** - *Istanbul* *Turkey* MMSI: 271002473 Official number: 5631	**431** 166 125	Class: TL (NV)	**1987-12 Skaalurens Skipsbyggeri AS — Rosendal** Yd No: 1583 Loa 38.82 Br ex - Dght 1.534 Lbp 36.41 Br md 9.47 Dpth 5.92 Welded, 1 dk	**(A37B2PS) Passenger Ship** Hull Material: Aluminium Alloy Passengers: unberthed: 449	**2 oil engines** with clutches, flexible couplings & sr geared to sc. shafts driving 2 Directional propellers Total Power: 3,020kW (4,106hp) 32.0kn M.T.U. 16V396TB83 2 x Vee 4 Stroke 16 Cy. 165 x 185 each-1510kW (2053bhp) MTU Friedrichshafen GmbH-Friedrichshafen AuxGen: 2 x 68kW 400V 50Hz a.c
9269934 *TCCU9* -	**ULUC KA** **Emden Denizcilik ve Tankercilik Ticaret AS** TRANS KA Tanker Management Co Ltd (TRANS KA Tanker Isletmeciligi Ltd Sti) *Istanbul* *Turkey* MMSI: 271000753 Official number: 741	**3,981** 1,600 5,468 T/cm 14.8	Class: BV	**2004-06 Celiktekne Sanayii ve Ticaret A.S. — Tuzla, Istanbul** Yd No: 47 Loa 107.45 (BB) Br ex - Dght 5.800 Lbp 99.80 Br md 16.00 Dpth 7.25 Welded, 1 dk	**(A12B2TR) Chemical/Products Tanker** Double Hull (13F) Liq: 6,336; Liq (Oil): 6,336 Cargo Heating Coils Compartments: 12 Wing Ta, ER 12 Cargo Pump (s): 12x175m³/hr Ice Capable	**1 oil engine** geared to sc. shaft driving 1 FP propeller Total Power: 2,720kW (3,698hp) 13.0kn MaK 8M25 1 x 4 Stroke 8 Cy. 255 x 400 2720kW (3698bhp) Caterpillar Motoren GmbH & Co. KG-Germany AuxGen: 3 x a.c Thrusters: 1 Tunnel thruster (f)
9490428 *TCYB9* -	**ULUCAK** *ex* Sanghrajka 1 *-2010* **Is Finansal Kiralama AS** Arkas Denizcilik ve Nakliyat AS (Arkas Shipping & Transport AS) *Izmir* *Turkey* MMSI: 271040610 Official number: 5115	*941* 688 1,450	Class: BV	**2009-03 Modest Infrastructure Ltd — Bhavnagar** Yd No: 305 Loa 63.60 Br ex 12.02 Dght 4.240 Lbp 60.30 Br md 12.00 Dpth 5.80 Welded, 1 dk	**(A13B2TP) Products Tanker** Double Hull (13F) Liq: 1,154; Liq (Oil): 1,154 Compartments: 12 Wing Ta, ER	**2 oil engines** reduction geared to sc. shaft driving 2 FP propellers Total Power: 894kW (1,216hp) 10.0kn Cummins KTA-19-M3 1 x 4 Stroke 6 Cy. 159 x 159 447kW (608bhp) Cummins India Ltd-India AuxGen: 2 x 200kW 50Hz a.c Thrusters: 1 Tunnel thruster (f)
9433523 *TCA2988* -	**ULUPINAR III** **Sanmar Denizcilik Makina ve Ticaret AS** - *Istanbul* *Turkey* MMSI: 271010634	**247** - -	Class: RI	**2008-09 Pirlant Shipyard — Tuzla** Yd No: 17 Loa 24.40 Br ex - Dght 3.000 Lbp 23.20 Br md 9.15 Dpth 4.04 Welded, 1 dk	**(B32A2ST) Tug**	**2 oil engines** reduction geared to sc. shafts driving 2 Z propellers Total Power: 2,428kW (3,302hp) 13.0kn Caterpillar 3512TA 2 x Vee 4 Stroke 12 Cy. 170 x 190 each-1214kW (1651bhp) Caterpillar Inc-USA
9604354 *TCZO9* -	**ULUPINAR XI** **Mersin Uluslararasi Liman Isletmeciligi AS (Mersin International Port)** - SatCom: Inmarsat C 427101141 *Istanbul* *Turkey* MMSI: 271042538 Official number: 10175	**247** 136 97	Class: RI	**2010-12 Pirlant Shipyard — Tuzla** Yd No: 27 Loa 24.39 Br ex - Dght 3.000 Lbp 23.20 Br md 9.15 Dpth 4.04 Welded, 1 dk	**(B32A2ST) Tug**	**2 oil engines** reduction geared to sc. shafts driving 2 Directional propellers Total Power: 2,460kW (3,344hp) 12.0kn Caterpillar 3512B-TA 2 x Vee 4 Stroke 12 Cy. 170 x 190 each-1230kW (1672bhp) Caterpillar Inc-USA AuxGen: 2 x 59kW a.c
9655901 *TCDV4* -	**ULUPINAR XV** **Sanmar Denizcilik Makina ve Ticaret AS** - *Istanbul* *Turkey* MMSI: 271043295 Official number: 10640	**247** 136 97	Class: RI	**2012-08 Sanmar Denizcilik Makina ve Ticaret — Istanbul** Yd No: 07 Loa 24.39 Br ex - Dght - Lbp 23.20 Br md 9.15 Dpth 4.04 Welded, 1 dk	**(B32A2ST) Tug**	**2 oil engines** reduction geared to sc. shafts driving 2 Directional propellers Total Power: 3,000kW (4,078hp) 13.0kn Caterpillar 3512B-HD 2 x Vee 4 Stroke 12 Cy. 170 x 215 each-1500kW (2039bhp) Caterpillar Inc-USA AuxGen: 2 x 74kW 380V 50Hz a.c Fuel: 73.0
9706023 *TCNW6* -	**ULUPINAR XVII** *launched as* Baus *-2014* *ex* Ulupinar Xvii *-2014* **Sanmar Denizcilik Makina ve Ticaret AS** Bukser og Berging AS *Istanbul* *Turkey* Official number: 2264	**248** 97 -	Class: RI	**2014-01 Sanmar Denizcilik Makina ve Ticaret — Istanbul** Yd No: 26 Loa 24.39 Br ex - Dght - Lbp 23.20 Br md 9.15 Dpth 4.04 Welded, 1 dk	**(B32A2ST) Tug**	**2 oil engines** reduction geared to sc. shafts driving 2 Z propellers Total Power: 3,300kW (4,486hp) 13.0kn Caterpillar 3512C 2 x Vee 4 Stroke 12 Cy. 170 x 215 each-1650kW (2243bhp) Caterpillar Inc-USA AuxGen: 2 x 86kW a.c
9327188 *UGTC* -	**ULUS BREEZE** **Ulusland 1 Maritime Co Ltd** Albros Shipping & Trading Ltd Co (Albros Denizcilik ve Ticaret Ltd Sti) *Taganrog* *Russia* MMSI: 273310040	**2,604** 1,413 3,732	Class: RS	**2006-01 Ceksan Tersanesi — Turkey** Yd No: 27 Loa 89.73 Br ex 15.76 Dght 4.460 Lbp 84.44 Br md 15.60 Dpth 5.75 Welded, 1 dk	**(A31A2GX) General Cargo Ship** Grain: 4,877 Compartments: 1 Ho, ER 1 Ha: ER	**1 oil engine** geared to sc. shaft driving 1 CP propeller Total Power: 1,290kW (1,754hp) 10.5kn MAN-B&W 6L21/31 1 x 4 Stroke 6 Cy. 210 x 310 1290kW (1754bhp) MAN B&W Diesel AG-Augsburg AuxGen: 2 x 160kW a.c, 1 x 216kW a.c Thrusters: 1 Thwart. FP thruster (f) Fuel: 240.0 (d.f.)

IMO / Call sign	Ship / Owner	Tonnage	Class	Construction	Type	Machinery
9297113 *UHPW* -	**ULUS PRIME** **Ulusland 1 Maritime Co Ltd** Albros Shipping & Trading Ltd Co (Albros Denizcilik ve Ticaret Ltd Sti) *Taganrog* *Russia* MMSI: 273438680 Official number: 030294	**2,614** 1,421 3,756	Class: RS	**2004-10 Çeksan Tersanesi — Turkey** Yd No: 20 Loa 89.73 Br ex 15.76 Dght 4.461 Lbp 84.44 Br md 15.60 Dpth 5.75 Welded, 1 dk	**(A31A2GX) General Cargo Ship** Grain: 4,877 Cranes: 1x14t	**1 oil engine** geared to sc. shaft driving 1 CP propeller Total Power: 1,290kW (1,754hp) 10.5kn MAN-B&W 6L21/31 1 x 4 Stroke 6 Cy. 210 x 310 1290kW (1754bhp) MAN B&W Diesel AG-West Germany AuxGen: 3 x 104kW a.c, 1 x 216kW a.c Fuel: 240.0 (d.f.)
9327176 *UBSH* -	**ULUS SKY** **Ulusland 1 Maritime Co Ltd** Albros Shipping & Trading Ltd Co (Albros Denizcilik ve Ticaret Ltd Sti) *Taganrog* *Russia* MMSI: 273319930	**2,607** 1,413 3,743	Class: RS	**2005-07 Çeksan Tersanesi — Turkey** Yd No: 26 Loa 89.73 Br ex 15.76 Dght 4.460 Lbp 84.44 Br md 15.60 Dpth 5.75 Welded, 1 dk	**(A31A2GX) General Cargo Ship** Grain: 4,877 Compartments: 1 Ho, ER	**1 oil engine** geared to sc. shaft driving 1 CP propeller Total Power: 1,290kW (1,754hp) 10.5kn MAN-B&W 6L21/31 1 x 4 Stroke 6 Cy. 210 x 310 1290kW (1754bhp) MAN B&W Diesel AG-Augsburg AuxGen: 3 x 104kW a.c, 1 x 216kW a.c Thrusters: 1 Thwart. FP thruster (f) Fuel: 240.0 (d.f.)
9297125 *UHPB* -	**ULUS STAR** **Ulusland 1 Maritime Co Ltd** Albros Shipping & Trading Ltd Co (Albros Denizcilik ve Ticaret Ltd Sti) *Taganrog* *Russia* MMSI: 273439680 Official number: 030307	**2,614** 1,421 3,737	Class: RS	**2005-03 Çeksan Tersanesi — Turkey** Yd No: 21 Loa 89.73 (BB) Br ex 15.76 Dght 4.460 Lbp 84.44 Br md 15.60 Dpth 5.75 Welded, 1 dk	**(A31A2GX) General Cargo Ship** Grain: 4,877 Compartments: 1 Ho, ER Ice Capable	**1 oil engine** geared to sc. shaft driving 1 CP propeller Total Power: 1,290kW (1,754hp) 10.5kn MAN-B&W 6L21/31 1 x 4 Stroke 6 Cy. 210 x 310 1290kW (1754bhp) MAN B&W Diesel AG-Augsburg AuxGen: 3 x 104kW, 1 x 216kW a.c Thrusters: 1 Thwart. FP thruster (f) Fuel: 240.0 (d.f.)
9361988 *UBPE3* -	**ULUS STREAM** **Ulusmarine Co Ltd** Albros Shipping & Trading Ltd Co (Albros Denizcilik ve Ticaret Ltd Sti) *Taganrog* *Russia* MMSI: 273313780	**2,604** 1,413 3,675	Class: RS	**2006-10 Çeksan Tersanesi — Turkey** Yd No: 29 Loa 89.61 (BB) Br ex 15.90 Dght 4.460 Lbp 84.44 Br md 15.60 Dpth 5.75 Welded, 1 dk	**(A31A2GX) General Cargo Ship** Grain: 4,740	**1 oil engine** reduction geared to sc. shaft driving 1 CP propeller Total Power: 1,470kW (1,999hp) 10.5kn MAN-B&W 6L28/32A 1 x 4 Stroke 6 Cy. 280 x 320 1470kW (1999bhp) MAN B&W Diesel A/S-Denmark AuxGen: 2 x 160kW a.c, 1 x 216kW a.c Thrusters: 1 Tunnel thruster (f) Fuel: 228.0 (d.f.)
9361976 *UGOM* -	**ULUS WIND** **Ulusmarine Co Ltd** Albros Shipping & Trading Ltd Co (Albros Denizcilik ve Ticaret Ltd Sti) *Taganrog* *Russia* MMSI: 273314540 Official number: 040440	**2,604** 1,413 3,689	Class: RS	**2006-06 Çeksan Tersanesi — Turkey** Yd No: 28 Loa 89.61 Br ex 15.95 Dght 4.460 Lbp 84.44 Br md 15.60 Dpth 5.75 Welded, 1 dk	**(A31A2GX) General Cargo Ship** Grain: 4,740 Compartments: 1 Ho, ER Ice Capable	**1 oil engine** reduction geared to sc. shaft driving 1 CP propeller Total Power: 1,470kW (1,999hp) 11.0kn MAN-B&W 6L28/32A 1 x 4 Stroke 6 Cy. 280 x 320 1470kW (1999bhp) MAN B&W Diesel A/S-Denmark AuxGen: 2 x 160kW a.c, 1 x 216kW a.c Fuel: 228.0 (d.f.)
8006799 - -	**ULUSAGHE** **South New Georgia Development Co** - *Honiara* *Solomon Islands*	*195* 120 250		**1981-07 Carpenters Industrial — Suva** Yd No: 26 Loa 27.01 Br ex - Dght 1.901 Lbp 23.73 Br md 7.50 Dpth 2.42 Welded	**(A36B2PL) Passenger/Landing Craft** Bow door/ramp	**2 oil engines** geared to sc. shafts driving 2 FP propellers Total Power: 250kW (340hp) Gardner 8LXB 2 x 4 Stroke 8 Cy. 121 x 152 each-125kW (170bhp) L. Gardner & Sons Ltd.-Manchester
7822160 *TCFQ* -	**ULUSOY-1** *ex* Falcon 1 *-1999* *ex* Xiao Shi Kou *-1999* **Karadeniz Roro ve Konteyner Tasimaciligi AS** Ulusoy Denizyollari Isletmeciligi AS (Ulusoy Sealines Management SA) *Istanbul* *Turkey* MMSI: 271000570	**13,867** 4,160 7,374	Class: LR (CC) **✠100A1** SS 05/2012 passenger/roll on - roll off cargo ship Ice Class 3 **✠LMC** **UMS** Eq.Ltr: E†; Cable: 577.5/64.0 U2	**1980-01 Kawasaki Heavy Industries Ltd — Sakaide KG** Yd No: 1315 Loa 146.55 (BB) Br ex 22.64 Dght 6.820 Lbp 130.00 Br md 22.60 Dpth 14.20 Welded, 2 dks	**(A36A2PR) Passenger/Ro-Ro Ship (Vehicles)** Passengers: 102 Quarter stern door/ramp (s. a.) Len: 34.00 Wid: 7.50 Swl: 100 Lane-Len: 948 Lane-Wid: 7.50 Lane-clr ht: 6.75 Trailers: 44 Bale: 18,900 TEU 435 Compartments: 1 Ho, ER Ice Capable	**1 oil engine** sr geared to sc. shaft driving 1 CP propeller Total Power: 7,760kW (10,550hp) 16.0kn MAN 10V52/55A 1 x Vee 4 Stroke 10 Cy. 520 x 550 7760kW (10550bhp) Kawasaki Heavy Industries Ltd-Japan AuxGen: 1 x 740kW 390V 50Hz a.c, 2 x 720kW 390V 50Hz a.c Thrusters: 1 Thwart. FP thruster (f) Fuel: 126.0 (d.f.) 644.0 (r.f.) 35.0pd
7822184 *TCFW* -	**ULUSOY-2** *ex* Falcon 2 *-1999* *ex* Bai He Kou *-1999* **Karadeniz Roro ve Konteyner Tasimaciligi AS** Ulusoy Denizyollari Isletmeciligi AS (Ulusoy Sealines Management SA) *Istanbul* *Turkey* MMSI: 271000571	**13,867** 4,160 7,374	Class: LR (TL) (CC) **✠100A1** SS 04/2009 passenger/roll on - roll off cargo ship Ice Class 3 **✠LMC** **UMS** Eq.Ltr: E†; Cable: 577.5/64.0 U2 (a)	**1980-05 Kawasaki Heavy Industries Ltd — Sakaide KG** Yd No: 1317 Loa 146.56 (BB) Br ex 22.64 Dght 6.810 Lbp 130.00 Br md 22.60 Dpth 14.20 Welded, 2 dks	**(A36A2PR) Passenger/Ro-Ro Ship (Vehicles)** Passengers: 102 Quarter stern door/ramp (s. a.) Len: 34.00 Wid: 7.50 Swl: 100 Lane-Len: 928 Lane-Wid: 7.50 Lane-clr ht: 6.75 Trailers: 42 Bale: 18,900 TEU 435 Compartments: 1 Ho, ER Ice Capable	**1 oil engine** sr geared to sc. shaft driving 1 CP propeller Total Power: 7,760kW (10,550hp) 16.0kn MAN 10V52/55A 1 x Vee 4 Stroke 10 Cy. 520 x 550 7760kW (10550bhp) Kawasaki Heavy Industries Ltd-Japan AuxGen: 1 x 740kW 390V 50Hz a.c, 2 x 720kW 390V 50Hz a.c Thrusters: 1 Thwart. FP thruster (f) Fuel: 126.0 (d.f.) 644.0 (r.f.) 35.0pd
8501464 *TCUV* -	**ULUSOY 5** *ex* Ulusoy-5 *-2011* *ex* UND Prenses *-2002* *ex* Mount Cameroon *-1995* *ex* Mercandian Nautic *-1989* **Ulusoy Deniz Tasimaciligi AS (Ulusoy Sea Transport SA)** Ulusoy Ro/Ro Isletmeleri AS (Ulusoy Ro/Ro Management SA) SatCom: Inmarsat C 427112240 *Istanbul* *Turkey* MMSI: 271000426 Official number: 6830	**19,689** 9,257 14,103	Class: LR (NV) **100A1** SS 08/2011 roll on - roll off cargo ship *IWS **LMC** **UMS**	**1987-12 Danyard A/S — Frederikshavn** Yd No: 423 Loa 163.81 (BB) Br ex - Dght 8.802 Lbp 148.62 Br md 23.51 Dpth 14.23 Welded, 3 dks	**(A35A2RR) Ro-Ro Cargo Ship** Passengers: cabins: 6; driver berths: 12 Stern door/ramp (p. a.) Len: 18.50 Wid: 7.30 Swl: 45 Stern door/ramp (s. a.) Len: 18.50 Wid: 7.30 Swl: 45 Side door/ramp (s) Len: 18.50 Wid: 7.30 Swl: 45 Lane-Len: 2760 Lane-Wid: 7.30 Lane-clr ht: 6.30 Trailers: 197 TEU 765 incl 72 ref C.	**1 oil engine** with flexible couplings & sr gearedto sc. shaft driving 1 CP propeller Total Power: 6,610kW (8,987hp) 16.0kn MaK 6M601AK 1 x 4 Stroke 6 Cy. 580 x 600 6610kW (8987bhp) Krupp MaK Maschinenbau GmbH-Kiel AuxGen: 1 x 1100kW 220/440V 60Hz a.c, 2 x 744kW 220/440V 60Hz a.c Thrusters: 1 Thwart. CP thruster (f); 1 Tunnel thruster (a) Fuel: 168.3 (d.f.) 897.8 (r.f.)
9458250 *TCSS9* -	**ULUSOY-8** **Ulusoy Denizyollari Isletmeciligi AS (Ulusoy Sealines Management SA)** - *Istanbul* *Turkey* MMSI: 271000973	**14,852** 7,662 22,000 T/cm 33.0	Class: BV	**2008-01 Zhejiang Pacific Shipbuilding Co Ltd — Wenling ZJ** Yd No: HQ-1001 Loa 159.90 Br ex - Dght 9.800 Lbp 149.80 Br md 24.00 Dpth 13.60 Welded, 1 dk	**(A21A2BC) Bulk Carrier** Grain: 29,100 Compartments: 5 Ho, ER 5 Ha: ER Cranes: 3x25t Ice Capable	**1 oil engine** driving 1 FP propeller Total Power: 5,180kW (7,043hp) 13.5kn MAN-B&W 7S35MC 1 x 2 Stroke 7 Cy. 350 x 1400 5180kW (7043bhp) STX Engine Co Ltd-South Korea
9498884 *TCTC7* -	**ULUSOY 9** *ex* New Century *-2008* **Ulusoy Denizcilik AS (Ulusoy Shipping SA)** Ulusoy Denizyollari Isletmeciligi AS (Ulusoy Sealines Management SA) *Istanbul* *Turkey* MMSI: 271002569 Official number: TUGS 1539	**8,557** 5,007 11,853	Class: BV (CC)	**2008-04 Zhoushan Zhaobao Shipbuilding & Repair Co Ltd — Zhoushan ZJ** Yd No: 066008 Loa 135.04 (BB) Br ex - Dght 8.000 Lbp 125.40 Br md 20.80 Dpth 11.00 Welded, 1 dk	**(A21A2BC) Bulk Carrier** Grain: 17,649 Compartments: 3 Ho, ER 3 Ha: (23.1 x 15.0) (24.5 x 15.0)ER (20.3 x 15.0) Cranes: 1x30t,2x25t	**1 oil engine** driving 1 FP propeller Total Power: 3,309kW (4,499hp) 11.0kn Hanshin LH46LA 1 x 4 Stroke 6 Cy. 460 x 880 3309kW (4499bhp) The Hanshin Diesel Works Ltd-Japan AuxGen: 3 x 448kW 400V 50Hz a.c, 1 x 350kW 400V 50Hz a.c Fuel: 611.0 14.0pd

9586411 *TCZU4* -	**ULUSOY 11** **Ulusoy Denizyollari Isletmeciligi AS (Ulusoy Sealines Management SA)** - *Istanbul* *Turkey* MMSI: 271042566 Official number: 26300	**43,717** 26,508 79,422 T/cm 71.9	Class: LR **✠100A1** SS 05/2011 bulk carrier CSR BC-A GRAB (20) Nos. 2, 4 & 6 holds may be empty ESP **ShipRight** (CM) *IWS LI Ice Class 1D Max/min draughts fwd 15.4/4.716m Max/min draights aft 15.702/6.934m Required power 5080.6kw, installed power 11620kw **✠LMC** **UMS** Eq.Ltr: Q†; Cable: 687.5/81.0 U3 (a)	**2011-05 Jiangsu Eastern Heavy Industry Co Ltd — Jingjiang JS** Yd No: 06C-015 Loa 229.00 (BB) Br ex 32.30 Dght 14.620 Lbp 222.00 Br md 32.26 Dpth 20.25 Welded, 1 dk	**(A21A2BC) Bulk Carrier** Grain: 97,000; Bale: 90,784 Compartments: 7 Ho, ER 7 Ha: ER Ice Capable	**1 oil engine** driving 1 FP propeller Total Power: 11,620kW (15,799hp) 14.0kn Wartsila 7RT-flex50 1 x 2 Stroke 7 Cy. 500 x 2050 11620kW (15799bhp) Diesel United Ltd.-Aioi AuxGen: 3 x 875kW 450V 60Hz a.c Boilers: AuxB (Comp) 8.2kgf/cm² (8.0bar)
9586423 *TCZU5* -	**ULUSOY-12** **Ulusoy Denizyollari Isletmeciligi AS (Ulusoy Sealines Management SA)** - *Istanbul* *Turkey* MMSI: 271042567 Official number: 26395	**43,717** 26,510 79,403 T/cm 71.9	Class: LR **✠100A1** SS 09/2011 bulk carrier CSR BC-A GRAB (20) Nos. 2, 4 & 6 holds may be empty ESP **ShipRight** (CM) *IWS LI Ice Class 1D Max/min draughts fwd 15.400/4.716m Max/min draughts aft 15.702/6.934m Power required 5081kw, power installed 11620kw **✠LMC** **UMS** Eq.Ltr: Q†; Cable: 687.5/81.0 U3 (a)	**2011-09 Jiangsu Eastern Heavy Industry Co Ltd — Jingjiang JS** Yd No: 06C-016 Loa 229.00 (BB) Br ex 32.30 Dght 14.620 Lbp 222.00 Br md 32.26 Dpth 20.25 Welded, 1 dk	**(A21A2BC) Bulk Carrier** Grain: 97,000; Bale: 90,784 Compartments: 7 Ho, ER 7 Ha: ER Ice Capable	**1 oil engine** driving 1 FP propeller Total Power: 11,620kW (15,799hp) 14.0kn Wartsila 7RT-flex50 1 x 2 Stroke 7 Cy. 500 x 2050 11620kW (15799bhp) Diesel United Ltd.-Aioi AuxGen: 3 x 700kW 450V 60Hz a.c Boilers: AuxB (Comp) 8.2kgf/cm² (8.0bar)
9506253 *TCUP3* -	**ULUSOY-14** **Ulusoy Lojistik Tasimacilik ve Konteyner Hizmetleri AS (Ulusoy Logistic Transportation & Container Services SA)** Ulusoy Denizyollari Isletmeciligi AS (Ulusoy Sealines Management SA) *Istanbul* *Turkey* MMSI: 271043164	**31,540** 9,463 15,000	Class: LR (NV) **100A1** SS 12/2012 TOC contemplated	**2012-12 Flensburger Schiffbau-Ges. mbH & Co. KG — Flensburg** Yd No: 753 Loa 208.30 (BB) Br ex - Dght 7.000 Lbp 197.39 Br md 26.00 Dpth 16.70 Welded, 3 dks	**(A35A2RR) Ro-Ro Cargo Ship** Stern door/ramp (centre) Len: 15.00 Wid: 17.00 Swl: 120 Lane-Len: 4094 Trailers: 283	**2 oil engines** reduction geared to sc. shafts driving 2 CP propellers Total Power: 19,200kW (26,104hp) 20.6kn MAN-B&W 8L48/60CR 2 x 4 Stroke 8 Cy. 480 x 600 each-9600kW (13052bhp) MAN B&W Diesel AG-Augsburg AuxGen: 2 x a.c, 2 x 1185kW a.c Thrusters: 1 Tunnel thruster (f)
9506265 *TCUP4* -	**ULUSOY-15** **Ulusoy Lojistik Tasimacilik ve Konteyner Hizmetleri AS (Ulusoy Logistic Transportation & Container Services SA)** Ulusoy Denizyollari Isletmeciligi AS (Ulusoy Sealines Management SA) *Istanbul* *Turkey* MMSI: 271043165	**31,540** 9,463 15,000	Class: LR (NV) **100A1** SS 01/2013 TOC contemplated	**2013-01 Flensburger Schiffbau-Ges. mbH & Co. KG — Flensburg** Yd No: 754 Loa 208.30 (BB) Br ex - Dght 7.000 Lbp 198.08 Br md 26.00 Dpth 16.70 Welded, 3 dks	**(A35A2RR) Ro-Ro Cargo Ship** Stern door/ramp (centre) Len: 15.00 Wid: 17.00 Swl: 120 Lane-Len: 4094 Trailers: 283	**2 oil engines** reduction geared to sc. shafts driving 2 CP propellers Total Power: 19,200kW (26,104hp) 20.6kn MAN-B&W 8L48/60CR 2 x 4 Stroke 8 Cy. 480 x 600 each-9600kW (13052bhp) MAN B&W Diesel AG-Augsburg AuxGen: 2 x 1185kW a.c, 2 x a.c Thrusters: 1 Tunnel thruster (f)
9019585 *SBRX* -	**ULVON** **Ornskoldsviks Buss AB** - *Ulvohamn* *Sweden* MMSI: 265585920	**172** 68 50		**1990-06 Moen Slip og Mekanisk Verksted AS — Kolvereid** Yd No: 35 Loa 28.00 Br ex - Dght 3.271 Lbp 24.00 Br md 7.20 Dpth 3.30 Welded	**(A36A2PR) Passenger/Ro-Ro Ship (Vehicles)** Passengers: unberthed: 200	**2 oil engines** driving 1 Directional propeller Total Power: 404kW (550hp) Scania DSI1440M 2 x Vee 4 Stroke 8 Cy. 127 x 140 each-202kW (275bhp) Saab Scania AB-Sweden Thrusters: 1 Thwart. FP thruster (f)
6524694 *LCTM* -	**ULVOS** *ex Nordhavn -1992* **Atle Dale P/R** - *Bergen* *Norway* MMSI: 257810500	**153** 45 203		**1965 AS Mjellem & Karlsen — Bergen** Yd No: 90 Loa 31.55 Br ex 6.71 Dght 2.763 Lbp 27.79 Br md 6.61 Dpth 3.26 Welded, 1 dk	**(A31A2GX) General Cargo Ship** Compartments: 1 Ho, ER 1 Ha: (5.4 x 2.8)ER Derricks: 1x4t	**1 oil engine** geared to sc. shaft driving 1 CP propeller Total Power: 416kW (566hp) Deutz SBA6M528 1 x 4 Stroke 6 Cy. 220 x 280 416kW (566bhp) Kloeckner Humboldt Deutz AG-West Germany AuxGen: 1 x 20kW 220V 50Hz a.c, 1 x 11kW 220V 50Hz a.c Fuel: 9.0 (d.f.)
8704860 *OWXU* -	**ULVSUND** **Government of The Kingdom of Denmark (Statens Veterinaere Institut)** - *Lindholm* *Denmark* MMSI: 219000804 Official number: A407	**235** 78 90	Class: BV	**1987 Soby Motorfabrik og Staalskibsvaerft A/S — Soby** Yd No: 70 Loa 30.21 Br ex - Dght 2.300 Lbp 30.03 Br md 9.01 Dpth 3.31 Welded, 1 dk	**(A37B2PS) Passenger Ship** Passengers: unberthed: 150 Ice Capable	**2 oil engines** driving 2 CP propellers Total Power: 564kW (766hp) 10.3kn Alpha 2 x 4 Stroke each-282kW (383bhp) MAN B&W Diesel A/S-Denmark
8996712 - -	**ULYSSE** **Government of The Republic of Tunisia (Ministere de l'Equipment)** - *Houmet Essouk* *Tunisia*	**236** 84 420	Class: BV (NV)	**2000-03 Societe de ConstructionsIndustrielles et Navales (SCIN) — Sfax** Yd No: 198 Loa 36.00 Br ex 11.03 Dght 1.630 Lbp 34.56 Br md 11.00 Dpth 3.00 Welded, 1 dk	**(A36A2PR) Passenger/Ro-Ro Ship (Vehicles)**	**4 oil engines** reduction geared to sc. shafts driving 4 Directional propellers Total Power: 552kW (752hp) Deutz F10L413F 4 x Vee 4 Stroke 10 Cy. 125 x 130 each-138kW (188bhp) Deutz AG-Koeln AuxGen: 1 x a.c
9175652 *FNUL* -	**ULYSSE** **Bourbon Offshore Surf SAS** - *Marseille* *France (FIS)* MMSI: 228050000 Official number: 923623N	**2,341** 702 2,514	Class: BV	**1998-11 Chantiers Piriou — Concarneau** Yd No: 197 Loa 69.66 Br ex - Dght 6.100 Lbp 61.50 Br md 17.20 Dpth 7.20 Welded, 1 dk	**(B21B20A) Anchor Handling Tug Supply** Passengers: berths: 30 Cranes: 1x5t	**4 oil engines** with clutches, flexible couplings & sr geared to sc. shafts driving 2 CP propellers Total Power: 11,476kW (15,604hp) Normo BRM-6 4 x 4 Stroke 6 Cy. 320 x 360 each-2869kW (3901bhp) Ulstein Bergen AS-Norway AuxGen: 2 x 1760kW 440/220V 60Hz a.c, 2 x 250kW 440/220V 60Hz a.c Thrusters: 1 Retract. directional thruster (f); 1 Thwart. FP thruster (f); 1 Tunnel thruster (a) Fuel: 1082.3 (d.f.) 47.0pd
9142459 *TSMU* -	**ULYSSE** *ex Ulyssee -1997* **Compagnie Tunisienne de Navigation SA (COTUNAV)** - SatCom: Inmarsat B 367224810 *La Goulette* *Tunisia* MMSI: 672248000 Official number: TG845	**17,907** 5,372 5,250 T/cm 32.6	Class: BV	**1997-07 SSW Faehr- und Spezialschiffbau GmbH — Bremerhaven** Yd No: 1093 Loa 161.50 (BB) Br ex - Dght 6.018 Lbp 146.00 Br md 25.80 Dpth 7.70 Welded, 4 dks, incl. 1 hoistable dk	**(A36A2PR) Passenger/Ro-Ro Ship (Vehicles)** Passengers: cabins: 50; berths: 100; driver berths: 100 Stern door/ramp Len: 12.00 Wid: 11.00 Swl: 132 Lane-Len: 1950 Trailers: 150 Ice Capable	**4 oil engines** with clutches, flexible couplings & sr geared to sc. shafts driving 2 CP propellers Total Power: 14,000kW (19,036hp) 20.0kn Sulzer 6ZAL40S 4 x 4 Stroke 6 Cy. 400 x 560 each-3500kW (4759bhp) Zaklady Urzadzen Technicznych'Zgoda' SA-Poland AuxGen: 2 x 650kW 230/400V 50Hz a.c, 2 x 1248kW 230/400V 50Hz a.c Thrusters: 2 Thwart. CP thruster (f) Fuel: 246.6 (d.f.) (Heating Coils) 997.2 (r.f.)

6618407 *5NLI* -	**ULYSSES** *ex* Abeille No. 14 *-2000* **GFL Marine Services Ltd** - *Nigeria* Official number: SR691	**232** 69 -	Class: (BV)	**1966 Muetzelfeldtwerft GmbH — Cuxhaven** Yd No: 171 Loa 33.23 Br ex 8.39 Dght 3.353 Lbp 29.57 Br md 8.01 Dpth 3.97 Welded, 1 dk	**(B32A2ST) Tug**	**1 oil engine** geared to sc. shaft driving 1 FP propeller Total Power: 736kW (1,001hp) 12.0kn Deutz SBV8M545 1 x 4 Stroke 8 Cy. 320 x 450 736kW (1001bhp) Kloeckner Humboldt Deutz AG-West Germany AuxGen: 3 x 85kW 220V d.c Fuel: 81.5 (d.f.)
1010959 *2FHQ5* -	**ULYSSES** **Gramvale Services Ltd** Fraser Worldwide SAM *Douglas* *Isle of Man (British)* MMSI: 235091361 Official number: 743901	**878** 263 190	Class: LR ✠**100A1** SS 04/2012 SSC Yacht, mono, G6 **LMC** Cable: 330.0/20.5 U3 (a)	**2012-04 Azimut-Benetti SpA — Livorno** Yd No: FB251 Loa 56.10 (BB) Br ex - Dght 3.100 Lbp 47.27 Br md 10.40 Dpth 5.45 Welded, 1 dk	**(X11A2YP) Yacht**	**2 oil engines** with clutches, flexible couplings & sr reverse geared to sc. shafts driving 2 FP propellers Total Power: 2,760kW (3,752hp) 16.0kn Caterpillar 3512B 2 x Vee 4 Stroke 12 Cy. 170 x 215 each-1380kW (1876bhp) Caterpillar Inc-USA AuxGen: 2 x 200kW 230V 50Hz a.c
9364203 *V2CB3* -	**ULYSSES** *ex* Maruba Pampero *-2010* *completed as* Ulysses *-2006* **Schiffahrtsgesellschaft ms 'Ulysses' mbH & Co KG** Hansa Shipping GmbH & Co KG *Saint John's* *Antigua & Barbuda* MMSI: 304969000 Official number: 4179	**27,061** 12,221 34,393	Class: GL	**2006-09 'Crist' Sp z oo — Gdansk** (Aft & pt cargo sections) Yd No: 381 **2006-09 SSW Schichau Seebeck Shipyard GmbH — Bremerhaven** (Fwd & pt cargo sections) Yd No: 2026 Loa 212.20 (BB) Br ex - Dght 11.400 Lbp 199.95 Br md 29.80 Dpth 16.70 Welded, 1 dk	**(A33A2CC) Container Ship (Fully Cellular)** Double Bottom Entire Compartment Length TEU 2496 C Ho 958 TEU C Dk 1538 TEU incl 400 ref C Cranes: 3x45t	**1 oil engine** driving 1 FP propeller Total Power: 21,771kW (29,600hp) 22.0kn MAN-B&W 7S70MC-C 1 x 2 Stroke 7 Cy. 700 x 2800 21771kW (29600bhp) H Cegielski Poznan SA-Poland AuxGen: 4 x 1200kW 450V a.c Thrusters: 1 Tunnel thruster (f)
9214991 *C4HP2* -	**ULYSSES** **Irish Ferries Ltd** Irish Ferries Ltd *Limassol* *Cyprus* MMSI: 209952000 Official number: 9214991	**50,938** 15,713 9,665	Class: LR ✠**100A1** CS 02/2011 roro cargo/passenger ferry *IWS LI Ice Class 1A Max draught midship 6.747m Max/min draught aft 6.747/5.813m Max/min draught forward 6.747/4.413m ✠**LMC** **UMS** Eq.Ltr: O†; Cable: 660.0/78.0 U3 (a)	**2001-02 Aker Finnyards Oy — Rauma** Yd No: 429 Loa 209.08 (BB) Br ex 31.84 Dght 6.400 Lbp 190.80 Br md 31.20 Dpth 9.90 Welded, 12 dks incl. 1 hoistable	**(A36A2PR) Passenger/Ro-Ro Ship (Vehicles)** Passengers: unberthed: 1647; cabins: 157; berths: 228 Bow door/ramp Len: 20.00 Wid: 6.00 Swl: - Stern door/ramp (p) Len: 8.00 Wid: 10.15 Swl: - Stern door/ramp (s) Len: 8.00 Wid: 10.15 Swl: - Lane-Len: 4106 Lane-Wid: 3.10 Lane-clr ht: 5.20 Cars: 1,342 Ice Capable	**4 oil engines** with clutches, flexible couplings & sr geared to sc. shafts driving 2 CP propellers Total Power: 31,200kW (42,420hp) 22.0kn MaK 9M43 4 x 4 Stroke 9 Cy. 430 x 610 each-7800kW (10605bhp) MaK Motoren GmbH & Co. KG-Kiel AuxGen: 4 x 2635kW 6600V 50Hz a.c, 3 x 1450kW 400V 50Hz a.c Boilers: 4 TOH (ex.g.) 11.2kgf/cm² (11.0bar), TOH (o.f.) 11.2kgf/cm² (11.0bar) Thrusters: 3 Thwart. CP thruster (f); 1 Tunnel thruster (a)
8878063 *HQWC8* -	**ULYSSES I** *ex* North Star *-2002* *ex* Gnat *-2002* **Pamela Maritime Co** - *San Lorenzo* *Honduras* MMSI: 334123000 Official number: L-3827804	*279* 84 -		**1970-04 Charles D. Holmes & Co. Ltd. — Beverley** Yd No: 1019 Converted From: Munitions Carrier-1970 Loa 34.10 Br ex - Dght - Lbp - Br md 8.50 Dpth 3.40 Welded, 1 dk	**(B34R2QY) Supply Tender**	**1 oil engine** geared to sc. shaft driving 1 FP propeller Total Power: 485kW (659hp) 12.0kn Blackstone ERS8M 1 x 4 Stroke 8 Cy. 222 x 292 485kW (659bhp) Lister Blackstone Marine Ltd.-Dursley
5372719 - -	**ULZAMA** - - -	*253* 114 -	Class: (BV)	**1958 Enrique Lorenzo y Cia SA — Vigo** Yd No: 232 Loa 37.98 Br ex 6.89 Dght 3.709 Lbp 33.38 Br md 6.80 Dpth 4.02 Riveted\Welded, 1 dk	**(B11A2FT) Trawler** 3 Ha:	**1 oil engine** driving 1 FP propeller Total Power: 515kW (700hp) 11.5kn Krupps 1 x 4 Stroke 8 Cy. 295 x 420 515kW (700bhp) La Maquinista Terrestre y Mar (MTM)-Spain Fuel: 48.5 (d.f.)
9281114 *HSB4608* -	**UM ADVANCER** *ex* Meothai 1 *-2013* *ex* Pacific Copper *-2011* *ex* Hadi XV *-2003* **Uniwise Offshore Ltd** Miclyn Express Offshore Pte Ltd *Bangkok* *Thailand* MMSI: 567437000 Official number: 540002267	**1,595** 478 1,780	Class: BV (AB)	**2003-01 Keppel Singmarine Pte Ltd — Singapore** Yd No: 258 Loa 60.00 Br ex - Dght 4.800 Lbp 53.90 Br md 16.00 Dpth 5.50 Welded, 1 dk	**(B21B20A) Anchor Handling Tug Supply**	**2 oil engines** reduction geared to sc. shafts driving 2 CP propellers Total Power: 4,050kW (5,506hp) 13.0kn Deutz SBV9M628 2 x 4 Stroke 9 Cy. 240 x 280 each-2025kW (2753bhp) Deutz AG-Koeln AuxGen: 2 x 350kW 440/240V 60Hz a.c, 2 x 450kW 440/240V 60Hz a.c Thrusters: 1 Tunnel thruster (f); 1 Tunnel thruster (a) Fuel: 486.9 (r.f.)
8711186 - -	**UM AL QURA** *ex* Erasun *-1993* - -	**278** 119 304	Class: (BV)	**1988-02 S.A. Balenciaga — Zumaya** Yd No: 326 Loa 39.60 Br ex - Dght 3.801 Lbp 32.60 Br md 8.80 Dpth 5.87 Welded, 1 dk	**(B11B2FV) Fishing Vessel** Ins: 320	**1 oil engine** driving 1 CP propeller Total Power: 736kW (1,001hp) 11.8kn M.T.M. TI829C 1 x 4 Stroke 8 Cy. 295 x 420 736kW (1001bhp) La Maquinista Terrestre y Mar (MTM)-Spain
8619443 *5NQY8* -	**UM BALWA** *ex* Al Badiyah *-2013* **Sea Transport Services Nigeria Ltd** Oceanic Shipping Services Pvt Ltd *Lagos* *Nigeria* MMSI: 657966000 Official number: 377863	**26,356** 8,643 35,644 T/cm 51.0	Class: LR ✠**100A1** SS 05/2009 Double Hull oil tanker MARPOL 13G (1) (c) ESP ✠**LMC** **UMS IGS** Eq.Ltr: M†; Cable: 632.5/73.0 U3	**1989-05 Samsung Shipbuilding & Heavy Industries Co Ltd — Geoje** Yd No: 1058 Loa 182.94 (BB) Br ex 32.23 Dght 9.766 Lbp 173.00 Br md 32.20 Dpth 16.53 Welded, 1 dk	**(A13B2TP) Products Tanker** Double Hull (13F) Liq: 44,801; Liq (Oil): 44,800 Compartments: 8 Ta, 1 Slop Ta, 2 Wing Slop Ta, ER 8 Cargo Pump (s): 8x750m³/hr Manifold: Bow/CM: 92.8m	**1 oil engine** driving 1 FP propeller Total Power: 6,716kW (9,131hp) 13.5kn B&W 5L60MC 1 x 2 Stroke 5 Cy. 600 x 1944 6716kW (9131bhp) Korea Heavy Industries & ConstrCo Ltd (HANJUNG)-South Korea AuxGen: 1 x 850kW 450V 60Hz a.c, 2 x 820kW 450V 60Hz a.c Boilers: e 11.2kgf/cm² (11.0bar), AuxB (o.f.) 9.2kgf/cm² (9.0bar) Fuel: 234.0 (d.f.) 2293.0 (r.f.) 23.5pd
9645310 - -	**UM QASR** *ex* Xing Hang Jun 2 *-2013* **General Company for Ports of Iraq (GCPI)** -	**9,251** 2,775 9,073	Class: (CC)	**2012-06 Zhejiang Fangyuan Ship Industry Co Ltd — Linhai ZJ** Yd No: FY201007 Loa 132.44 (BB) Br ex - Dght 6.800 Lbp 119.20 Br md 22.00 Dpth 9.20 Welded, 1 dk	**(B33B2DT) Trailing Suction Hopper Dredger**	**2 oil engines** reduction geared to sc. shafts driving 2 Propellers Total Power: 8,826kW (12,000hp) 13.0kn Daihatsu 8DKM-36 2 x 4 Stroke 8 Cy. 360 x 480 each-4413kW (6000bhp) Daihatsu Diesel Manufacturing Co Lt-Japan AuxGen: 2 x 2050kW 690V a.c, 2 x 560kW 400V a.c Thrusters: 1 Tunnel thruster (f)
9643362 *HSB4721* -	**UM SUPPORTER** *ex* PSV Shoveler *-2012* *ex* AHT Shoveler *-2012* **Uniwise Offshore Ltd** - *Bangkok* *Thailand* MMSI: 567467000	**2,259** 677 1,940	Class: BV (AB)	**2012-11 POET (China) Shipbuilding & Engineering Co Ltd — Taixing JS** (Hull) Yd No: (1475) **2012-11 Pacific Ocean Engineering & Trading Pte Ltd (POET) — Singapore** Yd No: 1475 Loa 66.00 (BB) Br ex 17.20 Dght 4.830 Lbp 58.50 Br md 16.00 Dpth 6.20 Welded, 1 dk	**(B21A20S) Platform Supply Ship** Cranes: 1	**2 oil engines** reduction geared to sc. shafts driving 2 CP propellers Total Power: 3,840kW (5,220hp) 10.5kn Yanmar 6EY26 2 x 4 Stroke 6 Cy. 260 x 385 each-1920kW (2610bhp) Yanmar Diesel Engine Co Ltd-Japan AuxGen: 2 x 900kW 440V 60Hz a.c, 3 x 590kW 440V 60Hz a.c Thrusters: 2 Tunnel thruster (f); 1 Tunnel thruster (a) Fuel: 618.0 (r.f.)
8958796 *YGSG*	**UMA KALADA** **Government of The Republic of Indonesia (Direktorat Jenderal Perhubungan Darat - Ministry of Land Communications)** PT ASDP Indonesia Ferry (Persero) - Angkutan Sungai Danau & Penyeberangan *Jakarta* *Indonesia* MMSI: 525019442	**496** 148 -	Class: KI	**1999-08 P.T. Adiluhung Sarana Segara Industri — Bangkalan** Loa 45.50 Br ex - Dght 2.240 Lbp 40.15 Br md 12.00 Dpth 3.20 Welded, 1 dk	**(A36A2PR) Passenger/Ro-Ro Ship (Vehicles)** Bow ramp (centre) Stern ramp (centre)	**2 oil engines** reduction geared to sc. shafts driving 2 FP propellers Total Power: 986kW (1,340hp) 10.5kn Yanmar 8LAAM-DTE 2 x Vee 4 Stroke 8 Cy. 148 x 165 each-493kW (670bhp) (made 1999) Yanmar Diesel Engine Co Ltd-Japan
8333518 - -	**UMALIA I** **Urmila & Co Pvt Ltd** - *Mumbai* *India* Official number: 1911	*410* 258 599	Class: IR (AB)	**1975-07 G.R. Engineering — Goa** Yd No: 101 Loa 47.50 Br ex - Dght 2.453 Lbp 46.00 Br md 10.25 Dpth 3.00 Welded, 1 dk	**(A31A2GX) General Cargo Ship**	**2 oil engines** reverse reduction geared to sc. shafts driving 2 FP propellers Total Power: 320kW (436hp) 7.0kn Cummins NT-743-M 2 x 4 Stroke 6 Cy. 130 x 152 each-160kW (218bhp) Kirloskar Cummins Ltd-India AuxGen: 2 x 3kW a.c Fuel: 10.0 (d.f.)

Vessel	Tonnage	Class	Builder / Dimensions	Type / Cargo	Machinery
8010946 **UMALKHAIR** *XUGS7* *ex* Zenith Focus *-2012* *ex* Fortuna *-1996* - *ex* Shinakisan Maru *-1995* **Red Sea Livestock Line SA** GMZ Ship Management Co SA SatCom: Inmarsat C 444052319 *Phnom Penh* *Cambodia* MMSI: 514072000 Official number: 0280233	**2,035** 1,162 2,996	Class: (BV) (NK)	**1980**-04 **Kanda Zosensho K.K. — Kawajiri** Yd No: 253 Loa 93.00 Br ex 12.32 Dght 5.492 Lbp 85.02 Br md 12.31 Dpth 6.91 Welded, 1 dk	**(A31A2GX) General Cargo Ship** Grain: 4,264; Bale: 3,936 Compartments: 1 Ho, ER 2 Ha: 2 (26.2 x 7.6)ER	**1 oil engine** driving 1 FP propeller Total Power: 2,354kW (3,200hp) 14.0kn Hanshin 6LU50A 1 x 4 Stroke 6 Cy. 500 x 800 2354kW (3200bhp) Hanshin Nainenki Kogyo-Japan AuxGen: 2 x 96kW 225V a.c Fuel: 32.5 (d.f.) 200.0 (r.f.) 9.0pd
8306826 **UMANG** *A8PF6* *ex* Sveti Vlaho *-2008* *ex* Thalassini Doxa *-1990* - *ex* Carol *-1987* *ex* Garoufalia *-1987* **Umang Shipping Services Ltd** ArcelorMittal Shipping Ltd *Monrovia* *Liberia* MMSI: 636013767 Official number: 13767	**25,063** 13,219 39,443 T/cm 49.1	Class: LR (CS) (JR) ✠ **100A1** SS 07/2012 bulk carrier strengthened for heavy cargoes, Nos. 2 & 4 holds may be empty container cargoes in cargo holds & on U dk and hatch covers ESP ESN-Hold 1 LI ✠ **LMC** **UMS** Eq.Ltr: L†; Cable: 632.5/70.0 U3 (a)	**1984**-04 **Hitachi Zosen Corp — Maizuru KY** Yd No: 4764 Loa 188.93 (BB) Br ex 30.66 Dght 11.024 Lbp 179.00 Br md 30.60 Dpth 16.01 Welded, 1 dk	**(A21A2BC) Bulk Carrier** Grain: 52,370; Bale: 51,323 TEU 1000 incl 50 ref C. Compartments: 5 Ho, ER 5 Ha: 5 (18.7 x 15.0)ER Cranes: 5x25t	**1 oil engine** driving 1 FP propeller Total Power: 9,562kW (13,000hp) 14.0kn B&W 6L67GBE 1 x 2 Stroke 6 Cy. 670 x 1700 9562kW (13000bhp) Hitachi Zosen Corp-Japan AuxGen: 3 x 660kW 450V 60Hz a.c Boilers: e 13.0kgf/cm² (12.7bar), AuxB (o.f.) 8.5kgf/cm² (8.3bar) Fuel: 243.0 (d.f.) 2241.5 (r.f.)
9600310 **UMANG** *AWDI* - **Government of The Republic of India (Navy Department)** - *India* MMSI: 419000808	**323** 97 -	Class: IR	**2013**-09 **Tebma Shipyards Ltd — Udupi** Yd No: 152 Loa 32.90 Br ex - Dght 4.000 Lbp - Br md 9.50 Dpth - Welded, 1 dk	**(B32A2ST) Tug**	**2 oil engines** reduction geared to sc. shafts driving 2 Propellers
9521411 **UMAR 1** *9HA2498* - **United Mariners Corp** CSM Denizcilik Ltd Sti (Chemfleet) *Valletta* *Malta* MMSI: 248751000 Official number: 9521411	**3,280** 1,458 4,916 T/cm 12.6	Class: BV	**2010**-05 **Torgem Gemi Insaat Sanayii ve Ticaret a.s. — Tuzla, Istanbul** Yd No: 79 Loa 96.75 (BB) Br ex - Dght 6.070 Lbp 94.00 Br md 15.00 Dpth 7.40 Welded, 1 dk	**(A12B2TR) Chemical/Products Tanker** Double Hull (13F) Liq: 5,021; Liq (Oil): 5,274 Cargo Heating Coils Compartments: 12 Wing Ta, ER 12 Cargo Pump (s): 12x150m³/hr Manifold: Bow/CM: 44.1m	**1 oil engine** reduction geared to sc. shaft driving 1 CP propeller Total Power: 1,960kW (2,665hp) 14.0kn MAN-B&W 8L28/32A 1 x 4 Stroke 8 Cy. 280 x 320 1960kW (2665bhp) STX Engine Co Ltd-South Korea AuxGen: 3 x 360kW 440V 60Hz a.c, 1 x 720kW 440V 60Hz a.c Thrusters: 1 Tunnel thruster (f) Fuel: 45.0 (d.f.) 220.0 (r.f.)
8851015 **UMATILLA** - - **Shaver Transportation Co** - *Portland, OR* *United States of America* MMSI: 367513210 Official number: 613398	*136* 93 -		**1979** **Nichols Boat & Barge — Vancouver, Wa** Yd No: P-22 Loa - Br ex - Dght - Lbp 18.41 Br md 7.32 Dpth 2.99 Welded, 1 dk	**(B32A2ST) Tug**	**1 oil engine** driving 1 FP propeller Total Power: 1,030kW (1,400hp)
8402864 **UMAY** *E5U2657* *ex* Lord Hinton *-2013* - **Umay Sea Services Ltd** Beyaz Denizcilik Ltd Sti *Avatiu* *Cook Islands* MMSI: 518710000 Official number: 1746	**14,201** 6,275 22,447 T/cm 34.2	✠ **100A1** SS 09/2010 ✠ **LMC** **UMS** Eq.Ltr: F†; Cable: 577.5/66.0 U2	**1986**-02 **Govan Shipbuilders Ltd — Glasgow** Yd No: 264 Loa 154.87 (BB) Br ex 24.54 Dght 9.016 Lbp 148.01 Br md 24.50 Dpth 13.52 Welded, 1 dk	**(A31A2GX) General Cargo Ship** Double Sides Entire Compartment Length Grain: 26,147; Bale: 25,522 Compartments: 4 Ho, ER 4 Ha: 2 (20.0 x 17.0)2 (19.2 x 17.0)ER	**1 oil engine** with clutches, flexible couplings & sr geared to sc. shaft driving 1 CP propeller Total Power: 4,354kW (5,920hp) 12.5kn Mirrlees KMR8MK3 1 x 4 Stroke 8 Cy. 400 x 457 4354kW (5920bhp) Mirrlees Blackstone Ltd-Dursley AuxGen: 1 x 1300kW 415V 50Hz a.c, 2 x 400kW 415V 50Hz a.c Thrusters: 1 Thwart. CP thruster (f); 1 Tunnel thruster (a) Fuel: 28.5 (d.f.) (Part Heating Coils) 292.0 (r.f.)
9217395 **UMAY** *YYV3751* - **Latin American Petroleum Services de Venezuela SA** Global Shipmanagement CA *Pampatar* *Venezuela* Official number: ARSH 11444	**167** 97	Class: BV (AB)	**2000**-05 **Yardimci Tersanesi A.S. — Tuzla** Yd No: 20 Loa 21.30 Br ex - Dght - Lbp 19.50 Br md 7.80 Dpth 3.15 Welded, 1 dk	**(B32A2ST) Tug**	**2 oil engines** reduction geared to sc. shafts driving 2 FP propellers Total Power: 1,566kW (2,130hp) 11.0kn Cummins KTA-38-M2 2 x Vee 4 Stroke 12 Cy. 159 x 159 each-783kW (1065bhp) Cummins Engine Co Ltd-United Kingdom
9476484 **UMBERTO D'AMATO** *ICRX* - **Perseveranza SpA di Navigazione** - *Naples* *Italy* MMSI: 247299600	**51,255** 31,192 93,263 T/cm 80.9	Class: AB RI	**2011**-09 **Jiangsu Newyangzi Shipbuilding Co Ltd — Jingjiang JS** Yd No: YZJ2006-839 Loa 229.20 (BB) Br ex - Dght 14.900 Lbp 222.00 Br md 38.00 Dpth 20.70 Welded, 1 dk	**(A21A2BC) Bulk Carrier** Grain: 110,300 Compartments: 7 Ho, ER 7 Ha: ER	**1 oil engine** driving 1 FP propeller Total Power: 13,560kW (18,436hp) 14.1kn MAN-B&W 6S60MC-C 1 x 2 Stroke 6 Cy. 600 x 2400 13560kW (18436bhp) AuxGen: 3 x 730kW a.c
8515972 **UMBOI** *P24070* - **Kambang Holding Ltd** Lutheran Shipping (LUSHIP) *Madang* *Papua New Guinea* Official number: 000377	*380* - 450	Class: (AB)	**1985**-11 **Singmarine Shipyard Pte Ltd — Singapore** Yd No: 049 Loa - Br ex - Dght 2.939 Lbp 41.08 Br md 8.50 Dpth 3.51 Welded, 1 dk	**(A31A2GX) General Cargo Ship** Compartments: 1 Ho, ER 1 Ha: (15.0 x 5.0)ER	**2 oil engines** reverse reduction geared to sc. shafts driving 2 FP propellers Total Power: 368kW (500hp) 10.0kn Gardner 8L3B 2 x 4 Stroke 8 Cy. 140 x 197 each-184kW (250bhp) L. Gardner & Sons Ltd.-Manchester AuxGen: 2 x 30kW a.c
9554652 **UMBRA** *ZCEB9* - **Beta Maritime Ltd II** - *Hamilton* *Bermuda (British)* MMSI: 310592000 Official number: 16562E	**464** 139 365	Class: LR (BV) **100A1** SS 05/2010 SSC Yacht mono G6 **LMC** **UMS**	**2010**-05 **Song Cam Shipyard — Haiphong** (Hull) Yd No: (547209) **2010**-05 **B.V. Scheepswerf Damen — Gorinchem** Yd No: 547209 Converted From: Supply Tender-2010 Loa 50.03 Br ex 9.20 Dght 3.200 Lbp 49.00 Br md 9.00 Dpth 4.70 Welded, 1 dk	**(X11A2YP) Yacht**	**4 oil engines** reduction geared to sc. shafts driving 4 FP propellers Total Power: 5,280kW (7,180hp) 25.0kn M.T.U. 12V4000M60 4 x Vee 4 Stroke 12 Cy. 165 x 190 each-1320kW (1795bhp) MTU Friedrichshafen GmbH-Friedrichshafen Thrusters: 2 Tunnel thruster (f)
7052571 **UMBRINA** *UAKE* - **MTR Co Ltd (OOO 'MTR')** - *Murmansk* *Russia* MMSI: 273210500 Official number: 700276	**604** 200 386	Class: (RS)	**1970**-09 **Yaroslavskiy Sudostroitelnyy Zavod — Yaroslavl** Yd No: 17 Converted From: Fishery Patrol Vessel Loa 54.23 Br ex 9.38 Dght 3.901 Lbp 48.87 Br md - Dpth 4.75 Welded, 1 dk	**(B12B2FC) Fish Carrier** Bale: 418 Compartments: 2 Ho, ER 2 Ha: 2 (1.5 x 1.6) Derricks: 1x2t	**1 oil engine** driving 1 FP propeller Total Power: 588kW (799hp) 11.8kn S.K.L. 8NVD48AU 1 x 4 Stroke 8 Cy. 320 x 480 588kW (799bhp) VEB Schwermaschinenbau "KarlLiebknecht" (SKL)-Magdeburg AuxGen: 3 x 100kW a.c Fuel: 158.0 (d.f.)
9672387 **UMBUL MAS** *POYJ* *ex* Boda 5 *-2012* - **PT Pelayaran Tempuran Emas Tbk (TEMAS Line)** - *Indonesia* MMSI: 525019101	**6,640** 3,718 8,180	Class: CC	**2012**-11 **Ningbo Boda Shipbuilding Co Ltd — Xiangshan County ZJ** Yd No: BD1205 Loa 119.90 (BB) Br ex - Dght 5.200 Lbp 115.00 Br md 21.80 Dpth 7.30 Welded, 1 dk	**(A33A2CC) Container Ship (Fully Cellular)** TEU 537	**1 oil engine** reduction geared to sc. shaft driving 1 FP propeller Total Power: 2,060kW (2,801hp) 10.5kn Thrusters: 1 Tunnel thruster (f)
8135617 **UME MARU** *JM5165* - **Sasebo City** - *Sasebo, Nagasaki* *Japan* Official number: 124748	*161* - 220		**1982**-05 **Maebata Zosen Tekko K.K. — Sasebo** Yd No: 150 Loa - Br ex - Dght 2.520 Lbp 27.31 Br md 6.80 Dpth 3.00 Welded, 1 dk	**(A14A2LO) Water Tanker**	**1 oil engine** driving 1 FP propeller
9184213 **UMEKO** *3FJP9* - **North Star Shipholding SA** COSCO Container Lines Co Ltd (COSCON) SatCom: Inmarsat C 435746110 *Panama* *Panama* MMSI: 357461000 Official number: 2636499D	**8,957** 4,132 9,515 T/cm 24.6	Class: NK	**1999**-05 **Kyokuyo Shipyard Corp — Shimonoseki YC** Yd No: 423 Loa 138.03 (BB) Br ex - Dght 7.817 Lbp 128.00 Br md 22.40 Dpth 11.30 Welded, 1 dk	**(A33A2CC) Container Ship (Fully Cellular)** TEU 564 C Ho 214 TEU C Dk 350 incl 222 ref C Compartments: 6 Cell Ho, ER 11 Ha: (12.6 x 13.6)Tappered 2 (12.6 x 8.3)Tappered 8 (12.6 x 8.3)ER	**1 oil engine** driving 1 FP propeller Total Power: 7,208kW (9,800hp) 17.5kn B&W 6S46MC-C 1 x 2 Stroke 6 Cy. 460 x 1932 7208kW (9800bhp) Kawasaki Heavy Industries Ltd-Japan Fuel: 41.4 (d.f.) (Heating Coils) 924.1 (r.f.) 36.0pd

IMO / Call sign	Name / Owner	Tonnage	Class	Build / Dimensions	Type / Capacity	Machinery
9254161 *JPKZ* TK1-1355	**UMESATO** **Toko Senpaku KK** *Tokyo* *Japan* MMSI: 432195000 Official number: 137101	*499* - 611 T/cm 4.5		**2001-11 Miho Zosensho K.K. — Shimizu** Yd No: 1495 Loa 64.65 (BB) Br ex 9.32 Dght 4.070 Lbp 58.00 Br md 9.30 Dpth 4.30 Welded, 1 dk	**(B12D2FP) Fishery Patrol Vessel**	**1 oil engine** with clutches, flexible couplings & sr reverse geared to sc. shaft driving 1 FP propeller Total Power: 1,839kW (2,500hp) 15.7kn Akasaka 6U28AK 1 x 4 Stroke 6 Cy. 280 x 380 1839kW (2500bhp) Akasaka Tekkosho KK (Akasaka DieselLtd)-Japan AuxGen: 2 x 240kW 220V 60Hz a.c Thrusters: 1 Thwart. FP thruster (f) Fuel: 276.4 (r.f.) (Heating Coils) 7.1pd
8103652 *3EX06* -	**UMG PLUTO** *ex* Nontalee *-2013* *ex* Siam Pavinee *-2008* *ex* Gillion *-2002* *ex* Bright Acme *-2002* *ex* Soyo Maru *-1997* **Mazuma Marine Inc** - *Panama* *Panama* MMSI: 356632000 Official number: 4537413	**2,539** 1,172 4,125	Class: (NK)	**1981-07 Imamura Zosen — Kure** Yd No: 273 Loa 96.25 (BB) Br ex 14.25 Dght 6.595 Lbp 89.01 Br md 14.00 Dpth 7.32 Welded, 1 dk	**(A13B2TP) Products Tanker** Liq: 4,299; Liq (Oil): 4,299 Compartments: 10 Ta, ER	**1 oil engine** driving 1 FP propeller Total Power: 2,427kW (3,300hp) 12.0kn Hanshin 6EL40 1 x 4 Stroke 6 Cy. 400 x 800 2427kW (3300bhp) The Hanshin Diesel Works Ltd-Japan AuxGen: 2 x 144kW 440V 60Hz a.c, 1 x 60kW 440V 60Hz a.c Fuel: 54.5 (d.f.) 303.0 (r.f.) 10.0pd
9382499 *9V9273* -	**UMGENI** *ex* Umzimvubu *-2011* *ex* Siyanda *-2011* **Unicorn Caspian Pte Ltd** Unicorn Shipping, a division of Grindrod Shipping (South Africa) (Pty) Ltd *Singapore* *Singapore* MMSI: 566043000 Official number: 396861	**11,271** 4,986 16,900 T/cm 28.1	Class: NV (BV)	**2011-07 Taizhou Sanfu Ship Engineering Co Ltd — Taizhou JS** Yd No: SF050203 Loa 144.00 (BB) Br ex - Dght 8.800 Lbp 135.60 Br md 23.00 Dpth 12.50 Welded, 1 dk	**(A12B2TR) Chemical/Products Tanker** Double Hull (13F) Liq: 18,896; Liq (Oil): 19,398 Cargo Heating Coils Compartments: 7 Wing Ta, 7 Wing Ta, 1 Wing Slop Ta, 1 Wing Slop Ta, ER 4 Cargo Pump (s): 4x500m³/hr Manifold: Bow/CM: 73.4m	**1 oil engine** driving 1 FP propeller Total Power: 4,378kW (5,952hp) 13.0kn MAN-B&W 6S35MC 1 x 2 Stroke 6 Cy. 350 x 1400 4378kW (5952bhp) STX Engine Co Ltd-South Korea AuxGen: 3 x 580kW 60Hz a.c Fuel: 650.0
8317681 *ZR2120* -	**UMHLALI** *ex* Bart Grove *-2011* **Transnet Ltd** Portnet Dredging Services *Durban* *South Africa* Official number: 351199	*315* 94 629	Class: (LR) ✠ Classed LR until 18/4/86	**1985-02 Dorbyl Marine Pty. Ltd. — Durban** Yd No: 8400 Loa 33.15 Br ex 10.11 Dght 6.079 Lbp 30.99 Br md 9.52 Dpth 4.12 Welded, 1 dk	**(B32A2ST) Tug**	**2 oil engines** with clutches, flexible couplings & sr geared to sc. shafts driving 2 Directional propellers Total Power: 2,400kW (3,264hp) 12.0kn MaK 6M322AK 2 x 4 Stroke 6 Cy. 240 x 330 each-1200kW (1632bhp) Krupp MaK Maschinenbau GmbH-Kiel AuxGen: 3 x 128kW 380/400V 50Hz a.c Fuel: 56.0 (d.f.) 11.5pd
9334715 *XJAR* -	**UMIAK I** **Fednav Ltd** *St John's, NL* *Canada* MMSI: 316013340 Official number: 828352	**22,462** 8,853 31,992 T/cm 44.8	Class: NV	**2006-04 Universal Shipbuilding Corp — Maizuru KY** Yd No: 10003 Loa 188.80 Br ex 26.64 Dght 11.714 Lbp 178.00 Br md 26.60 Dpth 15.70 Welded, 1 dk	**(A21A2BC) Bulk Carrier** Double Hull Grain: 30,170 TEU 152 Compartments: 5 Ho, ER 5 Ha: (19.2 x 15.8)ER 4 (13.6 x 15.8) Cranes: 1x50t,2x30t Ice Capable	**1 oil engine** driving 1 CP propeller Total Power: 21,770kW (29,598hp) 14.3kn MAN-B&W 7S70ME-C 1 x 2 Stroke 7 Cy. 700 x 2800 21770kW (29598bhp) Hitachi Zosen Corp-Japan AuxGen: 3 x a.c Fuel: 81.0 (d.f.) 2015.0 (r.f.)
8801591 - -	**UMIAVUT** *ex* Lindengracht *-2000* *ex* Kapitan Silin *-1992* *completed as* Newca *-1988* **Transport Umialarik Inc** Nunavut Eastern Arctic Shipping Inc (NEAS) *Bridgetown* *Barbados* MMSI: 314953764	**6,037** 3,602 9,682 T/cm 18.5	Class: BV (LR) (NV) (RS) ✠ Classed LR until 14/7/12	**1988-10 Miho Zosensho K.K. — Shimizu** Yd No: 1329 Loa 113.12 (BB) Br ex 19.23 Dght 8.532 Lbp 106.00 Br md 18.90 Dpth 11.28 Welded, 2 dks	**(A31A2GX) General Cargo Ship** Grain: 12,582; Bale: 11,528 TEU 564 C Ho 234 TEU C Dk 330 TEU incl 50 ref C. Compartments: 1 Ho, ER 2 Ha: (33.6 x 15.7) (35.7 x 15.7)ER Cranes: 2x50t	**1 oil engine** driving 1 CP propeller Total Power: 4,413kW (6,000hp) 12.5kn Hanshin 6LF58 1 x 4 Stroke 6 Cy. 580 x 1050 4413kW (6000bhp) The Hanshin Diesel Works Ltd-Japan AuxGen: 1 x 600kW 445V 60Hz a.c, 3 x 200kW 445V 60Hz a.c Boilers: TOH (o.f.) 10.2kgf/cm² (10.0bar), TOH (ex.g.) 10.2kgf/cm² (10.0bar)
8210041 *JG4290* -	**UMIGIRI** **Government of Japan (Ministry of Land, Infrastructure & Transport) (The Coastguard)** - *Tokyo* *Japan* Official number: 126168	*149* - -		**1983-02 Hitachi Zosen Corp — Kawasaki KN** Yd No: 117086 Loa 31.00 Br ex 6.32 Dght 1.150 Lbp 28.50 Br md 6.30 Dpth 3.30 Welded, 1 dk	**(B34H2SQ) Patrol Vessel** Hull Material: Aluminium Alloy	**2 oil engines** with clutches, flexible couplings & sr geared to sc. shafts driving 2 FP propellers Total Power: 3,472kW (4,720hp) 30.0kn M.T.U. 16V652TB71 2 x Vee 4 Stroke 16 Cy. 190 x 230 each-1736kW (2360bhp) Ikegai Tekkosho-Japan
8975976 *TCAS3* -	**UMIT-K** *ex* Umit K *-2012* **Karkan Denizcilik Nakliyati Sanayi ve Ticaret Ltd Sti** - *Istanbul* *Turkey* MMSI: 271002667 Official number: 6030	**743** 407 1,302	Class: TL	**1990-03 Yildirim Gemi Insaat Sanayii A.S. — Tuzla** Yd No: 24 Loa 53.40 Br ex - Dght 4.400 Lbp 47.65 Br md 10.05 Dpth 5.15 Welded, 1 dk	**(A31A2GX) General Cargo Ship** Derricks: 2	**1 oil engine** driving 1 Propeller Total Power: 294kW (400hp) 10.0kn S.K.L. 1 x 4 Stroke 294kW (400bhp) VEB Schwermaschinenbau "KarlLiebknecht" (SKL)-Magdeburg
9231078 *JPAT* -	**UMITAKA MARU** **Tokyo University of Marine Science & Technology (Tokyo Kaiyo-Daigaku)** - *Tokyo* *Japan* MMSI: 432187000 Official number: 136932	*1,886* - -	Class: FA	**2000-06 Mitsui Eng. & SB. Co. Ltd. — Tamano** Yd No: 1510 Loa 93.00 Br ex - Dght 5.800 Lbp 83.00 Br md 14.90 Dpth 8.90 Welded, 1 dk	**(B11B2FV) Fishing Vessel**	**1 oil engine** reduction geared to sc. shaft driving 1 CP propeller Total Power: 4,489kW (6,103hp) 17.4kn Niigata 6MG41HX 1 x 4 Stroke 6 Cy. 410 x 560 4489kW (6103bhp) Niigata Engineering Co Ltd-Japan AuxGen: 3 x 600kW 450V 60Hz a.c Thrusters: 1 Thwart. FP thruster (f) Fuel: 651.0 (d.f.) 20.3pd
8403208 *JL5243* -	**UMITAKA MARU No. 15** *ex* Daitei Maru No. 61 *-1995* *ex* Taisho Maru No. 51 *-1989* **Kamata Suisan KK** - SatCom: Inmarsat M 643186310 *Ofunato, Iwate* *Japan* MMSI: 432562000 Official number: 126413	*169* - -		**1984-03 Sanuki Shipbuilding & Iron Works Co Ltd — Mitoyo KG** Yd No: 1126 Loa 39.27 Br ex - Dght 2.615 Lbp 32.01 Br md 6.61 Dpth 2.90 Welded, 1 dk	**(B11B2FV) Fishing Vessel** Ins: 113 Compartments: 11 Ho, ER 11 Ha: ER	**1 oil engine** sr geared to sc. shaft driving 1 FP propeller Total Power: 669kW (910hp) Yanmar T250-ET 1 x 4 Stroke 6 Cy. 250 x 330 669kW (910bhp) Yanmar Diesel Engine Co Ltd-Japan
9646285 *JD3106* -	**UMIWAKA MARU** **Government of Japan (Ministry of Land, Infrastructure & Transport - Kinki Regional Development Bureau)** - *Kobe, Hyogo* *Japan* MMSI: 431002126 Official number: 141307	*198* - -		**2011-01 IHI Amtec Co Ltd — Aioi HG** Yd No: 5020 Loa 33.50 Br ex - Dght 2.640 Lbp 31.00 Br md 11.40 Dpth 4.20 Welded, 1 dk	**(B34G2SE) Pollution Control Vessel**	**2 oil engines** reduction geared to sc. shafts driving 2 Propellers Total Power: 2,640kW (3,590hp) 14.1kn M.T.U. 12V4000M60 2 x Vee 4 Stroke 12 Cy. 165 x 190 each-1320kW (1795bhp) MTU Friedrichshafen GmbH-Friedrichshafen
9299733 *A7MY* -	**UMLMA** **Qatar Shipping Co (Q Ship) SPC** *Doha* *Qatar* MMSI: 466241000 Official number: 223/2005	**57,243** 32,763 106,005 T/cm 91.9	Class: NV	**2006-01 Hyundai Samho Heavy Industries Co Ltd — Samho** Yd No: S303 Loa 243.96 Br ex 42.03 Dght 14.920 Lbp 234.00 Br md 42.00 Dpth 21.00 Welded, 1 dk	**(A13A2TV) Crude Oil Tanker** Double Hull (13F) Liq: 117,926; Liq (Oil): 117,926 Cargo Heating Coils Compartments: 12 Wing Ta, ER 3 Cargo Pump (s): 3x3000m³/hr Manifold: Bow/CM: 123.3m	**1 oil engine** driving 1 FP propeller Total Power: 13,548kW (18,420hp) 14.8kn MAN-B&W 6S60MC-C 1 x 2 Stroke 6 Cy. 600 x 2400 13548kW (18420bhp) Hyundai Heavy Industries Co Ltd-South Korea AuxGen: 3 x 740kW 440/220V 60Hz a.c
9522922 *A8XK7* -	**UMM AD DALKH** **Umm Ad Dalkh Shipping Co Inc** Abu Dhabi National Tanker Co (ADNATCO) SatCom: Inmarsat C 463709291 *Monrovia* *Liberia* MMSI: 636014919 Official number: 14919	**22,668** 12,334 36,490 T/cm 46.1	Class: NV	**2011-01 Hyundai Mipo Dockyard Co Ltd — Ulsan** Yd No: 6007 Loa 186.40 (BB) Br ex 27.83 Dght 10.900 Lbp 178.00 Br md 27.80 Dpth 15.60 Welded, 1 dk	**(A21A2BC) Bulk Carrier** Grain: 47,922; Bale: 47,692 Compartments: 5 Ho, ER 5 Ha: ER Cranes: 4x30t	**1 oil engine** driving 1 FP propeller Total Power: 7,860kW (10,686hp) 14.8kn MAN-B&W 6S46MC-C 1 x 2 Stroke 6 Cy. 460 x 1932 7860kW (10686bhp) Hyundai Heavy Industries Co Ltd-South Korea AuxGen: 3 x a.c

Identity / Name / Owner	Tonnage	Classification	Build / Dimensions	Type / Cargo	Machinery
9534781 **UMM AL AISH** *9KEL* *ex Qaruh -2011* - **Kuwait Oil Tanker Co SAK** - SatCom: Inmarsat C 444702531 *Kuwait* *Kuwait* MMSI: 447025000 Official number: KT1757	**162,625** 112,189 319,634 T/cm 178.8	Class: NV	**2011-02 Daewoo Shipbuilding & Marine Engineering Co Ltd — Geoje** Yd No: 5345 Loa 333.00 (BB) Br ex 60.04 Dght 22.520 Lbp 320.00 Br md 60.00 Dpth 30.50 Welded, 1 dk	**(A13A2TV) Crude Oil Tanker** Double Hull (13F) Liq: 341,517; Liq (Oil): 340,600 Compartments: 5 Ta, 10 Wing Ta, ER, 2 Wing Slop Ta 3 Cargo Pump (s): 3x5500m³/hr Manifold: Bow/CM: 164m	**1 oil engine** driving 1 FP propeller Total Power: 27,160kW (36,927hp) 15.3kn MAN-B&W 7S80ME-C 1 x 2 Stroke 7 Cy. 800 x 3200 27160kW (36927bhp) MAN Diesel A/S-Denmark AuxGen: 3 x 1200kW 440/220V 60Hz a.c Fuel: 1140.0 (d.f.) 7873.0 (r.f.)
9360829 **UMM AL AMAD** *V7OE6* - **J5 Nakilat No 7 Ltd** 'K' Line LNG Shipping (UK) Ltd SatCom: Inmarsat C 453800545 *Majuro* *Marshall Islands* MMSI: 538003073 Official number: 3073	**136,685** 44,082 121,730 T/cm 136.5	Class: AB	**2008-09 Daewoo Shipbuilding & Marine Engineering Co Ltd — Geoje** Yd No: 2253 Loa 315.00 (BB) Br ex - Dght 13.621 Lbp 303.57 Br md 50.00 Dpth 27.00 Welded, 1 dk	**(A11A2TN) LNG Tanker** Double Hull Liq (Gas): 206,958 6 x Gas Tank (s); 5 membrane (36% Ni.stl) pri horizontal, ER 10 Cargo Pump (s): 10x1500m³/hr Manifold: Bow/CM: 154m	**2 oil engines** driving 4 gen. Connecting to 1 elec. Motor driving 2 FP propellers Total Power: 33,178kW (45,108hp) 19.5kn MAN-B&W 6S70ME-C 2 x 2 Stroke 6 Cy. 700 x 2800 each-16589kW (22554bhp) Doosan Engine Co Ltd-South Korea AuxGen: 4 x 3860kW 6600V 60Hz a.c Fuel: 605.0 (d.f.) 8200.0 (r.f.)
7206330 **UMM AL ANBER** *A6E2759* *ex Geomaster -1996* - *ex Canada's Tomorrow -1990* *ex Merchant Navigator -1985* *ex Lady Tone -1983* *ex Lagan Bridge -1980* *ex Ilkka -1979* **E-Marine PJSC** - SatCom: Inmarsat A 1720604 *Abu Dhabi* *United Arab Emirates* MMSI: 470441000 Official number: 4518	**7,750** 2,325 2,670	Class: IR NV	**1972-06 Ankerlokken Verft Floro AS — Floro** Yd No: 89 Converted From: Diving Support Vessel-1996 Converted From: Ro-Ro Cargo Ship-1990 Loa 133.70 Br ex 20.45 Dght 6.180 Lbp 122.50 Br md 20.40 Dpth 12.50 Welded, 2 dks	**(B34D2SL) Cable Layer** Ice Capable	**2 oil engines** driving 2 CP propellers Total Power: 5,884kW (8,000hp) 18.0kn Pielstick 8PC2V-400 2 x 4 Stroke 8 Cy. 400 x 460 each-2942kW (4000bhp) Lindholmen Motor AB-Sweden AuxGen: 2 x 540kW 440V 60Hz a.c Thrusters: 2 Thwart. FP thruster (f) Fuel: 600.0 (r.f.) 24.0pd
9074652 **UMM AL ASHTAN** *ELUD4* - **Umm Al Ashtan Ltd** National Gas Shipping Co Ltd (NGSCO) SatCom: Inmarsat B 363658210 *Monrovia* *Liberia* MMSI: 636010647 Official number: 10647	**116,703** 35,010 73,100 T/cm 110.0	Class: LR ✠ **100A1** SS 08/2011 liquefied gas carrier ship type 2G Methane in independent type B spherical tanks, max. pressure 0.25 bar, min. temp. of minus 163~C *IWS LI ✠ **LMC** **UMS** Eq.Ltr: D*; Cable: 770.0/127.0 U2 (a)	**1997-05 Kvaerner Masa-Yards Inc — Turku** Yd No: 1333 Loa 290.14 (BB) Br ex 48.19 Dght 12.300 Lbp 275.00 Br md 48.10 Dpth 27.00 Welded, 1 dk	**(A11A2TN) LNG Tanker** Double Bottom Entire Compartment Length Liq (Gas): 137,000 4 x Gas Tank (s); 4 independent Kvaerner-Moss (alu) sph 8 Cargo Pump (s): 8x1375m³/hr	**1 Steam Turb** with flexible couplings & dr gearedto sc. shaft driving 1 FP propeller Total Power: 29,600kW (40,244hp) 19.5kn Mitsubishi MS40-2 1 x steam Turb 29600kW (40244shp) Mitsubishi Heavy Industries Ltd-Japan AuxGen: 3 x 2761kW 450V 60Hz a.c Boilers: 2 WTB (o.f.) 79.6kgf/cm² (78.1bar) Superheater 515°C 67.1kgf/cm² (65.8bar), sg 9.0kgf/cm² (8.8bar) Fuel: 730.0 (d.f.) 6298.0 (r.f.)
9494204 **UMM AL LULU-I** *A6E3011* - **Umm-Al Lulu-I Shipping Co Inc** Abu Dhabi National Tanker Co (ADNATCO) SatCom: Inmarsat C 447084810 *Abu Dhabi* *United Arab Emirates* MMSI: 470848000 Official number: 6145	**8,653** 4,670 15,161 T/cm 27.0	Class: LR (BV) **100A1** SS 05/2009 Double Hull oil and chemical tanker, Ship Type 2 ESP *IWS LI EP (bar above) **LMC** **UMS IGS**	**2009-05 TVK Gemi Yapim Sanayi ve Ticaret AS — Basiskele** Yd No: 05 Loa 139.94 Br ex 21.40 Dght 8.100 Lbp 134.70 Br md 21.00 Dpth 10.60 Welded, 1 dk	**(A12B2TR) Chemical/Products Tanker** Double Hull (13F) Liq: 16,450; Liq (Oil): 16,450 Compartments: 12 Wing Ta, 2 Wing Slop Ta, ER	**1 oil engine** sr geared to sc. shaft driving 1 FP propeller Total Power: 5,400kW (7,342hp) 14.0kn MaK 6M43C 1 x 4 Stroke 6 Cy. 430 x 610 5400kW (7342bhp) Caterpillar Motoren GmbH & Co. KG-Germany AuxGen: 3 x 746kW 440V 60Hz a.c Boilers: e (ex.g.) 10.2kgf/cm² (10.0bar), TOH (o.f.) 10.2kgf/cm² (10.0bar)
7812816 **UMM AL SHAIF** - - - -	*186* 105 307	Class: (LR) (AB) Classed LR until 16/4/97	**1978-08 Sing Koon Seng Pte Ltd — Singapore** Yd No: SKS475 Loa 30.00 Br ex 7.55 Dght 2.610 Lbp 28.00 Br md 7.31 Dpth 3.00 Welded, 1 dk	**(A13B2TP) Products Tanker** Compartments: 4 Ta, ER	**2 oil engines** reverse reduction geared to sc. shafts driving 2 FP propellers Total Power: 338kW (460hp) 10.0kn G.M. (Detroit Diesel) 8V-71-N 2 x Vee 2 Stroke 8 Cy. 108 x 127 each-169kW (230bhp) General Motors Detroit DieselAllison Divn-USA AuxGen: 1 x 96kW 415V 50Hz a.c
9308431 **UMM BAB** *SYGA* - **Sea Trade International Inc** Maran Gas Maritime Inc SatCom: Inmarsat Mini-M 764469622 *Piraeus* *Greece* MMSI: 240411000 Official number: 11439	**97,496** 29,249 84,659 T/cm 104.3	Class: LR ✠ **100A1** SS 11/2010 liquefied gas tanker, Ship Type 2G methane (LNG) in membrane tanks, max. vapour pressure 0.25 bar, minimum temp. minus 163 degree C *IWS LI EP (barred) **ShipRight** (SDA) ✠ **LMC** **UMS** Eq.Ltr: Z†; Cable: 742.5/102.0 U3 (a)	**2005-11 Daewoo Shipbuilding & Marine Engineering Co Ltd — Geoje** Yd No: 2228 Loa 285.47 (BB) Br ex 43.44 Dght 12.520 Lbp 274.40 Br md 43.40 Dpth 26.00 Welded, 1 dk	**(A11A2TN) LNG Tanker** Double Bottom Entire Compartment Length Liq (Gas): 143,708 4 x Gas Tank (s); 4 membrane (36% Ni.stl) pri horizontal 8 Cargo Pump (s): 8x1700m³/hr Manifold: Bow/CM: 144.6m	**1 Steam Turb** with flexible couplings & dr reverse geared to sc. shaft driving 1 FP propeller Total Power: 27,066kW (36,799hp) 19.1kn Kawasaki UA-400 1 x steam Turb 27066kW (36799shp) Kawasaki Heavy Industries Ltd-Japan AuxGen: 3 x 3500kW 6600V 60Hz a.c Boilers: wtdb (o.f.) 78.0kgf/cm² (76.5bar) Superheater 515°C 66.3kgf/cm² (65.0bar) Thrusters: 1 Thwart. CP thruster (f) Fuel: 436.4 (d.f.) 4799.0 (r.f.)
9593579 **UMM KHORAH** *A6E2732* - **A M Marine Transport International Cargo Est (Al Masaood)** - *Abu Dhabi* *United Arab Emirates* MMSI: 470451000 Official number: 0006740	**488** 146 409	Class: LR ✠ **100A1** SS 10/2011 Gulf area coastal service Eq.Ltr: J; Cable: 357.5/26.0 U2 (a)	**2011-10 Berjaya Dockyard Sdn Bhd — Miri** Yd No: 67 Loa 45.50 Br ex 10.92 Dght 2.400 Lbp 42.23 Br md 10.90 Dpth 3.20 Welded, 1 dk	**(A35D2RL) Landing Craft** Bow ramp (centre)	**2 oil engines** with clutches & sr geared to sc. shafts driving 2 FP propellers Total Power: 1,074kW (1,460hp) Caterpillar 3412C 2 x Vee 4 Stroke 12 Cy. 137 x 152 each-537kW (730bhp) Caterpillar Inc-USA AuxGen: 2 x 80kW 415V 50Hz a.c Thrusters: 1 Thwart. FP thruster (f)
9359454 **UMM LAQHAB** *V7CG8* - **Umm Laqhab LPG Shipping Co LLC** Phoenix Tankers Pte Ltd *Majuro* *Marshall Islands* MMSI: 538005256 Official number: 5256	**47,058** 15,944 54,538 T/cm 70.6	Class: NV	**2008-07 Hyundai Heavy Industries Co Ltd — Ulsan** Yd No: 1867 Loa 225.28 (BB) Br ex 36.63 Dght 12.024 Lbp 215.00 Br md 36.60 Dpth 22.02 Welded, 1 dk	**(A11B2TG) LPG Tanker** Double Hull Liq (Gas): 80,771 4 x Gas Tank (s); 4 independent (C.mn.stl) pri horizontal 10 Cargo Pump (s): 8x600m³/hr, 2x600m³/hr Manifold: Bow/CM: 109.5m	**1 oil engine** driving 1 FP propeller Total Power: 13,560kW (18,436hp) 16.8kn MAN-B&W 6S60MC-C 1 x 2 Stroke 6 Cy. 600 x 2400 13560kW (18436bhp) Hyundai Heavy Industries Co Ltd-South Korea AuxGen: 3 x a.c Fuel: 175.8 (d.f.) 2703.0 (r.f.)
9525857 **UMM SALAL** *9HA2682* - **UMM Salal Ltd** United Arab Shipping Co (UASC) *Valletta* *Malta* MMSI: 215237000 Official number: 9525857	**141,077** 75,670 145,327	Class: LR (GL) **100A1** SS 04/2011 container ship **ShipRight** (SDA, FDA) *IWS LI **LMC** **UMS**	**2011-04 Samsung Heavy Industries Co Ltd — Geoje** Yd No: 1876 Loa 365.93 (BB) Br ex - Dght 15.500 Lbp 349.50 Br md 48.20 Dpth 29.90 Welded, 1 dk	**(A33A2CC) Container Ship (Fully Cellular)** TEU 13296 C Ho 6428 Teu C Dk 6868 TEU incl 1000 ref C	**1 oil engine** driving 1 FP propeller Total Power: 71,760kW (97,565hp) 24.1kn MAN-B&W 12K98ME7 1 x 2 Stroke 12 Cy. 980 x 2660 71760kW (97565bhp) Doosan Engine Co Ltd-South Korea AuxGen: 1 x 3340kW 6600/2240V a.c, 1 x 7000kW 6600/2240V a.c, 1 x 6640kW 6600/2240V a.c, 3 x 4250kW 6600/2240V a.c Thrusters: 1 Tunnel thruster (f) Fuel: 344.0 (d.f.) 12258.0 (r.f.)

IMO / Call sign	Name / Owner / Manager / Flag	Tonnage	Classification	Builder / Dimensions	Type / Cargo	Machinery
9372731 *V7PW3* -	**UMM SLAL** **Qatar Gas Transport Co Ltd (Nakilat)** Shell International Trading & Shipping Co Ltd (STASCO) SatCom: Inmarsat C 453833441 *Majuro* *Marshall Islands* MMSI: 538003300 Official number: 3300	**163,922** 51,596 130,059 T/cm 163.3	Class: LR **✠100A1** SS 11/2008 liquefied gas tanker, Ship Type 2G methane (LNG) in membrane tanks maximum vapour pressure 0.25 bar minimum temperature minus 163 degree C **ShipRight** (SDA, FDA plus, CM) *IWS LI EP (A,B,O,P) **✠LMC UMS +Lloyd's RMC (LG)** **CCS** Eq.Ltr: E*; Cable: 770.0/117.0 U3 (a)	**2008-11 Samsung Heavy Industries Co Ltd — Geoje** Yd No: 1676 Loa 345.28 (BB) Br ex 53.83 Dght 12.200 Lbp 332.00 Br md 53.80 Dpth 27.00 Welded, 1 dk	**(A11A2TN) LNG Tanker** Double Hull Liq (Gas): 260,928 5 x Gas Tank (s); 5 membrane (s.stl) pri horizontal 10 Cargo Pump (s): 10x1400m³/hr Manifold: Bow/CM: 170.4m	**2 oil engines** driving 2 FP propellers Total Power: 37,880kW (51,502hp) 19.0kn MAN-B&W 7S70ME-C 2 x 2 Stroke 7 Cy. 700 x 2800 each-18940kW (25751bhp) Doosan Engine Co Ltd-South Korea AuxGen: 4 x 4300kW 6600V 60Hz a.c Boilers: e (ex.g.) 12.6kgf/cm² (12.4bar), WTAuxB (o.f.) 10.1kgf/cm² (9.9bar) Fuel: 586.7 (d.f.) 8126.0 (r.f.)
9206736 - -	**UMM SUQEEM** **Dubai Drydocks** - *Dubai* *United Arab Emirates* Official number: 4432	**424** 128 500	Class: NV	**1998-11 Dubai Drydocks — Dubai** Yd No: 9991 Loa 40.00 Br ex - Dght 2.350 Lbp 39.12 Br md 10.00 Dpth 3.00 Welded, 1 dk	**(B33A2DU) Dredger (unspecified)** Hopper: 250	**2 oil engines** gearing integral to driving 2 Z propellers Total Power: 412kW (560hp) Scania DSI11 2 x 4 Stroke 6 Cy. 127 x 145 each-206kW (280bhp) Scania AB-Sweden AuxGen: 2 x 136kW 220/380V 50Hz a.c
7428770 *H02413* -	**UMMAL KAIR** *ex* Ouzou *-2007* *ex* Nego Iron *-1981* **Delair Marine Corp** - *Panama* *Panama* MMSI: 372500000 Official number: 35371PEXT1	*485* 239 596	Class: IS (LR) (AB) Classed LR until 22/8/97	**1976-06 Singapore Shipbuilding & Engineering Pte Ltd — Singapore** Yd No: 114 Loa 49.79 Br ex 12.37 Dght 2.439 Lbp 44.89 Br md 12.20 Dpth 3.20 Welded, 1 dk	**(A35D2RL) Landing Craft** Bow door/ramp Compartments: 5 Ta, ER	**2 oil engines** reverse reduction geared to sc. shafts driving 2 FP propellers Total Power: 736kW (1,000hp) 8.8kn MWM TBD601-6 2 x 4 Stroke 6 Cy. 160 x 165 each-368kW (500bhp) Motoren Werke Mannheim AG (MWM)-West Germany AuxGen: 2 x 40kW 415V 50Hz a.c
9662605 *A9D3155* -	**UMMUSAWALI** **Arab Shipbuilding & Repair Yard Co (ASRY)** - *Bahrain* *Bahrain* MMSI: 408440000 Official number: BN6054	**244** 73 197	Class: AB	**2012-03 Arab Shipbuilding & Repair Yard Co (ASRY) — Hidd** Yd No: 6 Loa 25.80 Br ex - Dght 4.500 Lbp 21.91 Br md 9.50 Dpth 5.00 Welded, 1 dk	**(B32A2ST) Tug**	**2 oil engines** reduction geared to sc. shafts driving 2 Directional propellers Total Power: 2,648kW (3,600hp) Yanmar 8N21A-EN 2 x 4 Stroke 8 Cy. 210 x 290 each-1324kW (1800bhp) Yanmar Diesel Engine Co Ltd-Japan AuxGen: 2 x 130kW a.c Fuel: 100.0 (d.f.)
8303264 *YDLF* -	**UMSINI** **Government of The Republic of Indonesia (Direktorat Jenderal Perhubungan Laut - Ministry of Sea Communications)** PT Pelayaran Nasional Indonesia (PELNI) *Sorong* *Indonesia* MMSI: 525005009	*14,501* 6,787 3,434	Class: KI (GL)	**1985-01 Jos L Meyer GmbH & Co — Papenburg** Yd No: 612 Loa 144.02 (BB) Br ex - Dght 5.865 Lbp 130.03 Br md 23.41 Dpth 11.79 Welded, 3 dks, 4th dk fwd of machinery space	**(A37B2PS) Passenger Ship** Passengers: unberthed: 500; cabins: 212; berths: 1096 Grain: 1,250; Bale: 1,000 Compartments: 1 Ho, ER, 2 Tw Dk 1 Ha: (8.1 x 6.0)ER Cranes: 2x7t	**2 oil engines** with flexible couplings & sr gearedto sc. shafts driving 2 FP propellers Total Power: 10,878kW (14,790hp) 20.0kn MaK 6M601AK 2 x 4 Stroke 6 Cy. 580 x 600 each-5439kW (7395bhp) Krupp MaK Maschinenbau GmbH-Kiel AuxGen: 4 x 800kW 380V 50Hz a.c Thrusters: 1 Thwart. CP thruster (f) Fuel: 889.0 (d.f.) 61.0pd
8119807 *ZR2191* -	**UMSUNDUZI** *ex* Dupel Erasmus *-1981* **Transnet Ltd** Portnet Dredging Services *Durban* *South Africa* Official number: 351197	*295* 83 234	Class: (LR) ✠ Classed LR until 13/7/84	**1983-04 Dorbyl Marine Pty. Ltd. — Durban** Yd No: 7100 Loa 33.15 Br ex 10.11 Dght 6.079 Lbp 30.99 Br md 9.50 Dpth 4.09 Welded, 1 dk	**(B32A2ST) Tug**	**2 oil engines** with clutches, flexible couplings & sr geared to sc. shafts driving 2 Directional propellers Total Power: 2,400kW (3,264hp) 12.0kn MaK 6M332AK 2 x 4 Stroke 6 Cy. 240 x 330 each-1200kW (1632bhp) Krupp MaK Maschinenbau GmbH-Kiel AuxGen: 3 x 128kW 380/400V 50Hz a.c Fuel: 56.0 (d.f.) 11.5pd
7603382 *PLVB* -	**UMT-2** **PT UMW Marabunta Timber Ltd** - *Bitung* *Indonesia*	*170* 74 188	Class: (KI) (NK)	**1976-06 Wakayama Zosen — Kainan** Yd No: 523 Loa 35.62 Br ex - Dght 1.610 Lbp 32.52 Br md 8.81 Dpth 2.01 Riveted\Welded, 1 dk	**(A13B2TU) Tanker (unspecified)** Liq: 238; Liq (Oil): 238	**2 oil engines** geared to sc. shafts driving 2 FP propellers Total Power: 354kW (482hp) 8.5kn Yanmar 6BNGGE 2 x 4 Stroke 6 Cy. 155 x 180 each-177kW (241bhp) Yanmar Diesel Engine Co Ltd-Japan
7603394 *PLVC* -	**UMT-3** **PT UMW Marabunta Timber Ltd** - *Bitung* *Indonesia*	*170* 74 188	Class: (KI) (NK)	**1976-06 Wakayama Zosen — Kainan** Yd No: 524 Loa 35.62 Br ex - Dght 1.610 Lbp 32.52 Br md 8.81 Dpth 2.01 Riveted\Welded, 1 dk	**(A13B2TU) Tanker (unspecified)** Liq: 238; Liq (Oil): 238	**2 oil engines** geared to sc. shafts driving 2 FP propellers Total Power: 354kW (482hp) 8.5kn Yanmar 6BNGGE 2 x 4 Stroke 6 Cy. 155 x 180 each-177kW (241bhp) Yanmar Diesel Engine Co Ltd-Japan
9188104 *9V5833* -	**UMT 6** *ex* Surya Wira 6 *-2012* **CTS Consulting Pte Ltd** United Marine & Trading Co Ltd *Singapore* *Singapore* MMSI: 563004190 Official number: 388703	**165** 50 129	Class: NK	**2000-01 Super-Light Shipbuilding Contractor — Sibu** Yd No: 38 Loa 25.00 Br ex - Dght 2.712 Lbp 22.88 Br md 7.62 Dpth 3.30 Welded, 1 dk	**(B32A2ST) Tug**	**2 oil engines** reduction geared to sc. shafts driving 2 FP propellers Total Power: 1,074kW (1,460hp) 11.0kn Caterpillar 3412TA 2 x Vee 4 Stroke 12 Cy. 137 x 152 each-537kW (730bhp) Caterpillar Inc-USA Fuel: 125.0 (d.f.)
7615921 *ZR2052* -	**UMTWALUME** *ex* Coenie de Villiers *-2012* **Transnet Ltd** Portnet Dredging Services *Port Elizabeth* *South Africa* Official number: 351527	*431* 130 -	Class: (LR) ✠ Classed LR until 9/11/79	**1978-09 Dorman Long Vanderbijl Corp. Ltd. (DORBYL) — Durban** Yd No: 5000 Loa 36.40 Br ex 11.61 Dght 3.558 Lbp 34.45 Br md 11.00 Dpth 4.14 Welded, 1 dk	**(B32A2ST) Tug**	**2 oil engines** dr geared to sc. shafts driving 2 Directional propellers Total Power: 2,280kW (3,100hp) 12.0kn Niigata 8L25CX 2 x 4 Stroke 8 Cy. 250 x 320 each-1140kW (1550bhp) Niigata Engineering Co Ltd-Japan AuxGen: 3 x 104kW 380/400V 50Hz a.c
8607866 *TCBJ3* -	**UMUR BEY** **Istanbul Deniz Otobusleri Sanayi ve Ticaret AS (IDO)** - *Istanbul* *Turkey* MMSI: 271002469 Official number: 5570	**431** 166 125	Class: TL (NV)	**1987-04 Skaalurens Skipsbyggeri AS — Rosendal** Yd No: 1578 Loa 38.82 Br ex 9.71 Dght 1.550 Lbp 36.41 Br md 9.47 Dpth 3.92 Welded, 1 dk	**(A37B2PS) Passenger Ship** Hull Material: Aluminium Alloy Passengers: unberthed: 449	**2 oil engines** with clutches, flexible couplings & sr geared to sc. shafts driving 2 Directional propellers Total Power: 3,020kW (4,106hp) 32.0kn M.T.U. 16V396TB83 2 x Vee 4 Stroke 16 Cy. 165 x 185 each-1510kW (2053bhp) MTU Friedrichshafen GmbH-Friedrichshafen AuxGen: 2 x 68kW 400V 50Hz a.c Fuel: 9.0 (d.f.)
7643928 - -	**UMURGA** *ex* Leninskaya Kuznitsa *-1993* **Vostoktrans Co Ltd** -	**716** 214 395	Class: (RS)	**1977-03 Zavod "Leninskaya Kuznitsa" — Kiyev** Yd No: 1432 Loa 54.82 Br ex 9.96 Dght 4.141 Lbp 50.30 Br md - Dpth 5.03 Welded, 1 dk	**(B11A2FS) Stern Trawler** Ins: 414 Compartments: 2 Ho, ER 3 Ha: 3 (1.5 x 1.6) Derricks: 2x1.5t; Winches: 2 Ice Capable	**1 oil engine** driving 1 CP propeller Total Power: 736kW (1,001hp) 12.0kn S.K.L. 8NVD48A-2U 1 x 4 Stroke 8 Cy. 320 x 480 736kW (1001bhp) VEB Schwermaschinenbau "KarlLiebknecht" (SKL)-Magdeburg
8119819 *ZR2057* -	**UMVOTI** *ex* Bertie Groenewald *-1993* **Transnet Ltd** Portnet Dredging Services *Durban* *South Africa* MMSI: 601118000 Official number: 351196	*295* 83 629	Class: (LR) ✠ Classed LR until 13/7/84	**1983-06 Dorbyl Marine Pty. Ltd. — Durban** Yd No: 7200 Loa 33.15 Br ex 10.11 Dght 6.079 Lbp 30.31 Br md 9.52 Dpth 4.12 Welded, 1 dk	**(B32A2ST) Tug**	**2 oil engines** with clutches, flexible couplings & sr geared to sc. shafts driving 2 Directional propellers Total Power: 2,200kW (2,992hp) 12.0kn MaK 6M332AK 2 x 4 Stroke 6 Cy. 240 x 330 each-1100kW (1496bhp) Krupp MaK Maschinenbau GmbH-Kiel AuxGen: 3 x 128kW 380/400V 50Hz a.c Fuel: 56.0 (d.f.) 11.5pd
9557616 *UNDE* -	**UMYD** *ex* Sea Falcon I *-2013* **Circle Maritime Investment LLP** Caspian Offshore Construction LLP *Aqtau* *Kazakhstan* MMSI: 436000225	**168** 50 74	Class: BV	**2010-09 Damen Shipyards Singapore Pte Ltd — Singapore** (Hull) Yd No: (544814) **2010-09 B.V. Scheepswerf Damen — Gorinchem** Yd No: 544814 Loa 33.25 Br ex - Dght 1.940 Lbp 32.00 Br md 6.34 Dpth 3.30 Welded, 1 dk	**(B34J2SD) Crew Boat** Hull Material: Aluminium Alloy Passengers: unberthed: 80	**3 oil engines** reduction geared to sc. shafts driving 3 FP propellers Total Power: 2,460kW (3,345hp) Caterpillar C32 3 x Vee 4 Stroke 12 Cy. 145 x 162 each-820kW (1115bhp) Caterpillar Inc-USA AuxGen: 2 x 58kW 60Hz a.c Thrusters: 1 Tunnel thruster (f)

IMO / Call sign	Name / Owner / Manager / Port / Flag	Tonnage	Class	Built / Dimensions	Type / Details	Machinery
8119780 *ZR2124* -	**UMZUMBE** *ex* Otto Buhr **Transnet Ltd** Portnet Dredging Services *East London* *South Africa* Official number: 351606	*295* 83 629	Class: (LR) ✠ Classed LR until 6/1/84	**1982-10 Dorbyl Marine Pty. Ltd. — Durban** Yd No: 6900 Loa 33.15 Br ex 10.11 Dght 6.079 Lbp 30.99 Br md 9.50 Dpth 4.09 Welded, 1 dk	**(B32A2ST) Tug**	**2 oil engines** with clutches, flexible couplings & sr geared to sc. shafts driving 2 Directional propellers Total Power: 2,400kW (3,264hp) 12.0kn MaK 6M332AK 2 x 4 Stroke 6 Cy. 240 x 330 each-1200kW (1632bhp) Krupp MaK Maschinenbau GmbH-Kiel AuxGen: 3 x 128kW 380/400V 50Hz a.c Fuel: 56.0 (d.f.) 11.5pd
9356737 *TCTD2* -	**UN AKDENIZ** - **UN Ro-Ro Isletmeleri AS (UN Ro-Ro Management Inc)** Bluewater Ship Management Ltd *Istanbul* *Turkey* MMSI: 271002572	**29,004** 8,702 11,526	Class: NV	**2008-06 Flensburger Schiffbau-Ges. mbH & Co. KG — Flensburg** Yd No: 736 Loa 193.30 (BB) Br ex - Dght 6.450 Lbp 182.39 Br md 26.00 Dpth 16.70 Welded, 3 dks	**(A35A2RR) Ro-Ro Cargo Ship** Double Hull Stern door/ramp (centre) Len: 15.00 Wid: 17.00 Swl: 120 Lane-Len: 3726 Trailers: 254	**2 oil engines** reduction geared to sc. shafts driving 2 CP propellers Total Power: 16,798kW (22,838hp) 21.5kn MaK 9M43 2 x 4 Stroke 9 Cy. 430 x 610 each-8399kW (11419bhp) Caterpillar Motoren GmbH & Co. KG-Germany AuxGen: 2 x 1440kW a.c, 2 x 1600kW a.c Thrusters: 1 Tunnel thruster (f)
9506277 *TCVE4* -	**UN ISTANBUL** - **UN Ro-Ro Isletmeleri AS (UN Ro-Ro Management Inc)** - *Istanbul* *Turkey* MMSI: 271043303	**31,540** 9,463 15,000	Class: NV	**2013-04 Flensburger Schiffbau-Ges. mbH & Co. KG — Flensburg** Yd No: 755 Loa 208.20 (BB) Br ex - Dght 7.000 Lbp 198.08 Br md 26.00 Dpth 16.70 Welded, 3 dks	**(A35A2RR) Ro-Ro Cargo Ship** Stern door/ramp (centre) Len: 15.00 Wid: 17.00 Swl: 120 Lane-Len: 4094 Trailers: 283	**2 oil engines** reduction geared to sc. shafts driving 2 CP propellers Total Power: 19,200kW (26,104hp) 20.6kn MAN-B&W 8L48/60CR 2 x 4 Stroke 8 Cy. 480 x 600 each-9600kW (13052bhp) MAN B&W Diesel AG-Augsburg AuxGen: 2 x 1185kW a.c, 2 x a.c Thrusters: 1 Tunnel thruster (f)
8330944 *9GNU* -	**UN JIN** *ex* Izumi *-2002* *ex* Mizuho *-2000* *ex* Yoko *-2000* *ex* Yoko Maru *-1991* **Afko Fisheries Co Ltd** - SatCom: Inmarsat A 1335365 *Takoradi* *Ghana* Official number: 316987	**2,472** 962 2,549	Class: (KR) (NK)	**1984-12 Kinoura Zosen K.K. — Imabari** Yd No: 125 Loa 86.52 Br ex - Dght 4.971 Lbp 80.02 Br md 14.51 Dpth 5.01 Welded, 2 dks	**(A34A2GR) Refrigerated Cargo Ship** Ins: 3,436 Compartments: 3 Ho, ER 3 Ha: 3 (6.6 x 6.3)ER Derricks: 6x5t	**1 oil engine** driving 1 FP propeller Total Power: 1,912kW (2,600hp) 12.8kn Akasaka A37 1 x 4 Stroke 6 Cy. 370 x 720 1912kW (2600bhp) Akasaka Tekkosho KK (Akasaka DieselLtd)-Japan AuxGen: 2 x 448kW a.c
9356749 *TCTD3* -	**UN KARADENIZ** - **UN Ro-Ro Isletmeleri AS (UN Ro-Ro Management Inc)** Bluewater Ship Management Ltd *Istanbul* *Turkey* MMSI: 271002571	**29,004** 8,702 11,636	Class: NV	**2008-09 Flensburger Schiffbau-Ges. mbH & Co. KG — Flensburg** Yd No: 737 Loa 193.30 (BB) Br ex - Dght 6.450 Lbp 182.39 Br md 26.00 Dpth 16.70 Welded, 3 dks	**(A35A2RR) Ro-Ro Cargo Ship** Stern door/ramp (centre) Len: 15.00 Wid: 17.00 Swl: 120 Lane-Len: 3726 Trailers: 254	**2 oil engines** reduction geared to sc. shafts driving 2 CP propellers Total Power: 16,798kW (22,838hp) 21.5kn MaK 9M43 2 x 4 Stroke 9 Cy. 430 x 610 each-8399kW (11419bhp) Caterpillar Motoren GmbH & Co. KG-Germany AuxGen: 2 x 1440kW a.c, 2 x 1600kW a.c Thrusters: 1 Tunnel thruster (f)
9293428 *TCCU8* -	**UN MARMARA** - **UN Ro-Ro Isletmeleri AS (UN Ro-Ro Management Inc)** Bluewater Ship Management Ltd *Istanbul* *Turkey* MMSI: 271000748	**29,004** 8,702 11,400	Class: NV	**2005-06 Flensburger Schiffbau-Ges. mbH & Co. KG — Flensburg** Yd No: 727 Loa 193.00 (BB) Br ex 26.04 Dght 6.450 Lbp 182.39 Br md 26.00 Dpth 16.70 Welded, 3 dks	**(A35A2RR) Ro-Ro Cargo Ship** Passengers: driver berths: 12 Stern door/ramp (centre) Len: 15.00 Wid: 17.00 Swl: 120 Lane-Len: 3726 Trailers: 255	**2 oil engines** reduction geared to sc. shafts driving 2 CP propellers Total Power: 16,200kW (22,026hp) 21.5kn MaK 9M43 2 x 4 Stroke 9 Cy. 430 x 610 each-8100kW (11013bhp) Caterpillar Motoren GmbH & Co. KG-Germany AuxGen: 2 x 1080kW a.c, 2 x 1600kW a.c Thrusters: 1 Tunnel thruster (f)
9322425 *TCOD2* -	**UN PENDIK** - **UN Ro-Ro Isletmeleri AS (UN Ro-Ro Management Inc)** Bluewater Ship Management Ltd *Istanbul* *Turkey* MMSI: 271000792	**29,004** 8,702 11,400	Class: NV	**2005-10 Flensburger Schiffbau-Ges. mbH & Co. KG — Flensburg** Yd No: 728 Loa 193.00 (BB) Br ex - Dght 6.450 Lbp 182.39 Br md 26.00 Dpth 16.70 Welded, 3 dks	**(A35A2RR) Ro-Ro Cargo Ship** Passengers: driver berths: 12 Stern door/ramp (centre) Len: 15.00 Wid: 17.00 Swl: 120 Lane-Len: 3726 Trailers: 254	**2 oil engines** reduction geared to sc. shafts driving 2 CP propellers Total Power: 16,200kW (22,026hp) 21.5kn MaK 9M43 2 x 4 Stroke 9 Cy. 430 x 610 each-8100kW (11013bhp) Caterpillar Motoren GmbH & Co. KG-Germany AuxGen: 2 x 900kW 60Hz a.c, 2 x 1600kW 60Hz a.c Thrusters: 1 Tunnel thruster (f)
9322437 *TCOD3* -	**UN TRIESTE** - **UN Ro-Ro Isletmeleri AS (UN Ro-Ro Management Inc)** Bluewater Ship Management Ltd *Istanbul* *Turkey* MMSI: 271000793	**29,004** 8,702 11,400	Class: NV	**2006-01 Flensburger Schiffbau-Ges. mbH & Co. KG — Flensburg** Yd No: 729 Loa 193.00 (BB) Br ex - Dght 6.450 Lbp 182.39 Br md 26.00 Dpth 16.70 Welded, 3 dks	**(A35A2RR) Ro-Ro Cargo Ship** Passengers: driver berths: 12 Stern door/ramp (centre) Len: 15.00 Wid: 17.00 Swl: 120 Lane-Len: 3726 Trailers: 254	**2 oil engines** reduction geared to sc. shafts driving 2 CP propellers Total Power: 16,200kW (22,026hp) 21.5kn MaK 9M43 2 x 4 Stroke 9 Cy. 430 x 610 each-8100kW (11013bhp) Caterpillar Motoren GmbH & Co. KG-Germany AuxGen: 1 x 1080kW a.c, 1 x 900kW a.c, 2 x 1600kW a.c Thrusters: 1 Tunnel thruster (f)
9558361 *3EVV5* -	**UNA** - **Gea-Uniform Pte Ltd** Stellar Shipmanagement Services Pte Ltd *Panama* *Panama* MMSI: 370159000 Official number: 4489313A	**4,758** 2,321 7,419 T/cm 16.9	Class: BV	**2013-05 Nanjing Tianshun Shipbuilding Co Ltd — Nanjing JS** Yd No: 0607 Loa 115.00 Br ex - Dght 7.000 Lbp 109.24 Br md 17.60 Dpth 8.70 Welded, 1 dk	**(A12B2TR) Chemical/Products Tanker** Double Hull (13F)	**1 oil engine** reduction geared to sc. shaft driving 1 FP propeller Total Power: 3,310kW (4,500hp) 12.0kn Yanmar 8N330-EN 1 x 4 Stroke 8 Cy. 330 x 440 3310kW (4500bhp) Zibo Diesel Engine Factory-China
8846292 *YL2798* -	**UNA** *ex* Mrtk-0801 *-2012* **Varita Ltd (SIA 'Varita')** - *Riga* *Latvia* MMSI: 275425000 Official number: 0844	**117** 35 30	Class: (RS)	**1991-06 Sosnovskiy Sudostroitelnyy Zavod — Sosnovka** Yd No: 801 Loa 25.50 Br ex 7.00 Dght 2.390 Lbp 22.00 Br md - Dpth 3.30 Welded, 1 dk	**(B11A2FS) Stern Trawler** Ins: 64 Ice Capable	**1 oil engine** driving 1 FP propeller Total Power: 220kW (299hp) 9.5kn S.K.L. 6NVD26A-2 1 x 4 Stroke 6 Cy. 180 x 260 220kW (299bhp) SKL Motoren u. Systemtechnik AG-Magdeburg
8414324 *JI3188* -	**UNABARA** - **Nittetsu Butsuryu KK** - *Wakayama, Wakayama* *Japan* MMSI: 431301252 Official number: 126482	*199* - 229		**1984-10 Kochi Jyuko (Kaisei Zosen) K.K. — Kochi** Yd No: 1732 Loa 36.35 Br ex - Dght 3.503 Lbp 29.52 Br md 9.31 Dpth 4.12 Welded, 1 dk	**(B32A2ST) Tug**	**2 oil engines** Geared Integral to driving 2 Z propellers Total Power: 2,500kW (3,400hp) 13.5kn Niigata 6L28BXE 2 x 4 Stroke 6 Cy. 280 x 320 each-1250kW (1700bhp) Niigata Engineering Co Ltd-Japan
8003448 *J5MI2* -	**UNAL** - **Guinemar** - *Bissau* *Guinea-Bissau*	*120* - 200	Class: (BV)	**1980-12 Scheepswerf A. Baars Azn. B.V. — Sliedrecht** Yd No: 692 Loa - Br ex - Dght 1.001 Lbp 20.32 Br md 7.92 Dpth 1.81 Welded, 1 dk	**(A35D2RL) Landing Craft** Bow door/ramp	**1 oil engine** geared to sc. shaft driving 1 FP propeller Total Power: 216kW (294hp) Volvo Penta TMD121 1 x 4 Stroke 6 Cy. 130 x 150 216kW (294bhp) AB Volvo Penta-Sweden
9118642 *DSDG6* -	**UNAM FRONTIER** *ex* Faseco No. 101 *-2012* **Unam Chemical Carriers Ltd** - *Incheon* *South Korea* MMSI: 440102110 Official number: ICR-940705	**999** 701 2,385 T/cm 7.4	Class: KR	**1994-08 Koje Shipbuilding Co Ltd — Geoje** Yd No: 356 Loa 76.20 (BB) Br ex 11.83 Dght 5.239 Lbp 68.80 Br md 11.80 Dpth 5.70 Welded, 1 dk	**(A12B2TR) Chemical/Products Tanker** Double Bottom Entire Compartment Length Liq: 2,430; Liq (Oil): 2,430 Cargo Heating Coils Compartments: 10 Wing Ta, 2 Wing Slop Ta, ER 10 Cargo Pump (s): 10x125m³/hr Manifold: Bow/CM: 35m	**1 oil engine** with clutches, flexible couplings & sr geared to sc. shaft driving 1 FP propeller Total Power: 1,030kW (1,400hp) 12.4kn Niigata 6M28AFTE 1 x 4 Stroke 6 Cy. 280 x 480 1030kW (1400bhp) Ssangyong Heavy Industries Co Ltd-South Korea AuxGen: 2 x 220kW 445V a.c Fuel: 28.0 (d.f.) 63.0 (r.f.)
9121338 *DSDC9* -	**UNAM GLORY** *ex* Paragon *-2003* *ex* Jee Yang *-2001* *ex* Bando Sapphire *-1999* *ex* Dong Myung Sapphire *-1994* **Unam Chemical Carriers Ltd** - *Incheon* *South Korea* MMSI: 441035000 Official number: ICR-947771	**999** 701 2,372 T/cm 7.4	Class: KR	**1994-04 Koje Shipbuilding Co Ltd — Geoje** Yd No: 355 Loa 76.20 (BB) Br ex - Dght 5.239 Lbp 68.81 Br md 11.80 Dpth 5.70 Welded, 1 dk	**(A12B2TR) Chemical/Products Tanker** Double Bottom Entire Compartment Length Liq: 2,406; Liq (Oil): 2,555 Cargo Heating Coils Compartments: 6 Ta, 10 Wing Ta, 2 Wing Slop Ta, ER 2 Cargo Pump (s): 2x400m³/hr Manifold: Bow/CM: 34.2m	**1 oil engine** with clutches, flexible couplings & sr geared to sc. shaft driving 1 FP propeller Total Power: 1,261kW (1,714hp) 12.5kn Alpha 6L28/32 1 x 4 Stroke 6 Cy. 280 x 320 1261kW (1714bhp) STX Corp-South Korea AuxGen: 2 x 148kW 445V a.c Fuel: 32.0 (d.f.) 73.0 (r.f.)

9120437 DSFP5 -
UNAM MERCURY
ex Boghil *-2005* *ex* Daemyong *-2002*
ex Eastern Jin Joo *-1998*
Unam Chemical Carriers Ltd
-
SatCom: Inmarsat C 444066912
Incheon *South Korea*
MMSI: 440056000
Official number: ICR-950957
1,999 1,087 3,422 T/cm 9.8
Class: KR
1995-08 Banguhjin Engineering & Shipbuilding Co Ltd — Ulsan Yd No: 97
Loa 85.60 (BB) Br ex - Dght 5.636
Lbp 78.01 Br md 14.00 Dpth 6.60
Welded, 1 dk
(A12B2TR) Chemical/Products Tanker
Double Bottom Entire, Double Sides Partial
Liq: 3,670; Liq (Oil): 3,670
Cargo Heating Coils
Compartments: 10 Wing Ta, 2 Wing Slop Ta, ER
2 Cargo Pump (s): 2x400m³/hr
Manifold: Bow/CM: 47m
1 oil engine reduction geared to sc. shaft (s) driving 1 FP propeller
Total Power: 1,713kW (2,329hp) 13.6kn
Alpha 7L28/32A
1 x 4 Stroke 7 Cy. 280 x 320 1713kW (2329bhp)
Ssangyong Heavy Industries Co Ltd-South Korea
AuxGen: 2 x 250kW 480V a.c
Fuel: 53.0 (d.f.) 135.0 (r.f.)

9480306 DSQF4 -
UNAM POSEIDON
ex Samho Beryl *-2010*
Unam Chemical Carriers Ltd
-
SatCom: Inmarsat C 444055510
Incheon *South Korea*
MMSI: 441555000
Official number: ICR-084661
2,479 1,078 3,363 T/cm 10.1
Class: KR
2008-10 Samho Shipbuilding Co Ltd — Tongyeong Yd No: 1104
Loa 87.91 (BB) Br ex - Dght 5.813
Lbp 80.40 Br md 14.00 Dpth 7.30
Welded, 1 dk
(A12B2TR) Chemical/Products Tanker
Double Hull (13F)
Liq: 3,728; Liq (Oil): 3,728
Cargo Heating Coils
Compartments: 1 Ta, 8 Wing Ta, ER, 2 Wing Slop Ta
11 Cargo Pump (s): 11x200m³/hr
Manifold: Bow/CM: 46.1m
1 oil engine driving 1 FP propeller
Total Power: 2,205kW (2,998hp) 12.7kn
Hanshin LH38L
1 x 4 Stroke 6 Cy. 380 x 760 2205kW (2998bhp)
The Hanshin Diesel Works Ltd-Japan
AuxGen: 3 x 260kW 450V a.c
Thrusters: 1 Tunnel thruster (f)
Fuel: 47.0 (d.f.) 156.0 (r.f.)

9117428 DSDQ250 -
UNAM PRIDE
ex Jin Nam Fortune *-2010*
ex Fortune No. 9 *-2004* *ex* Pu Yang No. 1 *-1999*
Unam Chemical Carriers Ltd
-
Incheon *South Korea*
MMSI: 440000000
Official number: ICR-942543
698 - 1,963
Class: KR
1994-12 Haedong Shipbuilding Co Ltd — Tongyeong Yd No: 1007
Loa 79.80 (BB) Br ex - Dght 4.511
Lbp 72.80 Br md 11.00 Dpth 5.00
Welded, 1 dk
(A12B2TR) Chemical/Products Tanker
Liq: 2,067; Liq (Oil): 2,067
Manifold: Bow/CM: 40.4m
1 oil engine driving 1 FP propeller
Total Power: 1,030kW (1,400hp) 11.1kn
Niigata 6M28AET
1 x 4 Stroke 6 Cy. 280 x 480 1030kW (1400bhp)
Ssangyong Heavy Industries Co Ltd-South Korea

5372915 YXYY -
UNARE
PDV Marina SA
-
Puerto la Cruz *Venezuela*
Official number: AGSP-0678
279 139 -
Class: (AB)
1954 Gulfport Shipbuilding Corp. — Port Arthur, Tx Yd No: 466
Loa 32.42 Br ex 8.31 Dght 3.868
Lbp 30.56 Br md 8.26 Dpth 4.27
Welded, 1 dk
(B32A2ST) Tug
1 oil engine sr geared to sc. shaft driving 1 FP propeller
Total Power: 1,169kW (1,589hp)
General Motors 16-278-A
1 x Vee 2 Stroke 16 Cy. 222 x 267 1169kW (1589bhp)
(Re-engined ,made 1943, refitted 1954)
General Motors Corp-USA
AuxGen: 2 x 40kW, 1 x 35kW
Fuel: 94.5

9525871 9HA2953 -
UNAYZAH
Onayzah Ltd
United Arab Shipping Co (UASC)
Valletta *Malta*
MMSI: 256885000
Official number: 9525871
141,077 75,670 145,520
Class: LR (GL) SS 02/2012
100A1
container ship
ShipRight (SDA, FDA)
*IWS
LI
ECO (TOC)
LMC **UMS**
Cable: 770.0/122.0 U3 (a)
2012-02 Samsung Heavy Industries Co Ltd — Geoje Yd No: 1878
Loa 366.10 (BB) Br ex 48.33 Dght 15.500
Lbp 349.50 Br md 48.20 Dpth 29.80
Welded, 1 dk
(A33A2CC) Container Ship (Fully Cellular)
TEU 13296 C Ho 6428 Teu C Dk 6868 TEU incl 1000 ref C
Compartments: 7 Cell Ho, ER
1 oil engine driving 1 FP propeller
Total Power: 71,770kW (97,578hp) 24.1kn
MAN-B&W 12K98ME7
1 x 2 Stroke 12 Cy. 980 x 2660 71770kW (97578bhp)
Doosan Engine Co Ltd-South Korea
AuxGen: 3 x 4250kW 6600V 60Hz a.c
Boilers: e (ex.g.) 7.6kgf/cm² (7.5bar), e (ex.g.) 13.8kgf/cm² (13.5bar), WTAuxB (o.f.) 8.2kgf/cm² (8.0bar)
Thrusters: 1 Thwart. CP thruster (f)
Fuel: 344.0 (d.f.) 12258.0 (r.f.)

9526318 ZCXS6 -
UNBRIDLED
Neptunes Ltd
Nigel Burgess Ltd (BURGESS)
SatCom: Inmarsat C 431900167
George Town *Cayman Islands (British)*
MMSI: 319003900
Official number: 740775
803 240 234
Class: AB
2009-06 Trinity Yachts LLC — New Orleans LA Yd No: 039
Loa 58.23 Br ex 10.48 Dght 2.740
Lbp 52.62 Br md 10.06 Dpth 5.37
Welded, 1 dk
(X11A2YP) Yacht
Hull Material: Aluminium Alloy
2 oil engines reduction geared to sc. shafts driving 2 FP propellers
Total Power: 2,960kW (4,024hp)
Caterpillar 3512
2 x Vee 4 Stroke 12 Cy. 170 x 190 each-1480kW (2012bhp)
Caterpillar Inc-USA
AuxGen: 2 x 236kW a.c
Fuel: 110.0

8847674 - -
UNCLE BAYOU
ex Capt. Tom *-1999*
Jerry L Osborn Jr
-
Port O'Connor, TX *United States of America*
Official number: 916663
103 82 -
1987 Turn-Key Construction — New Iberia, La
Loa - Br ex - Dght -
Lbp 23.77 Br md 6.71 Dpth 2.74
Welded, 1 dk
(B11B2FV) Fishing Vessel
1 oil engine driving 1 FP propeller

7937525 WYA2662 -
UNCLE BILLY
ex Gems *-1999*
Snodgrass Brothers Inc
-
Port Isabel, TX *United States of America*
MMSI: 367174370
Official number: 597031
103 70 -
1978 Marine Mart, Inc. — Port Isabel, Tx Yd No: 175
L reg 19.69 Br ex 6.13 Dght -
Lbp - Br md - Dpth 3.43
Welded, 1 dk
(B11A2FT) Trawler
1 oil engine driving 1 FP propeller
Total Power: 268kW (364hp)
Caterpillar 3408PCTA
1 x Vee 4 Stroke 8 Cy. 137 x 152 268kW (364bhp)
Caterpillar Tractor Co-USA

7650701 DUA2016 -
UNCLE CHICK
ex Joffrei 2 *-1991*
ex Tatsuhiro Maru No. 11 *-1991*
Flor De Cana Shipping Inc
National Marine Corp
Manila *Philippines*
Official number: 00-0001173
499 380 1,189
Class: RI (NK)
1976 Kogushi Zosen K.K. — Okayama Yd No: 200
Loa 63.10 Br ex - Dght 4.046
Lbp 57.94 Br md 10.00 Dpth 4.50
Welded, 1 dk
(A13B2TU) Tanker (unspecified)
Liq: 1,261; Liq (Oil): 1,261
1 oil engine driving 1 FP propeller
Total Power: 1,030kW (1,400hp) 10.5kn
Hanshin 6LU32
1 x 4 Stroke 6 Cy. 320 x 510 1030kW (1400bhp)
The Hanshin Diesel Works Ltd-Japan
AuxGen: 3 x 42kW a.c
Fuel: 50.0 (d.f.)

8851120 WYT8897 -
UNCLE GEORGE
ex El Toro *-1998*
Marine Fueling Service Inc
-
Port Arthur, TX *United States of America*
Official number: 558222
147 100 -
1974 Bergeron Machine Shop — Braithwaite, La
Loa - Br ex - Dght -
Lbp 19.48 Br md 7.32 Dpth 2.99
Welded, 1 dk
(B32A2ST) Tug
1 oil engine driving 1 FP propeller
Total Power: 1,177kW (1,600hp)

9242388 TCCJ5 -
UND ATILIM
UN Ro-Ro Isletmeleri AS (UN Ro-Ro Management Inc)
Bluewater Ship Management Ltd
Istanbul *Turkey*
MMSI: 271000661
Official number: 7927
26,469 7,941 9,830
Class: NV
2002-01 Flensburger Schiffbau-Ges. mbH & Co. KG — Flensburg Yd No: 715
Loa 193.28 (BB) Br ex - Dght 7.400
Lbp 182.39 Br md 26.00 Dpth 16.70
Welded, 3 dks
(A35A2RR) Ro-Ro Cargo Ship
Passengers: driver berths: 12
Stern door/ramp (centre)
Len: 18.00 Wid: 17.00 Swl: 120
Lane-Len: 3214
Lane-Wid: 3.10
Lane-clr ht: 6.80
Trailers: 222
TEU 760 incl 60 ref C.
2 oil engines reduction geared to sc. shafts driving 2 CP propellers
Total Power: 16,200kW (22,026hp) 21.0kn
MaK 9M43
2 x 4 Stroke 9 Cy. 430 x 610 each-8100kW (11013bhp)
Caterpillar Motoren GmbH & Co. KG-Germany
AuxGen: 1 x 400kW 460V 60Hz a.c, 2 x 400kW 460V 60Hz a.c
Thrusters: 1 Thwart. CP thruster (f)
Fuel: 138.1 (d.f.) 1121.9 (r.f.) 60.9pd

9242390 TCCA6 -
UND BIRLIK
UN Ro-Ro Isletmeleri AS (UN Ro-Ro Management Inc)
Bluewater Ship Management Ltd
Istanbul *Turkey*
MMSI: 271000662
26,469 7,941 9,865
Class: NV
2002-03 Flensburger Schiffbau-Ges. mbH & Co. KG — Flensburg Yd No: 716
Loa 193.00 (BB) Br ex 26.04 Dght 6.450
Lbp 182.39 Br md 26.00 Dpth 16.70
Welded, 3 dks
(A35A2RR) Ro-Ro Cargo Ship
Passengers: driver berths: 12
Stern door/ramp (a)
Len: 18.00 Wid: 15.00 Swl: 120
Lane-Len: 3214
Lane-Wid: 3.10
Lane-clr ht: 6.80
Trailers: 222
TEU 709 incl 60 ref C.
2 oil engines reduction geared to sc. shafts driving 2 CP propellers
Total Power: 16,200kW (22,026hp) 21.6kn
MaK 9M43
2 x 4 Stroke 9 Cy. 430 x 610 each-8100kW (11013bhp)
Caterpillar Motoren GmbH & Co. KG-Germany
AuxGen: 1 x 400kW 460V 60Hz a.c, 2 x 400kW 460V 60Hz a.c
Thrusters: 1 Thwart. CP thruster (f)
Fuel: 138.1 (d.f.) (Heating Coils) 1121.9 (r.f.) 60.9pd

9215476 TCUY -
UND EGE
UN Ro-Ro Isletmeleri AS (UN Ro-Ro Management Inc)
Bluewater Ship Management Ltd
Istanbul *Turkey*
MMSI: 271000623
Official number: 7842
26,469 7,941 9,830
Class: NV
2001-06 Flensburger Schiffbau-Ges. mbH & Co. KG — Flensburg Yd No: 713
Loa 193.00 (BB) Br ex 26.04 Dght 7.400
Lbp 182.39 Br md 26.00 Dpth 16.70
Welded, 3 dks
(A35A2RR) Ro-Ro Cargo Ship
Passengers: berths: 12; driver berths: 12
Stern door/ramp (a)
Len: 18.00 Wid: 15.00 Swl: 120
Lane-Len: 3214
Lane-Wid: 3.10
Lane-clr ht: 6.80
Trailers: 222
TEU 709 incl 60 ref C.
2 oil engines with flexible couplings & reduction geared to sc shafts driving 2 CP propellers
Total Power: 16,200kW (22,026hp) 21.6kn
MaK 9M43
2 x 4 Stroke 9 Cy. 430 x 610 each-8100kW (11013bhp)
Caterpillar Motoren GmbH & Co. KG-Germany
AuxGen: 2 x 1600kW 230/440V 60Hz a.c, 2 x 1440kW 230/440V 60Hz a.c
Thrusters: 1 Thwart. CP thruster (f)
Fuel: 138.1 (d.f.) (Heating Coils) 1121.9 (r.f.) 60.9pd

5372939 - -
UNDA
ex Underley Queen *-1960*
Madeleine Llanos
Sea Harvester Shipping Co Ltd
Port of Spain *Trinidad & Tobago*
Official number: TT033006
113 52 -
Class: (LR)
✠ Classed LR until 5/60
1952-02 Henry Scarr Ltd. — Hessle Yd No: 684
Converted From: Trawler-1976
L reg 25.76 Br ex 6.56 Dght -
Lbp 25.61 Br md 6.51 Dpth 2.98
Welded, 1 dk
(B12A2FF) Fish Factory Ship
1 oil engine driving 1 FP propeller
Mirrlees TLSDMR
1 x 4 Stroke 6 Cy. 216 x 330
Mirrlees, Bickerton & Day-Stockport

7047320 *YDPY* -	**UNDAN** *ex* Challenge *-1984* **PT Baruna Raya Logistics** - *Jakarta* *Indonesia* MMSI: 525017022	**648** 195 1,024	Class: KI (AB)	**1970-09 Zigler Shipyards Inc — Jennings LA** Yd No: 210 Loa 51.82 Br ex - Dght 3.899 Lbp 47.70 Br md 11.59 Dpth 4.58 Welded, 1 dk	**(B21B20A) Anchor Handling Tug Supply**	**2 oil engines** reverse reduction geared to sc. shafts driving 2 FP propellers Total Power: 2,206kW (3,000hp) EMD (Electro-Motive) 12-645-E5 2 x Vee 2 Stroke 12 Cy. 230 x 254 each-1103kW (1500bhp) General Motors Corp.Electro-Motive Div.-La Grange AuxGen: 2 x 450V a.c Thrusters: 1 Thwart. FP thruster (f) Fuel: 225.5 (d.f.)
9430090 *5BWD2* -	**UNDARUM** **Seafund Shipping Co Ltd** Marlow Navigation Co Ltd *Limassol* *Cyprus* MMSI: 210296000	**7,170** 3,068 8,512	Class: GL (BV)	**2009-10 Yangfan Group Co Ltd — Zhoushan ZJ** Yd No: 2064 Loa 132.70 (BB) Br ex - Dght 7.650 Lbp 121.00 Br md 19.20 Dpth 10.50 Welded, 1 dk	**(A33A2CC) Container Ship (Fully Cellular)** TEU 704 incl 116 ref C Compartments: 2 Cell Ho, ER 2 Ha: ER Ice Capable	**1 oil engine** reduction geared to sc. shaft driving 1 CP propeller Total Power: 6,300kW (8,565hp) 17.0kn MaK 7M43 1 x 4 Stroke 7 Cy. 430 x 610 6300kW (8565bhp) Caterpillar Motoren GmbH & Co. KG-Germany AuxGen: 3 x 492kW 400V 50Hz a.c, 1 x 1200kW 400V 50Hz a.c Thrusters: 1 Tunnel thruster (f) Fuel: 704.0
8963210 *WDB8103* -	**UNDAUNTED** *ex* Krystal K *-1998* *ex* Kings Pointer *-1993* *ex* Undaunted (ATA-199) *-1963* *ex* Undaunted (ATR-126) *-1943* **Pere Marquette Shipping Co** - *Ludington, MI* *United States of America* MMSI: 366578000 Official number: 995467	**569** 170 -	Class: (AB)	**1943-01 Gulfport Boiler & Welding Works, Inc. — Port Arthur, Tx** Yd No: 244 Loa 43.58 Br ex - Dght 4.930 Lbp 42.26 Br md 10.08 Dpth 5.18 Welded, 1 dk	**(B32B2SA) Articulated Pusher Tug**	**2 oil engines** geared to sc. shafts driving 2 FP propellers Total Power: 1,104kW (1,500hp) 13.0kn General Motors 12-278A 2 x Vee 2 Stroke 12 Cy. 222 x 267 each-552kW (750bhp) General Motors Corp-USA AuxGen: 2 x 150kW a.c Fuel: 117.0 (d.f.)
7216763 - -	**UNDERSEA HUNTER** **Cazador Submarino SA** Undersea Hunter Inc *Costa Rica*	*148* 100 -		**1968 Sermons Shipyard — Tarpon Springs, Fl** Converted From: Research Vessel-1990 L reg 23.44 Br ex 7.32 Dght - Lbp - Br md - Dpth 3.41 Welded	**(A37A2PC) Passenger/Cruise** Passengers: cabins: 7; berths: 14	**1 oil engine** driving 1 FP propeller Total Power: 353kW (480hp) Caterpillar 1 x 4 Stroke 353kW (480bhp) Caterpillar Tractor Co-USA
9006112 *LXUN* -	**UNDINE** **CLdN ro-ro SA** Cobelfret Ferries NV *Luxembourg* *Luxembourg* MMSI: 253031000	**11,854** 3,556 7,225	Class: NV	**1991-12 Dalian Shipyard Co Ltd — Dalian LN** Yd No: R70/3 Loa 147.40 (BB) Br ex - Dght 5.331 Lbp 137.10 Br md 21.00 Dpth 12.50 Welded, 2 dks	**(A35A2RR) Ro-Ro Cargo Ship** Stern door/ramp (p) Len: 16.00 Wid: 7.70 Swl: 45 Stern door/ramp (s) Len: 11.00 Wid: 7.70 Swl: 45 Lane-Len: 1604 Lane-clr ht: 6.26 Trailers: 122 TEU 514 incl 44 ref C.	**2 oil engines** reduction geared to sc. shafts driving 2 CP propellers Total Power: 4,770kW (6,486hp) 13.0kn MaK 8M453C 2 x 4 Stroke 8 Cy. 320 x 420 each-2385kW (3243bhp) Krupp MaK Maschinenbau GmbH-Kiel AuxGen: 1 x 500kW 440V 60Hz a.c, 2 x 390kW 440V 60Hz a.c Thrusters: 1 Tunnel thruster (f) Fuel: 160.0 (d.f.) 754.9 (r.f.)
9240160 *SHJC* -	**UNDINE** **Rederi AB Wallship** Wallenius Marine AB SatCom: Inmarsat C 426588410 *Stockholm* *Sweden* MMSI: 265884000	**67,378** 28,512 28,388 T/cm 48.9	Class: LR ✠ **100A1** SS 01/2013 vehicle carrier movable decks Nos. 4, 6 & 8 dks strengthened for the carriage of roll on - roll off cargoes *IWS LI ✠ **LMC** **UMS** Eq.Ltr: R†; Cable: 747.5/84.0 U3 (a)	**2003-01 Daewoo Shipbuilding & Marine Engineering Co Ltd — Geoje** Yd No: 4431 **2006-01 Hyundai-Vinashin Shipyard Co Ltd — Ninh Hoa** (Additional cargo section) Lengthened-2006 Loa 227.90 (BB) Br ex 32.33 Dght 9.500 Lbp 219.30 Br md 32.26 Dpth 32.59 Welded, 12 dks incl 4 hoistable decks	**(A35B2RV) Vehicles Carrier** Side door/ramp (s) Len: 25.00 Wid: 5.00 Swl: 30 Quarter stern door & ramp (s. a.) Len: 45.00 Wid: 7.00 Swl: 105 Lane-Len: 5700 Cars: 7,100	**1 oil engine** driving 1 FP propeller Total Power: 16,358kW (22,240hp) 20.5kn B&W 8S60MC 1 x 2 Stroke 8 Cy. 600 x 2292 16358kW (22240bhp) Doosan Engine Co Ltd-South Korea AuxGen: 2 x 1400kW 450V 60Hz a.c, 1 x 1087kW 450V 60Hz a.c, 1 x 728kW 450V 60Hz a.c Boilers: AuxB (ex.g.) 9.0kgf/cm² (8.8bar), WTAuxB (o.f.) 9.0kgf/cm² (8.8bar) Thrusters: 2 Thwart. CP thruster (f)
9262912 *V7AN7* -	**UNDINE** *ex* Houyoshi Express *-2013* **Proton Marine Ltd** Product Shipping & Trading SA *Majuro* *Marshall Islands* MMSI: 538005033 Official number: 5033	**28,799** 12,945 47,999 T/cm 51.8	Class: BV (NK)	**2004-03 Iwagi Zosen Co Ltd — Kamijima EH** Yd No: 219 Loa 179.99 Br ex - Dght 12.480 Lbp 172.00 Br md 32.20 Dpth 19.05 Welded, 1 dk	**(A13B2TP) Products Tanker** Double Hull (13F) Liq: 57,424; Liq (Oil): 57,424 4 Cargo Pump (s)	**1 oil engine** driving 1 FP propeller Total Power: 9,480kW (12,889hp) 15.1kn MAN-B&W 6S50MC-C 1 x 2 Stroke 6 Cy. 500 x 2000 9480kW (12889bhp) Mitsui Engineering & Shipbuilding CLtd-Japan AuxGen: 3 x 420kW a.c Fuel: 2130.0
9659804 *DHDP2* -	**UNDINE** **Hohe Dune GmbH** *Rostock* *Germany* MMSI: 211590700 Official number: 4073	**189** 57 38	Class: GL	**2013-06 Poltramp Yard Sp z oo — Swinoujscie** Yd No: 84-11 Loa 24.93 Br ex - Dght 1.700 Lbp 21.30 Br md 7.00 Dpth 3.30 Welded, 1 dk	**(A37B2PS) Passenger Ship** Passengers: unberthed: 60	**2 oil engines** reduction geared to sc. shafts driving 2 Propellers Total Power: 450kW (612hp) 10.5kn John Deere 6068TFM75 2 x 4 Stroke 6 Cy. 106 x 127 each-225kW (306bhp)
7811666 - -	**UNECA XII** *ex* Jorge H *-1986* **Union de Empresas Constructoras del Caribe (UNECA)** - *Cuba*	*498* 224 502	Class: (LR) ✠ Classed LR until 17/10/90	**1979-05 van Doesburg Heeselt N.V. — Waardenburg** Yd No: 113 Loa 45.37 Br ex 12.50 Dght 2.159 Lbp 39.20 Br md 12.21 Dpth 2.80 Welded, 1 dk	**(A35D2RL) Landing Craft** Bow door/ramp	**2 oil engines** sr geared to sc. shafts driving 2 FP propellers Total Power: 706kW (960hp) G.M. (Detroit Diesel) 16V-71-N 2 x Vee 2 Stroke 16 Cy. 108 x 127 each-353kW (480bhp) General Motors Detroit DieselAllison Divn-USA AuxGen: 1 x 30kW 380V 50Hz a.c, 1 x 5kW 380V 50Hz a.c
8889579 *JJ3825* -	**UNEI MARU No. 7** **YK Yamani Kaiun** *Ieshima, Hyogo* *Japan* Official number: 132330	*499* - 999		**1995-07 Tokuoka Zosen K.K. — Naruto** Loa 71.00 Br ex - Dght 3.520 Lbp 65.00 Br md 13.50 Dpth 6.97 Welded, 1 dk	**(A24D2BA) Aggregates Carrier** Cranes: 1	**1 oil engine** driving 1 FP propeller Total Power: 1,912kW (2,600hp) 12.0kn Akasaka A37 1 x 4 Stroke 6 Cy. 370 x 720 1912kW (2600bhp) Akasaka Tekkosho KK (Akasaka DieselLtd)-Japan
9385403 *4XFL* -	**UNEX I** **United Petroleum Export Co Ltd (UNEX)** - *Haifa* *Israel* MMSI: 428016000 Official number: MS384	**855** 392 1,481	Class: GL (AB) (BV)	**2006-04 Guangdong Hope Yue Shipbuilding Industry Ltd — Guangzhou GD** Yd No: 2132 Loa 44.75 Br ex - Dght 4.900 Lbp 43.20 Br md 12.50 Dpth 6.10 Welded, 1 dk	**(B35E2TF) Bunkering Tanker** Double Hull (13F)	**2 oil engines** reduction geared to sc. shafts driving 2 FP propellers Total Power: 882kW (1,200hp) 9.0kn Caterpillar C18 2 x 4 Stroke 6 Cy. 145 x 183 each-441kW (600bhp) Caterpillar Inc-USA AuxGen: 3 x 99kW a.c
9417672 *4XGH* -	**UNEX II** **United Petroleum Export Co Ltd (UNEX)** - *Haifa* *Israel* MMSI: 428019000 Official number: MS386	**855** 392 1,472	Class: GL (AB) (BV)	**2006-12 Guangdong Hope Yue Shipbuilding Industry Ltd — Guangzhou GD** Yd No: 2139 Loa 44.75 Br ex - Dght 4.900 Lbp 43.20 Br md 12.50 Dpth 6.10 Welded, 1 dk	**(B35E2TF) Bunkering Tanker** Double Hull (13F)	**2 oil engines** reduction geared to sc. shafts driving 2 FP propellers Total Power: 882kW (1,200hp) 9.0kn Caterpillar C18 2 x 4 Stroke 6 Cy. 145 x 183 each-441kW (600bhp) Caterpillar Inc-USA
9611541 *D5AG7* -	**UNEX III** **Jasmine II Shipping Co Ltd** Bahia Grande SA SatCom: Inmarsat C 463711068 *Monrovia* *Liberia* MMSI: 636015372 Official number: 15372	**1,484** 635 2,100	Class: BV	**2011-07 Zhuhai Chenlong Shipyard Co Ltd — Zhuhai GD** Yd No: SI-019 Loa 55.00 Br ex - Dght 5.250 Lbp 52.19 Br md 15.00 Dpth 6.75 Welded, 1 dk	**(A13B2TP) Products Tanker** Double Hull (13F)	**2 oil engines** reduction geared to sc. shafts driving 2 FP propellers Total Power: 1,472kW (2,002hp) 9.0kn Caterpillar C32 2 x Vee 4 Stroke 12 Cy. 145 x 162 each-736kW (1001bhp) Caterpillar Inc-USA AuxGen: 2 x 215kW 50Hz a.c Fuel: 140.0
8980945 *ZCIZ4* -	**UNFORGETTABLE** **Unforgettable Maritime Ltd** - *George Town* *Cayman Islands (British)* MMSI: 319823000 Official number: 736873	**409** 123 -	Class: NV	**2003-08 Danyard Aalborg A/S — Aalborg** Yd No: 285 Loa 37.14 Br ex 8.20 Dght 2.100 Lbp 33.00 Br md 8.00 Dpth 4.35 Welded, 1 dk	**(X11A2YP) Yacht**	**2 oil engines** geared to sc. shafts driving 2 Propellers Total Power: 882kW (1,200hp) 12.0kn Caterpillar 3406E 2 x 4 Stroke 6 Cy. 137 x 165 each-441kW (600bhp) Caterpillar Inc-USA

9655705 *JZI0* -	**UNGARAN** **PT Baruna Raya Logistics** - *Jakarta* *Indonesia* MMSI: 525019646 Official number: 3632/BA	**1,727** 518 1,393	Class: AB	**2013-05 Fujian Southeast Shipyard — Fuzhou FJ** Yd No: DN59M-103 Loa 59.85 Br ex - Dght 4.600 Lbp 54.56 Br md 14.95 Dpth 6.10 Welded, 1 dk	**(B21B20A) Anchor Handling Tug Supply**	**2 oil engines** reduction geared to sc. shafts driving 2 Propellers Total Power: 2,984kW (4,058hp) 11.0kn Caterpillar 3516C 2 x Vee 4 Stroke 16 Cy. 170 x 190 each-1492kW (2029bhp) Caterpillar Inc-USA
8217764 *POWI* -	**UNGGUL** *ex Shinei Maru -2012* *ex Yoshu Maru No. 17 -2006* **PT Pelayaran Andalas Bahtera Baruna** - *Indonesia* MMSI: 525020186	*1,668* - 3,037		**1983-01 Ube Dockyard Co. Ltd. — Ube** Yd No: 175 Loa 82.02 Br ex 13.82 Dght 5.314 Lbp 76.03 Br md 13.81 Dpth 6.33 Welded, 1 dk	**(A24A2BT) Cement Carrier** Grain: 2,530 Compartments: 6 Ho, ER	**1 oil engine** with clutches, flexible couplings & sr reverse geared to sc. shaft driving 1 FP propeller Total Power: 1,618kW (2,200hp) 11.8kn Niigata 6M34AFT 1 x 4 Stroke 6 Cy. 340 x 620 1618kW (2200bhp) Niigata Engineering Co Ltd-Japan AuxGen: 2 x 240kW 450V 60Hz a.c Fuel: 20.0 (d.f.) 90.0 (r.f.) 7.5pd
9261841 *3EUQ6* -	**UNGIESHI** *ex St Mila -2014 ex FS Mila -2008* *ex Clipper Legacy -2003* **P'S Maritime Co Nigeria Ltd** - *Panama* *Panama* MMSI: 355413000 Official number: 45590PEXT	**6,516** 3,195 10,018 T/cm 19.5	Class: BV (NV) (AB)	**2003-01 Yardimci Tersanesi A.S. — Tuzla** Yd No: 26 Loa 118.37 (BB) Br ex 19.02 Dght 8.220 Lbp 112.06 Br md 19.00 Dpth 10.10 Welded, 1 dk	**(A12B2TR) Chemical/Products Tanker** Double Hull (13F) Liq: 10,956; Liq (Oil): 11,369 Cargo Heating Coils Compartments: 10 Wing Ta, 2 Ta, 2 Wing Slop Ta, ER 12 Cargo Pump (s): 12x200m³/hr Manifold: Bow/CM: 57m Ice Capable	**1 oil engine** driving 1 FP propeller Total Power: 4,443kW (6,041hp) 14.5kn B&W 6S35MC 1 x 2 Stroke 6 Cy. 350 x 1400 4443kW (6041bhp) AuxGen: 3 x 500kW 450V 60Hz a.c, 1 x 500kW 450V a.c Thrusters: 1 Thwart. CP thruster Fuel: 197.0 (d.f.) 602.0 (r.f.) 22.0pd
8840092 *V8V2022* -	**UNGKAYAH JATI** **QR Sdn Bhd** - *Bandar Seri Begawan* *Brunei*	**239** 120 270	Class: (GL)	**1990-12 Greenbay Marine Pte Ltd — Singapore** Yd No: 79 Loa - Br ex - Dght 2.198 Lbp 34.80 Br md 8.50 Dpth 3.00 Welded, 1 dk	**(A13B2TU) Tanker (unspecified)**	**2 oil engines** reduction geared to sc. shafts driving 2 Directional propellers Total Power: 354kW (482hp) 9.0kn Cummins NTA-855-M 2 x 4 Stroke 6 Cy. 140 x 152 each-177kW (241bhp) Cummins Engine Co Inc-USA AuxGen: 2 x 29kW 220/380V a.c
9615987 *FFZK* -	**UNGUNDJA** **Venus Offshore Pte Ltd** Bourbon Offshore Surf SAS *Marseille* *France (FIS)* MMSI: 228002600 Official number: 929958Z	**5,830** 1,749 4,849	Class: BV	**2011-06 Zhejiang Shipbuilding Co Ltd — Fenghua ZJ** Yd No: ZJ2001 Loa 100.20 Br ex - Dght 6.350 Lbp 95.60 Br md 21.00 Dpth 8.00 Welded, 1 dk	**(B22A2OR) Offshore Support Vessel** Cranes: 1x150t,1x15t	**7 diesel electric oil engines** driving 7 gen. each 1235kW 600V a.c Connecting to 3 elec. motors each (1685kW) driving 3 Azimuth electric drive units Total Power: 10,444kW (14,203hp) 10.0kn Cummins KTA-50-M2 3 x Vee 4 Stroke 16 Cy. 159 x 159 each-1492kW (2029bhp) Cummins Engine Co Inc-USA Cummins KTA-50-M2 4 x Vee 4 Stroke 16 Cy. 159 x 159 each-1492kW (2029bhp) Cummins Engine Co Inc-USA Thrusters: 2 Tunnel thruster (f); 1 Retract. directional thruster (f)
7207877 *HO2772* -	**UNI 8** *ex Renegade -2007 ex Petro Service -1996* **Uni-Star Shipping Inc** - *Panama* *Panama* Official number: 3345408	**499** 150 508	Class: (GL)	**1968-07 Burton Shipyard Co., Inc. — Port Arthur, Tx** Yd No: 432 Loa 51.82 Br ex - Dght 3.566 Lbp 48.27 Br md 12.19 Dpth 4.27 Welded, 1 dk	**(B21A2OS) Platform Supply Ship**	**2 oil engines** reduction geared to sc. shafts driving 2 FP propellers Total Power: 678kW (922hp) 9.0kn G.M. (Detroit Diesel) 16V-71 2 x Vee 2 Stroke 16 Cy. 108 x 127 each-339kW (461bhp) (new engine 1974) General Motors Detroit DieselAllison Divn-USA
9130535 *VRYW2* -	**UNI-ACCORD** *ex Cosco Redsea -2002 ex Uni-Accord -2001* **Evergreen Marine (Hong Kong) Ltd** Evergreen Marine Corp (Taiwan) Ltd (EVERGREEN LINE) *Hong Kong* *Hong Kong* MMSI: 477406000 Official number: HK-1080	**14,807** 4,849 15,511 T/cm 33.0	Class: NK	**1997-10 Evergreen Heavy Industrial Corp — Nagasaki NS** Yd No: 1019 Loa 165.00 (BB) Br ex 27.30 Dght 8.520 Lbp 150.00 Br md 27.10 Dpth 10.10 Welded, 1 dk	**(A33A2CC) Container Ship (Fully Cellular)** TEU 1164 C Ho 440 TEU C Dk 724 TEU incl 200 ref C. Compartments: 4 Cell Ho, ER 13 Ha: (12.6 x 10.6)2 (12.8 x 7.9)10 (12.8 x 10.5)ER	**1 oil engine** driving 1 FP propeller Total Power: 10,916kW (14,841hp) 18.7kn Sulzer 7RTA52U 1 x 2 Stroke 7 Cy. 520 x 1800 10916kW (14841bhp) Diesel United Ltd.-Aioi AuxGen: 4 x a.c Thrusters: 1 Thwart. FP thruster (f) Fuel: 2315.0 (r.f.)
9130547 *BKNR* -	**UNI-ACTIVE** **Evergreen International Storage & Transport Corp** Evergreen Marine Corp (Taiwan) Ltd (EVERGREEN LINE) SatCom: Inmarsat B 335190610 *Keelung* *Chinese Taipei* MMSI: 416340000 Official number: 013839	**14,807** 4,849 15,512 T/cm 33.0	Class: CR NK	**1998-01 Evergreen Shipyard Corp — Nagasaki NS** Yd No: 1021 Loa 165.00 (BB) Br ex 27.30 Dght 8.518 Lbp 150.00 Br md 27.10 Dpth 10.10 Welded, 1 dk	**(A33A2CC) Container Ship (Fully Cellular)** TEU 1164 C Ho 440 TEU C Dk 724 TEU incl 200 ref C. Compartments: 4 Cell Ho, ER 13 Ha: (12.6 x 10.6)2 (12.8 x 7.9)10 (12.8 x 10.5)ER	**1 oil engine** driving 1 FP propeller Total Power: 10,916kW (14,841hp) 18.7kn Sulzer 7RTA52U 1 x 2 Stroke 7 Cy. 520 x 1800 10916kW (14841bhp) Diesel United Ltd.-Aioi AuxGen: 3 x 1100kW 450V a.c Thrusters: 1 Thwart. CP thruster (f) Fuel: 148.0 (d.f.) (Heating Coils) 2207.0 (r.f.) 42.0pd
9130559 *BKNS* -	**UNI-ADROIT** **Evergreen International Storage & Transport Corp** Evergreen Marine Corp (Taiwan) Ltd (EVERGREEN LINE) SatCom: Inmarsat B 335460710 *Keelung* *Chinese Taipei* MMSI: 416341000 Official number: 013840	**14,807** 4,849 15,511 T/cm 33.0	Class: CR NK	**1998-04 Evergreen Shipyard Corp — Nagasaki NS** Yd No: 1022 Loa 165.00 (BB) Br ex 27.30 Dght 8.500 Lbp 150.00 Br md 27.10 Dpth 10.10 Welded, 1 dk	**(A33A2CC) Container Ship (Fully Cellular)** TEU 1164 C Ho 440 TEU C Dk 724 TEU incl 200 ref C. Compartments: 4 Cell Ho, ER 7 Ha: ER	**1 oil engine** driving 1 FP propeller Total Power: 10,916kW (14,841hp) 18.7kn Sulzer 7RTA52U 1 x 2 Stroke 7 Cy. 520 x 1800 10916kW (14841bhp) Diesel United Ltd.-Aioi AuxGen: 3 x 880kW 450V 60Hz a.c Thrusters: 1 Thwart. CP thruster (f) Fuel: 172.0 (d.f.) (Heating Coils) 2398.0 (r.f.) 45.0pd
9143348 *3FOM7* -	**UNI-AHEAD** **Gaining Enterprise SA** Evergreen Marine Corp (Taiwan) Ltd (EVERGREEN LINE) SatCom: Inmarsat B 335143810 *Panama* *Panama* MMSI: 351438000 Official number: 2505097CH	**14,796** 4,842 15,477 T/cm 33.0	Class: NK	**1997-08 China Shipbuilding Corp (CSBC) — Kaohsiung** Yd No: 642 Loa 165.01 (BB) Br ex - Dght 8.518 Lbp 150.00 Br md 27.10 Dpth 13.30 Welded, 1 dk	**(A33A2CC) Container Ship (Fully Cellular)** TEU 1164 C Ho 440 TEU C Dk 724 TEU incl 170 ref C. Compartments: 4 Cell Ho, ER 13 Ha: (12.6 x 10.6)2 (12.8 x 7.9)10 (12.8 x 10.5)ER	**1 oil engine** driving 1 FP propeller Total Power: 10,916kW (14,841hp) 18.7kn Sulzer 7RTA52U 1 x 2 Stroke 7 Cy. 520 x 1800 10916kW (14841bhp) Diesel United Ltd.-Aioi AuxGen: 4 x 850kW a.c Thrusters: 1 Thwart. FP thruster (f) Fuel: 2320.0 (r.f.)
9143336 *3FOJ7* -	**UNI-AMPLE** **Gaining Enterprise SA** Evergreen Marine Corp (Taiwan) Ltd (EVERGREEN LINE) SatCom: Inmarsat B 335143210 *Panama* *Panama* MMSI: 351432000 Official number: 2510097CH	**14,796** 4,842 15,477 T/cm 33.0	Class: NK	**1997-08 China Shipbuilding Corp (CSBC) — Kaohsiung** Yd No: 641 Loa 165.01 (BB) Br ex - Dght 8.518 Lbp 150.00 Br md 27.10 Dpth 13.30 Welded, 1 dk	**(A33A2CC) Container Ship (Fully Cellular)** TEU 1164 C Ho 440 TEU C Dk 724 TEU incl 170 ref C. Compartments: 4 Cell Ho 13 Ha: (12.6 x 10.6)2 (12.8 x 7.9)10 (12.8 x 10.5)ER	**1 oil engine** driving 1 FP propeller Total Power: 10,916kW (14,841hp) 18.7kn Sulzer 7RTA52U 1 x 2 Stroke 7 Cy. 520 x 1800 10916kW (14841bhp) Diesel United Ltd.-Aioi AuxGen: 4 x 850kW a.c Thrusters: 1 Thwart. FP thruster (f) Fuel: 2320.0 (r.f.)
9143350 *3FST7* -	**UNI-ANGEL** **Gaining Enterprise SA** Evergreen Marine Corp (Taiwan) Ltd (EVERGREEN LINE) SatCom: Inmarsat B 335160210 *Panama* *Panama* MMSI: 351602000 Official number: 2510797CH	**14,796** 4,842 15,477 T/cm 33.0	Class: NK	**1997-09 China Shipbuilding Corp (CSBC) — Kaohsiung** Yd No: 643 Loa 165.01 (BB) Br ex - Dght 8.518 Lbp 150.00 Br md 27.10 Dpth 13.30 Welded, 1 dk	**(A33A2CC) Container Ship (Fully Cellular)** TEU 1164 C Ho 440 TEU C Dk 724 TEU incl 170 ref C. Compartments: 4 Cell Ho 13 Ha:	**1 oil engine** driving 1 FP propeller Total Power: 10,916kW (14,841hp) 18.7kn Sulzer 7RTA52U 1 x 2 Stroke 7 Cy. 520 x 1800 10916kW (14841bhp) Diesel United Ltd.-Aioi AuxGen: 4 x 850kW a.c Thrusters: 1 Thwart. FP thruster (f) Fuel: 2320.0 (r.f.)
9130561 *3FPG8* -	**UNI-ARDENT** **Gaining Enterprise SA** Evergreen Marine Corp (Taiwan) Ltd (EVERGREEN LINE) SatCom: Inmarsat C 435285210 *Panama* *Panama* MMSI: 352852000 Official number: 2570898C	**14,807** 4,849 15,511 T/cm 33.0	Class: NK	**1998-07 Evergreen Shipyard Corp — Nagasaki NS** Yd No: 1023 Loa 165.00 (BB) Br ex 27.30 Dght 8.518 Lbp 150.00 Br md 27.10 Dpth 10.10 Welded, 1 dk	**(A33A2CC) Container Ship (Fully Cellular)** TEU 1164 C Ho 440 TEU C Dk 724 TEU incl 200 ref C. Compartments: 4 Cell Ho, ER 7 Ha: ER	**1 oil engine** driving 1 FP propeller Total Power: 10,916kW (14,841hp) 18.7kn Sulzer 7RTA52U 1 x 2 Stroke 7 Cy. 520 x 1800 10916kW (14841bhp) Diesel United Ltd.-Aioi AuxGen: 3 x 880kW 450V 60Hz a.c Thrusters: 1 Thwart. CP thruster (f) Fuel: 2315.0 (r.f.) (Heating Coils) 45.6pd

Number / Call sign	Name / Owner / Manager / Flag	Tonnage	Class	Builder / Dimensions	Type / Capacity	Machinery
9143362 *3FSV7* -	**UNI-ARISE** **Gaining Enterprise SA** Evergreen Marine Corp (Taiwan) Ltd (EVERGREEN LINE) SatCom: Inmarsat B 335160810 *Panama* Panama MMSI: 351608000 Official number: 2517298CH	**14,796** 4,842 15,477 T/cm 33.0	Class: NK	**1997-10 China Shipbuilding Corp (CSBC) — Kaohsiung** Yd No: 644 Loa 165.01 (BB) Br ex - Dght 8.518 Lbp 150.00 Br md 27.10 Dpth 13.30 Welded, 1 dk	**(A33A2CC) Container Ship (Fully Cellular)** TEU 1164 C Ho 440 TEU C Dk 724 TEU incl 170 ref C. Compartments: 4 Cell Ho 13 Ha:	**1 oil engine** driving 1 FP propeller Total Power: 10,916kW (14,841hp) 18.7kn Sulzer 7RTA52U 1 x 2 Stroke 7 Cy. 520 x 1800 10916kW (14841bhp) Diesel United Ltd.-Aioi AuxGen: 4 x 850kW a.c Thrusters: 1 Thwart. FP thruster (f) Fuel: 2320.0 (r.f.)
9130573 *3FVN8* -	**UNI-ASPIRE** **Gaining Enterprise SA** Evergreen Marine Corp (Taiwan) Ltd (EVERGREEN LINE) SatCom: Inmarsat B 335369510 *Panama* Panama MMSI: 353695000 Official number: 2593098C	**14,807** 4,849 15,511 T/cm 33.0	Class: NK	**1998-10 Evergreen Shipyard Corp — Nagasaki NS** Yd No: 1025 Loa 165.10 (BB) Br ex 27.30 Dght 8.518 Lbp 150.00 Br md 27.10 Dpth 10.10 Welded, 1 dk	**(A33A2CC) Container Ship (Fully Cellular)** TEU 1164 C Ho 440 TEU C Dk 724 TEU incl 200 ref C. Compartments: 4 Cell Ho, ER 13 Ha:	**1 oil engine** driving 1 FP propeller Total Power: 10,916kW (14,841hp) 18.7kn Sulzer 7RTA52U 1 x 2 Stroke 7 Cy. 520 x 1800 10916kW (14841bhp) Diesel United Ltd.-Aioi AuxGen: 4 x a.c Thrusters: 1 Thwart. CP thruster (f) Fuel: 2315.0 (r.f.)
9130585 *3FBD9* -	**UNI-ASSENT** **Gaining Enterprise SA** Evergreen Marine Corp (Taiwan) Ltd (EVERGREEN LINE) SatCom: Inmarsat B 335715710 *Panama* Panama MMSI: 357157000 Official number: 2609599C	**14,807** 4,849 15,511 T/cm 33.0	Class: NK	**1999-01 Evergreen Shipyard Corp — Nagasaki NS** Yd No: 1026 Loa 165.10 (BB) Br ex 27.30 Dght 8.518 Lbp 150.00 Br md 27.10 Dpth 10.10 Welded, 1 dk	**(A33A2CC) Container Ship (Fully Cellular)** TEU 1164 C Ho 440 TEU C Dk 724 TEU incl 200 ref C. 7 Ha: (12.6 x 10.6)6 (12.8 x -)	**1 oil engine** driving 1 FP propeller Total Power: 10,916kW (14,841hp) 18.7kn Sulzer 7RTA52U 1 x 2 Stroke 7 Cy. 520 x 1800 10916kW (14841bhp) Diesel United Ltd.-Aioi AuxGen: 3 x 880kW 450V 60Hz a.c Thrusters: 1 Thwart. CP thruster (f) Fuel: 172.0 (d.f.) (Heating Coils) 2398.6 (r.f.) 44.0pd
9130597 *3FHV9* -	**UNI-ASSURE** **Gaining Enterprise SA** Evergreen Marine Corp (Taiwan) Ltd (EVERGREEN LINE) *Panama* Panama MMSI: 357398000 Official number: 2628399CC	**14,807** 4,849 15,511 T/cm 33.0	Class: NK	**1999-04 Evergreen Shipyard Corp — Nagasaki NS** Yd No: 1027 Loa 165.10 (BB) Br ex 27.30 Dght 8.518 Lbp 150.00 Br md 27.10 Dpth 10.10 Welded, 1 dk	**(A33A2CC) Container Ship (Fully Cellular)** TEU 1164 C Ho 440 TEU C Dk 724 TEU incl 200 ref C.	**1 oil engine** driving 1 FP propeller Total Power: 10,916kW (14,841hp) 18.7kn Sulzer 7RTA52U 1 x 2 Stroke 7 Cy. 520 x 1800 10916kW (14841bhp) Diesel United Ltd.-Aioi AuxGen: 4 x a.c Thrusters: 1 Thwart. CP thruster (f) Fuel: 2315.0 (r.f.)
9310616 *VRII9* -	**UNI AUC ONE** *ex* Matariki Forest *-2011* **Karat Bulkship SA** Daiichi Chuo Kisen Kaisha *Hong Kong* Hong Kong MMSI: 477013600 Official number: HK-3057	**17,663** 10,133 28,709	Class: NK	**2007-06 Shin Kochi Jyuko K.K. — Kochi** Yd No: 7200 Loa 176.63 (BB) Br ex 26.00 Dght 9.633 Lbp 169.40 Br md 26.00 Dpth 13.60 Welded, 1 dk	**(A21A2BC) Bulk Carrier** Grain: 39,052; Bale: 37,976 Compartments: 5 Ho, ER 5 Ha: 4 (19.5 x 17.8)ER (17.9 x 12.8) Cranes: 4x30.5t	**1 oil engine** driving 1 FP propeller Total Power: 5,900kW (8,022hp) 14.5kn Mitsubishi 5UEC52LA 1 x 2 Stroke 5 Cy. 520 x 1600 5900kW (8022bhp) Kobe Hatsudoki KK-Japan AuxGen: 3 x 364kW a.c Fuel: 93.0 (d.f.) 1024.0 (r.f.)
8312071 *3FVZ5* -	**UNI-BROTHERS** *ex* Atlantic Cozumel *-2012* *ex* Alam Sempurna *-2009* *ex* Saint Laurent *-1991* **EGY United Lines Inc** Unimar Shipping Management SatCom: Inmarsat C 435541710 *Panama* Panama MMSI: 355417000 Official number: 38554PEXT1	**17,065** 10,334 27,650	Class: NK (AB)	**1984-02 Hitachi Zosen Corp — Onomichi HS (Innoshima Shipyard)** Yd No: 4768 Loa 178.21 (BB) Br ex 23.14 Dght 10.610 Lbp 167.21 Br md 23.11 Dpth 14.76 Welded, 1 dk	**(A21A2BC) Bulk Carrier** Grain: 38,568; Bale: 33,612 Compartments: 5 Ho, ER 5 Ha: (12.0 x 11.4)3 (19.2 x 11.4) (17.6 x 11.4)ER Cranes: 4x25t	**1 oil engine** driving 1 FP propeller Total Power: 7,061kW (9,600hp) 13.0kn Sulzer 6RTA58 1 x 2 Stroke 6 Cy. 580 x 1700 7061kW (9600bhp) Hitachi Zosen Corp-Japan AuxGen: 3 x 440kW 450V 60Hz a.c
9606546 *9VBD7* -	**UNI CHALLENGE** *launched as* Sleuth *-2012* **Joule Asset Management (Pte) Ltd** Apex Ship Management Pte Ltd *Singapore* Singapore MMSI: 566507000 Official number: 397847	**18,465** 10,371 29,078	Class: LR ✠ **100A1** SS 04/2012 bulk carrier CSR BC-A Nos 2 & 4 holds may be empty GRAB (20) ESP LI ✠ **LMC** Eq.Ltr: H†; Cable: 605.0/62.0 U3 (a)	**2012-04 Yangzhou Nakanishi Shipbuilding Co Ltd — Yizheng JS** Yd No: 012 Loa 170.00 (BB) Br ex 27.04 Dght 10.038 Lbp 163.60 Br md 27.00 Dpth 14.20 Welded, 1 dk	**(A21A2BC) Bulk Carrier** Grain: 39,988; Bale: 39,070 Compartments: 5 Ho, ER 5 Ha: ER Cranes: 4x30t	**1 oil engine** driving 1 FP propeller Total Power: 7,150kW (9,721hp) 14.2kn MAN-B&W 5S50MC 1 x 2 Stroke 5 Cy. 500 x 1910 7150kW (9721bhp) Kawasaki Heavy Industries Ltd-Japan AuxGen: 3 x 450kW 450V 60Hz a.c Boilers: AuxB (Comp) 7.0kgf/cm² (6.9bar)
9012848 *BKNK* -	**UNI-CHART** **Evergreen Marine Corp (Taiwan) Ltd (EVERGREEN LINE)** - SatCom: Inmarsat A 1355252 *Keelung* Chinese Taipei MMSI: 416102000 Official number: 11975	**12,405** 6,571 17,446 T/cm 32.3	Class: CR NK	**1992-06 Kanda Zosensho K.K. — Kawajiri** Yd No: 343 Loa 152.05 (BB) Br ex 25.65 Dght 9.539 Lbp 141.00 Br md 25.60 Dpth 12.70 Welded, 1 dk	**(A33A2CC) Container Ship (Fully Cellular)** TEU 1038 C Ho 422 TEU C Dk 616 TEU incl 94 ref C. Compartments: 4 Cell Ho, ER 13 Ha: (12.6 x 10.6)2 (12.8 x 7.9)10 (12.8 x 10.5)ER	**1 oil engine** driving 1 FP propeller Total Power: 8,496kW (11,551hp) 17.0kn B&W 7L50MC 1 x 2 Stroke 7 Cy. 500 x 1620 8496kW (11551bhp) Hitachi Zosen Corp-Japan AuxGen: 3 x 650kW 440V 60Hz a.c Thrusters: 1 Thwart. CP thruster (f) Fuel: 127.0 (d.f.) 1730.0 (r.f.) 32.0pd
9012874 *BKNN* -	**UNI-CONCERT** **Evergreen Marine Corp (Taiwan) Ltd (EVERGREEN LINE)** - SatCom: Inmarsat A 1355447 *Keelung* Chinese Taipei MMSI: 416105000 Official number: 011978	**12,405** 6,571 17,446 T/cm 32.3	Class: CR NK	**1993-05 Kanda Zosensho K.K. — Kawajiri** Yd No: 346 Loa 152.05 (BB) Br ex 25.65 Dght 9.539 Lbp 141.00 Br md 25.60 Dpth 12.70 Welded, 1 dk	**(A33A2CC) Container Ship (Fully Cellular)** TEU 1038 C Ho 422 TEU C Dk 616 TEU incl 94 ref C. Compartments: 4 Cell Ho, ER 13 Ha: (12.6 x 10.6)2 (12.8 x 7.9)10 (12.8 x 10.5)ER	**1 oil engine** driving 1 FP propeller Total Power: 8,496kW (11,551hp) 17.0kn B&W 7L50MC 1 x 2 Stroke 7 Cy. 500 x 1620 8496kW (11551bhp) Hitachi Zosen Corp-Japan AuxGen: 3 x 650kW 440V 60Hz a.c Thrusters: 1 Thwart. CP thruster (f) Fuel: 127.0 (d.f.) 1730.0 (r.f.) 32.0pd
9012850 *BKNL* -	**UNI-CORONA** **Evergreen Marine Corp (Taiwan) Ltd (EVERGREEN LINE)** - SatCom: Inmarsat A 1355270 *Keelung* Chinese Taipei MMSI: 416103000 Official number: 11976	**12,405** 6,571 17,446 T/cm 32.3	Class: CR NK	**1992-09 Kanda Zosensho K.K. — Kawajiri** Yd No: 344 Loa 152.05 (BB) Br ex 25.65 Dght 9.539 Lbp 141.00 Br md 25.60 Dpth 12.70 Welded, 1 dk	**(A33A2CC) Container Ship (Fully Cellular)** TEU 1038 C Ho 422 TEU C Dk 616 TEU incl 94 ref C. Compartments: 4 Cell Ho, ER 13 Ha: (12.6 x 10.6)2 (12.8 x 7.9)10 (12.8 x 10.5)ER	**1 oil engine** driving 1 FP propeller Total Power: 8,496kW (11,551hp) 16.0kn B&W 7L50MC 1 x 2 Stroke 7 Cy. 500 x 1620 8496kW (11551bhp) Hitachi Zosen Corp-Japan AuxGen: 3 x 650kW 450V 60Hz a.c Thrusters: 1 Thwart. CP thruster (f) Fuel: 127.0 (d.f.) 1729.6 (r.f.) 35.0pd
9012836 *BKNJ* -	**UNI-CROWN** **Evergreen Marine Corp (Taiwan) Ltd (EVERGREEN LINE)** - SatCom: Inmarsat A 1355240 *Keelung* Chinese Taipei MMSI: 416101000 Official number: 011974	**12,404** 6,571 17,446 T/cm 32.3	Class: CR NK	**1992-03 Kanda Zosensho K.K. — Kawajiri** Yd No: 342 Loa 152.05 (BB) Br ex 25.65 Dght 9.539 Lbp 141.00 Br md 25.60 Dpth 12.70 Welded, 1 dk	**(A33A2CC) Container Ship (Fully Cellular)** TEU 1038 C Ho 422 TEU C Dk 616 TEU incl 94 ref C. Compartments: 4 Cell Ho, ER 13 Ha: (12.6 x 10.6)2 (12.8 x 7.9)10 (12.8 x 10.5)ER	**1 oil engine** driving 1 FP propeller Total Power: 8,496kW (11,551hp) 17.0kn B&W 7L50MC 1 x 2 Stroke 7 Cy. 500 x 1620 8496kW (11551bhp) Hitachi Zosen Corp-Japan AuxGen: 3 x 650kW 440V 60Hz a.c Thrusters: 1 Thwart. CP thruster (f) Fuel: 127.0 (d.f.) 1730.0 (r.f.) 32.0pd
9118927 *9MQ02* -	**UNI CRYSTAL** *ex* Kiho Maru *-2006* **Uni Petroleum Pte Ltd** - *Port Klang* Malaysia MMSI: 533180027 Official number: 334599	**731** 300 1,020	Class: (NK)	**1995-03 Matsuura Tekko Zosen K.K. — Osakikamijima** Yd No: 386 Loa 69.29 Br ex - Dght 3.918 Lbp 64.50 Br md 10.00 Dpth 4.50 Welded, 1 dk	**(A13B2TP) Products Tanker** Liq: 1,149; Liq (Oil): 1,149 Compartments: 8 Ta, ER	**1 oil engine** driving 1 CP propeller Total Power: 1,324kW (1,800hp) Hanshin LH30LG 1 x 4 Stroke 6 Cy. 300 x 600 1324kW (1800bhp) The Hanshin Diesel Works Ltd-Japan Thrusters: 1 Thwart. FP thruster (f) Fuel: 60.0 (d.f.)

9266279 *HSB347* -	**UNI EXPRESS 2** *ex* Express 19 *-2006* *ex* Kaltim Maju *-2006* **Uniwise Offshore Ltd** Miclyn Express Offshore Pte Ltd *Bangkok* *Thailand* Official number: 490003270	**180** 54 60	Class: BV	**2002-03 Strategic Marine Pty Ltd — Fremantle WA** Yd No: H101 Loa 29.80 Br ex 7.52 Dght 1.130 Lbp 26.50 Br md 7.50 Dpth 2.60 Welded, 1 dk	**(B21A2OC) Crew/Supply Vessel** Hull Material: Aluminium Alloy Passengers: unberthed: 50	**3 oil engines** with clutches & reverse reduction geared to sc. shafts driving 3 FP propellers Total Power: 2,070kW (2,814hp) 25.0kn Caterpillar 3412E 3 x Vee 4 Stroke 12 Cy. 137 x 152 each-690kW (938bhp) Caterpillar Inc-USA AuxGen: 2 x 77kW 415/230V 50Hz a.c Fuel: 12.0 (d.f.)
9525039 *HSB3879* -	**UNI EXPRESS 9** **Uniwise Offshore Ltd** Miclyn Express Offshore Pte Ltd *Bangkok* *Thailand* MMSI: 567346000 Official number: 510083990	**205** 63 50	Class: BV	**2008-09 Marsun Co Ltd — Samut Prakan** Yd No: 215 Loa 36.00 Br ex 7.75 Dght 1.700 Lbp 32.50 Br md 7.60 Dpth 3.30 Welded, 1 dk	**(B21A2OC) Crew/Supply Vessel** Hull Material: Aluminium Alloy Passengers: unberthed: 90	**3 oil engines** geared to sc. shafts driving 3 FP propellers Total Power: 3,021kW (4,107hp) 21.0kn Cummins KTA-38-M2 3 x Vee 4 Stroke 12 Cy. 159 x 159 each-1007kW (1369bhp) Cummins Engine Co Ltd-United Kingdom AuxGen: 2 x 90kW 50Hz a.c
9525041 *HSB3880* -	**UNI EXPRESS 10** **Uniwise Offshore Ltd** Miclyn Express Offshore Pte Ltd *Bangkok* *Thailand* MMSI: 567347000 Official number: 510083982	**205** 63 50	Class: BV	**2008-09 Marsun Co Ltd — Samut Prakan** Yd No: 216 Loa 36.00 Br ex 7.75 Dght 1.700 Lbp 32.50 Br md 7.60 Dpth 3.30 Welded, 1 dk	**(B21A2OC) Crew/Supply Vessel** Hull Material: Aluminium Alloy Passengers: 90	**3 oil engines** geared to sc. shafts driving 3 FP propellers Total Power: 3,021kW (4,107hp) 21.0kn Cummins KTA-38-M2 3 x Vee 4 Stroke 12 Cy. 159 x 159 each-1007kW (1369bhp) Cummins Engine Co Ltd-United Kingdom AuxGen: 2 x 90kW 50Hz a.c
9525053 *HSB392* -	**UNI EXPRESS 11** **Uniwise Offshore Ltd** Miclyn Express Offshore Pte Ltd *Bangkok* *Thailand* MMSI: 567352000 Official number: 510085219	**205** 63 50	Class: BV	**2009-03 Marsun Co Ltd — Samut Prakan** Yd No: 217 Loa 36.00 Br ex 7.75 Dght 1.700 Lbp 32.50 Br md 7.60 Dpth 3.30 Welded, 1 dk	**(B21A2OC) Crew/Supply Vessel** Hull Material: Aluminium Alloy Passengers: 90	**3 oil engines** geared to sc. shafts driving 3 FP propellers Total Power: 3,357kW (4,563hp) 21.0kn Cummins KTA-38-M2 3 x Vee 4 Stroke 12 Cy. 159 x 159 each-1119kW (1521bhp) Cummins Engine Co Inc-USA AuxGen: 2 x 90kW 50Hz a.c
9525065 *HSB3924* -	**UNI EXPRESS 12** **Uniwise Offshore Ltd** Miclyn Express Offshore Pte Ltd *Bangkok* *Thailand* MMSI: 567353000 Official number: 510085227	**205** 63 50	Class: BV	**2009-03 Marsun Co Ltd — Samut Prakan** Yd No: 218 Loa 36.00 Br ex 7.75 Dght 1.700 Lbp 32.50 Br md 7.60 Dpth 3.30 Welded, 1 dk	**(B21A2OC) Crew/Supply Vessel** Hull Material: Aluminium Alloy Passengers: 90	**3 oil engines** reduction geared to sc. shafts driving 3 FP propellers Total Power: 3,357kW (4,563hp) 21.0kn Cummins KTA-38-M2 3 x Vee 4 Stroke 12 Cy. 159 x 159 each-1119kW (1521bhp) Cummins Engine Co Inc-USA AuxGen: 2 x 80kW 50Hz a.c
9525077 *HSB4205* -	**UNI EXPRESS 13** **Uniwise Offshore Ltd** Miclyn Express Offshore Pte Ltd SatCom: Inmarsat C 456700173 *Bangkok* *Thailand* MMSI: 567344000 Official number: 520080473	**205** 63 50	Class: BV	**2009-03 Marsun Co Ltd — Samut Prakan** Yd No: 219 Loa 36.00 Br ex 7.75 Dght 1.700 Lbp 32.50 Br md 7.60 Dpth 3.30 Welded, 1 dk	**(B21A2OC) Crew/Supply Vessel** Hull Material: Aluminium Alloy	**3 oil engines** geared to sc. shafts driving 3 FP propellers Total Power: 3,357kW (4,563hp) 21.0kn Cummins KTA-38-M2 3 x Vee 4 Stroke 12 Cy. 159 x 159 each-1119kW (1521bhp) Cummins Engine Co Ltd-United Kingdom AuxGen: 2 x 80kW 50Hz a.c
9525089 *HSB4206* -	**UNI EXPRESS 14** **Uniwise Offshore Ltd** Miclyn Express Offshore Pte Ltd *Bangkok* *Thailand* MMSI: 567345000 Official number: 520080481	**205** 63 50	Class: BV	**2009-04 Marsun Co Ltd — Samut Prakan** Yd No: 223 Loa 36.00 Br ex 7.75 Dght 1.700 Lbp 32.50 Br md 7.60 Dpth 3.30 Welded, 1 dk	**(B21A2OC) Crew/Supply Vessel** Hull Material: Aluminium Alloy	**3 oil engines** geared to sc. shafts driving 3 FP propellers Total Power: 3,357kW (4,563hp) 21.0kn Cummins KTA-38-M2 3 x Vee 4 Stroke 12 Cy. 159 x 159 each-1119kW (1521bhp) Cummins Engine Co Ltd-United Kingdom AuxGen: 2 x 80kW 50Hz a.c
9554377 *HSB4345* -	**UNI EXPRESS 15** **Uniwise Offshore Ltd** Miclyn Express Offshore Pte Ltd *Bangkok* *Thailand* MMSI: 567367000 Official number: 520083552	**205** 63 50	Class: BV	**2009-09 Marsun Co Ltd — Samut Prakan** Yd No: 224 Loa 36.00 Br ex 7.75 Dght 1.700 Lbp 31.60 Br md 7.60 Dpth 3.30 Welded, 1 dk	**(B21A2OC) Crew/Supply Vessel** Hull Material: Aluminium Alloy Passengers: unberthed: 90	**3 oil engines** reduction geared to sc. shafts driving 3 FP propellers Total Power: 3,021kW (4,107hp) 21.0kn Cummins KTA-38-M2 3 x Vee 4 Stroke 12 Cy. 159 x 159 each-1007kW (1369bhp) Cummins Engine Co Ltd-United Kingdom AuxGen: 2 x 80kW 50Hz a.c Fuel: 50.0
9554389 *HSB4346* -	**UNI EXPRESS 16** **Uniwise Offshore Ltd** Miclyn Express Offshore Pte Ltd *Bangkok* *Thailand* MMSI: 567368000 Official number: 520083560	**205** 63 50	Class: BV	**2009-09 Marsun Co Ltd — Samut Prakan** Yd No: 225 Loa 36.00 Br ex 7.75 Dght 1.700 Lbp 31.60 Br md 7.60 Dpth 3.30 Welded, 1 dk	**(B21A2OC) Crew/Supply Vessel** Hull Material: Aluminium Alloy Passengers: unberthed: 90	**3 oil engines** reduction geared to sc. shafts driving 3 FP propellers Total Power: 3,021kW (4,107hp) 21.0kn Cummins KTA-38-M2 3 x Vee 4 Stroke 12 Cy. 159 x 159 each-1007kW (1369bhp) Cummins Engine Co Ltd-United Kingdom AuxGen: 2 x 80kW 50Hz a.c Fuel: 50.0
9564293 *HSB4404* -	**UNI EXPRESS 17** **Uniwise Offshore Ltd** Miclyn Express Offshore Pte Ltd *Bangkok* *Thailand* MMSI: 567387000 Official number: 520084590	**205** 63 50	Class: BV	**2009-12 Marsun Co Ltd — Samut Prakan** Yd No: 228 Loa 36.00 Br ex 7.75 Dght 1.250 Lbp 32.50 Br md 7.60 Dpth 3.30 Welded, 1 dk	**(B21A2OC) Crew/Supply Vessel** Hull Material: Aluminium Alloy Passengers: 92	**3 oil engines** reduction geared to sc. shafts driving 3 FP propellers Total Power: 3,021kW (4,107hp) 21.0kn Cummins KTA-38-M2 3 x Vee 4 Stroke 12 Cy. 159 x 159 each-1007kW (1369bhp) Cummins Engine Co Inc-USA AuxGen: 2 x 90kW 380V 50Hz a.c Thrusters: 1 Tunnel thruster (f)
9610054 *HSB4548* -	**UNI EXPRESS 18** **Uniwise Offshore Ltd** Miclyn Express Offshore Pte Ltd *Bangkok* *Thailand* MMSI: 567418000 Official number: 540000134	**247** 74 120	Class: BV	**2011-02 Marsun Co Ltd — Samut Prakan** Yd No: 232 Loa 40.00 Br ex 8.65 Dght 1.700 Lbp 37.50 Br md 7.60 Dpth 3.60 Welded, 1 dk	**(B21A2OC) Crew/Supply Vessel** Hull Material: Aluminium Alloy Passengers: unberthed: 70	**3 oil engines** reduction geared to sc. shafts driving 3 FP propellers Total Power: 2,979kW (4,050hp) 18.0kn Cummins KTA-38-M2 3 x Vee 4 Stroke 12 Cy. 159 x 159 each-993kW (1350bhp) Cummins Engine Co Ltd-United Kingdom AuxGen: 2 x 80kW 50Hz a.c Fuel: 65.0 (d.f.)
9590462 *HSB4484* -	**UNI EXPRESS 19** *ex* Penguin 163 *-2010* **Uniwise Offshore Ltd** Miclyn Express Offshore Pte Ltd *Bangkok* *Thailand* MMSI: 567399000 Official number: 530002655	**236** 71 116	Class: BV (AB)	**2010-05 Penguin Shipyard International Pte Ltd — Singapore** Yd No: 163 Loa 36.00 Br ex - Dght 1.850 Lbp 33.20 Br md 7.60 Dpth 3.65 Welded, 1 dk	**(B21A2OC) Crew/Supply Vessel** Hull Material: Aluminium Alloy	**3 oil engines** reduction geared to sc. shafts driving 3 FP propellers Total Power: 3,021kW (4,107hp) 20.0kn Cummins KTA-38-M2 3 x Vee 4 Stroke 12 Cy. 159 x 159 each-1007kW (1369bhp) Cummins Engine Co Ltd-United Kingdom AuxGen: 2 x 80kW 50Hz a.c
9590474 *HSB4485* -	**UNI EXPRESS 20** *ex* Penguin 164 *-2010* **Uniwise Offshore Ltd** Miclyn Express Offshore Pte Ltd *Bangkok* *Thailand* MMSI: 567401000 Official number: 530002663	**236** 71 116	Class: BV (AB)	**2010-05 Penguin Shipyard International Pte Ltd — Singapore** Yd No: 164 Loa 36.00 Br ex Dght 1.850 Lbp 33.20 Br md 7.60 Dpth 3.65 Welded, 1 dk	**(B21A2OC) Crew/Supply Vessel** Hull Material: Aluminium Alloy	**3 oil engines** reduction geared to sc. shafts driving 3 FP propellers Total Power: 3,021kW (4,107hp) 20.0kn Cummins KTA-38-M2 3 x Vee 4 Stroke 12 Cy. 159 x 159 each-1007kW (1369bhp) Cummins Engine Co Ltd-United Kingdom AuxGen: 2 x 80kW 50Hz a.c Fuel: 61.0 (d.f.)
9280251 *HSB4744* -	**UNI EXPRESS 21** *ex* Express 28 *-2012* *ex* Abeer Thirty Eight *-2006* **Uniwise Offshore Ltd** Miclyn Express Offshore Pte Ltd *Bangkok* *Thailand* MMSI: 567000354	**243** 77 45	Class: BV (AB)	**2002-10 WaveMaster International Pty Ltd — Fremantle WA** Yd No: 180 Loa 34.00 Br ex 8.73 Dght 1.600 Lbp 31.35 Br md 8.50 Dpth 3.48 Welded, 1 Dk.	**(B21A2OC) Crew/Supply Vessel** Hull Material: Aluminium Alloy Passengers: unberthed: 120	**3 oil engines** geared to sc. shafts driving 3 FP propellers Total Power: 2,907kW (3,951hp) 30.0kn Cummins KTA-38-M2 3 x Vee 4 Stroke 12 Cy. 159 x 159 each-969kW (1317bhp) Cummins Engine Co Inc-USA AuxGen: 2 x 68kW 220V a.c

8325016 *3EFD3* -	**UNI FORTUNE** *ex* Han Rich *-2012* *ex* Bao Lian Shan *-2007* *ex* Oriental Cedar *-1999* **Star Bravo Co Ltd** Dalian Panocean International Ship Management Co Ltd *Panama* *Panama* MMSI: 356609000 Official number: 12782PEXT5	**3,992** 2,519 6,506	Class: PD (CC) (NK)	**1984-09 Dae Sun Shipbuilding & Engineering Co Ltd — Busan** Yd No: 281 Loa 109.05 Br ex 16.44 Dght 6.751 Lbp 101.43 Br md 16.41 Dpth 8.26 Welded, 1 dk	**(A31A2GX) General Cargo Ship** Grain: 8,593; Bale: 8,280 Compartments: 2 Ho, ER 2 Ha: (29.0 x 8.5) (30.0 x 8.5)ER Derricks: 4x20t	**1 oil engine** driving 1 FP propeller Total Power: 2,942kW (4,000hp) 12.5kn Hanshin 6EL44 1 x 4 Stroke 6 Cy. 440 x 880 2942kW (4000bhp) The Hanshin Diesel Works Ltd-Japan AuxGen: 2 x 160kW a.c
7727487 *3FEF5* -	**UNI-OCEAN** *ex* Hai Long No. 8 *-2010* *ex* Hai Bei *-2000* *ex* Kyokutoku Maru *-1998* - - *Panama* *Panama* Official number: 40906TT	**1,172** 656 2,121		**1978-06 Hakata Zosen K.K. — Imabari** Yd No: 187 Loa 67.50 Br ex - Dght - Lbp 63.10 Br md 12.50 Dpth 5.41 Riveted\Welded, 1 dk	**(A13B2TP) Products Tanker**	**1 oil engine** reduction geared to sc. shaft Total Power: 740kW (1,006hp) 10.0kn Akasaka 1 x 4 Stroke 740kW (1006bhp) (new engine 2010) Akasaka Tekkosho KK (Akasaka DieselLtd)-Japan
8150801 *DUH2164* -	**UNI ORIENT PEARL 1** *ex* Ocean Pearl I *-1998* *ex* Nadashige Maru *-1992* **Uni Orient Pearl Ventures Inc** *Cebu* *Philippines*	*248* 149 723	Class: (BV)	**1975-07 K.K. Murakami Zosensho — Naruto** Loa 57.26 Br ex - Dght 3.301 Lbp 54.01 Br md 9.50 Dpth 6.00 Welded, 1 dk	**(A31A2GX) General Cargo Ship**	**1 oil engine** driving 1 FP propeller Total Power: 566kW (770hp) 10.0kn Hanshin 1 x 4 Stroke 566kW (770bhp) The Hanshin Diesel Works Ltd-Japan
9202156 *3FCE9* -	**UNI-PACIFIC** - **Gaining Enterprise SA** Evergreen Marine Corp (Taiwan) Ltd (EVERGREEN LINE) SatCom: Inmarsat C 435713110 *Panama* *Panama* MMSI: 357131000 Official number: 2650799C	**17,887** 6,283 19,309	Class: NK	**1999-08 Evergreen Shipyard Corp — Nagasaki NS** Yd No: 1030 Loa 181.76 (BB) Br ex - Dght 9.019 Lbp 170.00 Br md 28.00 Dpth 13.90 Welded, 1 dk	**(A33A2CC) Container Ship (Fully Cellular)** TEU 1618 C Ho 530 TEU C Dk 1088 TEU incl 289 ref C. Compartments: 4 Cell Ho 8 Ha: (12.7 x 7.8) (12.7 x 19.2)6 (12.7 x 24.3)	**1 oil engine** driving 1 FP propeller Total Power: 10,916kW (14,841hp) 18.7kn Sulzer 7RTA52U 1 x 2 Stroke 7 Cy. 520 x 1800 10916kW (14841bhp) Diesel United Ltd.-Aioi AuxGen: 3 x 880kW 450V a.c Thrusters: 1 Thwart. FP thruster (f) Fuel: 333.5 (d.f.) 2327.9 (r.f.) 44.4pd
9202168 *3FCF9* -	**UNI-PATRIOT** - **Gaining Enterprise SA** Evergreen Marine Corp (Taiwan) Ltd (EVERGREEN LINE) *Panama* *Panama* MMSI: 357787000 Official number: 2660799C	**17,887** 6,283 19,309	Class: NK	**1999-10 Evergreen Shipyard Corp — Nagasaki NS** Yd No: 1031 Loa 181.72 (BB) Br ex - Dght 9.018 Lbp 170.00 Br md 28.00 Dpth 13.90 Welded, 1 dk	**(A33A2CC) Container Ship (Fully Cellular)** TEU 1618 C Ho 530 TEU C Dk 1088 TEU incl 289 ref C. Compartments: 4 Cell Ho 8 Ha: (12.7 x 7.8) (12.7 x 19.2)6 (12.7 x 24.3)	**1 oil engine** driving 1 FP propeller Total Power: 10,916kW (14,841hp) 18.7kn Sulzer 7RTA52U 1 x 2 Stroke 7 Cy. 520 x 1800 10916kW (14841bhp) Diesel United Ltd.-Aioi AuxGen: 3 x 880kW 450V a.c Thrusters: 1 Thwart. FP thruster (f) Fuel: 333.5 (d.f.) 2327.9 (r.f.) 44.4pd
9202182 *3FZE9* -	**UNI-PERFECT** - **Gaining Enterprise SA** Evergreen Marine Corp (Taiwan) Ltd (EVERGREEN LINE) *Panama* *Panama* MMSI: 357979000 Official number: 2699700B	**17,887** 6,283 19,309	Class: NK	**2000-04 Evergreen Shipyard Corp — Nagasaki NS** Yd No: 1033 Loa 181.76 (BB) Br ex - Dght 9.018 Lbp 170.00 Br md 28.00 Dpth 13.90 Welded, 1 dk	**(A33A2CC) Container Ship (Fully Cellular)** TEU 1618 C Ho 530 TEU C Dk 1088 TEU incl 289 ref C. Compartments: 4 Cell Ho 8 Ha: (12.7 x 7.8) (12.7 x 19.2)6 (12.7 x 24.3)	**1 oil engine** driving 1 FP propeller Total Power: 10,916kW (14,841hp) 18.7kn Sulzer 7RTA52U 1 x 2 Stroke 7 Cy. 520 x 1800 10916kW (14841bhp) Diesel United Ltd.-Aioi AuxGen: 3 x 880kW 450V a.c Thrusters: 1 Thwart. FP thruster (f) Fuel: 333.5 (d.f.) 2327.9 (r.f.) 44.4pd
9202170 *3FYQ9* -	**UNI-PHOENIX** - **Gaining Enterprise SA** Evergreen Marine Corp (Taiwan) Ltd (EVERGREEN LINE) *Panama* *Panama* MMSI: 357962000 Official number: 2692600C	**17,887** 6,283 19,309	Class: NK	**2000-01 Evergreen Shipyard Corp — Nagasaki NS** Yd No: 1032 Loa 181.76 (BB) Br ex - Dght 9.019 Lbp 170.00 Br md 28.00 Dpth 13.90 Welded, 1 dk	**(A33A2CC) Container Ship (Fully Cellular)** TEU 1618 C Ho 530 TEU C Dk 1088 TEU incl 256 ref C. Compartments: 4 Cell Ho 8 Ha: (12.7 x 7.8) (12.7 x 19.2)6 (12.7 x 24.3)	**1 oil engine** driving 1 FP propeller Total Power: 10,916kW (14,841hp) 18.7kn Sulzer 7RTA52U 1 x 2 Stroke 7 Cy. 520 x 1800 10916kW (14841bhp) Diesel United Ltd.-Aioi AuxGen: 3 x 880kW 450V a.c Thrusters: 1 Thwart. FP thruster (f) Fuel: 386.5 (d.f.) (Heating Coils) 2530.3 (r.f.) 41.6pd
9202209 *3FZG9* -	**UNI-POPULAR** - **Gaining Enterprise SA** Evergreen Marine Corp (Taiwan) Ltd (EVERGREEN LINE) *Panama* *Panama* MMSI: 357981000 Official number: 2730400C	**17,887** 6,283 19,309	Class: NK	**2000-10 Evergreen Shipyard Corp — Nagasaki NS** Yd No: 1036 Loa 181.76 (BB) Br ex - Dght 9.019 Lbp 170.00 Br md 28.00 Dpth 13.90 Welded, 1 dk	**(A33A2CC) Container Ship (Fully Cellular)** TEU 1618 C Ho 530 TEU C Dk 1088 TEU incl 256 ref C. Compartments: 4 Cell Ho 8 Ha: (12.7 x 7.8) (12.7 x 19.2)6 (12.7 x 24.3)	**1 oil engine** driving 1 FP propeller Total Power: 10,916kW (14,841hp) 18.7kn Sulzer 7RTA52U 1 x 2 Stroke 7 Cy. 520 x 1800 10916kW (14841bhp) Diesel United Ltd.-Aioi AuxGen: 3 x 880kW 450V a.c Thrusters: 1 Thwart. FP thruster (f) Fuel: 333.5 (d.f.) 2327.9 (r.f.) 44.4pd
9202223 *H3YG* -	**UNI-PREMIER** - **Gaining Enterprise SA** Evergreen Marine Corp (Taiwan) Ltd (EVERGREEN LINE) *Panama* *Panama* MMSI: 355902000 Official number: 2779701C	**17,887** 6,283 19,309	Class: NK	**2001-03 Evergreen Shipyard Corp — Nagasaki NS** Yd No: 1038 Loa 181.76 (BB) Br ex - Dght 9.018 Lbp 170.00 Br md 28.00 Dpth 13.90 Welded, 1 dk	**(A33A2CC) Container Ship (Fully Cellular)** TEU 1618 C Ho 530 TEU C Dk 1088 TEU incl 256 ref C. Compartments: 4 Cell Ho, ER 8 Ha: (12.7 x 7.8) (12.7 x 19.2)6 (12.7 x 24.3)	**1 oil engine** driving 1 FP propeller Total Power: 10,916kW (14,841hp) 18.7kn Sulzer 7RTA52U 1 x 2 Stroke 7 Cy. 520 x 1800 10916kW (14841bhp) Diesel United Ltd.-Aioi AuxGen: 3 x 880kW 450V a.c Thrusters: 1 Thwart. CP thruster (f) Fuel: 333.5 (d.f.) 2327.9 (r.f.) 44.4pd
9202235 *BKHB* -	**UNI-PROBITY** - **Evergreen Marine Corp (Taiwan) Ltd (EVERGREEN LINE)** - *Keelung* *Chinese Taipei* MMSI: 416456000 Official number: 015215	**17,887** 6,283 19,309	Class: CR NK	**2001-06 Evergreen Shipyard Corp — Nagasaki NS** Yd No: 1039 Loa 181.76 (BB) Br ex - Dght 9.018 Lbp 170.00 Br md 28.00 Dpth 13.90 Welded, 1 dk	**(A33A2CC) Container Ship (Fully Cellular)** TEU 1618 C Ho 530 TEU C Dk 1088 TEU incl 256 ref C. Compartments: 4 Cell Ho 8 Ha: (12.7 x 7.8) (12.7 x 19.2)6 (12.7 x 24.3)	**1 oil engine** driving 1 FP propeller Total Power: 10,916kW (14,841hp) 18.7kn Sulzer 7RTA52U 1 x 2 Stroke 7 Cy. 520 x 1800 10916kW (14841bhp) Diesel United Ltd.-Aioi AuxGen: 3 x 880kW 450V a.c Thrusters: 1 Thwart. FP thruster (f) Fuel: 333.5 (d.f.) 2327.9 (r.f.) 44.4pd
9202211 *BKJL* -	**UNI-PROMOTE** - **Evergreen Marine Corp (Taiwan) Ltd (EVERGREEN LINE)** - *Taipei* *Chinese Taipei* MMSI: 416453000 Official number: 015175	**17,887** 6,283 19,311	Class: CR NK	**2001-01 Evergreen Shipyard Corp — Nagasaki NS** Yd No: 1037 Loa 181.76 (BB) Br ex - Dght 9.019 Lbp 170.00 Br md 28.00 Dpth 13.90 Welded, 1 dk	**(A33A2CC) Container Ship (Fully Cellular)** TEU 1618 C Ho 530 TEU C Dk 1088 TEU incl 256 ref C. Compartments: 4 Cell Ho 8 Ha: (12.7 x 7.8) (12.7 x 19.2)6 (12.7 x 24.3)	**1 oil engine** driving 1 FP propeller Total Power: 10,916kW (14,841hp) 18.7kn Sulzer 7RTA52U 1 x 2 Stroke 7 Cy. 520 x 1800 10916kW (14841bhp) Diesel United Ltd.-Aioi AuxGen: 3 x 880kW 450V a.c Thrusters: 1 Thwart. CP thruster (f) Fuel: 333.5 (d.f.) 2327.9 (r.f.) 44.4pd
9202247 *BKHC* -	**UNI-PROSPER** - **Evergreen Marine Corp (Taiwan) Ltd (EVERGREEN LINE)** - *Keelung* *Chinese Taipei* MMSI: 416459000 Official number: 015251	**17,887** 6,283 19,309	Class: CR NK	**2001-09 Evergreen Shipyard Corp — Nagasaki NS** Yd No: 1050 Loa 181.76 (BB) Br ex - Dght 9.019 Lbp 170.00 Br md 28.00 Dpth 13.90 Welded, 1 dk	**(A33A2CC) Container Ship (Fully Cellular)** TEU 1618 C Ho 530 TEU C Dk 1088 TEU incl 256 ref C. Compartments: 4 Cell Ho 8 Ha: (12.7 x 7.8) (12.7 x 19.2)6 (12.7 x 24.3)	**1 oil engine** driving 1 FP propeller Total Power: 10,916kW (14,841hp) 18.7kn Sulzer 7RTA52U 1 x 2 Stroke 7 Cy. 520 x 1800 10916kW (14841bhp) Diesel United Ltd.-Aioi AuxGen: 3 x 880kW 450V a.c Thrusters: 1 Thwart. FP thruster (f) Fuel: 333.5 (d.f.) 2327.9 (r.f.) 44.4pd
9202194 *3FZF9* -	**UNI-PRUDENT** - **Gaining Enterprise SA** Evergreen Marine Corp (Taiwan) Ltd (EVERGREEN LINE) *Panama* *Panama* MMSI: 357980000 Official number: 2717900C	**17,887** 6,283 19,309	Class: NK	**2000-07 Evergreen Shipyard Corp — Nagasaki NS** Yd No: 1035 Loa 181.76 (BB) Br ex - Dght 9.018 Lbp 170.00 Br md 28.00 Dpth 13.90 Welded, 1 dk	**(A33A2CC) Container Ship (Fully Cellular)** TEU 1618 C Ho 530 TEU C Dk 1088 TEU incl 256 ref C. Compartments: 4 Cell Ho 8 Ha: (12.7 x 7.8) (12.7 x 19.2)6 (12.7 x 24.3)	**1 oil engine** driving 1 FP propeller Total Power: 10,916kW (14,841hp) 18.7kn Sulzer 7RTA52U 1 x 2 Stroke 7 Cy. 520 x 1800 10916kW (14841bhp) Diesel United Ltd.-Aioi AuxGen: 3 x 880kW 450V a.c Thrusters: 1 Thwart. FP thruster (f) Fuel: 333.5 (d.f.) 2327.9 (r.f.) 44.4pd
8113138 *XUSU7* -	**UNI-R** *ex* Sea Carrier *-2009* *ex* Privilege *-2008* *ex* Misty *-1999* *ex* Lex Naranjo *-1996* *ex* Ebano *-1989* **Sea Brothers Shipping Lines Inc** Unimar Shipping Management *Phnom Penh* *Cambodia* MMSI: 515157000 Official number: 0983126	**5,868** 3,022 8,150	Class: IV (LR) (GL) Classed LR until 17/11/04	**1983-05 SA Juliana Constructora Gijonesa — Gijon** Yd No: 284 Loa 119.51 Br ex 18.55 Dght 7.401 Lbp 110.01 Br md 18.51 Dpth 9.53 Welded, 1 dk	**(A31A2GX) General Cargo Ship** Grain: 10,541; Bale: 10,273 TEU 160 C.Ho 96/20' (40') C.Dk 64/20' (40') Compartments: 2 Ho, ER 2 Ha: 2 (25.9 x 10.7)ER Derricks: 2x50t,2x25t; Winches: 4	**1 oil engine** with flexible couplings & sr gearedto sc. shaft driving 1 FP propeller Total Power: 3,310kW (4,500hp) 13.3kn Werkspoor 6TM410 1 x 4 Stroke 6 Cy. 410 x 470 3310kW (4500bhp) Astilleros Espanoles SA (AESA)-Spain AuxGen: 3 x 260kW 380V 50Hz a.c Boilers: AuxB (Comp) 7.5kgf/cm² (7.4bar) Fuel: 90.5 (d.f.) 379.5 (r.f.)

IMO / Call sign	Name / Owner / Flag	Tonnage	Class	Builder / Dimensions	Type / Cargo	Machinery
8602581 *3ERM6* -	**UNI TRADER** *ex* Golden Trader *-2012* *ex* Sun East *-2008* *ex* Sinar Suchen *-1999* **Uni Trader International Shipping Co Ltd** Pan Ocean (International) Co Ltd *Panama* *Panama* MMSI: 370105000 Official number: 37326PEXT1	**6,324** 2,591 7,719	Class: PD (KR) (NK)	**1986-08 Usuki Iron Works Co Ltd — Usuki OT** Yd No: 1551 Loa 105.31 (BB) Br ex 18.72 Dght 7.346 Lbp 98.02 Br md 18.71 Dpth 12.85 Welded, 2 dks	**(A31A2GX) General Cargo Ship** Grain: 15,782; Bale: 14,276 2 Ha: (22.4 x 11.0) (31.5 x 11.0)ER Derricks: 4x20t	**1 oil engine** driving 1 FP propeller Total Power: 2,273kW (3,090hp) 12.0kn Ito M506EUS 1 x 4 Stroke 6 Cy. 500 x 880 2273kW (3090bhp) Ito Tekkosho-Japan AuxGen: 1 x 240kW 445V a.c
9539743 *VRFV4* -	**UNI WEALTH** *ex* Glory Wealth *-2009* **Glory Bulkship SA** Wealth Ocean Ship Management (Shanghai) Co Ltd *Hong Kong* *Hong Kong* MMSI: 477621200 Official number: HK-2527	**18,499** 10,335 29,256	Class: NK (KR)	**2009-11 Yangzhou Nakanishi Shipbuilding Co Ltd — Yizheng JS** Yd No: 101 Loa 169.99 (BB) Br ex 27.83 Dght 10.056 Lbp 163.60 Br md 27.00 Dpth 14.20 Welded, 1 dk	**(A21A2BC) Bulk Carrier** Grain: 39,988; Bale: 39,070 Compartments: 5 Ho, ER 5 Ha: 4 (20.1 x 17.6)ER (12.1 x 16.0) Cranes: 4x30t	**1 oil engine** driving 1 FP propeller Total Power: 7,150kW (9,721hp) 14.2kn MAN-B&W 5S50MC 1 x 2 Stroke 5 Cy. 500 x 1910 7150kW (9721bhp) Hitachi Zosen Corp-Japan Fuel: 1600.0
8514306 *9MPL7* -	**UNICA** *ex* Dong Jin *-2011* *ex* Han Joo *-2010* *ex* Matsuyama Maru No. 22 *-2010* **Panoil Tankers Sdn Bhd** Silverline Maritime Sdn Bhd *Port Klang* *Malaysia* MMSI: 533064100 Official number: 334391	**3,100** 1,320 5,499	Class: BV (KR) (NK)	**1985-10 Taihei Kogyo K.K. — Hashihama, Imabari** Yd No: 1827 Loa 100.92 (BB) Br ex - Dght 7.101 Lbp 94.77 Br md 15.02 Dpth 8.01 Welded, 1 dk	**(A13B2TP) Products Tanker** Double Hull (13F) Liq: 5,549; Liq (Oil): 5,549 Compartments: 8 Ta, ER	**1 oil engine** sr geared to sc. shaft driving 1 CP propeller Total Power: 2,427kW (3,300hp) 13.3kn Akasaka A41 1 x 4 Stroke 6 Cy. 410 x 800 2427kW (3300bhp) Akasaka Tekkosho KK (Akasaka DieselLtd)-Japan AuxGen: 4 x 185kW a.c Fuel: 82.2
8744729 *J8Y4072* -	**UNICA** *ex* Akhir 100 *-2010* **Rusadventure Ltd** Navilux SA *Kingstown* *St Vincent & The Grenadines* MMSI: 377319000 Official number: 40542	**195** 58 -		**2003 Cantieri di Pisa — Pisa** Yd No: 672 Loa 30.10 Br ex - Dght 1.800 Lbp - Br md 7.03 Dpth 3.74 Bonded, 1 dk	**(X11A2YP) Yacht** Hull Material: Reinforced Plastic	**2 oil engines** reduction geared to sc. shafts driving 2 Propellers Total Power: 2,942kW (4,000hp) 24.0kn M.T.U. 16V2000M91 2 x Vee 4 Stroke 16 Cy. 130 x 150 each-1471kW (2000bhp) MTU Friedrichshafen GmbH-Friedrichshafen
9228203 *DSMU2* -	**UNICO ANNA** *ex* Sunny Royal *-2010* **Unico Logistics Co Ltd** - *Jeju* *South Korea* MMSI: 441932000 Official number: JJR-102145	**17,433** 9,829 28,407 T/cm 39.3	Class: KR (NK)	**2000-11 Kanda Zosensho K.K. — Kawajiri** Yd No: 413 Loa 170.00 Br ex - Dght 9.767 Lbp 162.00 Br md 27.00 Dpth 13.80 Welded, 1 dk	**(A21A2BC) Bulk Carrier** Grain: 37,732; Bale: 36,683 Compartments: 5 Ho, ER 5 Ha: (14.1 x 15.0)4 (19.2 x 18.0)ER Cranes: 4x30t	**1 oil engine** driving 1 FP propeller Total Power: 5,884kW (8,000hp) 14.0kn Mitsubishi 5UEC52LA 1 x 2 Stroke 5 Cy. 520 x 1600 5884kW (8000bhp) Kobe Hatsudoki KK-Japan Fuel: 1220.0
9462768 *V7ZD2* -	**UNICO SIENNA** **Anna Maritime Ltd** Unico Logistics Co Ltd *Majuro* *Marshall Islands* MMSI: 538004794 Official number: 4794	**22,939** 11,624 34,328	Class: KR	**2012-09 Dae Sun Shipbuilding & Engineering Co Ltd — Busan** Yd No: 506 Loa 180.40 (BB) Br ex - Dght 9.916 Lbp 170.37 Br md 30.00 Dpth 14.40 Welded, 1 dk	**(A21A2BC) Bulk Carrier** Double Hull Grain: 46,594; Bale: 44,527 Compartments: 5 Ho, ER 5 Ha: 4 (20.0 x 20.4)ER (15.2 x 14.8) Cranes: 4x30t	**1 oil engine** driving 1 FP propeller Total Power: 6,480kW (8,810hp) 13.9kn MAN-B&W 6S42MC 1 x 2 Stroke 6 Cy. 420 x 1764 6480kW (8810bhp) STX Engine Co Ltd-South Korea Fuel: 1560.0
9161687 - -	**UNICO STELLA** *ex* Kalypso *-2014* *ex* Pilsum *-2006* *ex* Andhika Loreto *-2003* *ex* Corona Challenge *-2002* **Stella Merchant Marine Ltd** Unico Shipping Co Ltd *South Korea* MMSI: 440185000	**38,364** 24,847 73,762 T/cm 65.4	Class: KR (Class contemplated) (BV) (NV) (NK)	**1997-08 Sumitomo Heavy Industries Ltd. — Yokosuka Shipyard, Yokosuka** Yd No: 1228 Loa 225.00 (BB) Br ex - Dght 13.871 Lbp 216.00 Br md 32.25 Dpth 19.00 Welded, 1 dk	**(A21A2BC) Bulk Carrier** Double Bottom Entire Compartment Length Grain: 87,278 Compartments: 7 Ho, ER 7 Ha: (16.3 x 13.9)6 (16.3 x 15.0)ER	**1 oil engine** driving 1 FP propeller Total Power: 8,878kW (12,071hp) 14.5kn Sulzer 7RTA48T 1 x 2 Stroke 7 Cy. 480 x 2000 8878kW (12071bhp) Diesel United Ltd.-Aioi
8317447 *YQWU* -	**UNICOM 3** *ex* Queen of Evian *-2002* *ex* Ruby II *-1997* *ex* Kokura *-1995* *ex* Kyokuho Maru No. 11 *-1995* **Constant Oil Ltd** Unicom Holding SA *Constanta* *Romania* MMSI: 264900073 Official number: 2681	**999** 421 1,563	Class: (RI)	**1984-02 Teraoka Shipyard Co Ltd — Minamiawaji HG** Yd No: 232 Loa 69.91 Br ex - Dght 4.501 Lbp 65.03 Br md 11.02 Dpth 5.01 Welded, 1 dk	**(A12A2TC) Chemical Tanker** Liq: 1,600 Compartments: 10 Ta, ER	**1 oil engine** driving 1 CP propeller Total Power: 1,177kW (1,600hp) Hanshin 6LUN28 1 x 4 Stroke 6 Cy. 280 x 480 1177kW (1600bhp) The Hanshin Diesel Works Ltd-Japan AuxGen: 2 x 100kW 130/225V 60Hz a.c
9133393 *UBCG7* -	**UNICOM ALPHA** *ex* Polaris Alpha *-2009* *ex* Inzhener Shlem *-2006* **AzovTransTerminal Ltd** - *Taganrog* *Russia* MMSI: 273344230	**3,704** 1,242 3,710	Class: RS	**1995-06 AO Sudostroitelnyy Zavod "Kama" — Perm** Yd No: 501 Loa 125.60 Br ex 13.90 Dght 4.100 Lbp 120.50 Br md 13.50 Dpth 6.50 Welded, 1 dk	**(A22B2BR) Ore/Oil Carrier** Double Hull Grain: 2,538; Liq: 3,654; Liq (Oil): 3,654 Compartments: 12 Ta, ER	**2 oil engines** driving 2 FP propellers Total Power: 1,400kW (1,904hp) 11.0kn S.K.L. 6VDS24/24AL-1 2 x 4 Stroke 6 Cy. 240 x 240 each-700kW (952bhp) SKL Motoren u. Systemtechnik AG-Magdeburg AuxGen: 3 x 160kW a.c, 1 x 100kW a.c Thrusters: 1 Tunnel thruster (f) Fuel: 233.0 (d.f.)
7614159 - -	**UNICOM SEVEN** *ex* Baicoi *-2008* *ex* NR 4392 *-2008* **Jetrow Nigeria Ltd**	**832** 800 1,243	Class: (RN)	**1972 Santierul Naval Giurgiu — Giurgiu** Yd No: 4392 Loa 54.28 Br ex - Dght 3.620 Lbp 52.37 Br md 9.99 Dpth 4.95 Welded, 1 dk	**(B35E2TF) Bunkering Tanker** Liq: 1,358; Liq (Oil): 1,358 Compartments: 8 Ta, ER	**2 oil engines** geared to sc. shafts driving 2 FP propellers Total Power: 412kW (560hp) 6.5kn Maybach MB836BB 2 x 4 Stroke 8 Cy. 175 x 205 each-206kW (280bhp) Uzina 23 August Bucuresti-Bucuresti AuxGen: 2 x 100kW 400V 50Hz a.c Fuel: 17.5 (d.f.)
7213010 *HSDD* -	**UNICORD 1** *ex* Sumiyoshi Maru No. 35 *-1982* **The Unicord Investment (Thailand) Co Ltd** - *Bangkok* *Thailand* Official number: 261031650	*402* 190 -		**1972 Mie Shipyard Co. Ltd. — Yokkaichi** Yd No: 62 Loa - Br ex 8.64 Dght - Lbp 49.20 Br md 8.62 Dpth 3.92 Riveted\Welded, 1 dk	**(B11B2FV) Fishing Vessel**	**1 oil engine** driving 1 FP propeller Total Power: 1,545kW (2,101hp) Akasaka AH38 1 x 4 Stroke 6 Cy. 380 x 560 1545kW (2101bhp) Akasaka Tekkosho KK (Akasaka DieselLtd)-Japan
7051735 *WX9752* -	**UNICORN** *ex* Gunsmoke *-1982* *ex* Sliparound *-1977* *ex* Blue Danube *-1977* **Vineyard Highland Inc** - *Chilmark, MA* *United States of America* Official number: 509574	*101* 69 -		**1967 Rockport Yacht & Supply Co. (RYSCO) — Rockport, Tx** L reg 21.37 Br ex 6.56 Dght - Lbp - Br md - Dpth 2.39 Welded	**(B11B2FV) Fishing Vessel**	**1 oil engine** driving 1 FP propeller Total Power: 257kW (349hp)
7000906 *5NQK* -	**UNICORN** *ex* Soliman Reys *-2009* *ex* Deichtor *-1984* **Selly Fak Energy Services Ltd** - *Lagos* *Nigeria* MMSI: 657403000 Official number: SR1235	**553** 166 715	Class: GL	**1969 JG Hitzler Schiffswerft und Masch GmbH & Co KG — Lauenburg** Yd No: 710 Loa 54.20 Br ex 11.28 Dght 3.370 Lbp 49.67 Br md 11.00 Dpth 3.97 Welded, 1 dk	**(B21B20A) Anchor Handling Tug Supply** A-frames: 1; Derricks: 1x5t Ice Capable	**2 oil engines** reverse reduction geared to sc. shaft driving 2 FP propellers Total Power: 1,398kW (1,900hp) 11.3kn MWM TB12RS18/22 2 x Vee 4 Stroke 12 Cy. 180 x 220 each-699kW (950bhp) Motoren Werke Mannheim AG (MWM)-West Germany AuxGen: 3 x 112kW 380/220V 50Hz a.c Thrusters: 1 Thwart. FP thruster (f) Fuel: 323.0
9162136 - -	**UNICORN** - **Chung Ho Marine Co Ltd** - *Chinese Taipei*	*1,498* - 405		**1997-05 Mitsubishi Heavy Industries Ltd. — Shimonoseki** Yd No: 1032 Loa 100.56 Br ex 14.91 Dght 2.700 Lbp 90.02 Br md 14.90 Dpth 10.30 Welded, 2 dks	**(A36A2PR) Passenger/Ro-Ro Ship (Vehicles)** Passengers: unberthed: 423 Stern door/ramp Len: 6.00 Wid: 5.00 Swl: - Lorries: 5, Cars: 78	**4 oil engines** with clutches, flexible couplings & reduction geared to sc. shafts driving 4 Water jets Total Power: 26,008kW (35,360hp) 35.0kn M.T.U. 20V1163TB73 4 x Vee 4 Stroke 20 Cy. 230 x 280 each-6502kW (8840bhp) MTU Friedrichshafen GmbH-Friedrichshafen AuxGen: 2 x 550kW a.c Thrusters: 1 Thwart. CP thruster (f)

Identity	Ship / Owner	Tonnage	Classification	Construction / Dimensions	Type / Capacity	Machinery
9595931 *9V9497* -	**UNICORN** **New Unicorn Marine Pte Ltd** - SatCom: Inmarsat C 456643910 *Singapore* *Singapore* MMSI: 566439000 Official number: 397199	**32,987** 19,231 56,739 T/cm 58.8	Class: LR ✠ **100A1** SS 04/2012 bulk carrier CSR BC-A GRAB (20) Nos 2 & 4 holds may be empty ESP **ShipRight** (CM, ACS (B)) *IWS LI EP ✠ **LMC** **UMS** Cable: 632.5/73.0 U3 (a)	2012-04 **Jinling Shipyard — Nanjing JS** Yd No: JLZ9100409 Loa 189.99 (BB) Br ex 32.31 Dght 12.800 Lbp 185.00 Br md 32.26 Dpth 18.00 Welded, 1 dk	**(A21A2BC) Bulk Carrier** Grain: 71,634; Bale: 68,200 Compartments: 5 Ho, ER 5 Ha: ER Cranes: 4x30t	**1 oil engine** driving 1 FP propeller Total Power: 9,480kW (12,889hp) 14.2kn MAN-B&W 6S50MC-C 1 x 2 Stroke 6 Cy. 500 x 2000 9480kW (12889bhp) STX Engine Co Ltd-South Korea AuxGen: 3 x 600kW 450V 60Hz a.c Boilers: WTAuxB (Comp) 8.9kgf/cm² (8.7bar)
8515996 - -	**UNICORN 2** **Inlaks Ltd** - *Nigeria*	*143* 48 87	Class: (BV)	**1986-01 Astilleros Armon SA — Navia** Yd No: 115 Loa 25.56 Br ex - Dght 3.050 Lbp 21.21 Br md 6.96 Dpth 3.79 Welded, 1 dk	**(B11A2FS) Stern Trawler**	**1 oil engine** with clutches, flexible couplings & reverse reduction geared to sc. shaft driving 1 FP propeller Total Power: 397kW (540hp) 10.5kn Caterpillar 3412T 1 x Vee 4 Stroke 12 Cy. 137 x 152 397kW (540bhp) Caterpillar Tractor Co-USA AuxGen: 1 x 124kW 380V a.c
8516005 - -	**UNICORN 3** **Inlaks Ltd** - *Nigeria*	*142* 50 87	Class: (BV)	**1986-04 Astilleros Armon SA — Navia** Yd No: 116 Loa 25.56 Br ex - Dght 3.001 Lbp 21.21 Br md 6.96 Dpth 3.79 Welded, 1 dk	**(B11A2FS) Stern Trawler**	**1 oil engine** with clutches, flexible couplings & reverse reduction geared to sc. shaft driving 1 FP propeller Total Power: 397kW (540hp) 10.5kn Caterpillar 3412PCTA 1 x Vee 4 Stroke 12 Cy. 137 x 152 397kW (540bhp) Caterpillar Tractor Co-USA AuxGen: 1 x 124kW 380V a.c
8516029 - -	**UNICORN 5** **Inlaks Ltd** - *Port Harcourt* *Nigeria*	**143** 48 87	Class: (BV)	**1986-08 Astilleros Armon SA — Navia** Yd No: 118 Loa 25.56 Br ex - Dght 3.050 Lbp 21.21 Br md 6.96 Dpth 3.79 Welded, 1 dk	**(B11A2FS) Stern Trawler** Ins: 110	**1 oil engine** with clutches, flexible couplings & reverse reduction geared to sc. shaft driving 1 FP propeller Total Power: 397kW (540hp) 10.5kn Caterpillar 3412T 1 x Vee 4 Stroke 12 Cy. 137 x 152 397kW (540bhp) Caterpillar Tractor Co-USA AuxGen: 1 x 124kW 380V a.c
9385817 *3ENF9* -	**UNICORN BRAVO** **Unicorn Bravo SA** Wisdom Marine Lines SA *Panama* *Panama* MMSI: 351943000 Official number: 3337008A	**5,691** 3,197 8,759	Class: NK	2007-10 **Ben Kien Shipbuilding Industry Co — Haiphong** Yd No: HG-06-05 Loa 111.80 (BB) Br ex - Dght 7.600 Lbp 103.60 Br md 18.60 Dpth 9.65 Welded, 1 dk	**(A31A2GX) General Cargo Ship** Grain: 10,976; Bale: 10,461 Derricks: 4x30t	**1 oil engine** driving 1 FP propeller Total Power: 3,120kW (4,242hp) 12.5kn Hanshin LH46L 1 x 4 Stroke 6 Cy. 460 x 880 3120kW (4242bhp) The Hanshin Diesel Works Ltd-Japan AuxGen: 2 x 275kW a.c Fuel: 665.0
9235945 *H3MU* -	**UNICORN DOLPHIN** *ex Fu Yuan -2010* **Guma Navigation SA** Wisdom Marine Lines SA *Panama* *Panama* MMSI: 355509000 Official number: 2731500CH	**4,764** 2,856 7,528	Class: NK	2000-08 **Hakata Zosen K.K. — Imabari** Yd No: 623 Loa 101.23 Br ex - Dght 7.164 Lbp 94.00 Br md 19.00 Dpth 9.50 Welded, 1 dk	**(A31A2GX) General Cargo Ship** Grain: 9,959; Bale: 9,530 Compartments: 2 Ho, ER 2 Ha: (20.3 x 10.0) (35.0 x 10.0)ER Derricks: 3x30t	**1 oil engine** driving 1 FP propeller Total Power: 3,089kW (4,200hp) 12.0kn Mitsubishi 6UEC37LA 1 x 2 Stroke 6 Cy. 370 x 880 3089kW (4200bhp) Akasaka Tekkosho KK (Akasaka DieselLtd)-Japan AuxGen: 2 x 240kW 110/440V 60Hz a.c Fuel: 129.5 (d.f.) (Heating Coils) 393.8 (r.f.) 10.0pd
9191577 *3FGI9* -	**UNICORN EMERALD** *ex Siam Emerald -2010* **TG Finance Co Ltd** Wisdom Marine Lines SA SatCom: Inmarsat C 435733510 *Panama* *Panama* MMSI: 357335000 Official number: 2629699C	**6,079** 3,290 10,122 T/cm 15.6	Class: NK	1999-03 **Shin Kurushima Dockyard Co. Ltd. — Hashihama, Imabari** Yd No: 5017 Loa 113.33 Br ex - Dght 8.067 Lbp 107.00 Br md 19.40 Dpth 10.40 Welded, 1 dk	**(A21A2BC) Bulk Carrier** Grain: 11,061; Bale: 10,701 Compartments: 3 Ho, ER 3 Ha: (14.6 x 10.6)2 (20.0 x 15.4)ER Cranes: 2x30t; Derricks: 1x25t	**1 oil engine** driving 1 FP propeller Total Power: 3,884kW (5,281hp) 13.6kn B&W 6L35MC 1 x 2 Stroke 6 Cy. 350 x 1050 3884kW (5281bhp) Makita Corp-Japan AuxGen: 2 x 280kW a.c Fuel: 660.0
9438810 *3ESQ4* -	**UNICORN LOGGER** *ex Ha Long HLK-104 -2008* **Unicorn Logger SA** Wisdom Marine Lines SA SatCom: Inmarsat C 437039410 *Panama* *Panama* MMSI: 370394000 Official number: 3433808A	**5,691** 3,197 8,725	Class: NK	2008-08 **Ha Long Shipbuilding Co Ltd — Ha Long** Yd No: HLK-104 Loa 118.80 (BB) Br ex - Dght 7.500 Lbp 103.60 Br md 18.60 Dpth 9.65 Welded	**(A31A2GX) General Cargo Ship** Grain: 10,976; Bale: 10,461 Derricks: 4x30t	**1 oil engine** driving 1 FP propeller Total Power: 3,309kW (4,499hp) 12.5kn Hanshin LH46LA 1 x 4 Stroke 6 Cy. 460 x 880 3309kW (4499bhp) The Hanshin Diesel Works Ltd-Japan Fuel: 670.0
9370197 *3EPO5* -	**UNICORN OCEAN** **Takanawa Line Inc** Toyo Kaiun Co Ltd *Panama* *Panama* MMSI: 372193000 Official number: 3366008A	**41,662** 25,647 78,888	Class: NK	2008-03 **Sanoyas Hishino Meisho Corp — Kurashiki OY** Yd No: 1266 Loa 225.00 (BB) Br ex - Dght 14.379 Lbp 219.00 Br md 32.24 Dpth 19.90 Welded, 1 dk	**(A21A2BC) Bulk Carrier** Grain: 91,188 Compartments: 7 Ho, ER 7 Ha: ER	**1 oil engine** driving 1 FP propeller Total Power: 9,560kW (12,998hp) 14.5kn MAN-B&W 7S50MC-C 1 x 2 Stroke 7 Cy. 500 x 2000 9560kW (12998bhp) Mitsui Engineering & Shipbuilding CLtd-Japan AuxGen: 3 x a.c Fuel: 2480.0
7914016 *9MPV7* -	**UNICORN SATU** *ex Unity -2011 ex Vista Mariner -2005* *ex Nautica Tg. Pelepas -2004* *ex Burgundy -2002 ex Princess Adeliene -2001* *ex HL Venture -2000 ex Koki Maru No. 28 -1993* *ex Shomei Maru No. 51 -1991* **Axel Ship Management Pte Ltd** - *Port Klang* *Malaysia* Official number: 334452	**676** 419 1,147	Class: (NK)	1979-12 **Suzuki Shipyard Co. Ltd. — Yokkaichi** Yd No: 320 Loa - Br ex - Dght 4.003 Lbp 55.00 Br md 10.20 Dpth 4.60 Welded, 1 dk	**(A13B2TU) Tanker (unspecified)** Liq: 1,542; Liq (Oil): 1,542	**1 oil engine** driving 1 FP propeller Total Power: 883kW (1,201hp) Matsui MS245GTSC 1 x 4 Stroke 6 Cy. 245 x 470 883kW (1201bhp) Matsui Iron Works Co Ltd-Japan
8738940 *SPG2728* -	**UNICUS** **Ustka Tour SC** - *Ustka* *Poland*	**113** - 24	Class: PR	**1967 Zaklad Remontu Kutrow Tadeusz Chalecki — Ustka** Rebuilt-2004 Loa 29.35 Br ex - Dght 2.540 Lbp 23.78 Br md 6.00 Dpth 3.65 Welded, 1 dk	**(A37B2PS) Passenger Ship** Passengers: unberthed: 125	**1 oil engine** reduction geared to sc. shaft driving 1 Propeller Total Power: 279kW (379hp) Volvo Penta TAMD122A 1 x 4 Stroke 6 Cy. 130 x 150 279kW (379hp) AB Volvo Penta-Sweden
9010515 *HP9782* -	**UNIDAD** **Panama Canal Authority** - *Balboa* *Panama* Official number: 2755601C	**286** 85 -	Class: (AB)	**1990-03 Houma Fabricators Inc — Houma LA** Yd No: 95 Loa 32.01 Br ex - Dght 3.039 Lbp 27.20 Br md 10.80 Dpth 4.45 Welded, 1 dk	**(B32A2ST) Tug**	**2 oil engines** geared to sc. shafts driving 2 Directional propellers Total Power: 2,206kW (3,000hp) 12.0kn EMD (Electro-Motive) 12-645-E6 2 x Vee 2 Stroke 12 Cy. 230 x 254 each-1103kW (1500bhp) General Motors Corp.Electro-Motive Div.-La Grange AuxGen: 2 x 75kW a.c Thrusters: 2 Thwart. FP thruster (f) Fuel: 67.0 (d.f.)
9671905 *HSB4782* -	**UNIEXPRESS 22** **Uniwise Offshore Ltd** Miclyn Express Offshore Pte Ltd *Bangkok* *Thailand* MMSI: 567062500	**259** 78 133	Class: BV	**2013-03 PT Kim Seah Shipyard Indonesia — Batam** (Hull) Yd No: (200) **2013-02 Penguin Shipyard International Pte Ltd — Singapore** Yd No: 200 Loa 38.00 Br ex - Dght 1.890 Lbp 36.00 Br md 7.60 Dpth 3.65 Welded, 1 dk	**(B21A20C) Crew/Supply Vessel** Hull Material: Aluminium Alloy	**3 oil engines** reduction geared to sc. shafts driving 3 FP propellers Total Power: 2,424kW (3,297hp) 24.0kn Baudouin 12M26.2P2 3 x Vee 4 Stroke 12 Cy. 150 x 150 each-808kW (1099bhp) Societe des Moteurs Baudouin SA-France AuxGen: 2 x 92kW 415/220V 50Hz a.c Thrusters: 1 Tunnel thruster (f) Fuel: 65.0 (d.f.)
9671917 *HSB4783* -	**UNIEXPRESS 23** **Uniwise Offshore Ltd** Miclyn Express Offshore Pte Ltd *Bangkok* *Thailand* MMSI: 567062600	**259** 78 133	Class: BV	**2013-03 PT Kim Seah Shipyard Indonesia — Batam** (Hull) Yd No: (201) **2013-03 Penguin Shipyard International Pte Ltd — Singapore** Yd No: 201 Loa 38.00 Br ex 7.60 Dght 1.890 Lbp 36.00 Br md 7.60 Dpth 3.65 Welded, 1 dk	**(B21A20C) Crew/Supply Vessel** Hull Material: Aluminium Alloy	**3 oil engines** reduction geared to sc. shafts driving 3 FP propellers Total Power: 2,424kW (3,297hp) 24.0kn Baudouin 12M26.2P2 3 x Vee 4 Stroke 12 Cy. 150 x 150 each-808kW (1099bhp) Societe des Moteurs Baudouin SA-France AuxGen: 2 x 92kW 415/220V 50Hz a.c Thrusters: 1 Tunnel thruster (f)

9671929 *HSB4784* -	**UNIEXPRESS 24** **Uniwise Offshore Ltd** Miclyn Express Offshore Pte Ltd *Bangkok* *Thailand* MMSI: 567062700	**259** 78 133	Class: BV	**2013-04 PT Kim Seah Shipyard Indonesia — Batam** (Hull) Yd No: (202) **2013-04 Penguin Shipyard International Pte Ltd — Singapore** Yd No: 202 Loa 38.00 Br ex - Dght 1.890 Lbp 36.00 Br md 7.60 Dpth 3.65 Welded, 1 dk	**(B21A2OC) Crew/Supply Vessel** Hull Material: Aluminium Alloy Passengers: unberthed: 90	**3 oil engines** reduction geared to sc. shafts driving 3 FP propellers Total Power: 2,424kW (3,297hp) 24.0kn Baudouin 12M26.2P2 3 x Vee 4 Stroke 12 Cy. 150 x 150 each-808kW (1099bhp) Societe des Moteurs Baudouin SA-France AuxGen: 2 x 92kW 415/220V 50Hz a.c Thrusters: 1 Tunnel thruster (f) Fuel: 65.0
7937886 *YD4247* -	**UNIFOR 2** **PT Satya Djaya Raya Trading Co** - *Jakarta* *Indonesia*	*113* 34 -	Class: KI (NK)	**1979 Pan-United Shipping Pte Ltd — Singapore** Loa 23.02 Br ex - Dght 3.290 Lbp 21.62 Br md 7.00 Dpth 3.56 Welded, 1 dk	**(B32A2ST) Tug**	**2 oil engines** geared to sc. shafts driving 2 FP propellers Total Power: 626kW (852hp) 11.0kn Caterpillar D353SCAC 2 x 4 Stroke 6 Cy. 159 x 203 each-313kW (426bhp) Caterpillar Tractor Co-USA AuxGen: 2 x 25kW
7526405 *YGAI* -	**UNIKA** *ex South Wind -2001 ex Lampung -2001* *ex Nazly Loqo't -1979* *ex Tokujin Maru No. 18 -1975* - - *Semarang* *Indonesia*	**779** 398 1,228	Class: (LR) (KI) Classed LR until 31/3/96	**1972-07 K.K. Matsuura Zosensho — Osakikamijima** Yd No: 200 Converted From: Bulk Aggregates Carrier Lengthened-1983 Loa 62.57 (BB) Br ex 9.73 Dght 4.014 Lbp 58.76 Br md 9.50 Dpth 5.52 Welded, 2 dks	**(A31A2GX) General Cargo Ship** TEU 42 C.Ho 28/20' (40') C.Dk 14/20' (40') Compartments: 1 Ho, ER 1 Ha: (20.8 x -)ER Derricks: 2x5t	**1 oil engine** reverse reduction geared to sc. shaft driving 1 FP propeller Total Power: 883kW (1,201hp) 8.0kn Fuji 6S30BH 1 x 4 Stroke 6 Cy. 300 x 450 883kW (1201bhp) Fuji Diesel Co Ltd-Japan AuxGen: 2 x 24kW 225V 60Hz a.c
9621742 *9V9460* -	**UNIKA** **Panoil Tankers Pte Ltd** Panoil Petroleum Pte Ltd *Singapore* *Singapore* MMSI: 566129000 Official number: 397118	**1,474** 676 2,409 T/cm 6.9	Class: RI	**2012-01 Zhejiang Chengzhou Shipbuilding Co Ltd — Sanmen County ZJ** Yd No: CZ1008 Loa 72.50 (BB) Br ex 12.42 Dght 4.700 Lbp 67.00 Br md 12.40 Dpth 6.20 Welded, 1 dk	**(A13B2TP) Products Tanker** Double Hull (13F) Liq: 2,353; Liq (Oil): 2,353 Compartments: 10 Wing Ta, 1 Slop Ta, ER 2 Cargo Pump (s): 2x750m³/hr Manifold: Bow/CM: 38.1m	**2 oil engines** reduction geared to sc. shafts driving 2 FP propellers Total Power: 1,912kW (2,600hp) 11.1kn Daihatsu 6DKM-20 2 x 4 Stroke 6 Cy. 200 x 300 each-956kW (1300bhp) Anqing Marine Diesel Engine Works-China AuxGen: 1 x 100kW 400V 50Hz a.c Fuel: 106.0 (d.f.)
7722463 *6NOZ* -	**UNIKOREA No. 77** **Maxan Co Ltd** - *Incheon* *South Korea* Official number: IC0300-A877	*446* 222 540	Class: (KR)	**1977-11 KK Kanasashi Zosen — Shizuoka SZ** Yd No: 1231 Loa 55.94 Br ex - Dght 3.750 Lbp 49.51 Br md 8.81 Dpth 4.07 Welded, 1 dk	**(B11B2FV) Fishing Vessel** 3 Ha: (1.0 x 0.9) (1.9 x 1.9) (1.0 x 0.7)ER	**1 oil engine** driving 1 FP propeller Total Power: 993kW (1,350hp) 11.0kn Akasaka AH28 1 x 4 Stroke 6 Cy. 280 x 440 993kW (1350bhp) Akasaka Tekkosho KK (Akasaka DieselLtd)-Japan AuxGen: 2 x 200kW 225V a.c
7722487 *6NPA* -	**UNIKOREA No. 79** **Maxan Co Ltd** - SatCom: Inmarsat M 644082110 *Incheon* *South Korea* Official number: IC0300-A849	*446* 222 540	Class: (KR)	**1977-12 KK Kanasashi Zosen — Shizuoka SZ** Yd No: 1233 Loa 55.94 Br ex - Dght 3.750 Lbp 49.51 Br md 8.81 Dpth 4.07 Welded, 1 dk	**(B11B2FV) Fishing Vessel** 3 Ha: (1.0 x 0.9) (1.9 x 1.9) (1.0 x 0.7)ER	**1 oil engine** driving 1 FP propeller Total Power: 993kW (1,350hp) 11.0kn Akasaka AH28 1 x 4 Stroke 6 Cy. 280 x 440 993kW (1350bhp) Akasaka Tekkosho KK (Akasaka DieselLtd)-Japan AuxGen: 2 x 200kW 225V a.c
8510312 - -	**UNILINK II** *ex Yutoku Maru No. 7 -2002* **Unilink Shipping Corp** - *Cebu* *Philippines* Official number: CEB1006110	*222* 137 673		**1985-10 Sanuki Shipbuilding & Iron Works Co Ltd — Mitoyo KG** Yd No: 1153 Loa 58.48 (BB) Br ex - Dght 3.231 Lbp 53.01 Br md 9.31 Dpth 5.57 Welded, 1 dk	**(A31A2GX) General Cargo Ship** Bale: 1,168 Compartments: 1 Ho, ER 1 Ha: ER	**1 oil engine** sr geared to sc. shaft driving 1 FP propeller Total Power: 625kW (850hp) Niigata 6M26BFT 1 x 4 Stroke 6 Cy. 260 x 460 625kW (850bhp) Niigata Engineering Co Ltd-Japan
8101680 *WCY8622* -	**UNIMAK** *ex Unimak Enterprise -2002* *ex Spring Mist -1987* **Unimak Fisheries LLC** - *Seattle, WA* *United States of America* MMSI: 338138000 Official number: 637693	*990* 703 -	Class: (AB)	**1981-07 Halter Marine, Inc. — Moss Point, Ms** Yd No: 990 Converted From: Offshore Tug/Supply Ship-1987 Loa 56.09 Br ex - Dght 3.664 Lbp 54.87 Br md 12.20 Dpth 4.27 Welded, 1 dk	**(B11A2FS) Stern Trawler**	**2 oil engines** reverse reduction geared to sc. shafts driving 2 FP propellers Total Power: 1,854kW (2,520hp) 12.0kn EMD (Electro-Motive) 12-645-E2 2 x Vee 2 Stroke 12 Cy. 230 x 254 each-927kW (1260bhp) (Re-engined ,made 1980, Reconditioned & fitted 1981) General Motors Corp.Electro-Motive Div.-La Grange AuxGen: 2 x 99kW a.c Thrusters: 1 Thwart. FP thruster (f)
9155949 *ZDHE5* -	**UNIMAR** *ex Musketier -2005* **Atobatc Shipping AB & Islandview Shipping Co Ltd** Briese Shipping BV *Gibraltar* *Gibraltar (British)* MMSI: 236306000	**2,820** 1,548 4,085	Class: GL (BV)	**1997-07 Bodewes Scheepswerf "Volharding" Foxhol B.V. — Foxhol** Yd No: 334 Loa 89.72 (BB) Br ex - Dght 5.710 Lbp 84.98 Br md 13.60 Dpth 7.20 Welded, 1 dk	**(A31A2GX) General Cargo Ship** Grain: 5,508; Bale: 5,477 TEU 261 C.Ho 111/20' (40') C.Dk 150/20' (40') incl. 18 ref C. Compartments: 1 Ho, ER 1 Ha: (63.0 x 11.0)ER Ice Capable	**1 oil engine** with flexible couplings & reductiongeared to sc. shaft driving 1 CP propeller Total Power: 2,200kW (2,991hp) 13.0kn MaK 6M453C 1 x 4 Stroke 6 Cy. 320 x 420 2200kW (2991bhp) MaK Motoren GmbH & Co. KG-Kiel AuxGen: 1 x 240kW a.c, 1 x 136kW a.c Thrusters: 1 Thwart. FP thruster (f)
8976724 *YB4037* -	**UNION** *ex Nila Samudra III -2005* **PT Sabang Raya Indah** - *Jambi* *Indonesia*	**200** 116 -	Class: (KI)	**1978 P.T. Nila Kandi — Palembang** Loa 39.60 Br ex - Dght 2.570 Lbp 35.70 Br md 6.98 Dpth 3.02 Welded, 1 dk	**(A31A2GX) General Cargo Ship**	**1 oil engine** driving 1 FP propeller Total Power: 221kW (300hp) 10.0kn Yanmar 6M-T 1 x 4 Stroke 6 Cy. 200 x 240 221kW (300bhp) Yanmar Diesel Engine Co Ltd-Japan
9034975 *OROU* -	**UNION 5** **URS Belgie NV** Unie van Redding - en Sleepdienst NV (Union de Remorquage et de Sauvetage SA) (Towage & Salvage Union Ltd) *Antwerpen* *Belgium* MMSI: 205065000 Official number: 01 00319 1996	**290** 87 131	Class: BV	**1992-09 N.V. Scheepswerf van Rupelmonde — Rupelmonde** Yd No: 469 Loa 31.69 Br ex 10.05 Dght 3.792 Lbp 25.77 Br md 9.70 Dpth 4.76 Welded, 1 dk	**(B32A2ST) Tug**	**2 oil engines** with clutches, flexible couplings & sr geared to sc. shafts driving 2 Directional propellers Total Power: 2,652kW (3,606hp) 12.6kn A.B.C. 6MDZC 2 x 4 Stroke 6 Cy. 256 x 310 each-1326kW (1803bhp) Anglo Belgian Corp NV (ABC)-Belgium AuxGen: 2 x 120kW 380V 50Hz a.c Fuel: 95.0 (d.f.)
9034987 *OROV* -	**UNION 6** **URS Belgie NV** Unie van Redding - en Sleepdienst NV (Union de Remorquage et de Sauvetage SA) (Towage & Salvage Union Ltd) *Zeebrugge* *Belgium* MMSI: 205348000 Official number: 01 00320 1996	**288** 86 240	Class: BV	**1993-02 N.V. Scheepswerf van Rupelmonde — Rupelmonde** Yd No: 470 Loa 31.69 Br ex 10.05 Dght 4.277 Lbp 25.77 Br md 9.70 Dpth 4.76 Welded, 1 dk	**(B32A2ST) Tug**	**2 oil engines** with clutches & sr geared to sc. shafts driving 2 Directional propellers Total Power: 2,652kW (3,606hp) 12.6kn A.B.C. 6MDZC 2 x 4 Stroke 6 Cy. 256 x 310 each-1326kW (1803bhp) Anglo Belgian Corp NV (ABC)-Belgium AuxGen: 2 x 120kW 380V 50Hz a.c Fuel: 61.0 (d.f.)
9120164 *ORKU* -	**UNION 7** **Unie van Redding - en Sleepdienst NV (Union de Remorquage et de Sauvetage SA) (Towage & Salvage Union Ltd)** - *Antwerpen* *Belgium* MMSI: 205188000 Official number: 01 00126 1996	**398** 119 255	Class: LR ✠ **100A1** SS 06/2011 tug ✠ **LMC** **UMS** Eq.Ltr: G; Cable: 302.5/20.5 U2	**1996-06 Astilleros Armon SA — Navia** Yd No: 370 Loa 30.06 Br ex 11.04 Dght 3.337 Lbp 28.50 Br md 11.00 Dpth 4.50 Welded, 1 dk	**(B32A2ST) Tug**	**2 oil engines** gearing integral to driving 2 Voith-Schneider propellers Total Power: 3,002kW (4,082hp) 12.5kn Deutz SBV8M628 2 x 4 Stroke 8 Cy. 240 x 280 each-1501kW (2041bhp) Motoren Werke Mannheim AG (MWM)-Mannheim AuxGen: 2 x 144kW 380V 50Hz a.c, 1 x 72kW 380V 50Hz a.c Fuel: 155.0 (d.f.) 13.0pd
9120176 *ORKE* -	**UNION 8** **URS Belgie NV** Unie van Redding - en Sleepdienst NV (Union de Remorquage et de Sauvetage SA) (Towage & Salvage Union Ltd) *Antwerpen* *Belgium* MMSI: 205193000 Official number: 01 00382 1997	**398** 119 256	Class: LR ✠ **100A1** SS 12/2011 tug ✠ **LMC** **UMS** Eq.Ltr: G; Cable: 302.5/20.5 U2	**1996-12 Astilleros Armon SA — Navia** Yd No: 371 Loa 30.60 Br ex 11.04 Dght 3.337 Lbp 28.50 Br md 11.00 Dpth 4.50 Welded, 1 dk	**(B32A2ST) Tug**	**2 oil engines** gearing integral to driving 2 Voith-Schneider propellers Total Power: 3,000kW (4,078hp) 12.5kn Deutz SBV8M628 2 x 4 Stroke 8 Cy. 240 x 280 each-1500kW (2039bhp) Motoren Werke Mannheim AG (MWM)-Mannheim AuxGen: 2 x 144kW 380V 50Hz a.c, 1 x 72kW 380V 50Hz a.c Fuel: 162.0 (d.f.) 13.0pd

IMO / Call sign	Name / Owners / Flag	Tonnage	Class	Builder / Dimensions	Type / Cargo	Machinery
9120190 *ORKQ* -	**UNION 11** **Unie van Redding - en Sleepdienst NV (Union de Remorquage et de Sauvetage SA) (Towage & Salvage Union Ltd)** - *Antwerpen* *Belgium* MMSI: 205233000 Official number: 01 00385 1997	**398** 119 255	Class: LR ✠**100A1** SS 07/2012 tug ✠**LMC** **UMS** Eq.Ltr: G; Cable: 302.5/20.5 U2	**1997**-07 **Astilleros Armon SA — Navia** Yd No: 373 Loa 30.60 Br ex 11.04 Dght 3.337 Lbp 28.50 Br md 11.00 Dpth 4.50 Welded, 1 dk	**(B32A2ST) Tug**	**2 oil engines** gearing integral to driving 2 Voith-Schneider propellers Total Power: 3,000kW (4,078hp) 12.5kn Deutz SBV8M628 2 x 4 Stroke 8 Cy. 240 x 280 each-1500kW (2039bhp) Motoren Werke Mannheim AG (MWM)-Mannheim AuxGen: 2 x 144kW 380V 50Hz a.c, 1 x 72kW 380V 50Hz a.c Fuel: 162.0 (d.f.) 13.0pd
9365130 *ORNJ* -	**UNION AMBER** **URS Belgie NV** Unie van Redding - en Sleepdienst NV (Union de Remorquage et de Sauvetage SA) (Towage & Salvage Union Ltd) *Zeebrugge* *Belgium* MMSI: 205474000 Official number: 01 00649 2007	**311** 93 265	Class: BV	**2007**-02 **Astilleros Armon SA — Navia** Yd No: 647 Loa 25.00 Br ex - Dght 3.800 Lbp 20.94 Br md 11.20 Dpth 5.25 Welded, 1 dk	**(B32A2ST) Tug**	**2 oil engines** reduction geared to sc. shafts driving 2 Z propellers Total Power: 3,750kW (5,098hp) A.B.C. 8MDZC 2 x 4 Stroke 8 Cy. 256 x 310 each-1875kW (2549bhp) Anglo Belgian Corp NV (ABC)-Belgium AuxGen: 2 x 196kW a.c
9494814 *3EWK9* -	**UNION ANTON** *ex* Panther *-2010* **Babylon Shipping Co** Union Commercial Inc *Panama* *Panama* MMSI: 355873000 Official number: 4154710	**19,785** 10,395 32,077 T/cm 45.1	Class: NK	**2010**-02 **The Hakodate Dock Co Ltd — Hakodate HK** Yd No: 850 Loa 175.53 (BB) Br ex - Dght 9.640 Lbp 167.00 Br md 29.40 Dpth 13.70 Welded, 1 dk	**(A21A2BC) Bulk Carrier** Double Hull Grain: 42,620; Bale: 39,272 Compartments: 5 Ho, ER 5 Ha: ER Cranes: 4x30t	**1 oil engine** driving 1 FP propeller Total Power: 6,840kW (9,300hp) 14.4kn Mitsubishi 6UEC45LSE 1 x 2 Stroke 6 Cy. 450 x 1840 6840kW (9300bhp) Mitsubishi Heavy Industries Ltd-Japan AuxGen: 3 x 288kW a.c Fuel: 1250.0
8918564 *ORLA* -	**UNION BEAVER** *ex* Salvage Chief *-2001* **URS Salvage & Maritime Contracting NV** Unie van Redding - en Sleepdienst NV (Union de Remorquage et de Sauvetage SA) (Towage & Salvage Union Ltd) *Antwerpen* *Belgium* MMSI: 205087000 Official number: 01 00300 1996	**856** 256 615 T/cm 5.6	Class: BV	**1991**-06 **Fulton Marine N.V. — Ruisbroek** Yd No: 180 Loa 50.65 Br ex 12.78 Dght 2.690 Lbp 45.52 Br md 12.50 Dpth 4.00 Welded, 1 dk	**(B34P2QV) Salvage Ship** Cranes: 1x24.5t	**2 oil engines** with flexible couplings & dr geared to sc. shafts driving 2 FP propellers Total Power: 1,350kW (1,836hp) 6.3kn Caterpillar 3508TA 2 x Vee 4 Stroke 8 Cy. 170 x 190 each-675kW (918bhp) Caterpillar Inc-USA AuxGen: 1 x 184kW 220/380V 60Hz a.c, 1 x 160kW 220/380V 50Hz a.c, 1 x 50kW 220/380V 50Hz a.c Thrusters: 1 Thwart. FP thruster (f)
9605061 *V7XR3* -	**UNION BIENVENIDO** **Byzantium Shipholding SA** Union Commercial Inc *Majuro* *Marshall Islands* MMSI: 538004549 Official number: 4549	**17,019** 10,108 28,189 T/cm 39.7	Class: NK	**2012**-01 **I-S Shipyard Co Ltd — Imabari EH** Yd No: S-A057 Loa 169.37 (BB) Br ex - Dght 9.820 Lbp 160.40 Br md 27.20 Dpth 13.60 Welded, 1 dk	**(A21A2BC) Bulk Carrier** Grain: 37,320; Bale: 35,742 Compartments: 5 Ho, ER 5 Ha: 4 (19.2 x 17.6)ER (13.6 x 16.0) Cranes: 4x30.5t	**1 oil engine** driving 1 FP propeller Total Power: 5,850kW (7,954hp) 14.0kn MAN-B&W 6S42MC 1 x 2 Stroke 6 Cy. 420 x 1764 5850kW (7954bhp) Imex Co Ltd-Japan Fuel: 1530.0 22.0
9537537 *ORPS* -	**UNION BOXER** **Caixa d'Estalvis i Pensions de Barcelona (Caja de Ahorros y Pensiones de Barcelona) (La Caixa)** Unie van Redding - en Sleepdienst NV (Union de Remorquage et de Sauvetage SA) (Towage & Salvage Union Ltd) *Antwerpen* *Belgium* MMSI: 205575000 Official number: 01 00760 2010	**810** 243 527	Class: LR ✠**100A1** SS 07/2010 tug fire-fighting Ship 1 (2400m3/h) with water spray ✠**LMC** **UMS** Eq.Ltr: J; Cable: 357.5/26.0 U2 (a)	**2010**-07 **Astilleros Armon SA — Navia** Yd No: 675 Loa 40.65 Br ex 12.70 Dght 5.500 Lbp 31.91 Br md 12.70 Dpth 6.90 Welded, 1 dk	**(B21B20A) Anchor Handling Tug Supply**	**2 oil engines** gearing integral to driving 2 Directional propellers Total Power: 5,304kW (7,212hp) 14.0kn A.B.C. 12VDZC 2 x Vee 4 Stroke 12 Cy. 256 x 310 each-2652kW (3606bhp) Anglo Belgian Corp NV (ABC)-Belgium AuxGen: 3 x 296kW 400V 50Hz a.c Thrusters: 1 Thwart. FP thruster (f)
7026390 *DUA2140* -	**UNION BULK** *ex* Fuyo Maru *-1992* **Isla Cebu Maritime Inc** *Manila* *Philippines* Official number: MNLD001986	**1,089** 729 1,593	Class: (BV)	**1970**-07 **Narasaki Zosen KK — Muroran HK** Yd No: 705 Loa 65.38 Br ex 10.83 Dght 4.928 Lbp 60.00 Br md 10.80 Dpth 5.41 Welded, 1 dk	**(A24A2BT) Cement Carrier** Compartments: 3 Ho, ER	**1 oil engine** geared to sc. shaft driving 1 FP propeller Total Power: 883kW (1,201hp) 10.5kn Daihatsu 6DSM-26F 1 x 4 Stroke 6 Cy. 260 x 320 883kW (1201bhp) Daihatsu Kogyo-Japan AuxGen: 2 x 64kW 445V 60Hz a.c Fuel: 9.0 (d.f.) 35.0 (r.f.) 5.0pd
9314260 *OROB* -	**UNION CORAL** **Unie van Redding - en Sleepdienst NV (Union de Remorquage et de Sauvetage SA) (Towage & Salvage Union Ltd)** - *Zeebrugge* *Belgium* MMSI: 205414000 Official number: 01 00553 2004	**493** 147 92	Class: LR ✠**100A1** SS 09/2009 tug fire fighting Ship 1 (2400 cubic m/h) with water spray ✠**LMC** **UMS** Eq.Ltr: I; Cable: 330.0/24.0 U2 (a)	**2004**-09 **Astilleros Armon SA — Navia** Yd No: 610 Loa 33.00 Br ex 11.60 Dght 4.400 Lbp 28.70 Br md 11.00 Dpth 5.60 Welded, 1 dk	**(B32A2ST) Tug**	**2 oil engines** gearing integral to driving 2 Z propellers Total Power: 3,700kW (5,030hp) 13.0kn A.B.C. 8MDZC 2 x 4 Stroke 8 Cy. 256 x 310 each-1850kW (2515bhp) Anglo Belgian Corp NV (ABC)-Belgium AuxGen: 2 x 180kW 380/220V 50Hz a.c Fuel: 246.2 (r.f.) 11.0pd
9456537 *3FTY2* -	**UNION DEDE** **Barfly Shipping Inc** Union Commercial Inc SatCom: Inmarsat C 435658212 *Panama* *Panama* MMSI: 356582000 Official number: 4249111	**31,540** 18,765 55,733 T/cm 56.9	Class: NK	**2011**-02 **IHI Marine United Inc — Yokohama KN** Yd No: 3271 Loa 190.00 (BB) Br ex - Dght 12.740 Lbp 185.00 Br md 32.26 Dpth 18.10 Welded, 1 dk	**(A21A2BC) Bulk Carrier** Grain: 72,062; Bale: 67,062 Compartments: 5 Ho, ER 5 Ha: ER Cranes: 4x35t	**1 oil engine** driving 1 FP propeller Total Power: 8,890kW (12,087hp) 14.0kn Wartsila 6RT-flex50 1 x 2 Stroke 6 Cy. 500 x 2050 8890kW (12087bhp) Diesel United Ltd.-Aioi Fuel: 2478.0 (r.f.)
8412558 *J8B4225* -	**UNION DEMETER** *ex* Columbian Express *-2010* *ex* ALS Endeavour *-2001* *ex* Columbian Express *-1998* *ex* ALS Strength *-1997* *ex* Kriti Amber *-1988* *ex* ALS Strength *-1988* *ex* Kriti Amber *-1987* **Demeter Shipping Co Ltd** Tranglory Shipping Co Ltd *Kingstown* *St Vincent & The Grenadines* MMSI: 376549000 Official number: 10698	**12,963** 7,928 20,479 T/cm 30.2	Class: RI (LR) ✠ Classed LR until 16/6/11	**1986**-09 **Mitsubishi Heavy Industries Ltd. — Shimonoseki** Yd No: 877 Loa 146.51 (BB) Br ex 25.05 Dght 9.818 Lbp 140.01 Br md 25.01 Dpth 13.62 Welded, 2 dks, 2nd dk in way of Nos. 2, 3 & 4 holds only	**(A31A2GX) General Cargo Ship** Grain: 28,764; Bale: 26,553 TEU 692 C Ho 314 TEU C Dk 378 TEU incl 10 ref C. Compartments: 4 Ho, ER, 3 Tw Dk 7 Ha: 4 (25.6 x 8.0)3 (12.8 x 8.0)ER Cranes: 4x25t	**1 oil engine** driving 1 FP propeller Total Power: 6,540kW (8,892hp) 14.8kn Sulzer 6RTA48 1 x 2 Stroke 6 Cy. 480 x 1400 6540kW (8892bhp) Mitsubishi Heavy Industries Ltd-Japan AuxGen: 3 x 550kW 450V 60Hz a.c Boilers: e (ex.g.) 11.9kgf/cm² (11.7bar), AuxB (o.f.) 6.9kgf/cm² (6.8bar) Fuel: 197.0 (d.f.) 966.0 (r.f.) 22.0pd
9220548 *ORLK* -	**UNION DIAMOND** **Smit Transport Belgium NV** Unie van Redding - en Sleepdienst NV (Union de Remorquage et de Sauvetage SA) (Towage & Salvage Union Ltd) *Antwerpen* *Belgium* MMSI: 205349000 Official number: 01 00455 2001	**498** 149 -	Class: LR ✠**100A1** SS 06/2011 tug ✠**LMC** **UMS** Eq.Ltr: I; Cable: 330.0/24.0 U2 (a)	**2001**-06 **Astilleros Armon SA — Navia** Yd No: 511 Lengthened-2010 Loa 35.75 Br ex 11.60 Dght - Lbp 28.70 Br md 11.00 Dpth 4.40 Welded, 1 dk	**(B32A2ST) Tug**	**2 oil engines** gearing integral to driving 2 Z propellers Total Power: 3,700kW (5,030hp) 13.0kn A.B.C. 8DZC 2 x 4 Stroke 8 Cy. 256 x 310 each-1850kW (2515bhp) Anglo Belgian Corp NV (ABC)-Belgium AuxGen: 2 x 144kW 380V 50Hz a.c Thrusters: 1 Thwart. CP thruster (f) Fuel: 70.0 (d.f.) 15.0pd
9406441 *ORPR* -	**UNION EAGLE** **Unie van Redding - en Sleepdienst NV (Union de Remorquage et de Sauvetage SA) (Towage & Salvage Union Ltd)** URS Belgie NV *Antwerpen* *Belgium* MMSI: 205300000 Official number: 01 00769 2010	**439** 149 286	Class: LR ✠**100A1** SS 11/2010 tug ✠**LMC** **UMS** Eq.Ltr: H; Cable: 302.5/22.0 U2 (a)	**2010**-11 **Astilleros Armon Burela SA — Burela** (Hull) **2010**-11 **Astilleros Armon SA — Navia** Yd No: 662 Loa 28.50 Br ex 12.20 Dght 4.700 Lbp 22.87 Br md 12.20 Dpth 5.89 Welded, 1 dk	**(B32A2ST) Tug**	**2 oil engines** gearing integral to driving 2 Z propellers Total Power: 5,300kW (7,206hp) A.B.C. 12VDZC 2 x Vee 4 Stroke 12 Cy. 256 x 310 each-2650kW (3603bhp) Anglo Belgian Corp NV (ABC)-Belgium AuxGen: 2 x 160kW 400V 50Hz a.c
9314296 *OROE* -	**UNION EMERALD** **URS Belgie NV** Unie van Redding - en Sleepdienst NV (Union de Remorquage et de Sauvetage SA) (Towage & Salvage Union Ltd) *Antwerpen* *Belgium* MMSI: 205417000 Official number: 01 00607 2005	**493** 135 92	Class: LR ✠**100A1** SS 09/2010 tug fire fighting Ship 1 (2400 cubic m/h) with water spray ✠**LMC** **UMS** Eq.Ltr: I; Cable: 330.0/24.0 U2 (a)	**2005**-09 **Astilleros Armon SA — Navia** Yd No: 614 Loa 33.00 Br ex 11.60 Dght 4.400 Lbp 28.70 Br md 11.00 Dpth 5.60 Welded, 1 dk	**(B32A2ST) Tug**	**2 oil engines** geared to sc. shafts driving 2 Z propellers Total Power: 3,700kW (5,030hp) 13.4kn A.B.C. 8MDZC 1 x 4 Stroke 8 Cy. 256 x 310 1850kW (2515bhp) Anglo Belgian Corp NV (ABC)-Belgium AuxGen: 2 x 180kW 380/220V 50Hz a.c Fuel: 230.0 (d.f.)

8314756 *J8B4438* -	**UNION EMMA** *ex* Hopi Princess *-2012* *ex* African Sanderling *-2008* *ex* DS Attica *-2004* *ex* Albert Oldendorff *-2000* *ex* Attica *-1999* *ex* Vaimama *-1996* *ex* Attica *-1996* *ex* Ushuaia *-1995* *ex* Mostween 8 *-1992* *ex* Silver Gulf *-1989* **Carrie Shipping Co Ltd** Tranglory Shipping Co Ltd *Kingstown* *St Vincent & The Grenadines* MMSI: 375569000 Official number: 10911	**13,911** 7,162 20,412	Class: RI (LR) (AB) (GL) Classed LR until 16/1/12	**1984-05 Hayashikane Shipbuilding & Engineering Co Ltd — Shimonoseki YC** Yd No: 1277 Loa 153.50 (BB) Br ex 22.76 Dght 10.090 Lbp 145.01 Br md 22.71 Dpth 13.82 Welded, 2 dks	**(A31A2GX) General Cargo Ship** Grain: 25,754; Bale: 24,807 TEU 621 C Ho 381 TEU C Dk 216 TEU incl 24 ref C. Compartments: 4 Ho, ER 4 Ha: (18.8 x 10.0)3 (18.8 x 17.4)ER Cranes: 4x30t	**1 oil engine** driving 1 FP propeller Total Power: 7,162kW (9,737hp) B&W 1 x 2 Stroke 5 Cy. 600 x 1944 7162kW (9737bhp) Mitsui Engineering & Shipbuilding CLtd-Japan AuxGen: 3 x 640kW 450V 60Hz a.c Boilers: AuxB (Comp) 7.1kgf/cm² (7.0bar) Fuel: 124.5 (d.f.) 988.0 (r.f.) 25.5pd	15.0kn 5L60MC
9456549 *V7WB8* -	**UNION ERWIN** **Auster Shipmanagement Corp** Union Commercial Inc SatCom: Inmarsat C 453836431 *Majuro* *Marshall Islands* MMSI: 538004260 Official number: 4260	**31,540** 18,765 55,733 T/cm 56.9	Class: NK	**2011-04 IHI Marine United Inc — Yokohama KN** Yd No: 3272 Loa 190.00 (BB) Br ex - Dght 12.735 Lbp 185.00 Br md 32.26 Dpth 18.10 Welded, 1 dk	**(A21A2BC) Bulk Carrier** Grain: 72,062; Bale: 67,062 Compartments: 5 Ho, ER 5 Ha: ER Cranes: 4x35t	**1 oil engine** driving 1 FP propeller Total Power: 8,890kW (12,087hp) Wartsila 1 x 2 Stroke 6 Cy. 500 x 2050 8890kW (12087bhp) Diesel United Ltd.-Aioi	14.5kn 6RT-flex50
9449259 *SVBG4* -	**UNION EXPLORER** **European Carriers Inc** Union Marine Enterprises SA SatCom: Inmarsat C 424110210 *Piraeus* *Greece* MMSI: 241102000	**33,280** 19,342 57,700 T/cm 57.3	Class: LR ✠ **100A1** SS 06/2011 bulk carrier CSR BC-A GRAB (20) Nos. 2 & 4 holds may be empty ESP **ShipRight** (ACS (B),CM) *IWS LI ✠ **LMC** **UMS** Eq.Ltr: N†; Cable: 660.0/76.0 U3 (a)	**2011-06 STX (Dalian) Shipbuilding Co Ltd — Wafangdian LN** Yd No: D2023 Loa 190.00 (BB) Br ex 32.30 Dght 13.000 Lbp 183.30 Br md 32.26 Dpth 18.50 Welded, 1 dk	**(A21A2BC) Bulk Carrier** Grain: 71,850 Compartments: 5 Ho, ER 5 Ha: 4 (19.7 x 18.3)ER (18.0 x 18.3) Cranes: 4x36t	**1 oil engine** driving 1 FP propeller Total Power: 9,480kW (12,889hp) MAN-B&W 1 x 2 Stroke 6 Cy. 500 x 2000 9480kW (12889bhp) STX Engine Co Ltd-South Korea AuxGen: 3 x 625kW 450V 60Hz a.c Boilers: AuxB (Comp) 8.9kgf/cm² (8.7bar)	14.5kn 6S50MC-C
6728006 - -	**UNION EXPRESS** *ex* Lancaster *-1989* *ex* Nova Cura *-1989* *ex* Michiel *-1984* - -	*174* 64 -		**1967 Scheepswerf Metz B.V. — Urk** Yd No: 15 Lengthened-1972 Loa 35.51 Br ex 6.81 Dght - Lbp 31.48 Br md 6.71 Dpth 3.23 Welded, 1 dk	**(B11B2FV) Fishing Vessel**	**1 oil engine** driving 1 FP propeller Total Power: 1,589kW (2,160hp) Stork 1 x 4 Stroke 6 Cy. 280 x 300 1589kW (2160bhp) (new engine 1984) Stork Werkspoor Diesel BV-Netherlands Fuel: 30.5 (d.f.)	11.0kn 6DRO218K
9537525 *ORPP* -	**UNION FIGHTER** **Caixa d'Estalvis i Pensions de Barcelona (Caja de Ahorros y Pensiones de Barcelona) (La Caixa)** Unie van Redding - en Sleepdienst NV (Union de Remorquage et de Sauvetage SA) (Towage & Salvage Union Ltd) SatCom: Inmarsat C 420556610 *Antwerpen* *Belgium* MMSI: 205566000 Official number: 01 00747 2010	**810** 243 527	Class: LR ✠ **100A1** SS 03/2010 tug fire-fighting Ship 1 (2400 m3/h) with water spray ✠ **LMC** **UMS** Eq.Ltr: J; Cable: 357.5/26.0 U2 (a)	**2010-03 Astilleros Armon SA — Navia** Yd No: 674 Loa 40.65 Br ex 12.70 Dght 5.500 Lbp 31.91 Br md 12.70 Dpth 6.90 Welded, 1 dk	**(B21B20A) Anchor Handling Tug Supply**	**2 oil engines** gearing integral to driving 2 Directional propellers Total Power: 5,304kW (7,212hp) A.B.C. 2 x Vee 4 Stroke 12 Cy. 256 x 310 each-2652kW (3606bhp) Anglo Belgian Corp NV (ABC)-Belgium AuxGen: 3 x 296kW 400V 50Hz a.c Thrusters: 1 Thwart. FP thruster (f)	14.0kn 12VDZC
8631491 *XUJN3* -	**UNION FORTUNE** *ex* Xin Long *-2008* *ex* Koya Maru *-2005* **You Lian Shipping Co Ltd** Yantai Union International Ship Management Co Ltd *Phnom Penh* *Cambodia* MMSI: 515031000 Official number: 0888992	**1,880** 1,041 3,194		**1988 Y.K. Takasago Zosensho — Naruto** Converted From: Grab Dredger-2005 Lengthened-2005 Loa 84.37 Br ex 12.52 Dght 3.620 Lbp 56.00 Br md 12.50 Dpth 6.45 Welded, 1 dk	**(A31A2GX) General Cargo Ship**	**1 oil engine** driving 1 FP propeller Total Power: 736kW (1,001hp) Niigata 1 x 4 Stroke 6 Cy. 310 x 530 736kW (1001bhp) Niigata Engineering Co Ltd-Japan	11.0kn 6M31AGT
9121754 *3EUG* -	**UNION FORTUNE** *ex* Chem Pegasus *-2013* *ex* Kerim *-2010* *ex* Spring Leo *-2003* **Fortune Tankers Co Ltd** Global Marine Ship Management Co Ltd *Panama* *Panama* MMSI: 371858000 Official number: 45070PEXT	**9,544** 4,834 16,150 T/cm 25.5	Class: NK (NV) (AB)	**1995-07 Shin Kurushima Dockyard Co. Ltd. — Akitsu** Yd No: 2853 Converted From: Chemical Tanker-2005 Loa 138.62 (BB) Br ex 21.83 Dght 9.072 Lbp 130.68 Br md 21.80 Dpth 12.10 Welded, 1 dk	**(A12B2TR) Chemical/Products Tanker** Double Hull (13F) Liq: 15,848; Liq (Oil): 16,676 Cargo Heating Coils Compartments: 20 Wing Ta (s.stl), ER 20 Cargo Pump (s): 6x200m³/hr, 8x300m³/hr, 6x150m³/hr Manifold: Bow/CM: 72m	**1 oil engine** driving 1 FP propeller Total Power: 4,531kW (6,160hp) B&W 1 x 2 Stroke 7 Cy. 350 x 1050 4531kW (6160bhp) Makita Corp-Japan Fuel: 63.0 (d.f.) 900.0 (r.f.)	13.8kn 7L35MC
8656570 *XUFJ5* -	**UNION GLORY** *ex* Liao Yuan 21 *-2013* *ex* Shen Yu 12 *-2012* **Union Glory International Shipping Ltd** - *Phnom Penh* *Cambodia* MMSI: 515723100 Official number: 1310134	**8,344** 4,672 13,817	Class: UB	**2010-07 Ningbo Boda Shipbuilding Co Ltd — Xiangshan County ZJ** Yd No: 08004 Loa 140.19 Br ex - Dght 7.800 Lbp 131.81 Br md 20.00 Dpth 10.50 Welded, 1 dk	**(A21A2BC) Bulk Carrier** Grain: 17,964; Bale: 16,500 Cranes: 3x30t	**1 oil engine** reduction geared to sc. shaft driving 1 FP propeller Total Power: 2,665kW (3,623hp) Guangzhou 1 x 4 Stroke 6 Cy. 320 x 480 2665kW (3623bhp) Guangzhou Diesel Engine Factory CoLtd-China	6G32
8323575 *5NSK* -	**UNION GRACE** *ex* Chem Baltic *-2009* *ex* Baltic Sif *-2000* *ex* Shoun Marigold *-1989* **Akoto Ventures Nigeria Ltd** - *Nigeria* MMSI: 657517000	**4,509** 2,140 6,733 T/cm 16.8	Class: (LR) (NK) Classed LR until 21/4/10	**1984-11 Kochi Jyuko K.K. — Kochi** Yd No: 2357 Loa 113.34 (BB) Br ex 18.03 Dght 6.319 Lbp 104.00 Br md 18.00 Dpth 8.00 Welded, 1 dk	**(A12A2TC) Chemical Tanker** Double Bottom Entire Compartment Length Liq: 7,254 Cargo Heating Coils Compartments: 15 Ta, ER 4 Cargo Pump (s) Manifold: Bow/CM: 52.1m	**1 oil engine** driving 1 FP propeller Total Power: 2,992kW (4,068hp) B&W 1 x 2 Stroke 6 Cy. 350 x 1050 2992kW (4068bhp) Hitachi Zosen Corp-Japan AuxGen: 2 x 240kW 450V 60Hz a.c Boilers: e (ex.g.) 13.0kgf/cm² (12.7bar), AuxB (o.f.) 10.0kgf/cm² (9.8bar) Fuel: 139.5 (d.f.) 583.0 (r.f.) 13.5pd	12.0kn 6L35MC
9397121 *OROL* -	**UNION GRIZZLY** *launched as* Zeynep *-2007* **URS Belgie NV** Unie van Redding - en Sleepdienst NV (Union de Remorquage et de Sauvetage SA) (Towage & Salvage Union Ltd) *Antwerpen* *Belgium* MMSI: 205483000 Official number: 01 00667 2007	**473** 141 -	Class: BV (RI)	**2007-07 Dearsan Gemi Insaat ve Sanayii Koll. Sti. — Tuzla** Yd No: 2039 Loa 32.03 Br ex - Dght 4.300 Lbp - Br md 11.61 Dpth 5.37 Welded, 1 dk	**(B32A2ST) Tug**	**2 oil engines** gearing integral to driving 2 Z propellers Total Power: 3,536kW (4,808hp) A.B.C. 2 x 4 Stroke 8 Cy. 256 x 310 each-1768kW (2404bhp) Anglo Belgian Corp NV (ABC)-Belgium	13.0kn 8MDZC
9580106 *V7XG8* -	**UNION GROOVE** **Carbonero Maritime Co** Union Commercial Inc *Majuro* *Marshall Islands* MMSI: 538004477 Official number: 4477	**23,783** 11,639 35,064	Class: NK	**2012-01 SPP Shipbuilding Co Ltd — Tongyeong** Yd No: H4060 Loa 180.00 (BB) Br ex - Dght 9.916 Lbp 172.00 Br md 30.00 Dpth 14.70 Welded, 1 dk	**(A21A2BC) Bulk Carrier** Grain: 48,588; Bale: 46,384 Compartments: 5 Ho, ER 5 Ha: 4 (19.2 x 20.2)ER (16.4 x 18.4) Cranes: 4x35t	**1 oil engine** driving 1 FP propeller Total Power: 6,700kW (9,109hp) MAN-B&W 1 x 2 Stroke 5 Cy. 500 x 2000 6700kW (9109bhp) Doosan Engine Co Ltd-South Korea AuxGen: 3 x a.c Fuel: 1730.0	14.0kn 5S50MC-C8
9140475 *3FUA6* -	**UNION HARVEST** *ex* Gemini L *-2011* *ex* Sunrise Sakura *-2011* **Union Tankers Co Ltd** Global Marine Ship Management Co Ltd SatCom: Inmarsat C 435346110 *Panama* *Panama* MMSI: 353461000 Official number: 2351197E	**4,744** 2,033 7,506 T/cm 16.1	Class: NK	**1996-12 Shin Kurushima Dockyard Co. Ltd. — Akitsu** Yd No: 2908 Loa 108.02 (BB) Br ex 18.22 Dght 7.120 Lbp 99.00 Br md 18.20 Dpth 9.00 Welded, 1 dk	**(A12B2TR) Chemical/Products Tanker** Double Hull (13F) Liq: 8,647; Liq (Oil): 8,647 Part Cargo Heating Coils Compartments: 10 Wing Ta (s.stl), 7 Ta (s.stl), 2 Wing Slop Ta (s.stl), ER (s.stl) 16 Cargo Pump (s): 16x200m³/hr Manifold: Bow/CM: 54.1m	**1 oil engine** driving 1 FP propeller Total Power: 2,722kW (3,701hp) B&W 1 x 2 Stroke 5 Cy. 350 x 1050 2722kW (3701bhp) Makita Corp-Japan Thrusters: 1 Tunnel thruster (f) Fuel: 103.0 (d.f.) 483.0 (r.f.)	12.8kn 5L35MC

IMO / Call sign	Name / Owner / Manager / Port / Flag	Tonnage	Classification	Build / Dimensions	Type / Cargo	Machinery
9406439 *ORPQ* -	**UNION HAWK** **Unie van Redding - en Sleepdienst NV (Union de Remorquage et de Sauvetage SA) (Towage & Salvage Union Ltd)** URS Belgie NV *Antwerpen* *Belgium* MMSI: 205234000 Official number: 01 00765 2010	**439** 149 293	Class: LR **✠100A1** SS 09/2010 tug **✠LMC** **UMS** Cable: 302.5/22.0 U2 (a)	2010-09 **Astilleros Armon Burela SA — Burela** (Hull) 2010-09 **Astilleros Armon SA — Navia** Yd No: 661 Loa 28.50 Br ex 12.20 Dght 4.400 Lbp 22.87 Br md 12.20 Dpth 5.89 Welded, 1 dk	**(B32A2ST) Tug**	**2 oil engines** gearing integral to driving 2 Z propellers Total Power: 5,300kW (7,206hp) 13.0kn A.B.C. 12VDZC 2 x Vee 4 Stroke 12 Cy. 256 x 310 each-2650kW (3603bhp) Anglo Belgian Corp NV (ABC)-Belgium AuxGen: 2 x 160kW 400V 50Hz a.c
9365142 *ORNK* -	**UNION JADE** **URS Belgie NV** Unie van Redding - en Sleepdienst NV (Union de Remorquage et de Sauvetage SA) (Towage & Salvage Union Ltd) *Zeebrugge* *Belgium* MMSI: 205475000 Official number: 01 00664 2007	**311** 93 265	Class: BV	2007-06 **Astilleros Armon SA — Navia** Yd No: 648 Loa 25.00 Br ex - Dght 3.800 Lbp 20.94 Br md 11.20 Dpth 5.25 Welded, 1 dk	**(B32A2ST) Tug**	**2 oil engines** reduction geared to sc. shafts driving 2 Z propellers Total Power: 3,740kW (5,084hp) A.B.C. 8MDZC 2 x 4 Stroke 8 Cy. 256 x 310 each-1870kW (2542bhp) Anglo Belgian Corp NV (ABC)-Belgium AuxGen: 2 x 196kW a.c
9502714 *ORPF* -	**UNION KOALA** **URS Belgie NV** Unie van Redding - en Sleepdienst NV (Union de Remorquage et de Sauvetage SA) (Towage & Salvage Union Ltd) SatCom: Inmarsat C 420554610 *Antwerpen* *Belgium* MMSI: 205546000 Official number: 01 00724 2009	**479** 141 249	Class: BV	2009-06 **Dearsan Gemi Insaat ve Sanayii Koll. Sti. — Tuzla** Yd No: 2056 Loa 32.03 Br ex - Dght 4.300 Lbp 26.28 Br md 11.61 Dpth 5.37 Welded, 1 dk	**(B32A2ST) Tug**	**2 oil engines** reduction geared to sc. shafts driving 2 CP propellers Total Power: 3,788kW (5,150hp) 12.0kn A.B.C. 8MDZC 2 x 4 Stroke 8 Cy. 256 x 310 each-1894kW (2575bhp) Anglo Belgian Corp NV (ABC)-Belgium AuxGen: 2 x 199kW 50Hz a.c
9397119 *OROK* -	**UNION KODIAK** *launched as* Simay *-2007* **URS Belgie NV** Unie van Redding - en Sleepdienst NV (Union de Remorquage et de Sauvetage SA) (Towage & Salvage Union Ltd) *Antwerpen* *Belgium* MMSI: 205484000 Official number: 01 00654 2007	**473** 141 -	Class: BV (RI)	2007-05 **Dearsan Gemi Insaat ve Sanayii Koll. Sti. — Tuzla** Yd No: 2038 Loa 32.32 Br ex - Dght 4.300 Lbp 30.26 Br md 11.61 Dpth 5.37 Welded, 1 dk	**(B32A2ST) Tug**	**2 oil engines** gearing integral to driving 2 Z propellers Total Power: 3,536kW (4,808hp) 13.0kn A.B.C. 8MDZC 2 x 4 Stroke 8 Cy. 256 x 310 each-1768kW (2404bhp) Anglo Belgian Corp NV (ABC)-Belgium AuxGen: 2 x 150kW 400V 50Hz a.c
8609797 *3FCR3* -	**UNION LUCKY** *ex* High Sea *-2011* *ex* Geiyo Maru No. 36 *-2003* *ex* Tenjin Maru No. 21 *-1989* **Union Lucky Shipping Ltd** - *Panama* *Panama* MMSI: 373770000 Official number: 42794PEXT	**1,886** 1,168 3,780		1986-09 **Kochi Jyuko K.K. — Kochi** Yd No: 1931 Converted From: Bulk Aggregates Carrier-2003 Lengthened-2003 Loa 88.62 (BB) Br ex - Dght 5.300 Lbp 83.10 Br md 13.00 Dpth 6.81 Welded, 1 dk	**(A31A2GX) General Cargo Ship** Grain: 892 Compartments: 1 Ho, ER 1 Ha: (14.7 x 9.6)ER Cranes: 1	**1 oil engine** geared to sc. shaft driving 1 FP propeller Total Power: 1,324kW (1,800hp) 10.0kn Hanshin 6LU35G 1 x 4 Stroke 6 Cy. 350 x 550 1324kW (1800bhp) The Hanshin Diesel Works Ltd-Japan
9261487 *ORKJ* -	**UNION MANTA** **Smit Transport Belgium NV** Unie van Redding - en Sleepdienst NV (Union de Remorquage et de Sauvetage SA) (Towage & Salvage Union Ltd) *Antwerpen* *Belgium* MMSI: 205340000 Official number: 01 00488 2003	**3,164** 949 2,481	Class: LR (NV) **100A1** SS 03/2013 offshore tug/supply ship strengthened for heavy cargoes *IWS **LMC** **UMS** Eq.Ltr: V; Cable: 916.0/46.0 U3 (a)	2003-03 **Orskov Christensens Staalskibsvaerft A/S — Frederikshavn** Yd No: 232 Loa 75.50 Br ex 18.05 Dght 6.600 Lbp 64.40 Br md 18.00 Dpth 8.00 Welded, 1 dk	**(B21B20A) Anchor Handling Tug Supply** A-frames: 1x200t	**2 oil engines** geared to sc. shafts driving 2 CP propellers Total Power: 15,720kW (21,372hp) 15.0kn Wartsila 16V32 2 x Vee 4 Stroke 16 Cy. 320 x 350 each-7860kW (10686bhp) Wartsila Finland Oy-Finland AuxGen: 2 x 372kW 440/220V 60Hz a.c, 2 x 2240kW 440/220V 60Hz a.c Thrusters: 2 Thwart. CP thruster (f); 2 Thwart. CP thruster (a) Fuel: 96.0 (d.f.) 1334.0 (r.f.)
9628934 *SVBP5* -	**UNION MARINER** **Euroforum Marine Co Ltd** Union Marine Enterprises SA *Piraeus* *Greece* MMSI: 241222000	**44,647** 27,430 81,964 T/cm 71.9	Class: LR **✠100A1** SS 01/2013 bulk carrier CSR BC-A GRAB (20) Nos. 2, 4 & 6 holds may be empty ESP **ShipRight** (ABS (B), CM) *IWS LI **✠LMC** **UMS** Cable: 687.5/81.0 U3 (a)	2013-01 **COSCO (Dalian) Shipyard Co Ltd — Dalian LN** Yd No: N376 Loa 229.00 (BB) Br ex 32.29 Dght 14.500 Lbp 225.50 Br md 32.26 Dpth 20.25 Welded, 1 dk	**(A21A2BC) Bulk Carrier** Grain: 97,000; Bale: 90,784 Compartments: 7 Ho, ER 7 Ha: 5 (18.3 x 15.0) (15.7 x 15.1)ER (13.1 x 13.2)	**1 oil engine** driving 1 FP propeller Total Power: 11,900kW (16,179hp) 14.0kn MAN-B&W 5S60ME-C8 1 x 2 Stroke 5 Cy. 600 x 2400 11900kW (16179bhp) Hyundai Heavy Industries Co Ltd-South Korea AuxGen: 3 x 650kW 450V 60Hz a.c Boilers: AuxB (Comp) 9.2kgf/cm² (9.0bar)
9406415 *5BSE3* -	**UNION ONYX** **BW Marine (Cyprus) Ltd** Baggermaatschappij Boskalis BV *Limassol* *Cyprus* MMSI: 212163000	**493** 147 90	Class: LR **✠100A1** SS 09/2013 tug **✠LMC** **UMS** Eq.Ltr: I; Cable: 330.0/24.0 U2 (a)	2008-09 **Astilleros Armon SA — Navia** Yd No: 659 Loa 33.00 Br ex 11.60 Dght 4.400 Lbp 28.70 Br md 11.00 Dpth 5.60 Welded, 1 dk	**(B32A2ST) Tug**	**2 oil engines** gearing integral to driving 2 Directional propellers Total Power: 3,700kW (5,030hp) 13.0kn A.B.C. 8DZC 2 x 4 Stroke 8 Cy. 256 x 310 each-1850kW (2515bhp) Anglo Belgian Corp NV (ABC)-Belgium AuxGen: 2 x 180kW 380V 50Hz a.c
9502697 *ORPE* -	**UNION PANDA** *ex* Dearsan 2054 *-2009* **URS Belgie NV** Unie van Redding - en Sleepdienst NV (Union de Remorquage et de Sauvetage SA) (Towage & Salvage Union Ltd) *Antwerpen* *Belgium* MMSI: 205545000 Official number: 01 00716 2009	**479** 141 -	Class: BV	2009-01 **Dearsan Gemi Insaat ve Sanayii Koll. Sti. — Tuzla** Yd No: 2054 Loa 32.03 Br ex - Dght 4.300 Lbp 26.28 Br md 11.61 Dpth 5.37 Welded, 1 dk	**(B32A2ST) Tug**	**2 oil engines** reduction geared to sc. shafts driving 2 Propellers Total Power: 3,824kW (5,200hp) 13.0kn A.B.C. 8DZC 2 x 4 Stroke 8 Cy. 256 x 310 each-1912kW (2600bhp) Anglo Belgian Corp NV (ABC)-Belgium
9314272 *OROC* -	**UNION PEARL** **URS Belgie NV** Unie van Redding - en Sleepdienst NV (Union de Remorquage et de Sauvetage SA) (Towage & Salvage Union Ltd) *Zeebrugge* *Belgium* MMSI: 205415000 Official number: 01 00617 2005	**493** 147 92	Class: LR **✠100A1** SS 01/2010 tug, fire fighting ship 1 (2400 cubic m3/h) with water spray **✠LMC** **UMS** Eq.Ltr: I; Cable: 330.0/24.0 U2 (a)	2005-01 **Astilleros Armon SA — Navia** Yd No: 611 Loa 33.00 Br ex 11.60 Dght 4.400 Lbp 28.70 Br md 11.00 Dpth 5.60 Welded, 1 dk	**(B32A2ST) Tug**	**2 oil engines** gearing integral to driving 2 Z propellers Total Power: 3,700kW (5,030hp) 13.4kn A.B.C. 8MDZC 2 x 4 Stroke 8 Cy. 256 x 310 each-1850kW (2515bhp) Anglo Belgian Corp NV (ABC)-Belgium AuxGen: 2 x 180kW 380/220V 50Hz a.c Thrusters: 1 Thwart. FP thruster (f) Fuel: 230.0 (d.f.)
7808918 *5NKI* -	**UNION PRIDE** *ex* Triton *-2007* *ex* Parameshwari *-1997* *ex* Jag Prabhu *-1995* *ex* Princess Alka *-1987* *ex* Princess Chie *-1986* *ex* Chie Maru *-1985* **Union Pride Ltd** - *Nigeria* MMSI: 657211000 Official number: 377665	**4,358** 2,365 7,261 T/cm 16.0	Class: (BV) (RI) (IR) (NV) (NK)	1978-06 **Kurinoura Dockyard Co Ltd — Yawatahama EH** Yd No: 132 Loa 110.29 (BB) Br ex - Dght 6.889 Lbp 104.02 Br md 17.01 Dpth 8.21 Welded, 1 dk	**(A12B2TR) Chemical/Products Tanker** Double Bottom Entire Compartment Length Liq: 8,414; Liq (Oil): 8,414 Cargo Heating Coils Compartments: 5 Ta, ER, 10 Wing Ta 5 Cargo Pump (s): 3x250m³/hr, 2x500m³/hr Manifold: Bow/CM: 41m	**1 oil engine** driving 1 FP propeller Total Power: 3,309kW (4,499hp) 12.0kn Hanshin 6LU54 1 x 4 Stroke 6 Cy. 540 x 860 3309kW (4499bhp) The Hanshin Diesel Works Ltd-Japan AuxGen: 2 x 200kW 440V 60Hz a.c, 1 x 200kW 440V 60Hz a.c Fuel: 91.0 (d.f.) 576.0 (r.f.)
9242766 *ORQU* -	**UNION PRINCESS** *ex* Anglian Princess *-2012* **Smit Shipping Singapore Pte Ltd** Smit Transport Belgium NV *Antwerpen* *Belgium* MMSI: 205642000 Official number: 6662	**2,258** 677 1,890	Class: LR **✠100A1** SS 07/2012 offshore tug/supply ship, fire fighting Ship 1 (2400 cubic metre/hr) **✠LMC** **UMS** Eq.Ltr: S; Cable: 467.5/40.0 U3 (a)	2002-07 **Yantai Raffles Shipyard Co Ltd — Yantai SD** Yd No: YRF2000-109 Loa 67.40 Br ex - Dght 5.200 Lbp 57.20 Br md 15.50 Dpth 7.50 Welded, 1 dk	**(B21B20A) Anchor Handling Tug Supply**	**2 oil engines** with flexible couplings & sr geared to sc. shafts driving 2 FP propellers Total Power: 12,000kW (16,316hp) Wartsila 16V32D 2 x Vee 4 Stroke 16 Cy. 320 x 350 each-6000kW (8158bhp) Wartsila Finland Oy-Finland AuxGen: 2 x 2240kW 440V 60Hz a.c, 1 x 300kW 440V 60Hz a.c Thrusters: 2 Thwart. CP thruster (f); 1 Thwart. CP thruster (a)

IMO / Call sign	Name / Owner / Flag	Tonnage	Class	Builder / Dimensions	Type	Machinery
9104562 *SYMB* -	**UNION RANGER** *ex* Bulk Capella *-2003* **Mava Shipping Co Ltd** Union Marine Enterprises SA SatCom: Inmarsat A 1701432 *Piraeus* *Greece* MMSI: 240070000 Official number: 11191	**26,071** 14,872 45,621 T/cm 49.8	Class: NK	**1995**-06 **Tsuneishi Shipbuilding Co Ltd — Fukuyama HS** Yd No: 1051 Loa 185.74 (BB) Br ex 30.43 Dght 11.600 Lbp 177.00 Br md 30.40 Dpth 16.50 Welded, 1 dk	**(A21A2BC) Bulk Carrier** Grain: 57,180; Bale: 55,565 Compartments: 5 Ho, ER 5 Ha: (20.0 x 15.3)4 (20.8 x 15.3)ER Cranes: 4x30t	**1 oil engine** driving 1 FP propeller Total Power: 8,562kW (11,641hp) 14.0kn B&W 6S50MC 1 x 2 Stroke 6 Cy. 500 x 1910 8562kW (11641bhp) Mitsui Engineering & Shipbuilding CLtd-Japan Fuel: 1535.0 (r.f.)
9314284 *OROD* -	**UNION RUBY** - **URS Belgie NV** Unie van Redding - en Sleepdienst NV (Union de Remorquage et de Sauvetage SA) (Towage & Salvage Union Ltd) *Antwerpen* *Belgium* MMSI: 205416000 Official number: 01 00618 2005	**493** 147 -	Class: LR ✠**100A1** SS 05/2010 tug, fire fighting Ship 1 (2400m3/hr) with water spray ✠**LMC** **UMS** Eq.Ltr: I; Cable: 330.0/24.0 U2 (a)	**2005**-05 **Astilleros Armon SA — Navia** Yd No: 612 Loa 33.00 Br ex 11.60 Dght 4.400 Lbp 28.70 Br md 11.00 Dpth 5.60 Welded, 1 dk	**(B32A2ST) Tug**	**2 oil engines** gearing integral to driving 2 Z propellers Total Power: 3,700kW (5,030hp) 13.0kn A.B.C. 8MDZC 2 x 4 Stroke 8 Cy. 256 x 310 each-1850kW (2515bhp) Anglo Belgian Corp NV (ABC)-Belgium AuxGen: 2 x 180kW 380/220V 50Hz a.c Fuel: 230.0 (d.f.)
9220550 *ORLL* -	**UNION SAPPHIRE** - **Smit Transport Belgium NV** Unie van Redding - en Sleepdienst NV (Union de Remorquage et de Sauvetage SA) (Towage & Salvage Union Ltd) *Antwerpen* *Belgium* MMSI: 205001000 Official number: 01 00459 2001	**498** 149 -	Class: LR ✠**100A1** SS 08/2011 tug ✠**LMC** **UMS** Eq.Ltr: I; Cable: 330.0/24.0 U2 (a)	**2001**-08 **Astilleros Armon SA — Navia** Yd No: 512 Converted From: Tug-2010 Loa 35.75 Br ex 11.60 Dght - Lbp - Br md 11.00 Dpth 4.40 Welded, 1 dk	**(B21B20A) Anchor Handling Tug Supply**	**2 oil engines** gearing integral to driving 2 Z propellers Total Power: 3,700kW (5,030hp) 13.0kn A.B.C. 8DZC 2 x 4 Stroke 8 Cy. 256 x 310 each-1850kW (2515bhp) Anglo Belgian Corp NV (ABC)-Belgium AuxGen: 2 x 144kW 380V 50Hz a.c Thrusters: 1 Thwart. CP thruster (f) Fuel: 231.0 (d.f.) 17.5pd
9262742 *ORQW* -	**UNION SOVEREIGN** *ex* Anglian Sovereign *-2012* **Smit Shipping Singapore Pte Ltd** Smit Transport Belgium NV *Antwerpen* *Belgium* MMSI: 205644000 Official number: 6660	**2,263** 678 1,890	Class: LR ✠**100A1** SS 05/2013 offshore tug/supply vessel fire fighting Ship 1 (2400 cubic m/hr) ✠**LMC** **UMS** Eq.Ltr: S; Cable: 467.5/40.0 U3 (a)	**2003**-05 **Yantai Raffles Shipyard Co Ltd — Yantai SD** Yd No: YRF2001-127 Loa 67.40 Br ex - Dght 6.200 Lbp 57.20 Br md 15.50 Dpth 7.50 Welded, 1 dk	**(B21B20A) Anchor Handling Tug Supply**	**2 oil engines** with flexible couplings & sr geared to sc. shafts driving 2 CP propellers Total Power: 12,000kW (16,316hp) 12.0kn Wartsila 16V32 2 x Vee 4 Stroke 16 Cy. 320 x 400 each-6000kW (8158bhp) Wartsila Finland Oy-Finland AuxGen: 2 x 2240kW a.c, 1 x 300kW a.c Boilers: AuxB (o.f.) 3.3kgf/cm² (3.2bar) Thrusters: 2 Thwart. FP thruster (f); 1 Thwart. FP thruster (a) Fuel: 1200.0 (d.f.) 45.0pd
8882284 - -	**UNION STAR** *ex* Beng Lian 16 *-2012* *ex* Tomoe Maru No. 16 *-1994* **Miss Titin Martini** - *San Lorenzo* *Honduras* Official number: L-1725963	*170* 42 -		**1972 Kyoei Zosen KK — Mihara HS** Loa 30.00 Br ex - Dght 2.500 Lbp 27.46 Br md 7.80 Dpth 3.19 Welded, 1 dk	**(B32B2SP) Pusher Tug**	**1 oil engine** driving 1 FP propeller Total Power: 1,177kW (1,600hp) Yanmar 1 x 4 Stroke 1177kW (1600bhp) Yanmar Diesel Engine Co Ltd-Japan
7620445 *YBHH* -	**UNION STAR 3** *ex* Tanjung Dua *-1994* *ex* Adri VII *-1994* - - *Jakarta* *Indonesia* Official number: 1930/L	*771* 316 874	Class: (KI)	**1958**-12 **Cheoy Lee Shipyards Ltd — Hong Kong** Yd No: 688 Loa 55.48 Br ex 8.74 Dght 3.810 Lbp - Br md 8.41 Dpth 4.81 Riveted\Welded, 1 dk	**(A31A2GX) General Cargo Ship**	**1 oil engine** geared to sc. shaft driving 1 FP propeller Total Power: 466kW (634hp) Blackstone ERMGR6 1 x 4 Stroke 6 Cy. 222 x 292 466kW (634bhp) Lister Blackstone Marine Ltd.-Dursley
7405314 - -	**UNION STAR 7** *ex* PU 4601 *-1997* *ex* Munar I *-1993* *ex* PU 4601 *-1991* *ex* Tosa Maru *-1990* - -	**530** 159 1,112	Class: (NK)	**1974**-06 **Sanyo Zosen K.K. — Onomichi** Yd No: 683 Loa 37.00 Br ex 10.04 Dght 3.548 Lbp 34.00 Br md 10.00 Dpth 4.58 Riveted\Welded, 1 dk	**(B32B2SP) Pusher Tug**	**2 oil engines** driving 2 FP propellers Total Power: 3,384kW (4,600hp) 12.0kn Makita GSLH637 2 x 4 Stroke 6 Cy. 370 x 590 each-1692kW (2300bhp) Makita Tekkosho-Japan AuxGen: 2 x 120kW a.c
7357218 *HQTI4* -	**UNION STAR 8** *ex* Indra Sakti *-1996* **SYUFRI** - *San Lorenzo* *Honduras* Official number: L-0326761	**686** 419 1,106	Class: (KI) (AB)	**1974**-10 **Singapore Shipbuilding & Engineering Pte Ltd — Singapore** Yd No: B081 Loa 53.83 Br ex - Dght 3.231 Lbp 51.21 Br md 11.00 Dpth 3.81 Welded, 1 dk	**(A31A2GX) General Cargo Ship** Compartments: 2 Ho, ER 2 Ha: 2 (13.1 x 7.0)ER Cranes: 2	**2 oil engines** reverse reduction geared to sc. shafts driving 2 FP propellers Total Power: 698kW (950hp) 10.0kn M.T.U. 8R530TZ 2 x 4 Stroke 8 Cy. 175 x 220 each-349kW (475bhp) MTU Friedrichshafen GmbH-Friedrichshafen AuxGen: 2 x 56kW Fuel: 77.0 (d.f.)
7628540 *YGFE* -	**UNION STAR 20** *ex* Kota Silat III *-1996* *ex* Kota Silat VI *-1996* **PT Pelayaran Asia Lestari Lines** - *Batam* *Indonesia* Official number: 6T-743 541/PPM	*743* 402 1,000	Class: (KI)	**1976**-11 **P.T. Pakin — Jakarta** Yd No: 644 Loa 62.80 Br ex - Dght 3.701 Lbp 57.80 Br md 9.20 Dpth 4.40 Welded, 1 dk	**(A31A2GX) General Cargo Ship**	**1 oil engine** driving 1 FP propeller Total Power: 588kW (799hp) 11.0kn Yanmar 6G-DT 1 x 4 Stroke 6 Cy. 240 x 290 588kW (799bhp) (, fitted 2000) Yanmar Diesel Engine Co Ltd-Japan AuxGen: 1 x 30kW 220V a.c
8002262 *YGNN* -	**UNION STAR 27** *ex* Union Star 3 *-2000* *ex* Decienfuegos *-1997* *ex* Choyo Maru *-1993* **PT Bandar Inti Intan International** - *Batam* *Indonesia* Official number: 2000 PPM NO. 71/L	**1,224** 696 2,050	Class: KI	**1980**-03 **Yamanaka Zosen K.K. — Imabari** Yd No: 221 Loa 70.58 Br ex - Dght 6.100 Lbp 66.02 Br md 11.02 Dpth 6.13 Welded, 1 dk	**(A31A2GX) General Cargo Ship**	**1 oil engine** driving 1 FP propeller Total Power: 1,214kW (1,651hp) Nippon Hatsudoki HS6NV45 1 x 4 Stroke 6 Cy. 450 x 640 1214kW (1651bhp) Nippon Kokan KK (NKK Corp)-Japan
7362017 *YGNM* -	**UNION STAR 28** *ex* Chiang Roong *-1999* *ex* Tian Li Shan *-1997* *ex* Lindinger Jade *-1978* **PT Asia Mega Lines** - *Batam* *Indonesia* Official number: 2000 PPM N073/L	**2,777** 1,566 4,114	Class: (KI) (CC) (BV)	**1974**-11 **Husumer Schiffswerft — Husum** Yd No: 1423 Loa 91.45 (BB) Br ex 14.25 Dght 6.060 Lbp 83.45 Br md 14.20 Dpth 8.60 Welded, 2 dks	**(A31A2GX) General Cargo Ship** Grain: 6,351; Bale: 5,785 TEU 137 C.Ho 81/20' C.Dk 56/20' Compartments: 1 Ho, ER 2 Ha: (18.9 x 10.8) (25.2 x 10.8)ER Derricks: 2x20t,2x5t; Winches: 4 Ice Capable	**1 oil engine** geared to sc. shaft driving 1 FP propeller Total Power: 2,942kW (4,000hp) 14.3kn Deutz SBV8M540 1 x 4 Stroke 8 Cy. 370 x 400 2942kW (4000bhp) Kloeckner Humboldt Deutz AG-West Germany AuxGen: 3 x 160kW 380V 50Hz a.c Fuel: 303.0 (d.f.) 15.0pd
6521991 *HQVM3* -	**UNION STAR 38** *ex* Daiko Maru No. 8 *-2000* *ex* Daiko Maru No. 3 *-1999* **Sukamoto S Djaya** - *San Lorenzo* *Honduras* MMSI: 334910000 Official number: L-0327343	**723** 440 950		**1965**-06 **Kishimoto Zosen — Osakikamijima** Yd No: 180 Loa 55.61 Br ex 8.67 Dght 3.937 Lbp 51.01 Br md 8.62 Dpth 6.30 Welded, 1 dk	**(A31A2GX) General Cargo Ship** Compartments: 1 Ho, ER 1 Ha: (26.9 x 5.6)ER Derricks: 1x5t,1x3t; Winches: 4	**1 oil engine** driving 1 FP propeller Total Power: 1,030kW (1,400hp) 11.5kn Hanshin Z6VSH 1 x 4 Stroke 6 Cy. 280 x 450 1030kW (1400bhp) Hanshin Nainenki Kogyo-Japan AuxGen: 1 x 5kW 110V d.c, 1 x 3kW 110V d.c
6404806 *YGRT* -	**UNION STAR 42** *ex* Hero Queen *-2002* *ex* Hiap Tong *-1994* *ex* Tong Aik *-1992* *ex* Naga Jaya *-1991* *ex* Unggul I *-1986* *ex* Pelita Jaya *-1984* *ex* Misool *-1981* *ex* Palana *-1964* - - *Batam* *Indonesia* Official number: PPM 234/L	**1,201** 696 1,660	Class: (KI) (GL)	**1963 Angyalfold Shipyard, Hungarian Ship & Crane Works — Budapest** Yd No: 1945 Loa 75.54 Br ex - Dght 4.600 Lbp 69.00 Br md 11.50 Dpth 4.70 Welded, 1 dk	**(A31A2GX) General Cargo Ship** Grain: 2,193; Bale: 2,086 Compartments: 3 Ho, ER 3 Ha: 3 (8.6 x 5.6)ER Derricks: 1x10t,6x2.5t; Winches: 6	**1 oil engine** driving 1 FP propeller Total Power: 677kW (920hp) 10.8kn Lang 8LD315RF 1 x 4 Stroke 8 Cy. 315 x 450 677kW (920bhp) Lang Gepgyar-Budapest AuxGen: 1 x 224kW 230V d.c Fuel: 96.5 (d.f.)
7639460 *YGQL* -	**UNION STAR 47** *ex* Gemilang Utama *-2002* *ex* Kengma *-2002* *ex* Keisho Maru *-1997* **PT Pelayaran Armada Maritim Nusantara** - *Batam* *Indonesia* MMSI: 525000003 Official number: PPM 236/L	**1,487** 1,023 2,077	Class: KI	**1977**-02 **Yamanaka Zosen K.K. — Imabari** Yd No: 167 Loa 73.05 Br ex 12.04 Dght 3.450 Lbp 66.91 Br md 12.01 Dpth 5.00 Welded, 1 dk	**(A31A2GX) General Cargo Ship**	**1 oil engine** driving 1 FP propeller Total Power: 1,471kW (2,000hp) 11.0kn Hanshin 6LUD35 1 x 4 Stroke 6 Cy. 350 x 550 1471kW (2000bhp) Hanshin Nainenki Kogyo-Japan

No. / Call sign	Name / Owner / Manager / Flag	Tonnage	Class	Build / Dimensions	Type / Capacity	Machinery
8613695 *YGWA* -	**UNION STAR 57** *ex* Towa Maru *-2004* **PT Teguh Abadi Nusantara** - *Batam* *Indonesia* Official number: 2002PPM NO. 212/L	**475** 176 678	Class: (KI)	**1986-11 Uchida Zosen — Ise** Yd No: 846 Loa 51.97 Br ex - Dght 3.834 Lbp 47.02 Br md 8.81 Dpth 4.22 Welded, 1 dk	**(A12A2TC) Chemical Tanker** Liq: 452 Compartments: 6 Ta, ER	**1 oil engine** driving 1 FP propeller Total Power: 625kW (850hp) Niigata 6M26BGT 1 x 4 Stroke 6 Cy. 260 x 460 625kW (850bhp) Niigata Engineering Co Ltd-Japan
7113129 - -	**UNION STAR 62** *ex* Agel *-2002* *ex* Ageliki K *-1989* *ex* Sabrina *-1987* *ex* Montecristo *-1987* *ex* Collette *-1984* *ex* Gibhawk *-1983* *ex* Frigard *-1983* *ex* Horsa *-1980* *ex* Alice Bewa *-1976* **PT Sinar Mega Nusantara** - *Batam* *Indonesia* Official number: 2002 PPM NO. 245/L	**1,728** 1,009 2,650	Class: (GL) (BV) (NV)	**1971-09 Orskovs Staalskibsvaerft A/S — Frederikshavn** Yd No: 62 Loa 70.90 Br ex 13.03 Dght 5.671 Lbp 65.61 Br md 12.98 Dpth 6.76 Welded, 2 dks	**(A31A2GX) General Cargo Ship** Grain: 3,278; Bale: 2,890 TEU 64 C. 64/20' (40') Compartments: 1 Ho, ER 2 Ha: 2 (18.5 x 8.5)ER Cranes: 1x5t; Derricks: 2x5t; Winches: 4 Ice Capable	**1 oil engine** driving 1 CP propeller Total Power: 1,194kW (1,623hp) 12.0kn Alpha 12V23HU 1 x Vee 4 Stroke 12 Cy. 225 x 300 1194kW (1623bhp) Alpha Diesel A/S-Denmark AuxGen: 3 x 120kW 380V 50Hz a.c Fuel: 130.0 (d.f.) 5.0pd
8503759 *YB3394* -	**UNION STAR 82** *ex* Sanwa Maru *-2003* **PT Pelayaran Teguh Persada Kencana** - *Batam* *Indonesia* Official number: PPM 311/L	**493** 148 692	Class: (KI)	**1985-04 Uchida Zosen — Ise** Yd No: 836 Loa 50.63 Br ex - Dght 3.852 Lbp 46.00 Br md 8.72 Dpth 4.27 Welded, 1 dk	**(A12A2TC) Chemical Tanker** Liq: 455 Compartments: 3 Ta, ER	**1 oil engine** driving 1 FP propeller Total Power: 588kW (799hp) Yanmar MF24-UT 1 x 4 Stroke 6 Cy. 240 x 420 588kW (799bhp) Yanmar Diesel Engine Co Ltd-Japan
9538957 *V3TT7*	**UNION SUCCESS** *ex* African Coastal Two *-2010* **China National Electronics Import & Export Shandong Co** Senior Master International Ship Management Co Ltd *Belize City* *Belize* MMSI: 312173000 Official number: 611330040	**5,688** 3,144 7,500	Class: BV	**2010-11 Jiangsu Shenghua Shipbuilding Co Ltd — Zhenjiang JS** Yd No: 537 Loa 110.92 Br ex - Dght 6.960 Lbp 103.90 Br md 18.20 Dpth 9.00 Welded, 1 dk	**(A31A2GX) General Cargo Ship** Grain: 10,282 Compartments: 3 Ho, ER 3 Ha: ER Cranes: 2x45t Ice Capable	**1 oil engine** reduction geared to sc. shaft driving 1 FP propeller Total Power: 3,089kW (4,200hp) 12.4kn Chinese Std. Type GN8320ZC 1 x 4 Stroke 8 Cy. 320 x 380 3089kW (4200bhp) Ningbo CSI Power & Machinery GroupCo Ltd-China AuxGen: 2 x 440kW 400V 50Hz a.c, 1 x 120kW 400V 50Hz a.c
9406427 *5BSF3* -	**UNION TOPAZ** **BW Marine (Cyprus) Ltd** Baggermaatschappij Boskalis BV *Limassol* *Cyprus* MMSI: 212165000	**493** 147 90	Class: LR ✠ **100A1** SS 12/2008 tug ✠ **LMC** **UMS** Eq.Ltr: I; Cable: 330.0/24.0 U2 (a)	**2008-12 Astilleros Armon SA — Navia** Yd No: 660 Loa 33.00 Br ex 11.60 Dght 4.400 Lbp 28.70 Br md 11.00 Dpth 5.60 Welded, 1 dk	**(B32A2ST) Tug**	**2 oil engines** gearing integral to driving 2 Directional propellers Total Power: 3,700kW (5,030hp) 13.0kn A.B.C. 8DZC 2 x 4 Stroke 8 Cy. 256 x 310 each-1850kW (2515bhp) Anglo Belgian Corp NV (ABC)-Belgium AuxGen: 2 x 180kW 380V 50Hz a.c
9445710 *SVAX6* -	**UNION TRADER** **Melvin International SA** Union Marine Enterprises SA *Piraeus* *Greece* MMSI: 240982000 Official number: 11979	**33,280** 19,342 57,700 T/cm 57.3	Class: LR ✠ **100A1** SS 04/2010 bulk carrier CSR BC-A Nos. 2 & 4 holds may be empty GRAB (20) ESP LI *IWS **ShipRight** (CM, ACS (B)) ✠ **LMC** **UMS** Eq.Ltr: N†; Cable: 660.0/76.0 U3 (a)	**2010-04 STX (Dalian) Shipbuilding Co Ltd — Wafangdian LN** Yd No: D2004 Loa 190.00 (BB) Br ex 32.30 Dght 13.000 Lbp 183.30 Br md 32.26 Dpth 18.50 Welded, 1 dk	**(A21A2BC) Bulk Carrier** Grain: 71,850 Compartments: 5 Ho, ER 5 Ha: 4 (19.7 x 18.3)ER (18.0 x 18.3) Cranes: 4x30t	**1 oil engine** driving 1 FP propeller Total Power: 9,480kW (12,889hp) 14.5kn MAN-B&W 6S50MC-C 1 x 2 Stroke 6 Cy. 500 x 2000 9480kW (12889bhp) STX Engine Co Ltd-South Korea AuxGen: 3 x 625kW 450V 60Hz a.c Boilers: AuxB (Comp) 9.2kgf/cm² (9.0bar)
8418356 *6YRP2* -	**UNION TWO** *ex* Condor *-2011* *ex* Rose Bay *-2005* *ex* Ocean Rich *-2001* *ex* Citron Jade *-1996* *ex* Coral Star *-1989* **Shenghua Management Ltd** Dalian Shenghua Ship Management Co Ltd *Jamaica* MMSI: 339300750	**4,299** 2,696 6,846	Class: IB (KR) (NK)	**1985-05 Donghae Shipbuilding Co Ltd — Ulsan** Yd No: 8441 Loa 110.17 Br ex 16.44 Dght 6.746 Lbp 103.03 Br md 16.41 Dpth 8.56 Welded, 1 dk	**(A31A2GX) General Cargo Ship** Grain: 9,438; Bale: 8,426 Compartments: 2 Ho, ER 2 Ha: (29.7 x 8.5) (30.7 x 8.5)ER Derricks: 1x30t,1x20t,2x15t	**1 oil engine** driving 1 FP propeller Total Power: 2,942kW (4,000hp) 12.5kn Hanshin 6EL44 1 x 4 Stroke 6 Cy. 440 x 880 2942kW (4000bhp) The Hanshin Diesel Works Ltd-Japan AuxGen: 2 x 200kW 445V 60Hz a.c
9628946 *SVBX2* -	**UNION VOYAGER** **Marine Operators Co Ltd** Union Marine Enterprises SA *Piraeus* *Greece* MMSI: 241299000	**42,900** - 82,000 T/cm 71.9	Class: LR (Class contemplated) **100A1** 03/2014 Class contemplated	**2014-03 COSCO (Dalian) Shipyard Co Ltd — Dalian LN** Yd No: N377 Loa 229.00 (BB) Br ex - Dght 14.500 Lbp - Br md 32.26 Dpth 20.25 Welded, 1 dk	**(A21A2BC) Bulk Carrier** Grain: 97,000; Bale: 90,784 Compartments: 7 Ho, ER 7 Ha: 5 (18.3 x 15.0) (15.7 x 15.1)ER (13.1 x 13.2)	**1 oil engine** driving 1 FP propeller Total Power: 11,060kW (15,037hp) 14.0kn MAN-B&W 7S50MC-C 1 x 2 Stroke 7 Cy. 500 x 2000 11060kW (15037bhp) AuxGen: 3 x 650kW a.c
9537513 *ORPI* -	**UNION WARRIOR** **Caixa d'Estalvis i Pensions de Barcelona (Caja de Ahorros y Pensiones de Barcelona) (La Caixa)** Unie van Redding - en Sleepdienst NV (Union de Remorquage et de Sauvetage SA) (Towage & Salvage Union Ltd) *Antwerpen* *Belgium* MMSI: 205558000 Official number: 01 00738 2009	**810** 243 527	Class: LR ✠ **100A1** SS 11/2009 tug ✠ **LMC** **UMS** Eq.Ltr: J; Cable: 357.5/26.0 U2 (a)	**2009-11 Astilleros Armon SA — Navia** Yd No: 673 Loa 40.65 Br ex 12.70 Dght 5.500 Lbp 31.91 Br md 12.70 Dpth 6.90 Welded, 1 dk	**(B21B20A) Anchor Handling Tug Supply**	**2 oil engines** reduction geared to sc. shafts driving 2 Directional propellers Total Power: 5,304kW (7,212hp) 14.0kn A.B.C. 12VDZC 2 x Vee 4 Stroke 12 Cy. 256 x 310 each-2652kW (3606bhp) Anglo Belgian Corp NV (ABC)-Belgium AuxGen: 3 x 296kW 400V 50Hz a.c Thrusters: 1 Thwart. FP thruster (f)
9537549 *ORPZ* -	**UNION WRESTLER** **Unie van Redding - en Sleepdienst NV (Union de Remorquage et de Sauvetage SA) (Towage & Salvage Union Ltd)** - SatCom: Inmarsat C 420558610 *Antwerpen* *Belgium* MMSI: 205586000 Official number: 01 00775 2011	**810** 243 519	Class: LR ✠ **100A1** SS 01/2011 tug, fire-fighting Ship 1 (2400m3/h) with water spray ✠ **LMC** **UMS** Eq.Ltr: J; Cable: 357.5/26.0 U2 (a)	**2011-01 Astilleros Armon SA — Navia** Yd No: 676 Loa 40.65 Br ex - Dght 5.500 Lbp 31.91 Br md 12.70 Dpth 6.90 Welded, 1 dk	**(B21B20A) Anchor Handling Tug Supply**	**2 oil engines** with clutches, flexible couplings & reduction geared to sc. shafts driving 2 Directional propellers Total Power: 5,304kW (7,212hp) 14.0kn A.B.C. 12VDZC 2 x Vee 4 Stroke 12 Cy. 256 x 310 each-2652kW (3606bhp) Anglo Belgian Corp NV (ABC)-Belgium AuxGen: 3 x 296kW 400V 50Hz a.c Thrusters: 1 Thwart. FP thruster (f)
8926597 *YL2319* -	**UNIONS** *ex* Bella *-1996* **SIA Vetrasputni** - *Riga* *Latvia* MMSI: 275173000 Official number: 0805	**112** 33 30	Class: (RS)	**1994 Sosnovskiy Sudostroitelnyy Zavod — Sosnovka** Yd No: 848 Loa 25.45 Br ex 7.00 Dght 2.390 Lbp 22.00 Br md 6.80 Dpth 3.30 Welded, 1 dk	**(B11B2FV) Fishing Vessel** Grain: 64	**1 oil engine** driving 1 FP propeller Total Power: 220kW (299hp) 9.5kn S.K.L. 6NVD26A-3 1 x 4 Stroke 6 Cy. 180 x 260 220kW (299bhp) SKL Motoren u. Systemtechnik AG-Magdeburg AuxGen: 2 x 14kW a.c Fuel: 15.0 (d.f.)
8708957 *CBUS* -	**UNIONSUR** *ex* Union Sur I *-2004* *ex* Koyo Maru No. 8 *-2004* **Empresa de Desarrollo Pesquero de Chile Ltda (EMDEPES)** - SatCom: Inmarsat C 472599076 *Valparaiso* *Chile* MMSI: 725011900 Official number: 3112	**4,991** 1,497 4,993	Class: NK	**1988-04 Naikai Shipbuilding & Engineering Co Ltd — Onomichi HS (Setoda Shipyard)** Yd No: 526 Loa 104.80 (BB) Br ex 17.84 Dght 6.719 Lbp 96.76 Br md 17.80 Dpth 10.30 Welded, 2 dks	**(B11A2FG) Factory Stern Trawler** Bale: 398; Ins: 3,150; Liq: 57	**1 oil engine** driving 1 CP propeller Total Power: 5,590kW (7,600hp) 15.0kn B&W 10L35MC 1 x 2 Stroke 10 Cy. 350 x 1050 5590kW (7600bhp) Innoshima Machinery Co Ltd-Japan AuxGen: 2 x 1375kW 440V a.c Fuel: 396.5 (d.f.) 1615.5 (r.f.) 20.5pd
9145970 *3EAY6* -	**UNIORDER** *ex* Honesty Ocean *-2013* *ex* Sea Velvet *-2006* *ex* Axios *-2006* *ex* Flaxen Halo *-1999* **Uniwise Marine Corp** Galaxy Shipping Corp SatCom: Inmarsat C 437140810 *Panama* *Panama* MMSI: 371408000 Official number: 3190906C	**25,977** 16,173 47,240 T/cm 50.7	Class: NK	**1997-04 Oshima Shipbuilding Co Ltd — Saikai NS** Yd No: 10201 Loa 185.73 (BB) Br ex - Dght 11.778 Lbp 177.00 Br md 30.95 Dpth 16.40 Welded, 1 dk	**(A21A2BC) Bulk Carrier** Grain: 59,387; Bale: 58,239 Compartments: 5 Ho, ER 5 Ha: (17.1 x 15.6)4 (19.8 x 15.6)ER Cranes: 4x30t	**1 oil engine** driving 1 FP propeller Total Power: 7,392kW (10,050hp) 15.4kn Mitsubishi 6UEC50LSII 1 x 2 Stroke 6 Cy. 500 x 1950 7392kW (10050bhp) Mitsubishi Heavy Industries Ltd-Japan Fuel: 1660.0 (r.f.)

7031606 *YCLW* -	**UNIPAC 1** *ex* Senta 1 *-1995* *ex* Marigold *-1979* *ex* Nagayasu Maru *-1976* **PT Unitama Pacific Lines** - *Jakarta* *Indonesia* MMSI: 525016389	**3,409** 2,086 5,852	Class: KI (NK)	**1970-07 Imabari Shipbuilding Co Ltd — Imabari EH (Imabari Shipyard)** Yd No: 250 Loa 101.96 Br ex 16.34 Dght 6.536 Lbp 98.60 Br md 16.29 Dpth 8.16 Welded, 1 dk	**(A31A2GX) General Cargo Ship** Grain: 7,490; Bale: 7,213 Compartments: 2 Ho, ER 2 Ha: (27.1 x 8.3) (27.8 x 8.3)ER Derricks: 4x15t	**1 oil engine** driving 1 FP propeller Total Power: 2,648kW (3,600hp) 12.5kn Hanshin 6LU50A 1 x 4 Stroke 6 Cy. 500 x 800 2648kW (3600bhp) Hanshin Nainenki Kogyo-Japan AuxGen: 2 x 132kW 450V 60Hz a.c Fuel: 538.5 13.5pd
7334383 *YFPS* -	**UNIPAC 3** *ex* Rising Tide *-1976* *ex* Fortune Carrier *-1996* *ex* Ambassador *-1993* *ex* Pacific Gembira *-1992* *ex* Ambassador 7 *-1988* *ex* Siti Yuka *-1987* *ex* Kalimantan Dua *-1984* *ex* Brilliant *-1982* **PT Unitama Pacific Lines** - *Jakarta* *Indonesia* MMSI: 525016390	**3,746** 2,368 6,548	Class: KI (NK)	**1973-10 Imabari Shipbuilding Co Ltd — Imabari EH (Imabari Shipyard)** Yd No: 313 Loa 105.59 Br ex 16.39 Dght 6.838 Lbp 98.61 Br md 16.34 Dpth 8.39 Welded, 1 dk	**(A31A2GX) General Cargo Ship** Grain: 8,421; Bale: 8,000 Compartments: 2 Ho, ER 2 Ha: (27.2 x 8.3) (28.5 x 8.3)ER Derricks: 3x15t,1x10t	**1 oil engine** driving 1 FP propeller Total Power: 2,795kW (3,800hp) 12.7kn Hanshin 6LU50A 1 x 4 Stroke 6 Cy. 500 x 800 2795kW (3800bhp) Hanshin Nainenki Kogyo-Japan AuxGen: 2 x 132kW a.c Fuel: 530.5 12.5pd
8912259 *3EQS7* -	**UNIPLUS** *ex* Ocean Lily *-1999* **Uniwise Marine Corp** Galaxy Shipping Corp SatCom: Inmarsat A 1332725 *Panama* *Panama* MMSI: 355839000 Official number: 1859989E	**16,472** 9,915 28,024	Class: BV (NK)	**1989-09 Imabari Shipbuilding Co Ltd — Imabari EH (Imabari Shipyard)** Yd No: 479 Loa 166.63 (BB) Br ex 27.22 Dght 9.767 Lbp 158.00 Br md 27.20 Dpth 13.60 Welded, 1 dk	**(A21A2BC) Bulk Carrier** Grain: 36,894; Bale: 35,444 Compartments: 4 Ho, ER 4 Ha: 3 (24.8 x 17.6) (20.8 x 16.0)ER Cranes: 4x30.5t	**1 oil engine** driving 1 FP propeller Total Power: 5,740kW (7,804hp) 13.9kn B&W 5S50MC 1 x 2 Stroke 5 Cy. 500 x 1910 5740kW (7804bhp) Makita Diesel Co Ltd-Japan AuxGen: 2 x 400kW 450V 60Hz a.c, 1 x 300kW 450V 60Hz a.c
7434482 *HSB2441* -	**UNIQUE 6** *ex* Asean 2 *-1996* *ex* Sunrise *-1994* **Siam Lucky Marine Co Ltd** - *Bangkok* *Thailand* MMSI: 567164000 Official number: 391000135	**1,196** 358 1,099	Class: (NK)	**1976-06 Usuki Iron Works Co Ltd — Usuki OT** Yd No: 923 Loa 67.98 Br ex 11.43 Dght 4.001 Lbp 62.51 Br md 11.41 Dpth 5.01 Welded, 1 dk	**(A11B2TG) LPG Tanker** Liq (Gas): 1,320 2 x Gas Tank (s);	**1 oil engine** driving 1 FP propeller Total Power: 993kW (1,350hp) Akasaka AH28 1 x 4 Stroke 6 Cy. 280 x 440 993kW (1350bhp) Akasaka Tekkosho KK (Akasaka DieselLtd)-Japan
7930187 *HSCF2* -	**UNIQUE 9** *ex* Tokuyo Maru No. 5 *-1998* **Siam Lucky Marine Co Ltd** - *Bangkok* *Thailand* MMSI: 567165000 Official number: 411001568	**701** 499 746	Class: (NK)	**1980-07 Kishimoto Zosen K.K. — Kinoe** Yd No: 501 Loa 60.30 Br ex - Dght 4.038 Lbp 55.53 Br md 10.01 Dpth 4.63 Welded, 1 dk	**(A11B2TG) LPG Tanker** Liq (Gas): 1,157 2 x Gas Tank (s);	**1 oil engine** driving 1 FP propeller Total Power: 1,177kW (1,600hp) 11.8kn Akasaka DM33 1 x 4 Stroke 6 Cy. 330 x 500 1177kW (1600bhp) Akasaka Tekkosho KK (Akasaka DieselLtd)-Japan AuxGen: 2 x 250kW
7916272 *HSB2600* -	**UNIQUE 10** *ex* Neptune Gas *-1999* **Siam Lucky Marine Co Ltd** - *Bangkok* *Thailand* MMSI: 567126000 Official number: 421000051	**2,703** 811 3,066	Class: (NK)	**1979-11 Kishigami Zosen K.K. — Akitsu** Yd No: 1338 Loa 93.45 Br ex 14.43 Dght 5.266 Lbp 87.03 Br md 14.41 Dpth 6.51 Welded, 1 dk	**(A11B2TG) LPG Tanker** Liq (Gas): 2,511 2 x Gas Tank (s);	**1 oil engine** driving 1 FP propeller Total Power: 2,354kW (3,200hp) 13.3kn Akasaka DM46 1 x 4 Stroke 6 Cy. 460 x 720 2354kW (3200bhp) Akasaka Tekkosho KK (Akasaka DieselLtd)-Japan AuxGen: 2 x 352kW
9058660 *HSB2800* -	**UNIQUE 12** *ex* Sunrise Ethylene *-2001* **Siam Lucky Marine Co Ltd** - *Bangkok* *Thailand* MMSI: 567197000 Official number: 441001132	**1,063** 343 1,005 T/cm 5.8	Class: (NK)	**1993-01 Kurinoura Dockyard Co Ltd — Yawatahama EH** Yd No: 297 Loa 65.15 Br ex 11.52 Dght 4.211 Lbp 60.00 Br md 11.50 Dpth 5.20 Welded, 1 dk	**(A11B2TG) LPG Tanker** Liq (Gas): 1,306 3 x Gas Tank (s); , ER 4 Cargo Pump (s)	**1 oil engine** reverse geared to sc. shaft driving 1 CP propeller Total Power: 1,177kW (1,600hp) 11.5kn Hanshin LH28LG 1 x 4 Stroke 6 Cy. 280 x 530 1177kW (1600bhp) The Hanshin Diesel Works Ltd-Japan AuxGen: 3 x 164kW a.c Thrusters: 1 Thwart. CP thruster (f)
8613372 *HSB3011* -	**UNIQUE 14** *ex* Senbo Maru *-2002* **Siam Lucky Marine Co Ltd** - *Bangkok* *Thailand* MMSI: 567220000 Official number: 451001752	**1,324** 397 1,118	Class: (NK)	**1986-12 Kochi Jyuko (Eiho Zosen) K.K. — Kochi** Yd No: 1927 Loa 68.74 (BB) Br ex - Dght 3.901 Lbp 63.02 Br md 12.21 Dpth 5.21 Welded, 1 dk	**(A11B2TG) LPG Tanker** Liq (Gas): 1,320 2 x Gas Tank (s); 2 (stl) pri horizontal	**1 oil engine** driving 1 CP propeller Total Power: 780kW (1,060hp) 12.8kn Akasaka A28 1 x 4 Stroke 6 Cy. 280 x 550 780kW (1060bhp) Akasaka Tekkosho KK (Akasaka DieselLtd)-Japan AuxGen: 1 x 180kW 450V 60Hz a.c Fuel: 40.5 (d.f.) 166.5 (r.f.) 3.0pd
9226633 *VRXK4* -	**UNIQUE BRILLIANCE** **Mercury Navigation Corp Ltd** Unique Shipping (HK) Ltd SatCom: Inmarsat C 447797010 *Hong Kong* *Hong Kong* MMSI: 477970000 Official number: HK-0776	**88,702** 58,998 176,347 T/cm 119.5	Class: LR ✠ **100A1** SS 01/2012 bulk carrier strengthened for heavy cargoes, Nos. 2, 4, 6 & 8 holds may be empty ESP LI ESN **ShipRight** (SDA, FDA, CM) ✠ **LMC** **UMS** Eq.Ltr: W†; Cable: 742.5/95.0 U3 (a)	**2002-01 Nippon Kokan KK (NKK Corp) — Tsu ME** Yd No: 216 Loa 289.05 (BB) Br ex 45.04 Dght 17.850 Lbp 280.75 Br md 45.00 Dpth 24.10 Welded, 1 dk	**(A21A2BC) Bulk Carrier** Double Bottom Entire Compartment Length Grain: 194,291 Cargo Heating Coils Compartments: 9 Ho, ER 9 Ha: 9 (15.2 x 21.0)ER	**1 oil engine** driving 1 FP propeller Total Power: 14,710kW (20,000hp) 14.9kn MAN-B&W 6S70MC 1 x 2 Stroke 6 Cy. 700 x 2674 14710kW (20000bhp) Mitsui Engineering & Shipbuilding CLtd-Japan AuxGen: 3 x 560kW 220/440V 60Hz a.c Boilers: AuxB (Comp) 7.0kgf/cm² (6.9bar) Fuel: 235.0 (d.f.) (Heating Coils) 4915.0 (r.f.) 62.0pd
9374832 *VRCV5* -	**UNIQUE CARRIER** **Saturn Navigation Corp Ltd** Unique Shipping (HK) Ltd SatCom: Inmarsat C 447700723 *Hong Kong* *Hong Kong* MMSI: 477797700 Official number: HK-1906	**91,384** 58,745 177,876 T/cm 120.6	Class: AB	**2007-05 Shanghai Waigaoqiao Shipbuilding Co Ltd — Shanghai** Yd No: 1075 Loa 291.95 (BB) Br ex 45.05 Dght 18.300 Lbp 279.00 Br md 45.00 Dpth 24.80 Welded, 1 dk	**(A21A2BC) Bulk Carrier** Grain: 194,486; Bale: 183,425 Compartments: 9 Ho, ER 9 Ha: 7 (15.5 x 20.0)ER 2 (15.5 x 16.5)	**1 oil engine** driving 1 FP propeller Total Power: 16,860kW (22,923hp) 14.0kn MAN-B&W 6S70MC 1 x 2 Stroke 6 Cy. 700 x 2674 16860kW (22923bhp) Hudong Heavy Machinery Co Ltd-China AuxGen: 3 x 900kW a.c Fuel: 327.7 (d.f.) 4731.6 (r.f.)
9402809 *VRGN7* -	**UNIQUE DEVELOPER** **Vela Navigation Corp Ltd** Norient Product Pool ApS *Hong Kong* *Hong Kong* MMSI: 477748800 Official number: HK-2678	**26,914** 13,660 47,366 T/cm 50.3	Class: NK	**2010-05 Onomichi Dockyard Co Ltd — Onomichi HS** Yd No: 551 Loa 182.50 (BB) Br ex 32.23 Dght 12.617 Lbp 172.00 Br md 32.20 Dpth 18.10 Welded, 1 dk	**(A13B2TP) Products Tanker** Double Hull (13F) Liq: 52,467; Liq (Oil): 52,500 Cargo Heating Coils Compartments: 12 Wing Ta, 2 Wing Slop Ta, 1 Slop Ta, ER 4 Cargo Pump (s): 4x1000m³/hr Manifold: Bow/CM: 91.8m	**1 oil engine** driving 1 FP propeller Total Power: 8,580kW (11,665hp) 15.3kn MAN-B&W 6S50MC 1 x 2 Stroke 6 Cy. 500 x 1910 8580kW (11665bhp) Mitsui Engineering & Shipbuilding CLtd-Japan AuxGen: 3 x 480kW a.c Fuel: 120.0 (d.f.) 1589.0 (r.f.)
9425526 *VRGT8* -	**UNIQUE EXPLORER** **Wega Navigation Corp Ltd** Unique Shipping (HK) Ltd *Hong Kong* *Hong Kong* MMSI: 477786800 Official number: HK-2727	**28,465** 14,372 50,090 T/cm 52.1	Class: NK	**2010-07 Onomichi Dockyard Co Ltd — Onomichi HS** Yd No: 553 Loa 182.50 (BB) Br ex - Dght 12.917 Lbp 175.00 Br md 32.20 Dpth 18.40 Welded, 1 dk	**(A13B2TP) Products Tanker** Double Hull (13F) Liq: 52,112; Liq (Oil): 55,000 Cargo Heating Coils Compartments: 12 Wing Ta, ER, 2 Wing Slop Ta 4 Cargo Pump (s): 4x1000m³/hr Manifold: Bow/CM: 91m	**1 oil engine** driving 1 FP propeller Total Power: 8,580kW (11,665hp) 14.8kn MAN-B&W 6S50MC 1 x 2 Stroke 6 Cy. 500 x 1910 8580kW (11665bhp) Mitsui Engineering & Shipbuilding CLtd-Japan AuxGen: 3 x 460kW a.c Fuel: 150.0 (d.f.) 1700.0 (r.f.)
9425538 *VRHD8* -	**UNIQUE FIDELITY** **Yed Post Navigation Corp Ltd** Unique Shipping (HK) Ltd *Hong Kong* *Hong Kong* MMSI: 477881800 Official number: HK-2807	**28,465** 14,372 50,083 T/cm 52.1	Class: NK	**2010-09 Onomichi Dockyard Co Ltd — Onomichi HS** Yd No: 554 Loa 182.50 (BB) Br ex 32.23 Dght 12.917 Lbp 175.00 Br md 32.20 Dpth 18.40 Welded, 1 dk	**(A13B2TP) Products Tanker** Double Hull (13F) Liq: 52,124; Liq (Oil): 55,000 Cargo Heating Coils Compartments: 12 Wing Ta, 2 Wing Slop Ta, 1 Slop Ta, ER 4 Cargo Pump (s): 4x1000m³/hr Manifold: Bow/CM: 91.4m	**1 oil engine** driving 1 FP propeller Total Power: 8,580kW (11,665hp) 14.8kn MAN-B&W 6S50MC 1 x 2 Stroke 6 Cy. 500 x 1910 8580kW (11665bhp) Mitsui Engineering & Shipbuilding CLtd-Japan AuxGen: 3 x 460kW a.c Fuel: 147.0 (d.f.) 1700.0 (r.f.)
9540821 *VRJM6* -	**UNIQUE GUARDIAN** **Alpha Navigation Ltd** Norient Product Pool ApS *Hong Kong* *Hong Kong* MMSI: 477274100 Official number: HK-3290	**29,411** 13,762 50,475 T/cm 52.3	Class: NK	**2012-01 Onomichi Dockyard Co Ltd — Onomichi HS** Yd No: 564 Loa 182.50 (BB) Br ex 32.26 Dght 13.117 Lbp 175.00 Br md 32.20 Dpth 19.05 Welded, 1 dk	**(A12B2TR) Chemical/Products Tanker** Double Hull (13F) Liq: 51,987; Liq (Oil): 55,000 Cargo Heating Coils Compartments: 6 Wing Ta, 6 Wing Ta, 1 Wing Slop Ta, 1 Wing Slop Ta, 1 Slop Ta, ER 12 Cargo Pump (s): 12x600m³/hr Manifold: Bow/CM: 88.6m	**1 oil engine** driving 1 FP propeller Total Power: 9,480kW (12,889hp) 14.8kn MAN-B&W 6S50MC-C 1 x 2 Stroke 6 Cy. 500 x 2000 9480kW (12889bhp) Mitsui Engineering & Shipbuilding CLtd-Japan Fuel: 147.0 (d.f.) 2343.0 (r.f.)

9609914 *VRJM7* -	**UNIQUE HARMONY** **Castor Navigation Ltd** Unique Shipping (HK) Ltd *Hong Kong* *Hong Kong* MMSI: 477274200 Official number: HK-3291	**29,411** 13,762 50,471 T/cm 52.2	Class: NK	**2012-02 Onomichi Dockyard Co Ltd — Onomichi HS** Yd No: 589 Loa 182.50 (BB) Br ex - Dght 13.117 Lbp 175.00 Br md 32.20 Dpth 19.05 Welded, 1 dk	**(A12B2TR) Chemical/Products Tanker** Double Hull (13F) Liq: 54,079; Liq (Oil): 54,079	**1 oil engine** driving 1 FP propeller Total Power: 9,480kW (12,889hp) 14.8kn MAN-B&W 6S50MC-C 1 x 2 Stroke 6 Cy. 500 x 2000 9480kW (12889bhp) Mitsui Engineering & Shipbuilding CLtd-Japan Fuel: 2490.0
9540833 *VRLY6* -	**UNIQUE INFINITY** **Beta Navigation Ltd** Norient Product Pool ApS *Hong Kong* *Hong Kong* MMSI: 477000001 Official number: HK-3804	**29,479** 13,762 50,378 T/cm 52.2	Class: NK	**2013-05 Onomichi Dockyard Co Ltd — Onomichi HS** Yd No: 569 Loa 182.50 (BB) Br ex - Dght 13.117 Lbp 175.00 Br md 32.20 Dpth 19.05 Welded, 1 dk	**(A12B2TR) Chemical/Products Tanker** Double Hull (13F) Liq: 55,000; Liq (Oil): 55,000	**1 oil engine** driving 1 FP propeller Total Power: 9,480kW (12,889hp) 14.8kn MAN-B&W 6S50MC-C 1 x 2 Stroke 6 Cy. 500 x 2000 9480kW (12889bhp) Mitsui Engineering & Shipbuilding CLtd-Japan Fuel: 2490.0
6815316 - - -	**UNIQUE - R - I** *ex* Triano *-2006* - -	*330* 116 152	Class: (LR) ✠ Classed LR until 15/3/84	**1968-06 Geo T Davie & Sons Ltd — Levis QC** Yd No: 99 Converted From: Trawler-1987 Loa 39.98 Br ex 8.03 Dght - Lbp 35.06 Br md 7.93 Dpth 4.35 Welded, 1 dk	**(B11B2FV) Fishing Vessel** Ins: 220 Compartments: 1 Ho, ER 2 Ha: 2 (1.6 x 1.0)ER Derricks: 1x2t Ice Capable	**1 oil engine** driving 1 CP propeller Total Power: 552kW (750hp) Alpha 496V0 1 x 2 Stroke 6 Cy. 310 x 490 552kW (750bhp) Alpha Diesel A/S-Denmark AuxGen: 2 x 50kW 230V 60Hz a.c
5419103 *SUAU* - -	**UNISHIP I** *ex* Bowler *-1983* **Uniship Agency** - *Port Said* *Egypt* Official number: 2308	*217* 103 284 T/cm 2.2	Class: (LR) (BV) ✠ Classed LR until 10/70	**1963-09 R. Dunston (Hessle) Ltd. — Hessle** Yd No: S803 Loa 35.01 Br ex 7.50 Dght 2.344 Lbp 33.53 Br md 7.17 Dpth 2.75 Welded, 1 dk	**(A13B2TP) Products Tanker** Liq: 391; Liq (Oil): 391 Cargo Heating Coils Compartments: 2 Ta, ER 1 Cargo Pump (s): 1x250m³/hr	**1 oil engine** with flexible couplings & sr reverse geared to sc. shaft driving 1 FP propeller Total Power: 177kW (241hp) 8.5kn Kelvin T8 1 x 4 Stroke 8 Cy. 165 x 184 177kW (241bhp) Bergius Kelvin Co. Ltd.-Glasgow AuxGen: 1 x 30kW 220V d.c
9404522 *3EMT4* -	**UNISON** **Spring Navigation SA** Unison Marine Corp *Panama* *Panama* MMSI: 356814000 Official number: 3346308A	**7,375** 5,013 12,616	Class: NK	**2007-10 Yangzhou Longchuan Shipbuilding Co Ltd — Jiangdu JS** Yd No: 701 Loa 121.90 Br ex 20.63 Dght 8.320 Lbp 115.00 Br md 20.60 Dpth 11.00 Welded, 1 dk	**(A31A2GX) General Cargo Ship** Grain: 16,645; Bale: 16,125 Cranes: 2x30.7t; Derricks: 2x30t	**1 oil engine** driving 1 FP propeller Total Power: 3,600kW (4,895hp) 12.6kn Mitsubishi 6UEC37LA 1 x 2 Stroke 6 Cy. 370 x 880 3600kW (4895bhp) Akasaka Tekkosho KK (Akasaka DieselLtd)-Japan Fuel: 840.0
9172387 *BICX* -	**UNISON LEADER** *ex* Orient Carp *-2009* **Franklin Shipping (HK) Co Ltd** Unison Marine Corp *Keelung* *Chinese Taipei* MMSI: 416478000 Official number: 015402	**20,947** 11,740 35,366 T/cm 44.4	Class: NK	**1999-07 Kanasashi Heavy Industries Co Ltd — Toyohashi AI** Yd No: 3467 Loa 178.04 (BB) Br ex 28.03 Dght 10.582 Lbp 170.00 Br md 28.00 Dpth 15.00 Welded, 1 dk	**(A21A2BC) Bulk Carrier** Grain: 45,494; Bale: 43,941 Compartments: 5 Ho, ER 5 Ha: (16.8 x 14.4)4 (19.2 x 19.2)ER Cranes: 4x30.5t	**1 oil engine** driving 1 FP propeller Total Power: 7,061kW (9,600hp) 14.4kn Mitsubishi 6UEC52LA 1 x 2 Stroke 6 Cy. 520 x 1600 7061kW (9600bhp) Kobe Hatsudoki KK-Japan AuxGen: 2 x 400kW 450V 60Hz a.c Thrusters: 1 Thwart. FP thruster (f) Fuel: 122.0 (d.f.) (Heating Coils) 1268.0 (r.f.) 27.7pd
9579406 *VRJI3* -	**UNISON POWER** **Potential Shipping (HK) Co Ltd** Unison Marine Corp *Hong Kong* *Hong Kong* MMSI: 477167500 Official number: HK-3255	**24,735** 12,342 38,145	Class: LR ✠ **100A1** SS 01/2012 bulk carrier CSR BC-A GRAB (20) Nos. 2 & 4 holds may be empty ESP **ShipRight** (ACS (B),CM) *IWS LI ✠ **LMC** **UMS** Eq.Ltr: K†; Cable: 632.5/68.0 U3 (a)	**2012-01 STX Offshore & Shipbuilding Co Ltd — Changwon (Jinhae Shipyard)** Yd No: 1505 Loa 189.00 (BB) Br ex 30.04 Dght 10.350 Lbp 180.00 Br md 30.00 Dpth 15.00 Welded, 1 dk	**(A21A2BC) Bulk Carrier** Grain: 46,000 Compartments: 5 Ho, ER 5 Ha: ER Cranes: 4	**1 oil engine** driving 1 FP propeller Total Power: 7,560kW (10,279hp) 14.1kn MAN-B&W 7S42MC 1 x 2 Stroke 7 Cy. 420 x 1764 7560kW (10279bhp) STX Engine Co Ltd-South Korea AuxGen: 3 x 625kW 440V 60Hz a.c Boilers: AuxB (Comp) 8.9kgf/cm² (8.7bar)
9636357 *VRLH4* -	**UNISON SPARK** **Sublime Shipping (HK) Co Ltd** Unison Marine Corp *Hong Kong* *Hong Kong* MMSI: 477203900 Official number: HK-3666	**17,895** 10,231 28,436	Class: NK	**2013-01 Kitanihon Zosen K.K. — Hachinohe** Yd No: 561 Loa 170.00 (BB) Br ex - Dght 9.869 Lbp 162.00 Br md 26.60 Dpth 14.00 Welded, 1 dk	**(A21A2BC) Bulk Carrier** Grain: 39,687; Bale: 38,341 Compartments: 5 Ho, ER 5 Ha: ER Cranes: 4x30t	**1 oil engine** driving 1 FP propeller Total Power: 5,800kW (7,886hp) 14.5kn MAN-B&W 6S42MC 1 x 2 Stroke 6 Cy. 420 x 1764 5800kW (7886bhp) Fuel: 1870.0
9579391 *VRJI4* -	**UNISON STAR** **Unison Marine Corp** - SatCom: Inmarsat C 447719610 *Hong Kong* *Hong Kong* MMSI: 477196700 Official number: HK-3256	**24,735** 12,342 38,190	Class: LR ✠ **100A1** SS 11/2011 bulk carrier CSR BC-A GRAB (20) Nos. 2 & 4 holds may be empty ESP **ShipRight** (ACS (B),CM) *IWS LI ✠ **LMC** **UMS** Eq.Ltr: K†; Cable: 632.5/68.0 U3 (a)	**2011-11 STX Offshore & Shipbuilding Co Ltd — Changwon (Jinhae Shipyard)** Yd No: 1503 Loa 189.00 (BB) Br ex 30.36 Dght 10.350 Lbp 180.00 Br md 30.00 Dpth 15.00 Welded, 1 dk	**(A21A2BC) Bulk Carrier** Grain: 49,242; Bale: 47,578 Compartments: 5 Ho, ER 5 Ha: ER Cranes: 4x30t	**1 oil engine** driving 1 FP propeller Total Power: 7,560kW (10,279hp) 14.1kn MAN-B&W 7S42MC 1 x 2 Stroke 7 Cy. 420 x 1764 7560kW (10279bhp) STX Engine Co Ltd-South Korea AuxGen: 3 x 625kW 440V 60Hz a.c Boilers: AuxB (Comp) 8.9kgf/cm² (8.7bar)
9505687 *YLFZ* -	**UNISTAR** *ex* Emi Leader *-2013* **TonBerg Management Ltd** 'Unimanager' Ltd (SIA Unimanager) *Riga* *Latvia* MMSI: 275434000	**2,997** 1,621 4,498	Class: GL	**2009-06 Onega Shipyard Ltd. — Petrozavodsk** Yd No: 202 Loa 89.92 (BB) Br ex - Dght 5.810 Lbp 84.43 Br md 14.00 Dpth 7.15 Welded, 1 dk	**(A31A2GX) General Cargo Ship** Double Hull Grain: 5,500 Compartments: 1 Ho, ER 1 Ha: ER Ice Capable	**1 oil engine** reduction geared to sc. shaft driving 1 CP propeller Total Power: 1,950kW (2,651hp) 12.5kn Wartsila 6L26 1 x 4 Stroke 6 Cy. 260 x 320 1950kW (2651bhp) Wartsila Finland Oy-Finland AuxGen: 1 x 305kW 400V a.c, 2 x 180kW 400V a.c Thrusters: 1 Tunnel thruster (f)
9595280 - -	**UNISTAR 32399** **Thaumas Marine Ltd**	**496** 149 400	Class: NK	**2012-04 Pleasant Engineering Sdn Bhd — Sandakan** Yd No: 40397 Loa 45.00 Br ex - Dght 3.210 Lbp 40.00 Br md 11.00 Dpth 4.00 Welded, 1 dk	**(B34L2QU) Utility Vessel**	**2 oil engines** reduction geared to sc. shafts driving 2 FP propellers Total Power: 2,386kW (3,244hp) 12.0kn Cummins KTA-50-M2 2 x Vee 4 Stroke 16 Cy. 159 x 159 each-1193kW (1622bhp) Cummins Engine Co Inc-USA AuxGen: 2 x 280kW 415V 50Hz a.c Thrusters: 1 Tunnel thruster (f) Fuel: 260.0
9595292 *T2DJ4* -	**UNISTAR 32506** **Thaumas Marine Ltd** Pleasant Engineering Sdn Bhd *Funafuti* *Tuvalu* Official number: 26981212	**496** 149 401	Class: NK	**2013-10 Pleasant Engineering Sdn Bhd — Sandakan** Yd No: 40402 Loa 45.00 Br ex - Dght 3.212 Lbp 40.99 Br md 11.00 Dpth 4.00 Welded, 1 dk	**(B34L2QU) Utility Vessel**	**2 oil engines** reduction geared to sc. shafts driving 2 Propellers Total Power: 2,386kW (3,244hp) 12.0kn Cummins KTA-50-M2 2 x Vee 4 Stroke 16 Cy. 159 x 159 each-1193kW (1622bhp) Cummins Engine Co Inc-USA AuxGen: 2 x 280kW 415V 50Hz a.c Thrusters: 1 Tunnel thruster (f) Fuel: 265.0
7825057 *H03947* -	**UNIT NO. 1** *ex* Sun No. 1 *-2005* *ex* TT Star *-2005* *ex* Hao Shun 2 *-2002* *ex* Hao Da 2 *-2002* *ex* Ocean Ace *-1999* *ex* Explorer *-1999* *ex* Lake Blue *-1998* *ex* Toku Maru No. 18 *-1996* **Global Trading Enterprises SA** Dalian East Ocean Maritime Consulting Services Co Ltd *Panama* *Panama* MMSI: 371107000 Official number: 3176606	**1,232** 603 1,613		**1978-12 K.K. Matsuura Zosensho — Osakikamijima** Yd No: 263 Loa 70.10 Br ex 11.03 Dght 4.330 Lbp 65.00 Br md 11.00 Dpth 6.30 Welded, 2 dks	**(A31A2GX) General Cargo Ship**	**1 oil engine** driving 1 FP propeller Total Power: 1,177kW (1,600hp) 10.0kn Akasaka DM33 1 x 4 Stroke 6 Cy. 330 x 500 1177kW (1600bhp) Akasaka Tekkosho KK (Akasaka DieselLtd)-Japan

IMO / Call sign	Name, former names, owners, flag	Tonnage	Class	Builder / dimensions	Type / cargo	Machinery
7921277 *V4RT2* -	**UNIT STAR** *ex* Stone Town Lady *-2013* *ex* Mashalla II *-2008* *ex* Krishna *-2006* *ex* Anjasmoro *-2003* *ex* Tomoe 63 *-1982* **International Unit Shipping in Cooperation Inc** Aalam Alhamar General Trading LLC *St Kitts & Nevis* MMSI: 341751000 Official number: SKN 1002483	**3,653** 1,867 6,049 T/cm 13.4	Class: (NK) (KI)	**1980-03 Asakawa Zosen K.K. — Imabari** Yd No: 292 Loa 104.53 Br ex - Dght 6.844 Lbp 96.02 Br md 15.51 Dpth 7.90 Welded, 1 dk	**(A13B2TP) Products Tanker** Double Bottom Entire Compartment Length Liq: 6,539; Liq (Oil): 6,539 Compartments: 12 Wing Ta, ER 4 Cargo Pump (s): 4x400m³/hr Manifold: Bow/CM: 54m	**1 oil engine** driving 1 FP propeller Total Power: 2,795kW (3,800hp) 12.8kn Mitsubishi 6UET45/75C 1 x 2 Stroke 6 Cy. 450 x 750 2795kW (3800bhp) Akasaka Tekkosho KK (Akasaka DieselLtd)-Japan AuxGen: 3 x 160kW
8873647 - -	**UNITAMA 9** *ex* Robby 18 *-1982* **PT Unitama Adiusaha Shipping** - *Samarinda* *Indonesia*	**168** 100 -	Class: KI	**1991 PT Menumbar Kaltim — Samarinda** Loa 28.00 Br ex - Dght - Lbp 24.48 Br md 8.30 Dpth 3.33 Welded, 1 dk	**(B32A2ST) Tug**	**2 oil engines** driving 2 FP propellers Total Power: 832kW (1,132hp) Yanmar S165L-ST 2 x 4 Stroke 6 Cy. 165 x 210 each-416kW (566bhp) (made 1983) Yanmar Diesel Engine Co Ltd-Japan AuxGen: 2 x 36kW 220/380V a.c
8873659 - -	**UNITAMA 14** - **PT Unitama Adiusaha Shipping** - *Samarinda* *Indonesia*	**101** 60 -	Class: KI	**1991 PT Menumbar Kaltim — Samarinda** Loa 20.50 Br ex - Dght 1.750 Lbp 19.57 Br md 6.00 Dpth 2.10 Welded, 1 dk	**(B32A2ST) Tug**	**2 oil engines** driving 2 FP propellers Total Power: 588kW (800hp) Caterpillar 3408B 2 x Vee 4 Stroke 8 Cy. 137 x 152 each-294kW (400bhp) Caterpillar Inc-USA AuxGen: 2 x 6kW 110/220V a.c
8873611 - -	**UNITAMA 15** - **PT Unitama Adiusaha Shipping** - *Samarinda* *Indonesia*	**102** 61 -	Class: KI	**1992 PT Menumbar Kaltim — Samarinda** Loa 20.50 Br ex - Dght - Lbp 19.57 Br md 6.00 Dpth 2.10 Welded, 1 dk	**(B32A2ST) Tug**	**2 oil engines** reduction geared to sc. shafts driving 2 FP propellers Total Power: 692kW (940hp) Caterpillar 3408B 2 x Vee 4 Stroke 8 Cy. 137 x 152 each-346kW (470bhp) Caterpillar Inc-USA AuxGen: 2 x 6kW 110/220V a.c
8874835 - -	**UNITAMA 18** - **PT Unitama Adiusaha Shipping** - *Samarinda* *Indonesia*	**101** 60 -	Class: KI	**1993-01 PT Menumbar Kaltim — Samarinda** Loa 20.50 Br ex - Dght - Lbp 18.25 Br md 6.10 Dpth 2.10 Welded, 1 dk	**(B32A2ST) Tug**	**2 oil engines** driving 2 FP propellers Total Power: 692kW (940hp) Caterpillar 3408B 2 x Vee 4 Stroke 8 Cy. 137 x 152 each-346kW (470bhp) Caterpillar Inc-USA AuxGen: 2 x 6kW 138/220V a.c
8874847 - -	**UNITAMA 19** - **PT Unitama Adiusaha Shipping** - *Samarinda* *Indonesia*	**102** 61 -	Class: KI	**1993 PT Menumbar Kaltim — Samarinda** Loa 20.50 Br ex - Dght - Lbp 18.25 Br md 6.10 Dpth 2.10 Welded, 1 dk	**(B32A2ST) Tug**	**2 oil engines** driving 2 FP propellers Total Power: 692kW (940hp) 6.0kn Caterpillar 3408TA 2 x Vee 4 Stroke 8 Cy. 137 x 152 each-346kW (470bhp) Caterpillar Inc-USA AuxGen: 2 x 6kW 220V a.c
6806432 *HP9325* -	**UNITED** *ex* Mac Tide 65 *-1998* *ex* Jaramac 65 *-1993* *ex* J. Ray McDermott *-1984* **Bahman Trading Corp** *Panama* *Panama* Official number: 27284PEXT1	*293* 87 -	Class: (AB)	**1967 McDermott Shipyards Inc — Morgan City LA** Yd No: 145 Loa 42.68 Br ex - Dght 5.007 Lbp 40.42 Br md 10.37 Dpth 5.57 Welded, 1 dk	**(B32A2ST) Tug**	**2 oil engines** driving 2 FP propellers Total Power: 3,090kW (4,202hp) 14.0kn Enterprise DMR48 2 x 4 Stroke 8 Cy. 432 x 533 each-1545kW (2101bhp) Enterprise Engineering & MachineryCo-USA AuxGen: 2 x 100kW Fuel: 356.5
7406746 *D6DM4*	**UNITED** *ex* Laguna *-2011* *ex* Hibat Allah *-2008* *ex* Blue Eye *-2005* *ex* Amina *-2004* *ex* Blue Eye *-2002* *ex* Adriatic Star *-1999* *ex* Prime Vision *-1993* *ex* Lancasterbrook *-1990* *ex* Chelseastream *-1979* *ex* Lancasterbrook *-1977* **The United (Al-Motahida) Co for Export & Transport & Enterway Egypt Co for Shipping & Transport** Safe Sea Services Sarl *Moroni* *Union of Comoros* MMSI: 616487000 Official number: 1200564	**2,580** 1,299 3,700	Class: (LR) (PR) (KC) (BV) ✠ Classed LR until 1/93	**1975-11 Handel en Scheepsbouw Mij. Kramer & Booy B.V. — Kootstertille** Yd No: 190 Loa 93.60 Br ex 13.67 Dght 5.639 Lbp 84.51 Br md 13.61 Dpth 7.80 Welded, 1 dk & S dk	**(A31A2GX) General Cargo Ship** Grain: 4,864; Bale: 4,833 TEU 172 C. 172/20' Compartments: 1 Ho, ER 1 Ha: (51.8 x 10.3)ER Cranes: 2x12.5t	**1 oil engine** sr geared to sc. shaft driving 1 FP propeller Total Power: 2,317kW (3,150hp) 13.0kn Smit-Bolnes 307HDK 1 x 2 Stroke 7 Cy. 300 x 550 2317kW (3150bhp) Motorenfabriek Smit & Bolnes NV-Netherlands AuxGen: 2 x 150kW 380/440V 50Hz a.c Fuel: 313.0 (d.f.)
9130901 *5VCC5* -	**UNITED 2** *ex* Troy-Y *-2013* *ex* Mareike *-2012* *ex* Wellington Express *-2002* **The United (Al-Motahida) Co for Export & Transport & Enterway Egypt Co for Shipping & Transport** Safe Sea Services Sarl *Lome* *Togo* MMSI: 671364000 Official number: TG00438L	**5,544** 2,622 7,061	Class: (GL)	**1996-05 Peene-Werft GmbH — Wolgast** (Hull) Yd No: 439 **1996-05 Detlef Hegemann Rolandwerft GmbH & Co. KG — Berne** Yd No: 174 Loa 117.94 (BB) Br ex - Dght 7.540 Lbp 110.00 Br md 19.40 Dpth 9.45 Welded, 1 dk	**(A33A2CC) Container Ship (Fully Cellular)** TEU 597 C Ho 168 TEU C Dk 429 TEU incl 80 ref C. Compartments: 1 Ho, 2 Cell Ho, ER 3 Ha: ER Cranes: 2x40t Ice Capable	**1 oil engine** with flexible couplings & sr gearedto sc. shaft driving 1 CP propeller Total Power: 5,280kW (7,179hp) 16.5kn MAN 12V32/40 1 x Vee 4 Stroke 12 Cy. 320 x 400 5280kW (7179bhp) MAN B&W Diesel AG-Augsburg AuxGen: 1 x 710kW 440V 60Hz a.c, 2 x 360kW 440V 60Hz a.c Thrusters: 1 Thwart. FP thruster (f) Fuel: 94.0 (d.f.) 490.0 (r.f.) 20.3pd
9465215 *3EXX6* -	**UNITED ADVENTURE** - **Salvia Maritime SA** NS United Kaiun Kaisha Ltd *Panama* *Panama* MMSI: 356590000 Official number: 4352012	**92,379** 60,235 180,745	Class: NK	**2012-01 Tsuneishi Heavy Industries (Cebu) Inc — Balamban** Yd No: SC-164 Loa 291.90 (BB) Br ex - Dght 18.070 Lbp 286.90 Br md 45.00 Dpth 24.50 Welded, 1 dk	**(A21A2BC) Bulk Carrier** Grain: 200,998 Compartments: 9 Ho, ER 9 Ha: ER	**1 oil engine** driving 1 FP propeller Total Power: 17,690kW (24,051hp) 14.5kn MAN-B&W 7S65ME-C 1 x 2 Stroke 7 Cy. 650 x 2730 17690kW (24051bhp) Mitsui Engineering & Shipbuilding CLtd-Japan Fuel: 5690.0
9307085 *SVAJ7* -	**UNITED AMBASSADOR** - **United Ambassador Inc** Marine Management Services MC *Piraeus* *Greece* MMSI: 240824000 Official number: 11819	**42,010** 22,382 73,584 T/cm 67.1	Class: AB	**2007-06 New Century Shipbuilding Co Ltd — Jingjiang JS** Yd No: 0307315 Loa 228.60 (BB) Br ex 32.29 Dght 14.498 Lbp 219.70 Br md 32.26 Dpth 20.80 Welded, 1 dk	**(A13B2TP) Products Tanker** Double Hull (13F) Liq: 81,325; Liq (Oil): 84,527 Compartments: 12 Wing Ta, 3 Wing Slop Ta, ER 3 Cargo Pump (s): 3x2300m³/hr Manifold: Bow/CM: 112.1m	**1 oil engine** driving 1 FP propeller Total Power: 11,290kW (15,350hp) 14.7kn MAN-B&W 5S60MC-C 1 x 2 Stroke 5 Cy. 600 x 2400 11290kW (15350bhp) Hudong Heavy Machinery Co Ltd-China AuxGen: 3 x 900kW a.c Fuel: 205.7 (d.f.) 1889.1 (r.f.)
9307097 *SVAJ8* -	**UNITED BANNER** - **United Banner Inc** Marine Management Services MC *Piraeus* *Greece* MMSI: 240825000 Official number: 11820	**42,010** 22,382 73,584 T/cm 67.1	Class: AB	**2007-09 New Century Shipbuilding Co Ltd — Jingjiang JS** Yd No: 0307316 Loa 228.60 (BB) Br ex 32.29 Dght 14.498 Lbp 219.70 Br md 32.26 Dpth 20.80 Welded, 1 dk	**(A13B2TP) Products Tanker** Double Hull (13F) Liq: 81,325; Liq (Oil): 84,500 Cargo Heating Coils Compartments: 12 Wing Ta, 2 Wing Slop Ta, ER 3 Cargo Pump (s): 3x2300m³/hr Manifold: Bow/CM: 112.1m	**1 oil engine** driving 1 FP propeller Total Power: 11,290kW (15,350hp) 14.7kn MAN-B&W 5S60MC-C 1 x 2 Stroke 5 Cy. 600 x 2400 11290kW (15350bhp) Hudong Heavy Machinery Co Ltd-China Fuel: 250.0 (d.f.) 2000.0
9574236 *3EZG7* -	**UNITED BREEZE** - **Highland Maritime SA** NS United Kaiun Kaisha Ltd *Panama* *Panama* MMSI: 373667000 Official number: 4353512	**92,752** 60,504 181,325 T/cm 125.0	Class: NK	**2012-01 Imabari Shipbuilding Co Ltd — Saijo EH (Saijo Shipyard)** Yd No: 8112 Loa 291.98 (BB) Br ex - Dght 18.235 Lbp 283.80 Br md 45.00 Dpth 24.70 Welded, 1 dk	**(A21A2BC) Bulk Carrier** Grain: 201,243 Compartments: 9 Ho, ER 9 Ha: ER	**1 oil engine** driving 1 FP propeller Total Power: 18,660kW (25,370hp) 14.0kn MAN-B&W 6S70MC-C 1 x 2 Stroke 6 Cy. 700 x 2800 18660kW (25370bhp) Hitachi Zosen Corp-Japan Fuel: 5800.0
9307102 *SVAJ9* -	**UNITED CARRIER** - **United Courage Inc** Marine Management Services MC *Piraeus* *Greece* MMSI: 240826000 Official number: 11803	**42,010** 22,382 73,675 T/cm 67.1	Class: AB	**2007-09 New Century Shipbuilding Co Ltd — Jingjiang JS** Yd No: 0307317 Loa 228.60 (BB) Br ex 32.29 Dght 14.498 Lbp 219.70 Br md 32.26 Dpth 20.80 Welded, 1 dk	**(A13B2TP) Products Tanker** Double Hull (13F) Liq: 81,325; Liq (Oil): 84,500 Cargo Heating Coils Compartments: 12 Wing Ta, 3 Wing Slop Ta, ER 3 Cargo Pump (s): 3x2300m³/hr Manifold: Bow/CM: 112.1m	**1 oil engine** driving 1 FP propeller Total Power: 11,290kW (15,350hp) 14.7kn MAN-B&W 5S60MC-C 1 x 2 Stroke 5 Cy. 600 x 2400 11290kW (15350bhp) Hudong Heavy Machinery Co Ltd-China Fuel: 205.7 (d.f.) 1889.1 (r.f.)

IMO / Call sign	Name / Owner / Manager	Tonnage	Class	Builder / Dimensions	Type / Capacity	Machinery
9460916 *9VHC6* -	**UNITED CHALLENGER** **Ocean (Kamsarmax) Pte Ltd** Nippon Yusen Kabushiki Kaisha (NYK Line) SatCom: Inmarsat C 456584510 *Singapore* *Singapore* MMSI: 565845000 Official number: 393978	**43,152** 27,291 82,641 T/cm 70.2	Class: NK	**2008-04 Tsuneishi Holdings Corp Tsuneishi Shipbuilding Co — Fukuyama HS** Yd No: 1414 Loa 228.99 Br ex - Dght 14.429 Lbp 222.00 Br md 32.26 Dpth 20.03 Welded, 1 dk	**(A21A2BC) Bulk Carrier** Grain: 97,186 Compartments: 7 Ho, ER 7 Ha: ER	**1 oil engine** driving 1 FP propeller Total Power: 9,800kW (13,324hp) 14.5kn MAN-B&W 7S50MC-C 1 x 2 Stroke 7 Cy. 500 x 2000 9800kW (13324bhp) Mitsui Engineering & Shipbuilding CLtd-Japan AuxGen: 4 x 320kW a.c Fuel: 2870.0
9660023 *3FFL4* -	**UNITED CROWN** **NSM Shipping 1 SA** Bernhard Schulte Shipmanagement (India) Pvt Ltd *Panama* *Panama* MMSI: 353297000 Official number: 4529313	**92,752** 60,504 181,381	Class: NK	**2013-10 Koyo Dockyard Co Ltd — Mihara HS** Yd No: 2380 Loa 291.98 (BB) Br ex - Dght 18.237 Lbp 283.80 Br md 45.00 Dpth 24.70 Welded, 1 dk	**(A21A2BC) Bulk Carrier** Grain: 201,243 Compartments: 9 Ho, ER 9 Ha: ER	**1 oil engine** driving 1 FP propeller Total Power: 16,700kW (22,705hp) 14.5kn MAN-B&W 6S70MC-C 1 x 2 Stroke 6 Cy. 700 x 2800 16700kW (22705bhp) Hitachi Zosen Corp-Japan AuxGen: 3 x 600kW a.c Fuel: 5800.0
9546813 *3EZC9* -	**UNITED DIGNITY** **Xanadu Maritime SA** NS United Kaiun Kaisha Ltd *Panama* *Panama* MMSI: 373275000 Official number: 4529113	**92,146** 60,545 180,818	Class: NK	**2013-09 Japan Marine United Corp (JMU) — Kure HS** Yd No: 3308 Loa 292.00 (BB) Br ex - Dght 18.240 Lbp 285.00 Br md 45.00 Dpth 24.70 Welded, 1 dk	**(A21A2BC) Bulk Carrier** Grain: 202,568; Bale: 191,431 Compartments: 9 Ho, ER 9 Ha: ER	**1 oil engine** driving 1 FP propeller Total Power: 16,540kW (22,488hp) 15.0kn Wartsila 6RT-flex68 1 x 2 Stroke 6 Cy. 680 x 2720 16540kW (22488bhp) Diesel United Ltd.-Aioi AuxGen: 3 x 730kW a.c Fuel: 5412.0
9412309 *SVAW4* -	**UNITED DYNAMIC** **United Dynamic Inc** Marine Management Services MC SatCom: Inmarsat C 424096810 *Piraeus* *Greece* MMSI: 240968000 Official number: 12023	**85,522** 53,219 161,653 T/cm 122.3	Class: NV	**2010-09 New Times Shipbuilding Co Ltd — Jingjiang JS** Yd No: 0316306 Loa 274.20 (BB) Br ex 50.04 Dght 17.020 Lbp 264.00 Br md 50.00 Dpth 23.20 Welded, 1 dk	**(A13A2TV) Crude Oil Tanker** Double Hull (13F) Liq: 173,400; Liq (Oil): 173,400 Cargo Heating Coils Compartments: 12 Wing Ta, ER, 2 Wing Slop Ta 3 Cargo Pump (s): 3x4000m³/hr Manifold: Bow/CM: 139.5m	**1 oil engine** driving 1 FP propeller Total Power: 18,660kW (25,370hp) 15.3kn MAN-B&W 6S70MC-C 1 x 2 Stroke 6 Cy. 700 x 2800 18660kW (25370bhp) Hyundai Heavy Industries Co Ltd-South Korea AuxGen: 3 x 990kW a.c Fuel: 380.0 (d.f.) 4250.0 (r.f.)
9087661 *3FJX6* -	**UNITED EARNING** *ex Palma Prima -2013 ex Global Pallas -2010* *ex Selene -2001 ex Perak -2000* *ex Global Pallas -2000* **United Earnings Co Ltd** Billion Star Marine Services Ltd *Panama* *Panama* MMSI: 354687000 Official number: 45177TT	**5,404** 2,797 9,141	Class: NK	**1994-03 Higaki Zosen K.K. — Imabari** Yd No: 438 Loa 112.02 (BB) Br ex 18.62 Dght 7.790 Lbp 104.00 Br md 18.60 Dpth 9.20 Welded, 1 dk	**(A12A2TC) Chemical Tanker** Liq: 9,728 Compartments: 20 Ta, ER	**1 oil engine** driving 1 FP propeller Total Power: 3,354kW (4,560hp) 12.5kn B&W 6L35MC 1 x 2 Stroke 6 Cy. 350 x 1050 3354kW (4560bhp) The Hanshin Diesel Works Ltd-Japan Fuel: 705.0 (r.f.)
9419096 *SVAW5* -	**UNITED EMBLEM** **United Emblem Inc** Marine Management Services MC SatCom: Inmarsat C 424096910 *Piraeus* *Greece* MMSI: 240969000 Official number: 12037	**85,522** 53,242 161,724 T/cm 120.0	Class: NV	**2010-12 New Times Shipbuilding Co Ltd — Jingjiang JS** Yd No: 0316307 Loa 274.20 (BB) Br ex 50.04 Dght 17.020 Lbp 264.00 Br md 50.00 Dpth 23.20 Welded, 1 dk	**(A13A2TV) Crude Oil Tanker** Double Hull (13F) Liq: 173,900; Liq (Oil): 173,900 Cargo Heating Coils Compartments: 12 Wing Ta, ER, 2 Wing Slop Ta 3 Cargo Pump (s): 3x4000m³/hr Manifold: Bow/CM: 139.5m	**1 oil engine** driving 1 FP propeller Total Power: 18,660kW (25,370hp) 15.3kn MAN-B&W 6S70MC-C 1 x 2 Stroke 6 Cy. 700 x 2800 18660kW (25370bhp) Hyundai Heavy Industries Co Ltd-South Korea AuxGen: 3 x 990kW a.c Fuel: 380.0 (d.f.) 4250.0 (r.f.)
8705735 *ERVD*	**UNITED ENTERPRISE** *ex W. S. Enterprise -2010* *ex Antonio d'Alesio -2005* **Corni Maritime Inc** Olimpex Nigeria Ltd *Moldova* MMSI: 214182204	**22,652** 14,226 42,088 T/cm 12.0	Class: IS (AB) (RI)	**1990-12 Fincantieri-Cant. Nav. Italiani S.p.A. — Ancona** Yd No: 5871 Loa 183.56 (BB) Br ex 29.54 Dght 12.300 Lbp 170.00 Br md 29.50 Dpth 16.30 Welded, 1 dk	**(A13B2TP) Products Tanker** Double Bottom Entire Compartment Length Liq: 45,577; Liq (Oil): 45,577 Cargo Heating Coils Compartments: 5 Ta, 10 Wing Ta, ER 4 Cargo Pump (s): 4x1200m³/hr Manifold: Bow/CM: 98m	**1 oil engine** driving 1 FP propeller Total Power: 7,988kW (10,860hp) 14.5kn Sulzer 6RTA52 1 x 2 Stroke 6 Cy. 520 x 1800 7988kW (10860bhp) Fincantieri Cantieri NavaliItaliani SpA-Italy AuxGen: 4 x 900kW a.c Fuel: 553.1 (d.f.) 1289.5 (r.f.)
9412452 *SVAU7* -	**UNITED FORTITUDE** **Trade Sky Inc** Marine Management Services MC SatCom: Inmarsat C 424095210 *Piraeus* *Greece* MMSI: 240952000 Official number: 11984	**62,775** 34,934 112,719 T/cm 99.7	Class: AB	**2010-05 New Times Shipbuilding Co Ltd — Jingjiang JS** Yd No: 0311518 Loa 250.00 (BB) Br ex 44.04 Dght 14.800 Lbp 240.00 Br md 44.00 Dpth 21.00 Welded, 1 dk	**(A13A2TW) Crude/Oil Products Tanker** Double Hull (13F) Liq: 124,619; Liq (Oil): 130,053 Cargo Heating Coils Compartments: 12 Wing Ta, 2 Wing Slop Ta, ER 3 Cargo Pump (s): 3x3000m³/hr Manifold: Bow/CM: 122.5m	**1 oil engine** driving 1 FP propeller Total Power: 15,820kW (21,509hp) 15.0kn MAN-B&W 7S60MC-C 1 x 2 Stroke 7 Cy. 600 x 2400 15820kW (21509bhp) Hyundai Heavy Industries Co Ltd-South Korea AuxGen: 3 x 1125kW a.c Fuel: 210.0 (d.f.) 3100.0 (r.f.)
9461192 *9V9537* -	**UNITED FORTUNE** **United Fortune Carrier Pte Ltd** United Ocean Ship Management Pte Ltd SatCom: Inmarsat C 456623310 *Singapore* *Singapore* MMSI: 566233000 Official number: 397243	**43,012** 27,239 82,099 T/cm 70.2	Class: NK	**2011-09 Tsuneishi Shipbuilding Co Ltd — Fukuyama HS** Yd No: 1451 Loa 228.99 Br ex - Dght 14.430 Lbp 222.00 Br md 32.26 Dpth 20.05 Welded, 1 dk	**(A21A2BC) Bulk Carrier** Grain: 97,381 Compartments: 7 Ho, ER 7 Ha: ER	**1 oil engine** driving 1 FP propeller Total Power: 9,710kW (13,202hp) 14.5kn MAN-B&W 6S60MC-C 1 x 2 Stroke 6 Cy. 600 x 2400 9710kW (13202bhp) Mitsui Engineering & Shipbuilding CLtd-Japan Fuel: 3180.0
9602394 *9V9986* -	**UNITED GALAXY** **United Ocean (Hull No S-1527) Pte Ltd** Nippon Yusen Kabushiki Kaisha (NYK Line) *Singapore* *Singapore* MMSI: 566641000 Official number: 397828	**43,005** 27,239 82,169 T/cm 70.2	Class: NK	**2012-07 Tsuneishi Shipbuilding Co Ltd — Fukuyama HS** Yd No: 1527 Loa 229.00 (BB) Br ex 32.29 Dght 14.429 Lbp 222.00 Br md 32.26 Dpth 20.05 Welded, 1 dk	**(A21A2BC) Bulk Carrier** Grain: 97,381 Compartments: 7 Ho, ER 7 Ha: ER	**1 oil engine** driving 1 FP propeller Total Power: 9,710kW (13,202hp) 14.5kn MAN-B&W 6S60MC-C 1 x 2 Stroke 6 Cy. 600 x 2400 9710kW (13202bhp) Mitsui Engineering & Shipbuilding CLtd-Japan Fuel: 3190.0
9538256 *DSQG7* -	**UNITED GLORY** *ex Oriental Peace -2011* **United Merchant Marine Co Ltd** Taiyoung Shipping Co Ltd *Jeju* *South Korea* MMSI: 441572000 Official number: JJR-085336	**2,081** 890 3,593	Class: KR	**2008-12 Yangzhou Nakanishi Shipbuilding Co Ltd — Yizheng JS** Yd No: 728 Loa 84.90 Br ex 13.02 Dght 5.700 Lbp 79.20 Br md 13.00 Dpth 7.50 Welded, 1 dk	**(A31A2GX) General Cargo Ship** Compartments: 1 Ho, ER 1 Ha: ER (45.0 x 10.0)	**1 oil engine** driving 1 FP propeller Total Power: 1,618kW (2,200hp) 12.5kn Niigata 6M34BT 1 x 4 Stroke 6 Cy. 340 x 620 1618kW (2200bhp) Niigata Engineering Co Ltd-Japan AuxGen: 2 x 145kW 445V a.c
9419137 *SVAU8* -	**UNITED GRACE** **Trade Industrial Development Corp** Marine Management Services MC SatCom: Inmarsat C 424095310 *Piraeus* *Greece* MMSI: 240953000 Official number: 12001	**62,775** 34,934 112,777 T/cm 99.7	Class: AB	**2010-06 New Times Shipbuilding Co Ltd — Jingjiang JS** Yd No: 0311519 Loa 250.00 (BB) Br ex 44.04 Dght 14.800 Lbp 240.00 Br md 44.00 Dpth 21.00 Welded, 1 dk	**(A13A2TW) Crude/Oil Products Tanker** Double Hull (13F) Liq: 124,856; Liq (Oil): 127,452 Cargo Heating Coils Compartments: 12 Wing Ta, 2 Wing Slop Ta, ER 3 Cargo Pump (s): 3x3000m³/hr Manifold: Bow/CM: 122.5m	**1 oil engine** driving 1 FP propeller Total Power: 14,280kW (19,415hp) 15.0kn MAN-B&W 7S60MC-C 1 x 2 Stroke 7 Cy. 600 x 2400 14280kW (19415bhp) Doosan Engine Co Ltd-South Korea AuxGen: 3 x 1125kW a.c Fuel: 555.0 (d.f.) 2370.0 (r.f.)
9593335 *3EYC6* -	**UNITED HALO** **Ken Line SA** Yano Kaiun Co Ltd *Panama* *Panama* MMSI: 373256000 Official number: 42729TJ	**31,541** 18,765 55,848 T/cm 56.9	Class: NK	**2012-01 IHI Marine United Inc — Kure HS** Yd No: 3321 Loa 189.96 (BB) Br ex - Dght 12.735 Lbp 185.00 Br md 32.26 Dpth 18.10 Welded, 1 dk	**(A21A2BC) Bulk Carrier** Grain: 72,111; Bale: 67,062 Compartments: 5 Ho, ER 5 Ha: ER Cranes: 4x30t	**1 oil engine** driving 1 FP propeller Total Power: 8,890kW (12,087hp) 14.5kn Wartsila 6RT-flex50 1 x 2 Stroke 6 Cy. 500 x 2050 8890kW (12087bhp) Diesel United Ltd.-Aioi Fuel: 2490.0
9419151 *SVAW3* -	**UNITED HONOR** **United Honor Inc** Marine Management Services MC SatCom: Inmarsat C 424097010 *Piraeus* *Greece* MMSI: 240997000 Official number: 12016	**62,775** 34,934 112,795 T/cm 99.7	Class: AB	**2010-09 New Times Shipbuilding Co Ltd — Jingjiang JS** Yd No: 0311520 Loa 250.00 (BB) Br ex 44.04 Dght 14.819 Lbp 240.00 Br md 44.00 Dpth 21.00 Welded, 1 dk	**(A13A2TW) Crude/Oil Products Tanker** Double Hull (13F) Liq: 124,620; Liq (Oil): 124,620 Cargo Heating Coils Compartments: 12 Wing Ta, 2 Wing Slop Ta, ER 3 Cargo Pump (s): 3x3000m³/hr Manifold: Bow/CM: 122.5m	**1 oil engine** driving 1 FP propeller Total Power: 15,820kW (21,509hp) 15.0kn MAN-B&W 7S60MC-C 1 x 2 Stroke 7 Cy. 600 x 2400 15820kW (21509bhp) Hyundai Heavy Industries Co Ltd-South Korea AuxGen: 3 x 1125kW a.c Fuel: 580.8 (d.f.) 2226.8 (r.f.)

Ship / Owner	Tonnage	Class	Build / Dimensions	Type	Machinery
7508049 **UNITED I** *YD3129* *ex* PU 1503 *-2001* *ex* Jaffer III *-1991* - **PT Permata Samudera Abadi** - *Batam* *Indonesia*	*152* 45 163	Class: KI (AB)	**1976**-01 **Sing Koon Seng Pte Ltd — Singapore** Yd No: SKS282 Loa 25.91 Br ex 8.23 Dght 3.048 Lbp 23.91 Br md 7.62 Dpth 3.81 Welded, 1 dk	**(B32A2ST) Tug**	**2 oil engines** reverse reduction geared to sc. shafts driving 2 FP propellers Total Power: 832kW (1,132hp) 10.0kn Caterpillar D379TA 2 x Vee 4 Stroke 8 Cy. 159 x 203 each-416kW (566bhp) Caterpillar Tractor Co-USA AuxGen: 2 x 28kW
9419101 **UNITED IDEAL** *SVAW6* - **United Ideal Inc** Marine Management Services MC SatCom: Inmarsat C 424097110 *Piraeus* *Greece* MMSI: 240971000 Official number: 12040	**85,522** 53,205 161,762 T/cm 122.0	Class: NV	**2011**-01 **New Times Shipbuilding Co Ltd — Jingjiang JS** Yd No: 0316308 Loa 274.20 (BB) Br ex 50.04 Dght 17.020 Lbp 264.00 Br md 50.00 Dpth 23.20 Welded, 1 dk	**(A13A2TV) Crude Oil Tanker** Double Hull (13F) Liq: 173,900; Liq (Oil): 173,900 Cargo Heating Coils Compartments: 12 Wing Ta, 2 Wing Slop Ta, ER 3 Cargo Pump (s): 3x4000m³/hr Manifold: Bow/CM: 139m	**1 oil engine** driving 1 FP propeller Total Power: 18,660kW (25,370hp) 15.3kn MAN-B&W 6S70MC-C 1 x 2 Stroke 6 Cy. 700 x 2800 18660kW (25370bhp) Hyundai Heavy Industries Co Ltd-South Korea AuxGen: 3 x 990kW a.c Fuel: 380.0 (d.f.) 4250.0 (r.f.)
8942450 **UNITED II** *YD3148* *ex* FGA 118 *-2002* *ex* Oil Rig I *-1998* - *ex* Rig Tender Pipit *-1992* *ex* Sam Chuan No. 2 *-1985* **PT Wahana Mitra Bahari** - *Batam* *Indonesia*	**125** 37 -	Class: KI (NV)	**1975**-08 **Mukaishima Zoki Co. Ltd. — Onomichi** Yd No: 381 L reg 23.98 Br ex - Dght 2.577 Lbp 23.04 Br md 7.01 Dpth 3.00 Welded, 1 dk	**(B32A2ST) Tug**	**2 oil engines** reduction geared to sc. shafts driving 2 FP propellers Total Power: 1,176kW (1,598hp) Niigata 6L20AX 2 x 4 Stroke 6 Cy. 200 x 260 each-588kW (799bhp) Niigata Engineering Co Ltd-Japan
8218172 **UNITED III** *YD3196* *ex* Naga *-2003* - **PT Pelayaran Inti Sejahtera Maju** - *Batam* *Indonesia*	*125* 38 -	Class: KI (AB)	**1983**-06 **Pan-United Shipping Pte Ltd — Singapore** Yd No: P-34 Loa 23.00 Br ex - Dght 2.650 Lbp 21.40 Br md 7.01 Dpth 3.56 Welded, 1 dk	**(B32A2ST) Tug**	**2 oil engines** reverse reduction geared to sc. shafts driving 2 FP propellers Total Power: 810kW (1,102hp) 11.0kn Yanmar S165L-ST 2 x 4 Stroke 6 Cy. 165 x 210 each-405kW (551bhp) Yanmar Diesel Engine Co Ltd-Japan AuxGen: 2 x 28kW
9099999 **UNITED IX** - - **PT Pelayaran Inti Sejahtera Maju** - *Batam* *Indonesia*	**148** 45 124	Class: KI	**2007**-01 **PT Sumber Samudra Makmur — Batam** Loa 25.00 Br ex - Dght 2.590 Lbp 23.13 Br md 7.00 Dpth 3.60 Welded, 1 dk	**(B32A2ST) Tug**	**2 oil engines** reduction geared to sc. shafts driving 2 Propellers Total Power: 1,176kW (1,598hp) Caterpillar D398 2 x Vee 4 Stroke 12 Cy. 159 x 203 each-588kW (799bhp) Caterpillar Inc-USA
9432347 **UNITED JALUA** *A8RX8* - **ms 'United Jalua' Schifffahrtsgesellschaft mbH & Co KG** United Seven GmbH & Co KG *Monrovia* *Liberia* MMSI: 636091721 Official number: 91721	**32,578** 18,070 53,414 T/cm 57.3	Class: BV (NV)	**2010**-03 **Ha Long Shipbuilding Co Ltd — Ha Long** Yd No: HR-53-HL07 Loa 190.00 (BB) Br ex - Dght 12.620 Lbp 183.25 Br md 32.26 Dpth 17.50 Welded, 1 dk	**(A21A2BC) Bulk Carrier** Double Hull Grain: 65,900; Bale: 64,000 Compartments: 5 Ho, ER 5 Ha: 4 (21.6 x 22.4)ER (19.2 x 20.8) Cranes: 4x36t	**1 oil engine** driving 1 FP propeller Total Power: 9,480kW (12,889hp) 14.2kn MAN-B&W 6S50MC-C 1 x 2 Stroke 6 Cy. 500 x 2000 9480kW (12889bhp) Dalian Marine Diesel Co Ltd-China AuxGen: 3 x 680kW 440V 60Hz a.c Fuel: 215.0 (d.f.) 2000.0 (r.f.)
9440538 **UNITED JOURNEY** *V7AI9* *ex* Gan-Dignity *-2013* - **United Journey Inc** Marine Management Services MC *Majuro* *Marshall Islands* MMSI: 538005006 Official number: 5006	**62,571** 34,784 112,723 T/cm 99.0	Class: NV	**2010**-06 **SPP Plant & Shipbuilding Co Ltd — Sacheon** Yd No: S5043 Loa 249.96 (BB) Br ex 44.03 Dght 14.800 Lbp 239.00 Br md 44.00 Dpth 21.00 Welded, 1 dk	**(A13B2TP) Products Tanker** Double Hull (13F) Liq: 128,500; Liq (Oil): 128,500	**1 oil engine** driving 1 FP propeller Total Power: 14,280kW (19,415hp) 14.5kn MAN-B&W 6S60MC-C8 1 x 2 Stroke 6 Cy. 600 x 2400 14280kW (19415bhp) Doosan Engine Co Ltd-South Korea AuxGen: 3 x 900kW a.c
9392456 **UNITED JOURNEY** *9V7891* - **United (Kamsarmax) Pte Ltd** Nippon Yusen Kabushiki Kaisha (NYK Line) *Singapore* *Singapore* MMSI: 563355000 Official number: 394996	**43,152** 27,291 82,580 T/cm 70.2	Class: NK	**2009**-03 **Tsuneishi Holdings Corp Tsuneishi Shipbuilding Co — Fukuyama HS** Yd No: 1413 Loa 228.99 Br ex - Dght 14.429 Lbp 222.00 Br md 32.26 Dpth 20.03 Welded, 1 dk	**(A21A2BC) Bulk Carrier** Grain: 97,186 Compartments: 7 Ho, ER 7 Ha: ER	**1 oil engine** driving 1 FP propeller Total Power: 9,800kW (13,324hp) 14.5kn MAN-B&W 7S50MC-C 1 x 2 Stroke 7 Cy. 500 x 2000 9800kW (13324bhp) Mitsui Engineering & Shipbuilding CLtd-Japan Fuel: 2880.0
9290397 **UNITED KALAVRVTA** *V7EN7* *ex* SCF Byrranga *-2014* - **United Kalavryta Inc** Marine Management Services MC *Majuro* *Marshall Islands* MMSI: 538005501 Official number: 5501	**81,076** 52,045 159,156 T/cm 117.2	Class: AB	**2005**-02 **Hyundai Heavy Industries Co Ltd — Ulsan** Yd No: 1563 Loa 274.47 (BB) Br ex 48.04 Dght 17.072 Lbp 264.00 Br md 48.00 Dpth 23.10 Welded, 1 dk	**(A13A2TV) Crude Oil Tanker** Double Hull (13F) Liq: 167,931; Liq (Oil): 167,931 Cargo Heating Coils Compartments: 12 Wing Ta, 2 Wing Slop Ta, ER 3 Cargo Pump (s): 3x4000m³/hr Manifold: Bow/CM: 138m	**1 oil engine** driving 1 FP propeller Total Power: 18,623kW (25,320hp) 15.7kn MAN-B&W 6S70ME-C 1 x 2 Stroke 6 Cy. 700 x 2800 18623kW (25320bhp) Hyundai Heavy Industries Co Ltd-South Korea AuxGen: 3 x 850kW Fuel: 140.0 (d.f.) 3500.0 (r.f.)
9290385 **UNITED LEADERSHIP** *V7EN9* *ex* SCF Aldan *-2014* - **United Leadership Inc** Marine Management Services MC *Majuro* *Marshall Islands* MMSI: 538005502 Official number: 5502	**81,076** 52,045 159,062 T/cm 117.5	Class: AB	**2005**-02 **Hyundai Heavy Industries Co Ltd — Ulsan** Yd No: 1562 Loa 274.47 (BB) Br ex 48.04 Dght 17.072 Lbp 264.00 Br md 48.00 Dpth 23.10 Welded, 1 dk	**(A13A2TV) Crude Oil Tanker** Double Hull (13F) Liq: 167,931; Liq (Oil): 167,931 Cargo Heating Coils Compartments: 12 Wing Ta, ER, 2 Wing Slop Ta 3 Cargo Pump (s): 3x4000m³/hr Manifold: Bow/CM: 138m	**1 oil engine** driving 1 FP propeller Total Power: 18,623kW (25,320hp) 15.7kn MAN-B&W 6S70ME-C 1 x 2 Stroke 6 Cy. 700 x 2800 18623kW (25320bhp) Hyundai Heavy Industries Co Ltd-South Korea AuxGen: 3 x 850kW Fuel: 170.0 (d.f.) 3500.0 (r.f.)
9060962 **UNITED LION** *9V3740* - **United Richfield Maritime Pte Ltd** - *Singapore* *Singapore* Official number: 385300	*171* 51 -	Class: AB	**1992**-07 **Southern Ocean Shipbuilding Co Pte Ltd — Singapore** Yd No: 195 Loa - Br ex - Dght 2.390 Lbp 23.07 Br md 7.80 Dpth 3.00 Welded	**(B34L2QU) Utility Vessel**	**2 oil engines** geared to sc. shafts driving 2 FP propellers Total Power: 882kW (1,200hp) 11.0kn Yanmar S165L-ET 2 x 4 Stroke 6 Cy. 165 x 210 each-441kW (600bhp) Yanmar Diesel Engine Co Ltd-Japan AuxGen: 2 x 40kW a.c
9632600 **UNITED MADERAS** *D5AK5* - **Orange 24 GmbH & Co KG** United Seven GmbH & Co KG *Monrovia* *Liberia* MMSI: 636092324 Official number: 92324	**32,839** 19,559 58,000 T/cm 59.2	Class: BV	**2011**-11 **Yangzhou Dayang Shipbuilding Co Ltd — Yangzhou JS** Yd No: DY140 Loa 189.99 (BB) Br ex - Dght 12.950 Lbp 185.00 Br md 32.26 Dpth 18.00 Welded, 1 dk	**(A21A2BC) Bulk Carrier** Grain: 71,549; Bale: 69,760 Compartments: 5 Ho, ER 5 Ha: ER Cranes: 4x35t	**1 oil engine** driving 1 FP propeller Total Power: 8,700kW (11,829hp) 14.3kn MAN-B&W 6S50MC-C 1 x 2 Stroke 6 Cy. 500 x 2000 8700kW (11829bhp) Doosan Engine Co Ltd-South Korea AuxGen: 3 x 610kW 60Hz a.c Fuel: 2376.0
9530670 **UNITED MILOS** *A8RY5* - **Orange 22 GmbH & Co KG** United Seven GmbH & Co KG *Monrovia* *Liberia* MMSI: 636091726 Official number: 91726	**33,045** 20,121 57,802 T/cm 59.2	Class: BV (LR) ✠ Classed LR until 13/1/11	**2010**-09 **Zhejiang Shipbuilding Co Ltd — Fenghua ZJ** Yd No: 07-176 Loa 189.99 (BB) Br ex 32.30 Dght 12.950 Lbp 185.00 Br md 32.26 Dpth 18.00 Welded, 1 dk	**(A21A2BC) Bulk Carrier** Grain: 71,549; Bale: 69,760 Compartments: 5 Ho, ER 5 Ha: ER Cranes: 4x35t	**1 oil engine** driving 1 FP propeller Total Power: 9,480kW (12,889hp) 14.3kn MAN-B&W 6S50MC-C 1 x 2 Stroke 6 Cy. 500 x 2000 9480kW (12889bhp) Doosan Engine Co Ltd-South Korea AuxGen: 3 x 480kW 450V 60Hz a.c Boilers: AuxB (Comp) 9.2kgf/cm² (9.0bar)
9530682 **UNITED MIRAVALLES** *A8RY6* - **Orange 23 GmbH & Co KG** United Seven GmbH & Co KG SatCom: Inmarsat C 463708580 *Monrovia* *Liberia* MMSI: 636091727 Official number: 91727	**33,045** 20,112 57,802 T/cm 59.2	Class: BV (LR) ✠ Classed LR until 30/12/10	**2010**-12 **Zhejiang Shipbuilding Co Ltd — Fenghua ZJ** Yd No: 07-177 Loa 189.99 (BB) Br ex 32.30 Dght 12.950 Lbp 185.00 Br md 32.26 Dpth 18.00 Welded, 1 dk	**(A21A2BC) Bulk Carrier** Grain: 71,549; Bale: 69,760 Compartments: 5 Ho, ER 5 Ha: ER Cranes: 4x35t	**1 oil engine** driving 1 FP propeller Total Power: 9,480kW (12,889hp) 14.3kn MAN-B&W 6S50MC-C 1 x 2 Stroke 6 Cy. 500 x 2000 9480kW (12889bhp) Doosan Engine Co Ltd-South Korea AuxGen: 3 x 480kW 450V 60Hz a.c Boilers: AuxB (Comp) 9.2kgf/cm² (9.0bar)
9632612 **UNITED MOJANDA** *D5BB2* - **Orange 25 GmbH & Co KG** United Seven GmbH & Co KG *Monrovia* *Liberia* MMSI: 636092362 Official number: 92362	**32,839** 19,559 58,000 T/cm 59.2	Class: BV	**2012**-01 **Yangzhou Dayang Shipbuilding Co Ltd — Yangzhou JS** Yd No: DY141 Loa 189.99 (BB) Br ex 32.30 Dght 12.950 Lbp 185.00 Br md 32.26 Dpth 18.00 Welded, 1 dk	**(A21A2BC) Bulk Carrier** Grain: 71,549; Bale: 69,760 Compartments: 5 Ho, ER 5 Ha: ER Cranes: 4x35t	**1 oil engine** driving 1 FP propeller Total Power: 8,700kW (11,829hp) 14.3kn MAN-B&W 6S50MC-C 1 x 2 Stroke 6 Cy. 500 x 2000 8700kW (11829bhp) Doosan Engine Co Ltd-South Korea AuxGen: 3 x 610kW 60Hz a.c

7941394 - -	**UNITED No. 1** *ex* Seiho Maru No. 10 **Kosai Ishii & Kokichi Unozawa**	*196* 94 -	Class: (NK)	**1973-11 Y.K. Akamatsu Zosen — Uwajima** Loa 33.23 Br ex - Dght 1.507 Lbp 29.90 Br md 10.00 Dpth 2.49 Welded, 1 dk	**(B34B2SC) Crane Vessel** 1 Ha: (9.9 x 6.0)ER Derricks: 1x20t	**1 oil engine** driving 1 FP propeller Total Power: 353kW (480hp) 8.8kn Yanmar 6MAL-HT 1 x 4 Stroke 6 Cy. 200 x 240 353kW (480bhp) Yanmar Diesel Engine Co Ltd-Japan AuxGen: 1 x 16kW
7510925 *3FPW9* -	**UNITED No. 1** *ex* Hai Soon *-2001* *ex* Allwell Prosper *-1999* *ex* Saratorn *-1990* *ex* Yuwa Maru *-1986* **United International Shipping Ltd** - *Panama* *Panama* MMSI: 357664000 Official number: 2665300A	**2,297** 1,230 4,337	Class: PC (BV)	**1975-12 Hakata Zosen K.K. — Imabari** Yd No: 157 Loa 89.01 Br ex 14.03 Dght 5.995 Lbp 86.70 Br md 14.00 Dpth 6.48 Riveted\Welded, 1 dk	**(A13B2TP) Products Tanker** Liq: 4,508; Liq (Oil): 4,508 Compartments: 10 Ta, ER	**1 oil engine** driving 1 FP propeller Total Power: 2,060kW (2,801hp) 12.0kn Hanshin 6LUS40 1 x 4 Stroke 6 Cy. 400 x 640 2060kW (2801bhp) The Hanshin Diesel Works Ltd-Japan AuxGen: 2 x 144kW 440V a.c Fuel: 63.5 (d.f.) 168.5 (r.f.) 10.5pd
9060948 *9V3738* -	**UNITED PANTHER** **United Richfield Maritime Pte Ltd** - *Singapore* *Singapore* Official number: 385298	*171* 51 -	Class: AB	**1992-07 Southern Ocean Shipbuilding Co Pte Ltd — Singapore** Yd No: 193 Loa - Br ex - Dght 2.390 Lbp 23.07 Br md 7.80 Dpth 3.00 Welded	**(B34L2QU) Utility Vessel**	**2 oil engines** geared to sc. shafts driving 2 FP propellers Total Power: 882kW (1,200hp) 11.0kn Yanmar S165L-ET 2 x 4 Stroke 6 Cy. 165 x 210 each-441kW (600bhp) Yanmar Diesel Engine Co Ltd-Japan AuxGen: 2 x 40kW a.c
9401960 *9V8106* -	**UNITED SERENITY** **Ocean Promise Pte Ltd** Nippon Yusen Kabushiki Kaisha (NYK Line) SatCom: Inmarsat C 456453510 *Singapore* *Singapore* MMSI: 564535000 Official number: 395316	**42,931** 26,874 82,533	Class: NK	**2009-07 Oshima Shipbuilding Co Ltd — Saikai NS** Yd No: 10530 Loa 224.99 (BB) Br ex - Dght 14.526 Lbp 221.50 Br md 32.26 Dpth 20.05 Welded, 1 dk	**(A21A2BC) Bulk Carrier** Grain: 96,170; Bale: 94,244 Compartments: 7 Ho, ER 7 Ha: ER	**1 oil engine** driving 1 FP propeller Total Power: 9,378kW (12,750hp) 14.5kn MAN-B&W 5S60MC-C 1 x 2 Stroke 5 Cy. 600 x 2400 9378kW (12750bhp) Kawasaki Heavy Industries Ltd-Japan AuxGen: 3 x 400kW a.c Fuel: 2620.0
9185047 *ELYB2* -	**UNITED SPIRIT** **Kashima Naviera SA & Secure Shipping Co Ltd** Nissan Motor Car Carrier Co Ltd (Nissan Senyo Sen KK) *Monrovia* *Liberia* MMSI: 636011280 Official number: 11280	**37,949** 11,385 14,067 T/cm 41.0	Class: NK	**2000-04 Kanasashi Heavy Industries Co Ltd — Toyohashi AI** Yd No: 3495 Loa 174.98 (BB) Br ex - Dght 8.519 Lbp 166.00 Br md 29.20 Dpth 11.51 Welded, 11 dks, Nos. 2 & 4 hoistable	**(A35B2RV) Vehicles Carrier** Side door/ramp (s) Len: 17.10 Wid: 4.50 Swl: 16 Quarter stern door/ramp (s. a.) Len: 30.00 Wid: 7.00 Swl: 80 Lane-Wid: 6.56 Lane-clr ht: 4.80 Cars: 3,199	**1 oil engine** driving 1 FP propeller Total Power: 10,592kW (14,401hp) 18.9kn Mitsubishi 8UEC52LS 1 x 2 Stroke 8 Cy. 520 x 1850 10592kW (14401bhp) Kobe Hatsudoki KK-Japan AuxGen: 3 x 760kW 450V 60Hz a.c Thrusters: 1 Thwart. CP thruster (f) Fuel: 136.9 (d.f.) (Heating Coils) 2117.4 (r.f.) 41.0pd
9134751 - -	**UNITED SPIRIT 1** *ex* Audacity *-2011* **United Group Ltd (United Petroleum)** SatCom: Inmarsat C 467400176 *Tanzania* MMSI: 677001020	**2,965** 1,136 3,778 T/cm 11.0	Class: LR ✠ **100A1** SS 03/2012 Double Hull oil tanker ESP LI ✠ **LMC** **UMS** Eq.Ltr: S; Cable: 467.5/36.0 U3	**1997-03 Singmarine Dockyard & Engineering Pte Ltd — Singapore** Yd No: 215 Loa 88.60 (BB) Br ex 16.52 Dght 5.600 Lbp 82.20 Br md 16.50 Dpth 7.65 Welded, 1 dk	**(A13B2TP) Products Tanker** Double Hull (13F) Liq: 4,180; Liq (Oil): 4,180 Compartments: 5 Ta, ER, 1 Slop Ta 5 Cargo Pump (s): 5x550m³/hr	**1 oil engine** with clutches, flexible couplings & sr geared to sc. shaft driving 1 CP propeller Total Power: 2,000kW (2,719hp) 11.5kn Normo KRMB-9 1 x 4 Stroke 9 Cy. 250 x 300 2000kW (2719bhp) Ulstein Bergen AS-Norway AuxGen: 1 x 800kW 440V 60Hz a.c, 3 x 435kW 440V 60Hz a.c Boilers: HWH (o.f.) 3.6kgf/cm² (3.5bar) Thrusters: 1 Thwart. FP thruster (f)
9602409 *3FEN4* -	**UNITED SPLENDOUR** **United Ocean (Hull No S-1528) Pte Ltd** United Ocean Ship Management Pte Ltd *Panama* *Panama* MMSI: 372166000 Official number: 45389PEXT	**43,005** 27,239 82,129 T/cm 70.2	Class: NK	**2014-01 Tsuneishi Shipbuilding Co Ltd — Fukuyama HS** Yd No: 1528 Loa 228.99 Br ex 32.29 Dght 14.430 Lbp 222.54 Br md 32.26 Dpth 20.05 Welded, 1 dk	**(A21A2BC) Bulk Carrier** Grain: 97,000	**1 oil engine** driving 1 FP propeller Total Power: 9,800kW (13,324hp) 14.5kn MAN-B&W 6S60MC-C 1 x 2 Stroke 6 Cy. 600 x 2400 9800kW (13324bhp) Mitsui Engineering & Shipbuilding CLtd-Japan
9100097 *C6TE2* -	**UNITED STARS** *ex* United Purpose *-2003* **Erne Shipping Inc** Aegeus Shipping SA *Nassau* *Bahamas* MMSI: 311602000 Official number: 8000702	**26,756** 13,885 43,991 T/cm 55.9	Class: NK NV	**1995-01 Daewoo Heavy Industries Ltd — Geoje** Yd No: 1093 Loa 190.00 (BB) Br ex - Dght 11.221 Lbp 181.00 Br md 30.50 Dpth 16.60 Welded, 1 dk	**(A21A2BC) Bulk Carrier** Grain: 56,667; Bale: 54,931 Compartments: 5 Ho, ER 5 Ha: 5 (18.9 x 16.0)ER Cranes: 4x25t	**1 oil engine** driving 1 FP propeller Total Power: 7,135kW (9,701hp) 14.0kn B&W 5S50MC 1 x 2 Stroke 5 Cy. 500 x 1910 7135kW (9701bhp) Korea Heavy Industries & ConstrCo Ltd (HANJUNG)-South Korea AuxGen: 3 x 500kW 220/440V 60Hz a.c Fuel: 129.7 (d.f.) 1627.4 (r.f.) 30.0pd
5373476 *KJEH* -	**UNITED STATES** **SS United States Conservancy** - *New York, NY* *United States of America* Official number: 263934	*38,216* 19,352 13,016	Class: (AB)	**1952-03 Newport News Shipbuilding — Newport News, Va** Yd No: 488 Loa 301.76 Br ex 30.97 Dght 9.818 Lbp 276.66 Br md 30.94 Dpth 17.07 Welded, 3 dks	**(A37B2PS) Passenger Ship** Passengers: cabins: 691; berths: 1930 Bale: 4,191; Ins: 1,019	**4 Steam Turbs** dr geared to sc. shafts driving 4 FP propellers Total Power: 127,832kW (173,800hp) 30.0kn Westinghouse 4 x steam Turb each-31958kW (43450shp) Westinghouse Elec. & Mfg. Co.-Pittsburgh, Pa AuxGen: 6 x 1500kW Boilers: WTB (o.f.) Fuel: 12077.5 (r.f.)
8132988 *WBK2388* -	**UNITED STATES** *ex* Jessica Palmer *-1991* *ex* Atlantic King *-1988* *ex* Eleanor Eileen VII *-1980* **Boat United States Inc** - *New Bedford, MA* *United States of America* MMSI: 367198440 Official number: 618882	*144* 97 -		**1980 St Augustine Trawlers, Inc. — Saint Augustine, Fl** Loa 23.29 Br ex 6.53 Dght - Lbp - Br md - Dpth 3.38 Welded, 1 dk	**(B11B2FV) Fishing Vessel**	**1 oil engine** driving 1 FP propeller Total Power: 482kW (655hp) Caterpillar D379SCAC 1 x Vee 4 Stroke 8 Cy. 159 x 203 482kW (655bhp) Caterpillar Tractor Co-USA
9502752 *A8RY4* -	**UNITED TAKAWANGHA** *ex* Stella Jabbah *-2012* *completed as* Pretty Delta *-2010* **ms 'United Takawangha' Schifffahrtsgesellschaft mbH & Co KG** United Seven GmbH & Co KG *Monrovia* *Liberia* MMSI: 636091725 Official number: 91725	**22,402** 12,019 35,283	Class: BV	**2010-01 Nantong Changqingsha Shipyard — Rugao JS** Yd No: 0804 Loa 179.90 (BB) Br ex - Dght 10.800 Lbp 171.50 Br md 28.40 Dpth 15.00 Welded, 1 dk	**(A21A2BC) Bulk Carrier** Grain: 43,700 Compartments: 5 Ho, ER 5 Ha: ER Cranes: 4x30.5t	**1 oil engine** driving 1 FP propeller Total Power: 6,480kW (8,810hp) 14.5kn MAN-B&W 6S42MC 1 x 2 Stroke 6 Cy. 420 x 1764 6480kW (8810bhp) STX Engine Co Ltd-South Korea AuxGen: 3 x 465kW 60Hz a.c
9502740 *A8RY3* -	**UNITED TAMBORA** *ex* Stella Kuma *-2012* *launched as* Pretty Crown *-2009* **ms 'United Tambora' Schifffahrtsgesellschaft mbH & Co KG** United Seven GmbH & Co KG SatCom: Inmarsat C 463705898 *Monrovia* *Liberia* MMSI: 636091724 Official number: 91724	**22,402** 12,019 35,239	Class: BV	**2009-10 Nantong Changqingsha Shipyard — Rugao JS** Yd No: 0803 Loa 179.90 (BB) Br ex - Dght 10.800 Lbp 171.50 Br md 28.40 Dpth 15.00 Welded, 1 dk	**(A21A2BC) Bulk Carrier** Grain: 44,294 Compartments: 5 Ho, ER 5 Ha: ER Cranes: 4x30.5t	**1 oil engine** driving 1 FP propeller Total Power: 6,480kW (8,810hp) 14.5kn MAN-B&W 6S42MC 1 x 2 Stroke 6 Cy. 420 x 1764 6480kW (8810bhp) STX Engine Co Ltd-South Korea AuxGen: 3 x 465kW 60Hz a.c Fuel: 1516.0
9502764 *A8UB9* -	**UNITED TENORIO** **ms 'United Tenorio' Schifffahrtsgesellschaft mbH & Co KG** United Seven GmbH & Co KG *Monrovia* *Liberia* MMSI: 636091880 Official number: 91880	**22,402** 12,019 35,220	Class: BV	**2010-04 Nantong Changqingsha Shipyard — Rugao JS** Yd No: 0805 Loa 179.90 (BB) Br ex - Dght 10.800 Lbp 171.50 Br md 28.40 Dpth 15.00 Welded, 1 dk	**(A21A2BC) Bulk Carrier** Grain: 44,294 Compartments: 5 Ho, ER 5 Ha: ER Cranes: 4x30.5t	**1 oil engine** driving 1 FP propeller Total Power: 4,766kW (6,480hp) 14.5kn MAN-B&W 6S42MC 1 x 2 Stroke 6 Cy. 420 x 1764 4766kW (6480bhp) STX Engine Co Ltd-South Korea AuxGen: 3 x 465kW 60Hz a.c Fuel: 1500.0 25.0pd
9060950 *9V3739* -	**UNITED TIGER** **United Richfield Maritime Pte Ltd** - *Singapore* *Singapore* MMSI: 564980000 Official number: 385299	*171* 51 -	Class: AB	**1992-07 Southern Ocean Shipbuilding Co Pte Ltd — Singapore** Yd No: 194 Loa - Br ex - Dght 2.390 Lbp 23.07 Br md 7.80 Dpth 3.00 Welded	**(B34L2QU) Utility Vessel**	**2 oil engines** geared to sc. shafts driving 2 FP propellers Total Power: 882kW (1,200hp) 11.0kn Yanmar S165L-ET 2 x 4 Stroke 6 Cy. 165 x 210 each-441kW (600bhp) Yanmar Diesel Engine Co Ltd-Japan AuxGen: 2 x 40kW a.c

9659517 *S6NY6* -	**UNITED TRADER** *ex* Gmg 01 *-2013* **GMG Marine Singapore Pte Ltd** RK Offshore Management Pte Ltd *Singapore* *Singapore* MMSI: 566591000 Official number: 397875	**4,445** 1,963 6,841	Class: AB	2012-06 **Shantou Shipping Corp Shipbuilding & Repair Yard — Shantou GD** Yd No: GMG0738 Loa 100.50 (BB) Br ex 18.02 Dght 6.800 Lbp 95.10 Br md 18.00 Dpth 9.50 Welded, 1 dk	**(A13B2TP) Products Tanker** Double Hull (13F) Liq: 7,288; Liq (Oil): 7,288 Compartments: 5 Wing Ta, 5 Wing Ta, 1 Wing Slop Ta, 1 Wing Slop Ta, ER	**2 oil engines** reduction geared to sc. shaft (s) driving 2 FP propellers Total Power: 3,236kW (4,400hp) 13.5kn Daihatsu 6DKM-26 2 x 4 Stroke 6 Cy. 260 x 380 each-1618kW (2200bhp) Anqing Marine Diesel Engine Works-China AuxGen: 3 x 320kW a.c Fuel: 190.0 (d.f.) 300.0 (r.f.)
9286607 *3EFI7* -	**UNITED TREASURE** **Rams Shipping SA** Nippon Yusen Kabushiki Kaisha (NYK Line) *Panama* *Panama* MMSI: 355688000 Official number: 3194906A	**42,887** 27,547 82,926 T/cm 70.2	Class: NK	2006-07 **Tsuneishi Corp — Fukuyama HS** Yd No: 1304 Loa 228.99 Br ex - Dght 14.429 Lbp 222.00 Br md 32.26 Dpth 19.90 Welded, 1 dk	**(A21A2BC) Bulk Carrier** Grain: 97,233 Compartments: 7 Ho, ER 7 Ha: 6 (17.8 x 15.4)ER (16.2 x 13.8)	**1 oil engine** driving 1 FP propeller Total Power: 9,800kW (13,324hp) 14.5kn MAN-B&W 7S50MC-C 1 x 2 Stroke 7 Cy. 500 x 2000 9800kW (13324bhp) Mitsui Engineering & Shipbuilding CLtd-Japan AuxGen: 4 x 400kW a.c Fuel: 2590.0
9502726 *A8RX9* -	**UNITED TRISTAN DA CUNHA** *ex* Stella Gemma *-2012* *launched as* Pretty Asia *-2009* **ms 'United Tristan da Cunha' Schifffahrtsgesellschaft mbH & Co KG** United Seven GmbH & Co KG SatCom: Inmarsat C 463704778 *Monrovia* *Liberia* MMSI: 636091722 Official number: 91722	**22,402** 12,019 35,283	Class: BV	2009-05 **Nantong Changqingsha Shipyard — Rugao JS** Yd No: 0801 Loa 179.90 (BB) Br ex - Dght 10.800 Lbp 171.50 Br md 28.40 Dpth 15.00 Welded, 1 dk	**(A21A2BC) Bulk Carrier** Grain: 44,294 Compartments: 5 Ho, ER 5 Ha: ER Cranes: 4x30.5t	**1 oil engine** driving 1 FP propeller Total Power: 6,480kW (8,810hp) 14.5kn MAN-B&W 6S42MC 1 x 2 Stroke 6 Cy. 420 x 1764 6480kW (8810bhp) STX Engine Co Ltd-South Korea AuxGen: 3 x 465kW 60Hz a.c
9502738 *A8RY2* -	**UNITED TRONADOR** *ex* Stella Hamal *-2012* *launched as* Pretty Beam *-2009* **ms 'United Tronador' Schifffahrtsgesellschaft mbH & Co KG** United Seven GmbH & Co KG SatCom: Inmarsat C 463705528 *Monrovia* *Liberia* MMSI: 636091723 Official number: 91723	**22,402** 12,019 35,283	Class: BV	2009-08 **Nantong Changqingsha Shipyard — Rugao JS** Yd No: 0802 Loa 179.90 (BB) Br ex - Dght 10.800 Lbp 171.50 Br md 28.40 Dpth 15.00 Welded, 1 dk	**(A21A2BC) Bulk Carrier** Grain: 44,294 Compartments: 5 Ho, ER 5 Ha: ER Cranes: 4x30.5t	**1 oil engine** driving 1 FP propeller Total Power: 6,480kW (8,810hp) 14.5kn MAN-B&W 6S42MC 1 x 2 Stroke 6 Cy. 420 x 1764 6480kW (8810bhp) STX Engine Co Ltd-South Korea AuxGen: 3 x 465kW 60Hz a.c Fuel: 1500.0
9523471 *V7PH6* -	**UNITED VENTURE** *ex* Gmg 02 *-2013* *launched as* Mariana *-2012* **GMG Marine Singapore Pte Ltd** RK Offshore Management Pte Ltd *Majuro* *Marshall Islands* MMSI: 538003229 Official number: 3229	**5,034** 1,686 6,365 T/cm 16.1	Class: AB	2012-06 **Zhenjiang Sopo Shiprepair & Building Co Ltd — Zhenjiang JS** Yd No: SP12 Loa 99.60 (BB) Br ex 18.02 Dght 6.520 Lbp 94.00 Br md 18.00 Dpth 9.60 Welded, 1 dk	**(A12B2TR) Chemical/Products Tanker** Double Hull (13F) Liq: 7,254; Liq (Oil): 7,254 Compartments: 6 Wing Ta, 6 Wing Ta, 1 Wing Slop Ta, 1 Wing Slop Ta, ER	**1 oil engine** reduction geared to sc. shaft driving 1 Propeller Total Power: 2,970kW (4,038hp) 12.0kn MaK 9M25C 1 x 4 Stroke 9 Cy. 255 x 400 2970kW (4038bhp) Caterpillar Motoren GmbH & Co. KG-Germany AuxGen: 3 x 360kW a.c Fuel: 110.0 (d.f.) 297.6 (r.f.)
9634830 *3FAZ8* -	**UNITED WORLD** **United Ocean Hull No 1533 SA** United Ocean Ship Management Pte Ltd *Panama* *Panama* MMSI: 352816000 Official number: 45124PEXT	**43,005** 27,239 82,026 T/cm 70.2	Class: NK	2013-10 **Tsuneishi Shipbuilding Co Ltd — Fukuyama HS** Yd No: 1533 Loa 228.99 Br ex 32.29 Dght 14.400 Lbp 222.00 Br md 32.26 Dpth 20.05 Welded, 1 dk	**(A21A2BC) Bulk Carrier** Grain: 97,381 Compartments: 7 Ho, ER 7 Ha: 6 (17.8 x 15.4)ER (16.2 x 13.8)	**1 oil engine** driving 1 FP propeller Total Power: 9,710kW (13,202hp) 14.5kn MAN-B&W 6S60MC-C 1 x 2 Stroke 6 Cy. 600 x 2400 9710kW (13202bhp) Mitsui Engineering & Shipbuilding CLtd-Japan Fuel: 3190.0
9548172 *PMUQ* -	**UNITED-X** **PT Pelayaran Inti Sejahtera Maju** *Batam* *Indonesia* MMSI: 525016312 Official number: 2008 PPM No. 899/L	**953** 416 1,682	Class: KI	2008-10 **PT Sumber Samudra Makmur — Batam** Yd No: SSM-XI B Loa 55.06 Br ex - Dght 4.692 Lbp 51.60 Br md 11.66 Dpth 6.25 Welded, 1 dk	**(A13B2TP) Products Tanker** Double Hull (13F)	**2 oil engines** driving 2 Propellers Total Power: 1,220kW (1,658hp) Mitsubishi S6R2-MPTK 2 x 4 Stroke 6 Cy. 170 x 220 each-610kW (829bhp) Mitsubishi Heavy Industries Ltd-Japan
8628406 - -	**UNITED XI** **PT Pelayaran Inti Sejahtera Maju** *Batam* *Indonesia*	**245** 74 -	Class: KI	2010-07 **PT Sumber Samudra Makmur — Batam** Loa 29.30 Br ex - Dght 3.290 Lbp 27.16 Br md 8.20 Dpth 4.20 Welded, 1 dk	**(B32A2ST) Tug**	**2 oil engines** reduction geared to sc. shafts driving 2 Propellers AuxGen: 2 x 66kW 400/200V a.c
8121604 *S2BT* -	**UNITY** *ex* Banglar Shobha *-1999* *ex* Hiranand Star *-1987* **Zhoushan Yihai Shipping Co Ltd (Zhejiang Shipping Group)** *Chittagong* *Bangladesh* Official number: 156	**9,840** 6,373 15,552 T/cm 25.0	Class: (LR) ✠ Classed LR until 28/4/03	1984-06 **Astilleros Espanoles SA (AESA) — Bilbao** Yd No: 354 Loa 144.00 (BB) Br ex 21.47 Dght 8.965 Lbp 134.02 Br md 21.40 Dpth 12.20 Welded, 2 dks	**(A31A2GX) General Cargo Ship** Grain: 22,677; Bale: 20,715 TEU 401 C Ho 239 TEU C Dk 162 TEU Compartments: 4 Ho, ER, 4 Tw Dk 4 Ha: (13.5 x 8.0) (7.5 x 12.6)2 (20.2 x 12.6)ER Cranes: 3x25t	**1 oil engine** driving 1 FP propeller Total Power: 5,080kW (6,907hp) 14.0kn B&W 7L45GFCA 1 x 2 Stroke 7 Cy. 450 x 1200 5080kW (6907bhp) Astilleros Espanoles SA (AESA)-Spain AuxGen: 3 x 392kW 450V 60Hz a.c Boilers: AuxB (Comp) 6.4kgf/cm² (6.3bar) Fuel: 103.0 (d.f.) 1052.0 (r.f.) 21.5pd
1010181 *ZCYN6* -	**UNITY** *ex* Addiction *-2010* **Osicha Trading Ltd** Imperial Yachts SARL *George Town* *Cayman Islands (British)* MMSI: 319006800 Official number: 741452	**649** 194 170	Class: LR ✠ **100A1** SS 04/2009 SSC yacht, mono, G6 **LMC** **UMS** Cable: 338.0/20.5 U2 (a)	2009-04 **Damen Shipyards Gdynia SA — Gdynia** (Hull) Yd No: (455) 2009-04 **Amels BV — Vlissingen** Yd No: 455 Loa 52.30 Br ex 9.47 Dght 3.150 Lbp 44.86 Br md 9.00 Dpth 4.90 Welded, 4 dks	**(X11A2YP) Yacht** Hull Material: Aluminium Alloy	**2 oil engines** with clutches, flexible couplings & sr reverse geared to sc. shafts driving 2 FP propellers Total Power: 2,100kW (2,856hp) M.T.U. 16V2000M70 2 x Vee 4 Stroke 16 Cy. 130 x 150 each-1050kW (1428bhp) MTU Friedrichshafen GmbH-Friedrichshafen AuxGen: 2 x 155kW 400V 50Hz a.c Thrusters: 1 Thwart. FP thruster (f)
9003392 *AUTW* -	**UNITY** *ex* Da Li *-2007* *ex* Budi Teguh *-2006* *ex* Nedlloyd Main *-1998* *ex* Waterklerk *-1991* **Shreyas Shipping & Logistics Ltd** Orient Express Ship Management Ltd *Mumbai* *India* MMSI: 419696000 Official number: 3411	**12,103** 5,570 14,100	Class: IR (GL)	1990-03 **VEB Mathias-Thesen-Werft — Wismar** Yd No: 181 Loa 156.88 (BB) Br ex 22.90 Dght 8.616 Lbp 145.35 Br md 22.86 Dpth 11.20 Welded, 1 dk	**(A31A2GX) General Cargo Ship** Grain: 18,657; Bale: 18,500 TEU 1034 C Ho 364 TEU C Dk 670 TEU incl 60 ref C. Compartments: 3 Ho, ER 3 Ha: ER Cranes: 1x40t,2x25t Ice Capable	**1 oil engine** driving 1 FP propeller Total Power: 7,950kW (10,809hp) 16.0kn Sulzer 5RTA58 1 x 2 Stroke 5 Cy. 580 x 1700 7950kW (10809bhp) VEB Dieselmotorenwerk Rostock-Rostock AuxGen: 1 x 800kW 440V 60Hz a.c, 3 x 480kW 440V 60Hz a.c Thrusters: 1 Thwart. FP thruster (f) Fuel: 101.6 (d.f.) 929.7 (r.f.) 50.8pd
9459113 *D5AW8* -	**UNITY** **Turquoise Trading Inc** Cosmoship Management SA *Monrovia* *Liberia* MMSI: 636015461 Official number: 15461	**21,300** 11,884 34,398	Class: BV	2012-01 **Dae Sun Shipbuilding & Engineering Co Ltd — Busan** Yd No: 501 Loa 180.40 (BB) Br ex - Dght 9.900 Lbp 171.40 Br md 30.00 Dpth 14.40 Welded, 1 dk	**(A21A2BC) Bulk Carrier** Grain: 46,670; Bale: 44,517 Compartments: 5 Ho, ER 5 Ha: 4 (20.0 x 20.0)ER (15.2 x 14.8) Cranes: 4x30t	**1 oil engine** driving 1 FP propeller Total Power: 6,480kW (8,810hp) 13.9kn MAN-B&W 6S42MC 1 x 2 Stroke 6 Cy. 420 x 1764 6480kW (8810bhp) STX Engine Co Ltd-South Korea AuxGen: 3 x 600kW 60Hz a.c Fuel: 1810.0 26.0pd
9337767 *9V6610* -	**UNITY** **Sino International Shipping Pte Ltd** United Maritime Pte Ltd *Singapore* *Singapore* MMSI: 563158000 Official number: 390962	**499** 205 599	Class: CC	2005-07 **Ocean Leader Shipbuilding Co Ltd — Zhongshan GD** Yd No: 2004A001 Loa 42.89 Br ex - Dght 2.900 Lbp 40.07 Br md 10.80 Dpth 4.00 Welded, 1 dk	**(A13B2TU) Tanker (unspecified)** Double Hull (13F) Liq: 833; Liq (Oil): 833 Compartments: 5 Ta, ER	**2 oil engines** reduction geared to sc. shafts driving 2 FP propellers Total Power: 814kW (1,106hp) 9.0kn Cummins KTA-19-M600 2 x 4 Stroke 6 Cy. 159 x 159 each-407kW (553bhp) Chongqing Cummins Engine Co Ltd-China AuxGen: 2 x 80kW 415V a.c
9330965 *2HDH8* -	**UNITY** *ex* Julianne Iii *-2014* **Unity Fishing Co Ltd** - *United Kingdom* MMSI: 235102697	**850** 255 -	Class: NV	2005-10 **SIMEK AS — Flekkefjord** Yd No: 109 Loa 38.10 Br ex - Dght 6.630 Lbp 33.30 Br md 12.00 Dpth 7.80 Welded, 1 dk	**(B11A2FT) Trawler** Ice Capable	**1 oil engine** geared to sc. shaft driving 1 CP propeller Total Power: 3,001kW (4,080hp) Bergens B32: 40L6P 1 x 4 Stroke 6 Cy. 320 x 400 3001kW (4080bhp) Rolls Royce Marine AS-Norway AuxGen: 1 x a.c, 1 x a.c
7426459 - -	**UNITY 1** *ex* Howa Maru *-2007* *ex* Toyota Maru *-2004* *ex* Howa Maru No. 15 *-1992* - -	**753** 300 1,000		1975-04 **K.K. Ichikawa Zosensho — Ise** Yd No: 1325 Loa 53.80 Br ex 9.43 Dght 4.192 Lbp 49.51 Br md 9.40 Dpth 4.40 Riveted\Welded, 1 dk	**(A13B2TU) Tanker (unspecified)**	**1 oil engine** driving 1 FP propeller Total Power: 956kW (1,300hp) Hanshin 6LUN28G 1 x 4 Stroke 6 Cy. 280 x 480 956kW (1300bhp) Hanshin Nainenki Kogyo-Japan

No. / Call sign	Ship / Owner	Tonnage	Class	Builder / Dimensions	Type	Machinery
5324449 *DUNC7* -	**UNITY FAITH** *ex* Don Jose B *ex* Don Lucio B-1 *ex* Seisho Maru No. 5 *-1975* *ex* Shinyo Maru *-1976* **Unity Fishing & Development Corp** - *Manila* *Philippines* Official number: MNLD004333	*451* 205 -		**1955-09 Nipponkai Heavy Ind. Co. Ltd. — Toyama** Yd No: 60 Loa 52.28 Br ex 8.34 Dght - Lbp 46.72 Br md 8.31 Dpth 4.20 Welded, 1 dk	**(B11B2FV) Fishing Vessel**	**1 oil engine** driving 1 FP propeller Niigata M6D 1 x 4 Stroke 6 Cy. 370 x 520 Niigata Tekkosho-Japan
7506285 *DUTA2* -	**UNITY GALAXY** *ex* Prince Arnold *-2000* *ex* Kaio Maru No. 58 *-1999* **Unity Fishing & Development Corp** - *Manila* *Philippines* MMSI: 548062100 Official number: MNLD001054	*816* 386 749		**1975-03 KK Kanasashi Zosen — Shizuoka SZ** Yd No: 1192 Loa 62.11 Br ex 9.33 Dght 3.861 Lbp 53.70 Br md 9.30 Dpth 4.25 Welded, 1 dk	**(B11B2FV) Fishing Vessel**	**1 oil engine** driving 1 FP propeller Total Power: 1,618kW (2,200hp) Akasaka AH38 1 x 4 Stroke 6 Cy. 380 x 560 1618kW (2200bhp) Akasaka Tekkosho KK (Akasaka DieselLtd)-Japan
5153008 *DUND3* -	**UNITY HOPE** *ex* Don Ramon B 1 *-2000* *ex* Kanagawa Maru No. 5 *-1975* *ex* Hoko Maru No. 26 *-1970* **Unity Fishing & Development Corp** - *Manila* *Philippines* Official number: MNLD004387	*499* 313 552		**1954-12 Nippon Kokan KK (NKK Corp) — Shizuoka SZ** Yd No: 107 L reg 49.50 Br ex 8.41 Dght - Lbp 49.29 Br md 8.40 Dpth 4.30 Riveted\Welded, 1 dk	**(B11B2FV) Fishing Vessel** Compartments: 4 Ho, ER 4 Ha: 4 (1.3 x 1.3)ER	**1 oil engine** driving 1 FP propeller Total Power: 662kW (900hp) 10.5kn Akasaka UZ6S 1 x 4 Stroke 6 Cy. 420 x 600 662kW (900bhp) (made 1975, fitted 1975) The Hanshin Diesel Works Ltd-Japan AuxGen: 2 x 100kW 210V 50Hz a.c
7331111 *DUOZ8* -	**UNITY PEACE** *ex* Shichirui Maru No. 81 *-1996* *ex* Seizan Maru No. 81 *-1988* **Unity Fishing & Development Corp** - *Manila* *Philippines* Official number: MNLD009216	*469* 263 589		**1973 Maebata Zosen Tekko K.K. — Sasebo** Yd No: 104 Loa 55.48 Br ex 8.44 Dght 3.937 Lbp 48.49 Br md 8.41 Dpth 4.12 Welded, 1 dk	**(B12B2FC) Fish Carrier**	**1 oil engine** driving 1 FP propeller Total Power: 1,692kW (2,300hp) Hanshin 6LU38 1 x 4 Stroke 6 Cy. 380 x 580 1692kW (2300bhp) Hanshin Nainenki Kogyo-Japan
5364372 *DUND* -	**UNITY POLARIS** *ex* San Miguel Ag *-1988* *ex* Unity Mars *-2003* *ex* Don Carlos B-I *-2003* *ex* Tone Maru *-1972* **Pesca Maharlika Marine Resources Inc** - *Manila* *Philippines* Official number: MNLD004208	*467* 237 368		**1946-02 Mitsubishi Jukogyo — Shimonoseki** Yd No: 324 Loa 55.66 Br ex 8.21 Dght 3.887 Lbp 49.99 Br md 8.18 Dpth 4.50 Riveted	**(B11A2FT) Trawler**	**1 oil engine** driving 1 FP propeller Total Power: 552kW (750hp) Akasaka 1 x 4 Stroke 6 Cy. 350 x 520 552kW (750bhp) Akasaka Tekkosho KK (Akasaka DieselLtd)-Japan AuxGen: 2 x 90kW 220V d.c, 1 x 30kW 220V d.c
9597800 *3FFG5* -	**UNITY PRIDE** **Unity Shipping Panama Corp** Inter Ship Management Co Ltd *Panama* *Panama* MMSI: 370167000 Official number: 4339612	**44,102** 27,208 81,393 T/cm 71.0	Class: KR	**2011-11 Hyundai Samho Heavy Industries Co Ltd — Samho** Yd No: S562 Loa 229.00 (BB) Br ex - Dght 14.518 Lbp 223.00 Br md 32.25 Dpth 20.10 Welded, 1 dk	**(A21A2BC) Bulk Carrier** Grain: 95,700 Compartments: 7 Ho, ER 7 Ha: 6 (17.3 x 15.0)ER (17.3 x 12.0)	**1 oil engine** driving 1 FP propeller Total Power: 11,620kW (15,799hp) 14.9kn MAN-B&W 7S50MC-C8 1 x 2 Stroke 7 Cy. 500 x 2000 11620kW (15799bhp) Hyundai Heavy Industries Co Ltd-South Korea
6903539 *DYLB* -	**UNITY STAR** *ex* Monalinda 37 *-2004* *ex* Yushin Maru *-1982* *ex* Chosho Maru No. 12 *-1981* **Unity Fishing & Development Corp** - *Manila* *Philippines* Official number: MNLD000094	*444* 223 -		**1968 Miho Zosensho K.K. — Shimizu** Yd No: 675 Loa 54.82 Br ex 8.64 Dght 3.404 Lbp 48.98 Br md 8.62 Dpth 4.02 Welded, 1 dk	**(B11B2FV) Fishing Vessel**	**1 oil engine** driving 1 FP propeller Total Power: 1,103kW (1,500hp) Niigata 6M37AHS 1 x 4 Stroke 6 Cy. 370 x 540 1103kW (1500bhp) Niigata Engineering Co Ltd-Japan
7123277 *DUNF3* -	**UNITY TRUTH** *ex* Koryo Maru No. 51 *-2000* **Unity Fishing & Development Corp** - *Manila* *Philippines* Official number: MNLD000353	*474* 221 -		**1971 KK Kanasashi Zosen — Shizuoka SZ** Yd No: 1041 Loa 55.28 Br ex 8.67 Dght 3.404 Lbp 49.00 Br md 8.62 Dpth 3.89 Welded, 1 dk	**(B11B2FV) Fishing Vessel**	**1 oil engine** driving 1 FP propeller Total Power: 956kW (1,300hp) Hanshin 6LU32 1 x 4 Stroke 6 Cy. 320 x 510 956kW (1300bhp) Hanshin Nainenki Kogyo-Japan
5245708 *DUNB5* -	**UNITY WORLD** *ex* Big Mama *-2000* *ex* Ultra Star *-2002* *ex* Unity Juno *-2000* *ex* Frabal B *-2000* *ex* Nagasaki Maru No. 2 *-1969* **Royale Fishing Corp** - *Manila* *Philippines* Official number: MNLD004097	**353** 106 350		**1956 KK Kanasashi Zosen — Shizuoka SZ** Yd No: 222 Loa 46.61 (BB) Br ex 7.50 Dght 3.252 Lbp 42.02 Br md 7.47 Dpth 3.81 Riveted\Welded	**(B11B2FV) Fishing Vessel**	**1 oil engine** driving 1 FP propeller Total Power: 662kW (900hp) 11.0kn Akasaka YM6S 1 x 4 Stroke 6 Cy. 370 x 520 662kW (900bhp) Akasaka Tekkosho KK (Akasaka DieselLtd)-Japan
9578854 *9WKE9* -	**UNITYLINE 1** **Unityline Shipping Sdn Bhd** - *Kuching* *Malaysia* MMSI: 533004170 Official number: 333169	**326** 97 285	Class: BV	**2010-10 Sarawak Land Shipyard Sdn Bhd — Miri** Yd No: 13 Loa 31.00 Br ex - Dght 3.500 Lbp 27.99 Br md 9.15 Dpth 4.30 Welded, 1 dk	**(B32A2ST) Tug**	**2 oil engines** reduction geared to sc. shafts driving 2 FP propellers Total Power: 1,800kW (2,448hp) Chinese Std. Type 12V190 2 x Vee 4 Stroke 12 Cy. 190 x 210 each-900kW (1224bhp) Jinan Diesel Engine Co Ltd-China AuxGen: 2 x 78kW 50Hz a.c
8505771 - -	**UNIVERSAL 1** **Universal Fishing Co Ltd** - *Lagos* *Nigeria*	*140* 45 129	Class: (BV)	**1985-03 Astilleros Armon SA — Navia** Yd No: 109 Loa 24.01 Br ex 7.07 Dght 2.701 Lbp 20.91 Br md 6.95 Dpth 3.46 Welded, 1 dk	**(B11A2FS) Stern Trawler** Ins: 100	**1 oil engine** with clutches, flexible couplings & sr reverse geared to sc. shaft driving 1 FP propeller Total Power: 331kW (450hp) 10.0kn Caterpillar 3412TA 1 x Vee 4 Stroke 12 Cy. 137 x 152 331kW (450bhp) Caterpillar Tractor Co-USA
9272979 *HPPX* -	**UNIVERSAL ACE** **Hitoyoshi Maritima SA** Far-East Transport Co Ltd *Panama* *Panama* MMSI: 353288000 Official number: 2950004B	**40,280** 18,407 49,892	Class: NK	**2003-10 Imabari Shipbuilding Co Ltd — Marugame KG (Marugame Shipyard)** Yd No: 1389 Loa 199.91 (BB) Br ex - Dght 11.547 Lbp 193.00 Br md 32.20 Dpth 22.65 Welded, 1 dk	**(A24B2BW) Wood Chips Carrier** Grain: 102,307 Compartments: 6 Ho, ER 6 Ha: ER 6 (14.4 x 19.2) Cranes: 3x14.5t	**1 oil engine** driving 1 FP propeller Total Power: 7,829kW (10,644hp) 14.5kn Mitsubishi 6UEC50LSII 1 x 2 Stroke 6 Cy. 500 x 1950 7829kW (10644bhp) Kobe Hatsudoki KK-Japan Fuel: 2610.0
7722671 - -	**UNIVERSAL AMETHYST** *ex* Mitawaka Maru No. 58 *-1992* *ex* Fukuyoshi Maru No. 58 *-1990* **Zamboanga Universal Fishing Co** - *Zamboanga* *Philippines* Official number: ZAM2F00125	*158* 80 -		**1977-12 Nagasaki Zosen K.K. — Nagasaki** Yd No: 627 Loa 38.10 Br ex - Dght 2.701 Lbp 33.02 Br md 6.61 Dpth 3.18 Welded, 1 dk	**(B11B2FV) Fishing Vessel**	**1 oil engine** driving 1 FP propeller Total Power: 397kW (540hp) Hanshin 6LUS28G 1 x 4 Stroke 6 Cy. 280 x 440 397kW (540bhp) The Hanshin Diesel Works Ltd-Japan
9509243 *5BQB2* -	**UNIVERSAL AMSTERDAM** **Beheermaatschappij ms 'Universal Amsterdam' BV** Rederij C Vermeulen *Limassol* *Cyprus* MMSI: 212427000	**14,909** 7,874 22,108 T/cm 33.0	Class: CC (GL)	**2009-04 Zhejiang Hongxin Shipbuilding Co Ltd — Taizhou ZJ** Yd No: 2007-05 Loa 159.90 (BB) Br ex 24.10 Dght 9.800 Lbp 149.80 Br md 24.00 Dpth 13.60 Welded, 1 dk	**(A21A2BC) Bulk Carrier** Double Bottom Entire, Double Sides Partial Grain: 29,100; Bale: 28,940 Compartments: 5 Ho, ER 5 Ha: (13.5 x 16.0) (14.3 x 16.0) (17.3 x 16.0) (18.8 x 16.0)ER (12.8 x 16.0) Cranes: 3x30t Ice Capable	**1 oil engine** driving 1 FP propeller Total Power: 5,180kW (7,043hp) 13.5kn MAN-B&W 7S35MC 1 x 2 Stroke 7 Cy. 350 x 1400 5180kW (7043bhp) STX Engine Co Ltd-South Korea AuxGen: 3 x 440kW 450V 60Hz a.c
9509255 *5BTC2* -	**UNIVERSAL ANTWERP** **Beheermaatschappij Universal Antwerpen BV** Universal Shipping BV SatCom: Inmarsat C 421285510 *Limassol* *Cyprus* MMSI: 212855000	**14,909** 7,874 22,108 T/cm 33.0	Class: CC (GL)	**2009-07 Zhejiang Hongxin Shipbuilding Co Ltd — Taizhou ZJ** Yd No: 2007-06 Loa 159.90 (BB) Br ex 24.10 Dght 9.800 Lbp 149.80 Br md 24.00 Dpth 13.60 Welded, 1 dk	**(A21A2BC) Bulk Carrier** Double Bottom Entire, Double Sides Partial Grain: 29,100; Bale: 28,940 Compartments: 5 Ho, ER 5 Ha: (13.5 x 16.0) (14.3 x 16.0) (17.3 x 16.0) (18.8 x 16.0)ER (12.8 x 16.0) Cranes: 3x30t Ice Capable	**1 oil engine** driving 1 FP propeller Total Power: 5,180kW (7,043hp) 13.5kn MAN-B&W 7S35MC 1 x 2 Stroke 7 Cy. 350 x 1400 5180kW (7043bhp) STX Engine Co Ltd-South Korea AuxGen: 3 x 440kW 450V 60Hz a.c

9500819 *9HA2798* -	**UNIVERSAL BALTIMORE** **Beheersmaatschappij Universal Baltimore BV** Universal Shipping BV *Valletta* *Malta* MMSI: 215848000 Official number: 9500819	**33,042** 19,132 56,801 T/cm 58.8	Class: GL	**2011-12 Qingshan Shipyard — Wuhan HB** Yd No: 20060366 Loa 189.97 (BB) Br ex - Dght 12.800 Lbp 185.00 Br md 32.26 Dpth 18.00 Welded, 1 dk	**(A21A2BC) Bulk Carrier** Grain: 71,634; Bale: 68,200 Compartments: 5 Ho, ER 5 Ha: ER Cranes: 4x30t	**1 oil engine** driving 1 FP propeller Total Power: 9,480kW (12,889hp) 14.2kn MAN-B&W 6S50MC-C 1 x 2 Stroke 6 Cy. 500 x 2000 9480kW (12889bhp) STX (Dalian) Engine Co Ltd-China AuxGen: 3 x 600kW 450V a.c
9500821 *9HA2797* -	**UNIVERSAL BANGKOK** **Beheermaatschappij ms 'Universal Bangkok' BV** Universal Shipping BV SatCom: Inmarsat C 421582410 *Valletta* *Malta* MMSI: 215824000 Official number: 9500821	**33,042** 19,132 56,729 T/cm 58.8	Class: GL	**2012-04 Qingshan Shipyard — Wuhan HB** Yd No: 20060377 Loa 189.91 (BB) Br ex - Dght 12.800 Lbp 185.00 Br md 32.26 Dpth 18.00 Welded, 1 dk	**(A21A2BC) Bulk Carrier** Grain: 71,634; Bale: 68,200 Compartments: 5 Ho, ER 5 Ha: 4 (21.3 x 18.3)ER (18.9 x 18.3) Cranes: 4x30t	**1 oil engine** driving 1 FP propeller Total Power: 9,480kW (12,889hp) 14.2kn MAN-B&W 6S50MC-C 1 x 2 Stroke 6 Cy. 500 x 2000 9480kW (12889bhp) STX (Dalian) Engine Co Ltd-China AuxGen: 3 x 600kW 450V a.c
9500807 *9HA2728* -	**UNIVERSAL BARCELONA** **Beheermaatschappij ms 'Universal Barcelona' BV** Navig8 Bulk Asia Pte Ltd *Valletta* *Malta* MMSI: 215431000 Official number: 9500807	**33,042** 19,132 56,729 T/cm 58.8	Class: GL	**2011-04 Qingshan Shipyard — Wuhan HB** Yd No: 20060365 Loa 189.99 (BB) Br ex - Dght 12.800 Lbp 185.00 Br md 32.26 Dpth 18.00 Welded, 1 dk	**(A21A2BC) Bulk Carrier** Grain: 71,634; Bale: 68,200 Compartments: 5 Ho, ER 5 Ha: ER Cranes: 4x30t	**1 oil engine** driving 1 FP propeller Total Power: 9,480kW (12,889hp) 14.2kn MAN-B&W 6S50MC-C 1 x 2 Stroke 6 Cy. 500 x 2000 9480kW (12889bhp) STX Engine Co Ltd-South Korea AuxGen: 3 x 600kW 450V a.c
9158874 *9HQA8* -	**UNIVERSAL BRAVE** **Nereids Owning Co Ltd** Heidmar Inc SatCom: Inmarsat C 425627410 *Valletta* *Malta* MMSI: 256274000 Official number: 9158874	**156,692** 107,870 301,242 T/cm 168.1	Class: BV (KR) (AB)	**1997-09 Hyundai Heavy Industries Co Ltd — Ulsan** Yd No: 1053 Loa 331.00 (BB) Br ex Dght 22.150 Lbp 314.62 Br md 58.00 Dpth 31.00 Welded, 1 dk	**(A13A2TV) Crude Oil Tanker** Double Hull (13F) Liq: 331,629; Liq (Oil): 331,629 Compartments: 15 Ta, ER 3 Cargo Pump (s): 3x5000m³/hr Manifold: Bow/CM: 166.3m	**1 oil engine** driving 1 FP propeller Total Power: 23,538kW (32,002hp) 15.0kn B&W 7S80MC 1 x 2 Stroke 7 Cy. 800 x 3056 23538kW (32002bhp) Hyundai Heavy Industries Co Ltd-South Korea AuxGen: 3 x 950kW a.c
9494242 *LXEM* -	**UNIVERSAL BREMEN** **Beheermaatschappij ms 'Universal Bremen' BV** Universal Shipping BV SatCom: Inmarsat C 425344610 *Luxembourg* *Luxembourg* MMSI: 253466000	**33,042** 18,700 56,726 T/cm 58.8	Class: GL	**2010-12 Qingshan Shipyard — Wuhan HB** Yd No: 20060364 Loa 189.99 (BB) Br ex - Dght 12.800 Lbp 185.00 Br md 32.26 Dpth 18.00 Welded, 1 dk	**(A21A2BC) Bulk Carrier** Grain: 71,634; Bale: 68,200 Compartments: 5 Ho, ER 5 Ha: ER Cranes: 4x30t	**1 oil engine** driving 1 FP propeller Total Power: 9,480kW (12,889hp) 14.2kn MAN-B&W 6S50MC-C 1 x 2 Stroke 6 Cy. 500 x 2000 9480kW (12889bhp) STX Engine Co Ltd-South Korea AuxGen: 3 x 600kW 450V 60Hz a.c
9307645 *3EDY4* -	**UNIVERSAL CROWN** **Kamco No 18 Shipping Co SA** Hyundai Merchant Marine Co Ltd (HMM) SatCom: Inmarsat Mini-M 764572376 *Panama* *Panama* MMSI: 371727000 Official number: 3135006A	**163,465** 110,455 309,316 T/cm 185.7	Class: KR (NV)	**2005-12 Hyundai Heavy Industries Co Ltd — Ulsan** Yd No: 1638 Loa 333.12 (BB) Br ex 60.04 Dght 21.022 Lbp 319.00 Br md 60.00 Dpth 29.60 Welded, 1 dk	**(A13A2TV) Crude Oil Tanker** Double Hull (13F) Liq: 337,756; Liq (Oil): 337,756 Compartments: 5 Ta, 10 Wing Ta, 2 Wing Slop Ta, ER 3 Cargo Pump (s): 3x5000m³/hr Manifold: Bow/CM: 167.7m	**1 oil engine** driving 1 FP propeller Total Power: 28,729kW (39,060hp) 15.6kn Wartsila 7RT-flex84T 1 x 2 Stroke 7 Cy. 840 x 3150 28729kW (39060bhp) Hyundai Heavy Industries Co Ltd-South Korea Fuel: 510.0 (d.f.) 9698.0 (r.f.)
9644251 *9HA3061* -	**UNIVERSAL DURBAN** **Beheermaatschappij Universal Durban BV** Universal Shipping BV *Valletta* *Malta* MMSI: 229089000 Official number: 9644251	**15,732** 7,660 22,983	Class: CC	**2012-06 Zhejiang Hongxin Shipbuilding Co Ltd — Taizhou ZJ** Yd No: 2007-11 Loa 159.60 (BB) Br ex 24.44 Dght 9.800 Lbp 149.80 Br md 24.40 Dpth 14.00 Welded, 1 dk	**(A21A2BC) Bulk Carrier** Double Sides Entire Compartment Length Grain: 29,886 Compartments: 4 Ho, ER 4 Ha: 3 (21.0 x 15.0)ER (21.0 x 13.0) Cranes: 3x30t Ice Capable	**1 oil engine** driving 1 FP propeller Total Power: 5,180kW (7,043hp) 13.2kn MAN-B&W 7S35MC 1 x 2 Stroke 7 Cy. 350 x 1400 5180kW (7043bhp) STX Engine Co Ltd-South Korea AuxGen: 3 x 440kW 450V a.c
9286877 *HPYT* -	**UNIVERSAL GLORIA** **Universal Gloria Shipping SA** Taiyo Nippon Kisen Co Ltd *Panama* *Panama* MMSI: 356844000 Official number: 31754PEXT3	**48,191** 24,291 62,716 T/cm 72.0	Class: NK	**2004-02 Imabari Shipbuilding Co Ltd — Marugame KG (Marugame Shipyard)** Yd No: 1395 Loa 228.93 (BB) Br ex - Dght 11.418 Lbp 218.00 Br md 35.40 Dpth 21.60 Welded, 1 dk	**(A24B2BW) Wood Chips Carrier** Grain: 121,757 Compartments: 6 Ho, ER 6 Ha: 4 (21.6 x 17.6) (13.6 x 17.6)ER (20.0 x 17.6) Cranes: 3x14.5t	**1 oil engine** driving 1 FP propeller Total Power: 8,130kW (11,054hp) 14.0kn Mitsubishi 6UEC60LSII 1 x 2 Stroke 6 Cy. 600 x 2300 8130kW (11054bhp) Kobe Hatsudoki KK-Japan Fuel: 2600.0
7512686 *DXAK* -	**UNIVERSAL GRACE I** *ex* Yamasan Maru No. 5 *-1988* **BM Universal Marine & Fishing Corp** - *Manila* *Philippines* Official number: 230269	*169* 77 -		**1975-09 Kochi Jyuko K.K. — Kochi** Yd No: 1207 L reg 32.50 Br ex 6.41 Dght 2.490 Lbp 31.50 Br md 6.38 Dpth 2.90 Riveted\Welded, 1 dk	**(B11B2FV) Fishing Vessel**	**1 oil engine** driving 1 FP propeller Total Power: 736kW (1,001hp) Daihatsu 6DSM-22 1 x 4 Stroke 6 Cy. 220 x 280 736kW (1001bhp) Daihatsu Diesel Manufacturing Co Lt-Japan
9238583 *DYGN* -	**UNIVERSAL GREEN** **Cygnet Bulk Carriers SA** Mitsui OSK Lines Ltd (MOL) *Manila* *Philippines* MMSI: 548630000 Official number: MNLA000557	**46,515** 14,561 54,053	Class: NK	**2002-03 Sanoyas Hishino Meisho Corp — Kurashiki OY** Yd No: 1195 Loa 203.50 Br ex - Dght 10.818 Lbp 196.00 Br md 37.20 Dpth 22.30 Welded, 1 dk	**(A24B2BW) Wood Chips Carrier** Grain: 115,699 Compartments: 6 Ho, ER 6 Ha: 2 (16.2 x 22.5)2 (15.4 x 22.5)ER 2 (14.6 x 22.5) Cranes: 3x14.7t	**1 oil engine** driving 1 FP propeller Total Power: 9,121kW (12,401hp) 14.5kn B&W 6S50MC-C 1 x 2 Stroke 6 Cy. 500 x 2000 9121kW (12401bhp) Mitsui Engineering & Shipbuilding CLtd-Japan Fuel: 3030.0
8882650 - LA 585	**UNIVERSAL IV** **Universal Fishing Co Ltd** - *Lagos* *Nigeria*	*139* 89 -		**1989 Ocean Marine, Inc. — Bayou La Batre, Al** Yd No: 233 Loa - Br ex - Dght - Lbp - Br md - Dpth - Welded, 1 dk	**(B11B2FV) Fishing Vessel**	**1 oil engine** driving 1 FP propeller
8875580 - -	**UNIVERSAL MARINE I** *ex* Universal Marine *-2007* *ex* Joonsul T-1 *-2006* *ex* Hanyang T-1 *-1996* **Abbas Velayati, Ali Reza Mohammad** -	*164* 50 79	Class: (KR)	**1982 Inchon Engineering & Shipbuilding Corp — Incheon** Yd No: 8262 Loa 26.95 Br ex - Dght 2.800 Lbp 23.95 Br md 8.00 Dpth 3.50 Welded, 1 dk	**(B32A2ST) Tug**	**2 oil engines** driving 2 FP propellers Total Power: 1,472kW (2,002hp) 11.8kn Niigata 6M26AET 2 x 4 Stroke 6 Cy. 260 x 460 each-736kW (1001bhp) Niigata Engineering Co Ltd-Japan AuxGen: 2 x 43kW 225V a.c
9087556 *VRUT5* -	**UNIVERSAL MK 2001** **Tri-Cat (No 1) Ltd** Shun Tak-China Travel Ship Management Ltd (TurboJET) *Hong Kong* *Hong Kong* MMSI: 477303000 Official number: HK-0233	**605** 193 45	Class: NV	**1994-12 FBM Marine Ltd. — Cowes** Yd No: 1407 Loa 45.00 Br ex - Dght 1.570 Lbp 40.00 Br md 11.80 Dpth 4.76 Welded, 1 dk	**(A37B2PS) Passenger Ship** Hull Material: Aluminium Alloy Passengers: unberthed: 332	**2 Gas Turbs** geared to sc. shafts driving 2 Water jets 44.0kn Solar Turbines TAURUS 60 Solar Turbines Inc.-San Diego, Ca
9087568 *VRUT4* -	**UNIVERSAL MK 2002** **Tri-Cat (No 2) Ltd** Shun Tak-China Travel Ship Management Ltd (TurboJET) *Hong Kong* *Hong Kong* MMSI: 477304000 Official number: HK-0232	**605** 193 45	Class: NV	**1995-04 FBM Marine Ltd. — Cowes** Yd No: 1408 Loa 45.00 Br ex - Dght 1.620 Lbp 40.00 Br md 11.80 Dpth 4.76 Welded, 1 dk	**(A37B2PS) Passenger Ship** Hull Material: Aluminium Alloy Passengers: unberthed: 332	**2 Gas Turbs** 2 Gas Turbs. geared to sc. shafts driving 2 Water jets Total Power: 8,400kW (11,420hp) 44.0kn Solar Turbines TAURUS 60 2 x Gas Turb each-4200kW (5710shp) Solar Turbines Inc.-San Diego, Ca
9087570 *VRUV2* -	**UNIVERSAL MK 2003** **Tri-Cat (No 3) Ltd** Shun Tak-China Travel Ship Management Ltd (TurboJET) *Hong Kong* *Hong Kong* MMSI: 477324000 Official number: HK-0246	**605** 192 45	Class: NV	**1995-04 Babcock Rosyth Fabricators — Dunfermline** (Hull) **1995-04 FBM Marine Ltd. — Cowes** Yd No: 1409 Loa 45.00 Br ex - Dght 1.570 Lbp 44.90 Br md 11.80 Dpth 4.76 Welded, 1 dk	**(A37B2PS) Passenger Ship** Hull Material: Aluminium Alloy Passengers: unberthed: 304	**2 Gas Turbs** 2 Gas Turbs. geared to sc. shafts driving 2 Water jets Total Power: 8,400kW (11,420hp) 44.0kn Solar Turbines TAURUS 60 2 x Gas Turb each-4200kW (5710shp) Solar Turbines Inc.-San Diego, Ca

IMO / Call sign	Name / Owner / Manager	Tonnage	Class	Builder / Dimensions	Type	Machinery
9087582 *VRUY9* -	**UNIVERSAL MK 2004** **Tri-Cat (No 4) Ltd** Shun Tak-China Travel Ship Management Ltd (TurboJET) *Hong Kong* *Hong Kong* MMSI: 477384000 Official number: HK-0290	**610** 192 45	Class: NV	**1995-12 FBM Marine Ltd. — Cowes** Yd No: 1410 Loa 45.00 Br ex - Dght 1.620 Lbp 40.00 Br md 11.80 Dpth 4.76 Welded, 1 dk	**(A37B2PS) Passenger Ship** Hull Material: Aluminium Alloy Passengers: unberthed: 332	**2 Gas Turbs** 2 Gas Turbs. geared to sc. shafts driving 2 Water jets Total Power: 8,400kW (11,420hp) 44.0kn Solar Turbines TAURUS 60 2 x Gas Turb each-4200kW (5710shp) Solar Turbines Inc.-San Diego, Ca AuxGen: 2 x 85kW 220/415V 50Hz a.c Fuel: 16.0 2.5pd
9087594 *VRVA2* -	**UNIVERSAL MK 2005** **Tri-Cat (No 5) Ltd** Shun Tak-China Travel Ship Management Ltd (TurboJET) *Hong Kong* *Hong Kong* MMSI: 477385000 Official number: HK-0291	**610** 193 45	Class: NV	**1996-02 FBM Marine Ltd. — Cowes** Yd No: 1411 Loa 45.00 Br ex - Dght 1.620 Lbp 40.00 Br md 11.80 Dpth 4.76 Welded, 1 dk	**(A37B2PS) Passenger Ship** Hull Material: Aluminium Alloy Passengers: unberthed: 322	**2 Gas Turbs** 2 Gas Turbs. geared to sc.shafts driving 2 Water jets Total Power: 8,400kW (11,420hp) 45.0kn Solar Turbines TAURUS 60 2 x Gas Turb each-4200kW (5710shp) Solar Turbines Inc.-San Diego, Ca
9139206 *VRVD9* -	**UNIVERSAL MK 2006** **Tri-Cat (No 6) Ltd** Shun Tak-China Travel Ship Management Ltd (TurboJET) *Hong Kong* *Hong Kong* MMSI: 477509000 Official number: HK-0319	**610** 192 45	Class: NV	**1996-12 FBM Marine Ltd. — Cowes** Yd No: 1428 Loa 45.00 Br ex - Dght 1.620 Lbp 40.00 Br md 11.80 Dpth 4.76 Welded, 1 dk	**(A37B2PS) Passenger Ship** Hull Material: Aluminium Alloy Passengers: unberthed: 318	**2 Gas Turbs** reduction geared to sc. shafts driving 2 Water jets Total Power: 10,298kW (14,002hp) 47.0kn Solar Turbines TAURUS 60 2 x Gas Turb each-5149kW (7001shp) Solar Turbines Inc.-San Diego, Ca AuxGen: 2 x 101kW 220/425V 50Hz a.c Fuel: 16.0 (d.f.) 2.5pd
9139218 *VRVF6* -	**UNIVERSAL MK 2007** **Tri-Cat (No 7) Ltd** Shun Tak-China Travel Ship Management Ltd (TurboJET) *Hong Kong* *Hong Kong* MMSI: 477525000 Official number: HK-0330	**610** 192 36	Class: NV	**1996-12 FBM Marine Ltd. — Cowes** Yd No: 1429 Loa 45.00 Br ex - Dght 1.370 Lbp 40.00 Br md 11.80 Dpth 4.76 Welded, 1 dk	**(A37B2PS) Passenger Ship** Hull Material: Aluminium Alloy Passengers: unberthed: 318	**2 Gas Turbs** reduction geared to sc. shafts driving 2 Water jets Total Power: 10,298kW (14,002hp) 47.0kn Solar Turbines TAURUS 60 2 x Gas Turb each-5149kW (7001shp) Solar Turbines Inc.-San Diego, Ca AuxGen: 2 x 101kW 220/425V 50Hz a.c Fuel: 16.0 (d.f.) 2.5pd
9139220 *VRVL8* -	**UNIVERSAL MK 2008** **Tri-Cat (No 8) Ltd** Shun Tak-China Travel Ship Management Ltd (TurboJET) *Hong Kong* *Hong Kong* MMSI: 477545000 Official number: HK-0357	**609** 192 36	Class: NV	**1997-12 FBM-Aboitiz Marine Inc — Balamban** (Hull) Yd No: 1001 **1997-12 FBM Marine Ltd. — Cowes** Yd No: 1430 Loa 45.00 Br ex - Dght 1.370 Lbp 40.00 Br md 11.80 Dpth 4.76 Welded, 1 dk	**(A37B2PS) Passenger Ship** Hull Material: Aluminium Alloy Passengers: unberthed: 318	**2 Gas Turbs** reduction geared to sc. shafts driving 2 Water jets Total Power: 10,298kW (14,002hp) 45.0kn Solar Turbines TAURUS 60 2 x Gas Turb each-5149kW (7001shp) Solar Turbines Inc.-San Diego, Ca
9160188 *VRBJ2* -	**UNIVERSAL MK 2009** *ex* Sassacus *-2005* **Universal MK V Ltd** Shun Tak-China Travel Ship Management Ltd (TurboJET) *Hong Kong* *Hong Kong* MMSI: 477070100 Official number: HK-1598	**579** 97 36	Class: NV	**1997-09 Pequot River Shipworks Inc — New London CT** Yd No: PRS1 Loa 45.30 Br ex - Dght 1.750 Lbp 40.00 Br md 11.80 Dpth 4.75 Welded, 1 dk	**(A37B2PS) Passenger Ship** Hull Material: Aluminium Alloy Passengers: unberthed: 302	**2 Gas Turbs** 2 Gas Turbines geared to sc. shafts driving 2 Water jets Total Power: 10,298kW (14,002hp) 47.0kn Solar Turbines TAURUS 60 2 x Gas Turb each-5149kW (7001shp) Solar Turbines Inc.-San Diego, Ca
9182538 *VRBJ3* -	**UNIVERSAL MK 2010** *ex* Tatobam *-2005* **Universal MK VI Ltd** Shun Tak-China Travel Ship Management Ltd (TurboJET) *Hong Kong* *Hong Kong* MMSI: 477020900 Official number: HK-1599	**575** 187 44	Class: NV	**1999-04 Pequot River Shipworks Inc — New London CT** Yd No: PRS2 Loa 45.00 Br ex - Dght 1.750 Lbp 40.00 Br md 11.80 Dpth 4.78 Welded, 1 dk	**(A37B2PS) Passenger Ship** Hull Material: Aluminium Alloy Passengers: unberthed: 302	**2 Gas Turbs** 2 Gas Turbines geared to sc. shafts driving 2 Water jets Total Power: 10,298kW (14,002hp) 47.0kn Solar Turbines TAURUS 60 2 x Gas Turb each-5149kW (7001shp) Solar Turbines Inc.-San Diego, Ca AuxGen: 2 x 174kW 110/440V 60Hz a.c
9444209 *VRDD6* -	**UNIVERSAL MK 2011** *ex* New Ferry LXXXVII *-2008* **Wealth Trump Ltd** Shun Tak-China Travel Ship Management Ltd (TurboJET) *Hong Kong* *Hong Kong* MMSI: 477056200 Official number: HK-1972	**695** 230 58	Class: NV	**2008-08 North West Bay Ships Pty Ltd — Margate TAS** Yd No: 401 Loa 47.50 Br ex 12.13 Dght 1.620 Lbp 44.00 Br md 11.80 Dpth 3.80 Welded, 1 dk	**(A37B2PS) Passenger Ship** Hull Material: Aluminium Alloy Passengers: 418	**4 oil engines** geared to sc. shafts driving 4 Water jets Total Power: 9,280kW (12,616hp) 42.3kn M.T.U. 16V4000M70 4 x Vee 4 Stroke 16 Cy. 165 x 190 each-2320kW (3154bhp) MTU Friedrichshafen GmbH-Friedrichshafen AuxGen: 2 x a.c
9433676 *VRDD7* -	**UNIVERSAL MK 2012** *ex* New Ferry LXXXVIII *-2008* **Sunrise Field Ltd** Shun Tak-China Travel Ship Management Ltd (TurboJET) *Hong Kong* *Hong Kong* MMSI: 477056300 Official number: HK-1973	**695** 230 58	Class: NV	**2008-08 North West Bay Ships Pty Ltd — Margate TAS** Yd No: 402 Loa 47.50 (BB) Br ex 11.80 Dght 1.620 Lbp 44.00 Br md 11.75 Dpth 3.80 Welded, 1 dk	**(A37B2PS) Passenger Ship** Hull Material: Aluminium Alloy Passengers: unberthed: 430	**4 oil engines** geared to sc. shafts driving 4 Water jets Total Power: 9,280kW (12,616hp) 42.3kn M.T.U. 16V4000M70 4 x Vee 4 Stroke 16 Cy. 165 x 190 each-2320kW (3154bhp) MTU Friedrichshafen GmbH-Friedrichshafen AuxGen: 2 x a.c Fuel: 30.0 (r.f.)
9323209 *VRAB5* -	**UNIVERSAL MK 2016** *ex* New Ferry Lxxxv *-2013* **Wonder United Ltd** Shun Tak-China Travel Macau Ferries Ltd *Hong Kong* *Hong Kong* MMSI: 477320600 Official number: HK-1329	**695** 230 63	Class: NV	**2004-08 Image Marine Pty Ltd — Fremantle WA** Yd No: 148 Loa 47.50 (BB) Br ex 12.13 Dght 1.620 Lbp 44.00 Br md 11.80 Dpth 3.80 Welded, 1 dk	**(A37B2PS) Passenger Ship** Hull Material: Aluminium Alloy Passengers: unberthed: 430	**4 oil engines** geared to sc. shafts driving 4 Water jets Total Power: 9,280kW (12,616hp) 42.0kn M.T.U. 16V4000M70 4 x Vee 4 Stroke 16 Cy. 165 x 190 each-2320kW (3154bhp) MTU Friedrichshafen GmbH-Friedrichshafen AuxGen: 2 x 480V 50Hz a.c Fuel: 8.0 (d.f.)
9323211 *VRAB6* -	**UNIVERSAL MK 2017** *ex* New Ferry Lxxxvi *-2013* **Best Fiscal Holdings Ltd** Shun Tak-China Travel Macau Ferries Ltd *Hong Kong* *Hong Kong* MMSI: 477320700 Official number: HK-1330	**695** 230 54	Class: NV	**2004-08 Image Marine Pty Ltd — Fremantle WA** Yd No: 150 Loa 47.50 Br ex 12.13 Dght 1.621 Lbp 41.80 Br md 11.80 Dpth 3.80 Welded, 1 dk	**(A37B2PS) Passenger Ship** Hull Material: Aluminium Alloy Passengers: unberthed: 418	**4 oil engines** geared to sc. shafts driving 4 Water jets Total Power: 9,280kW (12,616hp) 42.0kn M.T.U. 16V4000M70 4 x Vee 4 Stroke 16 Cy. 165 x 190 each-2320kW (3154bhp) MTU Friedrichshafen GmbH-Friedrichshafen AuxGen: 2 x a.c
9251767 *9HA2521* -	**UNIVERSAL MK I** **MV 2208 Ltd** Societe Maritime Cote d'Azur SAS *Valletta* *Malta* MMSI: 248800000 Official number: 9251767	**841** 269 67	Class: NV	**2001-07 FBM Babcock Marine Ltd. — Dunfermline** Yd No: 2208 Loa 56.47 Br ex 13.00 Dght 1.660 Lbp 47.58 Br md 12.99 Dpth 4.75 Welded, 1 dk	**(A37B2PS) Passenger Ship** Hull Material: Aluminium Alloy Passengers: unberthed: 450	**4 oil engines** geared to sc. shafts driving 4 Water jets Total Power: 9,280kW (12,616hp) 42.0kn M.T.U. 16V4000M70 4 x Vee 4 Stroke 16 Cy. 165 x 190 each-2320kW (3154bhp) MTU Friedrichshafen GmbH-Friedrichshafen
9060376 *VRUG8* -	**UNIVERSAL MK I** **Woolaston Holdings Ltd** Shun Tak-China Travel Ship Management Ltd (TurboJET) *Hong Kong* *Hong Kong* MMSI: 477146000 Official number: HK-0111	**479** 159 100	Class: (NV)	**1992-12 Kvaerner Fjellstrand (S) Pte Ltd — Singapore** Yd No: 004 Loa 40.00 Br ex - Dght 2.400 Lbp - Br md 10.10 Dpth 3.97 Welded, 1 dk	**(A37B2PS) Passenger Ship** Hull Material: Aluminium Alloy Passengers: unberthed: 262	**2 oil engines** reduction geared to sc. shafts driving 2 Water jets Total Power: 3,920kW (5,330hp) 38.0kn M.T.U. 16V396TE74L 2 x Vee 4 Stroke 16 Cy. 165 x 185 each-1960kW (2665bhp) MTU Friedrichshafen GmbH-Friedrichshafen AuxGen: 2 x 81kW 400V 50Hz a.c
9060388 - -	**UNIVERSAL MK II** - -	**479** 159 100	Class: (NV)	**1992-12 Kvaerner Fjellstrand (S) Pte Ltd — Singapore** Yd No: 005 Loa 40.00 Br ex - Dght 2.400 Lbp 40.00 Br md 10.10 Dpth 3.97 Welded, 1 dk	**(A37B2PS) Passenger Ship** Hull Material: Aluminium Alloy Passengers: unberthed: 262	**2 oil engines** reduction geared to sc. shafts driving 2 Water jets Total Power: 3,920kW (5,330hp) 38.0kn M.T.U. 16V396TE74L 2 x Vee 4 Stroke 16 Cy. 165 x 185 each-1960kW (2665bhp) MTU Friedrichshafen GmbH-Friedrichshafen AuxGen: 2 x 81kW 400V 50Hz a.c

9060390 *VRUL9* -
UNIVERSAL MK III
Woolaston Holdings Ltd
Shun Tak-China Travel Ship Management Ltd (TurboJET)
Hong Kong *Hong Kong*
MMSI: 477210000
Official number: HK-0160
479 159 100 Class: (NV)
1993-10 Kvaerner Fjellstrand (S) Pte Ltd — Singapore Yd No: 010
Loa 40.00 Br ex 10.10 Dght 2.400
Lbp 40.00 Br md - Dpth 3.97
Welded, 1 dk
(A37B2PS) Passenger Ship
Hull Material: Aluminium Alloy
Passengers: unberthed: 262
2 oil engines geared to sc. shafts driving 2 Water jets
Total Power: 3,920kW (5,330hp) 38.0kn
M.T.U. 16V396TE74L
2 x Vee 4 Stroke 16 Cy. 165 x 185 each-1960kW (2665bhp)
MTU Friedrichshafen GmbH-Friedrichshafen

9236872 *VRWR5* -
UNIVERSAL MK V
ex New Ferry V -2013
Shun Tak-China Travel Macau Ferries Ltd
-
Hong Kong *Hong Kong*
MMSI: 477821000
Official number: HK-0623
489 176 40 Class: (NV)
2000-12 Damen Shipyards Singapore Pte Ltd — Singapore Yd No: 0041
Loa 40.00 Br ex - Dght 1.700
Lbp 35.00 Br md 10.10 Dpth 3.97
Welded, 1 dk
(A37B2PS) Passenger Ship
Hull Material: Aluminium Alloy
Passengers: unberthed: 409
2 oil engines reduction geared to sc. shafts driving 2 Water jets
Total Power: 5,120kW (6,962hp) 32.5kn
M.T.U. 16V396TE74L
2 x Vee 4 Stroke 16 Cy. 165 x 185 each-2560kW (3481bhp)
MTU Friedrichshafen GmbH-Friedrichshafen
AuxGen: 2 x 113kW a.c
Fuel: 6.0 (d.f.)

9259525 *VRXY5* -
UNIVERSAL MK2013
ex New Ferry Lxxxi -2014
Onfirst Holdings Ltd
Shun Tak-China Travel Macau Ferries Ltd
Hong Kong *Hong Kong*
MMSI: 477064000
Official number: HK-0890
714 234 55 Class: NV
2002-10 Austal Ships Pty Ltd — Fremantle WA Yd No: 144
Loa 47.50 Br ex - Dght 1.610
Lbp 44.00 Br md 11.80 Dpth 3.80
Welded
(A37B2PS) Passenger Ship
Hull Material: Aluminium Alloy
Passengers: unberthed: 414
4 oil engines geared to sc. shafts driving 4 Water jets
Total Power: 9,280kW (12,616hp) 42.5kn
M.T.U. 16V4000M70
4 x Vee 4 Stroke 16 Cy. 165 x 190 each-2320kW (3154bhp)
MTU Friedrichshafen GmbH-Friedrichshafen

9279848 *YDA4090* -
UNIVERSAL ML 9603
PT Cahaya Bintang Respati
-
Palembang *Indonesia*
110 33 - Class: KI
2002-04 Forward Shipbuilding Enterprise Sdn Bhd — Sibu
Loa 20.42 Br ex - Dght 2.400
Lbp 19.70 Br md 6.70 Dpth 2.90
Welded, 1 Dk.
(B32A2ST) Tug
2 oil engines geared to sc. shafts driving 2 FP propellers
Total Power: 716kW (974hp)
Caterpillar 3408TA
2 x Vee 4 Stroke 8 Cy. 137 x 152 each-358kW (487bhp)
Caterpillar Inc-USA
AuxGen: 2 x 27kW a.c

9086100 *YD4812* -
UNIVERSAL ML-11005
ex Kimtrans Aries -2001
PT Cahaya Bintang Respati
-
Palembang *Indonesia*
118 70 97 Class: KI (NK)
1993-08 Borneo Shipping & Timber Agencies Sdn Ltd — Bintulu Yd No: 9
Loa 23.00 Br ex - Dght 2.397
Lbp 21.77 Br md 6.70 Dpth 2.90
Welded, 1 dk
(B32A2ST) Tug
2 oil engines reduction geared to sc. shafts driving 2 FP propellers
Total Power: 790kW (1,074hp) 9.0kn
Yanmar 6LAAL-DT
2 x 4 Stroke 6 Cy. 148 x 165 each-395kW (537bhp)
Yanmar Diesel Engine Co Ltd-Japan
AuxGen: 2 x 16kW a.c

7214997 *HQDE8* -
UNIVERSAL No. 3
ex Yuryo Maru No. 51 -2001
Universal S de RL
Dong Hae Fisheries Co Ltd
San Lorenzo *Honduras*
Official number: L-1822207
265 126 301 Class: (KR)
1971 Niigata Engineering Co Ltd — Niigata NI Yd No: 1037
Loa 45.65 Br ex 7.93 Dght 3.150
Lbp 40.20 Br md 7.90 Dpth 3.51
Welded, 1 dk
(B11B2FV) Fishing Vessel
1 oil engine driving 1 FP propeller
Total Power: 625kW (850hp)
Niigata 6M28KHS
1 x 4 Stroke 6 Cy. 280 x 440 625kW (850bhp)
Niigata Engineering Co Ltd-Japan

8862404 *HQMM5* -
UNIVERSAL No. 4
ex Aiei Maru No. 5 -1993
Kochan Inc
-
San Lorenzo *Honduras*
Official number: L-0324883
484 203 548
1977-08 Y.K. Takasago Zosensho — Naruto
Loa 49.40 Br ex 8.00 Dght 3.200
Lbp 45.00 Br md - Dpth 5.00
Welded, 1 dk
(A31A2GX) General Cargo Ship
Compartments: 1 Ho, ER
1 Ha: (25.3 x 5.6)ER
1 oil engine driving 1 FP propeller
Total Power: 588kW (799hp) 10.0kn
Matsui 6M26KGHS
1 x 4 Stroke 6 Cy. 260 x 400 588kW (799bhp) (made 1977)
Matsui Iron Works Co Ltd-Japan

9002635 *H9IZ* -
UNIVERSAL PEACE
ex Emma Maersk -2004 ex Ellen Maersk -1997
KSF 1 International SA
Hyundai Merchant Marine Co Ltd (HMM)
SatCom: Inmarsat C 435343710
Panama *Panama*
MMSI: 353437000
Official number: 3045605B
158,475 95,332 299,700 T/cm 171.5 Class: KR (LR)
✠ Classed LR until 16/5/07
1995-05 Odense Staalskibsvaerft A/S — Munkebo (Lindo Shipyard) Yd No: 145
Loa 343.71 (BB) Br ex 56.44 Dght 21.600
Lbp 327.54 Br md 56.40 Dpth 30.41
Welded, 1 dk
(A13A2TV) Crude Oil Tanker
Double Hull (13F)
Liq: 321,162; Liq (Oil): 340,813
Compartments: 5 Ta, 10 Wing Ta, 2 Wing Slop Ta, ER
3 Cargo Pump (s): 3x5000m³/hr
Manifold: Bow/CM: 172.9m
1 oil engine driving 1 FP propeller
Total Power: 23,535kW (31,998hp) 14.0kn
Mitsubishi 8UEC75LSII
1 x 2 Stroke 8 Cy. 750 x 2800 23535kW (31998bhp)
Mitsubishi Heavy Industries Ltd-Japan
AuxGen: 3 x 780kW 440V 60Hz a.c
Boilers: 2 WTAuxB (o.f.) 18.4kgf/cm² (18.0bar), e (ex.g.) 23.5kgf/cm² (23.0bar)
Fuel: 383.0 (d.f.) 7921.0 (r.f.)

9370214 *3FCG9* -
UNIVERSAL PIONEER
Great Homes Maritime SA
Hokoku Marine Co Ltd
Panama *Panama*
MMSI: 372130000
Official number: 4120610
49,720 18,358 64,538 Class: NK
2010-01 Sanoyas Hishino Meisho Corp — Kurashiki OY Yd No: 1268
Loa 209.99 (BB) Br ex - Dght 12.029
Lbp 204.00 Br md 37.00 Dpth 22.85
Welded, 1 dk
(A24B2BW) Wood Chips Carrier
Grain: 123,617
Compartments: 6 Ho, ER
6 Ha: ER
Cranes: 3x15.5t
1 oil engine driving 1 FP propeller
Total Power: 9,488kW (12,900hp) 14.6kn
MAN-B&W 6S50MC-C
1 x 2 Stroke 6 Cy. 500 x 2000 9488kW (12900bhp)
Mitsui Engineering & Shipbuilding CLtd-Japan
Fuel: 3050.0

9158886 *9HPZ8* -
UNIVERSAL PRIME
Oceanids Owning Co Ltd
Heidmar Inc
SatCom: Inmarsat C 425627310
Valletta *Malta*
MMSI: 256273000
Official number: 9158886
156,692 107,870 299,985 T/cm 168.0 Class: BV (KR) (AB)
1997-11 Hyundai Heavy Industries Co Ltd — Ulsan Yd No: 1054
Loa 331.00 (BB) Br ex - Dght 22.222
Lbp 314.00 Br md 58.00 Dpth 27.57
Welded, 1 dk
(A13A2TV) Crude Oil Tanker
Double Hull (13F)
Liq: 331,629; Liq (Oil): 331,629
Compartments: 15 Ta, ER
3 Cargo Pump (s): 3x5000m³/hr
1 oil engine driving 1 FP propeller
Total Power: 23,538kW (32,002hp) 15.0kn
B&W 7S80MC
1 x 2 Stroke 7 Cy. 800 x 3056 23538kW (32002bhp)
Hyundai Heavy Industries Co Ltd-South Korea
AuxGen: 3 x 950kW a.c

7812402 - -
UNIVERSAL QUEEN
ex Soho Maru No. 63 -1988
BM Universal Marine & Fishing Corp
-
Manila *Philippines*
Official number: U0029
163 91 -
1978-08 Nagasaki Zosen K.K. — Nagasaki Yd No: 662
Loa 37.29 Br ex - Dght 2.371
Lbp 30.94 Br md 7.00 Dpth 2.77
Welded, 1 dk
(B11B2FV) Fishing Vessel
1 oil engine reduction geared to sc. shaft driving 1 FP propeller
Total Power: 883kW (1,201hp)
Daihatsu 6DSM-28
1 x 4 Stroke 6 Cy. 280 x 340 883kW (1201bhp)
Daihatsu Diesel Manufacturing Co Lt-Japan

9307633 *3EDV* -
UNIVERSAL QUEEN
High Virtue Shipping Co SA
Hyundai Merchant Marine Co Ltd (HMM)
SatCom: Inmarsat Mini-M 764546340
Panama *Panama*
MMSI: 371662000
Official number: 3128206A
163,465 110,455 309,373 T/cm 185.7 Class: KR (NV)
2005-11 Hyundai Heavy Industries Co Ltd — Ulsan Yd No: 1637
Loa 333.12 (BB) Br ex 60.04 Dght 21.000
Lbp 324.00 Br md 60.00 Dpth 29.60
Welded, 1 dk
(A13A2TV) Crude Oil Tanker
Double Hull (13F)
Liq: 337,756; Liq (Oil): 337,756
Compartments: 5 Ta, 10 Wing Ta, ER, 2 Wing Slop Ta
3 Cargo Pump (s): 3x5000m³/hr
Manifold: Bow/CM: 167.7m
1 oil engine driving 1 FP propeller
Total Power: 28,729kW (39,060hp) 15.6kn
Wartsila 7RT-flex84T
1 x 2 Stroke 7 Cy. 840 x 3150 28729kW (39060bhp)
Hyundai Heavy Industries Co Ltd-South Korea
AuxGen: 3 x 1120kW 450V 60Hz a.c
Fuel: 510.3 (d.f.) 9698.0 (r.f.)

8971205 *WBB8829* -
UNIVERSAL SURVEYOR
Fugro Properties Inc
Fugro GeoServices Inc
Patterson, LA *United States of America*
MMSI: 367074880
Official number: 627510
329 98 - Class: AB
1980-01 Universal Iron Works — Houma, La Yd No: 172
Loa - Br ex - Dght 2.940
Lbp 37.20 Br md 9.20 Dpth 3.10
Welded, 1 dk
(B31A2SR) Research Survey Vessel
A-frames: 1
2 oil engines reverse reduction geared to sc. shafts driving 2 FP propellers
Total Power: 896kW (1,218hp) 10.0kn
G.M. (Detroit Diesel) 16V-92
2 x Vee 2 Stroke 16 Cy. 123 x 127 each-448kW (609bhp)
General Motors Corp-USA
AuxGen: 2 x 60kW 208V 60Hz a.c

8882662 LA 584 -
UNIVERSAL V
Universal Fishing Co Ltd
-
Lagos *Nigeria*
139 89 -
1989 Ocean Marine, Inc. — Bayou La Batre, Al Yd No: 234
Loa - Br ex - Dght -
Lbp - Br md - Dpth -
Welded, 1 dk
(B11B2FV) Fishing Vessel
1 oil engine driving 1 FP propeller

8323850 *3EHD7* -
UNIVERSE FOREST
ex Vinashin Iron -2011
ex Washington Rainbow II -2006
Universe Forest Shipping Co Ltd
Greatsources Shipping Consultants Ltd
Panama *Panama*
MMSI: 372030000
Official number: 3231907B
13,881 8,411 22,828 T/cm 31.6 Class: NK
1984-07 Mitsubishi Heavy Industries Ltd. — Shimonoseki Yd No: 869
Loa 157.26 (BB) Br ex 23.04 Dght 9.908
Lbp 149.00 Br md 23.00 Dpth 13.62
Welded, 1 dk
(A21A2BC) Bulk Carrier
Grain: 30,170; Bale: 25,832
Compartments: 4 Ho, ER
4 Ha: (12.8 x 10.8)2 (19.2 x 12.4) (24.8 x 12.4)ER
Cranes: 4x25t
1 oil engine driving 1 FP propeller
Total Power: 4,780kW (6,499hp) 13.8kn
Mitsubishi 6UEC52LA
1 x 2 Stroke 6 Cy. 520 x 1600 4780kW (6499bhp)
Mitsubishi Heavy Industries Ltd-Japan
AuxGen: 3 x 485kW 450V 60Hz a.c
Fuel: 190.5 (d.f.) 976.5 (r.f.) 17.5pd

8852019 - -
UNIVERSE I
ex Father Stan -1992
Naviera Delrem SA de CV
-
Mexico
252 75 - Class: (BV)
1968-03 Industrial Steel & Machine Works — Gulfport, Ms
Loa 20.12 Br ex - Dght -
Lbp - Br md 8.56 Dpth 4.27
Welded, 1 dk
(B32B2SA) Articulated Pusher Tug
Grain: 6,325
1 oil engine driving 1 FP propeller
Total Power: 1,324kW (1,800hp) 8.5kn
Fairbanks, Morse 10-38D8-1/8
1 x 2 Stroke 10 Cy. 207 x 254 1324kW (1800bhp)
Fairbanks Morse & Co.-New Orleans, La

IMO / Call sign	Name / Owner	Tonnage	Class	Builder / Dimensions	Type	Machinery
8102919 *HLLG* -	**UNIVERSE KIM** *ex Granada -1986 ex Granada II -1986* - **Dongwon Industries Co Ltd** - SatCom: Inmarsat C 444055314 *Busan* *South Korea* MMSI: 440462000 Official number: 9510056-6260008	*981* 443 1,209	Class: KR	**1981-11 Campbell Industries — San Diego, Ca** Yd No: 133 Loa 67.52 Br ex 12.50 Dght 5.931 Lbp 59.72 Br md 12.27 Dpth 8.21 Welded, 2 dks	**(B11B2FV) Fishing Vessel** Grain: 662; Bale: 555; Ins: 1,390	**1 oil engine** reverse reduction geared to sc. shaft driving 1 FP propeller Total Power: 2,648kW (3,600hp) 15.0kn EMD (Electro-Motive) 20-645-E7 1 x Vee 2 Stroke 20 Cy. 230 x 254 2648kW (3600bhp) General Motors Corp.Electro-Motive Div.-La Grange AuxGen: 3 x 240kW 440V d.c Thrusters: 1 Thwart. FP thruster (f)
7641724 *V3ET* -	**UNIVERSO** *ex Oyster -1999 ex Jacob Neeltje -1990* *ex Hendrika -1980 ex Jacoba Maria -1980* **Glaxwell Financial Ltd** - *Belize City* *Belize* MMSI: 312363000 Official number: 159910042	**362** 140 -		**1970 Scheepsbouw- en Constructiebedr. K. Hakvoort N.V. — Monnickendam** Yd No: 129 Lengthened-1978 Loa 34.80 Br ex 7.60 Dght - Lbp - Br md 7.52 Dpth 3.71 Welded, 1 dk	**(B11A2FS) Stern Trawler**	**1 oil engine** driving 1 FP propeller Total Power: 964kW (1,311hp) 11.0kn Werkspoor 1 x 4 Stroke 8 Cy. 250 x 250 964kW (1311bhp) (new engine 1973) Stork Werkspoor Diesel BV-Netherlands
8919790 *ERSO* -	**UNIWIND** *ex Ranfoss -2008 ex Effort -2004* *ex Jana -2004 ex Somers Isles -2002* *ex Jana -1999* **Tardis Shipping Co Ltd** Info Market Srl *Moldova* MMSI: 214181915	**3,125** 1,619 3,000	Class: MG (GL)	**1990-12 Kroeger Werft GmbH & Co. KG — Schacht-Audorf** Yd No: 1524 Loa 89.54 (BB) Br ex 16.16 Dght 6.142 Lbp 81.50 Br md 16.00 Dpth 7.80 Welded, 1 dk	**(A31A2GX) General Cargo Ship** Grain: 5,851; Bale: 5,772; Ins: 34 TEU 260 C Ho 110 TEU C Dk 150 TEU incl 34 ref C. Compartments: 1 Cell Ho, ER 1 Ha: (51.4 x 13.2)ER	**1 oil engine** with clutches, flexible couplings & sr geared to sc. shaft driving 1 CP propeller Total Power: 2,640kW (3,589hp) 14.6kn Alpha 12V28/32 1 x Vee 4 Stroke 12 Cy. 280 x 320 2640kW (3589bhp) MAN B&W Diesel A/S-Denmark AuxGen: 1 x 392kW 220/380V a.c, 1 x 212kW 220/380V a.c, 1 x 104kW 220/380V a.c Thrusters: 1 Thwart. FP thruster (f)
9350305 *HSB3379* -	**UNIWISE CHONBURI** - **Uniwise Towage Ltd** Miclyn Express Offshore Pte Ltd *Bangkok* *Thailand* MMSI: 567000690 Official number: 490001113	**818** 345 300	Class: BV (LR) Classed LR until 1/11/13	**2006-07 Unithai Shipyard & Engineering, Ltd. — Si Racha** Yd No: 107 Loa 45.64 Br ex - Dght 4.800 Lbp 42.38 Br md 13.20 Dpth 6.00 Welded, 1 dk	**(B32A2ST) Tug** Cranes: 1x6t	**2 oil engines** gearing integral to driving 2 Z propellers Total Power: 3,678kW (5,000hp) Niigata 6L28HX 2 x 4 Stroke 6 Cy. 280 x 370 each-1839kW (2500bhp) Niigata Engineering Co Ltd-Japan AuxGen: 2 x 250kW a.c Thrusters: 1 Tunnel thruster (f)
9385283 *HSB3653* -	**UNIWISE PHUKET** *ex Unisvitzer Phuket -2014* *ex Svitzer Merlion -2007* *launched as Swissco Sky -2006* **Uniwise Towage Ltd** Miclyn Express Offshore Pte Ltd *Bangkok* *Thailand* MMSI: 567326000 Official number: 500052311	**499** 149 235	Class: BV (LR) Classed LR until 11/11/13	**2006-11 Guangzhou Panyu Lingshan Shipyard Ltd — Guangzhou GD** Yd No: 143 Loa 45.00 Br ex 11.25 Dght 3.412 Lbp 41.12 Br md 11.00 Dpth 4.00 Welded, 1 dk	**(B21B20A) Anchor Handling Tug Supply**	**2 oil engines** reduction geared to sc. shafts driving 2 FP propellers Total Power: 2,574kW (3,500hp) 12.0kn Caterpillar 3512B 2 x Vee 4 Stroke 12 Cy. 170 x 190 each-1287kW (1750bhp) Caterpillar Inc-USA AuxGen: 2 x 229kW a.c
9332573 *HSB3316* -	**UNIWISE RATCHABURI** *ex Swissco Sky -2005* **Uniwise Towage Ltd** Miclyn Express Offshore Pte Ltd *Bangkok* *Thailand* MMSI: 567047700 Official number: 480001860	**499** 150 235	Class: BV (LR) Classed LR until 26/11/13	**2005-03 Guangzhou Panyu Lingshan Shipyard Ltd — Guangzhou GD** Yd No: 115 Loa 45.00 Br ex 11.25 Dght 3.412 Lbp 41.11 Br md 11.00 Dpth 4.00 Welded, 1 dk	**(B32A2ST) Tug**	**2 oil engines** reduction geared to sc. shafts driving 2 FP propellers Total Power: 2,574kW (3,500hp) 12.0kn Caterpillar 3512B 2 x Vee 4 Stroke 12 Cy. 170 x 215 each-1287kW (1750bhp) Caterpillar Inc-USA
9351880 *HSB3277* -	**UNIWISE RAYONG** - **Uniwise Towage Ltd** Miclyn Express Offshore Pte Ltd *Bangkok* *Thailand* MMSI: 567000620 Official number: 480001195	**696** 209 680	Class: BV (LR) Classed LR until 11/11/13	**2005-03 ASL Shipyard Pte Ltd — Singapore** Yd No: 333 Loa 40.20 Br ex - Dght 5.200 Lbp 37.92 Br md 13.20 Dpth 6.00 Welded, 1 dk	**(B32A2ST) Tug**	**2 oil engines** reduction geared to sc. shafts driving 2 Directional propellers Total Power: 3,306kW (4,494hp) 13.0kn Niigata 6L28HX 2 x 4 Stroke 6 Cy. 280 x 370 each-1653kW (2247bhp) Niigata Engineering Co Ltd-Japan AuxGen: 2 x 245kW Thrusters: 1 Tunnel thruster (f)
9592408 *HSB4652* -	**UNIWISE SONGKHLA** *ex Unisvitzer Songkhla -2013* *ex Svitzer Alfa -2012* *ex Unisvitzer Songkhla -2011* **Uniwise Towage Ltd** Miclyn Express Offshore Pte Ltd *Bangkok* *Thailand* MMSI: 567453000 Official number: 5500-00411	**906** 271 -	Class: BV (LR) Classed LR until 15/11/13	**2011-07 Qingdao Qianjin Shipyard — Qingdao SD** Yd No: 6Z20801 Loa 45.64 Br ex - Dght 5.100 Lbp 38.70 Br md 13.20 Dpth 6.00 Welded, 1 dk	**(B32A2ST) Tug**	**2 oil engines** reduction geared to sc. shafts driving 2 Z propellers Total Power: 4,412kW (5,998hp) Niigata 8L28HX 2 x 4 Stroke 8 Cy. 280 x 370 each-2206kW (2999bhp) Niigata Engineering Co Ltd-Japan AuxGen: 2 x a.c
8627543 *UBWE4* -	**UNIX** *ex Kuroshio -2003 ex Kuroshio No. 3 -2003* **Gidrostroy JSC (A/O 'Gidrostroy')** - *Korsakov* *Russia* MMSI: 273344220	**473** 169 591	Class: RS	**1986-12 K.K. Kamishima Zosensho — Osakikamijima** Yd No: 181 Loa 51.36 Br ex 8.50 Dght 3.200 Lbp 46.12 Br md 8.50 Dpth 5.01 Welded, 1 dk	**(A31A2GX) General Cargo Ship**	**1 oil engine** driving 1 FP propeller Total Power: 515kW (700hp) 9.0kn Matsui 6M26KGHS 1 x 4 Stroke 6 Cy. 260 x 400 515kW (700bhp) Matsui Iron Works Co Ltd-Japan
8650136 *VMQ9529* -	**UNLIMITED** - **Edward Peter Fader, Gregory Laurence Prescott & Richard Francis Fader** - *Hobart, Tas* *Australia* MMSI: 503268900 Official number: 858931	**165** 50 55		**2008-12 Richardson Devine Marine Constructions Pty Ltd — Hobart TAS** Yd No: 048 Loa 24.60 Br ex - Dght 1.800 Lbp - Br md 8.00 Dpth 3.40 Welded, 1 dk	**(B21A20C) Crew/Supply Vessel** Hull Material: Aluminium Alloy Cranes: 1x3.5t	**2 oil engines** reduction geared to sc. shafts driving 2 Propellers Total Power: 1,640kW (2,230hp) 25.0kn Caterpillar C32 2 x Vee 4 Stroke 12 Cy. 145 x 162 each-820kW (1115bhp) Caterpillar Inc-USA Fuel: 25.0 (d.f.)
9334416 *TCON5* -	**UNLU 5** - **Emsan Denizcilik Sanayi ve Ticaret AS** - *Istanbul* *Turkey* MMSI: 271000854	**3,551** 1,802 5,346	Class: TL	**2006-06 Deniz Endustrisi A.S. — Tuzla, Istanbul** Yd No: 33 Loa 99.60 (BB) Br ex - Dght 6.130 Lbp 96.05 Br md 14.00 Dpth 8.00 Welded, 1 dk	**(A31A2GX) General Cargo Ship** Grain: 6,688; Bale: 6,523 Compartments: 2 Ho, ER 2 Ha: ER Derricks: 4x5t	**1 oil engine** geared to sc. shaft driving 1 FP propeller Total Power: 1,765kW (2,400hp) 10.0kn MaK 9M452AK 1 x 4 Stroke 9 Cy. 320 x 450 1765kW (2400bhp) Caterpillar Motoren GmbH & Co. KG-Germany Thrusters: 1 Thwart. FP thruster (f)
8512671 *D6EZ6* -	**UNO** *ex Harbour Service Uno -2009* **West Africa Bunkering Ltd** - *Union of Comoros* MMSI: 616778000	**1,518** 747 2,635	Class: (BV) (GL) (PR)	**1986-09 Jose Valina Lavandeira — La Coruna** Yd No: 22 Loa 72.01 Br ex - Dght 4.601 Lbp 67.01 Br md 13.21 Dpth 5.41 Welded, 1 dk	**(A13B2TP) Products Tanker**	**1 oil engine** with flexible couplings & sr gearedto sc. shaft driving 1 FP propeller Total Power: 912kW (1,240hp) Alpha 8L23/30 1 x 4 Stroke 8 Cy. 225 x 300 912kW (1240bhp) Construcciones Echevarria SA-Spain
8734358 *C6LZ3* -	**UNPLUGGED** *ex Sarabande -2005 ex Parsifal -2005* **Everbright Ltd** Camper & Nicholsons France SARL *Nassau* *Bahamas* MMSI: 308691000 Official number: 723476	**171** 51 -		**1992-01 Cant. Valdettaro Srl — Le Grazie** Yd No: 157 Loa 34.00 Br ex - Dght 2.800 Lbp 26.08 Br md 7.95 Dpth 3.90 Welded, 1 dk	**(X11A2YS) Yacht (Sailing)**	**1 oil engine** geared to sc. shaft driving 1 Propeller Total Power: 317kW (431hp) Caterpillar 3196TA 1 x 4 Stroke 6 Cy. 130 x 150 317kW (431bhp) Caterpillar Inc-USA
9115640 *JIVJ* FK1-113	**UNRYU MARU** - **Fukui Prefecture** - SatCom: Inmarsat C 443173110 *Obama, Fukui* *Japan* MMSI: 431731000 Official number: 128623	*499* 222 389		**1995-03 Yamanishi Corp — Ishinomaki MG** Yd No: 1008 Loa 56.67 Br ex 9.42 Dght 3.800 Lbp 48.50 Br md 9.40 Dpth 6.20 Welded, 1 dk	**(B34K2QT) Training Ship** Ins: 53	**1 oil engine** with clutches, flexible couplings & dr reverse geared to sc. shaft driving 1 CP propeller Total Power: 1,324kW (1,800hp) 12.5kn Niigata 6M31BFT 1 x 4 Stroke 6 Cy. 310 x 530 1324kW (1800bhp) Niigata Engineering Co Ltd-Japan AuxGen: 2 x 360kW 225V 60Hz a.c Thrusters: 1 Thwart. CP thruster (f) Fuel: 238.4 (d.f.) 4.4pd

7818391 *UAWZ* -	**UNS TRADER** *ex* Amina *-2012* *ex* River Lozva *-2003* *ex* Lozva *-2003* **BOAZ LLC** 'Lakor' Ltd (OOO 'Lakor') *Astrakhan* *Russia* MMSI: 273446260 Official number: 7818391	**1,532** 580 1,932	Class: RS	**1979-05 VEB Elbewerften Boizenburg/Rosslau — Rosslau** Yd No: 349 Loa 82.02 Br ex 11.80 Dght 3.600 Lbp 78.11 Br md 11.61 Dpth 4.00 Welded, 1 dk	**(A31A2GX) General Cargo Ship** TEU 70 C.Ho 34/20' C.Dk 36/20' Compartments: 2 Ho, ER 2 Ha: ER	**2 oil engines** driving 2 FP propellers Total Power: 882kW (1,200hp) S.K.L. 8VD36/24A-1 2 x 4 Stroke 8 Cy. 240 x 360 each-441kW (600bhp) VEB Schwermaschinenbau "KarlLiebknecht" (SKL)-Magdeburg Fuel: 73.0 (d.f.)
9404778 *3FRX6* -	**UNTA** **Yakumo Maritime SA** KK Kyowa Sansho SatCom: Inmarsat C 435357110 *Panama* *Panama* MMSI: 353571000 Official number: 4068709	**58,120** 33,870 106,563 T/cm 98.0	Class: NK	**2009-08 Oshima Shipbuilding Co Ltd — Saikai NS** Yd No: 10448 Loa 254.62 (BB) Br ex - Dght 13.465 Lbp 245.62 Br md 43.00 Dpth 19.39 Welded, 1 dk	**(A21A2BC) Bulk Carrier** Grain: 130,648; Bale: 127,298 Compartments: 7 Ho, ER 7 Ha: ER	**1 oil engine** driving 1 FP propeller Total Power: 12,268kW (16,680hp) 14.5kn MAN-B&W 6S60MC 1 x 2 Stroke 6 Cy. 600 x 2292 12268kW (16680bhp) Kawasaki Heavy Industries Ltd-Japan Fuel: 3500.0
5373696 *OIWP* -	**UNTERELBE** *ex* Ramona *-1999* *ex* Unterelbe *-1988* *ex* Frieda Jonas *-1959* *ex* Danzig *-1951* **JR Shipping Ky Kb** - *Porvoo* *Finland* MMSI: 230976000 Official number: 10045	**259** 109 420	Class: (GL)	**1939 Schiffswerft W. Holst — Hamburg** Yd No: 154 Lengthened-1961 Loa 46.72 Br ex 6.81 Dght 2.671 Lbp 42.50 Br md 6.75 Dpth 3.05 Riveted, 1 dk	**(A31A2GX) General Cargo Ship** Grain: 595; Bale: 538 Compartments: 1 Ho, ER 1 Ha:	**1 oil engine** driving 1 FP propeller Total Power: 147kW (200hp) 8.0kn Deutsche Werke MU36 1 x 4 Stroke 6 Cy. 215 x 360 147kW (200bhp) Deutsche Werke Kiel AG (DWK)-Kiel
9088275 *TCWH4* -	**UNYECEM 1** *ex* Cemsea *-2013* *ex* Flinterland *-2004* **Omsan Denizcilik AS** - *Istanbul* *Turkey* MMSI: 271043513	**2,827** 1,542 4,213 T/cm 11.2	Class: NK (BV)	**1994-01 Scheepswerf Ferus Smit BV — Westerbroek** Yd No: 296 Converted From: General Cargo Ship-2004 Loa 91.46 (BB) Br ex 13.62 Dght 6.340 Lbp 84.85 Br md 13.60 Dpth 7.90 Welded, 1 dk	**(A24A2BT) Cement Carrier** Grain: 5,610 Compartments: 1 Ho, ER 1 Ha: (62.5 x 10.9)ER Ice Capable	**1 oil engine** with flexible couplings & sr reverse geared to sc. shaft driving 1 FP propeller Total Power: 1,750kW (2,379hp) 10.5kn Stork-Werkspoor 6SW280 1 x 4 Stroke 6 Cy. 280 x 300 1750kW (2379bhp) Stork Wartsila Diesel BV-Netherlands AuxGen: 3 x 146kW 380/220V 50Hz a.c Thrusters: 1 Thwart. FP thruster (f) Fuel: 40.8 (d.f.) 259.3 (d.f.) 7.3pd
7629685 - -	**UNZEN** *ex* Unzen Maru *-1980* **Chiyoichi-Sep (FE) Pte Ltd** -	*161* 41 -	Class: (NK)	**1968 Watanabe Zosen KK — Imabari EH** Loa 26.55 Br ex 8.02 Dght 3.144 Lbp 24.00 Br md 8.00 Dpth 3.60 Welded, 1 dk	**(B32B2SP) Pusher Tug**	**2 oil engines** driving 2 FP propellers Total Power: 912kW (1,240hp) 10.3kn Daihatsu 6PSTBM-26D 2 x 4 Stroke 6 Cy. 260 x 320 each-456kW (620bhp) Daihatsu Kogyo-Japan AuxGen: 2 x 28kW Fuel: 21.5 5.0pd
8122684 *CBUN* -	**UNZEN** *ex* Unzen Maru *-1989* **Empresa de Desarrollo Pesquero de Chile Ltda (EMDEPES)** - SatCom: Inmarsat B 372526190 *Valparaiso* *Chile* MMSI: 725000261 Official number: 2587	*2,985* 1,279 3,630	Class: NK	**1982-07 Naikai Shipbuilding & Engineering Co Ltd — Onomichi HS (Taguma Shipyard)** Yd No: 475 Loa 91.86 Br ex 15.02 Dght 6.414 Lbp 85.24 Br md 15.00 Dpth 9.20 Welded, 2 dks	**(B11A2FS) Stern Trawler** Ins: 2,653 Compartments: 4 Ho, ER 4 Ha: 2 (1.5 x 2.1)2 (2.4 x 2.4) Derricks: 6x5t	**1 oil engine** driving 1 FP propeller Total Power: 3,236kW (4,400hp) 13.9kn B&W 5K45GFC 1 x 2 Stroke 5 Cy. 450 x 900 3236kW (4400bhp) Hitachi Zosen Corp-Japan AuxGen: 2 x 752kW 445V 60Hz a.c Fuel: 71.0 (d.f.) 959.5 (r.f.) 16.0pd
8720527 *JM5714* -	**UNZEN MARU** **Kamigoto Sogo Service KK** *Shinkamigoto, Nagasaki* *Japan* Official number: 130392	*196* - -		**1988-05 Keihin Dock Co Ltd — Yokohama** Yd No: 207 Loa 36.60 Br ex 8.82 Dght 2.600 Lbp 31.90 Br md 8.80 Dpth 3.70 Welded, 1 dk	**(B32A2ST) Tug**	**2 oil engines** geared to sc. shaft driving 1 FP propeller Total Power: 2,206kW (3,000hp) 13.2kn Yanmar T260-ET 2 x 4 Stroke 6 Cy. 260 x 330 each-1103kW (1500bhp) Yanmar Diesel Engine Co Ltd-Japan AuxGen: 2 x 60kW 225V 60Hz a.c
9417414 *V2EE8* -	**UOS CHALLENGER** **ATL Offshore GmbH & Co ms 'Norderney' KG** Hartmann Offshore GmbH & Co KG SatCom: Inmarsat C 430540710 *Saint John's* *Antigua & Barbuda* MMSI: 305407000 Official number: 4603	**2,922** 953 2,948	Class: AB	**2009-05 Fincantieri-Cant. Nav. Italiani S.p.A. — Palermo** Yd No: 6161 Loa 76.50 (BB) Br ex - Dght 6.850 Lbp 67.40 Br md 17.50 Dpth 8.00 Welded, 1 dk	**(B21B20A) Anchor Handling Tug Supply** Passengers: cabins: 30	**4 oil engines** reduction geared to sc. shafts driving 2 CP propellers Total Power: 12,000kW (16,316hp) 16.3kn MaK 6M32C 4 x 4 Stroke 6 Cy. 320 x 480 each-3000kW (4079bhp) Caterpillar Motoren GmbH & Co. KG-Germany AuxGen: 2 x 2240kW 440V 60Hz a.c, 2 x 470kW 440V 60Hz a.c Thrusters: 1 Tunnel thruster (f); 1 Retract. directional thruster (f); 1 Tunnel thruster (a) Fuel: 156.0 (d.f.) 1012.0 (r.f.) 23.0pd
9417426 *V2EN6* -	**UOS COLUMBIA** **ATL Offshore GmbH & Co 'Isle of Baltrum' KG** Hartmann Offshore GmbH & Co KG *Saint John's* *Antigua & Barbuda* MMSI: 305488000 Official number: 4677	**2,922** 953 3,005	Class: AB	**2009-10 Fincantieri-Cant. Nav. Italiani S.p.A. — Riva Trigoso** Yd No: 6162 Loa 76.50 (BB) Br ex - Dght 6.850 Lbp 67.40 Br md 17.50 Dpth 8.00 Welded, 1 dk	**(B21B20A) Anchor Handling Tug Supply**	**4 oil engines** reduction geared to sc. shafts driving 2 CP propellers Total Power: 12,000kW (16,316hp) 16.3kn MaK 6M32C 4 x 4 Stroke 6 Cy. 320 x 480 each-3000kW (4079bhp) Caterpillar Motoren GmbH & Co. KG-Germany AuxGen: 2 x 2240kW a.c, 2 x 470kW a.c Thrusters: 1 Tunnel thruster (f); 1 Tunnel thruster (a); 1 Retract. directional thruster (f)
9435088 *V2EQ7* -	**UOS DISCOVERY** **ATL Offshore GmbH & Co 'Isle of Langeoog' KG** Go Marine Group Pty Ltd *Saint John's* *Antigua & Barbuda* MMSI: 305518000 Official number: 4702	**2,922** 953 3,006	Class: AB	**2010-02 Fincantieri-Cant. Nav. Italiani S.p.A. — Riva Trigoso** Yd No: 6163 Loa 76.50 (BB) Br ex - Dght 6.850 Lbp 67.40 Br md 17.50 Dpth 8.00 Welded, 1 dk	**(B21B20A) Anchor Handling Tug Supply** Cranes: 1x5t	**4 oil engines** reduction geared to sc. shafts driving 2 CP propellers Total Power: 12,000kW (16,316hp) 16.3kn MaK 6M32C 4 x 4 Stroke 6 Cy. 320 x 480 each-3000kW (4079bhp) Caterpillar Motoren GmbH & Co. KG-Germany AuxGen: 2 x 2240kW 440V 60Hz a.c, 2 x 470kW 440V 60Hz a.c Thrusters: 1 Tunnel thruster (f); 1 Tunnel thruster (a); 1 Retract. directional thruster (f) Fuel: 1030.0
9439890 *V2EQ8* -	**UOS ENDEAVOUR** **ATL Offshore GmbH & Co 'Isle of Amrun' KG** Hartmann Offshore GmbH & Co KG SatCom: Inmarsat C 430551910 *Saint John's* *Antigua & Barbuda* MMSI: 305519000	**2,922** 953 2,948	Class: AB	**2010-03 Fincantieri-Cant. Nav. Italiani S.p.A. — La Spezia** Yd No: 6168 Loa 76.50 (BB) Br ex - Dght 6.850 Lbp 67.50 Br md 17.50 Dpth 8.00 Welded, 1 dk	**(B21B20A) Anchor Handling Tug Supply**	**4 oil engines** reduction geared to sc. shafts driving 2 CP propellers Total Power: 12,000kW (16,316hp) 16.3kn MaK 6M32C 4 x 4 Stroke 6 Cy. 320 x 480 each-3000kW (4079bhp) Caterpillar Motoren GmbH & Co. KG-Germany AuxGen: 2 x 2240kW a.c, 2 x 470kW a.c Thrusters: 1 Tunnel thruster (f); 1 Retract. directional thruster (f); 1 Tunnel thruster (a) Fuel: 1030.0
9439905 *V2ET6* -	**UOS ENTERPRISE** **ATL Offshore GmbH & Co 'Isle of Sylt' KG** Hartmann Offshore GmbH & Co KG *Saint John's* *Antigua & Barbuda* MMSI: 305547000 Official number: 4725	**2,922** 953 2,948	Class: AB	**2010-07 Fincantieri-Cant. Nav. Italiani S.p.A. — Palermo** Yd No: 6169 Loa 76.50 (BB) Br ex - Dght 6.850 Lbp 67.40 Br md 17.50 Dpth 8.00 Welded, 1 dk	**(B21B20A) Anchor Handling Tug Supply**	**4 oil engines** reduction geared to sc. shafts driving 2 CP propellers Total Power: 12,000kW (16,316hp) 16.3kn MaK 6M32C 4 x 4 Stroke 6 Cy. 320 x 480 each-3000kW (4079bhp) Caterpillar Motoren GmbH & Co. KG-Germany AuxGen: 2 x 2240kW a.c, 2 x 470kW a.c Thrusters: 1 Tunnel thruster (f); 1 Retract. directional thruster (f); 1 Tunnel thruster (a) Fuel: 1030.0

Ship / Owner	Tonnage / Class	Builder / Dimensions	Type	Machinery
9439917 **UOS EXPLORER** *V2ET8* - **ATL Offshore GmbH & Co 'Isle of Wangerooge' KG** Hartmann Offshore GmbH & Co KG *Saint John's* *Antigua & Barbuda* MMSI: 305549000 Official number: 4727	**2,922** Class: AB 953 3,005	**2010-03 Fincantieri-Cant. Nav. Italiani S.p.A. — Riva Trigoso** Yd No: 6171 Loa 76.50 (BB) Br ex - Dght 6.850 Lbp 67.40 Br md 17.50 Dpth 8.00 Welded, 1 dk	**(B21B20A) Anchor Handling Tug Supply** Cranes: 1x5t	**4 oil engines** reduction geared to sc. shafts driving 2 CP propellers Total Power: 12,000kW (16,316hp) 16.3kn MAN-B&W 6L32/40CD 4 x 4 Stroke 6 Cy. 320 x 400 each-3000kW (4079bhp) STX Engine Co Ltd-South Korea AuxGen: 2 x 2240kW a.c, 2 x 470kW a.c Thrusters: 1 Tunnel thruster (f); 1 Retract. directional thruster (f); 1 Tunnel thruster (a) Fuel: 1030.0
9439929 **UOS FREEDOM** *V2EX7* - **ATL Offshore GmbH & Co 'Isle of Neuwerk' KG** United Offshore Support GmbH & Co KG *Saint John's* *Antigua & Barbuda* MMSI: 305591000 Official number: 4758	**2,922** Class: AB 953 3,006	**2010-06 Fincantieri-Cant. Nav. Italiani S.p.A. — La Spezia** Yd No: 6172 Loa 76.50 (BB) Br ex - Dght 6.850 Lbp 67.40 Br md 17.50 Dpth 8.00 Welded, 1 dk	**(B21B20A) Anchor Handling Tug Supply**	**4 oil engines** reduction geared to sc. shafts driving 2 CP propellers Total Power: 12,000kW (16,316hp) 16.3kn MAN-B&W 6L32/40CD 4 x 4 Stroke 6 Cy. 320 x 400 each-3000kW (4079bhp) STX Engine Co Ltd-South Korea AuxGen: 2 x 2240kW a.c, 2 x 470kW a.c Thrusters: 1 Tunnel thruster (f); 1 Retract. directional thruster (f); 1 Tunnel thruster (a) Fuel: 1030.0
9439931 **UOS LIBERTY** *V2EX8* - **ATL Offshore GmbH & Co 'Isle of Usedom' KG** Hartmann Offshore GmbH & Co KG *Saint John's* *Antigua & Barbuda* MMSI: 305592000 Official number: 4759	**2,922** Class: AB 953 3,006	**2010-06 Fincantieri-Cant. Nav. Italiani S.p.A. — Riva Trigoso** Yd No: 6173 Loa 76.50 (BB) Br ex - Dght 6.850 Lbp 67.40 Br md 17.50 Dpth 8.00 Welded, 1 dk	**(B21B20A) Anchor Handling Tug Supply** Cranes: 1	**4 oil engines** reduction geared to sc. shafts driving 2 CP propellers Total Power: 12,000kW (16,316hp) 16.3kn MAN-B&W 6L32/40CD 4 x 4 Stroke 6 Cy. 320 x 400 each-3000kW (4079bhp) STX Engine Co Ltd-South Korea AuxGen: 2 x 2240kW a.c, 2 x 470kW a.c Thrusters: 1 Retract. directional thruster (f); 1 Tunnel thruster (f); 1 Tunnel thruster (a) Fuel: 1030.0
9439943 **UOS NAVIGATOR** *V2EZ2* - **ATL Offshore GmbH & Co 'Isle of Fehmarn' KG** United Offshore Support GmbH & Co KG *Saint John's* *Antigua & Barbuda* MMSI: 305607000 Official number: 4769	**2,922** Class: AB 953 3,006	**2010-10 Fincantieri-Cant. Nav. Italiani S.p.A. — Palermo** Yd No: 6174 Loa 76.50 (BB) Br ex - Dght 6.850 Lbp 67.40 Br md 17.50 Dpth 8.00 Welded, 1 dk	**(B21B20A) Anchor Handling Tug Supply**	**4 oil engines** reduction geared to sc. shafts driving 2 CP propellers Total Power: 12,000kW (16,316hp) 16.3kn MAN-B&W 6L32/40CD 4 x 4 Stroke 6 Cy. 320 x 400 each-3000kW (4079bhp) STX Engine Co Ltd-South Korea AuxGen: 2 x 2240kW a.c, 2 x 470kW a.c Thrusters: 1 Retract. directional thruster (f); 1 Tunnel thruster (f); 1 Tunnel thruster (a) Fuel: 1030.0
9439955 **UOS PATHFINDER** *V2EZ3* - **ATL Offshore GmbH & Co 'Isle of Memmert' KG** Hartmann Offshore GmbH & Co KG *Saint John's* *Antigua & Barbuda* MMSI: 305608000 Official number: 4770	**2,922** Class: AB 953 2,900	**2010-10 Fincantieri-Cant. Nav. Italiani S.p.A. — Palermo** Yd No: 6175 Loa 76.50 (BB) Br ex - Dght 6.850 Lbp 67.40 Br md 17.50 Dpth 8.00 Welded, 1 dk	**(B21B20A) Anchor Handling Tug Supply**	**4 oil engines** reduction geared to sc. shafts driving 2 CP propellers Total Power: 12,000kW (16,316hp) 16.3kn MAN-B&W 6L32/40CD 4 x 4 Stroke 6 Cy. 320 x 400 each-3000kW (4079bhp) STX Engine Co Ltd-South Korea AuxGen: 2 x 2240kW a.c, 2 x 470kW a.c Thrusters: 1 Retract. directional thruster (f); 1 Tunnel thruster (f); 1 Tunnel thruster (a)
9439967 **UOS VOYAGER** *V2EZ9* - **ATL Offshore GmbH & Co 'Isle of Mellum' KG** United Offshore Support GmbH & Co KG *Saint John's* *Antigua & Barbuda* MMSI: 305617000 Official number: 4776	**2,922** Class: AB 953 2,900	**2010-09 Fincantieri-Cant. Nav. Italiani S.p.A. — La Spezia** Yd No: 6176 Loa 76.50 (BB) Br ex - Dght 6.850 Lbp 67.40 Br md 17.50 Dpth 8.00 Welded, 1 dk	**(B21B20A) Anchor Handling Tug Supply**	**4 oil engines** reduction geared to sc. shafts driving 2 CP propellers Total Power: 12,000kW (16,316hp) 16.3kn MAN-B&W 6L32/40CD 4 x 4 Stroke 6 Cy. 320 x 400 each-3000kW (4079bhp) STX Engine Co Ltd-South Korea AuxGen: 2 x 2240kW a.c, 2 x 470kW a.c Thrusters: 1 Retract. directional thruster (f); 1 Tunnel thruster (f); 1 Tunnel thruster (a) Fuel: 1030.0
8723658 **UOTAS** - *ex Kintai -1995 ex Kintay -1992* - -	**359** Class: (RS) 107 129	**1988-07 Sudostroitelnyy Zavod "Avangard" — Petrozavodsk** Yd No: 613 Loa 35.72 Br ex 8.92 Dght 3.490 Lbp 31.00 Br md 8.80 Dpth 6.07 Welded, 2 dks	**(B11A2FS) Stern Trawler**	**1 oil engine** driving 1 FP propeller Total Power: 589kW (801hp) 10.9kn S.K.L. 6NVD48A-2U 1 x 4 Stroke 6 Cy. 320 x 480 589kW (801bhp) VEB Schwermaschinenbau "KarlLiebknecht" (SKL)-Magdeburg AuxGen: 2 x 200kW a.c Fuel: 82.0 (d.f.)
9667227 **UP AGATE** *3FYC9* - **Leeward Shipping Inc** UP Offshore Apoio Maritimo Ltda *Panama* *Panama* MMSI: 352426000 Official number: 45272PEXT2	**3,601** Class: AB 1,429 5,141	**2013-12 Fujian Mawei Shipbuilding Ltd — Fuzhou FJ** Yd No: 619-41 Loa 87.08 (BB) Br ex - Dght 5.900 Lbp 82.96 Br md 18.80 Dpth 7.40 Welded, 1 dk	**(B21A20S) Platform Supply Ship**	**4 diesel electric oil engines** driving 4 gen. Connecting to 2 elec. motors each (2000kW) driving 2 Azimuth electric drive units Total Power: 6,864kW (9,332hp) 12.0kn Cummins QSK60-M 4 x Vee 4 Stroke 16 Cy. 159 x 190 each-1716kW (2333bhp) Cummins Diesel International Ltd-USA Thrusters: 1 Tunnel thruster (f); 1 Retract. directional thruster (f) Fuel: 900.0 (d.f.)
9328455 **UP AGUA-MARINHA** *PPQX* - **UP Offshore Apoio Maritimo Ltda** - SatCom: Inmarsat C 471011076 *Rio de Janeiro* *Brazil* MMSI: 710001530 Official number: 3810515311	**2,927** Class: NV 1,371 4,119	**2006-02 Estaleiro Ilha S.A. (EISA) — Rio de Janeiro** Yd No: 481 Loa 84.60 (BB) Br ex - Dght 6.500 Lbp 74.20 Br md 16.60 Dpth 7.80 Welded, 1 dk	**(B21A20S) Platform Supply Ship**	**2 oil engines** reduction geared to sc. shafts driving 2 Directional propellers Total Power: 5,280kW (7,178hp) 14.0kn MaK 8M25 2 x 4 Stroke 8 Cy. 255 x 400 each-2640kW (3589bhp) Caterpillar Motoren GmbH & Co. KG-Germany AuxGen: 2 x 600kW 450V 60Hz a.c, 2 x 1400kW 450V 60Hz a.c Thrusters: 2 Tunnel thruster (f)
9443657 **UP AMBER** *3FMX5* - **Amber Shipping Inc** UP Offshore Apoio Maritimo Ltda *Panama* *Panama* MMSI: 352073000 Official number: 4515613	**2,917** Class: LR 1,183 ✠**100A1** SS 01/2013 4,167 offshore supply ship EP (B) ✠**LMC** **UMS** Eq.Ltr: V; Cable: 550.0/42.0 U3 (a)	**2013-01 Bharati Shipyard Ltd — Ratnagiri** Yd No: 382 Loa 84.60 (BB) Br ex 16.60 Dght 6.500 Lbp 74.20 Br md 16.54 Dpth 7.80 Welded, 1 dk	**(B21A20S) Platform Supply Ship**	**2 oil engines** gearing integral to driving 2 Directional propellers Total Power: 5,200kW (7,070hp) Wartsila 8L26 2 x 4 Stroke 8 Cy. 260 x 320 each-2600kW (3535bhp) Wartsila Finland Oy-Finland AuxGen: 2 x 1800kW 450V 60Hz a.c, 2 x 590kW 440V 60Hz a.c Thrusters: 2 Tunnel thruster (f)
9667239 **UP CORAL** *3EUW6* - **Jura Shipping Inc** UP Offshore Apoio Maritimo Ltda *Panama* *Panama* MMSI: 351816000 Official number: 45273PEXT1	**3,601** Class: AB 1,429 5,128	**2013-12 Fujian Mawei Shipbuilding Ltd — Fuzhou FJ** Yd No: 619-42 Loa 87.08 (BB) Br ex - Dght 5.900 Lbp 82.96 Br md 18.80 Dpth 7.40 Welded, 1 dk	**(B21A20S) Platform Supply Ship**	**4 diesel electric oil engines** driving 4 gen. Connecting to 2 elec. motors driving 2 Azimuth electric drive units Total Power: 6,864kW (9,332hp) 12.0kn Cummins QSK60-M 4 x Vee 4 Stroke 16 Cy. 159 x 190 each-1716kW (2333bhp) Cummins Diesel International Ltd-USA Thrusters: 1 Tunnel thruster (f); 1 Directional thruster (f) Fuel: 900.0 (d.f.)
9307619 **UP DIAMANTE** *PPUC* - **UP Offshore Apoio Maritimo Ltda** Oceanmarine SA *Rio de Janeiro* *Brazil* MMSI: 710003070 Official number: 3810518417	**2,927** Class: NV 1,371 4,201	**2007-03 Estaleiro Ilha S.A. (EISA) — Rio de Janeiro** Yd No: 483 Loa 84.60 (BB) Br ex 16.60 Dght 6.500 Lbp 74.20 Br md 16.16 Dpth 7.80 Welded, 1 dk	**(B21A20S) Platform Supply Ship**	**2 oil engines** gearing integral to driving 2 Directional propellers Total Power: 5,100kW (6,934hp) 14.0kn MaK 8M25 2 x 4 Stroke 8 Cy. 255 x 400 each-2550kW (3467bhp) Caterpillar Motoren GmbH & Co. KG-Germany AuxGen: 2 x 590kW 450V 60Hz a.c, 2 x 1400kW 450V 60Hz a.c Thrusters: 2 Tunnel thruster (f)

IMO / Call sign / Flag	Name / Owners	Tonnage	Classification	Build / Dimensions	Type	Machinery
9307700 *H9IJ* -	**UP ESMERALDA** **Packet Maritime Inc** Ravenscroft Ship Management Inc *Panama* *Panama* MMSI: 353398000 Official number: 3097705A	**2,919** 1,371 4,313	Class: LR ✠ **100A1** SS 05/2010 main deck strengthened for loads of 5 tonnes/m2 ✠ **LMC** **UMS** Eq.Ltr: V†; Cable: 495.0/42.0 U3 (a)	**2005-03 Jinling Shipyard — Nanjing JS** Yd No: 03-0601 Loa 84.60 (BB) Br ex 16.66 Dght 6.450 Lbp 74.20 Br md 16.60 Dpth 7.80 Welded, 1 dk	**(B21A20S) Platform Supply Ship**	**2 oil engines** gearing integral to driving 2 Directional propellers Total Power: 5,100kW (6,934hp) 14.0kn MaK 8M25 2 x 4 Stroke 8 Cy. 255 x 400 each-2550kW (3467bhp) Caterpillar Motoren GmbH & Co. KG-Germany AuxGen: 2 x 1400kW 450V 60Hz a.c, 2 x 590kW 450V 60Hz a.c Boilers: AuxB (o.f.) Thrusters: 2 Tunnel thruster (f) Fuel: 839.0 (d.f.)
9443645 *HP6294* -	**UP JADE** **Bayshore Shipping Inc** UP Offshore Apoio Maritimo Ltda *Panama* *Panama* MMSI: 357377000 Official number: 4422812	**2,917** 1,183 4,127	Class: LR ✠ **100A1** SS 05/2012 offshore supply ship EP (B) ✠ **LMC** **UMS** Eq.Ltr: V*; Cable: 550.0/42.0 U3 (a)	**2012-05 Bharati Shipyard Ltd — Ratnagiri** Yd No: 381 Loa 84.60 (BB) Br ex 16.60 Dght 6.500 Lbp 74.20 Br md 16.60 Dpth 7.80 Welded, 1 dk	**(B21A20S) Platform Supply Ship**	**2 oil engines** gearing integral to driving 2 Directional propellers Total Power: 5,200kW (7,070hp) 15.0kn Wartsila 8L26 2 x 4 Stroke 8 Cy. 260 x 320 each-2600kW (3535bhp) Wartsila Finland Oy-Finland AuxGen: 2 x 1800kW 450V 60Hz a.c, 2 x 590kW 440V 60Hz a.c Thrusters: 2 Thwart. CP thruster (f)
9557666 *3FUI* -	**UP JASPER** **Zubia Shipping Inc** Ravenscroft Ship Management Inc *Panama* *Panama* MMSI: 352874000 Official number: 4287911	**3,753** 1,595 4,900	Class: NV	**2011-06 Wison (Nantong) Heavy Industry Co Ltd — Nantong JS** Yd No: S112 Loa 87.40 Br ex - Dght 6.540 Lbp 80.50 Br md 19.00 Dpth 8.00 Welded, 1 dk	**(B21A20S) Platform Supply Ship**	**2 oil engines** reduction geared to sc. shafts driving 2 CP propellers Total Power: 5,968kW (8,114hp) 15.0kn EMD (Electro-Motive) 16-710-G7C 2 x Vee 2 Stroke 16 Cy. 230 x 279 each-2984kW (4057bhp) General Motors Corp.Electro-Motive Div.-La Grange AuxGen: 2 x a.c, 2 x a.c Thrusters: 2 Tunnel thruster (f); 2 Tunnel thruster (a)
9655494 *3FJE3* -	**UP OPAL** **Hanford Shipping Inc** UP Offshore Apoio Maritimo Ltda *Panama* *Panama* MMSI: 357188000 Official number: 45393PEXT	**3,601** 1,429 5,188	Class: AB	**2014-01 Fujian Mawei Shipbuilding Ltd — Fuzhou FJ** Yd No: 619-40 Loa 87.08 Br ex - Dght 5.900 Lbp 83.00 Br md 18.80 Dpth 7.40 Welded, 1 dk	**(B21A20S) Platform Supply Ship**	**4 oil engines** driving 4 gen. Connecting to 2 elec. motors driving 2 Propellers Total Power: 6,864kW (9,332hp) 12.0kn Cummins QSK60-M 4 x Vee 4 Stroke 16 Cy. 159 x 190 each-1716kW (2333bhp) Cummins Diesel International Ltd-USA Thrusters: 1 Tunnel thruster (f); 1 Retract. directional thruster (f)
9466099 *3FMX8* -	**UP PEARL** **Springwater Shipping Inc** UP Offshore Apoio Maritimo Ltda *Panama* *Panama* MMSI: 353765000 Official number: 4526413	**2,917** 1,183 4,200	Class: LR ✠ **100A1** SS 08/2013 offshore supply ship EP (B) ✠ **LMC** **UMS** Eq.Ltr: W; Cable: 522.0/46.0 U3 (a)	**2013-08 Bharati Shipyard Ltd — Ratnagiri** Yd No: 386 Loa 84.60 (BB) Br ex 16.60 Dght 6.500 Lbp 74.20 Br md 16.54 Dpth 7.80 Welded, 1 dk	**(B21A20S) Platform Supply Ship**	**2 oil engines** gearing integral to driving 2 Directional propellers Total Power: 5,280kW (7,178hp) Wartsila 8L26 2 x 4 Stroke 8 Cy. 260 x 320 each-2640kW (3589bhp) Wartsila Italia SpA-Italy AuxGen: 2 x 1800kW 440V 60Hz a.c, 2 x 590kW 440V 60Hz a.c Thrusters: 2 Retract. directional thruster (f)
9307621 *PPXR* -	**UP RUBI** **UP Offshore Apoio Maritimo Ltda** - SatCom: Inmarsat C 471011093 *Rio de Janeiro* *Brazil* MMSI: 710000144 Official number: 3813872033	**2,927** 1,371 4,227	Class: NV	**2009-08 Estaleiro Ilha S.A. (EISA) — Rio de Janeiro** Yd No: 484 Loa 84.60 (BB) Br ex 16.64 Dght 6.450 Lbp 74.20 Br md 16.60 Dpth 7.80 Welded, 1 dk	**(B21A20S) Platform Supply Ship**	**2 oil engines** gearing integral to driving 2 Directional propellers Total Power: 5,030kW (6,838hp) 14.0kn MaK 8M25 2 x 4 Stroke 8 Cy. 255 x 400 each-2515kW (3419bhp) Caterpillar Motoren GmbH & Co. KG-Germany AuxGen: 2 x 590kW 450V 60Hz a.c, 2 x 1400kW 450V 60Hz a.c Thrusters: 2 Tunnel thruster (f)
9307712 *3EBA6* -	**UP SAFIRA** **Padow Shipping Inc** Ravenscroft Ship Management Inc *Panama* *Panama* MMSI: 371039000 Official number: 3098605A	**2,919** 1,371 4,313	Class: LR ✠ **100A1** SS 06/2010 occasionally oil recovery duties main deck strengthened for loads of 5 tonnes/m2 ✠ **LMC** **UMS** Eq.Ltr: V†; Cable: 495.0/42.0 U3 (a)	**2005-06 Jinling Shipyard — Nanjing JS** Yd No: 03-0602 Loa 84.60 (BB) Br ex 16.66 Dght 6.450 Lbp 74.20 Br md 16.60 Dpth 7.80 Welded, 1 dk	**(B21A20S) Platform Supply Ship**	**2 oil engines** gearing integral to driving 2 Directional propellers Total Power: 5,100kW (6,934hp) 14.0kn MaK 8M25 2 x 4 Stroke 8 Cy. 255 x 400 each-2550kW (3467bhp) Caterpillar Motoren GmbH & Co. KG-Germany AuxGen: 2 x 1400kW 450V 60Hz a.c, 2 x 590kW 450V 60Hz a.c Thrusters: 2 Tunnel thruster (f) Fuel: 839.0 (d.f.)
9307607 *PPTI* -	**UP TOPAZIO** **UP Offshore Apoio Maritimo Ltda** - *Rio de Janeiro* *Brazil* MMSI: 710000215 Official number: 3810516104	**2,927** 1,371 4,208	Class: NV	**2006-07 Estaleiro Ilha S.A. (EISA) — Rio de Janeiro** Yd No: 482 Loa 84.60 (BB) Br ex 16.60 Dght 6.500 Lbp 74.20 Br md 16.60 Dpth 7.80 Welded, 1 dk	**(B21A20S) Platform Supply Ship**	**2 oil engines** gearing integral to driving 2 Directional propellers Total Power: 5,280kW (7,178hp) 14.0kn MaK 8M25 2 x 4 Stroke 8 Cy. 255 x 400 each-2640kW (3589bhp) Caterpillar Motoren GmbH & Co. KG-Germany AuxGen: 2 x 590kW 450V 60Hz a.c, 2 x 1400kW 450V 60Hz a.c Thrusters: 2 Tunnel thruster (f) Fuel: 839.0 (d.f.)
9557654 *H9EB* -	**UP TURQUOISE** **Glasgow Shipping Inc** Ravenscroft Ship Management Inc SatCom: Inmarsat C 437298610 *Panama* *Panama* MMSI: 372986000 Official number: 4251011	**3,753** 1,595 5,261	Class: NV	**2010-12 Wison (Nantong) Heavy Industry Co Ltd — Nantong JS** Yd No: S111 Loa 87.40 Br ex - Dght 6.650 Lbp 80.50 Br md 19.00 Dpth 8.00 Welded, 1 dk	**(B21A20S) Platform Supply Ship**	**2 oil engines** reduction geared to sc. shafts driving 2 CP propellers Total Power: 5,968kW (8,114hp) 15.0kn EMD (Electro-Motive) 16-710-G7B 2 x Vee 2 Stroke 16 Cy. 230 x 279 each-2984kW (4057bhp) General Motors Corp.Electro-Motive Div.-La Grange AuxGen: 2 x a.c, 2 x a.c Thrusters: 2 Tunnel thruster (f); 2 Tunnel thruster (a)
9115937 *V2AN1* -	**UPHUSEN** *ex Saar Bremen -1996* **W Bockstiegel GmbH & Co Reederei KG ms 'Uphusen'** W Bockstiegel Reederei GmbH & Co KG SatCom: Inmarsat C 430401384 *Saint John's* *Antigua & Barbuda* MMSI: 304010651 Official number: 2483	**2,846** 1,585 4,363	Class: GL	**1996-03 Bodewes' Scheepswerven B.V. — Hoogezand** Yd No: 573 Loa 90.40 Br ex - Dght 5.858 Lbp 84.70 Br md 13.70 Dpth 7.10 Welded, 1 dk	**(A31A2GX) General Cargo Ship** Double Bottom Entire Compartment Length Grain: 5,793 TEU 206 C. 206/20' Compartments: 1 Ho, ER 1 Ha: (64.6 x 10.6)ER Ice Capable	**1 oil engine** reduction geared to sc. shaft driving 1 CP propeller Total Power: 1,800kW (2,447hp) 11.5kn Deutz SBV9M628 1 x 4 Stroke 9 Cy. 240 x 280 1800kW (2447bhp) Motoren Werke Mannheim AG (MWM)-Mannheim AuxGen: 1 x 325kW 220/380V a.c, 2 x 136kW a.c Thrusters: 1 Tunnel thruster (f) Fuel: 206.0 (d.f.)
8727381 - -	**UPS-0108** *ex FCH-0108 -1995* **OOO 'Bazovyy Otraslevoy Uchebno-Trenazhernyy Tsentr'** -	**193** 57 37	Class: (RS)	**1986-12 Sosnovskiy Sudostroitelnyy Zavod — Sosnovka** Yd No: 108 Converted From: Work/Repair Vessel-1999 Loa 27.56 Br ex 6.76 Dght 2.980 Lbp 24.09 Br md - Dpth 3.69 Welded, 1 dk	**(B34K2QT) Training Ship**	**1 oil engine** driving 1 FP propeller Total Power: 285kW (387hp) 9.6kn S.K.L. 6NVD26A-3 1 x 4 Stroke 6 Cy. 180 x 260 285kW (387bhp) VEB Schwermaschinenbau "KarlLiebknecht" (SKL)-Magdeburg AuxGen: 2 x 75kW a.c Fuel: 30.0 (d.f.)
8923313 *JM4159* -	**UPUYU** **Miyako Ferry KK** - *Miyakojima, Okinawa* *Japan* Official number: 120864	*112* - -		**1996-11 K.K. Miho Zosensho — Osaka** Yd No: 345 Loa 28.60 Br ex - Dght 1.142 Lbp 24.62 Br md 7.53 Dpth 2.60 Welded, 1 dk	**(A37B2PS) Passenger Ship** Hull Material: Aluminium Alloy	**2 oil engines** geared to sc. shafts driving 2 FP propellers Total Power: 2,206kW (3,000hp) 29.1kn G.M. (Detroit Diesel) 12V-149-TI 2 x Vee 2 Stroke 12 Cy. 146 x 146 each-1103kW (1500bhp) General Motors Detroit DieselAllison Divn-USA AuxGen: 1 x 48kW 225V a.c Fuel: 5.2 (d.f.)
9158355 - -	**UQAAB** **Government of Abu Dhabi** - *United Arab Emirates*	**120** - -	Class: (LR) ✠	**1997-06 Abu Dhabi Ship Building PJSC — Abu Dhabi** (Assembled by) Yd No: 033C **1997-06 B.V. Scheepswerf Damen — Gorinchem** (Parts for assembly by) Yd No: 6128 Loa 19.70 (BB) Br ex 6.04 Dght 2.020 Lbp 17.32 Br md 6.00 Dpth 2.80 Welded, 1 dk	**(B32A2ST) Tug**	**2 oil engines** with clutches, flexible couplings & sr reverse geared to sc. shafts driving 2 FP propellers Total Power: 1,060kW (1,442hp) 10.8kn Caterpillar 3412TA 2 x Vee 4 Stroke 12 Cy. 137 x 152 each-530kW (721bhp) Caterpillar Inc-USA AuxGen: 2 x 22kW 440V 50Hz a.c

IMO / Call sign / Reg.	Name / Owner / Manager / Port / Flag	Tonnage	Class	Builder / Dimensions	Type	Machinery
7416210 *LW9771* -	**UR ERTZA** **Uromar SA** - SatCom: Inmarsat C 470139710 *Argentina* MMSI: 701000511 Official number: 0377	*403* 49 213	Class: (BV)	**1976-07 S.L. Ardeag — Bilbao** Yd No: 83 Loa 45.90 Br ex - Dght 4.620 Lbp 39.60 Br md 9.01 Dpth 6.58 Welded, 2 dks	**(B11A2FT) Trawler**	**1 oil engine** driving 1 FP propeller Total Power: 1,103kW (1,500hp) 12.3kn Mirrlees KLSSDM-6 1 x 4 Stroke 6 Cy. 381 x 508 1103kW (1500bhp) Mirrlees Blackstone (Stockport)Ltd.-Stockport Fuel: 183.0 (d.f.)
9312236 *ECGY* 3-BI-43-04	**UR ERTZA** **Urondo SA** - *Ondarroa* *Spain* MMSI: 224294000 Official number: 3-3/2004	**387** 116 135	Class: (BV)	**2004-12 Hijos de J. Barreras S.A. — Vigo** Yd No: 1631 Loa 39.00 Br ex - Dght 3.250 Lbp 30.60 Br md 8.80 Dpth 3.80 Welded, 1 dk	**(B11A2FS) Stern Trawler**	**1 oil engine** geared to sc. shaft driving 1 CP propeller Total Power: 1,040kW (1,414hp) Wartsila 6L20 1 x 4 Stroke 6 Cy. 200 x 280 1040kW (1414bhp) Wartsila Diesel S.A.-Bermeo
8843068 *UCFL* -	**URA-GUBA** **Energiya Fishing Collective (Rybolovetskiy Kolkhoz 'Energiya')** - *Murmansk* *Russia* MMSI: 273518000 Official number: 901891	**737** 221 414	Class: (RS)	**1991-04 Zavod "Leninskaya Kuznitsa" — Kiyev** Yd No: 1635 Loa 54.82 Br ex 10.15 Dght 4.140 Lbp 50.30 Br md - Dpth 5.00 Welded, 1dk	**(B11A2FS) Stern Trawler** Ins: 412 Ice Capable	**1 oil engine** driving 1 CP propeller Total Power: 852kW (1,158hp) 12.0kn S.K.L. 8NVD48A-2U 1 x 4 Stroke 8 Cy. 320 x 480 852kW (1158bhp) SKL Motoren u. Systemtechnik AG-Magdeburg AuxGen: 4 x 160kW a.c
8628121 - - -	**URABA** - -	*696* 619 1,220	Class: (LR) Classed LR until 3/11/02	**1969 Astilleros Magdalena Ltda. — Barranquilla** Deepened-1988 Loa 61.07 Br ex 11.02 Dght 2.990 Lbp 58.48 Br md 11.00 Dpth 3.86 Welded, 1 dk	**(A13B2TP) Products Tanker** Compartments: 8 Ta, ER	**2 oil engines** with clutches, hydraulic couplings & sr reverse geared to sc. shafts driving 2 FP propellers Total Power: 626kW (852hp) Cummins KT-19-M 1 x 4 Stroke 6 Cy. 159 x 159 313kW (426bhp) (new engine 1969) Cummins Engine Co Inc-USA Cummins KT-19-M 1 x 4 Stroke 6 Cy. 159 x 159 313kW (426bhp) (new engine 1997) Cummins Engine Co Inc-USA AuxGen: 2 x 60kW 220V 60Hz a.c
7388243 *LW7149* -	**URABAIN** **Vasgapesca SAIC** - SatCom: Inmarsat C 470100719 *Bahia Blanca* *Argentina* MMSI: 701000512 Official number: 0612	**948** 460 1,731	Class: (BV)	**1976-01 Enrique Lorenzo y Cia SA — Vigo** Yd No: 380 Loa 79.00 (BB) Br ex - Dght 5.201 Lbp 69.22 Br md 12.01 Dpth 7.62 Welded, 2 dks	**(B11A2FS) Stern Trawler**	**1 oil engine** driving 1 CP propeller Total Power: 1,986kW (2,700hp) 14.0kn Deutz RBV8M358 1 x 4 Stroke 8 Cy. 400 x 580 1986kW (2700bhp) Hijos de J Barreras SA-Spain Fuel: 558.5 (d.f.)
7387615 - -	**URACANE** *ex Corvaceiras -1999 ex Corbaceiras -1997* **Astipesca Bissau Lda** Astipesca SL *Bissau* *Guinea-Bissau*	*195* 85 -	Class: (BV)	**1974-12 Ast. Ojeda y Aniceto S.A. — Aviles** Yd No: 13 Loa 29.01 Br ex 7.93 Dght 3.277 Lbp 28.33 Br md 7.85 Dpth 5.52 Welded, 2 dks	**(B11B2FV) Fishing Vessel**	**1 oil engine** geared to sc. shaft driving 1 FP propeller Total Power: 552kW (750hp) 10.5kn Deutz SBA6M528 1 x 4 Stroke 6 Cy. 220 x 280 552kW (750bhp) Hijos de J Barreras SA-Spain Fuel: 80.5 (d.f.)
9323156 *5BZV3* -	**URAG ELBE** *ex Elbe -2014* **Vetria Shipping Co Ltd** Unterweser Reederei GmbH (URAG Unterweser Reederei GmbH) *Limassol* *Cyprus* MMSI: 210951000	**633** 190 242	Class: GL	**2006-04 Astilleros Zamakona SA — Santurtzi** Yd No: 615 Loa 37.06 Br ex - Dght 4.200 Lbp 34.70 Br md 12.50 Dpth 4.90 Welded, 1 dk	**(B32A2ST) Tug** Ice Capable	**2 oil engines** geared to sc. shafts driving 2 Voith-Schneider propellers Total Power: 5,280kW (7,178hp) 13.5kn MaK 8M25 2 x 4 Stroke 8 Cy. 255 x 400 each-2640kW (3589bhp) (made 2004) Caterpillar Motoren GmbH & Co. KG-Germany
9323168 *5BZX3* -	**URAG EMS** *ex Ems -2014* **Vetria Shipping Co Ltd** Unterweser Reederei GmbH (URAG Unterweser Reederei GmbH) *Limassol* *Cyprus* MMSI: 210774000	**633** 190 242	Class: GL	**2006-04 Astilleros Zamakona SA — Santurtzi** Yd No: 616 Loa 37.06 Br ex - Dght 4.200 Lbp 34.70 Br md 12.50 Dpth 4.90 Welded, 1 dk	**(B32A2ST) Tug** Ice Capable	**2 oil engines** geared to sc. shafts driving 2 Voith-Schneider propellers Total Power: 5,280kW (7,178hp) 13.5kn MaK 8M25 2 x 4 Stroke 8 Cy. 255 x 400 each-2640kW (3589bhp) (made 2005) Caterpillar Motoren GmbH & Co. KG-Germany AuxGen: 2 x 192kW a.c, 1 x 100kW a.c
9094298 *JD2163* -	**URAGA MARU** **Tokyo Kisen KK** - *Yokohama, Kanagawa* *Japan* Official number: 140228	*181* - -		**2005-10 Kanagawa Zosen — Kobe** Yd No: 540 Loa 40.00 Br ex - Dght 2.900 Lbp 35.25 Br md 8.60 Dpth 3.62 Welded, 1 dk	**(B32A2ST) Tug**	**2 oil engines** reduction geared to sc. shafts driving 2 Propellers Total Power: 2,942kW (4,000hp) Niigata 6L26HLX 2 x 4 Stroke 6 Cy. 260 x 350 each-1471kW (2000bhp) Niigata Engineering Co Ltd-Japan
9439204 *SVBB3*	**URAGA PRINCESS** **Prosperity Success SA** Tsakos Columbia Shipmanagement (TCM) SA *Piraeus* *Greece* MMSI: 241029000 Official number: 12004	**55,909** 29,810 105,344 T/cm 88.9	Class: LR ✠ **100A1** SS 07/2010 Double Hull oil tanker ESP **ShipRight** (SDA, FDA, CM) *IWS LI EP (B,P,S,Vc) ✠ **LMC** **UMS IGS** Eq.Ltr: R†; Cable: 687.5/84.0 U3 (a)	**2010-07 Sumitomo Heavy Industries Marine & Engineering Co., Ltd. — Yokosuka** Yd No: 1360 Loa 228.60 (BB) Br ex 42.03 Dght 14.808 Lbp 217.80 Br md 42.00 Dpth 21.50 Welded, 1 dk	**(A13A2TV) Crude Oil Tanker** Double Hull (13F) Liq: 98,688; Liq (Oil): 98,688 Cargo Heating Coils Compartments: 10 Wing Ta, 2 Wing Slop Ta, ER 3 Cargo Pump (s): 3x2500m³/hr Manifold: Bow/CM: 116.6m	**1 oil engine** driving 1 FP propeller Total Power: 12,350kW (16,791hp) 14.8kn MAN-B&W 6S60MC-C 1 x 2 Stroke 6 Cy. 600 x 2400 12350kW (16791bhp) Mitsui Engineering & Shipbuilding CLtd-Japan AuxGen: 3 x 800kW 450V 60Hz a.c Boilers: e (ex.g.) 22.2kgf/cm² (21.8bar), WTAuxB (o.f.) 18.6kgf/cm² (18.2bar) Fuel: 200.0 (d.f.) 2100.0 (r.f.)
8727226 - -	**URAGAN** *ex PTR-50 No. 15 -1988* **Khimtek Ltd** -	**187** 56 77	Class: (RS)	**1986-06 Astrakhanskaya Sudoverf im. "Kirova" — Astrakhan** Yd No: 15 Loa 31.85 Br ex 7.08 Dght 2.100 Lbp 27.80 Br md - Dpth 3.15 Welded, 1 dk	**(B12B2FC) Fish Carrier** Ins: 100	**1 oil engine** geared to sc. shaft driving 1 FP propeller Total Power: 221kW (300hp) 10.2kn Daldizel 6CHNSP18/22-300 1 x 4 Stroke 6 Cy. 180 x 220 221kW (300bhp) Daldizel-Khabarovsk AuxGen: 2 x 25kW a.c Fuel: 14.0 (d.f.)
8929898 - -	**URAGAN** **State Enterprise Makhachkala International Sea Commercial Port** - *Makhachkala* *Russia* Official number: 752711	*187* - 46	Class: (RS)	**1976 Gorokhovetskiy Sudostroitelnyy Zavod — Gorokhovets** Yd No: 339 Loa 29.30 Br ex 8.49 Dght 3.090 Lbp 27.00 Br md - Dpth 4.30 Welded, 1 dk	**(B32A2ST) Tug** Ice Capable	**2 oil engines** driving 2 CP propellers Total Power: 882kW (1,200hp) 11.4kn Russkiy 6D30/50-4-3 2 x 2 Stroke 6 Cy. 300 x 500 each-441kW (600bhp) Mashinostroitelnyy Zavod"Russkiy-Dizel"-Leningrad AuxGen: 2 x 30kW a.c Fuel: 36.0 (d.f.)
8858192 - -	**URAGAN** *ex BK-1225 -1988* **Real Estate Management Committee of St Petersburg City Executive Board** - *St Petersburg* *Russia*	*164* 49 46	Class: (RS)	**1967 "Petrozavod" — Leningrad** Yd No: 728 Loa 29.30 Br ex 8.49 Dght 3.090 Lbp 27.00 Br md - Dpth 4.35 Welded, 1 dk	**(B32A2ST) Tug** Ice Capable	**2 oil engines** driving 2 CP propellers Total Power: 882kW (1,200hp) 11.4kn Russkiy 6DR30/50-4-2 2 x 2 Stroke 6 Cy. 300 x 500 each-441kW (600bhp) Mashinostroitelnyy Zavod"Russkiy-Dizel"-Leningrad AuxGen: 2 x 25kW a.c
9397028 *UHKL* -	**URAGANNYY** **JSC 'Far Eastern Shipbuilding Leasing Co' (Dalnevostochnaya Sudostroitelnaya Lizingovaya Kompaniya)** 'Moryak Rybolov' Fishing Collective (Rybkolkhoz Moryak-Rybolov) *Nakhodka* *Russia* MMSI: 273313050	**117** 35 65	Class: (RS)	**2006-09 Dalnevostochnyy Zavod "Zvezda" — Bolshoy Kamen** Yd No: 01541 Loa 27.69 Br ex 8.10 Dght 2.430 Lbp 24.00 Br md 7.81 Dpth 3.13 Welded, 1 dk	**(B11A2FS) Stern Trawler** Ins: 82 Ice Capable	**1 oil engine** reduction geared to sc. shaft driving 1 CP propeller Total Power: 328kW (446hp) 9.3kn Caterpillar 3406 1 x 4 Stroke 6 Cy. 137 x 165 328kW (446bhp) Caterpillar Inc-USA AuxGen: 1 x 108kW a.c, 1 x 100kW a.c Fuel: 20.0 (d.f.)

7218838 *IOIR* - **URAGANO** **Carmine Novella** *Salerno* *Italy* Official number: 1588
196 99 -
1972 Cant. Nav. Fratelli Maccioni — Viareggio Yd No: 2
Loa 37.70 Br ex 7.14 Dght 2.159
Lbp 28.86 Br md 7.12 Dpth 3.59
Welded, 1 dk
(B11A2FT) Trawler
1 oil engine geared to sc. shaft driving 1 FP propeller
Total Power: 736kW (1,001hp)
Blackstone EWSL8M
1 x 4 Stroke 8 Cy. 222 x 292 736kW (1001bhp)
Lister Blackstone MirrleesMarine Ltd.-Dursley

8937651 - - **URAGO MARU** *ex Urago Maru No. 56 -1997* - -
282 - -
1973-07 Narasaki Zosen KK — Muroran HK
L reg 29.20 Br ex - Dght -
Lbp - Br md 6.20 Dpth 2.55
Welded, 1 dk
(B11B2FV) Fishing Vessel
1 oil engine driving 1 FP propeller
Total Power: 478kW (650hp) 10.5kn
Hanshin
1 x 4 Stroke 478kW (650bhp)
The Hanshin Diesel Works Ltd-Japan

8820767 *JH3114* - **URAGO MARU NO. 5** *ex Nichiei Maru No. 57 -2008* *ex Gorotake Maru No. 12 -1995* **Urago Suisan KK** *Nishinoshima, Shimane* *Japan* Official number: 130049
139 - -
1988-10 K.K. Watanabe Zosensho — Nagasaki Yd No: 1138
Loa 41.92 (BB) Br ex 7.32 Dght 3.200
Lbp 34.90 Br md 7.30 Dpth 3.40
Welded, 1 dk
(B11B2FV) Fishing Vessel
1 oil engine dr reverse geared to sc. shaft driving 1 CP propeller
Total Power: 736kW (1,001hp)
Yanmar T260-ET
1 x 4 Stroke 6 Cy. 260 x 330 736kW (1001bhp)
Yanmar Diesel Engine Co Ltd-Japan
Thrusters: 1 Thwart. FP thruster (a)

8015130 - - **URAGO MARU NO. 8** *ex Mandai Maru No. 17 -2010* *ex Nagahisa Maru No. 31 -1993* *ex Shichirui Maru No. 31 -1993* - -
196 - 275
1980-10 Tokushima Zosen K.K. — Fukuoka Yd No: 1356
Loa 42.30 (BB) Br ex - Dght 2.901
Lbp 38.03 Br md 7.12 Dpth 3.36
Welded, 1 dk
(B11B2FV) Fishing Vessel
1 oil engine driving 1 FP propeller
Total Power: 883kW (1,201hp) 12.0kn
Hanshin 6LU28
1 x 4 Stroke 6 Cy. 280 x 440 883kW (1201bhp)
Hanshin Nainenki Kogyo-Japan

8227367 *UHJZ* - **URAL** *ex Urals -2005 ex Ural -1993* *ex MRTK-1088 -1985* **Belryba Fishing Collective (Selskokhozyaystvennyy Proizvodstvennyy Kooperativ Rybolovetskiy Kolkhoz 'Belryba')** - *Murmansk* *Russia* Official number: 832969
119 35 23 Class: RS
1984-05 Sosnovskiy Sudostroitelnyy Zavod — Sosnovka Yd No: 659
Loa 25.45 Br ex 7.00 Dght 2.390
Lbp 22.00 Br md 6.80 Dpth 3.30
Welded, 1 dk
(B11B2FV) Fishing Vessel
Ice Capable
1 oil engine driving 1 FP propeller
Total Power: 221kW (300hp) 9.5kn
S.K.L. 6NVD26A-2
1 x 4 Stroke 6 Cy. 180 x 260 221kW (300bhp)
VEB Schwermaschinenbau "KarlLiebknecht" (SKL)-Magdeburg
AuxGen: 2 x 12kW
Fuel: 15.0 (d.f.)

7725386 *3ENK3* - **URAL** *ex Melih K -2013 ex Merdif 3 -2007* *ex Pella I -2004 ex Pella -2003* *ex Wesley D -1997 ex Marc Spyros -1997* *ex Mercandian Trader II -1992* **Uphill Shipping SA** Akdeniz Roro Deniz Tasimaciligi Turizm Sanayi ve Ticaret Ltd Sti *Panama* *Panama* MMSI: 354059000 Official number: 36322PEXT1
4,994 1,498 3,297 Class: MC TL (LR) (HR) (NV) Classed LR until 19/12/97
1980-09 Frederikshavn Vaerft A/S — Frederikshavn Yd No: 390
Loa 105.60 (BB) Br ex 18.98 Dght 4.973
Lbp 96.00 Br md 18.80 Dpth 10.55
Welded, 2 dks
(A35A2RR) Ro-Ro Cargo Ship
Stern door/ramp (centre)
Len: 15.40 Wid: 7.70 Swl: -
Side door/ramp (s. a.)
Len: 13.35 Wid: 4.30 Swl: -
Lane-Len: 870
Lane-Wid: 7.70
Lane-clr ht: 4.70
Cars: 450, Trailers: 63
Grain: 10,320; Bale: 10,188
TEU 256 C RoRo Dk 58 TEU C Dk 198 TEU incl 50 ref C.
1 oil engine sr geared to sc. shaft driving 1 CP propeller
Total Power: 3,960kW (5,384hp) 15.0kn
MaK 12M453AK
1 x Vee 4 Stroke 12 Cy. 320 x 420 3960kW (5384bhp)
Krupp MaK Maschinenbau GmbH-Kiel
AuxGen: 3 x 280kW 440V 60Hz a.c
Thrusters: 1 Thwart. FP thruster (f)
Fuel: 482.0 (d.f.) 13.0pd

6872883 *UHXU* - **URAN** *ex TM-332 -1992* **Morskoy Standart Co Ltd** - *Petropavlovsk-Kamchatskiy* *Russia* Official number: 580419
245 78 276 Class: RS
1958-12 VEB Elbewerft — Boizenburg Yd No: 332
Loa 42.96 Br ex 7.32 Dght 3.210
Lbp 38.25 Br md 7.30 Dpth 3.48
Welded, 1 dk
(A13B2TU) Tanker (unspecified)
Liq: 208; Liq (Oil): 208
Compartments: 1 Ho, 5 Ta, ER
1 Ha: (1.6 x 1.2)
1 oil engine driving 1 FP propeller
Total Power: 224kW (305hp) 8.0kn
S.K.L. 8NVD36-1U
1 x 4 Stroke 8 Cy. 240 x 360 224kW (305bhp) (new engine 1967)
VEB Schwermaschinenbau "KarlLiebknecht" (SKL)-Magdeburg
AuxGen: 2 x 60kW a.c
Fuel: 45.0 (d.f.)

8133700 - - **URAN** **Sevastopol Port Authority** - *Sevastopol* *Ukraine* Official number: 821080
149 101 20 Class: (RS)
1982 Ilyichyovskiy Sudoremontnyy Zavod im. "50-letiya SSSR" — Ilyichyovsk Yd No: 18
Loa 28.70 Br ex 6.35 Dght 1.480
Lbp 27.00 Br md - Dpth 2.50
Welded, 1 dk
(A37B2PS) Passenger Ship
Passengers: unberthed: 250
2 oil engines driving 2 FP propellers
Total Power: 220kW (300hp) 10.4kn
Barnaultransmash 3D6C
2 x 4 Stroke 6 Cy. 150 x 180 each-110kW (150bhp)
Barnaultransmash-Barnaul
AuxGen: 2 x 1kW
Fuel: 2.0 (d.f.)

8727408 *UBXE2* - **URAN** **Real Estate Management Committee of St Petersburg City Executive Board** JSC 'Port Fleet Ltd' (ZAO 'Portovyy Flot') *St Petersburg* *Russia* MMSI: 273446880 Official number: 860935
279 81 89 Class: RS
1987-05 Brodogradiliste 'Tito' — Belgrade Yd No: 1116
Loa 35.78 Br ex 9.49 Dght 3.280
Lbp 30.23 Br md - Dpth 4.94
Welded, 1 dk
(B32A2ST) Tug
Ice Capable
2 oil engines driving 1 CP propeller
Total Power: 1,854kW (2,520hp) 13.5kn
Sulzer 6ASL25D
2 x 4 Stroke 6 Cy. 250 x 300 each-927kW (1260bhp) in Yugoslavia
AuxGen: 1 x 150kW a.c

9190482 *SPS2396* - **URAN** **Fairplay Polska Sp z oo & Co Sp k** *Swinoujscie* *Poland* MMSI: 261269000 Official number: ROS/S/549
313 93 Class: PR (LR) ✠Classed LR until 25/11/02
2001-09 PO SevMash Predpriyatiye — Severodvinsk (Hull)
2001-09 B.V. Scheepswerf Damen — Gorinchem Yd No: 511703
Loa 30.82 Br ex 10.20 Dght 3.760
Lbp 26.62 Br md 9.40 Dpth 4.80
Welded, 1 dk
(B32A2ST) Tug
2 oil engines with clutches & sr geared to sc. shafts driving 2 Directional propellers
Total Power: 3,370kW (4,582hp) 12.4kn
Caterpillar 3516B-TA
2 x Vee 4 Stroke 16 Cy. 170 x 190 each-1685kW (2291bhp)
Caterpillar Inc-USA
AuxGen: 2 x 85kW 230/400V 50Hz a.c
Fuel: 115.8 (d.f.)

9315422 *YL2526* - **URAN** **AS PKL Flote** *Riga* *Latvia* MMSI: 275305000 Official number: 0140
144 44 46 Class: RS (NV)
2004-11 Stocznia Polnocna SA (Northern Shipyard) — Gdansk Yd No: B840/2
Loa 19.10 Br ex - Dght 4.200
Lbp 17.73 Br md 9.00 Dpth 3.80
Welded, 1 dk
(B32A2ST) Tug
Ice Capable
2 oil engines geared to sc. shafts driving 2 Z propellers
Total Power: 2,100kW (2,856hp) 10.0kn
Caterpillar 3512B
2 x Vee 4 Stroke 12 Cy. 170 x 190 each-1050kW (1428bhp)
Caterpillar Inc-USA

9234941 *JG5586* - **URANAMI** **Government of Japan (Ministry of Land, Infrastructure & Transport) (The Coastguard)** *Tokyo* *Japan* MMSI: 431301458 Official number: 136737
116 - -
2000-01 Sumidagawa Zosen K.K. — Tokyo Yd No: N10-86
Loa 35.00 Br ex - Dght 1.250
Lbp 32.00 Br md 6.50 Dpth 3.43
Welded, 1 dk
(B34H2SQ) Patrol Vessel
2 oil engines reduction geared to sc. shafts driving 2 FP propellers
Total Power: 2,942kW (4,000hp) 24.0kn
Niigata 12V16FX
2 x Vee 4 Stroke 12 Cy. 165 x 185 each-1471kW (2000bhp)
Niigata Engineering Co Ltd-Japan

9027673 - - **URANGUL V** **PT Daya Guna Samudera** *Surabaya* *Indonesia*
161 73 - Class: (KI)
1991-01 P.T. Gresik Jaya Dockyard — Gresik
L reg 32.00 Br ex - Dght 2.490
Lbp 29.25 Br md 7.30 Dpth 3.05
Welded, 1 dk
(B11B2FV) Fishing Vessel
1 oil engine geared to sc. shaft driving 1 Propeller
Total Power: 268kW (364hp) 10.0kn
Cummins KT-19-M
1 x 4 Stroke 6 Cy. 159 x 159 268kW (364bhp)
Cummins Engine Co Ltd-United Kingdom

9027685 - - **URANGUL VI** **PT Daya Guna Samudera** - *Surabaya* *Indonesia*
161 73 - Class: (KI)
1991-01 P.T. Gresik Jaya Dockyard — Gresik
L reg 32.00 Br ex - Dght 2.490
Lbp 29.25 Br md 7.30 Dpth 3.05
Welded, 1 dk
(B11B2FV) Fishing Vessel
1 oil engine geared to sc. shaft driving 1 Propeller
Total Power: 268kW (364hp) 10.0kn
Cummins KT-19-M
1 x 4 Stroke 6 Cy. 159 x 159 268kW (364bhp)
Cummins Engine Co Ltd-United Kingdom

9027697 - - **URANGUL VII** **PT Daya Guna Samudera** - *Surabaya* *Indonesia*
161 73 - Class: (KI)
1991-01 P.T. Gresik Jaya Dockyard — Gresik
L reg 32.00 Br ex - Dght 2.490
Lbp 29.25 Br md 7.30 Dpth 3.05
Welded, 1 dk
(B11B2FV) Fishing Vessel
1 oil engine geared to sc. shaft driving 1 Propeller
Total Power: 268kW (364hp) 10.0kn
Cummins KT-19-M
1 x 4 Stroke 6 Cy. 159 x 159 268kW (364bhp)
Cummins Engine Co Ltd-United Kingdom

IMO / Call sign	Name / Owner / Manager / Flag	Tonnage	Class	Builder / Dimensions	Type	Machinery
9013220 *IQSU* -	**URANIA** **SOPROMAR SpA** - SatCom: Inmarsat C 424738920 *Naples* *Italy* MMSI: 247498000 Official number: 275	**1,115** 334 470	Class: RI	**1992**-07 **Cant. Nav. M. Morini & C. — Ancona** Yd No: 227 Loa 61.30 (BB) Br ex 12.00 Dght 3.761 Lbp 52.50 Br md 11.10 Dpth 4.75 Welded, 1 dk	**(B31A2SR) Research Survey Vessel**	**2 oil engines** sr geared to sc. shafts driving 2 CP propellers Total Power: 2,000kW (2,720hp) 11.0kn MaK 6M332AK 2 x 4 Stroke 6 Cy. 240 x 330 each-1000kW (1360bhp) Krupp MaK Maschinenbau GmbH-Kiel AuxGen: 3 x 330kW 380V 50Hz a.c Thrusters: 1 Thwart. CP thruster (f) Fuel: 252.0 (d.f.) 7.5pd
9177480 *9HA3244* -	**URANIA** *ex* Oneida Princess *-2012* *ex* Gebe Oldendorff *-2008* *ex* J. Captain Trader *-2002* **ms Urania Schiffahrtsgesellschaft mbH & Co KG** Orion Bulkers GmbH & Co KG *Valletta* *Malta* MMSI: 229335000 Official number: 9177480	**14,762** 8,447 24,247 T/cm 34.2	Class: NK (LR) (BV) Classed LR until 12/3/13	**1998**-07 **Tsuneishi Heavy Industries (Cebu) Inc — Balamban** Yd No: SC-005 Loa 154.38 (BB) Br ex - Dght 9.730 Lbp 146.13 Br md 26.00 Dpth 13.35 Welded, 1 dk	**(A21A2BC) Bulk Carrier** Grain: 30,811; Bale: 30,088 Compartments: 4 Ho, ER 4 Ha: (19.2 x 12.7)3 (20.0 x 17.5)ER Cranes: 4x30t	**1 oil engine** driving 1 FP propeller Total Power: 5,185kW (7,050hp) 14.1kn B&W 7S35MC 1 x 2 Stroke 7 Cy. 350 x 1400 5185kW (7050bhp) Mitsui Engineering & Shipbuilding CLtd-Japan AuxGen: 3 x 400kW 450V 60Hz a.c Boilers: AuxB (Comp) 7.0kgf/cm² (6.9bar) Fuel: 1130.0 (r.f.)
9117818 *3FZA2* -	**URANIA** *ex* Daesan Pioneer No. 2 *-2008* **Amalthia Shipping Co Inc** Eurotank Maritime Management SA *Panama* *Panama* MMSI: 370859000 Official number: 4090309A	**1,997** 1,132 3,481 T/cm 8.5	Class: RI (KR)	**1994**-02 **Han-Il Shipbuilding Co Ltd — Tongyeong** Yd No: 9302 Loa 86.20 (BB) Br ex - Dght 5.622 Lbp 78.61 Br md 14.00 Dpth 6.60 Welded, 1 dk	**(A12A2TC) Chemical Tanker** Liq: 4,148 Cargo Heating Coils Compartments: 8 Wing Ta, ER 10 Cargo Pump (s): 10x100m³/hr Manifold: Bow/CM: 40.9m	**1 oil engine** reduction geared to sc. shaft driving 1 FP propeller Total Power: 1,714kW (2,330hp) 13.0kn Alpha 7L28/32A 1 x 4 Stroke 7 Cy. 280 x 320 1714kW (2330bhp) Hyundai Heavy Industries Co Ltd-South Korea AuxGen: 3 x 200kW 445V a.c
9616125 *SHFT* -	**URANIBORG** **Ventrafiken AB** - *Landskrona* *Sweden* MMSI: 265698740 Official number: TSS2010-1463-060302	**1,151** 345 158	Class: BV	**2012**-11 **'Crist' SA — Gdansk** (Hull) **2012**-11 **A/S Hvide Sande Skibs- og Baadebyggeri — Hvide Sande** Yd No: 124 Loa 49.95 Br ex 12.32 Dght 2.850 Lbp 47.00 Br md 12.00 Dpth 4.40 Welded, 1 dk	**(A36A2PR) Passenger/Ro-Ro Ship (Vehicles)** Passengers: unberthed: 394 Bow door/ramp (centre) Stern door/ramp (centre) Cars: 14 Ice Capable	**2 oil engines** reduction geared to sc. shafts driving 2 Directional propellers Total Power: 1,418kW (1,928hp) 11.5kn Caterpillar C32 ACERT 2 x Vee 4 Stroke 12 Cy. 145 x 162 each-709kW (964bhp) Caterpillar Inc-USA AuxGen: 2 x 170kW 50Hz a.c Fuel: 26.0 (d.f.)
7810650 - -	**URANO No. 3** *ex* Kintoku Maru *-1990* *ex* Kintoku Maru No. 12 *-1989* *ex* Miyaura Maru No. 8 *-1986* **Noriyuki Sugimoto** Je Yang Co Ltd	*255* 125 222	Class: (KR)	**1978**-09 **Sanuki Shipbuilding & Iron Works Co Ltd — Mitoyo KG** Yd No: 1003 Loa 44.46 Br ex - Dght 2.789 Lbp 37.80 Br md 7.41 Dpth 3.08 Riveted\Welded, 1 dk	**(B11B2FV) Fishing Vessel**	**1 oil engine** driving 1 FP propeller Total Power: 552kW (750hp) Niigata 6M26ZG 1 x 4 Stroke 6 Cy. 260 x 400 552kW (750bhp) Niigata Engineering Co Ltd-Japan
5050593 *IKWZ* -	**URANO S** *ex* Brasile *-1985* **Societa Anonima Italiana Lavori Edili Marittimi SpA (SAILEM)** - *Palermo* *Italy* Official number: 1031	*167* 17 -	Class: (RI)	**1961 Cant. del Tirreno — Genova** Yd No: 251 Loa 28.96 Br ex 7.32 Dght 3.720 Lbp 26.17 Br md 7.27 Dpth 4.20 Riveted\Welded, 1 dk	**(B32A2ST) Tug**	**1 oil engine** driving 1 FP propeller Total Power: 769kW (1,046hp) 12.0kn B&W 8-28VF-50 1 x 2 Stroke 8 Cy. 280 x 500 769kW (1046bhp) Cantieri Navali Riuniti-Italy AuxGen: 1 x 30kW 110V d.c, 1 x 10kW 110V d.c
9163207 *V7MA7* -	**URANUS** *ex* Cap Van Diemen *-2009* *ex* Uranus *-2006* *ex* Alianca Antuerpia *-2002* *ex* Uranus *-2001* **Alpha Ship GmbH & Co KG ms 'Uranus'** Alpha Shipmanagement GmbH & Co KG *Majuro* *Marshall Islands* MMSI: 538090293 Official number: 90293	**23,722** 9,843 29,210 T/cm 45.1	Class: GL	**1999**-02 **Stocznia Gdynia SA — Gdynia** Yd No: 8138/8 Loa 194.06 (BB) Br ex - Dght 11.500 Lbp 180.20 Br md 28.20 Dpth 16.80 Welded, 1 dk	**(A33A2CC) Container Ship (Fully Cellular)** TEU 1835 C Ho 780 TEU C Dk 1055 TEU incl 325 ref C. Compartments: 4 Cell Ho, ER 9 Ha: (18.5 x 13.2)Tappered 8 (12.8 x 23.6)ER Cranes: 3x45t	**1 oil engine** driving 1 FP propeller Total Power: 17,200kW (23,385hp) 21.3kn B&W 6L70MC 1 x 2 Stroke 6 Cy. 700 x 2268 17200kW (23385bhp) H Cegielski Poznan SA-Poland AuxGen: 2 x 1184kW 440/220V 60Hz a.c, 1 x 884kW 440/220V 60Hz a.c Thrusters: 1 Thwart. FP thruster (f) Fuel: 220.0 (d.f.) 2740.0 (r.f.) 85.0pd
9053919 *V2AQ3* -	**URANUS** *ex* Lucy Borchard *-2005* *ex* Gracechurch Sun *-2002* *ex* Uranus *-1997* **Reederei Heinz Corleis GmbH & Co KG ms 'Uranus'** Reederei Heinz Corleis KG SatCom: Inmarsat C 430401091 *Saint John's* *Antigua & Barbuda* MMSI: 304010957	**5,025** 2,520 6,541	Class: GL	**1992**-05 **J.J. Sietas KG Schiffswerft GmbH & Co. — Hamburg** Yd No: 1030 Loa 116.79 (BB) Br ex 18.15 Dght 6.858 Lbp 108.00 Br md 17.90 Dpth 8.80 Welded, 1 dk	**(A33A2CC) Container Ship (Fully Cellular)** Grain: 8,349; Bale: 8,071 TEU 510 C Ho 162 TEU C Dk 348 TEU incl 50 ref C. Compartments: 3 Ho, ER 3 Ha: ER	**1 oil engine** with flexible couplings & sr geared to sc. shaft driving 1 CP propeller Total Power: 6,330kW (8,606hp) 16.0kn MAN 6L48/60 1 x 4 Stroke 6 Cy. 480 x 600 6330kW (8606bhp) MAN B&W Diesel AG-Augsburg AuxGen: 1 x 800kW 220/380V a.c, 2 x 200kW 220/380V a.c Thrusters: 1 Thwart. FP thruster (f) Fuel: 513.0 (d.f.)
9064255 *BP2066* -	**URANUS** *ex* Albatross *-2003* *ex* Polar Star *-2000* **Hwa Chyi Shipping Co** - *Keelung* *Chinese Taipei* Official number: 014265	**446** 150 46	Class: CR	**1993**-03 **Mitsui Eng. & SB. Co. Ltd. — Tamano** Yd No: TH1623 Loa 43.20 Br ex - Dght 1.400 Lbp 37.80 Br md 10.80 Dpth 3.50 Welded	**(A37B2PS) Passenger Ship** Hull Material: Aluminium Alloy Passengers: unberthed: 300	**2 oil engines** geared to sc. shafts driving 2 FP propellers Total Power: 5,296kW (7,200hp) 36.8kn Pielstick 16PA4V200VGA 2 x Vee 4 Stroke 16 Cy. 200 x 210 each-2648kW (3600bhp) Niigata Engineering Co Ltd-Japan
8833233 - -	**URANUS** **Terramare Oy** - *Helsinki* *Finland* MMSI: 230991140 Official number: 12032	**520** 160 1,300	Class: (BV)	**1977**-03 **IHC Verschure BV — Amsterdam** Yd No: 879 Loa 58.04 Br ex - Dght 3.250 Lbp 58.04 Br md 9.53 Dpth 3.34 Welded, 1 dk	**(B34A2SH) Hopper, Motor** Hopper: 660 Compartments: 1 Ho, ER	**2 oil engines** driving 2 FP propellers Total Power: 480kW (652hp) Caterpillar 3406T 2 x 4 Stroke 6 Cy. 137 x 165 each-240kW (326bhp) Caterpillar Tractor Co-USA AuxGen: 2 x 3kW 24V d.c
8750792 *YJTG9* -	**URANUS** *ex* D. R. Stewart *-2013* **GVC Drilling Srl** - *Port Vila* *Vanuatu* MMSI: 577152000 Official number: 2215	**6,634** 1,990 -	Class: AB	**1980**-10 **Marathon LeTourneau Offshore Pte Ltd — Singapore** Yd No: 149 Loa - Br ex 60.96 Dght 4.570 Lbp 74.09 Br md - Dpth 7.92 Welded, 1 dk	**(Z11C4ZD) Drilling Rig, jack up** Passengers: berths: 86 Cranes: 3x50t,1x30t	**3 oil engines** Total Power: 3,903kW (5,306hp) EMD (Electro-Motive) 12-645-E8 1 x Vee 2 Stroke 12 Cy. 230 x 254 1103kW (1500bhp) General Motors Corp-USA EMD (Electro-Motive) 16-645-E8 2 x Vee 2 Stroke 16 Cy. 230 x 254 each-1400kW (1903bhp) General Motors Corp-USA AuxGen: 3 x 1400kW a.c
9541801 *PP8393* -	**URANUS** **Saveiros Camuyrano - Servicos Maritimos SA** - *Rio de Janeiro* *Brazil* MMSI: 710004470 Official number: 3813873340	**250** 75 112	Class: LR ✠ **100A1** SS 11/2009 tug Brazilian coastal service **LMC** **UMS** Eq.Ltr: F; Cable: 275.0/19.0 U2 (a)	**2009**-11 **Wilson, Sons SA — Guaruja** (Hull) Yd No: 110 **2009**-11 **B.V. Scheepswerf Damen — Gorinchem** Yd No: 512242 Loa 24.55 (BB) Br ex 11.70 Dght 5.350 Lbp 20.80 Br md 10.70 Dpth 4.50 Welded, 1 dk	**(B32A2ST) Tug**	**2 oil engines** gearing integral to driving 2 Directional propellers Total Power: 3,634kW (4,940hp) Caterpillar 3516B 2 x Vee 4 Stroke 16 Cy. 170 x 190 each-1817kW (2470bhp) Caterpillar Inc-USA AuxGen: 2 x 55kW 440V 60Hz a.c
9398539 *D5CY7* -	**URANUS** **Harms Offshore AHT 'Uranus' GmbH & Co KG** Harms Bergung Transport & Heavylift GmbH & Co KG *Monrovia* *Liberia* MMSI: 636092459 Official number: 92459	**3,732** 1,118 3,587	Class: GL	**2009**-10 **Muetzelfeldtwerft GmbH — Cuxhaven** Yd No: 256 Loa 74.36 Br ex - Dght 8.250 Lbp 66.65 Br md 18.50 Dpth 9.50 Welded, 1 dk	**(B21B20A) Anchor Handling Tug Supply** A-frames: 1x250t Ice Capable	**4 oil engines** reduction geared to sc. shafts driving 2 CP propellers Total Power: 18,000kW (24,472hp) 17.0kn MaK 9M32C 4 x 4 Stroke 9 Cy. 320 x 480 each-4500kW (6118bhp) Caterpillar Motoren GmbH & Co. KG-Germany AuxGen: 2 x 2000kW 400/230V 50Hz a.c, 2 x 400/230V 50Hz a.c Thrusters: 2 Thwart. CP thruster (f); 1 Thwart. CP thruster (a) Fuel: 148.0 (d.f.) 3112.0 (r.f.)
8994714 *PMSE* -	**URANUS 7** *ex* Uranus *-2009* *ex* Jin An 33 *-2005* *ex* Hailu 33 *-2005* **PT Foong Sun Shipping Indonesia** Foong Sun Shipping (Pte) Ltd *Jakarta* *Indonesia* MMSI: 525015433	**1,058** 686 1,778	Class: KI	**1984**-01 **Fu'an Far East Shipyard — Fu'an FJ** Yd No: JA8402 Loa 72.88 Br ex - Dght 4.200 Lbp 68.00 Br md 10.00 Dpth 5.40 Welded, 1 dk	**(A31A2GX) General Cargo Ship**	**1 oil engine** driving 1 Propeller Total Power: 735kW (999hp) Niigata 1 x 4 Stroke 735kW (999bhp) Niigata Engineering Co Ltd-Japan AuxGen: 1 x 140kW 225/130V a.c, 1 x 58kW 225/130V a.c

7927130 URANUS GAS
DSNG7
- **Duckyang Shipping Co Ltd**
-
Busan *South Korea*
MMSI: 441340000
Official number: BSR-039327

2,686 Class: KR (NK)
805
3,063
T/cm
11.1

1979-12 Kishigami Zosen K.K. — Akitsu
Yd No: 1340
Loa 93.44 (BB) Br ex 14.43 Dght 5.265
Lbp 87.03 Br md 14.40 Dpth 6.50
Welded, 1 dk

(A11B2TG) LPG Tanker
Double Hull
Liq (Gas): 2,510
2 x Gas Tank (s); 2 membrane (C.mn.stl) cyl horizontal
2 Cargo Pump (s): 2x150m³/hr
Manifold: Bow/CM: 41m

1 oil engine driving 1 FP propeller
Total Power: 2,354kW (3,200hp) 13.3kn
Akasaka DM46
1 x 4 Stroke 6 Cy. 460 x 720 2354kW (3200bhp)
Akasaka Tekkosho KK (Akasaka DieselLtd)-Japan
AuxGen: 2 x 176kW 445V a.c
Fuel: 93.0 (d.f.) (Heating Coils) 291.0 (r.f.)

9646297 URATA MARU
JD3122
- **Naikai Eisen KK**
-
Kobe, Hyogo *Japan*
MMSI: 431002066
Official number: 141336

206
-
-

2010-10 Keihin Dock Co Ltd — Yokohama
Yd No: 295
Loa 34.50 Br ex - Dght 2.990
Lbp 30.00 Br md 8.90 Dpth 4.00
Welded, 1 dk

(B32A2ST) Tug

2 oil engines reduction geared to sc. shafts driving 2 Z propellers
Total Power: 3,676kW (4,998hp) 14.7kn
Niigata 6L28HX
2 x 4 Stroke 6 Cy. 280 x 370 each-1838kW (2499bhp)
Niigata Engineering Co Ltd-Japan

9157351 URAWEE NAREE
HSB3319
ex J. Peace *-2005* *ex* Ocean Palm *-2002*
Precious Garnets Ltd
Great Circle Shipping Agency Ltd
Bangkok *Thailand*
MMSI: 567311000
Official number: 480003008

16,766 Class: NK
10,452
28,415

1997-04 Imabari Shipbuilding Co Ltd — Marugame KG (Marugame Shipyard)
Yd No: 1273
Loa 169.03 (BB) Br ex - Dght 9.760
Lbp 160.40 Br md 27.20 Dpth 13.60
Welded, 1 dk

(A21A2BC) Bulk Carrier
Grain: 37,523; Bale: 35,762
Compartments: 5 Ho, ER
5 Ha: (13.6 x 16.0)4 (19.2 x 17.6)ER
Cranes: 4x30.5t

1 oil engine driving 1 FP propeller
Total Power: 5,737kW (7,800hp) 13.9kn
B&W 5S50MC
1 x 2 Stroke 5 Cy. 500 x 1910 5737kW (7800bhp)
Hitachi Zosen Corp-Japan
Fuel: 1240.0

7856654 URAYUKI
JG3502
- **Government of Japan (Ministry of Land, Infrastructure & Transport) (The Coastguard)**
-
Tokyo *Japan*
MMSI: 431100014
Official number: 117703

123
-
-

1975-05 Mitsubishi Heavy Industries Ltd. — Shimonoseki Yd No: 756
Loa 26.00 Br ex 6.30 Dght 1.130
Lbp 24.50 Br md 6.29 Dpth 3.04
Welded, 1 dk

(B34H2SQ) Patrol Vessel
Hull Material: Aluminium Alloy

3 oil engines driving 3 FP propellers
Total Power: 2,208kW (3,003hp) 22.0kn
Mitsubishi 12DM20TK
3 x Vee 4 Stroke 12 Cy. 160 x 200 each-736kW (1001bhp)
Mitsubishi Heavy Industries Ltd-Japan
Fuel: 5.0 (d.f.)

8925220 URAZUKI
JG5466
ex Wakagumo *-2012*
Government of Japan (Ministry of Land, Infrastructure & Transport) (The Coastguard)
-
Tokyo *Japan*
Official number: 135827

101
-
-

1996-07 Ishihara Zosen — Takasago
Loa 33.00 Br ex - Dght 1.600
Lbp 30.50 Br md 6.30 Dpth 3.20
Welded, 1 dk

(B34H2SQ) Patrol Vessel

2 oil engines geared to sc. shafts driving 2 FP propellers
Total Power: 3,898kW (5,300hp) 30.0kn
M.T.U. 16V396TB94
2 x Vee 4 Stroke 16 Cy. 165 x 185 each-1949kW (2650bhp)
MTU Friedrichshafen GmbH-Friedrichshafen

8617615 URBAN SUCCESS
9WCX6
ex Penrider *-2011* *ex* Fukue Maru *-2000*
Urban Success Marine Sdn Bhd
-
Penang *Malaysia*
MMSI: 533651000
Official number: 328137

740
341
1,259

1987-02 Kurinoura Dockyard Co Ltd — Yawatahama EH Yd No: 233
Loa 59.67 Br ex 11.03 Dght 3.977
Lbp 54.62 Br md 11.00 Dpth 4.53
Welded, 1 dk

(A13B2TP) Products Tanker
Liq: 1,297; Liq (Oil): 1,297
Compartments: 10 Ta, ER

1 oil engine with clutches & reduction geared to sc. shaft driving 1 CP propeller
Total Power: 1,030kW (1,400hp)
Akasaka K28FD
1 x 4 Stroke 6 Cy. 280 x 480 1030kW (1400bhp)
Akasaka Tekkosho KK (Akasaka DieselLtd)-Japan

7826855 URD
OUYL2
ex Aktiv Marine *-1991* *ex* Boyana *-1990*
ex Seafreight Highway *-1989*
ex Easy Rider *-1985*
Stena Line Baltic A/S
-
Kalundborg *Denmark (DIS)*
MMSI: 219000776
Official number: A444

13,144 Class: LR (BV)
3,943 ✠**100A1** SS 12/2011
4,562 roro cargo and passenger ship
Ice Class 1C
LMC **UMS**

1981-06 Nuovi Cantieri Apuania SpA — Carrara
Yd No: 2119
Loa 171.05 (BB) Br ex 20.82 Dght 5.190
Lbp 155.75 Br md 20.21 Dpth 6.90
Welded, 2 dks

(A36A2PR) Passenger/Ro-Ro Ship (Vehicles)
Passengers: unberthed: 66; cabins: 49; berths: 120
Stern door/ramp (centre)
Len: 13.10 Wid: 12.30 Swl: -
Side door/ramp (s)
Lane-Len: 1598
Trailers: 69
Ice Capable

2 oil engines with clutches, flexible couplings & sr geared to sc. shafts driving 2 CP propellers
Total Power: 8,826kW (12,000hp) 17.5kn
Wartsila 12V32D
2 x Vee 4 Stroke 12 Cy. 320 x 350 each-4413kW (6000bhp) (new engine 1988)
Wartsila Diesel Oy-Finland
AuxGen: 3 x 700kW 220/450V 60Hz a.c
Thrusters: 3 Thwart. CP thruster (f)
Fuel: 183.0 (d.f.) 458.0 (r.f.) 42.0pd

7912111 URDANETA
YYT3498
- **Petroleos de Venezuela SA (PDVSA)**
-
Maracaibo *Venezuela*
Official number: AJZL - 10.810

149
48
-

1981-02 Tricomar C.A. — Maracaibo Yd No: 049
Loa - Br ex - Dght -
Lbp 22.41 Br md 7.95 Dpth 2.70
Welded, 1 dk

(B32A2ST) Tug

2 oil engines driving 2 FP propellers
Total Power: 1,288kW (1,752hp)

9404699 URDANETA TIDE
YJTD9
ex F. D. Irressistible *-2013*
Aqua Fleet Ltd
Tidewater Inc
Port Vila *Vanuatu*
MMSI: 577128000
Official number: 2190

2,305 Class: NV (RI)
848
3,105

2008-04 Cant. Nav. Rosetti — Ravenna Yd No: 89
Loa 72.00 Br ex - Dght 5.900
Lbp 66.80 Br md 16.00 Dpth 7.00
Welded, 1 dk

(B21A20S) Platform Supply Ship

2 oil engines reduction geared to sc. shafts driving 2 CP propellers
Total Power: 5,576kW (7,582hp) 14.0kn
GE Marine 16V228
2 x Vee 4 Stroke 16 Cy. 229 x 267 each-2788kW (3791bhp)
GE Marine Engines-Cincinnati, Oh
AuxGen: 2 x 300kW a.c, 2 x 1800kW a.c
Thrusters: 2 Tunnel thruster (f); 2 Tunnel thruster (a)

7800497 URECA XIII
-
ex Rusland *-2012* *ex* Smit Rusland *-2012*
Somagec Guinea Ecuatorial
SOMAGEC (Soc Marocaine de Genie Civil)
Malabo *Equatorial Guinea*

196 Class: BV
58
-

1979-07 BV Scheepswerf & Mfbk 'De Merwede' v/h van Vliet & Co — Hardinxveld
Yd No: 623
Loa 28.43 Br ex - Dght 3.310
Lbp 25.53 Br md 8.50 Dpth 3.38
Welded, 1 dk

(B32A2ST) Tug

2 oil engines reverse reduction geared to sc. shafts driving 2 CP propellers
Total Power: 1,398kW (1,900hp) 12.6kn
Kromhout 6F240
2 x 4 Stroke 6 Cy. 240 x 260 each-699kW (950bhp)
Stork Werkspoor Diesel BV-Netherlands
AuxGen: 3 x 37kW 380V a.c
Fuel: 161.5

7800461 UREKA XII
-
ex Zweden *-2012* *ex* Smit Zweden *-2012*
Somagec Guinea Ecuatorial
SOMAGEC (Soc Marocaine de Genie Civil)
Papua New Guinea

196 Class: BV
58
-

1979-02 BV Scheepswerf & Mfbk 'De Merwede' v/h van Vliet & Co — Hardinxveld
Yd No: 620
Loa 28.43 Br ex - Dght 3.310
Lbp 25.53 Br md 8.50 Dpth 3.38
Welded, 1 dk

(B32A2ST) Tug

2 oil engines reverse reduction geared to sc. shafts driving 2 CP propellers
Total Power: 1,398kW (1,900hp) 12.5kn
Kromhout 6F240
2 x 4 Stroke 6 Cy. 240 x 260 each-699kW (950bhp)
Stork Werkspoor Diesel BV-Netherlands
Fuel: 161.5

7800473 UREKA XIV
-
ex Finland *-2013* *ex* Smit Finland *-2012*
Somagec Guinea Ecuatorial
SOMAGEC (Soc Marocaine de Genie Civil)
Malabo *Equatorial Guinea*

196 Class: BV
58
-

1979-05 BV Scheepswerf & Mfbk 'De Merwede' v/h van Vliet & Co — Hardinxveld
Yd No: 621
Loa 28.43 Br ex - Dght 3.310
Lbp 25.53 Br md 8.50 Dpth 3.38
Welded, 1 dk

(B32A2ST) Tug

2 oil engines reverse reduction geared to sc. shafts driving 2 CP propellers
Total Power: 1,398kW (1,900hp) 12.5kn
Kromhout 6F240
2 x 4 Stroke 6 Cy. 240 x 260 each-699kW (950bhp)
Stork Werkspoor Diesel BV-Netherlands
Fuel: 161.5

8820482 UREYANA
PNFB
ex Sumiwaka Maru No. 11 *-2012*
PT Karsa Utama Line
-
Tanjung Priok *Indonesia*

941 Class: KI
318
1,761

1989-03 Kurinoura Dockyard Co Ltd — Yawatahama EH Yd No: 261
Loa 59.99 Br ex 12.82 Dght 4.550
Lbp 54.70 Br md 12.80 Dpth 6.40
Welded, 2 dks

(B33A2DG) Grab Dredger
Grain: 975
Compartments: 1 Ho, ER
1 Ha: ER

1 oil engine driving 1 FP propeller
Total Power: 736kW (1,001hp)
Niigata 6M30GT
1 x 4 Stroke 6 Cy. 300 x 530 736kW (1001bhp) (made 1988)
Niigata Engineering Co Ltd-Japan
AuxGen: 2 x 110kW 225V a.c, 1 x 40kW 225V a.c

9090292 URFALI CEMAL
TC9853
- **Harran Denizcilik Turz Sanayi Ticaret Ltd Sti**
S S Turizm ve Yolcu Deniz Tasiyicilar Kooperatifi (TURYOL)
Istanbul *Turkey*
Official number: 1419147

298
89
-

2000-06 Yilmaz Gemi Tersanesi — Karadeniz Eregli
Loa 40.30 Br ex - Dght 1.600
Lbp - Br md 8.50 Dpth 2.60
Welded, 1 dk

(A37B2PS) Passenger Ship

2 oil engines driving 2 Propellers
Total Power: 736kW (1,000hp) 14.0kn
Iveco Aifo
2 x 4 Stroke each-368kW (500bhp)
IVECO AIFO S.p.A.-Pregnana Milanese

8727288 URGA
YLKL
ex MRTK-1103 *-1986*
Vergi Ltd
-
Riga *Latvia*
MMSI: 275200000
Official number: 0786

112 Class: (RS)
33
30

1986-06 Sosnovskiy Sudostroitelnyy Zavod — Sosnovka Yd No: 697
Loa 25.45 Br ex 7.00 Dght 2.390
Lbp 22.00 Br md 6.80 Dpth 3.30
Welded, 1 dk

(B11A2FS) Stern Trawler
Ice Capable

1 oil engine driving 1 FP propeller
Total Power: 221kW (300hp) 9.5kn
S.K.L. 6NVD26A-3
1 x 4 Stroke 6 Cy. 180 x 260 221kW (300bhp)
VEB Schwermaschinenbau "KarlLiebknecht" (SKL)-Magdeburg

No. / Call sign	Name / Owner	Tonnage	Class	Builder / Dimensions	Type	Machinery
9541863 *UBJF6* -	**URGAL** - **Daltransugol Ltd (OOO 'Daltransugol')** - *Vanino* *Russia* MMSI: 273332910	**451** 347 136	Class: RS	**2008-11 OAO Leningradskiy Sudostroitelnyy Zavod 'Pella' — Otradnoye** Yd No: 609 Loa 28.50 Br ex 9.50 Dght 3.500 Lbp 26.50 Br md 9.28 Dpth 4.80 Welded, 1 dk	**(B32B2SP) Pusher Tug**	**2 oil engines** reduction geared to sc. shafts driving 2 Directional propellers Total Power: 2,982kW (4,054hp) 12.0kn Caterpillar 3516B-TA 2 x Vee 4 Stroke 16 Cy. 170 x 190 each-1491kW (2027bhp) Caterpillar Inc-USA Fuel: 82.0 (d.f.)
8411750 *EDJI* -	**URGOZO** - **Compania de Remolcadores Ibaizabal SA** - *Bilbao* *Spain* Official number: 5-12/1992	**170** 109 315		**1984-12 S.L. Ardeag — Bilbao** Yd No: 138 Loa 29.72 Br ex - Dght - Lbp 28.02 Br md 6.61 Dpth 3.31 Welded, 1 dk	**(A14A2LO) Water Tanker** Liq: 350 Compartments: 8 Ta, ER	**1 oil engine** geared to sc. shaft driving 1 FP propeller Total Power: 246kW (334hp) 6.0kn Caterpillar 3406T 1 x 4 Stroke 6 Cy. 137 x 165 246kW (334bhp) Caterpillar Tractor Co-USA
8810190 *HQWX4* -	**URGULL** *ex Orizon -2006 ex Hawk I -2005* *ex Orizon -1999 ex 21 Oktoobar II -1997* *launched as 21 Oktoobar Seconda -1989* **Urgora S de RL** - *San Lorenzo* *Honduras* MMSI: 334533000 Official number: L-2638197	**3,351** 1,005 3,202	Class: (BV) (RI)	**1989-07 Soc. Esercizio Cant. S.p.A. — Viareggio** Yd No: 791 Loa 98.80 (BB) Br ex 15.40 Dght 5.600 Lbp 90.31 Br md - Dpth 8.51 Welded	**(A34A2GR) Refrigerated Cargo Ship** Passengers: berths: 12 Ins: 3,000 Compartments: 4 Ho, ER 4 Ha: (3.8 x 3.7)3 (7.7 x 6.2)ER Cranes: 3x5t	**1 oil engine** geared to sc. shaft driving 1 FP propeller Total Power: 3,375kW (4,589hp) 15.5kn Wartsila 9R32D 1 x 4 Stroke 9 Cy. 320 x 350 3375kW (4589bhp) Wartsila Diesel Oy-Finland AuxGen: 2 x 834kW 380V 50Hz a.c
7347615 *OHMS* -	**URHO** - **Arctia Icebreaking Oy** - *Helsinki* *Finland* MMSI: 230290000 Official number: 10259	**7,525** 2,258 2,570		**1975-03 Oy Wartsila Ab — Helsinki** Yd No: 401 Loa 104.60 Br ex 23.80 Dght 8.300 Lbp 96.02 Br md 22.51 Dpth 12.12 Welded, 2 dks	**(B34C2SI) Icebreaker** Ice Capable	**5 diesel electric oil engines** driving 5 gen. Connecting to 4 elec. motors driving 2 CP propellers , 2 fwd Total Power: 17,100kW (23,250hp) 18.5kn Pielstick 12PC2-5V-400 5 x Vee 4 Stroke 12 Cy. 400 x 460 each-3420kW (4650bhp) Oy Wartsila Ab-Finland
8030685 *WRB5841* -	**URIC TIDE** - **Jackson Marine LLC** Tidewater Marine LLC *Morgan City, LA* *United States of America* Official number: 653839	**686** 205 1,200	Class: AB	**1982-12 Halter Marine, Inc. — Moss Point, Ms** Yd No: 1021 Loa - Br ex - Dght 3.664 Lbp 54.87 Br md 12.20 Dpth 4.27 Welded, 1 dk	**(B21A20S) Platform Supply Ship**	**2 oil engines** reverse reduction geared to sc. shafts driving 2 FP propellers Total Power: 1,838kW (2,498hp) 12.0kn Caterpillar D399SCAC 2 x Vee 4 Stroke 16 Cy. 159 x 203 each-919kW (1249bhp) Caterpillar Tractor Co-USA AuxGen: 2 x 135kW Thrusters: 1 Thwart. FP thruster (f)
7314541 - -	**URIEL** *ex Atlanti Kaei No. 25 -1998* *ex Kaei Maru No. 25 -1986* - -	*254* 127 -	Class: (KR)	**1973 Uchida Zosen — Ise** Yd No: 727 Loa - Br ex 8.03 Dght - Lbp 49.66 Br md 8.01 Dpth 3.46 Riveted\Welded, 1 dk	**(B11B2FV) Fishing Vessel**	**1 oil engine** driving 1 FP propeller Total Power: 736kW (1,001hp) Niigata 6L28X 1 x 4 Stroke 6 Cy. 280 x 440 736kW (1001bhp) Niigata Engineering Co Ltd-Japan AuxGen: 2 x 200kW 225V a.c
9141948 *JM6448* -	**URIZUN** - **Corporation for Advanced Transport & Technology & Kagoshima Niyaku Kairiku Unyu Co Ltd** Kagoshima Niyaku Kairiku Unyu Co Ltd *Kagoshima, Kagoshima* *Japan* MMSI: 431600613 Official number: 135420	*1,596* - 1,800	Class: NK	**1996-09 Honda Zosen — Saiki** Yd No: 885 Loa 110.03 Br ex - Dght 4.726 Lbp 102.00 Br md 17.20 Dpth 7.10 Welded, 1 dk	**(A31A2GX) General Cargo Ship** 1 Ha: (12.6 x 5.0)ER Cranes: 1x30t	**1 oil engine** reduction geared to sc. shaft driving 1 FP propeller Total Power: 5,958kW (8,100hp) 19.0kn Pielstick 12PC2-6V-400 1 x Vee 4 Stroke 12 Cy. 400 x 460 5958kW (8100bhp) Nippon Kokan KK (NKK Corp)-Japan Fuel: 280.0 (r.f.)
9665906 *JD3529* -	**URIZUN** - **Kaniyaku** - *Kagoshima, Kagoshima* *Japan* MMSI: 431004469 Official number: 141938	**1,561** - 2,482	Class: NK	**2013-04 Yamanishi Corp — Ishinomaki MG** Yd No: 1091 Loa 109.00 Br ex - Dght 4.920 Lbp 101.90 Br md 14.80 Dpth 4.95 Welded, 1 dk	**(A31A2GX) General Cargo Ship** Bale: 4,524 TEU 203 incl 60 ref C	**1 oil engine** driving 1 Propeller Total Power: 5,600kW (7,614hp) MAN-B&W 8S35MC 1 x 2 Stroke 8 Cy. 350 x 1400 5600kW (7614bhp) Fuel: 319.0
9221255 *JM6569* -	**URIZUN 21** - **Kagoshima Niyaku Kairiku Unyu Co Ltd** - *Kagoshima, Kagoshima* *Japan* MMSI: 431601973 Official number: 136418	*4,252* - 3,294	Class: NK	**2000-05 Yamanishi Corp — Ishinomaki MG** Yd No: 1021 Loa 132.16 (BB) Br ex - Dght 5.714 Lbp 120.00 Br md 20.00 Dpth 9.40 Welded	**(A35A2RR) Ro-Ro Cargo Ship** Quarter stern door/ramp (p) Len: 25.00 Wid: 7.00 Swl: - Lane-Len: 396 Cars: 41, Trailers: 33 Bale: 12,836 TEU 94 C. Dk. 94 TEU Cranes: 2x30t	**1 oil engine** reduction geared to sc. shaft driving 1 CP propeller Total Power: 9,929kW (13,499hp) 20.5kn Pielstick 18PC2-6V-400 1 x Vee 4 Stroke 18 Cy. 400 x 460 9929kW (13499bhp) Nippon Kokan KK (NKK Corp)-Japan AuxGen: 2 x 800kW a.c Thrusters: 1 Thwart. CP thruster (f) Fuel: 460.0 (r.f.) 39.6pd
5374250 *EHRU* -	**URKO** - **Cipriano Ojeda Perez** - *Bilbao* *Spain* Official number: 3-1704/	*143* 63 -		**1944 Cia Euskalduna de Construccion y Reparacion de Buques SA — Bilbao** L reg 26.22 Br ex 5.08 Dght - Lbp - Br md - Dpth - Welded	**(B11B2FV) Fishing Vessel**	**1 oil engine** driving 1 FP propeller Total Power: 306kW (416hp) 11.8kn B&W 6-24VF-37 1 x 2 Stroke 6 Cy. 240 x 370 306kW (416bhp) La Maquinista Terrestre y Mar (MTM)-Spain
8842583 *ERQP* -	**URLA** *ex Dolphin -2013 ex Dnepr-4 -2012* **Dupe Shipping Inc** Troy Denizcilik Turizm Ltd Sti (Troy Shipping & Tourism Co Ltd) *Giurgiulesti* *Moldova* MMSI: 214181716	**2,980** 906 3,332 T/cm 12.0	Class: BR (RS) (RR)	**1991-03 Slovenske Lodenice a.s. — Komarno** Yd No: 2338 Loa 116.03 Br ex 13.43 Dght 4.130 Lbp 111.20 Br md 13.00 Dpth 6.00 Welded, 1 dk	**(A31A2GX) General Cargo Ship** Grain: 4,064 TEU 102 C.Ho 62/20' (40') C.Dk 40/20' (40') Compartments: 3 Ho, ER 3 Ha: (11.6 x 10.1) (23.0 x 10.1) (24.0 x 10.1)ER	**2 oil engines** sr geared to sc. shafts driving 2 FP propellers Total Power: 1,030kW (1,400hp) 10.0kn Skoda 6L275A2 2 x 4 Stroke 6 Cy. 275 x 350 each-515kW (700bhp) CKD Praha-Praha AuxGen: 3 x 138kW a.c Thrusters: 1 Thwart. FP thruster (f) Fuel: 160.0 (d.f.) 7.5pd
9490430 *TCBX7* -	**URLA 1** *ex Sanghrajka 2 -2009* **Yapi Kredi Finansal Kiralama AO (Yapi Kredi Leasing AO)** Arkas Petrol Urunleri ve Ticaret AS (Arkas Bunkering & Trading SA) *Izmir* *Turkey* MMSI: 271040189 Official number: 5004	*934* 668 1,450	Class: BV	**2009-02 Modest Infrastructure Ltd — Bhavnagar** Yd No: 306 Loa 63.60 Br ex 12.02 Dght 4.000 Lbp 60.15 Br md 12.00 Dpth 5.80 Welded, 1 dk	**(A13B2TP) Products Tanker** Double Hull (13F) Liq: 1,403; Liq (Oil): 1,403 Compartments: 12 Wing Ta, ER	**2 oil engines** reduction geared to sc. shafts driving 2 FP propellers Total Power: 746kW (1,014hp) 10.0kn Cummins KTA-19-M3 2 x 4 Stroke 6 Cy. 159 x 159 each-373kW (507bhp) Cummins India Ltd-India AuxGen: 2 x 200kW 50Hz a.c Thrusters: 1 Tunnel thruster (f)
8023759 - -	**URMILA** - **Government of The People's Republic of Bangladesh (Ministry of Food)** - *Bangladesh*	*215* - 400		**1985-08 Highspeed Shipbuilding & Heavy Engineering Co Ltd — Dhaka** Yd No: 87 Loa - Br ex - Dght - Lbp 48.01 Br md 7.82 Dpth 2.52 Welded	**(A31A2GX) General Cargo Ship**	**1 oil engine** geared to sc. shaft driving 1 FP propeller Total Power: 287kW (390hp) Deutz SBA6M816 1 x 4 Stroke 6 Cy. 142 x 160 287kW (390bhp) Kloeckner Humboldt Deutz AG-West Germany
8314782 *YHRJ* -	**URMILA** *ex Alpheos -2003 ex Jackie -1987* **PT Apol Lestari** PT Arpeni Pratama Ocean Line Tbk *Jakarta* *Indonesia* MMSI: 525011060 Official number: 1536/PST	**35,119** 20,988 63,610 T/cm 63.0	Class: RI (AB)	**1984-10 Hitachi Zosen Corp — Onomichi HS (Innoshima Shipyard)** Yd No: 4756 Loa 224.52 (BB) Br ex 32.26 Dght 12.850 Lbp 215.02 Br md 32.20 Dpth 17.80 Welded, 1 dk	**(A21A2BC) Bulk Carrier** Grain: 82,926; Bale: 72,891 Compartments: 7 Ho, ER 7 Ha: (15.4 x 13.2)6 (15.2 x 13.2)ER Cranes: 4x25t	**1 oil engine** driving 1 FP propeller Total Power: 9,929kW (13,499hp) 14.0kn Sulzer 6RND76M 1 x 2 Stroke 6 Cy. 760 x 1550 9929kW (13499bhp) Hitachi Zosen Corp-Japan AuxGen: 3 x 600kW 450V 60Hz a.c
9312248 *ECGX* 3-BI-44-04	**URONDO** - **Urondo SA** - *Ondarroa* *Spain* MMSI: 224280000 Official number: 3-4/2004	**387** 116 135	Class: (BV)	**2004-12 Hijos de J. Barreras S.A. — Vigo** Yd No: 1632 Loa 39.00 Br ex - Dght 3.250 Lbp 30.60 Br md 8.80 Dpth 3.80 Welded, 1 dk	**(B11A2FS) Stern Trawler**	**1 oil engine** geared to sc. shaft driving 1 CP propeller Total Power: 1,040kW (1,414hp) Wartsila 6L20 1 x 4 Stroke 6 Cy. 200 x 280 1040kW (1414bhp) Wartsila Diesel S.A.-Bermeo

IMO / Call sign	Name / Owner	Tonnage	Class	Builder / Dimensions	Type	Machinery
6823193 *H03892* -	**URPECO DOS** *ex* Ugerri *-2005* *ex* Quo Vadis *-2000* **Sant Yago Tuna Fisheries NV** Jealsa Rianxeira SA *Panama* *Panama* Official number: 33129PEXT	**183** 54 -	Class: (BV)	**1968 Scheepswerf Ton Bodewes N.V. — Franeker** Yd No: F31 Converted From: Stern Trawler-1992 Lengthened-1973 Loa 32.75 Br ex 6.66 Dght 2.550 Lbp 29.27 Br md 6.58 Dpth 3.15 Welded, 1 dk	**(B21A20S) Platform Supply Ship**	**1 oil engine** driving 1 FP propeller Total Power: 772kW (1,050hp) Stork 1 x 772kW (1050bhp) (new engine 1981) Stork Werkspoor Diesel BV-Netherlands
6712643 *H04261* -	**URPECO UNO** *ex* Men Brial *-1995* *ex* Brakna *-1969* **Sant Yago Tuna Fisheries NV** Jealsa Rianxeira SA *Panama* *Panama* Official number: 3474009	**253** 76 122	Class: BV	**1967 Soc Industrielle et Commerciale de Consts Navales (SICCNa) — St-Malo** Yd No: 89 Loa 33.23 Br ex 7.93 Dght - Lbp 28.20 Br md 7.70 Dpth 5.95 Welded, 2 dks	**(B11A2FS) Stern Trawler** Ins: 163 Compartments: 1 Ho, ER 2 Ha: 2 (1.3 x 1.3)ER	**1 oil engine** reverse reduction geared to sc. shaft driving 1 FP propeller Total Power: 736kW (1,001hp) 11.5kn MGO 16V175BSHR 1 x Vee 4 Stroke 16 Cy. 175 x 180 736kW (1001bhp) (new engine 1972) Societe Alsacienne de ConstructionsMecaniques (SACM)-France AuxGen: 2 x 78kW 110/220V a.c, 1 x 30kW 110/220V a.c Fuel: 73.5 (d.f.)
7301049 - -	**URSA MAJOR** - -	**188** 56 -		**1973-03 Holland Launch N.V. — Zaandam** Yd No: 513 Loa 32.24 Br ex 7.40 Dght 3.099 Lbp 28.66 Br md 7.32 Dpth 3.61 Welded, 1 dk	**(B11A2FT) Trawler**	**1 oil engine** driving 1 FP propeller Total Power: 747kW (1,016hp) Kromhout 9F/SW240 1 x 4 Stroke 9 Cy. 240 x 260 747kW (1016bhp) Stork Werkspoor Diesel BV-Netherlands
9217589 *ICGI* -	**URSA MAJOR** **Ilva Servizi Marittimi SpA** - SatCom: Inmarsat C 424700397 *Genoa* *Italy* MMSI: 247061700 Official number: 113	**1,855** 556 1,100	Class: RI	**2001-11 Jiangsu Jiangyang Shipyard Group Co Ltd — Yangzhou JS** Yd No: CTC99180-PT1 Loa 48.00 Br ex - Dght 5.700 Lbp 44.40 Br md 18.00 Dpth 7.50 Welded, 1 dk	**(B32B2SP) Pusher Tug**	**2 oil engines** geared to sc. shafts driving 2 CP propellers Total Power: 13,120kW (17,838hp) Wartsila 16V32 2 x Vee 4 Stroke 16 Cy. 320 x 350 each-6560kW (8919bhp) Wartsila Finland Oy-Finland AuxGen: 2 x 800kW 400/230V 50Hz a.c
9217591 *ICGH* -	**URSA MINOR** *ex* Merak *-2004* **Ilva Servizi Marittimi SpA** - SatCom: Inmarsat C 424700487 *Genoa* *Italy* MMSI: 247082300 Official number: 104	**1,855** 556 1,100	Class: RI	**2003-03 Jiangsu Jiangyang Shipyard Group Co Ltd — Yangzhou JS** Yd No: CTC99180-PT2 Loa 48.00 Br ex - Dght 5.700 Lbp 44.40 Br md 18.00 Dpth 7.50 Welded, 1 dk	**(B32B2SA) Articulated Pusher Tug**	**2 oil engines** geared to sc. shafts driving 2 CP propellers Total Power: 13,120kW (17,838hp) Wartsila 16V32 2 x Vee 4 Stroke 16 Cy. 320 x 350 each-6560kW (8919bhp) Wartsila Finland Oy-Finland
7922348 *PICU* UK 37	**URSA MINOR** *ex* Helena Elizabeth *-2004* **J Romkes en Co CV** - *Urk* *Netherlands* MMSI: 245325000 Official number: 1836	**336** 101 -		**1980-05 Barkmeijer Stroobos B.V. — Stroobos** Yd No: 214 Loa 35.34 Br ex 7.60 Dght 2.899 Lbp 29.95 Br md 7.51 Dpth 3.92 Welded, 1 dk	**(B11B2FV) Fishing Vessel**	**1 oil engine** geared to sc. shaft driving 1 FP propeller Total Power: 1,052kW (1,430hp) Caterpillar 3516TA 1 x Vee 4 Stroke 16 Cy. 170 x 190 1052kW (1430bhp) Caterpillar Tractor Co-USA
7201897 *WYZ3785* -	**URSALA M** *ex* Quest *-1979* *ex* E. F. Henley *-1977* *ex* Smart Aleck *-1974* *ex* Hatteras I *-1974* **Kenneth Miller** - *Boston, MA* *United States of America* Official number: 525650	*123* 87 -		**1970 Hatteras Yachts, Inc. — New Bern, NC** L reg 19.73 Br ex - Dght - Lbp - Br md 6.71 Dpth 3.15 Bonded, 1 dk	**(B11B2FV) Fishing Vessel** Hull Material: Reinforced Plastic	**1 oil engine** driving 1 FP propeller Total Power: 268kW (364hp)
7352476 *V3AU3* -	**URSULA** *ex* Ursula Leonhardt *-2005* *ex* Satsuky *-1982* *ex* Juno I *-1976* **Starwar Shipping Co SA** Transadriatic doo *Belize City* *Belize* MMSI: 312227000 Official number: 140520149	**4,382** 2,226 6,874 T/cm 14.3	Class: RS (GL) (NK)	**1974-03 Imabari Shipbuilding Co Ltd — Imabari EH (Imabari Shipyard)** Yd No: 316 **1992 Estaleiros Navais de Viana do Castelo S.A. — Viana do Castelo** (Additional cargo section) Yd No: 168 Rebuilt-1992 Loa 104.10 Br ex 16.36 Dght 7.337 Lbp 97.70 Br md 15.96 Dpth 9.23 Welded, 1 dk	**(A31A2GX) General Cargo Ship** Grain: 8,007; Bale: 8,007 TEU 193 C. 193/20' Compartments: 3 Ho, ER 3 Ha: 3 (23.7 x 13.0)ER	**1 oil engine** driving 1 FP propeller Total Power: 2,795kW (3,800hp) 12.7kn Hanshin 6LU50A 1 x 4 Stroke 6 Cy. 500 x 800 2795kW (3800bhp) Hanshin Nainenki Kogyo-Japan AuxGen: 2 x 132kW 220/440V a.c Fuel: 648.0 (r.f.) 12.0pd
8137093 *DCRB* -	**URSULA** **Conradi GmbH** - *Greetsiel* *Germany* MMSI: 211359830 Official number: 3791	*143* 42 173		**1974 Schiffs- u. Bootswerft Luebbe Voss — Westerende-Kirchloog** Yd No: 53 Lengthened-1981 L reg 34.03 Br ex - Dght - Lbp - Br md 6.22 Dpth 2.45 Welded, 1 dk	**(B11B2FV) Fishing Vessel**	**1 oil engine** reverse reduction geared to sc. shaft driving 1 FP propeller Total Power: 221kW (300hp) Cummins KT-19-M 1 x 4 Stroke 6 Cy. 159 x 159 221kW (300bhp) (new engine 1986) Cummins Engine Co Inc-USA AuxGen: 1 x 86kW 220/380V a.c
9134672 *V7CG5* -	**URSULA** *ex* Ursula Rickmers *-2013* *ex* ZIM Sao Paulo II *-2012* *ex* Ursula Rickmers *-2001* **Pollux Navigation Ltd** Regal Agencies Corp *Majuro* *Marshall Islands* MMSI: 538005047 Official number: 5047	**16,801** 8,672 23,064 T/cm 37.1	Class: GL	**1997-08 Stocznia Szczecinska SA — Szczecin** Yd No: B170/3/8 Loa 184.00 (BB) Br ex - Dght 9.880 Lbp 171.94 Br md 25.30 Dpth 13.50 Welded, 1 dk	**(A33A2CC) Container Ship (Fully Cellular)** Grain: 29,744 TEU 1728 C Ho 632 TEU C Dk 1096 TEU incl 200 ref C. Compartments: 4 Cell Ho, ER 9 Ha: (12.5 x 13.0)8 (12.5 x 20.6)ER Cranes: 3x40t	**1 oil engine** driving 1 FP propeller Total Power: 13,328kW (18,121hp) 19.0kn Sulzer 6RTA62U 1 x 2 Stroke 6 Cy. 620 x 2150 13328kW (18121bhp) H Cegielski Poznan SA-Poland AuxGen: 3 x 1232kW 440/220V a.c Thrusters: 1 Tunnel thruster (f)
8983923 *WDD6528* -	**URSULA** *ex* Double Be *-2005* **Chau Thanh Dinh** - *Bayou La Batre, AL* *United States of America* MMSI: 367174090 Official number: 1130325	**171** 51 -		**2002** Yd No: 243 L reg 26.94 Br ex - Dght - Lbp - Br md 7.62 Dpth 3.96 Welded, 1 dk	**(B11B2FV) Fishing Vessel**	**1 oil engine** driving 1 Propeller
9480992 *PCMM* -	**URSULA ESSBERGER** **Ursula Essb BV** John T Essberger BV *Dordrecht* *Netherlands* MMSI: 246823000 Official number: 54672	**4,807** 1,442 5,322 T/cm 14.7	Class: BV	**2011-09 Eregli Gemi Insa Sanayi ve Ticaret AS — Karadeniz Eregli** Yd No: 25 Loa 99.40 (BB) Br ex - Dght 7.000 Lbp 93.70 Br md 16.50 Dpth 10.60 Welded, 1 dk	**(A12B2TR) Chemical/Products Tanker** Double Hull (13F) Liq: 6,198; Liq (Oil): 6,100 Cargo Heating Coils Compartments: 6 Wing Ta, 6 Wing Ta, ER 12 Cargo Pump (s): 12x150m³/hr Manifold: Bow/CM: 50m Ice Capable	**1 oil engine** reduction geared to sc. shaft driving 1 CP propeller Total Power: 4,000kW (5,438hp) 14.1kn MAN-B&W 8L32/40 1 x 4 Stroke 8 Cy. 320 x 400 4000kW (5438bhp) STX Engine Co Ltd-South Korea AuxGen: 3 x 620kW 60Hz a.c Thrusters: 1 Tunnel thruster (f) Fuel: 88.0 (d.f.) 438.0 (r.f.)
9269879 *YJVG6* -	**URSULA TIDE** **Green Fleet Ltd** Tidewater Marine International Inc *Port Vila* *Vanuatu* MMSI: 576301000 Official number: 1761	**494** 148 116	Class: AB	**2003-08** Yd No: 59 Loa 53.30 Br ex - Dght 3.350 Lbp 46.94 Br md 10.36 Dpth 4.27 Welded	**(B21A20C) Crew/Supply Vessel** Hull Material: Aluminium Alloy	**4 oil engines** reduction geared to sc. shafts driving 4 FP propellers Total Power: 5,368kW (7,300hp) 16.0kn Cummins KTA-50-M2 4 x Vee 4 Stroke 16 Cy. 159 x 159 each-1342kW (1825bhp) Cummins Engine Co Inc-USA AuxGen: 2 x 175kW a.c Fuel: 120.0

IMO / Call sign	Name / Owner / Manager / Port / Flag	Tonnage	Class	Builder / Dimensions	Type	Machinery
9367516 *V2DK5* -	**URSUS** **Harms Offshore AHT 'Ursus' GmbH & Co KG** Harms Bergung Transport & Heavylift GmbH & Co KG *Saint John's* *Antigua & Barbuda* MMSI: 305241000 Official number: 4463	**2,789** 836 3,216	Class: GL	**2008-04 Muetzelfeldtwerft GmbH — Cuxhaven** Yd No: 255 Loa 65.00 Br ex 18.80 Dght 7.500 Lbp 59.06 Br md 18.50 Dpth 8.50 Welded, 1 dk	**(B32A2ST) Tug** Passengers: 27 Ice Capable	**4 oil engines** reduction geared to sc. shafts driving 2 CP propellers Total Power: 13,800kW (18,762hp) MaK 6M32C 2 x 4 Stroke 6 Cy. 320 x 480 each-3060kW (4160bhp) Caterpillar Motoren GmbH & Co. KG-Germany MaK 8M32C 2 x 4 Stroke 8 Cy. 320 x 480 each-3840kW (5221bhp) Caterpillar Motoren GmbH & Co. KG-Germany AuxGen: 2 x 1200kW 400/230V 50Hz a.c, 2 x 500kW 400/230V 50Hz a.c Thrusters: 2 Thwart. CP thruster (f); 1 Thwart. CP thruster (a) Fuel: 150.0 (d.f.) 2400.0 (r.f.)
8805004 - -	**URSUS** *ex* Ocean Allenmar *-2012* *ex* Overseas Allenmar *-2009* *ex* Allenmar *-2005* *ex* Petrobulk Challenger *-1996* *ex* Osprey Challenger *-1996* *ex* Pacific Challenger *-1994* **Silvia Navigation SA** Altomare SA	**25,740** 11,222 41,570 T/cm 46.7	Class: (NV) (NK)	**1988-09 Koyo Dockyard Co Ltd — Mihara HS** Yd No: 2006 Loa 181.61 (BB) Br ex 30.03 Dght 11.770 Lbp 172.00 Br md 30.00 Dpth 18.40 Welded, 1 dk	**(A13B2TP) Products Tanker** Double Hull Liq: 49,417; Liq (Oil): 50,425 Cargo Heating Coils Compartments: 8 Ta, ER, 2 Slop Ta 4 Cargo Pump (s): 4x950m³/hr Manifold: Bow/CM: 93.8m	**1 oil engine** driving 1 FP propeller Total Power: 6,988kW (9,501hp) 14.2kn MAN-B&W 5S60MC 1 x 2 Stroke 5 Cy. 600 x 2292 6988kW (9501bhp) Mitsui Engineering & Shipbuilding CLtd-Japan AuxGen: 2 x 560kW Fuel: 108.1 (d.f.) 1592.4 (r.f.)
8634651 *OIRM* -	**URSUS** **K Jousmaa KY** - *Naantali* *Finland* Official number: 10462	**217** 66 99		**1979-07 Oy Navire Ab — Naantali** Yd No: 65 Loa 28.10 Br ex - Dght 1.500 Lbp - Br md 10.00 Dpth - Welded, 1 dk	**(A36A2PR) Passenger/Ro-Ro Ship (Vehicles)** Bow ramp Len: 12.00 Wid: - Swl: - Cranes: 1x12t	**2 oil engines** driving 2 Directional propellers Total Power: 344kW (468hp) 7.6kn Scania DSI11 2 x 4 Stroke 6 Cy. 127 x 145 each-172kW (234bhp) Saab Scania AB-Sweden
5422863 *IVHN* -	**URSUS** **VIPP Lavori SpA** - *Venice* *Italy* Official number: 612	*173* 50 -	Class: (RI)	**1963 Cant. Nav. Breda S.p.A. — Venezia** Yd No: 230 Loa 29.01 Br ex 7.35 Dght 3.048 Lbp 26.52 Br md 7.32 Dpth 3.74 Riveted\Welded, 1 dk	**(B32A2ST) Tug** Derricks: 1x2t	**1 oil engine** driving 1 FP propeller Total Power: 883kW (1,201hp) 12.5kn Deutz SBV8M545 1 x 4 Stroke 8 Cy. 320 x 450 883kW (1201bhp) Kloeckner Humboldt Deutz AG-West Germany AuxGen: 1 x 80kW 115/120V 50Hz a.c, 2 x 40kW 115V d.c
7424762 *LCJC* -	**URTER** *ex* Atlantic Vigour *-2008* *ex* Sea Transporter *-1987* *ex* Queen Supplier *-1987* **Haugaland Shipping AS** John K Haaland & Co AS *Haugesund* *Norway* MMSI: 258422000	**1,202** 360 1,155	Class: (NV)	**1974-10 Eid Verft AS — Nordfjordeid** (Hull) Yd No: 5 **1974-10 Smedvik Mek. Verksted AS — Tjorvaag** Yd No: 46 Converted From: Offshore Supply Ship-1988 Loa 57.82 Br ex 13.03 Dght 4.268 Lbp 50.09 Br md 13.00 Dpth 6.02 Welded, 2 dks	**(B11B2FV) Fishing Vessel**	**2 oil engines** driving 2 FP propellers Total Power: 2,206kW (3,000hp) 12.5kn EMD (Electro-Motive) 12-645-E8 2 x Vee 2 Stroke 12 Cy. 230 x 254 each-1103kW (1500bhp) General Motors Corp.Electro-Motive Div.-La Grange AuxGen: 2 x 163kW 440V 60Hz a.c, 1 x 56kW 440V 60Hz a.c Thrusters: 1 Thwart. FP thruster (f) Fuel: 366.0 (d.f.) 12.5pd
9293234 *HSGF2* -	**URU BHUM** **Regional Container Lines Public Co Ltd** RCL Shipmanagement Pte Ltd *Bangkok* *Thailand* MMSI: 567303000 Official number: 480000610	**24,955** 11,523 31,805	Class: GL	**2005-02 Mitsubishi Heavy Industries Ltd. — Nagasaki** Yd No: 2198 Loa 194.90 (BB) Br ex - Dght 11.400 Lbp 186.00 Br md 32.26 Dpth 16.80 Welded, 1 dk	**(A33A2CC) Container Ship (Fully Cellular)** TEU 2588 incl 300 ref C.	**1 oil engine** driving 1 FP propeller Total Power: 20,580kW (27,981hp) 22.3kn Mitsubishi 7UEC68LSE 1 x 2 Stroke 7 Cy. 680 x 2690 20580kW (27981bhp) Mitsubishi Heavy Industries Ltd-Japan AuxGen: 3 x 1400kW 450/230V 60Hz a.c Thrusters: 1 Tunnel thruster (f)
9293985 *OA4991* -	**URUBAMBA** *ex* STI Conqueror *-2012* *ex* Rose G *-2010* **Naviera Transoceanica SA** - SatCom: Inmarsat C 476000086 *Callao* *Peru* MMSI: 760000880	**25,431** 10,019 40,158 T/cm 48.9	Class: AB (BV) (RI)	**2005-09 ShinA Shipbuilding Co Ltd — Tongyeong** Yd No: 442 Loa 175.98 (BB) Br ex 31.03 Dght 11.115 Lbp 168.00 Br md 31.00 Dpth 17.20 Welded, 1 dk	**(A12B2TR) Chemical/Products Tanker** Double Hull (13F) Liq: 43,018; Liq (Oil): 43,018 Cargo Heating Coils Compartments: 12 Wing Ta, 2 Wing Slop Ta, ER 12 Cargo Pump (s): 12x500m³/hr Manifold: Bow/CM: 88.9m Ice Capable	**1 oil engine** driving 1 FP propeller Total Power: 8,580kW (11,665hp) 15.0kn MAN-B&W 6S50MC 1 x 2 Stroke 6 Cy. 500 x 1910 8580kW (11665bhp) Doosan Engine Co Ltd-South Korea AuxGen: 4 x 740kW 450/220V 60Hz a.c Thrusters: 1 Tunnel thruster (f) Fuel: 209.9 (d.f.) 1566.4 (r.f.)
7218711 - -	**URUBAMBA** *ex* Ocean Project *-2011* *ex* Rambo *-1997* *ex* 0601 *-1993* *ex* George E. Darby *-1992* *ex* Janie B *-1981* *ex* Cathy B *-1981* *ex* Nordic Offshore *-1981* **Trabajos Maritima SA (TRAMARSA)** -	**993** 297 1,208	Class: (AB)	**1972-07 Bel-Aire Shipyard Ltd — North Vancouver BC** Yd No: 222B Converted From: Offshore Tug/Supply Ship-1986 Loa 56.09 Br ex 14.03 Dght 4.417 Lbp 51.95 Br md 13.72 Dpth 5.03 Welded, 1 dk	**(B34M2QS) Search & Rescue Vessel** Ice Capable	**2 oil engines** reduction geared to sc. shafts driving 2 CP propellers Total Power: 3,884kW (5,280hp) 14.0kn English Electric 12RK3CM 2 x Vee 4 Stroke 12 Cy. 254 x 305 each-1942kW (2640bhp) Ruston Paxman Diesels Ltd.-Colchester Thrusters: 1 Tunnel thruster (f) Fuel: 588.0 (d.f.)
6615182 - -	**URUBAMBA 1** *ex* Tasa 21 *-1976* - -	*105* - -	Class: (AB)	**1965 Promecan Ingenieros S.A. — Callao** Yd No: 40 Loa - Br ex - Dght - Lbp 21.49 Br md 6.71 Dpth 3.51 Welded, 1 dk	**(B11A2FT) Trawler** Compartments: 1 Ho, ER 1 Ha: (1.9 x 3.3)	**1 oil engine** driving 1 CP propeller Total Power: 221kW (300hp) Normo Z4 1 x 2 Stroke 4 Cy. 300 x 360 221kW (300bhp) AS Bergens Mek Verksteder-Norway Fuel: 12.0 (d.f.)
6710243 - -	**URUBAMBA 2** *ex* Tasa 22 *-1976* - -	*150* - -	Class: (AB)	**1966 Promecan Ingenieros S.A. — Callao** Yd No: 66 Loa - Br ex 6.74 Dght - Lbp 21.49 Br md 6.71 Dpth 3.51 Welded, 1 dk	**(B11A2FT) Trawler** Compartments: 1 Ho, ER 1 Ha: (1.9 x 3.3)	**1 oil engine** driving 1 CP propeller Total Power: 221kW (300hp) Normo Z4 1 x 2 Stroke 4 Cy. 300 x 360 221kW (300bhp) AS Bergens Mek Verksteder-Norway Fuel: 12.0 (d.f.)
6710255 - -	**URUBAMBA 3** *ex* Tasa 23 *-1976* - -	*150* - -	Class: (AB)	**1966 Promecan Ingenieros S.A. — Callao** Yd No: 67 Loa 21.49 Br ex 6.74 Dght - Lbp - Br md 6.71 Dpth 3.51 Welded, 1 dk	**(B11A2FT) Trawler** Compartments: 1 Ho, ER 1 Ha: (1.9 x 3.3)	**1 oil engine** driving 1 CP propeller Total Power: 221kW (300hp) 9.0kn Normo Z4 1 x 2 Stroke 4 Cy. 300 x 360 221kW (300bhp) AS Bergens Mek Verksteder-Norway AuxGen: 2 x 50kW Fuel: 12.0 (d.f.)
6815029 - -	**URUBAMBA 4** *ex* Tasa 25 *-1976* - -	*150* - -	Class: (AB)	**1967 Promecan Ingenieros S.A. — Callao** Yd No: 97 Loa - Br ex 6.74 Dght - Lbp 21.49 Br md 6.71 Dpth 3.51 Welded, 1 dk	**(B11A2FT) Trawler** Compartments: 1 Ho, ER 1 Ha: (1.9 x 3.3)	**1 oil engine** driving 1 CP propeller Total Power: 221kW (300hp) Normo Z4 1 x 2 Stroke 4 Cy. 300 x 360 221kW (300bhp) AS Bergens Mek Verksteder-Norway Fuel: 12.0 (d.f.)
6912047 - -	**URUBAMBA 5** *ex* Ulises *-1976* - -	*158* 72 -	Class: (AB) (GL)	**1966 Promecan Ingenieros S.A. — Callao** Yd No: 60 Loa - Br ex 6.79 Dght - Lbp 21.47 Br md 6.71 Dpth 3.51 Welded	**(B11B2FV) Fishing Vessel** Compartments: 1 Ho, ER 1 Ha: (1.9 x 3.3)	**1 oil engine** reduction geared to sc. shaft driving 1 FP propeller Total Power: 279kW (379hp) 10.0kn Caterpillar D353SCAC 1 x 4 Stroke 6 Cy. 159 x 203 279kW (379bhp) Caterpillar Tractor Co-USA Fuel: 5.0
6727636 - -	**URUBAMBA 6** *ex* Golden Rose XI *-1976* *ex* Artefe 5 *-1970* - -	*105* - -	Class: (AB)	**1967 Promecan Ingenieros S.A. — Callao** Yd No: 79 Loa - Br ex 6.74 Dght - Lbp 21.47 Br md 6.71 Dpth 3.51 Welded, 1 dk	**(B11A2FT) Trawler** Compartments: 1 Ho, ER 1 Ha: (1.9 x 3.3)	**1 oil engine** sr reverse geared to sc. shaft driving 1 FP propeller Total Power: 279kW (379hp) Caterpillar D353SCAC 1 x 4 Stroke 6 Cy. 159 x 203 279kW (379bhp) Caterpillar Tractor Co-USA Fuel: 5.0 (d.f.)
6712497 - -	**URUBAMBA 8** *ex* Moquegua II *-1979* **Productos Marinos SA** - *Pisco* *Peru* Official number: PS-006407-PM	*154* 62 -	Class: (LR) ✠ Classed LR until 4/71	**1967-04 Fabricaciones Metallicas E.P.S. (FABRIMET) — Callao** Yd No: 349 Loa 25.20 Br ex 7.14 Dght 3.175 Lbp 21.49 Br md 7.01 Dpth 3.46 Welded, 1 dk	**(B11B2FV) Fishing Vessel**	**1 oil engine** reverse reduction geared to sc. shaft driving 1 FP propeller Total Power: 399kW (542hp) Caterpillar D353SCAC 1 x 4 Stroke 6 Cy. 159 x 203 399kW (542bhp) Caterpillar Tractor Co-USA

IMO / Call sign	Name / Owner	Tonnage	Class	Builder / Dimensions	Type	Machinery
6917451 - -	**URUBAMBA 9** *ex* Polaries *-1976* - -	*150* - -	Class: (AB)	**1966 Promecan Ingenieros S.A. — Callao** Yd No: 65 Loa - Br ex 6.74 Dght - Lbp 21.47 Br md 6.71 Dpth 3.51 Welded	**(B11A2FT) Trawler** Compartments: 1 Ho, ER 1 Ha: (1.9 x 3.3)	**1 oil engine** driving 1 FP propeller Total Power: 279kW (379hp) Caterpillar D353SCAC 1 x 4 Stroke 6 Cy. 159 x 203 279kW (379bhp) Caterpillar Tractor Co-USA
7008051 - -	**URUBAMBA 10** *ex* Sama 4 *-1976* - -	*150* - -	Class: (AB)	**1968 Metal Empresa S.A. — Callao** Yd No: L-1 Loa - Br ex 6.79 Dght - Lbp 21.49 Br md 6.71 Dpth 3.51 Welded, 1 dk	**(B11B2FV) Fishing Vessel** Compartments: 1 Ho, ER 1 Ha: (1.9 x 3.3)	**1 oil engine** driving 1 FP propeller Total Power: 279kW (379hp) Caterpillar D353SCAC 1 x 4 Stroke 6 Cy. 159 x 203 279kW (379bhp) Caterpillar Tractor Co-USA Fuel: 5.0
8650459 *PP8770* -	**URUCUM** - **Vale SA** - *Rio de Janeiro* *Brazil* Official number: 3813876730	**232** - -		**2010-09 H. Dantas Construcoes e Reparos Navais Ltda. — Aracaju** Loa - Br ex - Dght - Lbp - Br md - Dpth - Welded, 1 dk	**(B32A2ST) Tug**	**1 oil engine** driving 1 Propeller
7530250 *ZPPI* -	**URUGUAY FEEDER** *ex* Alexandra *-2006* *ex* Cuxhaven *-2000* **Lineas Feeder SA** - *Asuncion* *Paraguay* MMSI: 755463102	**2,245** 1,165 3,442	Class: (GL)	**1976-12 KG Norderwerft GmbH & Co. — Hamburg** (Hull) **1976-12 J.J. Sietas Schiffswerft — Hamburg** Yd No: 769 Loa 81.41 (BB) Br ex 13.44 Dght 6.001 Lbp 74.17 Br md 13.42 Dpth 7.50 Welded, 2 dks	**(A31A2GX) General Cargo Ship** Grain: 4,730; Bale: 4,415 TEU 162 C.Ho 86/20' C.Dk 76/20' incl. 20 ref C. Compartments: 1 Ho, ER 1 Ha: (50.4 x 10.2)ER Ice Capable	**1 oil engine** driving 1 FP propeller Total Power: 1,949kW (2,650hp) 13.8kn MaK 8M453AK 1 x 4 Stroke 8 Cy. 320 x 420 1949kW (2650bhp) MaK Maschinenbau GmbH-Kiel Thrusters: 1 Thwart. FP thruster (f)
9017264 *A8HP7* -	**URUGUAY STAR** *ex* Polar Uruguay *-2005* *ex* Hadrian *-1996* **Star Reefers Shipowning Inc** Star Reefers Poland Sp z oo *Monrovia* *Liberia* MMSI: 636012750 Official number: 12750	**10,629** 4,253 10,587 T/cm 25.4	Class: NV (LR) ✠ Classed LR until 10/12/08	**1993-06 Stocznia Gdanska SA — Gdansk** Yd No: B369/05 Loa 150.35 (BB) Br ex 22.64 Dght 9.100 Lbp 138.50 Br md 22.60 Dpth 13.25 Welded, 1dk, 2nd & 3rd dk in all holds, 4thdk in Nos. 2, 3 & 4 holds	**(A34A2GR) Refrigerated Cargo Ship** Ins: 14,843 TEU 220 C Ho 84 TEU C Dk 136 TEU incl 47 ref C Compartments: 4 Ho, ER, 1 Tw Dk in Fo'c's'l, 11 Tw Dk 4 Ha: 4 (12.4 x 8.5)ER Cranes: 2x32t,2x8t	**1 oil engine** driving 1 FP propeller Total Power: 11,400kW (15,499hp) 21.0kn Sulzer 6RTA62 1 x 2 Stroke 6 Cy. 620 x 2150 11400kW (15499bhp) Dieselmotorenwerk Rostock GmbH-Rostock AuxGen: 3 x 1000kW 440V 60Hz a.c Boilers: e (ex.g.) 8.7kgf/cm² (8.5bar), AuxB (o.f.) 8.7kgf/cm² (8.5bar) Fuel: 106.2 (d.f.) 1090.0 (r.f.) 57.4pd
9421673 *JD2338* -	**URUMA** - **Kyowa Marine Service KK (Kyowa Marine Service Co Ltd)** - *Uruma, Okinawa* *Japan* Official number: 140429	*193* - -		**2006-12 Kanagawa Zosen — Kobe** Yd No: 559 Loa 33.30 Br ex - Dght - Lbp 29.00 Br md 9.40 Dpth 3.98 Welded, 1 dk	**(B32A2ST) Tug**	**2 oil engines** reduction geared to sc. shafts driving 2 Propellers Total Power: 2,648kW (3,600hp) Niigata 6L28HX 2 x 4 Stroke 6 Cy. 280 x 370 each-1324kW (1800bhp) Niigata Engineering Co Ltd-Japan
9646182 *JD3073* -	**URUME** - **KK Komatsu Marine** - *Kure, Hiroshima* *Japan* Official number: 141254	*136* - -		**2010-07 K.K. Watanabe Zosensho — Nagasaki** L reg 14.50 Br ex - Dght - Lbp - Br md 12.19 Dpth 6.00 Welded, 1 dk	**(B32B2SP) Pusher Tug**	**2 oil engines** reduction geared to sc. shafts driving 2 Propellers Total Power: 1,324kW (1,800hp) Niigata 2 x each-662kW (900bhp) Niigata Engineering Co Ltd-Japan
9081538 *UHFU* -	**URUP** *ex* Dapkor-02 *-2002* **Morskie Linii Co Ltd** - *Petropavlovsk-Kamchatskiy* *Russia* MMSI: 273812800 Official number: 920356	**190** 57 78	Class: RS	**1992-11 OAO Astrakhanskaya Sudoverf — Astrakhan** Yd No: 104 Loa 31.85 Br ex 7.08 Dght 2.220 Lbp 27.94 Br md - Dpth 3.15 Welded, 1 dk	**(B12B2FC) Fish Carrier** Ins: 100 Ice Capable	**1 oil engine** geared to sc. shaft driving 1 FP propeller Total Power: 232kW (315hp) 10.3kn Daldizel 6CHSPN2A18-315 1 x 4 Stroke 6 Cy. 180 x 220 232kW (315bhp) Daldizel-Khabarovsk AuxGen: 2 x 25kW a.c Fuel: 14.0 (d.f.)
8000692 *CXLM* -	**URUPEZ II** - **Urupez SA** - *Piriapolis* *Uruguay*	*240* 97 300	Class: (BV) (NV)	**1981-04 B&W Skibsvaerft A/S — Copenhagen** Yd No: 904 Loa 32.59 (BB) Br ex 8.13 Dght 3.868 Lbp 27.21 Br md 7.90 Dpth 4.12 Welded, 1 dk	**(B11A2FS) Stern Trawler** Ins: 270; Liq: 55	**1 oil engine** driving 1 CP propeller Total Power: 566kW (770hp) 10.5kn Alpha 407-26VO 1 x 2 Stroke 7 Cy. 260 x 400 566kW (770bhp) B&W Alpha Diesel A/S-Denmark AuxGen: 2 x 50kW 220V 50Hz a.c
7406083 *ATNU* -	**URVASHI RANI** - **Eveready Industries India Ltd (EIIL)** - *Mumbai* *India* Official number: 1663	*185* 90 -	Class: (AB)	**1976-10 Mazagon Dock Ltd. — Mumbai** Yd No: 356 Loa 27.34 Br ex 8.06 Dght 2.901 Lbp 25.89 Br md 7.92 Dpth 3.64 Welded, 1 dk	**(B11A2FT) Trawler**	**1 oil engine** geared to sc. shaft driving 1 FP propeller Total Power: 625kW (850hp) 10.0kn Caterpillar D398SCAC 1 x Vee 4 Stroke 12 Cy. 159 x 203 625kW (850bhp) Caterpillar Tractor Co-USA AuxGen: 2 x 88kW
8943313 *UBQZ* -	**URYUM** - **JSC Moneron** - *Nevelsk* *Russia* MMSI: 273435850 Official number: 940311	**747** 224 1,220	Class: RS	**1997 ATVT Zavod "Leninska Kuznya" — Kyyiv** Yd No: 1691 Loa 54.82 Br ex 10.15 Dght 4.140 Lbp 50.30 Br md 9.80 Dpth 5.00 Welded, 1 dk	**(B11A2FS) Stern Trawler**	**1 oil engine** driving 1 FP propeller Total Power: 853kW (1,160hp) S.K.L. 8NVD48A-2U 1 x 4 Stroke 8 Cy. 320 x 480 853kW (1160bhp) SKL Motoren u. Systemtechnik AG-Magdeburg
7932898 *VRMN*	**URZELA** *ex* Princesa Voladora *-1981* *ex* Flying Princess *-1980* **Sinocross International Ltd** Shun Tak-China Travel Ship Management Ltd (TurboJET) *Hong Kong* *Hong Kong* MMSI: 477034000 Official number: 399441	**267** 97 -	Class: AB	**1976-03 Boeing Marine Systems — Seattle, Wa** Yd No: 0007 Loa 30.10 Br ex 9.50 Dght 1.505 Lbp 23.93 Br md 8.54 Dpth 2.60 Welded, 2 dks	**(A37B2PS) Passenger Ship** Hull Material: Aluminium Alloy Passengers: unberthed: 250	**2 Gas Turbs** dr geared to sc. shafts driving 2 Water jets Total Power: 5,442kW (7,398hp) 43.0kn Allison 501-K20A 2 x Gas Turb each-2721kW (3699shp) General Motors Detroit DieselAllison Divn-USA AuxGen: 2 x 50kW 440V 60Hz a.c Thrusters: 1 Thwart. FP thruster (f)
6804173 - -	**USA MARU No. 1** - - -	*300* 155 -		**1967 KK Kanasashi Zosen — Shizuoka SZ** Yd No: 772 Loa 46.31 Br ex 7.70 Dght 2.998 Lbp 41.00 Br md 7.68 Dpth 3.46 Welded, 1 dk	**(B11B2FV) Fishing Vessel**	**1 oil engine** driving 1 FP propeller Total Power: 588kW (799hp) Hanshin Z6WS 1 x 4 Stroke 6 Cy. 350 x 500 588kW (799bhp) Hanshin Nainenki Kogyo-Japan
8626070 *YGHM* -	**USAHA ABADI** *ex* K K 10 *-2001* *ex* Kannon Maru No. 8 *-1999* **PT Karya Terpadu Sejahtera** - *Jakarta* *Indonesia*	*389* 219 407	Class: KI	**1983-04 Y.K. Okajima Zosensho — Matsuyama** Loa 43.00 Br ex - Dght 3.310 Lbp 38.00 Br md 7.60 Dpth 5.00 Welded, 1 dk	**(A31A2GX) General Cargo Ship**	**1 oil engine** driving 1 FP propeller Total Power: 260kW (353hp) 10.3kn Matsui MU323CGHS 1 x 4 Stroke 3 Cy. 230 x 380 260kW (353bhp) Matsui Iron Works Co Ltd-Japan
9027738 - -	**USAHA ANUGERAH PERDANA** - **Fandy Wijaya Oeij** - *Samarinda* *Indonesia*	**340** 102 -	Class: KI	**2003-04 C.V. Dok & Galangan Kapal Perlun — Samarinda** Loa 47.10 Br ex - Dght - Lbp 43.30 Br md 9.00 Dpth 3.00 Welded, 1 dk	**(A35D2RL) Landing Craft** Bow ramp (centre)	**2 oil engines** geared to sc. shafts driving 2 Propellers Total Power: 618kW (840hp) Nissan RF10 2 x Vee 4 Stroke 10 Cy. 138 x 142 each-309kW (420bhp) (made 2002) Nissan Diesel Motor Co. Ltd.-Ageo AuxGen: 1 x 60kW 400/220V a.c, 1 x 13kW 400/220V a.c, 1 x 10kW 400/220V a.c
7943897 *YCDO* -	**USAHA MINA I** - **PT Usaha Mina** - *Jakarta* *Indonesia*	*518* 188 1,139	Class: (KI) (GL)	**1976 Kleen-n-Paint Shipbuilding & Engineering Pte — Singapore** Yd No: 128 Loa 49.50 Br ex 8.92 Dght 4.200 Lbp 48.00 Br md - Dpth 4.65 Welded, 1 dk	**(B11B2FV) Fishing Vessel** Ins: 455	**1 oil engine** driving 1 FP propeller Total Power: 758kW (1,031hp) 12.0kn MWM TBD440-8 1 x 4 Stroke 8 Cy. 230 x 270 758kW (1031bhp) Motoren Werke Mannheim AG (MWM)-West Germany AuxGen: 1 x 380kW
9027752 - -	**USDA JAYA** - **PT Kurnia Tunggal Nugraha** - *Dumai* *Indonesia*	**101** 60 -	Class: KI	**1985-01 PT Usda Seroja Jaya — Rengat** L reg 21.22 Br ex - Dght - Lbp 19.49 Br md 6.50 Dpth 2.20 Welded, 1 dk	**(B32A2ST) Tug**	**2 oil engines** geared to sc. shafts driving 2 Propellers Total Power: 368kW (500hp) Caterpillar 3406TA 2 x 4 Stroke 6 Cy. 137 x 165 each-184kW (250bhp) Caterpillar Tractor Co-USA

8827844 **USELL ALPHA**
-
ex Olympic No. 1 *-2006*
-
ex Sae Han Gang No. 1 *-1994*
C& Hanganland Co Ltd
-
Yeongdeungpo *South Korea*
Official number: ICR-860382

430
-
61

Class: (KR)

1986-10 **Seohae Shipbuilding & Engineering Co Ltd — Incheon**
Loa 61.00 Br ex - Dght 1.097
Lbp 53.50 Br md 11.00 Dpth 1.70
Welded, 1 dk

(A37B2PS) Passenger Ship

2 oil engines reduction geared to sc. shafts driving 2 FP propellers
Total Power: 328kW (446hp) 9.7kn
G.M. (Detroit Diesel) 6-71-N
2 x 2 Stroke 6 Cy. 108 x 127 each-164kW (223bhp) (made 1980, fitted 1992)
Detroit Diesel Corporation-Detroit, Mi
AuxGen: 2 x 180kW 445V a.c

8827856 **USELL BETA**
-
ex Olympic No. 2 *-2006*
-
ex Sae Han Gang No. 2 *-1994*
C& Hanganland Co Ltd
-
Yeongdeungpo *South Korea*
Official number: ICR-860390

302
-
61

Class: (KR)

1986-10 **Seohae Shipbuilding & Engineering Co Ltd — Incheon**
Loa 61.00 Br ex - Dght 0.898
Lbp 53.50 Br md 11.00 Dpth 1.70
Welded, 1 dk

(A37B2PS) Passenger Ship

2 oil engines reduction geared to sc. shafts driving 2 FP propellers
Total Power: 540kW (734hp) 7.0kn
Volvo Penta TAMD122A
2 x 4 Stroke 6 Cy. 130 x 150 each-270kW (367bhp)
AB Volvo Penta-Sweden
AuxGen: 2 x 208kW 445V a.c

8605545 **USHA**
VVPY
Sri Lakshmi Marine Products Ltd
-
-
India

121
-
-
-

1989-12 **Hooghly Dock & Port Engineers Ltd. — Haora** Yd No: 444
Loa - Br ex - Dght -
Lbp 23.53 Br md - Dpth -
Welded, 1 dk

(B11A2FS) Stern Trawler

1 oil engine geared to sc. shaft driving 1 FP propeller
Total Power: 405kW (551hp)
Caterpillar 3408TA
1 x Vee 4 Stroke 8 Cy. 137 x 152 405kW (551bhp)
Caterpillar Inc-USA

7320100 **USHBA**
4LEU
ex Zashchitnik *-1999*
-
Batumi Sea Port Ltd (Batumskiy Morskoy Port OOO)
-
Batumi *Georgia*
MMSI: 213242000
Official number: C-00060

264
-
83

Class: MG (RS)

1973-11 **Brodogradiliste 'Tito' Beograd - Brod 'Tito' — Belgrade** Yd No: 895
Loa 35.43 Br ex 9.21 Dght 3.140
Lbp 32.40 Br md 9.01 Dpth 4.52
Welded, 1 dk

(B32A2ST) Tug
Ice Capable

2 oil engines geared to sc. shaft driving 1 CP propeller
Total Power: 1,700kW (2,312hp) 13.0kn
B&W 7-26MTBF-40
2 x 4 Stroke 7 Cy. 260 x 400 each-850kW (1156bhp)
Titovi Zavodi 'Litostroj'-Yugoslavia
AuxGen: 2 x 100kW
Fuel: 43.0 (d.f.)

9054157 **USHIO MARU**
JD2672
HK1-300
Government of Japan (Ministry of Education, Culture, Sports, Science & Technology)
Hokkaido University - Fisheries Faculty (Hokkaido Daigaku Suisan Gakubu)
Hakodate, Hokkaido *Japan*
Official number: 128586

179
-
-

1992-09 **Sanuki Shipbuilding & Iron Works Co Ltd — Mitoyo KG** Yd No: 1226
Lengthened-2002
Loa 39.39 (BB) Br ex - Dght 2.500
Lbp 33.74 Br md 6.50 Dpth 3.00
Welded, 1 dk

(B31A2SR) Research Survey Vessel

1 oil engine sr geared to sc. shaft driving 1 CP propeller
Total Power: 736kW (1,001hp) 11.0kn
Yanmar M220-UN
1 x 4 Stroke 6 Cy. 220 x 300 736kW (1001bhp)
Yanmar Diesel Engine Co Ltd-Japan
AuxGen: 1 x 160kW a.c, 1 x 128kW a.c

6901907 **USHUAIA**
D6FH2
ex Malcolm Baldrige *-2001*
-
ex Researcher *-1988*
Ushuaia Adventure Corp
Antarpply SA
SatCom: Inmarsat C 461683610
Moroni *Union of Comoros*
MMSI: 616836000
Official number: 1200968

2,923
877
-

Class: IV (AB)

1970-06 **American Shipbuilding Co — Toledo OH** Yd No: 198
Loa 84.82 (BB) Br ex 15.70 Dght 5.010
Lbp 74.68 Br md 15.55 Dpth 7.62
Welded, 1 dk

(B31A2SR) Research Survey Vessel

2 oil engines sr geared to sc. shafts driving 2 CP propellers
Total Power: 2,412kW (3,280hp) 12.0kn
Alco 12V251E
2 x Vee 4 Stroke 12 Cy. 229 x 267 each-1206kW (1640bhp)
American Locomotive Co-USA
AuxGen: 3 x 500kW 450V 60Hz a.c
Thrusters: 1 Thwart. FP thruster (f)
Fuel: 861.5

7821831 **USL-1**
3FEM4
ex Crossway-I *-2011*
-
ex Neptune Thalassa *-2009*
ex Intra Highway *-1996*
ex Toyo Maru No. 23 *-1994*
Universal Shipping & Logistics Sarl
-
SatCom: Inmarsat C 435329810
Panama *Panama*
MMSI: 353298000
Official number: 23236PEXT4

6,655
1,997
2,873

Class: IS (NK)

1979-02 **Sasebo Heavy Industries Co. Ltd. — Sasebo Yard, Sasebo** Yd No: 275
Converted From: Vehicles Carrier-2011
Lengthened-1989
Loa 113.40 Br ex 16.02 Dght 5.116
Lbp 105.40 Br md 16.00 Dpth 8.00
Welded, 1 dk

(A38A2GL) Livestock Carrier
Cars: 560

1 oil engine geared to sc. shaft driving 1 FP propeller
Total Power: 3,309kW (4,499hp) 15.2kn
Hanshin 6LU50A
1 x 4 Stroke 6 Cy. 500 x 800 3309kW (4499bhp)
The Hanshin Diesel Works Ltd-Japan
AuxGen: 2 x 240kW 450V 60Hz a.c
Fuel: 119.5 (d.f.) 373.5 (r.f.) 10.5pd

8729444 **USMA**
UBDD
-
FCF Vskhody Kommunizma (Rybolovetskiy Kolkhoz 'Vskhody Kommunizma')
-
Murmansk *Russia*
MMSI: 273438550
Official number: 885033

730
219
414

Class: (RS)

1989-07 **Zavod "Leninskaya Kuznitsa" — Kiyev** Yd No: 1612
Loa 54.84 Br ex 10.15 Dght 4.141
Lbp 50.32 Br md 9.80 Dpth 5.01
Welded, 1 dk

(B11A2FS) Stern Trawler
Ins: 412
Ice Capable

1 oil engine driving 1 CP propeller
Total Power: 852kW (1,158hp) 12.0kn
S.K.L. 8NVD48A-2U
1 x 4 Stroke 8 Cy. 320 x 480 852kW (1158bhp)
VEB Schwermaschinenbau "KarlLiebknecht" (SKL)-Magdeburg
AuxGen: 4 x 160kW a.c
Fuel: 155.0 (d.f.)

9323364 **USMA**
V7LO2
-
Smiltene Navigation Inc
Latvian Shipping Co (Latvijas Kugnieciba)
Majuro *Marshall Islands*
MMSI: 538002776
Official number: 2776

30,641
15,318
52,684
T/cm
56.8

Class: LR (NV)
100A1 SS 07/2012
Double Hull oil and chemical tanker, Ship Type 2
ESP
LI
*IWS
SPM
Ice Class 1B at maximum draught of 12.798m
Max/min draughts fwd 12.798/5.918m
Max/min draughts aft 13.088/7.588m
Minimum power required 8716kw, installed power 9650kw
LMC **UMS IGS**

2007-07 **'3 Maj' Brodogradiliste dd — Rijeka** Yd No: 700
Loa 195.30 (BB) Br ex 32.24 Dght 12.000
Lbp 187.30 Br md 32.20 Dpth 17.80
Welded, 1 dk

(A12B2TR) Chemical/Products Tanker
Double Hull (13F)
Liq: 56,151; Liq (Oil): 56,151
Compartments: 12 Wing Ta, 2 Wing Slop Ta, ER
12 Cargo Pump (s): 12x550m³/hr
Manifold: Bow/CM: 97.2m
Ice Capable

1 oil engine driving 1 FP propeller
Total Power: 9,650kW (13,120hp) 14.0kn
Sulzer 7RTA48T-B
1 x 2 Stroke 7 Cy. 480 x 2000 9650kW (13120bhp)
'3 Maj' Motori i Dizalice dd-Croatia
AuxGen: 3 x 960kW 450V 60Hz a.c
Fuel: 161.5 (d.f.) 1510.5 (d.f.) 39.0pd

8800315 **USOLIE**
D5AZ6
ex Trident E *-2012* *ex* Trident Endeavor *-2011*
-
ex W-One *-2006* *ex* Antwerpia *-2004*
ex General Guisan *-1995*
Trident E Shipping SA
Harvester Shipmanagement Ltd
Monrovia *Liberia*
MMSI: 636015477
Official number: 15477

37,519
22,604
68,788
T/cm
67.0

Class: NK (LR) (NV)
Classed LR until 20/10/12

1990-03 **Hyundai Heavy Industries Co Ltd — Ulsan** Yd No: 629
Loa 225.00 (BB) Br ex 32.24 Dght 13.245
Lbp 215.63 Br md 32.21 Dpth 18.32
Welded, 1 dk

(A21A2BC) Bulk Carrier
Grain: 80,148; Bale: 76,407
Compartments: 7 Ho, ER
7 Ha: (14.4 x 12.0)6 (14.4 x 15.0)ER

1 oil engine driving 1 FP propeller
Total Power: 9,000kW (12,236hp) 14.5kn
B&W 6S60MC
1 x 2 Stroke 6 Cy. 600 x 2292 9000kW (12236bhp)
Hyundai Heavy Industries Co Ltd-South Korea
AuxGen: 2 x 550kW 440V 60Hz a.c
Boilers: WTAuxB (Comp) 9.2kgf/cm² (9.0bar)
Fuel: 200.0 (d.f.) 2900.0 (r.f.) 32.2pd

8026646 **USOLYE**
-
ex Lux Spirit *-1988* *ex* Josemi *-1987*
-
Commercial Fleet of Donbass Ltd
-

4,355
2,533
7,114

Class: UA (RS) (BV)

1982-10 **Sociedad Metalurgica Duro Felguera — Gijon** Yd No: 161
Loa 104.00 Br ex 16.53 Dght 7.570
Lbp 97.97 Br md 16.51 Dpth 9.70
Welded, 1 dk

(A31A2GX) General Cargo Ship
Grain: 8,914; Bale: 8,070
TEU 226 C.Ho 156/20' C.Dk 70/20'
Compartments: 2 Ho, ER
2 Ha: 2 (25.9 x 12.5)ER
Cranes: 1x8t; Derricks: 2x5t; Winches: 2

1 oil engine with flexible couplings & sr gearedto sc. shaft driving 1 FP propeller
Total Power: 2,944kW (4,003hp) 12.5kn
Deutz RBV12M350
1 x Vee 4 Stroke 12 Cy. 400 x 500 2944kW (4003bhp)
Hijos de J Barreras SA-Spain
AuxGen: 3 x 216kW 380V 50Hz a.c
Fuel: 72.5 (d.f.) (Heating Coils) 412.0 (r.f.) 12.5pd

8857447 **USPEH**
UGQD
ex GSH-16 *-2010*
-
True Diversified Industrial Corp JSC
-
Korsakov *Russia*
MMSI: 273894310

948
284
1,024

Class: (RS)

1985-07 **Santierul Naval Drobeta-Turnu Severin S.A. — Drobeta-Turnu S.** Yd No: 1160007
Converted From: Hopper-2000
Loa 56.19 Br ex 11.21 Dght 3.660
Lbp 53.20 Br md 11.19 Dpth 4.44
Welded, 1 dk

(A31A2GX) General Cargo Ship
Grain: 600
Compartments: 1 Ho, ER
1 Ha: (18.0 x 7.2)ER
Ice Capable

2 oil engines driving 2 FP propellers
Total Power: 574kW (780hp) 8.9kn
S.K.L. 6NVD26A-3
2 x 4 Stroke 6 Cy. 180 x 260 each-287kW (390bhp)
VEB Schwermaschinenbau "KarlLiebknecht" (SKL)-Magdeburg
Fuel: 120.0 (d.f.)

IMO / Call sign / Fishing no.	Name / Former names / Owner / Port / Flag	Tonnage / Class	Build / Dimensions	Type	Machinery
8320951 *UEGH* -	**USPEKH** *ex* Naga *-2010* *ex* Dc-1 *-2010* *ex* Naga *-2007* *ex* Prekrasnaya Elena *-2004* *ex* Sea Queen *-1997* *ex* Yahata Maru No. 28 *-1997* *ex* Kasuga Maru No. 77 *-1994* **Dmitriy Vladimirovich Dremlyga** - *Vladivostok* *Russia* MMSI: 273825030	**291** Class: RS 156 157	**1983-06 Takahashi Zosen Kogyo K.K. — Yokohama** Yd No: 172 Loa 42.85 (BB) Br ex 7.15 Dght 2.850 Lbp 36.21 Br md 7.15 Dpth 3.20 Welded, 1 dk	**(B11B2FV) Fishing Vessel** Ins: 166 Compartments: 2 Ho, ER 3 Ha: ER	**1 oil engine** with clutches, flexible couplings & dr reverse geared to sc. shaft driving 1 FP propeller Total Power: 647kW (880hp) Daihatsu 6DLM-24 1 x 4 Stroke 6 Cy. 240 x 320 647kW (880bhp) Daihatsu Diesel Manufacturing Co Lt-Japan
7395959 *UBPQ* -	**USSURI** *ex* Dae Sung Ho *-2003* *ex* Dae Sung *-2003* **Ussuri Co Ltd** - SatCom: Inmarsat C 427302640 *Vladivostok* *Russia* MMSI: 273449320 Official number: 744522	**3,728** Class: RS (KR) 1,254 2,858	**1975-03 Niigata Engineering Co Ltd — Niigata NI** Yd No: 1313 Loa 103.71 Br ex 16.01 Dght 6.060 Lbp 95.20 Br md 15.98 Dpth 9.89 Welded, 2 dks	**(B11A2FG) Factory Stern Trawler** Ins: 3,086 3 Ha: 3 (3.2 x 3.2) Derricks: 6x2.5t Ice Capable	**1 oil engine** driving 1 FP propeller Total Power: 3,310kW (4,500hp) 13.5kn Mitsubishi 6UET45/80D 1 x 2 Stroke 6 Cy. 450 x 800 3310kW (4500bhp) Akasaka Tekkosho KK (Akasaka DieselLtd)-Japan AuxGen: 3 x 500kW 445V a.c Fuel: 747.0 (d.f.)
9133185 *UCVT* -	**USSURI** **Far-Eastern Shipping Co (FESCO) (Dalnevostochnoye Morskoye Parokhodstvo)** - SatCom: Inmarsat C 427314710 *Vladivostok* *Russia* MMSI: 273147000 Official number: 950116	**6,263** Class: RS 2,755 7,212	**2002-04 AO Amurskiy Sudostroitelnyy Zavod — Komsomolsk-na-Amure** Yd No: 342 Lengthened-2006 Loa 129.10 (BB) Br ex 17.80 Dght 6.620 Lbp 119.40 Br md 17.75 Dpth 8.70 Welded, 1 dk	**(A31A2GX) General Cargo Ship** Grain: 9,272; Bale: 9,179 TEU 405 C. 405 TEU incl 10 Ref C Compartments: 3 Ho, ER 3 Ha: (25.6 x 14.0) (20.8 x 14.0)ER (19.2 x 14.0) Cranes: 2x12.5t Ice Capable	**1 oil engine** driving 1 CP propeller Total Power: 3,360kW (4,568hp) 13.0kn B&W 6DKRN35/105 1 x 2 Stroke 6 Cy. 350 x 1050 3360kW (4568bhp) AuxGen: 3 x 321kW 380V 50Hz a.c, 1 x 580kW 380V 50Hz a.c Thrusters: 1 Thwart. FP thruster (f) Fuel: 44.0 (d.f.) (Heating Coils) 286.0 (r.f.) 12.0pd
8934544 - -	**USSURIYSKIY ZALIV** - **Trading House Mortrans Co Ltd** Mortrans Co Ltd *Vladivostok* *Russia* MMSI: 273440750 Official number: 711815	*370* Class: RS 113 96	**1972-10 Kanonerskiy Sudoremontnyy Zavod — Leningrad** Yd No: 8 Loa 39.80 Br ex 10.20 Dght 2.800 Lbp 36.00 Br md 9.70 Dpth 4.20 Welded, 1 dk	**(A36A2PR) Passenger/Ro-Ro Ship (Vehicles)** Passengers: unberthed: 300 Ice Capable	**3 diesel electric oil engines** driving 3 gen. Connecting to 2 elec. motors each (312kW) driving 2 FP propellers Total Power: 663kW (900hp) 9.0kn Pervomaysk 6CH25/34-2 3 x 4 Stroke 6 Cy. 250 x 340 each-221kW (300bhp) Pervomaydizelmash (PDM)-Pervomaysk AuxGen: 3 x 30kW Fuel: 32.0 (d.f.)
7817543 *V5AD* L644	**UST-78** **Saddle Hill Namibia (Pty) Ltd** - *Luderitz* *Namibia* Official number: 92LB090	*107* Class: (PR) 33 69	**1979-05 Stocznia Ustka SA — Ustka** Yd No: B410/34 Loa 25.73 Br ex - Dght 2.893 Lbp 22.51 Br md 7.23 Dpth 3.51 Welded, 1 dk	**(B11A2FS) Stern Trawler**	**1 oil engine** geared to sc. shaft driving 1 CP propeller Total Power: 419kW (570hp) 11.0kn Sulzer 6AL20/24 1 x 4 Stroke 6 Cy. 200 x 240 419kW (570bhp) Puckie Zaklady Mechaniczne Ltd-Puck AuxGen: 1 x 32kW 400V a.c, 1 x 29kW 400V a.c
7807445 *V5UV* L702	**UST-80** **Agatha Bay Fishing** - *Luderitz* *Namibia* Official number: 93LB045	*107* Class: (PR) 33 68	**1978-09 Stocznia Ustka SA — Ustka** Yd No: B410/28 Loa 25.71 Br ex - Dght 2.900 Lbp 24.41 Br md 7.23 Dpth 3.48 Welded, 1 dk	**(B11A2FS) Stern Trawler**	**1 oil engine** geared to sc. shaft driving 1 CP propeller Total Power: 419kW (570hp) 11.0kn Sulzer 6AL20/24 1 x 4 Stroke 6 Cy. 200 x 240 419kW (570bhp) Puckie Zaklady Mechaniczne Ltd-Puck AuxGen: 1 x 32kW 400V a.c, 1 x 29kW 400V a.c
7806726 *V5UR* L852	**UST-81** **Karibib Visserye Beperk (Karibib Fisheries Pty Ltd)** Tunacor Ltd *Luderitz* *Namibia* Official number: 93LB036	*107* Class: (PR) 32 68	**1978-08 Stocznia Ustka SA — Ustka** Yd No: B410/27 Loa 25.82 Br ex - Dght 2.890 Lbp 24.41 Br md 7.21 Dpth 3.48 Welded, 1 dk	**(B11A2FS) Stern Trawler**	**1 oil engine** geared to sc. shaft driving 1 CP propeller Total Power: 419kW (570hp) 11.0kn Sulzer 6AL20/24 1 x 4 Stroke 6 Cy. 200 x 240 419kW (570bhp) Puckie Zaklady Mechaniczne Ltd-Puck AuxGen: 1 x 32kW 400V a.c, 1 x 29kW 400V a.c
7905950 *V5VO* L626	**UST-82** **Namcoast Co (Pty) Ltd** - *Luderitz* *Namibia* Official number: 92LB046	*107* Class: (PR) 33 68	**1979-09 Stocznia Ustka SA — Ustka** Yd No: B410/39 Loa 25.66 Br ex - Dght 2.890 Lbp 22.51 Br md 7.23 Dpth 3.48 Welded, 1 dk	**(B11A2FS) Stern Trawler**	**1 oil engine** geared to sc. shaft driving 1 CP propeller Total Power: 419kW (570hp) 10.8kn Sulzer 6AL20/24 1 x 4 Stroke 6 Cy. 200 x 240 419kW (570bhp) Puckie Zaklady Mechaniczne Ltd-Puck AuxGen: 1 x 32kW 400V a.c, 1 x 29kW 400V a.c
7905962 - L645	**UST-83** **Tunacor Fisheries Ltd** - *Luderitz* *Namibia* Official number: 92LB092	*107* Class: (PR) 33 68	**1979-11 Stocznia Ustka SA — Ustka** Yd No: B410/40 Loa 25.71 Br ex - Dght 2.890 Lbp 22.51 Br md 7.23 Dpth 3.48 Welded, 1 dk	**(B11A2FS) Stern Trawler**	**1 oil engine** geared to sc. shaft driving 1 CP propeller Total Power: 419kW (570hp) 11.0kn Sulzer 6AL20/24 1 x 4 Stroke 6 Cy. 200 x 240 419kW (570bhp) Puckie Zaklady Mechaniczne Ltd-Puck AuxGen: 1 x 32kW 400V a.c, 1 x 29kW 400V a.c
7606877 - -	**UST-86** **Karibib Visserye Beperk (Karibib Fisheries Pty Ltd)** Tunacor Ltd *Luderitz* *Namibia* Official number: 93LB038	*115* Class: (PR) 35 68	**1976-12 Stocznia Ustka SA — Ustka** Yd No: B410/10 Loa 25.84 Br ex 7.24 Dght 2.860 Lbp 22.51 Br md 7.19 Dpth 3.48 Welded, 1 dk	**(B11A2FT) Trawler**	**1 oil engine** reduction geared to sc. shaft driving 1 CP propeller Total Power: 419kW (570hp) 11.0kn Sulzer 6AL20/24 1 x 4 Stroke 6 Cy. 200 x 240 419kW (570bhp) Puckie Zaklady Mechaniczne Ltd-Puck AuxGen: 1 x 32kW 400V a.c, 1 x 29kW 400V a.c
7606889 - -	**UST-87** **Karibib Visserye Beperk (Karibib Fisheries Pty Ltd)** Tunacor Ltd *Luderitz* *Namibia*	*115* Class: (PR) 35 69	**1976-12 Stocznia Ustka SA — Ustka** Yd No: B410/09 Loa 25.81 Br ex 7.24 Dght 2.860 Lbp 22.51 Br md 7.19 Dpth 3.48 Welded, 1 dk	**(B11A2FT) Trawler**	**1 oil engine** reduction geared to sc. shaft driving 1 CP propeller Total Power: 419kW (570hp) 11.0kn Sulzer 6AL20/24 1 x 4 Stroke 6 Cy. 200 x 240 419kW (570bhp) Puckie Zaklady Mechaniczne Ltd-Puck AuxGen: 1 x 32kW 400V a.c, 1 x 29kW 400V a.c
7215381 *SPK2010* UST-97	**UST-97** **Kazimiera i Henryk Swiatek** - *Ustka* *Poland* MMSI: 261003310 Official number: ROG/S/694	*128* Class: (PR) 38 43	**1972-02 Gdynska Stocznia Remontowa — Gdynia** (Hull) Yd No: 338 **1972-02 Stocznia Ustka SA — Ustka** Yd No: B25s/A01 Loa 24.46 Br ex 6.61 Dght 2.500 Lbp 21.85 Br md 6.56 Dpth 3.38 Welded, 1 dk	**(B11B2FV) Fishing Vessel**	**1 oil engine** driving 1 CP propeller Total Power: 257kW (349hp) 10.5kn Wola 22H12A 1 x Vee 4 Stroke 12 Cy. 135 x 155 257kW (349bhp) Zaklady Mechaniczne 'PZL Wola' im MNowotki-Poalnd AuxGen: 2 x 4kW 30V d.c
8600375 *SPG2949* UST-116	**UST-116** *ex* DAR-316 *-2003* **Edmund Borecki** - *Ustka* *Poland* MMSI: 261004390 Official number: ROG/S/309	**166** Class: PR 50 126	**1990-11 Stocznia Ustka SA — Ustka** Yd No: B280/12 Loa 26.78 Br ex - Dght 3.200 Lbp 23.87 Br md 7.40 Dpth 3.66 Welded, 1dk	**(B11A2FS) Stern Trawler** Ins: 140	**1 oil engine** geared to sc. shaft driving 1 FP propeller Total Power: 419kW (570hp) 10.0kn Sulzer 6AL20/24 1 x 4 Stroke 6 Cy. 200 x 240 419kW (570bhp) Zaklady Przemyslu Metalowego 'HCegielski' SA-Poznan
7817531 *SPG2600* -	**UST-200** *ex* Wla-308 *-2013* *ex* UST-79 *-1996* **Przedsiebiorstwo Polowow I Uslug Rybackich 'Szkuner' (Fishing & Fishery Services Enterprise)** - *Wladyslawowo* *Poland* MMSI: 261021270	**141** Class: PR 42 68	**1979-02 Stocznia Ustka SA — Ustka** Yd No: B410/333 Loa 25.84 Br ex - Dght 3.201 Lbp 24.41 Br md 7.23 Dpth 3.48 Welded, 1 dk	**(B11A2FS) Stern Trawler**	**1 oil engine** geared to sc. shaft driving 1 CP propeller Total Power: 419kW (570hp) 11.0kn Sulzer 6AL20/24 1 x 4 Stroke 6 Cy. 200 x 240 419kW (570bhp) Puckie Zaklady Mechaniczne Ltd-Puck AuxGen: 1 x 32kW 400V a.c, 1 x 29kW 400V a.c
7931313 *V5US* L590	**UST-200** *launched as* UST-76 *-1980* **Saddle Hill Namibia (Pty) Ltd** - *Luderitz* *Namibia* Official number: 92LB072	*101* Class: (PR) 30 68	**1980-05 Stocznia Ustka SA — Ustka** Yd No: B410/48 Loa 25.76 Br ex 7.22 Dght 2.901 Lbp 24.36 Br md - Dpth 3.48 Welded, 1 dk	**(B11A2FS) Stern Trawler**	**1 oil engine** geared to sc. shaft driving 1 CP propeller Total Power: 419kW (570hp) 10.8kn Sulzer 6AL20/24 1 x 4 Stroke 6 Cy. 200 x 240 419kW (570bhp) Puckie Zaklady Mechaniczne Ltd-Puck AuxGen: 2 x 36kW 400V a.c

Ship / Owner	Tonnage / Class	Build / Dimensions	Type / Cargo	Machinery
7931325 **UST-201** *V5UT* *launched as* UST-77 *-1980* L589 **Tunacor Fisheries Ltd** - *Luderitz* *Namibia* Official number: 92LB073	*101* Class: (PR) 30 68	**1980-04 Stocznia Ustka SA — Ustka** Yd No: B410/49 Loa 25.68 Br ex 7.22 Dght 2.901 Lbp 24.36 Br md - Dpth 3.48 Welded, 1 dk	**(B11A2FS) Stern Trawler**	**1 oil engine** geared to sc. shaft driving 1 CP propeller Total Power: 419kW (570hp) 10.8kn Sulzer 6AL20/24 1 x 4 Stroke 6 Cy. 200 x 240 419kW (570bhp) Puckie Zaklady Mechaniczne Ltd-Puck AuxGen: 2 x 36kW 400V a.c
8008670 **UST-203** *SPK2146* *launched as* GDY-221 *-1981* UST-203 **B Mlynski, W Wojtkowiak, K Przewrocki & A Skroda** - *Ustka* *Poland* MMSI: 261001620 Official number: ROG/S/173	**135** Class: PR 40 79	**1981-07 Stocznia Ustka SA — Ustka** Yd No: B410/401 Loa 25.68 Br ex 7.22 Dght 2.980 Lbp 24.39 Br md - Dpth 3.48 Welded, 1 dk	**(B11A2FS) Stern Trawler**	**1 oil engine** geared to sc. shaft driving 1 CP propeller Total Power: 419kW (570hp) 11.0kn Sulzer 6AL20/24 1 x 4 Stroke 6 Cy. 200 x 240 419kW (570bhp) Puckie Zaklady Mechaniczne Ltd-Puck AuxGen: 2 x 36kW 400V a.c
8600325 **UST-204** *SPK2068* UST-204 **Przedsiebiorstwo Polowow I Uslug Rybackich 'Korab' (Fishing, Fish Processing & Trade)** - *Ustka* *Poland* MMSI: 261002530 Official number: ROG/S/174	*166* Class: PR 50 126	**1989-12 Stocznia Ustka SA — Ustka** Yd No: B280/07 Loa 26.77 Br ex - Dght 3.200 Lbp - Br md 7.41 Dpth 3.66 Welded, 1 dk	**(B11A2FS) Stern Trawler**	**1 oil engine** geared to sc. shaft driving 1 FP propeller Total Power: 419kW (570hp) 10.0kn Sulzer 6AL20/24 1 x 4 Stroke 6 Cy. 200 x 240 419kW (570bhp) Zaklady Przemyslu Metalowego 'HCegielski' SA-Poznan
7923718 **UST-IZHMA** *UFQA* - **Ust Izhma Co Ltd** Refrybflot Shipping Co SatCom: Inmarsat C 427320193 *Kaliningrad* *Russia* MMSI: 273810030 Official number: 802075	**5,105** Class: (RS) 1,833 4,991	**1981-10 Rauma-Repola Oy — Rauma** Yd No: 268 Loa 115.50 Br ex 17.02 Dght 6.410 Lbp 103.56 Br md 17.01 Dpth 8.51 Welded, 1 dk	**(A13B2TP) Products Tanker** Single Hull Bale: 203; Liq: 6,240; Liq (Oil): 6,240 Part Cargo Heating Coils Compartments: 1 Ho, 8 Ta, ER 1 Ha: (2.5 x 3.2)ER Ice Capable	**1 oil engine** driving 1 FP propeller Total Power: 2,465kW (3,351hp) 14.0kn B&W 5DKRN50/110-2 1 x 2 Stroke 5 Cy. 500 x 1100 2465kW (3351bhp) Bryanskiy Mashinostroitelnyy Zavod (BMZ)-Bryansk AuxGen: 3 x 264kW 380V 50Hz a.c Fuel: 543.0 (r.f.) 16.5pd
7923691 **UST-KAN** - - - -	**5,105** Class: (RS) 1,834 4,969	**1981-06 Rauma-Repola Oy — Rauma** Yd No: 266 Loa 115.50 Br ex 17.02 Dght 6.390 Lbp 105.01 Br md 17.01 Dpth 8.51 Welded, 1 dk	**(A13B2TP) Products Tanker** Bale: 203; Liq: 6,240; Liq (Oil): 6,240 Part Cargo Heating Coils Compartments: 1 Ho, 8 Ta, ER 1 Ha: (2.5 x 3.2)ER 2 Cargo Pump (s): 2x200m³/hr Ice Capable	**1 oil engine** driving 1 FP propeller Total Power: 2,465kW (3,351hp) 14.0kn B&W 5DKRN50/110-2 1 x 2 Stroke 5 Cy. 500 x 1100 2465kW (3351bhp) Bryanskiy Mashinostroitelnyy Zavod (BMZ)-Bryansk AuxGen: 3 x 264kW 380V 50Hz a.c Fuel: 543.0 (r.f.) 16.5pd
7636638 **UST-KARSK** *UGWQ* - **Eastern Shipping Co Ltd (Vostochnaya Sudokhodnaya Kompaniya OOO)** - SatCom: Inmarsat C 427320143 *Sovetskaya Gavan* *Russia* MMSI: 273812030 Official number: 792210	**5,105** Class: RS 1,834 4,969	**1979-12 Rauma-Repola Oy — Rauma** Yd No: 255 Loa 115.50 Br ex 17.02 Dght 6.390 Lbp 105.01 Br md 17.00 Dpth 8.51 Welded, 1 dk	**(A13B2TP) Products Tanker** Single Hull Bale: 203; Liq: 6,420; Liq (Oil): 6,420 Part Cargo Heating Coils Compartments: 1 Ho, 8 Ta, ER 1 Ha: (2.5 x 3.2)ER 2 Cargo Pump (s): 2x200m³/hr Ice Capable	**1 oil engine** driving 1 FP propeller Total Power: 2,465kW (3,351hp) 14.0kn B&W 5DKRN50/110-2 1 x 2 Stroke 5 Cy. 500 x 1100 2465kW (3351bhp) Bryanskiy Mashinostroitelnyy Zavod (BMZ)-Bryansk AuxGen: 3 x 264kW 380V 50Hz a.c Fuel: 88.0 (d.f.) (Part Heating Coils) 400.0 (r.f.) 16.5pd
8025886 **UST-LABINSK** - - - -	**5,105** Class: (RS) 1,834 4,969	**1982-02 Rauma-Repola Oy — Rauma** Yd No: 272 Loa 115.19 Br ex 17.05 Dght 6.390 Lbp 105.01 Br md 17.01 Dpth 8.51 Welded, 1 dk	**(A13B2TP) Products Tanker** Bale: 203; Liq: 6,420; Liq (Oil): 6,420 Part Cargo Heating Coils Compartments: 1 Ho, 8 Ta, ER 1 Ha: (2.5 x 3.2)ER Ice Capable	**1 oil engine** driving 1 FP propeller Total Power: 2,465kW (3,351hp) 14.0kn B&W 5DKRN50/110-2 1 x 2 Stroke 5 Cy. 500 x 1100 2465kW (3351bhp) Bryanskiy Mashinostroitelnyy Zavod (BMZ)-Bryansk AuxGen: 3 x 264kW 380V 50Hz a.c Fuel: 88.0 (d.f.) (Part Heating Coils) 400.0 (r.f.) 16.5pd
8839469 **USTRICHNYY** - - **Rybtransflot** -	**705** Class: (RS) 211 308	**1990-12 Khabarovskiy Sudostroitelnyy Zavod im Kirova — Khabarovsk** Yd No: 307 Loa 56.42 Br ex 9.53 Dght 4.141 Lbp 49.97 Br md - Dpth 5.01 Welded, 1 dk	**(B11B2FV) Fishing Vessel** Ins: 200 Ice Capable	**1 oil engine** driving 1 CP propeller Total Power: 736kW (1,001hp) 11.8kn S.K.L. 6NVD48A-2U 1 x 4 Stroke 6 Cy. 320 x 480 736kW (1001bhp) VEB Schwermaschinenbau "KarlLiebknecht" (SKL)-Magdeburg AuxGen: 4 x 200kW a.c
8884581 **USUKHCHAY** *4JLQ* *ex* MSK-4 *-1972* - **Specialized Sea Oil Fleet Organisation, Caspian Sea Oil Fleet, State Oil Co of the Republic of Azerbaijan** - *Baku* *Azerbaijan* MMSI: 423171100 Official number: DGR-0122	*816* Class: (RS) 112 348	**1972-01 Sudostroitelnyy Zavod "Krasnyye Barrikady" — Krasnyye Barrikady** Yd No: 4 Loa 54.95 Br ex 14.52 Dght 2.120 Lbp 51.50 Br md - Dpth 3.70 Welded, 1 dk	**(B34B2SC) Crane Vessel** Cranes: 1x25t	**2 oil engines** driving 2 FP propellers Total Power: 1,030kW (1,400hp) 11.0kn Russkiy 6DR30/50-6-1 2 x 2 Stroke 6 Cy. 300 x 500 each-515kW (700bhp) Mashinostroitelnyy Zavod"Russkiy-Dizel"-Leningrad AuxGen: 3 x 100kW a.c Fuel: 118.0 (d.f.)
9105554 **USUKI MARU No. 26** *JM6303* - **Yutaka Kaiun KK** - *Saiki, Oita* *Japan* Official number: 133582	*103* - 73	**1994-09 Shitanoe Shipbuilding Co Ltd — Usuki OT** Yd No: 1153 L reg 26.00 Br ex - Dght - Lbp - Br md 7.20 Dpth 3.20 Welded, 1 dk	**(B32A2ST) Tug**	**1 oil engine** driving 1 FP propeller Daihatsu 6DLM-24S 1 x 4 Stroke 6 Cy. 240 x 320 Daihatsu Diesel Manufacturing Co Lt-Japan
8501050 **USUMACINTA** - - **Government of Mexico (Secretaria de Communicaciones y Transportes Servicio de Transbordadores, Direccion General)** - *Tampico* *Mexico*	*127* Class: (AB) 116 50	**1983-06 Construcciones Navales de Tampico S.A. — Tampico** Yd No: 5 Loa - Br ex - Dght - Lbp 24.39 Br md 9.15 Dpth 1.86 Welded	**(A37B2PS) Passenger Ship**	**1 oil engine** driving 1 FP propeller Total Power: 405kW (551hp) Caterpillar 3408TA 1 x Vee 4 Stroke 8 Cy. 137 x 152 405kW (551bhp) Caterpillar Inc-USA
6620761 **USUMACINTA I** *HC2691* *ex* Pasa I *-1993* - **Empresa Pesquera Polar SA** - *Guayaquil* *Ecuador* Official number: P-00-0553	*164* Class: (LR) - ✠ Classed LR until 1/68 -	**1966-11 Fabricaciones Metallicas E.P.S. (FABRIMET) — Callao** Yd No: 332 Loa 25.20 Br ex 7.14 Dght 2.693 Lbp 21.49 Br md 7.01 Dpth 3.46 Welded, 1 dk	**(B11B2FV) Fishing Vessel**	**1 oil engine** reverse reduction geared to sc. shaft driving 1 FP propeller Total Power: 399kW (542hp) Caterpillar D353SCAC 1 x 4 Stroke 6 Cy. 159 x 203 399kW (542bhp) Caterpillar Tractor Co-USA
9422110 **UT GLORY** - - **The University of Transport Ho Ci Minh City** - *Saigon* *Vietnam* MMSI: 574580000	**1,498** Class: VR 707 2,399	**2007-03 Ben Kien Shipbuilding Industry Co — Haiphong** Yd No: TH-181 Loa 76.15 Br ex - Dght 4.750 Lbp 72.00 Br md 12.40 Dpth 5.70 Welded, 1 dk	**(A31A2GX) General Cargo Ship**	**1 oil engine** reduction geared to sc. shaft driving 1 FP propeller Total Power: 1,500kW (2,039hp) Chinese Std. Type G8300ZC 1 x 4 Stroke 8 Cy. 300 x 380 1500kW (2039bhp) Wuxi Antai Power Machinery Co Ltd-China
9369069 **UTA** *V2CJ9* - **ms 'Jop' Schiffahrtsgesellschaft mbH & Co KG** Intersee Schiffahrtsgesellschaft mbH & Co KG SatCom: Inmarsat C 430502410 *Saint John's* *Antigua & Barbuda* MMSI: 305024000	**7,878** Class: GL (LR) 3,909 ✠ Classed LR until 21/3/11 10,758	**2007-02 Damen Shipyards Yichang Co Ltd — Yichang HB** (Hull) **2007-02 B.V. Scheepswerf Damen — Gorinchem** Yd No: 7301 Loa 145.63 (BB) Br ex 18.29 Dght 7.350 Lbp 138.82 Br md 18.25 Dpth 10.30 Welded, 1 dk	**(A31A2GX) General Cargo Ship** Grain: 14,878 TEU 671 C Ho 302 C Dk 369 TEU incl 60 ref C. Compartments: 2 Ho, ER 2 Ha: (65.4 x 13.2)ER (39.0 x 13.2) Cranes: 2x60t Ice Capable	**1 oil engine** with flexible couplings & sr reverse geared to sc. shaft driving 1 CP propeller Total Power: 4,320kW (5,873hp) 14.2kn MaK 9M32C 1 x 4 Stroke 9 Cy. 320 x 480 4320kW (5873bhp) Caterpillar Motoren GmbH & Co. KG-Germany AuxGen: 1 x 760kW 400V 50Hz a.c, 3 x 350kW 380V 50Hz a.c Boilers: e (ex.g.) 10.2kgf/cm² (10.0bar), TOH (o.f.) 10.2kgf/cm² (10.0bar) Thrusters: 1 Thwart. FP thruster (f) Fuel: 52.0 (d.f.) 507.0 (r.f.)

IMO / Call sign / Flag	Name / Owner	Tonnage	Class	Builder / Dimensions	Type	Machinery
8415691 *E5U2824* -	**UTA** *ex* Andorra *-2001* *ex* Halina *-1997* *ex* Idun *-1989* *ex* Halina *-1988* **Uta Shipping Ltd** Wakes & Co Ltd SatCom: Inmarsat C 451800150 *Avatiu* *Cook Islands* MMSI: 518877000	**2,119** 1,085 3,042	Class: RI (GL) (BV)	**1984-12 J.J. Sietas KG Schiffswerft GmbH & Co. — Hamburg** Yd No: 962 Loa 92.11 (BB) Br ex 11.54 Dght 5.160 Lbp 89.21 Br md 11.31 Dpth 6.91 Welded, 2 dks	**(A31A2GX) General Cargo Ship** Grain: 4,060; Bale: 4,039 TEU 100 C.Ho 60/20' (40') C.Dk 40/20' (40') Compartments: 1 Ho, ER 1 Ha: (61.7 x 9.3)ER	**1 oil engine** sr reverse geared to sc. shaft driving 1 FP propeller Total Power: 599kW (814hp) 11.0kn Deutz SBV6M628 1 x 4 Stroke 6 Cy. 240 x 280 599kW (814bhp) Kloeckner Humboldt Deutz AG-West Germany AuxGen: 1 x 180kW 380V a.c, 1 x 61kW 380V a.c Thrusters: 1 Thwart. FP thruster (f) Fuel: 215.0 (d.f.)
8916683 - -	**UTARID** *ex* Kotohira Maru No. 3 *-2013* **PT Lindas Armada Indonesia** -	*494* - 1,250	Class: IZ	**1990-03 K.K. Miura Zosensho — Saiki** Yd No: 877 Loa - Br ex - Dght 4.141 Lbp 60.00 Br md 10.00 Dpth 4.40 Welded, 1 dk	**(B35E2TF) Bunkering Tanker**	**1 oil engine** driving 1 FP propeller Total Power: 1,177kW (1,600hp) Niigata 6M28HGT 1 x 4 Stroke 6 Cy. 280 x 480 1177kW (1600bhp) Niigata Engineering Co Ltd-Japan
8730508 *UHPE* -	**UTASHUD** - **Gorod 415 Ltd** - SatCom: Inmarsat C 427306335 *Petropavlovsk-Kamchatskiy* *Russia* MMSI: 273849800	**448** 134 207	Class: RS	**1989-11 Zavod 'Nikolayevsk-na-Amure' — Nikolayevsk-na-Amure** Yd No: 1270 Loa 44.89 Br ex 9.48 Dght 3.771 Lbp 39.37 Br md 9.30 Dpth 5.14 Welded	**(B11A2FS) Stern Trawler** Ins: 210 Ice Capable	**1 oil engine** driving 1 FP propeller Total Power: 588kW (799hp) 11.5kn S.K.L. 6NVD48A-2U 1 x 4 Stroke 6 Cy. 320 x 480 588kW (799bhp) VEB Schwermaschinenbau "KarlLiebknecht" (SKL)-Magdeburg AuxGen: 3 x 150kW a.c Fuel: 88.0 (d.f.)
9153408 *DGZO* -	**UTE OLTMANN** *ex* CP Rangitoto *-2006* *ex* Contship Rangitoto *-2005* *ex* Cielo di San Francisco *-2005* *ex* Ute Oltmann *-1999* **ms 'Ute Oltmann' Schiffahrtsgesellschaft mbH & Co KG** Schiffahrtsgesellschaft Oltmann mbH & Co KG *Hamburg* *Germany* MMSI: 211288580 Official number: 19018	**25,359** 12,733 33,964 T/cm 45.0	Class: GL	**1998-12 Volkswerft Stralsund GmbH — Stralsund** Yd No: 421 Loa 207.40 (BB) Br ex - Dght 11.420 Lbp 195.40 Br md 29.80 Dpth 16.40 Welded, 1 dk	**(A33A2CC) Container Ship (Fully Cellular)** Grain: 46,997 TEU 2474 C Ho 992 TEU C Dk 1482 TEU incl 320 ref C. Compartments: 5 Cell Ho, ER 10 Ha: ER Cranes: 3x45t	**1 oil engine** driving 1 FP propeller Total Power: 17,200kW (23,385hp) 20.9kn B&W 6L70MC 1 x 2 Stroke 6 Cy. 700 x 2268 17200kW (23385bhp) Dieselmotorenwerk Rostock GmbH-Rostock AuxGen: 2 x 1900kW 440V 60Hz a.c, 1 x 1400kW 440V 60Hz a.c Thrusters: 1 Thwart. CP thruster (f) Fuel: 212.0 (d.f.) (Heating Coils) 2313.0 (r.f.) 68.3pd
4500084 - -	**UTEC SURVEYOR** *ex* Goosander *-2006* **UTEC Survey Ltd**	**799** 240 -	Class: (LR) ✠	**1973-09 Robb Caledon Shipbuilders Ltd. — Scotland** Yd No: 513 Loa 60.25 Br ex 12.36 Dght 4.180 Lbp 48.80 Br md 12.20 Dpth 5.50 Welded, 1 dk	**(B34P2QV) Salvage Ship**	**1 oil engine** driving 1 CP propeller Total Power: 551kW (749hp) 10.0kn Paxman 16RPHM 1 x Vee 4 Stroke 16 Cy. 178 x 197 551kW (749bhp) Paxman Diesels Ltd.-Colchester AuxGen: 3 x 168kW
9548407 *DNPM* -	**UTHLANDE** - **Neue Pellwormer Dampfschiffahrts GmbH** - *Wyk auf Foehr* *Germany* MMSI: 211493380 Official number: 72981	**3,179** 990 499	Class: GL	**2010-05 J.J. Sietas KG Schiffswerft GmbH & Co. — Hamburg** Yd No: 1228 Loa 75.88 Br ex - Dght 1.850 Lbp 72.00 Br md 15.80 Dpth 3.40 Welded, 1 dk	**(A36A2PR) Passenger/Ro-Ro Ship (Vehicles)** Passengers: unberthed: 1184 Bow door (centre) Len: - Wid: 10.00 Swl: - Stern door (centre) Len: - Wid: 10.00 Swl: - Lane-Len: 340 Lane-Wid: 2.50 Lane-clr ht: 4.50 Cars: 75	**4 oil engines** reduction geared to sc. shafts driving 4 Voith-Schneider propellers 2 propellers aft, 2 fwd Total Power: 2,312kW (3,144hp) 12.0kn Caterpillar 3508C 4 x Vee 4 Stroke 8 Cy. 170 x 190 each-578kW (786bhp) Caterpillar Inc-USA AuxGen: 2 x 200kW 400V a.c Fuel: 66.0 (d.f.)
8100648 *DBCH* -	**UTHORN** - **Government of The Federal Republic of Germany (Bundesministerium fuer Forschung und Technologie)** Reederei F Laeisz (Bremerhaven) GmbH *Helgoland* *Germany* MMSI: 211216410	**274** 82 87	Class: GL	**1982-09 Schiffswerft Gebr Schloemer Oldersum — Moormerland** Yd No: 280 Loa 30.51 Br ex 8.59 Dght 2.650 Lbp 26.50 Br md 8.50 Dpth 3.36 Welded, 1 dk	**(B12D2FR) Fishery Research Vessel** Ice Capable	**2 oil engines** with clutches, flexible couplings & sr geared to sc. shafts driving 2 CP propellers Total Power: 464kW (630hp) 10.8kn MWM TBD232V12 2 x Vee 4 Stroke 12 Cy. 120 x 130 each-232kW (315bhp) Motoren Werke Mannheim AG (MWM)-West Germany
9265469 *ZR5137* -	**UTHUKELA** - **Transnet Ltd** Portnet Dredging Services *Durban* *South Africa* Official number: 20203	**378** 113 293	Class: (LR) ✠ Classed LR until 23/3/04	**2003-01 Southern African Shipyards (Pty.) Ltd. — Durban** Yd No: 304 Loa 30.80 Br ex 11.63 Dght 5.150 Lbp 28.50 Br md 11.00 Dpth 4.30 Welded, 1 dk	**(B32A2ST) Tug**	**2 oil engines** gearing integral to driving 2 Voith-Schneider propellers Total Power: 3,800kW (5,166hp) Ruston 6RK270M 2 x 4 Stroke 6 Cy. 270 x 305 each-1900kW (2583bhp) GEC Alsthom Ruston Diesels Ltd.-Newton-le-Willows AuxGen: 2 x 90kW 380V 50Hz a.c
7215769 - -	**UTILA EXPRESS II** *ex* Mary Maureen *-2004* **Henry Michael Rose Laurie** - *Honduras* Official number: S-3538005	*100* 41 -		**1966 Browns Shipyard, Inc. — Long Beach, Ms** L reg 21.10 Br ex 6.71 Dght - Lbp - Br md - Dpth 3.26 Welded	**(B11B2FV) Fishing Vessel**	**1 oil engine** driving 1 FP propeller Total Power: 243kW (330hp)
7041364 *3VHH* -	**UTIQUE** - **Government of The Republic of Tunisia (Office des Ports Nationaux Tunisiens)** - *Bizerte* *Tunisia* Official number: TG127	*226* - -	Class: (BV)	**1967 "Petrozavod" — Leningrad** Loa 29.32 Br ex 8.31 Dght 3.074 Lbp 26.98 Br md 7.95 Dpth 4.35 Welded, 1 dk	**(B32A2ST) Tug**	**2 oil engines** driving 2 CP propellers Total Power: 882kW (1,200hp) 11.3kn Russkiy 6DR30/50 2 x 2 Stroke 6 Cy. 300 x 500 each-441kW (600bhp) Mashinostroitelnyy Zavod"Russkiy-Dizel"-Leningrad AuxGen: 2 x 50kW 220V 50Hz a.c Fuel: 36.5 (d.f.)
6404739 *J8Y3725* -	**UTO** - **Eagle Shipping Ltd** Triton Shipping AB *Kingstown* *St Vincent & The Grenadines* MMSI: 375225000 Official number: 40195	**164** 50 45		**1964-02 Valmet Oy — Turku** Yd No: 282 Converted From: Training Vessel-2006 Converted From: Ferry (Passenger only)-1986 Loa 26.95 Br ex 6.91 Dght 2.801 Lbp 24.67 Br md 6.89 Dpth 4.04 Welded	**(X11A2YP) Yacht** Passengers: cabins: 6; berths: 12 Compartments: 1 Ho, ER 1 Ha: (1.5 x 2.0) Derricks: 2x2t; Winches: 2	**1 oil engine** driving 1 FP propeller Total Power: 303kW (412hp) 8.0kn Alpha 404-26VO 1 x 2 Stroke 4 Cy. 260 x 400 303kW (412bhp) (new engine ,made 1964) MAN B&W Diesel A/S-Denmark AuxGen: 1 x 8kW 400V 50Hz a.c, 1 x 2kW 400V 50Hz a.c, 1 x 1kW 400V 50Hz a.c Thrusters: 1 Thwart. FP thruster (f) Fuel: 10.0 (d.f.) 1.5pd
8030350 *SJYC* -	**UTO EXPRESS** *ex* Stadt Kappeln *-2002* *ex* Svea Lejon *-1994* **Uto Rederi AB** - *Uto* *Sweden* MMSI: 265530460	**225** 90 50		**1981-05 Marinteknik Verkstads AB — Oregrund** Yd No: B45 Loa 31.88 Br ex 6.74 Dght 1.720 Lbp 29.80 Br md 6.71 Dpth 2.37 Welded, 1 dk	**(A37B2PS) Passenger Ship** Hull Material: Aluminium Alloy	**2 oil engines** sr geared to sc. shaft driving 1 FP propeller Scania DSI1402M 2 x Vee 4 Stroke 8 Cy. 127 x 140 Saab Scania AB-Sweden
8889062 *JE3073* -	**UTO MARU** - **Aomori Ko Kanri Jimusho** - *Aomori, Aomori* *Japan* Official number: 130533	*196* - -		**1995-03 KK Kitahama Zosen Tekko — Aomori AO** Yd No: 108 Loa 32.01 Br ex - Dght 3.400 Lbp 28.00 Br md 9.00 Dpth 4.40 Welded, 1 dk	**(B32A2ST) Tug**	**2 oil engines** driving 2 FP propellers Total Power: 2,500kW (3,400hp) 12.0kn
7913919 - -	**UTOKU MARU No. 3** - - - *South Korea*	*159* - 278		**1979-08 Shimoda Dockyard Co. Ltd. — Shimoda** Yd No: 300 Loa 31.70 Br ex 7.24 Dght 2.450 Lbp 29.82 Br md 7.01 Dpth 2.67 Welded, 1 dk	**(A13B2TU) Tanker (unspecified)**	**1 oil engine** driving 1 FP propeller Total Power: 221kW (300hp) Matsui MU323CGHS 1 x 4 Stroke 3 Cy. 230 x 380 221kW (300bhp) Matsui Iron Works Co Ltd-Japan
7913921 - -	**UTOKU MARU No. 5** - - - *South Korea*	*296* - 560		**1979-10 Shimoda Dockyard Co. Ltd. — Shimoda** Yd No: 301 Loa 41.00 Br ex - Dght 3.250 Lbp 38.03 Br md 8.01 Dpth 3.51 Welded, 1 dk	**(A13B2TU) Tanker (unspecified)**	**1 oil engine** driving 1 FP propeller Total Power: 368kW (500hp) Matsui MU623CGHS 1 x 4 Stroke 6 Cy. 230 x 380 368kW (500bhp) Matsui Iron Works Co Ltd-Japan

8604266 *HOLS* -	**UTOPIA** *ex* New Hamanasu *-2002* **Utopia Line SA** Nishinihon Kisen Co Ltd *Panama* *Panama* MMSI: 355342000 Official number: 2879302B	**26,906** 8,072 6,473 T/cm 34.0	Class: NK	1987-03 **Ishikawajima-Harima Heavy Industries Co Ltd (IHI) — Aioi HG** Yd No: 2947 Loa 184.50 (BB) Br ex - Dght 6.784 Lbp 171.02 Br md 26.51 Dpth 14.25 Welded	**(A36A2PR) Passenger/Ro-Ro Ship (Vehicles)** Passengers: unberthed: 748; cabins: 47; berths: 172 Stern door/ramp (centre) Len: 7.65 Wid: 7.50 Swl: 40 Quarter stern door/ramp (s) Len: 16.00 Wid: 6.10 Swl: 40 Lane-Len: 1982 Lane-Wid: 3.00 Lane-clr ht: 4.20 Lorries: 150, Cars: 103	**2 oil engines** geared to sc. shafts driving 2 FP propellers Total Power: 21,844kW (29,700hp) 22.5kn Pielstick 9PC40L570 2 x 4 Stroke 9 Cy. 570 x 750 each-10922kW (14850bhp) Ishikawajima Harima Heavy IndustrieCo Ltd (IHI)-Japan AuxGen: 1 x 1400kW 450V 60Hz a.c Fuel: 128.0 (d.f.) 661.0 (r.f.) 52.0pd
1007263 *ZCNZ9* -	**UTOPIA** *ex* Utopia Dv *-2010* *ex* Utopia *-2005* **Utopia Enterprises Inc** Vessel Safety Management LLC *George Town* *Cayman Islands (British)* MMSI: 319326000 Official number: 737646	**1,564** 469 218	Class: LR ✠ **100A1** SS 08/2009 SSC Yacht (P), mono G6 ✠ **LMC** **UMS** Cable: 403.0/30.0 U2 (a)	2004-08 **Scheepswerf Slob B.V. — Papendrecht** (Hull) Yd No: 418 2004-08 **de Vries Scheepsbouw B.V. — Aalsmeer** Yd No: 667 Loa 71.60 (BB) Br ex 11.80 Dght 3.700 Lbp 59.48 Br md 11.20 Dpth 6.20 Welded, 1 dk	**(X11A2YP) Yacht**	**2 oil engines** with clutches, flexible couplings & sr reverse geared to sc. shafts driving 2 FP propellers Total Power: 2,984kW (4,058hp) 16.5kn Caterpillar 3516B-TA 2 x Vee 4 Stroke 16 Cy. 170 x 190 each-1492kW (2029bhp) Caterpillar Inc-USA AuxGen: 3 x 245kW 400V 50Hz a.c Thrusters: 1 Thwart. FP thruster (f); 2 Thwart. FP thruster (a)
9142801 - -	**UTOPIA** *ex* Baek Ryeong Island *-2011* **Daewang Industrial Co Ltd** Dong Yang Ferry Co Ltd *Mokpo* *South Korea* MMSI: 440322160 Official number: MPR-964354	**287** 168 53	Class: KR	1996-01 **Kvaerner Fjellstrand (S) Pte Ltd — Singapore** Yd No: 021 Loa 40.00 Br ex - Dght 1.740 Lbp - Br md 10.10 Dpth 3.97 Welded, 1 dk	**(A37B2PS) Passenger Ship** Hull Material: Aluminium Alloy Passengers: unberthed: 333	**2 oil engines** geared to sc. shafts driving 2 Water jets Total Power: 4,000kW (5,438hp) 35.0kn M.T.U. 16V396TE74L 2 x Vee 4 Stroke 16 Cy. 165 x 185 each-2000kW (2719bhp) MTU Friedrichshafen GmbH-Friedrichshafen
8604278 *H9FO* -	**UTOPIA 2** *ex* New Shirayuri *-2005* **Utopia Line SA** Nishinihon Kisen Co Ltd SatCom: Inmarsat C 435182010 *Panama* *Panama* MMSI: 351820000 Official number: 3096005A	*26,933* 8,080 6,434 T/cm 37.0	Class: NK	1987-04 **Ishikawajima-Harima Heavy Industries Co Ltd (IHI) — Aioi HG** Yd No: 2948 Loa 184.50 (BB) Br ex 26.52 Dght 6.784 Lbp 171.02 Br md 26.51 Dpth 14.25 Welded	**(A36A2PR) Passenger/Ro-Ro Ship (Vehicles)** Passengers: unberthed: 748; cabins: 47; berths: 172 Stern door/ramp (centre) Len: 7.65 Wid: 7.50 Swl: 40 Quarter stern door/ramp (s) Len: 16.00 Wid: 6.10 Swl: 40 Lane-Len: 1982 Lane-Wid: 3.00 Lane-clr ht: 4.20 Lorries: 150, Cars: 103	**2 oil engines** geared to sc. shafts driving 2 FP propellers Total Power: 21,846kW (29,702hp) 22.6kn Pielstick 9PC40L570 2 x 4 Stroke 9 Cy. 570 x 750 each-10923kW (14851bhp) Ishikawajima Harima Heavy IndustrieCo Ltd (IHI)-Japan AuxGen: 3 x 1400kW 450V 60Hz a.c Thrusters: 1 Thwart. CP thruster (f); 1 Tunnel thruster (a) Fuel: 128.0 (d.f.) 661.0 (r.f.) 60.0pd
8980244 *WDD2728* -	**UTOPIA III** *ex* Lady Linda *-2006* *ex* Bellini *-2001* **Market America Inc** - *Miami, FL* *United States of America* Official number: 1089708	**488** 146 -	Class: AB	1999-11 **Trinity Yachts LLC — New Orleans LA** Yd No: 011 Loa - Br ex - Dght - Lbp 39.62 Br md 7.92 Dpth 4.16 Welded, 1 dk	**(X11A2YP) Yacht** Hull Material: Aluminium Alloy Passengers: cabins: 5	**2 oil engines** reverse reduction geared to sc. shafts driving 2 Propellers Total Power: 3,310kW (4,500hp) 20.0kn Caterpillar 3512B 2 x Vee 4 Stroke 12 Cy. 170 x 190 each-1655kW (2250bhp) Caterpillar Inc-USA AuxGen: 2 x 99kW a.c Thrusters: 1 Tunnel thruster (f)
9045895 *3ESV8* -	**UTOPIA IV** *ex* Akatuki *-2009* *ex* New Akatsuki *-2008* **Utopia Line SA** Nishinihon Kisen Co Ltd *Panama* *Panama* MMSI: 370441000 Official number: 3494910	**14,250** 4,275 4,322	Class: NK	1992-07 **Hayashikane Dockyard Co Ltd — Nagasaki NS** Yd No: 995 Loa 145.61 (BB) Br ex - Dght 6.250 Lbp 132.00 Br md 22.00 Dpth 14.00 Welded	**(A36A2PR) Passenger/Ro-Ro Ship (Vehicles)** Passengers: unberthed: 534; cabins: 20; berths: 46; driver berths: 20 Quarter bow door/ramp (s) Quarter stern door/ramp (p) Quarter stern door/ramp (s) Lane-Len: 1460 Lane-clr ht: 5.40 Lorries: 70, Cars: 54	**2 oil engines** reduction geared to sc. shafts driving 2 FP propellers Total Power: 13,240kW (18,002hp) 21.5kn Pielstick 12PC2-6V-400 2 x Vee 4 Stroke 12 Cy. 400 x 460 each-6620kW (9001bhp) Diesel United Ltd.-Aioi AuxGen: 3 x 880kW a.c, 1 x 250kW a.c Thrusters: 1 Thwart. FP thruster (f); 1 Tunnel thruster (a) Fuel: 500.0 (r.f.) 51.3pd
9125956 *PCQC* -	**UTRECHT** *ex* Amsterdam *-2007* **Sleephopperzuiger Utrecht BV** Van Oord Ship Management BV SatCom: Inmarsat B 324560110 *Rotterdam* *Netherlands* MMSI: 245601000 Official number: 29387	**18,259** 5,477 23,000	Class: BV	1996-11 **Merwede Shipyard BV — Hardinxveld** Yd No: 670 Loa 154.30 Br ex - Dght 8.910 Lbp 141.65 Br md 28.00 Dpth 11.85 Welded, 1 dk	**(B33B2DT) Trailing Suction Hopper Dredger** Hopper: 18,292	**2 oil engines** with clutches & reduction geared to sc. shafts driving 2 CP propellers Total Power: 21,720kW (29,530hp) 15.6kn Wartsila 12V46 2 x Vee 4 Stroke 12 Cy. 460 x 580 each-10860kW (14765bhp) Wartsila Diesel Oy-Finland AuxGen: 2 x 9000kW a.c, 1 x 1200kW a.c Thrusters: 2 Thwart. CP thruster (f)
9540027 *5NJV2* -	**UTS** *ex* CS Enterprise *-2011* **UTM Dredging Ltd** - *Nigeria* MMSI: 657666000	**450** 135 -	Class: (BV)	2009-07 **Celtug Service Shipyard Sdn Bhd — Sibu** Yd No: 0614 Loa 36.00 Br ex - Dght 4.000 Lbp 31.50 Br md 10.40 Dpth 5.00 Welded, 1 dk	**(B32A2ST) Tug**	**2 oil engines** reduction geared to sc. shafts driving 2 FP propellers Total Power: 2,984kW (4,058hp) 10.0kn Cummins KTA-50-M2 2 x Vee 4 Stroke 16 Cy. 159 x 159 each-1492kW (2029bhp) Cummins Engine Co Ltd-United Kingdom Thrusters: 1 Tunnel thruster (f)
9334507 *LNDY* -	**UTSIRA** **Rutebaaten Utsira AS** - *Haugesund* *Norway* MMSI: 259395000	**1,513** 453 -		2005-01 **AS Rigas Kugu Buvetava (Riga Shipyard) — Riga** (Hull) Yd No: 1069/2 2005-01 **Blaalid AS — Raudeberg** Yd No: 32 Loa 48.20 (BB) Br ex - Dght - Lbp - Br md 12.40 Dpth 5.50 Welded, 1 dk	**(A36A2PR) Passenger/Ro-Ro Ship (Vehicles)** Passengers: unberthed: 150 Cars: 25	**2 oil engines** geared to sc. shafts driving 2 CP propellers Total Power: 2,206kW (3,000hp) 14.3kn MAN-B&W 6L21/31 2 x 4 Stroke 6 Cy. 210 x 310 each-1103kW (1500bhp) MAN B&W Diesel AG-Augsburg Thrusters: 1 Tunnel thruster (f)
7434676 *LAEL* -	**UTSTEIN** *ex* Eidfjord *-1987* **Norled AS** - *Stavanger* *Norway* MMSI: 257022700	**827** 277 250	Class: (NV)	1975-07 **AS Haugesunds Slip — Haugesund** Yd No: 18 Loa 64.32 Br ex 11.28 Dght 3.117 Lbp 58.50 Br md 11.23 Dpth 4.22 Welded, 1 dk	**(A36A2PR) Passenger/Ro-Ro Ship (Vehicles)** Passengers: unberthed: 390	**1 oil engine** driving 2 Propellers aft, 1 fwd Total Power: 1,011kW (1,375hp) 13.3kn Wichmann 5AXA 1 x 2 Stroke 5 Cy. 300 x 450 1011kW (1375bhp) Wichmann Motorfabrikk AS-Norway AuxGen: 2 x 72kW 220V 50Hz a.c
7713979 *JJ3065* -	**UTSUMI** *ex* Senho Maru *-1991* **Kambara Logistics Co Ltd** - *Fukuyama, Hiroshima* *Japan* Official number: 118821	*196* - -		1977-08 **Kanagawa Zosen — Kobe** Yd No: 177 Loa 30.30 Br ex - Dght 2.701 Lbp 25.51 Br md 8.62 Dpth 3.81 Welded, 1 dk	**(B32A2ST) Tug**	**2 oil engines** Geared Integral to driving 1 Propeller , 1 Z propeller Total Power: 1,912kW (2,600hp) 14.0kn Daihatsu 6DSM-26 2 x 4 Stroke 6 Cy. 260 x 320 each-956kW (1300bhp) Daihatsu Diesel Manufacturing Co Lt-Japan
7714076 - -	**UTSUMI No. 2** *ex* Ikuchi Maru *-1985* *ex* Mukaishima Maru No. 35 *-1984* **Yangpang Trading Co Ltd** - *Chinese Taipei*	*193* - 180		1977-11 **Kanbara Zosen K.K. — Onomichi** Yd No: 228 Loa 33.80 Br ex - Dght 2.200 Lbp 28.60 Br md 10.00 Dpth 2.90 Riveted\Welded, 1 dk	**(A36A2PR) Passenger/Ro-Ro Ship (Vehicles)** Passengers: unberthed: 146	**2 oil engines** driving 2 FP propellers Total Power: 192kW (262hp) Yanmar 6ML 2 x 4 Stroke 6 Cy. 200 x 240 each-96kW (131bhp) Yanmar Diesel Engine Co Ltd-Japan
9129861 - -	**UTTAMI** **West Bengal Surface Transport Corp** - *India*	*250* - -	Class: (IR)	1997-03 **Meroline Engineering Works — Haora** Yd No: 44 Loa - Br ex - Dght - Lbp 27.30 Br md 8.00 Dpth 2.50 Welded, 1 dk	**(A37B2PS) Passenger Ship**	**2 oil engines** geared to sc. shafts driving 2 Propellers Cummins N-495-M 2 x 4 Stroke 4 Cy. 130 x 152 Kirloskar Cummins Ltd-India
9015450 *V2NY* -	**UTTUM** *ex* Saar Antwerp *-1997* **Erwin Strahlmann** Reederei Erwin Strahlmann eK SatCom: Inmarsat C 430401115 *Saint John's* *Antigua & Barbuda* MMSI: 304010302 Official number: 2338	**1,662** 810 2,363	Class: GL	1993-06 **Rosslauer Schiffswerft GmbH — Rosslau** Yd No: 244 Loa 81.80 Br ex - Dght 4.349 Lbp 77.50 Br md 11.30 Dpth 5.52 Welded, 2 dks	**(A31A2GX) General Cargo Ship** Grain: 3,086; Bale: 3,070 TEU 80 C.Ho 48/20' C.Dk 32/20' Compartments: 1 Ho, ER 1 Ha: (52.0 x 9.0)ER Ice Capable	**1 oil engine** reverse reduction geared to sc. shaft driving 1 FP propeller Total Power: 960kW (1,305hp) 10.5kn Deutz SBV6M628 1 x 4 Stroke 6 Cy. 240 x 280 960kW (1305bhp) Motoren Werke Mannheim AG (MWM)-Mannheim AuxGen: 2 x 104kW 220/380V a.c Thrusters: 1 Thwart. FP thruster (f)

IMO / Call sign	Name / Owner / Port	Tonnage	Class	Builder / Dimensions	Type	Machinery
9193989 - -	**UTW CHALLENGE** *ex Pelican Challenge -2007* **UTM Dredging Ltd** *Nigeria*	**364** 109 303 T/cm 3.3	Class: (AB)	**1998**-06 **Penguin Boat International Ltd — Singapore** Yd No: 113 Loa 47.75 Br ex 9.20 Dght 2.450 Lbp 41.10 Br md 9.10 Dpth 3.85 Welded, 1 dk	**(B21A2OC) Crew/Supply Vessel**	**4 oil engines** with clutches & sr reverse geared to sc. shafts driving 4 FP propellers Total Power: 2,824kW (3,840hp) 24.0kn G.M. (Detroit Diesel) 16V-92-TA 4 x Vee 2 Stroke 16 Cy. 123 x 127 each-706kW (960bhp) General Motors Detroit DieselAllison Divn-USA AuxGen: 2 x 90kW 415V 50Hz a.c Thrusters: 1 Thwart. FP thruster (f)
7640914 *4JAX* -	**UTYOS** **Azerbaijan State Caspian Shipping Co (ASCSS)** *Baku* *Azerbaijan* Official number: DGR-0179	*1,074* 232 440	Class: (RS)	**1976 Khersonskiy Sudostroitelnyy Zavod — Kherson** Yd No: 1802 Loa 58.55 Br ex 12.68 Dght 4.687 Lbp 51.62 Br md - Dpth 5.90 Welded, 1 dk	**(B32A2ST) Tug** Derricks: 1x5t,1x1t Ice Capable	**2 diesel electric oil engines** driving 2 gen. each 1100kW Connecting to 1 elec. Motor of (1900kW) driving 1 FP propeller Total Power: 2,206kW (3,000hp) 13.3kn Kolomna 6CHN30/38 2 x 4 Stroke 6 Cy. 300 x 380 each-1103kW (1500bhp) Kolomenskiy Zavod-Kolomna AuxGen: 2 x 300kW a.c, 2 x 160kW Fuel: 302.0 (d.f.)
8226492 *UIAR* -	**UTYOS** **Zvezda-DISSK Co Ltd (Far-Eastern Engineering Shipbuilding Co)** *Vladivostok* *Russia* MMSI: 273819610 Official number: 822524	**1,160** 348 404	Class: RS	**1983**-11 **Yaroslavskiy Sudostroitelnyy Zavod — Yaroslavl** Yd No: 222 Loa 58.55 Br ex 12.67 Dght 4.690 Lbp 51.62 Br md - Dpth 5.90 Welded, 1 dk	**(B32A2ST) Tug** Derricks: 1x5t Ice Capable	**2 diesel electric oil engines** driving 2 gen. each 1100kW Connecting to 2 elec. motors each (950kW) driving 1 FP propeller Total Power: 2,206kW (3,000hp) 13.2kn Kolomna 6CHN30/38 2 x 4 Stroke 6 Cy. 300 x 380 each-1103kW (1500bhp) Kolomenskiy Zavod-Kolomna AuxGen: 2 x 300kW a.c, 2 x 160kW a.c Fuel: 295.0 (d.f.)
8629656 - -	**UVA** *ex Iris -2006* **C& Hangangland Co Ltd** - *Yeongdeungpo* *South Korea* Official number: ICR-860311	**135** - 32	Class: (KR)	**1986**-10 **Semo Co Ltd — Incheon** Yd No: 4 Loa 30.00 Br ex - Dght 1.215 Lbp 29.00 Br md 7.06 Dpth 1.44 Welded, 1 dk	**(A37B2PS) Passenger Ship**	**2 oil engines** driving 2 FP propellers Total Power: 442kW (600hp) 7.0kn Volvo Penta TMD122A 2 x 4 Stroke 6 Cy. 130 x 150 each-221kW (300bhp) AB Volvo Penta-Sweden AuxGen: 1 x 48kW 220V a.c
7121827 - -	**UVAZHITELNYY** **Twins Co Ltd (OOO'Tvins')** -	**206** 62 111	Class: (RS)	**1971**-07 **Sretenskiy Sudostroitelnyy Zavod — Sretensk** Yd No: 30 Loa 33.91 Br ex 7.09 Dght 3.100 Lbp 30.00 Br md - Dpth 3.69 Welded, 1 dk	**(B11B2FV) Fishing Vessel** Bale: 114 Compartments: 1 Ho, ER 1 Ha: (1.6 x 1.3) Derricks: 2x2t	**1 oil engine** driving 1 FP propeller 9.0kn S.K.L. 1 x 4 Stroke 8 Cy. 240 x 360 VEB Schwermaschinenbau "KarlLiebknecht" (SKL)-Magdeburg
7119290 *UHTC* -	**UVERENNYY** *ex Kristalnyy -2002* **BTO Vostokremstroy Co Ltd** *Vladivostok* *Russia*	**172** 51 102	Class: (RS)	**1971 Zavod 'Nikolayevsk-na-Amure' — Nikolayevsk-na-Amure** Yd No: 48 Loa 33.96 Br ex 7.09 Dght 2.900 Lbp 29.97 Br md 7.00 Dpth 3.69 Welded, 1 dk	**(B11B2FV) Fishing Vessel** Bale: 115 Compartments: 1 Ho, ER 1 Ha: (1.6 x 1.3) Derricks: 2x2t Ice Capable	**1 oil engine** driving 1 FP propeller Total Power: 224kW (305hp) 9.5kn S.K.L. 8NVD36-1U 1 x 4 Stroke 8 Cy. 240 x 360 224kW (305bhp) VEB Schwermaschinenbau "KarlLiebknecht" (SKL)-Magdeburg AuxGen: 1 x 75kW, 1 x 50kW Fuel: 24.0 (d.f.)
8975586 - -	**UVM 08** *ex Tensho Maru -2013* *ex Fukuei Maru No. 8 -2005* - - *Indonesia*	*103* - -		**1987**-08 **Maekawa Zosensho — Japan** L reg 25.26 Br ex - Dght - Lbp - Br md 7.20 Dpth 3.00 Welded, 1 dk	**(B32A2ST) Tug**	**1 oil engine** driving 1 Propeller Total Power: 883kW (1,201hp) Sumiyoshi S6UFGSS 1 x 4 Stroke 6 Cy. 260 x 400 883kW (1201bhp) Sumiyoshi Marine Diesel Co Ltd-Japan
9275892 *JL6678* -	**UWAKAI** **Uwakai Kisen KK** *Seiyo, Ehime* *Japan* MMSI: 431501741 Official number: 136572	*999* - 2,485	Class: NK	**2002**-10 **Hakata Zosen K.K. — Imabari** Yd No: 651 Loa 80.98 Br ex - Dght 5.144 Lbp 76.50 Br md 12.00 Dpth 5.75 Welded, 1 dk	**(A13B2TP) Products Tanker** Double Hull (13F) Liq: 2,744; Liq (Oil): 2,800	**1 oil engine** driving 1 FP propeller Total Power: 1,912kW (2,600hp) 12.5kn Hanshin LH36LAG 1 x 4 Stroke 6 Cy. 360 x 670 1912kW (2600bhp) The Hanshin Diesel Works Ltd-Japan Fuel: 121.0 (d.f.)
8879495 *JL6302* -	**UWAKAI No. 1** **KK Yamaya** - *Uwajima, Ehime* *Japan* MMSI: 431197000 Official number: 133938	*198* - 419		**1994**-12 **Mikami Zosen K.K. — Japan** Yd No: 333 Loa 46.85 Br ex - Dght 3.250 Lbp 40.70 Br md 7.80 Dpth 3.70 Welded, 1 dk	**(B11B2FV) Fishing Vessel**	**1 oil engine** driving 1 FP propeller Total Power: 736kW (1,001hp) 11.0kn Niigata 6M28HRGT 1 x 4 Stroke 6 Cy. 280 x 480 736kW (1001bhp) Niigata Engineering Co Ltd-Japan
8889206 *JL6305* -	**UWAKAI No. 2** **KK Yamaya** - *Uwajima, Ehime* *Japan* Official number: 134882	*198* - -		**1995**-04 **Mikami Zosen K.K. — Japan** L reg 41.00 Br ex - Dght - Lbp - Br md 7.80 Dpth 3.70 Welded, 1 dk	**(B11B2FV) Fishing Vessel**	**1 oil engine** driving 1 FP propeller Niigata 1 x 4 Stroke Niigata Engineering Co Ltd-Japan
9218325 *DBDI* -	**UWE JENS LORNSEN** **Government of The Federal Republic of Germany (Bundesminister fuer Verkehr-WSV)** - *Toenning* *Germany* MMSI: 211294830	**104** 31 14	Class: GL	**1999**-03 **Deutsche Binnenwerften GmbH — Berlin** Yd No: 3189 Loa 24.17 Br ex 6.80 Dght 1.300 Lbp 22.06 Br md 6.50 Dpth 2.50 Welded, 1 dk	**(B31A2SR) Research Survey Vessel**	**2 oil engines** geared to sc. shafts driving 2 Directional propellers Total Power: 550kW (748hp) 12.0kn M.T.U. 6R183TE72 2 x 4 Stroke 6 Cy. 128 x 142 each-275kW (374bhp) MTU Friedrichshafen GmbH-Friedrichshafen
5115317 *JWXW* -	**UWEX** *ex Finnsnes -1984* **A/S Betongspregning** Lars Nevra *Aalesund* *Norway*	**212** 63 -	Class: (NV)	**1958 Kaarbos Mek. Verksted AS — Harstad** Yd No: 23 Loa 28.77 Br ex 9.30 Dght - Lbp 26.70 Br md 8.01 Dpth 3.26 Welded, 1 dk	**(A36A2PR) Passenger/Ro-Ro Ship (Vehicles)** Passengers: unberthed: 160 Cars: 16	**1 oil engine** driving 1 FP propeller Total Power: 316kW (430hp) Wichmann 4ACA 1 x 2 Stroke 4 Cy. 280 x 420 316kW (430bhp) (made 1969, fitted 1970) Wichmann Motorfabrikk AS-Norway AuxGen: 1 x 10kW 220V 50Hz a.c
8847478 *YL2362* -	**UZAVA** *ex Uzhava -1992* **Ventspils Free Port Authority (Ventspils Brivostas Parvalde)** *Ventspils* *Latvia* Official number: 1002	**236** 127 440	Class: (RS)	**1982 Bakinskiy Sudostroitelnyy Zavod im Vano Sturua — Baku** Yd No: 353 Loa 35.17 Br ex 8.01 Dght 3.120 Lbp 33.25 Br md 7.60 Dpth 3.60 Welded, 1 dk	**(B34E2SW) Waste Disposal Vessel** Liq: 480; Liq (Oil): 480 Compartments: 10 Ta Ice Capable	**1 oil engine** geared to sc. shaft driving 1 FP propeller Total Power: 165kW (224hp) 8.1kn Daldizel 6CHNSP18/22 1 x 4 Stroke 6 Cy. 180 x 220 165kW (224bhp) Daldizel-Khabarovsk AuxGen: 1 x 50kW, 1 x 30kW Fuel: 13.0 (d.f.)
9323388 *V7LN7* -	**UZAVA** **Sigulda Navigation Inc** Latvian Shipping Co (Latvijas Kugnieciba) *Majuro* *Marshall Islands* MMSI: 538002774 Official number: 2774	**30,641** 15,297 52,650 T/cm 56.8	Class: LR (NV) **100A1** SS 01/2013 Double Hull oil and chemical tanker, Ship Type 2 ESP LI *IWS SPM Ice Class 1B at a draft of 12.798m Max/min draught fwd 12.798/5.918m Max/min draught aft 13.088/7.588m Minimum power required 8716kw, installed power 9650kw **LMC** **UMS IGS**	**2008**-01 **'3 Maj' Brodogradiliste dd — Rijeka** Yd No: 702 Loa 195.17 (BB) Br ex 32.24 Dght 12.500 Lbp 187.30 Br md 32.20 Dpth 17.80 Welded, 1 dk	**(A12B2TR) Chemical/Products Tanker** Double Hull (13F) Liq: 56,151; Liq (Oil): 57,330 Compartments: 12 Wing Ta, 2 Wing Slop Ta, ER 12 Cargo Pump (s): 12x550m³/hr Manifold: Bow/CM: 97.1m Ice Capable	**1 oil engine** driving 1 FP propeller Total Power: 9,650kW (13,120hp) 14.0kn Sulzer 7RTA48T-B 1 x 2 Stroke 7 Cy. 480 x 2000 9650kW (13120bhp) '3 Maj' Motori i Dizalice dd-Croatia AuxGen: 3 x 960kW 450V 60Hz a.c Fuel: 333.0 (d.f.) 2830.0 (r.f.)

7370014 *ZTUN* -	**UZAVOLO** *ex* R. H. Tarpey **Transnet Ltd** Portnet Dredging Services *Durban* *South Africa* Official number: 351131	*373* - -	Class: (LR) ✠ Classed LR until 21/11/75	**1974-05 James Brown & Hamer Ltd. — Durban** Yd No: 23 Loa 35.97 Br ex 11.59 Dght - Lbp 33.51 Br md 11.00 Dpth 4.14 Welded, 1 dk	**(B32A2ST) Tug**	**2 oil engines** geared to sc. shafts driving 2 Directional propellers Total Power: 2,898kW (3,940hp) Blackstone ESL16MK2 2 x Vee 4 Stroke 16 Cy. 222 x 292 each-1449kW (1970bhp) Mirrlees Blackstone (Stamford)Ltd.-Stamford AuxGen: 2 x 110kW 380/220V 50Hz a.c
7110907 *IQAU* -	**UZEDA CATANESE** *ex* Uzeda *ex* Audacia **Fratelli Giacalone e Gilante** - *Mazara del Vallo* *Italy* Official number: 186	*157* 76 61		**1971 Cant. Nav. Dante Castracani Srl — Ancona** Yd No: 79 Loa 30.51 Br ex 6.30 Dght 2.553 Lbp 23.02 Br md 6.28 Dpth 3.10 Welded, 1 dk	**(B11A2FT) Trawler**	**1 oil engine** driving 1 FP propeller Total Power: 346kW (470hp) 11.0kn MWM RH435AU 1 x 4 Stroke 8 Cy. 250 x 350 346kW (470bhp) Motoren Werke Mannheim AG (MWM)-West Germany
7646853 *4JDR* -	**UZEYIR HAJYBEYOV** *ex* Uzeir Gadzhibekov *-1994* **Azerbaijan State Caspian Shipping Co (ASCSS)** Meridian Shipping & Management LLC *Baku* *Azerbaijan* MMSI: 423065100 Official number: DGR-0025	**2,434** 994 3,135 T/cm 13.0	Class: (RS)	**1977-06 Sudostroitelnyy Zavod im Volodarskogo — Rybinsk** Yd No: 75 Loa 114.03 Br ex 13.21 Dght 3.650 Lbp 108.01 Br md 12.98 Dpth 5.52 Welded, 1 dk	**(A31A2GX) General Cargo Ship** Bale: 4,297 Compartments: 4 Ho, ER 4 Ha: (17.6 x 9.3)3 (18.0 x 9.3)ER Ice Capable	**2 oil engines** driving 2 FP propellers Total Power: 970kW (1,318hp) 10.8kn S.K.L. 6NVD48A-U 2 x 4 Stroke 6 Cy. 320 x 480 each-485kW (659bhp) VEB Schwermaschinenbau "KarlLiebknecht" (SKL)-Magdeburg AuxGen: 3 x 50kW Fuel: 102.0 (d.f.)
9121467 *TC7924* -	**UZMAR** **Uzmar-Uzmanlar Denizcilik Ticaret ve Sanayi Ltd Sti** - *Izmir* *Turkey* MMSI: 271015025	**135** 40 -	Class: LR ✠ **100A1** SS 11/2010 tug **LMC** Cable: 247.5/18.0 U2	**1995-11 Stocznia Tczew Sp z oo — Tczew** (Hull) **1995-11 B.V. Scheepswerf Damen — Gorinchem** Yd No: 6520 Loa 22.55 Br ex 7.45 Dght 3.180 Lbp 19.82 Br md 7.20 Dpth 3.74 Welded, 1 dk	**(B32A2ST) Tug**	**2 oil engines** with clutches, flexible couplings & sr reverse geared to sc. shafts driving 2 FP propellers Total Power: 2,026kW (2,754hp) 11.4kn Caterpillar 3512TA 2 x Vee 4 Stroke 12 Cy. 170 x 190 each-1013kW (1377bhp) Caterpillar Inc-USA AuxGen: 2 x 44kW 380V 50Hz a.c
8847258 *UDKD* TE-1378	**UZON** **Akros 2 JSC** Akros Fishing Co Ltd (A/O Akros) *Petropavlovsk-Kamchatskiy* *Russia* MMSI: 273848610 Official number: 900259	**831** 249 258	Class: RS	**1991-06 Yaroslavskiy Sudostroitelnyy Zavod — Yaroslavl** Yd No: 378 Loa 53.70 (BB) Br ex 10.71 Dght 4.400 Lbp 47.92 Br md 10.50 Dpth 6.00 Welded, 1 dk	**(B11A2FS) Stern Trawler** Ins: 248 Ice Capable	**1 oil engine** driving 1 CP propeller Total Power: 969kW (1,317hp) 12.6kn S.K.L. 8NVD48A-2U 1 x 4 Stroke 8 Cy. 320 x 480 969kW (1317bhp) SKL Motoren u. Systemtechnik AG-Magdeburg AuxGen: 1 x 300kW a.c, 3 x 150kW a.c
8112366 - -	**UZU** *ex* Lake Sonfon *-1990* **Government of Libya (Socialist Ports Co)** - *Tripoli* *Libya*	*121* 36 51	Class: (LR) ✠ Classed LR until 7/10/92	**1987-09 Scheepswerf Aalst/'t Gilde B.V. — Aalst (Nl)** (Hull) **1987-09 B.V. Scheepswerf Damen — Gorinchem** Yd No: 2709 Loa 25.66 Br ex 6.94 Dght 2.909 Lbp 23.17 Br md 6.61 Dpth 3.43 Welded, 1 dk	**(B32A2ST) Tug**	**2 oil engines** with clutches, flexible couplings & sr reverse geared to sc. shafts driving 2 FP propellers Total Power: 1,186kW (1,612hp) Deutz SBA12M816 2 x Vee 4 Stroke 12 Cy. 142 x 160 each-593kW (806bhp) Kloeckner Humboldt Deutz AG-West Germany AuxGen: 2 x 48kW 380V 50Hz a.c
8954271 - -	**V 96** **Metapsco (Cong Ty Co Phan Vat Tu Thiet Bi)** - *Saigon* *Vietnam* Official number: VNSG-1453-TD	**130** 64 170	Class: VR	**1995-01 76-Shipbuilding Enterprise — Ho Chi Minh City** Loa 34.10 Br ex 6.52 Dght 1.700 Lbp 31.00 Br md 6.50 Dpth 2.25 Welded, 1 dk	**(A13B2TU) Tanker (unspecified)**	**2 oil engines** driving 2 FP propellers Total Power: 132kW (180hp) 6.0kn Caterpillar 2 x 4 Stroke each-66kW (90bhp) Caterpillar Inc-USA AuxGen: 1 x 30kW a.c, 1 x 10kW a.c
6523951 - -	**V ADMIRAL KLOKACHEV** *ex* Smorbukk *-2012* *ex* Fenring *-1980* *ex* Askoy *-1979* **Sevastopol Transport Systems Ltd** - *Sevastopol* *Ukraine* MMSI: 272126100	**657** 244 -	Class: (NV)	**1965-03 Loland Motorverkstad AS — Leirvik i Sogn** Yd No: 21 Converted From: Ferry (Passenger/Vehicle)-1992 Lengthened-1992 Loa 51.50 Br ex 9.50 Dght 2.883 Lbp - Br md 9.25 Dpth 3.36 Welded, 1 dk	**(A37B2PS) Passenger Ship** Passengers: unberthed: 600	**1 oil engine** driving 2 Propellers 1 fwd and 1 aft Total Power: 883kW (1,201hp) 11.0kn Alpha 6L23/30A 1 x 4 Stroke 6 Cy. 225 x 300 883kW (1201bhp) (new engine 1992) MAN B&W Diesel A/S-Denmark
9201011 *EAWD* -	**V.B. ADRIATICO** **Remolcadores Boluda SA** Boluda Corporacion Maritima *Valencia* *Spain* MMSI: 224870000 Official number: 5-8/2001	**342** 103 190	Class: GL (LR) ✠ Classed LR until 26/2/12	**1999-11 Astilleros Zamakona SA — Santurtzi** Yd No: 440 Loa 30.20 Br ex 11.50 Dght 2.500 Lbp 28.00 Br md 11.00 Dpth 4.00 Welded, 1 dk	**(B32A2ST) Tug**	**2 oil engines** reduction geared to sc. shafts driving 2 Directional propellers Total Power: 3,040kW (4,134hp) MaK 8M20 2 x 4 Stroke 8 Cy. 200 x 300 each-1520kW (2067bhp) MaK Motoren GmbH & Co. KG-Kiel AuxGen: 2 x 160kW 380V 50Hz a.c
9319363 *ECLO* -	**V.B. ALMERIA** **Servicios Auxiliares de Puertos SA (SERTOSA)** - *Ceuta* *Spain* MMSI: 224215290 Official number: 1-2/2006	**237** 102 58	Class: BV	**2007-01 Union Naval Valencia SA (UNV) — Valencia** Yd No: 385 Loa 23.80 Br ex - Dght 4.000 Lbp 21.46 Br md 11.00 Dpth 4.72 Welded, 1 dk	**(B32A2ST) Tug**	**2 oil engines** geared to sc. shafts driving 2 Z propellers Total Power: 3,162kW (4,300hp) 12.5kn Caterpillar 3516B 2 x Vee 4 Stroke 16 Cy. 170 x 190 each-1581kW (2150bhp) Caterpillar Inc-USA
9289295 *ECFI* -	**V.B. ANDALUCIA** **Servicios Auxiliares de Puertos SA (SERTOSA)** - *Ceuta* *Spain* MMSI: 224117450 Official number: 5-2/2004	**374** 112 210	Class: BV	**2003-12 Union Naval Valencia SA (UNV) — Valencia** Yd No: 305 Loa - Br ex - Dght 3.450 Lbp 28.00 Br md 11.00 Dpth 4.00 Welded, 1 dk	**(B32A2ST) Tug**	**2 oil engines** geared to sc. shafts driving 2 Voith-Schneider propellers Total Power: 3,678kW (5,000hp) Deutz SBV9M628 2 x 4 Stroke 9 Cy. 240 x 280 each-1839kW (2500bhp) Deutz AG-Koeln
9257668 *EBWG* -	**V.B. ANIBAL** **Boluda Towage & Salvage SLU** Boluda Corporacion Maritima *Valencia* *Spain* MMSI: 224049240 Official number: 5-6/2001	**354** 106 190	Class: GL (LR) Classed LR until 11/1/12	**2002-03 Union Naval Valencia SA (UNV) — Valencia** Yd No: 299 Loa 29.50 Br ex - Dght 3.350 Lbp 28.00 Br md 11.00 Dpth 4.70 Welded, 1 dk	**(B32A2ST) Tug**	**2 oil engines** gearing integral to driving 2 Voith-Schneider propellers Total Power: 4,060kW (5,520hp) Caterpillar 3606TA 2 x 4 Stroke 6 Cy. 280 x 300 each-2030kW (2760bhp) Caterpillar Inc-USA AuxGen: 2 x 181kW 380V a.c
9245811 *EBVS* -	**V.B. ASDRUBAL** **Remolcadores de Cartagena SA (RECASA)** - *Cartagena* *Spain* MMSI: 224056980 Official number: 5-5/2001	**345** 106 190	Class: GL	**2002-06 Union Naval Valencia SA (UNV) — Valencia** Yd No: 293 Loa 29.50 Br ex - Dght 2.500 Lbp 28.00 Br md 11.00 Dpth 4.00 Welded, 1 dk	**(B32A2ST) Tug**	**2 oil engines** gearing integral to driving 2 Voith-Schneider propellers Total Power: 4,060kW (5,520hp) Caterpillar 3606TA 2 x 4 Stroke 6 Cy. 280 x 300 each-2030kW (2760bhp) Caterpillar Inc-USA
9122083 *HP4688* -	**V.B. ATLANTICO** *ex* Boa Odin *-1997* *ex* PM 177 *-1995* **Compania Maritima Mexicana SA de CV** Boluda Corporacion Maritima *Panama* *Panama* Official number: 4232811	**431** 129 240	Class: GL (AB)	**1994-03 President Marine Pte Ltd — Singapore** Yd No: 177 Loa 34.00 Br ex - Dght 4.000 Lbp 32.00 Br md 10.60 Dpth 4.96 Welded, 1 dk	**(B32A2ST) Tug**	**2 oil engines** reduction geared to sc. shafts driving 2 Directional propellers Total Power: 2,940kW (3,998hp) Nohab 6R25 2 x 4 Stroke 6 Cy. 250 x 300 each-1470kW (1999bhp) Wartsila Diesel AB-Sweden AuxGen: 2 x 120kW 415V 50Hz a.c Fuel: 200.0 (d.f.) 11.8pd
9052757 *LW2605* -	**V.B. AUSTRAL** *ex* Boluda Alisio *-2010* **Compania Maritima Austral SA** - *Buenos Aires* *Argentina* Official number: 02757	**231** 69 113	Class: (LR) (GL) Classed LR until 10/3/13	**1993-06 S.L. Ardeag — Bilbao** Yd No: 176 Lengthened-2005 L reg 29.94 Br ex - Dght 3.600 Lbp - Br md 8.60 Dpth 4.55 Welded, 1 dk	**(B32A2ST) Tug**	**2 oil engines** with clutches, flexible couplings & sr reverse geared to sc. shafts driving 2 CP propellers Total Power: 2,640kW (3,590hp) 12.0kn Caterpillar 3516TA 2 x Vee 4 Stroke 16 Cy. 170 x 190 each-1320kW (1795bhp) Caterpillar Inc-USA AuxGen: 2 x 80kW 220/380V a.c Thrusters: 1 Thwart. FP thruster (f)
9158018 *EAQX* -	**V.B. BALEAR** **Remolcadores y Barcazas de Las Palmas SA** Boluda Corporacion Maritima *Valencia* *Spain* MMSI: 224494000 Official number: 5-9/2001	**342** 102 190	Class: (LR) ✠ Classed LR until 25/5/05	**1998-05 Astilleros Zamakona SA — Santurtzi** Yd No: 393 Loa 30.20 Br ex 11.50 Dght 2.500 Lbp 28.00 Br md 11.00 Dpth 4.00 Welded, 1 dk	**(B32A2ST) Tug**	**2 oil engines** reduction geared to sc. shafts driving 2 Directional propellers Total Power: 3,040kW (4,134hp) 12.0kn MaK 8M20 2 x 4 Stroke 8 Cy. 200 x 300 each-1520kW (2067bhp) MaK Motoren GmbH & Co. KG-Kiel AuxGen: 2 x 160kW 380V 50Hz a.c

IMO / Call sign	Name / Owner	Tonnage	Class	Builder / Dimensions	Type	Machinery
9245809 *EAGC* -	**V.B. BORA** **Boluda Towage & Salvage SLU** Boluda Corporacion Maritima *Huelva* *Spain* MMSI: 224027840 Official number: 5-2/2001	**351** 105 156	Class: BV (LR) (GL) Classed LR until 1/11/13	**2001-07 Union Naval Valencia SA (UNV) — Valencia** Yd No: 292 Loa 29.50 Br ex - Dght 3.350 Lbp 28.00 Br md 11.00 Dpth 4.00 Welded, 1 dk	**(B32A2ST) Tug**	**2 oil engines** gearing integral to driving 2 Voith-Schneider propellers Total Power: 4,060kW (5,520hp) Caterpillar 3606TA 2 x 4 Stroke 6 Cy. 280 x 300 each-2030kW (2760bhp) Caterpillar Inc-USA
9402201 *EAOV* -	**V.B. BRAVO** **Auxiliar Maritima del Sur SA (AUXMASA)** - SatCom: Inmarsat C 422540110 *Santa Cruz de Tenerife* *Spain* MMSI: 225401000	**848** 254 450	Class: GL (AB)	**2009-11 Union Naval Valencia SA (UNV) — Valencia** Yd No: 389 Loa 35.46 Br ex - Dght 5.590 Lbp 31.49 Br md 13.00 Dpth 6.60 Welded, 1 dk	**(B32A2ST) Tug**	**2 oil engines** gearing integral to driving 2 Z propellers Total Power: 6,120kW (8,320hp) 13.0kn MAN-B&W 9L27/38 2 x 4 Stroke 9 Cy. 270 x 380 each-3060kW (4160bhp) MAN Diesel A/S-Denmark AuxGen: 2 x 220kW 400V 50Hz a.c Thrusters: 2 Directional thruster (f) Fuel: 320.0 (d.f.)
9313890 *ECFJ* -	**V.B. BRIO** **Boluda Towage & Salvage SLU** Boluda Corporacion Maritima *Valencia* *Spain* MMSI: 224121260 Official number: 5-2/2004	**369** 112 219	Class: BV	**2003-12 Union Naval Valencia SA (UNV) — Valencia** Yd No: 304 Loa 28.00 Br ex - Dght 3.790 Lbp 28.00 Br md 11.00 Dpth 4.00 Welded, 1 dk	**(B32A2ST) Tug**	**2 oil engines** gearing integral to driving 2 Voith-Schneider propellers Total Power: 4,046kW (5,500hp) Deutz SBV9M628 2 x 4 Stroke 9 Cy. 240 x 280 each-2023kW (2750bhp) Deutz AG-Koeln AuxGen: 2 x 145kW 400V 50Hz a.c
8107684 *HO2802* -	**V.B. BUCANERO** *ex* Punta Tarifa *-2007* **Tug Services Panama SA** Compania Maritima de Panama SA *Panama* *Panama* MMSI: 372738000 Official number: 3305207A	**309** 92 183	Class: LR ✠**100A1** SS 03/2009 tug ✠**LMC** **UMS** Eq.Ltr: G; Cable: 302.5/20.5 U2	**1982-07 Astilleros Luzuriaga SA — Pasaia** Yd No: 229 Loa 33.00 Br ex 9.63 Dght 4.671 Lbp 29.01 Br md 9.11 Dpth 5.52 Welded, 1 dk	**(B32A2ST) Tug**	**1 oil engine** with clutches, flexible couplings & sr geared to sc. shaft driving 1 CP propeller Total Power: 2,383kW (3,240hp) 13.0kn Sulzer 12ASV25/30 1 x Vee 4 Stroke 12 Cy. 250 x 300 2383kW (3240bhp) Astilleros Espanoles SA (AESA)-Spain AuxGen: 1 x 100kW 380V 50Hz a.c, 1 x 96kW 380V 50Hz a.c, 1 x 32kW 380V 50Hz a.c Fuel: 183.0 (d.f.) 8.0pd
8518388 *VWMR* -	**V. B. C. CHOLA** **VBC Exports Ltd** - *Visakhapatnam* *India*	*155* 47 80	Class: (IR) (NV)	**1987-05 Australian Shipbuilding Industries (WA) Pty Ltd — Fremantle WA** Yd No: 245 Loa 24.95 Br ex 7.42 Dght 3.010 Lbp 22.05 Br md - Dpth 3.00 Welded, 1 dk	**(B11A2FT) Trawler** Ins: 110	**1 oil engine** with clutches, flexible couplings & sr geared to sc. shaft driving 1 FP propeller Total Power: 373kW (507hp) Caterpillar 3412T 1 x Vee 4 Stroke 12 Cy. 137 x 152 373kW (507bhp) Caterpillar Inc-USA AuxGen: 2 x 63kW 415V 50Hz a.c
8628274 *VWMP* -	**V. B. C. GOWTAMI** **VBC Exports Ltd** - *Visakhapatnam* *India* Official number: 2214	*116* 35 73	Class: (AB) (IR)	**1987 Alcock, Ashdown & Co. Ltd. — Bhavnagar** Yd No: 137 Loa 23.50 Br ex - Dght 2.830 Lbp 20.35 Br md 7.31 Dpth 3.41 Welded, 1 dk	**(B11A2FT) Trawler**	**2 oil engines** sr geared to sc. shafts driving 2 FP propellers Total Power: 296kW (402hp) 9.5kn Caterpillar 3408TA 2 x Vee 4 Stroke 8 Cy. 137 x 152 each-148kW (201bhp) Caterpillar Inc-USA AuxGen: 2 x 40kW 440V 50Hz a.c
8518390 *VWMS* -	**V. B. C. PANDYA** **VBC Exports Ltd** - *Visakhapatnam* *India*	*155* 47 80	Class: (IR) (NV)	**1987-08 Australian Shipbuilding Industries (WA) Pty Ltd — Fremantle WA** Yd No: 246 Loa - Br ex 7.42 Dght 3.010 Lbp 24.92 Br md - Dpth 3.00 Welded, 1 dk	**(B11A2FT) Trawler**	**1 oil engine** sr geared to sc. shaft driving 1 FP propeller Total Power: 370kW (503hp) Caterpillar 3412T 1 x Vee 4 Stroke 12 Cy. 137 x 152 370kW (503bhp) Caterpillar Inc-USA AuxGen: 2 x 63kW 415V 50Hz a.c
8628286 *VWMQ* -	**V. B. C. SALIVAHAN** **VBC Exports Ltd** - *Visakhapatnam* *India* Official number: 2215	*116* 35 73	Class: (IR) (AB)	**1987 Alcock, Ashdown & Co. Ltd. — Bhavnagar** Yd No: 138 Loa 23.50 Br ex - Dght 2.830 Lbp 20.35 Br md 7.31 Dpth 3.41 Welded, 1 dk	**(B11A2FT) Trawler**	**2 oil engines** sr geared to sc. shafts driving 2 FP propellers Total Power: 296kW (402hp) 9.5kn Caterpillar 3408TA 2 x Vee 4 Stroke 8 Cy. 137 x 152 each-148kW (201bhp) Caterpillar Inc-USA AuxGen: 2 x 40kW 440V 50Hz a.c
9319375 *ECLW* -	**V.B. CADIZ** **Compania Valenciana de Remolcadores SA** - *Cadiz* *Spain* MMSI: 224215320 Official number: 1-1/2006	**237** 71 58	Class: BV	**2007-03 Union Naval Valencia SA (UNV) — Valencia** Yd No: 386 Loa 23.80 Br ex - Dght 4.000 Lbp 21.46 Br md 11.00 Dpth 4.72 Welded, 1 dk	**(B32A2ST) Tug**	**2 oil engines** geared to sc. shafts driving 2 Z propellers Total Power: 3,162kW (4,300hp) 12.5kn Caterpillar 3516B 2 x Vee 4 Stroke 16 Cy. 170 x 190 each-1581kW (2150bhp) Caterpillar Inc-USA
8906169 *HP6401* -	**V.B. CALIFORNIA** *ex* SPTA-2 *-2000* **Tug Services Panama SA** Compania Maritima de Panama SA *Panama* *Panama* MMSI: 373203000 Official number: 4410012	*331* 99 -	Class: GL (AB)	**1989-09 Astilleros Unidos de Mazatlan S.A. de C.V. (AUMAZ) — Mazatlan** (Assembled by) Yd No: 009 **1989-09 B.V. Scheepswerf Damen — Gorinchem** (Parts for assembly by) Yd No: 4708 Loa 32.10 Br ex - Dght 3.750 Lbp 30.52 Br md 9.00 Dpth 4.75 Welded, 1 dk	**(B32A2ST) Tug**	**2 oil engines** reverse reduction geared to sc. shafts driving 2 FP propellers Total Power: 2,354kW (3,200hp) Deutz SBV6M628 2 x 4 Stroke 6 Cy. 240 x 280 each-1177kW (1600bhp) Kloeckner Humboldt Deutz AG-West Germany AuxGen: 2 x 63kW a.c Fuel: 157.5 (d.f.)
9289271 *EATM* -	**V.B. CANARIAS** **Remolcadores y Barcazas de Tenerife SA** - *Santa Cruz de Tenerife* *Spain* MMSI: 224289000 Official number: 1-1/2003	**410** 123 335	Class: BV	**2003-12 Union Naval Valencia SA (UNV) — Valencia** Yd No: 336 Loa - Br ex - Dght 4.850 Lbp - Br md - Dpth - Welded, 1 dk	**(B32A2ST) Tug**	**2 oil engines** reduction geared to sc. shafts driving 2 Z propellers Total Power: 4,170kW (5,670hp) Deutz SBV9M628 2 x 4 Stroke 9 Cy. 240 x 280 each-2085kW (2835bhp) Deutz AG-Koeln AuxGen: 3 x 72kW a.c
9137272 *CXKF* -	**V.B. CARIBE** **Remolcadores y Lanchas SA** - *Montevideo* *Uruguay* MMSI: 770576209 Official number: 8223	**408** 122 612	Class: LR (GL) (AB) **100A1** SS 03/2012 Tug **LMC**	**1997-02 President Marine Pte Ltd — Singapore** Yd No: 210 Loa 34.00 Br ex - Dght 4.000 Lbp 31.52 Br md 10.58 Dpth 4.94 Welded, 1 dk	**(B32A2ST) Tug**	**2 oil engines** geared to sc. shafts driving 2 Directional propellers Total Power: 3,046kW (4,142hp) 12.0kn Nohab 6R25 2 x 4 Stroke 6 Cy. 250 x 300 each-1523kW (2071bhp) Wartsila Diesel AB-Sweden AuxGen: 2 x 120kW a.c Fuel: 203.0 (d.f.)
9111747 *EAKT* -	**V.B. CARTAGENA** **ING Lease (Espana) SA EFC** Remolcadores de Cartagena SA (RECASA) *Valencia* *Spain* MMSI: 224102970 Official number: 1-1/1995	**343** 102 200	Class: (GL) **100A1** SS 12/2010 tug, fire fighting Ship 1 (2700m3/h) **LMC** **UMS**	**1995-12 Astilleros Zamakona SA — Santurtzi** Yd No: 320 Loa 29.50 Br ex - Dght 2.990 Lbp 28.00 Br md 11.00 Dpth 4.00 Welded, 1 dk	**(B32A2ST) Tug**	**2 oil engines** gearing integral to driving 2 Voith-Schneider propellers Total Power: 3,060kW (4,160hp) 12.0kn MaK 9M20 2 x 4 Stroke 9 Cy. 200 x 300 each-1530kW (2080bhp) Krupp MaK Maschinenbau GmbH-Kiel AuxGen: 2 x 180kW 220/380V 50Hz a.c Fuel: 125.0 (d.f.)
7368126 *HO2374* -	**V.B. CHAGRES** *ex* Smit Jamaica *-2003* *ex* Piku *-2001* **Tug Services Panama SA** Compania Maritima de Panama SA *Panama* *Panama* MMSI: 355764000 Official number: 2828602B	**384** 115 304	Class: LR ✠**100A1** SS 07/2009 tug ✠**LMC** Eq.Ltr: (l) G; Cable: U2	**1974-04 B.V. Scheepswerven v/h H.H. Bodewes — Millingen a/d Rijn** Yd No: 712 Loa 35.90 Br ex 10.62 Dght 4.141 Lbp 32.14 Br md 10.01 Dpth 4.86 Welded, 1 dk	**(B32A2ST) Tug**	**2 oil engines** sr geared to sc. shafts driving 2 CP propellers Total Power: 2,834kW (3,854hp) 13.0kn Allen 9S37-E 2 x 4 Stroke 9 Cy. 325 x 370 each-1417kW (1927bhp) W. H. Allen, Sons & Co. Ltd.-Bedford AuxGen: 2 x 104kW 380V 50Hz a.c
9305374 *XCDZ5* -	**V.B. CHIHUAHUA** *completed as* Med Salvor *-2004* **Compania Maritima del Pacifico SA de CV** - *Coatzacoalcos* *Mexico* MMSI: 345030052	**382** 115 -	Class: GL (BV)	**2004-11 Torgem Gemi Insaat Sanayii ve Ticaret a.s. — Tuzla, Istanbul** Yd No: 72 Loa 32.00 Br ex - Dght 4.200 Lbp 30.14 Br md 11.00 Dpth 5.60 Welded, 1 dk	**(B32A2ST) Tug**	**2 oil engines** gearing integral to driving 2 Z propellers Total Power: 4,046kW (5,500hp) Deutz SBV9M628 2 x 4 Stroke 9 Cy. 240 x 280 each-2023kW (2750bhp) Deutz AG-Koeln AuxGen: 2 x 145kW
7419327 - -	**V.B. CHIRIQUI** *ex* Salou *-2001* - -	**260** 78 -	Class: (LR) (AB) ✠ Classed LR until 1/12/82	**1976-02 Const. Nav. del Sureste S.A. — Alicante** Yd No: 25 Loa 33.10 Br ex 8.74 Dght 4.239 Lbp 29.11 Br md 8.22 Dpth 4.81 Welded, 1 dk	**(B32A2ST) Tug**	**1 oil engine** sr geared to sc. shaft driving 1 CP propeller Total Power: 1,655kW (2,250hp) 12.0kn MWM TBD501-6 1 x 4 Stroke 6 Cy. 360 x 450 1655kW (2250bhp) Motoren Werke Mannheim AG (MWM)-West Germany AuxGen: 2 x 132kW 380V 50Hz a.c

IMO / Call sign	Name / Owner / Manager	Tonnage	Classification	Builder / Dimensions	Type	Machinery
9260665 *EBXM* -	**V.B. CIERZO** **Auxiliar Maritima del Sur SA (AUXMASA)** Boluda Corporacion Maritima *Huelva* *Spain* MMSI: 224056990 Official number: 5-4/2001	**354** 106 241	Class: BV (LR) (GL) Classed LR until 29/10/13	**2002**-07 **Union Naval Valencia SA (UNV) — Valencia** Yd No: 297 Loa 29.50 Br ex - Dght 3.258 Lbp 28.00 Br md 11.00 Dpth 4.70 Welded, 1 dk	**(B32A2ST) Tug**	**2 oil engines** gearing integral to driving 2 Voith-Schneider propellers Total Power: 3,870kW (5,262hp) Caterpillar 3606TA 2 x 4 Stroke 6 Cy. 280 x 300 each-1935kW (2631bhp) Caterpillar Inc-USA AuxGen: 2 x 150kW 380/220V 50Hz a.c Fuel: 6.0 (d.f.) 110.0 (r.f.)
9332353 *ECJW* -	**V.B. CONQUERIDOR** **Pastor Servicios Financieros Establecimiento Financiero de Credito SA (PSF)** Remolcadores Boluda SA *Valencia* *Spain* MMSI: 224182440 Official number: 1-4/2005	**395** 119 211	Class: GL (LR) Classed LR until 3/5/12	**2006**-05 **Union Naval Valencia SA (UNV) — Valencia** Yd No: 393 Loa 29.50 Br ex - Dght 3.440 Lbp 28.00 Br md 11.00 Dpth 4.00 Welded, 1 dk	**(B32A2ST) Tug**	**2 oil engines** geared to sc. shafts driving 2 Voith-Schneider propellers Total Power: 4,160kW (5,656hp) Wartsila 6L26 2 x 4 Stroke 6 Cy. 260 x 320 each-2080kW (2828bhp) Wartsila Finland Oy-Finland
9298026 *XCNF2* -	**V.B. CONTADORA** *ex* Morena I *-2011* *ex* V.B. Contadora *-2009* *ex* Quihnce *-2006* **Compania Maritima del Pacifico SA de CV** - *Mazatlan* *Mexico*	**358** 107 396	Class: GL (BV)	**2003**-12 **Astilleros Armon SA — Navia** Yd No: 585 Loa 30.00 Br ex - Dght 4.800 Lbp 26.80 Br md 9.85 Dpth 5.40 Welded, 1 dk	**(B32A2ST) Tug**	**2 oil engines** geared to sc. shafts driving 2 Z propellers Total Power: 2,942kW (4,000hp) Caterpillar 3516B-TA 2 x Vee 4 Stroke 16 Cy. 170 x 190 each-1471kW (2000bhp) Caterpillar Inc-USA
9181443 *XCVW* -	**V.B. CORAL** **Compania Maritima del Pacifico SA de CV** - *Ensenada* *Mexico*	**375** 112 452	Class: GL	**1999**-06 **Astilleros Zamakona SA — Santurtzi** Yd No: 436 Loa 30.25 Br ex 9.85 Dght 4.670 Lbp 26.80 Br md 9.80 Dpth 5.40 Welded, 1 dk	**(B32A2ST) Tug**	**2 oil engines** reduction geared to sc. shafts driving 2 Directional propellers Total Power: 3,100kW (4,214hp) 12.5kn MaK 8M20 2 x 4 Stroke 8 Cy. 200 x 300 each-1550kW (2107bhp) MaK Motoren GmbH & Co. KG-Kiel AuxGen: 2 x 165kW 380V 50Hz a.c Fuel: 151.7 (d.f.)
9306897 *ECIL* -	**V.B. FURIA** **Remolcadores Boluda SA** Boluda Corporacion Maritima *Valencia* *Spain* MMSI: 224161160 Official number: 1-2/2005	**395** 119 211	Class: GL (LR) (BV) Classed LR until 22/5/12	**2005**-07 **Union Naval Valencia SA (UNV) — Valencia** Yd No: 375 Loa 29.50 Br ex - Dght 3.400 Lbp 27.65 Br md 11.00 Dpth 4.00 Welded, 1 dk	**(B32A2ST) Tug**	**2 oil engines** geared to sc. shafts driving 2 Directional propellers Total Power: 4,050kW (5,506hp) Deutz SBV9M628 2 x 4 Stroke 9 Cy. 240 x 280 each-2025kW (2753bhp) Deutz AG-Koeln
7625665 *HO3197* -	**V.B. GAMBOA** *ex* Boluda Treinta *-2003* *ex* Dauphin *-1989* *ex* T.V. O. 1 *-1985* *ex* Dogue *-1982* *ex* Nasser *-1978* **Tug Services Panama SA** Compania Maritima de Panama SA *Panama* *Panama* Official number: 2977504B	**197** 59 -	Class: (BV) (GL) (RI) (AB)	**1977**-01 **Penang Shipbuilding Corp Sdn Bhd — Penang** Yd No: 14425 L reg 26.25 Br ex - Dght 3.001 Lbp 26.01 Br md 7.82 Dpth 3.92 Welded, 1 dk	**(B32A2ST) Tug**	**2 oil engines** reverse reduction geared to sc. shafts driving 2 FP propellers Total Power: 1,558kW (2,118hp) 11.0kn G.M. (Detroit Diesel) 16V-149-TI 2 x Vee 2 Stroke 16 Cy. 146 x 146 each-779kW (1059bhp) General Motors Detroit DieselAllison Divn-USA AuxGen: 2 x 48kW 220/380V a.c
9245823 *EBVU* -	**V.B. GLACIAL** **Remolcadores de Cartagena SA (RECASA)** - *Cartagena* *Spain* MMSI: 224049190 Official number: 5-4/2001	**354** 106 190	Class: GL (LR) Classed LR until 1/1/12	**2001**-12 **Union Naval Valencia SA (UNV) — Valencia** Yd No: 294 Loa 29.50 Br ex - Dght 3.350 Lbp 28.00 Br md 11.00 Dpth 4.00 Welded, 1 dk	**(B32A2ST) Tug**	**2 oil engines** gearing integral to driving 2 Voith-Schneider propellers Total Power: 4,060kW (5,520hp) 12.0kn Caterpillar 3606TA 2 x 4 Stroke 6 Cy. 280 x 300 each-2030kW (2760bhp) Caterpillar Inc-USA
9114892 *EAKX* -	**V.B. HUELVA** **ING Lease (Espana) SA EFC** Auxiliar Maritima del Sur SA (AUXMASA) *Huelva* *Spain* MMSI: 224333000 Official number: 1-1/1995	**342** 102 197	Class: LR ✠ **100A1** SS 12/2010 tug fire fighting ship 1 (2400 cubic metre/hr) *IWS ✠ **LMC** **UMS** Eq.Ltr: G; Cable: 275.0/19.0 U2	**1995**-12 **Astilleros Zamakona SA — Santurtzi** Yd No: 300 Loa 30.15 Br ex 11.45 Dght 2.500 Lbp 28.00 Br md 11.00 Dpth 4.00 Welded, 1 dk	**(B32A2ST) Tug**	**2 oil engines** gearing integral to driving 2 Voith-Schneider propellers Total Power: 2,840kW (3,862hp) 12.0kn Wartsila 8R22/26 2 x 4 Stroke 8 Cy. 220 x 260 each-1420kW (1931bhp) Wartsila Diesel S.A.-Bermeo AuxGen: 2 x 165kW 380V 50Hz a.c
9402184 *EBYJ* -	**V.B. JEREZ** **Servicios Auxiliares de Puertos SA (SERTOSA)** - *Ceuta* *Spain* MMSI: 224261230 Official number: 1-3/2006	**237** 102 57	Class: BV	**2007**-07 **Union Naval Valencia SA (UNV) — Valencia** Yd No: 387 Loa 23.80 Br ex - Dght 3.190 Lbp 21.46 Br md 11.00 Dpth 4.72 Welded, 1 dk	**(B32A2ST) Tug**	**2 oil engines** reduction geared to sc. shafts driving 2 Directional propellers Total Power: 3,132kW (4,258hp) 11.5kn Caterpillar 3516B 2 x Vee 4 Stroke 16 Cy. 170 x 190 each-1566kW (2129bhp) Caterpillar Inc-USA AuxGen: 2 x 85kW 400/230V 50Hz a.c
9402196 *EAVY* -	**V.B. LANZAROTE** **Remolcadores y Barcazas de Las Palmas SA** - *Las Palmas de Gran Canaria* *Spain* MMSI: 224261240 Official number: 1-1/2007	**237** 102 57	Class: BV	**2007**-07 **Union Naval Valencia SA (UNV) — Valencia** Yd No: 388 Loa 23.80 Br ex - Dght 3.190 Lbp 21.46 Br md 11.00 Dpth 4.72 Welded, 1 dk	**(B32A2ST) Tug**	**2 oil engines** reduction geared to sc. shafts driving 2 Directional propellers Total Power: 3,132kW (4,258hp) 11.5kn Caterpillar 3516B 2 x Vee 4 Stroke 16 Cy. 170 x 190 each-1566kW (2129bhp) Caterpillar Inc-USA AuxGen: 2 x 85kW 400/230V 50Hz a.c
9158006 *EAQV* -	**V.B. MEDITERRANEO** **Boluda Towage & Salvage SLU** Boluda Corporacion Maritima *Valencia* *Spain* MMSI: 224533000 Official number: 5-2/2001	**342** 103 190	Class: BV (Class contemplated) (LR) ✠ Classed LR until 25/5/05	**1998**-03 **Astilleros Zamakona SA — Santurtzi** Yd No: 392 Loa 30.20 Br ex 11.50 Dght 2.500 Lbp 28.00 Br md 11.00 Dpth 4.00 Welded, 1 dk	**(B32A2ST) Tug**	**2 oil engines** with clutches, flexible couplings & reduction geared to sc. shafts driving 2 Directional propellers Total Power: 3,040kW (4,134hp) 12.0kn MaK 8M20 2 x 4 Stroke 8 Cy. 200 x 300 each-1520kW (2067bhp) MaK Motoren GmbH & Co. KG-Kiel AuxGen: 2 x 160kW 380V 50Hz a.c
9241138 *CXGT* -	**V.B. MONTEVIDEO** *ex* Tecoman *-2005* **Remolcadores y Lanchas SA** - *Montevideo* *Uruguay* MMSI: 770576190 Official number: P773	**296** 88 -	Class: LR (BV) **100A1** SS 07/2010 tug **LMC** Cable: 220.0/19.0 U2 (a)	**2000**-07 **Guangzhou Fishing Vessel Shipyard — Guangzhou GD** Yd No: XY-2098 Loa 31.80 Br ex - Dght 3.200 Lbp 28.00 Br md 9.60 Dpth 4.15 Welded, 1 dk	**(B32A2ST) Tug**	**2 oil engines** reduction geared to sc. shafts driving 2 FP propellers Total Power: 2,352kW (3,198hp) 12.0kn Cummins KTA-50-M2 2 x Vee 4 Stroke 16 Cy. 159 x 159 each-1176kW (1599bhp) Cummins Engine Co Inc-USA AuxGen: 2 x 85kW 380V 50Hz a.c
9137260 *XCV1* -	**V.B. PACIFICO** **Compania Maritima del Pacifico SA de CV** - *Mazatlan* *Mexico*	**420** 122 225	Class: GL (AB)	**1997**-02 **President Marine Pte Ltd — Singapore** Yd No: 209 Loa 34.00 Br ex - Dght 4.000 Lbp 31.52 Br md 10.58 Dpth 4.94 Welded, 1dk	**(B32A2ST) Tug**	**2 oil engines** geared to sc. shafts driving 2 Directional propellers Total Power: 3,046kW (4,142hp) 12.0kn Nohab 6R25 2 x 4 Stroke 6 Cy. 250 x 300 each-1523kW (2071bhp) Wartsila Diesel AB-Sweden AuxGen: 2 x 120kW a.c Fuel: 203.0 (d.f.)
9319313 *EAAK* -	**V.B. PODER** **Remolcadores Boluda SA** Boluda Corporacion Maritima *Valencia* *Spain* MMSI: 224161170 Official number: 1-1/2005	**395** 119 211	Class: GL (LR) Classed LR until 22/2/12	**2005**-12 **Union Naval Valencia SA (UNV) — Valencia** Yd No: 377 Loa 29.50 Br ex - Dght 3.450 Lbp 28.00 Br md 11.00 Dpth 4.00 Welded, 1 dk	**(B32A2ST) Tug**	**2 oil engines** gearing integral to driving 2 Voith-Schneider propellers Total Power: 4,046kW (5,500hp) Deutz SBV9M628 2 x 4 Stroke 9 Cy. 240 x 280 each-2023kW (2750bhp) Deutz AG-Koeln
8008060 *LW2829* -	**V.B. RECOLETA** *ex* Uxmal *-2010* **Compania Maritima Austral SA** - *Buenos Aires* *Argentina* MMSI: 701006396	**235** 70 -	Class: (LR) (GL) (AB) Classed LR until 5/6/13	**1981**-08 **Scheepsbouw Alblas B.V. — Krimpen a/d IJssel** (Hull) **1981**-08 **B.V. Scheepswerf Damen — Gorinchem** Yd No: 3111 Loa 27.61 Br ex 8.01 Dght 3.450 Lbp 27.36 Br md 7.80 Dpth 4.05 Welded, 1 dk	**(B32A2ST) Tug**	**2 oil engines** with clutches, flexible couplings & sr reverse geared to sc. shafts driving 2 FP propellers Total Power: 1,654kW (2,248hp) 13.0kn Caterpillar D399SCAC 2 x Vee 4 Stroke 16 Cy. 159 x 203 each-827kW (1124bhp) Caterpillar Tractor Co-USA AuxGen: 2 x 55kW a.c

IMO / Call sign	Ship / Owner	Tonnage	Class	Build / Dimensions	Type	Machinery
9319351 *EAJN* -	**V.B. ROTA** - **Servicios Auxiliares de Puertos SA (SERTOSA)** - *Ceuta* *Spain* MMSI: 224097140 Official number: 1-1/2006	**237** 102 58	Class: BV	**2006-11 Union Naval Valencia SA (UNV) — Valencia** Yd No: 384 Loa 23.80 Br ex - Dght 4.000 Lbp 21.46 Br md 11.00 Dpth 4.72 Welded, 1 dk	**(B32A2ST) Tug**	**2 oil engines** geared to sc. shafts driving 2 Directional propellers Total Power: 3,162kW (4,300hp) 12.5kn Caterpillar 3516B 2 x Vee 4 Stroke 16 Cy. 170 x 190 each-1581kW (2150bhp) Caterpillar Inc-USA
9181431 *EAUL* -	**V.B. SARGAZOS** - **ING Lease (Espana) SA EFC** Compania Valenciana de Remolcadores SA SatCom: Inmarsat C 422452410 *Cadiz* *Spain* MMSI: 224524000 Official number: 1-2/1999	**375** 112 300	Class: GL (LR) Classed LR until 1/7/13	**1999-03 Astilleros Zamakona SA — Santurtzi** Yd No: 435 Loa 30.50 Br ex 10.50 Dght 4.000 Lbp 26.80 Br md 9.85 Dpth 5.40 Welded, 1 dk	**(B32A2ST) Tug**	**2 oil engines** reduction geared to sc. shafts driving 2 Directional propellers Total Power: 3,040kW (4,134hp) 12.0kn MaK 8M20 2 x 4 Stroke 8 Cy. 200 x 300 each-1520kW (2067bhp) MaK Motoren GmbH & Co. KG-Kiel AuxGen: 2 x 160kW 380V 50Hz a.c
9231860 *EBSP* -	**V.B. SIMUN** - **Servicios Auxiliares de Puertos SA (SERTOSA)** - *Ceuta* *Spain* MMSI: 224232000 Official number: 5-1/2001	**352** 105 190	Class: GL (LR) Classed LR until 22/8/13	**2001-05 Union Naval Valencia SA (UNV) — Valencia** Yd No: 290 Loa 29.50 Br ex - Dght 3.350 Lbp 28.00 Br md 11.00 Dpth 4.00 Welded, 1 dk	**(B32A2ST) Tug**	**2 oil engines** gearing integral to driving 2 Voith-Schneider propellers Total Power: 3,870kW (5,262hp) 12.0kn Caterpillar 3606TA 2 x 4 Stroke 6 Cy. 280 x 300 each-1935kW (2631bhp) Caterpillar Inc-USA
9319337 *XCEX2* -	**V.B. SINALOA** - **Compania Maritima del Pacifico SA de CV** - *Mazatlan* *Mexico*	**236** 71 60	Class: GL	**2005-03 Union Naval Valencia SA (UNV) — Valencia** Yd No: 379 Loa 23.80 Br ex - Dght 4.010 Lbp 21.46 Br md 11.00 Dpth 4.72 Welded, 1 dk	**(B32A2ST) Tug**	**2 oil engines** geared to sc. shafts driving 2 Z propellers Total Power: 3,162kW (4,300hp) 12.5kn Caterpillar 3516 2 x Vee 4 Stroke 16 Cy. 170 x 190 each-1581kW (2150bhp) Caterpillar Inc-USA
9231872 *EBSO* -	**V.B. SIROCO** - **Servicios Auxiliares de Puertos SA (SERTOSA)** - *Ceuta* *Spain* MMSI: 224231000 Official number: 5-2/2001	**352** 105 190	Class: GL (LR) Classed LR until 1/11/13	**2001-07 Union Naval Valencia SA (UNV) — Valencia** Yd No: 291 Loa 29.50 Br ex - Dght 3.350 Lbp 28.00 Br md 11.00 Dpth 4.00 Welded, 1 dk	**(B32A2ST) Tug**	**2 oil engines** gearing integral to driving 2 Voith-Schneider propellers Total Power: 3,870kW (5,262hp) 12.0kn Caterpillar 3606TA 2 x 4 Stroke 6 Cy. 280 x 300 each-1935kW (2631bhp) Caterpillar Inc-USA AuxGen: 2 x 320kW 220/380V 50Hz a.c Fuel: 150.0 (d.f.) 14.5pd
9332341 *ECJX* -	**V.B. SONADOR** - **Pastor Servicios Financieros Establecimiento Financiero de Credito SA (PSF)** Remolcadores Boluda SA *Valencia* *Spain* MMSI: 224182450 Official number: 1-3/2005	**395** 119 211	Class: GL (LR) Classed LR until 3/5/12	**2006-04 Union Naval Valencia SA (UNV) — Valencia** Yd No: 392 Loa 29.50 Br ex - Dght 3.440 Lbp 28.00 Br md 11.00 Dpth 4.00 Welded, 1 dk	**(B32A2ST) Tug**	**2 oil engines** geared to sc. shafts driving 2 Voith-Schneider propellers Total Power: 4,046kW (5,500hp) Wartsila 6L26 2 x 4 Stroke 6 Cy. 260 x 320 each-2023kW (2750bhp) Wartsila France SA-France
9319349 *XCEV9* -	**V.B. SONORA** - **Compania Maritima del Pacifico SA de CV** - *Tampico* *Mexico*	**236** 71 60	Class: GL	**2005-05 Union Naval Valencia SA (UNV) — Valencia** Yd No: 380 Loa 23.80 Br ex - Dght 4.010 Lbp 21.46 Br md 11.00 Dpth 4.72 Welded, 1 dk	**(B32A2ST) Tug**	**2 oil engines** geared to sc. shafts driving 2 Z propellers Total Power: 3,162kW (4,300hp) 12.5kn Caterpillar 3516 2 x Vee 4 Stroke 16 Cy. 170 x 190 each-1581kW (2150bhp) Caterpillar Inc-USA
9289269 *EADM* -	**V.B. SUPERNACHO** - **Remolques del Mediterraneo SA** - *Castellon de la Plana* *Spain* MMSI: 224121270 Official number: 1-1/2003	**410** 123 335	Class: BV	**2003-12 Union Naval Valencia SA (UNV) — Valencia** Yd No: 335 Loa 30.50 Br ex - Dght 4.850 Lbp - Br md 10.60 Dpth - Welded, 1 dk	**(B32A2ST) Tug**	**2 oil engines** geared to sc. shafts driving 2 Directional propellers Total Power: 4,046kW (5,500hp) Deutz SBV9M628 2 x 4 Stroke 9 Cy. 240 x 280 each-2023kW (2750bhp) Deutz AG-Koeln AuxGen: 3 x 72kW 50Hz a.c Fuel: 248.0 (d.f.)
7803310 *EAGD* -	**V.B. SUPLENTE** *ex Hoedic -2004* **Remolques del Mediterraneo SA** - *Castellon de la Plana* *Spain* MMSI: 224150720	*373* 112 -	Class: BV	**1979-09 Chantiers et Ateliers de La Perriere — Lorient** Yd No: 315 Loa 34.83 Br ex 9.81 Dght 3.171 Lbp 31.02 Br md 9.66 Dpth 4.12 Welded, 1 dk	**(B32A2ST) Tug**	**2 oil engines** geared to sc. shafts driving 2 Voith-Schneider propellers Total Power: 2,206kW (3,000hp) 13.3kn Crepelle 8SN2 2 x 4 Stroke 8 Cy. 260 x 280 each-1103kW (1500bhp) Crepelle et Cie-France AuxGen: 2 x 160kW 115/380V a.c
9319325 *XCEW1* -	**V.B. TAMAULIPAS** - **Compania Maritima del Pacifico SA de CV** - *Tampico* *Mexico*	**236** 71 60	Class: GL	**2005-03 Union Naval Valencia SA (UNV) — Valencia** Yd No: 378 Loa 23.80 Br ex - Dght 4.000 Lbp 21.46 Br md 11.00 Dpth 4.72 Welded, 1 dk	**(B32A2ST) Tug**	**2 oil engines** geared to sc. shafts driving 2 Z propellers Total Power: 3,162kW (4,300hp) 12.5kn Caterpillar 3516 2 x Vee 4 Stroke 16 Cy. 170 x 190 each-1581kW (2150bhp) Caterpillar Inc-USA
9201023 *EAXD* -	**V.B. TIRRENO** - **ING Lease (Espana) SA EFC** Boluda Corporacion Maritima *Valencia* *Spain* MMSI: 224465000 Official number: 5-3/2001	**342** 103 190	Class: GL (LR) ✠ Classed LR until 23/5/12	**2000-02 Astilleros Zamakona SA — Santurtzi** Yd No: 441 Loa 30.20 Br ex 11.50 Dght 2.500 Lbp 28.00 Br md 11.00 Dpth 4.00 Welded, 1 dk	**(B32A2ST) Tug**	**2 oil engines** reduction geared to sc. shafts driving 2 Directional propellers Total Power: 3,040kW (4,134hp) 12.0kn MaK 8M20 2 x 4 Stroke 8 Cy. 200 x 300 each-1520kW (2067bhp) MaK Motoren GmbH & Co. KG-Kiel AuxGen: 2 x 160kW 380V 50Hz a.c
9116539 *EAMJ* -	**V.B. VICENTA C** - **Remolcadores y Barcazas de Las Palmas SA** - *Valencia* *Spain* MMSI: 224256690 Official number: 1-1/1996	**203** 60 120	Class: GL	**1996-06 Astilleros Zamakona SA — Santurtzi** Yd No: 301 Loa 27.30 Br ex - Dght 2.999 Lbp 24.50 Br md 8.10 Dpth 4.35 Welded, 1 dk	**(B32A2ST) Tug**	**2 oil engines** reduction geared to sc. shafts driving 2 FP propellers Total Power: 2,028kW (2,758hp) 12.0kn Caterpillar 3512TA 2 x Vee 4 Stroke 12 Cy. 170 x 190 each-1014kW (1379bhp) Caterpillar Inc-USA AuxGen: 2 x 40kW 220/380V a.c
9313888 *ECFK* -	**V.B. VIGOR** - **Boluda Towage & Salvage SLU** Boluda Corporacion Maritima *Valencia* *Spain* MMSI: 224133320 Official number: 5-1/2004	**369** 112 210	Class: BV	**2003-12 Union Naval Valencia SA (UNV) — Valencia** Yd No: 303 Loa 29.50 Br ex - Dght 3.790 Lbp 27.93 Br md 11.00 Dpth 4.00 Welded, 1 dk	**(B32A2ST) Tug**	**2 oil engines** gearing integral to driving 2 Voith-Schneider propellers Total Power: 4,046kW (5,500hp) Deutz SBV9M628 2 x 4 Stroke 9 Cy. 240 x 280 each-2023kW (2750bhp) Deutz AG-Koeln AuxGen: 2 x 145kW 400/220V 50Hz a.c
9340831 - -	**V. BELTSOV** - **Federal State Unitary Enterprise 'Admiralty Shipyards' (FGUP 'Admiralteyskiye Verfi')** - *St Petersburg* *Russia* Official number: 040050	**188** 56 92	Class: (RS)	**2004-10 OAO Leningradskiy Sudostroitelnyy Zavod 'Pella' — Otradnoye** Yd No: 904 Loa 25.40 Br ex - Dght 3.180 Lbp 23.40 Br md 8.80 Dpth 4.30 Welded, 1 dk	**(B32A2ST) Tug**	**2 oil engines** reduction geared to sc. shafts driving 2 Directional propellers Total Power: 1,098kW (1,492hp) Cummins KTA-38-M1 2 x Vee 4 Stroke 12 Cy. 159 x 159 each-549kW (746bhp) Cummins Engine Co Ltd-United Kingdom
8984111 - -	**V. C. C.** *ex Frong 1 -2004* **VCC Inter Marine Service & Transport Co Ltd** - *Bangkok* *Thailand* Official number: 460000438	**482** 209 939		**2003-06 Nava Progress Co. Ltd. — Samut Prakan** L reg 49.50 Br ex - Dght - Lbp 47.00 Br md 9.00 Dpth 4.20 Welded, 1 dk	**(A13B2TP) Products Tanker** Double Hull (13F) Liq: 1,000; Liq (Oil): 1,000	**1 oil engine** driving 1 Propeller Total Power: 736kW (1,001hp) Mitsui 1 x 736kW (1001bhp) Mitsui Engineering & Shipbuilding CLtd-Japan
8990299 *HSB3250* -	**V. C. C. 2** - **VCC Inter Marine Service & Transport Co Ltd** - *Bangkok* *Thailand* Official number: 476100466	**351** 149 550		**2004 Navacharoenkij — Bangkok** Loa 47.10 Br ex 8.00 Dght - Lbp 43.00 Br md - Dpth 3.30 Welded, 1 dk	**(A13B2TP) Products Tanker** Double Hull (13F) Liq: 631; Liq (Oil): 631 2 Cargo Pump (s)	**1 oil engine** driving 1 Propeller Total Power: 560kW (761hp) Akasaka 1 x 4 Stroke 560kW (761bhp) Akasaka Tekkosho KK (Akasaka DieselLtd)-Japan

7812012 *EHXT* -	**V CENTENARIO** *ex* El Segundo *-1987* **Mariscos Rodriguez SA** - SatCom: Inmarsat C 422473910 *Las Palmas* *Spain (CSR)* MMSI: 224739000 Official number: 5/2002	**2,990** 897 2,235	Class: BV	**1986**-12 **Ast. de Huelva S.A. — Huelva** Yd No: 115 Converted From: Ro-Ro Cargo Ship Loa 84.73 (BB) Br ex 14.23 Dght 4.422 Lbp 78.86 Br md 14.20 Dpth 5.62 Welded, 3 dks	**(A34A2GR) Refrigerated Cargo Ship** Ins: 3,500 Compartments: 3 Ho, ER Cranes: 2x3t	**1 oil engine** with flexible couplings & sr gearedto sc. shaft driving 1 CP propeller Total Power: 1,596kW (2,170hp) 13.5kn Alpha 14V23L-VO 1 x Vee 4 Stroke 14 Cy. 225 x 300 1596kW (2170bhp) Construcciones Echevarria SA-Spain AuxGen: 3 x 280kW 440/220V 60Hz a.c Fuel: 1150.0
7717717 *HQLS2* -	**V. I. PRIDE** *ex* Bahama Pride *-2005* *ex* State Progress *-1977* **Wind Rose Maritime Co Ltd** Black Hawk Shipping Enterprise Inc *San Lorenzo* *Honduras* MMSI: 334383000 Official number: L-0728076	**646** 194 450	Class: HZ (AB)	**1977**-12 **Zigler Shipyards Inc — Jennings LA** Yd No: 256 Loa 54.87 Br ex 11.61 Dght 3.582 Lbp 49.69 Br md 11.59 Dpth 4.27 Welded, 1 dk	**(B21B20A) Anchor Handling Tug Supply**	**2 oil engines** reverse reduction geared to sc. shafts driving 2 FP propellers Total Power: 1,250kW (1,700hp) 11.0kn Caterpillar D398SCAC 2 x Vee 4 Stroke 12 Cy. 159 x 203 each-625kW (850bhp) Caterpillar Tractor Co-USA AuxGen: 2 x 75kW a.c Thrusters: 1 Thwart. FP thruster (f) Fuel: 160.0
9291274 *3EAT8*	**V. K. EDDIE** **Seven Seas Shipping Ltd** Tankers (UK) Agencies Ltd SatCom: Inmarsat C 435624510 *Panama* *Panama* MMSI: 356245000 Official number: 3077305A	**159,016** 100,899 305,261 T/cm 171.0	Class: LR ✠ **100A1** SS 05/2010 Double Hull oil tanker ESP *IWS LI NAV1 **ShipRight** (SDA, FDA, CM) ✠ **LMC** **UMS IGS** Eq.Ltr: D*; Cable: 770.0/114.0 U3 (a)	**2005**-05 **Daewoo Shipbuilding & Marine Engineering Co Ltd — Geoje** Yd No: 5298 Loa 332.00 (BB) Br ex 58.04 Dght 22.423 Lbp 320.28 Br md 58.00 Dpth 31.00 Welded, 1 dk	**(A13A2TV) Crude Oil Tanker** Double Hull (13F) Liq: 330,573; Liq (Oil): 330,573 Compartments: 5 Ta, 10 Wing Ta, 2 Wing Slop Ta, ER 3 Cargo Pump (s): 3x5000m^3/hr Manifold: Bow/CM: 163.5m	**1 oil engine** driving 1 FP propeller Total Power: 25,485kW (34,649hp) 15.2kn B&W 7S80MC 1 x 2 Stroke 7 Cy. 800 x 3056 25485kW (34649bhp) Doosan Engine Co Ltd-South Korea AuxGen: 3 x 1150kW 440/220V 60Hz a.c Boilers: e (ex.g.) 24.0kgf/cm^2 (23.5bar), WTAuxB (o.f.) 18.7kgf/cm^2 (18.3bar) Fuel: 382.9 (d.f.) 8712.8 (r.f.) 88.5pd
8303628 *HSB2567* -	**V. L. 3** *ex* Wako Maru *-1999* **VL Enterprise Co Ltd** - *Bangkok* *Thailand* MMSI: 567037000 Official number: 411000936	**1,290** 625 2,327	Class: (NK)	**1983**-11 **Hakata Zosen K.K. — Imabari** Yd No: 282 Loa 83.24 (BB) Br ex 12.03 Dght 5.300 Lbp 77.46 Br md 12.00 Dpth 5.75 Welded, 1 dk	**(A13B2TP) Products Tanker** Double Hull (13F) Liq: 2,273; Liq (Oil): 2,642 Compartments: 10 Wing Ta, ER 2 Cargo Pump (s): 2x750m^3/hr Manifold: Bow/CM: 37m	**1 oil engine** with clutches, flexible couplings & sr geared to sc. shaft driving 1 CP propeller Total Power: 1,250kW (1,700hp) 12.5kn Akasaka A34 1 x 4 Stroke 6 Cy. 340 x 660 1250kW (1700bhp) Akasaka Tekkosho KK (Akasaka DieselLtd)-Japan AuxGen: 2 x 120kW 440V 60Hz a.c, 1 x 40kW 440V 60Hz a.c Fuel: 34.5 (d.f.) (Heating Coils) 108.5 (r.f.) 5.5pd
8712881 *HSB2612* -	**V. L. 4** *ex* Eiwa Maru No. 35 *-1999* **VL Enterprise Co Ltd** - *Bangkok* *Thailand* MMSI: 567009800 Official number: 421000255	**1,017** 595 1,998		**1987**-11 **Shin Kurushima Dockyard Co. Ltd. — Hashihama, Imabari** Yd No: 2542 Loa 71.00 (BB) Br ex 12.02 Dght 4.701 Lbp 67.21 Br md 11.90 Dpth 5.31 Welded, 1 dk	**(A13B2TP) Products Tanker** Double Bottom Entire Compartment Length Liq: 2,231; Liq (Oil): 2,231 Compartments: 10 Ta, ER 2 Cargo Pump (s): 2x750m^3/hr Manifold: Bow/CM: 37m	**1 oil engine** reduction geared to sc. shaft driving 1 FP propeller Total Power: 1,030kW (1,400hp) 10.5kn Hanshin LH28G 1 x 4 Stroke 6 Cy. 280 x 460 1030kW (1400bhp) The Hanshin Diesel Works Ltd-Japan AuxGen: 2 x 107kW 225V 60Hz a.c Fuel: 69.5 (d.f.)
8805250 *HSB2785* -	**V. L. 5** *ex* Nissei Maru No. 31 *-2001* **VL Enterprise Co Ltd** - *Bangkok* *Thailand* MMSI: 567033900 Official number: 441000851	**1,228** 674 2,498 T/cm 7.9	Class: (NK)	**1988**-07 **Sasaki Shipbuilding Co Ltd — Osakikamijima HS** Yd No: 520 Loa 83.33 (BB) Br ex - Dght 4.950 Lbp 78.00 Br md 12.00 Dpth 5.85 Welded, 1 dk	**(A13B2TP) Products Tanker** Double Hull (13F) Liq: 2,892; Liq (Oil): 2,892 Compartments: 10 Ta, ER 2 Cargo Pump (s): 2x750m^3/hr	**1 oil engine** with clutches, flexible couplings & reduction geared to sc. shaft driving 1 CP propeller Total Power: 1,545kW (2,101hp) 13.1kn Hanshin 6EL32 1 x 4 Stroke 6 Cy. 320 x 640 1545kW (2101bhp) The Hanshin Diesel Works Ltd-Japan AuxGen: 3 x 128kW a.c
8816998 *HSB2893* -	**V. L. 6** *ex* Shoyo Maru *-2002* **VL Enterprise Co Ltd** - *Bangkok* *Thailand* MMSI: 567037700 Official number: 451000706	**1,042** 595 1,998 T/cm 6.4		**1988**-09 **Asakawa Zosen K.K. — Imabari** Yd No: 340 Loa 69.81 (BB) Br ex - Dght 4.922 Lbp 66.02 Br md 12.01 Dpth 5.01 Welded, 1 dk	**(A13B2TP) Products Tanker** Double Bottom Entire Compartment Length Liq: 2,187; Liq (Oil): 2,187 Cargo Heating Coils 2 Cargo Pump (s): 2x720m^3/hr	**1 oil engine** reverse geared to sc. shaft driving 1 FP propeller Total Power: 736kW (1,001hp) 12.5kn Akasaka A31R 1 x 4 Stroke 6 Cy. 310 x 600 736kW (1001bhp) Akasaka Tekkosho KK (Akasaka DieselLtd)-Japan
8712374 *HSB2922* -	**V. L. 7** *ex* Miyako Maru *-2002* **VL Enterprise Co Ltd** - *Bangkok* *Thailand* MMSI: 567038200 Official number: 451000730	**1,022** 502 1,966	Class: (NK)	**1987**-11 **Kurinoura Dockyard Co Ltd — Yawatahama EH** Yd No: 241 Loa 76.43 (BB) Br ex 11.43 Dght 4.676 Lbp 72.14 Br md 11.41 Dpth 5.16 Welded, 1 dk	**(A13B2TP) Products Tanker** Double Bottom Entire Compartment Length Liq: 2,223; Liq (Oil): 2,223 Compartments: 10 Wing Ta, ER 2 Cargo Pump (s): 2x750m^3/hr	**1 oil engine** driving 1 CP propeller Total Power: 1,324kW (1,800hp) 12.5kn Akasaka A31R 1 x 4 Stroke 6 Cy. 310 x 600 1324kW (1800bhp) Akasaka Tekkosho KK (Akasaka DieselLtd)-Japan AuxGen: 3 x 128kW Thrusters: 1 Thwart. CP thruster (f)
9047128 *HSB3152* -	**V. L. 8** *ex* Shinsei Maru *-2004* **VL Enterprise Co Ltd** - *Bangkok* *Thailand* MMSI: 567042100 Official number: 470001177	**3,274** 1,523 5,357 T/cm 13.4	Class: (LR) (NK) Classed LR until 14/9/09	**1992**-06 **Kanrei Zosen K.K. — Naruto** Yd No: 355 Loa 105.00 (BB) Br ex 15.40 Dght 6.416 Lbp 98.00 Br md 15.38 Dpth 7.50 Welded, 1 dk	**(A13B2TP) Products Tanker** Double Bottom Entire Compartment Length Bale: 17,837; Liq: 5,450; Liq (Oil): 5,450 Compartments: 10 Wing Ta, ER	**1 oil engine** driving 1 CP propeller Total Power: 2,942kW (4,000hp) 13.0kn Hanshin 6EL44 1 x 4 Stroke 6 Cy. 440 x 880 2942kW (4000bhp) The Hanshin Diesel Works Ltd-Japan AuxGen: 2 x 320kW 445V 60Hz a.c Boilers: e (ex.g.), WTAuxB (o.f.) Thrusters: 1 Thwart. CP thruster (f)
8820810 *HSB3445* -	**V. L. 10** *ex* Nisshun Maru *-2006* **VL Enterprise Co Ltd** - *Bangkok* *Thailand* MMSI: 567050200 Official number: 490001278	**1,846** 974 2,995	Class: (NK)	**1989**-01 **Yamanaka Zosen K.K. — Imabari** Yd No: 375 Loa 83.02 (BB) Br ex - Dght 5.680 Lbp 78.00 Br md 13.50 Dpth 6.50 Welded, 1 dk	**(A13B2TP) Products Tanker** Double Hull (13F)	**1 oil engine** driving 1 CP propeller Total Power: 1,811kW (2,462hp) 13.0kn Hanshin 6EL40 1 x 4 Stroke 6 Cy. 400 x 800 1811kW (2462bhp) The Hanshin Diesel Works Ltd-Japan Thrusters: 1 Thwart. FP thruster (f) Fuel: 183.0
9067099 *HSB3897* -	**V. L. 11** *ex* Koei Maru No. 7 *-2008* **VL Enterprise Co Ltd** - SatCom: Inmarsat C 456700216 *Bangkok* *Thailand* MMSI: 567054100 Official number: 5200-80685	**1,350** 658 2,494	Class: IR (NK)	**1993**-07 **Shin Kurushima Dockyard Co. Ltd. — Akitsu** Yd No: 2775 Loa 81.92 (BB) Br ex 12.22 Dght 5.070 Lbp 77.00 Br md 12.20 Dpth 5.65 Welded, 1 dk	**(A13B2TP) Products Tanker** Double Hull Liq: 2,406; Liq (Oil): 2,406 Compartments: 10 Wing Ta, ER 2 Cargo Pump (s): 2x750m^3/hr	**1 oil engine** driving 1 FP propeller Total Power: 1,470kW (1,999hp) 11.0kn Hanshin LH34L 1 x 4 Stroke 6 Cy. 340 x 640 1470kW (1999bhp) The Hanshin Diesel Works Ltd-Japan AuxGen: 3 x 140kW a.c Thrusters: 1 Tunnel thruster (f)
9134957 *HSB4460* -	**V. L. 12** *ex* Shoei Maru No. 7 *-2010* **VL Enterprise Co Ltd** - SatCom: Inmarsat C 456700349 *Bangkok* *Thailand* MMSI: 567061200 Official number: 530001586	**1,344** 639 2,498 T/cm 7.0	Class: IR (NK)	**1995**-11 **Hakata Zosen K.K. — Imabari** Yd No: 586 Loa 81.03 (BB) Br ex 12.02 Dght 5.141 Lbp 76.50 Br md 12.00 Dpth 5.75 Welded, 1 dk	**(A13B2TP) Products Tanker** Double Hull (13F) Liq: 2,338; Liq (Oil): 2,800 Compartments: 8 Wing Ta, 2 Wing Slop Ta, ER 2 Cargo Pump (s): 2x750m^3/hr Manifold: Bow/CM: 40.7m	**1 oil engine** driving 1 CP propeller Total Power: 1,491kW (2,027hp) 12.0kn Hanshin LH36LG 1 x 4 Stroke 6 Cy. 360 x 670 1491kW (2027bhp) The Hanshin Diesel Works Ltd-Japan AuxGen: 3 x 440V 60Hz a.c Thrusters: 1 Tunnel thruster (f) Fuel: 100.0 (d.f.)
9084712 *HSB4730* -	**V. L. 14** *ex* Ryoka Maru No. 5 *-1993* **VL Enterprise Co Ltd** - *Bangkok* *Thailand* MMSI: 567062200 Official number: 550003257	**1,074** 426 1,569 T/cm 5.4	Class: (NK)	**1993**-09 **Hakata Zosen K.K. — Imabari** Yd No: 555 Loa 68.90 (BB) Br ex - Dght 4.511 Lbp 65.00 Br md 11.50 Dpth 5.00 Welded, 1 dk	**(A13B2TP) Products Tanker** Double Hull (13F) Liq: 1,852; Liq (Oil): 1,852 Compartments: 10 Wing Ta, ER	**1 oil engine** driving 1 FP propeller Total Power: 1,471kW (2,000hp) 12.0kn Hanshin LH34LA 1 x 4 Stroke 6 Cy. 340 x 640 1471kW (2000bhp) The Hanshin Diesel Works Ltd-Japan Fuel: 70.0 (d.f.)
9201542 - -	**V. NIKOLAEV** *ex* V. Nikolayev *-2004* **Getpoint Shipping Ltd** Maloye Predpriyatiye 'Meridian'	**2,193** 658 2,084	Class: (RS)	**1998**-10 **AT Kyyivskyi Sudnobudivnyi-Sudnoremontnyi Zavod — Kyyiv** Yd No: 22 Loa 109.20 Br ex - Dght 3.300 Lbp - Br md 16.20 Dpth - Welded, 1 dk	**(A31A2GX) General Cargo Ship** 104 C. 104/20'	**2 oil engines** driving 2 FP propellers Total Power: 1,300kW (1,768hp) S.K.L. 8NVD48-2U 2 x 4 Stroke 8 Cy. 320 x 480 each-650kW (884bhp) SKL Motoren u. Systemtechnik AG-Magdeburg AuxGen: 1 x 58kW

6513865 - -	**V O S BISCAY** *ex Seaworker -2005* *ex Coulson Marine One -1997* *ex Frank Broderick -1996* **Adamac Industries Ltd** Adamac Marine Services Ltd (Adamac Group)	**2,310** 693 1,190	Class: (LR) (BV) Classed LR until 2/9/92	**1965-07 Yarrows Ltd — Victoria BC** Yd No: 278 Converted From: Supply Tender-1981 Loa 88.40 Br ex 17.53 Dght 3.048 Lbp 81.77 Br md 12.81 Dpth 6.86 Welded, 2 dks	**(B31A2SR) Research Survey Vessel** Bow door/ramp	**2 oil engines** with clutches, flexible couplings & reverse reduction geared to sc. shafts driving 2 FP propellers Total Power: 2,118kW (2,880hp) General Motors 16-278-A 2 x Vee 2 Stroke 16 Cy. 222 x 267 each-1059kW (1440bhp) (made 1944, fitted 1965) General Motors Corp-USA AuxGen: 3 x 150kW 480V 60Hz a.c Thrusters: 2 Thwart. FP thruster (a); 1 Water jet (f)
8408442 *ZPRY* -	**V USHAKOV** *ex Rolf Buck -2005* - - *Asuncion* *Paraguay*	**2,295** 1,000 2,591	Class: (GL)	**1985-09 Thyssen Nordseewerke GmbH — Emden** Yd No: 491 Loa 95.92 Br ex 14.23 Dght 4.058 Lbp 90.25 Br md 14.10 Dpth 6.74 Welded, 2 dks	**(A35A2RR) Ro-Ro Cargo Ship** Stern door/ramp (centre) Len: 7.50 Wid: 6.50 Swl: - Lane-Len: 468 Lane-clr ht: 5.46 Grain: 3,708; Bale: 3,667 TEU 180 C Ho 72 TEU C Dk 108 TEU Compartments: 1 Ho, ER 1 Ha: (57.2 x 10.5)ER Ice Capable	**1 oil engine** with clutches, flexible couplings & sr reverse geared to sc. shaft driving 1 FP propeller Total Power: 600kW (816hp) 10.0kn Deutz SBV9M628 1 x 4 Stroke 9 Cy. 240 x 280 600kW (816bhp) Kloeckner Humboldt Deutz AG-West Germany AuxGen: 2 x 150kW a.c Thrusters: 1 Thwart. FP thruster (f)
8946389 *UCWO* -	**V. USPENSKIY** *ex Volgo-Don 221 -2005* **Don River Shipping JSC (OAO 'Donrechflot')** LLC Rosshipcom *Taganrog* *Russia* MMSI: 273372100	**3,969** 1,362 5,379	Class: (RS) (RR)	**1978-09 Navashinskiy Sudostroitelnyy Zavod 'Oka' — Navashino** Yd No: 1126 Loa 138.30 Br ex 16.70 Dght 3.520 Lbp 132.06 Br md - Dpth 5.50 Welded, 1 dk	**(A31A2GX) General Cargo Ship** Grain: 6,370 Compartments: 2 Ho, ER 2 Ha: (44.4 x 13.1) (45.6 x 13.0)ER	**2 oil engines** driving 2 FP propellers Total Power: 1,324kW (1,800hp) 10.0kn Dvigatel Revolyutsii G-60 2 x 4 Stroke 6 Cy. 360 x 450 each-662kW (900bhp) Zavod "Dvigatel Revolyutsii"-Gorkiy AuxGen: 2 x 100kW a.c Fuel: 155.0 (d.f.)
9436018 *V7SW7* -	**V8 STEALTH** *ex Cape Antigua -2009* **Mayhem Crude Inc** Siva Ships International Pte Ltd SatCom: Inmarsat C 453834818 *Majuro* *Marshall Islands* MMSI: 538003737 Official number: 3737	**62,775** 34,934 112,871 T/cm 99.7	Class: AB	**2009-11 New Times Shipbuilding Co Ltd — Jingjiang JS** Yd No: 0311516 Loa 249.96 (BB) Br ex 44.04 Dght 14.819 Lbp 240.00 Br md 44.00 Dpth 21.00 Welded, 1 dk	**(A13A2TV) Crude Oil Tanker** Double Hull (13F) Liq: 124,398; Liq (Oil): 130,053 Cargo Heating Coils Compartments: 12 Wing Ta, 2 Wing Slop Ta, ER 3 Cargo Pump (s): 3x3000m³/hr Manifold: Bow/CM: 122.5m	**1 oil engine** driving 1 FP propeller Total Power: 15,820kW (21,509hp) 15.0kn MAN-B&W 7S60MC-C 1 x 2 Stroke 7 Cy. 600 x 2400 15820kW (21509bhp) Doosan Engine Co Ltd-South Korea AuxGen: 3 x 1125kW a.c Fuel: 170.0 (d.f.) 2500.0 (r.f.)
9436020 *V7TR8* -	**V8 STEALTH II** *ex Cape Avon -2010* **Diablo Fortune Inc** Siva Ships International Pte Ltd SatCom: Inmarsat C 453834926 *Majuro* *Marshall Islands* MMSI: 538003868 Official number: 3868	**62,775** 34,934 112,871 T/cm 99.7	Class: AB	**2010-05 New Times Shipbuilding Co Ltd — Jingjiang JS** Yd No: 0311517 Loa 250.00 (BB) Br ex 44.04 Dght 14.819 Lbp 240.00 Br md 44.00 Dpth 21.00 Welded, 1 dk	**(A13A2TW) Crude/Oil Products Tanker** Double Hull (13F) Liq: 124,963; Liq (Oil): 124,963 Cargo Heating Coils Compartments: 12 Wing Ta, 2 Wing Slop Ta, ER 3 Cargo Pump (s): 3x3000m³/hr Manifold: Bow/CM: 122.5m	**1 oil engine** driving 1 FP propeller Total Power: 15,820kW (21,509hp) 15.0kn MAN-B&W 7S60MC-C 1 x 2 Stroke 7 Cy. 600 x 2400 15820kW (21509bhp) Hyundai Heavy Industries Co Ltd-South Korea AuxGen: 3 x 900kW a.c Fuel: 160.0 (d.f.) 2430.0 (r.f.)
1000447 *ZCIP8* -	**VA BENE** *ex Only 4 U -2002 ex Petara -2002* *ex Anthea Pa -1999* **MV Glen Wyllin Ltd** *George Town* *Cayman Islands (British)* MMSI: 319854000 Official number: 722190	**496** 148 -	Class: LR **✠100A1** SS 12/2012 Yacht **LMC**	**1992-12 Kees Cornelissen Constructiebedrijf B.V. — Dreumel** Loa 43.80 Br ex 8.95 Dght 2.400 Lbp 41.80 Br md - Dpth 4.48 Welded, 1 dk	**(X11A2YP) Yacht**	**2 oil engines** geared to sc. shafts driving 2 FP propellers Total Power: 2,610kW (3,548hp) Caterpillar 3512TA 2 x Vee 4 Stroke 12 Cy. 170 x 190 each-1305kW (1774bhp) Caterpillar Inc-USA
5346100 *LMOD* -	**VAARVIND** *ex Gerlaug -1985 ex Suzanne Faroult -1967* *ex Cote de Grace -1959* **Marine Harvest Norway AS** *Floro* *Norway* MMSI: 257578950	*229* 102 291	Class: (BV)	**1950 Scheepsbouw Unie N.V. — Groningen** Loa 39.88 Br ex 6.71 Dght 2.591 Lbp 35.92 Br md 6.66 Dpth 2.87 Welded, 1 dk	**(A31A2GX) General Cargo Ship** 2 Ha: (6.5 x 3.9) (8.2 x 3.9) Derricks: 2x2t; Winches: 2	**1 oil engine** sr geared to sc. shaft driving 1 FP propeller Total Power: 268kW (364hp) 10.0kn G.M. (Detroit Diesel) 12V-71-N 1 x Vee 2 Stroke 12 Cy. 108 x 127 268kW (364bhp) (new engine 1969) General Motors Corp-USA Fuel: 28.5 (d.f.)
9196242 *PDAI* -	**VAASABORG** *ex Normed Hamburg -2004 ex Vaasaborg -2003* **Wagenborg Rederij BV** Wagenborg Shipping BV *Delfzijl* *Netherlands* MMSI: 246441000 Official number: 38269	**6,130** 3,424 8,700 T/cm 18.3	Class: BV	**2000-03 Bodewes Scheepswerf "Volharding" Foxhol B.V. — Foxhol** Yd No: 346 Loa 132.23 (BB) Br ex 15.95 Dght 7.060 Lbp 124.59 Br md 15.87 Dpth 9.65 Welded, 1 dk	**(A31A2GX) General Cargo Ship** Grain: 12,814 TEU 552 C.Ho 264/20' (40') C.Dk 288/20' (40') incl. 50 ref C Compartments: 2 Ho, ER 2 Ha: (40.0 x 13.2) (52.5 x 13.2)ER Ice Capable	**1 oil engine** with flexible couplings & sr gearedto sc. shaft driving 1 CP propeller Total Power: 3,960kW (5,384hp) 14.9kn Wartsila 6R38 1 x 4 Stroke 6 Cy. 380 x 475 3960kW (5384bhp) Wartsila NSD Nederland BV-Netherlands AuxGen: 1 x 650kW 440V 60Hz a.c, 2 x 240kW 440V 60Hz a.c Thrusters: 1 Thwart. FP thruster (f) Fuel: 40.0 (d.f.) (Heating Coils) 384.0 (r.f.) 20.0pd
9402691 *3FAN2* -	**VACAMONTE** *ex Priority -2012* **VT Vacamonte Inc** *Panama* *Panama* MMSI: 373151000 Official number: 4394512	**3,953** 1,940 6,891 T/cm 14.9	Class: LR (BV) **100A1** SS 07/2011 Double Hull Oil and Chemical Tanker, Ship Type 2 ESP *IWS LI Ice Class 1C FS Max/min draughts fwd 6.772/3.182m Max/min draughts aft 7.972/3.182m Power required 1825kw, power installed 2640kw **LMC** **UMS**	**2011-07 Rongcheng Xixiakou Shipyard Co Ltd — Rongcheng SD** Yd No: 06-037 Loa 103.00 (BB) Br ex 16.03 Dght 7.000 Lbp 96.50 Br md 16.00 Dpth 8.70 Welded, 1 dk	**(A12B2TR) Chemical/Products Tanker** Double Hull (13F) Liq: 6,661; Liq (Oil): 6,662 Cargo Heating Coils Compartments: 6 Wing Ta, 6 Wing Ta, 2 Wing Slop Ta, ER 3 Cargo Pump (s): 3x510m³/hr Manifold: Bow/CM: 54.5m Ice Capable	**1 oil engine** reduction geared to sc. shaft driving 1 CP propeller Total Power: 2,640kW (3,589hp) 11.7kn MaK 8M25C 1 x 4 Stroke 8 Cy. 255 x 400 2640kW (3589bhp) Caterpillar Motoren GmbH & Co. KG-Germany AuxGen: 1 x 600kW 440V a.c, 2 x 420kW 440V 60Hz a.c Thrusters: 1 Tunnel thruster (f) Fuel: 74.0 (d.f.) 309.0 (r.f.)
7305904 *CZ3678* -	**VACHON** **Canadian Acceptance Corp Ltd** La Compagnie Miniere Queber Cartier (Quebec Cartier Mining Co) *Quebec, QC* *Canada* MMSI: 316013092 Official number: 347867	*390* 18 272	Class: LR **✠100A1** CS 01/2011 tug Ice Class 3 **✠LMC** Eq.Ltr: (e) ; Cable: U1	**1973-07 Star Shipyards Ltd — New Westminster BC** Yd No: 408 Loa 30.99 Br ex 11.59 Dght 5.595 Lbp 29.44 Br md 10.98 Dpth 4.42 Welded, 1 dk	**(B32A2ST) Tug** Ice Capable	**2 oil engines** gearing integral to driving 2 Voith-Schneider propellers Total Power: 2,648kW (3,600hp) Alco 12V251E 2 x Vee 4 Stroke 12 Cy. 229 x 267 each-1324kW (1800bhp) Montreal Locomotive Works-Canada AuxGen: 2 x 75kW 450V 60Hz a.c
7742097 *OW2185* TN 349	**VADASTEINUR** **P/FVadasteinur** Birgir Simonsen *Torshavn* *Faeroe Islands (Danish)* MMSI: 231134000 Official number: D2439	**401** 120 -	Class: NV	**1977 p/f Torshavnar Skipasmidja — Torshavn** Yd No: 22 Loa 39.10 Br ex 8.54 Dght - Lbp 33.16 Br md 8.50 Dpth 3.99 Welded, 1 dk	**(B11B2FV) Fishing Vessel** Ins: 360 Ice Capable	**1 oil engine** geared to sc. shaft driving 1 CP propeller Deutz SBV6M628 1 x 4 Stroke 6 Cy. 240 x 280 Deutz AG-Koeln AuxGen: 3 x 64kW 380V 50Hz a.c
9663013 *AVSZ* -	**VADDEM** **Sesa Goa Ltd** *Mumbai* *India* MMSI: 419000538 Official number: 3991	**1,196** 494 2,027	Class: IR	**2012-10 Vinayaga Marine Petro Ltd — Thane** Yd No: 104 Loa 68.50 Br ex 13.22 Dght 3.500 Lbp 66.24 Br md 13.00 Dpth 4.40 Welded, 3 dks	**(A31A2GX) General Cargo Ship**	**2 oil engines** reduction geared to sc. shafts driving 2 FP propellers Total Power: 396kW (538hp) 10.0kn Volvo Penta D12MH 2 x 4 Stroke 6 Cy. 131 x 150 each-198kW (269bhp) AB Volvo Penta-Sweden
9032018 *SCFR* -	**VADDO** **Waxholms Angfartygs AB** *Vaxholm* *Sweden* MMSI: 265520420	**299** 118 50		**1992-03 Oskarshamns Varv AB — Oskarshamn** Yd No: 533 Loa - Br ex 7.52 Dght 1.280 Lbp 37.72 Br md 7.51 Dpth 2.78 Welded, 1 dk	**(A37B2PS) Passenger Ship** Hull Material: Aluminium Alloy Passengers: unberthed: 340	**3 oil engines** with clutches & sr geared to sc. shafts driving 3 FP propellers Total Power: 1,800kW (2,448hp) 22.0kn MAN D2842LYE 3 x Vee 4 Stroke 12 Cy. 128 x 142 each-600kW (816bhp) MAN Nutzfahrzeuge AG-Nuernberg AuxGen: 1 x 110kW 380V 50Hz a.c, 1 x 60kW 380V 50Hz a.c Thrusters: 1 Thwart. FP thruster (f)

IMO / Call sign	Name / Owner / Manager / Port / Flag	Tonnage	Class	Builder / Dimensions	Type / Cargo	Machinery
9427627 *SVAS7* -	**VADELA** **Ligaria Owning Co Ltd** Heidmar Inc SatCom: Inmarsat C 424092310 *Piraeus* *Greece* MMSI: 240923000 Official number: 11925	**83,545** 49,022 157,048 T/cm 112.7	Class: AB	**2009-09 Jiangsu Rongsheng Shipbuilding Co Ltd — Rugao JS** Yd No: 1016 Loa 274.50 (BB) Br ex 48.04 Dght 17.010 Lbp 264.00 Br md 48.00 Dpth 23.70 Welded, 1 dk	**(A13A2TV) Crude Oil Tanker** Double Hull (13F) Liq: 167,552; Liq (Oil): 167,554 Cargo Heating Coils Compartments: 12 Wing Ta, 2 Wing Slop Ta, ER 3 Cargo Pump (s): 3x3500m³/hr Manifold: Bow/CM: 138.8m	**1 oil engine** driving 1 FP propeller Total Power: 18,660kW (25,370hp) 15.1kn MAN-B&W 6S70MC-C 1 x 2 Stroke 6 Cy. 700 x 2800 18660kW (25370bhp) Doosan Engine Co Ltd-South Korea AuxGen: 3 x 940kW a.c Fuel: 260.0 (d.f.) 4490.0 (r.f.)
7623423 - -	**VADENI** **Black Sea Services Srl** *Braila* *Romania* Official number: 1249	**195** 61 49	Class: (RN)	**1975-02 Santierul Naval Braila — Braila** Yd No: 1121 Loa 29.30 Br ex 8.21 Dght 3.290 Lbp 27.00 Br md 8.20 Dpth 4.30 Welded, 1 dk	**(B32A2ST) Tug** Ice Capable	**2 oil engines** driving 2 CP propellers Total Power: 882kW (1,200hp) 12.5kn Russkiy 6DR30/50-4 2 x 2 Stroke 6 Cy. 300 x 500 each-441kW (600bhp) (made 1974) Mashinostroitelnyy Zavod"Russkiy-Dizel"-Leningrad AuxGen: 2 x 50kW 230V 50Hz a.c Fuel: 39.5 (d.f.)
9254977 *LAMK7* -	**VADERO HIGHLANDER** *ex* Clipper Highlander *-2008* *ex* Crescent Highlander *-2006* *ex* Montipora *-2004* *ex* Kerem D *-2003* **Rederi AB Vaderotank** Vadero Ship Management AB SatCom: Inmarsat C 425973710 *Oslo* *Norway (NIS)* MMSI: 259737000	**1,300** 600 1,862 T/cm 7.2	Class: BV	**2003-07 R.M.K. Tersanesi — Tuzla** Yd No: 48 Converted From: Chemical Tanker-2008 Loa 78.84 (BB) Br ex - Dght 4.270 Lbp 72.98 Br md 10.45 Dpth 5.10 Welded, 1 dk	**(A13B2TP) Products Tanker** Double Hull (13F) Liq: 2,145; Liq (Oil): 1,650 Cargo Heating Coils Compartments: 1 Ta, 8 Wing Ta, ER 9 Cargo Pump (s): 9x100m³/hr Ice Capable	**1 oil engine** reduction geared to sc. shaft driving 1 CP propeller Total Power: 1,140kW (1,550hp) 10.5kn MaK 6M20 1 x 4 Stroke 6 Cy. 200 x 300 1140kW (1550bhp) Caterpillar Motoren GmbH & Co. KG-Germany AuxGen: 2 x 240kW 440/230V 60Hz a.c, 1 x 250kW 440/230V 60Hz a.c Thrusters: 1 Tunnel thruster (f) Fuel: 80.0 (d.f.)
8307753 *3FOJ8* -	**VADIBEL** *ex* Progress *-2011* *ex* Sanmar Progress *-2002* *ex* Intrepid *-1995* *ex* Spring Condor *-1992* *ex* Sanko Condor *-1986* **Combined Mining & Shipping FZE** - *Panama* *Panama* MMSI: 352802000 Official number: 44922PEXTF1	**24,111** 13,019 41,098 T/cm 48.1	Class: (NK) (IR)	**1984-05 Oshima Shipbuilding Co Ltd — Saikai NS** Yd No: 10077 Loa 185.40 (BB) Br ex - Dght 11.102 Lbp 176.03 Br md 29.51 Dpth 15.83 Welded, 1 dk	**(A21A2BC) Bulk Carrier** Grain: 50,416; Bale: 49,443 Compartments: 5 Ho, ER 5 Ha: (14.4 x 15.0)4 (19.2 x 15.0)ER Cranes: 4x25t	**1 oil engine** driving 1 FP propeller Total Power: 6,377kW (8,670hp) 14.0kn Sulzer 6RTA58 1 x 2 Stroke 6 Cy. 580 x 1700 6377kW (8670bhp) Sumitomo Heavy Industries Ltd-Japan AuxGen: 3 x 420kW 450V 60Hz a.c Fuel: 216.0 (d.f.) (Heating Coils) 1651.0 (r.f.) 24.5pd
8805547 *UUSJ* -	**VADIM GLAZUNOV** **Ukrainian Danube Shipping Co** - *Izmail* *Ukraine* MMSI: 272897000 Official number: 875644	**2,060** 696 2,099	Class: (RS)	**1988-10 Osterreichische Schiffswerften AG Linz-Korneuburg — Korneuburg** Yd No: 770 Loa 91.90 (BB) Br ex 13.60 Dght 3.370 Lbp 84.90 Br md 13.40 Dpth 4.90 Welded, 2 dks	**(A34A2GR) Refrigerated Cargo Ship** Ins: 3,064 TEU 96 C.Ho 64/20' (40') C.Dk 32/20' incl. 24 ref C. Compartments: 2 Ho, ER 2 Ha: 2 (25.2 x 10.0)ER Cranes: 1 Ice Capable	**2 oil engines** driving 2 CP propellers Total Power: 1,950kW (2,652hp) 12.0kn Wartsila 8R22 2 x 4 Stroke 8 Cy. 220 x 240 each-975kW (1326bhp) Wartsila Diesel Oy-Finland AuxGen: 2 x 248kW Thrusters: 1 Thwart. FP thruster (f)
8422436 *UDBL* -	**VADIM POPOV** **Kamchatsk Territorial Administration for Hydrometeorology (Kamchatgidromet)** Kripto Co Ltd (OOO Kripto) SatCom: Inmarsat C 427320816 *Petropavlovsk-Kamchatskiy* *Russia* MMSI: 273432200 Official number: 851423	**693** 207 293	Class: (RS)	**1986-10 Valmetin Laivateollisuus Oy — Turku** Yd No: 369 Loa 49.90 Br ex 10.02 Dght 3.601 Lbp 44.95 Br md 10.01 Dpth 5.01 Welded, 1 dk	**(B31A2SR) Research Survey Vessel**	**1 oil engine** with clutches, flexible couplings & sr geared to sc. shaft driving 1 CP propeller Total Power: 986kW (1,341hp) 12.8kn Wartsila 824TS 1 x 4 Stroke 8 Cy. 240 x 310 986kW (1341bhp) Oy Wartsila Ab-Finland AuxGen: 1 x 160kW a.c, 1 x 160kW a.c Fuel: 90.0 (d.f.)
8422230 *4JKN* -	**VADIM SEYIDOV** *ex* Neftegaz-19 *-1993* **Specialized Sea Oil Fleet Organisation, Caspian Sea Oil Fleet, State Oil Co of the Republic of Azerbaijan** - *Baku* *Azerbaijan* MMSI: 423172100 Official number: DGR-0376	**2,737** 821 1,329	Class: RS	**1985-09 Stocznia Szczecinska im A Warskiego — Szczecin** Yd No: B92/19 Loa 81.16 Br ex 16.30 Dght 4.900 Lbp 71.45 Br md 15.97 Dpth 7.22 Welded, 2 dks	**(B21B20T) Offshore Tug/Supply Ship** 20 TEU C. Derricks: 1x12.5t Ice Capable	**2 oil engines** reduction geared to sc. shafts driving 2 CP propellers Total Power: 5,296kW (7,200hp) 15.3kn Sulzer 6ZL40/48 2 x 4 Stroke 6 Cy. 400 x 480 each-2648kW (3600bhp) Zaklady Przemyslu Metalowego 'HCegielski' SA-Poznan AuxGen: 3 x 384kW 400V 50Hz a.c Thrusters: 1 Thwart. FP thruster (f) Fuel: 399.0 (r.f.)
8100404 *UFQD* -	**VADIM TYURNEV** *ex* Sibirskiy-2127 *-2002* **JSC LORP (A/O 'LORP' - Lena United River Shipping Co) (Lenskoye Obyedinyonnoye Rechnoye Parokhodstvo)** Port of Yakutsk *Zhatay* *Russia* MMSI: 273383700 Official number: 209525	**2,870** - 4,865	Class: RR	**1982-06 Valmet Oy — Turku** Yd No: 390 Loa 128.19 Br ex 15.64 Dght 3.000 Lbp 125.00 Br md 15.41 Dpth 5.45 Welded, 1 dk	**(A31A2GX) General Cargo Ship** Bale: 4,800 TEU 142 C. 142/20' (40')	**2 oil engines** driving 2 FP propellers Total Power: 1,324kW (1,800hp) 10.0kn Dvigatel Revolyutsii 6CHRN36/45 2 x 4 Stroke 6 Cy. 360 x 450 each-662kW (900bhp) Zavod "Dvigatel Revolyutsii"-Gorkiy Thrusters: 1 Thwart. FP thruster (f)
9354038 *NWLE* -	**VADM. K. R. WHEELER** **Military Sealift Command (MSC)** - *Galliano, LA* *United States of America* MMSI: 369887000 Official number: 1195545	**5,565** 1,669 6,034	Class: AB	**2007-09 North American Shipbuilding LLC — Larose LA** Yd No: 228 Loa 106.07 (BB) Br ex - Dght 7.010 Lbp 98.15 Br md 21.33 Dpth 8.53 Welded, 1 dk	**(B21A20S) Platform Supply Ship**	**2 oil engines** geared to sc. shafts driving 2 FP propellers Total Power: 12,000kW (16,316hp) 16.0kn MaK 12M32C 2 x Vee 4 Stroke 12 Cy. 320 x 420 each-6000kW (8158bhp) Caterpillar Motoren GmbH & Co. KG-Germany AuxGen: 1 x 1360kW a.c, 2 x 3300kW a.c, 1 x 910kW a.c
7947685 *WTR3534* -	**VAERDAL** *ex* Aleutian Mistress *-2002* **Alaska Vaerdal LLC** United States Seafoods LLC *Seattle, WA* *United States of America* Official number: 611225	*199* 136 -		**1979 Marine Industries Northwest, Inc. — Tacoma, Wa** Yd No: 281 L reg 33.69 Br ex 9.71 Dght - Lbp - Br md - Dpth 3.31 Welded, 1 dk	**(B11B2FV) Fishing Vessel**	**1 oil engine** driving 1 FP propeller Total Power: 1,066kW (1,449hp)
9607382 *LCHE* -	**VAEROY** **Torghatten Nord AS** - *Tromso* *Norway* MMSI: 259988000	**5,695** 2,507 650	Class: NV	**2012-10 Remontowa Shipbuilding SA — Gdansk** (Hull) Yd No: B612/2 **2012-10 Gdanska Stocznia 'Remontowa' SA — Gdansk** Yd No: 2410/2 Loa 95.99 Br ex 17.40 Dght 4.000 Lbp 90.00 Br md 16.80 Dpth 5.50 Welded, 1 dk	**(A36A2PR) Passenger/Ro-Ro Ship (Vehicles)** Passengers: unberthed: 390 Bow door (f) Len: - Wid: 5.50 Swl: - Stern door (a) Len: - Wid: 11.50 Swl: - Cars: 120	**1 oil engine** reduction geared to sc. shaft driving 1 CP propeller Total Power: 5,200kW (7,070hp) 19.0kn Bergens C35: 40V12PG 1 x Vee 4 Stroke 12 Cy. 350 x 400 5200kW (7070bhp) Rolls Royce Marine AS-Norway Thrusters: 2 Tunnel thruster (f); 1 Tunnel thruster (a)
6804317 *LDYC* T-35-T	**VAEROYTRANS** *ex* Thales *-2011* *ex* Silverfors *-2008* *ex* Solvskjer *-2004* *ex* Solvar Viking *-1997* *ex* Liaskjeren *-1990* *ex* Storhav *-1989* *ex* Glomfjord *-1986* **Nordvesttrans AS** Marine Supply AS *Bodo* *Norway* MMSI: 257261000	**359** 111 -		**1967-10 Vaagland Baatbyggeri AS — Vaagland** Yd No: 74 Lengthened-1971 Loa 38.87 Br ex 7.68 Dght - Lbp 29.67 Br md 7.65 Dpth 3.81 Welded, 1 dk	**(B11B2FV) Fishing Vessel**	**1 oil engine** driving 1 FP propeller Total Power: 438kW (596hp) Alpha 407-24V0 1 x 2 Stroke 7 Cy. 240 x 400 438kW (596bhp) Alpha Diesel A/S-Denmark
9436226 *5BHU2* -	**VAESTERBOTTEN** *ex* Bip Bull *-2013* *ex* Uppland *-2013* *ex* Medonega *-2012* **3 Sommerwiese UG (haftungsbeschrankt)** Liberty One Shipmanagement GmbH & Co KG *Limassol* *Cyprus* MMSI: 212838000	**5,335** 2,566 6,804	Class: GL	**2008-09 Sainty Shipbuilding (Yangzhou) Corp Ltd — Yizheng JS** Yd No: 06STIG026 Loa 119.26 Br ex - Dght 6.280 Lbp 112.00 Br md 16.50 Dpth 8.30 Welded, 1 dk	**(A31A2GX) General Cargo Ship** TEU 331 incl 20 ref C. Compartments: 2 Ho, ER 2 Ha: ER Ice Capable	**1 oil engine** reduction geared to sc. shaft driving 1 CP propeller Total Power: 3,000kW (4,079hp) 13.5kn MAN-B&W 6L32/40 1 x 4 Stroke 6 Cy. 320 x 400 3000kW (4079bhp) STX Engine Co Ltd-South Korea AuxGen: 1 x 400kW 400V a.c, 2 x 225kW 400V a.c Thrusters: 1 Retract. directional thruster (f)

8422670 *UFZS* -	**VAFA** *ex Zarya -2006 ex STK-1010 -1993* **Vafa Wholesale Ltd (OOO Optovaya Firma 'Vafa')** - SatCom: Inmarsat C 427310416 *Astrakhan* *Russia* MMSI: 273370900	**1,575** 472 2,161	Class: RS (RR)	**1984-10 VEB Elbewerften Boizenburg/Rosslau — Rosslau** Yd No: 312/3459 Loa 82.70 Br ex - Dght 3.950 Lbp 78.10 Br md 11.60 Dpth 6.20 Welded, 1 dk	**(A31A2GX) General Cargo Ship** Grain: 1,870 Compartments: 2 Ho, ER 2 Ha: 2 (20.0 x 9.6)ER Ice Capable	**2 oil engines** driving 2 FP propellers Total Power: 882kW (1,200hp) 10.3kn S.K.L. 8NVDS36/24A-1 2 x 4 Stroke 8 Cy. 240 x 360 each-441kW (600bhp) VEB Schwermaschinenbau "KarlLiebknecht" (SKL)-Magdeburg Fuel: 95.0 (d.f.)
8422682 *UHCT* -	**VAFA-1** *ex Antares -2007 ex STK-1011 -1998* **Vafa Wholesale Ltd (OOO Optovaya Firma 'Vafa')** - SatCom: Inmarsat C 427300764 *Astrakhan* *Russia* MMSI: 273375800 Official number: 216360	**1,570** 471 2,159	Class: RS (RR)	**1984-12 VEB Elbewerften Boizenburg/Rosslau — Rosslau** Yd No: 313/3460 Loa 82.00 Br ex 12.00 Dght 3.960 Lbp 79.70 Br md 11.60 Dpth 6.20 Welded, 1 dk	**(A31A2GX) General Cargo Ship** Grain: 1,870 TEU 70 C. 70/20' incl. 10 ref C. Compartments: 2 Ho, ER 2 Ha: 2 (20.0 x 9.6)ER Ice Capable	**2 oil engines** driving 2 FP propellers Total Power: 882kW (1,200hp) 11.5kn S.K.L. 8NVDS36/24A-1 2 x 4 Stroke 8 Cy. 240 x 360 each-441kW (600bhp) VEB Schwermaschinenbau "KarlLiebknecht" (SKL)-Magdeburg Fuel: 80.0 (r.f.)
8869919 *EPBC4* -	**VAFA 2** *ex Raya -2013 ex Samur 5 -2011* *ex Ruza-6 -2001 ex ST-1324 -2001* **Vafa Piroz Shipping Co** Moje Sepide Atlas Co *Bandar Anzali* *Iran* MMSI: 422915000	**1,846** 554 2,755	Class: (RS)	**1988-05 Sudostroitelnyy Zavod im Volodarskogo — Rybinsk** Yd No: 04912 Loa 86.70 Br ex 12.30 Dght 4.100 Lbp 82.55 Br md 12.00 Dpth 3.50 Welded, 1 dk	**(A31A2GX) General Cargo Ship** Grain: 2,230 TEU 54 C.Ho 36/20' C.Dk 18/20' Compartments: 1 Ho, ER 2 Ha: 2 (19.8 x 9.0)ER Ice Capable	**2 oil engines** driving 2 FP propellers Total Power: 1,030kW (1,400hp) S.K.L. 6NVD48A-2U 2 x 4 Stroke 6 Cy. 320 x 480 each-515kW (700bhp) VEB Schwermaschinenbau "KarlLiebknecht" (SKL)-Magdeburg
8720371 *VJN297* -	**VAGABOND SPIRIT** *ex Queen Rokko -2005* **Poseidon Holdings Pty Ltd** - *Sydney, NSW* *Australia* Official number: 857870	*217* - -		**1988-07 Mitsui Eng. & SB. Co. Ltd. — Tamano** Yd No: 1609 L reg 30.80 Br ex 9.02 Dght 2.000 Lbp - Br md 9.00 Dpth 3.00 Welded, 1 dk	**(A37B2PS) Passenger Ship** Hull Material: Aluminium Alloy Passengers: unberthed: 236	**2 oil engines** geared to sc. shafts driving 2 FP propellers Total Power: 810kW (1,102hp) 30.0kn Yanmar 6AYM-ETE 2 x 4 Stroke 6 Cy. 155 x 180 each-405kW (551bhp) (new engine 2006) Yanmar Diesel Engine Co Ltd-Japan
7804962 *LIGY* -	**VAGAN** - **Torghatten Nord AS** - *Narvik* *Norway* MMSI: 258415000	**1,677** 775 100	Class: (NV)	**1979-05 Bolsones Verft AS — Molde** Yd No: 259 Loa 56.27 Br ex 11.61 Dght - Lbp 51.01 Br md - Dpth 4.20 Welded, 2 dks	**(A36A2PT) Passenger/Ro-Ro Ship (Vehicles/Rail)** Bow door & ramp Stern door & ramp Cars: 45	**1 oil engine** driving 1 FP propeller Total Power: 1,368kW (1,860hp) Alpha 12V23L-VO 1 x Vee 4 Stroke 12 Cy. 225 x 300 1368kW (1860bhp) Alpha Diesel A/S-Denmark AuxGen: 1 x 240kW 230V 50Hz a.c, 2 x 120kW 230V 50Hz a.c Thrusters: 1 Thwart. FP thruster (f)
9643594 *LG6774* AA-5-G	**VAGAN** - **Dagfinn Pettersen** - *Grimstad* *Norway* MMSI: 257282700	**100** - -		**2012-10 in Poland** (Hull) Yd No: (296) **2012-10 Vestvaerftet ApS — Hvide Sande** Yd No: 296 Loa 14.99 Br ex - Dght 2.800 Lbp - Br md 6.10 Dpth 2.80 Welded, 1 dk	**(B11A2FS) Stern Trawler**	**1 oil engine** driving 1 Propeller Total Power: 552kW (750hp) Volvo Penta D16 1 x 4 Stroke 6 Cy. 144 x 165 552kW (750bhp) AB Volvo Penta-Sweden Thrusters: 1 Thwart. FP thruster (f)
7804986 *LIIJ* -	**VAGGASVARRE** *ex Gjemnes -1993* **Bjorklids Ferjerederi AS** - *Tromso* *Norway* MMSI: 257059800	**772** 251 50	Class: (NV)	**1979-06 Johan Drage AS — Rognan** Yd No: 379 Loa 64.34 Br ex 11.54 Dght - Lbp 64.32 Br md 11.26 Dpth 4.27 Welded, 1 dk	**(A36A2PR) Passenger/Ro-Ro Ship (Vehicles)** Cars: 50	**1 oil engine** driving 1 Propeller , 1 fwd Total Power: 883kW (1,201hp) MWM TBD484-6 1 x 4 Stroke 6 Cy. 320 x 480 883kW (1201bhp) Motoren Werke Mannheim AG (MWM)-West Germany AuxGen: 2 x 72kW 220V 50Hz a.c
9148764 *SVA5594* -	**VAGIA II** *ex Vaya Ii -2012 ex Fairplay-22 -2011* **Aigaion Marine Ltd** Maritime Consortium of Thessaloniki Inc (MCT) *Thessaloniki* *Greece* MMSI: 241223000 Official number: GRC102000085	**496** 148 317	Class: LR (GL) **100A1** SS 05/2012 tug **LMC** **UMS**	**1998-04 Construcciones Navales Santodomingo SA — Vigo** Yd No: 613 Loa 34.75 (BB) Br ex - Dght 4.600 Lbp 32.14 Br md 10.80 Dpth 5.70 Welded, 1 dk	**(B32A2ST) Tug**	**2 oil engines** geared to sc. shafts driving 2 Directional propellers Total Power: 3,292kW (4,476hp) 13.0kn Deutz SBV8M628 2 x 4 Stroke 8 Cy. 240 x 280 each-1646kW (2238bhp) Motoren Werke Mannheim AG (MWM)-Mannheim AuxGen: 2 x 104kW 380/220V 50Hz a.c Thrusters: 1 Thwart. FP thruster (f)
7620342 *4JHA* -	**VAGIF** *ex Vaqiv -2011 ex Vagif -1997* **Azerbaijan State Caspian Shipping Co (ASCSS)** Meridian Shipping & Management LLC SatCom: Inmarsat C 442306610 *Baku* *Azerbaijan* MMSI: 423066100 Official number: DGR-0007	**3,714** 1,715 4,150 T/cm 15.2	Class: RS	**1976-07 Navashinskiy Sudostroitelnyy Zavod 'Oka' — Navashino** Yd No: 1069 Loa 123.50 Br ex 15.02 Dght 4.500 Lbp 112.50 Br md 14.99 Dpth 6.51 Welded, 1 dk	**(A31A2GX) General Cargo Ship** Grain: 6,070; Bale: 5,800 Compartments: 4 Ho, ER 4 Ha: 2 (11.9 x 8.3)2 (13.7 x 8.3)ER Cranes: 2x8t Ice Capable	**2 oil engines** driving 2 FP propellers Total Power: 1,472kW (2,002hp) 11.8kn Russkiy 8DR30/50-4 2 x 2 Stroke 8 Cy. 300 x 500 each-736kW (1001bhp) Mashinostroitelnyy Zavod"Russkiy-Dizel"-Leningrad AuxGen: 3 x 100kW Fuel: 202.0 (d.f.)
8207214 *4JDD* -	**VAGIF JAFAROV** *ex Alikhan Gagkayev -1994* **Specialized Sea Oil Fleet Organisation, Caspian Sea Oil Fleet, State Oil Co of the Republic of Azerbaijan** - *Baku* *Azerbaijan* MMSI: 423151100 Official number: DGR-0118	**2,971** 891 1,326	Class: RS	**1986-06 Brodogradiliste 'Titovo' — Kraljevica** Yd No: 463 Loa 98.99 Br ex 17.43 Dght 3.201 Lbp 92.40 Br md 17.01 Dpth 6.13 Welded, 1 dk	**(B34B2SC) Crane Vessel** Cranes: 1x100t	**2 oil engines** with flexible couplings & sr gearedto sc. shafts driving 2 FP propellers Total Power: 3,178kW (4,320hp) 11.3kn Sulzer 8ASL25/30 2 x 4 Stroke 8 Cy. 250 x 300 each-1589kW (2160bhp) Tvornica Dizel Motora 'Jugoturbina'-Yugoslavia AuxGen: 2 x 1100kW a.c, 4 x 200kW a.c Thrusters: 1 Thwart. FP thruster (f) Fuel: 479.0 (d.f.)
9376476 *UFXZ* -	**VAGIS** - **Rosneft JSC (A/O Komsomolskiy Neftepererabatyvayushchiy Zavod 'Rosneft')** - *Nakhodka* *Russia* MMSI: 273310540	**315** 94 106	Class: RS	**2007-11 AO Amurskiy Sudostroitelnyy Zavod — Komsomolsk-na-Amure** Yd No: 380 Loa 31.00 Br ex 10.30 Dght 3.300 Lbp 26.60 Br md 9.50 Dpth 4.80 Welded, 1 dk	**(B32A2ST) Tug** Ice Capable	**2 oil engines** reduction geared to sc. shafts driving 2 CP propellers Total Power: 2,610kW (3,548hp) 10.0kn Caterpillar 3512B-TA 2 x Vee 4 Stroke 12 Cy. 170 x 190 each-1305kW (1774bhp) Caterpillar Inc-USA AuxGen: 2 x 130kW a.c Fuel: 87.0 (d.f.)
5259412 *LLTC* -	**VAGSFJELL** *ex Nyborg -1997 ex A. Rose -1946* **Torgeirson AS** - *Bronnoysund* *Norway* MMSI: 257039600	**202** 93 305	Class: (LR) (BV) ✠ Classed LR until 9/29	**1924-11 Cochrane & Sons Ltd. — Selby** Yd No: 940 Converted From: Fishing Vessel-1924 Loa 39.30 Br ex 6.58 Dght - Lbp - Br md 6.57 Dpth 3.81 Riveted, 1 dk	**(A31A2GX) General Cargo Ship** Grain: 340 Compartments: 1 Ho, ER 1 Ha: (11.1 x 3.8) Derricks: 1; Winches: 1	**1 oil engine** driving 1 FP propeller Total Power: 250kW (340hp) 8.0kn Alpha 404-24VO 1 x 2 Stroke 4 Cy. 240 x 400 250kW (340bhp) (new engine 1940) Frederikshavn Jernstoberi ogMaskinfabrik-Denmark
9196723 *LJQB* -	**VAGSFJORD** - **Torghatten Nord AS** - *Tromso* *Norway* MMSI: 259560000	**177** 70 20		**1999 Oma Baatbyggeri AS — Stord** Yd No: 512 Loa 23.99 Br ex 10.00 Dght - Lbp 23.95 Br md 9.00 Dpth 4.50 Welded, 1 dk	**(A37B2PS) Passenger Ship** Hull Material: Aluminium Alloy Passengers: unberthed: 150	**2 oil engines** geared to sc. shafts driving 2 FP propellers Total Power: 1,498kW (2,036hp) M.T.U. 12V2000M70 2 x Vee 4 Stroke 12 Cy. 130 x 150 each-749kW (1018bhp) MTU Friedrichshafen GmbH-Friedrichshafen
9506837 *LCGE* -	**VAGSOY** - **Fjord1 AS** - *Floro* *Norway* MMSI: 258314500	**777** 233 350	Class: (NV)	**2009-06 UAB Vakaru Laivu Remontas (JSC Western Shiprepair) — Klaipeda** (Hull) Yd No: (62) **2009-06 Fiskerstrand Verft AS — Fiskarstrand** Yd No: 62 Loa 54.57 Br ex 14.00 Dght 3.300 Lbp 51.90 Br md 13.70 Dpth 4.80 Welded, 1 dk	**(A36A2PR) Passenger/Ro-Ro Ship (Vehicles)** Passengers: unberthed: 150 Bow ramp (centre) Stern ramp (centre) Cars: 42	**2 oil engines** reduction geared to sc. shaft driving 2 Directional propellers Total Power: 882kW (1,200hp) Scania DI16 M 2 x Vee 4 Stroke 8 Cy. 127 x 154 each-441kW (600bhp) Scania AB-Sweden AuxGen: 2 x 98kW a.c
8713823 *3YOK* -	**VAGSUND** *ex Torill -2011 ex Fehn Trader -2006* *ex Arklow Marsh -2004* **Bio Feeder AS** Maritime Management AS *Bergen* *Norway* MMSI: 259991000	**1,732** 783 2,183	Class: GL RI	**1988-05 Schiffs. Hugo Peters Wewelsfleth Peters & Co. GmbH — Wewelsfleth** Yd No: 636 Converted From: General Cargo Ship-2011 Loa 73.84 Br ex - Dght 4.373 Lbp 70.21 Br md 11.51 Dpth 5.41 Welded, 1 dk	**(B12D2FM) Fish Farm Support Vessel** Grain: 2,888; Bale: 2,853 TEU 31 C. 31/20' Compartments: 1 Ho, ER 1 Ha: (43.2 x 9.0)ER Ice Capable	**1 oil engine** with clutches, flexible couplings & sr reverse geared to sc. shaft driving 1 FP propeller Total Power: 749kW (1,018hp) 11.5kn MaK 6M332AK 1 x 4 Stroke 6 Cy. 240 x 330 749kW (1018bhp) Krupp MaK Maschinenbau GmbH-Kiel AuxGen: 3 x 43kW 380/220V 50Hz a.c Thrusters: 1 Thwart. FP thruster (f)

6815720 *LAIZ* M-495-SM	**VAGTRANS** *ex* Storund *-2007* *ex* Nils Holm *-2007* **Vagtrans AS** - *Sandnessjoen* *Norway* MMSI: 258274000 Official number: 17079	**469** 140 -	Class: NV	**1968-06 Smedvik Mek. Verksted AS — Tjorvaag** Yd No: 17 Loa 41.15 Br ex 8.26 Dght 4.380 Lbp 36.53 Br md 8.23 Dpth 4.40 Welded, 1 dk	**(B11B2FV) Fishing Vessel** Compartments: 6 Ta, ER 6 Ha: 6 (2.5 x 1.9)ER Derricks: 1; Winches: 1 Ice Capable	**1 oil engine** driving 1 FP propeller Total Power: 588kW (799hp) 12.0kn Wichmann 8ACA 1 x 2 Stroke 8 Cy. 280 x 420 588kW (799bhp) Wichmann Motorfabrikk AS-Norway AuxGen: 1 x 220V 50Hz a.c, 1 x 220V 50Hz a.c, 1 x 220V 50Hz a.c Thrusters: 1 Thwart. FP thruster (f); 1 Tunnel thruster (a)
5400449 *ES2361* EK-9802	**VAHASE** *ex* Tirana *-1998* *ex* Kapduva *-1990* *ex* Mallemukken *-1987* **MTU Keri Selts** - *Nasva* *Estonia* MMSI: 276315000 Official number: 398FL04	**147** 44 37	Class: (RS)	**1962-01 D. & Joh. Boot Scheepswerf "De Industrie" — Alphen a/d Rijn** Yd No: 1308 Loa 28.88 Br ex 6.53 Dght 3.300 Lbp 24.95 Br md 6.51 Dpth 3.31 Welded	**(B11B2FV) Fishing Vessel**	**1 oil engine** driving 1 FP propeller Total Power: 375kW (510hp) De Industrie 6D6 1 x 4 Stroke 6 Cy. 250 x 350 375kW (510bhp) NV Motorenfabriek 'De Industrie'-Netherlands
9193006 *VWCI* -	**VAHBIZ** - **Gol Offshore Ltd** - *Mumbai* *India* MMSI: 419413000 Official number: 2788	**292** 88 148	Class: IR (LR) Classed LR until 7/7/10	**1999-11 Bharati Shipyard Ltd — Ratnagiri** Yd No: 270 Loa 31.00 Br ex 9.62 Dght 4.800 Lbp 30.00 Br md 9.60 Dpth 3.90 Welded, 1 dk	**(B32A2ST) Tug** Passengers: berths: 9	**2 oil engines** with flexible couplings & geared to sc. shafts driving 2 Z propellers Total Power: 2,670kW (3,630hp) 10.0kn Normo KRMB-6 2 x 4 Stroke 6 Cy. 250 x 300 each-1335kW (1815bhp) Ulstein Bergen AS-Norway AuxGen: 2 x 60kW 415V 50Hz a.c Fuel: 80.0 (d.f.)
8657770 *AVQZ* -	**VAIDYANATH** - **United Shippers Ltd** - *Mumbai* *India* MMSI: 419000484 Official number: 3940	**1,054** 513 1,690	Class: IR	**2011-11 Vijai Marine Services — Goa** Yd No: 65 Loa 67.10 Br ex 12.01 Dght 3.200 Lbp 64.03 Br md 12.00 Dpth 4.35 Welded, 1 dk	**(A31A2GX) General Cargo Ship** Bale: 1,982 Compartments: 1 Ho, ER 1 Ha: ER	**2 oil engines** reduction geared to sc. shafts driving 2 FP propellers Total Power: 536kW (728hp) 8.2kn Cummins NT-855-M 2 x 4 Stroke 6 Cy. 140 x 152 each-268kW (364bhp) Cummins India Ltd-India
8228787 *UDNW* -	**VAIGALE** *ex* Timashevsk *-1992* **Marfish Co Ltd (A/O 'Marfish')** - *Kaliningrad* *Russia* Official number: 831491	**356** 107 138	Class: RS	**1984 Sudostroitelnyy Zavod "Avangard" — Petrozavodsk** Yd No: 416 Loa 35.74 Br ex 8.92 Dght 3.429 Lbp 31.00 Br md 8.80 Dpth 5.97 Welded, 1 dk	**(B11A2FS) Stern Trawler** Ins: 90 Ice Capable	**1 oil engine** driving 1 FP propeller Total Power: 589kW (801hp) S.K.L. 6NVD48A-2U 1 x 4 Stroke 6 Cy. 320 x 480 589kW (801bhp) VEB Schwermaschinenbau "KarlLiebknecht" (SKL)-Magdeburg AuxGen: 2 x 160kW Fuel: 35.0 (d.f.)
8990342 *LXVI* -	**VAIMITI** - **Navimar Services SA** Magellan Management & Consulting SA *Luxembourg* *Luxembourg* MMSI: 253203000 Official number: 6-44	**174** 52 135	Class: BV	**2003-07** Yd No: 130 Loa 39.30 Br ex - Dght 2.900 Lbp 36.20 Br md 8.35 Dpth 3.50 Welded, 1 dk	**(X11A2YS) Yacht (Sailing)** Hull Material: Aluminium Alloy Passengers: cabins: 4; berths: 10	**1 oil engine** geared to sc. shaft driving 1 CP propeller Total Power: 368kW (500hp) 12.5kn MAN D2866LXE 1 x 4 Stroke 6 Cy. 128 x 155 368kW (500bhp) MAN Nutzfahrzeuge AG-Nuernberg AuxGen: 1 x 45kW 380/220V 50Hz, 1 x 33kW 380/220V 50Hz
9082776 *VTLQ* -	**VAISHNAVI 1** - **Fishing Falcons Ltd** - SatCom: Inmarsat A 1640526 *Chennai* *India* Official number: F-MDR-007	*603* 182 398	Class: (IR) (KR)	**1992-12 Koje Shipbuilding Co Ltd — Geoje** Loa 53.89 (BB) Br ex 8.90 Dght 3.400 Lbp 48.05 Br md 8.70 Dpth 3.75 Welded, 1 dk	**(B11B2FV) Fishing Vessel** Ins: 688 Compartments: 2 Ho, ER 2 Ha: ER	**1 oil engine** driving 1 FP propeller Total Power: 1,030kW (1,400hp) 14.0kn Niigata 6M28AFTE 1 x 4 Stroke 6 Cy. 280 x 480 1030kW (1400bhp) Ssangyong Heavy Industries Co Ltd-South Korea
9082788 *VTLR* -	**VAISHNAVI 2** - **Fishing Falcons Ltd** - *Chennai* *India* Official number: F-MDR-008	*603* 182 427	Class: (IR) (KR)	**1992-12 Koje Shipbuilding Co Ltd — Geoje** Loa 53.89 (BB) Br ex 8.90 Dght 3.400 Lbp 48.05 Br md 8.70 Dpth 3.75 Welded, 1 dk	**(B11B2FV) Fishing Vessel** Ins: 688 Compartments: 2 Ho, ER 2 Ha: ER	**1 oil engine** driving 1 FP propeller Total Power: 1,030kW (1,400hp) 14.0kn Niigata 6M28AFTE 1 x 4 Stroke 6 Cy. 280 x 480 1030kW (1400bhp) Ssangyong Heavy Industries Co Ltd-South Korea
8004894 *ATIG* -	**VAISHNAVI-3** *ex* Habomai Maru No. 83 *-1994* **Fishing Falcons Ltd** - SatCom: Inmarsat A 1640733 *Visakhapatnam* *India* Official number: F-VSM-252	*314* 156 374	Class: (IR)	**1980-07 Miho Zosensho K.K. — Shimizu** Yd No: 1173 Loa 51.52 Br ex 8.62 Dght 3.250 Lbp 44.81 Br md 8.60 Dpth 3.61 Welded, 1 dk	**(B11B2FV) Fishing Vessel**	**1 oil engine** driving 1 FP propeller Total Power: 1,029kW (1,399hp) 11.5kn Hanshin 6LUN28AG 1 x 4 Stroke 6 Cy. 280 x 480 1029kW (1399bhp) Hanshin Nainenki Kogyo-Japan AuxGen: 2 x 200kW 225V 60Hz a.c
9662411 *AVQN* -	**VAITARNA** - **Shreeji Shipping Services (India) Ltd** - *Mumbai* *India* MMSI: 419000468 Official number: 3933	**170** 55 115	Class: IR	**2012-06 KP Marine Services Pvt Ltd — Jamnagar** Yd No: 101 Loa 23.95 Br ex - Dght 2.310 Lbp 22.36 Br md 8.00 Dpth 3.20 Welded, 2 dks	**(B32A2ST) Tug**	**2 oil engines** reduction geared to sc. shafts driving 2 FP propellers Total Power: 894kW (1,216hp) Cummins KTA-19-M3 2 x 4 Stroke 6 Cy. 159 x 159 each-447kW (608bhp) Cummins India Ltd-India
8318491 *VVK* -	**VAJRA** - **Government of The Republic of India (Coast Guard)** - *Mumbai* *India*	**1,400** 450 195 T/cm 5.1	Class: IR (AB)	**1988-12 Mazagon Dock Ltd. — Mumbai** Yd No: 785 Loa 74.10 Br ex 11.42 Dght 3.320 Lbp 69.02 Br md 11.40 Dpth 7.90 Welded, 2 dks	**(B34H2SQ) Patrol Vessel**	**2 oil engines** with clutches, flexible couplings & sr reverse geared to sc. shafts driving 2 CP propellers Total Power: 9,420kW (12,808hp) 14.0kn Pielstick 16PA6V280 2 x Vee 4 Stroke 16 Cy. 280 x 290 each-4710kW (6404bhp) SEMT Pielstick SA-France AuxGen: 4 x 213kW 415V 50Hz a.c, 1 x 160kW 160V 50Hz a.c Fuel: 140.0 (d.f.) 12.0pd
9063809 *ATNE* -	**VAJRA** - **Visakhapatnam Port Trust** - *Visakhapatnam* *India* Official number: 2564	**366** 110 157	Class: (IR)	**2000-03 The Shalimar Works (1980) Ltd — Haora** Yd No: 755 Loa 32.49 Br ex 10.10 Dght 3.010 Lbp 31.19 Br md 10.08 Dpth 4.00 Welded, 1 dk	**(B32A2ST) Tug**	**2 oil engines** gearing integral to driving 2 Voith-Schneider propellers Total Power: 2,500kW (3,400hp) 11.0kn Bergens KRMB-8 2 x 4 Stroke 8 Cy. 250 x 300 each-1250kW (1700bhp) Ulstein Bergen AS-Norway AuxGen: 2 x 88kW 415V 50Hz a.c Fuel: 58.0 (d.f.)
8885626 *WDF9672* -	**VAK 5** *ex* Grace *-2011* *ex* Princess Mary *-2011* **Vak Fisheries LLC** - *Honolulu, HI* *United States of America* MMSI: 367507610 Official number: 916945	*103* 82 -		**1988 National Fisherman's Cooperative — Biloxi, Ms** Yd No: 12 L reg 21.95 Br ex - Dght - Lbp - Br md 6.33 Dpth 2.19 Welded, 1 dk	**(B11B2FV) Fishing Vessel**	**1 oil engine** driving 1 FP propeller
5399016 *TCAT7* -	**VAKFIKEBIR-I** *ex* Ekinlik II *-1992* *ex* Ziya Kalkavan *-1990* *ex* Hamit Naci *-1955* *ex* Balik *-1955* *ex* Rinovia *-1955* *ex* Sesostris *-1955* **Durmusoglu Denizcilik Sanayi ve Ticaret AS** - *Istanbul* *Turkey* Official number: 888	*398* 270 725	Class: (LR) ✠ Classed LR until 5/53	**1916-02 Cook, Welton & Gemmell Ltd. — Beverley** Yd No: 320 Loa 53.45 Br ex 7.01 Dght 3.630 Lbp 51.20 Br md 7.00 Dpth 4.20 Riveted	**(B11A2FT) Trawler**	**1 oil engine** driving 1 FP propeller 9.0kn Polar 1 x 2 Stroke 5 Cy. 180 x 300 Atlas Diesel AB-Sweden
6801286 - -	**VAL** *ex* Dmitriy Donskoy *-2002* **Private Enterprise 'Valship'** -	*352* - 52	Class: (RS)	**1956 Bakinskiy Sudostroitelnyy Zavod im Vano Sturua — Baku** Yd No: 29 Loa 44.05 Br ex 8.36 Dght 2.210 Lbp 42.00 Br md - Dpth 3.52 Welded, 1 dk	**(B32A2ST) Tug**	**2 oil engines** driving 2 FP propellers Total Power: 882kW (1,200hp) 12.0kn Russkiy 6DR30/50 2 x 2 Stroke 6 Cy. 300 x 500 each-441kW (600bhp) (new engine 1965) Mashinostroitelnyy Zavod"Russkiy-Dizel"-Leningrad AuxGen: 2 x 100kW a.c, 1 x 50kW a.c Fuel: 59.0 (d.f.)

6917592 *IRMO* -	**VAL** *ex* Prompt *-1979* **Ocean Srl** - *Trieste* *Italy* Official number: 736	*139* 38 119	Class: RI (GL)	**1969 Schulte & Bruns Schiffswerft — Emden** Yd No: 256 Loa 27.79 Br ex 7.90 Dght 2.883 Lbp 24.49 Br md 7.50 Dpth 3.48 Welded, 1 dk	**(B32A2ST) Tug** Ice Capable	**1 oil engine** driving 1 CP propeller Total Power: 762kW (1,036hp) MaK 6M451AK 1 x 4 Stroke 6 Cy. 320 x 450 762kW (1036bhp) Atlas MaK Maschinenbau GmbH-Kiel
7116901 *IVHA* -	**VALAIS** *ex* Saint Tropez *-1978* **Vetor Srl** - SatCom: Inmarsat C 424740720 *Naples* *Italy* MMSI: 247230000 Official number: 739	**1,435** 689 2,227	Class: RI (BV)	**1971-07 Soc Nouvelle des Ats et Chs de La Rochelle-Pallice — La Rochelle** Yd No: 1206 Converted From: Oil Tanker-2005 Loa 81.31 Br ex 12.45 Dght 4.830 Lbp 74.81 Br md 12.40 Dpth 5.59 Welded, 1 dk	**(A12C2LW) Wine Tanker** Liq: 2,529; Liq (Oil): 2,529 Compartments: 28 Ta, ER	**1 oil engine** driving 1 FP propeller Total Power: 1,765kW (2,400hp) 13.0kn MaK 6MU551AK 1 x 4 Stroke 6 Cy. 450 x 550 1765kW (2400bhp) Atlas MaK Maschinenbau GmbH-Kiel AuxGen: 3 x 108kW 380V 50Hz a.c Fuel: 264.0 (d.f.) 7.0pd
9437749 *9BML* -	**VALASHT** - **Government of The Islamic Republic of Iran (Ports & Maritime Organisation)** - *Now Shahr* *Iran* MMSI: 422624000 Official number: 162	**151** 45 71	Class: (BV)	**2007-02 Shahid Tamjidi Marine Industries — Bandar Anzali** Yd No: 506323 Loa 25.00 Br ex 7.25 Dght 2.650 Lbp 23.35 Br md 7.20 Dpth 3.75 Welded, 1 dk	**(B32A2ST) Tug**	**2 oil engines** reduction geared to sc. shafts driving 2 Z propellers Total Power: 1,340kW (1,822hp) 10.6kn MAN D2842LE 2 x Vee 4 Stroke 12 Cy. 128 x 142 each-670kW (911bhp) MAN Nutzfahrzeuge AG-Nuernberg
9064281 *ELYY* -	**VALBELLA** *ex* Halla No. 5 *-2004* **Ocean Carriers Inc** John T Essberger GmbH & Co KG *Monrovia* *Liberia*	**5,286** 2,285 9,146	Class: LR (KR) **100A1** SS 11/2012 cement carrier *IWS **LMC** Eq.Ltr: X; Cable: 495.0/46.0 U3 (a)	**1992-12 Halla Engineering & Heavy Industries Ltd — Incheon** Yd No: 188 Loa 113.50 (BB) Br ex 17.82 Dght 7.712 Lbp 106.00 Br md 17.80 Dpth 10.00 Welded, 1 dk	**(A24A2BT) Cement Carrier** Grain: 8,068 Compartments: 2 Ho, ER	**1 oil engine** driving 1 FP propeller Total Power: 3,360kW (4,568hp) 14.6kn B&W 6L35MC 1 x 2 Stroke 6 Cy. 350 x 1050 3360kW (4568bhp) Hyundai Heavy Industries Co Ltd-South Korea AuxGen: 2 x 320kW 450V 60Hz a.c Boilers: AuxB (o.f.) 8.1kgf/cm² (7.9bar)
6423216 - DAK 700	**VALBERG** - **Nouvelle Chalucap SA** - *Dakar* *Senegal*	*156* 52 -	Class: (BV)	**1964 Ateliers & Chantiers de La Rochelle-Pallice — La Rochelle** Yd No: 5100 Loa 29.90 Br ex 6.76 Dght 2.921 Lbp 25.00 Br md 6.71 Dpth 3.56 Welded, 1 dk	**(B11A2FT) Trawler** Ins: 100 Compartments: 1 Ho, ER 2 Ha: 2 (0.9 x 1.0)ER Derricks: 1x3t	**1 oil engine** driving 1 FP propeller Total Power: 412kW (560hp) 11.0kn Deutz RBV6M536 1 x 4 Stroke 6 Cy. 270 x 360 412kW (560bhp) Kloeckner Humboldt Deutz AG-West Germany Fuel: 30.0 (d.f.)
8658138 *TFAW* IS 307	**VALBJORN** *ex* Gunnbjorn *-2010* *ex* Kristjan Thor *-2010* *ex* Gullthor *-2010* *ex* Haukur Bodvarsson *-2010* **Birnir Ehf** - *Bolungarvik* *Iceland* MMSI: 251159110 Official number: 1686	**263** 78 -		**1984-01 Hordur hf — Reykjanesbaer** Yd No: 0002 Loa 28.95 Br ex - Dght - Lbp 25.47 Br md 6.98 Dpth 5.00 Welded, 1 dk	**(B11A2FS) Stern Trawler**	**1 oil engine** reduction geared to sc. shaft driving 1 Propeller Total Power: 700kW (952hp) M.T.U. 1 x 700kW (952bhp) (new engine ,made 1984) MTU Friedrichshafen GmbH-Friedrichshafen
9422835 *IBUJ* -	**VALBRENTA** - **Navigazione Montanari SpA** - SatCom: Inmarsat C 424702842 *Trieste* *Italy* MMSI: 247276900	**60,185** 33,762 109,039 T/cm 91.3	Class: AB RI	**2009-10 Hudong-Zhonghua Shipbuilding (Group) Co Ltd — Shanghai** Yd No: H1523A Loa 243.00 (BB) Br ex 42.03 Dght 15.367 Lbp 233.00 Br md 42.00 Dpth 22.00 Welded, 1 dk	**(A13A2TV) Crude Oil Tanker** Double Hull (13F) Liq: 123,030; Liq (Oil): 123,030 Cargo Heating Coils Compartments: 12 Wing Ta, 2 Wing Slop Ta, ER 3 Cargo Pump (s): 3x2500m³/hr Manifold: Bow/CM: 119.5m	**1 oil engine** driving 1 FP propeller Total Power: 14,280kW (19,415hp) 14.7kn MAN-B&W 7S60MC 1 x 2 Stroke 7 Cy. 600 x 2292 14280kW (19415bhp) Hudong Heavy Machinery Co Ltd-China AuxGen: 3 x 680kW 60Hz a.c
9384112 *ICIA* -	**VALCADORE** - **Navigazione Montanari SpA** - SatCom: Inmarsat C 424701588 *Trieste* *Italy* MMSI: 247228200	**23,335** 9,628 37,481 T/cm 45.2	Class: BV RI	**2008-02 Hyundai Mipo Dockyard Co Ltd — Ulsan** Yd No: 2041 Loa 184.32 (BB) Br ex 27.43 Dght 11.316 Lbp 176.00 Br md 27.40 Dpth 17.20 Welded, 1 dk	**(A12B2TR) Chemical/Products Tanker** Double Hull (13F) Liq: 40,750; Liq (Oil): 40,750 Compartments: 12 Wing Ta, 2 Wing Slop Ta, ER 12 Cargo Pump (s): 10x500m³/hr, 2x300m³/hr Manifold: Bow/CM: 92.6m	**1 oil engine** driving 1 FP propeller Total Power: 7,860kW (10,686hp) 14.5kn MAN-B&W 6S46MC-C 1 x 2 Stroke 6 Cy. 460 x 1932 7860kW (10686bhp) Hyundai Heavy Industries Co Ltd-South Korea AuxGen: 3 x 960kW a.c Thrusters: 1 Tunnel thruster (f) Fuel: 132.0 (d.f.) 1017.0 (r.f.)
5339743 *ORIV* -	**VALCKE** *ex* Astroloog *-1986* *ex* Steenbank *-1972* **Government of The Kingdom of Belgium** - *Zeebrugge* *Belgium* MMSI: 205216000	*183* - -	Class: (BV)	**1960-12 N.V. Scheepswerven v/h H.H. Bodewes — Millingen a/d Rijn** Yd No: 560 Loa 30.38 Br ex 7.55 Dght 2.998 Lbp - Br md 7.22 Dpth 3.81 Welded, 1 dk	**(B32A2ST) Tug**	**2 diesel electric oil engines** Connecting to 1 elec. Motor driving 1 FP propeller 13.0kn Deutz SBA8M528 2 x 4 Stroke 8 Cy. 220 x 280 Kloeckner Humboldt Deutz AG-West Germany
9422005 *IBLI* -	**VALCONCA** - **Navigazione Montanari SpA** - SatCom: Inmarsat C 424702255 *Trieste* *Italy* MMSI: 247267500	**60,185** 33,762 109,060 T/cm 91.3	Class: AB RI	**2009-07 Hudong-Zhonghua Shipbuilding (Group) Co Ltd — Shanghai** Yd No: H1522A Loa 243.00 (BB) Br ex 42.03 Dght 15.367 Lbp 233.00 Br md 42.00 Dpth 22.00 Welded, 1 dk	**(A13A2TV) Crude Oil Tanker** Double Hull (13F) Liq: 123,030; Liq (Oil): 125,540 Cargo Heating Coils Compartments: 12 Wing Ta, 2 Wing Slop Ta, ER 3 Cargo Pump (s): 3x2500m³/hr Manifold: Bow/CM: 119.5m	**1 oil engine** driving 1 FP propeller Total Power: 13,570kW (18,450hp) 14.5kn MAN-B&W 7S60MC 1 x 2 Stroke 7 Cy. 600 x 2292 13570kW (18450bhp) Hudong Heavy Machinery Co Ltd-China AuxGen: 3 x 680kW a.c Fuel: 140.0 (d.f.) 2725.0 (r.f.)
9231705 *IBZL* -	**VALDAOSTA** - **Navigazione Montanari SpA** - *Trieste* *Italy* MMSI: 247067400	**19,408** 6,556 25,527 T/cm 41.0	Class: RI (BV) (AB)	**2002-07 ShinA Shipbuilding Co Ltd — Tongyeong** Yd No: 410 Loa 176.00 (BB) Br ex - Dght 9.000 Lbp 168.00 Br md 27.40 Dpth 15.00 Welded, 1 dk	**(A12B2TR) Chemical/Products Tanker** Double Hull (13F) Liq: 33,027; Liq (Oil): 33,550 Cargo Heating Coils Compartments: 12 Wing Ta, ER, 2 Wing Slop Ta 12 Cargo Pump (s): 12x450m³/hr Manifold: Bow/CM: 83.4m	**1 oil engine** driving 1 FP propeller Total Power: 7,134kW (9,699hp) 15.0kn B&W 5S50MC 1 x 2 Stroke 5 Cy. 500 x 1910 7134kW (9699bhp) Doosan Engine Co Ltd-South Korea AuxGen: 3 x 740kW a.c Thrusters: 1 Tunnel thruster (f)
9417335 *ICIL* -	**VALDARNO** - **Navigazione Montanari SpA** - 773130642 *Trieste* *Italy* MMSI: 247285900	**60,185** 33,762 108,914 T/cm 91.3	Class: AB RI	**2010-03 Hudong-Zhonghua Shipbuilding (Group) Co Ltd — Shanghai** Yd No: H1525A Loa 243.00 (BB) Br ex 42.03 Dght 15.367 Lbp 233.00 Br md 42.00 Dpth 22.00 Welded, 1 dk	**(A13A2TV) Crude Oil Tanker** Double Hull (13F) Liq: 123,030; Liq (Oil): 123,030 Compartments: 12 Wing Ta, ER, 2 Wing Slop Ta 3 Cargo Pump (s): 3x2500m³/hr Manifold: Bow/CM: 119.5m	**1 oil engine** driving 1 FP propeller Total Power: 14,280kW (19,415hp) 14.7kn MAN-B&W 7S60MC 1 x 2 Stroke 7 Cy. 600 x 2292 14280kW (19415bhp) Hudong Heavy Machinery Co Ltd-China Fuel: 139.5 (d.f.) 2839.0 (r.f.)
7343633 *OWCJ2* -	**VALDEMAR M** *ex* Viking Staffa *-2009* *ex* BUE Staffa *-2005* *ex* Alexandra Tide *-1999* *ex* Lady Alexandra *-1974* **KEM-Offshore ApS** - *Esbjerg* *Denmark (DIS)* MMSI: 219012732 Official number: D4424	**1,146** 343 1,196	Class: LR ✠**100A1** SS 05/2011 tug ✠**LMC** Eq.Ltr: M; Cable: U2	**1974-01 Allied Shipbuilders Ltd — North Vancouver BC** Yd No: 184 Converted From: Offshore Supply Ship-2008 Converted From: Offshore Tug/Supply Ship-1991 Loa 58.27 Br ex 13.14 Dght 5.112 Lbp 54.13 Br md 12.79 Dpth 6.00 Welded, 1 dk	**(B34L2QU) Utility Vessel** Cranes: 1x9.5t	**4 oil engines** sr geared to sc. shafts driving 2 CP propellers Total Power: 2,624kW (3,568hp) 10.0kn Nohab F26R 4 x 4 Stroke 6 Cy. 250 x 300 each-656kW (892bhp) AB NOHAB-Sweden AuxGen: 2 x 230kW 380V 50Hz a.c, 1 x 200kW 380V 50Hz a.c Thrusters: 1 Thwart. FP thruster (f) Fuel: 845.0 (d.f.)
8600258 *YL2755* -	**VALDEROY** *ex* Kjalken *-1994* *ex* Vestflud *-1991* **BraDava Ltd (SIA 'BraDava')** - *Ventspils* *Latvia* MMSI: 275412000 Official number: 1556	**395** 129 -		**1985-12 Longva Mek. Verksted AS — Gursken** Yd No: 20 Loa 27.41 Br ex - Dght 4.250 Lbp - Br md 8.01 Dpth 6.20 Welded, 1 dk	**(B11B2FV) Fishing Vessel**	**1 oil engine** geared to sc. shaft driving 1 FP propeller Total Power: 588kW (799hp) 11.5kn Cummins KT-38-M 1 x Vee 4 Stroke 12 Cy. 159 x 159 588kW (799bhp) Cummins Engine Co Inc-USA
9370020 *WDC5717* -	**VALDEZ SPIRIT** - **Stan Stephens Cruises Inc** - *Valdez, AK* *United States of America* MMSI: 367045440 Official number: 1168747	**215** 72 -		**2005-05 All American Marine Inc — Bellingham WA** Yd No: 820995D05 Loa 25.29 Br ex - Dght 0.960 Lbp - Br md 8.89 Dpth - Welded, 1 dk	**(A37B2PS) Passenger Ship** Hull Material: Aluminium Alloy Passengers: 149	**2 oil engines** reduction geared to sc. shafts driving 2 Propellers Total Power: 1,176kW (1,598hp) 20.0kn Lugger L6170A 2 x 4 Stroke 6 Cy. 170 x 170 each-588kW (799bhp) Alaska Diesel Electric Inc-USA

IMO / Call sign	Name / Owner	Tonnage	Class	Builder / Dimensions	Type	Machinery
9055802 *WCO7674* -	**VALDEZ STAR** **Prince William Sound Oil Spill Response Corp** Crowley Marine Services Inc *Juneau, AK* *United States of America* MMSI: 366888920 Official number: 972499	**357** 107 609	Class: AB	**1991**-03 **Goudy & Stevens — East Boothbay, Me** Yd No: 237 Loa 37.49 Br ex - Dght - Lbp 35.11 Br md 9.45 Dpth 4.12 Welded, 1 dk	**(B34G2SE) Pollution Control Vessel** Compartments: 4 Wing Ta, ER	**2 oil engines** sr geared to sc. shafts driving 2 FP propellers Total Power: 1,412kW (1,920hp) 8.0kn Caterpillar 3508TA 2 x Vee 4 Stroke 8 Cy. 170 x 190 each-706kW (960bhp) Caterpillar Inc-USA AuxGen: 2 x 75kW a.c
8302117 *TFAF* GK 195	**VALDIMAR** *ex* Vesturborg *-2000* *ex* Aarsheim Senior *-1997* *ex* Bommelgutt *-1987* **Thorbjorn Fiskanes hf** - SatCom: Inmarsat C 425142310 *Vogar* *Iceland* MMSI: 251423000 Official number: 2354	**569** 171 -	Class: (BV)	**1982**-07 **H. & E. Nordtveit Skipsbyggeri AS — Nordtveitgrend** Yd No: 73 Lengthened Loa 41.36 Br ex - Dght 6.550 Lbp 38.00 Br md 8.51 Dpth 3.33 Welded, 1 dk	**(B11B2FV) Fishing Vessel**	**1 oil engine** driving 1 CP propeller Total Power: 507kW (689hp) Callesen 6-427C-FOT 1 x 4 Stroke 6 Cy. 270 x 400 507kW (689bhp) Aabenraa Motorfabrik, HeinrichCallesen A/S-Denmark
8104515 *HC4479* -	**VALDIVIA** *ex* Hai *-2002* **Servicios Navales Fluvimar SA** Negocios Navieros y de Transporte Transneg SA *Guayaquil* *Ecuador* MMSI: 735057606 Official number: TN-00-0439	**2,025** 1,039 3,150 T/cm 8.5	Class: LR (GL) **100A1** SS 02/2012 oil tanker ESP Ice Class 1D **LMC** **UMS**	**1981**-12 **Sieghold Werft Bremerhaven GmbH & Co. — Bremerhaven** Yd No: 187 Loa 86.70 Br ex 12.62 Dght 5.762 Lbp 78.62 Br md 12.50 Dpth 6.35 Welded, 1 dk	**(A13B2TP) Products Tanker** Single Hull Liq: 4,047; Liq (Oil): 3,768 Compartments: 5 Ta, 8 Wing Ta, ER 3 Cargo Pump (s) Ice Capable	**1 oil engine** with flexible couplings & sr geared to sc. shaft driving 1 CP propeller Total Power: 1,760kW (2,393hp) 12.5kn MaK 8M452AK 1 x 4 Stroke 8 Cy. 320 x 450 1760kW (2393bhp) Krupp MaK Maschinenbau GmbH-Kiel AuxGen: 2 x 220kW a.c, 1 x 120kW a.c Fuel: 153.6 (r.f.)
6614970 - -	**VALDIVIA** *launched as* J. C. P.-R. 2 *-1967* **Arwad Full Marine SA** - *Panama* *Panama*	*298* 53 -	Class: (LR) ✠ Classed LR until 12/1/10	**1967**-04 **Sociedad Espanola de Construccion Naval SA — Puerto Real** Yd No: 130 Loa 36.10 Br ex 9.50 Dght 3.620 Lbp 32.16 Br md 9.00 Dpth 4.25 Welded, 1 dk	**(B32A2ST) Tug**	**2 oil engines** sr geared to sc. shaft driving 1 CP propeller Total Power: 1,214kW (1,650hp) 12.0kn Werkspoor TMABS276 2 x 4 Stroke 6 Cy. 270 x 500 each-607kW (825bhp) Naval Stork Werkspoor SA-Spain AuxGen: 2 x 45kW 220V d.c
9053115 *CBVL* -	**VALDIVIA** *ex* Parapola *-2006* **Sociedad Nacional Maritima SA (Sonamar)** - *Valparaiso* *Chile* MMSI: 725016500 Official number: 3158	**38,792** 21,279 68,232 T/cm 65.1	Class: LR (NV) **100A1** SS 02/2009 Double Hull oil tanker MARPOL 13G (1) (c) ESP Ice Class 1C **LMC** **UMS IGS** Eq.Ltr: Q†; Cable: 687.5/81.0 U3	**1994**-02 **ATVT Sudnobudivnyi Zavod "Zaliv" — Kerch** Yd No: 914 Loa 242.80 (BB) Br ex 32.64 Dght 13.639 Lbp 228.00 Br md 32.20 Dpth 18.00 Welded, 1 dk	**(A13A2TW) Crude/Oil Products Tanker** Double Hull (13F) Liq: 68,153; Liq (Oil): 68,153 Cargo Heating Coils Compartments: 14 Wing Ta, 2 Wing Slop Ta, ER 4 Cargo Pump (s): 4x1500m³/hr Manifold: Bow/CM: 124m Ice Capable	**1 oil engine** driving 1 FP propeller Total Power: 13,180kW (17,920hp) 14.5kn B&W 8L60MCE 1 x 2 Stroke 8 Cy. 600 x 1944 13180kW (17920bhp) AO Bryanskiy MashinostroitelnyyZavod (BMZ)-Bryansk AuxGen: 1 x 650kW 380V 50Hz a.c, 1 x 848kW 380V 50Hz a.c, 2 x 740kW 380V 50Hz a.c Boilers: AuxB (ex.g.) 6.9kgf/cm² (6.8bar) 5.6kgf/cm² (5.5bar), WTAuxB (o.f.) 18.6kgf/cm² (18.2bar), WTAuxB (o.f.) (fitted: 1994) 9.2kgf/cm² (9.0bar) Fuel: 420.0 (d.f.) (Heating Coils) 3534.0 (r.f.) 44.5pd
9333395 *V7LJ5* -	**VALDIVIA** **ms 'Nb 1273' Schiffahrtsges mbH & Co KG** MCC Transport Singapore Pte Ltd *Majuro* *Marshall Islands* MMSI: 538090268 Official number: 90268	**17,360** 9,038 22,229	Class: GL	**2006**-12 **Daewoo-Mangalia Heavy Industries S.A. — Mangalia** (Hull) Yd No: 4059 **2006**-12 **J.J. Sietas KG Schiffswerft GmbH & Co. — Hamburg** Yd No: 1273 Loa 178.57 (BB) Br ex - Dght 10.850 Lbp 167.50 Br md 27.60 Dpth 14.58 Welded, 1 dk	**(A33A2CC) Container Ship (Fully Cellular)** Double Hull TEU 1856 incl 385 ref C. Cranes: 3x45t Ice Capable	**1 oil engine** driving 1 FP propeller Total Power: 16,980kW (23,086hp) 20.0kn MAN-B&W 6L70ME-C 1 x 2 Stroke 6 Cy. 700 x 2360 16980kW (23086bhp) Manises Diesel Engine Co. S.A.-Valencia AuxGen: 4 x 1030kW 440/230V a.c Thrusters: 1 Tunnel thruster (f); 1 Tunnel thruster (a)
9262558 *9HNC7* -	**VALDIVIA** *ex* CSAV Genova *-2007* *ex* Valdivia *-2004* **ms 'Castilla' Schiffahrtsgesellschaft mbH & Co KG** FH Bertling Reederei GmbH *Valletta* *Malta* MMSI: 215391000 Official number: 8134	**24,918** 12,552 35,079	Class: NV	**2003**-06 **Jiangdu Yahai Shipbuilding Co Ltd — Jiangdu JS** Yd No: BC32000-003 Loa 188.40 (BB) Br ex 27.73 Dght 11.300 Lbp 177.03 Br md 27.68 Dpth 15.49 Welded, 1 dk	**(A31A2GX) General Cargo Ship** Grain: 45,069 TEU 1874 incl 100 ref C. Compartments: 5 Ho, ER 8 Ha: (12.8 x 20.0)7 (12.8 x 23.0)ER Cranes: 4x40t	**1 oil engine** driving 1 FP propeller Total Power: 8,730kW (11,869hp) 15.0kn Sulzer 6RTA48T-B 1 x 2 Stroke 6 Cy. 480 x 2000 8730kW (11869bhp) Yichang Marine Diesel Engine Co Ltd-China AuxGen: 3 x 600kW 60Hz a.c
7367392 *CB3159* -	**VALDIVIA IV** *ex* Loa 23 *-2001* *ex* Hustler *-1993* **Empresa Pesquera Tarapaca SA** - *Valparaiso* *Chile* MMSI: 725000830 Official number: 2895	**754** - -	Class: (AB)	**1974 Zigler Shipyards Inc — Jennings LA** Yd No: 234 Converted From: Fishing Vessel-2010 Converted From: Offshore Supply Ship-1993 Loa - Br ex 12.20 Dght 3.836 Lbp 54.77 Br md 12.17 Dpth 4.58 Welded, 1 dk	**(A35A2RR) Ro-Ro Cargo Ship** Stern ramp (a)	**2 oil engines** reverse reduction geared to sc. shafts driving 2 FP propellers Total Power: 1,654kW (2,248hp) 12.0kn Caterpillar D399SCAC 2 x Vee 4 Stroke 16 Cy. 159 x 203 each-827kW (1124bhp) Caterpillar Tractor Co-USA AuxGen: 2 x 90kW a.c Thrusters: 1 Tunnel thruster (f); 1 Tunnel thruster (a) Fuel: 368.0 (d.f.)
9340350 *9VHK8* -	**VALE** **Open Waters Vale Pte Ltd** Lloyd Fonds Singapore Pte Ltd SatCom: Inmarsat C 456500034 *Singapore* *Singapore* MMSI: 565588000 Official number: 393456	**8,539** 4,117 13,006 T/cm 23.2	Class: GL (AB)	**2007**-01 **INP Heavy Industries Co Ltd — Ulsan** Yd No: 1141 Loa 128.60 (BB) Br ex 21.65 Dght 8.714 Lbp 120.40 Br md 20.40 Dpth 11.50 Welded, 1 dk	**(A12B2TR) Chemical/Products Tanker** Double Hull (13F) Liq: 13,399; Liq (Oil): 14,074 Cargo Heating Coils Compartments: 12 Wing Ta, 2 Wing Slop Ta, ER 12 Cargo Pump (s): 12x200m³/hr Manifold: Bow/CM: 61.7m	**1 oil engine** driving 1 FP propeller Total Power: 4,440kW (6,037hp) 13.4kn MAN-B&W 6S35MC 1 x 2 Stroke 6 Cy. 350 x 1400 4440kW (6037bhp) STX Engine Co Ltd-South Korea AuxGen: 3 x 480kW a.c Thrusters: 1 Tunnel thruster (f) Fuel: 66.0 (d.f.) 675.9 (r.f.)
9575448 *V7XB3* -	**VALE BEIJING** **POS Maritime PZ SA** Pan Ocean Co Ltd *Majuro* *Marshall Islands* MMSI: 538004438 Official number: 4438	**199,959** 77,072 404,389 T/cm 217.0	Class: KR NV	**2011**-09 **STX Offshore & Shipbuilding Co Ltd — Changwon (Jinhae Shipyard)** Yd No: 1701 Loa 361.00 (BB) Br ex - Dght 23.022 Lbp 353.52 Br md 65.00 Dpth 30.50 Welded, 1 dk	**(A21B2BO) Ore Carrier** Grain: 246,730 Compartments: 7 Ho, ER 7 Ha: 5 (28.5 x 22.3) (28.5 x 20.5)ER (28.5 x 16.7)	**1 oil engine** driving 1 FP propeller Total Power: 29,260kW (39,782hp) 14.8kn MAN-B&W 7S80ME-C8 1 x 2 Stroke 7 Cy. 800 x 3200 29260kW (39782bhp) STX Engine Co Ltd-South Korea AuxGen: 3 x a.c Fuel: 12710.0
9488918 *9V9127* -	**VALE BRASIL** *launched as* Ore China *-2011* **Vale Shipping Holding Pte Ltd** Vale SA SatCom: Inmarsat C 456490510 *Singapore* *Singapore* MMSI: 564905000 Official number: 396661	**198,980** 67,993 402,347	Class: NV	**2011**-03 **Daewoo Shipbuilding & Marine Engineering Co Ltd — Geoje** Yd No: 1201 Loa 362.00 (BB) Br ex 65.06 Dght 23.020 Lbp 350.00 Br md 65.00 Dpth 30.40 Welded, 1 dk	**(A21B2BO) Ore Carrier** Grain: 238,000 Compartments: 7 Ho, ER 7 Ha: ER	**1 oil engine** driving 1 FP propeller Total Power: 31,500kW (42,827hp) 14.8kn MAN-B&W 7S80ME-C8 1 x 2 Stroke 7 Cy. 800 x 3200 31500kW (42827bhp) MAN Diesel A/S-Denmark AuxGen: 3 x 1200kW a.c
9532575 *9V9121* -	**VALE CAOFEIDIAN** **Vale Shipping Singapore Pte Ltd** Bernhard Schulte Shipmanagement (Singapore) Pte Ltd *Singapore* *Singapore* MMSI: 566863000 Official number: 396655	**201,384** 68,974 400,000	Class: NV	**2013**-07 **Jiangsu Rongsheng Shipbuilding Co Ltd — Rugao JS** Yd No: 1111 Loa 359.90 Br ex 65.06 Dght 23.000 Lbp 352.94 Br md 65.00 Dpth 30.40 Welded, 1 dk	**(A21B2BO) Ore Carrier** Grain: 230,000 Compartments: 7 Ho, ER 7 Ha: ER	**1 oil engine** driving 1 FP propeller Total Power: 31,640kW (43,018hp) 14.8kn Wartsila 7RT-flex82T 1 x 2 Stroke 7 Cy. 820 x 3375 31640kW (43018bhp) (new engine 2013) in China AuxGen: 3 x 1280kW a.c
9522972 *9V9115* -	**VALE CHINA** **Vale Shipping Singapore Pte Ltd** Vale SA SatCom: Inmarsat C 456620610 *Singapore* *Singapore* MMSI: 566206000 Official number: 396649	**201,384** 68,974 400,606	Class: NV	**2011**-11 **Jiangsu Rongsheng Shipbuilding Co Ltd — Rugao JS** Yd No: 1105 Loa 359.94 Br ex 65.05 Dght 23.000 Lbp 352.95 Br md 65.00 Dpth 30.40 Welded, 1 dk	**(A21B2BO) Ore Carrier** Grain: 230,000 Compartments: 7 Ho, ER 7 Ha: ER	**1 oil engine** driving 1 FP propeller Total Power: 31,640kW (43,018hp) 14.8kn Wartsila 7RT-flex82T 1 x 2 Stroke 7 Cy. 820 x 3375 31640kW (43018bhp) (new engine 2011) in China AuxGen: 3 x 1280kW a.c
9532525 *9V9117* -	**VALE DALIAN** **Vale Shipping Singapore Pte Ltd** Vale SA SatCom: Inmarsat C 456639310 *Singapore* *Singapore* MMSI: 566393000 Official number: 396651	**201,384** 68,974 400,398	Class: NV	**2012**-05 **Jiangsu Rongsheng Shipbuilding Co Ltd — Rugao JS** Yd No: 1107 Loa 360.00 (BB) Br ex 65.60 Dght 23.000 Lbp 350.96 Br md 65.00 Dpth 30.40 Welded, 1 dk	**(A21B2BO) Ore Carrier** Grain: 230,000 Compartments: 7 Ho, ER 7 Ha: ER	**1 oil engine** driving 1 FP propeller Total Power: 31,640kW (43,018hp) 14.8kn Wartsila 7RT-flex82T 1 x 2 Stroke 7 Cy. 820 x 3375 31640kW (43018bhp) (new engine 2012) in China AuxGen: 3 x 1280kW a.c

IMO / Call sign	Name / Owner	Tonnage	Class	Builder / Dimensions	Type	Machinery
9532513 *9V9116* -	**VALE DONGJIAKOU** **Vale Shipping Singapore Pte Ltd** Vale SA *Singapore* *Singapore* MMSI: 566371000 Official number: 396650	**201,384** 68,974 400,606	Class: NV	**2012-04 Jiangsu Rongsheng Shipbuilding Co Ltd — Rugao JS** Yd No: 1106 Loa 359.94 (BB) Br ex 65.05 Dght 23.020 Lbp 351.04 Br md 65.00 Dpth 30.40 Welded, 1 dk	**(A21B2BO) Ore Carrier** Grain: 230,000 Compartments: 7 Ho, ER 7 Ha: ER	**1 oil engine** driving 1 FP propeller Total Power: 31,640kW (43,018hp) 14.8kn Wartsila 7RT-flex82T 1 x 2 Stroke 7 Cy. 820 x 3375 31640kW (43018bhp) (new engine 2012) in China AuxGen: 3 x 1280kW a.c
9575462 *V7YY5* -	**VALE ESPIRITO SANTO** **POS Maritime UZ SA** Pan Ocean Co Ltd SatCom: Inmarsat C 453837862 *Majuro* *Marshall Islands* MMSI: 538004765 Official number: 4765	**199,959** 77,072 403,627 T/cm 217.0	Class: KR NV	**2012-09 STX (Dalian) Shipbuilding Co Ltd — Wafangdian LN** Yd No: 1703 Loa 361.00 (BB) Br ex 65.64 Dght 23.022 Lbp 353.50 Br md 65.00 Dpth 28.67 Welded, 1 dk	**(A21B2BO) Ore Carrier** Grain: 242,540 Compartments: 7 Ho, ER 7 Ha: 5 (28.5 x 22.3) (28.5 x 20.5)ER (28.5 x 16.7)	**1 oil engine** driving 1 FP propeller Total Power: 29,260kW (39,782hp) 14.8kn MAN-B&W 7S80ME-C8 1 x 2 Stroke 7 Cy. 800 x 3200 29260kW (39782bhp) STX Engine Co Ltd-South Korea AuxGen: 3 x a.c
9575486 *V7ZA5* -	**VALE FUJIYAMA** **POS Maritime RZ SA** Pan Ocean Co Ltd SatCom: Inmarsat C 453838152 *Majuro* *Marshall Islands* MMSI: 538004778 Official number: 4778	**199,959** 77,072 403,811 T/cm 217.0	Class: KR NV	**2012-11 STX Offshore & Shipbuilding Co Ltd — Changwon (Jinhae Shipyard)** Yd No: 1705 Loa 361.00 (BB) Br ex - Dght 23.022 Lbp 353.50 Br md 65.00 Dpth 28.67 Welded, 1 dk	**(A21B2BO) Ore Carrier** Grain: 246,730 Compartments: 7 Ho, ER 7 Ha: 5 (28.5 x 22.3) (28.5 x 20.5)ER (28.5 x 16.7)	**1 oil engine** driving 1 FP propeller Total Power: 29,260kW (39,782hp) 14.8kn MAN-B&W 7S80ME-C8 1 x 2 Stroke 7 Cy. 800 x 3200 29260kW (39782bhp) STX Engine Co Ltd-South Korea Fuel: 12650.0
9643398 *FICV* -	**VALE GRAND SUD** **Vale Nouvelle-Caledonie SAS** - *Noumea* *France* MMSI: 540011300	**583** 175 49	Class: BV	**2012-04 Austal Ships Pty Ltd — Fremantle WA** Yd No: 202 Loa 41.20 (BB) Br ex 11.00 Dght 2.000 Lbp 38.40 Br md 10.90 Dpth 6.80 Welded, 1 dk	**(A37B2PS) Passenger Ship** Hull Material: Aluminium Alloy Passengers: unberthed: 439	**4 oil engines** reduction geared to sc. shafts driving 4 Water jets Total Power: 5,760kW (7,832hp) 37.5kn M.T.U. 16V2000M72 4 x Vee 4 Stroke 16 Cy. 135 x 156 each-1440kW (1958bhp) MTU Friedrichshafen GmbH-Friedrichshafen AuxGen: 2 x 143kW 50Hz a.c
9532537 *9V9118* -	**VALE HEBEI** *completed as* Ore Zhanjiang *-2012* **Vale Shipping Singapore Pte Ltd** Vale SA SatCom: Inmarsat C 456646510 *Singapore* *Singapore* MMSI: 566465000 Official number: 396652	**201,384** 68,974 400,535	Class: NV	**2012-09 Jiangsu Rongsheng Shipbuilding Co Ltd — Rugao JS** Yd No: 1108 Loa 359.90 (BB) Br ex 65.05 Dght 23.000 Lbp 352.95 Br md 64.99 Dpth 30.40 Welded, 1 dk	**(A21B2BO) Ore Carrier** Grain: 230,000 Compartments: 7 Ho, ER 7 Ha: ER	**1 oil engine** driving 1 FP propeller Total Power: 31,640kW (43,018hp) 14.8kn Wartsila 7RT-flex82T 1 x 2 Stroke 7 Cy. 820 x 3375 31640kW (43018bhp) (new engine 2012) in China AuxGen: 3 x 1280kW a.c
9575474 *V7ZH3* -	**VALE INDONESIA** **POS Maritime VZ SA** Pan Ocean Co Ltd SatCom: Inmarsat C 453837991 *Majuro* *Marshall Islands* MMSI: 538004826 Official number: 4826	**199,959** 77,072 403,727 T/cm 216.9	Class: KR NV	**2012-10 STX (Dalian) Shipbuilding Co Ltd — Wafangdian LN** Yd No: 1704 Loa 361.00 (BB) Br ex - Dght 23.022 Lbp 353.50 Br md 65.00 Dpth 28.67 Welded, 1 dk	**(A21B2BO) Ore Carrier** Grain: 246,730 Compartments: 7 Ho, ER 7 Ha: 5 (28.5 x 22.3) (28.5 x 20.5)ER (28.5 x 16.7)	**1 oil engine** driving 1 FP propeller Total Power: 29,260kW (39,782hp) 14.8kn MAN-B&W 7S80ME-C8 1 x 2 Stroke 7 Cy. 800 x 3200 29260kW (39782bhp) STX Engine Co Ltd-South Korea Fuel: 12700.0
9572331 *9V9129* -	**VALE ITALIA** **Vale Shipping Enterprise Pte Ltd** Vale SA SatCom: Inmarsat C 456626110 *Singapore* *Singapore* MMSI: 566261000 Official number: 396663	**198,980** 67,993 400,000	Class: NV	**2011-10 Daewoo Shipbuilding & Marine Engineering Co Ltd — Geoje** Yd No: 1203 Loa 362.00 (BB) Br ex 65.06 Dght 23.020 Lbp 350.00 Br md 65.00 Dpth 30.40 Welded, 1 dk	**(A21B2BO) Ore Carrier** Grain: 238,000 Compartments: 7 Ho, ER 7 Ha: ER	**1 oil engine** driving 1 FP propeller Total Power: 31,500kW (42,827hp) 14.8kn MAN-B&W 7S80ME-C8 1 x 2 Stroke 7 Cy. 800 x 3200 31500kW (42827bhp) AuxGen: 3 x a.c
9532551 *9V9120* -	**VALE JIANGSU** **Vale Shipping Singapore Pte Ltd** Vale SA *Singapore* *Singapore* MMSI: 566587000 Official number: 396654	**201,384** 68,974 399,997	Class: NV	**2013-03 Jiangsu Rongsheng Shipbuilding Co Ltd — Rugao JS** Yd No: 1110 Loa 359.85 (BB) Br ex 65.05 Dght 23.000 Lbp 352.85 Br md 64.99 Dpth 30.40 Welded, 1 dk	**(A21B2BO) Ore Carrier** Grain: 230,000 Compartments: 7 Ho, ER 7 Ha: ER	**1 oil engine** driving 1 FP propeller Total Power: 31,640kW (43,018hp) 14.8kn Wartsila 7RT-flex82T 1 x 2 Stroke 7 Cy. 820 x 3375 31640kW (43018bhp) (new engine 2013) in China AuxGen: 3 x 1280kW a.c
9593969 *9V9133* -	**VALE KOREA** **Vale Shipping Holding Pte Ltd** Vale SA *Singapore* *Singapore* MMSI: 566777000 Official number: 396667	**198,980** 67,993 400,000	Class: NV	**2013-04 Daewoo Shipbuilding & Marine Engineering Co Ltd — Geoje** Yd No: 1214 Loa 362.00 (BB) Br ex 65.06 Dght 23.000 Lbp 350.00 Br md 65.00 Dpth 30.40 Welded, 1 dk	**(A21B2BO) Ore Carrier** Grain: 238,000 Compartments: 7 Ho, ER 7 Ha: ER	**1 oil engine** driving 1 FP propeller Total Power: 31,500kW (42,827hp) 14.8kn MAN-B&W 7S80ME-C8 1 x 2 Stroke 7 Cy. 800 x 3200 31500kW (42827bhp) MAN B&W Diesel A/S-Denmark AuxGen: 3 x a.c
9532587 *9V9122* -	**VALE LIANYUNGANG** **Vale Shipping Co Pte Ltd** Vale SA *Singapore* *Singapore* MMSI: 563254000 Official number: 396656	**201,384** 68,974 399,995	Class: NV	**2013-11 Jiangsu Rongsheng Shipbuilding Co Ltd — Rugao JS** Yd No: 1112 Loa 359.87 (BB) Br ex 65.05 Dght 23.000 Lbp 352.90 Br md 64.99 Dpth 30.40 Welded, 1 dk	**(A21B2BO) Ore Carrier** Grain: 230,000 Compartments: 7 Ho, ER 7 Ha: ER	**1 oil engine** driving 1 FP propeller Total Power: 31,640kW (43,018hp) 14.8kn Wartsila 7RT-flex82T 1 x 2 Stroke 7 Cy. 820 x 3375 31640kW (43018bhp) (new engine 2013) in China AuxGen: 3 x a.c
9566514 *V7ZP9* -	**VALE LIWA** *completed as* Yanqul *-2012* **Vale Liwa Maritime Transportation Co Ltd** Oman Shipping Co SAOC *Majuro* *Marshall Islands* MMSI: 538004889 Official number: 4889	**201,384** 68,974 400,314	Class: LR (NV) **100A1** SS 08/2012 ore carrier ESP strengthened for regular discharge by heavy grabs **ShipRight** (ACS (B)) *IWS LI **LMC** **UMS**	**2012-08 Jiangsu Rongsheng Shipbuilding Co Ltd — Rugao JS** Yd No: 1126 Loa 360.00 (BB) Br ex 65.60 Dght 23.000 Lbp 353.00 Br md 65.00 Dpth 30.40 Welded, 1 dk	**(A21B2BO) Ore Carrier** Grain: 230,000 Compartments: 7 Ho, ER 7 Ha: ER	**1 oil engine** driving 1 FP propeller Total Power: 31,640kW (43,018hp) 14.8kn Wartsila 7RT-flex82T 1 x 2 Stroke 7 Cy. 820 x 3375 31640kW (43018bhp) Hyundai Heavy Industries Co Ltd-South Korea AuxGen: 3 x 980kW 60Hz a.c
9674660 *PQ6871* -	**VALE MARAMBAIA** **Vale SA** - *Itacuruca* *Brazil*	**517** 155 270	Class: NV	**2013-06 Detroit Brasil Ltda — Itajai** Yd No: 365 Loa 46.45 Br ex 15.03 Dght 1.500 Lbp 44.25 Br md 15.00 Dpth 2.75 Welded, 1 dk	**(A36A2PR) Passenger/Ro-Ro Ship (Vehicles)**	**2 oil engines** reduction geared to sc. shafts driving 2 FP propellers Total Power: 894kW (1,216hp) Caterpillar C18 ACERT 2 x 4 Stroke 6 Cy. 145 x 183 each-447kW (608bhp) Caterpillar Inc-USA AuxGen: 2 x 99kW a.c Thrusters: 1 Tunnel thruster (f)
9575515 *V7BB5* -	**VALE MARANHAO** **POS Maritime LZ SA** Pan Ocean Co Ltd SatCom: Inmarsat C 453839065 *Majuro* *Marshall Islands* MMSI: 538005109 Official number: 5109	**199,959** 77,072 403,844 T/cm 217.0	Class: KR NV	**2013-08 STX Offshore & Shipbuilding Co Ltd — Changwon (Jinhae Shipyard)** Yd No: 1708 Loa 361.00 (BB) Br ex 65.64 Dght 23.000 Lbp 353.50 Br md 65.00 Dpth 28.67 Welded, 1 dk	**(A21B2BO) Ore Carrier** Grain: 243,730 Compartments: 7 Ho, ER 7 Ha: 5 (28.5 x 22.3) (28.5 x 20.5)ER (28.5 x 16.7)	**1 oil engine** driving 1 FP propeller Total Power: 29,260kW (39,782hp) 14.8kn MAN-B&W 7S80ME-C8 1 x 2 Stroke 7 Cy. 800 x 3200 29260kW (39782bhp) STX Engine Co Ltd-South Korea AuxGen: 3 x 1250kW a.c
9575450 *V7XR6* -	**VALE QINGDAO** **POS Maritime QZ SA** Pan Ocean Co Ltd SatCom: Inmarsat C 453837271 *Majuro* *Marshall Islands* MMSI: 538004553 Official number: 4553	**199,959** 77,072 403,919 T/cm 217.0	Class: KR NV	**2012-04 STX Offshore & Shipbuilding Co Ltd — Changwon (Jinhae Shipyard)** Yd No: 1702 Loa 361.00 (BB) Br ex - Dght 23.022 Lbp 353.50 Br md 65.00 Dpth 30.50 Welded, 1 dk	**(A21B2BO) Ore Carrier** Grain: 246,730 Compartments: 7 Ho, ER 7 Ha: 5 (28.5 x 22.3) (28.5 x 20.5)ER (28.5 x 16.7)	**1 oil engine** driving 1 FP propeller Total Power: 29,260kW (39,782hp) 14.8kn MAN-B&W 7S80ME-C8 1 x 2 Stroke 7 Cy. 800 x 3200 29260kW (39782bhp) STX Engine Co Ltd-South Korea AuxGen: 3 x a.c

IMO / Call sign	Name, owner, manager, flag	Tonnage	Class	Builder & dimensions	Type & capacity	Machinery
9566526 *V7ZR9* -	**VALE SAHAM** **Vale Saham Maritime Transportation Co Ltd** *Majuro* *Marshall Islands* MMSI: 538004900 Official number: 4900	**201,336** 71,039 400,694	Class: AB	**2013-01 Jiangsu Rongsheng Shipbuilding Co Ltd — Rugao JS** Yd No: 1127 Loa 360.00 (BB) Br ex 65.60 Dght 23.000 Lbp 353.00 Br md 65.00 Dpth 30.40 Welded, 1 dk	**(A21B2BO) Ore Carrier** Grain: 230,000 Compartments: 7 Ho, ER 7 Ha: ER	**1 oil engine** driving 1 FP propeller Total Power: 29,400kW (39,972hp) 14.8kn Wartsila 7RT-flex82T 1 x 2 Stroke 7 Cy. 820 x 3375 29400kW (39972bhp) Hyundai Heavy Industries Co Ltd-South Korea AuxGen: 3 x 1200kW a.c Fuel: 540.0 (d.f.) 10240.0 (r.f.)
9532549 *9V9119* -	**VALE SHANDONG** *ex Ore Dongjiakou -2012* *ex Jiangsu Rongsheng 1109 -2012* **Vale Shipping Co Pte Ltd** Vale SA *Singapore* *Singapore* MMSI: 566586000 Official number: 396653	**201,384** 68,974 400,000	Class: NV	**2012-12 Jiangsu Rongsheng Shipbuilding Co Ltd — Rugao JS** Yd No: 1109 Loa 359.93 Br ex 65.60 Dght 23.020 Lbp 352.95 Br md 65.00 Dpth 30.40 Welded, 1 dk	**(A21B2BO) Ore Carrier** Grain: 230,000 Compartments: 7 Ho, ER 7 Ha: ER	**1 oil engine** driving 1 FP propeller Total Power: 31,640kW (43,018hp) 14.8kn Wartsila 7RT-flex82T 1 x 2 Stroke 7 Cy. 820 x 3375 31640kW (43018bhp) in China AuxGen: 3 x 1280kW a.c
9566538 *V7ZR8* -	**VALE SHINAS** *launched as Wafi -2013* **Vale Shinas Maritime Transportation Co Ltd** Oman Shipping Co SAOC *Majuro* *Marshall Islands* MMSI: 538004899 Official number: 4899	**201,336** 71,039 400,420	Class: AB	**2013-03 Jiangsu Rongsheng Shipbuilding Co Ltd — Rugao JS** Yd No: 1128 Loa 360.00 (BB) Br ex 65.60 Dght 23.000 Lbp 353.00 Br md 65.00 Dpth 30.40 Welded, 1 dk	**(A21B2BO) Ore Carrier** Grain: 224,427 Compartments: 7 Ho, ER 7 Ha: ER	**1 oil engine** driving 1 FP propeller Total Power: 29,400kW (39,972hp) 14.8kn Wartsila 7RT-flex82T 1 x 2 Stroke 7 Cy. 820 x 3375 29400kW (39972bhp) Hyundai Heavy Industries Co Ltd-South Korea AuxGen: 3 x 1200kW a.c Fuel: 540.0 (d.f.) 10310.0 (r.f.)
9565065 *V7ZP8* -	**VALE SOHAR** *launched as Jazer -2012* **Vale Sohar Maritime Transportation Co Ltd** Oman Shipping Co SAOC *Majuro* *Marshall Islands* MMSI: 538004888 Official number: 4888	**201,384** 68,974 400,315	Class: LR (NV) **100A1** SS 09/2012 ore carrier ESP strengthend for regular discharge by heavy grabs **ShipRight** (ACS (B)) *IWS LI **LMC** **UMS**	**2012-09 Jiangsu Rongsheng Shipbuilding Co Ltd — Rugao JS** Yd No: 1125 Loa 360.00 (BB) Br ex 65.60 Dght 23.000 Lbp 353.02 Br md 65.00 Dpth 30.40 Welded, 1 dk	**(A21B2BO) Ore Carrier** Grain: 230,000 Compartments: 7 Ho, ER 7 Ha: ER	**1 oil engine** driving 1 FP propeller Total Power: 31,640kW (43,018hp) 14.8kn Wartsila 7RT-flex82T 1 x 2 Stroke 7 Cy. 820 x 3375 31640kW (43018bhp) Hyundai Heavy Industries Co Ltd-South Korea AuxGen: 3 x 980kW 60Hz a.c
9575498 *V7ZU6* -	**VALE TUBARAO** **POS Maritime WZ SA** Pan Ocean Co Ltd *Majuro* *Marshall Islands* MMSI: 538004918 Official number: 4918	**199,959** 77,072 403,784 T/cm 217.0	Class: KR NV	**2013-01 STX (Dalian) Shipbuilding Co Ltd — Wafangdian LN** Yd No: 1706 Loa 361.00 (BB) Br ex 65.64 Dght 22.000 Lbp 353.52 Br md 65.00 Dpth 28.67 Welded, 1 dk	**(A21B2BO) Ore Carrier** Grain: 246,730 Compartments: 7 Ho, ER 7 Ha: 5 (28.5 x 22.3) (28.5 x 20.5)ER (28.5 x 16.7)	**1 oil engine** driving 1 FP propeller Total Power: 29,260kW (39,782hp) 14.8kn MAN-B&W 7S80ME-C8 1 x 2 Stroke 7 Cy. 800 x 3200 29260kW (39782bhp) STX Engine Co Ltd-South Korea AuxGen: 3 x 450V a.c
9628180 *9HA3398* -	**VALENCE** **Terance Shipping Co** Costamare Shipping Co SA *Valletta* *Malta* MMSI: 229548000 Official number: 9628180	**95,390** 56,260 110,692	Class: AB AR (Class contemplated) GL (Class contemplated)	**2013-09 Sungdong Shipbuilding & Marine Engineering Co Ltd — Tongyeong** Yd No: 4023 Loa 299.95 (BB) Br ex - Dght 14.500 Lbp 288.50 Br md 48.20 Dpth 24.60 Welded, 1 dk	**(A33A2CC) Container Ship (Fully Cellular)** TEU 8827 incl 1462 ref C	**1 oil engine** driving 1 FP propeller Total Power: 47,430kW (64,486hp) 22.0kn MAN-B&W 9S90ME-C8 1 x 2 Stroke 9 Cy. 900 x 3188 47430kW (64486bhp) Hyundai Heavy Industries Co Ltd-South Korea AuxGen: 2 x 4350kW a.c, 2 x 3860kW a.c Thrusters: 1 Tunnel thruster (f) Fuel: 900.0 (d.f.) 8630.0 (r.f.)
9292254 *HOUU* -	**VALENCIA BRIDGE** **Aegir Navigation SA** 'K' Line Ship Management Co Ltd (KLSM) *Panama* *Panama* MMSI: 354608000 Official number: 3041905B	**54,519** 22,921 65,006 T/cm 82.5	Class: NK	**2004-12 Hyundai Heavy Industries Co Ltd — Ulsan** Yd No: 1577 Loa 294.12 (BB) Br ex - Dght 13.520 Lbp 283.33 Br md 32.20 Dpth 21.80 Welded, 1 dk	**(A33A2CC) Container Ship (Fully Cellular)** TEU 4738 incl 400 ref C	**1 oil engine** driving 1 FP propeller Total Power: 44,564kW (60,589hp) 23.5kn MAN-B&W 8K98MC-C 1 x 2 Stroke 8 Cy. 980 x 2400 44564kW (60589bhp) Hyundai Heavy Industries Co Ltd-South Korea AuxGen: 4 x 1995kW a.c Thrusters: 1 Thwart. CP thruster (f) Fuel: 7385.0
9108130 *ZCBD4* -	**VALENCIA EXPRESS** *ex CP Performer -2006* *ex Lykes Performer -2005* *ex Cast Prominence -2005* *ex Canmar Courage -2003* **Hapag-Lloyd Ships Ltd** Hapag-Lloyd AG SatCom: Inmarsat C 431007610 *Hamilton* *Bermuda (British)* MMSI: 310133000 Official number: 727394	**33,735** 14,270 34,330 T/cm 56.1	Class: NV (LR) ✠ Classed LR until 24/2/04	**1996-02 Daewoo Heavy Industries Ltd — Geoje** Yd No: 4038 Loa 216.13 (BB) Br ex 32.26 Dght 10.780 Lbp 204.00 Br md 32.20 Dpth 19.00 Welded, 1 dk	**(A33A2CC) Container Ship (Fully Cellular)** TEU 2400 C Ho 1134 TEU C Dk 1266 TEU incl 149 ref C. Compartments: ER, 6 Cell Ho 11 Ha: ER Ice Capable	**1 oil engine** driving 1 FP propeller Total Power: 20,930kW (28,456hp) 20.0kn Sulzer 7RTA72U 1 x 2 Stroke 7 Cy. 720 x 2500 20930kW (28456bhp) Hyundai Heavy Industries Co Ltd-South Korea AuxGen: 3 x 1750kW 450V 60Hz a.c Boilers: e (ex.g.) 9.2kgf/cm² (9.0bar), AuxB (o.f.) 7.1kgf/cm² (7.0bar), AuxB (o.f.) 8.0kgf/cm² (7.8bar) Thrusters: 1 Thwart. CP thruster (f)
9434266 *EAUZ* -	**VALENCIA KNUTSEN** **Norspan LNG VII AS** Knutsen OAS Shipping AS SatCom: Inmarsat C 422542010 *Santa Cruz de Tenerife* *Spain (CSR)* MMSI: 225420000	**110,920** 34,573 97,730	Class: NV	**2010-10 Daewoo Shipbuilding & Marine Engineering Co Ltd — Geoje** Yd No: 2274 Loa 290.00 (BB) Br ex - Dght 12.900 Lbp 279.00 Br md 45.80 Dpth 26.50 Welded, 1 dk	**(A11A2TN) LNG Tanker** Liq (Gas): 173,400 4 x Gas Tank (s); 4 membrane (36% Ni.stl) pri horizontal 8 Cargo Pump (s)	**4 diesel electric oil engines** driving 3 gen. each 9778kW 6600V a.c 1 gen. of 8889kW 6600V a.c Connecting to 2 elec. motors each (13600kW) driving 2 FP propellers Total Power: 43,650kW (59,345hp) 19.5kn Wartsila 12V50DF 3 x Vee 4 Stroke 12 Cy. 500 x 580 each-11400kW (15499bhp) Wartsila Italia SpA-Italy Wartsila 9L50DF 1 x 4 Stroke 9 Cy. 500 x 580 9450kW (12848bhp) Wartsila Italia SpA-Italy Fuel: 6100.0 (r.f.)
6906141 *ECDL* -	**VALENCIA PIDESA** *ex Valencia -2004 ex Boluda Valencia -1999* *ex Aznar Jose Luis -1989* **Pinturas y Desgasificaciones SL** - SatCom: Inmarsat C 422407311 *Huelva* *Spain* MMSI: 224073000	**338** 104 290	Class: (LR) (GL) ✠ Classed LR until 1/91	**1969-04 Astilleros de Murueta S.A. — Gernika-Lumo** Yd No: 90 Loa 37.32 Br ex 9.56 Dght 4.140 Lbp 31.73 Br md 8.91 Dpth 4.60 Welded, 1 dk	**(B32A2ST) Tug**	**2 oil engines** sr geared to sc. shaft driving 1 FP propeller Total Power: 1,472kW (2,002hp) 13.5kn Deutz SBA8M528 2 x 4 Stroke 8 Cy. 220 x 280 each-736kW (1001bhp) Kloeckner Humboldt Deutz AG-West Germany AuxGen: 2 x 100kW 220/380V 50Hz a.c, 1 x 45kW 220/380V a.c
7015901 *CSYD6* -	**VALENTE** *ex Nalon -2008 ex Lady Alma -1991* *ex Lady Sarah -1991* **Bay Point Maritime Inc** - *Lisbon* *Portugal* Official number: LX-37-RC	*263* - 170	Class: (LR) ✠ Classed LR until 22/10/08	**1970-07 R. Dunston (Hessle) Ltd. — Hessle** Yd No: S871 Loa 32.77 Br ex 9.53 Dght 4.287 Lbp 28.96 Br md 8.84 Dpth 4.88 Welded, 1 dk	**(B32A2ST) Tug**	**1 oil engine** reverse reduction geared to sc. shaft driving 1 FP propeller Total Power: 1,809kW (2,460hp) Ruston 9ATCM 1 x 4 Stroke 9 Cy. 318 x 368 1809kW (2460bhp) English Electric Diesels Ltd.Paxman Eng. Div.-Colchester AuxGen: 2 x 50kW 400V 50Hz a.c, 1 x 40kW 400V 50Hz a.c Fuel: 52.0 (d.f.)
9266437 *VQHD3* BS 8	**VALENTE** **Myti Mussels Ltd** - *Beaumaris* *United Kingdom* MMSI: 235830329 Official number: C17580	**388** 116 -	Class: LR ✠ **100A1** SS 02/2008 fishing vessel **LMC** Cable: 226.9/20.5 U2	**2003-02 'Crist' Sp z oo — Gdansk** (Hull) Yd No: C43/1 **2003-02 B.V. Scheepswerf Maaskant — Bruinisse** Yd No: 575 Loa 43.19 (BB) Br ex 9.29 Dght 1.150 Lbp 39.93 Br md 9.00 Dpth 3.30 Welded, 1 dk	**(B11A2FT) Trawler** Bale: 178	**2 oil engines** with clutches, flexible couplings & sr reverse geared to sc. shafts driving 2 FP propellers Total Power: 736kW (1,000hp) 11.0kn Caterpillar 3412E 2 x Vee 4 Stroke 12 Cy. 137 x 152 each-368kW (500bhp) Caterpillar Inc-USA AuxGen: 2 x 64kW 380V 50Hz a.c Thrusters: 1 Thwart. FP thruster (f)
9445124 *3ENQ2* -	**VALENTE ANGEL** **San Lorenzo Shipping SA** SMTECH Ship Management Co Ltd *Panama* *Panama* MMSI: 351454000 Official number: 3339108A	**16,960** 10,498 28,534 T/cm 39.6	Class: NK	**2007-11 Shimanami Shipyard Co Ltd — Imabari EH** Yd No: 511 Loa 169.30 (BB) Br ex - Dght 9.779 Lbp 160.40 Br md 27.20 Dpth 13.60 Welded, 1 dk	**(A21A2BC) Bulk Carrier** Grain: 37,523; Bale: 35,762 Compartments: 5 Ho, ER 5 Ha: 4 (19.2 x 17.6)ER (13.6 x 16.0) Cranes: 4x30.5t	**1 oil engine** driving 1 FP propeller Total Power: 5,850kW (7,954hp) 14.0kn MAN-B&W 6S42MC 1 x 2 Stroke 6 Cy. 420 x 1764 5850kW (7954bhp) Makita Corp-Japan AuxGen: 3 x 440kW 60Hz a.c Fuel: 1381.0 (r.f.)

IMO / Call sign	Name / Owner	Tonnage	Class	Builder / Dimensions	Type / Cargo	Machinery
9424637 *3EOC7* -	**VALENTE VENUS** **Floral Shipping Navigation SA** Nissho Odyssey Ship Management Pte Ltd *Panama* *Panama* MMSI: 354905000 Official number: 3351008A	**16,992** 8,186 28,401	Class: NK	**2008-01 Naikai Zosen Corp — Onomichi HS (Setoda Shipyard)** Yd No: 714 Loa 161.00 (BB) Br ex - Dght 9.880 Lbp 154.50 Br md 26.00 Dpth 14.00 Welded, 1 dk	**(A31A2GO) Open Hatch Cargo Ship** Double Hull Grain: 30,321 Compartments: 4 Ho, ER 4 Ha: ER Cranes: 3x30t	**1 oil engine** driving 1 FP propeller Total Power: 5,180kW (7,043hp) 13.0kn MAN-B&W 7S35MC 1 x 2 Stroke 7 Cy. 350 x 1400 5180kW (7043bhp) Hitachi Zosen Corp-Japan AuxGen: 3 x a.c Fuel: 926.0
5015622 *IPTK* -	**VALENTIA** *ex Anacapri -1997* **Overmar Srl** - *Naples* *Italy* Official number: 867	*197* 65 -	Class: (RI)	**1960 Cantiere Navale M & B Benetti — Viareggio** Yd No: 40 Loa 32.87 Br ex 8.03 Dght 3.171 Lbp 29.93 Br md 8.01 Dpth 4.02 Welded, 1 dk	**(B32A2ST) Tug** Derricks: 1x2t	**1 oil engine** geared to sc. shaft driving 1 FP propeller Total Power: 736kW (1,001hp) MAN G8V30/45ATL 1 x 4 Stroke 8 Cy. 300 x 450 736kW (1001bhp) Maschinenbau Augsburg Nuernberg (MAN)-Augsburg AuxGen: 1 x 20kW 220V d.c, 1 x 15kW 220V d.c Fuel: 59.0
9683714 - -	**VALENTIN GRUZDEV** **Gaztechleasing Ltd** Moscow River Shipping Co *Russia*	**5,075** 2,026 6,980	Class: RS (Class contemplated)	**2014-03 Sudostroitelnyy Zavod "Krasnoye Sormovo" — Nizhniy Novgorod** Yd No: 11 Loa 140.85 (BB) Br ex 16.86 Dght 4.200 Lbp 136.29 Br md 16.70 Dpth 6.00 Welded, 1 dk	**(A13B2TP) Products Tanker** Double Hull (13F) Liq: 7,828; Liq (Oil): 7,828	**2 oil engines** reduction geared to sc. shafts driving 2 Directional propellers Total Power: 2,400kW (3,264hp) 10.0kn Wartsila 6L20 2 x 4 Stroke 6 Cy. 200 x 280 each-1200kW (1632bhp) Wartsila Finland Oy-Finland
7333896 *H8QD* -	**VALENTIN I** *ex Tri Box -2008 ex Louise -1992* *ex Louise Smits -1984 ex Tobias Lonborg -1977* **Meloyro Shipping Co Ltd** Granince SA *Panama* *Panama* MMSI: 353201000 Official number: 32315PEXT1	**2,669** 1,270 3,786	Class: (LR) ✠ Classed LR until 1/6/04	**1973-12 N.V. Scheepsbouwwerf v/h de Groot & van Vliet — Bolnes** Yd No: 385 Loa 84.31 (BB) Br ex 14.41 Dght 6.325 Lbp 74.43 Br md 14.30 Dpth 8.77 Welded, 1 dk	**(A31A2GX) General Cargo Ship** Grain: 4,652 Compartments: 1 Ho, ER 1 Ha: (45.1 x 10.9)ER Cranes: 1x8t	**1 oil engine** driving 1 CP propeller Total Power: 1,839kW (2,500hp) 13.5kn Smit-Bolnes 307HDK 1 x 2 Stroke 7 Cy. 300 x 550 1839kW (2500bhp) Motorenfabriek Smit & Bolnes NV-Netherlands AuxGen: 3 x 160kW 380V 50Hz a.c Fuel: 335.5 (d.f.)
9057264 *9HNV8* -	**VALENTIN PIKUL** **NWS 3 Balt Shipping Co Ltd** JS North-Western Shipping Co (OAO 'Severo-Zapadnoye Parokhodstvo') *Valletta* *Malta* MMSI: 256196000 Official number: 9057264	**2,506** 1,185 2,917	Class: GL RS (LR) ✠ Classed LR until 26/8/04	**1994-10 OAO Volgogradskiy Sudostroitelnyy Zavod — Volgograd** Yd No: 203 Loa 89.50 Br ex 13.42 Dght 4.281 Lbp 84.90 Br md 13.20 Dpth 5.50 Welded, 1 dk	**(A31A2GX) General Cargo Ship** TEU 118 C. 118/20' Compartments: 2 Ho, ER 2 Ha: ER Ice Capable	**1 oil engine** with clutches, flexible couplings & sr reverse geared to sc. shaft driving 1 FP propeller Total Power: 1,740kW (2,366hp) 11.8kn Wartsila 12V22HF 1 x Vee 4 Stroke 12 Cy. 220 x 240 1740kW (2366bhp) Wartsila Diesel Oy-Finland AuxGen: 2 x 160kW 400V 50Hz a.c, 1 x 80kW 400V 50Hz a.c Thrusters: 1 Thwart. FP thruster (f)
7811654 *YVGS* -	**VALENTINA** *ex La Iguana -1987* **Inversiones y Suministros Amacuro CA (ISACA)** - *Ciudad Guayana* *Venezuela* Official number: ARSK-2501	*498* 224 502	Class: (LR) ✠ Classed LR until 26/8/92	**1979-01 van Doesburg Heeselt N.V. — Waardenburg** Yd No: 111 Loa 45.37 Br ex 12.50 Dght 2.159 Lbp 39.20 Br md 12.21 Dpth 2.80 Welded, 1 dk	**(A35D2RL) Landing Craft** Bow door/ramp Liq: 440; Liq (Oil): 440 TEU 36 C.Dk 36/20'	**2 oil engines** sr geared to sc. shafts driving 2 FP propellers Total Power: 1,030kW (1,400hp) G.M. (Detroit Diesel) 16V-71 2 x Vee 2 Stroke 16 Cy. 108 x 127 each-515kW (700bhp) General Motors Detroit DieselAllison Divn-USA AuxGen: 1 x 30kW 380V 50Hz a.c, 1 x 5kW 380V 50Hz a.c Fuel: 34.5 (d.f.)
9344722 *V7MK3* -	**VALENTINA** *ex Niledutch Louise -2011 ex Valentina -2010* **ms 'NB 1269' Schiffahrtsges mbH & Co KG** Peter Doehle Schiffahrts-KG *Majuro* *Marshall Islands* MMSI: 538090304 Official number: 90304	**17,360** 9,038 22,263	Class: GL	**2007-06 Daewoo-Mangalia Heavy Industries S.A. — Mangalia (Hull)** Yd No: 4061 **2007-06 J.J. Sietas KG Schiffswerft GmbH & Co. — Hamburg** Yd No: 1269 Loa 178.57 (BB) Br ex - Dght 10.858 Lbp 167.50 Br md 27.60 Dpth 14.58 Welded, 1 dk	**(A33A2CC) Container Ship (Fully Cellular)** TEU 1853 incl 385 ref C. Cranes: 3x45t Ice Capable	**1 oil engine** driving 1 FP propeller Total Power: 16,747kW (22,769hp) 21.0kn MAN-B&W 6L70ME-C 1 x 2 Stroke 6 Cy. 700 x 2360 16747kW (22769bhp) Manises Diesel Engine Co. S.A.-Valencia AuxGen: 4 x 1030kW 450/230V a.c Thrusters: 1 Tunnel thruster (f); 1 Tunnel thruster (a)
9504023 *3ERZ7* -	**VALENTINE** **New Eagle Shipping SA** Koyo Kaiun Asia Pte Ltd SatCom: Inmarsat Mini-M 764856137 *Panama* *Panama* MMSI: 370229000 Official number: 3417808B	**8,417** 4,735 14,214 T/cm 23.4	Class: NK	**2008-07 Asakawa Zosen K.K. — Imabari** Yd No: 563 Loa 134.16 (BB) Br ex 20.52 Dght 8.813 Lbp 125.00 Br md 20.50 Dpth 11.60 Welded, 1 dk	**(A12B2TR) Chemical/Products Tanker** Double Hull (13F) Liq: 15,596; Liq (Oil): 15,596 Cargo Heating Coils Compartments: 18 Wing Ta, 2 Wing Slop Ta, ER 18 Cargo Pump (s): 8x200m³/hr, 10x300m³/hr Manifold: Bow/CM: 61.7m	**1 oil engine** driving 1 FP propeller Total Power: 4,440kW (6,037hp) 13.9kn MAN-B&W 6S35MC 1 x 2 Stroke 6 Cy. 350 x 1400 4440kW (6037bhp) Makita Corp-Japan AuxGen: 3 x 480kW 450V 60Hz a.c Thrusters: 1 Tunnel thruster (f) Fuel: 82.0 (d.f.) 733.0 (r.f.)
9166625 *ONDL* -	**VALENTINE** **CLdN ro-ro SA** UBEM NV *Antwerpen* *Belgium* MMSI: 205461000 Official number: 02 00029 2010	**23,987** 7,196 9,729 T/cm 34.7	Class: LR ✠ **100A1** SS 02/2014 roll on - roll off cargo ship *IWS LI Ice Class 1C ✠ **LMC** **UMS** Eq.Ltr: I†; Cable: 608.6/64.0 U3	**1999-02 Kawasaki Heavy Industries Ltd — Sakaide KG** Yd No: 1485 Loa 162.49 (BB) Br ex 25.64 Dght 6.500 Lbp 150.00 Br md 25.20 Dpth 15.45 Welded, 4 dks including 2 superstructure decks	**(A35A2RR) Ro-Ro Cargo Ship** Stern door/ramp (centre) Len: 22.90 Wid: 21.70 Swl: 100 Lane-Len: 2307 Lorries: 157, Cars: 635 Ice Capable	**2 oil engines** with flexible couplings & sr gearedto sc. shafts driving 2 CP propellers Total Power: 9,840kW (13,378hp) 18.0kn MAN 7L40/54 2 x 4 Stroke 7 Cy. 400 x 540 each-4920kW (6689bhp) Kawasaki Heavy Industries Ltd-Japan AuxGen: 1 x 1700kW 450V 60Hz a.c, 2 x 800kW 450V 60Hz a.c Boilers: TOH (o.f.) 10.0kgf/cm² (9.8bar), TOH (ex.g.) 10.0kgf/cm² (9.8bar) Thrusters: 2 Thwart. FP thruster (f)
9161352 *J8B3738* -	**VALENTINE 2** *ex ENA Emperor -2007* **Valentine Maritime Co (Gulf) LLC** - SatCom: Inmarsat C 437573110 *Kingstown* *St Vincent & The Grenadines* MMSI: 375731000 Official number: 10211	**494** 148 367	Class: AB	**1998-11 Pandan Shipyard Pte Ltd — Singapore** Yd No: 1/96 Loa 39.60 Br ex - Dght 3.600 Lbp 35.20 Br md 10.00 Dpth 4.20 Welded, 1 dk	**(B32A2ST) Tug**	**2 oil engines** reverse reduction geared to sc. shafts driving 2 FP propellers Total Power: 2,942kW (4,000hp) Yanmar Z280A-EN 2 x 4 Stroke 6 Cy. 280 x 360 each-1471kW (2000bhp) Yanmar Diesel Engine Co Ltd-Japan AuxGen: 3 x 90kW 415V 50Hz a.c Thrusters: 1 Tunnel thruster (f) Fuel: 330.0
9204104 *A6E2924* -	**VALENTINE I** *ex Jaya Victor -2003* **Valentine Maritime Co (Gulf) LLC** - SatCom: Inmarsat C 447073111 *Abu Dhabi* *United Arab Emirates* MMSI: 470731000 Official number: 4885	**520** 156 380	Class: BV	**1998-09 Yantai Raffles Shipyard Co Ltd — Yantai SD** Yd No: YPZ97-91 Loa 41.80 Br ex - Dght 4.000 Lbp 37.40 Br md 11.40 Dpth 4.96 Welded, 1 dk	**(B21B20A) Anchor Handling Tug Supply** Passengers: berths: 18 Cranes: 1x8t	**2 oil engines** reduction geared to sc. shafts driving 2 FP propellers Total Power: 2,942kW (4,000hp) Yanmar Z280-EN 2 x 4 Stroke 6 Cy. 260 x 280 each-1471kW (2000bhp) Yanmar Diesel Engine Co Ltd-Japan AuxGen: 3 x 300kW 415V 50Hz a.c Thrusters: 1 Thwart. CP thruster (f)
9204099 *A6E2939* -	**VALENTINE III** *ex Jaya Valiant -2003* **Valentine Maritime Co (Gulf) LLC** - SatCom: Inmarsat C 447074610 *Abu Dhabi* *United Arab Emirates* MMSI: 470746000 Official number: 4914	**484** 145 422	Class: BV	**1998-08 Yantai Raffles Shipyard Co Ltd — Yantai SD** Yd No: YPZ97-90 Loa 38.80 Br ex - Dght 4.000 Lbp 36.00 Br md 11.40 Dpth 4.96 Welded, 1 dk	**(B21B20A) Anchor Handling Tug Supply** Passengers: berths: 18	**2 oil engines** reduction geared to sc. shafts driving 2 FP propellers Total Power: 2,942kW (4,000hp) Yanmar Z280A-EN 2 x 4 Stroke 6 Cy. 280 x 360 each-1471kW (2000bhp) Yanmar Diesel Engine Co Ltd-Japan AuxGen: 3 x 300kW 415V 50Hz a.c Thrusters: 1 Thwart. CP thruster (f)
7729485 *WCP8692* -	**VALENTINE MORAN** *ex Coastal Jacksonville -1996* *ex J. A. Belcher Sr. -1990* **Moran Towing Corp** - *Wilmington, DE* *United States of America* MMSI: 366939750 Official number: 589286	**350** 105 194	Class: AB	**1977-12 Bollinger Machine Shop & Shipyard, Inc. — Lockport, La** Yd No: 108 Loa - Br ex 9.78 Dght 3.849 Lbp 31.40 Br md 9.76 Dpth 4.27 Welded, 1 dk	**(B32A2ST) Tug**	**2 oil engines** reverse reduction geared to sc. shafts driving 2 FP propellers Total Power: 2,588kW (3,518hp) 12.0kn Alco 12V251E 2 x Vee 4 Stroke 12 Cy. 229 x 267 each-1294kW (1759bhp) (Re-engined ,made 1976, Reconditioned & fitted 1977) White Industrial Power Inc-USA AuxGen: 2 x 75kW
8912974 *UBUI8* -	**VALERI VASILIEV** *ex Hesperia -2012* **Key Developments SA** Azia Shipping Holding Ltd *St Petersburg* *Russia* MMSI: 273359470	**10,374** 4,439 13,565 T/cm 26.7	Class: RS (LR) ✠ Classed LR until 14/7/12	**1991-07 Rauma-Repola Offshore Oy — Pori** Yd No: RR-26 Loa 135.29 (BB) Br ex 21.63 Dght 8.190 Lbp 128.80 Br md 21.60 Dpth 11.00 Welded, 1 dk	**(A31A2GX) General Cargo Ship** Grain: 16,140 Compartments: 2 Ho, ER 2 Ha: ER Cranes: 3x30t	**1 oil engine** driving 1 CP propeller Total Power: 6,050kW (8,226hp) 14.0kn B&W 5L50MC 1 x 2 Stroke 5 Cy. 500 x 1620 6050kW (8226bhp) Mitsui Engineering & Shipbuilding CLtd-Japan AuxGen: 3 x 620kW 380V 50Hz a.c Boilers: e (ex.g.) 8.2kgf/cm² (8.0bar), AuxB (o.f.) 8.2kgf/cm² (8.0bar) Thrusters: 1 Thwart. CP thruster (f) Fuel: 98.1 (d.f.) 873.0 (r.f.) 21.5pd

IMO / Call sign	Name / Owner	Tonnage	Class	Build / Dimensions	Type / Capacity	Machinery
7351185 *ILFT* -	**VALERIA** *ex* Valeria Sa 60 *-2002* *ex* Valeria *-2000* **Severino Pesca SnC** - *Salerno* *Italy* Official number: 2549	**260** 81 -	Class: (RI)	**1976**-09 **Cant. Nav. Fratelli Maccioni — Viareggio** Yd No: 7 Loa 49.31 Br ex 7.78 Dght 3.501 Lbp 39.71 Br md 7.47 Dpth 4.07 Welded, 1 dk	**(B11A2FT) Trawler**	**1 oil engine** geared to sc. shaft driving 1 CP propeller Total Power: 897kW (1,220hp) Blackstone ESL8 1 x 4 Stroke 8 Cy. 222 x 292 897kW (1220bhp) Mirrlees Blackstone (Stamford)Ltd.-Stamford
8137794 *IPHM* -	**VALERIA C.** *ex* Benedetta Prima *-1983* **Valerio Ciavaglia e C** - *Ancona* *Italy* Official number: 492	*150* 53 -	Class: (RI)	**1981 Artemio Bugari Costruz. Nav. e Mecc. — Fano** Loa 27.74 Br ex 6.63 Dght 2.320 Lbp 22.15 Br md 6.61 Dpth 3.33 Welded, 1 dk	**(B11B2FV) Fishing Vessel**	**1 oil engine** driving 1 FP propeller Total Power: 485kW (659hp) S.K.L. 6NVD48-2U 1 x 4 Stroke 6 Cy. 320 x 480 485kW (659bhp) VEB Schwermaschinenbau "KarlLiebknecht" (SKL)-Magdeburg
7408598 - -	**VALERIAN URYVAYEV** - **Far Eastern Regional Hydrometeorological Research Institute** -	**734** 220 350	Class: (RS)	**1974**-03 **Khabarovskiy Sudostroitelnyy Zavod im Kirova — Khabarovsk** Yd No: 901 Loa 54.77 Br ex 9.53 Dght 4.190 Lbp 49.95 Br md 9.30 Dpth 5.19 Welded, 1 dk	**(B31A2SR) Research Survey Vessel** Bale: 68 Compartments: 1 Ho, ER 1 Ha: (2.7 x 1.7) Derricks: 2x1.5t; Winches: 2 Ice Capable	**1 oil engine** driving 1 CP propeller Total Power: 644kW (876hp) 11.8kn S.K.L. 6NVD48-2U 1 x 4 Stroke 6 Cy. 320 x 480 644kW (876bhp) VEB Schwermaschinenbau "KarlLiebknecht" (SKL)-Magdeburg Thrusters: 1 Thwart. FP thruster (f)
8805509 *URAZ* -	**VALERIAN ZORIN** - **Marine Technical Centre LLC** - *Izmail* *Ukraine* MMSI: 272893000 Official number: 863609	**2,060** 696 2,099	Class: UA (RS)	**1987**-12 **Osterreichische Schiffswerften AG Linz-Korneuburg — Korneuburg** Yd No: 766 Loa 91.90 (BB) Br ex 13.60 Dght 3.370 Lbp 84.90 Br md 13.40 Dpth 4.90 Welded, 2 dks	**(A34A2GR) Refrigerated Cargo Ship** Ins: 3,064 TEU 96 C.Ho 64/20' (40') C.Dk 32/20' incl. 24 ref C. Compartments: 2 Ho, ER 2 Ha: 2 (25.2 x 10.0)ER Cranes: 1x5t Ice Capable	**2 oil engines** driving 2 FP propellers Total Power: 1,950kW (2,652hp) 12.0kn Wartsila 8R22HF 2 x 4 Stroke 8 Cy. 220 x 240 each-975kW (1326bhp) Wartsila Diesel Oy-Finland AuxGen: 2 x 248kW Thrusters: 1 Thwart. FP thruster (f)
1010624 *J8Y4380* -	**VALERIE** *ex* Firebird *-2011* **Linkpoint Services Ltd** Kaalbye Shipping International Ltd *Kingstown* *St Vincent & The Grenadines* MMSI: 375551000 Official number: 40850	**2,595** 778 325	Class: LR ✠ **100A1** SS 06/2011 SSC Yacht (P), mono, G6 ✠ **LMC** **UMS** Cable: 440.0/34.0 U2 (a)	**2011**-06 **Kroeger Werft GmbH & Co. KG — Schacht-Audorf** Yd No: 13660 Loa 85.10 Br ex 14.28 Dght 3.800 Lbp 68.40 Br md 13.80 Dpth 7.00 Welded, 1 dk	**(X11A2YP) Yacht**	**2 oil engines** with clutches, flexible couplings & sr reverse geared to sc. shafts driving 2 FP propellers Total Power: 4,000kW (5,438hp) M.T.U. 16V4000M60 2 x Vee 4 Stroke 16 Cy. 165 x 190 each-2000kW (2719bhp) MTU Friedrichshafen GmbH-Friedrichshafen AuxGen: 2 x 280kW 400V 50Hz a.c, 1 x 448kW 400V 50Hz a.c Thrusters: 1 Thwart. CP thruster (f); 1 Water jet (a)
9427897 *V7PY8* -	**VALERIE** *launched as* Mandarin Sea *-2008* **Valerie Shipping Inc** Densan Deniz Nakliyat ve Sanayi AS (Densan Shipping Co Inc) *Majuro* *Marshall Islands* MMSI: 538003315 Official number: 3315	**32,957** 19,231 56,788 T/cm 58.8	Class: NV (BV)	**2008**-08 **Jiangsu Hantong Ship Heavy Industry Co Ltd — Tongzhou JS** Yd No: 007 Loa 189.99 (BB) Br ex - Dght 12.800 Lbp 185.00 Br md 32.26 Dpth 18.00 Welded, 1 dk	**(A21A2BC) Bulk Carrier** Grain: 71,634; Bale: 68,200 Compartments: 5 Ho, ER 5 Ha: ER Cranes: 4x36t	**1 oil engine** driving 1 FP propeller Total Power: 9,480kW (12,889hp) 14.2kn MAN-B&W 6S50MC-C 1 x 2 Stroke 6 Cy. 500 x 2000 9480kW (12889bhp) STX Engine Co Ltd-South Korea AuxGen: 3 x a.c
9315874 *A8JM3* -	**VALERIE SCHULTE** *ex* Kota Pemimpin *-2010* *ex* E. R. Malta *-2005* **ms 'Valerie Schulte' Shipping GmbH & Co KG** Ocean Shipmanagement GmbH *Monrovia* *Liberia* MMSI: 636091114 Official number: 91114	**28,927** 15,033 39,200 T/cm 56.7	Class: NV (GL)	**2005**-06 **Hyundai Mipo Dockyard Co Ltd — Ulsan** Yd No: 0404 Loa 222.17 (BB) Br ex 30.04 Dght 12.000 Lbp 210.00 Br md 30.00 Dpth 16.80 Welded, 1 dk	**(A33A2CC) Container Ship (Fully Cellular)** TEU 2824 C Ho 1026 TEU C Dk 1798 TEU incl 586 ref C.	**1 oil engine** driving 1 FP propeller Total Power: 25,270kW (34,357hp) 22.5kn MAN-B&W 7K80MC-C 1 x 2 Stroke 7 Cy. 800 x 2300 25270kW (34357bhp) Hyundai Heavy Industries Co Ltd-South Korea AuxGen: 4 x 1600kW 440/220V 60Hz a.c, 1 x a.c Thrusters: 1 Tunnel thruster (f) Fuel: 215.0 (d.f.) 3241.0 (r.f.) 92.0pd
8729690 *UAUA* -	**VALERIY DZHAPARIDZE** - **Kaliningrad Industry Fishing Company 'Fishing Fleet-FOR' Plc (OAO Kaliningradskaya Rybopromyshlennaya Kompaniya 'Rybflot-FOR')** JSC Fishing Fleet-FOR SatCom: Inmarsat A 1401420 *Kaliningrad* *Russia* MMSI: 273240600 Official number: 882510	**4,407** 1,322 1,810	Class: RS	**1989**-06 **GP Chernomorskiy Sudostroitelnyy Zavod — Nikolayev** Yd No: 577 Loa 104.50 Br ex 16.03 Dght 5.900 Lbp 96.40 Br md 16.00 Dpth 10.20 Welded, 2 dks	**(B11A2FG) Factory Stern Trawler** Bale: 420; Ins: 2,219 Ice Capable	**2 oil engines** reduction geared to sc. shaft driving 1 CP propeller Total Power: 5,148kW (7,000hp) 16.1kn Russkiy 6CHN40/46 2 x 4 Stroke 6 Cy. 400 x 460 each-2574kW (3500bhp) Mashinostroitelnyy Zavod"Russkiy-Dizel"-Leningrad AuxGen: 2 x 1600kW 220/380V 50Hz a.c, 3 x 200kW 220/380V 50Hz a.c Fuel: 1226.0 (d.f.) 23.0pd
8951293 - -	**VALERIY GORCHAKOV** *ex* Volgo-Don 5009 *-2005* **AZ Shipping & Trading FZE** Volgo-Balt Service	**4,628** 2,109 5,192		**1969 Santierul Naval Oltenita S.A. — Oltenita** Loa 138.80 Br ex 16.70 Dght 3.000 Lbp - Br md - Dpth 5.50 Welded, 1 dk	**(A31A2GX) General Cargo Ship** Grain: 6,270	**2 oil engines** driving 2 FP propellers Total Power: 1,324kW (1,800hp) 10.0kn Dvigatel Revolyutsii 6CHRN36/45 2 x 4 Stroke 6 Cy. 360 x 450 each-662kW (900bhp) Zavod "Dvigatel Revolyutsii"-Gorkiy
7945558 *UFUE* -	**VALERIY KALACHEV** *ex* Nefterudovoz-39m *-2009* **Optima Shipping Ltd** EWL-Transshipping LLC *Makhachkala* *Russia* MMSI: 273435610	**2,615** 1,144 3,345	Class: RS	**1981**-07 **Sudostroitelnyy Zavod "Kama" — Perm** Yd No: 838 Loa 118.93 Br ex 13.47 Dght 3.800 Lbp 112.84 Br md 13.00 Dpth 5.80 Welded, 1 dk	**(A22B2BR) Ore/Oil Carrier** Grain: 1,821; Liq: 3,556; Liq (Oil): 3,556 Compartments: 1 Ho, 8 Wing Ta, ER 1 Ha: (70.4 x 4.9)ER Ice Capable	**2 oil engines** driving 2 FP propellers Total Power: 970kW (1,318hp) 11.0kn S.K.L. 6NVD48A-U 2 x 4 Stroke 6 Cy. 320 x 480 each-485kW (659bhp) VEB Schwermaschinenbau "KarlLiebknecht" (SKL)-Magdeburg AuxGen: 3 x 100kW a.c Fuel: 77.0 (d.f.)
9231391 *UEAG* -	**VALERIY MASLAKOV** - **'Atoll-West' JSC Ltd** - *Petropavlovsk-Kamchatskiy* *Russia* MMSI: 273424250	**606** 181 349	Class: RS	**2003**-03 **Dalnevostochnyy Zavod "Zvezda" — Bolshoy Kamen** Yd No: 01521 Loa 42.24 Br ex - Dght 3.850 Lbp 38.90 Br md 9.50 Dpth 6.88 Welded, 1 dk	**(B11A2FS) Stern Trawler** Ins: 400	**1 oil engine** geared to sc. shaft driving 1 FP propeller Total Power: 919kW (1,249hp) 11.0kn Caterpillar 3512B 1 x Vee 4 Stroke 12 Cy. 170 x 190 919kW (1249bhp) Caterpillar Inc-USA
8841503 *9LC2130* -	**VALERIY ONISCHUK** *ex* Slavutich 11 *-2011* **Malcom Group Ltd** LLC 'Obogatitelnaya Fabrika' *Freetown* *Sierra Leone* MMSI: 667006037 Official number: SL106037	**1,471** 441 1,794	Class: RS	**1987**-07 **Kiyevskiy Sudostroitelnyy Sudoremontnyy Zavod — Kiyev** Yd No: 11 Shortened-2014 Loa 75.00 Br ex 16.22 Dght 3.240 Lbp 71.13 Br md 16.00 Dpth 4.00 Welded, 1 dk	**(A31A2GX) General Cargo Ship**	**2 oil engines** driving 2 FP propellers Total Power: 1,294kW (1,760hp) 9.0kn S.K.L. 8NVD48-2U 2 x 4 Stroke 8 Cy. 320 x 480 each-647kW (880bhp) VEB Schwermaschinenbau "KarlLiebknecht" (SKL)-Magdeburg Fuel: 500.0
8888862 *UREZ* -	**VALERIY PLATONOV** *ex* Trubezh *-2002* **'Ukrrichflot' Joint Stock Shipping Co** - *Kherson* *Ukraine* MMSI: 272292000	**3,995** 1,199 4,515		**1982**-11 **Santierul Naval Oltenita S.A. — Oltenita** Yd No: 5085 Loa 135.00 Br ex 16.70 Dght 3.170 Lbp 134.05 Br md 16.50 Dpth 5.50 Welded, 1 dk	**(A31A2GX) General Cargo Ship**	**2 oil engines** driving 2 FP propellers Total Power: 1,324kW (1,800hp) 10.0kn Dvigatel Revolyutsii 6CHRN36/45 2 x 4 Stroke 6 Cy. 360 x 450 each-662kW (900bhp) Zavod "Dvigatel Revolyutsii"-Gorkiy
8887222 - -	**VALERIY RYLOV** *ex* MSK-8 *-1977* **Turkmennefteflot** - *Turkmenbashy* *Turkmenistan* Official number: 762234	*817* 81 343	Class: (RS)	**1977 Sudostroitelnyy Zavod "Krasnyye Barrikady" — Krasnyye Barrikady** Yd No: 8 Loa 54.49 Br ex 14.48 Dght 2.160 Lbp 51.50 Br md - Dpth 3.70 Welded, 1 dk	**(B34B2SC) Crane Vessel**	**2 oil engines** driving 2 FP propellers Total Power: 1,030kW (1,400hp) 11.0kn Russkiy 6DR30/50-6-3 2 x 2 Stroke 6 Cy. 300 x 500 each-515kW (700bhp) Mashinostroitelnyy Zavod"Russkiy-Dizel"-Leningrad AuxGen: 3 x 100kW a.c Fuel: 118.0 (d.f.)
9226566 *UHGE* -	**VALERIY ZELENKO** *ex* Orahope *-2013* **Baltic Petroleum K/S** - *St Petersburg* *Russia* MMSI: 273333950	**2,631** 1,093 3,514 T/cm 10.7	Class: BV (NV)	**2002**-12 **Gemyat A.S. — Tuzla** Yd No: 49 Loa 92.86 (BB) Br ex 14.36 Dght 5.600 Lbp 86.65 Br md 14.10 Dpth 6.00 Welded, 1 dk	**(A12B2TR) Chemical/Products Tanker** Double Hull (13F) Liq: 3,897; Liq (Oil): 3,897 Cargo Heating Coils Compartments: 1 Ta, ER, 22 Wing Ta 3 Cargo Pump (s): 3x250m³/hr Manifold: Bow/CM: 53m Ice Capable	**1 oil engine** reduction geared to sc. shaft driving 1 CP propeller Total Power: 2,040kW (2,774hp) 13.0kn MAN-B&W 6L27/38 1 x 4 Stroke 6 Cy. 270 x 380 2040kW (2774bhp) MAN B&W Diesel A/S-Denmark AuxGen: 2 x 285kW 50Hz a.c, 1 x 350kW 50Hz a.c Thrusters: 1 Thwart. FP thruster (f) Fuel: 43.0 (d.f.) 324.0 (d.f.)

IMO / Call sign / Fishing no.	Name / Owner / Port / Flag	Tonnage	Class	Build / Dimensions	Type	Machinery
7414729 *HP7115* -	**VALERO SAN NICOLAS** *ex* Coastal San Nicolas *-2004* *ex* Vanguardia *-1993 ex* Vanguard *-1990* *ex* Westmar *-1987 ex* Murgen *-1987* **Valero Refining Co - Aruba NV** Valero Aruba Marine Services *Panama* *Panama* Official number: 2085893E	**295** 88 -	Class: (LR) ✠ Classed LR until 17/8/10	**1975-12 N.V. Scheepswerf van Rupelmonde — Rupelmonde** Yd No: 427 Loa 29.98 Br ex 10.16 Dght 4.261 Lbp 27.11 Br md 10.01 Dpth 4.81 Welded, 1 dk	**(B32A2ST) Tug**	**2 oil engines** reverse reduction geared to sc. shafts driving 2 FP propellers Total Power: 3,162kW (4,300hp) 12.0kn EMD (Electro-Motive) 12-645-E5 2 x Vee 2 Stroke 12 Cy. 230 x 254 each-1581kW (2150bhp) General Motors Corp.Electro-Motive Div.-La Grange AuxGen: 2 x 76kW 440V 60Hz a.c, 1 x 36kW 440V 60Hz a.c Fuel: 159.5 (d.f.)
8859328 *UCWJ* -	**VALERY KOKOV** *ex* Volzhskiy-43 *-2009* **Don River Shipping JSC (OAO 'Donrechflot')** *Taganrog* *Russia* MMSI: 273377000 Official number: 906024	**4,997** 2,299 5,361	Class: RS RR	**1991-07 Navashinskiy Sudostroitelnyy Zavod 'Oka' — Navashino** Yd No: 1045 Loa 138.45 Br ex 16.75 Dght 3.754 Lbp 135.00 Br md 16.50 Dpth 5.50 Welded, 1 dk	**(A31A2GX) General Cargo Ship** Grain: 6,440	**2 oil engines** driving 2 FP propellers Total Power: 1,766kW (2,402hp) 10.7kn Dvigatel Revolyutsii 6CHRN36/45 2 x 4 Stroke 6 Cy. 360 x 450 each-883kW (1201bhp) Zavod "Dvigatel Revolyutsii"-Gorkiy
8993576 *H03333* -	**VALEUREUX** **Association Theophile** *Panama* *Panama* Official number: 35938PEXT	**165** 49 -		**1959-01 Ch. Nav. Franco-Belges — Villeneuve-la-Garenne** Converted From: Tug-2005 Loa 28.25 Br ex 7.92 Dght - Lbp 25.30 Br md 7.60 Dpth 4.00 Welded, 1 dk	**(B32A2ST) Tug**	**1 oil engine** driving 1 Propeller Total Power: 771kW (1,048hp) MGO 16V175ASHR 1 x Vee 4 Stroke 16 Cy. 175 x 180 771kW (1048bhp) Societe Alsacienne de ConstructionsMecaniques (SACM)-France
8400103 *EQOX* -	**VALFAJR 2** **NITC** - *Bushehr* *Iran*	**419** 125 650	Class: (NV)	**1985-03 Costruz. Riparaz. Nav. Antonini S.p.A. — La Spezia** Yd No: 110 Loa 35.72 Br ex - Dght 4.660 Lbp 31.30 Br md 9.50 Dpth 5.11 Welded, 1 dk	**(B32A2ST) Tug**	**2 oil engines** with clutches, flexible couplings & sr geared to sc. shafts driving 2 CP propellers Total Power: 2,206kW (3,000hp) Deutz SBV8M628 2 x 4 Stroke 8 Cy. 240 x 280 each-1103kW (1500bhp) Kloeckner Humboldt Deutz AG-West Germany AuxGen: 2 x 260kW 380V 50Hz a.c, 1 x 125kW 380V 50Hz a.c Thrusters: 1 Thwart. CP thruster (f)
8400115 *EQOY* -	**VALFAJR 3** *ex* Marsea 3 *-2010 ex* Valfajr 3 *-2006* **Marine Logistics Solutions (MarSol) LLC** - *Bushehr* *Iran* Official number: 16821	**419** 125 555	Class: AS (CC) (NV)	**1985-05 Costruz. Riparaz. Nav. Antonini S.p.A. — La Spezia** Yd No: 111 Loa 35.72 Br ex - Dght 4.679 Lbp 31.30 Br md 9.50 Dpth 5.11 Welded, 1 dk	**(B32A2ST) Tug**	**2 oil engines** with clutches, flexible couplings & sr geared to sc. shafts driving 2 CP propellers Total Power: 2,206kW (3,000hp) Deutz SBV8M628 2 x 4 Stroke 8 Cy. 240 x 280 each-1103kW (1500bhp) Kloeckner Humboldt Deutz AG-West Germany AuxGen: 2 x 260kW 380V 50Hz a.c, 1 x 125kW 380V 50Hz a.c Thrusters: 1 Thwart. CP thruster (f)
9417309 *ICLM* -	**VALFOGLIA** **Navigazione Montanari SpA** SatCom: Inmarsat C 424723515 *Trieste* *Italy* MMSI: 247235700	**60,185** 33,762 109,060 T/cm 91.3	Class: AB RI	**2009-01 Hudong-Zhonghua Shipbuilding (Group) Co Ltd — Shanghai** Yd No: H1520A Loa 243.00 (BB) Br ex 42.08 Dght 15.350 Lbp 233.00 Br md 42.00 Dpth 22.00 Welded, 1 dk	**(A13A2TV) Crude Oil Tanker** Double Hull (13F) Liq: 123,604; Liq (Oil): 125,992 Part Cargo Heating Coils Compartments: 12 Wing Ta, 2 Wing Slop Ta, ER 3 Cargo Pump (s): 3x2500m³/hr Manifold: Bow/CM: 119.5m	**1 oil engine** driving 1 FP propeller Total Power: 14,280kW (19,415hp) 14.5kn MAN-B&W 7S60MC 1 x 2 Stroke 7 Cy. 600 x 2292 14280kW (19415bhp) Hyundai Heavy Industries Co Ltd-South Korea AuxGen: 3 x 680kW a.c Fuel: 139.0 (d.f.) 2724.0 (r.f.)
9384124 *ICKG* -	**VALGARDENA** **Navigazione Montanari SpA** SatCom: Inmarsat C 424702144 *Trieste* *Italy* MMSI: 247243800	**23,335** 9,628 37,481 T/cm 45.2	Class: BV RI	**2008-06 Hyundai Mipo Dockyard Co Ltd — Ulsan** Yd No: 2042 Loa 184.32 (BB) Br ex 27.43 Dght 11.316 Lbp 176.00 Br md 27.40 Dpth 17.20 Welded, 1 dk	**(A12B2TR) Chemical/Products Tanker** Double Hull (13F) Liq: 40,750; Liq (Oil): 40,750 Compartments: 12 Wing Ta, 2 Wing Slop Ta, ER 12 Cargo Pump (s): 2x300m³/hr, 10x500m³/hr Manifold: Bow/CM: 92.6m	**1 oil engine** driving 1 FP propeller Total Power: 7,860kW (10,686hp) 14.5kn MAN-B&W 6S46MC-C 1 x 2 Stroke 6 Cy. 460 x 1932 7860kW (10686bhp) Hyundai Heavy Industries Co Ltd-South Korea AuxGen: 3 x 900kW a.c Thrusters: 1 Tunnel thruster Fuel: 132.0 (d.f.) 1017.0 (r.f.)
9191084 *MY006* FR 268	**VALHALLA** **Freedom Fish Ltd, Tranquility BF7 LLP, & MCM Fishing Ltd** Peter & J Johnstone Ltd *Fraserburgh* *United Kingdom* MMSI: 232004160 Official number: C16561	**201** 67 -		**1999-07 Astilleros Armon SA — Navia** Yd No: 485 Lengthened-2012 Loa 25.60 (BB) Br ex - Dght 3.500 Lbp 23.34 Br md 7.00 Dpth 3.70 Welded, 1 dk	**(B11A2FT) Trawler** Bale: 90	**1 oil engine** reduction geared to sc. shaft driving 1 FP propeller Total Power: 515kW (700hp) Caterpillar 3412TA 1 x Vee 4 Stroke 12 Cy. 137 x 152 515kW (700bhp) Caterpillar Inc-USA
9381457 *HKBV1* -	**VALI** *ex* Svitzer Nabih Saleh *-2010* **Waves Razor** International Tugs SA (INTERTUG) *Cartagena de Indias* *Colombia* MMSI: 730089000 Official number: MC-05-632	**332** 99 142	Class: LR (AB) **100A1** SS 04/2011 tug **LMC** Cable: 302.0/20.0 U3 (a)	**2006-04 Jiangsu Wuxi Shipyard Co Ltd — Wuxi JS** (Hull) Yd No: (1205) **2006-04 Pacific Ocean Engineering & Trading Pte Ltd (POET) — Singapore** Yd No: 1205 Loa 28.00 Br ex - Dght 4.000 Lbp 22.94 Br md 9.80 Dpth 4.90 Welded, 1 dk	**(B32A2ST) Tug**	**2 oil engines** reduction geared to sc. shafts driving 2 Z propellers Total Power: 2,648kW (3,600hp) 12.0kn Yanmar 8N21A-EN 2 x 4 Stroke 8 Cy. 210 x 290 each-1324kW (1800bhp) Yanmar Diesel Engine Co Ltd-Japan AuxGen: 2 x 99kW a.c
9686962 *CA4365* -	**VALI** **Naviera Detroit Chile SA** Detroit Chile SA *Valparaiso* *Chile* MMSI: 725001072	**1,573** 472 1,932	Class: BV	**2013-12 Guangzhou Huangpu Shipbuilding Co Ltd — Guangzhou GD** Yd No: H3042 Loa 62.85 Br ex 13.77 Dght 5.010 Lbp 58.40 Br md 13.50 Dpth 5.80 Welded, 1 dk	**(B12C2FL) Live Fish Carrier (Well Boat)**	**2 oil engines** reduction geared to sc. shafts driving 2 FP propellers Total Power: 2,398kW (3,260hp) 12.0kn Chinese Std. Type CW12V200ZC 2 x Vee 4 Stroke 12 Cy. 200 x 270 each-1199kW (1630bhp) Weichai Power Co Ltd-China Fuel: 175.0
8985919 - -	**VALIA** **Maritime Atlantic Ltd** Atlantic Marine & Aviation LLP *London* *United Kingdom* Official number: 719721	**140** 42 -	Class: (AB)	**1985-07 Heesen Shipyards B.V. — Oss** Yd No: 6326 Loa 29.30 Br ex - Dght 2.700 Lbp 22.04 Br md 6.75 Dpth 3.06 Welded, 1 dk	**(X11A2YP) Yacht** Hull Material: Aluminium Alloy Passengers: cabins: 5; berths: 10	**3 oil engines** sr geared to sc. shafts driving 3 Propellers Total Power: 2,382kW (3,240hp) G.M. (Detroit Diesel) 12V-92-TA 3 x Vee 2 Stroke 12 Cy. 123 x 127 each-794kW (1080bhp) General Motors Detroit DieselAllison Divn-USA AuxGen: 2 x 44kW a.c Thrusters: 1 Thwart. FP thruster (f)
8967682 *WDA3995* -	**VALIANT** **Tedesco Shipping Co LLC** *Boston, MA* *United States of America* MMSI: 366804610 Official number: 1107465	**154** 61 -		**2001 Midship Marine, Inc. — New Orleans, La** Yd No: 289 Loa 29.56 Br ex - Dght 1.820 Lbp - Br md 6.09 Dpth 3.53 Welded, 1 dk	**(A37A2PC) Passenger/Cruise** Hull Material: Aluminium Alloy Passengers: cabins: 4; berths: 8	**1 oil engine** driving 1 FP propeller Total Power: 331kW (450hp) 11.0kn
9030503 *8PVI* -	**VALIANT** *ex* Lass Neptun *-2008 ex* Wolgast *-1994* *ex* Lass Neptun *-1993* *launched as* Neptun *-1993* **Faversham Ships Ltd** *Bridgetown* *Barbados* MMSI: 314281000	**1,513** 696 2,366	Class: GL	**1993-09 Rosslauer Schiffswerft GmbH — Rosslau** Yd No: 235 Loa 74.94 Br ex - Dght 4.352 Lbp 70.47 Br md 11.40 Dpth 5.50 Welded, 1 dk	**(A31A2GX) General Cargo Ship** Grain: 2,550; Bale: 2,550 Compartments: 1 Ho, ER 1 Ha: (48.0 x 9.0)ER Ice Capable	**2 oil engines** reverse reduction geared to sc. shafts driving 2 Directional propellers Total Power: 1,090kW (1,482hp) 11.0kn Cummins KT-38-M 2 x Vee 4 Stroke 12 Cy. 159 x 159 each-545kW (741bhp) Cummins Engine Co Ltd-United Kingdom AuxGen: 2 x 88kW 220/440V a.c Thrusters: 1 Thwart. FP thruster (f) Fuel: 65.0 (d.f.)
8744561 *9LY2243* -	**VALIANT** *ex* Yue Qing Yuan Huo 2999 *-2010* **Jaris Global Pte Ltd** *Freetown* *Sierra Leone* MMSI: 667003046 Official number: SL103046	**1,361** 408 -		**2005-03 in the People's Republic of China** Yd No: 090105000108 Loa 75.00 Br ex - Dght 2.600 Lbp - Br md 15.20 Dpth 4.50 Welded, 1 dk	**(A24D2BA) Aggregates Carrier**	**2 oil engines** reduction geared to sc. shafts driving 2 Propellers Total Power: 588kW (800hp) Chinese Std. Type 2 x 4 Stroke each-294kW (400bhp) in China
8744303 - -	**VALIANT** **Government of The United States of America (Department of The Navy)** - *United States of America*	**351** 105 116	Class: (AB)	**2010-01 J M Martinac Shipbuilding Corp — Tacoma WA** Yd No: 248 Loa 27.43 Br ex - Dght 3.400 Lbp 25.07 Br md 11.65 Dpth 5.03 Welded, 1 dk	**(B32A2ST) Tug**	**2 oil engines** reduction geared to sc. shafts driving 2 Z propellers Total Power: 2,700kW (3,670hp) Caterpillar 3512C 2 x Vee 4 Stroke 12 Cy. 170 x 215 each-1350kW (1835bhp) Caterpillar Inc-USA AuxGen: 2 x 135kW a.c Fuel: 98.0 (d.f.)

IMO / Call sign / Flag	Name / Owners	Tonnage	Class	Build	Type	Machinery
8003280 *WCY6766* -	**VALIANT** **Penn Tug & Barge Inc** Penn Maritime Inc SatCom: Inmarsat A 1502123 *Philadelphia, PA* *United States of America* MMSI: 369350000 Official number: 634811	**947** 284 -	Class: AB	**1981-04 McDermott Shipyards Inc — Amelia LA** Yd No: 258 Loa - Br ex - Dght 6.268 Lbp 39.63 Br md 13.12 Dpth 6.71 Welded, 1 dk	**(B32B2SA) Articulated Pusher Tug**	**2 oil engines** sr geared to sc. shafts driving 2 FP propellers Total Power: 5,884kW (8,000hp) 14.0kn MaK 6MU551AK 2 x 4 Stroke 6 Cy. 450 x 550 each-2942kW (4000bhp) Krupp MaK Maschinenbau GmbH-Kiel AuxGen: 2 x 300kW a.c
8217570 *XUSB7* -	**VALIANT** *ex* Ost *-2010* *ex* Bernes *-2007* *ex* Centavr *-2007* *ex* Tora Maru No. 52 *-2005* **Pharos Maritime Pte Ltd** - *Phnom Penh* *Cambodia* MMSI: 515987000 Official number: 0783632	*272* 81 -		**1983-02 Sanuki Shipbuilding & Iron Works Co Ltd — Mitoyo KG** Yd No: 1111 Converted From: Stern Trawler-2006 Loa 37.72 Br ex - Dght 2.471 Lbp 30.92 Br md 7.38 Dpth 4.60 Welded, 1 dk	**(A34A2GR) Refrigerated Cargo Ship** Ins: 94 Compartments: 1 Ho, ER 1 Ha: ER	**1 oil engine** driving 1 CP propeller Total Power: 956kW (1,300hp) 12.3kn Hanshin 6MUH28 1 x 4 Stroke 6 Cy. 280 x 340 956kW (1300bhp) The Hanshin Diesel Works Ltd-Japan AuxGen: 2 x 150kW 225V a.c
7005841 *WDD5776* -	**VALIANT** **Valiant Fisheries LLC** - SatCom: Inmarsat C 436758110 *Seattle, WA* *United States of America* MMSI: 367581000 Official number: 522574	*195* 132 -		**1969 Pacific Fishermen, Inc. — Seattle, Wa** Yd No: 277 Loa 27.74 Br ex 8.08 Dght - Lbp - Br md 7.93 Dpth 3.08 Welded, 1 dk	**(B11B2FV) Fishing Vessel**	**2 oil engines** driving 2 FP propellers Total Power: 1,030kW (1,400hp) G.M. (Detroit Diesel) 16V-71 2 x Vee 2 Stroke 16 Cy. 108 x 127 each-515kW (700bhp) General Motors Corp-USA
9293698 *MBLL8* -	**VALIANT** **Government of The United Kingdom (Home Office Border Force, Maritime & Aviation Operations)** - *United Kingdom* MMSI: 235745000	**238** 71 57	Class: (LR) **UMS** ✠ 30/4/05	**2004-04 Scheepswerf Made B.V. — Made** (Hull) **2004-04 B.V. Scheepswerf Damen — Gorinchem** Yd No: 549855 Loa 42.80 Br ex 7.11 Dght 2.520 Lbp 38.50 Br md 6.80 Dpth 3.77 Welded, 1 dk	**(B34H2SQ) Patrol Vessel**	**2 oil engines** with clutches, flexible couplings & dr reverse geared to sc. shafts driving 2 CP propellers Total Power: 4,176kW (5,678hp) Caterpillar 3516TA 2 x Vee 4 Stroke 16 Cy. 170 x 190 each-2088kW (2839bhp) Caterpillar Inc-USA AuxGen: 2 x 85kW 415V 50Hz a.c Thrusters: 1 Thwart. FP thruster (f)
9628178 *9HA3391* -	**VALIANT** **Sander Shipping Co** Costamare Shipping Co SA *Valletta* *Malta* MMSI: 229541000 Official number: 9628178	**95,390** 56,260 110,876	Class: GL	**2013-08 Sungdong Shipbuilding & Marine Engineering Co Ltd — Tongyeong** Yd No: 4022 Loa 300.05 (BB) Br ex - Dght 14.500 Lbp 288.46 Br md 48.20 Dpth 24.60 Welded, 1 dk	**(A33A2CC) Container Ship (Fully Cellular)** TEU 8827 incl 1462 ref C	**1 oil engine** driving 1 FP propeller Total Power: 47,430kW (64,486hp) 22.0kn MAN-B&W 9S90ME-C8 1 x 2 Stroke 9 Cy. 900 x 3188 47430kW (64486bhp) Thrusters: 1 Tunnel thruster (f)
8855580 - -	**VALIANT '84** **Noble House Seafoods Co Ltd** - *Georgetown* *Guyana* Official number: 0000372	*101* 69 -		**1984 Steiner Shipyard, Inc. — Bayou La Batre, Al** Loa 22.86 Br ex - Dght - Lbp 20.33 Br md 6.71 Dpth 3.32 Welded, 1 dk	**(B11A2FT) Trawler**	**1 oil engine** geared to sc. shaft driving 1 FP propeller Total Power: 268kW (364hp) Cummins KT-1150-M 1 x 4 Stroke 6 Cy. 159 x 159 268kW (364bhp) Cummins Engine Co Inc-USA
9610420 *V7YX6* -	**VALIANT ACE** **Valiant Shipholding Inc** MOL Ship Management Singapore Pte Ltd *Majuro* *Marshall Islands* MMSI: 538004759 Official number: 4759	**59,022** 18,289 18,143	Class: NK	**2012-08 Minaminippon Shipbuilding Co Ltd — Usuki OT** Yd No: 728 Loa 199.95 (BB) Br ex - Dght 9.816 Lbp 190.00 Br md 32.20 Dpth 34.20 Welded, 12 dks	**(A35B2RV) Vehicles Carrier** Side door/ramp (s) Quarter stern door/ramp (s. a.) Cars: 6,141	**1 oil engine** driving 1 FP propeller Total Power: 15,130kW (20,571hp) 20.0kn MAN-B&W 7S60MC-C 1 x 2 Stroke 7 Cy. 600 x 2400 15130kW (20571bhp) Mitsui Engineering & Shipbuilding CLtd-Japan Thrusters: 1 Tunnel thruster (f) Fuel: 2860.0
7396707 *A9D2656* -	**VALIANT EAGLE** *ex* Dubai Sun *-1997* *ex* Asie Trinidad *-1997* *ex* Smit Trinidad *-1990* *ex* Smit-Lloyd 24 *-1984* *ex* Broco Bird *-1979* **Al Jazeera Shipping Co** Al Jazeera Shipping Co WLL (AJS) SatCom: Inmarsat Mini-M 761473590 *Bahrain* *Bahrain* MMSI: 408713000 Official number: 2069	**1,096** 329 915	Class: BV (NV)	**1975-08 B.V. Scheepswerf "Waterhuizen" J. Pattje — Waterhuizen** Yd No: 311 Loa 58.86 Br ex 12.02 Dght 4.910 Lbp 51.31 Br md 11.99 Dpth 6.51 Welded, 2 dks	**(B21B20T) Offshore Tug/Supply Ship** Passengers: berths: 12	**2 oil engines** driving 2 CP propellers Total Power: 2,132kW (2,898hp) 12.0kn Alpha 10V23L-VO 2 x Vee 4 Stroke 10 Cy. 225 x 300 each-1066kW (1449bhp) Alpha Diesel A/S-Denmark AuxGen: 2 x 169kW 440V 60Hz a.c Thrusters: 1 Thwart. FP thruster (f) Fuel: 400.0 (d.f.) 12.0pd
8401432 *V7EG4* -	**VALIANT ENERGY** *ex* Energy Lord *-2014* *ex* Aries Lord *-2010* *ex* Active Lord *-2008* *ex* Gro Viking *-2003* *ex* Lord Supplier *-1990* **Valiant Maritime Co** Prime Gas Management Inc *Marshall Islands* MMSI: 538005465 Official number: 5465	**1,823** 547 1,800	Class: NV	**1984-12 Ulstein Hatlo AS — Ulsteinvik** Yd No: 189 Loa 65.21 Br ex - Dght 4.982 Lbp 57.71 Br md 15.51 Dpth 7.01 Welded, 2 dks	**(B21A20S) Platform Supply Ship**	**2 oil engines** reduction geared to sc. shafts driving 2 CP propellers Total Power: 4,902kW (6,664hp) 10.5kn Nohab F312V 2 x Vee 4 Stroke 12 Cy. 250 x 300 each-2451kW (3332bhp) Nohab Diesel AB-Sweden AuxGen: 2 x 1224kW 440V 60Hz a.c, 2 x 275kW 440V 60Hz a.c Thrusters: 2 Thwart. CP thruster (f); 1 Tunnel thruster (a)
9155858 *A9D2788* -	**VALIANT FALCON** *ex* Modalwan No. 5 *-2002* **Al Jazeera Shipping Co** Al Jazeera Shipping Co WLL (AJS) *Bahrain* *Bahrain* MMSI: 408730000 Official number: BN 8265	**115** 35 -	Class: BV (GL)	**1996-09 Seri Modalwan Sdn Bhd — Sandakan** Yd No: 036 L reg 21.58 Br ex Dght 2.938 Lbp 21.43 Br md 6.82 Dpth 3.50 Welded, 1 dk	**(B32A2ST) Tug**	**2 oil engines** reduction geared to sc. shafts driving 2 FP propellers Total Power: 702kW (954hp) 10.0kn Caterpillar 3408TA 2 x Vee 4 Stroke 8 Cy. 137 x 152 each-351kW (477bhp) Caterpillar Inc-USA AuxGen: 2 x 23kW 220/380V a.c
9447940 *VHLE* -	**VALIANT II** *ex* Valiant *-2011* *ex* Valiant II *-2011* *ex* Valiant *-2009* **Sino Tankers Pte Ltd** Teekay Shipping (Australia) Pty Ltd *Dampier, WA* *Australia* MMSI: 503619000 Official number: 858877	**499** 205 597	Class: CC	**2007-08 Ocean Leader Shipbuilding Co Ltd — Zhongshan GD** Yd No: 178 Loa 42.46 Br ex - Dght 2.880 Lbp 40.07 Br md 10.80 Dpth 4.00 Welded, 1 dk	**(B35E2TF) Bunkering Tanker** Double Hull (13F) Liq: 848; Liq (Oil): 848 Compartments: 10 Wing Ta, ER	**2 oil engines** reduction geared to sc. shafts driving 2 FP propellers Total Power: 814kW (1,106hp) 9.0kn Cummins KTA-19-M3 2 x 4 Stroke 6 Cy. 159 x 159 each-407kW (553bhp) Chongqing Cummins Engine Co Ltd-China AuxGen: 2 x 75kW 415/220V a.c
9587881 *VNPE* -	**VALIANT III** **Sino Tankers Pte Ltd** Teekay Shipping (Australia) Pty Ltd *Brisbane, Qld* *Australia* MMSI: 503649000 Official number: 859689	**942** 331 1,315	Class: CC	**2010-09 Yamen Shipyard Ltd — Jiangmen GD** Yd No: YM-09-001 Loa 53.50 Br ex - Dght 3.800 Lbp 50.50 Br md 12.00 Dpth 5.20 Welded, 1 dk	**(A13B2TP) Products Tanker** Double Hull (13F) Liq: 1,261; Liq (Oil): 1,261 Compartments: 5 Wing Ta, 5 Wing Ta, 1 Wing Slop Ta, 1 Wing Slop Ta, ER	**2 oil engines** reduction geared to sc. shafts driving 2 Propellers Total Power: 894kW (1,216hp) 8.5kn Cummins KTA-19-M3 2 x 4 Stroke 6 Cy. 159 x 159 each-447kW (608bhp) Chongqing Cummins Engine Co Ltd-China AuxGen: 2 x 200kW 400V a.c
7367378 *A9D2817* -	**VALIANT SERVICE** **Gulf Dragon Trading Co WLL** - *Bahrain* *Bahrain* MMSI: 408768000	**748** 224 -	Class: BV (AB)	**1974-01 Zigler Shipyards Inc — Jennings LA** Yd No: 232 Loa 56.70 Br ex - Dght 3.928 Lbp 49.54 Br md 11.59 Dpth 4.58 Welded, 1 dk	**(B21B20T) Offshore Tug/Supply Ship**	**2 oil engines** reverse reduction geared to sc. shafts driving 2 FP propellers Total Power: 2,354kW (3,200hp) EMD (Electro-Motive) 16-567-BC 1 x Vee 2 Stroke 16 Cy. 216 x 254 1177kW (1600bhp) (Re-engined ,made 1950, Reconditioned & fitted 1974) General Motors Corp-USA EMD (Electro-Motive) 16-567-BC 1 x Vee 2 Stroke 16 Cy. 216 x 254 1177kW (1600bhp) (Re-engined ,made 1950, Reconditioned & fitted 1977) General Motors Corp-USA AuxGen: 2 x 200kW Thrusters: 1 Thwart. FP thruster (f)

9112911 *D5AB8* -	**VALIANT STAR** *ex* Aquila Atmosphere *-2011* *ex* Alona *-2007* *ex* Georgia T *-2005* *launched as* Transworld-3 *-2002* **Acropole Maritime SA** Valiant Shipping SA SatCom: Inmarsat C 463710769 *Monrovia* *Liberia* MMSI: 636015346 Official number: 15346	**29,054** 16,082 48,640 T/cm 55.6	Class: RI (GL) (NV)	**2002-05 AO Baltiyskiy Zavod — Sankt-Peterburg** Yd No: 451 Loa 190.50 (BB) Br ex 32.01 Dght 11.850 Lbp 182.60 Br md 32.00 Dpth 16.40 Welded, 1 dk	**(A21A2BC) Bulk Carrier** Grain: 58,180; Bale: 56,412 Compartments: 5 Ho, ER 5 Ha: 4 (19.2 x 18.0)ER (18.4 x 16.0) Cranes: 4x32t	**1 oil engine** driving 1 FP propeller Total Power: 10,400kW (14,140hp) 13.8kn Sulzer 5RTA62U 1 x 2 Stroke 5 Cy. 620 x 2150 10400kW (14140bhp) H Cegielski Poznan SA-Poland AuxGen: 3 x 740kW 450/220V 60Hz a.c Fuel: 170.0 (d.f.) 1900.0 (r.f.) 33.5pd
8001050 - -	**VALIDO** - **Firmino Martins Ltda** - *Lisbon* *Portugal* Official number: LX148C	*199* - 150		**1983-05 Est. Navais da Figueira da Foz Lda. (FOZNAVE) — Figueira da Foz** Yd No: 044 Loa 33.91 Br ex 8.01 Dght 3.601 Lbp 28.61 Br md 7.80 Dpth 3.92 Welded, 1 dk	**(B11A2FS) Stern Trawler** Ins: 140 Compartments: 1 Ho, ER 1 Ha: ER	**1 oil engine** with clutches, flexible couplings & sr reverse geared to sc. shaft driving 1 CP propeller Total Power: 1,066kW (1,449hp) Alpha 10V23L-VO 1 x Vee 4 Stroke 10 Cy. 225 x 300 1066kW (1449bhp) B&W Alpha Diesel A/S-Denmark
7534995 *LW3369* -	**VALIENTE** *ex* Koyo Maru No. 2 *-1980* **Esparza SA** - *Buenos Aires* *Argentina* MMSI: 701006114 Official number: 02543	*470* 364 1,096 T/cm 4.2	Class: RI (BV)	**1966 Kurushima Dockyard Co. Ltd. — Imabari** Yd No: 367 Loa 57.95 Br ex 9.48 Dght 4.301 Lbp 52.46 Br md 9.45 Dpth 4.70 Welded, 1 dk	**(A13B2TP) Products Tanker** Liq: 1,342; Liq (Oil): 1,342 Cargo Heating Coils Compartments: 6 Ta, ER 2 Cargo Pump (s): 2x350m³/hr Manifold: Bow/CM: 35m	**1 oil engine** driving 1 FP propeller Total Power: 603kW (820hp) 10.5kn Akasaka TM6SS 1 x 4 Stroke 6 Cy. 300 x 440 603kW (820bhp) Akasaka Tekkosho KK (Akasaka DieselLtd)-Japan Fuel: 477.5 (d.f.) 3.0pd
9372951 *AULI* -	**VALIYAPANI** - **Government of The Republic of India (Administration of Union Territory of Lakshadweep)** The Shipping Corporation of India Ltd (SCI) *Kochi* *India* MMSI: 419066900 Official number: 3194	**396** 119 43	Class: IR (BV)	**2007-06 Penguin Shipyard International Pte Ltd — Singapore** Yd No: 142 Loa 34.91 Br ex 9.61 Dght 1.390 Lbp 33.51 Br md 9.60 Dpth 4.45 Welded, 1 dk	**(A37B2PS) Passenger Ship** Hull Material: Aluminium Alloy Passengers: unberthed: 154	**2 oil engines** reduction geared to sc. shafts driving 2 Water jets Total Power: 2,648kW (3,600hp) 25.0kn Cummins KTA-50-M2 2 x Vee 4 Stroke 16 Cy. 159 x 159 each-1324kW (1800bhp) Cummins Engine Co Inc-USA AuxGen: 2 x 99kW 415V 50Hz a.c Fuel: 24.4 (d.f.)
9526837 *HP3057* -	**VALKYRIA** - **Panama Tugs SA** - *Panama* *Panama* Official number: 4418412B	**285** 85 150	Class: LR (BV) **100A1** SS 03/2009 tug **LMC** **UMS**	**2009-03 Damen Shipyards Changde Co Ltd — Changde HN** (Hull) Yd No: (511549) **2009-03 B.V. Scheepswerf Damen — Gorinchem** Yd No: 511549 Loa 28.67 Br ex 10.43 Dght 4.800 Lbp 27.90 Br md 9.80 Dpth 4.60 Welded, 1 dk	**(B32A2ST) Tug**	**2 oil engines** reduction geared to sc. shafts driving 2 Z propellers Total Power: 3,372kW (4,584hp) Caterpillar 3516B-HD 2 x Vee 4 Stroke 16 Cy. 170 x 215 each-1686kW (2292bhp) Caterpillar Inc-USA AuxGen: 2 x 98kW 60Hz a.c
7504548 *SFKP* -	**VALKYRIA** - **Lulea Bogserbats AB** - *Lulea* *Sweden* MMSI: 265537680	**312** 93 -	Class: LR ✠ **100A1** SS 09/2009 tug Baltic coasting service Ice Class 1A Super ✠ **LMC** Eq.Ltr: (F) H; Cable: U2	**1977-09 AB Asi-Verken — Amal** Yd No: 118 Loa 32.90 Br ex 9.76 Dght 4.101 Lbp 28.58 Br md 9.30 Dpth 5.19 Welded, 1 dk	**(B32A2ST) Tug** Ice Capable	**1 oil engine** sr geared to sc. shaft driving 1 CP propeller Total Power: 2,589kW (3,520hp) 13.0kn Nohab F216V 1 x Vee 4 Stroke 16 Cy. 250 x 300 2589kW (3520bhp) AB Bofors NOHAB-Sweden AuxGen: 2 x 136kW 390V 50Hz a.c Thrusters: 1 Thwart. FP thruster (f)
7309663 *WX8041* -	**VALKYRIE** - **Jacobson Fishing Co Inc** - *New Bedford, MA* *United States of America* MMSI: 366244990 Official number: 507048	*197* 134 -		**1967 Goudy & Stevens — East Boothbay, Me** L reg 27.86 Br ex 7.07 Dght - Lbp - Br md - Dpth 3.92 Welded	**(B11A2FT) Trawler**	**1 oil engine** driving 1 FP propeller Total Power: 563kW (765hp) Caterpillar D398SCAC 1 x Vee 4 Stroke 12 Cy. 159 x 203 563kW (765bhp) Caterpillar Tractor Co-USA
9444754 *AUPT* -	**VALLARPADAM** - **Cochin Port Trust** - SatCom: Inmarsat C 441922330 *Kochi* *India* MMSI: 419073100 Official number: 3304	**449** 135 138	Class: IR	**2009-05 Tebma Shipyards Ltd — Chengalpattu** Yd No: 125 Loa 32.00 Br ex 10.85 Dght 2.860 Lbp 29.49 Br md 10.65 Dpth 4.74 Welded, 1 dk	**(B32A2ST) Tug**	**2 oil engines** reduction geared to sc. shafts driving 2 Voith-Schneider propellers Total Power: 3,240kW (4,406hp) Wartsila 9L20 2 x 4 Stroke 9 Cy. 200 x 280 each-1620kW (2203bhp) Wartsila Finland Oy-Finland AuxGen: 2 x a.c
9391488 *ICEG* -	**VALLE AZZURRA** - **Navigazione Montanari SpA** - *Trieste* *Italy* MMSI: 247226600	**29,987** 13,240 50,697 T/cm 51.9	Class: BV RI	**2007-12 SPP Shipbuilding Co Ltd — Tongyeong** Yd No: H1010 Loa 183.09 (BB) Br ex 32.23 Dght 13.017 Lbp 174.00 Br md 32.20 Dpth 19.13 Welded, 1 dk	**(A12B2TR) Chemical/Products Tanker** Double Hull (13F) Liq: 51,026; Liq (Oil): 52,145 Compartments: 12 Wing Ta, 2 Wing Slop Ta, ER 12 Cargo Pump (s): 12x600m³/hr Manifold: Bow/CM: 88.8m	**1 oil engine** driving 1 FP propeller Total Power: 9,494kW (12,908hp) 14.9kn Sulzer 7RTA48T-B 1 x 2 Stroke 7 Cy. 480 x 2000 9494kW (12908bhp) Yichang Marine Diesel Engine Co Ltd-China AuxGen: 3 x 900kW 440/220V 60Hz a.c Fuel: 200.0 (d.f.) 1457.8 (r.f.)
9387580 *ICEF* -	**VALLE BIANCA** - **Navigazione Montanari SpA** - *Trieste* *Italy* MMSI: 247218600	**29,987** 13,240 50,633 T/cm 51.9	Class: BV RI	**2007-11 SPP Shipbuilding Co Ltd — Tongyeong** Yd No: H1009 Loa 183.09 (BB) Br ex 32.23 Dght 13.017 Lbp 174.00 Br md 32.20 Dpth 19.10 Welded, 1 dk	**(A12B2TR) Chemical/Products Tanker** Double Hull (13F) Liq: 52,145; Liq (Oil): 52,067 Compartments: 12 Wing Ta, 2 Wing Slop Ta, ER 12 Cargo Pump (s): 12x600m³/hr Manifold: Bow/CM: 89.7m	**1 oil engine** driving 1 FP propeller Total Power: 9,485kW (12,896hp) 14.9kn Sulzer 7RTA48T-B 1 x 2 Stroke 7 Cy. 480 x 2000 9485kW (12896bhp) Yichang Marine Diesel Engine Co Ltd-China AuxGen: 3 x 900kW 450/220V 60Hz a.c Fuel: 200.0 (d.f.) 1535.0 (r.f.)
9220940 *IBTJ* -	**VALLE DI ANDALUSIA** - **Navigazione Montanari SpA** - *Trieste* *Italy* MMSI: 247046200	**25,063** 10,189 40,218 T/cm 49.3	Class: RI (BV) (AB)	**2001-12 Hyundai Mipo Dockyard Co Ltd — Ulsan** Yd No: 9926 Loa 176.00 (BB) Br ex - Dght 11.100 Lbp 168.00 Br md 31.00 Dpth 17.20 Welded, 1 dk	**(A12B2TR) Chemical/Products Tanker** Double Hull (13F) Liq: 37,065; Liq (Oil): 37,065 Compartments: 12 Wing Ta, ER 12 Cargo Pump (s): 12x450m³/hr	**1 oil engine** driving 1 FP propeller Total Power: 8,562kW (11,641hp) 14.5kn B&W 6S50MC 1 x 2 Stroke 6 Cy. 500 x 1910 8562kW (11641bhp) Hyundai Heavy Industries Co Ltd-South Korea AuxGen: 3 x 720kW a.c Thrusters: 1 Tunnel thruster (f)
9220914 *IBQW* -	**VALLE DI ARAGONA** - **Navigazione Montanari SpA** - *Trieste* *Italy* MMSI: 247015800	**25,063** 10,189 40,218 T/cm 49.3	Class: RI (BV) (AB)	**2001-03 Hyundai Mipo Dockyard Co Ltd — Ulsan** Yd No: 9916 Loa 176.00 (BB) Br ex - Dght 11.100 Lbp 168.00 Br md 31.00 Dpth 17.20 Welded, 1 dk	**(A12B2TR) Chemical/Products Tanker** Double Hull (13F) Liq: 42,561; Liq (Oil): 42,561 Cargo Heating Coils Compartments: 12 Wing Ta 12 Cargo Pump (s): 12x450m³/hr Manifold: Bow/CM: 88.8m	**1 oil engine** driving 1 FP propeller Total Power: 8,580kW (11,665hp) 14.5kn B&W 6S50MC 1 x 2 Stroke 6 Cy. 500 x 1910 8580kW (11665bhp) Hyundai Heavy Industries Co Ltd-South Korea AuxGen: 3 x 720kW a.c Thrusters: 1 Thwart. FP thruster (f)
9220926 *IBVD* -	**VALLE DI CASTIGLIA** - **Navigazione Montanari SpA** - *Trieste* *Italy* MMSI: 247029800	**25,063** 10,189 40,218 T/cm 49.3	Class: RI (BV) (AB)	**2001-06 Hyundai Mipo Dockyard Co Ltd — Ulsan** Yd No: 9917 Loa 176.00 (BB) Br ex - Dght 11.100 Lbp 168.00 Br md 31.00 Dpth 17.20 Welded, 1 dk	**(A12B2TR) Chemical/Products Tanker** Double Hull (13F) Liq: 42,564; Liq (Oil): 42,564 Cargo Heating Coils Compartments: 12 Wing Ta, 2 Wing Slop Ta, ER 12 Cargo Pump (s): 12x450m³/hr Manifold: Bow/CM: 88.8m	**1 oil engine** driving 1 FP propeller Total Power: 8,580kW (11,665hp) 14.5kn B&W 6S50MC 1 x 2 Stroke 6 Cy. 500 x 1910 8580kW (11665bhp) Hyundai Heavy Industries Co Ltd-South Korea AuxGen: 3 x 720kW 440/220V 60Hz a.c Thrusters: 1 Thwart. CP thruster (f) Fuel: 249.9 (d.f.) (Heating Coils) 1379.4 (r.f.)
9295311 *IBQM* -	**VALLE DI CORDOBA** - **Navigazione Montanari SpA** - *Trieste* *Italy* MMSI: 247129100 Official number: 38	**25,063** 8,300 40,200 T/cm 49.3	Class: RI (BV)	**2005-04 Hyundai Mipo Dockyard Co Ltd — Ulsan** Yd No: 0252 Loa 176.00 (BB) Br ex - Dght 11.100 Lbp 168.00 Br md 31.00 Dpth 17.20 Welded, 1 dk	**(A12B2TR) Chemical/Products Tanker** Double Hull (13F) Liq: 42,561; Liq (Oil): 42,561 Cargo Heating Coils Compartments: 12 Wing Ta, ER, 1 Slop Ta, 2 Wing Slop Ta 12 Cargo Pump (s): 12x450m³/hr Manifold: Bow/CM: 90m Ice Capable	**1 oil engine** driving 1 FP propeller Total Power: 8,580kW (11,665hp) 14.5kn B&W 6S50MC 1 x 2 Stroke 6 Cy. 500 x 1910 8580kW (11665bhp) Hyundai Heavy Industries Co Ltd-South Korea AuxGen: 3 x 720kW 440/220V 60Hz a.c Thrusters: 1 Thwart. CP thruster (f)

IMO / Call sign / Official No.	Name / Owner / Manager / Port	Tonnage	Class	Builder / Dimensions	Type / Cargo	Machinery
9292278 *IBPY* -	**VALLE DI GRANADA** **Navigazione Montanari SpA** - *Trieste* *Italy* MMSI: 247118700	**25,063** 8,269 40,218 T/cm 49.3	Class: RI (BV)	**2005-01 Hyundai Mipo Dockyard Co Ltd — Ulsan** Yd No: 0251 Loa 176.00 (BB) Br ex - Dght 11.115 Lbp - Br md 31.00 Dpth 17.20 Welded, 1 dk	**(A12B2TR) Chemical/Products Tanker** Double Hull (13F) Liq: 37,065; Liq (Oil): 37,065 Cargo Heating Coils Compartments: 12 Wing Ta, ER 12 Cargo Pump (s): 12x450m³/hr Manifold: Bow/CM: 90m Ice Capable	**1 oil engine** driving 1 FP propeller Total Power: 8,561kW (11,640hp) 14.5kn B&W 6S50MC 1 x 2 Stroke 6 Cy. 500 x 1910 8561kW (11640bhp) Hyundai Heavy Industries Co Ltd-South Korea AuxGen: 3 x 900kW 450/220V 60Hz a.c
9251547 *IBZP* -	**VALLE DI NAVARRA** **Navigazione Montanari SpA** - *Trieste* *Italy* MMSI: 247069700	**25,063** 8,269 40,218 T/cm 49.3	Class: RI (BV) (AB)	**2002-07 Hyundai Mipo Dockyard Co Ltd — Ulsan** Yd No: 0103 Loa 176.00 (BB) Br ex - Dght 11.100 Lbp 168.00 Br md 31.00 Dpth 17.20 Welded, 1 dk	**(A12B2TR) Chemical/Products Tanker** Double Hull (13F) Liq: 37,065; Liq (Oil): 37,065 Cargo Heating Coils Compartments: 12 Wing Ta, 2 Wing Slop Ta, ER 12 Cargo Pump (s): 12x450m³/hr	**1 oil engine** driving 1 FP propeller Total Power: 8,562kW (11,641hp) 14.5kn B&W 6S50MC 1 x 2 Stroke 6 Cy. 500 x 1910 8562kW (11641bhp) Hyundai Heavy Industries Co Ltd-South Korea AuxGen: 3 x 720kW a.c Thrusters: 1 Tunnel thruster (f)
9288942 *IBPC* -	**VALLE DI NERVION** **Navigazione Montanari SpA** - *Trieste* *Italy* MMSI: 247109500	**25,063** 8,300 40,218 T/cm 49.3	Class: RI (BV)	**2004-07 Hyundai Mipo Dockyard Co Ltd — Ulsan** Yd No: 0250 Loa 176.00 (BB) Br ex - Dght 11.100 Lbp 168.00 Br md 31.00 Dpth 17.20 Welded, 1 dk	**(A12B2TR) Chemical/Products Tanker** Double Hull (13F) Liq: 37,065; Liq (Oil): 37,065 Cargo Heating Coils Compartments: 12 Wing Ta, ER 12 Cargo Pump (s): 12x450m³/hr Manifold: Bow/CM: 90m	**1 oil engine** driving 1 FP propeller Total Power: 8,580kW (11,665hp) 14.5kn B&W 6S50MC 1 x 2 Stroke 6 Cy. 500 x 1910 8580kW (11665bhp) Hyundai Heavy Industries Co Ltd-South Korea
9220938 *IBTN* -	**VALLE DI SIVIGLIA** **Navigazione Montanari SpA** - *Trieste* *Italy* MMSI: 247042800	**25,063** 8,269 40,218 T/cm 49.3	Class: RI (BV) (AB)	**2001-09 Hyundai Mipo Dockyard Co Ltd — Ulsan** Yd No: 9925 Loa 176.00 (BB) Br ex - Dght 11.115 Lbp 168.00 Br md 31.00 Dpth 17.20 Welded, 1 dk	**(A12B2TR) Chemical/Products Tanker** Double Hull (13F) Liq: 42,950; Liq (Oil): 42,950 Cargo Heating Coils Compartments: 12 Wing Ta, 2 Wing Slop Ta, ER 12 Cargo Pump (s): 12x450m³/hr	**1 oil engine** driving 1 FP propeller Total Power: 8,580kW (11,665hp) 14.5kn B&W 6S50MC 1 x 2 Stroke 6 Cy. 500 x 1910 8580kW (11665bhp) Hyundai Heavy Industries Co Ltd-South Korea AuxGen: 3 x 720kW a.c Thrusters: 1 Tunnel thruster (f)
7415670 *EAGN* -	**VALLE FRAGA** **Jose Valle Vazquez** - *Santander* *Spain* MMSI: 224577000 Official number: 3-2551/	**241** 72 100		**1980-11 Sociedad Co-operativa de Ast. Ojeda y Aniceto — Aviles** Yd No: 24 Loa 31.75 Br ex 7.78 Dght 3.201 Lbp 27.03 Br md 7.03 Dpth 3.74 Welded, 1 dk	**(B11A2FT) Trawler**	**1 oil engine** geared to sc. shaft driving 1 FP propeller Total Power: 827kW (1,124hp) Caterpillar D399SCAC 1 x Vee 4 Stroke 16 Cy. 159 x 203 827kW (1124bhp) Caterpillar Tractor Co-USA
8328757 *9HTT3* -	**VALLENTINA** *ex* Professor Bubnov *-2009* **Vallentina Ship Management Ltd** Transyug Shipping Co Ltd SatCom: Inmarsat C 425696310 *Valletta* *Malta* MMSI: 256963000 Official number: 3136	**4,724** 1,959 5,020	Class: RS	**1984-11 Navashinskiy Sudostroitelnyy Zavod 'Oka' — Navashino** Yd No: 1703 Loa 124.42 Br ex 16.41 Dght 5.501 Lbp 113.92 Br md 15.82 Dpth 7.52 Welded, 1 dk	**(A31A2GX) General Cargo Ship** Grain: 5,800; Bale: 5,800 TEU 165 Compartments: 4 Ho 4 Ha: (13.3 x 10.6)3 (13.3 x 12.8)	**2 oil engines** driving 2 FP propellers Total Power: 2,200kW (2,992hp) 12.5kn Dvigatel Revolyutsii 6CHRNP36/45 2 x 4 Stroke 6 Cy. 360 x 450 each-1100kW (1496bhp) Zavod "Dvigatel Revolyutsii"-Gorkiy AuxGen: 3 x 200kW a.c Fuel: 465.0 (r.f.)
9251559 *IBZT* -	**VALLERMOSA** **Navigazione Montanari SpA** - *Trieste* *Italy* MMSI: 247078500	**25,063** 8,269 40,218 T/cm 49.0	Class: RI (BV) (AB)	**2003-01 Hyundai Mipo Dockyard Co Ltd — Ulsan** Yd No: 0104 Loa 176.00 (BB) Br ex - Dght 11.100 Lbp 168.00 Br md 31.00 Dpth 17.20 Welded, 1 dk	**(A12B2TR) Chemical/Products Tanker** Double Hull (13F) Liq: 37,065; Liq (Oil): 37,065 Cargo Heating Coils Compartments: 12 Wing Ta, ER 12 Cargo Pump (s): 12x450m³/hr	**1 oil engine** driving 1 FP propeller Total Power: 8,561kW (11,640hp) 14.5kn B&W 6S50MC 1 x 2 Stroke 6 Cy. 500 x 1910 8561kW (11640bhp) Hyundai Heavy Industries Co Ltd-South Korea AuxGen: 3 x 720kW a.c Thrusters: 1 Thwart. FP thruster (f)
9417311 *IBIZ* -	**VALLESINA** **Navigazione Montanari SpA** - SatCom: Inmarsat C 424726520 *Trieste* *Italy* MMSI: 247265500	**60,185** 33,762 109,060 T/cm 91.3	Class: AB RI	**2009-03 Hudong-Zhonghua Shipbuilding (Group) Co Ltd — Shanghai** Yd No: H1521A Loa 243.00 (BB) Br ex 42.03 Dght 15.350 Lbp 233.00 Br md 42.00 Dpth 22.00 Welded, 1 dk	**(A13A2TV) Crude Oil Tanker** Double Hull (13F) Liq: 123,029; Liq (Oil): 123,029 Cargo Heating Coils Compartments: 12 Wing Ta, 2 Wing Slop Ta, ER 3 Cargo Pump (s): 3x2500m³/hr Manifold: Bow/CM: 119.5m	**1 oil engine** driving 1 FP propeller Total Power: 13,570kW (18,450hp) 14.5kn MAN-B&W 7S60MC 1 x 2 Stroke 7 Cy. 600 x 2292 13570kW (18450bhp) Hudong Heavy Machinery Co Ltd-China AuxGen: 3 x 650kW a.c Fuel: 139.0 (d.f.) 2724.0 (r.f.)
9627837 *VRLF6* -	**VALLEY STAR** **CLC Ship Chartering-VII Co Ltd** Shanghai Hong Xiang Shipping Management Co Ltd *Hong Kong* *Hong Kong* MMSI: 477427900 Official number: HK-3652	**107,162** 68,519 205,123	Class: AB	**2013-06 Qingdao Yangfan Shipbuilding Co Ltd — Jimo SD** Yd No: BC205K-01 Loa 299.95 (BB) Br ex - Dght 18.250 Lbp 295.20 Br md 50.00 Dpth 24.75 Welded, 1 dk	**(A21A2BC) Bulk Carrier** Grain: 224,873 Compartments: 9 Ho, ER 9 Ha: ER	**1 oil engine** driving 1 FP propeller Total Power: 16,860kW (22,923hp) 14.5kn MAN-B&W 6S70MC-C8 1 x 2 Stroke 6 Cy. 700 x 2800 16860kW (22923bhp) Hyundai Heavy Industries Co Ltd-South Korea AuxGen: 3 x 900kW a.c Fuel: 514.0 (d.f.) 5520.0 (r.f.)
9512953 *9V7439* -	**VALLIANZ HOPE** *ex* Swissco Samson *-2011* **Vallianz Samson Pte Ltd** Newcruz Offshore Marine Pte Ltd *Singapore* *Singapore* MMSI: 564471000 Official number: 394168	**499** 149 -	Class: BV	**2008-12 Guangzhou Panyu Lingshan Shipyard Ltd — Guangzhou GD** Yd No: 170 Loa 40.00 Br ex - Dght 3.800 Lbp 34.90 Br md 11.80 Dpth 4.60 Welded, 1 dk	**(B21B20T) Offshore Tug/Supply Ship**	**2 oil engines** reduction geared to sc. shafts driving 2 FP propellers Total Power: 3,090kW (4,202hp) Caterpillar 3516B 2 x Vee 4 Stroke 16 Cy. 170 x 190 each-1545kW (2101bhp) Caterpillar Inc-USA Thrusters: 1 Tunnel thruster (f)
7333183 *WBA5522* -	**VALLY** **Shrimp Trawler Vally Inc** - *Port Isabel, TX* *United States of America* MMSI: 367131930 Official number: 543320	*103* 70 -		**1972 Marine Mart, Inc. — Port Isabel, Tx** L reg 19.69 Br ex 6.13 Dght - Lbp - Br md - Dpth 3.46 Welded	**(B11B2FV) Fishing Vessel**	**1 oil engine** driving 1 FP propeller Total Power: 247kW (336hp)
9438224 *3ETK5* -	**VALME B** **Singapore Tankers Pte Ltd** Compania Maritima de Panama SA SatCom: Inmarsat C 437059210 *Panama* *Panama* MMSI: 370592000 Official number: 3464009A	**5,034** 1,958 6,936 T/cm 15.6	Class: LR ✠ **100A1** SS 11/2013 Double Hull oil tanker, carriage of oils with a FP exceeding 60 degree C ESP LI ✠ **LMC** Eq.Ltr: X; Cable: 495.0/50.0 U2 (a)	**2008-11 Titan Quanzhou Shipyard Co Ltd — Hui'an County FJ** Yd No: H0006 Loa 99.36 Br ex 18.08 Dght 7.200 Lbp 94.00 Br md 18.00 Dpth 10.00 Welded, 1 dk	**(A13B2TP) Products Tanker** Double Hull (13F) Compartments: 10 Wing Ta, 2 Wing Slop Ta, ER	**2 oil engines** with clutches, flexible couplings & dr reverse geared to sc. shafts driving 2 FP propellers Total Power: 2,940kW (3,998hp) 11.5kn MAN-B&W 6L28/32A 2 x 4 Stroke 6 Cy. 280 x 320 each-1470kW (1999bhp) Zhenjiang Marine Diesel Works-China AuxGen: 2 x 360kW 400V 50Hz a.c Boilers: AuxB (o.f.) 7.7kgf/cm² (7.6bar) Thrusters: 1 Thwart. FP thruster (f)
8734695 *CUFN* PM-1291-N	**VALMITAO** *ex* Vila de Ribamar *-2008* **Sebastiao & Filhos Lda** - *Portimao* *Portugal* MMSI: 263577600	**593** 177 -		**2003 Astilleros Armon Vigo SA — Vigo** Loa 40.95 Br ex - Dght - Lbp 33.59 Br md 9.20 Dpth 3.90 Welded, 1 dk	**(B11B2FV) Fishing Vessel**	**1 oil engine** reduction geared to sc. shaft driving 1 Propeller Total Power: 633kW (861hp) Caterpillar 1 x 633kW (861bhp) Caterpillar Inc-USA
5353220 - -	**VALO** *ex* Tasman Bay *-2003* - - *Nuku'alofa* *Tonga*	**270** 81 340	Class: (LR) ✠ Classed LR until 5/57	**1952-04 Charles Hill & Sons Ltd. — Bristol** Yd No: 375 Loa 38.56 Br ex 8.74 Dght 2.845 Lbp 36.58 Br md 8.69 Dpth 3.20 Riveted\Welded, 1 dk	**(B33B2DG) Grab Hopper Dredger** Cranes: 1x5.5t; Winches: 2	**1 oil engine** sr geared to sc. shaft driving 1 FP propeller Total Power: 397kW (540hp) 9.0kn Ruston 6VEBXM 1 x 4 Stroke 6 Cy. 260 x 368 397kW (540bhp) Ruston & Hornsby Ltd.-Lincoln AuxGen: 2 x 30kW 220V d.c Fuel: 42.5 (d.f.)
9544310 *SIPR* -	**VALO** *ex* Aa 259 *-2010* **A/B Goteborg-Styrso Skargardstrafik** - *Gothenburg* *Sweden* MMSI: 265650970	**229** 78 19	Class: NV	**2010-04 Brodrene Aa AS — Hyen** Yd No: 259 Loa 27.00 Br ex 8.40 Dght 0.950 Lbp 25.17 Br md 8.00 Dpth 2.70 Bonded, 1 dk	**(A37B2PS) Passenger Ship** Hull Material: Carbon Fibre Sandwich Passengers: unberthed: 162	**2 oil engines** reduction geared to sc. shafts driving 2 CP propellers Total Power: 1,498kW (2,036hp) 27.0kn MAN D2842LE 2 x Vee 4 Stroke 12 Cy. 128 x 142 each-749kW (1018bhp) MAN Nutzfahrzeuge AG-Nuernberg AuxGen: 2 x 28kW 50Hz a.c Thrusters: 2 Tunnel thruster (f)

Ship	Tonnage	Class	Builder / Dimensions	Type / Cargo	Machinery
9198393 **VALOPOULA** *C6XE8* *ex* Pacific Trader *-2008* *ex* Falcon Trader *-2006* - *ex* Ludolf Oldendorff *-2005* **Valopoula Maritime Inc** Petrofin Ship Management Inc *Nassau* *Bahamas* MMSI: 311006700 Official number: 8001528	**26,010** 14,834 45,578 T/cm 49.8	Class: NK (LR) (BV) Classed LR until 1/8/08	**2000-05 Tsuneishi Heavy Industries (Cebu) Inc — Balamban** Yd No: SC-015 Loa 186.00 (BB) Br ex - Dght 11.620 Lbp 175.47 Br md 30.40 Dpth 16.50 Welded, 1 dk	**(A21A2BC) Bulk Carrier** Grain: 57,208; Bale: 55,564 Compartments: 5 Ho, ER 5 Ha: (20.0 x 15.3)4 (20.8 x 15.3)ER Cranes: 4x30t	**1 oil engine** driving 1 FP propeller Total Power: 7,171kW (9,750hp) 14.0kn MAN-B&W 6S50MC 1 x 2 Stroke 6 Cy. 500 x 1910 7171kW (9750bhp) Mitsui Engineering & Shipbuilding CLtd-Japan AuxGen: 3 x 400kW 440V 60Hz a.c Boilers: AuxB (Comp) 7.0kgf/cm² (6.9bar) Fuel: 63.0 (d.f.) 1555.0 (r.f.) 29.0pd
9226009 **VALOR** *ZDEX4* *ex* Valerie *-2011* - **Valor Maritime Ltd** Salmar Shipping Ltd *Gibraltar* *Gibraltar (British)* MMSI: 236041000 Official number: 734688	**12,814** 6,602 19,819 T/cm 32.4	Class: GL	**2002-12 Qingshan Shipyard — Wuhan HB** Yd No: 9901 Loa 164.34 (BB) Br ex - Dght 9.540 Lbp 155.39 Br md 23.00 Dpth 12.80 Welded, 1 dk	**(A12B2TR) Chemical/Products Tanker** Double Hull (13F) Liq: 21,930; Liq (Oil): 21,930 Cargo Heating Coils Compartments: 16 Wing Ta (s.stl), 2 Wing Slop Ta (s.stl), ER 16 Cargo Pump (s): 6x500m³/hr, 10x300m³/hr Manifold: Bow/CM: 78.8m Ice Capable	**1 oil engine** driving 1 CP propeller Total Power: 7,860kW (10,686hp) 15.5kn B&W 6S46MC-C 1 x 2 Stroke 6 Cy. 460 x 1932 7860kW (10686bhp) Yichang Marine Diesel Engine Co Ltd-China AuxGen: 2 x 910kW 450/230V 60Hz a.c, 1 x 100kW 450V 60Hz a.c Thrusters: 1 Tunnel thruster (f) Fuel: 336.1 (d.f.) (Heating Coils) 1084.0 (r.f.) 24.0pd
9628154 **VALOR** *9HA3347* - **Quentin Shipping Co** Costamare Shipping Co SA *Valletta* *Malta* MMSI: 229458000 Official number: 9628154	**95,390** 56,260 110,679	Class: GL	**2013-06 Sungdong Shipbuilding & Marine Engineering Co Ltd — Tongyeong** Yd No: 4020 Loa 300.01 (BB) Br ex - Dght 14.500 Lbp 288.46 Br md 48.20 Dpth 24.60 Welded, 1 dk	**(A33A2CC) Container Ship (Fully Cellular)** TEU 8827 incl 1462 ref C	**1 oil engine** driving 1 FP propeller Total Power: 47,430kW (64,486hp) 22.0kn MAN-B&W 9S90ME-C8 1 x 2 Stroke 9 Cy. 900 x 3188 47430kW (64486bhp) Thrusters: 1 Tunnel thruster (f)
9409924 **VALOR** *WDD8691* - **Baydelta Navigation Inc** Baydelta Maritime Ltd *San Francisco, CA* *United States of America* MMSI: 367301480 Official number: 1199816	**414** 124 -		**2007-07 Nichols Bros. Boat Builders, Inc. — Freeland, Wa** Yd No: S-149 Loa 30.50 Br ex - Dght - Lbp - Br md 12.20 Dpth 4.90 Welded, 1 dk	**(B32A2ST) Tug**	**2 oil engines** gearing integral to driving 2 Z propellers Total Power: 5,130kW (6,974hp) Caterpillar 3516C 2 x Vee 4 Stroke 16 Cy. 170 x 215 each-2565kW (3487bhp) Caterpillar Inc-USA AuxGen: 2 x 215kW a.c
9325154 **VALOR SW** *3EQW9* *ex* Lake Valor SW *-2011* - **Valor Pescadores SA Panama** Shih Wei Navigation Co Ltd *Panama* *Panama* MMSI: 353114000 Official number: 3397308A	**17,944** 10,748 29,818 T/cm 40.5	Class: NK (CR)	**2008-04 Shikoku Dockyard Co. Ltd. — Takamatsu** Yd No: 1037 Loa 170.70 (BB) Br ex - Dght 9.716 Lbp 163.50 Br md 27.00 Dpth 13.80 Welded, 1 dk	**(A21A2BC) Bulk Carrier** Grain: 40,031; Bale: 38,422 Compartments: 5 Ho, ER 5 Ha: ER Cranes: 4x30.5t	**1 oil engine** driving 1 FP propeller Total Power: 6,150kW (8,362hp) 14.3kn MAN-B&W 6S42MC 1 x 2 Stroke 6 Cy. 420 x 1764 6150kW (8362bhp) Mitsui Engineering & Shipbuilding CLtd-Japan AuxGen: 3 x 315kW a.c Fuel: 1575.0 24.5pd
9558397 **VALOROUS QUEEN** *9V9185* *launched as* Lady Kiho *-2011* - **Blue Wake Shipping Pte Ltd** Fairfield Chemical Carriers Inc SatCom: Inmarsat C 456620110 *Singapore* *Singapore* MMSI: 566201000 Official number: 396761	**11,994** 6,185 19,986 T/cm 30.2	Class: NK	**2011-09 Fukuoka Shipbuilding Co Ltd — Fukuoka FO** Yd No: 1289 Loa 146.19 (BB) Br ex 24.23 Dght 9.532 Lbp 138.10 Br md 24.20 Dpth 12.90 Welded, 1 dk	**(A12B2TR) Chemical/Products Tanker** Double Hull (13F) Liq: 21,813; Liq (Oil): 21,813 Cargo Heating Coils Compartments: 10 Wing Ta, 10 Wing Ta, ER 20 Cargo Pump (s): 12x300m³/hr, 8x200m³/hr Manifold: Bow/CM: 73.7m	**1 oil engine** driving 1 FP propeller Total Power: 6,150kW (8,362hp) 14.6kn MAN-B&W 6S42MC 1 x 2 Stroke 6 Cy. 420 x 1764 6150kW (8362bhp) Hitachi Zosen Corp-Japan AuxGen: 3 x 460kW 60Hz a.c Thrusters: 1 Tunnel thruster (f) Fuel: 111.0 (d.f.) 944.0 (r.f.)
6519754 **VALOSKAR** *SHCG* *ex* Kennedy *-2009* *ex* Sandettie *-2002* - *ex* Ronnfors *-2001* *ex* Amazon *-2000* *ex* Clipperton *-1997* *ex* Tunafors *-1976* **Valoskar AB** *Vrango* *Sweden* MMSI: 265803000	**217** 65 -	Class: (BV)	**1965 VEB Rosslauer Schiffswerft — Rosslau** Loa 32.03 Br ex 6.61 Dght 2.701 Lbp 27.06 Br md 6.58 Dpth 3.31 Welded, 1 dk	**(B11A2FT) Trawler** 2 Ha: 2 (1.6 x 1.2) Derricks: 1x2t; Winches: 1 Ice Capable	**1 oil engine** driving 1 FP propeller Total Power: 515kW (700hp) 12.0kn Nohab F26R 1 x 4 Stroke 6 Cy. 250 x 300 515kW (700bhp) Nydqvist & Holm AB-Sweden Fuel: 20.0 (d.f.)
8744535 **VALOUR** *9LY2242* *ex* Sui Dong Fang 086 *-2010* - **Jaris Global Pte Ltd** *Freetown* *Sierra Leone* MMSI: 667003045 Official number: SL103045	**1,423** 445 -		**2005-12 Guangzhou Baiyun Suijiang Shiprepair Yard — Guangzhou GD** Yd No: 090105000617 Loa 75.29 Br ex - Dght 3.850 Lbp - Br md 16.00 Dpth 4.55 Welded, 1 dk	**(A24D2BA) Aggregates Carrier**	**2 oil engines** reduction geared to sc. shafts driving 2 Propellers Total Power: 1,080kW (1,468hp) Chinese Std. Type 2 x 4 Stroke each-540kW (734bhp) Zibo Diesel Engine Factory-China
9231690 **VALPADANA** *IBZD* - **Navigazione Montanari SpA** - *Trieste* *Italy* MMSI: 247060700	**19,408** 6,556 25,583 T/cm 41.0	Class: RI (BV) (AB)	**2002-05 ShinA Shipbuilding Co Ltd — Tongyeong** Yd No: 409 Loa 176.00 (BB) Br ex - Dght 9.013 Lbp 168.00 Br md 27.40 Dpth 15.00 Welded, 1 dk	**(A12B2TR) Chemical/Products Tanker** Double Hull (13F) Liq: 33,027; Liq (Oil): 33,550 Cargo Heating Coils Compartments: 12 Wing Ta, ER, 2 Wing Slop Ta 12 Cargo Pump (s): 12x450m³/hr Manifold: Bow/CM: 83.4m	**1 oil engine** driving 1 FP propeller Total Power: 7,150kW (9,721hp) 15.0kn B&W 5S50MC 1 x 2 Stroke 5 Cy. 500 x 1910 7150kW (9721bhp) Doosan Engine Co Ltd-South Korea AuxGen: 3 x 780kW a.c Thrusters: 1 Thwart. FP thruster (f)
6522921 **VALPARAISO** *CPB868* *ex* Jutta-B *-2011* *ex* Hendrik *-1987* - *ex* Doris *-1978* *ex* Gebina *-1970* - - SatCom: Inmarsat C 472077710 *La Paz* *Bolivia* MMSI: 720777000 Official number: 0001-07 10 2 2 925	**637** 243 580	Class: (GL)	**1965-09 Martin Jansen GmbH & Co. KG Schiffsw. u. Masch. — Leer** Yd No: 73 Lengthened-1974 Loa 55.89 Br ex 8.77 Dght 3.058 Lbp 50.27 Br md 8.72 Dpth 5.29 Welded, 2 dks	**(A31A2GX) General Cargo Ship** 1 Ha: (31.3 x 5.0)ER Ice Capable	**1 oil engine** driving 1 FP propeller Total Power: 184kW (250hp) 9.5kn MaK 6MU451 1 x 4 Stroke 6 Cy. 320 x 450 184kW (250bhp) Maschinenbau Kiel AG (MaK)-Kiel
9417323 **VALPIAVE** *ICAV* - **Navigazione Montanari SpA** - 773130490 *Trieste* *Italy* MMSI: 247285300	**60,185** 33,762 109,060 T/cm 91.3	Class: AB RI	**2010-01 Hudong-Zhonghua Shipbuilding (Group) Co Ltd — Shanghai** Yd No: H1524A Loa 243.00 (BB) Br ex 42.03 Dght 15.367 Lbp 233.00 Br md 42.00 Dpth 22.00 Welded, 1 dk	**(A13A2TV) Crude Oil Tanker** Double Hull (13F) Liq: 123,030; Liq (Oil): 120,570 Cargo Heating Coils Compartments: 12 Wing Ta, 2 Wing Slop Ta, ER 3 Cargo Pump (s): 3x2500m³/hr Manifold: Bow/CM: 119.5m	**1 oil engine** driving 1 FP propeller Total Power: 14,280kW (19,415hp) 14.7kn MAN-B&W 7S60MC 1 x 2 Stroke 7 Cy. 600 x 2292 14280kW (19415bhp) Hudong Heavy Machinery Co Ltd-China AuxGen: 3 x 720kW a.c Fuel: 154.0 (d.f.) 2992.0 (r.f.)
1009730 **VALQUEST** *2CGK8* - **Cagayan D'Oro Ltd** Nigel Burgess Ltd (BURGESS) SatCom: Inmarsat C 423591766 *Douglas* *Isle of Man (British)* MMSI: 235072559 Official number: 741892	**240** - -	Class: LR ✠ **100A1** SS 08/2009 SSC Yacht, mono, G6 **LMC** **UMS** Cable: 275.0/19.0 U2 (a)	**2009-08 Bloemsma Van Breemen Shipyard — Makkum** Yd No: 140 Loa 40.75 Br ex 8.90 Dght 1.866 Lbp 35.25 Br md 8.48 Dpth 4.00 Welded, 1 dk	**(X11A2YS) Yacht (Sailing)** Hull Material: Aluminium Alloy	**1 oil engine** sr geared to sc. shaft driving 1 CP propeller Total Power: 533kW (725hp) 13.0kn Caterpillar C18 1 x 4 Stroke 6 Cy. 145 x 183 533kW (725bhp) Caterpillar Inc-USA AuxGen: 2 x 67kW 400V 50Hz a.c
9391505 **VALROSSA** *ICHI* - **Navigazione Montanari SpA** - SatCom: Inmarsat C 424701899 *Trieste* *Italy* MMSI: 247230300	**29,987** 13,240 50,344 T/cm 52.0	Class: BV RI	**2008-03 SPP Shipbuilding Co Ltd — Tongyeong** Yd No: H1012 Loa 183.09 (BB) Br ex 32.23 Dght 13.017 Lbp 174.00 Br md 32.20 Dpth 19.10 Welded, 1 dk	**(A12B2TR) Chemical/Products Tanker** Double Hull (13F) Liq: 52,145; Liq (Oil): 52,067 Compartments: 12 Wing Ta, 2 Wing Slop Ta, ER 12 Cargo Pump (s): 12x600m³/hr Manifold: Bow/CM: 89.7m	**1 oil engine** driving 1 FP propeller Total Power: 10,185kW (13,848hp) 14.9kn Wartsila 7RTA48T 1 x 2 Stroke 7 Cy. 480 x 2000 10185kW (13848bhp) Yichang Marine Diesel Engine Co Ltd-China AuxGen: 3 x 900kW 440/220V 60Hz a.c Fuel: 227.0 (d.f.) 1396.0 (r.f.)
9385178 **VALSESIA** *ICLK* - **Navigazione Montanari SpA** - SatCom: Inmarsat C 424702274 *Trieste* *Italy* MMSI: 247254800	**23,335** 9,628 37,481 T/cm 45.1	Class: BV RI	**2008-10 Hyundai Mipo Dockyard Co Ltd — Ulsan** Yd No: 2044 Loa 184.32 (BB) Br ex 27.43 Dght 11.316 Lbp 176.00 Br md 27.40 Dpth 17.20 Welded, 1 dk	**(A12B2TR) Chemical/Products Tanker** Double Hull (13F) Liq: 40,750; Liq (Oil): 43,396 Compartments: 12 Wing Ta, 2 Wing Slop Ta, ER 12 Cargo Pump (s): 10x500m³/hr, 2x300m³/hr Manifold: Bow/CM: 92.6m	**1 oil engine** driving 1 FP propeller Total Power: 7,860kW (10,686hp) 14.5kn MAN-B&W 6S46MC-C 1 x 2 Stroke 6 Cy. 460 x 1932 7860kW (10686bhp) Hyundai Heavy Industries Co Ltd-South Korea AuxGen: 3 x 900kW a.c Thrusters: 1 Tunnel thruster (f) Fuel: 132.0 (d.f.) 1017.0 (r.f.)

9292840 *IBPB* -	**VALTAMED** *launched as* Valtevere *-2004* **Navigazione Montanari SpA** - SatCom: Inmarsat C 424700271 *Trieste* *Italy* MMSI: 247114500 Official number: 36	83,669 48,975 158,609 T/cm 117.6	Class: RI (BV)	2004-09 **Daewoo Shipbuilding & Marine Engineering Co Ltd — Geoje** Yd No: 5251 Loa 274.00 (BB) Br ex 48.04 Dght 17.000 Lbp 264.00 Br md 48.00 Dpth 23.74 Welded, 1 dk	**(A13A2TV) Crude Oil Tanker** Double Hull (13F) Liq: 167,810; Liq (Oil): 171,089 Cargo Heating Coils Compartments: 6 Wing Ta, 6 Wing Ta, 1 Wing Slop Ta, 1 Wing Slop Ta, ER 3 Cargo Pump (s): 3x3700m^3/hr Manifold: Bow/CM: 134.1m	**1 oil engine** driving 1 FP propeller Total Power: 18,660kW (25,370hp) 14.0kn B&W 6S70MC-C 1 x 2 Stroke 6 Cy. 700 x 2800 18660kW (25370bhp) Doosan Engine Co Ltd-South Korea AuxGen: 3 x 950kW 450/220V 60Hz a.c Fuel: 274.0 (d.f.) 3955.0 (r.f.) 64.5pd
9384136 *ICKF* -	**VALTELLINA** **Navigazione Montanari SpA** - SatCom: Inmarsat C 424702146 *Trieste* *Italy* MMSI: 247243900	23,335 9,628 37,481 T/cm 45.2	Class: BV RI	2008-05 **Hyundai Mipo Dockyard Co Ltd — Ulsan** Yd No: 2043 Loa 184.32 (BB) Br ex 27.43 Dght 11.316 Lbp 176.00 Br md 27.40 Dpth 17.20 Welded, 1 dk	**(A12B2TR) Chemical/Products Tanker** Double Hull (13F) Liq: 40,750; Liq (Oil): 40,750 Compartments: 12 Wing Ta, 2 Wing Slop Ta, ER 12 Cargo Pump (s): 2x300m^3/hr, 10x500m^3/hr Manifold: Bow/CM: 92.6m	**1 oil engine** driving 1 FP propeller Total Power: 7,860kW (10,686hp) 14.5kn MAN-B&W 6S46MC-C 1 x 2 Stroke 6 Cy. 460 x 1932 7860kW (10686bhp) Hyundai Heavy Industries Co Ltd-South Korea AuxGen: 3 x 900kW a.c Thrusters: 1 Tunnel thruster (f) Fuel: 132.0 (d.f.) 1017.0 (r.f.)
9470131 *9HA2650* -	**VALUE** **Value Shipping Ltd** Genel Denizcilik Nakliyati AS (GEDEN LINES) *Valletta* *Malta* MMSI: 215137000 Official number: 9470131	61,336 35,873 115,984 T/cm 99.1	Class: NV	2011-07 **Samsung Heavy Industries Co Ltd — Geoje** Yd No: 1804 Loa 248.97 (BB) Br ex 43.83 Dght 15.000 Lbp 239.00 Br md 43.80 Dpth 21.00 Welded, 1 dk	**(A13A2TV) Crude Oil Tanker** Double Hull (13F) Liq: 123,650; Liq (Oil): 123,650 Cargo Heating Coils Compartments: 12 Wing Ta, 2 Wing Slop Ta, ER 3 Cargo Pump (s): 3x2800m^3/hr Manifold: Bow/CM: 123.7m	**1 oil engine** driving 1 FP propeller Total Power: 13,560kW (18,436hp) 15.3kn MAN-B&W 6S60MC-C 1 x 2 Stroke 6 Cy. 600 x 2400 13560kW (18436bhp) Doosan Engine Co Ltd-South Korea AuxGen: 3 x 800kW a.c Fuel: 220.0 (d.f.) 2900.0 (r.f.)
9628166 *9HA3355* -	**VALUE** **Raymond Shipping Co** Costamare Shipping Co SA *Valletta* *Malta* MMSI: 229467000 Official number: 9628166	95,390 56,260 110,643	Class: GL	2013-06 **Sungdong Shipbuilding & Marine Engineering Co Ltd — Tongyeong** Yd No: 4021 Loa 300.06 (BB) Br ex - Dght 14.500 Lbp 288.52 Br md 48.20 Dpth 24.60 Welded, 1 dk	**(A33A2CC) Container Ship (Fully Cellular)** TEU 8827 incl 1462 ref C	**1 oil engine** driving 1 FP propeller Total Power: 47,430kW (64,486hp) 22.0kn MAN-B&W 9S90ME-C8 1 x 2 Stroke 9 Cy. 900 x 3188 47430kW (64486bhp) Thrusters: 1 Tunnel thruster (f)
8223282 *9A6347* -	**VALUN** *ex* Koraku Maru *-1998* **Jadrolinija** - *Rijeka* *Croatia* MMSI: 238151000	3,078 1,327 514	Class: CS	1983-07 **Hayashikane Shipbuilding & Engineering Co Ltd — Nagasaki NS** Yd No: 915 Loa 81.82 Br ex - Dght 3.601 Lbp 76.71 Br md 15.10 Dpth 4.75 Welded	**(A36A2PR) Passenger/Ro-Ro Ship (Vehicles)** Passengers: unberthed: 730 Cars: 76, Trailers: 30	**2 oil engines** with clutches & sr geared to sc. shafts driving 2 FP propellers Total Power: 2,354kW (3,200hp) 13.0kn Daihatsu 6DSM-28 2 x 4 Stroke 6 Cy. 280 x 340 each-1177kW (1600bhp) Daihatsu Diesel Manufacturing Co Lt-Japan AuxGen: 2 x 264kW 225V 50Hz a.c Fuel: 30.0 (d.f.) 52.0 (r.f.)
7831020 - -	**VALUYSK** **Sakhalinskiy Rybak Fishing Collective (Rybolovetskiy Kolkhoz 'Sakhalinskiy Rybak')** -	739 221 332	Class: (RS)	1979-10 **Volgogradskiy Sudostroitelnyy Zavod — Volgograd** Yd No: 885 Loa 53.75 (BB) Br ex 10.72 Dght 4.290 Lbp 47.92 Br md - Dpth 6.02 Welded, 1 dk	**(B11A2FS) Stern Trawler** Ins: 218 Compartments: 1 Ho, ER 1 Ha: (1.6 x 1.6) Derricks: 2x1.5t Ice Capable	**1 oil engine** driving 1 FP propeller Total Power: 971kW (1,320hp) 12.8kn S.K.L. 8NVD48A-2U 1 x 4 Stroke 8 Cy. 320 x 480 971kW (1320bhp) VEB Schwermaschinenbau "KarlLiebknecht" (SKL)-Magdeburg
9391490 *ICHJ* -	**VALVERDE** **Navigazione Montanari SpA** - SatCom: Inmarsat C 424701587 *Trieste* *Italy* MMSI: 247227900	29,987 13,240 50,344 T/cm 51.9	Class: BV RI	2008-01 **SPP Shipbuilding Co Ltd — Tongyeong** Yd No: H1011 Loa 183.09 (BB) Br ex 32.23 Dght 13.016 Lbp 174.00 Br md 32.20 Dpth 19.10 Welded, 1 dk	**(A12B2TR) Chemical/Products Tanker** Double Hull (13F) Liq: 52,146; Liq (Oil): 51,026 Compartments: 12 Wing Ta, 2 Wing Slop Ta, Wing ER 12 Cargo Pump (s): 12x600m^3/hr Manifold: Bow/CM: 89.7m	**1 oil engine** driving 1 FP propeller Total Power: 9,485kW (12,896hp) 14.9kn Wartsila 7RTA48T 1 x 2 Stroke 7 Cy. 480 x 2000 9485kW (12896bhp) Yichang Marine Diesel Engine Co Ltd-China AuxGen: 3 x 900kW 440/220V 60Hz a.c Fuel: 140.0 (d.f.) 1396.0 (r.f.)
8945854 *DUA2340* -	**VALVINA 6** *ex* Dolman 2 *-2006* **Valvina Shipping Corp** - *Bacolod* *Philippines* Official number: 06-0000218	*460* 387 -		1987 **at Manila** L reg 55.32 Br ex - Dght - Lbp - Br md 10.57 Dpth 3.70 Welded, 1 dk	**(A13B2TU) Tanker (unspecified)**	**1 oil engine** driving 1 FP propeller Total Power: 368kW (500hp) Isuzu 1 x 4 Stroke 368kW (500bhp) Isuzu Marine Engine Inc-Japan
5233913 *HO5527* -	**VALVIRIA** *ex* Beverly B *-2008* *ex* American Endeavor *-1978* *ex* William A. Weber *-1977* *ex* Michael J. McAllister *-1977* *ex* Pottsville *-1961* **Suministros Marinos SA** - *Panama* *Panama* MMSI: 370518000 Official number: 3490509A	*298* 89 -	Class: (AB)	1952-02 **R.T.C. Shipbuilding Corp. — Camden, NJ** Yd No: 208 Loa 33.56 Br ex 7.95 Dght - Lbp 31.75 Br md 7.78 Dpth 3.97 Welded, 1 dk	**(B32A2ST) Tug**	**1 oil engine** sr geared to sc. shaft driving 1 FP propeller Total Power: 1,471kW (2,000hp) Fairbanks, Morse 10-38D8-1/8 1 x 2 Stroke 10 Cy. 207 x 254 1471kW (2000bhp) (Re-engined ,made 1944, refitted 1952) Fairbanks Morse & Co.-New Orleans, La Fuel: 114.0
8135100 *UFSH* -	**VAMA** *ex* Sergey Losev *-2012* *ex* Sormovskiy-46 *-1992* **Onego Shipping Co LLC** OSS Ltd *St Petersburg* *Russia* MMSI: 273343010	2,478 999 3,353	Class: RS	1983-03 **Sudostroitelnyy Zavod "Krasnoye Sormovo" — Gorkiy** Yd No: 75 Loa 114.03 Br ex 13.21 Dght 3.810 Lbp 107.60 Br md 13.00 Dpth 5.52 Welded, 1 dk	**(A31A2GX) General Cargo Ship** Bale: 4,297 Compartments: 4 Ho, ER 4 Ha: (17.6 x 9.3)3 (17.9 x 9.3)ER Ice Capable	**2 oil engines** driving 2 FP propellers Total Power: 970kW (1,318hp) 10.8kn S.K.L. 6NVD48-2U 2 x 4 Stroke 6 Cy. 320 x 480 each-485kW (659bhp) VEB Schwermaschinenbau "KarlLiebknecht" (SKL)-Magdeburg Fuel: 94.0 (d.f.)
8745008 - -	**VAMPY NO. 1** - -	130 35 -		1978-01 **O C Fergusson Ltd — Vancouver BC** L reg 22.10 Br ex - Dght - Lbp - Br md 6.71 Dpth 2.74 Welded, 1 dk	**(B11B2FV) Fishing Vessel**	**1 oil engine** reduction geared to sc. shaft driving 1 Propeller Total Power: 250kW (340hp) 11.0kn
9124691 *AWDG* -	**VAMSEE** *ex* Nichiasu Maru No. 2 *-2013* **Vamsee Shipping Carrier Pvt Ltd** - *India* MMSI: 419000806	*697* - 1,059	Class: IZ NK	1995-02 **Hakata Zosen K.K. — Imabari** Yd No: 577 Loa 69.81 Br ex - Dght 3.512 Lbp 65.00 Br md 11.50 Dpth 4.40 Welded, 1 dk	**(A13C2LA) Asphalt/Bitumen Tanker** Liq: 991; Liq (Oil): 991; Asphalt: 991	**1 oil engine** driving 1 FP propeller Total Power: 1,177kW (1,600hp) 11.5kn Hanshin LH31G 1 x 4 Stroke 6 Cy. 310 x 530 1177kW (1600bhp) The Hanshin Diesel Works Ltd-Japan AuxGen: 3 x 112kW a.c Fuel: 90.0 (d.f.)
8718342 *AUSU* -	**VAMSEE II** *ex* Ryoshin Maru *-2007* **Vamsee Shipping Carrier Pvt Ltd** Fleet Management Pvt Ltd *Visakhapatnam* *India* MMSI: 419681000 Official number: 3383	652 258 1,179 T/cm 5.0	Class: IR	1988-03 **Hakata Zosen K.K. — Imabari** Yd No: 370 Converted From: Chemical Tanker Loa 62.71 (BB) Br ex 10.02 Dght 4.600 Lbp 58.02 Br md 10.00 Dpth 4.95 Welded, 1 dk	**(A13B2TP) Products Tanker** Double Hull (13F) Liq: 1,119; Liq (Oil): 1,119 Cargo Heating Coils Compartments: 8 Wing Ta, ER 2 Cargo Pump (s): 2x300m^3/hr Manifold: Bow/CM: 30m	**1 oil engine** driving 1 CP propeller Total Power: 767kW (1,043hp) 10.0kn Hanshin LH28G 1 x 4 Stroke 6 Cy. 280 x 460 767kW (1043bhp) The Hanshin Diesel Works Ltd-Japan AuxGen: 2 x 120kW 225V 60Hz a.c Fuel: 70.0 (d.f.)
7322366 *D9EZ* -	**VAN CASTLE** *ex* Harumi Maru No. 1 *-1982* *ex* Shunkai Maru No. 1 *-1982* **Heung Hae Co Ltd** - *Incheon* *South Korea* Official number: ICR-730021	*166* 51 114	Class: (KR) (NK)	1973-04 **Hanasaki Zosensho K.K. — Yokosuka** Yd No: 158 Loa 29.50 Br ex 8.02 Dght 3.080 Lbp 27.30 Br md 8.00 Dpth 3.60 Welded, 1 dk	**(B32A2ST) Tug**	**2 oil engines** driving 2 FP propellers Total Power: 1,220kW (1,658hp) 11.0kn Niigata 6L20AX 2 x 4 Stroke 6 Cy. 200 x 260 each-610kW (829bhp) Niigata Engineering Co Ltd-Japan AuxGen: 2 x 46kW 225V a.c
9661998 - -	**VAN CASTLE** **Heung Hae Co Ltd** - *Incheon* *South Korea*	161 - -		2012-06 **DH Shipbuilding Co Ltd — Incheon** Yd No: 1102 Loa 29.50 Br ex 8.02 Dght 2.700 Lbp 25.30 Br md 8.00 Dpth 3.70 Welded, 1 dk	**(B32A2ST) Tug**	**2 oil engines** reduction geared to sc. shafts driving 2 Propellers Total Power: 1,190kW (1,618hp) Niigata 6L19HX 2 x 4 Stroke 6 Cy. 190 x 260 each-595kW (809bhp) Niigata Engineering Co Ltd-Japan
9657430 - -	**VAN CASTLE** **Heung Hae Co Ltd** - *Pyeongtaek* *South Korea* Official number: PTR-127303	*161* - 114	Class: KR	2012-04 **DH Shipbuilding Co Ltd — Incheon** Yd No: 1101 Loa 29.50 Br ex 8.02 Dght 2.910 Lbp 27.18 Br md 8.00 Dpth 3.70 Welded, 1 dk	**(B32A2ST) Tug**	**2 oil engines** reduction geared to sc. shafts driving 2 Propellers Total Power: 1,190kW (1,618hp) Niigata 6L19HX 2 x 4 Stroke 6 Cy. 190 x 260 each-595kW (809bhp) Niigata Engineering Co Ltd-Japan

6815471 *BVOB* -
VAN CHUNG No. 2
Van Chung Oceanic Development Co Ltd
-
Kaohsiung *Chinese Taipei*
287 150 107
Class: (CR)
1968 **Taiwan Machinery Manufacturing Corp. — Kaohsiung** Yd No: 1421
Loa 40.19 Br ex 7.12 Dght 2.693
Lbp 35.03 Br md 7.09 Dpth 3.18
Welded, 1 dk
(B11B2FV) Fishing Vessel
Ins: 260
Compartments: 3 Ho, ER
3 Ha: (1.0 x 2.1)2 (1.3 x 1.3)ER
Derricks: 1x1.5t; Winches: 1
1 oil engine driving 1 Directional propeller
Total Power: 552kW (750hp) 10.5kn
Niigata
1 x 4 Stroke 6 Cy. 280 x 440 552kW (750bhp)
Niigata Engineering Co Ltd-Japan
AuxGen: 2 x 80kW 220V 60Hz a.c

7213890 - -
VAN CHUNG No. 11
Van Chung Oceanic Development Co Ltd
-
Kaohsiung *Chinese Taipei*
216 152 -
Class: (CR)
1969 **Taiwan Machinery Manufacturing Corp. — Kaohsiung**
Loa 34.60 Br ex 6.53 Dght 2.439
Lbp 30.48 Br md 6.51 Dpth 2.85
Welded
(B11B2FV) Fishing Vessel
Compartments: 3 Ho, ER
3 Ha: 3 (1.2 x 1.2)ER
1 oil engine driving 1 FP propeller
Total Power: 331kW (450hp) 10.5kn
Niigata 6M26CHS
1 x 4 Stroke 6 Cy. 260 x 400 331kW (450bhp)
Niigata Engineering Co Ltd-Japan
AuxGen: 1 x 64kW a.c, 1 x 40kW a.c

7416791 *MNHL2* BM 362
VAN DIJCK
McLeod Trawlers Ltd
-
Brixham *United Kingdom*
MMSI: 232005410
Official number: B11898
203 60 -
1974-06 **N.V. Scheepswerven L. de Graeve — Zeebrugge**
Loa 33.53 Br ex - Dght -
Lbp 32.50 Br md 7.20 Dpth 4.20
Welded, 1 dk
(B11A2FT) Trawler
1 oil engine driving 1 FP propeller
Total Power: 736kW (1,001hp)
MaK 6M452AK
1 x 4 Stroke 6 Cy. 320 x 450 736kW (1001bhp)
MaK Maschinenbau GmbH-Kiel

8415782 *JVCQ4* -
VAN DON GRACE
ex Han Sprinter *-2009* *ex* JS Leader *-2008*
ex Viscount *-2005*
ex Pandang Timor Lima *-1999*
Hong Gay Shipping Co Ltd
-
Ulaanbaatar *Mongolia*
MMSI: 457303000
Official number: 26170985
6,342 2,312 6,716
Class: VR (KR) (NK)
1985-03 **Honda Zosen — Saiki** Yd No: 731
Loa 108.31 (BB) Br ex 18.04 Dght 6.625
Lbp 99.80 Br md 18.01 Dpth 12.22
Welded, 2 dks
(A35A2RR) Ro-Ro Cargo Ship
Quarter stern door/ramp (s)
Len: 17.00 Wid: 4.00 Swl: -
Cars: 155
Grain: 14,494; Bale: 13,019
Compartments: 2 Ho, ER
4 Ha: ER
Derricks: 4x25t
1 oil engine driving 2 gen. each 272kW 450V a.c driving 1 FP propeller
Total Power: 2,868kW (3,899hp) 12.8kn
Mitsubishi 6UEC37L
1 x 2 Stroke 6 Cy. 370 x 880 2868kW (3899bhp)
Kobe Hatsudoki KK-Japan
AuxGen: 2 x 272kW a.c

7309687 *WDD6201* -
VAN ELLIOTT
Van Elliott LLC
-
Kodiak, AK *United States of America*
Official number: 524557
120 82 -
1969 **at Freeport, Tx**
L reg 21.49 Br ex 6.76 Dght -
Lbp - Br md - Dpth 3.41
Welded
(B11B2FV) Fishing Vessel
1 oil engine driving 1 FP propeller
Total Power: 268kW (364hp)

7916959 *OPCA* Z 53
VAN EYCK
Irina's NV
-
Zeebrugge *Belgium*
MMSI: 205259000
Official number: 01 00313 1996
234 70 -
1981-03 **Scheepswerven West-Vlaamse N.V. — Oostkamp** Yd No: C99
Loa 34.29 Br ex 7.57 Dght 3.301
Lbp - Br md 7.51 Dpth 3.92
Welded, 1 dk
(B11A2FS) Stern Trawler
1 oil engine reduction geared to sc. shaft driving 1 FP propeller
Total Power: 596kW (810hp)
A.B.C. 6MDXC
1 x 4 Stroke 6 Cy. 242 x 320 596kW (810bhp)
Anglo Belgian Corp NV (ABC)-Belgium

8930366 - -
VAN HAI 09
ex Cai Rong *-1996*
Cai Rong-Quang Ninh Transport Co (Cong Ty Van Tai Cai Rong Quang Ninh)
-
Quang Ninh *Vietnam*
150 69 100
Class: (VR)
1966 **in the People's Republic of China**
L reg 37.00 Br ex - Dght 2.300
Lbp - Br md 6.20 Dpth 2.80
Welded, 1 dk
(A31A2GX) General Cargo Ship
1 oil engine reduction geared to sc. shaft driving 1 FP propeller
Total Power: 99kW (135hp)
Skoda 6L160
1 x 4 Stroke 6 Cy. 160 x 225 99kW (135bhp) (new engine 1988)
CKD Praha-Praha
AuxGen: 1 x 3kW a.c

9241009 *H3TQ* -
VAN HARMONY
ex MOL Harmony *-2009*
Olive Investment Corp SA
Northstar Ship Management Ltd
Panama *Panama*
MMSI: 353089000
Official number: 2777001C
13,267 7,391 18,078
Class: NK
2000-12 **Iwagi Zosen Co Ltd — Kamijima EH** Yd No: 193
Loa 161.85 (BB) Br ex - Dght 9.065
Lbp 150.00 Br md 25.60 Dpth 12.90
Welded, 1 dk
(A33A2CC) Container Ship (Fully Cellular)
TEU 1032 incl 156 ref C.
16 Ha: 2 (12.6 x 5.6)14 (12.6 x 10.7)ER
1 oil engine driving 1 FP propeller
Total Power: 11,440kW (15,554hp) 18.5kn
B&W 8S50MC
1 x 2 Stroke 8 Cy. 500 x 1910 11440kW (15554bhp)
Mitsui Engineering & Shipbuilding CLtd-Japan
AuxGen: 3 x a.c
Thrusters: 1 Tunnel thruster (f)
Fuel: 1315.0

9122320 *3WQZ* -
VAN HUNG
ex Pretty Billow *-2007*
Bien Dong Shipping Co Ltd (Bien Dong)
-
Haiphong *Vietnam*
MMSI: 574491000
Official number: VN-2311-VT
4,914 2,306 7,020 T/cm 16.6
Class: VR (NK)
1996-03 **Daedong Shipbuilding Co Ltd — Busan**
Loa 112.50 (BB) Br ex - Dght 6.712
Lbp 105.20 Br md 18.20 Dpth 8.70
Welded, 1 dk
(A33A2CC) Container Ship (Fully Cellular)
Bale: 8,214
TEU 420 C Ho 151 TEU C Dk 269 TEU incl 30 ref C
Compartments: 6 Cell Ho, ER
6 Ha: ER
Ice Capable
1 oil engine driving 1 FP propeller
Total Power: 3,354kW (4,560hp) 14.0kn
B&W 6L35MC
1 x 2 Stroke 6 Cy. 350 x 1050 3354kW (4560bhp)
Korea Heavy Industries & ConstrCo Ltd (HANJUNG)-South Korea

9561124 *XVJD* -
VAN KIEU 18
Van Kieu Co Ltd
-
SatCom: Inmarsat C 457493810
Haiphong *Vietnam*
MMSI: 574938000
999 651 1,901
Class: VR
2009-11 **Song Dao Shipyard — Nam Dinh** Yd No: DKTB-08
Loa 69.85 Br ex 11.27 Dght 4.290
Lbp 65.95 Br md 11.25 Dpth 5.20
Welded, 1 dk
(A21A2BC) Bulk Carrier
Grain: 2,433; Bale: 2,192
Compartments: 2 Ho, ER
2 Ha: ER 2 (18.2 x 7.0)
1 oil engine reduction geared to sc. shaft driving 1 FP propeller
Total Power: 662kW (900hp) 10.0kn
Chinese Std. Type 6210ZLC
1 x 4 Stroke 6 Cy. 210 x 290 662kW (900bhp)
Zibo Diesel Engine Factory-China
AuxGen: 2 x 35kW 400V a.c

9201578 *PAKB* -
VAN KINSBERGEN
Government of The Kingdom of The Netherlands (Ministerie van Defensie) (Commandant Zeemacht Nederland)
Defensie Materieel Organisatie
Den Helder *Netherlands*
MMSI: 244736000
Official number: 36171
528 158 -
Class: LR
✠ **100A1** SS 11/2009
LMC **UMS**
Cable: 165.0/24.0 U2 (a)
1999-11 **Vervako Heusden B.V. — Heusden** (Hull) Yd No: 3415
1999-11 **B.V. Scheepswerf Damen — Gorinchem** Yd No: 6914
Loa 41.58 Br ex - Dght 3.510
Lbp 37.05 Br md 9.20 Dpth 4.66
Welded, 1 dk
(B34H2SQ) Patrol Vessel
2 oil engines with clutches, flexible couplings & sr reverse geared to sc. shafts driving 2 FP propellers
Total Power: 1,156kW (1,572hp) 12.0kn
Caterpillar 3508TA
2 x Vee 4 Stroke 8 Cy. 170 x 190 each-578kW (786bhp)
Caterpillar Inc-USA
AuxGen: 2 x 260kW 440V 60Hz a.c
Thrusters: 1 Thwart. FP thruster (f)

8983583 *WDD2200* -
VAN LANG
Lang Huynh Inc
-
Garland, TX *United States of America*
MMSI: 367112240
Official number: 1128737
224 128 -
2002 **T.M. Jemison Construction Co., Inc. — Bayou La Batre, Al** Yd No: 174
L reg 28.43 Br ex - Dght -
Lbp - Br md 8.22 Dpth 4.26
Welded, 1 dk
(B11B2FV) Fishing Vessel
1 oil engine driving 1 Propeller

8939946 - -
VAN LANG II
ex Sea Commander II *-2007*
ex Diamondhead *-2001*
L & D Inc
-
Belle Chasse, LA *United States of America*
Official number: 1045464
175 58 -
1996 **La Force Shipyard Inc — Coden AL** Yd No: 202
L reg 26.43 Br ex - Dght -
Lbp - Br md 7.92 Dpth 3.72
Welded, 1 dk
(B11B2FV) Fishing Vessel
1 oil engine driving 1 FP propeller

8893544 - -
VAN LONG HAI
Trung Kien Co Ltd (Cong Ty Tnhh Trung Kien)
-
Haiphong *Vietnam*
Official number: VN-1130-VT
397 240 778
Class: (VR)
1994-01 **Ha Long Shipbuilding Engineering JSC — Haiphong**
Lengthened & Deepened-2000
Loa 49.12 Br ex 7.94 Dght 3.690
Lbp 45.07 Br md 7.72 Dpth 4.44
Welded, 1 dk
(A31A2GX) General Cargo Ship
Grain: 430
Compartments: 2 Ho, ER
1 Ha:
1 oil engine reduction geared to sc. shaft driving 1 FP propeller
Total Power: 232kW (315hp) 9.0kn
Daldizel 6CHNSP2A18/22
1 x 4 Stroke 6 Cy. 180 x 220 232kW (315bhp) (made 1972)
Daldizel-Khabarovsk
AuxGen: 1 x 5kW a.c

9107057 *3WPC* -
VAN LY
ex Yi Feng *-2006*
Bien Dong Shipping Co Ltd (Bien Dong)
-
Haiphong *Vietnam*
MMSI: 574443000
Official number: VN-2128-VT
4,879 2,465 6,832 T/cm 16.5
Class: VR (NK) (CC)
1994-03 **Dae Sun Shipbuilding & Engineering Co Ltd — Busan** Yd No: 406
Loa 113.00 (BB) Br ex - Dght 6.513
Lbp 103.00 Br md 19.00 Dpth 8.50
Welded, 1 dk
(A33A2CC) Container Ship (Fully Cellular)
TEU 357 C Ho 151 TEU C Dk 206 TEU
Compartments: 5 Cell Ho, ER
6 Ha: ER
1 oil engine driving 1 FP propeller
Total Power: 3,354kW (4,560hp) 14.0kn
B&W 6L35MC
1 x 2 Stroke 6 Cy. 350 x 1050 3354kW (4560bhp)
Ssangyong Heavy Industries Co Ltd-South Korea

No.	Name / Owner	Tonnage	Class	Builder / Dimensions	Type / Cargo	Machinery
9553141 *3FKC4* -	**VAN ORCHID** **Rupert Investment Corp** Northstar Ship Management Ltd *Panama* Panama MMSI: 372612000 Official number: 4100110	**17,018** 10,109 28,341 T/cm 39.7	Class: NK	**2009-11 Imabari Shipbuilding Co Ltd — Marugame KG (Marugame Shipyard)** Yd No: 1554 Loa 169.37 (BB) Br ex - Dght 9.819 Lbp 160.40 Br md 27.20 Dpth 13.60 Welded, 1 dk	**(A21A2BC) Bulk Carrier** Grain: 37,320; Bale: 35,742 Compartments: 5 Ho, ER 5 Ha: ER Cranes: 4x30.7t	**1 oil engine** driving 1 FP propeller Total Power: 5,850kW (7,954hp) 14.0kn MAN-B&W 6S42MC 1 x 2 Stroke 6 Cy. 420 x 1764 5850kW (7954bhp) Makita Corp-Japan AuxGen: 3 x a.c Fuel: 1246.0 (r.f.)
9266372 *XVCY* -	**VAN PHONG 1** *ex Maersk Priority -2010* *ex Unique Priority -2007* **Vietnam National Petroleum Corp (Tong Cong Ty Xang Dau) (PETROLIMEX)** - SatCom: Inmarsat C 457453410 *Saigon* Vietnam MMSI: 574534000 Official number: VNSG-2003-TD	**59,843** 31,327 105,636 T/cm 95.1	Class: NV VR	**2004-04 Daewoo Shipbuilding & Marine Engineering Co Ltd — Geoje** Yd No: 5258 Loa 248.00 (BB) Br ex 43.03 Dght 14.319 Lbp 238.30 Br md 43.00 Dpth 21.00 Welded, 1 dk	**(A13B2TP) Products Tanker** Double Hull (13F) Liq: 120,153; Liq (Oil): 120,153 Compartments: 12 Wing Ta, ER, 2 Wing Slop Ta 3 Cargo Pump (s): 3x2800m³/hr Manifold: Bow/CM: 124.5m	**1 oil engine** driving 1 FP propeller Total Power: 14,049kW (19,101hp) 15.2kn MAN-B&W 5S70MC 1 x 2 Stroke 5 Cy. 700 x 2674 14049kW (19101bhp) Doosan Engine Co Ltd-South Korea Fuel: 200.0 (d.f.) 3168.0 (r.f.)
9671204 *3WHC9* -	**VAN PHUC 126** **Van Phuc Co Ltd** - *Haiphong* Vietnam Official number: VN-3413-VT	**999** 657 1,967	Class: VR	**2012-07 Thanh Long Shipbuilding Industry Co Ltd — Haiphong** Yd No: S07-047.05 Loa 69.95 Br ex 10.83 Dght 4.570 Lbp 65.80 Br md 10.80 Dpth 5.50 Welded, 1 dk	**(A31A2GX) General Cargo Ship** Compartments: 2 Ho, ER 2 Ha: (16.0 x 7.0)ER (15.4 x 7.0)	**1 oil engine** reduction geared to sc. shaft driving 1 FP propeller Total Power: 600kW (816hp) 10.0kn Chinese Std. Type CW6200ZC 1 x 4 Stroke 6 Cy. 200 x 270 600kW (816bhp) Weichai Power Co Ltd-China AuxGen: 1 x 60kW 400V a.c Fuel: 44.0
9573842 *H9TX* -	**VAN STAR** **Beamer Investment Corp** Northstar Ship Management Ltd SatCom: Inmarsat C 435408410 *Panama* Panama MMSI: 354084000 Official number: 4262111	**34,778** 20,209 61,508 T/cm 61.4	Class: NK	**2011-03 Shin Kasado Dockyard Co Ltd — Kudamatsu YC** Yd No: K-022 Loa 199.98 (BB) Br ex - Dght 13.010 Lbp 195.00 Br md 32.24 Dpth 18.60 Welded, 1 dk	**(A21A2BC) Bulk Carrier** Grain: 77,674; Bale: 73,552 Compartments: 5 Ho, ER 5 Ha: 4 (23.5 x 19.0)ER (18.7 x 19.0) Cranes: 4x30.5t	**1 oil engine** driving 1 FP propeller Total Power: 8,450kW (11,489hp) 14.5kn MAN-B&W 6S50MC-C8 1 x 2 Stroke 6 Cy. 500 x 2000 8450kW (11489bhp) Hitachi Zosen Corp-Japan Fuel: 2565.0 (r.f.)
9023110 - -	**VAN TRANG 07** *ex Van Trang 07-Alci -2012* *ex Huu Nghi 05 -2005* **Huyen Trang Trading & Shipping Co Ltd** - *Haiphong* Vietnam MMSI: 574012062 Official number: VN-3504-VT	**499** 337 977	Class: VR	**2004-01 Mechanical Shipbuilding Aquatic Product Enterprise — Haiphong** Yd No: TB-07-1 Loa 56.00 Br ex 9.27 Dght 3.280 Lbp 53.27 Br md 9.25 Dpth 3.97 Welded, 1 dk	**(A31A2GX) General Cargo Ship**	**1 oil engine** driving 1 FP propeller Total Power: 300kW (408hp) S.K.L. 8NVD36-1U 1 x 4 Stroke 8 Cy. 240 x 360 300kW (408bhp) SKL Motoren u. Systemtechnik AG-Magdeburg
9358448 *3WMQ* -	**VAN TRANG 18-BIDV** *launched as Hoang Loc 17 -2005* **BIDV Leasing Co** Huyen Trang Trading & Shipping Co Ltd *Haiphong* Vietnam MMSI: 574506000 Official number: VN-2022-VT	**998** 654 1,790	Class: VR	**2005-12 Haiphong Mechanical & Trading Co. — Haiphong** Yd No: HT-42 Loa 69.61 Br ex 10.10 Dght 4.200 Lbp 66.43 Br md 10.08 Dpth 5.20 Welded, 1 dk	**(A31A2GX) General Cargo Ship** Grain: 2,443 Compartments: 2 Ho, ER 2 Ha: (15.9 x 6.8)ER (18.7 x 6.8)	**1 oil engine** reduction geared to sc. shaft driving 1 FP propeller Total Power: 530kW (721hp) 10.0kn Chinese Std. Type Z8170ZL 1 x 4 Stroke 8 Cy. 170 x 200 530kW (721bhp) Zibo Diesel Engine Factory-China AuxGen: 2 x 60kW 400V a.c
1004431 *VSBF5* -	**VAN TRIUMPH** **D T V Lieu** - SatCom: Inmarsat B 331016283 *Hamilton* Bermuda (British) Official number: 702178	**1,506** - -	Class: LR ✠ **100A1** SS 01/2012 Yacht ✠ **LMC** Eq.Ltr: L;	**1984-09 Supercraft (Hong Kong) Ltd. — Hong Kong** Yd No: 262 Loa 64.59 Br ex 11.28 Dght 5.420 Lbp 59.32 Br md - Dpth 7.25 Welded, 1 dk	**(X11A2YP) Yacht**	**2 oil engines** driving 2 FP propellers Total Power: 2,060kW (2,800hp) 14.5kn Yanmar 2 x 4 Stroke 6 Cy. 220 x 330 each-1030kW (1400bhp) Yanmar Diesel Engine Co Ltd-Japan Fuel: 252.7 (d.f.)
8998980 *3WIL* -	**VAN XUAN 18-ALCI** *ex Trung Duc 18 -2012* *ex Prosimex 16-Alci -2008* *ex Minh Hung 16-ALCI -2006* **Agriculture Leasing Co I** Trung Duc Trading & Transportation JSC (Cong Ty Co Phan TM VTB Trung Duc) *Haiphong* Vietnam MMSI: 574012374 Official number: VN-1664-VT	**1,097** 693 1,955	Class: VR	**2003-07 Trung Hai Private Enterprise — Haiphong** Loa 73.98 Br ex 10.82 Dght 4.300 Lbp 70.35 Br md 10.80 Dpth 5.10 Welded, 1 dk	**(A31A2GX) General Cargo Ship**	**1 oil engine** driving 1 Propeller Total Power: 736kW (1,001hp) S.K.L. 6NVD48A-2U 1 x 4 Stroke 6 Cy. 320 x 480 736kW (1001bhp) SKL Motoren u. Systemtechnik AG-Magdeburg
8852813 *V3QV6* -	**VANADIY** *ex Volgo-Don 5086 -1997* **Saluta Shipping Ltd** Kent Shipping & Chartering Ltd *Belize City* Belize Official number: 141220224	**3,994** 1,302 4,975	Class: (RS) (RR)	**1983-09 Santierul Naval Oltenita S.A. — Oltenita** Loa 138.80 Br ex 16.70 Dght 3.380 Lbp 132.22 Br md 16.50 Dpth 5.50 Welded, 1 dk	**(A31A2GX) General Cargo Ship** Grain: 6,270 Ice Capable	**2 oil engines** driving 2 FP propellers Total Power: 1,324kW (1,800hp) 10.0kn Dvigatel Revolyutsii 6CHRNP36/45 2 x 4 Stroke 6 Cy. 360 x 450 each-662kW (900bhp) Zavod "Dvigatel Revolyutsii"-Gorkiy
7344560 - -	**VANCHI** **Andaman & Nicobar Islands (Marine Engineer)** - *Kolkata* India Official number: 1767	**349** 105 101		**1985-04 Central Inland Water Transport Corp. Ltd. — Kolkata** Yd No: 358 Loa 33.00 Br ex 9.10 Dght 3.401 Lbp 29.95 Br md 9.01 Dpth 4.50 Welded, 1 dk	**(B32A2ST) Tug**	**2 oil engines** with clutches, flexible couplings & sr reverse geared to sc. shafts driving 2 FP propellers Total Power: 1,250kW (1,700hp) MAN G5V30/45ATL 2 x 4 Stroke 5 Cy. 300 x 450 each-625kW (850bhp) Garden Reach Shipbuilders &Engineers Ltd-India
9060106 - -	**VANCOUVER** **Shaver Transportation Co** - *Portland, OR* United States of America MMSI: 367513220 Official number: 990262	*158* 126 -		**1993-08 J M Martinac Shipbuilding Corp — Tacoma WA** Yd No: 238 Loa 22.89 Br ex - Dght 3.200 Lbp - Br md 8.53 Dpth 3.43 Welded, 1 dk	**(B32A2ST) Tug**	**2 oil engines** gearing integral to driving 2 Z propellers Total Power: 2,206kW (3,000hp) 12.4kn G.M. (Detroit Diesel) 16V-149-TI 2 x Vee 2 Stroke 16 Cy. 146 x 146 each-1103kW (1500bhp) General Motors Corp-USA AuxGen: 2 x 115kW a.c
9292230 *H8FE* -	**VANCOUVER BRIDGE** **Vancouver Bridge Shipholding SA** Kawasaki Kisen Kaisha Ltd (Kawasaki Kisen KK) ('K' Line) *Panama* Panama MMSI: 356413000 Official number: 3052905B	**54,519** 22,921 65,002 T/cm 82.5	Class: NK	**2005-01 Hyundai Heavy Industries Co Ltd — Ulsan** Yd No: 1579 Loa 294.12 (BB) Br ex - Dght 13.520 Lbp 283.33 Br md 32.20 Dpth 21.80 Welded, 1 dk	**(A33A2CC) Container Ship (Fully Cellular)** TEU 4738 incl 400 ref C	**1 oil engine** driving 1 FP propeller Total Power: 45,660kW (62,079hp) 23.5kn MAN-B&W 8K98MC-C 1 x 2 Stroke 8 Cy. 980 x 2400 45660kW (62079bhp) Hyundai Heavy Industries Co Ltd-South Korea AuxGen: 4 x 1995kW a.c Thrusters: 1 Thwart. CP thruster (f) Fuel: 7385.0
9450387 *9HA3490* -	**VANCOUVER EXPRESS** **KG ms 'CPO Bremen' Offen Reederei GmbH & Co** Reederei Claus-Peter Offen GmbH & Co KG *Valletta* Malta MMSI: 229655000 Official number: 9450387	**91,203** 55,360 103,773	Class: GL	**2009-12 Hyundai Heavy Industries Co Ltd — Ulsan** Yd No: 2075 Loa 334.07 (BB) Br ex - Dght 14.610 Lbp 319.00 Br md 42.80 Dpth 24.80 Welded, 1 dk	**(A33A2CC) Container Ship (Fully Cellular)** TEU 8580 C Ho 3832 TEU C Dk 4748 incl 700 ref C.	**1 oil engine** driving 1 FP propeller Total Power: 72,240kW (98,218hp) 25.6kn MAN-B&W 12K98MC-C 1 x 2 Stroke 12 Cy. 980 x 2400 72240kW (98218bhp) Hyundai Heavy Industries Co Ltd-South Korea AuxGen: 4 x 2699kW 6600/450V a.c Thrusters: 1 Tunnel thruster (f)
9213741 *PBCF* -	**VANCOUVERBORG** **Wagenborg Rederij BV** Wagenborg Shipping BV *Delfzijl* Netherlands MMSI: 245930000 Official number: 39383	**6,361** 3,099 9,850 T/cm 18.3	Class: BV	**2001-07 Daewoo-Mangalia Heavy Industries S.A. — Mangalia** (Hull) Yd No: 1029 **2001-07 Bodewes Scheepswerf "Volharding" Foxhol B.V. — Foxhol** Yd No: 501 Loa 132.20 (BB) Br ex - Dght 8.070 Lbp 123.84 Br md 15.87 Dpth 9.65 Welded, 1 dk	**(A31A2GX) General Cargo Ship** Grain: 12,855 TEU 552 C. 552/20' incl. 25 ref C. Compartments: 2 Ho, ER 2 Ha: (52.5 x 13.2)ER (39.9 x 13.2) Ice Capable	**1 oil engine** reduction geared to sc. shaft driving 1 CP propeller Total Power: 4,197kW (5,706hp) 15.0kn Wartsila 6R38 1 x 4 Stroke 6 Cy. 380 x 475 4197kW (5706bhp) Wartsila Nederland BV-Netherlands AuxGen: 2 x 244kW 400/230V 60Hz a.c

8410419 *HQUH7* -	**VANDA** *ex* Kinko Maru No. 10 *-1998* **Vanda Maritime Lines SA** Jurong Oceanic Trading Co Pte Ltd *San Lorenzo* *Honduras* MMSI: 334513000 Official number: L-1337126	**1,029** 584 1,861	Class: (NK)	**1984-10 Hakata Zosen K.K. — Imabari** Yd No: 300 Loa 77.17 (BB) Br ex - Dght 4.592 Lbp 72.01 Br md 11.21 Dpth 5.01 Welded, 1 dk	**(A13B2TP) Products Tanker** Liq: 2,190; Liq (Oil): 2,190 Compartments: 10 Ta, ER	**1 oil engine** driving 1 CP propeller Total Power: 1,324kW (1,800hp) 11.5kn Hanshin 6EL30 1 x 4 Stroke 6 Cy. 300 x 600 1324kW (1800bhp) The Hanshin Diesel Works Ltd-Japan
7322471 *DYDH* -	**VANDA 888** *ex* Sea Express *-1999* *ex* Tama Maru *-1988* *ex* Hakubasan Maru *-1986* **Frabelle Fishing Corp** - SatCom: Inmarsat A 1333255 *Manila* *Philippines* Official number: MNLD010349	**2,219** 900 3,071	Class: (KR) (NK)	**1973-08 Kyokuyo Shipbuilding & Iron Works Co Ltd — Shimonoseki YC** Yd No: 258 Loa 100.13 Br ex 14.05 Dght 6.016 Lbp 92.06 Br md 14.03 Dpth 7.01 Welded, 1 dk	**(A34A2GR) Refrigerated Cargo Ship** Ins: 3,256 Compartments: 3 Ho, ER 3 Ha: 3 (6.4 x 4.0)ER Derricks: 6x3t	**1 oil engine** driving 1 FP propeller Total Power: 3,310kW (4,500hp) 14.0kn Mitsubishi 6UET45/80D 1 x 2 Stroke 6 Cy. 450 x 800 3310kW (4500bhp) Akasaka Tekkosho KK (Akasaka DieselLtd)-Japan AuxGen: 2 x 400kW 445V 60Hz a.c Fuel: 234.0 (d.f.) 376.0 (r.f.) 16.0pd
8518443 - -	**VANDANA** - **Coastal Trawlers Ltd** - *Visakhapatnam* *India*	*155* 47 80	Class: (IR) (NV)	**1987-03 Australian Shipbuilding Industries (WA) Pty Ltd — Fremantle WA** Yd No: 257 Loa 24.95 Br ex 7.47 Dght 3.010 Lbp 22.05 Br md 7.42 Dpth 3.00 Welded, 1 dk	**(B11A2FT) Trawler** Ins: 110	**1 oil engine** with clutches, flexible couplings & sr geared to sc. shaft driving 1 FP propeller Total Power: 370kW (503hp) Caterpillar 3412T 1 x Vee 4 Stroke 12 Cy. 137 x 152 370kW (503bhp) Caterpillar Inc-USA AuxGen: 2 x 63kW 415V 50Hz a.c
8652574 *YD6853* -	**VANDO I** - **Samudera Pratama Abadi PT** - *Samarinda* *Indonesia*	**224** 68 -	Class: KI	**2005-12 PT Candi Pasifik — Samarinda** Loa 28.50 Br ex - Dght - Lbp 26.78 Br md 8.00 Dpth 3.95 Welded, 1 dk	**(B32A2ST) Tug**	**2 oil engines** reduction geared to sc. shafts driving 2 Propellers Total Power: 1,472kW (2,002hp) Caterpillar D398TA 2 x Vee 4 Stroke 12 Cy. 159 x 203 each-736kW (1001bhp) Caterpillar Inc-USA
5376313 *CSKU* -	**VANDOMA** *ex* ST-745 *-1986* **Government of The Republic of Portugal (Administracao dos Portos do Douro e Leixoes)** - *Leixoes* *Portugal* Official number: LX-976-EST	*150* 38 -	Class: (AB)	**1944 Tampa Marine Corp — Tampa FL** Yd No: 29 L reg 26.71 Br ex 6.99 Dght 2.890 Lbp - Br md - Dpth - Welded, 1 dk	**(B32A2ST) Tug**	**1 oil engine** driving 1 FP propeller Fairbanks, Morse 1 x 2 Stroke 6 Cy. 355 x 430 Fairbanks Morse & Co.-New Orleans, La
8919958 *JVXA4* -	**VANDON ACE** *ex* Yin Hu *-2012* *ex* New Splendor *-2003* **Hong Gay Shipping Co Ltd** - *Ulaanbaatar* *Mongolia* MMSI: 457648000 Official number: 31591290	**4,409** 2,806 7,204	Class: VR (NK)	**1990-10 Iwagi Zosen Co Ltd — Kamijima EH** Yd No: 136 Loa 106.86 (BB) Br ex - Dght 6.868 Lbp 100.00 Br md 17.60 Dpth 8.70 Welded	**(A31A2GX) General Cargo Ship** Grain: 9,701; Bale: 8,903 2 Ha: 2 (28.7 x 10.4)ER Derricks: 4x20t	**1 oil engine** driving 1 FP propeller Total Power: 2,942kW (4,000hp) 14.5kn B&W 6L35MC 1 x 2 Stroke 6 Cy. 350 x 1050 2942kW (4000bhp) Makita Corp-Japan AuxGen: 3 x 148kW a.c Fuel: 510.0 (r.f.)
8987113 *WDC2297* -	**VANE BROTHERS** *ex* Logan J *-2003* *ex* Marine Glory *-2003* *ex* Jennifer C *-2003* **Vane Line Bunkering Inc** - *Baltimore, MD* *United States of America* MMSI: 366990810 Official number: 643710	**197** 134 -		**1981 St Charles Steel Works Inc — Thibodaux, La** Yd No: 87 Loa 23.32 Br ex - Dght - Lbp - Br md 7.99 Dpth 3.57 Welded, 1 dk	**(B32B2SP) Pusher Tug**	**2 oil engines** geared to sc. shafts driving 2 Propellers Total Power: 1,472kW (2,002hp) Cummins KTA-38-M 2 x Vee 4 Stroke 12 Cy. 159 x 159 each-736kW (1001bhp) Cummins Engine Co Inc-USA
5376337 *SJGE* -	**VANERVIK** *ex* Havden *-2009* *ex* Lidan *-1994* *ex* Vanervik *-1979* *ex* Lidan *-1962* **Hans-Peter Ake Landstrom** - *Gothenburg* *Sweden* MMSI: 265506720	**127** 39 195	Class: (BV)	**1943 Sjotorps Varv & Mekaniska Verkstad — Sjotorp** Converted From: General Cargo Ship-1991 Loa 26.34 Br ex 6.89 Dght 2.998 Lbp 23.86 Br md 6.84 Dpth 2.90 Welded, 1 dk	**(X11B2QN) Sail Training Ship** Hull Material: Iron & Wood Passengers: unberthed: 35; berths: 28	**1 oil engine** eared to sc. shaft driving 1 FP propeller Total Power: 169kW (230hp) Scania DSI11 1 x 4 Stroke 6 Cy. 127 x 145 169kW (230bhp) (new engine 1969) AB Scania Vabis-Sweden
6805452 *D3UB* -	**VANESSA** *ex* Secil Teba *-1995* *ex* Germek *-1971* **Jar Lda** - *Luanda* *Angola* Official number: C-582	*1,199* 826 2,260	Class: RP (BV) (NV)	**1968-05 Kristiansands Mek. Verksted AS — Kristiansand** Yd No: 212 Loa 71.02 Br ex 11.54 Dght 5.328 Lbp 65.26 Br md 11.46 Dpth 6.30 Welded, 1 dk & S dk	**(A31A2GX) General Cargo Ship** Grain: 2,832; Bale: 2,492 Compartments: 2 Ho, ER 2 Ha: (16.7 x 7.0) (17.3 x 7.0)ER Derricks: 3x10t,3x5t; Winches: 4 Ice Capable	**1 oil engine** driving 1 FP propeller Total Power: 1,030kW (1,400hp) 12.5kn MaK 8MU451AK 1 x 4 Stroke 8 Cy. 320 x 450 1030kW (1400bhp) Atlas MaK Maschinenbau GmbH-Kiel AuxGen: 2 x 68kW 380V a.c Fuel: 142.0 (d.f.)
9669043 *WDG8798* -	**VANESSA** - **Offshore Liftboats LLC** - *New Orleans, LA* *United States of America* MMSI: 367581180	**761** - -		**2013-07 Halimar Shipyard LLC — Morgan City, La** Yd No: 173 Loa 35.10 Br ex 20.30 Dght 2.290 Lbp - Br md - Dpth 3.05 Welded, 1 dk	**(B22A2ZM) Offshore Construction Vessel, jack up** Cranes: 1x125t,1x30t	**2 oil engines** reduction geared to sc. shaft (s) driving 2 Propellers Total Power: 1,066kW (1,450hp) Caterpillar C18 2 x 4 Stroke 6 Cy. 145 x 183 each-533kW (725bhp) Caterpillar Inc-USA AuxGen: 2 x 150kW 60Hz a.c
9681637 *9WQP2* -	**VANESSA 9** - **Seabright Sdn Bhd** Sealink Sdn Bhd *Kuching* *Malaysia* Official number: 334932	**498** 149 512	Class: LR (Class contemplated) **100A1** 02/2014 Class contemplated	**2014-02 Sealink Shipyard Sdn Bhd — Miri** Yd No: 184 Loa 48.00 Br ex - Dght 2.500 Lbp 46.20 Br md 11.00 Dpth 3.50 Welded, 1 dk	**(B21B20A) Anchor Handling Tug Supply**	**2 oil engines** reduction geared to sc. shafts driving 2 Propellers Total Power: 2,420kW (3,290hp) Mitsubishi S12R-MPTK 2 x Vee 4 Stroke 12 Cy. 170 x 180 each-1210kW (1645bhp) Mitsubishi Heavy Industries Ltd-Japan
9449637 *9WHL2* -	**VANESSA 12** - **Sealink Sdn Bhd** - *Kuching* *Malaysia* MMSI: 533000763 Official number: 330998	**494** 148 516	Class: LR **100A1** SS 12/2013 offshore tug/supply ship ✠**LMC** Cable: 660.0/26.0 U2 (a)	**2008-12 Sealink Shipyard Sdn Bhd — Miri** Yd No: 164 Loa 48.00 Br ex - Dght 2.500 Lbp 46.20 Br md 11.00 Dpth 3.50 Welded, 1 dk	**(B21B20T) Offshore Tug/Supply Ship** Cranes: 1x1.9t	**2 oil engines** with clutches & sr reverse geared to sc. shafts driving 2 FP propellers Total Power: 1,790kW (2,434hp) 12.0kn Cummins KTA-38-M2 2 x Vee 4 Stroke 12 Cy. 159 x 159 each-895kW (1217bhp) Cummins Engine Co Inc-USA AuxGen: 2 x 150kW 415V 50Hz a.c Thrusters: 1 Thwart. FP thruster (f) Fuel: 517.0 (d.f.)
9480887 *9WHK7* -	**VANESSA 17** *completed as* Sealink Vanessa 17 *-2009* **Sealink Sdn Bhd** - SatCom: Inmarsat C 453300828 *Kuching* *Malaysia* MMSI: 533000797 Official number: 330997	**494** 148 519	Class: LR **100A1** SS 06/2009 offshore tug/supply ship ✠**LMC** Cable: 27.5/26.0 U2 (a)	**2009-06 Sealink Shipyard Sdn Bhd — Miri** Yd No: 165 Loa 48.00 Br ex 11.05 Dght 2.800 Lbp 46.20 Br md 11.00 Dpth 3.50 Welded, 1 dk	**(B21B20T) Offshore Tug/Supply Ship**	**2 oil engines** with clutches & sr reverse geared to sc. shafts driving 2 FP propellers Total Power: 2,984kW (4,058hp) Cummins KTA-50-M2 2 x Vee 4 Stroke 16 Cy. 159 x 159 each-1492kW (2029bhp) Cummins Engine Co Inc-USA AuxGen: 2 x 150kW 415V 50Hz a.c Thrusters: 1 Thwart. FP thruster (f)
9529164 *9WKD9* -	**VANESSA 18** - **Sealink Sdn Bhd** - *Kuching* *Malaysia* MMSI: 533980000 Official number: 333139	**494** 148 522	Class: LR **100A1** SS 03/2010 offshore tug/supply ship ✠**LMC** Cable: 357.5/26.0 U2 (a)	**2010-03 Sealink Shipyard Sdn Bhd — Miri** Yd No: 195 Loa 48.00 Br ex 11.05 Dght 3.400 Lbp 46.20 Br md 11.00 Dpth 3.50 Welded, 1 dk	**(B21B20A) Anchor Handling Tug Supply**	**2 oil engines** with clutches & sr reverse geared to sc. shafts driving 2 FP propellers Total Power: 2,536kW (3,448hp) Cummins KTA-50-M2 2 x Vee 4 Stroke 16 Cy. 159 x 159 each-1268kW (1724bhp) Cummins Engine Co Inc-USA AuxGen: 2 x 150kW 415V 50Hz a.c Thrusters: 1 Thwart. FP thruster (f)
8022107 *DUE2111* -	**VANESSA P 1** *ex* Santa Cruz *-2009* *ex* Kariyushi No. 3 *-1998* **Sta Cruz Shipping Services Corp** - *Lucena* *Philippines* Official number: 04-0000213	*129* 88 17		**1980-10 Suzuki Shipyard Co. Ltd. — Yokkaichi** Yd No: 351 Loa 25.30 Br ex - Dght 1.000 Lbp 24.01 Br md 5.40 Dpth 2.20 Welded, 1 dk	**(A37B2PS) Passenger Ship** Hull Material: Aluminium Alloy Passengers: unberthed: 200	**3 oil engines** geared to sc. shafts driving 3 FP propellers Total Power: 1,191kW (1,620hp) G.M. (Detroit Diesel) 12V-71 3 x Vee 2 Stroke 12 Cy. 108 x 127 each-397kW (540bhp) General Motors Corp-USA

IMO / Call sign	Name / Owner	Tonnage	Class	Builder / Dimensions	Type	Machinery
9529047 *9WKE3* -	**VANESSA XI** **Sealink Sdn Bhd** - SatCom: Inmarsat C 453301436 *Kuching* *Malaysia* MMSI: 533000989 Official number: 333141	**494** 148 509	Class: LR ✠ **100A1** SS 12/2010 offshore tug/supply ship ✠ **LMC** Eq.Ltr: E; Cable: 357.5/26.0 U2 (a)	**2010-12 Sealink Shipyard Sdn Bhd — Miri** Yd No: 174 Loa 48.00 (BB) Br ex 11.05 Dght 3.400 Lbp 46.20 Br md 11.00 Dpth 3.50 Welded, 1 dk	**(B21B20A) Anchor Handling Tug Supply**	**2 oil engines** with clutches & sr reverse geared to sc. shafts driving 2 FP propellers Total Power: 1,790kW (2,434hp) Cummins KTA-38-M2 2 x Vee 4 Stroke 12 Cy. 159 x 159 each-895kW (1217bhp) Cummins Engine Co Inc-USA AuxGen: 2 x 150kW 415V 50Hz a.c Thrusters: 1 Thwart. FP thruster (f)
9627095 *5BAF4* -	**VANGELIS** *launched as* Centrans Rhythm *-2014* **Global Eagle Shipping Ltd** Transmed Shipping Co Ltd *Limassol* *Cyprus* MMSI: 210934000 Official number: 9627095	**94,863** 59,646 179,910 T/cm 124.3	Class: NK (Class contemplated) (LR) ✠ Classed LR until 25/1/14	**2014-01 Qingdao Beihai Shipbuilding Heavy Industry Co Ltd — Qingdao SD** Yd No: BC18.0-30 Loa 295.00 (BB) Br ex 46.06 Dght 18.100 Lbp 285.00 Br md 46.00 Dpth 24.80 Welded, 1 dk	**(A21A2BC) Bulk Carrier** Grain: 201,953 Compartments: 9 Ho, ER 9 Ha: ER	**1 oil engine** driving 1 FP propeller Total Power: 18,660kW (25,370hp) 15.0kn MAN-B&W 6S70MC-C 1 x 2 Stroke 6 Cy. 700 x 2800 18660kW (25370bhp) Dalian Marine Diesel Co Ltd-China AuxGen: 3 x 900kW 450V 60Hz a.c Boilers: AuxB (Comp) 8.7kgf/cm² (8.5bar)
9385350 *ZCOX3* -	**VANGO** **Jennifer A Bonqratz** Van Tuyl Group Inc *George Town* *Cayman Islands (British)* MMSI: 319193000 Official number: 738543	**490** 147 99	Class: AB	**2006-03 Westport Shipyard, Inc. — Westport, Wa** Yd No: 5001 Loa 49.94 Br ex - Dght 2.360 Lbp 43.53 Br md 9.35 Dpth 4.17 Bonded, 1 dk	**(X11A2YP) Yacht** Hull Material: Reinforced Plastic	**2 oil engines** reduction geared to sc. shafts driving 2 FP propellers Total Power: 5,440kW (7,396hp) M.T.U. 16V4000M90 2 x Vee 4 Stroke 16 Cy. 165 x 190 each-2720kW (3698bhp) Detroit Diesel Corporation-Detroit, Mi
9224116 *2HBU7* -	**VANGUARD** *ex* Flinterhunze *-2013* *ex* Hunzedijk *-2005* **Windle Shipping Co Ltd** Faversham Ships Ltd *Peel* *Isle of Man (British)* MMSI: 235102352	**2,548** 1,428 3,300	Class: BV	**2001-01 Tille Scheepsbouw Kootstertille B.V. — Kootstertille** Yd No: 335 Loa 91.25 Br ex - Dght 4.720 Lbp 84.95 Br md 13.75 Dpth 6.25 Welded, 1 dk	**(A31A2GX) General Cargo Ship** Grain: 4,870 TEU 140 C. 140/20' Ice Capable	**1 oil engine** reduction geared to sc. shaft driving 1 FP propeller Total Power: 1,950kW (2,651hp) 13.0kn Wartsila 6L26 1 x 4 Stroke 6 Cy. 260 x 320 1950kW (2651bhp) Wartsila NSD Nederland BV-Netherlands
8114467 - -	**VANGUARD** *ex* Tensho Maru *-1995* - -	**997** 439 1,100		**1981-04 K.K. Miura Zosensho — Saiki** Yd No: 626 Loa 67.27 Br ex - Dght 3.710 Lbp 63.40 Br md 10.51 Dpth 6.02 Welded, 1 dk	**(A31A2GX) General Cargo Ship**	**1 oil engine** driving 1 FP propeller Total Power: 883kW (1,201hp) Hanshin 1 x 4 Stroke 6 Cy. 440 x 780 883kW (1201bhp) The Hanshin Diesel Works Ltd-Japan
7823413 *WTF5649* -	**VANGUARD** **Futura Fisheries Inc** - SatCom: Inmarsat C 430368410 *Kodiak, AK* *United States of America* MMSI: 303684000 Official number: 617802	**221** 66 800		**1980-01 Mid-Coast Marine, Inc. — Coos Bay, Or** Yd No: 9901 Loa 28.66 Br ex 8.06 Dght 2.744 Lbp 26.52 Br md 7.93 Dpth 3.41 Welded, 1 dk	**(B11B2FV) Fishing Vessel**	**2 oil engines** geared to sc. shafts driving 2 FP propellers Total Power: 588kW (800hp) Cummins NTA-855-M 2 x 4 Stroke 6 Cy. 140 x 152 each-294kW (400bhp) Cummins Engine Co Inc-USA
8960684 *SBDM* SD 622	**VANGUARD AV HAVSTENSUND** *ex* Fiona K *-2000* *ex* Westero *-1996* *ex* Gano *-1995* *ex* Gandor *-1995* *ex* Auster *-1995* *ex* Father Oliver *-1995* **SD 622 Vanguard AB** - *Havstenssund* *Sweden* MMSI: 266091000	**110** 33 -		**1983 in the Irish Republic** Loa 19.40 Br ex - Dght 2.900 Lbp - Br md 6.13 Dpth - Welded, 1 dk	**(B11B2FV) Fishing Vessel**	**1 oil engine** driving 1 FP propeller Total Power: 353kW (480hp) Caterpillar 1 x 4 Stroke 353kW (480bhp) Caterpillar Tractor Co-USA
8910237 *SW5999* -	**VANI** **Morgia Vanilia Naftiki Eteria** - *Piraeus* *Greece* MMSI: 237151600 Official number: 9497	*262* 158 402		**1990-03 "Naus" Shipyard Philippou Bros. S.A. — Piraeus** Yd No: 160 Loa 33.30 Br ex 7.05 Dght 2.750 Lbp 32.00 Br md - Dpth 3.20 Welded, 1 dk	**(A13B2TP) Products Tanker** Liq: 450; Liq (Oil): 450 Compartments: 6 Ta, ER	**2 oil engines** sr geared to sc. shafts driving 2 FP propellers Total Power: 242kW (330hp) Delfin UE680LM 2 x 4 Stroke 6 Cy. 127 x 146 each-121kW (165bhp) Puckie Zaklady Mechaniczne Ltd-Puck
7203479 *HSB2166* -	**VANICH** *ex* Wakamiya *-1987* *ex* Takachiho Maru No. 2 *-1985* **Sompong Keyurawichien** - *Bangkok* *Thailand* Official number: 301000608	*1,677* 968 3,470	Class: (NK)	**1971-12 Kyokuyo Shipbuilding & Iron Works Co Ltd — Shimonoseki YC** Yd No: 230 Loa 87.03 (BB) Br ex 12.83 Dght 5.855 Lbp 80.52 Br md 12.81 Dpth 6.35 Welded, 1 dk	**(A13B2TP) Products Tanker** Liq: 3,520; Liq (Oil): 3,520 Compartments: 4 Ta, ER	**1 oil engine** driving 1 FP propeller Total Power: 1,839kW (2,500hp) 11.8kn Hanshin Z6L46SH 1 x 4 Stroke 6 Cy. 460 x 680 1839kW (2500bhp) Hanshin Nainenki Kogyo-Japan AuxGen: 2 x 112kW 440V 60Hz a.c Fuel: 20.0 (d.f.) 100.0 (r.f.) 8.0pd
6613469 *DUUP* -	**VANILLA** *ex* Igloo Wind *-1989* *ex* Tingo *-1984* **Frabelle Fishing Corp** - *Manila* *Philippines* Official number: MNLD001020	*1,203* 722 1,575	Class: (LR) ✠ Classed LR until 28/4/93	**1966-07 Uudenkaupungin Telakka Oy (Nystads Varv Ab) — Uusikaupunki** Yd No: 245 Loa 73.82 (BB) Br ex 10.52 Dght 4.712 Lbp 66.55 Br md 10.51 Dpth 6.35 Welded, 2 dks	**(A34A2GR) Refrigerated Cargo Ship** Ins: 2,036 Compartments: 2 Ho, ER, 2 Tw Dk 4 Ha: (4.0 x 3.5) (5.3 x 4.3)2 (5.2 x 4.3)ER Derricks: 8x3t; Winches: 8	**1 oil engine** driving 1 FP propeller Total Power: 1,103kW (1,500hp) 13.5kn MaK 8M451AK 1 x 4 Stroke 8 Cy. 320 x 450 1103kW (1500bhp) Atlas MaK Maschinenbau GmbH-Kiel AuxGen: 3 x 108kW 450V 60Hz a.c Fuel: 148.0 (d.f.) 5.0pd
8406597 *A8GZ9* -	**VANIN** *ex* Vanino *-2006* **Castletown Enterprises Ltd** Kollintzas Marine Co SA SatCom: Inmarsat B 363702529 *Monrovia* *Liberia* MMSI: 636012685 Official number: 12685	**5,154** 1,741 6,237 T/cm 16.4	Class: (RS) (NV) (BV)	**1985-06 Rauma-Repola Oy — Rauma** Yd No: 287 Loa 113.01 Br ex 18.35 Dght 7.201 Lbp 105.34 Br md 18.31 Dpth 8.51 Welded, 1 dk	**(A13B2TP) Products Tanker** Double Bottom Entire Compartment Length Liq: 5,924; Liq (Oil): 5,924 Compartments: 3 Ta, 8 Wing Ta, ER, 2 Wing Slop Ta, 1 Slop Ta 11 Cargo Pump (s): 8x145m³/hr, 3x190m³/hr Manifold: Bow/CM: 48m Ice Capable	**1 oil engine** driving 1 FP propeller Total Power: 3,960kW (5,384hp) 15.0kn B&W 6DKRN45/120 1 x 2 Stroke 6 Cy. 450 x 1200 3960kW (5384bhp) Bryanskiy Mashinostroitelnyy Zavod (BMZ)-Bryansk AuxGen: 4 x 220kW 380V 50Hz a.c Fuel: 75.5 (d.f.) 623.0 (r.f.)
7053020 - -	**VANINDA NO. 22** *ex* Hansoo No. 1 *-2006* *ex* Tempo No. 306 *-1994* *ex* Tenyo Maru No. 83 *-1988* *ex* Kaiyo Maru No. 7 *-1982* *ex* Taiki Maru No. 2 *-1978* - -	*221* 82 -		**1970 Kyokuyo Shipbuilding & Iron Works Co Ltd — Shimonoseki YC** Yd No: 222 Loa 36.76 Br ex 6.63 Dght 2.693 Lbp 31.02 Br md 6.61 Dpth 3.10 Welded, 1 dk	**(B11B2FV) Fishing Vessel**	**1 oil engine** driving 1 FP propeller Total Power: 662kW (900hp) Niigata 6MG25BX 1 x 4 Stroke 6 Cy. 250 x 320 662kW (900bhp) Niigata Engineering Co Ltd-Japan
6818368 - -	**VANINDA No. 23** *ex* Namhaieo 001 *-1996* *ex* Tempo No. 201 *-1989* *ex* Tokuhiro Maru No. 81 *-1986* - -	*197* 66 150	Class: (KR)	**1968 Tokushima Zosen K.K. — Fukuoka** Yd No: 737 Loa 34.40 Br ex 6.71 Dght 3.039 Lbp 29.32 Br md 6.68 Dpth 3.15 Welded, 1 dk	**(B11A2FS) Stern Trawler**	**1 oil engine** driving 1 FP propeller Total Power: 515kW (700hp) 8.8kn Akasaka 6DH27SS 1 x 4 Stroke 6 Cy. 270 x 420 515kW (700bhp) Akasaka Tekkosho KK (Akasaka DieselLtd)-Japan AuxGen: 2 x 60kW 225V 50Hz a.c
8035180 - -	**VANINO** *ex* Lideka *-2004* *ex* Lydeka *-1997* *ex* Telets *-1992* - -	**746** 223 405	Class: (RS)	**1982-05 Zavod "Leninskaya Kuznitsa" — Kiyev** Yd No: 1507 Loa 54.82 Br ex 9.96 Dght 4.141 Lbp 50.29 Br md - Dpth 5.01 Welded, 1 dk	**(B11A2FS) Stern Trawler** Ins: 414 Compartments: 2 Ho 3 Ha: 3 (1.5 x 1.6) Derricks: 2x1.5t; Winches: 2 Ice Capable	**1 oil engine** driving 1 CP propeller Total Power: 736kW (1,001hp) 12.0kn S.K.L. 8NVD48AU 1 x 4 Stroke 8 Cy. 320 x 480 736kW (1001bhp) VEB Schwermaschinenbau "KarlLiebknecht" (SKL)-Magdeburg AuxGen: 4 x 160kW a.c Fuel: 182.0 (d.f.)
8724779 *UEYS* -	**VANINO** *ex* Nemunas *-2008* *ex* Vostok *-1992* **Tarvi Management Ltd** Baltic Tanker Co Ltd *St Petersburg* *Russia* MMSI: 273331620	**1,896** 713 2,739	Class: RS	**1986-06 Shipbuilding & Shiprepairing Yard 'Ivan Dimitrov' — Rousse** Yd No: 450 Loa 77.53 Br ex 14.34 Dght 4.990 Lbp 73.24 Br md 14.00 Dpth 6.50 Welded, 1dk	**(A13B2TP) Products Tanker** Liq: 2,677; Liq (Oil): 3,513 Compartments: 12 Ta, ER Ice Capable	**1 oil engine** driving 1 FP propeller Total Power: 883kW (1,201hp) 10.2kn S.K.L. 8NVD48A-2U 1 x 4 Stroke 8 Cy. 320 x 480 883kW (1201bhp) VEB Schwermaschinenbau "KarlLiebknecht" (SKL)-Magdeburg AuxGen: 2 x 160kW a.c

IMO / Call sign / Flag	Name / Owner	Tonnage	Class	Builder / Dimensions	Type / Capacity	Machinery
9054030 *UELB* -	**VANINONEFT** *ex Shinko V -2013 ex Shinko 23 -2013* *ex Shinko Maru No. 23 -2007* **Ost-Trans Co Ltd** LLC 'Bosfor-Bunker' *Vladivostok* *Russia* MMSI: 273350490	**723** 327 986	Class: RS (NK)	**1992-07 Kanmon Zosen K.K. — Shimonoseki** Yd No: 537 Converted From: Chemical Tanker-2013 Loa 66.01 (BB) Br ex 10.02 Dght 3.670 Lbp 62.00 Br md 10.00 Dpth 4.50 Welded, 1 dk	**(A13B2TP) Products Tanker** Liq: 1,008; Liq (Oil): 1,008 Compartments: 8 Ta, ER	**1 oil engine** reverse geared to sc. shaft driving 1 CP propeller Total Power: 736kW (1,001hp) 11.0kn Hanshin LH28G 1 x 4 Stroke 6 Cy. 280 x 460 736kW (1001bhp) The Hanshin Diesel Works Ltd-Japan AuxGen: 2 x 126kW a.c Fuel: 40.0 (d.f.)
7831032 *UCXP* -	**VANINSK** - **UTRF-Holding JSC (OAO 'UTRF-Holding')** - *Petropavlovsk-Kamchatskiy* *Russia* MMSI: 273841210 Official number: 791289	**739** 221 332	Class: (RS)	**1979 Volgogradskiy Sudostroitelnyy Zavod — Volgograd** Yd No: 886 Loa 53.75 (BB) Br ex 10.72 Dght 4.290 Lbp 47.92 Br md - Dpth 6.02 Welded, 1 dk	**(B11A2FS) Stern Trawler** Ins: 218 Compartments: 1 Ho, ER 1 Ha: (1.6 x 1.6) Derricks: 1x3.3t Ice Capable	**1 oil engine** driving 1 FP propeller Total Power: 971kW (1,320hp) 12.8kn S.K.L. 8NVD48A-2U 1 x 4 Stroke 8 Cy. 320 x 480 971kW (1320bhp) VEB Schwermaschinenbau "KarlLiebknecht" (SKL)-Magdeburg
7107352 - -	**VANKAREM** - **Sadko Shareholding Co (TOO 'Sadko')** -	**648** 194 313	Class: (RS)	**1970 Khabarovskiy Sudostroitelnyy Zavod im Kirova — Khabarovsk** Yd No: 197 Loa 54.23 Br ex 9.38 Dght 3.810 Lbp 48.80 Br md 9.30 Dpth 4.73 Welded, 1 dk	**(B11A2FT) Trawler** Ins: 284 Compartments: 2 Ho, ER 2 Ha: 2 (1.5 x 1.6) Derricks: 1x2t; Winches: 1 Ice Capable	**1 oil engine** driving 1 FP propeller Total Power: 588kW (799hp) 12.0kn S.K.L. 8NVD48AU 1 x 4 Stroke 8 Cy. 320 x 480 588kW (799bhp) VEB Schwermaschinenbau "KarlLiebknecht" (SKL)-Magdeburg AuxGen: 3 x 100kW Fuel: 140.0 (d.f.)
8977924 *MLZV6* -	**VANLIS III** - **Barbotte Ltd** A E Nomikos Shipping Investments Ltd *London* *United Kingdom* Official number: 718669	*223* 56 -	Class: AB	**1990-03 Baglietto S.p.A. — Varazze** Yd No: 10131/16 Loa 32.81 Br ex 7.40 Dght 2.630 Lbp 29.09 Br md 7.21 Dpth 3.67 Welded, 1 dk	**(X11A2YP) Yacht** Hull Material: Aluminium Alloy	**2 oil engines** geared to sc. shafts driving 2 Propellers Total Power: 2,946kW (4,006hp) M.T.U. 12V396TB93 2 x Vee 4 Stroke 12 Cy. 165 x 185 each-1473kW (2003bhp) MTU Friedrichshafen GmbH-Friedrichshafen AuxGen: 2 x 45kW
7928706 *9HA2082* -	**VANNA** *ex Tom Elba -2009 ex Helga Essberger -1992* **Marfa Tankers Ltd** Gaulos Shipping Co Ltd *Valletta* *Malta* MMSI: 249932000 Official number: 7928706	**1,958** 779 2,544 T/cm 8.9	Class: GL	**1980-10 Buesumer Werft GmbH — Buesum** (Hull) **1980-10 Schlichting-Werft GmbH — Luebeck** Yd No: 1424 Loa 80.81 (BB) Br ex 13.42 Dght 5.131 Lbp 74.14 Br md 13.39 Dpth 7.05 Welded, 1 dk.	**(A12B2TR) Chemical/Products Tanker** Double Hull (13F) Liq: 3,018; Liq (Oil): 3,018 Compartments: 16 Ta (s.stl), ER 16 Cargo Pump (s) Ice Capable	**1 oil engine** reduction geared to sc. shaft driving 1 CP propeller Total Power: 1,618kW (2,200hp) 12.3kn MaK 6M453AK 1 x 4 Stroke 6 Cy. 320 x 420 1618kW (2200bhp) Krupp MaK Maschinenbau GmbH-Kiel AuxGen: 1 x 240kW 440V 60Hz a.c, 2 x 228kW 220/440V 60Hz a.c Thrusters: 1 Thwart. FP thruster (f) Fuel: 148.0
9364502 *IFNT2* -	**VANNA C** - **Rimorchiatori Riuniti Panfido e Compagnia Srl** - *Venice* *Italy* MMSI: 247191300 Official number: VE773	*355* 55 190	Class: RI (AB)	**2007-05 Cantieri San Marco Srl — La Spezia** Yd No: 13 Loa 25.75 Br ex - Dght 3.240 Lbp 24.25 Br md 12.00 Dpth 4.40 Welded, 1 dk	**(B32A2ST) Tug**	**2 oil engines** reduction geared to sc. shafts driving 2 Propellers Total Power: 2,400kW (3,264hp) MaK 6M20 2 x 4 Stroke 6 Cy. 200 x 300 each-1200kW (1632bhp) Caterpillar Motoren GmbH & Co. KG-Germany
9002025 *SBNM* -	**VANO** - **Waxholms Angfartygs AB** - *Vaxholm* *Sweden* MMSI: 265520400	**299** 118 50		**1991-04 Oskarshamns Varv AB — Oskarshamn** (Hull) Yd No: 528 **1991-04 Djupviks Batvarv — Fagerfjall** Yd No: 350 Loa - Br ex 7.52 Dght 1.280 Lbp 37.72 Br md 7.51 Dpth 2.78 Welded, 1 dk	**(A37B2PS) Passenger Ship** Hull Material: Aluminium Alloy Passengers: unberthed: 340	**3 oil engines** with clutches & sr geared to sc. shafts driving 3 FP propellers Total Power: 1,764kW (2,397hp) 20.0kn MAN D2842LYE 3 x Vee 4 Stroke 12 Cy. 128 x 142 each-588kW (799bhp) MAN Nutzfahrzeuge AG-Nuernberg AuxGen: 1 x 110kW 380V 50Hz a.c, 1 x 60kW 380V 50Hz a.c
8997572 *2FBW2* B 74	**VANQUISH** - **Lenger Seafoods Ireland Ltd** Lenger Seafoods BV *Belfast* *United Kingdom* MMSI: 235089955 Official number: C19987	**246** 73 -		**2003-01 Steelkit Ltd. — Borth** Loa 24.80 Br ex - Dght - Lbp 23.14 Br md 8.54 Dpth 3.52 Welded, 1 dk	**(B11A2FS) Stern Trawler**	**1 oil engine** reduction geared to sc. shaft driving 1 Propeller Total Power: 392kW (533hp) Mitsubishi S6R2-MPTK 1 x 4 Stroke 6 Cy. 170 x 220 392kW (533bhp) Mitsubishi Heavy Industries Ltd-Japan
9116199 *PHCU* -	**VANQUISH** *ex Varmland -2005 launched as Wilhelm -1995* **Scheepvaartonderneming 'Gretina' BV** Holwerda Shipmanagement BV *Heerenveen* *Netherlands* MMSI: 246141000 Official number: 44193	**2,997** 1,398 4,624	Class: GL	**1995-06 J.J. Sietas KG Schiffswerft GmbH & Co. — Hamburg** Yd No: 1114 Loa 99.97 (BB) Br ex 16.74 Dght 5.950 Lbp 94.70 Br md 16.50 Dpth 7.63 Welded, 1 dk	**(A33A2CC) Container Ship (Fully Cellular)** Grain: 4,747; Bale: 4,458 TEU 326 incl 40 ref C. Compartments: 3 Ho, ER 3 Ha: (12.4 x 7.9)2 (24.9 x 13.1)ER Ice Capable	**1 oil engine** with flexible couplings & sr geared to sc. shaft driving 1 CP propeller Total Power: 3,250kW (4,419hp) 15.9kn MaK 8M32 1 x 4 Stroke 8 Cy. 320 x 480 3250kW (4419bhp) Krupp MaK Maschinenbau GmbH-Kiel Thrusters: 1 Thwart. FP thruster (f)
1008891 *ZCOX7* -	**VANQUISH** - **Wilkes Holdings Pty Ltd** - *George Town* *Cayman Islands (British)* MMSI: 319978000 Official number: 738546	**197** 59 47	Class: LR ✠ **100A1** SS 03/2011 SSC Yacht, mono HSC LDC G6 **LMC** Cable: 320.0/12.5 U2 (a)	**2006-03 Palmer Johnson Yachts LLC — Sturgeon Bay WI** Yd No: 240 Loa 36.50 Br ex 7.41 Dght 1.500 Lbp 30.48 Br md 7.40 Dpth 3.58 Welded, 1 dk	**(X11A2YP) Yacht**	**2 oil engines** with clutches, flexible couplings & sr reverse geared to sc. shafts driving 2 FP propellers Total Power: 4,080kW (5,548hp) M.T.U. 12V4000M90 2 x Vee 4 Stroke 12 Cy. 165 x 190 each-2040kW (2774bhp) MTU Friedrichshafen GmbH-Friedrichshafen AuxGen: 2 x 54kW 400V 50Hz a.c Thrusters: 1 Thwart. FP thruster (f)
9375135 *PHOW* -	**VANQUISH** - **Veka Compaan BV & Veka Global 3 BV** VMS Shipping BV *Werkendam* *Netherlands* MMSI: 244561000 Official number: 50497	**3,871** 1,333 4,800	Class: BV	**2012-04 Hangzhou Dongfeng Shipbuilding Co Ltd — Hangzhou ZJ** (Hull) Yd No: (740) **2012-04 Bijlsma Shipyard BV — Lemmer** Yd No: 740 Loa 99.97 (BB) Br ex - Dght 5.850 Lbp 93.24 Br md 15.85 Dpth 8.85 Welded, 1 dk	**(A31A2GX) General Cargo Ship** Grain: 6,648 TEU 354	**1 oil engine** reduction geared to sc. shaft driving 1 CP propeller Total Power: 3,280kW (4,459hp) 15.0kn Wartsila 8R32LN 1 x 4 Stroke 8 Cy. 320 x 350 3280kW (4459bhp) Wartsila Finland Oy-Finland AuxGen: 1 x 264kW 50Hz a.c, 1 x 680kW 50Hz a.c Thrusters: 1 Tunnel thruster (f); 1 Tunnel thruster (a) Fuel: 430.0
9633056 *WDF8434* -	**VANQUISH** - **Nelson Fishing Inc** - *Dartmouth, MA* *United States of America* MMSI: 367494810 Official number: 1230897	**297** - -		**2011-03 Williams Fabrication, Inc. — Coden, Al** Yd No: WF119 Loa 27.00 (BB) Br ex - Dght - Lbp - Br md 8.86 Dpth 4.29 Welded, 1 dk	**(B11B2FV) Fishing Vessel**	**1 oil engine** reduction geared to sc. shaft driving 1 Propeller Total Power: 746kW (1,014hp) Caterpillar 3508B 1 x Vee 4 Stroke 8 Cy. 170 x 190 746kW (1014bhp) Caterpillar Inc-USA Thrusters: 1 Thwart. FP thruster (f)
9451769 *9V8803* -	**VANSHI** - **Vanshi Shipping Pte Ltd** Adani Shipping Pte Ltd SatCom: Inmarsat C 456506011 *Singapore* *Singapore* MMSI: 565060000 Official number: 396261	**91,829** 59,082 175,337	Class: LR ✠ **100A1** SS 01/2011 bulk carrier CSR BC-A GRAB (25) Nos. 2, 4, 6 & 8 holds may be empty ESP **ShipRight** (CM, ACS (B)) *IWS LI ✠ **LMC** **UMS** Eq.Ltr: B*; Cable: 742.5/107.0 U3 (a)	**2011-01 HHIC-Phil Inc — Subic** Yd No: 025 Loa 289.80 (BB) Br ex 45.06 Dght 18.100 Lbp 279.00 Br md 45.00 Dpth 24.60 Welded, 1 dk	**(A21A2BC) Bulk Carrier** Grain: 198,000 Compartments: 9 Ho, ER 9 Ha: ER	**1 oil engine** driving 1 FP propeller Total Power: 18,660kW (25,370hp) 15.3kn MAN-B&W 6S70MC-C 1 x 2 Stroke 6 Cy. 700 x 2800 18660kW (25370bhp) Hyundai Heavy Industries Co Ltd-South Korea AuxGen: 3 x 760kW 450V 60Hz a.c Boilers: e (ex.g.) 12.0kgf/cm² (11.8bar), WTAuxB (o.f.) 9.2kgf/cm² (9.0bar)
9628192 *9HA3435* -	**VANTAGE** - **Undine Shipping Co** Costamare Shipping Co SA *Valletta* *Malta* MMSI: 229598000 Official number: 9628192	**95,390** 56,260 110,544	Class: AB	**2013-11 Sungdong Shipbuilding & Marine Engineering Co Ltd — Tongyeong** Yd No: 4024 Loa 299.95 (BB) Br ex - Dght 14.500 Lbp 288.50 Br md 48.20 Dpth 24.60 Welded, 1 dk	**(A33A2CC) Container Ship (Fully Cellular)** TEU 8827 incl 1462 ref C	**1 oil engine** driving 1 FP propeller Total Power: 47,430kW (64,486hp) 22.0kn MAN-B&W 9S90ME-C8 1 x 2 Stroke 9 Cy. 900 x 3188 47430kW (64486bhp) Hyundai Heavy Industries Co Ltd-South Korea AuxGen: 2 x 3860kW a.c, 2 x 4350kW a.c Thrusters: 1 Tunnel thruster (f) Fuel: 900.0 (d.f.) 8630.0 (r.f.)

9375111 **VANTAGE**
PBMC
-
Vantage CV
-
Werkendam *Netherlands*
MMSI: 244985000
Official number: 48535

3,871 Class: BV
1,333
3,650

2007-11 Oy Wartsila Ab — Vaasa (Hull launched by) Yd No: (738)
2007-11 Bijlsma Shipyard BV — Lemmer (Hull) Yd No: 738
Loa 99.97 (BB) Br ex - Dght 5.000
Lbp 91.55 Br md 15.85 Dpth 8.85
Welded, 1 dk

(A31A2GX) General Cargo Ship
TEU 354 incl 120 ref C.

1 oil engine reduction geared to sc. shaft driving 1 CP propeller
Total Power: 3,280kW (4,459hp) 15.0kn
Wartsila 8R32
1 x 4 Stroke 8 Cy. 320 x 350 3280kW (4459bhp)
Wartsila Finland Oy-Finland
AuxGen: 1 x 680kW 440V 50Hz a.c, 2 x 264kW 440V 50Hz a.c
Thrusters: 1 Tunnel thruster (f); 1 Tunnel thruster (a)

9242704 **VANTAGE**
LMHY3 *ex* Veritas Vantage *-2012*
- *launched as* Veritas Viking III *-2002*
Eidesvik Shipping AS
Eidesvik AS
Haugesund *Norway (NIS)*
MMSI: 257871000

8,186 Class: NV
2,455
3,984

2002-04 Stocznia Gdanska - Grupa Stoczni Gdynia SA — Gdansk (Hull) Yd No: 8248/01
2002-04 Mjellem & Karlsen Verft AS — Bergen Yd No: 155
Loa 93.45 (BB) Br ex 22.00 Dght 7.050
Lbp 81.30 Br md 22.00 Dpth 8.60
Welded

(B31A2SR) Research Survey Vessel
Cranes: 2x9t

2 oil engines reduction geared to sc. shafts driving 2 CP propellers
Total Power: 8,636kW (11,742hp) 11.3kn
MaK 9M32C
2 x 4 Stroke 9 Cy. 320 x 480 each-4318kW (5871bhp)
Caterpillar Motoren GmbH & Co. KG-Germany
AuxGen: 1 x 2200kW 440V 60Hz a.c, 2 x 2360kW 440V 60Hz a.c
Thrusters: 1 Retract. directional thruster (f); 1 Tunnel thruster (f); 1 Tunnel thruster (a)
Fuel: 2481.0 14.5pd

1011288 **VANTAGE**
ZGAZ8
-
The Blue Team Inc
-
George Town *Cayman Islands (British)*
MMSI: 319724000
Official number: 742944

395 Class: LR
- ✠ **100A1** SS 06/2010
- SSC
Yacht, mono
HSC
G6
Cable: 110.0/17.5 U2 (a)

2010-06 Palmer Johnson Yachts LLC — Sturgeon Bay WI Yd No: 259
Loa 45.70 Br ex 8.68 Dght 1.900
Lbp 38.10 Br md 8.38 Dpth 4.02
Welded, 1 dk

(X11A2YP) Yacht
Hull Material: Aluminium Alloy

2 oil engines with clutches, flexible couplings & sr reverse geared to sc. shafts driving 2 FP propellers
Total Power: 5,440kW (7,396hp) 26.8kn
M.T.U. 16V4000M90
2 x Vee 4 Stroke 16 Cy. 165 x 190 each-2720kW (3698bhp)
MTU Friedrichshafen GmbH-Friedrichshafen
AuxGen: 2 x 99kW 230V 50Hz a.c
Thrusters: 1 Thwart. FP thruster (f)

8986664 **VANTAGE**
WDB5965
-
Nelson Fishing Inc
-
Dartmouth, MA *United States of America*
MMSI: 366915690
Official number: 1150113

194
58
-

2003 Williams Fabrication, Inc. — Coden, Al Yd No: WF110
L reg 23.62 Br ex - Dght -
Lbp - Br md 7.31 Dpth 4.26
Welded, 1 dk

(B11B2FV) Fishing Vessel

1 oil engine driving 1 Propeller

9429338 **VANTEK 6**
9VNX4 *ex* Vanda *-2012*
- **Sentek Energy Pte Ltd**
Sentek Marine & Trading Pte Ltd
Singapore *Singapore*
MMSI: 563774000
Official number: 393086

4,419 Class: BV
1,976
6,300

2009-02 PT Dok dan Perkapalan Surabaya (Persero) — Surabaya Yd No: 06599
Loa 93.00 Br ex - Dght 7.200
Lbp 87.45 Br md 17.50 Dpth 9.00
Welded, 1 dk

(A13B2TP) Products Tanker
Double Hull (13F)
Liq: 6,950; Liq (Oil): 6,950
Compartments: 12 Wing Ta, ER

2 oil engines reduction geared to sc. shafts driving 2 FP propellers
Total Power: 3,680kW (5,004hp) 12.5kn
Yanmar 6EY26
2 x 4 Stroke 6 Cy. 260 x 385 each-1840kW (2502bhp)
Yanmar Diesel Engine Co Ltd-Japan
AuxGen: 2 x 320kW 60Hz a.c

8518613 **VANUATU FERRY**
- *ex* Moorea Ferry *-2014* *ex* New Himeji *-2001*
- **Vanuatu Ferry Ltd**

Port Vila *Vanuatu*

699 Class: (BV)
-
364

1986-03 Kochi Jyuko (Eiho Zosen) K.K. — Kochi Yd No: 1838
Loa 57.03 Br ex - Dght 3.112
Lbp 54.01 Br md 13.01 Dpth 9.02
Welded, 2 dks

(A36A2PR) Passenger/Ro-Ro Ship (Vehicles)
Passengers: unberthed: 488
Bow ramp
Stern ramp
Compartments: 1 Ho, ER
2 Ha: ER

2 oil engines driving 2 FP propellers
Total Power: 2,354kW (3,200hp) 14.5kn
Niigata 6M31AGTE
2 x 4 Stroke 6 Cy. 310 x 530 each-1177kW (1600bhp)
Niigata Engineering Co Ltd-Japan

8522016 **VANY**
- *ex* Brandi Sea *-2002* *ex* Orichi *-1995*
- **Talleres Navales del Golfo SA de CV**

1,898 Class: (RS)
569
690

1985-02 VEB Volkswerft Stralsund — Stralsund Yd No: 667
Loa 62.26 Br ex - Dght 5.131
Lbp 55.02 Br md 13.81 Dpth 9.22
Welded, 2 dks

(B11A2FS) Stern Trawler
Ins: 580
Ice Capable

2 oil engines sr geared to sc. shaft driving 1 CP propeller
Total Power: 1,766kW (2,402hp) 12.9kn
S.K.L. 8VD26/20AL-2
2 x 4 Stroke 8 Cy. 200 x 260 each-883kW (1201bhp)
VEB Schwermaschinenbau "KarlLiebknecht" (SKL)-Magdeburg
AuxGen: 1 x 640kW a.c, 3 x 568kW a.c, 1 x 260kW d.c

9448138 **VANY RICKMERS**
V7RX4
-
Onchan Navigation Ltd
Rickmers Shipmanagement (Singapore) Pte Ltd
Majuro *Marshall Islands*
MMSI: 538003594
Official number: 3594

47,090 Class: GL (NV)
14,315
12,300
T/cm
45.6

2010-02 Xiamen Shipbuilding Industry Co Ltd — Xiamen FJ Yd No: XSI460A
Loa 182.80 (BB) Br ex 31.53 Dght 9.000
Lbp 170.68 Br md 31.50 Dpth 31.80
Welded, 12 dks incl. 3 liftable dks.

(A35B2RV) Vehicles Carrier
Side door/ramp (s)
Len: 20.00 Wid: 4.70 Swl: 10
Quarter stern door/ramp (s. a.)
Len: 32.50 Wid: 7.50 Swl: 120
Cars: 4,943

1 oil engine driving 1 FP propeller
Total Power: 14,220kW (19,334hp) 20.0kn
MAN-B&W 9S50MC-C
1 x 2 Stroke 9 Cy. 500 x 2000 14220kW (19334bhp)
Hyundai Heavy Industries Co Ltd-South Korea
AuxGen: 2 x 1050kW 450V a.c, 1 x 750kW 450V a.c
Thrusters: 1 Tunnel thruster (f)
Fuel: 170.0 (d.f.) 3500.0 (r.f.) 57.0pd

8657471 **VAPOR**
9AA2945
- **Marijo Ercegovic**
-
Split *Croatia*
Official number: 5T-839

197 Class: CS
95
-

2005 Shipyard 'Viktor Lenac' dd — Rijeka Yd No: 051
Loa 30.40 Br ex - Dght 1.240
Lbp 25.70 Br md 7.50 Dpth 3.45
Welded, 1 dk

(A37B2PS) Passenger Ship

1 oil engine reduction geared to sc. shaft driving 1 FP propeller
Total Power: 219kW (298hp)
Iveco Aifo 8281 SRM32
1 x 219kW (298bhp)
IVECO AIFO S.p.A.-Pregnana Milanese

8835803 **VARAD**
-
- **Government of The Republic of India (Coast Guard)**
-
Mumbai *India*

1,367 Class: (IR) (AB)
410
191

1990-07 Goa Shipyard Ltd. — Goa Yd No: 1157
Loa 74.60 Br ex 11.39 Dght 3.240
Lbp 69.00 Br md 11.37 Dpth 7.89
Welded, 3 dk

(B34H2SQ) Patrol Vessel

2 oil engines driving 1 FP propeller
Total Power: 9,416kW (12,802hp) 22.0kn
Pielstick 16PA6V280
2 x Vee 4 Stroke 16 Cy. 280 x 290 each-4708kW (6401bhp)
Kirloskar Oil Engines Ltd-India
AuxGen: 4 x 212kW 415V 50Hz a.c, 1 x 159kW 415V 50Hz a.c
Fuel: 62.0 (d.f.)

9039626 **VARADA BLESSING**
9V8943 *ex* Dubai Titan *-2010* *ex* Titan Virgo *-2007*
- *ex* Folk Star *-2005* *ex* Siam *-2004*
Varada One Pte Ltd
Varada Ship Management Pte Ltd
SatCom: Inmarsat C 456433610
Singapore *Singapore*
MMSI: 564336000
Official number: 396422

156,539 Class: LR (NV)
108,433 **100A1** SS 05/2008
299,994 Double Hull oil tanker
T/cm ESP
171.2 **LMC** **UMS IGS**
Eq.Ltr: E*;
Cable: 770.0/117.0 U3 (a)

1993-05 Daewoo Shipbuilding & Heavy Machinery Ltd — Geoje Yd No: 5071
Loa 332.00 (BB) Br ex 58.00 Dght 22.022
Lbp 320.00 Br md 57.20 Dpth 30.40
Welded, 1 dk

(A13A2TV) Crude Oil Tanker
Double Hull
Liq: 332,781; Liq (Oil): 332,781
Compartments: 5 Ta, 10 Wing Ta, 2 Wing Slop Ta, ER
3 Cargo Pump (s): 3x5000m³/hr

1 oil engine not applicable driving 1 FP propeller
Total Power: 23,470kW (31,910hp) 15.0kn
B&W 7S80MC
1 x 2 Stroke 7 Cy. 800 x 3056 23470kW (31910bhp)
Korea Heavy Industries & ConstrCo Ltd (HANJUNG)-South Korea
AuxGen: 3 x 940kW 450V 60Hz a.c
Boilers: e (ex.g.) 24.0kgf/cm² (23.5bar), WTAuxB (o.f.) 17.9kgf/cm² (17.6bar)
Fuel: 323.2 (d.f.) 6737.2 (r.f.) 85.7pd

9468621 **VARADA BUZIOS**
9V9434
-
Varada Two Pte Ltd
Varada Ship Management Pte Ltd
Singapore *Singapore*
MMSI: 566101000
Official number: 397077

1,922 Class: NV
647
1,851

2011-07 ABG Shipyard Ltd — Surat Yd No: 325
Loa 63.40 Br ex 15.82 Dght 4.800
Lbp 56.52 Br md 15.80 Dpth 6.80
Welded, 1 dk

(B21B20A) Anchor Handling Tug Supply

2 oil engines reduction geared to sc. shafts driving 2 CP propellers
Total Power: 4,516kW (6,140hp) 10.5kn
General Electric 7FDM12
2 x Vee 4 Stroke 12 Cy. 229 x 267 each-2258kW (3070bhp)
General Electric Co.-Lynn, Ma
AuxGen: 2 x a.c, 2 x a.c
Thrusters: 2 Tunnel thruster (f)

9468633 **VARADA IBIZA**
9V9616
-
Varada Ten Pte Ltd
Varada Ship Management Pte Ltd
Singapore *Singapore*
MMSI: 566284000
Official number: 397356

1,931 Class: NV
647
1,500

2012-06 ABG Shipyard Ltd — Surat Yd No: 326
Loa 63.40 Br ex - Dght 4.800
Lbp 56.55 Br md 15.80 Dpth 6.80
Welded, 1 dk

(B21B20A) Anchor Handling Tug Supply

2 oil engines reduction geared to sc. shafts driving 2 CP propellers
Total Power: 4,516kW (6,140hp) 10.5kn
General Electric 7FDM12
2 x Vee 4 Stroke 12 Cy. 229 x 267 each-2258kW (3070bhp)
General Electric Co.-Lynn, Ma
AuxGen: 2 x a.c, 2 x a.c
Thrusters: 2 Tunnel thruster (f); 1 Tunnel thruster (a)

9369588 **VARADA ILHEUS**
5BQM3 *ex* Scan Superior *-2012*
- **Varada Three Shipping (Cyprus) Ltd**
Varada Marine Pte Ltd
Limassol *Cyprus*
MMSI: 210135000

1,969 Class: NV
591
1,575

2012-09 ABG Shipyard Ltd — Surat Yd No: 240
Loa 63.40 Br ex 15.83 Dght 4.600
Lbp 54.00 Br md 15.80 Dpth 6.80
Welded, 1 dk

(B21B20A) Anchor Handling Tug Supply

2 oil engines reduction geared to sc. shafts driving 2 CP propellers
Total Power: 4,780kW (6,498hp) 10.5kn
Bergens C25: 33L8P
2 x 4 Stroke 8 Cy. 250 x 330 each-2390kW (3249bhp)
Rolls Royce Marine AS-Norway
AuxGen: 3 x 425kW 440V 60Hz a.c
Thrusters: 1 Thwart. CP thruster (f)

IMO / Call sign	Name / Owner	Tonnage	Class	Builder / Dimensions	Type	Machinery
9468865 *9V9166* -	**VARADA IPANEMA** **Varada Two Pte Ltd** Varada Ship Management Pte Ltd SatCom: Inmarsat C 456380910 *Singapore* *Singapore* MMSI: 563809000 Official number: 396723	**1,922** 647 1,350	Class: NV	**2011-02 ABG Shipyard Ltd — Surat** Yd No: 324 Loa 63.40 Br ex - Dght 4.800 Lbp 56.52 Br md 15.80 Dpth 6.80 Welded, 1 dk	**(B21B20A) Anchor Handling Tug Supply**	**2 oil engines** reduction geared to sc. shafts driving 2 CP propellers Total Power: 4,516kW (6,140hp) 10.5kn GE Marine 12V228 2 x Vee 4 Stroke 12 Cy. 229 x 267 each-2258kW (3070bhp) General Electric Co.-Lynn, Ma AuxGen: 2 x 500kW a.c, 2 x a.c Thrusters: 2 Tunnel thruster (f); 1 Tunnel thruster (a)
9169536 *9V9369* -	**VARADA LALIMA** *ex Kythira -2011 ex Emerald Queen -2010* **Varada One Pte Ltd** Ledux Corporation *Singapore* *Singapore* MMSI: 566001000 Official number: 396975	**57,943** 31,693 107,176 T/cm 91.0	Class: NK	**1997-12 Koyo Dockyard Co Ltd — Mihara HS** Yd No: 2081 Loa 246.80 Br ex - Dght 14.798 Lbp 235.00 Br md 42.00 Dpth 21.30 Welded, 1 dk	**(A13A2TV) Crude Oil Tanker** Double Hull (13F) Liq: 122,296; Liq (Oil): 122,296 Cargo Heating Coils 3 Cargo Pump (s)	**1 oil engine** driving 1 FP propeller Total Power: 13,130kW (17,852hp) 14.6kn B&W 7S60MC 1 x 2 Stroke 7 Cy. 600 x 2292 13130kW (17852bhp) Hitachi Zosen Corp-Japan Fuel: 3960.0
9468657 *9V9952* -	**VARADA MARESIAS** **Varada Three Pte Ltd** Varada Ship Management Pte Ltd *Singapore* *Singapore* MMSI: 566459000 Official number: 397784	**1,931** 647 1,850	Class: NV	**2013-08 ABG Shipyard Ltd — Surat** Yd No: 328 Loa 63.40 Br ex - Dght 4.800 Lbp 56.55 Br md 15.80 Dpth 6.80 Welded, 1 dk	**(B21B20A) Anchor Handling Tug Supply**	**2 oil engines** reduction geared to sc. shafts driving 2 CP propellers Total Power: 4,516kW (6,140hp) 10.5kn General Electric 7FDM12 2 x Vee 4 Stroke 12 Cy. 229 x 267 each-2258kW (3070bhp) General Electric Co.-Lynn, Ma AuxGen: 2 x a.c, 2 x a.c
9591909 *9V9615* -	**VARADA QUEEN** **Varada Marine Pte Ltd** Nkrah Investments Ltd *Singapore* *Singapore* MMSI: 566283000 Official number: 397355	**1,291** 387 879	Class: AB	**2011-12 ABG Shipyard Ltd — Surat** Yd No: 346 Loa 53.00 Br ex 13.81 Dght 4.800 Lbp 45.00 Br md 13.80 Dpth 6.00 Welded, 1 dk	**(B21B20A) Anchor Handling Tug Supply**	**2 oil engines** reduction geared to sc. shafts driving 2 Propellers Total Power: 5,440kW (7,396hp) 11.0kn Wartsila 8L26 2 x 4 Stroke 8 Cy. 260 x 320 each-2720kW (3698bhp) Wartsila Italia SpA-Italy AuxGen: 2 x 750kW a.c, 2 x 350kW a.c Fuel: 740.0
9468645 *9V9951* -	**VARADA SANTOS** **Global Bulk Carriers Pte Ltd** Varada Ship Management Pte Ltd *Singapore* *Singapore* MMSI: 566458000 Official number: 397783	**1,931** 647 1,500	Class: NV	**2012-07 ABG Shipyard Ltd — Surat** Yd No: 327 Loa 63.40 Br ex - Dght 4.800 Lbp 56.50 Br md 15.80 Dpth 6.80 Welded, 1 dk	**(B21B20A) Anchor Handling Tug Supply**	**2 oil engines** reduction geared to sc. shafts driving 2 CP propellers Total Power: 4,516kW (6,140hp) 10.5kn General Electric 7FDM12 2 x Vee 4 Stroke 12 Cy. 229 x 267 each-2258kW (3070bhp) General Electric Co.-Lynn, Ma AuxGen: 2 x a.c, 2 x a.c Thrusters: 2 Tunnel thruster (f); 1 Tunnel thruster (a)
8818154 *MHBM9* -	**VARAGEN** **Orkney Islands Council** Orkney Ferries Ltd *Kirkwall* *United Kingdom* MMSI: 232000550 Official number: 710153	**928** 312 321	Class: LR ✠ **100A1** CS 01/2013 ferry U.K. coastal and Orkney Islands service ✠ **LMC** **UMS** Eq.Ltr: (J) ; Cable: 357.5/26.0 U3	**1989-06 Cochrane Shipbuilders Ltd. — Selby** Yd No: 162 Loa 49.95 Br ex 11.72 Dght 3.610 Lbp 45.75 Br md 11.40 Dpth 4.50 Welded, 1 dk	**(A36A2PR) Passenger/Ro-Ro Ship (Vehicles)** Passengers: unberthed: 144 Bow door & ramp Cars: 33	**2 oil engines** with clutches, flexible couplings & sr geared to sc. shafts driving 2 CP propellers Total Power: 1,580kW (2,148hp) 14.5kn Caterpillar 3512TA 2 x Vee 4 Stroke 12 Cy. 170 x 190 each-790kW (1074bhp) Caterpillar Inc-USA AuxGen: 2 x 80kW 415V 50Hz a.c Thrusters: 1 Thwart. FP thruster (f)
9088976 - -	**VARAHA** **Government of The Republic of India (Coast Guard)** - *India*	*1,367* 410 191	Class: (AB) (IR)	**1992-02 Goa Shipyard Ltd. — Goa** Yd No: 1158 Loa 74.60 Br ex 11.39 Dght 3.240 Lbp 69.00 Br md 11.37 Dpth 7.89 Welded, 1 dk	**(B34H2SQ) Patrol Vessel**	**2 oil engines** sr geared to sc. shafts driving 2 CP propellers Total Power: 9,416kW (12,802hp) 22.0kn Pielstick 16PA6V280 2 x Vee 4 Stroke 16 Cy. 280 x 290 each-4708kW (6401bhp) (made 1988) Kirloskar Oil Engines Ltd-India AuxGen: 4 x 213kW 415V 50Hz a.c, 1 x 159kW 415V 50Hz a.c
9113757 *VVPM* -	**VARAHI** **New Mangalore Port Trust** - *Mumbai* *India* MMSI: 419091800 Official number: 2621	**374** 112 141	Class: IR	**1995-11 Cochin Shipyard Ltd — Ernakulam** Yd No: BY-19 Loa 32.90 Br ex 9.99 Dght 3.160 Lbp 31.50 Br md 9.97 Dpth 4.25 Welded, 1 dk	**(B32A2ST) Tug**	**2 oil engines** gearing integral to driving 2 Voith-Schneider propellers Total Power: 2,540kW (3,454hp) 12.0kn Nohab 6R25 2 x 4 Stroke 6 Cy. 250 x 300 each-1270kW (1727bhp) Wartsila Diesel AB-Sweden AuxGen: 2 x 100kW 415V 50Hz a.c Fuel: 50.0 (d.f.)
7337919 *LNOA* N-260VV	**VARAK** **Nordland Havfiske AS** - *Aalesund* *Norway* MMSI: 258227000	**548** 164 -	Class: (NV)	**1974-04 Bodo Skipsverft & Mek. Verksted AS — Bodo** Yd No: 38 Loa 46.51 Br ex 9.00 Dght 4.470 Lbp 40.01 Br md 8.95 Dpth 6.51 Welded, 1 dk & S dk	**(B11A2FS) Stern Trawler** Ice Capable	**1 oil engine** driving 1 CP propeller Total Power: 1,103kW (1,500hp) MaK 8M451AK 1 x 4 Stroke 8 Cy. 320 x 450 1103kW (1500bhp) MaK Maschinenbau GmbH-Kiel AuxGen: 2 x 84kW 220V 50Hz a.c
9395044 *C4SQ2* -	**VARAMO** **Varamo Shipping Co Ltd** Marlow Navigation Co Ltd *Limassol* *Cyprus* MMSI: 210950000	**15,375** 5,983 18,322	Class: GL	**2007-02 Zhejiang Ouhua Shipbuilding Co Ltd — Zhoushan ZJ** Yd No: 2037 Loa 166.15 (BB) Br ex - Dght 9.500 Lbp 155.08 Br md 25.00 Dpth 14.20 Welded, 1 dk	**(A33A2CC) Container Ship (Fully Cellular)** TEU 1296 C Ho 472 TEU C Dk 824 TEU incl 390 ref C Cranes: 2x40t	**1 oil engine** driving 1 FP propeller Total Power: 11,200kW (15,228hp) 19.0kn MAN-B&W 8L58/64 1 x 4 Stroke 8 Cy. 580 x 640 11200kW (15228bhp) MAN B&W Diesel AG-Augsburg AuxGen: 4 x 1600kW 450/220V a.c Thrusters: 1 Tunnel thruster (f)
9089205 *TC9066* -	**VARAN 1** **Varan Denizcilik Turizm Sanayi ve Ticaret Ltd** S S Turizm ve Yolcu Deniz Tasiyicilar Kooperatifi (TURYOL) *Istanbul* *Turkey* MMSI: 271010301 Official number: 7153	*230* 114 -		**1997-01 at Karadeniz Eregli** Loa 36.25 Br ex - Dght 0.960 Lbp - Br md 9.00 Dpth 2.05 Welded, 1 dk	**(A37B2PS) Passenger Ship** Passengers: unberthed: 600	**2 oil engines** geared to sc. shafts driving 2 Propellers Total Power: 514kW (698hp) 11.0kn Wartsila 2 x each-257kW (349bhp) Wartsila Propulsion AS-Norway
8331687 *UCPN* -	**VARANDEY** **Kupets JSC (A/O 'Kupets')** - *Korsakov* *Russia* MMSI: 273118900	**1,491** 462 1,322	Class: RS	**1985-02 Sudoremontnyy Zavod "Krasnaya Kuznitsa" — Arkhangelsk** Yd No: 2 Loa 72.20 Br ex 13.02 Dght 2.999 Lbp 65.60 Br md - Dpth 4.40 Welded, 1 dk	**(A31A2GA) General Cargo Ship (with Ro-Ro facility)** Stern door/ramp (centre) Grain: 1,661 Compartments: 1 Ho, ER Cranes: 1x12t	**2 oil engines** driving 2 FP propellers Total Power: 1,060kW (1,442hp) 20.3kn S.K.L. 6VD26/20AL-1 2 x 4 Stroke 6 Cy. 200 x 260 each-530kW (721bhp) VEB Schwermaschinenbau "KarlLiebknecht" (SKL)-Magdeburg AuxGen: 3 x 100kW a.c Fuel: 140.0 (d.f.)
9402392 *UHLY* -	**VARANDEY** **LUKoil-Trans Co Ltd** - *Kaliningrad* *Russia* MMSI: 273343920	**7,338** 2,201 3,150	Class: RS	**2008-11 Keppel Singmarine Pte Ltd — Singapore** Yd No: 328 Loa 100.00 Br ex - Dght 10.500 Lbp 92.00 Br md 21.70 Dpth 13.30 Welded, 1 dk	**(B34C2SI) Icebreaker** Ice Capable	**4 diesel electric oil engines** driving 4 gen. Connecting to 2 elec. motors driving 2 Azimuth electric drive units Total Power: 23,040kW (31,324hp) 15.0kn Wartsila 12V32 4 x Vee 4 Stroke 12 Cy. 320 x 400 each-5760kW (7831bhp) Wartsila Finland Oy-Finland AuxGen: 1 x 936kW a.c, 1 x 320kW a.c Thrusters: 2 Tunnel thruster (f) Fuel: 2848.0
8927890 *UFBP* -	**VARAVINO** **Arctic Anchorage (Baza Reydovykh Arkticheskikh Plavsredstv - Arktikreyd Navigating Co)** - *Arkhangelsk* *Russia*	**155** 47 150	Class: RS	**1977 Sudoremontnyy Zavod "Krasnaya Kuznitsa" — Arkhangelsk** Yd No: 6 Loa 35.75 Br ex 7.40 Dght 1.710 Lbp 33.50 Br md 7.00 Dpth 2.40 Welded, 1 dk	**(A31C2GD) Deck Cargo Ship** Ice Capable	**1 oil engine** geared to sc. shaft driving 1 FP propeller Total Power: 165kW (224hp) 7.8kn Daldizel 6CHNSP18/22 1 x 4 Stroke 6 Cy. 180 x 220 165kW (224bhp) Daldizel-Khabarovsk AuxGen: 2 x 13kW a.c Fuel: 5.0 (d.f.)

7705051 *V3WO7* -	**VARDBERG** *ex* African Viking *-2005* *ex* Vardberg *-2002* *ex* Inda Explorer *-2001* *ex* Tilla II *-1998* *ex* Azu *-1994* **Vardberg Fisheries Inc** Maritim Management AS *Belize City* *Belize* MMSI: 312189000 Official number: 020520175	**2,628** 788 2,220	Class: NV (LR) ✠ Classed LR until 14/3/01	**1981-04 Soviknes Verft AS — Sovik** Yd No: 88 Loa 77.30 Br ex 14.23 Dght 6.590 Lbp 67.01 Br md 14.00 Dpth 9.40 Welded, 2 dks	**(B11A2FG) Factory Stern Trawler** Ins: 1,770	**1 oil engine** sr geared to sc. shaft driving 1 CP propeller Total Power: 4,000kW (5,438hp) 13.0kn Wartsila 12V32LN 1 x Vee 4 Stroke 12 Cy. 320 x 350 4000kW (5438bhp) Wartsila Finland Oy-Finland AuxGen: 3 x 500kW 440V 60Hz a.c Fuel: 621.5 (d.f.)
5417210 *XPPI* FD 436	**VARDBORG** *ex* Tummas T *-1980* *ex* Porkerisnes *-1970* **O C Joensen P/F** P/F Thor *Oyri* *Faeroe Islands (Danish)* MMSI: 231021000 Official number: D998	**274** 113 -	Class: NV	**1963-06 p/f Torshavnar Skipasmidja — Torshavn** Yd No: 9 Lengthened-1968 Loa 39.76 Br ex 7.04 Dght - Lbp 36.83 Br md 7.03 Dpth 5.92 Welded, 2 dks	**(B11B2FV) Fishing Vessel** Compartments: 1 Ho, ER 3 Ha: (0.9 x 1.0)2 (1.6 x 0.9)ER Derricks: 1x2t; Winches: 1	**1 oil engine** driving 1 CP propeller Total Power: 552kW (750hp) Volvo Penta D16 1 x 4 Stroke 6 Cy. 144 x 165 552kW (750bhp) (new engine 1981) AuxGen: 1 x 25kW 220V 50Hz a.c, 1 x 20kW 220V 50Hz a.c
9210622 *LLAE* -	**VARDEHORN** **Torghatten Nord AS** - *Tromso* *Norway* MMSI: 259650000	**2,299** 689 1,129	Class: (NV)	**1999-12 Stocznia Cenal Sp z oo — Gdansk** (Hull) Yd No: 111 **1999-12 Fiskerstrand Verft AS — Fiskarstrand** Yd No: 45 Loa 112.00 Br ex 16.30 Dght - Lbp 102.20 Br md 15.90 Dpth 5.00 Welded, 1 dk	**(A36A2PR) Passenger/Ro-Ro Ship (Vehicles)** Passengers: unberthed: 350 Bow door (centre) Stern door (centre) Cars: 120	**4 diesel electric oil engines** driving 4 gen. each 480kW Connecting to 2 elec. motors driving 2 Azimuth electric drive units contra-rotating propellers Total Power: 2,560kW (3,480hp) 13.5kn Mitsubishi S6R2-MPTK 4 x 4 Stroke 6 Cy. 170 x 220 each-640kW (870bhp) Mitsubishi Heavy Industries Ltd-Japan Fuel: 96.0 (d.f.)
8610710 *UBOI2* -	**VARDHOLM** *ex* Kongsfjord *-2006* **Yuzhno-Kurilskiy Rybokombinat Co Ltd** *Nevelsk* *Russia* MMSI: 273352760	**1,890** 567 870	Class: NV RS	**1987-03 Sterkoder Mek. Verksted AS — Kristiansund** Yd No: 110 Converted From: Stern Trawler-2007 Loa 56.90 Br ex - Dght 5.590 Lbp 48.42 Br md 13.01 Dpth 8.70 Welded, 2 dks	**(B31A2SR) Research Survey Vessel** Ins: 845 Cranes: 1x3t,1x2.5t Ice Capable	**1 oil engine** reduction geared to sc. shaft driving 1 CP propeller Total Power: 2,425kW (3,297hp) 11.0kn Normo KVMB-12 1 x Vee 4 Stroke 12 Cy. 250 x 300 2425kW (3297bhp) AS Bergens Mek Verksteder-Norway AuxGen: 1 x 1200kW 380/440V 50Hz a.c, 1 x 320kW 380/440V 50Hz a.c Thrusters: 1 Thwart. CP thruster (f) Fuel: 353.5 (d.f.) 6.0pd
8996920 *XPYJ* TN 711	**VARDIN** **Stiggjar P/F** - *Oyri* *Faeroe Islands (Danish)* MMSI: 231363000	**117** 35 -		**2005-04 Vestvaerftet ApS — Hvide Sande** Loa 18.75 (BB) Br ex - Dght - Lbp 15.95 Br md 6.20 Dpth 3.00 Welded, 1 dk	**(B11A2FS) Stern Trawler**	**1 oil engine** geared to sc. shaft driving 1 Propeller Total Power: 485kW (659hp) Caterpillar 3412E 1 x Vee 4 Stroke 12 Cy. 137 x 152 485kW (659bhp) Caterpillar Inc-USA Thrusters: 1 Thwart. FP thruster (f)
7822677 *LFZT* F-15-B	**VARDOVAERING** *ex* Fjordvaering *-1999* *ex* Mefjordvaering *-1997* *ex* Ryggefjord *-1987* *ex* J. M. Berntsen *-1979* **Kystfisk Berlevag AS** *Vardo* *Norway*	**201** 92 -	Class: (NV)	**1978-06 Liaseth Mek. Verksted AS — Hjorungavaag** Yd No: 8 Loa 27.44 Br ex - Dght 3.515 Lbp 24.13 Br md 6.76 Dpth 5.57 Welded, 2 dks	**(B11B2FV) Fishing Vessel** Compartments: 1 Ho, ER 1 Ha: Ice Capable	**1 oil engine** driving 1 FP propeller Total Power: 405kW (551hp) 11.0kn Alpha 405-26VO 1 x 2 Stroke 5 Cy. 260 x 400 405kW (551bhp) Alpha Diesel A/S-Denmark AuxGen: 2 x 44kW 230V 50Hz a.c Fuel: 32.0 3.0pd
7358054 - -	**VARE** *ex* Avare *-2014* **Exim Inc** - *Zanzibar* *Tanzania (Zanzibar)* Official number: 300023	**17,183** 11,170 28,903 T/cm 39.6	Class: AB	**1975-10 Verolme Estaleiros Reunidos do Brasil S.A. — Angra dos Reis** Yd No: 874 Converted From: Crude Oil Tanker-1998 Loa 175.90 (BB) Br ex 25.66 Dght 10.061 Lbp 168.03 Br md 25.63 Dpth 13.39 Welded, 1 dk	**(B22H2OF) FSO, Oil** Single Hull Liq: 32,822; Liq (Oil): 32,822 Cargo Heating Coils Compartments: 12 Ta, ER 4 Cargo Pump (s): 4x900m³/hr Manifold: Bow/CM: 86m	**1 oil engine** driving 1 FP propeller Total Power: 8,238kW (11,200hp) 16.0kn MAN K8Z70/120E 1 x 2 Stroke 8 Cy. 700 x 1200 8238kW (11200bhp) Mecanica Pesada SA-Brazil AuxGen: 3 x 550kW 440V 60Hz a.c Fuel: 170.5 (d.f.) (Heating Coils) 1972.0 (r.f.) 41.5pd
7941344 - -	**VARELA** - **Government of The Republic of Guinea-Bissau (Ministerio da Economia e Financas)** - *Bissau* *Guinea-Bissau*	*172* - -	Class: (BV)	**1980 Scheepswerf Ravestein BV — Deest** Yd No: 981 Loa - Br ex - Dght - Lbp 26.67 Br md 7.51 Dpth 2.49 Welded, 1 dk	**(A31A2GX) General Cargo Ship** Compartments: 2 Ho, ER 2 Ha: ER	**1 oil engine** with clutches, flexible couplings & sr geared to sc. shaft driving 1 Directional propeller Total Power: 353kW (480hp) Deutz F12L413F 1 x Vee 4 Stroke 12 Cy. 125 x 130 353kW (480bhp) Kloeckner Humboldt Deutz AG-West Germany AuxGen: 1 x 12kW 380V 50Hz a.c
9045376 *C6TS5* -	**VARG STAR** *ex* Varg *-2005* **Suerte Navigation Co Ltd** Estoril Navigation Ltd *Nassau* *Bahamas* MMSI: 311763000 Official number: 8000833	**38,792** 21,279 68,157 T/cm 66.6	Class: NV (RS)	**1992-03 ATVT Sudnobudivnyi Zavod "Zaliv" — Kerch** Yd No: 912 Loa 242.80 (BB) Br ex 32.64 Dght 13.640 Lbp 228.00 Br md 32.20 Dpth 18.00 Welded, 1 dk	**(A13A2TW) Crude/Oil Products Tanker** Double Hull (13F) Liq: 68,151; Liq (Oil): 68,151 Cargo Heating Coils Compartments: 14 Wing Ta, ER, 2 Wing Slop Ta 4 Cargo Pump (s): 4x1500m³/hr Manifold: Bow/CM: 124m Ice Capable	**1 oil engine** driving 1 FP propeller Total Power: 10,592kW (14,401hp) 13.5kn B&W 8L60MCE 1 x 2 Stroke 8 Cy. 600 x 1944 10592kW (14401bhp) AO Bryanskiy MashinostroitelnyyZavod (BMZ)-Bryansk AuxGen: 1 x 888kW 380V 50Hz a.c, 3 x 500kW 380V 50Hz a.c Fuel: 550.0 (d.f.) 3600.0 (r.f.) 53.5pd
7325564 *LMEU* -	**VARGOY** *ex* Gullholm *-1999* *ex* Lena *-1995* *ex* Vestland *-1989* *ex* Trans Oy *-1989* **Sjovarg AS** - *Namsos* *Norway* MMSI: 258434000	**907** 588 950	Class: BV (NV)	**1973-09 Fosen Mek. Verksteder AS — Rissa** Yd No: 10 Lengthened-1979 Loa 55.55 Br ex 11.03 Dght 3.772 Lbp 50.81 Br md 10.98 Dpth 5.62 Welded, 2 dks	**(A31A2GX) General Cargo Ship** Bale: 1,693 Compartments: 1 Ho, ER 1 Ha: (13.7 x 9.5) Derricks: 1x10t; Winches: 1 Ice Capable	**1 oil engine** driving 1 FP propeller Total Power: 441kW (600hp) 11.0kn Alpha 406-26VO 1 x 2 Stroke 6 Cy. 260 x 400 441kW (600bhp) Alpha Diesel A/S-Denmark AuxGen: 2 x 50kW 220V 50Hz a.c Fuel: 33.7
9606998 *YD3804* -	**VARIA USAHA 9** *ex* Tb. Varia Usaha 9 *-2010* **PT Varia Usaha Lintas Segara** - *Tanjung Priok* *Indonesia*	**189** 57 167	Class: KI (NK)	**2010-11 Kaibuok Shipyard (M) Sdn Bhd — Sibu** Yd No: 0723 Loa 26.00 Br ex - Dght 3.012 Lbp 24.36 Br md 8.00 Dpth 3.65 Welded, 1 dk	**(B32A2ST) Tug**	**2 oil engines** reduction geared to sc. shafts driving 2 FP propellers Total Power: 1,220kW (1,658hp) Yanmar 6AYM-ETE 2 x 4 Stroke 6 Cy. 155 x 180 each-610kW (829bhp) Yanmar Diesel Engine Co Ltd-Japan
9065247 *UHSL* -	**VARIANT** **Variant Fishing Co (Rybolovetskaya Firma 'Variant')** - SatCom: Inmarsat C 427300810 *Murmansk* *Russia* MMSI: 273415090 Official number: 912839	**877** 278 331	Class: RS	**1992-07 OAO Volgogradskiy Sudostroitelnyy Zavod — Volgograd** Yd No: 273 Loa 53.74 Br ex 10.71 Dght 4.600 Lbp 47.92 Br md - Dpth 6.00 Welded, 1 dk	**(B11A2FS) Stern Trawler** Ins: 360 Ice Capable	**1 oil engine** driving 1 FP propeller Total Power: 969kW (1,317hp) 12.8kn S.K.L. 8NVD48A-2U 1 x 4 Stroke 8 Cy. 320 x 480 969kW (1317bhp) SKL Motoren u. Systemtechnik AG-Magdeburg
9657090 *9HA3073* -	**VARIETY VOYAGER** *completed as* Harmony A *-2012* **Balanda Maritime Co** Naftiliaki Touristiki Maritime Co of Pleasure Yachts *Valletta* *Malta* MMSI: 229104000 Official number: 9657090	**1,593** 501 -	Class: RI	**2012-04 Emmanouil Psarros Shipyard — Piraeus** Yd No: 08013 Loa 65.95 Br ex - Dght 3.380 Lbp 54.67 Br md 11.50 Dpth 6.50 Welded, 1 dk	**(X11A2YP) Yacht** Passengers: cabins: 36; berths: 72	**2 oil engines** reduction geared to sc. shafts driving 2 Propellers Total Power: 2,760kW (3,752hp) 14.0kn Caterpillar 2 x 4 Stroke each-1380kW (1876bhp) Caterpillar Inc-USA
8652586 - -	**VARITA TRANSPORTASI 01** **PT Varita Majutama** - *Tanjung Priok* *Indonesia*	**170** 51 -	Class: KI	**2010-12 CV Sunjaya Abadi — Samarinda** Loa - Br ex - Dght 1.720 Lbp 33.70 Br md 7.50 Dpth 2.25 Welded, 1 dk	**(A35D2RL) Landing Craft** Bow ramp (centre)	**2 oil engines** reduction geared to sc. shafts driving 2 Propellers AuxGen: 2 x 40kW a.c
9488839 *TCYK2* -	**VARKAN AKDENIZ** *ex* Deha Vardal *-2010* **Varkan Akdeniz Gemi Insa Sanayi AS** CSM Denizcilik Ltd Sti (Chemfleet) *Istanbul* *Turkey* MMSI: 271041519	**7,366** 3,589 11,215 T/cm 22.5	Class: BV	**2010-10 Torgem Gemi Insaat Sanayii ve Ticaret a.s. — Tuzla, Istanbul** Yd No: 90 Loa 129.50 (BB) Br ex - Dght 8.150 Lbp 122.70 Br md 19.80 Dpth 10.40 Welded, 1 dk	**(A12B2TR) Chemical/Products Tanker** Double Hull (13F) Liq: 11,216; Liq (Oil): 11,216 Cargo Heating Coils Compartments: 12 Wing Ta, ER 12 Cargo Pump (s): 12x250m³/hr Manifold: Bow/CM: 65.1m Ice Capable	**1 oil engine** driving 1 CP propeller Total Power: 3,309kW (4,499hp) 13.5kn Hanshin LH46LA 1 x 4 Stroke 6 Cy. 460 x 880 3309kW (4499bhp) The Hanshin Diesel Works Ltd-Japan AuxGen: 1 x 720kW 440V 60Hz a.c, 3 x 482kW 440V 60Hz a.c Thrusters: 1 Tunnel thruster (f) Fuel: 103.0 (d.f.) 494.0 (r.f.)

Identity	Name / Owner	Tonnage	Class	Build	Type	Machinery
9433092 *TCSZ3* -	**VARKAN EGE** *launched as* Fevzi Vardal *-2008* **Varkan Ege Denizcilik Sanayi ve Ticaret AS** Veysel Vardal Gemicilik Denizcilik ve Ticaret AS *Istanbul* *Turkey* MMSI: 271002541 Official number: 1482	**2,222** 1,064 3,548 T/cm 10.3	Class: BV (AB)	**2008-02 Dentas Gemi Insaat ve Onarim Sanayii A.S. — Istanbul** Yd No: 91 Loa 88.31 (BB) Br ex - Dght 5.544 Lbp 82.25 Br md 13.50 Dpth 6.50 Welded, 1 dk	**(A12B2TR) Chemical/Products Tanker** Double Hull (13F) Liq: 3,751; Liq (Oil): 3,751 Cargo Heating Coils Compartments: 12 Wing Ta, ER 12 Cargo Pump (s): 12x100m³/hr Manifold: Bow/CM: 41.8m	**1 oil engine** reduction geared to sc. shaft driving 1 CP propeller Total Power: 1,850kW (2,515hp) 14.0kn MaK 6M25 1 x 4 Stroke 6 Cy. 255 x 400 1850kW (2515bhp) Caterpillar Motoren GmbH & Co. KG-Germany AuxGen: 2 x 336kW, 1 x 535kW Thrusters: 1 Tunnel thruster (f) Fuel: 36.0 (d.f.) 156.0 (r.f.)
9458145 *TCTN8* -	**VARKAN MARMARA** *completed as* Barbaros Vardal *-2009* **Varkan Gemi Insa Sanayi AS** Veysel Vardal Gemicilik Denizcilik ve Ticaret AS *Istanbul* *Turkey* MMSI: 271002685	**3,478** 1,506 4,865 T/cm 13.2	Class: BV	**2009-01 Dentas Gemi Insaat ve Onarim Sanayii A.S. — Istanbul** Yd No: 94 Loa 99.84 (BB) Br ex - Dght 6.100 Lbp 94.76 Br md 15.60 Dpth 7.60 Welded, 1 dk	**(A12B2TR) Chemical/Products Tanker** Double Hull (13F) Liq: 5,115; Liq (Oil): 5,115 Cargo Heating Coils Compartments: 10 Wing Ta, 2 Wing Slop Ta, ER 10 Cargo Pump (s): 10x185m³/hr Manifold: Bow/CM: 43.2m Ice Capable	**1 oil engine** driving 1 CP propeller Total Power: 2,205kW (2,998hp) 13.0kn MAN-B&W 9L28/32A 1 x 4 Stroke 9 Cy. 280 x 320 2205kW (2998bhp) STX Engine Co Ltd-South Korea AuxGen: 3 x 390kW 450V 60Hz a.c, 1 x 480kW 450V 60Hz a.c Thrusters: 1 Tunnel thruster (f) Fuel: 25.0 (d.f.) 209.0 (r.f.)
6814245 *YLKV* -	**VARMA** **Freeport of Riga Fleet (Rigas Brivostas Flote)** Freeport of Riga Authority (Rigas Brivostas Parvalde) SatCom: Inmarsat C 427518710 *Riga* *Latvia* MMSI: 275187000 Official number: 0367	**4,121** 1,236 4,968	Class: (BV)	**1968-12 Oy Wartsila Ab — Helsinki** Yd No: 387 Loa 86.52 Br ex 21.21 Dght 7.380 Lbp 80.75 Br md 21.04 Dpth 9.50 Welded, 2 dks	**(B34C2SI) Icebreaker** Cranes: 1x8t Ice Capable	**4 diesel electric oil engines** driving 4 gen. each 2400kW 400V d.c Connecting to 2 elec. motors 2 elec. motors driving 2 Propellers , 2 fwd Total Power: 10,164kW (13,820hp) 18.0kn Sulzer 8MH51 4 x 2 Stroke 8 Cy. 510 x 550 each-2541kW (3455bhp) Oy Wartsila Ab-Finland AuxGen: 4 x 337kW 380V 50Hz a.c Fuel: 548.5 (d.f.)
9028122 *OGOE* -	**VARMA** *ex* Turva *-2013* **Ky-Osterland Kb** *Nauvo* *Finland* MMSI: 230301000 Official number: 12433	**447** 135 -		**1977-07 Oy Laivateollisuus Ab — Turku** Yd No: 318 Converted From: Patrol Vessel-2006 Loa 48.35 Br ex 8.66 Dght 4.380 Lbp - Br md - Dpth 4.90 Welded, 1 dk	**(B32A2ST) Tug**	**2 oil engines** reduction geared to sc. shaft driving 1 Propeller Total Power: 1,480kW (2,012hp) 15.0kn Wartsila 6R24TS 2 x 4 Stroke 6 Cy. 240 x 310 each-740kW (1006bhp) (made 1977) Oy Wartsila Ab-Finland Thrusters: 1 Tunnel thruster (f)
1004443 *MFLB7* -	**VARMAR VE** **Gildoran Ltd,** Daska Maritime Ltd *Southampton* *United Kingdom* MMSI: 232193000 Official number: 711671	**687** 206	Class: LR ✠ **100A1** SS 03/2011 Yacht ✠ **LMC**	**1986-11 Jacht- en Scheepswerf C. van Lent & Zonen B.V. — Kaag** Yd No: 755 Loa 55.40 Br ex 9.40 Dght 3.200 Lbp 49.50 Br md 9.35 Dpth 5.30 Welded, 1 dk	**(X11A2YP) Yacht**	**2 oil engines** geared to sc. shafts driving 2 FP propellers Total Power: 2,310kW (3,140hp) Caterpillar 3516TA 2 x Vee 4 Stroke 16 Cy. 170 x 190 each-1155kW (1570bhp) Caterpillar Tractor Co-USA Fuel: 62.7 (d.f.)
8900945 *SMXZ* -	**VARMDO** **Waxholms Angfartygs AB** *Vaxholm* *Sweden* MMSI: 265520390	**298** 118 50		**1990-04 AB Nya Oskarshamns Varv — Oskarshamn** Yd No: 517 Loa 37.70 Br ex 7.52 Dght 1.280 Lbp 34.79 Br md 7.50 Dpth 2.78 Welded, 1 dk	**(A37B2PS) Passenger Ship** Hull Material: Aluminium Alloy Passengers: unberthed: 340	**3 oil engines** with clutches, flexible couplings & sr reverse geared to sc. shafts driving 3 FP propellers Total Power: 1,764kW (2,397hp) 22.0kn MAN D2842LE 3 x Vee 4 Stroke 12 Cy. 128 x 142 each-588kW (799bhp) MAN Nutzfahrzeuge AG-Nuernberg AuxGen: 1 x 105kW 380V 50Hz a.c, 1 x 60kW 380V 50Hz a.c
9120384 *LZFZ* -	**VARNA** *ex* Sondos *-2011* **Varnaferry OOD** Navigation Maritime Bulgare *Varna* *Bulgaria* MMSI: 207136000	**5,684** 1,752 4,577	Class: (BV) (RS)	**1994 OAO Sudostroitelnyy Zavod 'Okean' — Nikolayev** Yd No: 701 Loa 140.40 Br ex 16.60 Dght 4.500 Lbp 130.20 Br md 16.20 Dpth 8.10 Welded	**(A35A2RR) Ro-Ro Cargo Ship** Quarter stern door/ramp (s) Len: 14.00 Wid: 5.00 Swl: 60 Lane-Len: 650 TEU 220	**2 oil engines** driving 2 FP propellers Total Power: 2,942kW (4,000hp) 13.5kn B&W 6S26MC 2 x 2 Stroke 6 Cy. 260 x 980 each-1471kW (2000bhp) AO Bryanskiy MashinostroitelnyyZavod (BMZ)-Bryansk Fuel: 442.0 (d.f.)
9263540 *PBIB* -	**VARNADIEP** *launched as* Scan Leader *-2002* **Beheermaatschappij ms Varnadiep BV** Feederlines BV *Groningen* *Netherlands* MMSI: 244729000 Official number: 41486	**4,938** 2,631 7,250	Class: GL (LR) ✠ Classed LR until 1/9/12	**2002-10 Bodewes' Scheepswerven B.V. — Hoogezand** Yd No: 608 Loa 118.55 (BB) Br ex 15.43 Dght 7.050 Lbp 111.85 Br md 15.20 Dpth 8.44 Welded, 1 dk	**(A31A2GX) General Cargo Ship** Grain: 9,415 TEU 390 C Ho 174 TEU C Dk 216 TEU Compartments: 2 Ho, ER 2 Ha: (42.8 x 12.7)ER (39.0 x 12.7)	**1 oil engine** with clutches, flexible couplings & sr geared to sc. shaft driving 1 CP propeller Total Power: 3,800kW (5,166hp) 12.0kn MaK 8M32C 1 x 4 Stroke 8 Cy. 320 x 480 3800kW (5166bhp) Caterpillar Motoren GmbH & Co. KG-Germany AuxGen: 1 x 400kW 400V 50Hz a.c, 2 x 264kW 400V 50Hz a.c Boilers: HWH (o.f.) 3.6kgf/cm² (3.5bar) Thrusters: 1 Thwart. CP thruster (f)
9213739 *PBAH* -	**VARNEBANK** **BV Skagenship** Pot Scheepvaart BV SatCom: Inmarsat C 424417110 *Delfzijl* *Netherlands* MMSI: 244171000 Official number: 38949	**6,130** 3,424 8,727 T/cm 18.3	Class: BV	**2000-10 Bodewes Scheepswerf "Volharding" Foxhol B.V. — Foxhol** Yd No: 352 Loa 132.23 (BB) Br ex - Dght 7.050 Lbp 123.84 Br md 15.87 Dpth 9.65 Welded, 1 dk	**(A31A2GX) General Cargo Ship** Grain: 12,855 TEU 548 C. 548/20' incl. 50 ref C. Compartments: 2 Ho, ER 2 Ha: ER Ice Capable	**1 oil engine** reduction geared to sc. shaft driving 1 CP propeller Total Power: 3,960kW (5,384hp) 15.0kn MaK 8M32C 1 x 4 Stroke 8 Cy. 320 x 480 3960kW (5384bhp) Caterpillar Motoren GmbH & Co. KG-Germany AuxGen: 1 x 650kW 230/440V 60Hz a.c Fuel: 402.0 (d.f.)
7603734 *WCO4117* -	**VARON** *ex* George C. Tower *-1993* **Varon Inc** *Brownsville, TX* *United States of America* Official number: 555460	*103* 70 -		**1974 Marine Mart, Inc. — Port Isabel, Tx** Yd No: 131 L reg 19.69 Br ex - Dght - Lbp - Br md 6.13 Dpth 3.46 Welded, 1 dk	**(B11B2FV) Fishing Vessel**	**1 oil engine** driving 1 FP propeller Total Power: 268kW (364hp) Caterpillar D353TA 1 x 4 Stroke 6 Cy. 159 x 203 268kW (364bhp) Caterpillar Tractor Co-USA
8747666 *CSPB* -	**VAROSA** **Somague Engenharia SA** *Lisbon* *Portugal* MMSI: 263672270 Official number: LX412AL	**670** 201 -		**1977 FEAB-Karlstadverken — Karlstad** Yd No: 1977 Loa 55.00 Br ex - Dght 3.100 Lbp 52.46 Br md 11.00 Dpth 4.20 Welded, 1 dk	**(B34A2SH) Hopper, Motor**	**2 oil engines** reduction geared to sc. shafts driving 2 Propellers Total Power: 596kW (810hp) Cummins NTA-855-M 2 x 4 Stroke 6 Cy. 140 x 152 each-298kW (405bhp) Cummins Engine Co Inc-USA
7424023 *CA2611* -	**VARUA VAIKAVA** *ex* Clipper *-2008* *ex* Jenclipper *-2008* *ex* Aries Trigon *-1982* **Naviera GV SA** - *Valparaiso* *Chile* MMSI: 725000682 Official number: 3236	**569** 275 795	Class: BV	**1976-06 A/S Nordsoevaerftet — Ringkobing** Yd No: 116 Loa 49.69 Br ex 8.31 Dght 3.720 Lbp 44.43 Br md 8.28 Dpth 5.52 Welded, 2 dks	**(A31A2GX) General Cargo Ship** Grain: 1,302; Bale: 1,155 TEU 20 C. 20/20' Compartments: 1 Ho, ER 1 Ha: (24.6 x 5.0)ER Derricks: 2x5t; Winches: 2 Ice Capable	**1 oil engine** driving 1 FP propeller Total Power: 507kW (689hp) 10.0kn Callesen 6-427-FOT 1 x 4 Stroke 6 Cy. 270 x 400 507kW (689bhp) Aabenraa Motorfabrik, HeinrichCallesen A/S-Denmark Fuel: 66.0 (d.f.) 2.0pd
5376868 *VTLL* -	**VARUNA** **Government of The Republic of India (Director of Indo-Norwegian Project)** - *Kochi* *India* Official number: 1074	*160* 48 163	Class: IR	**1961 Ankerlokken Verft Floro AS — Floro** Yd No: 34 Loa 28.00 Br ex 6.89 Dght 3.302 Lbp 27.97 Br md 6.86 Dpth 3.43 Welded, 1 dk	**(B12D2FR) Fishery Research Vessel** Compartments: 1 Ho, ER Derricks: 1x1.5t	**1 oil engine** driving 1 FP propeller Total Power: 294kW (400hp) Wichmann 4ACA 1 x 2 Stroke 4 Cy. 280 x 420 294kW (400bhp) Wichmann Motorfabrikk AS-Norway AuxGen: 2 x 45kW Fuel: 36.5 (d.f.)
8318489 - -	**VARUNA** **Government of The Republic of India (Coast Guard)** - *Mumbai* *India*	**1,247** 750 195	Class: IR (AB)	**1988-02 Mazagon Dock Ltd. — Mumbai** Yd No: 784 Loa 74.12 Br ex 10.65 Dght 3.001 Lbp 69.02 Br md 10.61 Dpth 7.93 Welded, 2 dks	**(B34H2SQ) Patrol Vessel**	**2 oil engines** with clutches, flexible couplings & reduction geared to sc. shafts driving 2 CP propellers Total Power: 9,416kW (12,802hp) 25.0kn Pielstick 16PA6V280 2 x Vee 4 Stroke 16 Cy. 280 x 290 each-4708kW (6401bhp) SEMT Pielstick SA-France AuxGen: 4 x 212kW a.c
8737116 *YDA6254* -	**VARUNA** **PT Ansel Jaya Mandiri** - *Samarinda* *Indonesia*	**213** 64 -	Class: KI	**2008-09 PT Eka Multi Bahari — Samarinda** Loa 28.00 Br ex - Dght 2.800 Lbp 25.60 Br md 8.00 Dpth 3.75 Welded, 1 dk	**(B32A2ST) Tug**	**2 oil engines** driving 2 Propellers Total Power: 1,250kW (1,700hp) Caterpillar D398 2 x Vee 4 Stroke 12 Cy. 159 x 203 each-625kW (850bhp) Caterpillar Inc-USA

IMO No.	Name / Owner	Tonnage	Class	Builder / Dimensions	Type	Machinery
8738603 - -	**VARUNA 01** - **PT Ansel Jaya Mandiri** - *Samarinda* *Indonesia*	**213** 64 -	Class: KI	**2009**-04 **in Indonesia** Loa 28.00 Br ex - Dght - Lbp 26.40 Br md 8.00 Dpth 3.75 Welded, 1 dk	**(B32A2ST) Tug**	**2 oil engines** driving 2 Propellers Total Power: 1,716kW (2,334hp) Mitsubishi S12A2-MPTK 2 x Vee 4 Stroke 12 Cy. 150 x 160 each-858kW (1167bhp) Mitsubishi Heavy Industries Ltd-Japan
9314428 *YDA3197* -	**VARUNA ACE** *ex* Bina Ocean 7 *-2013* **PT Pelayaran Nasional Varuna Servicatama** - *Tanjungpinang* *Indonesia* MMSI: 525021104	**125** 38 108	Class: KI (GL) (NK)	**2004**-02 **Tuong Aik Shipyard Sdn Bhd — Sibu** Yd No: 2309 Loa 23.17 Br ex - Dght 2.388 Lbp 21.79 Br md 7.00 Dpth 2.90 Welded, 1 dk	**(B32A2ST) Tug**	**2 oil engines** geared to sc. shafts driving 2 FP propellers Total Power: 716kW (974hp) Caterpillar 3408TA 2 x Vee 4 Stroke 8 Cy. 137 x 152 each-358kW (487bhp) Caterpillar Inc-USA
9027776 - -	**VARUNA EXPRESS** *ex* Baruna 5 *-2013* **PT Rejeki Abadi Sakti** - *Samarinda* *Indonesia*	**111** 66 -	Class: KI	**1968**-07 **Lafco Inc — Lafayette LA** L reg 18.93 Br ex - Dght - Lbp 17.79 Br md 5.61 Dpth 2.99 Welded, 1 dk	**(B21A20C) Crew/Supply Vessel** Hull Material: Aluminium Alloy	**2 oil engines** driving 2 Propellers Total Power: 900kW (1,224hp) Volvo Penta TAMD162B 2 x 4 Stroke 6 Cy. 144 x 165 each-450kW (612bhp) AB Volvo Penta-Sweden
9664641 *AVVT* -	**VARUNI** - **Jindal ITF Ltd** - *Mumbai* *India* MMSI: 419000610 Official number: 4036	**1,368** 579 2,160	Class: IR	**2012**-10 **Dempo Engineering Works Ltd. — Goa** Yd No: 504 Loa 72.00 Br ex 14.02 Dght 3.000 Lbp 69.65 Br md 14.00 Dpth 4.25 Welded, 1 dk	**(A31A2GX) General Cargo Ship** Grain: 2,300 Compartments: 1 Ho, ER 1 Ha: ER	**2 oil engines** reduction geared to sc. shafts driving 2 FP propellers Total Power: 736kW (1,000hp) 9.9kn Volvo Penta D13MH 2 x 4 Stroke 6 Cy. 131 x 158 each-368kW (500bhp) AB Volvo Penta-Sweden
5379315 *UBCI5* -	**VARYAG** *ex* Viking *-2012* *ex* Grindal *-2004* *ex* Vestskjell *-1973* **Nord-Ost Oil Ltd** Rostranservis Ltd *Taganrog* *Russia* MMSI: 273355840	**397** 184 662 T/cm 2.0	Class: RS (NV)	**1956**-12 **AS Framnaes Mek. Vaerksted — Sandefjord** Yd No: 157 Converted From: Oil Tanker-2003 Lengthened-1980 Loa 53.72 Br ex 7.37 Dght 3.493 Lbp 49.90 Br md 7.35 Dpth 3.93 Welded, 2 dks	**(A12D2LV) Vegetable Oil Tanker** Liq: 719; Liq (Oil): 719 Cargo Heating Coils Compartments: 10 Wing Ta, ER 2 Cargo Pump (s): 2x140m³/hr Manifold: Bow/CM: 37m Ice Capable	**1 oil engine** driving 1 FP propeller Total Power: 403kW (548hp) 11.0kn Volvo Penta TAMD165A 1 x 4 Stroke 6 Cy. 144 x 165 403kW (548bhp) (new engine 1996) AB Volvo Penta-Sweden AuxGen: 1 x 38kW 110V d.c, 1 x 34kW 110V d.c
7500401 *UGTL* -	**VARZUGA** *ex* Uikku *-2003* **Murmansk Shipping Co (MSC)** - SatCom: Inmarsat C 427330528 *Murmansk* *Russia* MMSI: 273449450 Official number: 774814	**11,290** 4,937 16,038 T/cm 29.5	Class: RS (NV)	**1977**-10 **Werft Nobiskrug GmbH — Rendsburg** Yd No: 689 Loa 164.47 Br ex 22.26 Dght 9.500 Lbp 151.54 Br md 22.22 Dpth 12.02 Welded, 1 dk	**(A13A2TW) Crude/Oil Products Tanker** Double Hull (13F) Liq: 16,214; Liq (Oil): 16,214 Cargo Heating Coils Compartments: 8 Wing Ta, ER 8 Cargo Pump (s): 8x420m³/hr Manifold: Bow/CM: 34m Ice Capable	**4 diesel electric oil engines** driving 2 gen. each 4800kW a.c 1 gen. of 2300kW a.c 1 gen. of 1800kW a.c Connecting to 1 elec. Motor of (11400kW) driving 1 Azimuth electric drive unit Total Power: 14,190kW (19,292hp) 14.0kn MaK 12M282AK 1 x Vee 4 Stroke 12 Cy. 240 x 280 2400kW (3263bhp) (new engine 1993) MaK Motoren GmbH & Co. KG-Kiel Wartsila 12V22 1 x Vee 4 Stroke 12 Cy. 220 x 240 1950kW (2651bhp) (new engine 1993) Wartsila SACM Diesel SA-France Wartsila 12V32 2 x Vee 4 Stroke 12 Cy. 320 x 350 each-4920kW (6689bhp) (new engine 1993) Wartsila Diesel Oy-Finland Thrusters: 1 Thwart. FP thruster (f) Fuel: 1904.0 (r.f.) (Heating Coils)
9009554 *JG4973* -	**VASA** - **Hakone Kankosen KK** - *Hakone, Kanagawa* *Japan* Official number: 131918	*308* - 54		**1991**-02 **Hitachi Zosen Corp — Kawasaki KN** Yd No: 114857 Loa 35.67 (BB) Br ex 10.80 Dght 1.901 Lbp 29.00 Br md 10.00 Dpth 2.90 Welded, 1 dk	**(A37B2PS) Passenger Ship** Passengers: unberthed: 650	**1 oil engine** with clutches & geared to sc. shaft driving 1 FP propeller Total Power: 515kW (700hp) 10.5kn Akasaka MH23R 1 x 4 Stroke 6 Cy. 230 x 390 515kW (700bhp) Akasaka Tekkosho KK (Akasaka DieselLtd)-Japan AuxGen: 1 x 160kW a.c, 1 x 48kW a.c Thrusters: 1 Thwart. CP thruster (f)
9263552 *PHLB* -	**VASADIEP** *launched as* Scan Runner *-2002* **Beheermaatschappij ms 'Vasadiep' BV** Feederlines BV *Groningen* *Netherlands* MMSI: 244764000 Official number: 41614	**4,941** 2,786 7,875	Class: GL (LR) ✠ Classed LR until 18/3/04	**2002**-12 **Bodewes' Scheepswerven B.V. — Hoogezand** Yd No: 609 Loa 118.55 (BB) Br ex 15.43 Dght 7.050 Lbp 111.85 Br md 15.20 Dpth 8.44 Welded, 1 dk	**(A31A2GX) General Cargo Ship** Grain: 9,413 TEU 390 C Ho 174 TEU C Dk 216 TEU Compartments: 2 Ho, ER 2 Ha: (42.8 x 12.7)ER (39.0 x 12.7) Ice Capable	**1 oil engine** with clutches, flexible couplings & sr geared to sc. shaft driving 1 CP propeller Total Power: 3,840kW (5,221hp) 14.7kn MaK 8M32C 1 x 4 Stroke 8 Cy. 320 x 480 3840kW (5221bhp) Caterpillar Motoren GmbH & Co. KG-Germany AuxGen: 1 x 400kW 380/220V 50Hz a.c, 2 x 264kW 380/220V 50Hz a.c Boilers: HWH (o.f.) 3.6kgf/cm² (3.5bar) Thrusters: 1 Thwart. CP thruster (f) Fuel: 69.0 (d.f.) 533.0 (r.f.) 14.5pd
8222111 *MMFA7* -	**VASALAND** *ex* Oihonna *-2003* **Imperial RoRo Ltd** Imperial Ship Management AB *London* *United Kingdom* MMSI: 235035113 Official number: 911554	**20,544** 6,163 12,870 T/cm 32.5	Class: LR ✠ **100A1** SS 04/2009 Ice Class 1A Super Max draught midship 8.463m Max/min draught aft 8.463/6.013m Max/min draught forward 8.463/6.813m ✠ **LMC** **UMS** Eq.Ltr: I†; Cable: 605.0/64.0 U3	**1984**-04 **Rauma-Repola Oy — Rauma** Yd No: 284 Loa 155.00 (BB) Br ex 25.15 Dght 8.465 Lbp 146.01 Br md 24.96 Dpth 16.90 Welded, 2 dks	**(A35A2RR) Ro-Ro Cargo Ship** Passengers: cabins: 6; berths: 12 Stern door/ramp (a) Len: 12.00 Wid: 10.60 Swl: 70 Lane-Len: 2170 Lane-Wid: 2.80 Lane-clr ht: 6.20 Trailers: 164 Bale: 34,776 TEU 608 C RoRo Dk 422 C Dk 186 TEU incl 43 ref C Ice Capable	**2 oil engines** with clutches, flexible couplings & sr geared to sc. shaft driving 1 CP propeller Total Power: 13,198kW (17,944hp) 17.3kn Pielstick 12PC2-6V-400 2 x Vee 4 Stroke 12 Cy. 400 x 460 each-6599kW (8972bhp) Oy Wartsila Ab-Finland AuxGen: 3 x 1000kW 400V 50Hz a.c Boilers: 3 e 8.1kgf/cm² (7.9bar), AuxB (o.f.) 8.1kgf/cm² (7.9bar) Thrusters: 1 Thwart. CP thruster (f); 1 Tunnel thruster (a) Fuel: 90.0 (d.f.) 1189.0 (r.f.) 45.0pd
8862088 *UESS* -	**VASAN** *ex* 1656 *-1993* **Primorskaya Fishery Co Ltd (OOO 'Primorskaya Rybolovnaya Kompaniya')** - SatCom: Inmarsat C 427320928 *Nevelsk* *Russia* MMSI: 273452210 Official number: 910462	**726** 217 414	Class: RS	**1991**-11 **Zavod "Leninskaya Kuznitsa" — Kiyev** Yd No: 1656 Loa 54.82 Br ex 10.15 Dght 4.140 Lbp 50.30 Br md 9.80 Dpth 5.00 Welded, 1 dk	**(B11A2FS) Stern Trawler** Ice Capable	**1 oil engine** driving 1 FP propeller Total Power: 852kW (1,158hp) 12.0kn S.K.L. 8NVD48A-2U 1 x 4 Stroke 8 Cy. 320 x 480 852kW (1158bhp) (made 1991) SKL Motoren u. Systemtechnik AG-Magdeburg
9084633 *ATEJ* -	**VASAVADATTA** - **Welspun Maxsteel Ltd** - *Mumbai* *India* MMSI: 419029000 Official number: 2569	**1,874** 562 2,873	Class: IR	**1995**-01 **Magdalla Shipyard Pvt Ltd — Surat** Yd No: 127 Loa 82.00 Br ex 14.20 Dght 3.862 Lbp 78.59 Br md 14.00 Dpth 5.00 Welded, 1 dk	**(A31A2GX) General Cargo Ship** Grain: 1,867 Compartments: 1 Ho, ER 1 Ha: ER	**2 oil engines** with clutches, flexible couplings & sr reverse geared to sc. shafts driving 2 FP propellers Total Power: 1,274kW (1,732hp) 10.0kn Caterpillar 3508TA 2 x Vee 4 Stroke 8 Cy. 170 x 190 each-637kW (866bhp) Caterpillar Inc-USA AuxGen: 3 x 85kW 415V 50Hz a.c Fuel: 227.0 (d.f.)
7509548 - -	**VASCO** *ex* Dzhambul *-1997* **Cosmix Underwater Research Ltd** - *Philippines*	*156* 47 88	Class: (RS)	**1974 Zavod 'Nikolayevsk-na-Amure' — Nikolayevsk-na-Amure** Yd No: 108 Converted From: Fishing Vessel-1997 Loa 34.60 Br ex 7.09 Dght 2.899 Lbp - Br md 7.07 Dpth 3.66 Welded, 1 dk	**(A37B2PS) Passenger Ship** Bale: 115 Compartments: 1 Ho, ER 1 Ha: (1.6 x 1.3) Derricks: 2x2t; Winches: 2 Ice Capable	**1 oil engine** reduction geared to sc. shaft driving 1 FP propeller Total Power: 592kW (805hp) 9.5kn Cummins 1 x 4 Stroke 8 Cy. 592kW (805bhp) (new engine 2010) Cummins Engine Co Inc-USA
7904449 - -	**VASCO DA GAMA** *ex* Tenyu Maru No. 81 *-1996* **Shelfco 22 (Pty) Ltd** - *Walvis Bay* *Namibia* Official number: 2003WB004	**565** 205 -		**1979**-06 **Yamanishi Shipbuilding Co Ltd — Ishinomaki MG** Yd No: 861 Loa 49.66 Br ex - Dght 3.234 Lbp 42.96 Br md 8.21 Dpth 3.56 Welded, 1 dk	**(B11B2FV) Fishing Vessel**	**1 oil engine** driving 1 FP propeller Total Power: 809kW (1,100hp) 11.0kn Niigata 6L28X 1 x 4 Stroke 6 Cy. 280 x 440 809kW (1100bhp) Niigata Engineering Co Ltd-Japan

IMO / Call sign	Name / Owner	Tonnage	Class	Build / Dimensions	Type	Machinery
9187473 *LXVG* -	**VASCO DA GAMA** *ex* Da Jia Ma *-2012* *ex* Vasco Da Gama *-2010* **Vasco SA** - *Luxembourg* *Luxembourg* MMSI: 253193000	**36,567** 10,970 59,235	Class: BV (CC)	**2000**-06 **Thyssen Nordseewerke GmbH — Emden** Yd No: 525 Loa 201.00 (BB) Br ex 36.25 Dght 14.600 Lbp 178.00 Br md 36.20 Dpth 19.33 Welded, 1 dk	**(B33B2DT) Trailing Suction Hopper Dredger** Hopper: 33,125	**2 oil engines** with clutches, flexible couplings & sr geared to sc. shafts driving 2 CP propellers Total Power: 29,400kW (39,972hp) 16.5kn MAN 14V48/60 2 x Vee 4 Stroke 14 Cy. 480 x 600 each-14700kW (19986bhp) MAN B&W Diesel AG-Augsburg AuxGen: 2 x 9999kW 6000V 60Hz a.c, 2 x 2500kW 690V 60Hz a.c Thrusters: 2 Thwart. CP thruster (f); 2 Thwart. CP thruster (a) Fuel: 495.0 (d.f.) (Heating Coils) 3800.0 (r.f.) 120.0pd
8855578 *WBF3638* -	**VASCO DA GAMA** - **Westbank Corp** Daybrook Fisheries Inc *New Orleans, LA* *United States of America* MMSI: 367166240 Official number: 645397	*468* 318 -		**1982 Patterson Shipyard Inc. — Patterson, La** Yd No: 37 Loa - Br ex - Dght - Lbp 49.44 Br md 9.45 Dpth 3.44 Welded, 1 dk	**(B11B2FV) Fishing Vessel**	**1 oil engine** driving 1 FP propeller
6614750 *8QAJ* -	**VASCO MARKET** *ex* Ostra Pall *-1992* *ex* Tromoysund *-1986* **Happy Market Shipping Co Pvt Ltd** - *Male* *Maldives* Official number: 226-10T	*495* 242 762	Class: (NV) (HR)	**1966 AS Haugesunds Slip — Haugesund** Yd No: 7 Loa 62.79 Br ex 10.83 Dght 3.830 Lbp 55.61 Br md 10.72 Dpth 3.92 Welded, 1 dk & S dk	**(A31A2GX) General Cargo Ship** Grain: 1,982 Compartments: 1 Ho, ER 1 Ha: (8.3 x 3.9)ER Cranes: 1x5t; Derricks: 1x20t; Winches: 1 Ice Capable	**1 oil engine** driving 1 FP propeller Total Power: 993kW (1,350hp) 12.5kn Wichmann 9ACA 1 x 2 Stroke 9 Cy. 280 x 420 993kW (1350bhp) Wichmann Motorfabrikk AS-Norway AuxGen: 2 x 92kW 220V 50Hz a.c, 1 x 22kW 220V 50Hz a.c Fuel: 71.0 (d.f.) 3.5pd
8887650 - -	**VASIF HUSEYNOV** *ex* Reyd *-1993* **Azerbaijan State Caspian Shipping Co (ASCSS)** - *Baku* *Azerbaijan* Official number: DGR-0333	*136* 49 81	Class: RS	**1973**-10 **Astrakhan. SSZ im 10-iy God Oktyabrskoy Revolyutsii — Astrakhan** Yd No: 22 Loa 28.20 Br ex 7.30 Dght 2.770 Lbp 26.00 Br md 7.00 Dpth 3.75 Welded, 1 dk	**(B21B20T) Offshore Tug/Supply Ship** Ice Capable	**2 oil engines** driving 2 FP propellers Total Power: 442kW (600hp) 10.2kn Pervomaysk 6CHRP25/34 2 x 4 Stroke 6 Cy. 250 x 340 each-221kW (300bhp) Pervomaydizelmash (PDM)-Pervomaysk AuxGen: 2 x 50kW a.c Fuel: 10.0 (d.f.)
7508104 - -	**VASILIA EXPRESS** *ex* Caribe Dolphin C. I. *-1996* *ex* Tjigombong 1 *-1984* *ex* Kasim *-1979* - - -	*1,188* 457 1,439	Class: (KI) (AB)	**1976**-01 **Sing Koon Seng Pte Ltd — Singapore** Yd No: SKS303 Loa - Br ex - Dght 3.099 Lbp 70.11 Br md 13.42 Dpth 4.27 Welded, 1 dk	**(A35D2RL) Landing Craft** Bow door/ramp	**2 oil engines** geared to sc. shafts driving 2 FP propellers Total Power: 1,280kW (1,740hp) 11.0kn Deutz SBA6M528 2 x 4 Stroke 6 Cy. 220 x 280 each-640kW (870bhp) Kloeckner Humboldt Deutz AG-West Germany AuxGen: 2 x 90kW
7713527 - -	**VASILIJE** *ex* Borik *-2010* **Yu Briv doo** - *Kotor* *Montenegro*	*414* 219 170	Class: (CS) (JR)	**1978**-06 **Brodogradiliste 'Titovo' — Kraljevica** Yd No: 421 Converted From: Ferry (Passenger/Vehicle)-1978 Loa 44.56 Br ex 12.70 Dght 2.841 Lbp 39.22 Br md 12.41 Dpth 4.12 Welded, 1 dk	**(B34L2QU) Utility Vessel** Bow ramp (centre) Stern ramp (centre)	**4 oil engines** driving 4 CP propellers 2 fwd and 2 aft Total Power: 916kW (1,244hp) 9.5kn Scania DSI11 4 x 4 Stroke 6 Cy. 127 x 145 each-229kW (311bhp) (new engine 1993) Saab Scania AB-Sweden
8938071 - -	**VASILIKI** *ex* Pescarus 5 *-2006* *ex* IEP 6990 *-1983* **Ergomare SA** -	**119** 46 -	Class: (RN)	**1982 Santierul Naval Drobeta-Turnu Severin S.A. — Drobeta-Turnu S.** Yd No: 11435006 Loa 23.39 Br ex - Dght 2.320 Lbp 20.61 Br md 6.96 Dpth 3.30 Welded, 1 dk	**(B32A2ST) Tug**	**2 oil engines** driving 2 FP propellers Total Power: 410kW (558hp) 10.8kn Maybach MB836BB 2 x 4 Stroke 8 Cy. 175 x 205 each-205kW (279bhp) Uzina 23 August Bucuresti-Bucuresti AuxGen: 2 x 35kW 400V 50Hz a.c Fuel: 9.4 (d.f.)
8623999 *URHP* -	**VASILIY BOZHENKO** - **'Ukrrichflot' Joint Stock Shipping Co** - *Kherson* *Ukraine* MMSI: 272085000 Official number: 840109	**2,466** 988 3,135	Class: UA (RS)	**1984**-10 **Sudostroitelnyy Zavod "Krasnoye Sormovo" — Gorkiy** Yd No: 80 Loa 114.23 Br ex 13.21 Dght 3.423 Lbp 108.03 Br md 13.01 Dpth 5.54 Welded, 1 dk	**(A31A2GX) General Cargo Ship** Grain: 6,040; Bale: 5,770 Compartments: 4 Ta, ER 4 Ha: (17.6 x 9.3)3 (17.9 x 9.3)ER Ice Capable	**2 oil engines** driving 2 FP propellers Total Power: 970kW (1,318hp) 10.7kn S.K.L. 6NVD48A-2U 2 x 4 Stroke 6 Cy. 320 x 480 each-485kW (659bhp) VEB Schwermaschinenbau "KarlLiebknecht" (SKL)-Magdeburg AuxGen: 3 x 50kW a.c
8913277 *UBRW* -	**VASILIY GOLOVNIN** - **Murmansk Trawl Fleet Co (OAO 'Murmanskiy Tralovyy Flot')** - *Murmansk* *Russia* MMSI: 273845800 Official number: 913719	**1,928** 623 1,258	Class: RS (NV)	**1992**-06 **Sterkoder AS — Kristiansund** Yd No: 137 Loa 64.00 Br ex - Dght 5.780 Lbp 55.55 Br md 13.00 Dpth 8.85 Welded, 2 dks	**(B11A2FG) Factory Stern Trawler** Ice Capable	**1 oil engine** reduction geared to sc. shaft driving 1 FP propeller Total Power: 2,458kW (3,342hp) Wartsila 6R32 1 x 4 Stroke 6 Cy. 320 x 350 2458kW (3342bhp) Wartsila Diesel Oy-Finland AuxGen: 1 x 1304kW 380V 50Hz a.c, 2 x 336kW 380V 50Hz a.c Thrusters: 1 Thwart. FP thruster (f)
8723426 *UGWJ* -	**VASILIY GOLOVNIN** - **Far-Eastern Shipping Co (FESCO) (Dalnevostochnoye Morskoye Parokhodstvo)** - SatCom: Inmarsat A 1401727 *Vladivostok* *Russia* MMSI: 273149510 Official number: 861389	**13,514** 4,777 10,700	Class: RS	**1988**-12 **Khersonskiy Sudostroitelnyy Zavod — Kherson** Yd No: 5004 Loa 163.90 Br ex 22.46 Dght 9.000 Lbp 145.38 Br md 22.40 Dpth 12.00 Welded, 2 dk	**(A31A2GX) General Cargo Ship** Side door & ramp (s. a.) Grain: 15,590; Bale: 13,030; Ins: 424; Liq: 865 TEU 319 incl 28 ref C. Compartments: 5 Ho, ER 5 Ha: ER Cranes: 2x22.5t,3x12.5t Ice Capable	**2 diesel electric oil engines** driving 2 gen. each 5500kW d.c Connecting to 1 elec. Motor of (9300kW) driving 1 FP propeller Total Power: 11,460kW (15,582hp) 15.9kn Sulzer 12ZV40/48 2 x Vee 2 Stroke 12 Cy. 400 x 480 each-5730kW (7791bhp) Wartsila Diesel Oy-Finland AuxGen: 3 x 880kW 50Hz a.c Fuel: 830.0 (d.f.) 1440.0 (r.f.)
8908129 *UCMM* -	**VASILIY KALENOV** *ex* Pomor *-1995* **JSC Kamchatimpex** - SatCom: Inmarsat B 327309110 *Petropavlovsk-Kamchatskiy* *Russia* MMSI: 273848100 Official number: 910640	**7,765** 2,329 3,372	Class: RS	**1993**-02 **Volkswerft Stralsund GmbH — Stralsund** Yd No: 836 Loa 120.70 Br ex 19.03 Dght 6.620 Lbp 107.00 Br md 19.00 Dpth 12.22 Welded, 2 dks	**(B11A2FG) Factory Stern Trawler** Ins: 3,454 Ice Capable	**2 oil engines** with clutches, flexible couplings & sr geared to sc. shaft driving 1 CP propeller Total Power: 5,296kW (7,200hp) 15.0kn S.K.L. 6VDS48/42AL-2 2 x 4 Stroke 6 Cy. 420 x 480 each-2648kW (3600bhp) Maschinenbau Halberstadt GmbH-Halberstadt
6874829 *UBPE6* -	**VASILIY KIRILLOV** *ex* BK-1213 *-1967* **Rim Co Ltd** - *Sovetskaya Gavan* *Russia*	*182* 55 46	Class: RS	**1966**-05 **"Petrozavod" — Leningrad** Yd No: 709 Loa 29.30 Br ex 8.48 Dght 3.090 Lbp 27.00 Br md - Dpth 4.34 Welded, 1 dk	**(B32A2ST) Tug** Ice Capable	**2 oil engines** driving 2 CP propellers Total Power: 882kW (1,200hp) 11.5kn Russkiy 6D30/50-4-2 2 x 2 Stroke 6 Cy. 300 x 500 each-441kW (600bhp) (new engine 1977) Mashinostroitelnyy Zavod"Russkiy-Dizel"-Leningrad AuxGen: 2 x 25kW a.c Fuel: 43.0 (d.f.)
8036160 - -	**VASILIY KOSYAKOV** - **Ritmik Co Ltd (OOO Ritmik)** -	*245* 103 51	Class: (RS)	**1982**-06 **Nakhodkinskiy Sudoremontnyy Zavod — Nakhodka** Yd No: 25 Loa 38.41 Br ex 6.71 Dght 2.201 Lbp 34.50 Br md - Dpth 2.90 Welded, 1 dk	**(A37B2PS) Passenger Ship** Passengers: unberthed: 180 Ice Capable	**2 oil engines** geared to sc. shafts driving 2 FP propellers Total Power: 464kW (630hp) 12.5kn Daldizel 8CHNSP18/22 2 x 4 Stroke 8 Cy. 180 x 220 each-232kW (315bhp) Daldizel-Khabarovsk AuxGen: 3 x 13kW Fuel: 17.0 (d.f.)
8929783 - -	**VASILIY KRUGLOV** - **Azimut Ltd** - *Kaliningrad* *Russia* Official number: 752389	**182** 54 46	Class: (RS)	**1975 Gorokhovetskiy Sudostroitelnyy Zavod — Gorokhovets** Yd No: 332 Loa 29.30 Br ex 8.49 Dght 3.090 Lbp 27.00 Br md - Dpth 4.30 Welded, 1 dk	**(B32A2ST) Tug** Ice Capable	**2 oil engines** driving 2 CP propellers Total Power: 882kW (1,200hp) 11.4kn Russkiy 6D30/50-4-2 2 x 2 Stroke 6 Cy. 300 x 500 each-441kW (600bhp) Mashinostroitelnyy Zavod"Russkiy-Dizel"-Leningrad AuxGen: 2 x 30kW a.c Fuel: 36.0 (d.f.)

8607323 *UCUD* M-0009	**VASILIY LOZOVSKIY** **Strelets Co Ltd (OOO 'Strelets')** - SatCom: Inmarsat C 427300452 *Murmansk* *Russia* MMSI: 273527800 Official number: 893892	**7,765** 2,329 3,372	Class: RS	**1990**-05 **VEB Volkswerft Stralsund — Stralsund** Yd No: 823 Loa 120.47 Br ex 19.03 Dght 6.630 Lbp 108.12 Br md 19.02 Dpth 12.22 Welded, 1 dk	**(B11A2FG) Factory Stern Trawler** Ins: 3,454 Ice Capable	**2 oil engines** with clutches, flexible couplings & sr geared to sc. shaft driving 1 CP propeller Total Power: 5,296kW (7,200hp) 15.5kn S.K.L. 6VDS48/42AL-2 2 x 4 Stroke 6 Cy. 420 x 480 each-2648kW (3600bhp) VEB Maschinenbau Halberstadt-Halberstadt AuxGen: 2 x 1500kW a.c, 2 x 760kW a.c
8858647 *UILF* -	**VASILIY LUKANOV** **ZAO 'Aldzena' JSC** - *Khasanskiy* *Russia*	**359** 107 129	Class: RS	**1991**-10 **Sudostroitelnyy Zavod "Avangard" — Petrozavodsk** Yd No: 633 Loa 35.72 Br ex 8.92 Dght 3.470 Lbp 31.00 Br md 8.80 Dpth 6.07 Welded, 1 dk	**(B11A2FS) Stern Trawler** Ice Capable	**1 oil engine** driving 1 FP propeller Total Power: 588kW (799hp) 10.9kn S.K.L. 6NVD48A-2U 1 x 4 Stroke 6 Cy. 320 x 480 588kW (799bhp) SKL Motoren u. Systemtechnik AG-Magdeburg Fuel: 82.0 (d.f.)
7612486 *UCFZ* -	**VASILIY MALOV** *ex* Baltiyskiy-104 *-1981* **NWS Fourteen Balt Shipping Co Ltd** JS North-Western Shipping Co (OAO 'Severo-Zapadnoye Parokhodstvo') *St Petersburg* *Russia* MMSI: 273324400	**1,926** 936 2,557	Class: RS	**1978**-11 **Valmet Oy — Turku** Yd No: 368 Loa 95.00 Br ex 13.21 Dght 4.100 Lbp 90.20 Br md 13.01 Dpth 5.49 Welded, 1 dk	**(A31A2GX) General Cargo Ship** Bale: 3,475 TEU 83 C.Ho 48/20' C.Dk 35/20' Compartments: 3 Ho, ER 3 Ha: (16.5 x 8.3)2 (16.5 x 10.2)ER Ice Capable	**2 oil engines** reverse reduction geared to sc. shafts driving 2 FP propellers Total Power: 1,280kW (1,740hp) 12.5kn S.K.L. 6NVD48A-2U 2 x 4 Stroke 6 Cy. 320 x 480 each-640kW (870bhp) VEB Schwermaschinenbau "KarlLiebknecht" (SKL)-Magdeburg Thrusters: 1 Thwart. FP thruster (f) Fuel: 212.0 (r.f.)
8701038 *UIQL* -	**VASILIY POLESHCHUK** *ex* Vasilij Poleshchuk *-2001* **Euphrates Co Ltd** - *Nakhodka* *Russia* MMSI: 273429140	**12,410** 4,104 10,085	Class: RS (NV)	**1987**-03 **VEB Mathias-Thesen-Werft — Wismar** Yd No: 236 Loa 152.94 Br ex - Dght 8.290 Lbp 141.99 Br md 22.20 Dpth 13.60 Welded, 1 dk, 2nd & 3rd dk in holds only	**(B12B2FC) Fish Carrier** Ins: 13,326 Compartments: 4 Ho, ER, 8 Tw Dk 4 Ha: 4 (6.0 x 3.9)ER Derricks: 2x10t,7x5t Ice Capable	**1 oil engine** driving 1 FP propeller Total Power: 7,600kW (10,333hp) 15.0kn MAN K5SZ70/125BL 1 x 2 Stroke 5 Cy. 700 x 1250 7600kW (10333bhp) VEB Dieselmotorenwerk Rostock-Rostock AuxGen: 4 x 588kW 390V 50Hz a.c Fuel: 633.0 (d.f.) 3902.0 (r.f.) 41.5pd
9057288 *9HNH8* -	**VASILIY SHUKSHIN** **NWS 5 Balt Shipping Co Ltd** INOK NV *Valletta* *Malta* MMSI: 256179000 Official number: 9057288	**2,506** 1,185 2,792	Class: RS (LR) (GL) ✠ Classed LR until 6/8/05	**1995**-08 **OAO Volgogradskiy Sudostroitelnyy Zavod — Volgograd** Yd No: 205 Loa 89.50 Br ex 13.42 Dght 4.281 Lbp 84.90 Br md 13.20 Dpth 5.50 Welded, 1 dk	**(A31A2GX) General Cargo Ship** Grain: 3,330 TEU 128 C. 128/20' Compartments: 2 Ho, ER 2 Ha: ER Ice Capable	**1 oil engine** with clutches, flexible couplings & sr reverse geared to sc. shaft driving 1 FP propeller Total Power: 1,740kW (2,366hp) 11.8kn Wartsila 12V22HF 1 x Vee 4 Stroke 12 Cy. 220 x 240 1740kW (2366bhp) Wartsila Diesel Oy-Finland AuxGen: 2 x 160kW 400V 50Hz a.c, 1 x 80kW 400V 50Hz a.c Thrusters: 1 Thwart. FP thruster (f) Fuel: 240.0 (d.f.)
8885157 *V3RO5* -	**VASILIY TATISHCHEV** *ex* Volgo-Don 209 *-1994* **Saluta Shipping Ltd** Kent Shipping & Chartering Ltd *Belize City* *Belize* MMSI: 312409000 Official number: 141120198	**3,956** 1,291 5,009	Class: IV (RS) (RR)	**1977**-07 **Navashinskiy Sudostroitelnyy Zavod 'Oka' — Navashino** Yd No: 1120 Loa 138.30 Br ex 16.75 Dght 3.380 Lbp 135.00 Br md 16.50 Dpth 5.50 Welded, 1 dk	**(A31A2GX) General Cargo Ship** Grain: 6,370; Bale: 3,877 Compartments: 2 Ho, ER 2 Ha: (45.6 x 12.3) (45.0 x 12.3)ER	**2 oil engines** driving 2 FP propellers Total Power: 1,324kW (1,800hp) 10.5kn Dvigatel Revolyutsii 6CHRN36/45 2 x 4 Stroke 6 Cy. 360 x 450 each-662kW (900bhp) Zavod "Dvigatel Revolyutsii"-Gorkiy AuxGen: 2 x 100kW Fuel: 145.0 (d.f.)
7226536 *UAXD* -	**VASILIY TEPLOV** **Ust-Khayryuzovskiy Fish Cannery Plant (Ust-Khayryuzovskiy Rybokonservnyy Zavod)** - SatCom: Inmarsat C 427330145 *Petropavlovsk-Kamchatskiy* *Russia* MMSI: 273413300	**172** 51 100	Class: RS	**1972**-07 **Astrakhanskaya Sudoverf im. "Kirova" — Astrakhan** Yd No: 35 Loa 34.02 Br ex 7.09 Dght 2.900 Lbp 31.19 Br md 7.00 Dpth 3.69 Welded, 1 dk	**(B11B2FV) Fishing Vessel** Bale: 95 Compartments: 1 Ho, ER 1 Ha: (1.6 x 1.3) Derricks: 2x2t Ice Capable	**1 oil engine** driving 1 FP propeller Total Power: 224kW (305hp) 9.0kn S.K.L. 8NVD36-1U 1 x 4 Stroke 8 Cy. 240 x 360 224kW (305bhp) VEB Schwermaschinenbau "KarlLiebknecht" (SKL)-Magdeburg AuxGen: 1 x 75kW a.c, 1 x 50kW a.c Fuel: 19.0 (d.f.)
9372547 *UEVN* -	**VASILY DINKOV** **Loteria Shipping Co Ltd** Unicom Management Services (St Petersburg) Ltd *St Petersburg* *Russia* MMSI: 273345020 Official number: 070060	**49,597** 21,075 72,722 T/cm 80.4	Class: AB RS	**2008**-01 **Samsung Heavy Industries Co Ltd — Geoje** Yd No: 1660 Loa 257.29 Br ex 34.06 Dght 14.000 Lbp 234.70 Br md 34.00 Dpth 21.00 Welded, 1 dk	**(A13A2TS) Shuttle Tanker** Double Hull (13F) Liq: 84,641; Liq (Oil): 84,641 Cargo Heating Coils Compartments: 10 Wing Ta, 2 Wing Slop Ta, ER 10 Cargo Pump (s): 10x800m³/hr Manifold: Bow/CM: 119.9m Ice Capable	**3 diesel electric oil engines** driving 1 gen. of 4200kW 440V a.c 2 gen. each 11200kW 440V a.c Connecting to 2 elec. motors each (10000kW) driving 2 Azimuth electric drive units Total Power: 27,550kW (37,456hp) 15.7kn Wartsila 16V38 2 x Vee 4 Stroke 16 Cy. 380 x 475 each-11600kW (15771bhp) Wartsila Italia SpA-Italy Wartsila 6L38 1 x 4 Stroke 6 Cy. 380 x 475 4350kW (5914bhp) Wartsila Italia SpA-Italy Thrusters: 1 Thwart. FP thruster (f) Fuel: 296.6 (d.f.) 3401.2 (r.f.)
8721181 *UBHE* HA-6126	**VASILYEVSKIY OSTROV** **JSC 'Tralflot'** - SatCom: Inmarsat A 1401535 *Petropavlovsk-Kamchatskiy* *Russia* MMSI: 273811060 Official number: 883829	**4,407** 1,322 1,810	Class: RS	**1988**-10 **GP Chernomorskiy Sudostroitelnyy Zavod — Nikolayev** Yd No: 571 Loa 104.50 Br ex 16.03 Dght 5.900 Lbp 96.40 Br md 16.00 Dpth 10.20 Welded, 2 dks	**(B11A2FG) Factory Stern Trawler** Ice Capable	**2 oil engines** geared to sc. shaft driving 1 CP propeller Total Power: 5,152kW (7,004hp) 16.1kn Russkiy 6CHN40/46 2 x 4 Stroke 6 Cy. 400 x 460 each-2576kW (3502bhp) Mashinostroitelnyy Zavod"Russkiy-Dizel"-Leningrad AuxGen: 2 x 1600kW a.c, 3 x 200kW a.c
8710833 - -	**VASK ONCE** *ex* Peix Del Mar Once *-2001* **Eurorim Industries Sem** - *Nouadhibou* *Mauritania* Official number: NDB 857	**364** 109 172	Class: (BV)	**1988**-02 **Astilleros Zamakona SA — Santurtzi** Yd No: 149 Loa 36.71 Br ex - Dght 3.401 Lbp 31.68 Br md 8.31 Dpth 5.41 Welded, 1 dk	**(B11A2FS) Stern Trawler** Ins: 277	**1 oil engine** with flexible couplings & sr geared to sc. shaft driving 1 FP propeller Total Power: 780kW (1,060hp) Caterpillar 3512TA 1 x Vee 4 Stroke 12 Cy. 170 x 190 780kW (1060bhp) Caterpillar Inc-USA
8927905 *UFBC* -	**VASKOVO** **Arctic Anchorage (Baza Reydovykh Arkticheskikh Plavsredstv - Arktikreyd Navigating Co)** - *Arkhangelsk* *Russia*	*145* 47 158	Class: RS	**1978 Sudoremontnyy Zavod "Krasnaya Kuznitsa" — Arkhangelsk** Yd No: 9 Loa 35.75 Br ex 7.40 Dght 1.710 Lbp 33.50 Br md 7.20 Dpth 2.40 Welded, 1 dk	**(A31C2GD) Deck Cargo Ship** Ice Capable	**1 oil engine** geared to sc. shaft driving 1 FP propeller Total Power: 165kW (224hp) 7.8kn Daldizel 6CHNSP18/22 1 x 4 Stroke 6 Cy. 180 x 220 165kW (224bhp) Daldizel-Khabarovsk AuxGen: 2 x 13kW a.c Fuel: 5.0 (d.f.)
8969094 *SX6656* -	**VASOS K** **Porthmia Kefallinias Naftiki Eteria** Taxiarchis Sea Lines Group *Piraeus* *Greece* MMSI: 237357700 Official number: 10431	**478** 189 -	Class: PR	**1997 in Greece** Loa 56.00 Br ex - Dght - Lbp - Br md 14.00 Dpth - Welded, 1 dk	**(A37B2PS) Passenger Ship**	**1 oil engine** driving 1 FP propeller Total Power: 603kW (820hp)
5040433 *SV5008* -	**VASOULA** *ex* Doxa *-1996* *ex* Gamma *-1982* *ex* BP Zest *-1980* *ex* Ben Harold Smith *-1976* **Thalassopouli Maritime Co** - *Piraeus* *Greece* MMSI: 237099800 Official number: 7897	*325* 162 328	Class: (LR) ✠ Classed LR until 1/82	**1952**-09 **Rowhedge Ironworks Co. Ltd. — Rowhedge** Yd No: 742 Loa 41.46 Br ex 7.95 Dght 2.306 Lbp 40.24 Br md 7.93 Dpth 2.90 Riveted\Welded, 1 dk	**(A13B2TU) Tanker (unspecified)** Liq: 396; Liq (Oil): 396 Compartments: 4 Ta, ER	**1 oil engine** driving 1 FP propeller Total Power: 228kW (310hp) 8.5kn Polar M44I 1 x 2 Stroke 4 Cy. 250 x 420 228kW (310bhp) British Polar Engines Ltd.-Glasgow AuxGen: 1 x 15kW 110V d.c Fuel: 10.0 (d.f.) 1.5pd
7113375 *SXQK* -	**VASSILIKI** *ex* Lindfjord *-1997* *ex* Stor *-1980* **Petronavia Shipping Co** Andriamar Shipping Inc *Piraeus* *Greece* MMSI: 239512000 Official number: 10498	**2,026** 1,015 3,184 T/cm 9.0	Class: (GL)	**1971**-07 **C. Luehring — Brake** Yd No: 7101 Loa 86.72 Br ex 12.53 Dght 5.690 Lbp 78.59 Br md 12.51 Dpth 6.35 Welded, 1 dk	**(A13B2TP) Products Tanker** Liq: 3,726; Liq (Oil): 3,726 Compartments: 11 Ta, ER 1 Cargo Pump (s): 1x228m³/hr Ice Capable	**1 oil engine** sr geared to sc. shaft driving 1 FP propeller Total Power: 1,324kW (1,800hp) 12.0kn MaK 8M452AK 1 x 4 Stroke 8 Cy. 320 x 450 1324kW (1800bhp) Atlas MaK Maschinenbau GmbH-Kiel

IMO / Call sign	Name / Owner	Tonnage	Class	Builder / Dimensions	Type	Machinery
5424512 *HQQH7* -	**VASSILIKO BAY** *ex* Albatros I *-1991* *ex* Vassiliko Bay *-2003* *ex* Marina Bay *-1991* *ex* Anna Marina *-1990* *ex* Frances *-1989* *ex* Cariba *-1988* *ex* Eastholm *-1986* *ex* Anne Sobye *-1984* *ex* Lankenauersand *-1972* **Olympic Navigation SA** - *San Lorenzo* *Honduras* MMSI: 334596000 Official number: L-0315937	**998** 605 1,101	Class: (HR) (GL)	**1963 Elsflether Werft AG — Elsfleth** Yd No: 339 Loa 68.10 Br ex 10.44 Dght 3.810 Lbp 61.42 Br md 10.42 Dpth 5.80 Welded, 1 dk	**(A31A2GX) General Cargo Ship** Grain: 2,265; Bale: 1,981 Compartments: 2 Ho, ER 2 Ha: 2 (15.0 x 6.0)ER Ice Capable	**1 oil engine** driving 1 FP propeller Total Power: 780kW (1,060hp) 9.5kn Deutz RBV8M545 1 x 4 Stroke 8 Cy. 320 x 450 780kW (1060bhp) Kloeckner Humboldt Deutz AG-West Germany AuxGen: 2 x 30kW 230V d.c
7606932 *5VAU9* -	**VASSILIO XVIII** *ex* Vassilios XVIII *-2010* *ex* Virtue *-2000* *ex* Belopolye *-1995* *ex* Essi Baltic *-1984* *ex* Johot *-1979* **NV Lihansa io** NV Sanahil io SatCom: Inmarsat C 467115110 *Lome* *Togo* MMSI: 671151000	**1,471** 677 2,575 T/cm 7.1	Class: (BV) (RS) (NV)	**1977-05 Aukra Bruk AS — Aukra** Yd No: 60 Loa 69.68 Br ex 12.73 Dght 5.700 Lbp 64.40 Br md 12.70 Dpth 6.61 Welded, 1 dk	**(A13B2TP) Products Tanker** Liq: 5,329; Liq (Oil): 5,329; Asphalt: 5,329 Cargo Heating Coils Compartments: 16 Ta, ER 3 Cargo Pump (s) Ice Capable	**1 oil engine** driving 1 FP propeller Total Power: 971kW (1,320hp) 11.5kn S.K.L. 8NVD48A-2 1 x 4 Stroke 8 Cy. 320 x 480 971kW (1320bhp) VEB Schwermaschinenbau "KarlLiebknecht" (SKL)-Magdeburg AuxGen: 3 x 132kW 380V 50Hz a.c Fuel: 132.0 (d.f.) 4.5pd
9041502 *J8B2485* -	**VASSILIOS XXI** *ex* Taisei Maru *-2002* **Continental Shipmanagement Inc** Vassilios Shipmanagement SA *Kingstown* *St Vincent & The Grenadines* MMSI: 377077000 Official number: 8957	**3,262** 1,497 4,920 T/cm 12.7	Class: BV (NK)	**1992-01 Higaki Zosen K.K. — Imabari** Yd No: 401 Loa 103.19 (BB) Br ex 15.31 Dght 6.335 Lbp 95.80 Br md 15.00 Dpth 7.50 Welded, 1 dk	**(A13B2TP) Products Tanker** Liq: 5,450; Liq (Oil): 5,450 Compartments: 10 Wing Ta, ER 2 Cargo Pump (s)	**1 oil engine** driving 1 CP propeller Total Power: 2,942kW (4,000hp) 13.5kn Akasaka A45 1 x 4 Stroke 6 Cy. 450 x 880 2942kW (4000bhp) Akasaka Tekkosho KK (Akasaka DieselLtd)-Japan AuxGen: 4 x 240kW a.c Thrusters: 1 Thwart. CP thruster (f)
9256872 *P3ST9* -	**VASSOS** **Avstes Shipping Corp** Safety Management Overseas SA *Limassol* *Cyprus* MMSI: 210256000 Official number: 9256872	**40,002** 26,101 76,015 T/cm 67.8	Class: LR ✠ **100A1** SS 02/2014 bulk carrier strengthened for heavy cargoes, Nos. 2, 4 and 6 holds may be empty ESP ESN *IWS LI **ShipRight** (SDA, FDA, CM) EP (B) ✠ **LMC** **UMS** Eq.Ltr: O†; Cable: 660.0/78.0 U3 (a)	**2004-02 Tsuneishi Corp — Fukuyama HS** Yd No: 1248 Loa 225.00 (BB) Br ex 32.30 Dght 14.013 Lbp 217.00 Br md 32.26 Dpth 19.30 Welded, 1 dk	**(A21A2BC) Bulk Carrier** Grain: 91,300 Compartments: 7 Ho, ER 7 Ha: 6 (17.3 x 15.4)ER (15.6 x 12.8)	**1 oil engine** driving 1 FP propeller Total Power: 8,550kW (11,625hp) 14.5kn B&W 6S60MC 1 x 2 Stroke 6 Cy. 600 x 2292 8550kW (11625bhp) Mitsui Engineering & Shipbuilding CLtd-Japan AuxGen: 3 x 600kW 450V 60Hz a.c Boilers: AuxB (Comp) 7.1kgf/cm² (7.0bar)
8950536 - -	**VAST EXPLORER** *ex* Guardian II *-2001* *ex* Camille Eugene Pouliot *-2001* **Nolan Associates LLC** - *Provincetown, MA* *United States of America* Official number: 1129492	*106* 85 -		**1983 Industries Raymond Inc — Sept-Iles QC** L reg 20.10 Br ex - Dght - Lbp - Br md 6.00 Dpth 3.00 Welded, 1 dk	**(B31A2SR) Research Survey Vessel** Hull Material: Aluminium Alloy	**2 oil engines** driving 2 FP propellers Total Power: 994kW (1,352hp) 21.0kn
8405220 *XUGZ6* -	**VAST OCEAN** *ex* Heng Tong *-2010* *ex* Maritime Master *-2010* *ex* Ocean Master *-1992* **Win Trade Worldwide Ltd** Shenghao Marine (Hong Kong) Ltd *Phnom Penh* *Cambodia* MMSI: 515907000 Official number: 1384164	**15,850** 9,110 26,320	Class: PD (NK)	**1984-12 Kurushima Dockyard Co. Ltd. — Onishi** Yd No: 2305 Loa 160.00 (BB) Br ex - Dght 10.372 Lbp 150.00 Br md 25.40 Dpth 14.20 Welded, 1 dk	**(A21A2BC) Bulk Carrier** Grain: 33,139; Bale: 31,879 Compartments: 4 Ho, ER 4 Ha: (17.6 x 11.5) (20.8 x 13.1) (22.4 x 13.1) (21.6 x 13.1)ER Cranes: 4x25t	**1 oil engine** driving 1 FP propeller Total Power: 5,296kW (7,200hp) 13.7kn Mitsubishi 6UEC52HA 1 x 2 Stroke 6 Cy. 520 x 1250 5296kW (7200bhp) Kobe Hatsudoki KK-Japan AuxGen: 2 x 400kW a.c Fuel: 1320.0 (r.f.)
9115030 *3FVX4* -	**VAST OCEAN 1** *ex* Sea Sapphire *-2013* *ex* Kobe Queen *-2005* **Hao Yang Shipping (HK) Ltd** Weihai Yunhao International Ship Management Co Ltd SatCom: Inmarsat C 435478810 *Panama* *Panama* MMSI: 354788000 Official number: 2197195E	**7,657** 2,708 9,038 T/cm 18.5	Class: NK	**1995-02 Higaki Zosen K.K. — Imabari** Yd No: 451 Loa 114.11 (BB) Br ex - Dght 7.432 Lbp 105.40 Br md 19.60 Dpth 13.20 Welded, 2 dks	**(A31A2GX) General Cargo Ship** Grain: 16,606; Bale: 14,781 TEU 40 Compartments: 2 Ho, ER 2 Ha: (20.3 x 12.6) (33.6 x 12.6)ER Cranes: 2x25t; Derricks: 1x25t	**1 oil engine** driving 1 FP propeller Total Power: 3,884kW (5,281hp) 12.8kn B&W 6L35MC 1 x 2 Stroke 6 Cy. 350 x 1050 3884kW (5281bhp) Mitsui Engineering & Shipbuilding CLtd-Japan Fuel: 580.0 (r.f.)
7856513 - -	**VAST POWER** *ex* Vast Power I *-2006* *ex* Kurikoma Maru *-1997* **PT Pelayaran Gema Tirta Sarana** - *Balikpapan* *Indonesia*	*175* 105 -	Class: (KI)	**1968-02 Yokohama Yacht Co Ltd — Yokohama KN** Yd No: 578 Loa 26.80 Br ex - Dght 2.380 Lbp 24.50 Br md 7.00 Dpth 3.41 Welded, 1 dk	**(B32B2SP) Pusher Tug**	**2 oil engines** driving 2 FP propellers Total Power: 588kW (800hp) 10.5kn Daihatsu 6PSHTBM-20 2 x 4 Stroke 6 Cy. each-294kW (400bhp) Daihatsu Diesel Manufacturing Co Lt-Japan
7342495 *9MGX8* -	**VASTA JATI** *ex* Nico Sattahip *-2006* *ex* Nico Satwa *-2001* *ex* Trojan Tide *-1991* **Vastalux Sdn Bhd** - *Port Klang* *Malaysia* MMSI: 533960000 Official number: 332301	**1,318** 395 1,174	Class: (LR) (NV) ✠ Classed LR until 13/3/91	**1975-03 Hall, Russell & Co. Ltd. — Aberdeen** Yd No: 966 Loa 58.32 Br ex 13.09 Dght 4.776 Lbp 52.68 Br md 12.81 Dpth 5.95 Welded, 2 dks	**(B21B20T) Offshore Tug/Supply Ship** Liq: 170 Compartments: 4 Ta, ER	**2 oil engines** driving 2 CP propellers Total Power: 4,230kW (5,752hp) 13.0kn EMD (Electro-Motive) 16-645-E5 2 x Vee 2 Stroke 16 Cy. 230 x 254 each-2115kW (2876bhp) General Motors Corp-USA AuxGen: 3 x 250kW 415V 60Hz a.c Thrusters: 1 Thwart. FP thruster (f) Fuel: 386.0 (d.f.)
5377135 *SFUK* -	**VASTAN** *ex* Nya Svartsjolandet *-1991* **Waxholms Angfartygs AB** - *Vaxholm* *Sweden* MMSI: 265522440	**166** 69 -		**1900 Motala Verkstad — Motala** Yd No: 414 Loa 32.47 Br ex 5.91 Dght 3.101 Lbp - Br md 5.90 Dpth - Riveted, 1 dk	**(A37B2PS) Passenger Ship** Passengers: unberthed: 340	**1 oil engine** driving 1 CP propeller Total Power: 687kW (934hp) 12.0kn Alpha 405-26VO 1 x 2 Stroke 5 Cy. 260 x 400 312kW (424bhp) (new engine 1966) Alpha Diesel A/S-Denmark AuxGen: 1 x 48kW a.c, 1 x 33kW a.c Fuel: 6.0 (d.f.) 1.7pd
6600618 *SITA* -	**VASTANVIK** - **Vestanvik Shipping Ltd** Eureka Shipping Ltd *Slite* *Sweden* MMSI: 265191000	**2,256** 738 3,282	Class: BV (LR) ✠ Classed LR until 26/4/10	**1966-03 Wartsila-Koncernen, AB Crichton-Vulcan — Turku** Yd No: 1132 Loa 90.48 Br ex 13.03 Dght 5.773 Lbp 82.05 Br md 13.01 Dpth 7.60 Welded, 1 dk	**(A24A2BT) Cement Carrier** Grain: 2,713 Compartments: 2 Ho, ER Ice Capable	**1 oil engine** sr geared to sc. shaft driving 1 CP propeller Total Power: 2,060kW (2,801hp) Nohab F312V 1 x Vee 4 Stroke 12 Cy. 250 x 300 2060kW (2801bhp) (new engine 1986) Wartsila Diesel Oy-Finland AuxGen: 2 x 300kW 400V 50Hz a.c Thrusters: 1 Thwart. FP thruster (f)
9328443 *IIXW2* -	**VASTASO** - **Rimorchiatori Laziali Impresa di Salvataggio e Rimorchi SpA** - SatCom: Inmarsat C 424703092 *Naples* *Italy* MMSI: 247289200	**448** 134 373	Class: RI	**2005-07 Cant. Nav. Rosetti — Ravenna** Yd No: 59 Loa 35.31 Br ex - Dght 4.760 Lbp 29.63 Br md 10.80 Dpth 5.60 Welded, 1 dk	**(B32A2ST) Tug**	**2 oil engines** geared to sc. shafts driving 2 Directional propellers Total Power: 4,082kW (5,550hp) 12.5kn Deutz SBV9M628 2 x 4 Stroke 9 Cy. 240 x 280 each-2041kW (2775bhp) Deutz AG-Koeln AuxGen: 2 x a.c Thrusters: 1 Tunnel thruster (f)
9568251 *SJDE* GG 181	**VASTERLAND** - **Vasterland AB** - *Hono* *Sweden* MMSI: 266322000	**228** - -		**2009-09 Stocznia Remontowa 'Nauta' SA — Gdynia** (Hull) **2010 Vestvaerftet ApS — Hvide Sande** Yd No: 283 Loa 23.99 (BB) Br ex - Dght - Lbp - Br md 7.70 Dpth 6.10 Welded, 1 dk	**(B11A2FS) Stern Trawler**	**1 oil engine** driving 1 Propeller Thrusters: 1 Tunnel thruster (f)

IMO / Call sign	Name / Owner / Flag	Tonnage	Class	Builder / Dimensions	Type	Machinery
8322765 *SKNM* -	**VASTFJORD** *ex* Westfjord *-2013* *ex* Shannon *-2012* *ex* Pernille *-2012* **Vastfjord Fiskeri AB** - *Foto* *Sweden* MMSI: 266352000	**499** 245 -		**1984-11 Johs Kristensen Skibsbyggeri A/S — Hvide Sande** Yd No: 169 Loa 37.83 Br ex 9.71 Dght - Lbp 32.47 Br md 9.61 Dpth 6.71 Welded, 2 dks	**(B11A2FS) Stern Trawler** Ins: 619	**1 oil engine** with clutches, flexible couplings & sr geared to sc. shaft driving 1 CP propeller Total Power: 809kW (1,100hp) 11.5kn Alpha 6T23L-KVO 1 x 4 Stroke 6 Cy. 225 x 300 809kW (1100bhp) B&W Alpha Diesel A/S-Denmark AuxGen: 2 x 64kW 380V 50Hz a.c Thrusters: 1 Thwart. FP thruster (f)
9005235 *JVCY5* -	**VASTIKA IV** *ex* Zap *-2013* *ex* Yiomaral *-2012* *ex* Dundee *-2004* *ex* Golar Dundee *-2001* **Garbin Navigation Ltd** Sambouk Shipping FZC *Ulaanbaatar* *Mongolia* MMSI: 457900051	**156,096** 101,762 299,085 T/cm 170.4	Class: (NV)	**1993-01 Daewoo Shipbuilding & Heavy Machinery Ltd — Geoje** Yd No: 5063 Conv to DH-2011 Loa 332.00 (BB) Br ex 58.00 Dght 22.022 Lbp 320.00 Br md 56.00 Dpth 28.10 Welded, 1 dk	**(A13A2TV) Crude Oil Tanker** Double Hull (13F) Liq: 309,259; Liq (Oil): 350,000 Compartments: 14 Wing Ta, 2 Wing Slop Ta, ER 3 Cargo Pump (s): 3x5500m³/hr Manifold: Bow/CM: 168.5m	**1 oil engine** driving 1 FP propeller Total Power: 26,079kW (35,457hp) 15.5kn Sulzer 7RTA84M 1 x 2 Stroke 7 Cy. 840 x 2900 26079kW (35457bhp) Korea Heavy Industries & ConstrCo Ltd (HANJUNG)-South Korea AuxGen: 3 x 1200kW 220/440V 60Hz a.c Fuel: 300.0 (d.f.) 6900.0 (r.f.)
8976932 *SLKZ* -	**VASTRA BANKEN** *ex* Grundkallen *-1923* *ex* Kopparstenarne *-1911* **Rolf Elis Wiklund** - *Norrtalje* *Sweden*	**209** 69 -		**1901 Bergsunds Mekaniska Verkstads AB — Stockholm** Converted From: Lightship-1970 Loa 28.10 Br ex - Dght 3.120 Lbp - Br md 6.99 Dpth - Riveted, 1 dk	**(A37B2PS) Passenger Ship**	**1 oil engine** driving 1 CP propeller Total Power: 129kW (175hp) 8.0kn Bolinders 1 x 2 Stroke 2 Cy. 129kW (175bhp) (new engine 1923) J & C G Bolinders MekaniskaVerkstad AB-Sweden
5377173 - -	**VASTTANK** *ex* Vastmanland *-1952* *ex* Sigvard *-1952* - -	*223* 110 275	Class: (GL)	**1907 P. Larsson — Torrskog** Converted From: General Cargo Ship-1952 Loa 31.86 Br ex 6.81 Dght 2.720 Lbp 30.38 Br md 6.76 Dpth 3.03 Riveted, 1 dk	**(A13B2TU) Tanker (unspecified)**	**1 oil engine** reduction geared to sc. shaft driving 1 FP propeller Total Power: 221kW (300hp) Volvo Penta TAMD120AK 1 x 4 Stroke 6 Cy. 130 x 150 221kW (300bhp) (new engine 1975) AB Volvo Penta-Sweden
7723481 *3DPN* -	**VASUA** - **Government of The Republic of The Fiji Islands** - *Suva* *Fiji* Official number: 332644	*238* 97 259	Class: (AB)	**1978-09 Marine Builders Pte Ltd — Singapore** Yd No: 1029 Loa 33.00 Br ex - Dght - Lbp 30.51 Br md 8.50 Dpth 2.47 Welded, 1 dk	**(A35D2RL) Landing Craft** Bow door/ramp	**2 oil engines** geared to sc. shafts driving 2 FP propellers Total Power: 302kW (410hp) G.M. (Detroit Diesel) 6-71-TI 2 x 2 Stroke 6 Cy. 108 x 127 each-151kW (205bhp) Detroit Diesel Corporation-Detroit, Mi AuxGen: 2 x 30kW
9328235 - -	**VASUDHA** - **Tartous General Port Co** - *Syria*	**270** - 85		**2003-09 Bharati Shipyard Ltd — Ratnagiri** Yd No: 287 Loa - Br ex - Dght - Lbp - Br md - Dpth - Welded, 1 dk	**(B32A2ST) Tug**	**2 oil engines** geared to sc. shafts driving 2 Propellers
7325954 *D6GK6* -	**VASYL FRANKO** *ex* Tacoronte *-2012* *launched as* Helios *-1974* **Eastern Logistics Co Ltd SA** - *Moroni* *Union of Comoros* MMSI: 616999079	**201** 60 135	Class: (LR) ✠ Classed LR until 10/89	**1974-01 Astilleros de Santander SA (ASTANDER) — El Astillero** Yd No: 90 Loa 31.91 Br ex 8.84 Dght 3.499 Lbp 28.50 Br md 8.60 Dpth 4.09 Welded, 1 dk	**(B32A2ST) Tug**	**1 oil engine** dr geared to sc. shaft driving 1 CP propeller Total Power: 1,324kW (1,800hp) MWM TBD500-6 1 x 4 Stroke 6 Cy. 360 x 450 1324kW (1800bhp) Fabrica de San Carlos SA-Spain AuxGen: 2 x 80kW 380V 50Hz a.c, 1 x 20kW 380V 50Hz a.c
7311496 *UCDC* -	**VATAN-1** *ex* Sormovskiy-27 *-2003* **Media Shipping Inc** VTS-Trans Co Ltd (IP OOO 'VTS-Trans') *Astrakhan* *Russia* MMSI: 273431760 Official number: 720392	**2,457** 952 3,134	Class: RS	**1973-01 Sudostroitelnyy Zavod "Krasnoye Sormovo" — Gorkiy** Yd No: 37 Loa 114.03 Br ex 13.21 Dght 3.650 Lbp 108.01 Br md 13.00 Dpth 5.52 Welded, 1 dk	**(A31A2GX) General Cargo Ship** Bale: 4,297 Compartments: 4 Ho, ER 4 Ha: (17.6 x 9.3)3 (18.1 x 9.3)ER Ice Capable	**2 oil engines** driving 2 FP propellers Total Power: 970kW (1,318hp) 10.8kn S.K.L. 6NVD48A-U 2 x 4 Stroke 6 Cy. 320 x 480 each-485kW (659bhp) VEB Schwermaschinenbau "KarlLiebknecht" (SKL)-Magdeburg AuxGen: 3 x 50kW Fuel: 94.0 (d.f.)
9037290 *TCCC9* -	**VATAN L** *ex* Obahan C *-2007* *ex* Delight *-2003* **Clean Shipping Ltd** Armador Gemi Isletmecilig Ticaret Ltd Sti (Armador Shipping) *Istanbul* *Turkey* MMSI: 271000694	**6,167** 3,146 9,205 T/cm 17.9	Class: BV	**2002-02 Santierul Naval Damen Galati S.A. — Galati** Yd No: 863 Loa 130.76 (BB) Br ex - Dght 8.100 Lbp 121.00 Br md 17.70 Dpth 10.20 Welded, 1 dk	**(A31A2GX) General Cargo Ship** Grain: 11,197; Bale: 10,669 TEU 900 C. 900/20' Compartments: 3 Ho, ER 3 Ha: (30.2 x 13.0) (16.8 x 8.0)ER (29.5 x 13.0) Cranes: 3	**1 oil engine** reduction geared to sc. shaft driving 1 CP propeller Total Power: 3,840kW (5,221hp) 15.0kn MaK 8M32C 1 x 4 Stroke 8 Cy. 320 x 480 3840kW (5221bhp) Caterpillar Motoren GmbH & Co. KG-Germany AuxGen: 1 x 600kW 400/230V 50Hz a.c, 2 x 450kW 400/230V 50Hz a.c Thrusters: 1 Tunnel thruster (f)
6800878 *8QHV* -	**VATTARU** *ex* Taurus *-1986* *ex* Hung Hom *-1976* **Central Atolls Shipping Ltd** Maldives National Shipping Ltd *Male* *Maldives* Official number: 78/10-T	*262* 66 -	Class: (LR) ✠ Classed LR until 20/1/89	**1968-02 Hong Kong & Whampoa Dock Co Ltd — Hong Kong** Yd No: 1057 Loa 32.54 Br ex 9.02 Dght 3.633 Lbp 28.20 Br md 8.54 Dpth 4.27 Welded, 1 dk	**(B32A2ST) Tug**	**1 oil engine** sr reverse geared to sc. shaft driving 1 FP propeller Total Power: 1,177kW (1,600hp) 12.0kn Crossley HGP8 1 x 2 Stroke 8 Cy. 267 x 343 1177kW (1600bhp) Crossley Premier Engines Ltd.-Manchester AuxGen: 2 x 20kW 220V d.c Fuel: 77.0 (d.f.)
5377252 - -	**VAUBAN** - **Institut de Recherche pour le Developpement (IRD)** - *Noumea* *France* Official number: 318049	*110* 84 -	Class: (BV)	**1951 H C Stuelcken Sohn — Hamburg** Converted From: Fishing Vessel-1965 Loa 22.51 Br ex 6.23 Dght - Lbp 21.49 Br md 6.20 Dpth 3.20 Welded, 1 dk	**(B12D2FR) Fishery Research Vessel** 1 Ha: (0.6 x 0.5)	**1 oil engine** driving 1 FP propeller Total Power: 228kW (310hp) 12.0kn Deutz RBA8M528 1 x 4 Stroke 8 Cy. 220 x 280 228kW (310bhp) (new engine 1957) Kloeckner Humboldt Deutz AG-West Germany Fuel: 15.5 (d.f.)
9633044 *WDF8318* -	**VAUD J** - **Vaud J Inc** - *Cape May, NJ* *United States of America* MMSI: 367493590 Official number: 1231259	**206** - -		**2011-05 T.M. Jemison Construction Co., Inc. — Bayou La Batre, Al** Yd No: 200 Loa 28.65 Br ex - Dght - Lbp 25.20 Br md 7.92 Dpth 4.11 Welded, 1 dk	**(B11B2FV) Fishing Vessel**	**1 oil engine** driving 1 Propeller
1010387 *ZGBG98* -	**VAVA II** - **Lighthouse Marine Ltd** - *George Town* *Cayman Islands (British)* MMSI: 319808000 Official number: 743498	**3,933** 1,179 -	Class: LR ✠ **100A1** SS 02/2012 passenger ship *IWS ✠ **LMC** **UMS** Eq.Ltr: U; Cable: 467.5/40.0 U3 (a)	**2012-02 Babcock Marine Appledore — Bideford** (Hull) **2012-02 Devonport Engineering Consortium Ltd — Plymouth** Yd No: 055 Loa 96.83 Br ex 17.21 Dght 4.790 Lbp 95.00 Br md 16.00 Dpth 8.50 Welded, 1 dk	**(X11A2YP) Yacht** Passengers: 36	**4 oil engines** with clutches, flexible couplings & sr geared to sc. shafts driving 2 CP propellers Total Power: 8,770kW (11,922hp) 18.5kn M.T.U. 12V4000M71 2 x Vee 4 Stroke 12 Cy. 165 x 190 each-1920kW (2610bhp) MTU Friedrichshafen GmbH-Friedrichshafen M.T.U. 16V4000M71 2 x Vee 4 Stroke 16 Cy. 165 x 190 each-2465kW (3351bhp) MTU Friedrichshafen GmbH-Friedrichshafen AuxGen: 3 x 520kW 400V 50Hz a.c Thrusters: 3 Thwart. FP thruster (f)
9206815 *FW6863* -	**VAVAU** - **Bora Bora Navettes (Bora Bora Shuttles)** - *Bora-Bora* *France* MMSI: 546001350	**290** - 20	Class: BV	**1998-07 NQEA Australia Pty Ltd — Cairns QLD** Yd No: 202 Loa - Br ex - Dght 1.070 Lbp 27.00 Br md 7.00 Dpth 2.09 Welded, 1 dk	**(A37B2PS) Passenger Ship** Hull Material: Aluminium Alloy Passengers: unberthed: 115	**2 oil engines** geared to sc. shafts driving 2 FP propellers Total Power: 630kW (856hp) 22.0kn Caterpillar 3196DI 2 x 4 Stroke 6 Cy. 130 x 150 each-315kW (428bhp) Caterpillar Inc-USA
8941767 *UCPT* -	**VAVAY** *ex* Sakhfrakht-1 *-2002* *ex* Shinpaku Maru No. 2 *-1992* *ex* Marunaka Maru No. 8 *-1992* *ex* Hokuten Maru No. 18 *-1992* *ex* Shoichi Maru No. 57 *-1992* **Albatros JSC (A/O 'Albatros')** - *Nevelsk* *Russia* MMSI: 273898200 Official number: 763720	**198** 89 142	Class: RS	**1976-01 K.K. Otsuchi Kogyo — Otsuchi** Loa 36.90 Br ex 6.20 Dght 2.240 Lbp 33.14 Br md - Dpth 2.55 Welded, 1 dk	**(B11A2FT) Trawler** Ins: 133 Compartments: 3 Ho 3 Ha: 3 (1.2 x 1.2)	**1 oil engine** driving 1 FP propeller Total Power: 487kW (662hp) 9.0kn Niigata 6M26KGHS 1 x 4 Stroke 6 Cy. 260 x 400 487kW (662bhp) Niigata Engineering Co Ltd-Japan AuxGen: 1 x 250kW a.c Fuel: 89.0 (d.f.)

Identity / Owner	Tonnage	Class	Builder / Dimensions	Type	Machinery
9058282 **VAXO** *SDWE* - **Waxholms Angfartygs AB** - *Vaxholm* *Sweden* MMSI: 265520430	**299** 118 50		**1993-05 Oskarshamns Varv AB — Oskarshamn** Yd No: 541 Loa 37.70 Br ex 7.52 Dght 1.280 Lbp - Br md 7.51 Dpth 2.78 Welded, 1 dk	**(A37B2PS) Passenger Ship** Hull Material: Aluminium Alloy Passengers: 340	**3 oil engines** with clutches, flexible couplings & sr reverse geared to sc. shafts driving 3 FP propellers Total Power: 1,815kW (2,469hp) MAN D2842LYE 3 x Vee 4 Stroke 12 Cy. 128 x 142 each-605kW (823bhp) MAN Nutzfahrzeuge AG-Nuernberg Thrusters: 1 Thwart. FP thruster (f)
9202871 **VAYA CON DIOS** *OPUV* Z 526 **De Flamingo BVBA** - *Zeebrugge* *Belgium* MMSI: 205316000 Official number: 01 00399 1998	**351** 105 -		**1999-06 'Crist' Sp z oo — Gdansk** (Hull) **1999-06 Scheepswerf van der Werff en Visser — Irnsum** Yd No: 298 Loa 36.11 (BB) Br ex - Dght - Lbp 32.29 Br md 8.11 Dpth 4.60 Welded, 1 dk	**(B11A2FT) Trawler**	**1 oil engine** sr reverse geared to sc. shaft driving 1 FP propeller Total Power: 853kW (1,160hp) MaK 9M20 1 x 4 Stroke 9 Cy. 200 x 300 853kW (1160bhp) MaK Motoren GmbH & Co. KG-Kiel AuxGen: 2 x 125kW 50Hz a.c Thrusters: 1 Thwart. FP thruster (f)
8898568 **VAYENGA** *UGNK* - **Hermes Co Ltd-Murmansk (OOO 'Germes')** - *Murmansk* *Russia*	**117** 35 30	Class: (RS)	**1993-05 Sosnovskiy Sudostroitelnyy Zavod — Sosnovka** Yd No: 839 Loa 25.50 Br ex 7.00 Dght 2.390 Lbp 22.00 Br md 6.80 Dpth 3.30 Welded, 1 dk	**(B11A2FS) Stern Trawler** Ice Capable	**1 oil engine** driving 1 FP propeller Total Power: 220kW (299hp) 9.5kn S.K.L. 6NVD26A-2 1 x 4 Stroke 6 Cy. 180 x 260 220kW (299bhp) SKL Motoren u. Systemtechnik AG-Magdeburg AuxGen: 2 x 14kW a.c Fuel: 15.0 (d.f.)
8834768 **VAYGACH** *UAAM* - *ex* SPA-014 *-1999* **District State Unitary Enterprise 'Chukotsnab' (Gosudarstvennoe Unitarnoe Predpriyatie - Chukotskiy Avtonomnyy Okrug 'Chukotsnab')** - *Anadyr* *Russia*	**162** 48 167	Class: RS	**1990-08 Sudoremontnyy Zavod "Yakor" — Sovetskaya Gavan** Yd No: 855 Loa 35.84 Br ex 7.21 Dght 1.851 Lbp 33.63 Br md 7.20 Dpth 2.42 Welded, 1 dk	**(A31C2GD) Deck Cargo Ship** Ice Capable	**1 oil engine** geared to sc. shaft driving 1 FP propeller Total Power: 230kW (313hp) 8.7kn Daldizel 6CHNSP18/22-300 1 x 4 Stroke 6 Cy. 180 x 220 230kW (313bhp) Daldizel-Khabarovsk AuxGen: 1 x 14kW, 1 x 13kW Fuel: 56.0 (d.f.)
8417493 **VAYGACH** *UBNY* - **Government of The Russian Federation** Federal State Unitary Enterprise 'Atomflot' SatCom: Inmarsat C 427300985 *Murmansk* *Russia* MMSI: 273133100 Official number: 851419	**20,791** 6,237 3,581 T/cm 37.0	Class: RS	**1990-08 Wartsila Marine Industries Inc — Helsinki (Helsingin Telakka)** Yd No: 475 Loa 149.70 Br ex 29.20 Dght 9.002 Lbp 136.32 Br md 28.87 Dpth 15.68 Welded, 1 dk	**(B34C2SI) Icebreaker** Cranes: 1x20t,1x16t,1x12t,1x10t Ice Capable	**3 diesel electric oil engines & 2 turbo electric Steam Turbs** driving 3 gen. each 2320kW 6300V a.c 2 gen. each 18400kW 6300V a.c Connecting to 3 elec. motors each (12000kW) driving 3 FP propellers Total Power: 43,880kW (59,661hp) 18.2kn Wartsila 6R22 3 x 4 Stroke 6 Cy. 220 x 240 each-2360kW (3209bhp) Wartsila Diesel Oy-Finland Russkiy 2 x steam Turb each-18400kW (25017shp) in the U.S.S.R. AuxGen: 3 x 2432kW 400V 50Hz a.c, 2 x 2000kW 400V 50Hz a.c Boilers: NR 30.0kgf/cm² (29.4bar) Superheater 300°C 30.0kgf/cm² (29.4bar) Thrusters: 3 Thwart. FP thruster (a) Fuel: 900.0 (d.f.)
8937168 **VAYNOVO** - - **JSC 'Nord Vey' (A/O 'Nord Vey')** - *Arkhangelsk* *Russia*	**155** 47 158	Class: (RS)	**1976 Sudoremontnyy Zavod "Krasnaya Kuznitsa" — Arkhangelsk** Yd No: 1 Loa 35.75 Br ex 7.40 Dght 1.710 Lbp 33.50 Br md 7.00 Dpth 2.40 Welded, 1 dk	**(A31C2GD) Deck Cargo Ship** Ice Capable	**1 oil engine** geared to sc. shaft driving 1 FP propeller Total Power: 165kW (224hp) 7.8kn Daldizel 6CHNSP18/22 1 x 4 Stroke 6 Cy. 180 x 220 165kW (224bhp) Daldizel-Khabarovsk AuxGen: 2 x 13kW Fuel: 5.0 (d.f.)
9664677 **VAYUPUTRA** *AVVW* - **Jindal ITF Ltd** - *Mumbai* *India* MMSI: 419000613 Official number: 4039	**1,368** 579 2,214	Class: IR	**2012-11 Dempo Engineering Works Ltd. — Goa** Yd No: 507 Loa 72.00 Br ex 14.02 Dght 3.000 Lbp 69.65 Br md 14.00 Dpth 4.25 Welded, 1 dk	**(A31A2GX) General Cargo Ship** Grain: 2,300 Compartments: 1 Ho, ER 1 Ha: ER	**2 oil engines** reduction geared to sc. shafts driving 2 FP propellers Total Power: 736kW (1,000hp) 9.3kn Volvo Penta D13MH 2 x 4 Stroke 6 Cy. 131 x 158 each-368kW (500bhp) AB Volvo Penta-Sweden
8722484 **VAYVARA** - - *ex* Vaivara *-2000* *ex* MRTK-0695 *-1992* **NV Mishin** - *Kaliningrad* *Russia* Official number: 850191	**117** 35 30	Class: RS	**1986-05 Sosnovskiy Sudostroitelnyy Zavod — Sosnovka** Yd No: 695 Loa 25.50 Br ex 7.00 Dght 2.390 Lbp 22.00 Br md 6.80 Dpth 3.30 Welded, 1 dk	**(B11A2FS) Stern Trawler** Grain: 64 Ice Capable	**1 oil engine** driving 1 FP propeller Total Power: 221kW (300hp) 9.5kn S.K.L. 6NVD26A-2 1 x 4 Stroke 6 Cy. 180 x 260 221kW (300bhp) VEB Schwermaschinenbau "KarlLiebknecht" (SKL)-Magdeburg AuxGen: 2 x 12kW Fuel: 15.0 (d.f.)
9393747 **VB ADROIT** *FNQN* - **Boluda France SAS** Boluda Dunkerque *Dunkirk* *France* MMSI: 228293600 Official number: 924447	**342** 102 -	Class: BV	**2008-09 Chantiers Piriou — Concarneau** Yd No: C285 Loa 30.30 Br ex 11.00 Dght 4.500 Lbp 29.00 Br md 10.40 Dpth 4.32 Welded, 1 dk	**(B32A2ST) Tug**	**2 oil engines** reduction geared to sc. shafts driving 2 Directional propellers Total Power: 3,536kW (4,808hp) 11.0kn A.B.C. 8MDZC 2 x 4 Stroke 8 Cy. 256 x 310 each-1768kW (2404bhp) Anglo Belgian Corp NV (ABC)-Belgium AuxGen: 2 x 90kW 240V 50Hz a.c Fuel: 75.0
9158020 **VB ALBORAN** *EARA* - **Credit Agricole Leasing Sucursal en Espana** Remolcadores y Barcazas de Las Palmas SA *Algeciras* *Spain* MMSI: 224550000 Official number: 1-1/1998	**342** 102 566	✠ **100A1** SS 09/2012 tug (fire fighting ship 1 (2400 cubic/metre) with water spray) ✠ **LMC** **UMS** Eq.Ltr: G; Cable: 302.5/20.5 U2	**1998-06 Astilleros Zamakona SA — Santurtzi** Yd No: 394 Loa 30.20 Br ex 11.50 Dght 5.800 Lbp 28.00 Br md 11.00 Dpth 4.00 Welded, 1 dk	**(B32A2ST) Tug**	**2 oil engines** reduction geared to sc. shafts driving 2 Directional propellers Total Power: 3,040kW (4,134hp) 12.0kn MaK 8M20 2 x 4 Stroke 8 Cy. 200 x 300 each-1520kW (2067bhp) MaK Motoren GmbH & Co. KG-Kiel AuxGen: 2 x 160kW 380V 50Hz a.c Fuel: 136.0 (d.f.)
9289348 **VB. ALGECIRAS** *ECCR* - **Boat Service SA** - *Algeciras* *Spain* MMSI: 224121250 Official number: 5-1/2004	**374** 112 210	Class: BV	**2003-12 Union Naval Valencia SA (UNV) — Valencia** Yd No: 337 Loa 29.50 Br ex - Dght 3.790 Lbp 28.00 Br md 11.00 Dpth 4.00 Welded, 1 dk	**(B32A2ST) Tug**	**2 oil engines** geared to sc. shafts driving 2 Directional propellers Total Power: 4,050kW (5,506hp) Deutz SBV9M628 2 x 4 Stroke 9 Cy. 240 x 280 each-2025kW (2753bhp) Deutz AG-Koeln
7613014 **VB ARTICO** *HP9983* - *ex* Shamal *-2000* **Boluda Internacional SA** - SatCom: Inmarsat C 422457920 *Panama* *Panama* MMSI: 352896000 Official number: 2721000C	**978** 293 941	Class: GL (AB)	**1976-10 Matsuura Tekko Zosen K.K. — Osakikamijima** Yd No: 258 Loa 55.00 Br ex 11.23 Dght 4.817 Lbp 50.02 Br md 11.21 Dpth 5.21 Welded, 1 dk	**(B32A2ST) Tug**	**2 oil engines** reverse reduction geared to sc. shaft driving 2 FP propellers Total Power: 7,356kW (10,002hp) 14.5kn Stork-Werkspoor 16SW280 2 x Vee 4 Stroke 16 Cy. 280 x 300 each-3678kW (5001bhp) (, fitted 2002) Stork Werkspoor Diesel BV-Netherlands AuxGen: 3 x 240kW 440V a.c Thrusters: 1 Thwart. FP thruster (f)
8022652 **VB AZUA** - - *ex* Trece De Julio *-2012* **Compania Maritima del Pacifico SA de CV** - *Santo Domingo* *Dominican Rep.* Official number: RRM-V84-4010SDG	*222* 64 -	Class: (GL) (AB)	**1981-12 Scheepswerf Ton Bodewes B.V. — Franeker** (Hull) Yd No: F79 **1981-12 B.V. Scheepswerf Damen — Gorinchem** Yd No: 3121 Loa 30.26 Br ex 8.26 Dght 3.310 Lbp 27.36 Br md 7.80 Dpth 4.07 Welded, 1 dk	**(B32A2ST) Tug**	**2 oil engines** with clutches, flexible couplings & sr reverse geared to sc. shaft driving 2 FP propellers Total Power: 1,654kW (2,248hp) Caterpillar D399SCAC 2 x Vee 4 Stroke 16 Cy. 159 x 203 each-827kW (1124bhp) Caterpillar Tractor Co-USA AuxGen: 2 x 55kW a.c
7113583 **VB BARAHONA** - - *ex* VB Huracan *-2012* *ex* Hoeksebank *-2002* **Glasgow Society & Co SA** Remolcadores y Barcazas del Caribe SA *Santo Domingo* *Dominican Rep.* Official number: RM-H24-2016 SDG	**274** 82 -	Class: (AB)	**1971 N.V. Scheepswerven v/h H.H. Bodewes — Millingen a/d Rijn** Yd No: 695 Loa 32.95 Br ex 9.58 Dght 4.673 Lbp 31.30 Br md 9.52 Dpth 3.81 Welded, 1 dk	**(B32A2ST) Tug**	**2 oil engines** driving 2 CP propellers Total Power: 2,060kW (2,800hp) 12.0kn Kromhout 6FFHD240 2 x 4 Stroke 6 Cy. 240 x 260 each-1030kW (1400bhp) (new engine 1981) Stork Werkspoor Diesel BV-Netherlands AuxGen: 1 x 76kW a.c, 1 x 64kW a.c

IMO / Call sign / Flag	Name / Owner / Port	Tonnage	Class	Built / Builder / Dimensions	Type	Machinery
9293040 *FVFB* -	**VB BARFLEUR** *ex* Abeille Barfleur *-2008* **Boluda France SAS** Boluda Le Havre *Le Havre* *France* MMSI: 228179700 Official number: 896392	**329** - -	Class: BV	**2003-09 Chantiers Piriou — Concarneau** Yd No: 259 Loa 30.30 Br ex - Dght 4.500 Lbp - Br md 10.40 Dpth 4.32 Welded, 1 dk	**(B32A2ST) Tug**	**2 oil engines** geared to sc. shafts driving 2 Directional propellers Total Power: 3,532kW (4,802hp) 11.0kn A.B.C. 8MDZC 2 x 4 Stroke 8 Cy. 256 x 310 each-1766kW (2401bhp) Anglo Belgian Corp NV (ABC)-Belgium AuxGen: 2 x 90kW a.c Thrusters: 1 Tunnel thruster (f) Fuel: 101.0 (d.f.)
7224552 - -	**VB BAYAHIBE** *ex* Boluda Cuarenta *-2010* *ex* Martes *-1986* **Remolcadores y Barcazas del Caribe SA** -	*263* 7 138	Class: (LR) (GL) ✠ Classed LR until 2/91	**1972-10 Sociedad Metalurgica Duro Felguera — Gijon** Yd No: 73 Loa 32.21 Br ex 8.84 Dght 3.753 Lbp 28.17 Br md 8.41 Dpth 4.32 Welded, 1 dk	**(B32A2ST) Tug**	**1 oil engine** dr geared to sc. shaft driving 1 CP propeller Total Power: 1,846kW (2,510hp) 12.5kn Caterpillar 3606TA 1 x 4 Stroke 6 Cy. 280 x 300 1846kW (2510bhp) (new engine 1990) Caterpillar Inc-USA AuxGen: 2 x 80kW 220/380V 50Hz a.c, 1 x 60kW 220/380V 50Hz a.c
9395850 *FNUW* -	**VB BOUGAINVILLE** **Boluda La Reunion** - *La Reunion* *France* MMSI: 660004100 Official number: 928784	**289** 86 -	Class: BV	**2008-11 Damen Shipyards Changde Co Ltd — Changde HN** (Hull) Yd No: (511542) **2008-11 B.V. Scheepswerf Damen — Gorinchem** Yd No: 511542 Loa 28.67 Br ex - Dght 3.610 Lbp 27.90 Br md 9.80 Dpth 4.60 Welded, 1 dk	**(B32A2ST) Tug**	**2 oil engines** reduction geared to sc. shafts driving 2 Directional propellers Total Power: 3,676kW (4,998hp) Caterpillar 3516B-HD 2 x Vee 4 Stroke 16 Cy. 170 x 215 each-1838kW (2499bhp) Caterpillar Inc-USA
8207680 - -	**VB BOXER** *ex* ZP Caymus *-2012* **Remolcadores y Barcazas de Las Palmas SA** - *Castellon de la Plana* *Spain* MMSI: 225439000 Official number: CP2 3 12	**272** 81 337	Class: BV (AB)	**1982-06 Valley Shipbuilding, Inc. — Brownsville, Tx** Yd No: 114 Loa 28.50 Br ex - Dght 5.060 Lbp 26.93 Br md 10.37 Dpth 3.81 Welded, 1 dk	**(B32A2ST) Tug**	**2 oil engines** sr geared to sc. shafts driving 2 Directional propellers Total Power: 2,354kW (3,200hp) 8.0kn Alpha 7SL28L-VO 2 x 4 Stroke 7 Cy. 280 x 320 each-1177kW (1600bhp) B&W Holeby Diesel A/S-Denmark AuxGen: 2 x 135kW 460V 60Hz a.c Fuel: 202.0 (d.f.) 13.0pd
9071260 - -	**VB BRACO** *ex* Deilginis *-2013* **Boluda Corporacion Maritima** - *Spain* MMSI: 224624000	**335** 100 -	Class: BV	**1997-03 Astilleros Zamakona SA — Santurtzi** Yd No: 375 Loa - Br ex - Dght 2.500 Lbp 28.00 Br md 11.00 Dpth 4.00 Welded	**(B32A2ST) Tug**	**2 oil engines** reduction geared to sc. shafts driving 2 Voith-Schneider propellers Total Power: 2,560kW (3,480hp) 12.0kn Caterpillar 3516TA 2 x Vee 4 Stroke 16 Cy. 170 x 190 each-1280kW (1740bhp) Caterpillar Inc-USA AuxGen: 2 x 85kW 380V 50Hz a.c Fuel: 115.0 (d.f.)
9357341 *FMHX* -	**VB BRETAGNE** *ex* SD Seine *-2011* *ex* Med Firat *-2005* **Boluda Corporacion Maritima** - *St-Nazaire* *France* MMSI: 228234700	**389** 117 -	Class: BV	**2005-11 Usmed Gemi Insa Sanayi ve Ticaret AS — Karadeniz Eregli** Yd No: 17 Loa 32.00 Br ex - Dght 3.710 Lbp 28.40 Br md 10.50 Dpth 5.30 Welded, 1 dk	**(B32A2ST) Tug**	**2 oil engines** gearing integral to driving 2 Z propellers Total Power: 3,600kW (4,894hp) Wartsila 9L20 2 x 4 Stroke 9 Cy. 200 x 280 each-1800kW (2447bhp) Wartsila Finland Oy-Finland
7621633 *XCSH9* -	**VB BRIOSO** *ex* Dordtsebank *-2011* **Compania Maritima del Pacifico SA de CV** - *Salina Cruz* *Mexico* Official number: 20031481229	**292** 87 179	Class: GL (AB)	**1977-06 B.V. Scheepswerven v/h H.H. Bodewes — Millingen a/d Rijn** Yd No: 736 Loa 34.32 Br ex 9.58 Dght 3.210 Lbp 30.82 Br md 9.20 Dpth 4.98 Welded, 1 dk	**(B32A2ST) Tug**	**2 oil engines** geared to sc. shafts driving 2 CP propellers Total Power: 2,500kW (3,400hp) 12.0kn Kromhout 9FDHD240 2 x 4 Stroke 9 Cy. 240 x 260 each-1250kW (1700bhp) Stork Werkspoor Diesel BV-Netherlands Fuel: 107.5 (d.f.)
8207692 *EACR* -	**VB BULLDOG** *ex* ZP Chandon *-2012* **Boluda Internacional SA** - *Castellon de la Plana* *Spain* MMSI: 225434000	**272** 81 337	Class: BV (AB)	**1982-09 Valley Shipbuilding, Inc. — Brownsville, Tx** Yd No: 115 Loa 28.50 Br ex - Dght 5.060 Lbp 26.93 Br md 10.37 Dpth 3.81 Welded, 1 dk	**(B32A2ST) Tug**	**2 oil engines** sr geared to sc. shafts driving 2 Z propellers Total Power: 2,354kW (3,200hp) 12.5kn Alpha 7SL28L-VO 2 x 4 Stroke 7 Cy. 280 x 320 each-1177kW (1600bhp) B&W Holeby Diesel A/S-Denmark AuxGen: 2 x 250kW 460V 50Hz a.c Fuel: 202.0 (d.f.) 13.0pd
7503489 - -	**VB CABO ROJO** *ex* Provencal 2 *-2012* **Remolcadores y Barcazas del Caribe SA**	*287* - -	Class: (BV)	**1976-10 Chantiers et Ateliers de La Perriere — Lorient** Yd No: 306 Loa 31.42 Br ex - Dght 3.652 Lbp 29.01 Br md 8.81 Dpth 4.35 Welded, 1 dk	**(B32A2ST) Tug**	**2 oil engines** geared to sc. shafts driving 2 FP propellers Total Power: 1,838kW (2,498hp) 12.0kn Crepelle 8SN1 2 x 4 Stroke 8 Cy. 260 x 280 each-919kW (1249bhp) Crepelle et Cie-France
9393694 *FNMR* -	**VB CAMARGUE** *ex* Abeille Camargue *-2008* **Boluda France SAS** Boluda Marseilla Fos *Marseille* *France* MMSI: 228279900 Official number: 925826H	**342** - -	Class: BV	**2007-09 Chantiers Piriou — Concarneau** Yd No: C280 Loa 30.30 Br ex - Dght 4.700 Lbp 29.00 Br md 10.40 Dpth 4.32 Welded, 1 dk	**(B32A2ST) Tug**	**2 oil engines** reduction geared to sc. shafts driving 2 Directional propellers Total Power: 3,718kW (5,055hp) 11.0kn A.B.C. 8DZC 2 x 4 Stroke 8 Cy. 256 x 310 each-1768kW (2404bhp) Anglo Belgian Corp NV (ABC)-Belgium
9471410 *EAHF* -	**VB CAMPEADOR** **Naviera Boluda Fos SL** - *Santa Cruz de Tenerife* *Spain (CSR)* MMSI: 224443000	**413** 124 335	Class: BV	**2010-05 Union Naval Valencia SA (UNV) — Valencia** Yd No: 475 Loa 30.50 Br ex - Dght 4.400 Lbp 26.80 Br md 11.00 Dpth 5.80 Welded, 1 dk	**(B32A2ST) Tug**	**2 oil engines** reduction geared to sc. shafts driving 2 Z propellers Total Power: 3,650kW (4,962hp) Caterpillar 3516C-HD 2 x Vee 4 Stroke 16 Cy. 170 x 215 each-1825kW (2481bhp) Caterpillar Inc-USA
9395848 *FNUV* -	**VB CARTIER** **Boluda La Reunion** - *La Reunion* *France* MMSI: 660003900 Official number: 928785	**289** 86 -	Class: BV	**2008-11 Damen Shipyards Changde Co Ltd — Changde HN** (Hull) Yd No: (511541) **2008-11 B.V. Scheepswerf Damen — Gorinchem** Yd No: 511541 Loa 28.67 Br ex - Dght 3.610 Lbp 27.90 Br md 9.80 Dpth 4.60 Welded, 1 dk	**(B32A2ST) Tug**	**2 oil engines** reduction geared to sc. shafts driving 2 Directional propellers Total Power: 3,676kW (4,998hp) Caterpillar 3516B-HD 2 x Vee 4 Stroke 16 Cy. 170 x 215 each-1838kW (2499bhp) Caterpillar Inc-USA
9366718 *CNA4276* -	**VB CIRES** *ex* Abeille Cires *-2009* **Boluda Tanger Med** - *Tangier* *Morocco* MMSI: 242903000	**285** 88 153	Class: BV	**2007-03 Santierul Naval Damen Galati S.A. — Galati** (Hull) Yd No: 1090 **2007-03 B.V. Scheepswerf Damen — Gorinchem** Yd No: 511524 Loa 28.75 Br ex 10.42 Dght 3.910 Lbp 25.79 Br md 9.80 Dpth 4.60 Welded, 1 dk	**(B32A2ST) Tug**	**2 oil engines** reduction geared to sc. shafts driving 2 Directional propellers Total Power: 3,618kW (4,920hp) Caterpillar 3516B-HD 2 x Vee 4 Stroke 16 Cy. 170 x 215 each-1809kW (2460bhp) Caterpillar Inc-USA AuxGen: 2 x 83kW 400V 50Hz a.c
8017372 *EABI* -	**VB COCO** *ex* Escota *-2011* **Remolcadores de Cartagena SA (RECASA)** - *Santander* *Spain* Official number: 1-10/1992	*168* 36 76	Class: (GL) (AB) **100A1** SS 07/2009 tug **LMC** **UMS** Eq.Ltr: B; Cable: 220.0/18.0 U2 (a)	**1981-02 Ast. de Tarragona — Tarragona** Yd No: 213 Loa 25.02 Br ex - Dght 3.499 Lbp 22.13 Br md 8.41 Dpth 3.50 Welded, 1 dk	**(B32A2ST) Tug**	**1 oil engine** reduction geared to sc. shaft driving 1 CP propeller Total Power: 1,900kW (2,583hp) 12.0kn Caterpillar 3606TA 1 x 4 Stroke 6 Cy. 280 x 300 1900kW (2583bhp) (new engine 2001) Caterpillar Inc-USA AuxGen: 2 x 85kW 220V 50Hz a.c Thrusters: 1 Tunnel thruster (f)
7931973 *HO3768* -	**VB COIBA** *ex* Coria *-2004* **Tug Services Panama SA** Compania Maritima de Panama SA *Panama* *Panama* MMSI: 357751000 Official number: 3264807A	*335* 100 190	Class: (LR) ✠ Classed LR until 13/10/10	**1982-07 Union Naval de Levante SA (UNL) — Barcelona** Yd No: 67 Loa 33.30 Br ex 9.48 Dght 4.031 Lbp 28.71 Br md 9.01 Dpth 4.81 Welded, 1 dk	**(B32A2ST) Tug**	**1 oil engine** with flexible couplings & sr gearedto sc. shaft driving 1 CP propeller Total Power: 2,383kW (3,240hp) 12.5kn Sulzer 12ASV25/30 1 x Vee 4 Stroke 12 Cy. 250 x 300 2383kW (3240bhp) Astilleros Espanoles SA (AESA)-Spain AuxGen: 2 x 128kW 380V 50Hz a.c

IMO / Call sign	Name / Owner / Flag	Tonnage	Class	Builder / Dimensions	Type	Machinery
9471422 *HP7575* -	**VB CORSARIO** **Naviera Boluda Fos SL** - *Panama* *Panama* MMSI: 373045000 Official number: 4381812	**413** 124 335	Class: BV	**2010-05 Union Naval Valencia SA (UNV) — Valencia** Yd No: 476 Loa 30.50 Br ex - Dght 4.400 Lbp 26.80 Br md 11.00 Dpth 5.80 Welded, 1 dk	**(B32A2ST) Tug**	**2 oil engines** reduction geared to sc. shafts driving 2 Z propellers Total Power: 4,700kW (6,390hp) 13.0kn Caterpillar 3516C-HD 2 x Vee 4 Stroke 16 Cy. 170 x 215 each-2350kW (3195bhp) Caterpillar Inc-USA AuxGen: 3 x 98kW 60Hz a.c Fuel: 220.0 (d.f.)
9393759 *FNRD* -	**VB CRAU** **Boluda France SAS** Boluda Marseilla Fos *Marseille* *France* MMSI: 228299700 Official number: 925827J	**342** 102 -	Class: BV	**2009-01 Chantiers Piriou — Concarneau** Yd No: C286 Loa 30.30 Br ex 11.00 Dght 4.500 Lbp 29.47 Br md 10.40 Dpth 4.32 Welded, 1 dk	**(B32A2ST) Tug**	**2 oil engines** reduction geared to sc. shafts driving 2 Directional propellers Total Power: 3,890kW (5,288hp) 11.0kn A.B.C. 8DZC 2 x 4 Stroke 8 Cy. 256 x 310 each-1945kW (2644bhp) Anglo Belgian Corp NV (ABC)-Belgium AuxGen: 2 x 90kW 50Hz a.c
9370161 *CNA4275* -	**VB DALIA** *ex* Abeille Dalia *-2009* **Boluda Tanger Med** - *Tangier* *Morocco* MMSI: 242904000	**285** 88 -	Class: BV	**2007-03 Santierul Naval Damen Galati S.A. — Galati** (Hull) Yd No: 1091 **2007-03 B.V. Scheepswerf Damen — Gorinchem** Yd No: 511525 Loa 28.75 Br ex 10.43 Dght 3.910 Lbp 25.79 Br md 9.80 Dpth 4.60 Welded, 1 dk	**(B32A2ST) Tug**	**2 oil engines** reduction geared to sc. shafts driving 2 Directional propellers Total Power: 3,618kW (4,920hp) Caterpillar 3516B-TA 2 x Vee 4 Stroke 16 Cy. 170 x 190 each-1809kW (2460bhp) Caterpillar Inc-USA
9202754 *FW9208* -	**VB DEAUVILLE** *ex* Abeille Deauville *-2008* **Boluda France SAS** Boluda Le Havre *Le Havre* *France* MMSI: 227006770 Official number: 896364	**487** 146 260	Class: BV	**2000-10 Alstom Leroux Naval SA — St-Malo** Yd No: 644 Loa 37.42 Br ex - Dght 5.200 Lbp 35.50 Br md 10.60 Dpth 4.80 Welded, 1 dk	**(B32A2ST) Tug**	**2 oil engines** reduction geared to sc. shafts driving 2 Directional propellers Total Power: 3,680kW (5,004hp) 12.5kn A.B.C. 8MDZC 2 x 4 Stroke 8 Cy. 256 x 310 each-1840kW (2502bhp) Anglo Belgian Corp NV (ABC)-Belgium AuxGen: 2 x 168kW 380/220V 50Hz a.c Thrusters: 1 Thwart. FP thruster (f) Fuel: 142.0 (d.f.)
9393761 *FNRE* -	**VB ESTEREL** **Boluda France SAS** - *Marseille* *France* MMSI: 228299600 Official number: 928788C	**336** 102 -	Class: BV	**2009-02 Chantiers Piriou — Concarneau** Yd No: C287 Loa 30.30 Br ex 11.00 Dght 4.500 Lbp 29.00 Br md 10.40 Dpth 4.32 Welded, 1 dk	**(B32A2ST) Tug**	**2 oil engines** reduction geared to sc. shafts driving 2 Directional propellers Total Power: 3,536kW (4,808hp) 11.0kn A.B.C. 8DZC 2 x 4 Stroke 8 Cy. 256 x 310 each-1768kW (2404bhp) Anglo Belgian Corp NV (ABC)-Belgium
9202728 *FW9209* -	**VB FECAMP** *ex* Abeille Fecamp *-2008* **Boluda France SAS** Boluda Le Havre *Le Havre* *France* MMSI: 227006760 Official number: 896362	**487** 146 275	Class: BV	**2000-04 Alstom Leroux Naval SA — St-Malo** Yd No: 641 Loa 37.42 Br ex - Dght 5.200 Lbp 35.50 Br md 10.60 Dpth 4.80 Welded, 1 dk	**(B32A2ST) Tug**	**2 oil engines** geared to sc. shafts driving 2 Directional propellers Total Power: 3,680kW (5,004hp) 12.5kn A.B.C. 8MDZC 2 x 4 Stroke 8 Cy. 256 x 310 each-1840kW (2502bhp) Anglo Belgian Corp NV (ABC)-Belgium AuxGen: 2 x 168kW 380/220V 50Hz a.c Thrusters: 1 Thwart. FP thruster (f) Fuel: 142.0 (d.f.)
9189536 *J8B4152* -	**VB FILAO** *ex* VB Mafate *-2009* *ex* Abeille Mafate *-2009* **Abeille Mafate** Ivoirienne de Remorquage et de Sauvetage (IRES) *Kingstown* *St Vincent & The Grenadines* MMSI: 376844000 Official number: 10625	**267** 80 -	Class: BV	**1998-11 Chantiers Piriou — Concarneau** Yd No: 200 Loa - Br ex - Dght - Lbp 27.30 Br md 9.70 Dpth 4.01 Welded, 1 dk	**(B32A2ST) Tug**	**2 oil engines** geared to sc. shafts driving 2 FP propellers Total Power: 2,508kW (3,410hp) 12.0kn A.B.C. 6MDZC 2 x 4 Stroke 6 Cy. 256 x 310 each-1254kW (1705bhp) Anglo Belgian Corp NV (ABC)-Belgium Fuel: 74.0 (d.f.)
7621621 *3FWB4* -	**VB FURIOSO** *ex* Sandettiebank *-2011* **Tug Services Panama SA** Compania Maritima de Panama SA *Panama* *Panama* Official number: 4290311	**292** 204 179	Class: BV (AB)	**1977-04 B.V. Scheepswerven v/h H.H. Bodewes — Millingen a/d Rijn** Yd No: 735 Loa 34.32 Br ex 9.58 Dght 3.210 Lbp 30.78 Br md 9.20 Dpth 4.98 Welded, 1 dk	**(B32A2ST) Tug**	**2 oil engines** geared to sc. shafts driving 2 CP propellers Total Power: 2,206kW (3,000hp) 12.0kn Kromhout 9FDHD240 2 x 4 Stroke 9 Cy. 240 x 260 each-1103kW (1500bhp) Stork Werkspoor Diesel BV-Netherlands AuxGen: 2 x 76kW a.c
9202730 *FW9206* -	**VB GASCOGNE** *ex* Abeille Gascogne *-2008* **Boluda France SAS** Boluda Le Havre *Le Havre* *France* MMSI: 227023200 Official number: 896363	**487** 146 235	Class: BV	**2000-06 Alstom Leroux Naval SA — St-Malo** Yd No: 642 Loa 37.42 Br ex - Dght 5.500 Lbp 35.50 Br md 10.60 Dpth 4.80 Welded, 1 dk	**(B32A2ST) Tug**	**2 oil engines** geared to sc. shafts driving 2 Directional propellers Total Power: 3,680kW (5,004hp) 12.5kn A.B.C. 8MDZC 2 x 4 Stroke 8 Cy. 256 x 310 each-1840kW (2502bhp) Anglo Belgian Corp NV (ABC)-Belgium AuxGen: 2 x 168kW 380/220V 50Hz a.c Thrusters: 1 Thwart. FP thruster (f) Fuel: 142.0 (d.f.)
9357286 *EAFD* -	**VB GOLDEN** *ex* SD Gironde *-2011* *ex* Med Dicle *-2006* **Caen Enterprises SL** Remolques del Mediterraneo SA *Castellon de la Plana* *Spain* MMSI: 224364000	**389** 117 -	Class: BV	**2006-03 Medyilmaz Gemi Sanayi ve Ticaret AS — Karadeniz Eregli** Yd No: 28 Loa 32.00 Br ex - Dght 3.710 Lbp 28.40 Br md 10.50 Dpth 5.30 Welded, 1 dk	**(B32A2ST) Tug**	**2 oil engines** gearing integral to driving 2 Z propellers Total Power: 3,600kW (4,894hp) 11.0kn Wartsila 9L20 2 x 4 Stroke 9 Cy. 200 x 280 each-1800kW (2447bhp) Wartsila Finland Oy-Finland
7430486 - -	**VB HIGUEY** *ex* Icor *-2006* *ex* Kerhuon *-2001* **Remolcadores y Barcazas del Caribe SA** Boluda Corporacion Maritima	*278* 20 -	Class: (BV)	**1980-02 Scheepsbouwwerf Slob B.V. — Sliedrecht** Yd No: 299 Loa 31.78 Br ex - Dght 4.720 Lbp 28.55 Br md 9.03 Dpth 4.88 Welded, 1 dk	**(B32A2ST) Tug**	**1 oil engine** geared to sc. shaft driving 1 FP propeller Total Power: 1,765kW (2,400hp) 13.0kn MWM TBD441V16 1 x Vee 4 Stroke 16 Cy. 230 x 270 1765kW (2400bhp) Motoren Werke Mannheim AG (MWM)-West Germany
7015987 *FWIC* -	**VB IROISE** *ex* Abeille Iroise *-2009* *ex* Ingenieur Maxime Hesse *-1994* **Boluda France SAS** Boluda Brest *Brest* *France* MMSI: 227004620 Official number: 332394	*135* - -	Class: BV	**1969 SOCARENAM — Calais** Loa 25.51 Br ex 7.93 Dght 3.404 Lbp 23.02 Br md 7.50 Dpth 3.89 Welded, 1 dk	**(B32A2ST) Tug**	**1 oil engine** reduction geared to sc. shaft driving 1 FP propeller Total Power: 1,030kW (1,400hp) 12.0kn MaK 6M451AK 1 x 4 Stroke 6 Cy. 320 x 450 1030kW (1400bhp) Atlas MaK Maschinenbau GmbH-Kiel AuxGen: 2 x 48kW 220V 50Hz a.c
9189524 *J8B4153* -	**VB IROKO** *ex* VB Cilaos *-2009* *ex* Abeille Cilaos *-2009* **Abeille Cilaos** Ivoirienne de Remorquage et de Sauvetage (IRES) *Kingstown* *St Vincent & The Grenadines* MMSI: 377732000 Official number: 10626	**267** 80 -	Class: BV	**1998-11 Chantiers Piriou — Concarneau** Yd No: 199 Loa - Br ex - Dght - Lbp 27.30 Br md 9.70 Dpth 4.01 Welded, 1 dk	**(B32A2ST) Tug**	**2 oil engines** geared to sc. shafts driving 2 Directional propellers Total Power: 2,508kW (3,410hp) A.B.C. 6MDZC 2 x 4 Stroke 6 Cy. 256 x 310 each-1254kW (1705bhp) Anglo Belgian Corp NV (ABC)-Belgium Fuel: 74.0 (d.f.)
9640798 *XCAB9* -	**VB JALISCO** **Compania Maritima del Pacifico SA de CV** - *Ensenada* *Mexico* MMSI: 345020028	**472** 141 282	Class: LR **✠100A1** SS 09/2013 tug fire-fighting Ship 1 (2400m3/h) with water spray **✠LMC** Eq.Ltr: H; Cable: 302.5/22.0 U2 (a)	**2013-09 Guangdong Yuexin Ocean Engineering Co Ltd — Guangzhou GD** Yd No: 3178 Loa 33.15 Br ex 12.23 Dght 4.300 Lbp 25.87 Br md 11.60 Dpth 5.36 Welded, 1 dk	**(B32A2ST) Tug**	**2 oil engines** gearing integral to driving 2 Directional propellers Total Power: 4,000kW (5,438hp) Caterpillar 3516C-HD 2 x Vee 4 Stroke 16 Cy. 170 x 215 each-2000kW (2719bhp) Caterpillar Inc-USA AuxGen: 2 x 110kW 415V 50Hz a.c
8875322 - -	**VB JARAGUA** *ex* Sanergy Jaya *-2007* **Remolcadores y Barcazas del Caribe SA** -	**336** 101 -	Class: (AB)	**1994-07 Jaya Shipbuilding & Engineering Pte Ltd — Singapore** Yd No: 801 Loa 29.50 Br ex - Dght 4.221 Lbp 27.68 Br md 9.80 Dpth 4.20 Welded, 1 dk	**(B32A2ST) Tug**	**2 oil engines** dr geared to sc. shafts driving 2 Directional propellers Total Power: 1,986kW (2,700hp) Wartsila 6R20 2 x 4 Stroke 6 Cy. 200 x 280 each-993kW (1350bhp) Wartsila Diesel Oy-Finland AuxGen: 2 x 90kW a.c Fuel: 124.0 (d.f.)

IMO / Call sign	Name / Owner	Tonnage	Class	Build / Dimensions	Type	Machinery
7503477 *J8B4774* -	**VB KARITE** *ex* Marseillais 17 *-2013* **Boluda France SAS** Ivoirienne de Remorquage et de Sauvetage (IRES) *Kingstown St Vincent & The Grenadines* MMSI: 375101000 Official number: 11247	**287** 84 -	Class: (BV)	**1976-09 Chantiers et Ateliers de La Perriere — Lorient** Yd No: 305 Loa 31.42 Br ex - Dght 3.652 Lbp 29.01 Br md 8.80 Dpth 4.35 Welded, 1 dk	**(B32A2ST) Tug**	**2 oil engines** geared to sc. shafts driving 2 FP propellers Total Power: 1,838kW (2,498hp) 12.0kn Crepelle 8SN2 2 x 4 Stroke 8 Cy. 260 x 280 each-919kW (1249bhp) Crepelle et Cie-France
9192557 *FW9205* -	**VB LA HEVE** *ex* Abeille La Heve *-2000* **Boluda France SAS** Boluda Le Havre *Le Havre France* MMSI: 227006810 Official number: 896360	**313** 93 335	Class: BV	**1999-09 Alstom Leroux Naval SA — St-Malo** (Hull launched by) Yd No: 635 **1999-09 Alstom Leroux Naval SA — Lanester** (Hull completed by) Loa 30.00 Br ex 10.90 Dght 5.100 Lbp 28.50 Br md 10.40 Dpth 3.80 Welded, 1 dk	**(B32A2ST) Tug**	**2 oil engines** reduction geared to sc. shafts driving 2 Z propellers Total Power: 2,600kW (3,534hp) 12.0kn A.B.C. 6MDZC 2 x 4 Stroke 6 Cy. 256 x 310 each-1300kW (1767bhp) Anglo Belgian Corp NV (ABC)-Belgium AuxGen: 2 x 144kW 400V 50Hz a.c Fuel: 56.0 (d.f.)
9524114 *EADP* -	**VB LLEVANT** *ex* Eugenia *-2012* **Pastor Servicios Financieros Establecimiento Financiero de Credito SA (PSF)** Boluda Corporacion Maritima *Valencia Spain* MMSI: 225437000	**381** 113 300	Class: RI	**2011-06 Union Naval Valencia SA (UNV) — Valencia** Yd No: 478 Loa 29.50 Br ex - Dght 3.600 Lbp 28.00 Br md 11.00 Dpth 4.30 Welded, 1 dk	**(B32A2ST) Tug**	**2 oil engines** reduction geared to sc. shafts driving 2 Voith-Schneider propellers Total Power: 4,560kW (6,200hp) GE Marine 12V228 2 x Vee 4 Stroke 12 Cy. 229 x 267 each-2280kW (3100bhp) General Electric Co.-Lynn, Ma
9122813 *FKVD* -	**VB MAHAVEL** *ex* Abeille Mahavel *-2009* **Boluda France SAS** Boluda La Reunion *Saint-Denis France* MMSI: 227004200 Official number: 850024	**315** 94 90	Class: BV	**1995-12 Manche Industrie Marine — Dieppe** Yd No: 519 Loa 29.90 Br ex 9.95 Dght 3.240 Lbp 27.76 Br md 9.70 Dpth 4.03 Welded, 1 dk	**(B32A2ST) Tug**	**2 oil engines** with hydraulic couplings & sr geared to sc. shafts driving 2 Directional propellers Total Power: 2,470kW (3,358hp) 11.5kn Deutz SBV6M628 2 x 4 Stroke 6 Cy. 240 x 280 each-1235kW (1679bhp) Motoren Werke Mannheim AG (MWM)-Mannheim
9344629 *CNA4277* -	**VB MALABATA** *ex* Abeille Malabata *-2009* **Boluda Tanger Med** - *Tangier Morocco* MMSI: 242905000	**289** 86 -	Class: BV	**2007-01 Santierul Naval Damen Galati S.A. — Galati** (Hull) Yd No: 1079 **2007-01 B.V. Scheepswerf Damen — Gorinchem** Yd No: 511520 Loa 28.75 Br ex 10.43 Dght 3.610 Lbp 25.79 Br md 9.80 Dpth 4.60 Welded, 1 dk	**(B32A2ST) Tug**	**2 oil engines** geared to sc. shafts driving 2 Directional propellers Total Power: 3,678kW (5,000hp) Caterpillar 3516B 2 x Vee 4 Stroke 16 Cy. 170 x 190 each-1839kW (2500bhp) Caterpillar Inc-USA AuxGen: 2 x 84kW 400V 50Hz a.c Fuel: 82.1 (r.f.)
7810026 *HP5559* -	**VB MICHOACAN** *ex* VB Corsario *-2008* *ex* Kinross *-2007* *ex* Fuji Maru *-1981* **Tug Services Panama SA** Compania Maritima de Panama SA *Panama Panama* Official number: 4224411	**347** 104 -	Class: LR **100A1** SS 09/2011 tug near continental trading area **LMC** Eq.Ltr: (E) ; Cable: 300.0/26.0 U2	**1978-08 Sagami Zosen Tekko K.K. — Yokosuka** Yd No: 197 Loa 36.35 Br ex 9.83 Dght 4.131 Lbp 30.26 Br md 9.61 Dpth 4.20 Welded, 1 dk	**(B32A2ST) Tug**	**2 oil engines** gearing integral to driving 2 Z propellers Total Power: 2,354kW (3,200hp) 11.5kn Niigata 8L28BX 2 x 4 Stroke 8 Cy. 280 x 320 each-1177kW (1600bhp) Niigata Engineering Co Ltd-Japan AuxGen: 2 x 80kW 220V 60Hz a.c
9333876 *EAOE* -	**VB MUSCLE** *ex* Rt Antonie *-2011* **RT Antonie Ltd** Remolques del Mediterraneo SA *Castellon de la Plana Spain* MMSI: 225427000	**343** 102 136	Class: GL (LR) ✠ Classed LR until 12/4/12	**2006-02 ASL Shipyard Pte Ltd — Singapore** Yd No: 501 Loa 28.30 Br ex 11.70 Dght 3.100 Lbp 26.10 Br md 11.20 Dpth 5.24 Welded, 1 dk	**(B32A2ST) Tug**	**3 oil engines** gearing integral to driving 3 Z propellers Total Power: 3,930kW (5,343hp) Wartsila 8L20 3 x 4 Stroke 8 Cy. 200 x 280 each-1310kW (1781bhp) Wartsila Finland Oy-Finland AuxGen: 2 x 90kW 400V 50Hz a.c Fuel: 110.0 (d.f.) 18.0pd
9357274 *FMIA* -	**VB NANTES** *ex* SD Loire *-2011* *completed as* Med Meric *-2005* **Boluda Corporacion Maritima** - *St-Nazaire France* MMSI: 228234900	**389** 117 -	Class: BV	**2005-12 Medyilmaz Gemi Sanayi ve Ticaret AS — Karadeniz Eregli** Yd No: 27 Loa 32.00 Br ex - Dght 3.710 Lbp 28.40 Br md 10.50 Dpth 5.30 Welded, 1 dk	**(B32A2ST) Tug**	**2 oil engines** reduction geared to sc. shafts driving 2 Z propellers Total Power: 3,240kW (4,406hp) 11.0kn Wartsila 9L20 2 x 4 Stroke 9 Cy. 200 x 280 each-1620kW (2203bhp) Wartsila Finland Oy-Finland
9264374 *6WKB* -	**VB NORA** *ex* Temeraire *-2010* *ex* Honce *-2005* **Union des Remorqueurs de Dakar (URD)** - *Dakar Senegal* MMSI: 663076000	**358** 107 -	Class: BV	**2002-05 Astilleros Armon SA — Navia** Yd No: 551 Loa 28.29 Br ex - Dght 4.200 Lbp 26.80 Br md 9.85 Dpth 5.40 Welded, 1 dk	**(B32A2ST) Tug**	**2 oil engines** with clutches, flexible couplings & sr geared to sc. shafts driving 2 Directional propellers Total Power: 2,942kW (4,000hp) Caterpillar 3516B 2 x Vee 4 Stroke 16 Cy. 170 x 190 each-1471kW (2000bhp) Caterpillar Inc-USA
9393709 *FLEF* -	**VB OCTEVILLE** *ex* Abeille Octeville *-2009* **Boluda France SAS** Boluda Le Havre *Le Havre France* MMSI: 228284800 Official number: 000752	**342** 102 -	Class: BV	**2007-12 Chantiers Piriou — Concarneau** Yd No: C281 Loa 30.30 Br ex - Dght 4.500 Lbp - Br md 10.40 Dpth 4.32 Welded, 1 dk	**(B32A2ST) Tug**	**2 oil engines** reduction geared to sc. shafts driving 2 Directional propellers Total Power: 3,900kW (5,302hp) 11.0kn A.B.C. 8DZC 2 x 4 Stroke 8 Cy. 256 x 310 each-1950kW (2651bhp) Anglo Belgian Corp NV (ABC)-Belgium Thrusters: 1 Tunnel thruster (f)
9002051 *FV6093* -	**VB OLERON** *ex* VB Le Havre *-2011* *ex* Abeille Le Havre *-2009* **Boluda France SAS** Boluda La Rochelle *La Rochelle France* MMSI: 227005260 Official number: 698251	**287** 8 90	Class: BV	**1991-06 Manche Industrie Marine — Dieppe** Yd No: 512 Loa 30.60 Br ex - Dght 4.801 Lbp 28.30 Br md 9.95 Dpth - Welded, 1 dk	**(B32A2ST) Tug**	**2 oil engines** with clutches & sr geared to sc. shafts driving 2 Directional propellers Total Power: 2,140kW (2,910hp) 11.5kn Deutz SBV6M628 2 x 4 Stroke 6 Cy. 240 x 280 each-1070kW (1455bhp) Kloeckner Humboldt Deutz AG-Germany
7217901 *FSGN* -	**VB PIRIAC** *ex* Abeille Piriac *-2009* *ex* Abeille No. 8 *-1992* **Boluda France SAS** Boluda Brest *St-Nazaire France* MMSI: 228025000 Official number: 188707	*299* - 133	Class: BV	**1972 Ch. de la Garonne — Bordeaux** Yd No: 1134 Loa 33.00 Br ex 9.73 Dght 4.960 Lbp 30.00 Br md 9.33 Dpth 4.14 Welded, 1 dk	**(B32A2ST) Tug**	**2 oil engines** gearing integral to driving 2 Voith-Schneider propellers Total Power: 1,986kW (2,700hp) 12.3kn AGO 240G8LS 2 x 4 Stroke 8 Cy. 240 x 220 each-993kW (1350bhp) Societe Alsacienne de ConstructionsMecaniques (SACM)-France AuxGen: 1 x 112kW a.c
8521153 *FT3888* -	**VB POULIGUEN** *ex* Abeille Pouliguen *-2009* *ex* Francia *-1997* **Boluda France SAS** Les Abeilles Nantes *St-Nazaire France* MMSI: 227004660 Official number: 915941	*198* 40 145	Class: BV (RI)	**1988-07 Cant. Navale "Ferrari" S.p.A. — La Spezia** Yd No: 57 Loa 26.85 Br ex 9.12 Dght 3.160 Lbp 26.01 Br md 9.10 Dpth 3.90 Welded, 1 dk	**(B32A2ST) Tug**	**2 oil engines** with clutches & sr geared to sc. shafts driving 2 Directional propellers Total Power: 2,370kW (3,222hp) 10.8kn Deutz SBV6M628 2 x 4 Stroke 6 Cy. 240 x 280 each-1185kW (1611bhp) Kloeckner Humboldt Deutz AG-West Germany AuxGen: 2 x 38kW 220/380V 50Hz a.c Fuel: 36.0 (d.f.) 11.0pd
9032123 *FQRZ* -	**VB PROVENCE** *ex* Abeille Provence *-2008* **Boluda France SAS** - *Marseille France* MMSI: 227272000 Official number: 850433J	*498* - -	Class: BV (LR) ✠ Classed LR until 1/8/01	**1993-01 Saint-Malo Naval — St-Malo** (Hull) Yd No: 614 **1993-01 Manche Industrie Marine — Dieppe** Loa 35.50 Br ex 11.58 Dght 3.740 Lbp 32.50 Br md 11.50 Dpth 4.40 Welded, 1 dk	**(B32A2ST) Tug**	**2 oil engines** gearing integral to driving 2 Voith-Schneider propellers Total Power: 3,700kW (5,030hp) 12.0kn Caterpillar 3606TA 2 x 4 Stroke 6 Cy. 280 x 300 each-1850kW (2515bhp) Caterpillar Inc-USA AuxGen: 2 x 125kW 380V 50Hz a.c Fuel: 153.0 (d.f.)
9393735 *FNQP* -	**VB PUISSANT** *ex* V.B. Trouville *-2010* **Boluda France SAS** Societe des Remorqueurs du Port Autonome de Marseille *Dunkirk France* MMSI: 228293700 Official number: 896417	**342** 102 -	Class: BV	**2008-09 Chantiers Piriou — Concarneau** Yd No: C284 Loa 30.30 Br ex 11.00 Dght 4.500 Lbp 29.00 Br md 10.40 Dpth 4.32 Welded, 1 dk	**(B32A2ST) Tug**	**2 oil engines** reduction geared to sc. shafts driving 2 Directional propellers Total Power: 3,536kW (4,808hp) 11.0kn A.B.C. 8MDZC 2 x 4 Stroke 8 Cy. 256 x 310 each-1768kW (2404bhp) Anglo Belgian Corp NV (ABC)-Belgium Thrusters: 1 Tunnel thruster (f)

Ship	Tonnage / Class	Builder & dimensions	Type	Machinery
7387043 - - **VB PUNTA CANA** *ex* V.B. Punta Cana *-2008* *ex* Montduber *-2008* **Remolcadores y Barcazas del Caribe SA** - *Santo Domingo* *Dominican Rep.*	*245* 37 - Class: (LR) ✠ Classed LR until 1/1/12	**1976**-07 **Sociedad Metalurgica Duro Felguera — Gijon** Yd No: 117 Loa 31.96 Br ex 9.73 Dght 4.084 Lbp 28.02 Br md 9.21 Dpth 4.73 Welded, 1 dk	**(B32A2ST) Tug**	**1 oil engine** sr geared to sc. shaft driving 1 CP propeller Total Power: 1,765kW (2,400hp) 13.0kn MWM RHS345SU 1 x 4 Stroke 6 Cy. 360 x 450 1765kW (2400bhp) (made 1973, fitted 1976) Fabrica de San Carlos SA-Spain AuxGen: 3 x 84kW 380V 50Hz a.c
8821436 - - **VB PUNTA DEL ESTE** *ex* Smit Bahama *-2010* *ex* Kitano Maru *-1998* **Monteverde Compania Naviera SA** Remolcadores y Lanchas SA *Uruguay*	**355** 106 - Class: (BV)	**1989**-03 **Sagami Zosen Tekko K.K. — Yokosuka** Yd No: 239 Loa 36.22 Br ex 9.82 Dght 3.900 Lbp 31.50 Br md 9.80 Dpth 4.40 Welded	**(B32A2ST) Tug**	**2 oil engines** with clutches, flexible couplings & dr geared to sc. shafts driving 2 FP propellers Total Power: 2,648kW (3,600hp) 11.0kn Niigata 6L28HX 2 x 4 Stroke 6 Cy. 280 x 370 each-1324kW (1800bhp) Niigata Engineering Co Ltd-Japan
9393711 *FNOF* - **VB RHONE** *launched as* Abeille Rhone *-2008* **Boluda France SAS** Boluda Marseilla Fos *Marseille* *France* MMSI: 228287800 Official number: 925829L	**342** 102 - Class: BV	**2008**-05 **Chantiers Piriou — Concarneau** Yd No: C282 Loa 30.30 Br ex - Dght 4.500 Lbp 29.46 Br md 10.40 Dpth 4.32 Welded, 1 dk	**(B32A2ST) Tug**	**2 oil engines** reduction geared to sc. shafts driving 2 Directional propellers Total Power: 3,900kW (5,302hp) 11.0kn A.B.C. 8DZC 2 x 4 Stroke 8 Cy. 256 x 310 each-1950kW (2651bhp) Anglo Belgian Corp NV (ABC)-Belgium
8718768 *EASM* - **VB RISBAN** *ex* Abeille Risban *-2008* *ex* Abeille No. 15 *-1995* **Boluda France SAS** Boat Service SA *Las Palmas de Gran Canaria* *Spain* MMSI: 224046000 Official number: 1-1/2009	*264* 7 - Class: BV	**1988**-09 **Scheepswerf Bijlholt B.V. — Foxhol** (Hull) Yd No: 651 **1988**-09 **B.V. Scheepswerf Damen — Gorinchem** Yd No: 4802 Loa 29.70 Br ex 9.95 Dght 3.700 Lbp 27.21 Br md 9.25 Dpth 4.90 Welded, 1 dk	**(B32A2ST) Tug**	**2 oil engines** geared to sc. shafts driving 2 Directional propellers Total Power: 2,160kW (2,936hp) 12.0kn Deutz SBV6M628 2 x 4 Stroke 6 Cy. 240 x 280 each-1080kW (1468bhp) Kloeckner Humboldt Deutz AG-West Germany AuxGen: 2 x 93kW 380V 50Hz a.c Fuel: 54.0 (d.f.)
8317473 *8QDB* - **VB RULER** *ex* Wave Ruler *-2009* *ex* Sumiho Maru No. 21 *-1999* *ex* Jingu Maru No. 8 *-1989* **A A A Trading Co** - *Male* *Maldives* MMSI: 455239000 Official number: C6689A	**956** 361 1,000	**1983**-08 **Shitanoe Shipbuilding Co Ltd — Usuki OT** Yd No: 1031 Loa 66.30 Br ex - Dght - Lbp 62.01 Br md 10.32 Dpth 6.02 Welded, 1 dk	**(A31A2GX) General Cargo Ship**	**1 oil engine** driving 1 FP propeller Total Power: 736kW (1,001hp) Niigata 6M28AFTE 1 x 4 Stroke 6 Cy. 280 x 480 736kW (1001bhp) Niigata Engineering Co Ltd-Japan
9002075 *FV6095* - **VB SAINT BREVIN** *ex* VB Honfleur *-2009* *ex* Abeille Honfleur *-2009* **Boluda France SAS** Boluda Nantes Saint Nazaire *St-Nazaire* *France* MMSI: 227005280 Official number: 698253	**287** 94 90 Class: BV	**1991**-12 **Manche Industrie Marine — Dieppe** Yd No: 514 Loa 30.60 Br ex 9.95 Dght 2.990 Lbp 28.30 Br md 9.70 Dpth 4.03 Welded, 1 dk	**(B32A2ST) Tug**	**2 oil engines** with clutches & sr geared to sc. shafts driving 2 Directional propellers Total Power: 2,140kW (2,910hp) 11.5kn Deutz SBV6M628 2 x 4 Stroke 6 Cy. 240 x 280 each-1070kW (1455bhp) Kloeckner Humboldt Deutz AG-Germany AuxGen: 3 x 96kW 380/220V 50Hz a.c Fuel: 60.0 (d.f.)
9002063 *FV6094* - **VB SAINT MARC** *ex* VB Etretat *-2009* *ex* Abeille Etretat *-2009* **Boluda France SAS** Boluda Nantes Saint Nazaire *St-Nazaire* *France* MMSI: 227005270 Official number: 698252	**287** 94 90 Class: BV	**1991**-07 **Manche Industrie Marine — Dieppe** Yd No: 513 Loa 30.60 Br ex - Dght 2.990 Lbp 28.30 Br md 9.70 Dpth 4.03 Welded, 1 dk	**(B32A2ST) Tug**	**2 oil engines** with clutches & sr geared to sc. shafts driving 2 Directional propellers Total Power: 2,140kW (2,910hp) 11.5kn Deutz SBV6M628 2 x 4 Stroke 6 Cy. 240 x 280 each-1070kW (1455bhp) Kloeckner Humboldt Deutz AG-Germany AuxGen: 3 x 96kW 220/380V 50Hz a.c
9202742 *FW9207* - **VB SAINTE ADRESSE** *ex* Abeille Sainte Adresse *-2008* **Boluda France SAS** Boluda Le Havre *Le Havre* *France* MMSI: 227006780 Official number: 896365	**487** 146 260 Class: BV	**2000**-10 **Alstom Leroux Naval SA — St-Malo** Yd No: 643 Loa 36.82 Br ex - Dght 5.500 Lbp 33.90 Br md 10.60 Dpth 5.60 Welded, 1 dk	**(B32A2ST) Tug**	**2 oil engines** reduction geared to sc. shafts driving 2 Directional propellers Total Power: 3,680kW (5,004hp) 12.5kn A.B.C. 8MDZC 2 x 4 Stroke 8 Cy. 256 x 310 each-1840kW (2502bhp) Anglo Belgian Corp NV (ABC)-Belgium AuxGen: 2 x 168kW 380/220V 50Hz a.c Thrusters: 1 Thwart. FP thruster (f) Fuel: 142.0 (d.f.)
7237274 - - **VB SAMANA** *ex* VB Tifon *-2008* *ex* Steenbank *-2002* **Remolcadores y Barcazas del Caribe SA** - *Santo Domingo* *Dominican Rep.* Official number: RM-T94-2017 SDG	*274* 82 - Class: (AB)	**1972**-12 **B.V. Scheepswerven v/h H.H. Bodewes — Millingen a/d Rijn** Yd No: 705 Loa 33.25 Br ex 9.58 Dght - Lbp 31.32 Br md 9.21 Dpth 3.81 Welded, 1 dk	**(B32A2ST) Tug**	**2 oil engines** driving 2 FP propellers Total Power: 1,912kW (2,600hp) 11.5kn Kromhout 6FFHD240 2 x 4 Stroke 6 Cy. 240 x 260 each-956kW (1300bhp) Stork Werkspoor Diesel BV-Netherlands AuxGen: 1 x 90kW 380V 50Hz a.c, 1 x 80kW 380V 50Hz a.c
8017346 *EAFX* - **VB SOLEA** *ex* Elkiti *-2008* **Boluda Towage & Salvage SLU** Boluda Corporacion Maritima SatCom: Inmarsat C 422500145 *Tarragona* *Spain* MMSI: 224142950 Official number: 1-2/1992	*162* - 92 Class: (AB)	**1981**-06 **S.A. Balenciaga — Zumaya** Yd No: 301 Loa 26.83 Br ex - Dght 3.350 Lbp 24.01 Br md 7.92 Dpth 3.97 Welded, 1 dk	**(B32A2ST) Tug**	**1 oil engine** reverse reduction geared to sc. shaft driving 1 CP propeller Total Power: 1,471kW (2,000hp) 12.0kn MaK 8M332AK 1 x 4 Stroke 8 Cy. 240 x 330 1471kW (2000bhp) Krupp MaK Maschinenbau GmbH-Kiel AuxGen: 2 x 84kW
8615590 *6WJQ* - **VB SOMONE** *ex* Marseillais 4 *-2010* **Union des Remorqueurs de Dakar (URD)** - *Dakar* *Senegal*	**290** 87 - Class: BV	**1987**-10 **C.E.R.N.A.T. — Nantes** Yd No: 43355 Loa 31.02 Br ex - Dght 2.671 Lbp 27.84 Br md 9.20 Dpth 3.61 Welded, 1 dk	**(B32A2ST) Tug**	**2 oil engines** with flexible couplings & sr gearedto sc. shafts driving 2 Directional propellers Total Power: 2,000kW (2,720hp) 11.0kn MaK 6M332AK 2 x 4 Stroke 6 Cy. 240 x 330 each-1000kW (1360bhp) Krupp MaK Maschinenbau GmbH-Kiel AuxGen: 2 x 80kW 380V 50Hz a.c Fuel: 53.0 (d.f.)
9344617 *CNA4278* - **VB SPARTEL** *ex* Abeille Spartel *-2009* **Boluda Tanger Med** - *Tangier* *Morocco* MMSI: 242906000	**289** 86 - Class: BV	**2007**-01 **Santierul Naval Damen Galati S.A. — Galati** (Hull) Yd No: 1078 **2007**-01 **B.V. Scheepswerf Damen — Gorinchem** Yd No: 511519 Loa 28.75 Br ex 10.43 Dght 3.900 Lbp 25.79 Br md 9.80 Dpth 4.60 Welded, 1 dk	**(B32A2ST) Tug**	**2 oil engines** geared to sc. shafts driving 2 Directional propellers Total Power: 3,678kW (5,000hp) Caterpillar 3516B 2 x Vee 4 Stroke 16 Cy. 170 x 190 each-1839kW (2500bhp) Caterpillar Inc-USA AuxGen: 2 x 84kW 400V 50Hz a.c
9395836 *FHXE* - **VB SUPERENZO** *ex* Abeille Vespucci *-2008* **Boluda France SAS** - *Le Havre* *France* MMSI: 228011900	**289** 86 - Class: BV	**2008**-01 **Damen Shipyards Changde Co Ltd — Changde HN** (Hull) Yd No: (511540) **2008**-01 **B.V. Scheepswerf Damen — Gorinchem** Yd No: 511540 Loa 28.67 Br ex 10.43 Dght 3.610 Lbp 25.90 Br md 9.80 Dpth 4.60 Welded, 1 dk	**(B32A2ST) Tug**	**2 oil engines** reduction geared to sc. shafts driving 2 Z propellers Total Power: 3,372kW (4,584hp) Caterpillar 3516B-HD 2 x Vee 4 Stroke 16 Cy. 170 x 215 each-1686kW (2292bhp) Caterpillar Inc-USA AuxGen: 2 x 80kW 400/230V 50Hz a.c Fuel: 96.5 (r.f.)
9395824 *XCKD3* - **VB TABASCO** *ex* Abeille Magellan *-2009* **Compania Maritima del Pacifico SA de CV** - *Mazatlan* *Mexico* MMSI: 345020023	**289** 86 - Class: GL (BV)	**2008**-01 **Damen Shipyards Changde Co Ltd — Changde HN** (Hull) **2008**-01 **B.V. Scheepswerf Damen — Gorinchem** Yd No: 511539 Loa 28.67 Br ex 10.43 Dght 3.610 Lbp 25.79 Br md 9.80 Dpth 4.60 Welded, 1 dk	**(B32A2ST) Tug**	**2 oil engines** reduction geared to sc. shafts driving 2 Z propellers Total Power: 3,678kW (5,000hp) Caterpillar 3516B-HD 2 x Vee 4 Stroke 16 Cy. 170 x 215 each-1839kW (2500bhp) Caterpillar Inc-USA AuxGen: 2 x 80kW 400/230V 50Hz a.c Fuel: 96.5 (r.f.)

IMO / Call sign	Name / Owner	Tonnage	Class	Builder / Dimensions	Type	Machinery
8207707 - -	**VB TECKEL** *ex* ZP Montali *-2013* *launched as* ZP Mayacamas *-1985* **Servicios Auxiliares de Puertos SA (SERTOSA)** - *Castellon de la Plana* *Spain* Official number: CP2212	**272** 81 337	Class: AB	**1985 Cameron Shipbuilders, Inc. — Brownsville, Tx** Yd No: 116 Loa 28.50 Br ex - Dght 5.060 Lbp 26.93 Br md 10.37 Dpth 3.81 Welded, 1 dk	**(B32A2ST) Tug**	**2 oil engines** sr geared to sc. shafts driving 2 Directional propellers Total Power: 2,354kW (3,200hp) 8.0kn Alpha 7SL28L-VO 2 x 4 Stroke 7 Cy. 280 x 320 each-1177kW (1600bhp) MAN B&W Diesel A/S-Denmark AuxGen: 2 x 135kW 460V 50Hz a.c Fuel: 202.0 (d.f.) 13.0pd
9181429 *EATB* -	**VB TENERIFE** **ING Lease (Espana) SA EFC** Remolcadores y Barcazas de Tenerife SA *Santa Cruz de Tenerife* *Spain* MMSI: 224474000 Official number: 1-3/1998	**375** 112 326	Class: BV (Class contemplated) LR ✠ **100A1** SS 01/2009 tug (fire fighting ship 1 (2400 cubic metre/hr) with water spray) *IWS ✠ **LMC** **UMS** Eq.Ltr: G; Cable: 302.5/20.5 U2	**1999-01 Astilleros Zamakona SA — Santurtzi** Yd No: 434 Loa 30.50 Br ex 10.50 Dght 4.200 Lbp 26.80 Br md 9.85 Dpth 5.40 Welded, 1 dk	**(B32A2ST) Tug**	**2 oil engines** with clutches, flexible couplings & sr geared to sc. shafts driving 2 Directional propellers Total Power: 3,040kW (4,134hp) 9.0kn MaK 8M20 2 x 4 Stroke 8 Cy. 200 x 300 each-1520kW (2067bhp) MaK Motoren GmbH & Co. KG-Kiel AuxGen: 2 x 165kW 380V 50Hz a.c Fuel: 220.0 (d.f.) 17.0pd
8207719 *HP4232* -	**VB TERRIER** *ex* ZP Montelena *-2012* **Kotug Vijf BV** Sleepdienst Adriaan Kooren BV (Tugboat Company Adriaan Kooren) - KOTUG *Panama* *Panama* MMSI: 372263000 Official number: 43988PEXTF	**222** 66 337	Class: BV (AB)	**1982-12 Valley Shipbuilding, Inc. — Brownsville, Tx** Yd No: 117 Loa 28.50 Br ex - Dght 5.060 Lbp 27.12 Br md 10.38 Dpth 3.81 Welded, 1 dk	**(B32A2ST) Tug**	**2 oil engines** sr geared to sc. shafts driving 2 Directional propellers Total Power: 2,356kW (3,204hp) 8.0kn Alpha 7SL28L-VO 2 x 4 Stroke 7 Cy. 280 x 320 each-1178kW (1602bhp) B&W Holeby Diesel A/S-Denmark AuxGen: 2 x 135kW 460V 50Hz a.c Fuel: 202.0 (d.f.) 13.0pd
9456898 *ECAD* -	**VB TITAN** **Remolcadores Boluda SA** Boluda Corporacion Maritima *Valencia* *Spain* MMSI: 224096000	**644** 266 266	Class: BV	**2010-04 Union Naval Valencia SA (UNV) — Valencia** Yd No: 473 Loa 32.00 Br ex - Dght 5.600 Lbp 30.60 Br md 14.00 Dpth 4.40 Welded, 1 dk	**(B32A2ST) Tug**	**2 oil engines** reduction geared to sc. shafts driving 2 Voith-Schneider propellers Total Power: 5,300kW (7,206hp) 12.5kn MAN-B&W 8L27/38 2 x 4 Stroke 8 Cy. 270 x 380 each-2650kW (3603bhp) MAN B&W Diesel AG-Augsburg AuxGen: 2 x 130kW 440V 50Hz a.c Fuel: 115.0 (d.f.)
9456903 *EAKY* -	**VB TRON** **Remolcadores Boluda SA** Boluda Corporacion Maritima SatCom: Inmarsat C 422424811 *Valencia* *Spain* MMSI: 224248000	**644** 266 266	Class: BV	**2010-06 Union Naval Valencia SA (UNV) — Valencia** Yd No: 474 Loa 32.00 Br ex - Dght 5.600 Lbp 30.60 Br md 14.00 Dpth 4.40 Welded, 1 dk	**(B32A2ST) Tug**	**2 oil engines** reduction geared to sc. shafts driving 2 Voith-Schneider propellers Total Power: 5,440kW (7,396hp) MAN-B&W 8L27/38 2 x 4 Stroke 8 Cy. 270 x 380 each-2720kW (3698bhp) MAN B&W Diesel AG-Augsburg AuxGen: 2 x 130kW 440V 50Hz a.c Fuel: 115.0 (d.f.)
9393723 *FNOI* -	**VB YPORT** **Boluda France SAS** Boluda Corporacion Maritima *Le Havre* *France* MMSI: 228287900 Official number: 000750	**342** 102 -	Class: BV	**2008-05 Chantiers Piriou — Concarneau** Yd No: C283 Loa 30.30 Br ex - Dght 4.500 Lbp 29.46 Br md 10.40 Dpth 4.32 Welded, 1 dk	**(B32A2ST) Tug**	**2 oil engines** reduction geared to sc. shafts driving 2 Z propellers Total Power: 3,900kW (5,302hp) 11.0kn A.B.C. 8DZC 2 x 4 Stroke 8 Cy. 256 x 310 each-1950kW (2651bhp) Anglo Belgian Corp NV (ABC)-Belgium
9341249 *XCAE3* -	**VB YUCATAN** *ex* Baek Du *-2013* **Compania Maritima del Pacifico SA de CV** - *Ensenada* *Mexico* MMSI: 345020500	**366** - -	Class: GL (KR)	**2004-12 Yeunsoo Shipbuilding Co Ltd — Janghang** Yd No: 18 Loa 34.60 Br ex - Dght 3.500 Lbp 30.00 Br md 9.50 Dpth 4.10 Welded, 1 dk	**(B32A2ST) Tug**	**2 oil engines** reduction geared to sc. shafts driving 2 CP propellers Total Power: 3,264kW (4,438hp) M.T.U. 16V4000M60 2 x Vee 4 Stroke 16 Cy. 165 x 190 each-1632kW (2219bhp) MTU Friedrichshafen GmbH-Friedrichshafen
9314454 *LMMJ* -	**VEA** **Vea AS** Didrik T Vea *Kopervik* *Norway* MMSI: 257284000	*1,475* 442 -	Class: NV	**2004-01 Stocznia Polnocna SA (Northern Shipyard) — Gdansk** Yd No: B309/1 Loa 60.38 Br ex 12.62 Dght 5.602 Lbp 54.38 Br md 12.60 Dpth 8.10 Welded, 1 dk	**(B11B2FV) Fishing Vessel**	**1 oil engine** geared to sc. shaft driving 1 CP propeller Total Power: 3,000kW (4,079hp) MaK 6M32C 1 x 4 Stroke 6 Cy. 320 x 480 3000kW (4079bhp) Caterpillar Motoren GmbH & Co. KG-Germany AuxGen: 2 x a.c, 1 x a.c Thrusters: 1 Tunnel thruster (f)
7403562 - - -	**VEABAS** *ex* Borgoygutt *-1992* *ex* Sjannoy *-1989* - -	**976** 550 -	Class: (NV)	**1975-03 Sandnessjoen Slip & Mek. Verksted — Sandnessjoen** Yd No: 31 Lengthened-1983 Loa 62.72 Br ex 9.53 Dght 6.217 Lbp 54.96 Br md 9.50 Dpth 7.62 Welded, 2 dks	**(B11A2FT) Trawler** Compartments: 1 Ho, 6 Ta, ER 7 Ha: (2.5 x 1.6)6 (0.9 x 1.6) Cranes: 1x5t,1x2t Ice Capable	**1 oil engine** driving 1 FP propeller Total Power: 1,416kW (1,925hp) Wichmann 7AXA 1 x 2 Stroke 7 Cy. 300 x 450 1416kW (1925bhp) Wichmann Motorfabrikk AS-Norway AuxGen: 3 x 108kW 220V 50Hz a.c Thrusters: 1 Thwart. FP thruster (f); 1 Tunnel thruster (a)
8870061 *LCFH* R-1-K	**VEAGUTT** *ex* Heringshai *-2008* **Fiskeriselskapet Norli AS** - *Kopervik* *Norway* MMSI: 259388000	**185** 74 -	Class: (GL)	**1993 Johs Kristensen Skibsbyggeri A/S — Hvide Sande** Yd No: 202 Loa 23.71 Br ex - Dght - Lbp - Br md 7.20 Dpth 3.80 Welded, 1 dk	**(B11B2FV) Fishing Vessel**	**1 oil engine** reduction geared to sc. shaft driving 1 FP propeller Total Power: 411kW (559hp) 11.0kn MWM TBD604BL6 1 x 4 Stroke 6 Cy. 170 x 195 411kW (559bhp) Motoren Werke Mannheim AG (MWM)-Mannheim
9293454 *3EBR8* -	**VECCHIO BRIDGE** **Wealth Line Inc** Fukujin Kisen KK (Fukujin Kisen Co Ltd) *Panama* *Panama* MMSI: 371208000 Official number: 3088305A	**54,519** 22,921 64,983 T/cm 82.5	Class: NK	**2005-07 Hyundai Heavy Industries Co Ltd — Ulsan** Yd No: 1593 Loa 294.12 (BB) Br ex - Dght 13.520 Lbp 283.33 Br md 32.20 Dpth 21.80 Welded, 1 dk	**(A33A2CC) Container Ship (Fully Cellular)** TEU 4738 incl 400 ref C	**1 oil engine** driving 1 FP propeller Total Power: 45,660kW (62,079hp) 23.5kn MAN-B&W 8K98MC-C 1 x 2 Stroke 8 Cy. 980 x 2400 45660kW (62079bhp) Hyundai Heavy Industries Co Ltd-South Korea AuxGen: 4 x 1995kW a.c Thrusters: 1 Thwart. CP thruster (f) Fuel: 7385.0
7052583 *UCLH* -	**VECHE** *ex* Mirfan *-1991* **A/O Soyma** - *Murmansk* *Russia* MMSI: 273429400 Official number: 700933	*629* 220 393	Class: (RS)	**1970 Zavod "Leninskaya Kuznitsa" — Kiyev** Yd No: 1334 Loa 54.82 Br ex 9.96 Dght 4.080 Lbp 50.29 Br md - Dpth 5.01 Welded, 1 dk	**(B11A2FS) Stern Trawler** Ins: 400 Compartments: 2 Ho, ER 3 Ha: 3 (1.5 x 1.6) Derricks: 2x1.5t; Winches: 2 Ice Capable	**1 oil engine** driving 1 CP propeller Total Power: 736kW (1,001hp) 12.0kn S.K.L. 8NVD48AU 1 x 4 Stroke 8 Cy. 320 x 480 736kW (1001bhp) VEB Schwermaschinenbau "KarlLiebknecht" (SKL)-Magdeburg
9395068 *PBMW* -	**VECHT TRADER** *ex* Medatlantic *-2008* **Vecht Trader Beheer BV** Reider Shipping BV *Winschoten* *Netherlands* MMSI: 245591000 Official number: 52215	**15,375** 5,983 18,349	Class: GL	**2007-05 Zhejiang Ouhua Shipbuilding Co Ltd — Zhoushan ZJ** Yd No: 2039 Loa 166.15 (BB) Br ex - Dght 9.500 Lbp 155.08 Br md 25.00 Dpth 14.20 Welded, 1 dk	**(A33A2CC) Container Ship (Fully Cellular)** TEU 1284 C Ho 472 C Dk 812 TEU incl 390 ref C. Cranes: 2x45t	**1 oil engine** reduction geared to sc. shaft driving 1 CP propeller Total Power: 11,200kW (15,228hp) 19.0kn MAN-B&W 8L58/64 1 x 4 Stroke 8 Cy. 580 x 640 11200kW (15228bhp) MAN B&W Diesel AG-Augsburg AuxGen: 4 x 2000kW 450/230V a.c Thrusters: 1 Tunnel thruster (f)
9160334 *V2EM4* -	**VECHTBORG** **ms 'Niobe' Schifffahrtsgesellschaft mbH + Co KG** Esmeralda Schiffahrts- Verwaltungsgesellschaft mbH *Saint John's* *Antigua & Barbuda* MMSI: 305477000 Official number: 4667	**6,130** 3,424 8,664 T/cm 18.3	Class: AB (BV)	**1998-09 Bodewes Scheepswerf "Volharding" Foxhol B.V. — Foxhol** Yd No: 331 Loa 132.20 (BB) Br ex - Dght 7.050 Lbp 123.84 Br md 15.87 Dpth 9.65 Welded, 1 dk	**(A31A2GX) General Cargo Ship** Grain: 12,855 TEU 552 C.Ho 264/20' C.Dk 288/20' incl. 25 ref C. Compartments: 2 Ho, ER 2 Ha: ER Ice Capable	**1 oil engine** with flexible couplings & sr gearedto sc. shaft driving 1 CP propeller Total Power: 3,960kW (5,384hp) 15.5kn Wartsila 6R38 1 x 4 Stroke 6 Cy. 380 x 475 3960kW (5384bhp) Wartsila NSD Nederland BV-Netherlands AuxGen: 1 x 650kW 230/440V 60Hz a.c, 2 x 244kW 230/440V 60Hz a.c Thrusters: 1 Thwart. CP thruster (f) Fuel: 50.0 (d.f.) 455.0 (r.f.) 19.0pd

IMO / Call sign	Name, Owner, Manager, Port, Flag	Tonnage	Classification	Builder, Dimensions	Type, Cargo	Machinery	Speed / Engine
9224142 *A8ZO9* -	**VECHTDIEP** **Vechtdiep Shipping Co Ltd** Feederlines BV *Monrovia* *Liberia* MMSI: 636015265 Official number: 15265	**4,938** 2,631 7,200	Class: LR ✠ **100A1** SS 12/2010 strengthened for heavy cargoes container cargoes in holds and on upper deck hatch covers Ice Class 1A (Finnish-Swedish Ice Class Rules 1985) Max draught midship 7.197m Max/min draught aft 7.197/4.367m Max/min draught fwd 7.197/1.837m Power required 2864kw, installed 3840kw ✠ **LMC** **UMS** Eq.Ltr: W; Cable: 498.4/44.0 U3 (a)	**2000**-12 **Bodewes' Scheepswerven B.V. — Hoogezand** Yd No: 593 Loa 118.55 (BB) Br ex 15.43 Dght 6.700 Lbp 111.85 Br md 15.20 Dpth 8.45 Welded, 1 dk	**(A31A2GX) General Cargo Ship** Grain: 9,415 TEU 281 C Ho 166 TEU C Dk 115 TEU. Compartments: 2 Ho, ER 2 Ha: (39.0 x 12.7) (42.8 x 12.7)ER Ice Capable	**1 oil engine** with clutches, flexible couplings & sr geared to sc. shaft driving 1 CP propeller Total Power: 3,840kW (5,221hp) MaK 1 x 4 Stroke 8 Cy. 320 x 480 3840kW (5221bhp) MaK Motoren GmbH & Co. KG-Kiel AuxGen: 1 x 400kW 400V 50Hz a.c, 2 x 264kW 400V 50Hz a.c Boilers: HWH (o.f.) 3.6kgf/cm² (3.5bar) Thrusters: 1 Thwart. CP thruster (f) Fuel: 442.0 (r.f.)	12.0kn 8M32
9626168 *2GAS9* -	**VECTIS CASTLE** **Carisbrooke Shipping (CV 23) BV** Carisbrooke Shipping Ltd *Cowes* *United Kingdom* MMSI: 235095837 Official number: 918798	**7,227** 3,124 10,203 T/cm 20.2	Class: BV GL	**2013**-01 **Jiangsu Yangzijiang Shipbuilding Co Ltd — Jiangyin JS** Yd No: YZJ2011-1000 Loa 123.95 Br ex - Dght 7.930 Lbp 121.70 Br md 17.40 Dpth 11.40 Welded, 1 dk	**(A31A2GX) General Cargo Ship** Grain: 12,655 TEU 494 C Ho 244 TEU C Ha 250 TEU Compartments: 2 Ho, ER 2 Ha: (57.4 x 13.8)ER (25.2 x 13.8) Cranes: 2x80t Ice Capable	**1 oil engine** reduction geared to sc. shaft driving 1 CP propeller Total Power: 3,000kW (4,079hp) MaK 1 x 4 Stroke 6 Cy. 320 x 480 3000kW (4079bhp) Caterpillar Motoren GmbH & Co. KG-Germany AuxGen: 1 x 420kW a.c Thrusters: 1 Tunnel thruster (f) Fuel: 222.0 (d.f.) 252.0 (r.f.)	12.7kn 6M32C
9594286 *2FBR8* -	**VECTIS EAGLE** **Super Greenship BV** Carisbrooke Shipping Ltd *Cowes* *United Kingdom* MMSI: 235089915 Official number: 917982	**6,190** 2,619 8,690 T/cm 17.7	Class: BV GL	**2012**-01 **Jiangsu Yangzijiang Shipbuilding Co Ltd — Jiangyin JS** Yd No: YZJ2010-931 Loa 109.95 Br ex - Dght 8.000 Lbp 105.90 Br md 17.40 Dpth 11.40 Welded, 1 dk	**(A31A2GX) General Cargo Ship** Grain: 10,648 TEU 377 C Ho 204 TEU C Dk 173 TEU Compartments: 1 Ho, ER 1 Ha: ER (76.3 x 13.8) Cranes: 2x80t Ice Capable	**1 oil engine** reduction geared to sc. shaft driving 1 CP propeller Total Power: 2,400kW (3,263hp) MaK 1 x 4 Stroke 6 Cy. 320 x 480 2400kW (3263bhp) Caterpillar Motoren GmbH & Co. KG-Germany AuxGen: 1 x 420kW a.c, 2 x 400kW a.c Thrusters: 1 Thwart. CP thruster (f) Fuel: 222.0 (d.f.) 255.0 (r.f.)	15.0kn 6M32C
9594298 *2FBR7* -	**VECTIS FALCON** **Super Greenship BV** Carisbrooke Shipping Ltd *Cowes* *United Kingdom* MMSI: 235089914 Official number: 918105	**6,190** 2,619 8,555 T/cm 17.7	Class: BV GL	**2012**-03 **Jiangsu Yangzijiang Shipbuilding Co Ltd — Jiangyin JS** Yd No: YZJ2010-932 Loa 109.95 Br ex - Dght 8.000 Lbp 107.70 Br md 17.40 Dpth 11.40 Welded, 1 dk	**(A31A2GX) General Cargo Ship** Grain: 10,648 TEU 377 C Ho 204 TEU C Dk 173 TEU Compartments: 1 Ho, ER 1 Ha: ER (76.3 x 13.8) Cranes: 2x80t Ice Capable	**1 oil engine** reduction geared to sc. shaft driving 1 CP propeller Total Power: 2,400kW (3,263hp) MaK 1 x 4 Stroke 6 Cy. 320 x 480 2400kW (3263bhp) Caterpillar Motoren GmbH & Co. KG-Germany AuxGen: 1 x 420kW a.c, 2 x 400kW a.c Thrusters: 1 Thwart. CP thruster (f) Fuel: 238.0 (d.f.) 277.0 (r.f.)	12.3kn 6M32C
9594303 *2FBR6* -	**VECTIS HARRIER** **Super Greenship BV** Carisbrooke Shipping Ltd *Douglas* *Isle of Man (British)* MMSI: 235089913 Official number: 743913	**6,190** 2,619 8,556 T/cm 17.7	Class: BV GL	**2012**-05 **Jiangsu Yangzijiang Shipbuilding Co Ltd — Jiangyin JS** Yd No: YZJ2010-939 Loa 109.95 Br ex - Dght 8.000 Lbp 107.70 Br md 17.40 Dpth 11.40 Welded, 1 dk	**(A31A2GX) General Cargo Ship** Grain: 10,648 TEU 377 C Ho 204 TEU C Dk 173 TEU Compartments: 1 Ho, ER 1 Ha: ER (76.3 x 13.8) Cranes: 2x80t Ice Capable	**1 oil engine** reduction geared to sc. shaft driving 1 CP propeller Total Power: 2,400kW (3,263hp) MaK 1 x 4 Stroke 6 Cy. 320 x 480 2400kW (3263bhp) Caterpillar Motoren GmbH & Co. KG-Germany AuxGen: 1 x 420kW a.c, 2 x 400kW a.c Thrusters: 1 Thwart. CP thruster (f) Fuel: 227.0 (d.f.) 277.0 (r.f.)	12.3kn 6M32C
9626156 *2GAS8* -	**VECTIS ISLE** **Northern Shipmanagement BV** Carisbrooke Shipping Ltd *Douglas* *Isle of Man (British)* MMSI: 235095836 Official number: 743960	**7,227** 3,124 10,199 T/cm 20.2	Class: GL	**2012**-12 **Jiangsu Yangzijiang Shipbuilding Co Ltd — Jiangyin JS** Yd No: YZJ2011-999 Loa 123.96 Br ex - Dght 7.930 Lbp 121.70 Br md 17.40 Dpth 11.40 Welded, 1 dk	**(A31A2GX) General Cargo Ship** Grain: 12,754 TEU 494 C Ho 244 TEU C Dk 250 TEU Compartments: 2 Ho, ER 2 Ha: (57.4 x 13.8)ER (25.2 x 13.8) Cranes: 2x80t Ice Capable	**1 oil engine** reduction geared to sc. shaft driving 1 CP propeller Total Power: 3,000kW (4,079hp) MaK 1 x 4 Stroke 6 Cy. 320 x 480 3000kW (4079bhp) Caterpillar Motoren GmbH & Co. KG-Germany AuxGen: 2 x 400kW a.c, 1 x 420kW a.c Thrusters: 1 Tunnel thruster (f) Fuel: 222.0 (d.f.) 252.0 (r.f.)	12.3kn 6M32C
8903040 *D6DB6* -	**VECTIS ISLE** *ex* Lesley-Jane C *-1993* *completed as* Union Mercury *-1991* **Tonga Management Inc** South River Shipping Co Ltd SatCom: Inmarsat C 461640910 *Moroni* *Union of Comoros* MMSI: 616409000 Official number: 1200478	**2,237** 1,244 3,222	Class: IV (GL)	**1990**-12 **Cochrane Shipbuilders Ltd. — Selby** Yd No: 166 Loa 99.73 Br ex - Dght 4.746 Lbp 96.00 Br md 12.50 Dpth 6.35 Welded, 1 dk	**(A31A2GX) General Cargo Ship** Grain: 4,575; Bale: 4,447 TEU 114 C.Ho 86/20' C.Dk 28/20' Compartments: 2 Ho, ER 1 Ha: (70.2 x 10.1)ER	**1 oil engine** with clutches, flexible couplings & sr geared to sc. shaft driving 1 CP propeller Total Power: 1,018kW (1,384hp) Alpha 1 x 4 Stroke 8 Cy. 225 x 300 1018kW (1384bhp) MAN B&W Diesel A/S-Denmark AuxGen: 1 x 324kW 220/380V a.c, 3 x 84kW 220/380V a.c Thrusters: 1 Thwart. FP thruster (f)	11.2kn 8L23/30
9594315 *2FBR5* -	**VECTIS OSPREY** **Super Greenship BV** Carisbrooke Shipping Ltd SatCom: Inmarsat C 423508910 *Douglas* *Isle of Man (British)* MMSI: 235089912 Official number: 743926	**6,190** 2,619 8,685 T/cm 17.7	Class: BV GL	**2012**-06 **Jiangsu Yangzijiang Shipbuilding Co Ltd — Jiangyin JS** Yd No: YZJ2010-940 Loa 109.94 Br ex - Dght 8.000 Lbp 107.70 Br md 17.40 Dpth 11.40 Welded, 1 dk	**(A31A2GX) General Cargo Ship** Grain: 10,688 TEU 377 C Ho 204 TEU C Dk 173 TEU Compartments: 1 Ho, ER 1 Ha: ER (76.6 x 13.8) Cranes: 2x80t Ice Capable	**1 oil engine** reduction geared to sc. shaft driving 1 CP propeller Total Power: 2,400kW (3,263hp) MaK 1 x 4 Stroke 6 Cy. 320 x 480 2400kW (3263bhp) AuxGen: 1 x 420kW a.c, 2 x 400kW a.c Thrusters: 1 Thwart. CP thruster (f) Fuel: 227.0 (d.f.) 277.0 (r.f.)	12.3kn 6M32C
9626132 *2FVR8* -	**VECTIS PRIDE** **Carisbrooke Shipping 10 000 BV** Carisbrooke Shipping Ltd *Douglas* *Isle of Man (British)* MMSI: 235094625 Official number: 743949	**7,227** 3,124 10,234 T/cm 20.2	Class: BV (GL)	**2012**-08 **Jiangsu Yangzijiang Shipbuilding Co Ltd — Jiangyin JS** Yd No: YZJ2011-997 Loa 123.96 Br ex - Dght 7.930 Lbp 121.70 Br md 17.40 Dpth 11.40 Welded, 1 dk	**(A31A2GX) General Cargo Ship** Grain: 12,655 TEU 494 C Ho 244 TEU C Dk 250 TEU Compartments: 2 Ho, ER 2 Ha: (57.4 x 13.8)ER (25.2 x 13.8) Cranes: 2x80t Ice Capable	**1 oil engine** reduction geared to sc. shaft driving 1 CP propeller Total Power: 3,000kW (4,079hp) MaK 1 x 4 Stroke 6 Cy. 320 x 480 3000kW (4079bhp) Caterpillar Motoren GmbH & Co. KG-Germany AuxGen: 1 x 440kW a.c Thrusters: 1 Tunnel thruster (f) Fuel: 222.0 (d.f.) 255.0 (r.f.)	12.3kn 6M32C
9626144 *2FVR9* -	**VECTIS PROGRESS** **Carisbrooke Shipping 10 000 BV** Carisbrooke Shipping Ltd *Douglas* *Isle of Man (British)* MMSI: 235094626 Official number: 743948	**7,227** 3,124 10,260 T/cm 20.2	Class: BV (GL)	**2012**-10 **Jiangsu Yangzijiang Shipbuilding Co Ltd — Jiangyin JS** Yd No: YZJ2011-998 Loa 123.96 Br ex - Dght 7.930 Lbp 121.70 Br md 17.40 Dpth 11.40 Welded, 1 dk	**(A31A2GX) General Cargo Ship** Grain: 12,655 TEU 494 C Ho 244 TEU C Dk 250 TEU Compartments: 2 Ho, ER 2 Ha: (57.4 x 13.8)ER (25.2 x 13.8) Cranes: 2x80t Ice Capable	**1 oil engine** reduction geared to sc. shaft driving 1 CP propeller Total Power: 3,000kW (4,079hp) MaK 1 x 4 Stroke 6 Cy. 320 x 480 3000kW (4079bhp) Caterpillar Motoren GmbH & Co. KG-Germany AuxGen: 1 x 420kW a.c Thrusters: 1 Tunnel thruster (f) Fuel: 222.0 (d.f.) 255.0 (r.f.)	12.3kn 6M32C
6717760 *CGBW* - -	**VECTOR** **Government of Canada (Canadian Coast Guard)** *Ottawa, ON* *Canada* MMSI: 316115000 Official number: 328079	*516* 187 184	Class: (LR) ✠ Classed LR until 2/3/79	**1967**-11 **Yarrows Ltd — Victoria BC** Yd No: 293 Loa 39.63 Br ex 9.66 Dght 3.048 Lbp 35.97 Br md 9.45 Dpth 4.35 Welded, 1 dk, 2nd dk fwd of mchy. space	**(B31A2SR) Research Survey Vessel** Cranes: 1x4.5t,1x1t	**4 oil engines** geared to sc. shaft driving 1 CP propeller Total Power: 604kW (820hp) G.M. (Detroit Diesel) 4 x 2 Stroke 6 Cy. 108 x 127 each-151kW (205bhp) Detroit Diesel Corporation-Detroit, Mi AuxGen: 3 x 100kW 460V 60Hz a.c Thrusters: 1 Water jet (f) Fuel: 66.0 (d.f.)	10.0kn 6-71-TI
6873746 - -	**VECTOR** *ex* Vikhr *-2006* *ex* BK-1211 *-1966* **Universal Stevedore Co LLC** *Temryuk* *Russia*	**164** 54 46	Class: RS (RR)	**1965**-12 **"Petrozavod" — Leningrad** Yd No: 706 Loa 29.30 Br ex 8.49 Dght 3.090 Lbp 25.20 Br md 8.30 Dpth 4.35 Welded, 1 dk	**(B32A2ST) Tug**	**2 oil engines** driving 2 CP propellers Total Power: 882kW (1,200hp) Russkiy 2 x 2 Stroke 6 Cy. 300 x 500 each-441kW (600bhp) Mashinostroitelnyy Zavod"Russkiy-Dizel"-Leningrad	11.4kn 6DR30/50-4

IMO / Call sign / Official no.	Name / Former names / Owner / Manager / Port / Flag	Tonnage	Classification	Builder / Dimensions	Type / Cargo	Machinery
7638935 *HP4112* -	**VECTOR** *ex* Kansa *-2008* *ex* Kao Fong *-2000* *ex* Asif I *-1991* *ex* Aiwa Maru *-1989* **Golden Giant Oil Co Ltd** SM Lito Shipmanagement Pte Ltd *Panama* *Panama* Official number: 4495413	**909** 560 1,586 T/cm 6.0	Class: IS (BV)	**1977-04 Higaki Zosen K.K. — Imabari** Yd No: 190 Loa 67.55 Br ex - Dght 4.380 Lbp 63.50 Br md 11.00 Dpth 5.01 Welded, 1 dk	**(A13B2TP) Products Tanker** Liq: 2,210; Liq (Oil): 2,210 Compartments: 10 Ta, ER 2 Cargo Pump (s)	**1 oil engine** driving 1 FP propeller Total Power: 1,324kW (1,800hp) 11.9kn Makita GSLH633 1 x 4 Stroke 6 Cy. 330 x 530 1324kW (1800bhp) Makita Diesel Co Ltd-Japan
7216907 *OJLN* FIN-128-K	**VEDERLAX** *ex* Della Strada *-2006* *ex* Ambassador *-1995* *ex* Heritage *-1994* **Ab Kotka Fiskeri - Kotkan Kalastus Oy** - SatCom: Inmarsat C 423096710 *Kotka* *Finland* MMSI: 230967000 Official number: 12349	**382** 115 -		**1972 Scheepswerf Vooruit B.V. — Zaandam** Yd No: 339 Loa 40.58 Br ex 7.24 Dght - Lbp - Br md 7.19 Dpth 3.81 Welded, 1 dk	**(B11B2FV) Fishing Vessel**	**1 oil engine** geared to sc. shaft driving 1 FP propeller Total Power: 552kW (750hp) Blackstone EWSL6 1 x 4 Stroke 6 Cy. 222 x 292 552kW (750bhp) Lister Blackstone MirrleesMarine Ltd.-Dursley
8739009 *LAWB* -	**VEDEROY** *ex* Bergo *-2008* **Kriminalomsorgen Region Sor** - *Horten* *Norway* MMSI: 259674000	**147** 45 -		**1991-01 Oy Lun-Mek Ab — Mariehamn** Yd No: 16 Loa 20.30 Br ex - Dght - Lbp - Br md 5.95 Dpth 3.10 Welded, 1 dk	**(A36A2PR) Passenger/Ro-Ro Ship (Vehicles)** Passengers: unberthed: 60 Stern ramp (a) Cars: 2	**2 oil engines** reduction geared to sc. shafts driving 2 Propellers Total Power: 350kW (476hp) 10.0kn
6730073 - -	**VEDETTE** - **Sherman & Ovid Stoll** - *Georgetown* *Guyana* Official number: 0000260	*399* 246 780	Class: (BV)	**1967 N.V. Scheepswerf Bodewes Gruno — Foxhol** Yd No: 221 Loa 54.11 Br ex 9.25 Dght 3.379 Lbp 49.08 Br md 9.15 Dpth 3.46 Welded, 1 dk & S dk	**(A31A2GX) General Cargo Ship** Grain: 1,363; Bale: 1,222 Compartments: 1 Ho, ER 2 Ha: (12.1 x 5.4) (14.2 x 5.4)ER Derricks: 2x3t; Winches: 2	**1 oil engine** driving 1 FP propeller Total Power: 276kW (375hp) 10.0kn Brons 6GV 1 x Vee 2 Stroke 6 Cy. 220 x 380 276kW (375bhp) NV Appingedammer Bronsmotorenfabrie-Netherlands
9195729 *2DTN5* -	**VEDETTE** *ex* Petra *-2010* **Faversham Ships Ltd** - SatCom: Inmarsat C 423592499 *Peel* *Isle of Man (British)* MMSI: 235081933 Official number: 736479	**2,545** 1,460 3,850	Class: GL (LR) ✠ Classed LR until 20/8/10	**2000-12 Daewoo-Mangalia Heavy Industries S.A. — Mangalia** (Hull) Yd No: 1014 **2000-12 B.V. Scheepswerf Damen Bergum — Bergum** Yd No: 368 Loa 88.78 Br ex - Dght 5.420 Lbp 84.99 Br md 12.50 Dpth 7.02 Welded, 1 dk	**(A31A2GX) General Cargo Ship** Grain: 5,320 TEU 193 C Ho 113 TEU C Dk 80 TEU Compartments: 1 Ho, ER 1 Ha: (62.7 x 10.1)ER	**1 oil engine** with clutches, flexible couplings & sr reverse geared to sc. shaft driving 1 FP propeller Total Power: 1,520kW (2,067hp) 10.5kn MaK 8M20 1 x 4 Stroke 8 Cy. 200 x 300 1520kW (2067bhp) Caterpillar Motoren GmbH & Co. KG-Germany AuxGen: 1 x 258kW 400V 50Hz a.c, 1 x 100kW 400V 50Hz a.c Boilers: HWH (o.f.) (fitted: 2000) 5.1kgf/cm² (5.0bar) Thrusters: 1 Thwart. FP thruster (f) Fuel: 46.2 (d.f.) 130.3 (r.f.)
9032680 *AVFE* -	**VEDIKA PREM** *ex* Dynamic Express *-2010* **Mercator Ltd** - *Mumbai* *India* MMSI: 419000109 Official number: 3687	**25,644** 11,349 42,253 T/cm 47.7	Class: IR (NK)	**1993-05 Minaminippon Shipbuilding Co Ltd — Usuki OT** Yd No: 623 Loa 179.80 (BB) Br ex 31.34 Dght 11.567 Lbp 171.00 Br md 31.30 Dpth 17.80 Welded, 1 dk	**(A13B2TP) Products Tanker** Double Hull (13F) Liq: 47,501; Liq (Oil): 48,471 Cargo Heating Coils Compartments: 9 Ta, 2 Slop Ta, ER 4 Cargo Pump (s): 4x950m³/hr Manifold: Bow/CM: 92m	**1 oil engine** driving 1 FP propeller Total Power: 9,378kW (12,750hp) 14.8kn B&W 5S60MC 1 x 2 Stroke 5 Cy. 600 x 2292 9378kW (12750bhp) Mitsui Engineering & Shipbuilding CLtd-Japan AuxGen: 3 x 500kW a.c Fuel: 156.0 (d.f.) 1649.0 (r.f.)
8724133 *UCKN* -	**VEDUSHCHIY** - **SK Portovyy Flot Ltd** - *Nakhodka* *Russia* Official number: 831190	**228** - 86	Class: RS	**1985-09 Brodogradiliste 'Tito' — Belgrade** Yd No: 1102 Loa 35.23 Br ex 9.01 Dght 3.160 Lbp 30.00 Br md 9.00 Dpth 4.50 Welded, 1 dk	**(B32A2ST) Tug** Ice Capable	**2 oil engines** driving 1 CP propeller Total Power: 1,860kW (2,528hp) 11.5kn Sulzer 6ASL25/30 2 x 4 Stroke 6 Cy. 250 x 300 each-930kW (1264bhp) Tvornica Dizel Motora 'Jugoturbina'-Yugoslavia AuxGen: 2 x 100kW a.c
9277333 *PHBQ* -	**VEELERDIEP** *ex* OSC Rotterdam *-2011* *ex* UAL Rotterdam *-2009* *ex* Veelerdiep *-2004* **Beheermaatschappij ms Veelerdiep BV** Feederlines BV *Groningen* *Netherlands* MMSI: 245009000 Official number: 42546	**5,057** 2,681 7,762	Class: LR ✠ **100A1** SS 09/2009 strengthened for heavy cargoes, container cargoes in holds and on upper deck hatch covers Ice Class 1A FS at a draught of 7.200m Max/min draughts fwd 7.200/1.837m Max/min draughts aft 7.200/4.367m ✠ **LMC** **UMS** Eq.Ltr: W; Cable: 550.0/44.0 U3 (a)	**2004-09 ATVT Sudnobudivnyi Zavod "Zaliv" — Kerch** (Hull) Yd No: (623) **2004-09 Bodewes' Scheepswerven B.V. — Hoogezand** Yd No: 623 Loa 119.98 (BB) Br ex 15.43 Dght 7.050 Lbp 113.65 Br md 15.20 Dpth 8.50 Welded, 1 dk	**(A31A2GX) General Cargo Ship** Grain: 9,415 TEU 390 C Ho 174 TEU C Dk 216 TEU Compartments: 2 Ho, ER 2 Ha: ER Cranes: 2 Ice Capable	**1 oil engine** with clutches, flexible couplings & sr geared to sc. shaft driving 1 CP propeller Total Power: 3,840kW (5,221hp) 14.0kn MaK 8M32C 1 x 4 Stroke 8 Cy. 320 x 480 3840kW (5221bhp) Caterpillar Motoren GmbH & Co. KG-Germany AuxGen: 1 x 400kW 400V 50Hz a.c, 3 x 290kW 400V 50Hz a.c Boilers: TOH (ex.g.) 10.2kgf/cm² (10.0bar), TOH (o.f.) 10.2kgf/cm² (10.0bar) Thrusters: 1 Thwart. CP thruster (f)
9102992 *PHEO* -	**VEENDAM** - **HAL Nederland NV** Holland America Line NV SatCom: Inmarsat C 424650610 *Rotterdam* *Netherlands* MMSI: 246506000 Official number: 47153	**57,092** 26,819 6,604	Class: LR ✠ **100A1** CS 05/2011 passenger ship *IWS ✠ **LMC** Eq.Ltr: P†; Cable: 660.0/78.0 U3	**1996-05 Fincantieri-Cant. Nav. Italiani S.p.A. (Breda) — Venezia** Yd No: 5954 Loa 219.21 (BB) Br ex 30.83 Dght 7.716 Lbp 185.00 Br md 30.80 Dpth 19.13 Welded, 5 dks	**(A37A2PC) Passenger/Cruise** Passengers: cabins: 633; berths: 1613	**5 diesel electric oil engines** driving 2 gen. each 9540kW 6600V a.c 3 gen. each 6340kW 6600V a.c Connecting to 2 elec. motors each (12000kW) driving 2 CP propellers Total Power: 33,924kW (46,123hp) 20.0kn Sulzer 12ZAV40S 2 x Vee 4 Stroke 12 Cy. 400 x 560 each-8640kW (11747bhp) Fincantieri Cantieri NavaliItaliani SpA-Italy Sulzer 8ZAL40S 3 x 4 Stroke 8 Cy. 400 x 560 each-5548kW (7543bhp) Fincantieri Cantieri NavaliItaliani SpA-Italy Boilers: 5 e (ex.g.) 12.2kgf/cm² (12.0bar), 2 AuxB (o.f.) 9.8kgf/cm² (9.6bar) Thrusters: 2 Thwart. CP thruster (f); 1 Thwart. CP thruster (a) Fuel: 129.5 (d.f.) 1812.3 (r.f.)
9346718 *PBQQ* -	**VEENDIJK** - **Beheermaatschappij ms 'Veendijk' BV** Navigia Shipmanagement BV SatCom: Inmarsat C 424469410 *Groningen* *Netherlands* MMSI: 244694000 Official number: 49411	**2,984** 1,598 4,891	Class: GL (BV)	**2009-06 Chowgule & Co Pvt Ltd — Goa** Yd No: 178 Loa 89.95 (BB) Br ex - Dght 6.220 Lbp 84.94 Br md 14.40 Dpth 7.85 Welded, 1 dk	**(A31A2GX) General Cargo Ship** Grain: 5,818 Compartments: 1 Ho, ER 1 Ha: ER (62.3 x 11.7)	**1 oil engine** reduction geared to sc. shaft driving 1 CP propeller Total Power: 1,986kW (2,700hp) 11.5kn MaK 6M25 1 x 4 Stroke 6 Cy. 255 x 400 1986kW (2700bhp) Caterpillar Motoren GmbH & Co. KG-Germany AuxGen: 1 x 312kW 400V 50Hz a.c, 2 x 168kW 400V 50Hz a.c Thrusters: 1 Tunnel thruster (f) Fuel: 35.0 (d.f.) 280.0 (r.f.)
9523500 *A8WR4* -	**VEENUS** - **Gregarious Estates Inc** Ship Management Services Inc *Monrovia* *Liberia* MMSI: 636014812 Official number: 14812	**43,753** 27,351 79,200 T/cm 71.9	Class: NV	**2011-08 COSCO (Dalian) Shipyard Co Ltd — Dalian LN** Yd No: N215 Loa 229.00 (BB) Br ex - Dght 14.620 Lbp 222.00 Br md 32.26 Dpth 20.25 Welded, 1 dk	**(A21A2BC) Bulk Carrier** Grain: 97,000; Bale: 90,784 Compartments: 7 Ho, ER 7 Ha: ER Cranes: 4x35t	**1 oil engine** driving 1 FP propeller Total Power: 11,060kW (15,037hp) 14.0kn MAN-B&W 7S50MC-C 1 x 2 Stroke 7 Cy. 500 x 2000 11060kW (15037bhp) Doosan Engine Co Ltd-South Korea AuxGen: 3 x a.c
8007406 - -	**VEER** - **Government of The Republic of India (Coast Guard)** - *India*	*995* - 195	Class: IR	**1986-05 Mazagon Dock Ltd. — Mumbai** Yd No: 574 Loa 74.10 Br ex 10.64 Dght 3.001 Lbp 69.00 Br md 10.60 Dpth 7.90 Welded, 2 dks	**(B34H2SQ) Patrol Vessel**	**2 oil engines** with clutches, flexible couplings & sr geared to sc. shafts driving 2 FP propellers Total Power: 9,414kW (12,800hp) Pielstick 16PA6V280 2 x Vee 4 Stroke 16 Cy. 280 x 290 each-4707kW (6400bhp) Alsthom Atlantique-France
8928193 *ES2151* EK-9227	**VEERE** *ex* MRTK-0611 *-1988* **Kaabeltau Ltd (OU Kaabeltau)** - *Nasva* *Estonia* MMSI: 276174000 Official number: 399FK17	**117** 35 30	Class: (RS)	**1981-04 Sosnovskiy Sudostroitelnyy Zavod — Sosnovka** Yd No: 611 Loa 25.50 Br ex 7.00 Dght 2.390 Lbp 22.00 Br md 6.80 Dpth 3.30 Welded, 1 dk	**(B11A2FS) Stern Trawler** Compartments: 1 Ho 1 Ha: (1.4 x 1.5) Ice Capable	**1 oil engine** driving 1 FP propeller Total Power: 221kW (300hp) 9.5kn S.K.L. 6NVD26A-2 1 x 4 Stroke 6 Cy. 180 x 260 221kW (300bhp) VEB Schwermaschinenbau "KarlLiebknecht" (SKL)-Magdeburg AuxGen: 2 x 12kW a.c Fuel: 15.0 (d.f.)

9184653 *V2ON5* -	**VEERSEBORG** *ex* Matfen *-2007* *ex* Veerseborg *-2004* **Reederei Frank Dahl ms 'Veerseborg' GmbH & Co KG** Reederei Frank Dahl eK SatCom: Inmarsat C 430460611 *Saint John's* *Antigua & Barbuda* MMSI: 304606000	**6,130** 3,424 8,736 T/cm 18.3	Class: GL (BV)	**1998-12 Bodewes Scheepswerf "Volharding" Foxhol B.V. — Foxhol** Yd No: 345 Loa 132.20 (BB) Br ex - Dght 7.050 Lbp 123.84 Br md 15.87 Dpth 9.65 Welded, 1 dk	**(A31A2GX) General Cargo Ship** Grain: 12,604 TEU 552 C Ho 128/40'+ 8/20' C.Dk 132/40'+ 24/20' incl. 49 ref C Compartments: 2 Ho, ER 2 Ha: (39.9 x 13.2) (52.4 x 13.2)ER Ice Capable	**1 oil engine** reduction geared to sc. shaft driving 1 CP propeller Total Power: 3,647kW (4,958hp) 14.0kn Wartsila 6R38 1 x 4 Stroke 6 Cy. 380 x 475 3647kW (4958bhp) Wartsila NSD Nederland BV-Netherlands AuxGen: 2 x 260kW 440V 60Hz a.c Thrusters: 1 Thwart. CP thruster (f) Fuel: 40.0 (d.f.) 391.0 (r.f.) 18.0pd
9229075 *A8ZP3* -	**VEERSEDIEP** **Lingediep Shipping Co Ltd** Feederlines BV *Monrovia* *Liberia* MMSI: 636015267 Official number: 15267	**4,938** 2,631 7,250	Class: LR ✠ **100A1** SS 09/2011 strengthened for heavy cargoes, container cargoes in holds and on upper deck hatch covers Ice Class 1A (Finnish-Swedish Ice Class Rules 1985) Max draught midship 7.222m Max/min draught aft 7.197/4.367m Max/min draught fwd 7.197/1.837m Power required 2864kw, installed 3840kw ✠ **LMC** **UMS** Eq.Ltr: W; Cable: 499.3/44.0 U3 (a)	**2001-09 Bodewes' Scheepswerven B.V. — Hoogezand** Yd No: 605 Loa 118.55 (BB) Br ex 15.43 Dght 7.060 Lbp 111.85 Br md 15.20 Dpth 8.44 Welded, 1 dk	**(A31A2GX) General Cargo Ship** Grain: 9,415 TEU 390 C Ho 174 TEU C Dk 216 TEU incl 20 ref C Compartments: 2 Ho, ER 2 Ha: (39.0 x 12.7) (42.8 x 12.7)ER Ice Capable	**1 oil engine** with clutches, flexible couplings & sr geared to sc. shaft driving 1 CP propeller Total Power: 3,840kW (5,221hp) 12.0kn MaK 8M32 1 x 4 Stroke 8 Cy. 320 x 480 3840kW (5221bhp) MaK Motoren GmbH & Co. KG-Kiel AuxGen: 2 x 264kW 400V 50Hz a.c Boilers: HWH (o.f.) 3.6kgf/cm^2 (3.5bar) Thrusters: 1 Thwart. FP thruster (f) Fuel: 70.5 (d.f.) 515.2 (r.f.)
9246140 *PBCX* -	**VEERSEDIJK** **Beheermaatschappij ms Veersedijk II BV** Navigia Shipmanagement BV *Groningen* *Netherlands* MMSI: 244268000 Official number: 39497	**6,420** 3,240 8,441	Class: GL	**2001-08 Detlef Hegemann Rolandwerft GmbH & Co. KG — Berne** Yd No: 194 Loa 132.23 (BB) Br ex - Dght 7.350 Lbp 125.50 Br md 19.40 Dpth 9.45 Welded, 1 dk	**(A33A2CC) Container Ship (Fully Cellular)** Grain: 10,477 TEU 707 C Ho 204 TEU C Dk 503 TEU incl 150 ref C. Compartments: 3 Cell Ho, ER 3 Ha: (25.6 x 13.2)2 (25.6 x 15.8)ER Ice Capable	**1 oil engine** reduction geared to sc. shaft driving 1 CP propeller Total Power: 7,200kW (9,789hp) 18.4kn MaK 8M43 1 x 4 Stroke 8 Cy. 430 x 610 7200kW (9789bhp) Caterpillar Motoren GmbH & Co. KG-Germany AuxGen: 1 x 700kW a.c, 2 x 480kW a.c, 1 x 428kW a.c Thrusters: 1 Thwart. FP thruster (f)
9135937 - -	**VEERU** **Maldives Port Authority** - *Male* *Maldives* Official number: 271-01-T	**121** 37 19	Class: (LR) ✠ Classed LR until 5/7/00	**1997-04 Goa Shipyard Ltd. — Goa** Yd No: 1173 Loa 23.75 Br ex 7.20 Dght 2.200 Lbp 20.00 Br md 7.00 Dpth 3.05 Welded, 1 dk	**(B32A2ST) Tug**	**2 oil engines** reduction geared to sc. shafts driving 2 Directional propellers Total Power: 530kW (720hp) 10.5kn Cummins KT-1150-M 2 x 4 Stroke 6 Cy. 159 x 159 each-265kW (360bhp) Kirloskar Cummins Ltd-India AuxGen: 2 x 44kW 380V 50Hz a.c
7315337 *LLHK* -	**VEFSNA** *ex* Storfjord *-2009* **Boreal Transport Nord AS** - *Sandnessjoen* *Norway* MMSI: 257382400	**744** 272 -	Class: (NV)	**1973-05 Smedvik Mek. Verksted AS — Tjorvaag** Yd No: 38 Loa 64.47 Br ex 11.13 Dght 3.036 Lbp 58.98 Br md 11.10 Dpth 4.22 Welded, 1 dk	**(A36A2PR) Passenger/Ro-Ro Ship (Vehicles)** Passengers: 300 Bow door & ramp Stern ramp Cars: 50	**1 oil engine** driving 2 Propellers aft, 1 fwd Total Power: 919kW (1,249hp) 14.0kn Wichmann 5AXA 1 x 2 Stroke 5 Cy. 300 x 450 919kW (1249bhp) Wichmann Motorfabrikk AS-Norway AuxGen: 2 x 72kW 220V 50Hz a.c
6508107 *SMYC* -	**VEGA** **Gute Bogser og Marin Service AB** - *Valleviken* *Sweden* MMSI: 265283000	**458** 137 -		**1964 AB Asi-Verken — Amal** Yd No: 68 Loa 43.58 Br ex 9.83 Dght 3.201 Lbp 37.50 Br md 9.81 Dpth 4.50 Welded, 1 dk	**(B34Q2QX) Lighthouse Tender**	**1 oil engine** driving 1 FP propeller Total Power: 1,214kW (1,651hp) 12.0kn Polar MN16S 1 x 2 Stroke 6 Cy. 340 x 570 1214kW (1651bhp) Nydqvist & Holm AB-Sweden
7850959 - -	**VEGA** *ex* Arima Maru *-2005* **Harbor Star Shipping Services Inc** - *Batangas* *Philippines* Official number: 04-0000915	*204* 120 60		**1977-11 Hikari Kogyo K.K. — Yokosuka** Yd No: 290 Loa 28.38 Br ex - Dght 2.610 Lbp 25.00 Br md 8.59 Dpth 3.48 Welded, 1 dk	**(B32A2ST) Tug**	**2 oil engines** driving 2 FP propellers Total Power: 1,544kW (2,100hp) 11.0kn Daihatsu 8PSHTCM-26D 2 x 4 Stroke 8 Cy. 260 x 320 each-772kW (1050bhp) Daihatsu Diesel Manufacturing Co Lt-Japan
8135112 - -	**VEGA** **Crimean Hydrogeological Expidition (Krymskaya Gidrogeologicheskaya Ekspeditsiya)** -	**170** 51 124	Class: (RS)	**1983 Astrakhanskaya Sudoverf im. "Kirova" — Astrakhan** Yd No: 159 Converted From: Fishing Vessel Loa 34.02 Br ex 7.09 Dght 3.140 Lbp 29.98 Br md - Dpth 3.66 Welded, 1 dk	**(A31A2GX) General Cargo Ship** Compartments: 1 Ho, ER 1 Ha: (1.6 x 1.3) Derricks: 2x2t; Winches: 2 Ice Capable	**1 oil engine** driving 1 CP propeller Total Power: 224kW (305hp) 9.5kn S.K.L. 8NVD36-1U 1 x 4 Stroke 8 Cy. 240 x 360 224kW (305bhp) VEB Schwermaschinenbau "KarlLiebknecht" (SKL)-Magdeburg
8516756 *V3PP7* -	**VEGA** *ex* Henriette *-2005* *ex* Katja *-2000* *ex* Dafi *-1999* *ex* Mete *-1999* *ex* Suzie *-1995* *ex* Six Madun *-1995* **Fora Maritime Corp** Voda Denizcilik Ic ve Dis Ticaret Ltd Sti (Voda Shipping) *Belize City* *Belize* MMSI: 312579000	**1,949** 1,036 3,346	Class: NK (RS) (GL)	**1985-12 B.V. Scheepswerf Damen — Gorinchem** Yd No: 8202 Loa 89.31 (BB) Br ex 12.53 Dght 4.840 Lbp 85.50 Br md 12.51 Dpth 6.35 Welded, 2 dks	**(A31A2GX) General Cargo Ship** Grain: 3,950 TEU 158 C.Ho 78/20' (40') C.Dk 80/20' (40') Compartments: 1 Ho, ER 1 Ha: (63.3 x 10.1)ER Ice Capable	**1 oil engine** with clutches, flexible couplings & sr reverse geared to sc. shaft driving 1 FP propeller Total Power: 1,000kW (1,360hp) 10.0kn MaK 6M332AK 1 x 4 Stroke 6 Cy. 240 x 330 1000kW (1360bhp) Krupp MaK Maschinenbau GmbH-Kiel Thrusters: 1 Thwart. FP thruster (f) Fuel: 170.0 (d.f.)
8328874 - -	**VEGA** *ex* Naval Primero *-2010* *ex* Trasumar VII *-2010* *ex* F. P. T. 7 *-1992* *ex* Antifer *-1986* **SERMAR** - *Havana* *Cuba*	**591** 184 1,448		**1969 A. Vuijk & Zonen's Scheepswerven N.V. — Capelle a/d IJssel** Converted From: Hopper/Grab Dredger-1992 Converted From: Hopper-1992 Converted From: Unknown Function-1973 Loa 56.40 Br ex 10.04 Dght 3.500 Lbp 55.60 Br md 10.00 Dpth 5.00 Welded, 1 dk	**(B33B2DT) Trailing Suction Hopper Dredger** Hopper: 627	**2 oil engines** geared to sc. shafts driving 2 FP propellers Total Power: 760kW (1,034hp) 8.0kn Cummins KT-19-M 2 x 4 Stroke 6 Cy. 159 x 159 each-380kW (517bhp) (new engine 2010) Cummins Engine Co Inc-USA Thrusters: 1 Tunnel thruster (f)
8411736 *CUSG* -	**VEGA** **Sociedade de Pescas do Algarve Lda (PESCAL)** - SatCom: Inmarsat C 426327810 *Portimao* *Portugal* Official number: PM-253-C	**132** 58 72	Class: (BV) (RP)	**1986-11 Est. Navais da Figueira da Foz Lda. (FOZNAVE) — Figueira da Foz** Yd No: 061 Loa 24.01 Br ex 7.40 Dght 3.000 Lbp 20.00 Br md 7.36 Dpth 3.50 Welded, 1 dk	**(B11A2FS) Stern Trawler** Ins: 95	**1 oil engine** driving 1 CP propeller Total Power: 368kW (500hp) GUASCOR E318T-SP 1 x Vee 4 Stroke 12 Cy. 150 x 150 368kW (500bhp) Gutierrez Ascunce Corp (GUASCOR)-Spain
9183582 *C6VW2* -	**VEGA** *ex* Sonia *-2013* *ex* Taintless *-2006* *ex* Hellas Renaissance *-2005* **Magnificent Shipping Inc** Super-Eco Tankers Management Inc *Nassau* *Bahamas* MMSI: 311223000 Official number: 8001282	**27,645** 12,616 46,217 T/cm 50.7	Class: NV	**1999-06 Hyundai Heavy Industries Co Ltd — Ulsan** Yd No: 1168 Loa 183.24 (BB) Br ex - Dght 12.220 Lbp 175.49 Br md 32.20 Dpth 18.20 Welded, 1 dk	**(A13A2TW) Crude/Oil Products Tanker** Double Hull (13F) Liq: 50,715; Liq (Oil): 52,120 Part Cargo Heating Coils Compartments: 12 Wing Ta, 2 Wing Slop Ta, ER 12 Cargo Pump (s): 12x600m^3/hr Manifold: Bow/CM: 92m	**1 oil engine** driving 1 FP propeller Total Power: 7,679kW (10,440hp) 14.2kn MAN-B&W 6S50MC 1 x 2 Stroke 6 Cy. 500 x 1910 7679kW (10440bhp) Hyundai Heavy Industries Co Ltd-South Korea AuxGen: 3 x 830kW 440V 60Hz a.c Fuel: 219.0 (d.f.) (Heating Coils) 1388.0 (r.f.) 34.6pd
9183063 *IFXV* -	**VEGA** **Tripmare Srl** - SatCom: Inmarsat C 424725320 *Trieste* *Italy* MMSI: 247295000 Official number: 56	**360** - 109	Class: RI	**1998-07 Astilleros Armon SA — Navia** Yd No: 425 Loa 30.00 Br ex - Dght 4.700 Lbp 26.80 Br md 9.85 Dpth 5.40 Welded, 1 dk	**(B32A2ST) Tug**	**2 oil engines** reduction geared to sc. shafts driving 2 Directional propellers Total Power: 3,000kW (4,078hp) MaK 9M20 2 x 4 Stroke 9 Cy. 200 x 300 each-1500kW (2039bhp) MaK Motoren GmbH & Co. KG-Kiel AuxGen: 2 x 160kW 380V 50Hz a.c Thrusters: 1 Thwart. FP thruster (f)
9033359 *UFKP* -	**VEGA** *ex* Shinko Maru *-2004* **Fair Wind Co Ltd (OOO 'Poputnyy Veter')** - *Petropavlovsk-Kamchatskiy* *Russia* MMSI: 273448760 Official number: 905996	**737** 221 725	Class: RS	**1991-06 K.K. Miura Zosensho — Saiki** Yd No: 1011 Loa 57.30 Br ex 10.20 Dght 3.601 Lbp 52.02 Br md 10.01 Dpth 4.53 Welded, 1 dk	**(A12A2TC) Chemical Tanker** Double Bottom Entire Compartment Length 2 Cargo Pump (s): 2x150m^3/hr Ice Capable	**1 oil engine** geared to sc. shaft driving 1 FP propeller Total Power: 883kW (1,201hp) 11.6kn Hanshin LH26G 1 x 4 Stroke 6 Cy. 260 x 440 883kW (1201bhp) Hanshin Nainenki Kogyo-Japan AuxGen: 2 x 104kW 225V a.c, 1 x 24kW 225V a.c Fuel: 88.0 (d.f.) 3.5pd

IMO / Call sign / Fishing No.	Name / Owner / Port / Flag	Tonnage	Class	Build / Dimensions	Type	Machinery
8935093 - -	**VEGA** *ex* BK-1253 **Vanino Marine Trading Port JSC (Vaninskiy Morskoy Torgovyy Port OAO)** -	*187* - 46	Class: (RS)	**1971**-05 **"Petrozavod" — Leningrad** Yd No: 781 Loa 29.30 Br ex 8.49 Dght 3.090 Lbp 27.00 Br md - Dpth 4.34 Welded, 1 dk	**(B32A2ST) Tug** Ice Capable	**2 oil engines** driving 2 CP propellers Total Power: 882kW (1,200hp) 11.4kn Russkiy 6D30/50-4-2 2 x 2 Stroke 6 Cy. 300 x 500 each-441kW (600bhp) Mashinostroitelnyy Zavod"Russkiy-Dizel"-Leningrad AuxGen: 2 x 25kW Fuel: 42.0 (d.f.)
8898271 *UHOM* M-0184	**VEGA** **Vega JSC** - *Murmansk* *Russia* MMSI: 273211900 Official number: 921236	**936** 281 433	Class: RS	**1993 AO Yaroslavskiy Sudostroitelnyy Zavod — Yaroslavl** Yd No: 390 Loa 53.70 Br ex 10.72 Dght 4.650 Lbp 47.92 Br md 10.50 Dpth 6.00 Welded, 1 dk	**(B11A2FS) Stern Trawler** Ins: 254 Ice Capable	**1 oil engine** driving 1 CP propeller Total Power: 970kW (1,319hp) 12.6kn S.K.L. 8NVD48A-2U 1 x 4 Stroke 8 Cy. 320 x 480 970kW (1319bhp) SKL Motoren u. Systemtechnik AG-Magdeburg AuxGen: 1 x 300kW a.c, 3 x 150kW a.c Fuel: 192.0 (d.f.)
8724822 *UFSW* -	**VEGA** **Kamagro Co Ltd** - *Petropavlovsk-Kamchatskiy* *Russia* MMSI: 273424010 Official number: 842513	**702** 210 473	Class: RS	**1987**-04 **SSZ im. "Oktyabrskoy Revolyutsii" — Blagoveshchensk** Yd No: 304 Loa 53.80 Br ex 9.70 Dght 3.230 Lbp 49.40 Br md 9.40 Dpth 4.20 Welded, 1dk	**(B35E2TF) Bunkering Tanker**	**1 oil engine** driving 1 FP propeller Total Power: 441kW (600hp) 10.0kn Russkiy 6DR30/50-5-3 1 x 2 Stroke 6 Cy. 300 x 500 441kW (600bhp) Mashinostroitelnyy Zavod"Russkiy-Dizel"-Leningrad AuxGen: 2 x 100kW a.c, 1 x 50kW a.c
8730596 - -	**VEGA** **Port Fleet-99 SLtd (Portovi Flot-99)** - *Varna* *Bulgaria* Official number: 338	**182** 54 57	Class: BR (RS)	**1989**-12 **Gorokhovetskiy Sudostroitelnyy Zavod — Gorokhovets** Loa 29.32 Br ex 8.62 Dght 3.401 Lbp 27.01 Br md - Dpth 4.32 Welded, 1 dk	**(B32A2ST) Tug** Ice Capable	**2 oil engines** driving 2 CP propellers Total Power: 1,180kW (1,604hp) 11.5kn Pervomaysk 8CHNP25/34 2 x 4 Stroke 8 Cy. 250 x 340 each-590kW (802bhp) Pervomaydizelmash (PDM)-Pervomaysk AuxGen: 2 x 50kW a.c
8744224 *EROE* -	**VEGA** *ex* Sarisa *-2012* *ex* Barge 100036 *-2010* **Fix Trading & Shipping Ltd Corp** Yagmur Deniz Tasimaciligi Ticaret Ltd Sti *Giurgiulesti* *Moldova* MMSI: 214181505	**2,516** 959 3,733	Class: BR	**1996**-12 **Marine Company Inc** Yd No: 100036 Converted From: General Cargo Barge, Non-propelled-2010 Loa 115.06 Br ex - Dght 3.680 Lbp 110.50 Br md 13.19 Dpth 5.50 Welded, 1 dk	**(A31A2GX) General Cargo Ship**	**2 oil engines** reduction geared to sc. shafts driving 2 FP propellers Total Power: 1,030kW (1,400hp) Skoda 6L275A2 2 x 4 Stroke 6 Cy. 275 x 350 each-515kW (700bhp) CKD Praha-Praha
8836728 - -	**VEGA** - **Government of The Republic of Italy (Ministero dei Transporti e della Navigazione)-ISP TEC-Nucleo Operativo di Venezia** - SatCom: Inmarsat M 624700232 *Italy*	*1,751* 1,070 -	Class: (RI)	**1990**-02 **Fincantieri-Cant. Nav. Italiani S.p.A. — La Spezia** Yd No: 5849 Loa 80.70 Br ex 11.82 Dght 4.300 Lbp 71.51 Br md 11.80 Dpth 5.60 Welded, 2 dks	**(B34G2SE) Pollution Control Vessel**	**2 oil engines** driving 2 FP propellers Total Power: 5,840kW (7,940hp) GMT BL230.16V 2 x Vee 4 Stroke 16 Cy. 230 x 310 each-2920kW (3970bhp) Fincantieri Cantieri Navaliltaliani SpA-Italy
9225433 *V7MA3* -	**VEGA** *ex* Maersk Valparaiso *-2008* *completed as* Vega *-2001* **Rooi Santu Shipping NV** Alpha Shipmanagement GmbH & Co KG *Majuro* *Marshall Islands* MMSI: 538090289 Official number: 90289	**23,722** 9,843 29,098 T/cm 45.1	Class: GL	**2001**-02 **Stocznia Gdynia SA — Gdynia** Yd No: 8138/12 Loa 194.06 (BB) Br ex - Dght 11.500 Lbp 180.20 Br md 28.20 Dpth 16.80 Welded, 1 dk	**(A33A2CC) Container Ship (Fully Cellular)** TEU 1835 C Ho 780 TEU C Dk 1055 TEU incl 440 ref C. Compartments: 4 Cell Ho, ER 9 Ha: (18.5 x 13.2)Tappered (12.8 x 13.2)7 (12.8 x 23.6)ER Cranes: 3x45t	**1 oil engine** driving 1 FP propeller Total Power: 17,200kW (23,385hp) 21.3kn B&W 6L70MC 1 x 2 Stroke 6 Cy. 700 x 2268 17200kW (23385bhp) H Cegielski Poznan SA-Poland AuxGen: 2 x 1184kW 440/220V 60Hz a.c, 2 x 884kW 440/220V 60Hz a.c Thrusters: 1 Thwart. CP thruster (f) Fuel: 230.0 (d.f.) (Heating Coils) 2700.0 (r.f.) 75.0pd
9197052 *3FGA9* -	**VEGA** **Rising Sun Line SA** Shinsei Kaiun Co Ltd SatCom: Inmarsat C 427310370 *Panama* *Panama* MMSI: 357322000 Official number: 2629199C	**9,340** 5,138 10,947 T/cm 24.3	Class: NK	**1999**-03 **Fukuoka Shipbuilding Co Ltd — Fukuoka FO** Yd No: 1206 Loa 145.48 (BB) Br ex 22.23 Dght 9.014 Lbp 135.40 Br md 22.20 Dpth 13.10 Welded, 4 dks	**(A34A2GR) Refrigerated Cargo Ship** Ins: 14,714 TEU 176 C Ho 24 TEU C Dk 152 TEU incl 76 ref C Compartments: 4 Ho, ER, 11 Tw Dk 4 Ha: (6.5 x 7.4)3 (8.2 x 7.4)ER Cranes: 2x35t	**1 oil engine** driving 1 FP propeller Total Power: 11,004kW (14,961hp) 22.6kn Mitsubishi 8UEC50LSII 1 x 2 Stroke 8 Cy. 500 x 1950 11004kW (14961bhp) Kobe Hatsudoki KK-Japan AuxGen: 3 x 1100kW 450V 60Hz a.c Fuel: 149.2 (d.f.) (Heating Coils) 1620.0 (r.f.) 46.0pd
9293703 *AUVB* -	**VEGA** *ex* Bula Z3 *-2009* **Kei-Rsos Maritime Ltd** - *Visakhapatnam* *India* MMSI: 419075600 Official number: 3442	**299** 90 137	Class: IR (KI) (AB)	**2003**-05 **Jiangsu Wuxi Shipyard Co Ltd — Wuxi JS** Yd No: 1150 Loa 27.00 Br ex 9.81 Dght 3.400 Lbp 21.40 Br md 9.80 Dpth 4.85 Welded, 1 dk	**(B32A2ST) Tug**	**2 oil engines** geared to sc. shafts driving 2 FP propellers Total Power: 2,648kW (3,600hp) Yanmar 8N21A-EN 2 x 4 Stroke 8 Cy. 210 x 290 each-1324kW (1800bhp) Yanmar Diesel Engine Co Ltd-Japan
9375343 *ES2646* -	**VEGA** **PKL AS (PKL Ltd)** - *Tallinn* *Estonia* MMSI: 276641000 Official number: 1T06E04	**144** 44 52	Class: RS (NV)	**2006**-05 **Marine Projects Ltd Sp z oo — Gdansk** Yd No: 024/PKL3 Loa 19.10 Br ex - Dght 3.050 Lbp 17.30 Br md 9.00 Dpth 3.80 Welded, 1 dk	**(B32A2ST) Tug** Ice Capable	**2 oil engines** reduction geared to sc. shafts driving 2 Directional propellers Total Power: 2,088kW (2,838hp) 11.5kn Caterpillar 3512B 2 x Vee 4 Stroke 12 Cy. 170 x 190 each-1044kW (1419bhp) Caterpillar Inc-USA AuxGen: 1 x 70kW a.c Fuel: 41.0 (d.f.)
9541916 *PP7207* -	**VEGA** **Saveiros Camuyrano - Servicos Maritimos SA** - *Rio de Janeiro* *Brazil* MMSI: 710001820 Official number: 3813872025	**250** 75 112	Class: LR ✠**100A1** SS 06/2009 tug Brazilian coastal service **LMC** **UMS** Eq.Ltr: F; Cable: 275.0/19.0 U2 (a)	**2009**-06 **Wilson, Sons SA — Guaruja** (Hull) Yd No: 089 **2009**-05 **B.V. Scheepswerf Damen — Gorinchem** Yd No: 512228 Loa 24.55 Br ex 11.70 Dght 5.350 Lbp 20.80 Br md 10.70 Dpth 4.60 Welded, 1 dk	**(B32A2ST) Tug**	**2 oil engines** reduction geared to sc. shafts driving 2 Directional propellers Total Power: 4,200kW (5,710hp) Caterpillar 3516B-TA 2 x Vee 4 Stroke 16 Cy. 170 x 190 each-2100kW (2855bhp) Caterpillar Inc-USA AuxGen: 2 x 55kW 440V 60Hz a.c
9076507 *UHBJ* -	**VEGA-1** **Banivess Ltd (TOO 'Banivess')** IP Staroshko NA *Taganrog* *Russia*	**104** 31 58	Class: (RS)	**1992**-08 **AO Azovskaya Sudoverf — Azov** Yd No: 1058 Loa 26.50 Br ex 6.59 Dght 2.360 Lbp 22.90 Br md 6.50 Dpth 3.05 Welded, 1 dk	**(B11A2FS) Stern Trawler**	**1 oil engine** geared to sc. shaft driving 1 FP propeller Total Power: 165kW (224hp) 9.3kn Daldizel 6CHNSP18/22 1 x 4 Stroke 6 Cy. 180 x 220 165kW (224bhp) Daldizel-Khabarovsk AuxGen: 2 x 30kW a.c Fuel: 9.0 (d.f.)
7331044 *C9KD* -	**VEGA 2** **Entreposto Frigorifico de Pesca de Mocambique Ltda** - *Quelimane* *Mozambique*	*149* 48 124		**1973**-09 **Kanmon Zosen K.K. — Shimonoseki** Yd No: 319 Loa 29.14 Br ex 6.84 Dght 2.598 Lbp 25.18 Br md 6.81 Dpth 3.00 Welded, 1 dk	**(B11A2FT) Trawler**	**1 oil engine** geared to sc. shaft driving 1 FP propeller Total Power: 368kW (500hp) Daihatsu 6PSTCM-22 1 x 4 Stroke 6 Cy. 220 x 280 368kW (500bhp) Daihatsu Diesel Manufacturing Co Lt-Japan
7353937 *C9KX* -	**VEGA 3** **Entreposto Frigorifico de Pesca de Mocambique Ltda** - *Quelimane* *Mozambique*	*149* 48 125	Class: IS	**1973**-11 **Kanmon Zosen K.K. — Shimonoseki** Yd No: 320 Loa 29.14 Br ex 6.84 Dght 2.598 Lbp 25.20 Br md 6.81 Dpth 3.00 Welded, 1 dk	**(B11A2FT) Trawler**	**1 oil engine** geared to sc. shaft driving 1 FP propeller Total Power: 368kW (500hp) Daihatsu 6PSTCM-22 1 x 4 Stroke 6 Cy. 220 x 280 368kW (500bhp) Daihatsu Diesel Manufacturing Co Lt-Japan
7722504 *C9PT* Q-67	**VEGA 5** **Entreposto Frigorifico de Pesca de Mocambique Ltda** - *Quelimane* *Mozambique*	*148* 48 125		**1978**-03 **Kanmon Zosen K.K. — Shimonoseki** Yd No: 334 Loa 29.11 Br ex - Dght 2.598 Lbp 25.23 Br md 6.81 Dpth 3.03 Welded, 1 dk	**(B11A2FS) Stern Trawler**	**1 oil engine** geared to sc. shaft driving 1 FP propeller Total Power: 368kW (500hp) Daihatsu 6PSTCM-22 1 x 4 Stroke 6 Cy. 220 x 280 368kW (500bhp) Daihatsu Diesel Manufacturing Co Lt-Japan
7722516 *C9PU* Q-68	**VEGA 6** **Entreposto Frigorifico de Pesca de Mocambique Ltda** - *Quelimane* *Mozambique*	*148* 48 125		**1978**-03 **Kanmon Zosen K.K. — Shimonoseki** Yd No: 335 Loa 29.11 Br ex - Dght 2.598 Lbp 25.23 Br md 6.81 Dpth 3.03 Welded, 1 dk	**(B11A2FS) Stern Trawler**	**1 oil engine** geared to sc. shaft driving 1 FP propeller Total Power: 368kW (500hp) Daihatsu 6PSTCM-22 1 x 4 Stroke 6 Cy. 220 x 280 368kW (500bhp) Daihatsu Diesel Manufacturing Co Lt-Japan

7920883 - Q-69	**VEGA 7** **Entreposto Frigorifico de Pesca de Mocambique Ltda** - *Quelimane* *Mozambique*	*149* 48 125		**1979-11 Kanmon Zosen K.K. — Shimonoseki** Yd No: 353 Loa 29.11 Br ex 6.84 Dght 2.598 Lbp 25.20 Br md 6.81 Dpth 3.00 Welded, 1 dk	**(B11A2FT) Trawler**	**1 oil engine** driving 1 FP propeller Total Power: 368kW (500hp) 10.3kn Daihatsu 6PSHTCM-22 1 x 4 Stroke 6 Cy. 220 x 280 368kW (500bhp) Daihatsu Diesel Manufacturing Co Lt-Japan
7920895 *C9QN* Q-70	**VEGA 8** **Entreposto Frigorifico de Pesca de Mocambique Ltda** - *Quelimane* *Mozambique*	*149* 48 125		**1979-11 Kanmon Zosen K.K. — Shimonoseki** Yd No: 354 Loa 29.11 Br ex 6.84 Dght 2.598 Lbp 25.20 Br md 6.81 Dpth 3.00 Welded, 1 dk	**(B11A2FT) Trawler**	**1 oil engine** driving 1 FP propeller Total Power: 368kW (500hp) 10.3kn Daihatsu 6PSHTCM-22 1 x 4 Stroke 6 Cy. 220 x 280 368kW (500bhp) Daihatsu Diesel Manufacturing Co Lt-Japan
7929451 *C9QW* Q-72	**VEGA 10** **Entreposto Frigorifico de Pesca de Mocambique Ltda** - *Quelimane* *Mozambique*	*148* 49 -		**1980-05 Kanmon Zosen K.K. — Shimonoseki** Yd No: 357 Loa 29.14 Br ex 6.81 Dght 2.601 Lbp 25.00 Br md 6.80 Dpth 3.03 Welded, 1 dk	**(B11A2FT) Trawler**	**1 oil engine** driving 1 FP propeller Total Power: 368kW (500hp) 10.3kn Daihatsu 6DS-22 1 x 4 Stroke 6 Cy. 220 x 280 368kW (500bhp) Daihatsu Diesel Manufacturing Co Lt-Japan
7929463 *5RQY* -	**VEGA 11** **Societe Malgache De Pecherie (SOMAPECHE)** - *Mahajanga* *Madagascar*	*148* 49 -		**1980-05 Kanmon Zosen K.K. — Shimonoseki** Yd No: 358 Loa 29.14 Br ex 6.81 Dght 2.601 Lbp 25.00 Br md 6.80 Dpth 3.03 Welded, 1 dk	**(B11A2FT) Trawler**	**1 oil engine** driving 1 FP propeller Total Power: 368kW (500hp) 10.3kn Daihatsu 6DS-22 1 x 4 Stroke 6 Cy. 220 x 280 368kW (500bhp) Daihatsu Diesel Manufacturing Co Lt-Japan
7929475 *C9QX* Q-74	**VEGA 12** **Entreposto Frigorifico de Pesca de Mocambique Ltda** - *Quelimane* *Mozambique*	*148* 49 -		**1980-05 Kanmon Zosen K.K. — Shimonoseki** Yd No: 359 Loa 29.14 Br ex 6.81 Dght 2.601 Lbp 25.00 Br md 6.80 Dpth 3.03 Welded, 1 dk	**(B11A2FT) Trawler**	**1 oil engine** driving 1 FP propeller Total Power: 368kW (500hp) 10.3kn Daihatsu 6DS-22 1 x 4 Stroke 6 Cy. 220 x 280 368kW (500bhp) Daihatsu Diesel Manufacturing Co Lt-Japan
9301081 *A8ZB3* -	**VEGA ALPHA** *ex* Hr Magician *-2012* *ex* SITC Express *-2011* *launched as* Beluga Magician *-2005* **Vega Beteiligungsgesellschaft Alpha mbH & Co KG** Vega-Reederei Friedrich Dauber GmbH & Co KG *Monrovia* *Liberia* MMSI: 636092238 Official number: 92238	**8,971** 4,776 10,746 T/cm 27.3	Class: GL	**2005-11 OAO Damen Shipyards Okean — Nikolayev** (Hull) Yd No: 9113 **2005-11 Volharding Shipyards B.V. — Foxhol** Yd No: 565 Loa 154.85 (BB) Br ex - Dght 6.974 Lbp 144.80 Br md 21.50 Dpth 9.30 Welded, 1 dk	**(A33A2CC) Container Ship (Fully Cellular)** Double Bottom Entire Compartment Length TEU 917 C Ho 267 TEU C Dk 650 TEU incl 200 ref C. Compartments: 4 Cell Ho, ER 4 Ha: 2 (28.7 x 19.0) (12.7 x 19.0)ER (25.9 x 19.0) Ice Capable	**1 oil engine** geared to sc. shaft driving 1 CP propeller Total Power: 7,999kW (10,875hp) 14.0kn MaK 8M43 1 x 4 Stroke 8 Cy. 430 x 610 7999kW (10875bhp) Caterpillar Motoren GmbH & Co. KG-Germany AuxGen: 2 x 432kW a.c, 1 x 1150kW a.c Thrusters: 1 Thwart. CP thruster (f) Fuel: 93.5 (d.f.) 703.0 (r.f.)
9429170 *A8SX9* -	**VEGA AQUARIUS** **ms Vega Aquarius Schifffahrtsgesellschaft mbH & Co KG** Vega-Reederei GmbH & Co KG *Monrovia* *Liberia* MMSI: 636091790 Official number: 91790	**32,957** 19,231 57,000 T/cm 58.8	Class: BV	**2010-01 Taizhou Kouan Shipbuilding Co Ltd — Taizhou JS** Yd No: KA101 Loa 189.99 (BB) Br ex - Dght 12.800 Lbp 185.00 Br md 32.26 Dpth 18.00 Welded, 1 dk	**(A21A2BC) Bulk Carrier** Double Hull Grain: 71,634; Bale: 68,200 Compartments: 5 Ho, ER 5 Ha: ER Cranes: 4x30t	**1 oil engine** driving 1 FP propeller Total Power: 8,400kW (11,421hp) 14.5kn MAN-B&W 6S50MC-C 1 x 2 Stroke 6 Cy. 500 x 2000 8400kW (11421bhp) STX Engine Co Ltd-South Korea AuxGen: 3 x 480kW 450V 60Hz a.c
9508299 *A8RJ7* -	**VEGA AQUILA** *launched as* Solitas H *-2009* **ms Vega Aquila Schifffahrtsgesellschaft mbH & Co KG** Vega-Reederei GmbH & Co KG *Monrovia* *Liberia* MMSI: 636091664 Official number: 91664	**9,961** 4,900 12,015	Class: BV (GL)	**2009-01 Yangfan Group Co Ltd — Zhoushan ZJ** Yd No: 2093 Loa 139.08 (BB) Br ex - Dght 8.800 Lbp 129.00 Br md 22.60 Dpth 11.80 Welded, 1 dk	**(A33A2CC) Container Ship (Fully Cellular)** TEU 957 C Ho 312 TEU C Dk 645 TEU incl 252 ref C. Ice Capable	**1 oil engine** reduction geared to sc. shaft driving 1 CP propeller Total Power: 9,600kW (13,052hp) 18.0kn MAN-B&W 8L48/60B 1 x 4 Stroke 8 Cy. 480 x 600 9600kW (13052bhp) MAN B&W Diesel AG-Augsburg AuxGen: 1 x 2000kW 450V a.c, 2 x 910kW 450V a.c Thrusters: 1 Tunnel thruster (f); 1 Tunnel thruster (a)
9488188 *V2EV2* -	**VEGA ARIES** **ms Vega Aries Schiffahrtsgesellschaft MbH & Co KG** Vega-Reederei Friedrich Dauber GmbH & Co KG *Saint John's* *Antigua & Barbuda* MMSI: 305569000	**33,005** 19,231 57,000 T/cm 58.8	Class: BV	**2010-04 Taizhou Kouan Shipbuilding Co Ltd — Taizhou JS** Yd No: KA102 Loa 189.99 (BB) Br ex - Dght 12.800 Lbp 185.00 Br md 32.26 Dpth 18.00 Welded, 1 dk	**(A21A2BC) Bulk Carrier** Grain: 71,634; Bale: 70,557 Compartments: 5 Ho, ER 5 Ha: ER Cranes: 4x30t	**1 oil engine** driving 1 FP propeller Total Power: 9,960kW (13,542hp) 14.6kn MAN-B&W 6S50MC-C 1 x 2 Stroke 6 Cy. 500 x 2000 9960kW (13542bhp) STX Engine Co Ltd-South Korea AuxGen: 3 x 600kW 450V 60Hz a.c
9347786 *D5EL7* -	**VEGA AURIGA** *ex* Medbay *-2013* *ex* MCC Sinag *-2010* *ex* Medbay *-2008* **ms 'Vega Auriga' Schiffahrtsgesellschaft mbH & Co KG** Vega-Reederei Friedrich Dauber GmbH & Co KG *Monrovia* *Liberia* MMSI: 636092508 Official number: 92508	**9,981** 4,900 11,809	Class: GL	**2006-10 Yangfan Group Co Ltd — Zhoushan ZJ** Yd No: 2027 Loa 139.13 (BB) Br ex - Dght 8.800 Lbp 129.00 Br md 22.60 Dpth 11.80 Welded, 1 dk	**(A33A2CC) Container Ship (Fully Cellular)** TEU 966 C Ho 312 TEU C Dk 654 TEU incl 252 ref C Cranes: 2x45t	**1 oil engine** reduction geared to sc. shaft driving 1 CP propeller Total Power: 9,600kW (13,052hp) 18.0kn MAN-B&W 8L48/60B 1 x 4 Stroke 8 Cy. 480 x 600 9600kW (13052bhp) MAN B&W Diesel AG-Augsburg AuxGen: 1 x 2000kW 450/230V a.c, 2 x 900kW 450/230V a.c Thrusters: 1 Tunnel thruster (f); 1 Tunnel thruster (f)
9403437 *A8KR2* -	**VEGA AZURIT** **ms Vega Azurit Schifffahrtsgesellschaft mbH & Co KG** Vega-Reederei GmbH & Co KG *Monrovia* *Liberia* MMSI: 636091206 Official number: 91206	**9,957** 5,020 13,684 T/cm 28.0	Class: BV (GL)	**2008-04 Taizhou Kouan Shipbuilding Co Ltd — Taizhou JS** Yd No: KA409 Loa 147.81 (BB) Br ex 23.45 Dght 8.510 Lbp 140.30 Br md 23.25 Dpth 11.50 Welded, 1 dk	**(A33A2CC) Container Ship (Fully Cellular)** Grain: 16,067; Bale: 16,067 TEU 1118 C Ho 334 TEU C Dk 784 incl 240 ref C Compartments: 5 Ho, ER 7 Ha: 6 (12.6 x 18.8)ER (14.0 x 10.4) Cranes: 2x45t Ice Capable	**1 oil engine** reduction geared to sc. shaft driving 1 CP propeller Total Power: 9,730kW (13,229hp) 19.6kn MAN-B&W 7L58/64CD 1 x 4 Stroke 7 Cy. 580 x 640 9730kW (13229bhp) MAN B&W Diesel AG-Augsburg AuxGen: 3 x 570kW 450V 60Hz a.c, 1 x 550kW 450V 60Hz a.c Thrusters: 1 Tunnel thruster (f)
9308613 *D5DF8* -	**VEGA BETA** *ex* Colleen *-2012* *ex* Melfi Cristobal *-2011* *ex* Dole Guatemala *-2009* *completed as* Colleen *-2006* **Vega Beteiligungsgesellschaft Beta mbH & Co KG** Vega-Reederei Friedrich Dauber GmbH & Co KG *Monrovia* *Liberia* MMSI: 636092465 Official number: 92465	**9,981** 4,900 11,836	Class: GL	**2006-01 Yangfan Group Co Ltd — Zhoushan ZJ** Yd No: 2020 Loa 139.00 (BB) Br ex - Dght 8.800 Lbp 129.00 Br md 22.60 Dpth 11.80 Welded, 1 dk	**(A33A2CC) Container Ship (Fully Cellular)** Double Hull TEU 957 incl 240 ref C. Cranes: 2x45t	**1 oil engine** geared to sc. shaft driving 1 CP propeller Total Power: 9,600kW (13,052hp) 18.8kn MAN-B&W 8L48/60B 1 x 4 Stroke 8 Cy. 480 x 600 9600kW (13052bhp) Thrusters: 2 Thwart. CP thruster (f)
9319595 *D5DU7* -	**VEGA CARINA** *ex* Pauline *-2013* **ms 'Vega Carina' Schifffahrtsgesellschaft mbH & Co KG** Vega-Reederei GmbH & Co KG *Monrovia* *Liberia* MMSI: 636092491 Official number: 92491	**9,981** 4,900 11,834	Class: GL	**2006-04 Yangfan Group Co Ltd — Zhoushan ZJ** Yd No: 2022 Loa 139.10 (BB) Br ex - Dght 8.800 Lbp 129.00 Br md 22.60 Dpth 11.80 Welded, 1 dk	**(A33A2CC) Container Ship (Fully Cellular)** Double Bottom Entire Compartment Length TEU 957 incl 252 ref C. Cranes: 2x45t	**1 oil engine** geared to sc. shaft driving 1 CP propeller Total Power: 9,600kW (13,052hp) 18.8kn MAN-B&W 8L48/60B 1 x 4 Stroke 8 Cy. 480 x 600 9600kW (13052bhp) MAN B&W Diesel AG-Augsburg AuxGen: 1 x 2000kW 450/230V a.c, 2 x 910kW 450/230V a.c Thrusters: 1 Thwart. CP thruster (f); 1 Thwart. CP thruster (f)
9680786 *V7CA7* -	**VEGA CHALLENGER** **Vega Challenger AS** Vega Offshore Management AS *Majuro* *Marshall Islands* MMSI: 538005229 Official number: 5229	**1,686** 506 1,296	Class: AB	**2013-09 Fujian Southeast Shipyard — Fuzhou FJ** Yd No: FN601-10 Loa 59.25 Br ex 14.95 Dght 4.950 Lbp 52.20 Br md 14.95 Dpth 6.10 Welded, 1 dk	**(B21B20A) Anchor Handling Tug Supply**	**2 oil engines** reduction geared to sc. shafts driving 2 CP propellers Total Power: 3,840kW (5,220hp) 11.0kn Caterpillar 3516C-HD 1 x Vee 4 Stroke 16 Cy. 170 x 215 1920kW (2610bhp) Caterpillar Inc-USA AuxGen: 2 x 800kW a.c, 2 x 450kW a.c Fuel: 520.0

IMO / Call sign	Name / Owner / Manager / Port / Flag	Tonnage	Class	Builder / Dimensions	Type / Capacities	Machinery
9680774 *V7CA5* -	**VEGA CHASER** **Vega Chaser AS** Vega Offshore Management AS *Majuro* *Marshall Islands* MMSI: 538005227 Official number: 5227	**1,686** 506 1,310	Class: AB	**2013-09 Fujian Southeast Shipyard — Fuzhou FJ** Yd No: FN601-9 Loa 59.25 Br ex 14.95 Dght 4.950 Lbp 52.20 Br md 14.95 Dpth 6.10 Welded, 1 dk	**(B21B20A) Anchor Handling Tug Supply**	**2 oil engines** reduction geared to sc.shafts driving 2 CP propellers Total Power: 3,840kW (5,220hp) 11.0kn Caterpillar 3516C-HD 1 x Vee 4 Stroke 16 Cy. 170 x 215 1920kW (2610bhp) Caterpillar Inc-USA AuxGen: 2 x 800kW a.c, 2 x 350kW a.c Fuel: 520.0
9651357 *LAQG7* -	**VEGA CORONA** *ex SK Line 72 -2012* **Vega Corona AS** Vega Offshore Management AS *Kristiansand* *Norway (NIS)* MMSI: 257977000	**1,678** 504 1,430	Class: AB	**2012-09 Fujian Funing Shipyard Industry Co Ltd — Fu'an FJ** Yd No: SK72 Loa 59.25 Br ex - Dght 4.950 Lbp 52.20 Br md 14.95 Dpth 6.10 Welded, 1 dk	**(B21B20A) Anchor Handling Tug Supply**	**2 oil engines** reduction geared to sc. shafts driving 2 CP propellers Total Power: 3,788kW (5,150hp) 11.0kn Caterpillar 3516C-HD 2 x Vee 4 Stroke 16 Cy. 170 x 215 each-1894kW (2575bhp) Caterpillar Inc-USA AuxGen: 2 x 800kW a.c, 2 x 350kW a.c Fuel: 520.0
9651345 *LAQF7* -	**VEGA CRUSADER** *ex SK Line 71 -2012* **Vega Crusader AS** Vega Offshore Management AS *Kristiansand* *Norway (NIS)* MMSI: 257974000	**1,678** 504 1,456	Class: AB	**2012-08 Fujian Funing Shipyard Industry Co Ltd — Fu'an FJ** Yd No: SK71 Loa 59.27 Br ex - Dght 4.950 Lbp 52.16 Br md 14.95 Dpth 6.10 Welded, 1 dk	**(B21B20A) Anchor Handling Tug Supply**	**2 oil engines** reduction geared to sc. shafts driving 2 CP propellers Total Power: 3,840kW (5,220hp) 11.0kn Caterpillar 3516C-HD 2 x Vee 4 Stroke 16 Cy. 170 x 215 each-1920kW (2610bhp) Caterpillar Inc-USA AuxGen: 2 x 800kW a.c, 2 x 350kW a.c Thrusters: 2 Tunnel thruster (f)
9358527 *A8IH3* -	**VEGA DAVOS** **SIC ms 'Vega Davos' Schiffbeteiligungs GmbH & Co KG** Vega-Reederei Friedrich Dauber GmbH & Co KG *Monrovia* *Liberia* MMSI: 636090977 Official number: 90977	**7,464** 3,097 8,272 T/cm 22.0	Class: BV (GL)	**2006-04 Fujian Mawei Shipbuilding Ltd — Fuzhou FJ** Yd No: 437-18 Loa 129.52 (BB) Br ex - Dght 7.400 Lbp 120.34 Br md 20.60 Dpth 10.80 Welded, 1 dk	**(A33A2CC) Container Ship (Fully Cellular)** Double Bottom Entire Compartment Length TEU 698 C Ho 226 TEU C Dk 472 TEU incl 120 ref C. Compartments: 4 Cell Ho, ER 4 Ha: (12.5 x 15.8)2 (25.4 x 15.8)ER (6.4 x 10.7) Ice Capable	**1 oil engine** reduction geared to sc. shaft driving 1 CP propeller Total Power: 7,200kW (9,789hp) 15.9kn MaK 8M43C 1 x 4 Stroke 8 Cy. 430 x 610 7200kW (9789bhp) Caterpillar Motoren GmbH & Co. KG-Germany AuxGen: 1 x 1000kW 440/230V a.c, 3 x 450kW 450/230V a.c Thrusters: 1 Thwart. CP thruster (f) Fuel: 648.0 (d.f.)
7927960 *VOCQ* -	**VEGA DESGAGNES** *ex Bacalan -2001 ex Acila -1999* *ex Shelltrans -1994* **Royal Bank of Canada (Banque Royale du Canada) (RBC)** Transport Desgagnes Inc *Quebec, QC* *Canada* MMSI: 316003770 Official number: 822171	**8,806** 3,279 11,548 T/cm 25.5	Class: LR (BV) ✠ **100A1** SS 05/2012 oil tanker ESP Ice Class 1A ✠ **LMC** **UMS** Eq.Ltr: C†; Cable: 550.0/52.0 U3	**1982-03 Valmet Oy — Helsinki** Yd No: 307 Loa 140.80 Br ex 21.24 Dght 7.314 Lbp 132.82 Br md 21.21 Dpth 10.70 Welded, 1 dk	**(A13B2TP) Products Tanker** Double Hull Liq: 13,471; Liq (Oil): 13,471 Compartments: 8 Wing Ta, 1 Slop Ta, 2 Wing Slop Ta, ER 8 Cargo Pump (s): 8x250m³/hr Manifold: Bow/CM: 63m Ice Capable	**2 oil engines** reverse reduction geared to sc. shaft driving 1 CP propeller Total Power: 5,560kW (7,560hp) 12.5kn Wartsila 9R32 2 x 4 Stroke 9 Cy. 320 x 350 each-2780kW (3780bhp) Oy Wartsila Ab-Finland AuxGen: 2 x 1900kW 380/220V 60Hz a.c, 2 x 330kW 380/220V 60Hz a.c Thrusters: 1 Thwart. FP thruster (f) Fuel: 110.4 (d.f.) (Part Heating Coils) 601.1 (r.f.) 27.0pd
9532094 *7JHY* -	**VEGA DREAM** **SMFL Orchid Co Ltd** New Asian Shipping Co Ltd SatCom: Inmarsat C 443277110 *Tokyo* *Japan* MMSI: 432771000 Official number: 141323	**91,468** 57,660 174,713 T/cm 122.0	Class: NK	**2010-07 Namura Shipbuilding Co Ltd — Imari SG** Yd No: 331 Loa 289.98 (BB) Br ex - Dght 18.029 Lbp 280.00 Br md 45.00 Dpth 24.70 Welded, 1 dk	**(A21A2BC) Bulk Carrier** Grain: 199,507; Bale: 195,968 Compartments: 9 Ho, ER 9 Ha: 7 (16.2 x 20.2) (16.2 x 15.1)ER (15.3 x 16.8)	**1 oil engine** driving 1 FP propeller Total Power: 16,860kW (22,923hp) 14.8kn MAN-B&W 6S70MC-C 1 x 2 Stroke 6 Cy. 700 x 2800 16860kW (22923bhp) Hitachi Zosen Corp-Japan AuxGen: 3 x 600kW a.c Fuel: 5137.0 (r.f.)
9655731 *LAQY7* -	**VEGA EMTOLI** *ex Bute -2013* **Vega Emtoli AS** Vega Offshore Management AS *Kristiansand* *Norway (NIS)* MMSI: 258026000	**1,695** 508 1,352	Class: AB	**2013-01 Fujian Southeast Shipyard — Fuzhou FJ** Yd No: FN601-5 Loa 59.25 Br ex - Dght 4.950 Lbp 52.20 Br md 14.95 Dpth 6.10 Welded, 1 dk	**(B21B20A) Anchor Handling Tug Supply**	**2 oil engines** reduction geared to sc. shafts driving 2 CP propellers Total Power: 3,840kW (5,220hp) 11.0kn Caterpillar 3516C-HD 2 x Vee 4 Stroke 16 Cy. 170 x 215 each-1920kW (2610bhp) Caterpillar Inc-USA AuxGen: 2 x 800kW a.c, 2 x 438kW a.c Fuel: 520.0
9330238 *D5EV4* -	**VEGA EPSILON** *ex Amazon River -2013 ex Papuan Gulf -2009* *launched as Amazon River -2007* **Vega Beteiligungsgesellschaft Epsilon mbH & Co KG** Vega-Reederei Friedrich Dauber GmbH & Co KG *Monrovia* *Liberia* MMSI: 636092525 Official number: 92525	**9,940** 5,020 13,619 T/cm 28.0	Class: GL	**2007-01 Qingshan Shipyard — Wuhan HB** Yd No: 20040312 Loa 147.84 (BB) Br ex 23.45 Dght 8.510 Lbp 140.30 Br md 23.25 Dpth 11.50 Welded, 1 dk	**(A33A2CC) Container Ship (Fully Cellular)** Double Bottom Partial Compartment Length Grain: 16,000; Bale: 16,000 TEU 1092 C Ho 334 TEU C Dk 758 TEU incl 220 ref C Compartments: 5 Cell Ho, ER Cranes: 1x45t,1x40t	**1 oil engine** reduction geared to sc. shaft driving 1 CP propeller Total Power: 9,730kW (13,229hp) 19.6kn MAN-B&W 7L58/64 1 x 4 Stroke 7 Cy. 580 x 640 9730kW (13229bhp) MAN B&W Diesel AG-Augsburg AuxGen: 1 x 2000kW 450V 60Hz a.c, 3 x 570kW 450V 60Hz a.c Thrusters: 1 Thwart. FP thruster (f) Fuel: 200.0 (d.f.) 1200.0 (r.f.)
9336359 *V2BU6* -	**VEGA FYNEN** **ms 'Vega Fynen' Schiffahrts GmbH & Co KG** MCC Transport Singapore Pte Ltd *Saint John's* *Antigua & Barbuda* MMSI: 304931000	**9,957** 5,020 13,742 T/cm 28.0	Class: BV (GL)	**2006-06 Kouan Shipbuilding Industry Co — Taizhou JS** Yd No: KA405 Loa 147.87 (BB) Br ex 23.43 Dght 8.500 Lbp 140.30 Br md 23.25 Dpth 11.50 Welded, 1 dk	**(A33A2CC) Container Ship (Fully Cellular)** Grain: 16,000; Bale: 16,000 TEU 1118 C Ho 334 TEU C Dk 784 incl 240 ref C Compartments: 5 Ho, ER 7 Ha: 6 (12.6 x 18.8)ER (14.0 x 10.4) Cranes: 2x45t Ice Capable	**1 oil engine** reduction geared to sc. shaft driving 1 CP propeller Total Power: 9,730kW (13,229hp) 19.6kn MAN-B&W 7L58/64 1 x 4 Stroke 7 Cy. 580 x 640 9730kW (13229bhp) MAN B&W Diesel AG-Augsburg AuxGen: 1 x 1400kW 450/230V a.c, 3 x 570kW 450/230V a.c Thrusters: 1 Tunnel thruster (f)
9336347 *V2BP4* -	**VEGA GOTLAND** **ms 'Vega Gotland' Schiffahrtsges mbH & Co KG** Vega-Reederei Friedrich Dauber GmbH & Co KG *Saint John's* *Antigua & Barbuda* MMSI: 304889000 Official number: 4079	**9,957** 5,020 13,806 T/cm 28.0	Class: BV (GL)	**2006-01 Kouan Shipbuilding Industry Co — Taizhou JS** Yd No: KA404 Loa 147.87 (BB) Br ex 23.43 Dght 8.510 Lbp 140.30 Br md 23.25 Dpth 11.50 Welded, 1 dk	**(A33A2CC) Container Ship (Fully Cellular)** Grain: 16,000; Bale: 16,000 TEU 1118 C Ho 334 TEU C Dk 784 incl 220 ref C Compartments: 5 Ho, ER 7 Ha: 6 (12.6 x 18.8)ER (14.0 x 10.4) Cranes: 2x45t Ice Capable	**1 oil engine** reduction geared to sc. shaft driving 1 CP propeller Total Power: 9,730kW (13,229hp) 19.0kn MAN-B&W 7L58/64 1 x 4 Stroke 7 Cy. 580 x 640 9730kW (13229bhp) MAN B&W Diesel AG-Augsburg AuxGen: 3 x 570kW 450V a.c, 1 x 1400kW 450V a.c Thrusters: 1 Tunnel thruster (f)
9497440 *A8UN7* -	**VEGA GRANAT** **ms 'Vega Pollux' Schiffahrtsgesellschaft mbH & Co KG** Vega-Reederei Friedrich Dauber GmbH & Co KG *Monrovia* *Liberia* MMSI: 636091919 Official number: 91919	**19,994** 10,883 31,780 T/cm 42.6	Class: BV GL	**2011-11 Fujian Mawei Shipbuilding Ltd — Fuzhou FJ** Yd No: 451-7 Loa 177.48 (BB) Br ex - Dght 10.200 Lbp 168.00 Br md 28.20 Dpth 14.20 Welded, 1 dk	**(A21A2BC) Bulk Carrier** Grain: 42,006; Bale: 39,906 Compartments: 5 Ho, ER 5 Ha: 4 (19.2 x 16.8)ER (19.4 x 15.2) Cranes: 4x30t Ice Capable	**1 oil engine** driving 1 FP propeller Total Power: 6,300kW (8,565hp) 13.7kn Mitsubishi 6UEC43LSII 1 x 2 Stroke 6 Cy. 430 x 1500 6300kW (8565bhp) Mitsubishi Heavy Industries Ltd-Japan AuxGen: 3 x 500kW 450V 60Hz a.c
8655966 *IFVV* -	**VEGA I** **LMD SpA** - *Chioggia* *Italy* MMSI: 247196500 Official number: CI3346	**499** 236 808	Class: (RI)	**1995 CiEsse Srl — Scafati** Yd No: 46/94 Loa 49.52 Br ex 11.52 Dght 2.500 Lbp 48.63 Br md 11.50 Dpth 2.80 Welded, 1 dk	**(B33B2DG) Grab Hopper Dredger**	**2 oil engines** reduction geared to sc. shafts driving 2 Propellers Total Power: 760kW (1,034hp) Cummins KT-19-M 2 x 4 Stroke 6 Cy. 159 x 159 each-380kW (517bhp) Cummins Engine Co Inc-USA
7235575 *A6E2885* -	**VEGA I** *ex BUE Shuna -2000 ex Skua -1999* *ex Hornbeck Skua -1997* *ex Seaboard Skua -1995 ex Hawk -1991* *ex Red Hawk -1991 ex Maersk Helper -1981* **Ecomar AG LLC** Akron Trade & Transport *Sharjah* *United Arab Emirates* MMSI: 470689000 Official number: 4807	**698** 210 757	Class: RI (GL) (BV)	**1972-06 Rolandwerft Dockbetrieb GmbH Ganspe — Berne** (Hull launched by) Yd No: 982 **1972-06 Aarhus Flydedok A/S — Aarhus** (Hull completed by) Yd No: 152 Converted From: Offshore Tug/Supply Ship-1991 Loa 53.48 Br ex 11.23 Dght 3.480 Lbp 50.02 Br md 11.04 Dpth 4.02 Welded, 1 dk	**(B21A20S) Platform Supply Ship** Compartments: 8 Ta, 1 Ho, ER Derricks: 1x3t; Winches: 1 Ice Capable	**2 oil engines** driving 2 FP propellers Total Power: 2,796kW (3,802hp) 13.0kn MaK 8MU452AK 2 x 4 Stroke 8 Cy. 320 x 450 each-1398kW (1901bhp) MaK Maschinenbau GmbH-Kiel AuxGen: 3 x 128kW 220/380V 50Hz a.c Thrusters: 1 Thwart. FP thruster (f) Fuel: 81.5 (d.f.)

Identity / Owner	Tonnage / Class	Builder / Dimensions	Type / Cargo	Machinery
9081435 **VEGA II** *9HIR6* *ex* Vega *-1999* - **Vega 2 Navigation Ltd** Legpromexport Ltd SatCom: Inmarsat C 435732210 *Valletta* *Malta* MMSI: 248573000 Official number: 6576	**2,676** Class: RS 909 2,968	**1992-08 Krasnoyarskiy Sudostroitelnyy Zavod — Krasnoyarsk** Yd No: 4 Loa 113.30 Br ex 15.34 Dght 3.160 Lbp 109.29 Br md - Dpth 5.00 Welded, 1 dk	**(A31A2GX) General Cargo Ship** Grain: 4,380 TEU 104 C.Ho 32/20' C.Dk 72/20' Compartments: 4 Ho, ER 4 Ha: 4 (15.5 x 10.9)ER Cranes: 1x8t,1x8t Ice Capable	**2 oil engines** driving 2 FP propellers Total Power: 1,030kW (1,400hp) S.K.L. 6NVD48A-2U 2 x 4 Stroke 6 Cy. 320 x 480 each-515kW (700bhp) SKL Motoren u. Systemtechnik AG-Magdeburg
9547491 **VEGA II** *HP5182* *ex* Blue Vega *-2012* *ex* Drejo (Y301) *-2008* - **Michael Larsen** - *Panama* *Panama* MMSI: 371845000 Official number: 4073409A	**104** 84 -	**1969-01 A/S Svendborg Skibsvaerft — Svendborg** Yd No: 127 Converted From: Patrol Vessel, Naval-2008 Loa 25.64 Br ex - Dght 2.700 Lbp - Br md 6.00 Dpth 3.20 Welded, 1 dk	**(B22G20Y) Standby Safety Vessel**	**1 oil engine** geared to sc. shaft driving 1 Propeller Total Power: 368kW (500hp) 9.5kn Alpha 405-26VO 1 x 2 Stroke 5 Cy. 260 x 400 368kW (500bhp) Alpha Diesel A/S-Denmark AuxGen: 2 x 32kW a.c
9655676 **VEGA INRUDA** *LARY7* - **Vega Inruda AS** Vega Offshore Management AS *Kristiansand* *Norway (NIS)* MMSI: 258756000	**1,727** Class: AB 518 1,401	**2013-04 Fujian Southeast Shipyard — Fuzhou FJ** Yd No: DN59M-100 Loa 59.85 Br ex 15.15 Dght 5.000 Lbp 52.80 Br md 14.95 Dpth 6.10 Welded, 1 dk	**(B21B20A) Anchor Handling Tug Supply**	**2 oil engines** reduction geared to sc. shafts driving 2 Propellers Total Power: 3,840kW (5,220hp) 11.0kn Caterpillar 3516C-HD 2 x Vee 4 Stroke 16 Cy. 170 x 215 each-1920kW (2610bhp) Caterpillar Inc-USA AuxGen: 2 x 800kW a.c, 2 x 383kW a.c Fuel: 450.0 (d.f.)
9651321 **VEGA JAANCA** *LASL7* *ex* SK Line 69 *-2013* - **Vega Jaanca AS** Vega Offshore Management AS *Kristiansand* *Norway (NIS)* MMSI: 258889000	**1,695** Class: AB 508 1,360	**2012-12 Fujian Southeast Shipyard — Fuzhou FJ** Yd No: SK69 Loa 59.25 Br ex - Dght 4.950 Lbp 52.20 Br md 14.95 Dpth 6.10 Welded, 1 dk	**(B21B20A) Anchor Handling Tug Supply**	**2 oil engines** reduction geared to sc. shafts driving 2 CP propellers Total Power: 3,840kW (5,220hp) 11.0kn Caterpillar 3516C-HD 2 x Vee 4 Stroke 16 Cy. 170 x 215 each-1920kW (2610bhp) Caterpillar Inc-USA AuxGen: 2 x 800kW a.c, 2 x 444kW a.c Fuel: 520.0
9651307 **VEGA JUNIZ** *LAQX7* *ex* SK Line 67 *-2012* - **Vega Juniz AS** Thome Offshore Management Pte Ltd *Kristiansand* *Norway (NIS)* MMSI: 258022000	**1,695** Class: AB 508 1,317	**2012-09 Fujian Southeast Shipyard — Fuzhou FJ** Yd No: SK67 Loa 59.25 Br ex - Dght 4.950 Lbp 52.20 Br md 14.95 Dpth 6.10 Welded, 1 dk	**(B21B20A) Anchor Handling Tug Supply**	**2 oil engines** reduction geared to sc. shafts driving 2 CP propellers Total Power: 3,840kW (5,220hp) 11.0kn Caterpillar 3516B-HD 2 x Vee 4 Stroke 16 Cy. 170 x 215 each-1920kW (2610bhp) Caterpillar Inc-USA AuxGen: 2 x 800kW a.c, 2 x 444kW a.c Fuel: 540.0
9330252 **VEGA KAPPA** *D5EV5* *ex* Vaal River *-2013* *ex* Yingchow *-2012* - *ex* Pacific Fighter *-2012* *ex* Vaal River *-2011* *ex* Tiger Power *-2011* *ex* Vaal River *-2009* **Vega Beteiligungsgesellschaft Kappa mbH & Co KG** Vega-Reederei Friedrich Dauber GmbH & Co KG *Monrovia* *Liberia* MMSI: 636092526 Official number: 92526	**9,940** Class: GL 5,020 13,705 T/cm 28.0	**2007-12 Qingshan Shipyard — Wuhan HB** Yd No: 20040314 Loa 147.87 (BB) Br ex 23.45 Dght 8.510 Lbp 140.30 Br md 23.25 Dpth 11.50 Welded, 1 dk	**(A33A2CC) Container Ship (Fully Cellular)** Grain: 16,000; Bale: 16,000 TEU 1118 C Ho 334 TEU C Dk 784 incl 220 ref C Compartments: 5 Cell Ho, ER Cranes: 1x45t,1x40t	**1 oil engine** reduction geared to sc. shaft driving 1 CP propeller Total Power: 9,730kW (13,229hp) 19.6kn MAN-B&W 7L58/64 1 x 4 Stroke 7 Cy. 580 x 640 9730kW (13229bhp) MAN B&W Diesel AG-Augsburg AuxGen: 3 x 570kW 60Hz a.c, 1 x 2000kW 60Hz a.c Thrusters: 1 Thwart. FP thruster (f) Fuel: 200.0 (d.f.) 1200.0 (r.f.)
9477684 **VEGA LEA** *A8VU8* - **ms 'Vega Lea' Schifffahrtsgesellschaft mbH & Co KG** Vega-Reederei GmbH & Co KG SatCom: Inmarsat C 463708327 *Monrovia* *Liberia* MMSI: 636092045 Official number: 92045	**32,638** Class: NV (BV) 18,070 53,716 T/cm 57.3	**2010-07 Chengxi Shipyard Co Ltd — Jiangyin JS** Yd No: CX4238 Loa 190.00 (BB) Br ex - Dght 12.620 Lbp 180.05 Br md 32.26 Dpth 17.50 Welded, 1 dk	**(A21A2BC) Bulk Carrier** Grain: 65,900; Bale: 64,000 Compartments: 5 Ho, ER 5 Ha: 4 (21.3 x 18.3)ER (18.9 x 18.3) Cranes: 4x36t	**1 oil engine** driving 1 FP propeller Total Power: 9,480kW (12,889hp) 14.2kn MAN-B&W 6S50MC-C 1 x 2 Stroke 6 Cy. 500 x 2000 9480kW (12889bhp) Hudong Heavy Machinery Co Ltd-China AuxGen: 3 x 540kW 450V 60Hz a.c
9213818 **VEGA LEADER** *H3NW* - **Aires del Mar Co SA** Far-East Transport Co Ltd *Panama* *Panama* MMSI: 355948000 Official number: 2733300CH	**51,496** Class: NK 15,449 16,396 T/cm 47.2	**2000-09 Sumitomo Heavy Industries Ltd. — Yokosuka Shipyard, Yokosuka** Yd No: 1262 Loa 180.00 (BB) Br ex - Dght 9.625 Lbp 170.00 Br md 32.26 Dpth 34.60 Welded, 12 dks, incl 3 hoistable	**(A35B2RV) Vehicles Carrier** Side door/ramp (s) Len: 20.00 Wid: 4.20 Swl: 15 Quarter stern door/ramp (s. a.) Len: 35.00 Wid: 13.50 Swl: 100 Lane-Wid: 8.00 Lane-clr ht: 5.10 Cars: 4,323	**1 oil engine** driving 1 FP propeller Total Power: 13,540kW (18,409hp) 19.3kn Sulzer 7RTA62 1 x 2 Stroke 7 Cy. 620 x 2150 13540kW (18409bhp) Diesel United Ltd.-Aioi AuxGen: 3 x 1200kW 440V 60Hz a.c Thrusters: 1 Thwart. CP thruster (f); 1 Thwart. CP thruster (a) Fuel: 250.7 (d.f.) (Heating Coils) 2735.3 (r.f.) 54.2pd
9477696 **VEGA LIBRA** *A8VU9* - **ms 'Vega Libra' Schifffahrtsgesellschaft mbH & Co KG** Vega-Reederei GmbH & Co KG *Monrovia* *Liberia* MMSI: 636092046 Official number: 92046	**32,557** Class: NV 18,070 53,743 T/cm 57.3	**2010-09 Chengxi Shipyard Co Ltd — Jiangyin JS** Yd No: CX4239 Loa 190.00 (BB) Br ex - Dght 12.620 Lbp 180.05 Br md 32.26 Dpth 17.50 Welded, 1 dk	**(A21A2BC) Bulk Carrier** Grain: 65,900; Bale: 64,000 Compartments: 5 Ho, ER 5 Ha: 4 (21.3 x 18.3)ER (18.9 x 18.3) Cranes: 4x36t	**1 oil engine** driving 1 FP propeller Total Power: 9,480kW (12,889hp) 14.2kn MAN-B&W 6S50MC-C 1 x 2 Stroke 6 Cy. 500 x 2000 9480kW (12889bhp) Hudong Heavy Machinery Co Ltd-China AuxGen: 3 x 540kW 450V 60Hz a.c
9364356 **VEGA LUNA** *A8JG7* *ex* Turtle Bay *-2013* - **ms 'Vega Luna' Schifffahrtsgesellschaft mbH & Co KG** Vega-Reederei GmbH & Co KG *Monrovia* *Liberia* MMSI: 636091087 Official number: 91087	**9,940** Class: GL 5,020 13,715 T/cm 28.0	**2006-11 Qingshan Shipyard — Wuhan HB** Yd No: 20040321 Loa 147.87 (BB) Br ex - Dght 8.500 Lbp 140.30 Br md 23.25 Dpth 11.50 Welded, 1 dk	**(A33A2CC) Container Ship (Fully Cellular)** Grain: 16,000; Bale: 16,000 TEU 1118 C Ho 334 TEU C Dk 784 TEU incl 220 ref C Cranes: 2x45t	**1 oil engine** reduction geared to sc. shaft driving 1 CP propeller Total Power: 9,730kW (13,229hp) 19.6kn MAN-B&W 7L58/64 1 x 4 Stroke 7 Cy. 580 x 640 9730kW (13229bhp) MAN B&W Diesel AG-Augsburg AuxGen: 1 x 2000kW 450/220V a.c, 3 x 575kW 450/220V a.c Thrusters: 1 Tunnel thruster (f)
9364344 **VEGA LUPUS** *A8JG6* *ex* Tampa Bay *-2013* *ex* St. John Spirit *-2010* - *ex* Tampa Bay *-2009* **ms 'Vega Lupus' Schifffahrtsgesellschaft mbH & Co KG** Vega-Reederei Friedrich Dauber GmbH & Co KG *Monrovia* *Liberia* MMSI: 636091086 Official number: 91086	**9,940** Class: GL 5,020 13,690 T/cm 28.0	**2006-06 Qingshan Shipyard — Wuhan HB** Yd No: 20040320 Loa 147.87 (BB) Br ex - Dght 8.500 Lbp 140.30 Br md 23.25 Dpth 11.50 Welded, 1 dk	**(A33A2CC) Container Ship (Fully Cellular)** Grain: 16,000; Bale: 16,000 TEU 1118 C Ho 334 TEU C Dk 784 incl 220 ref C Cranes: 2x45t	**1 oil engine** reduction geared to sc. shaft driving 1 CP propeller Total Power: 9,730kW (13,229hp) 19.6kn MAN-B&W 7L58/64 1 x 4 Stroke 7 Cy. 580 x 640 9730kW (13229bhp) MAN B&W Diesel AG-Augsburg AuxGen: 1 x 2000kW 450/220V a.c, 3 x 575kW 450/220V a.c Thrusters: 1 Tunnel thruster (f)
7520530 **VEGA MARIE** *WYT9689* *ex* Bold Lady *-2001* *ex* Miss Edith Z *-1974* - **Boat Dakota Inc** - *Seattle, WA* *United States of America* Official number: 553377	*114* 77 -	**1973 S & R Boat Builders, Inc. — Bayou La Batre, Al** L reg 21.98 Br ex 6.76 Dght - Lbp - Br md - Dpth 3.38 Welded, 1 dk	**(B11B2FV) Fishing Vessel**	**1 oil engine** driving 1 FP propeller Total Power: 257kW (349hp)
9497438 **VEGA MARS** *A8UN8* - **ms 'Vega Mars' Schifffahrtsgesellschaft mbH & Co KG** Vega-Reederei Friedrich Dauber GmbH & Co KG *Monrovia* *Liberia* MMSI: 636091920 Official number: 91920	**19,994** Class: BV GL 10,883 31,728 T/cm 42.6	**2011-05 Fujian Mawei Shipbuilding Ltd — Fuzhou FJ** Yd No: 451-6 Loa 177.36 (BB) Br ex - Dght 10.200 Lbp 167.94 Br md 28.20 Dpth 14.20 Welded, 1 dk	**(A21A2BC) Bulk Carrier** Grain: 42,700 Compartments: 5 Ho, ER 5 Ha: 4 (19.2 x 16.8)ER (19.4 x 15.2) Cranes: 4x30t Ice Capable	**1 oil engine** driving 1 FP propeller Total Power: 6,300kW (8,565hp) 13.7kn Mitsubishi 6UEC43LSII 1 x 2 Stroke 6 Cy. 430 x 1500 6300kW (8565bhp) Yichang Marine Diesel Engine Co Ltd-China AuxGen: 3 x 500kW 450V 60Hz a.c
9403463 **VEGA MERCURY** *A8PT9* - **Vega Mercury Schifffahrtsgesellschaft mbH & Co KG** Vega-Reederei GmbH & Co KG *Monrovia* *Liberia* MMSI: 636091602 Official number: 91602	**9,957** Class: BV (GL) 5,020 13,702 T/cm 28.0	**2009-03 Taizhou Kouan Shipbuilding Co Ltd — Taizhou JS** Yd No: KA412 Loa 147.81 (BB) Br ex - Dght 8.510 Lbp 140.30 Br md 23.25 Dpth 11.50 Welded, 1 dk	**(A33A2CC) Container Ship (Fully Cellular)** Grain: 16,067; Bale: 16,067 TEU 1118 C Ho 334 TEU C Dk 784 incl 220 ref C Compartments: 5 Ho, ER 7 Ha: ER Cranes: 2x45t Ice Capable	**1 oil engine** reduction geared to sc. shaft driving 1 CP propeller Total Power: 9,730kW (13,229hp) 19.6kn MAN-B&W 7L58/64CD 1 x 4 Stroke 7 Cy. 580 x 640 9730kW (13229bhp) MAN B&W Diesel AG-Augsburg AuxGen: 3 x 570kW 450V a.c Thrusters: 1 Tunnel thruster (f)

9497452 *A8UN5* -
VEGA NEPTUNE
ms 'Vega Neptune' Schifffahrtsgesellschaft mbH & Co KG
Vega-Reederei GmbH & Co KG
Monrovia *Liberia*
MMSI: 636091917
Official number: 91917
19,994 10,883 31,796 T/cm 42.6
Class: BV GL
2012-01 Fujian Mawei Shipbuilding Ltd — Fuzhou FJ Yd No: 451-8
Loa 177.43 (BB) Br ex - Dght 10.200
Lbp 169.02 Br md 28.20 Dpth 14.20
Welded, 1 dk
(A21A2BC) Bulk Carrier
Grain: 42,700
Compartments: 5 Ho, ER
5 Ha: 4 (19.2 x 16.8)ER (19.4 x 15.2)
Cranes: 4x30t
Ice Capable
1 oil engine driving 1 FP propeller
Total Power: 6,300kW (8,565hp) 13.7kn
Mitsubishi 6UEC43LSII
1 x 2 Stroke 6 Cy. 430 x 1500 6300kW (8565bhp)
Mitsubishi Heavy Industries Ltd-Japan
AuxGen: 3 x 500kW 450V 60Hz a.c

9449687 *A8QD2* -
VEGA NIKOLAS
ms 'Vega Nikolas' Schifffahrtsgesellschaft mbH & Co KG
Vega-Reederei GmbH & Co KG
Monrovia *Liberia*
MMSI: 636091613
Official number: 91613
9,996 4,900 11,807
Class: BV (GL)
2008-06 Yangfan Group Co Ltd — Zhoushan ZJ Yd No: 2061
Loa 139.17 (BB) Br ex - Dght 8.800
Lbp 129.00 Br md 22.60 Dpth 11.80
Welded, 1 dk
(A33A2CC) Container Ship (Fully Cellular)
TEU 957 incl 256 ref C
Cranes: 2x45t
Ice Capable
1 oil engine reduction geared to sc. shaft driving 1 CP propeller
Total Power: 9,600kW (13,052hp) 18.1kn
MAN-B&W 8L48/60B
1 x 4 Stroke 8 Cy. 480 x 600 9600kW (13052bhp)
MAN B&W Diesel AG-Augsburg
AuxGen: 1 x 2000kW 450V a.c, 2 x 728kW 450V a.c
Thrusters: 1 Tunnel thruster (f); 1 Tunnel thruster (f)

9330226 *D5EU5* -
VEGA OMEGA
ex Vento Di Levante *-2014*
ex Surinam River *-2012*
ex Vento Di Maestrale *-2011* *ex* Eagle 2 *-2008*
completed as Surinam River *-2006*
Vega Beteiligungsgesellschaft Omega mbH & Co KG
Vega-Reederei Friedrich Dauber GmbH & Co KG
Monrovia *Liberia*
MMSI: 636092523
Official number: 92523
9,940 5,020 13,639 T/cm 28.0
Class: GL
2006-08 Qingshan Shipyard — Wuhan HB Yd No: 20040311
Loa 147.87 (BB) Br ex 23.45 Dght 8.510
Lbp 140.30 Br md 23.25 Dpth 11.50
Welded, 1 dk
(A33A2CC) Container Ship (Fully Cellular)
Grain: 16,000; Bale: 16,000
TEU 1102 C Ho 334 TEU C Dk 768 incl 220 ref C
Compartments: 5 Cell Ho, ER
Cranes: 1x45t,1x40t
1 oil engine reduction geared to sc. shaft driving 1 CP propeller
Total Power: 9,730kW (13,229hp) 19.6kn
MAN-B&W 7L58/64
1 x 4 Stroke 7 Cy. 580 x 640 9730kW (13229bhp)
MAN B&W Diesel AG-Augsburg
AuxGen: 3 x 570kW 60Hz a.c, 1 x 2000kW 60Hz a.c
Thrusters: 1 Thwart. FP thruster (f)
Fuel: 200.0 (d.f.) 1200.0 (r.f.)

9308596 *V2BK5* -
VEGA POLLUX
ex Helene *-2012*
ms 'Vega Pollux' Schifffahrtsgesellschaft mbH & Co KG
Vega-Reederei Friedrich Dauber GmbH & Co KG
Saint John's *Antigua & Barbuda*
MMSI: 304846000
Official number: 4035
9,981 4,900 11,788
Class: GL
2005-10 Yangfan Group Co Ltd — Zhoushan ZJ Yd No: 2018
Loa 139.10 (BB) Br ex - Dght 8.800
Lbp 129.00 Br md 22.60 Dpth 11.80
Welded, 1 dk
(A33A2CC) Container Ship (Fully Cellular)
TEU 974 C Ho 218 TEU C Dk 756 TEU incl 240 ref C
Cranes: 2x45t
1 oil engine geared to sc. shaft driving 1 CP propeller
Total Power: 9,600kW (13,052hp) 18.8kn
MAN-B&W 8L48/60B
1 x 4 Stroke 8 Cy. 480 x 600 9600kW (13052bhp)
AuxGen: 2 x 850kW 440/220V 60Hz a.c, 1 x 2100kW 440/220V 60Hz a.c
Thrusters: 1 Tunnel thruster (f); 1 Tunnel thruster (f)

8822832 *D3N2012* -
VEGA Q
Oceanpesca Srl di Giuseppe Quinci
-
Luanda *Angola*
Official number: C-610-AC
445 133 -
Class: (RI)
1988 SINAM s.r.l. — Mazara del Vallo Yd No: 4
Loa 41.40 Br ex - Dght 3.290
Lbp 32.50 Br md 8.80 Dpth 6.18
Welded, 1 dk
(B11B2FV) Fishing Vessel
1 oil engine geared to sc. shaft driving 1 FP propeller
Total Power: 990kW (1,346hp)
Blackstone ESL8MK2
1 x 4 Stroke 8 Cy. 222 x 292 990kW (1346bhp)
Mirrlees Blackstone (Stockport)Ltd.-Stockport

9336866 *3EIO9* -
VEGA ROSE
Rosex Co Ltd
Fednav Ltd
Panama *Panama*
MMSI: 372351000
Official number: 3250207A
30,847 18,103 55,711 T/cm 56.1
Class: NK
2007-01 Kawasaki Shipbuilding Corp — Kobe HG Yd No: 1568
Loa 189.90 (BB) Br ex 32.26 Dght 12.520
Lbp 185.00 Br md 32.26 Dpth 17.80
Welded, 1 dk
(A21A2BC) Bulk Carrier
Grain: 69,450; Bale: 66,368
Compartments: 5 Ho, ER
5 Ha: 4 (20.5 x 18.6)ER (17.8 x 18.6)
Cranes: 4x30.5t
1 oil engine driving 1 FP propeller
Total Power: 8,201kW (11,150hp) 14.6kn
MAN-B&W 6S50MC-C
1 x 2 Stroke 6 Cy. 500 x 2000 8201kW (11150bhp)
Kawasaki Heavy Industries Ltd-Japan
AuxGen: 3 x a.c
Fuel: 1790.0

9403449 *A8PO5* -
VEGA SACHSEN
completed as State Waratah *-2008*
launched as Vega Sachsen *-2008*
ms Vega Sachsen Schifffahrtsgesellschaft mbH & Co KG
Vega-Reederei GmbH & Co KG
Monrovia *Liberia*
MMSI: 636091585
Official number: 91585
9,957 5,020 13,742 T/cm 28.0
Class: BV (GL)
2008-07 Taizhou Kouan Shipbuilding Co Ltd — Taizhou JS Yd No: KA410
Loa 147.81 (BB) Br ex 23.45 Dght 8.510
Lbp 140.30 Br md 23.25 Dpth 11.50
Welded, 1 dk
(A33A2CC) Container Ship (Fully Cellular)
Grain: 16,067; Bale: 16,067
TEU 1118 C Ho 334 TEU C Dk 784 incl 240 ref C
Compartments: 5 Ho, ER
7 Ha: 6 (12.6 x 18.8)ER (14.0 x 10.4)
Cranes: 2x45t
Ice Capable
1 oil engine reduction geared to sc. shaft driving 1 CP propeller
Total Power: 9,730kW (13,229hp) 19.6kn
MAN-B&W 7L58/64CD
1 x 4 Stroke 7 Cy. 580 x 640 9730kW (13229bhp)
MAN B&W Diesel AG-Augsburg
AuxGen: 3 x 570kW 450V a.c
Thrusters: 1 Tunnel thruster (f)

9491616 *A8RK2* -
VEGA SAGITTARIUS
ms 'Vega Sagittarius' Schifffahrtsgesellschaft mbH & Co KG
Vega-Reederei GmbH & Co KG
Monrovia *Liberia*
MMSI: 636091667
Official number: 91667
9,750 4,900 11,811
Class: GL
2012-01 Yangfan Group Co Ltd — Zhoushan ZJ Yd No: 2096
Loa 139.17 (BB) Br ex - Dght 8.800
Lbp 129.00 Br md 22.60 Dpth 11.80
Welded, 1 dk
(A33A2CC) Container Ship (Fully Cellular)
TEU 957 incl 256 ref C
Cranes: 2x45t
1 oil engine reduction geared to sc. shaft driving 1 CP propeller
Total Power: 9,600kW (13,052hp) 18.8kn
MAN-B&W 8L48/60B
1 x 4 Stroke 8 Cy. 480 x 600 9600kW (13052bhp)
MAN B&W Diesel AG-Augsburg
AuxGen: 1 x 2000kW a.c, 2 x 910kW a.c
Thrusters: 1 Tunnel thruster (f); 1 Tunnel thruster (f)

9403451 *A8PT8* -
VEGA SATURN
ms Vega Saturn Schifffahrtsgesellschaft mbH & Co KG
Vega-Reederei GmbH & Co KG
Monrovia *Liberia*
MMSI: 636091601
Official number: 91601
9,957 5,020 13,621 T/cm 28.0
Class: BV (GL)
2008-10 Taizhou Kouan Shipbuilding Co Ltd — Taizhou JS Yd No: KA411
Loa 148.00 (BB) Br ex - Dght 8.510
Lbp 140.30 Br md 23.25 Dpth 11.50
Welded, 1 dk
(A33A2CC) Container Ship (Fully Cellular)
Grain: 16,067; Bale: 16,067
TEU 1118 C Ho 334 TEU C Dk 784 incl 240 ref C
Compartments: 5 Ho, ER
7 Ha: 6 (12.6 x 18.8)ER (14.0 x 10.4)
Cranes: 1x45t,1x40t
Ice Capable
1 oil engine reduction geared to sc. shaft driving 1 CP propeller
Total Power: 9,730kW (13,229hp) 19.6kn
MAN-B&W 7L58/64CD
1 x 4 Stroke 7 Cy. 580 x 640 9730kW (13229bhp)
MAN B&W Diesel AG-Augsburg
AuxGen: 3 x 570kW 60Hz a.c, 1 x 550kW 450V 60Hz a.c
Thrusters: 1 Tunnel thruster (f)
Fuel: 1639.0 (r.f.)

9491599 *A8RJ8* -
VEGA SCORPIO
ms 'Vega Scorpio' Schifffahrtsgesellschaft GmbH & Co KG
Vega-Reederei Friedrich Dauber GmbH & Co KG
Monrovia *Liberia*
MMSI: 636091665
Official number: 91665
9,999 4,900 11,768
Class: BV (GL)
2010-06 Yangfan Group Co Ltd — Zhoushan ZJ Yd No: 2094
Loa 139.10 (BB) Br ex - Dght 8.800
Lbp 129.00 Br md 22.60 Dpth -
Welded, 1 dk
(A33A2CC) Container Ship (Fully Cellular)
TEU 957 incl 256 ref C
Compartments: 4 Cell Ho, ER
Cranes: 2x45t
Ice Capable
1 oil engine reduction geared to sc. shaft driving 1 CP propeller
Total Power: 9,600kW (13,052hp) 18.1kn
MAN-B&W 8L48/60B
1 x 4 Stroke 8 Cy. 480 x 600 9600kW (13052bhp)
MAN B&W Diesel AG-Augsburg
AuxGen: 1 x 2000kW 440V a.c, 2 x 900kW 440V a.c
Thrusters: 1 Tunnel thruster (a); 1 Tunnel thruster (f)

9330240 *D5EV6* -
VEGA SIGMA
ex Orinoco River *-2013*
Vega Beteiligungsgesellschaft Sigma mbH & Co KG
Vega-Reederei Friedrich Dauber GmbH & Co KG
Monrovia *Liberia*
MMSI: 636092527
Official number: 92527
9,940 5,020 13,689 T/cm 28.0
Class: GL
2007-12 Qingshan Shipyard — Wuhan HB Yd No: 20040313
Loa 147.84 (BB) Br ex 23.45 Dght 8.510
Lbp 140.30 Br md 23.25 Dpth 11.50
Welded, 1 dk
(A33A2CC) Container Ship (Fully Cellular)
Grain: 15,990; Bale: 15,990
TEU 1118 C Ho 334 TEU C Dk 784 incl 240 ref C
Compartments: 5 Cell Ho, ER
Cranes: 1x45t,1x40t
1 oil engine reduction geared to sc. shaft driving 1 CP propeller
Total Power: 9,730kW (13,229hp) 19.6kn
MAN-B&W 7L58/64
1 x 4 Stroke 7 Cy. 580 x 640 9730kW (13229bhp)
MAN B&W Diesel AG-Augsburg
AuxGen: 3 x 570kW 60Hz a.c, 1 x 2000kW 60Hz a.c
Thrusters: 1 Thwart. FP thruster (f)
Fuel: 199.8 (d.f.) 1140.0 (r.f.)

9629407 *3FPM7* -
VEGA SKY
Chijin Shipping SA
Kambara Kisen Co Ltd
Panama *Panama*
MMSI: 351664000
Official number: 4487113
9,996 4,492 12,587
Class: GL NV
2013-05 Tsuneishi Group (Zhoushan) Shipbuilding Inc — Daishan County ZJ Yd No: SS-130
Loa 142.98 (BB) Br ex - Dght 7.400
Lbp 140.00 Br md 22.60 Dpth 11.30
Welded, 1 dk
(A33A2CC) Container Ship (Fully Cellular)
TEU 1000
1 oil engine driving 1 FP propeller
Total Power: 8,580kW (11,665hp) 18.6kn
MAN-B&W 6S50MC
1 x 2 Stroke 6 Cy. 500 x 1910 8580kW (11665bhp)
Mitsui Engineering & Shipbuilding CLtd-Japan
AuxGen: 3 x a.c
Thrusters: 1 Tunnel thruster (f)

9235476 *H9LO* -
VEGA SPRING
ex Iver Spring *-2005*
Inter-Breeze International SA
Handytankers K/S
Panama *Panama*
MMSI: 354986000
Official number: 2814201C
15,042 6,073 22,780 T/cm 32.7
Class: NK
2001-09 Kitanihon Zosen K.K. — Hachinohe Yd No: 330
Loa 153.20 (BB) Br ex 25.03 Dght 10.017
Lbp 144.00 Br md 25.00 Dpth 15.20
Welded, 1 dk
(A12B2TR) Chemical/Products Tanker
Double Hull (13F)
Liq: 25,760; Liq (Oil): 26,891
Compartments: 10 Wing Ta, 2 Wing Slop Ta, ER
10 Cargo Pump (s): 10x500m³/hr
Manifold: Bow/CM: 73.9m
1 oil engine driving 1 FP propeller
Total Power: 7,081kW (9,627hp) 14.5kn
Mitsubishi 6UEC52LA
1 x 2 Stroke 6 Cy. 520 x 1600 7081kW (9627bhp)
Akasaka Tekkosho KK (Akasaka DieselLtd)-Japan
AuxGen: 3 x 550kW a.c
Fuel: 141.0 (d.f.) (Heating Coils) 1318.0 (r.f.)

IMO / Call sign	Name / Owner / Manager / Flag	Tonnage	Class	Builder / Dimensions	Type / Cargo	Machinery
9384203 *A8NA8* -	**VEGA STAR** **Vela International Marine Ltd** - SatCom: Inmarsat Mini-M 764852576 *Monrovia* *Liberia* MMSI: 636013448 Official number: 13448	**162,252** 111,896 319,429 T/cm 178.7	Class: LR ✠ **100A1** SS 06/2013 Double Hull oil tanker ESP **ShipRight** (SDA, FDA Plus, CM) LI *IWS SPM ✠ **LMC** **UMS IGS** Eq.Ltr: E*; Cable: 770.0/117.0 U3 (a)	**2008-06 Daewoo Shipbuilding & Marine Engineering Co Ltd — Geoje** Yd No: 5303 Loa 333.00 (BB) Br ex 60.04 Dght 22.524 Lbp 320.00 Br md 60.00 Dpth 30.50 Welded, 1 dk	**(A13A2TV) Crude Oil Tanker** Double Hull (13F) Liq: 340,988; Liq (Oil): 340,988 Compartments: 5 Ta, 10 Wing Ta, 2 Wing Slop Ta, ER 3 Cargo Pump (s): 3x5500m³/hr Manifold: Bow/CM: 164.2m	**1 oil engine** driving 1 FP propeller Total Power: 29,340kW (39,891hp) 15.3kn MAN-B&W 6S90MC-C 1 x 2 Stroke 6 Cy. 900 x 3188 29340kW (39891bhp) Doosan Engine Co Ltd-South Korea AuxGen: 2 x 1600kW 450V 60Hz a.c, 1 x 1400kW 450V 60Hz a.c Boilers: e (ex.g.) 27.5kgf/cm² (27.0bar), WTAuxB (o.f.) 22.4kgf/cm² (22.0bar) Fuel: 360.0 (d.f.) 7778.4 (r.f.)
9061588 *XVFR* -	**VEGA STAR** *ex Little Lady P -2003 ex Ken Ei -2000* **Vietnam Ocean Shipping JSC (VOSCO) (Cong Ty Co Phan Van Tai Bien Viet Nam)** - SatCom: Inmarsat A 1346317 *Haiphong* *Vietnam* MMSI: 574304000 Official number: VN-1683-VT	**13,713** 7,721 22,035	Class: NK VR	**1994-05 Saiki Heavy Industries Co Ltd — Saiki OT** (Hull) Yd No: 1032 **1994-05 Onomichi Dockyard Co Ltd — Onomichi HS** Yd No: 379 Loa 157.50 (BB) Br ex - Dght 9.109 Lbp 148.00 Br md 25.00 Dpth 12.70 Welded, 1 dk	**(A21A2BC) Bulk Carrier** Grain: 29,254; Bale: 28,299 Compartments: 4 Ho, ER 4 Ha: (20.0 x 17.5)3 (20.8 x 17.5)ER Cranes: 4x30t	**1 oil engine** driving 1 FP propeller Total Power: 5,296kW (7,200hp) 14.0kn Mitsubishi 6UEC45LA 1 x 2 Stroke 6 Cy. 450 x 1350 5296kW (7200bhp) Akasaka Tekkosho KK (Akasaka DieselLtd)-Japan Fuel: 925.0 (r.f.)
9358539 *A8IH4* -	**VEGA STOCKHOLM** **ms 'Vega Stockholm' Schiffahrts GmbH & Co KG** Vega-Reederei Friedrich Dauber GmbH & Co KG *Monrovia* *Liberia* MMSI: 636090978 Official number: 90978	**7,464** 3,097 8,306 T/cm 22.0	Class: BV (GL)	**2006-12 Fujian Mawei Shipbuilding Ltd — Fuzhou FJ** Yd No: 437-19 Loa 129.62 (BB) Br ex - Dght 7.400 Lbp 120.34 Br md 20.60 Dpth 10.80 Welded, 1 dk	**(A33A2CC) Container Ship (Fully Cellular)** Double Bottom Entire Compartment Length TEU 698 C Ho 226 TEU C Dk 472 TEU incl 120 ref C. Compartments: 4 Cell Ho, ER 4 Ha: (12.5 x 15.8)2 (25.4 x 15.8)ER (6.4 x 10.7) Ice Capable	**1 oil engine** reduction geared to sc. shaft driving 1 CP propeller Total Power: 7,200kW (9,789hp) 15.9kn MaK 8M43C 1 x 4 Stroke 8 Cy. 430 x 610 7200kW (9789bhp) Caterpillar Motoren GmbH & Co. KG-Germany AuxGen: 1 x 1000kW 450/230V a.c, 3 x 450kW 450/230V a.c Thrusters: 1 Tunnel thruster (f)
9493731 *A8SY3* -	**VEGA TAURUS** **ms 'Vega Taurus' Schifffahrtsgesellschaft mbH & Co KG** Vega-Reederei Friedrich Dauber GmbH & Co KG *Monrovia* *Liberia* MMSI: 636091792 Official number: 91792	**33,044** 19,231 57,000 T/cm 58.8	Class: BV	**2010-07 Taizhou Kouan Shipbuilding Co Ltd — Taizhou JS** Yd No: KA103 Loa 189.99 (BB) Br ex - Dght 12.800 Lbp 185.00 Br md 32.26 Dpth 18.00 Welded, 1 dk	**(A21A2BC) Bulk Carrier** Grain: 71,634; Bale: 70,557 Compartments: 5 Ho, ER 5 Ha: ER Cranes: 4x30t	**1 oil engine** driving 1 FP propeller Total Power: 9,960kW (13,542hp) 14.6kn MAN-B&W 6S50MC-C 1 x 2 Stroke 6 Cy. 500 x 2000 9960kW (13542bhp) STX Engine Co Ltd-South Korea AuxGen: 3 x 600kW 450V 60Hz a.c
9192040 *V2BG8* -	**VEGA TOPAS** *ex Cape Coldbek -2004* **FHH Fonds Nr 25 ms 'Vega Topas' GmbH & Co Containerschiff KG** Vega-Reederei Friedrich Dauber GmbH & Co KG *Saint John's* *Antigua & Barbuda* MMSI: 304693000	**9,030** 4,222 10,968 T/cm 25.1	Class: BV (GL)	**1999-04 Xiamen Shipyard — Xiamen FJ** Yd No: MX438G Loa 135.65 (BB) Br ex - Dght 8.635 Lbp 125.00 Br md 22.50 Dpth 11.20 Welded, 1 dk	**(A33A2CC) Container Ship (Fully Cellular)** Grain: 15,554 TEU 834 C Ho 286 TEU C Dk 548 TEU incl 80 ref C. Compartments: 5 Cell Ho, ER 5 Ha: ER Ice Capable	**1 oil engine** driving 1 FP propeller Total Power: 7,900kW (10,741hp) 18.5kn MAN-B&W 5S50MC-C 1 x 2 Stroke 5 Cy. 500 x 2000 7900kW (10741bhp) Hudong Heavy Machinery Co Ltd-China AuxGen: 3 x 760kW 440V 60Hz a.c Thrusters: 1 Thwart. FP thruster (f) Fuel: 83.8 (d.f.) (Heating Coils) 902.9 (r.f.) 28.0pd
9259343 *HPNF* -	**VEGA TRADER** **Cedar Shipping Navigation SA** Mitsui OSK Lines Ltd (MOL) SatCom: Inmarsat C 435183710 *Panama* *Panama* MMSI: 351837000 Official number: 2944103B	**159,813** 97,102 299,985 T/cm 180.0	Class: NK	**2003-09 Universal Shipbuilding Corp — Nagasu KM (Ariake Shipyard)** Yd No: 4996 Loa 332.98 (BB) Br ex 60.04 Dght 20.808 Lbp 320.00 Br md 60.00 Dpth 29.40 Welded, 1 dk	**(A13A2TV) Crude Oil Tanker** Double Hull (13F) Liq: 334,448; Liq (Oil): 334,448 Compartments: 5 Ta, 10 Wing Ta, ER 4 Cargo Pump (s): 3x5000m³/hr, 1x2500m³/hr Manifold: Bow/CM: 163.6m	**1 oil engine** driving 1 FP propeller Total Power: 27,160kW (36,927hp) 15.8kn MAN-B&W 7S80MC-C 1 x 2 Stroke 7 Cy. 800 x 3200 27160kW (36927bhp) Hitachi Zosen Corp-Japan AuxGen: 3 x a.c Fuel: 606.0 (d.f.) 6863.0 (r.f.)
9204116 *V2AP2* -	**VEGA TURMALIN** *ex MOL Fortitude -2009* *ex P&O Nedlloyd Malindi -2005 ex Leo J -2002* **FHH Fonds Nr 21 ms 'Vega Turmalin' GmbH & Co Containerschiff KG** Vega-Reederei Friedrich Dauber GmbH & Co KG SatCom: Inmarsat B 330454310 *Saint John's* *Antigua & Barbuda* MMSI: 304010932 Official number: 3500	**12,004** 6,750 14,065	Class: BV (GL)	**1999-06 Tianjin Xingang Shipyard — Tianjin** Yd No: 320 Loa 149.15 (BB) Br ex - Dght 9.700 Lbp 140.50 Br md 23.10 Dpth 13.20 Welded, 1 dk	**(A33A2CC) Container Ship (Fully Cellular)** Grain: 19,772 TEU 1116 C Dk 458 TEU C Dk 658 TEU incl 196 ref C. Compartments: 5 Cell Ho, ER 7 Ha: Cranes: 2x45t Ice Capable	**1 oil engine** driving 1 FP propeller Total Power: 10,880kW (14,792hp) 19.0kn Sulzer 8RTA48T-B 1 x 2 Stroke 8 Cy. 480 x 2000 10880kW (14792bhp) Hudong Heavy Machinery Co Ltd-China AuxGen: 3 x 740kW 440V 60Hz a.c Thrusters: 1 Thwart. FP thruster (f)
9497426 *A8UN6* -	**VEGA VENUS** **ms 'Vega Venus' Schifffahrtsgesellschaft mbH & Co KG** Vega-Reederei Friedrich Dauber GmbH & Co KG SatCom: Inmarsat C 463709763 *Monrovia* *Liberia* MMSI: 636091918 Official number: 91918	**19,994** 10,883 31,754 T/cm 42.6	Class: BV (GL)	**2011-03 Fujian Mawei Shipbuilding Ltd — Fuzhou FJ** Yd No: 451-5 Loa 177.43 (BB) Br ex - Dght 10.200 Lbp 169.02 Br md 28.20 Dpth 14.20 Welded, 1 dk	**(A21A2BC) Bulk Carrier** Grain: 42,700 Compartments: 5 Ho, ER 5 Ha: (19.2 x 16.8)ER (19.4 x 15.2) Cranes: 4x30t	**1 oil engine** driving 1 FP propeller Total Power: 6,300kW (8,565hp) 13.7kn Mitsubishi 6UEC43LSII 1 x 2 Stroke 6 Cy. 430 x 1500 6300kW (8565bhp) Yichang Marine Diesel Engine Co Ltd-China AuxGen: 3 x 500kW 450V 60Hz a.c
9491604 *A8RJ9* -	**VEGA VIRGO** **ms 'Vega Virgo' Schifffahrtsgesellschaft GmbH & Co KG** Vega-Reederei Friedrich Dauber GmbH & Co KG *Monrovia* *Liberia* MMSI: 636091666 Official number: 91666	**9,999** 4,900 11,768	Class: BV GL	**2011-10 Yangfan Group Co Ltd — Zhoushan ZJ** Yd No: 2095 Loa 139.26 (BB) Br ex - Dght 8.800 Lbp 129.00 Br md 22.60 Dpth 11.80 Welded, 1 dk	**(A33A2CC) Container Ship (Fully Cellular)** TEU 957 incl 256 ref C Compartments: 4 Cell Ho, ER Cranes: 2x45t	**1 oil engine** reduction geared to sc. shaft driving 1 CP propeller Total Power: 9,600kW (13,052hp) 18.1kn MAN-B&W 8L48/60B 1 x 4 Stroke 8 Cy. 480 x 600 9600kW (13052bhp) MAN B&W Diesel AG-Augsburg AuxGen: 2 x 910kW a.c, 1 x 2000kW a.c Thrusters: 1 Tunnel thruster (f); 1 Tunnel thruster (a)
9256468 *C6FV3* -	**VEGA VOYAGER** **CM Pacific Maritime Corp** Chevron Tankers Ltd *Nassau* *Bahamas* MMSI: 311486000 Official number: 9000060	**58,088** 30,727 104,864 T/cm 91.2	Class: AB	**2003-11 Samsung Heavy Industries Co Ltd — Geoje** Yd No: 1417 Loa 243.54 (BB) Br ex - Dght 14.772 Lbp 234.88 Br md 42.00 Dpth 21.30 Welded, 1 dk	**(A13A2TV) Crude Oil Tanker** Double Hull (13F) Liq: 113,314; Liq (Oil): 120,000 Cargo Heating Coils Compartments: 12 Wing Ta, 2 Wing Slop Ta, ER 3 Cargo Pump (s): 3x2800m³/hr Manifold: Bow/CM: 120.4m	**1 oil engine** driving 1 FP propeller Total Power: 13,549kW (18,421hp) 14.5kn B&W 6S60MC-C 1 x 2 Stroke 6 Cy. 600 x 2400 13549kW (18421bhp) Doosan Engine Co Ltd-South Korea AuxGen: 3 x 740kW a.c Fuel: 163.0 (d.f.) 3512.2 (r.f.)
9385439 *A8KR3* -	**VEGA ZIRKON** *ex X-Press Monte Bianco -2008* *launched as Vega Zirkon -2007* **ms 'Vega Zirkon' Schifffahrtsgesellschaft mbH & Co KG** Vega-Reederei Friedrich Dauber GmbH & Co KG *Monrovia* *Liberia* MMSI: 636091207 Official number: 91207	**7,170** 3,068 8,524	Class: BV	**2007-04 Yangfan Group Co Ltd — Zhoushan ZJ** Yd No: 2043 Loa 132.70 (BB) Br ex - Dght 7.650 Lbp 121.00 Br md 19.20 Dpth 10.50 Welded, 1 dk	**(A33A2CC) Container Ship (Fully Cellular)** TEU 706 incl 118 ref C. Compartments: 3 Cell Ho, ER 3 Ha: 2 (25.2 x 16.0)ER (12.6 x 10.8)	**1 oil engine** reduction geared to sc. shaft driving 1 CP propeller Total Power: 6,300kW (8,565hp) 17.0kn MaK 7M43C 1 x 4 Stroke 7 Cy. 430 x 610 6300kW (8565bhp) Caterpillar Motoren GmbH & Co. KG-Germany AuxGen: 1 x 1200kW 400/220V 50Hz a.c, 2 x 450kW 400/220V 50Hz a.c Thrusters: 1 Tunnel thruster (f)

IMO / Call sign / Fishing no.	Name / Owner	Tonnage	Class	Builder / Dimensions	Type / Cargo	Machinery
9317808 *PBHV* -	**VEGADIEP** *ex* UAL Ghana *-2012* *ex* Osc Vegadiep *-2011* *ex* UAL Coburg *-2010* **Beheermaatschappij ms Vegadiep BV** Feederlines BV *Groningen* *Netherlands* MMSI: 245579000 Official number: 42794	**5,057** 2,681 7,763	Class: LR ✠ **100A1** SS 02/2010 strengthened for heavy cargoes, container cargoes in all holds and on upper deck hatch covers Ice Class 1A (Finnish-Swedish Ice Class Rules 1985) at 7.20m draught Max/min draught fwd 7.20/1.837m Max/min draught aft 7.20/4.367m Power required 2864kw, installed 3840kw ✠ **LMC** **UMS** Eq.Ltr: W; Cable: 550.0/44.0 U3 (a)	**2005-02 ATVT Sudnobudivnyi Zavod "Zaliv" — Kerch** (Hull) Yd No: (643) **2005-02 Bodewes' Scheepswerven B.V. — Hoogezand** Yd No: 643 Loa 119.98 (BB) Br ex 15.43 Dght 7.050 Lbp 113.65 Br md 15.20 Dpth 8.50 Welded, 1 dk	**(A31A2GX) General Cargo Ship** Grain: 9,415 TEU 390 C Ho 174 TEU C Dk 216 TEU Compartments: 2 Ho, 2 Tw Dk, ER 2 Ha: ER Cranes: 2x60t Ice Capable	**1 oil engine** with clutches, flexible couplings & sr geared to sc. shaft driving 1 CP propeller Total Power: 3,840kW (5,221hp) 14.0kn MaK 8M32C 1 x 4 Stroke 8 Cy. 320 x 480 3840kW (5221bhp) Caterpillar Motoren GmbH & Co. KG-Germany AuxGen: 1 x 400kW 400V 50Hz a.c, 3 x 290kW 400V 50Hz a.c Boilers: TOH (ex.g.) 10.2kgf/cm² (10.0bar), TOH (o.f.) 10.2kgf/cm² (10.0bar) Thrusters: 1 Thwart. CP thruster (f)
8706208 *A8RM3* -	**VEGAS** *ex* Overseas Vega *-2009* *ex* Vega *-2006* **Sheridan Management Inc** Delfi SA *Monrovia* *Liberia* MMSI: 636014125 Official number: 14125	**22,972** 12,995 39,710 T/cm 44.9	Class: BV (AB)	**1989-06 Hyundai Heavy Industries Co Ltd — Ulsan** Yd No: 611 Loa 185.96 (BB) Br ex 27.46 Dght 12.219 Lbp 177.00 Br md 27.43 Dpth 17.00 Welded, 1 dk	**(A13A2TW) Crude/Oil Products Tanker** Double Sides Entire Compartment Length Liq: 45,124; Liq (Oil): 47,059 Compartments: 7 Ta, 2 Wing Slop Ta, ER 4 Cargo Pump (s): 4x1000m³/hr Manifold: Bow/CM: 94.5m	**1 oil engine** driving 1 FP propeller Total Power: 7,967kW (10,832hp) 14.0kn MAN-B&W 6S50MC 1 x 2 Stroke 6 Cy. 500 x 1910 7967kW (10832bhp) Hyundai Heavy Industries Co Ltd-South Korea AuxGen: 3 x 500kW a.c Fuel: 145.1 (d.f.) 1297.1 (r.f.)
8226583 *ZR2743* PQ 750	**VEGKOP** - **Foodcorp (Pty) Ltd** - *Cape Town* *South Africa* MMSI: 601821000 Official number: 350723	*150* 45 -		**1974 Dorman Long Swan Hunter (Pty.) Ltd. — Cape Town** Loa - Br ex - Dght - Lbp 27.21 Br md 7.10 Dpth 3.28 Welded	**(B11B2FV) Fishing Vessel**	**1 oil engine** driving 1 FP propeller Total Power: 353kW (480hp) 12.0kn Caterpillar 3408TA 1 x Vee 4 Stroke 8 Cy. 137 x 152 353kW (480bhp) Caterpillar Tractor Co-USA
9111711 *LHLH* -	**VEGTIND** - **Torghatten Trafikkselskap AS** - *Bronnoysund* *Norway* MMSI: 257133600	**210** 65 18	Class: (NV)	**1994-12 Rosendal Verft AS — Rosendal** Yd No: 264 Loa 29.00 Br ex 8.20 Dght 1.400 Lbp 27.22 Br md 8.00 Dpth 3.05 Welded, 1 dk	**(A37B2PS) Passenger Ship** Hull Material: Aluminium Alloy Passengers: unberthed: 100	**2 oil engines** geared to sc. shafts driving 2 FP propellers Total Power: 1,878kW (2,554hp) 32.0kn Mitsubishi S12R-MPTA 2 x Vee 4 Stroke 12 Cy. 170 x 180 each-939kW (1277bhp) Mitsubishi Heavy Industries Ltd-Japan AuxGen: 2 x 52kW a.c Fuel: 3.0 (d.f.)
8818427 - -	**VEGUETA** - **Sindicato Pesquero del Peru SA (SIPESA)** - *Pisco* *Peru* Official number: PS-006243-PM	*274* 124 266		**1991 Factoria Naval S.A. — Callao** Yd No: 08 Loa 33.55 Br ex 7.85 Dght - Lbp - Br md 7.70 Dpth 4.00 Welded	**(B11B2FV) Fishing Vessel**	**1 oil engine** with clutches, flexible couplings & dr reverse geared to sc. shaft driving 1 FP propeller Total Power: 420kW (571hp) Caterpillar 3508TA 1 x Vee 4 Stroke 8 Cy. 170 x 190 420kW (571bhp) Caterpillar Inc-USA
9525443 *ECLD* -	**VEHINTICINCO** - **Santander Lease SA EFC (Bansalease SA)** Remolques Unidos SL *Santander* *Spain* MMSI: 224943140	**428** 128 100	Class: BV	**2010-07 Astilleros Armon SA — Navia** Yd No: 689 Loa 31.50 Br ex - Dght 4.600 Lbp 27.30 Br md 11.20 Dpth 5.40 Welded, 1 dk	**(B32A2ST) Tug**	**2 oil engines** reduction geared to sc. shafts driving 2 Directional propellers Total Power: 5,050kW (6,866hp) 12.0kn Caterpillar 3516C 2 x Vee 4 Stroke 16 Cy. 170 x 215 each-2525kW (3433bhp) Caterpillar Inc-USA AuxGen: 2 x 86kW 50Hz a.c Thrusters: 1 Tunnel thruster (f)
9525431 *ECPB* -	**VEHINTICUATRO** - **Santander Lease SA EFC (Bansalease SA)** Remolques Unidos SL *Santander* *Spain* MMSI: 224230000	**428** 128 413	Class: BV	**2010-02 Astilleros Armon SA — Navia** Yd No: 688 Loa 32.50 Br ex - Dght 4.400 Lbp 27.30 Br md 11.20 Dpth 5.40 Welded, 1 dk	**(B32A2ST) Tug**	**2 oil engines** reduction geared to sc. shafts driving 2 Directional propellers Total Power: 5,050kW (6,866hp) 12.0kn Caterpillar 3516C 2 x Vee 4 Stroke 16 Cy. 170 x 215 each-2525kW (3433bhp) Caterpillar Inc-USA Thrusters: 1 Tunnel thruster (f)
9664079 *EAFS* -	**VEHINTISIETE** - **Remolques Unidos SL** - *Santander* *Spain* MMSI: 225442000	**440** - -	Class: GL	**2013-03 Astilleros Armon SA — Navia** Yd No: 710 Loa 33.00 Br ex - Dght 4.400 Lbp 27.00 Br md 11.20 Dpth 5.40 Welded, 1 dk	**(B32A2ST) Tug**	**2 oil engines** reduction geared to sc. shafts driving 2 Directional propellers Total Power: 4,480kW (6,092hp) M.T.U. 16V4000M63L 2 x Vee 4 Stroke 16 Cy. 170 x 210 each-2240kW (3046bhp) MTU Friedrichshafen GmbH-Friedrichshafen
9152894 *LIKG* M-6-HO	**VEIDAR 1** *ex* Leinefisk *-2010* **Veidar AS** - *Aalesund* *Norway* MMSI: 259380000	**879** 263 416	Class: NV	**1996-12 Solstrand AS — Tomrefjord** Yd No: 60 Loa 43.20 (BB) Br ex - Dght 4.150 Lbp 39.55 Br md 10.50 Dpth 7.10 Welded, 1 dk	**(B11B2FV) Fishing Vessel** Ins: 480 Ice Capable	**1 oil engine** reduction geared to sc. shaft driving 1 FP propeller Total Power: 1,118kW (1,520hp) 12.8kn Caterpillar 3512TA 1 x Vee 4 Stroke 12 Cy. 170 x 190 1118kW (1520bhp) Caterpillar Inc-USA AuxGen: 2 x 240kW 230/380V 50Hz a.c Thrusters: 1 Thwart. FP thruster (f)
8959116 *LFPA* R-69-K	**VEIDING** *ex* Veavik *-1996* *ex* Vesthavn *-1996* **Veiding AS** - *Haugesund* *Norway* MMSI: 257816500	**178** 53 -		**1969-06 Bolsones Verft AS — Molde** Yd No: 222 Loa 26.25 Br ex - Dght 3.050 Lbp - Br md 6.10 Dpth 5.23 Welded, 1 dk	**(B12D2FR) Fishery Research Vessel**	**1 oil engine** driving 1 FP propeller Total Power: 313kW (426hp) 10.0kn Caterpillar 1 x 4 Stroke 313kW (426bhp) Caterpillar Tractor Co-USA
9255086 *LLSD* -	**VEIDNES** - **Polarsild AS** - *Sandnessjoen* *Norway* MMSI: 259237000	**695** 237 650		**2002-07 AS Rigas Kugu Buvetava (Riga Shipyard) — Riga** (Hull) **2002-07 Sletta Baatbyggeri AS — Mjosundet** Yd No: 98 Loa 41.60 (BB) Br ex - Dght 4.850 Lbp 37.00 Br md 9.70 Dpth 5.10 Welded, 1 dk	**(B12C2FL) Live Fish Carrier (Well Boat)** Liq: 650	**1 oil engine** driving 1 CP propeller Total Power: 1,324kW (1,800hp) A.B.C. 6DZC 1 x 4 Stroke 6 Cy. 256 x 310 1324kW (1800bhp) Anglo Belgian Corp NV (ABC)-Belgium AuxGen: 1 x 350kW Thrusters: 1 Tunnel thruster (f)
6812493 *JWZZ* SF-73-F	**VEIVAG** *ex* Skjongholm Junior *-2011* *ex* Skjongholm *-2010* *ex* Skjongholm Junior *-1995* *ex* Nesbakk *-1995* *ex* Geir *-1978* **Britt Janne AS** - *Floro* *Norway* MMSI: 258258000	**176** 70 -		**1968 Fiskerstrand Slip & Mek. Verksted AS — Fiskarstrand** Yd No: 11 Loa 26.65 Br ex 6.74 Dght - Lbp 22.51 Br md 6.71 Dpth 3.51 Welded, 1 dk & S dk	**(B11B2FV) Fishing Vessel**	**1 oil engine** driving 1 FP propeller Total Power: 324kW (441hp) 10.5kn Alpha 404-26VO 1 x 2 Stroke 4 Cy. 260 x 400 324kW (441bhp) Alpha Diesel A/S-Denmark
9640346 - -	**VEJUNAS** - **Government of The Republic of Lithuania (Ministry of Environment)** - *Klaipeda* *Lithuania*	**160** - -		**2012-02 Baltic Workboats AS — Kaarma** Yd No: 90093 Loa 23.90 Br ex 8.20 Dght 1.500 Lbp - Br md 8.00 Dpth 3.40 Welded, 1 dk	**(B31A2SR) Research Survey Vessel**	**2 oil engines** reduction geared to sc. shaft (s) driving 2 Propellers Total Power: 604kW (822hp) 12.0kn Agco Sisu Diesel 84CTA 2 x 4 Stroke 6 Cy. 111 x 145 each-302kW (411bhp) AGCO Sisu Power Inc-Finland Thrusters: 1 Tunnel thruster (f)
8504088 *OITM* -	**VEKARA** *ex* Sami-Petteri *-1985* **Mopro Oy** - *Savonlinna* *Finland* MMSI: 230325000 Official number: 10573	**1,656** 712 2,700		**1979 Oy Navire Ab — Naantali** Yd No: 67 Converted From: General Cargo Barge, Non-propelled-1985 Loa 80.70 Br ex 12.60 Dght 4.350 Lbp 77.70 Br md 12.40 Dpth 5.01 Welded, 1 dk	**(A35D2RL) Landing Craft** Bow door/ramp Grain: 3,050 Compartments: 1 Ho, ER 1 Ha: ER	**2 oil engines** with clutches, flexible couplings & sr reverse geared to sc. shafts driving 2 FP propellers Total Power: 808kW (1,098hp) Wizeman WM424LT 2 x Vee 4 Stroke 12 Cy. 142 x 128 each-404kW (549bhp) J. Wizemann GmbH & Co.-Remseck Thrusters: 1 Thwart. FP thruster (f)

8104539 **VELA** **1,939** Class: (GL)
J7CB3 *ex Diadem -2009 ex Helm Trader -2004* 885
\- *ex Tramp -2004 ex Breitenburg -2004* 2,890
ex Keitum -1995 ex Jule -1994
ex Balder -1993 ex Jule -1988
Vela Sky Shipping Co Ltd
Atrica-Marine Ltd
Portsmouth *Dominica*
MMSI: 325529000

1982-01 J.J. Sietas KG Schiffswerft GmbH & Co. — Hamburg Yd No: 873
Loa 87.97 (BB) Br ex 11.33 Dght 4.671
Lbp 85.30 Br md 11.31 Dpth 4.88
Welded, 2 dks

(A31A2GX) General Cargo Ship
Grain: 3,806; Bale: 3,781
TEU 90 C.Ho 54/20' C.Dk 36/20'
Compartments: 1 Ho, ER
1 Ha: (55.9 x 9.3)ER

1 oil engine sr reverse geared to sc. shaft driving 1 FP propeller
Total Power: 735kW (999hp) 11.5kn
Deutz SBV8M628
1 x 4 Stroke 8 Cy. 240 x 280 735kW (999bhp)
Kloeckner Humboldt Deutz AG-West Germany
AuxGen: 2 x 152kW 220/380V 50Hz a.c
Thrusters: 1 Thwart. FP thruster (f)
Fuel: 45.0 (d.f.) 140.0 (r.f.) 5.0pd

8742513 **VELA** **225** Class: (RS)
J8Y2469 *ex Alla -2013 ex Aria -2010* 67
\- *ex Murphy's Law -2010 ex Marilyn -2010* 47
ex Janet -2010
Olvia Shipping Ltd
Kaalbye Yacht LLC
Kingstown *St Vincent & The Grenadines*
MMSI: 377681000
Official number: 4938

1987-12 Broward Marine Inc — Fort Lauderdale FL Yd No: 501
Loa 40.03 Br ex 6.44 Dght 1.160
Lbp 36.00 Br md 6.09 Dpth 2.98
Welded, 1 dk

(X11A2YP) Yacht
Hull Material: Aluminium Alloy

2 oil engines reduction geared to sc. shafts driving 2 FP propellers
Total Power: 2,060kW (2,800hp) 14.0kn
MAN D2862LE
2 x Vee 4 Stroke 12 Cy. 128 x 157 each-1030kW (1400bhp) (new engine 1987)
MAN Nutzfahrzeuge AG-Nuernberg

9047465 **VELA** *209* Class: (RP)
CUEB 84
LX-89-N **Sociedade de Pesca do Miradouro Lda** 314
\-
SatCom: Inmarsat C 426382810
Aveiro *Portugal*
MMSI: 263828000
Official number: A-3586-N

1992-06 Polyships S.A. — Vigo Yd No: 100005
Loa 30.10 Br ex 8.30 Dght 3.100
Lbp 26.00 Br md 8.00 Dpth 4.20
Bonded, 1 dk

(B11A2FS) Stern Trawler
Hull Material: Reinforced Plastic
Ins: 175

1 oil engine with clutches & sr geared to sc. shaft driving 1 CP propeller
Total Power: 519kW (706hp) 11.0kn
Caterpillar 3508TA
1 x Vee 4 Stroke 8 Cy. 170 x 190 519kW (706bhp)
Caterpillar Inc-USA

9573177 **VELA** **250** Class: LR
PP9310 75 ✠**100A1** SS 12/2010
\- **Saveiros Camuyrano - Servicos Maritimos SA** 112 tug, Brazilian coastal service
LMC **UMS**
Rio de Janeiro *Brazil* Eq.Ltr: F;
MMSI: 710007040 Cable: 275.0/19.0 U2 (a)
Official number: 3813879992

2010-12 Wilson, Sons SA — Guaruja (Hull) Yd No: 115
2010-12 B.V. Scheepswerf Damen — Gorinchem Yd No: 512239
Loa 24.55 Br ex 11.70 Dght 5.350
Lbp 20.80 Br md 10.70 Dpth 4.60
Welded, 1 dk

(B32A2ST) Tug

2 oil engines gearing integral to driving 2 Directional propellers
Total Power: 4,200kW (5,710hp)
Caterpillar 3516B
2 x Vee 4 Stroke 16 Cy. 170 x 190 each-2100kW (2855bhp)
Caterpillar Inc-USA
AuxGen: 2 x 59kW 220V 60Hz a.c

9330628 **VELA** **32,583** Class: NV
LACD7 *launched as Graiglas -2007* 18,070
\- **V Bulk KS** 53,565
Seven Seas Carriers AS T/cm
Bergen *Norway (NIS)* 57.3
MMSI: 258868000

2007-06 Nam Trieu Shipbuilding Industry Co. Ltd. — Haiphong Yd No: HR-53-NT01
Loa 190.00 (BB) Br ex - Dght 12.620
Lbp 183.25 Br md 32.26 Dpth 17.50
Welded, 1 dk

(A21A2BC) Bulk Carrier
Double Hull
Grain: 65,945; Bale: 64,626
Compartments: 5 Ho, ER
5 Ha: 4 (21.6 x 22.4)ER (19.2 x 20.8)
Cranes: 4x36t

1 oil engine driving 1 FP propeller
Total Power: 9,481kW (12,890hp) 14.2kn
MAN-B&W 6S50MC-C
1 x 2 Stroke 6 Cy. 500 x 2000 9481kW (12890bhp)
AuxGen: 3 x 680kW 440V 60Hz a.c
Fuel: 215.0 (d.f.) 2000.0 (r.f.) 34.5pd

8656817 **VELA 1** **928**
9LY2547 519
\- **Hoh Tel Eight Ltd** -
Seabird Ship Management Inc
Freetown *Sierra Leone*
MMSI: 667003350
Official number: SL103350

2007-07 Fuzhou Gaishan Shipyard — Fuzhou FJ
Loa 60.00 Br ex - Dght -
Lbp - Br md 11.80 Dpth 3.50
Welded, 1 dk

(B33A2DS) Suction Dredger

2 oil engines reduction geared to sc. shafts driving 2 Propellers
Total Power: 480kW (652hp)
Weifang WD618C
2 x 4 Stroke 6 Cy. 126 x 155 each-240kW (326bhp)
Weichai Power Co Ltd-China

8665167 **VELA 3** **1,489** Class: SL
\- *ex Hong Xiang 62 -2013* 878
\- **Charlie Three Ltd** -
\-
Quanzhou, Fujian *China*
Official number: CN20093133402

2009-12 Fujian Guo'an Shipbuilding Industry Co Ltd — Longhai FJ
Loa 70.50 Br ex - Dght -
Lbp 66.50 Br md 12.80 Dpth 4.60
Welded, 1 dk

(A31A2GX) General Cargo Ship

2 oil engines driving 2 Propellers
Total Power: 900kW (1,224hp)
Chinese Std. Type N6170ZLC
2 x 4 Stroke 6 Cy. 170 x 200 each-450kW (612bhp)
Ningbo CSI Power & Machinery GroupCo Ltd-China

8733990 **VELA GALLEGO DOS** **114**
EA3200 *ex Sigue Vela Gallego -2000* 34
3-CT-42-97 **Antonio, Gines & Jose Vela Gallego & Fernando Vela Garcia** -
\-
Cartagena *Spain*
Official number: 3-2/1997

1997 Nicolas Casas SL — Adra
Loa 24.00 Br ex - Dght 2.410
Lbp - Br md 6.40 Dpth 2.85
Bonded, 1 dk

(B11A2FS) Stern Trawler
Hull Material: Reinforced Plastic

1 oil engine driving 1 Propeller
Total Power: 160kW (218hp) 10.0kn

9480966 **VELA OCEAN** **30,006** Class: NK
S6RW4 *ex Pleasant Sky -2012* 18,486
\- **Diamond Star Shipping Pte Ltd** 53,549
Synergy Marine Pte Ltd T/cm
Singapore *Singapore* 55.3
MMSI: 566650000
Official number: 397896

2008-05 Iwagi Zosen Co Ltd — Kamijima EH Yd No: 296
Loa 189.90 Br ex - Dght 12.300
Lbp 182.00 Br md 32.26 Dpth 17.30
Welded, 1 dk

(A21A2BC) Bulk Carrier
Grain: 68,927; Bale: 65,526
Compartments: 5 Ho, ER
5 Ha: ER
Cranes: 4x30.5t

1 oil engine driving 1 FP propeller
Total Power: 9,480kW (12,889hp) 15.0kn
MAN-B&W 6S50MC-C
1 x 2 Stroke 6 Cy. 500 x 2000 9480kW (12889bhp)
Mitsui Engineering & Shipbuilding CLtd-Japan
AuxGen: 4 x 348kW a.c
Fuel: 2090.0

6708018 **VELAMEEN** *117* Class: IR
ATDT *ex Hessatral -1967* 51
\- **Government of The Republic of India (Director of Indo-Norwegian Project)** -
India
Official number: 1277

1960 Aukra Bruk AS — Aukra Yd No: 11
Loa 23.88 Br ex 6.20 Dght -
Lbp 21.01 Br md - Dpth 3.41
Welded, 1 dk

(B11A2FS) Stern Trawler
1 Ha: (1.9 x 1.4)

1 oil engine driving 1 FP propeller
Total Power: 353kW (480hp)
Caterpillar D379SCAC
1 x Vee 4 Stroke 8 Cy. 159 x 203 353kW (480bhp) (new engine 1966)
Caterpillar Tractor Co-USA

9455741 **VELEBIT** **30,638** Class: BV (NV)
9AA7659 15,286
\- **Fontana Shipping Co Ltd** 52,554
Tankerska Plovidba dd T/cm
Zadar *Croatia* 56.8
MMSI: 238295000

2011-04 '3 Maj' Brodogradiliste dd — Rijeka Yd No: 711
Loa 195.09 (BB) Br ex 32.24 Dght 12.500
Lbp 187.30 Br md 32.20 Dpth 17.80
Welded, 1 dk

(A12B2TR) Chemical/Products Tanker
Double Hull (13F)
Liq: 56,189; Liq (Oil): 56,189
Cargo Heating Coils
Compartments: 6 Wing Ta, 6 Wing Ta, 2 Wing Slop Ta, ER
12 Cargo Pump (s): 12x550m³/hr
Manifold: Bow/CM: 96.8m

1 oil engine driving 1 FP propeller
Total Power: 10,185kW (13,848hp) 14.0kn
Wartsila 7RTA48T
1 x 2 Stroke 7 Cy. 480 x 2000 10185kW (13848bhp)
'3 Maj' Motori i Dizalice dd-Croatia
AuxGen: 3 x 1190kW 450V 60Hz a.c
Fuel: 200.0 (d.f.) 1550.0 (r.f.)

7738503 **VELERO IV** *198*
WDD6435 134
\- **Velero IV Charters LLC**
\-
Seattle, WA *United States of America*
MMSI: 367172910
Official number: 255750

1948 National Iron Works — San Diego, Ca Yd No: 154
Converted From: Fishing Vessel-1972
Loa 33.53 Br ex - Dght 3.963
Lbp - Br md 8.23 Dpth -
Welded, 1 dk

(B12D2FR) Fishery Research Vessel

1 oil engine driving 1 FP propeller
Total Power: 441kW (600hp) 9.0kn

8724183 **VELES** **187** Class: (RS)
UAFI *ex Ostrovnoy -2014 ex Monino -2005* 56
\- *launched as PTR-50 No. 3 -1986* 95
Barenz-Francht Co Ltd
\-
Arkhangelsk *Russia*
Official number: 841690

1985-07 Astrakhanskaya Sudoverf im. "Kirova" — Astrakhan Yd No: 3
Loa 31.85 Br ex 7.08 Dght 2.220
Lbp 27.80 Br md 6.90 Dpth 3.15
Welded, 1 dk

(B12B2FC) Fish Carrier
Ins: 100

1 oil engine geared to sc. shaft driving 1 FP propeller
Total Power: 221kW (300hp) 10.2kn
Daldizel 6CHNSP18/22-300
1 x 4 Stroke 6 Cy. 180 x 220 221kW (300bhp)
Daldizel-Khabarovsk
AuxGen: 2 x 25kW
Fuel: 14.0 (d.f.)

8845676 **VELES** **448** Class: (RS)
HO3944 *ex Veles I -2005 ex Dayma -2005* 134
\- *ex Argus -2003 ex Tamara Shabashova -2001* 207
ex Beringovskiy -1999
Veles Co SA
\-
Panama *Panama*
MMSI: 371105000
Official number: 33280PEXT1

1991-06 Zavod 'Nikolayevsk-na-Amure' — Nikolayevsk-na-Amure Yd No: 1279
Loa 44.88 Br ex 9.47 Dght 3.770
Lbp 39.37 Br md 9.30 Dpth 5.13
Welded, 1 dk

(B11A2FS) Stern Trawler
Ins: 210
Ice Capable

1 oil engine driving 1 FP propeller
Total Power: 588kW (799hp) 11.5kn
S.K.L. 6NVD48A-2U
1 x 4 Stroke 6 Cy. 320 x 480 588kW (799bhp)
SKL Motoren u. Systemtechnik AG-Magdeburg
AuxGen: 3 x 150kW a.c

8857980 **VELES** **2,432** Class: UA
ERHA *ex City of Sochi -2000 ex Omskiy-25 -1992* 757
\- **Delf Services LLC** 3,060
Niesco Shipping Co Ltd (Nikolayev Association of External Economic Cooperation 'NIIKA')
SatCom: Inmarsat C 421400155
Moldova
MMSI: 214180801

1982 Krasnoyarskiy Sudostroitelnyy Zavod — Krasnoyarsk Yd No: 29
Loa 108.40 Br ex 15.00 Dght 3.000
Lbp - Br md 14.80 Dpth 5.00
Welded, 1 dk

(A31A2GX) General Cargo Ship

2 oil engines driving 2 FP propellers
Total Power: 522kW (710hp) 8.0kn
S.K.L. 6NVD48A-2U
2 x 4 Stroke 6 Cy. 320 x 480 each-261kW (355bhp)
VEB Schwermaschinenbau "KarlLiebknecht" (SKL)-Magdeburg

IMO / Call sign / Flag	Name / Owner	Tonnage	Class	Builder / Dimensions	Type / Capacity	Machinery
8118334 *UBFG7* -	**VELEZH** *ex* Moana *-2013* *ex* Tsunetoyo Maru *-2002* *ex* Tsunetoyo *-1981* **Blue Ribbon Co Ltd** - *Korsakov* *Russia* MMSI: 273345630	**1,120** 694 1,314	Class: RS	**1981-10 Kochi Jyuko (Kaisei Zosen) K.K. — Kochi** Yd No: 1485 Loa 67.31 Br ex - Dght 4.020 Lbp 64.01 Br md 11.51 Dpth 5.41 Welded, 1 dk	**(A31A2GX) General Cargo Ship**	**1 oil engine** driving 1 FP propeller Total Power: 736kW (1,001hp) 10.0kn Makita GNLH6275 1 x 4 Stroke 6 Cy. 275 x 450 736kW (1001bhp) Makita Diesel Co Ltd-Japan Fuel: 74.0
6524670 *LACY* -	**VELFJORD** - **Marine Harvest Norway AS** - *Bronnoysund* *Norway*	**153** 54	Class: (NV)	**1965 Sandnessjoen Slip & Mek. Verksted — Sandnessjoen** Yd No: 11 Loa 27.79 Br ex 8.03 Dght 2.509 Lbp 24.52 Br md 8.01 Dpth 3.31 Welded, 1 dk	**(A36A2PR) Passenger/Ro-Ro Ship (Vehicles)** Passengers: unberthed: 100 Cars: 9	**2 oil engines** geared to sc. shaft driving 1 FP propeller Total Power: 294kW (400hp) Volvo Penta TMD100A 2 x 4 Stroke 6 Cy. 121 x 140 each-147kW (200bhp) AB Volvo Penta-Sweden
8657483 *9AA7302* -	**VELI BRIJUN** - **Javna Ustanova Nacionalni Park Brijuni (Brijuni National Park)** - *Pula* *Croatia* Official number: 1T-211	**241** 111 -	Class: CS (Class contemplated)	**2010-09 Remontno Brodogradiliste Sibenik doo — Sibenik** Loa 29.80 Br ex - Dght 2.063 Lbp 27.00 Br md 8.00 Dpth 3.33 Welded, 1 dk	**(A37B2PS) Passenger Ship**	**2 oil engines** reduction geared to sc. shafts driving 2 FP propellers Total Power: 500kW (680hp) Isuzu UM6SD1TCX 1 x 4 Stroke 6 Cy. 118 x 145 250kW (340bhp) Isuzu Marine Seizo KK-Japan Isuzu UMSD1TCX 1 x 4 Stroke 6 Cy. 118 x 145 250kW (340bhp) Isuzu Marine Seizo KK-Japan
8139209 - -	**VELI KAPTAN** - **Munir Alp Kezer** - *Turkey* Official number: 4916	*226* 152 -		**1981 at Karadeniz Eregli** Loa - Br ex - Dght - Lbp 29.21 Br md 8.54 Dpth 2.60 Welded, 1 dk	**(A37B2PS) Passenger Ship**	**2 oil engines** driving 2 FP propellers Total Power: 216kW (294hp)
9630004 *D5FB3* -	**VELIKIY NOVGOROD** - **Boreray Shipping Ltd** OAO 'SOVCOMFLOT' (SCF Sovcomflot Group) *Monrovia* *Liberia* MMSI: 636016219 Official number: 16219	**113,876** 34,632 93,486	Class: LR RS ✠ **100A1** SS 01/2014 liquefied gas tanker, Ship Type 2G* methane in membrane tanks, maximum vapour pressure 0.25bar minimum temperature minus 163 degree C **ShipRight** (SDA, ACS (B)) *IWS LI ECO (BWT, GW, IHM, OW, P) ✠ **LMC** **UMS** Eq.Ltr: B*; Cable: 752.0/107.0 U3	**2014-01 STX Offshore & Shipbuilding Co Ltd — Changwon (Jinhae Shipyard)** Yd No: 1910 Loa 299.90 (BB) Br ex 45.80 Dght 12.500 Lbp 288.00 Br md 45.48 Dpth 26.00 Welded, 1 dk	**(A11A2TN) LNG Tanker** Double Hull Liq (Gas): 170,471 4 x Gas Tank (s); 4 membrane Gas Transport horizontal Ice Capable	**4 diesel electric oil engines** driving 2 gen. each 8700kW 6600V a.c 2 gen. each 7700kW 6600V a.c Connecting to 2 elec. motors each (11700kW) driving 2 FP propellers Total Power: 34,000kW (46,226hp) 19.5kn MAN-B&W 8L51/60DF 2 x 4 Stroke 8 Cy. 510 x 600 each-8000kW (10877bhp) STX Engine Co Ltd-South Korea MAN-B&W 9L51/60DF 2 x 4 Stroke 9 Cy. 510 x 600 each-9000kW (12236bhp) STX Engine Co Ltd-South Korea AuxGen: 1 x 1800kW 6600V 60Hz a.c Boilers: e (ex.g.) 10.7kgf/cm² (10.5bar)238°C , WTAuxB (o.f.) 11.2kgf/cm² (11.0bar) Thrusters: 1 Thwart. CP thruster (f) Fuel: 7121.0
6871499 *ESBB* -	**VELISE** *ex* Ipiki *-1992* **JSC Verneriin (OU Verneriin)** - *Tallinn* *Estonia* MMSI: 276100000 Official number: 199MB05	**333** 99 155	Class: (RS)	**1961 Sudostroitelnyy Zavod "Baltiya" — Klaypeda** Yd No: 214 Loa 43.59 Br ex 7.65 Dght 2.990 Lbp 39.05 Br md 7.60 Dpth 3.97 Welded, 1 dk	**(B11B2FV) Fishing Vessel** Bale: 214 Compartments: 2 Ho, ER 3 Ha: 2 (2.2 x 1.5) (1.8 x 0.6) Derricks: 1x2t,1x1.5t Ice Capable	**1 oil engine** driving 1 FP propeller Total Power: 294kW (400hp) 10.5kn S.K.L. 6NVD48 1 x 4 Stroke 6 Cy. 320 x 480 294kW (400bhp) (, fitted 1967) VEB Schwermaschinenbau "KarlLiebknecht" (SKL)-Magdeburg AuxGen: 2 x 57kW Fuel: 51.0 (d.f.)
9506966 *9V8359* -	**VELOCITY 2411** - **Topniche Marine Pte Ltd** - *Singapore* *Singapore* Official number: 395650	**272** 82 314	Class: BV (GL)	**2009-12 Sapor Shipbuilding Industries Sdn Bhd — Sibu** Yd No: SAPOR 34 Loa 30.20 Br ex - Dght 3.800 Lbp 27.20 Br md 9.00 Dpth 4.60 Welded, 1 dk	**(B32A2ST) Tug**	**2 oil engines** reverse reduction geared to sc. shafts driving 2 FP propellers Total Power: 1,790kW (2,434hp) Cummins KTA-38-M2 2 x Vee 4 Stroke 12 Cy. 159 x 159 each-895kW (1217bhp) Cummins Engine Co Inc-USA AuxGen: 2 x 80kW 400V a.c
9587295 *9V8548* -	**VELOCITY 3212** - **Topniche Shipping Pte Ltd** - *Singapore* *Singapore* MMSI: 563785000 Official number: 395942	**374** 112 -	Class: BV	**2010-10 Yangzhou Topniche Shipbuilding Co Ltd — Yangzhou JS** Yd No: TG-01 Loa 34.50 Br ex 9.90 Dght 3.800 Lbp 30.65 Br md 9.50 Dpth 4.60 Welded, 1 dk	**(B32A2ST) Tug**	**2 oil engines** reduction geared to sc. shafts driving 2 FP propellers Total Power: 2,984kW (4,058hp) 11.5kn Cummins KTA-50-M2 2 x Vee 4 Stroke 16 Cy. 159 x 159 each-1492kW (2029bhp) Cummins Engine Co Ltd-United Kingdom
9587300 *9V8549* -	**VELOCITY 3213** - **Topniche Shipping Pte Ltd** - SatCom: Inmarsat C 456381010 *Singapore* *Singapore* MMSI: 563810000 Official number: 395943	**374** 112 -	Class: BV	**2011-01 Yangzhou Topniche Shipbuilding Co Ltd — Yangzhou JS** Yd No: TG-02 Loa 34.50 Br ex 9.90 Dght 3.650 Lbp 30.65 Br md 9.50 Dpth 4.60 Welded, 1 dk	**(B32A2ST) Tug**	**2 oil engines** reduction geared to sc. shafts driving 2 FP propellers Total Power: 2,984kW (4,058hp) Cummins KTA-50-M2 2 x Vee 4 Stroke 16 Cy. 159 x 159 each-1492kW (2029bhp) Cummins Engine Co Ltd-United Kingdom
9031961 *SWEC* -	**VELOPOULA** - **Velopoula Special Maritime Enterprise (ENE)** Eletson Corp SatCom: Inmarsat C 423789910 *Piraeus* *Greece* MMSI: 237899000 Official number: 9991	**39,265** 17,954 66,895 T/cm 67.4	Class: LR (NV) **100A1** SS 01/2013 Double Hull oil tanker ESP LI **LMC** **UMS IGS** Eq.Ltr: 0†; Cable: 660.0/78.0 U3	**1993-01 Hyundai Heavy Industries Co Ltd — Ulsan** Yd No: 772 Loa 228.00 (BB) Br ex 32.40 Dght 13.217 Lbp 216.49 Br md 32.20 Dpth 19.70 Welded, 1 dk	**(A13A2TW) Crude/Oil Products Tanker** Double Hull Liq: 71,532; Liq (Oil): 71,532 Cargo Heating Coils Compartments: 14 Wing Ta, 2 Wing Slop Ta, ER 3 Cargo Pump (s): 3x2000m³/hr Manifold: Bow/CM: 115m	**1 oil engine** driving 1 FP propeller Total Power: 7,963kW (10,826hp) 14.7kn B&W 6L60MC 1 x 2 Stroke 6 Cy. 600 x 1944 7963kW (10826bhp) Hyundai Heavy Industries Co Ltd-South Korea AuxGen: 1 x 750kW 450V 60Hz a.c, 2 x 600kW 450V 60Hz a.c Boilers: 2 AuxB (o.f.) 18.4kgf/cm² (18.0bar) Fuel: 134.2 (d.f.) (Heating Coils) 1894.7 (r.f.) 36.2pd
9317066 *LMQW* -	**VELOX** - **Bugsertjeneste II AS KS** Ostensjo Rederi AS *Haugesund* *Norway* MMSI: 259514000	**643** 192 481	Class: NV	**2005-02 Astilleros Gondan SA — Castropol** Yd No: 428 Loa 38.27 (BB) Br ex 14.72 Dght 6.900 Lbp 33.29 Br md 14.00 Dpth 5.53 Welded, 1 dk	**(B32A2ST) Tug**	**2 oil engines** geared to sc. shafts driving 2 Voith-Schneider propellers Total Power: 4,880kW (6,634hp) 12.0kn Bergens C25: 33L9P 2 x 4 Stroke 9 Cy. 250 x 330 each-2440kW (3317bhp) Rolls Royce Marine AS-Norway AuxGen: 2 x 136kW 400/220V 50Hz a.c Fuel: 194.0 (d.f.)
9224104 *2GUL9* -	**VELOX** *ex* Flinterlinge *-2013* *ex* Lingedijk *-2005* **Atlas Navigation Co Ltd** Faversham Ships Ltd *Peel* *Isle of Man (British)* MMSI: 235100629 Official number: 736482	**2,548** 1,428 3,300	Class: GL (BV)	**2000-10 Tille Scheepsbouw Kootstertille B.V. — Kootstertille** Yd No: 334 Loa 91.25 Br ex - Dght 4.920 Lbp 84.99 Br md 13.75 Dpth 6.25 Welded, 1 dk	**(A31A2GX) General Cargo Ship** Grain: 5,196 TEU 126 C. 126/20' Compartments: 1 Ho, ER 1 Ha: (62.0 x 10.0)ER Ice Capable	**1 oil engine** with flexible couplings & reduction geared to sc. shaft driving 1 CP propeller Total Power: 1,950kW (2,651hp) 13.0kn Wartsila 6L26 1 x 4 Stroke 6 Cy. 260 x 320 1950kW (2651bhp) Wartsila NSD Nederland BV-Netherlands AuxGen: 1 x 300kW 230/400V a.c, 1 x 100kW 230/400V 50Hz a.c Thrusters: 1 Thwart. FP thruster (f) Fuel: 229.6 (d.f.)
9277319 *PBLP* -	**VELSERDIEP** *ex* Onego Trader *-2010* *completed as* Velserdiep *-2004* **Beheermaatschappij ms Velserdiep BV** Feederlines BV *Groningen* *Netherlands* MMSI: 244484000 Official number: 41846	**5,057** 2,631 7,250	Class: GL (LR) ✠ Classed LR until 23/2/13	**2003-12 ATVT Sudnobudivnyi Zavod "Zaliv" — Kerch** (Hull) Yd No: (619) **2003-12 Bodewes' Scheepswerven B.V. — Hoogezand** Yd No: 619 Loa 119.98 (BB) Br ex 15.43 Dght 7.050 Lbp 113.65 Br md 15.20 Dpth 8.44 Welded, 1 dk	**(A31A2GX) General Cargo Ship** Grain: 9,415 TEU 390 C Ho 174 TEU C Dk 216 TEU Compartments: 2 Ho, ER 2 Ha: ER Cranes: 2x40t	**1 oil engine** with clutches, flexible couplings & sr geared to sc. shaft driving 1 CP propeller Total Power: 3,840kW (5,221hp) 14.7kn MaK 8M32C 1 x 4 Stroke 8 Cy. 320 x 480 3840kW (5221bhp) Caterpillar Motoren GmbH & Co. KG-Germany AuxGen: 1 x 400kW 400V 50Hz a.c, 2 x 259kW 400V 50Hz a.c Boilers: TOH (ex.g.) 10.2kgf/cm² (10.0bar), TOH (o.f.) 10.2kgf/cm² (10.0bar) Thrusters: 1 Thwart. CP thruster (f)

IMO / Call sign	Name / Owner / Manager / Flag	Tonnage	Class	Built / Dimensions	Type / Capacity	Machinery
9346691 *PBIC* -	**VELSERDIJK** **Beheermaatschappij ms Velserdijk II BV** Navigia Shipmanagement BV *Groningen* *Netherlands* MMSI: 244865000 Official number: 49576	**2,984** 1,598 4,450	Class: GL (BV)	**2008-08 Chowgule & Co Pvt Ltd — Goa** Yd No: 176 Loa 89.95 (BB) Br ex Dght 6.220 Lbp 84.94 Br md 14.40 Dpth 7.85 Welded, 1 dk	**(A31A2GX) General Cargo Ship** Grain: 5,818 Compartments: 1 Ho, ER 1 Ha: ER (62.3 x 11.7)	**1 oil engine** reduction geared to sc. shaft driving 1 CP propeller Total Power: 1,986kW (2,700hp) 11.5kn MaK 6M25 1 x 4 Stroke 6 Cy. 255 x 400 1986kW (2700bhp) Caterpillar Motoren GmbH & Co. KG-Germany AuxGen: 2 x 168kW 400V 50Hz a.c Thrusters: 1 Tunnel thruster (f) Fuel: 40.0 (d.f.) 290.0 (r.f.)
9494008 *2FSG6* -	**VELSHEDA** **ms 'Velsheda' Schiffahrtsgesellschaft mbH & Co KG** Orion Bulkers GmbH & Co KG *Douglas* *Isle of Man (British)* MMSI: 235093794 Official number: DR0187	**43,022** 27,239 82,172 T/cm 70.2	Class: NK	**2012-08 Tsuneishi Group (Zhoushan) Shipbuilding Inc — Daishan County ZJ** Yd No: SS-050 Loa 229.00 (BB) Br ex - Dght 14.430 Lbp 222.00 Br md 32.26 Dpth 20.05 Welded, 1 dk	**(A21A2BC) Bulk Carrier** Grain: 97,380 Compartments: 7 Ho, ER 7 Ha: ER	**1 oil engine** driving 1 FP propeller Total Power: 9,710kW (13,202hp) 14.5kn MAN-B&W 6S60MC-C 1 x 2 Stroke 6 Cy. 600 x 2400 9710kW (13202bhp) Mitsui Engineering & Shipbuilding CLtd-Japan Fuel: 3180.0
1006001 *MWVT6*	**VELSHEDA** **Tarbat Investments Ltd** Strawberry Marketing UK Ltd *Guernsey* *Guernsey* MMSI: 234429000 Official number: 162792	**104** 31 -	Class: LR ✠ **100A1** SS 06/2011 Yacht **LMC**	**1933 Camper & Nicholsons (Yachts) Ltd. — Gosport** Yd No: 400 Loa - Br ex - Dght 4.780 Lbp - Br md - Dpth - Welded, 1 dk	**(X11A2YP) Yacht**	**1 oil engine** with flexible couplings & sr geared to sc. shaft driving 1 FP propeller Total Power: 305kW (415hp) M.T.U. 6R183TE72 1 x 4 Stroke 6 Cy. 128 x 142 305kW (415bhp) (, fitted 1997) MTU Friedrichshafen GmbH-Friedrichshafen AuxGen: 2 x 36kW 400V 50Hz a.c
8846979 - -	**VELTA** *ex* Venta *-1992* **Transoil Co Ltd** - *St Petersburg* *Russia*	**878** 595 1,580	Class: (RS)	**1971 Shipbuilding & Shiprepairing Yard 'Ivan Dimitrov' — Rousse** Yd No: 87 Loa 59.69 Br ex 10.80 Dght 4.780 Lbp - Br md - Dpth 5.52 Welded, 1 dk	**(B35E2TF) Bunkering Tanker** Ice Capable	**2 oil engines** driving 2 FP propellers Total Power: 588kW (800hp) 8.7kn S.K.L. 8NVD36-1U 2 x 4 Stroke 8 Cy. 240 x 360 each-294kW (400bhp) VEB Schwermaschinenbau "KarlLiebknecht" (SKL)-Magdeburg AuxGen: 1 x 34kW a.c, 2 x 25kW a.c
6622123 *IVJZ* -	**VELTRO** **Oceanpesca Srl di Giuseppe Quinci** - *Mazara del Vallo* *Italy* Official number: 159	*191* 94 362	Class: (RI)	**1966 Cant. Navalmeccanico di Senigallia S.p.A. — Senigallia** Yd No: 22 Loa 36.00 Br ex 6.79 Dght 3.239 Lbp 31.50 Br md 6.76 Dpth 3.59 Riveted\Welded, 1 dk	**(B11A2FT) Trawler**	**1 oil engine** driving 1 FP propeller Total Power: 331kW (450hp) MaK 6M451AK 1 x 4 Stroke 6 Cy. 320 x 450 331kW (450bhp) Atlas MaK Maschinenbau GmbH-Kiel
9225940 - -	**VELUSUMANA** **Government of The Democratic Socialist Republic of Sri Lanka (Ports Authority)** - *Colombo* *Sri Lanka*	**320** 96 181	Class: LR ✠ **100A1** SS 05/2011 tug Sri Lanka coastal service ✠ **LMC** Eq.Ltr: F; Cable: 275.0/19.0 U2 (a)	**2001-05 Colombo Dockyard Ltd. — Colombo** Yd No: 154 Loa 30.50 Br ex 9.84 Dght 3.800 Lbp 29.50 Br md 9.60 Dpth 4.48 Welded, 1 dk	**(B32A2ST) Tug**	**2 oil engines** with clutches, flexible couplings & sr geared to sc. shafts driving 2 Directional propellers Total Power: 1,440kW (1,958hp) 10.5kn Wartsila 4L20 2 x 4 Stroke 4 Cy. 200 x 280 each-720kW (979bhp) Wartsila Finland Oy-Finland AuxGen: 2 x 120kW 440V 50Hz a.c Fuel: 48.0 (d.f.)
9598282 *5BRA3* -	**VELVET** **Zeggi Shipping Ltd** Navarone SA *Limassol* *Cyprus* MMSI: 210914000 Official number: 9598282	**19,943** - 32,860	Class: GL	**2012-09 Yangfan Group Co Ltd — Zhoushan ZJ** Yd No: 2173 Loa 177.41 Br ex - Dght 10.200 Lbp 168.00 Br md 28.20 Dpth 14.20 Welded, 1 dk	**(A21A2BC) Bulk Carrier** Grain: 42,700 Compartments: 5 Ho, ER 5 Ha: ER Cranes: 4x30t Ice Capable	**1 oil engine** driving 1 FP propeller Total Power: 6,480kW (8,810hp) 14.2kn MAN-B&W 6S42MC 1 x 2 Stroke 6 Cy. 420 x 1764 6480kW (8810bhp) STX (Dalian) Engine Co Ltd-China
8802686 *EIIC3* SO 750	**VELVET CHORD II** **Atlantic Trawlers Ltd** - *Sligo* *Irish Republic* Official number: 404463	**216** 65 -		**1988-11 Scheepswerf Made B.V. — Made** (Hull) **1988-11 B.V. Scheepswerf Damen — Gorinchem** Yd No: 4172 Loa 23.21 Br ex - Dght 3.201 Lbp - Br md 7.12 Dpth - Welded, 1 dk	**(B11A2FS) Stern Trawler**	**1 oil engine** with clutches, flexible couplings & sr geared to sc. shaft driving 1 FP propeller Total Power: 526kW (715hp) Caterpillar 3508TA 1 x Vee 4 Stroke 8 Cy. 170 x 190 526kW (715bhp) Caterpillar Inc-USA
9036868 *9HWD7* -	**VEMAOIL XI** *ex* Jolly Falcon *-2004* *ex* Yuwa Maru *-2002* **Abbey Shipping Ltd** Queensway Navigation Co Ltd SatCom: Inmarsat C 421563110 *Valletta* *Malta* MMSI: 215631000 Official number: 8845	**3,207** 1,273 5,260 T/cm 12.6	Class: NK (VR)	**1991-08 Shin Kurushima Dockyard Co. Ltd. — Akitsu** Yd No: 2718 Conv to DH-2006 Loa 105.02 (BB) Br ex 15.50 Dght 6.750 Lbp 97.00 Br md 15.50 Dpth 7.90 Welded, 1 dk	**(A13B2TP) Products Tanker** Double Hull (13F) Liq: 4,563; Liq (Oil): 5,500 Cargo Heating Coils Compartments: 8 Wing Ta, 2 Wing Slop Ta, ER 2 Cargo Pump (s): 2x1700m³/hr Manifold: Bow/CM: 53.5m	**1 oil engine** driving 1 CP propeller Total Power: 2,185kW (2,971hp) 13.0kn B&W 6S26MC 1 x 2 Stroke 6 Cy. 260 x 980 2185kW (2971bhp) The Hanshin Diesel Works Ltd-Japan AuxGen: 3 x 340kW a.c Thrusters: 1 Thwart. CP thruster (f) Fuel: 61.5 (d.f.) 146.9 (r.f.)
9078414 *9HA2016* -	**VEMAOIL XIV** *ex* Orange Sun *-2010* *ex* Showa Maru No. 5 *-2009* **Navamar Marine Corp** Queensway Navigation Co Ltd SatCom: Inmarsat C 424981210 *Valletta* *Malta* MMSI: 249812000 Official number: 9078414	**2,992** 1,267 4,997	Class: NK	**1993-09 Kurinoura Dockyard Co Ltd — Yawatahama EH** Yd No: 310 Converted From: Products Tanker-1993 Loa 105.00 (BB) Br ex 15.23 Dght 6.450 Lbp 97.00 Br md 15.20 Dpth 7.50 Welded, 1 dk	**(A12B2TR) Chemical/Products Tanker** Double Hull Liq: 5,450; Liq (Oil): 5,450 Compartments: 10 Ta, ER 2 Cargo Pump (s): 2x1500m³/hr Manifold: Bow/CM: 26m	**1 oil engine** driving 1 CP propeller Total Power: 2,940kW (3,997hp) 13.9kn Hanshin 6LF50 1 x 4 Stroke 6 Cy. 500 x 800 2940kW (3997bhp) The Hanshin Diesel Works Ltd-Japan AuxGen: 1 x 360kW 445V 60Hz a.c, 2 x 200kW 445V 60Hz a.c Thrusters: 1 Thwart. CP thruster (f) Fuel: 67.0 (d.f.) 228.0 (r.f.) 13.0pd
9005613 *9HHM7* -	**VEMAOIL XX** *ex* Oriental Energy *-2002* *ex* Hikari Maru No. 11 *-2002* **Sea Ruby Maritime Co Ltd** Queensway Navigation Co Ltd SatCom: Inmarsat C 421524210 *Valletta* *Malta* MMSI: 215242000 Official number: 7775	**3,321** 1,319 4,958 T/cm 13.1	Class: NK	**1990-10 Naikai Shipbuilding & Engineering Co Ltd — Onomichi HS (Setoda Shipyard)** Yd No: 562 Conv to DH-2005 Loa 105.24 (BB) Br ex 15.52 Dght 6.574 Lbp 97.60 Br md 15.52 Dpth 7.50 Welded, 1 dk	**(A13B2TP) Products Tanker** Double Hull (13F) Liq: 4,725; Liq (Oil): 5,528 Compartments: 10 Wing Ta, ER 2 Cargo Pump (s): 2x1500m³/hr Manifold: Bow/CM: 52m	**1 oil engine** geared to sc. shaft driving 1 CP propeller Total Power: 2,942kW (4,000hp) 13.3kn Hanshin 6EL44 1 x 4 Stroke 6 Cy. 440 x 880 2942kW (4000bhp) The Hanshin Diesel Works Ltd-Japan AuxGen: 2 x 400kW a.c Thrusters: 1 Thwart. CP thruster (f) Fuel: 36.2 (d.f.) 179.7 (r.f.) 10.8pd
9081071 *9HMS9* -	**VEMAOIL XXI** *ex* Jian She 31 *-2008* **Sea Ydrias Shipping Co** Queensway Navigation Co Ltd SatCom: Inmarsat C 424919210 *Valletta* *Malta* MMSI: 249192000 Official number: 9081071	**5,971** 2,799 9,927	Class: BV (LR) ✠ Classed LR until 10/6/99	**1994-09 Daedong Shipbuilding Co Ltd — Busan** Yd No: 391 Loa 115.00 (BB) Br ex 18.22 Dght 8.014 Lbp 107.38 Br md 18.20 Dpth 10.72 Welded, 1 dk	**(A13B2TP) Products Tanker** Double Hull (13F) Liq: 10,566; Liq (Oil): 10,566 Compartments: 10 Ta, ER	**1 oil engine** driving 1 FP propeller Total Power: 3,352kW (4,557hp) 12.5kn B&W 6L35MC 1 x 2 Stroke 6 Cy. 350 x 1050 3352kW (4557bhp) Ssangyong Heavy Industries Co Ltd-South Korea AuxGen: 2 x 440kW 445V 60Hz a.c
9078098 *9HXU9* -	**VEMAOIL XXIII** *ex* Sunrise Iris *-2009* **Sea Islands Shipping Co Ltd** Queensway Navigation Co Ltd SatCom: Inmarsat C 424967711 *Valletta* *Malta* MMSI: 249677000 Official number: 9078098	**4,893** 2,487 8,256 T/cm 16.7	Class: NK	**1994-01 Fukuoka Shipbuilding Co Ltd — Fukuoka FO** Yd No: 1177 Loa 110.50 (BB) Br ex - Dght 7.496 Lbp 102.00 Br md 18.20 Dpth 9.30 Welded, 1 dk	**(A12A2TC) Chemical Tanker** Double Hull Liq: 8,920 Cargo Heating Coils Compartments: 6 Ta (s.stl), Wing ER, 9 Wing Ta, 1 Slop Ta, ER 16 Cargo Pump (s): 10x200m³/hr, 4x100m³/hr, 2x150m³/hr Manifold: Bow/CM: 54.9m	**1 oil engine** driving 1 FP propeller Total Power: 3,089kW (4,200hp) 14.0kn Mitsubishi 6UEC37LA 1 x 2 Stroke 6 Cy. 370 x 880 3089kW (4200bhp) Akasaka Tekkosho KK (Akasaka DieselLtd)-Japan AuxGen: 3 x 400kW 450V 60Hz a.c Thrusters: 1 Thwart. CP thruster (f) Fuel: 118.0 (d.f.) (Heating Coils) 576.0 (r.f.) 12.9pd
9087867 *9HSA7* -	**VEMAOIL XXV** *ex* Koyo Maru *-2003* **Sea Ivory Maritime Co Ltd** Queensway Navigation Co Ltd SatCom: Inmarsat C 421552010 *Valletta* *Malta* MMSI: 215520000 Official number: 8473	**3,586** 1,538 5,196 T/cm 13.0	Class: NK	**1993-12 Kurinoura Dockyard Co Ltd — Yawatahama EH** Yd No: 312 Loa 104.70 (BB) Br ex 15.40 Dght 6.681 Lbp 97.00 Br md 15.40 Dpth 8.00 Welded, 1 dk	**(A13B2TP) Products Tanker** Double Hull (13F) Liq: 5,011; Liq (Oil): 5,597 Cargo Heating Coils Compartments: 8 Wing Ta, 2 Wing Slop Ta, ER 2 Cargo Pump (s): 2x2500m³/hr Manifold: Bow/CM: 51.8m	**1 oil engine** driving 1 CP propeller Total Power: 2,942kW (4,000hp) 13.4kn Akasaka A45 1 x 4 Stroke 6 Cy. 450 x 880 2942kW (4000bhp) Akasaka Tekkosho KK (Akasaka DieselLtd)-Japan AuxGen: 1 x 480kW a.c, 2 x 320kW a.c Thrusters: 1 Thwart. FP thruster (f) Fuel: 58.8 (d.f.) 260.5 (r.f.)

Number / Call sign	Name / Owner	Tonnage	Class	Builder / Dimensions	Type	Machinery
9045364 *IRYC* -	**VEMAR** *launched as* Rioni *-1991* **Vetor Srl** - *Naples* *Italy* MMSI: 247160100 Official number: 1823	*153* 101 15 T/cm 1.1	Class: RI (RS)	**1991 Zavod im. "Ordzhonikidze" — Poti** Yd No: 128 Loa - Br ex - Dght 1.010 Lbp 34.50 Br md 5.80 Dpth 3.50 Welded, 1 dk	**(A37B2PS) Passenger Ship** Hull Material: Aluminium Alloy Passengers: unberthed: 155	**2 oil engines** with flexible couplings & sr geared to sc. shafts driving 2 FP propellers Total Power: 2,100kW (2,856hp) 33.0kn M.T.U. 12V396TC82 2 x Vee 4 Stroke 12 Cy. 165 x 185 each-1050kW (1428bhp) MTU Friedrichshafen GmbH-Friedrichshafen AuxGen: 3 x 20kW 24V d.c
9136058 *9HA3113* -	**VEMASPIRIT** *ex* Eagle Charlotte *-2012* **Sea Ocean Maritime Ltd** Queensway Navigation Co Ltd *Valletta* *Malta* MMSI: 229157000 Official number: 9136058	**57,949** 31,560 107,169 T/cm 91.0	Class: LR (NK) **100A1** SS 11/2012 Double Hull oil tanker ESP LI **LMC** **UMS IGS** Eq.Ltr: U†; Cable: 715.0/90.0 U3 (a)	**1997-11 Koyo Dockyard Co Ltd — Mihara HS** Yd No: 2072 Loa 246.80 (BB) Br ex 42.00 Dght 14.761 Lbp 235.00 Br md 41.97 Dpth 21.30 Welded, 1 dk	**(A13A2TV) Crude Oil Tanker** Double Hull (13F) Liq: 118,566; Liq (Oil): 118,566 Cargo Heating Coils Compartments: 6 Wing Ta, 4 Ta, 1 Slop Ta, 2 Wing Slop Ta, ER 3 Cargo Pump (s): 3x2500m³/hr Manifold: Bow/CM: 124m	**1 oil engine** driving 1 FP propeller Total Power: 13,128kW (17,849hp) 14.6kn B&W 7S60MC 1 x 2 Stroke 7 Cy. 600 x 2292 13128kW (17849bhp) Mitsui Engineering & Shipbuilding CLtd-Japan AuxGen: 3 x 750kW 440V 60Hz a.c Boilers: e (ex.g.) 23.2kgf/cm² (22.8bar), WTAuxB (o.f.) 16.8kgf/cm² (16.5bar) Fuel: 386.0 (d.f.) (Heating Coils) 2924.0 (r.f.) 49.0pd
9029700 - -	**VENAD** - **Cochin Port Trust** - *Kochi* *India*	**273** 82 108	Class: IR	**1996-07 Goodwill Engineering Works — Pondicherry** Yd No: 15 Loa 33.00 Br ex 10.02 Dght 1.810 Lbp 31.00 Br md 10.00 Dpth 3.00 Welded, 1 dk	**(B34G2SE) Pollution Control Vessel** Cranes: 1x12.5t	**2 oil engines** geared to sc. shaft driving 2 Voith-Schneider propellers Total Power: 702kW (954hp) 9.0kn Cummins KTA-1150-M 2 x 4 Stroke 6 Cy. 159 x 159 each-351kW (477bhp) Kirloskar Oil Engines Ltd-India AuxGen: 2 x 88kW 415V 50Hz a.c Fuel: 35.0 (d.f.)
7417185 *XCVV* -	**VENADO** *ex* Helios *-2001* *ex* Pargo *-1995* *ex* Hope Tide *-1993* **Naviera Mexicana JM SA de CV** Naviera Mexicana Neptuno SA de CV *Ciudad del Carmen* *Mexico* MMSI: 345070060 Official number: 0401029135-3	*680* 206 -	Class: GL (AB)	**1975-05 Halter Marine, Inc. — Moss Point, Ms** Yd No: 481 Loa 54.23 Br ex 11.59 Dght 3.644 Lbp 50.45 Br md 11.56 Dpth 4.25 Welded, 1 dk	**(B21A20S) Platform Supply Ship**	**2 oil engines** reverse reduction geared to sc. shafts driving 2 FP propellers Total Power: 1,654kW (2,248hp) 12.0kn Caterpillar D399SCAC 2 x Vee 4 Stroke 16 Cy. 159 x 203 each-827kW (1124bhp) Caterpillar Tractor Co-USA AuxGen: 2 x 99kW a.c Thrusters: 1 Thwart. FP thruster (f) Fuel: 148.5 (d.f.)
7039268 *D6CE7* -	**VENALY** *ex* Doris *-2004* *ex* Kirre *-1999* *ex* Sovetskiy Pogranichnik *-1997* **Verpa Marketing SA** - *Moroni* *Union of Comoros* MMSI: 616238000 Official number: 1200285	**1,798** 965 2,360	Class: (RS)	**1970 Sudostroitelnyy Zavod 'Okean' — Nikolayev** Yd No: 203 Loa 82.00 Br ex 12.53 Dght 5.120 Lbp 74.91 Br md 12.48 Dpth 6.02 Welded, 1 dk	**(A31A2GX) General Cargo Ship** Grain: 2,980; Bale: 2,870 Compartments: 3 Ho, ER 3 Ha: 3 (10.7 x 8.0)ER Cranes: 2x8t Ice Capable	**1 oil engine** driving 1 FP propeller Total Power: 1,839kW (2,500hp) 12.8kn Skoda 6L525IIPS 1 x 4 Stroke 6 Cy. 525 x 720 1839kW (2500bhp) CKD Praha-Praha Fuel: 135.0 (r.f.)
8419453 *HSB3189* -	**VENAS 20** *ex* Big Sea 11 *-2012* *ex* Top Helmsman No. 1 *-2005* *ex* Nichizan Maru *-1998* **MU Oil Partnership** - *Bangkok* *Thailand* Official number: 470001410	**997** 614 1,908	Class: (CC)	**1985-02 Kishigami Zosen K.K. — Akitsu** Yd No: 1785 Loa 76.26 (BB) Br ex - Dght 4.500 Lbp 70.01 Br md 11.41 Dpth 5.01 Welded, 1 dk	**(A13B2TP) Products Tanker** Liq: 2,294; Liq (Oil): 2,294 Compartments: 12 Ta, ER	**1 oil engine** driving 1 CP propeller Total Power: 1,324kW (1,800hp) 12.7kn Hanshin 6EL30 1 x 4 Stroke 6 Cy. 300 x 600 1324kW (1800bhp) The Hanshin Diesel Works Ltd-Japan
8507470 *9HLL4* -	**VENATOR** *ex* Kartal 7 *-2002* *ex* Gimo One *-2000* *ex* Kartal 7 *-1994* **Santomar Shipping Co Ltd** Menkent Shipping Co Ltd SatCom: Inmarsat C 424914710 *Valletta* *Malta* MMSI: 249147000 Official number: 4218	**4,896** 2,761 7,310	Class: RS (AB)	**1986-07 Sedef Gemi Endustrisi A.S. — Gebze** Yd No: 52 Loa 106.84 (BB) Br ex 16.64 Dght 7.601 Lbp 97.62 Br md 16.62 Dpth 9.53 Welded, 1 dk	**(A31A2GX) General Cargo Ship** Grain: 9,854; Bale: 9,656 Compartments: 2 Ho, ER 2 Ha: ER	**1 oil engine** sr geared to sc. shaft driving 1 CP propeller Total Power: 2,942kW (4,000hp) 13.0kn Hanshin 6EL44 1 x 4 Stroke 6 Cy. 440 x 880 2942kW (4000bhp) The Hanshin Diesel Works Ltd-Japan AuxGen: 1 x 224kW a.c, 2 x 216kW a.c, 1 x 60kW a.c
7742231 *LW4750* -	**VENCEDOR** *ex* ATA-236 *-1994* **Maruba SCA Empresa de Navegacion Maritima** - *Argentina* Official number: 02468	*461* 161 -	Class: (AB)	**1947-06 Gulfport Boiler & Welding Works, Inc. — Port Arthur, Tx** Yd No: 265 Loa - Br ex - Dght 4.579 Lbp 41.00 Br md 10.06 Dpth 5.19 Welded, 1 dk	**(B32A2ST) Tug**	**2 diesel electric oil engines** Connecting to 2 elec. motors driving 1 FP propeller Total Power: 1,104kW (1,500hp) General Motors 12-278A 2 x Vee 2 Stroke 12 Cy. 222 x 267 each-552kW (750bhp) General Motors Corp-USA
8128664 *C6UO5* -	**VENCEREMOS** *ex* Gdansk *-2012* *ex* Norsul Rio *-2005* *ex* Rio Trombetas *-1998* *launched as* Genesio Pires *-1984* **Partrederiet Risholmen Shipping DA** SMT Shipmanagement & Transport Gdynia Ltd Sp z oo *Nassau* *Bahamas* Official number: 8001015	**34,837** 20,990 63,671 T/cm 63.7	Class: BV (NV) (AB)	**1984-12 Ishikawajima do Brasil Est. S.A. (ISHIBRAS) — Rio de Janeiro** Yd No: 142 Converted From: Bulk Carrier-2007 Loa 224.98 (BB) Br ex 32.26 Dght 12.943 Lbp 215.40 Br md 32.21 Dpth 17.81 Welded, 1 dk	**(A23A2BD) Bulk Carrier, Self-discharging** Grain: 75,460 Compartments: 7 Ho, ER 7 Ha: (12.8 x 15.4)6 (16.0 x 15.4)ER Gantry cranes: 1x40t	**1 oil engine** driving 1 FP propeller Total Power: 9,738kW (13,240hp) 13.0kn Sulzer 6RLB76 1 x 2 Stroke 6 Cy. 760 x 1600 9738kW (13240bhp) Ishikawajima do Brasil Estaleiros S (ISHIBRAS)-Brazil AuxGen: 1 x 800kW 450V 60Hz a.c, 3 x 600kW 450V 60Hz a.c Fuel: 314.0 (d.f.) 3482.0 (r.f.) 42.0pd
9517587 *YYV3609* -	**VENCEREMOS** - **Government of The Republic of Venezuela (Instituto Nacional de los Espacios Acuaticos e Insulares (INEA))** Global Shipping Agentes Navieros CA *La Guaira* *Venezuela* MMSI: 775994270	**176** 52	Class: LR ✠**100A** SS 03/2010 tug **LMC** Eq.Ltr: D; Cable: 247.5/17.5 U2 (a)	**2010-03 Damex Shipbuilding & Engineering AVV — Santiago de Cuba** (Assembled by) Yd No: 509833 **2010-03 B.V. Scheepswerf Damen — Gorinchem** (Parts for assembly by) Yd No: 509833 Loa 26.09 Br ex 7.94 Dght 3.440 Lbp 23.96 Br md 7.90 Dpth 4.05 Welded, 1 dk	**(B32A2ST) Tug**	**2 oil engines** with clutches, flexible couplings & sr geared to sc. shafts driving 2 FP propellers Total Power: 2,610kW (3,548hp) Caterpillar 3512B-HD 2 x Vee 4 Stroke 12 Cy. 170 x 190 each-1305kW (1774bhp) Caterpillar Inc-USA AuxGen: 2 x 75kW 400V 60Hz a.c
9646091 *LCYN* -	**VENDLA** - **Vendla AS** Maritime Management AS *Bergen* *Norway* MMSI: 258944000	**2,987** 896 3,100	Class: NV	**2013-08 Maritim Shipyard Sp z oo — Gdansk** (Hull) Yd No: (35) **2013-08 Fitjar Mek. Verksted AS — Fitjar** Yd No: 35 Loa 76.40 (BB) Br ex - Dght 8.300 Lbp 67.20 Br md 15.60 Dpth 9.30 Welded, 1 dk	**(B11B2FV) Fishing Vessel** Ice Capable	**1 oil engine** reduction geared to sc. shaft driving 1 CP propeller Total Power: 4,000kW (5,438hp) MaK 8M32C 1 x 4 Stroke 8 Cy. 320 x 480 4000kW (5438bhp) Caterpillar Motoren GmbH & Co. KG-Germany Thrusters: 1 Tunnel thruster (f); 1 Tunnel thruster (a)
9171022 *LJTP* H-40-AV	**VENDLA II** *ex* Vendla *-2013* **Vendla AS** - SatCom: Inmarsat C 425964010 *Bergen* *Norway* MMSI: 259640000	**1,773** 531 1,600	Class: NV	**1999-09 UAB Vakaru Laivu Remontas (JSC Western Shiprepair) — Klaipeda** (Hull) Yd No: K001 **1999-09 Karmsund Maritime Service AS — Kopervik** Yd No: 14 Loa 68.10 Br ex - Dght 7.150 Lbp 60.00 Br md 12.60 Dpth 8.40 Welded, 1 dk	**(B11B2FV) Fishing Vessel** Ice Capable	**1 oil engine** reduction geared to sc. shaft driving 1 CP propeller Total Power: 3,837kW (5,217hp) MaK 8M32 1 x 4 Stroke 8 Cy. 320 x 480 3837kW (5217bhp) MaK Motoren GmbH & Co. KG-Kiel Thrusters: 2 Thwart. FP thruster (f)
9573672 *A8YI6* -	**VENDOME STREET** *ex* Pacific Garnet *-2013* **Arpege SA** Zodiac Maritime Agencies Ltd SatCom: Inmarsat C 463709536 *Monrovia* *Liberia* MMSI: 636015064 Official number: 15064	**28,778** 12,680 47,879 T/cm 51.8	Class: NK (AB)	**2011-03 Iwagi Zosen Co Ltd — Kamijima EH** Yd No: 291 Loa 179.99 (BB) Br ex - Dght 12.588 Lbp 172.00 Br md 32.20 Dpth 19.05 Welded, 1 dk	**(A13A2TW) Crude/Oil Products Tanker** Double Hull (13F) Liq: 54,946; Liq (Oil): 53,803 Compartments: 8 Wing Ta, 8 Wing Ta, 1 Wing Slop Ta, 1 Wing Slop Ta, ER	**1 oil engine** driving 1 FP propeller Total Power: 9,480kW (12,889hp) 15.0kn MAN-B&W 6S50MC-C 1 x 2 Stroke 6 Cy. 500 x 2000 9480kW (12889bhp) Mitsui Engineering & Shipbuilding CLtd-Japan AuxGen: 3 x 900kW a.c Fuel: 140.0 (d.f.) 2220.0 (r.f.)
8870853 *ES2290* -	**VENE** *ex* Baltiets *-2013* **Baltiyskiy Ship Repairing Yard JSC** MPV Management Ltd *Tallinn* *Estonia* MMSI: 276364000 Official number: 199TJ10	*187* - 46	Class: (RS)	**1971-12 "Petrozavod" — Leningrad** Yd No: 798 Loa 29.30 Br ex 8.49 Dght 3.400 Lbp 27.00 Br md 8.30 Dpth 4.35 Welded, 1 dk	**(B32A2ST) Tug**	**2 oil engines** driving 2 CP propellers Total Power: 882kW (1,200hp) 11.4kn Russkiy 6DR30/50-4-2 2 x 2 Stroke 6 Cy. 300 x 500 each-441kW (600bhp) Mashinostroitelnyy Zavod"Russkiy-Dizel"-Leningrad AuxGen: 2 x 25kW a.c Fuel: 36.0 (d.f.)

IMO / Call sign	Name / Owner	Tonnage	Class	Builder / Dimensions	Type	Machinery
6519259 - -	**VENE** *ex* Audacieux *-1995* **Union des Remorqueurs de Dakar (URD)** - *Dakar* *Senegal*	*207* - -	Class: (BV)	**1965 Ziegler Freres — Dunkerque** Yd No: 151 Loa 32.29 Br ex 8.67 Dght 2.998 Lbp 29.01 Br md 8.01 Dpth 3.99 Riveted\Welded, 1 dk	**(B32A2ST) Tug** 1 Ha: (19.6 x 11.2)	**1 oil engine** driving 1 FP propeller Total Power: 919kW (1,249hp) 13.0kn Werkspoor 1 x 4 Stroke 8 Cy. 330 x 600 919kW (1249bhp) Ziegler Freres-Dunkerque AuxGen: 2 x 48kW 110V d.c
9438212 *3ETK6* -	**VENEBUNKER 7** **Singapore Tankers Pte Ltd** Compania Maritima de Panama SA *Panama* *Panama* MMSI: 370593000 Official number: 3464109A	**5,034** 1,958 6,963 T/cm 15.6	Class: LR ✠ **100A1** SS 10/2013 Double Hull oil tanker carriage of oils with FP exceeding 60 degree C ESP LI ✠ **LMC** Eq.Ltr: X; Cable: 495.0/50.0 U2 (a)	**2008-10 Titan Quanzhou Shipyard Co Ltd — Hui'an County FJ** Yd No: H0005 Loa 99.36 (BB) Br ex 18.08 Dght 7.000 Lbp 94.00 Br md 18.00 Dpth 10.00 Welded, 1 dk	**(A13B2TP) Products Tanker** Double Hull (13F) Compartments: 10 Wing Ta, 2 Wing Slop Ta, ER	**2 oil engines** with clutches, flexible couplings & dr reverse geared to sc. shafts driving 2 FP propellers Total Power: 2,940kW (3,998hp) 11.5kn MAN-B&W 6L28/32A 2 x 4 Stroke 6 Cy. 280 x 320 each-1470kW (1999bhp) Zhenjiang Marine Diesel Works-China AuxGen: 2 x 360kW 400V 50Hz a.c Boilers: AuxB (o.f.) Thrusters: 1 Thwart. FP thruster (f)
7502306 *YYJX* -	**VENEBUNKER UNO** *ex* Campeche *-2004* **Compania Maritima de Venezuela VBCA** - *Puerto Cabello* *Venezuela*	*1,203* 899 2,796	Class: (LR) (BV) ✠ Classed LR until 9/3/79	**1977-11 Ast. de Mallorca S.A. — Palma de Mallorca** Yd No: 219 Loa 68.50 Br ex - Dght 4.800 Lbp - Br md 11.50 Dpth 5.80 Welded, 1 dk	**(B35E2TF) Bunkering Tanker**	**2 oil engines** driving 2 Voith-Schneider propellers Total Power: 882kW (1,200hp) 8.0kn Baudouin DNP12M 2 x Vee 4 Stroke 12 Cy. 150 x 150 each-441kW (600bhp) Internacional Diesel S.A.-Zumaya
7807548 *HO2184* -	**VENECIA EXPRESS** *ex* Cape Charlie *-2000* *ex* Sea Horse *-2000* **Marine Investors Ltd Corp** - *Panama* *Panama* MMSI: 356094000 Official number: 29138PEXT	**563** 169 1,000	Class: (AB)	**1978-06 Halter Marine, Inc. — Chalmette, La** Yd No: 736 Loa 49.33 Br ex 11.61 Dght - Lbp 48.80 Br md 11.59 Dpth 3.97 Welded, 1 dk	**(B21B20T) Offshore Tug/Supply Ship**	**2 oil engines** reverse reduction geared to sc. shafts driving 2 FP propellers Total Power: 1,324kW (1,800hp) 12.0kn G.M. (Detroit Diesel) 16V-149 2 x Vee 2 Stroke 16 Cy. 146 x 146 each-662kW (900bhp) General Motors Detroit DieselAllison Divn-USA AuxGen: 2 x 75kW a.c Thrusters: 1 Thwart. FP thruster (f)
8805573 - -	**VENEDIKT ANDREEV** **Ukrainian Danube Shipping Co** - *Izmail* *Ukraine* MMSI: 272896000 Official number: 864391	**2,060** 696 2,099	Class: UA (RS)	**1988-05 Osterreichische Schiffswerften AG Linz-Korneuburg — Linz** Yd No: 1364 Loa 91.90 (BB) Br ex 13.60 Dght 3.370 Lbp 84.90 Br md 13.40 Dpth 4.90 Welded, 2 dks	**(A34A2GR) Refrigerated Cargo Ship** Ins: 3,064 TEU 96 C. 96/20' incl. 24 ref C. Compartments: 2 Ho, ER 2 Ha: 2 (25.2 x 10.0)ER Cranes: 1 Ice Capable	**2 oil engines** driving 2 CP propellers Total Power: 1,950kW (2,652hp) 12.0kn Wartsila 8R22HF 2 x 4 Stroke 8 Cy. 220 x 240 each-975kW (1326bhp) Wartsila Diesel Oy-Finland AuxGen: 2 x 248kW Thrusters: 1 Thwart. FP thruster (f)
6525789 - -	**VENERA** - -	*113* 41	Class: (LR) (BR) ✠ Classed LR until 12/67	**1965-12 Angyalfold Shipyard, Hungarian Ship & Crane Works — Budapest** Yd No: 2085 Loa 28.45 Br ex 6.91 Dght 3.010 Lbp 26.07 Br md 6.51 Dpth 3.36 Welded, 1 dk	**(B32A2ST) Tug**	**1 oil engine** with flexible coupling driving 1 FP propeller Total Power: 736kW (1,001hp) S.K.L. 6NVD48A-2U 1 x 4 Stroke 6 Cy. 320 x 480 736kW (1001bhp) (new engine 1982) VEB Schwermaschinenbau "KarlLiebknecht" (SKL)-Magdeburg AuxGen: 2 x 75kW 220V a.c, 1 x 15kW 220V a.c
8869268 *ILLW* -	**VENERE** *ex* Saronic Moon *-1997* **Adriatic Shipping Lines Srl** - *Naples* *Italy* MMSI: 247069200	**190** 97 -	Class: (RI)	**1993 Derzhavne Vyrobnyche Obednannya Illichivskyi SRZ — Illichivsk** Loa - Br ex - Dght - Lbp 35.91 Br md 6.90 Dpth 2.90 Welded, 1 dk	**(A37B2PS) Passenger Ship**	**3 oil engines** geared to sc. shafts driving 3 FP propellers Total Power: 1,081kW (1,469hp) Barnaultransmash 3D6N-235 2 x 4 Stroke 6 Cy. 150 x 180 each-173kW (235bhp) AO Barnaultransmash-Barnaul Zvezda M401A 1 x Vee 4 Stroke 12 Cy. 180 x 200 735kW (999bhp) AO "Zvezda"-Sankt-Peterburg AuxGen: 1 x 30kW 220V 50Hz a.c
9298040 *9HA2108* -	**VENERE** *launched as* Merope Star *-2004* **Venere Scheepvaart BV** Maritime Performances BV SatCom: Inmarsat C 424996910 *Valletta* *Malta* MMSI: 249969000 Official number: 9298040	**2,708** 820 3,090 T/cm 9.6	Class: RI (BV)	**2004-11 Cant. Nav. de Poli S.p.A. — Pellestrina** Yd No: 196 Loa 74.94 (BB) Br ex - Dght 6.600 Lbp 69.70 Br md 14.20 Dpth 7.50 Welded, 1 dk	**(A11B2TG) LPG Tanker** Double Bottom Entire Compartment Length Liq (Gas): 2,940 2 x Gas Tank (s); 2 independent (C.mn.stl) cyl horizontal 4 Cargo Pump (s): 4x250m³/hr Manifold: Bow/CM: 41.6m	**4 diesel electric oil engines** driving 4 gen. each 800kW 440V a.c Connecting to 2 elec. motors each (1050kW) driving 2 Directional propellers twin propellers Total Power: 3,200kW (4,352hp) 13.0kn Yanmar 6N21AL-SV 4 x 4 Stroke 6 Cy. 210 x 290 each-800kW (1088bhp) Yanmar Diesel Engine Co Ltd-Japan AuxGen: 1 x 128kW 440/220V 60Hz a.c Thrusters: 1 Tunnel thruster (f) Fuel: 86.0 (d.f.) 270.0 (r.f.)
8946066 *DUA2267* -	**VENESSA** **Asian Shipping Corp** - *Manila* *Philippines* Official number: 00-0000393	*493* 294 -		**1990 at Manila** L reg 63.00 Br ex - Dght - Lbp - Br md 14.00 Dpth 3.54 Welded, 1 dk	**(A35D2RL) Landing Craft** Bow ramp (f) Len: 7.93 Wid: 7.93 Swl: -	**2 oil engines** reverse reduction geared to sc. shaft driving 2 FP propellers Total Power: 654kW (890hp) 6.0kn Caterpillar 2 x 4 Stroke each-327kW (445bhp) Caterpillar Inc-USA
8014930 *D6FL4* -	**VENESSA** *ex* Jurong *-1997* *ex* Esso Jurong *-1994* **Indian Ocean Maritime Ltd** Alba Petroleum Ltd SatCom: Inmarsat C 461688810 *Moroni* *Union of Comoros* MMSI: 616888000	**3,421** 1,976 5,449 T/cm 13.0	Class: (AB)	**1981-02 Shimoda Dockyard Co. Ltd. — Shimoda** Yd No: 313 Loa 107.07 Br ex - Dght 6.200 Lbp 100.01 Br md 15.02 Dpth 7.32 Welded, 1 dk	**(A13B2TP) Products Tanker** Single Hull Liq: 6,627; Liq (Oil): 6,763 Part Cargo Heating Coils Compartments: 12 Wing Ta, ER 4 Cargo Pump (s): 4x200m³/hr Manifold: Bow/CM: 52m	**1 oil engine** driving 1 FP propeller Total Power: 2,354kW (3,200hp) 12.0kn Akasaka DM46 1 x 4 Stroke 6 Cy. 460 x 720 2354kW (3200bhp) Akasaka Tekkosho KK (Akasaka DieselLtd)-Japan AuxGen: 2 x 240kW
9260914 *D5DR5* -	**VENETIKO** *ex* Ace Ireland *-2013* *ex* APL Ireland *-2012* **Lindner Shipping Co** Costamare Shipping Co SA *Monrovia* *Liberia* MMSI: 636015952 Official number: 15952	**66,462** 25,614 67,009	Class: NK	**2003-01 Koyo Dockyard Co Ltd — Mihara HS** Yd No: 2141 Loa 279.70 (BB) Br ex 40.10 Dght 14.021 Lbp 262.00 Br md 40.00 Dpth 24.00 Welded, 1 dk	**(A33A2CC) Container Ship (Fully Cellular)** TEU 5928 incl 588 ref C. 17 Ha: (6.5 x 15.7) (13.5 x 25.8)10 (12.6 x 36.2)2 (13.0 x 36.2) (12.7 x 36.2)2 (14.1 x 11.2)ER	**1 oil engine** driving 1 FP propeller Total Power: 57,200kW (77,769hp) 24.7kn MAN-B&W 10K98MC 1 x 2 Stroke 10 Cy. 980 x 2660 57200kW (77769bhp) Mitsui Engineering & Shipbuilding CLtd-Japan AuxGen: 4 x 2200kW 440/220V 60Hz a.c, 1 x 2100kW 440/220V 60Hz a.c Thrusters: 1 Thwart. CP thruster (f) Fuel: 10640.0
6917322 *CUWV* A-2011-C	**VENEZA DE PORTUGAL** **Sociedade de Pesca de Arrasto de Aveiro Lda** - *Aveiro* *Portugal*	*182* 56 -	Class: (LR) ✠ Classed LR until 9/71	**1969-06 Estaleiros Sao Jacinto S.A. — Aveiro** Yd No: 82 Loa 32.01 Br ex 7.45 Dght 2.750 Lbp 27.08 Br md 7.21 Dpth 3.41 Riveted\Welded	**(B11A2FS) Stern Trawler**	**1 oil engine** driving 1 CP propeller Total Power: 600kW (816hp) MaK 6MU451A 1 x 4 Stroke 6 Cy. 320 x 450 600kW (816bhp) Atlas MaK Maschinenbau GmbH-Kiel AuxGen: 2 x 28kW 380V 50Hz a.c
7726093 *5IM500* -	**VENEZIA** *ex* Kenan I *-2009* *ex* Alioth *-2007* *ex* Estefox *-2006* *ex* Felix *-2004* *ex* Leveche *-1994* *ex* Pacifico *-1994* *ex* Eve Pacific *-1993* *ex* Svea Pacific *-1993* *ex* Burro *-1988* *ex* Burro Bulk *-1986* *ex* Astillero *-1986* *ex* Cabados *-1985* *ex* Duro Ocho *-1982* **Mantion Shipping Ltd** B & B Shipping Co *Zanzibar* *Tanzania (Zanzibar)* MMSI: 677040000 Official number: 300240	**2,610** 1,482 4,510	Class: MG (LR) (GL) ✠ Classed LR until 20/11/95	**1980-01 Sociedad Metalurgica Duro Felguera — Gijon** Yd No: 149 Loa 86.81 (BB) Br ex 14.36 Dght 6.763 Lbp 79.30 Br md 14.30 Dpth 8.35 Welded, 1 dk	**(A31A2GX) General Cargo Ship** Grain: 4,898; Bale: 4,842 TEU 127 C.Ho. 82/20' (40') C.Dk. 45/20' (40') Compartments: 2 Ho, ER 2 Ha: (25.0 x 10.6) (18.6 x 10.6)ER Cranes: 2x12.5t Ice Capable	**1 oil engine** sr geared to sc. shaft driving 1 CP propeller Total Power: 2,207kW (3,001hp) 12.0kn Deutz SBV6M540 1 x 4 Stroke 6 Cy. 370 x 400 2207kW (3001bhp) Hijos de J Barreras SA-Spain AuxGen: 1 x 270kW 380V 50Hz a.c, 2 x 140kW 380V 50Hz a.c Fuel: 390.0 (d.f.) 2.2pd
9231743 *VRDI6* -	**VENEZIA** *ex* Hanjin Venezia *-2013* *ex* MSC Venezia *-2010* *ex* Hanjin Venezia *-2008* *ex* Cosco Busan *-2008* *ex* Hanjin Cairo *-2006* **Regal Stone Ltd** Synergy Management Ltd SatCom: Inmarsat C 447701059 *Hong Kong* *Hong Kong* MMSI: 477968900 Official number: HK-2012	**65,131** 34,078 68,086 T/cm 89.6	Class: GL	**2001-12 Hyundai Heavy Industries Co Ltd — Ulsan** Yd No: 1381 Loa 274.68 (BB) Br ex - Dght 14.000 Lbp 263.00 Br md 40.00 Dpth 24.20 Welded, 1 dk	**(A33A2CC) Container Ship (Fully Cellular)** TEU 5551 C Ho 2603 TEU C Dk 2948 TEU incl 500 ref C. Compartments: ER, 7 Cell Ho	**1 oil engine** driving 1 FP propeller Total Power: 57,100kW (77,633hp) 25.9kn MAN-B&W 10K98MC-C 1 x 2 Stroke 10 Cy. 980 x 2400 57100kW (77633bhp) Hyundai Heavy Industries Co Ltd-South Korea AuxGen: 4 x 2000kW 440/220V a.c Thrusters: 1 Thwart. FP thruster (f) Fuel: 405.0 (d.f.) (Heating Coils) 7833.0 (r.f.) 230.0pd

IMO / Call sign	Name / Owner / Manager	Tonnage	Class	Built / Dimensions	Type	Machinery
9229946 *IFBC* -	**VENEZIA 1** **Azienda del Consorzio Trasporti Veneziano (ACTV)** - *Venice* *Italy*	**129** 84 130	Class: RI	**2000**-02 **Cant. Nav. Rosetti — Ravenna** Yd No: 003 Loa 30.40 Br ex - Dght - Lbp 27.50 Br md 5.65 Dpth 2.30 Welded, 1 dk	**(A37B2PS) Passenger Ship** Passengers: unberthed: 330	**2 oil engines** driving 2 FP propellers Total Power: 294kW (400hp) Iveco Aifo 8210M 2 x 4 Stroke 6 Cy. 137 x 156 each-147kW (200bhp) IVECO AIFO S.p.A.-Pregnana Milanese
9229958 *IFBB* -	**VENEZIA 2** **Azienda del Consorzio Trasporti Veneziano (ACTV)** - *Venice* *Italy*	**129** 84 130	Class: RI	**2000**-02 **Cant. Nav. Rosetti — Ravenna** Yd No: 004 Loa 30.40 Br ex - Dght - Lbp 27.50 Br md 5.65 Dpth 2.30 Welded, 1 dk	**(A37B2PS) Passenger Ship** Passengers: unberthed: 330	**2 oil engines** driving 2 FP propellers Total Power: 294kW (400hp) Iveco Aifo 8210M 2 x 4 Stroke 6 Cy. 137 x 156 each-147kW (200bhp) IVECO AIFO S.p.A.-Pregnana Milanese
9229960 *IFBA* -	**VENEZIA 3** **Azienda del Consorzio Trasporti Veneziano (ACTV)** - *Venice* *Italy* Official number: 8781	**129** 84 130	Class: RI	**2000**-03 **Cant. Nav. Rosetti — Ravenna** Yd No: 005 Loa 30.40 Br ex - Dght - Lbp 27.50 Br md 5.65 Dpth 2.30 Welded, 1 dk	**(A37B2PS) Passenger Ship** Passengers: unberthed: 330	**2 oil engines** driving 2 FP propellers Total Power: 294kW (400hp) Iveco Aifo 8210M 2 x 4 Stroke 6 Cy. 137 x 156 each-147kW (200bhp) IVECO AIFO S.p.A.-Pregnana Milanese
9235751 *IFCZ* -	**VENEZIA 4** **Azienda del Consorzio Trasporti Veneziano (ACTV)** - *Venice* *Italy* Official number: 8793	**129** 84 131	Class: RI	**2000**-03 **Cant. Nav. Rosetti — Ravenna** Yd No: 002 Loa 30.40 Br ex - Dght - Lbp 27.50 Br md 5.65 Dpth 2.30 Welded, 1 dk	**(A37B2PS) Passenger Ship** Passengers: unberthed: 330	**2 oil engines** driving 2 FP propellers Total Power: 294kW (400hp) Iveco Aifo 8210M 2 x 4 Stroke 6 Cy. 137 x 156 each-147kW (200bhp) IVECO AIFO S.p.A.-Pregnana Milanese
9235763 *IFCY* -	**VENEZIA 5** **Azienda del Consorzio Trasporti Veneziano (ACTV)** - *Venice* *Italy* Official number: 8797	**129** 84 131	Class: RI	**2000**-04 **Cant. Nav. Rosetti — Ravenna** Yd No: 006 Loa 30.40 Br ex - Dght - Lbp 27.50 Br md 5.65 Dpth 2.30 Welded, 1 dk	**(A37B2PS) Passenger Ship** Passengers: unberthed: 330	**2 oil engines** driving 2 FP propellers Total Power: 294kW (400hp) Iveco Aifo 8210M 2 x 4 Stroke 6 Cy. 137 x 156 each-147kW (200bhp) IVECO AIFO S.p.A.-Pregnana Milanese
9150327 *PBRQ* -	**VENEZIA D** *ex* Jo Venezia D. *-2006* *ex* Venezia D *-2003* **Venezia Shipping BV** Maritime Performances BV *Rotterdam* *Netherlands* MMSI: 246347000 Official number: 51608	**6,875** 3,291 10,127 T/cm 20.5	Class: RI (BV)	**1998**-02 **Cant. Nav. de Poli S.p.A. — Pellestrina** Yd No: 162 Loa 127.72 (BB) Br ex 19.02 Dght 7.850 Lbp 115.20 Br md 19.00 Dpth 9.91 Welded, 1 dk	**(A12B2TR) Chemical/Products Tanker** Double Hull (13F) Liq: 10,535; Liq (Oil): 10,559 Cargo Heating Coils Compartments: 1 Wing Ta, 19 Wing Ta (s.stl), ER, 4 Wing Slop Ta 20 Cargo Pump (s): 14x200m³/hr, 6x100m³/hr Manifold: Bow/CM: 62m Ice Capable	**1 oil engine** with flexible couplings & sr gearedto sc. shaft driving 1 CP propeller Total Power: 5,280kW (7,179hp) 13.0kn Wartsila 8L38 1 x 4 Stroke 8 Cy. 380 x 475 5280kW (7179bhp) Wartsila NSD Nederland BV-Netherlands AuxGen: 1 x 1240kW 440/220V 60Hz a.c, 3 x 884kW 440/220V 60Hz a.c Thrusters: 1 Tunnel thruster (f) Fuel: 129.0 (d.f.) (Heating Coils) 671.0 (r.f.) 21.0pd
8137914 *IKZQ* -	**VENEZIA PRIMA** **Tiozzo Gianfranco Srl** - *Venice* *Italy* MMSI: 247213900 Official number: VE8944	*637* 364 -	Class: (RI)	**1975 Cant. Nav. Vittoria — Adria** Yd No: 184 Loa 55.30 Br ex 9.83 Dght 3.660 Lbp 51.72 Br md 9.81 Dpth 3.81 Welded, 1 dk	**(B34A2SH) Hopper, Motor**	**2 oil engines** driving 2 FP propellers Total Power: 714kW (970hp) MWM TBD601-6K 2 x 4 Stroke 6 Cy. 160 x 165 each-357kW (485bhp) Motoren Werke Mannheim AG (MWM)-West Germany
8137938 *IKZR* -	**VENEZIA SECONDA** **Merceron TP** - *Genoa* *Italy* MMSI: 247232900 Official number: 8834	*615* 364 -	Class: BV (Class contemplated) RI (Class contemplated)	**1975 Cant. Nav. Vittoria — Adria** Yd No: 185 Loa 55.29 Br ex 9.83 Dght 3.230 Lbp 51.72 Br md 9.81 Dpth 3.81 Welded, 1 dk	**(B34A2SH) Hopper, Motor**	**2 oil engines** driving 2 FP propellers Total Power: 714kW (970hp) MWM TBD601-6K 2 x 4 Stroke 6 Cy. 160 x 165 each-357kW (485bhp) Motoren Werke Mannheim AG (MWM)-West Germany
7742243 - -	**VENGADOR** *ex* ATA-237 *-2003* **RUA Remolcadores Unidos Argentinos SAM y C** - *Argentina* Official number: 02556	**461** 161 -	Class: (AB)	**1947**-06 **Gulfport Boiler & Welding Works, Inc. — Port Arthur, Tx** Yd No: 266 Loa - Br ex - Dght 4.579 Lbp 41.00 Br md 10.06 Dpth 5.19 Welded, 1 dk	**(B32A2ST) Tug**	**2 diesel electric oil engines** Connecting to 2 elec. motors driving 1 FP propeller Total Power: 1,104kW (1,500hp) 14.0kn General Motors 12-278A 2 x Vee 2 Stroke 12 Cy. 222 x 267 each-552kW (750bhp) General Motors Corp-USA AuxGen: 2 x 60kW d.c
8126850 *UHOG* -	**VENGERY** *ex* Crowley Alliance *-2007* *ex* Tackler *-2006* *ex* Maersk Tackler *-2005* *ex* Tawaki *-1990* *ex* Federal Atlantic *-1988* *ex* Seaforth Atlantic *-1986* **Femcoborg II BV** FEMCO-Management Ltd (OOO 'FEMKO-Menedzhment') *Kholmsk* *Russia* MMSI: 273318630	**1,672** 591 1,477	Class: RS (LR) ✠ Classed LR until 16/10/09	**1983**-08 **Hyundai Heavy Industries Co Ltd — Ulsan** Yd No: 0710 Loa 68.69 Br ex 14.86 Dght 5.885 Lbp 62.72 Br md 14.51 Dpth 6.91 Welded, 1 dk	**(B21B20A) Anchor Handling Tug Supply** Ice Capable	**4 oil engines** with clutches, flexible couplings & sr geared to sc. shafts driving 2 CP propellers Total Power: 8,824kW (11,996hp) Normo KVMB-12 4 x Vee 4 Stroke 12 Cy. 250 x 300 each-2206kW (2999bhp) AS Bergens Mek Verksteder-Norway AuxGen: 2 x 1256kW 450V 60Hz a.c, 2 x 248kW 450V 60Hz a.c, 1 x 75kW 450V 60Hz a.c Thrusters: 2 Thwart. CP thruster (f); 1 Tunnel thruster (a) Fuel: 367.5 (d.f.) 636.5 (r.f.)
9588782 *3YJO* -	**VENGSOY** *launched as* Nengsoy *-2011* **Torghatten Nord AS** - *Tromso* *Norway* MMSI: 257067000	**987** 296 132	Class: NV	**2011**-11 **Remontowa Shipbuilding SA — Gdansk** (Hull) Yd No: B611/1 **2011**-11 **Gdanska Stocznia 'Remontowa' SA — Gdansk** Yd No: B2399/1 Loa 40.60 Br ex - Dght 3.000 Lbp 38.21 Br md 12.40 Dpth 4.70 Welded, 1 dk	**(A36A2PR) Passenger/Ro-Ro Ship (Vehicles)** Passengers: unberthed: 147 Bow door/ramp (centre) Stern door/ramp (centre) Vehicles: 21	**1 oil engine** reduction geared to sc. shaft driving 1 CP propeller Total Power: 1,081kW (1,470hp) Caterpillar C32 ACERT 1 x Vee 4 Stroke 12 Cy. 145 x 162 1081kW (1470bhp) Caterpillar Inc-USA AuxGen: 2 x a.c Thrusters: 1 Tunnel thruster (f)
8661111 *ZCPL9* -	**VENI VIDI VICI** **VVV Charters Ltd** Magellan Management & Consulting SA *George Town* *Cayman Islands (British)* Official number: 739174	**265** 79 -	Class: BV	**2006**-07 **Overmarine SpA — Viareggio** Yd No: 130/07 Loa 39.00 Br ex - Dght 3.110 Lbp 34.87 Br md 7.76 Dpth 4.15 Bonded, 1 dk	**(X11A2YP) Yacht** Hull Material: Reinforced Plastic	**2 oil engines** reduction geared to sc. shafts driving 2 Water jets Total Power: 5,440kW (7,396hp) 34.0kn M.T.U. 16V4000M90 2 x Vee 4 Stroke 16 Cy. 165 x 190 each-2720kW (3698bhp) MTU Friedrichshafen GmbH-Friedrichshafen
9179634 *V7GA6* -	**VENICE** **Venice Shipping Co Ltd** Scorpio Commercial Management SAM *Majuro* *Marshall Islands* MMSI: 538002060 Official number: 2060	**43,822** 26,307 81,408 T/cm 81.0	Class: AB	**2001**-06 **'3 Maj' Brodogradiliste dd — Rijeka** Yd No: 674 Loa 240.40 Br ex - Dght 13.320 Lbp 230.00 Br md 36.40 Dpth 18.10 Welded, 1 dk	**(A13A2TV) Crude Oil Tanker** Double Hull (13F) Liq: 86,626; Liq (Oil): 86,626 Compartments: 12 Wing Ta, ER 12 Cargo Pump (s): 12x900m³/hr Manifold: Bow/CM: 81m Ice Capable	**1 oil engine** driving 1 FP propeller Total Power: 12,200kW (16,587hp) 14.5kn Sulzer 6RTA62U 1 x 2 Stroke 6 Cy. 620 x 2150 12200kW (16587bhp) '3 Maj' Motori i Dizalice dd-Croatia AuxGen: 3 x 1360kW 220/440V 60Hz a.c Thrusters: 1 Thwart. FP thruster (f) Fuel: 363.0 (d.f.) 3090.0 (r.f.)
9283306 *SXFK* -	**VENICE** *ex* Maersk Pristine *-2007* **Hyperion Owning Co Ltd** TMS Tankers Ltd SatCom: Inmarsat Mini-M 761149889 *Piraeus* *Greece* MMSI: 240671000 Official number: 11633	**61,724** 32,726 109,637 T/cm 91.4	Class: LR ✠ **100A1** SS 11/2009 Double Hull oil tanker ESP *IWS SPM LI **ShipRight** (SDA, FDA, CM) ✠ **LMC** **UMS IGS** Eq.Ltr: U†; Cable: 715.0/92.0 U3 (a)	**2004**-11 **Dalian New Shipbuilding Heavy Industries Co Ltd — Dalian LN** Yd No: PC1100-16 Loa 244.60 (BB) Br ex 42.03 Dght 15.517 Lbp 233.00 Br md 42.00 Dpth 22.20 Welded, 1 dk	**(A13A2TW) Crude/Oil Products Tanker** Double Hull (13F) Liq: 117,921; Liq (Oil): 117,921 Cargo Heating Coils Compartments: 12 Wing Ta, 2 Wing Slop Ta, ER 3 Cargo Pump (s): 3x3000m³/hr Manifold: Bow/CM: 122.2m	**1 oil engine** driving 1 FP propeller Total Power: 15,540kW (21,128hp) 15.3kn Sulzer 7RTA62U 1 x 2 Stroke 7 Cy. 620 x 2150 15540kW (21128bhp) Dalian Marine Diesel Works-China AuxGen: 3 x 780kW 450V 60Hz a.c Boilers: AuxB (ex.g.) 8.2kgf/cm² (8.0bar), WTAuxB New (o.f.) 18.4kgf/cm² (18.0bar) Fuel: 330.0 (d.f.) 3241.0 (r.f.)

9293442 *3EAU3* -	**VENICE BRIDGE** **GOD Shipping SA** Doun Kisen KK (Doun Kisen Co Ltd) *Panama* *Panama* MMSI: 352798000 Official number: 3086905A	**54,519** 22,921 64,989 T/cm 82.5	Class: NK	**2005-05 Hyundai Heavy Industries Co Ltd — Ulsan** Yd No: 1592 Loa 294.12 (BB) Br ex - Dght 13.520 Lbp 283.33 Br md 32.20 Dpth 21.80 Welded, 1 dk	**(A33A2CC) Container Ship (Fully Cellular)** TEU 4738 incl 400 ref C	**1 oil engine** driving 1 FP propeller Total Power: 41,129kW (55,919hp) 23.5kn MAN-B&W 8K98MC-C 1 x 2 Stroke 8 Cy. 980 x 2400 41129kW (55919bhp) Hyundai Heavy Industries Co Ltd-South Korea AuxGen: 4 x 1995kW a.c Thrusters: 1 Thwart. CP thruster (f) Fuel: 7385.0
9159919 - -	**VENICE CARNIVAL** *ex Seaflight 3 -2002 ex Katran-3 -2000* **Top Line Istra doo** Columbus doo *Lome* *Togo*	**135** 53 15	Class: (CS) (RI) (RS)	**1996-07 OAO Volgogradskiy Sudostroitelnyy Zavod — Volgograd** Yd No: S-603 Loa 34.50 Br ex 10.30 Dght 1.140 Lbp 30.93 Br md 5.80 Dpth 1.80 Welded, 1 dk	**(A37B2PS) Passenger Ship**	**2 oil engines** geared to sc. shafts driving 2 FP propellers Total Power: 2,520kW (3,426hp) 34.0kn M.T.U. 12V396TE74 2 x Vee 4 Stroke 12 Cy. 165 x 185 each-1260kW (1713bhp) MTU Friedrichshafen GmbH-Friedrichshafen AuxGen: 2 x 8kW a.c Fuel: 2.0 (d.f.)
9005364 *D5BW7* -	**VENIE** *ex Northern Crusader -2012* *ex Monika Viking -1997* **Management 2 Shipping Co Ltd** FEMCO-Management Ltd (OOO 'FEMKO-Menedzhment') *Monrovia* *Liberia* MMSI: 636015621 Official number: 15621	**2,335** 924 2,783	Class: NV	**1992-09 UDL Engineering Pte Ltd — Singapore** Yd No: 8640 Loa 73.60 Br ex - Dght 6.856 Lbp 63.60 Br md 16.40 Dpth 8.00 Welded, 2 dks	**(B21B20A) Anchor Handling Tug Supply**	**4 oil engines** dr geared to sc. shafts driving 2 CP propellers Total Power: 11,326kW (15,400hp) 12.0kn Wartsila 6R32E 2 x 4 Stroke 6 Cy. 320 x 350 each-2427kW (3300bhp) Wartsila Diesel Oy-Finland Wartsila 8R32E 2 x 4 Stroke 8 Cy. 320 x 350 each-3236kW (4400bhp) Wartsila Diesel Oy-Finland AuxGen: 2 x 1800kW 440V 60Hz a.c, 2 x 288kW 440V 60Hz a.c Thrusters: 1 Thwart. CP thruster (f); 1 Retract. directional thruster (f); 1 Tunnel thruster (a) Fuel: 900.0 (d.f.) 10.0pd
9206231 *JD2740* -	**VENILIA** **Corporation for Advanced Transport & Technology & Higashi Nihon Ferry Co Ltd** Higashi Nihon Ferry Co Ltd *Muroran, Hokkaido* *Japan* MMSI: 431800389 Official number: 132897	*6,558* - 3,485	Class: (NK)	**1999-03 Mitsubishi Heavy Industries Ltd. — Shimonoseki** Yd No: 1059 Loa 134.60 Br ex - Dght 5.721 Lbp 125.00 Br md 21.00 Dpth 12.03 Welded	**(A36A2PR) Passenger/Ro-Ro Ship (Vehicles)** Passengers: unberthed: 450 Lane-Len: 670 Cars: 14, Trailers: 67	**2 oil engines** reduction geared to sc. shafts driving 2 FP propellers Total Power: 11,768kW (16,000hp) 19.4kn Pielstick 12PC2-6V-400 2 x Vee 4 Stroke 12 Cy. 400 x 460 each-5884kW (8000bhp) Nippon Kokan KK (NKK Corp)-Japan AuxGen: 3 x 880kW 450V 60Hz a.c Fuel: 509.0 (r.f.) 43.7pd
7933610 - -	**VENKA M** - - -	*185* 126 -		**1979 Bender Welding & Machine Co Inc — Mobile AL** L reg 25.30 Br ex 7.35 Dght - Lbp - Br md - Dpth 3.43 Welded, 1 dk	**(B11B2FV) Fishing Vessel**	**2 oil engines** driving 2 FP propellers Total Power: 536kW (728hp) Caterpillar 3408TA 2 x Vee 4 Stroke 8 Cy. 137 x 152 each-268kW (364bhp) Caterpillar Tractor Co-USA
7002693 - -	**VENKAT** *ex Michael B -1971* **Chennai Port Trust** - *Chennai* *India*	*194* 91 450	Class: (BV) (IR)	**1969 Kanagawa Zosen — Kobe** Yd No: 92 Loa 30.71 Br ex 8.95 Dght 3.425 Lbp 27.01 Br md 8.41 Dpth 3.99 Riveted\Welded, 1 dk	**(B32A2ST) Tug**	**2 oil engines** driving 2 FP propellers Total Power: 2,648kW (3,600hp) 12.0kn Nippon Hatsudoki HS6NV138 2 x 4 Stroke 6 Cy. 380 x 540 each-1324kW (1800bhp) Nippon Hatsudoki-Japan AuxGen: 2 x 32kW 210V 50Hz a.c, 1 x 9kW 210V 50Hz a.c
8701650 *VVMM* -	**VENKATESHWARA** **Venkateshwara Fisheries Pvt Ltd** - *Chennai* *India* Official number: 2212	**127** 38 74	Class: (IR)	**1987-01 Chowgule & Co Pvt Ltd — Goa** Yd No: 91 Loa 24.01 Br ex 7.40 Dght 2.636 Lbp 20.02 Br md 7.21 Dpth 3.41 Welded, 1 dk	**(B11A2FS) Stern Trawler** Ins: 45	**1 oil engine** with clutches & sr reverse geared to sc. shaft driving 1 FP propeller Total Power: 331kW (450hp) 10.3kn Caterpillar 3412T 1 x Vee 4 Stroke 12 Cy. 137 x 152 331kW (450bhp) Caterpillar Inc-USA AuxGen: 2 x 16kW 415V 50Hz a.c Fuel: 53.0 (d.f.)
9277345 *PHBK* -	**VENNENDIEP** *ex Onego Traveller -2010* **Beheermaatschappij ms Vennendiep BV** Feederlines BV *Groningen* *Netherlands* MMSI: 245913000 Official number: 42547	**5,057** 2,681 7,750	Class: GL (LR) ✠ Classed LR until 13/5/12	**2004-07 ATVT Sudnobudivnyi Zavod "Zaliv" — Kerch (Hull)** Yd No: (624) **2004-07 Bodewes' Scheepswerven B.V. — Hoogezand** Yd No: 624 Loa 119.98 (BB) Br ex 15.43 Dght 7.050 Lbp 113.65 Br md 15.20 Dpth 8.45 Welded, 1 dk	**(A31A2GX) General Cargo Ship** Grain: 9,415 TEU 390 C Ho 174 TEU C Dk 216 TEU Compartments: 2 Ho, ER 2 Ha: ER Cranes: 2x40t Ice Capable	**1 oil engine** with clutches, flexible couplings & sr geared to sc. shaft driving 1 CP propeller Total Power: 3,840kW (5,221hp) 14.0kn MaK 8M32C 1 x 4 Stroke 8 Cy. 320 x 480 3840kW (5221bhp) Caterpillar Motoren GmbH & Co. KG-Germany AuxGen: 1 x 400kW 400V 50Hz a.c, 3 x 290kW 400V 50Hz a.c Boilers: HWH (o.f.) 3.6kgf/cm² (3.5bar) Thrusters: 1 Thwart. CP thruster (f)
9564449 *OWFG* -	**VENO FAERGEN** **Veno Faergefart v/Struer Kommune** - *Veno* *Denmark* MMSI: 219014579 Official number: A532	**269** 80 115	Class: (BV)	**2010-08 A/S Hvide Sande Skibs- og Baadebyggeri — Hvide Sande** Yd No: 122 Loa 41.40 Br ex 9.20 Dght 2.200 Lbp 31.20 Br md 9.00 Dpth 3.40 Welded, 1 dk	**(A36A2PR) Passenger/Ro-Ro Ship (Vehicles)** Passengers: unberthed: 75 Bow ramp (centre) Stern ramp (centre) Cars: 11	**2 oil engines** reduction geared to sc. shafts driving 2 Z propellers Total Power: 512kW (696hp) Volvo Penta D12MH 2 x 4 Stroke 6 Cy. 131 x 150 each-256kW (348bhp) AB Volvo Penta-Sweden
8847571 *YL2361* -	**VENTA** **Ventspils Free Port Authority (Ventspils Brivostas Parvalde)** - *Ventspils* *Latvia* Official number: 1020	**193** 85 326	Class: (RS)	**1978 Bakinskiy Sudostroitelnyy Zavod im Vano Sturua — Baku** Yd No: 321 Loa 29.17 Br ex 8.01 Dght 3.120 Lbp 28.50 Br md 7.58 Dpth 3.60 Welded, 1 dk	**(B34G2SE) Pollution Control Vessel** Liq: 336; Liq (Oil): 336 Compartments: 8 Ta Ice Capable	**1 oil engine** geared to sc. shaft driving 1 FP propeller Total Power: 165kW (224hp) 7.5kn Daldizel 6CHNSP18/22 1 x 4 Stroke 6 Cy. 180 x 220 165kW (224bhp) (made 1976) Daldizel-Khabarovsk AuxGen: 1 x 50kW a.c, 1 x 30kW a.c Fuel: 12.0 (d.f.)
9074729 *LYSV* -	**VENTA** *ex Dual Confidence -2008* *ex Pacific Frontier -2006 ex Stellar Glory -2002* **AB 'Lietuvos Juru Laivininkyste' (LJL) (Lithuanian Shipping Co)** *Klaipeda* *Lithuania* MMSI: 277375000 Official number: 798	**15,899** 9,465 24,202 T/cm 35.0	Class: BV (NK)	**1995-07 Imabari Shipbuilding Co Ltd — Imabari EH (Imabari Shipyard)** Yd No: 522 Loa 159.92 (BB) Br ex - Dght 9.801 Lbp 149.80 Br md 26.00 Dpth 13.50 Welded, 1 dk	**(A31A2GX) General Cargo Ship** Grain: 30,540; Bale: 30,260 TEU 415 Compartments: 4 Ho, ER 4 Ha: (18.4 x 17.6)3 (24.8 x 22.0)ER Cranes: 3x30t	**1 oil engine** driving 1 FP propeller Total Power: 7,134kW (9,699hp) 14.0kn B&W 5S50MC 1 x 2 Stroke 5 Cy. 500 x 1910 7134kW (9699bhp) Hitachi Zosen Corp-Japan AuxGen: 3 x 560kW 450V 60Hz a.c Fuel: 176.0 (d.f.) 1541.0 (r.f.) 26.7pd
8812150 *LW8366* -	**VENTARON 1** *ex Vieirasa Once -2009 ex Vieira Once -2006* *ex Alvamar Cuatro -2002* **Atunera Argentina SA** *Mar del Plata* *Argentina* MMSI: 701006046 Official number: 0479	**1,002** 410 1,300	Class: BV	**1989-09 Astilleros de Murueta S.A. — Gernika-Lumo** Yd No: 165 Loa 66.50 (BB) Br ex 11.22 Dght 4.652 Lbp 58.56 Br md 11.21 Dpth 4.73 Welded	**(B11A2FG) Factory Stern Trawler** Ins: 1,400 Ice Capable	**1 oil engine** with flexible couplings & sr geared to sc. shaft driving 1 CP propeller Total Power: 1,467kW (1,995hp) 13.0kn Wartsila 6R32 1 x 4 Stroke 6 Cy. 320 x 350 1467kW (1995bhp) Construcciones Echevarria SA-Spain
9143324 *CBVT* -	**VENTISQUERO** **Pesquera San Jose SA** *Valparaiso* *Chile* MMSI: 725000880 Official number: 2906	**1,447** 472 1,956	Class: LR ✠ **100A1** SS 04/2012 fishing vessel **LMC** Cable: 412.5/34.0 U2	**1997-03 Ast. y Maestranzas de la Armada (ASMAR Chile) — Talcahuano** Yd No: 73 Loa 66.00 Br ex - Dght 6.750 Lbp 60.40 Br md 12.00 Dpth 8.00 Welded, 2 dks	**(B11A2FT) Trawler**	**1 oil engine** with clutches, flexible couplings & sr geared to sc. shaft driving 1 CP propeller Total Power: 3,690kW (5,017hp) 13.0kn Wartsila 9R32 1 x 4 Stroke 9 Cy. 320 x 350 3690kW (5017bhp) Wartsila Diesel Oy-Finland AuxGen: 1 x 1810kW 380V 50Hz a.c, 2 x 400kW 380V 50Hz a.c Thrusters: 1 Thwart. FP thruster (f); 1 Tunnel thruster (a)
9082623 *3FHD6* -	**VENTO** *ex African Jaguar -2013* *ex Handy Roseland -2005* **Estate Maritime Co** Thetis Shipholding SA *Panama* *Panama* MMSI: 357677000 Official number: 45477PEXT	**16,041** 9,280 26,477 T/cm 37.9	Class: BV (LR) ✠ Classed LR until 8/4/05	**1996-03 Guangzhou Shipyard International Co Ltd — Guangzhou GD** Yd No: 3130010 Loa 168.68 (BB) Br ex 26.03 Dght 9.520 Lbp 160.00 Br md 26.00 Dpth 13.30 Welded, 1 dk	**(A21A2BC) Bulk Carrier** Grain: 33,858; Bale: 32,700 Compartments: 5 Ho, ER 5 Ha: (13.9 x 13.1)4 (19.3 x 13.1)ER Cranes: 4x30t	**1 oil engine** driving 1 FP propeller Total Power: 6,074kW (8,258hp) 14.0kn MAN-B&W 5L50MC 1 x 2 Stroke 5 Cy. 500 x 1620 6074kW (8258bhp) Hudong Shipyard-China AuxGen: 3 x 456kW 450V 60Hz a.c Boilers: AuxB (Comp) 6.6kgf/cm² (6.5bar) Fuel: 1156.0

9300659 *TCPS8* -	**VENTO DI BORA** *ex* Gabriel A *-2007* **Limar Liman ve Gemi Isletmeleri AS (Limar Port & Ship Operators SA)** Arkas Denizcilik ve Nakliyat AS (Arkas Shipping & Transport AS) *Izmir* *Turkey* MMSI: 271001018 Official number: 117	**14,193** 4,960 17,264	Class: AB (GL)	**2004-09 Detlef Hegemann Rolandwerft GmbH & Co. KG — Berne** Yd No: 224 Loa 155.60 (BB) Br ex - Dght 9.500 Lbp 146.60 Br md 24.50 Dpth 14.20 Welded, 1 dk	**(A33A2CC) Container Ship (Fully Cellular)** TEU 1221 C Ho 476 TEU C Dk 745 TEU incl 178 ref C. Compartments: 4 Cell Ho, ER Ice Capable	**1 oil engine** driving 1 FP propeller Total Power: 11,060kW (15,037hp) 18.3kn B&W 7S50MC-C 1 x 2 Stroke 7 Cy. 500 x 2000 11060kW (15037bhp) AuxGen: 3 x 780kW 450/230V 60Hz a.c Thrusters: 1 Thwart. CP thruster (f)
9362724 *V2DN9* -	**VENTO DI PONENTE** *ex* Macao Strait *-2013* *ex* BG Freight Atlantic *-2013* *ex* Macao Strait *-2012* *ex* Niledutch Qingdao *-2011* *completed as* Macao Strait *-2008* **ms 'Macao Strait' GmbH & Co KG** Carsten Rehder Schiffsmakler und Reederei GmbH & Co KG *Saint John's* *Antigua & Barbuda* MMSI: 305276000 Official number: 4493	**21,018** 8,836 25,903	Class: GL	**2008-06 Taizhou Kouan Shipbuilding Co Ltd — Taizhou JS** Yd No: KA508 Loa 179.69 (BB) Br ex 27.65 Dght 10.700 Lbp 167.20 Br md 27.60 Dpth 15.90 Welded, 1 dk	**(A33A2CC) Container Ship (Fully Cellular)** TEU 1794 C Ho 740 TEU C Dk 1054 TEU incl 319 ref C Cranes: 2x40t	**1 oil engine** driving 1 FP propeller Total Power: 16,664kW (22,656hp) 20.5kn MAN-B&W 7S60MC-C 1 x 2 Stroke 7 Cy. 600 x 2400 16664kW (22656bhp) Hudong Heavy Machinery Co Ltd-China AuxGen: 2 x 1710kW 450V a.c, 1 x 1330kW 450V a.c Thrusters: 1 Tunnel thruster (f)
9377690 *D5FH9* -	**VENTO DI TRAMONTANA** *ex* Manatee *-2013* *ex* Cala Pantera *-2013* **Los Halillos Shipping Co SA** Seachange Maritime (Singapore) Pte Ltd *Monrovia* *Liberia* MMSI: 636016269 Official number: 16269	**17,518** 8,004 21,416	Class: NK	**2006-11 Imabari Shipbuilding Co Ltd — Imabari EH (Imabari Shipyard)** Yd No: 621 Loa 171.99 (BB) Br ex 27.60 Dght 9.516 Lbp 160.00 Br md 27.60 Dpth 14.00 Welded, 1 dk	**(A33A2CC) Container Ship (Fully Cellular)** TEU 1577 TEU incl 192 ref C Cranes: 3x45t	**1 oil engine** driving 1 FP propeller Total Power: 15,820kW (21,509hp) 19.7kn MAN-B&W 7S60MC-C 1 x 2 Stroke 7 Cy. 600 x 2400 15820kW (21509bhp) Mitsui Engineering & Shipbuilding CLtd-Japan AuxGen: 3 x a.c Thrusters: 1 Tunnel thruster (f) Fuel: 2180.0
9101508 *9HA3208* -	**VENTO DI TRAMONTANA** *ex* Novia *-2013* *ex* Melfi Iberia *-2010* *ex* Cala Providencia *-2008* *ex* Novia *-2004* *ex* P&O Nedlloyd Slauerhoff *-2003* *ex* P&O Nedlloyd Mombasa *-2002* *ex* Novia *-2001* *ex* Sea Novia *-1997* *launched as* Novia *-1995* **ms 'Novia' Schiffahrtsgellschaft mbH & Co KG** Herm Dauelsberg GmbH & Co KG *Valletta* *Malta* MMSI: 229291000 Official number: 9101508	**14,936** 7,550 20,100 T/cm 65.8	Class: GL	**1995-05 Kvaerner Warnow Werft GmbH — Rostock** Yd No: 432 Loa 167.03 (BB) Br ex - Dght 9.830 Lbp 156.71 Br md 25.00 Dpth 13.40 Welded, 1 dk	**(A33A2CC) Container Ship (Fully Cellular)** Grain: 26,102 TEU 1452 C Ho 534 TEU C Dk 918 TEU incl 209 ref C. Compartments: 6 Cell Ho, ER 8 Ha: ER Cranes: 3x45t	**1 oil engine** driving 1 FP propeller Total Power: 11,130kW (15,132hp) 19.0kn Sulzer 7RTA58 1 x 2 Stroke 7 Cy. 580 x 1700 11130kW (15132bhp) Dieselmotorenwerk Rostock GmbH-Rostock AuxGen: 1 x 1000kW 220/440V 60Hz a.c, 3 x 904kW 220/440V 60Hz a.c Thrusters: 1 Thwart. CP thruster (f) Fuel: 174.3 (d.f.) 1239.9 (r.f.) 52.5pd
8129591 *UAEB* -	**VENTSPILS** - **Ventspils Marine Ltd** Russian Inspector's & Marine Surveyor's Corp (RIMSCO) *Vladivostok* *Russia* MMSI: 273449750 Official number: 820507	**5,154** 1,741 6,297 T/cm 16.4	Class: RS	**1983-09 Rauma-Repola Oy — Rauma** Yd No: 279 Loa 113.01 Br ex 18.32 Dght 7.200 Lbp 105.34 Br md 18.30 Dpth 8.51 Welded, 1 dk	**(A13B2TP) Products Tanker** Double Bottom Entire Compartment Length Liq: 5,943; Liq (Oil): 5,943 Part Cargo Heating Coils Compartments: 3 Ta, 8 Wing Ta, ER 11 Cargo Pump (s): 3x190m³/hr, 8x145m³/hr Manifold: Bow/CM: 50m Ice Capable	**1 oil engine** driving 1 FP propeller Total Power: 4,350kW (5,914hp) 15.0kn B&W 6L45GFCA 1 x 2 Stroke 6 Cy. 450 x 1200 4350kW (5914bhp) Bryanskiy Mashinostroitelnyy Zavod (BMZ)-Bryansk AuxGen: 4 x 200kW 380V 50Hz a.c Fuel: 623.0 (r.f.) 17.3pd
9219599 *YLAQ* -	**VENTSPILS** - **AS PKL Flote** - *Ventspils* *Latvia* MMSI: 275057000 Official number: 1041	**305** 91 246	Class: RS (LR) ✠ Classed LR until 10/6/10	**2000-06 Damen Shipyards Gdynia SA — Gdynia** (Hull) **2000-06 B.V. Scheepswerf Damen — Gorinchem** Yd No: 511701 Loa 29.80 Br ex - Dght 3.840 Lbp - Br md 9.40 Dpth 4.80 Welded, 1 dk	**(B32A2ST) Tug** Ice Capable	**2 oil engines** reduction geared to sc. shafts driving 2 Directional propellers Total Power: 2,610kW (3,548hp) 12.3kn Caterpillar 3516B-TA 2 x Vee 4 Stroke 16 Cy. 170 x 190 each-1305kW (1774bhp) Caterpillar Inc-USA AuxGen: 2 x 50kW 380V 50Hz a.c Fuel: 115.0 (d.f.)
7407908 *YYGZ* -	**VENTUARI** *ex* Larry Z *-1997* *ex* Marjorie R *-1997* **Pesquera Ventuari CA** - *Puerto Sucre* *Venezuela* MMSI: 775610060 Official number: APNN-7022	**1,350** 409 -	Class: RP	**1974-03 Campbell Industries — San Diego, Ca** Yd No: 98 Lengthened-1987 Loa 73.76 Br ex - Dght 5.817 Lbp 70.57 Br md 12.20 Dpth 8.27 Welded, 1 dk	**(B11B2FV) Fishing Vessel**	**1 oil engine** driving 1 FP propeller Total Power: 2,648kW (3,600hp) 17.0kn EMD (Electro-Motive) 20-645-E7B 1 x Vee 2 Stroke 20 Cy. 230 x 254 2648kW (3600bhp) General Motors Corp-USA
8915859 - -	**VENTURA** *ex* Valkyrie Venturer *-1997* **Udeen Pty Ltd** - *Brisbane, Qld* *Australia* Official number: 853611	*150* - -		**1989-12 Port Lincoln Ship Construction Pty Ltd — Port Lincoln SA** Yd No: V15 Loa 19.70 Br ex 7.18 Dght 3.125 Lbp 17.00 Br md 7.00 Dpth 3.50 Welded	**(B11A2FT) Trawler**	**1 oil engine** sr reverse geared to sc. shaft driving 1 FP propeller Total Power: 368kW (500hp) Cummins KT-19-M 1 x 4 Stroke 6 Cy. 159 x 159 368kW (500bhp) Cummins Engine Co Inc-USA
9346756 *9HKL8* -	**VENTURA** - **Ambassador Shipping Corp** TMS Dry Ltd SatCom: Inmarsat C 425608010 *Valletta* *Malta* MMSI: 256080000 Official number: 9906	**88,930** 58,083 174,316 T/cm 119.0	Class: AB	**2006-05 Shanghai Waigaoqiao Shipbuilding Co Ltd — Shanghai** Yd No: 1040 Loa 289.00 (BB) Br ex 45.05 Dght 18.120 Lbp 278.20 Br md 45.00 Dpth 24.50 Welded, 1 dk	**(A21A2BC) Bulk Carrier** Grain: 193,247; Bale: 183,425 Compartments: 9 Ho, ER 9 Ha: 7 (15.5 x 20.0)ER 2 (15.5 x 16.5)	**1 oil engine** driving 1 FP propeller Total Power: 16,860kW (22,923hp) 14.5kn MAN-B&W 6S70MC 1 x 2 Stroke 6 Cy. 700 x 2674 16860kW (22923bhp) Hudong Heavy Machinery Co Ltd-China AuxGen: 3 x 750kW Fuel: 322.5 (d.f.) 4508.5 (r.f.)
9333175 *ZCDT2* -	**VENTURA** - **Carnival Plc (Carnival UK)** - SatCom: Inmarsat C 431056210 *Hamilton* *Bermuda (British)* MMSI: 310562000 Official number: 737911	**116,017** 85,255 8,044	Class: LR (RI) ✠ **100A1** CS 03/2013 passenger ship **ShipRight** (SDA, CM) *IWS ✠ **LMC** **CCS** Eq.Ltr: Z†; Cable: 742.5/102.0 U3 (a)	**2008-03 Fincantieri-Cant. Nav. Italiani S.p.A. — Monfalcone** Yd No: 6132 Loa 288.61 (BB) Br ex 36.05 Dght 8.500 Lbp 242.31 Br md 35.99 Dpth 11.41 Welded, 8 dks plus 9 non continuous dks	**(A37A2PC) Passenger/Cruise** Passengers: cabins: 1546; berths: 3597	**6 diesel electric oil engines** driving 4 gen. each 12240kW 11000V a.c 2 gen. each 8160kW 11000V a.c Connecting to 2 elec. motors each (21000kW) driving 2 FP propellers Total Power: 67,220kW (91,390hp) 22.0kn Wartsila 12V46C 4 x Vee 4 Stroke 12 Cy. 460 x 580 each-12604kW (17136bhp) Wartsila Italia SpA-Italy Wartsila 8L46C 2 x 4 Stroke 8 Cy. 460 x 580 each-8402kW (11423bhp) Wartsila Italia SpA-Italy Boilers: e (ex.g.) 11.7kgf/cm² (11.5bar), e (ex.g.) 11.7kgf/cm² (11.5bar), WTAuxB (o.f.) 10.9kgf/cm² (10.7bar) Thrusters: 3 Thwart. CP thruster (f); 3 Thwart. CP thruster (a)
9312729 *V2GM2* -	**VENTURA** *ex* Julia *-2013* *launched as* Emma *-2006* **E Strahlmann GmbH & Co Reederei KG ms 'Ventura'** Reederei Erwin Strahlmann eK *Saint John's* *Antigua & Barbuda* MMSI: 305994000	**3,870** 2,132 5,780 T/cm 13.0	Class: GL (BV)	**2006-12 Maritim Shipyard Sp z oo — Gdansk** (Hull) **2006-12 Niestern Sander B.V. — Delfzijl** Yd No: 830 Loa 106.12 (BB) Br ex - Dght 6.140 Lbp 100.05 Br md 14.40 Dpth 8.10 Welded, 1 dk	**(A31A2GX) General Cargo Ship** Grain: 7,645 TEU 240 C Ho 136 TEU C Dk 104 TEU Compartments: 2 Ho, ER 2 Ha: ER 2 (37.5 x 11.7) Ice Capable	**1 oil engine** reduction geared to sc. shaft driving 1 CP propeller Total Power: 2,700kW (3,671hp) 12.0kn MaK 9M25 1 x 4 Stroke 9 Cy. 255 x 400 2700kW (3671bhp) Caterpillar Motoren GmbH & Co. KG-Germany AuxGen: 1 x 350kW 400/230V 50Hz a.c, 2 x 150kW 400/230V 50Hz a.c Thrusters: 1 Tunnel thruster (f) Fuel: 88.0 (d.f.) 245.0 (r.f.)
9679347 *ZJL8707* -	**VENTURA** - **Aviemore Assets Ltd** Alfa Bravo Srl *British Virgin Islands* MMSI: 378365000 Official number: 744478	**496** 148 -	Class: AB	**2013-04 Heesen Shipyards B.V. — Oss** Yd No: 16050 Loa 49.80 Br ex - Dght 2.500 Lbp 44.00 Br md 8.50 Dpth 3.80 Welded, 1 dk	**(X11A2YP) Yacht** Hull Material: Aluminium Alloy	**2 oil engines** reverse reduction geared to sc. shafts driving 2 FP propellers Total Power: 5,440kW (7,396hp) M.T.U. 16V4000M90 2 x Vee 4 Stroke 16 Cy. 165 x 190 each-2720kW (3698bhp) MTU Friedrichshafen GmbH-Friedrichshafen AuxGen: 2 x 99kW a.c Thrusters: 1 Tunnel thruster (f)

Identity	Tonnage / Class	Builder / Dimensions	Type	Machinery
7230977 **VENTURA II** *WCR8907* *ex* Lois U. Wetmore *-2001* *ex* Clearview IV *-2001* - *ex* Matco IV *-2001* **Pete Dupuy** - *Los Angeles, CA* *United States of America* MMSI: 338502000 Official number: 536620	*166* 121 -	**1971 Rockport Yacht & Supply Co. (RYSCO) — Rockport, Tx** Loa 26.52 Br ex 7.04 Dght 3.658 Lbp - Br md - Dpth 3.51 Welded	**(B11B2FV) Fishing Vessel**	**1 oil engine** driving 1 FP propeller Total Power: 493kW (670hp)
8855566 **VENTURE** *WDC6136* - **Nordic Inc** - *New Bedford, MA* *United States of America* MMSI: 367051880 Official number: 942988	*194* 131 -	**1988 Rodriguez Boat Builders, Inc. — Coden, Al** Yd No: 80 Loa - Br ex - Dght - Lbp 26.00 Br md 7.77 Dpth 3.99 Welded, 1 dk	**(B11B2FV) Fishing Vessel**	**1 oil engine** driving 1 FP propeller
8843305 **VENTURE** - - **Venture Trading Co Ltd** - *Turks Islands* *Turks & Caicos Islands (British)* Official number: 720555	*105* 70 -	**1951 United States Coast Guard Yard — Baltimore, Md** Converted From: Patrol Vessel Loa - Br ex 5.79 Dght - Lbp 28.96 Br md - Dpth 3.65 Welded, 1 dk	**(A31A2GX) General Cargo Ship**	**2 oil engines** driving 2 FP propellers Total Power: 514kW (698hp) 12.0kn G.M. (Detroit Diesel) 8V-71 2 x Vee 2 Stroke 8 Cy. 108 x 127 each-257kW (349bhp) Detroit Diesel Corporation-Detroit, Mi
9020390 **VENTURE** *MNMS9* *ex* Lynn May *-1999* *ex* Victoria May *-1994* LK 641 **Venture Fishing Co Ltd** LHD Ltd SatCom: Inmarsat C 423329010 *Lerwick* *United Kingdom* MMSI: 235002051 Official number: B12204	**227** 82 82	**1991-07 James N. Miller & Sons Ltd. — St. Monans** Yd No: 1044 Loa 24.70 Br ex 7.42 Dght 3.800 Lbp 21.20 Br md 7.35 Dpth 4.00 Welded, 1 dk	**(B11B2FV) Fishing Vessel** Ins: 160	**1 oil engine** with clutches, flexible couplings & sr reverse geared to sc. shaft driving 1 FP propeller Total Power: 388kW (528hp) 10.5kn Deutz SBA12M816 1 x Vee 4 Stroke 12 Cy. 142 x 160 388kW (528bhp) Motoren Werke Mannheim AG (MWM)-Mannheim
9480849 **VENTURE G** *HP2217* - **Rederij Groen BV** - *Panama* *Panama* MMSI: 370941000 Official number: 4013309B	**1,076** Class: NV (AB) 322 1,126	**2008-09 Sealink Engineering & Slipway Sdn Bhd — Miri** Yd No: 163 Loa 53.80 Br ex 13.83 Dght 3.800 Lbp 50.00 Br md 13.80 Dpth 4.50 Welded, 1 dk	**(B21A2OS) Platform Supply Ship** Cranes: 1x10t	**2 oil engines** reduction geared to sc. shafts driving 2 CP propellers Total Power: 2,386kW (3,244hp) 10.0kn Cummins KTA-50-M2 2 x Vee 4 Stroke 16 Cy. 159 x 159 each-1193kW (1622bhp) Cummins Engine Co Inc-USA AuxGen: 3 x 245kW 415V 50Hz a.c Thrusters: 1 Thwart. FP thruster (f) Fuel: 190.0 (d.f.) 830.0 (r.f.)
9222182 **VENTURE II** *ZNS09* BF 326 **Venture II Fishing Co Ltd** - *Banff* *United Kingdom* MMSI: 235002690 Official number: C17393	**468** 263 -	**2001-07 Richards Dry Dock & Engineering Ltd — Great Yarmouth** (Hull) **2001-07 Macduff Shipyards Ltd — Macduff** Yd No: 608 Loa 28.00 (BB) Br ex - Dght 6.200 Lbp 23.99 Br md 9.50 Dpth 7.20 Welded, 1 dk	**(B11A2FT) Trawler** Ins: 230	**1 oil engine** reduction geared to sc. shaft driving 1 CP propeller Total Power: 1,058kW (1,438hp) 13.0kn MaK 8M20 1 x 4 Stroke 8 Cy. 200 x 300 1058kW (1438bhp) MaK Motoren GmbH & Co. KG-Kiel Thrusters: 1 Thwart. FP thruster (f) Fuel: 84.0 (d.f.)
8405517 **VENTURE K** - *launched as* Tanimbar 1 *-1985* - **Sanford Ltd** - SatCom: Inmarsat C 451200144 *Napier* *New Zealand* Official number: 875270	*129* 62 -	**1985-08 K Shipyard Construction Co — Fremantle WA** Yd No: 81 Loa 25.33 Br ex - Dght 3.052 Lbp - Br md 6.41 Dpth 3.66 Welded, 1 dk	**(B11A2FT) Trawler** Ins: 82	**1 oil engine** sr reverse geared to sc. shaft driving 1 FP propeller Total Power: 349kW (475hp) 9.0kn Mercedes Benz OM424A 1 x Vee 4 Stroke 12 Cy. 128 x 142 349kW (475bhp) Daimler Benz AG-West Germany AuxGen: 1 x 120kW 415V 50Hz a.c Fuel: 55.0 (d.f.) 1.5pd
9483279 **VENTURE PEARL** *D5CT5* - **PT Pann (Persero)** HBC Hamburg Bulk Carriers GmbH & Co KG *Monrovia* *Liberia* MMSI: 636015777 Official number: 15777	**32,672** Class: NK (NV) 18,529 55,639 T/cm 57.1	**2012-08 Hyundai-Vinashin Shipyard Co Ltd — Ninh Hoa** Yd No: S-010 Loa 187.88 (BB) Br ex - Dght 12.868 Lbp 182.50 Br md 32.26 Dpth 18.30 Welded, 1 dk	**(A21A2BC) Bulk Carrier** Grain: 70,733; Bale: 69,550 Compartments: 5 Ho, ER 5 Ha: ER Cranes: 4x30t	**1 oil engine** driving 1 FP propeller Total Power: 8,820kW (11,992hp) 14.5kn MAN-B&W 6S50MC-C8 1 x 2 Stroke 6 Cy. 500 x 2000 8820kW (11992bhp) Hyundai Heavy Industries Co Ltd-South Korea AuxGen: 3 x 640kW a.c Fuel: 1920.0
9197301 **VENTURE SEA** *VCVZ* **3260819 Nova Scotia Ltd** Secunda Canada LP *Halifax, NS* *Canada* MMSI: 316250000 Official number: 820661	**2,235** Class: NV 670 2,680	**1998-08 Halter Marine Pascagoula, Inc. — Pascagoula, Ms** Yd No: B100 Loa 73.45 Br ex 15.88 Dght 5.713 Lbp 67.59 Br md 15.85 Dpth 6.71 Welded, 1 dk	**(B21B20A) Anchor Handling Tug Supply** Cranes: 1x5t	**4 oil engines** reduction geared to sc. shafts driving 2 CP propellers Total Power: 9,040kW (12,292hp) 10.8kn EMD (Electro-Motive) 16-645-F7B 4 x Vee 2 Stroke 16 Cy. 230 x 254 each-2260kW (3073bhp) General Motors Corp.Electro-Motive Div.-La Grange AuxGen: 2 x 1600kW 110/460V 60Hz a.c, 1 x a.c Thrusters: 2 Thwart. FP thruster (f); 1 Thwart. FP thruster (a) Fuel: 880.0
9245794 **VENTURE SPIRIT** *VRYU3* - **Wah Kwong Satellite Technology Co Ltd** Wah Kwong Ship Management (Hong Kong) Ltd SatCom: Inmarsat C 447740910 *Hong Kong* *Hong Kong* MMSI: 477409000 Official number: HK-1065	**159,456** Class: BV 95,323 298,330 T/cm 181.0	**2003-06 Universal Shipbuilding Corp — Nagasu KM (Ariake Shipyard)** Yd No: 4989 Loa 332.94 (BB) Br ex - Dght 21.130 Lbp 321.34 Br md 60.00 Dpth 29.55 Welded, 1 dk	**(A13A2TV) Crude Oil Tanker** Double Hull (13F) Liq: 331,823; Liq (Oil): 331,823 Compartments: 5 Ta, 10 Wing Ta, 2 Wing Slop Ta, ER 3 Cargo Pump (s): 3x5500m³/hr Manifold: Bow/CM: 164.2m	**1 oil engine** driving 1 FP propeller Total Power: 25,485kW (34,649hp) 15.6kn MAN-B&W 7S80MC 1 x 2 Stroke 7 Cy. 800 x 3056 25485kW (34649bhp) Hitachi Zosen Corp-Japan AuxGen: 3 x 760kW 440/115V 60Hz a.c Fuel: 450.0 (d.f.) 7500.0 (r.f.)
9369150 **VENTURE SW** *3ELC3* - **Fortunate Maritime SA** Shih Wei Navigation Co Ltd *Panama* *Panama* MMSI: 372909000 Official number: 3291307A	**7,271** Class: BV 4,859 12,500	**2007-06 Higaki Zosen K.K. — Imabari** Yd No: 603 Loa 127.82 Br ex - Dght 8.170 Lbp 119.83 Br md 19.60 Dpth 11.00 Welded, 1 dk	**(A31A2GX) General Cargo Ship** Grain: 17,150 Compartments: 3 Ho, ER 3 Ha: ER Cranes: 2; Derricks: 1	**1 oil engine** driving 1 FP propeller Total Power: 3,900kW (5,302hp) 13.3kn MAN-B&W 6L35MC 1 x 2 Stroke 6 Cy. 350 x 1050 3900kW (5302bhp) Makita Corp-Japan AuxGen: 2 x 320kW 440V 60Hz a.c
8510673 **VENTURER** *LAZD5* *ex* CGG Venturer *-2006* *ex* Polar Venturer *-2006* - *ex* Thales Venturer *-2003* *ex* Seisventurer *-2001* **Ostervold Seismikk AS** Geofield Ship Management Services SAS *Bergen* *Norway (NIS)* MMSI: 257239000	**3,935** Class: NV 1,180 2,000	**1986-05 Drammen Slip & Verksted — Drammen** Yd No: 101 Lengthened-1992 Loa 89.55 Br ex 14.41 Dght 4.970 Lbp 82.61 Br md 14.40 Dpth 7.50 Welded, 4 dks	**(B31A2SR) Research Survey Vessel** Ice Capable	**2 oil engines** reduction geared to sc. shafts driving 2 CP propellers Total Power: 3,308kW (4,498hp) 14.0kn Normo KRGB-9 2 x 4 Stroke 9 Cy. 250 x 300 each-1654kW (2249bhp) AS Bergens Mek Verksteder-Norway AuxGen: 3 x 1570kW 380V 50Hz a.c, 1 x 287kW 380V 50Hz a.c Thrusters: 1 Thwart. FP thruster (f)
8619754 **VENTURER** *ZDLP1* *ex* Ixia *-1998* *ex* Cabu Primero *-1992* - **Petrel Fishing Co Ltd** Pescapuerta SA *Stanley* *Falkland Islands (British)* MMSI: 740354000 Official number: 730448	**1,881** Class: BV (LR) 659 ✠ Classed LR until 7/92 2,119	**1988-12 Construcciones Navales Santodomingo SA — Vigo** Yd No: 589 Loa 84.20 Br ex 12.78 Dght 6.301 Lbp 75.00 Br md 12.51 Dpth 7.37 Welded, 2 dks	**(B11A2FS) Stern Trawler** Ice Capable	**1 oil engine** with flexible couplings & sr geared to sc. shaft driving 1 CP propeller Total Power: 1,802kW (2,450hp) MaK 6M453AK 1 x 4 Stroke 6 Cy. 320 x 420 1802kW (2450bhp) Krupp MaK Maschinenbau GmbH-Kiel AuxGen: 1 x 500kW 380V 50Hz a.c, 2 x 372kW 380V 50Hz a.c, 1 x 135kW 380V 50Hz a.c
8108717 **VENTURER** *V4SV2* *ex* OSA Venturer *-2013* *ex* Lancelot Cliff *-1992* - *ex* British Piper *-1990* *ex* Balder Hansa *-1986* **Roxford Enterprises SA** Canadian Global Sea Carriers Inc *St Kitts & Nevis* MMSI: 341958000 Official number: SKN1002515	**1,334** Class: AB (GL) (NV) 400 1,917	**1982-12 Kroegerwerft Rendsburg GmbH — Schacht-Audorf** Yd No: 1507 Loa 64.67 Br ex - Dght 5.909 Lbp 56.42 Br md 13.81 Dpth 6.91 Welded, 2 dks	**(B21B20A) Anchor Handling Tug Supply**	**2 oil engines** with clutches, flexible couplings & sr geared to sc. shafts driving 2 CP propellers Total Power: 5,400kW (7,342hp) 15.5kn MaK 9M453AK 2 x 4 Stroke 9 Cy. 320 x 420 each-2700kW (3671bhp) Krupp MaK Maschinenbau GmbH-Kiel AuxGen: 2 x 640kW 220/440V 60Hz a.c, 2 x 245kW 220/440V 60Hz a.c Thrusters: 1 Thwart. CP thruster (f) Fuel: 794.0 (d.f.) 28.0pd

7315313 *H05062* -	**VENTURER** *ex* Viking Venturer *-2008* *ex* Cam Venturer *-1995* *ex* Mehamn *-1990* *ex* Mehamntral *-1982* **Seaport International Shipping Co Ltd** Seaport International Shipping Co LLC *Panama* *Panama* MMSI: 351959000 Official number: 37077PEXT	**524** 158 -	Class: (NV)	**1973**-04 **Kaarbos Mek. Verksted AS — Harstad** Yd No: 74 Converted From: Stern Trawler-1984 Loa 41.03 Br ex 9.22 Dght 4.436 Lbp 35.03 Br md 9.17 Dpth 6.51 Welded, 2 dks	**(B22G20Y) Standby Safety Vessel** Ice Capable	**1 oil engine** driving 1 CP propeller Total Power: 1,103kW (1,500hp) 6.0kn Wichmann 6AXA 1 x 2 Stroke 6 Cy. 300 x 450 1103kW (1500bhp) Wichmann Motorfabrikk AS-Norway AuxGen: 2 x 112kW 220V 50Hz a.c Thrusters: 1 Thwart. FP thruster (f) Fuel: 72.0 (d.f.)
5270698 - -	**VENTURER II** *ex* Paris Bretagne *-1985* - -	*281* 80 -	Class: (BV)	**1962 Chantiers et Ateliers de La Perriere — Lorient** Loa 36.30 Br ex 8.26 Dght 3.068 Lbp 31.73 Br md 8.13 Dpth 3.97 Welded, 2 dks	**(B11A2FS) Stern Trawler**	**1 oil engine** driving 1 FP propeller Total Power: 688kW (935hp) 12.3kn Deutz SBA12M528 1 x Vee 4 Stroke 12 Cy. 220 x 280 688kW (935bhp) (new engine 1968) Kloeckner Humboldt Deutz AG-West Germany Fuel: 87.0 (d.f.)
9389631 *9MGZ8* -	**VENTURES TUAH DUA** **Bumi Armada Navigation Sdn Bhd** - *Port Klang* *Malaysia* MMSI: 533000517 Official number: 332321	**663** 199 443	Class: AB	**2007**-03 **Nam Cheong Dockyard Sdn Bhd — Miri** Yd No: 530 Loa 42.50 Br ex - Dght 4.000 Lbp 41.00 Br md 11.60 Dpth 5.00 Welded, 1 dk	**(B21B20A) Anchor Handling Tug Supply**	**2 oil engines** reduction geared to sc. shafts driving 2 Propellers Total Power: 2,942kW (4,000hp) Yanmar 6EY26 2 x 4 Stroke 6 Cy. 260 x 385 each-1471kW (2000bhp) Yanmar Diesel Engine Co Ltd-Japan AuxGen: 2 x 280kW a.c Fuel: 310.0 (r.f.)
9389629 *9WIJ2* -	**VENTURES TUAH SATU** **Bumi Armada Navigation Sdn Bhd** - *Port Klang* *Malaysia* MMSI: 533637000 Official number: 332229	**1,234** 370 1,300	Class: AB	**2006**-12 **Nam Cheong Dockyard Sdn Bhd — Miri** Yd No: 529 Loa 59.20 Br ex - Dght 4.300 Lbp 57.70 Br md 13.80 Dpth 5.50 Welded, 1 dk	**(B21B20T) Offshore Tug/Supply Ship**	**2 oil engines** reduction geared to sc. shafts driving 2 Propellers Total Power: 3,840kW (5,220hp) Yanmar 6EY26 2 x 4 Stroke 6 Cy. 260 x 385 each-1920kW (2610bhp) Yanmar Diesel Engine Co Ltd-Japan AuxGen: 2 x 280kW a.c Fuel: 643.1 (d.f.)
9095814 *H04889* -	**VENTURIA** *ex* Mariano Dos *-2008* **Mr Kazem Hamdavi** - *Panama* *Panama* Official number: 3428908A	**497** 149 481		**1994**-09 **Parola Marine Service & Supply Co. — Manila** Yd No: 191 Loa 54.00 Br ex 11.02 Dght 3.460 Lbp 50.80 Br md 11.00 Dpth 3.95 Welded, 1 dk	**(B21A20S) Platform Supply Ship**	**2 oil engines** geared to sc. shafts driving 2 Propellers Total Power: 2,169kW (2,949hp) MWM TBD440-8 2 x 4 Stroke 8 Cy. 230 x 270 each-919kW (1249bhp) (made 1985) Motoren Werke Mannheim AG (MWM)-Mannheim
9320283 - -	**VENTURILLA** **Government of Bermuda (Department of Marine & Ports Services)** - *Hamilton* *Bermuda (British)*	*174* 118 18	Class: LR ✠ **100A1** SS 06/2009 SSC passenger catamaran HSC G2 for inter island service in Bermuda **LMC** **UMS** Cable: 110.0/14.0 U1	**2004**-06 **North West Bay Ships Pty Ltd — Margate TAS** Yd No: 8 Loa 23.56 Br ex 7.87 Dght 0.940 Lbp 20.77 Br md 7.66 Dpth 2.45 Welded, 1 dk	**(A37B2PS) Passenger Ship** Hull Material: Aluminium Alloy Passengers: unberthed: 177	**4 oil engines** geared to sc. shafts driving 4 Water jets Total Power: 2,100kW (2,856hp) 30.0kn M.T.U. 8V2000M70 4 x Vee 4 Stroke 8 Cy. 130 x 150 each-525kW (714bhp) MTU Friedrichshafen GmbH-Friedrichshafen AuxGen: 2 x 25kW 230V 60Hz a.c
8821022 *MLEY5* LK 75	**VENTUROUS** *ex* Venture *-1999* **Venturous Fishing Co Ltd** - SatCom: Inmarsat C 423324610 *Lerwick* *United Kingdom* MMSI: 232007300 Official number: B10814	**244** 147 -		**1989**-07 **R. Dunston (Hessle) Ltd. — Hessle** Yd No: H972 Loa 26.19 Br ex - Dght - Lbp 23.00 Br md 7.51 Dpth 4.15 Welded, 2 dks	**(B11A2FS) Stern Trawler**	**1 oil engine** with clutches, flexible couplings & sr geared to sc. shaft driving 1 CP propeller Total Power: 625kW (850hp) Alpha 5L23/30 1 x 4 Stroke 5 Cy. 225 x 300 625kW (850bhp) MAN B&W Diesel A/S-Denmark
8834809 *SW8264* -	**VENUS** *ex* Alina 1 *-1992* *ex* Floks-1 *-1990* **Ionia Shipping Co** - *Agios Nikolaos, Kea* *Greece* MMSI: 237012900 Official number: 01	**144** 95 65	Class: RS	**1990**-08 **Ilyichyovskiy Sudoremontnyy Zavod im. "50-letiya SSSR" — Ilyichyovsk** Yd No: 122 Loa 37.62 Br ex 6.90 Dght 1.850 Lbp 34.02 Br md 6.72 Dpth 2.93 Welded, 1 dk	**(A37B2PS) Passenger Ship** Passengers: unberthed: 295	**2 oil engines** reduction geared to sc. shafts driving 2 FP propellers Total Power: 720kW (978hp) 16.5kn Cummins VT-1710-M 1 x Vee 4 Stroke 12 Cy. 140 x 152 360kW (489bhp) (made 1969, fitted 1990) Cummins Engine Co Ltd-United Kingdom Cummins VT-1710-M 1 x Vee 4 Stroke 12 Cy. 140 x 152 360kW (489bhp) (made 1972, fitted 1990) Cummins Engine Co Ltd-United Kingdom
8936657 - -	**VENUS** **Jackson Marine LLC** Tidewater de Mexico S de RL de CV	**138** 42 -	Class: AB	**1984**-01 **Aluminum Boats, Inc. — Crown Point, La** Yd No: 293 Loa - Br ex - Dght - Lbp 31.69 Br md 7.31 Dpth 3.35 Welded, 1 dk	**(B34J2SD) Crew Boat** Hull Material: Aluminium Alloy	**3 oil engines** reverse reduction geared to sc. shafts driving 3 FP propellers Total Power: 1,566kW (2,130hp) 20.0kn G.M. (Detroit Diesel) 12V-92-TA 3 x Vee 2 Stroke 12 Cy. 123 x 127 each-522kW (710bhp) General Motors Detroit DieselAllison Divn-USA AuxGen: 2 x 40kW a.c
9114567 *JD2733* -	**VENUS** **Seiko Kaiun KK** - *Muroran, Hokkaido* *Japan* MMSI: 431800044 Official number: 128514	*7,198* - 3,096	Class: (NK)	**1995**-03 **Mitsubishi Heavy Industries Ltd. — Shimonoseki** Yd No: 1000 Loa 136.60 (BB) Br ex 22.40 Dght 5.721 Lbp 125.00 Br md 21.00 Dpth 12.09 Welded	**(A36A2PR) Passenger/Ro-Ro Ship (Vehicles)** Passengers: unberthed: 484; cabins: 34; berths: 116 Bow door/ramp Len: 8.40 Wid: 4.50 Swl: - Stern door/ramp Len: 8.80 Wid: 5.50 Swl: - Quarter bow door/ramp (s) Len: 13.45 Wid: 6.50 Swl: - Lane-Len: 785 Lorries: 95, Cars: 20	**2 oil engines** with flexible couplings & sr geared to sc. shafts driving 2 FP propellers Total Power: 13,388kW (18,202hp) 20.0kn Pielstick 14PC2-6V-400 2 x Vee 4 Stroke 14 Cy. 400 x 460 each-6694kW (9101bhp) Nippon Kokan KK (NKK Corp)-Japan AuxGen: 3 x 780kW a.c Thrusters: 1 Thwart. CP thruster (f) Fuel: 391.0 (d.f.) 47.9pd
9017599 *JM6078* -	**VENUS** **Kyushu Yusen KK** - *Fukuoka, Fukuoka* *Japan* Official number: 132635	*163* - 34		**1991**-03 **Kawasaki Heavy Industries Ltd — Kobe HG** Yd No: F009 Loa 30.33 Br ex - Dght 1.560 Lbp 23.99 Br md 8.53 Dpth 2.59 Welded	**(A37B2PS) Passenger Ship** Hull Material: Aluminium Alloy Passengers: unberthed: 263	**2 Gas Turbs** geared to sc. shafts driving 2 Water jets Total Power: 5,590kW (7,600hp) 43.0kn Allison 501-KF 2 x Gas Turb each-2795kW (3800shp) General Motors Detroit DieselAllison Divn-USA AuxGen: 2 x 50kW 450V 60Hz a.c
1011836 *ZGCS8* -	**VENUS** **Aqua Ltd** Vessel Safety Management LLC *George Town* *Cayman Islands (British)* MMSI: 319327000 Official number: 743794	**1,876** 562 231	Class: LR ✠ **100A1** SS 12/2012 SSC Yacht, mono, G6 ✠ **LMC** **UMS** Cable: 400.0/26.0 U3	**2012**-12 **Jacht- en Scheepswerf Gouwerok B.V. — Aalsmeer** (Hull) Yd No: 427 **2012**-12 **de Vries Scheepsbouw B.V. — Aalsmeer** Yd No: 684 Loa 78.20 Br ex 11.80 Dght 3.000 Lbp 75.75 Br md 11.80 Dpth 5.30 Welded, 1 dk	**(X11A2YP) Yacht**	**2 oil engines** with flexible couplings & sr geared to sc. shafts driving 2 CP propellers Total Power: 5,120kW (6,962hp) 20.0kn M.T.U. 16V4000M73 2 x Vee 4 Stroke 16 Cy. 170 x 190 each-2560kW (3481bhp) MTU Friedrichshafen GmbH-Friedrichshafen AuxGen: 3 x 424kW 400V 50Hz a.c Thrusters: 1 Thwart. FP thruster (f); 1 Thwart. FP thruster (a)
7022899 *ERDU* -	**VENUS** *ex* Fatema M *-2008* *ex* Moro 5 *-2008* *ex* Lirica *-2005* *ex* Larita *-2001* *ex* Engenes *-1990* *ex* Bergmann *-1989* *ex* Frengen *-1986* *ex* Egin *-1984* **Marine Shipping Lines Inc** - *Giurgiulesti* *Moldova* MMSI: 214180421	**1,055** 510 1,400	Class: (LR) (BV) Classed LR until 2/12/04	**1970**-06 **Frederikshavn Vaerft og Tordok A/S — Frederikshavn** Yd No: 307 Loa 64.60 Br ex 11.03 Dght 4.130 Lbp 58.00 Br md 11.00 Dpth 6.20 Welded, 1 dk	**(A31A2GX) General Cargo Ship** Grain: 2,549; Bale: 2,296 Compartments: 1 Ho, ER 1 Ha: (31.6 x 8.0)ER Ice Capable	**1 oil engine** sr geared to sc. shaft driving 1 CP propeller Total Power: 653kW (888hp) 11.0kn Blackstone EWSL8 1 x 4 Stroke 8 Cy. 222 x 292 653kW (888bhp) Lister Blackstone MirrleesMarine Ltd.-Dursley AuxGen: 2 x 70kW 380V 50Hz a.c, 1 x 65kW 380V 50Hz a.c Fuel: 61.0 (d.f.) 3.5pd

7223223 *TFKT* HF 519	**VENUS** *ex Juni -1986* **HB Grandi hf** SatCom: Inmarsat C 425102910 *Hafnarfjordur* *Iceland* MMSI: 251029000 Official number: 1308	**1,779** 534 793	Class: LR ✠**100A1** SS 02/2010 stern trawler Ice Class 2 ✠**LMC** Eq.Ltr: M; Cable: U2	**1973-05 Astilleros Luzuriaga SA — Pasaia** Yd No: 112 Lengthened-1994 Loa 77.66 Br ex 11.71 Dght 4.801 Lbp 68.21 Br md 11.60 Dpth 7.52 Welded, 2 dks	**(B11A2FS) Stern Trawler** Ice Capable	**1 oil engine** sr geared to sc. shaft driving 1 CP propeller Total Power: 2,133kW (2,900hp) 16.0kn MaK 8M453AK 1 x 4 Stroke 8 Cy. 320 x 420 2133kW (2900bhp) (new engine 1980) Krupp MaK Maschinenbau GmbH-Kiel AuxGen: 2 x 380kW 380V 50Hz a.c, 1 x 136kW 380V 50Hz a.c Boilers: db 8.1kgf/cm² (7.9bar)
7607168 *XPZE* KG 386	**VENUS** *ex Ekliptika -1986 ex Oyliner -2005* **Ekliptika P/F** Christian Guttorm Mathisen *Sandavagur* *Faeroe Islands (Danish)*	**391** 145 -		**1977-03 Kystvaagen Slip & Baatbyggeri — Kristiansund** Yd No: 37 Lengthened-1978 Loa 30.97 Br ex 7.52 Dght 3.099 Lbp 22.38 Br md 7.50 Dpth 6.00 Welded, 2 dks	**(B11B2FV) Fishing Vessel**	**1 oil engine** geared to sc. shaft driving 1 FP propeller Total Power: 515kW (700hp) G.M. (Detroit Diesel) 16V-71-N 1 x Vee 2 Stroke 16 Cy. 108 x 127 515kW (700bhp) General Motors Detroit DieselAllison Divn-USA
8105806 *D9XG* -	**VENUS** *ex Miyo Maru -1991* **Han Chang Industrial Co Ltd** *Pyeongtaek* *South Korea* Official number: PTR-912329	**175** - 116	Class: KR	**1981-06 Kanagawa Zosen — Kobe** Yd No: 225 Loa 31.50 Br ex 8.62 Dght 2.601 Lbp 26.62 Br md 8.60 Dpth 3.81 Welded, 1 dk	**(B32A2ST) Tug**	**2 oil engines** driving 2 FP propellers Total Power: 1,766kW (2,402hp) Niigata 6L25BX 2 x 4 Stroke 6 Cy. 250 x 320 each-883kW (1201bhp) Niigata Engineering Co Ltd-Japan
7942441 *5IM480* -	**VENUS** *ex Skipper -2007 ex Skipper K -2004* *ex Maria L -2002 ex Seawave -2000* *ex Hirsova -1997* **Zahranos Shipping Co SA** Zahra Maritime Services Co *Zanzibar* *Tanzania (Zanzibar)* MMSI: 677038000 Official number: 300220	**5,930** 3,535 9,034	Class: BR (PR) (GL) (RN)	**1980-07 Santierul Naval Braila — Braila** Yd No: 1196 Loa 130.72 (BB) Br ex 17.71 Dght 8.100 Lbp 121.03 Br md 17.70 Dpth 10.20 Welded, 2 dks	**(A31A2GX) General Cargo Ship** Grain: 11,980; Bale: 11,067 Compartments: 4 Ho, ER 4 Ha: (11.9 x 5.9)3 (13.6 x 9.9)ER Cranes: 4x5t Ice Capable	**1 oil engine** driving 1 FP propeller Total Power: 4,487kW (6,101hp) 13.0kn Sulzer 6RD68 1 x 2 Stroke 6 Cy. 680 x 1250 4487kW (6101bhp) Zaklady Przemyslu Metalowego 'HCegielski' SA-Poznan AuxGen: 3 x 200kW 220/380V 50Hz a.c Fuel: 1148.0
8619924 *9A2475* -	**VENUS** **Jadranski Pomorski Servis dd** *Rijeka* *Croatia*	*195* 58 100	Class: CS (JR)	**1988-12 Brodogradiliste 'Titovo' — Kraljevica** Yd No: 475 Loa 29.85 Br ex - Dght 3.550 Lbp 25.65 Br md 8.00 Dpth 4.10 Welded, 1 dk	**(B32A2ST) Tug**	**1 oil engine** sr geared to sc. shaft driving 1 FP propeller Total Power: 2,220kW (3,018hp) Sulzer 12ASV25/30 1 x Vee 4 Stroke 12 Cy. 250 x 300 2220kW (3018bhp) Tvornica Dizel Motora 'Jugoturbina'-Yugoslavia AuxGen: 2 x 80kW 400V 50Hz a.c Thrusters: 1 Thwart. FP thruster (f) Fuel: 58.7 (d.f.) 9.0pd
8621886 - -	**VENUS** *ex Yusho Maru -2000* **Bengal Shipping Line Ltd** - *Chittagong* *Bangladesh* Official number: C.1377	**495** 289 1,114	Class: (NK)	**1984 Shitanoe Shipbuilding Co Ltd — Usuki OT** Yd No: 1037 Loa 66.30 Br ex - Dght 2.820 Lbp 62.01 Br md 10.30 Dpth 6.00 Welded, 1 dk	**(A31A2GX) General Cargo Ship**	**1 oil engine** reduction geared to sc. shaft driving 1 FP propeller Total Power: 736kW (1,001hp) 10.5kn Hanshin 6LU26G 1 x 4 Stroke 6 Cy. 260 x 440 736kW (1001bhp) The Hanshin Diesel Works Ltd-Japan
8300042 - -	**VENUS** *ex An Yang -2012 ex Tai Rong 12 -2010* *ex Jing Hai 2 -2008 ex Jian She 3 -2008* - -	*2,990* 1,476 5,280	Class: (CC)	**1984-03 Hudong Shipyard — Shanghai** Yd No: 1124 Loa 107.42 Br ex - Dght 6.420 Lbp 98.00 Br md 15.00 Dpth 7.49 Welded, 1 dk	**(A13B2TP) Products Tanker** Single Hull Liq: 6,283; Liq (Oil): 6,283	**1 oil engine** driving 1 FP propeller Total Power: 2,207kW (3,001hp) 13.0kn Hudong 6ESDZ43/82B 1 x 2 Stroke 6 Cy. 430 x 820 2207kW (3001bhp) Hudong Shipyard-China
9553232 *C6A09* -	**VENUS** *ex Federica -2013* **Golden Stavraetos Maritime Inc** Super-Eco Tankers Management Inc *Nassau* *Bahamas* MMSI: 311000108	**32,987** 19,242 56,568 T/cm 58.8	Class: LR ✠**100A1** SS 06/2012 bulk carrier CSR BC-A GRAB (20) Nos. 2 & 4 holds may be empty ESP **ShipRight** (CM) *IWS LI ✠**LMC** **UMS** Eq.Ltr: M†; Cable: 632.5/73.0 U3 (a)	**2012-06 COSCO (Zhoushan) Shipyard Co Ltd — Zhoushan ZJ** Yd No: N194 Loa 189.99 (BB) Br ex 32.30 Dght 12.800 Lbp 185.60 Br md 32.26 Dpth 18.00 Welded, 1 dk	**(A21A2BC) Bulk Carrier** Grain: 71,634; Bale: 68,200 Compartments: 5 Ho, ER 5 Ha: ER Cranes: 4x30t	**1 oil engine** driving 1 FP propeller Total Power: 9,480kW (12,889hp) 14.2kn MAN-B&W 6S50MC-C 1 x 2 Stroke 6 Cy. 500 x 2000 9480kW (12889bhp) Hyundai Engine & Machinery Co Ltd-South Korea AuxGen: 3 x 600kW 450V 60Hz a.c Boilers: AuxB (Comp) 9.0kgf/cm² (8.8bar)
8632756 *JJ3507* -	**VENUS 2** *ex Falcon -1999 ex Jet No. 8 -1996* **Kyushu Yusen KK** SatCom: Inmarsat A 1204530 *Fukuoka, Fukuoka* *Japan* Official number: 129169	*163* - -		**1985-06 Boeing Marine Systems — Seattle, Wa** Yd No: 0026 Loa 27.43 Br ex - Dght 1.300 Lbp 24.18 Br md 8.53 Dpth 2.59 Welded, 1 dk	**(A37B2PS) Passenger Ship** Hull Material: Aluminium Alloy Passengers: unberthed: 282	**2 Gas Turbs** dr geared to sc. shafts driving 2 Water jets Total Power: 5,444kW (7,402hp) 43.0kn Allison 501-K20B 2 x Gas Turb each-2722kW (3701shp) General Motors Detroit DieselAllison Divn-USA AuxGen: 2 x 50kW 440V 60Hz a.c Thrusters: 1 Thwart. FP thruster (f)
8513857 *3EVZ8* -	**VENUS 09** *ex Viet My -2012 ex Shosen Maru -2007* *ex Seisen Maru -1998* **Quynh Anh Trading Co Ltd** Nhat Viet Transportation Corp SatCom: Inmarsat C 437301110 *Panama* *Panama* MMSI: 373011000 Official number: 4372812	**1,344** 512 1,294	Class: VR (NK)	**1985-10 Kochi Jyuko (Eiho Zosen) K.K. — Kochi** Yd No: 1850 Loa 71.51 (BB) Br ex - Dght 4.665 Lbp 65.03 Br md 12.01 Dpth 5.41 Welded, 1 dk	**(A11B2TG) LPG Tanker** Liq (Gas): 1,928 2 x Gas Tank (s);	**1 oil engine** driving 1 CP propeller Total Power: 1,471kW (2,000hp) 12.0kn Akasaka A34 1 x 4 Stroke 6 Cy. 340 x 660 1471kW (2000bhp) Akasaka Tekkosho KK (Akasaka DieselLtd)-Japan AuxGen: 3 x 180kW a.c
9482952 - -	**VENUS 15** **Uthai Pakcharoen** - *Bangkok* *Thailand* Official number: 490001422	**205** 67 -		**2006-06 Kasem Sontirak — Samut Prakan** Loa 30.00 Br ex - Dght - Lbp 27.26 Br md 7.50 Dpth 4.00 Welded, 1 dk	**(A13B2TU) Tanker (unspecified)** Double Hull (13F)	**1 oil engine** driving 1 Propeller Total Power: 704kW (957hp) Cummins 1 x 4 Stroke 704kW (957bhp) Cummins Engine Co Inc-USA
8202549 *HSB2422* -	**VENUS 19** *ex Big Sea 19 -2012 ex Big Sea 5 -2006* *ex Masayoshi Maru No. 2 -1995* **MU Oil Partnership** - *Bangkok* *Thailand* Official number: 381001799	*699* 519 1,743		**1982-03 Sasaki Shipbuilding Co Ltd — Osakikamijima HS** Yd No: 355 Loa 69.86 (BB) Br ex - Dght 4.540 Lbp 65.03 Br md 11.02 Dpth 5.01 Welded, 1 dk	**(A13B2TP) Products Tanker** Compartments: 10 Ta, ER	**1 oil engine** reverse reduction geared to sc. shaft driving 1 FP propeller Total Power: 1,324kW (1,800hp) Hanshin 6EL30G 1 x 4 Stroke 6 Cy. 300 x 600 1324kW (1800bhp) The Hanshin Diesel Works Ltd-Japan
7714868 *HSB2452* -	**VENUS 21** *ex Big Sea 6 -2012 ex Irene VII -1996* *ex Kosho Maru -1989* **MU Oil Partnership** - *Thailand* Official number: 391000737	**1,328** 872 2,582	Class: (NV)	**1978-06 Sasaki Shipbuilding Co Ltd — Osakikamijima HS** Yd No: 318 Loa 79.10 (BB) Br ex - Dght 5.190 Lbp 74.02 Br md 12.04 Dpth 5.55 Welded, 1 dk	**(A13B2TP) Products Tanker**	**1 oil engine** driving 1 FP propeller Total Power: 1,618kW (2,200hp) 12.0kn Hanshin 6LU38 1 x 4 Stroke 6 Cy. 380 x 580 1618kW (2200bhp) Hanshin Nainenki Kogyo-Japan AuxGen: 2 x 100kW 445V 60Hz a.c
9414450 *2HHT8* -	**VENUS BAY** *ex Fengli 11 -2014* **PNR Marine Trading XII LLC** Synergy Maritime Pvt Ltd *Douglas* *Isle of Man (British)* MMSI: 235103765 Official number: 744983	**19,999** 10,419 30,003 T/cm 43.5	Class: AB	**2012-07 Tsuji Heavy Industries (Jiangsu) Co Ltd — Zhangjiagang JS** Yd No: NB0022 Loa 178.70 (BB) Br ex - Dght 9.816 Lbp 170.00 Br md 28.00 Dpth 14.00 Welded, 1 dk	**(A21A2BC) Bulk Carrier** Grain: 40,639; Bale: 38,602 Compartments: 5 Ho, ER 5 Ha: 4 (20.8 x 21.0)ER (16.6 x 15.0) Cranes: 4x30t	**1 oil engine** driving 1 FP propeller Total Power: 6,232kW (8,473hp) 14.0kn MAN-B&W 6S42MC 1 x 2 Stroke 6 Cy. 420 x 1764 6232kW (8473bhp) STX Engine Co Ltd-South Korea AuxGen: 3 x 550kW a.c Fuel: 123.0 (d.f.) 1314.0 (r.f.)

IMO / Call sign	Name / Owners / Flag	Tonnage	Class	Builder / Dimensions	Type / Cargo	Machinery
8813609 *A8LX5* -	**VENUS C** *ex* YT Venus *-2007* *ex* Australian Express *-2003* *ex* Premier *-1998* **Xin Hai Hui Shipping Corp** Orient International Logistics Holding Shanghai Newseas Navigation Co Ltd *Monrovia* *Liberia* MMSI: 636013286 Official number: 13286	**9,949** 5,492 14,867	Class: NK	**1989-06 Shin Kurushima Dockyard Co. Ltd. — Onishi** Yd No: 2618 Loa 150.43 (BB) Br ex - Dght 8.235 Lbp 142.00 Br md 22.60 Dpth 11.10 Welded, 1 dk	**(A33A2CC) Container Ship (Fully Cellular)** TEU 760 incl 200 ref C Compartments: 5 Ho, ER 2 Ha: (7.0 x 8.0) (12.6 x 8.0)ER 11 Wing Ha: 11 (12.6 x 8.0)	**1 oil engine** driving 1 FP propeller Total Power: 7,061kW (9,600hp) 18.5kn Mitsubishi 6UEC52LA 1 x 2 Stroke 6 Cy. 520 x 1600 7061kW (9600bhp) Kobe Hatsudoki KK-Japan Fuel: 1435.0 (r.f.)
9393682 *3ESD* -	**VENUS GLORY** **Avance Gas 3 Inc** Northern Marine Management Ltd *Panama* *Panama* MMSI: 370263000 Official number: 3467109B	**48,654** 17,273 54,474 T/cm 70.9	Class: NV	**2008-07 Daewoo Shipbuilding & Marine Engineering Co Ltd — Geoje** Yd No: 2323 Loa 226.00 (BB) Br ex 36.63 Dght 11.400 Lbp 215.00 Br md 36.60 Dpth 22.20 Welded, 1 dk	**(A11B2TG) LPG Tanker** Double Bottom Partial Compartment Length Liq (Gas): 83,000 4 x Gas Tank (s); 4 independent (C.mn.stl) pri horizontal 8 Cargo Pump (s): 8x600m³/hr Manifold: Bow/CM: 114.2m	**1 oil engine** driving 1 FP propeller Total Power: 13,560kW (18,436hp) 17.0kn MAN-B&W 6S60MC-C 1 x 2 Stroke 6 Cy. 600 x 2400 13560kW (18436bhp) Doosan Engine Co Ltd-South Korea AuxGen: 3 x 1500kW a.c Fuel: 290.0 (d.f.) 3000.0 (r.f.)
9593347 *H0HJ* -	**VENUS HALO** **Tanagra Shipping SA** Yano Kaiun Co Ltd *Panama* *Panama* MMSI: 373362000 Official number: 4360512	**31,541** 18,765 55,848 T/cm 56.9	Class: NK	**2012-02 IHI Marine United Inc — Kure HS** Yd No: 3322 Loa 190.00 (BB) Br ex - Dght 12.740 Lbp 185.00 Br md 32.26 Dpth 18.10 Welded, 1 dk	**(A21A2BC) Bulk Carrier** Grain: 72,062; Bale: 67,062 Compartments: 5 Ho, ER 5 Ha: ER Cranes: 4x30t	**1 oil engine** driving 1 FP propeller Total Power: 8,890kW (12,087hp) 14.5kn Wartsila 6RT-flex50 1 x 2 Stroke 6 Cy. 500 x 2050 8890kW (12087bhp) Diesel United Ltd.-Aioi Fuel: 2490.0
9468786 *5BDU3* -	**VENUS HERITAGE** **Maxdeka Shipping Corp** Safety Management Overseas SA SatCom: Inmarsat C 421213910 *Limassol* *Cyprus* MMSI: 212139000	**50,617** 31,470 95,650	Class: AB (NK)	**2010-12 Imabari Shipbuilding Co Ltd — Marugame KG (Marugame Shipyard)** Yd No: 1583 Loa 234.98 (BB) Br ex - Dght 14.400 Lbp 227.00 Br md 38.00 Dpth 19.90 Welded, 1 dk	**(A21A2BC) Bulk Carrier** Grain: 109,476 Compartments: 7 Ho, ER 7 Ha: ER	**1 oil engine** driving 1 FP propeller Total Power: 12,950kW (17,607hp) 14.5kn MAN-B&W 6S60MC-C 1 x 2 Stroke 6 Cy. 600 x 2400 12950kW (17607bhp) Hitachi Zosen Corp-Japan AuxGen: 3 x 500kW 450V 60Hz a.c Fuel: 310.0 (d.f.) 3750.0 (r.f.)
9591600 *5BKT3* -	**VENUS HISTORY** **Shikoku Friendship Shipping Co** Safety Management Overseas SA *Limassol* *Cyprus* MMSI: 209941000 Official number: 9591600	**50,647** 31,579 95,692	Class: AB	**2011-09 Imabari Shipbuilding Co Ltd — Marugame KG (Marugame Shipyard)** Yd No: 1579 Loa 234.98 (BB) Br ex - Dght 14.400 Lbp 227.00 Br md 38.00 Dpth 19.90 Welded, 1 dk	**(A21A2BC) Bulk Carrier** Grain: 109,476 Compartments: 7 Ho, ER 7 Ha: ER	**1 oil engine** driving 1 FP propeller Total Power: 12,950kW (17,607hp) 14.5kn MAN-B&W 6S60MC-C 1 x 2 Stroke 6 Cy. 600 x 2400 12950kW (17607bhp) Mitsui Engineering & Shipbuilding CLtd-Japan AuxGen: 3 x 500kW a.c Fuel: 308.0 (d.f.) 3749.0 (r.f.)
9604952 *5BNP3* -	**VENUS HORIZON** **Maxenteka Shipping Corp** Safety Management Overseas SA SatCom: Inmarsat C 420978610 *Limassol* *Cyprus* MMSI: 209786000 Official number: 9604952	**50,647** 31,567 95,755	Class: AB	**2012-02 Imabari Shipbuilding Co Ltd — Marugame KG (Marugame Shipyard)** Yd No: 1594 Loa 234.98 (BB) Br ex - Dght 14.450 Lbp 227.00 Br md 38.00 Dpth 19.90 Welded, 1 dk	**(A21A2BC) Bulk Carrier** Grain: 109,477 Compartments: 7 Ho, ER 7 Ha: ER	**1 oil engine** driving 1 FP propeller Total Power: 12,950kW (17,607hp) 14.5kn MAN-B&W 6S60MC-C 1 x 2 Stroke 6 Cy. 600 x 2400 12950kW (17607bhp) Mitsui Engineering & Shipbuilding CLtd-Japan AuxGen: 3 x 500kW a.c Fuel: 308.0 (d.f.) 3748.0 (r.f.)
8721193 *J8B2251* -	**VENUS I** *ex* Vecmilgravis *-2001* *ex* Vetsmilgravis *-1992* **Trachurus Fishing (Pty) Ltd** - *Kingstown* *St Vincent & The Grenadines* MMSI: 375714000 Official number: 8723	**4,407** 1,322 1,810	Class: RS	**1988-04 GP Chernomorskiy Sudostroitelnyy Zavod — Nikolayev** Yd No: 568 Loa 104.50 Br ex 16.03 Dght 5.900 Lbp 96.40 Br md 16.00 Dpth 10.20 Welded, 2 dks	**(B11A2FG) Factory Stern Trawler** Ice Capable	**2 oil engines** reduction geared to sc. shaft driving 1 CP propeller Total Power: 5,148kW (7,000hp) 16.1kn Russkiy 6CHN40/46 2 x 4 Stroke 6 Cy. 400 x 460 each-2574kW (3500bhp) Mashinostroitelnyy Zavod"Russkiy-Dizel"-Leningrad AuxGen: 2 x 1600kW 220/380V 50Hz a.c, 3 x 200kW 220/380V 50Hz a.c Fuel: 1226.0 (d.f.) 23.0pd
8741480 *HP9337* -	**VENUS II** *ex* Kirstine *-2013* *ex* Laeso *-2010* **MichaelLarsen** - *Panama* *Panama* MMSI: 370046000 Official number: 4523613	**145** 43 -		**1973-03 A/S Svendborg Skibsvaerft — Svendborg** Yd No: 143 Converted From: Patrol Vessel-2010 Loa 31.26 Br ex 7.42 Dght - Lbp 26.26 Br md 7.40 Dpth 3.15 Welded, 1 dk	**(B22A20R) Offshore Support Vessel**	**1 oil engine** reduction geared to sc. shaft driving 1 Propeller Total Power: 588kW (799hp) 11.0kn Alpha 408-26VO 1 x 2 Stroke 8 Cy. 260 x 400 588kW (799bhp) Alpha Diesel A/S-Denmark
9392341 *3FSL* -	**VENUS LEADER** *ex* Dream Planet *-2010* **Encantada Maritima SA** NYK Shipmanagement Pte Ltd *Panama* *Panama* MMSI: 370779000 Official number: 4182410	**42,487** 12,747 15,031	Class: NK	**2010-06 Shin Kurushima Dockyard Co. Ltd. — Onishi** Yd No: 5521 Loa 186.03 Br ex - Dght 8.524 Lbp 181.00 Br md 28.20 Dpth 29.43 Welded, 9 dks plus 2 movable dks	**(A35B2RV) Vehicles Carrier** Side door/ramp (s) Quarter stern door/ramp (s. a.) Cars: 4,115	**1 oil engine** driving 1 FP propeller Total Power: 11,441kW (15,555hp) 19.4kn MAN-B&W 8S50MC 1 x 2 Stroke 8 Cy. 500 x 1910 11441kW (15555bhp) Mitsui Engineering & Shipbuilding CLtd-Japan AuxGen: 3 x 800kW a.c Thrusters: 1 Tunnel thruster (f) Fuel: 2300.0 (r.f.)
7507538 *D8UP* -	**VENUS No. 1** **Hanryeo Development Co Ltd** - *Tongyeong* *South Korea* Official number: TM12040	*151* 82 23	Class: (KR)	**1974 Busan Shipbuilding Co Ltd — Busan** Loa 31.30 Br ex 6.02 Dght - Lbp 30.00 Br md 6.00 Dpth 3.00 Welded, 1 dk	**(A37B2PS) Passenger Ship**	**2 oil engines** driving 2 FP propellers Total Power: 2,060kW (2,800hp) 21.0kn M.T.U. 2 x Vee 4 Stroke 16 Cy. 160 x 180 each-1030kW (1400bhp) MTU Friedrichshafen GmbH-Friedrichshafen AuxGen: 2 x 40kW 240V a.c
9277747 *P3TH9* -	**VENUS R** *ex* Nordvenus *-2011* **Nordvenus Shipping Co Ltd** Reederei Nord Ltd *Limassol* *Cyprus* MMSI: 212084000 Official number: 9277747	**42,432** 21,815 74,999 T/cm 68.6	Class: NV (LR) ✠ Classed LR until 6/5/04	**2004-03 Hyundai Heavy Industries Co Ltd — Ulsan** Yd No: 1511 Loa 228.19 (BB) Br ex 32.23 Dght 14.426 Lbp 219.00 Br md 32.20 Dpth 20.90 Welded, 1 dk	**(A13B2TP) Products Tanker** Double Hull (13F) Liq: 82,053; Liq (Oil): 82,053 Compartments: 12 Wing Ta, 2 Wing Slop Ta, ER 12 Cargo Pump (s): 12x900m³/hr Manifold: Bow/CM: 111.5m	**1 oil engine** driving 1 FP propeller Total Power: 13,548kW (18,420hp) 16.0kn MAN-B&W 6S60MC-C 1 x 2 Stroke 6 Cy. 600 x 2400 13548kW (18420bhp) Hyundai Heavy Industries Co Ltd-South Korea AuxGen: 3 x 800kW 450V 60Hz a.c Boilers: e (ex.g.) 16.3kgf/cm² (16.0bar), WTAuxB (o.f.) 12.2kgf/cm² (12.0bar) Fuel: 248.1 (d.f.) 2386.5 (r.f.)
9260251 *H9RN* -	**VENUS SEVEN** **Venus Marine Co Ltd SA** Santoku Senpaku Co Ltd *Panama* *Panama* MMSI: 353405000 Official number: 2823502B	**4,030** 1,774 4,999	Class: NK	**2001-12 Kegoya Dock K.K. — Kure** Yd No: 1068 Loa 92.80 Br ex - Dght 6.613 Lbp 84.60 Br md 16.00 Dpth 10.75 Welded, 1 dk	**(A31A2GX) General Cargo Ship** Grain: 9,289; Bale: 8,240 2 Ha: (25.9 x 11.5) (14.0 x 11.5) Cranes: 1x35t,1x30t; Derricks: 1x30t	**1 oil engine** driving 1 FP propeller Total Power: 2,427kW (3,300hp) 12.5kn Hanshin LH41L 1 x 4 Stroke 6 Cy. 410 x 800 2427kW (3300bhp) The Hanshin Diesel Works Ltd-Japan
9505900 *A8YD8* -	**VENUS SPIRIT** **Secure Shipping Co Ltd** Nissan Motor Car Carrier Co Ltd (Nissan Senyo Sen KK) SatCom: Inmarsat C 463709358 *Monrovia* *Liberia* MMSI: 636015032 Official number: 15032	**45,959** 13,788 13,951	Class: NK	**2011-01 Naikai Zosen Corp — Onomichi HS (Setoda Shipyard)** Yd No: 736 Loa 183.00 (BB) Br ex - Dght 8.970 Lbp 170.00 Br md 30.20 Dpth 28.80 Welded, 1 dk	**(A35B2RV) Vehicles Carrier** Side door/ramp (s) Quarter stern door/ramp (s. a.) Cars: 5,007	**1 oil engine** driving 1 FP propeller Total Power: 12,210kW (16,601hp) 20.0kn MAN-B&W 6S60MC-C 1 x 2 Stroke 6 Cy. 600 x 2400 12210kW (16601bhp) Hitachi Zosen Corp-Japan Thrusters: 1 Tunnel thruster (f) Fuel: 2408.0 (r.f.)
9477646 *3FWK2* -	**VENUS TRIUMPH** **Seashore Shipping Maritime SA** Unitra Maritime Co Ltd SatCom: Inmarsat C 435492510 *Panama* *Panama* MMSI: 354925000 Official number: 4061609A	**9,680** 4,168 13,006	Class: NK	**2009-07 Honda Zosen — Saiki** Yd No: 1061 Loa 120.00 (BB) Br ex - Dght 8.990 Lbp 111.50 Br md 21.20 Dpth 14.30 Welded, 1 dk	**(A31A2GX) General Cargo Ship** Grain: 20,025; Bale: 19,344 Compartments: 2 Ho, 2 Tw Dk, ER 2 Ha: ER 2 (29.3 x 15.0) Cranes: 2x78t	**1 oil engine** driving 1 FP propeller Total Power: 4,200kW (5,710hp) 12.5kn MAN-B&W 6S35MC 1 x 2 Stroke 6 Cy. 350 x 1400 4200kW (5710bhp) Makita Corp-Japan Fuel: 900.0

8217219 *J8VP9* -	**VENUZS** *ex* Amalia *-1999* *ex* Bravery *-1995* *ex* Orchid *-1993* *ex* Tokei Maru *-1986* **Venuzs Shipping Ltd** Jiangsu Fareast Shipping Co Ltd *Kingstown* *St Vincent & The Grenadines* MMSI: 376278000 Official number: 7951	**13,397** 7,818 22,403	Class: NK	**1983-04 K.K. Uwajima Zosensho — Uwajima** Yd No: 2245 Loa 160.00 (BB) Br ex - Dght 9.970 Lbp 150.02 Br md 24.60 Dpth 13.62 Welded, 1 dk	**(A31A2GX) General Cargo Ship** Grain: 28,657; Bale: 27,444 Compartments: 4 Ho, ER 4 Ha: (19.2 x 11.2)3 (24.8 x 12.8)ER Cranes: 2x26t; Derricks: 2x25.5t	**1 oil engine** driving 1 FP propeller Total Power: 5,002kW (6,801hp) 14.2kn Mitsubishi 6UEC52HA 1 x 2 Stroke 6 Cy. 520 x 1250 5002kW (6801bhp) Kobe Hatsudoki KK-Japan AuxGen: 2 x 400kW 450V 60Hz a.c Fuel: 173.0 (d.f.) 1049.0 (r.f.) 20.0pd
7368748 *LNWN* -	**VEOY** - **Fjord1 AS** - *Molde* *Norway* MMSI: 257028700	**1,870** 613 467	Class: (NV)	**1974-05 Hjorungavaag Verksted AS — Hjorungavaag** Yd No: 20 Loa 74.99 Br ex 12.50 Dght 3.099 Lbp 66.20 Br md 11.99 Dpth 4.53 Welded, 1 dk	**(A36A2PR) Passenger/Ro-Ro Ship (Vehicles)** Bow door & ramp Stern ramp	**2 oil engines** driving 2 FP propellers Total Power: 1,838kW (2,498hp) 14.0kn Wichmann 5AXA 2 x 2 Stroke 5 Cy. 300 x 450 each-919kW (1249bhp) Wichmann Motorfabrikk AS-Norway AuxGen: 2 x 104kW 220V 50Hz a.c Thrusters: 1 Thwart. FP thruster (f) Fuel: 77.0 (d.f.) 4.0pd
8892021 *UFLL* -	**VEPR** *ex* Sap *-2013* *ex* OT-2439 *-1996* *ex* Halong *-1996* **Nitek SAP Shipping Ltd** Nitek Corp *Novorossiysk* *Russia*	**841** 252 -	Class: (RS)	**1986-12 Angyalfold Shipyard, Ganz Danubius Shipyard — Budapest** Yd No: 1945 Loa 51.65 Br ex 12.02 Dght 2.300 Lbp 50.00 Br md 11.60 Dpth 3.30 Welded, 1 dk	**(B32B2SP) Pusher Tug**	**2 oil engines** driving 2 FP propellers Total Power: 1,766kW (2,402hp) 11.9kn Dvigatel Revolyutsii 6CHRN36/45 2 x 4 Stroke 6 Cy. 360 x 450 each-883kW (1201bhp) Zavod "Dvigatel Revolyutsii"-Gorkiy AuxGen: 2 x 150kW a.c Fuel: 188.0 (d.f.)
8660428 *ZGBQ6* -	**VERA** *ex* Mangusta 105/30 *-2011* **Nikita** SARL Arrow Services Monaco *George Town* *Cayman Islands (British)* Official number: 743571	**167** 50 -		**2008 Overmarine SpA — Viareggio** Yd No: 105/30 Loa 33.00 Br ex - Dght 2.850 Lbp 27.85 Br md 6.90 Dpth 3.80 Bonded, 1 dk	**(X11A2YP) Yacht** Hull Material: Reinforced Plastic Passengers: 8; cabins: 4	**2 oil engines** reduction geared to sc. shafts driving 2 Propellers Total Power: 3,580kW (4,868hp) 31.0kn M.T.U. 16V2000M93 2 x Vee 4 Stroke 16 Cy. 135 x 156 each-1790kW (2434bhp) MTU Friedrichshafen GmbH-Friedrichshafen
1006415 *SVA2154* -	**VERA** *ex* Splendido *-2008* *ex* Airwaves *-2007* *launched as* Endeavour *-1999* **Aegean Yachting MCPY** Aegean Agency SA *Piraeus* *Greece* MMSI: 240806000 Official number: 11786	**887** 266 180	Class: LR ✠ **100A1** SS 08/2012 Yacht ✠ **LMC** Eq.Ltr: K; Cable: 357.6/28.0 U2 (a)	**1999-08 Schiffs- u. Yachtwerft Abeking & Rasmussen GmbH & Co. — Lemwerder** Yd No: 6426 Loa 52.00 Br ex 10.65 Dght 3.500 Lbp 46.50 Br md 10.30 Dpth 6.15 Welded, 1 dk	**(X11A2YP) Yacht**	**2 oil engines** with clutches, flexible couplings & sr reverse geared to sc. shafts driving 2 FP propellers Total Power: 2,796kW (3,802hp) 16.0kn Caterpillar 3516TA 2 x Vee 4 Stroke 16 Cy. 170 x 190 each-1398kW (1901bhp) Caterpillar Inc-USA AuxGen: 2 x 160kW 400V 50Hz a.c Thrusters: 1 Thwart. FP thruster (f)
1004950 *SY2409* -	**VERA** *ex* Multiple *-2002* **Aegean Yachting EPE** - *Piraeus* *Greece* MMSI: 239949000 Official number: 11005	*233* 69 135	Class: (LR) Cable: 302.0/16.0 YY ✠ Classed LR until 29/1/03	**1997-10 Cantieri di Pisa — Pisa** Yd No: 642 Loa 38.00 Br ex - Dght 1.488 Lbp 32.30 Br md 7.90 Dpth 3.45 Bonded, 1 dk	**(X11A2YP) Yacht** Hull Material: Reinforced Plastic	**2 oil engines** with clutches, flexible couplings & sr reverse geared to sc. shafts driving 2 FP propellers Total Power: 4,184kW (5,688hp) MWM TBD604BV16 2 x Vee 4 Stroke 16 Cy. 170 x 195 each-2092kW (2844bhp) Motoren Werke Mannheim AG (MWM)-Mannheim Thrusters: 1 Thwart. FP thruster (f); 1 Tunnel thruster (a)
9233064 *EAZR* 3-VILL-14-	**VERA** - **Alvarez e Hijos SA** Salvador Alvarez San Pedro *Santa Eugenia de Ribeira* *Spain* Official number: 3-4/2000	**326** - -		**2001-03 Montajes Cies S.L. — Vigo** Yd No: 88 Loa - Br ex - Dght - Lbp 26.00 Br md 7.50 Dpth 3.50 Welded, 1 dk	**(B11B2FV) Fishing Vessel**	**1 oil engine** reduction geared to sc. shaft driving 1 FP propeller Total Power: 451kW (613hp) Caterpillar 3512TA 1 x Vee 4 Stroke 12 Cy. 170 x 190 451kW (613bhp) Caterpillar Inc-USA
9202118 *TCYF3* -	**VERA 9** *ex* Island Oasis *-2010* **Vera Denizcilik AS** Horizon Gemi Isletmeciligi Sanayi ve Ticaret AS *Istanbul* *Turkey* MMSI: 271040831	**26,989** 15,619 46,681 T/cm 51.4	Class: NK	**1999-04 Mitsui Eng. & SB. Co. Ltd. — Tamano** Yd No: 1502 Loa 189.80 (BB) Br ex - Dght 11.620 Lbp 181.00 Br md 31.00 Dpth 16.50 Welded, 1 dk	**(A21A2BC) Bulk Carrier** Grain: 59,820; Bale: 57,237 Compartments: 5 Ho, ER 5 Ha: (17.6 x 17.2)4 (20.8 x 17.2)ER Cranes: 4x30.5t	**1 oil engine** driving 1 FP propeller Total Power: 8,165kW (11,101hp) 14.0kn B&W 6S50MC 1 x 2 Stroke 6 Cy. 500 x 1910 8165kW (11101bhp) Mitsui Engineering & Shipbuilding CLtd-Japan Fuel: 1690.0
9221140 *WDC3027* -	**VERA BISSO** - **Bisso Offshore LLC** E N Bisso & Son Inc *New Orleans, LA* *United States of America* MMSI: 367001730 Official number: 1086279	**416** 124 -	Class: (AB)	**1999-11 Bollinger Machine Shop & Shipyard, Inc. — Lockport, La** Yd No: 342 Loa 31.82 Br ex - Dght 4.880 Lbp 29.87 Br md 12.19 Dpth 5.25 Welded, 1 dk	**(B32A2ST) Tug**	**2 oil engines** reverse reduction geared to sc. shafts driving 2 FP propellers Total Power: 3,384kW (4,600hp) EMD (Electro-Motive) 16-645-E6 2 x Vee 2 Stroke 16 Cy. 230 x 254 each-1692kW (2300bhp) General Motors Corp.Electro-Motive Div.-La Grange
7346582 - -	**VERA CRUZ** - -	*1,034* 539 377	Class: (LR) ✠ Classed LR until 7/9/84	**1975-12 Estaleiros EBIN/So SA — Porto Alegre** Yd No: 58 Loa 71.02 Br ex 13.92 Dght 2.693 Lbp 63.35 Br md 13.50 Dpth 4.50 Welded, 1 dk	**(A36A2PR) Passenger/Ro-Ro Ship (Vehicles)** Passengers: unberthed: 590	**2 oil engines** sr geared to sc. shafts driving 2 CP propellers Total Power: 1,236kW (1,680hp) MAN G7V235/330ATL 2 x 4 Stroke 7 Cy. 235 x 330 each-618kW (840bhp) Mecanica Pesada SA-Brazil AuxGen: 2 x 140kW 225V 60Hz a.c Thrusters: 1 Thwart. FP thruster (f) Fuel: 48.0 (d.f.)
9178044 *A8ZY6* -	**VERA CRUZ** *ex* Potrero *-2011* *ex* Potrero Del Llano II *-2011* *ex* Torm Agnete *-2005* *ex* Zorca *-2004* **Lysistrati SA** Avin International SA *Monrovia* *Liberia* MMSI: 636015320 Official number: 15320	**28,546** 12,369 47,165 T/cm 90.9	Class: NV (NK)	**1999-05 Onomichi Dockyard Co Ltd — Onomichi HS** Yd No: 437 Loa 182.50 Br ex 32.30 Dght 12.666 Lbp 172.00 Br md 32.20 Dpth 19.10 Welded, 1 dk	**(A13B2TP) Products Tanker** Double Hull (13F) Liq: 53,000; Liq (Oil): 53,000 Cargo Heating Coils Compartments: 14 Wing Ta, 2 Wing Slop Ta, ER 4 Cargo Pump (s): 4x1000m³/hr	**1 oil engine** driving 1 FP propeller Total Power: 8,562kW (11,641hp) 15.3kn B&W 6S50MC 1 x 2 Stroke 6 Cy. 500 x 1910 8562kW (11641bhp) Mitsui Engineering & Shipbuilding CLtd-Japan
9290177 *CQID* -	**VERA D** *ex* Maersk Vera Cruz *-2009* *launched as* Pyxis *-2004* **Aspera Schiffahrtsgesellschaft mbH & Co KG** Peter Doehle Schiffahrts-KG *Madeira* *Portugal (MAR)* MMSI: 255805553 Official number: TEMP171M	**17,188** 9,038 22,513	Class: GL	**2004-10 Daewoo-Mangalia Heavy Industries S.A. — Mangalia** (Hull) Yd No: 4045 **2004-10 J.J. Sietas KG Schiffswerft GmbH & Co. — Hamburg** Yd No: 1205 Loa 178.57 (BB) Br ex - Dght 10.850 Lbp 167.50 Br md 27.60 Dpth 14.58 Welded, 1 dk	**(A33A2CC) Container Ship (Fully Cellular)** TEU 1678 C Ho 638 TEU C Dk 1040 TEU incl 400 ref C. Cranes: 3x45t	**1 oil engine** driving 1 FP propeller Total Power: 16,918kW (23,002hp) 20.0kn B&W 6L70MC 1 x 2 Stroke 6 Cy. 700 x 2268 16918kW (23002bhp) Manises Diesel Engine Co. S.A.-Valencia AuxGen: 4 x 1040kW 450/230V 60Hz a.c Thrusters: 1 Thwart. CP thruster (a); 1 Thwart. CP thruster (f)
9432220 *DFUT2* -	**VERA RAMBOW** - **Reederei Rambow GmbH & Co ms 'Vera Rambow' KG** Wilfried Rambow KG SatCom: Inmarsat C 421862710 *Hamburg* *Germany* MMSI: 218627000 Official number: 21988	**17,488** 8,125 17,888	Class: GL	**2008-09 J.J. Sietas KG Schiffswerft GmbH & Co. — Hamburg** Yd No: 1265 Loa 168.11 (BB) Br ex - Dght 9.620 Lbp 155.40 Br md 26.80 Dpth 14.00 Welded, 1 dk	**(A33A2CC) Container Ship (Fully Cellular)** TEU 1421 C Ho 1133 TEU C Dk 288 TEU incl 300 ref C 1 Ha: (27.3 x 23.1) Ice Capable	**1 oil engine** reduction geared to sc. shaft driving 1 CP propeller Total Power: 11,200kW (15,228hp) 19.5kn MAN-B&W 8L58/64CE 1 x 4 Stroke 8 Cy. 580 x 640 11200kW (15228bhp) MAN B&W Diesel AG-Augsburg AuxGen: 1 x 2288kW a.c, 3 x 1088kW a.c Thrusters: 1 Tunnel thruster (f); 1 Tunnel thruster (a) Fuel: 207.0 (d.f.) 1175.0 (r.f.)
9123506 *3FQR5* -	**VERA STAR** *ex* Costa *-2013* *ex* Castor *-2012* *ex* Iberian Bridge *-1998* *ex* Castor *-1997* **Vera Shipping Ltd** Kadir Colak Denizcilik Turizm ve Ticaret AS *Panama* *Panama* MMSI: 373490000 Official number: 4505313	**4,178** 2,282 5,905 T/cm 15.6	Class: GL	**1996-02 Scheepswerf Pattje B.V. — Waterhuizen** Yd No: 390 Loa 110.57 (BB) Br ex - Dght 6.050 Lbp 102.75 Br md 15.90 Dpth 8.00 Welded, 1 dk	**(A33A2CC) Container Ship (Fully Cellular)** Grain: 7,787 TEU 448 C Ho 156 TEU C Dk 292 TEU incl 40 ref C. Compartments: 1 Ho, 2 Cell Ho, ER 3 Ha: (6.4 x 10.6) (25.6 x 13.2) (38.3 x 13.2)ER Ice Capable	**1 oil engine** with flexible couplings & sr gearedto sc. shaft driving 1 CP propeller Total Power: 3,520kW (4,786hp) 14.5kn MaK 8M32 1 x 4 Stroke 8 Cy. 320 x 480 3520kW (4786bhp) Krupp MaK Maschinenbau GmbH-Kiel AuxGen: 1 x 500kW 220/440V 60Hz a.c, 2 x 270kW 220/440V 60Hz a.c Thrusters: 1 Thwart. FP thruster (f) Fuel: 52.0 (d.f.) 378.0 (r.f.)

8611219 **VERA SU**
H9YA *ex* Rantum *-2014* *ex* Waldtraut B *-2002*
\- **Vera Shipping Ltd**
Kadir Colak Denizcilik Turizm ve Ticaret AS
Panama *Panama*
MMSI: 351299000
Official number: 45681PEXT

1,984 Class: GL
1,056
3,217

1989-10 IHC Holland NV Beaver Dredgers — Sliedrecht (Hull) Yd No: 10296
1989-10 B.V. Scheepswerf Damen — Gorinchem Yd No: 8209
Loa 89.30 Br ex - Dght 4.703
Lbp 85.50 Br md 12.50 Dpth 6.35
Welded, 1 dk

(A31A2GX) General Cargo Ship
Grain: 3,983; Bale: 3,907
TEU 158 C.Ho 78/20' C.Dk 80/20'
Compartments: 1 Ho, ER
1 Ha: (63.4 x 10.1)ER
Ice Capable

1 oil engine with flexible couplings & sr reverse geared to sc. shaft driving 1 FP propeller
Total Power: 927kW (1,260hp) 11.0kn
Deutz SBV6M628
1 x 4 Stroke 6 Cy. 240 x 280 927kW (1260bhp)
Kloeckner Humboldt Deutz AG-West Germany
AuxGen: 2 x 84kW 220/380V 50Hz a.c, 1 x 38kW 220/380V 50Hz a.c
Thrusters: 1 Thwart. FP thruster (f)

6418792 **VERACRUZ**
\-
\- **Fernando Quintana Garcia**
\-
Alvarado *Mexico*

140
\-
\-

1965-02 N.V. Scheepsbouwbedrijf v/h Th.J. Fikkers — Foxhol (Hull) Yd No: 104
1965-02 Scheepswerf Haak N.V. — Zaandam Yd No: 899
Loa 26.01 Br ex 7.47 Dght 2.515
Lbp 23.02 Br md 7.21 Dpth 2.95
Welded

(B11A2FT) Trawler

2 oil engines geared to sc. shaft driving 1 FP propeller
Caterpillar
1 x 4 Stroke
Caterpillar Tractor Co-USA

9234501 **VERACRUZ**
XCFQ3 *ex* Amatlan Ii *-2011* *ex* Elka Baluni *-2005*
\- *ex* Baluni *-2004*
Buques Tanque del Pacifico SA de CV
Naviera del Pacifico SA de CV
Salina Cruz *Mexico*
MMSI: 345200008
Official number: 9234501

30,770 Class: LR (AB) (CS)
11,067 **100A1** SS 07/2012
45,467 oil and chemical tanker, Ship Type 1
T/cm ESP
53.0 LI
LMC **UMS**

2002-07 Brodosplit - Brodogradiliste doo — Split Yd No: 430
Loa 188.90 (BB) Br ex 32.23 Dght 11.200
Lbp 180.00 Br md 32.20 Dpth 19.15
Welded, 1 dk

(A12B2TR) Chemical/Products Tanker
Double Hull (13F)
Liq: 55,420; Liq (Oil): 55,420
Compartments: 14 Wing Ta (s.stl), ER
17 Cargo Pump (s)

1 oil engine driving 1 FP propeller
Total Power: 10,849kW (14,750hp) 16.0kn
MAN-B&W 6S60MC
1 x 2 Stroke 6 Cy. 600 x 2292 10849kW (14750bhp)
Hyundai Heavy Industries Co Ltd-South Korea

5378440 **VERAGUAS**
HO2538 *ex* Seremoek *-1961* *ex* Chelmer *-1949*
\- **Compania de Transportes Edna SA**
\-
Panama *Panama*
Official number: 29066

206 Class: (LR)
112 ✠ Classed LR until 3/60
197

1948-01 A E Goodwin Ltd — Port Kembla NSW
Loa 37.65 Br ex 7.78 Dght 2.331
Lbp 35.31 Br md 7.32 Dpth 2.75
Welded, 1 dk

(A31A2GX) General Cargo Ship

2 oil engines driving 2 FP propellers
8.0kn
Ruston 6VCBM
2 x 4 Stroke 6 Cy. 203 x 273
Commonwealth Government MarineEngine Works-Australia
Fuel: 69.5

9363572 **VERAGUAS I**
HO4369
\- **Panama Canal Authority**
\-
Panama *Panama*
MMSI: 370483000
Official number: 3274407A

327 Class: (LR)
98 ✠ Classed LR until 2/3/08
135

2006-12 Hin Lee (Zhuhai) Shipyard Co Ltd — Zhuhai GD (Hull) Yd No: 112
2006-12 Cheoy Lee Shipyards Ltd — Hong Kong Yd No: 4894
Loa 27.40 Br ex 12.35 Dght 5.200
Lbp 22.85 Br md 11.65 Dpth 5.00
Welded, 1 dk

(B32A2ST) Tug

2 oil engines gearing integral to driving 2 Z propellers
Total Power: 3,600kW (4,894hp) 12.8kn
Wartsila 9L20
2 x 4 Stroke 9 Cy. 200 x 280 each-1800kW (2447bhp)
Wartsila France SA-France
AuxGen: 2 x 175kW 208V 60Hz a.c

7375868 **VERANO**
YJTN8 *ex* Apollo *-2014* *ex* Viento Del Sur *-2013*
\- *ex* Shinkai Maru *-2000*
Nuevo Mar Co Ltd
Insung Corp
Port Vila *Vanuatu*
Official number: 2264

3,979 Class: KR (NK)
1,214
3,535

1975-03 Shikoku Dockyard Co. Ltd. — Takamatsu Yd No: 781
Loa 100.60 Br ex 16.03 Dght 6.216
Lbp 93.23 Br md 16.01 Dpth 10.01
Riveted\Welded, 2 dks pt 3rd dk

(B11A2FG) Factory Stern Trawler
Ins: 3,046
2 Ha: 2 (2.9 x 2.9)ER
Derricks: 6x5t
Ice Capable

1 oil engine driving 1 FP propeller
Total Power: 3,678kW (5,001hp) 14.0kn
Mitsubishi 7UET45/80D
1 x 2 Stroke 7 Cy. 450 x 800 3678kW (5001bhp)
Kobe Hatsudoki KK-Japan
AuxGen: 3 x 720kW 450V 60Hz a.c
Fuel: 402.0 (d.f.) 1063.0 (r.f.) 20.0pd

9055266 **VERASPER**
UBPO
\- **Akros Fishing Co Ltd (A/O Akros)**
\-
SatCom: Inmarsat A 1407214
Petropavlovsk-Kamchatskiy *Russia*
MMSI: 273847700

1,315 Class: RS (NV)
395
851

1994-06 Elbewerft Boizenburg GmbH — Boizenburg Yd No: 108
Loa 52.50 Br ex 11.59 Dght 5.426
Lbp 45.54 Br md 11.50 Dpth 8.05
Welded, 2 dks

(B11B2FV) Fishing Vessel
Ins: 850
Ice Capable

1 oil engine with flexible couplings & sr geared to sc. shaft driving 1 CP propeller
Total Power: 1,060kW (1,441hp)
MAN-B&W 8L23/30A
1 x 4 Stroke 8 Cy. 225 x 300 1060kW (1441bhp)
MAN B&W Diesel A/S-Denmark
AuxGen: 1 x 560kW a.c, 2 x 291kW a.c
Thrusters: 1 Thwart. FP thruster (f)
Fuel: 300.0 (d.f.)

8717271 **VERAZ**
LW7365
\- **Pesquera Veraz SA**
\-
SatCom: Inmarsat C 470100512
Mar del Plata *Argentina*
MMSI: 701000711
Official number: 0144

116 Class: (RI)
76
116

1988-04 Ast. Naval Federico Contessi y Cia. S.A. — Mar del Plata Yd No: 48
Loa 28.28 Br ex - Dght 2.901
Lbp 25.02 Br md 6.41 Dpth 3.31
Welded, 1 dk

(B11B2FV) Fishing Vessel
Ins: 160

1 oil engine driving 1 FP propeller
Total Power: 444kW (604hp)
Cummins VTA-28-M2
1 x Vee 4 Stroke 12 Cy. 140 x 152 444kW (604bhp)
Cummins Engine Co Inc-USA

9338539 **VERDANT ISLAND**
3EHG7
\- **Ambitious Line SA**
Shikishima Kisen KK
Panama *Panama*
MMSI: 372073000
Official number: 3220906A

19,822 Class: NK
10,953
32,119
T/cm
45.1

2006-10 The Hakodate Dock Co Ltd — Hakodate HK Yd No: 809
Loa 175.53 (BB) Br ex - Dght 9.640
Lbp 167.00 Br md 29.40 Dpth 13.70
Welded, 1 dk

(A21A2BC) Bulk Carrier
Double Hull
Grain: 42,620; Bale: 41,095
Compartments: 5 Ho, ER
5 Ha: ER
Cranes: 4x30t

1 oil engine driving 1 FP propeller
Total Power: 6,840kW (9,300hp) 14.4kn
Mitsubishi 6UEC52LA
1 x 2 Stroke 6 Cy. 520 x 1600 6840kW (9300bhp)
Kobe Hatsudoki KK-Japan
AuxGen: 3 x 360kW a.c
Fuel: 1360.0

8512657 **VERDEL**
LW9866
\- **Ibermar SA**
\-
SatCom: Inmarsat C 470149910
San Antonio Oeste *Argentina*
MMSI: 701045000
Official number: 0175

1,605 Class: BV
533
1,400

1987-07 Construcciones Navales P Freire SA — Vigo Yd No: 291
Loa 74.00 (BB) Br ex - Dght 5.281
Lbp 64.83 Br md 12.51 Dpth 7.68
Welded, 2 dks

(B11A2FS) Stern Trawler
Ins: 2,000

1 oil engine with flexible couplings & sr gearedto sc. shaft driving 1 CP propeller
Total Power: 1,471kW (2,000hp)
Deutz SBV6M358
1 x 4 Stroke 6 Cy. 400 x 580 1471kW (2000bhp)
Hijos de J Barreras SA-Spain

8017164 **VERDEMILHO**
CUOZ
\- **Pescarias Rio Novo do Principe RL**
\-
Aveiro *Portugal*
MMSI: 263500102
Official number: A-3139C

174 Class: (LR) (GL)
99 ✠
109

1982-11 Estaleiros Navais de Viana do Castelo S.A. — Viana do Castelo Yd No: 116
Loa 28.63 Br ex - Dght 2.901
Lbp 24.01 Br md 7.41 Dpth 3.41
Welded, 1 dk

(B11A2FT) Trawler
Ins: 100
Compartments: 2 Ho, ER
2 Ha:

1 oil engine with clutches, flexible couplings & sr reverse geared to sc. shaft driving 1 FP propeller
Total Power: 552kW (750hp)
Stork DRO218K
1 x 4 Stroke 8 Cy. 210 x 300 552kW (750bhp)
Stork Werkspoor Diesel BV-Netherlands
AuxGen: 2 x 48kW 220/380V 50Hz a.c
Fuel: 49.5 (d.f.)

6606650 **VERDI**
V5KE *ex* Luroy *-1995* *ex* Marna Hepso *-1991*
L864 **Namib Fisheries**
\-
Walvis Bay *Namibia*
Official number: 96WB011

570 Class: (NV)
233
\-

1966-01 AS Hommelvik Mek. Verksted — Hommelvik Yd No: 101
Lengthened-1968
Loa 51.74 Br ex 8.26 Dght 4.376
Lbp 40.04 Br md 8.23 Dpth 4.65
Welded, 1 dk

(B11B2FV) Fishing Vessel
Compartments: 2 Ho, ER
3 Ha: (2.5 x 3.1) (2.5 x 2.7) (2.5 x 3.2)ER
Derricks: 1x3t; Winches: 1

1 oil engine geared to sc. shaft driving 1 FP propeller
Total Power: 1,765kW (2,400hp)
Alpha 8L28/32A
1 x 4 Stroke 8 Cy. 280 x 320 1765kW (2400bhp) (new engine 1990)
MAN B&W Diesel A/S-Denmark
AuxGen: 1 x 72kW 220V 50Hz a.c, 1 x 30kW 220V 50Hz a.c
Thrusters: 1 Thwart. FP thruster (f); 1 Tunnel thruster (a)

5338567 **VERDI**
CB5074 *ex* Radek *-1992* *ex* Ligrunn *-1990*
\- *ex* K. Vaage *-1988* *ex* H. K. M. *-1966*
\- *ex* Star VIII *-1965*
South Pacific Korp SA (SPK)
\-
Valparaiso *Chile*
MMSI: 725000293
Official number: 2788

812 Class: (LR) (NV)
271 *Classed BC until 10/65
\-

1948-10 Smith's Dock Ltd. — South Bank, Middlesbrough Yd No: 1177
Converted From: Whale-catcher-1965
Lengthened-1975
Loa 54.43 Br ex 8.41 Dght 4.115
Lbp 44.02 Br md 8.39 Dpth 4.72
Welded, 1 dk

(B11B2FV) Fishing Vessel
Compartments: 1 Ho, ER
1 Ha: (1.9 x 0.9)ER

1 oil engine driving 1 FP propeller
Total Power: 1,545kW (2,101hp) 10.5kn
Wichmann 7AXA
1 x 2 Stroke 7 Cy. 300 x 450 1545kW (2101bhp) (new engine 1978)
Wichmann Motorfabrikk AS-Norway
AuxGen: 2 x 220kW 230V 50Hz a.c

9157002 **VERDI**
V2AP4
\- **Hansa Befrachtungs GmbH**
GEFO Gesellschaft fur Oeltransporte mbH
Saint John's *Antigua & Barbuda*
MMSI: 304070935
Official number: 3502

2,195 Class: GL
832
3,079
T/cm
10.0

1999-06 Ceske Lodenice a.s. — Usti nad Labem (Hull)
1999-06 Scheepswerf K Damen BV — Hardinxveld Yd No: 712
Loa 93.99 (BB) Br ex - Dght 4.650
Lbp 89.30 Br md 12.50 Dpth 6.35
Welded, 1 dk

(A12B2TR) Chemical/Products Tanker
Double Hull (13F)
Liq: 3,162; Liq (Oil): 3,150
Compartments: 24 Wing Ta, 2 Wing Slop Ta, ER
12 Cargo Pump (s): 10x120m³/hr, 2x70m³/hr
Manifold: Bow/CM: 53m
Ice Capable

1 oil engine reduction geared to sc. shaft driving 1 CP propeller
Total Power: 1,980kW (2,692hp) 13.0kn
Alpha 8L28/32A
1 x 4 Stroke 8 Cy. 280 x 320 1980kW (2692bhp)
MAN B&W Diesel A/S-Denmark
AuxGen: 1 x 360kW 450V a.c, 2 x 215kW 450V a.c
Thrusters: 1 Tunnel thruster (f)
Fuel: 17.0 (d.f.) 208.0 (r.f.)

Identity / Owner	Tonnage	Class	Builder / Dimensions	Type / Capacity	Machinery
9440980 **VERDI** *3FFE7* *ex* GL Primera *-2013* - **Gasport Shipping Inc** Arminter SAM *Panama* *Panama* MMSI: 353862000 Official number: 4492913	**32,415** 19,353 58,758 T/cm 57.4	Class: RI (NK)	**2007-10 Tsuneishi Group (Zhoushan) Shipbuilding Inc — Daishan County ZJ** Yd No: SS-041 Loa 189.99 (BB) Br ex - Dght 12.828 Lbp 185.60 Br md 32.26 Dpth 18.00 Welded, 1 dk	**(A21A2BC) Bulk Carrier** Grain: 72,360; Bale: 70,557 Compartments: 5 Ho, ER 5 Ha: ER Cranes: 4x30t	**1 oil engine** driving 1 FP propeller Total Power: 8,400kW (11,421hp) 14.5kn MAN-B&W 6S50MC-C 1 x 2 Stroke 6 Cy. 500 x 2000 8400kW (11421bhp) Mitsui Engineering & Shipbuilding CLtd-Japan AuxGen: 3 x 480kW a.c Fuel: 2540.0
7855492 **VERDUN UTAMA I** *YEOW* *ex* Kowa Maru *-1991* - **PT Arghaniaga Pancatunggal** *Banjarmasin* *Indonesia*	*422* 156 600	Class: KI	**1975-12 Mategata Zosen K.K. — Namikata** Loa 49.70 Br ex - Dght 3.260 Lbp 46.23 Br md 8.32 Dpth 3.79 Welded, 1 dk	**(A13B2TU) Tanker (unspecified)**	**1 oil engine** geared to sc. shaft driving 1 FP propeller Total Power: 552kW (750hp) 10.5kn Yanmar 6UA-UT 1 x 4 Stroke 6 Cy. 200 x 240 552kW (750bhp) Yanmar Diesel Engine Co Ltd-Japan
9334480 **VEREINA** *V7PU5* *ex* Casanna *-2008* - **Keybridge Shipping Ltd** Columbia Shipmanagement Ltd *Majuro* *Marshall Islands* MMSI: 538003289 Official number: 3289	**16,418** 9,565 27,112	Class: NK	**2008-08 Ente Administrador Astilleros Rio Santiago — Ensenada (Arg)** Yd No: 75 Loa 165.50 (BB) Br ex - Dght 9.606 Lbp 158.00 Br md 27.00 Dpth 13.30 Welded, 1 dk	**(A21A2BC) Bulk Carrier** Grain: 34,811; Bale: 34,182 Compartments: 5 Ho, ER 5 Ha: ER Cranes: 4x30.5t	**1 oil engine** driving 1 FP propeller Total Power: 5,369kW (7,300hp) 14.4kn MAN-B&W 5L50MC 1 x 2 Stroke 5 Cy. 500 x 1620 5369kW (7300bhp) Mitsui Engineering & Shipbuilding CLtd-Japan AuxGen: 3 x 320kW 440V 60Hz a.c Fuel: 1305.0
7223649 **VEREMOS** - - - -	*226* 85 -	Class: (BV)	**1973 Ast. Neptuno — Valencia** Yd No: 44 Loa 30.92 Br ex - Dght 3.302 Lbp 26.01 Br md 7.50 Dpth 3.81 Welded, 1 dk	**(B11A2FT) Trawler**	**1 oil engine** driving 1 FP propeller Total Power: 485kW (659hp) 10.5kn Poyaud A12150SRHM 1 x Vee 4 Stroke 12 Cy. 150 x 180 485kW (659bhp) Societe Surgerienne de ConstructionMecaniques-France
9149938 **VERES** *J8B3784* *ex* Midland 4 *-2007* *ex* Ileksa *-2005* - *ex* Pannon River *-2000* **Panama Skippers & Managers Inc** Transport-Company Firm 'Vernal' *Kingstown* *St Vincent & The Grenadines* MMSI: 377101000 Official number: 10257	**4,955** 1,645 6,207 T/cm 20.0	Class: RS	**1996-06 Sudostroitelnyy Zavod "Krasnoye Sormovo" — Nizhniy Novgorod** Yd No: 19610/37 Loa 140.00 Br ex 16.65 Dght 4.670 Lbp 134.00 Br md 16.40 Dpth 6.70 Welded, 1 dk	**(A31A2GX) General Cargo Ship** Grain: 6,843; Bale: 6,785	**2 oil engines** driving 2 FP propellers Total Power: 1,942kW (2,640hp) 10.0kn S.K.L. 8NVDS48A-3U 2 x 4 Stroke 8 Cy. 320 x 480 each-971kW (1320bhp) SKL Motoren u. Systemtechnik AG-Magdeburg AuxGen: 3 x 150kW a.c Thrusters: 1 Thwart. FP thruster (f) Fuel: 417.0 (r.f.)
7733826 **VERESHCHAGINO** *EOKZ* - **National Academy of Sciences of Ukraine** Pic Shipping Ltd (OOO 'Pik Shipping') *Illichevsk* *Ukraine* MMSI: 272014500 Official number: 773073	*746* 227 395	Class: (RS)	**1978-08 Zavod "Leninskaya Kuznitsa" — Kiyev** Yd No: 1450 Loa 54.82 Br ex 9.96 Dght 4.141 Lbp 49.30 Br md 9.80 Dpth 5.01 Welded, 1 dk	**(A31A2GX) General Cargo Ship** Ins: 414 Compartments: 2 Ho, ER 3 Ha: 3 (1.5 x 1.6) Derricks: 2x1.3t; Winches: 2 Ice Capable	**1 oil engine** driving 1 CP propeller Total Power: 736kW (1,001hp) 12.0kn S.K.L. 8NVD48A-2U 1 x 4 Stroke 8 Cy. 320 x 480 736kW (1001bhp) VEB Schwermaschinenbau "KarlLiebknecht" (SKL)-Magdeburg Fuel: 154.0 (d.f.)
8746181 **VERGE LORETO SEGONA** *EBTE* 3-AT-41-03 **Aresteus SL** *Villajoyosa* *Spain* Official number: 3-1/2003	**104** - -		**2003-12 Asfibe S.A. — Benicarlo** Loa 24.85 (BB) Br ex - Dght - Lbp 21.50 Br md 6.15 Dpth 3.55 Bonded, 1 dk	**(B11A2FS) Stern Trawler** Hull Material: Reinforced Plastic	**1 oil engine** driving 1 Propeller Total Power: 367kW (499hp)
8331584 **VERGI** *YL2402* *ex* MRTK-0660 *-1985* EK-0660 **Vergi Ltd** *Riga* *Latvia* MMSI: 275072000 Official number: 0829	**117** 35 26	Class: (RS)	**1984 Sosnovskiy Sudostroitelnyy Zavod — Sosnovka** Yd No: 660 Loa 25.50 Br ex 7.00 Dght 2.390 Lbp 22.00 Br md 6.80 Dpth 3.30 Welded, 1 dk	**(B11B2FV) Fishing Vessel** Grain: 64 Compartments: 1 Ho, ER 1 Ha: (1.3 x 1.5)ER Ice Capable	**1 oil engine** driving 1 FP propeller Total Power: 221kW (300hp) 9.5kn S.K.L. 6NVD26A-2 1 x 4 Stroke 6 Cy. 180 x 260 221kW (300bhp) VEB Schwermaschinenbau "KarlLiebknecht" (SKL)-Magdeburg AuxGen: 2 x 12kW Fuel: 15.0 (d.f.)
7938945 **VERGINE DEL ROSARIO** *INFM* - **Cooperativa Pescatori La Tonnara** *Salerno* *Italy* Official number: 577	**245** 72 -	Class: RI	**1977 Cant. Nav. Ugo Codecasa S.p.A. — Viareggio** Yd No: 31 Loa 44.33 Br ex 7.52 Dght 3.150 Lbp 35.36 Br md 7.51 Dpth 4.02 Welded, 1 dk	**(B11B2FV) Fishing Vessel**	**1 oil engine** driving 1 FP propeller Total Power: 1,081kW (1,470hp) Sulzer 6ASL25/30 1 x 4 Stroke 6 Cy. 250 x 300 1081kW (1470bhp) Maschinenbau Augsburg Nuernberg (MAN)-Augsburg AuxGen: 2 x 96kW 220V 50Hz a.c
7237004 **VERICA** *DTBG3* *ex* Ocean No. 2 *-2013* - *ex* Sea Queen No. 2 *-2005* *ex* Kim's Marine No. 212 *-1989* *ex* Daitoku Maru No. 31 *-1985* *ex* Kyowa Maru No. 23 *-1978* **Daeyoung Fisheries Co Ltd** *Busan* *South Korea* MMSI: 441114000 Official number: 0108004-6260002	*724* 213 405	Class: KR	**1972 Yamanishi Shipbuilding Co Ltd — Ishinomaki MG** Yd No: 705 Loa 55.50 Br ex 9.02 Dght 3.523 Lbp 49.87 Br md 9.00 Dpth 5.74 Welded, 2 dks	**(B11A2FT) Trawler**	**1 oil engine** driving 1 FP propeller Total Power: 1,986kW (2,700hp) 13.0kn Akasaka AH40 1 x 4 Stroke 6 Cy. 400 x 600 1986kW (2700bhp) Akasaka Tekkosho KK (Akasaka DieselLtd)-Japan AuxGen: 2 x 200kW 225V a.c
6610675 **VERICA** *YYP2248* - **Terminales Maracaibo CA** *Maracaibo* *Venezuela* Official number: AJZL-07902	*142* 43 -	Class: (AB)	**1965 Equitable Equipment Co. — Madisonville, La** Yd No: 1384 Loa 25.91 Br ex 7.78 Dght 2.439 Lbp 23.78 Br md 7.32 Dpth 3.15 Welded, 1 dk	**(B32A2ST) Tug**	**2 oil engines** sr reverse geared to sc. shafts driving 2 FP propellers Total Power: 1,126kW (1,530hp) Caterpillar D398TA 2 x Vee 4 Stroke 12 Cy. 159 x 203 each-563kW (765bhp) Caterpillar Tractor Co-USA AuxGen: 2 x 40kW
9401128 **VERIGE** *9AA6988* - **United Shipping Services Eleven Inc** Uljanik Shipmanagement Inc *Pula* *Croatia* MMSI: 238265000 Official number: 01-1686-1-074177	**30,638** 15,319 52,606 T/cm 56.8	Class: CS LR (NV) **100A1** SS 03/2010 Double Hull oil and chemical tanker, Ship Type 2* ESP LI *IWS SPM Ice Class 1B FS at a draught of 12.798m Max/min draughts fwd 12.798/5.918m Max/min draughts aft 13.088/7.588m Power required 8716kw, power installed 9650kw **LMC** **UMS IGS**	**2010-03 '3 Maj' Brodogradiliste dd — Rijeka** Yd No: 709 Loa 195.12 (BB) Br ex 32.24 Dght 12.500 Lbp 187.30 Br md 32.20 Dpth 17.80 Welded, 1 dk	**(A12B2TR) Chemical/Products Tanker** Double Hull (13F) Liq: 56,190; Liq (Oil): 56,190 Compartments: 12 Wing Ta, 2 Wing Slop Ta, ER 12 Cargo Pump (s): 12x550m³/hr Manifold: Bow/CM: 97.2m Ice Capable	**1 oil engine** driving 1 FP propeller Total Power: 10,185kW (13,848hp) 14.0kn Wartsila 7RTA48T 1 x 2 Stroke 7 Cy. 480 x 2000 10185kW (13848bhp) '3 Maj' Motori i Dizalice dd-Croatia AuxGen: 3 x 1190kW a.c Fuel: 200.0 (d.f.) 1550.0 (r.f.)
9136931 **VERILA** *9HYH9* *ex* Lark *-2007* *ex* Gloire *-2006* - *ex* Blue Gemini *-2003* **Verila Maritime Ltd** Navigation Maritime Bulgare *Valletta* *Malta* MMSI: 249698000 Official number: 9136931	**14,431** 8,741 23,723 T/cm 33.7	Class: NK	**1996-09 Shin Kurushima Dockyard Co. Ltd. — Onishi** Yd No: 2896 Loa 150.52 (BB) Br ex - Dght 9.566 Lbp 143.00 Br md 26.00 Dpth 13.20 Welded, 1 dk	**(A21A2BC) Bulk Carrier** Grain: 31,249; Bale: 30,169 Compartments: 4 Ho, ER 4 Ha: (17.9 x 12.8)3 (19.5 x 17.8)ER Cranes: 4x30.5t	**1 oil engine** driving 1 FP propeller Total Power: 5,296kW (7,200hp) 14.0kn Mitsubishi 6UEC45LA 1 x 2 Stroke 6 Cy. 450 x 1350 5296kW (7200bhp) Kobe Hatsudoki KK-Japan AuxGen: 3 x 400kW a.c Fuel: 765.0 (r.f.) 19.0pd
9565194 **VERINA** *EAFZ* - **Lico Leasing SA EFC** Remolques Gijoneses SA *Gijon* *Spain* MMSI: 225425000	**785** 235 627	Class: BV	**2011-04 Astilleros Armon SA — Navia** Yd No: 687 Loa 37.00 Br ex - Dght 5.200 Lbp 32.00 Br md 14.00 Dpth 6.70 Welded, 1 dk	**(B32A2ST) Tug**	**2 oil engines** reduction geared to sc. shafts driving 2 Directional propellers Total Power: 5,940kW (8,076hp) MaK 9M25C 2 x 4 Stroke 9 Cy. 255 x 400 each-2970kW (4038bhp) Caterpillar Motoren GmbH & Co. KG-Germany AuxGen: 2 x 175kW 50Hz a.c

Ship	Tonnage / Class	Builder / Dimensions	Type	Machinery
7019610 **VERING** *DUA2208* *ex* Sung Kong *ex* Ikoma Maru *-1973* - **Malayan Towage & Salvage Corp (SALVTUG)** - *Manila* *Philippines* Official number: MNLD007736	*216* Class: (LR) 103 Classed LR until 3/89 -	**1970 Kanagawa Zosen — Kobe** Yd No: 100 Loa 31.70 Br ex 8.95 Dght 3.506 Lbp 27.01 Br md 8.40 Dpth 4.02 Welded, 1 dk	**(B32A2ST) Tug**	**2 oil engines** driving 2 CP propellers Total Power: 2,206kW (3,000hp) 12.0kn Nippon Hatsudoki HS6NVA38 2 x 4 Stroke 6 Cy. 380 x 540 each-1103kW (1500bhp) Nippon Hatsudoki-Japan AuxGen: 2 x 32kW 210V 50Hz a.c
7531008 **VERITAS** - *ex* Salveritas *-1995* - *ex* Takusei Maru No. 31 *-1980* **Master Divers Pvt Ltd (Marine & Underwater Services)** Ocean Carriers Ltd	**587** Class: (NK) 177 534	**1976-03 Matsuura Tekko Zosen K.K. — Osakikamijima** Yd No: 254 Loa 50.50 Br ex 10.04 Dght 3.990 Lbp 45.73 Br md 10.01 Dpth 4.42 Welded, 1 dk	**(B32A2ST) Tug** 1 Ha: (2.2 x 1.9)	**2 oil engines** sr geared to sc. shafts driving 2 FP propellers Total Power: 4,118kW (5,598hp) 14.0kn Fuji 8L32X 2 x 4 Stroke 8 Cy. 320 x 380 each-2059kW (2799bhp) Fuji Diesel Co Ltd-Japan AuxGen: 2 x 176kW
9138745 **VERITAS-H** *V2AL2* *ex* Regulus *-1997* *ex* Veritas-H *-1996* **ms Veritas-H Hinsch Schiffahrts GmbH & Co KG** Reederei Hinsch GmbH & Co KG SatCom: Inmarsat C 430401376 *Saint John's* *Antigua & Barbuda* MMSI: 304010625 Official number: 2466	**2,899** Class: GL 1,390 3,931	**1995-12 Elbewerft Boizenburg GmbH — Boizenburg** (Hull) Yd No: 229 **1995-12 Motorenwerk Bremerhaven GmbH (MWB) — Bremerhaven** Yd No: 229 Loa 99.26 (BB) Br ex 16.44 Dght 4.900 Lbp 93.95 Br md 16.20 Dpth 6.40 Welded, 1 dk	**(A33A2CC) Container Ship (Fully Cellular)** Grain: 4,440; Bale: 4,300 TEU 340 C Ho 82 TEU C Dk 258 TEU incl 40 ref C. Compartments: 2 Ho, ER 2 Ha: ER	**1 oil engine** with clutches, flexible couplings & sr geared to sc. shaft driving 1 CP propeller Total Power: 2,589kW (3,520hp) 14.0kn MaK 8M453C 1 x 4 Stroke 8 Cy. 320 x 420 2589kW (3520bhp) Krupp MaK Maschinenbau GmbH-Kiel Thrusters: 1 Thwart. FP thruster (f)
9173599 **VERITAS VIKING** *LMIB3* *ex* Veritas Viking I *-2003* *ex* Veritas Viking *-2001* **Eidesvik Shipping AS** Eidesvik AS *Haugesund* *Norway (NIS)* MMSI: 259517000	**7,886** Class: NV 2,365 5,200	**1998-05 Halsnoy Verft AS — Hoylandsbygd** (Hull) **1998-05 Mjellem & Karlsen Verft AS — Bergen** Yd No: 149 Loa 93.35 (BB) Br ex - Dght 7.220 Lbp 81.30 Br md 22.00 Dpth 8.60 Welded, 1 dk	**(B31A2SR) Research Survey Vessel**	**2 oil engines** with clutches, flexible couplings & reduction geared to sc. shafts driving 2 CP propellers Total Power: 8,640kW (11,746hp) 15.5kn MaK 9M32 2 x 4 Stroke 9 Cy. 320 x 480 each-4320kW (5873bhp) MaK Motoren GmbH & Co. KG-Kiel AuxGen: 2 x 2360kW 220/440V 60Hz a.c, 1 x 500kW 220/440V 60Hz a.c Thrusters: 1 Retract. directional thruster (f); 1 Thwart. FP thruster (f); 1 Tunnel thruster (a) Fuel: 2043.0 (d.f.) 20.0pd
9505388 **VERITY** *9VVD7* - **HL Resources Pte Ltd** Hong Lam Marine Pte Ltd *Singapore* *Singapore* MMSI: 563432000 Official number: 393597	**7,284** Class: BV 3,490 11,306 T/cm 19.1	**2008-10 Yangzhou Kejin Shipyard Co Ltd — Jiangdu JS** Yd No: 07035 Loa 130.20 (BB) Br ex 18.60 Dght 8.000 Lbp 122.97 Br md 18.60 Dpth 10.80 Welded, 1 dk	**(A12B2TR) Chemical/Products Tanker** Double Hull (13F) Liq: 12,720; Liq (Oil): 12,720 Part Cargo Heating Coils Compartments: 12 Wing Ta, ER, 2 Wing Slop Ta 12 Cargo Pump (s): 8x300m³/hr, 4x200m³/hr Manifold: Bow/CM: 62.8m	**1 oil engine** reduction geared to sc. shaft driving 1 FP propeller Total Power: 3,300kW (4,487hp) 13.0kn Daihatsu 6DKM-36 1 x 4 Stroke 6 Cy. 360 x 480 3300kW (4487bhp) Daihatsu Diesel Manufacturing Co Lt-Japan AuxGen: 3 x 500kW 450V 60Hz a.c Thrusters: 1 Tunnel thruster (f) Fuel: 78.0 (d.f.) 677.0 (r.f.)
9229178 **VERITY** *MGDL2* *ex* Union Mercury *-2008* *ex* Estime *-2004* - **Faversham Ships Ltd** - *Douglas* *Isle of Man (British)* MMSI: 235007990 Official number: 737445	**2,601** Class: GL (BV) 1,428 3,360	**2001-06 Tille Scheepsbouw Kootstertille B.V. — Kootstertille** Yd No: 336 Loa 91.25 (BB) Br ex - Dght 5.213 Lbp 84.65 Br md 13.75 Dpth 6.25 Welded, 1 dk	**(A31A2GX) General Cargo Ship** Grain: 5,168 TEU 142 C.Ho 102/20' (40') C.Dk 40/20' (40') Compartments: 1 Ho, ER 1 Ha: (62.0 x 10.0)ER Ice Capable	**1 oil engine** with flexible couplings & sr geared to sc. shaft driving 1 CP propeller Total Power: 1,710kW (2,325hp) 13.0kn MaK 9M20C 1 x 4 Stroke 9 Cy. 200 x 300 1710kW (2325bhp) (new engine 2009) Caterpillar Motoren GmbH & Co. KG-Germany AuxGen: 1 x 312kW 400V 50Hz a.c, 2 x 124kW 380V 50Hz a.c Thrusters: 1 Thwart. FP thruster (f) Fuel: 212.0 (d.f.) 7.7pd
7611262 **VERKHNETORETSKOE** - *ex* Savran *-1999* -	**744** Class: GM (RS) 223 618	**1975-11 Volgogradskiy Sudostroitelnyy Zavod — Volgograd** Yd No: 864 Converted From: Stern Trawler-1996 Loa 53.70 (BB) Br ex 10.70 Dght 4.650 Lbp 48.04 Br md - Dpth 6.02 Welded, 1 dk	**(A31A2GX) General Cargo Ship** Grain: 476 Compartments: 1 Ho, ER 1 Ha: (9.9 x 3.0) Ice Capable	**1 oil engine** driving 1 CP propeller Total Power: 971kW (1,320hp) 12.8kn S.K.L. 8NVD48A-2U 1 x 4 Stroke 8 Cy. 320 x 480 971kW (1320bhp) (new engine 1982) VEB Schwermaschinenbau "KarlLiebknecht" (SKL)-Magdeburg Thrusters: 1 Thwart. FP thruster (f); 1 Tunnel thruster (a)
8841694 **VERLAINE** *XUAZ5* *ex* Volgo-Balt 223 *-2010* - **Verlaine Shipping Ltd** Mes Marine Ltd Corp *Phnom Penh* *Cambodia* MMSI: 514437000 Official number: 1080518	**2,457** Class: UA (RS) (RR) 1,191 2,893	**1980-04 Zavody Tazkeho Strojarstva (ZTS) — Komarno** Yd No: 1954 Loa 114.00 Br ex 13.20 Dght 3.640 Lbp 110.00 Br md 13.00 Dpth 5.50 Welded, 1dk	**(A31A2GX) General Cargo Ship** Grain: 4,720	**2 oil engines** driving 2 FP propellers Total Power: 1,030kW (1,400hp) Skoda 6L275A2 2 x 4 Stroke 6 Cy. 275 x 350 each-515kW (700bhp) CKD Praha-Praha
8705204 **VERLAINE** *FHIT* CC 683110 **Verlaine Sarl** - *Concarneau* *France* MMSI: 227557000 Official number: 683110	*160* 35 -	**1986-09 Chantiers Navals Vergoz — Concarneau** Loa 24.01 Br ex 6.84 Dght - Lbp 21.21 Br md 6.81 Dpth 3.51 Welded, 1 dk	**(B11A2FS) Stern Trawler** Ins: 90	**1 oil engine** with clutches, flexible couplings & sr geared to sc. shaft driving 1 CP propeller Total Power: 478kW (650hp) A.B.C. 6MDXS 1 x 4 Stroke 6 Cy. 242 x 320 478kW (650bhp) Anglo Belgian Corp NV (ABC)-Belgium
8724597 **VERMAN** - - **Kandalaksha Commercial Sea Port (Kandalakshskiy Moskoy Torgovyy Port)** - *Kandalaksha* *Russia* Official number: 841142	**182** Class: RS 54 57	**1985-04 Gorokhovetskiy Sudostroitelnyy Zavod — Gorokhovets** Yd No: 208 Loa 29.30 Br ex 8.60 Dght 3.400 Lbp 27.00 Br md 8.24 Dpth 4.30 Welded, 1 dk	**(B32A2ST) Tug** Ice Capable	**2 oil engines** driving 2 CP propellers Total Power: 1,180kW (1,604hp) 11.5kn Pervomaysk 8CHNP25/34 2 x 4 Stroke 8 Cy. 250 x 340 each-590kW (802bhp) Pervomaydizelmash (PDM)-Pervomaysk AuxGen: 2 x 50kW a.c
9189952 **VERMILION ENERGY** *A8ZY3* *ex* Vermilion Express *-2011* - **Vermilion Energy Inc** LL Energy SA *Monrovia* *Liberia* MMSI: 636015318 Official number: 15318	**56,245** Class: NK 32,479 106,131 T/cm 88.4	**1999-01 Namura Shipbuilding Co Ltd — Imari SG** Yd No: 974 Loa 240.99 (BB) Br ex - Dght 14.923 Lbp 232.00 Br md 42.00 Dpth 21.20 Welded, 1 dk	**(A13B2TP) Products Tanker** Double Hull (13F) Liq: 122,028; Liq (Oil): 122,028 Compartments: 12 Wing Ta, ER 3 Cargo Pump (s): 3x2500m³/hr	**1 oil engine** driving 1 FP propeller Total Power: 12,284kW (16,701hp) 15.0kn Sulzer 7RTA58T 1 x 2 Stroke 7 Cy. 580 x 2416 12284kW (16701bhp) Mitsubishi Heavy Industries Ltd-Japan AuxGen: 3 x 500kW a.c Fuel: 2732.0 (r.f.) 42.0pd
9397080 **VERMILION FIRST** *3FBK2* - **Comosa Building & Pluto Navigation SA** Daiichi Chuo Kisen Kaisha *Panama* *Panama* MMSI: 357786000 Official number: 4136410A	**46,025** Class: NK 13,808 49,999 T/cm 70.3	**2010-01 Mitsubishi Heavy Industries Ltd. — Nagasaki** Yd No: 2243 Loa 230.00 (BB) Br ex 36.63 Dght 10.810 Lbp 219.00 Br md 36.60 Dpth 20.80 Welded, 1 dk	**(A11B2TG) LPG Tanker** Double Bottom Entire Compartment Length Liq (Gas): 77,323 5 x Gas Tank (s); 4 independent pri horizontal, ER 8 Cargo Pump (s): 8x550m³/hr Manifold: Bow/CM: 113.7m	**1 oil engine** driving 1 FP propeller Total Power: 12,360kW (16,805hp) 16.4kn Mitsubishi 7UEC60LSII 1 x 2 Stroke 7 Cy. 600 x 2300 12360kW (16805bhp) Mitsubishi Heavy Industries Ltd-Japan AuxGen: 3 x a.c Fuel: 310.0 (d.f.) 2500.0 (r.f.)
7016620 **VERNA TRADER** *H03154* *ex* Chilibre *-2003* *ex* Golden Owl *-1974* - **Laguna Alta SA** - *Panama* *Panama* Official number: 00434PEXT11	*1,911* Class: (LR) (AB) 1,329 Classed LR until 1/9/10 3,678 T/cm 11.6	**1970-03 Bethlehem Steel Corp. — Beaumont, Tx** Yd No: 4854 Loa 79.25 Br ex 16.82 Dght 4.747 Lbp 77.35 Br md 16.77 Dpth 5.19 Welded, 1 dk	**(A13B2TP) Products Tanker** Single Hull Liq: 4,610; Liq (Oil): 4,610 Compartments: 12 Ta, ER 2 Cargo Pump (s): 2x150m³/hr	**2 oil engines** geared to sc. shafts driving 2 FP propellers Total Power: 1,500kW (2,040hp) 8.0kn Caterpillar D398TA 2 x Vee 4 Stroke 12 Cy. 159 x 203 each-750kW (1020bhp) Caterpillar Tractor Co-USA AuxGen: 2 x 75kW Fuel: 13.5 (d.f.)
9381469 **VERNICOS MASTER** *SVA2352* *ex* Stadt Master *-2009* *ex* PW Kappa *-2007* - **Antaios Maritime Co** Argonaftis Anonymos Naftiki Eteria *Piraeus* *Greece* MMSI: 240917000 Official number: 11869	**318** Class: LR (AB) 95 **100A1** SS 11/2011 162 **tug** **LMC**	**2006-11 Jiangsu Wuxi Shipyard Co Ltd — Wuxi JS** (Hull) Yd No: (1213) **2006-11 Pacific Ocean Engineering & Trading Pte Ltd (POET) — Singapore** Yd No: 1213 Loa 27.70 Br ex - Dght 4.000 Lbp 22.94 Br md 9.80 Dpth 4.90 Welded, 1 dk	**(B32A2ST) Tug**	**2 oil engines** reduction geared to sc. shafts driving 2 Z propellers Total Power: 2,648kW (3,600hp) Yanmar 8N21A-EN 2 x 4 Stroke 8 Cy. 210 x 290 each-1324kW (1800bhp) Yanmar Diesel Engine Co Ltd-Japan AuxGen: 2 x 99kW a.c Fuel: 170.0 (d.f.)

9067611 *SVA3846* -	**VERNICOS MERMAID** *ex* Svitzer Mermaid *-2012* *ex* Avonwise *-2006* *ex* Ferdinando *-2001* *ex* San Ferdinando *-2001* *ex* Citta della Spezia *-1996* **Santa Marina Maritime Co** Vernicos Tugs & Salvage *Piraeus* *Greece* MMSI: 241188000 Official number: 12111	*305* 91 233	Class: LR (BV) (AB) (RI) **100A1** SS 06/2013 tug, fire fighting Ship 1 (2600 m3/h) **LMC**	**1993-11 B.V. Scheepswerf Damen Bergum — Bergum** (Hull) **1993-11 B.V. Scheepswerf Damen — Gorinchem** Yd No: 7904 Loa 31.06 Br ex 10.00 Dght 4.450 Lbp 28.02 Br md 9.40 Dpth 4.80 Welded, 1 dk	**(B32A2ST) Tug**	**2 oil engines** geared to sc. shafts driving 2 Directional propellers Total Power: 2,940kW (3,998hp) Nohab 6R25 2 x 4 Stroke 6 Cy. 250 x 300 each-1470kW (1999bhp) Wartsila Diesel AB-Sweden Thrusters: 1 Thwart. FP thruster (f)
5378725 - -	**VERNIKOU IRINI** *ex* Agia Irini *-2002* *ex* Vernicos Irini *-1988* *ex* ST-755 *-1988* **Northern Greece Tugs Maritime Co** -	*141* 60 -	Class: (AB)	**1944 Continental Shipbuilding Corp. — Brooklyn, NY** Yd No: 4 Loa 26.70 Br ex 7.07 Dght 2.858 Lbp 24.67 Br md 7.01 Dpth 3.15 Welded, 1 dk	**(B32A2ST) Tug**	**1 oil engine** driving 1 FP propeller Fuel: 51.0 (d.f.)
8847480 - -	**VERNIY** *ex* Antares *-2005* *ex* Orions *-2003* *ex* Antares *-2002* *ex* Orions *-2001* *ex* Orion *-1992* **Shakuda-Invest Ltd** *Kerch* *Ukraine*	**263** 78 83	Class: RS	**1969 Brodogradiliste 'Tito' — Belgrade** Yd No: 234 Loa 35.48 Br ex 9.21 Dght 4.300 Lbp 31.45 Br md 9.02 Dpth 4.52 Welded, 1 dk	**(B32A2ST) Tug** Ice Capable	**2 oil engines** driving 2 CP propellers Total Power: 1,704kW (2,316hp) 13.6kn B&W 7-26MTBF-40 2 x 4 Stroke 7 Cy. 260 x 400 each-852kW (1158bhp) Titovi Zavodi 'Litostroj'-Yugoslavia AuxGen: 2 x 100kW a.c, 1 x 25kW a.c
8724585 - -	**VERNYY** - **Orion-98 Co Ltd** - *Magadan* *Russia*	**182** 54 57	Class: RS	**1985-05 Gorokhovetskiy Sudostroitelnyy Zavod — Gorokhovets** Yd No: 207 Loa 29.30 Br ex 8.60 Dght 3.400 Lbp 27.00 Br md 8.24 Dpth 4.30 Welded, 1 dk	**(B32A2ST) Tug** Ice Capable	**2 oil engines** driving 2 CP propellers Total Power: 1,180kW (1,604hp) 11.5kn Pervomaysk 8CHNP25/34 2 x 4 Stroke 8 Cy. 250 x 340 each-590kW (802bhp) Pervomaydizelmash (PDM)-Pervomaysk AuxGen: 2 x 50kW a.c
8009052 *HP9751* -	**VERO B** *ex* Elena B *-2007* *ex* Dakar Bridge *-2007* *ex* Art 2 *-2005* *ex* Dart 2 *-2005* *ex* Bazias 2 *-1995* *ex* Balder Hav *-1985* **Boluda Lines SA** - *Panama* *Panama* MMSI: 372653000 Official number: 4037809A	**9,080** 2,724 4,700	Class: RI (BV) (RN) (GL) (NV)	**1984-11 Santierul Naval Galati S.A. — Galati** Yd No: 768 Loa 120.01 (BB) Br ex - Dght 5.316 Lbp 111.18 Br md 21.00 Dpth 12.50 Welded, 2 dks	**(A35A2RR) Ro-Ro Cargo Ship** Passengers: cabins: 6; driver berths: 12 Stern door/ramp (p) Len: 17.50 Wid: 7.70 Swl: 50 Stern door/ramp (s) Len: 12.50 Wid: 7.70 Swl: 57 Lane-Len: 1225 Lane-Wid: 7.50 Lane-clr ht: 6.20 Cars: 49, Trailers: 94 TEU 394 C Roro Dk 186 TEU C Dk 208 TEU incl 44 ref C.	**2 oil engines** sr geared to sc. shafts driving 2 CP propellers Total Power: 5,300kW (7,206hp) 15.5kn MaK 9M453AK 2 x 4 Stroke 9 Cy. 320 x 420 each-2650kW (3603bhp) Krupp MaK Maschinenbau GmbH-Kiel AuxGen: 1 x 525kW 440V 60Hz a.c, 2 x 425kW 440V 60Hz a.c Thrusters: 1 Thwart. CP thruster (f) Fuel: 171.0 (d.f.) 745.5 (r.f.) 24.5pd
5233999 - -	**VERONA** *ex* Bronx *-1990* *ex* Cove Point *-1990* *ex* Michael Moran *-1975* *ex* Maj. Gen. J.B. Aleshire *-1975* *ex* Dolphin *-1975* *ex* Hamburg American Line No. 3 *-1975* *ex* Dolphin *-1975* **Maritime Salvage Solutions**	*288* 196 -	Class: (AB)	**1913 Staten Island SB. Co. — Port Richmond, NY** Yd No: 601 Loa 35.06 Br ex 8.41 Dght 4.382 Lbp 34.45 Br md 8.39 Dpth 4.78 Riveted\Welded, 1 dk	**(B32A2ST) Tug**	**1 diesel electric oil engine** driving 1 gen. of 1210kW 525V d.c Connecting to 1 elec. Motor driving 1 FP propeller Total Power: 1,287kW (1,750hp) General Motors 16-278-A 1 x Vee 2 Stroke 16 Cy. 222 x 267 1287kW (1750bhp) (made 1944, fitted 1960) General Motors Corp-USA AuxGen: 1 x 30kW 125V d.c Fuel: 108.5 (d.f.)
8705254 *V2UN* -	**VERONA** *ex* Martyna *-2005* *ex* Marjesco *-2004* *ex* Unitas H *-1996* **Marlen Shipping Co Ltd** UAB Juru Agentura 'Forsa' *Saint John's* *Antigua & Barbuda* MMSI: 304011006	**2,184** 1,061 3,304	Class: GL	**1988-02 Schiffswerft und Maschinenfabrik Cassens GmbH — Emden** Yd No: 174 Loa 82.63 Br ex 12.70 Dght 5.280 Lbp 79.13 Br md 12.60 Dpth 6.66 Welded, 1 dk	**(A31A2GX) General Cargo Ship** Grain: 4,078 TEU 138 C.Ho 45/20' C.Dk 93/20' Compartments: 1 Ho, ER 1 Ha: (54.0 x 10.3)ER Ice Capable	**1 oil engine** with flexible couplings & sr gearedto sc. shaft driving 1 CP propeller Total Power: 1,100kW (1,496hp) 11.5kn MWM TBD444-6 1 x 4 Stroke 6 Cy. 230 x 320 1100kW (1496bhp) Motoren Werke Mannheim AG (MWM)-West Germany AuxGen: 1 x 200kW 220/380V 50Hz a.c, 1 x 64kW 220/380V 50Hz a.c Thrusters: 1 Thwart. CP thruster (f) Fuel: 103.5 (d.f.) 4.5pd
9190858 *LARI7* -	**VERONA** - **SCC Shipowning I AS** Siem Car Carriers AS *Oslo* *Norway (NIS)* MMSI: 258649000	**37,237** 11,172 12,778	Class: BV NV	**2000-08 'Uljanik' Brodogradiliste dd — Pula** Yd No: 425 Loa 176.70 (BB) Br ex - Dght 8.766 Lbp 165.00 Br md 31.10 Dpth 28.00 Welded	**(A35B2RV) Vehicles Carrier** Side door (s) Len: - Wid: - Swl: 25 Quarter stern door & ramp (s. a.) Len: - Wid: - Swl: 100 Cars: 4,632	**1 oil engine** driving 1 FP propeller Total Power: 11,060kW (15,037hp) 19.5kn B&W 7S50MC-C 1 x 2 Stroke 7 Cy. 500 x 2000 11060kW (15037bhp) 'Uljanik' Strojogradnja dd-Croatia Thrusters: 1 Tunnel thruster (f); 1 Tunnel thruster (a)
7211854 *HO3714* -	**VERONA I** *ex* Scorpio *-2004* *ex* Helix *-2002* *ex* Ursa *-2000* *ex* Ursa Minor *-1998* *ex* Berendina *-1981* **GloMar Holding BV** - *Panama* *Panama* MMSI: 353634000 Official number: 32624PEXT2	**212** 50 -		**1972-07 Holland Launch N.V. — Zaandam** Yd No: 508 Converted From: Trawler-1998 Loa 32.25 Br ex 7.40 Dght 2.720 Lbp 28.85 Br md 7.29 Dpth 3.62 Welded, 1 dk	**(B22G2OY) Standby Safety Vessel**	**1 oil engine** driving 1 FP propeller Total Power: 747kW (1,016hp) Kromhout 9FBHD240 1 x 4 Stroke 9 Cy. 240 x 260 747kW (1016bhp) Stork Werkspoor Diesel BV-Netherlands AuxGen: 2 x 44kW a.c
5329865 *LLOO* -	**VERONICA** *ex* Froysjo *-1987* *ex* Sirahav *-1979* *ex* Reiher *-1955* **Havfangst AS** - *Hammerfest* *Norway* MMSI: 257101400	*125* 63 152	Class: (GL)	**1914 J.S. Figee — Vlaardingen** Converted From: Stern Trawler-1979 Converted From: General Cargo Ship Lengthened-1925 Loa 30.03 Br ex 6.66 Dght 2.718 Lbp 26.83 Br md 6.61 Dpth 2.95 Riveted, 1 dk	**(A24D2BA) Aggregates Carrier** Grain: 198 Compartments: 1 Ho, ER 1 Ha: (7.6 x 2.9)ER Derricks: 1x2t; Winches: 1	**1 oil engine** reverse reduction geared to sc. shaft driving 1 FP propeller Total Power: 373kW (507hp) Cummins KTA-19-M 1 x 4 Stroke 6 Cy. 159 x 159 373kW (507bhp) (new engine 1990) Cummins Engine Co Inc-USA
8108212 - -	**VERONICA** *ex* El Padrino *-1955* **Pesquera Los Compadres De Guaymas SA** - *Guaymas* *Mexico*	*121* 77 -		**1980 Astilleros Navarro — Guaymas** Yd No: P-62 Loa - Br ex - Dght - Lbp 19.41 Br md 6.21 Dpth 3.61 Welded, 1 dk	**(B11A2FT) Trawler**	**1 oil engine** geared to sc. shaft driving 1 FP propeller Total Power: 313kW (426hp) Caterpillar D353SCAC 1 x 4 Stroke 6 Cy. 159 x 203 313kW (426bhp) Caterpillar Tractor Co-USA
8653695 *IFNU* 02CA01075	**VERONICA** **Lecca Bruno** - *Sant'Antioco* *Italy*	**175** - -		**1999-01 Cant. Nav. di Ortona — Ortona** Loa 29.20 Br ex - Dght - Lbp 23.52 Br md - Dpth - Welded, 1 dk	**(B11B2FV) Fishing Vessel**	**1 oil engine** driving 1 Propeller Total Power: 662kW (900hp)
9111515 *SFED* -	**VERONICA** *ex* Fredrika af Graso *-1994* **Government of The Kingdom of Sweden (Vagverket Farjerederiet)** - *Vaxholm* *Sweden* MMSI: 265546930	**375** 132 700		**1972 in Sweden** Lengthened-1994 Loa 64.00 Br ex - Dght 3.500 Lbp - Br md 14.50 Dpth - Welded, 1 dk	**(A36A2PR) Passenger/Ro-Ro Ship (Vehicles)** Passengers: unberthed: 300 Cars: 62	**2 oil engines** driving 2 FP propellers Total Power: 960kW (1,306hp) Mitsubishi S6R2-MPTK 2 x 4 Stroke 6 Cy. 170 x 220 each-480kW (653bhp) Mitsubishi Heavy Industries Ltd-Japan
9202455 *EIJC3* -	**VERONICA** *ex* Ostanger *-2010* *ex* Gitte Henning *-2008* **Atlantic Dawn Ltd** - SatCom: Inmarsat C 425000274 *Dublin* *Irish Republic* MMSI: 250002036 Official number: 404632	**1,198** 447 1,700	Class: NV	**2000-05 Stocznia Cenal Sp z oo — Gdansk** (Hull) Yd No: 113 **2000-05 Karstensens Skibsvaerft A/S — Skagen** Yd No: 381 Loa 55.90 (BB) Br ex - Dght 4.700 Lbp 49.80 Br md 11.50 Dpth 5.20 Welded, 1 dk	**(B11A2FS) Stern Trawler** Bale: 1,500	**1 oil engine** geared to sc. shaft driving 1 FP propeller Total Power: 3,840kW (5,221hp) MaK 8M32 1 x 4 Stroke 8 Cy. 320 x 480 3840kW (5221bhp) MaK Motoren GmbH & Co. KG-Kiel Thrusters: 2 Thwart. FP thruster (f); 1 Tunnel thruster (a)
9263992 *XCLM* -	**VERONICA** - **Otto Candies LLC** Oceanografia SA de CV *Ciudad del Carmen* *Mexico* MMSI: 345070063 Official number: 0401132525-8	**365** 109 -	Class: AB	**2002-01 Austal USA LLC — Mobile AL** Yd No: 262 Loa 45.80 Br ex - Dght 2.200 Lbp 40.60 Br md 8.20 Dpth 3.80 Welded, 1 dk	**(B21A2OC) Crew/Supply Vessel** Hull Material: Aluminium Alloy	**4 oil engines** reverse reduction geared to sc. shafts driving 4 Water jets Total Power: 3,028kW (4,116hp) 26.5kn Caterpillar 3508B-TA 4 x Vee 4 Stroke 8 Cy. 170 x 190 each-757kW (1029bhp) Caterpillar Inc-USA AuxGen: 2 x 65kW a.c

8996475 *SLRE* GG-352	**VERONICA AV FISKEBACK** *ex* Polaris *-2010* **Fiskeri AB Ginneton** - *Fiskeback* Sweden MMSI: 266332000	**185** 55 -		2003-01 **Vestvaerftet ApS — Hvide Sande** Yd No: 234 Loa 23.50 (BB) Br ex 7.01 Dght 3.300 Lbp - Br md 7.00 Dpth 5.62 Welded, 1 dk	**(B11B2FV) Fishing Vessel**	**1 oil engine** geared to sc. shaft driving 1 Propeller Total Power: 511kW (695hp) Caterpillar 3508B 1 x Vee 4 Stroke 8 Cy. 170 x 190 511kW (695bhp) Caterpillar Inc-USA Thrusters: 1 Thwart. FP thruster (f)
9348625 *CQNP* -	**VERONICA B** *ex* Ruiloba *-2009* **Confidence Trade SL** Boluda Lines SA *Madeira* *Portugal (MAR)* MMSI: 255803950	**14,016** 6,524 18,091	Class: GL RI (LR) ✠ Classed LR until 16/9/10	2007-07 **Hijos de J. Barreras S.A. — Vigo** Yd No: 1651 Loa 159.80 (BB) Br ex 24.80 Dght 9.500 Lbp 143.00 Br md 24.80 Dpth 14.00 Welded, 1 dk	**(A33A2CC) Container Ship (Fully Cellular)** TEU 1267 C Ho 517 TEU C Dk 750 TEU incl 170 ref C Compartments: 8 Cell Ho, ER 8 Ha: ER	**1 oil engine** with clutches, flexible couplings & sr reverse geared to sc. shaft driving 1 CP propeller Total Power: 10,395kW (14,133hp) 18.0kn Wartsila 9L46D 1 x 4 Stroke 9 Cy. 460 x 580 10395kW (14133bhp) Wartsila Diesel S.A.-Bermeo AuxGen: 3 x 804kW 400V 50Hz a.c, 1 x 1600kW 400V 50Hz a.c Boilers: e (ex.g.) 9.2kgf/cm² (9.0bar), AuxB (o.f.) 9.2kgf/cm² (9.0bar) Thrusters: 2 Thwart. FP thruster (f)
7101009 *HO2011* -	**VERONICA I** *ex* Emmanuel I *-2000* *ex* Emmanuel *-1998* *ex* St. Giuse *-1998* *ex* Phu Yen *-1991* *ex* Manuel M *-1991* **John Marck** - *Panama* *Panama* Official number: 28834PEXT	*120* 80 -		**1969 at Freeport, Tx** Converted From: Fishing Vessel L reg 20.80 Br ex 6.91 Dght - Lbp 20.64 Br md 6.89 Dpth 3.56 Welded	**(A31A2GX) General Cargo Ship**	**1 oil engine** driving 1 FP propeller Total Power: 268kW (364hp) 10.0kn
9285328 *MEPV6* -	**VERONICA PG** *ex* W-O Topa *-2010* *ex* Veronica PG *-2007* *launched as* Topa *-2004* **Nordica Schiffahrts GmbH & Co KG ms 'Helsinki'** Pritchard-Gordon Tankers Ltd *Douglas* *Isle of Man (British)* MMSI: 235007440 Official number: 9285328	**6,688** 2,869 10,632 T/cm 22.8	Class: LR ✠ **100A1** SS 06/2009 Double Hull oil & chemical tanker, Ship Type 2 in association with an approved list of defined cargoes ESP LI ✠ **LMC** **UMS** Eq.Ltr: Z; Cable: 526.6/48.0 U3 (a)	2004-06 **OAO Damen Shipyards Okean — Nikolayev** (Hull) Yd No: 108 2004-06 **Bodewes Scheepswerf "Volharding" Foxhol B.V. — Foxhol** Yd No: 558 Loa 126.95 (BB) Br ex - Dght 6.800 Lbp 121.40 Br md 19.60 Dpth 9.35 Welded, 1 dk	**(A12B2TR) Chemical/Products Tanker** Double Hull (13F) Liq: 10,948; Liq (Oil): 10,948 Cargo Heating Coils Compartments: 12 Wing Ta, 2 Wing Slop Ta, ER 12 Cargo Pump (s): 12x250m³/hr Manifold: Bow/CM: 62m	**1 oil engine** with clutches, flexible couplings & sr geared to sc. shaft driving 1 CP propeller Total Power: 3,840kW (5,221hp) 13.5kn MaK 8M32C 1 x 4 Stroke 8 Cy. 320 x 480 3840kW (5221bhp) Caterpillar Motoren GmbH & Co. KG-Germany AuxGen: 1 x 752kW 415V 50Hz a.c, 3 x 370kW 415V 50Hz a.c Boilers: TOH (o.f.) 10.2kgf/cm² (10.0bar), TOH (ex.g.) 10.2kgf/cm² (10.0bar) Thrusters: 1 Thwart. CP thruster (f) Fuel: 121.0 (d.f.) 401.0 (r.f.)
8644979 - -	**VERONIKI** *ex* Agios Georgios *-2004* **Van Baerle International** -	*259* 32 352	Class: IV (HR)	**1966 Th. Zervas & Sons — Piraeus** Loa 52.90 Br ex 11.68 Dght 1.360 Lbp 45.50 Br md 11.65 Dpth 2.21 Welded, 1 dk	**(A36A2PR) Passenger/Ro-Ro Ship (Vehicles)**	**1 oil engine** geared to sc. shaft driving 1 Propeller Total Power: 537kW (730hp) Caterpillar 1 x 4 Stroke 6 Cy. 537kW (730bhp) Caterpillar Tractor Co-USA AuxGen: 2 x 88kW 380V 50Hz a.c
7701562 *SX6630* -	**VERONIKI DIO** *ex* Chiccogas *-1998* *ex* Kaitos *-1991* *ex* New Star *-1989* *ex* Newmarket *-1988* *ex* Kyoseki Maru No. 3 *-1987* **Stefanaus Shipping Co** - *Piraeus* *Greece* MMSI: 237005500 Official number: 10533	**1,110** 401 1,047	Class: RI (HR) (NK)	1977-09 **Naikai Shipbuilding & Engineering Co Ltd — Onomichi HS (Taguma Shipyard)** Yd No: 417 Loa 65.28 Br ex - Dght 4.439 Lbp 60.20 Br md 11.41 Dpth 5.16 Welded, 1 dk	**(A11B2TG) LPG Tanker** Liq (Gas): 1,504 2 x Gas Tank (s); 2 cyl horizontal	**1 oil engine** driving 1 FP propeller Total Power: 1,545kW (2,101hp) 12.5kn Hanshin 6LU38 1 x 4 Stroke 6 Cy. 380 x 580 1545kW (2101bhp) Hanshin Nainenki Kogyo-Japan AuxGen: 3 x 141kW a.c
8626123 *SY6044* -	**VERONIKI III** *ex* Berkah Selatan *-2005* *ex* Hakusei Maru No. 65 *-2004* **Veronaus Shipping Co** - SatCom: Inmarsat C 424038810 *Piraeus* *Greece* MMSI: 240388000 Official number: 11410	**445** 150 482	Class: HR (KI)	**1984 K.K. Mochizuki Zosensho — Osakikamijima** Yd No: 126 Loa 51.44 Br ex - Dght 3.000 Lbp 47.00 Br md 8.81 Dpth 3.71 Welded, 1 dk	**(A11B2TG) LPG Tanker** Liq (Gas): 450	**1 oil engine** driving 1 FP propeller Total Power: 625kW (850hp) 10.5kn Niigata 6M26AGT 1 x 4 Stroke 6 Cy. 260 x 460 625kW (850bhp) Niigata Engineering Co Ltd-Japan
9572070 *V7WJ3* -	**VERONIQUE D** - **Veronique Shipping Inc** Densan Deniz Nakliyat ve Sanayi AS (Densan Shipping Co Inc) *Majuro* *Marshall Islands* MMSI: 538004314 Official number: 4314	**33,139** 19,125 58,698 T/cm 59.5	Class: NV	2012-01 **Nantong COSCO KHI Ship Engineering Co Ltd (NACKS) — Nantong JS** Yd No: 087 Loa 197.00 (BB) Br ex 32.32 Dght 12.650 Lbp 193.96 Br md 32.26 Dpth 18.10 Welded, 1 dk	**(A21A2BC) Bulk Carrier** Grain: 73,614; Bale: 70,963 Compartments: 5 Ho, ER 5 Ha: ER Cranes: 4x30t	**1 oil engine** driving 1 FP propeller Total Power: 9,960kW (13,542hp) 14.5kn MAN-B&W 6S50MC-C 1 x 2 Stroke 6 Cy. 500 x 2000 9960kW (13542bhp) AuxGen: 3 x 600kW a.c
9649146 *FIFU* -	**VERRAZANE** - **SNC Diderot Financement 4** Geogas Trading SA *Marseille* *France (FIS)* MMSI: 228032700	**23,160** 6,947 26,120	Class: BV	2013-10 **Hyundai Mipo Dockyard Co Ltd — Ulsan** Yd No: 8097 Loa 173.70 (BB) Br ex 28.04 Dght 10.400 Lbp 167.52 Br md 28.00 Dpth 17.80 Welded, 1 dk	**(A11B2TG) LPG Tanker** Liq (Gas): 35,566	**1 oil engine** driving 1 FP propeller Total Power: 9,290kW (12,631hp) 16.4kn MAN-B&W 6S50ME-B8 1 x 2 Stroke 6 Cy. 500 x 2000 9290kW (12631bhp) Hyundai Heavy Industries Co Ltd-South Korea AuxGen: 2 x 1100kW 60Hz a.c, 1 x 900kW 60Hz a.c Fuel: 1760.0
9292175 *HOKN* -	**VERRAZANO BRIDGE** - **Scorpio Line Shipping SA** 'K' Line Ship Management Co Ltd (KLSM) *Panama* *Panama* MMSI: 353111000 Official number: 3041105B	**54,519** 22,921 65,038 T/cm 82.5	Class: NK	2004-11 **Hyundai Heavy Industries Co Ltd — Ulsan** Yd No: 1575 Loa 294.12 (BB) Br ex - Dght 13.520 Lbp 283.33 Br md 32.20 Dpth 21.80 Welded, 1 dk	**(A33A2CC) Container Ship (Fully Cellular)** TEU 4738 incl 400 ref C	**1 oil engine** driving 1 FP propeller Total Power: 44,584kW (60,616hp) 23.5kn MAN-B&W 8K98MC-C 1 x 2 Stroke 8 Cy. 980 x 2400 44584kW (60616bhp) Hyundai Heavy Industries Co Ltd-South Korea AuxGen: 4 x 1995kW a.c Thrusters: 1 Thwart. CP thruster (f) Fuel: 7385.0
7931014 *3BLI* -	**VERRAZZANO 1800** - **Port Louis Maritime Corp** - *Port Louis* *Mauritius* MMSI: 645160000 Official number: MR160	**1,872** 561 3,512	Class: BV	1979-07 **Sing Koon Seng Pte Ltd — Singapore** Yd No: SKS501 Loa 80.02 Br ex - Dght 4.501 Lbp 78.75 Br md 14.51 Dpth 5.52 Welded, 1 dk	**(B34A2SH) Hopper, Motor** Hopper: 2,000	**2 oil engines** driving 2 FP propellers Total Power: 1,440kW (1,958hp) Deutz SBA16M816 2 x Vee 4 Stroke 16 Cy. 142 x 160 each-720kW (979bhp) Kloeckner Humboldt Deutz AG-West Germany
7931519 - -	**VERTEX** - - -	*277* - 113	Class: (LR) ✠ Classed LR until 9/6/06	1981-08 **Gul Engineering Pte Ltd — Singapore** Yd No: 6006 Loa 33.51 Br ex 9.48 Dght 2.852 Lbp 30.99 Br md 9.16 Dpth 4.20 Welded, 1 dk	**(B32A2ST) Tug**	**2 oil engines** gearing integral to driving 2 Voith-Schneider propellers Total Power: 2,162kW (2,940hp) Kromhout 9FEHD240 2 x 4 Stroke 9 Cy. 240 x 260 each-1081kW (1470bhp) Stork Werkspoor Diesel BV-Netherlands AuxGen: 2 x 70kW 400V 50Hz a.c
7823621 - -	**VERTEX** *ex* Marriott International *-2009* *ex* Dragon Sea *-2000* *ex* Eastern Star *-1998* *ex* Hua Dong *-1996* *ex* Tenkai Maru *-1993* - - *San Lorenzo* *Honduras*	**3,310** 1,514 5,999	Class: (CC) (NK)	1979-10 **Miyoshi Shipbuilding Co Ltd — Uwajima EH** Yd No: 250 Loa 98.02 Br ex 15.52 Dght 6.960 Lbp 91.34 Br md 15.51 Dpth 7.83 Welded, 1 dk	**(A12B2TR) Chemical/Products Tanker** Liq: 5,504; Liq (Oil): 5,504 Cargo Heating Coils	**1 oil engine** driving 1 FP propeller Total Power: 2,942kW (4,000hp) 13.0kn Hanshin 6LU50A 1 x 4 Stroke 6 Cy. 500 x 800 2942kW (4000bhp) The Hanshin Diesel Works Ltd-Japan AuxGen: 2 x 280kW 445V 60Hz a.c Fuel: 78.0 (d.f.) 531.0 (r.f.) 12.0pd
1011147 *V7UX3* -	**VERTIGO** - **Maritime Asset Ventures (MI) Ltd** Nigel Burgess Ltd (BURGESS) *Bikini* *Marshall Islands* MMSI: 538080075 Official number: 80075	**837** 251 -	Class: LR ✠ **100A1** SS 05/2011 SSC Yacht, mono, G6 **UMS** Cable: 137.5/17.5 U2 (a)	2011-05 **Alloy Yachts — Auckland** Yd No: 41 Loa 68.36 Br ex 12.54 Dght 2.200 Lbp 56.36 Br md 12.54 Dpth 5.90 Welded, 1 dk	**(X11A2YS) Yacht (Sailing)** Hull Material: Aluminium Alloy	**2 oil engines** with clutches, flexible couplings & sr reverse geared to sc. shafts driving 2 CP propellers Total Power: 2,162kW (2,940hp) 19.0kn Caterpillar C32 ACERT 2 x Vee 4 Stroke 12 Cy. 145 x 162 each-1081kW (1470bhp) Caterpillar Inc-USA AuxGen: 2 x 200kW 400V 50Hz a.c Thrusters: 1 Thwart. FP thruster (f); 1 Thwart. FP thruster (a)

9721164 *JZRY* -	**VERTIKAL** *ex* Bo Yuan Sheng *-2013* **PT Salam Pacific Indonesia Lines** - *Surabaya* *Indonesia* MMSI: 525018239	**5,569** 3,118 8,031	Class: KI (Class contemplated)	**2013-10 Linhai Jianghai Shipbuilding Co Ltd — Linhai ZJ** Yd No: JH1206 Loa 118.10 Br ex - Dght 6.150 Lbp 110.90 Br md 18.20 Dpth 8.20 Welded, 1 dk	**(A31A2GX) General Cargo Ship**	**1 oil engine** driving 1 Propeller Total Power: 2,574kW (3,500hp) Yanmar 6N330-EN 1 x 4 Stroke 6 Cy. 330 x 440 2574kW (3500bhp) Yanmar Diesel Engine Co Ltd-Japan
9222053 *PECT* ZZ 9	**VERTROUWEN** - **S L Schot & Zn** - *Zierikzee* *Netherlands* MMSI: 244250000 Official number: 37923	**332** 99 -		**2000-07 'Crist' Sp z oo — Gdansk** (Hull) Yd No: C41/1 **2000-07 B.V. Scheepswerf Maaskant — Bruinisse** Yd No: 562 Loa 41.18 Br ex - Dght 1.000 Lbp 38.77 Br md 10.00 Dpth 2.65 Welded, 1 dk	**(B11B2FV) Fishing Vessel**	**2 oil engines** geared to sc. shafts driving 2 FP propellers Total Power: 918kW (1,248hp) Caterpillar 3412TA 2 x Vee 4 Stroke 12 Cy. 137 x 152 each-459kW (624bhp) Caterpillar Inc-USA
5019056 *PEUY* -	**VERTROUWEN** *ex* Hydra *-2008* *ex* Horne *-1987* *ex* Vega V *-1985* *ex* Annelies *-1978* **Visserijbedrijf de Rousant BV** - *Zoutkamp* *Netherlands* MMSI: 244737000 Official number: 2336	**316** 135 -	Class: (GL)	**1962 Stader Schiffswerft GmbH — Stade** Yd No: 196 Converted From: General Cargo Ship Lengthened & Deepened-1968 Loa 48.47 Br ex 7.35 Dght 2.510 Lbp 45.22 Br md 7.27 Dpth 2.93 Welded, 1 dk	**(B11A2FT) Trawler** Grain: 580; Bale: 525 1 Ha: (25.9 x 4.8)ER Ice Capable	**1 oil engine** reduction geared to sc. shaft driving 1 FP propeller Total Power: 169kW (230hp) 8.0kn Deutz RA6M528 1 x 4 Stroke 6 Cy. 220 x 280 169kW (230bhp) Kloeckner Humboldt Deutz AG-West Germany
7011046 *MKTF5* DS 11	**VERTROUWEN** *ex* Albatros *-1988* *ex* Jannetje Hoekman *-1984* *ex* Koningin Juliana *-1981* *ex* Vertrouwen *-1974* **Scott Trawlers Ltd** - *Dumfries* *United Kingdom* MMSI: 234209000 Official number: B10005	*144* 76 -		**1968 T. van den Beldt Thz., Scheeps. "Voorwaarts" — West-Graftdijk** Yd No: 427 Loa 26.24 Br ex - Dght - Lbp 23.30 Br md 6.43 Dpth 2.85 Welded, 1 dk	**(B11B2FV) Fishing Vessel**	**1 oil engine** driving 1 FP propeller Total Power: 441kW (600hp) Bolnes 6NL190 1 x 2 Stroke 6 Cy. 190 x 350 441kW (600bhp) NV Machinefabriek 'Bolnes' v/h JHvan Cappellen-Netherlands
7931284 *PIGE* GO 37	**VERTROUWEN** *ex* Andries de Vries *-1992* **BV Visserijbedrijf GO 37** - *Goedereede* *Netherlands* MMSI: 246107000 Official number: 1918	**373** 111 -		**1981-05 Stocznia Remontowa 'Nauta' SA — Gdynia** (Hull) Yd No: 393 **1981-05 B.V. Scheepswerf Maaskant — Stellendam** Yd No: 393 Loa 40.01 Br ex 8.00 Dght 3.520 Lbp - Br md - Dpth 4.69 Welded, 1 dk	**(B11A2FT) Trawler**	**1 oil engine** geared to sc. shaft driving 1 FP propeller Total Power: 1,471kW (2,000hp) Stork-Wartsila 6SW28 1 x 4 Stroke 6 Cy. 280 x 300 1471kW (2000bhp) (new engine 1997) Stork Wartsila Diesel BV-Netherlands
8128561 *DQQI* NG4	**VERTROUWEN** *ex* Teunis Van Atje *-2009* *ex* Atje-Helena *-1996* **Fischkutter 'Niedersachsen' GmbH See- und Flussfischerei** - *Jemgum* *Germany* Official number: 4823	**113** 33 -		**1982 Scheepswerf Veldthuis B.V. — Zuidbroek** Yd No: 309 Loa 24.93 Br ex - Dght 2.330 Lbp 23.91 Br md 6.03 Dpth 2.78 Welded, 1 dk	**(B11A2FT) Trawler**	**1 oil engine** driving 1 FP propeller Total Power: 368kW (500hp) Mitsubishi S6R-MPTA 1 x 4 Stroke 6 Cy. 170 x 180 368kW (500bhp) Mitsubishi Heavy Industries Ltd-Japan
9065455 *PIFT* TX 68	**VERTROUWEN** - **P A Van de Vis** - SatCom: Inmarsat C 424456710 *Texel* *Netherlands* MMSI: 244567000 Official number: 24728	**438** 131 598		**1993-09 Scheepswerf Haak B.V. — Zaandam** Yd No: 992 Loa 41.15 Br ex 8.70 Dght 4.080 Lbp 36.50 Br md 8.50 Dpth 5.30 Welded, 1 dk	**(B11A2FT) Trawler** Ins: 116	**1 oil engine** with flexible couplings & sr reverse geared to sc. shaft driving 1 FP propeller Total Power: 1,470kW (1,999hp) 14.3kn Caterpillar 3606TA 1 x 4 Stroke 6 Cy. 280 x 300 1470kW (1999bhp) Caterpillar Inc-USA Thrusters: 1 Thwart. FP thruster (f)
9585546 *9AA8040* -	**VERUDA** - **United Shipping Services Nine Inc** Uljanik Shipmanagement Inc SatCom: Inmarsat C 423829710 *Rijeka* *Croatia* MMSI: 238297000	**30,092** - 51,886	Class: BV CS	**2011-10 'Uljanik' Brodogradiliste dd — Pula** Yd No: 488 Loa 189.99 (BB) Br ex - Dght 12.350 Lbp 182.00 Br md 32.24 Dpth 17.10 Welded, 1 dk	**(A21A2BC) Bulk Carrier** Grain: 64,500 Compartments: 5 Ho, ER 5 Ha: ER Cranes: 4x30t	**1 oil engine** driving 1 FP propeller Total Power: 8,600kW (11,693hp) 14.2kn MAN-B&W 6S50MC-C 1 x 2 Stroke 6 Cy. 500 x 2000 8600kW (11693bhp) 'Uljanik' Strojogradnja dd-Croatia AuxGen: 3 x 620kW 60Hz a.c Fuel: 1703.0 (r.f.)
8300963 *IBUD* -	**VERVE** *ex* Dutch Pilot *-2009* *ex* Jacqueline Broere *-1993* **Zoom Srl** - SatCom: Inmarsat C 424702750 *Palermo* *Italy* MMSI: 247274400 Official number: 217 RI	**2,137** 858 3,052 T/cm 10.4	Class: RI (LR) ✠ Classed LR until 4/7/09	**1984-04 Verolme Scheepswerf Heusden B.V. — Heusden** (Aft section) Yd No: 996 **1993-06 "Welgelegen" Scheepswerf en Machinefabriek B.V. — Harlingen** (Fwd & cargo sections) Converted From: Chemical Tanker-2009 New forept-1993 Loa 91.18 Br ex 13.70 Dght 5.012 Lbp 88.16 Br md 13.61 Dpth 6.00 Welded, 1 dk	**(A12B2TR) Chemical/Products Tanker** Double Hull (13F) Liq: 3,080; Liq (Oil): 3,080 Cargo Heating Coils Compartments: 2 Wing Slop Ta (s.stl), 12 Wing Ta (s.stl), ER 12 Cargo Pump (s): 12x100m³/hr Manifold: Bow/CM: 43m	**1 oil engine** with flexible couplings & sr geared to sc. shaft driving 1 CP propeller Total Power: 1,365kW (1,856hp) 12.3kn Wartsila 4R32 1 x 4 Stroke 4 Cy. 320 x 350 1365kW (1856bhp) Oy Wartsila Ab-Finland AuxGen: 2 x 260kW 440V 60Hz a.c, 1 x 240kW 440V 60Hz a.c Boilers: 2 AuxB (o.f.) 10.2kgf/cm² (10.0bar), AuxB (e.g.) 14.3kgf/cm² (14.0bar) Thrusters: 1 Thwart. FP thruster (f) Fuel: 46.0 (d.f.) 117.0 (r.f.) 6.0pd
6413003 *IVKC* -	**VERVECE** - **Rimorchiatori Napoletani Srl** - *Naples* *Italy* Official number: 940	*193* 55 -	Class: (RI)	**1964 Cantiere Navale M & B Benetti — Viareggio** Yd No: 61 Loa 28.66 Br ex 7.73 Dght 3.460 Lbp 25.86 Br md 7.70 Dpth 4.02 Riveted\Welded, 1 dk	**(B32A2ST) Tug**	**1 oil engine** geared to sc. shaft driving 1 CP propeller Total Power: 772kW (1,050hp) 12.0kn MAN G8V30/45ATL 1 x 4 Stroke 8 Cy. 300 x 450 772kW (1050bhp) Maschinenbau Augsburg Nuernberg (MAN)-Augsburg AuxGen: 1 x 20kW d.c, 1 x 15kW 220V d.c
7011008 *GCVJ* P 845	**VERWACHTING** - **Saltire Seafoods Ltd** - *Portsmouth* *United Kingdom* MMSI: 232007210 Official number: A20461	**139** 85 -		**1969-01 van Goor's Scheepswerf en Mfbk N.V. — Monnickendam** Yd No: 637 Loa 28.10 Br ex - Dght - Lbp 26.75 Br md 7.04 Dpth 2.85 Welded, 1 dk	**(B11B2FV) Fishing Vessel**	**1 oil engine** geared to sc. shaft driving 1 FP propeller Total Power: 441kW (600hp) Daewoo V222TIH 1 x Vee 4 Stroke 12 Cy. 128 x 142 441kW (600bhp) (new engine 2009) Doosan Infracore Co Ltd-South Korea
7365617 *PIGF* UK 176	**VERWACHTING** *ex* Soli Deo Gloria *-1982* **C Post & Zonen** - *Urk* *Netherlands* MMSI: 245771000 Official number: 1941	*189* 70 -		**1975-05 Scheepsbouw- en Constructiebedr. K. Hakvoort B.V. — Monnickendam** Yd No: 141 Loa 33.63 Br ex - Dght - Lbp 28.35 Br md 7.50 Dpth 3.89 Welded, 1 dk	**(B11B2FV) Fishing Vessel**	**1 oil engine** driving 1 FP propeller Total Power: 736kW (1,001hp) De Industrie 6D7HDN 1 x 4 Stroke 6 Cy. 305 x 460 736kW (1001bhp) B.V. Motorenfabriek "De Industrie"-Alphen a/d Rijn
8805901 *PIFV* TX 63	**VERWACHTING** *ex* Missouri *-1995* *ex* Catjan *-1994* **Lenger Seafoods BV** - *Texel* *Netherlands* MMSI: 244525000	**311** 93 -		**1988-02 Scheepsbouw en Machinefabriek De Greuns B.V. — Leeuwarden** Yd No: 5940 Loa 43.72 Br ex - Dght 1.200 Lbp 41.84 Br md 11.82 Dpth 1.60 Welded, 1 dk	**(B11B2FV) Fishing Vessel**	**1 oil engine** reduction geared to sc. shaft driving 1 FP propeller Total Power: 400kW (544hp) Scania DSI14 1 x Vee 4 Stroke 8 Cy. 127 x 140 400kW (544bhp) (new engine 1998) Scania AB-Sweden
8933356 *YD6577* -	**VES FAIR 10** - **PT Perusahaan Pelayaran Rusianto Bersaudara** - *Samarinda* *Indonesia*	**296** 89 -	Class: (BV)	**1997-08 Fujian Fishing Vessel Shipyard — Fuzhou FJ** Yd No: 124 Loa 31.80 Br ex - Dght 3.000 Lbp 29.34 Br md 9.00 Dpth 4.27 Welded, 1 dk	**(B32A2ST) Tug**	**2 oil engines** geared to sc. shafts driving 2 FP propellers Total Power: 1,766kW (2,402hp) 12.5kn Cummins KTA-38-M2 2 x Vee 4 Stroke 12 Cy. 159 x 159 each-883kW (1201bhp) Cummins Engine Co Ltd-United Kingdom AuxGen: 2 x 75kW 400V 50Hz a.c Fuel: 204.0 (d.f.)
9198707 *YD6921* -	**VES FAIR 12** - **PT Perusahaan Pelayaran Rusianto Bersaudara** - *Samarinda* *Indonesia*	**177** 54 355	Class: KI (BV)	**1998-08 Fujian Southeast Shipyard — Fuzhou FJ** Yd No: 134 Loa 28.15 Br ex 8.40 Dght 2.880 Lbp 24.60 Br md 7.80 Dpth 3.60 Welded, 1 dk	**(B32A2ST) Tug**	**2 oil engines** geared to sc. shafts driving 2 FP propellers Total Power: 882kW (1,200hp) Cummins KTA-19-M3 2 x 4 Stroke 6 Cy. 159 x 159 each-441kW (600bhp) Cummins Engine Co Inc-USA AuxGen: 2 x 40kW a.c

IMO / Call sign	Name / Owner	Tonnage	Class	Build / Dimensions	Type	Machinery
5055385 *YYEJ* -	**VESCA R-1** *ex* Conchita *-1979* *ex* Burede *-1971* *ex* Debora Moran *-1958* *ex* Burede *-1957* **Venecia Ship Services CA (VESCA)** - *Maracaibo* *Venezuela* Official number: AJZL-1291	*190* 104 -	Class: (AB)	**1949 Gulfport Shipbuilding Corp. — Port Arthur, Tx** Yd No: 355 Loa 31.15 Br ex 7.62 Dght 3.515 Lbp 29.27 Br md 7.32 Dpth 3.81 Welded, 1 dk	**(B32A2ST) Tug**	**1 oil engine** sr reverse geared to sc. shaft driving 1 FP propeller Total Power: 905kW (1,230hp) 11.5kn General Motors 12-278A 1 x Vee 2 Stroke 12 Cy. 222 x 267 905kW (1230bhp) General Motors Corp-USA AuxGen: 2 x 30kW
6701747 *YVV2003* -	**VESCA R-5** *ex* Seaman *-1978* **Venecia Ship Services CA (VESCA)** - *Puerto Cabello* *Venezuela* Official number: ADKN-1412	*324* 81 -	Class: (LR) ✠ Classed LR until 4/87	**1967-01 Charles D. Holmes & Co. Ltd. — Beverley** Yd No: 1004 Loa 32.49 Br ex 9.38 Dght 4.242 Lbp 28.96 Br md 8.84 Dpth 4.58 Welded, 1 dk	**(B32A2ST) Tug** 1 Ha: (1.4 x 1.8) Derricks: 1x5t	**2 oil engines** sr reverse geared to sc. shafts driving 2 FP propellers Total Power: 1,766kW (2,402hp) 13.0kn Ruston 6ARM 2 x 4 Stroke 6 Cy. 260 x 368 each-883kW (1201bhp) Ruston & Hornsby Ltd.-Lincoln AuxGen: 1 x 78kW 220V d.c, 2 x 75kW 220V d.c, 1 x 42kW 220V d.c Fuel: 122.0 (d.f.)
6706694 *YVV2005* -	**VESCA R-6** *ex* Superman *-1978* **Venecia Ship Services CA (VESCA)** - *Puerto Cabello* *Venezuela* Official number: ADKN-1413	*324* 81 -	Class: (LR) ✠ Classed LR until 6/11/85	**1967-04 Charles D. Holmes & Co. Ltd. — Beverley** Yd No: 1005 Loa 32.49 Br ex 9.38 Dght 3.995 Lbp 28.96 Br md 8.84 Dpth 4.58 Welded, 1 dk	**(B32A2ST) Tug**	**2 oil engines** sr reverse geared to sc. shafts driving 2 FP propellers Total Power: 1,766kW (2,402hp) 13.0kn Ruston 6ARM 2 x 4 Stroke 6 Cy. 260 x 368 each-883kW (1201bhp) Ruston & Hornsby Ltd.-Lincoln AuxGen: 1 x 78kW 220V d.c, 2 x 75kW 220V d.c, 1 x 42kW 220V d.c Fuel: 122.0 (d.f.)
7035535 *YVV2344* -	**VESCA R-9** *ex* Betty G *-1996* **Venecia Ship Services CA (VESCA)** - *Puerto Cabello* *Venezuela* Official number: ADKN-2710	*199* 48 -	Class: (AB)	**1968 Halter Marine Services, Inc. — New Orleans, La** Yd No: 202 Loa - Br ex 8.84 Dght 3.836 Lbp 31.73 Br md 8.69 Dpth 4.12 Welded, 1 dk	**(B32A2ST) Tug**	**2 oil engines** reverse reduction geared to sc. shafts driving 2 FP propellers Total Power: 2,206kW (3,000hp) EMD (Electro-Motive) 16-645-E5 2 x Vee 2 Stroke 16 Cy. 230 x 254 each-1103kW (1500bhp) (new engine 1976) General Motors Corp.Electro-Motive Div.-La Grange AuxGen: 2 x 95kW Fuel: 289.5
7501089 *YVV2555* -	**VESCA R-18** *ex* Tridente *-1997* *ex* Largo Remo *-1996* **Venecia Ship Services CA (VESCA)** - *Puerto Cabello* *Venezuela* Official number: ADKN-3161	*231* 138 -	Class: AB	**1976-09 Matton Shipyard Co., Inc. — Cohoes, NY** Yd No: 342 Loa 32.19 Br ex 8.82 Dght 4.133 Lbp 30.59 Br md 8.55 Dpth 4.78 Welded, 1 dk	**(B32A2ST) Tug**	**2 oil engines** reverse reduction geared to sc. shafts driving 2 FP propellers Total Power: 2,206kW (3,000hp) 12.0kn EMD (Electro-Motive) 12-645-E2 2 x Vee 2 Stroke 12 Cy. 230 x 254 each-1103kW (1500bhp) General Motors Corp.Electro-Motive Div.-La Grange AuxGen: 2 x 75kW
7819383 *YVV2656* -	**VESCA R-20** *ex* Montego Bay *-1998* **Venecia Ship Services CA (VESCA)** - *Puerto Cabello* *Venezuela* Official number: ADKN-3271	*187* 120 -	Class: (NV)	**1979-11 P. Hoivolds Mek. Verksted AS — Kristiansand** Yd No: 67 Loa 29.67 Br ex - Dght 3.344 Lbp 26.22 Br md 8.01 Dpth 3.87 Welded, 1 dk	**(B32A2ST) Tug**	**1 oil engine** driving 1 FP propeller Total Power: 2,059kW (2,799hp) EMD (Electro-Motive) 16-645-E6 1 x Vee 2 Stroke 16 Cy. 230 x 254 2059kW (2799bhp) General Motors Corp.Electro-Motive Div.-La Grange AuxGen: 2 x 105kW 380V 50Hz a.c Thrusters: 1 Thwart. FP thruster (f)
7819395 *YVV2618* -	**VESCA R-21** *ex* Port Antonio *-1998* **Venecia Ship Services CA (VESCA)** - *Puerto Cabello* *Venezuela* Official number: ADKN-3260	*187* -	Class: (NV)	**1980-03 P. Hoivolds Mek. Verksted AS — Kristiansand** Yd No: 68 Loa 27.16 Br ex - Dght 3.201 Lbp 26.73 Br md 8.01 Dpth 3.87 Welded, 1 dk	**(B32A2ST) Tug**	**1 oil engine** driving 1 FP propeller Total Power: 2,115kW (2,876hp) EMD (Electro-Motive) 16-645-E7 1 x Vee 2 Stroke 16 Cy. 230 x 254 2115kW (2876bhp) General Motors Corp-USA AuxGen: 2 x 105kW 380V 50Hz a.c Thrusters: 1 Thwart. FP thruster (f)
8892320 *UHZE* -	**VESEGONSK** - **JSC 'Lesosibirsk Port' (OAO Lesosibirskiy Port)** JSC Yenisey River Shipping Co (A/O Yeniseyskoye Parokhodstvo) *Taganrog* *Russia* MMSI: 273313400 Official number: 140267	**1,652** 622 2,064	Class: RR	**1965-12 Zavody Tazkeho Strojarstva (ZTS) — Komarno** Yd No: 2054 Loa 103.60 Br ex 12.40 Dght 2.780 Lbp 100.05 Br md 12.20 Dpth 4.90 Welded, 1 dk	**(A31A2GX) General Cargo Ship**	**2 oil engines** driving 2 FP propellers Total Power: 772kW (1,050hp) Skoda 6L275PN 2 x 4 Stroke 6 Cy. 275 x 360 each-386kW (525bhp) Skoda-Praha
8767161 - -	**VESLEFRIKK B** *ex* West Vision *-1987* **Statoil Norge AS** - *Norway*	*39,230* 11,769 -		**1987-01 Daewoo Shipbuilding & Heavy Machinery Ltd — Geoje** Loa 107.50 Br ex - Dght - Lbp - Br md 79.00 Dpth - Welded, 1 dk	**(Z11C3ZA) Accommodation Platform, semi submersible**	**1 oil engine** driving 1 Propeller
5378957 *LHNA* -	**VESLEGUT** *ex* Frode Junior *-2000* *ex* Eide Junior *-1981* *ex* Ulla Brith *-1974* *ex* Bolgagutt *-1972* *ex* Veslegut *-1969* *ex* Almirante Goni *-1969* **Veslegut AS** - *Harstad* *Norway* MMSI: 257343500	**173** 67 224	Class: (NV)	**1912 AS Framnaes Mek. Vaerksted — Sandefjord** Yd No: 88 Converted From: Whale-catcher-1948 Loa 36.05 Br ex 6.13 Dght 3.658 Lbp - Br md 6.10 Dpth 3.84 Riveted, 1 dk	**(A31A2GX) General Cargo Ship** Grain: 200 Compartments: 1 Ho, ER 1 Ha: (9.9 x 3.9) Derricks: 1x2t; Winches: 1	**1 oil engine** driving 1 FP propeller Total Power: 416kW (566hp) 11.0kn Caterpillar D379B 1 x Vee 4 Stroke 8 Cy. 159 x 203 416kW (566bhp) (new engine 1967) Caterpillar Tractor Co-USA Fuel: 10.0 (d.f.) 2.0pd
6812584 *V5JF* L178	**VESLEMARI** - **Namibian Fishing Industries Ltd (Namfish)** - *Luderitz* *Namibia* Official number: 91LB071	*382* 166 356	Class: (NV)	**1968 Ateliers & Chantiers de Dunkerque et Bordeaux (France-Gironde) — Bordeau** Yd No: 278 Lengthened-1977 Loa 45.52 Br ex 8.16 Dght - Lbp - Br md 8.11 Dpth 4.50 Welded, 1 dk	**(B12E2FX) Seal Catcher** Compartments: 5 Ho, ER 7 Ha: Derricks: 1x3t,1x2t; Winches: 1	**1 oil engine** driving 1 FP propeller Total Power: 1,103kW (1,500hp) MaK 1 x 4 Stroke 6 Cy. 320 x 450 1103kW (1500bhp) Atlas MaK Maschinenbau GmbH-Kiel AuxGen: 2 x 52kW 220V 50Hz a.c Thrusters: 1 Thwart. FP thruster (f); 1 Tunnel thruster (a)
7922867 *LJCU* -	**VESLEO II** *ex* Silverfjord *-1969* **BFTF Eiendom AS** Nadir Hvaler Fjordcruise AS *Fredrikstad* *Norway* MMSI: 259491000	**189** 61 49		**1980-05 Marinteknik Verkstads AB — Oregrund** Yd No: B43 Loa 33.05 Br ex 6.71 Dght 1.140 Lbp 31.20 Br md 6.20 Dpth 2.82 Welded, 1 dk	**(A37B2PS) Passenger Ship** Hull Material: Aluminium Alloy Passengers: 250	**2 oil engines** geared to sc. shafts driving 2 FP propellers Total Power: 588kW (800hp) Scania DSI1440M 2 x Vee 4 Stroke 8 Cy. 127 x 140 each-294kW (400bhp) Saab Scania AB-Sweden
7928550 - -	**VESNA-STAR** - **Fiona Holdings Pty Ltd** - *Port Adelaide, SA* *Australia* Official number: 385638	*180* 148 -	Class: (NV)	**1981-04 Kali Boat Building Pty Ltd — Port Adelaide SA** Yd No: 26 Loa 25.02 Br ex 7.55 Dght - Lbp 22.46 Br md 7.41 Dpth 3.92 Welded, 1 dk	**(B11B2FV) Fishing Vessel**	**1 oil engine** geared to sc. shaft driving 1 FP propeller Total Power: 640kW (870hp) MWM TBD602V12 1 x Vee 4 Stroke 12 Cy. 160 x 165 640kW (870bhp) Motoren Werke Mannheim AG (MWM)-West Germany AuxGen: 1 x 112kW 415V 50Hz a.c, 1 x 48kW 415V 50Hz a.c
9376713 *LXVH* -	**VESPERTINE** - **Shiplux III SA** EuroShip Services Ltd *Luxembourg* *Luxembourg* MMSI: 253417000	**25,593** 6,960 14,483	Class: LR ✠ **100A1** SS 02/2010 roll on-roll cargo ship *IWS LI ✠ **LMC** **UMS** Eq.Ltr: L†; Cable: 624.2/70.0 U3 (a)	**2010-02 Flensburger Schiffbau-Ges. mbH & Co. KG — Flensburg** Yd No: 740 Loa 195.40 (BB) Br ex 26.22 Dght 7.400 Lbp 186.22 Br md 26.20 Dpth 18.15 Welded, 3 dks	**(A35A2RR) Ro-Ro Cargo Ship** Passengers: 12 Stern door/ramp (centre) Len: 14.19 Wid: 21.60 Swl: 174 Lane-Len: 2907 Lane-clr ht: 7.00 Trailers: 190	**1 oil engine** with flexible couplings & sr geared to sc. shaft driving 1 CP propeller Total Power: 10,800kW (14,684hp) 18.5kn MaK 12M43C 1 x Vee 4 Stroke 12 Cy. 430 x 610 10800kW (14684bhp) Caterpillar Motoren GmbH & Co. KG-Germany AuxGen: 2 x 920kW 450V 60Hz a.c, 1 x 3000kW 450V 60Hz a.c Boilers: TOH (o.f.) 13.3kgf/cm² (13.0bar), TOH (ex.g.) 15.3kgf/cm² (15.0bar) Thrusters: 1 Thwart. CP thruster (f); 1 Thwart. CP thruster (a) Fuel: 110.0 (d.f.) 1100.0 (r.f.)

Identity	Name / Owner	Tonnage	Class	Construction	Type / Capacity	Machinery
7941710 - -	**VEST** **Sevastopol Port Authority** - *Sevastopol* *Ukraine* Official number: 800135	*149* 101 20	Class: (RS)	**1980 Ilyichyovskiy Sudoremontnyy Zavod im. "50-letiya SSSR" — Ilyichyovsk** Yd No: 7 Loa 28.70 Br ex 6.35 Dght 1.480 Lbp 27.00 Br md - Dpth 2.50 Welded, 1 dk	**(A37B2PS) Passenger Ship** Passengers: unberthed: 250	**2 oil engines** driving 2 FP propellers Total Power: 220kW (300hp) 10.4kr Barnaultransmash 3D6C 2 x 4 Stroke 6 Cy. 150 x 180 each-110kW (150bhp) Barnaultransmash-Barnaul AuxGen: 2 x 1kW Fuel: 2.0 (d.f.)
5153395 *XPE5603* -	**VEST** *ex* Oleto *-1972* *ex* Holger Andreasen *-1968* *ex* Christa Griese *-1960* **BV Shallow Shipping** - *Aalborg* *Denmark (DIS)* MMSI: 219001226	**300** 180 475	Class: (BV)	**1951-07 Orenstein-Koppel u. Luebecker Maschinenbau AG — Luebeck** Yd No: 451 Lengthened-1965 Lengthened-1955 Loa 43.60 Br ex 7.52 Dght 2.833 Lbp - Br md 7.47 Dpth 3.15 Riveted\Welded, 1 dk	**(A31A2GX) General Cargo Ship** Grain: 680; Bale: 623 Compartments: 1 Ho, ER 2 Ha: (8.0 x 4.7) (14.8 x 4.7)ER Derricks: 2x15t,1x2t Ice Capable	**1 oil engine** driving 1 FP propeller Total Power: 313kW (426hp) 8.5kn Alpha 405-24VO 1 x 2 Stroke 5 Cy. 240 x 400 313kW (426bhp) (new engine 1963) Alpha Diesel A/S-Denmark AuxGen: 3 x 24kW Fuel: 29.5 (d.f.)
7314254 *UDMX* -	**VESTA** *ex* Kintoku Maru No. 83 *-1996* **Firma Moreprodukt Co Ltd** - *Nevelsk* *Russia* MMSI: 273568100	**279** 83 85	Class: (RS)	**1973 Narasaki Zosen KK — Muroran HK** Yd No: 837 Loa 37.72 Br ex 7.42 Dght 2.280 Lbp 33.02 Br md 7.40 Dpth 4.70 Welded, 2 dks	**(B11B2FV) Fishing Vessel**	**1 oil engine** driving 1 CP propeller Total Power: 1,250kW (1,700hp) 10.5kn Daihatsu 6DSM-28FS 1 x 4 Stroke 6 Cy. 280 x 340 1250kW (1700bhp) (new engine 1977) Daihatsu Diesel Manufacturing Co Lt-Japan AuxGen: 2 x 130kW a.c Fuel: 40.0 (d.f.)
7804209 *ITLA* -	**VESTA** **Sardegna Regionale Marittima SpA (SAREMAR)** - *Cagliari* *Italy* MMSI: 247045400 Official number: 550	*1,386* 754 572	Class: RI	**1981-06 Cant. Nav. "Luigi Orlando" — Livorno** Yd No: 152 Loa 69.59 (BB) Br ex 14.03 Dght 3.610 Lbp 64.29 Br md 14.00 Dpth 4.81 Welded, 2 dks	**(A36A2PR) Passenger/Ro-Ro Ship (Vehicles)** Passengers: unberthed: 1200 Bow door/ramp Stern door/ramp	**2 oil engines** reverse reduction geared to sc. shafts driving 2 CP propellers Total Power: 3,706kW (5,038hp) 16.5kn GMT B230.12V 2 x Vee 4 Stroke 12 Cy. 230 x 270 each-1853kW (2519bhp) Grandi Motori Trieste-Italy Thrusters: 1 Thwart. FP thruster (f) Fuel: 95.5 (d.f.) 15.0pd
8033156 - -	**VESTA** *ex* Yelena Litvinova *-2003* **Adevalosh Shipping Ltd** Tramp Shipping Co Ltd	**2,478** 917 3,134	Class: (RS)	**1981 Sudostroitelnyy Zavod im Volodarskogo — Rybinsk** Yd No: 86 Loa 114.08 Br ex 13.21 Dght 3.671 Lbp 108.03 Br md 13.00 Dpth 5.54 Welded, 1 dk	**(A31A2GX) General Cargo Ship** Bale: 4,297 Compartments: 4 Ho, ER 4 Ha: (17.6 x 9.3)3 (17.9 x 9.3)ER Ice Capable	**2 oil engines** driving 2 FP propellers Total Power: 970kW (1,318hp) 10.8kn S.K.L. 6NVD48-2U 2 x 4 Stroke 6 Cy. 320 x 480 each-485kW (659bhp) VEB Schwermaschinenbau "KarlLiebknecht" (SKL)-Magdeburg
8881759 *UFMB* -	**VESTA** *ex* Salantai *-2003* *ex* Julija *-1998* *ex* Artemovsk *-1998* **OOO Transportnaya Firma 'Persepolis' (Transport-Forwarding Company 'Persepolis')** - *Taganrog* *Russia* MMSI: 273447950	**1,503** 722 2,183	Class: (RS) (PR)	**1966-12 Zavody Tazkeho Strojarstva (ZTS) — Komarno** Yd No: 1171 Shortened-1995 Loa 85.06 Br ex 12.40 Dght 3.500 Lbp 80.20 Br md 12.20 Dpth 4.90 Welded, 1 dk	**(A31A2GX) General Cargo Ship** Compartments: 3 Ho, ER 3 Ha: ER	**2 oil engines** driving 2 FP propellers Total Power: 772kW (1,050hp) 10.0kn Skoda 6L275PN 2 x 4 Stroke 6 Cy. 275 x 360 each-386kW (525bhp) Skoda-Praha
9185102 *SJXT* -	**VESTA** **A/B Goteborg-Styrso Skargardstrafik** - *Gothenburg* *Sweden* MMSI: 265509950	**347** 144 50		**1998-12 Batservice Holding AS — Mandal** Yd No: 19 Loa 34.40 Br ex - Dght 2.450 Lbp 32.20 Br md 7.80 Dpth 3.80 Welded, 1 dk	**(A37B2PS) Passenger Ship** Passengers: unberthed: 450	**2 oil engines** geared to sc. shafts driving 2 CP propellers Total Power: 750kW (1,020hp) Volvo Penta TAMD163A 2 x 4 Stroke 6 Cy. 144 x 165 each-375kW (510bhp) AB Volvo Penta-Sweden
9383730 *V3JO2* -	**VESTA** **Vesta Management Services Ltd** Mys Nikolaevsky Ltd *Belize City* *Belize* MMSI: 312773000 Official number: 070630099	**7,008** 4,161 10,975 T/cm 20.9	Class: RS	**2006-01 Taizhou Haibin Shipbuilding & Repairing Co Ltd — Sanmen County ZJ** Yd No: HBCCS-04-25 Loa 132.60 Br ex - Dght 7.320 Lbp 122.10 Br md 18.60 Dpth 9.50 Welded, 1 dk	**(A31A2GX) General Cargo Ship** Grain: 13,950 Compartments: 3 Ho, ER 3 Ha: (25.4 x 12.6)ER 2 (25.4 x 12.6)	**1 oil engine** reduction geared to sc. shafts driving 1 FP propeller Total Power: 2,868kW (3,899hp) 14.0kn Pielstick 6PC2-5L 1 x 4 Stroke 6 Cy. 400 x 460 2868kW (3899bhp) Shaanxi Diesel Heavy Industry Co Lt-China AuxGen: 3 x 200kW a.c Fuel: 453.0 11.0pd
9504152 *PCMK* -	**VESTANHAV** **Feran II Shipping Co BV & Erik Thun AB** Erik Thun AB (Thunship Management Holland) *Delfzijl* *Netherlands* MMSI: 246279000	**6,069** 3,100 10,036 T/cm 18.3	Class: BV	**2012-01 Scheepswerf Ferus Smit BV — Westerbroek** Yd No: 401 Loa 123.30 (BB) Br ex 16.00 Dght 7.660 Lbp 117.93 Br md 15.85 Dpth 10.46 Welded, 1 dk	**(A31A2GE) General Cargo Ship, Self-discharging** Grain: 11,197 Compartments: 2 Ho, ER 2 Ha: (38.5 x 13.2)ER (38.5 x 13.2) Cranes: 1 Ice Capable	**1 oil engine** reduction geared to sc. shaft driving 1 CP propeller Total Power: 3,840kW (5,221hp) 14.1kn Wartsila 8L32 1 x 4 Stroke 8 Cy. 320 x 400 3840kW (5221bhp) Wartsila Finland Oy-Finland AuxGen: 1 x 384kW 440V 60Hz a.c, 2 x 350kW 440V 60Hz a.c Thrusters: 1 Tunnel thruster (f) Fuel: 75.0 (d.f.) 362.0 (r.f.)
5125166 *LMGN* -	**VESTAS** *ex* Guro *-1974* *ex* Gabriel Faroult *-1964* **Terje Ziemele** - *Haugesund* *Norway*	*199* 99 300	Class: (BV)	**1949 Scheepswerf "De Waal" N.V. — Zaltbommel** Yd No: 628 Loa 39.35 Br ex 6.71 Dght 2.553 Lbp 36.00 Br md 6.63 Dpth 2.85 Riveted, 1 dk	**(A31A2GX) General Cargo Ship** Grain: 382; Bale: 340 Compartments: 1 Ho, ER 2 Ha: (6.6 x 3.9) (8.3 x 3.9)ER Derricks: 2x3t; Winches: 2	**1 oil engine** driving 1 FP propeller Total Power: 386kW (525hp) 10.0kn G.M. (Detroit Diesel) 12V-71-N 1 x Vee 2 Stroke 12 Cy. 108 x 127 386kW (525bhp) (new engine 1968) General Motors Corp-USA AuxGen: 2 x 1kW 24V d.c Fuel: 13.0 (d.f.)
9032472 *LHBI* R-6-SK	**VESTAVIND** *ex* Glomfjord *-2010* **Nesvaag Havfiske AS** - *Egersund* *Norway* MMSI: 259127000 Official number: 20911	**371** 111 126	Class: NV	**1992-08 Stocznia Ustka SA — Ustka** Yd No: B295/01 Loa 33.80 Br ex 8.15 Dght 4.018 Lbp 26.30 Br md 8.00 Dpth 6.20 Welded	**(B11A2FS) Stern Trawler**	**1 oil engine** geared to sc. shaft driving 1 FP propeller Total Power: 780kW (1,060hp) Caterpillar 3512TA 1 x Vee 4 Stroke 12 Cy. 170 x 190 780kW (1060bhp) Caterpillar Inc-USA AuxGen: 2 x 125kW 380V 50Hz a.c Thrusters: 1 Thwart. FP thruster (f)
9577666 *LHRX* SF-2-V	**VESTBAS** *ex* Ringbas *-2013* *launched as* Gambler *-2010* **Vestbas AS** - *Fosnavaag* *Norway* MMSI: 257445000	**499** 149 500		**2010-03 AO Yaroslavskiy Sudostroitelnyy Zavod — Yaroslavl** (Hull launched by) Yd No: 403 **2010-03 Lyng AS — Deknepollen** (Hull completed by) Yd No: 1 Loa 34.07 (BB) Br ex - Dght 3.400 Lbp 28.00 Br md 9.50 Dpth 5.02 Welded, 1 dk	**(B11B2FV) Fishing Vessel**	**1 oil engine** reduction geared to sc. shaft driving 1 Propeller Total Power: 960kW (1,305hp) MAN-B&W 6L23/30A 1 x 4 Stroke 6 Cy. 225 x 300 960kW (1305bhp) MAN Diesel A/S-Denmark
7104166 *OXMC2* -	**VESTBORG** *ex* Valborg *-2013* *ex* Taladi *-2006* *ex* Sonja Hove *-1993* *ex* Stevnsland *-1983* *ex* Mor-Sines *-1976* *ex* Ruth Klint *-1972* **Sandship ApS** P/F Sandgrevstur *Copenhagen* *Denmark (DIS)* MMSI: 219000035 Official number: D1764	**1,106** 421 1,060	Class: BV	**1971-08 Frederikshavn Vaerft og Tordok A/S — Frederikshavn** Yd No: 306 Loa 64.62 (BB) Br ex 11.03 Dght 3.910 Lbp 56.98 Br md 11.00 Dpth 6.20 Welded, 2 dks	**(A31A2GX) General Cargo Ship** Grain: 2,532; Bale: 2,263 Compartments: 1 Ho, ER 1 Ha: (32.4 x 8.2)ER Ice Capable	**1 oil engine** sr geared to sc. shaft driving 1 CP propeller Total Power: 662kW (900hp) 11.0kn Alpha 409-26VO 1 x 2 Stroke 9 Cy. 260 x 400 662kW (900bhp) (new engine 1973) Alpha Diesel A/S-Denmark AuxGen: 2 x 45kW 380V 50Hz a.c Fuel: 63.5 (d.f.) 3.0pd
7502021 *E5U2070* -	**VESTBORG** *ex* Aunborg *-2010* *ex* Jamie *-1998* *ex* Marico *-1995* *ex* Gina P *-1993* *ex* Kwintebank *-1992* *ex* Els Teekman *-1984* **Vestbulk AS** Lighthouse Ship Management AS SatCom: Inmarsat C 451812010 *Rarotonga* *Cook Islands* MMSI: 518120000 Official number: 1146	**1,086** 598 1,564	Class: IV (GL)	**1976-07 Scheepswerf "Voorwaarts" B.V. — Hoogezand** Yd No: 217 Loa 65.82 Br ex 10.80 Dght 4.301 Lbp 59.97 Br md 10.72 Dpth 5.11 Welded, 1 dk	**(A31A2GX) General Cargo Ship** Grain: 2,031; Bale: 1,986 Compartments: 1 Ho, ER 1 Ha: (37.1 x 8.2)ER Gantry cranes: 1	**1 oil engine** driving 1 FP propeller Total Power: 736kW (1,001hp) 14.5kn Brons 8GV-H 1 x Vee 2 Stroke 8 Cy. 220 x 380 736kW (1001bhp) NV Appingedammer Bronsmotorenfabrie-Netherlands AuxGen: 2 x 50kW 380V 50Hz a.c Fuel: 127.0 (d.f.) 4.0pd

8656984 *LMCW* SF-50-G	**VESTBRIS** **PR Vestbris DA** *Bergen* *Norway*	**278** 83 -		**2002 Mundal Baat AS — Saebovaagen** Yd No: 34 Loa 30.00 Br ex - Dght 4.600 Lbp - Br md 7.50 Dpth 6.10 Bonded, 1 dk	**(B11B2FV) Fishing Vessel** Hull Material: Reinforced Plastic	**1 oil engine** driving 1 Propeller
8704042 *LJDT* M-85-A	**VESTBUEN** *ex* Jonina *-1998* *ex* Glodanes *-1991* **A/S Havstal** - *Aalesund* *Norway* MMSI: 257531600	**161** 64 -	Class: (NV)	**1988-03 Herfjord Slip & Verksted AS — Revsnes i Fosna** (Hull) **1988-03 Moen Slip AS — Kolvereid** Yd No: 31 Loa 22.00 Br ex - Dght - Lbp 19.00 Br md 7.00 Dpth 5.85 Welded, 2 dks	**(B11B2FV) Fishing Vessel** Ins: 82	**1 oil engine** driving 1 FP propeller Total Power: 346kW (470hp) Mitsubishi S6A2-MTK 1 x 4 Stroke 6 Cy. 150 x 160 346kW (470bhp) Mitsubishi Heavy Industries Ltd-Japan
8010219 *WSK2063* -	**VESTERAALEN** **Vesteraalen LLC** *Seattle, WA* *United States of America* MMSI: 367563000 Official number: 611642	*195* 136 -		**1979-09 Western Maritime, Inc. — Tacoma, Wa** Yd No: 101 Loa 38.10 Br ex 9.99 Dght - Lbp 34.14 Br md 9.76 Dpth 5.49 Welded, 1 dk	**(B11A2FS) Stern Trawler** Cranes: 1x11t	**1 oil engine** reverse reduction geared to sc. shaft driving 1 FP propeller Total Power: 901kW (1,225hp) Caterpillar D399SCAC 1 x Vee 4 Stroke 16 Cy. 159 x 203 901kW (1225bhp) Caterpillar Tractor Co-USA AuxGen: 2 x 260kW, 1 x 55kW
8019368 *LLZY* -	**VESTERALEN** **Hurtigruten ASA** *Tromso* *Norway* MMSI: 258478000 Official number: 19839	**6,261** 2,257 900	Class: NV	**1983-02 Kaarbos Mek. Verksted AS — Harstad** Yd No: 101 Loa 108.55 (BB) Br ex - Dght 4.601 Lbp 96.02 Br md 16.51 Dpth 8.84 Welded, 3 dks	**(A32A2GF) General Cargo/Passenger Ship** Passengers: unberthed: 90; berths: 320 Side door/ramp (p) Len: 9.00 Wid: - Swl: - Cars: 40 Cranes: 1x15t Ice Capable	**2 oil engines** driving 2 FP propellers Total Power: 4,708kW (6,400hp) 17.5kn Normo KVMB-16 2 x Vee 4 Stroke 16 Cy. 250 x 300 each-2354kW (3200bhp) AS Bergens Mek Verksteder-Norway AuxGen: 2 x 598kW 380V 50Hz a.c, 1 x 385kW 380V 50Hz a.c Thrusters: 2 Thwart. FP thruster (f)
9163013 *CBVG* -	**VESTERVEG** *ex* Conquest *-2006* **South Pacific Korp SA (SPK)** SatCom: Inmarsat C 472500023 *Valparaiso* *Chile* MMSI: 725004270 Official number: 3175	**1,451** 435 750	Class: NV	**1997-06 Stocznia Remontowa 'Nauta' SA — Gdynia** (Hull) Yd No: TN60/2 **1997-06 Kopervik Slip AS — Kopervik** Yd No: 8 Loa 60.00 Br ex 12.03 Dght - Lbp 52.20 Br md 12.00 Dpth 8.00 Welded, 1 dk	**(B11A2FT) Trawler**	**1 oil engine** reduction geared to sc. shaft driving 1 FP propeller Total Power: 5,417kW (7,365hp) Caterpillar 3616TA 1 x Vee 4 Stroke 16 Cy. 280 x 300 5417kW (7365bhp) Caterpillar Inc-USA
9028641 *LCDZ* H-10-K	**VESTERVIK** *ex* Haugvaering *-2009* *ex* Sotrabas *-2002* *ex* Larsegutt *-1999* **Bergland ANS** - *Bergen* *Norway* MMSI: 257714500	**117** 46 -		**1990-01 Mjosundet Baatbyggeri AS — Mjosundet** Yd No: 126 Loa 21.31 Br ex - Dght - Lbp - Br md 6.40 Dpth 3.96 Welded, 1 dk	**(B11B2FV) Fishing Vessel**	**1 oil engine** reduction geared to sc. shaft driving 1 Propeller Total Power: 297kW (404hp) 10.0kn Scania DS14 1 x Vee 4 Stroke 8 Cy. 127 x 140 297kW (404bhp) Saab Scania AB-Sweden Thrusters: 1 Thwart. FP thruster (f)
8647878 *LLWG* SF-11-A	**VESTERVON** *ex* Boen Junior *-2011* **Vestoy AS** - *Floro* *Norway* MMSI: 257578600	**424** 133 -		**2002 Havyard Eid AS — Nordfjordeid** Yd No: 060 Loa 36.90 Br ex - Dght - Lbp 33.03 Br md 8.50 Dpth 5.08 Welded, 1 dk	**(B11B2FV) Fishing Vessel**	**1 oil engine** driving 1 Propeller
7613492 *LKDQ* SF-5-B	**VESTFART** *ex* Heroytral *-1997* *ex* Karolos *-1984* **P/R Vestfart ANS** Okonomisenteret AS SatCom: Inmarsat Mini-M 761598756 *Floro* *Norway* MMSI: 257166000 Official number: 19616	**811** 243 -	Class: NV	**1977-09 Th Hellesoy Skipsbyggeri AS — Lofallstrand** Yd No: 96 Lengthened-2010 Loa 52.20 (BB) Br ex 9.62 Dght 6.311 Lbp 41.80 Br md 9.60 Dpth 7.58 Welded, 2 dks	**(B11A2FT) Trawler** Ice Capable	**1 oil engine** driving 1 CP propeller Total Power: 2,310kW (3,141hp) MAN-B&W 7L27/38 1 x 4 Stroke 7 Cy. 270 x 380 2310kW (3141bhp) (new engine 2005) MAN B&W Diesel A/S-Denmark AuxGen: 2 x 500kW 50Hz a.c Thrusters: 1 Thwart. FP thruster (f); 1 Tunnel thruster (a) Fuel: 94.0
5338543 - -	**VESTFART II** *ex* Vestfart *-1997* *ex* Clupea *-1967* *ex* Star VI *-1965* - -	**730** 219 -	Class: (NV)	**1948 Hall, Russell & Co. Ltd. — Aberdeen** Yd No: 812 Converted From: Whale-catcher-1967 Loa 51.95 Br ex 9.05 Dght 5.068 Lbp 45.01 Br md 9.00 Dpth 5.49 Riveted\Welded, 2 dks	**(B11B2FV) Fishing Vessel** Compartments: 4 Ho, 4 Ta, ER 4 Ha: (2.6 x 2.9)2 (2.7 x 1.7) (1.7 x 2.9) 4 Wing Ha: 2 (2.3 x 1.3)2 (1.1 x 0.9) Derricks: 1x5t,1x2t; Winches: 2	**1 oil engine** driving 1 FP propeller Total Power: 809kW (1,100hp) 12.0kn MaK 1 x 4 Stroke 6 Cy. 320 x 450 809kW (1100bhp) (new engine 1967) Atlas MaK Maschinenbau GmbH-Kiel AuxGen: 2 x 166kW 220V 50Hz a.c, 1 x 72kW 220V 50Hz a.c Thrusters: 1 Thwart. FP thruster (f); 1 Tunnel thruster (a)
8015893 *LJMS* F-53-G	**VESTFISK** *ex* Vestliner *-1999* *ex* Nordkyn Pioner *-1996* *ex* Holmeset Senior *-1991* **Vestfisk AS** Merkantil Tjenester AS SatCom: Inmarsat C 425759950 *Aalesund* *Norway* MMSI: 257599500	**526** 157 -		**1980-12 Vaagland Baatbyggeri AS — Vaagland** (Hull) Yd No: 100 **1980-12 Solstrand Slip & Baatbyggeri AS — Tomrefjord** Yd No: 29 Loa 31.20 Br ex 8.51 Dght - Lbp 26.55 Br md - Dpth 4.02 Welded, 1 dk	**(B11B2FV) Fishing Vessel**	**1 oil engine** driving 1 CP propeller Total Power: 508kW (691hp) 10.0kn Callesen 6-427-FOT 1 x 4 Stroke 6 Cy. 270 x 400 508kW (691bhp) Aabenraa Motorfabrik, HeinrichCallesen A/S-Denmark Fuel: 32.0 (d.f.) 2.0pd
8417651 *LNHD* -	**VESTFJORD** **Kystverket Rederi** - *Aalesund* *Norway* MMSI: 257061400	**267** 80 250		**1984-06 Vaagland Baatbyggeri AS — Vaagland** Yd No: 108 Loa 31.02 Br ex 8.21 Dght 3.350 Lbp 26.01 Br md 8.01 Dpth 4.91 Welded, 1 dk	**(B32A2ST) Tug**	**1 oil engine** geared to sc. shaft driving 1 Directional propeller Total Power: 497kW (676hp) 10.0kn Callesen 5-427-EOTK 1 x 4 Stroke 5 Cy. 270 x 400 497kW (676bhp) Aabenraa Motorfabrik, HeinrichCallesen A/S-Denmark AuxGen: 1 x 56kW 220V 50Hz a.c, 1 x 40kW 220V 50Hz a.c Thrusters: 1 Thwart. FP thruster (f) Fuel: 46.0 (d.f.) 1.5pd
9052692 *PGFG* -	**VESTFJORD** *ex* Lotus *-2011* *ex* Nescio *-2001* **Fonnes Rederi AS** Wagenborg Shipping BV *Delfzijl* *Netherlands* MMSI: 246162000 Official number: 21875	**1,596** 874 2,280	Class: BV	**1993-07 Scheepswerf Bijlsma BV — Wartena** Yd No: 664 Loa 82.00 Br ex 11.10 Dght 4.160 Lbp 76.95 Br md 11.00 Dpth 5.20 Welded, 1 dk	**(A31A2GX) General Cargo Ship** Grain: 3,240 TEU 128 C. 128/20' Compartments: 1 Ho, ER 2 Ha: (26.8 x 10.3) (25.5 x 10.3)ER Ice Capable	**1 oil engine** driving 1 FP propeller Total Power: 942kW (1,281hp) 11.0kn Caterpillar 3512TA 1 x Vee 4 Stroke 12 Cy. 170 x 190 942kW (1281bhp) Caterpillar Inc-USA Fuel: 136.0 (d.f.)
8917338 *IBII* -	**VESTFOLD** **Caronte & Tourist Lines Srl** - *Reggio Calabria* *Italy* MMSI: 247455000 Official number: 38	**8,383** 4,362 2,131	Class: RI (NV)	**1991-03 Kaldnes AS — Tonsberg** (Hull) Yd No: 67 **1991-03 Tronderverftet AS — Hommelvik** Yd No: 67 Loa 120.00 Br ex - Dght 4.500 Lbp 112.00 Br md 19.00 Dpth 6.00 Welded, 2 dks	**(A36A2PR) Passenger/Ro-Ro Ship (Vehicles)** Passengers: unberthed: 700 Bow door/ramp Stern door/ramp Lane-Len: 300 Cars: 250 Ice Capable	**4 oil engines** with clutches & reduction geared to sc. shafts driving 4 Directional propellers 2 fwd and 2 aft Total Power: 5,280kW (7,180hp) 14.7kn Alpha 6L28/32A 4 x 4 Stroke 6 Cy. 280 x 320 each-1320kW (1795bhp) MAN B&W Diesel A/S-Denmark Fuel: 241.6 (d.f.) 16.0pd
8211849 *AVST* -	**VESTFONN** **Baker Hughes Oilfield Services India Pvt Ltd** - *Mumbai* *India* MMSI: 419000532 Official number: 3985	**3,753** 1,125 2,505	Class: IR NV	**1983-03 Ankerlokken Verft Forde AS — Forde** Yd No: 20 Converted From: Pipe Carrier-1985 Loa 81.97 Br ex - Dght 4.925 Lbp 76.21 Br md 18.01 Dpth 7.12 Welded, 2 dks	**(B22F20W) Well Stimulation Vessel**	**2 oil engines** with clutches, flexible couplings & sr geared to sc. shafts driving 2 CP propellers Total Power: 4,502kW (6,120hp) 14.5kn Nohab F212V 2 x Vee 4 Stroke 12 Cy. 250 x 300 each-2251kW (3060bhp) Nohab Diesel AB-Sweden AuxGen: 2 x 1520kW 440V 60Hz a.c, 2 x 244kW 440V 60Hz a.c Thrusters: 2 Thwart. FP thruster (f); 2 Tunnel thruster (a)
6411873 - -	**VESTFRAKT** *ex* Senera *-1996* *ex* Arenes *-1974* *ex* Vesta *-1974* - -	**148** 65 188	Class: (BV)	**1916 Gebr. J.S. & G. Figee — Vlaardingen** Lengthened-1956 Loa 34.14 Br ex 6.66 Dght 3.352 Lbp 31.09 Br md 6.63 Dpth 3.36 Riveted, 1 dk	**(B11B2FV) Fishing Vessel** Grain: 227 Compartments: 1 Ho, ER 1 Ha: (9.6 x 3.5)ER Derricks: 1x4t; Winches: 1	**1 oil engine** driving 1 FP propeller Total Power: 294kW (400hp) 10.0kn Caterpillar D353SCAC 1 x 4 Stroke 6 Cy. 159 x 203 294kW (400bhp) (new engine 1965) Caterpillar Tractor Co-USA

IMO / Call sign / Fishing no.	Name / Former names / Owner / Manager / Port / Flag	Tonnage	Classification	Builder / Dimensions	Type / Cargo	Machinery / Speed
8870334 *LINI* -	**VESTFRAKT** *ex* Sea Star *-2008* *ex* Seloyvaering *-1997* *ex* Martin Junior *-1995* *ex* Brudanes *-1994* *ex* Rano *-1994* **Vestfrakt AS** - *Bergen* *Norway* MMSI: 257089400	**142** 45 -		**1966 Bentsen & Sonner Slip & Mek. Verksted — Sogne** Yd No: 12 Loa 30.00 Br ex - Dght - Lbp - Br md 6.20 Dpth 3.65 Welded, 1 dk	**(A31A2GX) General Cargo Ship**	**1 oil engine** geared to sc. shaft driving 1 FP propeller Total Power: 294kW (400hp) 9.0kn Caterpillar 3406TA 1 x 4 Stroke 6 Cy. 137 x 165 294kW (400bhp) (new engine 1996) Caterpillar Inc-USA Thrusters: 1 Thwart. FP thruster (f)
7739997 *LMEA* -	**VESTGAR** *ex* Fredsbudet *-2007* *ex* Vestgar Senior *-1980* *ex* Vestgar *-1979* **Oygardsbatane AS** - *Bergen* *Norway* MMSI: 257120400	**220** 66 -		**1957 P. Hoivolds Mek. Verksted AS — Kristiansand** Yd No: 12 Loa 35.23 Br ex 6.38 Dght - Lbp - Br md - Dpth 3.00 Welded	**(A32A2GF) General Cargo/Passenger Ship** Passengers: unberthed: 252	**1 oil engine** driving 1 FP propeller Total Power: 353kW (480hp) 12.0kn Wichmann 6ACA 1 x 2 Stroke 6 Cy. 280 x 420 353kW (480bhp) Wichmann Motorfabrikk AS-Norway
9139555 *OW2038* VN 700	**VESTHAV** *ex* Vesturhavid *-2006* *ex* Oysund *-2001* **Atlantic Seafarm P/F** - *Vagur* *Faeroe Islands (Danish)* MMSI: 231136000	**460** 160 430		**1997-02 Aas Mek. Verksted AS — Vestnes** Yd No: 144 Lengthened-2013 Loa 39.18 Br ex - Dght - Lbp 35.13 Br md 8.00 Dpth 5.11 Welded, 1 dk	**(B12B2FC) Fish Carrier**	**1 oil engine** geared to sc. shaft driving 1 FP propeller Total Power: 823kW (1,119hp) Caterpillar 3508TA 1 x Vee 4 Stroke 8 Cy. 170 x 190 823kW (1119bhp) Caterpillar Inc-USA Thrusters: 1 Thwart. FP thruster (f); 1 Tunnel thruster (a)
9202699 *LLRH* -	**VESTHAV** *ex* Kaspryba 3 *-2014* **Magnarson AS** - *Bergen* *Norway*	**1,041** 322 524	Class: LR (RS) **100A1** SS 02/2008 fishing vessel Icelandic coastal service in sea areas with wave height 3 per cent probability of exceeding 8.5m and not more than 200 miles away from place of refuge **LMC** **UMS** Cable: 357.5/24.0 U3 (a)	**1999-09 Peene-Werft GmbH — Wolgast** Yd No: 445 Loa 49.95 (BB) Br ex 11.36 Dght 3.800 Lbp 43.60 Br md 11.20 Dpth 5.20 Welded, 1 dk	**(B11B2FV) Fishing Vessel** Ins: 600 Ice Capable	**1 oil engine** with flexible couplings & sr gearedto sc. shaft driving 1 CP propeller Total Power: 930kW (1,264hp) 11.0kn MaK 6M20 1 x 4 Stroke 6 Cy. 200 x 300 930kW (1264bhp) MaK Motoren GmbH & Co. KG-Kiel AuxGen: 2 x 480kW a.c Fuel: 246.0 (d.f.)
8725058 *XUCL2* -	**VESTIMAR** *ex* Sergiy Skadovskiy *-2010* *ex* Vladimir Molodtsov *-2000* **Vestimar Investments Ltd** MD Shipping Co *Phnom Penh* *Cambodia* MMSI: 515695000 Official number: 1085649	**2,466** 988 3,135	Class: RS (RR)	**1985-08 Sudostroitelnyy Zavod "Krasnoye Sormovo" — Gorkiy** Yd No: 84 Loa 114.02 Br ex 13.22 Dght 3.670 Lbp 110.76 Br md 13.00 Dpth 5.50 Welded, 1 dk	**(A31A2GX) General Cargo Ship**	**2 oil engines** driving 1 FP propeller Total Power: 970kW (1,318hp) 10.7kn S.K.L. 6NVD48A-2U 2 x 4 Stroke 6 Cy. 320 x 480 each-485kW (659bhp) VEB Schwermaschinenbau "KarlLiebknecht" (SKL)-Magdeburg AuxGen: 3 x 50kW a.c
8516885 *OXPO* -	**VESTKYSTEN** - **Denmark Ministry of Food, Agriculture & Fisheries (Ministeriet for Fodevare, Landbrug og Fiskeri) (Fiskeridirektoratet)** - SatCom: Inmarsat C 421947715 *Thyboron* *Denmark* MMSI: 219477000 Official number: D3093	**657** 197 126 T/cm 3.7	Class: NV	**1987-03 Marstal Staalskibsvaerft og Maskinfabrik A/S — Marstal** Yd No: 109 Loa 49.92 Br ex - Dght 3.201 Lbp 44.02 Br md 10.01 Dpth 4.53 Welded, 1 dk	**(B12D2FP) Fishery Patrol Vessel**	**2 oil engines** with clutches, flexible couplings & dr geared to sc. shaft driving 1 CP propeller Total Power: 798kW (1,084hp) 12.0kn Alpha 6L23/30 2 x 4 Stroke 6 Cy. 225 x 300 each-399kW (542bhp) MAN B&W Diesel A/S-Denmark AuxGen: 1 x 424kW 380V 50Hz a.c, 2 x 224kW 380V 50Hz a.c, 1 x 84kW 380V 50Hz a.c Thrusters: 1 Thwart. CP thruster (f); 1 Tunnel thruster (a) Fuel: 80.0 (d.f.) 4.0pd
8412857 *OZ2120* -	**VESTLAND** *ex* Kevin S. *-2011* *ex* Emsland *-2008* **Eidsvaag AS** JMB Bjerrum & Jensen ApS *Streymnes* *Faeroe Islands (Danish)* MMSI: 231823000	**1,561** 735 1,624	Class: BV (Class contemplated) GL	**1984-12 Krupp Ruhrorter Schiffswerft GmbH — Duisburg** Yd No: 719 Shortened-2011 Loa 69.63 Br ex 12.65 Dght 4.158 Lbp 64.15 Br md 12.62 Dpth 5.31 Welded, 2 dks	**(A31A2GX) General Cargo Ship** Grain: 3,183 Compartments: 1 Ho, ER 1 Ha: (40.3 x 10.2)ER Gantry cranes: 1 Ice Capable	**1 oil engine** with flexible couplings & sr reverse geared to sc. shaft driving 1 FP propeller Total Power: 1,000kW (1,360hp) 10.0kn MaK 6M332AK 1 x 4 Stroke 6 Cy. 240 x 330 1000kW (1360bhp) Krupp MaK Maschinenbau GmbH-Kiel AuxGen: 2 x 96kW 380V 50Hz a.c Thrusters: 1 Tunnel thruster (f); 1 Tunnel thruster (a) Fuel: 128.0 (d.f.) 5.0pd
6909985 *SGCF* SIN 272	**VESTLAND** *ex* Zaima *-2009* *ex* Rigel *-1987* *ex* Polar *-1982* *ex* Timor II *-1974* **Roland Pettersson** - *Kappelshamn* *Sweden* MMSI: 265754000	**256** 77 -	Class: (BV)	**1968 VEB Rosslauer Schiffswerft — Rosslau** Yd No: S.750/21 Loa 35.01 Br ex 6.61 Dght 2.699 Lbp 29.57 Br md 6.58 Dpth 3.31 Welded, 1 dk	**(B11B2FV) Fishing Vessel** Grain: 146 Compartments: 2 Ho, ER 4 Ha: 4 (1.2 x 1.2)ER Derricks: 1x3t,1x1.5t Ice Capable	**1 oil engine** driving 1 FP propeller Total Power: 662kW (900hp) 12.0kn Nohab F26R 1 x 4 Stroke 6 Cy. 250 x 300 662kW (900bhp) Nydqvist & Holm AB-Sweden Fuel: 24.0 (d.f.)
9644342 *C6AL7* -	**VESTLAND CETUS** - **Vestland PSV AS** Vestland Offshore Holding AS *Nassau* *Bahamas* MMSI: 311000082	**4,552** 1,839 4,260	Class: NV	**2013-02 Maritim Shipyard Sp z oo — Gdansk** (Hull) Yd No: (1687) **2013-02 Fjellstrand AS — Omastrand** Yd No: 1687 Loa 85.60 (BB) Br ex 20.60 Dght 7.141 Lbp 77.70 Br md 19.98 Dpth 8.60 Welded, 1 dk	**(B21A20S) Platform Supply Ship** Ice Capable	**4 diesel electric oil engines** driving 4 gen. Connecting to 2 elec. motors each (2300kW) driving 2 Azimuth electric drive units Total Power: 6,600kW (8,972hp) 15.0kn Wartsila 9L20 4 x 4 Stroke 9 Cy. 200 x 280 each-1650kW (2243bhp) Wartsila Nederland BV-Netherlands Thrusters: 2 Tunnel thruster (f); 1 Retract. directional thruster (f)
9653989 *C6AM8* -	**VESTLAND MIRA** - **Vestland PSV AS** Ocean Europe AS *Bahamas* MMSI: 311000091	**3,361** 1,361 4,000	Class: NV	**2012-10 Cemre Muhendislik Gemi Insaat Sanayi ve Ticaret Ltd Sti — Altinova** (Hull) Yd No: (110) **2012-10 Havyard Leirvik AS — Leirvik i Sogn** Yd No: 110 Loa 86.00 (BB) Br ex 18.20 Dght 6.370 Lbp 74.40 Br md 17.60 Dpth 7.70 Welded, 1 dk	**(B21A20S) Platform Supply Ship**	**4 oil engines** driving 4 gen. each 1560kW a.c Connecting to 2 elec. motors each (1600kW) driving 2 Azimuth electric drive units Total Power: 7,060kW (9,600hp) 12.5kn Caterpillar 3512C 4 x Vee 4 Stroke 12 Cy. 170 x 215 each-1765kW (2400bhp) Caterpillar Inc-USA Thrusters: 3 Thwart. CP thruster (f)
9620982 *LCRU* -	**VESTLAND MISTRAL** - **Vestland PSV AS** - *Bergen* *Norway* MMSI: 257803000	**4,344** 1,800 4,900	Class: NV	**2012-06 Stocznia Gdansk SA — Gdansk** (Hull) Yd No: 253/2 **2012-06 Hellesoy Verft AS — Lofallstrand** Yd No: 149 Loa 85.00 (BB) Br ex - Dght 7.160 Lbp 77.70 Br md 20.00 Dpth 8.60 Welded, 1 dk	**(B21A20S) Platform Supply Ship** Ice Capable	**4 diesel electric oil engines** driving 4 gen. each 1825kW 690V a.c Connecting to 2 elec. motors each (2300kW) driving 2 Azimuth electric drive units Total Power: 7,680kW (10,440hp) 12.5kn Caterpillar 3516B-HD 4 x Vee 4 Stroke 16 Cy. 170 x 215 each-1920kW (2610bhp) Caterpillar Inc-USA Thrusters: 1 Retract. directional thruster (f); 1 Tunnel thruster (f); 1 Tunnel thruster (a) Fuel: 900.0
8211100 *J7AX9* -	**VESTLANDIA** *ex* Green Igloo *-2006* *ex* Frio Skagen *-1996* *ex* Vestlandia *-1993* **Navares International Corp** Norfos Shipping Ltd (Norfos Shipping OU) SatCom: Inmarsat C 432522310 *Portsmouth* *Dominica* MMSI: 325223000 Official number: 50224	**1,313** 559 1,525	Class: LR (BV) **100A1** SS 02/2013 Ice Class 1B **LMC** **UMS RMC** Eq.Ltr: M; Cable: 440.0/32.0 U2	**1983-02 p/f Skala Skipasmidja — Skali** Yd No: 39 Loa 67.32 Br ex - Dght 4.401 Lbp 60.00 Br md 12.01 Dpth 6.51 Welded, 2 dks	**(A34A2GR) Refrigerated Cargo Ship** Ins: 2,106 Compartments: 2 Ho, ER 2 Ha: 2 (7.2 x 4.6)ER Cranes: 1x20t Ice Capable	**1 oil engine** reduction geared to sc. shaft driving 1 CP propeller Total Power: 1,765kW (2,400hp) 13.7kn Nohab F312V 1 x Vee 4 Stroke 12 Cy. 250 x 300 1765kW (2400bhp) Nohab Diesel AB-Sweden AuxGen: 1 x 392kW 220/380V 60Hz a.c, 2 x 175kW 220/380V 60Hz a.c Thrusters: 1 Thwart. CP thruster (f) Fuel: 209.0 (d.f.)
9382669 *TFMK* VE 444	**VESTMANNAEY** - **Bergur-Huginn hf** - *Vestmannaeyjar* *Iceland* MMSI: 251344000 Official number: 2444	**486** - 221	Class: LR ✠ **100A1** SS 03/2012 stern trawler ✠ **LMC** Cable: 2.6/26.0 U2 (a)	**2007-03 'Crist' Sp z oo — Gdansk** Yd No: B29/1 Loa 28.95 (BB) Br ex - Dght 5.150 Lbp 25.31 Br md 10.40 Dpth 6.60 Welded, 1 dk	**(B11A2FS) Stern Trawler** Ice Capable	**1 oil engine** with clutches, flexible couplings & sr reverse geared to sc. shaft driving 1 CP propeller Total Power: 956kW (1,300hp) 11.5kn Yanmar 6N21A-EV 1 x 4 Stroke 6 Cy. 210 x 290 956kW (1300bhp) Yanmar Diesel Engine Co Ltd-Japan AuxGen: 1 x 520kW 380V 50Hz a.c, 1 x 312kW 380V 50Hz a.c

8825901 *OW2097* VN 360	**VESTMENNINGUR** *ex San Vestman -2002 ex Hadegisklettur -1994* **P/F Medalsbrekka** *Vestmanna* *Faeroe Islands (Danish)* MMSI: 231106000	**364** 116 -	Class: NV	**1989-07 p/f Torshavnar Skipasmidja — Torshavn** Yd No: 29 Lengthened-2006 Loa 34.60 (BB) Br ex 8.50 Dght 4.300 Lbp 29.15 Br md - Dpth 4.30 Welded	**(B11A2FS) Stern Trawler**	**1 oil engine** driving 1 FP propeller Total Power: 959kW (1,304hp) MWM TBD440-8 1 x 4 Stroke 8 Cy. 230 x 270 959kW (1304bhp) Motoren Werke Mannheim AG (MWM)-West Germany AuxGen: 1 x 99kW 380V 50Hz a.c, 1 x 68kW 380V 50Hz a.c
5369633 *LJVL* -	**VESTRA** *ex Trygge -1966* **Skyssbaatservice Torgeir Vareberg** - *Aalesund* *Norway* MMSI: 257055600	**126** 37 -	Class: (NV)	**1938-06 AS Storviks Mek. Verksted — Kristiansund** Loa 28.38 Br ex 7.65 Dght 2.337 Lbp - Br md 7.60 Dpth 3.20 Riveted, 1 dk	**(A37B2PS) Passenger Ship** Passengers: unberthed: 99	**1 oil engine** driving 1 FP propeller Total Power: 338kW (460hp) 10.0kn Callesen 4-427-DOT 1 x 4 Stroke 4 Cy. 270 x 400 338kW (460bhp) (new engine 1966) Aabenraa Motorfabrik, HeinrichCallesen A/S-Denmark Fuel: 7.0 (d.f.) 1.5pd
6400525 *TFVR* BA 063	**VESTRI** *ex Grettir -2006 ex Olafur Ingi -1983* *ex Steinanes -1981 ex Saedis -1977* *ex Sigurdur Jonsson -1976* **Vestri Ehf** *Patreksfjordur* *Iceland* MMSI: 251250110 Official number: 0182	**293** 87 122	Class: (NV)	**1963-11 Karmsund Verft & Mek. Verksted — Avaldsnes** Yd No: 3 Loa 30.64 Br ex 6.74 Dght 3.315 Lbp 28.78 Br md 6.71 Dpth 5.43 Riveted\Welded, 1 dk	**(B11B2FV) Fishing Vessel** Compartments: 1 Ho, ER 1 Ha: (2.7 x 1.5)ER Derricks: 1x3t; Winches: 1 Ice Capable	**1 oil engine** geared to sc. shaft driving 1 FP propeller Total Power: 441kW (600hp) Blackstone ESS6 1 x 4 Stroke 6 Cy. 222 x 292 441kW (600bhp) Lister Blackstone Marine Ltd.-Dursley AuxGen: 1 x 28kW 220V d.c, 1 x 25kW 220V d.c
8504155 *LGAK* R-92-K	**VESTSKJAER** *ex Sun Lady -1992 ex Prevail -1992* **Vestskjaer AS** - *Haugesund* *Norway* MMSI: 257548500	**140** 56		**1986-02 James N. Miller & Sons Ltd. — St. Monans** Yd No: 1023 Loa 23.02 Br ex 7.17 Dght - Lbp 19.99 Br md 7.10 Dpth 4.02 Welded, 1 dk	**(B11A2FS) Stern Trawler** Ins: 144	**1 oil engine** with clutches, flexible couplings & sr geared to sc. shaft driving 1 CP propeller Total Power: 485kW (659hp) Kelvin TBSC8 1 x 4 Stroke 8 Cy. 165 x 184 485kW (659bhp) Kelvin Diesels Ltd., GECDiesels-Glasgow
9171307 *LJCM* SF-22-S	**VESTSTEINEN** *ex Froyanes Junior -2004* **Veststeinen AS** Merkantil Tjenester AS *Maaloy* *Norway* MMSI: 259489000	**897** 311 560	Class: NV	**1998-03 SC Santierul Naval SA Braila — Braila** (Hull) Yd No: 1387 **1998-03 Baatbygg AS — Raudeberg** Yd No: 001 Loa 46.58 Br ex - Dght - Lbp 41.50 Br md 10.00 Dpth 4.60 Welded, 1 dk	**(B11B2FV) Fishing Vessel** Ins: 694 Ice Capable	**1 oil engine** reduction geared to sc. shaft driving 1 FP propeller Total Power: 1,104kW (1,501hp) Caterpillar 3512TA 1 x Vee 4 Stroke 12 Cy. 170 x 190 1104kW (1501bhp) Caterpillar Inc-USA AuxGen: 2 x 300kW 220/440V 60Hz a.c Thrusters: 1 Thwart. FP thruster (f)
6608012 *LDRM* -	**VESTTANK** *ex Lissamar -2003 ex Bergentank -1997* *ex Esso 5 -1993* **Oytank AS** Oytank Bunkerservice AS *Aalesund* *Norway* MMSI: 257063600 Official number: 16410	**143** 86 244 T/cm 1.0	Class: NV	**1965 Johan Drage AS — Rognan** Yd No: 360 Loa 28.48 Br ex 7.01 Dght 3.030 Lbp 25.99 Br md 7.00 Dpth 3.26 Welded, 1 dk	**(A13B2TP) Products Tanker** Compartments: 6 Ta, ER 2 Cargo Pump (s): 2x150m³/hr Manifold: Bow/CM: 12m	**1 oil engine** driving 1 FP propeller Total Power: 180kW (245hp) 10.0kn Caterpillar D343TA 1 x 4 Stroke 6 Cy. 137 x 165 180kW (245bhp) Caterpillar Tractor Co-USA AuxGen: 1 x 12kW 220V 50Hz a.c, 1 x a.c Fuel: 9.0 (d.f.) 1.0pd
9217137 *LLDH* M-7-MO	**VESTTIND** *ex Polaris -2007* **Nordland Havfiske AS** Havfisk ASA *Aalesund* *Norway* MMSI: 259683000	**2,243** 672 -	Class: NV	**2000-05 SC Santierul Naval SA Braila — Braila** (Hull) Yd No: 1400 **2000-05 Myklebust Mek. Verksted AS — Gursken** Yd No: 27 Loa 60.00 Br ex - Dght 5.850 Lbp 52.80 Br md 14.00 Dpth 8.65 Welded, 1 dk	**(B11A2FS) Stern Trawler** Ins: 860 Ice Capable	**1 oil engine** geared to sc. shaft driving 1 CP propeller Total Power: 5,520kW (7,505hp) Wartsila 9R32 1 x 4 Stroke 9 Cy. 320 x 350 5520kW (7505bhp) Wartsila NSD Finland Oy-Finland AuxGen: 1 x 2300kW a.c, 1 x 1520kW a.c Thrusters: 1 Thwart. FP thruster (f)
6509474 *CXTQ* -	**VESTTIND II** *ex Vesttind -1995* **Frigorifico Pesquero del Uruguay SA (FRIPUR)** - *Montevideo* *Uruguay*	*291* 85 -	Class: (NV)	**1965-03 AS Fredriksstad Mek. Verksted — Fredrikstad** Yd No: 385 Lengthened-1977 Loa 45.65 Br ex 8.23 Dght 4.128 Lbp 40.34 Br md 8.18 Dpth 6.30 Welded, 2 dks	**(B11A2FS) Stern Trawler** Ins: 239 Compartments: 1 Ho, ER 2 Ha: (2.7 x 2.4) (5.2 x 2.4)ER Derricks: 1x3t; Winches: 2	**1 oil engine** driving 1 FP propeller Total Power: 1,103kW (1,500hp) Wichmann 5AXA 1 x 2 Stroke 5 Cy. 300 x 450 1103kW (1500bhp) (new engine 1977) Wichmann Motorfabrikk AS-Norway AuxGen: 2 x 120kW 220V 50Hz a.c
9020986 *OW2493* VN 459	**VESTURBUGVIN** **P/F Vesturbugvin** Danial i Skalum *Vestmanna* *Faeroe Islands (Danish)* Official number: D3400	**535** 160 -	Class: NV	**1991-12 p/f Torshavnar Skipasmidja — Torshavn** Yd No: 33 Loa 36.20 (BB) Br ex 9.80 Dght - Lbp 31.00 Br md 9.50 Dpth 4.60 Welded, 2 dks	**(B11A2FS) Stern Trawler** Ins: 205; Liq: 129 Ice Capable	**1 oil engine** with clutches, flexible couplings & sr geared to sc. shaft driving 1 CP propeller Total Power: 1,029kW (1,399hp) MWM TBD440-8K 1 x 4 Stroke 8 Cy. 230 x 270 1029kW (1399bhp) Motoren Werke Mannheim AG (MWM)-Mannheim AuxGen: 1 x 404kW 380V 50Hz a.c, 1 x 200kW 380V 50Hz a.c
6403448 *XPPE* FD 101	**VESTURHAVID** *ex Strandingur -2007* **H K O P/F** - *Vestmanna* *Faeroe Islands (Danish)* MMSI: 231167000 Official number: D1021	**327** 98	Class: NV	**1963 p/f Skala Skipasmidja — Skali** Yd No: 2 Loa 36.76 Br ex 7.55 Dght 3.815 Lbp 32.21 Br md 7.32 Dpth 3.87 Welded, 2 dks	**(B11B2FV) Fishing Vessel** Compartments: 2 Ho, ER 3 Ha: (1.2 x 1.2) (1.3 x 1.2) (1.8 x 1.2)ER Derricks: 1; Winches: 1	**1 oil engine** geared to sc. shaft driving 1 CP propeller Total Power: 368kW (500hp) Grenaa 6F24 1 x 4 Stroke 6 Cy. 240 x 300 368kW (500bhp) (new engine 1986) A/S Grenaa Motorfabrik-Denmark AuxGen: 2 x 60kW 220V 50Hz a.c
7014359 *XPUU* VN 307	**VESTURLAND** **P/F Thor** - *Hosvik* *Faeroe Islands (Danish)* MMSI: 231126000 Official number: D1766	**295** 95 165	Class: NV	**1970 p/f Torshavnar Skipasmidja — Torshavn** Yd No: 15 Loa 33.96 Br ex 7.35 Dght 3.576 Lbp 28.71 Br md 7.32 Dpth 3.81 Welded, 1 dk	**(B11B2FV) Fishing Vessel** Passengers: berths: 12 Ins: 225 Compartments: 1 Ho, ER 1 Ha: (2.9 x 1.9)ER Derricks: 1x1.5t; Winches: 1 Ice Capable	**1 oil engine** reduction geared to sc. shaft driving 1 CP propeller Total Power: 690kW (938hp) 11.0kn Alpha 6L23/30 1 x 4 Stroke 6 Cy. 225 x 300 690kW (938bhp) (new engine 1983) B&W Alpha Diesel A/S-Denmark AuxGen: 2 x 96kW 380/220V 50Hz a.c Fuel: 35.0 (d.f.)
8704834 *OW2336* VA 404	**VESTURLEIKI** *ex Beinir -2007 ex Haanseeraq -2006* *ex Grinnoy -2005 ex Rossvik -1998* *ex Salleq -1997* **P/F Vesturleiki** - *Torshavn* *Faeroe Islands (Danish)* MMSI: 231090000	**724** 272 -	Class: NV	**1988-06 Danyard Aalborg A/S — Aalborg** (Hull) **1988-06 Johs Kristensen Skibsbyggeri A/S — Hvide Sande** Yd No: 187 Loa 42.10 Br ex - Dght 4.600 Lbp 36.00 Br md 10.41 Dpth 4.63 Welded, 2 dks	**(B11A2FS) Stern Trawler** Ins: 300 Ice Capable	**1 oil engine** reverse reduction geared to sc. shaft driving 1 FP propeller Total Power: 1,320kW (1,795hp) Alpha 6L28/32 1 x 4 Stroke 6 Cy. 280 x 320 1320kW (1795bhp) MAN B&W Diesel A/S-Denmark AuxGen: 1 x 720kW 380V 50Hz a.c, 2 x 431kW 380V 50Hz a.c
8616063 - -	**VESTURSKIN** - -	**567** 120 -	Class: (NV)	**1986-03 p/f Skala Skipasmidja — Skali** Yd No: 47 Loa 41.03 Br ex - Dght - Lbp 36.56 Br md 8.86 Dpth 6.46 Welded, 2 dks	**(B11A2FS) Stern Trawler** Ice Capable	**1 oil engine** geared to sc. shaft driving 1 FP propeller Total Power: 1,499kW (2,038hp) Nohab F38V 1 x Vee 4 Stroke 8 Cy. 250 x 300 1499kW (2038bhp) Wartsila Diesel AB-Sweden AuxGen: 1 x 632kW 440V 50Hz a.c, 1 x 144kW 440V 50Hz a.c, 1 x 108kW 440V 50Hz a.c
8216631 *XPRB* TN 330	**VESTURSKIN** *ex Kallsevni -2009 ex Hamrasvanur -2002* *ex Oddeyrin -1996* **P/F Nofa** - *Torshavn* *Faeroe Islands (Danish)* MMSI: 231215000	**475** 143 140	Class: NV	**1986-12 Slippstodin h/f — Akureyri** Yd No: 66 Loa 38.80 Br ex - Dght 3.960 Lbp 35.26 Br md 8.11 Dpth 5.24 Welded, 1 dk	**(B11A2FS) Stern Trawler** Ins: 250 Compartments: 1 Ho, ER 1 Ha: (2.0 x 1.8) Ice Capable	**1 oil engine** with clutches, flexible couplings & sr geared to sc. shaft driving 1 CP propeller Total Power: 728kW (990hp) 12.0kn Normo LDM-6 1 x 4 Stroke 6 Cy. 250 x 300 728kW (990bhp) AS Bergens Mek Verksteder-Norway AuxGen: 2 x 248kW 380V 50Hz a.c, 1 x 152kW 380V 50Hz a.c
8414130 *OW2372* VA 181	**VESTURTUGVA** *ex Vestmenningur II -1999* *ex Vestmenningur -1999* **P/F Hysisa** Halvdan Gudmundsen *Sandavagur* *Faeroe Islands (Danish)* MMSI: 231173000 Official number: D2916	**306** 138 -	Class: NV	**1985-09 p/f Torshavnar Skipasmidja — Torshavn** Yd No: 26 Loa 32.45 Br ex - Dght 4.001 Lbp 28.71 Br md 8.01 Dpth 6.18 Welded, 2 dks	**(B11A2FS) Stern Trawler**	**1 oil engine** driving 1 FP propeller Total Power: 869kW (1,181hp) MWM TBD440-6 1 x 4 Stroke 6 Cy. 230 x 270 869kW (1181bhp) Motoren Werke Mannheim AG (MWM)-West Germany AuxGen: 2 x 72kW 380V 50Hz a.c

8318427 XPRA TN 320
VESTURVARDI
ex Grimur Kamban *-2009* *ex* Nokkvi *-2002*
P/F Nofa
-
Torshavn *Faeroe Islands (Danish)*
MMSI: 231214000
502 151 220 Class: NV
1987-02 Slippstodin h/f — Akureyri Yd No: 67
Loa 38.70 Br ex - Dght -
Lbp 35.25 Br md 8.11 Dpth 5.24
Welded, 1 dk
(B11A2FS) Stern Trawler
Ins: 250
Ice Capable
1 oil engine with clutches, flexible couplings & sr geared to sc. shaft driving 1 CP propeller
Total Power: 783kW (1,065hp) 12.0kn
Normo LDM-6
1 x 4 Stroke 6 Cy. 250 x 300 783kW (1065bhp)
AS Bergens Mek Verksteder-Norway
AuxGen: 2 x 184kW 380V 50Hz a.c, 1 x 152kW 380V 50Hz a.c

8609357 OW2420 VA 200
VESTURVON
Pesquera Ancora SL
-
SatCom: Inmarsat C 423104220
Sorvagur *Faeroe Islands (Danish)*
MMSI: 231042000
Official number: D3108
2,114 643 1,100 Class: NV
1987-03 Aukra Industrier AS — Aukra Yd No: 79
Loa 65.51 (BB) Br ex - Dght 5.620
Lbp 57.21 Br md 13.01 Dpth 8.32
Welded, 3 dks
(B11A2FG) Factory Stern Trawler
Ice Capable
1 oil engine driving 1 FP propeller
Total Power: 2,998kW (4,076hp)
Wartsila 8R32D
1 x 4 Stroke 8 Cy. 320 x 350 2998kW (4076bhp)
Wartsila Diesel Oy-Finland
AuxGen: 1 x 1440kW 380V 50Hz a.c, 2 x 616kW 380V 50Hz a.c
Thrusters: 1 Thwart. CP thruster (f)

8962357 LGSR T-94-S
VESTVAERING
ex Seilsjo *-2006* *ex* Vikmark Senior *-2005*
ex Styrk *-1999* *ex* Signal *-1999*
ex Meilandstinn *-1999* *ex* Meilandstind *-1999*
ex Telstar *-1999*
Ole Johan Korneliussen
-
Svolvaer *Norway*
MMSI: 257817500
106 42 -
1965 Kr.K. Frostad & Sonner — Tomrefjord Yd No: 18
Loa 21.31 Br ex - Dght 3.500
Lbp - Br md 5.95 Dpth 3.81
Welded, 1 dk
(B11B2FV) Fishing Vessel
1 oil engine geared to sc. shaft driving 1 FP propeller
Total Power: 405kW (551hp) 8.5kn
Grenaa 6F24T
1 x 4 Stroke 6 Cy. 240 x 300 405kW (551bhp) (new engine 1977)
A/S Grenaa Motorfabrik-Denmark
Thrusters: 1 Thwart. FP thruster (f); 1 Tunnel thruster (a)

8934922 LJEF -
VESTVEG TO
Sibelco Nordic AS
-
Sortland *Norway*
MMSI: 257077700
133 39 -
1962 Kaarbos Mek. Verksted AS — Harstad Yd No: 37
Loa 29.09 Br ex - Dght -
Lbp - Br md - Dpth -
Welded, 1 dk
(A36A2PR) Passenger/Ro-Ro Ship (Vehicles)
1 oil engine driving 1 FP propeller
Total Power: 200kW (272hp)
General Motors
1 x 200kW (272bhp)
General Motors Corp-USA
AuxGen: 2 x 220V a.c
Fuel: 4.5 (d.f.)

8512102 JXAM H-12-AV
VESTVIKING
ex Slaatteroy *-2003*
P/R Johrema ANS
Hans Reidar Njastad
SatCom: Inmarsat C 425838110
Bergen *Norway*
MMSI: 258381000
Official number: 20187
1,492 468 - Class: NV
1986-03 Th Hellesoy Skipsbyggeri AS — Lofallstrand Yd No: 112
Loa 62.95 Br ex 11.99 Dght 4.500
Lbp 55.20 Br md - Dpth 5.52
Welded, 2 dks
(B11B2FV) Fishing Vessel
Ins: 1,800
Ice Capable
1 oil engine driving 1 FP propeller
Total Power: 2,354kW (3,200hp)
Wichmann WX28V8
1 x Vee 4 Stroke 8 Cy. 280 x 360 2354kW (3200bhp)
Wichmann Motorfabrikk AS-Norway
AuxGen: 1 x 1280kW 220V 60Hz a.c, 2 x 252kW 220V 60Hz a.c
Thrusters: 1 Thwart. FP thruster (f)

8209743 ZDGI4 -
VESTVIND
ex Rita *-2011* *ex* Sea Waal *-2006*
ex Triton Navigator *-2001* *ex* Lys Crown *-1999*
ex Ettina *-1997*
Vestbulk AS
Lighthouse Ship Management AS
Gibraltar *Gibraltar (British)*
MMSI: 236250000
1,843 950 2,064 Class: GL RI
1985-12 Schiffswerft und Maschinenfabrik Cassens GmbH — Emden Yd No: 165
Loa 80.02 Br ex 12.70 Dght 4.150
Lbp 75.21 Br md 12.62 Dpth 5.31
Welded, 1 dk
(A31A2GX) General Cargo Ship
Grain: 3,292
TEU 102 C.Ho 62/20' (40') C.Dk 40/20' (40')
Compartments: 1 Ho, ER
1 Ha: (51.3 x 10.1)ER
Ice Capable
1 oil engine with flexible couplings & sr gearedto sc. shaft driving 1 FP propeller
Total Power: 1,000kW (1,360hp) 10.5kn
MaK 6M332AK
1 x 4 Stroke 6 Cy. 240 x 330 1000kW (1360bhp)
Krupp MaK Maschinenbau GmbH-Kiel
AuxGen: 2 x 96kW 380V 50Hz a.c
Thrusters: 1 Thwart. FP thruster (f)
Fuel: 104.0 (d.f.) 5.0pd

8219516 ITIN -
VESUVIO
Rimorchiatori Napoletani Srl
-
Naples *Italy*
MMSI: 247034300
Official number: 1424
199 72 145 Class: RI
1983-05 Cantiere Navale di Pesaro SpA (CNP) — Pesaro Yd No: 53
Loa 33.54 Br ex 9.28 Dght 3.757
Lbp 29.01 Br md 8.58 Dpth 4.27
Welded, 1 dk
(B32A2ST) Tug
1 oil engine sr reverse geared to sc. shaft driving 1 CP propeller
Total Power: 1,622kW (2,205hp) 13.0kn
MAN G8V30/45ATL
1 x 4 Stroke 8 Cy. 300 x 450 1622kW (2205bhp)
Maschinenbau Augsburg Nuernberg (MAN)-Augsburg

9276432 IJPV -
VESUVIO JET
Navigazione Libera del Golfo Srl
-
Naples *Italy*
MMSI: 247091800
528 334 56 Class: RI
2003-06 Rodriquez Cantieri Navali SpA — Messina Yd No: 306
Loa 50.46 Br ex 8.80 Dght 1.280
Lbp 43.00 Br md 8.78 Dpth 4.20
Welded, 1 dk
(A37B2PS) Passenger Ship
Hull Material: Aluminium Alloy
Passengers: 444
3 oil engines geared to sc. shafts driving 3 Water jets
Total Power: 6,000kW (8,157hp) 36.0kn
M.T.U. 16V396TE74L
3 x Vee 4 Stroke 16 Cy. 165 x 185 each-2000kW (2719bhp)
MTU Friedrichshafen GmbH-Friedrichshafen

6802462 - -
VETEN
ex Guriev *-2009*
Fizuli D Abdullayev
-
Baku *Azerbaijan*
1,002 392 176 Class: RS
1963 'Georgi Dimitrov' Shipyard — Varna Yd No: 530
Converted From: Ferry (Passenger only)-2010
Loa 63.81 Br ex 9.33 Dght 3.001
Lbp 57.80 Br md 9.28 Dpth 5.87
Welded, 1 dk
(X11A2YP) Yacht
Cranes: 1x1t; Derricks: 3x1t; Winches: 3
1 oil engine driving 1 FP propeller
Total Power: 736kW (1,001hp) 12.3kn
S.K.L. 8NVD48
1 x 4 Stroke 8 Cy. 320 x 480 736kW (1001bhp)
VEB Schwermaschinenbau "KarlLiebknecht" (SKL)-Magdeburg
Fuel: 35.0 (d.f.)

8894586 - -
VETHELKHAIR 901
ex Tweizegtt 901 *-2009*
Etablissement Abdellani Ould Noueigued
-
Nouadhibou *Mauritania*
317 95 - Class: (RI)
1995 Yantai Fishing Vessel Shipyard — Yantai SD
Loa - Br ex - Dght 3.053
Lbp 38.60 Br md 7.80 Dpth 3.90
Welded, 1 dk
(B11B2FV) Fishing Vessel
1 oil engine geared to sc. shaft driving 1 FP propeller
Total Power: 662kW (900hp)
Chinese Std. Type 8300
1 x 4 Stroke 8 Cy. 300 x 380 662kW (900bhp)
Zibo Diesel Engine Factory-China
AuxGen: 2 x 90kW 220/440V 50Hz a.c

8894603 - -
VETHELKHAIR 904
ex Tweizegtt 904 *-2009*
Etablissement Abdellani Ould Noueigued
-
Nouadhibou *Mauritania*
317 95 - Class: (RI)
1995 Yantai Fishing Vessel Shipyard — Yantai SD
Loa - Br ex - Dght 3.053
Lbp 38.68 Br md 7.80 Dpth 3.90
Welded, 1 dk
(B11B2FV) Fishing Vessel
1 oil engine geared to sc. shaft driving 1 FP propeller
Total Power: 662kW (900hp)
Chinese Std. Type 8300
1 x 4 Stroke 8 Cy. 300 x 380 662kW (900bhp)
Zibo Diesel Engine Factory-China
AuxGen: 2 x 90kW 220/440V 50Hz a.c

8924587 - -
VETHELKHAIR 905
ex Tweizegtt 905 *-2009*
Etablissement Abdellani Ould Noueigued
-
Nouadhibou *Mauritania*
317 95 - Class: (RI)
1995 Yantai Fishing Vessel Shipyard — Yantai SD
Loa - Br ex - Dght 3.053
Lbp 38.68 Br md 7.80 Dpth 3.90
Welded, 1 dk
(B11B2FV) Fishing Vessel
1 oil engine geared to sc. shaft driving 1 FP propeller
Total Power: 662kW (900hp)
Chinese Std. Type 8300
1 x 4 Stroke 8 Cy. 300 x 380 662kW (900bhp)
Zibo Diesel Engine Factory-China
AuxGen: 2 x 90kW 220/440V 50Hz a.c

8932211 - -
VETHELKHAIR 906
ex Tweizegtt 906 *-2009*
Etablissement Abdellani Ould Noueigued
-
Nouadhibou *Mauritania*
Official number: 75376
317 95 - Class: (RI)
1995-03 Yantai Fishing Vessel Shipyard — Yantai SD
Loa - Br ex - Dght 3.053
Lbp 38.60 Br md 7.80 Dpth 3.90
Welded, 1 dk
(B11B2FV) Fishing Vessel
1 oil engine geared to sc. shaft driving 1 FP propeller
Total Power: 662kW (900hp)
Chinese Std. Type 8300
1 x 4 Stroke 8 Cy. 300 x 380 662kW (900bhp)
Zibo Diesel Engine Factory-China
AuxGen: 2 x 90kW 220/440V 50Hz a.c

8924599 - -
VETHELKHAIR 907
ex Tweizegtt 907 *-2009*
Etablissement Abdellani Ould Noueigued
-
Nouadhibou *Mauritania*
317 95 - Class: (RI)
1995 Yantai Fishing Vessel Shipyard — Yantai SD
Loa - Br ex - Dght 3.053
Lbp 38.68 Br md 7.80 Dpth 3.90
Welded, 1 dk
(B11B2FV) Fishing Vessel
1 oil engine geared to sc. shaft driving 1 FP propeller
Total Power: 662kW (900hp)
Chinese Std. Type 8300
1 x 4 Stroke 8 Cy. 300 x 380 662kW (900bhp)
Zibo Diesel Engine Factory-China
AuxGen: 2 x 90kW 220/440V 50Hz a.c

9264348 LLVB -
VETLEFJORD
ex Fjordlys *-2003*
Fjord1 AS
-
Floro *Norway*
MMSI: 257931650
142 43 38
2003-06 Batservice Mandal AS — Mandal (Hull)
2003-06 Oma Baatbyggeri AS — Stord Yd No: 517
Loa 25.75 Br ex - Dght 1.100
Lbp 23.95 Br md 9.00 Dpth 3.40
Welded, 1 dk
(A36A2PR) Passenger/Ro-Ro Ship (Vehicles)
Hull Material: Aluminium Alloy
Passengers: unberthed: 60
Cars: 8
2 oil engines geared to sc. shafts driving 2 FP propellers
Total Power: 1,220kW (1,658hp) 28.0kn
M.T.U. 12V183TE72
2 x Vee 4 Stroke 12 Cy. 128 x 142 each-610kW (829bhp)
MTU Friedrichshafen GmbH-Friedrichshafen

8139120 UAWF AG-1361
VETLUGA
JSC Arkhangelsk Trawl Fleet (A/O 'Arkhangelskiy Tralflot')
-
Murmansk *Russia*
MMSI: 273295700
1,734 677 966 Class: RS
1983-09 Sudostroitelnyy Zavod "Baltiya" — Klaypeda Yd No: 361
Lengthened-1990
Loa 69.80 Br ex 13.03 Dght 4.873
Lbp 63.20 Br md 13.00 Dpth 8.89
Welded, 2 dks
(B11A2FS) Stern Trawler
Bale: 95; Ins: 500
Compartments: 2 Ho, 1 Ta, ER
2 Ha: (1.2 x 1.3) (1.9 x 1.9)
Ice Capable
1 oil engine driving 1 FP propeller
Total Power: 1,618kW (2,200hp) 13.0kn
Skoda 6L525IIPS
1 x 4 Stroke 6 Cy. 525 x 720 1618kW (2200bhp)
CKD Praha-Praha
Fuel: 264.0 (d.f.)

IMO No. / Call sign	Ship name / Owner / Port	Tonnage	Class	Builder / Dimensions	Type / Capacity	Machinery
8137811 *IQIU* -	**VETOR 944** *ex* Isola di Palmarola *-1982* **Vetor Srl** - *Naples* *Italy* MMSI: 247160200 Official number: 1867	*140* 90 -	Class: RI	**1981 Feodosiyskoye Sudostroitelnoye Obyedineniye "More" — Feodosiya** Loa 35.18 Br ex 6.02 Dght 1.120 Lbp 30.00 Br md 6.00 Dpth 1.81 Welded, 1 dk	**(A37B2PS) Passenger Ship** Passengers: unberthed: 114	**2 oil engines** driving 2 FP propellers Total Power: 1,942kW (2,640hp) Isotta Fraschini ID36SS12V 2 x Vee 4 Stroke 12 Cy. 170 x 170 each-971kW (1320bhp) (new engine 1984) Isotta Fraschini SpA-Italy
6360696 *INVR* -	**VETOR QUINTO** *ex* Vetor *-1975* *ex* Bellona *-1973* *ex* Thuntank *-1967* **Vetor Srl** - *Naples* *Italy* MMSI: 247222900 Official number: 1863	*498* 241 944	Class: RI (NV)	**1963 Grotvaagen Verft AS — Kyrksaeterora** Yd No: 27 Loa 62.03 Br ex 9.48 Dght 3.738 Lbp 55.33 Br md 9.45 Dpth 4.07 Welded, 1 dk	**(A12C2LW) Wine Tanker** Liq: 1,218 Compartments: 8 Ta, ER	**1 oil engine** driving 1 FP propeller Total Power: 588kW (799hp) 11.5kn Deutz RBV6M545 1 x 4 Stroke 6 Cy. 320 x 450 588kW (799bhp) Kloeckner Humboldt Deutz AG-West Germany AuxGen: 1 x 68kW 380V 50Hz a.c, 1 x 44kW 380V 50Hz a.c, 1 x 20kW 380V 50Hz a.c
7833107 *XUDZ2* -	**VETRA** *ex* Sormovskiy-41 *-2011* **Commerce Properties Inc** MD Shipping Co SatCom: Inmarsat C 451549110 *Phnom Penh* *Cambodia* MMSI: 515491000 Official number: 1180882	**2,478** 999 3,353	Class: RS	**1980-07 Sudostroitelnyy Zavod "Krasnoye Sormovo" — Gorkiy** Yd No: 65 Loa 114.03 Br ex 13.21 Dght 3.810 Lbp 110.76 Br md 13.00 Dpth 5.50 Welded, 1 dk	**(A31A2GX) General Cargo Ship** Bale: 4,297 Compartments: 4 Ho, ER 4 Ha: (17.6 x 9.3)3 (17.9 x 9.3)ER Ice Capable	**2 oil engines** driving 2 FP propellers Total Power: 970kW (1,318hp) 10.8kn S.K.L. 6NVD48A-2U 2 x 4 Stroke 6 Cy. 320 x 480 each-485kW (659bhp) VEB Schwermaschinenbau "KarlLiebknecht" (SKL)-Magdeburg Fuel: 84.0 (d.f.)
8729406 *UHCB* -	**VETROVOY** - **Sea Resources Co Ltd (A/O 'Morskiye Resursy')** - *Nevelsk* *Russia* MMSI: 273844200 Official number: 890199	**448** 134 207	Class: RS	**1989-08 Zavod 'Nikolayevsk-na-Amure' — Nikolayevsk-na-Amure** Yd No: 1267 Loa 44.89 Br ex - Dght 3.771 Lbp 39.37 Br md 9.48 Dpth 5.14 Welded, 1 dk	**(B11A2FS) Stern Trawler** Ins: 210 Ice Capable	**1 oil engine** driving 1 FP propeller Total Power: 588kW (799hp) 11.5kn S.K.L. 6NVD48A-2U 1 x 4 Stroke 6 Cy. 320 x 480 588kW (799bhp) VEB Schwermaschinenbau "KarlLiebknecht" (SKL)-Magdeburg AuxGen: 3 x 150kW a.c
9079303 *9HIQ8* -	**VEYSEL VARDAL** - **VV Shipping Co Ltd** Veysel Vardal Gemicilik Denizcilik ve Ticaret AS *Valletta* *Malta* MMSI: 256020000 Official number: 9848	**2,108** 1,147 3,265	Class: BV (AB)	**1993-06 Iyi Deniz (Tuncer Denizyaranli) — Tuzla** Yd No: 38 Loa 84.35 Br ex - Dght 5.400 Lbp 78.00 Br md 14.00 Dpth 6.20 Welded, 1 dk	**(A12D2LV) Vegetable Oil Tanker**	**1 oil engine** driving 1 FP propeller Total Power: 1,471kW (2,000hp) 11.5kn Hanshin 6EL32 1 x 4 Stroke 6 Cy. 320 x 640 1471kW (2000bhp) The Hanshin Diesel Works Ltd-Japan AuxGen: 3 x 215kW 380V 50Hz a.c Fuel: 180.0 (d.f.) 5.5pd
8228634 *UBNV* -	**VEZUVSK** *ex* Khiva *-2006* **Atlantica Co Ltd** - *Nevelsk* *Russia* MMSI: 273565900 Official number: 843158	**722** 217 414	Class: RS	**1984-10 Zavod "Leninskaya Kuznitsa" — Kiyev** Yd No: 1547 Loa 54.84 Br ex 9.96 Dght 4.140 Lbp 50.30 Br md 9.80 Dpth 5.01 Welded, 1 dk	**(B11A2FS) Stern Trawler** Ins: 412 Compartments: 2 Ho Ice Capable	**1 oil engine** driving 1 CP propeller Total Power: 852kW (1,158hp) 12.0kn S.K.L. 8NVD48A-2U 1 x 4 Stroke 8 Cy. 320 x 480 852kW (1158bhp) VEB Schwermaschinenbau "KarlLiebknecht" (SKL)-Magdeburg AuxGen: 4 x 160kW a.c Fuel: 180.0 (d.f.)
9486271 *3EPI5* -	**VF GLORY** *ex* B&M Reach *-2008* **Transport & Chartering Corp (VIETFRACHT)** - *Panama* *Panama* MMSI: 353838000 Official number: 3395608A	**6,491** 2,844 8,442	Class: (CC)	**2008-01 Chongqing Dongfeng Ship Industry Co — Chongqing** Yd No: K06-1007 Loa 117.80 Br ex 18.03 Dght 7.000 Lbp 111.40 Br md 18.00 Dpth 10.40 Welded, 1 dk	**(A31A2GX) General Cargo Ship** Grain: 11,914; Bale: 11,914 Compartments: 2 Ho, ER 2 Ha: ER 2 (32.2 x 15.0) Cranes: 2x35t Ice Capable	**1 oil engine** reduction geared to sc. shaft driving 1 Propeller Total Power: 2,574kW (3,500hp) 11.8kn Yanmar 6N330-EN 1 x 4 Stroke 6 Cy. 330 x 440 2574kW (3500bhp) Qingdao Zichai Boyang Diesel EngineCo Ltd-China AuxGen: 3 x 250kW 400V a.c
9365192 *IJJA* -	**VF M01** - **Government of The Republic of Italy (Ministry of the Interior - Fire Department)** - *Augusta* *Italy*	**140** 53 -		**2005 Cant. Nav. F. Giacalone — Mazara del Vallo** Yd No: 119 Loa 28.45 Br ex - Dght 1.850 Lbp - Br md 7.00 Dpth - Welded, 1 dk	**(B34F2SF) Fire Fighting Vessel**	**2 oil engines** reduction geared to sc. shaftS driving 2 Propellers Total Power: 1,618kW (2,200hp) MAN D2842LE 2 x Vee 4 Stroke 12 Cy. 128 x 142 each-809kW (1100bhp) MAN Nutzfahrzeuge AG-Nuernberg
8647907 *IJCU* -	**VF M02** - **Government of The Republic of Italy (Ministry of the Interior - Fire Department)** - *Italy* MMSI: 247154800	**128** 75 -		**2006-01 Cant. Nav. F. Giacalone — Mazara del Vallo** Yd No: 120 Loa 28.45 Br ex - Dght 1.850 Lbp - Br md 7.00 Dpth - Welded, 1 dk	**(B34F2SF) Fire Fighting Vessel**	**2 oil engines** reduction geared to sc. shafts driving 2 Propellers Total Power: 1,618kW (2,200hp) MAN D2842LE 2 x Vee 4 Stroke 12 Cy. 128 x 142 each-809kW (1100bhp) MAN Nutzfahrzeuge AG-Nuernberg
8647919 *IJOC* -	**VF M03** - **Government of The Republic of Italy (Ministry of the Interior - Fire Department)** - *Italy*	**128** 75 -		**2006-01 Cant. Nav. F. Giacalone — Mazara del Vallo** Yd No: 121 Loa 28.45 Br ex - Dght 1.850 Lbp - Br md 7.00 Dpth - Welded, 1 dk	**(B34F2SF) Fire Fighting Vessel**	**2 oil engines** reduction geared to sc. shafts driving 2 Propellers Total Power: 1,618kW (2,200hp) MAN D2842LE 2 x Vee 4 Stroke 12 Cy. 128 x 142 each-809kW (1100bhp) MAN Nutzfahrzeuge AG-Nuernberg
8647921 *IJSR* -	**VF M04** - **Government of The Republic of Italy (Ministry of the Interior - Fire Department)** - *Italy*	**128** 75 -		**2006-01 Cant. Nav. F. Giacalone — Mazara del Vallo** Yd No: 122 Loa 28.45 Br ex - Dght 1.850 Lbp - Br md 7.00 Dpth - Welded, 1 dk	**(B34F2SF) Fire Fighting Vessel**	**2 oil engines** reduction geared to sc. shafts driving 2 Propellers Total Power: 1,618kW (2,200hp) MAN D2842LE 2 x Vee 4 Stroke 12 Cy. 128 x 142 each-809kW (1100bhp) MAN Nutzfahrzeuge AG-Nuernberg
8647933 - -	**VF M05** - **Government of The Republic of Italy (Ministry of the Interior - Fire Department)** - *Italy*	**128** 75 -		**2009-01 Cant. Nav. F. Giacalone — Mazara del Vallo** Yd No: 130 Loa 28.45 Br ex - Dght 1.850 Lbp - Br md 7.00 Dpth - Welded, 1 dk	**(B34F2SF) Fire Fighting Vessel**	**2 oil engines** reduction geared to sc. shafts driving 2 Propellers MAN D2842LE 2 x Vee 4 Stroke 12 Cy. 128 x 142 MAN Nutzfahrzeuge AG-Nuernberg
8647945 *IJRX* -	**VF M06** - **Government of The Republic of Italy (Ministry of the Interior - Fire Department)** - *Italy*	**128** 75 -		**2009-01 Cant. Nav. F. Giacalone — Mazara del Vallo** Yd No: 131 Loa 28.45 Br ex - Dght 1.850 Lbp - Br md 7.00 Dpth - Welded, 1 dk	**(B34F2SF) Fire Fighting Vessel**	**2 oil engines** reduction geared to sc. shafts driving 2 Propellers Total Power: 1,618kW (2,200hp) MAN D2842LE 2 x Vee 4 Stroke 12 Cy. 128 x 142 each-809kW (1100bhp) MAN Nutzfahrzeuge AG-Nuernberg
8647957 *IJUJ* -	**VF M07** - **Government of The Republic of Italy (Ministry of the Interior - Fire Department)** - *Italy*	**128** 75 -		**2009-01 Cant. Nav. F. Giacalone — Mazara del Vallo** Yd No: 132 Loa 28.45 Br ex - Dght 1.850 Lbp - Br md 7.00 Dpth - Welded, 1 dk	**(B34F2SF) Fire Fighting Vessel**	**2 oil engines** reduction geared to sc. shafts driving 2 Propellers Total Power: 1,618kW (2,200hp) MAN D2842LE 2 x Vee 4 Stroke 12 Cy. 128 x 142 each-809kW (1100bhp) MAN Nutzfahrzeuge AG-Nuernberg
9640499 *UBFI2* -	**VF TANKER-1** - **OJSC 'VEB-Leasing'** VF Tanker Ltd SatCom: Inmarsat C 427305352 *St Petersburg* *Russia* MMSI: 273351450	**5,075** 2,026 7,022	Class: RS	**2012-05 Sudostroitelnyy Zavod "Krasnoye Sormovo" — Nizhniy Novgorod** Yd No: 1 Loa 140.85 (BB) Br ex 16.86 Dght 4.200 Lbp 136.29 Br md 16.70 Dpth 6.00 Welded, 1 dk	**(A13B2TP) Products Tanker** Double Hull (13F) Liq: 7,828; Liq (Oil): 8,100 Compartments: 6 Wing Ta, 2 Wing Slop Ta, Wing ER 2 Cargo Pump (s): 2x200m³/hr Ice Capable	**2 oil engines** reduction geared to sc. shaft (s) driving 2 Directional propellers Total Power: 2,160kW (2,936hp) 10.0kn Wartsila 6L20 2 x 4 Stroke 6 Cy. 200 x 280 each-1080kW (1468bhp) Wartsila Finland Oy-Finland AuxGen: 3 x 296kW a.c Thrusters: 1 Thwart. FP thruster (f) Fuel: 311.0 (d.f.)
9640504 *UBFI3* -	**VF TANKER-2** - **OJSC 'VEB-Leasing'** VF Tanker Ltd *St Petersburg* *Russia* MMSI: 273352450	**5,075** 2,026 7,019	Class: RS	**2012-05 Sudostroitelnyy Zavod "Krasnoye Sormovo" — Nizhniy Novgorod** Yd No: 2 Loa 140.85 (BB) Br ex 16.86 Dght 4.200 Lbp 136.29 Br md 16.70 Dpth 6.00 Welded, 1 dk	**(A13B2TP) Products Tanker** Double Hull (13F) Liq: 7,828; Liq (Oil): 8,100 Compartments: 6 Wing Ta, 2 Wing Slop Ta, ER 2 Cargo Pump (s): 2x200m³/hr Ice Capable	**2 oil engines** reduction geared to sc. shaft (s) driving 2 Directional propellers Total Power: 2,160kW (2,936hp) 10.0kn Wartsila 6L20 2 x 4 Stroke 6 Cy. 200 x 280 each-1080kW (1468bhp) Wartsila Finland Oy-Finland AuxGen: 3 x 296kW a.c Thrusters: 1 Thwart. FP thruster (f) Fuel: 311.0 (d.f.)

IMO / Call sign	Name / Owner / Manager	Tonnage / Class	Built / Builder / Dimensions	Type / Cargo	Machinery
9640516 *UBFI4* -	**VF TANKER-3** **OJSC 'VEB-Leasing'** VF Tanker Ltd *St Petersburg* *Russia* MMSI: 273353450	**5,075** Class: RS 2,026 7,004	**2012-05 Sudostroitelnyy Zavod "Krasnoye Sormovo" — Nizhniy Novgorod** Yd No: 3 Loa 140.85 (BB) Br ex 16.86 Dght 4.200 Lbp 136.29 Br md 16.70 Dpth 6.00 Welded, 1 dk	**(A13B2TP) Products Tanker** Double Hull (13F) Liq: 7,828; Liq (Oil): 8,100 Compartments: 6 Wing Ta, 2 Wing Slop Ta, Wing ER 6 Cargo Pump (s): 6x200m³/hr Ice Capable	**2 oil engines** reduction geared to sc. shaft (s) driving 2 Directional propellers Total Power: 2,160kW (2,936hp) 10.0kn Wartsila 6L20 2 x 4 Stroke 6 Cy. 200 x 280 each-1080kW (1468bhp) Wartsila Finland Oy-Finland AuxGen: 3 x 296kW a.c Thrusters: 1 Thwart. FP thruster (f) Fuel: 311.0 (d.f.)
9640528 *UBFI5* -	**VF TANKER-4** **OJSC 'VEB-Leasing'** VF Tanker Ltd *St Petersburg* *Russia* MMSI: 273354450	**5,075** Class: RS 2,026 7,031	**2012-06 Sudostroitelnyy Zavod "Krasnoye Sormovo" — Nizhniy Novgorod** Yd No: 4 Loa 140.85 (BB) Br ex 16.86 Dght 4.200 Lbp 136.29 Br md 16.70 Dpth 6.00 Welded, 1 dk	**(A13B2TP) Products Tanker** Double Hull (13F) Liq: 7,828; Liq (Oil): 8,100 Compartments: 6 Wing Ta, 2 Wing Slop Ta, Wing ER 2 Cargo Pump (s): 2x200m³/hr	**2 oil engines** reduction geared to sc. shaft (s) driving 2 Directional propellers Total Power: 2,160kW (2,936hp) 10.0kn Wartsila 6L20 2 x 4 Stroke 6 Cy. 200 x 280 each-1080kW (1468bhp) Wartsila Finland Oy-Finland AuxGen: 3 x 296kW a.c Thrusters: 1 Thwart. FP thruster (f) Fuel: 311.0 (d.f.)
9640530 *UBFI6* -	**VF TANKER-5** **OJSC 'VEB-Leasing'** VF Tanker Ltd SatCom: Inmarsat C 427305458 *St Petersburg* *Russia* MMSI: 273355450	**5,075** Class: RS 2,026 7,032	**2012-07 Sudostroitelnyy Zavod "Krasnoye Sormovo" — Nizhniy Novgorod** Yd No: 5 Loa 140.85 (BB) Br ex 16.86 Dght 4.200 Lbp 136.29 Br md 16.70 Dpth 6.00 Welded, 1 dk	**(A13B2TP) Products Tanker** Double Hull (13F) Liq: 7,828; Liq (Oil): 8,100 Compartments: 6 Wing Ta, 2 Wing Slop Ta, ER 2 Cargo Pump (s): 2x200m³/hr	**2 oil engines** reduction geared to sc. shaft (s) driving 2 Directional propellers Total Power: 2,160kW (2,936hp) 10.0kn Wartsila 6L20 2 x 4 Stroke 6 Cy. 200 x 280 each-1080kW (1468bhp) Wartsila Finland Oy-Finland AuxGen: 3 x 296kW a.c Thrusters: 1 Thwart. FP thruster (f) Fuel: 311.0 (d.f.)
9640542 *UBMI7* -	**VF TANKER-6** ex Krasnoye Sormovo 6 *-2012* **OJSC 'VEB-Leasing'** VF Tanker Ltd *St Petersburg* *Russia* MMSI: 273359560	**5,075** Class: RS 2,026 7,033	**2012-08 Sudostroitelnyy Zavod "Krasnoye Sormovo" — Nizhniy Novgorod** Yd No: 6 Loa 140.85 (BB) Br ex 16.86 Dght 4.200 Lbp 136.29 Br md 16.70 Dpth 6.00 Welded, 1 dk	**(A13B2TP) Products Tanker** Double Hull (13F) Liq: 7,828; Liq (Oil): 8,100 Compartments: 6 Wing Ta, 2 Wing Slop Ta, ER 2 Cargo Pump (s): 2x200m³/hr Ice Capable	**2 oil engines** reduction geared to sc. shaft (s) driving 2 Directional propellers Total Power: 2,160kW (2,936hp) 10.0kn Wartsila 6L20 2 x 4 Stroke 6 Cy. 200 x 280 each-1080kW (1468bhp) Wartsila Finland Oy-Finland AuxGen: 3 x 296kW a.c Thrusters: 1 Thwart. FP thruster (f) Fuel: 311.0
9640554 *UBMI8* -	**VF TANKER-7** **OJSC 'VEB-Leasing'** VF Tanker Ltd *St Petersburg* *Russia* MMSI: 273350660	**5,075** Class: RS 2,026 7,036	**2012-09 Sudostroitelnyy Zavod "Krasnoye Sormovo" — Nizhniy Novgorod** Yd No: 7 Loa 140.85 (BB) Br ex 16.86 Dght 4.200 Lbp 136.29 Br md 16.70 Dpth 6.00 Welded, 1 dk	**(A13B2TP) Products Tanker** Double Hull (13F) Liq: 7,828; Liq (Oil): 8,100 Compartments: 6 Wing Ta, 2 Wing Slop Ta, Wing ER 2 Cargo Pump (s): 2x200m³/hr	**2 oil engines** reduction geared to sc. shafts driving 2 Directional propellers Total Power: 2,160kW (2,936hp) 10.0kn Wartsila 6L20 2 x 4 Stroke 6 Cy. 200 x 280 each-1080kW (1468bhp) Wartsila Finland Oy-Finland AuxGen: 3 x 296kW a.c Thrusters: 1 Thwart. FP thruster (f) Fuel: 310.0
9640566 *UGBI* -	**VF TANKER-8** **OJSC 'VEB-Leasing'** VF Tanker Ltd *St Petersburg* *Russia* MMSI: 273358860	**5,075** Class: RS 2,026 7,017	**2012-10 Sudostroitelnyy Zavod "Krasnoye Sormovo" — Nizhniy Novgorod** Yd No: 8 Loa 140.85 (BB) Br ex 16.86 Dght 4.200 Lbp 136.29 Br md 16.70 Dpth 6.00 Welded, 1 dk	**(A13B2TP) Products Tanker** Double Hull (13F) Liq: 7,828; Liq (Oil): 8,100 Compartments: 6 Wing Ta, 2 Wing Slop Ta, Wing ER 2 Cargo Pump (s): 2x200m³/hr Ice Capable	**2 oil engines** reduction geared to sc. shaft (s) driving 2 Directional propellers Total Power: 2,400kW (3,264hp) 10.0kn Wartsila 6L20 2 x 4 Stroke 6 Cy. 200 x 280 each-1200kW (1632bhp) Wartsila Finland Oy-Finland AuxGen: 3 x 296kW a.c Thrusters: 1 Thwart. FP thruster (f) Fuel: 310.0
9640578 *UBSI5* -	**VF TANKER-9** **OJSC 'VEB-Leasing'** VF Tanker Ltd *St Petersburg* *Russia* MMSI: 273355270	**5,075** Class: RS 2,026 7,020	**2012-11 Sudostroitelnyy Zavod "Krasnoye Sormovo" — Nizhniy Novgorod** Yd No: 9 Loa 140.85 (BB) Br ex 16.85 Dght 4.200 Lbp 136.29 Br md 16.80 Dpth 6.00 Welded, 1 dk	**(A13B2TP) Products Tanker** Double Hull (13F) Liq: 7,828; Liq (Oil): 8,100 Compartments: 6 Wing Ta, 2 Wing Slop Ta, Wing ER 2 Cargo Pump (s): 2x200m³/hr Ice Capable	**2 oil engines** reduction geared to sc. shaft (s) driving 2 Directional propellers Total Power: 1,766kW (2,402hp) 10.0kn Wartsila 6L20 2 x 4 Stroke 6 Cy. 200 x 280 each-883kW (1201bhp) Wartsila Finland Oy-Finland AuxGen: 3 x 296kW a.c Thrusters: 1 Thwart. FP thruster (f) Fuel: 310.0
9645009 *UBRI8* -	**VF TANKER-11** **VF Tanker-Invest Ltd** VF Tanker Ltd *St Petersburg* *Russia* MMSI: 273357860	**5,075** Class: RS 2,035 6,980	**2012-07 OAO Okskaya Sudoverf — Navashino** Yd No: 2701 Loa 140.85 (BB) Br ex 16.86 Dght 4.200 Lbp 137.10 Br md 16.70 Dpth 6.00 Welded, 1 dk	**(A13B2TP) Products Tanker** Double Hull (13F) Liq: 7,828; Liq (Oil): 7,828 Compartments: 3 Wing Ta, 3 Wing Ta, ER	**2 oil engines** reduction geared to sc. shaft driving 2 Directional propellers Total Power: 2,400kW (3,264hp) 10.0kn Wartsila 6L20 2 x 4 Stroke 6 Cy. 200 x 280 each-1200kW (1632bhp) AuxGen: 3 x 284kW a.c Thrusters: 1 Tunnel thruster (f) Fuel: 310.0
9645011 *UBSI2* -	**VF TANKER-12** **VF Tanker-Invest Ltd** VF Tanker Ltd *St Petersburg* *Russia* MMSI: 273358170	**5,075** Class: RS 2,026 7,025	**2012-08 OAO Okskaya Sudoverf — Navashino** Yd No: 2702 Loa 140.85 (BB) Br ex 16.86 Dght 4.200 Lbp 137.10 Br md 16.70 Dpth 6.00 Welded, 1 dk	**(A13B2TP) Products Tanker** Double Hull (13F) Liq: 7,828; Liq (Oil): 7,828 Cargo Heating Coils Compartments: 6 Ta, ER Ice Capable	**2 oil engines** reduction geared to sc. shafts driving 2 Directional propellers Total Power: 2,400kW (3,264hp) 10.0kn Wartsila 6L20 2 x 4 Stroke 6 Cy. 200 x 280 each-1200kW (1632bhp) AuxGen: 3 x 284kW a.c Thrusters: 1 Tunnel thruster (f)
9645023 *UBSI3* -	**VF TANKER-13** **VF Tanker-Invest Ltd** VF Tanker Ltd *St Petersburg* *Russia* MMSI: 273359170	**5,075** Class: RS 2,026 7,026	**2012-10 OAO Okskaya Sudoverf — Navashino** Yd No: 2703 Loa 140.85 (BB) Br ex 16.86 Dght 4.200 Lbp 137.10 Br md 16.70 Dpth 6.00 Welded, 1 dk	**(A13B2TP) Products Tanker** Double Hull (13F) Liq: 7,828; Liq (Oil): 7,828 Compartments: 6 Ta, ER Ice Capable	**2 oil engines** reduction geared to sc. shafts driving 2 Directional propellers Total Power: 2,400kW (3,264hp) 10.0kn Wartsila 6L20 2 x 4 Stroke 6 Cy. 200 x 280 each-1200kW (1632bhp) Wartsila Finland Oy-Finland AuxGen: 3 x 284kW a.c Thrusters: 1 Tunnel thruster (f) Fuel: 380.0 (d.f.)
9645035 *UBSI4* -	**VF TANKER-14** **VF Tanker-Invest Ltd** VF Tanker Ltd *St Petersburg* *Russia* MMSI: 273350270	**5,075** Class: RS 2,026 7,025	**2012-11 OAO Okskaya Sudoverf — Navashino** Yd No: 2704 Loa 140.85 (BB) Br ex 16.86 Dght 4.200 Lbp 137.10 Br md 16.80 Dpth 6.00 Welded, 1 dk	**(A13B2TP) Products Tanker** Double Hull (13F) Liq: 7,828; Liq (Oil): 7,828 Cargo Heating Coils Compartments: 6 Ta, ER Ice Capable	**2 oil engines** reduction geared to sc. shafts driving 2 Directional propellers Total Power: 2,400kW (3,264hp) 10.0kn Wartsila 6L20 2 x 4 Stroke 6 Cy. 200 x 280 each-1200kW (1632bhp) Wartsila Finland Oy-Finland AuxGen: 3 x 284kW a.c Thrusters: 1 Tunnel thruster (f) Fuel: 311.0
9645047 *UBUV* -	**VF TANKER-15** **VF Tanker-Invest Ltd** VF Tanker Ltd *St Petersburg* *Russia* MMSI: 273353180	**5,075** Class: RS 2,026 7,026	**2012-12 OAO Okskaya Sudoverf — Navashino** Yd No: 2705 Loa 140.85 (BB) Br ex 16.86 Dght 4.200 Lbp 137.10 Br md 16.70 Dpth 6.00 Welded, 1 dk	**(A13B2TP) Products Tanker** Double Hull (13F) Liq: 7,828; Liq (Oil): 7,828 Cargo Heating Coils Compartments: 6 Ta, ER Ice Capable	**2 oil engines** reduction geared to sc. shafts driving 2 Directional propellers Total Power: 2,400kW (3,264hp) 10.0kn Wartsila 6L20 2 x 4 Stroke 6 Cy. 200 x 280 each-1200kW (1632bhp) Wartsila Finland Oy-Finland AuxGen: 3 x 284kW a.c Thrusters: 1 Tunnel thruster (f) Fuel: 310.0
9645059 *UDML* -	**VF TANKER-16** **VF Tanker Ltd** - *St Petersburg* *Russia* MMSI: 273354680	**5,075** Class: RS 2,025 7,033	**2013-05 OAO Okskaya Sudoverf — Navashino** Yd No: 2706 Loa 140.85 (BB) Br ex 16.86 Dght 4.200 Lbp 137.10 Br md 16.70 Dpth 6.00 Welded, 1 dk	**(A13B2TP) Products Tanker** Double Hull (13F) Liq: 7,828; Liq (Oil): 7,828 Compartments: 6 Ta, ER	**2 oil engines** reduction geared to sc. shafts driving 2 Directional propellers Total Power: 2,400kW (3,264hp) 10.0kn Wartsila 6L20 2 x 4 Stroke 6 Cy. 200 x 280 each-1200kW (1632bhp) AuxGen: 3 x 292kW a.c Thrusters: 1 Tunnel thruster (f) Fuel: 310.0

IMO / Call sign / Flag	Name / Owner	Tonnage	Class	Build / Dimensions	Type / Cargo	Machinery
9645061 *UDHR* -	**VF TANKER-17** **VF Tanker-Invest Ltd** VF Tanker Ltd *St Petersburg* *Russia* MMSI: 273355680	**5,075** 2,026 7,013	Class: RS	**2013-04 OAO Okskaya Sudoverf — Navashino** Yd No: 2707 Loa 140.85 (BB) Br ex 16.86 Dght 4.200 Lbp 137.10 Br md 16.70 Dpth 6.00 Welded, 1 dk	**(A12B2TR) Chemical/Products Tanker** Double Hull (13F) Liq: 7,828; Liq (Oil): 7,828 Compartments: 6 Ta, ER	**2 oil engines** reduction geared to sc. shafts driving 2 Directional propellers Total Power: 2,400kW (3,264hp) 10.0kn Wartsila 6L20 2 x 4 Stroke 6 Cy. 200 x 280 each-1200kW (1632bhp) Wartsila Finland Oy-Finland AuxGen: 2 x 284kW a.c Thrusters: 1 Tunnel thruster (f) Fuel: 310.0
9645073 *UAYV* -	**VF TANKER-18** **VF Tanker-Invest Ltd** VF Tanker Ltd *St Petersburg* *Russia* MMSI: 273357390	**5,075** 2,026 7,025	Class: RS	**2013-06 OAO Okskaya Sudoverf — Navashino** Yd No: 2708 Loa 140.85 (BB) Br ex 16.86 Dght 4.200 Lbp 137.10 Br md 16.70 Dpth 6.00 Welded, 1 dk	**(A13B2TP) Products Tanker** Double Hull (13F) Liq: 7,828; Liq (Oil): 7,828 Compartments: 6 Ta, ER	**2 oil engines** reduction geared to sc. shafts driving 2 Directional propellers Total Power: 2,400kW (3,264hp) 10.0kn Wartsila 6L20 2 x 4 Stroke 6 Cy. 200 x 280 each-1200kW (1632bhp) Wartsila Finland Oy-Finland Thrusters: 1 Tunnel thruster (f) Fuel: 311.0 (d.f.)
9645085 *UAYF* -	**VF TANKER-19** **VF Tanker-Invest Ltd** VF Tanker Ltd *St Petersburg* *Russia* MMSI: 273356390	**5,075** 2,026 7,016	Class: RS	**2013-07 OAO Okskaya Sudoverf — Navashino** Yd No: 2709 Loa 140.85 (BB) Br ex 16.86 Dght 4.200 Lbp 137.10 Br md 16.70 Dpth 6.00 Welded, 1 dk	**(A12B2TR) Chemical/Products Tanker** Double Hull (13F) Liq: 7,828; Liq (Oil): 7,828 Compartments: 6 Ta, ER	**2 oil engines** reduction geared to sc. shafts driving 2 Directional propellers Total Power: 2,400kW (3,264hp) 10.0kn Wartsila 6L20 2 x 4 Stroke 6 Cy. 200 x 280 each-1200kW (1632bhp) Wartsila Finland Oy-Finland AuxGen: 3 x 284kW a.c Thrusters: 1 Tunnel thruster (f) Fuel: 311.0 (d.f.)
9645097 *UAYW* -	**VF TANKER-20** **VF Tanker Ltd** - *St Petersburg* *Russia* MMSI: 273358390	**5,075** 2,026 7,031	Class: RS	**2013-07 OAO Okskaya Sudoverf — Navashino** Yd No: 2710 Loa 140.85 (BB) Br ex 16.86 Dght 4.200 Lbp 137.10 Br md 16.70 Dpth 6.00 Welded, 1 dk	**(A13B2TP) Products Tanker** Double Hull (13F) Liq: 7,828; Liq (Oil): 7,828 Cargo Heating Coils Compartments: 6 Ta, ER Ice Capable	**2 oil engines** reduction geared to sc. shafts driving 2 Directional propellers Total Power: 2,400kW (3,264hp) 10.0kn Wartsila 6L20 2 x 4 Stroke 6 Cy. 200 x 280 each-1200kW (1632bhp) Wartsila Finland Oy-Finland AuxGen: 3 x 284kW a.c Thrusters: 1 Tunnel thruster (f) Fuel: 300.0
9645102 *UAYY* -	**VF TANKER-21** **VF Tanker Ltd** - *St Petersburg* *Russia* MMSI: 273359390	**5,075** 2,026 7,029	Class: RS	**2013-09 OAO Okskaya Sudoverf — Navashino** Yd No: 2711 Loa 140.85 (BB) Br ex 16.86 Dght 4.200 Lbp 137.10 Br md 16.70 Dpth 6.00 Welded, 1 dk	**(A13B2TP) Products Tanker** Double Hull (13F) Liq: 7,828; Liq (Oil): 7,828 Cargo Heating Coils Compartments: 7 Ta, ER Ice Capable	**2 oil engines** reduction geared to sc. shafts driving 2 Directional propellers Total Power: 2,400kW (3,264hp) 10.0kn Wartsila 6L20 2 x 4 Stroke 6 Cy. 200 x 280 each-1200kW (1632bhp) Wartsila Finland Oy-Finland AuxGen: 3 x 284kW a.c Thrusters: 1 Tunnel thruster (f) Fuel: 300.0 (d.f.)
9645114 *UHTZ* -	**VF TANKER-22** **VF Tanker-Invest Ltd** VF Tanker Ltd *St Petersburg* *Russia* MMSI: 273333670	**5,075** 2,028 7,030	Class: RS	**2013-10 OAO Okskaya Sudoverf — Navashino** Yd No: 2712 Loa 140.85 (BB) Br ex 16.86 Dght 4.200 Lbp 137.10 Br md 16.70 Dpth 6.00 Welded, 1 dk	**(A13B2TP) Products Tanker** Double Hull (13F) Liq: 7,828; Liq (Oil): 7,828 Cargo Heating Coils Compartments: 6 Wing Ta, 6 Wing Ta, ER Ice Capable	**2 oil engines** reduction geared to sc. shafts driving 2 Directional propellers Total Power: 2,400kW (3,264hp) 10.0kn Wartsila 6L20 2 x 4 Stroke 6 Cy. 200 x 280 each-1200kW (1632bhp) Wartsila Finland Oy-Finland AuxGen: 3 x 284kW a.c Thrusters: 1 Tunnel thruster (f) Fuel: 310.0
8503814 *YYKN* -	**VFM ALITA** *ex* MSC Maxie *-2011* *ex* Mekong Swift *-2005* *ex* Sepik River *-2000* *ex* Baltimar Nereus *-2000* *ex* Lirena *-1997* *ex* Azapa *-1996* *ex* Lirena *-1995* *ex* Pacheco *-1992* *ex* ScanDutch Corsica *-1990* *ex* Pacheco *-1989* *ex* Gracechurch Gem *-1989* *ex* Pacheco *-1988* *ex* Gerrans Bay *-1987* *ex* Pacheco *-1986* **Compania Naviera Maxie SA** Venezuela Feeder Maritime CA SatCom: Inmarsat C 477531910 *Puerto Cabello* *Venezuela* MMSI: 775319000 Official number: ADKN - 4214	**3,790** 2,097 4,250 T/cm 13.6	Class: (LR) (BV) ✠ Classed LR until 3/11/10	**1986-01 E.J. Smit & Zoon's Scheepswerven B.V. — Westerbroek** Yd No: 831 Loa 106.61 (BB) Br ex 16.13 Dght 6.350 Lbp 98.00 Br md 15.85 Dpth 8.51 Welded, 1 dk	**(A31A2GX) General Cargo Ship** Double Sides Entire Compartment Length Grain: 7,138 TEU 354 C Ho 144 TEU C Dk 210 TEU incl 20 ref C. Compartments: 1 Ho, ER 3 Ha: (12.5 x 12.0)2 (25.3 x 12.0)ER Cranes: 2x35t Ice Capable	**1 oil engine** sr geared to sc. shaft driving 1 CP propeller Total Power: 3,000kW (4,079hp) 14.8kn Wartsila 8R32 1 x 4 Stroke 8 Cy. 320 x 350 3000kW (4079bhp) Oy Wartsila Ab-Finland AuxGen: 3 x 272kW 440V 60Hz a.c Thrusters: 1 Thwart. FP thruster (f) Fuel: 106.0 (d.f.) 341.0 (r.f.) 11.5pd
9164859 *3FRS4* -	**VFM ANDRES** *ex* Yong Cai *-2013* **CIA Naviera VFM Andres SA** Venezuela Feeder Maritime CA *Panama* *Panama* MMSI: 353033000 Official number: 44988PEXT	**9,810** 4,397 14,080 T/cm 28.0	Class: (LR) (CC) Classed LR until 15/2/14	**1998-12 Peene-Werft GmbH — Wolgast** Yd No: 485 Loa 135.50 (BB) Br ex - Dght 9.050 Lbp 127.04 Br md 24.50 Dpth 12.20 Welded, 1 dk	**(A31A2GX) General Cargo Ship** Grain: 14,700 TEU 810 C Ho 300 TEU C Dk 510 TEU incl 200 ref C. Compartments: 4 Cell Ho, ER 4 Ha: (12.6 x 10.4)2 (12.6 x 20.4) (39.9 x 20.4)ER Cranes: 2x40t Ice Capable	**1 oil engine** driving 1 CP propeller Total Power: 9,360kW (12,726hp) 17.1kn Sulzer 6RTA52U 1 x 2 Stroke 6 Cy. 520 x 1800 9360kW (12726bhp) Dieselmotorenwerk Rostock GmbH-Rostock AuxGen: 3 x 600kW 450V 60Hz a.c Thrusters: 1 Thwart. CP thruster (f) Fuel: 200.0 (d.f.) (Heating Coils) 1000.0 (r.f.) 33.0pd
9164861 *YYNI* -	**VFM EDUARDO** *ex* Yong Da *-2013* **CIA Naviera VFM Eduardo SA** Venezuela Feeder Maritime CA *Venezuela* MMSI: 775348000	**9,810** 4,397 14,082 T/cm 28.0	Class: (LR) (CC) Classed LR until 19/2/14	**1999-04 Peene-Werft GmbH — Wolgast** Yd No: 486 Loa 135.50 (BB) Br ex - Dght 9.050 Lbp 127.40 Br md 24.50 Dpth 12.20 Welded, 1 dk	**(A31A2GX) General Cargo Ship** Grain: 14,700 TEU 810 C Ho 300 TEU C Dk 510 TEU incl 200 ref C. Compartments: 4 Ho, ER 4 Ha: (12.6 x 10.4)2 (12.6 x 20.4) (39.9 x 20.4)ER Cranes: 2x40t Ice Capable	**1 oil engine** driving 1 CP propeller Total Power: 9,360kW (12,726hp) 17.1kn Sulzer 6RTA52U 1 x 2 Stroke 6 Cy. 520 x 1800 9360kW (12726bhp) Dieselmotorenwerk Rostock GmbH-Rostock AuxGen: 1 x 1400kW 450V 60Hz a.c, 3 x 600kW 450V 60Hz a.c Thrusters: 1 Thwart. CP thruster (f) Fuel: 172.6 (d.f.) (Heating Coils) 920.0 (r.f.) 36.0pd
7126176 *DUH2052* -	**VG 1** *ex* Andy Two *-2013* *ex* Princess Joan *-2010* *ex* Tachibana *-1987* **Vicent Vda De Garcia** - *Cebu* *Philippines* Official number: CEB1001285	*148* 100 27	Class: (NK)	**1971 KK Izumi Zosensho — Kitakyushu** Yd No: 124 Loa 31.98 Br ex 6.23 Dght 2.328 Lbp 29.01 Br md 6.20 Dpth 2.67 Welded, 1 dk	**(A37B2PS) Passenger Ship** Passengers: 160	**1 oil engine** driving 1 FP propeller Total Power: 441kW (600hp) 12.0kn Niigata 6L20AX 1 x 4 Stroke 6 Cy. 200 x 260 441kW (600bhp) Niigata Engineering Co Ltd-Japan AuxGen: 2 x 20kW a.c
9489675 *H04770* -	**VI-NAIS** **Coast Shipline Ltd** MMS Shipmanagement Inc *Panama* *Panama* MMSI: 356907000 Official number: 3478709	**487** 146 587		**2007-11 Russell Portier, Inc. — Chauvin, La** Yd No: 157 Loa 57.92 Br ex 11.62 Dght 2.260 Lbp 54.88 Br md 11.59 Dpth 3.05 Welded, 1 dk	**(A35A2RR) Ro-Ro Cargo Ship** Bow ramp (centre)	**2 oil engines** geared to sc. shafts driving 2 Propellers Total Power: 1,250kW (1,700hp) 10.0kn Caterpillar 2 x 4 Stroke each-625kW (850bhp) Caterpillar Inc-USA
6705298 - -	**VIA** *ex* Key *-2003* *ex* Bremer Saturn *-1984* **-** -	**1,219** 531 1,115	Class: (GL)	**1967-02 Schiffbau Gesellschaft Unterweser AG — Bremerhaven** Yd No: 457 Loa 68.15 Br ex 10.90 Dght 3.757 Lbp 62.03 Br md 10.80 Dpth 6.18 Welded, 2 dks	**(A31A2GX) General Cargo Ship** Grain: 2,586; Bale: 2,392 Compartments: 1 Ho, ER 2 Ha: (19.8 x 7.0) (11.9 x 7.0)ER Cranes: 1x7t Ice Capable	**1 oil engine** driving 1 FP propeller Total Power: 736kW (1,001hp) 11.8kn Deutz RBV6M545 1 x 4 Stroke 6 Cy. 320 x 450 736kW (1001bhp) Kloeckner Humboldt Deutz AG-West Germany AuxGen: 2 x 70kW 230/440V 50Hz a.c Fuel: 48.0 (d.f.)

IMO / Call sign / Fishing no.	Name / Owner / Port	Tonnage	Class	Builder / Dimensions	Type / Capacity	Machinery
9019066 *ICNL* -	**VIA ADRIATICO** **Compagnia Italiana Di Navigazione Srl** - *Palermo* *Italy* MMSI: 247000400 Official number: 142	**14,398** 4,319 7,330 T/cm 27.7	Class: RI (LR) ✠ Classed LR until 7/4/94	**1992-11 Tille Scheepsbouw B.V. (Frisian Shipyard) — Harlingen (Hull)** Yd No: 5 286 **1992-11 van der Giessen-de Noord BV — Krimpen a/d IJssel** Yd No: 958 Loa 150.38 (BB) Br ex 23.43 Dght 6.015 Lbp 137.33 Br md 23.40 Dpth 13.40 Welded, 2 dks	**(A36A2PR) Passenger/Ro-Ro Ship (Vehicles)** Passengers: cabins: 25; berths: 74; driver berths: 74 Stern door/ramp Len: 12.00 Wid: 15.50 Swl: 100 Lane-Len: 1650 Lane-clr ht: 4.90 Trailers: 141	**2 oil engines** with flexible couplings & sr geared to sc. shafts driving 2 CP propellers Total Power: 18,000kW (24,472hp) 18.5kn Sulzer 8ZAL40S 2 x 4 Stroke 8 Cy. 400 x 560 each-9000kW (12236bhp) Zaklady Urzadzen Technicznych'Zgoda' SA-Poland AuxGen: 2 x 800kW 440V 60Hz a.c, 2 x 800kW 440V 60Hz a.c Thrusters: 1 Thwart. CP thruster (f)
9334088 *CBVU* -	**VIA AUSTRALIS** **Transportes Maritimos Via Australis SA** Navarino Administradora de Naves SA *Valparaiso* *Chile* MMSI: 725003280 Official number: 3133	*2,716* 898 307	Class: AB	**2005-10 Astilleros y Servicios Navales S.A. (ASENAV) — Valdivia** Yd No: 145 Loa 72.30 Br ex - Dght 2.740 Lbp 63.60 Br md 13.40 Dpth 4.50 Welded, 1 dk	**(A37A2PC) Passenger/Cruise** Passengers: cabins: 64; berths: 136	**2 oil engines** geared to sc. shafts driving 2 FP propellers Total Power: 1,250kW (1,700hp) Cummins KTA-38-M0 2 x Vee 4 Stroke 12 Cy. 159 x 159 each-625kW (850bhp) Cummins Engine Co Inc-USA Thrusters: 1 Tunnel thruster (f)
8812186 *FGPJ* CC 752564	**VIA AVENIR** **Compagnie Saupiquet** - SatCom: Inmarsat C 422812810 *Concarneau* *France* MMSI: 228128000 Official number: 752564	*1,283* 644 1,886	Class: BV	**1990-10 Campbell Industries — San Diego, Ca** Yd No: 147 Loa 78.34 (BB) Br ex 13.69 Dght 5.560 Lbp 68.28 Br md 13.56 Dpth 5.64 Welded, 1 dk	**(B11B2FV) Fishing Vessel** Ins: 1,643	**1 oil engine** with clutches, flexible couplings & sr geared to sc. shaft driving 1 FP propeller Total Power: 3,089kW (4,200hp) Caterpillar 3612TA 1 x Vee 4 Stroke 12 Cy. 280 x 300 3089kW (4200bhp) Caterpillar Inc-USA Thrusters: 1 Thwart. FP thruster (f)
9017862 *FGRS* CC 791294	**VIA EUROS** *ex* Rio Mare *-1995* **Compagnie Saupiquet** - SatCom: Inmarsat B 322816820 *Concarneau* *France* MMSI: 228168000 Official number: 791294	**1,780** 534 1,361	Class: BV (RI)	**1991-11 Campbell Industries — San Diego, Ca** Yd No: 149 Loa - Br ex - Dght 5.540 Lbp 68.33 Br md 13.26 Dpth 8.13 Welded	**(B11B2FV) Fishing Vessel** Ins: 1,644	**1 oil engine** with clutches, flexible couplings & sr geared to sc. shaft driving 1 FP propeller Total Power: 3,089kW (4,200hp) 17.5kn Caterpillar 3612TA 1 x Vee 4 Stroke 12 Cy. 280 x 300 3089kW (4200bhp) Caterpillar Inc-USA AuxGen: 3 x 376kW 380V 50Hz a.c Thrusters: 1 Thwart. FP thruster (f)
7125108 *FHBJ* CC 622908	**VIA HARMATAN** *ex* Harmattan *-1985* *ex* Agustin Primero *-1978* **Compagnie Saupiquet** - SatCom: Inmarsat B 322784620 *Concarneau* *France* MMSI: 227846000 Official number: 622908	*1,359* 708 1,459	Class: BV	**1972 Maritima de Axpe S.A. — Bilbao** Yd No: 64 Loa 64.60 Br ex 12.83 Dght 5.995 Lbp 58.65 Br md 12.81 Dpth 8.56 Welded, 2 dks	**(B11A2FT) Trawler**	**1 oil engine** driving 1 FP propeller Total Power: 2,207kW (3,001hp) 15.0kn MaK 6MU551AK 1 x 4 Stroke 6 Cy. 450 x 550 2207kW (3001bhp) MaK Maschinenbau GmbH-Kiel Fuel: 404.0 (d.f.)
7411258 *9LD2472* -	**VIA MARE** *ex* Begonia *-2005* *ex* European Pathfinder *-2002* *ex* Panther *-1998* *ex* European Clearway *-1996* **Akgunler Isletmeleri Sti Ltd** - *Freetown* *Sierra Leone* MMSI: 667005172 Official number: SL105172	**8,023** 2,406 3,927	Class: BV (LR) (NV) ✠ Classed LR until 29/10/93	**1976-01 Schichau-Unterweser AG — Bremerhaven** Yd No: 2263 Loa 118.15 Br ex 21.60 Dght 5.032 Lbp 111.56 Br md 19.91 Dpth 11.66 Welded, 2 dks	**(A36A2PR) Passenger/Ro-Ro Ship (Vehicles)** Passengers: unberthed: 53; berths: 54; driver berths: 54 Bow door/ramp Stern door/ramp Lane-Len: 1000 Cars: 30, Trailers: 76 Ice Capable	**2 oil engines** with clutches, flexible couplings & sr geared to sc. shafts driving 2 CP propellers Total Power: 8,386kW (11,402hp) 18.4kn Werkspoor 9TM410 2 x 4 Stroke 9 Cy. 410 x 470 each-4193kW (5701bhp) Stork Werkspoor Diesel BV-Netherlands AuxGen: 4 x 552kW 400V 50Hz a.c Thrusters: 2 Thwart. FP thruster (f)
9017850 *FGRY* CC 790948	**VIA MISTRAL** **Compagnie Saupiquet** - SatCom: Inmarsat B 322816720 *Concarneau* *France* MMSI: 228167000 Official number: 790948	*1,284* 645 1,500	Class: BV	**1991-06 Campbell Industries — San Diego, Ca** Yd No: 148 Loa 77.88 (BB) Br ex 13.71 Dght 5.540 Lbp 67.88 Br md 13.68 Dpth 8.00 Welded	**(B11B2FV) Fishing Vessel** Ins: 1,644	**1 oil engine** with clutches, flexible couplings & sr geared to sc. shaft driving 1 FP propeller Total Power: 3,089kW (4,200hp) 17.5kn Caterpillar 3612TA 1 x Vee 4 Stroke 12 Cy. 280 x 300 3089kW (4200bhp) Caterpillar Inc-USA Thrusters: 1 Thwart. FP thruster (f)
6708719 - -	**VIA ZEPHIR** *ex* Ancolie *-1992* *ex* Tonton Pierre *-1977* *ex* Ar Gueveur *-1974* *ex* Guidimaka *-1968* - -	**252** 75 122	Class: (BV)	**1967 Soc Industrielle et Commerciale de Consts Navales (SICCNa) — St-Malo** Yd No: 86 Loa 33.25 Br ex 7.93 Dght 3.001 Lbp 28.20 Br md 7.50 Dpth 5.95 Welded, 2 dks	**(B11B2FV) Fishing Vessel** Grain: 163 Compartments: 1 Ho, ER 2 Ha: 2 (1.3 x 1.3)ER	**1 oil engine** driving 1 FP propeller Total Power: 736kW (1,001hp) 12.5kn MGO 16V175ASHR 1 x Vee 4 Stroke 16 Cy. 175 x 180 736kW (1001bhp) (new engine 1974) Societe Alsacienne de ConstructionsMecaniques (SACM)-France Fuel: 73.5 (d.f.)
9010723 *EPBI* -	**VIANA** *ex* Iran Ghadeer *-2010* **Khazar Sea Shipping Lines** - SatCom: Inmarsat C 442211010 *Bandar Anzali* *Iran* MMSI: 422111000	**3,638** 1,235 3,955	Class: (RS) (NV)	**1992-08 Rousse Shipyard Ltd — Rousse** Yd No: 381 Loa 128.25 Br ex 13.60 Dght 4.250 Lbp 122.00 Br md 13.40 Dpth 6.20 Welded, 1 dk	**(A31A2GX) General Cargo Ship** TEU 116 C. 116/20' Compartments: 4 Ho, ER 4 Ha: (19.1 x 10.1)3 (19.1 x 12.7)ER Ice Capable	**2 oil engines** sr geared to sc. shafts driving 2 FP propellers Total Power: 1,762kW (2,396hp) 10.7kn S.K.L. 8NVD48A-2U 2 x 4 Stroke 8 Cy. 320 x 480 each-881kW (1198bhp) SKL Motoren u. Systemtechnik AG-Magdeburg AuxGen: 2 x 80kW 380V 50Hz a.c Thrusters: 1 Thwart. FP thruster (f) Fuel: 279.0 (d.f.)
8918356 *UUJE* -	**VIANA DO CASTELO** **Ukrainian Danube Shipping Co** - SatCom: Inmarsat C 427214110 *Izmail* *Ukraine* MMSI: 272141000 Official number: 920430	**2,977** 1,490 4,050	Class: UA (RS)	**1992-10 Estaleiros Navais de Viana do Castelo S.A. — Viana do Castelo** Yd No: 173 Loa 88.45 Br ex 15.68 Dght 5.678 Lbp 82.30 Br md 15.50 Dpth 7.10 Welded, 1 dk	**(A31A2GX) General Cargo Ship** Grain: 5,076 TEU 199 C. 199/20' Compartments: 2 Ho, ER 2 Ha: 2 (25.2 x 12.6)ER Cranes: 4x8t Ice Capable	**1 oil engine** with flexible couplings & sr geared to sc. shaft driving 1 CP propeller Total Power: 1,985kW (2,699hp) 12.0kn Wartsila 6R32 1 x 4 Stroke 6 Cy. 320 x 350 1985kW (2699bhp) Wartsila Diesel Oy-Finland Thrusters: 1 Thwart. FP thruster (f)
7386013 *EGNS* -	**VIANTO TERCERO** **Armadora Parleros SL** - *Santander* *Spain* Official number: 3-2482/	**142** 71 -		**1974-09 Astilleros de Santander SA (ASTANDER) — El Astillero** Yd No: 92 Loa 28.40 Br ex - Dght - Lbp 24.41 Br md 6.29 Dpth 3.36 Welded, 1 dk	**(B11A2FT) Trawler**	**1 oil engine** driving 1 FP propeller Total Power: 552kW (750hp) 10.5kn Baudouin DNP12M 1 x Vee 4 Stroke 12 Cy. 150 x 150 552kW (750bhp) Internacional Diesel S.A.-Zumaya
8505408 *JWTU* SF-33-G	**VIBEKE HELENE** *ex* Meilandstind *-2008* *ex* Kamoyfisk *-2000* *ex* Langegovaering *-1991* **Vibeke Helene AS** Egil Uthaug *Bergen* *Norway* MMSI: 257801500	**222** 85 -		**1985-10 Aas Skipsbyggeri AS — Vestnes** Yd No: 124 Loa - Br ex - Dght 3.201 Lbp 22.86 Br md - Dpth - Welded, 1 dk	**(B11B2FV) Fishing Vessel**	**1 oil engine** geared to sc. shaft driving 1 FP propeller Total Power: 530kW (721hp) Mitsubishi S8N-MPTA 1 x 4 Stroke 8 Cy. 160 x 180 530kW (721bhp) Mitsubishi Heavy Industries Ltd-Japan
9048885 *SCRX* -	**VIBERO** **Waxholms Angfartygs AB** *Vaxholm* *Sweden* MMSI: 265520410	**299** 118 50		**1993-03 Oskarshamns Varv AB — Oskarshamn** Yd No: 537 Loa 37.70 Br ex 7.52 Dght 1.280 Lbp - Br md 7.51 Dpth 2.78 Welded, 1 dk	**(A37B2PS) Passenger Ship** Hull Material: Aluminium Alloy Passengers: 340	**3 oil engines** with clutches, flexible couplings & sr reverse geared to sc. shafts driving 3 FP propellers Total Power: 1,764kW (2,397hp) 20.0kn MAN D2842LYE 3 x Vee 4 Stroke 12 Cy. 128 x 142 each-588kW (799bhp) MAN Nutzfahrzeuge AG-Nuernberg AuxGen: 1 x 110kW 380V 50Hz a.c, 1 x 60kW 380V 50Hz a.c Thrusters: 1 Thwart. FP thruster (f)
7344118 *ATTF* -	**VIBHA II** **Bombay Marine Engineering Works Pvt Ltd** *Mormugao* *India* Official number: MRH540	*410* 258 590	Class: IR (AB)	**1975-06 Bombay Marine Engineering Works Pvt. Ltd. — Mumbai** Yd No: 7 Loa 47.50 Br ex - Dght 2.380 Lbp 46.00 Br md 10.25 Dpth 3.00 Welded, 1 dk	**(A31A2GX) General Cargo Ship** Compartments: 1 Ho, ER 1 Ha: (25.2 x 7.0)ER	**2 oil engines** driving 2 FP propellers Total Power: 356kW (484hp) 7.0kn Kirloskar 2 x 4 Stroke 8 Cy. 175 x 220 each-178kW (242bhp) Kirloskar Oil Engines Ltd-India AuxGen: 2 x 4kW
7723261 - -	**VIBHA IV** **Bombay Marine Engineering Works Pvt Ltd** *Mumbai* *India*	*500* 250 700	Class: IR	**1979-05 Bombay Marine Engineering Works Pvt. Ltd. — Mumbai** Yd No: 17 Loa 51.11 Br ex 10.27 Dght 2.252 Lbp 48.11 Br md 10.25 Dpth 3.00 Welded, 1 dk	**(A31A2GX) General Cargo Ship**	**2 oil engines** driving 2 FP propellers Total Power: 346kW (470hp) Kirloskar NRTO-6-M 2 x 4 Stroke 6 Cy. 130 x 152 each-173kW (235bhp) Kirloskar Oil Engines Ltd-India

IMO/Call sign	Name, owners, registry	Tonnage	Class	Builder, dimensions	Type, cargo	Machinery
9189718 *9HLX9* -	**VIBORA** *ex* Orient Success *-2008* **Vibora Marine SA** Medlink Management SA SatCom: Inmarsat C 424914910 *Valletta* *Malta* MMSI: 249149000 Official number: 9189718	**4,947** 2,774 7,224	Class: NK	**1999**-03 Yd No: 02 Loa 99.90 Br ex - Dght 6.314 Lbp 93.50 Br md 19.50 Dpth 8.50 Welded, 1 dk	**(A31A2GX) General Cargo Ship** Grain: 9,779; Bale: 8,909 Compartments: 2 Ho, ER 2 Ha: (24.5 x 11.2) (30.1 x 11.2)ER Derricks: 2x30t,2x25t	**1 oil engine** driving 1 FP propeller Total Power: 3,884kW (5,281hp) 12.3kn B&W 6L35MC 1 x 2 Stroke 6 Cy. 350 x 1050 3884kW (5281bhp) Hitachi Zosen Corp-Japan AuxGen: 2 x 330kW a.c Fuel: 570.0
7372969 *LW6129* -	**VIBRADOR** *ex* Masuei Maru No. 31 *-1992* *ex* Nichifuku Maru *-1981* **Maruba SCA Empresa de Navegacion Maritima** - *Buenos Aires* *Argentina* MMSI: 701006260 Official number: 02477	*250* 72 420	Class: (NK)	**1974**-03 **Kanagawa Zosen — Kobe** Yd No: 132 Loa 33.30 Br ex 9.20 Dght 3.616 Lbp 29.01 Br md 9.17 Dpth 4.20 Riveted\Welded, 1 dk	**(B32A2ST) Tug**	**2 oil engines** geared to sc. shafts driving 2 FP propellers Total Power: 2,354kW (3,200hp) 13.5kn Niigata 8MG25BX 2 x 4 Stroke 8 Cy. 250 x 320 each-1177kW (1600bhp) Niigata Engineering Co Ltd-Japan AuxGen: 2 x 64kW Fuel: 30.0 (d.f.)
1010002 *2BQE2* -	**VIBRANT CURIOSITY** **Vibrant Curiosity Ltd** - SatCom: Inmarsat C 423597583 *London* *United Kingdom* MMSI: 235068366 Official number: 915551	**2,822** 846 -	Class: LR ✠ **100A1** SS 05/2009 SSC Yacht (P), mono, G6 ✠ **LMC** **UMS** Cable: 440.0/34.0 U3 (a)	**2009**-05 **Zwijnenburg BV — Krimpen a/d IJssel** (Hull) Yd No: (704) **2009**-05 **Aluship Technology Sp z oo — Gdansk** (Upper part) Yd No: (704) **2009**-05 **Oceanco Shipyards (Alblasserdam) B.V. — Alblasserdam** Yd No: 704 Loa 85.43 (BB) Br ex 13.80 Dght 3.950 Lbp 76.03 Br md 13.78 Dpth 7.10 Welded, 1 dk	**(X11A2YP) Yacht**	**2 oil engines** with clutches, flexible couplings & sr reverse geared to sc. shafts driving 2 FP propellers Total Power: 7,200kW (9,790hp) M.T.U. 16V595TE70 2 x Vee 4 Stroke 16 Cy. 190 x 210 each-3600kW (4895bhp) MTU Friedrichshafen GmbH-Friedrichshafen AuxGen: 3 x 308kW 400V 50Hz a.c Thrusters: 1 Thwart. FP thruster (f); 1 Directional thruster (a)
8635241 *CZ9716* -	**VIC INGRAHAM** **Northern Transportation Co Ltd** - *Vancouver, BC* *Canada* Official number: 344735	*711* 483 -		**1970**-10 **Allied Shipbuilders Ltd — North Vancouver BC** Yd No: 173 Loa 47.09 Br ex - Dght 1.143 Lbp - Br md 15.24 Dpth 2.89 Welded, 1 dk	**(B32B2SP) Pusher Tug**	**4 oil engines** reduction geared to sc. shafts driving 4 FP propellers Total Power: 3,312kW (4,504hp) Caterpillar D399TA 4 x Vee 4 Stroke 16 Cy. 159 x 203 each-828kW (1126bhp) Caterpillar Tractor Co-USA AuxGen: 2 x 100kW 440V 60Hz a.c Fuel: 200.0 (d.f.)
9579171 *ZGAF5* -	**VICA** **Vica Maritime Ltd** - *George Town* *Cayman Islands (British)* MMSI: 319015400 Official number: 742382	**456** 136 -	Class: AB	**2010**-02 **Azimut-Benetti SpA — Viareggio** Yd No: BV014 Loa 43.60 Br ex 9.26 Dght 2.630 Lbp 36.00 Br md 8.96 Dpth 4.64 Bonded, 1 dk	**(X11A2YP) Yacht** Hull Material: Reinforced Plastic	**2 oil engines** reverse reduction geared to sc. shafts driving 2 Propellers Total Power: 1,940kW (2,638hp) Caterpillar C32 ACERT 2 x Vee 4 Stroke 12 Cy. 145 x 162 each-970kW (1319bhp) Caterpillar Inc-USA AuxGen: 2 x 115kW a.c Fuel: 57.0 (r.f.)
9026069 *XVEJ* -	**VICCO-09** *ex* Van Long 2 *-2008* **Vinashin Investment & Construction Co Ltd** - *Haiphong* *Vietnam* Official number: VN-1849-TK	**148** 44 -	Class: VR	**2003**-12 **in Vietnam** Yd No: LT-03-01 Loa 27.70 Br ex 7.42 Dght 2.300 Lbp 25.78 Br md 7.20 Dpth 3.20 Welded, 1 dk	**(B32A2ST) Tug**	**2 oil engines** geared to sc. shafts driving 2 FP propellers Total Power: 832kW (1,132hp) 8.0kn Caterpillar 2 x 4 Stroke 6 Cy. 158 x 180 each-416kW (566bhp) Caterpillar Inc-USA
9680554 *TCPO2* -	**VICE** **Polimar Denizcilik Muhendislik ve TurizmTicaret Ltd Sti** - *Istanbul* *Turkey* MMSI: 271043580	**495** - 806	Class: BV	**2013**-06 **Istanbul Tersanecilik ve Denizcilik Sanayi Tic Ltd Sti — Istanbul (Tuzla** Yd No: 14 Loa 49.99 Br ex - Dght 2.890 Lbp 48.27 Br md 9.50 Dpth 4.00 Welded, 1 dk	**(A13B2TP) Products Tanker** Double Hull (13F) Liq: 810; Liq (Oil): 810 Compartments: 5 Wing Ta, 5 Wing Ta, ER	**2 oil engines** reduction geared to sc. shafts driving 2 FP propellers Total Power: 736kW (1,000hp) 8.0kn Yanmar 6HYM-WET 2 x 4 Stroke 6 Cy. 133 x 165 each-368kW (500bhp) Yanmar Diesel Engine Co Ltd-Japan AuxGen: 2 x 120kW 60Hz a.c Fuel: 26.0 (d.f.)
9600724 - -	**VICE ADMIRAL OWUSU-ANSAH** **Government of The Republic of Ghana (Ports & Harbours Authority)** - *Takoradi* *Ghana* Official number: GSR0139	**294** 88 176	Class: LR ✠ **100A1** SS 12/2012 tug **LMC** **UMS** Eq.Ltr: H; Cable: 275.0/19.0 U2 (a)	**2012**-12 **Damen Shipyards Changde Co Ltd — Changde HN** (Hull) Yd No: (511576) **2012**-12 **B.V. Scheepswerf Damen — Gorinchem** Yd No: 511576 Loa 28.67 Br ex 10.43 Dght 3.750 Lbp 26.86 Br md 9.80 Dpth 4.60 Welded, 1 dk	**(B32A2ST) Tug**	**2 oil engines** gearing integral to driving 2 Z propellers Total Power: 3,728kW (5,068hp) Caterpillar 3516C 2 x Vee 4 Stroke 16 Cy. 170 x 190 each-1864kW (2534bhp) Caterpillar Inc-USA AuxGen: 2 x 86kW 400V 50Hz a.c
7825928 *HO3236* -	**VICEITAS** **Banco Internacional de Panama SA** - *Panama* *Panama*	*150* 41 110		**1979**-11 **Ast. Picsa S.A. — Callao** Yd No: 433 Loa 21.72 Br ex - Dght - Lbp 19.54 Br md 6.71 Dpth 2.75 Welded, 1 dk	**(B11B2FV) Fishing Vessel**	**1 oil engine** driving 1 FP propeller Total Power: 202kW (275hp) Caterpillar D353TA 1 x 4 Stroke 6 Cy. 159 x 203 202kW (275bhp) Caterpillar Tractor Co-USA
9642112 *2FUP8* -	**VICEM** *ex* Le Caprice V *-2013* **Solar Yachting Ltd** Vicem Yachts Inc *Douglas* *Isle of Man (British)*	**457** 137 55	Class: RI	**2013**-02 **Vicem Yachts Sanayi ve Ticaret AS — Antalya** Yd No: 001 Loa 46.08 Br ex - Dght - Lbp 38.00 Br md 8.83 Dpth 4.23 Bonded, 1 dk	**(X11A2YP) Yacht** Hull Material: Reinforced Plastic	**2 oil engines** reduction geared to sc. shafts driving 2 Propellers Total Power: 5,440kW (7,396hp) M.T.U. 16V4000M90 2 x Vee 4 Stroke 16 Cy. 165 x 190 each-2720kW (3698bhp) MTU Friedrichshafen GmbH-Friedrichshafen
9231121 *A8VI8* -	**VICENTE** *ex* Hyundai Rhino *-2012* *ex* CCNI Antartico *-2008* *ex* CSAV Genova *-2004* *ex* Cape Dorchester *-2003* **OCEAN Multipurpose Schifffahrtsunternehmen GmbH & Co KG** NSC Shipping GmbH & Cie KG *Monrovia* *Liberia* MMSI: 636092006 Official number: 92006	**23,132** 9,375 30,490 T/cm 46.7	Class: GL	**2002**-10 **Dalian Shipyard Co Ltd — Dalian LN** Yd No: MC300-2 Loa 192.90 (BB) Br ex - Dght 11.200 Lbp 182.00 Br md 27.80 Dpth 15.50 Welded, 1 dk	**(A31A2GX) General Cargo Ship** Grain: 34,773 TEU 1842 C Ho 786 TEU C Dk 1056 TEU incl 150 ref C. Compartments: 5 Ho, ER, 5 Tw Dk 9 Ha: Cranes: 2x100t,2x50t Ice Capable	**1 oil engine** driving 1 FP propeller Total Power: 15,750kW (21,414hp) 19.4kn B&W 7S60MC-C 1 x 2 Stroke 7 Cy. 600 x 2400 15750kW (21414bhp) Dalian Marine Diesel Works-China AuxGen: 1 x 1060kW 440/220V a.c, 2 x 910kW 440/220V a.c Thrusters: 1 Thwart. FP thruster (f) Fuel: 2620.0 (r.f.) 62.0pd
6518279 *D4GL* -	**VICENTE** *ex* Vis *-2011* *ex* Vicente *-2011* *ex* Vis *-2011* *ex* Sydfyn *-1976* **Tuninha Transporte Maritimo SA** - *Sao Vicente* *Cape Verde* MMSI: 617078000	*894* 425 200	Class: IS (CS) (JR) (BV)	**1965**-03 **Flensburger Schiffbau-Ges. mbH — Flensburg** Yd No: 608 Loa 57.00 Br ex 14.94 Dght 3.361 Lbp 51.01 Br md 14.91 Dpth 4.12 Welded, 2 dks & S dk	**(A36A2PR) Passenger/Ro-Ro Ship (Vehicles)** Passengers: 500	**2 oil engines** driving 2 CP propellers Total Power: 1,794kW (2,440hp) 12.0kn MAN G9V30/45ATL 2 x 4 Stroke 9 Cy. 300 x 450 each-897kW (1220bhp) Bremer Vulkan AG Schiffbau u.Maschinenfabrik-Bremen AuxGen: 4 x 118kW 400V 50Hz a.c Fuel: 49.0 (d.f.) 10.0pd
9130781 - -	**VICENTE** *ex* Toanui *-2011* *ex* Athena F *-2010* *ex* Bold Venture *-2005* *ex* Via Libeccio *-2002* **Advance Solution Services Ltd** -	**3,722** 1,117 3,709	Class: (BV)	**1996**-12 **Hijos de J. Barreras S.A. — Vigo** Yd No: 1548 Loa 107.50 (BB) Br ex - Dght 6.800 Lbp 94.50 Br md 16.60 Dpth 10.08 Welded, 2 dks	**(B11B2FV) Fishing Vessel** Ins: 3,200 Compartments: 1 Ho 3 Ha:	**6 diesel electric oil engines** driving 6 gen. each 1280kW 690V Connecting to 1 elec. Motor of (6200kW) driving 1 FP propeller Total Power: 7,680kW (10,440hp) 19.0kn Caterpillar 3516TA 6 x Vee 4 Stroke 16 Cy. 170 x 190 each-1280kW (1740bhp) Caterpillar Inc-USA AuxGen: 1 x 630kW 400/230V 50Hz a.c Thrusters: 1 Thwart. FP thruster (f); 1 Tunnel thruster (a)
7503960 - -	**VICENTE BARREIRO** - -	*394* 179 269	Class: (BV)	**1976**-08 **Astilleros Gondan SA — Castropol** Yd No: 140 Loa 41.41 Br ex 8.59 Dght 3.971 Lbp 36.10 Br md 8.51 Dpth 6.18 Welded, 2 dks	**(B11A2FT) Trawler**	**1 oil engine** geared to sc. shaft driving 1 FP propeller Total Power: 883kW (1,201hp) 11.3kn A.B.C. 8MDXC 1 x 4 Stroke 8 Cy. 242 x 320 883kW (1201bhp) Anglo Belgian Co NV (ABC)-Belgium Fuel: 185.5 (d.f.)
9389320 *XCSM6* -	**VICENTE GUERRERO II** *ex* Ocean Chariot *-2012* **Petroleos Mexicanos SA (PEMEX) Refinacion Gerencia de Transportacion Maritima** - *Coatzacoalcos* *Mexico* MMSI: 345030015	**29,304** 12,017 46,925 T/cm 52.2	Class: NV	**2009**-12 **Hyundai Mipo Dockyard Co Ltd — Ulsan** Yd No: 2051 Loa 183.21 (BB) Br ex 32.24 Dght 12.200 Lbp 174.00 Br md 32.20 Dpth 18.80 Welded, 1 dk	**(A12B2TR) Chemical/Products Tanker** Double Hull (13F) Liq: 51,922; Liq (Oil): 51,922 Cargo Heating Coils Compartments: 12 Wing Ta, 2 Wing Slop Ta, ER 12 Cargo Pump (s): 12x600m³/hr Manifold: Bow/CM: 92.2m	**1 oil engine** driving 1 FP propeller Total Power: 9,960kW (13,542hp) 14.5kn MAN-B&W 6S50MC-C 1 x 2 Stroke 6 Cy. 500 x 2000 9960kW (13542bhp) Hyundai Heavy Industries Co Ltd-South Korea AuxGen: 3 x a.c

IMO / Call sign	Name / Owner / Flag	Tonnage	Class	Builder / Dimensions	Type	Machinery
9082518 *LW9770* -	**VICENTE LUIS** *ex* Gianfranco *-2010* **PIEA SA** - *Argentina* MMSI: 701000522 Official number: 01075	**118** 73 110		**1995-09 SANYM S.A. — Buenos Aires** Yd No: 99 Loa - Br ex - Dght 3.000 Lbp 26.50 Br md 6.50 Dpth 3.30 Welded	**(B11A2FS) Stern Trawler** Ins: 165	**1 oil engine** geared to sc. shaft driving 1 FP propeller Total Power: 397kW (540hp) 10.0kn Caterpillar 3412TA 1 x Vee 4 Stroke 12 Cy. 137 x 152 397kW (540bhp) Caterpillar Inc-USA
9599559 - -	**VICHAMA** **Trabajos Maritima SA (TRAMARSA)** - *Callao* *Peru* MMSI: 760000630 Official number: CO-038681-EM	**272** 81 107	Class: AB	**2011-04 Jiangsu Wuxi Shipyard Co Ltd — Wuxi JS** Yd No: WX611 Loa 26.50 Br ex - Dght 3.500 Lbp 23.85 Br md 9.80 Dpth 4.50 Welded, 1 dk	**(B32A2ST) Tug**	**2 oil engines** reduction geared to sc. shafts driving 2 Directional propellers Total Power: 3,282kW (4,462hp) Caterpillar 3516B 2 x Vee 4 Stroke 16 Cy. 170 x 190 each-1641kW (2231bhp) Caterpillar Inc-USA AuxGen: 2 x 95kW a.c
6914148 *4JAC* -	**VICHEGDA** *ex* Vychegda *-1997* **Baki Sea Fishing Port (Baki Deniz Baliq Limani ASC - OAO 'Bakinskiy Morskoy Rybnyy Port')** - *Baku* *Azerbaijan* Official number: DGR-0403	*1,115* 426 650	Class: (RS)	**1969-09 VEB Mathias-Thesen-Werft — Wismar** Yd No: 140 Loa 65.72 Br ex 11.13 Dght 3.620 Lbp 59.82 Br md 11.10 Dpth 5.36 Welded, 2 dks	**(B11B2FV) Fishing Vessel** Ins: 1,150 Compartments: 2 Ho, ER 2 Ha: 2 (2.3 x 2.3)ER Cranes: 2x2t Ice Capable	**1 oil engine** driving 1 FP propeller Total Power: 647kW (880hp) 11.0kn S.K.L. 8NVD48-2U 1 x 4 Stroke 8 Cy. 320 x 480 647kW (880bhp) VEB Schwermaschinenbau "KarlLiebknecht" (SKL)-Magdeburg AuxGen: 2 x 272kW 380V a.c, 1 x 192kW 380V a.c Fuel: 170.0 (d.f.)
8891247 *CNA4052* -	**VICHIALO** - - *Morocco*	**183** - -		**1995 Astilleros Armon Burela SA — Burela** Yd No: 47 Loa - Br ex - Dght - Lbp - Br md - Dpth - Welded, 1 dk	**(B11B2FV) Fishing Vessel**	**1 oil engine** driving 1 FP propeller
9171668 *CBVH* -	**VICHUQUEN II** *ex* Vichuquen *-2001* **Alimentos Marinos SA (ALIMAR)** - *Valparaiso* *Chile* MMSI: 725005100 Official number: 2934	**1,694** - 2,200		**1997-11 Ast. y Maestranzas de la Armada (ASMAR Chile) — Talcahuano** Yd No: 78 Loa - Br ex - Dght - Lbp 70.00 Br md 12.60 Dpth 8.10 Welded, 1 dk	**(B11B2FV) Fishing Vessel**	**1 oil engine** reduction geared to sc. shaft driving 1 CP propeller Total Power: 3,972kW (5,400hp) 17.0kn MWM TBD645L9 1 x 4 Stroke 9 Cy. 330 x 450 3972kW (5400bhp) Deutz AG-Koeln AuxGen: 1 x 2200kW a.c, 2 x 400kW a.c
6511219 *WDD5722* -	**VICKI K** *ex* Eastward *-2013* **Charca Fish VIII LLC** - *San Diego, CA* *United States of America* MMSI: 367162580 Official number: 639319	**307** 92 249	Class: (AB)	**1964 Sturgeon Bay Shipbuilding & Dry Dock Corp — Sturgeon Bay WI** Yd No: 264 Converted From: Research Vessel Loa 35.82 Br ex 8.74 Dght 3.957 Lbp 31.88 Br md 8.69 Dpth 4.20 Welded, 1 dk	**(B11B2FV) Fishing Vessel** 4 Ha: 2 (1.3 x 0.9) (7.3 x -) (7.3 x 7.3) Derricks: 1x5t	**1 oil engine** driving 1 CP propeller Total Power: 471kW (640hp) 10.5kn Fairbanks, Morse 1 x 2 Stroke 8 Cy. 133 x 184 471kW (640bhp) Fairbanks Morse & Co.-New Orleans, La AuxGen: 2 x 100kW 225V 60Hz a.c Fuel: 84.5 (d.f.)
9257826 *WDA6093* -	**VICKI M. MCALLISTER** **McAllister Towing & Transportation Co Inc (MT & T)** - *New York, NY* *United States of America* MMSI: 366828620 Official number: 1112731	**281** 84 -	Class: AB	**2001-09 Eastern Shipbuilding Group — Panama City, Fl** Yd No: 787 Loa 29.90 Br ex - Dght 3.660 Lbp 25.20 Br md 11.00 Dpth 4.50 Welded, 1 dk	**(B32A2ST) Tug**	**2 oil engines** gearing integral to driving 2 Z propellers Total Power: 3,390kW (4,610hp) 13.0kn EMD (Electro-Motive) 12-645-E7B 2 x Vee 2 Stroke 12 Cy. 230 x 254 each-1695kW (2305bhp) General Motors Corp.Electro-Motive Div.-La Grange AuxGen: 2 x 99kW a.c
8958526 *WDD7516* -	**VICKIE II** *ex* Bob Cat *-2006* **Hiwall Inc** - *Wanchese, NC* *United States of America* MMSI: 367187480 Official number: 1073368	**116** 35 -		**1998 Ocean Marine, Inc. — Bayou La Batre, Al** Yd No: 346 L reg 22.67 Br ex - Dght - Lbp - Br md 7.01 Dpth 3.71 Welded, 1 dk	**(B11B2FV) Fishing Vessel**	**1 oil engine** driving 1 FP propeller
9269855 *YJVY2* -	**VICKIE TIDE** **Twenty Grand Marine Service LLC** Tidewater Marine LLC *Port Vila* *Vanuatu* MMSI: 576264000 Official number: 1884	**494** 148 116	Class: AB	**2003-01** Yd No: 56 Loa 53.31 Br ex - Dght 3.350 Lbp 46.94 Br md 10.36 Dpth 4.25 Welded, 1 Dk.	**(B21A2OC) Crew/Supply Vessel** Hull Material: Aluminium Alloy Passengers: unberthed: 175	**4 oil engines** geared to sc. shafts driving 4 FP propellers Total Power: 5,368kW (7,300hp) 16.0kn Cummins KTA-50-M2 4 x Vee 4 Stroke 16 Cy. 159 x 159 each-1342kW (1825bhp) Cummins Engine Co Inc-USA AuxGen: 2 x 175kW a.c Thrusters: 1 Tunnel thruster (f) Fuel: 111.6 (r.f.)
6524498 - -	**VICKY** - -	*105* - -	Class: (LR) ✠ Classed LR until 9/70	**1965-08 Fabricaciones Metallicas E.P.S. (FABRIMET) — Callao** Yd No: 293 Loa 22.36 Br ex 6.91 Dght 3.887 Lbp 19.13 Br md 6.63 Dpth 3.18 Welded, 1 dk	**(B11B2FV) Fishing Vessel**	**1 oil engine** reverse reduction geared to sc. shaft driving 1 FP propeller Total Power: 162kW (220hp) General Motors 6-110 1 x 2 Stroke 6 Cy. 127 x 142 162kW (220bhp) General Motors Corp-USA
1009778 *2COY4* -	**VICKY** **Smith Solemar Charter Ltd** Ocean Management GmbH *London* *United Kingdom* MMSI: 235074591 Official number: 915809	**879** 263 30	Class: LR ✠ **100A1** SS 06/2009 SSC Yacht, mono LDC G6 **LMC** **UMS** Cable: 330.0/20.5 U2 (a)	**2009-06 Baglietto S.p.A. — Varazze** Yd No: 10201 Loa 59.40 Br ex - Dght 3.000 Lbp 53.55 Br md 10.70 Dpth 5.03 Welded, 1 dk	**(X11A2YP) Yacht** Hull Material: Aluminium Alloy	**2 oil engines** with clutches, flexible couplings & sr geared to sc. shafts driving 2 FP propellers Total Power: 5,440kW (7,396hp) M.T.U. 16V4000M90 2 x Vee 4 Stroke 16 Cy. 165 x 190 each-2720kW (3698bhp) MTU Friedrichshafen GmbH-Friedrichshafen AuxGen: 2 x 175kW 400V 50Hz a.c Thrusters: 1 Thwart. FP thruster (f)
1011135 *ZGCI3* -	**VICKY** **Continental Maritime Ltd** Nigel Burgess Ltd (BURGESS) *George Town* *Cayman Islands (British)* MMSI: 319243000 Official number: 743711	**1,730** 519 200	Class: LR ✠ **100A1** SS 06/2012 SSC Yacht, mono, G6 ✠ **LMC** **UMS** Cable: 385.0/26.0 U3 (a)	**2012-06 Celikyat Insaa Sanayi ve Ticaret AS — Basiskele (Hull)** Yd No: (54) **2012-06 Proteksan-Turquoise Yachts Inc — Istanbul (Pendik)** Yd No: 54 Loa 72.65 Br ex 12.14 Dght 4.100 Lbp 61.84 Br md 12.00 Dpth 7.00 Welded, 1 dk	**(X11A2YP) Yacht**	**2 oil engines** with clutches, flexible couplings & sr reverse geared to sc. shafts driving 2 FP propellers Total Power: 3,650kW (4,962hp) 18.0kn Caterpillar 3516B 2 x Vee 4 Stroke 16 Cy. 170 x 190 each-1825kW (2481bhp) Caterpillar Inc-USA AuxGen: 4 x 200kW 400V 50Hz a.c Thrusters: 1 Thwart. FP thruster (f)
7428304 - -	**VICKY** *ex* Strilvaer *-1984* *ex* Finnvaer *-1983* *ex* Frovaer *-1973* *ex* Nordmore *-1973* **Bjorn Bjornstad** -	*120* 50 -	Class: (NV)	**1952-11 AS Stord Verft — Stord** Yd No: 17 L reg 24.24 Br ex 5.82 Dght - Lbp - Br md 5.80 Dpth 3.10 Welded, 1 dk	**(A37B2PS) Passenger Ship** Passengers: unberthed: 100	**1 oil engine** driving 1 FP propeller Total Power: 268kW (364hp) G.M. (Detroit Diesel) 12V-71-N 1 x Vee 2 Stroke 12 Cy. 108 x 127 268kW (364bhp) (new engine 1975) General Motors Detroit DieselAllison Divn-USA Fuel: 5.0 (d.f.) 1.5pd
5239199 *8RMK* -	**VICKY B** *ex* Mona Rosa *-2006* *ex* Hanny *-2005* *ex* Wiebke I *-1997* *ex* Mona Rosa *-1990* **Friendship Shipping Co Inc** - *Georgetown* *Guyana* MMSI: 750000022 Official number: 0000413	**319** 163 477	Class: (GL)	**1960 Alfred Hagelstein Masch. u. Schiffswerft — Luebeck** Yd No: 600 Loa 45.34 Br ex 8.54 Dght 2.696 Lbp 43.11 Br md 8.50 Dpth 3.23 Riveted\Welded, 1 dk	**(A31A2GX) General Cargo Ship** Grain: 580; Bale: 534 Compartments: 1 Ho, ER 1 Ha: (20.5 x 5.4)ER Derricks: 2x2t; Winches: 2 Ice Capable	**1 oil engine** reverse reduction geared to sc. shaft driving 1 FP propeller Total Power: 221kW (300hp) 10.0kn Deutz SBA6M528 1 x 4 Stroke 6 Cy. 220 x 280 221kW (300bhp) Kloeckner Humboldt Deutz AG-West Germany
7922324 *H3VL* -	**VICKY B** *ex* Nevado *-2001* **Excelsior Shipping Co Ltd (Panama) SA** Compania Maritima de Panama SA *Panama* *Panama* MMSI: 354138000 Official number: 2789401CH	**3,193** 1,054 4,942	Class: GL (NV)	**1980-06 Tangen Verft AS — Kragero (Hull)** Yd No: 73 **1980-06 Vaagen Verft AS — Kyrksaeterora** (Hull completed by) Yd No: 45 **1980-06 AS Akers Mekaniske Verksted — Oslo** Yd No: 820 Conv to DH-2008 Loa 103.99 Br ex 20.44 Dght 3.790 Lbp 100.01 Br md 20.41 Dpth 6.30 Welded, 1 dk	**(A13B2TP) Products Tanker** Double Hull (13F) Liq: 5,750; Liq (Oil): 5,950 Compartments: 4 Wing Ta, 4 Wing Ta, ER	**2 oil engines** geared to sc. shafts driving 2 FP propellers Total Power: 1,728kW (2,350hp) 11.0kn Normo LDMB-6 2 x 4 Stroke 6 Cy. 250 x 300 each-864kW (1175bhp) AS Bergens Mek Verksteder-Norway AuxGen: 3 x 268kW 440V 60Hz a.c

IMO / Call sign / Reg.	Name / Owner / Manager	Tonnage	Class	Builder / Dimensions	Type / Cargo	Machinery
9329198 *EAYM* 3-VI-52-04	**VICMAR UN** **Miguel Angel Vicente Sobrino & Argimira Martinez Rodriguez** - *La Guardia* *Spain* Official number: 3-2/2004	**142** 42 -		**2004**-11 **Montajes Cies S.L. — Vigo** Yd No: 102 Loa 24.30 Br ex - Dght 2.300 Lbp 18.00 Br md 6.20 Dpth 4.90 Welded, 1 dk	**(B11A2FS) Stern Trawler**	**1 oil engine** geared to sc. shaft driving 1 FP propeller Total Power: 199kW (271hp) 11.0kn Cummins KTA-19-M 1 x 4 Stroke 6 Cy. 159 x 159 199kW (271bhp) Cummins Engine Co Inc-USA
7611212 *UCXO* -	**VICOUNT** *ex* Bratya Nobel *-2006* *ex* Neftec-1 *-2000* *ex* Nefterudovoz-19M *-1998* **Brandex Group Ltd** Metship Ltd *Astrakhan* *Russia* MMSI: 273450650	**2,613** 1,159 3,345	Class: RS	**1975**-12 **Sudostroitelnyy Zavod "Kama" — Perm** Yd No: 818 Loa 118.93 Br ex 13.47 Dght 3.800 Lbp 110.00 Br md 13.00 Dpth 5.80 Welded, 1 dk	**(A22B2BR) Ore/Oil Carrier** Grain: 1,821; Liq: 3,556; Liq (Oil): 3,556 Compartments: 1 Ho, 8 Wing Ta, ER 1 Ha: (70.4 x 4.9)ER Ice Capable	**2 oil engines** driving 2 FP propellers Total Power: 970kW (1,318hp) 11.0kn S.K.L. 6NVD48A-U 2 x 4 Stroke 6 Cy. 320 x 480 each-485kW (659bhp) VEB Schwermaschinenbau "KarlLiebknecht" (SKL)-Magdeburg AuxGen: 3 x 100kW a.c Fuel: 77.0 (d.f.)
9321885 *3EAT6* -	**VICTOIRE** **Gaz Pacifique SAS** Oceangas Services Australia Pty Ltd SatCom: Inmarsat C 437100810 *Panama* *Panama* MMSI: 371008000 Official number: 3091105B	**3,759** 1,127 3,854 T/cm 11.9	Class: NK (BV)	**2005**-05 **Shitanoe Shipbuilding Co Ltd — Usuki OT** Yd No: 1240 Loa 86.00 (BB) Br ex 16.02 Dght 6.219 Lbp 82.00 Br md 16.00 Dpth 8.00 Welded, 1 dk	**(A11B2TG) LPG Tanker** Double Hull Liq (Gas): 3,869 2 x Gas Tank (s); 2 independent (C.mn.stl) cyl horizontal 2 Cargo Pump (s): 2x300m³/hr Manifold: Bow/CM: 42m	**1 oil engine** driving 1 FP propeller Total Power: 3,398kW (4,620hp) 13.5kn Mitsubishi 6UEC33LSII 1 x 2 Stroke 6 Cy. 330 x 1050 3398kW (4620bhp) Akasaka Tekkosho KK (Akasaka DieselLtd)-Japan AuxGen: 3 x 480kW 450/220V 60Hz a.c Thrusters: 1 Tunnel thruster (f) Fuel: 159.0 (d.f.) 461.0 (r.f.)
7522370 *YDPC* -	**VICTOR** *ex* Wanuaku *-1984* *ex* Okishima Maru *-1984* **PT Alexindo Yakin Prima** - *Jakarta* *Indonesia* MMSI: 525016488	**1,244** 694 1,743	Class: KI	**1976**-03 **Sasaki Shipbuilding Co Ltd — Osakikamijima HS** Yd No: 302 Loa 70.50 Br ex 11.03 Dght 4.570 Lbp 65.00 Br md 11.02 Dpth 6.33 Welded, 2 dks	**(A31A2GX) General Cargo Ship**	**1 oil engine** driving 1 FP propeller Total Power: 1,324kW (1,800hp) Akasaka AH33 1 x 4 Stroke 6 Cy. 330 x 500 1324kW (1800bhp) Akasaka Tekkosho KK (Akasaka DieselLtd)-Japan
7651585 *YHAM* -	**VICTOR** *ex* Chang Shing No. 7 *-2003* *ex* Chang Shing *-1994* *ex* Koei Maru No. 16 *-1989* *ex* Fukuyoshi Maru No. 2 *-1982* **PT Tirtamas Surya Segara** - *Jakarta* *Indonesia*	**686** 203 650	Class: KI	**1973**-11 **Oyama Zosen Tekko K.K. — Japan** Converted From: Bulk Aggregates Carrier-2003 Loa 52.00 Br ex - Dght 3.601 Lbp 46.70 Br md 10.51 Dpth 5.62 Welded, 2dks	**(A31A2GX) General Cargo Ship** 1 Ha: (15.6 x 8.3)ER	**1 oil engine** geared to sc. shaft driving 1 FP propeller Total Power: 809kW (1,100hp) 10.0kn Otsuka SODHS6A30 1 x 4 Stroke 6 Cy. 300 x 460 809kW (1100bhp) KK Otsuka Diesel-Japan
8807246 - -	**VICTOR** **Uniline Shipping Pte Ltd** JR Orion Services Pte Ltd	**1,680** 977 3,190 T/cm 10.1	Class: NK	**1988**-01 **Hong Lam Marine Pte Ltd — Singapore** Yd No: 1 Loa 73.00 Br ex - Dght 4.831 Lbp 70.50 Br md 15.00 Dpth 5.80 Welded, 1 dk	**(A13B2TP) Products Tanker** Liq: 3,577; Liq (Oil): 3,577 Cargo Heating Coils Compartments: 10 Wing Ta, ER 2 Cargo Pump (s)	**2 oil engines** with clutches, flexible couplings & epicyclic geared to sc. shafts driving 2 Directional propellers Total Power: 1,544kW (2,100hp) 10.0kn Daihatsu 2 x 4 Stroke 8 Cy. 260 x 320 each-772kW (1050bhp) Daihatsu Diesel Manufacturing Co Lt-Japan AuxGen: 3 x 56kW a.c Fuel: 140.0 (r.f.)
8985543 *OXBW2* -	**VICTOR** *ex* Wilcarry *-2006* *ex* V-2 *-2006* **JD Crafts A/S** JD-Contractor A/S *Struer* *Denmark (DIS)* MMSI: 219010747 Official number: M992	**215** 64 -	Class: BV	**1981 Boele's Scheepswerven en Machinefabriek B.V. — Bolnes** Yd No: 1069 Loa 43.15 Br ex - Dght 1.180 Lbp 41.96 Br md 9.38 Dpth 1.99 Welded, 1 dk	**(A31C2GD) Deck Cargo Ship** Cranes: 1x16t	**2 oil engines** gearing integral to driving 2 Directional propellers Total Power: 500kW (680hp) 7.0kn Scania D19-60M 2 x 4 Stroke 6 Cy. 115 x 144 each-250kW (340bhp) Saab Scania AB-Sweden AuxGen: 1 x 160kW 240V 60Hz a.c
9302401 *VHS6216* -	**VICTOR BJ** **Tony's Tuna International Pty Ltd** - *Port Adelaide, SA* *Australia* Official number: 857657	**220** - -		**2004**-08 **Adelaide Ship Const International Pty Ltd — Port Adelaide SA** Yd No: 321 Loa 24.00 Br ex - Dght 3.500 Lbp - Br md 8.00 Dpth - Welded, 1 dk	**(B12D2FU) Fishery Support Vessel** Cranes: 1x12t	**1 oil engine** reduction geared to sc. shaft driving 1 FP propeller Total Power: 449kW (610hp) 10.0kn Caterpillar 3412 1 x Vee 4 Stroke 12 Cy. 137 x 152 449kW (610bhp) Caterpillar Inc-USA
8502066 *UBCH8* -	**VICTOR CHERTKOV** *ex* Tuyuq *-2011* *ex* Reval *-2010* *ex* Mariel *-2003* *ex* Kapitan Khabalov *-1998* **Kamchatka Shipping Co Ltd (KASCO)** - *Petropavlovsk-Kamchatskiy* *Russia* MMSI: 273351420	**6,395** 2,823 7,148	Class: RS (GL)	**1991**-03 **Malta Shipbuilding Co. Ltd. — Marsa** (Assembled by) Yd No: 169 **1991**-03 **Malta Drydocks — Cospicua** (Parts for assembly by) Yd No: 169 Loa 131.63 Br ex 19.40 Dght 7.401 Lbp 122.03 Br md 19.31 Dpth 8.82 Welded, 1 dk	**(A31A2GX) General Cargo Ship** Grain: 9,898; Bale: 9,393 TEU 274 C. 274/20' Compartments: 4 Ho, ER 4 Ha: ER Cranes: 4x12.5t Ice Capable	**1 oil engine** driving 1 FP propeller Total Power: 4,690kW (6,377hp) 14.8kn B&W 7L45GBE 1 x 2 Stroke 7 Cy. 450 x 1200 4690kW (6377bhp) Zaklady Przemyslu Metalowego 'HCegielski' SA-Poznan
8826424 *UCLW* -	**VICTOR GAVRILOV** *ex* Kamchatskiy Shelf *-2010* *ex* Panastar *-2002* *ex* Kamchatskiy Shelf *-1997* **Collective Farm Fishery V Lenin (Rybolovetskiy Kolkhoz Imeni V I Lenina)** - *Petropavlovsk-Kamchatskiy* *Russia* MMSI: 273847200	**8,289** 2,486 2,886	Class: RS	**1990**-02 **Sudostroitelnyy Zavod 'Okean' — Nikolayev** Yd No: 601 Loa 126.30 Br ex 18.20 Dght 5.710 Lbp 118.00 Br md - Dpth 7.30 Welded	**(B12A2FF) Fish Factory Ship** Grain: 304; Ins: 2,797; Liq: 353 Ice Capable	**1 oil engine** driving 1 FP propeller Total Power: 2,648kW (3,600hp) 12.8kn S.K.L. 6VD48/42AL-2 1 x 4 Stroke 6 Cy. 420 x 480 2648kW (3600bhp) VEB Schwermaschinenbau "KarlLiebknecht" (SKL)-Magdeburg AuxGen: 3 x 800kW a.c
9101041 *UIEZ* -	**VICTOR GUBANOU** *ex* Tsunami *-2011* **North Astarta Co Ltd (OOO 'Severnaya Astarta')** - SatCom: Inmarsat C 427321037 *Petropavlovsk-Kamchatskiy* *Russia* MMSI: 273816900	**779** 233 414	Class: (RS)	**1993**-06 **ATVT Zavod "Leninska Kuznya" — Kyyiv** Yd No: 1667 Loa 54.82 Br ex 10.15 Dght 4.140 Lbp 50.30 Br md 9.80 Dpth 5.00 Welded, 1 dk	**(B11A2FS) Stern Trawler** Ins: 412 Compartments: 2 Ho 3 Ha: 3 (1.5 x 1.6) Derricks: 2x1t Ice Capable	**1 oil engine** driving 1 CP propeller Total Power: 852kW (1,158hp) 12.0kn S.K.L. 8NVD48A-2U 1 x 4 Stroke 8 Cy. 320 x 480 852kW (1158bhp) SKL Motoren u. Systemtechnik AG-Magdeburg
7360655 *9HYZ7* -	**VICTOR HENSEN** *ex* La Cour *-2004* *ex* Victor Hensen *-2001* **mv 'Victor Hensen' GmbH & Co KG** Hempel Shipping GmbH *Valletta* *Malta* MMSI: 215729000 Official number: 9052	**464** 139 -	Class: GL	**1975**-05 **Schichau-Unterweser AG — Bremerhaven** Yd No: 2257 Converted From: Fishing Vessel-2001 Loa 39.22 (BB) Br ex 9.50 Dght 3.071 Lbp 34.02 Br md 9.43 Dpth 4.40 Welded, 1 dk	**(B31A2SR) Research Survey Vessel** Ice Capable	**2 oil engines** reduction geared to sc. shaft driving 1 CP propeller Total Power: 706kW (960hp) 12.3kn M.T.U. 6R362TB61 2 x 4 Stroke 6 Cy. 160 x 180 each-353kW (480bhp) MTU Friedrichshafen GmbH-Friedrichshafen AuxGen: 1 x 300kW 380/220V 50Hz a.c, 1 x 196kW 380/220V 50Hz a.c Thrusters: 1 Tunnel thruster (f)
9525704 *ORQA* -	**VICTOR HORTA** **Fortis Lease NV** DEME Building Materials NV *Antwerpen* *Belgium* MMSI: 205604000 Official number: 01 00786 2011	**5,666** 1,699 8,198	Class: BV	**2011**-06 **IHC Dredgers BV — Kinderdijk** Yd No: CO1257 Loa 99.90 (BB) Br ex - Dght 7.160 Lbp 92.50 Br md 20.80 Dpth 9.21 Welded, 1 dk	**(B33B2DT) Trailing Suction Hopper Dredger** Hopper: 5,000	**2 oil engines** reduction geared to sc. shaft (s) driving 2 CP propellers Total Power: 5,400kW (7,342hp) 17.0kn Wartsila 6L26 2 x 4 Stroke 6 Cy. 260 x 320 each-2700kW (3671bhp) Wartsila France SA-France AuxGen: 1 x 1450kW 690V 60Hz a.c, 1 x 324kW 690V 60Hz a.c Thrusters: 1 Tunnel thruster (f) Fuel: 752.0
9157806 *FGD2660* -	**VICTOR HUGO** *ex* Salten *-2003* **Compagnie des Iles de La Manche** Compagnie Maritime Anglo-Normande *Cherbourg* *France* MMSI: 227010940 Official number: 922517	**387** 121 34	Class: BV (NV)	**1997**-05 **Kvaerner Fjellstrand AS — Omastrand** Yd No: 1641 Loa 35.00 Br ex - Dght 1.600 Lbp 34.40 Br md 10.10 Dpth 3.94 Welded, 1 dk	**(A37B2PS) Passenger Ship** Hull Material: Aluminium Alloy Passengers: unberthed: 199	**4 oil engines** reduction geared to sc. shafts driving 2 FP propellers Total Power: 2,560kW (3,480hp) 32.7kn M.T.U. 12V183TE92 4 x Vee 4 Stroke 12 Cy. 128 x 142 each-640kW (870bhp) MTU Friedrichshafen GmbH-Friedrichshafen AuxGen: 2 x 62kW 230/400V 50Hz a.c

5018399 *5NLC* -	**VICTOR I** *ex* Ebun I *-2008* *ex* Shantha *-2006* *ex* Anastasios II *-2005* *ex* Agios Rafael *-1999* *ex* Sfakia *-1997* *ex* Abdullah *-1982* *ex* Anna Broere *-1975* **Sadax Services Ltd** - *Nigeria* Official number: 377671	**558** 242 803	Class: (LR) ✠ Classed LR until 14/4/99	**1961-07 D.W. Kremer Sohn — Elmshorn** Yd No: 1091 Loa 59.31 Br ex 8.69 Dght 3.506 Lbp 54.89 Br md 8.60 Dpth 3.74 Riveted\Welded, 1 dk	**(A13B2TU) Tanker (unspecified)** Liq: 934; Liq (Oil): 934 Compartments: 10 Ta, ER	**1 oil engine** driving 1 FP propeller Total Power: 478kW (650hp) 11.0kn Deutz RBV6M545 1 x 4 Stroke 6 Cy. 320 x 450 478kW (650bhp) Kloeckner Humboldt Deutz AG-West Germany AuxGen: 1 x 8kW 115V d.c, 2 x 8kW 110V d.c Fuel: 68.5 (d.f.) 3.0pd
8841840 *WU8860* -	**VICTOR J ALTMAN** *ex* Rosemary McAllister *-2006* *ex* Trans World *-1980* - - *Duluth, MN* *United States of America* Official number: 297886	*195* 49 -		**1965 Gulfport Shipbuilding Corp. — Port Arthur, Tx** Yd No: 579 Loa - Br ex - Dght 3.870 Lbp 30.56 Br md 8.25 Dpth 4.27 Welded, 1 dk	**(B32A2ST) Tug**	**1 oil engine** driving 1 FP propeller Total Power: 1,206kW (1,640hp) EMD (Electro-Motive) 16-567-BC 1 x Vee 2 Stroke 16 Cy. 216 x 254 1206kW (1640bhp) General Motors Corp-USA
9301421 *C4UK2*	**VICTOR KONETSKY** - **Vimena Trading Ltd** SCF Unicom Singapore Pte Ltd SatCom: Inmarsat C 420911010 *Limassol* *Cyprus* MMSI: 209110000 Official number: 9301421	**60,434** 28,502 101,018 T/cm 92.5	Class: NV	**2005-12 Hyundai Heavy Industries Co Ltd — Ulsan** Yd No: 1603 Loa 246.88 (BB) Br ex - Dght 14.520 Lbp 234.00 Br md 42.00 Dpth 21.60 Welded, 1 dk	**(A13A2TV) Crude Oil Tanker** Double Hull (13F) Liq: 112,823; Liq (Oil): 112,823 Cargo Heating Coils Compartments: 12 Wing Ta, 2 Wing Slop Ta, ER 3 Cargo Pump (s): 3x2500m³/hr Manifold: Bow/CM: 123.5m Ice Capable	**1 oil engine** driving 1 CP propeller Total Power: 16,402kW (22,300hp) 14.5kn MAN-B&W 7S60ME-C 1 x 2 Stroke 7 Cy. 600 x 2400 16402kW (22300bhp) Hyundai Heavy Industries Co Ltd-South Korea AuxGen: 3 x 1045kW 220/450V 60Hz a.c Fuel: 366.5 (d.f.) 3090.5 (r.f.) 63.0pd
7709784 *PMYA* -	**VICTOR SATU** *ex* Anelly *-2009* *ex* Nippo Maru No. 80 *-1993* **PT Victor Dua Tiga Sarana** - *Tanjung Priok* *Indonesia*	**1,791** 697 2,448	Class: KI (NK)	**1977-11 Tokushima Zosen Sangyo K.K. — Komatsushima** Yd No: 527 Loa 85.18 Br ex - Dght 5.235 Lbp 78.52 Br md 17.00 Dpth 6.08 Riveted\Welded, 1 dk	**(A13B2TP) Products Tanker** Liq: 2,920; Liq (Oil): 2,920	**1 oil engine** driving 1 FP propeller Total Power: 1,912kW (2,600hp) 13.0kn Hanshin 6LUS40 1 x 4 Stroke 6 Cy. 400 x 640 1912kW (2600bhp) Hanshin Nainenki Kogyo-Japan AuxGen: 2 x 132kW 445V 60Hz a.c Fuel: 27.5 (d.f.) 132.0 (r.f.) 8.0pd
7400998 *P2V4991* -	**VICTORIA** *ex* Arnhem Bay *-1996* *ex* Albany *-1989* **Bismark Maritime Ltd** - *Lae* *Papua New Guinea* MMSI: 553111171 Official number: 000664	*338* 151 355	Class: PA (LR) ✠ Classed LR until 3/8/96	**1975-10 Dillingham Shipyards (WA) Pty Ltd — Fremantle WA** Yd No: 229 Lengthened Loa 49.38 Br ex 10.19 Dght 2.280 Lbp 42.47 Br md 10.00 Dpth 2.75 Welded, 1 dk	**(A35D2RL) Landing Craft** Bow door/ramp (centre) Len: 7.50 Wid: 5.00 Swl: - Grain: 582; Liq: 406; Liq (Oil): 406 TEU 40 incl 10 ref C Compartments: 6 Ta, 1 Ho, ER	**2 oil engines** reverse reduction geared to sc. shafts driving 2 FP propellers Total Power: 672kW (914hp) 10.0kn Caterpillar D343SCAC 2 x 4 Stroke 6 Cy. 137 x 165 each-336kW (457bhp) Caterpillar Tractor Co-USA AuxGen: 1 x 98kW 415V 50Hz a.c, 1 x 72kW 415V 50Hz a.c Fuel: 84.5 (d.f.)
5115379 *OGWN* -	**VICTORIA** *ex* Johanna V *-1998* *ex* Fiona *-1995* **BF-Cargo Oy Ab** - *Turku* *Finland* MMSI: 230966000 Official number: 11063	**388** 160 480	Class: (BV)	**1953 Martenshoekster Scheepsbouw N.V. — Hoogezand** Yd No: 78 Loa 48.27 Br ex 7.80 Dght 2.871 Lbp 41.51 Br md 7.75 Dpth 3.10 Riveted, 1 dk	**(A31A2GX) General Cargo Ship** Grain: 736; Bale: 697 Compartments: 1 Ho, ER 2 Ha: 2 (11.5 x 4.9)ER Derricks: 2x2t; Winches: 2	**1 oil engine** driving 1 FP propeller Total Power: 221kW (300hp) 9.0kn Brons 5ED 1 x 4 Stroke 5 Cy. 290 x 450 221kW (300bhp) NV Appingedammer Bronsmotorenfabrie-Netherlands Fuel: 20.5 (d.f.)
5379822 *LFGJ* -	**VICTORIA** - **Skien Dalen Skipsselskab AS** - *Skien* *Norway* MMSI: 257196600	**127** 54 -		**1882-01 AS Akers Mekaniske Verksted — Oslo** Yd No: 95 Loa 30.82 Br ex 5.49 Dght 2.134 Lbp - Br md 5.45 Dpth 2.93 Riveted, 1 dk	**(A37B2PS) Passenger Ship** Hull Material: Iron Passengers: 150	**1 oil engine** driving 1 FP propeller Total Power: 178kW (242hp) 11.0kn G.M. (Detroit Diesel) 8V-71-N 1 x Vee 2 Stroke 8 Cy. 108 x 127 178kW (242bhp) (new engine 1966) General Motors Detroit DieselAllison Divn-USA
6918845 *HC4762* -	**VICTORIA** *ex* Paradise Sound *-2007* *ex* Tower Duchess *-1984* **Servicios Portuarios SA Seaservice** - *Puerto Ayora* *Ecuador* MMSI: 735057713 Official number: TN-01-0214	**276** 132 430	Class: (LR) ✠ Classed LR until 5/84	**1969-06 Clelands Shipbuilding Co. Ltd. — Wallsend** Yd No: 305 Loa 41.86 Br ex 7.73 Dght 2.699 Lbp 39.37 Br md 7.62 Dpth 3.38 Welded, 1 dk	**(A31A2GX) General Cargo Ship** Grain: 550; Bale: 494 Compartments: 1 Ho, ER 1 Ha: (24.0 x 4.9)ER	**2 oil engines** reverse reduction geared to sc. shaft driving 2 FP propellers Total Power: 464kW (630hp) 9.3kn Volvo Penta 2 x 4 Stroke each-232kW (315bhp) (new engine 2007, fitted 2007) AB Volvo Penta-Sweden AuxGen: 3 x 1kW 24V d.c Fuel: 10.0 (d.f.)
8509404 - -	**VICTORIA** *ex* Ocean Credit *-2005* **East Way LLC** -	**4,181** 1,898 4,977	Class: RS (NV)	**1986-03 Hayashikane Shipbuilding & Engineering Co Ltd — Nagasaki NS** Yd No: 935 Loa 100.21 (BB) Br ex - Dght 6.351 Lbp 100.01 Br md 17.01 Dpth 8.11 Welded, 1 dk	**(A31A2GX) General Cargo Ship** Grain: 6,447 Compartments: 3 Ho, ER 3 Ha: ER Cranes: 1x30t,2x16t	**1 oil engine** driving 1 FP propeller Total Power: 3,354kW (4,560hp) B&W 6L35MC 1 x 2 Stroke 6 Cy. 350 x 1050 3354kW (4560bhp) Hitachi Zosen Corp-Japan AuxGen: 3 x 400kW 440V 60Hz a.c
8604058 *V3BN2* -	**VICTORIA** *ex* Mai *-2008* *ex* Oceaan IV *-2005* *ex* Tetman Hette *-1996* **Span-Ice Ehf** Uthafsskip ehf *Belize City* *Belize* MMSI: 312060000 Official number: 140520147	**3,938** 1,314 2,836	Class: NV (LR) ✠ Classed LR until 23/6/08	**1988-06 Stocznia Gdanska im Lenina — Gdansk** Yd No: B674/01 Loa 93.63 Br ex 15.96 Dght 6.501 Lbp 84.97 Br md 15.88 Dpth 10.01 Welded, 2 dks	**(B11A2FG) Factory Stern Trawler** Ins: 3,200 Ice Capable	**1 oil engine** with clutches, flexible couplings & sr geared to sc. shaft driving 1 CP propeller Total Power: 3,679kW (5,002hp) 15.5kn Sulzer 8ZAL40S 1 x 4 Stroke 8 Cy. 400 x 480 3679kW (5002bhp) Zaklady Urzadzen Technicznych'Zgoda' SA-Poland AuxGen: 1 x 1200kW 400V 50Hz a.c, 2 x 760kW 400V 50Hz a.c Boilers: e (ex.g.) 5.5kgf/cm² (5.4bar), e (ex.g.) (fitted: 1988) 8.7kgf/cm² (8.5bar), (AuxB (o.f.)) (5.1kgf/cm² (5.0bar))
7827859 *UCEV* -	**VICTORIA** *ex* Tory *-2012* *ex* Viktoriya *-2010* *ex* Kofuku Maru No. 68 *-1995* **Government of The Russian Federation (Territorial Department of Federal Agency on Management of Federal Property at Leningrad Oblast)** - *Kholmsk* *Russia* MMSI: 273412800	**291** 110 235	Class: (RS)	**1978-12 Kidoura Shipyard Co Ltd — Kesennuma MG** Yd No: 363 Loa 39.30 Br ex - Dght 2.301 Lbp 32.31 Br md 7.03 Dpth 2.70 Welded, 1 dk	**(B11B2FV) Fishing Vessel**	**1 oil engine** driving 1 FP propeller Total Power: 441kW (600hp) Niigata 6M26ZG 1 x 4 Stroke 6 Cy. 260 x 400 441kW (600bhp) Niigata Engineering Co Ltd-Japan Fuel: 205.0 (d.f.)
7802770 *SGWN* -	**VICTORIA** *ex* Veronica *-1982* **Lulea Bogserbats AB** - *Lulea* *Sweden* MMSI: 265537040	**239** 71 -	Class: LR ✠ **100A1** SS 04/2011 tug Ice Class 1A FS at a draught of 4.212m Max/min draughts fwd 3.712/3.492m Max/min draughts aft 4.712/3.992m Power required 949kw, power installed 1942kw Baltic Sea service ✠ **LMC** **UMS** Eq.Ltr: H; Cable: 302.5/22.0 U2	**1979-06 AB Asi-Verken — Amal** Yd No: 126 Loa 27.46 Br ex 9.91 Dght 4.245 Lbp 24.80 Br md 9.52 Dpth 4.91 Welded, 1 dk	**(B32A2ST) Tug** Ice Capable	**1 oil engine** sr geared to sc. shaft driving 1 CP propeller Total Power: 1,942kW (2,640hp) Polar SF112VS-F 1 x Vee 4 Stroke 12 Cy. 250 x 300 1942kW (2640bhp) AB Bofors NOHAB-Sweden AuxGen: 2 x 76kW 400V 50Hz a.c
8828226 *4XJO* -	**VICTORIA** *ex* Victoria 2000 *-2009* *ex* Dierna *-1999* **Gal Yam Marine Works Ltd** - *Israel* MMSI: 428030000	**571** 171 -	Class: (RN)	**1985-10 Santierul Naval Oltenita S.A. — Oltenita** Loa 37.33 Br ex - Dght 2.800 Lbp 34.00 Br md 11.67 Dpth 4.61 Welded, 1dk	**(A37B2PS) Passenger Ship**	**1 oil engine** driving 1 FP propeller Total Power: 519kW (706hp) 22.4kn S.K.L. 6VD18/15 1 x 4 Stroke 6 Cy. 150 x 180 519kW (706bhp) VEB Schwermaschinenbau "KarlLiebknecht" (SKL)-Magdeburg AuxGen: 2 x 56kW 400V 50Hz a.c

IMO / Call sign	Name / Owner	Tonnage	Class	Builder / Dimensions	Type / Cargo	Machinery
8727719 *4LBX* -	**VICTORIA** *ex* Dnestr-3 *-2011* *ex* Shprot *-2004* **Alioni 2011 Ltd** - *Poti* *Georgia* Official number: C-01589	**104** 41 58	Class: MG (RS)	**1985-10 Azovskaya Sudoverf — Azov** Yd No: 1003 Loa 26.50 Br ex 6.59 Dght 2.360 Lbp 22.90 Br md - Dpth 3.05 Welded, 1 dk	**(B11A2FS) Stern Trawler**	**1 oil engine** geared to sc. shaft driving 1 FP propeller Total Power: 165kW (224hp) 9.3kn Daldizel 6CHNSP18/22 1 x 4 Stroke 6 Cy. 180 x 220 165kW (224bhp) Daldizel-Khabarovsk AuxGen: 2 x 30kW Fuel: 7.0 (d.f.)
8960282 *WDB5400* -	**VICTORIA** *ex* Sea Angel III *-2001* **Ocean Emperess Inc** - *New Orleans, LA* *United States of America* MMSI: 366909230 Official number: 1094947	*106* 106 -		**2000 Kannin Pham — Slidell** Loa 22.56 Br ex - Dght - Lbp - Br md 6.55 Dpth 3.05 Welded, 1 dk	**(B11B2FV) Fishing Vessel**	**1 oil engine** driving 1 FP propeller
9140097 *YJQE9* -	**VICTORIA** **Navisa Maritima SA** Kobe Shipping Co Ltd *Port Vila* *Vanuatu* MMSI: 576420000 Official number: 1929	**2,717** 1,161 3,050	Class: NK	**1996-01 KK Kanasashi — Shizuoka SZ** Yd No: 3373 Loa 91.48 (BB) Br ex - Dght 5.518 Lbp 84.98 Br md 14.50 Dpth 8.60 Welded, 1 dk	**(A34A2GR) Refrigerated Cargo Ship** Ins: 4,279 Compartments: 1 Wing Yes 3 Ha: 3 (3.2 x 3.2)ER Derricks: 6x3t	**1 oil engine** driving 1 FP propeller Total Power: 1,471kW (2,000hp) 12.7kn B&W 6S26MC 1 x 2 Stroke 6 Cy. 260 x 980 1471kW (2000bhp) The Hanshin Diesel Works Ltd-Japan Thrusters: 1 Thwart. CP thruster (f) Fuel: 820.0 (r.f.)
9091179 *HC2035* -	**VICTORIA** **Agencia Naviera Agnamar SA** Negocios Navieros y de Transporte Transneg SA *Guayaquil* *Ecuador* Official number: TN-00-0035	*102* 44 -		**1991-10 Varadero Mariduena — Guayaquil** Loa 25.33 Br ex 6.25 Dght 1.310 Lbp 24.00 Br md 6.20 Dpth 1.61 Welded, 1 dk	**(B35E2TF) Bunkering Tanker**	**1 oil engine** driving 1 Propeller Total Power: 245kW (333hp) G.M. (Detroit Diesel) 1 x 2 Stroke 245kW (333bhp) General Motors Detroit DieselAllison Divn-USA
9121950 *V4UO* -	**VICTORIA** *ex* Mag Victory *-2012* *ex* Coral *-2008* *ex* Truestar 8 *-2004* *ex* Island 9 *-2003* *ex* Ngee Tai No. 1 *-2001* **Trans Victoria Marine Inc** - *Basseterre* *St Kitts & Nevis* MMSI: 341533000 Official number: SKN 1001533	**2,287** 687 4,173	Class: IS (NK)	**1994-10 Fong Syn Shipyard Sdn Bhd — Sibu** Yd No: 60 Loa 80.40 Br ex - Dght 3.904 Lbp 75.48 Br md 19.40 Dpth 5.20 Welded, 1 dk	**(A31A2GX) General Cargo Ship** Grain: 4,900; Bale: 4,410 Compartments: 2 Ho, ER 2 Ha: ER	**2 oil engines** reduction geared to sc. shafts driving 2 FP propellers Total Power: 1,472kW (2,002hp) 10.0kn Wartsila UD25V12M5D 2 x Vee 4 Stroke 12 Cy. 150 x 180 each-736kW (1001bhp) SACM Diesel SA-France AuxGen: 3 x a.c Fuel: 119.0
9078426 *UBRF3* -	**VICTORIA** *ex* Shinpo Maru No. 2 *-2008* **Shipping Co Mercury Co Ltd** - SatCom: Inmarsat C 427302418 *Vladivostok* *Russia* MMSI: 273330720	**1,526** 833 1,100	Class: RS	**1993-08 Kurinoura Dockyard Co Ltd — Yawatahama EH** Yd No: 316 Loa 59.78 Br ex 11.02 Dght 4.053 Lbp 54.60 Br md 11.00 Dpth 4.50 Welded, 1 dk	**(A13B2TP) Products Tanker** Compartments: 8 Ta, ER Ice Capable	**1 oil engine** reverse geared to sc. shaft driving 1 FP propeller Total Power: 1,030kW (1,400hp) Hanshin LH28G 1 x 4 Stroke 6 Cy. 280 x 460 1030kW (1400bhp) The Hanshin Diesel Works Ltd-Japan
9049499 *ZGCQ9* -	**VICTORIA** *ex* Ohana *-2012* **Midwest Marketing Ltd** - *Bloody Bay* *Cayman Islands (British)* MMSI: 319043500 Official number: 743685	**297** 90 52	Class: AB	**2004-06 Perini Navi SpA (Divisione Picchiotti) — Viareggio** Yd No: 2055 Loa 43.44 Br ex - Dght 3.600 Lbp 35.28 Br md 9.43 Dpth 5.20 Welded, 1 dk	**(X11A2YS) Yacht (Sailing)** Hull Material: Aluminium Alloy Passengers: cabins: 5; berths: 12	**2 oil engines** reduction geared to sc. shafts driving 2 Propellers Total Power: 880kW (1,196hp) 10.0kn Deutz BF8M1015MC 2 x Vee 4 Stroke 8 Cy. 132 x 145 each-440kW (598bhp) Deutz AG-Koeln
9290074 *V2BQ5* -	**VICTORIA** **ms 'Victoria' Schiffahrts GmbH & Co Reederei KG** Intersee Schiffahrtsgesellschaft mbH & Co KG SatCom: Inmarsat C 430458710 *Saint John's* *Antigua & Barbuda* MMSI: 304587000 Official number: 4089	**7,767** 3,856 10,500 T/cm 23.2	Class: GL (LR) ✠ Classed LR until 15/12/10	**2004-01 B.V. Scheepswerf Damen Hoogezand — Foxhol** Yd No: 838 **2004-01 Damen Shipyards Yichang Co Ltd — Yichang HB** (Hull) Loa 145.63 (BB) Br ex 18.36 Dght 7.360 Lbp 139.38 Br md 18.25 Dpth 10.30 Welded, 1 dk	**(A31A2GX) General Cargo Ship** Grain: 14,695; Bale: 13,975 TEU 679 C Ho 302 TEU C Dk 377 TEU incl 60 ref C. Cranes: 2x60t Ice Capable	**1 oil engine** with flexible couplings & sr geared to sc. shaft driving 1 CP propeller Total Power: 4,320kW (5,873hp) 14.8kn MaK 9M32C 1 x 4 Stroke 9 Cy. 320 x 480 4320kW (5873bhp) Caterpillar Motoren GmbH & Co. KG-Germany AuxGen: 1 x 440kW 400V 50Hz a.c, 3 x 350kW 400V 50Hz a.c Boilers: TOH (ex.g.) 10.2kgf/cm² (10.0bar), TOH (o.f.) 10.2kgf/cm² (10.0bar) Thrusters: 1 Thwart. CP thruster (f) Fuel: 300.0 (r.f.)
9290165 *CQIB* -	**VICTORIA** *ex* Maersk Victoria *-2009* *launched as* Palomar *-2004* **Aspera Schiffahrtsgesellschaft mbH & Co KG** Peter Doehle Schiffahrts-KG *Madeira* *Portugal (MAR)* MMSI: 255805551 Official number: TEMP169M	**17,188** 9,038 22,506	Class: GL	**2004-08 Daewoo-Mangalia Heavy Industries S.A. — Mangalia** (Hull) Yd No: 4044 **2004-08 J.J. Sietas KG Schiffswerft GmbH & Co. — Hamburg** Yd No: 1204 Loa 178.57 (BB) Br ex - Dght 10.850 Lbp 167.50 Br md 27.60 Dpth 14.58 Welded, 1 dk	**(A33A2CC) Container Ship (Fully Cellular)** TEU 1678 C Ho 638 TEU C Dk 1040 TEU incl 400 ref C. Cranes: 3x45t	**1 oil engine** driving 1 FP propeller Total Power: 16,918kW (23,002hp) 20.0kn B&W 6L70MC 1 x 2 Stroke 6 Cy. 700 x 2268 16918kW (23002bhp) Manises Diesel Engine Co. S.A.-Valencia AuxGen: 4 x 1040kW 450/230V 60Hz a.c Thrusters: 1 Thwart. CP thruster (f); 1 Thwart. CP thruster (a)
9295892 *DFJD* -	**VICTORIA** *ex* India Rose *-2008* **'Victoria' Fischereigesellschaft GmbH** Nicklasson Fiskeri AB SatCom: Inmarsat C 421816210 *Cuxhaven* *Germany* MMSI: 218162000 Official number: 1032	**499** 149 250	Class: NV	**2004-12 Stal-Rem SA — Gdansk** (Hull) Yd No: B332/1 **2004-12 Karstensens Skibsvaerft A/S — Skagen** Yd No: 395 Loa 37.05 (BB) Br ex 10.30 Dght 5.000 Lbp 31.65 Br md 10.00 Dpth 6.50 Welded, 1 dk	**(B11B2FV) Fishing Vessel**	**1 oil engine** geared to sc. shaft driving 1 CP propeller Total Power: 1,720kW (2,339hp) MAN-B&W 8L21/31 1 x 4 Stroke 8 Cy. 210 x 310 1720kW (2339bhp) MAN B&W Diesel AG-Augsburg AuxGen: 1 x 500kW a.c, 1 x a.c Thrusters: 1 Tunnel thruster (f)
9287857 *XCWR* -	**VICTORIA** **Otto Candies LLC** - *Ciudad del Carmen* *Mexico* MMSI: 345070093 Official number: 0401149325-3	**257** 77 165	Class: AB	**2002-11 Swiftships Shipbuilders LLC — Morgan City LA** Yd No: 545 Loa 45.72 Br ex - Dght 1.910 Lbp 40.00 Br md 8.08 Dpth 3.58 Welded, 1 dk	**(B21A2OC) Crew/Supply Vessel** Hull Material: Aluminium Alloy	**4 oil engines** reverse reduction geared to sc. shafts driving 4 Water jets Total Power: 3,136kW (4,264hp) Caterpillar 3508B-TA 4 x Vee 4 Stroke 8 Cy. 170 x 190 each-784kW (1066bhp) Caterpillar Inc-USA AuxGen: 2 x 65kW a.c
9398591 *HC5351* -	**VICTORIA** *ex* Sampurna *-2012* *ex* Sampurna Abidin *-2012* *ex* Feng Hai You 1 *-2007* **Servamain SA** - *Guayaquil* *Ecuador* MMSI: 735059140	**4,032** 1,975 6,412 T/cm 14.9	Class: LR (AB) (CC) **100A1** SS 07/2011 Double Hull oil tanker ESP **LMC**	**2007-01 Zhejiang Dongpeng Shipbuilding & Repair Co Ltd — Zhoushan ZJ** Yd No: 05-02 Loa 113.08 (BB) Br ex 15.72 Dght 6.900 Lbp 105.60 Br md 15.70 Dpth 8.80 Welded, 1 dk	**(A13B2TP) Products Tanker** Double Hull (13F) Liq: 6,690; Liq (Oil): 4,410 Cargo Heating Coils Compartments: 10 Wing Ta, 2 Wing Slop Ta, ER 2 Cargo Pump (s): 2x750m³/hr Manifold: Bow/CM: 56.2m	**1 oil engine** reduction geared to sc. shaft driving 1 FP propeller Total Power: 1,942kW (2,640hp) 11.3kn Chinese Std. Type G8300ZC 1 x 4 Stroke 8 Cy. 300 x 380 1942kW (2640bhp) Wuxi Antai Power Machinery Co Ltd-China AuxGen: 2 x 150kW 400V a.c
9365415 *D6ER8* -	**VICTORIA** *ex* Vera 777 *-2008* *ex* Xin Long Zhou 155 *-2005* **Samtex Alliance Ltd** - *Union of Comoros* MMSI: 616715000	**3,043** 1,940 5,000	Class: IV	**2005-06 Zhejiang Jiantiao Shipyard Co Ltd — Sanmen County ZJ** Loa 99.80 (BB) Br ex - Dght 5.550 Lbp 92.90 Br md 15.80 Dpth 7.10 Welded, 1 dk	**(A31A2GX) General Cargo Ship** Grain: 6,427 Compartments: 2 Ho, ER 2 Ha: (27.9 x 10.1)ER (26.8 x 10.1)	**1 oil engine** driving 1 FP propeller Total Power: 1,765kW (2,400hp) 11.0kn Chinese Std. Type G8300ZC 1 x 4 Stroke 8 Cy. 300 x 380 1765kW (2400bhp) Ningbo CSI Power & Machinery GroupCo Ltd-China
9462665 *LXRI* -	**VICTORIA** **Trivisa SA** Jan De Nul Luxembourg SA *Luxembourg* *Luxembourg* MMSI: 253181000	**2,392** 717 3,400	Class: BV	**2010-06 Tianjin Xinhe Shipbuilding Heavy Industry Co Ltd — Tianjin** Yd No: SB710 Loa 80.00 (BB) Br ex - Dght 4.500 Lbp 76.40 Br md 17.20 Dpth 5.85 Welded, 1 dk	**(B34A2SH) Hopper, Motor** Hopper: 1,800	**2 oil engines** reduction geared to sc. shafts driving 2 Z propellers Total Power: 1,566kW (2,130hp) 11.0kn Caterpillar 3508C 2 x Vee 4 Stroke 8 Cy. 170 x 190 each-783kW (1065bhp) Caterpillar Inc-USA Thrusters: 1 Tunnel thruster (f)
6826808 - -	**VICTORIA 1** *ex* Amaro *-2012* *ex* Maro G *-2011* *ex* Tuana *-2008* *ex* Halikarnas 2 *-2003* *ex* Halik *-1998* *ex* Seydi Reis *-1997* **Oilgate Global Concept Ltd** -	**497** 359 982	Class: (LR) (TL) ✠ Classed LR until 3/91	**1968-12 Denizcilik Anonim Sirketi Beykoz Tersanesi — Beykoz** Yd No: 12 Loa 61.00 Br ex 9.33 Dght 3.500 Lbp 57.84 Br md 9.30 Dpth 4.12 Welded, 1 dk	**(A13B2TU) Tanker (unspecified)** Liq: 1,363; Liq (Oil): 1,363 Compartments: 8 Ta, ER	**1 oil engine** driving 1 FP propeller Total Power: 552kW (750hp) 10.0kn Deutz RBV6M545 1 x 4 Stroke 6 Cy. 320 x 450 552kW (750bhp) Kloeckner Humboldt Deutz AG-West Germany AuxGen: 2 x 15kW 110V d.c, 1 x 8kW 110V d.c Fuel: 30.5 (d.f.) 3.0pd

9244594 *9WCX7* -	**VICTORIA 2** **Sealink Pacific Sdn Bhd** Sealink Sdn Bhd *Kuching* *Malaysia* MMSI: 533578000 Official number: 328143	**499** 149 483	Class: AB	**2000-12 Sealink Shipyard Sdn Bhd — Miri** Yd No: 107 Loa 49.80 Br ex - Dght 2.400 Lbp 47.03 Br md 10.90 Dpth 2.80 Welded, 1 dk	**(A35D2RL) Landing Craft** Bow ramp (centre)	**2 oil engines** with clutches, flexible couplings & sr geared to sc. shafts driving 2 FP propellers Total Power: 904kW (1,230hp) 10.5kn Caterpillar 3412TA 2 x Vee 4 Stroke 12 Cy. 137 x 152 each-452kW (615bhp) Caterpillar Inc-USA AuxGen: 2 x 80kW 415V 50Hz a.c Thrusters: 1 Thwart. FP thruster (f)
9608594 *3WKG9* -	**VICTORIA 03** *launched as* Star 88 *-2014* **Duong Huy Co Ltd** - *Haiphong* *Vietnam* MMSI: 574001970 Official number: VN-3591-VT	**2,995** 1,860 5,242	Class: VR	**2014-01 Hoang Phong Shipbuilding JSC — Xuan Truong** Yd No: S52-33 Loa 91.94 Br ex 15.33 Dght 6.300 Lbp 84.97 Br md 15.30 Dpth 7.90 Welded, 1 dk	**(A31A2GX) General Cargo Ship** Grain: 6,590; Bale: 6,058 Compartments: 2 Ho, ER 2 Ha: (21.1 x 10.0)ER (20.3 x 10.0) Cranes: 2x10t	**1 oil engine** reduction geared to sc. shaft driving 1 FP propeller Total Power: 1,765kW (2,400hp) 11.0kn Chinese Std. Type G8300ZC 1 x 4 Stroke 8 Cy. 300 x 380 1765kW (2400bhp) Ningbo CSI Power & Machinery GroupCo Ltd-China AuxGen: 2 x 150kW 400V a.c
9608570 *3WKN9* -	**VICTORIA 05** *ex* Sunrise 15 *-2014* *ex* Sunlight 15 *-2013* *ex* MR05 *-2012* **Duong Huy Co Ltd** - *Haiphong* *Vietnam* MMSI: 574002020 Official number: VN-3593-VT	**2,995** 1,860 5,240	Class: VR	**2013-09 Hoang Phong Shipbuilding JSC — Xuan Truong** Yd No: S52-38 Loa 91.94 Br ex 15.33 Dght 6.300 Lbp 84.97 Br md 15.30 Dpth 7.90 Welded, 1 dk	**(A31A2GX) General Cargo Ship** Grain: 6,590; Bale: 6,058 Compartments: 2 Ho, ER 2 Ha: (21.1 x 10.0)ER (20.3 x 10.0) Cranes: 2x10t	**1 oil engine** reduction geared to sc. shaft driving 1 Propeller Total Power: 2,000kW (2,719hp) 12.0kn Chinese Std. Type G8300ZC 1 x 4 Stroke 8 Cy. 300 x 380 2000kW (2719bhp)
9613903 *9WOF3* -	**VICTORIA 8** *ex* Sealink Victoria 8 *-2012* **Sealink Sdn Bhd** Sea Swift Pty Ltd *Kuching* *Malaysia* MMSI: 533004840 Official number: 334678	**488** 146 854	Class: LR ✠ **100A1** SS 01/2012 Eq.Ltr: J; Cable: 357.5/26.0 U2 (a)	**2012-01 Sealink Shipyard Sdn Bhd — Miri** Yd No: 207 Loa 45.50 Br ex 10.92 Dght 2.400 Lbp 42.23 Br md 10.90 Dpth 3.20 Welded, 1 dk	**(A35D2RL) Landing Craft** Bow ramp (centre)	**2 oil engines** with clutches & sr geared to sc. shafts driving 2 FP propellers Total Power: 1,074kW (1,460hp) 10.0kn Caterpillar 3412C-TA 2 x Vee 4 Stroke 12 Cy. 137 x 152 each-537kW (730bhp) Caterpillar Inc-USA AuxGen: 2 x 80kW 415V 50Hz a.c Thrusters: 1 Thwart. FP thruster (f)
9684483 *9WPW7* -	**VICTORIA 9** **Seabright Sdn Bhd** Sealink Sdn Bhd *Kuching* *Malaysia* Official number: 334870	**494** 165 382	Class: AB	**2013-11 Sealink Shipyard Sdn Bhd — Miri** Yd No: 237 Loa 45.00 Br ex - Dght 2.200 Lbp 41.20 Br md 10.00 Dpth 3.60 Welded, 1 dk	**(A35D2RL) Landing Craft** Bow ramp (centre)	**2 oil engines** reduction geared to sc. shafts driving 2 FP propellers Total Power: 894kW (1,216hp) Cummins KTA-19-M3 2 x 4 Stroke 6 Cy. 159 x 159 each-447kW (608bhp) Cummins Engine Co Inc-USA AuxGen: 2 x 100kW a.c
8818221 *PMNL* -	**VICTORIA-11** *ex* Woo Bong *-2009* *ex* Toho Maru *-1995* **PT Bahari Nusantara** - *Makassar* *Indonesia*	**2,292** 1,401 4,114	Class: KI (KR) (NK)	**1988-09 Murakami Hide Zosen K.K. — Imabari** Yd No: 287 Loa 89.90 Br ex 14.02 Dght 6.350 Lbp 84.50 Br md 14.00 Dpth 7.00 Welded, 1 dk	**(A13B2TP) Products Tanker** Liq: 4,949; Liq (Oil): 4,949 Cargo Heating Coils Compartments: 8 Wing Ta, ER 2 Cargo Pump (s): 2x1500m³/hr Manifold: Bow/CM: 45m	**1 oil engine** driving 1 CP propeller Total Power: 1,323kW (1,799hp) 11.0kn Hanshin 6EL35 1 x 4 Stroke 6 Cy. 350 x 700 1323kW (1799bhp) The Hanshin Diesel Works Ltd-Japan AuxGen: 2 x 422kW 445V 60Hz a.c, 1 x 105kW 445V a.c Thrusters: 1 Thwart. CP thruster (a) Fuel: 171.0 (d.f.) 6.5pd
8838477 - - -	**VICTORIA 77** *ex* Shoho Maru No. 58 *-1995* - -	*124* 42 -		**1976 Narasaki Zosen KK — Muroran HK** L reg 32.30 Br ex - Dght 4.000 Lbp - Br md 7.30 Dpth 4.40 Welded, 1 dk	**(B11B2FV) Fishing Vessel**	**1 oil engine** driving 1 FP propeller Total Power: 397kW (540hp) Niigata 1 x 4 Stroke 397kW (540bhp) Niigata Engineering Co Ltd-Japan
6826080 - - -	**VICTORIA A** *ex* Cabrillo *-1990* - -	*1,007* 204 -	Class: (GL)	**1968-07 J M Martinac Shipbuilding Corp — Tacoma WA** Yd No: 174 L reg 50.30 Br ex 10.83 Dght 4.790 Lbp - Br md 10.45 Dpth 5.56 Welded	**(B11B2FV) Fishing Vessel**	**1 oil engine** reduction geared to sc. shaft driving 1 FP propeller Total Power: 2,058kW (2,798hp) 14.8kn EMD (Electro-Motive) 16-645-E... 1 x Vee 2 Stroke 16 Cy. 230 x 254 2058kW (2798bhp) Electro Motive Div. Gen. Motors-La Grange, Illinois AuxGen: 1 x 3000kW 440V a.c, 2 x 200kW 440V a.c
7383736 - - -	**VICTORIA A** *ex* Ana Maria F *-1990* *ex* Connie F *-1996* - -	*1,022* 270 900	Class: (LR) ✠ Classed LR until 21/9/94	**1989-04 SIMA Serv. Ind. de la Marina Chimbote (SIMACH) — Chimbote** Yd No: 398 Loa 51.52 Br ex 11.02 Dght 5.537 Lbp 46.94 Br md 10.67 Dpth 5.69 Welded, 2 dks	**(B11B2FV) Fishing Vessel** Ins: 755	**1 oil engine** with clutches, flexible couplings & dr reverse geared to sc. shaft driving 1 FP propeller Total Power: 1,405kW (1,910hp) MAN G9V30/45AT... 1 x 4 Stroke 9 Cy. 300 x 450 1405kW (1910bhp) (made 1974) Maschinenbau Augsburg Nuernberg (MAN)-Augsburg AuxGen: 3 x 252kW 440V 60Hz a.c Thrusters: 1 Thwart. FP thruster (f)
8711784 *YYIH* -	**VICTORIA B** *ex* Anastasia *-1998* *ex* Ilyichyovets-1 *-1997* **Excelsior Shipping Co Ltd (Panama) SA** Compania Maritima de Venezuela VBCA *Puerto la Cruz* *Venezuela* MMSI: 775062000 Official number: AGSP-2402	**1,826** 952 3,389	Class: (GL) (RS)	**1988-03 Shipbuilding & Shiprepairing Yard 'Ivan Dimitrov' — Rousse** Yd No: 462 Loa 77.53 Br ex 14.34 Dght 5.335 Lbp 73.20 Br md 14.00 Dpth 6.50 Welded, 1 dk	**(A13B2TP) Products Tanker** Liq: 3,513; Liq (Oil): 3,513 Compartments: 12 Ta, ER Ice Capable	**1 oil engine** sr geared to sc. shaft driving 1 FP propeller Total Power: 885kW (1,203hp) 9.0kn S.K.L. 8NVD48A-2... 1 x 4 Stroke 8 Cy. 320 x 480 885kW (1203bhp) VEB Schwermaschinenbau "KarlLiebknecht" (SKL)-Magdeburg AuxGen: 2 x 150kW a.c Thrusters: 1 Thwart. CP thruster (f)
9293466 *3ECG9* -	**VICTORIA BRIDGE** **Victoria Bridge Shipping SA** 'K' Line Ship Management Co Ltd (KLSM) *Panama* *Panama* MMSI: 371345000 Official number: 3109805B	**54,519** 22,921 64,986 T/cm 82.5	Class: NK	**2005-08 Hyundai Heavy Industries Co Ltd — Ulsan** Yd No: 1594 Loa 294.12 (BB) Br ex - Dght 13.520 Lbp 283.33 Br md 32.20 Dpth 21.80 Welded, 1 dk	**(A33A2CC) Container Ship (Fully Cellular)** TEU 4738 incl 400 ref C	**1 oil engine** driving 1 FP propeller Total Power: 45,660kW (62,079hp) 23.5kn MAN-B&W 8K98MC-... 1 x 2 Stroke 8 Cy. 980 x 2400 45660kW (62079bhp) Hyundai Heavy Industries Co Ltd-South Korea AuxGen: 4 x 1995kW a.c Thrusters: 1 Thwart. CP thruster (f) Fuel: 7385.0
9373539 *MTQS* -	**VICTORIA C** **Carisbrooke Shipping 634 Ltd** Carisbrooke Shipping Ltd *Cowes* *United Kingdom* MMSI: 235056276 Official number: 913648	**2,990** 1,686 4,998 T/cm 11.4	Class: BV	**2007-11 Construcciones Navales P Freire SA — Vigo** Yd No: 634 Loa 89.80 (BB) Br ex - Dght 6.300 Lbp 84.70 Br md 14.50 Dpth 7.35 Welded, 1 dk	**(A31A2GX) General Cargo Ship** Grain: 6,080 Compartments: 1 Ho, ER 1 Ha: ER	**1 oil engine** reduction geared to sc. shaft driving 1 CP propeller Total Power: 1,980kW (2,692hp) 12.5kn MaK 6M2... 1 x 4 Stroke 6 Cy. 255 x 400 1980kW (2692bhp) Caterpillar Motoren GmbH & Co. KG-Germany AuxGen: 1 x 168kW 440/220V 50Hz a.c, 1 x 312kW 440/220V 50Hz a.c Thrusters: 1 Tunnel thruster (f) Fuel: 50.0 (d.f.) 200.0 (r.f.) 8.0pd
8520757 *PJAO* -	**VICTORIA CLIPPER** **Clipper Navigation Inc** - *Willemstad* *Curacao* MMSI: 306258000 Official number: 1986-C-1111	*431* 146 -	Class: NV	**1986-04 Fjellstrand AS — Omastrand** Yd No: 1572 Loa 40.42 Br ex 9.45 Dght 1.570 Lbp 36.58 Br md 9.43 Dpth 3.97 Welded, 1 dk	**(A37B2PS) Passenger Ship** Hull Material: Aluminium Alloy Passengers: unberthed: 330	**2 oil engines** geared to sc. shafts driving 2 Water jets Total Power: 3,078kW (4,184hp) M.T.U. 16V396TB8... 2 x Vee 4 Stroke 16 Cy. 165 x 185 each-1539kW (2092bhp) MTU Friedrichshafen GmbH-Friedrichshafen AuxGen: 2 x 60kW 220V 60Hz a.c
8745096 *WAP4478* -	**VICTORIA CLIPPER III** *ex* Audubon Express *-1994* **Clipper Navigation Inc** - *Seattle, WA* *United States of America* MMSI: 366902890 Official number: 965831	**235** 105 -		**1990-07 Gladding-Hearn SB. Duclos Corp. — Somerset, Ma** Yd No: P-272 Loa 26.06 Br ex - Dght - Lbp - Br md 8.69 Dpth 2.28 Welded, 1 dk	**(A37B2PS) Passenger Ship** Hull Material: Aluminium Alloy	**2 oil engines** reduction geared to sc. shafts driving 2 Propellers Total Power: 1,766kW (2,402hp) G.M. (Detroit Diesel) 16V-149-T... 2 x Vee 2 Stroke 16 Cy. 146 x 146 each-883kW (1201bhp) General Motors Detroit DieselAllison Divn-USA

IMO / Call sign	Name / Owner	Tonnage	Class	Builder / Dimensions	Type	Machinery
9059999 *C6YL9* -	**VICTORIA CLIPPER IV** **Clipper Navigation Inc** *Nassau* *Bahamas* MMSI: 311037800 Official number: 8001762	**478** 162 50	Class: NV	**1993-02 Kvaerner Fjellstrand AS — Omastrand** Yd No: 1615 Loa 40.00 Br ex - Dght 1.830 Lbp 36.00 Br md 10.10 Dpth 4.01 Welded	**(A37B2PS) Passenger Ship** Hull Material: Aluminium Alloy Passengers: unberthed: 324	**2 oil engines** geared to sc. shafts driving 2 Water jets Total Power: 4,000kW (5,438hp) 31.0kn M.T.U. 16V396TE74 2 x Vee 4 Stroke 16 Cy. 165 x 185 each-2000kW (2719bhp) MTU Friedrichshafen GmbH-Friedrichshafen AuxGen: 2 x 81kW 460V 60Hz a.c
9021813 *LXVC* -	**VICTORIA D** *ex* Victoria T *-2006* **Societe Financiere DBG** Luxembourg Marine Services SA (LMS) *Luxembourg* *Luxembourg* MMSI: 253303000	**100** 30 -	Class: BV	**1994-12 Construction Navale Bordeaux SA (CNB) — Bordeaux** Yd No: 15 Loa 31.66 Br ex 7.49 Dght 1.150 Lbp 26.90 Br md 7.48 Dpth 3.45 Welded, 1 dk	**(X11A2YS) Yacht (Sailing)** Hull Material: Aluminium Alloy Passengers: cabins: 6; berths: 10	**1 oil engine** geared to sc. shaft driving 1 Propeller Total Power: 257kW (349hp) 7.0kn Cummins 6CTA8.3-M2 1 x 4 Stroke 6 Cy. 114 x 135 257kW (349bhp) Cummins Engine Co Inc-USA
8996944 *ZCGP7* -	**VICTORIA DEL MAR** *ex* Bodacious *-2005* *ex* White Heaven III *-2005* **Victoria Del Mar Holdings Inc** Fairport Inc (Fairport Yacht Support) *George Town* *Cayman Islands (British)* MMSI: 319900000 Official number: 735459	**341** 102 -	Class: LR (GL) **100A1** SS 06/2013 SSC Yacht, mono, G6 **LMC**	**2001-06 Moonen Shipyards B.V. — 's-Hertogenbosch** Yd No: 171 Loa 35.05 (BB) Br ex - Dght 3.560 Lbp 31.40 Br md 8.00 Dpth 4.75 Welded, 1 dk	**(X11A2YP) Yacht** Passengers: cabins: 5; berths: 10	**2 oil engines** geared to sc. shafts driving 2 Propellers Total Power: 1,000kW (1,360hp) 12.0kn Caterpillar 3412 2 x Vee 4 Stroke 12 Cy. 137 x 152 each-500kW (680bhp) Caterpillar Inc-USA
9589229 *VRIJ2* -	**VICTORIA HARBOUR** **Hope Bulkship SA** Wealth Ocean Ship Management (Shanghai) Co Ltd *Hong Kong* *Hong Kong* MMSI: 477514700 Official number: HK-3058	**18,465** 10,365 29,100	Class: LR ✠ **100A1** SS 05/2011 bulk carrier CSR BC-A Nos. 2 & 4 holds may be empty GRAB (20) ESP LI ✠ **LMC** Eq.Ltr: H†; Cable: 605.0/62.0 U3 (a)	**2011-05 Yangzhou Nakanishi Shipbuilding Co Ltd — Yizheng JS** Yd No: 010 Loa 170.00 (BB) Br ex - Dght 10.038 Lbp 163.60 Br md 27.00 Dpth 14.20 Welded, 1 dk	**(A21A2BC) Bulk Carrier** Grain: 39,988; Bale: 39,070 Compartments: 5 Ho, ER 5 Ha: ER Cranes: 4x30t	**1 oil engine** driving 1 FP propeller Total Power: 5,730kW (7,791hp) 14.2kn MAN-B&W 5S50MC 1 x 2 Stroke 5 Cy. 500 x 1910 5730kW (7791bhp) AuxGen: 3 x 450kW 450V 60Hz a.c Boilers: AuxB (Comp) 7.1kgf/cm² (7.0bar)
7338834 *V3PT8* -	**VICTORIA HUNT** *ex* Carl Ray *-2007* **Banana Enterprises Ltd** *Belize City* *Belize* MMSI: 312236000 Official number: 011111795	*182* 124 -	Class: (AB)	**1968 McDermott Shipyards Inc — Morgan City LA** Yd No: 154 Loa - Br ex - Dght 4.293 Lbp 33.41 Br md 9.45 Dpth 4.73 Welded, 1 dk	**(B32A2ST) Tug**	**2 oil engines** reverse reduction geared to sc. shafts driving 2 FP propellers Total Power: 1,654kW (2,248hp) 12.0kn Caterpillar D399TA 2 x Vee 4 Stroke 16 Cy. 159 x 203 each-827kW (1124bhp) Caterpillar Tractor Co-USA AuxGen: 2 x 60kW 125V 60Hz a.c Fuel: 212.5 (d.f.)
9063184 - -	**VICTORIA I** **Changjiang Shipping Co** SatCom: Inmarsat A 1572362 *China*	*278* - 158	Class: (CC)	**1994-06 Jiangxi Jiangzhou Shipyard — Ruichang JX** Yd No: A429 Loa - Br ex - Dght - Lbp - Br md - Dpth - Welded	**(A37B2PS) Passenger Ship** Passengers: unberthed: 168	**2 oil engines** geared to sc. shafts driving 2 FP propellers Total Power: 1,472kW (2,002hp) Daihatsu 6DSM-22 2 x 4 Stroke 6 Cy. 220 x 280 each-736kW (1001bhp) Shaanxi Diesel Engine Factory-China
8747757 - -	**VICTORIA I** **Pereira Argentina SA** *Argentina* Official number: 0554	*107* - -		**1985-05 Ast. Naval Federico Contessi y Cia. S.A. — Mar del Plata** Loa 25.28 Br ex - Dght - Lbp - Br md 6.35 Dpth 3.32 Welded, 1 dk	**(B11B2FV) Fishing Vessel**	**1 oil engine** driving 1 Propeller
8738938 *SPS2368* -	**VICTORIA I** *ex* Maryna *-2000* **Jozef & Halina Skiba** *Dziwnow* *Poland* MMSI: 261002250	**103** 42 -	Class: PR	**1967-09 Gdanska Stocznia Rzeczna — Gdansk** Yd No: 120/7 Loa 21.56 Br ex - Dght 1.750 Lbp 20.47 Br md 5.82 Dpth 3.05 Welded, 1 dk	**(A37B2PS) Passenger Ship** Passengers: unberthed: 176	**1 oil engine** driving 1 Propeller Total Power: 121kW (165hp) 8.0kn Delfin UE680LM 1 x 4 Stroke 6 Cy. 127 x 146 121kW (165bhp) Puckie Zaklady Mechaniczne Ltd-Puck
9510539 *PMSS* -	**VICTORIA I** **PT Lumoso Pratama Line** *Jakarta* *Indonesia* MMSI: 525016387 Official number: 2009 PST NO. 5577/L	**32,355** 18,118 55,060	Class: NK (BV)	**2009-01 Zhejiang Jiantiao Shipyard Co Ltd — Sanmen County ZJ** Yd No: JT0701 Loa 189.98 (BB) Br ex - Dght 12.800 Lbp 182.00 Br md 32.26 Dpth 18.00 Welded, 1 dk	**(A21A2BC) Bulk Carrier** Grain: 67,601; Bale: 64,220 Compartments: 5 Ho, ER 5 Ha: ER Cranes: 4x30t	**1 oil engine** driving 1 FP propeller Total Power: 9,480kW (12,889hp) 14.7kn MAN-B&W 6S50MC-C 1 x 2 Stroke 6 Cy. 500 x 2000 9480kW (12889bhp) STX Engine Co Ltd-South Korea AuxGen: 3 x 560kW 60Hz a.c Fuel: 2330.0
9281281 *ESRP* -	**VICTORIA I** **Tallink Group Ltd (AS Tallink Grupp)** *Tallinn* *Estonia* MMSI: 276496000 Official number: 5P04C03	**40,975** 24,797 4,930 T/cm 41.6	Class: BV	**2004-03 Aker Finnyards Oy — Rauma** Yd No: 434 Loa 192.90 (BB) Br ex 35.20 Dght 6.600 Lbp 175.20 Br md 29.00 Dpth 15.40 Welded, 12 dks	**(A36A2PR) Passenger/Ro-Ro Ship (Vehicles)** Passengers: unberthed: 254; cabins: 739; berths: 2246 Bow ramp (centre) Len: 18.00 Wid: 4.70 Swl: - Stern ramp1 (p) 1 (s) Len: 11.75 Wid: 8.40 Swl: - Lane-Len: 1030 Lane-Wid: 3.10 Lane-clr ht: 4.90 Ice Capable	**4 oil engines** geared to sc. shafts driving 2 CP propellers Total Power: 26,240kW (35,676hp) 22.0kn Wartsila 16V32 4 x Vee 4 Stroke 16 Cy. 320 x 350 each-6560kW (8919bhp) Wartsila Finland Oy-Finland AuxGen: 3 x 2368kW 690/380V 50Hz a.c, 1 x 2160kW 690/380V 50Hz a.c Thrusters: 2 Thwart. CP thruster (f) Fuel: 187.0 (d.f.) 1418.0 (r.f.) 50.0pd
9063196 - -	**VICTORIA II** **Changjiang Shipping Co** - *China*	*278* - 158		**1995-01 Jiangxi Jiangzhou Shipyard — Ruichang JX** Yd No: A430 Loa - Br ex - Dght - Lbp - Br md - Dpth - Welded, 1 dk	**(A37B2PS) Passenger Ship** Passengers: unberthed: 168	**2 oil engines** geared to sc. shafts driving 2 FP propellers Total Power: 1,472kW (2,002hp) Daihatsu 6DSM-22 2 x 4 Stroke 6 Cy. 220 x 280 each-736kW (1001bhp) Shaanxi Diesel Engine Factory-China
8612574 *LW6554* -	**VICTORIA II** **Crestas SA** SatCom: Inmarsat C 470124010 *Puerto Madryn* *Argentina* MMSI: 701000869 Official number: 0556	**116** 72 145	Class: (RI)	**1987-01 Ast. Naval Federico Contessi y Cia. S.A. — Mar del Plata** Yd No: 45 Loa 28.25 Br ex - Dght 2.901 Lbp 25.00 Br md 6.41 Dpth 3.31 Welded, 1 dk	**(B11A2FS) Stern Trawler** Ins: 133	**1 oil engine** with flexible couplings & reductiongeared to sc. shaft driving 1 FP propeller Total Power: 441kW (600hp) 11.0kn Caterpillar 3412TA 1 x Vee 4 Stroke 12 Cy. 137 x 152 441kW (600bhp) Caterpillar Tractor Co-USA
9063201 - -	**VICTORIA III** **Changjiang Shipping Co** - *China*	*278* - 158		**1996-08 Jiangxi Jiangzhou Shipyard — Ruichang JX** Yd No: A431 Loa - Br ex - Dght - Lbp - Br md - Dpth - Welded, 1 dk	**(A37B2PS) Passenger Ship** Passengers: unberthed: 168	**2 oil engines** geared to sc. shafts driving 2 FP propellers Total Power: 1,472kW (2,002hp) Daihatsu 6DSM-22 2 x 4 Stroke 6 Cy. 220 x 280 each-736kW (1001bhp) Shaanxi Diesel Engine Factory-China
9390965 *2BYK3* -	**VICTORIA KOSAN** **Lauritzen Kosan Singapore Pte Ltd** Lauritzen Kosan A/S SatCom: Inmarsat C 423591662 *Douglas* *Isle of Man (British)* MMSI: 235070466 Official number: 740876	**7,465** 2,239 8,556 T/cm 18.7	Class: BV (NV)	**2009-07 Sekwang Heavy Industries Co Ltd — Ulsan** Yd No: 1172 Loa 115.00 (BB) Br ex 18.90 Dght 8.675 Lbp 108.10 Br md 18.60 Dpth 10.60 Welded, 1 dk	**(A11B2TG) LPG Tanker** Double Bottom Entire Compartment Length Liq (Gas): 8,055 3 x Gas Tank (s); 2 independent (5% Ni.stl) cyl horizontal, ER 2 Cargo Pump (s): 2x480m³/hr Manifold: Bow/CM: 58.2m	**1 oil engine** driving 1 CP propeller Total Power: 5,920kW (8,049hp) 15.7kn MAN-B&W 8S35MC 1 x 2 Stroke 8 Cy. 350 x 1400 5920kW (8049bhp) MAN Diesel A/S-Denmark AuxGen: 3 x 665kW 450V 60Hz a.c, 1 x 1200kW 450V 60Hz a.c Thrusters: 1 Tunnel thruster (f) Fuel: 104.0 (d.f.) 957.0 (r.f.) 31.0pd
9458896 *V3MD2* -	**VICTORIA-M** **Donawill Holdings Ltd** *Belize City* *Belize* MMSI: 312131000	**252** 76 46	Class: RS (NV)	**2009-12 OAO Moskovskiy Sudostroitelnyy i Sudoremontnyy Zavod — Moscow** Yd No: 311 Loa 31.39 Br ex 7.61 Dght 2.080 Lbp 28.47 Br md 7.51 Dpth 3.97 Welded, 1 dk	**(X11A2YP) Yacht**	**2 oil engines** driving 2 FP propellers Total Power: 714kW (970hp) 11.0kn Caterpillar C18 2 x 4 Stroke 6 Cy. 145 x 183 each-357kW (485bhp) (made 2009) Caterpillar Inc-USA AuxGen: 2 x 50kW a.c Fuel: 35.0 (d.f.)

9578244 *DIPB2* -	**VICTORIA MATHIAS** *launched as* Seabreeze I *-2011* **RWE Seabreeze I GmbH & Co KG** NSB Niederelbe Schiffahrtsgesellschaft mbH & Co KG *Bremerhaven* *Germany* MMSI: 218766000 Official number: 1014	**11,730** 8,190 6,314	Class: GL	**2011-12 Daewoo Shipbuilding & Marine Engineering Co Ltd — Geoje** Yd No: 3303 Loa 120.77 Br ex - Dght 5.000 Lbp 100.00 Br md 40.00 Dpth 8.00 Welded, 1 dk	**(B22A2ZM) Offshore Construction Vessel, jack up** Cranes: 1x1000t	**4 diesel electric oil engines** driving 4 gen. Connecting to 2 elec. motors each (1600kW) driving 2 Directional propellers 7.5kn Thrusters: 2 Retract. directional thruster (f); 2 Retract. directional thruster (a)
9596246 - -	**VICTORIA MAY** - -	**228** 82 -		**2011-10 Macduff Shipyards Ltd — Macduff** Yd No: 650 Loa 24.27 (BB) Br ex - Dght - Lbp - Br md 7.00 Dpth - Welded, 1 dk	**(B11A2FT) Trawler**	**1 oil engine** reduction geared to sc. shaft driving 1 CP propeller Total Power: 634kW (862hp) Cummins KTA-38-M0 1 x Vee 4 Stroke 12 Cy. 159 x 159 634kW (862bhp) Cummins Engine Co Ltd-United Kingdom
8014368 - -	**VICTORIA No. 8** *ex* Chopes No. 1 *-1992* *ex* Tenryu Maru No. 11 *-1992* - SatCom: Inmarsat A 1337305 *Indonesia*	**585** 175 365		**1980-11 Miho Zosensho K.K. — Shimizu** Yd No: 1182 Loa 50.53 Br ex - Dght 2.678 Lbp 43.52 Br md 8.58 Dpth 3.59 Welded, 1 dk	**(B11B2FV) Fishing Vessel**	**1 oil engine** reduction geared to sc. shaft driving 1 FP propeller Total Power: 809kW (1,100hp) Akasaka DM28AFD 1 x 4 Stroke 6 Cy. 280 x 460 809kW (1100bhp) Akasaka Tekkosho KK (Akasaka DieselLtd)-Japan
8914867 - -	**VICTORIA NO. 11** *ex* Zhongyuan Yu 11 *-2005* *ex* Heisei Maru No. 1 *-2005* - -	*349* - -		**1989-10 Fujishin Zosen K.K. — Kamo** Yd No: 552 Loa 69.78 (BB) Br ex - Dght 4.510 Lbp 60.00 Br md 10.70 Dpth 6.96 Welded, 2 dks	**(B11B2FV) Fishing Vessel**	**1 oil engine** with clutches & reverse geared to sc. shaft driving 1 FP propeller Total Power: 973kW (1,323hp) Niigata 6M31AFTE 1 x 4 Stroke 6 Cy. 310 x 530 973kW (1323bhp) Niigata Engineering Co Ltd-Japan Thrusters: 1 Thwart. FP thruster (f)
7631925 *6NHG* -	**VICTORIA No. 102** *ex* Chun Yang No. 102 *-1983* **Dong Ho Deep Sea Fisheries Co Ltd** - *Busan* *South Korea* Official number: BS02-A965	*394* 204 430	Class: (KR)	**1975 Korea Tacoma Marine Industries Ltd — Changwon** Loa 52.61 Br ex - Dght 3.489 Lbp 47.27 Br md 8.41 Dpth 3.81 Welded, 1 dk	**(B11B2FV) Fishing Vessel** Ins: 528 3 Ha: (1.0 x 1.2)2 (1.6 x 1.6)ER	**1 oil engine** driving 1 FP propeller Total Power: 736kW (1,001hp) 12.0kn Yanmar 6GL-UT 1 x 4 Stroke 6 Cy. 240 x 290 736kW (1001bhp) Yanmar Diesel Engine Co Ltd-Japan AuxGen: 2 x 176kW 225V a.c
8714308 *LW2604* -	**VICTORIA P** *ex* Spitsbergen *-2003* *ex* Qilalugaq *-1996* **Pesquera Santa Elena SAI y C** - SatCom: Inmarsat C 470108124 *Buenos Aires* *Argentina* MMSI: 701000587 Official number: 02246	*474* 189 -	Class: (NV)	**1988-04 Hjorungavaag Verksted AS — Hjorungavaag** Yd No: 45 Loa 38.46 Br ex - Dght 4.700 Lbp 32.11 Br md 9.61 Dpth 6.91 Welded, 2 dks	**(B11A2FS) Stern Trawler** Ins: 300 Ice Capable	**1 oil engine** geared to sc. shaft driving 1 FP propeller Total Power: 974kW (1,324hp) Wartsila 6R22 1 x 4 Stroke 6 Cy. 220 x 240 974kW (1324bhp) Wartsila Diesel Oy-Finland AuxGen: 2 x 306kW 380V 50Hz a.c
8502561 *V3JT2* -	**VICTORIA R** *ex* Victoria *-2013* *ex* Ignacy Daszynski *-2012* **World Shipping Ltd** Sadent Shipping Ltd *Belize City* *Belize* MMSI: 312798000 Official number: 291330157	**21,437** 12,477 33,580 T/cm 42.6	Class: UV (PR)	**1988-01 Stocznia Szczecinska im A Warskiego — Szczecin** Yd No: B545/03 Loa 195.23 (BB) Br ex - Dght 10.651 Lbp 185.02 Br md 25.32 Dpth 15.12 Welded, 1 dk	**(A21A2BC) Bulk Carrier** Grain: 43,824 Compartments: 5 Ho, ER 5 Ha: 2 (26.4 x 12.8)3 (20.0 x 12.8)ER	**1 oil engine** driving 1 FP propeller Total Power: 7,322kW (9,955hp) 14.6kn Sulzer 6RTA58 1 x 2 Stroke 6 Cy. 580 x 1700 7322kW (9955bhp) Zaklady Przemyslu Metalowego 'HCegielski' SA-Poznan AuxGen: 3 x 504kW a.c
8983595 *WDA8437* -	**VICTORIA ROSE** - **Victoria Rose Inc** - *Port Lavaca, TX* *United States of America* MMSI: 366854340 Official number: 1126157	**140** 42 -		**2002 T.M. Jemison Construction Co., Inc. — Bayou La Batre, Al** Yd No: 175 L reg 24.14 Br ex - Dght - Lbp - Br md 7.31 Dpth 3.65 Welded, 1 dk	**(B11B2FV) Fishing Vessel**	**1 oil engine** driving 1 Propeller
9350721 *LYTD* -	**VICTORIA SEAWAYS** *ex* Lisco Maxima *-2012* *launched as* Forza *-2009* **LISCO Maxima Shipping Ltd** AB DFDS Seaways SatCom: Inmarsat C 427740810 *Klaipeda* *Lithuania* MMSI: 277408000 Official number: 813	**25,518** 11,568 8,500	Class: RI	**2009-03 Nuovi Cantieri Apuania SpA — Carrara** Yd No: 1241 Loa 198.99 (BB) Br ex 27.00 Dght 6.400 Lbp 176.92 Br md 26.60 Dpth 15.30 Welded, 1 Dk	**(A36A2PR) Passenger/Ro-Ro Ship (Vehicles)** Passengers: unberthed: 116; cabins: 114; berths: 399 Stern door/ramp (p. a.) Stern door/ramp (s. a.) Lane-Len: 2600	**2 oil engines** geared to sc. shafts driving 2 CP propellers Total Power: 24,000kW (32,630hp) 23.0kn Wartsila 12V46 2 x Vee 4 Stroke 12 Cy. 460 x 580 each-12000kW (16315bhp) Wartsila France SA-France AuxGen: 3 x a.c Thrusters: 2 Tunnel thruster (f)
9132650 *VRAY9* -	**VICTORIA SPIRIT** *ex* African Joy *-2013* *ex* Super Ace *-2008* *ex* Super Rubin *-2005* **African Joy Shipping Ltd** Asia Maritime Pacific (Shanghai) Ltd *Hong Kong* *Hong Kong* MMSI: 477993500 Official number: HK-1517	**15,932** 9,568 26,482 T/cm 37.1	Class: NK	**1996-02 Imabari Shipbuilding Co Ltd — Imabari EH (Imabari Shipyard)** Yd No: 518 Loa 169.51 (BB) Br ex - Dght 9.789 Lbp 160.40 Br md 25.50 Dpth 13.65 Welded, 1 dk	**(A21A2BC) Bulk Carrier** Grain: 35,944; Bale: 34,172 Compartments: 5 Ho, ER 5 Ha: (12.8 x 16.0)4 (19.2 x 17.0)ER Cranes: 4x30.5t	**1 oil engine** driving 1 FP propeller Total Power: 5,443kW (7,400hp) 14.0kn Mitsubishi 5UEC50LS 1 x 2 Stroke 5 Cy. 500 x 1950 5443kW (7400bhp) Akasaka Tekkosho KK (Akasaka DieselLtd)-Japan Fuel: 1170.0 (r.f.)
7737468 *TJAQ* D 269	**VICTORIA STAR** - **Compagnie de Peche et de Mareyage (COPEMAR)** - *Douala* *Cameroon*	*176* 91 -		**1977 Esmadan ApS — Esbjerg** Yd No: 95 Loa 31.70 Br ex - Dght - Lbp 27.51 Br md 6.91 Dpth 3.46 Welded, 1 dk	**(B11B2FV) Fishing Vessel**	**1 oil engine** geared to sc. shaft driving 1 FP propeller Total Power: 368kW (500hp) Grenaa 6F24 1 x 4 Stroke 6 Cy. 240 x 300 368kW (500bhp) A/S Grenaa Motorfabrik-Denmark
7029122 - -	**VICTORIA STAR** *ex* Lady McKell *-1998* **Lady Mckell Pleasure Cruises Pty Ltd** Melbourne Star Cruises Pty Ltd *Melbourne, Vic* *Australia* Official number: 343913	*339* 184 15	Class: (LR) ✠ Classed LR until 11/10/74	**1970-09 New South Wales Govt Engineering & Shbldg Undertaking — Newcastle NSW** Yd No: 88 Converted From: Ferry (Passenger only)-1999 Loa 38.66 Br ex 9.35 Dght 2.058 Lbp 35.31 Br md 8.84 Dpth 3.05 Welded, 1 dk	**(A37B2PS) Passenger Ship** Passengers: unberthed: 570	**1 oil engine** driving 1 FP propeller Total Power: 375kW (510hp) 11.0kn MWM RH435AU 1 x 4 Stroke 8 Cy. 250 x 350 375kW (510bhp) Motoren Werke Mannheim AG (MWM)-West Germany AuxGen: 2 x 19kW 415V 50Hz a.c Fuel: 11.5 (d.f.)
9265574 *V2BG6* -	**VICTORIA STRAIT** - **ms 'Victoria Strait' GmbH & Co KG** Carsten Rehder Schiffsmakler und Reederei GmbH & Co KG *Saint John's* *Antigua & Barbuda* MMSI: 304439000 Official number: 4000	**9,966** 5,046 13,760	Class: NV	**2002-12 Jinling Shipyard — Nanjing JS** Yd No: 01-0101 Loa 147.87 (BB) Br ex 23.55 Dght 8.506 Lbp 140.30 Br md 23.25 Dpth 11.50 Welded, 1 dk	**(A33A2CC) Container Ship (Fully Cellular)** Grain: 16,150 TEU 1118 C Ho 334 TEU C Dk 784 TEU incl 220 ref C Compartments: 5 Cell Ho, ER 7 Ha: ER 6 (12.6 x 18.0) (14.0 x 10.4) Cranes: 2x40t Ice Capable	**1 oil engine** geared to sc. shaft driving 1 CP propeller Total Power: 9,730kW (13,229hp) 20.0kn MAN 7L58/64 1 x 4 Stroke 7 Cy. 580 x 640 9730kW (13229bhp) AuxGen: 1 x 1400kW 440V 60Hz a.c, 3 x 610kW a.c Thrusters: 1 Thwart. FP thruster (f)
8810982 *9V6052* -	**VICTORIA STRIKE** *ex* Tyson I *-2002* *ex* Hoei Maru *-2001* **Uni Petroleum Pte Ltd** - *Singapore* *Singapore* MMSI: 564285000 Official number: 389298	**741** 299 1,064	Class: NK	**1988-12 Hakata Zosen K.K. — Imabari** Yd No: 380 Loa 65.40 Br ex - Dght 3.754 Lbp 58.02 Br md 10.01 Dpth 4.53 Welded, 1 dk	**(A13B2TP) Products Tanker**	**1 oil engine** with clutches & sr geared to sc. shaft driving 1 FP propeller Total Power: 956kW (1,300hp) Hanshin LH28 1 x 4 Stroke 6 Cy. 280 x 460 956kW (1300bhp) The Hanshin Diesel Works Ltd-Japan Fuel: 95.0 (r.f.)
9437189 *A8XA2* -	**VICTORIA TRADER** - **ms 'Victoria Trader' Schiffahrts UG (haftungsbeschrankt) & Co KG** Hermann Buss GmbH & Cie KG *Monrovia* *Liberia* MMSI: 636092103 Official number: 92103	**15,334** 5,983 18,471	Class: GL	**2008-09 Zhejiang Ouhua Shipbuilding Co Ltd — Zhoushan ZJ** Yd No: 505 Loa 166.13 (BB) Br ex - Dght 9.500 Lbp 155.08 Br md 25.00 Dpth 14.20 Welded, 1 dk	**(A33A2CC) Container Ship (Fully Cellular)** TEU 1296 C Ho 472 TEU C Dk 824 TEU incl 390 ref C	**1 oil engine** reduction geared to sc. shaft driving 1 CP propeller Total Power: 11,120kW (15,119hp) 19.0kn MAN-B&W 8L58/64 1 x 4 Stroke 8 Cy. 580 x 640 11120kW (15119bhp) MAN B&W Diesel AG-Augsburg AuxGen: 3 x 1600kW 450V a.c Thrusters: 1 Tunnel thruster (f)

IMO / Call sign	Name / Owner	Tonnage	Class	Builder / Dimensions	Type	Machinery
8004002 - -	**VICTORIA V** *ex* Suburban *-2004* *ex* Grand Pacific I *-2004* *ex* Sakae Maru No. 28 *-2004* **Floronel Shipping Corp** - *Philippines*	*486* - 1,451		**1980**-06 **Asakawa Zosen K.K. — Imabari** Yd No: 296 Loa 68.92 Br ex - Dght 4.201 Lbp 64.01 Br md 11.50 Dpth 6.20 Welded, 2 dks	**(A31A2GX) General Cargo Ship**	**1 oil engine** driving 1 FP propeller Total Power: 1,177kW (1,600hp) Akasaka DM33 1 x 4 Stroke 6 Cy. 330 x 500 1177kW (1600bhp) Akasaka Tekkosho KK (Akasaka DieselLtd)-Japan
7728699 *3ELW8* -	**VICTORIA VI** *ex* Victoria *-2007* *ex* Nor Hav *-2005* *ex* Nordhav *-2002* *ex* Cres *-1998* **Cargo-Link A/S** - SatCom: Inmarsat C 435267810 *Panama* *Panama* MMSI: 352678000 Official number: 3368608	**5,846** 1,763 4,476	Class: IV (LR) (HR) (CS) (JR) ✠ Classed LR until 15/6/07	**1980**-06 **Brodogradiliste 'Titovo' — Kraljevica** Yd No: 423 Loa 103.00 (BB) Br ex 19.72 Dght 6.598 Lbp 89.90 Br md 19.50 Dpth 12.20 Welded, 2 dks	**(A35A2RR) Ro-Ro Cargo Ship** Passengers: cabins: 6; driver berths: 12 Stern door/ramp (centre) Len: 5.00 Wid: 9.98 Swl: 40 Lane-Len: 804 Lane-Wid: 3.00 Lane-clr ht: 4.80 Trailers: 69 Grain: 11,140; Bale: 5,629 TEU 247 C RoRo Dk 117 TEU C Dk 130 TEU Compartments: 1 Ho, ER 3 Ha: (25.2 x 12.8) (12.5 x 12.8) (12.5 x 7.7)ER Cranes: 2x25t	**1 oil engine** with flexible couplings & sr geared to sc. shaft driving 1 CP propeller Total Power: 4,800kW (6,526hp) 16.0kn Sulzer 8ZAL40S 1 x 4 Stroke 8 Cy. 400 x 560 4800kW (6526bhp) (new engine 2005) Wartsila Switzerland Ltd-Switzerland AuxGen: 1 x 672kW 400V 50Hz a.c, 2 x 400kW 400V 50Hz a.c Boilers: AuxB (o.f.) 5.9kgf/cm² (5.8bar), AuxB (ex.g.) (fitted: 1980) 5.9kgf/cm² (5.8bar) Thrusters: 1 Thwart. FP thruster (f) Fuel: 120.0 (d.f.) 580.0 (r.f.) 25.5pd
9614103 *3EVY8* -	**VICTORIA VII** *ex* Victoria IV *-2012* **Jianghai Shipping Group Ltd** - SatCom: Inmarsat C 435551210 *Panama* *Panama* MMSI: 373294000 Official number: 4402512	**32,355** 18,118 55,000	Class: BV	**2011**-07 **Zhejiang Jiantiao Shipyard Co Ltd — Sanmen County ZJ** Yd No: JT0704 Loa 189.98 (BB) Br ex - Dght 12.800 Lbp 182.00 Br md 32.26 Dpth 18.00 Welded, 1 dk	**(A21A2BC) Bulk Carrier** Grain: 67,601 Compartments: 5 Ho, ER 5 Ha: ER Cranes: 4x30t	**1 oil engine** driving 1 FP propeller Total Power: 9,480kW (12,889hp) 14.0kn MAN-B&W 6S50MC-C 1 x 2 Stroke 6 Cy. 500 x 2000 9480kW (12889bhp) STX Engine Co Ltd-South Korea AuxGen: 3 x 600kW 60Hz a.c Fuel: 2180.0
9234276 *PBDS* -	**VICTORIABORG** **Wagenborg Rederij BV** Wagenborg Shipping BV SatCom: Inmarsat C 424602910 *Delfzijl* *Netherlands* MMSI: 246029000 Official number: 39594	**6,361** 3,099 9,850 T/cm 18.3	Class: BV	**2001**-12 **Daewoo-Mangalia Heavy Industries S.A. — Mangalia** (Hull) Yd No: 1030 **2001**-12 **Bodewes Scheepswerf "Volharding" Foxhol B.V. — Foxhol** Yd No: 502 Loa 132.20 (BB) Br ex - Dght 8.070 Lbp 123.84 Br md 15.87 Dpth 9.65 Welded, 1 dk	**(A31A2GX) General Cargo Ship** Grain: 12,855 TEU 552 C. 552/20' incl. 25 ref C. Compartments: 2 Ho, ER 2 Ha: (52.5 x 13.2)ER (39.9 x 13.2) Ice Capable	**1 oil engine** reduction geared to sc. shaft driving 1 CP propeller Total Power: 4,197kW (5,706hp) 15.0kn Wartsila 6R38 1 x 4 Stroke 6 Cy. 380 x 475 4197kW (5706bhp) Wartsila Nederland BV-Netherlands AuxGen: 2 x 244kW 400/230V 60Hz a.c
9351153 *PHMM* -	**VICTORIADIEP** *ex* OSC Victoriadiep *-2011* *launched as* Victoriadiep *-2007* **Beheermaatschappij ms 'Victoriadiep' BV** Feederlines BV *Groningen* *Netherlands* MMSI: 245054000 Official number: 51546	**5,057** 2,681 7,750	Class: LR ✠ **100A1** SS 12/2012 strengthened for heavy cargoes, container cargoes in all holds and on all hatch covers Ice Class 1A FS at a draught of 7.197m Max/min draughts fwd 7.197/1.837m Max/min draughts aft 7.197/4.367m Required power 3171kw, installed power 3840kw ✠ **LMC** **UMS** Eq.Ltr: W; Cable: 495.0/44.0 U3 (a)	**2007**-12 **ATVT Sudnobudivnyi Zavod "Zaliv" — Kerch** (Hull) Yd No: (658) **2007**-12 **Bodewes' Scheepswerven B.V. — Hoogezand** Yd No: 658 Loa 119.80 (BB) Br ex 15.43 Dght 7.050 Lbp 113.65 Br md 15.20 Dpth 8.50 Welded, 1 dk	**(A31A2GX) General Cargo Ship** Grain: 9,415 TEU 390 C Ho 174 TEU C Dk 216 TEU Compartments: 2 Ho, ER 2 Ha: (44.3 x 12.7)ER (39.0 x 12.7) Cranes: 2x40t Ice Capable	**1 oil engine** with clutches, flexible couplings & sr geared to sc. shaft driving 1 CP propeller Total Power: 3,840kW (5,221hp) 14.0kn MaK 8M32 1 x 4 Stroke 8 Cy. 320 x 480 3840kW (5221bhp) Caterpillar Motoren GmbH & Co. KG-Germany AuxGen: 3 x 259kW 400V 50Hz a.c, 1 x 400kW 400V 50Hz a.c Boilers: HWH (o.f.) 3.6kgf/cm² (3.5bar) Thrusters: 1 Thwart. CP thruster (f)
9180205 *VHAG* -	**VICTORIAN RELIANCE** *ex* Evolution *-1999* **Commonwealth Bank of Australia** Toll Transport Pty Ltd *Melbourne, Vic* *Australia* MMSI: 503086000 Official number: 856086	**20,343** 6,103 11,000 T/cm 28.7	Class: NV	**1999**-05 **Samsung Heavy Industries Co Ltd — Geoje** Yd No: 1250 Loa 184.00 (BB) Br ex - Dght 6.350 Lbp 172.37 Br md 23.60 Dpth 8.10 Welded, 2 dks	**(A35A2RR) Ro-Ro Cargo Ship** Passengers: cabins: 6; berths: 12; driver berths: 12 Stern door/ramp (centre) Len: 17.00 Wid: 18.60 Swl: - Lane-Len: 2378 Lane-Wid: 3.00 Lane-clr ht: 6.80 Trailers: 177 TEU 592 C RoRo Dk 383 TEU C Dk 209 TEU incl 153 ref C.	**4 oil engines** reduction geared to sc. shaft (s) driving 2 CP propellers Total Power: 15,360kW (20,884hp) 19.5kn Wartsila 8L32 4 x 4 Stroke 8 Cy. 320 x 400 each-3840kW (5221bhp) Wartsila NSD Finland Oy-Finland AuxGen: 2 x 1200kW 440V 60Hz a.c, 2 x 960kW 440V 60Hz a.c Thrusters: 2 Tunnel thruster (f) Fuel: 156.0 (d.f.) (Heating Coils) 755.0 (r.f.) 63.5pd
8829646 *ELJE2* -	**VICTORIANA** *ex* Pacific Challenge *-1989* **Victoriana Maritime Panama SA** Virtue Shipping & Enterprises (HK) Ltd *Monrovia* *Liberia* Official number: 8497	*166* 85 -	Class: BV	**1986 Wanganui Boats N.Z. Ltd. — Wanganui** L reg 26.22 Br ex 7.50 Dght - Lbp - Br md - Dpth 3.50 Welded, 1 dk	**(A37B2PS) Passenger Ship** Hull Material: Aluminium Alloy	**2 oil engines** driving 2 FP propellers Total Power: 260kW (354hp) 12.0kn Caterpillar 3208TA 2 x Vee 4 Stroke 8 Cy. 114 x 127 each-130kW (177bhp) Caterpillar Tractor Co-USA
9184029 *ONDO* -	**VICTORINE** **HSBC Leasing SA** UBEM NV *Antwerpen* *Belgium* MMSI: 205509000 Official number: 01 00675 2007	**23,987** 7,196 9,755 T/cm 34.7	Class: LR ✠ **100A1** SS 03/2010 roll on - roll off cargo ship LI *IWS Ice Class 1C ✠ **LMC** **UMS** Eq.Ltr: I†; Cable: 605.0/64.0 U3 (a)	**2000**-03 **Kawasaki Heavy Industries Ltd — Sakaide KG** Yd No: 1491 Loa 162.49 (BB) Br ex 25.64 Dght 6.500 Lbp 150.00 Br md 25.20 Dpth 15.45 Welded, 4 dks	**(A35A2RR) Ro-Ro Cargo Ship** Passengers: berths: 12; driver berths: 12 Stern door/ramp (centre) Len: 22.92 Wid: 21.72 Swl: 100 Lane-Len: 2307 Lane-Wid: 2.94 Cars: 635, Trailers: 157 Ice Capable	**2 oil engines** with flexible couplings & sr gearedto sc. shafts driving 2 CP propellers Total Power: 9,840kW (13,378hp) 17.8kn MAN 7L40/54 2 x 4 Stroke 7 Cy. 400 x 540 each-4920kW (6689bhp) Kawasaki Heavy Industries Ltd-Japan AuxGen: 1 x 1700kW 450V 60Hz a.c, 2 x 800kW 450V 60Hz a.c Boilers: TOH (o.f.) 10.0kgf/cm² (9.8bar), TOH (ex.g.) 10.0kgf/cm² (9.8bar) Thrusters: 2 Thwart. FP thruster (f) Fuel: 60.0 (d.f.) (Heating Coils) 1570.0 (r.f.) 42.8pd
8923131 *NVIC* -	**VICTORIOUS** **Military Sealift Command (MSC)** *Norfolk, VA* *United States of America* MMSI: 367838000 Official number: CG03068	**3,347** 1,004 2,700	Class: AB	**1991**-08 **McDermott Shipyards Inc — Amelia LA** Yd No: 279 Loa 71.47 Br ex - Dght 7.870 Lbp 57.91 Br md 24.38 Dpth 14.85 Welded, 1 dk	**(B31A2SR) Research Survey Vessel** Ice Capable	**4 diesel electric oil engines** driving 4 gen. each 830kW Connecting to 2 elec. motors each (588kW) driving 2 FP propellers Total Power: 4,472kW (6,080hp) 10.0kn Caterpillar 3512TA 4 x Vee 4 Stroke 12 Cy. 170 x 190 each-1118kW (1520bhp) Caterpillar Inc-USA AuxGen: 1 x 300kW a.c
9473262 *CFN5313* -	**VICTORIOUS** **McAsphalt Marine Transportation Ltd** SatCom: Inmarsat C 431697673 *Toronto, ON* *Canada* MMSI: 316013946 Official number: 833294	**1,299** 389 -	Class: LR ✠ **100A1** SS 06/2009 tug Ice Class 1D at draught of 5.614m Max/min draught fwd 5.614/4.016m Max/min draught aft 5.614/4.016m Protected waters service at ports in the Great Lakes and River St. Lawrance when acting in uncoupled mode. Unrestricted when acting in coupled mode with barge having suitable anchoring equipment on board for the combined unit ✠ **LMC** **UMS** Eq.Ltr: 0; Cable: 15.2/24.0 U3 (a)	**2009**-06 **Penglai Bohai Shipyard Co Ltd — Penglai SD** Yd No: PBZ07-84 Loa 37.18 Br ex 13.51 Dght 5.500 Lbp 35.51 Br md 13.49 Dpth 8.00 Welded, 1 dk	**(B32B2SA) Articulated Pusher Tug** Ice Capable	**2 oil engines** with flexible couplings & sr geared to sc. shafts driving 2 CP propellers Total Power: 3,960kW (5,384hp) 10.5kn MaK 6M25 2 x 4 Stroke 6 Cy. 255 x 400 each-1980kW (2692bhp) Caterpillar Motoren GmbH & Co. KG-Germany AuxGen: 2 x 425kW 440V 60Hz a.c Boilers: e (ex.g.) 10.2kgf/cm² (10.0bar), TOH (o.f.) 10.2kgf/cm² (10.0bar) Fuel: 52.0 (d.f.) 379.0 (r.f.)

IMO / Call sign	Name / Owners / Flag	Tonnage	Class	Builder / Dimensions	Type / Capacity	Machinery
8611661 *PKSI* -	**VICTORIOUS 5** *ex* Laut Teduh 5 *-2009* *ex* DVD No. I *-2000* *ex* Yong Lian *-1998* *ex* DVD No. I *-1997* *ex* Mercandia VI *-1995* *launched as* Superflex Juliet *-1990* **PT Bukit Samudera Perkasa** - *Tanjung Priok* *Indonesia*	**4,280** 1,576 1,283	Class: KI (LR) (NV) ✠ Classed LR until 12/3/91	**1990-03 North East Shipbuilders Ltd. — Southwick, Sunderland** Yd No: 10 Loa 95.81 (BB) Br ex 17.00 Dght 3.601 Lbp 89.34 Br md 15.00 Dpth 9.85 Welded, 2 dks	**(A36A2PR) Passenger/Ro-Ro Ship (Vehicles)** Passengers: unberthed: 303 Bow door/ramp Len: 4.50 Wid: 4.00 Swl: - Stern door/ramp Len: 4.50 Wid: 4.00 Swl: - Quarter bow ramp (s. upr) Len: 6.00 Wid: 3.50 Swl: - Quarter stern ramp (p. upr) Len: 6.00 Wid: 3.50 Swl: - Lane-Len: 684 Lane-Wid: 3.50 Lane-clr ht: 4.20 Lorries: 16, Cars: 85	**10 diesel electric oil engines** driving 10 gen. each 275kW 440V a.c Connecting to 4 elec. motors each (550kW) driving 4 Directional propellers Total Power: 2,950kW (4,010hp) 12.8kn Cummins NTA-855-M 10 x 4 Stroke 6 Cy. 140 x 152 each-295kW (401bhp) Cummins Engine Co Inc-USA Fuel: 120.0 (d.f.) 12.0pd
9610406 *3FTR4* -	**VICTORIOUS ACE** - **White Bear Maritime Ltd** Mitsui OSK Lines Ltd (MOL) SatCom: Inmarsat C 435654110 *Panama* *Panama* MMSI: 356541000 Official number: 4306511	**59,022** 18,290 18,396	Class: NK	**2011-09 Minaminippon Shipbuilding Co Ltd — Usuki OT** Yd No: 719 Loa 199.95 (BB) Br ex - Dght 9.820 Lbp 190.00 Br md 32.20 Dpth 14.70 Welded, 12 dks	**(A35B2RV) Vehicles Carrier** Side door/ramp (s) Quarter stern door/ramp (s. a.) Cars: 6,163	**1 oil engine** driving 1 FP propeller Total Power: 15,130kW (20,571hp) 20.6kn MAN-B&W 7S60MC-C 1 x 2 Stroke 7 Cy. 600 x 2400 15130kW (20571bhp) Mitsui Engineering & Shipbuilding CLtd-Japan Thrusters: 1 Tunnel thruster (f) Fuel: 2860.0
9273375 *MERS9* -	**VICTORIUS** - **Coral Seaways Marine SA** Enterprises Shipping & Trading SA SatCom: Inmarsat C 423500748 *Douglas* *Isle of Man (British)* MMSI: 235007480 Official number: 737153	**87,720** 54,606 171,314	Class: BV	**2004-06 Hyundai Samho Heavy Industries Co Ltd — Samho** Yd No: S193 Loa 289.00 (BB) Br ex - Dght 17.750 Lbp 279.30 Br md 45.00 Dpth 24.10 Welded, 1 dk	**(A21A2BC) Bulk Carrier** Double Hull Grain: 188,500; Bale: 179,499 Compartments: 9 Ho, ER 9 Ha: 7 (15.4 x 20.6)ER 2 (15.4 x 17.2)	**1 oil engine** driving 1 FP propeller Total Power: 16,860kW (22,923hp) 14.6kn B&W 6S70MC 1 x 2 Stroke 6 Cy. 700 x 2674 16860kW (22923bhp) Hyundai Heavy Industries Co Ltd-South Korea
9238325 *V2DS8* -	**VICTORY** *ex* Leopold Oldendorff *-2006* *ex* IVS Victory *-2003* **Masuria Pearl Shipping GmbH & Co KG** Aquila Maritime Management GmbH & Co KG SatCom: Inmarsat C 430532810 *Saint John's* *Antigua & Barbuda* MMSI: 305328000 Official number: 4531	**22,072** 11,132 34,676 T/cm 44.0	Class: AB (GL)	**2002-09 Tianjin Xingang Shipyard — Tianjin** Yd No: 332 Loa 179.28 (BB) Br ex - Dght 10.650 Lbp 173.04 Br md 28.00 Dpth 15.20 Welded, 1 dk	**(A21A2BC) Bulk Carrier** Double Hull Grain: 44,021; Bale: 42,721 Compartments: 5 Ho, ER 5 Ha: 3 (20.8 x 19.6)ER 2 (20.0 x 14.0) Cranes: 4x30t Ice Capable	**1 oil engine** driving 1 FP propeller Total Power: 7,650kW (10,401hp) 14.0kn Sulzer 6RTA48T-B 1 x 2 Stroke 6 Cy. 480 x 2000 7650kW (10401bhp) Yichang Marine Diesel Engine Co Ltd-China AuxGen: 3 x 560kW 450V 60Hz a.c Fuel: 119.0 (d.f.) 1741.0 (r.f.) 28.4pd
9380233 *JD2345* -	**VICTORY** - **Hakone Kankosen KK** - *Hakone, Kanagawa* *Japan* Official number: 140441	*282* - 420		**2007-02 Universal Shipbuilding Corp — Yokohama KN (Keihin Shipyard)** Yd No: 0029 Loa 35.00 Br ex - Dght 1.900 Lbp 29.91 Br md 10.00 Dpth 2.89 Welded, 1 dk	**(A37B2PS) Passenger Ship**	**2 oil engines** reduction geared to sc. shafts driving 2 Propellers Total Power: 868kW (1,180hp) Mitsubishi S6B3-MPTK 2 x 4 Stroke 6 Cy. 135 x 170 each-434kW (590bhp) Mitsubishi Heavy Industries Ltd-Japan
9593232 *CQNV* -	**VICTORY** - **An Do Fe Shipping Management Srl** - *Madeira* *Portugal (MAR)* MMSI: 255804260 Official number: MAR1402	**495** 148 400	Class: BV	**2011-03 Yong Choo Kui Shipyard Sdn Bhd — Sibu** Yd No: 28007 Loa 38.00 Br ex - Dght 4.500 Lbp 33.71 Br md 10.80 Dpth 5.00 Welded, 1 dk	**(B32A2ST) Tug**	**2 oil engines** reduction geared to sc. shafts driving 2 FP propellers Total Power: 3,788kW (5,150hp) Caterpillar 3516B 2 x Vee 4 Stroke 16 Cy. 170 x 190 each-1894kW (2575bhp) Caterpillar Inc-USA AuxGen: 3 x 245kW 50Hz a.c Thrusters: 1 Tunnel thruster (f)
9478781 *E5U2349* -	**VICTORY** *ex* Victory V *-2010* *ex* Victory *-2008* *ex* O'ptasia *-2007* *completed as* Ploes *-2007* **Ginny Worldwide Co Inc** - *Cook Islands Yacht Squadron* *Cook Islands* MMSI: 518399000 Official number: 1438	**498** 149 -	Class: BV (AB)	**2007-05 Lamda Nafs Shipyards SA — Piraeus** Yd No: 102061 Loa 51.84 Br ex - Dght 2.600 Lbp 43.97 Br md 9.20 Dpth 5.00 Welded, 1 dk	**(X11A2YP) Yacht**	**2 oil engines** reduction geared to sc. shafts driving 2 FP propellers Total Power: 1,576kW (2,142hp) M.T.U. 12V2000M70 2 x Vee 4 Stroke 12 Cy. 130 x 150 each-788kW (1071bhp) MTU Friedrichshafen GmbH-Friedrichshafen
9702376 *WDG6857* -	**VICTORY** - **Wahl Fisheries LLC** - *Reedsport, OR* *United States of America* MMSI: 367561420 Official number: 1237586	**365** - -		**2013-05 Fred Wahl Marine Construction Inc — Reedsport, Or** Yd No: 11-114-37 Loa 35.00 (BB) Br ex - Dght 2.460 Lbp - Br md 9.44 Dpth 3.38 Welded, 1 dk	**(B11B2FV) Fishing Vessel**	**1 oil engine** reduction geared to sc. shaft driving 1 Propeller Total Power: 533kW (725hp) Caterpillar C18 1 x 4 Stroke 6 Cy. 145 x 183 533kW (725bhp) Caterpillar Inc-USA
8003292 *WDD8849* -	**VICTORY** - **Black Creek Shipping Co Inc** - SatCom: Inmarsat A 1502124 *Cleveland, OH* *United States of America* MMSI: 367303550 Official number: 637185	**947** 284 -	Class: (AB)	**1981-06 McDermott Shipyards Inc — Amelia LA** Yd No: 259 Converted From: Pusher Tug-2008 Loa 42.68 Br ex 13.72 Dght 6.268 Lbp 39.63 Br md 13.12 Dpth 6.71 Welded, 1 dk	**(B32B2SA) Articulated Pusher Tug**	**2 oil engines** sr geared to sc. shafts driving 2 FP propellers Total Power: 2,898kW (3,940hp) 14.0kn MaK 6MU551AK 2 x 4 Stroke 6 Cy. 450 x 550 each-1449kW (1970bhp) Krupp MaK Maschinenbau GmbH-Kiel AuxGen: 2 x 200kW 460V 50Hz a.c
7313327 - -	**VICTORY** *ex* Miyazaki Maru *-1987* **Delsan Transport Lines Inc** - *Cebu* *Philippines*	*294* 128 -		**1973 KK Kanasashi Zosen — Shizuoka SZ** Yd No: 1103 Loa 48.60 Br ex 7.65 Dght 3.099 Lbp 46.46 Br md 7.62 Dpth 3.56 Welded, 1 dk	**(B11B2FV) Fishing Vessel**	**1 oil engine** driving 1 FP propeller Total Power: 956kW (1,300hp) Niigata 6L25BX 1 x 4 Stroke 6 Cy. 250 x 320 956kW (1300bhp) Niigata Engineering Co Ltd-Japan
7411117 *P2V5113* -	**VICTORY** *ex* Biloela *-2008* *ex* Willunga *-1983* *ex* Privateer *-1978* **Pacific Towing (PNG) Pty Ltd** - *Port Moresby* *Papua New Guinea* MMSI: 553111513	*247* - -	Class: (LR) ✠ Classed LR until 23/1/05	**1975-02 Carrington Slipways Pty Ltd — Newcastle NSW** Yd No: 99 Loa 29.01 Br ex 9.96 Dght 3.988 Lbp 24.80 Br md 9.71 Dpth 4.70 Welded, 1 dk	**(B32A2ST) Tug**	**2 oil engines** reverse reduction geared to sc. shafts driving 2 FP propellers Total Power: 1,838kW (2,498hp) 12.0kn Blackstone ESL8MK2 2 x 4 Stroke 8 Cy. 222 x 292 each-919kW (1249bhp) Mirrlees Blackstone (Stamford)Ltd.-Stamford AuxGen: 2 x 50kW 415V 50Hz a.c
7050298 - -	**VICTORY** *ex* David Le *-1993* *ex* Arthur M *-1993* - -	*111* 75 -		**1968 Capell Marine, Inc. — Freeport, Tx** Yd No: 68-1 L reg 21.43 Br ex 6.76 Dght - Lbp - Br md - Dpth 3.46 Welded	**(B11B2FV) Fishing Vessel**	**1 oil engine** driving 1 FP propeller Total Power: 268kW (364hp)
8910706 *AWCV* -	**VICTORY** *ex* Rasim Akar *-2013* *ex* Aditi *-2007* *ex* Champion Express *-2005* *ex* Hawaiian Express *-2003* **Seven Islands Shipping Ltd** - *Mumbai* *India* MMSI: 419000795 Official number: 4097	**18,260** 8,145 29,998 T/cm 38.0	Class: BV IR (NV) (NK)	**1990-03 Minaminippon Shipbuilding Co Ltd — Usuki OT** Yd No: 609 Conv to DH-2010 Loa 167.00 (BB) Br ex 27.43 Dght 10.257 Lbp 159.00 Br md 27.40 Dpth 15.55 Welded, 1 dk	**(A12B2TR) Chemical/Products Tanker** Double Hull (13F) Liq: 32,523; Liq (Oil): 43,531 Cargo Heating Coils Compartments: 5 Ta, 4 Wing Ta, ER, 2 Wing Slop Ta 4 Cargo Pump (s): 4x750m³/hr Manifold: Bow/CM: 84.5m	**1 oil engine** driving 1 FP propeller Total Power: 6,664kW (9,060hp) 14.3kn B&W 6S50MC 1 x 2 Stroke 6 Cy. 500 x 1910 6664kW (9060bhp) Mitsui Engineering & Shipbuilding CLtd-Japan AuxGen: 3 x 343kW 450V 60Hz a.c Fuel: 153.6 (d.f.) 1637.0 (r.f.) 24.4pd
8883393 - -	**VICTORY** *ex* Taisei Maru No. 32 *-1994* *ex* Taiei Maru *-1994* - -	*474* 296 792		**1976 Ishida Zosen Kogyo YK — Onomichi HS** Loa 48.86 Br ex - Dght - Lbp 44.45 Br md 10.00 Dpth 5.41 Welded, 1 dk	**(A31A2GX) General Cargo Ship**	**1 oil engine** driving 1 FP propeller Total Power: 809kW (1,100hp) 10.0kn Hanshin 6LU28G 1 x 4 Stroke 6 Cy. 280 x 440 809kW (1100bhp) The Hanshin Diesel Works Ltd-Japan

9165293 VICTORY
V7ZU3
-
ex Overseas Maremar *-2013* *ex* Maremar *-2005*
ex Alam Belia *-2002*
Maremar Tanker LLC
OSG Ship Management (GR) Ltd
Majuro *Marshall Islands*
MMSI: 538004915
Official number: 4915

28,400 12,377 47,236 T/cm 50.3
Class: LR (AB)
100A1 SS 04/2013
Double Hull oil tanker
ESP
LI
LMC **UMS IGS**
Cable: 577.5/73.0 U3 (a)

1998-04 Onomichi Dockyard Co Ltd — Onomichi HS Yd No: 430
Loa 182.50 (BB) Br ex 32.23 Dght 12.667
Lbp 172.00 Br md 32.20 Dpth 19.10
Welded, 1 dk

(A13B2TP) Products Tanker
Double Hull (13F)
Liq: 50,335; Liq (Oil): 50,335
Cargo Heating Coils
Compartments: 2 Ta, 12 Wing Ta, 2 Wing Slop Ta, ER
4 Cargo Pump (s): 4x1000m³/hr
Manifold: Bow/CM: 92.9m

1 oil engine driving 1 FP propeller
Total Power: 8,683kW (11,805hp) 15.3kn
MAN-B&W 6S50MC
1 x 2 Stroke 6 Cy. 500 x 1910 8683kW (11805bhp)
Mitsui Engineering & Shipbuilding CLtd-Japan
AuxGen: 3 x 420kW 450V 60Hz a.c
Boilers: e (ex.g.) 21.4kgf/cm² (21.0bar), WTAuxB (o.f.) 18.4kgf/cm² (18.0bar)
Fuel: 112.0 (d.f.) 1350.0 (r.f.) 48.0pd

9097707 VICTORY 1
YD3405
-
PT Wahana Mitra Bahari
-
Batam *Indonesia*

201 61 -
Class: KI

2007-04 PT Sumber Samudra Makmur — Batam
Loa 27.00 Br ex - Dght -
Lbp 24.76 Br md 8.20 Dpth 4.00
Welded, 1 dk

(B32A2ST) Tug

2 oil engines reduction geared to sc. shafts driving 2 Propellers
Total Power: 1,104kW (1,500hp)
Yanmar 6MHL-UT
2 x 4 Stroke 6 Cy. 200 x 240 each-552kW (750bhp)
Yanmar Diesel Engine Co Ltd-Japan

8312227 VICTORY 2
JVPS4
-
ex Bu Yon 2 *-2011* *ex* He Hua *-2005*
ex MMM Merisa *-2004* *ex* Merisa *-2002*
ex Embo *-1995*
Korea Buyon Shipping Co
-
SatCom: Inmarsat C 445745610
Ulaanbaatar *Mongolia*
MMSI: 457456000
Official number: 29721183

5,463 2,257 7,226
Class: SC (KC) (NK) (KI)

1983-09 Imai Shipbuilding Co Ltd — Kochi KC Yd No: 522
Loa 98.18 (BB) Br ex - Dght 7.549
Lbp 89.95 Br md 18.00 Dpth 13.00
Welded, 2 dks

(A31A2GX) General Cargo Ship
Grain: 13,001; Bale: 12,103
Compartments: 2 Ho, ER
2 Ha: (22.2 x 9.8) (24.7 x 9.8)ER
Derricks: 2x30t,2x25t

1 oil engine driving 1 FP propeller
Total Power: 3,354kW (4,560hp) 12.0kn
B&W 6L35MC
1 x 2 Stroke 6 Cy. 350 x 1050 3354kW (4560bhp)
Hitachi Zosen Corp-Japan
AuxGen: 2 x 240kW

8415433 VICTORY 3
9LY2420
-
ex Light *-2011* *ex* Bu Yon 1 *-2006*
ex Revival *-2004* *ex* Phoenix *-2003*
Ever Ocean Shipping Agency Co Ltd
Sea Star Ship Co Ltd
Freetown *Sierra Leone*
MMSI: 667003223
Official number: SL103223

3,026 1,741 4,650
Class: PD UB (KC) (KR) (NK)

1984-04 Yamanaka Zosen K.K. — Imabari Yd No: 278
Loa 91.42 (BB) Br ex - Dght 6.189
Lbp 84.92 Br md 15.02 Dpth 6.51
Welded, 1 dk

(A31A2GX) General Cargo Ship
Grain: 6,983; Bale: 6,721
Compartments: 2 Ho, ER
2 Ha: (13.3 x 10.3) (27.3 x 10.3)ER
Cranes: 2x15t

1 oil engine driving 1 FP propeller
Total Power: 1,471kW (2,000hp) 10.5kn
Makita LS38
1 x 4 Stroke 6 Cy. 380 x 700 1471kW (2000bhp)
Makita Diesel Co Ltd-Japan
AuxGen: 2 x 120kW 445V a.c

8415263 VICTORY 6
PMQF
-
ex Victory *-2009* *ex* Jyohei Maru *-2002*
ex Taisei Maru No. 18 *-1991*
PT Pelayaran Prima Jaya Samudra
Foong Sun Shipping (Pte) Ltd
Jakarta *Indonesia*
MMSI: 525015394

675 435 660
Class: KI

1985-01 Hamamoto Zosensho K.K. — Tokushima Yd No: 665
Loa 56.28 Br ex - Dght 3.040
Lbp 53.66 Br md 9.20 Dpth 5.64
Welded, 1 dk

(A31A2GX) General Cargo Ship
Compartments: 1 Ho, ER
1 Ha: ER

1 oil engine sr geared to sc. shaft driving 1 FP propeller
Total Power: 441kW (600hp)
Yanmar T220-UT
1 x 4 Stroke 6 Cy. 220 x 280 441kW (600bhp)
Yanmar Diesel Engine Co Ltd-Japan

9067142 VICTORY 8
-
-
ex Tenjin Maru No. 3 *-2012*
-
-
Indonesia

499 - 1,300

1993-09 Shinhama Dockyard Co. Ltd. — Anan Yd No: 827
Loa 76.43 Br ex - Dght -
Lbp 70.50 Br md 12.00 Dpth 7.10
Welded, 1 dk

(A31A2GX) General Cargo Ship
Grain: 2,969; Bale: 2,694
Compartments: 1 Ho
1 Ha: (40.3 x 9.6)

1 oil engine reverse geared to sc. shaft driving 1 FP propeller
Total Power: 736kW (1,001hp) 11.0kn
Akasaka A31R
1 x 4 Stroke 6 Cy. 310 x 600 736kW (1001bhp)
Akasaka Tekkosho KK (Akasaka DieselLtd)-Japan

9284635 VICTORY 622
-
-
-
-
China

800 1,550

2003-01 Huanghai Shipbuilding Co Ltd — Rongcheng SD
Loa 65.00 Br ex - Dght 3.700
Lbp 59.50 Br md 10.00 Dpth 4.60
Welded, 1 dk

(A13B2TP) Products Tanker
Double Hull (13F)
Liq: 982; Liq (Oil): 982

1 oil engine reduction geared to sc. shafts driving 1 Propeller
Total Power: 750kW (1,020hp) 11.5kn
Chinese Std. Type LB6250ZLC
1 x 4 Stroke 6 Cy. 250 x 320 750kW (1020bhp)
Zibo Diesel Engine Factory-China
Fuel: 61.0 (r.f.)

7520360 VICTORY AT SEA
WYU8412
-
ex Point Break *-2012* *ex* Christie R *-2005*
Victory at Sea Christian Adventure Retreats Inc
-
Crescent City, CA *United States of America*
Official number: 553235

119 81 -

1973 St Charles Steel Works Inc — Thibodaux, La
Converted From: Trawler-2005
Loa - Br ex - Dght -
Lbp 20.99 Br md 6.63 Dpth 3.46
Welded, 1 dk

(X11A2YP) Yacht

1 oil engine driving 1 FP propeller
Total Power: 246kW (334hp)

9009724 VICTORY EXPRESS
9MFF8
-
ex Sanyo Maru No. 31 *-2006*
Victory Supply Sdn Bhd
-
Port Klang *Malaysia*
MMSI: 533016400
Official number: 332401

739 329 1,200

1990-09 Matsuura Tekko Zosen K.K. — Osakikamijima Yd No: 360
Loa 63.86 (BB) Br ex - Dght 4.252
Lbp 58.00 Br md 10.00 Dpth 4.50
Welded, 1 dk

(A13B2TP) Products Tanker
Compartments: 8 Ta, ER

1 oil engine reverse geared to sc. shaft driving 1 FP propeller
Total Power: 956kW (1,300hp)
Hanshin 6LUN28ARG
1 x 4 Stroke 6 Cy. 280 x 480 956kW (1300bhp)
The Hanshin Diesel Works Ltd-Japan

9318838 VICTORY-G
3ECY4
-
ex Sealink Victoria 3 *-2006*
Rederij Groen BV
-
SatCom: Inmarsat C 435479110
Panama *Panama*
MMSI: 354791000
Official number: 3280307A

1,058 317 1,125
Class: NV (AB)

2004-06 Sealink Shipyard Sdn Bhd — Miri Yd No: 112
Loa 53.80 Br ex - Dght 3.810
Lbp 50.00 Br md 13.80 Dpth 4.50
Welded, 1 dk

(B21A2OS) Platform Supply Ship

2 oil engines reverse reduction geared to sc. shafts driving 2 FP propellers
Total Power: 2,350kW (3,196hp) 8.0kn
Caterpillar 3512B
2 x Vee 4 Stroke 12 Cy. 170 x 190 each-1175kW (1598bhp)
Caterpillar Inc-USA
AuxGen: 2 x 260kW 440V 50Hz a.c, 1 x 85kW
Thrusters: 1 Thwart. FP thruster (f)

8314811 VICTORY HOPE
XUHD4
-
ex Ocean Baby *-2011* *ex* New Anhui *-2008*
ex Sea Partizan *-2005*
ex Express Partizan *-2004* *ex* Atlas *-2000*
ex Anangel Atlas *-1996*
ex Columbus Singapore *-1990*
ex Anangel Atlas *-1989*
Step Shipping Ltd
Shenghao Marine (Hong Kong) Ltd
Phnom Penh *Cambodia*
MMSI: 514826000
Official number: 1384243

10,511 6,280 17,249
Class: PD (LR) (NK) (NV) (AB)
Classed LR until 24/10/08

1984-07 Ishikawajima-Harima Heavy Industries Co Ltd (IHI) — Tokyo Yd No: 2866
Loa 145.52 (BB) Br ex 21.04 Dght 9.460
Lbp 137.72 Br md 21.01 Dpth 13.11
Welded, 1 dk, 2nd dk portable

(A31A2GX) General Cargo Ship
Grain: 21,269; Bale: 21,096
TEU 558 C Ho 334 TEU C Dk 224 TEU
Compartments: 5 Ho, ER
5 Ha: (15.0 x 9.9) (12.7 x 15.6)3 (15.0 x 15.6)ER
Cranes: 5x20t

1 oil engine with clutches, flexible couplings & sr reverse geared to sc. shaft driving 1 CP propeller
Total Power: 3,972kW (5,400hp) 14.5kn
Pielstick 10PC2-6V-400
1 x Vee 4 Stroke 10 Cy. 400 x 460 3972kW (5400bhp)
Ishikawajima Harima Heavy IndustrieCo Ltd (IHI)-Japan
AuxGen: 1 x 550kW 450V 60Hz a.c, 1 x 190kW 450V 60Hz a.c
Fuel: 128.0 (d.f.) 732.5 (r.f.) 17.5pd

7353420 VICTORY I
-
-
ex Fajar-I *-2005* *ex* Sabang Marindo I *-2005*
ex Karimun I *-1995* *ex* Junei Maru No. 5 *-1993*
-
-
Indonesia

251 76 -

1973-11 Shikoku Dockyard Co. Ltd. — Takamatsu Yd No: 765
Loa 28.99 Br ex 8.51 Dght 2.794
Lbp 26.50 Br md 8.49 Dpth 3.89
Riveted\Welded, 1 dk

(B32A2ST) Tug

2 oil engines driving 2 FP propellers
Total Power: 1,912kW (2,600hp) 9.0kn
Daihatsu 6DSM-26
2 x 4 Stroke 6 Cy. 260 x 320 each-956kW (1300bhp)
Daihatsu Diesel Manufacturing Co Lt-Japan

8977572 VICTORY II
H03624
-
ex Chun Jin No. 1 *-2004* *ex* Chin Wen *-2003*
Hon Le Fishery Co Ltd
-
Panama *Panama*
Official number: 32378PEXT

263 123 -

1983 Fong Kuo Shipbuilding Co Ltd — Kaohsiung
L reg 35.12 Br ex - Dght -
Lbp - Br md 6.50 Dpth 2.55
Welded, 1 dk

(B11A2FT) Trawler

1 oil engine driving 1 FP propeller
Total Power: 405kW (551hp)
Niigata
1 x 4 Stroke 405kW (551bhp)
Niigata Engineering Co Ltd-Japan

7014531 VICTORY III
-
-
ex Victory *-2003* *ex* Challenger *-2003*
Colman & Donohue
-

100 - -

1970-04 R. Dunston (Hessle) Ltd. — Hessle Yd No: S869
Loa 23.71 Br ex - Dght 2.830
Lbp - Br md 6.74 Dpth -
Welded, 1 dk

(B11B2FV) Fishing Vessel

1 oil engine driving 1 FP propeller
Total Power: 313kW (426hp)
Cummins
1 x 4 Stroke 313kW (426bhp) (new engine 1970)
Cummins Engine Co Inc-USA

8412730 VICTORY III
VZW2021
-
launched as QC 33 *-1985*
Colin Archibald Boreham
-
Rockhampton, Qld *Australia*
MMSI: 503029900
Official number: 851855

396 152 100
Class: (NV)

1985-07 SBF Shipbuilders (1977) Pty Ltd — Fremantle WA Yd No: OC.CA
Loa 31.81 Br ex 12.91 Dght -
Lbp 29.01 Br md 12.50 Dpth 3.00
Welded, 1 dk

(A37B2PS) Passenger Ship
Hull Material: Aluminium Alloy
Passengers: unberthed: 450

2 oil engines with clutches & sr reverse geared to sc. shafts driving 2 FP propellers
Total Power: 782kW (1,064hp)
MWM TBD234V16
2 x Vee 4 Stroke 16 Cy. 128 x 140 each-391kW (532bhp)
Motoren Werke Mannheim AG (MWM)-West Germany

9395628 C6XG4 -	**VICTORY LEADER** **Victory Ray Ltd** Ray Car Carriers Ltd *Nassau* *Bahamas* MMSI: 311008700 Official number: 8001544	**49,675** 14,903 13,363	Class: NV	**2010-04 Ha Long Shipbuilding Co Ltd — Ha Long** Yd No: CR4900-HL01 Loa 189.30 (BB) Br ex 32.29 Dght 9.100 Lbp 177.73 Br md 32.26 Dpth 36.56 Welded, 13 dks	**(A35B2RV) Vehicles Carrier** Side door/ramp (s) Len: 22.00 Wid: 6.55 Swl: - Quarter stern door/ramp (s. a.) Len: 28.00 Wid: 7.00 Swl: - Cars: 4,914	**1 oil engine** driving 1 FP propeller Total Power: 13,560kW (18,436hp) 19.8kn MAN-B&W 6S60MC-C 1 x 2 Stroke 6 Cy. 600 x 2400 13560kW (18436bhp) MAN Diesel A/S-Denmark AuxGen: 3 x 1600kW a.c Thrusters: 1 Tunnel thruster (f); 1 Tunnel thruster (a)
8126082 YFZO -	**VICTORY PRIMA** *ex* Victory I *-1999* *ex* Botany Triad *-1995* *ex* Inn Ma *-1991* *ex* Botany Triad *-1990* **PT Citra Bintang Familindo** - *Jakarta* *Indonesia* MMSI: 525020006	**3,570** 1,983 5,989 T/cm 13.4	Class: KI (LR) (NK) Classed LR until 21/10/98	**1982-03 K.K. Taihei Kogyo — Akitsu** Yd No: 1478 Loa 101.81 Br ex - Dght 6.785 Lbp 94.01 Br md 16.01 Dpth 8.21 Welded, 1 dk	**(A13B2TP) Products Tanker** Single Hull Liq: 7,285; Liq (Oil): 7,285 Cargo Heating Coils Compartments: 12 Wing Ta, ER 4 Cargo Pump (s): 2x500m^3/hr, 2x200m^3/hr Manifold: Bow/CM: 46m	**1 oil engine** sr geared to sc. shaft driving 1 FP propeller Total Power: 2,001kW (2,721hp) 12.5kn Akasaka DM46 1 x 4 Stroke 6 Cy. 460 x 720 2001kW (2721bhp) Akasaka Tekkosho KK (Akasaka DieselLtd)-Japan AuxGen: 2 x 221kW 450V 60Hz a.c Fuel: 68.0 (d.f.) 430.0 (r.f.) 10.0pd
7518678 XUMY8 -	**VICTORY STAR** *ex* R H H 2 *-1990* *ex* Victory Star *-1995* *ex* Taihei Maru *-1990* **New Matac Sdn Bhd** - *Phnom Penh* *Cambodia* MMSI: 515144000 Official number: 0976026	**309** 111 600	Class: UB (BV)	**1976-07 Nishii Dock Co. Ltd. — Nansei** Yd No: 281 Loa 48.20 Br ex 7.85 Dght 3.101 Lbp 44.00 Br md 7.82 Dpth 3.30 Welded, 1 dk	**(A13B2TU) Tanker (unspecified)** Compartments: 6 Ta, ER 2 Cargo Pump (s): 2x150m^3/hr	**1 oil engine** driving 1 FP propeller Total Power: 441kW (600hp) 10.4kn Hanshin 6L26BSH 1 x 4 Stroke 6 Cy. 260 x 400 441kW (600bhp) Hanshin Nainenki Kogyo-Japan AuxGen: 1 x 32kW 220V 60Hz a.c
9172595 DSNR9 -	**VICTORY STAR** - **Nam Sung Shipping Co Ltd** - *Jeju* *South Korea* MMSI: 440245000 Official number: JJR-049678	**7,401** 3,371 9,157	Class: KR	**1998-06 ShinA Shipbuilding Co Ltd — Tongyeong** Yd No: 394 Loa 127.00 (BB) Br ex - Dght 7.410 Lbp 118.34 Br md 20.00 Dpth 10.70 Welded, 1 dk	**(A33A2CC) Container Ship (Fully Cellular)** TEU 706 incl 100 ref C 10 Ha: 2 (12.9 x 5.2)8 (12.5 x 7.9)ER	**1 oil engine** driving 1 FP propeller Total Power: 5,590kW (7,600hp) 16.5kn B&W 8S35MC 1 x 2 Stroke 8 Cy. 350 x 1400 5590kW (7600bhp) Ssangyong Heavy Industries Co Ltd-South Korea AuxGen: 3 x 540kW 440/220V a.c Thrusters: 1 Tunnel thruster (f) Fuel: 84.0 (d.f.) 526.0 (r.f.)
8028060 YCSA -	**VICTORY UNION** *ex* Irenes Vigor *-2006* *ex* Global Vigor *-2002* *ex* Irenes Vigor *-1997* *ex* Oakby *-1997* *ex* Continental Reliance *-1992* **PT Jaya Samudra Karunia** - *Jakarta* *Indonesia* MMSI: 525015146	**35,622** 21,992 70,000 T/cm 63.6	Class: KI (NV) (AB)	**1983-06 Hyundai Heavy Industries Co Ltd — Ulsan** Yd No: 186 Loa 224.36 (BB) Br ex 32.26 Dght 14.040 Lbp 215.00 Br md 32.20 Dpth 18.00 Welded, 1 dk	**(A21A2BC) Bulk Carrier** Grain: 74,952; Bale: 71,760 Compartments: 7 Ho, ER 7 Ha: 7 (16.0 x 13.2)ER	**1 oil engine** driving 1 FP propeller Total Power: 10,813kW (14,701hp) 16.5kn B&W 7L67GFCA 1 x 2 Stroke 7 Cy. 670 x 1700 10813kW (14701bhp) Hyundai Engine & Machinery Co Ltd-South Korea AuxGen: 3 x 540kW 450V 60Hz a.c Fuel: 284.0 (d.f.) (Heating Coils) 3383.0 (r.f.) 39.5pd
8110875 - -	**VICTRESS** **Howard & Compania Sociedad en Comandita Simple** - *Isla de San Andres* *Colombia* Official number: MC-07-0174	**1,095** 599 1,622	Class: (BV)	**1982-04 Niestern Sander B.V. — Delfzijl** Yd No: 507 Loa 66.15 Br ex 11.56 Dght 4.461 Lbp 59.97 Br md 11.35 Dpth 5.26 Welded, 1 dk	**(A31A2GX) General Cargo Ship** Grain: 2,227; Bale: 2,151 Compartments: 1 Ho, ER 1 Ha: (33.7 x 7.8)ER	**1 oil engine** driving 1 FP propeller Total Power: 868kW (1,180hp) 11.0kn MaK 6M452AK 1 x 4 Stroke 6 Cy. 320 x 450 868kW (1180bhp) Krupp MaK Maschinenbau GmbH-Kiel AuxGen: 2 x 60kW 380V 50Hz a.c, 1 x 32kW 380V 50Hz a.c
9030498 8PVG -	**VICTRESS** *ex* Lass Uranus *-2008* *launched as* Uranus *-1992* **Faversham Ships Ltd** - *Bridgetown* *Barbados* MMSI: 314279000	**1,512** 696 2,386	Class: GL	**1992-07 Rosslauer Schiffswerft GmbH — Rosslau** Yd No: 234 Loa 74.94 Br ex - Dght 4.352 Lbp 70.47 Br md 11.40 Dpth 5.50 Welded, 1 dk	**(A31A2GX) General Cargo Ship** Grain: 2,550; Bale: 2,550 Compartments: 1 Ho, ER 1 Ha: (48.0 x 9.0)ER Ice Capable	**2 oil engines** reverse reduction geared to sc. shafts driving 2 Directional propellers Total Power: 1,090kW (1,482hp) 10.0kn Cummins KT-38-M 2 x Vee 4 Stroke 12 Cy. 159 x 159 each-545kW (741bhp) Cummins Engine Co Ltd-United Kingdom AuxGen: 2 x 88kW 220/440V a.c Thrusters: 1 Thwart. FP thruster (f) Fuel: 65.0 (d.f.)
9371775 H9SC -	**VICUNA** **Vicuna Shipping Inc** Naviera Ultranav Ltda *Panama* *Panama* MMSI: 352317000 Official number: 4238011	**13,666** 6,687 22,062 T/cm 32.9	Class: LR ✠ **100A1** SS 05/2013 Double Hull oil and chemical tanker, Ship Type 1 CR (s.stl) SG 1.85 Maximum temperature 70 degree C ESP **ShipRight** (SDA, FDA plus, CM) *IWS LI SPM ✠ **LMC** **UMS IGS** Eq.Ltr: G; Cable: 660.0/60.0 U3 (a)	**2008-05 Factorias Vulcano SA — Vigo** Yd No: 489 Loa 161.12 (BB) Br ex 23.04 Dght 9.950 Lbp 149.80 Br md 23.00 Dpth 13.40 Welded, 1 dk	**(A12B2TR) Chemical/Products Tanker** Double Hull (13F) Liq: 23,400; Liq (Oil): 23,400 Compartments: 7 Ta, 20 Wing Ta, 2 Wing Slop Ta, ER 27 Cargo Pump (s): 24x175m^3/hr, 3x300m^3/hr Manifold: Bow/CM: 78.8m	**1 oil engine** driving 1 CP propeller Total Power: 8,730kW (11,869hp) 15.0kn Wartsila 6RTA48T 1 x 2 Stroke 6 Cy. 480 x 2000 8730kW (11869bhp) Wartsila Finland Oy-Finland AuxGen: 3 x 875kW 450V 60Hz a.c, 1 x 900kW 440V 60Hz a.c Boilers: e (ex.g.) 10.2kgf/cm^2 (10.0bar), sg (o.f.) 8.2kgf/cm^2 (8.0bar), WTAuxB (o.f.) 13.3kgf/cm^2 (13.0bar) Thrusters: 1 Thwart. CP thruster (f) Fuel: 564.0 (d.f.) 1038.0 (r.f.)
7128631 - PS9074	**VIDA** *ex* Ica 7 *-1995* *ex* Santa Elena XXV *-1975* **Pesquera Ondina SA** - *Pisco* *Peru* Official number: PS-011281-PM	*307* 137 -	Class: (GL)	**1971 Metal Empresa S.A. — Callao** Yd No: L-34 Loa 36.63 Br ex 8.01 Dght - Lbp - Br md - Dpth 3.99 Welded, 1 dk	**(B11B2FV) Fishing Vessel**	**1 oil engine** geared to sc. shaft driving 1 FP propeller Total Power: 633kW (861hp) 12.0kn Caterpillar D398TA 1 x Vee 4 Stroke 12 Cy. 159 x 203 633kW (861bhp) Caterpillar Tractor Co-USA AuxGen: 1 x 14kW 110V a.c
9098830 EAXF 3-HU-312-9	**VIDAL BOCANEGRA CUARTO** **Mariscos Rodriguez SA** - SatCom: Inmarsat C 422405410 *Huelva* *Spain* MMSI: 224054000 Official number: 3-12/1999	**275** 82 -	Class: BV	**2000-01 Astilleros La Parrilla S.A. — San Esteban de Pravia** Yd No: 154 Loa 32.53 Br ex - Dght 3.560 Lbp 28.20 Br md 7.70 Dpth 5.60 Welded, 1 dk	**(B11B2FV) Fishing Vessel**	**1 oil engine** driving 1 FP propeller Total Power: 1,230kW (1,672hp) 11.0kn Caterpillar 3512B-TA 1 x Vee 4 Stroke 12 Cy. 170 x 190 1230kW (1672bhp) (made 1999) Caterpillar Inc-USA
7004457 EAFW -	**VIDAL CUARTO** *ex* Senecozulua *-2010* **Maria Alcira Marino Lijo** - *Pasaia* *Spain* MMSI: 224123820 Official number: 5-1/2004	*388* 224 580	Class: (LR) ✠ Classed LR until 20/9/95	**1970-04 Enrique Lorenzo y Cia SA — Vigo** Yd No: 347 Loa 43.72 Br ex 9.25 Dght 3.099 Lbp 41.03 Br md 9.00 Dpth 3.36 Welded, 1 dk	**(B34A2SH) Hopper, Motor**	**1 oil engine** reverse reduction geared to sc. shaft driving 1 FP propeller Total Power: 302kW (411hp) Stork 5DR21 1 x 4 Stroke 5 Cy. 210 x 300 302kW (411bhp) Naval Stork Werkspoor SA-Spain AuxGen: 1 x 25kW 220V d.c, 1 x 10kW 220V d.c
7013135 EAKJ -	**VIDAL TERCERO** *ex* Freundschaft *-1994* **Maria Alcira Marino Lijo** - *Vilagarcia de Arousa* *Spain* Official number: 5-1/1994	**279** 83 -	Class: (DS) (GL)	**1956 VEB Elbewerft — Boizenburg** Yd No: 1802 Loa 47.96 Br ex 8.34 Dght 2.701 Lbp 46.66 Br md 8.03 Dpth 3.00 Welded, 1 dk	**(B34A2SH) Hopper, Motor**	**1 oil engine** driving 1 FP propeller Total Power: 147kW (200hp) 6.0kn S.K.L. 6NVD36 1 x 4 Stroke 6 Cy. 240 x 360 147kW (200bhp) VEB Schwermaschinenbau "KarlLiebknecht" (SKL)-Magdeburg AuxGen: 1 x 16kW 220V, 1 x 7kW 220V
8845743 UEDZ -	**VIDANOVO** **Flagman Co Ltd** - SatCom: Inmarsat C 427320838 *Magadan* *Russia* MMSI: 273820420 Official number: 903789	**498** 149 207	Class: RS	**1991-06 Zavod 'Nikolayevsk-na-Amure' — Nikolayevsk-na-Amure** Yd No: 1280 Loa 44.88 Br ex 9.47 Dght 3.770 Lbp 39.37 Br md 9.30 Dpth 5.13 Welded, 1 dk	**(B11A2FS) Stern Trawler** Ins: 210 Ice Capable	**1 oil engine** driving 1 FP propeller Total Power: 588kW (799hp) 11.5kn S.K.L. 6NVD48A-2U 1 x 4 Stroke 6 Cy. 320 x 480 588kW (799bhp) SKL Motoren u. Systemtechnik AG-Magdeburg AuxGen: 3 x 150kW a.c

IMO / Call sign	Name / Owner / Manager / Flag	Tonnage	Class	Build / Dimensions	Type	Machinery
9655315 *DDWP2* -	**VIDAR** **Naviera Trans Wind SL** HOCHTIEF Solutions AG *Hamburg* *Germany* MMSI: 218657000 Official number: 23714	**18,886** 5,665 8,265	Class: NV	**2013-12 'Crist' SA — Gdansk** Yd No: 130 Loa 140.29 Br ex 41.24 Dght 6.600 Lbp 133.22 Br md 40.99 Dpth 9.51 Welded, 1 dk	**(Z11C4ZM) Support Platform, jack up** Passengers: 90 Cranes: 1x1200t	**6 diesel electric oil engines** driving 6 gen. each 5438kW a.c Connecting to 4 elec. motors each (2600kW) driving 4 Azimuth electric drive units Total Power: 24,000kW (32,628hp) 10.0kn MaK 8M32C 6 x 4 Stroke 8 Cy. 320 x 480 each-4000kW (5438bhp) Caterpillar Motoren GmbH & Co. KG-Germany Thrusters: 3 Tunnel thruster (f)
9199646 *UBDJ6* -	**VIDAR VIKING** **Viking Supply Ships 5 ApS** Viking Supply Ships AS *Kholmsk* *Russia* MMSI: 273356480	**3,382** 1,145 2,600	Class: NV RS	**2001-02 Havyard Leirvik AS — Leirvik i Sogn** Yd No: 284 Loa 83.70 Br ex 18.04 Dght 7.220 Lbp 77.86 Br md 18.00 Dpth 8.52 Welded, 1 dk	**(B21B20A) Anchor Handling Tug Supply** Liq: 4,295 Cranes: 1x12t Ice Capable	**4 oil engines** reduction geared to sc. shafts driving 2 CP propellers Total Power: 13,440kW (18,274hp) 12.0kn MaK 6M32 2 x 4 Stroke 6 Cy. 320 x 480 each-2880kW (3916bhp) MaK Motoren GmbH & Co. KG-Kiel MaK 8M32 2 x 4 Stroke 8 Cy. 320 x 480 each-3840kW (5221bhp) MaK Motoren GmbH & Co. KG-Kiel AuxGen: 2 x 2640kW 690/400V 50Hz a.c, 2 x 400kW 690/400V 50Hz a.c Thrusters: 1 Retract. directional thruster (f); 1 Thwart. FP thruster (f); 1 Tunnel thruster (a) Fuel: 1000.0 (d.f.)
8915524 *V2QK4* -	**VIDFOSS** *ex* Ice Bird *-2014* *ex* San Carlos Pride *-1993* *ex* Ice Clipper *-1992* **Goda Line Ltd** The Iceland Steamship Co Ltd (Eimskip Island Ehf) (Eimskip Ehf) SatCom: Inmarsat C 430584610 *Saint John's* *Antigua & Barbuda* MMSI: 305846000	**3,625** 1,663 3,546	Class: NV (LR) ✠ Classed LR until 24/2/14	**1990-10 Aarhus Flydedok A/S — Aarhus** Yd No: 193 Loa 92.90 (BB) Br ex 15.37 Dght 5.600 Lbp 84.37 Br md 15.10 Dpth 10.50 Welded, 2 dks, 3rd dk in holds 1 & 2	**(A34A2GR) Refrigerated Cargo Ship** Side doors (s) Ins: 5,130 TEU 42 C.Dk 34/20' (40') incl. 7 ref C. Compartments: 2 Ho, ER, 4 Tw Dk 2 Ha: 2 (6.2 x 7.5)ER Cranes: 2x4t	**1 oil engine** reduction geared to sc. shaft driving 1 CP propeller Total Power: 2,190kW (2,978hp) 13.3kn B&W 6S26MC 1 x 2 Stroke 6 Cy. 260 x 980 2190kW (2978bhp) MAN B&W Diesel A/S-Denmark AuxGen: 1 x 504kW 380V 50Hz a.c, 3 x 312kW 380V 50Hz a.c Boilers: HWH (o.f.) 12.2kgf/cm² (12.0bar) Thrusters: 1 Thwart. CP thruster (f)
8840339 *PNRV* -	**VIDI NO. 1** *ex* Za No. 3 *-2010* *ex* Fukujin Maru No. 10 *-2010* **PT Aliet Sakatha Bahtera Rahayu** - *Tanjung Priok* *Indonesia*	*1,263* 757 -	Class: KI	**1990-03 Kimura Zosen K.K. — Kure** Converted From: Bulk Aggregates Carrier-2010 Lengthened-2010 Loa 73.81 Br ex - Dght 4.300 Lbp 65.96 Br md 11.50 Dpth 5.60 Welded, 1 dk	**(A31A2GX) General Cargo Ship** Compartments: 1 Ho, ER 1 Ha: (18.2 x 9.0)ER	**1 oil engine** driving 1 FP propeller Total Power: 662kW (900hp) 11.0kn Daihatsu 6DLM-28S 1 x 4 Stroke 6 Cy. 280 x 360 662kW (900bhp) Daihatsu Diesel Manufacturing Co Lt-Japan
8609682 - -	**VIDNOE** *ex* Erfolg *-2010* *ex* Poseidon No. 1 *-2009* *ex* Koei Maru No. 5 *-2007* **IBN Co Ltd** -	**490** 239 380	Class: IS	**1986-10 Goriki Zosensho — Ise** Yd No: 883 Converted From: Fishing Vessel-1986 Loa 52.79 Br ex - Dght 3.420 Lbp 45.60 Br md 8.60 Dpth 3.76 Welded, 1 dk	**(A34A2GR) Refrigerated Cargo Ship** Ins: 443	**1 oil engine** geared to sc. shaft driving 1 CP propeller Total Power: 736kW (1,001hp) 11.5kn Akasaka K28FD 1 x 4 Stroke 6 Cy. 280 x 480 736kW (1001bhp) Akasaka Tekkosho KK (Akasaka DieselLtd)-Japan
7408471 - -	**VIEIRASA CATORCE** *ex* Alvamar Tres *-2000* *launched as* Joaquin Moyano *-1980* **Sociedad Pescasur SA**	**238** 146 194	Class: (BV)	**1980-04 Astilleros Gondan SA — Castropol** Yd No: 134 Loa 37.83 Br ex 8.08 Dght 3.601 Lbp 35.21 Br md 8.01 Dpth 3.92 Welded, 1 dk	**(B11A2FT) Trawler**	**1 oil engine** geared to sc. shaft driving 1 FP propeller Total Power: 883kW (1,201hp) 10.5kn Deutz SBA12M528 1 x Vee 4 Stroke 12 Cy. 220 x 280 883kW (1201bhp) Hijos de J Barreras SA-Spain Fuel: 133.0 (d.f.)
6917334 *6WFJ* DAK-1093	**VIEIRASA CINCO** - **Vieira Mar** - *Dakar* *Senegal*	*472* 212 498	Class: (LR) ✠ Classed LR until 11/7/01	**1970-09 Construcciones Navales P Freire SA — Vigo** Yd No: 52 Loa 49.15 Br ex 9.05 Dght 4.052 Lbp 42.02 Br md 9.00 Dpth 4.37 Welded, 1 dk	**(B11A2FT) Trawler** Ins: 453	**1 oil engine** driving 1 FP propeller Total Power: 809kW (1,100hp) 12.0kn MWM TBD484-6 1 x 4 Stroke 6 Cy. 320 x 480 809kW (1100bhp) (made 1967, fitted 1970) Motoren Werke Mannheim AG (MWM)-West Germany AuxGen: 1 x 120kW 220V 50Hz a.c, 1 x 60kW 220V 50Hz a.c
8712673 - -	**VIEIRASA DIECIOCHO** *ex* Shunyo Maru No. 178 *-2010* **Vieira Argentina SA** - *Argentina* Official number: 02563	*999* 335 959		**1987-11 Miho Zosensho K.K. — Shimizu** Yd No: 1316 Loa 70.19 (BB) Br ex 10.62 Dght 4.152 Lbp 60.10 Br md 10.61 Dpth 6.96 Welded	**(B11B2FV) Fishing Vessel** Ins: 1,434	**1 oil engine** with clutches, flexible couplings & sr geared to sc. shaft driving 1 FP propeller Total Power: 1,324kW (1,800hp) Akasaka K31FD 1 x 4 Stroke 6 Cy. 310 x 530 1324kW (1800bhp) Akasaka Tekkosho KK (Akasaka DieselLtd)-Japan Thrusters: 1 Thwart. CP thruster (f)
8801149 *LW9722* -	**VIEIRASA DIECISEIS** *ex* Alvamar Seis *-2005* *ex* Monteferro *-1995* **Vieira Argentina SA** Eduardo Vieira SA SatCom: Inmarsat C 470126410 *Puerto Deseado* *Argentina* MMSI: 701000800 Official number: 0240	**277** 72 353	Class: (LR) (BV) ✠ Classed LR until 16/4/99	**1989-01 Astilleros Armon SA — Navia** Yd No: 188 Loa 39.00 Br ex 9.11 Dght 3.950 Lbp 32.50 Br md 9.00 Dpth 4.00 Welded, 2 dks	**(B11A2FS) Stern Trawler** Ins: 390	**1 oil engine** with clutches, flexible couplings & sr reverse geared to sc. shaft driving 1 FP propeller Total Power: 1,118kW (1,520hp) 10.5kn Caterpillar 3512TA 1 x Vee 4 Stroke 12 Cy. 170 x 190 1118kW (1520bhp) Caterpillar Inc-USA AuxGen: 2 x 155kW 380V 50Hz a.c Fuel: 198.5 (d.f.)
8515116 - -	**VIEIRASA DIECISIETE** *ex* Kaneshige Maru No. 25 *-2010* **Vieira Argentina SA** - *Argentina* Official number: 02568	**746** 344 799		**1985-12 Yamanishi Shipbuilding Co Ltd — Ishinomaki MG** Yd No: 917 Loa 61.10 (BB) Br ex 9.82 Dght 4.011 Lbp 53.00 Br md 9.80 Dpth 6.46 Welded, 2 dks	**(B11B2FV) Fishing Vessel**	**1 oil engine** with clutches, flexible couplings & sr reverse geared to sc. shaft driving 1 FP propeller Total Power: 1,030kW (1,400hp) Akasaka DM28AKFD 1 x 4 Stroke 6 Cy. 280 x 460 1030kW (1400bhp) Akasaka Tekkosho KK (Akasaka DieselLtd)-Japan
8714516 *LW8902* -	**VIEIRASA QUINCE** *ex* Alvamar Cinco *-2008* *ex* Pisco *-1993* **Vieira Argentina SA** - *Puerto Deseado* *Argentina* MMSI: 701006060 Official number: 0179	**449** 202 328	Class: (BV)	**1989-05 Enrique Lorenzo y Cia SA — Vigo** Yd No: 434 Loa 40.00 (BB) Br ex 9.52 Dght 4.370 Lbp 35.23 Br md 9.50 Dpth 6.15 Welded, 2 dks	**(B11A2FS) Stern Trawler** Ins: 410	**1 oil engine** with flexible couplings & sr gearedto sc. shaft driving 1 CP propeller Total Power: 927kW (1,260hp) 11.4kn Deutz SBV6M628 1 x 4 Stroke 6 Cy. 240 x 280 927kW (1260bhp) Hijos de J Barreras SA-Spain AuxGen: 2 x 160kW 380V a.c
7212298 *6WFH* DAK-1094	**VIEIRASA SEIS** - **Vieira Mar** - *Dakar* *Senegal*	*481* 221 627	Class: (BV)	**1972 Construcciones Navales P Freire SA — Vigo** Yd No: 69 Loa 53.37 Br ex - Dght 4.001 Lbp 43.11 Br md 9.00 Dpth 4.40 Welded, 2 dks	**(B11A2FT) Trawler**	**1 oil engine** driving 1 FP propeller Total Power: 846kW (1,150hp) 11.0kn MWM TBD484-8 1 x 4 Stroke 8 Cy. 320 x 480 846kW (1150bhp) Motoren Werke Mannheim AG (MWM)-West Germany Fuel: 229.5 (d.f.)
6422195 *V5VI* L528	**VIEIRASA TRES** - **Cadilu Fishing (Pty) Ltd** - SatCom: Inmarsat C 465901093 *Luderitz* *Namibia* MMSI: 659047000 Official number: 92LB078	*1,135* 341 1,156	Class: (LR) ✠ Classed LR until 15/6/94	**1965-05 Maritima de Axpe S.A. — Bilbao** Yd No: 4 Lengthened-1968 Loa 70.06 Br ex 10.55 Dght 4.700 Lbp 62.26 Br md 10.51 Dpth 7.30 Welded, 2 dks	**(B11A2FS) Stern Trawler** Ins: 1,393	**1 oil engine** driving 1 FP propeller Total Power: 1,361kW (1,850hp) 14.0kn Werkspoor TMABS398 1 x 4 Stroke 8 Cy. 390 x 680 1361kW (1850bhp) Hijos de J Barreras SA-Spain
8852253 *WAE9107* -	**VIEKODA BAY** **f/v Viekoda Bay LLC** - *Kodiak, AK* *United States of America* MMSI: 303407000 Official number: 939078	*192* 130 -		**1988 Frank J Abena III — Santa Rosa CA** Loa - Br ex - Dght - Lbp 28.83 Br md 8.90 Dpth 2.53 Welded, 1 dk	**(B11B2FV) Fishing Vessel**	**1 oil engine** driving 1 FP propeller

Ship / Owner	Tonnage	Class	Builder / Dimensions	Type	Machinery
9318670 **VIEN DONG 3** *3WGP* - **Vietnam Sea Transport & Chartering Co (VITRANSCHART) (Cong Ty Van Tai Bien Va Thue Tau Vietnam)** - SatCom: Inmarsat C 457425610 *Saigon* *Vietnam* MMSI: 574256000 Official number: VNSG-1703-TH	**4,095** 2,448 6,523	Class: NK VR	**2004-06 Bach Dang Shipyard — Haiphong** Yd No: 208 Loa 102.79 Br ex 17.02 Dght 6.957 Lbp 94.50 Br md 17.00 Dpth 8.80 Welded, 1 dk	**(A31A2GX) General Cargo Ship** Grain: 8,610; Bale: 8,159 Compartments: 2 Ho, ER 2 Ha: (25.9 x 10.9)ER (25.4 x 10.9) Derricks: 4x25t	**1 oil engine** driving 1 FP propeller Total Power: 2,648kW (3,600hp) 12.5kn Hanshin LH41LA 1 x 4 Stroke 6 Cy. 410 x 800 2648kW (3600bhp) The Hanshin Diesel Works Ltd-Japan AuxGen: 2 x 265kW 440V 60Hz a.c Fuel: 80.0 (d.f.) 372.0 (r.f.) 11.0pd
9391555 **VIEN DONG 5** *3WPB* - **Vietnam Sea Transport & Chartering Co (VITRANSCHART) (Cong Ty Van Tai Bien Va Thue Tau Vietnam)** - *Saigon* *Vietnam* MMSI: 574380000 Official number: VNSG-1791-TH	**4,124** 2,472 6,509	Class: NK VR	**2006-10 Saigon Shipbuilding Industry Co — Ho Chi Minh City** Yd No: 213 Loa 102.84 (BB) Br ex 17.00 Dght 6.957 Lbp 94.50 Br md 17.00 Dpth 8.80 Welded, 2 dks	**(A31A2GX) General Cargo Ship** Grain: 8,610; Bale: 8,159 Compartments: 2 Ho, ER 2 Ha: (25.9 x 10.0)ER (23.5 x 10.0) Derricks: 4x25t	**1 oil engine** driving 1 FP propeller Total Power: 2,648kW (3,600hp) 12.5kn Hanshin LH41LA 1 x 4 Stroke 6 Cy. 410 x 800 2648kW (3600bhp) The Hanshin Diesel Works Ltd-Japan AuxGen: 2 x 240kW 440V a.c Fuel: 410.0
9023665 **VIEN DONG 08** *3WDJ* *ex Hoang Hoa 08 -2010* - **Far Eastern Trading Transportation JSC** - *Haiphong* *Vietnam* Official number: VN-1471-VT	**377** 247 555	Class: VR	**1996-01 Nam Ha Shipyard — Nam Ha** Loa 46.38 Br ex 7.51 Dght 3.000 Lbp 44.00 Br md 7.49 Dpth 3.75 Welded, 1 dk	**(A31A2GX) General Cargo Ship**	**1 oil engine** driving 1 Propeller Total Power: 199kW (271hp) Skoda 6L160 1 x 4 Stroke 6 Cy. 160 x 225 199kW (271bhp) CKD Praha-Praha
8656441 **VIEN DONG 38-ALCI** *XVUY* *completed as Huy Hieu 09-ALCI -2009* - **Agriculture Leasing Co I** Vien Dong Trading JSC *Haiphong* *Vietnam*	**1,599** 1,088 3,148	Class: VR	**2009-07 Haiphong Shipyard — Haiphong** Yd No: THB-30-12 Loa 79.80 Br ex 12.82 Dght 5.060 Lbp 74.80 Br md 12.80 Dpth 6.20 Welded, 1 dk	**(A31A2GX) General Cargo Ship** Grain: 3,950 Compartments: 2 Ho, ER 2 Ha: ER 2 (20.4 x 8.0)	**1 oil engine** reduction geared to sc. shaft driving 1 FP propeller Total Power: 1,100kW (1,496hp) 10.0kn Chinese Std. Type 8300ZLC 1 x 4 Stroke 8 Cy. 300 x 380 1100kW (1496bhp) Zibo Diesel Engine Factory-China
6702789 **VIENNA** *5NAJ* - **Ibru Sea Foods Ltd** - *Lagos* *Nigeria* Official number: 321519	*166* 54 -		**1965 Schiffswerft Korneuburg A.G. — Korneuburg** Yd No: 651 Loa 23.60 Br ex 6.35 Dght 2.572 Lbp 19.99 Br md 6.30 Dpth 3.20 Welded, 1 dk	**(B11A2FT) Trawler** Ins: 63	**1 oil engine** driving 1 FP propeller Total Power: 353kW (480hp) 10.5kn MWM 1 x Vee 4 Stroke 12 Cy. 140 x 180 353kW (480bhp) Motoren Werke Mannheim AG (MWM)-West Germany
9450416 **VIENNA EXPRESS** *DGWF2* - **Hapag-Lloyd AG** - SatCom: Inmarsat C 421835510 *Hamburg* *Germany* MMSI: 218355000 Official number: 22414	**93,750** 37,699 103,648 T/cm 122.0	Class: GL	**2010-01 Hyundai Heavy Industries Co Ltd — Ulsan** Yd No: 2095 Loa 335.08 (BB) Br ex - Dght 14.610 Lbp 319.00 Br md 42.80 Dpth 24.50 Welded, 1 dk	**(A33A2CC) Container Ship (Fully Cellular)** TEU 8749 incl 730 ref C.	**1 oil engine** driving 1 FP propeller Total Power: 57,200kW (77,769hp) 25.2kn MAN-B&W 12K98ME 1 x 2 Stroke 12 Cy. 980 x 2660 57200kW (77769bhp) Hyundai Heavy Industries Co Ltd-South Korea AuxGen: 1 x 6880kW 6600/690V a.c, 1 x 5145kW 6600/690V a.c, 2 x 3894kW 6600/690V a.c, 2 x 2934kW 6600/690V a.c Thrusters: 1 Tunnel thruster (f)
9593713 **VIENNA WOOD N** *VRHS6* - **Leo Navigation Inc** AM Nomikos Transworld Maritime Agencies SA SatCom: Inmarsat C 447703328 *Hong Kong* *Hong Kong* MMSI: 477051600 Official number: HK-2926	**31,540** 18,765 55,768 T/cm 56.9	Class: NK	**2011-02 IHI Marine United Inc — Yokohama KN** Yd No: 3327 Loa 190.00 (BB) Br ex - Dght 12.735 Lbp 185.00 Br md 32.26 Dpth 18.10 Welded, 1 dk	**(A21A2BC) Bulk Carrier** Grain: 72,062; Bale: 67,062 Compartments: 5 Ho, ER 5 Ha: 4 (20.9 x 18.6)ER (14.6 x 18.6) Cranes: 4x30t	**1 oil engine** driving 1 FP propeller Total Power: 8,890kW (12,087hp) 14.5kn Wartsila 6RT-flex50 1 x 2 Stroke 6 Cy. 500 x 2050 8890kW (12087bhp) Diesel United Ltd.-Aioi Fuel: 200.0 (d.f.) 1880.0 (r.f.)
9362176 **VIENNE** *PONQ* *ex T Fortuner -2012* - *ex Hiep Thang 10-Bidv -2009* **PT Gemilang Raya Maritim** - *Jakarta* *Indonesia*	**1,266** 821 2,204	Class: KI (VR)	**2006-04 Haiphong Mechanical & Trading Co. — Haiphong** Yd No: 0406 Loa 75.84 Br ex 10.87 Dght 4.500 Lbp 72.56 Br md 10.85 Dpth 5.57 Welded, 1 dk	**(A31A2GX) General Cargo Ship**	**1 oil engine** reduction geared to sc. shaft driving 1 FP propeller Total Power: 647kW (880hp) S.K.L. 8NVD48-2U 1 x 4 Stroke 8 Cy. 320 x 480 647kW (880bhp) SKL Motoren u. Systemtechnik AG-Magdeburg AuxGen: 2 x 80kW 400V a.c
9068902 **VIEQUES II** *WDD3935* - **Puerto Rico Ports Authority** - *San Juan, PR* *United States of America* MMSI: 367138260 Official number: 1041579	**493** 203 -		**1996-01 Breaux Bay Craft, Inc. — Loreauville, La** Yd No: 1695 L reg 38.67 Br ex - Dght - Lbp - Br md 9.00 Dpth 3.65 Welded, 1 dk	**(A37B2PS) Passenger Ship** Hull Material: Aluminium Alloy	**1 oil engine** driving 1 Propeller
7368190 **VIER GEBROEDERS** *PJJW* SA114 *ex Lummetje -1980* **Sufish NV** - *Willemstad* *Curacao* MMSI: 306035000 Official number: 1991-C-1301	*255* 96 -	Class: (BV)	**1974-03 T. van Duijvendijk's Scheepswerven B.V. — Alphen/Rijn** Yd No: 1348 Loa 34.98 Br ex 7.75 Dght 3.201 Lbp 30.87 Br md 7.70 Dpth 4.20 Welded, 1 dk	**(B11B2FV) Fishing Vessel**	**1 oil engine** driving 1 FP propeller Total Power: 912kW (1,240hp) De Industrie 8D70 1 x 4 Stroke 8 Cy. 305 x 460 912kW (1240bhp) B.V. Motorenfabriek "De Industrie"-Alphen a/d Rijn
9217840 **VIER GEBROEDERS** *PCHA* TH 48 **Gebr W J de Jonge** - *Tholen* *Netherlands* MMSI: 245345000 Official number: 37584	**312** 93		**2000-04 Gebr. Kooiman B.V. Scheepswerf en Machinefabriek — Zwijndrecht** Yd No: 160 Loa 41.25 Br ex - Dght - Lbp - Br md 10.00 Dpth 2.80 Welded, 1 dk	**(B11B2FV) Fishing Vessel**	**2 oil engines** geared to sc. shafts driving 2 FP propellers Total Power: 918kW (1,248hp) Caterpillar 3412T 2 x Vee 4 Stroke 12 Cy. 137 x 152 each-459kW (624bhp) Caterpillar Inc-USA
9561203 **VIER NAVIGATOR** *YERQ* - *ex Dorie -2011* **PT Vierlines** - *Jakarta* *Indonesia* Official number: 3264/PST	**289** 87 246	Class: KI (AB)	**2011-05 Wuhu Dajiang Shipbuilding Co Ltd — Wuhu AH** Yd No: SWM1026 Loa 32.00 Br ex - Dght 3.800 Lbp 30.14 Br md 9.20 Dpth 4.60 Welded, 1 dk	**(B32A2ST) Tug**	**2 oil engines** reduction geared to sc. shafts driving 2 FP propellers Total Power: 2,350kW (3,196hp) Caterpillar 3512B 2 x Vee 4 Stroke 12 Cy. 170 x 190 each-1175kW (1598bhp) Caterpillar Inc-USA AuxGen: 2 x 99kW a.c Fuel: 260.0 (d.f.)
8723696 **VIERA** *UAGR* *ex Zarasay -1999 ex Zarasai -1996* - *ex Zarasay -1992* **Marshal Zhukov Co Ltd** - *Petropavlovsk-Kamchatskiy* *Russia* MMSI: 273455940	**366** 107 124	Class: RS	**1986-06 Sudostroitelnyy Zavod "Avangard" — Petrozavodsk** Yd No: 603 Loa 35.72 Br ex 8.92 Dght 3.470 Lbp 31.00 Br md - Dpth 6.07 Welded, 2 dks	**(B11A2FS) Stern Trawler** Ice Capable	**1 oil engine** driving 1 FP propeller Total Power: 589kW (801hp) 10.9kn S.K.L. 6NVD48A-2U 1 x 4 Stroke 6 Cy. 320 x 480 589kW (801bhp) VEB Schwermaschinenbau "KarlLiebknecht" (SKL)-Magdeburg AuxGen: 2 x 200kW a.c
8403492 **VIERGE DE L'OCEAN** *FHBO* SM 584781 *ex Lapart Bihen -1992* **Hamon** - *St-Malo* *France* MMSI: 227330000 Official number: 584781	**156** 38 -		**1985-04 Ch. Normands Reunis — Courseulles-sur-Mer** (Hull) **1985-04 Ateliers et Chantiers de La Manche — Dieppe** Yd No: 1327 Loa 23.02 Br ex 7.40 Dght - Lbp 19.82 Br md - Dpth 3.92 Welded, 1 dk	**(B11A2FS) Stern Trawler** Ins: 80	**1 oil engine** driving 1 FP propeller Total Power: 441kW (600hp) Baudouin 12P15.2SR 1 x Vee 4 Stroke 12 Cy. 150 x 150 441kW (600bhp) Societe des Moteurs Baudouin SA-France
8847179 **VIERGE MARIE** *EI8467* DA 32 *ex Glorieuse Vierge Marie -2006* **Tomas Whelahan** - *Drogheda* *Irish Republic* MMSI: 250000546 Official number: 403986	*141* 42 -		**1988-12 Chantiers Piriou — Concarneau** Yd No: 127 Loa 22.40 Br ex - Dght - Lbp 20.40 Br md 7.00 Dpth 3.44 Welded, 1 dk	**(B11A2FT) Trawler**	**1 oil engine** geared to sc. shaft driving 1 CP propeller Total Power: 1,210kW (1,645hp) 10.0kn Mitsubishi S12R-MPTK 1 x Vee 4 Stroke 12 Cy. 170 x 180 1210kW (1645bhp) (new engine 1998) Mitsubishi Heavy Industries Ltd-Japan

IMO / Call sign	Name / Owner / Port	Tonnage	Class	Builder / Dimensions	Type / Cargo	Machinery
7388566 *LW6049* -	**VIERNES SANTO** **Pesquera Santa Cruz SA** - *Puerto Deseado* *Argentina* MMSI: 701006001 Official number: 0668	**240** 140 -	Class: (BV)	**1975-03 Construcciones Navales Santodomingo SA — Vigo** Yd No: 505 Loa 29.19 Br ex 7.55 Dght 3.379 Lbp 25.48 Br md 7.50 Dpth 5.41 Welded, 1 dk	**(B11A2FS) Stern Trawler** Grain: 180 Compartments: 1 Ho, ER	**1 oil engine** geared to sc. shaft driving 1 FP propeller Total Power: 588kW (799hp) 11.0kn Deutz SBA8M528 1 x 4 Stroke 8 Cy. 220 x 280 588kW (799bhp) Kloeckner Humboldt Deutz AG-West Germany Fuel: 115.0 (d.f.)
8662555 *9LY2630* -	**VIET 8** *ex* Xiang Zhang Jia Jie Gong 0010 *-2013* *ex* Wan Liu An Fu 018 *-2010* **Big Fame Investment Ltd** Sunrise International Shipping Co Ltd *Freetown* *Sierra Leone* MMSI: 667003433 Official number: SL103433	**666** 200 -	Class: ZC	**2007-06 Taoyuan Sanchagang Shipyard — Taoyuan County HN** Loa 55.50 Br ex 10.10 Dght 2.450 Lbp 53.90 Br md 10.00 Dpth 3.65 Welded, 1 dk	**(B33A2DB) Bucket Ladder Dredger**	**2 oil engines** reduction geared to sc. shafts driving 2 Propellers Total Power: 536kW (728hp) Cummins NT-855-M 2 x 4 Stroke 6 Cy. 140 x 152 each-268kW (364bhp)
8662543 *9LY2636* -	**VIET 66** *ex* Jie Shun Da 22 *-2013* **HK Dragon Flying Int'l Trading Ltd** - *Freetown* *Sierra Leone* MMSI: 667003439 Official number: SL103439	**1,678** 939 3,057	Class: SL (Class contemplated) ZC	**2002-06 Guangzhou Panyu Yuefeng Shiprepair & Building Yard — Guangzhou GD** Loa 67.50 Br ex 16.30 Dght 3.380 Lbp 63.75 Br md 16.00 Dpth 4.00 Welded, 1 dk	**(A24D2BA) Aggregates Carrier**	**2 oil engines** reduction geared to sc. shafts driving 2 Propellers Total Power: 678kW (922hp) Cummins 1 x 339kW (461bhp) Chongqing Cummins Engine Co Ltd-China Cummins KT-19-M 1 x 4 Stroke 6 Cy. 159 x 159 339kW (461bhp) Chongqing Cummins Engine Co Ltd-China
8662608 *9LY2634* -	**VIET 86** *ex* Yue Du Cheng Huo 9011 *-2013* **HK Dragon Flying Int'l Trading Ltd** - *Freetown* *Sierra Leone* MMSI: 667003437 Official number: SL103437	**1,588** 889 3,302	Class: SL (Class contemplated) ZC	**2006-01 Guangzhou Panyu Nansha Xianglong Dockyard — Guangzhou GD** Loa 73.00 Br ex 15.50 Dght 3.450 Lbp 69.50 Br md 15.20 Dpth 4.50 Welded, 1 dk	**(A24D2BA) Aggregates Carrier**	**2 oil engines** reduction geared to sc. shafts driving 2 Propellers Total Power: 662kW (900hp) Chinese Std. Type 6190ZLC 2 x 4 Stroke 6 Cy. 190 x 210 each-331kW (450bhp) Jinan Diesel Engine Co Ltd-China
8662189 *9LY2635* -	**VIET 168** *ex* Tian Li 78 *-2013* **HK Dragon Flying Int'l Trading Ltd** - *Freetown* *Sierra Leone* MMSI: 667003438 Official number: SL103438	**1,688** 945 -	Class: SL (Class contemplated)	**2006-06 Qingyuan Qingcheng Yongli Shipyard — Qingyuan GD** Loa 74.87 Br ex 15.47 Dght - Lbp 70.40 Br md 15.20 Dpth 4.60 Welded, 1 dk	**(A24D2BA) Aggregates Carrier**	**2 oil engines** reduction geared to sc. shafts driving 2 FP propellers Total Power: 814kW (1,106hp) 8.0kn Cummins KTA-19-M600 2 x 4 Stroke 6 Cy. 159 x 159 each-407kW (553bhp) Chongqing Cummins Engine Co Ltd-China
8868094 - -	**VIET ANH** *ex* VP 10 *-2006* *ex* Sam Son 28 *-2000* *ex* Ngoai Thuong 04 *-1997* **Nam Anh Long Ltd** - *Saigon* *Vietnam*	**425** 246 600	Class: VR	**1987-01 Fishing Shipbuilding & Repairing Enterprise — Vietnam** Converted From: General Cargo Ship-2004 Lengthened & Widened & Deepened-2004 Loa 49.58 Br ex 8.70 Dght 3.150 Lbp 47.02 Br md 8.40 Dpth 4.25 Welded, 1 dk	**(A13B2TU) Tanker (unspecified)** Grain: 484 Compartments: 2 Ho, ER	**1 oil engine** reduction geared to sc. shaft driving 1 FP propeller Total Power: 103kW (140hp) Yanmar 5KDGGE 1 x 4 Stroke 5 Cy. 145 x 170 103kW (140bhp) (made 1977) Yanmar Diesel Engine Co Ltd-Japan
7337103 *H09296* -	**VIET DUC VII** *ex* Mr. Adam *-1974* **Camarao Fishing Corp** - *Panama* *Panama* Official number: 483274	*134* 97 -		**1973 at Mobile, Al** L reg 23.47 Br ex - Dght - Lbp - Br md 6.84 Dpth 3.41 Welded	**(B11A2FT) Trawler**	**1 oil engine** driving 1 FP propeller Total Power: 268kW (364hp) Caterpillar D353SCAC 1 x 4 Stroke 6 Cy. 159 x 203 268kW (364bhp) Caterpillar Tractor Co-USA
7301647 - -	**VIET DUC XI** *ex* Lady Celia *-1974* - - -	*135* 98 -		**1972 Marine Builders, Inc. — Mobile, Al** L reg 23.47 Br ex - Dght - Lbp - Br md 6.84 Dpth 3.41 Welded	**(B11B2FV) Fishing Vessel**	**1 oil engine** driving 1 FP propeller Total Power: 195kW (265hp)
9046875 *3WDV* -	**VIET GAS** *ex* Capella Gas *-2000* **International Gas Products Shipping JSC (Gas Shipping JSC)** - SatCom: Inmarsat C 457415910 *Saigon* *Vietnam* MMSI: 574159149 Official number: VNSG-1927-TG	**1,683** 505 1,601 T/cm 7.6	Class: NK VR	**1992-12 Murakami Hide Zosen K.K. — Imabari** Yd No: 341 Loa 78.03 Br ex - Dght 4.463 Lbp 72.00 Br md 12.60 Dpth 5.50 Welded, 1 dk	**(A11B2TG) LPG Tanker** Liq (Gas): 1,807 2 x Gas Tank (s); 2 independent (C.mn.stl) cyl horizontal 2 Cargo Pump (s): 2x150m³/hr	**1 oil engine** driving 1 FP propeller Total Power: 1,618kW (2,200hp) 12.0kn Akasaka A34 1 x 4 Stroke 6 Cy. 340 x 660 1618kW (2200bhp) Akasaka Tekkosho KK (Akasaka DieselLtd)-Japan AuxGen: 2 x 240kW a.c Fuel: 170.0 (d.f.)
8014095 - -	**VIET GAS 03** *ex* Koho Maru No. 11 *-2005* **Viet Hai Shipping & Real Properties Corp** - *Vietnam* MMSI: 574633000	*494* 304 567	Class: (NK)	**1980-10 Kochi Jyuko (Eiho Zosen) K.K. — Kochi** Yd No: 1401 Loa 52.96 Br ex - Dght 3.633 Lbp 48.54 Br md 9.30 Dpth 4.02 Welded, 1 dk	**(A11B2TG) LPG Tanker** Liq (Gas): 747 2 x Gas Tank (s);	**1 oil engine** driving 1 FP propeller Total Power: 956kW (1,300hp) 11.0kn Akasaka DM28R 1 x 4 Stroke 6 Cy. 280 x 460 956kW (1300bhp) Akasaka Tekkosho KK (Akasaka DieselLtd)-Japan AuxGen: 2 x 144kW
8650007 *XVYE* -	**VIET HAI 06** **Viet Hai Co Ltd** - *Haiphong* *Vietnam* MMSI: 574012459 Official number: VN-2867-VT	**1,599** 1,102 3,160	Class: VR	**2009-04 Cuong Thinh JSC — Haiphong** Yd No: THB-30 Loa 79.80 Br ex 12.82 Dght 5.040 Lbp 74.80 Br md 12.80 Dpth 6.20 Welded, 1 dk	**(A31A2GX) General Cargo Ship** Grain: 3,950 Compartments: 2 Dp Ta, ER 2 Ha: ER 2 (20.4 x 8.0)	**1 oil engine** reduction geared to sc. shaft driving 1 FP propeller Total Power: 735kW (999hp) 10.0kn Chinese Std. Type 8300ZLC 1 x 4 Stroke 8 Cy. 300 x 380 735kW (999bhp) Zibo Diesel Engine Factory-China Fuel: 50.0
9469479 *3WLC9* -	**VIET HAI STAR** *ex* Thanh Hai 28 *-2005* **Viet Hai Co Ltd** - SatCom: Inmarsat C 457449510 *Haiphong* *Vietnam* MMSI: 574495000 Official number: VN-3550-VT	**2,363** 1,449 4,062	Class: VR	**2007-12 Nam Ha Shipyard — Nam Ha** Yd No: LD/TH-07 Loa 87.50 (BB) Br ex 13.62 Dght 5.900 Lbp 81.20 Br md 13.60 Dpth 7.40 Welded, 1 dk	**(A31A2GX) General Cargo Ship** Grain: 5,279; Bale: 4,799 Compartments: 2 Ho, ER 2 Ha: ER Cranes: 2x10t	**1 oil engine** reduction geared to sc. shaft driving 1 FP propeller Total Power: 1,500kW (2,039hp) 11.0kn Chinese Std. Type G8300ZC 1 x 4 Stroke 8 Cy. 300 x 380 1500kW (2039bhp) Zibo Diesel Engine Factory-China AuxGen: 2 x a.c Fuel: 240.0
9026045 - -	**VIET HUNG 01-ALCI** - **Agriculture Leasing Co I** - *Haiphong* *Vietnam* MMSI: 574658000	**299** 209 522	Class: VR	**2003-12 in Vietnam** Yd No: H-168 Loa 46.70 Br ex 8.22 Dght 2.580 Lbp 44.10 Br md 8.00 Dpth 3.20 Welded, 1 dk	**(A31A2GX) General Cargo Ship** Grain: 742; Bale: 714 Compartments: 2 Ho, ER 2 Ha: (12.0 x 5.0)ER (8.5 x 5.0)	**2 oil engines** geared to sc. shafts driving 2 FP propellers Total Power: 198kW (270hp) 9.0kn Skoda 6L160 2 x 4 Stroke 6 Cy. 160 x 225 each-99kW (135bhp) CKD Praha-Praha
9555462 *XVMI* -	**VIET HUNG 09** - **Vu Viet Hung Co Ltd** - *Haiphong* *Vietnam* MMSI: 574012591	**1,742** 1,061 3,151	Class: VR	**2010-05 Huy Van Private Enterprise — Kim Thanh** Yd No: TB-02-15-SD2 Converted From: General Cargo Ship-2010 Loa 87.68 Br ex - Dght 4.800 Lbp 82.53 Br md 12.60 Dpth 6.48 Welded, 1 dk	**(A13B2TP) Products Tanker** Double Hull (13F) Compartments: 10 Wing Ta, ER	**1 oil engine** reduction geared to sc. shaft driving 1 FP propeller Total Power: 735kW (999hp) 12.0kn Chinese Std. Type 8300ZLC 1 x 4 Stroke 8 Cy. 300 x 380 735kW (999bhp) Zibo Diesel Engine Factory-China AuxGen: 2 x 88kW 400V 50Hz a.c
9563847 *XVBH* -	**VIET HUY 09** - **Viet Huy Co Ltd** Tu Cuong Co Ltd SatCom: Inmarsat C 457495410 *Haiphong* *Vietnam* MMSI: 574954000	**1,400** 889 2,574	Class: VR	**2009-08 Minh Khai Shipyard — Truc Ninh** Yd No: TKT-516D Loa 75.90 Br ex 11.86 Dght 4.850 Lbp 71.00 Br md 11.84 Dpth 5.90 Welded, 1 dk	**(A21A2BC) Bulk Carrier** Grain: 3,288; Bale: 2,962 Compartments: 2 Ho, ER 2 Ha: ER 2 (17.1 x 7.8)	**1 oil engine** reduction geared to sc. shaft driving 1 FP propeller Total Power: 698kW (949hp) 11.0kn Chinese Std. Type CW6200ZC 1 x 4 Stroke 6 Cy. 200 x 270 698kW (949bhp) Weifang Diesel Engine Factory-China AuxGen: 2 x 62kW 400V a.c
9010034 *3WPY* -	**VIET LONG** *ex* San Yang *-2006* *ex* Unison Praise *-1996* **Eastern Dragon Shipping Co Ltd (EDSCO) (Cong Ty Van Tai Bien Dong Long)** - *Haiphong* *Vietnam* MMSI: 574371000 Official number: VN-2089-VT	**5,551** 2,351 7,044	Class: NK VR	**1991-09 Shin Kochi Jyuko K.K. — Kochi** Yd No: 7012 Loa 98.17 (BB) Br ex - Dght 7.427 Lbp 89.95 Br md 18.80 Dpth 12.90 Welded, 2 dks	**(A31A2GX) General Cargo Ship** Grain: 13,789; Bale: 12,611 Compartments: 2 Ho, ER 2 Ha: 2 (20.3 x 12.7)ER Derricks: 2x30t,2x25t	**1 oil engine** driving 1 FP propeller Total Power: 2,427kW (3,300hp) 12.4kn Hanshin 6EL40 1 x 4 Stroke 6 Cy. 400 x 800 2427kW (3300bhp) The Hanshin Diesel Works Ltd-Japan AuxGen: 3 x 164kW a.c Fuel: 525.0 (r.f.)

IMO / Call sign	Name / Owner / Port	Tonnage	Class	Builder / Dimensions	Type	Machinery
8122995 - -	**VIET PHONG** *ex* Hakusei Maru No. 2 *-2004* **An Pha Petrol Group JSC**	*498* - 566	Class: (NK)	**1982-03 Shirahama Zosen K.K. — Honai** Yd No: 106 Loa 54.51 Br ex - Dght 3.552 Lbp 50.02 Br md 9.42 Dpth 4.02 Welded, 1 dk	**(A11B2TG) LPG Tanker** Liq (Gas): 763	**1 oil engine** sr geared to sc. shaft driving 1 FP propeller Total Power: 736kW (1,001hp) 10.5kn Daihatsu 6DSM-26A 1 x 4 Stroke 6 Cy. 260 x 300 736kW (1001bhp) Daihatsu Diesel Manufacturing Co Lt-Japan
9621089 *3WCR9* -	**VIET PHU 09** **Viet Phu JSC** - *Haiphong* *Vietnam* MMSI: 574000950	**1,316** 816 2,368	Class: VR	**2012-06 Nguyen Van Tuan Mechanical Shipbuilding IPE — Kien Xuong** Yd No: THB-14-04 Loa 74.70 Br ex 11.23 Dght 4.750 Lbp 70.00 Br md 11.20 Dpth 5.85 Welded, 1 dk	**(A31A2GX) General Cargo Ship** Compartments: 2 Ho, ER 2 Ha: (18.7 x 7.6)ER (19.2 x 7.6)	**1 oil engine** reduction geared to sc. shaft driving 1 FP propeller Total Power: 698kW (949hp) 12.0kn Chinese Std. Type CW6200ZC 1 x 4 Stroke 6 Cy. 200 x 270 698kW (949bhp) Weichai Power Co Ltd-China Fuel: 32.0
8656398 *XVYG* -	**VIET PHUC 08** **Viet Phuc Co Ltd** - *Haiphong* *Vietnam* Official number: VN-2857-VT	**1,599** 1,088 3,156	Class: VR	**2009-04 Nam Trieu Shipbuilding Industry Co. Ltd. — Haiphong** Yd No: THB-30-67 Loa 79.80 Br ex 12.82 Dght 5.040 Lbp 74.80 Br md 12.80 Dpth 6.20 Welded, 1 dk	**(A31A2GX) General Cargo Ship** Grain: 5,244 Compartments: 2 Ho, ER 2 Ha: ER 2 (20.4 x 8.0)	**1 oil engine** reduction geared to sc. shaft driving 1 FP propeller Total Power: 1,100kW (1,496hp) 10.5kn Chinese Std. Type 8300ZLC 1 x 4 Stroke 8 Cy. 300 x 380 1100kW (1496bhp) Zibo Diesel Engine Factory-China
8852916 *WDE3658* -	**VIET PRIDE** *ex* Capt. le *-2004* **Le & Le Inc** - *Biloxi, MS* *United States of America* MMSI: 367342380 Official number: 698893	*202* 138 -		**1986 M.M. Flechas Shipyard — Pascagoula, Ms** Loa - Br ex - Dght - Lbp 26.15 Br md 8.05 Dpth 3.72 Welded, 1 dk	**(B11B2FV) Fishing Vessel**	**1 oil engine** driving 1 FP propeller
9599743 *3WKX9* -	**VIET STAR** *launched as* Nam Long *-2014* **Viet Star Co Ltd** - *Haiphong* *Vietnam* MMSI: 574002040	**2,998** - 4,986		**2014-03 Khien Ha Trading Co Ltd — Haiphong** Yd No: HT-169.10 Loa 90.98 Br ex - Dght 6.850 Lbp 84.26 Br md 15.60 Dpth 8.65 Welded, 1 dk	**(A31A2GX) General Cargo Ship**	**1 oil engine** reduction geared to sc. shaft driving 1 FP propeller Total Power: 2,000kW (2,719hp) Chinese Std. Type G8300ZC 1 x 4 Stroke 8 Cy. 300 x 380 2000kW (2719bhp) in China
8667282 - -	**VIET THAI 126** **Agribank Leasing Co II** Viet Thai Shipping Co Ltd (Cong Ty Tnhh Van Bien Viet Thai) *Haiphong* *Vietnam* Official number: VN-2199-VT	**1,598** 1,062 3,155	Class: VR	**2007-04 Haiphong Mechanical & Trading Co. — Haiphong** Yd No: THB-11-01 Loa 79.80 Br ex 12.82 Dght 5.100 Lbp 74.80 Br md 12.80 Dpth 6.08 Welded, 1 dk	**(A31A2GX) General Cargo Ship** Grain: 3,409 Compartments: 2 Ho, ER 2 Ha: ER 2 (20.4 x 8.4)	**1 oil engine** driving 1 FP propeller 1.0kn Chinese Std. Type CW8200ZC 1 x 4 Stroke 8 Cy. 200 x 270 Weifang Diesel Engine Factory-China
9561693 - -	**VIET THANG 36** **Viet Thang Trading Co** - *Vietnam* MMSI: 574002140	**2,998** - 5,050		**2013-11 Vu Hat Duong JSC — Hai Duong** Yd No: S52-05 Loa 91.94 Br ex - Dght 6.300 Lbp 84.97 Br md 15.30 Dpth 7.90 Welded, 1 dk	**(A31A2GX) General Cargo Ship** Grain: 6,590; Bale: 6,058 Compartments: 2 Ho, ER 2 Ha: (21.1 x 10.0)ER (20.3 x 10.0) Cranes: 2x10t	**1 oil engine** reduction geared to sc. shaft driving 1 FP propeller Total Power: 1,765kW (2,400hp) 12.0kn Chinese Std. Type G8300ZC 1 x 4 Stroke 8 Cy. 300 x 380 1765kW (2400bhp) in China
9269312 *3WCC9* -	**VIET THANG 68** *ex* Ocean 28 *-2014* *ex* Hoang Cuong 28 *-2012* *ex* Viet Gas 02 *-2012* *ex* Hoang Cuong 28 *-2011* *ex* Viet Gas 02 *-2010* **Viet Thang Shipping & Trading Joint Stock Co** - *Haiphong* *Vietnam* MMSI: 574226000 Official number: VN-3491-VT	**2,777** 1,519 2,650	Class: VR	**2002-08 Ha Long Shipbuilding Co Ltd — Ha Long** Yd No: HT-01 Loa 92.17 Br ex 14.04 Dght 5.000 Lbp 84.90 Br md 14.00 Dpth 6.50 Welded, 1 dk	**(A11B2TG) LPG Tanker** Liq (Gas): 2,500	**1 oil engine** driving 1 FP propeller Total Power: 2,795kW (3,800hp) Mitsubishi 6UET45/75 1 x 2 Stroke 6 Cy. 450 x 750 2795kW (3800bhp) Kobe Hatsudoki KK-Japan
9632454 *3WCM9* -	**VIET THANG 126** *ex* Viet Thang 18 *-2011* **Truong Thanh JSC** - *Haiphong* *Vietnam* Official number: VN-3271-VT	**1,599** 1,032 3,233	Class: VR	**2011-05 Hang Giang Co Ltd — Haiphong** Yd No: S.32-76 Loa 78.63 Br ex 12.62 Dght 5.350 Lbp 73.60 Br md 12.60 Dpth 6.48 Welded, 1 dk	**(A31A2GX) General Cargo Ship** Bale: 3,313 Compartments: 2 Ho, ER 2 Ha: ER 2 (19.8 x 8.4)	**1 oil engine** driving 1 FP propeller Total Power: 735kW (999hp) 10.0kn S.K.L. 8NVD48A-1U 1 x 4 Stroke 8 Cy. 320 x 480 735kW (999bhp) (made 1989, fitted 2011) VEB Schwermaschinenbau "KarlLiebknecht" (SKL)-Magdeburg AuxGen: 2 x 52kW 400V a.c Fuel: 84.0 (d.f.)
8941171 - -	**VIET THANH** *ex* Billy *-2011* *ex* Lady Anna *-2011* - *New Iberia, LA* *United States of America* Official number: 1055886	**160** 48 -		**1997 Ocean Marine, Inc. — Bayou La Batre, Al** Yd No: 328 L reg 27.92 Br ex - Dght - Lbp - Br md 7.62 Dpth 4.05 Welded, 1 dk	**(B11B2FV) Fishing Vessel**	**1 oil engine** driving 1 FP propeller
9502403 *XVSH* -	**VIET THUAN 06** *ex* Truong Phat 18 *-2009* **Truong Nguyen Bus Transport Import - Export Co Ltd** - SatCom: Inmarsat C 457439910 *Haiphong* *Vietnam* MMSI: 574399000	**1,599** 1,081 3,029	Class: VR	**2008-08 Marine Service Co. No. 1 — Haiphong** Yd No: TKC 48A-10SD Loa 74.52 Br ex 12.62 Dght 5.250 Lbp 70.90 Br md 12.60 Dpth 6.30 Welded, 1 dk	**(A31A2GX) General Cargo Ship** Bale: 3,975 Compartments: 2 Ho, ER 2 Ha: (18.0 x 8.0)ER (20.9 x 8.0)	**1 oil engine** reduction geared to sc. shaft driving 1 FP propeller Total Power: 736kW (1,001hp) 10.5kn Chinese Std. Type 8300ZLC 1 x 4 Stroke 8 Cy. 300 x 380 736kW (1001bhp) Zibo Diesel Engine Factory-China AuxGen: 2 x 84kW 400V a.c
9352901 *3WML* -	**VIET THUAN 08** *ex* Phu An 46 *-2008* **Viet Thuan Transport Co Ltd** - *Haiphong* *Vietnam* MMSI: 574575000 Official number: VN-1969-VT	**1,199** 787 2,311	Class: VR	**2005-07 Mechanical Shipbuilding Aquatic Product Enterprise — Haiphong** Yd No: DH-04-08 Loa 69.99 Br ex 11.82 Dght 4.850 Lbp 66.15 Br md 11.80 Dpth 5.90 Welded, 1 dk	**(A31A2GX) General Cargo Ship**	**1 oil engine** reduction geared to sc. shaft driving 1 FP propeller Total Power: 736kW (1,001hp) S.K.L. 6NVD48A-2U 1 x 4 Stroke 6 Cy. 320 x 480 736kW (1001bhp) (made 1973) SKL Motoren u. Systemtechnik AG-Magdeburg
9544841 *XVVN* -	**VIET THUAN 18** **Viet Thuan Co Ltd** - *Haiphong* *Vietnam* MMSI: 574671000	**1,599** 1,074 3,072	Class: VR	**2009-04 Nam Trieu Shipbuilding Industry Co. Ltd. — Haiphong** Yd No: TKT-129M-SD Loa 79.60 Br ex 12.82 Dght 5.050 Lbp 74.80 Br md 12.80 Dpth 6.10 Welded, 1 dk	**(A31A2GX) General Cargo Ship** Bale: 3,405 Compartments: 2 Ho, ER 2 Ha: ER 2 (20.4 x 8.4)	**1 oil engine** reduction geared to sc. shaft driving 1 FP propeller Total Power: 720kW (979hp) 10.0kn Chinese Std. Type CW8200ZC 1 x 4 Stroke 8 Cy. 200 x 270 720kW (979bhp) (made 2007) Weichai Power Co Ltd-China AuxGen: 2 x 64kW 400V 50Hz a.c
8656453 - -	**VIET THUAN 26** **An Thang Co Ltd** - *Haiphong* *Vietnam* MMSI: 574012524	**999** 545 1,829	Class: VR	**2009-12 Hoang Tung Trading JSC — Nam Sach** Yd No: TKT579 Loa 65.00 Br ex 12.02 Dght 3.450 Lbp 62.50 Br md 12.00 Dpth 4.30 Welded, 1 dk	**(A31A2GX) General Cargo Ship** Compartments: 3 Ho, ER 3 Ha: (13.0 x 9.1) (12.8 x 9.1)ER (11.8 x 9.1)	**2 oil engines** reduction geared to sc. shafts driving 2 FP propellers Total Power: 510kW (694hp) Chinese Std. Type R6160ZC 2 x 4 Stroke 6 Cy. 160 x 225 each-255kW (347bhp) Weifang Diesel Engine Factory-China AuxGen: 2 x 18kW 400V a.c
9622186 *3WAJ9* -	**VIET THUAN 35** **Viet Thuan Transport Co Ltd** - *Haiphong* *Vietnam* Official number: VN-3159-VT	**999** 447 1,930	Class: VR	**2010-08 Kim Son Shipbuilding & Transport Co — Dong Trieu** Loa 68.30 Br ex 12.62 Dght 3.500 Lbp 64.75 Br md 12.60 Dpth 4.20 Welded, 1 dk	**(A31A2GX) General Cargo Ship** Compartments: 2 Ho, ER 2 Ha: ER 2 (17.1 x 8.6)	**2 oil engines** reduction geared to sc. shafts driving 2 FP propellers Total Power: 510kW (694hp) 10.0kn Chinese Std. Type 6160ZC 2 x 4 Stroke 6 Cy. 160 x 225 each-255kW (347bhp) Weichai Power Co Ltd-China AuxGen: 2 x 30kW 400V a.c
9557707 *3WFT* -	**VIET THUAN 36** **Viet Thuan Co Ltd** - *Haiphong* *Vietnam* MMSI: 574981000	**1,599** 1,064 3,067	Class: VR	**2009-12 Kim Son Shipbuilding & Transport Co — Dong Trieu** Yd No: DKTB02-25 Loa 79.60 Br ex 12.82 Dght 5.050 Lbp 74.80 Br md 12.80 Dpth 6.10 Welded, 1 dk	**(A31A2GX) General Cargo Ship** Bale: 3,405 Compartments: 2 Ho, ER 2 Ha: ER 2 (20.4 x 8.4)	**1 oil engine** reduction geared to sc. shaft driving 1 FP propeller Total Power: 720kW (979hp) 14.0kn Chinese Std. Type CW8200ZC 1 x 4 Stroke 8 Cy. 200 x 270 720kW (979bhp) Weichai Power Co Ltd-China AuxGen: 2 x 99kW 400V a.c Fuel: 30.0 (d.f.)

IMO / Call sign	Name / Owner / Port	Tonnage / Class	Build / Dimensions	Type / Cargo	Machinery
8667294 *3WRT* -	**VIET THUAN 37** **Viet Thuan Co Ltd** - *Haiphong* *Vietnam* Official number: VN-2295-VT	**1,598** 1,062 3,155 Class: VR	**2008-05 Haiphong Mechanical & Trading Co. — Haiphong** Yd No: THB-11-03 Loa 79.80 Br ex 12.83 Dght 5.100 Lbp 74.80 Br md 12.80 Dpth 6.08 Welded, 1 dk	**(A31A2GX) General Cargo Ship** Grain: 3,409 Compartments: 2 Ho, ER 2 Ha: ER 2 (20.4 x 8.4)	**1 oil engine** driving 1 FP propeller 10.0kn Chinese Std. Type CW8200ZC 1 x 4 Stroke 8 Cy. 200 x 270 Weichai Power Co Ltd-China
9525510 *XVKG* -	**VIET THUAN 68** *ex* Hai Phuong 26 *-2008* **Agriculture Leasing Co I** Viet Thuan Transport Co Ltd SatCom: Inmarsat C 457439710 *Haiphong* *Vietnam* MMSI: 574012248	**1,599** 1,072 3,095 Class: VR	**2008-04 Haiphong Mechanical & Trading Co. — Haiphong** Yd No: VNB02-01 Loa 79.60 Br ex - Dght 5.150 Lbp 74.80 Br md 12.80 Dpth 6.10 Welded, 1 dk	**(A31A2GX) General Cargo Ship** Grain: 3,943 Compartments: 2 Ho, ER 2 Ha: ER 2 (20.4 x 8.4)	**1 oil engine** reduction geared to sc. shaft driving 1 FP propeller Total Power: 735kW (999hp) 12.0kn Chinese Std. Type 8300ZLC 1 x 4 Stroke 8 Cy. 300 x 380 735kW (999bhp) Zibo Diesel Engine Factory-China AuxGen: 2 x 110kW 400V a.c
8508838 *3WBO* -	**VIET TIN 01** *ex* Healthy Falcon *-2008* *ex* Eiwa Maru *-1998* **Viet Trust Shipping Corp (Cong Ty Co Phan Van Tai Viet Tin)** - SatCom: Inmarsat C 457405610 *Saigon* *Vietnam* MMSI: 574056046 Official number: VNSG-1468-TC	**2,998** 1,599 5,453 Class: VR (NK)	**1985-01 Taihei Kogyo K.K. — Hashihama, Imabari** Yd No: 1757 Loa 104.53 (BB) Br ex - Dght 6.719 Lbp 96.02 Br md 15.61 Dpth 7.80 Welded, 1 dk	**(A13B2TP) Products Tanker** Single Hull Liq: 5,549; Liq (Oil): 5,549 Cargo Heating Coils Compartments: 8 Ta, ER	**1 oil engine** driving 1 CP propeller Total Power: 2,059kW (2,799hp) 12.5kn Akasaka A38 1 x 4 Stroke 6 Cy. 380 x 740 2059kW (2799bhp) Akasaka Tekkosho KK (Akasaka DieselLtd)-Japan AuxGen: 3 x 200kW a.c Thrusters: 1 Thwart. FP thruster (f)
9147916 *XVAN* -	**VIET TIN LUCKY** *ex* Woo Young *-2009* **Viet Trust Shipping Corp (Cong Ty Co Phan Van Tai Viet Tin)** - *Saigon* *Vietnam* MMSI: 574937000 Official number: VNSG-1966-TD	**4,573** 2,137 6,693 T/cm 16.5 Class: KR VR	**1996-04 Shinyoung Shipbuilding Industry Co Ltd — Yeosu** Yd No: 184 Loa 109.90 (BB) Br ex - Dght 6.713 Lbp 102.00 Br md 18.20 Dpth 8.50 Welded, 1 dk	**(A12B2TR) Chemical/Products Tanker** Double Hull Liq: 7,475; Liq (Oil): 7,475 Cargo Heating Coils Compartments: 12 Wing Ta, 2 Wing Slop Ta, ER 12 Cargo Pump (s): 12x180m³/hr Manifold: Bow/CM: 54.7m	**1 oil engine** driving 1 FP propeller Total Power: 3,354kW (4,560hp) 14.5kn B&W 6L35MC 1 x 2 Stroke 6 Cy. 350 x 1050 3354kW (4560bhp) (made 1994) Ssangyong Heavy Industries Co Ltd-South Korea AuxGen: 3 x 320kW 445V a.c Thrusters: 1 Tunnel thruster (f) Fuel: 80.0 360.0 (r.f.)
9023201 - -	**VIET TRUNG 05** **Hai Son Co Ltd** - *Haiphong* *Vietnam*	**344** 323 666 Class: VR	**2003-06 Nam Trieu Shipbuilding Industry Co. Ltd. — Haiphong** Yd No: TKT-071NC Lengthened-2005 Loa 50.85 Br ex 8.20 Dght 2.850 Lbp 47.33 Br md 7.90 Dpth 3.50 Welded, 1 dk	**(A31A2GX) General Cargo Ship**	**1 oil engine** driving 1 Propeller Total Power: 224kW (305hp) 8.0kn S.K.L. 6NVD36-1U 1 x 4 Stroke 6 Cy. 240 x 360 224kW (305bhp) SKL Motoren u. Systemtechnik AG-Magdeburg
9027001 - -	**VIET TRUNG 10-ALCI** *ex* Thanh Trung 18-Alci *-2009* **Agriculture Leasing Co I** Viet Trung Trading Transport & Investment JSC *Haiphong* *Vietnam* MMSI: 574012508	**499** 296 1,012 Class: VR	**2004-01 Nam Trieu Shipbuilding Industry Co. Ltd. — Haiphong** Yd No: HP-0323 Loa 56.45 Br ex 9.02 Dght 3.450 Lbp 52.70 Br md 9.00 Dpth 4.10 Welded, 1 dk	**(A31A2GX) General Cargo Ship**	**1 oil engine** geared to sc. shaft driving 1 FP propeller Total Power: 425kW (578hp) 10.0kn S.K.L. 8NVD36A-1U 1 x 4 Stroke 8 Cy. 240 x 360 425kW (578bhp) SKL Motoren u. Systemtechnik AG-Magdeburg
8653645 *3WDX9* -	**VIET TRUNG 36** *completed as* Trang Thanh 27 *-2012* **Hai Son Co Ltd** - *Haiphong* *Vietnam* MMSI: 574012104	**499** 331 885 Class: VR	**2007-06 Haiphong Mechanical & Trading Co. — Haiphong** Yd No: THB-19 Loa 57.00 Br ex - Dght 3.260 Lbp 53.48 Br md 9.00 Dpth 3.97 Welded, 1 dk	**(A31A2GX) General Cargo Ship** Grain: 1,120 Compartments: 2 Ho, ER 2 Ha: (14.5 x 5.0)ER (16.5 x 5.0)	**1 oil engine** reduction geared to sc. shaft driving 1 FP propeller Total Power: 441kW (600hp) 10.0kn Chinese Std. Type 8170ZCA 1 x 4 Stroke 8 Cy. 170 x 200 441kW (600bhp) (new engine 2011) Weichai Power Co Ltd-China AuxGen: 2 x 20kW 380V a.c Fuel: 15.0
8746454 *3WYW* -	**VIET TRUNG 45** *ex* Hoang Hieu 15 *-2010* **Hai Son Co Ltd** - SatCom: Inmarsat C 457400048 *Haiphong* *Vietnam* MMSI: 574000930	**499** 325 942 Class: VR	**2008-03 Thang Loi Enterprise — Kim Thanh** Yd No: TKT457C Loa 57.07 Br ex - Dght 3.380 Lbp 53.32 Br md 9.00 Dpth 4.05 Welded, 1 dk	**(A31A2GX) General Cargo Ship**	**1 oil engine** reduction geared to sc. shaft driving 1 Propeller Total Power: 441kW (600hp) Weifang 8170ZC 1 x 4 Stroke 8 Cy. 170 x 200 441kW (600bhp) Weifang Diesel Engine Factory-China
8839134 - -	**VIET XO 03** **Halong Fishery Complex Enterprise (Xi Nghiep Lien Hiep Thuy San Ha Long)** - *Haiphong* *Vietnam*	*648* 210 395 Class: (VR)	**1972 Zavod "Leninskaya Kuznitsa" — Kiyev** Loa 54.75 Br ex - Dght 4.100 Lbp - Br md 9.82 Dpth 5.00 Welded, 1 dk	**(B11A2FS) Stern Trawler** Ins: 562	**1 oil engine** driving 1 FP propeller Total Power: 736kW (1,001hp) 11.0kn S.K.L. 8NVD48A-2U 1 x 4 Stroke 8 Cy. 320 x 480 736kW (1001bhp) VEB Schwermaschinenbau "KarlLiebknecht" (SKL)-Magdeburg AuxGen: 2 x 150kW a.c, 2 x 100kW a.c
8839146 *XVWD* -	**VIET XO 04** **Halong Fishery Complex Enterprise (Xi Nghiep Lien Hiep Thuy San Ha Long)** - *Haiphong* *Vietnam*	*648* 210 395 Class: (VR)	**1973 Zavod "Leninskaya Kuznitsa" — Kiyev** Loa 54.75 Br ex - Dght 4.100 Lbp - Br md 9.87 Dpth 5.00 Welded, 1 dk	**(B11A2FS) Stern Trawler** Ins: 562	**1 oil engine** driving 1 FP propeller Total Power: 736kW (1,001hp) 11.0kn S.K.L. 8NVD48A-2U 1 x 4 Stroke 8 Cy. 320 x 480 736kW (1001bhp) VEB Schwermaschinenbau "KarlLiebknecht" (SKL)-Magdeburg AuxGen: 2 x 150kW a.c, 2 x 100kW a.c
8839158 - -	**VIET XO 06** **Halong Fishery Complex Enterprise (Xi Nghiep Lien Hiep Thuy San Ha Long)** - *Haiphong* *Vietnam*	*648* 210 395 Class: (VR)	**1973 Zavod "Leninskaya Kuznitsa" — Kiyev** Loa 54.82 Br ex - Dght 4.100 Lbp - Br md 9.80 Dpth 5.00 Welded, 1 dk	**(B11A2FS) Stern Trawler** Ins: 562	**1 oil engine** driving 1 FP propeller Total Power: 736kW (1,001hp) 11.0kn S.K.L. 8NVD48A-2U 1 x 4 Stroke 8 Cy. 320 x 480 736kW (1001bhp) VEB Schwermaschinenbau "KarlLiebknecht" (SKL)-Magdeburg AuxGen: 2 x 150kW a.c, 2 x 100kW a.c
8839160 - -	**VIET XO 07** **Halong Fishery Complex Enterprise (Xi Nghiep Lien Hiep Thuy San Ha Long)** - *Haiphong* *Vietnam*	**492** 147 395 Class: (VR)	**1978 Zavod "Leninskaya Kuznitsa" — Kiyev** Loa 54.82 Br ex - Dght 4.100 Lbp - Br md 9.80 Dpth 5.00 Welded, 1 dk	**(B11A2FS) Stern Trawler** Ins: 562	**1 oil engine** driving 1 FP propeller Total Power: 736kW (1,001hp) 11.0kn S.K.L. 8NVD48A-2U 1 x 4 Stroke 8 Cy. 320 x 480 736kW (1001bhp) VEB Schwermaschinenbau "KarlLiebknecht" (SKL)-Magdeburg AuxGen: 2 x 150kW a.c, 2 x 100kW a.c
8839201 - -	**VIET XO 11** **Halong Fishery Complex Enterprise (Xi Nghiep Lien Hiep Thuy San Ha Long)** - *Haiphong* *Vietnam*	**665** 200 395 Class: (VR)	**1979 Zavod "Leninskaya Kuznitsa" — Kiyev** Loa 54.82 Br ex - Dght 4.100 Lbp - Br md 9.80 Dpth 5.00 Welded, 1 dk	**(B11A2FS) Stern Trawler** Ins: 562	**1 oil engine** driving 1 FP propeller Total Power: 736kW (1,001hp) 11.0kn S.K.L. 8NVD48A-2U 1 x 4 Stroke 8 Cy. 320 x 480 736kW (1001bhp) VEB Schwermaschinenbau "KarlLiebknecht" (SKL)-Magdeburg AuxGen: 2 x 150kW a.c, 2 x 100kW a.c
8330346 - -	**VIETROSKO 02** *ex* Kolkhida-2 *-2003* **Sai Thanh Transport Co Ltd (Cong Ty Trach Nhiem Huu Han Van tai Thanh)** - *Saigon* *Vietnam*	**130** 39 16 Class: VR (RS)	**1984 Zavod im. "Ordzhonikidze" — Poti** Yd No: 102 Loa 34.50 Br ex 10.30 Dght 1.110 Lbp - Br md - Dpth 1.80 Welded, 1 dk	**(A37B2PS) Passenger Ship** Hull Material: Aluminium Alloy Passengers: unberthed: 155	**2 oil engines** geared to sc. shafts driving 2 FP propellers Total Power: 1,920kW (2,610hp) 34.0kn M.T.U. 12V396 2 x Vee 4 Stroke 12 Cy. 165 x 185 each-960kW (1305bhp) MTU Friedrichshafen GmbH-Friedrichshafen
9438339 *3WMB9* -	**VIETSUN FORTUNE** *ex* Bo Hai *-2014* **Beyond Motorship Ltd** Dandong Marine Shipping Co Ltd *Vietnam* MMSI: 574002180	**5,272** 2,309 7,991 Class: (CC)	**2007-04 Huanghai Shipbuilding Co Ltd — Rongcheng SD** Yd No: HCY-34 Loa 117.00 Br ex - Dght 6.450 Lbp 110.00 Br md 19.70 Dpth 8.50 Welded, 1 dk	**(A31A2GX) General Cargo Ship** Grain: 9,608; Bale: 9,608 TEU 602 C Ho 197 TEC C Dk 405 TEU. Compartments: 3 Ho, ER 3 Ha: (25.4 x 15.0) (31.9 x 15.0)ER (19.5 x 15.0) Ice Capable	**2 oil engines** reduction geared to sc. shafts driving 2 FP propellers Total Power: 5,000kW (6,798hp) 13.8kn Daihatsu 8DKM-28 2 x 4 Stroke 8 Cy. 280 x 390 each-2500kW (3399bhp) Shaanxi Diesel Heavy Industry Co Lt-China AuxGen: 3 x 256kW 400V a.c

IMO / Call sign	Ship / Owner / Port	Tonnage	Class	Builder / Dimensions	Type	Machinery
9264219 *3WJS9* -	**VIETSUN PACIFIC** *ex* Inga H. *-2013* *ex* PAC Palawan *-2007* **Vietsun Corp** - *Saigon* *Vietnam* MMSI: 574001850 Official number: 27/2012/TT	**5,593** 3,149 7,057	Class: GL VR (AB)	**2003-01 Jiangsu Yangzijiang Shipbuilding Co Ltd — Jiangyin JS** Yd No: 01YZJ-640C43 Loa 124.19 (BB) Br ex - Dght 6.450 Lbp 118.20 Br md 18.20 Dpth 8.40 Welded, 1 dk	**(A33A2CC) Container Ship (Fully Cellular)** TEU 639 incl 60 ref C. Cranes: 2x45t	**1 oil engine** reduction geared to sc. shaft driving 1 CP propeller Total Power: 4,320kW (5,873hp) 16.0kn MaK 9M32 1 x 4 Stroke 9 Cy. 320 x 480 4320kW (5873bhp) Caterpillar Motoren GmbH & Co. KG-Germany AuxGen: 3 x 370kW 440V a.c, 1 x 500kW 440V a.c Thrusters: 1 Tunnel thruster (f)
8811730 *IWZN* -	**VIGATA** *ex* Citta Di Catania *-2011* **Compagnia Trasporti Petrolio Srl** Pietro Barbaro SpA *Palermo* *Italy* Official number: 1357	*198* 41 186	Class: RI	**1988-12 Cooperativa Metallurgica Ing G Tommasi Srl — Ancona** Yd No: 57 Loa 31.27 Br ex 9.16 Dght 3.680 Lbp 28.01 Br md 8.50 Dpth 4.25 Welded, 1 dk	**(B32A2ST) Tug**	**1 oil engine** with flexible couplings & sr geared to sc. shaft driving 1 CP propeller Total Power: 1,838kW (2,499hp) 13.0kn Nohab 8V25 1 x Vee 4 Stroke 8 Cy. 250 x 300 1838kW (2499bhp) Wartsila Diesel AB-Sweden AuxGen: 2 x 80kW 380V 50Hz a.c, 1 x 37kW 26V d.c Fuel: 80.0 (d.f.) 9.7pd
9355989 *C6ZV7* -	**VIGEO ADEBOLA** *ex* Siem Danis *-2012* **Island Shippers Ltd** Vestland Marine Sp z oo *Nassau* *Bahamas* MMSI: 311067600	**2,465** 859 3,555	Class: NV	**2006-07 SC Aker Braila SA — Braila** (Hull) Yd No: 1083 **2006-07 Aker Yards AS Aukra — Aukra** Yd No: 120 Loa 73.40 (BB) Br ex 16.63 Dght 6.500 Lbp 64.00 Br md 16.60 Dpth 7.60 Welded, 1 dk	**(B21A20S) Platform Supply Ship**	**2 oil engines** reduction geared to sc. shafts driving 2 CP propellers Total Power: 4,060kW (5,520hp) 14.0kn Caterpillar 3606 2 x 4 Stroke 6 Cy. 280 x 300 each-2030kW (2760bhp) Caterpillar Inc-USA AuxGen: 2 x 1300kW 60Hz a.c, 2 x 345kW 60Hz a.c Thrusters: 2 Tunnel thruster (f); 2 Tunnel thruster (a) Fuel: 1016.5 (r.f.)
9053177 *C6XZ6* -	**VIGEO OLUFUNKE** *ex* Lady Margaret *-2007* *ex* Shelf Challenger *-2002* **Vigeo Shipping Ltd** Vestland Marine Sp z oo *Nassau* *Bahamas* MMSI: 311026800 Official number: 8001685	**1,759** 527 1,903	Class: NV	**1993-12 Transfield Shipbuilding WA — Fremantle WA** Yd No: 297 Loa 67.40 Br ex 15.30 Dght 6.012 Lbp 56.40 Br md 15.00 Dpth 7.10 Welded, 1 dk	**(B21B20A) Anchor Handling Tug Supply**	**2 oil engines** with flexible couplings & sr geared to sc. shafts driving 2 CP propellers Total Power: 7,260kW (9,870hp) 12.0kn Deutz SBV16M628 2 x Vee 4 Stroke 16 Cy. 240 x 280 each-3630kW (4935bhp) Motoren Werke Mannheim AG (MWM)-Mannheim AuxGen: 2 x 390kW 440V 60Hz a.c, 2 x a.c Thrusters: 2 Thwart. FP thruster (f); 1 Tunnel thruster (a)
9173719 *OJIQ* -	**VIGGEN** - **Alands Landskapsregering** - *Mariehamn* *Finland* MMSI: 230914000 Official number: 55153	**1,512** 513 265	Class: LR (NV) **100A1** SS 04/2013 passenger and vehicle ferry Ice Class 1A Min draught fwd 3.3m Min draught aft 3.3m Coastal service within 50 miles from port of refuge **LMC** **UMS** Cable: 247.0/34.0	**1998-09 Uudenkaupungin Tyovene Oy — Uusikaupunki** Yd No: 97/98 Loa 53.50 Br ex - Dght 4.000 Lbp 47.50 Br md 12.25 Dpth 5.45 Welded, 1dk plus port & stbd hoistable dk.	**(A36A2PR) Passenger/Ro-Ro Ship (Vehicles)** Passengers: unberthed: 300 Bow door/ramp (centre) Len: 4.40 Wid: 4.00 Swl: 56 Stern ramp (centre) Len: 4.40 Wid: 4.00 Swl: 56 Lane-Len: 130 Lane-Wid: 4.00 Lane-clr ht: 4.25 Cars: 58 Ice Capable	**2 oil engines** with flexible couplings & sr geared to sc. shaft driving 1 CP propeller Total Power: 2,640kW (3,590hp) 14.0kn Wartsila 8R20 2 x 4 Stroke 8 Cy. 200 x 280 each-1320kW (1795bhp) Wartsila NSD Finland Oy-Finland AuxGen: 2 x 136kW 400V 50Hz a.c Thrusters: 1 Thwart. FP thruster (f); 1 Thwart. FP thruster (a) Fuel: 70.0 (d.f.)
8308496 *VWRS* -	**VIGHNAHARTA** *ex* SCI-05 *-2013* **Glory Shipmanagement Pvt Ltd** - *Mumbai* *India* MMSI: 419259000 Official number: 2042	**1,310** 393 1,819	Class: IR (NV)	**1984-12 Robin Shipyard Pte Ltd — Singapore** Yd No: 338 Loa 58.60 Br ex 13.01 Dght 5.936 Lbp 51.62 Br md 12.98 Dpth 6.76 Welded, 2 dks	**(B21B20A) Anchor Handling Tug Supply**	**4 oil engines** with clutches, flexible couplings & sr geared to sc. shafts driving 2 CP propellers Total Power: 3,972kW (5,400hp) Daihatsu 6DSM-26A 4 x 4 Stroke 6 Cy. 260 x 300 each-993kW (1350bhp) Daihatsu Diesel Manufacturing Co Lt-Japan AuxGen: 2 x 680kW 380V 50Hz a.c, 2 x 245kW 380V 50Hz a.c Thrusters: 1 Thwart. CP thruster (f)
9660700 *AVQP* -	**VIGHNESHWAR** - **United Shippers Ltd** - *Mumbai* *India* MMSI: 419000470 Official number: 3929	**1,063** 514 1,700	Class: IR	**2012-05 Dempo Engineering Works Ltd. — Goa** Yd No: 503 Loa 67.10 Br ex 12.02 Dght 3.200 Lbp 64.03 Br md 12.00 Dpth 4.35 Welded, 1 dk	**(A31A2GX) General Cargo Ship** Bale: 1,982 Compartments: 1 Ho, ER 1 Ha: ER	**2 oil engines** reduction geared to sc. shafts driving 2 FP propellers Total Power: 804kW (1,094hp) 10.0kn Cummins NT-855-M 2 x 4 Stroke 6 Cy. 140 x 152 each-402kW (547bhp) Cummins India Ltd-India
8015659 *AWAC* -	**VIGHNRAJ** *ex* Sopot *-2013* *ex* Arctic *-1994* *ex* Cast Husky *-1994* **Sula Shipping & Logistics Pvt Ltd** - *Mumbai* *India* MMSI: 419000723 Official number: 4076	**40,504** 23,339 70,912 T/cm 69.5	Class: BV IR (NV)	**1982-09 Hyundai Heavy Industries Co Ltd — Ulsan** Yd No: 178 Converted From: Bulk Carrier-2006 Loa 234.63 (BB) Br ex 32.26 Dght 13.477 Lbp 225.00 Br md 32.21 Dpth 18.60 Welded, 1 dk	**(A23A2BD) Bulk Carrier, Self-discharging** Grain: 84,895 Compartments: 7 Ho, ER 7 Ha: (12.6 x 14.1)3 (29.3 x 18.8)3 (15.1 x 18.8)ER Gantry cranes: 2x45t Ice Capable	**1 oil engine** driving 1 FP propeller Total Power: 10,010kW (13,610hp) 13.0kn Sulzer 4RLA90 1 x 2 Stroke 4 Cy. 900 x 1900 10010kW (13610bhp) Hyundai Heavy Industries Co Ltd-South Korea AuxGen: 3 x 570kW 440V 60Hz a.c Fuel: 262.0 (d.f.) 2028.5 (r.f.)
8027406 *PBNX* -	**VIGILANT** - **Gardline Holding (Netherlands) BV** Tranship BV *Den Helder* *Netherlands* MMSI: 244891000 Official number: 52500	**1,365** 409 388	Class: LR ✠ **100A1** SS 02/2012 ✠ **LMC** **UMS** Eq.Ltr: M; Cable: U2 (a)	**1982-09 Ferguson-Ailsa Ltd — Port Glasgow** Yd No: 487 Converted From: Fishery Patrol Vessel-2010 Loa 71.40 Br ex 11.71 Dght 4.760 Lbp 64.01 Br md 11.60 Dpth 7.40 Welded, 2 dks	**(B31A2SR) Research Survey Vessel**	**2 oil engines** with clutches, flexible couplings & sr geared to sc. shafts driving 2 CP propellers Total Power: 4,148kW (5,640hp) 14.0kn Ruston 12RKCM 2 x Vee 4 Stroke 12 Cy. 254 x 305 each-2074kW (2820bhp) Ruston Diesels Ltd.-Newton-le-Willows AuxGen: 3 x 195kW 415V 50Hz a.c Thrusters: 1 Thwart. CP thruster (f) Fuel: 203.0 (d.f.) 9.0pd
7806477 *WYB6987* -	**VIGILANT** - **Kirby Ocean Transport Co** - SatCom: Inmarsat C 430313510 *Wilmington, DE* *United States of America* MMSI: 366998170 Official number: 599311	**815** 244 -	Class: AB	**1978-11 Main Iron Works, Inc. — Houma, La** Yd No: 339 Loa 41.64 Br ex 12.22 Dght 5.606 Lbp 38.71 Br md 12.20 Dpth 5.97 Welded, 1 dk	**(B32A2ST) Tug**	**2 oil engines** reverse reduction geared to sc. shafts driving 2 FP propellers Total Power: 4,118kW (5,598hp) 13.0kn EMD (Electro-Motive) 16-645-E7B 2 x Vee 2 Stroke 16 Cy. 230 x 254 each-2059kW (2799bhp) General Motors Corp.Electro-Motive Div.-La Grange AuxGen: 2 x 98kW
5273949 *5VKY* -	**VIGILANT** *ex* Pengarth *-1997* **Togo Oil & Marine (TOM) Sarl** - *Lome* *Togo* Official number: 84	*160* - -	Class: (LR) ✠ Classed LR until 8/91	**1962-09 Charles Hill & Sons Ltd. — Bristol** Yd No: 438 Loa 28.66 Br ex 7.95 Dght 3.264 Lbp 26.22 Br md 7.62 Dpth 3.66 Riveted\Welded, 1 dk	**(B32A2ST) Tug**	**1 oil engine** sr reverse geared to sc. shaft driving 1 FP propeller Total Power: 794kW (1,080hp) 10.5kn Ruston 6ATCM 1 x 4 Stroke 6 Cy. 318 x 368 794kW (1080bhp) Ruston & Hornsby Ltd.-Lincoln AuxGen: 2 x 30kW 220V d.c Fuel: 28.5 (d.f.)
6809484 *5VSN4* -	**VIGILANT** *ex* Brandon Bay *-2005* **Togo Oil & Marine (TOM) Sarl** - *Lome* *Togo*	**299** 89 153	Class: (LR) ✠ Classed LR until 4/7/01	**1968-08 Charles D. Holmes & Co. Ltd. — Beverley** Yd No: 1009 Loa 39.35 Br ex 9.12 Dght - Lbp 35.59 Br md 8.69 Dpth 4.27 Welded, 1 dk	**(B32A2ST) Tug**	**1 oil engine** with flexible couplings & sr reverse geared to sc. shaft driving 1 FP propeller Total Power: 1,854kW (2,521hp) 12.5kn Mirrlees KMR-6 1 x 4 Stroke 6 Cy. 381 x 457 1854kW (2521bhp) Mirrlees National Ltd.-Stockport AuxGen: 1 x 75kW 220V d.c, 2 x 55kW 220V d.c
9131979 *EIPX* SO 709	**VIGILANT** *ex* Brendelen *-2004* **Ocean Trawlers Ltd** - SatCom: Inmarsat B 325006610 *Sligo* *Irish Republic* MMSI: 250000096 Official number: 403032	**786** 272 -	Class: NV	**1995-09 Flekkefjord Slipp & Maskinfabrikk AS AS — Flekkefjord** Yd No: 156 Lengthened-1998 Loa 58.00 (BB) Br ex - Dght 6.700 Lbp 52.80 Br md 11.00 Dpth 7.90 Welded, 1 dk	**(B11A2FS) Stern Trawler** Ins: 880	**1 oil engine** reduction geared to sc. shaft driving 1 CP propeller Total Power: 2,708kW (3,682hp) 13.0kn Caterpillar 3608TA 1 x 4 Stroke 8 Cy. 280 x 300 2708kW (3682hp) Caterpillar Inc-USA AuxGen: 1 x 1400kW a.c Thrusters: 1 Thwart. FP thruster (f); 1 Tunnel thruster (a)

IMO / Call sign	Name / Owner	Tonnage	Class	Builder / Dimensions	Type	Machinery
9265603 *4DEX3* -	**VIGILANT** *ex* Cheung Chau *-2013* **Malayan Towage & Salvage Corp (SALVTUG)** - *Manila* *Philippines* MMSI: 548026500 Official number: M: TG-000072	**295** 88 170	Class: LR ✠**100A1** SS 09/2012 tug ✠**LMC** Eq.Ltr: F; Cable: 302.5/22.0 U2 (a)	**2002-09 Kegoya Dock K.K. — Kure** Yd No: 1073 Loa 29.00 Br ex - Dght 3.900 Lbp 23.50 Br md 9.50 Dpth 4.70 Welded, 1 dk	**(B32A2ST) Tug**	**2 oil engines** gearing integral to driving 2 Z propellers Total Power: 2,942kW (4,000hp) 13.3kn Yanmar 6N260-EN 2 x 4 Stroke 6 Cy. 260 x 360 each-1471kW (2000bhp) Yanmar Diesel Engine Co Ltd-Japan AuxGen: 2 x 80kW 380V 50Hz a.c Fuel: 137.2
9276353 *ZITI4* -	**VIGILANT** **Government of The United Kingdom (Home Office Border Force, Maritime & Aviation Operations)** - *United Kingdom* MMSI: 235521000	**238** 71 57	Class: (LR) ✠ 27/7/04	**2003-04 Scheepswerf Made B.V. — Made** (Hull) Yd No: (549854) **2003-04 B.V. Scheepswerf Damen — Gorinchem** Yd No: 549854 Loa 42.80 Br ex 7.11 Dght 2.140 Lbp 38.50 Br md 6.80 Dpth 3.77 Welded, 1 dk	**(B34H2SQ) Patrol Vessel**	**2 oil engines** with clutches, flexible couplings & sr reverse geared to sc. shafts driving 2 CP propellers Total Power: 4,176kW (5,678hp) 25.0kn Caterpillar 3516B-TA 2 x Vee 4 Stroke 16 Cy. 170 x 190 each-2088kW (2839bhp) Caterpillar Inc-USA AuxGen: 2 x 85kW 415V 50Hz a.c Thrusters: 1 Thwart. FP thruster (f)
9409948 *WDE2719* -	**VIGILANT** **General Electric Capital Corp** Baydelta Maritime Ltd *San Francisco, CA* *United States of America* MMSI: 367328780 Official number: 1205479	**414** 124 -		**2008-02 Nichols Bros. Boat Builders, Inc. — Freeland, Wa** Yd No: S-151 Loa 30.50 Br ex - Dght - Lbp - Br md 12.20 Dpth 4.90 Welded, 1 dk	**(B32A2ST) Tug**	**2 oil engines** gearing integral to driving 2 Z propellers Total Power: 5,130kW (6,974hp) Caterpillar 3516C 2 x Vee 4 Stroke 16 Cy. 170 x 215 each-2565kW (3487bhp) Caterpillar Inc-USA AuxGen: 2 x 215kW a.c
8994178 *CFB3996* -	**VIGILANT I** *ex* Glenlivet II *-2001* *ex* Canadian Franko *-1982* *ex* Glenlivet II *-1977* *ex* Glenlivet (W-43) *-1975* **Nadro Marine Services Ltd** - *Chatham, ON* *Canada* MMSI: 316001876 Official number: 179311	**111** 43 -		**1944-01 Russel Brothers Ltd — Owen Sound ON** L reg 23.46 Br ex - Dght 2.750 Lbp - Br md 6.39 Dpth 3.11 Welded, 1 dk	**(B32A2ST) Tug**	**2 oil engines** reverse reduction geared to sc. shafts driving 2 Propellers Total Power: 1,082kW (1,472hp) 11.0kn G.M. (Detroit Diesel) 16V-71 2 x Vee 2 Stroke 16 Cy. 108 x 127 each-541kW (736bhp) (new engine 2003) General Motors Detroit DieselAllison Divn-USA AuxGen: 1 x 471kW 208V 60Hz a.c, 1 x 25kW 208V 60Hz a.c Fuel: 22.4 (d.f.) 5.0pd
6422420 - -	**VIGILANTE** *ex* Cayolle *-1976* - -	*156* 52 -	Class: (BV)	**1964 Ateliers & Chantiers de La Rochelle-Pallice — La Rochelle** Yd No: 5082 Loa 29.90 Br ex 6.76 Dght - Lbp 25.00 Br md 6.71 Dpth 3.56 Welded, 1 dk	**(B11A2FT) Trawler** 2 Ha: 2 (1.0 x 1.0) Derricks: 1x3t; Winches: 1	**1 oil engine** driving 1 FP propeller Total Power: 412kW (560hp) 11.0kn Deutz RBV6M536 1 x 4 Stroke 6 Cy. 270 x 360 412kW (560bhp) Kloeckner Humboldt Deutz AG-West Germany Fuel: 35.5 (d.f.)
9212541 *IFDU* -	**VIGNOLE** **Azienda del Consorzio Trasporti Veneziano (ACTV)** - *Venice* *Italy*	**129** 84 124	Class: RI	**2000-10 Cant. Nav. S.M.E.B. S.p.A. — Messina** Yd No: 182 Loa 30.40 Br ex - Dght 1.460 Lbp 27.50 Br md 5.65 Dpth 2.30 Welded, 1 dk	**(A37B2PS) Passenger Ship**	**2 oil engines** with flexible couplings & reductiongeared to sc. shafts driving 2 FP propellers Total Power: 294kW (400hp) Iveco Aifo 8210M 2 x 4 Stroke 6 Cy. 137 x 156 each-147kW (200bhp) IVECO AIFO S.p.A.-Pregnana Milanese
9533646 *3FCU3* -	**VIGO** *ex* Stanford Hobby *-2012* **Naviera Ftapias Galicia SL** - *Panama* *Panama* MMSI: 372642000 Official number: 4496213A	**3,689** 1,106 5,125	Class: AB	**2012-02 Fujian Mawei Shipbuilding Ltd — Fuzhou FJ** Yd No: 619-10 Loa 87.08 (BB) Br ex - Dght 6.050 Lbp 82.96 Br md 18.80 Dpth 7.40 Welded, 1 dk	**(B21A2OS) Platform Supply Ship**	**4 diesel electric oil engines** driving 4 gen. each 1600kW a.c Connecting to 2 elec. motors each (2000kW) driving 2 Azimuth electric drive units Total Power: 7,300kW (9,924hp) 12.0kn Cummins QSK60-M 4 x Vee 4 Stroke 16 Cy. 159 x 190 each-1825kW (2481bhp) Cummins Engine Co Inc-USA Thrusters: 1 Thwart. CP thruster (f); 1 Retract. directional thruster (f) Fuel: 975.0 (d.f.)
8746741 *CPA862* -	**VIGO 1** *ex* Moi Soon Satu *-2010* **Transvision Sdn Bhd** - *La Paz* *Bolivia* MMSI: 720763000 Official number: 691012913	**499** 318 -		**1999-06 in Malaysia** Yd No: 3 Loa 49.38 Br ex - Dght - Lbp - Br md 9.75 Dpth 3.96 Welded, 1 dk	**(A31A2GX) General Cargo Ship**	**2 oil engines** reduction geared to sc. shafts driving 2 Propellers Total Power: 514kW (698hp) Caterpillar 2 x 4 Stroke each-257kW (349bhp) Caterpillar Inc-USA
9707247 *3FNX9* -	**VIGOR** **Global Epic Roads Sdn Bhd** - *Panama* *Panama* MMSI: 371458000 Official number: 45183PEXT1	**1,173** 352 -	Class: BV	**2013-12 Guangzhou Panyu Lingshan Shipyard Ltd — Guangzhou GD** Yd No: 249 Loa 56.20 Br ex - Dght 4.750 Lbp 49.20 Br md 13.80 Dpth 5.50 Welded, 1 dk	**(B21B20T) Offshore Tug/Supply Ship**	**2 oil engines** reduction geared to sc. shafts driving 2 FP propellers Total Power: 3,090kW (4,202hp) 12.5kn Caterpillar 3516C 2 x Vee 4 Stroke 16 Cy. 170 x 190 each-1545kW (2101bhp) Caterpillar Inc-USA AuxGen: 3 x 275kW 50Hz a.c Fuel: 600.0
9383508 *3EXV3* -	**VIGOR SW** **Vigor Pescadores SA Panama** Shih Wei Navigation Co Ltd SatCom: Inmarsat C 435272110 *Panama* *Panama* MMSI: 352721000 Official number: 4039209A	**20,236** 10,947 32,228 T/cm 43.8	Class: NK (CR)	**2009-05 Kanda Zosensho K.K. — Kawajiri** Yd No: 495 Loa 177.13 (BB) Br ex - Dght 10.020 Lbp 168.50 Br md 28.40 Dpth 14.25 Welded, 1 dk	**(A31A2GO) Open Hatch Cargo Ship** Double Hull Grain: 42,595; Bale: 41,124 Compartments: 5 Ho, ER 5 Ha: ER Cranes: 4x30.5t	**1 oil engine** driving 1 FP propeller Total Power: 5,627kW (7,650hp) 14.3kn Mitsubishi 6UEC52LA 1 x 2 Stroke 6 Cy. 520 x 1600 5627kW (7650bhp) Kobe Hatsudoki KK-Japan AuxGen: 3 x 440kW a.c Fuel: 1750.0
7312593 *IRFV* -	**VIGORE** **San Cataldo SpA** - *Cagliari* *Italy* Official number: 386	**227** 68 -	Class: RI	**1973 Soc. Esercizio Cant. Sud — Napoli** Yd No: 141 Loa 31.37 Br ex 8.64 Dght 3.836 Lbp 28.00 Br md 8.60 Dpth 4.27 Welded, 1 dk	**(B32A2ST) Tug**	**1 oil engine** driving 1 CP propeller Total Power: 1,405kW (1,910hp) MAN G9V30/45ATL 1 x 4 Stroke 9 Cy. 300 x 450 1405kW (1910bhp) Maschinenbau Augsburg Nuernberg (MAN)-Augsburg
9191943 *ZDIK3* -	**VIGOROSO** *launched as* Kar Cengizhan *-2007* **ShipCom Bereederungs GmbH & Co Betriebs-KG ms 'Scaldis'** ShipCom Bereederungs GmbH SatCom: Inmarsat C 423645110 *Gibraltar* *Gibraltar (British)* MMSI: 236451000	**4,244** 2,370 5,555	Class: GL	**2007-08 Slovenske Lodenice a.s. — Komarno** (Hull launched by) Yd No: 5103 **2007-08 Turkiye Gemi Sanayii A.S. — Pendik** (Hull completed by) Loa 99.98 (BB) Br ex - Dght 6.100 Lbp 94.64 Br md 16.50 Dpth 8.00 Welded, 1 dk	**(A31A2GX) General Cargo Ship** Grain: 7,835; Bale: 7,810 TEU 357 C Ho 141 TEU C Dk 216 TEU Compartments: 1 Ho, ER Ice Capable	**1 oil engine** reduction geared to sc. shaft driving 1 CP propeller Total Power: 3,500kW (4,759hp) 13.0kn MAN-B&W 7L32/40 1 x 4 Stroke 7 Cy. 320 x 400 3500kW (4759bhp) MAN B&W Diesel AG-Augsburg AuxGen: 1 x 600kW 380/220V a.c, 2 x 360kW 380/220V a.c Thrusters: 1 Tunnel thruster (f)
9203344 *IYZZ* -	**VIGOROSO** **Capieci SpA Navigazione Rimorchiatori e Salvataggio** - SatCom: Inmarsat C 424759230 *Naples* *Italy* MMSI: 247545000	**315** 94 100	Class: RI	**1999-06 Cooperativa Ing G Tommasi Cantiere Navale Srl — Ancona** Yd No: 90 Loa 30.00 Br ex - Dght 4.000 Lbp 26.30 Br md 10.00 Dpth 5.00 Welded, 1 dk	**(B32A2ST) Tug**	**2 oil engines** driving 2 FP propellers Total Power: 2,560kW (3,480hp) Nohab 6R25 2 x 4 Stroke 6 Cy. 250 x 300 each-1280kW (1740bhp) Wartsila NSD Finland Oy-Finland
9546239 *V7ZQ2* -	**VIGOROUS** **Vigorous Trading & Shipping Co** Lamda Maritime SA *Majuro* *Marshall Islands* MMSI: 538004890 Official number: 4890	**23,432** 10,758 33,500 T/cm 48.8	Class: NV	**2013-05 Samjin Shipbuilding Industries Co Ltd — Weihai SD** Yd No: 1040 Loa 180.00 (BB) Br ex - Dght 9.800 Lbp 170.00 Br md 30.00 Dpth 14.70 Welded, 1 dk	**(A21A2BC) Bulk Carrier** Double Hull Grain: 46,284; Bale: 45,570 Compartments: 5 Ho, ER 5 Ha: ER Cranes: 4x35t	**1 oil engine** driving 1 FP propeller Total Power: 8,580kW (11,665hp) 14.0kn MAN-B&W 6S50MC 1 x 2 Stroke 6 Cy. 500 x 1910 8580kW (11665bhp) Doosan Engine Co Ltd-South Korea AuxGen: 3 x 640kW a.c
7048025 *WDC6824* -	**VIGOROUS** *ex* Debbie Lynn *-1993* *ex* Donna *-1993* *ex* Ruth M *-1974* **C Seaman Seafood Ltd** - *New York, NY* *United States of America* MMSI: 367061820 Official number: 518181	*121* 82 -		**1969 Barbour Boat Works Inc. — New Bern, NC** L reg 24.57 Br ex - Dght - Lbp - Br md 6.41 Dpth 3.26 Welded, 1 dk	**(B11B2FV) Fishing Vessel**	**1 oil engine** driving 1 FP propeller Total Power: 257kW (349hp)

8423480 *WYP2674* -	**VIGOROUS** *ex* Vaga (YTB-374) *-1973* **Crowley Marine Services Inc** Crowley Maritime Corp *San Francisco, CA* *United States of America* Official number: 553114	*187* 127 -		**1944-05 Gulfport Boiler & Welding Works, Inc. — Port Arthur, Tx** Yd No: 234 Loa - Br ex - Dght 3.306 Lbp 29.27 Br md 7.32 Dpth 3.81 Welded, 1 dk	**(B32A2ST) Tug**	**1 oil engine** driving 1 FP propeller
5422930 *CB2944* -	**VIGRI** - **Empresa Pesquera Coquimbo Dos Ltda** - *Valparaiso* *Chile* MMSI: 725008200 Official number: 2394	*208* - -		**1963 Bolsones Verft AS — Molde** Yd No: 192 Loa 30.48 Br ex 6.86 Dght 3.315 Lbp 27.46 Br md - Dpth 3.51 Welded, 1 dk	**(B11A2FT) Trawler**	**1 oil engine** driving 1 FP propeller Total Power: 375kW (510hp) Caterpillar D379SCAC 1 x Vee 4 Stroke 8 Cy. 159 x 203 375kW (510bhp) Caterpillar Tractor Co-USA
9048691 *TFDM* RE 71	**VIGRI** - **Ogurvik hf** - SatCom: Inmarsat C 425106210 *Reykjavik* *Iceland* MMSI: 251062110 Official number: 2184	**2,157** 647 2,236	Class: LR ✠ **100A1** SS 10/2012 stern trawler Ice Class 1D hull in accordance Ice Class 1B ✠ **LMC** Cable: 449.5/36.0 U2	**1992-10 Flekkefjord Slipp & Maskinfabrikk AS AS — Flekkefjord** Yd No: 145 Loa 66.50 (BB) Br ex 13.32 Dght - Lbp 59.40 Br md 13.00 Dpth 5.97 Welded, 2 dks	**(B11A2FS) Stern Trawler** Ins: 1,250 Ice Capable	**1 oil engine** with clutches, flexible couplings & sr geared to sc. shaft driving 1 CP propeller Total Power: 3,000kW (4,079hp) 14.0kn Wartsila 8R32D 1 x 4 Stroke 8 Cy. 320 x 350 3000kW (4079bhp) Wartsila Diesel Oy-Finland AuxGen: 1 x 1760kW 440V 60Hz a.c, 2 x 720kW 440V 60Hz a.c Fuel: 110.8 (d.f.) 334.6 (r.f.) 7.5pd
8869505 *ES2501* -	**VIGRI** - **BLRT Grupp AS** - *Tallinn* *Estonia* MMSI: 276482000 Official number: 1T00C22	*201* 74 307	Class: (RS)	**1980 Svetlovskiy Sudoremontnyy Zavod — Svetlyy** Yd No: 3 Loa 29.45 Br ex 7.58 Dght 3.120 Lbp 28.50 Br md - Dpth 3.60 Welded, 1 dk	**(B34G2SE) Pollution Control Vessel** Liq: 336; Liq (Oil): 336 Compartments: 8 Ta Ice Capable	**1 oil engine** geared to sc. shaft driving 1 FP propeller Total Power: 165kW (224hp) 7.5kn Daldizel 6CHNSP18/22 1 x 4 Stroke 6 Cy. 180 x 220 165kW (224bhp) Daldizel-Khabarovsk AuxGen: 1 x 50kW, 1 x 25kW Fuel: 11.0 (d.f.)
8006828 *OINV* -	**VIIKARI** - **Finntugs Oy** - *Kotka* *Finland* MMSI: 230992970 Official number: 10669	**330** 99 128	Class: AB (LR) ✠ Classed LR until 16/6/10	**1981-09 Rauma-Repola Oy — Savonlinna** Yd No: 448 Loa 32.92 Br ex 10.37 Dght 4.906 Lbp 30.03 Br md 10.01 Dpth 5.72 Welded, 1 dk	**(B32A2ST) Tug** Ice Capable	**1 oil engine** with clutches, flexible couplings & sr geared to sc. shaft driving 1 CP propeller Total Power: 2,880kW (3,916hp) 12.0kn Wartsila 9R32 1 x 4 Stroke 9 Cy. 320 x 350 2880kW (3916bhp) Oy Wartsila Ab-Finland AuxGen: 2 x 136kW 390V 50Hz a.c Thrusters: 1 Thwart. FP thruster (f)
8228244 *ES2412* -	**VIIKING** *ex* Chernomorets-33 *-1992* **Eesti Veesiehitus Ltd (Eesti Veesiehituse AS)** - *Tallinn* *Estonia* MMSI: 276342000 Official number: 199TI09	**782** 235 412	Class: RS	**1984-08 Zavod im. "Ordzhonikidze" — Sevastopol** Yd No: 33 Loa 40.67 Br ex 20.21 Dght 2.050 Lbp 38.42 Br md 20.00 Dpth 3.41 Welded, 1 dk	**(B34B2SC) Crane Vessel** Ice Capable	**2 diesel electric oil engines** driving 2 gen. each 331kW Connecting to 2 elec. motors each (220kW) driving 2 Voith-Schneider propellers Total Power: 662kW (900hp) Pervomaysk 6CHN25/34 2 x 4 Stroke 6 Cy. 250 x 340 each-331kW (450bhp) Pervomaydizelmash (PDM)-Pervomaysk Fuel: 50.0 (d.f.)
8711760 *ES2084* -	**VIIMSI** *ex* Viymsi *-1992* **NT Marine Ltd (AS NT Marine)** - *Tallinn* *Estonia* MMSI: 276297000 Official number: 1T00F32	**1,896** 743 2,786	Class: RS	**1987-12 Shipbuilding & Shiprepairing Yard 'Ivan Dimitrov' — Rousse** Yd No: 460 Conv to DH-2007 Loa 77.53 Br ex 14.54 Dght 4.980 Lbp 73.24 Br md 14.02 Dpth 6.50 Welded, 1 dk	**(A13B2TP) Products Tanker** Double Hull (13F) Liq: 2,538; Liq (Oil): 2,538 Cargo Heating Coils Compartments: 12 Ta, ER	**1 oil engine** sr geared to sc. shaft driving 1 FP propeller Total Power: 882kW (1,199hp) 10.2kn S.K.L. 8NVD48A-2U 1 x 4 Stroke 8 Cy. 320 x 480 882kW (1199bhp) VEB Schwermaschinenbau "KarlLiebknecht" (SKL)-Magdeburg AuxGen: 2 x 150kW a.c Thrusters: 1 Thwart. CP thruster (f)
8037255 *ATSC* -	**VIJAYA LAKSHMI** - **Pron Magnate Pvt Ltd** - *Visakhapatnam* *India* Official number: 1765	*116* 79 57	Class: (IR) (AB)	**1978 Ingenieria y Maq. Especializada S.A. (IMESA) — Salina Cruz** Loa 23.17 Br ex - Dght 2.240 Lbp 21.39 Br md 7.33 Dpth 3.28 Welded, 1 dk	**(B11B2FV) Fishing Vessel**	**1 oil engine** sr geared to sc. shaft driving 1 FP propeller Total Power: 279kW (379hp) 8.5kn Caterpillar D353TA 1 x 4 Stroke 6 Cy. 159 x 203 279kW (379bhp) Caterpillar Tractor Co-USA AuxGen: 2 x 10kW 120V 50Hz a.c Fuel: 39.5 (d.f.)
9141429 - -	**VIJAYABAHU** - **Government of The Democratic Socialist Republic of Sri Lanka (Ports Authority)** - *Colombo* *Sri Lanka*	**393** 117 156	Class: LR ✠ **100A1** SS 04/2012 tug Sri Lanka coastal service ✠ **LMC** Eq.Ltr: (G) ; Cable: 302.5/20.5 U2	**1997-04 Colombo Dockyard Ltd. — Colombo** Yd No: 120 Loa 32.92 Br ex 10.10 Dght 3.920 Lbp 28.15 Br md 9.80 Dpth 5.30 Welded, 1 dk	**(B32A2ST) Tug**	**2 oil engines** with clutches, flexible couplings & dr geared to sc. shafts driving 2 Directional propellers Total Power: 3,016kW (4,100hp) Wartsila 9L20 2 x 4 Stroke 9 Cy. 200 x 280 each-1508kW (2050bhp) Wartsila Diesel Oy-Finland AuxGen: 2 x 145kW 380V 50Hz a.c, 1 x 50kW 380V 50Hz a.c
9523263 *ZGAH5* -	**VIJAYANAGAR** - **TSC1521 Shipping SA** Taiyo Nippon Kisen Co Ltd *George Town* *Cayman Islands (British)* MMSI: 319016900 Official number: 742397	**43,012** 27,239 82,167 T/cm 70.2	Class: NK	**2010-02 Tsuneishi Holdings Corp Tsuneishi Shipbuilding Co — Tadotsu KG** Yd No: 1521 Loa 228.99 (BB) Br ex - Dght 14.430 Lbp 222.00 Br md 32.26 Dpth 20.05 Welded, 1 dk	**(A21A2BC) Bulk Carrier** Grain: 97,294 Compartments: 7 Ho, ER 7 Ha: ER	**1 oil engine** driving 1 FP propeller Total Power: 9,710kW (13,202hp) 14.5kn MAN-B&W 6S60MC-C 1 x 2 Stroke 6 Cy. 600 x 2400 9710kW (13202bhp) Mitsui Engineering & Shipbuilding CLtd-Japan AuxGen: 3 x a.c Fuel: 2870.0
9230696 - -	**VIJAYLAXMI** - - - *India*	**800** - 1,100		**2000-08 Bright Engineers — Mumbai** Yd No: 101 Loa 65.00 Br ex - Dght - Lbp 60.50 Br md 12.00 Dpth 4.00 Welded, 1 dk	**(A13B2TP) Products Tanker** Double Hull	**2 oil engines** driving 2 FP propellers Total Power: 390kW (530hp)
7623370 - -	**VIJELIA** *ex* NR 4641 *-1992* - -	**141** 98 -	Class: (RN)	**1971 Zavod im. "Ordzhonikidze" — Poti** Loa 33.46 Br ex 9.56 Dght 1.700 Lbp 30.00 Br md 6.01 Dpth 1.81 Welded, 1 dk	**(A37B2PS) Passenger Ship** Hull Material: Aluminium Alloy Passengers: unberthed: 141	**2 oil engines** geared to sc. shafts driving 2 FP propellers Total Power: 1,472kW (2,002hp) 31.0kn Zvezda M401A-1 2 x Vee 4 Stroke 12 Cy. 180 x 200 each-736kW (1001bhp) "Zvezda"-Leningrad AuxGen: 1 x 5kW 28V d.c, 2 x 1kW 28V d.c Fuel: 3.0 (d.f.)
8603602 *VTQM* -	**VIJETA** - **Coastal Trawlers Ltd** - *Mumbai* *India* Official number: 2341	*180* 57 138	Class: (IR) (AB)	**1988-05 Bharati Shipyard Ltd — Ratnagiri** Yd No: 196 Loa 27.00 (BB) Br ex 7.83 Dght 2.700 Lbp 23.50 Br md 7.50 Dpth 3.50 Welded, 1 dk	**(B11A2FT) Trawler** Ins: 100	**1 oil engine** with clutches, flexible couplings & sr reverse geared to sc. shaft driving 1 FP propeller Total Power: 405kW (551hp) Caterpillar 3412TA 1 x Vee 4 Stroke 12 Cy. 137 x 152 405kW (551bhp) Caterpillar Inc-USA
9159347 *HSEE2* -	**VIJITRA NAREE** *ex* Tiger Falcon *-2004* **Precious Orchids Ltd** Great Circle Shipping Agency Ltd *Bangkok* *Thailand* MMSI: 567291000 Official number: 470004094	**17,879** 9,914 28,646	Class: NK	**1997-08 Naikai Zosen Corp — Onomichi HS (Setoda Shipyard)** Yd No: 623 Loa 171.93 (BB) Br ex - Dght 9.573 Lbp 164.90 Br md 27.00 Dpth 13.60 Welded, 1 dk	**(A31A2GO) Open Hatch Cargo Ship** Grain: 38,320; Bale: 36,801 Compartments: 5 Ho, ER 5 Ha: (12.7 x 16.0)4 (20.1 x 17.6)ER Cranes: 4x30t	**1 oil engine** driving 1 FP propeller Total Power: 5,392kW (7,331hp) 14.0kn B&W 5S50MC 1 x 2 Stroke 5 Cy. 500 x 1910 5392kW (7331bhp) Hitachi Zosen Corp-Japan Fuel: 1430.0
7905247 *LHTT* R-48-U	**VIKANOY** *ex* Nordkappfisk *-1997* *ex* Sirafisk *-1993* *ex* Meilandstind *-1986* **Havbor AS** - *Hammerfest* *Norway* MMSI: 259263000	**242** 77 -		**1979-02 Solstrand Slip & Baatbyggeri AS — Tomrefjord** Yd No: 27 Loa 27.21 Br ex 7.62 Dght - Lbp 23.98 Br md 7.61 Dpth 6.28 Welded, 1 dk	**(B11B2FV) Fishing Vessel**	**1 oil engine** geared to sc. shaft driving 1 FP propeller Total Power: 596kW (810hp) Grenaa 6FR24TK 1 x 4 Stroke 6 Cy. 240 x 300 596kW (810bhp) A/S Grenaa Motorfabrik-Denmark Thrusters: 1 Thwart. FP thruster (f); 1 Tunnel thruster (a)
7734246 - -	**VIKEN** *ex* American Patriot *-1979* **Merenkulkulaitos (Finnish Maritime Administration) (FMA)** Saaristomeren Merenkulkupiiri	*192* 131 -		**1977 at Mobile, Al** L reg 25.03 Br ex - Dght - Lbp - Br md 7.35 Dpth 3.41 Welded, 1 dk	**(B11B2FV) Fishing Vessel**	**1 oil engine** driving 1 FP propeller Total Power: 537kW (730hp)

IMO / Call sign / Flag	Name / Owner / Port	Tonnage	Class	Built / Dimensions	Type	Machinery
8707604 *SLRH* -	**VIKEN AV EDSVIK** *ex Carmita -2000* **SD 437 i Edsvik AB** - *Grebbestad* *Sweden* MMSI: 266088000	*125* 37 -		**1987-01 Ronnangs Svets AB — Ronnang** Yd No: 112 Loa 20.43 Br ex - Dght 4.492 Lbp 16.79 Br md 6.58 Dpth - Welded	**(B11A2FS) Stern Trawler**	**1 oil engine** driving 1 FP propeller Total Power: 530kW (721hp) Caterpillar 3412TA 1 x Vee 4 Stroke 12 Cy. 137 x 152 530kW (721bhp) Caterpillar Tractor Co-USA
8313881 *EORV* -	**VIKHR- 1** **National JSC 'Chernomorneftegaz'** - *Chernomorskiy* *Ukraine* MMSI: 272875500 Official number: 831383	**2,009** 603 425	Class: (RS)	**1983-12 Stocznia Polnocna im Bohaterow Westerplatte — Gdansk** Yd No: B98/01 Loa 72.29 Br ex 14.36 Dght 4.701 Lbp 63.00 Br md 14.00 Dpth 6.41 Welded, 1 dk	**(B34F2SF) Fire Fighting Vessel**	**2 oil engines** geared to sc. shafts driving 2 FP propellers Sulzer 16ASV25/30 2 x Vee 4 Stroke 16 Cy. 250 x 300 Zaklady Przemyslu Metalowego 'HCegielski' SA-Poznan
8404587 *4JFC* -	**VIKHR- 3** **Specialized Sea Oil Fleet Organisation, Caspian Sea Oil Fleet, State Oil Co of the Republic of Azerbaijan** - *Baku* *Azerbaijan* MMSI: 423180100 Official number: DGR-0306	**2,008** 602 425	Class: RS	**1984-06 Stocznia Polnocna im Bohaterow Westerplatte — Gdansk** Yd No: B98/03 Loa 72.29 Br ex 14.36 Dght 4.701 Lbp 63.00 Br md 14.01 Dpth 6.41 Welded, 1 dk	**(B34F2SF) Fire Fighting Vessel** Ice Capable	**2 oil engines** geared to sc. shafts driving 2 FP propellers Sulzer 16ASV25/30 2 x Vee 4 Stroke 16 Cy. 250 x 300 Zaklady Przemyslu Metalowego 'HCegielski' SA-Poznan Fuel: 167.0 (d.f.)
8404604 *4JAU* -	**VIKHR- 5** **Azerbaijan State Caspian Shipping Co (ASCSS)** - *Baku* *Azerbaijan* MMSI: 423181100 Official number: DGR-0305	**2,008** 602 382	Class: RS	**1984-11 Stocznia Polnocna im Bohaterow Westerplatte — Gdansk** Yd No: B98/05 Loa 72.30 Br ex 14.36 Dght 4.700 Lbp 63.00 Br md 14.01 Dpth 6.40 Welded, 1 dk	**(B34F2SF) Fire Fighting Vessel** Ice Capable	**2 oil engines** geared to sc. shafts driving 2 CP propellers Total Power: 4,320kW (5,874hp) 16.0kn Sulzer 16ASV25/30 2 x Vee 4 Stroke 16 Cy. 250 x 300 each-2160kW (2937bhp) Zaklady Przemyslu Metalowego 'HCegielski' SA-Poznan AuxGen: 2 x 600kW a.c, 3 x 400kW a.c Fuel: 167.0 (d.f.)
8422199 *4JAT* -	**VIKHR- 7** **Specialized Sea Oil Fleet Organisation, Caspian Sea Oil Fleet, State Oil Co of the Republic of Azerbaijan** - *Baku* *Azerbaijan* MMSI: 423149100 Official number: DGR-0282	**2,008** 602 382	Class: RS	**1985-04 Stocznia Polnocna im Bohaterow Westerplatte — Gdansk** Yd No: B98/07 Loa 72.30 Br ex 14.36 Dght 4.700 Lbp 63.00 Br md 14.01 Dpth 6.40 Welded, 1 dk	**(B34F2SF) Fire Fighting Vessel** Ice Capable	**2 oil engines** geared to sc. shafts driving 2 CP propellers Total Power: 4,320kW (5,874hp) 16.0kn Sulzer 16ASV25/30 2 x Vee 4 Stroke 16 Cy. 250 x 300 each-2160kW (2937bhp) Zaklady Przemyslu Metalowego 'HCegielski' SA-Poznan AuxGen: 2 x 600kW a.c, 3 x 400kW a.c Fuel: 186.0 (d.f.)
8422204 *4JHJ* -	**VIKHR- 8** **Azerbaijan State Caspian Shipping Co (ASCSS)** - *Baku* *Azerbaijan* MMSI: 423182100	**2,008** 602 382	Class: RS	**1985-05 Stocznia Polnocna im Bohaterow Westerplatte — Gdansk** Yd No: B98/08 Loa 72.30 Br ex 14.36 Dght 5.090 Lbp 63.00 Br md 14.00 Dpth 6.40 Welded, 2 dks	**(B34F2SF) Fire Fighting Vessel** Ice Capable	**2 oil engines** geared to sc. shafts driving 2 CP propellers Total Power: 4,320kW (5,874hp) 16.0kn Sulzer 16ASV25/30 2 x Vee 4 Stroke 16 Cy. 250 x 300 each-2160kW (2937bhp) Zaklady Przemyslu Metalowego 'HCegielski' SA-Poznan AuxGen: 2 x 600kW a.c, 3 x 400kW a.c
8422216 *4JFD* -	**VIKHR-9** *ex Vixr- 9 -2010 ex Vikhr- 9 -1997* **Specialized Sea Oil Fleet Organisation, Caspian Sea Oil Fleet, State Oil Co of the Republic of Azerbaijan** - *Baku* *Azerbaijan* MMSI: 423183100 Official number: DGR-0262	**2,008** 602 382	Class: (RS)	**1986-03 Stocznia Polnocna im Bohaterow Westerplatte — Gdansk** Yd No: B98/09 Loa 72.32 Br ex 14.36 Dght 4.700 Lbp 63.00 Br md 14.01 Dpth 6.41 Welded	**(B34F2SF) Fire Fighting Vessel** Ice Capable	**2 oil engines** geared to sc. shafts driving 2 CP propellers Total Power: 4,320kW (5,874hp) 16.0kn Sulzer 16ASV25/30 2 x Vee 4 Stroke 16 Cy. 250 x 300 each-2160kW (2937bhp) Zaklady Przemyslu Metalowego 'HCegielski' SA-Poznan AuxGen: 2 x 600kW a.c, 3 x 400kW a.c Fuel: 186.0 (d.f.)
8511471 - -	**VIKHR-10** **Azerbaijan State Caspian Shipping Co (ASCSS)** -	**2,008** 602 317	Class: (RS)	**1986-05 Stocznia Polnocna im Bohaterow Westerplatte — Gdansk** Yd No: B98/10 Loa 72.32 Br ex 14.36 Dght 4.601 Lbp 63.02 Br md 14.01 Dpth 6.41 Welded, 1 dk	**(B34F2SF) Fire Fighting Vessel** Ice Capable	**2 oil engines** geared to sc. shafts driving 2 CP propellers Total Power: 4,320kW (5,874hp) 16.0kn Sulzer 16ASV25/30 2 x Vee 4 Stroke 16 Cy. 250 x 300 each-2160kW (2937bhp) Zaklady Przemyslu Metalowego 'HCegielski' SA-Poznan AuxGen: 2 x 600kW a.c, 3 x 400kW a.c
8521294 *4JXL* -	**VIKHR-11** *ex Vixr-11 -2010 ex Vikhr-11 -1997* **Specialized Sea Oil Fleet Organisation, Caspian Sea Oil Fleet, State Oil Co of the Republic of Azerbaijan** - *Baku* *Azerbaijan* MMSI: 423184100 Official number: DGR-0332	**2,008** 602 382	Class: RS	**1986-07 Stocznia Polnocna im Bohaterow Westerplatte — Gdansk** Yd No: B98/11 Loa 72.30 Br ex 14.36 Dght 4.700 Lbp 63.02 Br md 14.03 Dpth 6.43 Welded	**(B34F2SF) Fire Fighting Vessel** Ice Capable	**2 oil engines** geared to sc. shafts driving 2 CP propellers Total Power: 4,320kW (5,874hp) 16.0kn Sulzer 16ASV25/30 2 x Vee 4 Stroke 16 Cy. 250 x 300 each-2160kW (2937bhp) Zaklady Przemyslu Metalowego 'HCegielski' SA-Poznan AuxGen: 2 x 600kW a.c, 3 x 400kW a.c
8601771 - -	**VIKHR-13** *ex Vixr-13 -2010 ex Vikhr-13 -1997* **Specialized Sea Oil Fleet Organisation, Caspian Sea Oil Fleet, State Oil Co of the Republic of Azerbaijan**	**2,008** 602 382	Class: (RS)	**1987-06 Stocznia Polnocna im Bohaterow Westerplatte — Gdansk** Yd No: B98/13 Loa 72.30 Br ex 14.36 Dght 4.700 Lbp 63.00 Br md 14.01 Dpth 6.40 Welded	**(B34F2SF) Fire Fighting Vessel** Ice Capable	**2 oil engines** geared to sc. shafts driving 2 CP propellers Total Power: 4,320kW (5,874hp) 16.0kn Sulzer 16ASV25/30 2 x Vee 4 Stroke 16 Cy. 250 x 300 each-2160kW (2937bhp) Zaklady Przemyslu Metalowego 'HCegielski' SA-Poznan AuxGen: 2 x 600kW a.c, 3 x 400kW a.c
9360075 *UEEO* -	**VIKHREVOY** **Baltic Tugs (Cyprus) Ltd** Baltic Tug Ltd (OOO 'Baltiyskie Buksiry') *St Petersburg* *Russia* MMSI: 273315070	**198** 59 110	Class: RS (LR) ✠ Classed LR until 1/10/08	**2006-06 Damen Shipyards Gdynia SA — Gdynia** (Hull) Yd No: 510813 **2006-06 B.V. Scheepswerf Damen — Gorinchem** Yd No: 510813 Loa 25.86 Br ex 8.94 Dght 3.900 Lbp 22.75 Br md 8.90 Dpth 4.30 Welded, 1 dk	**(B32A2ST) Tug** Ice Capable	**2 oil engines** gearing integral to driving 2 Directional propellers Total Power: 2,610kW (3,548hp) 11.0kn Caterpillar 3512B-TA 2 x Vee 4 Stroke 12 Cy. 170 x 190 each-1305kW (1774bhp) Caterpillar Inc-USA AuxGen: 2 x 84kW 400V 50Hz a.c Fuel: 74.0 (d.f.)
5338763 - -	**VIKI LYNE II** *ex David Wilson -1978 ex Admiral Hardy -1968* *ex Star of Devon -1963* **Nebulous Holdings Inc** - *Victoria, BC* *Canada* Official number: 302240	*224* 72 -	Class: (LR) ✠ Classed LR until 10/3/78	**1961-01 P K Harris & Sons Ltd — Bideford** Yd No: 131 L reg 33.01 Br ex 7.29 Dght 3.048 Lbp 32.47 Br md 7.24 Dpth 3.66 Welded, 1 dk	**(B11A2FT) Trawler**	**1 oil engine** with clutch driving 1 CP propeller Total Power: 515kW (700hp) Polar MN14 1 x 2 Stroke 4 Cy. 340 x 570 515kW (700bhp) British Polar Engines Ltd.-Glasgow AuxGen: 2 x 220kW
5420293 *UEIK* -	**VIKING** *ex Viking Naja -2006 ex Hargo -1990* *ex Karl-Erik -1990 ex Hermes -1984* **Joint Stock Northern Shipping Co (A/O 'Severnoye Morskoye Parokhodstvo') (NSC ARKHANGELSK)** - *Arkhangelsk* *Russia* Official number: 632651	**218** 65 150	Class: RS (LR) (NV) ✠ Classed LR until 9/92	**1963-05 AB Asi-Verken — Amal** Yd No: 64 Loa 29.44 Br ex 8.44 Dght 3.897 Lbp 26.85 Br md 8.31 Dpth 4.60 Welded, 1 dk	**(B32A2ST) Tug** Ice Capable	**2 oil engines** with fluid couplings & sr reverse geared to sc. shafts driving 2 CP propellers Total Power: 1,176kW (1,598hp) 13.0kn Hedemora V8A/12 2 x Vee 4 Stroke 8 Cy. 185 x 210 each-588kW (799bhp) Hedemora Diesel AB-Sweden AuxGen: 2 x 70kW 380V 50Hz a.c Thrusters: 1 Thwart. FP thruster (f) Fuel: 58.0 (d.f.)
6618550 - -	**VIKING** *ex Modena -1987 ex Embdena -1987* *ex Suntis -1985 ex Germann -1978* *ex Germa -1968* **Viking Trader Ltd** -	**299** 171 791	Class: (GL)	**1966-01 C Cassens Schiffswerft — Emden** Yd No: 75 Loa 54.34 Br ex 9.53 Dght 3.409 Lbp 49.92 Br md 9.50 Dpth 5.49 Welded, 1 dk & S dk	**(A31A2GX) General Cargo Ship** Grain: 1,529; Bale: 1,393 1 Ha: (28.0 x 6.2)ER Derricks: 2x2t Ice Capable	**1 oil engine** driving 1 FP propeller Total Power: 588kW (799hp) 10.0kn MWM TD484-6 1 x 4 Stroke 6 Cy. 320 x 480 588kW (799bhp) Motoren Werke Mannheim AG (MWM)-West Germany
7011606 *UBMO* -	**VIKING** *ex Stevns Icebird -2013 ex Rauni -1999* *ex Skuld -1995* **Alliance Co Ltd** - *St Petersburg* *Russia* MMSI: 273350380	**291** 87 150	Class: RS (BV)	**1970-06 A/S Svendborg Skibsvaerft — Svendborg** (Hull launched by) Yd No: 133 **1970-06 Aarhus Flydedok og Maskinkompagni A/S — Aarhus** (Hull completed by) Yd No: 142 Loa 31.81 Br ex 9.63 Dght 3.900 Lbp 28.81 Br md 9.59 Dpth 4.65 Welded, 1 dk	**(B32A2ST) Tug** Compartments: 1 Ho, ER 1 Ha: (1.2 x 2.1) Ice Capable	**2 oil engines** geared to sc. shaft driving 1 CP propeller Total Power: 2,060kW (2,800hp) 13.0kn MaK 6M452AK 2 x 4 Stroke 6 Cy. 320 x 450 each-1030kW (1400bhp) Atlas MaK Maschinenbau GmbH-Kiel AuxGen: 1 x 180kW 380V 50Hz a.c, 1 x 150kW 380V 50Hz a.c Thrusters: 1 Thwart. CP thruster (f) Fuel: 152.5 (d.f.)

6825696 *9AA4723* -	**VIKING** *ex* Renata I *-2007* *ex* Christiane II *-2001* *ex* Viking I *-1999* *ex* Viking *-1991* **TUO "Mankul" vl Luka Bjelanovic** - *Zadar* *Croatia* MMSI: 238425840	**314** Class: CS (GL) 111 73	**1968 Husumer Schiffswerft — Husum** Yd No: 1264 Loa 40.19 Br ex 7.83 Dght 2.058 Lbp 35.72 Br md 7.80 Dpth 3.13 Welded, 1 dk	**(A37B2PS) Passenger Ship** Passengers: unberthed: 405 Ice Capable	**2 oil engines** reduction geared to sc. shaft driving 2 CP propellers aft, 1 fwd Total Power: 734kW (998hp) 14.0kn MAN R8V16/18TL 2 x 4 Stroke 8 Cy. 160 x 180 each-367kW (499bhp) Maschinenbau Augsburg Nuernberg (MAN)-Augsburg AuxGen: 2 x 39kW 400V 50Hz a.c Fuel: 13.0 (d.f.)
7511527 *UELN* A1-0077	**VIKING** *ex* Olafur Jonsson *-1998* **Yagry Co Ltd (OOO 'Yagry')** - *Murmansk* *Russia* MMSI: 273433220	**1,067** Class: RS (LR) 320 ✠ Classed LR until 27/2/10 265	**1976-12 Stocznia im Komuny Paryskiej — Gdynia** Yd No: B402/01 Lengthened-1990 Loa 63.23 Br ex 10.83 Dght 4.547 Lbp 43.82 Br md 10.77 Dpth 6.99 Welded, 2 dks	**(B11A2FS) Stern Trawler** Ins: 430 Compartments: 1 Ho, ER Ice Capable	**1 oil engine** sr geared to sc. shaft driving 1 CP propeller Total Power: 1,618kW (2,200hp) 14.5kn Sulzer 12ASV25/30 1 x Vee 4 Stroke 12 Cy. 250 x 300 1618kW (2200bhp) Zaklady Przemyslu Metalowego 'HCegielski' SA-Poznan AuxGen: 1 x 320kW 380V 50Hz a.c, 1 x 200kW 380V 50Hz a.c Fuel: 44.0 (d.f.) 124.0 (r.f.)
7511814 *WTT5010* -	**VIKING** - **Viking LP** - SatCom: Inmarsat C 436748910 *Seattle, WA* *United States of America* MMSI: 366222300 Official number: 565017	*416* 124 -	**1975-05 Marine Construction & Design Co. (MARCO) — Seattle, Wa** Yd No: 271 L reg 32.37 Br ex 8.87 Dght - Lbp - Br md 8.82 Dpth 3.38 Welded, 1 dk	**(B11A2FT) Trawler**	**1 oil engine** driving 1 FP propeller Total Power: 827kW (1,124hp) 13.0kn Caterpillar 1 x 4 Stroke 827kW (1124bhp) Caterpillar Tractor Co-USA
7309780 *WDF8358* -	**VIKING** *ex* Wm. Fraser *-1998* *ex* F 48 *-1998* **Viking Fisheries Inc** - *Seattle, WA* *United States of America* MMSI: 367494020 Official number: 276959	*167* 62 -	**1943 Birchfield Boiler, Inc. — Tacoma, Wa** Yd No: 7 Converted From: General Cargo Ship L reg 27.74 Br ex - Dght - Lbp - Br md 6.41 Dpth 2.57 Welded, 1 dk	**(B12A2FF) Fish Factory Ship**	**1 oil engine** driving 1 FP propeller Total Power: 221kW (300hp)
7235202 *WDB5552* -	**VIKING** *ex* Robin Alario *-1992* **K-Sea Operating LLC** - *New York, NY* *United States of America* MMSI: 366910880 Official number: 541711	**608** Class: AB 182 -	**1972-08 McDermott Shipyards Inc — Morgan City LA** Yd No: 175 Loa - Br ex - Dght 5.004 Lbp 40.42 Br md 10.37 Dpth 5.57 Welded, 1 dk	**(B32A2ST) Tug**	**2 oil engines** reverse reduction geared to sc. shafts driving 2 FP propellers Total Power: 3,090kW (4,202hp) EMD (Electro-Motive) 12-645-E5 2 x Vee 2 Stroke 12 Cy. 230 x 254 each-1545kW (2101bhp) General Motors Corp-USA AuxGen: 2 x 100kW a.c Fuel: 470.5 (d.f.)
7390337 *H03646* -	**VIKING** *ex* Mega Ton *-2008* *ex* Mega Tide *-2002* *ex* Pearcy Eagle *-1991* *ex* Mega Tide *-1989* *ex* Dearborn 202 *-1983* **Singh J** - *Panama* *Panama* MMSI: 356243000 Official number: 32419PEXT4	**891** Class: (BV) 267 2,022	**1976-02 Burton Shipyard Co., Inc. — Port Arthur, Tx** Yd No: 513 Loa 60.99 Br ex 12.25 Dght 4.879 Lbp 56.75 Br md 12.20 Dpth 5.49 Welded, 1 dk	**(B21B20T) Offshore Tug/Supply Ship** Ice Capable	**2 oil engines** sr geared to sc. shafts driving 2 CP propellers Total Power: 5,296kW (7,200hp) 15.5kn Alco 18V251F 2 x Vee 4 Stroke 18 Cy. 229 x 267 each-2648kW (3600bhp) White Industrial Power Inc-USA AuxGen: 2 x 200kW 208V 60Hz a.c Thrusters: 1 Thwart. FP thruster (f)
8300157 - -	**VIKING** *ex* Jotunheim *-2004* *ex* Viking *-1996* *ex* Star Viking *-1992* **Derri Shipping Inc** Seatrans Service LLC Official number: 11425	**1,962** Class: RS (NV) 828 1,700	**1983-10 p/f Skala Skipasmidja — Skali** Yd No: 40 Loa 77.63 Br ex 13.20 Dght 4.355 Lbp 69.60 Br md 13.01 Dpth 7.12 Welded, 2 dks	**(A35A2RR) Ro-Ro Cargo Ship** Stern ramp Len: 8.50 Wid: 5.40 Swl: - Side door/ramp (s) Len: 6.00 Wid: 7.00 Swl: - Grain: 3,341; Bale: 3,114; Ins: 1,376 TEU 42 Cranes: 1x25t Ice Capable	**1 oil engine** sr geared to sc. shaft driving 1 CP propeller Total Power: 2,019kW (2,745hp) 13.8kn Alpha 12U28L-VO 1 x Vee 4 Stroke 12 Cy. 280 x 320 2019kW (2745bhp) B&W Alpha Diesel A/S-Denmark AuxGen: 1 x 450kW 380V 50Hz a.c, 2 x 184kW 380V 50Hz a.c Thrusters: 1 Thwart. FP thruster (f) Fuel: 48.5 (d.f.) 155.5 (r.f.) 9.0pd
7944994 - -	**VIKING** - **Ronald E Eachus** - *Mobile, AL* *United States of America* Official number: 606625	*183* 124 -	**1979 Coastal Engineering Co. — Moss Point, Ms** Yd No: 104 L reg 24.18 Br ex 7.37 Dght - Lbp - Br md - Dpth 3.74 Welded, 1 dk	**(B11B2FV) Fishing Vessel**	**1 oil engine** driving 1 FP propeller Total Power: 441kW (600hp)
9431903 *PIHD* -	**VIKING** - **Koerts International Towage Service (KITS)** - SatCom: Inmarsat C 424503912 *Delfzijl* *Netherlands* MMSI: 245039000 Official number: 50496	**332** Class: BV 99 245	**2008-02 Gebr. Kooiman B.V. Scheepswerf en Machinefabriek — Zwijndrecht** Yd No: 177 Loa 30.50 Br ex 10.79 Dght 3.750 Lbp 27.76 Br md 10.50 Dpth 4.10 Welded, 1 dk	**(B32A2ST) Tug** Cranes: 1	**2 oil engines** reduction geared to sc. shafts driving 2 FP propellers Total Power: 4,478kW (6,088hp) Mitsubishi S12U-MPTK 2 x Vee 4 Stroke 12 Cy. 240 x 260 each-2239kW (3044bhp) Mitsubishi Heavy Industries Ltd-Japan AuxGen: 2 x 96kW 50Hz a.c Thrusters: 1 Tunnel thruster (f) Fuel: 175.0 (d.f.)
9139517 *9WDT8* -	**VIKING 23** *ex* Tonle Sap 1 *-1999* **Tamex Timber Sdn Bhd** - *Kuching* *Malaysia* Official number: 329242	**157** Class: NK 48 99	**1995-08 Sarawak Slipways Sdn Bhd — Miri** Yd No: 182 L reg 24.57 Br ex - Dght 2.250 Lbp 24.57 Br md 7.25 Dpth 2.83 Welded, 1 dk	**(B32A2ST) Tug**	**2 oil engines** reduction geared to sc. shafts driving 2 FP propellers Total Power: 988kW (1,344hp) 9.5kn Caterpillar 3412TA 2 x Vee 4 Stroke 12 Cy. 137 x 152 each-494kW (672bhp) Caterpillar Inc-USA Fuel: 60.0 (d.f.)
9150793 *9WDZ9* -	**VIKING 25** *ex* Bon Eureka 2 *-2005* **Tinjar Transport Sdn Bhd** - *Kuching* *Malaysia* Official number: 329326	**118** Class: GL 36 -	**1996-03 P.T. Batamas Jala Nusantara — Batam** Yd No: 002 Loa 23.17 Br ex - Dght 2.402 Lbp - Br md 6.70 Dpth 3.00 Welded, 1 dk	**(B32A2ST) Tug**	**2 oil engines** reduction geared to sc. shafts driving 2 FP propellers Total Power: 700kW (952hp) 10.0kn Caterpillar 3408B 2 x Vee 4 Stroke 8 Cy. 137 x 152 each-350kW (476bhp) (made 1995) Caterpillar Inc-USA AuxGen: 2 x 20kW a.c
8923985 *9WFD5* -	**VIKING 26** *ex* Tonle Sap 4 *-2005* **Tamex Timber Sdn Bhd** - *Kuching* *Malaysia* Official number: 329413	**157** Class: NK 48 99	**1996-12 Sarawak Slipways Sdn Bhd — Miri** Yd No: 193 Loa 26.60 Br ex - Dght 2.250 Lbp 24.57 Br md 7.25 Dpth 2.83 Welded, 1 dk	**(B32A2ST) Tug**	**2 oil engines** reduction geared to sc. shafts driving 2 FP propellers Total Power: 988kW (1,344hp) 9.5kn Caterpillar 3412TA 2 x Vee 4 Stroke 12 Cy. 137 x 152 each-494kW (672bhp) Caterpillar Inc-USA Fuel: 60.0 (d.f.)
9139529 *P2V5255* -	**VIKING 27** *ex* Tonle Sap 2 *-2002* **Sharrington Ltd** - *Port Moresby* *Papua New Guinea* Official number: 001087	**157** Class: (NK) 48 99	**1995-08 Sarawak Slipways Sdn Bhd — Miri** Yd No: 183 L reg 26.60 Br ex - Dght 2.250 Lbp 24.57 Br md 7.25 Dpth 2.83 Welded, 1 dk	**(B32A2ST) Tug**	**2 oil engines** reduction geared to sc. shafts driving 2 FP propellers Total Power: 988kW (1,344hp) 9.5kn Caterpillar 3412TA 2 x Vee 4 Stroke 12 Cy. 137 x 152 each-494kW (672bhp) Caterpillar Inc-USA
9164067 - -	**VIKING 28** *ex* Tonle Sap 5 *-2002* - -	**157** Class: (NK) 48 102	**1997-01 Sarawak Slipways Sdn Bhd — Miri** Yd No: 194 L reg 26.60 Br ex - Dght 2.250 Lbp 24.57 Br md 7.25 Dpth 2.83 Welded, 1 dk	**(B32A2ST) Tug**	**2 oil engines** reduction geared to sc. shafts driving 2 FP propellers Total Power: 988kW (1,344hp) 9.5kn Caterpillar 3412TA 2 x Vee 4 Stroke 12 Cy. 137 x 152 each-494kW (672bhp) Caterpillar Inc-USA
9134830 *9WFM3* -	**VIKING 30** *ex* Bon Eureka 1 *-2003* **Tamex Timber Sdn Bhd** - *Kuching* *Malaysia* MMSI: 533000388 Official number: 329542	**106** Class: GL 32 96	**1995-12 P.T. Batamas Jala Nusantara — Batam** Yd No: 001 Loa 22.00 Br ex - Dght 2.508 Lbp - Br md 6.20 Dpth 3.08 Welded, 1 dk	**(B32A2ST) Tug**	**2 oil engines** reduction geared to sc. shafts driving 2 FP propellers Total Power: 474kW (644hp) 8.0kn Caterpillar 3406TA 2 x 4 Stroke 6 Cy. 137 x 165 each-237kW (322bhp) (made 1995) Caterpillar Inc-USA AuxGen: 2 x 16kW a.c

IMO / Call sign / Flag no.	Name / Former names / Owner / Manager / Port / Flag	Tonnage	Class	Builder / Dimensions	Type	Machinery
8888068 *9WFQ9* -	**VIKING 31** **Tamex Timber Sdn Bhd** - *Kuching* *Malaysia* Official number: 329621	**152** 46 -	Class: BV	**1992-01 Piasau Slipways Sdn Bhd — Miri** Yd No: 62 Loa 26.60 Br ex - Dght 2.150 Lbp 24.48 Br md 7.25 Dpth 2.75 Welded, 1 dk	**(B32A2ST) Tug**	**2 oil engines** geared to sc. shafts driving 2 Propellers Total Power: 750kW (1,020hp) Caterpillar 3412 2 x Vee 4 Stroke 12 Cy. 137 x 152 each-375kW (510bhp) Caterpillar Inc-USA
9481049 *9V7985* -	**VIKING AMBER** **Gram Car Carriers Pte Ltd** P D Gram & Co AS *Singapore* *Singapore* MMSI: 563255000 Official number: 395134	**39,362** 13,317 12,471	Class: NV	**2010-09 Nantong Mingde Heavy Industry Co Ltd — Tongzhou JS** Yd No: 33000PCTC-01 Loa 167.25 (BB) Br ex 28.03 Dght 8.600 Lbp 158.64 Br md 28.00 Dpth 30.09 Welded, 11 dks. incl. 2 liftable dks.	**(A35B2RV) Vehicles Carrier** Side door/ramp (s) Len: 23.75 Wid: 6.70 Swl: 20 Quarter stern door/ramp (s. a.) Len: 31.50 Wid: 7.00 Swl: 80 Cars: 4,200	**1 oil engine** driving 1 FP propeller Total Power: 11,060kW (15,037hp) 18.0kn MAN-B&W 7S50ME-C 1 x 2 Stroke 7 Cy. 500 x 2000 11060kW (15037bhp) Hyundai Heavy Industries Co Ltd-South Korea AuxGen: 3 x 970kW a.c Thrusters: 1 Thwart. CP thruster (f) Fuel: 200.0 (d.f.) 2360.0 (r.f.)
9366809 *LAJX* -	**VIKING ATHENE** **Eidesvik Shipping AS** Eidesvik AS *Haugesund* *Norway* MMSI: 258793000	**2,469** 904 3,546	Class: NV	**2006-11 OAO Sudostroitelnyy Zavod "Severnaya Verf" — St.-Peterburg** (Hull) Yd No: 795 **2006-11 West Contractors AS — Olensvaag** Yd No: 27 Loa 73.40 (BB) Br ex - Dght 6.450 Lbp 64.00 Br md 16.60 Dpth 7.60 Welded, 1 dk	**(B21A20S) Platform Supply Ship**	**2 oil engines** reduction geared to sc. shafts driving 2 CP propellers Total Power: 4,900kW (6,662hp) 12.0kn MaK 8M25 2 x 4 Stroke 8 Cy. 255 x 400 each-2450kW (3331bhp) Caterpillar Motoren GmbH & Co. KG-Germany AuxGen: 2 x 400kW 450/230V 60Hz a.c, 2 x 1440kW 450/230V 60Hz a.c Thrusters: 2 Tunnel thruster (f); 2 Tunnel thruster (a)
9306914 *LMSZ* -	**VIKING AVANT** **Eidesvik MPSV AS** Eidesvik AS *Haugesund* *Norway* MMSI: 258403000	**6,545** 1,963 6,200	Class: NV	**2004-12 SC Aker Tulcea SA — Tulcea** (Hull) Yd No: 309 **2004-12 Aker Langsten AS — Tomrefjord** Yd No: 197 Loa 92.17 (BB) Br ex 20.40 Dght 7.240 Lbp 84.80 Br md 20.40 Dpth 9.00 Welded, 1 dk	**(B21A20S) Platform Supply Ship** Ice Capable	**4 diesel electric oil engines** driving 4 gen. each 1800kW 690V a.c Connecting to 2 elec. motors each (3000kW) driving 2 Azimuth electric drive units Total Power: 7,200kW (9,788hp) 16.0kn Caterpillar 3516B 4 x Vee 4 Stroke 16 Cy. 170 x 190 each-1800kW (2447bhp) Caterpillar Inc-USA Thrusters: 2 Tunnel thruster (f); 1 Retract. directional thruster (f)
7713008 *CNA4694* -	**VIKING BANK** *ex* Quo Vadis *-2012* *ex* Morten Einar *-2006* *ex* Ostanger *-2004* *ex* Jon Sigurdsson *-2003* *ex* Kings Cross *-1996* *ex* Torbas *-1987* **Ghali-de-Peche SNC** *Dakhla* *Morocco* MMSI: 242138100 Official number: 12-82	**972** 291 999	Class: NV	**1978-04 Molde Verft AS — Hjelset** (Hull launched by) Yd No: (154) **1978-04 Ulstein Hatlo AS — Ulsteinvik** (Hull completed by) Yd No: 154 Converted From: Standby Safety Vessel-1987 Converted From: Fishing Vessel-1982 Loa 56.05 (BB) Br ex 10.42 Dght 6.030 Lbp 50.30 Br md 10.41 Dpth 7.45 Welded, 2 dks	**(B11B2FV) Fishing Vessel** Compartments: 15 Ta, ER Cranes: 1x3t,1x1.5t Ice Capable	**1 oil engine** geared to sc. shaft driving 1 Directional propeller Total Power: 2,427kW (3,300hp) 16.0kn Deutz SBV6M540 1 x 4 Stroke 6 Cy. 370 x 400 2427kW (3300bhp) Kloeckner Humboldt Deutz AG-West Germany AuxGen: 1 x 1016kW 380V 50Hz a.c, 2 x 168kW 380V 50Hz a.c Thrusters: 1 Thwart. FP thruster (f); 1 Tunnel thruster (a) Fuel: 129.5 (d.f.)
9221516 *EAWJ* VI-5-1913-	**VIKING BAY** **Copemar SA** SatCom: Inmarsat B 322334210 *Vigo* *Spain* MMSI: 224342000 Official number: 3-13/1999	**626** 188 -	Class: BV	**1999-12 Astilleros Armon Burela SA — Burela** Yd No: 125 Loa 43.50 Br ex - Dght 3.800 Lbp 36.50 Br md 9.20 Dpth 4.12 Welded, 1 dk	**(B11B2FV) Fishing Vessel**	**1 oil engine** geared to sc. shaft driving 1 FP propeller Total Power: 533kW (725hp) 10.0kn Wartsila 6L20 1 x 4 Stroke 6 Cy. 200 x 280 533kW (725bhp) Wartsila Diesel S.A.-Bermeo
7419250 *H04314* -	**VIKING BOY** *ex* Edda Jarl *-1977* **Sinopec Star Petroleum Co Ltd** China Petroleum & Chemical Corp (Sinopec) *Panama* *Panama* MMSI: 371878000 Official number: 3184106B	**1,560** 468 1,219	Class: NV	**1976-10 Astilleros de Santander SA (ASTANDER) — El Astillero** Yd No: 115 Lengthened-1986 Loa 72.22 Br ex 13.82 Dght 4.843 Lbp 56.39 Br md 13.80 Dpth 6.91 Welded, 2 dks	**(B21B20T) Offshore Tug/Supply Ship**	**2 oil engines** reduction geared to sc. shafts driving 2 CP propellers Total Power: 7,354kW (9,998hp) 13.0kn Wichmann 10AXAG 2 x 2 Stroke 10 Cy. 300 x 450 each-3677kW (4999bhp) (new engine 1986) Wichmann Motorfabrikk AS-Norway AuxGen: 2 x 640kW 440V 60Hz a.c, 2 x 133kW 440V 60Hz a.c Thrusters: 2 Thwart. CP thruster (f)
8945725 *DUAU* -	**VIKING C** **Dona Industries Corp** - *Lucena* *Philippines*	*134* 57 -		**1986 at Manila** L reg 21.47 Br ex - Dght - Lbp - Br md 6.25 Dpth 2.26 Welded, 1 dk	**(B11B2FV) Fishing Vessel**	**1 oil engine** driving 1 FP propeller Total Power: 257kW (349hp) Isuzu 1 x 4 Stroke 257kW (349bhp) Isuzu Marine Engine Inc-Japan
7803114 *VG2867* -	**VIKING CAVALIER** *ex* Ocean Cavalier *-2008* **Leader Fishing Ltd** - *Vancouver, BC* *Canada* Official number: 384020	*124* 39 142		**1978-06 Allied Shipbuilders Ltd — North Vancouver BC** Yd No: 209 Loa 23.78 Br ex 7.12 Dght - Lbp 21.75 Br md 6.86 Dpth 3.69 Welded, 1 dk	**(B11B2FV) Fishing Vessel**	**1 oil engine** geared to sc. shaft driving 1 FP propeller Total Power: 386kW (525hp) Caterpillar 3412TA 1 x Vee 4 Stroke 12 Cy. 137 x 152 386kW (525bhp) Caterpillar Tractor Co-USA
9188790 *ELXJ7* -	**VIKING CHANCE** *ex* Modern Chance *-2011* **Onslow Shipping Corp I Inc** OSM Ship Management Pte Ltd SatCom: Inmarsat C 463678380 *Monrovia* *Liberia* MMSI: 636011177 Official number: 11177	**33,863** 10,240 10,834	Class: NV (KR)	**1999-08 ShinA Shipbuilding Co Ltd — Tongyeong** Yd No: 398 Loa 164.00 (BB) Br ex 28.06 Dght 8.716 Lbp 155.00 Br md 28.00 Dpth 12.65 Welded, 10 dks incl. 2 hoistable	**(A35B2RV) Vehicles Carrier** Side door/ramp (s) Len: 7.80 Wid: 3.50 Swl: 20 Quarter stern door/ramp (s. a.) Len: 5.40 Wid: 7.00 Swl: 80 Lane-Wid: 3.50 Lane-clr ht: 5.03 Cars: 3,578	**1 oil engine** driving 1 FP propeller Total Power: 9,985kW (13,576hp) 18.5kn B&W 7S50MC 1 x 2 Stroke 7 Cy. 500 x 1910 9985kW (13576bhp) Hyundai Heavy Industries Co Ltd-South Korea AuxGen: 3 x 760kW 220/440V 60Hz a.c Thrusters: 1 Tunnel thruster (f) Fuel: 93.5 (d.f.) (Heating Coils) 2363.7 (r.f.) 44.0pd
8719188 *SEAI* -	**VIKING CINDERELLA** *ex* Cinderella *-2003* **SF Line Ab (Viking Line Abp)** - *Stockholm* *Sweden* MMSI: 266027000	**46,398** 29,223 4,228 T/cm 41.5	Class: NV	**1989-10 Wartsila Marine Industries Inc — Turku** Yd No: 1302 Loa 191.00 (BB) Br ex 35.84 Dght 6.600 Lbp 169.00 Br md 29.00 Dpth 14.65 Welded, 11 dks, 5 in superstructure	**(A36A2PR) Passenger/Ro-Ro Ship (Vehicles)** Passengers: cabins: 914; berths: 2766; driver berths: 44 Bow door & ramp Len: 16.01 Wid: 7.40 Swl: 45 Stern door/ramp Len: 9.25 Wid: 7.40 Swl: 45 Lane-Len: 1800 Lane-Wid: 7.00 Lane-clr ht: 4.80 Cars: 480 Ice Capable	**4 oil engines** with clutches, flexible couplings & sr geared to sc. shafts driving 2 CP propellers Total Power: 28,780kW (39,128hp) 22.0kn Sulzer 12ZAV40S 4 x Vee 4 Stroke 12 Cy. 400 x 560 each-7195kW (9782bhp) Wartsila Diesel Oy-Finland AuxGen: 4 x 590kW 660V 50Hz a.c Thrusters: 2 Thwart. CP thruster (f) Fuel: 45.0 (d.f.) 1240.0 (r.f.) 15.0pd
9407689 *9V7984* -	**VIKING CONSTANZA** **Gram Car Carriers Pte Ltd** OSM Ship Management Pte Ltd *Singapore* *Singapore* MMSI: 565150000 Official number: 395133	**20,209** 6,062 4,696	Class: NV (BV)	**2010-06 Kyokuyo Shipyard Corp — Shimonoseki YC** Yd No: 488 Loa 140.00 (BB) Br ex - Dght 6.100 Lbp 131.00 Br md 22.50 Dpth 22.95 Welded, 8 dks. incl. 1 hoistable dk.	**(A35B2RV) Vehicles Carrier** Stern door/ramp (centre) Len: 15.90 Wid: 7.00 Swl: 75 Quarter stern door/ramp (s. a.) Len: 16.30 Wid: 5.00 Swl: 30 Cars: 2,000 Ice Capable	**2 oil engines** reduction geared to sc. shafts driving 1 CP propeller Total Power: 12,000kW (16,316hp) 18.5kn MaK 6M43C 1 x 4 Stroke 6 Cy. 430 x 610 6000kW (8158bhp) Caterpillar Motoren GmbH & Co. KG-Germany AuxGen: 2 x 490kW a.c, 1 x 2400kW a.c Thrusters: 1 Tunnel thruster (f)
9481051 *9V7986* -	**VIKING CORAL** **Gram Car Carriers Pte Ltd** OSM Ship Management Pte Ltd SatCom: Inmarsat C 456489310 *Singapore* *Singapore* MMSI: 564893000 Official number: 395135	**39,362** 13,317 12,588	Class: NV	**2011-02 Nantong Mingde Heavy Industry Co Ltd — Tongzhou JS** Yd No: 33000PCTC-02 Loa 167.23 (BB) Br ex 28.03 Dght 8.600 Lbp 158.64 Br md 28.00 Dpth 30.09 Welded, 11 dks. incl. 2 liftable dks.	**(A35B2RV) Vehicles Carrier** Side door/ramp (s) Len: 23.75 Wid: 6.70 Swl: 20 Quarter stern door/ramp (s. a.) Len: 31.50 Wid: 7.00 Swl: 80 Cars: 4,200	**1 oil engine** driving 1 FP propeller Total Power: 11,060kW (15,037hp) 18.0kn MAN-B&W 7S50ME-C 1 x 2 Stroke 7 Cy. 500 x 2000 11060kW (15037bhp) Hyundai Heavy Industries Co Ltd-South Korea AuxGen: 3 x 970kW a.c Thrusters: 1 Tunnel thruster (f) Fuel: 200.0 (d.f.) 2360.0 (r.f.)
9481075 *9V7988* -	**VIKING DIAMOND** **Gram Car Carriers Pte Ltd** OSM Ship Management Pte Ltd SatCom: Inmarsat C 456608310 *Singapore* *Singapore* MMSI: 566083000 Official number: 395137	**39,362** 13,317 12,572	Class: NV	**2011-08 Nantong Mingde Heavy Industry Co Ltd — Tongzhou JS** Yd No: 33000PCTC-04 Loa 167.24 (BB) Br ex 28.01 Dght 8.600 Lbp 158.64 Br md 28.00 Dpth 30.09 Welded, 11 dks. incl.2 liftable dks.	**(A35B2RV) Vehicles Carrier** Side door/ramp (s) Len: 23.75 Wid: 6.70 Swl: 20 Quarter stern door/ramp (s. a.) Len: 31.50 Wid: 7.00 Swl: 80 Cars: 4,200	**1 oil engine** driving 1 FP propeller Total Power: 11,060kW (15,037hp) 18.0kn MAN-B&W 7S50ME-C 1 x 2 Stroke 7 Cy. 500 x 2000 11060kW (15037bhp) Hyundai Heavy Industries Co Ltd-South Korea AuxGen: 3 x 970kW a.c Thrusters: 1 Tunnel thruster (f) Fuel: 200.0 (d.f.) 2360.0 (r.f.)

9188817 *VRHE9* -	**VIKING DRIVE** *ex* Modern Drive *-2010* **Gramcar Shipping (HK) Ltd** OSM Ship Management Pte Ltd *Hong Kong* Hong Kong MMSI: 477852700 Official number: HK-2816	33,831 10,241 10,817	Class: NV (NK) (KR)	**2000-03 ShinA Shipbuilding Co Ltd — Tongyeong** Yd No: 400 Loa 164.00 (BB) Br ex 28.06 Dght 7.800 Lbp 155.00 Br md 28.00 Dpth 29.25 Welded, 10 dks incl. 2 hoistable	**(A35B2RV) Vehicles Carrier** Side door/ramp (s) Len: 17.00 Wid: 3.50 Swl: 20 Quarter stern door/ramp (s. a.) Len: 28.00 Wid: 7.00 Swl: 80 Cars: 2,967	**1 oil engine** driving 1 FP propeller Total Power: 9,989kW (13,581hp) 18.5kn B&W 7S50MC 1 x 2 Stroke 7 Cy. 500 x 1910 9989kW (13581bhp) Hyundai Heavy Industries Co Ltd-South Korea AuxGen: 3 x 760kW 220/440V 60Hz a.c Thrusters: 1 Thwart. FP thruster (f) Fuel: 102.0 (d.f.) (Heating Coils) 2230.0 (r.f.) 40.0pd
9244568 *LLTN* -	**VIKING DYNAMIC** **Viking Dynamic AS** Eidesvik AS *Haugesund* Norway MMSI: 258591000	3,524 1,057 4,505	Class: NV	**2002-06 Aker Aukra AS — Aukra** Yd No: 104 Loa 90.20 (BB) Br ex - Dght 6.970 Lbp 77.20 Br md 19.00 Dpth 8.40 Welded, 1 dk	**(B21A20S) Platform Supply Ship**	**5 diesel electric oil engines** driving 5 gen. each 1825kW 690V a.c Connecting to 2 elec. motors each (3000kW) driving 2 Azimuth electric drive units contra rotating azimuth thrusters Total Power: 9,505kW (12,925hp) 12.0kn Caterpillar 3516B 5 x Vee 4 Stroke 16 Cy. 170 x 190 each-1901kW (2585bhp) Caterpillar Inc-USA Thrusters: 2 Thwart. FP thruster (f); 1 Directional thruster (f) Fuel: 1403.0
9344954 *A8IH5* -	**VIKING EAGLE** *ex* Hansa Lauenburg *-2013* **Rum Shipping Ltd** Goodwood Ship Management Pte Ltd *Monrovia* Liberia MMSI: 636015923 Official number: 15923	18,327 10,908 23,482 T/cm 38.0	Class: GL	**2006-01 Guangzhou Wenchong Shipyard Co Ltd — Guangzhou GD** Yd No: 319 Loa 175.47 (BB) Br ex - Dght 10.905 Lbp 165.00 Br md 27.40 Dpth 14.30 Welded, 1 dk	**(A33A2CC) Container Ship (Fully Cellular)** Double Bottom Entire Compartment Length TEU 1740 C Ho 700 TEU C Dk 1040 TEU incl 300 ref C Compartments: 5 Cell Ho, ER Cranes: 2x40t	**1 oil engine** driving 1 FP propeller Total Power: 16,660kW (22,651hp) 19.5kn MAN-B&W 7S60MC-C 1 x 2 Stroke 7 Cy. 600 x 2400 16660kW (22651bhp) Hudong Heavy Machinery Co Ltd-China AuxGen: 2 x 1400kW 450/220V a.c Thrusters: 1 Tunnel thruster (f) Fuel: 170.0 (d.f.) 1700.0 (r.f.)
9514987 *9V7990* -	**VIKING EMERALD** **Gram Car Carriers II Pte Ltd** OSM Ship Management Pte Ltd *Singapore* Singapore MMSI: 566485000 Official number: 395139	39,454 13,317 12,500	Class: NV	**2012-05 Nantong Mingde Heavy Industry Co Ltd — Tongzhou JS** Yd No: 33000PCTC-06 Loa 167.25 (BB) Br ex 28.01 Dght 8.600 Lbp 158.81 Br md 28.00 Dpth 30.09 Welded, 11 dks. incl. 2 liftable dks.	**(A35B2RV) Vehicles Carrier** Side door/ramp (s) Len: 23.75 Wid: 6.70 Swl: 20 Quarter stern door/ramp (s. a.) Len: 31.50 Wid: 7.00 Swl: 80 Cars: 4,200	**1 oil engine** driving 1 FP propeller Total Power: 11,060kW (15,037hp) 18.0kn MAN-B&W 7S50ME-C 1 x 2 Stroke 7 Cy. 500 x 2000 11060kW (15037bhp) Hyundai Heavy Industries Co Ltd-South Korea AuxGen: 3 x 970kW a.c Thrusters: 1 Tunnel thruster (f) Fuel: 200.0 (d.f.) 2360.0 (r.f.)
6806602 *WX9219* -	**VIKING EMPIRE** *ex* Mud Lump *-1991* *ex* Jaramac 73 *-1990* *ex* Mud Lump *-1987* **Empire Alaska Seafoods Inc** - *Seattle, WA* United States of America Official number: 503515	*277* 188 -		**1966 McDermott Shipyards Inc — Morgan City LA** Yd No: 134 Converted From: Utility Vessel, Offshore Converted From: Fishing Vessel-1971 Loa 51.82 Br ex 10.75 Dght 3.757 Lbp 49.94 Br md 10.67 Dpth 4.27 Welded, 1 dk	**(B11B2FV) Fishing Vessel**	**2 oil engines** driving 2 FP propellers Total Power: 1,250kW (1,700hp) G.M. (Detroit Diesel) 16V-71 2 x Vee 2 Stroke 16 Cy. 108 x 127 each-625kW (850bhp) General Motors Detroit DieselAllison Divn-USA
9258442 *LLVY* -	**VIKING ENERGY** *ex* Stril Pioner *-2003* **Eidesvik Shipping AS** Eidesvik AS *Haugesund* Norway MMSI: 258390000	5,073 1,521 6,013	Class: NV	**2003-09 Maritim Shipyard Sp z oo — Gdansk** (Hull) **2003-09 Kleven Verft AS — Ulsteinvik** Yd No: 303 Loa 94.90 (BB) Br ex 20.62 Dght 7.890 Lbp 81.60 Br md 20.50 Dpth 9.60 Welded, 1 dk	**(B21A20S) Platform Supply Ship**	**4 diesel electric oil engines** driving 4 gen. each 1920kW 690V a.c Connecting to 2 elec. motors each (3000kW) & gearing integral to driving 2 Azimuth electric drive units contra-rotating propellers Total Power: 8,040kW (10,932hp) 16.0kn Wartsila 6R32DF 4 x 4 Stroke 6 Cy. 320 x 350 each-2010kW (2733bhp) Wartsila Finland Oy-Finland Thrusters: 2 Tunnel thruster (f); 1 Retract. directional thruster (f) Fuel: 86.0 (LNG)
8802404 *CFG7403* -	**VIKING ENTERPRISE** *ex* Kristinn Fridriksson *-2004* *ex* Geiri Peturs *-2004* *ex* Sverri Olason *-1997* **Viking Seafoods Ltd** *Vancouver, BC* Canada Official number: 826780	272 99 -	Class: BV	**1989-07 Poul Ree A/S — Stokkemarke** (Hull) **1989-07 p/f Vags Skipasmidja — Vagur** Yd No: 9 Loa 40.65 Br ex - Dght 4.150 Lbp 35.35 Br md 8.50 Dpth 6.55 Welded	**(B11A2FS) Stern Trawler** Ice Capable	**1 oil engine** driving 1 FP propeller Total Power: 1,500kW (2,039hp) Nohab F38V 1 x Vee 4 Stroke 8 Cy. 250 x 300 1500kW (2039bhp) Wartsila Diesel Oy-Finland
9150042 - -	**VIKING EXPLORER** - -	241 72 123		**1996-05 OCEA SA — Les Sables-d'Olonne** Yd No: 029 Loa 24.95 (BB) Br ex 10.15 Dght 2.391 Lbp 23.90 Br md 10.00 Dpth 3.85 Welded, 1 dk	**(B11B2FV) Fishing Vessel** Hull Material: Aluminium Alloy	**2 oil engines** with clutches, flexible couplings & sr reverse geared to sc. shafts driving 2 FP propellers Total Power: 558kW (758hp) Baudouin 6M26SR 2 x 4 Stroke 6 Cy. 150 x 150 each-279kW (379bhp) Societe des Moteurs Baudouin SA-France
7411985 *HP8664* -	**VIKING EXPLORER** *ex* Joan Salton *-1998* *ex* Punta Libeccio *-1996* *ex* Spray Fish *-1988* **Payette Ships (US) Inc** - *Panama* Panama Official number: 25291PEXT2	243 72 200	Class: (RI) (BV)	**1975-08 Chantiers et Ateliers de La Perriere — Lorient** Yd No: 302 Loa 41.15 Br ex 7.57 Dght 3.001 Lbp 38.49 Br md 7.50 Dpth 3.79 Welded, 1 dk	**(B21B20A) Anchor Handling Tug Supply** Passengers: berths: 12	**2 oil engines** driving 2 CP propellers Total Power: 1,766kW (2,402hp) 15.0kn MGO 16V175ASHR 2 x Vee 4 Stroke 16 Cy. 175 x 180 each-883kW (1201bhp) Societe Alsacienne de ConstructionsMecaniques (SACM)-France AuxGen: 2 x 102kW 220/380V 50Hz a.c Thrusters: 1 Thwart. FP thruster (f) Fuel: 69.0 (d.f.)
7934248 *WRC8693* -	**VIKING EXPLORER** **Royal Viking Inc** Trident Seafoods Corp *Seattle, WA* United States of America MMSI: 303648000 Official number: 605228	*193* 131 -		**1979 Dakota Creek Industries Inc — Anacortes WA** L reg 33.99 Br ex 9.76 Dght - Lbp - Br md - Dpth 3.26 Welded, 1 dk	**(B11B2FV) Fishing Vessel**	**1 oil engine** driving 1 FP propeller Total Power: 827kW (1,124hp) Caterpillar D399SCAC 1 x Vee 4 Stroke 16 Cy. 159 x 203 827kW (1124bhp) Caterpillar Tractor Co-USA
9623025 *LDGT* -	**VIKING FIGHTER** **Viking Fighter AS** Maritime Logistic Services AS *Stavanger* Norway MMSI: 257838000	3,580 1,322 4,000	Class: NV	**2012-07 STX OSV Tulcea SA — Tulcea** (Hull) **2012-07 STX OSV Brattvaag — Brattvaag** Yd No: 783 Loa 81.70 (BB) Br ex 18.04 Dght 6.500 Lbp 74.00 Br md 18.00 Dpth 7.80 Welded, 1 dk	**(B21A20S) Platform Supply Ship** Ice Capable	**4 diesel electric oil engines** driving 2 gen. each 1780kW 690V a.c 2 gen. each 1187kW 690V a.c Connecting to 2 elec. motors each (1600kW) driving 2 Azimuth electric drive units Total Power: 5,400kW (7,342hp) 12.5kn Wartsila 6L20 2 x 4 Stroke 6 Cy. 200 x 280 each-1080kW (1468bhp) Wartsila Finland Oy-Finland Wartsila 9L20 2 x 4 Stroke 9 Cy. 200 x 280 each-1620kW (2203bhp) Wartsila Finland Oy-Finland Thrusters: 1 Retract. directional thruster (f); 1 Tunnel thruster (f)
9606900 *OJPQ* -	**VIKING GRACE** **SF Line Ab (Viking Line Abp)** - SatCom: Inmarsat C 423062910 *Mariehamn* Finland MMSI: 230629000	57,565 38,039 6,107	Class: LR ✠ **100A1** SS 01/2013 passenger and vehicle ferry **ShipRight** (SDA, CM, ACS (B)) movable decks *IWS LI Ice Class 1AS FS at a draught of 7.165m Max/min draughts fwd 7.165/6.165m Max/min draughts aft 7.165/6.165m Power required 10221kw, power installed 21000kw ✠ **LMC** **UMS** Eq.Ltr: R†; Cable: 687.0/84.0 U3 (a)	**2013-01 STX Finland Oy — Turku** Yd No: 1376 Loa 218.21 (BB) Br ex 32.42 Dght 7.015 Lbp 200.02 Br md 31.80 Dpth 18.60 Welded, 2 dks	**(A36A2PR) Passenger/Ro-Ro Ship (Vehicles)** Passengers: cabins: 880; berths: 2800 Bow door/ramp (centre) Len: 21.00 Wid: 6.00 Swl: - Stern door/ramp (centre) Lane-Len: 2375 Cars: 450 Ice Capable	**4 diesel electric oil engines** driving 4 gen. each 7372kW a.c Connecting to 2 elec. motors each (10500kW) driving 2 FP propellers Total Power: 30,400kW (41,332hp) 21.8kn Wartsila 8L50DF 4 x 4 Stroke 8 Cy. 500 x 580 each-7600kW (10333bhp) Wartsila Italia SpA-Italy Boilers: e (ex.g.) 10.2kgf/cm² (10.0bar), AuxB (o.f.) 9.4kgf/cm² (9.2bar) Thrusters: 2 Thwart. CP thruster (f); 1 Thwart. CP thruster (a)

5018246 **VIKING I**
- *ex* Viking *ex* Ann Arbor No. 7 *-1965*
- **Viking I LLC**
K & K Warehousing Inc
Menominee, MI *United States of America*
Official number: 224430

2,713 Class: (AB)
1,287
-

1925 Manitowoc Shipbuilding Co — Manitowoc WI Yd No: 214
Loa 109.73 Br ex 17.12 Dght 5.477
Lbp 106.08 Br md 17.07 Dpth 6.56
Riveted, 2 dks

(A36A2PR) Passenger/Ro-Ro Ship (Vehicles)
Passengers: 375

4 diesel electric oil engines driving 4 gen. each 1226kW 750V d.c Connecting to 4 elec. motors driving 2 FP propellers
Total Power: 4,500kW (6,120hp)
EMD (Electro-Motive) 16-567-BC
4 x Vee 2 Stroke 16 Cy. 216 x 254 each-1125kW (1530bhp) (new engine 1965)
General Motors Corp-USA
AuxGen: 3 x 300kW 450V 60Hz a.c
Thrusters: 1 Thwart. FP thruster (f)

9189512 **VIKING II**
LCKW3 *ex* Veritas Viking II *-1999*
- **Eidesvik Shipping AS**
Eidesvik AS
Haugesund *Norway (NIS)*
MMSI: 259569000

7,764 Class: NV
2,329
4,410

1999-06 Stocznia Gdanska - Grupa Stoczni Gdynia SA — Gdansk (Hull) Yd No: 201/1
1999-06 Mjellem & Karlsen Verft AS — Bergen Yd No: 150
Loa 93.35 (BB) Br ex - Dght 7.050
Lbp 81.30 Br md 22.00 Dpth 8.60
Welded, 1 dk

(B31A2SR) Research Survey Vessel

2 oil engines reduction geared to sc. shafts driving 2 CP propellers
Total Power: 8,640kW (11,746hp) 11.5kn
MaK 9M32
2 x 4 Stroke 9 Cy. 320 x 480 each-4320kW (5873bhp)
MaK Motoren GmbH & Co. KG-Kiel
AuxGen: 2 x 2360kW 440V 60Hz a.c, 1 x 420kW 440V 60Hz a.c
Thrusters: 1 Thwart. FP thruster (f); 1 Retract. directional thruster (f)
Fuel: 1777.9 (r.f.)

7945948 **VIKING III**
- *ex* Haneda Maru *-1982*
-
-
-

125
41
-

1966-09 Kurushima Dockyard Co. Ltd. — Imabari Yd No: 378
Loa 26.57 Br ex - Dght 2.720
Lbp 23.50 Br md 7.00 Dpth 3.20
Welded, 1 dk

(B32A2ST) Tug

2 oil engines driving 2 CP propellers
Total Power: 956kW (1,300hp) 11.8kn
Nippon Hatsudoki HS6NV229
2 x 4 Stroke 6 Cy. 290 x 430 each-478kW (650bhp)
Nippon Hatsudoki-Japan

7048051 **VIKING KING**
WY7687
- **Northern Reefer Co Inc**
-
Seattle, WA *United States of America*
Official number: 522596

179
122
-

1969 John A. Martinolich Shipbuilding Corp. — Tacoma, Wa
L reg 22.93 Br ex 7.75 Dght -
Lbp - Br md - Dpth 3.31
Welded

(B11B2FV) Fishing Vessel

1 oil engine driving 1 FP propeller
Total Power: 533kW (725hp)

9409675 **VIKING LADY**
LAWZ
- **Eidesvik Shipping AS**
Eidesvik AS
SatCom: Inmarsat C 425996810
Haugesund *Norway*
MMSI: 259968000

6,111 Class: NV
1,834
6,200

2009-04 Torlak Gemi Insaat Sanayi ve Ticaret A.S. — Tuzla (Hull) Yd No: 57
2009-04 West Contractors AS — Olensvaag Yd No: 30
Loa 92.20 (BB) Br ex 21.00 Dght 7.624
Lbp 84.80 Br md 20.40 Dpth 9.60
Welded, 1 dk

(B21A2OS) Platform Supply Ship
Cranes: 1x10t
Ice Capable

4 diesel electric oil engines driving 4 gen. each 1950kW 690V a.c Connecting to 2 elec. motors each (2300kW) & gearing integral to driving 2 Azimuth electric drive units
Total Power: 8,040kW (10,932hp) 16.0kn
Wartsila 6R32DF
4 x 4 Stroke 6 Cy. 320 x 350 each-2010kW (2733bhp)
Wartsila Finland Oy-Finland
AuxGen: 1 x 320kW a.c
Thrusters: 1 Retract. directional thruster (f); 2 Tunnel thruster (f)
Fuel: 400.0 (LNG)

1005576 **VIKING LEGACY**
MMCE4 *ex* Greybeard *-2003*
- **Orcades Viking Ltd**
Green Marine (Orkney) Ltd
Stromness *United Kingdom*
MMSI: 235010950
Official number: 906798

159 Class: (LR) (BV)
47 ✠ Classed LR until 1/12/04
-

1997-06 Farocean Marine Pty Ltd — Cape Town Yd No: 116
Loa 26.82 Br ex 6.60 Dght 3.750
Lbp 25.68 Br md 6.40 Dpth 3.80
Welded, 2 dks

(X11A2YP) Yacht

2 oil engines with flexible couplings & sr reverse geared to sc. shafts driving 2 FP propellers
Total Power: 588kW (800hp) 12.0kn
Caterpillar 3406TA
2 x 4 Stroke 6 Cy. 137 x 165 each-294kW (400bhp)
Caterpillar Inc-USA
AuxGen: 2 x 37kW 380V 50Hz a.c
Thrusters: 1 Thwart. FP thruster (f)

8730546 **VIKING MADSALEX**
OVSR2 *ex* DSV Explore *-1999* *ex* Drive Explore *-1997*
ex Rikke Diver *-1997* *ex* Wels *-1992*
- *ex* Els *-1992*
Dykkerselskabet Viking AS
-
Svendborg *Denmark (DIS)*
MMSI: 220267000
Official number: H1184

127 Class: (GL) (RS)
38
52

1989-09 Sosnovskiy Sudostroitelnyy Zavod — Sosnovka Yd No: 766
Loa 25.50 Br ex 7.00 Dght 2.200
Lbp 22.00 Br md 6.80 Dpth 3.30
Welded

(B34R2QY) Supply Tender
Ins: 64
Ice Capable

1 oil engine reverse reduction geared to sc. shaft driving 1 FP propeller
Total Power: 220kW (299hp) 10.0kn
S.K.L. 6NVD26A-2
1 x 4 Stroke 6 Cy. 180 x 260 220kW (299bhp)
VEB Schwermaschinenbau "KarlLiebknecht" (SKL)-Magdeburg
AuxGen: 2 x 14kW a.c

9128491 **VIKING MARLIN**
-
- -
-

100
-
75

1995-07 OCEA SA — Les Sables-d'Olonne Yd No: 26
Loa - (BB) Br ex - Dght -
Lbp - Br md - Dpth -
Welded, 1 dk

(B11B2FV) Fishing Vessel
Hull Material: Aluminium Alloy

2 oil engines with clutches, flexible couplings & sr reverse geared to sc. shafts driving 2 FP propellers
Total Power: 640kW (870hp)
Wartsila UD19L6M4D
2 x 4 Stroke 6 Cy. 127 x 145 each-320kW (435bhp)
Wartsila SACM Diesel SA-France

9169574 **VIKING MONARCH**
MXHW8 *ex* Solstice Ii *-1992*
BF 56 **Norlantic Marine Ltd**
-
Kirkwall *United Kingdom*
MMSI: 232116000
Official number: C16409

611
183
-

1998-06 Ailsa Troon Ltd — Troon Yd No: 576
Loa 40.00 Br ex - Dght 6.000
Lbp 32.60 Br md 10.50 Dpth 7.25
Welded, 1 dk

(B11A2FS) Stern Trawler
Ins: 440

1 oil engine reduction geared to sc. shaft driving 1 CP propeller
Total Power: 1,960kW (2,665hp) 12.5kn
Alpha 8L28/32A
1 x 4 Stroke 8 Cy. 280 x 320 1960kW (2665bhp)
MAN B&W Diesel A/S-Denmark
AuxGen: 1 x 800kW a.c, 2 x 400kW a.c
Thrusters: 1 Thwart. FP thruster (f)

8733914 **VIKING MOON**
-
- **Westfjord Fishing Ltd, Pathfinder Fishing Ltd & Pacific National Fishing Ltd**
-
Vancouver, BC *Canada*
Official number: 817566

213
118
-

1994-12 Sylte Shipyard Ltd — Maple Ridge BC
L reg 24.54 Br ex - Dght -
Lbp - Br md 7.46 Dpth 6.28
Welded, 1 dk

(B11A2FS) Stern Trawler
Hull Material: Aluminium Alloy

1 oil engine driving 1 Propeller
Total Power: 448kW (609hp) 10.0kn

9297797 **VIKING NEREUS**
LDEQ *ex* Malaviya Nineteen *-2012*
- **Viking Surf AS**
Eidesvik AS
Haugesund *Norway*
MMSI: 257835000

2,151 Class: NV (IR)
1,047
3,302

2004-01 SC Aker Braila SA — Braila (Hull) Yd No: 1423
2004-01 Aker Aukra AS — Aukra Yd No: 113
Loa 72.00 Br ex 16.04 Dght 5.810
Lbp 65.90 Br md 16.00 Dpth 7.00
Welded, 1 dk

(B21A2OS) Platform Supply Ship
Cranes: 1x3t

2 oil engines geared to sc. shafts driving 2 CP propellers
Total Power: 4,016kW (5,460hp) 13.0kn
Bergens KRMB-9
2 x 4 Stroke 9 Cy. 250 x 300 each-2008kW (2730bhp)
Rolls Royce Marine AS-Norway
AuxGen: 2 x 260kW 440V 60Hz a.c, 2 x 1280kW 440V 60Hz a.c
Thrusters: 2 Tunnel thruster (f); 1 Tunnel thruster (a)
Fuel: 760.0 (r.f.)

9514999 **VIKING OCEAN**
9V8008
- **Gram Car Carriers II Pte Ltd**
OSM Ship Management Pte Ltd
Singapore *Singapore*
MMSI: 566613000
Official number: 395169

39,454 Class: NV
13,317
12,500

2012-09 Nantong Mingde Heavy Industry Co Ltd — Tongzhou JS Yd No: 33000PCTC-07
Loa 167.25 (BB) Br ex - Dght 8.600
Lbp 158.81 Br md 28.00 Dpth 30.09
Welded, 11 dks. incl. 2 liftable dks.

(A35B2RV) Vehicles Carrier
Side door/ramp (s)
Len: 23.75 Wid: 6.70 Swl: 20
Quarter stern door/ramp (s. a.)
Len: 31.50 Wid: 7.00 Swl: 80
Cars: 4,200

1 oil engine driving 1 FP propeller
Total Power: 11,060kW (15,037hp) 18.0kn
MAN-B&W 7S50ME-C
1 x 2 Stroke 7 Cy. 500 x 2000 11060kW (15037bhp)
Hyundai Heavy Industries Co Ltd-South Korea
AuxGen: 3 x a.c
Thrusters: 1 Tunnel thruster (f)

9398876 **VIKING ODESSA**
9V7982
- **Gram Car Carriers Pte Ltd**
OSM Ship Management Pte Ltd
SatCom: Inmarsat C 456444610
Singapore *Singapore*
MMSI: 564446000
Official number: 395131

20,216 Class: NV (BV)
6,064
4,693

2009-08 Kyokuyo Shipyard Corp — Shimonoseki YC Yd No: 485
Loa 140.00 (BB) Br ex - Dght 6.100
Lbp 131.00 Br md 22.50 Dpth 22.95
Welded, 8 dks. incl. 1 hoistable dk.

(A35B2RV) Vehicles Carrier
Stern door/ramp (centre)
Len: 15.90 Wid: 7.00 Swl: 75
Quarter stern door/ramp (s. a.)
Len: 16.30 Wid: 5.00 Swl: 30
Cars: 2,000
Ice Capable

2 oil engines reduction geared to sc. shaft driving 1 CP propeller
Total Power: 12,000kW (16,316hp) 18.5kn
MaK 6M43C
1 x 4 Stroke 6 Cy. 430 x 610 6000kW (8158bhp)
Caterpillar Motoren GmbH & Co. KG-Germany
AuxGen: 2 x 490kW a.c, 1 x 2400kW a.c
Thrusters: 1 Tunnel thruster (f)

IMO / Call sign / Flag	Name / Owner / Manager / Port	Tonnage	Class	Build / Dimensions	Type / Cargo	Machinery
9413535 *LFKP* -	**VIKING POSEIDON** **Eidesvik OCV AS** Eidesvik AS SatCom: Inmarsat C 425987310 *Haugesund* *Norway* MMSI: 259873000	**11,719** 3,516 8,700	Class: NV	**2009-01 Maritim Shipyard Sp z oo — Gdansk** (Hull) Yd No: (281) **2009-01 Ulstein Verft AS — Ulsteinvik** Yd No: 281 Loa 130.00 Br ex 25.03 Dght 7.800 Lbp 122.10 Br md 25.00 Dpth 10.00 Welded, 1 dk	**(B22A20R) Offshore Support Vessel** Cranes: 1x250t	**6 diesel electric oil engines** driving 4 gen. each 2700kW a.c 2 gen. each 1450kW a.c Connecting to 2 elec. motors each (3500kW) driving 2 Azimuth electric drive units Total Power: 15,300kW (20,802hp) 14.5kn MaK 9M20C 2 x 4 Stroke 9 Cy. 200 x 300 each-1710kW (2325bhp) Caterpillar Motoren GmbH & Co. KG-Germany MaK 9M25C 4 x 4 Stroke 9 Cy. 255 x 400 each-2970kW (4038bhp) Caterpillar Motoren GmbH & Co. KG-Germany Thrusters: 2 Tunnel thruster (f); 1 Retract. directional thruster (f); 1 Retract. directional thruster (a) Fuel: 2830.0 (d.f.)
8989147 - -	**VIKING PRIDE** **Leader Fishing Ltd** - *Vancouver, BC* *Canada* MMSI: 316011441 Official number: 812341	**105** 40 -		**1989 RivTow Straits Ltd — Vanvouver BC** L reg 21.92 Br ex - Dght - Lbp - Br md 6.70 Dpth 3.44 Welded, 1 dk	**(B11B2FV) Fishing Vessel**	**1 oil engine** driving 1 Propeller Total Power: 596kW (810hp) 10.0kn
9596296 *LDCE* -	**VIKING PRINCE** **Eidesvik Supply AS** Eidesvik AS *Haugesund* *Norway* MMSI: 257787000	**5,381** 1,626 6,150	Class: NV	**2012-03 Kleven Verft AS — Ulsteinvik** Yd No: 346 Loa 89.60 (BB) Br ex - Dght 7.600 Lbp 79.20 Br md 21.00 Dpth 9.60 Welded, 1 dk	**(B21A20S) Platform Supply Ship** Ice Capable	**4 diesel electric oil engines** driving 4 gen. Connecting to 2 elec. motors each (2450kW) driving 2 Azimuth electric drive units contra rotating propellers Total Power: 7,380kW (10,034hp) Wartsila 6L20 2 x 4 Stroke 6 Cy. 200 x 280 each-1080kW (1468bhp) Wartsila Finland Oy-Finland Wartsila 6L34DF 2 x 4 Stroke 6 Cy. 340 x 400 each-2610kW (3549bhp) Wartsila Finland Oy-Finland Thrusters: 2 Tunnel thruster (f); 1 Retract. directional thruster (f) Fuel: 230.0 (LNG) 820.0
9611840 *LDDE* -	**VIKING PRINCESS** **Eidesvik Shipping AS** Eidesvik AS *Haugesund* *Norway*	**5,381** 1,626 6,150	Class: NV	**2012-09 Kleven Verft AS — Ulsteinvik** Yd No: 347 Loa 89.60 (BB) Br ex - Dght 7.600 Lbp 79.20 Br md 21.00 Dpth 9.60 Welded, 1 dk	**(B21A20S) Platform Supply Ship** Ice Capable	**4 diesel electric oil engines** driving 2 gen. each 2008kW 690V a.c 2 gen. each 811kW 690V a.c Connecting to 2 elec. motors each (2450kW) driving 2 Azimuth electric drive units contra rotating propellers Total Power: 7,380kW (10,034hp) Wartsila 6L20 2 x 4 Stroke 6 Cy. 200 x 280 each-1080kW (1468bhp) Wartsila Finland Oy-Finland Wartsila 6L34DF 1 x 4 Stroke 6 Cy. 340 x 400 2610kW (3549bhp) Wartsila Finland Oy-Finland Thrusters: 1 Tunnel thruster (f); 1 Retract. directional thruster (f); 1 Tunnel thruster (a)
9136967 *VRCX4* -	**VIKING PRINCESS** *ex* Prince Maru No. 2 *-2007* **Karianne Shipping Ltd** Hisamoto Kisen Co Ltd (Hisamoto Kisen KK) *Hong Kong* *Hong Kong* MMSI: 477898200 Official number: HK-1921	**9,827** 3,444 3,995	Class: NK	**1996-01 Usuki Shipyard Co Ltd — Usuki OT** Yd No: 1635 Loa 117.00 (BB) Br ex - Dght 5.962 Lbp 106.00 Br md 20.00 Dpth 6.15 Welded, 1 dk	**(A35B2RV) Vehicles Carrier** Quarter stern door/ramp (p. a.) Quarter stern door/ramp (s. a.) Cars: 797	**1 oil engine** driving 1 FP propeller Total Power: 5,980kW (8,130hp) 17.5kn B&W 6L42MC 1 x 2 Stroke 6 Cy. 420 x 1360 5980kW (8130bhp) Hitachi Zosen Corp-Japan AuxGen: 2 x 600kW 450V a.c Thrusters: 1 Thwart. CP thruster (f) Fuel: 381.0 (r.f.) 23.6pd
6603751 - -	**VIKING PUMA** *ex* Cam Puma *-1996* *ex* Sea Guard *-1987* *ex* Nyegg *-1981* *launched as* Stalegg *-1966* - -	**457** 146 -	Class: (NV)	**1966-03 Kleven Mek Verksted AS — Ulsteinvik** Yd No: 11 Converted From: Fishing Vessel-1982 Lengthened-1971 Loa 48.44 Br ex 7.65 Dght 4.168 Lbp 43.95 Br md 7.62 Dpth 4.27 Welded, 1 dk	**(B22G20Y) Standby Safety Vessel** Compartments: 2 Ho, 3 Ta, ER 5 Ha: (2.2 x 2.5) (1.8 x 2.7)2 (1.5 x 2.7) (3.1 x 2.5)ER Derricks: 1x3t; Winches: 1	**1 oil engine** driving 1 FP propeller Total Power: 625kW (850hp) 12.0kn MaK 6M451AK 1 x 4 Stroke 6 Cy. 320 x 450 625kW (850bhp) Maschinenbau Kiel AG (MaK)-Kiel AuxGen: 1 x 128kW 220V 50Hz a.c, 1 x 59kW 220V 50Hz a.c, 1 x 38kW 220V 50Hz a.c Thrusters: 1 Thwart. FP thruster (f); 1 Tunnel thruster (a)
7309792 *WX8727* -	**VIKING QUEEN** **Icicle Seafoods Inc** - SatCom: Inmarsat C 436777710 *Petersburg, AK* *United States of America* Official number: 508212	**215** 64 -		**1967 Pacific Fishermen, Inc. — Seattle, Wa** L reg 25.64 Br ex 7.93 Dght - Lbp - Br md - Dpth 3.08 Welded, 1 dk	**(B11B2FV) Fishing Vessel**	**1 oil engine** driving 1 FP propeller Total Power: 500kW (680hp)
9372901 *LAWA* -	**VIKING QUEEN** **Eidesvik Shipping AS** Eidesvik AS SatCom: Inmarsat C 425886510 *Haugesund* *Norway* MMSI: 258865000	**6,111** 1,834 6,200	Class: NV	**2008-02 'Crist' Sp z oo — Gdansk** (Hull) Yd No: B493 **2008-02 West Contractors AS — Olensvaag** Yd No: 29 Loa 92.20 (BB) Br ex 21.00 Dght 7.624 Lbp 84.80 Br md 20.40 Dpth 9.60 Welded, 1 dk	**(B21A20S) Platform Supply Ship** Passengers: berths: 25 Cranes: 1x10t Ice Capable	**4 diesel electric oil engines** driving 4 gen. each 1950kW 690V a.c Connecting to 2 elec. motors each (2200kW) & gearing integral to driving 2 Azimuth electric drive units Total Power: 9,200kW (12,508hp) 16.0kn Wartsila 6L32DF 4 x 4 Stroke 6 Cy. 320 x 350 each-2300kW (3127bhp) Wartsila Finland Oy-Finland Thrusters: 2 Tunnel thruster (f); 1 Retract. directional thruster (f) Fuel: 400.0 (LNG)
7432068 *OZMM2* -	**VIKING R** *ex* Koraalzee *-1988* **RN Shipping A/S** Rohde Nielsen A/S *Grenaa* *Denmark (DIS)* MMSI: 219000219 Official number: D3687	**1,102** 330 -	Class: BV	**1975-07 Scheepswerf en Machinefabriek "De Liesbosch" B.V. — Nieuwegein** Yd No: 145 Converted From: Hopper Loa 66.71 Br ex - Dght 4.301 Lbp 57.26 Br md 11.85 Dpth 4.75 Welded, 1 dk	**(B33B2DT) Trailing Suction Hopper Dredger** Hopper: 1,010	**2 oil engines** reverse reduction geared to sc. shafts driving 2 FP propellers Total Power: 882kW (1,200hp) 9.0kn Bolnes 5DNL120/500 1 x 2 Stroke 5 Cy. 190 x 350 441kW (600bhp) 'Bolnes' Motorenfabriek BV-Netherlands Bolnes 5DNL150/600 1 x 2 Stroke 5 Cy. 190 x 350 441kW (600bhp) 'Bolnes' Motorenfabriek BV-Netherlands AuxGen: 2 x 275kW 380/220V 50Hz a.c Thrusters: 1 Thwart. FP thruster (f) Fuel: 118.0 (d.f.)
9336660 *3ELF9* -	**VIKING RIVER** **Fractal Marine Corp** Kawasaki Kisen Kaisha Ltd (Kawasaki Kisen KK) ('K' Line) *Panama* *Panama* MMSI: 372938000 Official number: 3306507A	**25,937** 7,782 29,536 T/cm 44.7	Class: NK	**2007-07 Daewoo Shipbuilding & Marine Engineering Co Ltd — Geoje** Yd No: 2314 Loa 180.00 (BB) Br ex 29.20 Dght 10.422 Lbp 173.43 Br md 29.20 Dpth 18.20 Welded, 1 dk	**(A11B2TG) LPG Tanker** Double Bottom Entire Compartment Length Liq (Gas): 38,898 3 x Gas Tank (s); 3 independent (C.mn.stl) cyl horizontal 6 Cargo Pump (s): 6x465m³/hr Manifold: Bow/CM: 92.3m	**1 oil engine** driving 1 FP propeller Total Power: 9,480kW (12,889hp) 16.4kn MAN-B&W 6S50MC-C 1 x 2 Stroke 6 Cy. 500 x 2000 9480kW (12889bhp) Doosan Engine Co Ltd-South Korea
9305439 *ZR8020* -	**VIKING RUBY** *ex* Seawin Ruby *-2009* **Viking Fishing Co (Deep Sea) Pty Ltd (Viking Fishing Group)** - *Cape Town* *South Africa* MMSI: 601072800 Official number: 10734	**151** 45 75	Class: (BV)	**2003-09 Fujian Southeast Shipyard — Fuzhou FJ** Yd No: 2002-16 Loa 24.46 Br ex 7.20 Dght 2.500 Lbp 21.50 Br md 7.00 Dpth 3.25 Welded, 1 dk	**(B11B2FV) Fishing Vessel**	**1 oil engine** geared to sc. shaft driving 1 FP propeller Total Power: 485kW (659hp) Cummins QSK19-M 1 x 4 Stroke 6 Cy. 159 x 159 485kW (659bhp) Cummins Engine Co Inc-USA
5364267 *LKRU* -	**VIKING SAGA** *ex* Ringnes *-2004* *ex* Vildanden *-1990* *ex* Snapp *-1986* *ex* Tomma *-1963* **Fjordservice Sogn og Fjordane AS** - *Oslo* *Norway* MMSI: 257371700	*111* 40 -	Class: (NV)	**1942 Kristiansands Mek. Verksted AS — Kristiansand** Yd No: 174 Rebuilt-1985 Loa 27.86 Br ex 5.61 Dght 1.855 Lbp - Br md 5.57 Dpth 2.01 Riveted\Welded, 1 dk	**(A37B2PS) Passenger Ship** Passengers: unberthed: 183	**2 oil engines** driving 2 FP propellers Total Power: 338kW (460hp) 12.0kn MWM 2 x 4 Stroke 6 Cy. 180 x 260 each-169kW (230bhp) (new engine 1954) Motoren Werke Mannheim AG (MWM)-West Germany AuxGen: 1 x 10kW 220V 50Hz a.c

9515008 *9V8009* -	**VIKING SEA** **Gram Car Carriers Pte Ltd** P D Gram & Co AS *Singapore* *Singapore* MMSI: 566614000 Official number: 395170	**39,454** Class: NV 13,317 10,600	2012-11 **Nantong Mingde Heavy Industry Co Ltd — Tongzhou JS** Yd No: 33000PCTC-08 Loa 167.25 (BB) Br ex - Dght 8.600 Lbp 158.64 Br md 28.00 Dpth 30.09 Welded, 11 dks. incl. 2 liftable dks.	**(A35B2RV) Vehicles Carrier** Side door/ramp (s) Len: 23.75 Wid: 6.70 Swl: 20 Quarter stern door/ramp (s. a.) Len: 31.50 Wid: 7.00 Swl: 80 Cars: 4,200	**1 oil engine** driving 1 FP propeller Total Power: 11,060kW (15,037hp) 18.0kn MAN-B&W 7S50ME-C 1 x 2 Stroke 7 Cy. 500 x 2000 11060kW (15037bhp) Hyundai Heavy Industries Co Ltd-South Korea AuxGen: 3 x a.c Thrusters: 1 Tunnel thruster (f)
7823994 *UUA08* -	**VIKING SINEUS** *ex* Mikhail Lomonosov *-2009* **Viking Ukraine Ltd** Viking River Cruises AG *Kherson* *Ukraine* Official number: 2-306367	*5,182* 3,932 555	1979-11 **VEB Elbewerften Boizenburg/Rosslau — Boizenburg** Yd No: 338 Loa 124.95 Br ex 16.69 Dght 4.530 Lbp 117.89 Br md 16.68 Dpth - Welded, 4 dks	**(A37A2PC) Passenger/Cruise** Passengers: berths: 360	**3 oil engines** driving 3 FP propellers Total Power: 2,208kW (3,003hp) Dvigatel Revolyutsii 6CHN36/45 3 x 4 Stroke 6 Cy. 360 x 450 each-736kW (1001bhp) Zavod "Dvigatel Revolyutsii"-Gorkiy
6602745 *CXXA* -	**VIKING SKY** *ex* Gulf Grenadier *-1990* **Encomar SA** - *Montevideo* *Uruguay* MMSI: 770576144 Official number: 7965	*513* Class: (LR) 244 ✠ Classed LR until 6/69 -	1966-05 **Bathurst Marine Ltd — Georgetown PE** Yd No: 12 Loa 39.32 Br ex 8.56 Dght - Lbp 33.23 Br md 8.54 Dpth 6.56 Welded, 2 dks	**(B11A2FS) Stern Trawler**	**1 oil engine** sr geared to sc. shaft driving 1 CP propeller Total Power: 780kW (1,060hp) 10.0kn Normo LSMC-6 1 x 4 Stroke 6 Cy. 250 x 300 780kW (1060bhp) AS Bergens Mek Verksteder-Norway AuxGen: 2 x 40kW 220V 60Hz a.c
7629269 *CZ6393* -	**VIKING SPIRIT** **Grim Estates Ltd** - *Vancouver, BC* *Canada* MMSI: 316004832 Official number: 369682	*100* 43 -	1975 **Shore Boat Builders Ltd — Richmond BC** L reg 18.48 Br ex 6.10 Dght - Lbp - Br md - Dpth 3.43 Welded, 1 dk	**(B11A2FS) Stern Trawler** Hull Material: Aluminium Alloy	**1 oil engine** driving 1 FP propeller Total Power: 279kW (379hp) 11.0kn Caterpillar D353TA 1 x 4 Stroke 6 Cy. 159 x 203 279kW (379bhp) Caterpillar Tractor Co-USA
7817206 *E5WY* -	**VIKING SPIRIT** *ex* Neeltje Cornelis *-1997* *ex* Zes Gebroeders *-1984* **Brightwater Pacific Ltd** - SatCom: Inmarsat C 451299063 *Avatiu* *Cook Islands* MMSI: 518000004 Official number: CI 01/02	**275** 82 -	1979-06 **W. Visser & Zoon B.V. Werf "De Lastdrager" — Den Helder** Yd No: 90 Loa 37.14 Br ex 7.70 Dght 3.090 Lbp 33.05 Br md 7.51 Dpth 4.12 Welded, 1 dk	**(B11B2FV) Fishing Vessel**	**1 oil engine** reverse reduction geared to sc. shaft driving 1 FP propeller Total Power: 1,103kW (1,500hp) Kromhout 9F/SW240 1 x 4 Stroke 9 Cy. 240 x 260 1103kW (1500bhp) Stork Werkspoor Diesel BV-Netherlands
7810832 *VG4139* -	**VIKING STAR** **Westfjord Fishing Ltd** - *Vancouver, BC* *Canada* MMSI: 316003331 Official number: 391345	*138* 57 -	1978-11 **Allied Shipbuilders Ltd — North Vancouver BC** Yd No: 210 Loa 24.24 Br ex 7.04 Dght - Lbp 22.56 Br md 7.01 Dpth 3.69 Welded	**(B11B2FV) Fishing Vessel**	**1 oil engine** reverse reduction geared to sc. shaft driving 1 FP propeller Total Power: 386kW (525hp) Caterpillar 3412PCTA 1 x Vee 4 Stroke 12 Cy. 137 x 152 386kW (525bhp) Caterpillar Tractor Co-USA
8991554 *ATAP* -	**VIKING STAR** **Viking Lighterage & Cargo Handlers Pvt Ltd** K V Rao *Navlakhi* *India* MMSI: 419028100 Official number: GMB/NLK/45	**306** Class: IR 92 325	1998 **Neptune Marine Pvt. Ltd. — Mumbai** Yd No: 013 Loa 42.50 Br ex 9.18 Dght 1.800 Lbp 41.50 Br md 9.00 Dpth 2.96 Welded, 1 dk	**(A13B2TU) Tanker (unspecified)** Liq: 428; Liq (Oil): 428	**2 oil engines** geared to sc. shafts driving 2 Propellers Total Power: 346kW (470hp) 8.5kn Cummins NT-743-M 2 x 4 Stroke 6 Cy. 130 x 152 each-173kW (235bhp) Kirloskar Oil Engines Ltd-India AuxGen: 2 x 24kW 415V 50Hz a.c Fuel: 13.0 (d.f.)
8661379 *HP5435* -	**VIKING STARLINER** *ex* M. S. Shahan *-1964* **Comercializadora Vacamonte SA** - *Panama* *Panama* Official number: 44683PEXT1	**287** 110 -	1963-01 **Blount Marine Corp. — Warren, RI** Yd No: 90 Loa 32.32 Br ex - Dght 2.550 Lbp 29.82 Br md 8.54 Dpth 3.08 Welded, 1 dk	**(A37B2PS) Passenger Ship** Passengers: unberthed: 300	**3 oil engines** reduction geared to sc. shafts driving 3 Propellers 10.0kn G.M. (Detroit Diesel) 12V-71 3 x Vee 2 Stroke 12 Cy. 108 x 127 General Motors Detroit DieselAllison Divn-USA
7919858 *CZ7642* -	**VIKING STORM** *ex* Gail Bernice *-1964* *ex* Simstar *-1985* **Leader Fishing Ltd** - *Vancouver, BC* *Canada* MMSI: 316005448 Official number: 800025	*246* 115 231	1981-03 **Benson Bros Shipbuilding Co (1960) Ltd — New Westminster BC** Yd No: 41 Loa 29.27 Br ex - Dght 2.439 Lbp 27.44 Br md 8.23 Dpth 3.05 Welded, 1 dk	**(B11B2FV) Fishing Vessel**	**1 oil engine** geared to sc. shaft driving 1 FP propeller Total Power: 335kW (455hp) Cummins VT-28-M2 1 x Vee 4 Stroke 12 Cy. 140 x 152 335kW (455bhp) Cummins Engine Co Inc-USA
8950940 - -	**VIKING SUPER STAR** *ex* Wave Dancer *-2005* *ex* Super Squirrel II *-1992* **462 Starlite Inc** - *Montauk, NY* *United States of America* MMSI: 367071160 Official number: 567912	*188* 90 -	1975-01 **Gulf Craft Inc — Patterson LA** Yd No: 197 L reg 29.30 Br ex - Dght - Lbp - Br md 7.50 Dpth 2.90 Welded, 1 dk	**(B11B2FV) Fishing Vessel** Hull Material: Aluminium Alloy	**1 oil engine** driving 1 FP propeller 10.0kn General Motors General Motors Corp-USA
5404342 *CXZO* -	**VIKING SUR** *ex* Western Horizon *-2000* *ex* G. B. Reed *-2000* **Talivent SA** - *Montevideo* *Uruguay* MMSI: 770576015 Official number: 8041	*769* Class: (LR) 363 ✠ Classed LR until 1/5/73 -	1962-11 **Yarrows Ltd — Victoria BC** Yd No: 215 Loa 54.11 Br ex 9.86 Dght 3.734 Lbp 50.14 Br md 9.76 Dpth 4.88 Riveted\Welded, 1 dk, 2nd dk except in mchy. space	**(B12D2FR) Fishery Research Vessel** Compartments: 2 Ho, ER 2 Ha: (1.8 x 1.3) (1.3 x 1.3) Cranes: 1x5t,2x2t; Winches: 2	**1 oil engine** with hydraulic coupling driving 1 CP propeller Total Power: 736kW (1,001hp) 12.0kn Alpha 498-VO 1 x 2 Stroke 8 Cy. 310 x 490 736kW (1001bhp) Alpha Diesel A/S-Denmark AuxGen: 2 x 120kW 440V 60Hz a.c Fuel: 203.0 (d.f.)
9257606 *YJSA5* -	**VIKING SURF** **Boldini SA** Navegacao Sao Miguel Ltda *Port Vila* *Vanuatu* MMSI: 577084000 Official number: 2149	**2,417** Class: RI (NV) 1,088 3,640	2003-01 **Stocznia Polnocna SA (Northern Shipyard) — Gdansk** (Hull) Yd No: B836/1 2003-01 **West Contractors AS — Olensvaag** Yd No: 19 Loa 70.40 (BB) Br ex - Dght 6.500 Lbp 64.00 Br md 16.60 Dpth 7.60 Welded, 1 dk	**(B21A20S) Platform Supply Ship**	**2 oil engines** reduction geared to sc. shafts driving 2 CP propellers Total Power: 4,900kW (6,662hp) MaK 8M25 2 x 4 Stroke 8 Cy. 255 x 400 each-2450kW (3331bhp) Caterpillar Motoren GmbH & Co. KG-Germany AuxGen: 2 x 345kW a.c, 2 x 1440kW a.c Thrusters: 1 Thwart. FP thruster (f); 1 Retract. directional thruster (f); 1 Thwart. FP thruster (a)
9316440 *YJRZ8* -	**VIKING THAUMAS** **Boldini SA** Navegacao Sao Miguel Ltda *Port Vila* *Vanuatu* MMSI: 577083000 Official number: 2148	**2,451** Class: RI (NV) 913 3,550	2005-07 **'Crist' Sp z oo — Gdansk** (Hull) Yd No: B74 2005-07 **West Contractors AS — Olensvaag** Yd No: 25 Loa 73.40 (BB) Br ex - Dght 6.500 Lbp 64.00 Br md 16.60 Dpth 7.60 Welded, 1 dk	**(B21A20S) Platform Supply Ship** Double Bottom Entire Compartment Length Cranes: 1x3t	**2 oil engines** geared to sc. shafts driving 2 FP propellers Total Power: 4,800kW (6,526hp) 14.5kn MaK 8M25 2 x 4 Stroke 8 Cy. 255 x 400 each-2400kW (3263bhp) Caterpillar Motoren GmbH & Co. KG-Germany AuxGen: 2 x 350kW a.c, 2 x 1440kW 450V 60Hz a.c Thrusters: 2 Tunnel thruster (f); 1 Tunnel thruster (a)
7914559 *WDB3671* -	**VIKING TIDE** *ex* Ensco Viking *-2003* *ex* Blue Chip *-1996* *ex* Tahitian Express *-1990* *ex* Tahitian Command *-1989* **Twenty Grand Offshore Inc** Tidewater Marine LLC *New Orleans, LA* *United States of America* MMSI: 366890020 Official number: 614763	*681* Class: AB 204 1,200	1979-11 **Halter Marine, Inc. — Moss Point, Ms** Yd No: 850 Loa 54.87 Br ex - Dght 3.640 Lbp 51.85 Br md 12.20 Dpth 4.27 Welded, 1 dk	**(B21B20T) Offshore Tug/Supply Ship**	**2 oil engines** reverse reduction geared to sc. shafts driving 2 FP propellers Total Power: 1,434kW (1,950hp) 12.0kn EMD (Electro-Motive) 8-645-E6 2 x Vee 2 Stroke 8 Cy. 230 x 254 each-717kW (975bhp) General Motors Corp.Electro-Motive Div.-La Grange AuxGen: 2 x 150kW Thrusters: 1 Thwart. FP thruster (f)
7823035 - -	**VIKING TIDE** *ex* Angela Lynn *-2008* **Leader Fishing Ltd** - *Vancouver, BC* *Canada* Official number: 391847	*115* 48 -	1979-03 **Allied Shipbuilders Ltd — North Vancouver BC** Yd No: 216 Loa 24.31 Br ex 7.01 Dght - Lbp 22.03 Br md 6.99 Dpth 3.69 Welded, 1 dk	**(B11B2FV) Fishing Vessel**	**1 oil engine** reverse reduction geared to sc. shaft driving 1 FP propeller Total Power: 382kW (519hp) 11.0kn Caterpillar 3412TA 1 x Vee 4 Stroke 12 Cy. 137 x 152 382kW (519bhp) Caterpillar Tractor Co-USA

IMO / Call sign	Name / Owner	Tonnage	Classification	Builder / Dimensions	Type	Machinery
7208572 *PNWP* -	**VIKING VANGUARD** *ex* Cam Viking *-1995* *ex* Biggas *-1991* **PT Bahari Lines Indonesia** - *Jakarta* *Indonesia*	**604** 182 520	Class: KI (NV)	**1972**-05 **Sterkoder Mek. Verksted AS — Kristiansund** Yd No: 25 Converted From: Stern Trawler-1991 Loa 47.20 Br ex 9.02 Dght 4.490 Lbp 41.80 Br md 9.00 Dpth 5.20 Welded, 2 dks	**(B22G20Y) Standby Safety Vessel** Compartments: 1 Ho, ER 1 Ha: (2.2 x 1.9)ER Ice Capable	**1 oil engine** driving 1 FP propeller Total Power: 883kW (1,201hp) 12.5kn Wichmann 8ACA 1 x 2 Stroke 8 Cy. 280 x 420 883kW (1201bhp) Wichmann Motorfabrikk AS-Norway AuxGen: 2 x 100kW 220V 50Hz a.c Thrusters: 1 Directional thruster (f) Fuel: 51.0 (d.f.) 5.0pd
9165554 *LIUG3* -	**VIKING VANQUISH** *ex* Viking Poseidon *-2007* **Eidesvik MPSV AS** Eidesvik AS SatCom: Inmarsat B 325948210 *Haugesund* *Norway (NIS)* MMSI: 259482000	**8,621** 2,586 5,767	Class: NV	**1998**-03 **Kvaerner Kleven AS — Ulsteinvik** Yd No: 273 Converted From: Offshore Supply Ship-2007 Loa 93.45 (BB) Br ex 22.20 Dght 6.870 Lbp 81.30 Br md 22.00 Dpth 8.60 Welded, 1 dk	**(B31A2SR) Research Survey Vessel** Cranes: 1x26t Ice Capable	**2 oil engines** reduction geared to sc. shafts driving 2 CP propellers Total Power: 7,920kW (10,768hp) Wichmann 12V28B 2 x Vee 2 Stroke 12 Cy. 280 x 360 each-3960kW (5384bhp) Wartsila NSD Finland Oy-Finland AuxGen: 2 x 3040kW 690/440V 60Hz a.c, 2 x 370kW 440/690V 60Hz a.c Thrusters: 1 Thwart. CP thruster (f); 1 Thwart. CP thruster (f); 1 Retract. directional thruster (f); 2 Tunnel thruster (a)
8907034 *LNXF3* -	**VIKING VISION** *ex* Veritas Vision *-2007* *ex* Sara II *-2007* *ex* Visjon *-1999* *ex* Sara II *-1998* *ex* Gijon *-1998* **Eidesvik Shipping AS** Eidesvik AS SatCom: Inmarsat C 425967110 *Haugesund* *Norway (NIS)* MMSI: 259671000	**9,811** 3,920 5,539	Class: NV	**1993**-05 **Naval Gijon S.A. (NAGISA) — Gijon** Yd No: 502 Converted From: Stern Trawler-2007 Loa 105.00 (BB) Br ex 20.03 Dght 8.524 Lbp 89.50 Br md 20.00 Dpth 14.70 Welded, 3 dks	**(B31A2SR) Research Survey Vessel** Passengers: berths: 70 Grain: 1,170; Bale: 330; Ins: 4,100 Ice Capable	**1 oil engine** reduction geared to sc. shaft driving 1 CP propeller Total Power: 5,921kW (8,050hp) 14.5kn Wartsila 16V32D 1 x Vee 4 Stroke 16 Cy. 320 x 350 5921kW (8050bhp) Echevarria Wartsila Diesel S.A.-Bermeo AuxGen: 1 x 2560kW 380V 50Hz a.c, 2 x 960kW 380V 50Hz a.c Thrusters: 1 Tunnel thruster (f); 2 Directional thruster (a)
8139364 *HO3606* -	**VIKING X** *ex* Viking *-2004* *ex* Diana *-1983* *ex* Hermina E Goedkoop *-1983* **Remolcatuna SL** - *Panama* *Panama* Official number: 3216006A	**123** 36 -	Class: (BV)	**1957 Arnhemsche Scheepsbouw Mij NV — Arnhem** Yd No: 384 Loa 26.90 Br ex 6.63 Dght 2.620 Lbp 26.50 Br md - Dpth 3.20 Welded, 1 dk	**(B32A2ST) Tug**	**2 oil engines** driving 2 FP propellers Total Power: 882kW (1,200hp) 10.0kn S.K.L. 8VDS29/24AL-2 2 x 4 Stroke 8 Cy. 240 x 290 each-441kW (600bhp) VEB Schwermaschinenbau "KarlLiebknecht" (SKL)-Magdeburg
9375654 *ESKC* -	**VIKING XPRS** **SF Line Ab (Viking Line Abp)** - *Tallinn* *Estonia* MMSI: 276813000 Official number: 5P14A01	**35,918** 14,216 5,184	Class: LR ✠ **100A1** SS 04/2012 passenger and vehicle ferry *IWS LI Ice Class 1AS FS at draught of 6.90m Max/min draught fwd 6.90/5.75m Max/min draught aft 6.90/5.75m Required power 6911kw, installed power 40000kw ✠ **LMC** **UMS** Eq.Ltr: K†; Cable: 633.0/68.0 U3 (a)	**2008**-04 **Aker Yards Oy — Helsinki** Yd No: 1358 Loa 185.00 (BB) Br ex 28.32 Dght 6.750 Lbp 170.00 Br md 27.70 Dpth 9.50 Welded, 7 dks plus 3 non-continuous dks.	**(A36A2PR) Passenger/Ro-Ro Ship (Vehicles)** Passengers: unberthed: 1768; cabins: 238; berths: 732 Bow door/ramp (centre) Len: 5.00 Wid: 5.20 Swl: - Quarter stern door/ramp (centre) Len: 5.00 Wid: 18.40 Swl: 236 Lane-Len: 1000 Cars: 240 Ice Capable	**4 oil engines** with clutches, flexible couplings & sr geared to sc. shafts driving 2 CP propellers Total Power: 40,000kW (54,384hp) 25.0kn Wartsila 8L46F 4 x 4 Stroke 8 Cy. 460 x 580 each-10000kW (13596bhp) Wartsila Finland Oy-Finland AuxGen: 3 x 1000kW 400V 50Hz a.c Boilers: e (ex.g.) 8.5kgf/cm² (8.3bar), AuxB (o.f.) 7.4kgf/cm² (7.3bar) Thrusters: 2 Thwart. CP thruster (f); 1 Thwart. CP thruster (a) Fuel: 141.0 (d.f.) 930.0 (r.f.)
9604184 *PCOR* -	**VIKINGBANK** **D P Pot** Pot Scheepvaart BV *Delfzijl* *Netherlands* MMSI: 244855000	**7,367** 3,688 11,850	Class: BV	**2012**-04 **Scheepswerf Ferus Smit BV — Westerbroek** Yd No: 406 Loa 142.65 Br ex 16.05 Dght 7.730 Lbp 139.43 Br md 15.87 Dpth 10.78 Welded, 1 dk	**(A31A2GX) General Cargo Ship** Grain: 14,267 Compartments: 2 Ho, ER 2 Ha: (63.6 x 13.2)ER (41.0 x 13.2) Ice Capable	**1 oil engine** reduction geared to sc. shaft driving 1 CP propeller Total Power: 4,000kW (5,438hp) 14.5kn MaK 8M32C 1 x 4 Stroke 8 Cy. 320 x 480 4000kW (5438bhp) Caterpillar Motoren GmbH & Co. KG-Germany AuxGen: 2 x 310kW 50Hz a.c Thrusters: 1 Tunnel thruster (f) Fuel: 590.0
9381380 *PHMN* -	**VIKINGDIEP** **Beheermaatschappij ms Vikingdiep BV** Feederlines BV *Groningen* *Netherlands* MMSI: 245067000 Official number: 46831	**5,040** 2,681 7,750	Class: GL (LR) ✠ Classed LR until 17/4/12	**2008**-01 **Hangzhou Dongfeng Shipbuilding Co Ltd — Hangzhou ZJ** (Hull) Yd No: 2004-50 **2008**-01 **Bodewes' Scheepswerven B.V. — Hoogezand** Yd No: 780 **2008**-01 **All Ships Outfitting & Repairs — Krimpen a/d Lek** (Hull completed by) Yd No: 260 Loa 119.98 (BB) Br ex 15.43 Dght 7.050 Lbp 113.35 Br md 15.20 Dpth 8.45 Welded, 1 dk	**(A31A2GX) General Cargo Ship** Grain: 9,415 TEU 390 C Ho 174 TEU C Dk 216 TEU Compartments: 2 Ho, ER 2 Ha: (42.8 x 12.7)ER (39.0 x 12.7) Ice Capable	**1 oil engine** with clutches, flexible couplings & sr geared to sc. shaft driving 1 CP propeller Total Power: 3,840kW (5,221hp) 12.0kn MaK 8M32C 1 x 4 Stroke 8 Cy. 320 x 480 3840kW (5221bhp) Caterpillar Motoren GmbH & Co. KG-Germany AuxGen: 1 x 348kW 400V 50Hz a.c, 2 x 264kW 400V 50Hz a.c Boilers: HWH (o.f.) 3.6kgf/cm² (3.5bar) Thrusters: 1 Thwart. CP thruster (f)
9036038 *LEVF* -	**VIKINGEN** **Norled AS** Tide ASA *Bergen* *Norway* MMSI: 257029700	**2,631** 844 100	Class: (NV)	**1992**-07 **Slipen Mek. Verksted AS — Sandnessjoen** (Hull) Yd No: 45 **1992**-07 **Kaarboverkstedet AS — Harstad** Yd No: 45 Loa 84.00 Br ex 15.50 Dght 3.346 Lbp 70.80 Br md 15.00 Dpth 5.00 Welded, 2 dks	**(A36A2PR) Passenger/Ro-Ro Ship (Vehicles)** Passengers: unberthed: 399	**2 oil engines** with clutches, flexible couplings & sr geared to sc. shaft driving 2 CP propellers 1 fwd and 1 aft Total Power: 4,798kW (6,524hp) Wichmann 8V28B 2 x Vee 4 Stroke 8 Cy. 280 x 360 each-2399kW (3262bhp) Wartsila Wichmann Diesel AS-Norway AuxGen: 2 x 235kW 230V 50Hz a.c
5030828 - -	**VIKINGFJORD** *ex* Mercator *-2011* *ex* Mathilda *-2007* *ex* Galtesund *-2003* *ex* Vikingfjord *-2001* *ex* Trondelag *-1989* *ex* Aure *-1964* **PM Varustamo Oy** - *Pernio* *Finland* Official number: 12286	**531** 198 100	Class: (NV)	**1950**-07 **AS Stord Verft — Stord** Yd No: 9 Loa 49.20 Br ex 7.68 Dght 3.506 Lbp - Br md 7.62 Dpth 5.57 Riveted\Welded, 2 dks	**(B34K2QT) Training Ship** Compartments: 1 Ho, ER 1 Ha: (4.8 x 1.9) Derricks: 2x0.5t	**1 oil engine** driving 1 FP propeller Total Power: 809kW (1,100hp) 12.0kn MaK 8M451AK 1 x 4 Stroke 8 Cy. 320 x 450 809kW (1100bhp) (made 1966, fitted 1973) Atlas MaK Maschinenbau GmbH-Kiel AuxGen: 2 x 45kW 220V 50Hz a.c, 2 x 37kW 380V d.c Fuel: 20.5 (d.f.) 5.0pd
8020599 *MCMF3* -	**VIKINGLAND** *ex* Aurora *-2012* *ex* Arcturus *-1991* **Classic Shipping Ltd** Imperial Ship Management AB *London* *United Kingdom* MMSI: 235006670 Official number: 918652	**20,381** 6,114 13,030 T/cm 32.5	Class: LR ✠ **100A1** CS 10/2011 Ice Class 1A Super Max draught midship 8.463m Max/min draught aft 8.463/6.813m Max/min draught forward 8.463/6.013m ✠ **LMC** **UMS** Eq.Ltr: I†; Cable: 605.0/64.0 U3	**1982**-06 **Rauma-Repola Oy — Rauma** Yd No: 270 Loa 155.02 (BB) Br ex 25.15 Dght 8.465 Lbp 146.01 Br md 24.96 Dpth 16.92 Welded, 2 dks	**(A35A2RR) Ro-Ro Cargo Ship** Passengers: cabins: 7; berths: 12 Stern door/ramp (centre) Len: 15.00 Wid: 10.90 Swl: - Lane-Len: 2170 Lane-Wid: 2.80 Lane-clr ht: 6.20 Trailers: 164 Bale: 34,776 TEU 608 C RoRo Dk 422 C Dk 186 TEU incl 60 ref C Ice Capable	**2 oil engines** with clutches, flexible couplings & sr geared to sc. shaft driving 1 CP propeller Total Power: 13,200kW (17,946hp) 18.5kn Pielstick 12PC2-6V-400 2 x Vee 4 Stroke 12 Cy. 400 x 460 each-6600kW (8973bhp) Oy Wartsila Ab-Finland AuxGen: 2 x 1000kW 400V 50Hz a.c, 1 x 1170kW 400V 50Hz a.c Boilers: 2 e 8.1kgf/cm² (7.9bar), AuxB (o.f.) 8.1kgf/cm² (7.9bar) Thrusters: 1 Thwart. CP thruster (f); 1 Thwart. CP thruster (a) Fuel: 90.0 (d.f.) 1189.0 (r.f.) 48.5pd
8428167 - -	**VIKINGS** **P P Enterprises** - *Zamboanga* *Philippines* Official number: ZAM2D0014J	*156* 87		**1984 at Zamboanga** Loa - Br ex 6.63 Dght - Lbp 32.52 Br md 6.61 Dpth 2.70 Welded, 1 dk	**(A32A2GF) General Cargo/Passenger Ship** Passengers: unberthed: 180	**1 oil engine** driving 1 FP propeller Total Power: 282kW (383hp)
5380417 *TFJL* AK 100	**VIKINGUR** **HB Grandi hf** - SatCom: Inmarsat C 425105310 *Akranes* *Iceland* MMSI: 251053110 Official number: 0220	**1,170** 351 1,449	Class: LR ✠ **100A1** SS 09/2011 trawler ✠ **LMC** Eq.Ltr: g†; Cable: SQ	**1960**-10 **AG Weser, Werk Seebeck — Bremerhaven** Yd No: 870 Deepened-1977 Loa 72.52 (BB) Br ex 10.39 Dght 7.400 Lbp 66.10 Br md 10.30 Dpth 7.90 Welded, 2 dks	**(B11A2FT) Trawler** Compartments: 3 Ho, ER 3 Ha: 3 (3.5 x 3.5)ER Ice Capable	**1 oil engine** with hydraulic coupling driving 1 CP propeller Total Power: 2,339kW (3,180hp) Alpha 12U28L-VO 1 x Vee 4 Stroke 12 Cy. 280 x 320 2339kW (3180bhp) (new engine 1981) B&W Alpha Diesel A/S-Denmark Boilers: db 6.9kgf/cm² (6.8bar) Thrusters: 1 Thwart. FP thruster (f); 1 Thwart. FP thruster (a)

6727363 *OW2188* -	**VIKINGUR** *ex* Vassoyfisk *-2000* *ex* Rani *-1995* *ex* Martin Ronning *-1976* *ex* Kjonno *-1976* **Viking Seafood P/F** Brandur Jacobsen *Strendur* *Faeroe Islands (Danish)* MMSI: 231117000	**181** 54 330	Class: (NV)	**1967 N.V. Scheepswerf "Voorwaarts" v/h E.J. Hijlkema — Hoogezand** Yd No: 195 Loa 32.62 Br ex 7.01 Dght 2.826 Lbp 29.52 Br md 7.00 Dpth 3.10 Welded, 1 dk	**(A31A2GX) General Cargo Ship** Grain: 374; Bale: 354 Compartments: 1 Ho, ER 1 Ha: (13.1 x 4.2)ER Derricks: 1x3t; Winches: 1	**1 oil engine** driving 1 FP propeller Total Power: 239kW (325hp) 9.5kn Caterpillar D353TA 1 x 4 Stroke 6 Cy. 159 x 203 239kW (325bhp) Caterpillar Tractor Co-USA AuxGen: 2 x 3kW 24V d.c Fuel: 12.0 (d.f.) 1.5pd
8962826 *TFII* -	**VIKINGUR** *ex* Isafold *-2013* *ex* Dickson *-2008* *ex* Gote *-2001* **Sjavarferdir Ehf** - *Vestmannaeyjar* *Iceland* MMSI: 251484110 Official number: 2777	**178** 53 -	Class: (NV)	**1971 AB Asi-Verken — Amal** Yd No: 92 Converted From: Training Vessel-2008 Converted From: Fire-fighting Vessel-2001 Loa 29.94 Br ex 7.16 Dght 2.600 Lbp - Br md 7.00 Dpth 2.70 Welded, 1 dk	**(A37B2PS) Passenger Ship**	**2 oil engines** driving 2 FP propellers Total Power: 882kW (1,200hp) 12.5kn Deutz SBF12M716 2 x Vee 4 Stroke 12 Cy. 135 x 160 each-441kW (600bhp) Kloeckner Humboldt Deutz AG-West Germany Thrusters: 1 Thwart. FP thruster (f)
8503838 *9HYT8* -	**VIKKI** *ex* Victoria I *-2007* *ex* Viktoriya I *-2005* *ex* Dor *-2003* *ex* Costinesti *-2002* **Sea Moon Shipping Ltd** Pic Shipping Ltd (OOO 'Pik Shipping') *Valletta* *Malta* MMSI: 256620000 Official number: 8503838	**5,949** 3,424 8,750	Class: RS (RN)	**1985-08 Santierul Naval Braila — Braila** Yd No: 1284 Loa 130.70 (BB) Br ex - Dght 8.102 Lbp 120.98 Br md 17.74 Dpth 10.26 Welded, 2 dks	**(A31A2GX) General Cargo Ship** Grain: 11,980; Bale: 11,067 Compartments: 4 Ho, ER 4 Ha: (6.0 x 11.8)3 (9.9 x 13.6)ER Cranes: 4x5t Ice Capable	**1 oil engine** driving 1 FP propeller Total Power: 4,487kW (6,101hp) 13.0kn Sulzer 5RD68 1 x 2 Stroke 5 Cy. 680 x 1250 4487kW (6101bhp) Zaklady Przemyslu Metalowego 'HCegielski' SA-Poznan AuxGen: 3 x 200kW 400V 50Hz a.c
9111759 *C6UL5* -	**VIKLAND** *ex* Havila Fame *-2008* *ex* Smit-Lloyd Fame *-2005* **Vestland Seismic AS** Vestland Marine Sp z oo *Nassau* *Bahamas* MMSI: 311947000 Official number: 8000986	**2,959** 888 2,580	Class: NV	**1995-03 Italthai Marine Co., Ltd. — Samut Prakan** Yd No: 96 Converted From: Offshore Supply Ship-2008 Loa 71.70 Br ex 16.30 Dght 5.611 Lbp 61.40 Br md 15.80 Dpth 7.00 Welded, 1 dk	**(B31A2SR) Research Survey Vessel** Cranes: 1	**2 oil engines** with clutches, flexible couplings & sr geared to sc. shafts driving 2 CP propellers Total Power: 3,960kW (5,384hp) 12.0kn Alpha 8L28/32 2 x 4 Stroke 8 Cy. 280 x 320 each-1980kW (2692bhp) MAN B&W Diesel A/S-Denmark AuxGen: 2 x 1200kW 440/220V 60Hz a.c, 2 x 324kW 440/220V 60Hz a.c Thrusters: 2 Thwart. CP thruster (f); 1 Tunnel thruster (a); 1 Directional thruster (f) Fuel: 899.0 (d.f.) 8.5pd
6808662 *LLMF* -	**VIKNA** *ex* Geisnes *-1992* **FosenNamsos Sjo AS** - *Namsos* *Norway* MMSI: 257078700	**111** 33 -	Class: (NV)	**1967 Lysosund Mek. Verksted — Lysoysundet** Yd No: 12 Loa 26.52 Br ex 7.52 Dght - Lbp 24.69 Br md - Dpth 3.20 Welded, 1 dk	**(A36A2PR) Passenger/Ro-Ro Ship (Vehicles)** Passengers: unberthed: 95 Bow door/ramp Stern door/ramp Derricks: 1x1.5t; Winches: 1	**1 oil engine** driving 1 CP propeller Total Power: 221kW (300hp) 10.0kn Caterpillar D343TA 1 x 4 Stroke 6 Cy. 137 x 165 221kW (300bhp) Caterpillar Tractor Co-USA AuxGen: 1 x 25kW 230V a.c, 1 x 15kW 230V a.c Thrusters: 1 Thwart. FP thruster (f) Fuel: 9.0 (d.f.) 1.0pd
9593268 *3YMR* -	**VIKNATRANS** - **Polartind AS** Norsk Fisketransport AS *Sandnessjoen* *Norway* MMSI: 259826000	**1,318** 395 1,500	Class: (NV)	**2011-09 AS Rigas Kugu Buvetava (Riga Shipyard) — Riga** (Hull) Yd No: 132 **2011-09 Aas Mek. Verksted AS — Vestnes** Yd No: 187 Loa 62.07 (BB) Br ex - Dght 4.590 Lbp 56.64 Br md 12.00 Dpth 5.10 Welded, 1 dk	**(B12C2FL) Live Fish Carrier (Well Boat)**	**1 oil engine** reduction geared to sc. shaft driving 1 FP propeller Total Power: 1,324kW (1,800hp) 13.0kn Caterpillar 3512B 1 x Vee 4 Stroke 12 Cy. 170 x 190 1324kW (1800bhp) Caterpillar Inc-USA Thrusters: 1 Tunnel thruster (f); 1 Tunnel thruster (a)
9139658 *2DYE8* -	**VIKNES** *ex* Camilla Christine *-2004* **Island Innovations Ltd** - *Lerwick* *United Kingdom* MMSI: 235082944 Official number: 917051	**296** 88 450	Class: BV	**1996-02 Sletta Baatbyggeri AS — Mjosundet** Yd No: 77 Loa 36.20 Br ex - Dght - Lbp 32.00 Br md 8.00 Dpth 4.20 Welded, 1 dk	**(B12B2FC) Fish Carrier**	**1 oil engine** reduction geared to sc. shaft driving 1 FP propeller Total Power: 1,119kW (1,521hp) Caterpillar 3508TA 1 x Vee 4 Stroke 8 Cy. 170 x 190 1119kW (1521bhp) Caterpillar Inc-USA
6721876 *SHCR* -	**VIKTOR** *ex* Boy *-1987* *ex* Tor *-1984* **Svitzer Sverige AB** - *Gothenburg* *Sweden* MMSI: 265606890	**101** 30 -		**1966 Furusunds Varv — Hogmarso** Loa 22.69 Br ex 7.01 Dght 4.201 Lbp - Br md 6.99 Dpth - Welded, 1 dk	**(B32A2ST) Tug**	**1 oil engine** driving 1 FP propeller Total Power: 640kW (870hp) 11.0kn Alpha 496VO 1 x 2 Stroke 6 Cy. 310 x 490 640kW (870bhp) (made 1962, fitted 1966) Alpha Diesel A/S-Denmark Fuel: 22.5 (d.f.) 0.5pd
6923747 - -	**VIKTOR** *ex* Kommunalnik *-2006* **Dunayspetsbut** -	**204** 61 71	Class: (RS)	**1969-08 VEB Schiffswerft "Edgar Andre" — Magdeburg** Yd No: 7020 Loa 34.73 Br ex 8.23 Dght 2.969 Lbp 30.41 Br md 8.21 Dpth 3.87 Welded, 1 dk	**(B32A2ST) Tug** Ice Capable	**1 oil engine** driving 1 CP propeller Total Power: 551kW (749hp) 11.0kn S.K.L. 6NVD48A-2U 1 x 4 Stroke 6 Cy. 320 x 480 551kW (749bhp) VEB Schwermaschinenbau "KarlLiebknecht" (SKL)-Magdeburg AuxGen: 2 x 42kW Fuel: 46.0 (d.f.)
9610810 *D5BN6* -	**VIKTOR BAKAEV** - **Streymoy Shipping Ltd** SCF Novoship JSC (Novorossiysk Shipping Co) *Monrovia* *Liberia* MMSI: 636015565 Official number: 15565	**66,855** 35,252 118,175 T/cm 104.9	Class: LR ✠ **100A1** SS 05/2013 Double Hull oil tanker CSR ESP **ShipRight** tanker CSR ESP **ShipRight** G,I,O,P,Vc) Ice Class 1CFS at draught of 14.60m Max/min draught fwd 14.60/6.10m Max/min draught aft 14.60/6.10m Required power 13350kw, installed power 13350kw ✠ **LMC** **UMS IGS** Eq.Ltr: W†; Cable: 745.3/95.0 U3 (a)	**2013-05 Daewoo Shipbuilding & Marine Engineering Co Ltd — Geoje** Yd No: 5387 Loa 249.90 (BB) Br ex 46.04 Dght 14.625 Lbp 243.00 Br md 46.00 Dpth 21.20 Welded, 1 dk	**(A13A2TW) Crude/Oil Products Tanker** Double Hull (13F) Liq: 131,862; Liq (Oil): 131,862 Compartments: 5 Ta, 10 Wing Ta, 2 Wing Slop Ta, ER Ice Capable	**1 oil engine** driving 1 FP propeller Total Power: 13,350kW (18,151hp) 15.7kn MAN-B&W 6S60MC-C8 1 x 2 Stroke 6 Cy. 600 x 2400 13350kW (18151bhp) Doosan Engine Co Ltd-South Korea AuxGen: 3 x 1600kW 450V 60Hz a.c Boilers: e (ex.g.) 14.3kgf/cm² (14.0bar), WTAuxB (o.f.) 11.2kgf/cm² (11.0bar)
7801908 *UBVT* -	**VIKTOR BORISOV** *ex* Sosnogorsk *-2012* *ex* Sibirskiy-2108 *-1999* **Donmaster Co Ltd** - *Taganrog* *Russia* MMSI: 273341110 Official number: 794112	**3,415** 1,024 3,484	Class: RS	**1980-12 Valmet Oy — Turku** Yd No: 377 Loa 128.23 Br ex 15.65 Dght 3.170 Lbp 125.02 Br md 15.41 Dpth 5.47 Welded, 1 dk	**(A31A2GX) General Cargo Ship** Bale: 4,700 Ice Capable	**2 oil engines** driving 2 FP propellers Total Power: 1,324kW (1,800hp) 10.2kn Dvigatel Revolyutsii 6CHRNP36/45 2 x 4 Stroke 6 Cy. 360 x 450 each-662kW (900bhp) Zavod "Dvigatel Revolyutsii"-Gorkiy AuxGen: 3 x 100kW a.c, 1 x 50kW a.c Thrusters: 1 Thwart. FP thruster (f) Fuel: 251.0 (d.f.)
8422448 *UAJX* -	**VIKTOR BUYNITSKIY** - **State Institution Murmansk Administration for Hydrometeorology & Environmental Monitoring** - SatCom: Inmarsat C 427300961 *Murmansk* *Russia* MMSI: 273453300 Official number: 851353	**693** 207 293	Class: RS	**1986-11 Valmetin Laivateollisuus Oy — Turku** Yd No: 370 Converted From: Cruise Ship-2006 Converted From: Research Vessel-1999 Loa 49.90 Br ex 10.02 Dght 3.601 Lbp 44.95 Br md 10.00 Dpth 5.00 Welded	**(B31A2SR) Research Survey Vessel** Passengers: berths: 35	**1 oil engine** with clutches, flexible couplings & sr geared to sc. shaft driving 1 CP propeller Total Power: 985kW (1,339hp) 12.8kn Wartsila 824TS 1 x 4 Stroke 8 Cy. 240 x 310 985kW (1339bhp) Oy Wartsila Ab-Finland AuxGen: 1 x 160kW a.c, 2 x 100kW a.c Fuel: 90.0 (d.f.)

Identity	Ship / Owner	Tonnage	Class	Construction	Type	Machinery
9657791 *UBIL4* -	**VIKTOR CHERNOMYRDIN** **Department of Property Relations of the Yamal-Nenets Autonomous District (Departament imushchestvennykh otnosheniy Yamalo-Nenetskogo avtonomnogo okruga)** Severrechflot JSC *St Petersburg* *Russia* MMSI: 273353850	**228** 86 20	Class: BV (Class contemplated) RS	**2013-09 Zelenodolskiy Sudostroitelnyy Zavod — Zelenodolsk** Yd No: 212 Loa 34.60 Br ex 6.80 Dght 0.910 Lbp 32.80 Br md 6.60 Dpth 2.50 Welded, 1 dk	**(A37B2PS) Passenger Ship** Hull Material: Aluminium Alloy Passengers: unberthed: 130	**2 oil engines** reduction geared to sc. shafts driving 2 Water jets Total Power: 2,880kW (3,916hp) 40.0kn M.T.U. 16V2000M72 2 x Vee 4 Stroke 16 Cy. 135 x 156 each-1440kW (1958bhp) MTU Friedrichshafen GmbH-Friedrichshafen Fuel: 8.0 (d.f.)
8709664 *UERW* -	**VIKTOR KIBENOK** **State Enterprise Makhachkala International Sea Commercial Port** Nord Shipping Ltd *Makhachkala* *Russia* MMSI: 273427250	**4,185** 1,397 6,321 T/cm 20.0	Class: (RS)	**1988-11 'Ilya Boyadzhiev' Shipyard — Bourgas** Yd No: 106 Loa 125.06 (BB) Br ex 16.63 Dght 4.830 Lbp 120.56 Br md - Dpth 6.92 Welded, 1 dk	**(A13B2TP) Products Tanker** Double Bottom Entire Compartment Length Liq: 5,827; Liq (Oil): 5,827 Cargo Heating Coils Compartments: 12 Wing Ta, ER 2 Cargo Pump (s): 2x850m³/hr Manifold: Bow/CM: 85m Ice Capable	**2 oil engines** sr reverse geared to sc. shafts driving 2 FP propellers Total Power: 2,206kW (3,000hp) 11.5kn Dvigatel Revolyutsii 6CHRNP36/45 2 x 4 Stroke 6 Cy. 360 x 450 each-1103kW (1500bhp) Zavod "Dvigatel Revolyutsii"-Gorkiy AuxGen: 4 x 160kW a.c Fuel: 269.0 (d.f.)
8953370 *UEPV* -	**VIKTOR KLIMOV** **Zapbaltrybvod (ZAO 'Zapbaltrybvod')** - *Kaliningrad* *Russia*	**104** 31 58	Class: RS (Class contemplated)	**1999 Sudoverf — Rybinsk** Yd No: 27 Loa 26.50 Br ex 6.50 Dght 2.320 Lbp 23.61 Br md - Dpth 3.05 Welded, 1 dk	**(B11A2FS) Stern Trawler** Compartments: 1 Ho 1 Ha: (1.0 x 1.4)	**1 oil engine** geared to sc. shaft driving 1 FP propeller Total Power: 232kW (315hp) 9.5kn Daldizel 6CHSP18/22 1 x 4 Stroke 6 Cy. 180 x 220 232kW (315bhp) Daldizel-Khabarovsk AuxGen: 2 x 25kW Fuel: 9.0 (d.f.)
8421896 *URKT* -	**VIKTOR LEKAREV** *ex Sivash -1999* **JSC Chernomortekhflot** - *Odessa* *Ukraine* MMSI: 272512000	**2,081** 624 583	Class: (RS)	**1984-06 VEB Schiffswerft Neptun — Rostock** Yd No: 107/1450 Loa 79.96 Br ex 14.42 Dght 3.752 Lbp 70.90 Br md 14.40 Dpth 5.21 Welded, 1 dk	**(B33A2DB) Bucket Ladder Dredger** Ice Capable	**2 diesel electric oil engines** Connecting to 2 elec. motors each (570kW) driving 2 FP propellers Total Power: 1,706kW (2,320hp) 8.8kn S.K.L. 6NVDS48A-2U 1 x 4 Stroke 6 Cy. 320 x 480 736kW (1001bhp) VEB Schwermaschinenbau "KarlLiebknecht" (SKL)-Magdeburg S.K.L. 8NVDS48A-2 1 x 4 Stroke 8 Cy. 320 x 480 970kW (1319bhp) VEB Schwermaschinenbau "KarlLiebknecht" (SKL)-Magdeburg AuxGen: 2 x 440kW, 1 x 200kW Fuel: 276.0 (r.f.)
8929795 - -	**VIKTOR LYAGIN** **Chernomorskiy Shipbuilding Yard JSC (Chernomorskiy Sudostroitelnyy Zavod)** - *Nikolayev* *Ukraine* MMSI: 272708000 Official number: 790817	*187* - 46	Class: (RS)	**1980 Gorokhovetskiy Sudostroitelnyy Zavod — Gorokhovets** Yd No: 385 Loa 29.30 Br ex 8.49 Dght 3.090 Lbp 27.00 Br md 8.00 Dpth 4.30 Welded, 1 dk	**(B32A2ST) Tug** Ice Capable	**2 oil engines** driving 2 CP propellers Total Power: 882kW (1,200hp) 11.4kn Russkiy 6D30/50-4-3 2 x 2 Stroke 6 Cy. 300 x 500 each-441kW (600bhp) Mashinostroitelnyy Zavod"Russkiy-Dizel"-Leningrad AuxGen: 2 x 30kW a.c Fuel: 45.0 (d.f.)
8325339 *UAVH* -	**VIKTOR MIRONOV** **JSC Arkhangelsk Trawl Fleet (A/O 'Arkhangelskiy Tralflot')** - *Arkhangelsk* *Russia* MMSI: 273297600	**3,832** 1,149 1,990	Class: RS	**1984-05 Stocznia Gdanska im Lenina — Gdansk** Yd No: B408/26 Converted From: Stern Trawler-2008 Loa 94.01 Br ex 15.92 Dght 6.220 Lbp 85.02 Br md 15.91 Dpth 10.01 Welded, 2 dks	**(B12B2FC) Fish Carrier** Ins: 1,947 Compartments: 3 Ho, ER 4 Ha: (0.6 x 0.6)3 (2.4 x 2.1) Derricks: 6x3t Ice Capable	**1 oil engine** geared to sc. shaft driving 1 FP propeller Total Power: 3,825kW (5,200hp) 15.8kn Sulzer 8ZL40/48 1 x 4 Stroke 8 Cy. 400 x 480 3825kW (5200bhp) Zaklady Urzadzen Technicznych'Zgoda' SA-Poland AuxGen: 1 x 1200kW 400V 50Hz a.c, 1 x 760kW 400V 50Hz a.c, 2 x 350kW 320V 50Hz a.c Fuel: 1491.0 (r.f.)
8927864 - -	**VIKTOR MUHORTOV** *ex Primorets -2011* **Government of The Russian Federation** Federal State Unitary Enterprise Rosmorport *Posyet* *Russia*	*226* - 46	Class: RS	**1969-05 "Petrozavod" — Leningrad** Yd No: 746 Loa 29.30 Br ex 8.49 Dght 3.090 Lbp 27.00 Br md 8.31 Dpth 4.35 Welded, 1 dk	**(B32A2ST) Tug** Ice Capable	**2 oil engines** driving 2 CP propellers Total Power: 882kW (1,200hp) 11.4kn Russkiy 6D30/50-4-2 2 x 2 Stroke 6 Cy. 300 x 500 each-441kW (600bhp) Mashinostroitelnyy Zavod"Russkiy-Dizel"-Leningrad AuxGen: 2 x 25kW a.c Fuel: 36.0 (d.f.)
8872538 *3EVY4* -	**VIKTOR TARATIN** *ex Volzhskiy-31 -2002* **Baltasar Shipping SA** Transverde Freight SA *Panama* *Panama* MMSI: 355646000 Official number: 4103710	**4,997** 2,298 5,415	Class: RS (RR)	**1989-12 Navashinskiy Sudostroitelnyy Zavod 'Oka' — Navashino** Yd No: 1033 Loa 138.30 Br ex 16.70 Dght 3.750 Lbp 132.20 Br md 16.50 Dpth 5.50 Welded, 1 dk	**(A31A2GX) General Cargo Ship** Grain: 6,440 Compartments: 4 Ho, ER 4 Ha: (25.3 x 13.2) (24.7 x 13.2) (19.5 x 13.2)ER (18.1 x 13.2)	**2 oil engines** driving 2 FP propellers Total Power: 1,766kW (2,402hp) 10.0kn Dvigatel Revolyutsii 6CHRN36/45 2 x 4 Stroke 6 Cy. 360 x 450 each-883kW (1201bhp) Zavod "Dvigatel Revolyutsii"-Gorkiy AuxGen: 2 x 100kW a.c, 1 x 50kW Fuel: 145.0 (d.f.)
9301407 *C4EU2* -	**VIKTOR TITOV** **Castellario Shipmanagement Ltd** SCF Unicom Singapore Pte Ltd SatCom: Inmarsat Mini-M 764565437 *Limassol* *Cyprus* MMSI: 209595000 Official number: 9301407	**60,434** 28,502 100,899 T/cm 92.4	Class: NV	**2005-11 Hyundai Heavy Industries Co Ltd — Ulsan** Yd No: 1601 Loa 246.88 (BB) Br ex 42.04 Dght 14.520 Lbp 234.00 Br md 42.00 Dpth 21.60 Welded, 1 dk	**(A13A2TW) Crude/Oil Products Tanker** Double Hull (13F) Liq: 112,823; Liq (Oil): 115,103 Cargo Heating Coils Compartments: 12 Wing Ta, 2 Wing Slop Ta, ER 3 Cargo Pump (s): 3x2500m³/hr Manifold: Bow/CM: 123.3m Ice Capable	**1 oil engine** driving 1 CP propeller Total Power: 16,600kW (22,569hp) 15.2kn MAN-B&W 7S60ME-C 1 x 2 Stroke 7 Cy. 600 x 2400 16600kW (22569bhp) Hyundai Heavy Industries Co Ltd-South Korea AuxGen: 3 x 1045kW 440/220V 60Hz a.c Fuel: 366.0 (d.f.) (Heating Coils) 3088.0 (r.f.) 65.0pd
8131934 *UCJX* -	**VIKTOR TKACHYOV** **Murmansk Shipping Co (MSC)** - SatCom: Inmarsat Mini-M 761322576 *Murmansk* *Russia* MMSI: 273136400 Official number: 811017	**14,141** 6,365 19,274	Class: RS	**1981-12 VEB Warnowwerft Warnemuende — Rostock** Yd No: 146 Loa 162.11 Br ex 22.92 Dght 9.881 Lbp 154.90 Br md 22.86 Dpth 13.52 Welded, 1 dk	**(A21A2BC) Bulk Carrier** Grain: 26,216; Bale: 22,245 TEU 442 C Ho 282 TEU C Dk 160 TEU Compartments: 6 Ho, ER 6 Ha: (12.8 x 10.8)5 (12.8 x 13.5)ER Cranes: 6x12.5t Ice Capable	**1 oil engine** driving 1 FP propeller Total Power: 8,238kW (11,200hp) 15.3kn MAN K8Z70/120E 1 x 2 Stroke 8 Cy. 700 x 1200 8238kW (11200bhp) VEB Dieselmotorenwerk Rostock-Rostock AuxGen: 4 x 400kW 380V 50Hz a.c Fuel: 441.0 (d.f.) 1257.0 (r.f.)
9369849 *LAFM* -	**VIKTORIA LADY** *ex Aspoy -2009* **Fosnavaag Wellboat AS** - *Fosnavaag* *Norway* MMSI: 259162000	**1,186** 355 700	Class: NV	**2006-12 Solstrand AS — Tomrefjord** Yd No: 78 Loa 51.60 (BB) Br ex 12.83 Dght 6.000 Lbp 49.35 Br md 12.80 Dpth 6.75 Welded, 1 dk	**(B12C2FL) Live Fish Carrier (Well Boat)** Ice Capable	**1 oil engine** reduction geared to sc. shafts driving 1 CP propeller Total Power: 1,920kW (2,610hp) Yanmar 6EY26 1 x 4 Stroke 6 Cy. 260 x 385 1920kW (2610bhp) Yanmar Diesel Engine Co Ltd-Japan AuxGen: 2 x 408kW a.c, 1 x 1400kW a.c Thrusters: 1 Tunnel thruster (f); 1 Tunnel thruster (a) Fuel: 86.0
9521801 *LCLO* -	**VIKTORIA VIKING** **Fosnavaag Wellboat AS** - *Fosnavaag* *Norway* MMSI: 259385000	**1,214** 364 1,460		**2009-11 AS Rigas Kugu Buvetava (Riga Shipyard) — Riga** (Hull) Yd No: 123 **2009-11 Aas Mek. Verksted AS — Vestnes** Yd No: 185 Loa 57.07 (BB) Br ex - Dght 4.900 Lbp 51.44 Br md 12.00 Dpth 5.10 Welded, 1 dk	**(B12C2FL) Live Fish Carrier (Well Boat)**	**1 oil engine** reduction geared to sc. shaft driving 1 FP propeller Total Power: 1,324kW (1,800hp) 14.0kn Caterpillar 3512B-TA 1 x Vee 4 Stroke 12 Cy. 170 x 190 1324kW (1800bhp) Caterpillar Inc-USA AuxGen: 2 x 515kW a.c Thrusters: 1 Tunnel thruster (f); 1 Tunnel thruster (a)
8035130 *UCHI* -	**VIKTORIYA** *ex Saaremaa -1995* **Sigma Marine Technology Co Ltd (OOO 'Sigma Marin Tekhnolodzhi')** - *Sovetskaya Gavan* *Russia* MMSI: 273524100	**845** 258 389	Class: RS	**1982 Zavod "Leninskaya Kuznitsa" — Kiyev** Yd No: 1508 Loa 54.82 Br ex 9.96 Dght 4.141 Lbp 50.30 Br md 9.80 Dpth 5.01 Welded, 1 dk	**(B11A2FS) Stern Trawler** Ins: 414 Compartments: 2 Ho, ER 3 Ha: 3 (1.5 x 1.6) Derricks: 2x1.5t; Winches: 2 Ice Capable	**1 oil engine** driving 1 CP propeller Total Power: 736kW (1,001hp) 12.0kn S.K.L. 8NVD48-2U 1 x 4 Stroke 8 Cy. 320 x 480 736kW (1001bhp) VEB Schwermaschinenbau "KarlLiebknecht" (SKL)-Magdeburg Fuel: 154.0 (d.f.)

No. / Call sign	Name / Owner	Tonnage	Class	Build / Dimensions	Type	Machinery
8507573 *UBBI5* K-2180	**VIKTORIYA** *ex* Miyajima Maru *-1991* **Baltiyskiy Briz Ltd** - *Kaliningrad* Russia MMSI: 273356740	**9,814** 2,994 6,591	Class: RS (NK)	**1986**-05 **Hitachi Zosen Corp — Onomichi HS (Innoshima Shipyard)** Yd No: 4819 Loa 140.87 Br ex 20.00 Dght 6.524 Lbp 130.00 Br md - Dpth 12.10 Welded, 2 dks	**(B11A2FG) Factory Stern Trawler** Grain: 2,400; Ins: 3,036; Liq: 131 Ice Capable	**1 oil engine** with clutches, flexible couplings & sr geared to sc. shaft driving 1 CP propeller Total Power: 4,965kW (6,750hp) 16.0kn Pielstick 9PC2-6L-400 1 x 4 Stroke 9 Cy. 400 x 460 4965kW (6750bhp) Ishikawajima Harima Heavy IndustrieCo Ltd (IHI)-Japan AuxGen: 3 x 1500kW a.c Thrusters: 1 Thwart. CP thruster (f)
8858661 - -	**VIKTORIYA** - **Odissey Joint Venture (S/P 'Odissey')** -	**446** 133 207	Class: (RS)	**1992**-08 **AO Zavod 'Nikolayevsk-na-Amure' — Nikolayevsk-na-Amure** Yd No: 1288 Loa 44.88 Br ex 9.47 Dght 3.770 Lbp 39.37 Br md - Dpth 5.13 Welded, 1 dk	**(B11A2FS) Stern Trawler** Ice Capable	**1 oil engine** driving 1 FP propeller Total Power: 588kW (799hp) 11.5kn S.K.L. 6NVD48A-2U 1 x 4 Stroke 6 Cy. 320 x 480 588kW (799bhp) SKL Motoren u. Systemtechnik AG-Magdeburg
8930835 - -	**VIKTORIYA** *ex* SLV-01 *-2005* **Firma 'Kristall'** - *Tuapse* Russia	*202* 81 323	Class: RS	**1979**-09 **Svetlovskiy Sudoremontnyy Zavod — Svetlyy** Yd No: 1 Loa 29.17 Br ex 8.15 Dght 3.120 Lbp 28.50 Br md 7.58 Dpth 3.60 Welded, 1 dk	**(B34G2SE) Pollution Control Vessel** Liq: 336; Liq (Oil): 336 Compartments: 8 Ta Ice Capable	**1 oil engine** geared to sc. shaft driving 1 FP propeller Total Power: 165kW (224hp) 7.5kn Daldizel 6CHNSP18/22 1 x 4 Stroke 6 Cy. 180 x 220 165kW (224bhp) Daldizel-Khabarovsk AuxGen: 1 x 50kW a.c, 1 x 25kW a.c Fuel: 14.0 (d.f.)
8866890 *UEEW* -	**VIKTORIYA-120** *ex* Volgo-Balt 13 *-1999* **Turash Co** - *Astrakhan* Russia MMSI: 273456120 Official number: 93018	**2,406** 1,005 2,893	Class: RR	**1964 Astrakhanskaya Sudoverf im. "Kirova" — Astrakhan** Loa 114.02 Br ex 13.23 Dght 3.610 Lbp 110.15 Br md 13.00 Dpth 5.50 Welded, 1 dk	**(A31A2GX) General Cargo Ship** Grain: 4,512; Bale: 2,600 Compartments: 4 Ho 4 Ha: 4 (16.4 x 9.3)	**2 oil engines** driving 2 FP propellers Total Power: 970kW (1,318hp) S.K.L. 6NVD48-2U 2 x 4 Stroke 6 Cy. 320 x 480 each-485kW (659bhp) VEB Schwermaschinenbau "KarlLiebknecht" (SKL)-Magdeburg
8901559 *UDKA* SI-2133	**VIKTORIYA I** *ex* Victoria *-1993* **Akros Fishing Co Ltd (A/O Akros)** - SatCom: Inmarsat A 140511114 *Petropavlovsk-Kamchatskiy* Russia MMSI: 273847900 Official number: 922076	**1,923** 620 1,258	Class: RS (NV)	**1992**-12 **Sterkoder AS — Kristiansund** Yd No: 133 Loa 64.00 Br ex 13.00 Dght 5.780 Lbp 55.55 Br md - Dpth 8.85 Welded, 2 dks	**(B11A2FG) Factory Stern Trawler** Grain: 130; Ins: 950 Ice Capable	**1 oil engine** reduction geared to sc. shaft driving 1 FP propeller Total Power: 2,457kW (3,341hp) Wartsila 6R32E 1 x 4 Stroke 6 Cy. 320 x 350 2457kW (3341bhp) Wartsila Diesel Oy-Finland AuxGen: 1 x 1304kW 380V 50Hz a.c, 2 x 336kW 380V 50Hz a.c Thrusters: 1 Thwart. FP thruster (f)
8897136 *UEMG* -	**VIKTORIYA II** *ex* Victorya II *-2000* *ex* Viktoriya I *-1995* **'Moryak Rybolov' Fishing Collective (Rybkolkhoz Moryak-Rybolov)** - *Nakhodka* Russia Official number: 931129	**359** 107 129	Class: RS	**1995**-05 **OAO Sudostroitelnyy Zavod "Avangard" — Petrozavodsk** Yd No: 647 Loa 35.72 Br ex 9.00 Dght 3.490 Lbp 31.00 Br md 8.92 Dpth 6.07 Welded, 1 dk	**(B11A2FS) Stern Trawler** Ice Capable	**1 oil engine** driving 1 FP propeller Total Power: 589kW (801hp) 10.9kn S.K.L. 6NVDS48A-2U 1 x 4 Stroke 6 Cy. 320 x 480 589kW (801bhp) SKL Motoren u. Systemtechnik AG-Magdeburg AuxGen: 3 x 200kW a.c Fuel: 82.0 (d.f.)
8871235 - -	**VIKTORS** *ex* Viktor *-1992* - -	*176* - 17		**1992 in Russia** Loa 34.62 Br ex 9.49 Dght 2.350 Lbp - Br md - Dpth 6.26 Welded, 1 dk	**(A37B2PS) Passenger Ship**	**2 oil engines** driving 2 FP propellers Total Power: 1,472kW (2,002hp) 35.0kn Zvezda M400 2 x Vee 4 Stroke 12 Cy. 180 x 200 each-736kW (1001bhp) AO "Zvezda"-Sankt-Peterburg
8722379 *ESUH* EK-1003	**VIKTORY** *ex* Mrtk-0724 *-2010* **OU Novirina Kalaparadiis** - SatCom: Inmarsat C 427679010 *Narva-Joesuu* Estonia MMSI: 276790000 Official number: 1F10G03	**117** 35 30	Class: (RS)	**1987**-10 **Sosnovskiy Sudostroitelnyy Zavod — Sosnovka** Yd No: 724 Loa 25.50 Br ex 7.00 Dght 2.390 Lbp 22.00 Br md - Dpth 3.30 Welded, 1 dk	**(B11A2FS) Stern Trawler** Ice Capable	**1 oil engine** driving 1 FP propeller Total Power: 221kW (300hp) 9.5kn S.K.L. 6NVD26A-2 1 x 4 Stroke 6 Cy. 180 x 260 221kW (300bhp) VEB Schwermaschinenbau "KarlLiebknecht" (SKL)-Magdeburg
8126484 - -	**VIKUS** - **Servicios Tecnicos Maritimos SRL** - *Callao* Peru Official number: CO-000058-SM	*101* - -	Class: (LR) (BV) ✠ Classed LR until 13/5/97	**1982**-10 **John Manly Shipyard Ltd — Vancouver BC** Yd No: 581 Loa 23.04 Br ex 7.85 Dght 3.520 Lbp 20.27 Br md 7.32 Dpth 3.56 Welded, 1 dk	**(B32A2ST) Tug**	**2 oil engines** with clutches, flexible couplings & sr reverse geared to sc. shafts driving 2 FP propellers Total Power: 994kW (1,352hp) G.M. (Detroit Diesel) 12V-149-NA 2 x Vee 2 Stroke 12 Cy. 146 x 146 each-497kW (676bhp) General Motors Detroit DieselAllison Divn-USA AuxGen: 2 x 25kW 220V 60Hz a.c
9404443 *A8VU4* -	**VIL ATLANTIC** *ex* Salta *-2010* **VIL Atlantic GmbH & Co KG** Peter Doehle Schiffahrts-KG *Monrovia* Liberia MMSI: 636092044 Official number: 92044	**24,165** 12,245 37,852 T/cm 50.0	Class: LR ✠ **100A1** SS 02/2010 bulk carrier BC-A strengthened for heavy cargoes, Nos. 2 & 4 holds may be empty all holds strengthened for regular discharge by heavy grabs ESP **ShipRight** (SDA, FDA, CM) *IWS LI Ice Class 1C FS at draught of 10.634m Max/min draught fwd 10.634/4.19m Max/min draught aft 10.634/6.24m Required power 6054kw, installed power 7368kw ✠ **LMC** **UMS** Eq.Ltr: J†; Cable: 597.1/66.0 U3 (a)	**2010**-02 **Jiangsu Eastern Heavy Industry Co Ltd — Jingjiang JS** Yd No: 06C-003 Loa 189.91 (BB) Br ex 28.55 Dght 10.440 Lbp 183.00 Br md 28.49 Dpth 15.10 Welded, 1 dk	**(A21A2BC) Bulk Carrier** Grain: 48,957; Bale: 47,872 Compartments: 5 Ho, ER 5 Ha: ER Cranes: 4x30t Ice Capable	**1 oil engine** driving 1 FP propeller Total Power: 8,730kW (11,869hp) 14.0kn Wartsila 6RTA48T 1 x 2 Stroke 6 Cy. 480 x 2000 8730kW (11869bhp) Wartsila Diesel S.A.-Bermeo AuxGen: 3 x 600kW 450V 60Hz a.c Boilers: AuxB (Comp) 8.0kgf/cm² (7.8bar)
9492402 *A8ZF6* -	**VIL BALTIC** *ex* Wuhan *-2011* **VIL Baltic GmbH & Co KG** Peter Doehle Schiffahrts-KG *Monrovia* Liberia MMSI: 636092251 Official number: 92251	**33,044** 19,231 57,021 T/cm 58.8	Class: LR (BV) **100A1** SS 05/2010 bulk carrier CSR BC-A GRAB (20) Nos. 2 & 4 holds may be empty ESP *IWS LI **LMC** **UMS** Cable: 633.5/73.0 U3 (a)	**2010**-05 **Qingshan Shipyard — Wuhan HB** Yd No: 20060352 Loa 189.99 (BB) Br ex 32.28 Dght 12.800 Lbp 185.00 Br md 32.26 Dpth 18.00 Welded, 1 dk	**(A21A2BC) Bulk Carrier** Grain: 71,634; Bale: 68,200 Compartments: 5 Ho, ER 5 Ha: ER Cranes: 4x30t	**1 oil engine** driving 1 FP propeller Total Power: 9,480kW (12,889hp) 14.2kn MAN-B&W 6S50MC-C 1 x 2 Stroke 6 Cy. 500 x 2000 9480kW (12889bhp) STX Engine Co Ltd-South Korea AuxGen: 2 x 720kW 450V 60Hz a.c, 1 x 600kW 450V 60Hz a.c Boilers: AuxB (o.f.) 9.2kgf/cm² (9.0bar)
7921746 *8QAH* -	**VILA ALI** *ex* Kyoritsu Maru No. 5 *-1991* **Villa Shipping & Trading Co Pvt Ltd** - *Male* Maldives MMSI: 455118000 Official number: C5050A	*932* 587 682		**1979**-05 **Sokooshi Zosen K.K. — Osakikamijima** Yd No: 256 Lengthened-1982 Loa 59.11 Br ex - Dght 3.009 Lbp 57.92 Br md 9.61 Dpth 6.20 Welded, 1 dk	**(A31A2GX) General Cargo Ship**	**1 oil engine** driving 1 FP propeller Total Power: 883kW (1,201hp) Niigata 1 x 4 Stroke 883kW (1201bhp) Niigata Engineering Co Ltd-Japan
5070713 *8QLQ* -	**VILA BAANI** *ex* Quince Marianne *-1990* *ex* Sun Mount *-1981* *ex* Chiyo Maru *-1975* **Qasim Ibrahim** - *Male* Maldives Official number: 163/10-T	*455* 256 685	Class: (NK)	**1962**-07 **Fukushima Zosen Ltd. — Matsue** Yd No: 170 Loa 54.21 Br ex 7.65 Dght 3.447 Lbp 49.51 Br md 7.60 Dpth 3.81 Riveted\Welded, 1 dk	**(A13B2TU) Tanker (unspecified)** Liq: 929; Liq (Oil): 929 Compartments: 4 Ta, ER	**1 oil engine** driving 1 FP propeller Total Power: 441kW (600hp) 10.5kn Kinoshita 1 x 4 Stroke 6 Cy. 300 x 420 441kW (600bhp) Kinoshita Tekkosho-Japan AuxGen: 1 x 8kW 105V d.c, 1 x 5kW 105V d.c, 1 x 3kW 105V d.c Fuel: 29.5 2.5pd

IMO / Call sign	Name / Former names / Owner / Port / Flag	Tonnage	Class	Builder / Dimensions	Type	Machinery	
7801439 *8QA0* -	**VILA BURU** *ex* Ryusho Maru *-1992* **Villa Shipping & Trading Co Pvt Ltd** - *Male* *Maldives* MMSI: 455125000 Official number: C5054A	*137* 51 220		**1978**-03 **Nakamura Shipbuilding & Engine Works Co. Ltd. — Yanai** Yd No: 137 Loa 32.50 Br ex - Dght 2.930 Lbp 29.50 Br md 6.50 Dpth 3.00 Welded, 1 dk	**(A13B2TU) Tanker (unspecified)**	**1 oil engine** geared to sc. shaft driving 1 FP propeller Total Power: 221kW (300hp) Matsui 1 x 4 Stroke 6 Cy. 230 x 380 221kW (300bhp) Matsui Iron Works Co Ltd-Japan	MU623BA
8613528 - -	**VILA BURU-2** *ex* Kaiyu *-2008* *ex* Maruoka Maru No. 3 *-2006* **Villa Shipping & Trading Co Pvt Ltd**	*178* - 445		**1987**-04 **Koa Sangyo KK — Takamatsu KG** Yd No: 527 Loa 41.61 Br ex - Dght 3.177 Lbp 37.52 Br md 7.51 Dpth 3.31 Welded, 1 dk	**(A12A2TC) Chemical Tanker** Liq: 210 Compartments: 4 Ta, ER	**1 oil engine** driving 1 FP propeller Total Power: 368kW (500hp) Hanshin 1 x 4 Stroke 6 Cy. 240 x 400 368kW (500bhp) The Hanshin Diesel Works Ltd-Japan	6L24GS
8211045 *8QFP* -	**VILA DHAURU** *ex* Seiko Maru No. 16 *-2006* *ex* Victoria V *-1995* *ex* Victoria *-1994* **Aariya Investment Co Pvt Ltd** Villa Shipping & Trading Co Pvt Ltd *Male* *Maldives* MMSI: 455302000 Official number: C8303A	**1,954** 789 2,235	Class: NK	**1983**-01 **Wakamatsu Zosen K.K. — Kitakyushu** Yd No: 330 Loa 83.26 Br ex - Dght 5.021 Lbp 76.99 Br md 13.26 Dpth 7.83 Welded, 2 dks	**(A34A2GR) Refrigerated Cargo Ship** Ins: 2,783 2 Ha: 2 (3.8 x 3.8)ER Derricks: 2x5t,2x3t	**1 oil engine** driving 1 FP propeller Total Power: 2,427kW (3,300hp) Hanshin 1 x 4 Stroke 6 Cy. 400 x 800 2427kW (3300bhp) The Hanshin Diesel Works Ltd-Japan AuxGen: 2 x 360kW a.c Fuel: 660.0 (r.f.)	14.0kn 6EL40
7714698 *8QNY* -	**VILA DHUNI** *ex* Taiko Maru No. 3 *-1988* *ex* Taihaku Maru No. 8 *-1987* **Qasim Ibrahim** - *Male* *Maldives* MMSI: 455220000 Official number: P5051A	**312** 133 550		**1977**-09 **Oka Zosen Tekko K.K. — Ushimado** Yd No: 247 Loa - Br ex - Dght 3.301 Lbp 42.02 Br md 7.80 Dpth 3.41 Welded, 1 dk	**(A13B2TU) Tanker (unspecified)**	**1 oil engine** driving 1 FP propeller Total Power: 588kW (799hp) Yanmar 1 x 4 Stroke 6 Cy. 240 x 290 588kW (799bhp) Yanmar Diesel Engine Co Ltd-Japan	6GL-HT
8120143 *WCY3150* -	**VILA DO CONDE** *ex* Susan Marie II *-2001* *ex* Howard Reed *-2001* **Vila do Conde Inc** - *Cape May, NJ* *United States of America* Official number: 615610	*167* 114 -		**1979**-12 **Quality Marine, Inc. — Bayou La Batre, Al** Yd No: 132 L reg 24.88 Br ex - Dght - Lbp - Br md 7.32 Dpth 3.87 Welded, 1 dk	**(B11A2FS) Stern Trawler**	**1 oil engine** driving 1 FP propeller Total Power: 401kW (545hp) Caterpillar 1 x Vee 4 Stroke 8 Cy. 159 x 203 401kW (545bhp) Caterpillar Tractor Co-USA	D379TA
9207259 *CUOW7* SA-543-C	**VILA DO INFANTE** - **Americo Serafim** - *Portugal* MMSI: 263401270	**128** - -		**1999**-10 **Estaleiros Navais Lda. (ASTINAVA) — Figueira da Foz** (Hull) Yd No: GP-015 **1999**-10 **Andres Cajeao Alonso (Gestinaval S.L.) — Cudillero** Yd No: 337 Loa 25.40 Br ex - Dght 2.950 Lbp 20.63 Br md 6.60 Dpth 3.47 Welded, 1 dk	**(B11B2FV) Fishing Vessel** Bale: 99	**1 oil engine** geared to sc. shaft driving 1 FP propeller Total Power: 331kW (450hp) Baudouin 1 x Vee 4 Stroke 12 Cy. 150 x 150 331kW (450bhp) Societe des Moteurs Baudouin SA-France	12M26SR
8214645 - -	**VILA MOOSUN** *ex* Eastern Star I *-2006* *ex* Eastern Star *-2005* *ex* Anchorage *-2003* *ex* Adventure *-1999* *ex* Anchorage *-1998* *ex* Miyoshima Maru *-1992* **Aariya Investment Co Pvt Ltd** Villa Shipping & Trading Co Pvt Ltd	**3,321** 1,534 3,788	Class: (KR) (NK)	**1982**-12 **Kishimoto Zosen K.K. — Kinoe** Yd No: 525 Loa 102.44 Br ex - Dght 6.414 Lbp 94.01 Br md 15.02 Dpth 9.43 Welded, 3 dks	**(A34A2GR) Refrigerated Cargo Ship** Ins: 4,462 Compartments: 3 Ho, ER 3 Ha: (6.4 x 5.6)2 (6.5 x 5.6)ER Derricks: 6x5t	**1 oil engine** driving 1 FP propeller Total Power: 3,347kW (4,551hp) Mitsubishi 1 x 2 Stroke 7 Cy. 370 x 880 3347kW (4551bhp) Akasaka Tekkosho KK (Akasaka DieselLtd)-Japan AuxGen: 2 x 480kW 445V 60Hz a.c Fuel: 52.5 (d.f.) 687.5 (r.f.) 15.0pd	15.1kn 7UEC37/88H
8969446 *WDC8664* -	**VILA NOVA DO CORVO I** *ex* Vila Nova do Corvo *-2005* *ex* St. Joseph II *-2005* **Vila Fishing Corp** - *New Bedford, MA* *United States of America* MMSI: 367091040 Official number: 1110463	**198** 59 -		**2001** Yd No: 195 L reg 26.94 Br ex - Dght - Lbp - Br md 7.92 Dpth 3.81 Welded, 1 dk	**(B11B2FV) Fishing Vessel**	**1 oil engine** driving 1 FP propeller	
8019710 *WDD4766* -	**VILA NOVA DO CORVO II** *ex* Sandra Lee *-2006* *ex* Cajun Love *-2006* **Vila Nova do Corvo II Inc** - *New Bedford, MA* *United States of America* MMSI: 367148770 Official number: 618384	**202** 60 -		**1980** **Marine Builders, Inc. — Mobile, Al** Yd No: 122 L reg 27.16 Br ex - Dght - Lbp - Br md 8.08 Dpth 3.97 Welded, 1 dk	**(B11A2FS) Stern Trawler**	**2 oil engines** driving 2 FP propellers G.M. (Detroit Diesel) 2 x Vee 2 Stroke 12 Cy. 123 x 127 General Motors Detroit DieselAllison Divn-USA AuxGen: 2 x 40kW	12V-92-TA
7504574 - -	**VILA REAL** - **Pereira Mendes & Companhia Lda** - *Portugal*	*189* 64 -	Class: (BV)	**1975** **Soc. Argibay de Const. Navais e Mecanicas S.A.R.L. — Alverca** Yd No: 132 Loa 33.99 Br ex 7.78 Dght 3.506 Lbp 30.26 Br md 7.75 Dpth 5.62 Welded, 2 dks	**(B11A2FS) Stern Trawler**	**1 oil engine** geared to sc. shaft driving 1 CP propeller Total Power: 736kW (1,001hp) Deutz 1 x 4 Stroke 8 Cy. 220 x 280 736kW (1001bhp) Kloeckner Humboldt Deutz AG-West Germany Fuel: 77.5 (d.f.)	SBA8M528
9367310 - -	**VILA TUG 2** *ex* Abadi 6 *-2005* **Villa Shipping (S) Pte Ltd** Villa Shipping & Trading Co Pvt Ltd	**179** 54	Class: (GL)	**2005**-12 **SC Yii Brothers Shipyard Sdn Bhd — Sibu** Yd No: 112 Loa 25.00 Br ex 8.12 Dght 3.000 Lbp 22.75 Br md 8.10 Dpth 3.60 Welded, 1 dk	**(B32A2ST) Tug**	**2 oil engines** reverse reduction geared to sc. shafts driving 2 FP propellers Total Power: 1,248kW (1,696hp) Caterpillar 2 x Vee 4 Stroke 12 Cy. 145 x 162 each-624kW (848bhp) Caterpillar Inc-USA AuxGen: 2 x 50kW 415/230V a.c	11.0kn 3412D
7702279 - -	**VILA TUG 3** *ex* Dae Ryong *-2008* *ex* Dong Young *-1991* **Villa Shipping (S) Pte Ltd** Villa Shipping & Trading Co Pvt Ltd	*261* 63 189	Class: (KR)	**1976**-12 **Dae Sun Shipbuilding & Engineering Co Ltd — Busan** Yd No: 194 Loa 30.99 Br ex - Dght 3.101 Lbp 29.42 Br md 9.01 Dpth 3.81 Welded, 1 dk	**(B32A2ST) Tug**	**2 oil engines** driving 2 FP propellers Total Power: 1,104kW (1,500hp) Sumiyoshi 2 x 4 Stroke 6 Cy. 300 x 450 each-552kW (750bhp) Sumiyoshi Tekkosho-Japan AuxGen: 2 x 64kW 220V a.c	14.3kn S6HPSS
9411496 - -	**VILA TUG 4** *ex* Fordeco 71 *-2008* **Villa Shipping (S) Pte Ltd** -	**196** 59 -	Class: GL (NK)	**2006**-09 **Jana Seribu Shipbuilding (M) Sdn Bhd — Sibu** Yd No: 2021 Loa 26.00 Br ex - Dght 3.012 Lbp 23.95 Br md 8.00 Dpth 3.65 Welded, 1 dk	**(B32A2ST) Tug**	**2 oil engines** reduction geared to sc. shafts driving 2 FP propellers Total Power: 1,220kW (1,658hp) Yanmar 2 x 4 Stroke 6 Cy. 155 x 180 each-610kW (829bhp) Yanmar Diesel Engine Co Ltd-Japan AuxGen: 2 x 40kW 415/230V 50Hz a.c	10.0kn 6AYM-ETE
8998978 *8QF0* -	**VILA UFULI** *ex* Sea Lord 1 *-2006* **Villa Shipping & Trading Co Pvt Ltd** - *Male* *Maldives* MMSI: 455301000 Official number: C8272A	*266* 141 -		**2000**-09 **Santiago Shipyard — Consolacion** Loa 50.29 Br ex - Dght 2.000 Lbp 46.00 Br md 9.75 Dpth 2.43 Welded, 1 dk	**(A35D2RL) Landing Craft** Bow ramp (f)	**2 oil engines** driving 2 Propellers Total Power: 810kW (1,102hp) Yanmar 2 x 4 Stroke 6 Cy. each-405kW (551bhp) Yanmar Diesel Engine Co Ltd-Japan	6UBTU2
7231816 *HQLP3* -	**VILA VIDHUVARU** *ex* Hakusei Maru No. 15 *-1990* **Villa Shipping & Trading Co Pvt Ltd** - *San Lorenzo* *Honduras* Official number: L-0324749	**647** 239 920 T/cm 4.1	Class: (BV)	**1971** **Fukae Zosen K.K. — Etajima** Yd No: 131 Loa 57.21 Br ex 9.43 Dght 3.798 Lbp 51.01 Br md 9.40 Dpth 4.40 Welded, 2 dks	**(A11B2TG) LPG Tanker** Liq (Gas): 948 2 x Gas Tank (s); 2 Cargo Pump (s): 2x225m³/hr	**1 oil engine** driving 1 FP propeller Total Power: 883kW (1,201hp) Sumiyoshi 1 x 4 Stroke 6 Cy. 310 x 480 883kW (1201bhp) Sumiyoshi Marine Diesel Co Ltd-Japan AuxGen: 2 x 40kW 225V 60Hz a.c	12.4kn S631SS
7930395 *8QAK* -	**VILA VIYU** *ex* Tsurushio Maru No. 12 *-1992* *ex* Shinei Maru No. 8 *-1987* **Villa Shipping & Trading Co Pvt Ltd** - *Male* *Maldives* MMSI: 455121000 Official number: C5053A	*199* 126 400		**1980**-05 **KK Ura Kyodo Zosensho — Awaji HG** Yd No: 203 Loa - Br ex - Dght - Lbp 42.02 Br md 7.51 Dpth 3.41 Welded, 1 dk	**(A13B2TU) Tanker (unspecified)**	**1 oil engine** driving 1 FP propeller Total Power: 552kW (750hp) Hanshin 1 x 4 Stroke 6 Cy. 200 x 240 552kW (750bhp) Hanshin Nainenki Kogyo-Japan	

IMO No. / Call sign	Ship / Owner	Tonnage	Class	Builder / Dimensions	Type	Machinery
8734839 *EBRC* 3-ST-44-00	**VILABOA UNO** **Pesqueras Vilaboa SL** - *Santander* *Spain* Official number: 3-4/2000	224 67 -		2000-01 **Industrias Navales A Xunqueira SL — Moana** Loa 28.50 Br ex - Dght 3.000 Lbp 25.00 Br md 7.40 Dpth 3.55 Welded, 1 dk	**(B11A2FS) Stern Trawler**	**1 oil engine** driving 1 Propeller Total Power: 279kW (379hp)
7221990 *EAPZ* -	**VILACHAN** *launched as* Valle *-1972* **Monte Ventoso SA** - *Vigo* *Spain* Official number: 3-9272/	380 114 -	Class: (BV)	1972-08 **Construcciones Navales Santodomingo SA — Vigo** Yd No: 408 Lengthened-1980 Loa 38.54 Br ex 8.03 Dght 3.801 Lbp 34.93 Br md 8.01 Dpth 5.92 Welded, 2 dks	**(B11A2FT) Trawler**	**1 oil engine** driving 1 FP propeller Total Power: 588kW (799hp) 11.5kn Deutz SBA8M528 1 x 4 Stroke 8 Cy. 220 x 280 588kW (799bhp) Kloeckner Humboldt Deutz AG-West Germany Fuel: 129.5 (d.f.)
9529293 *9HA2697* -	**VILAMOURA** **Olympian Apollo Owners Inc** TMS Tankers Ltd SatCom: Inmarsat Mini-M 765059313 *Valletta* *Malta* MMSI: 215287000 Official number: 9529293	81,380 51,274 158,621 T/cm 119.6	Class: AB	2011-03 **Samsung Heavy Industries Co Ltd — Geoje** Yd No: 1887 Loa 274.37 (BB) Br ex 48.04 Dght 17.020 Lbp 264.00 Br md 48.00 Dpth 23.20 Welded, 1 dk	**(A13A2TV) Crude Oil Tanker** Double Hull (13F) Liq: 167,400; Liq (Oil): 167,400 Cargo Heating Coils Compartments: 12 Wing Ta, 2 Wing Slop Ta, ER 3 Cargo Pump (s): 3x4000m³/hr Manifold: Bow/CM: 137m	**1 oil engine** driving 1 FP propeller Total Power: 17,298kW (23,518hp) 15.5kn MAN-B&W 6S70MC-C 1 x 2 Stroke 6 Cy. 700 x 2800 17298kW (23518bhp) Doosan Engine Co Ltd-South Korea AuxGen: 3 x 900kW a.c Fuel: 200.0 (d.f.) 3900.0 (r.f.)
8847569 - -	**VILAND** *ex* Saka *-2007* *ex* Gauya *-1992* **Verdius Ltd** Delta Co Ltd *Russia*	1,896 1,014 3,389	Class: (RS)	1983 **Shipbuilding & Shiprepairing Yard 'Ivan Dimitrov' — Rousse** Yd No: 425 Loa 77.53 Br ex 14.34 Dght 5.400 Lbp 73.24 Br md 14.02 Dpth 6.50 Welded, 1 dk	**(A13B2TP) Products Tanker** Single Hull Part Cargo Heating Coils	**1 oil engine** driving 1 FP propeller Total Power: 883kW (1,201hp) 10.0kn S.K.L. 8NVD48A-2U 1 x 4 Stroke 8 Cy. 320 x 480 883kW (1201bhp) (made 1982) VEB Schwermaschinenbau "KarlLiebknecht" (SKL)-Magdeburg AuxGen: 2 x 150kW a.c, 1 x 50kW a.c Thrusters: 1 Tunnel thruster (f)
9311787 *V2DV3* -	**VILANO** *ex* Cap Vilano *-2013* *completed as* Fesco Barguzin *-2006* **ms 'Vilano' Schiffahrts GmbH & Co KG** Reederei Harmstorf & Co Thomas Meier-Hedde GmbH & Co KG *Saint John's* *Antigua & Barbuda* MMSI: 305345000 Official number: 4550	28,372 13,574 37,882 T/cm 56.8	Class: GL	2006-08 **Aker MTW Werft GmbH — Wismar** (Aft section) Yd No: 123 2006-08 **Aker Warnemuende Operations GmbH — Rostock** (Fwd section) Loa 221.69 (BB) Br ex - Dght 11.400 Lbp 209.62 Br md 29.80 Dpth 16.40 Welded, 1 dk	**(A33A2CC) Container Ship (Fully Cellular)** TEU 2742 C Ho 1112 TEU C Dk 1630 TEU incl 400 ref C Cranes: 3x45t	**1 oil engine** driving 1 FP propeller Total Power: 21,769kW (29,597hp) 21.9kn MAN-B&W 7L70MC-C 1 x 2 Stroke 7 Cy. 700 x 2360 21769kW (29597bhp) H Cegielski Poznan SA-Poland AuxGen: 3 x a.c Thrusters: 1 Tunnel thruster (f)
7731218 - -	**VILCO 17** *ex* John & Kossie *-2006* **R H V Inc** - *Corpus Christi, TX* *United States of America* Official number: 582919	*127* 87 -		1977 **Desco Marine — Saint Augustine, Fl** Yd No: 221-F L reg 20.97 Br ex 6.74 Dght - Lbp - Br md - Dpth 3.81 Bonded, 1 dk	**(B11B2FV) Fishing Vessel** Hull Material: Reinforced Plastic	**1 oil engine** driving 1 FP propeller Total Power: 268kW (364hp) Caterpillar 1 x 4 Stroke 268kW (364bhp) Caterpillar Tractor Co-USA
7905481 *ERUQ* -	**VILENA** *ex* Mesarya *-2013* *ex* Isis *-2012* *ex* Osiris I *-1993* *ex* Horus *-1988* *ex* Sexto Reefer *-1986* *ex* El Sexto *-1986* **Baron Group Assets Ltd** Vival Marine Ltd *Moldova* MMSI: 214182117	2,622 811 2,762	Class: (RS) (BV)	1981-02 **Astilleros Construcciones SA — Meira** Yd No: 162 Loa 74.71 Br ex 14.38 Dght 5.540 Lbp 68.99 Br md 14.22 Dpth 9.71 Welded, 3 dks	**(A35A2RR) Ro-Ro Cargo Ship** Stern door & ramp Cars: 207 Ins: 4,038 Compartments: 1 Ho, ER 2 Ha: 2 (5.5 x 4.5)ER Cranes: 2x3.3t	**1 oil engine** with flexible couplings & sr gearedto sc. shaft driving 1 CP propeller Total Power: 1,545kW (2,101hp) 12.0kn Alpha 14V23L-VO 1 x Vee 4 Stroke 14 Cy. 225 x 300 1545kW (2101bhp) Construcciones Echevarria SA-Spain AuxGen: 3 x 280kW 440V 60Hz a.c Fuel: 305.0 (d.f.)
9435375 *UBXF3* -	**VILESH RIVER** **Armada Trading-14 Co Ltd** Palmali Gemicilik ve Acentelik AS (Palmali Shipping & Agency) SatCom: Inmarsat C 427302731 *Taganrog* *Russia* MMSI: 273332530	4,681 2,273 7,073	Class: RS	2009-05 **Sudostroitelnyy Zavod "Krasnoye Sormovo" — Nizhniy Novgorod** Yd No: 07005 Loa 139.95 Br ex 16.83 Dght 4.600 Lbp 134.50 Br md 16.60 Dpth 6.00 Welded, 1 dk	**(A13B2TP) Products Tanker** Double Hull (13F) Liq: 7,833; Liq (Oil): 7,833 Cargo Heating Coils Compartments: 6 Ta, ER 6 Cargo Pump (s): 6x150m³/hr Ice Capable	**2 oil engines** reduction geared to sc. shafts driving 2 Directional propellers Total Power: 2,160kW (2,936hp) 10.5kn Wartsila 6L20 2 x 4 Stroke 6 Cy. 200 x 280 each-1080kW (1468bhp) Wartsila Finland Oy-Finland AuxGen: 3 x 292kW a.c Thrusters: 1 Tunnel thruster (f)
7833119 *J8B4518* -	**VILGA** *ex* Sormovskiy-42 *-2011* **Milena Trading Ltd** Baltic Maritime Bureau Ltd *Kingstown* *St Vincent & The Grenadines* MMSI: 377609000 Official number: 10991	2,478 999 3,353	Class: (RS)	1980-07 **Sudostroitelnyy Zavod "Krasnoye Sormovo" — Gorkiy** Yd No: 66 Loa 114.03 Br ex 13.21 Dght 3.810 Lbp 108.03 Br md 13.00 Dpth 5.52 Welded, 1 dk	**(A31A2GX) General Cargo Ship** Bale: 4,297 Compartments: 4 Ho, ER 4 Ha: (17.6 x 9.3)3 (17.9 x 9.3)ER Ice Capable	**2 oil engines** driving 2 FP propellers Total Power: 970kW (1,318hp) 10.8kn S.K.L. 6NVD48-2U 2 x 4 Stroke 6 Cy. 320 x 480 each-485kW (659bhp) VEB Schwermaschinenbau "KarlLiebknecht" (SKL)-Magdeburg Fuel: 84.0 (d.f.)
9109811 *UFQL* -	**VILGA** *ex* Saratov City *-2013* *launched as* Liko-5 *-1995* **Investtransgroup Ltd** - *Astrakhan* *Russia* MMSI: 273447490 Official number: 931492	2,878 863 3,085	Class: RS	1995-11 **Rousse Shipyard Ltd — Rousse** Yd No: 530 Loa 122.83 Br ex 15.30 Dght 3.150 Lbp 115.28 Br md 14.80 Dpth 5.20 Welded, 1 dk	**(A13B2TP) Products Tanker** Double Hull (13F) Liq: 3,488; Liq (Oil): 3,488 Compartments: 10 Ta, ER 2 Cargo Pump (s) Ice Capable	**2 oil engines** driving 2 FP propellers Total Power: 1,280kW (1,740hp) 10.0kn S.K.L. 6NVD48A-2U 2 x 4 Stroke 6 Cy. 320 x 480 each-640kW (870bhp) SKL Motoren u. Systemtechnik AG-Magdeburg AuxGen: 3 x 100kW a.c Thrusters: 1 Thwart. CP thruster (f) Fuel: 167.0 (d.f.)
9223136 *TFCM* EA 011	**VILHELM TORSTEINSSON** **Samherji hf** - *Akureyri* *Iceland* MMSI: 251451000 Official number: 2410	3,239 1,062 3,860	Class: NV	2000-08 **Stocznia Polnocna SA (Northern Shipyard) — Gdansk** (Hull) Yd No: B310/01 2000-08 **Kleven Verft AS — Ulsteinvik** Yd No: 290 Loa 79.00 (BB) Br ex - Dght 8.200 Lbp 70.00 Br md 16.00 Dpth 9.50 Welded, 2 dks	**(B11A2FS) Stern Trawler** Ins: 1,180 Ice Capable	**1 oil engine** sr geared to sc. shaft driving 1 CP propeller Total Power: 4,060kW (5,520hp) 15.0kn Wartsila 12V32 1 x Vee 4 Stroke 12 Cy. 320 x 350 4060kW (5520bhp) Wartsila NSD Finland Oy-Finland AuxGen: 1 x 2500kW 230/440V 60Hz a.c, 1 x 1091kW 230/440V 60Hz a.c, 1 x 544kW 230/440V 60Hz a.c Thrusters: 1 Thwart. FP thruster (f); 1 Tunnel thruster (a) Fuel: 750.8 (d.f.) 15.0pd
8826199 *UDYS* -	**VILIGA** *ex* Virsaytis *-2000* *ex* Virsaitis *-1999* *ex* Auseklis *-1992* **MAG-SEA International** - SatCom: Inmarsat C 427321038 *Magadan* *Russia* MMSI: 273436430 Official number: 892476	776 232 414	Class: RS	1989-12 **Zavod "Leninskaya Kuznitsa" — Kiyev** Yd No: 1620 Loa 54.82 Br ex 10.15 Dght 4.140 Lbp 50.30 Br md - Dpth 5.00 Welded	**(B11A2FS) Stern Trawler** Ins: 824 Ice Capable	**1 oil engine** driving 1 CP propeller Total Power: 852kW (1,158hp) 12.0kn S.K.L. 8NVD48A-2U 1 x 4 Stroke 8 Cy. 320 x 480 852kW (1158bhp) VEB Schwermaschinenbau "KarlLiebknecht" (SKL)-Magdeburg AuxGen: 4 x 160kW a.c
8918382 *URWK* -	**VILKOVO** **Ukrainian Danube Shipping Co** - SatCom: Inmarsat C 427214210 *Izmail* *Ukraine* MMSI: 272142000 Official number: 921970	2,977 1,219 4,050	Class: RS UA	1993-07 **Estaleiros Navais de Viana do Castelo S.A. — Viana do Castelo** Yd No: 176 Loa 88.45 (BB) Br ex 15.52 Dght 5.670 Lbp 82.30 Br md 15.50 Dpth 7.10 Welded, 1 dk	**(A31A2GX) General Cargo Ship** Grain: 5,076 TEU 199 Compartments: 2 Ho, ER 2 Ha: 2 (25.2 x 12.6)ER Ice Capable	**1 oil engine** with flexible couplings & sr gearedto sc. shaft driving 1 CP propeller Total Power: 1,985kW (2,699hp) 12.0kn Wartsila 6R32 1 x 4 Stroke 6 Cy. 320 x 350 1985kW (2699bhp) Wartsila Diesel Oy-Finland Thrusters: 1 Thwart. FP thruster (f)
9126417 *9V5112* -	**VILLA** *ex* Merlion *-2011* **Tomiura Nippon Chartering Pte Ltd** Transocean Oil Pte Ltd *Singapore* *Singapore* MMSI: 563001831 Official number: 386482	1,264 777 2,395 T/cm 7.8	Class: NK	1995-04 **Greenbay Marine Pte Ltd — Singapore** Yd No: 92 Loa 66.00 Br ex - Dght 4.513 Lbp 61.72 Br md 13.00 Dpth 5.60 Welded, 1 dk	**(B35E2TF) Bunkering Tanker** Single Hull Liq: 2,586; Liq (Oil): 2,586 Compartments: 8 Wing Ta, ER 2 Cargo Pump (s): 2x300m³/hr	**2 oil engines** geared to sc. shafts driving 2 FP propellers Total Power: 1,060kW (1,442hp) 10.0kn Mitsubishi S6R2-MTK 2 x 4 Stroke 6 Cy. 170 x 220 each-530kW (721bhp) Mitsubishi Heavy Industries Ltd-Japan Fuel: 124.0 (d.f.)

8219918 *IBVK* -
VILLA
Rete Ferroviaria Italiana (RFI)
-
Catania *Italy*
MMSI: 247052100
Official number: 247
5,619 2,577 2,435 T/cm 5.8 Class: RI
1985-05 Fincantieri-Cant. Nav. Italiani S.p.A. — Palermo Yd No: 919
Loa 145.01 Br ex 18.42 Dght 5.868
Lbp 138.61 Br md 18.41 Dpth 7.73
Welded, 2 dks
(A36A2PT) Passenger/Ro-Ro Ship (Vehicles/Rail)
Passengers: unberthed: 1500
Bow door
Stern door/ramp
Len: 6.00 Wid: 4.50 Swl: -
Lane-Len: 454
Lane-clr ht: 4.75
Cars: 170, Rail Wagons: 45
4 oil engines with flexible couplings & sr gearedto sc. shafts driving 2 CP propellers
Total Power: 8,800kW (11,964hp) 19.0kn
GMT B420.6L
4 x 4 Stroke 6 Cy. 420 x 500 each-2200kW (2991bhp)
Fincantieri Cantieri NavaliItaliani SpA-Italy
AuxGen: 4 x 900kW 440V 60Hz a.c
Thrusters: 1 Thwart. CP thruster (f); 1 Tunnel thruster (a)
Fuel: 567.5 (d.f.)

7382641 *JXNW* -
VILLA
Kystverket Rederi
-
Aalesund *Norway*
MMSI: 258150000
554 166 356 Class: (NV)
1975-06 Sigbjorn Iversen — Flekkefjord Yd No: 32
Loa 41.81 Br ex 10.04 Dght 3.849
Lbp 37.62 Br md 10.00 Dpth 4.91
Welded, 1 dk
(B34Q2QL) Buoy & Lighthouse Tender
Compartments: 1 Ho, ER
1 Ha: (8.6 x 5.2)ER
Derricks: 1x6t
Ice Capable
1 oil engine driving 1 FP propeller
Total Power: 919kW (1,249hp) 12.0kn
Wichmann 5AXA
1 x 2 Stroke 5 Cy. 300 x 450 919kW (1249bhp)
Wichmann Motorfabrikk AS-Norway
Thrusters: 1 Thwart. FP thruster (f)

5380534 *HO2661* -
VILLA
ex Sjarmor *-1986* *ex* Villa *-1975*
Jayton Enterprises Inc
-
Panama *Panama*
Official number: 13020PEXT1
249 86 - Class: (NV)
1920 J. Storviks Mek. Verksted — Kristiansund Yd No: 10
Converted From: Buoy Tender
Lengthened-1955
Loa 39.53 Br ex 6.20 Dght 2.744
Lbp 36.61 Br md 6.18 Dpth 3.38
Riveted, 1 dk
(B22G2OY) Standby Safety Vessel
Compartments: 1 Ho, ER
Derricks: 1x5t,1x1.5t; Winches: 1
1 oil engine driving 1 FP propeller
Total Power: 235kW (320hp)
Wichmann 4ACA
1 x 2 Stroke 4 Cy. 280 x 420 235kW (320bhp) (new engine 1959)
Wichmann Motorfabrikk AS-Norway

9248629 *V5VD* -
VILLA DE HIO
Seawork Fish Processors (Pty) Ltd
-
Walvis Bay *Namibia*
825 248 -
2002-02 Montajes Cies S.L. — Vigo Yd No: 68
L reg 43.49 Br ex - Dght -
Lbp 41.00 Br md 9.60 Dpth 4.30
Welded, 1 dk
(B11A2FS) Stern Trawler
1 oil engine geared to sc. shaft driving 1 FP propeller
Total Power: 853kW (1,160hp)
Wartsila 8L20
1 x 4 Stroke 8 Cy. 200 x 280 853kW (1160bhp)
Wartsila Diesel S.A.-Bermeo

9175365 *EADK* 3-CA-33-97
VILLA DE MARIN
ex Playa la Caleta *-2005*
Pesquerias Nores Marin SL
-
Cadiz *Spain*
MMSI: 224468000
Official number: 3-3/1997
547 164 - Class: BV
1998-02 Astilleros Armon SA — Navia Yd No: 443
Loa - Br ex - Dght 3.750
Lbp 32.50 Br md 9.20 Dpth 4.00
Welded, 1 dk
(B11A2FS) Stern Trawler
1 oil engine driving 1 CP propeller
Total Power: 1,140kW (1,550hp) 10.0kn
MaK 6M20
1 x 4 Stroke 6 Cy. 200 x 300 1140kW (1550bhp)
MaK Motoren GmbH & Co. KG-Kiel

9098244 *ECCU* 3-VI-55-03
VILLA DE PITANXO
Pesquerias Nores Marin SL
-
SatCom: Inmarsat C 422481911
Vigo *Spain*
MMSI: 224819000
Official number: 3-5/2003
825 248 1,120 Class: BV
2004-01 Montajes Cies S.L. — Vigo Yd No: 76
Loa 50.30 Br ex - Dght 4.250
Lbp 42.14 Br md 9.70 Dpth 6.85
Welded, 2 dks
(B11A2FS) Stern Trawler
1 oil engine reduction geared to sc. shaft driving 1 CP propeller
Total Power: 1,529kW (2,079hp) 10.0kn
Wartsila 9L20
1 x 4 Stroke 9 Cy. 200 x 280 1529kW (2079bhp)
Wartsila Diesel S.A.-Bermeo

7386025 *EGSV* -
VILLA DE SARGADELOS
ex Isla de San Cipriano *-2005*
Pesquera Parrocha SL
-
SatCom: Inmarsat A 1351215
Celeiro *Spain*
MMSI: 224005650
Official number: 3-2950/
138 71 -
1974-12 Astilleros de Santander SA (ASTANDER) — El Astillero Yd No: 93
Loa 28.40 Br ex - Dght -
Lbp 24.39 Br md 6.30 Dpth 3.33
Welded, 1 dk
(B11A2FT) Trawler
1 oil engine driving 1 FP propeller
Total Power: 427kW (581hp)
Werkspoor
1 x 4 Stroke 427kW (581bhp)
Fabrica de San Carlos SA-Spain

5380613 - -
VILLA-FLORIDA
Government of The Republic of Paraguay (Ministerio de Obras Publicas y Communicaciones)
-
Asuncion *Paraguay*
153 55 Class: (LR) ✠ Classed LR until 6/63
1962-09 Indunaval S.A. — Bilbao Yd No: 45
Loa 30.33 Br ex 9.73 Dght -
Lbp 30.00 Br md 8.21 Dpth 2.21
Welded, 1 dk
(A37B2PS) Passenger Ship
2 oil engines sr reverse geared to sc. shafts driving 2 FP propellers
MWM
2 x 4 Stroke 6 Cy. 140 x 180
MWM AG Lieferwerk MuenchenSueddeutsche Bremsen-Muenchen

5380625 - -
VILLA HAYES
Government of The Republic of Paraguay (Ministerio de Obras Publicas y Communicaciones)
-
Asuncion *Paraguay*
200 69 -
1960 Nippon Kokan KK (NKK Corp) — Shizuoka SZ Yd No: 177
Loa 33.43 Br ex 10.37 Dght 1.512
Lbp 33.00 Br md 9.96 Dpth 2.21
Welded, 1 dk
(A37B2PS) Passenger Ship
2 oil engines driving 2 FP propellers
Hanshin
2 x 4 Stroke 6 Cy. 200 x 300
Hanshin Nainenki Kogyo-Japan

9098256 *ECCT* 3-VI-56-03
VILLA NORES
Pesquerias Nores Marin SL
-
SatCom: Inmarsat C 422482011
Vigo *Spain*
MMSI: 224820000
Official number: 3-6/2003
825 248 1,120 Class: BV
2004-01 Montajes Cies S.L. — Vigo Yd No: 77
Loa 50.30 Br ex - Dght 4.250
Lbp 42.14 Br md 9.70 Dpth 6.85
Welded, 2 dks
(B11A2FS) Stern Trawler
1 oil engine geared to sc. shaft driving 1 CP propeller
Total Power: 1,529kW (2,079hp) 10.0kn
Wartsila 9L20
1 x 4 Stroke 9 Cy. 200 x 280 1529kW (2079bhp)
Wartsila Diesel S.A.-Bermeo

7929126 *ITJA* -
VILLA SAN GIOVANNI
Caronte & Tourist SpA
-
Reggio Calabria *Italy*
MMSI: 247054600
Official number: 260
1,396 399 2,500 Class: RI
1980-12 Cantiere Navale Visentini di Visentini F e C SAS — Porto Viro Yd No: 141
Loa 94.19 Br ex 17.00 Dght 3.810
Lbp 86.01 Br md 16.50 Dpth 5.06
Welded, 1 dk
(A36A2PR) Passenger/Ro-Ro Ship (Vehicles)
Passengers: unberthed: 600
Bow door/ramp
Len: - Wid: 7.80 Swl: -
Stern door/ramp
Len: - Wid: 7.80 Swl: -
Lane-Len: 320
Lane-clr ht: 4.40
Lorries: 52, Cars: 120, Trailers: 18
2 oil engines driving 2 FP propellers
Total Power: 3,678kW (5,000hp)
Nohab F212V
2 x Vee 4 Stroke 12 Cy. 250 x 300 each-1839kW (2500bhp)
Nohab Diesel AB-Sweden

7101308 *HQBV5* -
VILLA ST. NICOLAS
ex Charleen B *-1987*
Marie Jose Lucar & Ilardo Vassor
-
San Lorenzo *Honduras*
Official number: L-0321802
173 117 -
1957 Platzer Shipyard — Houston, Tx
L reg 27.95 Br ex 7.32 Dght -
Lbp - Br md - Dpth 2.42
Welded, 1 dk
(B21A2OC) Crew/Supply Vessel
2 oil engines driving 2 FP propellers
Total Power: 442kW (600hp)
General Motors
2 x 2 Stroke each-221kW (300bhp)
General Motors Corp-USA

8945440 - -
VILLAFLOR 10
Navotas Shipyard & Fishing Corp
-
Manila *Philippines*
Official number: MNLD000963
115 56 -
1974 at Manila
L reg 23.57 Br ex - Dght -
Lbp - Br md 6.11 Dpth 2.71
Welded, 1 dk
(B11B2FV) Fishing Vessel
1 oil engine driving 1 FP propeller
Total Power: 625kW (850hp)
Rolls Royce
1 x 4 Stroke 625kW (850bhp)
Rolls Royce PLC-Coventry

8945476 - -
VILLAFLOR 13
Navotas Shipyard & Fishing Corp
-
Manila *Philippines*
Official number: MNLD002799
125 68 -
1975 at Manila
L reg 29.26 Br ex - Dght -
Lbp - Br md 5.85 Dpth 2.03
Welded, 1 dk
(B11B2FV) Fishing Vessel
1 oil engine driving 1 FP propeller
Total Power: 368kW (500hp)

7322782 - -
VILLAFLOR 15
ex Kinsei Maru No. 26 *-1989*
ex Fukuei Maru No. 8 *-1983*
ex Eisho Maru No. 23 *-1980*
Navotas Shipyard & Fishing Corp
-
Manila *Philippines*
Official number: MNLD001945
181 107 -
1973 Usuki Iron Works Co Ltd — Usuki OT Yd No: 882
Loa 38.44 Br ex 6.53 Dght 2.693
Lbp 34.27 Br md 6.51 Dpth 3.08
Welded, 1 dk
(B11B2FV) Fishing Vessel
1 oil engine driving 1 FP propeller
Total Power: 809kW (1,100hp)
Akasaka AH27
1 x 4 Stroke 6 Cy. 270 x 420 809kW (1100bhp)
Akasaka Tekkosho KK (Akasaka DieselLtd)-Japan

IMO / Call sign	Name / Owner	Tonnage	Class	Builder / Dimensions	Type	Machinery
9181340 *JH3457* -	**VILLAGGIO ITALIA** *ex* Reina Pelra *-2006* - - *Nagoya, Aichi* *Japan* Official number: 135637	*171* - -		**1997-07 Kanbara Zosen K.K. — Onomichi** Yd No: 495 Loa 27.70 Br ex - Dght 1.500 Lbp 24.00 Br md 6.60 Dpth 2.39 Welded, 1 dk	**(A37B2PS) Passenger Ship**	**1 oil engine** geared to sc. shaft driving 1 FP propeller Total Power: 445kW (605hp) 10.0kn M.T.U. 8V183TE92 1 x Vee 4 Stroke 8 Cy. 128 x 142 445kW (605bhp) MTU Friedrichshafen GmbH-Friedrichshafen
8910653 *LW8870* -	**VILLARINO** *ex* Sumiyoshi Maru No. 58 *-2003* *ex* Sumiyoshi Maru No. 81 *-2002* **Pesca Austral SA** - *Argentina* MMSI: 701000684 Official number: 02178	*957* - 1,005		**1989-12 Miho Zosensho K.K. — Shimizu** Yd No: 1351 Loa 70.19 (BB) Br ex - Dght 4.206 Lbp 60.10 Br md 10.60 Dpth 7.00 Welded, 1 dk	**(B11B2FV) Fishing Vessel** Ins: 1,472	**1 oil engine** with clutches & sr geared to sc. shaft driving 1 FP propeller Total Power: 1,324kW (1,800hp) Niigata 6M31AGTE 1 x 4 Stroke 6 Cy. 310 x 530 1324kW (1800bhp) Niigata Engineering Co Ltd-Japan
8911401 *EA3372* 3-GI-42194	**VILLASELAN** **D F Jacinto Gonzalez** - *Aviles* *Spain* Official number: 3-2194/	**172** 51 80		**1989-11 Astilleros Gondan SA — Castropol** Yd No: 294 Loa 27.00 Br ex 6.63 Dght 3.060 Lbp 22.90 Br md 6.50 Dpth 3.20 Welded, 1 dk	**(B11B2FV) Fishing Vessel** Ins: 100	**1 oil engine** with clutches, flexible couplings & sr geared to sc. shaft driving 1 FP propeller Total Power: 346kW (470hp) 10.0kn Poyaud UD25V12M3 1 x Vee 4 Stroke 12 Cy. 150 x 180 346kW (470bhp) Poyaud S.S.C.M.-Surgeres Fuel: 60.0 (d.f.)
7423615 *IRAA* -	**VILLASMUNDO** **Augustea Imprese Marittime e di Salvataggi SpA** - *Augusta* *Italy* MMSI: 247213500 Official number: 40	*215* 25 160	Class: RI	**1976-10 Bacino di Carenaggio S.p.A. — Trapani** Yd No: 7 Loa 31.02 Br ex 8.64 Dght 3.803 Lbp 28.02 Br md 8.62 Dpth 4.68 Welded, 1 dk	**(B32A2ST) Tug**	**1 oil engine** geared to sc. shaft driving 1 CP propeller Total Power: 1,442kW (1,961hp) MAN G8V30/45ATL 1 x 4 Stroke 8 Cy. 300 x 450 1442kW (1961bhp) Maschinenbau Augsburg Nuernberg (MAN)-Augsburg AuxGen: 3 x 96kW 440V 60Hz a.c
8857148 *OJFF* -	**VILLE** *ex* Aalto 5 *-1996* *ex* Volna 5 *-1992* **Sillanpaa Shipping Ltd Oy** OY Sillanpaa Trading Ltd *Naantali* *Finland* MMSI: 230347000 Official number: 10030	**473** 142 563	Class: BV (RS)	**1985-09 Deggendorfer Werft u. Eisenbau GmbH — Deggendorf** Yd No: 773 Converted From: Hopper-1992 Loa 51.50 Br ex 9.85 Dght 2.200 Lbp 50.00 Br md - Dpth 3.00 Welded, 1 dk	**(A31C2GD) Deck Cargo Ship** Ice Capable	**2 oil engines** driving 2 Directional propellers Total Power: 348kW (474hp) 7.5kn Deutz F12L413F 2 x Vee 4 Stroke 12 Cy. 125 x 130 each-174kW (237bhp) Kloeckner Humboldt Deutz AG-West Germany
7210630 - -	**VILLE D'ABIDJAN** *ex* Amalia *-2007* *ex* Carnival II *-2004* *ex* Lana Hana *-2000* *ex* Western Cay *-2000* *ex* Unitedgeo II *-1972* - -	**195** 132 -		**1966 Mangone Shipbuilding Co. — Houston, Tx** Yd No: 72 Converted From: Offshore Supply Ship Loa - Br ex 8.54 Dght 3.150 Lbp 35.13 Br md 8.53 Dpth 3.66 Welded, 1 dk	**(B31A2SR) Research Survey Vessel**	**2 oil engines** driving 2 FP propellers Total Power: 1,030kW (1,400hp) G.M. (Detroit Diesel) 16V-71 2 x Vee 2 Stroke 16 Cy. 108 x 127 each-515kW (700bhp) General Motors Detroit DieselAllison Divn-USA
9096624 *FMIC* ST 924880	**VILLE D'AGDE IV** **Fortassier** - *Sete* *France* Official number: 924880	**299** - -		**2005-01 Chantier Naval Martinez — Saint-Cyprien** Loa 40.00 (BB) Br ex - Dght 3.560 Lbp - Br md 9.00 Dpth - Bonded, 1 dk	**(B11B2FV) Fishing Vessel** Hull Material: Reinforced Plastic Ins: 182	**1 oil engine** driving 1 Propeller Total Power: 858kW (1,167hp) 17.0kn Mitsubishi 1 x 4 Stroke 858kW (1167bhp) Mitsubishi Heavy Industries Ltd-Japan Thrusters: 1 Thwart. FP thruster (f)
9125607 *C4ZS2* -	**VILLE D'AQUARIUS** *ex* Lykes Tiger *-2003* *ex* Ville d'Aquarius *-2002* **Global Ship Lease 2 Ltd** CMA CGM SA (The French Line) *Limassol* *Cyprus* MMSI: 210949000	**40,465** 22,910 49,229 T/cm 70.1	Class: BV (GL)	**1996-12 Daewoo Heavy Industries Ltd — Geoje** Yd No: 4043 Loa 259.35 (BB) Br ex - Dght 12.244 Lbp 259.00 Br md 32.20 Dpth 19.00 Welded, 1 dk	**(A33A2CC) Container Ship (Fully Cellular)** TEU 3961 incl 150 ref C. 14 Ha:	**1 oil engine** driving 1 FP propeller Total Power: 32,423kW (44,082hp) 24.0kn Sulzer 8RTA84C 1 x 2 Stroke 8 Cy. 840 x 2400 32423kW (44082bhp) Korea Heavy Industries & ConstrCo Ltd (HANJUNG)-South Korea AuxGen: 3 x 1175kW 440/220V 60Hz a.c Thrusters: 1 Thwart. CP thruster (f)
9270842 *FZCE* -	**VILLE DE BORDEAUX** **Seaplane One SAS** Louis Dreyfus Armateurs SAS *Bordeaux* *France* MMSI: 228084000 Official number: 904459	**21,528** 5,382 5,291	Class: BV	**2004-04 Jinling Shipyard — Nanjing JS** Yd No: 02-0401 Loa 154.15 (BB) Br ex - Dght 6.600 Lbp 138.00 Br md 24.00 Dpth 21.85 Welded, 2 dks	**(A35A2RR) Ro-Ro Cargo Ship** Passengers: driver berths: 12 Stern door/ramp (a) Len: 22.00 Wid: 14.00 Swl: 220 Lane-Len: 2160	**2 oil engines** sr geared to sc. shafts driving 2 CP propellers Total Power: 16,800kW (22,842hp) 21.0kn MaK 9M43 2 x 4 Stroke 9 Cy. 430 x 610 each-8400kW (11421bhp) Caterpillar Motoren GmbH & Co. KG-Germany AuxGen: 2 x 1500kW a.c, 2 x 1400kW a.c Thrusters: 2 Tunnel thruster (f) Fuel: 252.8 (d.f.) 952.9 (r.f.)
8822909 - -	**VILLE DE CANNES** *ex* Georges Cadoudal *-1990* - - -	*337* 212 -	Class: (BV)	**1985 Chantier J Chauvet — Paimboeuf** Loa 35.53 Br ex 8.98 Dght 1.390 Lbp 30.24 Br md - Dpth 3.15 Welded, 2 dks	**(B34J2SD) Crew Boat**	**2 oil engines** driving 2 FP propellers Total Power: 380kW (516hp) 10.0kn Volvo Penta 2 x 4 Stroke each-190kW (258bhp) AB Volvo Penta-Sweden AuxGen: 2 x 72kW 380V a.c Fuel: 13.0 (d.f.)
6509589 *5TAA* NDB 315	**VILLE DE CHINGUETTI No. 1** *ex* Inase Maru No. 1 *-1980* **Parimco SA** - *Nouadhibou* *Mauritania*	*285* 107 -	Class: (KR)	**1964 Nichiro Zosen K.K. — Hakodate** Yd No: 166 Loa 45.62 Br ex 7.90 Dght 3.404 Lbp 39.60 Br md 7.85 Dpth 3.87 Welded, 1 dk	**(B11A2FS) Stern Trawler** Ins: 311 2 Ha: 2 (1.4 x 1.4)ER	**1 oil engine** driving 1 FP propeller Total Power: 736kW (1,001hp) 11.0kn Niigata 1 x 4 Stroke 6 Cy. 350 x 500 736kW (1001bhp) Niigata Engineering Co Ltd-Japan
9153678 *C6WS8* -	**VILLE DE DUBAI** *ex* Ilona *-1997* **K/S Silver Valley** CMA CGM SA (The French Line) *Nassau* *Bahamas* MMSI: 311006000 Official number: 8001453	**9,068** 4,186 11,116	Class: AB (GL)	**1996-12 Qingshan Shipyard — Wuhan HB** Yd No: QSJ95-01 Loa 132.00 (BB) Br ex - Dght 8.686 Lbp - Br md 22.80 Dpth 11.20 Welded, 1 dk	**(A31A2GX) General Cargo Ship** Double Bottom Entire Compartment Length Grain: 14,059 TEU 847 C Ho 279 TEU C Dk 568 TEU incl 50 ref C. 6 Ha: 6 (12.7 x 20.4)ER Cranes: 2x35t Ice Capable	**1 oil engine** reduction geared to sc. shaft driving 1 CP propeller Total Power: 8,400kW (11,421hp) 17.5kn MAN 8L48/60 1 x 4 Stroke 8 Cy. 480 x 600 8400kW (11421bhp) MAN B&W Diesel AG-Augsburg AuxGen: 1 x 600kW 220/380V 50Hz a.c, 2 x 500kW 220/380V 50Hz a.c, 1 x 248kW 220/380V 50Hz a.c Thrusters: 1 Thwart. FP thruster (f) Fuel: 961.0 (r.f.)
7209356 - -	**VILLE DE SIMA** *ex* Armor *-2011* *ex* Ar Vro *-2010* *ex* Trident I *-1987* *ex* Belle de Dinard *-1986* *ex* Karmsund *-1976* **Mohamed Djaanfari & Mohamed Anriffa**	*195* 109 -	Class: (BV) (NV)	**1972 Westermoen Hydrofoil AS — Mandal** Yd No: 22 Loa 26.67 Br ex 9.02 Dght 1.201 Lbp 24.62 Br md 9.01 Dpth 2.77 Welded, 1 dk	**(A37B2PS) Passenger Ship** Hull Material: Aluminium Alloy Passengers: unberthed: 140	**2 oil engines** driving 2 FP propellers Total Power: 1,618kW (2,200hp) 28.0kn M.T.U. 12V493TY60 2 x Vee 4 Stroke 12 Cy. 175 x 205 each-809kW (1100bhp) MTU Friedrichshafen GmbH-Friedrichshafen AuxGen: 1 x 10kW 220V 50Hz a.c
8001074 *CNA2258* -	**VILLE DE TANGER** *ex* Ferreira da Cunha *-1992* **Tanger Peche SA** - SatCom: Inmarsat C 424228010 *Tangier* *Morocco*	*194* 68 110	Class: (BV)	**1981-07 Estaleiros Navais do Mondego S.A. — Figueira da Foz** Yd No: 193 Loa 34.50 Br ex 7.83 Dght 3.001 Lbp 29.32 Br md 7.60 Dpth 3.61 Welded, 1 dk	**(B11A2FS) Stern Trawler**	**1 oil engine** sr geared to sc. shaft driving 1 CP propeller Total Power: 1,067kW (1,451hp) 12.5kn Alpha 10V23L-VO 1 x Vee 4 Stroke 10 Cy. 225 x 300 1067kW (1451bhp) B&W Alpha Diesel A/S-Denmark AuxGen: 1 x 80kW 220/380V a.c, 1 x 56kW 220/380V a.c
7027849 - -	**VILLE DE TUNIS** *ex* Amour des Iles XII *-1996* *ex* Bugel Eussa *-1987* **Abdelhamid Bouali** - *Tunis* *Tunisia*	*130* 39 122	Class: (BV)	**1969 At. & Ch. C. Auroux — Arcachon** Yd No: 291 Loa 29.49 Br ex 6.23 Dght 1.880 Lbp 27.01 Br md 6.18 Dpth 3.10 Welded, 1 dk	**(A32A2GF) General Cargo/Passenger Ship** Passengers: 250 Compartments: 1 Ho, ER 1 Ha: (1.9 x 1.9) Derricks: 1x1.5t; Winches: 1	**2 oil engines** reduction geared to sc. shafts driving 2 FP propellers Total Power: 1,874kW (2,548hp) 16.8kn Baudouin 2 x Vee 4 Stroke each-937kW (1274bhp) (new engine 1986) Societe des Moteurs Baudouin SA-France AuxGen: 2 x 15kW 220/380V 50Hz a.c
9125619 *C4ZZ2* -	**VILLE D'ORION** *ex* ANL California *-2003* *ex* Ville d'Orion *-2003* **Global Ship Lease 1 Ltd** CMA CGM SA (The French Line) *Limassol* *Cyprus* MMSI: 212817000	**40,465** 22,910 49,208 T/cm 70.1	Class: BV (GL)	**1997-01 Daewoo Heavy Industries Ltd — Geoje** Yd No: 4044 Loa 259.35 (BB) Br ex - Dght 12.000 Lbp 244.00 Br md 32.20 Dpth 19.00 Welded, 1 dk	**(A33A2CC) Container Ship (Fully Cellular)** TEU 3961 incl 150 ref C. 14 Ha:	**1 oil engine** driving 1 FP propeller Total Power: 32,423kW (44,082hp) 23.7kn Sulzer 8RTA84C 1 x 2 Stroke 8 Cy. 840 x 2400 32423kW (44082bhp) Korea Heavy Industries & ConstrCo Ltd (HANJUNG)-South Korea AuxGen: 3 x 1175kW 440/220V 60Hz a.c Thrusters: 1 Thwart. CP thruster (f)

IMO / Call sign	Ship / Owner	Tonnage	Class	Builder / Dimensions	Type	Machinery
9534664 *8QGW* -	**VILLINGILI ALAKA** **Addu Investments Pvt Ltd** Aberdeen Marina Club Ltd *Male* *Maldives* Official number: 408-10-T	**288** 86 -	Class: (BV)	**2008-08 Marine Expert (Zhaoqing) Xijiang Shipyard Co Ltd — Zhaoqing GD** Yd No: MES018 Loa 34.50 Br ex - Dght 2.200 Lbp 30.80 Br md 7.50 Dpth 3.30 Welded, 1 dk	**(B34R2QY) Supply Tender**	**2 oil engines** reduction geared to sc. shafts driving 2 FP propellers Total Power: 892kW (1,212hp) 12.0kn Cummins 2 x 4 Stroke each-446kW (606bhp) Cummins Engine Co Inc-USA
9216250 *OYVY2* -	**VILLUM CLAUSEN** **Nordea Finans Sverige AB** Danske Faerger A/S SatCom: Inmarsat C 421965312 *Ronne* *Denmark (DIS)* MMSI: 219653000 Official number: A492	**6,402** 1,921 485	Class: BV (NV)	**2000-02 Austal Ships Pty Ltd — Fremantle WA** Yd No: 96 Loa 86.60 Br ex - Dght 3.200 Lbp 74.10 Br md 24.00 Dpth 7.30 Bonded, 1 dk	**(A36A2PR) Passenger/Ro-Ro Ship (Vehicles)** Hull Material: Aluminium Alloy Passengers: unberthed: 1037 Lane-Len: 837 Lane-clr ht: 4.40 Cars: 186	**2 Gas Turbs** reduction geared to sc. shafts driving 4 Water jets Total Power: 36,000kW (48,946hp) 41.0kn GE Marine LM2500 2 x Gas Turb each-18000kW (24473shp) GE Marine Engines-Cincinnati, Oh AuxGen: 4 x 370kW a.c Thrusters: 2 Thwart. FP thruster (f)
9181089 *DFGH* -	**VILM** **Land Mecklenburg-Vorpommern eV** Bitunamel Feldmann GmbH *Rostock* *Germany* MMSI: 211298240 Official number: 3796	**590** 177 680	Class: (GL)	**1999-05 Oderwerft GmbH — Eisenhuettenstadt** Yd No: 2612 Loa 48.15 Br ex - Dght 2.794 Lbp 46.25 Br md 10.20 Dpth 3.65 Welded, 1 dk	**(B34G2SE) Pollution Control Vessel** Liq: 500; Liq (Oil): 500 Ice Capable	**2 oil engines** geared to sc. shafts driving 2 Directional propellers Total Power: 894kW (1,216hp) 9.0kn Cummins KTA-19-M3 2 x 4 Stroke 6 Cy. 159 x 159 each-447kW (608bhp) Cummins Engine Co Inc-USA
6706060 - -	**VILMA** *ex* Anne Marina *-1974* **Transportes Costeiros Internacionais de Cabo Verde** -	*299* 190 620	Class: RP (BV)	**1967 Frederikshavn Vaerft og Tordok A/S — Frederikshavn** Yd No: 263 Loa 48.01 Br ex 9.22 Dght 3.350 Lbp 42.52 Br md 9.15 Dpth 3.59 Welded, 1 dk	**(A31A2GX) General Cargo Ship** Grain: 957; Bale: 822 Compartments: 1 Ho, ER 2 Ha: 2 (10.8 x 4.9)ER Derricks: 2x3t; Winches: 2	**1 oil engine** driving 1 CP propeller Total Power: 313kW (426hp) 9.5kn Alpha 405-26VO 1 x 2 Stroke 5 Cy. 260 x 400 313kW (426bhp) Alpha Diesel A/S-Denmark AuxGen: 2 x 30kW 380V 50Hz a.c Fuel: 30.5 (d.f.)
8311900 *LYAI* -	**VILNIUS SEAWAYS** *ex* Vilnius *-2011* *ex* Vilnyus *-1991* **AB DFDS Seaways** - *Klaipeda* *Lithuania* MMSI: 277093000 Official number: 619	**22,341** 6,702 9,341	Class: LR (RS) **100A1** SS 04/2013 roll on - roll off cargo and passenger ship Ice Class 1B **LMC** **CCS** Eq.Ltr: I†; Cable: 605.0/73.0 U2	**1987-10 VEB Mathias-Thesen-Werft — Wismar** Yd No: 323 Loa 190.93 (BB) Br ex 28.00 Dght 6.500 Lbp 172.66 Br md 26.01 Dpth 15.20 Welded, 1 dk	**(A36A2PT) Passenger/Ro-Ro Ship (Vehicles/Rail)** Passengers: cabins: 51; berths: 120; driver berths: 24 Stern door Len: 30.00 Wid: 3.70 Swl: - Lane-Len: 1539 Lane-Wid: 3.70 Trailers: 107 Ice Capable	**4 oil engines** with flexible couplings & sr geared to sc. shafts driving 2 CP propellers Total Power: 10,592kW (14,400hp) 15.8kn S.K.L. 6VDS48/42AL-2 4 x 4 Stroke 6 Cy. 420 x 480 each-2648kW (3600bhp) VEB Schwermaschinenbau "KarlLiebknecht" (SKL)-Magdeburg AuxGen: 2 x 1500kW 380V 50Hz a.c, 3 x 1140kW 400V 50Hz a.c Boilers: 4 e (ex.g.) 10.2kgf/cm² (10.0bar), WTAuxB (o.f.) 10.2kgf/cm² (10.0bar) Thrusters: 2 Thwart. CP thruster (f); 1 Thwart. CP thruster (a) Fuel: 103.0 (d.f.) (Heating Coils) 577.0 (r.f.) 45.0pd
8227056 *UFJN* MG-1362	**VILNYUS** **Polar Research Institute of Marine Fisheries Oceanography NM Knipovich** - *Murmansk* *Russia* MMSI: 273210600 Official number: 831561	**1,409** 422 484	Class: RS	**1984 Sudostroitelnyy Zavod "Baltiya" — Klaypeda** Yd No: 362 Loa 59.03 (BB) Br ex 13.02 Dght 4.873 Lbp 52.02 Br md 13.00 Dpth 8.89 Welded, 2 dks	**(B11A2FS) Stern Trawler** Ice Capable	**1 oil engine** driving 1 FP propeller Total Power: 1,618kW (2,200hp) Skoda 6L525IIPS 1 x 4 Stroke 6 Cy. 525 x 720 1618kW (2200bhp) CKD Praha-Praha Fuel: 300.0 (d.f.)
7210551 - -	**VILTIS** *ex* Vertikalas *-1995* *ex* Vertikal *-1992* **Ivor Trading Ltd** -	**700** 210 398	Class: (RS)	**1972 Zavod "Leninskaya Kuznitsa" — Kiyev** Yd No: 1354 Loa 54.82 Br ex 9.96 Dght 4.109 Lbp 50.29 Br md - Dpth 5.03 Welded, 1 dk	**(B11A2FS) Stern Trawler** Ins: 400 Compartments: 2 Ho, ER 3 Ha: 3 (1.5 x 1.6) Derricks: 2x1.5t; Winches: 2 Ice Capable	**1 oil engine** driving 1 CP propeller Total Power: 736kW (1,001hp) 12.0kn S.K.L. 8NVD48AU 1 x 4 Stroke 8 Cy. 320 x 480 736kW (1001bhp) VEB Schwermaschinenbau "KarlLiebknecht" (SKL)-Magdeburg AuxGen: 2 x 160kW, 2 x 100kW Fuel: 200.0 (d.f.)
8901444 *UEZG* TI-2122	**VILYUCHINSKIY** **Akros Fishing Co Ltd (A/O Akros)** - SatCom: Inmarsat A 1401743 *Petropavlovsk-Kamchatskiy* *Russia* MMSI: 273843810 Official number: 903435	**1,944** 592 1,255	Class: RS (NV)	**1990-09 Sterkoder Mek. Verksted AS — Kristiansund** Yd No: 122 Loa 64.05 (BB) Br ex - Dght 5.780 Lbp 55.55 Br md 13.00 Dpth 5.95 Welded	**(B11A2FG) Factory Stern Trawler** Grain: 130; Ins: 930 Ice Capable	**1 oil engine** reduction geared to sc. shaft driving 1 CP propeller Total Power: 2,458kW (3,342hp) 14.0kn Wartsila 6R32E 1 x 4 Stroke 6 Cy. 320 x 350 2458kW (3342bhp) Wartsila Diesel Oy-Finland AuxGen: 1 x 1304kW 380V 50Hz a.c, 2 x 336kW 380V 50Hz a.c Thrusters: 1 Thwart. FP thruster (f)
8408662 *T3WR* -	**VIMARU ACE** *ex* Ho Mao *-2010* *ex* Patria *-2004* *ex* Sungreen *-1991* *ex* Clipper Maestro *-1987* **Eastern Dragon Shipping Co Ltd (EDSCO) (Cong Ty Van Tai Bien Dong Long)** - *Tarawa* *Kiribati* MMSI: 529330000 Official number: K-13851030	**5,586** 3,160 8,880	Class: VR (CR) (NK)	**1985-02 Kochi Jyuko K.K. — Kochi** Yd No: 2387 Loa 115.19 (BB) Br ex - Dght 7.621 Lbp 103.99 Br md 18.61 Dpth 9.81 Welded, 1 dk	**(A21A2BC) Bulk Carrier** Grain: 10,914; Bale: 10,494 Compartments: 3 Ho, ER 3 Ha: (13.7 x 10.2) (25.5 x 10.2) (18.7 x 10.2)ER Derricks: 4x25t	**1 oil engine** sr geared to sc. shaft driving 1 FP propeller Total Power: 3,347kW (4,551hp) 12.9kn Mitsubishi 7UEC37H-II 1 x 2 Stroke 7 Cy. 370 x 880 3347kW (4551bhp) Akasaka Tekkosho KK (Akasaka DieselLtd)-Japan AuxGen: 3 x 227kW a.c
9168403 *XVYS* -	**VIMARU PEARL** *ex* El Toro *-2009* *ex* Unicorn No. 2 *-2007* **Eastern Dragon Shipping Co Ltd (EDSCO) (Cong Ty Van Tai Bien Dong Long)** - SatCom: Inmarsat C 457496310 *Haiphong* *Vietnam* MMSI: 574963000 Official number: VN-3029-VT	**5,185** 3,269 8,889 T/cm 16.4	Class: NK VR	**1997-10 Nishi Shipbuilding Co Ltd — Imabari EH** Yd No: 406 Loa 100.61 (BB) Br ex - Dght 8.144 Lbp 94.50 Br md 19.00 Dpth 10.30 Welded, 1 dk	**(A31A2GX) General Cargo Ship** Grain: 11,171; Bale: 10,331 Compartments: 2 Ho, ER 2 Ha: 2 (25.9 x 10.4)ER Derricks: 4x30t	**1 oil engine** driving 1 FP propeller Total Power: 3,884kW (5,281hp) 13.0kn B&W 6L35MC 1 x 2 Stroke 6 Cy. 350 x 1050 3884kW (5281bhp) Makita Corp-Japan AuxGen: 2 x 240kW 440V 60Hz a.c Fuel: 77.0 (d.f.) (Heating Coils) 497.0 (r.f.) 14.0pd
7942192 *USPI* -	**VIMBA** *ex* RS-300 No. 137 *-2007* **'Odessarybvod'** - *Illichevsk* *Ukraine* Official number: 802624	*163* 39 88	Class: (RS)	**1981 Astrakhanskaya Sudoverf im. "Kirova" — Astrakhan** Yd No: 137 Loa 34.01 Br ex 7.09 Dght 2.899 Lbp 29.98 Br md - Dpth 3.69 Welded, 1 dk	**(B11B2FV) Fishing Vessel** Bale: 115 Compartments: 1 Ho, ER 1 Ha: (1.6 x 1.3) Derricks: 2x2t; Winches: 2 Ice Capable	**1 oil engine** driving 1 CP propeller Total Power: 224kW (305hp) 9.5kn S.K.L. 8VD36/24-1 1 x 4 Stroke 8 Cy. 240 x 360 224kW (305bhp) VEB Schwermaschinenbau "KarlLiebknecht" (SKL)-Magdeburg
6926153 *SDLF* -	**VINA** *ex* Windia *-2006* *ex* Flensia *-1995* *ex* Eystein *-1995* *ex* Iris I *-1994* *ex* Iris *-1993* *ex* Tor Baltic *-1976* *ex* Iris *-1975* **Petersen & Sorensen Motorvaerksted A/S** - *Ljustero* *Sweden* MMSI: 265393000	**1,303** 736 2,226	Class: (GL)	**1969-07 Husumer Schiffswerft — Husum** Yd No: 1239 Loa 76.31 Br ex 11.94 Dght 4.396 Lbp 68.28 Br md 11.92 Dpth 6.41 Welded, 2 dks	**(A31A2GX) General Cargo Ship** Grain: 2,842; Bale: 2,643 TEU 72 C. 72/20' Compartments: 1 Ho, ER 1 Ha: (43.8 x 7.6)ER Ice Capable	**1 oil engine** driving 1 FP propeller Total Power: 1,103kW (1,500hp) 13.0kn Deutz RBV8M545 1 x 4 Stroke 8 Cy. 320 x 450 1103kW (1500bhp) (made 1969, fitted 2011) Kloeckner Humboldt Deutz AG-West Germany
5245227 *HQBF6* -	**VINA** *ex* Reihan *-1975* *ex* Rima *-1983* *ex* Towal *-1982* *ex* Maha *-1979* *ex* Astir *-1978* *ex* Naerebout *-1972* **Erba Maritime SAZF** - *San Lorenzo* *Honduras* Official number: L-0321593	*399* 253 935	Class: (LR) (BV) ✠ Classed LR until 31/10/80	**1957-08 N.V. Scheepswerf "Waterhuizen" J. Pattje — Waterhuizen** Yd No: 229 Loa 60.30 Br ex 9.38 Dght 3.650 Lbp 55.00 Br md 9.20 Dpth 4.07 Riveted\Welded, 1 dk	**(A31A2GX) General Cargo Ship** Grain: 1,178; Bale: 1,089 Compartments: 1 Ho, ER 2 Ha: 2 (12.8 x 4.9)ER Derricks: 2x3t; Winches: 2	**1 oil engine** driving 1 FP propeller Total Power: 460kW (625hp) 10.0kn Smit-Bolnes 305HD 1 x 2 Stroke 5 Cy. 300 x 550 460kW (625bhp) L Smit & Zoon's Scheeps &Werktuigbouw NV-Netherlands AuxGen: 2 x 10kW 110V d.c, 1 x 5kW 110V d.c Fuel: 63.0 (d.f.)

IMO / Call sign	Name, owner, flag	Tonnage	Class	Builder & dimensions	Type & capacity	Machinery
7712896 *OVJJ2* -	**VINA** *ex Mina -2010 ex Scan Mina -2006* *ex Jaxlinn -2005 ex Nordvag -2004* *ex Trans Vag -2001* **JD Crafts A/S** JD-Contractor A/S *Struer* *Denmark (DIS)* MMSI: 220474000 Official number: D4206	**2,065** 664 1,251	Class: RI (NV)	**1979-04 Loland Verft AS — Leirvik i Sogn** Yd No: 43 Loa 76.71 Br ex 14.03 Dght 4.942 Lbp 69.80 Br md 14.01 Dpth 9.43 Welded, 1 dk & S dk	**(A31B2GP) Palletised Cargo Ship** Side door/ramp (s) Cars: 50 Bale: 2,764 TEU 36 C. 36/20' Compartments: 2 Ho, ER 2 Ha: (5.4 x 4.9) (12.9 x 4.9)ER Cranes: 1x5t; Derricks: 1x75t; Winches: 1 Ice Capable	**1 oil engine** driving 1 CP propeller Total Power: 1,471kW (2,000hp) 12.0kn Wichmann 6AXA 1 x 2 Stroke 6 Cy. 300 x 450 1471kW (2000bhp) Wichmann Motorfabrikk AS-Norway AuxGen: 2 x 132kW 220V 50Hz a.c Thrusters: 1 Thwart. FP thruster (f) Fuel: 107.5 (r.f.) 7.0pd
9310965 - -	**VINABUNKER 05** *ex Guo Hui -2013* - - *Vietnam* MMSI: 574012722	**1,212** 539 1,833	Class: BV (Class contemplated) (CC)	**2004-01 Guangxi Wuzhou Shipyard — Wuzhou GX** Yd No: 2003007 Loa 54.95 Br ex - Dght 4.100 Lbp 52.10 Br md 15.00 Dpth 5.30 Welded, 1 dk	**(A12A2TC) Chemical Tanker** Double Hull Liq: 1,940 Compartments: 8 Wing Ta, ER 2 Cargo Pump (s) Manifold: Bow/CM: 16m	**2 oil engines** reduction geared to sc. shafts driving 2 FP propellers Total Power: 787kW (1,070hp) 8.0kn Cummins KTA-19-M600 2 x 4 Stroke 6 Cy. 159 x 159 each-380kW (517bhp) Chongqing Cummins Engine Co Ltd-China AuxGen: 2 x 80kW 400V a.c
8894237 - -	**VINACHIMEX 02** **Vietnam Chemicals Import Export Co (VINACHIMEX) (Cong Ty Vat Tu Xnk Hoa Chat)** - *Haiphong* *Vietnam*	**327** 184 400	Class: (VR)	**1986 Tam Bac Shipyard — Haiphong** Loa 53.80 Br ex - Dght 2.550 Lbp 48.30 Br md 7.60 Dpth 3.20 Welded, 1 dk	**(A31A2GX) General Cargo Ship** Grain: 715 Compartments: 2 Ho, ER 2 Ha: 2 (9.0 x 5.0)ER	**1 oil engine** driving 1 FP propeller Total Power: 224kW (305hp) 10.0kn S.K.L. 6NVD36-1U 1 x 4 Stroke 6 Cy. 240 x 360 224kW (305bhp) VEB Schwermaschinenbau "KarlLiebknecht" (SKL)-Magdeburg AuxGen: 2 x 30kW a.c
9573282 *3WNC* -	**VINACOMIN 01** **Vinacomin Waterway Transport JSC** - SatCom: Inmarsat C 457499010 *Haiphong* *Vietnam* MMSI: 574990000 Official number: VN-3063-VT	**1,599** 1,099 2,913	Class: VR	**2009-12 Song Ninh Co-operative — Vietnam** Yd No: THB-11-31 Loa 79.80 Br ex 12.82 Dght 4.900 Lbp 74.80 Br md 12.80 Dpth 6.08 Welded, 1 dk	**(A21A2BC) Bulk Carrier** Grain: 3,937; Bale: 3,547 Compartments: 2 Ho, ER 2 Ha: ER 2 (20.4 x 8.4)	**1 oil engine** reduction geared to sc. shaft driving 1 FP propeller Total Power: 1,080kW (1,468hp) 10.0kn Chinese Std. Type CW12V200ZC 1 x Vee 4 Stroke 12 Cy. 200 x 270 1080kW (1468bhp) Weifang Diesel Engine Factory-China AuxGen: 2 x 93kW 400V 50Hz a.c
9573294 *XVEP* -	**VINACOMIN 02** **Vinacomin Waterway Transport JSC** - SatCom: Inmarsat C 457499968 *Haiphong* *Vietnam* MMSI: 574000180 Official number: VN-3107-VT	**1,599** 1,099 2,913	Class: VR	**2010-04 Song Ninh Co-operative — Vietnam** Yd No: THB-11-32 Loa 79.80 Br ex 12.82 Dght 4.900 Lbp 74.80 Br md 12.80 Dpth 6.08 Welded, 1 dk	**(A21A2BC) Bulk Carrier** Grain: 4,058; Bale: 3,656 Compartments: 2 Ho, ER 2 Ha: ER 2 (20.4 x 8.4)	**1 oil engine** reduction geared to sc. shaft driving 1 FP propeller Total Power: 1,080kW (1,468hp) 10.0kn Chinese Std. Type CW12V200ZC 1 x Vee 4 Stroke 12 Cy. 200 x 270 1080kW (1468bhp) (made 2007) Weichai Power Co Ltd-China AuxGen: 2 x 93kW 400V a.c
9698563 *3WKU9* -	**VINACOMIN 05** *launched as Song Ninh 05 -2013* **Vietnam National Coal-Mineral Industry Holding Corp Ltd** - *Haiphong* *Vietnam* MMSI: 574001990 Official number: VN-3634-VT	**1,599** 1,032 3,097	Class: VR	**2013-10 Hoang Tien Shipbuilding Industry JSC — Truc Ninh** (Hull launched by) Yd No: S32-74 **2013-10 TKV Shipbuilding & Mechanical Co — Ha Long** (Hull completed by) Yd No: S32-74 Loa 78.63 (BB) Br ex 12.62 Dght 5.220 Lbp 73.58 Br md 12.60 Dpth 6.48 Welded, 1 dk	**(A31A2GX) General Cargo Ship**	**1 oil engine** reduction geared to sc. shafts driving 1 FP propeller Total Power: 1,080kW (1,468hp) Chinese Std. Type CW12V200ZC 1 x Vee 4 Stroke 12 Cy. 200 x 270 1080kW (1468bhp) AuxGen: 2 x 75kW 400V a.c
9581813 *3WBO9* -	**VINACOMIN HALONG** **Vinacomin Waterway Transport JSC** - SatCom: Inmarsat C 457400034 *Haiphong* *Vietnam* MMSI: 574000800 Official number: VN-3259-VT	**5,405** 2,693 7,770	Class: VR	**2011-03 TKV Shipbuilding & Mechanical Co — Ha Long** Yd No: VHX4122.04 Loa 116.50 Br ex - Dght 6.800 Lbp 107.20 Br md 17.20 Dpth 9.20 Welded, 1 dk	**(A21A2BC) Bulk Carrier** Grain: 10,413 Compartments: 3 Ho, ER 3 Ha: ER 3 (16.9 x 11.2) Cranes: 2x15t	**1 oil engine** reduction geared to sc. shaft driving 1 FP propeller Total Power: 2,574kW (3,500hp) 12.0kn Yanmar 6N330-EN 1 x 4 Stroke 6 Cy. 330 x 440 2574kW (3500bhp) Qingdao Zichai Boyang Diesel EngineCo Ltd-China AuxGen: 3 x 205kW 400V a.c Fuel: 670.0
9581772 *XVFA* -	**VINACOMIN HANOI** **Vinacomin Waterway Transport JSC** - SatCom: Inmarsat C 457499967 *Haiphong* *Vietnam* MMSI: 574000190 Official number: VN-3165-VT	**5,570** 3,140 7,764	Class: VR	**2010-06 TKV Shipbuilding & Mechanical Co — Ha Long** Yd No: VHX4122 Loa 116.50 (BB) Br ex 17.24 Dght 6.800 Lbp 107.20 Br md 17.20 Dpth 9.20 Welded, 1 dk	**(A21A2BC) Bulk Carrier** Grain: 10,413 Compartments: 3 Ho, ER 3 Ha: ER 3 (16.9 x 11.2) Cranes: 2x15t	**1 oil engine** reduction geared to sc. shaft driving 1 FP propeller Total Power: 2,574kW (3,500hp) 12.0kn Yanmar 6N330-EN 1 x 4 Stroke 6 Cy. 330 x 440 2574kW (3500bhp) Qingdao Zichai Boyang Diesel EngineCo Ltd-China AuxGen: 3 x 240kW 400V a.c Fuel: 650.0
8866539 - -	**VINAFCO 01** *ex Hoa Hong 01 -1994 ex Song Lo 10 -1990* **Vietnam Freight Forwarding Corp (VINAFCO) (Cong Ty Dich Vu Van Tai Trung Uong)** - *Haiphong* *Vietnam*	**200** 75 200	Class: (VR)	**1990 Song Lo Shipyard — Vinh Phu** Loa 40.25 Br ex - Dght 2.200 Lbp - Br md 6.20 Dpth 2.80 Welded, 1 dk	**(A31A2GX) General Cargo Ship** Grain: 242 2 Ha: 2 (9.0 x 4.0)ER	**1 oil engine** reduction geared to sc. shaft driving 1 FP propeller Total Power: 99kW (135hp) 9.0kn Skoda 6L160 1 x 4 Stroke 6 Cy. 160 x 225 99kW (135bhp) Skoda-Praha AuxGen: 1 x 16kW a.c
9124914 *3WFH* -	**VINAFCO 25** *ex Lady Star -2003 ex Uno Spirit -2000* **Vietnam Freight Forwarding Corp (VINAFCO) (Cong Ty Dich Vu Van Tai Trung Uong)** - *Haiphong* *Vietnam* MMSI: 574187177 Official number: VN-5166-VT	**4,159** 1,893 5,778	Class: VR (NK)	**1995-08 Shin Kurushima Dockyard Co. Ltd. — Akitsu** Yd No: 2856 Loa 97.49 (BB) Br ex 18.42 Dght 6.018 Lbp 89.95 Br md 18.40 Dpth 9.20 Welded, 1 dk	**(A31A2GX) General Cargo Ship** Grain: 8,690; Bale: 8,264 TEU 200 C. 200/20' (40') incl. 30 ref C. Compartments: 2 Ho, ER 2 Ha: (18.9 x 10.4) (37.8 x 10.4)ER	**1 oil engine** driving 1 FP propeller Total Power: 2,059kW (2,799hp) 12.0kn Akasaka A38 1 x 4 Stroke 6 Cy. 380 x 740 2059kW (2799bhp) Akasaka Tekkosho KK (Akasaka DieselLtd)-Japan
9509889 *XVWA* -	**VINAKANSAI 01** **Phu Hai Long JSC (Dargon JSC)** - *Haiphong* *Vietnam* MMSI: 574400000	**2,999** 1,980 5,188	Class: VR	**2008-08 Hanoi Shipyard — Hanoi** Yd No: HT-40C Loa 97.12 Br ex 15.63 Dght 6.450 Lbp 90.20 Br md 15.60 Dpth 8.10 Welded, 1 dk	**(A31A2GX) General Cargo Ship** Grain: 6,763; Bale: 6,014 Compartments: 2 Ho, ER 2 Ha: (23.1 x 9.0)ER (23.4 x 9.0) Cranes: 3x12.5t	**1 oil engine** reduction geared to sc. shaft driving 1 FP propeller Total Power: 2,000kW (2,719hp) 11.0kn Chinese Std. Type G8300ZC 1 x 4 Stroke 8 Cy. 300 x 380 2000kW (2719bhp) Ningbo CSI Power & Machinery GroupCo Ltd-China AuxGen: 3 x 180kW 400V a.c Fuel: 290.0
9405459 *3WBV9* -	**VINALINES BRAVE** *ex Nord Brave -2011* **Vietnam National Shipping Lines (VINALINES) (Tong Cong Ty Hang Hai Viet Nam)** Vinalines Shipping Co (VLC) *Haiphong* *Vietnam* MMSI: 574000840 Official number: VN-49.TT-VT	**29,965** 18,486 53,529 T/cm 55.3	Class: BV VR (LR) (NK) Classed LR until 27/1/11	**2007-07 Iwagi Zosen Co Ltd — Kamijima EH** Yd No: 259 Loa 189.90 (BB) Br ex - Dght 12.300 Lbp 182.00 Br md 32.26 Dpth 17.30 Welded, 1 dk	**(A21A2BC) Bulk Carrier** Grain: 68,927; Bale: 65,526 Compartments: 5 Ho, ER 5 Ha: ER Cranes: 4x30.5t	**1 oil engine** driving 1 FP propeller Total Power: 9,480kW (12,889hp) 15.0kn MAN-B&W 6S50MC-C 1 x 2 Stroke 6 Cy. 500 x 2000 9480kW (12889bhp) Mitsui Engineering & Shipbuilding CLtd-Japan Fuel: 2100.0
9330288 *3ETI4* -	**VINALINES DIAMOND** *ex El Lobo -2008* **Vietnam National Shipping Lines (VINALINES) (Tong Cong Ty Hang Hai Viet Nam)** Vinalines Container Shipping Co (VCSC) *Panama* *Panama* MMSI: 370569000 Official number: 3452608A	**9,957** 5,020 13,719 T/cm 28.0	Class: GL	**2007-05 Taizhou Kouan Shipbuilding Co Ltd — Taizhou JS** Yd No: KA403 Loa 147.89 (BB) Br ex 23.43 Dght 8.510 Lbp 140.30 Br md 23.25 Dpth 11.50 Welded, 1 dk	**(A33A2CC) Container Ship (Fully Cellular)** Grain: 16,067; Bale: 16,067 TEU 1118 C Ho 334 TEU C Dk 784 incl 240 ref C Compartments: 5 Ho, ER 7 Ha: 6 (12.6 x 18.0)ER (14.0 x 10.4) Cranes: 2x45t	**1 oil engine** reduction geared to sc. shaft driving 1 CP propeller Total Power: 9,730kW (13,229hp) 19.6kn MAN-B&W 7L58/64 1 x 4 Stroke 7 Cy. 580 x 640 9730kW (13229bhp) MAN B&W Diesel AG-Augsburg AuxGen: 1 x 1400kW 450V a.c, 3 x 570kW 450V a.c Thrusters: 1 Tunnel thruster (f)
9018751 *3ENB9* -	**VINALINES FORTUNA** *ex Vinalines Saigon -2009 ex Liberator -2007* *ex Ocean Orchid -2001* **Vietnam National Shipping Lines (VINALINES) (Tong Cong Ty Hang Hai Viet Nam)** VINALINES Ho Chi Minh City *Panama* *Panama* MMSI: 354273000 Official number: 3410408A	**15,867** 8,931 26,369 T/cm 37.7	Class: NK VR	**1991-11 The Hakodate Dock Co Ltd — Hakodate HK** Yd No: 744 Loa 167.20 (BB) Br ex - Dght 9.540 Lbp 160.00 Br md 26.00 Dpth 13.30 Welded, 1 dk	**(A21A2BC) Bulk Carrier** Grain: 33,768; Bale: 32,655 Compartments: 5 Ho, ER 5 Ha: (13.8 x 13.1)4 (19.2 x 13.1)ER Cranes: 4x30.5t	**1 oil engine** driving 1 FP propeller Total Power: 5,826kW (7,921hp) 14.2kn B&W 6L50MCE 1 x 2 Stroke 6 Cy. 500 x 1620 5826kW (7921bhp) Mitsui Engineering & Shipbuilding CLtd-Japan AuxGen: 2 x 692kW a.c Fuel: 1055.0 (r.f.)

9577317 *XVGE* -	**VINALINES FREEDOM** **Vietnam National Shipping Lines (VINALINES) (Tong Cong Ty Hang Hai Viet Nam)** Vinalines Shipping Co (VLC) *Haiphong* *Vietnam* MMSI: 574000160 Official number: VN-3177-VT	**8,216** 5,295 13,279	Class: NK VR	**2010-05 Ha Long Shipbuilding Co Ltd — Ha Long** Yd No: HL-20 Loa 136.40 Br ex 20.23 Dght 8.350 Lbp 126.00 Br md 20.20 Dpth 11.30 Welded, 1 dk	**(A21A2BC) Bulk Carrier** Grain: 18,601; Bale: 17,744 Compartments: 4 Ho, ER 4 Ha: (18.7 x 11.4)2 (18.4 x 11.4)ER (18.3 x 10.8) Derricks: 4x25t	**1 oil engine** driving 1 FP propeller Total Power: 3,964kW (5,389hp) 13.2kn Mitsubishi 7UEC33LSII 1 x 2 Stroke 7 Cy. 330 x 1050 3964kW (5389bhp) Akasaka Tekkosho KK (Akasaka DieselLtd)-Japan AuxGen: 2 x 355kW 450V 50Hz a.c Fuel: 710.0 (r.f.)
9337339 *3WRA* -	**VINALINES GALAXY** *ex* Lidong *-2007* **Vietnam National Shipping Lines (VINALINES) (Tong Cong Ty Hang Hai Viet Nam)** Vinalines Shipping Co (VLC) SatCom: Inmarsat C 457400210 *Haiphong* *Vietnam* MMSI: 574002000 Official number: VN-2435-TD	**30,042** 13,312 50,530 T/cm 51.9	Class: NV VR	**2007-02 SPP Shipbuilding Co Ltd — Tongyeong** Yd No: H1004 Loa 183.00 (BB) Br ex 32.23 Dght 13.020 Lbp 174.00 Br md 32.20 Dpth 19.10 Welded, 1 dk	**(A12B2TR) Chemical/Products Tanker** Double Hull (13F) Liq: 52,147; Liq (Oil): 53,547 Cargo Heating Coils Compartments: 12 Wing Ta, 2 Wing Slop Ta, ER 12 Cargo Pump (s): 12x600m³/hr Manifold: Bow/CM: 92m	**1 oil engine** driving 1 FP propeller Total Power: 9,488kW (12,900hp) 14.8kn Sulzer 7RTA48T-B 1 x 2 Stroke 7 Cy. 480 x 2000 9488kW (12900bhp) Brodosplit Tvornica Dizel Motoradoo-Croatia AuxGen: 3 x 776kW 450V a.c Fuel: 270.0 (d.f.) 1640.0 (r.f.)
9050668 *3WVX* -	**VINALINES GLOBAL** *ex* Jag Akshay *-2008* *ex* Maritime King *-2007* *ex* Maritime Omi *-2000* **Vietnam National Shipping Lines (VINALINES) (Tong Cong Ty Hang Hai Viet Nam)** VINALINES Ho Chi Minh City *Saigon* *Vietnam* MMSI: 574131000 Official number: VNSG-1886-TH	**38,479** 24,924 73,350 T/cm 65.2	Class: NK VR (NV) (IR)	**1994-01 Oshima Shipbuilding Co Ltd — Saikai NS** Yd No: 10161 Loa 225.00 (BB) Br ex - Dght 13.874 Lbp 217.00 Br md 32.26 Dpth 19.00 Welded, 1 dk	**(A21A2BC) Bulk Carrier** Grain: 88,234; Bale: 86,527 Compartments: 7 Ho, ER 7 Ha: (16.6 x 12.3)6 (16.6 x 15.4)ER Cranes: 4x30t	**1 oil engine** driving 1 FP propeller Total Power: 9,047kW (12,300hp) 14.8kn Sulzer 6RTA62 1 x 2 Stroke 6 Cy. 620 x 2150 9047kW (12300bhp) Diesel United Ltd.-Aioi AuxGen: 3 x 385kW 440V 60Hz a.c Fuel: 167.0 (d.f.) 2477.0 (r.f.)
9337303 *XVQK* -	**VINALINES GLORY** *ex* Morning *-2007* **Vietnam National Shipping Lines (VINALINES) (Tong Cong Ty Hang Hai Viet Nam)** Thome Ship Management Pte Ltd *Haiphong* *Vietnam* MMSI: 574475000 Official number: VN-27TT-TD	**30,042** 13,312 50,530 T/cm 51.9	Class: NV VR	**2006-08 SPP Shipbuilding Co Ltd — Tongyeong** Yd No: H1001 Loa 183.00 (BB) Br ex 32.24 Dght 13.017 Lbp 174.00 Br md 32.20 Dpth 19.11 Welded, 1 dk	**(A12B2TR) Chemical/Products Tanker** Double Hull (13F) Liq: 52,151; Liq (Oil): 52,151 Cargo Heating Coils Compartments: 12 Wing Ta, 2 Wing Slop Ta, ER 12 Cargo Pump (s): 12x600m³/hr Manifold: Bow/CM: 92m	**1 oil engine** driving 1 FP propeller Total Power: 8,061kW (10,960hp) 14.9kn Sulzer 7RTA48T-B 1 x 2 Stroke 7 Cy. 480 x 2000 8061kW (10960bhp) Wartsila Switzerland Ltd-Switzerland AuxGen: 3 x 900kW 440/220V 60Hz a.c Fuel: 181.0 (d.f.) 1635.0 (r.f.)
9159414 *3FNK7* -	**VINALINES GREEN** *ex* Dubai Guardian *-2009* *ex* Rubin Cygnus *-2003* **Vietnam National Shipping Lines (VINALINES) (Tong Cong Ty Hang Hai Viet Nam)** VINALINES Haiphong SatCom: Inmarsat M 635138210 *Panama* *Panama* MMSI: 351382000 Official number: 2506497CH	**25,939** 16,173 47,271 T/cm 50.7	Class: NK	**1997-09 Oshima Shipbuilding Co Ltd — Saikai NS** Yd No: 10212 Loa 185.73 (BB) Br ex - Dght 11.778 Lbp 177.00 Br md 30.95 Dpth 16.40 Welded, 1 dk	**(A21A2BC) Bulk Carrier** Grain: 59,387; Bale: 58,239 Compartments: 5 Ho, ER 5 Ha: (17.1 x 15.6)4 (19.8 x 15.6)ER Cranes: 4x30t	**1 oil engine** driving 1 FP propeller Total Power: 7,039kW (9,570hp) 14.3kn Mitsubishi 6UEC50LSII 1 x 2 Stroke 6 Cy. 500 x 1950 7039kW (9570bhp) Mitsubishi Heavy Industries Ltd-Japan AuxGen: 3 x 480kW a.c Fuel: 1558.0 (r.f.) 25.0pd
9335458 *3WQD* -	**VINALINES MIGHTY** **Vietnam National Shipping Lines (VINALINES) (Tong Cong Ty Hang Hai Viet Nam)** Vinalines Shipping Co (VLC) *Haiphong* *Vietnam* MMSI: 574473000 Official number: VN-25.TT-VT	**14,851** 7,158 22,625	Class: NK VR	**2007-07 Bach Dang Shipyard — Haiphong** Yd No: BV-03 Loa 153.20 (BB) Br ex 26.00 Dght 9.517 Lbp 143.00 Br md 26.00 Dpth 13.75 Welded, 1 dk	**(A21A2BC) Bulk Carrier** Grain: 29,157; Bale: 28,964 Compartments: 5 Ho, ER 5 Ha: (11.2 x 15.0)3 (15.0 x 15.0)ER (10.5 x 13.2) Cranes: 4x30.7t	**1 oil engine** driving 1 FP propeller Total Power: 6,230kW (8,470hp) 13.5kn Mitsubishi 7UEC45LA 1 x 2 Stroke 7 Cy. 450 x 1350 6230kW (8470bhp) Akasaka Tekkosho KK (Akasaka DieselLtd)-Japan AuxGen: 3 x 426kW a.c Fuel: 1650.0
9047013 *3WQT* -	**VINALINES OCEAN** *ex* Ambassador *-2007* *ex* Ocean Lydia *-2002* **Vietnam National Shipping Lines (VINALINES) (Tong Cong Ty Hang Hai Viet Nam)** VINALINES Ho Chi Minh City SatCom: Inmarsat C 457451710 *Saigon* *Vietnam* MMSI: 574517000 Official number: VNSG-1838-TH	**15,884** 8,992 26,465 T/cm 37.7	Class: NK VR	**1993-05 The Hakodate Dock Co Ltd — Hakodate HK** Yd No: 749 Loa 167.20 (BB) Br ex 26.03 Dght 9.500 Lbp 160.00 Br md 26.00 Dpth 13.20 Welded, 1 dk	**(A21A2BC) Bulk Carrier** Grain: 33,918; Bale: 32,682 Compartments: 5 Ho, ER 5 Ha: (13.8 x 13.1)4 (19.2 x 13.1)ER Cranes: 4x30.5t	**1 oil engine** driving 1 FP propeller Total Power: 5,737kW (7,800hp) 14.4kn Mitsubishi 6UEC52LA 1 x 2 Stroke 6 Cy. 520 x 1600 5737kW (7800bhp) Kobe Hatsudoki KK-Japan AuxGen: 3 x 400kW 450V 60Hz a.c Fuel: 148.3 (d.f.) (Part Heating Coils) 1045.5 (r.f.) 22.1pd
9167514 *3WPJ* -	**VINALINES PIONEER** *ex* Unicorn Brilliant *-2007* *ex* Tokyo Glory *-2004* *ex* Heung-A Inchon *-2001* **Vietnam National Shipping Lines (VINALINES) (Tong Cong Ty Hang Hai Viet Nam)** Vinalines Container Shipping Co (VCSC) *Haiphong* *Vietnam* MMSI: 574453000 Official number: VN-2155-VT	**6,875** 3,363 9,088	Class: NK VR	**1998-03 Shin Kochi Jyuko K.K. — Kochi** Yd No: 7101 Loa 120.84 (BB) Br ex - Dght 7.528 Lbp 111.60 Br md 20.20 Dpth 10.40 Welded, 1 dk	**(A33A2CC) Container Ship (Fully Cellular)** TEU 588 C Ho 252 TEU C Dk 336 TEU incl 100 ref C Compartments: 4 Cell Ho, ER 6 Ha: (12.6 x 10.7)5 (12.6 x 15.9)ER Cranes: 2x36t	**1 oil engine** driving 1 FP propeller Total Power: 5,590kW (7,600hp) 15.6kn B&W 8S35MC 1 x 2 Stroke 8 Cy. 350 x 1400 5590kW (7600bhp) Makita Corp-Japan AuxGen: 6 x 450kW 450V 60Hz a.c Thrusters: 1 Thwart. CP thruster (f) Fuel: 147.9 (d.f.) (Heating Coils) 680.9 (r.f.) 22.1pd
9168269 *XVRV* -	**VINALINES SKY** *ex* Adria *-2007* *ex* Star Sea Bridge *-2005* **Vietnam National Shipping Lines (VINALINES) (Tong Cong Ty Hang Hai Viet Nam)** VINALINES Haiphong *Haiphong* *Vietnam* MMSI: 574483000 Official number: VN-2398-VT	**24,953** 13,547 42,717 T/cm 48.8	Class: NK VR (GL) (BV)	**1997-10 Ishikawajima-Harima Heavy Industries Co Ltd (IHI) — Tokyo** Yd No: 3097 Loa 181.50 (BB) Br ex - Dght 11.350 Lbp 172.00 Br md 30.50 Dpth 16.40 Welded, 1 dk	**(A21A2BC) Bulk Carrier** Grain: 52,852; Bale: 52,379 Compartments: 5 Ho, ER 5 Ha: (15.2 x 12.8)4 (19.2 x 15.2)ER Cranes: 1x30t,3x27t	**1 oil engine** driving 1 FP propeller Total Power: 6,990kW (9,504hp) 15.5kn Sulzer 6RTA48T 1 x 2 Stroke 6 Cy. 480 x 2000 6990kW (9504bhp) Diesel United Ltd.-Aioi AuxGen: 3 x 570kW a.c Fuel: 1670.0
9052329 *3WXQ* -	**VINALINES STAR** *ex* Senator *-2007* *ex* Sleek Ocean *-2002* *ex* Columbia Bay *-2001* **Vietnam National Shipping Lines (VINALINES) (Tong Cong Ty Hang Hai Viet Nam)** Vinalines Shipping Co (VLC) *Saigon* *Vietnam* MMSI: 574521000 Official number: VNSG-1837-TH	**15,884** 8,992 26,456 T/cm 37.7	Class: NK VR	**1993-08 The Hakodate Dock Co Ltd — Hakodate HK** Yd No: 750 Loa 167.20 (BB) Br ex 26.03 Dght 9.524 Lbp 160.00 Br md 26.00 Dpth 13.20 Welded, 1 dk	**(A21A2BC) Bulk Carrier** Grain: 33,918; Bale: 32,682 Compartments: 5 Ho, ER 5 Ha: (13.8 x 13.1)4 (19.2 x 13.1)ER Cranes: 4x30.5t	**1 oil engine** driving 1 FP propeller Total Power: 5,737kW (7,800hp) 14.4kn Mitsubishi 6UEC52LA 1 x 2 Stroke 6 Cy. 520 x 1600 5737kW (7800bhp) Kobe Hatsudoki KK-Japan AuxGen: 3 x 400kW a.c Fuel: 1240.0 (r.f.)
9331878 *3WAM9* -	**VINALINES SUNRISE** *ex* Sunny Glory *-2010* **Vietnam National Shipping Lines (VINALINES) (Tong Cong Ty Hang Hai Viet Nam)** VINALINES Haiphong *Haiphong* *Vietnam* MMSI: 574000580 Official number: VN-40.TT-VT	**31,236** 18,504 56,057 T/cm 55.8	Class: NK VR	**2006-12 Mitsui Eng. & SB. Co. Ltd. — Tamano** Yd No: 1636 Loa 189.99 (BB) Br ex - Dght 12.570 Lbp 182.00 Br md 32.26 Dpth 17.90 Welded, 1 dk	**(A21A2BC) Bulk Carrier** Grain: 70,811; Bale: 68,083 Compartments: 5 Ho, ER 5 Ha: 4 (21.1 x 18.9)ER (17.6 x 18.9) Cranes: 4x30t	**1 oil engine** driving 1 FP propeller Total Power: 9,480kW (12,889hp) 14.5kn MAN-B&W 6S50MC-C 1 x 2 Stroke 6 Cy. 500 x 2000 9480kW (12889bhp) Mitsui Engineering & Shipbuilding CLtd-Japan Fuel: 2260.0
9140554 *3WAS9* -	**VINALINES TRADER** *ex* Beilun Seal *-2010* *ex* Torm Baltic *-2009* *ex* Navios Minerva *-2002* **Vietnam National Shipping Lines (VINALINES) (Tong Cong Ty Hang Hai Viet Nam)** SatCom: Inmarsat C 457464910 *Haiphong* *Vietnam* MMSI: 574649000 Official number: VN3319VT	**36,592** 23,057 69,614 T/cm 65.6	Class: NK VR (LR) Classed LR until 25/9/10	**1997-04 Tsuneishi Shipbuilding Co Ltd — Fukuyama HS** Yd No: 1096 Loa 225.00 (BB) Br ex 32.20 Dght 13.257 Lbp 215.00 Br md 32.20 Dpth 18.30 Welded, 1 dk	**(A21A2BC) Bulk Carrier** Grain: 81,809 Compartments: 7 Ho, ER 7 Ha: (14.3 x 12.8)6 (16.8 x 14.4)ER	**1 oil engine** driving 1 FP propeller Total Power: 8,910kW (12,114hp) 14.0kn B&W 6S60MC 1 x 2 Stroke 6 Cy. 600 x 2292 8910kW (12114bhp) Mitsui Engineering & Shipbuilding CLtd-Japan AuxGen: 2 x 400kW 450V 60Hz a.c Boilers: AuxB (Comp) 7.0kgf/cm² (6.9bar) Fuel: 186.8 (d.f.) 2746.0 (r.f.)
9472062 *3WVE* -	**VINALINES UNITY** **Vietnam National Shipping Lines (VINALINES) (Tong Cong Ty Hang Hai Viet Nam)** Vinalines Shipping Co (VLC) SatCom: Inmarsat C 457400510 *Haiphong* *Vietnam* MMSI: 574005000 Official number: VN-40.TT-VT	**14,851** 7,158 22,723	Class: NK VR	**2007-12 Bach Dang Shipyard — Haiphong** Yd No: BV-05 Loa 153.20 (BB) Br ex 26.04 Dght 9.500 Lbp 143.00 Br md 26.00 Dpth 13.75 Welded, 1 dk	**(A21A2BC) Bulk Carrier** Double Hull Grain: 29,157; Bale: 28,964 Compartments: 5 Ho, ER 5 Ha: (11.2 x 15.0)3 (15.0 x 15.0)ER (10.5 x 13.2) Cranes: 4x30.7t	**1 oil engine** driving 1 FP propeller Total Power: 6,230kW (8,470hp) 13.5kn Mitsubishi 7UEC45LA 1 x 2 Stroke 7 Cy. 450 x 1350 6230kW (8470bhp) Akasaka Tekkosho KK (Akasaka DieselLtd)-Japan AuxGen: 3 x 426kW a.c Fuel: 1650.0

8741894 *XVTA* -	**VINASHIN BACH DANG 01** **Bach Dang Shipyard (Nha May Dong Tau Bach Dang)** - *Haiphong* *Vietnam*	**138** 41 57	Class: VR	**2009-07 Bach Dang Shipyard — Haiphong** Yd No: LT-15.01 Loa 24.50 Br ex 7.22 Dght 2.200 Lbp 22.86 Br md 7.00 Dpth 3.10 Welded, 1 dk	**(B32A2ST) Tug**	**2 oil engines** reduction geared to sc. shafts driving 2 FP propellers Total Power: 736kW (1,000hp) 8.0kn Yanmar 6HYM-ETE 2 x 4 Stroke 6 Cy. 133 x 165 each-368kW (500bhp) Yanmar Diesel Engine Co Ltd-Japan AuxGen: 2 x 61kW 380V a.c Fuel: 36.0 (d.f.)
8741909 *XVBK* -	**VINASHIN BACH DANG 02** **Bach Dang Shipyard (Nha May Dong Tau Bach Dang)** - *Haiphong* *Vietnam*	**138** 41 58	Class: VR	**2009-07 Bach Dang Shipyard — Haiphong** Yd No: LT-15.02 Loa 24.50 Br ex 7.02 Dght 2.200 Lbp 22.86 Br md 7.00 Dpth 3.10 Welded, 1 dk	**(B32A2ST) Tug**	**2 oil engines** reduction geared to sc. shafts driving 2 FP propellers Total Power: 736kW (1,000hp) 8.0kn Yanmar 6HYM-ETE 2 x 4 Stroke 6 Cy. 133 x 165 each-368kW (500bhp) Yanmar Diesel Engine Co Ltd-Japan AuxGen: 2 x 61kW 380V a.c Fuel: 36.0 (d.f.)
9430583 *3WKT9* -	**VINASHIN EXPRESS 01** **Bien Dong Shipping Co Ltd (Bien Dong)** - *Haiphong* *Vietnam*	**16,174** 8,675 23,321 T/cm 37.1	Class: GL	**2013-06 Bach Dang Shipyard — Haiphong** Yd No: B-170-V/22 Loa 184.14 Br ex - Dght 9.880 Lbp 171.97 Br md 25.28 Dpth 13.50 Welded, 1 dk	**(A33A2CC) Container Ship (Fully Cellular)** TEU 1730	**1 oil engine** driving 1 FP propeller Total Power: 13,324kW (18,115hp) 19.7kn Wartsila 6RTA62U 1 x 2 Stroke 6 Cy. 620 x 2150 13324kW (18115bhp) H Cegielski Poznan SA-Poland Thrusters: 1 Tunnel thruster (f)
9379557 *3WOW* -	**VINASHIN INCO 09** *ex* Nam Viet-Alci *-2007* *ex* Hoa Phat 02-ALCI *-2007* *launched as* Hoang Giang 27 *-2006* **Vinashin Investment & Mineral JSC (VINASHIN INCO)** - SatCom: Inmarsat C 457447910 *Haiphong* *Vietnam* MMSI: 574479000 Official number: VN-2072-VT	**1,598** 1,010 3,069	Class: VR	**2006-09 Ha Long Shipbuilding Engineering JSC — Haiphong** Yd No: HN-25A-2 Loa 79.94 Br ex 12.62 Dght 5.300 Lbp 74.80 Br md 12.60 Dpth 6.48 Welded, 1 dk	**(A31A2GX) General Cargo Ship** Grain: 3,900; Bale: 3,723 Compartments: 2 Ho, ER 2 Ha: ER 2 (18.6 x 7.6) Cranes: 1x8t	**1 oil engine** reduction geared to sc. shaft driving 1 FP propeller Total Power: 1,103kW (1,500hp) 9.0kn Chinese Std. Type 8300 1 x 4 Stroke 8 Cy. 300 x 380 1103kW (1500bhp) (made 2005) Zibo Diesel Engine Factory-China
9345178 *3WLE* -	**VINASHIN INCO 36** *ex* Truong Minh Alci *-2007* *ex* Victory 08 *-2007* **Vinashin Investment & Mineral JSC (VINASHIN INCO)** - SatCom: Inmarsat C 457429211 *Haiphong* *Vietnam* MMSI: 574292000 Official number: VN-2441-VT	**2,399** 1,398 3,960	Class: VR	**2005-03 LISEMCO — Haiphong** Loa 86.20 Br ex 13.63 Dght 5.950 Lbp 80.10 Br md 13.60 Dpth 7.30 Welded, 1 dk	**(A31A2GX) General Cargo Ship** Grain: 5,098; Bale: 5,000 Compartments: 2 Ho, ER 2 Ha: (20.3 x 8.4)ER (18.6 x 8.4) Cranes: 2x8t	**1 oil engine** reduction geared to sc. shaft driving 1 FP propeller Total Power: 1,470kW (1,999hp) 11.5kn MAN-B&W 6L28/32A 1 x 4 Stroke 6 Cy. 280 x 320 1470kW (1999bhp) Zhenjiang Marine Diesel Works-China AuxGen: 2 x 150kW 400V a.c
9122332 *3WRO* -	**VINASHIN LINER 1** *ex* Pretty Ripple *-2007* **Vinashin Ocean Shipping Co Ltd** - *Haiphong* *Vietnam* MMSI: 574568000 Official number: VN-2353-VT	**4,914** 2,306 7,040 T/cm 16.6	Class: VR (NK)	**1996-04 Daedong Shipbuilding Co Ltd — Busan** Yd No: 405 Loa 112.50 (BB) Br ex - Dght 6.712 Lbp 105.20 Br md 18.20 Dpth 8.70 Welded, 1 dk	**(A33A2CC) Container Ship (Fully Cellular)** Bale: 8,214 TEU 420 C Ho 151 TEU C Dk 269 TEU incl 30 ref C. Compartments: 6 Cell Ho, ER 6 Ha: ER Ice Capable	**1 oil engine** driving 1 FP propeller Total Power: 3,354kW (4,560hp) 14.0kn B&W 6L35MC 1 x 2 Stroke 6 Cy. 350 x 1050 3354kW (4560bhp) Korea Heavy Industries & ConstrCo Ltd (HANJUNG)-South Korea
9128984 *3WTG* -	**VINASHIN LINER 2** *ex* Heung-A Seoul *-2007* **Vinashin Ocean Shipping Co Ltd** - SatCom: Inmarsat C 457400410 *Haiphong* *Vietnam* MMSI: 574004000 Official number: VN-35.TT-VT	**4,914** 2,452 7,040	Class: VR (KR)	**1996-06 Daedong Shipbuilding Co Ltd — Busan** Yd No: 408 Loa 112.50 (BB) Br ex - Dght 6.712 Lbp 105.00 Br md 18.20 Dpth 8.70 Welded, 1 dk	**(A33A2CC) Container Ship (Fully Cellular)** TEU 420 C Ho 151 TEU C Dk 269 TEU incl 30 ref C Compartments: 5 Cell Ho, ER 5 Ha: ER	**1 oil engine** driving 1 FP propeller Total Power: 3,884kW (5,281hp) 14.5kn B&W 6L35MC 1 x 2 Stroke 6 Cy. 350 x 1050 3884kW (5281bhp) Hyundai Heavy Industries Co Ltd-South Korea Thrusters: 1 Thwart. CP thruster (f)
9385568 *3WOE* -	**VINASHIN ORIENT** **Hai Duong Shipbuilding Industry JSC** - *Haiphong* *Vietnam* MMSI: 574346000 Official number: VN-2077-VT	**6,195** 2,684 8,300	Class: VR (GL)	**2006-04 Ben Kien Shipbuilding Industry Co — Haiphong** Yd No: Q-84-01 Loa 115.00 Br ex 20.83 Dght 7.100 Lbp 109.00 Br md 20.80 Dpth 9.20 Welded, 2 dks	**(A31A2GX) General Cargo Ship** Grain: 9,597 TEU 564 Compartments: 3 Ho, ER 3 Ha: ER	**1 oil engine** reduction geared to sc. shaft driving 1 CP propeller Total Power: 5,760kW (7,831hp) 16.5kn MAN-B&W 8L40/54 1 x 4 Stroke 8 Cy. 400 x 540 5760kW (7831bhp) MAN B&W Diesel AG-Augsburg AuxGen: 2 x 443kW 400V a.c Fuel: 619.0
9387061 *XVJP* -	**VINASHIN ROSE** **Vietnam Shipbuilding Industry Corp (VINASHIN)** Vinashin Ocean Shipping Co Ltd *Haiphong* *Vietnam* MMSI: 574354000	**230** 85 25	Class: VR (BV)	**2006-10 Tam Bac Shipyard — Haiphong** Loa 30.04 Br ex - Dght 1.200 Lbp 28.17 Br md 8.50 Dpth 2.79 Welded, 1 dk	**(A37B2PS) Passenger Ship** Hull Material: Aluminium Alloy	**2 oil engines** reduction geared to sc. shafts driving 2 FP propellers Total Power: 2,760kW (3,752hp) 30.0kn Cummins KTA-50-M2 2 x Vee 4 Stroke 16 Cy. 159 x 159 each-1380kW (1876bhp) Cummins Engine Co Inc-USA AuxGen: 2 x 74kW 380V a.c
9527362 - -	**VINASHIN SOUTHERN 6** *ex* Lao Deun Thaley 01 *-2012* **Cam Ranh Shipbuilding Co Ltd** - *Saigon* *Vietnam*	**14,580** 5,670 19,678	Class: VR	**2012-06 Cam Ranh Shipbuilding Industry Co — Cam Ranh** Yd No: (H170B) Loa 165.45 Br ex 25.04 Dght 7.800 Lbp 156.00 Br md 25.00 Dpth 12.00 Welded, 1 dk	**(A21A2BC) Bulk Carrier** Grain: 25,260; Bale: 28,964 Compartments: 6 Ho, ER 6 Ha: 3 (15.4 x 12.4)2 (14.7 x 12.4)ER (13.8 x 12.4) Cranes: 3x25t	**2 oil engines** reduction geared to sc. shafts driving 2 FP propellers Total Power: 4,412kW (5,998hp) 10.5kn Guangzhou 8320ZC 2 x 4 Stroke 8 Cy. 320 x 440 each-2206kW (2999bhp) Guangzhou Diesel Engine Factory CoLtd-China AuxGen: 2 x 155kW 400V a.c
9142095 *XVXF* -	**VINASHIP DIAMOND** *ex* Baltic Ranger *-2009* *ex* Pacific Bangxin *-2009* *ex* Addu Star *-2007* *ex* Glory Island *-2004* **Vinaship JSC** - *Haiphong* *Vietnam* MMSI: 574904000 Official number: VN-03TT-VT	**14,397** 8,314 24,034	Class: NK VR	**1996-11 Kanda Zosensho K.K. — Kawajiri** Yd No: 373 Loa 153.50 (BB) Br ex - Dght 9.553 Lbp 146.00 Br md 25.80 Dpth 13.30 Welded, 1 dk	**(A21A2BC) Bulk Carrier** Grain: 31,101; Bale: 30,101 Compartments: 4 Ho, ER 4 Ha: ER Cranes: 4x30t	**1 oil engine** driving 1 FP propeller Total Power: 5,296kW (7,200hp) 13.8kn Mitsubishi 6UEC45LA 1 x 2 Stroke 6 Cy. 450 x 1350 5296kW (7200bhp) Akasaka Tekkosho KK (Akasaka DieselLtd)-Japan AuxGen: 2 x 400kW 450V a.c Fuel: 982.0 (r.f.) 20.5pd
9468956 *3WSS* -	**VINASHIP GOLD** **Vinaship JSC** - *Haiphong* *Vietnam* MMSI: 574634000 Official number: VN- 2695-VT	**8,216** 5,295 13,245	Class: NK VR	**2008-04 Ha Long Shipbuilding Co Ltd — Ha Long** Yd No: HL-14 Loa 136.40 Br ex - Dght 8.365 Lbp 126.00 Br md 20.20 Dpth 11.30 Welded, 1 dk	**(A31A2GX) General Cargo Ship** Grain: 18,601; Bale: 17,744 Compartments: 4 Ho, ER 4 Ha: (18.7 x 11.4)2 (18.4 x 11.4)ER (18.3 x 10.8) Derricks: 5x25t	**1 oil engine** driving 1 FP propeller Total Power: 3,965kW (5,391hp) 13.2kn Mitsubishi 7UEC33LSII 1 x 2 Stroke 7 Cy. 330 x 1050 3965kW (5391bhp) Akasaka Tekkosho KK (Akasaka DieselLtd)-Japan AuxGen: 2 x 355kW 450V a.c Fuel: 710.0
8512865 *3EME3* -	**VINASHIP OCEAN** *ex* Cement Express *-2007* *ex* Kimolian Earth *-2006* *ex* Hafnia *-1995* **Vinaship JSC** - *Panama* *Panama* MMSI: 357202000 Official number: 3360308A	**7,110** 4,381 12,367	Class: NK VR	**1986-01 K.K. Taihei Kogyo — Akitsu** Yd No: 1825 Loa 121.80 (BB) Br ex - Dght 8.302 Lbp 116.01 Br md 20.01 Dpth 11.03 Welded, 1 dk	**(A21A2BC) Bulk Carrier** Grain: 15,052; Bale: 14,435 Compartments: 3 Ho, ER 3 Ha: (16.8 x 10.2) (28.7 x 10.2) (18.9 x 10.2)ER Derricks: 4x25.4t	**1 oil engine** driving 1 FP propeller Total Power: 3,016kW (4,101hp) 13.0kn Mitsubishi 5UEC45LA 1 x 2 Stroke 5 Cy. 450 x 1350 3016kW (4101bhp) Kobe Hatsudoki KK-Japan AuxGen: 3 x 176kW a.c Fuel: 500.0 (r.f.)
9114488 *3WLV* -	**VINASHIP PEARL** *ex* Mercury Frontier *-2009* *ex* Ocean Rose *-2004* *ex* Sea Frontier *-1999* **Vinaship JSC** - *Haiphong* *Vietnam* MMSI: 574987000 Official number: VN-3402-VT	**14,602** 8,402 24,241	Class: NK (VR)	**1996-01 The Hakodate Dock Co Ltd — Hakodate HK** Yd No: 760 Loa 157.26 (BB) Br ex - Dght 9.548 Lbp 144.99 Br md 26.00 Dpth 13.34 Welded, 1 dk	**(A21A2BC) Bulk Carrier** Grain: 30,910; Bale: 29,817 Compartments: 4 Ho, ER 4 Ha: 3 (21.6 x 13.1) (18.5 x 13.1)ER Cranes: 3x30.5t,1x25t	**1 oil engine** driving 1 FP propeller Total Power: 5,296kW (7,200hp) 15.5kn Mitsubishi 6UEC45LA 1 x 2 Stroke 6 Cy. 450 x 1350 5296kW (7200bhp) Akasaka Tekkosho KK (Akasaka DieselLtd)-Japan Fuel: 1080.0 (r.f.)

IMO / Call sign	Name / Owner	Tonnage	Class	Builder / Dimensions	Type / Cargo	Machinery
9168350 *3WZI* -	**VINASHIP SEA** *ex* Eternal Island *-2010* *ex* Alfonso *-2005* **Vinaship JSC** - *Haiphong* *Vietnam* MMSI: 574620000	**18,108** 10,015 27,841	Class: NK VR	**1998-01 Naikai Zosen Corp — Onomichi HS (Setoda Shipyard)** Yd No: 627 Loa 169.03 (BB) Br ex - Dght 9.670 Lbp 162.00 Br md 27.00 Dpth 13.80 Welded, 1 dk	**(A31A2GO) Open Hatch Cargo Ship** Grain: 36,255; Bale: 34,926 Compartments: 5 Ho, ER 5 Ha: (12.6 x 18.4)3 (20.8 x 22.8) (19.2 x 22.8)ER Cranes: 4x30t	**1 oil engine** driving 1 FP propeller Total Power: 6,546kW (8,900hp) 14.4kn B&W 5S50MC 1 x 2 Stroke 5 Cy. 500 x 1910 6546kW (8900bhp) Hitachi Zosen Corp-Japan Fuel: 1370.0
9122887 *3WCQ9* -	**VINASHIP STAR** *ex* Seven Ocean *-2011* *ex* C. S. Ocean *-2006* **Vinaship JSC** - *Haiphong* *Vietnam* MMSI: 574824000 Official number: VN-51.TT-VT	**15,438** 8,180 23,948	Class: NK VR	**1996-08 Kanda Zosensho K.K. — Kawajiri** Yd No: 370 Loa 158.50 (BB) Br ex - Dght 9.417 Lbp 151.00 Br md 25.80 Dpth 13.30 Welded, 1 dk	**(A31A2GX) General Cargo Ship** Grain: 29,463; Bale: 28,768 Compartments: 4 Ho, ER 4 Ha: (22.4 x 14.3)3 (24.0 x 20.2)ER Cranes: 4x30t	**1 oil engine** driving 1 FP propeller Total Power: 5,980kW (8,130hp) 15.2kn B&W 6L42MC 1 x 2 Stroke 6 Cy. 420 x 1360 5980kW (8130bhp) Mitsui Engineering & Shipbuilding CLtd-Japan Fuel: 1465.0 (r.f.)
9240287 *XVBM* -	**VINAWACO-TK 01** - **Government of The Socialist Republic of Vietnam (Union of Waterways Administrations Ministry of Communication & Transport)** - *Haiphong* *Vietnam* Official number: VN-1377-TK	**139** 42 134	Class: VR (NK)	**2000-10 Sing Kiong Hong Dockyard Sdn Bhd — Sibu** Yd No: 7497 Loa 23.50 Br ex 7.52 Dght 3.012 Lbp 21.58 Br md 7.30 Dpth 3.50 Welded, 1 dk	**(B32A2ST) Tug**	**2 oil engines** reduction geared to sc. shafts driving 2 FP propellers Total Power: 912kW (1,240hp) Cummins KTA-19-M3 2 x 4 Stroke 6 Cy. 159 x 159 each-456kW (620bhp) Cummins Engine Co Inc-USA AuxGen: 2 x 40kW 400V 50Hz a.c Fuel: 85.0 (d.f.)
8501335 - -	**VINAY I** - - - *Nigeria*	*139* 89 -		**1984-12 Quality Shipyards Inc — Houma LA** Yd No: 177 Loa 27.16 Br ex - Dght - Lbp - Br md - Dpth - Welded, 1 dk	**(B11A2FT) Trawler**	**1 oil engine** driving 1 FP propeller Total Power: 460kW (625hp) Caterpillar 3412PCTA 1 x Vee 4 Stroke 12 Cy. 137 x 152 460kW (625bhp) Caterpillar Tractor Co-USA
9298557 *3EEV2* -	**VINCA** - **Asahi Marine (Panama) SA** Shinyo Kaiun Co Ltd *Panama* *Panama* MMSI: 371821000 Official number: 3148706A	**30,053** 18,207 52,447 T/cm 55.5	Class: NK	**2006-03 Tsuneishi Heavy Industries (Cebu) Inc — Balamban** Yd No: SC-058 Loa 189.99 (BB) Br ex - Dght 12.059 Lbp 182.00 Br md 32.26 Dpth 17.00 Welded, 1 dk	**(A21A2BC) Bulk Carrier** Grain: 67,756; Bale: 65,601 Compartments: 5 Ho, ER 5 Ha: 4 (21.3 x 18.4)ER (20.4 x 18.4) Cranes: 4x30t	**1 oil engine** driving 1 FP propeller Total Power: 7,800kW (10,605hp) 14.5kn MAN-B&W 6S50MC 1 x 2 Stroke 6 Cy. 500 x 1910 7800kW (10605bhp) Kawasaki Heavy Industries Ltd-Japan Fuel: 159.0 (d.f.) 2143.0 (r.f.) 27.0pd
7217133 *WDG2188* -	**VINCENT D. TIBBETTS, JR.** *ex* Daley *-1985* **Boston Towing & Transportation Co Inc** - *New York, NY* *United States of America* MMSI: 367513050 Official number: 539033	*181* 123 -	Class: (AB)	**1972-04 Southern SB. Corp. — Slidell, La** Yd No: 96 Loa 29.27 Br ex 9.00 Dght 3.963 Lbp 28.10 Br md 8.54 Dpth 4.58 Welded, 1 dk	**(B32A2ST) Tug**	**2 oil engines** reverse reduction geared to sc. shafts driving 2 FP propellers Total Power: 2,206kW (3,000hp) EMD (Electro-Motive) 12-645-E5 2 x Vee 2 Stroke 12 Cy. 230 x 254 each-1103kW (1500bhp) General Motors Corp-USA AuxGen: 2 x 60kW 210V 60Hz a.c Fuel: 110.5 (d.f.)
8749391 - -	**VINCENT I** - **PT Pelayaran Nasional Mitra Samudera Perkasa** - *Jambi* *Indonesia*	**166** 50 -	Class: KI	**2008-01 PT Talang Duku Makmur — Jambi** Loa 25.00 Br ex - Dght - Lbp 23.32 Br md 7.50 Dpth 3.40 Welded, 1 dk	**(B32A2ST) Tug**	**2 oil engines** reduction geared to sc. shafts driving 2 Propellers Total Power: 1,766kW (2,402hp) Yanmar M220-EN 2 x 4 Stroke 6 Cy. 220 x 300 each-883kW (1201bhp) Yanmar Diesel Engine Co Ltd-Japan AuxGen: 2 x 74kW 380V a.c
9292266 *H3WJ* -	**VINCENT THOMAS BRIDGE** - **VT Bridge Maritima SA** Kawasaki Kisen Kaisha Ltd (Kawasaki Kisen KK) ('K' Line) *Panama* *Panama* MMSI: 351968000 Official number: 3051605B	**54,519** 22,921 65,023 T/cm 82.5	Class: NK	**2005-01 Hyundai Heavy Industries Co Ltd — Ulsan** Yd No: 1578 Loa 294.12 (BB) Br ex - Dght 13.520 Lbp 283.33 Br md 32.20 Dpth 21.80 Welded, 1 dk	**(A33A2CC) Container Ship (Fully Cellular)** TEU 4738 incl 400 ref C	**1 oil engine** driving 1 FP propeller Total Power: 41,129kW (55,919hp) 23.5kn MAN-B&W 8K98MC-C 1 x 2 Stroke 8 Cy. 980 x 2400 41129kW (55919bhp) Hyundai Heavy Industries Co Ltd-South Korea AuxGen: 4 x 1995kW a.c Thrusters: 1 Thwart. CP thruster (f) Fuel: 7385.0
7020334 *IRFG* -	**VINCENTE** - **Moby SpA** - *Cagliari* *Italy* Official number: 351	**223** 66 -	Class: RI	**1970 Cant. Nav. Pellegrino — Napoli** Yd No: 140 Loa 31.37 Br ex 8.64 Dght 3.836 Lbp 28.00 Br md 8.62 Dpth 4.27 Welded, 1 dk	**(B32A2ST) Tug**	**1 oil engine** reduction geared to sc. shaft driving 1 CP propeller Total Power: 1,405kW (1,910hp) 10.8kn MAN G9V30/45ATL 1 x 4 Stroke 9 Cy. 300 x 450 1405kW (1910bhp) Maschinenbau Augsburg Nuernberg (MAN)-Augsburg
7337971 - -	**VINCENTO-V** *ex* Kengarags *-2001* - -	**671** 237 470	Class: (RS)	**1973-03 Khabarovskiy Sudostroitelnyy Zavod im Kirova — Khabarovsk** Yd No: 803 Loa 55.00 Br ex 9.50 Dght 4.179 Lbp - Br md - Dpth 5.16 Welded, 1 dk	**(B12B2FC) Fish Carrier** Ins: 648 Compartments: 2 Ho, ER 2 Ha: 2 (2.9 x 2.9) Derricks: 2x3.3t,2x1.5t; Winches: 4 Ice Capable	**1 oil engine** driving 1 FP propeller Total Power: 971kW (1,320hp) 11.5kn S.K.L. 6NVD48-2U 1 x 4 Stroke 6 Cy. 320 x 480 971kW (1320bhp) VEB Schwermaschinenbau "KarlLiebknecht" (SKL)-Magdeburg
7811264 - -	**VINCENZA GIACALONE** *ex* Elvia Prima *-2001* **Pietro Giacalone E Co** - *Mazara del Vallo* *Italy*	*120* - -		**1981-06 Cant. Nav. SIMAR S.p.A. — Trapani** Yd No: 1 Loa 27.51 Br ex 6.61 Dght 2.410 Lbp 21.59 Br md 6.58 Dpth 3.13 Welded, 1 dk	**(B11A2FS) Stern Trawler**	**1 oil engine** geared to sc. shaft driving 1 FP propeller Deutz SBA12M816 1 x Vee 4 Stroke 12 Cy. 142 x 160 Kloeckner Humboldt Deutz AG-West Germany
9452933 *IFGD2* -	**VINCENZO COSENTINO** *ex* C. 19F *-2006* **Eureco Srl** - *Palermo* *Italy* MMSI: 247160300 Official number: 207	**688** 414 1,000	Class: RI	**2006-04 in Italy** Yd No: 1312 Loa 46.70 Br ex - Dght 2.450 Lbp 43.51 Br md 15.02 Dpth 3.20 Welded, 1 dk	**(A31C2GD) Deck Cargo Ship**	**2 oil engines** reduction geared to sc. shafts driving 2 Directional propellers Total Power: 765kW (1,040hp) GUASCOR F180TA-SP 2 x 4 Stroke 6 Cy. 152 x 165 each-382kW (519bhp) Gutierrez Ascunce Corp (GUASCOR)-Spain
9144732 *ICFQ* -	**VINCENZO FLORIO** - **Compagnia Italiana Di Navigazione Srl** - *Naples* *Italy* MMSI: 247441000	**31,041** 12,885 100	Class: RI	**1999-06 Cant. Navale "Ferrari" S.p.A. — La Spezia** Yd No: 225 Loa 181.68 (BB) Br ex - Dght 6.800 Lbp 166.50 Br md 26.80 Dpth 14.35 Welded, 1 dk	**(A36A2PR) Passenger/Ro-Ro Ship (Vehicles)** Passengers: unberthed: 200; cabins: 289; berths: 1000 Stern door/ramp (p. a.) Len: 11.80 Wid: 7.50 Swl: - Stern door/ramp (s. a.) Len: 11.80 Wid: 9.30 Swl: - Lane-Len: 2000 Lane-clr ht: 4.50 Cars: 608	**2 oil engines** geared to sc. shafts driving 2 CP propellers Total Power: 24,000kW (32,630hp) 23.0kn Wartsila 12V46C 2 x Vee 4 Stroke 12 Cy. 460 x 580 each-12000kW (16315bhp) Wartsila NSD Finland Oy-Finland Thrusters: 2 Thwart. FP thruster (f)
6417437 *IRBB* -	**VINCENZO IV** *ex* Lerici Primo *-1997* *ex* Schelde I *-1997* **Impresa di Costruzioni CEM Srl** - *Naples* *Italy* Official number: 10657	*113* 18 -	Class: RI (BV)	**1964 Arnhemsche Scheepsbouw Mij NV — Arnhem** Yd No: 423 Loa 27.67 Br ex 6.86 Dght 2.800 Lbp 24.62 Br md 6.30 Dpth 3.19 Welded, 1 dk	**(B32A2ST) Tug**	**1 oil engine** driving 1 FP propeller Total Power: 552kW (750hp) 11.5kn Deutz RBV6M545 1 x 4 Stroke 6 Cy. 320 x 450 552kW (750bhp) Kloeckner Humboldt Deutz AG-West Germany Fuel: 11.5 (d.f.)
9291145 *IKSR* -	**VINCENZO M** *ex* Med Salvor *-2003* **Eureco Srl** - *Naples* *Italy* MMSI: 247097100	**380** 117 -	Class: RI (BV)	**2003-04 Yilmaz Gemi Tersanesi — Karadeniz Eregli** Yd No: 11 Loa 32.07 Br ex - Dght 4.300 Lbp 29.90 Br md 10.50 Dpth 5.30 Welded, 1 dk	**(B32A2ST) Tug**	**2 oil engines** geared to sc. shafts driving 2 Directional propellers Total Power: 3,090kW (4,202hp) 11.0kn Caterpillar 3516B 2 x Vee 4 Stroke 16 Cy. 170 x 190 each-1545kW (2101bhp) Caterpillar Inc-USA AuxGen: 2 x 120kW a.c Fuel: 200.0

IMO / Call sign	Name / Owner	Tonnage	Class	Build / Dimensions	Type	Machinery
8620002 *IWSP* -	**VINCENZO MARTELLOTTA** **Whitehead Alenia Sistemi Subacquei Spa (WASS)** - *Livorno* *Italy* Official number: 9915	*381* 184 340	Class: (RI)	**1988**-12 **Cant. Nav. Picchiotti SpA — Viareggio** Yd No: 576 Loa 43.04 (BB) Br ex 7.88 Dght 3.790 Lbp 38.80 Br md 7.75 Dpth 4.15 Welded, 1 dk	**(B31A2SR) Research Survey Vessel**	**2 oil engines** with clutches, flexible couplings & sr reverse geared to sc. shafts driving 2 FP propellers Total Power: 2,590kW (3,522hp) 17.0kn Isotta Fraschini ID36SS16V 2 x Vee 4 Stroke 16 Cy. 170 x 170 each-1295kW (1761bhp) Isotta Fraschini SpA-Italy AuxGen: 2 x 200kW 380V 50Hz a.c Thrusters: 1 Thwart. CP thruster (f); 1 Thwart. CP thruster (a) Fuel: 32.0 (d.f.) 10.5pd
7512507 *IPGD* -	**VINCENZO ONORATO** **Moby SpA** - SatCom: Inmarsat C 424757930 *Cagliari* *Italy* MMSI: 247117000 Official number: 478	**387** 116 -	Class: RI	**1976**-12 **Cant. Nav. A. Giorgetti — Viareggio** Yd No: 24 Loa 35.21 Br ex 9.89 Dght 4.706 Lbp 31.42 Br md 9.85 Dpth 4.86 Welded, 1 dk	**(B32A2ST) Tug**	**2 oil engines** geared to sc. shaft driving 1 CP propeller Total Power: 3,244kW (4,410hp) MAN G9V30/45ATL 2 x 4 Stroke 9 Cy. 300 x 450 each-1622kW (2205bhp) Maschinenbau Augsburg Nuernberg (MAN)-Augsburg
7204344 *SKYV* -	**VINDHEM** *ex* Vindhem af Sundsvall *-1988* *ex* Sundet *-1984* *ex* Romo *-1983* *ex* Kalmarin *-1979* **Polena Rederi AB** - *Stockholm* *Sweden* MMSI: 265663480	**369** 151 54	Class: (BV)	**1971**-07 **Kalmar Varv AB — Kalmar** Yd No: 429 Loa 30.21 Br ex 8.46 Dght 1.804 Lbp 25.51 Br md - Dpth 4.91 Welded, 1 dk	**(A37B2PS) Passenger Ship** Passengers: 250	**2 oil engines** reduction geared to sc. shafts driving 2 FP propellers Total Power: 662kW (900hp) 13.0kn M.T.U. 6R493TY60 2 x 4 Stroke 6 Cy. 175 x 205 each-331kW (450bhp) MTU Friedrichshafen GmbH-Friedrichshafen Fuel: 7.0 (d.f.) 3.0pd
9165566 *FW3808* -	**VINDILIS** **Government of The Republic of France (Departement du Morbihan)** Compagnie Oceane *Vannes* *France* MMSI: 227003750 Official number: 911723	**1,299** 589 162	Class: BV	**1998**-03 **Con. Mec. de Normandie — Cherbourg** Yd No: 1723 Loa 48.00 Br ex - Dght 2.730 Lbp 43.70 Br md 12.50 Dpth 4.60 Welded, 1 dk	**(A36A2PR) Passenger/Ro-Ro Ship (Vehicles)** Passengers: unberthed: 462 Lorries: 3, Cars: 30	**2 oil engines** geared to sc. shafts driving 2 Directional propellers Total Power: 1,980kW (2,692hp) 12.5kn Wartsila 6L20 2 x 4 Stroke 6 Cy. 200 x 280 each-990kW (1346bhp) Wartsila NSD Finland Oy-Finland
7720398 *SFRA* -	**VINDOGA** **Waxholms Angfartygs AB** - *Vaxholm* *Sweden* MMSI: 265522520	**221** 78 40		**1978**-04 **Gotaverken Finnboda AB — Stockholm** Yd No: 401 Loa 27.51 Br ex 7.19 Dght 3.252 Lbp 26.52 Br md - Dpth 3.51 Welded, 1 dk	**(A37B2PS) Passenger Ship** Passengers: unberthed: 233	**1 oil engine** geared to sc. shaft driving 1 CP propeller Total Power: 405kW (551hp) 11.0kn Hedemora V6A/9 1 x Vee 4 Stroke 6 Cy. 185 x 210 405kW (551bhp) Hedemora Diesel AB-Sweden
9520950 *HBLL* -	**VINDONISSA** **Zenith Shipping AG** Reederei Zurich AG *Basel* *Switzerland* MMSI: 269038000 Official number: 206	**32,315** 19,458 58,110 T/cm 57.4	Class: NK	**2012**-02 **Tsuneishi Group (Zhoushan) Shipbuilding Inc — Daishan County ZJ** Yd No: SS-074 Loa 189.99 (BB) Br ex - Dght 12.826 Lbp 185.60 Br md 32.26 Dpth 18.00 Welded, 1 dk	**(A21A2BC) Bulk Carrier** Grain: 72,689; Bale: 70,122 Compartments: 5 Ho, ER 5 Ha: ER Cranes: 4x30t	**1 oil engine** driving 1 FP propeller Total Power: 8,400kW (11,421hp) 14.5kn MAN-B&W 6S50MC-C 1 x 2 Stroke 6 Cy. 500 x 2000 8400kW (11421bhp) Mitsui Engineering & Shipbuilding CLtd-Japan Fuel: 2380.0
9513191 *V7XY8* -	**VINE 1** *ex* Naftobulk VII *-2012* **Vine Shipping Inc** Wallem Commercial Services Ltd *Majuro* *Marshall Islands* MMSI: 538004603 Official number: 4603	**5,751** 3,069 8,200	Class: RI	**2009**-07 **Terme Tersanesi AS — Terme** Yd No: 1 Loa 122.20 Br ex - Dght 7.770 Lbp 114.30 Br md 16.39 Dpth 9.90 Welded, 1 dk	**(A31A2GX) General Cargo Ship**	**1 oil engine** driving 1 FP propeller Total Power: 2,620kW (3,562hp) 11.5kn Hyundai Himsen 9H25/33P 1 x 4 Stroke 9 Cy. 250 x 330 2620kW (3562bhp) Hyundai Heavy Industries Co Ltd-South Korea
9372640 *9HZK8* -	**VINE 2** *ex* Naftocement XV *-2011* **Vine Shipping Inc** Naftotrade Shipping & Commercial SA *Valletta* *Malta* MMSI: 256640000 Official number: 9372640	**9,299** 3,244 12,500	Class: RI	**2007**-06 **Selah Makina Sanayi ve Ticaret A.S. — Tuzla, Istanbul** Yd No: 48 Loa 133.93 (BB) Br ex - Dght 8.280 Lbp 122.30 Br md 20.60 Dpth 10.50 Welded, 1 dk	**(A24A2BT) Cement Carrier**	**1 oil engine** rduction geared to sc. shaft driving 1 CP propeller Total Power: 5,737kW (7,800hp) 14.5kn Wartsila 8L38B 1 x 4 Stroke 8 Cy. 380 x 475 5737kW (7800bhp) Wartsila Finland Oy-Finland
9397494 *9HBJ9* -	**VINE 3** *ex* Naftocement XVII *-2011* **Vine Shipping Inc** Naftotrade Shipping & Commercial SA *Valletta* *Malta* MMSI: 256740000 Official number: 9397494	**4,073** 1,433 5,800	Class: RI (KR)	**2007**-06 **Nantong Tongshun Shiprepair & Building Co Ltd — Nantong JS** Yd No: TS05118 Loa 102.40 (BB) Br ex - Dght 6.500 Lbp 95.00 Br md 17.00 Dpth 8.90 Welded, 1 dk	**(A24A2BT) Cement Carrier**	**1 oil engine** driving 1 FP propeller Total Power: 2,427kW (3,300hp) 12.1kn Hanshin LH41L 1 x 4 Stroke 6 Cy. 410 x 800 2427kW (3300bhp) The Hanshin Diesel Works Ltd-Japan Thrusters: 1 Tunnel thruster (f) Fuel: 100.0 (d.f.) 300.0 (r.f.) 10.0pd
9587207 *LACP7* -	**VINGA** **Mowinckel Suezmax Tankers AS** Mowinckel Ship Management AS *Bergen* *Norway (NIS)* MMSI: 257792000	**81,453** 51,377 158,982 T/cm 119.2	Class: NV	**2012**-06 **Samsung Heavy Industries Co Ltd — Geoje** Yd No: 1916 Loa 274.23 (BB) Br ex 48.04 Dght 17.000 Lbp 264.00 Br md 48.00 Dpth 23.20 Welded, 1 dk	**(A13A2TV) Crude Oil Tanker** Double Hull (13F) Liq: 167,400; Liq (Oil): 167,400 Cargo Heating Coils Compartments: 12 Wing Ta, 2 Wing Slop Ta, ER 3 Cargo Pump (s): 3x4000m³/hr Manifold: Bow/CM: 137m	**1 oil engine** driving 1 FP propeller Total Power: 18,660kW (25,370hp) 15.5kn MAN-B&W 6S70ME-C 1 x 2 Stroke 6 Cy. 700 x 2800 18660kW (25370bhp) MAN Diesel A/S-Denmark AuxGen: 3 x 900kW a.c Fuel: 130.0 (d.f.) 3400.0 (r.f.)
7393690 *CB2638* -	**VINGA** *ex* Vingaborg *-1983* **South Pacific Korp SA (SPK)** - *Valparaiso* *Chile* MMSI: 725000077 Official number: 2365	*566* 180 -	Class: (NV)	**1974**-07 **Flekkefjord Slipp & Maskinfabrikk AS AS — Flekkefjord** Yd No: 115 Loa 49.23 Br ex 9.56 Dght - Lbp 42.98 Br md 9.53 Dpth 7.32 Welded, 1 dk & S dk	**(B11A2FT) Trawler** Ice Capable	**1 oil engine** driving 1 CP propeller Total Power: 1,287kW (1,750hp) Wichmann 7AXA 1 x 2 Stroke 7 Cy. 300 x 450 1287kW (1750bhp) Wichmann Motorfabrikk AS-Norway AuxGen: 2 x 132kW 220V 50Hz a.c, 1 x 60kW 220V 50Hz a.c Thrusters: 1 Thwart. FP thruster (f); 1 Thwart. FP thruster (a)
9200158 *OZ2136* -	**VINGA SAFIR** *ex* Yaren *-2005* **Sp/f SOL Tankers** Swedia Rederi AB *Torshavn* *Faeroe Islands (Danish)* MMSI: 231141000	**1,685** 715 2,713 T/cm 8.3	Class: GL (TL)	**2000**-06 **Torlak Gemi Insaat Sanayi ve Ticaret A.S. — Tuzla** Yd No: 18 Conv to DH-2005 Loa 79.10 (BB) Br ex 12.80 Dght 5.180 Lbp 71.00 Br md 12.20 Dpth 6.20 Welded, 1 dk	**(A13B2TP) Products Tanker** Double Hull (13F) Liq: 2,618; Liq (Oil): 2,618 Cargo Heating Coils Compartments: 10 Ta, 1 Slop Ta, ER 3 Cargo Pump (s): 1x200m³/hr, 2x325m³/hr Manifold: Bow/CM: 35.5m Ice Capable	**1 oil engine** reduction geared to sc. shaft driving 1 CP propeller Total Power: 1,499kW (2,038hp) 11.5kn MaK 8M20 1 x 4 Stroke 8 Cy. 200 x 300 1499kW (2038bhp) MaK Motoren GmbH & Co. KG-Kiel AuxGen: 2 x 228kW 220/380V 50Hz a.c, 1 x 120kW 220/380V 50Hz a.c Thrusters: 1 Tunnel thruster (f)
8967395 *SLBQ* GG 173	**VINGAFJORD AV HONO** **Vingafjord Fiskeri AB** - *Hono* *Sweden* MMSI: 266068000	**113** 33 -		**2000 Tjornvarvet AB Ronnang — Ronnang** Yd No: 127 L reg 18.49 Br ex - Dght 2.710 Lbp - Br md 6.57 Dpth - Welded, 1 dk	**(B11A2FS) Stern Trawler**	**1 oil engine** driving 1 FP propeller Total Power: 552kW (750hp) Mitsubishi 1 x 552kW (750bhp) Mitsubishi Heavy Industries Ltd-Japan
9195822 *OZ2131* -	**VINGAREN** *ex* Lone Bres *-2012* **Sp/f Ackaren** Berndtssons Rederi AB *Torshavn* *Faeroes (FAS)* MMSI: 231844000	**2,876** 1,585 4,748	Class: LR ✠ **100A1** SS 09/2009 strengthened for heavy cargoes container cargoes in holds and on hatch covers Ice Class 1A (Finnish-Swedish Ice Class Rules 1985) at a draught of 6.19m Max/min draughts fwd 6.19/2.75m Max/min draughts aft 6.19/2.75m **LMC** **UMS** Eq.Ltr: 0†; Cable: 474.0/36.0 U3	**2000**-02 **B.V. Scheepswerf Damen Hoogezand — Foxhol** Yd No: 737 **2000**-02 **Santierul Naval Damen Galati S.A. — Galati** (Hull) Yd No: 942 Loa 88.94 (BB) Br ex 13.20 Dght 6.300 Lbp 84.99 Br md 13.17 Dpth 7.15 Welded, 1 dk	**(A31A2GX) General Cargo Ship** Grain: 5,717 TEU 213 C.Ho 117/20' C.Dk 96/20' Compartments: 1 Ho, ER 1 Ha: (62.5 x 11.0)ER Ice Capable	**1 oil engine** with clutches, flexible couplings & reverse reduction geared to sc. shaft driving 1 CP propeller Total Power: 2,400kW (3,263hp) 12.0kn MaK 8M25 1 x 4 Stroke 8 Cy. 255 x 400 2400kW (3263bhp) MaK Motoren GmbH & Co. KG-Kiel AuxGen: 1 x 360kW 400V 50Hz a.c, 2 x 135kW 400V 50Hz a.c Thrusters: 1 Thwart. FP thruster (f) Fuel: 35.1 (d.f.) 192.6 (d.f.) 9.5pd

6721101 *SGND* GG 690
VINGASAND *ex* Vingasand Av Fiskeback *-2011* *ex* Sette Mari *-1979* *ex* Sandettie *-1978* *ex* Ryvingen *-1975* *ex* Birgitte Engholm *-1972* *ex* Palermo *-1971*
Daniel Johansson
-
Fiskeback *Sweden*
MMSI: 265704000
234 / 72 / - Class: (BV) (NV)
1967 Kalmar Varv AB — Kalmar Yd No: 418
Loa 33.86 Br ex 7.35 Dght 3.506
Lbp 30.03 Br md 7.32 Dpth 3.66
Welded, 1 dk
(B11B2FV) Fishing Vessel
Compartments: 2 Ho, ER
3 Ha: (0.9 x 1.2)2 (1.5 x 1.2)ER
Derricks: 1x3t,2x0.3t; Winches: 1
Ice Capable
1 oil engine driving 1 CP propeller
Total Power: 809kW (1,100hp)
MWM
1 x 4 Stroke 6 Cy. 320 x 480 809kW (1100bhp)
Motoren Werke Mannheim AG (MWM)-West Germany
AuxGen: 1 x 21kW 110V d.c, 1 x 12kW 110V d.c
Fuel: 35.5 (d.f.) 2.5pd

8702757 *SCPZ* GG500
VINGASKAR AV STYRSO *ex* Saenes Jr. *-2004* *ex* Saenes *-1995*
Vingaskar Fiskeri AB
-
Styrso *Sweden*
MMSI: 266134000
253 / 68 / -
1987-10 Ronnangs Svets AB — Ronnang
Yd No: 114
Loa 24.16 Br ex - Dght -
Lbp 23.68 Br md 7.01 Dpth 3.54
Welded, 1 dk
(B11A2FS) Stern Trawler
1 oil engine geared to sc. shaft driving 1 FP propeller
Total Power: 662kW (900hp)
Caterpillar 3508B
1 x Vee 4 Stroke 8 Cy. 170 x 190 662kW (900bhp)
Caterpillar Inc-USA

8901717 *JG4912* -
VINGT ET UN
-
Vingt et Un Cruise KK
-
Tokyo *Japan*
MMSI: 431000431
Official number: 131933
1,717 / - / 351
1989-09 Mitsubishi Heavy Industries Ltd. — Shimonoseki Yd No: 933
Loa 64.83 Br ex 13.02 Dght 3.000
Lbp 55.00 Br md 13.00 Dpth 4.70
Welded
(A37B2PS) Passenger Ship
Passengers: 690
2 oil engines with clutches, flexible couplings & sr geared to sc. shafts driving 2 CP propellers
Total Power: 882kW (1,200hp) 11.5kn
Yanmar S165L-ET
2 x 4 Stroke 6 Cy. 165 x 210 each-441kW (600bhp)
Yanmar Diesel Engine Co Ltd-Japan
AuxGen: 3 x 360kW 450V a.c
Thrusters: 1 Thwart. CP thruster (f)

9616814 *LCNQ* -
VINGTOR
-
Norled AS
-
Stavanger *Norway*
MMSI: 257151900
457 / 152 / 40 Class: NV
2012-04 Oma Baatbyggeri AS — Stord Yd No: 530
Loa 35.15 Br ex - Dght 1.600
Lbp 32.75 Br md 10.60 Dpth 3.65
Welded, 1 dk
(A37B2PS) Passenger Ship
Hull Material: Aluminium Alloy
Passengers: unberthed: 290
4 oil engines reduction geared to sc. shafts driving 4 Water jets
Total Power: 3,236kW (4,400hp) 34.0kn
M.T.U. 10V2000M72
4 x Vee 4 Stroke 10 Cy. 135 x 156 each-809kW (1100bhp)
MTU Friedrichshafen GmbH-Friedrichshafen
AuxGen: 2 x a.c

9581801 *3WAA* -
VINH 02
-
Nghe An Vinashin Transport Shipbuilding Industry JSC (NAVISHINCO)
-
Haiphong *Vietnam*
MMSI: 574000590
2,976 / 1,837 / 5,466 Class: VR
2010-09 Cat Tuong Shipyard — Truc Ninh Yd No: HP714.03
Loa 92.85 Br ex 15.32 Dght 6.450
Lbp 84.95 Br md 15.30 Dpth 7.90
Welded, 1 dk
(A21A2BC) Bulk Carrier
Grain: 6,645; Bale: 5,986
Compartments: 2 Ho, ER
2 Ha: ER 2 (20.3 x 9.4)
1 oil engine reduction geared to sc. shaft driving 1 FP propeller
Total Power: 1,765kW (2,400hp) 12.0kn
Chinese Std. Type G8300ZC
1 x 4 Stroke 8 Cy. 300 x 380 1765kW (2400bhp)
Ningbo CSI Power & Machinery GroupCo Ltd-China
AuxGen: 2 x 170kW 400V a.c

9251236 *XVEK* -
VINH AN
-
Vietnam Ocean Shipping JSC (VOSCO) (Cong Ty Co Phan Van Tai Bien Viet Nam)
-
Haiphong *Vietnam*
MMSI: 574182172
Official number: VN-2465-VT
4,089 / 2,448 / 6,665 Class: NK VR
2001-11 Bach Dang Shipyard — Haiphong Yd No: 203
Loa 102.79 (BB) Br ex - Dght 6.957
Lbp 94.54 Br md 17.00 Dpth 8.80
Welded, 1 dk
(A31A2GX) General Cargo Ship
Grain: 8,807; Bale: 8,356
Compartments: 2 Ho, ER
2 Ha: (25.4 x 10.9) (25.9 x 10.9)ER
Derricks: 4x15t
1 oil engine driving 1 FP propeller
Total Power: 2,648kW (3,600hp) 12.4kn
Hanshin LH41LA
1 x 4 Stroke 6 Cy. 410 x 800 2648kW (3600bhp)
The Hanshin Diesel Works Ltd-Japan
AuxGen: 2 x 265kW a.c
Fuel: 69.0 (d.f.) (Heating Coils) 340.0 (r.f.) 9.5pd

8915172 *XVFM* -
VINH HOA *ex* Asian Saffron *-2002* *ex* Asian Lilac *-1998* *ex* Sun Glory *-1998* *ex* Sound Royal *-1995* *ex* Southern Cross *-1991*
Vietnam Ocean Shipping JSC (VOSCO) (Cong Ty Co Phan Van Tai Bien Viet Nam)
SatCom: Inmarsat B 335713810
Haiphong *Vietnam*
MMSI: 574200000
Official number: VN-1501-VT
5,506 / 2,273 / 7,371 Class: VR (NK)
1989-09 Nishi Shipbuilding Co Ltd — Imabari EH Yd No: 355
Loa 97.13 (BB) Br ex 18.02 Dght 7.864
Lbp 89.95 Br md 18.00 Dpth 13.00
Welded, 2 dks
(A31A2GX) General Cargo Ship
Grain: 12,821; Bale: 11,896
Compartments: 2 Ho, ER
2 Ha: (19.8 x 10.2) (26.0 x 10.2)ER
Cranes: 4x25t
1 oil engine driving 1 FP propeller
Total Power: 2,427kW (3,300hp) 12.0kn
Hanshin 6EL40
1 x 4 Stroke 6 Cy. 400 x 800 2427kW (3300bhp)
The Hanshin Diesel Works Ltd-Japan
AuxGen: 3 x 148kW a.c
Fuel: 735.0 (r.f.)

9276212 *XVFL* -
VINH HUNG
-
Vietnam Ocean Shipping JSC (VOSCO) (Cong Ty Co Phan Van Tai Bien Viet Nam)
-
Haiphong *Vietnam*
MMSI: 574206000
Official number: VN-2466-VT
4,089 / 2,488 / 6,665 Class: NK VR
2002-06 Bach Dang Shipyard — Haiphong Yd No: 204
Loa 102.79 Br ex 17.02 Dght 6.957
Lbp 94.50 Br md 17.00 Dpth 8.80
Welded, 1 dk
(A31A2GX) General Cargo Ship
Grain: 8,807; Bale: 8,356
Compartments: 2 Ho, ER
2 Ha: (25.4 x 10.9) (25.9 x 10.9)ER
Derricks: 4x15t
1 oil engine driving 1 FP propeller
Total Power: 2,648kW (3,600hp) 12.4kn
Hanshin LH41LA
1 x 4 Stroke 6 Cy. 410 x 800 2648kW (3600bhp)
The Hanshin Diesel Works Ltd-Japan
AuxGen: 2 x 265kW a.c
Fuel: 69.0 (d.f.) (Heating Coils) 340.0 (r.f.) 9.5pd

9647332 *3WDB9* -
VINH KHANG 01
-
Vinh Khang Service Trading Co Ltd
-
Saigon *Vietnam*
211 / 63 / 176 Class: VR
2011-05 Duc Tai Thinh Co Ltd — Nhon Trach Yd No: TKC45-08E
Loa 27.99 Br ex 8.00 Dght 2.900
Lbp 24.70 Br md 7.80 Dpth 3.80
Welded, 1 dk
(B32A2ST) Tug
2 oil engines reduction geared to sc. shafts driving 2 FP propellers
Total Power: 2,238kW (3,042hp)
Cummins KTA-38-M2
2 x Vee 4 Stroke 12 Cy. 159 x 159 each-1119kW (1521bhp)
Cummins Engine Co Inc-USA
Fuel: 80.0 (d.f.)

9693032 *3WJP9* -
VINH KHANG 02
-
Vinh Khang Service Trading Co Ltd
-
Saigon *Vietnam*
Official number: 22/2012/TT
115 / 35 / 72 Class: VR
2012-12 Falcon Shipbuilding & Repair JSC — Ho Chi Minh City
Loa 23.74 Br ex 6.70 Dght 2.500
Lbp 21.58 Br md 6.50 Dpth 3.10
Welded, 1 dk
(B32A2ST) Tug
2 oil engines reduction geared to sc. shafts driving 2 FP propellers
Total Power: 1,194kW (1,624hp)
Cummins QSK19-M
2 x 4 Stroke 6 Cy. 159 x 159 each-597kW (812bhp)
Cummins Engine Co Inc-USA
AuxGen: 2 x 20kW 380V a.c

8613126 *3WDR* -
VINH PHUOC *ex* Kumul Queen *-1990*
Vietnam Ocean Shipping JSC (VOSCO) (Cong Ty Co Phan Van Tai Bien Viet Nam)
-
SatCom: Inmarsat C 457401310
Haiphong *Vietnam*
MMSI: 574013003
Official number: VN-2467-VT
7,166 / 3,322 / 12,307 Class: VR (NK)
1988-01 Shin Kurushima Dockyard Co. Ltd. — Akitsu Yd No: 1917
Loa 121.80 (BB) Br ex - Dght 8.308
Lbp 116.01 Br md 20.01 Dpth 11.03
Welded, 1 dk
(A21A2BC) Bulk Carrier
Grain: 15,127; Bale: 14,639
Compartments: 3 Ho, ER
3 Ha: ER
Derricks: 4x25t
1 oil engine driving 1 FP propeller
Total Power: 3,016kW (4,101hp) 13.2kn
Mitsubishi 5UEC45LA
1 x 2 Stroke 5 Cy. 450 x 1350 3016kW (4101bhp)
Kobe Hatsudoki KK-Japan
AuxGen: 3 x 176kW a.c
Fuel: 580.0 (r.f.)

9223007 *3WFG* -
VINH THUAN
-
Vietnam Ocean Shipping JSC (VOSCO) (Cong Ty Co Phan Van Tai Bien Viet Nam)
-
Haiphong *Vietnam*
MMSI: 574144134
Official number: VN-2474-VT
4,143 / 2,504 / 6,592 Class: NK VR
1999-12 Bach Dang Shipyard — Haiphong Yd No: 202
Loa 102.79 Br ex 17.03 Dght 6.957
Lbp 94.50 Br md 17.00 Dpth 8.80
Welded, 1 dk
(A31A2GX) General Cargo Ship
Grain: 8,807; Bale: 8,356
Compartments: 2 Ho, ER
1 Ha: (23.4 x 10.9)ER
Derricks: 4x15t
1 oil engine driving 1 FP propeller
Total Power: 2,648kW (3,600hp) 12.5kn
Hanshin LH41LA
1 x 4 Stroke 6 Cy. 410 x 800 2648kW (3600bhp)
The Hanshin Diesel Works Ltd-Japan
AuxGen: 1 x 260kW a.c
Fuel: 80.0 (d.f.) 372.0 (r.f.)

9608532 - -
VINH THUAN 09
-
Ngoc Anh Shipping JSC
-
Haiphong *Vietnam*
MMSI: 574012585
1,599 / 1,014 / 3,221 Class: VR
2010-12 Duc Manh Co Ltd — Kinh Mon Yd No: S07-008.07
Loa 78.60 Br ex 12.62 Dght 5.350
Lbp 73.60 Br md 12.60 Dpth 6.48
Welded, 1 dk
(A31A2GX) General Cargo Ship
Bale: 3,381
Compartments: 2 Ho, ER
2 Ha: (19.2 x 8.4)ER (19.8 x 8.4)
1 oil engine geared to sc. shaft driving 1 FP propeller
Total Power: 441kW (600hp) 10.0kn
Chinese Std. Type 6300ZC
1 x 4 Stroke 6 Cy. 300 x 380 441kW (600bhp)
Ningbo CSI Power & Machinery GroupCo Ltd-China
AuxGen: 2 x 84kW 400V a.c

8937601 *FOBL* -
VINI VINI VI
-
Ching Francis
-
Papeete *France*
MMSI: 227124700
154 / - / - Class: (BV)
1997 Chantier Naval du Pacifique Sud (CNPS) — Papeete Yd No: 953
Loa - Br ex - Dght 3.250
Lbp 24.80 Br md 7.40 Dpth 3.96
Welded, 1 dk
(B11B2FV) Fishing Vessel
1 oil engine reduction geared to sc. shaft driving 1 FP propeller
Total Power: 331kW (450hp) 10.0kn
Wartsila UD25L6M
1 x 4 Stroke 6 Cy. 150 x 180 331kW (450bhp)
Wartsila NSD France SA-France
AuxGen: 2 x 168kW 440V 60Hz a.c

ID / Call sign	Name / Owner / Flag	Tonnage	Class	Builder / Dimensions	Type	Machinery
8518170 IXWJ -	**VINICIO BARRETTA** **Impresa Fratelli Barretta Domenico e Giovanni SNC** - SatCom: Inmarsat C 424744720 *Brindisi* *Italy* MMSI: 247605000 Official number: 56	**359** 107 263	Class: RI	**1987-11 Bacino di Carenaggio S.p.A. — Trapani** Yd No: 14 Loa 33.51 Br ex 9.83 Dght 4.412 Lbp 30.08 Br md 9.81 Dpth 5.01 Welded, 1 dk	**(B32A2ST) Tug**	**1 oil engine** sr geared to sc. shafriving 1 CP propeller Total Power: 2,400kW (3,263hp) 8M453AK MaK 1 x 4 Stroke 8 Cy. 320 x 420 ?0kW (3263bhp) Krupp MaK Maschinenbau Gr-Kiel Thrusters: 1 Thwart. FP thruster
9489194 9AA7771 -	**VINJERAC** **Fontana Shipping Co Ltd** Tankerska Plovidba dd SatCom: Inmarsat C 423829610 *Zadar* *Croatia* MMSI: 238296000	**30,638** 15,218 52,554 T/cm 56.0	Class: BV CS (NV)	**2011-10 '3 Maj' Brodogradiliste dd — Rijeka** Yd No: 712 Loa 195.10 (BB) Br ex 32.24 Dght 12.500 Lbp 187.30 Br md 32.20 Dpth 17.80 Welded, 1 dk	**(A12B2TR) Chemical/Products Tanker** Double Hull (13F) Liq: 56,190; Liq (Oil): 56,190 Compartments: 12 Wing Ta, 2 Wing Slop Ta, ER 12 Cargo Pump (s): 12x550m³/hr Manifold: Bow/CM: 96.8m Ice Capable	**1 oil engine** driving 1 FP proper Total Power: 10,185kW (13,8?hp) 14.0kn Wartsila 7RTA48T 1 x 2 Stroke 7 Cy. 480 x ?0 10185kW (13848bhp) '3 Maj' Motori i Dizalice cCroatia AuxGen: 3 x 960kW 450V 6z a.c Fuel: 193.0 (d.f.) 1570.0 (r.
5116127 OICE -	**VINKERI II** *ex* Flatoy *-1973* *ex* Fjordbussen *-1954* **Nurmeksen Pikapalvelu, Matti Turunen ja Kumpp Kommandiittiyhtio** *Nurmes* *Finland* Official number: 11144	**127** 46 -		**1941-03 Kristiansands Mek. Verksted AS — Kristiansand** Yd No: 172 Loa 28.07 Br ex 5.62 Dght 1.850 Lbp 24.57 Br md 5.59 Dpth 2.01 Riveted\Welded, 1 dk	**(A37B2PS) Passenger Ship** Passengers: unberthed: 120	**2 oil engines** driving 2 FFopellers Total Power: 438kW (596 11.0kn G.M. (Detroit Diesel) 6V-92-TA 2 x Vee 2 Stroke 6 Cy23 x 127 each-219kW (298bhp) (new engine 1949) General Motors CorpSA
9216389 LAHC7 -	**VINLAND** **Ugland Shipping AS** Canship Ugland Ltd SatCom: Inmarsat C 425985110 *Grimstad* *Norway (NIS)* MMSI: 259851000	**76,567** 34,691 125,827 T/cm 112.1	Class: AB	**2000-08 Samsung Heavy Industries Co Ltd — Geoje** Yd No: 1293 Loa 271.80 (BB) Br ex 46.00 Dght 15.347 Lbp 257.80 Br md 46.00 Dpth 22.60 Welded, 1 dk	**(A13A2TS) Shuttle Tanker** Double Hull (13F) Liq: 133,870; Liq (Oil): 137,514 Cargo Heating Coils Compartments: 12 Wing Ta, 2 Wing Slop Ta, ER 8 Cargo Pump (s): 4x4000m³/hr, 4x1000m³/hr Manifold: Bow/CM: 134m Ice Capable	**2 oil engines** driving 2P propellers Total Power: 19,978k(27,162hp) 14.6kn MAN-B&W 7S50MC 2 x 2 Stroke 7 Cy. 0 x 1910 each-9989kW (13581bhp) HSD Engine Co LtSouth Korea AuxGen: 2 x 2250kW440V 60Hz a.c, 2 x 3000kW 440V 60Hz a.c Thrusters: 2 ThwarP thruster (f) Fuel: 270.0 (d.f.) 30.0 (r.f.)
9071129 - -	**VINLANDER** *ex* Jacob Heilmann II *-2004* *ex* Newfoundland Tradition *-2000* **Jacob Heilmann II Management Inc** - *St John's, NL* *Canada* MMSI: 316012240 Official number: 816224	**387** 116 -		**1992 Glovertown Shipyards Ltd — Glovertown NL** Loa - Br ex - Dght - Lbp 29.28 Br md 7.38 Dpth 6.96 Welded, 1 dk	**(B11B2FV) Fishing Vessel**	**1 oil engine** gear to sc. shaft driving 1 FP propeller Total Power: 473((643hp) 11.0kn Mitsubishi S6R2-MTK 1 x 4 Stroke 6y. 170 x 220 473kW (643bhp) Mitsubishi Hey Industries Ltd-Japan
7800100 H8RO -	**VINLANDIA** *ex* Nando *-2004* *ex* Nabeul *-1995* **Leechcroft Investments Ltd** Sicilnavi Srl *Panama* *Panama* MMSI: 353830000 Official number: 3051005C	**2,808** 1,063 3,847	Class: RI (BV)	**1979-03 Ernst Menzer-Werft — Geesthacht** Yd No: 508 Loa 103.40 (BB) Br ex 14.69 Dght 5.541 Lbp 86.72 Br md 14.51 Dpth 6.61 Welded, 1 dk	**(A12A2TC) Chemical Tanker** Liq: 3,300 Compartments: 16 Ta, ER 10 Cargo Pump (s): 10x100m³/hr Ice Capable	**1 oil engine** rerse reduction geared to sc. shaft driving 1 FP propeller Total Power: ?648kW (3,600hp) 13.8kn MaK 9M453AK 1 x 4 Stro 9 Cy. 320 x 420 2648kW (3600bhp) MaK Masinenbau GmbH-Kiel
8227068 USHY -	**VINOGRADNOYE** **Linart Ltd (OOO 'Linart')** - *Sevastopol* *Ukraine* MMSI: 272007400 Official number: 832066	**734** 220 414	Class: (RS)	**1984-01 Zavod "Leninskaya Kuznitsa" — Kiyev** Yd No: 1533 Loa 54.84 Br ex 9.96 Dght 4.111 Lbp 50.29 Br md - Dpth 5.01 Welded, 1 dk	**(B11A2FS) Stern Trawler**	**1 oil engir** driving 1 CP propeller Total Powe 736kW (1,001hp) 12.0kn S.K.L. 8NVD48A-2U 1 x 4 Soke 8 Cy. 320 x 480 736kW (1001bhp) VEB Scwermaschinenbau "KarlLiebknecht" (SKL)-agdeburg AuxGen: x 160kW Fuel: 180 (d.f.)
8228414 UHGC -	**VINOGRADOVKA** **'Moryak Rybolov' Fishing Collective (Rybkolkhoz Moryak-Rybolov)** - *Nakhodka* *Russia* MMSI: 273823400 Official number: 832920	**816** 221 332	Class: (RS)	**1984 Volgogradskiy Sudostroitelnyy Zavod — Volgograd** Yd No: 219 Loa 53.75 (BB) Br ex 10.72 Dght 4.290 Lbp 47.92 Br md 10.50 Dpth 6.02 Welded, 1 dk	**(B11A2FS) Stern Trawler** Ins: 218 Compartments: 1 Ho, ER 1 Ha: (1.6 x 1.6) Derricks: 2x1.5t Ice Capable	**1 oil enine** driving 1 CP propeller Total Pover: 971kW (1,320hp) 12.7kn S.K.L. 8NVD48A-2U 1 x 4 Stroke 8 Cy. 320 x 480 971kW (1320bhp) VEBSchwermaschinenbau "KarlLiebknecht" (SKL)-Magdeburg AuxGen: 1 x 300kW, 3 x 160kW Fuel: 184.0 (d.f.)
8923026 WDA9686 -	**VINTON CROSBY** *ex* N. Joseph Guidry *-2002* **Crosby Marine Transportation LLC** Crosby Tugs LLC *New Orleans, LA* *United States of America* MMSI: 366867850 Official number: 566645	**359** 107 -	Class: (AB)	**1975 Bobben Fabricators, Inc. — Harvey, La** Yd No: 3 Loa - Br ex - Dght 4.240 Lbp 30.33 Br md 9.44 Dpth 4.76 Welded, 1 dk	**(B32A2ST) Tug**	**2 oil engines** reverse reduction geared to sc. shafts driving 2 FP propellers Total Power: 2,206kW (3,000hp) 12.0kn Brons 12GV-H 2 x Vee 2 Stroke 12 Cy. 220 x 380 each-1103kW (1500bhp) NV Appingedammer Bronsmotorenfabrie-Netherlands AuxGen: 2 x 75kW a.c
6711479 HO8454 -	**VIOLA** *ex* Solgunn *-2002* *ex* Rost *-1997* *ex* Hilmir II *-1990* *ex* Hilmir *-1980* *ex* Fylkir *-1969* **Westship Pty Ltd** - *Panama* *Panama* Official number: 4337312	**539** 162 -	Class: (NV)	**1967-04 N.V. Scheepswerf Gebr. van der Werf — Deest** Yd No: 326 Lengthened-1972 Loa 41.71 Br ex 7.62 Dght 3.770 Lbp 39.40 Br md 7.60 Dpth 3.96 Welded, 1 dk	**(B11A2FT) Trawler** Winches: 1 Ice Capable	**1 oil engine** reduction geared to sc. shaft driving 1 CP propeller Total Power: 980kW (1,332hp) 13.5kn Alpha 10V23L-VO 1 x Vee 4 Stroke 10 Cy. 225 x 300 980kW (1332bhp) (new engine 1977) Alpha Diesel A/S-Denmark AuxGen: 1 x 332kW 220V 50Hz a.c Thrusters: 1 Thwart. FP thruster (f); 1 Tunnel thruster (a)
9403061 D5EQ6 -	**VIOLA** *ex* Furness Melbourne *-2013* **Wenaas Shipping AS** Nordic Shipping AS *Monrovia* *Liberia* MMSI: 636016135 Official number: 16135	**32,387** 19,450 58,729 T/cm 57.4	Class: AB	**2008-09 Tsuneishi Heavy Industries (Cebu) Inc — Balamban** Yd No: SC-088 Loa 190.00 (BB) Br ex - Dght 12.800 Lbp 185.60 Br md 32.26 Dpth 18.00 Welded, 1 dk	**(A21A2BC) Bulk Carrier** Grain: 72,360; Bale: 70,557 Compartments: 5 Ho, ER 5 Ha: ER Cranes: 4x30t	**1 oil engine** driving 1 FP propeller Total Power: 8,400kW (11,421hp) 14.5kn MAN-B&W 6S50MC-C 1 x 2 Stroke 6 Cy. 500 x 2000 8400kW (11421bhp) Mitsui Engineering & Shipbuilding CLtd-Japan AuxGen: 3 x 480kW a.c Fuel: 156.0 (d.f.) 1923.0 (r.f.)
9379076 V2PT4 -	**VIOLA** **Sargamassa Shipping Co Ltd** Klingenberg Bereederungs- und Befrachtungs GmbH & Co KG *Saint John's* *Antigua & Barbuda* MMSI: 305197000 Official number: 2976	**6,479** 3,300 8,152	Class: GL	**2008-04 Hangzhou Dongfeng Shipbuilding Co Ltd — Hangzhou ZJ** Yd No: 2005-04 Loa 123.17 (BB) Br ex - Dght 7.091 Lbp 114.41 Br md 20.80 Dpth 9.20 Welded, 1 dk	**(A31A2GX) General Cargo Ship** TEU 713 C Ho 204 TEU C Dk 509 TEU incl 125 ref C. Cranes: 2x45t Ice Capable	**1 oil engine** reduction geared to sc. shaft driving 1 CP propeller Total Power: 5,400kW (7,342hp) 17.0kn MaK 6M43 1 x 4 Stroke 6 Cy. 430 x 610 5400kW (7342bhp) Caterpillar Motoren GmbH & Co. KG-Germany AuxGen: 2 x 576kW 400V a.c, 1 x 740kW 400V a.c Thrusters: 1 Tunnel thruster (f)
8329957 - -	**VIOLAINE** **Dragages & Travaux Publics** *Libreville* *Gabon*	*261* 137 400	Class: (BV)	**1982 SFEDTP — Abidjan** Loa 44.38 Br ex - Dght 1.401 Lbp 38.71 Br md 10.00 Dpth 2.49 Welded, 1 dk	**(A37B2PS) Passenger Ship**	**2 oil engines** driving 2 FP propellers Total Power: 422kW (574hp) Baudouin 2 x Vee 4 Stroke 8 Cy. 150 x 150 each-211kW (287bhp) Societe des Moteurs Baudouin SA-France
9429285 SVAU5 -	**VIOLANDO** *ex* Crude Delta *-2009* **Violando 1 Special Maritime Enterprise (ENE)** Andriaki Shipping Co Ltd SatCom: Inmarsat C 424095510 *Andros* *Greece* MMSI: 240955000 Official number: 606	**84,735** 54,305 164,763 T/cm 123.2	Class: NV	**2009-09 Hyundai Samho Heavy Industries Co Ltd — Samho** Yd No: S390 Loa 274.19 (BB) Br ex 50.04 Dght 17.170 Lbp 264.00 Br md 50.00 Dpth 23.10 Welded, 1 dk	**(A13A2TV) Crude Oil Tanker** Double Hull (13F) Liq: 173,672; Liq (Oil): 173,672 Cargo Heating Coils Compartments: 12 Wing Ta, 2 Wing Slop Ta, ER 3 Cargo Pump (s): 3x4000m³/hr Manifold: Bow/CM: 136.5m	**1 oil engine** driving 1 FP propeller Total Power: 18,660kW (25,370hp) 15.5kn MAN-B&W 6S70MC-C 1 x 2 Stroke 6 Cy. 700 x 2800 18660kW (25370bhp) Hyundai Heavy Industries Co Ltd-South Korea AuxGen: 3 x 756kW a.c Fuel: 279.1 (d.f.) 4505.5 (r.f.)

9474292 **VIOLET** **4,908** Class: (BV)
9HPA9 2,229
\- **Chem-Ist Sping Ltd** 7,080
Chemmarine Shipping Ltd T/cm
SatCom: Inmarsat C 424930112 16.3
Valletta *Malta*
MMSI: 249300
Official number: 9474292

2008-09 **in** **Turkey** Yd No: 10
Loa 109.92 (BB) Br ex 17.20 Dght 7.096
Lbp 103.18 Br md 17.20 Dpth 8.80
Welded, 1 dk

(A12B2TR) Chemical/Products Tanker
Double Hull (13F)
Liq: 6,920; Liq (Oil): 6,920
Cargo Heating Coils
Compartments: 12 Wing Ta, 2 Wing Slop Ta, ER
12 Cargo Pump (s): 12x200m³/hr
Manifold: Bow/CM: 55.9m

1 oil engine reduction geared to sc. shaft driving 1 CP propeller
Total Power: 3,500kW (4,759hp) 13.5kn
MAN-B&W 7L32/40CD
1 x 4 Stroke 7 Cy. 320 x 400 3500kW (4759bhp)
STX Engine Co Ltd-South Korea
AuxGen: 3 x 590kW 440V 60Hz a.c, 1 x 1200kW 440V 60Hz a.c
Thrusters: 1 Tunnel thruster (f)
Fuel: 80.0 (d.f.) 460.0 (r.f.)

9314935 **VIOLET** **28,927** Class: GL (BV)
VRCP8 *ex CMA CGM Vi -2012* 15,033
\- **Resplendent Sp Ltd** 39,155
Univan Ship Manement Ltd T/cm
Hong Kong *Hong Kong* 56.7
MMSI: 47779160
Official number: HK1861

2006-01 **Hyundai Mipo Dockyard Co Ltd — Ulsan** Yd No: 0421
Loa 222.15 (BB) Br ex - Dght 12.000
Lbp 210.00 Br md 30.00 Dpth 16.80
Welded, 1 dk

(A33A2CC) Container Ship (Fully Cellular)
TEU 2824 C Ho 1026 TEU C Dk 1798 TEU incl 586 ref C
Compartments: 6 Cell Ho, ER

1 oil engine driving 1 FP propeller
Total Power: 25,228kW (34,300hp) 23.0kn
MAN-B&W 7K80MC-C
1 x 2 Stroke 7 Cy. 800 x 2300 25228kW (34300bhp)
Hyundai Heavy Industries Co Ltd-South Korea
AuxGen: 4 x 1600kW 440/220V a.c
Thrusters: 1 Thwart. CP thruster (f)
Fuel: 215.0 (d.f.) 3241.0 (r.f.)

9263629 **VIOLET** **320**
\- -
\- **S & Z Lukin Pty Ltd** -
\-
Australia

2002-11 **Adelaide Ship Const International Pty Ltd — Port Adelaide SA** Yd No: 288
Loa 30.80 Br ex - Dght 4.500
Lbp - Br md 9.00 Dpth 4.85
Welded, 1 dk

(B11B2FV) Fishing Vessel

1 oil engine geared to sc. shaft driving 1 FP propeller
Total Power: 941kW (1,279hp)
Caterpillar 3512B
1 x Vee 4 Stroke 12 Cy. 170 x 190 941kW (1279bhp)
Caterpillar Inc-USA

9154000 **VIOLET 1** **20,573** Class: NK
3FFR8 *ex Violet -2013 ex Sho Maru -2013* 7,644
\- **IMS Ltd** 30,952
SC 'Innovative Ukraine' T/cm
Panama *Panama* 41.4
MMSI: 352900000
Official number: 2553198

1998-02 **Minaminippon Shipbuilding Co Ltd — Usuki OT** Yd No: 647
Loa 175.00 (BB) Br ex 27.73 Dght 10.016
Lbp 166.00 Br md 27.70 Dpth 16.00
Welded, 1 dk

(A12B2TR) Chemical/Products Tanker
Double Hull (13F)
Liq: 33,232; Liq (Oil): 37,662
Manifold: Bow/CM: 88.6m

1 oil engine driving 1 FP propeller
Total Power: 7,944kW (10,801hp) 15.0kn
Mitsubishi 6UEC52LS
1 x 2 Stroke 6 Cy. 520 x 1850 7944kW (10801bhp)
Kobe Hatsudoki KK-Japan
Fuel: 169.0 (d.f.) 2250.0 (r.f.)

9395630 **VIOLET ACE** **49,708** Class: NV
C6XG3 14,913
\- **Violet Ray Ltd** 13,370
Ray Car Carriers Ltd
SatCom: Inmarsat C 431100094
Nassau *Bahamas*
MMSI: 311008600
Official number: 8001543

2011-03 **Ha Long Shipbuilding Co Ltd — Ha Long** Yd No: CR4900-HL02
Loa 189.30 (BB) Br ex 32.29 Dght 9.100
Lbp 177.73 Br md 32.26 Dpth 14.10
Welded, 13 dks

(A35B2RV) Vehicles Carrier
Side door/ramp (s)
Len: 22.00 Wid: 6.55 Swl: -
Quarter stern door/ramp (s. a.)
Len: 28.00 Wid: 7.00 Swl: -
Cars: 4,914

1 oil engine driving 1 FP propeller
Total Power: 13,560kW (18,436hp) 19.8kn
MAN-B&W 6S60MC-C
1 x 2 Stroke 6 Cy. 600 x 2400 13560kW (18436bhp)
MAN Diesel A/S-Denmark
AuxGen: 3 x 1600kW a.c
Thrusters: 1 Tunnel thruster (f); 1 Tunnel thruster (a)

7125859 **VIOLETITA I** *172* Class: (LR)
HC2473 *ex Don Julio -2013 ex Pizarro -1986* - ✠ Classed LR until 8/90
\- *ex Sol VI -1975* 249
Nancoro SA

Guayaquil *Ecuador*
Official number: P-00-0642

1971-11 **Fabricaciones Metallicas E.P.S. (FABRIMET) — Callao** Yd No: 427
Loa 31.22 Br ex 7.80 Dght 3.315
Lbp 26.70 Br md 7.68 Dpth 3.69
Welded

(B11B2FV) Fishing Vessel

1 oil engine sr reverse geared to sc. shaft driving 1 FP propeller
Total Power: 416kW (566hp) 11.0kn
Caterpillar D379TA
1 x Vee 4 Stroke 8 Cy. 159 x 203 416kW (566bhp)
Caterpillar Tractor Co-USA
AuxGen: 1 x 1kW 24V d.c
Fuel: 11.0 (d.f.)

8663028 **VIOLETITA II** **291**
\- -
\- **Peandres SA** -
\-
Manta *Ecuador*
Official number: P -00-00857

2008-11 **Varadero Mariduena — Guayaquil**
L reg 39.27 Br ex - Dght 2.960
Lbp - Br md 8.66 Dpth 4.33
Welded, 1 dk

(B11B2FV) Fishing Vessel

2 oil engines reduction geared to sc. shafts driving 2 Propellers
Cummins
Cummins Engine Co Inc-USA

8663030 **VIOLETITA III** **625**
\- 187
\- **Peandres SA** -
\-
Manta *Ecuador*
Official number: P -00-00879

2012-08 **Varadero Mariduena — Guayaquil**
Loa 47.70 Br ex - Dght 2.760
Lbp 41.66 Br md 9.05 Dpth 6.84
Welded, 1 dk

(B11B2FV) Fishing Vessel

1 oil engine reduction geared to sc. shaft driving 1 Propeller
Total Power: 1,230kW (1,672hp)
Caterpillar 3512
1 x Vee 4 Stroke 12 Cy. 170 x 190 1230kW (1672bhp)
Caterpillar Inc-USA

9344710 **VIOLETTA** **17,360** Class: GL
V7LR4 *ex Dal Madagascar -2010 ex Violetta -2009* 9,038
\- *ex CMA CGM Providencia -2008* 22,267
ex MOL Drakensberg -2007
launched as Violetta -2007
ms 'Nb 1268' Schiffahrtsges mbH & Co KG
Peter Doehle Schiffahrts-KG
Majuro *Marshall Islands*
MMSI: 538090271
Official number: 90271

2007-02 **Daewoo-Mangalia Heavy Industries S.A. — Mangalia** (Hull) Yd No: 4060
2007-02 **J.J. Sietas KG Schiffswerft GmbH & Co. — Hamburg** Yd No: 1268
Loa 178.57 (BB) Br ex - Dght 10.858
Lbp 167.50 Br md 27.60 Dpth 14.58
Welded, 1 dk

(A33A2CC) Container Ship (Fully Cellular)
TEU 1853 TEU incl 385 ref C
Cranes: 3x45t
Ice Capable

1 oil engine driving 1 FP propeller
Total Power: 16,980kW (23,086hp) 21.0kn
MAN-B&W 6L70ME-C
1 x 2 Stroke 6 Cy. 700 x 2360 16980kW (23086bhp)
Manises Diesel Engine Co. S.A.-Valencia
AuxGen: 4 x 1028kW 450/230V
Thrusters: 1 Tunnel thruster (f)

9333369 **VIONA** **17,360** Class: GL
CQIC *ex Emirates Dar Es Salaam -2013* 9,038
\- *ex Viona -2012 ex Safmarine Mbashe -2009* 22,248
launched as Viona -2006
ms 'Nb 1270' Schiffahrtsges mbH & Co KG
Peter Doehle Schiffahrts-KG
Madeira *Portugal (MAR)*
MMSI: 255805552
Official number: TEMP170M

2006-03 **Daewoo-Mangalia Heavy Industries S.A. — Mangalia** (Hull) Yd No: 4056
2006-03 **J.J. Sietas KG Schiffswerft GmbH & Co. — Hamburg** Yd No: 1270
Loa 178.57 (BB) Br ex 28.20 Dght 10.858
Lbp 167.50 Br md 27.60 Dpth 14.58
Welded, 2 dks

(A33A2CC) Container Ship (Fully Cellular)
Grain: 30,025
TEU 1853 incl 385 ref C.
Cranes: 3x45t
Ice Capable

1 oil engine driving 1 FP propeller
Total Power: 16,980kW (23,086hp) 20.0kn
MAN-B&W 6L70ME-C
1 x 2 Stroke 6 Cy. 700 x 2360 16980kW (23086bhp)
Manises Diesel Engine Co. S.A.-Valencia
AuxGen: 4 x 1028kW 450/230V a.c
Thrusters: 1 Thwart. CP thruster (f); 1 Tunnel thruster (a)

6928228 **VIOR** **3,264** Class: (LR)
5NBA5 *ex Avior -2000 ex Ekfjord -1988* 2,089 ✠ Classed LR until 10/3/04
\- *ex Amity -1977 ex Pointe du Toulinguet -1976* 6,000
ex Amity -1975 ex Thuntank 5 -1972 T/cm
Petromar Nigeria Ltd 12.6

Lagos *Nigeria*
Official number: 377170

1970-02 **Goole SB. & Repairing Co. Ltd. — Goole** Yd No: 566
Deepened-1977
Loa 98.30 Br ex 14.41 Dght 7.411
Lbp 93.20 Br md 14.33 Dpth 9.30
Welded, 1 dk

(A12B2TR) Chemical/Products Tanker
Single Hull
Liq: 7,255; Liq (Oil): 7,255
Cargo Heating Coils
Compartments: 14 Ta, ER
2 Cargo Pump (s)
Ice Capable

1 oil engine sr geared to sc. shaft driving 1 CP propeller
Total Power: 2,133kW (2,900hp) 12.5kn
Ruston 6AT350
1 x 4 Stroke 6 Cy. 350 x 368 2133kW (2900bhp) (new engine 1987)
Ruston Diesels Ltd.-Newton-le-Willows
AuxGen: 2 x 120kW 380V 50Hz a.c, 1 x 150kW 380V 50Hz a.c
Boilers: 2 AuxB (o.f.) 10.2kgf/cm² (10.0bar)
Fuel: 299.5 (r.f.) 11.0pd

8629761 **VIP** **117** Class: (KR)
D8GM *ex Korea No. 1 -2005 ex New Young Jin -1994* -
\- **Hyundai Marine Development Co** 22

Incheon *South Korea*
Official number: ICR-854075

1985-07 **Korea Tacoma Marine Industries Ltd — Changwon** Yd No: 10004
Loa 32.70 Br ex - Dght 1.166
Lbp 30.00 Br md 6.00 Dpth 3.18
Welded, 1 dk

(A37B2PS) Passenger Ship

2 oil engines reduction geared to sc. shafts driving 2 FP propellers
Total Power: 956kW (1,300hp) 16.0kn
G.M. (Detroit Diesel) 12V-
2 x Vee 2 Stroke 12 Cy. 108 x 127 each-478kW (650bhp)
Detroit Diesel Eng. Co.-Detroit, Mi
AuxGen: 1 x 40kW 445V a.c, 1 x 40kW 445V d.c

9685047 **VIP ASIA JAYA** **1,176** Class: KI (Class contemplated) RI
\- 353 (Class contemplated)
\- **PT Victoria Internusa Perkasa** 2,100
\-
Batam *Indonesia*
Official number: 688588

2013-12 **P.T. Bandar Victory Shipyard — Batam** Yd No: 458
Loa 74.42 Br ex - Dght -
Lbp 72.00 Br md 15.85 Dpth 3.66
Welded, 1 dk

(A35D2RL) Landing Craft
Bow ramp (centre)

2 oil engines reduction geared to sc. shafts driving 2 Propellers
Total Power: 970kW (1,318hp) 10.0kn
Yanmar 6AYM-W
2 x 4 Stroke 6 Cy. 155 x 180 each-485kW (659bhp)
Yanmar Diesel Engine Co Ltd-Japan

9678783 **VIP JAYA** **858** Class: KI
YECB 258
\- **PT Victoria Internusa Perkasa** 2,000
\-
Batam *Indonesia*
MMSI: 525021273
Official number: GT 858 no. 4505/ppm

2012-11 **P.T. Bandar Victory Shipyard — Batam** Yd No: 374
Loa 68.50 Br ex - Dght 3.000
Lbp 60.87 Br md 16.45 Dpth 3.66
Welded, 1 dk

(A35D2RL) Landing Craft
Bow ramp (centre)

2 oil engines reduction geared to sc. shafts driving 2 Propellers
Total Power: 970kW (1,318hp)
Yanmar
2 x 4 Stroke each-485kW (659bhp)
Yanmar Diesel Engine Co Ltd-Japan

7114422 **VIPAN** **241** Class: (GL)
SGKZ *ex Ternan I -2003 ex Ternan -1982* 75
\- *ex Wiking -1970* 42
Styrsobolaget AB

Gothenburg *Sweden*
MMSI: 265547240

1960-03 **Schiffswerft Hugo Peters — Wewelsfleth** Yd No: 507
Loa 36.61 Br ex 7.52 Dght 2.245
Lbp 31.02 Br md 7.50 Dpth 3.05
Welded, 1 dk

(A37B2PS) Passenger Ship
Ice Capable

1 oil engine driving 1 FP propeller
Total Power: 552kW (750hp)
Deutz RBV6M
1 x 4 Stroke 6 Cy. 320 x 450 552kW (750bhp)
Kloeckner Humboldt Deutz AG-West Germany

IMO / Call sign	Name / Owner	Tonnage	Class	Build / Dimensions	Type / Capacity	Machinery
9144055 *A8LT9* -	**VIPAVA** *ex* Isolde *-2008* *ex* Glen Maye *-2006* *ex* Allipen *-2005* **Genshipping Corp** Peter Doehle Schiffahrts-KG *Monrovia* *Liberia* MMSI: 636014062 Official number: 14062	**25,537** 15,927 46,570 T/cm 49.9	Class: AB	**1998**-12 **Oshima Shipbuilding Co Ltd — Saikai NS** Yd No: 10229 Loa 183.00 (BB) Br ex 30.95 Dght 11.788 Lbp 174.30 Br md - Dpth 16.40 Welded, 1 dk	**(A21A2BC) Bulk Carrier** Double Bottom Entire Compartment Length Grain: 58,209; Bale: 57,083 Compartments: 5 Ho, ER 5 Ha: 2 (17.1 x 15.6)3 (19.8 x 15.6)ER Cranes: 4x30t	**1 oil engine** driving 1 FP propeller Total Power: 7,594kW (10,325hp) 14.3kn Sulzer 6RTA48T 1 x 2 Stroke 6 Cy. 480 x 2000 7594kW (10325bhp) Diesel United Ltd.-Aioi AuxGen: 3 x 440kW 450V 60Hz a.c Fuel: 125.0 (d.f.) (Heating Coils) 1727.0 (r.f.) 29.1pd
8945763 - -	**VIPER** **Joyce Launch & Tug Co Inc** - *Manila* *Philippines* Official number: V0091	*150* 82 -		**1987 Navotas Industrial Corp — Manila** L reg 27.17 Br ex - Dght - Lbp - Br md 6.60 Dpth 3.30 Welded, 1 dk	**(B32A2ST) Tug**	**1 oil engine** driving 1 FP propeller Total Power: 331kW (450hp) Akasaka 1 x 4 Stroke 331kW (450bhp) Akasaka Tekkosho KK (Akasaka DieselLtd)-Japan
7620122 - -	**VIRA** *ex* Volna *-2009* *ex* Kogas *-2000* *ex* Tomas *-1999* *ex* Ramygala *-1996* *ex* Aleksandr Kulik *-1992* **Sea King SA** -	**864** 259 603	Class: (RS) (PR)	**1976**-07 **Yaroslavskiy Sudostroitelnyy Zavod — Yaroslavl** Yd No: 324 Loa 53.73 (BB) Br ex 10.70 Dght 4.950 Lbp 47.92 Br md 10.50 Dpth 6.00 Welded, 1 dk	**(B11A2FS) Stern Trawler** Ins: 218 Compartments: 1 Ho, ER 2 Ha: 2 (1.6 x 1.6) Derricks: 2x1.5t; Winches: 2 Ice Capable	**1 oil engine** driving 1 CP propeller Total Power: 971kW (1,320hp) 12.5kn S.K.L. 8NVD48A-2U 1 x 4 Stroke 8 Cy. 320 x 480 971kW (1320bhp) VEB Schwermaschinenbau "KarlLiebknecht" (SKL)-Magdeburg AuxGen: 1 x 300kW, 5 x 160kW, 2 x 135kW Thrusters: 1 Thwart. FP thruster (f); 1 Tunnel thruster (a) Fuel: 194.0 (d.f.)
9293246 *HSGG2* -	**VIRA BHUM** **Regional Container Lines Public Co Ltd** RCL Shipmanagement Pte Ltd *Bangkok* *Thailand* MMSI: 567304000 Official number: 480001022	**24,955** 11,523 31,300	Class: GL	**2005**-04 **Mitsubishi Heavy Industries Ltd. — Nagasaki** Yd No: 2199 Loa 194.90 (BB) Br ex - Dght 11.400 Lbp 186.00 Br md 32.26 Dpth 16.80 Welded, 1 dk	**(A33A2CC) Container Ship (Fully Cellular)** TEU 2588 incl 300 ref C.	**1 oil engine** driving 1 FP propeller Total Power: 20,580kW (27,981hp) 21.5kn Mitsubishi 7UEC68LSE 1 x 2 Stroke 7 Cy. 680 x 2690 20580kW (27981bhp) Mitsubishi Heavy Industries Ltd-Japan AuxGen: 3 x 1400kW 450/230V 60Hz a.c Thrusters: 1 Tunnel thruster (f)
9411824 *PCOY* -	**VIRAGE** **Virage CV** VMS Shipping BV *Werkendam* *Netherlands* MMSI: 246870000 Official number: 50553	**2,281** 1,170 3,200	Class: BV	**2012**-06 **NSC Marine Corp — China** (Hull) Yd No: (771) **2012**-06 **Bijlsma Shipyard BV — Lemmer** Yd No: 771 Loa 88.97 Br ex - Dght 5.050 Lbp 84.99 Br md 11.80 Dpth 6.70 Welded, 1 dk	**(A31A2GX) General Cargo Ship** Grain: 4,502 Compartments: 1 Ho, ER 1 Ha: ER (63.0 x 9.6)	**1 oil engine** reduction geared to sc. shaft driving 1 CP propeller Total Power: 1,440kW (1,958hp) 11.0kn Wartsila 8L20 1 x 4 Stroke 8 Cy. 200 x 280 1440kW (1958bhp) Wartsila Finland Oy-Finland Fuel: 250.0
7805162 *LIPA* -	**VIRAK** **Torghatten Nord AS** - *Narvik* *Norway* MMSI: 257377500	**1,532** 521 491	Class: (NV)	**1979**-09 **Skjervoy Skipsverft AS — Skjervoy** Yd No: 6 Lengthened-1988 Loa 76.36 Br ex 11.26 Dght 3.100 Lbp 54.01 Br md - Dpth 4.20 Welded, 1 dk	**(A36A2PR) Passenger/Ro-Ro Ship (Vehicles)** Passengers: unberthed: 360 Bow door/ramp Stern door/ramp Lane-Len: 59 Lane-Wid: 2.50 Lane-clr ht: 4.50 Cars: 82	**1 oil engine** driving 2 CP propellers aft, 1 fwd Total Power: 955kW (1,298hp) 12.0kn Normo LDMB-8 1 x 4 Stroke 8 Cy. 250 x 300 955kW (1298bhp) AS Bergens Mek Verksteder-Norway Fuel: 37.5 (d.f.) 4.0pd
9227546 - -	**VIRAMASHA II** **Viramasha Shipping Pvt Ltd** - *India*	**455** 391 800	Class: (RI)	**2000**-09 **United Marine Fabricators — Kalwa** Yd No: 11 Loa 49.85 Br ex - Dght 2.500 Lbp 46.60 Br md 11.00 Dpth 3.30 Welded, 1 dk	**(A31A2GX) General Cargo Ship**	**2 oil engines** geared to sc. shafts driving 2 FP propellers Total Power: 256kW (348hp) Cummins NT-743-M 2 x 4 Stroke 6 Cy. 130 x 152 each-128kW (174bhp) Cummins India Ltd-India
8951566 - -	**VIRAMESHWAR** - - *Mumbai* *India*	*400* - 750	Class: (BV)	**1998 United Marine Fabricators — Kalwa** Yd No: 13 Loa 46.00 Br ex - Dght 2.500 Lbp 44.30 Br md 11.00 Dpth 3.30 Welded, 1 dk	**(A31A2GX) General Cargo Ship**	**2 oil engines** driving 2 FP propellers 7.0kn Cummins 2 x 4 Stroke Cummins India Ltd-India
7388061 - -	**VIRGEN DE BELLA** *ex* Senemar III *-1991* *ex* Alvarez Entrena Decimo *-1982* **Continental Armadores de Pesca SA (CONARPESA)** -	*273* 107 -	Class: (BV)	**1974**-06 **Construcciones Navales P Freire SA — Vigo** Yd No: 88 Loa 38.44 Br ex - Dght 3.310 Lbp 33.86 Br md 7.24 Dpth 3.92 Welded, 1 dk	**(B11A2FT) Trawler** Grain: 265 Compartments: 2 Ho, ER	**1 oil engine** driving 1 FP propeller Total Power: 809kW (1,100hp) 11.8kn MWM TD484-6 1 x 4 Stroke 6 Cy. 320 x 480 809kW (1100bhp) Motoren Werke Mannheim AG (MWM)-West Germany AuxGen: 3 x 106kW 220/380V a.c Fuel: 130.5 (d.f.)
9279264 *YYNG* -	**VIRGEN DE COROMOTO** *ex* Dolphin Jet *-2013* *ex* Tanger Jet II *-2012* *ex* Spirit of Ontario 1 *-2007* **Bolivaria de Puertos SA** - *Pampatar* *Venezuela* MMSI: 775513000	**6,242** 1,873 491	Class: GL	**2004**-02 **Austal Ships Pty Ltd — Fremantle WA** Yd No: 251 Loa 86.60 Br ex - Dght 3.232 Lbp 74.15 Br md 23.75 Dpth 7.60 Welded, 1 dk	**(A36A2PR) Passenger/Ro-Ro Ship (Vehicles)** Hull Material: Aluminium Alloy Passengers: 900 Bow door/ramp (centre) Stern door/ramp (centre) Len: 21.50 Wid: - Swl: - Cars: 238	**4 oil engines** geared to sc. shafts driving 4 Water jets Total Power: 32,800kW (44,596hp) 42.0kn M.T.U. 20V8000M70 4 x Vee 4 Stroke 20 Cy. 265 x 315 each-8200kW (11149bhp) MTU Friedrichshafen GmbH-Friedrichshafen AuxGen: 4 x 300kW 480/208V a.c
7388059 *LW9733* -	**VIRGEN DE LA CINTA** *ex* Senemar II *-1991* *ex* Alvarez Entrena Noveno *-1982* **Alpesca SA** - SatCom: Inmarsat C 470129710 *Puerto Madryn* *Argentina* MMSI: 701000634 Official number: 0283	**204** 49 -	Class: (BV)	**1974**-05 **Construcciones Navales P Freire SA — Vigo** Yd No: 87 Loa 38.44 Br ex 7.27 Dght 3.595 Lbp 33.86 Br md 7.24 Dpth 3.92 Welded, 1 dk	**(B11A2FT) Trawler** Grain: 265 Compartments: 2 Ho, ER	**1 oil engine** driving 1 FP propeller Total Power: 809kW (1,100hp) 11.7kn MWM TD484-6 1 x 4 Stroke 6 Cy. 320 x 480 809kW (1100bhp) Motoren Werke Mannheim AG (MWM)-West Germany AuxGen: 3 x 106kW 220/380V a.c Fuel: 130.5 (d.f.)
6512885 *LW4499* -	**VIRGEN DE LA ESTRELLA** **Transhue SA** - *Mar del Plata* *Argentina* Official number: 01757	**939** 682 813	Class: (LR) ✠ Classed LR until 21/6/89	**1965**-10 **Maritima de Axpe S.A. — Bilbao** Yd No: 5 Loa 61.80 Br ex 10.55 Dght 4.700 Lbp 54.01 Br md 10.51 Dpth 7.29 Welded, 2 dks	**(B11A2FS) Stern Trawler** Ins: 1,026	**1 oil engine** driving 1 FP propeller Total Power: 1,361kW (1,850hp) 15.0kn Werkspoor TMABS398 1 x 4 Stroke 8 Cy. 390 x 680 1361kW (1850bhp) Hijos de J Barreras SA-Spain
5137547 *HC4520* -	**VIRGEN DE MONSERRATE** *ex* Pinzon *-1989* *ex* Stril Flower *-1978* *ex* Gula *-1977* **Arvitres SA** - *Guayaquil* *Ecuador* Official number: TN-00-0309	*423* 179 -	Class: (NV)	**1954 AS Mjellem & Karlsen — Bergen** Yd No: 74 Loa 46.33 Br ex 8.64 Dght 3.801 Lbp 41.74 Br md 8.59 Dpth 3.23 Welded, 2 dks	**(A32A2GF) General Cargo/Passenger Ship** Passengers: unberthed: 116; berths: 34 2 Ha: 2 (3.5 x 2.2)	**1 oil engine** driving 1 FP propeller Total Power: 485kW (659hp) 10.0kn Deutz RBV8M545 1 x 4 Stroke 8 Cy. 320 x 450 485kW (659bhp) Kloeckner Humboldt Deutz AG-West Germany Fuel: 39.0 (d.f.) 2.5pd
9233715 *DUE222* -	**VIRGEN DE PENAFRANCIA II** *ex* Cheonghaejin Car Ferry No. 2 *-1977* *ex* Soan Ferry No. 2 *-2003* *ex* Sinkwang Ferry No. 3 *-2000* **DBP Leasing Corp** - *Lucena* *Philippines* Official number: 04-0000872	**184** 158 44	Class: (KR)	**1997**-07 **Packcheon Shipbuilding & Engineering Co Ltd — Mokpo** Yd No: 96-122 Loa 42.50 Br ex - Dght 1.406 Lbp 34.90 Br md 7.00 Dpth 2.10 Welded, 1 dk	**(A36A2PR) Passenger/Ro-Ro Ship (Vehicles)**	**2 oil engines** reduction geared to sc. shafts driving 2 FP propellers Total Power: 750kW (1,020hp) 12.1kn Volvo Penta TAMD162C 2 x 4 Stroke 6 Cy. 144 x 165 each-375kW (510bhp) AB Volvo Penta-Sweden
9183659 *4DEL7* -	**VIRGEN DE PENAFRANCIA V** *ex* Star Cebu City *-2000* *ex* Hanlim Ferry No. 5 *-2010* *ex* Sinhan Ferry 2 Ho *-2009* *ex* Dae Yang Express Ferry *-2000* **DBP Leasing Corp** All-Star Shipping Group Inc *Batangas* *Philippines* Official number: 00-0000307	*375* 113 124	Class: (KR)	**1997**-12 **Han-Il Shipbuilding & Engineering Co Ltd — Mokpo** Yd No: 97-01 Loa 49.50 Br ex - Dght 1.609 Lbp 41.00 Br md 8.20 Dpth 2.30 Welded	**(A37B2PS) Passenger Ship**	**2 oil engines** geared to sc. shafts driving 2 FP propellers Total Power: 824kW (1,120hp) 13.8kn M.T.U. 12V183 2 x Vee 4 Stroke 12 Cy. 128 x 142 each-412kW (560bhp) Daewoo Heavy Industries Ltd-South Korea AuxGen: 2 x 140kW 220V a.c

IMO / Call sign / Official no.	Name / Owner / Port	Tonnage	Classification	Build / Dimensions	Type / Cargo	Machinery
7332177 *LW2622* -	**VIRGEN DEL CARMEN** *ex* Senemar V *-1991* *ex* Alvarez Entrena Doce *-1982* **Frigorifico Siracusa SA** - *Puerto Madryn* *Argentina* MMSI: 701000503 Official number: 0550	**204** 49 -	Class: (BV)	**1973-01 Ast. de Huelva S.A. — Huelva** Loa 38.66 Br ex 7.27 Dght 3.595 Lbp 33.28 Br md 7.24 Dpth 3.89 Welded, 1 dk	**(B11A2FT) Trawler**	**1 oil engine** driving 1 FP propeller Total Power: 809kW (1,100hp) 11.9kn MWM TD484-6 1 x 4 Stroke 6 Cy. 320 x 480 809kW (1100bhp) Motoren Werke Mannheim AG (MWM)-West Germany AuxGen: 2 x 168kW 220/380V a.c Fuel: 125.0 (d.f.)
9017252 *HP5588* -	**VIRGEN DEL CARMEN B** *ex* Emerald Star *-2011* **Pantor Holdings SA** Transgas Shipping Lines SAC SatCom: Inmarsat C 435500211 *Panama* *Panama* MMSI: 355002000 Official number: 4358212	**6,072** 2,076 7,572 T/cm 15.5	Class: RI	**1992-11 INMA SpA — La Spezia** (Hull) Yd No: 3140 **1992-11 Nuovi Cantieri Apuania SpA — Carrara** Yd No: 1178 Loa 112.24 (BB) Br ex - Dght 8.513 Lbp 103.03 Br md 17.60 Dpth 9.81 Welded, 1 dk	**(A11B2TG) LPG Tanker** Double Bottom Entire Compartment Length Liq (Gas): 7,393 3 x Gas Tank (s); 3 independent (s.stl) dcy horizontal 8 Cargo Pump (s): 8x250m³/hr Manifold: Bow/CM: 59.9m	**1 oil engine** sr geared to sc. shaft driving 1 CP propeller Total Power: 5,431kW (7,384hp) 14.5kn Wartsila 6R46 1 x 4 Stroke 6 Cy. 460 x 580 5431kW (7384bhp) Wartsila Diesel Oy-Finland AuxGen: 3 x 785kW 440V 60Hz a.c Fuel: 106.0 (d.f.) 564.0 (r.f.) 23.4pd
9264829 *ECAV* 3-CO-22-01	**VIRGEN DEL FARO** **Alfredo Cotelo Garcia y otros** - *La Coruna* *Spain* Official number: 3-2/2001	**235** - 152		**2003-02 Astilleros y Talleres Ferrolanos S.A. (ASTAFERSA) — Ferrol** Yd No: 354 Loa 30.00 Br ex - Dght 3.200 Lbp 25.00 Br md 7.20 Dpth 3.50 Welded, 1 dk	**(B11A2FS) Stern Trawler**	**1 oil engine** geared to sc. shaft driving 1 FP propeller Total Power: 368kW (500hp) 11.0kn GUASCOR 1 x 4 Stroke 368kW (500bhp) Gutierrez Ascunce Corp (GUASCOR)-Spain
6600046 *HKLA* -	**VIRGEN DEL ROCIO** *launched as* J. C. P.-D. 2 *-1966* **Sociedad Portuaria Regional de Barranquilla SA** - *Barranquilla* *Colombia* MMSI: 730057000 Official number: MC-03-0116	**1,555** 657 3,320	Class: LR **100A1** SS 04/2013 hopper dredger Columbian coastal service **LMC** Cable: 385.0/33.0 U2 (a)	**1966-09 Sociedad Espanola de Construccion Naval SA — Sestao** Yd No: 132 Loa 76.64 Br ex 12.62 Dght 4.585 Lbp 68.40 Br md 12.60 Dpth 5.40 Welded, 1 dk	**(B33B2DT) Trailing Suction Hopper Dredger** Hopper: 1,000	**2 oil engines** driving 2 FP propellers Total Power: 1,618kW (2,200hp) 12.0kn Werkspoor TMABS278 2 x 4 Stroke 8 Cy. 270 x 500 each-809kW (1100bhp) Naval Stork Werkspoor SA-Spain AuxGen: 4 x 120kW 380V 50Hz a.c Thrusters: 2 Thwart. FP thruster (f)
7129348 *LW9923* -	**VIRGEN DEL ROCIO** *ex* Senemar I *-1991* *ex* Alvarez Entrena Septimo *-1982* **Alpesca SA** - SatCom: Inmarsat C 470151810 *Puerto Madryn* *Argentina* MMSI: 701000761 Official number: 0194	**196** 97 -	Class: (BV)	**1972 Construcciones Navales P Freire SA — Vigo** Yd No: 71 Loa 36.94 Br ex 7.40 Dght - Lbp 31.55 Br md 7.24 Dpth 3.92 Welded, 1 dk	**(B11A2FT) Trawler** Ins: 220 Compartments: 2 Ho, ER	**1 oil engine** sr geared to sc. shaft driving 1 FP propeller Total Power: 607kW (825hp) 10.4kn Werkspoor TMAB276 1 x 4 Stroke 6 Cy. 270 x 500 607kW (825bhp) Naval Stork Werkspoor SA-Spain AuxGen: 3 x 32kW 220/380V a.c Fuel: 99.5 (d.f.)
9600748 *HP4549* -	**VIRGEN DEL VALLE** - **MMG Tugs, Boats & Barge Services Corp** - *Panama* *Panama* MMSI: 373832000 Official number: 4500713	**294** 88 147	Class: LR ✠ **100A1** SS 09/2012 tug, fire fighting Ship 1 (2400m3/h) **LMC** **UMS** Eq.Ltr: H; Cable: 220.0/19.0 U2 (a)	**2012-09 Song Cam Shipyard — Haiphong** (Hull) Yd No: (511578) **2012-09 B.V. Scheepswerf Damen — Gorinchem** Yd No: 511578 Loa 28.67 Br ex 10.43 Dght 4.800 Lbp 25.78 Br md 9.80 Dpth 4.60 Welded, 1 dk	**(B32A2ST) Tug**	**2 oil engines** gearing integral to driving 2 Z propellers Total Power: 3,728kW (5,068hp) Caterpillar 3516B-HD 2 x Vee 4 Stroke 16 Cy. 170 x 215 each-1864kW (2534bhp) Caterpillar Inc-USA AuxGen: 2 x 86kW 400V 50Hz a.c
9670913 *J8B4905* -	**VIRGEN DEL VALLE** *ex* Virgin Del Valle *-2014* **Petroleos de Venezuela SA (PDVSA)** - *Kingstown* *St Vincent & The Grenadines* MMSI: 376999000 Official number: 11378	**294** 88 140	Class: LR ✠ **100A1** SS 01/2014 tug, fire-fighting Ship 1 (2400m3/h) *IWS **LMC** **UMS** Eq.Ltr: F; Cable: 275.0/19.0 U2 (a)	**2014-01 Santierul Naval Damen Galati S.A. — Galati** (Hull) Yd No: 1242 **2014-01 B.V. Scheepswerf Damen — Gorinchem** Yd No: 512327 Loa 28.67 Br ex 10.43 Dght 3.700 Lbp 27.90 Br md 9.80 Dpth 4.60 Welded, 1 dk	**(B32A2ST) Tug**	**2 oil engines** reduction geared to sc. shafts driving 2 Directional propellers Total Power: 3,728kW (5,068hp) Caterpillar 3516C-HD 2 x Vee 4 Stroke 16 Cy. 170 x 215 each-1864kW (2534bhp) Caterpillar Inc-USA AuxGen: 2 x 86kW 400V 50Hz a.c
9235866 *YYNE* -	**VIRGEN DEL VALLE II** *ex* Euroferrys Pacifica *-2013* **Bolivaria de Puertos SA** Seamaster Marine Group CA *Pampatar* *Venezuela* MMSI: 775512000	**8,766** 2,630 766	Class: GL	**2001-04 Austal Ships Pty Ltd — Fremantle WA** Yd No: 114 Loa 101.40 (BB) Br ex - Dght 4.300 Lbp 88.70 Br md 26.65 Dpth 9.40 Welded, 3 dks, incl 1 Hoistable	**(A36A2PR) Passenger/Ro-Ro Ship (Vehicles)** Hull Material: Aluminium Alloy Passengers: unberthed: 951 Bow door/ramp (centre) Len: 11.88 Wid: 9.90 Swl: - Stern door/ramp (centre) Len: 7.80 Wid: 10.60 Swl: - Lane-Len: 1190 Lane-Wid: 3.50 Lane-clr ht: 4.60 Cars: 96, Trailers: 16	**4 oil engines** reduction geared to sc. shafts driving 4 Water jets Total Power: 28,800kW (39,156hp) 37.0kn Caterpillar 3618 4 x Vee 4 Stroke 18 Cy. 280 x 300 each-7200kW (9789bhp) Caterpillar Inc-USA AuxGen: 4 x 240kW a.c Fuel: 140.0 (d.f.) 127.2pd
7109049 *LW4379* -	**VIRGEN MARIA** *ex* Vierge Marie *-1977* **Luis Solimeno & Hijos SA** - *Mar del Plata* *Argentina* Official number: 0541	*704* 464 406	Class: (BV)	**1971 Soc Industrielle et Commerciale de Consts Navales (SICCNa) — St-Malo** Yd No: 114 Loa 50.73 Br ex 10.32 Dght 4.801 Lbp 44.86 Br md 10.22 Dpth 8.62 Welded, 2 dks	**(B11A2FT) Trawler** Compartments: 1 Ho, ER 2 Ha: 2 (1.3 x 0.9)ER	**1 oil engine** sr geared to sc. shaft driving 1 FP propeller Total Power: 1,324kW (1,800hp) 14.0kn Crepelle 12PSN 1 x Vee 4 Stroke 12 Cy. 260 x 280 1324kW (1800bhp) Crepelle et Cie-France AuxGen: 1 x 250kW, 2 x 120kW, 1 x 75kW Fuel: 178.5 (d.f.)
8903208 *3FVG5* -	**VIRGEN MARIA B** *ex* Sapphire Star *-2011* *ex* Gold *-1991* **Water Edge Investment Corp** Transgas Shipping Lines SAC SatCom: Inmarsat C 435140010 *Panama* *Panama* MMSI: 351400000 Official number: 4355612	**7,297** 2,189 4,825 T/cm 19.7	Class: RI (AB)	**1991-10 Soc. Esercizio Cant. S.p.A. — Viareggio** Yd No: 764 Loa 122.15 (BB) Br ex - Dght 8.600 Lbp 110.44 Br md 19.50 Dpth 11.50 Welded, 1 dk	**(A11B2TH) LPG/Chemical Tanker** Double Hull Liq: 6,777; Liq (Gas): 6,120 6 x Gas Tank (s); 6 (s.stl) 36 Cargo Pump (s): 21x180m³/hr, 15x97m³/hr Manifold: Bow/CM: 61m Ice Capable	**1 oil engine** sr geared to sc. shaft driving 1 CP propeller Total Power: 5,430kW (7,383hp) 15.0kn Wartsila 6R46 1 x 4 Stroke 6 Cy. 460 x 580 5430kW (7383bhp) Wartsila Diesel Oy-Finland AuxGen: 1 x 900kW a.c, 3 x 705kW a.c Thrusters: 1 Tunnel thruster (f) Fuel: 90.0 (d.f.) 916.0 (r.f.)
9055890 *LW9250* -	**VIRGEN MARIA INMACULADA** - **Baldimar SA** - *Mar del Plata* *Argentina* MMSI: 701000825 Official number: 0369	**121** 88 111		**1992-12 SANYM S.A. — Buenos Aires** Yd No: 89 Loa 26.50 Br ex - Dght 2.920 Lbp 23.90 Br md 6.50 Dpth 3.30 Welded, 1 dk	**(B11A2FS) Stern Trawler** Ins: 165	**1 oil engine** with clutches, flexible couplings & reverse reduction geared to sc. shaft driving 1 FP propeller Total Power: 397kW (540hp) 10.0kn Caterpillar 3412TA 1 x Vee 4 Stroke 12 Cy. 137 x 152 397kW (540bhp) Caterpillar Inc-USA
9276133 *EAUO* 3-HU-311-0	**VIRGEN MILAGRO R** - **Mariscos Rodriguez SA** - *Huelva* *Spain* MMSI: 224148000 Official number: 3-11/2001	**273** 81 421	Class: BV	**2002-07 Astilleros La Parrilla S.A. — San Esteban de Pravia** Yd No: 176 Loa - Br ex - Dght - Lbp - Br md - Dpth - Welded, 1 dk	**(B11B2FV) Fishing Vessel**	**1 oil engine** geared to sc. shaft driving 1 FP propeller Total Power: 397kW (540hp) Caterpillar 3512TA 1 x Vee 4 Stroke 12 Cy. 170 x 190 397kW (540bhp) Caterpillar Inc-USA
9264831 *EALO* 3-CO-27-02	**VIRGEN SEGUNDA** - **Pesquerias Ninons SL** - *La Coruna* *Spain* MMSI: 224111190 Official number: 3-7/2002	**254** 76 -		**2004-05 Astilleros Armon Burela SA — Burela** Yd No: 180 Loa 31.30 Br ex - Dght 3.450 Lbp 26.00 Br md 7.50 Dpth 3.50 Welded, 1 dk	**(B11A2FS) Stern Trawler** Ins: 158	**1 oil engine** with clutches, flexible couplings & sr reverse geared to sc.shaft driving 1 FP propeller Total Power: 441kW (600hp) 11.0kn GUASCOR F480TA-SP 1 x Vee 4 Stroke 16 Cy. 152 x 165 441kW (600bhp) Gutierrez Ascunce Corp (GUASCOR)-Spain
9264843 *ECGV* 3-CO-26-02	**VIRGEN TERCERA** - **Jose Veiga Blanco y otros SL** - *La Coruna* *Spain* MMSI: 224136380 Official number: 3-6/2002	**254** 76 112		**2004-12 Astilleros Armon Burela SA — Burela** Yd No: 181 Loa 31.30 Br ex - Dght 3.300 Lbp 26.00 Br md 7.50 Dpth 3.50 Welded, 1 dk	**(B11A2FS) Stern Trawler** Bale: 158	**1 oil engine** geared to sc. shaft driving 1 FP propeller Total Power: 456kW (620hp) 10.0kn GUASCOR F480TA-SP 1 x Vee 4 Stroke 16 Cy. 152 x 165 456kW (620bhp) Gutierrez Ascunce Corp (GUASCOR)-Spain

7373456 **VIRGIN C**
- *ex* Granada *-1997* *ex* Atlanta No. 1 *-1995*
- *ex* Amapola *-1994* *ex* Camellia I *-1990*
- *ex* Yuki Maru No. 28 *-1988*
- *ex* Wakashio Maru No. 28 *-1985*

254 / 125 / 325 — Class: (RI) (KR)

1974-02 Kochiken Zosen — Kochi Yd No: 455
Loa 46.30 Br ex 7.93 Dght 2.972
Lbp 40.20 Br md 7.90 Dpth 3.50
Riveted\Welded, 1 dk

(B11B2FV) Fishing Vessel

1 oil engine driving 1 FP propeller
Total Power: 736kW (1,001hp) 6M28KGHS
Niigata
1 x 4 Stroke 6 Cy. 280 x 440 736kW (1,0..hp)
Niigata Engineering Co Ltd-Japan
AuxGen: 2 x 220kW 220V 60Hz a.c

7233682 **VIRGINIA**
IVYT
- *ex* Paradisier *-1989* *ex* Aigrette V *-1985*
- **Morello Lorenzo**
- *La Maddalena* *Italy*
- Official number: 1725

137 / 79 / 25 — Class: RI (BV)

1972 Chantier Andre Merre — Nort-sur-Erdre
Loa 26.83 Br ex 7.01 Dght 1.740
Lbp 24.01 Br md 6.84 Dpth 2.85
Welded, 1 dk

(A37B2PS) Passenger Ship
Passengers: unberthed: 180

2 oil engines reduction geared to sc. s.. driving 2 FP propellers 12.0kn
Total Power: 632kW (860hp) DNP12M
Baudouin
2 x Vee 4 Stroke 12 Cy. 150 x 150 -316kW (430bhp)
Societe des Moteurs Baudouin SA ..ce

7639264 **VIRGINIA**
- *ex* Choei Maru *-1994*
- **Golden Horse Enterprise Inc**
- *Indonesia*

199 / 134 / 691

1977-12 Oka Zosen Tekko K.K. — Ushimado Yd No: 246
Loa - Br ex - Dght -
Lbp 49.00 Br md 9.11 Dpth 5.11
Riveted\Welded, 1 dk

(A31A2GX) General Cargo Ship

1 oil engine driving 1 FP propeller
Total Power: 736kW (1,001hp) 6L28X
Niigata
1 x 4 Stroke 6 Cy. 280 x 440 7.. (1001bhp)
Niigata Engineering Co Ltd-Ja..

8972637 **VIRGINIA**
- *ex* Florida *-2009* *ex* Ibrahim Xhatufa *-2009*
- **Santana Marine Ltd**
- *Zanzibar* *Tanzania (Zanzibar)*
- Official number: 300011

219 / 96 / 250

1988 Kantieri Detar "Durres" — Durres
Loa 34.00 Br ex - Dght 2.740
Lbp - Br md 7.25 Dpth 3.20
Welded, 1 dk

(A31A2GX) General Cargo Ship

1 oil engine geared to sc. shaft ..ng 1 FP propeller
S.K.L. 8NVD36A-1U
1 x 4 Stroke 8 Cy. 240 x 36.
VEB Schwermaschinenbau "Liebknecht"
(SKL)-Magdeburg

9289568 **VIRGINIA**
A8HA3
- *ex* APL Virginia *-2010*
- **ms 'Virginia' Schifffahrts GmbH & Co KG**
- NSC Schifffahrtsgesellschaft mbH & Cie KG
- *Monrovia* *Liberia*
- MMSI: 636090869
- Official number: 90869

54,592 / 34,532 / 66,644 — Class: GL

2005-06 Hyundai Samho Heavy Industries Co Ltd — Samho Yd No: S225
Loa 294.16 (BB) Br ex - Dght 13.650
Lbp 283.20 Br md 32.20 Dpth 22.10
Welded, 1 dk

(A33A2CC) Container Ship (Fully Cellular)
TEU 5018 C Ho 2266 TEU C Dk 2752 TEU incl 450 ref C.

1 oil engine driving 1 FP pr.. 25.0kn
Total Power: 45,778kW (62..hp) 8RTA96C
Sulzer
1 x 2 Stroke 8 Cy. 960 ..0 45778kW (62240bhp)
Hyundai Heavy Industr.. ..o Ltd-South Korea
AuxGen: 4 x 1800kW 45.. ..0V 60Hz a.c
Thrusters: 1 Tunnel thru.. (f)

9223186 **VIRGINIA**
V7YK5
- **Galitera Shipping Corp**
- Kassian Maritime Navigation Agency Ltd
- *Majuro* *Marshall Islands*
- MMSI: 538004678
- Official number: 4678

28,029 / 16,731 / 50,175 / T/cm 53.5
Class: LR
✠ **100A1** SS 04/2011
bulk carrier
strengthened for heavy cargoes, Nos. 2 & 4 holds may be empty
ESP
ESN
LI
ShipRight (SDA, FDA, CM)
✠ **LMC** **UMS**
Eq.Ltr: L;
Cable: 634.5/70.0 U3 (a)

2001-04 Mitsui Eng. & SB. Co. Ltd., Chiba Works — Ichihara Yd No: 1521
Loa 189.90 (BB) Br ex 32.30 Dght 11.925
Lbp 181.00 Br md 32.26 Dpth 16.90
Welded, 1 dk

(A21A2BC) Bulk Carrier
Double Bottom Entire Compartment Length
Grain: 63,216
Compartments: 5 Ho, ER
5 Ha: (17.6 x 18.0)4 (20.2 x 18.0)ER
Cranes: 4x30t

1 oil engine driving 1 F..opeller 15.7kn
Total Power: 8,090kW (..99hp) 6S50MC-C
MAN-B&W
1 x 2 Stroke 6 Cy. 5.. 2000 8090kW (10999bhp)
Mitsui Engineering .. ..hipbuilding CLtd-Japan
AuxGen: 3 x 480kW 4.. 60Hz a.c, 1 x 120kW 440V 60Hz a.c
Boilers: AuxB (Comp) ..kgf/cm² (6.9bar)
Fuel: 107.0 (d.f.) (He.. ..g Coils) 1693.0 (r.f.) 27.0pd

9292242 **VIRGINIA BRIDGE**
HOKP
- **Manatee Navigation SA**
- 'K' Line Ship Management Co Ltd (KLSM)
- *Panama* *Panama*
- MMSI: 353764000
- Official number: 3044005B

54,519 / 22,921 / 64,990 / T/cm 82.5 — Class: NK

2004-12 Hyundai Heavy Industries Co Ltd — Ulsan Yd No: 1576
Loa 294.12 (BB) Br ex - Dght 13.520
Lbp 283.33 Br md 32.20 Dpth 21.80
Welded, 1 dk

(A33A2CC) Container Ship (Fully Cellular)
TEU 4738 incl 400 ref C

1 oil engine drivi.. 1 FP propeller 23.5kn
Total Power: 44,..kW (60,616hp) 8K98MC-C
MAN-B&W
1 x 2 Stroke .. 980 x 2400 44584kW (60616bhp)
Hyundai Hea.. ..ndustries Co Ltd-South Korea
AuxGen: 4 x 1..kW a.c
Thrusters: 1 Th.. ..rt. CP thruster (f)
Fuel: 7385.0

9151668 **VIRGINIA D**
- **Autoridad Portuaria de Bilbao**
- *Spain*

150 / - / 100

1996-07 Astilleros Zamakona SA — Santurtzi Yd No: 391
Loa - Br ex - Dght -
Lbp - Br md - Dpth -
Welded, 1 dk

(A36A2PR) Passenger/Ro-Ro Ship (Vehicles)

1 oil engine ..ing 1 FP propeller

7940479 **VIRGINIA DARE**
WDE4421
- **Harbor Seafood Corp**
- *Norfolk, VA* *United States of America*
- Official number: 602653

165 / 112 / -

1979 Quality Marine, Inc. — Theodore, Al Yd No: 89
L reg 24.88 Br ex 7.32 Dght -
Lbp - Br md - Dpth 3.84
Welded, 1 dk

(B11B2FV) Fishing Vessel

1 oil engi.. ..geared to sc. shaft driving 1 FP propeller
Total Pow.. ..533kW (725hp) D348SCAC
Caterpill..
1 x Ve.. Stroke 12 Cy. 137 x 165 533kW (725bhp)
Caterp.. ..r Tractor Co-USA

8331352 **VIRGINIA DEL MAR**
- *ex* Ofelia *-1984*

274 / 53 / -

1977 Mitchel Duane Phares — Los Angeles, La
L reg 31.22 Br ex 8.54 Dght -
Lbp - Br md - Dpth 3.79
Welded, 2 dks

(B11B2FV) Fishing Vessel

1 oil en.. ..e driving 1 FP propeller 12.0kn
Total P.. ..er: 530kW (721hp) 12V-71-N
G.M. ..troit Diesel)
1 x .. 2 Stroke 12 Cy. 108 x 127 530kW (721bhp)
De.. ..t Diesel Eng. Co.-Detroit, Mi

8135681 **VIRGINIA G**
H03031
- *ex* Virginia del Cristo *-1999* *ex* Blue Wave *-1999*
- *ex* Kotobuki Maru *-1995*
- **Penn Masters Inc**
- Penn Lilac Trading SA
- *Panama* *Panama*
- MMSI: 356991000
- Official number: 2941803C

857 / 456 / 1,390

1982 Shitanoe Shipbuilding Co Ltd — Usuki OT Yd No: 1023
Lengthened-1988
Loa 65.00 Br ex - Dght 4.200
Lbp 60.00 Br md 10.00 Dpth 4.60
Welded, 1 dk

(A13B2TP) Products Tanker
Liq: 1,720; Liq (Oil): 1,720

1 oi.. ..gine driving 1 FP propeller 11.0kn
Tota.. ..ower: 882kW (1,199hp)

7939339 **VIRGINIA GENTLEMAN**
WSX7955
- **S Antonio Corp**
- *Norfolk, VA* *United States of America*
- Official number: 600797

168 / 114 / -

1978 Quality Marine, Inc. — Bayou La Batre, Al
L reg 24.88 Br ex 7.32 Dght -
Lbp - Br md - Dpth 3.84
Welded, 1 dk

(B11B2FV) Fishing Vessel

..il engine driving 1 FP propeller
..tal Power: 533kW (725hp) D348SCAC
..aterpillar
1 x Vee 4 Stroke 12 Cy. 137 x 165 533kW (725bhp)
Caterpillar Tractor Co-USA

8404264 **VIRGINIA KALIKASAN**
DUH3239
- *ex* Frida *-2011* *ex* Norden *-1995*
- **APO Cement Corp**
- Orophil Shipmanagement Corp
- *Cebu* *Philippines*
- MMSI: 548460100
- Official number: CEB1008641

5,707 / 1,856 / 7,682 / T/cm 17.8
Class: LR
✠ **100A1** SS 03/2010
Ice Class 2
✠ **LMC** **UMS**
Eq.Ltr: W; Cable: 495.0/50.0 U2

1985-08 Dannebrog Vaerft A/S — Aarhus Yd No: 187
Loa 118.93 Br ex 17.43 Dght 7.101
Lbp 111.72 Br md 17.40 Dpth 8.31
Welded, 1 dk

(A24A2BT) Cement Carrier
Grain: 6,714
Compartments: 4 Wing Ho, ER
Ice Capable

1 oil engine with flexible couplings & sr gearedto sc. shaft driving 1 CP propeller
Total Power: 3,601kW (4,896hp) 14.0kn
MaK 8M35
1 x 4 Stroke 8 Cy. 350 x 380 3601kW (4896bhp)
Krupp MaK Maschinenbau GmbH-Kiel
AuxGen: 4 x 428kW 380V 50Hz a.c, 1 x 406kW 380V 50Hz a.c
Boilers: TOH (o.f.) 10.2kgf/cm² (10.0bar), TOH (ex.g.) 10.2kgf/cm² (10.0bar)
Thrusters: 1 Thwart. CP thruster (f); 1 Tunnel thruster (a)
Fuel: 54.5 (d.f.) 228.0 (r.f.) 15.5pd

8038352 **VIRGINIA LYNN**
- *ex* Theresa *-1993* *ex* D. E. C. O. XXXI *-1993*
- **Virginia Lynn Commercial Fishing**
- *Manahawkin, NJ* *United States of America*
- Official number: 625459

147 / 114 / -

1980 St Augustine Trawlers, Inc. — Saint Augustine, Fl Yd No: S-24
L reg 19.76 Br ex 6.71 Dght -
Lbp - Br md - Dpth 3.13
Welded, 1 dk

(B11B2FV) Fishing Vessel

1 oil engine driving 1 FP propeller
Total Power: 382kW (519hp) 3412TA
Caterpillar
1 x Vee 4 Stroke 12 Cy. 137 x 152 382kW (519bhp)
Caterpillar Tractor Co-USA

8986212 **VIRGINIA MARIE**
WDD3352
- **Trebloc Seafood Inc**
- *Manomet, MA* *United States of America*
- MMSI: 367129260
- Official number: 1144678

103 / 82 / -

2003-01 Master Marine, Inc. — Bayou La Batre, Al Yd No: 314
L reg 21.33 Br ex - Dght -
Lbp - Br md 6.70 Dpth 3.04
Welded, 1 dk

(B11B2FV) Fishing Vessel

1 oil engine driving 1 Propeller

8749169 **VIRGINIA MIA**
J8Y3970
- **Virginia Mia Ltd**
- Magellan Management & Consulting SA
- *Kingstown* *St Vincent & The Grenadines*
- MMSI: 375637000
- Official number: 40440

141 / 42 / -

2001 Astilleros Astondoa SA — Santa Pola Yd No: A-95-GLXN08
Loa 27.40 Br ex - Dght -
Lbp 22.50 Br md 6.10 Dpth 3.00
Bonded, 1 dk

(X11A2YP) Yacht
Hull Material: Reinforced Plasti..

2 oil engines driving 2 Propellers 18.0kn
M.T.U.
2 x 4 Stroke
MTU Friedrichshafen GmbH-Friedrichshafen

IMO / Call sign	Name / Owner / Port / Flag	Tonnage	Class	Build / Dimensions	Type	Machinery
8224016 *ERST* -	**RGINA-N** Sampow Palm *-2012* *ex* Choyang Ace *-2007* Angul No. 21 *-2006* *ex* Seo Joo *-2004* **hid Al Zary Ships Supply LLC** *iulesti* *Moldova* N: 214181920	**1,598** 809 3,517	Class: (KR)	**1982-05 Banguhjin Engineering & Shipbuilding Co Ltd — Ulsan** Yd No: 26 Loa 82.23 Br ex - Dght 5.684 Lbp 74.02 Br md 12.81 Dpth 6.13 Welded, 1 dk	**(A13B2TP) Products Tanker** Liq: 3,859; Liq (Oil): 3,859 Compartments: 10 Ta, ER	**1 oil engine** driving 1 FP propeller Total Power: 1,324kW (1,800hp) 10.5kn Hanshin 6LU35 1 x 4 Stroke 6 Cy. 350 x 550 1324kW (1800bhp) Ssangyong Heavy Industries Co Ltd-South Korea AuxGen: 2 x 200kW 225V a.c
7948615 *WDE3474* -	**VIIA QUEEN** **Glster Seafood of VA Inc** - *NewNews, VA* *United States of America* MMS7339590 Officiamber: 612888	*166* 112 -		**1979 Quality Marine, Inc. — Theodore, Al** Yd No: 121 L reg 24.88 Br ex 7.32 Dght - Lbp - Br md - Dpth 3.84 Welded, 1 dk	**(B11B2FV) Fishing Vessel**	**1 oil engine** geared to sc. shaft driving 1 FP propeller Total Power: 533kW (725hp) Caterpillar D348SCAC 1 x Vee 4 Stroke 12 Cy. 137 x 165 533kW (725bhp) Caterpillar Tractor Co-USA
8990689 *WSX8135* -	**VIRGIEEL** **Gabrielige Corp** - *Montauk,* *United States of America* Official nu: 603390	*165* 112 -		**1979 Quality Marine, Inc. — Bayou La Batre, Al** L reg 24.87 Br ex - Dght - Lbp - Br md 7.32 Dpth 3.96 Welded, 1 dk	**(B11B2FV) Fishing Vessel**	**1 oil engine** geared to sc. shaft driving 1 Propeller Caterpillar 1 x 4 Stroke Caterpillar Tractor Co-USA
8855528 *WSX8006* -	**VIRGINIA SS** **Virginia Sarisheries Inc** - *New Bedford,* *United States of America* Official numbe2713	*167* 113 -		**1979 at Bayou La Batre, Al** Loa - Br ex - Dght - Lbp 24.87 Br md 7.32 Dpth 3.87 Welded, 1 dk	**(B11B2FV) Fishing Vessel**	**1 oil engine** driving 1 FP propeller Total Power: 533kW (725hp)
8426224 *DVUJ* -	**VIRGINIA VI** *ex* Viva Penafran *-1995* **Virginia Chua** - *Batangas* *Philippines*	*265* 151 -		**1972 Viva Shipping Lines Inc. — Lucena** Loa 51.82 Br ex 8.26 Dght 2.210 Lbp 46.46 Br md 8.22 Dpth 2.47 Welded, 1 dk	**(A32A2GF) General Cargo/Passenger Ship** Passengers: 597	**1 oil engine** driving 1 FP propeller
7939212 *WDE3332* -	**VIRGINIA WAVE** **Virginia Wave Inc** - *Newport News, VA* *United States of America* MMSI: 367337570 Official number: 60061	*168* 114 -		**1978 Quality Marine, Inc. — Theodore, Al** Yd No: 88 L reg 24.88 Br ex 7.32 Dght - Lbp - Br md - Dpth 3.84 Welded, 1 dk	**(B11B2FV) Fishing Vessel**	**1 oil engine** driving 1 FP propeller Total Power: 533kW (725hp) Caterpillar D348SCAC 1 x Vee 4 Stroke 12 Cy. 137 x 165 533kW (725bhp) Caterpillar Tractor Co-USA
8800509 *WDE6697* -	**VIRGINIA WAVE** *ex* Monomoy *-2013* *ex*on & Danielle *-2005* **Virginia Wave Inc** - *Newport News, VA* *ited States of America* MMSI: 367383510 Official number: 692922	*171* 116 -		**1985 La Force Shipyard Inc — Coden AL** Yd No: 27 Loa 28.05 Br ex - Dght - Lbp 25.35 Br md 7.31 Dpth 4.02 Welded, 1 dk	**(B11B2FV) Fishing Vessel**	**1 oil engine** driving 1 FP propeller Total Power: 530kW (721hp) Caterpillar 3412TA 1 x Vee 4 Stroke 12 Cy. 137 x 152 530kW (721bhp) Caterpillar Tractor Co-USA
9234290 *PBDL* -	**VIRGINIABORG** **Virginiaborg BV** Wagenborg Shipping BV *Delfzijl* *Netherlands* MMSI: 244632000 Official number: 39591	**6,361** 3,615 9,600 T/cm 18.3	Class: BV	**2001-09 Daewoo-Mangalia Heavy Industries S.A. — Mangalia** (Hull) Yd No: 1032 **2001-09 Bodewes Scheepswerf "Volharding" Foxhol B.V. — Foxhol** Yd No: 505 Loa 132.20 (BB) Br ex - Dght 8.070 Lbp 124.56 Br md 15.87 Dpth 11.15 Welded, 1 dk	**(A31A2GX) General Cargo Ship** Grain: 12,855 TEU 552 C. 552/20' incl. 25 ref C. Compartments: 2 Ho, ER 2 Ha: (39.3 x 13.2) (52.5 x 13.2)ER Ice Capable	**1 oil engine** reduction geared to sc. shaft driving 1 CP propeller Total Power: 3,960kW (5,384hp) 15.0kn Wartsila 6R38 1 x 4 Stroke 6 Cy. 380 x 475 3960kW (5384bhp) Wartsila Nederland BV-Netherlands AuxGen: 1 x 650kW 230/440V 60Hz a.c, 2 x 244kW 230/440V 60Hz a.c Thrusters: 1 Thwart. FP thruster (f) Fuel: 43.0 (d.f.) 418.0 (r.f.)
9439216 *PHNS* -	**VIRGINIADIEP** *ex* UAL Cyprus *-2012* *completed as* Virginiadiep *-2008* **Beheermaatschappij ms Virginiap BV** Feederlines BV SatCom: Inmarsat C 424444110 *Groningen* *Netherlands* MMSI: 244441000 Official number: 51669	**4,990** 2,648 7,796	Class: GL (BV)	**2008-04 Bodewes' Scheepswerven B.V. — Hoogezand** (Aft & pt cargo sections) Yd No: 787 **2008-04 Partner Shipyard Sp z oo — Szczecin** (Fwd & pt cargo sections) Yd No: (787) Loa 118.55 (BB) Br ex - Dght 7.050 Lbp 110.73 Br md 15.20 Dpth 8.45 Welded, 1 dk	**(A31A2GX) General Cargo Ship** Double Bottom Entire Compartment Length Grain: 9,415 TEU 348 incl 20 ref C Compartments: 1 Ho, ER Cranes: 2x60t	**1 oil engine** reduction geared to sc. shaft driving 1 CP propeller Total Power: 3,840kW (5,221hp) 14.7kn MaK 8M32C 1 x 4 Stroke 8 Cy. 320 x 480 3840kW (5221bhp) Caterpillar Motoren GmbH & Co. KG-Germany AuxGen: 1 x 348kW 400V a.c, 2 x 264kW 400V a.c Thrusters: 1 Tunnel thruster (f) Fuel: 82.0 (d.f.) 556.0 (r.f.)
8034564 - -	**VIRGINIAN** - - *United States America*	*120* - -		**1981-10 St Augustine Trawlers, Inc. — Saint Augustine, Fl** Loa 26.22 Br ex - Dght - Lbp - Br md - Dpth - Welded, 1 dk	**(B11B2FV) Fishing Vessel**	**1 oil engine** driving 1 FP propeller Total Power: 382kW (519hp) Caterpillar 3412TA 1 x Vee 4 Stroke 12 Cy. 137 x 152 382kW (519bhp) Caterpillar Tractor Co-USA
1004493 *ZCAL7* -	**VIRGINIAN** **Editallied Ltd** - SatCom: Inmarsat B 331018198 *Hamilton* *Bermuda ritish)* MMSI: 310181000 Official number: 715348	**1,027** 308	Class: LR ✠ **100A1** SS 12/2010 Yacht ✠ **LMC** Eq.Ltr: K;	**1990-12 Jacht- en Scheepswerf C. van Lent & Zonen B.V. — Kaag** Yd No: 765 Loa 62.23 Br ex 10.20 Dght 3.250 Lbp 54.72 Br md - Dpth 5.40 Welded, 1 dk	**(X11A2YP) Yacht**	**2 oil engines** geared to sc. shafts driving 2 FP propellers Total Power: 2,400kW (3,264hp) MAN 12V20/27 2 x Vee 4 Stroke 12 Cy. 200 x 270 each-1200kW (1632bhp) MAN B&W Diesel AG-Augsburg Fuel: 112.5 (d.f.)
8869220 - -	**VIRGINIJA** *ex* Bazalts *-2008* **Bojic Vladan, Obrt za Ribarstvo** - *Split* *Croja*	**117** 35 30	Class: (RS)	**1977 Sosnovskiy Sudostroitelnyy Zavod — Sosnovka** Yd No: 3259 Loa 25.42 Br ex 7.00 Dght 2.390 Lbp 22.97 Br md 6.80 Dpth 3.30 Welded, 1 dk	**(B11A2FS) Stern Trawler**	**1 oil engine** driving 1 FP propeller Total Power: 221kW (300hp) 10.0kn S.K.L. 6NVD26A-2 1 x 4 Stroke 6 Cy. 180 x 260 221kW (300bhp) VEB Schwermaschinenbau "KarlLiebknecht" (SKL)-Magdeburg
8921755 *JD2664* -	**VIRGO** - - *Hakodate, Hokkaido* *Japa* MMSI: 431800321 Official number: 128578	*6,706* - 3,359		**1990-09 Mitsubishi Heavy Industries Ltd. — Shimonoseki** Yd No: 941 Loa 134.60 (BB) Br ex 22.41 Dght 5.720 Lbp 125.00 Br md 21.00 Dpth 12.03 Welded	**(A36A2PR) Passenger/Ro-Ro Ship (Vehicles)** Passengers: 600 Lane-Len: 900 Lorries: 88, Cars: 20	**2 oil engines** with clutches, flexible couplings & sr reverse geared to sc. shafts driving 2 FP propellers Total Power: 13,388kW (18,202hp) 20.0kn Pielstick 14PC2-6V-400 2 x Vee 4 Stroke 14 Cy. 400 x 460 each-6694kW (9101bhp) Nippon Kokan KK (NKK Corp)-Japan AuxGen: 3 x 779kW, 1 x 110kW Thrusters: 1 Thwart. CP thruster (f)
6804537 *UFVF* -	**VIRGO** *ex* Fajal II *-1999* *ex* Brix *-1990* *ex* Gorce *-1987* *ex* Alecto *-1973* **Fis Ltd** - *Novorossiysk* *Russia* MMSI: 273446230	**1,007** 314 1,392	Class: (RS) (PR) (NV)	**1967-09 Soviknes Verft AS — Sovik** Yd No: 68 Loa 68.59 Br ex 11.54 Dght 3.741 Lbp 63.71 Br md 11.50 Dpth 5.69 Welded, 1 dk & S dk	**(B35E2TF) Bunkering Tanker** Liq: 1,542; Liq (Oil): 1,542 Cargo Heating Coils Compartments: 8 Ta, ER Ice Capable	**1 oil engine** driving 1 CP propeller Total Power: 772kW (1,050hp) 11.0kn MWM TBD484-6 1 x 4 Stroke 6 Cy. 320 x 480 772kW (1050bhp) Motoren Werke Mannheim AG (MWM)-West Germany AuxGen: 3 x 50kW 220V 60Hz a.c Fuel: 65.5 (d.f.) 4.0pd
7371367 *D6CJ2* -	**VIRGO** *ex* Tortuga *-2009* *ex* Captain Yamak *-2004* *ex* Haj Khaled *-2003* *ex* Draco *-2001* *ex* Sea Champ *-1996* *ex* Knight *-1995* *ex* Seven Daffodil *-1980* *ex* Georgia Merry *-1978* *ex* Sun Deneb *-1977* **Veltex (GB) Ltd** Ofra Shipping Ltd *Moroni* *Union of Comoros* MMSI: 616270000 Official number: 1200320	**941** 601 1994 cm .1	Class: IV (PR) (KR) (NK)	**1975-02 Ujina Zosensho — Hiroshima** Yd No: 541 Loa 128.76 Br ex 19.64 Dght 8.252 Lbp 120.00 Br md 19.59 Dpth 10.49 Welded, 1 dk	**(A21A2BC) Bulk Carrier** Grain: 14,108; Bale: 13,747 Compartments: 3 Ho, ER 3 Ha: (17.6 x 9.8) (30.1 x 9.8) (18.2 x 9.8)ER Derricks: 1x20t,3x15t	**1 oil engine** driving 1 FP propeller Total Power: 4,928kW (6,700hp) 13.2kn Ito M558HUS 1 x 4 Stroke 8 Cy. 550 x 900 4928kW (6700bhp) Ito Tekkosho-Japan AuxGen: 2 x 240kW 445V a.c Fuel: 1249.5 21.5pd

IMO / Call sign	Name / Owner / Manager	Tonnage	Class	Builder / Dimensions	Type / Cargo	Machinery
8653889 - -	**VIRGO** **Pelayaran Salim Samudra Pacific Line** - *Samarinda* *Indonesia*	**202** 61 -	Class: KI -	**2011-02 PT Candi Pasifik — Samarinda** Loa 28.50 Br ex - Dght 2.590 Lbp 26.44 Br md 8.00 Dpth 3.90 Welded, 1 dk	**(B32A2ST) Tug**	**2 oil engines** reduction geared to sc. shafts driving 2 FP propellers Total Power: 1,002kW (1,362hp) Yanmar 6LAH-STE3 2 x 4 Stroke 6 Cy. 150 x 165 each-501kW (681bhp) Yanmar Diesel Engine Co Ltd-Japan AuxGen: 2 x 90kW 400V a.c
9605815 - -	**VIRGO** **Government of Mexico (Secretaria de Comunicaciones y Transportes, Sub-Secretaria de Operacion, Direccion General de Marina Mercante, Direccion de Senalamiento Maritimo)** - *Mexico*	**313** 79 -	Class: GL	**2010-12 Servicios Navales e Industriales SA de CV (SENI) — Mazatlan** Yd No: 007 Loa 35.06 Br ex - Dght - Lbp 33.50 Br md 10.50 Dpth - Welded, 1 dk	**(B34Q2QB) Buoy Tender**	**2 oil engines** reduction geared to sc. shafts driving 2 FP propellers Total Power: 1,066kW (1,450hp) Caterpillar C18 2 x 4 Stroke 6 Cy. 145 x 183 each-533kW (725bhp) Caterpillar Inc-USA
9323302 *3EAT4* -	**VIRGO** **Virgo Shipping Ltd SA** Shinsung Shipping Co Ltd *Panama* *Panama* MMSI: 371006000 Official number: 3078805A	**4,562** 2,166 6,725	Class: KR	**2005-05 21st Century Shipbuilding Co Ltd — Tongyeong** Yd No: 207 Loa 109.47 (BB) Br ex - Dght 6.763 Lbp 102.00 Br md 16.60 Dpth 8.70 Welded, 1 dk	**(A31A2GX) General Cargo Ship** 3 Ha: 2 (29.4 x 11.1)	**1 oil engine** driving 1 FP propeller Total Power: 2,806kW (3,815hp) 13.7kn B&W 7S26MC 1 x 2 Stroke 7 Cy. 260 x 980 2806kW (3815bhp) STX Engine Co Ltd-South Korea AuxGen: 2 x 280kW 450V 60Hz a.c
9544578 *9V7713* -	**VIRGO 9** *ex* Maspapua 77 *-2009* **Kian Hup Holding Pte Ltd** KK Wong Marine Services *Singapore* *Singapore* MMSI: 563012090 Official number: 394675	**150** 45 128	Class: NK	**2009-02 Tuong Aik Shipyard Sdn Bhd — Sibu** Yd No: 2822 Loa 23.90 Br ex - Dght 2.860 Lbp 21.74 Br md 7.32 Dpth 3.35 Welded, 1 dk	**(B32A2ST) Tug**	**2 oil engines** reduction geared to sc. shafts driving 2 Propellers Total Power: 970kW (1,318hp) Yanmar 6AYM-STE 2 x 4 Stroke 6 Cy. 155 x 180 each-485kW (659bhp) Yanmar Diesel Engine Co Ltd-Japan AuxGen: 2 x 56kW a.c Fuel: 110.0
9576600 - -	**VIRGO 19** - -	**149** 45 103	Class: (NK)	**2010-02 Tuong Aik Shipyard Sdn Bhd — Sibu** Yd No: 2919 Loa 23.50 Br ex - Dght 2.710 Lbp 21.56 Br md 7.32 Dpth 3.20 Welded, 1 dk	**(B32A2ST) Tug**	**2 oil engines** reduction geared to sc. shafts driving 2 Propellers Total Power: 970kW (1,318hp) Yanmar 6AYM-STE 2 x 4 Stroke 6 Cy. 155 x 180 each-485kW (659bhp) Yanmar Diesel Engine Co Ltd-Japan Fuel: 100.0 (d.f.)
9576612 - -	**VIRGO 29** - -	**149** 45 102	Class: (NK)	**2010-03 Tuong Aik Shipyard Sdn Bhd — Sibu** Yd No: 2920 Loa 23.50 Br ex - Dght 2.712 Lbp 21.56 Br md 7.32 Dpth 3.20 Welded, 1 dk	**(B32A2ST) Tug**	**2 oil engines** reduction geared to sc. shafts driving 2 FP propellers Total Power: 970kW (1,318hp) Yanmar 6AYM-STE 2 x 4 Stroke 6 Cy. 155 x 180 each-485kW (659bhp) Yanmar Diesel Engine Co Ltd-Japan Fuel: 100.0 (d.f.)
8329232 - -	**VIRGO 97** *ex* Sun Trader *-2012* **PT Samudera Pratama Jaya** - *Ambon* *Indonesia*	*162* 95 -	Class: KI	**1980 PT Dwi Warna Shipyard — Samarinda** Loa 35.51 Br ex - Dght 1.401 Lbp 34.29 Br md 7.38 Dpth 1.76 Welded, 1 dk	**(A35D2RL) Landing Craft** Bow door/ramp	**2 oil engines** geared to sc. shafts driving 2 FP propellers Total Power: 242kW (330hp) Yanmar 6KDGGE 2 x 4 Stroke 6 Cy. 145 x 170 each-121kW (165bhp) Yanmar Diesel Engine Co Ltd-Japan
9515096 *3FFX7* -	**VIRGO COLOSSUS** *completed as* 0 Jizo *-2012* **Cygnus Line Shipping SA** - *Panama* *Panama* MMSI: 373926000 Official number: 4421212	**33,922** 19,947 61,616 T/cm 60.0	Class: NK	**2012-09 Oshima Shipbuilding Co Ltd — Saikai NS** Yd No: 10576 Loa 199.98 (BB) Br ex - Dght 12.850 Lbp 196.00 Br md 32.26 Dpth 18.33 Welded, 1 dk	**(A21A2BC) Bulk Carrier** Double Hull Grain: 76,913; Bale: 75,312 Compartments: 5 Ho, ER 5 Ha: ER Cranes: 4x30t	**1 oil engine** driving 1 FP propeller Total Power: 8,201kW (11,150hp) 14.5kn MAN-B&W 6S50MC-C 1 x 2 Stroke 6 Cy. 500 x 2000 8201kW (11150bhp) Kawasaki Heavy Industries Ltd-Japan Fuel: 2010.0
8515465 *HP6369* -	**VIRGO GAS** *ex* Oncor *-2012* *ex* Gongora *-2011* **Versatile Holdings Inc** Transgas Shipping Lines SAC *Panama* *Panama* MMSI: 353455000 Official number: 4272111A	**2,796** 839 3,659 T/cm 10.3	Class: BV (RI)	**1987-09 Ast. Reunidos del Nervion S.A. — Bilbao** Yd No: 502 Loa 84.60 (BB) Br ex - Dght 6.600 Lbp 78.60 Br md 14.50 Dpth 8.80 Welded, 1 dk	**(A11B2TG) LPG Tanker** Double Bottom Entire Compartment Length Liq (Gas): 3,216 3 x Gas Tank (s); 1 independent (C.mn.stl) dcy horizontal, 1 independent (C.mn.stl) dcy transverse, 1 independent (C.mn.stl) dcy horizontal 5 Cargo Pump (s): 5x90m³/hr Manifold: Bow/CM: 40.6m Ice Capable	**1 oil engine** sr geared to sc. shaft driving 1 CP propeller Total Power: 2,515kW (3,419hp) 14.0kn Alpha 12V28/32 1 x Vee 4 Stroke 12 Cy. 280 x 320 2515kW (3419bhp) Construcciones Echevarria SA-Spain AuxGen: 2 x 400kW 440/220V 60Hz, 1 x 264kW 440/220V 60Hz Fuel: 108.0 (d.f.) 247.0 (r.f.)
9273894 *H3YE* -	**VIRGO LEADER** **ANZ Bank New Zealand Ltd** NYK Shipmanagement Pte Ltd SatCom: Inmarsat C 435657710 *Panama* *Panama* MMSI: 356577000 Official number: 2998504C	**61,854** 18,557 20,111 T/cm 55.6	Class: NK	**2004-06 Imabari Shipbuilding Co Ltd — Marugame KG (Marugame Shipyard)** Yd No: 1421 Loa 199.94 (BB) Br ex - Dght 10.016 Lbp 190.00 Br md 32.26 Dpth 34.80 Welded, 12 dks	**(A35B2RV) Vehicles Carrier** Side door/ramp (s) Len: 20.00 Wid: 4.20 Swl: 15 Quarter stern door/ramp (s. a.) Len: 35.00 Wid: 8.00 Swl: 80 Cars: 5,415 Compartments: 12 Wing RoRo Dk	**1 oil engine** driving 1 FP propeller Total Power: 15,540kW (21,128hp) 20.0kn Mitsubishi 8UEC60LSII 1 x 2 Stroke 8 Cy. 600 x 2300 15540kW (21128bhp) Kobe Hatsudoki KK-Japan AuxGen: 4 x 1070kW 440/220V 60Hz a.c Thrusters: 1 Tunnel thruster (f) Fuel: 3280.0
9541875 *3FMO8* -	**VIRGO PHOENIX** **Granship Co SA** Wooil Marine Co Ltd *Panama* *Panama* MMSI: 370795000 Official number: 4006809B	**3,376** 1,462 4,410 T/cm 11.9	Class: KR	**2008-11 KK Onishigumi Zosensho — Mihara HS** Yd No: 361 Loa 95.99 (BB) Br ex 15.02 Dght 6.463 Lbp 89.99 Br md 15.00 Dpth 8.20 Welded, 1 dk	**(A12B2TR) Chemical/Products Tanker** Double Hull (13F) Liq: 4,972; Liq (Oil): 4,972 Cargo Heating Coils Compartments: 10 Wing Ta, 2 Wing Slop Ta, ER 10 Cargo Pump (s): 10x150m³/hr Manifold: Bow/CM: 48.6m	**1 oil engine** driving 1 FP propeller Total Power: 3,089kW (4,200hp) 13.5kn Hanshin LH46L 1 x 4 Stroke 6 Cy. 460 x 880 3089kW (4200bhp) The Hanshin Diesel Works Ltd-Japan AuxGen: 3 x 360kW 450V a.c Thrusters: 1 Tunnel thruster (f) Fuel: 64.0 (d.f.) 273.0 (r.f.)
9029360 - -	**VIRGO POWER** **PT Virgo Samudera Jaya** - *Banjarmasin* *Indonesia* Official number: IIA 2212/L	**215** 65 -	Class: (KI)	**2003-07 P.T. Budi Karya Persada — Banjarmasin** L reg 28.00 Br ex - Dght 2.480 Lbp 25.87 Br md 8.50 Dpth 3.50 Welded, 1 dk	**(B32A2ST) Tug**	**2 oil engines** geared to sc. shafts driving 2 Propellers Total Power: 1,766kW (2,402hp) Caterpillar D399 2 x Vee 4 Stroke 16 Cy. 159 x 203 each-883kW (1201bhp) Caterpillar Inc-USA
8730857 - -	**VIRGO POWER 3** **PT Virgo Samudera Jaya** - *Tanjung Priok* *Indonesia*	**278** 84 264	Class: KI	**2008-05 PT Karya Teknik Utama — Batam** Loa 28.05 Br ex - Dght 3.290 Lbp 25.74 Br md 8.60 Dpth 4.30 Welded, 1 dk	**(B32A2ST) Tug**	**2 oil engines** reduction geared to sc. shafts driving 2 Propellers Total Power: 1,618kW (2,200hp) 10.0kn Yanmar 12LAK (M)-STE2 2 x Vee 4 Stroke 12 Cy. 150 x 165 each-809kW (1100bhp) Yanmar Diesel Engine Co Ltd-Japan AuxGen: 2 x 77kW 400/220V a.c
8651518 - -	**VIRGO POWER 08** **PT Virgo Samudera Jaya** - *Banjarmasin* *Indonesia*	**211** 64 -	Class: KI	**2010-08 C.V. Mercusuar Mandiri — Batam** Loa 29.00 Br ex - Dght 2.990 Lbp 26.88 Br md 8.00 Dpth 3.70 Welded, 1 dk	**(B32A2ST) Tug**	**2 oil engines** reduction geared to sc. shafts driving 2 FP propellers Total Power: 1,220kW (1,658hp) Mitsubishi S6R2-MPTK 2 x 4 Stroke 6 Cy. 170 x 220 each-610kW (829bhp) Mitsubishi Heavy Industries Ltd-Japan AuxGen: 2 x 30kW 400V a.c
9068615 *YD6539*	**VIRGO POWER I** *ex* Marina Falcon *-2003* *ex* Kotoku Maru No. 13 *-1997* *ex* Kyokuei Maru No. 3 *-1980* **PT Virgo Samudera Jaya** - *Banjarmasin* *Indonesia*	**133** 40 -	Class: KI	**1972-08 Hongawara Zosen K.K. — Fukuyama** Loa 27.50 Br ex - Dght 2.500 Lbp 25.00 Br md 7.00 Dpth 3.10 Welded, 1 dk	**(B32A2ST) Tug**	**1 oil engine** driving 1 Propeller Total Power: 1,471kW (2,000hp) 12.0kn Yanmar 6Z-ET 1 x 4 Stroke 6 Cy. 280 x 340 1471kW (2000bhp) Yanmar Diesel Engine Co Ltd-Japan AuxGen: 2 x 64kW a.c

IMO / Call sign	Name / Owner / Manager	Tonnage	Class	Builder / Dimensions	Type	Machinery
8999518 - -	**VIRGO SAMUDERA** **PT Virgo Samudera Jaya** *Banjarmasin* *Indonesia* Official number: IIA 2124/L	**216** 129 -	Class: KI	**1998-12 P.T. Kacaba Marga Marina — Batam** L reg 23.80 Br ex - Dght - Lbp 21.30 Br md 7.60 Dpth 3.70 Welded, 1 dk	**(B32A2ST) Tug**	**2 oil engines** geared to sc. shafts driving 2 Propellers Total Power: 882kW (1,200hp) Yanmar 6MAL-DT 2 x 4 Stroke 6 Cy. 200 x 240 each-441kW (600bhp) (made 1976, fitted 1998) Yanmar Diesel Engine Co Ltd-Japan
8892540 - -	**VIRGO SEJATI** **PT Virgo Samudera Jaya** *Banjarmasin* *Indonesia*	*112* 67 -	Class: (KI)	**1993-01 P.T. Budi Karya Persada — Banjarmasin** Loa 23.35 Br ex - Dght 2.400 Lbp 21.30 Br md 6.90 Dpth 2.90 Welded, 1 dk	**(B32A2ST) Tug**	**2 oil engines** driving 2 FP propellers Total Power: 692kW (940hp) Caterpillar 3408TA 2 x Vee 4 Stroke 8 Cy. 137 x 152 each-346kW (470bhp) Caterpillar Inc-USA
8746583 - -	**VIRGO SEJATI 26** **PT Virgo Samudera Jaya** *Balikpapan* *Indonesia*	**139** 42 -	Class: KI	**2009-08 P.T. Rejeki Abadi Sakti — Samarinda** Loa 24.00 Br ex - Dght 2.990 Lbp 22.60 Br md 7.00 Dpth 3.10 Welded, 1 dk	**(B32A2ST) Tug**	**2 oil engines** reduction geared to sc. shafts driving 2 Propellers Total Power: 1,220kW (1,658hp) Yanmar 6AYM-ETE 2 x 4 Stroke 6 Cy. 155 x 180 each-610kW (829bhp) Yanmar Diesel Engine Co Ltd-Japan AuxGen: 2 x 74kW 400V a.c
8746416 - -	**VIRGO SEJATI 27** **PT Virgo Samudera Jaya** *Balikpapan* *Indonesia*	**139** 42 -	Class: KI	**2009-08 P.T. Rejeki Abadi Sakti — Samarinda** Loa 24.00 Br ex - Dght 2.990 Lbp 22.60 Br md 7.00 Dpth 3.10 Welded, 1 dk	**(B32A2ST) Tug**	**2 oil engines** reduction geared to sc. shafts driving 2 Propellers Total Power: 1,220kW (1,658hp) Yanmar 6AYM-ETE 2 x 4 Stroke 6 Cy. 155 x 180 each-610kW (829bhp) Yanmar Diesel Engine Co Ltd-Japan AuxGen: 2 x 74kW 400V a.c
9027790 - -	**VIRGO SEJATI VI** **PT Virgo Samudera Jaya** *Banjarmasin* *Indonesia*	**174** 52 -	Class: KI	**1994-11 P.T. Budi Karya Persada — Banjarmasin** L reg 28.50 Br ex - Dght 1.990 Lbp 26.10 Br md 7.50 Dpth 3.50 Welded, 1 dk	**(B32A2ST) Tug**	**2 oil engines** geared to sc. shafts driving 2 Propellers Total Power: 988kW (1,344hp) Caterpillar 3412D 2 x Vee 4 Stroke 12 Cy. 145 x 162 each-494kW (672bhp) Caterpillar Inc-USA
9027788 - -	**VIRGO SEJATI VII** **PT Virgo Samudera Jaya** *Banjarmasin* *Indonesia*	**197** 60 -	Class: (KI)	**1996-05 P.T. Budi Karya Persada — Banjarmasin** L reg 28.50 Br ex - Dght 2.500 Lbp 26.85 Br md 7.30 Dpth 3.50 Welded, 1 dk	**(B32A2ST) Tug**	**1 oil engine** geared to sc. shaft driving 1 Propeller Total Power: 941kW (1,279hp) 10.0kn Caterpillar 3512TA 1 x Vee 4 Stroke 12 Cy. 170 x 190 941kW (1279bhp) Caterpillar Inc-USA
9484728 *A8QM3* -	**VIRGO STAR** **Vela International Marine Ltd** Vela International Marine Ltd SatCom: Inmarsat C 463708136 *Monrovia* *Liberia* MMSI: 636013961 Official number: 13961	**162,863** 111,897 319,141 T/cm 178.7	Class: NV	**2010-06 Daewoo Shipbuilding & Marine Engineering Co Ltd — Geoje** Yd No: 5320 Loa 333.00 (BB) Br ex 60.04 Dght 22.500 Lbp 320.00 Br md 60.00 Dpth 30.50 Welded, 1 dk	**(A13A2TV) Crude Oil Tanker** Double Hull (13F) Liq: 340,500; Liq (Oil): 340,500 Compartments: 5 Ta, 10 Wing Ta, 2 Wing Slop Ta, ER 3 Cargo Pump (s): 3x5500m³/hr Manifold: Bow/CM: 163.4m	**1 oil engine** driving 1 FP propeller Total Power: 29,340kW (39,891hp) 15.3kn MAN-B&W 6S90MC-C 1 x 2 Stroke 6 Cy. 900 x 3188 29340kW (39891bhp) Doosan Engine Co Ltd-South Korea AuxGen: 2 x 1250kW a.c, 1 x 1250kW a.c Fuel: 350.0 (d.f.) 8255.0 (r.f.)
9332810 *D5FI3* -	**VIRGO SUN** *ex* Pacific Apollo *-2013* **Hebdol Shipping Inc** Zodiac Maritime Agencies Ltd *Monrovia* *Liberia* MMSI: 636016272 Official number: 16272	**59,164** 36,052 115,577 T/cm 93.3	Class: LR (AB) **100A1** SS 03/2012 Double Hull oil tanker ESP *IWS LI **LMC** **UMS IGS**	**2007-03 Sasebo Heavy Industries Co. Ltd. — Sasebo Yard, Sasebo** Yd No: 740 Loa 243.80 (BB) Br ex 42.04 Dght 15.620 Lbp 234.00 Br md 42.00 Dpth 21.50 Welded, 1 dk	**(A13A2TV) Crude Oil Tanker** Double Hull (13F) Liq: 124,074; Liq (Oil): 124,074 Cargo Heating Coils Compartments: 12 Wing Ta, 2 Wing Slop Ta, ER 3 Cargo Pump (s): 3x2500m³/hr Manifold: Bow/CM: 120m	**1 oil engine** driving 1 FP propeller Total Power: 11,700kW (15,907hp) 15.0kn MAN-B&W 6S60MC-C 1 x 2 Stroke 6 Cy. 600 x 2400 11700kW (15907bhp) Mitsui Engineering & Shipbuilding CLtd-Japan AuxGen: 3 x 700kW a.c Fuel: 72.0 (d.f.) 3228.0 (r.f.)
8613839 *A8VU6* -	**VIRINI PREM** *ex* Prem Prachi *-2010* *ex* Sea Voyager *-2005* *ex* Fernando Tapias *-2000* *ex* Silvia Tapias *-1996* *ex* Golar Rosemary *-1993* **Mercator Offshore (P) Pte Ltd** Mercator Ltd *Monrovia* *Liberia* MMSI: 636014671 Official number: 14671	**79,536** 58,182 183,257 T/cm 111.8	Class: LR (IR) (BV) (NV) **OI100AT** SS 11/2010 floating storage and offloading unit for service at the Ebok Field, offshore Nigeria OIWS LI **OMC** **IGS** Eq.Ltr: Y†; Cable: 742.5/97.0 U3 (a)	**1988-06 Daewoo Shipbuilding & Heavy Machinery Ltd — Geoje** Yd No: 5020 Converted From: Crude Oil/Products Tanker-2010 Loa 267.01 (BB) Br ex - Dght 19.017 Lbp 256.01 Br md 46.21 Dpth 23.83 Welded, 1 dk	**(B22H2OF) FSO, Oil** Double Sides Entire Compartment Length Liq: 166,549; Liq (Oil): 166,549 Cargo Heating Coils Compartments: 7 Ta, ER, 2 Slop Ta 3 Cargo Pump (s) Manifold: Bow/CM: 134m	**1 oil engine** driving 1 FP propeller Total Power: 15,401kW (20,939hp) 14.5kn MAN-B&W 6S70MC 1 x 2 Stroke 6 Cy. 700 x 2674 15401kW (20939bhp) Hyundai Engine & Machinery Co Ltd-South Korea AuxGen: 3 x 800kW 450V 60Hz a.c Boilers: AuxB (o.f.) (fitted: 1988) 18.3kgf/cm² (17.9bar) Fuel: 300.0 (d.f.) 3765.0 (r.f.) 55.0pd
8230481 *J8B3557* -	**VIRMA 2** *ex* Volgo-Balt 234 *-2006* **Stream Sand Ltd** OSS Ltd SatCom: Inmarsat C 437638410 *Kingstown* *St Vincent & The Grenadines* MMSI: 376384000 Official number: 10030	**2,516** 1,147 3,510	Class: RS (RR)	**1981-04 Zavody Tazkeho Strojarstva (ZTS) — Komarno** Yd No: 1965 Loa 113.87 Br ex 13.20 Dght 3.860 Lbp 110.52 Br md 13.00 Dpth 5.50 Welded, 1 dk	**(A31A2GX) General Cargo Ship** Grain: 4,720 Compartments: 4 Ho, ER 4 Ha: (18.2 x 9.5)3 (19.5 x 9.5)ER Ice Capable	**2 oil engines** driving 2 FP propellers Total Power: 1,030kW (1,400hp) 10.8kn Skoda 6L275A2 2 x 4 Stroke 6 Cy. 275 x 350 each-515kW (700bhp) Skoda-Praha Fuel: 120.0 (d.f.)
8414386 *XUDD4* -	**VIRT** *ex* Rubin *-2011* *ex* Dax *-2010* *ex* Rex *-2004* *ex* Nelma *-2004* *ex* Koyo Maru No. 15 *-2003* **Gaya Investment SA** East Shine Shipping Co Ltd *Phnom Penh* *Cambodia* MMSI: 515517000 Official number: 1184790	**570** 232 468		**1984-10 Niigata Engineering Co Ltd — Niigata NI** Yd No: 1827 Loa 54.01 (BB) Br ex - Dght 3.390 Lbp 47.91 Br md 8.72 Dpth 3.76 Welded, 1 dk	**(B11B2FV) Fishing Vessel**	**1 oil engine** with clutches, flexible couplings & sr geared to sc. shaft driving 1 CP propeller Total Power: 736kW (1,001hp) 11.0kn Niigata 6M28AFTE 1 x 4 Stroke 6 Cy. 280 x 480 736kW (1001bhp) Niigata Engineering Co Ltd-Japan AuxGen: 1 x 280kW 445V 60Hz a.c Thrusters: 1 Thwart. FP thruster (a) Fuel: 50.5 (d.f.) 244.5 (r.f.) 3.0pd
9103740 *MGLJ3* -	**VIRTSU** **K/S Difko Virtsu** Tschudi Ship Management AS *Douglas* *Isle of Man (British)* MMSI: 232414000 Official number: 737458	**2,658** 1,216 3,285	Class: LR ✠ **100A1** SS 12/2010 container cargoes in hold & on hatch covers Ice Class 1A (Finnish - Swedish Ice Class Rules 1985) Max draught midship 4.73m Max/min draught aft 4.73/3.50m Max/min draught forward 4.73/2.60m ✠ **LMC** **UMS** Eq.Ltr: T; Cable: 472.1/38.0 U3	**1995-12 Santierul Naval Galati S.A. — Galati** (Hull) Yd No: 891 **1995-12 Scheepswerf Bijlholt B.V. — Foxhol** Yd No: 705 Loa 90.67 (BB) Br ex 15.85 Dght 4.630 Lbp 84.99 Br md 15.80 Dpth 5.80 Welded, 1 dk	**(A31A2GX) General Cargo Ship** Double Sides Entire Compartment Length Grain: 3,990; Bale: 3,990 TEU 266 C.Ho 80/20' C.Dk 186/20' incl. 20 ref C. Compartments: 1 Ho, ER 1 Ha: (57.5 x 12.8)ER Ice Capable	**1 oil engine** with flexible couplings & sr geared to sc. shaft driving 1 CP propeller Total Power: 3,280kW (4,459hp) 12.5kn Wartsila 8R32E 1 x 4 Stroke 8 Cy. 320 x 350 3280kW (4459bhp) Wartsila Diesel Oy-Finland AuxGen: 1 x 350kW 380V 50Hz a.c, 2 x 180kW 380V 50Hz a.c Thrusters: 1 Thwart. CP thruster (f) Fuel: 32.2 (d.f.) 174.0 (r.f.) 12.0pd
8213938 *HP3809* -	**VIRTUE** *ex* Jeddah 17 *-2012* **Expert Marine Services Ltd** *Panama* *Panama* MMSI: 373510000 Official number: 4515213	**407** 112 271	Class: (LR) (NV) ✠ Classed LR until 20/3/87	**1983-07 Tille Scheepsbouw B.V. — Kootstertille** Yd No: 237 Loa 34.02 Br ex 11.28 Dght 3.376 Lbp 32.47 Br md 11.00 Dpth 3.97 Welded, 1 dk	**(B32A2ST) Tug**	**2 oil engines** gearing integral to driving 2 Voith-Schneider propellers Total Power: 2,208kW (3,002hp) 12.0kn Deutz SBV6M628 2 x 4 Stroke 6 Cy. 240 x 280 each-1104kW (1501bhp) Kloeckner Humboldt Deutz AG-West Germany AuxGen: 2 x 120kW 440V 60Hz a.c Thrusters: 2 Thwart. FP thruster (f) Fuel: 120.0 (d.f.)
8502339 *EIDC6* DA 80	**VIRTUOUS** *ex* Le Grand Louis *-2007* **D & N Kirwan** *Drogheda* *Irish Republic* Official number: 404154	**163** - -		**1984-11 Chantiers Piriou — Concarneau** Loa - Br ex - Dght - Lbp 23.42 Br md 7.21 Dpth 3.87 Welded, 1 dk	**(B11A2FS) Stern Trawler**	**1 oil engine** driving 1 FP propeller Baudouin 12P15.2SR 1 x Vee 4 Stroke 12 Cy. 150 x 150 Societe des Moteurs Baudouin SA-France
9577252 *2DSR6* FR 253	**VIRTUOUS** *ex* Parkol 028 *-2010* **Virtuous LLP** Westward Fishing Co *Fraserburgh* *United Kingdom* Official number: C19715	**210** 98 -		**2010-08 Parkol Marine Engineering Ltd — Whitby** Yd No: 028 Loa 23.30 (BB) Br ex - Dght - Lbp - Br md 7.20 Dpth 4.28 Welded, 1 dk	**(B11A2FS) Stern Trawler**	**1 oil engine** reduction geared to sc. shaft driving 1 Propeller Total Power: 610kW (829hp) Mitsubishi S6R2-MPTK 1 x 4 Stroke 6 Cy. 170 x 220 610kW (829bhp) Mitsubishi Heavy Industries Ltd-Japan Thrusters: 1 Tunnel thruster (f)

IMO / Call sign / Reg.	Name / Owner / Port	Tonnage	Class	Builder / Dimensions	Type	Machinery
9493690 *C6XX6* -	**VIRTUOUS STRIKER** **Chartley World Inc** Enterprises Shipping & Trading SA SatCom: Inmarsat C 431101057 *Nassau* *Bahamas* MMSI: 311025100 Official number: 8001669	**33,044** 19,231 56,822 T/cm 58.8	Class: BV	**2011-01 Jinling Shipyard — Nanjing JS** Yd No: 07-0410 Loa 189.99 (BB) Br ex - Dght 12.800 Lbp 185.00 Br md 32.26 Dpth 18.00 Welded, 1 dk	**(A21A2BC) Bulk Carrier** Grain: 71,634; Bale: 68,200 Compartments: 5 Ho, ER 5 Ha: ER Cranes: 4x30t	**1 oil engine** driving 1 FP propeller Total Power: 9,480kW (12,889hp) 14.2kn MAN-B&W 6S50MC-C 1 x 2 Stroke 6 Cy. 500 x 2000 9480kW (12889bhp) Doosan Engine Co Ltd-South Korea AuxGen: 3 x 700kW 60Hz a.c
9477048 *SPKN* -	**VIRTUS** **'WUZ' Port & Maritime Services Co Ltd ('WUZ' Sp z oo Przedsiebiorstwo Uslug Portowych i Morskich)** - *Gdansk* *Poland* MMSI: 261482000	**334** - 100	Class: PR	**2009-01 Gdanska Stocznia 'Remontowa' SA — Gdansk** Yd No: B848/1 Loa 31.20 Br ex - Dght 4.800 Lbp 28.36 Br md 10.50 Dpth 4.85 Welded, 1 dk	**(B32A2ST) Tug**	**2 oil engines** reduction geared to sc. shafts driving 2 Z propellers Caterpillar 2 x 4 Stroke Caterpillar Inc-USA
9596131 *ESJP* EK-1001	**VIRU** **AS DGM Shipping** - SatCom: Inmarsat C 427678711 *Tallinn* *Estonia* MMSI: 276787000 Official number: 1F10B01	**117** 35 40	Class: RS	**2010-02 Sosnovskiy Sudostroitelnyy Zavod — Sosnovka** Yd No: 862 Loa 25.50 Br ex 7.00 Dght 2.390 Lbp 22.00 Br md 6.80 Dpth 3.30 Welded, 1 dk	**(B11A2FS) Stern Trawler** Ins: 64 Compartments: 1 Ho, ER 1 Ha: ER	**1 oil engine** reduction geared to sc. shaft driving 1 FP propeller Total Power: 216kW (294hp) 9.5kn Volvo Penta D12MH 1 x 4 Stroke 6 Cy. 131 x 150 216kW (294bhp) AB Volvo Penta-Sweden AuxGen: 1 x 28kW a.c Fuel: 15.0 (d.f.)
5382219 *HQUU4* -	**VIRU** *ex* Georgios L *-1999* *ex* Katerina *-1997* *ex* Viru *-1965* *ex* Deni *-1958* *ex* Hinderika *-1932* *ex* Margrietha *-1928* *ex* Helder *-1928* **Denbrea Marine Corp** - *San Lorenzo* *Honduras* Official number: L-0327291	*219* 112 284	Class: (BV)	**1917 R. Brandsma & Zonen — Franeker** Yd No: 14 Loa 35.41 Br ex 6.71 Dght 2.750 Lbp - Br md 6.66 Dpth 3.04 Riveted, 1 dk	**(A31A2GX) General Cargo Ship** Bale: 230 Compartments: 1 Ho, ER 2 Ha: ER Derricks: 2x0.5t; Winches: 2	**1 oil engine** reduction geared to sc. shaft driving 1 FP propeller Total Power: 287kW (390hp) 7.0kn Scania DI14 M 1 x Vee 4 Stroke 8 Cy. 127 x 140 287kW (390bhp) (, fitted 1991) Saab Scania AB-Sweden Fuel: 7.0 (d.f.)
9095204 *EAMS* 3-VILL-12-	**VIRXE DO MAR** **Santamaria Alvarez Jose Manuel** - *Santa Eugenia de Ribeira* *Spain* Official number: 3-2/2006	**199** 60 -		**2006-06 Astilleros Armon Burela SA — Burela** Yd No: 270 Loa 27.50 Br ex - Dght 3.300 Lbp 22.00 Br md 7.50 Dpth - Welded, 1 dk	**(B11A2FS) Stern Trawler**	**1 oil engine** driving 1 Propeller Total Power: 364kW (495hp)
9338357 *EBVQ* 3-LU-22-05	**VIRXEN DA BLANCA** **Jose Antonio y Eugenio Lopez Abaz** - *Burela* *Spain* MMSI: 224071000 Official number: 3-2/2005	**241** 72 -		**2005-06 Astilleros Armon Burela SA — Burela** Yd No: 210 Loa 29.00 Br ex - Dght 3.000 Lbp 23.55 Br md 7.00 Dpth 3.50 Welded, 1 dk	**(B11B2FV) Fishing Vessel**	**1 oil engine** geared to sc. shaft driving 1 FP propeller Total Power: 294kW (400hp) 10.0kn Caterpillar 1 x 4 Stroke 294kW (400bhp) Caterpillar Inc-USA AuxGen: 2 x 175kW 380V 50Hz a.c
8958849 - -	**VISA** **PT Coral Mas** - *Jakarta* *Indonesia*	**228** 136 -	Class: KI	**2000-02 P.T. Dok & Perkapalan Air Kantung — Bangka** Loa 24.20 Br ex - Dght 3.000 Lbp 22.00 Br md 8.50 Dpth 5.20 Welded, 1 dk	**(B32A2ST) Tug**	**2 oil engines** reduction geared to sc. shafts driving 2 FP propellers Total Power: 780kW (1,060hp) 8.0kn Yanmar 6LAA-UTE 2 x 4 Stroke 6 Cy. 148 x 165 each-390kW (530bhp) Yanmar Diesel Engine Co Ltd-Japan
7047502 *XVVE* -	**VISAL 02** *ex* Constellation *-1989* *ex* Preakness *-1989* **Vietnam Union Salvage Corp (Xi Nghiep Lien Hiep Truc Vot Cuu Ho)** - *Da Nang* *Vietnam* MMSI: 574999007 Official number: VNDN-128-TL	**543** 163 -	Class: VR	**1969 Burton Shipyard Co., Inc. — Port Arthur, Tx** Yd No: 448 Loa 53.02 Br ex 12.50 Dght 3.850 Lbp 48.16 Br md 12.25 Dpth 4.57 Welded, 1 dk	**(B21A20S) Platform Supply Ship**	**2 oil engines** driving 2 FP propellers Total Power: 2,942kW (4,000hp) 12.0kn EMD (Electro-Motive) 16-567-C 2 x Vee 2 Stroke 16 Cy. 216 x 254 each-1471kW (2000bhp) General Motors Corp.Electro-Motive Div.-La Grange AuxGen: 2 x 96kW a.c Thrusters: 1 Tunnel thruster (f)
7047605 - -	**VISAL 4** *ex* Emu *-1989* *ex* Reliance *-1985* *ex* Apollo *-1985* - -	*272* 185 -	Class: (KI)	**1969 Halter Marine Fabricators, Inc. — Moss Point, Ms** Yd No: 223 Loa - Br ex 11.59 Dght 3.379 Lbp 47.43 Br md 11.54 Dpth 3.81 Welded, 1 dk	**(B21A20S) Platform Supply Ship**	**2 oil engines** driving 2 FP propellers Total Power: 1,176kW (1,598hp) Stork DR0218K 2 x 4 Stroke 8 Cy. 210 x 300 each-588kW (799bhp) Stork Werkspoor Diesel BV-Netherlands
8829751 *XVEI* -	**VISAL 8** *ex* Seagull *-2002* *ex* Harvest Gold *-1996* *ex* Belait Rose *-1994* **Enterprise of Salvage & Transport No 1 (Xi Nghiep Truc Vot Cuu Ho Va Van Tai 1)** - *Saigon* *Vietnam* Official number: VNSG-1639-DV	**265** 80 185	Class: VR (BV) (GL)	**1986 Greenbay Marine Pte Ltd — Singapore** Yd No: 55 Loa 32.00 Br ex 10.30 Dght 1.600 Lbp 29.76 Br md 10.00 Dpth 2.80 Welded, 1 dk	**(B21A20S) Platform Supply Ship**	**2 oil engines** geared to sc. shafts driving 2 FP propellers Total Power: 930kW (1,264hp) Caterpillar 3412TA 2 x Vee 4 Stroke 12 Cy. 137 x 152 each-465kW (632bhp) Caterpillar Tractor Co-USA AuxGen: 2 x 136kW 220/415V a.c
7623899 *T3SV* -	**VISAL SAIGON** *ex* Future One *-2009* *ex* Vos Hunter *-2009* *ex* DEA Hunter *-2008* *ex* Acadian Mistral *-2001* *ex* Offshore Hunter *-1986* *ex* Kongsholm *-1984* *ex* Normand Hunter *-1984* **Vietnam Salvage Co** - *Tarawa* *Kiribati* MMSI: 529237000 Official number: K-16791324	**1,317** 395 1,971	Class: VR (LR) ✠ Classed LR until 13/8/09	**1979-09 Marystown Shipyard Ltd — Marystown NL** Yd No: 25 Loa 64.40 Br ex 14.10 Dght 5.900 Lbp 58.53 Br md 13.80 Dpth 6.90 Welded, 1 dk, 1 part dk fwd & aft of ER	**(B21B20A) Anchor Handling Tug Supply**	**2 oil engines** with clutches, flexible couplings & sr geared to sc. shafts driving 2 CP propellers Total Power: 5,400kW (7,342hp) 15.0kn Wichmann 9AXAG 2 x 2 Stroke 9 Cy. 300 x 450 each-2700kW (3671bhp) Wichmann Motorfabrikk AS-Norway AuxGen: 2 x 170kW 440V 60Hz a.c, 1 x 56kW 440V 60Hz a.c Thrusters: 1 Thwart. CP thruster (f) Fuel: 750.0 (d.f.)
9226841 *PBDO* -	**VISAREND** **Government of The Kingdom of The Netherlands (Rijkswaterstaat Directie Noordzee)** - *Rijswijk, Zuid Holland* *Netherlands* MMSI: 245844000 Official number: 38383	**247** 71 250	Class: LR ✠**100A1** SS 12/2011 SSC patrol, mono HSC G4, service from an EC port ✠**LMC** **UMS** Cable: 137.5/16.0 U2 (a)	**2001-12 Scheepswerf Made B.V. — Made** (Hull) Yd No: 00028 **2001-12 B.V. Scheepswerf Damen — Gorinchem** Yd No: 549850 Loa 42.80 Br ex 7.10 Dght 2.600 Lbp 38.30 Br md 6.80 Dpth 3.77 Welded, 1 dk	**(B34H2SQ) Patrol Vessel**	**2 oil engines** with clutches, flexible couplings & sr reverse geared to sc. shafts driving 2 CP propellers Total Power: 4,176kW (5,678hp) 22.5kn Caterpillar 3516TA 2 x Vee 4 Stroke 16 Cy. 170 x 190 each-2088kW (2839bhp) Caterpillar Inc-USA AuxGen: 2 x 145kW 400V 50Hz a.c Thrusters: 1 Thwart. FP thruster (f) Fuel: 27.6 (d.f.)
9223784 *SGPH* -	**VISBY** **Rederi AB Gotland** Destination Gotland AB *Visby* *Sweden* MMSI: 265865000	**29,746** 9,505 4,730	Class: LR ✠**100A1** SS 01/2013 passenger/vehicle ferry *IWS EP LI Ice Class 1A at 6.562m draught Max/min draught forward 6.562/3.362m Max/min draught aft 6.562/3.362m ✠**LMC** **UMS** Eq.Ltr: I†; Cable: 601.0/66.0 U3 (a)	**2003-01 Guangzhou Shipyard International Co Ltd — Guangzhou GD** Yd No: 9130004 Loa 195.80 (BB) Br ex 25.64 Dght 6.550 Lbp 176.00 Br md 25.00 Dpth 9.30 Welded, 4 dks	**(A36A2PR) Passenger/Ro-Ro Ship (Vehicles)** Passengers: unberthed: 1100; cabins: 112; berths: 400 Bow ramp (centre) Len: 21.00 Wid: 6.20 Swl: - Stern ramp (wing) Len: 21.00 Wid: 4.80 Swl: - Stern door/ramp (centre) Len: 15.00 Wid: 11.00 Swl: - Side ramp (wing) Len: 4.80 Wid: 4.80 Swl: - Lane-Len: 1800 Cars: 520 Ice Capable	**4 oil engines** with clutches, flexible couplings & sr geared to sc. shafts driving 2 CP propellers Total Power: 50,400kW (68,524hp) 28.5kn Wartsila 12V46C 4 x Vee 4 Stroke 12 Cy. 460 x 580 each-12600kW (17131bhp) Wartsila Finland Oy-Finland AuxGen: 2 x 1460kW 440V 60Hz a.c, 3 x 1460kW 440V 60Hz a.c Boilers: TOH (o.f.) 10.2kgf/cm² (10.0bar), TOH (ex.g.) 10.2kgf/cm² (10.0bar) Thrusters: 2 Thwart. FP thruster (f) Fuel: 92.0 (d.f.) 1296.0 (r.f.) 200.0pd

9198197 *SMVK* -	**VISCARIA** - **Lulea Bogserbats AB** - *Lulea* *Sweden* MMSI: 265518260	**603** 181 451	Class: LR ✠ **100A1** SS 11/2010 tug Ice Class 1AS ✠ **LMC** **UMS** Eq.Ltr: J; Cable: 357.5/24.0 U3 (a)	**2000-11 Moen Slip AS — Kolvereid** Yd No: 44 Loa 35.75 Br ex 12.28 Dght 5.600 Lbp 32.00 Br md 12.00 Dpth 6.70 Welded, 1 dk	**(B32A2ST) Tug** Ice Capable	**1 oil engine** with clutches, flexible couplings & sr geared to sc. shaft driving 1 CP propeller Total Power: 4,410kW (5,996hp) 12.2kn Wartsila 12V32 1 x Vee 4 Stroke 12 Cy. 320 x 350 4410kW (5996bhp) Wartsila Finland Oy-Finland AuxGen: 2 x 196kW 380V 50Hz a.c Thrusters: 1 Thwart. FP thruster (f); 1 Tunnel thruster (a) Fuel: 117.0 (d.f.) 21.0pd
7330052 *LATC4* -	**VISCARIA** *ex Jurgen -1993 ex Jurgen Wehr -1993* *ex Jurgen W -1978 ex Jurgen Wehr -1977* **Rederiaktieselskabet Nyborg** A K Aagesen & Partners AS *Kristiansand* *Norway (NIS)* MMSI: 258897000 Official number: N01313	**1,859** 558 2,437	Class: NV (GL)	**1973-03 J.J. Sietas Schiffswerft — Hamburg** Yd No: 701 Converted From: General Cargo Ship-1994 Lengthened-1981 Loa 82.76 Br ex 11.84 Dght 4.753 Lbp 77.70 Br md 11.79 Dpth 6.61 Welded, 1 dk	**(A13C2LA) Asphalt/Bitumen Tanker** Liq: 1,451; Liq (Oil): 1,451; Asphalt: 1,451 Cargo Heating Coils Compartments: 4 Ta, ER 2 Cargo Pump (s): 2x200m^3/hr Ice Capable	**1 oil engine** reduction geared to sc. shaft driving 1 FP propeller Total Power: 993kW (1,350hp) 12.0kn Deutz SBA12M528 1 x Vee 4 Stroke 12 Cy. 220 x 280 993kW (1350bhp) Kloeckner Humboldt Deutz AG-West Germany AuxGen: 2 x 60kW 380V 50Hz a.c Fuel: 139.0 (d.f.)
7921411 - -	**VISDEMCO** *ex Propane Maru No. 2 -2000* - -	*696* - 793	Class: (NK)	**1979-12 Kurinoura Dockyard Co Ltd — Yawatahama EH** Yd No: 148 Loa 62.90 Br ex - Dght 3.885 Lbp 57.51 Br md 10.00 Dpth 4.40 Welded, 1 dk	**(A11B2TG) LPG Tanker** Liq (Gas): 1,173 2 x Gas Tank (s);	**1 oil engine** driving 1 FP propeller Total Power: 1,177kW (1,600hp) 12.0kn Akasaka DM33 1 x 4 Stroke 6 Cy. 330 x 500 1177kW (1600bhp) Akasaka Tekkosho KK (Akasaka DieselLtd)-Japan AuxGen: 3 x 368kW Fuel: 112.0 (d.f.) 4.0pd
7101499 *XVAF* -	**VISDEMCO 01** *ex Matsuyoshi -1994* *ex Matsuyoshi Maru No. 5 -1993* **Trung Kien Co Ltd (Cong Ty Tnhh Trung Kien)** - *Haiphong* *Vietnam* Official number: VN-1342-VT	**445** 243 1,130	Class: VR	**1970 K.K. Matsuura Zosensho — Osakikamijima** Yd No: 161 Lengthened-2001 Loa 59.44 Br ex 8.03 Dght 4.000 Lbp 56.17 Br md 8.01 Dpth 5.00 Welded, 1 dk	**(A31A2GX) General Cargo Ship** Grain: 936 1 Ha: (26.0 x 5.8)ER	**1 oil engine** driving 1 FP propeller Total Power: 559kW (760hp) Mitsubishi 12DE20MT 1 x Vee 4 Stroke 12 Cy. 150 x 200 559kW (760bhp) Mitsubishi Heavy Industries Ltd-Japan
9498743 *ICNA* -	**VISEMAR ONE** - **Visemar di Navigazione Srl** - SatCom: Inmarsat Mini-M 765040687 *Bari* *Italy* MMSI: 247281400	**26,375** 8,994 8,702	Class: RI	**2010-04 Cantiere Navale Visentini Srl — Porto Viro** Yd No: 223 Loa 186.40 (BB) Br ex Dght 6.850 Lbp 177.40 Br md 25.60 Dpth 9.15 Welded, 1 dk	**(A36A2PR) Passenger/Ro-Ro Ship (Vehicles)** Passengers: unberthed: 291; berths: 276 Stern door/ramp (centre) Len: 17.00 Wid: 13.80 Swl: - Lane-Len: 2860 Lane-clr ht: 4.80 Cars: 70	**2 oil engines** reduction geared to sc. shafts driving 2 CP propellers Total Power: 21,600kW (29,368hp) 23.5kn MAN-B&W 9L48/60B 2 x 4 Stroke 9 Cy. 480 x 600 each-10800kW (14684bhp) MAN B&W Diesel AG-Augsburg AuxGen: 2 x 1800kW 440/220V 60Hz a.c, 2 x 1800kW 440/220V 60Hz a.c Thrusters: 2 Tunnel thruster (f) Fuel: 312.0 (d.f.) 1158.0 (r.f.) 91.0pd
9360491 *CQMH* -	**VISEU** - **Lico Leasing SA EFC** Naveiro Transportes Maritimos (Madeira) Lda *Madeira* *Portugal (MAR)* MMSI: 255803370	**2,956** 1,558 4,672	Class: GL (Class contemplated) (LR) ✠ Classed LR until 18/12/12	**2008-12 OAO Khersonskiy Sudostroitelnyy Zavod — Kherson** (Hull) Yd No: (151) **2008-12 Factoria Naval de Marin S.A. — Marin** Yd No: 151 Loa 89.50 (BB) Br ex 13.70 Dght 6.000 Lbp 83.40 Br md 13.70 Dpth 8.00 Welded, 1 dk	**(A31A2GX) General Cargo Ship** Grain: 5,578 TEU 111 Compartments: 1 Ho, ER 1 Ha: ER (60.5 x 11.0)	**1 oil engine** with clutches, flexible couplings & dr reverse geared to sc. shaft driving 1 CP propeller Total Power: 1,850kW (2,515hp) 12.0kn MaK 6M25 1 x 4 Stroke 6 Cy. 255 x 400 1850kW (2515bhp) Caterpillar Motoren GmbH & Co. KG-Germany AuxGen: 2 x 184kW 380V 50Hz a.c, 1 x 448kW 380V 50Hz a.c Boilers: HWH (o.f.) 6.1kgf/cm^2 (6.0bar), HWH (ex.g.) 6.1kgf/cm^2 (6.0bar) Thrusters: 1 Thwart. FP thruster (f)
9648037 *AVPA* -	**VISHAL HIRA** - **V M Salgaocar & Brother Pvt Ltd** - *Panaji* *India* MMSI: 419000395 Official number: PNJ-626	**5,386** 1,616 1,500	Class: AB (Class contemplated) IR	**2012-10 Nantong Tongmao Shipbuilding Co Ltd — Rugao JS** Yd No: TM1011 Loa 92.38 Br ex 28.02 Dght 3.510 Lbp 88.52 Br md 28.00 Dpth 6.52 Welded, 1 dk	**(A31A2GE) General Cargo Ship, Self-discharging** Compartments: 1 Ho, ER 1 Ha: ER	**2 oil engines** geared to sc. shafts driving 2 Directional propellers Total Power: 1,920kW (2,610hp) MAN-B&W 6L23/30A 2 x 4 Stroke 6 Cy. 225 x 300 each-960kW (1305bhp) STX Engine Co Ltd-South Korea Fuel: 600.0
9091789 - -	**VISHAL NIKHIL** - - *Mormugao* *India* Official number: MRH 653	**1,111** 980 1,950	Class: (IR) (AB)	**1987-06 G.R. Engineering — Goa** Yd No: 5 Loa 65.00 Br ex 12.52 Dght 3.200 Lbp 62.00 Br md 12.50 Dpth 4.20 Welded, 1 dk	**(A31A2GX) General Cargo Ship**	**2 oil engines** sr geared to sc. shafts driving 2 Propellers 8.0kn Russkiy 2 x Vee 4 Stroke 12 Cy. 120 x 160 Mashinostroitelnyy Zavod"Russkiy-Dizel"-Sankt-Peterburg
9664691 *AVVY* -	**VISHAMBAR** - **Jindal ITF Ltd** - *Mumbai* *India* MMSI: 419000615 Official number: 4041	**1,368** 579 2,100	Class: IR	**2013-03 Dempo Engineering Works Ltd. — Goa** Yd No: 509 Loa 72.00 Br ex 14.02 Dght 3.000 Lbp 69.65 Br md 14.00 Dpth 4.25 Welded, 1 dk	**(A31A2GX) General Cargo Ship** Grain: 2,300	**2 oil engines** reduction geared to sc. shafts driving 2 FP propellers Total Power: 1,176kW (1,598hp) 12.0kn Volvo Penta D13MH 2 x 4 Stroke 6 Cy. 131 x 158 each-588kW (799bhp) AB Volvo Penta-Sweden
9515046 *AVLW* -	**VISHVA ANAND** - **The Shipping Corporation of India Ltd (SCI)** - SatCom: Inmarsat C 441923953 *Mumbai* *India* MMSI: 419000310 Official number: 3847	**44,007** 26,658 80,655 T/cm 71.9	Class: IR LR ✠ **100A1** SS 07/2012 bulk carrier CSR BC-A GRAB (20) Nos. 2, 4 & 6 holds may be empty ESP **ShipRight** (CM,ACS (B)) *IWS LI ✠ **LMC** **UMS** Eq.Ltr: Q†; Cable: 687.5/81.0 U3 (a)	**2012-07 STX (Dalian) Shipbuilding Co Ltd — Wafangdian LN** Yd No: D1085 Loa 229.00 (BB) Br ex 32.29 Dght 14.450 Lbp 222.00 Br md 32.24 Dpth 20.10 Welded, 1 dk	**(A21A2BC) Bulk Carrier** Grain: 95,149 Compartments: 7 Ho, ER 7 Ha: ER	**1 oil engine** driving 1 FP propeller Total Power: 11,060kW (15,037hp) 14.2kn MAN-B&W 7S50MC-C8 1 x 2 Stroke 7 Cy. 500 x 2000 11060kW (15037bhp) STX Engine Co Ltd-South Korea AuxGen: 3 x 625kW 450V 60Hz a.c Boilers: WTAuxB (o.f.) 9.2kgf/cm^2 (9.0bar) Fuel: 300.0 (d.f.) 2430.0 (r.f.)
9464778 *AVHR* -	**VISHVA BANDHAN** - **The Shipping Corporation of India Ltd (SCI)** - *Mumbai* *India* MMSI: 419000177 Official number: 3748	**33,185** 18,769 57,196 T/cm 57.3	Class: IR NV	**2011-12 STX (Dalian) Shipbuilding Co Ltd — Wafangdian LN** Yd No: D2044 Loa 190.00 (BB) Br ex 32.30 Dght 13.000 Lbp 183.31 Br md 32.26 Dpth 18.50 Welded, 1 dk	**(A21A2BC) Bulk Carrier** Grain: 71,850 Compartments: 5 Ho, ER 5 Ha: ER Cranes: 4x30t	**1 oil engine** driving 1 FP propeller Total Power: 9,960kW (13,542hp) 14.5kn MAN-B&W 6S50MC-C 1 x 2 Stroke 6 Cy. 500 x 2000 9960kW (13542bhp) STX Engine Co Ltd-South Korea AuxGen: 3 x a.c
9603893 *AVLR* -	**VISHVA CHETNA** - **The Shipping Corporation of India Ltd (SCI)** - *Mumbai* *India* MMSI: 419000303 Official number: 3842	**44,864** 27,954 82,000	Class: BV IR	**2013-05 Jiangsu Eastern Heavy Industry Co Ltd — Jingjiang JS** Yd No: JEHIC10-061 Loa 229.00 (BB) Br ex - Dght 14.450 Lbp 225.50 Br md 32.26 Dpth 20.05 Welded, 1 dk	**(A21A2BC) Bulk Carrier** Grain: 97,000; Bale: 90,784 Compartments: 7 Ho, ER 7 Ha: ER	**1 oil engine** driving 1 FP propeller Total Power: 11,900kW (16,179hp) 14.0kn MAN-B&W 5S60MC-C8 1 x 2 Stroke 5 Cy. 600 x 2400 11900kW (16179bhp) AuxGen: 3 x 600kW a.c
9487914 *AVHT* -	**VISHVA DIKSHA** - **The Shipping Corporation of India Ltd (SCI)** - *Mumbai* *India* MMSI: 419000179 Official number: 3750	**33,185** 18,769 57,133 T/cm 57.3	Class: IR NV	**2012-05 STX (Dalian) Shipbuilding Co Ltd — Wafangdian LN** Yd No: D2050 Loa 189.99 (BB) Br ex 32.30 Dght 13.020 Lbp 183.31 Br md 32.26 Dpth 18.50 Welded, 1 dk	**(A21A2BC) Bulk Carrier** Grain: 71,956; Bale: 70,111 Compartments: 5 Ho, ER 5 Ha: ER Cranes: 4x36t	**1 oil engine** driving 1 FP propeller Total Power: 9,480kW (12,889hp) 14.0kn MAN-B&W 6S50MC-C 1 x 2 Stroke 6 Cy. 500 x 2000 9480kW (12889bhp) STX (Dalian) Engine Co Ltd-China AuxGen: 3 x 625kW 450V 60Hz a.c Fuel: 160.0 (d.f.) 1854.0 (r.f.)
9487897 *AVHP* -	**VISHVA EKTA** - **The Shipping Corporation of India Ltd (SCI)** - *Mumbai* *India* MMSI: 419000175 Official number: 3746	**33,185** 18,769 57,099 T/cm 57.3	Class: IR NV	**2012-01 STX (Dalian) Shipbuilding Co Ltd — Wafangdian LN** Yd No: D2047 Loa 190.04 (BB) Br ex 32.30 Dght 13.000 Lbp 183.31 Br md 32.26 Dpth 18.50 Welded, 1 dk	**(A21A2BC) Bulk Carrier** Grain: 71,956; Bale: 69,525 Compartments: 5 Ho, ER 5 Ha: ER Cranes: 4x30t	**1 oil engine** driving 1 FP propeller Total Power: 9,480kW (12,889hp) 14.5kn MAN-B&W 6S50MC-C 1 x 2 Stroke 6 Cy. 500 x 2000 9480kW (12889bhp) STX Engine Co Ltd-South Korea AuxGen: 3 x a.c

9603881 *AVLQ* -	**VISHVA JYOTI** **The Shipping Corporation of India Ltd (SCI)** - *Mumbai* *India* MMSI: 419000302 Official number: 3841	**44,864** 27,954 81,895 T/cm 71.9	Class: BV IR	**2012-12 Jiangsu Eastern Heavy Industry Co Ltd — Jingjiang JS** Yd No: JEHIC10-060 Loa 228.95 (BB) Br ex 32.27 Dght 14.470 Lbp 225.17 Br md 32.26 Dpth 20.04 Welded, 1 dk	**(A21A2BC) Bulk Carrier** Grain: 95,568; Bale: 90,784 Compartments: 7 Ho, ER 7 Ha: (15.7 x 15.0)5 (17.4 x 15.0)ER (14.8 x 12.8)	**1 oil engine** driving 1 FP propeller Total Power: 9,800kW (13,324hp) 14.0kn MAN-B&W 5S60MC-C8 1 x 2 Stroke 5 Cy. 600 x 2400 9800kW (13324bhp) Jiangsu Antai Power Machinery Co Lt-China AuxGen: 3 x 615kW 60Hz a.c Fuel: 270.0 (d.f.) 2943.0 (r.f.)
9624017 *AVMH* -	**VISHVA MALHAR** **The Shipping Corporation of India Ltd (SCI)** - *Mumbai* *India* MMSI: 419000321 Official number: 3858	**33,032** 19,231 56,616 T/cm 58.8	Class: BV IR	**2011-08 Yangzhou Guoyu Shipbuilding Co Ltd — Yangzhou JS** Yd No: GY812 Loa 189.99 (BB) Br ex - Dght 12.800 Lbp 185.00 Br md 32.26 Dpth 18.00 Welded, 1 dk	**(A21A2BC) Bulk Carrier** Grain: 71,634; Bale: 68,200 Compartments: 5 Ho, ER 5 Ha: ER Cranes: 4x36t	**1 oil engine** driving 1 FP propeller Total Power: 9,480kW (12,889hp) 14.5kn Wartsila 6RT-flex50 1 x 2 Stroke 6 Cy. 500 x 2050 9480kW (12889bhp) Qingdao Qiyao Wartsila MHI LinshanMarine Diesel Co Ltd (QMD)-China AuxGen: 3 x 600kW 60Hz a.c Fuel: 2400.0
9464742 *AVHQ* -	**VISHVA NIDHI** **The Shipping Corporation of India Ltd (SCI)** - SatCom: Inmarsat C 441923048 *Mumbai* *India* MMSI: 419000176 Official number: 3747	**33,170** 18,769 57,144 T/cm 57.3	Class: IR NV	**2011-09 STX (Dalian) Shipbuilding Co Ltd — Wafangdian LN** Yd No: D2037 Loa 189.99 (BB) Br ex 32.30 Dght 13.000 Lbp 183.28 Br md 32.26 Dpth 18.50 Welded, 1 dk	**(A21A2BC) Bulk Carrier** Grain: 71,850 Compartments: 5 Ho, ER 5 Ha: ER Cranes: 4x30t	**1 oil engine** driving 1 FP propeller Total Power: 9,960kW (13,542hp) 14.5kn MAN-B&W 6S50MC-C 1 x 2 Stroke 6 Cy. 500 x 2000 9960kW (13542bhp) STX Engine Co Ltd-South Korea AuxGen: 3 x a.c
9533490 *AVLZ* -	**VISHVA PREETI** **The Shipping Corporation of India Ltd (SCI)** - *Mumbai* *India* MMSI: 419000313 Official number: 3850	**44,007** 26,658 80,250 T/cm 71.9	Class: IR LR ✠ **100A1** SS 10/2012 bulk carrier CSR BC-A GRAB (20) Nos. 2, 4 & 6 holds may be empty ESP **ShipRight** (CM,ACS (B)) *IWS LI ✠ **LMC** **UMS** Eq.Ltr: Q†; Cable: 687.5/81.0 U3 (a)	**2012-10 STX (Dalian) Shipbuilding Co Ltd — Wafangdian LN** Yd No: D1087 Loa 229.03 (BB) Br ex 32.72 Dght 14.450 Lbp 222.00 Br md 32.24 Dpth 20.11 Welded, 1 dk	**(A21A2BC) Bulk Carrier** Grain: 95,149 Compartments: 7 Ho, ER 7 Ha: ER	**1 oil engine** driving 1 FP propeller Total Power: 11,060kW (15,037hp) 14.6kn MAN-B&W 7S50MC-C 1 x 2 Stroke 7 Cy. 500 x 2000 11060kW (15037bhp) STX (Dalian) Engine Co Ltd-China AuxGen: 3 x 625kW 450V 60Hz a.c Boilers: WTAuxB (Comp) 9.2kgf/cm² (9.0bar) Fuel: 300.0 (d.f.) 2430.0 (r.f.)
9464766 *AVHO* -	**VISHVA PRERNA** **The Shipping Corporation of India Ltd (SCI)** - SatCom: Inmarsat C 441923148 *Mumbai* *India* MMSI: 419000174 Official number: 3745	**33,185** 18,769 57,161 T/cm 57.3	Class: IR NV	**2011-11 STX (Dalian) Shipbuilding Co Ltd — Wafangdian LN** Yd No: D2041 Loa 190.00 (BB) Br ex 32.30 Dght 13.000 Lbp 183.30 Br md 32.26 Dpth 18.50 Welded, 1 dk	**(A21A2BC) Bulk Carrier** Grain: 71,850 Compartments: 5 Ho, ER 5 Ha: ER Cranes: 4x30t	**1 oil engine** driving 1 FP propeller Total Power: 9,960kW (13,542hp) 14.5kn MAN-B&W 6S50MC-C 1 x 2 Stroke 6 Cy. 500 x 2000 9960kW (13542bhp) STX Engine Co Ltd-South Korea AuxGen: 3 x a.c
9604005 *AVLS* -	**VISHVA UDAY** **The Shipping Corporation of India Ltd (SCI)** - *Mumbai* *India* MMSI: 419000304 Official number: 3843	**44,861** 27,954 82,000 T/cm 71.9	Class: BV IR	**2013-11 Jiangsu Eastern Heavy Industry Co Ltd — Jingjiang JS** Yd No: JEHIC10-062 Loa 229.00 (BB) Br ex - Dght 14.450 Lbp 225.15 Br md 32.26 Dpth 20.05 Welded, 1 dk	**(A21A2BC) Bulk Carrier** Grain: 98,740; Bale: 90,784 Compartments: 7 Ho, ER 7 Ha: 6 (17.4 x 15.0)ER (14.8 x 12.8)	**1 oil engine** driving 1 FP propeller Total Power: 9,800kW (13,324hp) 14.0kn MAN-B&W 5S60MC-C8 1 x 2 Stroke 5 Cy. 600 x 2400 9800kW (13324bhp) Jiangsu Antai Power Machinery Co Lt-China AuxGen: 3 x 615kW 60Hz a.c Fuel: 119.0 (d.f.) 2943.0 (r.f.)
9533505 *AVLY* -	**VISHVA VIJAY** **The Shipping Corporation of India Ltd (SCI)** - *Mumbai* *India* MMSI: 419000312 Official number: 3849	**44,010** 26,658 80,312 T/cm 71.9	Class: IR LR ✠ **100A1** SS 10/2012 bulk carrier CSR BC-A GRAB (20) Nos. 2, 4 & 6 holds may be empty ESP **ShipRight** (CM,ACS (B)) *IWS LI ✠ **LMC** **UMS** Eq.Ltr: Q†; Cable: 687.5/81.0 U3 (a)	**2012-10 STX (Dalian) Shipbuilding Co Ltd — Wafangdian LN** Yd No: D1088 Loa 229.00 (BB) Br ex 32.29 Dght 14.450 Lbp 222.01 Br md 32.24 Dpth 20.10 Welded, 1 dk	**(A21A2BC) Bulk Carrier** Grain: 95,149 Compartments: 7 Ho, ER 7 Ha: ER	**1 oil engine** driving 1 FP propeller Total Power: 11,060kW (15,037hp) 14.5kn MAN-B&W 7S50MC-C 1 x 2 Stroke 7 Cy. 500 x 2000 11060kW (15037bhp) STX (Dalian) Engine Co Ltd-China AuxGen: 3 x 625kW 450V 60Hz a.c Boilers: WTAuxB (Comp) 9.1kgf/cm² (8.9bar) Fuel: 300.0 (d.f.) 2430.0 (r.f.)
9621699 *AVMI* -	**VISHVA VIJETA** **The Shipping Corporation of India Ltd (SCI)** - *Mumbai* *India* MMSI: 419000322 Official number: 3859	**33,032** 19,231 56,800 T/cm 58.8	Class: BV IR	**2011-07 Yangzhou Guoyu Shipbuilding Co Ltd — Yangzhou JS** Yd No: GY813 Loa 189.99 (BB) Br ex - Dght 12.800 Lbp 185.00 Br md 32.26 Dpth 18.00 Welded, 1 dk	**(A21A2BC) Bulk Carrier** Grain: 71,634; Bale: 68,200 Compartments: 5 Ho, ER 5 Ha: 4 (21.3 x 18.3)ER (18.9 x 18.3) Cranes: 4x36t	**1 oil engine** driving 1 FP propeller Total Power: 9,480kW (12,889hp) 14.2kn Wartsila 6RT-flex50 1 x 2 Stroke 6 Cy. 500 x 2050 9480kW (12889bhp) Qingdao Qiyao Wartsila MHI LinshanMarine Diesel Co Ltd (QMD)-China AuxGen: 3 x 600kW 60Hz a.c Fuel: 120.0 (d.f.) 2200.0 (r.f.)
9487902 *AVHS* -	**VISHVA VIKAS** **The Shipping Corporation of India Ltd (SCI)** - *Mumbai* *India* MMSI: 419000178 Official number: 3749	**33,185** 18,769 57,128 T/cm 57.3	Class: IR NV	**2012-03 STX (Dalian) Shipbuilding Co Ltd — Wafangdian LN** Yd No: D2049 Loa 189.99 (BB) Br ex 32.29 Dght 13.000 Lbp 183.30 Br md 32.26 Dpth 18.50 Welded, 1 dk	**(A21A2BC) Bulk Carrier** Grain: 71,903; Bale: 70,111 Compartments: 5 Ho, ER 5 Ha: ER Cranes: 4x30t	**1 oil engine** driving 1 FP propeller Total Power: 9,960kW (13,542hp) 14.5kn MAN-B&W 6S50MC-C 1 x 2 Stroke 6 Cy. 500 x 2000 9960kW (13542bhp) STX Engine Co Ltd-South Korea AuxGen: 3 x a.c
9533488 *AVLX* -	**VISHVA VINAY** **The Shipping Corporation of India Ltd (SCI)** - *Mumbai* *India* MMSI: 419000311 Official number: 3848	**44,007** 26,658 80,139 T/cm 71.9	Class: IR LR ✠ **100A1** SS 08/2012 bulk carrier CSR BC-A GRAB (20) Nos. 2, 4 & 6 holds may be empty ESP **ShipRight** (CM,ACS (B)) *IWS LI ✠ **LMC** **UMS** Eq.Ltr: Q†; Cable: 687.5/81.0 U3 (a)	**2012-08 STX (Dalian) Shipbuilding Co Ltd — Wafangdian LN** Yd No: D1086 Loa 229.00 (BB) Br ex 32.29 Dght 14.450 Lbp 222.00 Br md 32.24 Dpth 20.10 Welded, 1 dk	**(A21A2BC) Bulk Carrier** Grain: 95,172 Compartments: 7 Ho, ER 7 Ha: ER	**1 oil engine** driving 1 FP propeller Total Power: 11,060kW (15,037hp) 14.2kn MAN-B&W 7S50MC-C 1 x 2 Stroke 7 Cy. 500 x 2000 11060kW (15037bhp) STX (Dalian) Engine Co Ltd-China AuxGen: 3 x 625kW 450V 60Hz a.c Boilers: WTAuxB (o.f.) 9.2kgf/cm² (9.0bar)
9098919 - -	**VISHWASAGAR** **Streamline Shipping Co Ltd** - *Panaji* *India*	**1,164** 1,000 2,000	Class: BV	**2004-10 Shaun Holding Pvt. Ltd. — Goa** Yd No: XV Loa - Br ex - Dght 3.200 Lbp 68.50 Br md 13.00 Dpth 4.20 Welded, 1 dk	**(A31A2GX) General Cargo Ship**	**1 oil engine** driving 1 Propeller Total Power: 794kW (1,080hp)
8960505 - -	**VISION** - -	**175** 53 -	Class: GL	**1999-01 PT ASL Shipyard Indonesia — Batam** Yd No: 162/98 L reg 23.10 Br ex - Dght - Lbp - Br md 10.00 Dpth 2.90 Welded, 1 dk	**(B32A2ST) Tug**	**3 oil engines** reverse reduction geared to sc. shafts driving 3 FP propellers Total Power: 849kW (1,155hp) 8.0kn Caterpillar 3406TA 3 x 4 Stroke 6 Cy. 137 x 165 each-283kW (385bhp) Caterpillar Inc-USA AuxGen: 2 x 80kW 380V a.c

8514239 *3EEG2* -	**VISION** *ex* Samsun Ambition *-2009* *ex* Countess I *-2008* *ex* North Countess *-2006* *ex* Louisiana Rainbow *-1991* *ex* North Countess *-1990* *ex* Louisiana Rainbow *-1989* **Ambition Shipping SA** STX Marine Service Co Ltd *Panama* *Panama* MMSI: 371889000 Official number: 3274207B	**36,600** 23,399 70,280 T/cm 64.5	Class: LR (NK) **100A1** SS 10/2011 bulk carrier strengthened for heavy cargoes, Nos. 2, 4 & 6 holds may be empty ESP ESN-Hold 1 **LMC** **UMS** Eq.Ltr: O†; Cable: 660.0/78.0 U3 (a)	**1986-10 Sanoyas Corp — Kurashiki OY** Yd No: 1080 Loa 225.00 (BB) Br ex - Dght 13.274 Lbp 217.02 Br md 32.28 Dpth 18.32 Welded, 1 dk	**(A21A2BC) Bulk Carrier** Grain: 81,839; Bale: 78,529 Compartments: 7 Ho, ER 7 Ha: (16.7 x 13.3)6 (16.7 x 15.0)ER	**1 oil engine** driving 1 FP propeller Total Power: 7,050kW (9,585hp) 14.0kn Mitsubishi 6UEC60LA 1 x 2 Stroke 6 Cy. 600 x 1900 7050kW (9585bhp) Mitsubishi Heavy Industries Ltd-Japan AuxGen: 3 x 390kW 450V 60Hz a.c Boilers: e 10.9kgf/cm² (10.7bar), AuxB (o.f.) 6.9kgf/cm² (6.8bar) Fuel: 121.0 (d.f.) 2274.5 (r.f.) 31.5pd
9542609 *WDF6306* -	**VISION** **Vessel Management Services Inc** Intrepid Ship Management Inc *San Francisco, CA* *United States of America* MMSI: 366904000 Official number: 1217331	**1,052** 315 600	Class: AB	**2011-07 Moss Point Marine, Inc. — Escatawpa, Ms** Yd No: 1984 Loa 41.15 Br ex - Dght 5.800 Lbp 38.97 Br md 12.80 Dpth 6.70 Welded, 1 dk	**(B32B2SA) Articulated Pusher Tug**	**2 oil engines** reduction geared to sc. shafts driving 2 CP propellers Total Power: 8,160kW (11,094hp) Wartsila 8L32 2 x 4 Stroke 8 Cy. 320 x 400 each-4080kW (5547bhp) Wartsila Finland Oy-Finland AuxGen: 2 x 425kW 60Hz a.c
9332717 *9VNT8* -	**VISION** *ex* Qc Vision *-2009* **SJ Shipping Pte Ltd** QC Container Line Ltd *Singapore* *Singapore* MMSI: 565298000 Official number: 392570	**9,957** 5,032 13,796 T/cm 28.0	Class: GL	**2006-11 Jinling Shipyard — Nanjing JS** Yd No: 04-0413 Loa 147.87 (BB) Br ex 23.55 Dght 8.510 Lbp 140.30 Br md 23.25 Dpth 11.50 Welded, 1 dk	**(A33A2CC) Container Ship (Fully Cellular)** Grain: 16,000; Bale: 16,000 TEU 1118 C Ho 334 TEU C Dk 784 incl 240 ref C Compartments: 5 Cell Ho, ER Cranes: 2x40t	**1 oil engine** reduction geared to sc. shaft driving 1 CP propeller Total Power: 9,730kW (13,229hp) 19.6kn MAN-B&W 7L58/64 1 x 4 Stroke 7 Cy. 580 x 640 9730kW (13229bhp) MAN B&W Diesel AG-Augsburg AuxGen: 3 x 570kW 440/220V a.c, 1 x 1400kW 440/220V a.c Thrusters: 1 Tunnel thruster (f)
8983155 *WDB3311* -	**VISION I** **VT Halter Marine Inc** *Gulfport, MS* *United States of America* MMSI: 366885670 Official number: 1138291	*121* 96 -		**2003 Halter Marine, Inc. — U.S.A.** Yd No: 8011 L reg 19.65 Br ex - Dght - Lbp - Br md 8.53 Dpth 2.04 Welded, 1 dk	**(B32A2ST) Tug**	**1 oil engine** driving 1 Propeller
9314038 *MGKA6* BF 190	**VISION II** *ex* Amethyst *-2008* **MB Vision LLP** - *Banff* *United Kingdom* MMSI: 235008200 Official number: C18331	**163** 55 -		**2004-12 Richards Dry Dock & Engineering Ltd — Great Yarmouth** (Hull) **2004-12 Macduff Shipyards Ltd — Macduff** Yd No: 627 Loa 18.60 Br ex - Dght - Lbp - Br md 6.80 Dpth 3.80 Welded, 1 dk	**(B11A2FS) Stern Trawler**	**1 oil engine** geared to sc. shaft driving 1 Propeller Total Power: 217kW (295hp) Caterpillar 3412 1 x Vee 4 Stroke 12 Cy. 137 x 152 217kW (295bhp) Caterpillar Inc-USA
9658757 - BF 191	**VISION III** **Vision LLP** Westward Fishing Co *Banff* *United Kingdom*	**227** - -		**2014-03 Macduff Shipyards Ltd — Macduff** Yd No: 656 Loa 23.00 (BB) Br ex - Dght - Lbp - Br md 7.30 Dpth - Welded, 1 dk	**(B11A2FT) Trawler**	**1 oil engine** reduction geared to sc. shaft driving 1 Propeller Total Power: 610kW (829hp) Mitsubishi S6R2-MPTK 1 x 4 Stroke 6 Cy. 170 x 220 610kW (829bhp) Mitsubishi Heavy Industries Ltd-Japan
9116876 *C6SE8* -	**VISION OF THE SEAS** **Vision of the Seas Inc** Royal Caribbean Cruises Ltd (RCCL) *Nassau* *Bahamas* MMSI: 311321000 Official number: 8000405	**78,717** 46,263 5,000	Class: NV	**1998-04 Chantiers de l'Atlantique — St-Nazaire** Yd No: F31 Loa 279.00 (BB) Br ex 35.60 Dght 7.900 Lbp 234.71 Br md 32.20 Dpth 22.00 Welded, 1 dk	**(A37A2PC) Passenger/Cruise** Passengers: cabins: 998; berths: 2435	**4 diesel electric oil engines** driving 4 gen. each 12600kW 6600V a.c Connecting to 2 elec. motors each (17000kW) driving 2 FP propellers Total Power: 50,400kW (68,524hp) 22.3kn Wartsila 12V46C 4 x Vee 4 Stroke 12 Cy. 460 x 580 each-12600kW (17131bhp) Wartsila NSD Finland Oy-Finland Thrusters: 2 Thwart. FP thruster (f); 1 Tunnel thruster (a) Fuel: 182.1 (d.f.) (Heating Coils) 2019.6 (r.f.) 220.0pd
8660193 *9WGN3* -	**VISION STAR** **Daily Venture Sdn Bhd** - *Kuching* *Malaysia* Official number: 330713	**131** 40 -	Class: MY	**2006-04 Tung Lung Shipbuilding — Sibu** Loa 22.98 Br ex - Dght - Lbp - Br md 7.25 Dpth 2.93 Welded, 1 dk	**(B32A2ST) Tug**	**2 oil engines** reduction geared to sc. shafts driving 2 Propellers Total Power: 1,002kW (1,362hp) Yanmar 6LAH-STE3 2 x 4 Stroke 6 Cy. 150 x 165 each-501kW (681bhp) Yanmar Diesel Engine Co Ltd-Japan
8811572 *UACD8* -	**VISMAR** **Far-Eastern Metallozagotovitelnaya Co LLC** Admiralty Ltd SatCom: Inmarsat C 427305377 *Vladivostok* *Russia* MMSI: 273351650 Official number: 906414	**1,296** 600 1,021	Class: RS	**1990-12 VEB Elbewerften Boizenburg/Rosslau — Rosslau** Yd No: 223 Loa 82.00 Br ex 11.41 Dght 2.500 Lbp 78.65 Br md 11.20 Dpth 3.60 Welded, 1dk	**(A34A2GR) Refrigerated Cargo Ship** Ins: 257 TEU 26 C. 26/20'	**2 oil engines** driving 2 FP propellers Total Power: 1,472kW (2,002hp) 9.8kn S.K.L. 6NVD48A-2U 2 x 4 Stroke 6 Cy. 320 x 480 each-736kW (1001bhp) VEB Schwermaschinenbau "KarlLiebknecht" (SKL)-Magdeburg
7928251 *ZDJS2* -	**VISNES** *ex* Aasnes *-2010* *ex* Medallion *-2002* **Sarunto AS** Tornborg Shipping AS *Gibraltar* *Gibraltar (British)* MMSI: 236561000	**3,136** 1,368 4,015	Class: BV (NV)	**1981-05 A/S Svendborg Skibsvaerft — Svendborg** Yd No: 165 Loa 94.21 Br ex 15.45 Dght 5.912 Lbp 85.93 Br md 15.40 Dpth 8.30 Welded, 2 dks	**(A31A2GX) General Cargo Ship** Grain: 5,493 TEU 130 C. 130/20' (40') Compartments: 1 Ho, ER 1 Ha: (53.7 x 11.2)ER Cranes: 1 Ice Capable	**1 oil engine** with flexible couplings & sr gearedto sc. shaft driving 1 FP propeller Total Power: 1,949kW (2,650hp) 13.5kn MaK 8M453AK 1 x 4 Stroke 8 Cy. 320 x 420 1949kW (2650bhp) Krupp MaK Maschinenbau GmbH-Kiel Thrusters: 1 Tunnel thruster (f)
9098907 *ECGO* 3-CO-22-04	**VISPON** **Plana y Compania SL** - *La Coruna* *Spain* MMSI: 224125140 Official number: 3-2/2004	**277** 83 98	Class: (BV)	**2004-09 Astilleros Armon Burela SA — Burela** Yd No: 228 Loa 31.40 (BB) Br ex - Dght 3.970 Lbp 26.13 Br md 8.50 Dpth 5.75 Welded, 1 dk	**(B11A2FS) Stern Trawler**	**1 oil engine** driving 1 CP propeller Total Power: 356kW (484hp) 11.0kn Caterpillar 3512B 1 x Vee 4 Stroke 12 Cy. 170 x 190 356kW (484bhp) (made 2003) Caterpillar Inc-USA
9285586 *FVHE* -	**VISSOLELA** **Bourbon Offshore Surf SAS** - SatCom: Inmarsat C 422832970 *Marseille* *France (FIS)* MMSI: 228329700 Official number: 924396D	**3,770** 1,143 3,320	Class: BV	**2004-06 Scheepswerf De Hoop Lobith B.V. — Lobith** Yd No: 393 Loa 77.30 Br ex - Dght 6.100 Lbp 70.91 Br md 18.00 Dpth 7.40 Welded, 1 dk	**(B22A2OR) Offshore Support Vessel** A-frames: 1x54t; Cranes: 1x40t	**4 diesel electric oil engines** driving 4 gen. Connecting to 2 elec. motors each (1800kW) driving 2 Azimuth electric drive units Total Power: 5,620kW (7,640hp) 10.0kn Caterpillar 3512B 4 x Vee 4 Stroke 12 Cy. 170 x 190 each-1405kW (1910bhp) Caterpillar Inc-USA Thrusters: 1 Thwart. CP thruster (f); 1 Retract. directional thruster (f)
6726553 *UAYH* -	**VIST** *ex* Vorotynsk *-1999* *ex* Elisey Drokin *-1997* *ex* Morskoy-9 *-1992* **OOO Transportnaya Firma 'Persepolis' (Transport-Forwarding Company 'Persepolis')** - *Astrakhan* *Russia* MMSI: 273420620	**1,595** 806 2,610	Class: (RS)	**1968-01 Oy Laivateollisuus Ab — Turku** Yd No: 249 Loa 87.87 Br ex 12.43 Dght 4.100 Lbp 81.91 Br md 12.35 Dpth 5.23 Welded, 1 dk	**(A31A2GX) General Cargo Ship** Bale: 2,831 Compartments: 3 Ho, ER 3 Ha: 3 (13.7 x 8.2)ER Ice Capable	**2 oil engines** driving 2 FP propellers Total Power: 1,030kW (1,400hp) 11.8kn Russkiy 6DR30/50-6-3 2 x 2 Stroke 6 Cy. 300 x 500 each-515kW (700bhp) Mashinostroitelnyy Zavod"Russkiy-Dizel"-Leningrad
9010711 *EPBF* -	**VISTA** *ex* Iran Baseer *-2010* **Khazar Sea Shipping Lines** - SatCom: Inmarsat C 442210710 *Bandar Anzali* *Iran* MMSI: 422107000	**3,638** 1,235 3,955	Class: (RS) (NV)	**1991-06 Shipbuilding & Shiprepairing Yard 'Ivan Dimitrov' — Rousse** Yd No: 380 Loa 128.25 Br ex - Dght 6.200 Lbp 121.90 Br md 13.40 Dpth 9.00 Welded, 1 dk	**(A31A2GX) General Cargo Ship** TEU 116 C. 116/20' Compartments: 4 Ho, ER 4 Ha: ER Ice Capable	**2 oil engines** driving 2 FP propellers Total Power: 1,762kW (2,396hp) 10.7kn S.K.L. 8NVD48A-2U 2 x 4 Stroke 8 Cy. 320 x 480 each-881kW (1198bhp) (made 1985, fitted 1991) VEB Schwermaschinenbau "KarlLiebknecht" (SKL)-Magdeburg AuxGen: 2 x 80kW 380V 50Hz a.c Thrusters: 1 Thwart. FP thruster (f) Fuel: 279.0 (d.f.)

No. / Call sign	Name / Owner / Flag	Tonnage	Class	Builder / Dimensions	Type / Cargo	Machinery
8606410 *JVMB4* -	**VISTA 7** *ex* Oriental Brave *-2011* *ex* Astrid *-2008* *ex* Hosei Pearl *-2007* *ex* Cedar Tree *-2001* **MK Vista Shipping & Business Co Ltd** - *Ulaanbaatar* *Mongolia* MMSI: 457416000 Official number: 28951186	**4,359** 1,922 5,400	Class: (RI) (NK)	**1986**-06 **Hakata Zosen K.K. — Imabari** Yd No: 335 Loa 97.52 Br ex 18.27 Dght 5.715 Lbp 89.52 Br md 18.20 Dpth 9.20 Welded, 2 dks	**(A31A2GX) General Cargo Ship** Grain: 9,301; Bale: 8,955 Compartments: 2 Ho, ER 2 Ha: (18.2 x 10.8) (32.2 x 10.8)ER Cranes: 2x25t; Derricks: 1x20t	**1 oil engine** driving 1 FP propeller Total Power: 1,103kW (1,500hp) 13.5kn Akasaka A28 1 x 4 Stroke 6 Cy. 280 x 550 1103kW (1500bhp) Akasaka Tekkosho KK (Akasaka DieselLtd)-Japan Fuel: 505.0 (r.f.)
8017176 *CUOU* -	**VISTA ALEGRE** **Pescarias Rio Novo do Principe RL** - *Aveiro* *Portugal* MMSI: 263500101 Official number: A-3148C	*174* 99 120	Class: (LR) ✠	**1983**-08 **Estaleiros Navais de Viana do Castelo S.A. — Viana do Castelo** Yd No: 117 Loa 28.63 Br ex - Dght 2.901 Lbp 24.01 Br md 7.41 Dpth 3.41 Welded, 1 dk	**(B11A2FT) Trawler** Ins: 100 Compartments: 2 Ho, ER 2 Ha:	**1 oil engine** with clutches, flexible couplings & sr reverse geared to sc. shaft driving 1 FP propeller Total Power: 552kW (750hp) Stork DR0218K 1 x 4 Stroke 8 Cy. 210 x 300 552kW (750bhp) Stork Werkspoor Diesel BV-Netherlands AuxGen: 2 x 48kW 380V 50Hz a.c Fuel: 49.5 (d.f.)
8227977 *3EKR5* -	**VISTA I** *ex* Marshal Chuykov *-2007* **Doran Maritime SA** Akron Trade & Transport *Panama* *Panama* MMSI: 372801000 Official number: 3348908A	**37,884** 21,237 67,980 T/cm 64.9	Class: NV (RS)	**1984**-06 **Sudostroitelnyy Zavod "Zaliv" — Kerch** Yd No: 904 Loa 242.81 (BB) Br ex 32.24 Dght 13.620 Lbp 228.02 Br md 32.21 Dpth 18.01 Welded, 1 dk	**(A13A2TW) Crude/Oil Products Tanker** Double Hull Liq: 69,544; Liq (Oil): 69,544 Cargo Heating Coils Compartments: 14 Wing Ta, ER, 2 Wing Slop Ta 4 Cargo Pump (s): 4x1500m³/hr Manifold: Bow/CM: 123.8m Ice Capable	**1 oil engine** driving 1 FP propeller Total Power: 12,356kW (16,799hp) 13.0kn B&W 7DKRN80/160 1 x 2 Stroke 7 Cy. 800 x 1600 12356kW (16799bhp) Bryanskiy Mashinostroitelnyy Zavod (BMZ)-Bryansk AuxGen: 1 x 800kW 220/400V 50Hz a.c, 3 x 500kW 220/400V 50Hz a.c Fuel: 603.8 (d.f.) 3425.7 (r.f.)
9056806 *3FGQ* -	**VISTA III** *ex* Nikator *-2013* **Charme Marine SA** Akron Trade & Transport *Panama* *Panama* MMSI: 357343000 Official number: 45418PEXT	**81,162** 42,510 142,674 T/cm 109.9	Class: AB RI	**1994**-01 **Ishikawajima-Harima Heavy Industries Co Ltd (IHI) — Chita AI** Yd No: 3036 Loa 274.30 (BB) Br ex 44.55 Dght 16.927 Lbp 263.30 Br md 44.50 Dpth 24.70 Welded, 1 dk	**(A13A2TV) Crude Oil Tanker** Double Hull (13F) Liq: 160,260; Liq (Oil): 160,260 Cargo Heating Coils Compartments: 12 Wing Ta, ER, 2 Wing Slop Ta 3 Cargo Pump (s): 3x3500m³/hr Manifold: Bow/CM: 138m	**1 oil engine** driving 1 FP propeller Total Power: 14,483kW (19,691hp) 14.3kn Sulzer 6RTA72 1 x 2 Stroke 6 Cy. 720 x 2500 14483kW (19691bhp) Diesel United Ltd.-Aioi Fuel: 137.0 (d.f.) (Heating Coils) 4232.0 (r.f.)
8417467 *HSUC* -	**VISUD SAKORN** **Government of The Kingdom of Thailand (Marine Department)** - SatCom: Inmarsat A 1567133 *Bangkok* *Thailand* MMSI: 567002000 Official number: 29103953	**1,089** 326 688	Class: (LR) ✠ Classed LR until 8/6/99	**1986**-04 **A/S Nordsovaerftet — Ringkobing** Yd No: 181 Loa 61.19 Br ex 11.18 Dght 3.501 Lbp 54.77 Br md 11.00 Dpth 6.61 Welded, 2 dks	**(B34K2QT) Training Ship**	**1 oil engine** sr geared to sc. shaft driving 1 CP propeller Total Power: 810kW (1,101hp) 12.0kn Alpha 6T23L-VO 1 x 4 Stroke 6 Cy. 225 x 300 810kW (1101bhp) MAN B&W Diesel A/S-Denmark AuxGen: 3 x 184kW 380V 50Hz a.c Fuel: 195.0 (d.f.) 119.0 (r.f.) 4.0pd
9155975 *V2BN* -	**VISURGIS** **ShipCom Bereederungs GmbH & Co Betriebs-KG ms 'Visurgis'** ShipCom Bereederungs GmbH SatCom: Inmarsat C 430433010 *Saint John's* *Antigua & Barbuda* MMSI: 304330000	**2,853** 1,527 4,156	Class: GL	**1997**-12 **Bodewes Scheepswerf "Volharding" Foxhol B.V. — Foxhol** Yd No: 340 Converted From: General Cargo Ship-2012 Loa 89.80 (BB) Br ex - Dght 5.713 Lbp - Br md 13.60 Dpth 7.20 Welded, 1 dk	**(A31A2GX) General Cargo Ship** Grain: 5,582 TEU 252 C Ho 102 TEU C Dk 150 TEU Compartments: 1 Ho, ER 1 Ha: (62.9 x 11.0)ER Ice Capable	**1 oil engine** reduction geared to sc. shaft driving 1 CP propeller Total Power: 2,147kW (2,919hp) 11.5kn MaK 6M453C 1 x 4 Stroke 6 Cy. 320 x 420 2147kW (2919bhp) MaK Motoren GmbH & Co. KG-Kiel AuxGen: 1 x 648kW 380/220V a.c, 2 x 146kW 380/220V a.c Thrusters: 1 Thwart. FP thruster (f) Fuel: 200.0 (d.f.)
8906303 *V2TV* -	**VITA** *ex* Emja *-2004* **Gemini Maritime Co Ltd** Alpha Shipping Co SIA SatCom: Inmarsat Mini-M 761378285 *Saint John's* *Antigua & Barbuda* MMSI: 304010455 Official number: 2625	**2,497** 1,547 4,161 T/cm 10.6	Class: LR ✠**100A1** SS 09/2010 Ice Class 1B at draught of 5.637m Max/min draught aft 5.637/4.011m Max/min draught fwd 5.637/2.011m Power required 1572kw, installed 1690kw ✠**LMC** **UMS** Eq.Ltr: P; Cable: 400.0/32.0 U3	**1990**-12 **Scheepswerf Bijlsma BV — Wartena** (Hull) Yd No: 653 **1990**-12 **Scheepswerf Ferus Smit BV — Westerbroek** Yd No: 279 Loa 88.29 (BB) Br ex 13.21 Dght 5.459 Lbp 84.90 Br md 13.17 Dpth 7.00 Welded, 1 dk	**(A31A2GX) General Cargo Ship** Grain: 5,210 TEU 96 C.Ho 96/20' Compartments: 1 Ho, ER 2 Ha: 2 (26.0 x 10.2)ER Ice Capable	**1 oil engine** with flexible couplings & sr geared to sc. shaft driving 1 CP propeller Total Power: 1,690kW (2,298hp) 12.0kn Nohab 8V25 1 x Vee 4 Stroke 8 Cy. 250 x 300 1690kW (2298bhp) Wartsila Diesel AB-Sweden AuxGen: 1 x 140kW 380V 50Hz a.c, 1 x 220kW 380V 50Hz a.c Thrusters: 1 Water jet (f)
6870328 *UUGA* -	**VITA** *ex* Abava *-1992* **Firma 'Polakr'** - *Sevastopol* *Ukraine* Official number: 570258	**251** 75 195	Class: (RS)	**1957 VEB Volkswerft Stralsund — Stralsund** Yd No: 4470 Loa 39.15 Br ex 7.40 Dght 3.180 Lbp - Br md - Dpth 3.48 Welded, 1 dk	**(B11B2FV) Fishing Vessel** Ins: 167 Compartments: 2 Ho, ER 2 Ha: 2 (1.2 x 1.2) Derricks: 1x1.5t Ice Capable	**1 oil engine** driving 1 FP propeller Total Power: 294kW (400hp) 10.5kn S.K.L. 6NVD48-1U 1 x 4 Stroke 6 Cy. 320 x 480 294kW (400bhp) (, fitted 1970) VEB Schwermaschinenbau "KarlLiebknecht" (SKL)-Magdeburg AuxGen: 1 x 57kW, 1 x 42kW Fuel: 25.0 (d.f.)
7024940 *UIVR* -	**VITA** *ex* Volgo-Balt 8 *-1998* **ZAO 'Tekhnotreyd MT'** - *St Petersburg* *Russia* MMSI: 273452810	**2,406** 1,024 3,230	Class: (RS) (RR)	**1964 Sudostroitelnyy Zavod "Krasnoye Sormovo" — Gorkiy** Loa 114.02 Br ex 13.22 Dght 3.690 Lbp 110.15 Br md 13.01 Dpth 5.50 Welded, 1dk	**(A31A2GX) General Cargo Ship** Grain: 4,510 Compartments: 4 Ho, ER 4 Ha: 4 (16.5 x 9.5)ER	**2 oil engines** driving 2 FP propellers Total Power: 970kW (1,318hp) 10.0kn S.K.L. 6NVD48A-2U 2 x 4 Stroke 6 Cy. 320 x 480 each-485kW (659bhp) VEB Schwermaschinenbau "KarlLiebknecht" (SKL)-Magdeburg
8930495 *HQUB2* -	**VITA II** *ex* Sterebogen *-2004* *ex* Sunrise III *-2004* *ex* Viterburg *-2004* **Dynamic Shipping & Trading SA** - *San Lorenzo* *Honduras* Official number: L-0126443	*160* 72 -		**1991**-01 **Moskovskiy Sudostroitelnyy i Sudoremontnyy Zavod — Moscow** Loa 36.13 Br ex - Dght 1.360 Lbp - Br md 6.86 Dpth - Welded, 1 dk	**(A37B2PS) Passenger Ship**	**2 oil engines** driving 2 FP propellers Total Power: 300kW (408hp) Barnaultransmash 2 x 4 Stroke each-150kW (204bhp) Barnaultransmash-Barnaul
9233583 *9HA2036* -	**VITAGRACE** *ex* Yomoshio *-2009* **Grace Navigation Co Ltd** Vita Management SA *Valletta* *Malta* MMSI: 249840000 Official number: 9233583	**39,126** 25,373 75,921	Class: NK	**2001**-08 **Kanasashi Heavy Industries Co Ltd — Toyohashi AI** Yd No: 3536 Loa 224.99 (BB) Br ex - Dght 14.029 Lbp 217.00 Br md 32.26 Dpth 19.30 Welded, 1 dk	**(A21A2BC) Bulk Carrier** Grain: 90,165; Bale: 86,476 Compartments: 7 Ho, ER 7 Ha: (16.2 x 12.8)6 (18.7 x 14.0)ER	**1 oil engine** driving 1 FP propeller Total Power: 9,340kW (12,699hp) 14.5kn B&W 7S50MC-C 1 x 2 Stroke 7 Cy. 500 x 2000 9340kW (12699bhp) Mitsui Engineering & Shipbuilding CLtd-Japan AuxGen: 3 x 400kW 450V a.c Fuel: 2814.0 (r.f.)
9318357 *9HA2802* -	**VITAHORIZON** *ex* F. D. Cris De Angelis *-2011* **Horizon Navigation Ltd** Vita Management SA *Valletta* *Malta* MMSI: 215892000 Official number: 9318357	**40,488** 25,884 74,483 T/cm 67.0	Class: NK (AB) (RI)	**2007**-03 **Hudong-Zhonghua Shipbuilding (Group) Co Ltd — Shanghai** Yd No: H1343A Loa 225.00 (BB) Br ex - Dght 14.270 Lbp 217.00 Br md 32.26 Dpth 19.60 Welded, 1 dk	**(A21A2BC) Bulk Carrier** Grain: 91,717; Bale: 89,882 Compartments: 7 Ho, ER 7 Ha: ER	**1 oil engine** driving 1 FP propeller Total Power: 8,990kW (12,223hp) 14.0kn MAN-B&W 5S60MC-C 1 x 2 Stroke 5 Cy. 600 x 2400 8990kW (12223bhp) Hudong Heavy Machinery Co Ltd-China AuxGen: 3 x 530kW a.c Fuel: 120.0 (d.f.) 2700.0
9583225 *9HA2993* -	**VITAKOSMOS** **Kosmos Shipping Co Ltd** Vita Management SA SatCom: Inmarsat C 422901610 *Valletta* *Malta* MMSI: 229016000 Official number: 9583225	**43,022** 27,239 82,177 T/cm 70.2	Class: NK	**2012**-03 **Tsuneishi Group (Zhoushan) Shipbuilding Inc — Daishan County ZJ** Yd No: SS-107 Loa 228.99 (BB) Br ex 32.29 Dght 14.430 Lbp 222.00 Br md 32.26 Dpth 20.05 Welded, 1 dk	**(A21A2BC) Bulk Carrier** Grain: 97,381 Compartments: 7 Ho, ER 7 Ha: ER	**1 oil engine** driving 1 FP propeller Total Power: 9,710kW (13,202hp) 14.5kn MAN-B&W 6S60MC-C 1 x 2 Stroke 6 Cy. 600 x 2400 9710kW (13202bhp) Mitsui Engineering & Shipbuilding CLtd-Japan Fuel: 3180.0
8944836 *DUA2111* -	**VITAL 355** **Eva Shipping Corp** - *Cebu* *Philippines* Official number: CEB1000478	*247* 158 -		**1988 at Cebu** L reg 38.54 Br ex - Dght - Lbp - Br md 6.46 Dpth 3.10 Welded, 1 dk	**(A31A2GX) General Cargo Ship**	**1 oil engine** driving 1 FP propeller Total Power: 221kW (300hp)

Ship	Tonnage	Class	Builder / Dimensions	Type	Machinery
8322985 **VITAL STAR** - *ex* Golden Trinity *-2011* *ex* Pelita Luna *-2011* - *ex* Akademi I *-2005* *ex* Shinsei Maru *-1994* **Vital Cargo Pte Ltd** -	**2,645** 1,310 3,678	Class: (NK)	**1984-01 Higaki Zosen K.K. — Imabari** Yd No: 312 Converted From: Training Vessel-2005 Converted From: General Cargo Ship-1995 Loa 86.04 Br ex - Dght 5.725 Lbp 80.02 Br md 14.51 Dpth 8.51 Welded, 2 dks	**(A31A2GX) General Cargo Ship** Grain: 5,787; Bale: 5,524 Compartments: 2 Ho, ER 2 Ha: (15.6 x 8.0) (26.0 x 8.0)ER Derricks: 1x15t,2x10t	**1 oil engine** driving 1 FP propeller Total Power: 1,471kW (2,000hp) 11.0kn Hanshin 6ELS32 1 x 4 Stroke 6 Cy. 320 x 640 1471kW (2000bhp) The Hanshin Diesel Works Ltd-Japan AuxGen: 2 x 120kW 450V 60Hz a.c Fuel: 49.0 (d.f.) 259.5 (r.f.) 7.0pd
9639373 **VITALITY** *9V9848* - **United Maritime Pte Ltd** - *Singapore* *Singapore* MMSI: 566680000 Official number: 397658	**3,828** 1,765 5,702	Class: NK	**2012-11 Yangzhou Kejin Shipyard Co Ltd — Jiangdu JS** Yd No: 08096 Loa 88.90 Br ex - Dght 7.214 Lbp 83.50 Br md 17.30 Dpth 9.60 Welded, 1 dk	**(A13B2TP) Products Tanker** Double Hull (13F) Liq: 6,147; Liq (Oil): 6,147	**2 oil engines** reduction geared to sc. shafts driving 2 FP propellers Total Power: 2,702kW (3,674hp) 12.4kn Yanmar 6EY22 2 x 4 Stroke 6 Cy. 220 x 320 each-1351kW (1837bhp) Yanmar Diesel Engine Co Ltd-Japan Fuel: 290.0
9236638 **VITALITY** *P3JP9* *ex* CMA CGM Vitality *-2006* *ex* Laconikos *-2004* - *ex* MOL Santiago *-2004* *ex* Laconikos *-2002* **Rexanax Shipping Co Ltd** Dioryx Maritime Corp *Limassol* *Cyprus* MMSI: 210090000 Official number: 9236638	**27,093** 12,686 34,622 T/cm 51.1	Class: BV (LR) ✠ Classed LR until 28/3/10	**2002-09 STX Shipbuilding Co Ltd — Changwon (Jinhae Shipyard)** Yd No: 1076 Loa 210.00 (BB) Br ex 30.17 Dght 11.500 Lbp 198.80 Br md 30.10 Dpth 16.70 Welded, 1 dk	**(A33A2CC) Container Ship (Fully Cellular)** TEU 2622 C Ho 1078 TEU C Dk 1544 TEU incl 440 ref C. Compartments: 5 Cell Ho, ER 5 Ha: ER Cranes: 4x40t	**1 oil engine** driving 1 FP propeller Total Power: 24,815kW (33,738hp) 22.1kn B&W 8S70MC-C 1 x 2 Stroke 8 Cy. 700 x 2800 24815kW (33738bhp) Doosan Engine Co Ltd-South Korea AuxGen: 4 x 1400kW 450V 60Hz a.c Boilers: AuxB (Comp) 6.9kgf/cm² (6.8bar) Thrusters: 1 Thwart. CP thruster (f)
8710352 **VITALIY SHMYKOV** *UBOJ9* *ex* Washington *-2013* - **OOO 'Interrybflot'** - *Vladivostok* *Russia* MMSI: 273356290	**6,154** 3,565 7,190	Class: RS (NK)	**1988-04 Imabari Shipbuilding Co Ltd — Imabari EH (Imabari Shipyard)** Yd No: 470 Loa 137.55 (BB) Br ex 18.02 Dght 7.615 Lbp 129.00 Br md 18.00 Dpth 10.50 Welded, 1 dk	**(A34A2GR) Refrigerated Cargo Ship** Ins: 7,614 TEU 40 Compartments: 4 Ho, ER 4 Ha: 4 (7.7 x 6.4)ER Derricks: 8x5t,2x1t	**1 oil engine** driving 1 FP propeller Total Power: 5,701kW (7,751hp) 17.0kn B&W 5L50MC 1 x 2 Stroke 5 Cy. 500 x 1620 5701kW (7751bhp) Mitsui Engineering & Shipbuilding CLtd-Japan Fuel: 1070.0 (r.f.)
8606915 **VITALY FEDEROV** - *ex* Kandova *-1995* - **Sorelo Shipping Co Ltd** -	**1,895** 568 690	Class: (RS)	**1986-10 VEB Volkswerft Stralsund — Stralsund** Yd No: 723 Loa 62.25 Br ex 13.82 Dght 5.220 Lbp 55.00 Br md 13.81 Dpth 9.20 Welded, 2 dks	**(B11A2FS) Stern Trawler** Ins: 580 Ice Capable	**2 oil engines** sr geared to sc. shaft driving 1 CP propeller Total Power: 1,766kW (2,402hp) 12.9kn S.K.L. 8VD26/20AL-2 2 x 4 Stroke 8 Cy. 200 x 260 each-883kW (1201bhp) VEB Schwermaschinenbau "KarlLiebknecht" (SKL)-Magdeburg AuxGen: 1 x 640kW a.c, 3 x 568kW a.c, 1 x 260kW a.c
8518572 **VITALY VANUKHIN** *UBZK9* *ex* Paradise Bay *-2013* *ex* Nordic Swan *-2008* - *ex* Leng *-1999* **S&P LLC** Petropavlovsk-Kamchatskiy Shipping Co *Vostochnyy* *Russia* MMSI: 273321440	**7,090** 3,555 10,628 T/cm 21.5	Class: RS (GL)	**1986-07 Schiffswerft u. Masch. Paul Lindenau GmbH & Co. KG — Kiel** Yd No: 219 Loa 134.65 (BB) Br ex - Dght 8.257 Lbp 125.33 Br md 19.64 Dpth 10.67 Welded, 1 dk	**(A13B2TP) Products Tanker** Double Hull Liq: 11,918; Liq (Oil): 11,918 Cargo Heating Coils Compartments: 15 Ta, 2 Slop Ta, ER 4 Cargo Pump (s) Manifold: Bow/CM: 63m Ice Capable	**1 oil engine** with clutches & sr geared to sc. shaft driving 1 CP propeller Total Power: 4,001kW (5,440hp) 14.0kn MaK 8M551AK 1 x 4 Stroke 8 Cy. 450 x 550 4001kW (5440bhp) Krupp MaK Maschinenbau GmbH-Kiel AuxGen: 1 x 640kW a.c, 3 x 520kW a.c Thrusters: 1 Thwart. FP thruster (f)
1010997 **VITAMIN** *ZCYF* - **Jullen Global Ltd** Verpeka Yacht Brokerage *George Town* *Cayman Islands (British)* MMSI: 319003700 Official number: 741382	**223** 66 -	Class: LR ✠ **100A1** SS 02/2009 SSC Yacht, mono HSC G6 Cable: 320.0/16.0 U2 (a)	**2009-02 Palmer Johnson Yachts LLC — Sturgeon Bay WI** Yd No: 254 Loa 36.50 Br ex 7.41 Dght 1.720 Lbp 30.48 Br md 7.40 Dpth 3.58 Welded, 1 dk	**(X11A2YP) Yacht** Hull Material: Aluminium Alloy	**2 oil engines** with clutches, flexible couplings & sr reverse geared to sc. shafts driving 2 FP propellers Total Power: 4,080kW (5,548hp) 28.0kn M.T.U. 12V4000M90 2 x Vee 4 Stroke 12 Cy. 165 x 190 each-2040kW (2774bhp) MTU Friedrichshafen GmbH-Friedrichshafen AuxGen: 2 x 70kW 400V 50Hz a.c Thrusters: 1 Thwart. FP thruster (f)
8921511 **VITAMIN** *HO8032* *ex* Heisei Maru *-2013* - **Fgas Petrol JSC** - *Panama* *Panama* MMSI: 351745000 Official number: 4535413	**997** 397 1,091	Class: IB (Class contemplated) (NK)	**1990-10 Shinhama Dockyard Co. Ltd. — Anan** Yd No: 803 Loa 61.95 (BB) Br ex 12.02 Dght 4.062 Lbp 58.00 Br md 12.00 Dpth 4.90 Welded, 1 dk	**(A11B2TG) LPG Tanker** Liq (Gas): 1,507 2 x Gas Tank (s); 2 independent (C.mn.stl) dcy horizontal 4 Cargo Pump (s): 4x200m³/hr	**1 oil engine** driving 1 CP propeller Total Power: 1,324kW (1,800hp) 12.0kn Akasaka A31 1 x 4 Stroke 6 Cy. 310 x 600 1324kW (1800bhp) Akasaka Tekkosho KK (Akasaka DieselLtd)-Japan AuxGen: 2 x 225kW 440V 60Hz a.c Fuel: 53.0 (d.f.) 94.0 (r.f.) 5.5pd
8511249 **VITAMIN GAS** *HP5228* *ex* Daesan Gas *-2013* *ex* Kum Kang No. 1 *-2008* - *ex* Lake Star *-2004* *ex* Koho Maru No. 15 *-2003* **Fgas Petrol JSC** - *Panama* *Panama* MMSI: 355620000 Official number: 45480PEXT1	**1,067** 375 1,061	Class: IB (KR) (NK)	**1985-11 Sanyo Zosen K.K. — Onomichi** Yd No: 1011 Loa 65.99 Br ex 12.80 Dght 4.214 Lbp 61.02 Br md 11.02 Dpth 4.81 Welded, 1 dk	**(A11B2TG) LPG Tanker** Liq (Gas): 1,403 2 x Gas Tank (s); 2 independent (C.mn.stl) cyl horizontal Manifold: Bow/CM: 29.5m	**1 oil engine** driving 1 CP propeller Total Power: 1,324kW (1,800hp) 12.5kn Hanshin 6EL30 1 x 4 Stroke 6 Cy. 300 x 600 1324kW (1800bhp) The Hanshin Diesel Works Ltd-Japan AuxGen: 2 x 144kW 450V 60Hz a.c, 1 x 32kW 450V 60Hz a.c Fuel: 30.5 (d.f.) (Heating Coils) 87.5 (r.f.) 6.0pd
7909011 **VITAMIN GAS** *JVMM3* *ex* Star Four I *-2001* - *ex* Izumi Maru No. 55 *-1998* **Quynh Anh Trading Co Ltd** Nhat Viet Transportation Corp *Ulaanbaatar* *Mongolia* MMSI: 457875000 Official number: 20340679	**1,139** 425 1,135 T/cm 6.2	Class: VR (NK)	**1979-11 Miyoshi Shipbuilding Co Ltd — Uwajima EH** Yd No: 256 Loa 67.49 Br ex 11.23 Dght 4.341 Lbp 62.01 Br md 11.21 Dpth 5.11 Welded, 1 dk	**(A11B2TG) LPG Tanker** Liq (Gas): 1,606 2 x Gas Tank (s); 2 Cargo Pump (s) Manifold: Bow/CM: 27.2m	**1 oil engine** driving 1 FP propeller Total Power: 1,618kW (2,200hp) 12.0kn Akasaka DM38AR 1 x 4 Stroke 6 Cy. 380 x 600 1618kW (2200bhp) Akasaka Tekkosho KK (Akasaka DieselLtd)-Japan AuxGen: 2 x 288kW
9470492 **VITAOCEAN** *3FQO2* - **Ocean Shipping International SA** Vita Management SA *Panama* *Panama* MMSI: 355402000 Official number: 4528213	**43,013** 27,239 82,250 T/cm 70.2	Class: NK	**2013-07 Tsuneishi Shipbuilding Co Ltd — Tadotsu KG** Yd No: 1479 Loa 228.99 Br ex - Dght 14.429 Lbp 222.00 Br md 32.26 Dpth 20.05 Welded, 1 dk	**(A21A2BC) Bulk Carrier** Grain: 97,381 Compartments: 7 Ho, ER 7 Ha: ER 7 (17.8 x 15.4)	**1 oil engine** driving 1 FP propeller Total Power: 9,710kW (13,202hp) 14.5kn MAN-B&W 6S60MC-C 1 x 2 Stroke 6 Cy. 600 x 2400 9710kW (13202bhp) Mitsui Engineering & Shipbuilding CLtd-Japan AuxGen: 3 x a.c Fuel: 3184.0
9074016 **VITAPRIDE** *9HCU7* *ex* East Fortune *-2001* - **Akropolis Shipping Co Ltd** Vita Management SA *Valletta* *Malta* MMSI: 215115000 Official number: 7497	**35,884** 23,407 69,153 T/cm 64.4	Class: NK	**1993-11 Imabari Shipbuilding Co Ltd — Marugame KG (Marugame Shipyard)** Yd No: 1218 Loa 224.98 (BB) Br ex - Dght 13.295 Lbp 215.00 Br md 32.20 Dpth 18.30 Welded, 1 dk	**(A21A2BC) Bulk Carrier** Grain: 82,025 Compartments: 7 Ho, ER 7 Ha: (13.0 x 12.8)4 (17.9 x 14.4) (16.3 x 14.4) (14.7 x 14.4)ER	**1 oil engine** driving 1 FP propeller Total Power: 10,246kW (13,930hp) 14.8kn Sulzer 6RTA62 1 x 2 Stroke 6 Cy. 620 x 2150 10246kW (13930bhp) Mitsubishi Heavy Industries Ltd-Japan AuxGen: 4 x 343kW a.c Fuel: 2440.0 (r.f.)
8833934 **VITAS** *YL2347* *ex* Scholmac-4 *-1992* - **MTK Group SIA** - *Liepaja* *Latvia* MMSI: 275162000 Official number: 2114	**117** 35 30	Class: (RS)	**1990-08 Sosnovskiy Sudostroitelnyy Zavod — Sosnovka** Yd No: 783 Loa 25.51 Br ex 7.00 Dght 2.391 Lbp 22.03 Br md - Dpth 3.31 Welded, 1 dk	**(B11A2FS) Stern Trawler** Ins: 64	**1 oil engine** driving 1 FP propeller Total Power: 220kW (299hp) 9.5kn S.K.L. 6NVD26A-2 1 x 4 Stroke 6 Cy. 180 x 260 220kW (299bhp) VEB Schwermaschinenbau "KarlLiebknecht" (SKL)-Magdeburg
9231377 **VITASPIRIT** *9HZA9* *ex* Chorus *-2009* - **Odyssey Navigation Co Ltd** Vita Management SA *Valletta* *Malta* MMSI: 249662000 Official number: 9231377	**38,732** 25,807 74,269	Class: NK (NV)	**2001-07 Oshima Shipbuilding Co Ltd — Saikai NS** Yd No: 10313 Loa 225.00 (BB) Br ex - Dght 13.921 Lbp 216.00 Br md 32.26 Dpth 18.90 Welded, 1 dk	**(A21A2BC) Bulk Carrier** Grain: 89,344; Bale: 87,774 Compartments: 7 Ho, ER 7 Ha: ER 7 (15.5 x 15.9)	**1 oil engine** driving 1 FP propeller Total Power: 8,944kW (12,160hp) 14.0kn MAN-B&W 7S50MC-C 1 x 2 Stroke 7 Cy. 500 x 2000 8944kW (12160bhp) Kawasaki Heavy Industries Ltd-Japan Fuel: 2570.0
8331699 **VITEBSK** - - -	**1,402** 422 484	Class: (RS)	**1985 Sudostroitelnyy Zavod "Baltiya" — Klaypeda** Yd No: 364 Loa 59.00 Br ex 13.02 Dght 4.873 Lbp 55.00 Br md - Dpth 8.90 Welded, 2 dks	**(B11A2FS) Stern Trawler** Bale: 95; Ins: 500 Compartments: 2 Ho, 1 Ta, ER 2 Ha: (1.2 x 1.3) (1.9 x 1.9) Ice Capable	**1 oil engine** driving 1 CP propeller Total Power: 1,618kW (2,200hp) 13.2kn Skoda 6L525IIPS 1 x 4 Stroke 6 Cy. 525 x 720 1618kW (2200bhp) CKD Praha-Praha AuxGen: 1 x 500kW a.c, 2 x 150kW a.c

9505390 **VITESSE**
9MQB7
-
HL Epsilon Sdn Bhd
Hong Lam Marine Pte Ltd
Port Klang *Malaysia*
MMSI: 533130928
Official number: 334491

7,284
3,490
11,284
T/cm
19.1

Class: BV

2008-11 Yangzhou Kejin Shipyard Co Ltd — Jiangdu JS Yd No: 07036
Loa 130.20 (BB) Br ex 18.62 Dght 8.000
Lbp 122.10 Br md 18.60 Dpth 10.80
Welded, 1 dk

(A12B2TR) Chemical/Products Tanker
Double Hull (13F)
Liq: 12,621; Liq (Oil): 12,621
Part Cargo Heating Coils
Compartments: 14 Wing Ta, ER
14 Cargo Pump (s): 2x100m³/hr, 4x200m³/hr, 8x300m³/hr
Manifold: Bow/CM: 61.1m

1 oil engine reduction geared to sc. shaft driving 1 FP propeller
Total Power: 3,309kW (4,499hp) 13.0kn
Daihatsu 6DKM-36
1 x 4 Stroke 6 Cy. 360 x 480 3309kW (4499bhp)
Daihatsu Diesel Manufacturing Co Lt-Japan
Thrusters: 1 Tunnel thruster (f)
Fuel: 78.0 (d.f.) 677.0 (r.f.)

9322009 **VITIM**
5BJR2
-
ex Fesco Vitim *-2013* *ex* CMA CGM Volga *-2011*
ex FESCO Vitim *-2008*
Mar Space Shipping Co Ltd
Far-Eastern Shipping Co (FESCO)
(Dalnevostochnoye Morskoye Parokhodstvo)
Limassol *Cyprus*
MMSI: 212456000
Official number: 9322009

16,803
8,648
22,749
T/cm
37.1

Class: GL RS

2008-08 Stocznia Szczecinska Nowa Sp z oo — Szczecin Yd No: B170/V/1
Loa 183.98 (BB) Br ex - Dght 9.850
Lbp 171.94 Br md 25.30 Dpth 13.50
Welded, 1 dk

(A33A2CC) Container Ship (Fully Cellular)
Grain: 29,816
TEU 1728 C Ho 634 TEI C Dk 1094 TEU incl 200 ref C
Cranes: 3x45t
Ice Capable

1 oil engine driving 1 FP propeller
Total Power: 13,320kW (18,110hp) 19.5kn
Wartsila 6RTA62U
1 x 2 Stroke 6 Cy. 620 x 2150 13320kW (18110bhp)
H Cegielski Poznan SA-Poland
AuxGen: 3 x 1096kW 450/220V a.c
Thrusters: 1 Tunnel thruster (f)
Fuel: 134.0 (d.f.) 2060.0 (r.f.) 61.0pd

6807046 **VITIM**
UARR
-
ex Albo *-2012* *ex* Punta Ala *-2001*
ex Isebek *-1988* *ex* Alchimist Hamburg *-1979*
AzovTransTerminal Ltd
-
Taganrog *Russia*
MMSI: 273444950

1,530
761
2,254
T/cm
8.7

Class: RS (RI) (GL)

1968-03 Ernst Menzer-Werft — Geesthacht
Yd No: 483
Lengthened-1979
Loa 85.43 (BB) Br ex 11.23 Dght 4.360
Lbp 82.78 Br md 11.21 Dpth 4.96
Welded, 1 dk

(A12B2TR) Chemical/Products Tanker
Liq: 2,805; Liq (Oil): 2,805
Cargo Heating Coils
Compartments: 4 Ta, 8 Ta (s.stl), ER
12 Cargo Pump (s): 2x190m³/hr, 10x70m³/hr
Manifold: Bow/CM: 22m
Ice Capable

1 oil engine driving 1 FP propeller
Total Power: 1,103kW (1,500hp) 12.0kn
MaK 8MU451AK
1 x 4 Stroke 8 Cy. 320 x 450 1103kW (1500bhp)
Atlas MaK Maschinenbau GmbH-Kiel
AuxGen: 3 x 60kW 220/380V 50Hz a.c

8954910 **VITIM**
UBIH9
-
ex Altair *-2005*
ex Krasnoyarskiy Sudostroitel *-2001*
Tabatha Shipping Inc
Azia Shipping Holding Ltd
Vanino *Russia*
MMSI: 273353130

3,281
1,124
5,139

Class: RS

1973 Krasnoyarskiy Sudostroitelnyy Zavod — Krasnoyarsk
Loa 108.40 Br ex 15.80 Dght 4.740
Lbp 102.14 Br md 14.82 Dpth 7.41
Welded, 1 dk

(A31A2GX) General Cargo Ship
Compartments: 3 Ho, ER
4 Ha: ER 4 (10.9 x 15.6)
Ice Capable

2 oil engines driving 2 FP propellers
Total Power: 1,030kW (1,400hp) 9.0kn
S.K.L. 6NVD48A-2U
2 x 4 Stroke 6 Cy. 320 x 480 each-515kW (700bhp)
VEB Schwermaschinenbau "KarlLiebknecht" (SKL)-Magdeburg
AuxGen: 3 x 50kW a.c
Fuel: 84.0 (d.f.)

9006289 **VITIN**
OZ2150
-
ex Black Sea *-2013* *ex* Sunrise *-2005*
ex Stadt Wilhelmshaven *-1992*
launched as Castor *-1992*
P/F Sandgrevstur
-
Faeroes (FAS)
MMSI: 231114000

2,449
1,380
3,710

Class: RI (GL)

1992-04 Peene-Werft GmbH — Wolgast
Yd No: 403
Loa 87.83 (BB) Br ex 12.81 Dght 5.468
Lbp 81.00 Br md 12.80 Dpth 7.10
Welded, 1 dk

(A31A2GX) General Cargo Ship
Grain: 4,666; Bale: 4,635
TEU 180 C. 180/20' incl. 6 ref C.
Compartments: 1 Ho, ER
1 Ha: (56.6 x 10.2)ER

1 oil engine with flexible couplings & sr geared to sc. shaft driving 1 FP propeller
Total Power: 1,450kW (1,971hp) 10.0kn
Deutz SBV8M628
1 x 4 Stroke 8 Cy. 240 x 280 1450kW (1971bhp)
Motoren Werke Mannheim AG (MWM)-Mannheim
AuxGen: 2 x 168kW 220/380V 50Hz a.c
Thrusters: 1 Directional thruster (f)

9000613 **VITIS**
3FKC6
-
ex Dutch Navigator *-2013*
Ondamar Shipping Ltd
Sicilnavi Srl
Panama *Panama*
MMSI: 352099000
Official number: 45409PEXT

4,297
1,799
6,221
T/cm
15.0

Class: LR
✠ **100A1** SS 10/2011
chemical tanker, Ship Type 2, MARPOL 20.1.3
CR (s.stl)
SG 1.86
ESP
LI
Ice Class 1D at a draught of 6.35m
Max/min draughts fwd 6.60/2.75m
Max/min draughts aft n/a
Power required 1369kw, power installed 3375kw
✠ **LMC** **UMS**
Eq.Ltr: U;
Cable: 495.0/46.0 U3 (a)

1991-09 Verolme Scheepswerf Heusden B.V. — Heusden Yd No: 1024
Lengthened-1998
Loa 118.02 Br ex 17.10 Dght 6.201
Lbp 111.23 Br md 17.00 Dpth 8.70
Welded, 1 dk

(A12A2TC) Chemical Tanker
Double Hull (13F)
Liq: 6,384
Compartments: 20 Wing Ta (s.stl), ER, 2 Wing Slop Ta (s.stl)
22 Cargo Pump (s): 22x100m³/hr
Manifold: Bow/CM: 67.7m
Ice Capable

1 oil engine with flexible couplings & sr reverse geared to sc. shaft driving 1 CP propeller
Total Power: 3,375kW (4,589hp) 15.0kn
Wartsila 9R32D
1 x 4 Stroke 9 Cy. 320 x 350 3375kW (4589bhp)
Wartsila Diesel Oy-Finland
AuxGen: 1 x 500kW 440V 60Hz a.c, 2 x 400kW 440V 60Hz a.c
Boilers: 2 TOH (ex.g.) 10.2kgf/cm² (10.0bar), TOH (o.f.) 10.2kgf/cm² (10.0bar)
Thrusters: 1 Thwart. FP thruster (f)
Fuel: 66.0 (d.f.) (Part Heating Coils) 317.0 (r.f.)

8016586 **VITO C. II**
-
-
Vito C Corp
-
Gloucester, MA *United States of America*
Official number: 614860

186
121
-

1979
Loa 29.27 Br ex - Dght -
Lbp - Br md 7.56 Dpth 3.89
Welded, 1 dk

(B11A2FS) Stern Trawler

1 oil engine reverse reduction geared to sc. shaft driving 1 FP propeller
Total Power: 625kW (850hp)
Caterpillar D398SCAC
1 x Vee 4 Stroke 12 Cy. 159 x 203 625kW (850bhp)
Caterpillar Tractor Co-USA

7942855 **VITOL**
-
-
ex Yeon Chun *-2007* *ex* Merak *-2007*
Mibor Co Ltd
LG Marine Co Ltd

760
228
393

Class: (RS)

1981 Zavod "Leninskaya Kuznitsa" — Kiyev
Yd No: 1492
Loa 54.82 Br ex 9.96 Dght 5.000
Lbp 50.29 Br md - Dpth 5.06
Welded, 1 dk

(B11A2FS) Stern Trawler
Bale: 414
Compartments: 2 Ho, ER
3 Ha: 3 (1.5 x 1.6)
Derricks: 2x1.3t
Ice Capable

1 oil engine driving 1 FP propeller
Total Power: 736kW (1,001hp) 12.0kn
S.K.L. 8NVD48A-2U
1 x 4 Stroke 8 Cy. 320 x 480 736kW (1001bhp)
VEB Schwermaschinenbau "KarlLiebknecht" (SKL)-Magdeburg

6420264 **VITORIA**
PP2746
-
Log-In Logistica Intermodal SA
-
Vitoria *Brazil*

150
-
-

Class: (LR)
✠ Classed LR until 11/7/11

1965-09 Industrias Reunidas Caneco SA — Rio de Janeiro Yd No: 155
Loa 32.16 Br ex 8.54 Dght 3.696
Lbp 28.00 Br md 8.01 Dpth 4.09
Welded, 1 dk

(B32A2ST) Tug

1 oil engine reverse reduction geared to sc. shaft driving 1 FP propeller
Total Power: 1,177kW (1,600hp)
EMD (Electro-Motive) 16-567-BC
1 x Vee 2 Stroke 16 Cy. 216 x 254 1177kW (1600bhp)
General Motors Corp-USA

9445150 **VITORIA 10000**
V7UE3
-
launched as Petrobras Ii 10000 *-2010*
Drill Ship International BV
Schahin Engenharia SA
Majuro *Marshall Islands*
MMSI: 538003934
Official number: 3934

60,331
18,099
61,042

Class: BV (AB)

2010-07 Samsung Heavy Industries Co Ltd — Geoje Yd No: 1766
Loa 228.00 Br ex - Dght 13.000
Lbp 219.40 Br md 42.00 Dpth 19.00
Welded, 1 dk

(B22B2OD) Drilling Ship

6 diesel electric oil engines driving 6 gen. each 7000kW 11000V a.c Connecting to 3 elec. motors each (4500kW) driving 3 Azimuth electric drive units
Total Power: 48,000kW (65,262hp) 12.0kn
Wartsila 16V32
6 x Vee 4 Stroke 16 Cy. 320 x 400 each-8000kW (10877bhp)
Wartsila Finland Oy-Finland
Thrusters: 3 Retract. directional thruster (f)
Fuel: 6170.0 (d.f.)

7328061 **VITORIA LIFT 1**
H09292
-
ex Eide Lift 2 *-2010* *ex* Sudopodyom-1 *-1998*
Technip Ships (Netherlands) BV
-
Panama *Panama*
MMSI: 355720000
Official number: 4437212

1,495
448
1,675

Class: (NV) (GL) (RS)

1973-06 Howaldtswerke-Deutsche Werft AG (HDW) — Hamburg Yd No: 70
Loa 54.35 Br ex 24.01 Dght 2.699
Lbp 52.50 Br md 23.96 Dpth 5.41
Welded, 1 dk

(B34B2SC) Crane Vessel
Cranes: 1x400t
Ice Capable

4 oil engines driving 4 Propellers 2 fwd & 2 aft
Total Power: 748kW (1,016hp) 7.6kn
Deutz SBF6M716
4 x 4 Stroke 6 Cy. 135 x 160 each-187kW (254bhp)
Kloeckner Humboldt Deutz AG-West Germany
AuxGen: 2 x 152kW a.c, 1 x 76kW a.c
Fuel: 24.0 (d.f.)

8650461 **VITORIA LX**
PP9223
-
Vale SA
-
Rio de Janeiro *Brazil*
Official number: 3813879119

232
-
-

2011-07 H. Dantas Construcoes e Reparos Navais Ltda. — Aracaju
Loa - Br ex - Dght -
Lbp - Br md - Dpth -
Welded, 1 dk

(B32A2ST) Tug

1 oil engine driving 1 Propeller

7616793 *OYDC2* -	**VITUS** *ex* Rauma IV *-1989* *ex* Wilhelm Hackman *-1984* **Andtri Towing ApS** - *Halsskov* *Denmark (DIS)* MMSI: 220392000 Official number: H1035	*138* 17 177	Class: (LR) ✠ Classed LR until 26/5/87	**1978-06 Rauma-Repola Oy — Savonlinna** Yd No: 410 Loa 25.71 Br ex 7.52 Dght 2.952 Lbp 23.42 Br md 7.50 Dpth 3.51 Welded, 1 dk	**(B32A2ST) Tug** Ice Capable	**1 oil engine** sr geared to sc. shaft driving 1 CP propeller Total Power: 736kW (1,001hp) 13.0kn Wartsila 624TS 1 x 4 Stroke 6 Cy. 240 x 310 736kW (1001bhp) Oy Wartsila Ab-Finland AuxGen: 2 x 32kW 380V 50Hz a.c
8901432 *UDKG* TI-2121	**VITUS BERING** **Murmansk Gubernia Fleet Co (OAO 'Murmanskiy Gubernskiy Flot')** - SatCom: Inmarsat A 1401364 *Murmansk* *Russia* MMSI: 273841710 Official number: 895775	**1,944** 592 1,255	Class: RS (NV)	**1990-04 Sterkoder Mek. Verksted AS — Kristiansund** Yd No: 121 Loa 64.05 (BB) Br ex - Dght 5.780 Lbp 55.55 Br md 13.00 Dpth 5.95 Welded	**(B11A2FG) Factory Stern Trawler** Grain: 130; Ins: 930 Ice Capable	**1 oil engine** reduction geared to sc. shaft driving 1 CP propeller Total Power: 2,458kW (3,342hp) 14.0kn Wartsila 6R32E 1 x 4 Stroke 6 Cy. 320 x 350 2458kW (3342bhp) Wartsila Diesel Oy-Finland AuxGen: 1 x 1304kW 380V 50Hz a.c, 2 x 336kW 380V 50Hz a.c Thrusters: 1 Thwart. FP thruster (f)
9613549 *UBGJ9* -	**VITUS BERING** **Dafne Line Shipping Co Ltd** Unicom Management Services (St Petersburg) Ltd *St Petersburg* *Russia* MMSI: 273358680	**7,487** 2,246 4,158	Class: RS (LR) ✠ Classed LR until 21/3/14	**2012-12 Arctech Helsinki Shipyard Oy — Helsinki** Yd No: 506 Loa 99.90 Br ex 21.26 Dght 7.900 Lbp 91.38 Br md 21.23 Dpth 11.00 Welded, 2 dk	**(B21B20T) Offshore Tug/Supply Ship** Cranes: 1x9.5t Ice Capable	**4 diesel electric oil engines** driving 2 gen. each 5530kW 3300V a.c 2 gen. each 2765kW 3300V a.c Connecting to 2 elec. motors each (6500kW) driving 2 Directional propellers Total Power: 18,000kW (24,474hp) 16.0kn Wartsila 12V32 2 x Vee 4 Stroke 12 Cy. 320 x 400 each-6000kW (8158bhp) Wartsila Finland Oy-Finland Wartsila 6L32 2 x 4 Stroke 6 Cy. 320 x 400 each-3000kW (4079bhp) Wartsila Finland Oy-Finland Boilers: e (ex.g.) 10.5kgf/cm² (10.3bar), AuxB (o.f.) 7.3kgf/cm² (7.2bar) Thrusters: 2 Thwart. CP thruster (f) Fuel: 2330.0 (d.f.)
9573062 *LXVB* -	**VITUS BERING** **Vitus Bering SA** Ondernemingen Jan De Nul NV (Jan De Nul Group) *Luxembourg* *Luxembourg* MMSI: 253494000	**8,048** 2,414 11,800	Class: BV	**2012-05 STX Offshore & Shipbuilding Co Ltd — Busan** Yd No: 5057 Loa 119.10 (BB) Br ex - Dght 8.150 Lbp 104.25 Br md 23.00 Dpth 10.80 Welded, 1 dk	**(B33B2DT) Trailing Suction Hopper Dredger** Hopper: 7,500	**2 oil engines** reducton geared to sc. shafts driving 2 CP propellers Total Power: 8,000kW (10,876hp) 13.7kn MAN-B&W 8L32/40 2 x 4 Stroke 8 Cy. 320 x 400 each-4000kW (5438bhp) MAN B&W Diesel AG-Augsburg AuxGen: 2 x 3852kW 50Hz a.c, 1 x 800kW 50Hz a.c Thrusters: 1 Tunnel thruster (f) Fuel: 1060.0
8923179 - -	**VITYAZ** *ex* BK-1251 *-1984* **Azimut Ltd** - *Kaliningrad* *Russia* Official number: 702002	**182** 54 46	Class: (RS)	**1970-11 "Petrozavod" — Leningrad** Yd No: 778 Loa 29.30 Br ex 8.49 Dght 3.090 Lbp 27.00 Br md - Dpth 4.34 Welded, 1 dk	**(B32A2ST) Tug** Ice Capable	**2 oil engines** driving 2 CP propellers Total Power: 882kW (1,200hp) 11.4kn Russkiy 6D30/50-4-2 2 x 2 Stroke 6 Cy. 300 x 500 each-441kW (600bhp) Mashinostroitelnyy Zavod"Russkiy-Dizel"-Leningrad AuxGen: 2 x 25kW a.c Fuel: 36.0 (d.f.)
8923181 - -	**VITYAZ** *ex* BK-1201 *-1984* **Specialized Oktyabrsk Sea Port (GP Spetsializirovannyy Morskoy Port Oktyabrsk)** - *Nikolayev* *Ukraine* Official number: 710090	*187* - 46	Class: (RS)	**1971 "Petrozavod" — Leningrad** Yd No: 791 Loa 29.30 Br ex 8.49 Dght 3.090 Lbp 27.00 Br md - Dpth 4.34 Welded, 1 dk	**(B32A2ST) Tug** Ice Capable	**2 oil engines** driving 2 CP propellers Total Power: 882kW (1,200hp) 11.4kn Russkiy 6D30/50-4-3 2 x 2 Stroke 6 Cy. 300 x 500 each-441kW (600bhp) Mashinostroitelnyy Zavod"Russkiy-Dizel"-Leningrad AuxGen: 2 x 25kW a.c Fuel: 36.0 (d.f.)
8724121 - -	**VITYAZ** - **Ust-Dunaysk Port (Ust-Dunayskiy MTP)** - *Izmail* *Ukraine* MMSI: 272881800 Official number: 842477	**228** - 86	Class: (RS)	**1985-12 Brodogradiliste 'Tito' — Belgrade** Yd No: 1103 Loa 35.23 Br ex 9.01 Dght 3.160 Lbp 30.00 Br md - Dpth 4.50 Welded, 1 dk	**(B32A2ST) Tug** Ice Capable	**2 oil engines** driving 1 CP propeller Total Power: 1,854kW (2,520hp) 11.5kn Sulzer 6ASL25/30 2 x 4 Stroke 6 Cy. 250 x 300 each-927kW (1260bhp) in Yugoslavia AuxGen: 2 x 100kW a.c
8727109 *UHGZ* -	**VITYAZ** *ex* Trud *-2003* **Compass Co Ltd** - *Vladivostok* *Russia* MMSI: 273817110 Official number: 861514	**794** 238 332	Class: (RS)	**1987-08 Volgogradskiy Sudostroitelnyy Zavod — Volgograd** Yd No: 240 Converted From: Stern Trawler-2002 Loa 53.74 Br ex 10.71 Dght 4.400 Lbp 47.92 Br md 10.50 Dpth 6.00 Welded, 1 dk	**(B11A2FS) Stern Trawler** Ice Capable	**1 oil engine** driving 1 CP propeller Total Power: 971kW (1,320hp) 12.7kn S.K.L. 8NVD48A-2U 1 x 4 Stroke 8 Cy. 320 x 480 971kW (1320bhp) VEB Schwermaschinenbau "KarlLiebknecht" (SKL)-Magdeburg AuxGen: 1 x 300kW a.c, 3 x 160kW a.c, 2 x 135kW a.c
7367603 *UIWK* -	**VITYAZ** *ex* Temp *-2012* **JSC 'Vostokbunker'** - *Vladivostok* *Russia*	**275** 82 83	Class: RS	**1974-03 Brodogradiliste 'Tito' Beograd - Brod 'Tito' — Belgrade** Yd No: 898 Loa 35.45 Br ex 9.21 Dght 3.150 Lbp 30.00 Br md 9.00 Dpth 4.52 Welded, 1 dk	**(B32A2ST) Tug** Ice Capable	**2 oil engines** geared to sc. shaft driving 1 CP propeller Total Power: 2,280kW (3,100hp) 13.0kn B&W 7-26MTBF-40 2 x 4 Stroke 7 Cy. 260 x 400 each-1140kW (1550bhp) Titovi Zavodi 'Litostroj'-Yugoslavia AuxGen: 2 x 100kW a.c Fuel: 64.0 (d.f.)
6873849 *UDQI* -	**VITYAZ** *ex* MB-6104 *-1967* *ex* BK-410 *-1967* **Ust-Kamchatsk Port Authority** - *Petropavlovsk-Kamchatskiy* *Russia* Official number: 631150	**118** 35 57	Class: RS	**1964 VEB Schiffswerft "Edgar Andre" — Magdeburg** Yd No: 6104 Loa 28.87 Br ex 6.78 Dght 2.620 Lbp 25.62 Br md 6.50 Dpth 3.00 Welded, 1 dk	**(B32A2ST) Tug** Ice Capable	**1 oil engine** driving 1 FP propeller Total Power: 294kW (400hp) 10.5kn S.K.L. 6NVD48-1U 1 x 4 Stroke 6 Cy. 320 x 480 294kW (400bhp) (, fitted 1980) VEB Schwermaschinenbau "KarlLiebknecht" (SKL)-Magdeburg AuxGen: 2 x 60kW Fuel: 25.0 (d.f.)
6873734 - -	**VITYAZ** *ex* MB-6124 *-1967* **1 May Fishing Collective (Rybolovetskiy Kolkhoz imeni 1 Maya)** - *Kerch* *Ukraine* Official number: 650109	**118** 35 36	Class: (RS)	**1966 VEB Schiffswerft "Edgar Andre" — Magdeburg** Yd No: 6124 Loa 28.88 Br ex 6.52 Dght 2.550 Lbp 25.55 Br md - Dpth 3.16 Welded, 1 dk	**(B32A2ST) Tug** Ice Capable	**1 oil engine** driving 1 FP propeller Total Power: 294kW (400hp) 10.0kn S.K.L. 6NVD48 1 x 4 Stroke 6 Cy. 320 x 480 294kW (400bhp) VEB Schwermaschinenbau "KarlLiebknecht" (SKL)-Magdeburg AuxGen: 2 x 27kW Fuel: 26.0 (d.f.)
7124439 *UGJM* -	**VITYAZ** *ex* Kavalerovo *-2011* **Elbrus Co Ltd** - *Nakhodka* *Russia* MMSI: 273822100	**735** 220 393	Class: RS	**1971-09 Zavod "Leninskaya Kuznitsa" — Kiyev** Yd No: 1349 Loa 54.82 Br ex 9.96 Dght 4.080 Lbp 50.29 Br md 9.80 Dpth 5.03 Welded, 1 dk	**(B11A2FS) Stern Trawler** Ins: 400 Compartments: 2 Ho, ER 3 Ha: 3 (1.5 x 1.6) Derricks: 2x1.5t; Winches: 2 Ice Capable	**1 oil engine** driving 1 CP propeller Total Power: 736kW (1,001hp) 12.0kn S.K.L. 8NVD48AU 1 x 4 Stroke 8 Cy. 320 x 480 736kW (1001bhp) VEB Schwermaschinenbau "KarlLiebknecht" (SKL)-Magdeburg AuxGen: 4 x 100kW Fuel: 141.0 (d.f.)
8125703 *UGYE* -	**VITYAZ** *ex* Blue Wave *-2005* *ex* Ruby *-2001* *ex* Donghwa No. 7 *-1996* *ex* Sankoh *-1994* *ex* Sanko Maru *-1987* **Alisa Co Ltd** - SatCom: Inmarsat C 427301110 *Vladivostok* *Russia* MMSI: 273447380 Official number: 814848	**1,553** 546 1,999	Class: RS (KR) (BV)	**1981-12 Kogushi Zosen K.K. — Okayama** Yd No: 231 Converted From: Chemical/Products Tanker-2005 Loa 77.95 Br ex - Dght 4.763 Lbp 72.00 Br md 12.70 Dpth 5.50 Welded, 1 dk	**(A13B2TP) Products Tanker** Liq: 2,045; Liq (Oil): 2,045 Compartments: 12 Wing Ta, ER 6 Cargo Pump (s): 6x130m³/hr	**1 oil engine** driving 1 FP propeller Total Power: 1,618kW (2,200hp) 14.0kn Hanshin 6ELS32 1 x 4 Stroke 6 Cy. 320 x 640 1618kW (2200bhp) The Hanshin Diesel Works Ltd-Japan AuxGen: 2 x 176kW 450V a.c Fuel: 162.0 (d.f.)

IMO / Call sign	Name, owner, port	Tonnage	Class	Built	Type	Machinery
8606654 *UBAK* -	**VITYAZ** *ex* Okainiai *-1999* *ex* Okaynyay *-1992* **OOO 'Nord Piligrim'** - *Murmansk* *Russia* MMSI: 273437550 Official number: 851584	**1,896** 568 690	Class: RS	**1986-01 VEB Volkswerft Stralsund — Stralsund** Yd No: 697 Loa 62.25 Br ex 13.82 Dght 5.220 Lbp 55.00 Br md 13.81 Dpth 9.20 Welded, 2 dks	**(B11A2FS) Stern Trawler** Ins: 580 Ice Capable	**2 oil engines** sr geared to sc. shaft driving 1 CP propeller Total Power: 1,764kW (2,398hp) 12.9kn S.K.L. 8VD26/20AL-2 2 x 4 Stroke 8 Cy. 200 x 260 each-882kW (1199bhp) VEB Schwermaschinenbau "KarlLiebknecht" (SKL)-Magdeburg AuxGen: 1 x 640kW a.c, 3 x 568kW a.c, 1 x 260kW a.c Fuel: 364.0 (d.f.)
8866400 - -	**VITZ** *ex* Mary *-2006* *ex* Pan Mary II *-1995* *ex* Fukuei Maru *-1993* **East Star Co Ltd** -	**368** 158 430		**1977 K.K. Saidaiji Zosensho — Okayama** Loa 42.00 Br ex - Dght 2.800 Lbp 38.00 Br md 7.80 Dpth 4.60 Welded, 1 dk	**(A31A2GX) General Cargo Ship**	**1 oil engine** driving 1 FP propeller Total Power: 368kW (500hp) 9.0kn Matsui 1 x 4 Stroke 368kW (500bhp) Matsui Iron Works Co Ltd-Japan
8733304 *ZR4880* -	**VIVA** - **Pioneer Fishing Ltd** - *Mossel Bay* *South Africa* MMSI: 601056900 Official number: 10711	*143* 43 -		**2007-01 Tallie Marine Pty Ltd — St Helena Bay** Loa 19.40 Br ex - Dght 2.400 Lbp - Br md 7.20 Dpth 3.60 Bonded, 1 dk	**(B11B2FV) Fishing Vessel** Hull Material: Reinforced Plastic	**1 oil engine** driving 1 Propeller 9.0kn
8203995 *HSB2499* -	**VIVA** *ex* Shinko Maru No. 38 *-1999* **Mahachai Marine Oil Co Ltd** NCA Marine Consultants Co Ltd *Thailand* Official number: 447400198	*944* 338 1,439		**1982-07 Kanmon Zosen K.K. — Shimonoseki** Yd No: 363 Loa 70.52 Br ex - Dght 4.360 Lbp 65.03 Br md 10.61 Dpth 5.01 Welded, 1 dk	**(A13B2TP) Products Tanker** Liq: 1,287; Liq (Oil): 1,287 Compartments: 8 Ta, ER	**1 oil engine** driving 1 FP propeller Total Power: 1,324kW (1,800hp) Hanshin 6EL30 1 x 4 Stroke 6 Cy. 300 x 600 1324kW (1800bhp) The Hanshin Diesel Works Ltd-Japan
7414066 *AVDD* -	**VIVA** *ex* Statesman Service *-2010* **Prince Marine Transport Services Pvt Ltd** Amba Shipping & Logistics Pvt Ltd *Mumbai* *India* MMSI: 419093800 Official number: 3650	**999** 299 975	Class: IR (AB)	**1975-09 Bel-Aire Shipyard Ltd — North Vancouver BC** Yd No: 240A Loa 61.98 Br ex 12.27 Dght 4.385 Lbp 56.70 Br md 12.20 Dpth 5.19 Welded, 1 dk	**(B21B20T) Offshore Tug/Supply Ship** Ice Capable	**2 oil engines** reverse reduction geared to sc. shafts driving 2 FP propellers Total Power: 4,230kW (5,752hp) 10.0kn EMD (Electro-Motive) 16-645-E6 2 x Vee 2 Stroke 16 Cy. 230 x 254 each-2115kW (2876bhp) Electro Motive Div. Gen. Motors-La Grange, Illinois AuxGen: 2 x 200kW a.c Thrusters: 1 Thwart. FP thruster (f)
8122385 *3EGN7* -	**VIVA 106** *ex* Chi Lai *-2008* *ex* Tsurusaki *-1993* **Viva Marine SA** Hua Fu International Group SA SatCom: Inmarsat C 435253312 *Panama* *Panama* MMSI: 352533000 Official number: 1843889F	**3,574** 1,673 4,183	Class: (NK)	**1982-03 Kitanihon Zosen K.K. — Hachinohe** Yd No: 171 Loa 99.01 (BB) Br ex 16.03 Dght 6.701 Lbp 89.92 Br md 16.00 Dpth 7.12 Welded, 3 dks	**(A34A2GR) Refrigerated Cargo Ship** Ins: 5,229 Compartments: 3 Ho, ER 3 Ha: 3 (6.5 x 5.0)ER Derricks: 3x5t	**1 oil engine** driving 1 FP propeller Total Power: 3,972kW (5,400hp) 15.5kn Mitsubishi 6UEC45/115H 1 x 2 Stroke 6 Cy. 450 x 1150 3972kW (5400bhp) Akasaka Tekkosho KK (Akasaka DieselLtd)-Japan AuxGen: 2 x 560kW 445V 60Hz a.c Fuel: 97.0 (d.f.) 668.5 (r.f.) 19.0pd
9611486 - -	**VIVA CASTLE** - **Heung Hae Co Ltd** - *Incheon* *South Korea* MMSI: 440011170 Official number: ICR-102888	**260** - 153	Class: KR	**2010-06 DH Shipbuilding Co Ltd — Incheon** Yd No: 0901 Loa 36.70 Br ex 9.82 Dght 3.509 Lbp 32.00 Br md 9.80 Dpth 4.50 Welded, 1 dk	**(B32A2ST) Tug**	**2 oil engines** reduction geared to sc. shafts driving 2 Propellers Total Power: 3,676kW (4,998hp) 15.0kn Niigata 6L28HX 2 x 4 Stroke 6 Cy. 280 x 370 each-1838kW (2499bhp) Niigata Engineering Co Ltd-Japan
7353054 *YFMF* -	**VIVA III** *ex* Cerlang *-1996* *ex* Fukuyu Maru *-1987* *ex* Eizo Maru No. 21 *-1983* *ex* Jingu Maru *-1979* **PT Trinoviza Indah Kencana** - *Pontianak* *Indonesia*	**1,207** 597 2,080	Class: (KI)	**1973-07 Murakami Hide Zosen K.K. — Imabari** Yd No: 110 Loa 74.70 Br ex 11.00 Dght 5.106 Lbp 70.01 Br md 10.98 Dpth 5.49 Riveted\Welded, 1 dk	**(A13B2TP) Products Tanker**	**1 oil engine** driving 1 FP propeller Total Power: 1,545kW (2,101hp) 12.3kn Hanshin 6LU38 1 x 4 Stroke 6 Cy. 380 x 580 1545kW (2101bhp) Hanshin Nainenki Kogyo-Japan
8895140 - -	**VIVA LADY OF LOURDES** *ex* Sazanami *-1979* **Viva Shipping Lines Co Inc** - *Batangas* *Philippines* Official number: MNLD000414	*152* 43 -		**1978-03 K.K. Miho Zosensho — Osaka** Loa 25.95 Br ex - Dght 0.980 Lbp 23.25 Br md 5.80 Dpth 2.60 Welded, 1 dk	**(A37B2PS) Passenger Ship** Hull Material: Aluminium Alloy Passengers: unberthed: 150	**2 oil engines** driving 2 FP propellers Total Power: 1,618kW (2,200hp) 25.0kn M.T.U. 2 x 4 Stroke each-809kW (1100bhp) Ikegai Tekkosho-Japan
9539133 *V7YN2* -	**VIVA MAS** *ex* Aquasition *-2012* *ex* Coco Loco *-2010* **Mas Yates Ltd** Brooks Smith *Bikini* *Marshall Islands* MMSI: 538070849 Official number: 70849	**247** 74 -	Class: LR (AB) **100A1** SS 05/2008 SSC Yacht, G6 **LMC**	**2008-05 Broward Marine Inc — Dania FL** Yd No: 602 Loa 33.67 Br ex - Dght - Lbp - Br md 7.19 Dpth 3.35 Welded, 1 dk	**(X11A2YP) Yacht** Hull Material: Aluminium Alloy	**2 oil engines** geared to sc. shafts driving 2 Propellers Total Power: 2,942kW (4,000hp) M.T.U. 16V2000M91 2 x Vee 4 Stroke 16 Cy. 130 x 150 each-1471kW (2000bhp) Detroit Diesel Corporation-Detroit, Mi AuxGen: 2 x 65kW a.c
7331460 *DUE2006* -	**VIVA PENAFRANCIA** *ex* Tamataka Maru No. 52 *-2010* **Viva Shipping Lines Co Inc** - *Batangas* *Philippines* Official number: BAT5000815	*494* 222 -		**1973 Sanuki Shipbuilding & Iron Works Co Ltd — Mitoyo KG** Yd No: 716 Loa - Br ex 10.42 Dght - Lbp 47.02 Br md 10.39 Dpth 3.51 Riveted\Welded, 1 dk	**(A37B2PS) Passenger Ship** Passengers: 784	**2 oil engines** driving 2 FP propellers Total Power: 1,472kW (2,002hp) Makita FSHC629 2 x 4 Stroke 6 Cy. 290 x 440 each-736kW (1001bhp) Makita Tekkosho-Japan
7126009 *DUE2076* -	**VIVA PENAFRANCIA 3** *ex* Sweet Pearl *-2010* *ex* Ocean Pearl *-1989* *ex* Ashizuri *-1988* **Viva Shipping Lines Co Inc** - *Philippines* Official number: BAT5000816	*1,275* 659 403		**1971-09 Usuki Iron Works Co Ltd — Usuki OT** Yd No: 815 Loa 69.70 Br ex 13.64 Dght 3.112 Lbp 63.00 Br md 13.62 Dpth 4.50 Welded, 2 dks	**(A36A2PR) Passenger/Ro-Ro Ship (Vehicles)** Passengers: 802	**2 oil engines** driving 2 FP propellers Total Power: 2,942kW (4,000hp) 16.0kn Niigata 6MQG31EZ 2 x 4 Stroke 6 Cy. 310 x 380 each-1471kW (2000bhp) Niigata Engineering Co Ltd-Japan
6908254 *DUE2075* -	**VIVA PENAFRANCIA 5** *ex* Sweet Pride *-1994* *ex* Hiyama *-1989* *ex* Hiyama No. 2 *-1987* *ex* Soya Maru No. 8 *-1983* *ex* Otaru Maru *-1982* *ex* Seikan Maru No. 5 *-1981* **Viva Shipping Lines Co Inc** - *Batangas* *Philippines* Official number: BAT5001087	*710* 360 455		**1968 Taguma Zosen KK — Onomichi HS** Yd No: 69 Loa 67.98 Br ex 14.20 Dght 3.048 Lbp 63.02 Br md 14.18 Dpth 4.40 Riveted\Welded, 1 dk	**(A37B2PS) Passenger Ship** Passengers: 900	**2 oil engines** geared to sc. shafts driving 2 FP propellers Total Power: 1,956kW (2,660hp) 15.5kn Daihatsu 8PSTCM-30 2 x 4 Stroke 8 Cy. 300 x 380 each-978kW (1330bhp) Daihatsu Kogyo-Japan AuxGen: 2 x 64kW 225V a.c Fuel: 61.0 3.5pd
6829197 - -	**VIVA PENAFRANCIA 8** *ex* Cerina *-1994* *ex* Sweet Marine *-1994* *ex* Taikan Maru No. 3 *-1988* **Viva Shipping Lines Co Inc** - *Batangas* *Philippines* Official number: BAT5000997	*913* 441 282		**1968 Shimoda Dockyard Co. Ltd. — Shimoda** Yd No: 158 Loa 60.56 Br ex 12.83 Dght 2.871 Lbp 56.49 Br md 12.81 Dpth 3.94 Welded, 1 dk	**(A36A2PT) Passenger/Ro-Ro Ship (Vehicles/Rail)** Passengers: 762	**2 oil engines** driving 2 FP propellers Total Power: 1,104kW (1,500hp) 11.3kn Daihatsu 8PSHTCM-26D 2 x 4 Stroke 8 Cy. 260 x 320 each-552kW (750bhp) Daihatsu Kogyo-Japan AuxGen: 2 x 72kW Fuel: 42.5
7225398 *DUA2068* -	**VIVA SAN JOSE** *ex* Hatsuhi No. 3 *-1995* **Viva Shipping Lines Co Inc** - *Batangas* *Philippines* Official number: MNLD001117	*364* 219 125		**1972 Nakamura Shipbuilding & Engine Works Co. Ltd. — Matsue** Yd No: 108 Loa 38.36 Br ex 8.54 Dght 2.299 Lbp 33.51 Br md 8.51 Dpth 3.15 Welded, 1 dk	**(A36A2PR) Passenger/Ro-Ro Ship (Vehicles)** Passengers: 300	**1 oil engine** driving 1 FP propeller Total Power: 736kW (1,001hp) 11.5kn Daihatsu 8PSHTCM-26F 1 x 4 Stroke 8 Cy. 260 x 320 736kW (1001bhp) Daihatsu Diesel Manufacturing Co Lt-Japan AuxGen: 1 x 10kW 22V a.c
6814611 *DUE2007* -	**VIVA STA. MARIA** *ex* Sea Bridge No. 111 *-1995* *ex* Soya Maru No. 7 *-1985* *ex* Seikan Maru No. 2 *-1981* **Viva Shipping Lines Co Inc** - *Batangas* *Philippines* Official number: BAT5000041	*742* 248 455		**1968 Taguma Zosen KK — Onomichi HS** Yd No: 62 Loa 67.98 Br ex 14.20 Dght 3.048 Lbp 63.02 Br md 11.99 Dpth 4.47 Riveted\Welded, 1 dk	**(A37B2PS) Passenger Ship** Passengers: 866	**2 oil engines** driving 2 FP propellers Total Power: 1,956kW (2,660hp) 15.5kn Daihatsu 8PSTM-30 2 x 4 Stroke 8 Cy. 300 x 380 each-978kW (1330bhp) Daihatsu Kogyo-Japan

IMO / Call sign	Name / Owner / Flag	Tonnage	Class	Builder / Dimensions	Type / Cargo	Machinery
9623829 *3FNY3* -	**VIVACE** **Lodestar Shipping & Navigation SA** Kawasaki Kisen Kaisha Ltd (Kawasaki Kisen KK) ('K' Line) SatCom: Inmarsat C 437358010 *Panama* *Panama* MMSI: 373580000 Official number: 4404512	40,354 24,954 74,933 T/cm 67.3	Class: NK	**2012-07 Sasebo Heavy Industries Co. Ltd. — Sasebo Yard, Sasebo** Yd No: 806 Loa 225.00 (BB) Br ex 32.25 Dght 14.136 Lbp 218.00 Br md 32.20 Dpth 19.80 Welded, 1 dk	**(A21A2BC) Bulk Carrier** Double Hull Grain: 90,771; Bale: 88,783 Compartments: 7 Ho, ER 7 Ha: 6 (17.0 x 14.4)ER (15.3 x 12.8)	**1 oil engine** driving 1 FP propeller Total Power: 8,700kW (11,829hp) 14.5kn MAN-B&W 7S50MC-C8 1 x 2 Stroke 7 Cy. 500 x 2000 8700kW (11829bhp) Mitsui Engineering & Shipbuilding CLtd-Japan Fuel: 2730.0
9203708 *V4MF2* -	**VIVARA** *ex* OMG Kolpino *-2009* *ex* Moksheim *-2008* **New Marine Technologies Group Ltd** Nautilus Shipping & Trading Group Co SatCom: Inmarsat C 434118410 *Basseterre* *St Kitts & Nevis* MMSI: 341184000 Official number: SKN 1002322	5,659 2,363 6,847 T/cm 17.1	Class: GL IS (Class contemplated) (BV) (NV)	**2000-04 OAO Sudostroitelnyy Zavod "Severnaya Verf" — St.-Peterburg** (Hull launched by) Yd No: 437 **2000-04 Stocznia Marynarki Wojennej SA (Naval Shipyard Gdynia) — Gdynia** (Hull completed by) Yd No: NS109/2 Loa 109.70 Br ex - Dght 7.044 Lbp 99.90 Br md 17.80 Dpth 9.00 Welded, 1 dk	**(A31A2GX) General Cargo Ship** Grain: 7,859; Bale: 7,758 TEU 342 C.Ho 138/20' C.Dk 204/20' incl. 20 ref C. Compartments: 3 Ho, ER 3 Ha: (12.0 x 12.8)Tappered 2 (25.4 x 12.8)ER Ice Capable	**1 oil engine** driving 1 FP propeller Total Power: 3,360kW (4,568hp) 12.5kn B&W 6L35MC 1 x 2 Stroke 6 Cy. 350 x 1050 3360kW (4568bhp) AO Bryanskiy MashinostroitelnyyZavod (BMZ)-Bryansk AuxGen: 3 x 320kW 220/380V 50Hz a.c Thrusters: 1 Thwart. CP thruster (f) Fuel: 67.3 (d.f.) (Heating Coils) 344.3 (r.f.) 13.5pd
9429546 *LAXB* -	**VIVAX** *launched as* Sanmar Eskort 80-1 *-2008* **Bugsertjeneste II AS KS** Ostensjo Rederi AS SatCom: Inmarsat C 425857713 *Haugesund* *Norway* MMSI: 258577000	485 146 187	Class: AB	**2008-09 Gemsan Gemi Insa ve Gemi Isletmeciligi San. Ltd. — Tuzla** Yd No: 36 Loa 33.10 Br ex - Dght 6.100 Lbp 30.10 Br md 12.00 Dpth 5.36 Welded, 1 dk	**(B32A2ST) Tug** Passengers: cabins: 4	**2 oil engines** reduction geared to sc. shafts driving 2 Z propellers Total Power: 4,800kW (6,526hp) 13.5kn Wartsila 8L26 2 x 4 Stroke 8 Cy. 260 x 320 each-2400kW (3263bhp) Wartsila Finland Oy-Finland AuxGen: 2 x 140kW 380V 50Hz a.c Thrusters: 1 Tunnel thruster (f) Fuel: 159.0 (d.f.)
1009754 *ZCXN3* -	**VIVE LA VIE** *launched as* Bounty Hunter *-2008* **Vive La Vie Ltd** Luerssen Logistics *George Town* *Cayman Islands (British)* MMSI: 319540000 Official number: 740721	1,277 383 186	Class: LR ✠ **100A1** SS 06/2013 SSC Yacht, mono, G6 ✠ **LMC** **UMS** Cable: 332.0/24.0 U3 (a)	**2008-06 Luerssen Bardenfleth GmbH & Co KG — Berne** (Hull) Yd No: 13649 **2008-06 Fr. Luerssen Werft GmbH & Co. — Bremen** Yd No: 13649 Loa 59.40 Br ex 11.42 Dght 3.360 Lbp 48.72 Br md 11.10 Dpth 6.30 Welded, 1 dk	**(X11A2YP) Yacht**	**2 oil engines** with clutches, flexible couplings & sr reverse geared to sc. shafts driving 2 FP propellers Total Power: 2,908kW (3,954hp) Caterpillar 3512B 2 x Vee 4 Stroke 12 Cy. 170 x 190 each-1454kW (1977bhp) Caterpillar Inc-USA AuxGen: 3 x 280kW 400V 50Hz a.c Thrusters: 1 Thwart. FP thruster (f)
9157181 *VVSC* -	**VIVEK** **Mumbai Port Trust** *Mumbai* *India* Official number: 2703	1,316 395 1,428	Class: (IR) (BV)	**1997-06 Mazagon Dock Ltd. — Mumbai** Yd No: 23001 Loa 64.60 Br ex 13.73 Dght 3.860 Lbp 60.20 Br md 13.51 Dpth 4.70 Welded, 1 dk	**(B33B2DU) Hopper/Dredger (unspecified)** Hopper: 850 Cranes: 2x15t	**2 oil engines** geared to sc. shafts driving 2 CP propellers Total Power: 1,530kW (2,080hp) 10.4kn Wartsila 6L20 2 x 4 Stroke 6 Cy. 200 x 280 each-765kW (1040bhp) Wartsila Diesel Oy-Finland AuxGen: 2 x 360kW 415V 50Hz a.c, 1 x 360kW 415V 50Hz a.c Fuel: 140.0 (d.f.)
9082673 - -	**VIVEKANANDA** **Poompuhar Shipping Corp Ltd** - *Kanniyakumari* *India* Official number: KK-10	*113* 34 12	Class: (IR)	**1992-05 Anderson Marine Pvt. Ltd. — Goa** Yd No: 027 Loa 24.25 Br ex - Dght 0.900 Lbp 21.67 Br md 6.00 Dpth 2.10 Welded, 1 dk	**(A37B2PS) Passenger Ship**	**1 oil engine** geared to sc. shaft driving 1 FP propeller Total Power: 270kW (367hp) 10.0kn Ruston 1 x 4 Stroke 270kW (367bhp) Ruston & Hornsby (India) Ltd-India
9154414 - -	**VIVER ATUN DOS** - -	249 74 310		**1997-03 Rodman Polyships S.A. — Vigo** Yd No: 110002 Loa 33.95 Br ex - Dght 3.500 Lbp 31.45 Br md 8.00 Dpth 4.20 Bonded, 1 dk	**(B12B2FC) Fish Carrier** Hull Material: Reinforced Plastic	**1 oil engine** reduction geared to sc. shaft driving 1 FP propeller Total Power: 306kW (416hp) 13.0kn Mitsubishi S6R2-MPTA 1 x 4 Stroke 6 Cy. 170 x 220 306kW (416bhp) Mitsubishi Heavy Industries Ltd-Japan
9154402 *EALW* -	**VIVER ATUN UNO** **Viver Atun Cartagena SA** - *Cartagena* *Spain* MMSI: 224129000 Official number: 4-6/1996	249 74 310		**1996-09 Rodman Polyships S.A. — Vigo** Yd No: 110001 Loa 33.95 Br ex - Dght 3.500 Lbp 31.45 Br md 8.00 Dpth 4.20 Bonded, 1 dk	**(B12B2FC) Fish Carrier** Hull Material: Reinforced Plastic	**1 oil engine** reduction geared to sc. shaft driving 1 FP propeller Total Power: 306kW (416hp) 13.0kn Mitsubishi S6R2-MPTA 1 x 4 Stroke 6 Cy. 170 x 220 306kW (416bhp) Mitsubishi Heavy Industries Ltd-Japan
6600682 *HP7787* -	**VIVEROS II** *ex* Bacalac Transport *-1994* *ex* Kirstie of Kishorn *-1979* *ex* Fixity *-1976* **Desarrollo Del Darien SA** - *Panama* *Panama* Official number: 23286PEXT1	*200* 125 329	Class: (LR) ✠ Classed LR until 30/8/85	**1966-01 Fellows & Co Ltd — Great Yarmouth** Yd No: 375 Loa 35.82 Br ex 7.70 Dght - Lbp 33.61 Br md 7.62 Dpth 2.90 Riveted\Welded, 1 dk	**(A31A2GX) General Cargo Ship** Grain: 440; Bale: 395 Compartments: 1 Ho, ER 1 Ha: (16.1 x 5.1)ER Derricks: 1x1t; Winches: 1	**1 oil engine** sr reverse geared to sc. shaft driving 1 FP propeller Total Power: 243kW (330hp) 9.0kn Blackstone ERS4M 1 x 4 Stroke 4 Cy. 222 x 292 243kW (330bhp) Lister Blackstone Marine Ltd.-Dursley AuxGen: 1 x 24V d.c Fuel: 9.5 (d.f.)
7814553 *HO3443* -	**VIVEROS VI** *ex* Cape X *-2004* *ex* Halliburton 222 *-2004* **Clean Waters de Panama SA** - *Panama* *Panama* MMSI: 357528000 Official number: 3055005C	760 228 700	Class: (AB)	**1979-08 Halter Marine, Inc. — New Orleans, La** Yd No: 735 Loa 56.39 Br ex - Dght 3.658 Lbp 51.85 Br md 12.20 Dpth 4.27 Welded, 1 dk	**(B21A20S) Platform Supply Ship**	**2 oil engines** reverse reduction geared to sc. shafts driving 2 FP propellers Total Power: 1,250kW (1,700hp) 12.0kn Caterpillar D398SCAC 2 x Vee 4 Stroke 12 Cy. 159 x 203 each-625kW (850bhp) (Re-engined) Caterpillar Tractor Co-USA AuxGen: 2 x 99kW Thrusters: 1 Thwart. FP thruster (f)
9254719 *VRIV9* -	**VIVIAN** *ex* Medi Rotterdam *-2011* **Trend Shipping Ltd** Hong Kong Continue Shipping Co Ltd *Hong Kong* *Hong Kong* MMSI: 477353600 Official number: HK-3164	38,854 25,197 75,735 T/cm 65.8	Class: NK	**2002-05 Sanoyas Hishino Meisho Corp — Kurashiki OY** Yd No: 1198 Loa 225.00 (BB) Br ex 32.30 Dght 13.995 Lbp 217.00 Br md 32.26 Dpth 19.30 Welded, 1 dk	**(A21A2BC) Bulk Carrier** Double Bottom Entire Compartment Length Grain: 89,250 Compartments: 7 Ho, ER 7 Ha: (16.3 x 13.4)6 (17.1 x 15.0)ER	**1 oil engine** driving 1 FP propeller Total Power: 8,973kW (12,200hp) 14.5kn B&W 7S50MC-C 1 x 2 Stroke 7 Cy. 500 x 2000 8973kW (12200bhp) Mitsui Engineering & Shipbuilding CLtd-Japan AuxGen: 3 x 400kW 450V 60Hz a.c Fuel: 151.0 (d.f.) (Heating Coils) 2691.0 (r.f.) 30.5pd
5010103 *HP8924* -	**VIVIANE II** *ex* 902 *-1997* *ex* Alexander Mackenzie *-1988* **Balladier Shipping SA** - *Panama* *Panama* Official number: 26039MFLA	487 204 244	Class: (LR) ✠ Classed LR until 23/6/78	**1950-07 Burrard Dry Dock Co Ltd — North Vancouver BC** Yd No: 266 Loa 45.73 Br ex 9.20 Dght 3.163 Lbp 42.63 Br md 9.15 Dpth 4.12 Riveted\Welded, 1 dk	**(B34Q2QL) Buoy & Lighthouse Tender** Compartments: 1 Ho, ER 1 Ha: (3.2 x 2.4) Derricks: 1x10t,1x0.5t Ice Capable	**2 oil engines** driving 2 FP propellers Total Power: 736kW (1,000hp) 10.0kn Vivian 2 x 4 Stroke 10 Cy. 230 x 305 each-368kW (500bhp) Vivian Engine Works Ltd-Canada AuxGen: 2 x 100kW 108/215V d.c
9491848 *TCYC4* -	**VIVIEN A** **Arkas Konteyner Tasimacilik AS (Arkas Container Transport SA)** Arkas Denizcilik ve Nakliyat AS (Arkas Shipping & Transport AS) *Izmir* *Turkey* MMSI: 271040635	26,195 12,700 34,973 T/cm 45.0	Class: GL	**2010-05 Volkswerft Stralsund GmbH — Stralsund** Yd No: 483 Loa 210.45 (BB) Br ex - Dght 11.400 Lbp 198.74 Br md 29.80 Dpth 16.40 Welded, 1 dk	**(A33A2CC) Container Ship (Fully Cellular)** TEU 2478 C Ho 992 TEU C Dk 1486 TEU incl 488 ref C Cranes: 3x45t Ice Capable	**1 oil engine** driving 1 FP propeller Total Power: 21,770kW (29,598hp) 21.9kn MAN-B&W 7L70ME-C 1 x 2 Stroke 7 Cy. 700 x 2360 21770kW (29598bhp) Doosan Engine Co Ltd-South Korea AuxGen: 3 x 1805kW 450V a.c Thrusters: 1 Tunnel thruster (f)
8970823 *YL2791* -	**VIVITA** *ex* Mars 1 *-2012* *ex* KM-0861 *-2006* **Gamma-A SIA** - *Liepaja* *Latvia* MMSI: 275423000 Official number: 2146	117 30 30	Class: (RS)	**2001-11 Sosnovskiy Sudostroitelnyy Zavod — Sosnovka** Yd No: 861 Loa 25.50 Br ex 7.00 Dght 2.390 Lbp 22.00 Br md 6.80 Dpth 3.30 Welded, 1 dk	**(B11A2FS) Stern Trawler** Grain: 64 Ice Capable	**1 oil engine** reduction geared to sc. shaft driving 1 FP propeller Total Power: 354kW (481hp) 10.0kn Caterpillar 3406E 1 x 4 Stroke 6 Cy. 137 x 165 354kW (481bhp) (made 1999) Caterpillar Inc-USA AuxGen: 2 x 16kW Fuel: 12.0 (d.f.)

IMO / Call sign	Name / Owner	Tonnage	Class	Builder / Dimensions	Type	Machinery
8650904 *H09384* -	**VIVRE-G** *ex Domenico Pappalardo -2011* **Rederij Groen BV** *Panama* *Panama* MMSI: 373250000 Official number: 4351412	**328** 98 -	Class: UV (RI)	**2004 Cant. Nav. di Ortona — Ortona** Converted From: Fishing Vessel-2011 Loa 32.72 (BB) Br ex 8.10 Dght 1.670 Lbp - Br md - Dpth 2.22 Welded, 1 dk	**(B22G20Y) Standby Safety Vessel**	**2 oil engines** reduction geared to sc. shafts driving 2 FP propellers Total Power: 2,542kW (3,456hp) 15.0kn GUASCOR SF480TA-SP 2 x Vee 4 Stroke 16 Cy. 152 x 165 each-1271kW (1728bhp) Gutierrez Ascunce Corp (GUASCOR)-Spain AuxGen: 2 x 180kW a.c Thrusters: 1 Tunnel thruster (f); 1 Tunnel thruster (a) Fuel: 60.0
8958655 *WDE5096* -	**VIXEN** **Vixen LLC** Oregon Seafood Producers Inc *Reedsport, OR* *United States of America* Official number: 1063312	**180** 54 -		**1998 Fred Wahl Marine Construction Inc — Reedsport, Or** Yd No: 98-98-8 Loa 29.87 Br ex - Dght - Lbp - Br md 7.92 Dpth 2.83 Welded, 1 dk	**(B11B2FV) Fishing Vessel**	**2 oil engines** reduction geared to sc. shafts driving 2 FP propellers Total Power: 706kW (960hp) Cummins N14-M 2 x 4 Stroke 6 Cy. 140 x 152 each-353kW (480bhp) Cummins Engine Co Inc-USA
9134701 *3FHT3* -	**VIYA** *ex Cape Spear -2013 ex Nirint Star -2011* *ex Cape Spear -2009 ex MSC Coimbra -2002* *ex Cape Spear -2001* **MTN Shipping & Trading Corp** Akar Deniz Tasimaciligi ve Ticaret AS *Panama* *Panama* MMSI: 351976000 Official number: 44729PEXT	**10,925** 5,548 13,623 T/cm 28.4	Class: BV (GL)	**1997-12 Stocznia Szczecinska SA — Szczecin** Yd No: B190/1/6 Loa 151.47 (BB) Br ex - Dght 8.250 Lbp 142.21 Br md 24.00 Dpth 11.10 Welded, 1 dk	**(A33A2CC) Container Ship (Fully Cellular)** Double Bottom Entire Compartment Length TEU 1158 C Ho 381 TEU C Dk 777 TEU incl 90 ref C. Compartments: 4 Cell Ho, ER 7 Ha: ER Cranes: 2x40t Ice Capable	**1 oil engine** with flexible couplings & sr gearedto sc. shaft driving 1 CP propeller Total Power: 9,730kW (13,229hp) 18.5kn MAN 7L58/64 1 x 4 Stroke 7 Cy. 580 x 640 9730kW (13229bhp) MAN B&W Diesel AG-Augsburg AuxGen: 1 x 870kW 220/440V 60Hz a.c, 2 x 580kW 220/440V 60Hz a.c Thrusters: 1 Thwart. FP thruster (f) Fuel: 163.0 (d.f.) 1196.0 (r.f.) 38.0pd
7320710 *UHNL* -	**VIZANTIN** *ex Sormovskiy-28 -2010* *ex Manfred Pauls -2005* *ex Sormovskiy-28 -2000* **Ladoga Shipping Co Ltd (OOO Sudokhodnaya Kompaniya 'Ladoga')** *Astrakhan* *Russia* MMSI: 273420740	**2,491** 1,083 3,346	Class: RS	**1973 Sudostroitelnyy Zavod "Krasnoye Sormovo" — Gorkiy** Yd No: 38 Loa 114.03 Br ex 13.21 Dght 3.810 Lbp 108.01 Br md 13.00 Dpth 5.52 Welded, 1 dk	**(A31A2GX) General Cargo Ship** Bale: 4,297 Compartments: 4 Ho, ER 4 Ha: (17.6 x 9.3)3 (18.0 x 9.3) Ice Capable	**2 oil engines** driving 2 FP propellers Total Power: 970kW (1,318hp) 10.8kn S.K.L. 6NVD48A-U 2 x 4 Stroke 6 Cy. 320 x 480 each-485kW (659bhp) VEB Schwermaschinenbau "KarlLiebknecht" (SKL)-Magdeburg AuxGen: 4 x 50kW Fuel: 94.0 (d.f.)
7604764 - -	**VIZCAINO** - -	*296* 190 330		**1976-05 Atlantic Marine — Jacksonville, Fl** Yd No: 4162 Loa 32.92 Br ex 8.84 Dght 3.671 Lbp 29.27 Br md 8.79 Dpth 4.78 Welded, 1 dk	**(B11B2FV) Fishing Vessel** Compartments: 2 Ho, ER Derricks: 2	**1 oil engine** reverse reduction geared to sc. shaft driving 1 FP propeller Total Power: 588kW (799hp) 9.0kn G.M. (Detroit Diesel) 12V-149 1 x Vee 2 Stroke 12 Cy. 146 x 146 588kW (799bhp) General Motors Detroit DieselAllison Divn-USA AuxGen: 1 x 50kW 216V
9206308 *EAXB* -	**VIZCONDE DE EZA** *ex Segepesca Uno -2000* **Government of Spain (Ministerio de Pesca, Secretaria General de Pesca Maritima)** - *Santa Cruz de Tenerife* *Spain (CSR)* MMSI: 224582000 Official number: 8-1/1999	**1,401** 420 -	Class: BV	**2000-06 Montajes Cies S.L. — Vigo** Yd No: 83 Loa 52.70 Br ex - Dght 4.950 Lbp 45.00 Br md 13.00 Dpth 5.06 Welded, 1 dk	**(B12D2FR) Fishery Research Vessel** Ice Capable	**2 diesel electric oil engines** driving 2 gen. Connecting to 2 elec. motors driving 2 FP propellers Total Power: 1,802kW (2,450hp) GUASCOR 2 x 4 Stroke each-901kW (1225bhp) Gutierrez Ascunce Corp (GUASCOR)-Spain
8657495 *9AA6749* -	**VJEKO** **UTO Silva** *Split* *Croatia* Official number: 5T-1020	**171** 74 -	Class: CS	**2009 Poseidon - Obrt za Proizvodnju i Popravak Plovila — Kastel Stafilic** Yd No: 108 Loa 29.90 Br ex - Dght - Lbp 22.84 Br md 7.30 Dpth 3.53 Welded, 1 dk	**(A37B2PS) Passenger Ship**	**1 oil engine** reduction geared to sc. shaft driving 1 FP propeller Total Power: 425kW (578hp) Caterpillar 3408C 1 x Vee 4 Stroke 8 Cy. 137 x 152 425kW (578bhp) Caterpillar Inc-USA
9683661 *3ETW7* -	**VL PIONEER** **Hi Gold Ocean Kmarine No 11A SA** Hyundai Ocean Service Co Ltd *Panama* *Panama* MMSI: 352489000 Official number: 45706SC	**161,367** 111,506 321,000 T/cm 180.0	Class: KR LR (Class contemplated) **100A1** 04/2014	**2014-04 Hyundai Samho Heavy Industries Co Ltd — Samho** Yd No: S692 Loa 333.08 (BB) Br ex - Dght - Lbp - Br md 60.00 Dpth 27.80 Welded, 1 dk	**(A13A2TV) Crude Oil Tanker** Double Hull (13F)	**1 oil engine** driving 1 FP propeller 15.5kn
8215883 *ORSK* -	**VLAANDEREN I** *ex Lesse II -1992* **Baggerwerken Decloedt en Zoon NV** *Zeebrugge* *Belgium* MMSI: 205050000 Official number: 01 00069 1996	**2,039** 611 2,883	Class: BV	**1983-08 Scheepswerf en Machinefabriek "De Liesbosch" B.V. — Nieuwegein** Yd No: 186 Loa 78.16 Br ex - Dght 4.350 Lbp 74.50 Br md 14.51 Dpth 5.26 Welded, 1 dk	**(B33B2DT) Trailing Suction Hopper Dredger** Hopper: 2,065	**2 oil engines** sr geared to sc. shafts driving 2 CP propellers Total Power: 2,500kW (3,400hp) 10.8kn Bolnes 10DNL170/600 2 x 2 Stroke 10 Cy. 190 x 350 each-1250kW (1700bhp) 'Bolnes' Motorenfabriek BV-Netherlands AuxGen: 1 x 580kW 380/220V 50Hz a.c, 2 x 152kW 380/220V 50Hz a.c Thrusters: 1 Thwart. FP thruster (f) Fuel: 174.0
9198173 *ORLW* -	**VLAANDEREN VII** **Baggerwerken Decloedt en Zoon NV** - *Ostend* *Belgium* MMSI: 205251000 Official number: 01 00400 1998	**941** 282 1,790	Class: BV	**1998-09 Daewoo-Mangalia Heavy Industries S.A. — Mangalia** (Hull) **1998-09 Neptune Shipyards BV — Aalst (Nl)** Yd No: 243 Loa 65.08 Br ex 11.91 Dght 3.000 Lbp 61.90 Br md 11.80 Dpth 4.30 Welded, 1 dk	**(B34A2SH) Hopper, Motor**	**2 oil engines** geared to sc. shafts driving 2 Directional propellers Total Power: 780kW (1,060hp) 8.5kn Cummins KTA-19-M 2 x 4 Stroke 6 Cy. 159 x 159 each-390kW (530bhp) Cummins Engine Co Inc-USA AuxGen: 2 x 48kW 440V 50Hz a.c Fuel: 55.0 (d.f.) 3.2pd
9198214 *ORLX* -	**VLAANDEREN VIII** **Baggerwerken Decloedt en Zoon NV** - *Ostend* *Belgium* MMSI: 205252000 Official number: 01 00401 1998	**941** 282 1,790	Class: BV	**1998-09 Daewoo-Mangalia Heavy Industries S.A. — Mangalia** (Hull) **1998-09 Neptune Shipyards BV — Aalst (Nl)** Yd No: 244 Loa 65.08 Br ex 11.91 Dght 3.000 Lbp 61.90 Br md 11.80 Dpth 4.30 Welded, 1 dk	**(B34A2SH) Hopper, Motor**	**2 oil engines** geared to sc. shafts driving 2 Directional propellers Total Power: 780kW (1,060hp) 8.5kn Cummins KTA-19-M 2 x 4 Stroke 6 Cy. 159 x 159 each-390kW (530bhp) Cummins Engine Co Inc-USA AuxGen: 2 x 48kW 440V 50Hz a.c Fuel: 55.0 (d.f.) 3.2pd
7704552 *FNJV* -	**VLAANDEREN XIX** **Societe de Dragage Internationale (SDI)** - *Marseille* *France (FIS)* MMSI: 226274000 Official number: 924622	**2,970** 891 3,000	Class: BV	**1978-02 IHC Smit BV — Kinderdijk** Yd No: 896 Loa 99.90 Br ex - Dght 4.801 Lbp 74.88 Br md 18.51 Dpth 5.97 Welded, 1 dk	**(B33A2DC) Cutter Suction Dredger** Liq: 1,800	**2 diesel electric oil engines** driving 2 gen. Connecting to 2 elec. motors driving 2 Directional propellers Total Power: 5,148kW (7,000hp) 8.0kn Mirrlees KMR-6 2 x 4 Stroke 6 Cy. 381 x 457 each-2574kW (3500bhp) Mirrlees Blackstone (Stockport)Ltd.-Stockport
7026479 *ORYN* -	**VLAANDEREN XVIII** **Baggerwerken Decloedt en Zoon NV** - *Zeebrugge* *Belgium* MMSI: 205042000 Official number: 01 00071 1996	**9,640** 3,463 16,385	Class: BV	**1970-09 IHC Smit NV — Kinderdijk** Yd No: 754 Loa 124.06 Br ex 23.04 Dght 8.281 Lbp 115.53 Br md 23.02 Dpth 11.00 Welded, 1 dk	**(B33B2DT) Trailing Suction Hopper Dredger** Hopper: 11,301 Compartments: 2 Ho, ER	**2 oil engines** with flexible couplings & geared to sc. shafts driving 2 CP propellers Total Power: 10,448kW (14,206hp) 14.0kn Deutz SBV12M640 2 x Vee 4 Stroke 12 Cy. 370 x 400 each-5224kW (7103bhp) (new engine 1985) Kloeckner Humboldt Deutz AG-West Germany AuxGen: 2 x 706kW 380/220V a.c, 3 x 258kW 380/220V a.c Fuel: 525.0
8106977 *J8B3816* -	**VLAANDEREN XX** *ex D. O. S. 11 -1992 ex Vlaanderen XX -1988* **Middle East Dredging Co QSC (MEDCO)** Dredging, Environmental & Marine Engineering NV (DEME Group) *Kingstown* *St Vincent & The Grenadines* MMSI: 376297000 Official number: 10289	**5,934** 1,780 7,160	Class: BV	**1982-06 IHC Smit BV — Kinderdijk** Yd No: C01149 Loa 106.03 Br ex 21.49 Dght 5.850 Lbp 101.02 Br md 21.42 Dpth 7.57 Welded, 1 dk	**(B33B2DT) Trailing Suction Hopper Dredger** Hopper: 5,072 Compartments: 1 Ho, ER 1 Ha: ER Cranes: 1x8.5t	**2 oil engines** sr geared to sc. shafts driving 2 CP propellers Total Power: 9,710kW (13,202hp) 14.4kn Deutz SBV12M540 2 x Vee 4 Stroke 12 Cy. 370 x 400 each-4855kW (6601bhp) Kloeckner Humboldt Deutz AG-West Germany Thrusters: 1 Tunnel thruster (f)

IMO / Call sign	Name / Owner	Tonnage	Class	Build / Dimensions	Type	Machinery
8881357 *UAKG* -	**VLAD ORION** **Oklend JSC** - SatCom: Inmarsat C 427320093 *Petropavlovsk-Kamchatskiy* *Russia* MMSI: 273815000 Official number: 920267	**2,489** 746 935	Class: RS	**1994-07 AB "Baltijos" Laivu Statykla — Klaipeda** Yd No: 819 Loa 85.06 Br ex 13.04 Dght 4.040 Lbp 75.95 Br md 13.00 Dpth 6.50 Welded, 1 dk	**(A34A2GR) Refrigerated Cargo Ship** Ins: 1,245 Compartments: 2 Ho, ER 2 Ha: 2 (2.2 x 3.4)ER Cranes: 1x3.2t Ice Capable	**1 oil engine** driving 1 FP propeller Total Power: 852kW (1,158hp) 11.3kn S.K.L. 8NVD48A-2U 1 x 4 Stroke 8 Cy. 320 x 480 852kW (1158bhp) SKL Motoren u. Systemtechnik AG-Magdeburg
8957273 - -	**VLAD PRIMORYE** *ex* Liao Da Gan Yu 8713 *-2000* **Fasco Rybflot JSC** -	**115** 39 85	Class: (RS)	**1999-05 Rongcheng Shipbuilding Industry Co Ltd — Rongcheng SD** Yd No: Y040199522 Loa 34.00 Br ex - Dght 2.100 Lbp 29.62 Br md 6.00 Dpth 2.70 Welded, 1 dk	**(B11B2FV) Fishing Vessel** Grain: 130	**1 oil engine** geared to sc. shaft driving 1 CP propeller Total Power: 220kW (299hp) 11.5kn Chinese Std. Type Z6170ZL 1 x 4 Stroke 6 Cy. 170 x 200 220kW (299bhp) Zibo Diesel Engine Factory-China AuxGen: 2 x 12kW Fuel: 42.0 (d.f.)
6828234 - - - -	**VLADI** *ex* Jin Sung -1 *-2000* *ex* Myeong Jin *-1999* *ex* Hwa Sung No. 11 *-1997* *ex* Kanei Maru No. 8 *-1997* - -	**291** 89 -		**1968 Uchida Zosen — Ise** Yd No: 663 Loa - Br ex 7.32 Dght 3.099 Lbp 38.84 Br md 7.29 Dpth 3.48 Riveted\Welded, 1 dk	**(B11B2FV) Fishing Vessel**	**1 oil engine** driving 1 FP propeller Total Power: 736kW (1,001hp) Hanshin 6LU32 1 x 4 Stroke 6 Cy. 320 x 510 736kW (1001bhp) Hanshin Nainenki Kogyo-Japan
9313589 *UHSW* -	**VLADIMIR** **Armator Co Ltd** Navigator LLC *St Petersburg* *Russia* MMSI: 273445480	**4,378** 1,313 5,600 T/cm 22.0	Class: RS	**2004-06 Sudostroitelnyy Zavod "Krasnoye Sormovo" — Nizhniy Novgorod** Yd No: 19614/5 Loa 141.00 Br ex 16.90 Dght 3.740 Lbp 134.88 Br md 16.80 Dpth 6.10 Welded, 1 dk	**(A13B2TP) Products Tanker** Double Hull (13F) Liq: 6,587; Liq (Oil): 6,721 Cargo Heating Coils Compartments: 12 Wing Ta, ER, 1 Slop Ta 2 Cargo Pump (s): 2x250m³/hr Manifold: Bow/CM: 70m Ice Capable	**2 oil engines** reduction geared to sc. shafts driving 2 FP propellers Total Power: 1,860kW (2,528hp) 10.0kn Wartsila 6L20 2 x 4 Stroke 6 Cy. 200 x 280 each-930kW (1264bhp) Wartsila Finland Oy-Finland Thrusters: 1 Tunnel thruster (f)
9354533 *5BSL2* -	**VLADIMIR** *ex* Fesco Vladimir *-2013* **Star Warm Shipping Co Ltd** Far-Eastern Shipping Co (FESCO) (Dalnevostochnoye Morskoye Parokhodstvo) SatCom: Inmarsat C 420977711 *Limassol* *Cyprus* MMSI: 209777000 Official number: 9354533	**16,803** 8,648 22,708 T/cm 37.1	Class: GL RS	**2009-05 Stocznia Szczecinska Nowa Sp z oo — Szczecin** Yd No: B170/V/3 Loa 183.97 (BB) Br ex - Dght 9.889 Lbp 171.94 Br md 25.30 Dpth 13.50 Welded, 1 dk	**(A33A2CC) Container Ship (Fully Cellular)** TEU 1728 C Ho 634 TEI C Dk 1094 TEU incl 200 ref C Compartments: 4 Cell Ho, ER 9 Ha: ER Cranes: 3x45t Ice Capable	**1 oil engine** driving 1 FP propeller Total Power: 13,320kW (18,110hp) 19.5kn Wartsila 6RTA62U 1 x 2 Stroke 6 Cy. 620 x 2150 13320kW (18110bhp) H Cegielski Poznan SA-Poland AuxGen: 3 x 1096kW 450/220V a.c Thrusters: 1 Tunnel thruster (f)
8701868 *UBDF7* -	**VLADIMIR ATLASOV** *ex* Shunsho Maru No. 8 *-2008* **Global Shipping Co Ltd** Midglen Logistics Sakhalin LLC *Korsakov* *Russia* MMSI: 273335210	**678** 203 700	Class: RS	**1987-02 Shitanoe Shipbuilding Co Ltd — Usuki OT** Yd No: 1066 Loa 59.01 (BB) Br ex 9.53 Dght 3.280 Lbp 54.31 Br md 9.50 Dpth 5.52 Welded, 1 dk	**(A31A2GX) General Cargo Ship** Compartments: 2 Ho, ER 2 Ha: ER	**1 oil engine** geared to sc. shaft driving 1 FP propeller Total Power: 552kW (750hp) Hanshin 6LB26RG 1 x 4 Stroke 6 Cy. 260 x 440 552kW (750bhp) The Hanshin Diesel Works Ltd-Japan
8721210 *UGBB* -	**VLADIMIR BABICH** **Okeanrybflot JSC (A/O 'Okeanrybflot')** - *Petropavlovsk-Kamchatskiy* *Russia* MMSI: 273842020 Official number: 852360	**4,407** 1,322 1,810	Class: RS	**1986-07 GP Chernomorskiy Sudostroitelnyy Zavod — Nikolayev** Yd No: 553 Loa 104.50 Br ex 16.03 Dght 5.900 Lbp 96.40 Br md 16.00 Dpth 10.20 Welded, 2 dks	**(B11A2FG) Factory Stern Trawler** Bale: 420; Ins: 2,219 Ice Capable	**2 oil engines** reduction geared to sc. shaft driving 1 CP propeller Total Power: 5,148kW (7,000hp) 16.1kn Russkiy 6CHN40/46 2 x 4 Stroke 6 Cy. 400 x 460 each-2574kW (3500bhp) Mashinostroitelnyy Zavod"Russkiy-Dizel"-Leningrad AuxGen: 2 x 1600kW 220/380V 50Hz a.c, 3 x 200kW 220/380V 50Hz a.c Fuel: 1226.0 (d.f.)
8116295 *UFNH* -	**VLADIMIR BRODYUK** **Daltransflot Co Ltd** - *Vladivostok* *Russia* MMSI: 273516600 Official number: 810885	**3,816** 1,144 1,796	Class: RS	**1982 Stocznia Gdanska im Lenina — Gdansk** Yd No: B408/21 Loa 93.91 Br ex 15.92 Dght 5.670 Lbp 85.02 Br md 15.91 Dpth 10.01 Welded, 2 dks	**(B11A2FG) Factory Stern Trawler** Ins: 1,947; Liq: 39 Compartments: 3 Ho, ER 4 Ha: (0.6 x 0.6)3 (2.4 x 2.1) Derricks: 6x3t Ice Capable	**1 oil engine** geared to sc. shaft driving 1 FP propeller Total Power: 3,825kW (5,200hp) 15.8kn Sulzer 8ZL40/48 1 x 4 Stroke 8 Cy. 400 x 480 3825kW (5200bhp) Zaklady Urzadzen Technicznych'Zgoda' SA-Poland AuxGen: 1 x 1200kW 400V 50Hz a.c, 1 x 760kW 400V 50Hz a.c, 2 x 350kW 320V 50Hz a.c Fuel: 1319.0 (r.f.)
7646891 - -	**VLADIMIR GOLUZENKO** **Terneyles JSC (OAO 'Terneyles')** - *Vladivostok* *Russia* MMSI: 273440950 Official number: 760296	*245* 75 51	Class: RS	**1977-09 Nakhodkinskiy Sudoremontnyy Zavod — Nakhodka** Yd No: 6 Loa 38.42 Br ex 6.71 Dght 2.180 Lbp 33.98 Br md 6.70 Dpth 2.90 Welded, 1 dk	**(A37B2PS) Passenger Ship** Passengers: unberthed: 100 Ice Capable	**2 oil engines** reduction geared to sc. shaft (s) driving 2 FP propellers Total Power: 464kW (630hp) Daldizel 8CHNSP18/22 2 x 4 Stroke 8 Cy. 180 x 220 each-232kW (315bhp) AuxGen: 1 x 14kW, 2 x 13kW Fuel: 20.0 (d.f.)
8228177 *UEVF* - -	**VLADIMIR GUSAROV** *ex* BK-1200-40B *-1984* **JSC Ltd 'Magadanskiy Morskoy Torgoviy Port' (JSC Ltd 'Magadan Marine Commerical Port')** - *Magadan* *Russia* Official number: 811962	*180* 54 46	Class: RS	**1981-11 Gorokhovetskiy Sudostroitelnyy Zavod — Gorokhovets** Yd No: 406 Loa 29.30 Br ex 8.49 Dght 3.090 Lbp 27.00 Br md 8.30 Dpth 4.35 Welded, 1 dk	**(B32A2ST) Tug** Ice Capable	**2 oil engines** driving 2 CP propellers Total Power: 882kW (1,200hp) Russkiy 6DR30/50-4 2 x 2 Stroke 6 Cy. 300 x 500 each-441kW (600bhp) (made 1980) Mashinostroitelnyy Zavod"Russkiy-Dizel"-Leningrad AuxGen: 2 x 30kW a.c Fuel: 36.0 (d.f.)
8127804 *UGTP* - -	**VLADIMIR IGNATYUK** *ex* Arctic Kalvik *-2003* *ex* Kalvik *-1997* **Murmansk Shipping Co (MSC)** - *Murmansk* *Russia* MMSI: 273448450 Official number: 825556	**4,391** 1,317 2,113	Class: RS (LR) ✠ Classed LR until 30/6/04	**1983-07 Burrard Yarrows Corp — Victoria BC** Yd No: 554 Loa 88.02 Br ex 17.82 Dght 8.290 Lbp 75.39 Br md 17.51 Dpth 10.01 Welded, 1 dk	**(B34C2SI) Icebreaker** Passengers: berths: 34 Liq: 102 Cranes: 2x5t Ice Capable	**4 oil engines** sr geared to sc. shafts driving 2 CP propellers Total Power: 17,060kW (23,196hp) 15.4kn Werkspoor 8TM410 4 x 4 Stroke 8 Cy. 410 x 470 each-4265kW (5799bhp) Stork Werkspoor Diesel BV-Netherlands AuxGen: 2 x 1000kW 460V 60Hz a.c, 2 x 750kW 460V 60Hz a.c Thrusters: 1 Thwart. CP thruster (a); 1 Water jet (f) Fuel: 1686.0 (d.f.)
7116638 - -	**VLADIMIR KAMANIN** *ex* 11 *-1998* *ex* Vladimir Kamanin *-1996* **OOO 'Silen'** -	**170** 51 77	Class: (RS)	**1968-06 Astrakhanskaya Sudoverf im. "Kirova" — Astrakhan** Yd No: 15 Converted From: Fishing Vessel Loa 33.46 Br ex 6.68 Dght 2.631 Lbp 29.19 Br md - Dpth 3.54 Welded, 1 dk	**(B31A2SR) Research Survey Vessel** Compartments: 1 Ho, ER 1 Ha: (1.3 x 1.9) Ice Capable	**1 oil engine** driving 1 FP propeller Total Power: 224kW (305hp) 9.0kn S.K.L. 8NVD36-1U 1 x 4 Stroke 8 Cy. 240 x 360 224kW (305bhp) VEB Schwermaschinenbau "KarlLiebknecht" (SKL)-Magdeburg AuxGen: 1 x 50kW, 2 x 20kW Fuel: 20.0 (d.f.)
8955225 *UBYF4* -	**VLADIMIR KOMAROV** *ex* Georgia *-2008* *ex* Antivari *-2004* *ex* Kolkhida-39 *-2000* **Yuzhnyie Transportnye Linii Ltd** - *Novorossiysk* *Russia* MMSI: 273337630	**155** 46 17	Class: RS (BV)	**1999-12 Zavod im. "Ordzhonikidze" — Poti** Yd No: 139 Loa 34.50 Br ex 10.30 Dght 1.120 Lbp 33.46 Br md - Dpth 5.80 Welded, 1 dk	**(A37B2PS) Passenger Ship** Hull Material: Aluminium Alloy	**2 oil engines** geared to sc. shafts driving 2 FP propellers Total Power: 1,920kW (2,610hp) M.T.U. 12V396TC82 2 x Vee 4 Stroke 12 Cy. 165 x 185 each-960kW (1305bhp) MTU Friedrichshafen GmbH-Friedrichshafen
8729743 *UUA03* -	**VLADIMIR LUGOVSKOY** **State Enterprise 'Yalta Sea Trade Port'** - *Yalta* *Ukraine* MMSI: 272099900 Official number: 884747	**205** 62 31	Class: (RS)	**1989-03 Ilyichyovskiy Sudoremontnyy Zavod im. "50-letiya SSSR" — Ilyichyovsk** Yd No: 17 Loa 37.60 Br ex 7.21 Dght 1.690 Lbp 34.01 Br md - Dpth 2.90 Welded, 1 dk	**(A37B2PS) Passenger Ship** Passengers: unberthed: 250	**3 oil engines** reduction geared to sc. shafts driving 3 FP propellers Total Power: 960kW (1,306hp) 16.5kn Barnaultransmash 3D6C 2 x 4 Stroke 6 Cy. 150 x 180 each-110kW (150bhp) Barnaultransmash-Barnaul Zvezda M401A-1 1 x Vee 4 Stroke 12 Cy. 180 x 200 740kW (1006bhp) "Zvezda"-Leningrad

9014884 **VLADIMIR MYASNIKOV**
UBNI5 *ex* Atlas *-2012* *ex* Atlasgracht *-2012*
\- **Kamchatka Shipping Co Ltd (KASCO)**
\-
Petropavlovsk-Kamchatskiy *Russia*
MMSI: 273357660

7,949 Class: RS (LR)
4,157 ✠ Classed LR until 11/7/12
12,150

1991-08 Tille Scheepsbouw B.V. (Frisian Shipyard) — Harlingen (Assembled by) Yd No: 282
1991-08 Tille Scheepsbouw B.V. — Kootstertille (Parts for assembly by) Yd No: 282
Loa 129.80 (BB) Br ex 19.03 Dght 8.610
Lbp 120.60 Br md 18.90 Dpth 11.65
Welded, 1 dk, 2nd dk in hold only

(A31A2GX) General Cargo Ship
Grain: 14,870; Bale: 14,870
TEU 679 C Ho 273 TEU C Dk 406 TEU incl 30 ref C.
Compartments: 1 Ho, ER, 1 Tw Dk
3 Ha: (25.2 x 15.8)2 (26.6 x 15.8)ER
Cranes: 3x40t

1 oil engine with flexible couplings & sr geared to sc. shaft driving 1 CP propeller
Total Power: 4,920kW (6,689hp) 14.0kn
Wartsila 12V32E
1 x Vee 4 Stroke 12 Cy. 320 x 350 4920kW (6689bhp)
Wartsila Diesel Oy-Finland
AuxGen: 1 x 320kW 440V 60Hz a.c, 3 x 320kW 440V 60Hz a.c
Boilers: TOH (o.f.) 10.2kgf/cm² (10.0bar), TOH (ex.g.) 10.2kgf/cm² (10.0bar)
Thrusters: 1 Thwart. CP thruster (f)

8108406 **VLADIMIR NAZOR**
9A2171
\- **Jadrolinija**
\-
Rijeka *Croatia*
MMSI: 238113240
Official number: 2T-465

1,686 Class: CS (JR)
675
1,125

1986-05 Brodogradiliste 'Titovo' — Kraljevica Yd No: 444
Loa 86.59 Br ex 14.51 Dght 3.012
Lbp 79.91 Br md 14.30 Dpth 5.31
Welded, 1 dk

(A36A2PR) Passenger/Ro-Ro Ship (Vehicles)
Bow door & ramp
Stern ramp

2 oil engines reduction geared to sc. shafts driving 2 CP propellers
Total Power: 1,620kW (2,202hp)
Alpha 6S28LU
2 x 4 Stroke 6 Cy. 280 x 320 each-810kW (1101bhp)
MAN B&W Diesel A/S-Denmark
Thrusters: 1 Thwart. CP thruster (f)

7610995 **VLADIMIR OSIPTSOV**
USCQ *ex* Victoriya *-2008* *ex* Lyudmila *-2007*
\- *ex* Victoria *-2002* *ex* Ivan Koroteyev *-2002*
SRZ Ltd
Commercial Fleet of Donbass Ltd
Mariupol *Ukraine*
MMSI: 272826000

6,641 Class: (RS)
3,259
8,455

1975 Vyborgskiy Sudostroitelnyy Zavod — Vyborg Yd No: 709
Loa 136.81 (BB) Br ex 17.84 Dght 7.900
Lbp 124.97 Br md 17.73 Dpth 10.39
Welded, 2 dks

(A31A2GX) General Cargo Ship
Grain: 11,350; Bale: 10,650; Liq: 300
Compartments: 1 Dp Ta in Hold, 4 Ho, ER, 4 Tw Dk
4 Ha: (9.8 x 8.0)3 (18.9 x 12.8)ER
Derricks: 4x20t; Winches: 16
Ice Capable

1 oil engine driving 1 FP propeller
Total Power: 4,928kW (6,700hp) 16.5kn
B&W 5K62EF
1 x 2 Stroke 5 Cy. 620 x 1400 4928kW (6700bhp)
Bryanskiy Mashinostroitelnyy Zavod (BMZ)-Bryansk
AuxGen: 3 x 240kW 400V 50Hz a.c
Fuel: 160.0 (d.f.) 880.0 (r.f.)

8606587 **VLADIMIR PARSHIN**
EOHF
\- **Ukraine Marine Ecology Research Centre**
\-
SatCom: Inmarsat A 1404642
Odessa *Ukraine*
MMSI: 272506000
Official number: 880784

752 Class: (RS)
226
272

1989-06 Oy Laivateollisuus Ab — Turku Yd No: 379
Loa 49.92 Br ex 10.02 Dght 3.601
Lbp 44.51 Br md 10.00 Dpth 5.00
Welded

(B31A2SR) Research Survey Vessel
Bale: 149

1 oil engine with clutches, flexible couplings & sr geared to sc. shaft driving 1 CP propeller
Total Power: 985kW (1,339hp) 12.8kn
Wartsila 824TS
1 x 4 Stroke 8 Cy. 240 x 310 985kW (1339bhp)
Wartsila Diesel Oy-Finland
AuxGen: 1 x 160kW a.c, 2 x 150kW a.c

8935940 **VLADIMIR PASHKIN**
\- *ex* SRP-150-1 *-1974*
\- **Alfa-Marin Co Ltd**
\-
Nakhodka *Russia*
Official number: 730233

173 Class: RS
57
163

1974-10 Sudoremontnyy Zavod "Yakor" — Sovetskaya Gavan Yd No: 698/1
Loa 35.75 Br ex 7.50 Dght 1.710
Lbp 33.48 Br md 7.22 Dpth 2.42
Welded, 1 dk

(A31C2GD) Deck Cargo Ship
Ice Capable

1 oil engine geared to sc. shaft driving 1 FP propeller
Total Power: 165kW (224hp) 7.8kn
Daldizel 6CHNSP18/22
1 x 4 Stroke 6 Cy. 180 x 220 165kW (224bhp)
Daldizel-Khabarovsk
AuxGen: 1 x 12kW, 1 x 10kW
Fuel: 5.0 (d.f.)

8709676 **VLADIMIR PRAVIK**
UEMU
\- **Ukrtanker Co ('Ukrtanker' Kompaniya)**
Astrakhan *Russia*
MMSI: 273426250

4,185 Class: (RS)
1,397
6,321
T/cm
20.0

1987-09 'Ilya Boyadzhiev' Shipyard — Bourgas Yd No: 105
Loa 125.16 (BB) Br ex 16.64 Dght 4.830
Lbp 120.56 Br md 16.62 Dpth 6.94
Welded, 1 dk

(A13B2TP) Products Tanker
Double Bottom Entire Compartment Length
Liq: 5,827; Liq (Oil): 5,827
Compartments: 6 Wing Ta, ER
2 Cargo Pump (s): 2x850m³/hr
Manifold: Bow/CM: 85m

2 oil engines sr geared to sc. shafts driving 2 FP propellers
Total Power: 2,206kW (3,000hp) 11.5kn
Dvigatel Revolyutsii 6CHRNP36/45
2 x 4 Stroke 6 Cy. 360 x 450 each-1103kW (1500bhp)
Zavod "Dvigatel Revolyutsii"-Gorkiy
AuxGen: 4 x 160kW a.c

7741471 **VLADIMIR RODIK**
UHSH
\- **Trading House Mortrans Co Ltd**
Mortrans Co Ltd
Vladivostok *Russia*
MMSI: 273310940
Official number: 781589

245 Class: RS
103
51

1979-04 Nakhodkinskiy Sudoremontnyy Zavod — Nakhodka Yd No: 11
Loa 38.41 Br ex 6.71 Dght 2.201
Lbp 34.50 Br md 6.70 Dpth 2.90
Welded, 1 dk

(A37B2PS) Passenger Ship
Passengers: unberthed: 180
Ice Capable

2 oil engines geared to sc. shafts driving 2 FP propellers
Total Power: 464kW (630hp) 12.5kn
Daldizel 8CHNSP18/22
2 x 4 Stroke 8 Cy. 180 x 220 each-232kW (315bhp)
Daldizel-Khabarovsk
AuxGen: 4 x 13kW
Fuel: 20.0 (d.f.)

8947632 **VLADIMIR SAFONOV**
UGVT
\- **TINRO Centre - Pacific Research Fisheries Centre**
\-
Vladivostok *Russia*
MMSI: 273418710

480 Class: RS
144
176

1998-11 AO Zavod 'Nikolayevsk-na-Amure' — Nikolayevsk-na-Amure Yd No: 1309
Loa 39.52 Br ex 9.30 Dght 3.770
Lbp 39.37 Br md - Dpth 5.14
Welded, 1 dk

(B11A2FS) Stern Trawler
Ins: 139

1 oil engine driving 1 FP propeller
Total Power: 589kW (801hp) 11.4kn
S.K.L. 6NVD48A-2U
1 x 4 Stroke 6 Cy. 320 x 480 589kW (801bhp)
SKL Motoren u. Systemtechnik AG-Magdeburg
AuxGen: 3 x 160kW a.c
Fuel: 88.0 (d.f.)

8923624 **VLADIMIR SHUMAKOV**
\- *ex* Neptun-2 *-1997*
\- **Real Estate Management Committee of St Petersburg City Executive Board**
Baltmarin Co
St Petersburg *Russia*
MMSI: 273447870
Official number: 730642

950 Class: (RS)
495
1,634

1974-06 Shipbuilding & Shiprepairing Yard 'Ivan Dimitrov' — Rousse Yd No: 101
Loa 60.55 Br ex 11.00 Dght 4.760
Lbp 56.67 Br md - Dpth 5.50
Welded, 1 dk

(B35E2TF) Bunkering Tanker
Liq: 1,701; Liq (Oil): 1,701
Cargo Heating Coils
Compartments: 13 Ta, ER
Ice Capable

2 oil engines driving 2 FP propellers
Total Power: 448kW (610hp) 8.7kn
S.K.L. 8NVD36-1U
2 x 4 Stroke 8 Cy. 240 x 360 each-224kW (305bhp)
VEB Schwermaschinenbau "KarlLiebknecht" (SKL)-Magdeburg
AuxGen: 1 x 34kW a.c, 2 x 25kW a.c
Fuel: 6.0 (d.f.)

8907101 **VLADIMIR STARZHINSKIY**
UFEL *ex* Poseidon *-2011*
\- *ex* Vladimir Starzhinskiy *-2004*
JSC 'Roliz'
Vladivostok *Russia*
MMSI: 273814310

7,805 Class: RS (NV)
3,920
6,435

1993-04 Factorias Vulcano SA — Vigo Yd No: 504
Loa 105.00 (BB) Br ex 20.64 Dght 9.150
Lbp 89.50 Br md 20.00 Dpth 14.70
Welded, 3 dks

(B11A2FG) Factory Stern Trawler
Passengers: berths: 125
Ins: 5,500

1 oil engine reduction geared to sc. shaft driving 1 CP propeller
Total Power: 5,921kW (8,050hp) 14.5kn
Wartsila 16V32D
1 x Vee 4 Stroke 16 Cy. 320 x 350 5921kW (8050bhp)
Construcciones Echevarria SA-Spain
AuxGen: 1 x 2560kW 220/380V 50Hz a.c, 2 x 960kW 220/380V 50Hz a.c
Thrusters: 1 Thwart. FP thruster (f)
Fuel: 95.0 (d.f.) 1355.0 (r.f.)

7333731 **VLADIMIR SUKHOTSKIY**
UCHQ
\- **Government of The Russian Federation (Federal State Unitary Hydrographic Department of Ministry of Transport of Russian Federation)**
\-
SatCom: Inmarsat C 427300761
Vostochnyy *Russia*
MMSI: 273198000
Official number: 732652

1,212 Class: (RS)
363
644

1974-01 Oy Laivateollisuus Ab — Turku Yd No: 294
Loa 68.23 Br ex 11.89 Dght 4.150
Lbp 60.00 Br md 11.87 Dpth 6.00
Welded, 2 dks

(B31A2SR) Research Survey Vessel
Bale: 445
Compartments: 2 Ho, ER
2 Ha: (5.8 x 3.8) (2.0 x 1.7)ER
Cranes: 1x5t,1x2t
Ice Capable

1 oil engine driving 1 CP propeller
Total Power: 1,618kW (2,200hp) 13.5kn
Deutz SBV6M358
1 x 4 Stroke 6 Cy. 400 x 580 1618kW (2200bhp)
Kloeckner Humboldt Deutz AG-West Germany
Fuel: 264.0 (d.f.)

9311622 **VLADIMIR TIKHONOV**
A8IA6
\- **Bassett Oceanway Ltd**
Unicom Management Services (Cyprus) Ltd
SatCom: Inmarsat C 463791341
Monrovia *Liberia*
MMSI: 636012814
Official number: 12814

87,146 Class: NV
51,548
162,397
T/cm
126.6

2006-06 Daewoo Shipbuilding & Marine Engineering Co Ltd — Geoje Yd No: 5273
Loa 280.50 (BB) Br ex 50.06 Dght 16.524
Lbp 270.00 Br md 50.00 Dpth 23.00
Welded, 1 dk

(A13A2TW) Crude/Oil Products Tanker
Double Hull (13F)
Liq: 178,034; Liq (Oil): 178,034
Cargo Heating Coils
Compartments: 12 Wing Ta, 2 Wing Slop Ta, ER
3 Cargo Pump (s): 3x3700m³/hr
Manifold: Bow/CM: 136.3m
Ice Capable

1 oil engine driving 1 CP propeller
Total Power: 21,770kW (29,598hp) 15.5kn
MAN-B&W 7S70ME-C
1 x 2 Stroke 7 Cy. 700 x 2800 21770kW (29598bhp)
Doosan Engine Co Ltd-South Korea
AuxGen: 3 x 1037kW a.c
Thrusters: 1 Tunnel thruster (f)
Fuel: 294.0 (d.f.) 4067.0 (r.f.)

9353785 **VLADIMIR USKOV**
\-
\-
\-
Temryuk *Russia*

143 Class: RR (RS)
45
36

2005-08 Sosnovskiy Sudostroitelnyy Zavod — Sosnovka Yd No: 867
Loa 25.45 Br ex - Dght 2.390
Lbp 22.00 Br md 7.00 Dpth 3.30
Welded, 1 dk

(B11A2FS) Stern Trawler

1 oil engine driving 1 FP propeller 10.0kn

8517114 **VLADIMIR VYSOTSKIY**
UFGF
\- **North Eastern Shipping Co Ltd (NESCO Ltd) (OOO 'Severo-Vostochnoye Morskoye Parokhodstvo')**
\-
SatCom: Inmarsat A 1402166
Magadan *Russia*
MMSI: 273152400
Official number: 863863

10,949 Class: RS
3,567
16,970
T/cm
28.0

1988-09 Brodogradiliste '3 Maj' — Rijeka Yd No: 647
Loa 151.50 (BB) Br ex 22.43 Dght 9.360
Lbp 142.60 Br md 22.40 Dpth 12.15
Welded, 1 dk

(A13B2TP) Products Tanker
Single Hull
Liq: 20,071; Liq (Oil): 20,071
Cargo Heating Coils
Compartments: 6 Ta, 10 Wing Ta, ER
16 Cargo Pump (s): 16x250m³/hr
Manifold: Bow/CM: 73m
Ice Capable

2 oil engines with clutches, flexible couplings & dr geared to sc. shaft driving 1 CP propeller
Total Power: 5,738kW (7,802hp) 12.0kn
Pielstick 6PC2-6L-400
2 x 4 Stroke 6 Cy. 400 x 460 each-2869kW (3901bhp)
Tvornica Dizel Motora '3 Maj'-Yugoslavia
AuxGen: 2 x 1360kW a.c, 2 x 512kW a.c
Thrusters: 1 Thwart. CP thruster (f)

7607273 *UDID* -	**VLADIMIR ZAGOSKIN** *ex* Roar Kristensen *-2005* *ex* Syltefjord *-2000* *ex* Nessefjord *-1990* *ex* Martin and Phillip *-1985* *ex* Andenesfisk III *-1979* **Sea Community JSC (ZAO 'Morskoye Sodruzhestvo')** - *Murmansk* *Russia* MMSI: 273450850	**568** 197 240	Class: NV RS	**1977-03 AS Storviks Mek. Verksted — Kristiansund** Yd No: 78 Loa 46.54 Br ex 9.02 Dght 4.533 Lbp 40.01 Br md 9.00 Dpth 6.51 Welded, 2 dks	**(B11A2FS) Stern Trawler** Ice Capable	**1 oil engine** driving 1 FP propeller Total Power: 1,103kW (1,500hp) 12.5kn MaK 8M452AK 1 x 4 Stroke 8 Cy. 320 x 450 1103kW (1500bhp) MaK Maschinenbau GmbH-Kiel AuxGen: 2 x 248kW 220V 50Hz a.c Fuel: 101.0 (d.f.)
9618719 *UBMK5* -	**VLADIMIR ZAKHARENKO** **JSC 'Goznak-Leasing'** Anship LLC *Novorossiysk* *Russia* MMSI: 273332380 Official number: 04301540	**5,686** 3,321 7,240	Class: RS	**2014-03 OAO Sudostroitelnyy Zavod 'Lotos' — Narimanov** Yd No: 301 Loa 139.95 (BB) Br ex 16.70 Dght 4.700 Lbp 133.68 Br md 16.50 Dpth 6.00 Welded, 1 dk	**(A31A2GX) General Cargo Ship** Double Hull Grain: 10,920 Compartments: 3 Ho, ER 3 Ha: (50.0 x 12.7) (23.4 x 12.7)ER (21.4 x 12.7)	**2 oil engines** reduction geared to sc. shafts driving 2 FP propellers Total Power: 2,160kW (2,936hp) 11.5kn Wartsila 6L20 2 x 4 Stroke 6 Cy. 200 x 280 each-1080kW (1468bhp) AuxGen: 2 x a.c Thrusters: 1 Thwart. FP thruster (f)
9310018 *UEKQ* -	**VLADISLAV STRIZHOV** **Gazprom JSC & Gazprom Neft Shelf** OOO Gazflot *Murmansk* *Russia* MMSI: 273312530	**5,871** 1,762 3,867	Class: RS (NV)	**2006-03 DP Sudnobudivnyi Zavod im. "61 Kommunara" — Mykolayiv** (Hull) Yd No: 3310 **2006-03 Havyard Leirvik AS — Leirvik i Sogn** Yd No: 082 Loa 99.30 Br ex - Dght 8.500 Lbp 83.30 Br md 19.00 Dpth 10.50 Welded, 1 dk	**(B21B20A) Anchor Handling Tug Supply** Bale: 239; Liq: 3,158 Cranes: 1x10t Ice Capable	**4 diesel electric oil engines** driving 2 gen. each 6000kW a.c 2 gen. each 3995kW a.c Connecting to 2 elec. motors driving 2 Azimuth electric drive units Total Power: 19,990kW (27,180hp) 15.0kn Wartsila 12V32 2 x Vee 4 Stroke 12 Cy. 320 x 400 each-6000kW (8158bhp) Wartsila Finland Oy-Finland Wartsila 8L32 2 x 4 Stroke 8 Cy. 320 x 400 each-3995kW (5432bhp) Wartsila Finland Oy-Finland Thrusters: 2 Tunnel thruster (f) Fuel: 1474.0
9669081 *UBOI3* -	**VLADIVOSTOK** - - *Vladivostok* *Russia* MMSI: 273354760 Official number: 784	**257** 92 33	Class: RS (Class contemplated)	**2012-06 Pacifico Marine Ltd (OOO Pasifiko Marin) — Vladivostok** Yd No: CD342/02 Loa 28.00 Br ex - Dght 1.800 Lbp - Br md 8.10 Dpth 3.00 Bonded, 1 dk	**(A37B2PS) Passenger Ship** Hull Material: Reinforced Plastic	**2 oil engines** reduction geared to sc. shafts driving 2 Propellers Total Power: 2,060kW (2,800hp) MAN D2862LE 2 x Vee 4 Stroke 12 Cy. 128 x 157 each-1030kW (1400bhp) MAN Nutzfahrzeuge AG-Nuernberg
9060429 *UHDC* -	**VLADIVOSTOK** *ex* Igor *-2004* **JSC Turnif (A/O 'Turnif')** - SatCom: Inmarsat B 327312310 *Vladivostok* *Russia* MMSI: 273819700 Official number: 911287	**4,407** 1,322 1,820	Class: RS (NV)	**1992-11 DAHK Chernomorskyi Sudnobudivnyi Zavod — Mykolayiv** Yd No: 602 Loa 104.50 Br ex 16.03 Dght 5.900 Lbp 96.40 Br md 16.00 Dpth 10.20 Welded	**(B11A2FG) Factory Stern Trawler** Grain: 420; Ins: 2,219 Ice Capable	**2 oil engines** reduction geared to sc. shaft driving 1 CP propeller Total Power: 5,148kW (7,000hp) 16.1kn Russkiy 6CHN40/46 2 x 4 Stroke 6 Cy. 400 x 460 each-2574kW (3500bhp) Mashinostroitelnyy Zavod"Russkiy-Dizel"-Sankt-Peterburg AuxGen: 2 x 1600kW 220/380V 50Hz a.c, 3 x 200kW 220/380V 50Hz a.c Fuel: 1226.0 (d.f.) 23.0pd
9130145 *P3BJ8* -	**VLADIVOSTOK** **Bodyguard Shipping Co Ltd** Far-Eastern Shipping Co (FESCO) (Dalnevostochnoye Morskoye Parokhodstvo) *Limassol* *Cyprus* MMSI: 209389000 Official number: 9130145	**16,575** 8,817 23,200 T/cm 37.1	Class: GL	**1998-06 Stocznia Szczecinska SA — Szczecin** Yd No: B170/4/2 Loa 184.10 (BB) Br ex - Dght 9.880 Lbp 171.94 Br md 25.30 Dpth 13.50 Welded, 1 dk	**(A33A2CC) Container Ship (Fully Cellular)** Grain: 29,744 TEU 1748 C Ho 634 TEU C Dk 1114 TEU incl 150 ref C. Compartments: 4 Cell Ho, ER 9 Ha: (12.5 x 13.0)8 (12.5 x 20.6)ER	**1 oil engine** driving 1 FP propeller Total Power: 13,328kW (18,121hp) 19.0kn Sulzer 6RTA62U 1 x 2 Stroke 6 Cy. 620 x 2150 13328kW (18121bhp) H Cegielski Poznan SA-Poland AuxGen: 3 x 1096kW 440/220V a.c Thrusters: 1 Tunnel thruster (f)
9585015 *HP5468* -	**VLADMIR M** *ex* Tanya *-2011* **Zircon Holding & Finance Inc** Norfes-Marine Service Co Ltd *Panama* *Panama* MMSI: 354470000 Official number: 4308811	**8,887** 4,507 13,000	Class: BV	**2010-12 Zhoushan Penglai Shiprepairing & Building Co Ltd — Daishan County ZJ** Yd No: PL0709 Loa 138.60 (BB) Br ex - Dght 7.900 Lbp 129.80 Br md 20.40 Dpth 11.02 Welded, 1 dk	**(A21A2BC) Bulk Carrier** Grain: 16,759 Compartments: 4 Ho, ER 4 Ha: ER Cranes: 2x25t Ice Capable	**1 oil engine** reduction geared to sc. shaft driving 1 FP propeller Total Power: 4,050kW (5,506hp) 12.6kn Wartsila 6L38 1 x 4 Stroke 6 Cy. 380 x 475 4050kW (5506bhp) Wartsila Italia SpA-Italy AuxGen: 3 x 332kW 50Hz a.c
9656149 *CFN5920* -	**VLADYKOV** **Government of Canada (Ministry of Fisheries & Oceans)** Government of Canada (Canadian Coast Guard) *Ottawa, ON* *Canada* MMSI: 316021844 Official number: 836307	**254** 190 -	Class: BV	**2012-06 Chantier Meridien Industrie Inc — Matane QC** Yd No: 008 Loa 25.00 Br ex - Dght - Lbp 23.50 Br md 9.22 Dpth 3.82 Welded, 1 dk	**(B12D2FR) Fishery Research Vessel** A-frames: 1	**2 oil engines** reduction geared to sc. shafts driving 2 FP propellers Total Power: 894kW (1,216hp) 9.0kn Caterpillar C18 ACERT 2 x 4 Stroke 6 Cy. 145 x 183 each-447kW (608bhp) Caterpillar Inc-USA AuxGen: 2 x 136kW 60Hz a.c Thrusters: 1 Tunnel thruster (f) Fuel: 41.0 (d.f.)
6912231 *EOTW* -	**VLAS CHUBAR** **Globus-RS Ltd** - *Kherson* *Ukraine* MMSI: 272089000 Official number: 670456	**1,994** - 2,128	Class: (RS)	**1967-07 Gorokhovetskiy Sudostroitelnyy Zavod — Gorokhovets** Yd No: 423 Loa 96.02 Br ex 13.21 Dght 3.271 Lbp - Br md - Dpth 5.49 Welded, 1 dk	**(A31A2GX) General Cargo Ship** Bale: 3,467 Compartments: 3 Ho, ER 3 Ha: 3 (16.4 x 9.7)ER Ice Capable	**2 oil engines** driving 2 FP propellers Total Power: 970kW (1,318hp) 10.0kn S.K.L. 6NVD48A-U 2 x 4 Stroke 6 Cy. 320 x 480 each-485kW (659bhp) (, fitted 1978) VEB Schwermaschinenbau "KarlLiebknecht" (SKL)-Magdeburg AuxGen: 2 x 50kW Fuel: 111.0 (d.f.)
9546124 *V7PJ6* -	**VLAZAKIS I** **Yerba Buena** Efshipping Co SA Panama SatCom: Inmarsat C 435835082 *Majuro* *Marshall Islands* MMSI: 538003242 Official number: 3242	**33,044** 19,231 57,022 T/cm 58.8	Class: BV	**2010-01 COSCO (Dalian) Shipyard Co Ltd — Dalian LN** Yd No: 570-2 Loa 189.99 (BB) Br ex - Dght 12.800 Lbp 185.64 Br md 32.26 Dpth 18.00 Welded, 1 dk	**(A21A2BC) Bulk Carrier** Grain: 71,634; Bale: 68,200 Compartments: 5 Ho, ER 5 Ha: 4 (21.3 x 18.3)ER (12.9 x 18.3) Cranes: 4x30t	**1 oil engine** driving 1 FP propeller Total Power: 9,480kW (12,889hp) 14.2kn MAN-B&W 6S50MC-C 1 x 2 Stroke 6 Cy. 500 x 2000 9480kW (12889bhp) Dalian Marine Diesel Co Ltd-China AuxGen: 3 x 600kW 60Hz a.c Fuel: 140.0 (d.f.) 2200.0 (r.f.)
8744420 *ZR7812* -	**VLEIGANS** **Arno-Louis Visserye BK** - *Cape Town* *South Africa* MMSI: 601103500 Official number: 10902	**132** - -		**2008-01 Tallie Marine Pty Ltd — St Helena Bay** Loa 21.03 Br ex - Dght 2.400 Lbp - Br md 7.20 Dpth 3.60 Bonded, 1 dk	**(B11B2FV) Fishing Vessel** Hull Material: Reinforced Plastic	**2 oil engines** reduction geared to sc. shafts driving 2 Propellers Caterpillar 2 x 4 Stroke Caterpillar Inc-USA
9554781 *PCIX* -	**VLIEBORG** **Scheepvaartonderneming Vlieborg BV** Wagenborg Shipping BV *Delfzijl* *Netherlands* MMSI: 246625000	**7,367** 3,688 11,850	Class: BV	**2012-09 Scheepswerf Ferus Smit BV — Westerbroek** Yd No: 407 Loa 142.65 Br ex 16.50 Dght 7.730 Lbp 139.43 Br md 15.87 Dpth 10.78 Welded, 1 dk	**(A31A2GX) General Cargo Ship** Grain: 14,267 Compartments: 2 Ho, ER 2 Ha: (63.6 x 13.2)ER (41.0 x 13.2) Ice Capable	**1 oil engine** reduction geared to sc. shaft driving 1 FP propeller Total Power: 3,050kW (4,147hp) 14.5kn MaK 9M25C 1 x 4 Stroke 9 Cy. 255 x 400 3050kW (4147bhp) Caterpillar Motoren GmbH & Co. KG-Germany AuxGen: 2 x 332kW 50Hz a.c, 1 x 655kW 50Hz a.c Thrusters: 1 Tunnel thruster (f) Fuel: 590.0

IMO / Call sign	Name / Owner / Registry	Tonnage	Class	Builder / Dimensions	Type / Capacity	Machinery
9224154 *A8ZP2* -	**VLIEDIEP** **Vliediep Shipping Co Ltd** Feederlines BV *Monrovia* *Liberia* MMSI: 636015266 Official number: 15266	**4,938** 2,631 7,200	Class: LR ✠ **100A1** SS 05/2011 strengthened for heavy cargoes, container cargoes in hold and on upper deck hatch covers Ice Class 1A (Finnish-Swedish Ice Class Rules 1985) Max draught midship 7.208m Max/min draught aft 7.197/4.367m Max/min draught fwd 7.197/1.837m Power required 2864kw, installed 3840kw ✠ **LMC** **UMS** Eq.Ltr: W; Cable: 498.4/44.0 U3 (a)	**2001-05 Bodewes' Scheepswerven B.V. — Hoogezand** Yd No: 604 Loa 118.55 Br ex 15.43 Dght 6.700 Lbp 111.85 Br md 15.20 Dpth 8.44 Welded, 1 dk	**(A31A2GX) General Cargo Ship** Grain: 9,415 TEU 390 C Ho 174 TEU C Dk 216 TEU Compartments: 2 Ho, ER 2 Ha: (39.0 x 12.7) (42.8 x 12.7)ER Ice Capable	**1 oil engine** with clutches, flexible couplings & sr geared to sc. shaft driving 1 CP propeller Total Power: 3,840kW (5,221hp) 12.0kr MaK 8M32 1 x 4 Stroke 8 Cy. 320 x 480 3840kW (5221bhp) MaK Motoren GmbH & Co. KG-Kiel AuxGen: 1 x 400kW 400V 50Hz a.c, 2 x 264kW 400V 50Hz a.c Boilers: HWH (o.f.) 3.6kgf/cm² (3.5bar) Thrusters: 1 Thwart. CP thruster (f)
9303716 *PD2749* -	**VLIELAND** **Wilbar Shipping BV** BV Rederij G Doeksen en Zonen SatCom: Inmarsat C 424437612 *Terschelling* *Netherlands* MMSI: 244090796 Official number: 42937	**3,990** 872 333		**2005-04 FBMA Marine Inc — Balamban** Yd No: 1018 Loa 67.84 (BB) Br ex 17.25 Dght 2.600 Lbp 62.64 Br md 17.00 Dpth 5.00 Welded, 1 dk	**(A36A2PR) Passenger/Ro-Ro Ship (Vehicles)** Passengers: unberthed: 1300 Lane-Len: 300 Lane-Wid: 2.25 Lane-clr ht: 2.60 Cars: 59	**4 oil engines** reverse reduction geared to sc. shafts driving 4 FP propellers Total Power: 2,984kW (4,056hp) 15.1kr Caterpillar 3508E 4 x Vee 4 Stroke 8 Cy. 170 x 190 each-746kW (1014bhp) Caterpillar Inc-USA Thrusters: 2 Tunnel thruster (f); 2 Tunnel thruster (f) Fuel: 39.0 (d.f.)
9313814 *PBFD* -	**VLIELAND** **Vlieland Shipping CV** Kustvaart Harlingen BV *Harlingen* *Netherlands* MMSI: 244376000 Official number: 42937	**3,990** 2,208 6,000	Class: BV	**2005-09 Scheepswerf Ferus Smit BV — Westerbroek** Yd No: 361 Loa 110.78 (BB) Br ex - Dght 6.090 Lbp 105.45 Br md 14.00 Dpth 8.73 Welded, 1 dk	**(A31A2GX) General Cargo Ship** Grain: 7,946; Bale: 7,946 Compartments: 2 Ho, ER 2 Ha: (50.8 x 11.5)ER (27.5 x 11.5) Ice Capable	**1 oil engine** geared to sc. shaft driving 1 CP propeller Total Power: 2,640kW (3,589hp) 13.0kr MaK 8M25 1 x 4 Stroke 8 Cy. 255 x 400 2640kW (3589bhp) Caterpillar Motoren GmbH & Co. KG-Germany AuxGen: 1 x 424kW 400/230V 50Hz a.c, 2 x 140kW 400/230V 50Hz a.c Thrusters: 1 Tunnel thruster (f) Fuel: 46.0 (d.f.) 350.0 (r.f.)
5101938 *V3QN2* -	**VLIEREE** *ex* Ella *-1966* **Van Ouwerkerk Vastgoed BV** Zand & Grinthandel van Ouwerkerk BV *Belize City* *Belize* MMSI: 312102000 Official number: 701120022	**1,097** 329 1,500	Class: IV (LR) (BV) ✠ Classed LR until 8/1/82	**1955-05 Scheepsbouw Unie N.V. — Groningen** Yd No: 263 Converted From: General Cargo Ship-1982 Lengthened & Widened-1982 Loa 75.67 Br ex - Dght 4.271 Lbp 70.54 Br md 10.00 Dpth 5.36 Welded, 1 dk	**(B33B2DT) Trailing Suction Hopper Dredger** Hopper: 600 Ice Capable	**1 oil engine** driving 1 FP propeller Total Power: 515kW (700hp) 9.0kr MaK MAU423A 1 x 4 Stroke 8 Cy. 290 x 420 515kW (700bhp) Maschinenbau Kiel AG (MaK)-Kiel AuxGen: 2 x 88kW 220/380V 50Hz a.c, 2 x 44kW 220/380V 50Hz a.c Fuel: 48.0 (d.f.)
8802650 *PBWM* -	**VLIESTROOM** **Government of The Kingdom of The Netherlands (Rijkswaterstaat Directie Noordzee)** - *Hellevoetsluis* *Netherlands* MMSI: 244964000 Official number: 2382	**288** 86 133	Class: BV	**1988-01 Machinefabriek D.E. Gorter B.V. — Hoogezand** (Hull) **1988-01 B.V. Scheepswerf Damen — Gorinchem** Yd No: 4490 Loa 38.00 Br ex - Dght 1.700 Lbp 34.70 Br md 8.70 Dpth 2.75 Welded, 1 dk	**(B34Q2QB) Buoy Tender** Cranes: 1x7.5t Ice Capable	**2 oil engines** with clutches, flexible couplings & dr reverse geared to sc. shaft driving 1 FP propeller Total Power: 580kW (788hp) 10.0k Deutz SBA8M816 2 x 4 Stroke 8 Cy. 142 x 160 each-290kW (394bhp) Kloeckner Humboldt Deutz AG-West Germany AuxGen: 2 x 140kW 380V 50Hz a.c Thrusters: 1 Thwart. FP thruster (f)
9395109 *PBBS* -	**VLIET TRADER** *ex* Medpacific *-2008* **Vliet Trader Beheer BV** Reider Shipping BV *Winschoten* *Netherlands* MMSI: 245780000 Official number: 52629	**15,375** 5,983 18,278	Class: GL	**2007-11 Zhejiang Ouhua Shipbuilding Co Ltd — Zhoushan ZJ** Yd No: 2043 Loa 166.15 (BB) Br ex - Dght 9.500 Lbp 155.08 Br md 25.00 Dpth 14.20 Welded, 1 dk	**(A33A2CC) Container Ship (Fully Cellular)** TEU 1296 C Ho 472 C Dk 824 TEU incl 390 ref C. Cranes: 2x45t	**1 oil engine** reduction geared to sc. shaft driving 1 FP propeller Total Power: 11,200kW (15,228hp) 19.0kr MAN-B&W 8L58/64 1 x 4 Stroke 8 Cy. 580 x 640 11200kW (15228bhp) MAN B&W Diesel AG-Augsburg AuxGen: 4 x 1600kW 450/220V a.c Thrusters: 1 Tunnel thruster (f)
9160346 *V2EM6* -	**VLISTBORG** **ms 'Metta' Schifffahrtsgesellschaft mbH + Co KG** Esmeralda Schiffahrts- Verwaltungsgesellschaft mbH *Saint John's* *Antigua & Barbuda* MMSI: 305479000 Official number: 4669	**6,130** 3,424 8,664 T/cm 18.3	Class: AB (BV)	**1999-04 Bodewes Scheepswerf "Volharding" Foxhol B.V. — Foxhol** Yd No: 332 Loa 132.20 (BB) Br ex - Dght 7.050 Lbp 123.84 Br md 15.87 Dpth 9.65 Welded, 1 dk	**(A31A2GX) General Cargo Ship** Grain: 12,855 TEU 552 C. 552/20' incl. 25 ref C. Ice Capable	**1 oil engine** sr. geared to sc. shaft driving 1 CP propeller Total Power: 3,960kW (5,384hp) 14.0kr Wartsila 6R38 1 x 4 Stroke 6 Cy. 380 x 475 3960kW (5384bhp) Wartsila NSD Nederland BV-Netherlands AuxGen: 2 x 260kW 440V 60Hz a.c Thrusters: 1 Thwart. CP thruster (f) Fuel: 42.1 (d.f.) (Heating Coils) 461.7 (r.f.) 22.5pd
9414187 *PHLX* -	**VLISTDIEP** *ex* OSC Vlistdiep *-2011* *launched as* Vlistdiep *-2007* **Beheermaatschappij ms Vlistdiep BV** Feederlines BV *Groningen* *Netherlands* MMSI: 244928000 Official number: 51298	**4,990** 2,648 7,781	Class: GL (BV)	**2007-09 Bodewes' Scheepswerven B.V. — Hoogezand** Yd No: 785 Loa 118.55 (BB) Br ex - Dght 7.050 Lbp 111.85 Br md 15.20 Dpth 8.45 Welded, 1 dk	**(A31A2GX) General Cargo Ship** Grain: 9,415 TEU 390 C Ho 174 TEU C Dk 216 TEU incl 20 ref C. Compartments: 2 Ho, ER 2 Ha: (54.0 x 12.6)ER (27.7 x 12.6) Cranes: 2x40t	**1 oil engine** reduction geared to sc. shafts driving 1 CP propeller Total Power: 3,840kW (5,221hp) 14.7k MaK 8M32C 1 x 4 Stroke 8 Cy. 320 x 480 3840kW (5221bhp) Caterpillar Motoren GmbH & Co. KG-Germany AuxGen: 3 x 264kW a.c, 1 x 348kW a.c Thrusters: 1 Tunnel thruster (f)
5330967 - -	**VLORA V** *ex* Thiaki *-1999* *ex* Corfu Rose *-1984* *ex* Isola d'Elba *-1984* *ex* Skane *-1966* **Far East Maritime SA**	*499* 155 303	Class: (HR) (GL) (RI)	**1961-07 Martin Jansen GmbH & Co. KG Schiffsw. u. Masch. — Leer** Yd No: 45 Loa 56.06 Br ex 10.70 Dght 3.234 Lbp 51.01 Br md 10.39 Dpth 4.09 Welded, 1 dk	**(A36A2PR) Passenger/Ro-Ro Ship (Vehicles)** Passengers: unberthed: 200	**2 oil engines** driving 2 FP propellers Total Power: 970kW (1,318hp) Deutz 2 x 4 Stroke 8 Cy. 310 x 450 each-485kW (659bhp) Kloeckner Humboldt Deutz AG-West Germany AuxGen: 3 x 60kW 380V 50Hz a.c Fuel: 20.5 (d.f.)
8858104 *E5U2829* -	**VM FORAR** *ex* Omskiy-130 *-2014* *ex* Olga *-2006* *ex* Omskiy-130 *-1999* **Forar Ltd** Vesmec Makina Sanayi Mumessillik Danismanlik ve Ticaret Ltd Sti *Avatiu* *Cook Islands* MMSI: 518882000	**2,528** 983 3,070	Class: RS	**1987-10 Santierul Naval Oltenita S.A. — Oltenita** Yd No: 267 Loa 108.40 Br ex 15.00 Dght 3.260 Lbp 105.00 Br md 14.80 Dpth 5.00 Welded, 1 dk	**(A31A2GX) General Cargo Ship** Grain: 4,383	**2 oil engines** driving 2 FP propellers Total Power: 1,030kW (1,400hp) 10.0k S.K.L. 6NVD48A-2 2 x 4 Stroke 6 Cy. 320 x 480 each-515kW (700bhp) VEB Schwermaschinenbau "KarlLiebknecht" (SKL)-Magdeburg
9147629 *9V9476* -	**VM HANDLER** *ex* Lamnalco Finch *-2010* *ex* Britoil 22 *-1999* **VM Marine International Pte Ltd** VM Marine International Ltd *Singapore* *Singapore* MMSI: 566124000 Official number: 397136	**443** 133 350	Class: BV (AB)	**1996-12 Fujian Fishing Vessel Shipyard — Fuzhou FJ** Yd No: H8006 Loa 37.00 Br ex - Dght 4.000 Lbp 34.69 Br md 10.60 Dpth 4.95 Welded, 1 dk	**(B21B20A) Anchor Handling Tug Supply** Passengers: berths: 14	**2 oil engines** geared to sc. shafts driving 2 FP propellers Total Power: 2,984kW (4,058hp) 11.5k Yanmar 8Z280-E 2 x 4 Stroke 8 Cy. 280 x 360 each-1492kW (2029bhp) Yanmar Diesel Engine Co Ltd-Japan AuxGen: 2 x 300kW 380V 50Hz a.c Thrusters: 1 Tunnel thruster (f) Fuel: 200.0 (d.f.)
9257254 *9V5788* -	**VM LEADER** *ex* Britoil 48 *-2011* **VM Marine International Pte Ltd** - *Singapore* *Singapore* MMSI: 564960000 Official number: 388571	**1,021** 306 702	Class: AB	**2002-01 Jiangsu Wuxi Shipyard Co Ltd — Wuxi JS** Yd No: H8037 Loa 48.00 Br ex - Dght 6.200 Lbp 39.00 Br md 13.00 Dpth 6.00 Welded, 1 dk	**(B21B20A) Anchor Handling Tug Supply**	**2 oil engines** geared to sc. shafts driving 2 CP propellers Total Power: 5,926kW (8,057hp) 12.0k MaK 6M32 2 x 4 Stroke 6 Cy. 320 x 480 each-2942kW (4000bhp) Caterpillar Motoren GmbH & Co. KG-Germany AuxGen: 3 x 400kW 380V 50Hz a.c Thrusters: 1 Thwart. CP thruster (f) Fuel: 781.0 (d.f.) 22.0pd

9336646 *9V9834* -	**VM LEGEND** *ex* BOA Magnitor *-2011* *ex* Miclyn Magnitor *-2007* **VM Offshore Pte Ltd** VM Marine International Pte Ltd *Singapore* *Singapore* MMSI: 566394000 Official number: 397643	**1,047** 314 586	Class: LR ✠ **100A1** SS 08/2011 tug, fire fighting Ship 1 (2400 m3/h with water spray) ✠ **LMC** **UMS** Eq.Ltr: M; Cable: 192.5/32.0 U2 (a)	**2006-08 Nautica Nova Shipbuilding & Engineering Sdn Bhd — Butterworth** Yd No: A0267 Loa 48.00 Br ex 13.05 Dght 5.200 Lbp 40.56 Br md 13.00 Dpth 6.00 Welded, 1 dk	**(B21B20A) Anchor Handling Tug Supply**	**2 oil engines** with clutches, flexible couplings & sr reverse geared to sc. shafts driving 2 CP propellers Total Power: 5,080kW (6,906hp) 11.0kn MaK 8M25 2 x 4 Stroke 8 Cy. 255 x 400 each-2540kW (3453bhp) Caterpillar Motoren GmbH & Co. KG-Germany AuxGen: 3 x 430kW 415V 50Hz a.c Thrusters: 1 Thwart. CP thruster (f)
8857916 *E5U2828* -	**VM PASHA** *ex* Omskiy-131 *-2014* **Katana Industry Ltd** Vesmec Makina Sanayi Mumessillik Danismanlik ve Ticaret Ltd Sti *Avatiu* *Cook Islands* MMSI: 518881000	**2,528** 983 3,070	Class: RS	**1987-11 Santierul Naval Oltenita S.A. — Oltenita** Yd No: 268 Loa 108.40 Br ex 15.00 Dght 3.260 Lbp 105.00 Br md - Dpth 5.00 Welded, 1 dk	**(A31A2GX) General Cargo Ship**	**2 oil engines** driving 2 FP propellers Total Power: 1,030kW (1,400hp) 10.0kn S.K.L. 6NVD48A-2U 2 x 4 Stroke 6 Cy. 320 x 480 each-515kW (700bhp) VEB Schwermaschinenbau "KarlLiebknecht" (SKL)-Magdeburg
9605657 *9V8473* -	**VM POWER** *ex* WOS 5505 *-2012* **VM Offshore Pte Ltd** VM Marine International Pte Ltd *Singapore* *Singapore* MMSI: 566225000 Official number: 395833	**499** 149 336	Class: AB	**2012-01 Jiangsu Wuxi Shipyard Co Ltd — Wuxi JS** Yd No: H8074 Loa 40.00 Br ex - Dght 4.400 Lbp 36.80 Br md 11.40 Dpth 4.95 Welded, 1 dk	**(B21B20A) Anchor Handling Tug Supply**	**2 oil engines** reduction geared to sc. shafts driving 2 FP propellers Total Power: 3,840kW (5,220hp) Caterpillar 3516B-HD 2 x Vee 4 Stroke 16 Cy. 170 x 215 each-1920kW (2610bhp) Caterpillar Inc-USA AuxGen: 3 x 245kW a.c Thrusters: 1 Tunnel thruster (f) Fuel: 350.0 (d.f.)
9466673 *9V7244* -	**VM PRIDE** *ex* WOS 5503 *-2010* **VM Offshore Pte Ltd** VM Marine International Pte Ltd *Singapore* *Singapore* MMSI: 565702000 Official number: 393402	**499** 149 336	Class: AB	**2008-01 Jiangsu Wuxi Shipyard Co Ltd — Wuxi JS** Yd No: H8061 Loa 40.00 Br ex 11.42 Dght 4.400 Lbp 36.80 Br md 11.40 Dpth 4.95 Welded, 1 dk	**(B21B20A) Anchor Handling Tug Supply** Passengers: berths: 18	**2 oil engines** geared to sc. shafts driving 2 FP propellers Total Power: 3,680kW (5,004hp) Yanmar 6EY26 2 x 4 Stroke 6 Cy. 260 x 385 each-1840kW (2502bhp) Yanmar Diesel Engine Co Ltd-Japan AuxGen: 3 x 245kW 380V 50Hz a.c Thrusters: 1 Tunnel thruster (f) Fuel: 297.8 (d.f.)
9605669 *9V8474* -	**VM PRUDENT** *ex* WOS 5506 *-2012* **VM Offshore Pte Ltd** VM Marine International Pte Ltd *Singapore* *Singapore* MMSI: 566226000 Official number: 395834	**499** 149 336	Class: AB	**2012-01 Jiangsu Wuxi Shipyard Co Ltd — Wuxi JS** Yd No: H8075 Loa 40.00 Br ex 11.42 Dght 4.400 Lbp 36.80 Br md 11.40 Dpth 4.95 Welded, 1 dk	**(B21B20A) Anchor Handling Tug Supply**	**2 oil engines** geared to sc. shafts driving 2 FP propellers Total Power: 3,840kW (5,220hp) 13.0kn Caterpillar 3516B-HD 2 x Vee 4 Stroke 16 Cy. 170 x 215 each-1920kW (2610bhp) Caterpillar Inc-USA AuxGen: 3 x 400kW a.c Thrusters: 1 Tunnel thruster (f) Fuel: 350.0 (d.f.)
5303897 *VC4510* -	**VM/S HERCULES** *ex* S. L. S. Hercules *-1976* **Government of Canada (The St Lawrence Seaway Management Corp)** - *Montreal, QC* *Canada* MMSI: 316002166 Official number: 319256	*2,108* 1,282 2,107	Class: (LR) ✠ Classed LR until 26/10/04	**1962-11 Marine Industries Ltee (MIL) — Sorel QC** Yd No: 278 Loa 60.97 Br ex 22.86 Dght 4.265 Lbp 60.36 Br md 22.26 Dpth 5.69 Welded, 1 dk	**(B34B2SC) Crane Vessel** Cranes: 1x250t,1x50t Ice Capable	**2 oil engines** with flexible couplings & sr gearedto sc. shafts driving 2 Directional propellers aft, 1 fwd Total Power: 1,206kW (1,640hp) 4.0kn AuxGen: 1 x 175kW 575V 60Hz a.c
9590424 *HP5447* -	**VM SUPPORTER** - **Savannah Offshore Ltd Inc** VM Marine International Ltd *Panama* *Panama* MMSI: 373568000 Official number: 4417112	**1,446** 433 -	Class: BV	**2011-12 Eastern Marine Shipbuilding Sdn Bhd — Sibu** Yd No: 90 Loa 59.84 Br ex 16.00 Dght 4.500 Lbp 53.84 Br md 13.80 Dpth 5.50 Welded, 1 dk	**(B22A20R) Offshore Support Vessel**	**2 oil engines** reduction geared to sc. shafts driving 2 FP propellers Total Power: 2,386kW (3,244hp) 11.0kn Cummins KTA-50-M2 2 x Vee 4 Stroke 16 Cy. 159 x 159 each-1193kW (1622bhp) Cummins Engine Co Ltd-United Kingdom AuxGen: 3 x 245kW 50Hz a.c Fuel: 510.0
8828135 *AVGP* -	**VMS 3** *ex* Aos 7 *-2010* *ex* Uni Express 7 *-2008* *ex* Uniwise Laemchabang *-2006* *ex* Avonbeg *-2002* *ex* Alia *-1989* **Vinayak Marine Services Pvt Ltd** - *Mumbai* *India* MMSI: 419000149 Official number: 3724	**140** 40 36	Class: IR (BV)	**1981 Camcraft, Inc. — Marrero, La** Yd No: 254 Loa 33.60 Br ex - Dght 2.200 Lbp 30.19 Br md 7.13 Dpth 3.29 Welded, 1 dk	**(B21A20C) Crew/Supply Vessel**	**3 oil engines** reduction geared to sc. shafts driving 3 FP propellers Total Power: 1,491kW (2,028hp) 20.0kn G.M. (Detroit Diesel) 12V-71 3 x Vee 2 Stroke 12 Cy. 108 x 127 each-497kW (676bhp) General Motors Detroit DieselAllison Divn-USA AuxGen: 2 x 32kW 208V a.c
8849361 *AWCR* -	**VMS 21** *ex* Express 34 *-2013* *ex* Avonpark *-2005* *ex* Seabulk Arzanah *-2002* *ex* Gray Spear *-1997* **Vinayak Marine Services Pvt Ltd** - *Mumbai* *India* MMSI: 419000791 Official number: 4092	**154** 46 93	Class: IR (BV) (AB)	**1991-03 Aluminum Boats, Inc. — Crown Point, La** Yd No: A-025 Loa 30.55 Br ex - Dght 2.740 Lbp 29.51 Br md 7.92 Dpth 3.66 Welded, 1 dk	**(B21A20C) Crew/Supply Vessel** Hull Material: Aluminium Alloy	**3 oil engines** reverse reduction geared to sc. shafts driving 3 FP propellers Total Power: 1,125kW (1,530hp) 20.0kn G.M. (Detroit Diesel) 12V-71 3 x Vee 2 Stroke 12 Cy. 108 x 127 each-375kW (510bhp) Detroit Diesel Corporation-Detroit, Mi AuxGen: 2 x 40kW a.c
7703106 *GKCT* -	**VN PARTISAN** *ex* Vos Prince *-2011* *ex* DEA Prince *-2008* *ex* North Prince *-2007* *ex* Sun Prince *-1989* *ex* Falderntor *-1989* **Partisan Ltd** V Navy SAS SatCom: Inmarsat C 423405610 *Aberdeen* *United Kingdom* MMSI: 234056000 Official number: 714160	**2,342** 702 2,250	Class: NV (GL)	**1978-03 Hermann Suerken GmbH & Co. KG — Papenburg** Yd No: 295 Loa 78.87 (BB) Br ex 15.24 Dght 6.459 Lbp 77.91 Br md 15.21 Dpth 6.81 Welded, 1 dk	**(B21A20S) Platform Supply Ship** Ice Capable	**2 oil engines** geared to sc. shafts driving 2 CP propellers Total Power: 4,414kW (6,002hp) 15.0kn Deutz SBV6M540 2 x 4 Stroke 6 Cy. 370 x 400 each-2207kW (3001bhp) Kloeckner Humboldt Deutz AG-West Germany AuxGen: 2 x 350kW 440V 60Hz a.c Thrusters: 2 Tunnel thruster (f); 2 Tunnel thruster (a)
7633832 *ILBR* -	**VN REBEL** *ex* Vos Zefiro *-2011* *ex* Grecale Terzo *-2008* *ex* O. I. L. Supply 2 *-1986* **Libra Investments Sarl** V Navy SAS SatCom: Inmarsat C 424701011 *Catania* *Italy* MMSI: 247010300 Official number: 29	*499* 149 516	Class: RI (BV)	**1977-05 Singapore Shipbuilding & Engineering Pte Ltd — Singapore** Yd No: 122 Loa 44.96 Br ex - Dght 2.590 Lbp 42.63 Br md 11.00 Dpth 3.43 Welded, 1 dk	**(B21B20T) Offshore Tug/Supply Ship** Liq: 180; Liq (Oil): 180 Compartments: 6 Ta, ER Cranes: 1x7.5t	**2 oil engines** geared to sc. shafts driving 2 FP propellers Total Power: 1,596kW (2,170hp) 13.0kn Kromhout 6FDHD240 2 x 4 Stroke 6 Cy. 240 x 260 each-798kW (1085bhp) Stork Werkspoor Diesel BV-Netherlands AuxGen: 2 x 166kW 415/220V 50Hz a.c Thrusters: 1 Water jet (f) Fuel: 90.0 (d.f.)
8952144 *5NL02* -	**VNC FORTUNE** *ex* Demas Fortune *-2013* *ex* Willy 4003 *-2005* *ex* Red Finch *-2005* *ex* Point au'Fer *-1983* **VNC Offshore Ltd** - *Lagos* *Nigeria* MMSI: 657413000 Official number: SR1243	**425** 127 -	Class: AB	**1980-06 Halter Marine, Inc. — Mobile, Al** Yd No: 874 Loa - Br ex - Dght 3.370 Lbp 39.62 Br md 9.75 Dpth 3.65 Welded, 1 dk	**(B21A20S) Platform Supply Ship**	**2 oil engines** reverse reduction geared to sc. shafts driving 2 FP propellers Total Power: 1,030kW (1,400hp) G.M. (Detroit Diesel) 12V-149-TI 2 x Vee 2 Stroke 12 Cy. 146 x 146 each-515kW (700bhp) General Motors Corp-USA AuxGen: 2 x 75kW Thrusters: 1 Thwart. FP thruster (f) Fuel: 100.0
8831687 - -	**VNIMATELNYY** - **Sudoremont-Zapad (OGUP)** - *Kaliningrad* *Russia* Official number: 891558	**182** 54 57	Class: RS	**1990-06 Gorokhovetskiy Sudostroitelnyy Zavod — Gorokhovets** Yd No: 244 Loa 29.32 Br ex 8.62 Dght 3.401 Lbp 27.01 Br md 8.30 Dpth 4.32 Welded, 1 dk	**(B32A2ST) Tug** Ice Capable	**2 oil engines** driving 2 CP propellers Total Power: 1,180kW (1,604hp) 11.5kn Pervomaysk 8CHNP25/34 2 x 4 Stroke 8 Cy. 250 x 340 each-590kW (802bhp) Pervomaydizelmash (PDM)-Pervomaysk

IMO / Call sign	Name / Owner / Manager / Port / Flag	Tonnage	Class	Built / Dimensions	Type / Capacity	Machinery	Speed / Engine model
9503691 *3WIK9* - -	**VNL RUBY** **Vietnam National Shipping Lines (VINALINES) (Tong Cong Ty Hang Hai Viet Nam)** - *Haiphong* *Vietnam* MMSI: 574001630 Official number: VN-145DD-VT	**20,887** 9,500 25,795	Class: GL VR	**2012-12 Ha Long Shipbuilding Co Ltd — Ha Long** Yd No: HV-02 Loa 179.72 (BB) Br ex - Dght 10.700 Lbp 167.22 Br md 27.62 Dpth 15.90 Welded, 1 dk	**(A33A2CC) Container Ship (Fully Cellular)** TEU 1794 incl 319 ref C	**1 oil engine** driving 1 FP propeller Total Power: 15,785kW (21,461hp) Mitsubishi 1 x 2 Stroke 7 Cy. 600 x 2200 15785kW (21461bhp) Mitsubishi Heavy Industries Ltd-Japan	20.1kn 7UEC60LSE
8614637 - -	**VO DAVI** **Kowalsky** - *Brazil*	*100* - -		**1988-08 Empresa Brasileira de Construcao Naval S.A. (EBRASA) — Itajai** Yd No: 177 Loa - Br ex - Dght - Lbp - Br md - Dpth - Welded, 1 dk	**(B11A2FT) Trawler**	**1 oil engine** driving 1 FP propeller	
9154555 *3FEQ8* -	**VOC DAISY** *ex* Golden Daisy *-2002* **Middleburg Properties Ltd** J P Samartzis Maritime Enterprises Co SA *Panama* *Panama* MMSI: 371554000 Official number: 2545598CH	**25,807** 16,061 47,183 T/cm 50.7	Class: NV	**1998-02 Oshima Shipbuilding Co Ltd — Saikai NS** Yd No: 10221 Loa 185.73 (BB) Br ex - Dght 11.777 Lbp 177.00 Br md 30.95 Dpth 16.40 Welded, 1 dk	**(A21A2BC) Bulk Carrier** Grain: 58,999; Bale: 57,851 Compartments: 6 Ho, ER 6 Ha: (10.8 x 15.6)5 (14.4 x 15.6)ER Cranes: 4x30t	**1 oil engine** driving 1 FP propeller Total Power: 7,076kW (9,621hp) Sulzer 1 x 2 Stroke 6 Cy. 480 x 2000 7076kW (9621bhp) Diesel United Ltd.-Aioi AuxGen: 3 x 600kW 100/440V 60Hz a.c Fuel: 130.0 (d.f.) 1519.0 (r.f.) 28.0pd	14.0kn 6RTA48T
9154567 *3FPP7* -	**VOC ROSE** *ex* Golden Rose *-2002* **Reese Development Inc** J P Samartzis Maritime Enterprises Co SA *Panama* *Panama* MMSI: 371555000 Official number: 2556098D	**25,807** 16,061 47,183 T/cm 50.7	Class: NV	**1998-04 Oshima Shipbuilding Co Ltd — Saikai NS** Yd No: 10222 Loa 185.73 (BB) Br ex - Dght 11.777 Lbp 177.00 Br md 30.95 Dpth 16.40 Welded, 1 dk	**(A21A2BC) Bulk Carrier** Grain: 58,999; Bale: 57,851 Compartments: 6 Ho, ER 6 Ha: (10.8 x 15.6)5 (14.4 x 15.6)ER Cranes: 4x30t	**1 oil engine** driving 1 FP propeller Total Power: 7,076kW (9,621hp) Sulzer 1 x 2 Stroke 6 Cy. 480 x 2000 7076kW (9621bhp) Diesel United Ltd.-Aioi AuxGen: 3 x 600kW 100/440V 60Hz a.c Fuel: 130.0 (d.f.) 1519.0 (r.f.) 28.0pd	14.0kn 6RTA48T
7045085 - -	**VODITEL** **I T Pacific Ltd** Japan Avalon Ltd	**597** 194 315	Class: (RS)	**1969 Khabarovskiy Sudostroitelnyy Zavod im Kirova — Khabarovsk** Yd No: 184 Loa 54.23 Br ex 9.38 Dght 3.810 Lbp 48.72 Br md 9.22 Dpth 4.73 Welded, 1 dk	**(B11A2FT) Trawler** Ins: 284 Compartments: 2 Ho, ER 2 Ha: 2 (1.5 x 1.6) Derricks: 1x2t; Winches: 1 Ice Capable	**1 oil engine** driving 1 FP propeller Total Power: 588kW (799hp) S.K.L. 1 x 4 Stroke 8 Cy. 320 x 480 588kW (799bhp) VEB Schwermaschinenbau "KarlLiebknecht" (SKL)-Magdeburg AuxGen: 3 x 100kW Fuel: 140.0 (d.f.)	11.8kn 8NVD48AU
8230572 *UAKV* -	**VODLA 2** *ex* Volgo-Balt 243 *-2011* **Volgobalt Ship LLC** OSS Ltd *St Petersburg* *Russia* MMSI: 273328100	**2,457** 1,010 3,220	Class: RS (RR)	**1983-02 Zavody Tazkeho Strojarstva (ZTS) — Komarno** Yd No: 1974 Loa 114.00 Br ex 13.23 Dght 3.640 Lbp 110.52 Br md 13.01 Dpth 5.50 Welded, 1 dk	**(A31A2GX) General Cargo Ship** Grain: 4,720 Compartments: 4 Ho, ER 4 Ha: (18.6 x 11.2)2 (18.8 x 11.2) (20.3 x 11.2)ER	**2 oil engines** driving 2 FP propellers Total Power: 1,030kW (1,400hp) Skoda 2 x 4 Stroke 6 Cy. 275 x 350 each-515kW (700bhp) Skoda-Praha Fuel: 110.0 (d.f.)	10.8kn 6L275A2
7828762 - -	**VODOLAZ TEREKHOV** **Sakhalin Basin Emergency-Rescue Department (Sakhalinskoye Basseynovoye Avariyno-Spasatelnoye Upravleniye)** -	**295** 88 44	Class: (RS)	**1979-07 Gorokhovetskiy Sudostroitelnyy Zavod — Gorokhovets** Yd No: 607 Loa 41.00 Br ex 8.16 Dght 2.001 Lbp 37.00 Br md - Dpth 3.56 Welded, 1 dk	**(B22A2OV) Diving Support Vessel** Derricks: 1x2.5t Ice Capable	**2 oil engines** geared to sc. shafts driving 2 FP propellers Total Power: 440kW (598hp) Barnaultransmash 2 x Vee 4 Stroke 12 Cy. 150 x 180 each-220kW (299bhp) Barnaultransmash-Barnaul AuxGen: 2 x 50kW, 1 x 30kW Fuel: 17.0 (d.f.)	12.3kn 3D12A
8725400 - - -	**VODOLEY-2** *ex* SPPP-17 *-2011* **Belykh BM** - *Murmansk* *Russia* MMSI: 273424050 Official number: 782312	**109** 33 248	Class: RS	**1979-05 Sudoremontnyy Zavod "Krasnaya Kuznitsa" — Arkhangelsk** Yd No: 17 Converted From: Water Tanker-2006 Loa 35.75 Br ex 7.40 Dght 2.110 Lbp 33.50 Br md 7.20 Dpth 2.40 Welded, 1 dk	**(B35E2TF) Bunkering Tanker** Liq: 226; Liq (Oil): 226 Compartments: 3 Ta, ER Ice Capable	**1 oil engine** geared to sc. shaft driving 1 FP propeller Total Power: 165kW (224hp) Daldizel 1 x 4 Stroke 6 Cy. 180 x 220 165kW (224bhp) Daldizel-Khabarovsk AuxGen: 2 x 14kW Fuel: 5.0 (d.f.)	7.8kn 6CHNSP18/22
8884268 - -	**VODOLEY-4** **Azerbaijan State Caspian Shipping Co (ASCSS)** -	*637* 162 565	Class: (RS)	**1978 Khersonskiy Sudostroitelnyy Zavod — Kherson** Yd No: 4 Loa 53.84 Br ex 9.70 Dght 3.430 Lbp 49.40 Br md - Dpth 4.20 Welded, 1 dk	**(A14A2LO) Water Tanker**	**1 oil engine** driving 1 FP propeller Total Power: 441kW (600hp) Russkiy 1 x 2 Stroke 6 Cy. 300 x 500 441kW (600bhp) Mashinostroitelnyy Zavod"Russkiy-Dizel"-Leningrad AuxGen: 2 x 100kW a.c Fuel: 45.0 (d.f.)	10.0kn 6DR30/50-5-3
8008163 *2CRL5* -	**VOE CHIEF** *ex* Cudarebo *-2009* **Delta Marine Ltd** - *Lerwick* *United Kingdom* MMSI: 235075142 Official number: 916157	**131** 53 -	Class: LR ✠ **100A1** SS 11/2008 tug **LMC** Eq.Ltr: (F) ; Cable: 247.5/19.0 U2	**1980-09 Scheepswerf Ton Bodewes B.V. — Franeker** (Hull) Yd No: F76 **1980-09 B.V. Scheepswerf Damen — Gorinchem** Yd No: 3113 Loa 26.19 Br ex 8.06 Dght 3.250 Lbp 22.92 Br md 7.82 Dpth 4.07 Welded, 1 dk	**(B32A2ST) Tug**	**2 oil engines** with clutches, flexible couplings & sr reverse geared to sc. shafts driving 2 FP propellers Total Power: 2,060kW (2,800hp) Caterpillar 2 x Vee 4 Stroke 16 Cy. 159 x 203 each-1030kW (1400bhp) Caterpillar Tractor Co-USA AuxGen: 2 x 50kW 220V 50Hz a.c Fuel: 78.5 (d.f.)	D399TA
9639983 *2FEP6* -	**VOE EARL** **Delta Marine Ltd** - *Lerwick* *United Kingdom* MMSI: 235090599 Official number: 918098	**200** 200	Class: BV	**2012-01 Safe Co Ltd Sp z oo — Gdynia** (Hull) Yd No: (571655) **2012-01 B.V. Scheepswerf Damen Hardinxveld — Hardinxveld-Giessendam** Yd No: 571655 Loa 24.07 Br ex - Dght 3.750 Lbp 23.11 Br md 12.95 Dpth 4.00 Welded, 1 dk	**(B34L2QU) Utility Vessel** Cranes: 2x10.5t	**2 oil engines** reduction geared to sc. shafts driving 2 FP propellers Total Power: 2,850kW (3,874hp) Caterpillar 2 x Vee 4 Stroke 12 Cy. 170 x 215 each-1425kW (1937bhp) Caterpillar Inc-USA AuxGen: 2 x 93kW 50Hz a.c Thrusters: 2 Tunnel thruster (f) Fuel: 120.0 (d.f.)	11.0kn 3512C
9429974 *MSBB3* -	**VOE JARL** **Delta Marine Ltd** - *Lerwick* *United Kingdom* MMSI: 235055168 Official number: 913263	**255** 76 220	Class: BV	**2007-06 in Poland** (Hull) **2007-06 B.V. Scheepswerf Damen Hardinxveld — Hardinxveld-Giessendam** Yd No: 1560 Loa 26.00 Br ex - Dght 2.250 Lbp 23.92 Br md 11.50 Dpth 3.50 Welded, 1 dk	**(B34L2QU) Utility Vessel** Cranes: 2x10.5t	**3 oil engines** sr geared to sc. shafts driving 3 FP propellers Total Power: 1,902kW (2,586hp) Cummins 3 x Vee 4 Stroke 12 Cy. 159 x 159 each-634kW (862bhp) Cummins Engine Co Inc-USA AuxGen: 2 x 88kW a.c Thrusters: 1 Water jet (f) Fuel: 90.0	10.0kn KTA-38-M0
9106405 *MSVZ3* -	**VOE VENTURE** **Robert Spanswick** Delta Marine Ltd *Lerwick* *United Kingdom* MMSI: 235021489 Official number: 725763	**121** - -	Class: (BV)	**1994-04 Delta Shipyard Sliedrecht BV — Sliedrecht** Yd No: 897 Loa 22.42 Br ex - Dght 1.900 Lbp 18.00 Br md 8.00 Dpth 2.50 Welded	**(B34L2QU) Utility Vessel** Cranes: 1x7t	**2 oil engines** reduction geared to sc. shafts driving 2 FP propellers Total Power: 650kW (884hp) G.M. (Detroit Diesel) 2 x Vee 2 Stroke 12 Cy. 108 x 127 each-325kW (442bhp) General Motors Corp-USA	12V-71-TA
9331139 *MHWM4* -	**VOE VIKING** **Delta Marine Ltd** - *Lerwick* *United Kingdom* MMSI: 235008930 Official number: 910311	**161** - -	Class: BV	**2005-06 ZPUH Magra — Gdynia** (Hull) Yd No: (501563) **2005-06 B.V. Scheepswerf Damen — Gorinchem** Yd No: 501563 **2005-06 B.V. Scheepswerf Damen Hardinxveld — Hardinxveld-Giessendam** (Hull completed by) Yd No: 571563 Loa 26.00 Br ex - Dght 2.200 Lbp 23.90 Br md 11.54 Dpth 3.50 Welded, 1 dk	**(B34L2QU) Utility Vessel** Cranes: 2x10t	**3 oil engines** with clutches, flex coup & geared to sc. shafts driving 3 FP propellers Total Power: 1,770kW (2,406hp) Cummins 3 x Vee 4 Stroke 12 Cy. 159 x 159 each-590kW (802bhp) Cummins Engine Co Inc-USA AuxGen: 2 x 70kW 380/220V 50Hz a.c Thrusters: 1 Water jet (f) Fuel: 98.0 (d.f.)	9.5kn KTA-38-M0
6727973 *9A7288* -	**VOGA** *ex* Salvatore Lobianco *-2001* *ex* Luiciotta *-1976* **Neven Cvitanovic** - *Split* *Croatia* Official number: 5R-245	**171** 51 -	Class: CS (RI)	**1967 Cooperativa Metallurgica Ing G Tommasi Srl — Ancona** Yd No: 5 Converted From: Fishing Vessel-1991 Loa 30.69 Br ex 6.99 Dght 3.182 Lbp 25.10 Br md 6.96 Dpth 3.38 Welded, 1 dk	**(B31A2SR) Research Survey Vessel** Compartments: 1 Ho, ER	**1 oil engine** driving 1 FP propeller Total Power: 478kW (650hp) Ansaldo 1 x 4 Stroke 4 Cy. 320 x 420 478kW (650bhp) SA Ansaldo Stabilimento Meccaniche-Italy	10.2kn 324SR

IMO / Call sign	Name / Owner / Manager / Flag	Tonnage	Class	Builder / Dimensions	Type / Cargo	Machinery
9490454 A8XP8 -	**VOGE CHALLENGER** *ex* Jin Ha Wei *-2010* **ms 'King Harvey' Schiffahrts GmbH & Co KG** Bereederungsgesellschaft H Vogemann GmbH & Co KG SatCom: Inmarsat C 463709073 *Monrovia* *Liberia* MMSI: 636092146 Official number: 92146	**43,507** 27,692 79,648 T/cm 71.9	Class: GL (LR) ✠ Classed LR until 16/12/10	**2010-12 New Century Shipbuilding Co Ltd — Jingjiang JS** Yd No: 0108008 Loa 228.97 (BB) Br ex 32.32 Dght 14.620 Lbp 221.94 Br md 32.26 Dpth 20.25 Welded, 1 dk	**(A21A2BC) Bulk Carrier** Grain: 98,377; Bale: 90,784 Compartments: 7 Ho, ER 7 Ha: ER	**1 oil engine** driving 1 FP propeller Total Power: 11,060kW (15,037hp) 14.0kn MAN-B&W 7S50MC-C 1 x 2 Stroke 7 Cy. 500 x 2000 11060kW (15037bhp) Hyundai Heavy Industries Co Ltd-South Korea AuxGen: 3 x 700kW 450V 60Hz a.c Boilers: AuxB (Comp) 9.4kgf/cm^2 (9.2bar)
9420851 A8RQ9 -	**VOGE DIGNITY** **ms 'Voge Dignity' GmbH & Co KG** Bereederungsgesellschaft H Vogemann GmbH & Co KG SatCom: Inmarsat C 463704496 *Monrovia* *Liberia* MMSI: 636091700 Official number: 91700	**24,066** 11,100 38,334 T/cm 46.4	Class: NV	**2009-05 Guangzhou Shipyard International Co Ltd — Guangzhou GD** Yd No: 06130016 Loa 182.90 (BB) Br ex - Dght 11.600 Lbp 174.49 Br md 27.40 Dpth 16.80 Welded, 1 dk	**(A12B2TR) Chemical/Products Tanker** Double Hull (13F) Liq: 37,963; Liq (Oil): 44,414 Cargo Heating Coils Compartments: 10 Wing Ta, 2 Wing Slop Ta, ER 10 Cargo Pump (s): 10x540m^3/hr Manifold: Bow/CM: 91.3m	**1 oil engine** driving 1 FP propeller Total Power: 9,960kW (13,542hp) 14.2kn MAN-B&W 6S50MC-C 1 x 2 Stroke 6 Cy. 500 x 2000 9960kW (13542bhp) AuxGen: 3 x 920kW a.c Thrusters: 1 Tunnel thruster (f) Fuel: 80.0 (d.f.) 1050.0 (r.f.)
9541318 A8WC5 -	**VOGE ENTERPRISE** **ms 'Voge Enterprise' GmbH & Co KG** Bereederungsgesellschaft H Vogemann GmbH & Co KG SatCom: Inmarsat C 463709268 *Monrovia* *Liberia* MMSI: 636092066 Official number: 92066	**43,692** 27,797 79,410 T/cm 71.9	Class: GL (LR) ✠ Classed LR until 23/2/11	**2011-02 COSCO (Dalian) Shipyard Co Ltd — Dalian LN** Yd No: N273 Loa 229.04 (BB) Br ex - Dght 14.620 Lbp 222.03 Br md 32.26 Dpth 20.25 Welded, 1 dk	**(A21A2BC) Bulk Carrier** Grain: 96,500; Bale: 90,784 Compartments: 7 Ho, ER 7 Ha: ER	**1 oil engine** driving 1 FP propeller Total Power: 11,060kW (15,037hp) 14.0kn MAN-B&W 7S50MC-C 1 x 2 Stroke 7 Cy. 500 x 2000 11060kW (15037bhp) Doosan Engine Co Ltd-South Korea AuxGen: 3 x 730kW 450V 60Hz a.c Boilers: WTAuxB (Comp) 9.2kgf/cm^2 (9.0bar)
9123702 A8LO4 -	**VOGE EVA** *ex* Clipper Beaufort *-2007* *ex* Sea Amelita *-2003* **ms 'Voge Eva' GmbH & Co KG** Bereederungsgesellschaft H Vogemann GmbH & Co KG *Monrovia* *Liberia* MMSI: 636091282 Official number: 91282	**14,762** 8,420 23,407 T/cm 34.2	Class: LR (NK) **100A1** SS 05/2012 bulk carrier ESP ESN LI **LMC** Eq.Ltr: F†; Cable: 577.5/58.0 U3 (a)	**1997-05 Tsuneishi Heavy Industries (Cebu) Inc — Balamban** Yd No: SC-001 Loa 154.38 (BB) Br ex - Dght 9.518 Lbp 146.13 Br md 26.00 Dpth 13.35 Welded, 1 dk	**(A21A2BC) Bulk Carrier** Grain: 30,811; Bale: 30,089 Compartments: 4 Ho, ER 4 Ha: (19.2 x 12.7)2 (20.0 x 17.5) (20.8 x 17.5)ER Cranes: 4x30t	**1 oil engine** driving 1 FP propeller Total Power: 5,185kW (7,050hp) 14.1kn B&W 7S35MC 1 x 2 Stroke 7 Cy. 350 x 1400 5185kW (7050bhp) Mitsui Engineering & Shipbuilding CLtd-Japan AuxGen: 2 x 400kW 450V 60Hz a.c Boilers: AuxB (Comp) 7.1kgf/cm^2 (7.0bar)
9117600 A8MV6 -	**VOGE FANTASY** *ex* Pacific Fantasy *-2013* *ex* DS Fantasy *-2004* *ex* Cielo di Spagna *-2001* *ex* Clipper Fantasy *-2000* *ex* Paipote *-1998* *ex* Clipper Fantasy *-1997* *ex* Paipote *-1997* *ex* Clipper Fantasy *-1996* **ms 'Voge Fantasy' GmbH & Co KG** Bereederungsgesellschaft H Vogemann GmbH & Co KG *Monrovia* *Liberia* MMSI: 636092534 Official number: 92534	**19,354** 9,614 29,538 T/cm 41.0	Class: LR (AB) **100A1** SS 02/2011 TOC contemplated	**1996-01 Dalian Shipyard Co Ltd — Dalian LN** Yd No: MC280-1 Loa 181.00 (BB) Br ex 26.06 Dght 10.020 Lbp 172.00 Br md 26.00 Dpth 14.40 Welded, 1 dk	**(A31A2GX) General Cargo Ship** Grain: 36,311; Bale: 35,452 TEU 1130 C Ho 680 TEU C Dk 450 TEU incl 12 ref C. Compartments: 5 Ho, ER 5 Ha: (19.2 x 15.2)Tappered 2 (25.2 x 22.5) (19.3 x 22.5) (19.2 x 12.8)Tappered ER Cranes: 5x30t	**1 oil engine** driving 1 FP propeller Total Power: 6,400kW (8,701hp) 14.5kn B&W 5S50MC 1 x 2 Stroke 5 Cy. 500 x 1910 6400kW (8701bhp) Dalian Marine Diesel Works-China AuxGen: 1 x 500kW 440V 60Hz a.c, 2 x 500kW 440V 60Hz a.c Fuel: 146.0 (d.f.) 1238.0 (r.f.) 26.0pd
9168154 A8MV5 -	**VOGE FIESTA** *ex* Fiesta *-2013* *ex* DS Fiesta *-2006* *ex* Clipper Fiesta *-2001* **ms 'Voge Fiesta' GmbH & Co KG** Bereederungsgesellschaft H Vogemann GmbH & Co KG *Monrovia* *Liberia* Official number: 92540	**19,354** 9,614 29,516 T/cm 41.0	Class: AB	**1997-04 Dalian Shipyard Co Ltd — Dalian LN** Yd No: MC280-6 Loa 181.00 (BB) Br ex - Dght 10.030 Lbp 170.72 Br md 26.00 Dpth 14.40 Welded, 1 dk	**(A31A2GX) General Cargo Ship** Grain: 36,311; Bale: 35,452 TEU 1130 C Ho 680 TEU C Dk 450 TEU incl 12 ref C. Compartments: 5 Ho, ER 5 Ha: (19.2 x 15.2)Tappered 2 (25.2 x 22.5) (19.3 x 22.5) (19.2 x 12.8)Tappered ER Cranes: 5x30t	**1 oil engine** driving 1 FP propeller Total Power: 6,400kW (8,701hp) 14.5kn B&W 5S50MC 1 x 2 Stroke 5 Cy. 500 x 1910 6400kW (8701bhp) Dalian Marine Diesel Works-China AuxGen: 1 x 500kW 440V 60Hz a.c, 2 x 500kW 440V 60Hz a.c Fuel: 146.0 (d.f.) 1238.0 (r.f.) 26.0pd
9149689 A8OX7 -	**VOGE FREEWAY** *ex* Clipper Freeway *-2013* *ex* Freeway *-2007* *ex* DS Freeway *-2007* *ex* Mirande *-2004* **ms 'Voge Freeway' GmbH & Co KG** Bereederungsgesellschaft H Vogemann GmbH & Co KG *Monrovia* *Liberia* MMSI: 636092541 Official number: 92541	**18,597** 9,065 29,227 T/cm 41.0	Class: LR (BV) **100A1** SS 03/2013 TOC contemplated	**1998-03 Dalian Shipyard Co Ltd — Dalian LN** Yd No: MC280-10 Loa 181.00 (BB) Br ex 26.06 Dght 10.040 Lbp 172.00 Br md 26.00 Dpth 14.40 Welded, 1 dk	**(A31A2GX) General Cargo Ship** Grain: 36,000; Bale: 35,452 TEU 1172 C Ho 722 TEU C Dk 450 TEU incl 12 ref C. Compartments: 5 Ho, ER 5 Ha: ER Cranes: 5x30t	**1 oil engine** driving 1 FP propeller Total Power: 6,400kW (8,701hp) 14.0kn B&W 5S50MC 1 x 2 Stroke 5 Cy. 500 x 1910 6400kW (8701bhp) Dalian Marine Diesel Works-China AuxGen: 2 x 500kW 220/440V 60Hz a.c, 1 x 382kW 220/440V 60Hz a.c Fuel: 169.5 (d.f.) 1346.0 (r.f.) 23.5pd
9175913 A8TZ9 -	**VOGE LENA** *ex* Blue Aries *-2009* **ms 'Voge Lena' GmbH & Co KG** Bereederungsgesellschaft H Vogemann GmbH & Co KG SatCom: Inmarsat C 463706641 *Monrovia* *Liberia* MMSI: 636091871 Official number: 91871	**14,446** 8,548 23,612 T/cm 33.5	Class: LR (NK) **100A1** SS 08/2013 bulk carrier ESP LI **LMC**	**1998-08 KK Kanasashi — Toyohashi AI** Yd No: 2971 Loa 150.52 (BB) Br ex - Dght 9.564 Lbp 143.00 Br md 26.00 Dpth 13.20 Welded, 1 dk	**(A21A2BC) Bulk Carrier** Grain: 30,583; Bale: 29,929 Compartments: 4 Ho, ER 4 Ha: (17.9 x 12.8)3 (19.5 x 17.8)ER Cranes: 4x30.5t	**1 oil engine** driving 1 FP propeller Total Power: 5,296kW (7,200hp) 14.0kn Mitsubishi 6UEC45LA 1 x 2 Stroke 6 Cy. 450 x 1350 5296kW (7200bhp) Kobe Hatsudoki KK-Japan Fuel: 990.0
9339181 9HKR8 -	**VOGE MASTER** *ex* Avore *-2007* **ms 'Voge Master' GmbH & Co KG** Bereederungsgesellschaft H Vogemann GmbH & Co KG *Valletta* *Malta* MMSI: 256089000 Official number: 9339181	**88,930** 58,083 174,093 T/cm 119.0	Class: GL (AB)	**2006-03 Shanghai Waigaoqiao Shipbuilding Co Ltd — Shanghai** Yd No: 1041 Loa 289.00 (BB) Br ex 45.05 Dght 18.120 Lbp 278.20 Br md 45.00 Dpth 24.65 Welded, 1 dk	**(A21A2BC) Bulk Carrier** Grain: 193,247; Bale: 183,425 Compartments: 9 Ho, ER 9 Ha: 7 (15.5 x 20.0)ER 2 (15.5 x 16.5)	**1 oil engine** driving 1 FP propeller Total Power: 16,860kW (22,923hp) 14.5kn MAN-B&W 6S70MC 1 x 2 Stroke 6 Cy. 700 x 2674 16860kW (22923bhp) Dalian Marine Diesel Works-China AuxGen: 3 x 750kW a.c Fuel: 534.1 (d.f.) 4508.5 (r.f.)
9154866 A8LO3 -	**VOGE PAUL** *ex* Clipper Bounteous *-2007* *ex* Joint Spirit *-2003* *ex* Sea Harvest *-1998* **ms 'Voge Paula' GmbH & Co KG** Bereederungsgesellschaft H Vogemann GmbH & Co KG *Monrovia* *Liberia* MMSI: 636091281 Official number: 91281	**14,762** 8,420 23,494 T/cm 34.2	Class: LR (NK) **100A1** SS 01/2013 bulk carrier ESP LI **LMC** Eq.Ltr: F†; Cable: 577.5/58.0 U3 (a)	**1998-01 Tsuneishi Heavy Industries (Cebu) Inc — Balamban** Yd No: SC-003 Loa 154.38 (BB) Br ex - Dght 9.518 Lbp 146.00 Br md 26.00 Dpth 13.35 Welded, 1 dk	**(A21A2BC) Bulk Carrier** Grain: 30,811; Bale: 30,089 Compartments: 4 Ho, ER 4 Ha: (19.2 x 12.7)2 (20.0 x 17.5) (20.8 x 17.5)ER Cranes: 4x30t	**1 oil engine** driving 1 FP propeller Total Power: 5,185kW (7,050hp) 13.0kn B&W 7S35MC 1 x 2 Stroke 7 Cy. 350 x 1400 5185kW (7050bhp) Ssangyong Heavy Industries Co Ltd-South Korea AuxGen: 2 x 400kW 450V 60Hz a.c Boilers: AuxB (Comp) 7.0kgf/cm^2 (6.9bar)
9154854 A8LO2 -	**VOGE RENATE** *ex* Clipper Breeze *-2007* *ex* Joint Bright *-2003* *ex* Sea Splendor *-1998* **Maxim Sea Shipping Inc** Bereederungsgesellschaft H Vogemann GmbH & Co KG *Monrovia* *Liberia* MMSI: 636015492 Official number: 15492	**14,762** 8,420 23,407 T/cm 34.2	Class: LR (NK) **100A1** SS 09/2012 bulk carrier ESP LI **LMC** Eq.Ltr: F†; Cable: 577.5/58.0 U3 (a)	**1997-09 Tsuneishi Heavy Industries (Cebu) Inc — Balamban** Yd No: SC-002 Loa 154.38 (BB) Br ex - Dght 9.518 Lbp 146.13 Br md 26.00 Dpth 13.35 Welded, 1 dk	**(A21A2BC) Bulk Carrier** Grain: 30,811; Bale: 30,089 Compartments: 4 Ho, ER 4 Ha: (19.2 x 12.7)2 (20.0 x 17.5) (20.8 x 17.5)ER Cranes: 4x30t	**1 oil engine** driving 1 FP propeller Total Power: 5,185kW (7,050hp) 14.9kn B&W 7S35MC 1 x 2 Stroke 7 Cy. 350 x 1400 5185kW (7050bhp) Mitsui Engineering & Shipbuilding CLtd-Japan AuxGen: 2 x 400kW 450V 60Hz a.c Boilers: AuxB (Comp) 7.1kgf/cm^2 (7.0bar)
9420863 A8RR2 -	**VOGE TRUST** **ms 'Voge Trust' GmbH & Co KG** Bereederungsgesellschaft H Vogemann GmbH & Co KG SatCom: Inmarsat C 463706066 *Monrovia* *Liberia* MMSI: 636091701 Official number: 91701	**24,066** 11,100 38,349 T/cm 46.4	Class: NV	**2009-10 Guangzhou Shipyard International Co Ltd — Guangzhou GD** Yd No: 06130017 Loa 182.86 (BB) Br ex - Dght 11.600 Lbp 174.50 Br md 27.40 Dpth 16.80 Welded, 1 dk	**(A12B2TR) Chemical/Products Tanker** Double Hull (13F) Liq: 37,963; Liq (Oil): 44,414 Cargo Heating Coils Compartments: 10 Wing Ta, 2 Wing Slop Ta, ER 12 Cargo Pump (s): 10x540m^3/hr, 2x300m^3/hr Manifold: Bow/CM: 91.3m	**1 oil engine** driving 1 FP propeller Total Power: 9,960kW (13,542hp) 14.2kn MAN-B&W 6S50MC-C 1 x 2 Stroke 6 Cy. 500 x 2000 9960kW (13542bhp) AuxGen: 3 x 910kW a.c Thrusters: 1 Tunnel thruster (f) Fuel: 80.0 (d.f.) 1035.0 (r.f.)

9077109 *A8MU8* -	**VOGE WEST** *ex* Xinshi Hai *-2008* *ex* Brazilian Venture *-2001* **ms 'Voge West' GmbH & Co KG** Bereederungsgesellschaft H Vogemann GmbH & Co KG *Monrovia* *Liberia* MMSI: 636091375 Official number: 91375	**38,236** 23,142 70,728 T/cm 64.7	Class: NV (BV)	**1995-04 Ind. Verolme-Ishibras S.A. (IVI) (Est. Ishibras) — Rio** Yd No: 170 Loa 225.00 (BB) Br ex 32.30 Dght 13.721 Lbp 215.40 Br md 32.26 Dpth 19.15 Welded, 1 dk	**(A21A2BC) Bulk Carrier** Grain: 85,094 Compartments: 7 Ho, ER 7 Ha: (12.8 x 15.4)6 (16.0 x 15.4)ER	**1 oil engine** driving 1 FP propeller Total Power: 8,091kW (11,001hp) 14.0kr Sulzer 6RTA62 1 x 2 Stroke 6 Cy. 620 x 2150 8091kW (11001bhp) Hyundai Heavy Industries Co Ltd-South Korea AuxGen: 3 x 450kW 450V 60Hz a.c Fuel: 323.6 (d.f.) 1956.0 (r.f.) 30.0pd
9122095 *A8FT5* -	**VOGECARRIER** *ex* Eurotrader *-2004* *ex* Cherokee *-2000* **ms 'Vogecarrier' GmbH & Co KG** Bereederungsgesellschaft H Vogemann GmbH & Co KG SatCom: Inmarsat C 463704949 *Monrovia* *Liberia* MMSI: 636090804 Official number: 90804	**85,706** 55,394 164,303 T/cm 115.1	Class: LR **✠100A1** SS 07/2011 bulk carrier strengthened for heavy cargoes, any hold may be empty ESP LI ESN-Hold 1 **ShipRight** (SDA, FDA, CM) **✠LMC** **UMS** Eq.Ltr: Z†; Cable: 742.5/100.0 U3	**1996-07 Astilleros Espanoles SA (AESA) — Puerto Real** Yd No: 75 Loa 289.00 (BB) Br ex 43.25 Dght 18.867 Lbp 279.60 Br md 43.20 Dpth 24.20 Welded, 1 dk	**(A21A2BC) Bulk Carrier** Grain: 183,800 Compartments: 9 Ho, ER 9 Ha: (13.1 x 15.9)Tappered 7 (15.8 x 20.8) (15.8 x 12.0)ER	**1 oil engine** driving 1 FP propeller Total Power: 15,931kW (21,660hp) 15.0kn B&W 6S70MC 1 x 2 Stroke 6 Cy. 700 x 2674 15931kW (21660bhp) Manises Diesel Engine Co. S.A.-Valencia AuxGen: 3 x 650kW 450V 60Hz a.c Boilers: e (ex.g.) 9.1kgf/cm² (8.9bar), AuxB (o.f.) 7.0kgf/cm² (6.9bar)
8603107 *DRLP* -	**VOGELSAND** **Government of The Federal Republic of Germany (Bundesministerium fuer Verteidigung)** Marinestutzpunkt Wilhelmshaven *Wilhelmshaven* *Germany* MMSI: 211212120 Official number: 493	**278** 83 60	Class: GL	**1987-04 O & K Tagebau u. Schiffstechnik — Luebeck** Yd No: 778 Loa 30.26 Br ex 9.15 Dght 4.352 Lbp 28.02 Br md 9.11 Dpth 3.66 Welded, 1 dk	**(B32A2ST) Tug** Ice Capable	**2 oil engines** with flexible couplings & sr gearedto sc. shafts driving 2 Directional propellers Total Power: 1,640kW (2,230hp) Deutz SBV6M628 2 x 4 Stroke 6 Cy. 240 x 280 each-820kW (1115bhp) Kloeckner Humboldt Deutz AG-West Germany
9218820 *DBHI* -	**VOGELSAND** **Government of The Federal Republic of Germany (Wasser- und Schiffahrtsamt Cuxhaven)** - *Cuxhaven* *Germany* MMSI: 211349270	**251** 75 -	Class: GL	**2001-04 AO Pribaltiyskiy Sudostroitelnyy Zavod "Yantar" — Kaliningrad** (Hull) **2001-04 Fr Fassmer GmbH & Co KG — Berne** Yd No: 98/1/5821 Loa 34.05 Br ex - Dght 2.400 Lbp 31.00 Br md 8.60 Dpth 3.65 Welded, 1 dk	**(B31A2SR) Research Survey Vessel**	**1 oil engine** geared to sc. shaft driving 1 CP propeller Total Power: 740kW (1,006hp) 12.0kn M.T.U. 8V4000M60 1 x Vee 4 Stroke 8 Cy. 165 x 190 740kW (1006bhp) MTU Friedrichshafen GmbH-Friedrichshafen AuxGen: 1 x 280kW a.c
9475301 *9HA3074* -	**VOGERUNNER** **Vogerunner Shipping Inc** Bereederungsgesellschaft H Vogemann GmbH & Co KG *Valletta* *Malta* MMSI: 229105000	**89,603** 58,437 176,838 T/cm 121.7	Class: GL (NK)	**2008-12 Namura Shipbuilding Co Ltd — Imari SG** Yd No: 302 Loa 288.97 (BB) Br ex - Dght 17.930 Lbp 279.00 Br md 45.00 Dpth 24.40 Welded, 1 dk	**(A21A2BC) Bulk Carrier** Grain: 198,963; Bale: 195,968 Compartments: 9 Ho, ER 9 Ha: ER	**1 oil engine** driving 1 FP propeller Total Power: 16,860kW (22,923hp) 15.2kn MAN-B&W 6S70MC 1 x 2 Stroke 6 Cy. 700 x 2674 16860kW (22923bhp) Mitsui Engineering & Shipbuilding CLtd-Japan AuxGen: 3 x 480kW 450V a.c
9287807 *V2OW7* -	**VOHBURG** *ex* Jsv Yaiza *-2010* *ex* Vohburg *-2009* *ex* Geestdijk *-2008* **Jorg Kopping Dritte Bereederungs GmbH & Co ms 'Vohburg' KG** Kopping Reederei GmbH & Co KG *Saint John's* *Antigua & Barbuda* MMSI: 305773000	**7,852** 3,363 9,296 T/cm 24.6	Class: GL	**2005-03 B.V. Scheepswerf Damen Hoogezand — Foxhol** Yd No: 845 **2005-03 Santierul Naval Damen Galati S.A. — Galati** (Hull) Yd No: (845) Loa 140.56 (BB) Br ex 22.00 Dght 7.330 Lbp 130.00 Br md 21.80 Dpth 9.50 Welded, 1 dk	**(A33A2CC) Container Ship (Fully Cellular)** Grain: 11,668 TEU 812 C Ho 206 TEU C Dk 606 TEU incl 180 ref C. Ice Capable	**1 oil engine** geared to sc. shaft driving 1 CP propeller Total Power: 8,400kW (11,421hp) 18.0kn MaK 9M43 1 x 4 Stroke 9 Cy. 430 x 610 8400kW (11421bhp) Caterpillar Motoren GmbH & Co. KG-Germany AuxGen: 1 x 1500kW 440/220V 60Hz a.c, 2 x 455kW 440/220V 60Hz a.c Thrusters: 1 Tunnel thruster (f); 1 Tunnel thruster (a)
9298973 *A8FX2* -	**VOIDOMATIS** **Dominique Trading Corp** Pleiades Shipping Agents SA *Monrovia* *Liberia* MMSI: 636012508 Official number: 12508	**35,711** 16,707 61,325 T/cm 64.5	Class: LR **✠100A1** SS 03/2010 Double Hull oil tanker ESP *IWS LI **ShipRight** (SDA, FDA, CM) **✠LMC** **UMS IGS** Eq.Ltr: N*; Cable: 670.0/76.0 U3 (a)	**2005-03 Sumitomo Heavy Industries Marine & Engineering Co., Ltd. — Yokosuka** Yd No: 1311 Loa 213.36 (BB) Br ex 32.29 Dght 12.280 Lbp 206.56 Br md 32.26 Dpth 18.50 Welded, 1 dk	**(A13A2TV) Crude Oil Tanker** Double Hull (13F) Liq: 64,006; Liq (Oil): 64,006 Compartments: 10 Wing Ta, 2 Wing Slop Ta, ER 3 Cargo Pump (s): 3x2000m³/hr Manifold: Bow/CM: 102.9m	**1 oil engine** driving 1 FP propeller Total Power: 10,010kW (13,610hp) 15.0kn B&W 7S50MC 1 x 2 Stroke 7 Cy. 500 x 1910 10010kW (13610bhp) Mitsui Engineering & Shipbuilding CLtd-Japan AuxGen: 3 x 560kW 440/220V 60Hz a.c Boilers: e (ex.g.) 22.0kgf/cm² (21.6bar), WTAuxB (o.f.) 18.4kgf/cm² (18.0bar) Fuel: 235.0 (d.f.) 2153.0 (r.f.) 41.0pd
5383158 *OHLW* -	**VOIMA** **JM Voima Oy** Arctia Shipping Oy *Helsinki* *Finland* MMSI: 230291000 Official number: 12308	**4,159** 1,248 4,486		**1954-03 Wartsila-Koncernen, Ab Sandvikens Skeppsdocka & MV — Helsinki** Yd No: 349 Loa 83.52 Br ex 19.41 Dght 6.749 Lbp 79.81 Br md - Dpth - Welded, 2 dks	**(B34C2SI) Icebreaker** Ice Capable	**6 diesel electric oil engines** driving 4 Propellers 2 fwd and 2 aft Total Power: 12,840kW (17,460hp) Wartsila 16V22 6 x Vee 4 Stroke 16 Cy. 220 x 240 each-2140kW (2910bhp) (new engine 1979) Oy Wartsila Ab-Finland Fuel: 172.5 (d.f.)
7623746 - -	**VOINICUL** - -	**829** - -	Class: (RN)	**1966 Santierul Naval Oltenita S.A. — Oltenita** Loa 52.32 Br ex - Dght 4.609 Lbp 47.17 Br md 11.03 Dpth 5.82 Welded, 1 dk	**(B34P2QV) Salvage Ship** Derricks: 1x5t; Winches: 1 Ice Capable	**2 diesel electric oil engines** driving 2 gen. each 760kW Connecting to 1 elec. Motor driving 1 FP propeller Total Power: 1,398kW (1,900hp) 14.0kn Penza 6CHN31.8/33 2 x 4 Stroke 6 Cy. 318 x 330 each-699kW (950bhp) Penzdizelmash-Penza AuxGen: 2 x 100kW 220V d.c, 2 x 57kW 220V d.c Fuel: 294.5 (d.f.)
9044700 *9HNQ7* -	**VOLA 1** *ex* Vola *-2003* **Vola Maritime Ltd** Navigation Maritime Bulgare *Valletta* *Malta* MMSI: 215408000 Official number: 8169	**13,851** 6,832 21,395 T/cm 26.1	Class: GL (BR)	**1992-11 Varna Shipyard AD — Varna** Yd No: 453 Loa 168.42 Br ex - Dght 8.450 Lbp 159.00 Br md 25.00 Dpth 11.50 Welded, 1 dk	**(A21A2BC) Bulk Carrier** Grain: 27,878 Compartments: 5 Ho, ER 5 Ha: (9.1 x 13.0)4 (18.6 x 14.3)ER Cranes: 3x16t Ice Capable	**1 oil engine** driving 1 FP propeller Total Power: 5,884kW (8,000hp) 13.1kn B&W 8L42MC 1 x 2 Stroke 8 Cy. 420 x 1360 5884kW (8000bhp) AO Bryanskiy MashinostroitelnyyZavod (BMZ)-Bryansk AuxGen: 3 x 412kW 390V 50Hz a.c Fuel: 215.0 (d.f.) 1513.0 (r.f.) 26.5pd
6512122 *V3PP8* -	**VOLANS** *ex* Lady Anita *-1970* **Standard Union Ltd** Trinity Offshore Pte Ltd *Belize City* *Belize* MMSI: 312849000	**540** 162 620	Class: BV	**1965-03 Verolme Scheepswerf Heusden N.V. — Heusden** Yd No: 726 Loa 48.72 Br ex 10.06 Dght 2.998 Lbp 45.70 Br md 10.01 Dpth 3.81 Welded, 1 dk	**(B34L2QU) Utility Vessel** A-frames: 1x10t	**2 oil engines** reduction geared to sc. shafts driving 2 FP propellers Total Power: 1,250kW (1,700hp) 12.3kn Kromhout 8FHD240 2 x 4 Stroke 8 Cy. 240 x 260 each-625kW (850bhp) Stork Werkspoor Diesel BV-Netherlands AuxGen: 2 x 180kW 380/220V 50Hz a.c Thrusters: 1 Tunnel thruster (f); 1 Tunnel thruster (a) Fuel: 167.0 (d.f.)
9298856 *A6E3103* -	**VOLANS** *ex* SE Mariam 1 *-2004* **Mubarak Marine LLC** - *Dubai* *United Arab Emirates* MMSI: 470945000 Official number: 5438	**247** 74 148	Class: LR **✠100A1** SS 09/2012 tug **✠LMC** Eq.Ltr: F; Cable: 275.0/19.0 U2 (a)	**2004-03 PT Nanindah Mutiara Shipyard — Batam** Yd No: T117 Loa 29.00 Br ex 9.02 Dght 3.680 Lbp 26.50 Br md 9.00 Dpth 4.25 Welded, 1 dk	**(B32A2ST) Tug**	**2 oil engines** with clutches, flexible couplings & sr reverse geared to sc. shafts driving 2 FP propellers Total Power: 1,766kW (2,402hp) Yanmar M220-EN 2 x 4 Stroke 6 Cy. 220 x 300 each-883kW (1201bhp) Yanmar Diesel Engine Co Ltd-Japan AuxGen: 2 x 164kW 415V 50Hz a.c Thrusters: 1 Thwart. FP thruster (f)
9341835 *PS8176* -	**VOLANS** **Saveiros Camuyrano - Servicos Maritimos SA** - *Santos* *Brazil* MMSI: 710002080 Official number: 4010817470	**374** 112 336	Class: LR **✠100A1** SS 06/2011 tug, fire fighting Ship 1 (2400 m3/h) with water spray **LMC** **UMS** Eq.Ltr: H; Cable: 302.5/22.0 U2 (a)	**2006-06 Wilson, Sons SA — Guaruja** (Hull) Yd No: 082 **2006-06 B.V. Scheepswerf Damen — Gorinchem** Yd No: 511209 Loa 32.22 Br ex 11.70 Dght 4.250 Lbp 29.01 Br md 10.60 Dpth 5.00 Welded, 1 dk	**(B32A2ST) Tug**	**2 oil engines** geared to sc. shafts driving 2 Directional propellers Total Power: 4,280kW (5,820hp) 13.0kn Caterpillar 3516B-TA 2 x Vee 4 Stroke 16 Cy. 170 x 190 each-2140kW (2910bhp) Caterpillar Inc-USA AuxGen: 2 x 99kW 440V 60Hz a.c

101405 *UHY8*	**VOLANS-1** *ex* Rezon-1 *-2008* *ex* Sakhmoreprodukt-1 *-1997* **Ocean Shipping Co Ltd SA** - *Phnom Penh* *Cambodia* MMSI: 514051000 Official number: 0893058	**446** 133 207	Class: (RS)	**1993**-09 **AO Zavod 'Nikolayevsk-na-Amure' — Nikolayevsk-na-Amure** Yd No: 1296 Converted From: Fish Carrier-2008 Converted From: Stern Trawler-2007 Loa 44.88 Br ex 9.47 Dght 3.770 Lbp 39.37 Br md - Dpth 5.13 Welded, 1 dk	**(A31A2GX) General Cargo Ship** Ins: 210 Compartments: 1 Ho 1 Ha: (2.1 x 2.1) Derricks: 4x3t Ice Capable	**1 oil engine** driving 1 FP propeller Total Power: 589kW (801hp) 11.5kn S.K.L. 6NVD48A-2U 1 x 4 Stroke 6 Cy. 320 x 480 589kW (801bhp) SKL Motoren u. Systemtechnik AG-Magdeburg
381237 *EKZ6*	**VOLANS LEADER** **Catalina Shipping SA** Shoei Kisen Kaisha Ltd SatCom: Inmarsat C 437288410 *Panama* *Panama* MMSI: 372884000 Official number: 3306407	**61,775** 18,533 20,168 T/cm 55.6	Class: NK	**2007**-07 **Imabari Shipbuilding Co Ltd — Marugame KG (Marugame Shipyard)** Yd No: 1480 Loa 199.94 (BB) Br ex - Dght 10.016 Lbp 190.00 Br md 32.26 Dpth 34.80 Welded, 12 dks	**(A35B2RV) Vehicles Carrier** Side door/ramp (s) Len: 20.00 Wid: 4.20 Swl: 15 Quarter stern door/ramp (s. a.) Len: 35.00 Wid: 8.00 Swl: 80 Cars: 5,415	**1 oil engine** driving 1 FP propeller Total Power: 16,360kW (22,243hp) 20.0kn Mitsubishi 8UEC60LSII 1 x 2 Stroke 8 Cy. 600 x 2300 16360kW (22243bhp) Kobe Hatsudoki KK-Japan Thrusters: 1 Tunnel thruster (f) Fuel: 3275.0
399533 *EJT5*	**VOLANTIS** **Volstad Maritime DIS I AS** Volstad Maritime AS SatCom: Inmarsat C 437261510 *Panama* *Panama* MMSI: 372615000 Official number: 3439908A	**7,530** 2,260 6,555	Class: NV	**2008**-03 **LandskronaVarvet AB — Landskrona** (Hull) **2008**-03 **Fosen Mek. Verksteder AS — Rissa** Yd No: 78 Loa 106.60 (BB) Br ex - Dght 7.300 Lbp 91.20 Br md 22.00 Dpth 9.60 Welded, 1 dk	**(B22A20R) Offshore Support Vessel** Cranes: 1x150t,1x10t	**6 diesel electric oil engines** driving 2 gen. each 3440kW 690V a.c 4 gen. each 1710kW 690V a.c Connecting to 2 elec. motors each (3000kW) driving 2 Directional propellers Total Power: 13,720kW (18,654hp) 14.0kn Caterpillar 3612 2 x Vee 4 Stroke 12 Cy. 280 x 300 each-3440kW (4677bhp) Caterpillar Inc-USA MaK 9M20 4 x 4 Stroke 9 Cy. 200 x 300 each-1710kW (2325bhp) Caterpillar Motoren GmbH & Co. KG-Germany Thrusters: 1 Thwart. CP thruster (f); 2 Directional thruster (f); 1 Thwart. CP thruster (a) Fuel: 1955.0 (d.f.)
209738	**VOLAZARA** **Societe d'Explotation du Port de Toamasina (SEPT)** - *Toamasina* *Madagascar*	**183** 54 -	Class: BV	**2000**-12 **FGUP Mashinostroitelnoye Predp 'Zvyozdochka' — Severodvinsk** (Hull) **2000**-12 **B.V. Scheepswerf Damen — Gorinchem** Yd No: 7001 Loa 26.09 Br ex 7.99 Dght 3.220 Lbp 25.23 Br md 7.95 Dpth 4.05 Welded, 1 dk	**(B32A2ST) Tug**	**2 oil engines** reduction geared to sc. shafts driving 2 FP propellers Total Power: 2,028kW (2,758hp) Caterpillar 3512TA 2 x Vee 4 Stroke 12 Cy. 170 x 190 each-1014kW (1379bhp) Caterpillar Inc-USA
348558 *CKH*	**VOLCAN DE TABURIENTE** **Maritima de Sotavento SL** Naviera Armas SA SatCom: Inmarsat C 422427710 *Santa Cruz de Tenerife* *Spain (CSR)* MMSI: 224277000 Official number: 12/2005	**12,895** 3,869 1,400	Class: BV	**2006**-06 **Hijos de J. Barreras S.A. — Vigo** Yd No: 1650 Loa 130.45 (BB) Br ex - Dght 5.000 Lbp 115.45 Br md 21.60 Dpth 7.50 Welded, 1 dk	**(A36A2PR) Passenger/Ro-Ro Ship (Vehicles)** Passengers: 1500 Bow door/ramp (centre) Len: 13.00 Wid: 4.00 Swl: - Stern door/ramp (s. a.) Len: 9.50 Wid: 6.00 Swl: - Side door/ramp (p. a.) Len: 9.50 Wid: 6.00 Swl: - Lane-Len: 448 Cars: 110, Trailers: 28	**4 oil engines** geared to sc. shafts driving 2 CP propellers Total Power: 18,000kW (24,472hp) 22.5kn MaK 9M32 4 x 4 Stroke 9 Cy. 320 x 480 each-4500kW (6118bhp) Caterpillar Motoren GmbH & Co. KG-Germany AuxGen: 2 x 900kW a.c Thrusters: 2 Tunnel thruster (f)
360506 *AOG*	**VOLCAN DE TAMADABA** **Maritima de Barlovento SL** Naviera Armas SA SatCom: Inmarsat C 422495710 *Las Palmas* *Spain (CSR)* MMSI: 224957000 Official number: 2/2006	**19,976** 6,051 3,350	Class: BV	**2007**-05 **Hijos de J. Barreras S.A. — Vigo** Yd No: 1653 Loa 154.51 (BB) Br ex - Dght 5.800 Lbp 137.00 Br md 24.20 Dpth 13.55 Welded	**(A36A2PR) Passenger/Ro-Ro Ship (Vehicles)** Passengers: unberthed: 760; cabins: 56; berths: 206 Stern door/ramp (p. a.) Len: 8.00 Wid: 16.00 Swl: - Stern door/ramp (s. a.) Len: 8.00 Wid: 16.00 Swl: - Lane-Len: 1870 Lane-Wid: 3.00 Cars: 174, Trailers: 57	**2 oil engines** reduction geared to sc. shafts driving 2 CP propellers Total Power: 23,406kW (31,822hp) 23.0kn Wartsila 12V46 2 x Vee 4 Stroke 12 Cy. 460 x 580 each-11703kW (15911bhp) Wartsila Diesel S.A.-Bermeo AuxGen: 2 x 1200kW 400V 50Hz a.c, 2 x 1200kW 400V 50Hz a.c Thrusters: 2 Tunnel thruster (f) Fuel: 76.5 (d.f.) 584.3 (r.f.) 91.0pd
281322 *CFE*	**VOLCAN DE TAMASITE** **Naviera de Jandia SL** Naviera Armas SA SatCom: Inmarsat C 422409310 *Las Palmas* *Spain (CSR)* MMSI: 224093000 Official number: 1/2004	**17,343** 5,203 3,500	Class: BV	**2004**-06 **Hijos de J. Barreras S.A. — Vigo** Yd No: 1625 Loa 142.45 (BB) Br ex - Dght 6.000 Lbp 125.00 Br md 24.20 Dpth 13.55 Welded	**(A36A2PR) Passenger/Ro-Ro Ship (Vehicles)** Passengers: unberthed: 1466 Stern door/ramp (centre) Len: 16.00 Wid: 8.00 Swl: 108 Lane-Len: 1279 Lane-Wid: 3.00 Cars: 403	**2 oil engines** geared to sc. shafts driving 2 CP propellers Total Power: 15,604kW (21,216hp) 21.0kn Wartsila 8L46 2 x 4 Stroke 8 Cy. 460 x 580 each-7802kW (10608bhp) Wartsila Diesel S.A.-Bermeo AuxGen: 2 x 1200kW 50Hz a.c, 2 x 1080kW 50Hz a.c Thrusters: 2 Tunnel thruster (f) Fuel: 90.0 (d.f.) 620.0 (r.f.)
081588 *AGW*	**VOLCAN DE TAUCE** **Anarafe SL** Naviera Armas SA SatCom: Inmarsat C 422476110 *Santa Cruz de Tenerife* *Spain (CSR)* MMSI: 224761000 Official number: 16/1998	**9,807** 2,942 4,226	Class: BV	**1995**-04 **Hijos de J. Barreras S.A. — Vigo** Yd No: 1544 Loa 120.00 (BB) Br ex 19.52 Dght 5.300 Lbp 107.00 Br md 19.50 Dpth 6.80 Welded, 3 dks	**(A36A2PR) Passenger/Ro-Ro Ship (Vehicles)** Passengers: unberthed: 174; cabins: 19; berths: 76 Stern door/ramp Len: 15.00 Wid: 3.95 Swl: - Stern door/ramp Len: 15.00 Wid: 3.00 Swl: - Stern door/ramp Len: 15.00 Wid: 6.00 Swl: - Lane-Len: 1023 Lane-clr ht: 4.50 Trailers: 62 Bale: 12,015 Compartments: 3 Ho, ER	**2 oil engines** reduction geared to sc. shafts driving 2 CP propellers Total Power: 6,800kW (9,246hp) 18.0kn MWM TBD645L6 2 x 4 Stroke 6 Cy. 330 x 450 each-3400kW (4623bhp) Hijos de J Barreras SA-Spain AuxGen: 2 x 500kW a.c, 2 x 500kW a.c Thrusters: 2 Thwart. FP thruster (f) Fuel: 138.0 (d.f.) 1196.0 (r.f.)
335161 *CLA*	**VOLCAN DE TENEGUIA** *ex* Clara Del Mar *-2011* **Caflaja SL** - SatCom: Inmarsat C 422531710 *Santa Cruz de Tenerife* *Spain (CSR)* MMSI: 225317000 Official number: 4/2006	**11,197** 3,359 7,341	Class: GL	**2007**-10 **Fujian Mawei Shipbuilding Ltd — Fuzhou FJ** Yd No: 433-3 Loa 145.00 (BB) Br ex - Dght 6.000 Lbp 136.70 Br md 22.00 Dpth 13.90 Welded, 3 dks	**(A35A2RR) Ro-Ro Cargo Ship** Stern door/ramp (a) Len: - Wid: - Swl: 50 Lane-Len: 1509 Trailers: 104 TEU 500 incl 125 ref C Ice Capable	**1 oil engine** reduction geared to sc. shaft driving 1 CP propeller Total Power: 6,000kW (8,158hp) 16.5kn MaK 12M32C 1 x Vee 4 Stroke 12 Cy. 320 x 420 6000kW (8158bhp) Caterpillar Motoren GmbH & Co. KG-Germany AuxGen: 1 x 1440kW 450/220V a.c, 3 x 500kW 450/220V a.c Thrusters: 1 Tunnel thruster (f); 1 Tunnel thruster (a)
398890 *CNO*	**VOLCAN DE TIJARAFE** **Naviera Tamadaba SLU** Naviera Armas SA SatCom: Inmarsat C 422469210 *Santa Cruz de Tenerife* *Spain (CSR)* MMSI: 224692000 Official number: 10/2008	**19,976** 6,051 3,400	Class: BV	**2008**-04 **Hijos de J. Barreras S.A. — Vigo** Yd No: 1654 Loa 154.51 (BB) Br ex - Dght 5.800 Lbp 137.00 Br md 24.20 Dpth 13.55 Welded	**(A36A2PR) Passenger/Ro-Ro Ship (Vehicles)** Passengers: unberthed: 760; berths: 206 Stern door & ramp (a) Len: 16.00 Wid: 8.00 Swl: - Lane-Len: 1870 Lane-Wid: 3.00 Cars: 174, Trailers: 57	**2 oil engines** reduction geared to sc. shafts driving 2 CP propellers Total Power: 23,406kW (31,822hp) 21.7kn Wartsila 12V46 2 x Vee 4 Stroke 12 Cy. 460 x 580 each-11703kW (15911bhp) Wartsila Diesel S.A.-Bermeo AuxGen: 2 x 1200kW 400V 50Hz a.c, 2 x 1200kW 400V 50Hz a.c Thrusters: 2 Thwart. CP thruster (f) Fuel: 76.5 (d.f.) 584.3 (r.f.)
281334 *CHT*	**VOLCAN DE TIMANFAYA** **Naviera Armas SA** - SatCom: Inmarsat C 422414510 *Las Palmas* *Spain (CSR)* MMSI: 224145000 Official number: 10/2004	**17,343** 5,300 3,500	Class: BV	**2005**-04 **Hijos de J. Barreras S.A. — Vigo** Yd No: 1626 Loa 142.45 (BB) Br ex - Dght 5.700 Lbp 125.00 Br md 24.20 Dpth 13.55 Welded	**(A36A2PR) Passenger/Ro-Ro Ship (Vehicles)** Passengers: unberthed: 950 Stern door/ramp (centre) Len: 16.00 Wid: 8.00 Swl: 108 Lane-Len: 1279 Lane-Wid: 3.00 Cars: 403	**2 oil engines** reduction geared to sc. shafts driving 2 CP propellers Total Power: 16,804kW (22,846hp) 21.0kn Wartsila 8L46 2 x 4 Stroke 8 Cy. 460 x 580 each-8402kW (11423bhp) Wartsila Diesel S.A.-Bermeo AuxGen: 2 x 1200kW 50Hz a.c, 2 x 1080kW 50Hz a.c Thrusters: 2 Tunnel thruster (f) Fuel: 90.0 (d.f.) 620.0 (r.f.)

Number / Call sign	Name / Owner	Tonnage	Class	Builder / Dimensions	Type	Machinery
9506291 *EAGJ* -	**VOLCAN DE TINAMAR** **Caixa d'Estalvis i Pensions de Barcelona (Caja de Ahorros y Pensiones de Barcelona) (La Caixa)** Naviera Armas SA SatCom: Inmarsat C 422542310 *Las Palmas* *Spain (CSR)* MMSI: 225423000	**29,514** - 11,980	Class: BV	**2011-06 Hijos de J. Barreras S.A. — Vigo** Yd No: 1667 Loa 175.70 (BB) Br ex - Dght 6.400 Lbp 159.00 Br md 26.40 Dpth 14.94 Welded, 1 dk	**(A36A2PR) Passenger/Ro-Ro Ship (Vehicles)** Passengers: berths: 1500 Stern door/ramp (p. a.) Stern door/ramp (s. a.) Cars: 350	**4 oil engines** reduction geared to sc. shafts driving 2 CP propellers Total Power: 33,600kW (45,684hp) 24.0k MAN-B&W 7L48/60C 4 x 4 Stroke 7 Cy. 480 x 600 each-8400kW (11421bhp) MAN B&W Diesel AG-Augsburg AuxGen: 3 x 1000kW 400V 50Hz a.c, 2 x 1500kW 400V 50Hz a.c Thrusters: 2 Tunnel thruster (f)
9268411 *ECCK* -	**VOLCAN DE TINDAYA** **Maritima de las Islas SL** Naviera Armas SA SatCom: Inmarsat C 422412710 *Las Palmas* *Spain (CSR)* MMSI: 224127000 Official number: 1/2003	**3,715** 1,114 420	Class: BV	**2003-06 Hijos de J. Barreras S.A. — Vigo** Yd No: 1617 Loa 78.10 (BB) Br ex - Dght 3.300 Lbp 65.50 Br md 15.50 Dpth 15.20 Welded	**(A36A2PR) Passenger/Ro-Ro Ship (Vehicles)** Passengers: 682 Bow ramp (centre) Len: 10.00 Wid: 4.20 Swl: - Stern door/ramp (p) Len: 6.50 Wid: 5.50 Swl: - Stern door/ramp (s) Len: 6.50 Wid: 5.50 Swl: - Lane-Len: 110 Cars: 140	**2 oil engines** geared to sc. shafts driving 2 CP propellers Total Power: 5,200kW (7,070hp) 16.0k Wartsila 6L2 2 x 4 Stroke 6 Cy. 260 x 320 each-2600kW (3535bhp) Wartsila Diesel S.A.-Bermeo AuxGen: 2 x 550kW 400V 50Hz a.c, 2 x 625kW 400V 50Hz a.c Thrusters: 2 Thwart. CP thruster (f) Fuel: 170.0 (r.f.)
9506289 *EAIE* -	**VOLCAN DEL TEIDE** **Naviera Bruma AIE** Naviera Armas SA SatCom: Inmarsat C 422541610 *Santa Cruz de Tenerife* *Spain (CSR)* MMSI: 225416000	**29,514** - 11,980	Class: BV	**2011-01 Hijos de J. Barreras S.A. — Vigo** Yd No: 1666 Loa 175.70 (BB) Br ex - Dght 6.700 Lbp 159.00 Br md 26.40 Dpth 14.94 Welded, 1 dk	**(A36A2PR) Passenger/Ro-Ro Ship (Vehicles)** Passengers: berths: 1500 Stern door/ramp (p. a.) Stern door/ramp (s. a.) Lane-Len: 2010 Cars: 350	**4 oil engines** reduction geared to sc. shafts driving 2 CP propellers Total Power: 33,600kW (45,684hp) 24.0k MAN-B&W 7L48/60C 4 x 4 Stroke 7 Cy. 480 x 600 each-8400kW (11421bhp) MAN B&W Diesel AG-Augsburg AuxGen: 3 x 1000kW 400V 50Hz a.c, 2 x 1500kW 400V 50Hz a.c Thrusters: 2 Tunnel thruster (f) Fuel: 130.0 (d.f.) 900.0 (r.f.)
9254898 *LLPN* -	**VOLDA** **Fjord1 AS** - *Molde* *Norway* MMSI: 258505000	**1,986** 596 655	Class: (NV)	**2002-06 Gdanska Stocznia 'Remontowa' SA — Gdansk** Yd No: 827 Loa 87.60 Br ex - Dght 3.850 Lbp 86.40 Br md 16.40 Dpth 5.35 Welded, 1 dk	**(A36A2PR) Passenger/Ro-Ro Ship (Vehicles)** Passengers: unberthed: 300 Bow door (f) Len: 5.00 Wid: 10.50 Swl: - Stern door (a) Len: 5.00 Wid: 9.60 Swl: - Lane-Len: 56 Cars: 85	**2 oil engines** reduction geared to sc. shafts driving 2 Directional propellers 1 propeller aft, 1 fwd Total Power: 2,500kW (3,400hp) 12.5kn Caterpillar 3512TA 2 x Vee 4 Stroke 12 Cy. 170 x 190 each-1250kW (1700bhp) Caterpillar Inc-USA AuxGen: 2 x 170kW 50Hz a.c Fuel: 100.0 (d.f.)
9570553 *LKUB* F-80-M	**VOLDNES** **Ryggefjord Fiskebaatrederi AS** - *Hammerfest* *Norway* MMSI: 259937000	**498** 149 500		**2011-08 AO Yaroslavskiy Sudostroitelnyy Zavod — Yaroslavl (Hull)** Yd No: 404 **2011-08 Blaalid AS — Raudeberg** Yd No: 35 Loa 34.07 (BB) Br ex - Dght 4.920 Lbp 28.00 Br md 9.50 Dpth 6.60 Welded, 1 dk	**(B11B2FV) Fishing Vessel**	**1 oil engine** reduction geared to sc. shaft driving 1 CP propeller Mitsubishi 1 x 4 Stroke Mitsubishi Heavy Industries Ltd-Japan Thrusters: 1 Thwart. FP thruster (f)
9156515 *PCHM* -	**VOLENDAM** **HAL Antillen NV** Holland America Line NV SatCom: Inmarsat C 424596810 *Rotterdam* *Netherlands* MMSI: 245968000 Official number: 37008	**61,214** 31,371 6,150	Class: LR (RI) ✠ **100A1** CS 10/2009 passenger ship *IWS ✠ **LMC** Eq.Ltr: Rt; Cable: 687.5/84.0 U3 (a)	**1999-10 Fincantieri-Cant. Nav. Italiani S.p.A. (Breda) — Venezia** Yd No: 6035 Loa 237.91 (BB) Br ex 32.28 Dght 8.100 Lbp 202.75 Br md 32.25 Dpth 11.00 Welded, 5 dks plus 7 superstructure decks	**(A37A2PC) Passenger/Cruise** Passengers: cabins: 720; berths: 1824	**5 diesel electric oil engines** driving 5 gen. each 8400kW 6600V Connecting to 2 elec. motors each (13000kW) driving 2 CP propellers Total Power: 43,200kW (58,735hp) 22.0kn Sulzer 12ZAV40S 5 x Vee 4 Stroke 12 Cy. 400 x 560 each-8640kW (11747bhp) Grandi Motori Trieste-Italy Boilers: 5 e (ex.g.) 13.3kgf/cm² (13.0bar), 2 AuxB (o.f.) 10.4kgf/cm² (10.2bar) Thrusters: 2 Thwart. CP thruster (f); 2 Thwart. CP thruster (a) Fuel: 144.0 (d.f.) 2796.0 (r.f.)
8724573 - -	**VOLEVOY** **Vladivostok Sea Fishing Port (OAO 'Vladivostokskiy Morskoy Rybnyy Port')** - *Vladivostok* *Russia*	**182** 54 57	Class: RS	**1986-12 Gorokhovetskiy Sudostroitelnyy Zavod — Gorokhovets** Yd No: 221 Loa 29.30 Br ex 8.60 Dght 3.400 Lbp 27.00 Br md 8.24 Dpth 4.30 Welded, 1 dk	**(B32A2ST) Tug** Ice Capable	**2 oil engines** driving 2 CP propellers Total Power: 1,180kW (1,604hp) 11.5kn Pervomaysk 8CHNP25/34 2 x 4 Stroke 8 Cy. 250 x 340 each-590kW (802bhp) Pervomaydizelmash (PDM)-Pervomaysk AuxGen: 2 x 590kW a.c
8723282 *UDZS* -	**VOLGA** **Kamchatka Logistic Centre Co Ltd** - *Petropavlovsk-Kamchatskiy* *Russia* MMSI: 273313620 Official number: 870138	**2,393** 717 901	Class: (RS)	**1988-12 Sudostroitelnyy Zavod "Baltiya" — Klaypeda** Yd No: 801 Loa 85.06 Br ex 13.04 Dght 4.040 Lbp 76.95 Br md - Dpth 6.50 Welded, 1 dk	**(B11B2FV) Fishing Vessel** Ins: 1,245 Ice Capable	**1 oil engine** driving 1 FP propeller Total Power: 852kW (1,158hp) 11.3kn S.K.L. 8NVD48A-2U 1 x 4 Stroke 8 Cy. 320 x 480 852kW (1158bhp) VEB Schwermaschinenbau "KarlLiebknecht" (SKL)-Magdeburg AuxGen: 2 x 534kW a.c, 1 x 220kW a.c Fuel: 238.0 (d.f.)
8847260 *3EZN4* -	**VOLGA** **Baltasar Shipping SA** CJSC 'Onegoship' *Panama* *Panama* MMSI: 356841000 Official number: 4092709	**4,966** 1,776 6,277	Class: RS	**1991-08 Sudostroitelnyy Zavod "Krasnoye Sormovo" — Gorkiy** Yd No: 19610/13 Loa 139.81 Br ex 16.56 Dght 4.680 Lbp 134.00 Br md 16.40 Dpth 6.70 Welded, 1 dk	**(A31A2GX) General Cargo Ship** Grain: 6,843; Bale: 6,785 TEU 140 C.Dk 140/20' Compartments: 4 Ho, ER 4 Ha: 4 (18.7 x 11.8)ER	**2 oil engines** driving 2 FP propellers Total Power: 1,940kW (2,638hp) 10.0kn S.K.L. 8NVD48A-3U 2 x 4 Stroke 8 Cy. 320 x 480 each-970kW (1319bhp) SKL Motoren u. Systemtechnik AG-Magdeburg AuxGen: 3 x 150kW a.c Thrusters: 1 Thwart. FP thruster (f) Fuel: 417.0 (d.f.) (Heating Coils)
8982761 *UEDM* -	**VOLGA** **Casptransform Dredging Co Ltd (OOO Dnouglubitelnaya Kompaniya 'Kasptransform')** - *Astrakhan* *Russia* MMSI: 273441230 Official number: 822986	**1,016** - 192	Class: (RS)	**1983-06 in Czechoslovakia** Yd No: 18 Loa 76.60 Br ex 10.80 Dght 1.900 Lbp 64.53 Br md 10.55 Dpth 3.00 Welded, 1 dk	**(B33A2DS) Suction Dredger**	**2 oil engines** driving 2 FP propellers
9133197 *UCRA* -	**VOLGA-35** **Eurasian Shipping Co** Navigator LLC *St Petersburg* *Russia* MMSI: 273342000	**4,955** 1,663 5,885 T/cm 20.0	Class: RS	**1995-09 Sudostroitelnyy Zavod "Krasnoye Sormovo" — Nizhniy Novgorod** Yd No: 19610/35 Loa 139.90 Br ex 16.56 Dght 4.500 Lbp 134.00 Br md 16.40 Dpth 6.70 Welded, 1 dk	**(A31A2GX) General Cargo Ship** Grain: 6,843; Bale: 6,785 Ice Capable	**2 oil engines** driving 2 FP propellers Total Power: 1,940kW (2,638hp) 10.0kn S.K.L. 8NVD48A-3U 2 x 4 Stroke 8 Cy. 320 x 480 each-970kW (1319bhp) SKL Motoren u. Systemtechnik AG-Magdeburg AuxGen: 3 x 150kW a.c Fuel: 417.0 (d.f.)
9252905 *UBYH8* -	**VOLGA-44** **Eurasian Shipping Co** Navigator LLC *St Petersburg* *Russia* MMSI: 273357540	**4,953** 1,776 6,207 T/cm 20.0	Class: GL (RS)	**2001-05 Sudostroitelnyy Zavod "Krasnoye Sormovo" — Nizhniy Novgorod** Yd No: 44 Loa 139.93 Br ex 16.56 Dght 4.680 Lbp 134.00 Br md 16.40 Dpth 6.70 Welded, 1 dk	**(A31A2GX) General Cargo Ship** Grain: 6,843; Bale: 6,785 Ice Capable	**2 oil engines** driving 2 FP propellers Total Power: 2,200kW (2,992hp) 10.0kn S.K.L. 8NVD48A-3U 2 x 4 Stroke 8 Cy. 320 x 480 each-1100kW (1496bhp) SKL Motoren u. Systemtechnik AG-Magdeburg Thrusters: 1 Thwart. FP thruster (f)
8624278 *V4SK2* -	**VOLGA-4001** *ex* Aksoy *-2013* *ex* Umba *-2008* *ex* Volga-4001 *-1997* **Volga Maritime Ltd** Albros Shipping & Trading Ltd Co (Albros Denizcilik ve Ticaret Ltd Sti) *Basseterre* *St Kitts & Nevis* MMSI: 341862000 Official number: SKN1002503	**4,911** 1,776 5,845	Class: RS	**1986-03 Sudostroitelnyy Zavod "Krasnoye Sormovo" — Gorkiy** Yd No: 19610/01 Loa 139.81 Br ex 16.56 Dght 4.470 Lbp 134.00 Br md - Dpth 6.70 Welded, 1 dk	**(A31A2GX) General Cargo Ship** Grain: 6,843; Bale: 6,785 TEU 140 C.Dk 140/20' Compartments: 4 Ho, ER 4 Ha: 4 (18.7 x 11.8)ER Ice Capable	**2 oil engines** driving 2 FP propellers Total Power: 1,940kW (2,638hp) 10.0kn S.K.L. 8NVDS48A-3U 2 x 4 Stroke 8 Cy. 320 x 480 each-970kW (1319bhp) VEB Schwermaschinenbau "KarlLiebknecht" (SKL)-Magdeburg AuxGen: 3 x 150kW a.c Thrusters: 1 Thwart. FP thruster (f) Fuel: 417.0 (d.f.) (Heating Coils)

IMO / Call sign	Name, owner, flag	Tonnage	Class	Builder	Type	Machinery
624292 4RG2	**VOLGA-4002** **Volga Maritime Ltd** Albros Shipping & Trading Ltd Co (Albros Denizcilik ve Ticaret Ltd Sti) *Basseterre* *St Kitts & Nevis* MMSI: 341648000 Official number: SKN 1002470	**4,911** 1,776 5,845	Class: RS	**1987-07 Sudostroitelnyy Zavod "Krasnoye Sormovo" — Gorkiy** Yd No: 19610/02 Loa 139.81 Br ex 16.56 Dght 4.470 Lbp 134.00 Br md 16.40 Dpth 6.70 Welded, 1 dk	**(A31A2GX) General Cargo Ship** Grain: 6,843; Bale: 6,785 TEU 140 C.Dk 140/20' Compartments: 4 Ho, ER 4 Ha: 4 (18.7 x 11.8)ER Ice Capable	**2 oil engines** driving 2 FP propellers Total Power: 1,940kW (2,638hp) 10.0kn S.K.L. 8NVDS48A-3U 2 x 4 Stroke 8 Cy. 320 x 480 each-970kW (1319bhp) VEB Schwermaschinenbau "KarlLiebknecht" (SKL)-Magdeburg AuxGen: 3 x 150kW a.c Thrusters: 1 Thwart. FP thruster (f) Fuel: 417.0 (d.f.) (Heating Coils)
720216 DCB	**VOLGA-4004** **Baltasar Shipping SA** CJSC 'Onegoship' *St Petersburg* *Russia* MMSI: 273335100 Official number: 4154510	**4,911** 1,776 6,277	Class: RS	**1988-05 Sudostroitelnyy Zavod "Krasnoye Sormovo" — Gorkiy** Yd No: 19610/04 Loa 139.81 Br ex 16.56 Dght 4.680 Lbp 134.00 Br md 16.40 Dpth 6.70 Welded, 1 dk	**(A31A2GX) General Cargo Ship** Grain: 6,843; Bale: 6,785 TEU 140 C.Dk 140/20' Compartments: 4 Ho, ER 4 Ha: 4 (18.7 x 11.8)ER Ice Capable	**2 oil engines** driving 2 FP propellers Total Power: 1,940kW (2,638hp) 10.0kn S.K.L. 8NVD48A-3U 2 x 4 Stroke 8 Cy. 320 x 480 each-970kW (1319bhp) VEB Schwermaschinenbau "KarlLiebknecht" (SKL)-Magdeburg AuxGen: 3 x 150kW a.c Thrusters: 1 Thwart. FP thruster (f) Fuel: 417.0 (d.f.) (Heating Coils)
720230 4UI2	**VOLGA-4006** **Volga Maritime Ltd** Albros Shipping & Trading Ltd Co (Albros Denizcilik ve Ticaret Ltd Sti) *Basseterre* *St Kitts & Nevis* MMSI: 341447000 Official number: SKN 1002555	**4,911** 1,776 6,277	Class: BV (RS)	**1988-03 Sudostroitelnyy Zavod "Krasnoye Sormovo" — Gorkiy** Yd No: 19610/06 Loa 139.81 Br ex 16.56 Dght 4.680 Lbp 134.00 Br md 16.40 Dpth 6.70 Welded, 1 dk	**(A31A2GX) General Cargo Ship** Grain: 6,843; Bale: 6,785 TEU 140 C.Dk 140/20' Compartments: 4 Ho, ER 4 Ha: 4 (18.7 x 11.8)ER Ice Capable	**2 oil engines** driving 2 FP propellers Total Power: 1,940kW (2,638hp) 10.0kn S.K.L. 8NVD48A-3U 2 x 4 Stroke 8 Cy. 320 x 480 each-970kW (1319bhp) VEB Schwermaschinenbau "KarlLiebknecht" (SKL)-Magdeburg AuxGen: 3 x 150kW a.c Thrusters: 1 Thwart. FP thruster (f) Fuel: 417.0 (d.f.) (Heating Coils)
728816 GQL	**VOLGA-4007** **Baltasar Shipping SA** CJSC 'Onegoship' *St Petersburg* *Russia* MMSI: 273356200	**4,911** 1,778 6,277	Class: RS	**1989-05 Sudostroitelnyy Zavod "Krasnoye Sormovo" — Gorkiy** Yd No: 19610/07 Loa 139.81 Br ex 16.56 Dght 4.470 Lbp 134.00 Br md 16.40 Dpth 6.70 Welded, 1 dk	**(A31A2GX) General Cargo Ship** Grain: 6,843; Bale: 6,785 TEU 140 C.Dk 140/20' Compartments: 4 Ho, ER 4 Ha: 4 (18.7 x 11.8)ER Ice Capable	**2 oil engines** driving 2 FP propellers Total Power: 1,940kW (2,638hp) 10.0kn S.K.L. 8NVD48A-3U 2 x 4 Stroke 8 Cy. 320 x 480 each-970kW (1319bhp) VEB Schwermaschinenbau "KarlLiebknecht" (SKL)-Magdeburg AuxGen: 3 x 150kW a.c Thrusters: 1 Thwart. FP thruster (f) Fuel: 417.0 (d.f.) (Heating Coils)
629294 FEW9	**VOLGA-4009** **Baltasar Shipping SA** CJSC 'Onegoship' *Panama* *Panama* MMSI: 370424000 Official number: 4101010	**4,966** 1,778 5,985	Class: RS	**1990-05 Sudostroitelnyy Zavod "Krasnoye Sormovo" — Gorkiy** Yd No: 19610/10 Loa 139.81 Br ex 16.56 Dght 4.450 Lbp 134.00 Br md 16.40 Dpth 6.70 Welded, 1 dk	**(A31A2GX) General Cargo Ship** Grain: 6,843; Bale: 6,785 TEU 140 C.Dk 140/20' Compartments: 4 Ho, ER 4 Ha: 4 (18.7 x 11.8)ER Ice Capable	**2 oil engines** driving 2 FP propellers Total Power: 1,938kW (2,634hp) 10.0kn S.K.L. 8NVD48A-3U 2 x 4 Stroke 8 Cy. 320 x 480 each-969kW (1317bhp) VEB Schwermaschinenbau "KarlLiebknecht" (SKL)-Magdeburg AuxGen: 3 x 150kW a.c Thrusters: 1 Thwart. FP thruster (f)
847038 BNJ	**VOLGA-4011** **Amur Shipping Co** - SatCom: Inmarsat C 427320826 *Nikolayevsk-na-Amure* *Russia* MMSI: 273358200 Official number: 903115	**4,966** 1,673 5,985	Class: RS	**1991-09 Sudostroitelnyy Zavod "Krasnoye Sormovo" — Gorkiy** Yd No: 19610/14 Loa 139.81 Br ex 16.56 Dght 4.450 Lbp 134.00 Br md 16.40 Dpth 6.70 Welded, 1 dk	**(A31A2GX) General Cargo Ship** Grain: 6,843; Bale: 6,785 TEU 140 C.Dk 140/20' Compartments: 4 Ho, ER 4 Ha: 4 (18.7 x 11.8)ER Ice Capable	**2 oil engines** driving 2 FP propellers Total Power: 1,942kW (2,640hp) 19.1kn S.K.L. 8NVD48A-3U 2 x 4 Stroke 8 Cy. 320 x 480 each-971kW (1320bhp) SKL Motoren u. Systemtechnik AG-Magdeburg AuxGen: 3 x 160kW 400V 50Hz a.c Thrusters: 1 Thwart. FP thruster (f) Fuel: 170.0 (d.f.)
720228 4TJ2	**VOLGA-4051** *ex* Sumanus *-2013* *ex* Volga-4005 *-1998* **Volga Maritime Ltd** Albros Shipping & Trading Ltd Co (Albros Denizcilik ve Ticaret Ltd Sti) *Basseterre* *St Kitts & Nevis* MMSI: 341140000 Official number: SKN 1002530	**4,911** 1,776 6,261	Class: BV (RS)	**1988-08 Sudostroitelnyy Zavod "Krasnoye Sormovo" — Gorkiy** Yd No: 19610/05 Loa 139.89 Br ex 16.56 Dght 4.680 Lbp 133.95 Br md 16.56 Dpth 6.70 Welded, 1 dk	**(A31A2GX) General Cargo Ship** Grain: 6,843; Bale: 6,785 TEU 140 C.Dk 140/20' Compartments: 4 Ho, ER 4 Ha: 4 (18.7 x 11.8)ER Ice Capable	**2 oil engines** driving 2 FP propellers Total Power: 1,940kW (2,638hp) 10.0kn S.K.L. 8NVD48A-3U 2 x 4 Stroke 8 Cy. 320 x 480 each-970kW (1319bhp) VEB Schwermaschinenbau "KarlLiebknecht" (SKL)-Magdeburg AuxGen: 3 x 150kW a.c Thrusters: 1 Thwart. FP thruster (f) Fuel: 417.0 (d.f.) (Heating Coils)
728490 4TC2	**VOLGA-4052** *ex* Lady Mina *-2013* *ex* Midland 2 *-2008* *ex* Rabros *-2002* **Volga Maritime Ltd** Albros Shipping & Trading Ltd Co (Albros Denizcilik ve Ticaret Ltd Sti) *Basseterre* *St Kitts & Nevis* Official number: SKN1002523	**4,966** 1,781 5,984	Class: BV (RS)	**1989-09 Sudostroitelnyy Zavod "Krasnoye Sormovo" — Gorkiy** Yd No: 19610/08 Loa 139.89 Br ex 16.56 Dght 4.541 Lbp 133.95 Br md 16.40 Dpth 6.70 Welded, 1 dk	**(A31A2GX) General Cargo Ship** Grain: 6,843; Bale: 6,785 TEU 140 C.Dk 140/20' Compartments: 4 Ho, ER 4 Ha: 4 (18.7 x 11.8)ER Ice Capable	**2 oil engines** driving 2 FP propellers Total Power: 1,940kW (2,638hp) 10.0kn S.K.L. 8NVD48A-3U 2 x 4 Stroke 8 Cy. 320 x 480 each-970kW (1319bhp) VEB Schwermaschinenbau "KarlLiebknecht" (SKL)-Magdeburg AuxGen: 3 x 150kW a.c Thrusters: 1 Thwart. FP thruster (f) Fuel: 180.4 (d.f.) 6.5pd
745656 BVA4	**VOLGA-FLOT 1** *ex* Volzhskiy-1 *-2002* **VF Tanker Ltd** - *Nizhniy Novgorod* *Russia* MMSI: 273393300 Official number: V-01-33	**3,977** 1,265 5,212	Class: RR	**1982 Navashinskiy Sudostroitelnyy Zavod 'Oka' — Navashino** Yd No: 1003 Loa 138.70 Br ex 16.70 Dght 3.600 Lbp 132.21 Br md 16.50 Dpth 5.50 Welded, 1 dk	**(A13B2TP) Products Tanker** Double Hull (13F)	**2 oil engines** driving 2 Propellers Total Power: 1,764kW (2,398hp) 9.0kn
745668 BVA5	**VOLGA-FLOT 2** *ex* Volzhskiy-2 *-2002* **VF Tanker Ltd** - *Nizhniy Novgorod* *Russia* MMSI: 273394300 Official number: V-01-34	**3,977** 1,265 5,212	Class: RR	**1982 Navashinskiy Sudostroitelnyy Zavod 'Oka' — Navashino** Yd No: 1004 Loa 138.70 Br ex 16.70 Dght 3.600 Lbp 132.21 Br md 16.50 Dpth 5.50 Welded, 1 dk	**(A13B2TP) Products Tanker** Double Hull (13F)	**2 oil engines** driving 2 Propellers 9.0kn
745670 BVA6	**VOLGA-FLOT 3** *ex* Baskunchak *-1983* **VF Tanker Ltd** - *Nizhniy Novgorod* *Russia* MMSI: 273395300 Official number: V-01-41	**3,977** 1,265 5,212	Class: RR	**1983 Navashinskiy Sudostroitelnyy Zavod 'Oka' — Navashino** Yd No: 1005 Loa 138.70 Br ex 16.70 Dght 3.600 Lbp 132.21 Br md 16.50 Dpth 5.50 Welded, 1 dk	**(A13B2TP) Products Tanker** Double Hull (13F)	**2 oil engines** driving 2 Propellers 9.0kn
745682 BVA7	**VOLGA-FLOT 4** *ex* Volzhskiy-4 *-1983* **VF Tanker Ltd** - *Nizhniy Novgorod* *Russia* MMSI: 273396300 Official number: V-01-35	**3,977** 1,265 5,212	Class: RR	**1983 Navashinskiy Sudostroitelnyy Zavod 'Oka' — Navashino** Yd No: 1006 Loa 138.70 Br ex 16.70 Dght 3.600 Lbp 132.21 Br md 16.50 Dpth 5.50 Welded, 1 dk	**(A13B2TP) Products Tanker** Double Hull (13F)	**2 oil engines** driving 2 Propellers 9.0kn
745694 BVA8	**VOLGA-FLOT 5** *ex* Volzhskiy-5 *-1983* **VF Tanker Ltd** - *Nizhniy Novgorod* *Russia* MMSI: 273397300 Official number: V-01-36	**3,977** 1,265 5,212	Class: RR	**1983 Navashinskiy Sudostroitelnyy Zavod 'Oka' — Navashino** Yd No: 1007 Loa 138.70 Br ex 16.70 Dght 3.600 Lbp 132.21 Br md 16.50 Dpth 5.50 Welded, 1 dk	**(A13B2TP) Products Tanker** Double Hull (13F)	**2 oil engines** driving 2 Propellers 9.0kn
745709 BVA9	**VOLGA-FLOT 6** *ex* Volzhskiy-9 *-1983* **VF Tanker Ltd** - *Nizhniy Novgorod* *Russia* MMSI: 273398300 Official number: V-01-37	**3,977** 1,265 5,212	Class: RR	**1984 Navashinskiy Sudostroitelnyy Zavod 'Oka' — Navashino** Yd No: 1011 Loa 138.70 Br ex 16.70 Dght 3.600 Lbp 132.21 Br md 16.50 Dpth 5.50 Welded, 1 dk	**(A13B2TP) Products Tanker** Double Hull (13F)	**2 oil engines** driving 2 Propellers 9.0kn

8745711 *UBWA2* -	**VOLGA-FLOT 7** *ex* Volzhskiy-11 **VF Tanker Ltd** - *Nizhniy Novgorod* *Russia* MMSI: 273399300 Official number: V-01-38	**3,977** 1,265 5,212	Class: RR	**1985 Navashinskiy Sudostroitelnyy Zavod 'Oka' — Navashino** Yd No: 1013 Loa 138.70 Br ex 16.70 Dght 3.600 Lbp 132.21 Br md 16.50 Dpth 5.50 Welded, 1 dk	**(A13B2TP) Products Tanker** Double Hull (13F)	**2 oil engines** driving 2 Propellers	9.0kn
8745723 *UBWA3* -	**VOLGA-FLOT 8** *ex* Volzhskiy-12 **VF Tanker Ltd** - *Nizhniy Novgorod* *Russia* MMSI: 273390400 Official number: V-01-39	**3,977** 1,265 5,212	Class: RR	**1985 Navashinskiy Sudostroitelnyy Zavod 'Oka' — Navashino** Yd No: 1014 Loa 138.70 Br ex 16.70 Dght 3.600 Lbp 132.21 Br md 16.50 Dpth 5.50 Welded, 1 dk	**(A13B2TP) Products Tanker** Double Hull (13F)	**2 oil engines** driving 2 Propellers	9.0kn
8745072 *UBWA4* -	**VOLGA-FLOT 9** *ex* Volzhskiy-19 *-2001* **VF Tanker Ltd** - *Nizhniy Novgorod* *Russia* MMSI: 273391400 Official number: V-01-40	**3,977** 1,265 5,212	Class: RR	**1987 Navashinskiy Sudostroitelnyy Zavod 'Oka' — Navashino** Yd No: 1021 Converted From: General Cargo Ship-1987 Loa 138.70 Br ex 16.70 Dght 3.600 Lbp 132.21 Br md 16.50 Dpth 5.50 Welded, 1 dk	**(A13B2TP) Products Tanker**	**2 oil engines** driving 2 Propellers Total Power: 1,766kW (2,402hp) Dvigatel Revolyutsii 2 x 4 Stroke 6 Cy. 360 x 450 each-883kW (1201bhp) Zavod "Dvigatel Revolyutsii"-Gorkiy	9.0kn 6CHN36/45
5286398 *HP6279* -	**VOLGA I** *ex* Paloma Reefer *-1995* *ex* Puente Castrelos *-1991* **Valinia Trading Corp** - *Panama* *Panama* Official number: 20885PEXT1	*454* 285 539	Class: (BV)	**1961 Construcciones Navales P Freire SA — Vigo** Yd No: 1 Loa 49.56 Br ex 8.03 Dght 3.201 Lbp 44.99 Br md 8.01 Dpth 4.20 Riveted, 1 dk	**(A31A2GX) General Cargo Ship** Grain: 575 Compartments: 2 Ho, ER 2 Ha: 2 (8.5 x 5.0)ER Derricks: 4x2.5t	**1 oil engine** driving 1 FP propeller Total Power: 883kW (1,201hp) Krupps 1 x 4 Stroke 6 Cy. 400 x 460 883kW (1201bhp) Fried. Krupp Dieselmotoren GmbH-Essen AuxGen: 2 x 25kW 220V 50Hz a.c, 1 x 20kW 220V 50Hz a.c, 1 x 5kW 220V 50Hz a.c Fuel: 85.5 (d.f.)	11.5kn
9631072 *PCSQ* -	**VOLGABORG** - **Eems Beheer V BV** Wagenborg Shipping BV *Delfzijl* *Netherlands* MMSI: 246900000	**7,367** 3,688 11,850	Class: BV	**2013-04 Scheepswerf Ferus Smit BV — Westerbroek** Yd No: 408 Loa 142.65 Br ex - Dght 7.730 Lbp 139.43 Br md 15.87 Dpth 10.78 Welded, 1 dk	**(A31A2GX) General Cargo Ship** Grain: 14,258 Compartments: 2 Ho, ER 2 Ha: (63.6 x 13.2)ER (41.0 x 13.2) Ice Capable	**1 oil engine** reduction geared to sc. shaft driving 1 CP propeller Total Power: 3,000kW (4,079hp) MaK 1 x 4 Stroke 9 Cy. 255 x 400 3000kW (4079bhp) Caterpillar Motoren GmbH & Co. KG-Germany AuxGen: 1 x 680kW 50Hz a.c, 2 x 332kW 50Hz a.c Thrusters: 1 Tunnel thruster (f) Fuel: 590.0	14.7kn 9M25C
8230077 *UCGP* -	**VOLGO-BALT 106** - **OOO 'Zenit' Maritime Finance Co** 'St Petersburg' Shipping Co Ltd *St Petersburg* *Russia* MMSI: 273459650	*2,457* 1,429 2,907	Class: RR	**1969-04 Zavody Tazkeho Strojarstva (ZTS) — Komarno** Yd No: 1306 Loa 114.00 Br ex 13.23 Dght 3.640 Lbp 110.00 Br md 13.01 Dpth 5.50 Welded, 1 dk	**(A31A2GX) General Cargo Ship**	**2 oil engines** driving 2 FP propellers Total Power: 1,030kW (1,400hp) Skoda 2 x 4 Stroke 6 Cy. 275 x 350 each-515kW (700bhp) CKD Praha-Praha Fuel: 106.0 (d.f.)	6L275A2
7226134 *ERPK* -	**VOLGO-BALT 121** - **Fapiola Shipping SA** Poseidon Ltd *Giurgiulesti* *Moldova* MMSI: 214181611	**2,457** 1,010 3,265	Class: UA (RS) (RR)	**1970 Zavody Tazkeho Strojarstva (ZTS) — Komarno** Yd No: 1321 Loa 114.00 Br ex 13.23 Dght 3.640 Lbp 110.00 Br md 13.01 Dpth 5.50 Welded, 1 dk	**(A31A2GX) General Cargo Ship** Grain: 4,720 Compartments: 4 Ho, ER 4 Ha: (18.6 x 11.2)2 (18.8 x 11.2) (20.3 x 11.2)ER	**2 oil engines** driving 2 FP propellers Total Power: 1,000kW (1,359hp) Skoda 2 x 4 Stroke 6 Cy. 275 x 350 each-485kW (659bhp) Skoda-Praha	10.8kn 6L275IIPN
8851390 *UBNL* -	**VOLGO-BALT 136** - **Neva-Balt Co Ltd** - *St Petersburg* *Russia* MMSI: 273314210	**2,457** 1,010 3,294	Class: RS (RR)	**1971-03 Zavody Tazkeho Strojarstva (ZTS) — Komarno** Yd No: 1336 Loa 113.80 Br ex 13.23 Dght 3.640 Lbp 110.00 Br md 13.00 Dpth 5.50 Welded, 1 dk	**(A31A2GX) General Cargo Ship** Grain: 4,730 Compartments: 4 Ho, ER 4 Ha: (17.9 x 9.4)2 (18.9 x 9.4) (19.2 x 9.4)ER	**2 oil engines** driving 2 FP propellers Total Power: 1,030kW (1,400hp) Skoda 2 x 4 Stroke 6 Cy. 275 x 350 each-515kW (700bhp) CKD Praha-Praha	10.0kn 6L275A2
8862791 *UBOG* -	**VOLGO-BALT 138** - **OOO 'Zenit' Maritime Finance Co** 'St Petersburg' Shipping Co Ltd *St Petersburg* *Russia* MMSI: 273458650	**2,457** 1,010 3,165	Class: RR	**1971-05 Zavody Tazkeho Strojarstva (ZTS) — Komarno** Yd No: 1338 Loa 114.00 Br ex 13.23 Dght 3.450 Lbp 110.00 Br md 13.01 Dpth 5.50 Welded, 1 dk	**(A31A2GX) General Cargo Ship** Grain: 4,730 Compartments: 4 Ho, ER 4 Ha: (17.9 x 9.4)2 (18.9 x 9.4) (19.2 x 9.4)ER	**2 oil engines** driving 2 FP propellers Total Power: 1,030kW (1,400hp) Skoda 2 x 4 Stroke 6 Cy. 275 x 350 each-515kW (700bhp) CKD Praha-Praha	10.0kn 6L275IIIPN
8230209 *UBYY* -	**VOLGO-BALT 153** - **AI Ship Management Co Ltd** Youg Electronics Ltd (OOO 'Yug Elektroniks') *Russia* MMSI: 273365100	**2,457** 1,010 3,170	Class: IS (RR)	**1971-01 Zavody Tazkeho Strojarstva (ZTS) — Komarno** Yd No: 1353 Loa 114.00 Br ex 13.23 Dght 3.640 Lbp 107.35 Br md 13.01 Dpth 5.50 Welded, 1 dk	**(A31A2GX) General Cargo Ship** Grain: 4,750	**2 oil engines** driving 2 FP propellers Total Power: 1,030kW (1,400hp) Skoda 2 x 4 Stroke 6 Cy. 275 x 350 each-515kW (700bhp) CKD Praha-Praha Fuel: 110.0 (d.f.)	6L275IIIPN
8867442 *UBPI9* -	**VOLGO-BALT 156** *ex* Anton *-2012* *ex* Enely *-1997* *ex* Central *-1997* *ex* Volgo-Balt 156 *-1993* **Gervessa Shipping Co Ltd** Arcus Shipping Co Ltd *Russia* MMSI: 273356860	**2,498** 1,048 3,143	Class: (RS)	**1972-04 Zavody Tazkeho Strojarstva (ZTS) — Komarno** Yd No: 1356 Loa 114.00 Br ex 13.80 Dght 3.640 Lbp 110.00 Br md 13.01 Dpth 5.50 Welded, 1 dk	**(A31A2GX) General Cargo Ship** Grain: 4,720 Compartments: 4 Ho 4 Ha: 4 (14.0 x 9.0)	**2 oil engines** driving 2 FP propellers Total Power: 1,030kW (1,400hp) Skoda 2 x 4 Stroke 6 Cy. 275 x 350 each-515kW (700bhp) CKD Praha-Praha AuxGen: 2 x 80kW a.c Fuel: 106.0 (d.f.)	10.0kn 6L275IIIPN
8231019 *9LC2022* -	**VOLGO-BALT 179** - **Comet Shipping Inc** Seatrans Co Ltd *Freetown* *Sierra Leone* MMSI: 667243000 Official number: SL100243	**2,457** 1,134 3,506	Class: UA (RS) (RR)	**1973-12 Zavody Tazkeho Strojarstva (ZTS) — Komarno** Yd No: 1907 Loa 114.00 Br ex 13.23 Dght 3.840 Lbp 110.52 Br md 13.01 Dpth 5.50 Welded, 1 dk	**(A31A2GX) General Cargo Ship** Grain: 4,720 Compartments: 4 Ho, ER 4 Ha: (18.6 x 11.2)2 (18.8 x 11.2) (20.3 x 11.2)ER	**2 oil engines** driving 2 FP propellers Total Power: 1,030kW (1,400hp) Skoda 2 x 4 Stroke 6 Cy. 275 x 350 each-515kW (700bhp) Skoda-Praha	10.0kn 6L275A2
8857928 *UAPU* -	**VOLGO-BALT 190** - **Baltwave 190 Ltd** Baltic TransService Ltd *Taganrog* *Russia* MMSI: 273318700	**2,457** 1,134 3,474	Class: RS	**1975-10 Zavody Tazkeho Strojarstva (ZTS) — Komarno** Yd No: 1918 Loa 113.87 Br ex 13.23 Dght 3.860 Lbp 110.00 Br md 13.01 Dpth 5.50 Welded, 1 dk	**(A31A2GX) General Cargo Ship** Grain: 4,720 Compartments: 4 Ho, ER 4 Ha: (11.6 x 11.2)3 (19.8 x 11.2)ER	**2 oil engines** driving 2 FP propellers Total Power: 1,030kW (1,400hp) Skoda 2 x 4 Stroke 6 Cy. 275 x 350 each-515kW (700bhp) Skoda-Praha	10.0kn 6L275A2
8230302 *XUGN6* -	**VOLGO-BALT 193** - **Svir Shipping Co Inc** Private Enterprise 'Valship' *Phnom Penh* *Cambodia* MMSI: 515604000 Official number: 1376188	**2,516** 1,147 3,509	Class: (RS) (RR)	**1976-03 Zavody Tazkeho Strojarstva (ZTS) — Komarno** Yd No: 1921 Loa 114.00 Br ex 13.23 Dght 3.640 Lbp 110.52 Br md 13.01 Dpth 5.50 Welded, 1 dk	**(A31A2GX) General Cargo Ship** Grain: 4,720	**2 oil engines** driving 2 FP propellers Total Power: 1,030kW (1,400hp) Skoda 2 x 4 Stroke 6 Cy. 275 x 350 each-515kW (700bhp) Skoda-Praha Fuel: 110.0 (d.f.)	6L275A2
8865999 *UFVS* -	**VOLGO-BALT 195** - **Neva-Balt Co Ltd** - *St Petersburg* *Russia* MMSI: 273332400 Official number: 763542	**2,516** 1,021 3,180	Class: RS (RR)	**1976-03 Zavody Tazkeho Strojarstva (ZTS) — Komarno** Yd No: 1923 Loa 114.00 Br ex 13.23 Dght 3.640 Lbp 110.00 Br md 13.01 Dpth 5.50 Welded, 1 dk	**(A31A2GX) General Cargo Ship**	**2 oil engines** driving 2 FP propellers Total Power: 1,030kW (1,400hp) Skoda 2 x 4 Stroke 6 Cy. 275 x 350 each-515kW (700bhp) CKD Praha-Praha	6L275A2
8841606 *UBPI7* -	**VOLGO-BALT 200M** *ex* Spadina *-2012* *ex* Volgo-Balt 200 *-2002* **Onego Shipping LLC** - *St Petersburg* *Russia* MMSI: 273354860	**2,892** 1,669 3,180	Class: RS (RR)	**1977-07 Zavody Tazkeho Strojarstva (ZTS) — Komarno** Yd No: 1929 Loa 114.00 Br ex 13.20 Dght 3.640 Lbp 110.00 Br md - Dpth 5.50 Welded, 1 dk	**(A31A2GX) General Cargo Ship**	**2 oil engines** driving 2 FP propellers Total Power: 1,030kW (1,400hp) Skoda 2 x 4 Stroke 6 Cy. 275 x 350 each-515kW (700bhp) CKD Praha-Praha	6L275A2

IMO / Call sign	Name / Owner / Manager	Tonnage	Class	Build	Type / Capacity	Machinery
8841618 *V4NH*	**VOLGO-BALT 202** **Baltwave 202 Ltd** Navicor Ltd *Basseterre* *St Kitts & Nevis* MMSI: 341344000 Official number: SKN 1001344	**2,516** 1,147 3,498	Class: (RS) (RR)	**1977-03 Zavody Tazkeho Strojarstva (ZTS) — Komarno** Yd No: 1931 Loa 114.00 Br ex 13.20 Dght 3.860 Lbp 107.55 Br md - Dpth 5.50 Welded, 1 dk	**(A31A2GX) General Cargo Ship** Ice Capable	**2 oil engines** driving 2 FP propellers Total Power: 1,030kW (1,400hp) Skoda 6L275A2 2 x 4 Stroke 6 Cy. 275 x 350 each-515kW (700bhp) CKD Praha-Praha
8841620 *XUVS7* -	**VOLGO-BALT 203** **Berona International Ltd** SIA 'Als Ship Management' *Phnom Penh* *Cambodia* MMSI: 515153000 Official number: 0977122	**2,516** 1,147 3,498	Class: IC UA (RS) (RR)	**1977-03 Zavody Tazkeho Strojarstva (ZTS) — Komarno** Yd No: 1932 Loa 113.87 Br ex 13.20 Dght 3.860 Lbp 110.00 Br md 13.00 Dpth 5.50 Welded, 1 dk	**(A31A2GX) General Cargo Ship** Grain: 3,520 Compartments: 3 Ho, ER 3 Ha: 2 (19.7 x 9.5)ER (18.8 x 9.5)	**2 oil engines** driving 2 FP propellers Total Power: 1,030kW (1,400hp) 10.0kn Skoda 6L275A2 2 x 4 Stroke 6 Cy. 275 x 350 each-515kW (700bhp) CKD Praha-Praha Fuel: 110.0 (d.f.)
8230338 *XURN9* -	**VOLGO-BALT 205** **Nuova Partners Ltd** Richmar Logistic & Chartering Ltd *Phnom Penh* *Cambodia* MMSI: 515165000 Official number: 0977160	**2,516** 1,196 3,498	Class: IC UA (RS) (RR)	**1977-09 Zavody Tazkeho Strojarstva (ZTS) — Komarno** Yd No: 1934 Loa 113.87 Br ex 13.18 Dght 3.860 Lbp 110.00 Br md 13.00 Dpth 5.50 Welded, 1 dk	**(A31A2GX) General Cargo Ship** Grain: 4,750	**2 oil engines** driving 2 FP propellers Total Power: 1,030kW (1,400hp) 10.0kn Skoda 6L275A2 2 x 4 Stroke 6 Cy. 275 x 350 each-515kW (700bhp) Skoda-Praha Fuel: 110.0 (d.f.)
8230340 *V4KO* -	**VOLGO-BALT 206** **Baltwave 206 Ltd** Navicor Ltd *Basseterre* *St Kitts & Nevis* MMSI: 341273000 Official number: SKN 1001273	**2,516** 1,147 3,492	Class: RS (RR)	**1977-11 Zavody Tazkeho Strojarstva (ZTS) — Komarno** Yd No: 1935 Loa 114.00 Br ex 13.23 Dght 3.600 Lbp 110.52 Br md 13.01 Dpth 5.50 Welded, 1 dk	**(A31A2GX) General Cargo Ship** Grain: 4,720 Compartments: 4 Ho, ER 4 Ha: (18.6 x 11.2) (18.8 x 11.2) (18.8 x 11.1) (20.3 x 11.1)ER	**2 oil engines** driving 2 FP propellers Total Power: 1,030kW (1,400hp) 10.0kn Skoda 6L275A2 2 x 4 Stroke 6 Cy. 275 x 350 each-515kW (700bhp) Skoda-Praha Fuel: 110.0 (d.f.)
8230364 *UBLP* -	**VOLGO-BALT 208** **Donmaster Co Ltd** - *Taganrog* *Russia* MMSI: 273332300 Official number: 771055	**2,516** 1,021 3,191	Class: RS (RR)	**1978-03 Zavody Tazkeho Strojarstva (ZTS) — Komarno** Yd No: 1937 Loa 114.00 Br ex 13.23 Dght 3.640 Lbp 110.52 Br md 13.01 Dpth 5.50 Welded, 1 dk	**(A31A2GX) General Cargo Ship** Grain: 4,720 Compartments: 4 Ho, ER 4 Ha: (18.6 x 11.2)2 (18.8 x 11.2) (20.3 x 11.2)ER	**2 oil engines** driving 2 FP propellers Total Power: 1,030kW (1,400hp) 10.0kn Skoda 6L275A2 2 x 4 Stroke 6 Cy. 275 x 350 each-515kW (700bhp) Skoda-Praha Fuel: 110.0 (d.f.)
8230376 *UESJ* -	**VOLGO-BALT 210** **JSC 'Transonega'** Transonega-Shipping JSC (A/O Transonega-Shipping) *Kaliningrad* *Russia* MMSI: 273433720 Official number: 773900	**2,516** 1,021 3,165	Class: RS	**1978-04 Zavody Tazkeho Strojarstva (ZTS) — Komarno** Yd No: 1939 Loa 113.92 Br ex 13.18 Dght 3.640 Lbp 110.45 Br md 13.00 Dpth 5.50 Welded, 1 dk	**(A31A2GX) General Cargo Ship** Grain: 4,750	**2 oil engines** driving 2 FP propellers Total Power: 1,030kW (1,400hp) 10.0kn Skoda 6L275A2 2 x 4 Stroke 6 Cy. 275 x 350 each-515kW (700bhp) Skoda-Praha AuxGen: 2 x 100kW a.c Fuel: 110.0 (d.f.)
8841632 *V4OE* -	**VOLGO-BALT 213** **Baltwave 213 Ltd** Orbital Ship Management Co *Basseterre* *St Kitts & Nevis* MMSI: 341367000	**2,516** 1,147 3,492	Class: RS (RR)	**1978-08 Zavody Tazkeho Strojarstva (ZTS) — Komarno** Yd No: 1943 Loa 114.00 Br ex 13.20 Dght 3.850 Lbp 107.55 Br md - Dpth 5.50 Welded, 1dk	**(A31A2GX) General Cargo Ship** Grain: 4,700	**2 oil engines** driving 2 FP propellers Total Power: 1,030kW (1,400hp) Skoda 6L275A2 2 x 4 Stroke 6 Cy. 275 x 350 each-515kW (700bhp) CKD Praha-Praha
8841644 *V4WD* -	**VOLGO-BALT 214** **Baltwave 214 Ltd** Albros Shipping & Trading Ltd Co (Albros Denizcilik ve Ticaret Ltd Sti) *Basseterre* *St Kitts & Nevis* MMSI: 341574000	**2,516** 1,147 3,492	Class: RS	**1978-09 Zavody Tazkeho Strojarstva (ZTS) — Komarno** Yd No: 1944 Loa 113.87 Br ex 13.23 Dght 3.850 Lbp 107.55 Br md 13.01 Dpth 5.50 Welded, 1 dk	**(A31A2GX) General Cargo Ship** Grain: 4,720 Compartments: 4 Ho, ER 4 Ha: 2 (19.7 x 9.5) (19.5 x 9.5)ER (18.8 x 9.5)	**2 oil engines** driving 2 FP propellers Total Power: 1,030kW (1,400hp) Skoda 6L275A2 2 x 4 Stroke 6 Cy. 275 x 350 each-515kW (700bhp) CKD Praha-Praha
8841656 *UDCK* -	**VOLGO-BALT 216** **Donmaster Shipping Co** Donmaster Co Ltd *St Petersburg* *Russia* MMSI: 273331200	**2,516** 1,263 3,187	Class: RS	**1978-11 Zavody Tazkeho Strojarstva (ZTS) — Komarno** Yd No: 1946 Loa 113.79 Br ex 13.23 Dght 3.630 Lbp 110.00 Br md 13.01 Dpth 5.50 Welded, 1 dk	**(A31A2GX) General Cargo Ship** Grain: 4,700	**2 oil engines** driving 2 FP propellers Total Power: 1,030kW (1,400hp) 10.8kn Skoda 6L275A2 2 x 4 Stroke 6 Cy. 275 x 350 each-515kW (700bhp) CKD Praha-Praha AuxGen: 2 x 100kW a.c, 1 x 50kW a.c Fuel: 110.0 (d.f.)
8230417 *V3RN3* -	**VOLGO-BALT 217** **Nordix Partners Ltd** - *Belize City* *Belize* Official number: 361320129	**2,516** 1,021 3,455	Class: (RS) (RR)	**1979-06 Zavody Tazkeho Strojarstva (ZTS) — Komarno** Yd No: 1947 Loa 113.85 Br ex 13.19 Dght 3.860 Lbp 110.52 Br md 13.00 Dpth 5.50 Welded, 1 dk	**(A31A2GX) General Cargo Ship** Grain: 4,720 Compartments: 4 Ho, ER 4 Ha: (18.2 x 9.5)3 (19.5 x 9.5)ER Ice Capable	**2 oil engines** driving 2 FP propellers Total Power: 1,030kW (1,400hp) 10.8kn Skoda 6L275A2 2 x 4 Stroke 6 Cy. 275 x 350 each-515kW (700bhp) Skoda-Praha Fuel: 120.0 (d.f.)
8728074 *ENDS*	**VOLGO-BALT 218** **Kherson Port Authority** - *Ukraine* MMSI: 272027000	**2,516** 959 2,893	Class: RR	**1979-01 Zavody Tazkeho Strojarstva (ZTS) — Komarno** Yd No: 1948 Loa 113.85 Br ex 13.19 Dght 3.530 Lbp 110.52 Br md - Dpth 5.50 Welded, 1 dk	**(A31A2GX) General Cargo Ship** Grain: 4,720 Compartments: 4 Ho, ER 4 Ha: (18.2 x 9.5)3 (19.5 x 9.5)ER	**2 oil engines** driving 2 FP propellers Total Power: 1,030kW (1,400hp) 10.8kn Skoda 6L275A2 2 x 4 Stroke 6 Cy. 275 x 350 each-515kW (700bhp) CKD Praha-Praha
8841357 *V4WB* -	**VOLGO-BALT 219** **Baltwave 219 Ltd** Navicor Ltd *Basseterre* *St Kitts & Nevis* MMSI: 341572000 Official number: SKN 1001572	**2,457** 1,010 3,180	Class: (RS) (RR)	**1979-10 Zavody Tazkeho Strojarstva (ZTS) — Komarno** Yd No: 1950 Loa 114.00 Br ex 13.20 Dght 3.640 Lbp 110.00 Br md 13.00 Dpth 5.50 Welded, 1 dk	**(A31A2GX) General Cargo Ship** Grain: 4,700	**2 oil engines** driving 2 FP propellers Total Power: 1,030kW (1,400hp) Skoda 6L275A2 2 x 4 Stroke 6 Cy. 275 x 350 each-515kW (700bhp) CKD Praha-Praha
8841668 *V3QF6* -	**VOLGO-BALT 220** **DelMare Ltd** Drybulk Denizcilik Hizmetleri ve Ticaret Ltd Sti (Drybulk Shipping & Trading Co Ltd) *Belize City* *Belize* MMSI: 312794000 Official number: 141120216	**2,516** 1,021 3,187	Class: RS	**1979-07 Zavody Tazkeho Strojarstva (ZTS) — Komarno** Yd No: 1951 Loa 114.00 Br ex 13.20 Dght 3.640 Lbp 107.43 Br md 13.00 Dpth 5.50 Welded, 1 dk	**(A31A2GX) General Cargo Ship** Grain: 4,720 Compartments: 4 Ho, ER 4 Ha: (18.6 x 9.5) (19.5 x 9.5)2 (19.7 x 9.5)ER	**2 oil engines** driving 2 FP propellers Total Power: 1,030kW (1,400hp) 10.0kn Skoda 6L275A2 2 x 4 Stroke 6 Cy. 275 x 350 each-515kW (700bhp) CKD Praha-Praha AuxGen: 2 x 80kW a.c Fuel: 110.0 (d.f.)
8841711 *V4BF2* -	**VOLGO-BALT 226** **Azov 226 Shipping Co Ltd** Orbital Ship Management Co *Basseterre* *St Kitts & Nevis* MMSI: 341740000 Official number: SKN 1002021	**2,516** 1,147 3,187	Class: (RS) (RR)	**1980-10 Zavody Tazkeho Strojarstva (ZTS) — Komarno** Yd No: 1957 Loa 114.00 Br ex 13.20 Dght 3.640 Lbp 107.43 Br md - Dpth 5.50 Welded, 1 dk	**(A31A2GX) General Cargo Ship** Grain: 4,700	**2 oil engines** driving 2 FP propellers Total Power: 1,030kW (1,400hp) Skoda 6L275A2 2 x 4 Stroke 6 Cy. 275 x 350 each-515kW (700bhp) CKD Praha-Praha
8841723 *XUAH5*	**VOLGO-BALT 227** **Primavera Marine Co** Orbital Ship Management Co *Phnom Penh* *Cambodia* MMSI: 514337000 Official number: 0980460	**2,516** 1,021 3,180	Class: RS (RR)	**1980-11 Zavody Tazkeho Strojarstva (ZTS) — Komarno** Yd No: 1958 Loa 113.87 Br ex 13.23 Dght 3.640 Lbp 110.00 Br md 13.01 Dpth 5.50 Welded, 1 dk	**(A31A2GX) General Cargo Ship** Grain: 4,700	**2 oil engines** driving 2 FP propellers Total Power: 1,030kW (1,400hp) Skoda 6L275A2 2 x 4 Stroke 6 Cy. 275 x 350 each-515kW (700bhp) CKD Praha-Praha
8841747 *UHZF* -	**VOLGO-BALT 229** **Transintershipping Co Ltd** CJSC 'Onegoship' *St Petersburg* *Russia* MMSI: 273336300 Official number: 803843	**2,516** 1,021 3,180	Class: RS (RR)	**1981-07 Zavody Tazkeho Strojarstva (ZTS) — Komarno** Yd No: 1960 Loa 113.87 Br ex 13.02 Dght 3.640 Lbp 107.35 Br md 13.00 Dpth 5.50 Welded, 1 dk	**(A31A2GX) General Cargo Ship** Grain: 4,700 Ice Capable	**2 oil engines** driving 2 FP propellers Total Power: 1,030kW (1,400hp) 10.0kn Skoda 6L275A2 2 x 4 Stroke 6 Cy. 275 x 350 each-515kW (700bhp) CKD Praha-Praha AuxGen: 2 x 80kW a.c

Identity	Name / Owner	Tonnage / Class	Builder / Dimensions	Type / Capacity	Machinery
8230443 *UHZC* -	**VOLGO-BALT 230** **CJSC 'Farvater'** CJSC 'Onegoship' *St Petersburg* *Russia* MMSI: 273337300	**2,516** Class: RS (RR) 1,021 3,180	1981-03 **Zavody Tazkeho Strojarstva (ZTS) — Komarno** Yd No: 1961 Loa 114.00 Br ex 13.23 Dght 3.640 Lbp 110.52 Br md 13.01 Dpth 5.50 Welded, 1 dk	**(A31A2GX) General Cargo Ship** Grain: 4,720 Compartments: 4 Ho, ER 4 Ha: (18.6 x 11.2)2 (18.8 x 11.2) (20.3 x 11.2)ER	**2 oil engines** driving 2 FP propellers Total Power: 1,030kW (1,400hp) 10.0kr Skoda 6L275A2 2 x 4 Stroke 6 Cy. 275 x 350 each-515kW (700bhp) CKD Praha-Praha Fuel: 110.0 (d.f.)
8230455 *UHZZ* -	**VOLGO-BALT 231** **CJSC 'Farvater'** Alien Shipping Ltd SatCom: Inmarsat C 427300891 *St Petersburg* *Russia* MMSI: 273338300 Official number: 811322	**2,516** Class: RS (RR) 1,021 3,180	1981-07 **Zavody Tazkeho Strojarstva (ZTS) — Komarno** Yd No: 1962 Loa 114.00 Br ex 13.23 Dght 3.640 Lbp 110.52 Br md 13.01 Dpth 5.50 Welded, 1 dk	**(A31A2GX) General Cargo Ship** Grain: 4,720 Compartments: 4 Ho, ER 4 Ha: (18.6 x 11.2)2 (18.8 x 11.2) (20.3 x 11.2)ER	**2 oil engines** driving 2 FP propellers Total Power: 1,030kW (1,400hp) 10.0kn Skoda 6L275A2 2 x 4 Stroke 6 Cy. 275 x 350 each-515kW (700bhp) Skoda-Praha Fuel: 110.0 (d.f.)
8230467 *UHYP* -	**VOLGO-BALT 232** **Donmaster Co Ltd** - *Taganrog* *Russia* MMSI: 273339300 Official number: 811337	**2,600** Class: RS (RR) 1,087 3,208	1981-07 **Zavody Tazkeho Strojarstva (ZTS) — Komarno** Yd No: 1963 Loa 114.00 Br ex 13.23 Dght 3.640 Lbp 110.52 Br md 13.01 Dpth 5.50 Welded, 1 dk	**(A31A2GX) General Cargo Ship** Grain: 4,720 Compartments: 4 Ho, ER 4 Ha: (18.6 x 11.2)2 (18.8 x 11.2) (20.3 x 11.2)ER	**2 oil engines** driving 2 FP propellers Total Power: 1,030kW (1,400hp) 10.0kn Skoda 6L275A2 2 x 4 Stroke 6 Cy. 275 x 350 each-515kW (700bhp) CKD Praha-Praha Fuel: 110.0 (d.f.)
8230493 *V4DU2* -	**VOLGO-BALT 235** **Azov 235 Co** Orbital Ship Management Co *Basseterre* *St Kitts & Nevis* MMSI: 341977000	**2,516** Class: RS (RR) 1,147 3,187	1981-03 **Zavody Tazkeho Strojarstva (ZTS) — Komarno** Yd No: 1966 Loa 114.00 Br ex 13.23 Dght 3.640 Lbp 110.52 Br md 13.01 Dpth 5.50 Welded, 1 dk	**(A31A2GX) General Cargo Ship** Grain: 4,720 Compartments: 4 Ho, ER 4 Ha: (18.6 x 11.2)2 (18.8 x 11.2) (20.3 x 11.2)ER Ice Capable	**2 oil engines** driving 2 FP propellers Total Power: 1,030kW (1,400hp) 10.0kn Skoda 6L275IIIPN 2 x 4 Stroke 6 Cy. 275 x 350 each-515kW (700bhp) Skoda-Praha AuxGen: 2 x 80kW a.c Fuel: 110.0 (d.f.)
8230508 *V3OT3* -	**VOLGO-BALT 236** **Ivory Bay Ltd** AzimutTrans Ltd SatCom: Inmarsat C 431280911 *Belize City* *Belize* MMSI: 312809000 Official number: 141120207	**2,516** Class: RS (RR) 1,021 3,209	1982-03 **Zavody Tazkeho Strojarstva (ZTS) — Komarno** Yd No: 1967 Loa 114.00 Br ex 13.26 Dght 3.640 Lbp 107.43 Br md 13.00 Dpth 5.50 Welded, 1 dk	**(A31A2GX) General Cargo Ship** Grain: 4,720 Compartments: 4 Ho, ER 4 Ha: (18.6 x 11.2)2 (18.8 x 11.2) (20.3 x 11.2)ER	**2 oil engines** driving 2 FP propellers Total Power: 1,030kW (1,400hp) 10.0kn Skoda 6L275A2 2 x 4 Stroke 6 Cy. 275 x 350 each-515kW (700bhp) Skoda-Praha Fuel: 110.0 (d.f.)
8230510 *UIBV* -	**VOLGO-BALT 237** **Pallada JSC** AzimutTrans Ltd *St Petersburg* *Russia* MMSI: 273339800 Official number: 811375	**2,516** Class: RS (RR) 1,021 3,210	1983-06 **Zavody Tazkeho Strojarstva (ZTS) — Komarno** Yd No: 1968 Loa 114.00 Br ex 13.23 Dght 3.640 Lbp 110.52 Br md 13.01 Dpth 5.50 Welded, 1 dk	**(A31A2GX) General Cargo Ship** Grain: 4,720 Compartments: 4 Ho, ER 4 Ha: (18.6 x 11.2)2 (18.8 x 11.2) (20.3 x 11.2)ER	**2 oil engines** driving 2 FP propellers Total Power: 1,030kW (1,400hp) 10.0kn Skoda 6L275A2 2 x 4 Stroke 6 Cy. 275 x 350 each-515kW (700bhp) Skoda-Praha Fuel: 110.0 (d.f.)
8230534 *XUGH4* -	**VOLGO-BALT 239** **Vikaria SA** Private Enterprise 'Valship' *Phnom Penh* *Cambodia* MMSI: 515927296	**2,600** Class: RS (RR) 1,093 3,510	1982-03 **Zavody Tazkeho Strojarstva (ZTS) — Komarno** Yd No: 1970 Loa 114.00 Br ex 13.23 Dght 3.860 Lbp 110.00 Br md 13.01 Dpth 5.50 Welded, 1 dk	**(A31A2GX) General Cargo Ship** Grain: 4,720 Compartments: 4 Ho, ER 4 Ha: (18.6 x 11.2)2 (18.8 x 11.2) (20.3 x 11.2)ER	**2 oil engines** driving 2 FP propellers Total Power: 1,030kW (1,400hp) 10.0kn Skoda 6L275A2 2 x 4 Stroke 6 Cy. 275 x 350 each-515kW (700bhp) Skoda-Praha Fuel: 110.0 (d.f.)
8230546 *UDCN* -	**VOLGO-BALT 240** **Donmaster Co Ltd** - *Taganrog* *Russia* MMSI: 273334200 Official number: 821377	**2,600** Class: RS (RR) 1,093 3,217	1982-03 **Zavody Tazkeho Strojarstva (ZTS) — Komarno** Yd No: 1971 Loa 114.00 Br ex 13.23 Dght 3.640 Lbp 110.52 Br md 13.01 Dpth 5.50 Welded, 1 dk	**(A31A2GX) General Cargo Ship** Grain: 4,720 Compartments: 4 Ho, ER 4 Ha: (18.6 x 11.2)2 (18.8 x 11.2) (20.3 x 11.2)ER	**2 oil engines** driving 2 FP propellers Total Power: 1,030kW (1,400hp) 10.0kn Skoda 6L275A2 2 x 4 Stroke 6 Cy. 275 x 350 each-515kW (700bhp) Skoda-Praha Fuel: 123.0 (d.f.)
8230558 *V3ML5* -	**VOLGO-BALT 241** **River Shipping & Trading Corp** OOO 'VolgaComFlot' *Belize City* *Belize* MMSI: 312152000 Official number: 370920050	**2,516** Class: RS (RR) 1,021 3,150	1983 **Zavody Tazkeho Strojarstva (ZTS) — Komarno** Yd No: 1972 Loa 113.86 Br ex 13.19 Dght 3.640 Lbp 110.52 Br md 13.00 Dpth 5.50 Welded, 1 dk	**(A31A2GX) General Cargo Ship** Grain: 4,720 Compartments: 4 Ho, ER 4 Ha: (18.2 x 9.5)3 (19.5 x 9.5)ER	**2 oil engines** driving 2 FP propellers Total Power: 1,030kW (1,400hp) 9.6kn Skoda 6L275A2 2 x 4 Stroke 6 Cy. 275 x 350 each-515kW (700bhp) Skoda-Praha AuxGen: 2 x 80kW a.c Fuel: 123.0 (d.f.)
8230560 *ERQF* -	**VOLGO-BALT 242** **Sea Logistics International Ltd** Black Sea Azov-Service Ltd *Giurgiulesti* *Moldova* MMSI: 214181706	**2,894** Class: RS (RR) 1,661 3,472	1982-03 **Zavody Tazkeho Strojarstva (ZTS) — Komarno** Yd No: 1973 Loa 113.86 Br ex 13.19 Dght 3.860 Lbp 110.52 Br md 13.00 Dpth 5.50 Welded, 1 dk	**(A31A2GX) General Cargo Ship** Grain: 4,720 Compartments: 4 Ho, ER 4 Ha: (18.2 x 9.5)3 (19.5 x 9.5)ER	**2 oil engines** driving 2 FP propellers Total Power: 1,030kW (1,400hp) 10.8kn Skoda 6L275A2 2 x 4 Stroke 6 Cy. 275 x 350 each-515kW (700bhp) Skoda-Praha Fuel: 123.0 (d.f.)
8230584 *UAKW* -	**VOLGO-BALT 244** **Western Shipping Co JSC (OAO Zapadnoye Parokhodstvo - 'ZAPADFLOT')** - *Kaliningrad* *Russia* MMSI: 273327100 Official number: 821317	**2,457** Class: RS (RR) 1,010 3,248	1983-01 **Zavody Tazkeho Strojarstva (ZTS) — Komarno** Yd No: 1975 Loa 114.00 Br ex 13.23 Dght 3.630 Lbp 107.20 Br md 13.01 Dpth 5.50 Welded, 1 dk	**(A31A2GX) General Cargo Ship** Grain: 4,720 Compartments: 4 Ho, ER 4 Ha: (18.6 x 11.2)2 (18.8 x 11.2) (20.3 x 11.2)ER Ice Capable	**2 oil engines** driving 2 FP propellers Total Power: 1,030kW (1,400hp) 10.8kn Skoda 6L275A2 2 x 4 Stroke 6 Cy. 275 x 350 each-515kW (700bhp) Skoda-Praha Fuel: 110.0 (d.f.)
8230596 *UIDG* -	**VOLGO-BALT 245** **CJSC 'Farvater'** Alien Shipping Ltd *St Petersburg* *Russia* MMSI: 273331900	**2,516** Class: RS (RR) 1,021 3,180	1983-07 **Zavody Tazkeho Strojarstva (ZTS) — Komarno** Yd No: 1976 Loa 114.00 Br ex 13.23 Dght 3.640 Lbp 110.52 Br md 13.01 Dpth 5.50 Welded, 1 dk	**(A31A2GX) General Cargo Ship** Grain: 4,720	**2 oil engines** driving 2 FP propellers Total Power: 1,030kW (1,400hp) 10.0kn Skoda 6L275A2 2 x 4 Stroke 6 Cy. 275 x 350 each-515kW (700bhp) Skoda-Praha Fuel: 110.0 (d.f.)
8728050 *UCZA* -	**VOLGO-BALT 246** **JSC Northern River Shipping Lines** Mellord SA *Arkhangelsk* *Russia* MMSI: 273362100 Official number: 802677	**2,600** Class: RS (RR) 1,087 3,171	1983-05 **Zavody Tazkeho Strojarstva (ZTS) — Komarno** Yd No: 1977 Loa 113.00 Br ex 13.19 Dght 3.640 Lbp 110.57 Br md 13.00 Dpth 5.50 Welded, 1 dk	**(A31A2GX) General Cargo Ship** Grain: 4,720 Compartments: 4 Ho, ER 4 Ha: (18.0 x 9.2)2 (19.0 x 9.2) (18.8 x 9.2)ER	**2 oil engines** driving 2 FP propellers Total Power: 1,030kW (1,400hp) 10.8kn Skoda 6L275A2 2 x 4 Stroke 6 Cy. 275 x 350 each-515kW (700bhp) CKD Praha-Praha
8728024 *V3MH6* -	**VOLGO-BALT 248** **Stradon Foreign Trade SA** Valmar Oil Ltd *Belize City* *Belize* MMSI: 312128000 Official number: 370920053	**2,516** Class: RS (RR) 1,021 3,193	1984-01 **Zavody Tazkeho Strojarstva (ZTS) — Komarno** Yd No: 1979 Loa 113.85 Br ex 13.19 Dght 3.640 Lbp 110.52 Br md 13.00 Dpth 5.50 Welded, 1 dk	**(A31A2GX) General Cargo Ship** Grain: 4,720 Compartments: 4 Ho, ER 4 Ha: (18.2 x 9.5)3 (19.5 x 9.5)ER	**2 oil engines** driving 2 FP propellers Total Power: 1,030kW (1,400hp) 10.8kn Skoda 6L275A2 2 x 4 Stroke 6 Cy. 275 x 350 each-515kW (700bhp) CKD Praha-Praha Fuel: 120.0 (d.f.)
8863329 *UGBW* -	**VOLGO-DON 80** **JSC Volga Shipping (OAO Sudokhodnaya Kompaniya 'Volzhskoye Parokhodstvo')** - *Nizhniy Novgorod* *Russia* MMSI: 273377600 Official number: V-05-934	**3,904** Class: RR 1,663 5,150	1967 **Navashinskiy Sudostroitelnyy Zavod 'Oka' — Navashino** Yd No: 1004 Loa 138.30 Br ex 16.70 Dght 3.430 Lbp 135.00 Br md 16.50 Dpth 5.50 Welded, 1 dk	**(A31A2GX) General Cargo Ship** Grain: 6,270 Compartments: 2 Ho, ER 2 Ha: (44.4 x 13.1) (44.4 x 13.0)ER	**2 oil engines** driving 2 FP propellers Total Power: 1,324kW (1,800hp) 10.0kn Dvigatel Revolyutsii 6CHRN36/45 2 x 4 Stroke 6 Cy. 360 x 450 each-662kW (900bhp) Zavod "Dvigatel Revolyutsii"-Gorkiy AuxGen: 2 x 110kW a.c Fuel: 122.0 (d.f.)
8960177 *UGBY* -	**VOLGO-DON 85** **JSC Volga Shipping (OAO Sudokhodnaya Kompaniya 'Volzhskoye Parokhodstvo')** - *Volzhskiy* *Russia* MMSI: 273379600 Official number: V-04-430	**3,904** Class: RR 1,663 5,150	1967 **Navashinskiy Sudostroitelnyy Zavod 'Oka' — Navashino** Yd No: 1005 Loa 138.30 Br ex 16.70 Dght 3.430 Lbp 135.00 Br md 16.50 Dpth 5.50 Welded, 1 dk	**(A31A2GX) General Cargo Ship** Grain: 6,270	**2 oil engines** driving 2 FP propellers Total Power: 1,324kW (1,800hp) 10.0kn Dvigatel Revolyutsii 6CHRN36/45 2 x 4 Stroke 6 Cy. 360 x 450 each-662kW (900bhp) Zavod "Dvigatel Revolyutsii"-Gorkiy

IMO / Call sign	Ship / Owner / Port	Tonnage	Class	Built / Dimensions	Type / Capacity	Machinery
960189	**VOLGO-DON 90** **JSC Volga Shipping (OAO Sudokhodnaya Kompaniya 'Volzhskoye Parokhodstvo')** - *Volzhskiy* *Russia*	**3,904** 1,663 5,162	Class: RR	**1967 Navashinskiy Sudostroitelnyy Zavod 'Oka' — Navashino** Loa 138.30 Br ex - Dght 3.430 Lbp - Br md 16.70 Dpth 5.50 Welded, 1 dk	**(A31A2GX) General Cargo Ship** Grain: 6,270	**2 oil engines** driving 2 Propellers Total Power: 1,324kW (1,800hp) 10.0kn Dvigatel Revolyutsii 6CHRN36/45 2 x 4 Stroke 6 Cy. 360 x 450 each-662kW (900bhp) Zavod "Dvigatel Revolyutsii"-Gorkiy
960191	**VOLGO-DON 95** **JSC Volga Shipping (OAO Sudokhodnaya Kompaniya 'Volzhskoye Parokhodstvo')** - *Nizhniy Novgorod* *Russia* MMSI: 273332820 Official number: V-11-3614	**3,904** 1,663 5,150	Class: RR	**1968 Navashinskiy Sudostroitelnyy Zavod 'Oka' — Navashino** Yd No: 1007 Loa 138.30 Br ex 16.70 Dght 3.430 Lbp 135.00 Br md 16.50 Dpth 5.50 Welded, 1 dk	**(A31A2GX) General Cargo Ship** Grain: 6,270	**2 oil engines** driving 2 FP propellers Total Power: 1,324kW (1,800hp) 10.0kn Dvigatel Revolyutsii 6CHRN36/45 2 x 4 Stroke 6 Cy. 360 x 450 each-662kW (900bhp) Zavod "Dvigatel Revolyutsii"-Gorkiy
8960206	**VOLGO-DON 97** **JSC Volga Shipping (OAO Sudokhodnaya Kompaniya 'Volzhskoye Parokhodstvo')** - *Volzhskiy* *Russia*	**3,904** 1,663 5,162	Class: RR	**1968 Navashinskiy Sudostroitelnyy Zavod 'Oka' — Navashino** Loa 138.80 Br ex - Dght 3.000 Lbp - Br md 16.70 Dpth 5.50 Welded, 1 dk	**(A31A2GX) General Cargo Ship** Grain: 6,270	**2 oil engines** driving 2 Propellers Total Power: 1,324kW (1,800hp) 10.0kn Dvigatel Revolyutsii 6CHRN36/45 2 x 4 Stroke 6 Cy. 360 x 450 each-662kW (900bhp) Zavod "Dvigatel Revolyutsii"-Gorkiy
8960218 -	**VOLGO-DON 99** **JSC Volga Shipping (OAO Sudokhodnaya Kompaniya 'Volzhskoye Parokhodstvo')** - *Volzhskiy* *Russia*	**3,904** 1,663 5,162	Class: RR	**1968 Navashinskiy Sudostroitelnyy Zavod 'Oka' — Navashino** Loa 138.80 Br ex - Dght 3.000 Lbp - Br md 16.70 Dpth 5.50 Welded, 1 dk	**(A31A2GX) General Cargo Ship** Grain: 6,270	**2 oil engines** driving 2 Propellers Total Power: 1,324kW (1,800hp) 10.0kn Dvigatel Revolyutsii 6CHRN36/45 2 x 4 Stroke 6 Cy. 360 x 450 each-662kW (900bhp) Zavod "Dvigatel Revolyutsii"-Gorkiy
8956190 -	**VOLGO-DON 101** **JSC Volga Shipping (OAO Sudokhodnaya Kompaniya 'Volzhskoye Parokhodstvo')** - SatCom: Inmarsat C 427330484 *Nizhniy Novgorod* *Russia* MMSI: 273370600 Official number: V-04-432	**3,904** 1,663 5,150	Class: RR	**1968 Navashinskiy Sudostroitelnyy Zavod 'Oka' — Navashino** Yd No: 1012 Loa 138.30 Br ex 16.70 Dght 3.430 Lbp 135.00 Br md 16.50 Dpth 5.50 Welded, 1 dk	**(A31A2GX) General Cargo Ship** Grain: 6,270 Compartments: 2 Ho, ER 2 Ha: 2 (44.4 x 13.1)ER	**2 oil engines** driving 2 FP propellers Total Power: 1,324kW (1,800hp) 10.0kn Dvigatel Revolyutsii 6CHRN36/45 2 x 4 Stroke 6 Cy. 360 x 450 each-662kW (900bhp) Zavod "Dvigatel Revolyutsii"-Gorkiy AuxGen: 2 x 110kW Fuel: 122.0 (d.f.)
8956205 UGBZ	**VOLGO-DON 103** **JSC Volga Shipping (OAO Sudokhodnaya Kompaniya 'Volzhskoye Parokhodstvo')** - *Nizhniy Novgorod* *Russia* MMSI: 273370700 Official number: V-04-433	**3,904** 1,663 5,150	Class: RR	**1969 Navashinskiy Sudostroitelnyy Zavod 'Oka' — Navashino** Yd No: 1013 Loa 138.30 Br ex 16.70 Dght 3.430 Lbp 135.00 Br md 16.50 Dpth 5.50 Welded, 1 dk	**(A31A2GX) General Cargo Ship** Grain: 6,270 Compartments: 2 Ho, ER 2 Ha: 2 (44.4 x 13.1)ER	**2 oil engines** driving 2 FP propellers Total Power: 1,324kW (1,800hp) 10.0kn Dvigatel Revolyutsii 6CHRN36/45 2 x 4 Stroke 6 Cy. 360 x 450 each-662kW (900bhp) Zavod "Dvigatel Revolyutsii"-Gorkiy AuxGen: 2 x 110kW Fuel: 122.0 (d.f.)
8956231 UAGZ5 -	**VOLGO-DON 109** **JSC Volga Shipping (OAO Sudokhodnaya Kompaniya 'Volzhskoye Parokhodstvo')** - SatCom: Inmarsat C 427330486 *St Petersburg* *Russia* MMSI: 273347310 Official number: V-04-434	**3,904** 1,663 5,150	Class: RR	**1969 Navashinskiy Sudostroitelnyy Zavod 'Oka' — Navashino** Yd No: 1015 Loa 138.30 Br ex 16.70 Dght 3.430 Lbp 135.00 Br md 16.50 Dpth 5.50 Welded, 1 dk	**(A31A2GX) General Cargo Ship** Grain: 6,270 Compartments: 2 Ho, ER 2 Ha: 2 (44.4 x 13.1)ER	**2 oil engines** driving 2 FP propellers Total Power: 1,324kW (1,800hp) 10.0kn Dvigatel Revolyutsii 6CHRN36/45 2 x 4 Stroke 6 Cy. 360 x 450 each-662kW (900bhp) Zavod "Dvigatel Revolyutsii"-Gorkiy AuxGen: 2 x 110kW Fuel: 122.0 (d.f.)
8956243 UAVC6 -	**VOLGO-DON 111** **VF Cargo Transportation Ltd** JSC Volga Shipping (OAO Sudokhodnaya Kompaniya 'Volzhskoye Parokhodstvo') *St Petersburg* *Russia* MMSI: 273430580 Official number: V-05-945	*3,904* 1,663 5,150	Class: RR	**1969 Navashinskiy Sudostroitelnyy Zavod 'Oka' — Navashino** Yd No: 1016 Loa 138.30 Br ex 16.70 Dght 3.430 Lbp 135.00 Br md 16.50 Dpth 5.50 Welded, 1 dk	**(A31A2GX) General Cargo Ship** Grain: 6,270 Compartments: 2 Ho, ER 2 Ha: 2 (44.4 x 13.1)ER	**2 oil engines** driving 2 FP propellers Total Power: 1,324kW (1,800hp) 10.0kn Dvigatel Revolyutsii 6CHRN36/45 2 x 4 Stroke 6 Cy. 360 x 450 each-662kW (900bhp) Zavod "Dvigatel Revolyutsii"-Gorkiy AuxGen: 2 x 110kW Fuel: 122.0 (d.f.)
8959984 UAWC2 -	**VOLGO-DON 121** **JSC Volga Shipping (OAO Sudokhodnaya Kompaniya 'Volzhskoye Parokhodstvo')** - *Nizhniy Novgorod* *Russia* MMSI: 273431580 Official number: V-04-856	*3,904* 1,663 5,150	Class: RR	**1970 Navashinskiy Sudostroitelnyy Zavod 'Oka' — Navashino** Yd No: 1021 Loa 138.30 Br ex 16.70 Dght 3.430 Lbp 135.00 Br md 16.50 Dpth 5.50 Welded, 1 dk	**(A31A2GX) General Cargo Ship** Grain: 6,270 Compartments: 2 Ho, ER 2 Ha: 2 (44.4 x 13.1)ER	**2 oil engines** driving 2 FP propellers Total Power: 1,324kW (1,800hp) 10.0kn Dvigatel Revolyutsii 6CHRN36/45 2 x 4 Stroke 6 Cy. 360 x 450 each-662kW (900bhp) Zavod "Dvigatel Revolyutsii"-Gorkiy AuxGen: 2 x 110kW a.c Fuel: 122.0 (d.f.)
8959996 UAWC3 -	**VOLGO-DON 123** **JSC Volga Shipping (OAO Sudokhodnaya Kompaniya 'Volzhskoye Parokhodstvo')** - *Nizhniy Novgorod* *Russia* MMSI: 273432580 Official number: V-04-852	*3,904* 1,663 5,150	Class: RR	**1970 Navashinskiy Sudostroitelnyy Zavod 'Oka' — Navashino** Yd No: 1022 Loa 138.30 Br ex 16.70 Dght 3.430 Lbp 135.00 Br md 16.50 Dpth 5.50 Welded, 1 dk	**(A31A2GX) General Cargo Ship** Grain: 6,270 Compartments: 2 Ho, ER 2 Ha: 2 (44.4 x 13.1)ER	**2 oil engines** driving 2 FP propellers Total Power: 1,324kW (1,800hp) 10.0kn Dvigatel Revolyutsii 6CHRN36/45 2 x 4 Stroke 6 Cy. 360 x 450 each-662kW (900bhp) Zavod "Dvigatel Revolyutsii"-Gorkiy AuxGen: 2 x 110kW a.c Fuel: 122.0 (d.f.)
8960024 - -	**VOLGO-DON 131** **JSC Volga Shipping (OAO Sudokhodnaya Kompaniya 'Volzhskoye Parokhodstvo')** - SatCom: Inmarsat C 427330487 *Nizhniy Novgorod* *Russia* MMSI: 273440350 Official number: V-04-855	**3,904** 1,663 5,150	Class: RR	**1970 Navashinskiy Sudostroitelnyy Zavod 'Oka' — Navashino** Yd No: 1026 Loa 138.30 Br ex 16.70 Dght 3.430 Lbp - Br md 16.50 Dpth 5.50 Welded, 1 dk	**(A31A2GX) General Cargo Ship** Grain: 6,270 Compartments: 2 Ho, ER 2 Ha: 2 (44.4 x 13.1)ER	**2 oil engines** driving 2 FP propellers Total Power: 1,324kW (1,800hp) 10.0kn Dvigatel Revolyutsii 6CHRN36/45 2 x 4 Stroke 6 Cy. 360 x 450 each-662kW (900bhp) Zavod "Dvigatel Revolyutsii"-Gorkiy AuxGen: 2 x 110kW a.c Fuel: 122.0 (d.f.)
8938318 - -	**VOLGO-DON 133** **JSC Volga Shipping (OAO Sudokhodnaya Kompaniya 'Volzhskoye Parokhodstvo')** - SatCom: Inmarsat C 427330488 *Nizhniy Novgorod* *Russia* MMSI: 273348210 Official number: V-04-853	**3,904** 1,663 5,150	Class: RR	**1971 Navashinskiy Sudostroitelnyy Zavod 'Oka' — Navashino** Yd No: 1027 Loa 138.30 Br ex 16.70 Dght 3.430 Lbp 135.00 Br md 16.50 Dpth 5.50 Welded, 1 dk	**(A31A2GX) General Cargo Ship** Grain: 6,270 Compartments: 2 Ho, ER 2 Ha: 2 (44.4 x 13.1)ER	**2 oil engines** driving 2 FP propellers Total Power: 1,324kW (1,800hp) 10.0kn Dvigatel Revolyutsii 6CHRN36/45 2 x 4 Stroke 6 Cy. 360 x 450 each-662kW (900bhp) Zavod "Dvigatel Revolyutsii"-Gorkiy AuxGen: 2 x 110kW a.c Fuel: 122.0 (d.f.)
8960036 - -	**VOLGO-DON 135** **JSC Volga Shipping (OAO Sudokhodnaya Kompaniya 'Volzhskoye Parokhodstvo')** - SatCom: Inmarsat C 427322723 *Nizhniy Novgorod* *Russia* MMSI: 273342210 Official number: V-05- 863	**3,904** 1,663 5,150	Class: RR	**1971 Navashinskiy Sudostroitelnyy Zavod 'Oka' — Navashino** Yd No: 1028 Loa 138.30 Br ex 16.70 Dght 3.430 Lbp 135.00 Br md 16.50 Dpth 5.50 Welded, 1 dk	**(A31A2GX) General Cargo Ship** Grain: 6,270 Compartments: 2 Ho, ER 2 Ha: 2 (44.4 x 13.1)ER	**2 oil engines** driving 2 FP propellers Total Power: 1,324kW (1,800hp) 10.0kn Dvigatel Revolyutsii 6CHRN36/45 2 x 4 Stroke 6 Cy. 360 x 450 each-662kW (900bhp) Zavod "Dvigatel Revolyutsii"-Gorkiy AuxGen: 2 x 110kW a.c Fuel: 122.0 (d.f.)
8959661 - -	**VOLGO-DON 141** **VF Cargo Transportation Ltd** JSC Volga Shipping (OAO Sudokhodnaya Kompaniya 'Volzhskoye Parokhodstvo') SatCom: Inmarsat C 427350917 *Nizhniy Novgorod* *Russia* MMSI: 273359840 Official number: V-05-864	*3,904* 1,663 5,150	Class: RR	**1971 Navashinskiy Sudostroitelnyy Zavod 'Oka' — Navashino** Yd No: 1031 Loa 138.30 Br ex 16.70 Dght 3.490 Lbp 135.00 Br md 16.50 Dpth 5.50 Welded, 1 dk	**(A31A2GX) General Cargo Ship** Grain: 6,270 Compartments: 2 Ho, ER 2 Ha: 2 (44.4 x 13.1)ER	**2 oil engines** driving 2 FP propellers Total Power: 1,324kW (1,800hp) 10.0kn Dvigatel Revolyutsii 6CHRN36/45 2 x 4 Stroke 6 Cy. 360 x 450 each-662kW (900bhp) Zavod "Dvigatel Revolyutsii"-Gorkiy AuxGen: 2 x 110kW a.c Fuel: 122.0 (d.f.)

IMO / Call sign	Name / Owner	Tonnage	Class	Built / Dimensions	Type	Machinery
8959673 - -	**VOLGO-DON 147** **JSC Volga Shipping (OAO Sudokhodnaya Kompaniya 'Volzhskoye Parokhodstvo')** - SatCom: Inmarsat C 427330489 *Nizhniy Novgorod* *Russia* MMSI: 273346210 Official number: V-05-938	**3,904** 1,663 5,150	Class: RR	**1972 Navashinskiy Sudostroitelnyy Zavod 'Oka' — Navashino** Yd No: 1034 Loa 138.30 Br ex 16.70 Dght 3.430 Lbp 135.00 Br md 16.50 Dpth 5.50 Welded, 1 dk	**(A31A2GX) General Cargo Ship** Grain: 6,270 Compartments: 2 Ho, ER 2 Ha: 2 (44.4 x 13.1)ER	**2 oil engines** driving 2 FP propellers Total Power: 1,324kW (1,800hp) 10.0k Dvigatel Revolyutsii 6CHRN36/4 2 x 4 Stroke 6 Cy. 360 x 450 each-662kW (900bhp) Zavod "Dvigatel Revolyutsii"-Gorkiy AuxGen: 2 x 110kW a.c Fuel: 122.0 (d.f.)
8959697 - -	**VOLGO-DON 153** **JSC Volga Shipping (OAO Sudokhodnaya Kompaniya 'Volzhskoye Parokhodstvo')** - SatCom: Inmarsat C 427330494 *Nizhniy Novgorod* *Russia* MMSI: 273341210 Official number: V-05-939	**3,904** 1,663 5,150	Class: RR	**1972 Navashinskiy Sudostroitelnyy Zavod 'Oka' — Navashino** Yd No: 1037 Loa 138.30 Br ex 16.70 Dght 3.430 Lbp 135.00 Br md 16.50 Dpth 5.50 Welded, 1 dk	**(A31A2GX) General Cargo Ship** Grain: 6,270 Compartments: 2 Ho, ER 2 Ha: 2 (44.4 x 13.1)ER	**2 oil engines** driving 2 FP propellers Total Power: 1,324kW (1,800hp) 10.0k Dvigatel Revolyutsii 6CHRN36/4 2 x 4 Stroke 6 Cy. 360 x 450 each-662kW (900bhp) Zavod "Dvigatel Revolyutsii"-Gorkiy AuxGen: 2 x 110kW a.c Fuel: 122.0 (d.f.)
8866008 *UAXC5* -	**VOLGO-DON 157** **JSC Volga Shipping (OAO Sudokhodnaya Kompaniya 'Volzhskoye Parokhodstvo')** - *Nizhniy Novgorod* *Russia* MMSI: 273350500 Official number: V-05-1021	*3,904* 1,663 5,150	Class: RR	**1973 Navashinskiy Sudostroitelnyy Zavod 'Oka' — Navashino** Yd No: 1094 Loa 138.30 Br ex 16.70 Dght 3.430 Lbp 135.00 Br md 16.50 Dpth 5.50 Welded, 1 dk	**(A31A2GX) General Cargo Ship** Grain: 6,270 Compartments: 2 Ho, ER 2 Ha: (44.4 x 13.1) (44.4 x 13.0)ER	**2 oil engines** driving 2 FP propellers Total Power: 1,324kW (1,800hp) 10.0k Dvigatel Revolyutsii 6CHRN36/4 2 x 4 Stroke 6 Cy. 360 x 450 each-662kW (900bhp) Zavod "Dvigatel Revolyutsii"-Gorkiy AuxGen: 2 x 110kW a.c Fuel: 122.0 (d.f.)
8959702 - -	**VOLGO-DON 159** **JSC Volga Shipping (OAO Sudokhodnaya Kompaniya 'Volzhskoye Parokhodstvo')** - SatCom: Inmarsat C 427330495 *Nizhniy Novgorod* *Russia* MMSI: 273344210 Official number: V-05-939	**3,904** 1,663 5,150	Class: RR	**1973 Navashinskiy Sudostroitelnyy Zavod 'Oka' — Navashino** Yd No: 1095 Loa 138.80 Br ex 16.70 Dght 3.430 Lbp - Br md 16.50 Dpth 5.50 Welded, 1 dk	**(A31A2GX) General Cargo Ship** Grain: 6,270 Compartments: 2 Ho, ER 2 Ha: (44.4 x 13.1) (44.4 x 13.0)ER	**2 oil engines** driving 2 FP propellers Total Power: 1,324kW (1,800hp) 10.0k Dvigatel Revolyutsii 6CHRN36/4 2 x 4 Stroke 6 Cy. 360 x 450 each-662kW (900bhp) Zavod "Dvigatel Revolyutsii"-Gorkiy AuxGen: 2 x 110kW a.c Fuel: 122.0 (d.f.)
8949422 - -	**VOLGO-DON 161** **JSC Volga Shipping (OAO Sudokhodnaya Kompaniya 'Volzhskoye Parokhodstvo')** - SatCom: Inmarsat C 427330496 *St Petersburg* *Russia* MMSI: 273441650 Official number: V-05-940	**3,904** 1,663 5,150	Class: RR	**1973 Navashinskiy Sudostroitelnyy Zavod 'Oka' — Navashino** Yd No: 1096 Loa 138.30 Br ex 16.70 Dght 3.430 Lbp 135.00 Br md 16.50 Dpth 5.50 Welded, 1 dk	**(A31A2GX) General Cargo Ship** Grain: 6,270 Compartments: 2 Ho, ER 2 Ha: 2 (44.4 x 13.1)ER	**2 oil engines** driving 2 FP propellers Total Power: 1,324kW (1,800hp) 10.0k Dvigatel Revolyutsii 6CHRN36/4 2 x 4 Stroke 6 Cy. 360 x 450 each-662kW (900bhp) Zavod "Dvigatel Revolyutsii"-Gorkiy AuxGen: 2 x 110kW Fuel: 122.0 (d.f.)
8959714 *UAXC7* -	**VOLGO-DON 163** **JSC Volga Shipping (OAO Sudokhodnaya Kompaniya 'Volzhskoye Parokhodstvo')** - *Nizhniy Novgorod* *Russia* MMSI: 273442650 Official number: V-05-947	**3,904** 1,663 5,150	Class: RR	**1973 Navashinskiy Sudostroitelnyy Zavod 'Oka' — Navashino** Yd No: 1097 Loa 138.80 Br ex 16.70 Dght 3.430 Lbp - Br md 16.50 Dpth 5.50 Welded, 1 dk	**(A31A2GX) General Cargo Ship** Grain: 6,270 Compartments: 2 Ho, ER 2 Ha: (44.4 x 13.1) (44.4 x 13.0)ER	**2 oil engines** driving 2 FP propellers Total Power: 1,324kW (1,800hp) 10.0k Dvigatel Revolyutsii 6CHRN36/4 2 x 4 Stroke 6 Cy. 360 x 450 each-662kW (900bhp) Zavod "Dvigatel Revolyutsii"-Gorkiy AuxGen: 2 x 110kW a.c Fuel: 122.0 (d.f.)
8959738 *UECG* -	**VOLGO-DON 169** **JSC Volga Shipping (OAO Sudokhodnaya Kompaniya 'Volzhskoye Parokhodstvo')** - *Nizhniy Novgorod* *Russia* MMSI: 273443910 Official number: V-06-1768	**3,904** 1,663 5,150	Class: RR	**1974 Navashinskiy Sudostroitelnyy Zavod 'Oka' — Navashino** Yd No: 1100 Loa 138.30 Br ex 16.70 Dght 3.430 Lbp 135.00 Br md 16.50 Dpth 5.50 Welded, 1 dk	**(A31A2GX) General Cargo Ship** Grain: 6,270 Compartments: 2 Ho, ER 2 Ha: 2 (44.4 x 13.1)ER	**2 oil engines** driving 2 FP propellers Total Power: 1,324kW (1,800hp) 10.0k Dvigatel Revolyutsii 6CHRN36/4 2 x 4 Stroke 6 Cy. 360 x 450 each-662kW (900bhp) Zavod "Dvigatel Revolyutsii"-Gorkiy AuxGen: 2 x 110kW a.c Fuel: 122.0 (d.f.)
8959740 *UGCC* -	**VOLGO-DON 171** **JSC Volga Shipping (OAO Sudokhodnaya Kompaniya 'Volzhskoye Parokhodstvo')** - SatCom: Inmarsat C 427330029 *Nizhniy Novgorod* *Russia* MMSI: 273372500 Official number: V-04-812	*3,904* 1,663 5,150	Class: RR	**1974 Navashinskiy Sudostroitelnyy Zavod 'Oka' — Navashino** Yd No: 1101 Loa 138.30 Br ex 16.70 Dght 3.430 Lbp 135.00 Br md 16.50 Dpth 5.50 Welded, 1 dk	**(A31A2GX) General Cargo Ship** Grain: 6,270 Compartments: 2 Ho, ER 2 Ha: 2 (44.4 x 13.1)ER	**2 oil engines** driving 2 FP propellers Total Power: 1,324kW (1,800hp) 10.0k Dvigatel Revolyutsii 6CHRN36/4 2 x 4 Stroke 6 Cy. 360 x 450 each-662kW (900bhp) Zavod "Dvigatel Revolyutsii"-Gorkiy AuxGen: 2 x 110kW a.c Fuel: 122.0 (d.f.)
8864024 - -	**VOLGO-DON 173** **JSC Volga Shipping (OAO Sudokhodnaya Kompaniya 'Volzhskoye Parokhodstvo')** - SatCom: Inmarsat C 427330499 *Nizhniy Novgorod* *Russia* MMSI: 273346310 Official number: V-05-944	**3,904** 1,663 5,150	Class: RR	**1974 Navashinskiy Sudostroitelnyy Zavod 'Oka' — Navashino** Yd No: 1102 Loa 138.80 Br ex 16.70 Dght 3.430 Lbp 135.00 Br md 16.50 Dpth 5.50 Welded, 1 dk	**(A31A2GX) General Cargo Ship** Grain: 6,270 Compartments: 2 Ho, ER 2 Ha: 2 (44.4 x 13.1)ER	**2 oil engines** driving 2 FP propellers Total Power: 1,324kW (1,800hp) 10.0k Dvigatel Revolyutsii 6CHRN36/4 2 x 4 Stroke 6 Cy. 360 x 450 each-662kW (900bhp) Zavod "Dvigatel Revolyutsii"-Gorkiy AuxGen: 2 x 110kW a.c Fuel: 122.0 (d.f.)
8959594 *UDYE* -	**VOLGO-DON 175** **JSC Volga Shipping (OAO Sudokhodnaya Kompaniya 'Volzhskoye Parokhodstvo')** - *Nizhniy Novgorod* *Russia* MMSI: 273444650 Official number: V-04-429	*3,904* 1,663 5,162	Class: RR	**1974 Navashinskiy Sudostroitelnyy Zavod 'Oka' — Navashino** Yd No: 1103 Loa 138.30 Br ex 16.70 Dght 3.430 Lbp 135.00 Br md 16.50 Dpth 5.50 Welded, 1 dk	**(A31A2GX) General Cargo Ship** Grain: 6,270 Compartments: 2 Ho, ER 2 Ha: 2 (44.4 x 13.1)ER	**2 oil engines** driving 2 FP propellers Total Power: 1,324kW (1,800hp) 10.0k Dvigatel Revolyutsii 6CHRN36/4 2 x 4 Stroke 6 Cy. 360 x 450 each-662kW (900bhp) Zavod "Dvigatel Revolyutsii"-Gorkiy Fuel: 122.0 (d.f.)
8959609 - -	**VOLGO-DON 177** **JSC Volga Shipping (OAO Sudokhodnaya Kompaniya 'Volzhskoye Parokhodstvo')** - *Nizhniy Novgorod* *Russia* MMSI: 273345310 Official number: V-04-435	*3,904* 1,663 5,162	Class: RR	**1975 Navashinskiy Sudostroitelnyy Zavod 'Oka' — Navashino** Yd No: 1104 Loa 138.30 Br ex 16.70 Dght 3.430 Lbp 135.00 Br md 16.50 Dpth 5.50 Welded, 1 dk	**(A31A2GX) General Cargo Ship** Grain: 6,270 Compartments: 2 Ho, ER 2 Ha: 2 (44.4 x 13.1)ER	**2 oil engines** driving 2 FP propellers Total Power: 1,324kW (1,800hp) 10.0k Dvigatel Revolyutsii 6CHRN36/4 2 x 4 Stroke 6 Cy. 360 x 450 each-662kW (900bhp) Zavod "Dvigatel Revolyutsii"-Gorkiy AuxGen: 2 x 110kW a.c Fuel: 122.0 (d.f.)
8959611 - -	**VOLGO-DON 179** **VF Cargo Transportation Ltd** JSC Volga Shipping (OAO Sudokhodnaya Kompaniya 'Volzhskoye Parokhodstvo') SatCom: Inmarsat C 427330513 *Nizhniy Novgorod* *Russia* MMSI: 273344310 Official number: V-04-814	*3,904* 1,663 5,162	Class: RR	**1975 Navashinskiy Sudostroitelnyy Zavod 'Oka' — Navashino** Yd No: 1105 Loa 138.30 Br ex 16.70 Dght 3.430 Lbp 135.00 Br md 16.50 Dpth 5.50 Welded, 1 dk	**(A31A2GX) General Cargo Ship** Grain: 6,270 Compartments: 2 Ho, ER 2 Ha: 2 (44.4 x 13.1)ER	**2 oil engines** driving 2 FP propellers Total Power: 1,324kW (1,800hp) 10.0k Dvigatel Revolyutsii 6CHRN36/4 2 x 4 Stroke 6 Cy. 360 x 450 each-662kW (900bhp) Zavod "Dvigatel Revolyutsii"-Gorkiy AuxGen: 2 x 110kW a.c Fuel: 122.0 (d.f.)
8746521 - -	**VOLGO-DON 181** **VF Cargo Transportation Ltd** JSC Volga Shipping (OAO Sudokhodnaya Kompaniya 'Volzhskoye Parokhodstvo') SatCom: Inmarsat C 427330492 *Nizhniy Novgorod* *Russia* MMSI: 273343310 Official number: V-05-945	**3,904** 1,663 5,162	Class: RR	**1975 Navashinskiy Sudostroitelnyy Zavod 'Oka' — Navashino** Yd No: 1106 Loa 138.30 Br ex 16.70 Dght 3.430 Lbp 135.00 Br md 16.50 Dpth 5.50 Welded, 1 dk	**(A31A2GX) General Cargo Ship** Grain: 6,270	**2 oil engines** driving 2 FP propellers Total Power: 1,324kW (1,800hp) 10.0k Dvigatel Revolyutsii 6CHRN36/4 2 x 4 Stroke 6 Cy. 360 x 450 each-662kW (900bhp) Zavod "Dvigatel Revolyutsii"-Gorkiy

IMO / Call sign	Ship / Owner / Manager	Tonnage	Class	Build	Type / Capacity	Machinery
8959635 *UAZC2* -	**VOLGO-DON 187** **VF Cargo Transportation Ltd** JSC Volga Shipping (OAO Sudokhodnaya Kompaniya 'Volzhskoye Parokhodstvo') SatCom: Inmarsat C 427330493 *Nizhniy Novgorod* *Russia* MMSI: 273347210 Official number: V-05-865	*3,904* 1,663 5,150	Class: RR	**1975 Navashinskiy Sudostroitelnyy Zavod 'Oka' — Navashino** Yd No: 1109 Loa 138.30 Br ex 16.70 Dght 3.430 Lbp 135.00 Br md 16.50 Dpth 5.50 Welded, 1 dk	**(A31A2GX) General Cargo Ship** Grain: 6,270 Compartments: 2 Ho, ER 2 Ha: 2 (44.4 x 13.1)ER	**2 oil engines** driving 2 FP propellers Total Power: 1,324kW (1,800hp) 10.0kn Dvigatel Revolyutsii 6CHRN36/45 2 x 4 Stroke 6 Cy. 360 x 450 each-662kW (900bhp) Zavod "Dvigatel Revolyutsii"-Gorkiy AuxGen: 2 x 110kW a.c Fuel: 122.0 (d.f.)
8864036 *UGMB* -	**VOLGO-DON 189** **VF Cargo Transportation Ltd** JSC Volga Shipping (OAO Sudokhodnaya Kompaniya 'Volzhskoye Parokhodstvo') SatCom: Inmarsat C 427330514 *Nizhniy Novgorod* *Russia* MMSI: 273445650 Official number: V-05-942	*3,904* 1,663 5,162	Class: RR	**1975 Navashinskiy Sudostroitelnyy Zavod 'Oka' — Navashino** Yd No: 1110 Loa 138.30 Br ex 16.70 Dght 3.430 Lbp 135.00 Br md 16.50 Dpth 5.50 Welded, 1 dk	**(A31A2GX) General Cargo Ship** Grain: 6,270 Compartments: 2 Ho, ER 2 Ha: 2 (44.4 x 13.1)ER	**2 oil engines** driving 2 FP propellers Total Power: 1,324kW (1,800hp) 10.0kn Dvigatel Revolyutsii 6CHRN36/45 2 x 4 Stroke 6 Cy. 360 x 450 each-662kW (900bhp) Zavod "Dvigatel Revolyutsii"-Gorkiy AuxGen: 2 x 110kW a.c Fuel: 122.0 (d.f.)
8959647 *UGCD* -	**VOLGO-DON 197** **VF Cargo Transportation Ltd** JSC Volga Shipping (OAO Sudokhodnaya Kompaniya 'Volzhskoye Parokhodstvo') SatCom: Inmarsat C 427330515 *Nizhniy Novgorod* *Russia* MMSI: 273373500 Official number: V-05-874	*3,904* 1,663 5,162	Class: RR	**1976 Navashinskiy Sudostroitelnyy Zavod 'Oka' — Navashino** Yd No: 1114 Loa 138.30 Br ex 16.70 Dght 3.430 Lbp 135.00 Br md 16.50 Dpth 5.50 Welded, 1 dk	**(A31A2GX) General Cargo Ship** Grain: 6,270 Compartments: 2 Ho, ER 2 Ha: 2 (44.4 x 13.1)ER	**2 oil engines** driving 2 FP propellers Total Power: 1,324kW (1,800hp) 10.0kn Dvigatel Revolyutsii 6CHRN36/45 2 x 4 Stroke 6 Cy. 360 x 450 each-662kW (900bhp) Zavod "Dvigatel Revolyutsii"-Gorkiy AuxGen: 2 x 110kW a.c Fuel: 122.0 (d.f.)
8863094 - -	**VOLGO-DON 199** **VF Cargo Transportation Ltd** JSC Volga Shipping (OAO Sudokhodnaya Kompaniya 'Volzhskoye Parokhodstvo') SatCom: Inmarsat C 427330516 *Nizhniy Novgorod* *Russia* MMSI: 273342310 Official number: V-04-813	*3,904* 1,663 5,162	Class: RR	**1976 Navashinskiy Sudostroitelnyy Zavod 'Oka' — Navashino** Yd No: 1115 Loa 138.30 Br ex 16.70 Dght 3.430 Lbp 135.00 Br md 16.50 Dpth 5.50 Welded, 1 dk	**(A31A2GX) General Cargo Ship** Grain: 6,270 Compartments: 2 Ho, ER 2 Ha: 2 (44.4 x 13.1)ER	**2 oil engines** driving 2 FP propellers Total Power: 1,324kW (1,800hp) 10.0kn Dvigatel Revolyutsii 6CHRN36/45 2 x 4 Stroke 6 Cy. 360 x 450 each-662kW (900bhp) Zavod "Dvigatel Revolyutsii"-Gorkiy AuxGen: 2 x 110kW a.c Fuel: 122.0 (d.f.)
8866010 *UCWF* -	**VOLGO-DON 203** **LLC Rosshipcom** Rosshipcom Marine Ltd SatCom: Inmarsat C 427337310 *Taganrog* *Russia* MMSI: 273373000	**4,980** 2,316 5,859	Class: RS (RR)	**1977-04 Navashinskiy Sudostroitelnyy Zavod 'Oka' — Navashino** Yd No: 1117 Loa 138.30 Br ex 16.70 Dght 3.770 Lbp 131.04 Br md 16.50 Dpth 5.50 Welded, 1 dk	**(A31A2GX) General Cargo Ship** Grain: 6,370 Compartments: 2 Ho, ER 2 Ha: (44.4 x 13.1) (45.6 x 13.0)ER	**2 oil engines** driving 2 FP propellers Total Power: 1,324kW (1,800hp) 10.0kn Dvigatel Revolyutsii 6CHRN36/45 2 x 4 Stroke 6 Cy. 360 x 450 each-662kW (900bhp) Zavod "Dvigatel Revolyutsii"-Gorkiy Fuel: 158.0 (d.f.)
8959166 *UCWG* -	**VOLGO-DON 205** **Volgo-Don 219 Shipping Ltd** Volga-Don Shipping JSC (A/O 'Volgo-Donskoye Parokhodstvo') SatCom: Inmarsat C 427322655 *Russia* MMSI: 273374000	**3,959** 1,399 4,019	Class: RR	**1977 Navashinskiy Sudostroitelnyy Zavod 'Oka' — Navashino** Yd No: 1118 Loa 138.30 Br ex 16.75 Dght 2.870 Lbp 135.00 Br md 16.50 Dpth 5.50 Welded, 1 dk	**(A31A2GX) General Cargo Ship** Grain: 6,270 Compartments: 2 Ho, ER 2 Ha: (44.4 x 13.1) (45.6 x 13.0)ER	**2 oil engines** driving 2 FP propellers Total Power: 1,324kW (1,800hp) 10.0kn Dvigatel Revolyutsii 6CHRN36/45 2 x 4 Stroke 6 Cy. 360 x 450 each-662kW (900bhp) Zavod "Dvigatel Revolyutsii"-Gorkiy Fuel: 158.0 (d.f.)
8959178 *V3QY4* -	**VOLGO-DON 207** **Saluta Shipping Ltd** Kent Shipping & Chartering Ltd SatCom: Inmarsat C 431265412 *Belize City* *Belize* MMSI: 312654000 Official number: 141120211	**3,991** 1,197 4,585	Class: IV (RS) (RR)	**1977 Navashinskiy Sudostroitelnyy Zavod 'Oka' — Navashino** Yd No: 1119 Loa 138.30 Br ex 16.70 Dght 3.170 Lbp 135.00 Br md 16.50 Dpth 5.50 Welded, 1 dk	**(A31A2GX) General Cargo Ship** Grain: 6,370 Compartments: 2 Ho, ER 2 Ha: (44.4 x 13.1) (45.6 x 13.0)ER	**2 oil engines** driving 2 FP propellers Total Power: 1,324kW (1,800hp) 10.0kn Dvigatel Revolyutsii 6CHRN36/45 2 x 4 Stroke 6 Cy. 360 x 450 each-662kW (900bhp) Zavod "Dvigatel Revolyutsii"-Gorkiy AuxGen: 3 x 100kW a.c Fuel: 145.0 (d.f.)
8959180 *UCWQ* -	**VOLGO-DON 211** **Don River Shipping JSC (OAO 'Donrechflot')** - *Taganrog* *Russia* MMSI: 273374100 Official number: 186744	**4,963** 2,316 5,100	Class: RS (RR)	**1977-10 Navashinskiy Sudostroitelnyy Zavod 'Oka' — Navashino** Yd No: 1121 Loa 138.30 Br ex 16.70 Dght 3.770 Lbp 135.00 Br md - Dpth 5.50 Welded, 1 dk	**(A31A2GX) General Cargo Ship** Grain: 6,370 Compartments: 2 Ho, ER 2 Ha: (44.4 x 13.0) (45.6 x 13.0)ER	**2 oil engines** driving 2 FP propellers Total Power: 1,324kW (1,800hp) 10.7kn Dvigatel Revolyutsii 6CHRN36/45 2 x 4 Stroke 6 Cy. 360 x 450 each-662kW (900bhp) Zavod "Dvigatel Revolyutsii"-Gorkiy Fuel: 158.0 (d.f.)
8959192 *UCWH* -	**VOLGO-DON 213** **Don River Shipping JSC (OAO 'Donrechflot')** - *Taganrog* *Russia* MMSI: 273375000 Official number: 186754	**4,963** 2,316 5,657	Class: RS (RR)	**1977-11 Navashinskiy Sudostroitelnyy Zavod 'Oka' — Navashino** Yd No: 1122 Loa 138.30 Br ex 16.70 Dght 3.770 Lbp 135.00 Br md - Dpth 5.50 Welded, 1 dk	**(A31A2GX) General Cargo Ship** Grain: 6,370 Compartments: 2 Ho, ER 2 Ha: (44.4 x 13.0) (45.6 x 13.0)ER	**2 oil engines** driving 2 FP propellers Total Power: 1,324kW (1,800hp) 10.7kn Dvigatel Revolyutsii 6CHRN36/45 2 x 4 Stroke 6 Cy. 360 x 450 each-662kW (900bhp) Zavod "Dvigatel Revolyutsii"-Gorkiy Fuel: 158.0 (d.f.)
8959207 *UCWN* -	**VOLGO-DON 219** *ex* Kapitan Polivenko *-2006* *ex* Volgo-Don 219 *-2002* **Don River Shipping JSC (OAO 'Donrechflot')** SatCom: Inmarsat C 427322247 *Taganrog* *Russia* MMSI: 273371100	**3,992** 1,401 5,338	Class: RS (RR)	**1978-07 Navashinskiy Sudostroitelnyy Zavod 'Oka' — Navashino** Yd No: 1125 Loa 138.30 Br ex 16.70 Dght 3.520 Lbp 131.22 Br md 16.50 Dpth 5.50 Welded, 1 dk	**(A31A2GX) General Cargo Ship** Grain: 6,370 Compartments: 2 Ho, ER 2 Ha: (44.4 x 13.0) (45.6 x 13.0)ER	**2 oil engines** driving 2 FP propellers Total Power: 1,324kW (1,800hp) 10.0kn Dvigatel Revolyutsii 6CHRN36/45 2 x 4 Stroke 6 Cy. 360 x 450 each-662kW (900bhp) Zavod "Dvigatel Revolyutsii"-Gorkiy Fuel: 158.0 (d.f.)
8954958 *UCWP* -	**VOLGO-DON 225** **Don River Shipping JSC (OAO 'Donrechflot')** - *Taganrog* *Russia* MMSI: 273373100	**3,969** 1,191 4,051	Class: RR	**1979 Navashinskiy Sudostroitelnyy Zavod 'Oka' — Navashino** Yd No: 1128 Loa 138.30 Br ex 16.50 Dght 2.870 Lbp 131.30 Br md - Dpth 5.50 Welded, 1 dk	**(A31A2GX) General Cargo Ship** Grain: 6,398 Compartments: 2 Ho, ER 2 Ha: (44.4 x 13.1) (45.6 x 13.0)ER	**2 oil engines** driving 2 FP propellers Total Power: 1,324kW (1,800hp) 10.0kn Dvigatel Revolyutsii 6CHRN36/45 2 x 4 Stroke 6 Cy. 360 x 450 each-662kW (900bhp) Zavod "Dvigatel Revolyutsii"-Gorkiy AuxGen: 2 x 100kW a.c Fuel: 155.0 (d.f.)
8959154 *UCWI* -	**VOLGO-DON 235** **Don River Shipping JSC (OAO 'Donrechflot')** - *Taganrog* *Russia* MMSI: 273376000	**4,963** 2,316 5,618	Class: RS (RR)	**1979-12 Navashinskiy Sudostroitelnyy Zavod 'Oka' — Navashino** Yd No: 1133 Loa 138.74 Br ex 16.50 Dght 3.770 Lbp 135.00 Br md - Dpth 5.50 Welded, 1 dk	**(A31A2GX) General Cargo Ship** Grain: 6,400 Compartments: 2 Ho, ER 2 Ha: (44.4 x 13.1) (45.6 x 13.0)ER	**2 oil engines** driving 2 FP propellers Total Power: 1,324kW (1,800hp) 10.0kn Dvigatel Revolyutsii 6CHRN36/45 2 x 4 Stroke 6 Cy. 360 x 450 each-662kW (900bhp) Zavod "Dvigatel Revolyutsii"-Gorkiy AuxGen: 2 x 100kW a.c Fuel: 158.0 (d.f.)
8872526 *UFMI* -	**VOLGO-DON 236** **LLC Rosshipcom** - SatCom: Inmarsat C 427310074 *Taganrog* *Russia* MMSI: 273377700	**2,990** 962 3,853	Class: RS (RR)	**1980-04 Navashinskiy Sudostroitelnyy Zavod 'Oka' — Navashino** Yd No: 1134 Loa 107.10 Br ex 16.70 Dght 3.690 Lbp 103.80 Br md 16.50 Dpth 5.50 Welded, 1 dk	**(A31A2GX) General Cargo Ship** Grain: 4,045 Compartments: 2 Ho, ER 2 Ha: 2 (28.8 x 13.2)ER Ice Capable	**2 oil engines** driving 2 FP propellers Total Power: 1,324kW (1,800hp) 10.0kn Dvigatel Revolyutsii 6CHRN36/45 2 x 4 Stroke 6 Cy. 360 x 450 each-662kW (900bhp) Zavod "Dvigatel Revolyutsii"-Gorkiy AuxGen: 2 x 100kW a.c, 1 x 50kW a.c Fuel: 159.0 (d.f.)
8899031 *UBHH* -	**VOLGO-DON 238** **LLC Rosshipcom** - SatCom: Inmarsat C 427310552 *Taganrog* *Russia* MMSI: 273346000	**2,968** 961 3,853	Class: (RS)	**1980-07 Navashinskiy Sudostroitelnyy Zavod 'Oka' — Navashino** Yd No: 1136 Loa 107.10 Br ex 16.70 Dght 3.690 Lbp 103.80 Br md 16.50 Dpth 5.50 Welded, 1 dk	**(A31A2GX) General Cargo Ship** Grain: 4,045 TEU 56 C. 56/20' Compartments: 2 Ho, ER 4 Ha: 4 (13.8 x 13.2)ER Ice Capable	**2 oil engines** driving 2 FP propellers Total Power: 1,324kW (1,800hp) 10.0kn Dvigatel Revolyutsii 6CHRN36/45 2 x 4 Stroke 6 Cy. 360 x 450 each-662kW (900bhp) Zavod "Dvigatel Revolyutsii"-Gorkiy AuxGen: 2 x 100kW a.c, 1 x 50kW a.c Fuel: 182.0 (d.f.)

IMO / Call sign	Ship / Owner	Tonnage	Class	Built / Dimensions	Type / Cargo	Machinery
8951310 *UBGG4* -	**VOLGO-DON 5011** *ex* Eridan I *-2010* *ex* Volgo-Don 5011 *-2000* **Don River Shipping JSC (OAO 'Donrechflot')** *Russia* MMSI: 273340830	**3,994** 1,198 5,180	Class: RR (UA)	**1969-01 Santierul Naval Oltenita S.A. — Oltenita** Yd No: 11 Loa 138.30 Br ex 16.70 Dght 3.500 Lbp 135.00 Br md 16.50 Dpth 5.52 Welded, 1 dk	**(A31A2GX) General Cargo Ship** Grain: 6,270 Compartments: 2 Ho, ER 2 Ha: (44.0 x 13.1) (44.0 x 12.3)ER	**2 oil engines** driving 2 FP propellers Total Power: 1,324kW (1,800hp) 11.0kr Dvigatel Revolyutsii 6CHRN36/45 2 x 4 Stroke 6 Cy. 360 x 450 each-662kW (900bhp) Zavod "Dvigatel Revolyutsii"-Gorkiy
8951322 - -	**VOLGO-DON 5012** **JSC Volga Shipping (OAO Sudokhodnaya Kompaniya 'Volzhskoye Parokhodstvo')** - SatCom: Inmarsat C 427330517 *Nizhniy Novgorod* *Russia* MMSI: 273341310 Official number: V-04-794	*3,919* 1,685 5,152	Class: RR	**1969 Santierul Naval Oltenita S.A. — Oltenita** Yd No: 432 Loa 138.30 Br ex 16.70 Dght 3.460 Lbp 135.00 Br md 16.50 Dpth 5.50 Welded, 1 dk	**(A31A2GX) General Cargo Ship** Grain: 6,270 Compartments: 2 Ho, ER 2 Ha: 2 (44.4 x 13.1)ER	**2 oil engines** driving 2 FP propellers Total Power: 1,324kW (1,800hp) 10.0kr Dvigatel Revolyutsii 6CHRN36/45 2 x 4 Stroke 6 Cy. 360 x 450 each-662kW (900bhp) Zavod "Dvigatel Revolyutsii"-Gorkiy AuxGen: 2 x 100kW Fuel: 185.0 (d.f.)
8937285 *UDSN* -	**VOLGO-DON 5015** **JSC Volga Shipping (OAO Sudokhodnaya Kompaniya 'Volzhskoye Parokhodstvo')** - SatCom: Inmarsat C 427330518 *St Petersburg* *Russia* MMSI: 273377500 Official number: V-04-791	*3,919* 1,685 5,152	Class: RR	**1969 Santierul Naval Oltenita S.A. — Oltenita** Yd No: 442 Loa 138.30 Br ex 16.70 Dght 3.460 Lbp 135.00 Br md 16.50 Dpth 5.50 Welded, 1 dk	**(A31A2GX) General Cargo Ship** Grain: 6,270 Compartments: 2 Ho, ER 2 Ha: 2 (44.4 x 13.1)ER	**2 oil engines** driving 2 FP propellers Total Power: 1,324kW (1,800hp) 10.8kr Dvigatel Revolyutsii 6CHRNP36/45 2 x 4 Stroke 6 Cy. 360 x 450 each-662kW (900bhp) Zavod "Dvigatel Revolyutsii"-Gorkiy AuxGen: 2 x 100kW Fuel: 160.0 (d.f.)
8951358 - -	**VOLGO-DON 5016** **JSC Volga Shipping (OAO Sudokhodnaya Kompaniya 'Volzhskoye Parokhodstvo')** - SatCom: Inmarsat C 427330519 *Nizhniy Novgorod* *Russia* MMSI: 273340310 Official number: V-04-792	*3,919* 1,685 5,152	Class: RR	**1969 Santierul Naval Oltenita S.A. — Oltenita** Yd No: 443 Loa 138.30 Br ex 16.70 Dght 3.430 Lbp 135.00 Br md 16.50 Dpth 5.50 Welded, 1 dk	**(A31A2GX) General Cargo Ship** Grain: 6,270 Compartments: 2 Ho, ER 2 Ha: 2 (44.4 x 13.1)ER	**2 oil engines** driving 2 FP propellers Total Power: 1,324kW (1,800hp) 10.0kr Dvigatel Revolyutsii 6CHRN36/45 2 x 4 Stroke 6 Cy. 360 x 450 each-662kW (900bhp) Zavod "Dvigatel Revolyutsii"-Gorkiy AuxGen: 2 x 100kW Fuel: 185.0 (d.f.)
8937297 *UFBM* -	**VOLGO-DON 5017** *ex* Toliman *-2010* *ex* Linda II *-2003* *ex* Volgo-Don 5017 *-2000* - - *Russia* MMSI: 273445940	**3,994** 1,439 5,180	Class: (RS) (RR)	**1969-12 Santierul Naval Oltenita S.A. — Oltenita** Yd No: 5017 Loa 138.80 Br ex 16.70 Dght 3.500 Lbp 131.20 Br md - Dpth 5.50 Welded, 1 dk	**(A31A2GX) General Cargo Ship** Grain: 6,270 Compartments: 2 Ho, ER 2 Ha: 2 (44.4 x 13.1)ER	**2 oil engines** driving 2 FP propellers Total Power: 1,324kW (1,800hp) 10.8kr Dvigatel Revolyutsii 6CHRNP36/45 2 x 4 Stroke 6 Cy. 360 x 450 each-662kW (900bhp) Zavod "Dvigatel Revolyutsii"-Gorkiy AuxGen: 2 x 100kW Fuel: 160.0 (d.f.)
8937704 *UACY9* -	**VOLGO-DON 5019** **JSC Volga Shipping (OAO Sudokhodnaya Kompaniya 'Volzhskoye Parokhodstvo')** - *Nizhniy Novgorod* *Russia* MMSI: 273433580 Official number: V-04-793	**3,919** 1,685 5,152	Class: RR	**1970-04 Santierul Naval Oltenita S.A. — Oltenita** Yd No: 447 Loa 138.30 Br ex 16.70 Dght 3.430 Lbp 135.00 Br md 16.50 Dpth 5.50 Welded, 1 dk	**(A31A2GX) General Cargo Ship** Grain: 6,270 Compartments: 2 Ho, ER 2 Ha: 2 (44.4 x 13.1)ER	**2 oil engines** driving 2 FP propellers Total Power: 1,324kW (1,800hp) 10.0kr Dvigatel Revolyutsii 6CHRN36/45 2 x 4 Stroke 6 Cy. 360 x 450 each-662kW (900bhp) Zavod "Dvigatel Revolyutsii"-Gorkiy AuxGen: 2 x 100kW Fuel: 185.0 (d.f.)
8955873 *V3QQ5* -	**VOLGO-DON 5021** **Saluta Shipping Ltd** Sailtrade Denizcilik ve Ticaret Ltd Sti SatCom: Inmarsat C 431269210 *Belize City* *Belize* MMSI: 312692000 Official number: 141120214	**3,940** 1,182 3,960	Class: IV RR	**1970 Santierul Naval Oltenita S.A. — Oltenita** Yd No: 449 Loa 138.30 Br ex 16.70 Dght 2.950 Lbp 135.00 Br md 16.50 Dpth 5.50 Welded, 1 dk	**(A31A2GX) General Cargo Ship** Grain: 6,270 Compartments: 2 Ho, ER 2 Ha: (45.0 x 12.3) (44.4 x 12.3)ER	**2 oil engines** driving 2 FP propellers Total Power: 1,324kW (1,800hp) 10.0kr Dvigatel Revolyutsii 6CHRN36/45 2 x 4 Stroke 6 Cy. 360 x 450 each-662kW (900bhp) Zavod "Dvigatel Revolyutsii"-Gorkiy AuxGen: 2 x 100kW Fuel: 122.0 (d.f.)
8871508 *UBAG5* -	**VOLGO-DON 5038** *ex* Coral *-2012* *ex* Korall *-2010* *ex* Coral *-2009* *ex* Castor *-2006* *ex* Volgo-Don 5038 *-2004* **Don River Shipping JSC (OAO 'Donrechflot')** - *Taganrog* *Russia* MMSI: 273338930	**3,994** 1,439 5,150	Class: RS	**1972 Santierul Naval Oltenita S.A. — Oltenita** Yd No: 471 Loa 138.90 Br ex 16.70 Dght 3.000 Lbp - Br md - Dpth 5.50 Welded, 1 dk	**(A31A2GX) General Cargo Ship** Grain: 6,270 Compartments: 2 Ho, ER 2 Ha: ER Ice Capable	**2 oil engines** driving 2 FP propellers Total Power: 1,324kW (1,800hp) 10.0kr Dvigatel Revolyutsii 6CHRNP36/45 2 x 4 Stroke 6 Cy. 360 x 450 each-662kW (900bhp) Zavod "Dvigatel Revolyutsii"-Gorkiy
8955885 *UGPM* -	**VOLGO-DON 5041** - - *Taganrog* *Russia* MMSI: 273450260	**3,940** 1,270 3,934	Class: RS (RR)	**1972 Santierul Naval Oltenita S.A. — Oltenita** Yd No: 474 Loa 138.30 Br ex 16.70 Dght 3.380 Lbp 135.00 Br md 16.50 Dpth 5.50 Welded, 1 dk	**(A31A2GX) General Cargo Ship** Grain: 6,270 Compartments: 2 Ho, ER 2 Ha: (45.0 x 12.3) (44.4 x 12.3)ER Ice Capable	**2 oil engines** driving 2 FP propellers Total Power: 1,324kW (1,800hp) 10.0kr Dvigatel Revolyutsii 6CHRN36/45 2 x 4 Stroke 6 Cy. 360 x 450 each-662kW (900bhp) Zavod "Dvigatel Revolyutsii"-Gorkiy AuxGen: 2 x 100kW Fuel: 122.0 (d.f.)
8866321 *UGWY* -	**VOLGO-DON 5043** *ex* Orion *-2009* *ex* Volgo-Don 5043 *-1999* **Don River Shipping JSC (OAO 'Donrechflot')** - *Russia* MMSI: 273316500	**3,994** 1,198 3,640	Class: IS (RS)	**1972 Santierul Naval Oltenita S.A. — Oltenita** Yd No: 463 Loa 138.80 Br ex 16.70 Dght 2.707 Lbp - Br md - Dpth 5.50 Welded, 1 dk	**(A31A2GX) General Cargo Ship** Grain: 6,270 Compartments: 2 Ho, ER 2 Ha: ER	**2 oil engines** driving 2 FP propellers Total Power: 1,324kW (1,800hp) 11.0kr Dvigatel Revolyutsii 6CHRNP36/45 2 x 4 Stroke 6 Cy. 360 x 450 each-662kW (900bhp) Zavod "Dvigatel Revolyutsii"-Gorkiy AuxGen: 2 x 100kW a.c Fuel: 123.0 (d.f.)
8955897 - -	**VOLGO-DON 5044** **JSC Volga Shipping (OAO Sudokhodnaya Kompaniya 'Volzhskoye Parokhodstvo')** - SatCom: Inmarsat C 427330520 *Nizhniy Novgorod* *Russia* MMSI: 273443650 Official number: V-04-790	*3,904* 1,663 5,152	Class: RR	**1973 Santierul Naval Oltenita S.A. — Oltenita** Yd No: 478 Loa 138.30 Br ex 16.70 Dght 3.460 Lbp 135.00 Br md 16.50 Dpth 5.50 Welded, 1 dk	**(A31A2GX) General Cargo Ship** Grain: 6,270 Compartments: 2 Ho, ER 2 Ha: 2 (44.4 x 13.1)ER	**2 oil engines** driving 2 FP propellers Total Power: 1,324kW (1,800hp) 10.0kr Dvigatel Revolyutsii 6CHRN36/45 2 x 4 Stroke 6 Cy. 360 x 450 each-662kW (900bhp) Zavod "Dvigatel Revolyutsii"-Gorkiy AuxGen: 2 x 100kW Fuel: 185.0 (d.f.)
8867208 *UFZB* -	**VOLGO-DON 5046** **JSC Volga Shipping (OAO Sudokhodnaya Kompaniya 'Volzhskoye Parokhodstvo')** - *Gorodets* *Russia* MMSI: 273341300 Official number: 178003	**3,989** 1,196 5,150	Class: RR	**1975 Santierul Naval Oltenita S.A. — Oltenita** Loa 138.80 Br ex 16.70 Dght 2.790 Lbp - Br md - Dpth 5.50 Welded, 1 dk	**(A31A2GX) General Cargo Ship** Grain: 6,270 Compartments: 2 Ho, ER 2 Ha: ER	**2 oil engines** driving 2 FP propellers Total Power: 1,324kW (1,800hp) 10.0kr Dvigatel Revolyutsii 6CHRNP36/45 2 x 4 Stroke 6 Cy. 360 x 450 each-662kW (900bhp) Zavod "Dvigatel Revolyutsii"-Gorkiy
8872734 *UAPE* -	**VOLGO-DON 5065** **North-Western Fleet (A/O 'Severo-Zapadnyy Flot')** - *St Petersburg* *Russia* MMSI: 273436820	**3,958** 1,187 5,152	Class: RR	**1976-11 Santierul Naval Oltenita S.A. — Oltenita** Yd No: 513 Loa 138.80 Br ex 16.70 Dght 3.500 Lbp 131.20 Br md - Dpth 5.50 Welded, 1 dk	**(A31A2GX) General Cargo Ship** Grain: 6,270 2 Ha: 2 (44.0 x 13.1)ER	**2 oil engines** driving 2 FP propellers Total Power: 1,324kW (1,800hp) 10.0kn Dvigatel Revolyutsii 6CHRNP36/45 2 x 4 Stroke 6 Cy. 360 x 450 each-662kW (900bhp) Zavod "Dvigatel Revolyutsii"-Gorkiy
8874342 *UAOQ* -	**VOLGO-DON 5076** **North-Western Fleet (A/O 'Severo-Zapadnyy Flot')** - SatCom: Inmarsat C 427351720 *St Petersburg* *Russia* MMSI: 273433620 Official number: 191014	**3,958** 1,187 3,962	Class: RR	**1980 Santierul Naval Oltenita S.A. — Oltenita** Yd No: 106 Loa 138.00 Br ex 16.70 Dght 2.890 Lbp 135.00 Br md 16.50 Dpth 5.50 Welded, 1 dk	**(A31A2GX) General Cargo Ship** Grain: 6,270 2 Ha: 2 (44.0 x 13.1)ER	**2 oil engines** driving 2 FP propellers Total Power: 1,324kW (1,800hp) 10.0kn Dvigatel Revolyutsii 6CHRNP36/45 2 x 4 Stroke 6 Cy. 360 x 450 each-662kW (900bhp) Zavod "Dvigatel Revolyutsii"-Gorkiy

8866618 *UAON* -	**VOLGO-DON 5077** **North-Western Fleet (A/O 'Severo-Zapadnyy Flot')** - SatCom: Inmarsat C 427351721 *St Petersburg* *Russia* MMSI: 273434620 Official number: 191015	**3,958** Class: RR 1,187 3,962	**1980 Santierul Naval Oltenita S.A. — Oltenita** Yd No: 107 Loa 138.80 Br ex 16.70 Dght 2.890 Lbp 131.20 Br md 16.50 Dpth 5.50 Welded, 1 dk	**(A31A2GX) General Cargo Ship** Grain: 6,270 Compartments: 2 Ho, ER 2 Ha: ER	**2 oil engines** driving 2 FP propellers Total Power: 1,324kW (1,800hp) 10.0kn Dvigatel Revolyutsii 6CHRNP36/45 2 x 4 Stroke 6 Cy. 360 x 450 each-662kW (900bhp) Zavod "Dvigatel Revolyutsii"-Gorkiy
8852784 *UBEH2* -	**VOLGO-DON 5079** *ex* Delaware *-2011* *ex* Tiras *-2004* *ex* Volgo-Don 5079 *-1993* **Samara Shipping Co** - SatCom: Inmarsat C 427304788 *Astrakhan* *Russia* MMSI: 273359420	**3,972** Class: RS 1,407 5,258	**1980-12 Santierul Naval Oltenita S.A. — Oltenita** Yd No: 109 Loa 138.30 Br ex 16.70 Dght 3.520 Lbp 135.00 Br md 16.50 Dpth 5.50 Welded, 1 dk	**(A31A2GX) General Cargo Ship** Grain: 6,270 Compartments: 2 Ho, ER 2 Ha: ER	**2 oil engines** driving 2 FP propellers Total Power: 1,324kW (1,800hp) 10.0kn Dvigatel Revolyutsii 6CHRNP36/45 2 x 4 Stroke 6 Cy. 360 x 450 each-662kW (900bhp) Zavod "Dvigatel Revolyutsii"-Gorkiy
8866620 *UAPD* -	**VOLGO-DON 5080** **Vosnesenye Shipping Co** North-Western Fleet (A/O 'Severo-Zapadnyy Flot') *St Petersburg* *Russia* MMSI: 273433920 Official number: 191018	**3,958** Class: RR 1,187 3,962	**1981 Santierul Naval Oltenita S.A. — Oltenita** Yd No: 110 Loa 138.80 Br ex 16.70 Dght 2.890 Lbp 135.00 Br md 16.50 Dpth 5.50 Welded, 1 dk	**(A31A2GX) General Cargo Ship** Grain: 6,270 Compartments: 2 Ho, ER 2 Ha: ER	**2 oil engines** driving 2 FP propellers Total Power: 1,324kW (1,800hp) 10.0kn Dvigatel Revolyutsii 6CHRNP36/45 2 x 4 Stroke 6 Cy. 360 x 450 each-662kW (900bhp) Zavod "Dvigatel Revolyutsii"-Gorkiy
8943208 *UAOM* -	**VOLGO-DON 5084** **North-Western Fleet (A/O 'Severo-Zapadnyy Flot')** - *St Petersburg* *Russia* MMSI: 273435620 Official number: 191022	**3,958** Class: RR 1,187 3,962	**1982 Santierul Naval Oltenita S.A. — Oltenita** Yd No: 194 Loa 138.80 Br ex 16.70 Dght 2.890 Lbp 135.00 Br md - Dpth 5.50 Welded, 1 dk	**(A31A2GX) General Cargo Ship** Grain: 6,270 Compartments: 2 Ho, ER 2 Ha: 2 (44.4 x 13.1)ER	**2 oil engines** driving 2 FP propellers Total Power: 1,324kW (1,800hp) 10.3kn Dvigatel Revolyutsii 6CHRN36/45 2 x 4 Stroke 6 Cy. 360 x 450 each-662kW (900bhp) Zavod "Dvigatel Revolyutsii"-Gorkiy AuxGen: 2 x 100kW Fuel: 162.0 (d.f.)
8866632 *UEJV* -	**VOLGO-DON 5088** **North-Western Fleet (A/O 'Severo-Zapadnyy Flot')** - SatCom: Inmarsat C 427351724 *St Petersburg* *Russia* MMSI: 273436620 Official number: 191026	**3,958** Class: RR 1,187 3,962	**1984 Santierul Naval Oltenita S.A. — Oltenita** Yd No: 198 Loa 138.80 Br ex 16.70 Dght 2.890 Lbp 135.00 Br md 16.50 Dpth 5.50 Welded, 1 dk	**(A31A2GX) General Cargo Ship** Grain: 6,270 2 Ha: 2 (44.0 x 13.1)ER	**2 oil engines** driving 2 FP propellers Total Power: 1,324kW (1,800hp) 10.0kn Dvigatel Revolyutsii 6CHRNP36/45 2 x 4 Stroke 6 Cy. 360 x 450 each-662kW (900bhp) Zavod "Dvigatel Revolyutsii"-Gorkiy
8852825 *UBII* -	**VOLGO-DON 5091** **North-Western Fleet (A/O 'Severo-Zapadnyy Flot')** JS North-Western Shipping Co (OAO 'Severo-Zapadnoye Parokhodstvo') *St Petersburg* *Russia* MMSI: 273437620 Official number: 191029	**3,978** Class: RR (RS) 1,198 3,352	**1986-07 Santierul Naval Oltenita S.A. — Oltenita** Yd No: 201 Loa 138.30 Br ex 16.70 Dght 2.890 Lbp 135.00 Br md 16.50 Dpth 5.50 Welded, 1 dk	**(A31A2GX) General Cargo Ship** Grain: 6,270	**2 oil engines** driving 2 FP propellers Total Power: 1,324kW (1,800hp) 10.8kn Dvigatel Revolyutsii 6CHRNP36/45 2 x 4 Stroke 6 Cy. 360 x 450 each-662kW (900bhp) Zavod "Dvigatel Revolyutsii"-Gorkiy AuxGen: 2 x 100kW a.c Fuel: 1604.0 (d.f.)
8852837 *UAOV* -	**VOLGO-DON 5105** **North-Western Fleet (A/O 'Severo-Zapadnyy Flot')** - *St Petersburg* *Russia* MMSI: 273438620 Official number: 191045	**3,973** Class: RR 1,191 3,352	**1989 Santierul Naval Oltenita S.A. — Oltenita** Yd No: 412 Loa 138.80 Br ex 16.70 Dght 2.890 Lbp 135.00 Br md - Dpth 5.50 Welded, 1 dk	**(A31A2GX) General Cargo Ship** Grain: 6,270 Compartments: 2 Ho, ER 2 Ha: (44.4 x 13.1) (44.4 x 13.0)ER	**2 oil engines** driving 2 FP propellers Total Power: 1,324kW (1,800hp) 10.0kn Dvigatel Revolyutsii 6CHRN36/45 2 x 4 Stroke 6 Cy. 360 x 450 each-662kW (900bhp) Zavod "Dvigatel Revolyutsii"-Gorkiy Fuel: 185.0 (d.f.)
8925385 *UANA3* -	**VOLGONEFT-32** **Transpetro Reka Shipping Co Ltd** Vision Flot Co Ltd (OOO 'Vizhn Flot') *Astrakhan* *Russia*	**3,463** 1,039 4,100	**1968 Shipbuilding & Shiprepairing Yard 'Ivan Dimitrov' — Rousse** Yd No: 512 Loa 132.60 Br ex 16.90 Dght 3.000 Lbp 128.68 Br md 16.50 Dpth 5.50 Welded, 1 dk	**(A13B2TP) Products Tanker**	**2 oil engines** driving 2 FP propellers Total Power: 1,472kW (2,002hp) 10.5kn S.K.L. 8NVD48AU 2 x 4 Stroke 8 Cy. 320 x 480 each-736kW (1001bhp) VEB Schwermaschinenbau "KarlLiebknecht" (SKL)-Magdeburg
8925397 *UFWS* -	**VOLGONEFT-36** **Volgatransservis Zao** - *Russia* MMSI: 273317170	**3,463** 1,039 4,500	**1969 Shipbuilding & Shiprepairing Yard 'Ivan Dimitrov' — Rousse** Yd No: 516 Loa 132.60 Br ex - Dght 3.000 Lbp 128.60 Br md 16.50 Dpth 5.50 Welded, 1 dk	**(A13B2TP) Products Tanker**	**2 oil engines** driving 2 FP propellers Total Power: 1,472kW (2,002hp) 10.5kn S.K.L. 8NVD48AU 2 x 4 Stroke 8 Cy. 320 x 480 each-736kW (1001bhp) VEB Schwermaschinenbau "KarlLiebknecht" (SKL)-Magdeburg
8925402 *UFKL* -	**VOLGONEFT-42** **Transpetro-Volga JSC (A/O 'Transpetro-Volga')** - *Taganrog* *Russia* MMSI: 273314170	**3,566** 1,760 5,000	**1970 Shipbuilding & Shiprepairing Yard 'Ivan Dimitrov' — Rousse** Loa - Br ex - Dght 3.200 Lbp 128.60 Br md 16.50 Dpth 5.50 Welded, 1 dk	**(A13B2TP) Products Tanker**	**2 oil engines** driving 2 FP propellers Total Power: 1,472kW (2,002hp) 10.2kn S.K.L. 8NVD48AU 2 x 4 Stroke 8 Cy. 320 x 480 each-736kW (1001bhp) VEB Schwermaschinenbau "KarlLiebknecht" (SKL)-Magdeburg
7038317 *UABC4* -	**VOLGONEFT-53** **JSC Trans-Flot** - *Russia* MMSI: 273311960	*3,519* Class: RR 1,952 5,067	**1966-01 Shipbuilding & Shiprepairing Yard 'Ivan Dimitrov' — Rousse** Yd No: 788 Loa 132.59 Br ex 16.51 Dght 3.582 Lbp 128.61 Br md - Dpth 5.49 Welded, 1 dk	**(A13B2TP) Products Tanker** Compartments: 12 Ta, ER	**2 oil engines** driving 2 FP propellers Total Power: 1,472kW (2,002hp) 10.5kn S.K.L. 8NVD48AU 2 x 4 Stroke 8 Cy. 320 x 480 each-736kW (1001bhp) VEB Schwermaschinenbau "KarlLiebknecht" (SKL)-Magdeburg
8891998 *UBBG* -	**VOLGONEFT-101** - - *St Petersburg* *Russia* MMSI: 273277000 Official number: 161626	**3,463** Class: RR 1,039 4,550	**1971 Shipbuilding & Shiprepairing Yard 'Ivan Dimitrov' — Rousse** Yd No: 526 Loa 132.60 Br ex 16.90 Dght 3.130 Lbp 123.00 Br md - Dpth 5.50 Welded, 1 dk	**(A13B2TP) Products Tanker** Double Hull Liq: 4,800; Liq (Oil): 4,800 Compartments: 8 Ta, ER 2 Cargo Pump (s): 2x450m³/hr	**2 oil engines** driving 2 FP propellers Total Power: 1,472kW (2,002hp) 11.0kn S.K.L. 8NVD48A-2U 2 x 4 Stroke 8 Cy. 320 x 480 each-736kW (1001bhp) (new engine 1980) VEB Schwermaschinenbau "KarlLiebknecht" (SKL)-Magdeburg AuxGen: 3 x 100kW Fuel: 80.0 (d.f.)
8888769 *UBCE* -	**VOLGONEFT-102** **JSC Volzhski Oil Shipping Co 'Volgotanker'** - *Astrakhan* *Russia* MMSI: 273274000 Official number: 161627	**3,473** Class: RR 1,161 4,768	**1971-07 Shipbuilding & Shiprepairing Yard 'Ivan Dimitrov' — Rousse** Yd No: 527 Loa 132.60 Br ex 16.90 Dght 3.530 Lbp 123.70 Br md - Dpth 5.50 Welded, 1 dk	**(A13B2TP) Products Tanker** Liq: 5,672; Liq (Oil): 5,672 Compartments: 8 Ta, ER	**2 oil engines** driving 2 FP propellers Total Power: 1,472kW (2,002hp) 11.0kn S.K.L. 8NVD48A-2U 2 x 4 Stroke 8 Cy. 320 x 480 each-736kW (1001bhp) (new engine 1994) VEB Schwermaschinenbau "KarlLiebknecht" (SKL)-Magdeburg AuxGen: 3 x 100kW Fuel: 80.0 (d.f.)
8230601 *UBIA* -	**VOLGONEFT-103** **JSC Volzhski Oil Shipping Co 'Volgotanker'** - *Astrakhan* *Russia* MMSI: 273278100 Official number: 161628	**3,471** Class: RR 1,041 4,550	**1972-07 Shipbuilding & Shiprepairing Yard 'Ivan Dimitrov' — Rousse** Yd No: 528 Loa 132.60 Br ex 16.90 Dght 3.330 Lbp 123.70 Br md - Dpth 5.50 Welded, 1 dk	**(A13B2TP) Products Tanker** Double Hull (13F) Liq: 5,672; Liq (Oil): 5,672 Cargo Heating Coils Compartments: 8 Ta, ER	**2 oil engines** driving 2 FP propellers Total Power: 1,472kW (2,002hp) 10.9kn S.K.L. 8NVD48AU 2 x 4 Stroke 8 Cy. 320 x 480 each-736kW (1001bhp) VEB Schwermaschinenbau "KarlLiebknecht" (SKL)-Magdeburg AuxGen: 3 x 100kW a.c Fuel: 82.0 (d.f.)

Ship	Name / Owner	Tonnage	Class	Build / Dimensions	Type / Cargo	Machinery	Speed / Engine model
8230613 *UICX* -	**VOLGONEFT-104** **Transpetro Reka Shipping Co Ltd** Vision Flot Co Ltd (OOO 'Vizhn Flot') *Rostov-na-Donu* *Russia* MMSI: 273432720	**3,463** 1,041 4,550	Class: RR	**1972**-07 **Shipbuilding & Shiprepairing Yard 'Ivan Dimitrov' — Rousse** Yd No: 529 Loa 132.60 Br ex 16.90 Dght 3.580 Lbp 123.70 Br md - Dpth 5.50 Welded, 1 dk	**(A13B2TP) Products Tanker** Liq: 5,672; Liq (Oil): 5,672 Cargo Heating Coils Compartments: 8 Ta, ER	**2 oil engines** driving 2 FP propellers Total Power: 1,440kW (1,958hp) Skoda 2 x 4 Stroke 6 Cy. 350 x 500 each-720kW (979bhp) (new engine 1985) Skoda-Praha AuxGen: 3 x 100kW a.c Fuel: 82.0 (d.f.)	10.9kn 6L350IIPN
8727915 - -	**VOLGONEFT-105** *ex* Volgoneft-94M *-1972* **Middle Volga Shipping Co** - *Russia*	**3,463** 1,039 4,190	Class: RR	**1972**-01 **Shipbuilding & Shiprepairing Yard 'Ivan Dimitrov' — Rousse** Yd No: 530 Loa 132.60 Br ex 16.90 Dght 3.130 Lbp 123.68 Br md - Dpth 5.50 Welded, 1 dk	**(A13B2TP) Products Tanker** Liq: 5,683; Liq (Oil): 5,683 Cargo Heating Coils Compartments: 8 Ta, ER	**2 oil engines** driving 2 FP propellers Total Power: 1,472kW (2,002hp) S.K.L. 2 x 4 Stroke 8 Cy. 320 x 480 each-736kW (1001bhp) VEB Schwermaschinenbau "KarlLiebknecht" (SKL)-Magdeburg AuxGen: 3 x 100kW a.c Fuel: 82.0 (d.f.)	11.1kn 8NVD48AU
8230663 - -	**VOLGONEFT-111** **Middle Volga Shipping Co** - *Russia*	**3,463** 1,039 4,190	Class: RR	**1973 Shipbuilding & Shiprepairing Yard 'Ivan Dimitrov' — Rousse** Yd No: 46 Loa 132.60 Br ex 16.90 Dght 3.130 Lbp 123.70 Br md - Dpth 5.50 Welded, 1 dk	**(A13B2TP) Products Tanker** Liq: 5,672; Liq (Oil): 5,672 Cargo Heating Coils Compartments: 8 Ta, ER	**2 oil engines** driving 2 FP propellers Total Power: 1,472kW (2,002hp) S.K.L. 2 x 4 Stroke 8 Cy. 320 x 480 each-736kW (1001bhp) VEB Schwermaschinenbau "KarlLiebknecht" (SKL)-Magdeburg AuxGen: 3 x 100kW a.c Fuel: 82.0 (d.f.)	10.9kn 8NVD48AU
8925426 - -	**VOLGONEFT-117** **Middle Volga Shipping Co** - *Russia*	**3,566** 1,760 4,100	Class: RR	**1974 Shipbuilding & Shiprepairing Yard 'Ivan Dimitrov' — Rousse** Yd No: 52 Loa 132.60 Br ex 16.90 Dght 3.000 Lbp 128.60 Br md 16.50 Dpth 5.50 Welded, 1 dk	**(A13B2TP) Products Tanker** Liq: 5,672; Liq (Oil): 5,672 Compartments: 8 Ta, ER	**2 oil engines** driving 2 FP propellers Total Power: 1,472kW (2,002hp) S.K.L. 2 x 4 Stroke 8 Cy. 320 x 480 each-736kW (1001bhp) VEB Schwermaschinenbau "KarlLiebknecht" (SKL)-Magdeburg AuxGen: 3 x 100kW a.c Fuel: 82.0 (d.f.)	10.5kn 8NVD48AU
8936891 *UFMC* -	**VOLGONEFT-134** **Navigator LLC** - *St Petersburg* *Russia* MMSI: 273426530 Official number: 161672	**3,493** 1,090 4,747	Class: RR	**1977 Shipbuilding & Shiprepairing Yard 'Ivan Dimitrov' — Rousse** Yd No: 69 Loa 132.40 Br ex 16.90 Dght 3.000 Lbp 123.70 Br md - Dpth 5.50 Welded, 1 dk	**(A13B2TP) Products Tanker** Double Hull Liq: 4,594; Liq (Oil): 4,594 Compartments: 8 Ta, ER 2 Cargo Pump (s): 2x450m³/hr	**2 oil engines** driving 2 FP propellers Total Power: 1,472kW (2,002hp) S.K.L. 2 x 4 Stroke 8 Cy. 320 x 480 each-736kW (1001bhp) VEB Schwermaschinenbau "KarlLiebknecht" (SKL)-Magdeburg AuxGen: 3 x 100kW Fuel: 82.0 (d.f.)	10.9kn 8NVD48AU
8863020 *UHZX* -	**VOLGONEFT-141** **JSC Volzhski Oil Shipping Co 'Volgotanker'** - SatCom: Inmarsat C 427310426 *Astrakhan* *Russia* MMSI: 273342400 Official number: 161692	**3,463** 1,132 4,750	Class: RR	**1978**-07 **Shipbuilding & Shiprepairing Yard 'Ivan Dimitrov' — Rousse** Yd No: 76 Loa 132.60 Br ex 16.90 Dght 3.490 Lbp 123.60 Br md - Dpth 5.50 Welded, 1 dk	**(A13B2TP) Products Tanker** Double Hull (13F) Liq: 5,747; Liq (Oil): 5,747 Compartments: 8 Ta, ER	**2 oil engines** driving 2 FP propellers Total Power: 1,472kW (2,002hp) S.K.L. 2 x 4 Stroke 8 Cy. 320 x 480 each-736kW (1001bhp) VEB Schwermaschinenbau "KarlLiebknecht" (SKL)-Magdeburg AuxGen: 3 x 100kW a.c Fuel: 82.0 (d.f.)	11.1kn 8NVD48AU
8864751 *UHQY* -	**VOLGONEFT-143** **JSC Volzhski Oil Shipping Co 'Volgotanker'** - *Astrakhan* *Russia* MMSI: 273348000 Official number: 161694	*3,463* 1,132 4,750	Class: RR	**1979**-07 **Shipbuilding & Shiprepairing Yard 'Ivan Dimitrov' — Rousse** Yd No: 78 Loa 132.60 Br ex 16.90 Dght 3.490 Lbp 123.60 Br md - Dpth 5.50 Welded, 1 dk	**(A13B2TP) Products Tanker** Liq: 5,747; Liq (Oil): 5,747 Cargo Heating Coils Compartments: 8 Ta, ER	**2 oil engines** driving 2 FP propellers Total Power: 1,472kW (2,002hp) S.K.L. 2 x 4 Stroke 8 Cy. 320 x 480 each-736kW (1001bhp) VEB Schwermaschinenbau "KarlLiebknecht" (SKL)-Magdeburg AuxGen: 3 x 100kW Fuel: 82.0 (d.f.)	11.1kn 8NVD48AU
8862777 *UBIL* -	**VOLGONEFT-144** **JSC Volzhski Oil Shipping Co 'Volgotanker'** - *Astrakhan* *Russia* MMSI: 273279100 Official number: 161695	**3,471** 1,132 4,750	Class: RR	**1979**-07 **Shipbuilding & Shiprepairing Yard 'Ivan Dimitrov' — Rousse** Yd No: 79 Loa 132.60 Br ex 16.90 Dght 3.490 Lbp 123.68 Br md - Dpth 5.50 Welded, 1 dk	**(A13B2TP) Products Tanker** Double Hull (13F) Liq: 5,747; Liq (Oil): 5,747 Compartments: 8 Ta, ER	**2 oil engines** driving 2 FP propellers Total Power: 1,472kW (2,002hp) S.K.L. 2 x 4 Stroke 8 Cy. 320 x 480 each-736kW (1001bhp) VEB Schwermaschinenbau "KarlLiebknecht" (SKL)-Magdeburg AuxGen: 3 x 110kW a.c Fuel: 82.0 (d.f.)	11.1kn 8NVD48AU
8867064 *UFQI* -	**VOLGONEFT-145** **JSC Volzhski Oil Shipping Co 'Volgotanker'** - *Astrakhan* *Russia* MMSI: 273274200 Official number: 161696	**3,463** 1,132 4,750	Class: RR	**1979 Shipbuilding & Shiprepairing Yard 'Ivan Dimitrov' — Rousse** Yd No: 80 Loa 132.60 Br ex 16.90 Dght 3.490 Lbp 123.70 Br md - Dpth 5.50 Welded, 1 dk	**(A13B2TP) Products Tanker** Liq: 5,747; Liq (Oil): 5,747 Compartments: 8 Ta, ER	**2 oil engines** driving 2 FP propellers Total Power: 1,472kW (2,002hp) S.K.L. 2 x 4 Stroke 8 Cy. 320 x 480 each-736kW (1001bhp) VEB Schwermaschinenbau "KarlLiebknecht" (SKL)-Magdeburg AuxGen: 3 x 100kW Fuel: 82.0 (d.f.)	11.1kn 8NVD48AU
8892007 *UBIM* -	**VOLGONEFT-147** *ex* Inline 147 *-2013* *ex* Volgoneft-147 *-2009* **Middle Volga Shipping Co** - *Rostov-na-Donu* *Russia*	**3,515** 1,121 4,337	Class: RS	**1979**-11 **Shipbuilding & Shiprepairing Yard 'Ivan Dimitrov' — Rousse** Yd No: 82 Loa 132.00 Br ex 16.90 Dght 3.470 Lbp 123.00 Br md - Dpth 5.50 Welded, 1 dk	**(A13B2TP) Products Tanker** Liq: 5,747; Liq (Oil): 5,747 Compartments: 8 Ta, ER Ice Capable	**2 oil engines** driving 2 FP propellers Total Power: 1,472kW (2,002hp) S.K.L. 2 x 4 Stroke 8 Cy. 320 x 480 each-736kW (1001bhp) VEB Schwermaschinenbau "KarlLiebknecht" (SKL)-Magdeburg AuxGen: 3 x 100kW a.c Fuel: 82.0 (d.f.)	11.0kn 8NVD48AU
8864763 *UIKB* -	**VOLGONEFT-151** **JSC Volzhski Oil Shipping Co 'Volgotanker'** - *Astrakhan* *Russia* MMSI: 273344400 Official number: 161710	*3,463* 1,132 4,190	Class: RR	**1980**-07 **Shipbuilding & Shiprepairing Yard 'Ivan Dimitrov' — Rousse** Yd No: 86 Loa 132.60 Br ex 16.90 Dght 3.130 Lbp 122.70 Br md - Dpth 5.50 Welded, 1 dk	**(A13B2TP) Products Tanker** Double Hull (13F) Liq: 5,747; Liq (Oil): 5,747 Compartments: 8 Ta, ER	**2 oil engines** driving 2 FP propellers Total Power: 1,472kW (2,002hp) S.K.L. 2 x 4 Stroke 8 Cy. 320 x 480 each-736kW (1001bhp) VEB Schwermaschinenbau "KarlLiebknecht" (SKL)-Magdeburg AuxGen: 3 x 100kW a.c Fuel: 82.0 (d.f.)	11.1kn 8NVD48AU
8867088 *UHWU* -	**VOLGONEFT-153** **JSC Volzhski Oil Shipping Co 'Volgotanker'** - *Astrakhan* *Russia* MMSI: 273345400 Official number: 161712	*3,463* 1,132 4,750	Class: RR	**1980 Shipbuilding & Shiprepairing Yard 'Ivan Dimitrov' — Rousse** Yd No: 88 Loa 132.60 Br ex 16.90 Dght 3.530 Lbp 123.06 Br md - Dpth 5.50 Welded, 1 dk	**(A13B2TP) Products Tanker** Double Hull (13F) Liq: 5,672; Liq (Oil): 5,672 Compartments: 8 Ta, ER 2 Cargo Pump (s): 2x500m³/hr	**2 oil engines** driving 2 FP propellers Total Power: 1,472kW (2,002hp) S.K.L. 2 x 4 Stroke 8 Cy. 320 x 480 each-736kW (1001bhp) VEB Schwermaschinenbau "KarlLiebknecht" (SKL)-Magdeburg AuxGen: 3 x 100kW a.c Fuel: 80.0 (d.f.)	11.0kn 8NVD48AU
8867143 *UHPX* -	**VOLGONEFT-165** **Morchartering Ltd** Oil Marine Group *Astrakhan* *Russia* MMSI: 273342100 Official number: 161739	**4,059** 1,956 6,574	Class: RS (RR)	**1982**-09 **Shipbuilding & Shiprepairing Yard 'Ivan Dimitrov' — Rousse** Yd No: 100 Loa 138.00 Br ex 16.82 Dght 4.460 Lbp 134.20 Br md 16.50 Dpth 5.50 Welded, 1 dk	**(A13B2TP) Products Tanker** Liq: 6,500; Liq (Oil): 6,500 Compartments: 12 Ta, ER	**2 oil engines** driving 2 FP propellers Total Power: 1,764kW (2,398hp) S.K.L. 2 x 4 Stroke 8 Cy. 320 x 480 each-882kW (1199bhp) VEB Schwermaschinenbau "KarlLiebknecht" (SKL)-Magdeburg Fuel: 188.0 (d.f.)	11.0kn 8NVDS48A-2U
8934219 *V3PU6* -	**VOLGONEFT-205** **VL205 Ltd** - *Belize City* *Belize* Official number: 361120101	**3,518** 1,760 4,500	Class: RR	**1970 Volgogradskiy Sudostroitelnyy Zavod — Volgograd** Yd No: 901 Loa 132.60 Br ex 16.90 Dght 3.300 Lbp 123.06 Br md 16.90 Dpth 5.50 Welded, 1 dk	**(A13B2TP) Products Tanker** Liq: 5,565; Liq (Oil): 5,565 Compartments: 8 Ta, ER	**2 oil engines** driving 2 FP propellers Total Power: 1,472kW (2,002hp) S.K.L. 2 x 4 Stroke 8 Cy. 320 x 480 each-736kW (1001bhp) VEB Schwermaschinenbau "KarlLiebknecht" (SKL)-Magdeburg AuxGen: 3 x 100kW Fuel: 90.0 (d.f.)	10.9kn 8NVD48AU

8231033 **VOLGONEFT-207**
UABC3
-
Oil Marine Group
-
St Petersburg *Russia*
MMSI: 273448590
Official number: 089678

3,463 Class: RR
1,074
4,660

1969-07 **Volgogradskiy Sudostroitelnyy Zavod — Volgograd** Yd No: 903
Loa 132.60 Br ex 16.90 Dght 3.400
Lbp 124.40 Br md - Dpth 5.50
Welded, 1 dk

(A13B2TP) Products Tanker
Liq: 5,672; Liq (Oil): 5,672
Cargo Heating Coils
Compartments: 8 Ta, ER

2 oil engines driving 2 FP propellers
Total Power: 1,472kW (2,002hp) 10.9kn
S.K.L. 8NVD48AU
2 x 4 Stroke 8 Cy. 320 x 480 each-736kW (1001bhp) (new engine 1985)
VEB Schwermaschinenbau "KarlLiebknecht" (SKL)-Magdeburg
AuxGen: 3 x 100kW
Fuel: 82.0 (d.f.)

8925438 **VOLGONEFT-209**
UFWX
-
-
-
St Petersburg *Russia*
MMSI: 273427530
Official number: 3473

3,566 Class: RR
1,760
4,650

1969 **Volgogradskiy Sudostroitelnyy Zavod — Volgograd** Yd No: 905
Loa 132.60 Br ex 16.90 Dght 3.200
Lbp 123.68 Br md 16.52 Dpth 5.51
Welded, 1 dk

(A13B2TP) Products Tanker
Double Hull
Liq: 5,000; Liq (Oil): 5,000
Cargo Heating Coils
Compartments: 8 Ta, ER
2 Cargo Pump (s): 2x450m³/hr

2 oil engines driving 2 FP propellers
Total Power: 1,472kW (2,002hp) 9.0kn
S.K.L. 8NVD48AU
2 x 4 Stroke 8 Cy. 320 x 480 each-736kW (1001bhp)
VEB Schwermaschinenbau "KarlLiebknecht" (SKL)-Magdeburg
AuxGen: 3 x 100kW
Fuel: 90.0 (d.f.)

8934233 **VOLGONEFT-215**
V3PC7
-
Tilso Trading Ltd
-
Belize City *Belize*
Official number: 361120102

3,518 Class: RR
1,760
4,500

1970 **Volgogradskiy Sudostroitelnyy Zavod — Volgograd** Yd No: 911
Loa 132.60 Br ex 16.90 Dght 3.300
Lbp 123.06 Br md 16.90 Dpth 5.50
Welded, 1 dk

(A13B2TP) Products Tanker
Liq: 5,565; Liq (Oil): 5,565
Compartments: 8 Ta, ER

2 oil engines driving 2 FP propellers
Total Power: 1,472kW (2,002hp) 10.9kn
S.K.L. 8NVD48AU
2 x 4 Stroke 8 Cy. 320 x 480 each-736kW (1001bhp)
VEB Schwermaschinenbau "KarlLiebknecht" (SKL)-Magdeburg
AuxGen: 3 x 100kW
Fuel: 90.0 (d.f.)

8925414 **VOLGONEFT-217**
-
Middle Volga Shipping Co
-
Russia

3,463 Class: RR
1,039
4,150

1970 **Shipbuilding & Shiprepairing Yard 'Ivan Dimitrov' — Rousse** Yd No: 912
Loa 132.60 Br ex 16.90 Dght 3.000
Lbp 123.06 Br md - Dpth 5.50
Welded, 1 dk

(A13B2TP) Products Tanker
Liq: 5,565; Liq (Oil): 5,565
Compartments: 8 Ta, ER

2 oil engines driving 2 FP propellers
Total Power: 1,472kW (2,002hp) 10.5kn
S.K.L. 8NVD48AU
2 x 4 Stroke 8 Cy. 320 x 480 each-736kW (1001bhp)
VEB Schwermaschinenbau "KarlLiebknecht" (SKL)-Magdeburg
AuxGen: 3 x 100kW
Fuel: 90.0 (d.f.)

8934271 **VOLGONEFT-229**
V3QN8
-
VL229 Ltd
-
Belize City *Belize*
Official number: 361120103

3,518 Class: RR
1,760
4,500

1972-01 **Volgogradskiy Sudostroitelnyy Zavod — Volgograd** Yd No: 925
Loa 132.60 Br ex 16.90 Dght 3.500
Lbp 123.06 Br md 16.90 Dpth 5.50
Welded, 1 dk

(A13B2TP) Products Tanker
Liq: 5,565; Liq (Oil): 5,565
Compartments: 8 Ta, ER

2 oil engines driving 2 FP propellers
Total Power: 1,472kW (2,002hp) 10.9kn
S.K.L. 8NVD48AU
2 x 4 Stroke 8 Cy. 320 x 480 each-736kW (1001bhp)
VEB Schwermaschinenbau "KarlLiebknecht" (SKL)-Magdeburg
AuxGen: 3 x 100kW
Fuel: 90.0 (d.f.)

8727991 **VOLGONEFT-247**
UFWV
-
-
-
St Petersburg *Russia*
MMSI: 273270100
Official number: 89996

3,475 Class: RR
1,039
4,550

1975-06 **Volgogradskiy Sudostroitelnyy Zavod — Volgograd** Yd No: 944
Loa 132.40 Br ex 16.90 Dght 3.330
Lbp 125.60 Br md 16.50 Dpth 5.60
Welded, 1 dk

(A13B2TP) Products Tanker
Double Hull
Liq: 5,655; Liq (Oil): 5,655
Cargo Heating Coils
Compartments: 8 Ta, ER
2 Cargo Pump (s): 2x450m³/hr

2 oil engines driving 2 FP propellers
Total Power: 1,472kW (2,002hp) 10.2kn
S.K.L. 8NVD48A-2U
2 x 4 Stroke 8 Cy. 320 x 480 each-736kW (1001bhp) (new engine 1985)
VEB Schwermaschinenbau "KarlLiebknecht" (SKL)-Magdeburg
AuxGen: 3 x 100kW
Fuel: 76.0 (d.f.)

8231045 **VOLGONEFT-250**
UFQT
-
JSC Volzhski Oil Shipping Co 'Volgotanker'
-
Astrakhan *Russia*
MMSI: 273340600
Official number: 89999

3,463 Class: RR
1,039
4,125

1975-07 **Volgogradskiy Sudostroitelnyy Zavod — Volgograd** Yd No: 947
Loa 132.60 Br ex 16.90 Dght 3.130
Lbp 113.70 Br md - Dpth 5.50
Welded, 1 dk

(A13B2TP) Products Tanker
Double Hull (13F)
Liq: 5,672; Liq (Oil): 5,672
Cargo Heating Coils
Compartments: 8 Ta, ER

2 oil engines driving 2 FP propellers
Total Power: 1,472kW (2,002hp) 10.9kn
S.K.L. 8NVD48AU
2 x 4 Stroke 8 Cy. 320 x 480 each-736kW (1001bhp)
VEB Schwermaschinenbau "KarlLiebknecht" (SKL)-Magdeburg
AuxGen: 3 x 100kW a.c
Fuel: 82.0 (d.f.)

8231057 **VOLGONEFT-251**
UFMS
-
JSC Volzhski Oil Shipping Co 'Volgotanker'
-
Astrakhan *Russia*
MMSI: 273349500
Official number: 182999

3,463 Class: RR
1,132
4,125

1975-07 **Volgogradskiy Sudostroitelnyy Zavod — Volgograd** Yd No: 948
Loa 132.60 Br ex 16.90 Dght 3.490
Lbp 123.70 Br md - Dpth 5.50
Welded, 1 dk

(A13B2TP) Products Tanker
Liq: 5,672; Liq (Oil): 5,672
Cargo Heating Coils
Compartments: 8 Ta, ER

2 oil engines driving 2 FP propellers
Total Power: 1,472kW (2,002hp) 10.9kn
S.K.L. 8NVD48AU
2 x 4 Stroke 8 Cy. 320 x 480 each-736kW (1001bhp)
VEB Schwermaschinenbau "KarlLiebknecht" (SKL)-Magdeburg
AuxGen: 3 x 100kW a.c
Fuel: 82.0 (d.f.)

8230845 **VOLGONEFT-252**
UABX
-
Morchartering Ltd
Oil Marine Group
Astrakhan *Russia*
MMSI: 273275000

4,059 Class: RS (RR)
1,161
4,805

1976-07 **Volgogradskiy Sudostroitelnyy Zavod — Volgograd** Yd No: 949
Loa 132.60 Br ex 16.90 Dght 4.460
Lbp 125.42 Br md 16.50 Dpth 5.50
Welded, 1 dk

(A13B2TP) Products Tanker
Liq: 5,672; Liq (Oil): 5,672
Cargo Heating Coils
Compartments: 8 Ta, ER

2 oil engines driving 2 FP propellers
Total Power: 1,472kW (2,002hp) 10.9kn
S.K.L. 8NVD48AU
2 x 4 Stroke 8 Cy. 320 x 480 each-736kW (1001bhp)
VEB Schwermaschinenbau "KarlLiebknecht" (SKL)-Magdeburg
AuxGen: 3 x 100kW a.c
Thrusters: 1 Tunnel thruster (f)
Fuel: 82.0 (d.f.)

8231069 **VOLGONEFT-254**
UIKC
-
JSC Volzhski Oil Shipping Co 'Volgotanker'
-
Astrakhan *Russia*
MMSI: 273347300
Official number: 183074

3,463 Class: RR
1,039
4,125

1976-07 **Volgogradskiy Sudostroitelnyy Zavod — Volgograd** Yd No: 102
Loa 132.60 Br ex 16.90 Dght 3.130
Lbp 123.70 Br md - Dpth 5.50
Welded, 1 dk

(A13B2TP) Products Tanker
Double Hull (13F)
Liq: 5,672; Liq (Oil): 5,672
Cargo Heating Coils
Compartments: 8 Ta, ER

2 oil engines driving 2 FP propellers
Total Power: 1,472kW (2,002hp) 10.9kn
S.K.L. 8NVD48AU
2 x 4 Stroke 8 Cy. 320 x 480 each-736kW (1001bhp)
VEB Schwermaschinenbau "KarlLiebknecht" (SKL)-Magdeburg
AuxGen: 3 x 100kW a.c
Fuel: 82.0 (d.f.)

8230869 **VOLGONEFT-255**
UBIY
-
JSC Volzhski Oil Shipping Co 'Volgotanker'
-
Astrakhan *Russia*
MMSI: 273271200
Official number: 183075

3,463 Class: RR
1,132
4,125

1976-07 **Volgogradskiy Sudostroitelnyy Zavod — Volgograd** Yd No: 103
Loa 132.60 Br ex 16.90 Dght 3.130
Lbp 123.70 Br md - Dpth 5.50
Welded, 1 dk

(A13B2TP) Products Tanker
Liq: 5,672; Liq (Oil): 5,672
Cargo Heating Coils
Compartments: 8 Ta, ER

2 oil engines driving 2 FP propellers
Total Power: 1,472kW (2,002hp) 10.9kn
S.K.L. 8NVD48A-2U
2 x 4 Stroke 8 Cy. 320 x 480 each-736kW (1001bhp)
VEB Schwermaschinenbau "KarlLiebknecht" (SKL)-Magdeburg
AuxGen: 3 x 100kW a.c
Fuel: 82.0 (d.f.)

8231071 **VOLGONEFT-256**
UABW
-
Morchartering Ltd
Oil Marine Group
Astrakhan *Russia*
MMSI: 273276100

4,059 Class: RS (RR)
1,140
4,806

1976-11 **Volgogradskiy Sudostroitelnyy Zavod — Volgograd** Yd No: 104
Loa 132.60 Br ex 16.90 Dght 3.500
Lbp 123.70 Br md 16.50 Dpth 5.50
Welded, 1 dk

(A13B2TP) Products Tanker
Double Hull (13F)
Liq: 5,672; Liq (Oil): 5,672
Cargo Heating Coils
Compartments: 8 Ta, ER

2 oil engines driving 2 FP propellers
Total Power: 1,472kW (2,002hp) 10.9kn
S.K.L. 8NVD48A-2U
2 x 4 Stroke 8 Cy. 320 x 480 each-736kW (1001bhp)
VEB Schwermaschinenbau "KarlLiebknecht" (SKL)-Magdeburg
AuxGen: 3 x 100kW a.c
Fuel: 82.0 (d.f.)

8230871 **VOLGONEFT-259**
UFTN
-
JSC Volzhski Oil Shipping Co 'Volgotanker'
-
Astrakhan *Russia*
MMSI: 273348500

3,463 Class: RR
1,132
4,125

1977-07 **Volgogradskiy Sudostroitelnyy Zavod — Volgograd** Yd No: 107
Loa 132.60 Br ex 16.90 Dght 3.490
Lbp 123.70 Br md - Dpth 5.50
Welded, 1 dk

(A13B2TP) Products Tanker
Liq: 5,672; Liq (Oil): 5,672
Cargo Heating Coils
Compartments: 8 Ta, ER

2 oil engines driving 2 FP propellers
Total Power: 1,472kW (2,002hp) 10.9kn
S.K.L. 8NVD48AU
2 x 4 Stroke 8 Cy. 320 x 480 each-736kW (1001bhp)
VEB Schwermaschinenbau "KarlLiebknecht" (SKL)-Magdeburg
AuxGen: 3 x 100kW a.c
Fuel: 82.0 (d.f.)

IMO / Call sign	Name / Owner	Tonnage / Class	Build	Type	Machinery
8230883 *UFTM* -	**VOLGONEFT-260** **JSC Volzhski Oil Shipping Co 'Volgotanker'** - *Astrakhan* *Russia* MMSI: 273347500	**3,463** Class: RR 1,132 4,125	**1977-07 Volgogradskiy Sudostroitelnyy Zavod — Volgograd** Yd No: 108 Loa 132.60 Br ex 16.90 Dght 3.490 Lbp 123.70 Br md - Dpth 5.50 Welded, 1 dk	**(A13B2TP) Products Tanker** Double Hull (13F) Liq: 5,672; Liq (Oil): 5,672 Cargo Heating Coils Compartments: 8 Ta, ER	**2 oil engines** driving 2 FP propellers Total Power: 1,472kW (2,002hp) 10.9kn S.K.L. 8NVD48AU 2 x 4 Stroke 8 Cy. 320 x 480 each-736kW (1001bhp) VEB Schwermaschinenbau "KarlLiebknecht" (SKL)-Magdeburg AuxGen: 3 x 100kW a.c Fuel: 82.0 (d.f.)
8230895 *UFTL* -	**VOLGONEFT-261** **JSC Volzhski Oil Shipping Co 'Volgotanker'** - *Astrakhan* *Russia* MMSI: 273346500	**3,463** Class: RR 1,132 4,125	**1977-07 Volgogradskiy Sudostroitelnyy Zavod — Volgograd** Yd No: 110 Loa 132.60 Br ex 16.90 Dght 3.490 Lbp 123.70 Br md - Dpth 5.50 Welded, 1 dk	**(A13B2TP) Products Tanker** Double Hull (13F) Liq: 5,672; Liq (Oil): 5,672 Cargo Heating Coils Compartments: 8 Ta, ER	**2 oil engines** driving 2 FP propellers Total Power: 1,472kW (2,002hp) 10.9kn S.K.L. 8NVD48AU 2 x 4 Stroke 8 Cy. 320 x 480 each-736kW (1001bhp) VEB Schwermaschinenbau "KarlLiebknecht" (SKL)-Magdeburg AuxGen: 3 x 100kW a.c Fuel: 82.0 (d.f.)
8230900 *UFTJ* -	**VOLGONEFT-262** **JSC Volzhski Oil Shipping Co 'Volgotanker'** - *Astrakhan* *Russia* MMSI: 273345500	**3,475** Class: RR 1,132 4,750	**1978-07 Volgogradskiy Sudostroitelnyy Zavod — Volgograd** Yd No: 111 Loa 132.60 Br ex 16.90 Dght 3.400 Lbp 124.70 Br md - Dpth 5.50 Welded, 1 dk	**(A13B2TP) Products Tanker** Double Hull (13F) Liq: 5,672; Liq (Oil): 5,672 Cargo Heating Coils Compartments: 8 Ta, ER	**2 oil engines** driving 2 FP propellers Total Power: 1,472kW (2,002hp) 10.9kn S.K.L. 8NVD48AU 2 x 4 Stroke 8 Cy. 320 x 480 each-736kW (1001bhp) VEB Schwermaschinenbau "KarlLiebknecht" (SKL)-Magdeburg AuxGen: 3 x 100kW a.c Fuel: 82.0 (d.f.)
8230912 *UFTI* -	**VOLGONEFT-263** **Roschartering CJSC** - SatCom: Inmarsat C 427310243 *Astrakhan* *Russia* MMSI: 273344500	**3,475** Class: RS (RR) 1,113 4,701	**1978-07 Volgogradskiy Sudostroitelnyy Zavod — Volgograd** Yd No: 112 Loa 132.60 Br ex 16.90 Dght 3.460 Lbp 124.70 Br md 16.50 Dpth 5.50 Welded, 1 dk	**(A13B2TP) Products Tanker** Liq: 5,672; Liq (Oil): 5,672 Cargo Heating Coils Compartments: 8 Ta, ER	**2 oil engines** driving 2 FP propellers Total Power: 1,472kW (2,002hp) 10.9kn S.K.L. 8NVD48AU 2 x 4 Stroke 8 Cy. 320 x 480 each-736kW (1001bhp) (made 1977) VEB Schwermaschinenbau "KarlLiebknecht" (SKL)-Magdeburg AuxGen: 3 x 100kW a.c Fuel: 82.0 (d.f.)
8230924 *UFED* -	**VOLGONEFT-264** **JSC Volzhski Oil Shipping Co 'Volgotanker'** - *Astrakhan* *Russia*	**3,475** Class: RR 1,132 4,750	**1978-07 Volgogradskiy Sudostroitelnyy Zavod — Volgograd** Yd No: 113 Loa 132.60 Br ex 16.90 Dght 3.490 Lbp 124.70 Br md - Dpth 5.50 Welded, 1 dk	**(A13B2TP) Products Tanker** Double Hull (13F) Liq: 5,672; Liq (Oil): 5,672 Cargo Heating Coils Compartments: 8 Ta, ER	**2 oil engines** driving 2 FP propellers Total Power: 1,472kW (2,002hp) 10.9kn S.K.L. 8NVD48AU 2 x 4 Stroke 8 Cy. 320 x 480 each-736kW (1001bhp) VEB Schwermaschinenbau "KarlLiebknecht" (SKL)-Magdeburg AuxGen: 3 x 100kW a.c Fuel: 82.0 (d.f.)
8230936 *UFTH* -	**VOLGONEFT-265** **JSC Volzhski Oil Shipping Co 'Volgotanker'** - *Astrakhan* *Russia* MMSI: 273343500	**3,475** Class: RR 1,132 4,750	**1978-07 Volgogradskiy Sudostroitelnyy Zavod — Volgograd** Yd No: 114 Loa 132.60 Br ex 16.90 Dght 3.490 Lbp 124.70 Br md - Dpth 5.50 Welded, 1 dk	**(A13B2TP) Products Tanker** Double Hull (13F) Liq: 5,672; Liq (Oil): 5,672 Cargo Heating Coils Compartments: 8 Ta, ER	**2 oil engines** driving 2 FP propellers Total Power: 1,472kW (2,002hp) 10.9kn S.K.L. 8NVD48AU 2 x 4 Stroke 8 Cy. 320 x 480 each-736kW (1001bhp) VEB Schwermaschinenbau "KarlLiebknecht" (SKL)-Magdeburg AuxGen: 3 x 100kW a.c Fuel: 82.0 (d.f.)
8230948 *UFTG* -	**VOLGONEFT-266** **JSC Volzhski Oil Shipping Co 'Volgotanker'** - *Astrakhan* *Russia* MMSI: 273342500	**3,475** Class: RR 1,132 4,750	**1978-07 Volgogradskiy Sudostroitelnyy Zavod — Volgograd** Yd No: 115 Loa 132.60 Br ex 16.90 Dght 3.490 Lbp 124.70 Br md - Dpth 5.50 Welded, 1 dk	**(A13B2TP) Products Tanker** Liq: 5,672; Liq (Oil): 5,672 Cargo Heating Coils Compartments: 8 Ta, ER	**2 oil engines** driving 2 FP propellers Total Power: 1,472kW (2,002hp) 10.9kn S.K.L. 8NVD48AU 2 x 4 Stroke 8 Cy. 320 x 480 each-736kW (1001bhp) VEB Schwermaschinenbau "KarlLiebknecht" (SKL)-Magdeburg AuxGen: 3 x 100kW a.c Fuel: 82.0 (d.f.)
8230950 *UIBP* -	**VOLGONEFT-267** **JSC Volzhski Oil Shipping Co 'Volgotanker'** - *Astrakhan* *Russia* MMSI: 273341500	**3,473** Class: RR 1,149 4,750	**1979-07 Volgogradskiy Sudostroitelnyy Zavod — Volgograd** Yd No: 116 Loa 132.60 Br ex 16.90 Dght 3.490 Lbp 124.70 Br md - Dpth 5.50 Welded, 1 dk	**(A13B2TP) Products Tanker** Liq: 5,672; Liq (Oil): 5,672 Cargo Heating Coils Compartments: 8 Ta, ER	**2 oil engines** driving 2 FP propellers Total Power: 1,472kW (2,002hp) 10.9kn S.K.L. 8NVD48A-2U 2 x 4 Stroke 8 Cy. 320 x 480 each-736kW (1001bhp) VEB Schwermaschinenbau "KarlLiebknecht" (SKL)-Magdeburg AuxGen: 3 x 100kW a.c Fuel: 82.0 (d.f.)
8230962 *UBGY* -	**VOLGONEFT-268** **Roschartering CJSC** Oil Marine Group SatCom: Inmarsat C 427310247 *Astrakhan* *Russia* MMSI: 273340500 Official number: 790997	**3,475** Class: RS (RR) 1,132 4,701	**1979-07 Volgogradskiy Sudostroitelnyy Zavod — Volgograd** Yd No: 117 Loa 132.60 Br ex 16.90 Dght 3.460 Lbp 124.70 Br md 16.50 Dpth 5.50 Welded, 1 dk	**(A13B2TP) Products Tanker** Liq: 5,672; Liq (Oil): 5,672 Cargo Heating Coils Compartments: 8 Ta, ER	**2 oil engines** driving 2 FP propellers Total Power: 1,472kW (2,002hp) 10.9kn S.K.L. 8NVD48AU 2 x 4 Stroke 8 Cy. 320 x 480 each-736kW (1001bhp) VEB Schwermaschinenbau "KarlLiebknecht" (SKL)-Magdeburg AuxGen: 3 x 100kW a.c Fuel: 82.0 (d.f.)
8230974 *UBGA* -	**VOLGONEFT-269** **JSC Volzhski Oil Shipping Co 'Volgotanker'** - *Astrakhan* *Russia* MMSI: 273349400	**3,475** Class: RR 1,132 4,750	**1979-07 Volgogradskiy Sudostroitelnyy Zavod — Volgograd** Yd No: 118 Loa 132.60 Br ex 16.90 Dght 3.490 Lbp 124.70 Br md - Dpth 5.50 Welded, 1 dk	**(A13B2TP) Products Tanker** Double Hull (13F) Liq: 5,672; Liq (Oil): 5,672 Cargo Heating Coils Compartments: 8 Ta, ER	**2 oil engines** driving 2 FP propellers Total Power: 1,472kW (2,002hp) 10.9kn S.K.L. 8NVD48AU 2 x 4 Stroke 8 Cy. 320 x 480 each-736kW (1001bhp) VEB Schwermaschinenbau "KarlLiebknecht" (SKL)-Magdeburg AuxGen: 3 x 100kW a.c Fuel: 82.0 (d.f.)
8230986 *UBIS* -	**VOLGONEFT-270** **JSC Volzhski Oil Shipping Co 'Volgotanker'** - SatCom: Inmarsat B 327328011 *Astrakhan* *Russia* MMSI: 273348400	**3,475** Class: RR 1,132 4,750	**1979-07 Volgogradskiy Sudostroitelnyy Zavod — Volgograd** Yd No: 119 Loa 132.60 Br ex 16.90 Dght 3.490 Lbp 124.70 Br md - Dpth 5.50 Welded, 1 dk	**(A13B2TP) Products Tanker** Double Hull (13F) Liq: 5,672; Liq (Oil): 5,672 Cargo Heating Coils Compartments: 8 Ta, ER	**2 oil engines** driving 2 FP propellers Total Power: 1,472kW (2,002hp) 10.9kn S.K.L. 8NVD48AU 2 x 4 Stroke 8 Cy. 320 x 480 each-736kW (1001bhp) VEB Schwermaschinenbau "KarlLiebknecht" (SKL)-Magdeburg AuxGen: 3 x 100kW a.c Fuel: 82.0 (d.f.)
9021722 *PHBS* HD 36	**VOLHARDING** *ex Westerems -2006* **Rederij Zijlstra BV** - *Den Helder* *Netherlands* MMSI: 245813000 Official number: 42789	**167** Class: (GL) 50 -	**1991-07 Scheepswerf Visser B.V. — Den Helder** Yd No: 134 Loa 23.97 Br ex 6.75 Dght 3.000 Lbp 21.47 Br md 6.70 Dpth 4.00 Welded, 1 dk	**(B11A2FT) Trawler** Ins: 100	**1 oil engine** with flexible couplings & reduction geared to sc. shaft driving 1 FP propeller Total Power: 294kW (400hp) 9.0kn MWM TBD604BL6 1 x 4 Stroke 6 Cy. 170 x 195 294kW (400bhp) Motoren Werke Mannheim AG (MWM)-Mannheim Thrusters: 1 Thwart. FP thruster (f)
8024002 *UDUT* -	**VOLK ARKTIKI** *ex Arctic Wolf -2005 ex Sea Fox -1999* *ex Russian Viking -1997 ex Ran -1996* *ex Ilimmaasaq -1991* **Dimas Co Ltd (OOO 'Dimas')** - *Petropavlovsk-Kamchatskiy* *Russia* MMSI: 273539310	**1,196** Class: NV RS 359 245	**1982-12 Orskov Christensens Staalskibsvaerft A/S — Frederikshavn** Yd No: 124 Converted From: Stern Trawler-1985 Loa 57.08 (BB) Br ex - Dght 4.616 Lbp 52.48 Br md 11.61 Dpth 6.91 Welded, 2 dks	**(B11A2FG) Factory Stern Trawler** Ins: 679 Compartments: 1 Ho, ER 1 Ha: ER Ice Capable	**1 oil engine** with flexible couplings & sr gearedto sc. shaft driving 1 CP propeller Total Power: 1,471kW (2,000hp) Alpha 16V23L-VO 1 x Vee 4 Stroke 16 Cy. 225 x 300 1471kW (2000bhp) B&W Alpha Diesel A/S-Denmark AuxGen: 2 x 312kW 380V 50Hz a.c Fuel: 271.0 (d.f.)
7529885 *9LD2494* -	**VOLKAN** *ex Isla De Los Volcanes -2012 ex Luberon -1987* **Akgunler Isletmeleri Sti Ltd** - *Freetown* *Sierra Leone* MMSI: 667005194	**3,304** Class: BV (GL) 991 1,600	**1977-12 Soc Nouvelle des Ats et Chs de La Rochelle-Pallice — La Rochelle** Yd No: 1225 Loa 90.71 Br ex 14.00 Dght 4.452 Lbp 82.02 Br md 13.81 Dpth 4.50 Welded, 2 dks	**(A35A2RR) Ro-Ro Cargo Ship** Lane-Len: 348 Cars: 200 Grain: 8,344; Bale: 6,996	**1 oil engine** reduction geared to sc. shaft driving 1 CP propeller Total Power: 1,765kW (2,400hp) 13.5kn Pielstick 8PA6L280 1 x 4 Stroke 8 Cy. 280 x 290 1765kW (2400bhp) Alsthom Atlantique-France AuxGen: 1 x 240kW 220/380V a.c, 2 x 152kW 220/380V a.c Fuel: 156.5 (d.f.)

LR/IMO No. / Call sign / Flag	Name / Former names / Owner / Manager / Port / Official number	Tonnages	Class	Builder / Dimensions	Type / Cargo	Machinery
8846709 - -	**VOLKHOV** *ex* Iru *-2001* **Investtransgroup Ltd** - *St Petersburg* *Russia* Official number: 7601924	**223** 66 224	Class: RS	**1977 Bakinskiy Sudostroitelnyy Zavod im Vano Sturua — Baku** Yd No: 313 Loa 29.17 Br ex 8.01 Dght 2.750 Lbp 28.60 Br md 7.58 Dpth 3.60 Welded, 1 dk	**(B34G2SE) Pollution Control Vessel** Liq: 336; Liq (Oil): 336 Compartments: 8 Ta Ice Capable	**1 oil engine** geared to sc. shaft driving 1 FP propeller Total Power: 165kW (224hp) 7.5kn Daldizel 6CHNSP18/22 1 x 4 Stroke 6 Cy. 180 x 220 165kW (224bhp) Daldizel-Khabarovsk AuxGen: 1 x 50kW, 1 x 30kW Fuel: 11.0 (d.f.)
9284544 *C6AO8* -	**VOLME** *ex* Star Bergen *-2007* **United Shipping Services Four Inc** Uljanik Shipmanagement Inc *Nassau* *Bahamas* MMSI: 311000107	**29,414** 17,601 52,949	Class: BV (NK) (CS)	**2004-10 Oshima Shipbuilding Co Ltd — Saikai NS** Yd No: 10376 Loa 188.50 (BB) Br ex - Dght 12.163 Lbp 179.00 Br md 32.26 Dpth 17.15 Welded, 1 dk	**(A21A2BC) Bulk Carrier** Double Hull Grain: 66,416; Bale: 65,295 Compartments: 5 Ho, ER 5 Ha: (18.6 x 18.6)2 (21.4 x 18.6) (22.3 x 18.6)ER (16.7 x 18.6) Cranes: 4x30t	**1 oil engine** driving 1 FP propeller Total Power: 7,686kW (10,450hp) 14.5kn B&W 6S50MC-C 1 x 2 Stroke 6 Cy. 500 x 2000 7686kW (10450bhp) Mitsui Engineering & Shipbuilding CLtd-Japan
7630555 - -	**VOLNOGORSK** **Akros Fishing Co Ltd (A/O Akros)** -	**172** 51 89	Class: (RS)	**1976 Sretenskiy Sudostroitelnyy Zavod — Sretensk** Yd No: 90 Loa 33.96 Br ex 7.09 Dght 2.899 Lbp 30.00 Br md - Dpth 3.69 Welded, 1 dk	**(B11B2FV) Fishing Vessel** Grain: 115 Compartments: 1 Ho, ER 1 Ha: (1.3 x 1.6) Derricks: 2x2t; Winches: 2 Ice Capable	**1 oil engine** driving 1 FP propeller Total Power: 224kW (305hp) 9.0kn S.K.L. 8NVD36-1U 1 x 4 Stroke 8 Cy. 240 x 360 224kW (305bhp) VEB Schwermaschinenbau "KarlLiebknecht" (SKL)-Magdeburg
5387350 - -	**VOLO** *ex* Lars Bagger *-2009* *ex* Ulsnaes *-1989* *ex* Welf *-1989* - -	**326** 149 469	Class: (BV) (GL)	**1957-07 Muetzelfeldtwerft GmbH — Cuxhaven** Yd No: 148 Loa 44.86 Br ex 8.26 Dght 2.890 Lbp 39.88 Br md 8.23 Dpth 3.20 Riveted\Welded, 1 dk	**(A31A2GX) General Cargo Ship** Grain: 600; Bale: 538 Compartments: 1 Ho, ER 1 Ha: (19.2 x 4.8)ER Derricks: 2x2t Ice Capable	**1 oil engine** driving 1 FP propeller Total Power: 221kW (300hp) 9.0kn MaK MSU423 1 x 4 Stroke 6 Cy. 290 x 420 221kW (300bhp) Maschinenbau Kiel AG (MaK)-Kiel
8722159 - -	**VOLOCHAYEVSKIY** **Tunaycha Co Ltd (OOO 'Tunaycha')**	**738** 221 332	Class: (RS)	**1988-04 Volgogradskiy Sudostroitelnyy Zavod — Volgograd** Yd No: 244 Loa 53.74 (BB) Br ex - Dght 4.400 Lbp 47.92 Br md 10.71 Dpth 6.00 Welded, 1 dk	**(B11A2FS) Stern Trawler** Ice Capable	**1 oil engine** driving 1 CP propeller Total Power: 970kW (1,319hp) 12.7kn S.K.L. 8NVD48A-2U 1 x 4 Stroke 8 Cy. 320 x 480 970kW (1319bhp) VEB Schwermaschinenbau "KarlLiebknecht" (SKL)-Magdeburg AuxGen: 1 x 300kW a.c, 3 x 160kW a.c, 2 x 135kW a.c
7630567 *UHID* -	**VOLODARSK** **Rybokonservnyy Zavod Avacha Ltd** - *Petropavlovsk-Kamchatskiy* *Russia* MMSI: 273826500	**172** 51 89	Class: RS	**1976 Sretenskiy Sudostroitelnyy Zavod — Sretensk** Yd No: 89 Loa 33.96 Br ex 7.09 Dght 2.899 Lbp 30.00 Br md 7.00 Dpth 3.69 Welded, 1 dk	**(B11B2FV) Fishing Vessel** Bale: 96 Compartments: 1 Ho, ER 1 Ha: (1.3 x 1.6) Derricks: 2x2t; Winches: 2 Ice Capable	**1 oil engine** driving 1 FP propeller Total Power: 224kW (305hp) 9.0kn S.K.L. 8NVD36-1U 1 x 4 Stroke 8 Cy. 240 x 360 224kW (305bhp) VEB Schwermaschinenbau "KarlLiebknecht" (SKL)-Magdeburg AuxGen: 1 x 86kW, 1 x 60kW, 1 x 32kW Fuel: 20.0 (d.f.)
9363974 *UUAN6* -	**VOLODYMYR BONDAR** **Bug-5 Shipping Ltd** 'Ukrrichflot' Joint Stock Shipping Co *Kherson* *Ukraine* MMSI: 272526000	**5,197** 2,796 6,315	Class: RS	**2006-11 OAO Damen Shipyards Okean — Nikolayev** Yd No: 9123 Loa 127.30 Br ex 16.82 Dght 4.860 Lbp 121.10 Br md 16.60 Dpth 6.70 Welded, 1 dk	**(A31A2GX) General Cargo Ship** Grain: 9,880 TEU 331 Compartments: 3 Ho, ER 3 Ha: 2 (25.6 x 13.0)ER (32.8 x 13.0)	**1 oil engine** reduction geared to sc. shaft driving 1 CP propeller Total Power: 1,935kW (2,631hp) 11.2kn MAN-B&W 9L21/31 1 x 4 Stroke 9 Cy. 210 x 310 1935kW (2631bhp) MAN B&W Diesel A/S-Denmark AuxGen: 2 x 236kW 380V 50Hz a.c, 1 x 312kW 380V 50Hz a.c Thrusters: 1 Thwart. FP thruster (f) Fuel: 228.0 (d.f.) 10.0pd
9670872 *UUAX3* -	**VOLODYMYR IVANOV** **Port of Yuzhnyy** - *Ukraine* MMSI: 272700000	**453** 135 255	Class: (RS)	**2012-12 Song Cam Shipyard — Haiphong** (Hull completed by) Yd No: (512514) **2012-12 Santierul Naval Damen Galati S.A. — Galati** (Hull launched by) Yd No: (512514) **2012* B.V. Scheepswerf Damen — Gorinchem** Yd No: 512514 Loa 32.70 Br ex 12.82 Dght 4.200 Lbp 28.84 Br md 12.20 Dpth 5.35 Welded, 1 dk	**(B32A2ST) Tug**	**2 oil engines** reduction geared to sc. shafts driving 2 Directional propellers Total Power: 3,090kW (4,202hp) Caterpillar 3516C-HD 2 x Vee 4 Stroke 16 Cy. 170 x 215 each-1545kW (2101bhp) Caterpillar Inc-USA AuxGen: 2 x 100kW a.c Fuel: 130.0 (d.f.)
8844062 *UTJW* -	**VOLODYMYR SHARKOV** *ex* Irpen *-2002* **'Ukrrichflot' Joint Stock Shipping Co** - SatCom: Inmarsat C 427229411 *Kherson* *Ukraine* MMSI: 272294000 Official number: 191027	*3,995* 1,199 4,515	Class: UA	**1985 Santierul Naval Oltenita S.A. — Oltenita** Yd No: 199 Loa 138.80 Br ex 16.70 Dght 3.170 Lbp - Br md 16.50 Dpth 5.50 Welded, 1 dk	**(A31A2GX) General Cargo Ship** Grain: 6,270	**2 oil engines** driving 2 FP propellers Total Power: 1,324kW (1,800hp) 10.0kn Dvigatel Revolyutsii 6CHRN36/45 2 x 4 Stroke 6 Cy. 360 x 450 each-662kW (900bhp) Zavod "Dvigatel Revolyutsii"-Gorkiy
8926303 - -	**VOLOSHSKIY** **Nikolayev Clay Works (Nikolayevskiy Glinozemnyy Zavod)** - *Nikolayev* *Ukraine* Official number: 770902	*205* 77 326	Class: (RS)	**1978 Bakinskiy Sudostroitelnyy Zavod im Vano Sturua — Baku** Yd No: 319 Loa 29.17 Br ex 8.01 Dght 3.120 Lbp 28.50 Br md - Dpth 3.60 Welded, 1 dk	**(B34G2SE) Pollution Control Vessel** Liq: 336; Liq (Oil): 336 Compartments: 8 Ta Ice Capable	**1 oil engine** geared to sc. shaft driving 1 FP propeller Total Power: 168kW (228hp) 7.5kn Daldizel 6CHNSP18/22 1 x 4 Stroke 6 Cy. 180 x 220 168kW (228bhp) Daldizel-Khabarovsk AuxGen: 1 x 50kW a.c, 1 x 30kW a.c Fuel: 15.0 (d.f.)
1007976 *ZCNN3* -	**VOLPINI** *ex* Larissa *-2013* **La Volpe Ltd** New Wave Captains EURL (Sunseeker Superyacht Management) *George Town* *Cayman Islands (British)* MMSI: 319129000 Official number: 737341	**659** 197 116	Class: LR ✠ **100A1** SS 07/2009 SSC Yacht, mono, G6 ✠ **LMC** Cable: 440.0/20.0 U2 (a)	**2004-07 Amels Holland BV — Makkum** Yd No: 445 Loa 47.50 (BB) Br ex 9.25 Dght - Lbp 43.25 Br md 9.00 Dpth 5.10 Welded, 1 dk	**(X11A2YP) Yacht**	**2 oil engines** with clutches, flexible couplings & sr reverse geared to sc. shafts driving 2 FP propellers Total Power: 1,576kW (2,142hp) M.T.U. 12V2000M70 2 x Vee 4 Stroke 12 Cy. 130 x 150 each-788kW (1071bhp) MTU Friedrichshafen GmbH-Friedrichshafen AuxGen: 2 x 160kW 400V 50Hz a.c Thrusters: 1 Thwart. FP thruster (f)
6928864 *UUAS9* -	**VOLSHEBNIK** *ex* Wizard *-2011* *ex* Towing Wizard *-2003* *ex* Hollygarth *-1997* **Serena Sea Navigation Co** Tech Project LLC *Odessa* *Ukraine* MMSI: 272648000 Official number: 979	**347** 104 162	Class: HR (LR) ✠ Classed LR until 3/5/02	**1969-12 Appledore Shipbuilders Ltd — Bideford** Yd No: A.S. 68 Loa 36.56 Br ex 10.01 Dght 3.963 Lbp 31.70 Br md 9.45 Dpth 4.65 Welded, 1 dk	**(B32A2ST) Tug**	**2 oil engines** dr geared to sc. shaft driving 1 CP propeller Total Power: 2,486kW (3,380hp) 14.0kn Ruston 6ATCM 2 x 4 Stroke 6 Cy. 318 x 368 each-1243kW (1690bhp) English Electric Diesels Ltd.-Glasgow AuxGen: 2 x 100kW 440V 60Hz a.c Fuel: 87.5 (d.f.)
9652818 *3YYB* -	**VOLSTAD** **Volstad AS** Volstad Shipping AS *Aalesund* *Norway* MMSI: 258874000	**3,430** 1,036 1,500	Class: NV	**2013-06 Tersan Tersanecilik ve Tasimacilik AS — Istanbul (Tuzla)** Yd No: 1020 Loa 74.70 (BB) Br ex - Dght 6.360 Lbp 66.00 Br md 15.40 Dpth 6.16 Welded, 1 dk	**(B11A2FS) Stern Trawler** Ice Capable	**1 oil engine** reduction geared to sc. shaft driving 1 CP propeller Total Power: 4,500kW (6,118hp) Wartsila 9L32 1 x 4 Stroke 9 Cy. 320 x 400 4500kW (6118bhp) Wartsila Finland Oy-Finland AuxGen: 1 x a.c, 1 x a.c, 1 x a.c Thrusters: 1 Tunnel thruster (f)
9390549 *LADV* -	**VOLSTAD PRINCESS** **Volstad Shipping AS** - SatCom: Inmarsat C 425729611 *Aalesund* *Norway* MMSI: 257296000	**4,277** 1,283 4,867	Class: NV	**2008-05 SC Aker Tulcea SA — Tulcea** (Hull) Yd No: 374 **2008-05 Aker Yards AS Brattvaag — Brattvaag** Yd No: 129AYB Loa 93.40 (BB) Br ex - Dght 6.850 Lbp 82.20 Br md 19.20 Dpth 8.50 Welded, 1 dk	**(B21A2OS) Platform Supply Ship** Ice Capable	**5 diesel electric oil engines** driving 4 gen. each 1900kW a.c 1 gen. of 950kW a.c Connecting to 2 elec. motors each (3500kW) driving 2 Azimuth electric drive units Total Power: 8,550kW (11,624hp) 16.0kn Caterpillar 3508B 1 x Vee 4 Stroke 8 Cy. 170 x 190 950kW (1292bhp) Caterpillar Inc-USA Caterpillar 3516B 4 x Vee 4 Stroke 16 Cy. 170 x 190 each-1900kW (2583bhp) Caterpillar Inc-USA Thrusters: 2 Tunnel thruster (f); 1 Retract. directional thruster (f) Fuel: 1174.0 (d.f.)

IMO / Call sign	Name / Owner	Tonnage / Class	Builder / Dimensions	Type	Machinery
9363778 *LNZN* -	**VOLSTAD SUPPLIER** **Volstad Shipping AS** - SatCom: Inmarsat C 425910510 *Aalesund* *Norway* MMSI: 259105000	**4,201** Class: NV 1,260 5,100	**2007-10 SC Aker Tulcea SA — Tulcea** (Hull) Yd No: 356 **2007-10 Aker Yards AS Brattvaag — Brattvaag** Yd No: 118 Loa 93.40 (BB) Br ex - Dght 6.850 Lbp 82.20 Br md 19.20 Dpth 8.40 Welded, 1 dk	**(B21A2OS) Platform Supply Ship** Ice Capable	**4 diesel electric oil engines** driving 4 gen. each 1825kW a.c Connecting to 2 elec. motors each (3500kW) driving 2 Azimuth electric drive units Total Power: 7,600kW (10,332hp) 15.0kn Caterpillar 3516B 4 x Vee 4 Stroke 16 Cy. 170 x 190 each-1900kW (2583bhp) Caterpillar Inc-USA Thrusters: 2 Tunnel thruster (f); 1 Retract. directional thruster (f) Fuel: 1174.0 (d.f.)
9533373 *9HA2303* -	**VOLSTAD SURVEYOR** **Volstad Shipping AS** - *Valletta* *Malta* MMSI: 248290000 Official number: 9533373	**4,398** Class: NV 1,320 1,350	**2010-05 Yildirim Gemi Insaat Sanayii A.S. — Tuzla** (Hull) Yd No: 115 **0000* Construcciones Navales P Freire SA — Vigo** Yd No: 701 Loa 85.30 (BB) Br ex - Dght 6.800 Lbp 76.18 Br md 18.00 Dpth 9.10 Welded, 1 dk	**(B31A2SR) Research Survey Vessel** Cranes: 1x70t Ice Capable	**4 diesel electric oil engines** driving 4 gen. Connecting to 2 elec. motors each (2200kW) driving 2 Azimuth electric drive units Total Power: 7,300kW (9,924hp) Caterpillar 3516B 4 x Vee 4 Stroke 16 Cy. 170 x 190 each-1825kW (2481bhp) Caterpillar Inc-USA AuxGen: 2 x 1825kW a.c Thrusters: 2 Tunnel thruster (f); 1 Retract. directional thruster (f) Fuel: 1100.0 (d.f.)
9363728 *LNXU* -	**VOLSTAD VIKING** *launched as* Arctic Viking *-2007* **Volstad Shipping AS** - *Aalesund* *Norway* MMSI: 259498000	**4,183** Class: NV 1,254 4,940	**2007-04 SC Aker Tulcea SA — Tulcea** (Hull) Yd No: 349 **2007-04 Aker Yards AS Brattvaag — Brattvaag** Yd No: 116 Loa 93.40 (BB) Br ex 19.20 Dght 6.850 Lbp 82.20 Br md 19.20 Dpth 8.40 Welded, 1 dk	**(B21A2OS) Platform Supply Ship** Ice Capable	**4 diesel electric oil engines** driving 4 gen. each 1825kW a.c Connecting to 2 elec. motors each (3500kW) driving 2 Azimuth electric drive units Total Power: 6,744kW (9,168hp) 15.0kn Caterpillar 3516B-HD 4 x Vee 4 Stroke 16 Cy. 170 x 215 each-1686kW (2292bhp) Caterpillar Inc-USA AuxGen: 1 x a.c Thrusters: 2 Tunnel thruster (f); 1 Retract. directional thruster (f) Fuel: 1174.0 (d.f.)
8323604 *9GII* -	**VOLTA GLORY** *ex* Wan Shun *-2007* *ex* Enyoh Maru *-2003* **Panofi Co Ltd** Silla Co Ltd *Takoradi* *Ghana* MMSI: 627047000 Official number: GSR 0047	**2,829** Class: (NK) 1,626 3,988	**1983-12 Kochi Jyuko (Eiho Zosen) K.K. — Kochi** Yd No: 1637 Loa 93.88 Br ex - Dght 6.117 Lbp 86.52 Br md 16.01 Dpth 8.26 Welded, 2 dks	**(A34A2GR) Refrigerated Cargo Ship** Ins: 3,957 Compartments: 3 Ho, ER 3 Ha: 3 (7.1 x 6.0)ER Derricks: 6x3t	**1 oil engine** driving 1 FP propeller Total Power: 2,438kW (3,315hp) 14.0kn Mitsubishi 6UEC37H 1 x 2 Stroke 6 Cy. 370 x 880 2438kW (3315bhp) Kobe Hatsudoki KK-Japan AuxGen: 2 x 500kW 450V 60Hz a.c Fuel: 167.0 (d.f.) 677.5 (r.f.) 11.0pd
9140102 *9GRG* -	**VOLTA VICTORY** *ex* Ryuta Maru *-2009* *ex* Shinryuta Maru *-2008* *ex* Ishizuchi *-2005* **Panofi Co Ltd** Sea Road Shipping & Agency Co Ltd *Takoradi* *Ghana* MMSI: 627084000 Official number: GSR 0084	**2,716** Class: (NK) 1,161 3,043	**1996-03 KK Kanasashi — Shizuoka SZ** Yd No: 3376 Loa 91.48 (BB) Br ex - Dght 5.518 Lbp 84.98 Br md 14.50 Dpth 8.60 Welded, 1 dk	**(B12B2FC) Fish Carrier** Ins: 4,276 Compartments: 3 Ho, ER 3 Ha: 3 (2.6 x 2.6)ER Derricks: 6x3t	**1 oil engine** driving 1 FP propeller Total Power: 2,405kW (3,270hp) 14.0kn B&W 6S26MC 1 x 2 Stroke 6 Cy. 260 x 980 2405kW (3270bhp) Makita Corp-Japan AuxGen: 2 x 388kW a.c Fuel: 875.0 (r.f.) 9.8pd
7921473 - -	**VOLTAIRE** **Austfish Pty Ltd** - *Fremantle, WA* *Australia* Official number: 375263	*169* 74 -	**1979-06 Australian Shipbuilding Industries (WA) Pty Ltd — Fremantle WA** Yd No: 164 Loa 25.02 Br ex 7.01 Dght - Lbp 23.73 Br md 6.80 Dpth 4.25 Welded, 1 dk	**(B11A2FT) Trawler**	**1 oil engine** reverse reduction geared to sc. shaft driving 1 FP propeller Total Power: 375kW (510hp) Yanmar 6ML-DT 1 x 4 Stroke 6 Cy. 200 x 240 375kW (510bhp) Yanmar Diesel Engine Co Ltd-Japan
8963117 *EZDR* -	**VOLTAR** *ex* Chernomorets-5 *-2007* **Voltar Shipping Ltd** Krystal Marine Ltd (OOO 'Krystall Marin') *Turkmenbashy* *Turkmenistan* MMSI: 434115800	**854** Class: RS 232 386	**1968-12 Zavod im. "Ordzhonikidze" — Sevastopol** Yd No: 5 Loa 40.66 Br ex 20.21 Dght 2.000 Lbp 40.00 Br md 20.00 Dpth 3.40 Welded, 1 dk	**(B34B2SC) Crane Vessel** Cranes: 1x100t Ice Capable	**2 diesel electric oil engines** driving 2 gen. each 331kW Connecting to 2 elec. motors each (220kW) driving 2 Voith-Schneider propellers Total Power: 662kW (900hp) 6.0kn Pervomaysk 6CHN25/34 2 x 4 Stroke 6 Cy. 250 x 340 each-331kW (450bhp) Pervomaydizelmash (PDM)-Pervomaysk AuxGen: 1 x 50kW a.c Fuel: 55.0 (d.f.)
6922157 *9A3035* -	**VOLUJA** *ex* Aldebaran *-1993* *ex* Balder *-1968* *ex* ST-775 *-1968* *ex* DPC 45 *-1947* **Darislav & Dragislav Kustura** *Split* *Croatia* MMSI: 238103540 Official number: 5R-201	**149** Class: CS (JR) (AB) 45 -	**1943 Decatur Iron & Steel Co. — Decatur, Al** Yd No: 45 Converted From: Tug-1993 Loa 26.85 Br ex 7.35 Dght 2.982 Lbp 24.74 Br md 7.29 Dpth 3.26 Welded, 1 dk	**(B11A2FS) Stern Trawler**	**1 oil engine** driving 1 FP propeller Total Power: 515kW (700hp) 11.0kn EMD (Electro-Motive) 8-567 1 x Vee 2 Stroke 8 Cy. 216 x 254 515kW (700bhp) General Motors Corp-USA AuxGen: 2 x 30kW 120V a.c
8202991 *WDB5556* -	**VOLUNTEER** *ex* Energy Altair *-2003* **Kirby Offshore Marine LLC** K-Sea Operating LLC *New York, NY* *United States of America* MMSI: 366910930 Official number: 653464	**595** Class: AB 178 -	**1982-12 Bollinger Machine Shop & Shipyard, Inc. — Lockport, La** Yd No: 158 Converted From: Tug Loa - Br ex - Dght 5.160 Lbp 36.58 Br md 11.29 Dpth 5.49 Welded, 1 dk	**(B32B2SA) Articulated Pusher Tug**	**2 oil engines** reverse reduction geared to sc. shafts driving 2 FP propellers Total Power: 3,574kW (4,860hp) 12.0kn Alco 12V251E 2 x Vee 4 Stroke 12 Cy. 229 x 267 each-1787kW (2430bhp) Alco Power Inc-USA AuxGen: 2 x 99kW
8003838 *VNW5689* -	**VOLVOX ANGLIA** *ex* Argo *-1989* **Van Oord Overig Materieel I BV** WA Shell Sands Pty Ltd *Fremantle, WA* *Australia* MMSI: 503000000 Official number: 857711	**1,107** Class: BV (GL) 332 1,829	**1980-06 Hermann Suerken GmbH & Co. KG — Papenburg** Yd No: 305 Loa 66.62 Br ex 12.32 Dght 3.620 Lbp 60.03 Br md 12.01 Dpth 4.53 Welded, 1 dk	**(B33B2DT) Trailing Suction Hopper Dredger** Hopper: 1,200	**2 oil engines** reduction geared to sc. shafts driving 2 FP propellers Total Power: 906kW (1,232hp) 8.0kn Caterpillar 3412T 2 x Vee 4 Stroke 12 Cy. 137 x 152 each-453kW (616bhp) Caterpillar Tractor Co-USA AuxGen: 2 x 82kW 380V 50Hz a.c Thrusters: 1 Tunnel thruster (f)
9174737 *PFBG* -	**VOLVOX ASIA** *ex* Goryo Ho No. 5 *-2002* **Sleephopperzuigers I BV** Van Oord Ship Management BV *Rotterdam* *Netherlands* MMSI: 244517000 Official number: 41992	**12,030** Class: BV 3,609 17,299	**1999-06 Hyundai Heavy Industries Co Ltd — Ulsan** Yd No: HC82 Loa 139.00 (BB) Br ex - Dght 9.020 Lbp 127.00 Br md 26.00 Dpth 11.00 Welded, 1 dk	**(B33B2DT) Trailing Suction Hopper Dredger** Liq: 10,291; Hopper: 10,834	**2 oil engines** geared to sc. shafts driving 2 CP propellers Total Power: 14,256kW (19,382hp) 15.0kn MAN-B&W 18V32/40 2 x Vee 4 Stroke 18 Cy. 320 x 400 each-7128kW (9691bhp) Hyundai Heavy Industries Co Ltd-South Korea AuxGen: 4 x 1695kW 440/220V 60Hz a.c Thrusters: 2 Tunnel thruster (f)
9187019 *PGBI* -	**VOLVOX ATALANTA** **Sleephopperzuigers II BV** Van Oord Ship Management BV SatCom: Inmarsat C 424598410 *Gorinchem* *Netherlands* MMSI: 245984000 Official number: 35312	**4,370** Class: BV 1,311 6,230	**1999-01 IHC Holland NV Dredgers — Kinderdijk** Yd No: CO1220 Loa 92.92 (BB) Br ex 17.02 Dght 6.160 Lbp 84.95 Br md 17.00 Dpth 8.60 Welded, 1 dk	**(B33B2DT) Trailing Suction Hopper Dredger** Hopper: 4,500	**2 oil engines** with clutches, flexible couplings & sr reverse geared to sc. shafts driving 2 CP propellers Total Power: 3,870kW (5,262hp) 12.0kn Deutz SBV9M628 2 x 4 Stroke 9 Cy. 240 x 280 each-1935kW (2631bhp) Deutz AG-Koeln Thrusters: 1 Thwart. FP thruster (f) Fuel: 290.0 (d.f.)
8304567 *AWEW* -	**VOLVOX DELTA** **Van Oord Middle East Ltd** Van Oord Ship Management BV *Mumbai* *India* MMSI: 419000848 Official number: 4127	**8,089** Class: IR (BV) 2,426 10,915	**1984-07 IHC Smit BV — Kinderdijk** Yd No: CO1167 Loa 117.18 Br ex - Dght 7.170 Lbp 110.47 Br md 21.71 Dpth 9.12 Welded, 1 dk	**(B33B2DT) Trailing Suction Hopper Dredger** Hopper: 7,788 Cranes: 1x20t Ice Capable	**2 oil engines** with clutches, flexible couplings & sr geared to sc. shafts driving 2 CP propellers Total Power: 10,140kW (13,786hp) 15.3kn Werkspoor 9TM410 2 x 4 Stroke 9 Cy. 410 x 470 each-5070kW (6893bhp) Stork Werkspoor Diesel BV-Netherlands AuxGen: 2 x 3400kW 660/380V a.c, 2 x 408kW 660/380V a.c Thrusters: 2 Thwart. FP thruster (f) Fuel: 1596.0

9055541 *PIIF* -	**VOLVOX IBERIA** **Sleephopperzuigers I BV** Van Oord Ship Management BV SatCom: Inmarsat C 424610910 *Gorinchem* *Netherlands* MMSI: 246109000 Official number: 23855	**5,365** 1,618 8,933	Class: BV	**1993-06 IHC Holland NV Dredgers — Kinderdijk** Yd No: C01200 Loa 96.90 Br ex - Dght 7.450 Lbp 91.96 Br md 19.60 Dpth 9.60 Welded, 1 dk	**(B33B2DT) Trailing Suction Hopper Dredger** Hopper: 6,038	**2 oil engines** with clutches & sr geared to sc. shafts driving 2 FP propellers Total Power: 7,060kW (9,598hp) 13.8kn Stork-Werkspoor 12SW280 2 x Vee 4 Stroke 12 Cy. 280 x 300 each-3530kW (4799bhp) Stork Wartsila Diesel BV-Netherlands Thrusters: 1 Thwart. FP thruster (f); 1 Tunnel thruster (a)
9268370 *PBJI* -	**VOLVOX OLYMPIA** **Sleephopperzuigers II BV** Van Oord Ship Management BV *Gorinchem* *Netherlands* MMSI: 244011000 Official number: 40972	**4,967** 1,490 6,355	Class: BV	**2003-05 van der Giessen-de Noord BV — Krimpen a/d IJssel** (Hull) Yd No: 990 **2003-05 IHC Holland NV Dredgers — Kinderdijk** Yd No: C01236 Loa 97.75 (BB) Br ex 19.92 Dght 6.560 Lbp 84.95 Br md 19.90 Dpth 8.20 Welded, 1 dk	**(B33B2DT) Trailing Suction Hopper Dredger** Hopper: 4,871	**2 oil engines** geared to sc. shafts driving 2 CP propellers Total Power: 3,766kW (5,120hp) 12.5kn Wartsila 6L26A 2 x 4 Stroke 6 Cy. 260 x 320 each-1883kW (2560bhp) Wartsila Finland Oy-Finland AuxGen: 1 x 544kW 440/220V 50Hz a.c, 1 x 800kW 440/220V 50Hz a.c Thrusters: 1 Thwart. CP thruster (f) Fuel: 412.0 (d.f.)
9164110 *PGBG* -	**VOLVOX TERRANOVA** **Sleephopperzuigers I BV** Van Oord Ship Management BV SatCom: Inmarsat C 424599210 *Gorinchem* *Netherlands* MMSI: 245992000 Official number: 34043	**19,994** 5,998 30,234	Class: BV	**1999-01 IHC Holland NV Dredgers — Kinderdijk** Yd No: C01214 Loa 164.10 (BB) Br ex 29.03 Dght 9.600 Lbp 154.00 Br md 29.00 Dpth 12.80 Welded, 1 dk	**(B33B2DT) Trailing Suction Hopper Dredger** Hopper: 20,000 Cranes: 1x45t	**3 oil engines** with clutches, flexible couplings & sr reverse geared to sc. shafts driving 2 CP propellers Total Power: 28,580kW (38,858hp) 17.3kn Wartsila 18V38 2 x Vee 4 Stroke 18 Cy. 380 x 475 each-10800kW (14684bhp) Wartsila NSD Nederland BV-Netherlands Wartsila 9L38 1 x 4 Stroke 9 Cy. 380 x 475 5900kW (8022bhp) Wartsila NSD Nederland BV-Netherlands AuxGen: 1 x 1350kW 50Hz a.c Thrusters: 2 Thwart. FP thruster (f); 1 Tunnel thruster (a) Fuel: 524.0 (d.f.) 4286.0 (r.f.)
8102488 *PS9563* -	**VOLZEE** *ex* Sylvia *-1988* *launched as* Sea Splitter 2 *-1980* **Enterpa Engenharia Ltda** - *Brazil* MMSI: 710000282	**756** 226 1,320	Class: (BV)	**1980 A. Vuijk & Zonen's Scheepswerven B.V. — Capelle a/d IJssel** Yd No: 886 Loa 58.32 Br ex - Dght 3.660 Lbp 54.33 Br md 11.00 Dpth 3.76 Welded, 2 dks	**(B33B2DT) Trailing Suction Hopper Dredger** Hopper: 750	**2 oil engines** geared to sc. shafts driving 2 FP propellers Total Power: 810kW (1,102hp) 9.5kn Deutz SBA12M816 2 x Vee 4 Stroke 12 Cy. 142 x 160 each-405kW (551bhp) Kloeckner Humboldt Deutz AG-West Germany Thrusters: 2 Directional thruster Fuel: 53.0 (d.f.) 9.5pd
8883226 *UCBQ* -	**VOLZHSKIY-7** **VF International Transportation Ltd Co (OOO 'VF Zagranperevozki')** Volga-Neva Ltd *St Petersburg* *Russia* MMSI: 273319100	**3,070** 1,059 3,709	Class: RS	**1984-07 Navashinskiy Sudostroitelnyy Zavod 'Oka' — Navashino** Yd No: 1009 Shortened Loa 107.40 Br ex 16.70 Dght 3.690 Lbp 101.20 Br md 16.50 Dpth 5.50 Welded, 1 dk	**(A31A2GX) General Cargo Ship** Grain: 4,403 Compartments: 2 Ho, ER 2 Ha: 2 (28.8 x 13.3)ER Ice Capable	**2 oil engines** driving 2 FP propellers Total Power: 1,766kW (2,402hp) 10.8kn Dvigatel Revolyutsii 6CHRN36/45 2 x 4 Stroke 6 Cy. 360 x 450 each-883kW (1201bhp) Zavod "Dvigatel Revolyutsii"-Gorkiy AuxGen: 2 x 100kW a.c Fuel: 170.0 (d.f.)
8883238 *UCBR* -	**VOLZHSKIY-8** **VF International Transportation Ltd Co (OOO 'VF Zagranperevozki')** Volga-Neva Ltd *St Petersburg* *Russia* MMSI: 273310200 Official number: 845944	**3,070** 1,059 3,709	Class: (RS)	**1984-07 Navashinskiy Sudostroitelnyy Zavod 'Oka' — Navashino** Yd No: 1010 Shortened Loa 107.40 Br ex 16.70 Dght 3.690 Lbp 101.20 Br md 16.50 Dpth 5.50 Welded, 1 dk	**(A31A2GX) General Cargo Ship** Grain: 4,403 Compartments: 2 Ho, ER 2 Ha: 2 (28.8 x 13.3)ER Ice Capable	**2 oil engines** driving 2 FP propellers Total Power: 1,766kW (2,402hp) 10.8kn Dvigatel Revolyutsii 6CHRN36/45 2 x 4 Stroke 6 Cy. 360 x 450 each-883kW (1201bhp) Zavod "Dvigatel Revolyutsii"-Gorkiy AuxGen: 2 x 100kW a.c Fuel: 170.0 (d.f.)
8874354 *UCBS* -	**VOLZHSKIY-10** **VF International Transportation Ltd Co (OOO 'VF Zagranperevozki')** JS North-Western Shipping Co (OAO 'Severo-Zapadnoye Parokhodstvo') SatCom: Inmarsat C 427300130 *St Petersburg* *Russia* MMSI: 273311200 Official number: 846020	**3,070** 1,002 3,888	Class: RS	**1984-11 Navashinskiy Sudostroitelnyy Zavod 'Oka' — Navashino** Yd No: 1012 Shortened-1995 Loa 107.40 Br ex 16.70 Dght 3.800 Lbp 101.20 Br md 16.50 Dpth 5.50 Welded, 1 dk	**(A31A2GX) General Cargo Ship** Grain: 4,403 Compartments: 2 Ho, ER 2 Ha: 2 (28.8 x 13.3)ER	**2 oil engines** driving 2 FP propellers Total Power: 1,766kW (2,402hp) 10.8kn Dvigatel Revolyutsii 6CHRN36/45 2 x 4 Stroke 6 Cy. 360 x 450 each-883kW (1201bhp) Zavod "Dvigatel Revolyutsii"-Gorkiy AuxGen: 2 x 100kW a.c Fuel: 175.0 (d.f.)
8986353 *V3SH6* -	**VOLZHSKIY-14** **Papa Shipping Co Ltd** Kent Shipping & Chartering Ltd *Belize City* *Belize* Official number: 141220248	**4,055** 1,216 4,978	Class: RR	**1985 Navashinskiy Sudostroitelnyy Zavod 'Oka' — Navashino** Yd No: 1016 Loa 139.00 Br ex 16.70 Dght 3.870 Lbp 135.00 Br md 16.50 Dpth 5.50 Welded, 1 dk	**(A31A2GX) General Cargo Ship** Grain: 9,648	**2 oil engines** driving 2 Propellers Total Power: 1,764kW (2,398hp) 10.6kn Dvigatel Revolyutsii 6CHRN36/45 2 x 4 Stroke 6 Cy. 360 x 450 each-882kW (1199bhp) Zavod "Dvigatel Revolyutsii"-Gorkiy
8986377 *V3SQ6* -	**VOLZHSKIY-18** **Quebec Shipping Co Ltd** Kent Shipping & Chartering Ltd *Belize City* *Belize* Official number: 141220249	**4,055** 1,216 4,978	Class: RR	**1986 Navashinskiy Sudostroitelnyy Zavod 'Oka' — Navashino** Yd No: 1020 Loa 139.00 Br ex 16.70 Dght 3.870 Lbp 135.00 Br md 16.50 Dpth 5.50 Welded, 1 dk	**(A31A2GX) General Cargo Ship** Grain: 9,648	**2 oil engines** driving 2 Propellers Total Power: 1,766kW (2,402hp) 10.6kn Dvigatel Revolyutsii 6CHN36/45 2 x 4 Stroke 6 Cy. 360 x 450 each-883kW (1201bhp) Zavod "Dvigatel Revolyutsii"-Gorkiy
8955641 *UGPY* -	**VOLZHSKIY-33** *ex* Dmitriy Varvarin *-2009* *ex* Volzhskiy-33 *-2009* **Baltasar Shipping SA** Orion Shipping Co *St Petersburg* *Russia* MMSI: 273450450	**4,998** 2,298 5,375	Class: RS	**1990-04 Navashinskiy Sudostroitelnyy Zavod 'Oka' — Navashino** Yd No: 1035 Loa 138.30 Br ex 16.70 Dght 3.750 Lbp 135.00 Br md 16.50 Dpth 5.50 Welded, 1 dk	**(A31A2GX) General Cargo Ship** Grain: 9,356; Bale: 9,356 Compartments: 4 Ho, ER 4 Ha: (18.6 x 13.3) (25.2 x 13.3) (24.8 x 13.3) (19.0 x 13.3)ER Ice Capable	**2 oil engines** driving 2 FP propellers Total Power: 1,764kW (2,398hp) 10.7kn Dvigatel Revolyutsii 6CHRN36/45 2 x 4 Stroke 6 Cy. 360 x 450 each-882kW (1199bhp) Zavod "Dvigatel Revolyutsii"-Gorkiy
8850906 *UCFY* -	**VOLZHSKIY-40** **North-Western Fleet (A/O 'Severo-Zapadnyy Flot')** - *St Petersburg* *Russia* MMSI: 273439520	**5,205** 2,735 4,178	Class: RS RR	**1991-03 Navashinskiy Sudostroitelnyy Zavod 'Oka' — Navashino** Loa 138.00 Br ex 16.75 Dght 3.120 Lbp 136.00 Br md 16.50 Dpth 5.50 Welded, 1 dk	**(A31A2GX) General Cargo Ship** Grain: 6,440	**2 oil engines** driving 2 FP propellers Total Power: 1,766kW (2,402hp) 11.0kn Dvigatel Revolyutsii 6CHRN36/45 2 x 4 Stroke 6 Cy. 360 x 450 each-883kW (1201bhp) Zavod "Dvigatel Revolyutsii"-Gorkiy
8873489 *UBEW* -	**VOLZHSKIY-44** **North-Western Fleet (A/O 'Severo-Zapadnyy Flot')** - *St Petersburg* *Russia* MMSI: 273430620	**5,205** 2,735 6,050	Class: RS RR	**1991-07 Navashinskiy Sudostroitelnyy Zavod 'Oka' — Navashino** Loa 138.45 Br ex 16.75 Dght 4.100 Lbp 136.00 Br md 16.00 Dpth 5.50 Welded, 1 dk	**(A31A2GX) General Cargo Ship** Grain: 6,340; Bale: 6,340	**2 oil engines** driving 2 FP propellers Total Power: 1,766kW (2,402hp) 10.6kn Dvigatel Revolyutsii 6CHRN36/45 2 x 4 Stroke 6 Cy. 360 x 450 each-883kW (1201bhp) Zavod "Dvigatel Revolyutsii"-Gorkiy AuxGen: 2 x 100kW a.c Fuel: 199.0 (d.f.)
8862703 *UBNI* -	**VOLZHSKIY 45** *ex* Azov Grace *-2010* *ex* River Cat *-2005* *ex* Ekaterina *-1999* *ex* Yekaterina *-1997* *ex* Volzhskiy-45 *-1997* **Don River Shipping JSC (OAO 'Donrechflot')** - SatCom: Inmarsat C 427302226 *Taganrog* *Russia* MMSI: 273310130	**5,213** 1,228 6,003	Class: RS (RR)	**1991-07 Navashinskiy Sudostroitelnyy Zavod 'Oka' — Navashino** Yd No: 1047 Loa 138.40 Br ex 16.70 Dght 4.100 Lbp 136.00 Br md 16.50 Dpth 5.50 Welded, 1 dk	**(A31A2GX) General Cargo Ship** Grain: 6,340; Bale: 6,340 Compartments: 2 Ho, ER 2 Ha: 2 (44.4 x 13.3)ER Ice Capable	**2 oil engines** driving 2 FP propellers Total Power: 1,766kW (2,402hp) 10.0kn Dvigatel Revolyutsii 6CHRN36/45 2 x 4 Stroke 6 Cy. 360 x 450 each-883kW (1201bhp) Zavod "Dvigatel Revolyutsii"-Gorkiy AuxGen: 2 x 100kW Fuel: 145.0 (d.f.)
8933564 *UBEV* -	**VOLZHSKIY-47** **North-Western Fleet (A/O 'Severo-Zapadnyy Flot')** - *St Petersburg* *Russia* MMSI: 273431620	**4,189** 1,362 5,017	Class: RS RR	**1991 Navashinskiy Sudostroitelnyy Zavod 'Oka' — Navashino** Yd No: 1049 Loa 138.45 Br ex 16.75 Dght 3.500 Lbp 136.00 Br md 16.50 Dpth 5.50 Welded, 1 dk	**(A31A2GX) General Cargo Ship** Grain: 6,440	**2 oil engines** driving 2 FP propellers Total Power: 1,764kW (2,398hp) 10.0kn Dvigatel Revolyutsii 6CHRN36/45 2 x 4 Stroke 6 Cy. 360 x 450 each-882kW (1199bhp) Zavod "Dvigatel Revolyutsii"-Gorkiy AuxGen: 2 x 100kW a.c Fuel: 145.0 (d.f.)

Ship	Tonnage	Class	Builder / Dimensions	Type / Cargo	Machinery
8945086 **VOLZHSKIY 49** *UBHG5* *ex* Mercia *-2010* *ex* Sikvin *-2005* - *ex* Seaqueen *-2004* *ex* Neptun *-2002* *ex* Neptun II *-2000* *ex* Neptun *-1999* *ex* Nuai Ismailov *-1999* *ex* Volzhskiy-49 *-1999* **Don River Shipping JSC (OAO 'Donrechflot')** LLC Rosshipcom SatCom: Inmarsat C 427322681 *Taganrog* *Russia* MMSI: 273345930	**5,088** 2,361 5,346	Class: RS	**1992-10 OAO Navashinskiy Sudostroitelnyy Zavod 'Oka' — Navashino** Yd No: 1051 Loa 138.45 Br ex 16.70 Dght 3.800 Lbp 131.54 Br md 16.50 Dpth 5.50 Welded, 1 dk	**(A31A2GX) General Cargo Ship** Grain: 6,340 Compartments: 2 Ho, ER 2 Ha: 2 (44.4 x 13.3)ER	**2 oil engines** driving 2 FP propellers Total Power: 1,764kW (2,398hp) 10.0kr Dvigatel Revolyutsii 6CHRN36/45 2 x 4 Stroke 6 Cy. 360 x 450 each-882kW (1199bhp) Zavod "Dvigatel Revolyutsii"-Nizhniy Novgorod AuxGen: 2 x 100kW a.c Fuel: 145.0 (d.f.)
8873324 **VOLZHSKIY-50** *UIBL* - **North-Western Fleet (A/O 'Severo-Zapadnyy Flot')** - *St Petersburg* *Russia* MMSI: 273432620	**4,197** 575 4,178	Class: RS RR	**1992 OAO Navashinskiy Sudostroitelnyy Zavod 'Oka' — Navashino** Yd No: 1052 Loa 138.40 Br ex 16.75 Dght 3.120 Lbp 136.00 Br md 16.00 Dpth 5.50 Welded, 1 dk	**(A31A2GX) General Cargo Ship** Grain: 6,440	**2 oil engines** driving 2 FP propellers Total Power: 1,600kW (2,176hp) 11.6kn Dvigatel Revolyutsii 6CHRNP36/45 2 x 4 Stroke 6 Cy. 360 x 450 each-800kW (1088bhp) Zavod "Dvigatel Revolyutsii"-Nizhniy Novgorod AuxGen: 2 x 100kW a.c
8413344 **VOMBIE** - - **Compania Nationale de Navigation Interieure** - *Libreville* *Gabon*	*131* 73 62	Class: (BV)	**1985-07 Astilleros Gondan SA — Castropol** Yd No: 248 Loa 27.03 Br ex 7.04 Dght 1.401 Lbp 24.26 Br md 7.01 Dpth 2.01 Welded, 1 dk	**(A32A2GF) General Cargo/Passenger Ship** Passengers: unberthed: 50 Bow ramp (centre) Bale: 64 Compartments: 1 Ho, ER 1 Ha:	**2 oil engines** sr reverse geared to sc. shafts driving 2 FP propellers Total Power: 604kW (822hp) GUASCOR E212TA-SP 2 x Vee 4 Stroke 8 Cy. 150 x 150 each-302kW (411bhp) Gutierrez Ascunce Corp (GUASCOR)-Spain AuxGen: 2 x 48kW 380V 50Hz a.c
7225984 **VOMMOLBUEN** *CPA801* *ex* Froyfisk *-1996* *ex* Vestfisk Senior *-1994* - *ex* Vestfisk *-1993* *ex* Seifrakt *-1988* *ex* Tex *-1985* **Saumon de France** - *La Paz* *Bolivia* Official number: 690612781	**112** 60 -		**1956 Hollen Skipsverft — Sogne** Yd No: 129 Converted From: Fishing Vessel-1996 Lengthened-1972 Loa 28.53 Br ex 5.82 Dght - Lbp - Br md 5.80 Dpth 3.05 Welded, 1 dk	**(B12C2FL) Live Fish Carrier (Well Boat)**	**1 oil engine** driving 1 FP propeller Total Power: 313kW (426hp) Caterpillar D353SCAC 1 x 4 Stroke 6 Cy. 159 x 203 313kW (426bhp) (new engine 1975) Caterpillar Tractor Co-USA
6515837 **VON** *OW2463* *ex* Burgundia *-2013* *ex* Bofjord *-2000* - *ex* Arne Marius *-1990* *ex* Rodvin *-1987* *ex* Leiking *-1985* *ex* Stevnsland *-1974* **P/F Sandgrevstur** - *Runavik* *Faeroe Islands (Danish)* MMSI: 231522000	**399** 190 560	Class: BV	**1965 Husumer Schiffswerft — Husum** Yd No: 1224 Loa 48.21 Br ex 8.67 Dght 3.112 Lbp 43.21 Br md 8.62 Dpth 3.59 Riveted\Welded, 1 dk	**(A31A2GX) General Cargo Ship** Grain: 712; Bale: 635 Compartments: 1 Ho, ER 1 Ha: (22.1 x 5.0)ER Derricks: 2x3t; Winches: 2 Ice Capable	**1 oil engine** driving 1 FP propeller Total Power: 294kW (400hp) 10.3kn Callesen 5-427-EO 1 x 4 Stroke 5 Cy. 270 x 400 294kW (400bhp) Aabenraa Motorfabrik, HeinrichCallesen A/S-Denmark AuxGen: 2 x 32kW 380V a.c
9282754 **VONAR** *LMCJ* - **Finnoy Fiskeriselskap AS** - *Aalesund* *Norway* MMSI: 257582600	**1,319** 396 -	Class: NV	**2002-12 Societatea Comerciala Severnav S.A. — Drobeta-Turnu Severin (Hull)** Yd No: 154 **2002-12 Larsnes Mek. Verksted AS — Larsnes** Yd No: 40 Loa 49.60 Br ex 11.00 Dght 4.850 Lbp 44.00 Br md 10.60 Dpth 7.80 Welded	**(B11B2FV) Fishing Vessel** Bale: 405 Ice Capable	**1 oil engine** reduction geared to sc. shaft driving 1 FP propeller Total Power: 1,100kW (1,496hp) A.B.C. 6MDZC 1 x 4 Stroke 6 Cy. 256 x 310 1100kW (1496bhp) Anglo Belgian Corp NV (ABC)-Belgium
9179373 **VOORNEBORG** *PCGI* - **Wagenborg Rederij BV** Wagenborg Shipping BV *Delfzijl* *Netherlands* MMSI: 245491000 Official number: 38024	**6,130** 3,424 8,734 T/cm 18.3	Class: BV	**1999-11 Bodewes Scheepswerf "Volharding" Foxhol B.V. — Foxhol** Yd No: 344 Loa 132.23 (BB) Br ex 15.95 Dght 7.050 Lbp 123.84 Br md 15.87 Dpth 9.65 Welded, 1 dk	**(A31A2GX) General Cargo Ship** Grain: 12,814 TEU 552 C.Ho 264/20' (40') C.Dk 288/20' (40') incl. 50 ref C Compartments: 2 Ho, ER 2 Ha: (40.0 x 13.2) (52.5 x 13.2)ER Ice Capable	**1 oil engine** with flexible couplings & sr gearedto sc. shaft driving 1 CP propeller Total Power: 3,960kW (5,384hp) 14.9kn Wartsila 6R38 1 x 4 Stroke 6 Cy. 380 x 475 3960kW (5384bhp) Wartsila NSD Nederland BV-Netherlands AuxGen: 1 x 650kW 440V 60Hz a.c, 2 x 240kW 440V 60Hz a.c Thrusters: 1 Thwart. FP thruster (f) Fuel: 40.0 (d.f.) (Heating Coils) 384.0 (r.f.) 20.0pd
9346706 **VOORNEDIJK** *PBOW* - **Beheermaatschappij ms 'Voornedijk' BV** Navigia Shipmanagement BV *Groningen* *Netherlands* MMSI: 244971000 Official number: 49577	**2,984** 1,598 4,891	Class: GL (BV)	**2009-01 Chowgule & Co Pvt Ltd — Goa** Yd No: 177 Loa 89.95 (BB) Br ex - Dght 6.220 Lbp 84.94 Br md 14.40 Dpth 7.85 Welded, 1 dk	**(A31A2GX) General Cargo Ship** Grain: 5,818 Compartments: 1 Ho, ER 1 Ha: ER (62.3 x 11.7)	**1 oil engine** reduction geared to sc. shaft driving 1 CP propeller Total Power: 1,986kW (2,700hp) 11.5kn MaK 6M25 1 x 4 Stroke 6 Cy. 255 x 400 1986kW (2700bhp) Caterpillar Motoren GmbH & Co. KG-Germany AuxGen: 2 x 168kW 400V 50Hz a.c, 1 x 312kW 400V 50Hz a.c Thrusters: 1 Tunnel thruster (f) Fuel: 35.0 (d.f.) 280.0 (r.f.)
7028441 **VOR** *CBVO* *ex* Pioner *-2008* *ex* Melton Pioneer *-1981* - *ex* Windle Surf *-1979* *ex* Zepconcorde *-1976* *ex* Anneliese Bos *-1973* **Detroit Chile SA** - *Valparaiso* *Chile* MMSI: 725000629 Official number: 3203	**1,357** 638 1,754	Class: (BV) (GL)	**1970-10 Schiffswerft Korneuburg A.G. — Korneuburg** Yd No: 694 Loa 76.21 Br ex 11.89 Dght 4.240 Lbp 69.02 Br md 11.80 Dpth 6.05 Welded, 2 dks	**(A31A2GX) General Cargo Ship** Grain: 3,102; Bale: 2,722 Compartments: 1 Ho, ER 1 Ha: (43.8 x 7.7)ER Cranes: 1 Ice Capable	**1 oil engine** driving 1 FP propeller Total Power: 1,140kW (1,550hp) 12.0kn Caterpillar 3516TA 1 x Vee 4 Stroke 16 Cy. 170 x 190 1140kW (1550bhp) (new engine 1993) Caterpillar Inc-USA AuxGen: 3 x 75kW 220/380V 50Hz a.c Fuel: 101.5 (d.f.)
9382671 **VORDUR** *TFVD* *launched as* Gjogur *-2007* EA 748 **Gjogur hf** - *Grenivik* *Iceland* MMSI: 251269000 Official number: 2740	**486** 146 221	Class: LR ✠ **100A1** SS 06/2012 stern trawler ✠ **LMC** Cable: 2.6/26.0 U2 (a)	**2007-06 'Crist' Sp z oo — Gdansk** Yd No: B29/2 Loa 28.95 (BB) Br ex 10.40 Dght 5.150 Lbp 25.31 Br md 10.40 Dpth 6.60 Welded, 1 dk	**(B11A2FS) Stern Trawler** Ice Capable	**1 oil engine** with flexible couplings & sr geared to sc. shaft driving 1 CP propeller Total Power: 956kW (1,300hp) 11.5kn Yanmar 6N21A-EV 1 x 4 Stroke 6 Cy. 210 x 290 956kW (1300bhp) Yanmar Diesel Engine Co Ltd-Japan AuxGen: 1 x 312kW 380V 50Hz a.c, 1 x 520kW 380V 50Hz a.c
7401447 **VORIMU No. 1** - *ex* Harima *-1996* *ex* Aoki Maru No. 61 *-1994* - *ex* Bulldozer Maru No. 61 *-1994* - -	**777** 233 449		**1975-03 K.K. Miura Zosensho — Saiki** Yd No: 507 Loa 32.01 Br ex 13.01 Dght 4.979 Lbp 30.00 Br md 12.98 Dpth 6.51 Welded, 1 dk	**(B32B2SP) Pusher Tug**	**2 oil engines** driving 2 FP propellers Total Power: 4,414kW (6,002hp) 13.3kn Niigata 6MG40X 2 x 4 Stroke 6 Cy. 400 x 600 each-2207kW (3001bhp) Niigata Engineering Co Ltd-Japan
9130406 **VORINGEN** *LHSG* - **Norled AS** Tide ASA *Bergen* *Norway* MMSI: 257262600	**103** 41 -		**1995-06 Oma Baatbyggeri AS — Stord** Yd No: 507 Loa 19.80 (BB) Br ex 8.30 Dght 1.200 Lbp 19.60 Br md 8.00 Dpth 2.45 Welded, 1 dk	**(A37B2PS) Passenger Ship** Hull Material: Aluminium Alloy Passengers: unberthed: 80	**2 oil engines** with clutches, flexible couplings & reduction geared to sc. shafts driving 2 CP propellers Total Power: 1,470kW (1,998hp) 30.0kn M.T.U. 12V183TE92 2 x Vee 4 Stroke 12 Cy. 128 x 142 each-735kW (999bhp) MTU Friedrichshafen GmbH-Friedrichshafen AuxGen: 1 x 12kW 230V 50Hz a.c Fuel: 3.5 (d.f.) 0.2pd
8867428 **VORNAKS** *XUGD6* *ex* Aleksa *-2013* *ex* Santa Elena *-2010* - *ex* Dakota *-2003* *ex* Cherokee *-1999* *ex* Volgo-Balt 161 *-1994* **Vornaks Holding Ltd** Poseidon Ltd *Phnom Penh* *Cambodia* MMSI: 515206000	**2,576** 1,196 3,595	Class: UA (RS)	**1972-07 Zavody Tazkeho Strojarstva (ZTS) — Komarno** Yd No: 1361 Loa 114.00 Br ex 13.20 Dght 3.640 Lbp 110.00 Br md 13.00 Dpth 5.50 Welded, 1 dk	**(A31A2GX) General Cargo Ship** Grain: 4,720 Compartments: 3 Ho, ER 4 Ha: (18.0 x 9.5)ER 3 (19.0 x 9.5)	**2 oil engines** driving 2 FP propellers Total Power: 1,400kW (1,904hp) 11.0kn Skoda 6-275B8L 2 x 4 Stroke 6 Cy. 275 x 330 each-700kW (952bhp) (new engine 1984) CKD Praha-Praha AuxGen: 2 x 80kW a.c Fuel: 210.0 (d.f.)
9322011 **VORONEZH** *5BNG2* *ex* Fesco Voronezh *-2013* - *ex* CMA CGM Neva *-2011* *ex* Fesco Voronezh *-2009* **Lightview Shipping Co Ltd** Far-Eastern Shipping Co (FESCO) (Dalnevostochnoye Morskoye Parokhodstvo) *Limassol* *Cyprus* MMSI: 212357000	**16,803** 8,648 23,063 T/cm 37.1	Class: GL RS	**2008-11 Stocznia Szczecinska Nowa Sp z oo — Szczecin** Yd No: B170/V/2 Loa 184.70 (BB) Br ex - Dght 9.850 Lbp 171.94 Br md 25.30 Dpth 13.50 Welded, 1 dk	**(A33A2CC) Container Ship (Fully Cellular)** Grain: 29,816 TEU 1728 C Ho 634 TEI C Dk 1094 TEU incl 200 ref C Cranes: 3x45t Ice Capable	**1 oil engine** driving 1 FP propeller Total Power: 13,320kW (18,110hp) 19.5kn Wartsila 6RTA62U 1 x 2 Stroke 6 Cy. 620 x 2150 13320kW (18110bhp) H Cegielski Poznan SA-Poland AuxGen: 3 x 1100kW 440/220V a.c Thrusters: 1 Tunnel thruster (f)

IMO / Call sign / Flag	Name / Owner / Manager / Port	Tonnage	Class	Built / Dimensions	Type / Capacities	Machinery
7630579 *UDIP* -	**VOROTYNETS** **Priboy Co Ltd** - *Petropavlovsk-Kamchatskiy* *Russia*	**172** 51 89	Class: RS	**1976-08 Sretenskiy Sudostroitelnyy Zavod — Sretensk** Yd No: 91 Loa 33.96 Br ex 7.09 Dght 2.899 Lbp 30.00 Br md 7.00 Dpth 3.69 Welded, 1 dk	**(B11B2FV) Fishing Vessel** Ins: 96 Compartments: 1 Ho, ER 1 Ha: (1.3 x 1.6) Derricks: 2x2t; Winches: 2 Ice Capable	**1 oil engine** driving 1 FP propeller Total Power: 224kW (305hp) 9.0kn S.K.L. 8NVD36-1U 1 x 4 Stroke 8 Cy. 240 x 360 224kW (305bhp) VEB Schwermaschinenbau "KarlLiebknecht" (SKL)-Magdeburg AuxGen: 1 x 86kW, 1 x 60kW, 1 x 28kW Fuel: 20.0 (d.f.)
9525508 *2CVS9* -	**VORTEX** **Boreas Shipping Ltd** Ostensjo Rederi AS *Southampton* *United Kingdom* MMSI: 235076195 Official number: 916696	**839** 252 570	Class: NV	**2010-06 Astilleros Gondan SA — Castropol** Yd No: 447 Loa 37.50 Br ex 14.60 Dght 4.780 Lbp 34.58 Br md 14.00 Dpth 6.80 Welded, 1 dk	**(B32A2ST) Tug**	**2 oil engines** geared to sc. shafts driving 2 Voith-Schneider propellers Total Power: 4,002kW (5,442hp) 13.5kn Wartsila 8L26 2 x 4 Stroke 8 Cy. 260 x 320 each-2001kW (2721bhp) Wartsila Finland Oy-Finland AuxGen: 2 x 139kW a.c
9145645 *LYSC* -	**VORUTA** *ex* Theodor Oldendorff *-2006* **AB 'Lietuvos Juru Laivininkyste' (LJL) (Lithuanian Shipping Co)** - *Klaipeda* *Lithuania* MMSI: 277338000 Official number: 761	**12,192** 5,862 17,789	Class: NK (LR) (BV) ✠ Classed LR until 25/3/06	**1998-12 P.T. PAL Indonesia — Surabaya** Yd No: 150 Loa 141.35 (BB) Br ex 22.54 Dght 9.470 Lbp 134.77 Br md 22.50 Dpth 12.85 Welded, 1 dk	**(A31A2GX) General Cargo Ship** Double Hull Grain: 20,704; Bale: 19,909 Compartments: 4 Ho, ER 4 Ha: (14.0 x 13.0)3 (18.0 x 16.0)ER Cranes: 3x25t Ice Capable	**1 oil engine** driving 1 CP propeller Total Power: 4,900kW (6,662hp) 12.5kn B&W 7S35MC 1 x 2 Stroke 7 Cy. 350 x 1400 4900kW (6662bhp) MAN B&W Diesel A/S-Denmark AuxGen: 1 x 828kW 415V 50Hz a.c, 2 x 828kW 380V 50Hz a.c Boilers: TOH (o.f.) 10.2kgf/cm² (10.0bar), TOH (ex.g.) 10.2kgf/cm² (10.0bar) Thrusters: 1 Thwart. FP thruster (f) Fuel: 600.0 (d.f.)
9552161 *9V8665* -	**VOS ACHILLES** **Offshore Support Vessels 11 Pte Ltd** Vroon Offshore Services Pte Ltd SatCom: Inmarsat C 456578311 *Singapore* *Singapore* MMSI: 565783000 Official number: 396078	**1,678** 503 1,338	Class: AB	**2011-02 Fujian Southeast Shipyard — Fuzhou FJ** Yd No: DN59M-74 Loa 59.25 Br ex - Dght 4.950 Lbp 52.20 Br md 14.95 Dpth 6.10 Welded, 1 dk	**(B21B20A) Anchor Handling Tug Supply** Cranes: 1x3t	**2 oil engines** reduction geared to sc. shafts driving 2 CP propellers Total Power: 3,840kW (5,220hp) 10.0kn Caterpillar 3516B-HD 2 x Vee 4 Stroke 16 Cy. 170 x 215 each-1920kW (2610bhp) Caterpillar Inc-USA AuxGen: 2 x 350kW a.c, 2 x 800kW a.c Thrusters: 1 Tunnel thruster (f); 1 Tunnel thruster (a)
9552173 *9V8666* -	**VOS APHRODITE** **Offshore Support Vessels 11 Pte Ltd** Vroon Offshore Italia Srl *Singapore* *Singapore* MMSI: 563818000 Official number: 396079	**1,678** 503 1,337	Class: AB	**2011-03 Fujian Southeast Shipyard — Fuzhou FJ** Yd No: DN59M-75 Loa 59.25 Br ex - Dght 4.950 Lbp 52.20 Br md 14.95 Dpth 6.10 Welded, 1 dk	**(B21B20A) Anchor Handling Tug Supply**	**2 oil engines** reduction geared to sc. shafts driving 2 CP propellers Total Power: 3,840kW (5,220hp) 10.0kn Caterpillar 3516B-HD 2 x Vee 4 Stroke 16 Cy. 170 x 215 each-1920kW (2610bhp) Caterpillar Inc-USA AuxGen: 2 x 800kW a.c, 2 x 350kW a.c Thrusters: 1 Tunnel thruster (f); 1 Tunnel thruster (a) Fuel: 520.0
9552185 *ZDNV4* -	**VOS APOLLO** **Vroon BV** - *Gibraltar* *Gibraltar (British)* MMSI: 236642000	**1,678** 503 1,324	Class: AB	**2011-09 Fujian Southeast Shipyard — Fuzhou FJ** Yd No: DN59M-76 Loa 59.25 Br ex - Dght 4.950 Lbp 52.20 Br md 14.95 Dpth 6.10 Welded, 1 dk	**(B21B20A) Anchor Handling Tug Supply**	**2 oil engines** reduction geared to sc. shafts driving 2 CP propellers Total Power: 3,840kW (5,220hp) 10.0kn Caterpillar 3516B-HD 2 x Vee 4 Stroke 16 Cy. 170 x 215 each-1920kW (2610bhp) Caterpillar Inc-USA AuxGen: 2 x 800kW a.c, 2 x 350kW a.c Thrusters: 1 Tunnel thruster (f); 1 Tunnel thruster (a)
9552197 *9V8668* -	**VOS ARES** **Offshore Support Vessels 12 Pte Ltd** Vroon Offshore Services Pte Ltd *Singapore* *Singapore* MMSI: 566293000 Official number: 396081	**1,678** 503 1,319	Class: AB	**2012-01 Fujian Southeast Shipyard — Fuzhou FJ** Yd No: DN59M-77 Loa 59.25 Br ex - Dght 4.950 Lbp 52.20 Br md 14.95 Dpth 6.10 Welded, 1 dk	**(B21B20A) Anchor Handling Tug Supply**	**2 oil engines** reduction geared to sc. shafts driving 2 CP propellers Total Power: 3,840kW (5,220hp) 10.0kn Caterpillar 3516B-HD 2 x Vee 4 Stroke 16 Cy. 170 x 215 each-1920kW (2610bhp) Caterpillar Inc-USA AuxGen: 2 x 800kW a.c, 2 x 350kW a.c Thrusters: 1 Tunnel thruster (f); 1 Tunnel thruster (a)
9552202 *9V8669* -	**VOS ARTEMIS** **Offshore Support Vessels 12 Pte Ltd** Vroon Offshore Services Pte Ltd *Singapore* *Singapore* MMSI: 566290000 Official number: 396082	**1,678** 503 1,308	Class: AB	**2011-11 Fujian Southeast Shipyard — Fuzhou FJ** Yd No: DN59M-78 Loa 59.25 Br ex - Dght 4.950 Lbp 52.20 Br md 14.95 Dpth 6.10 Welded, 1 dk	**(B21B20A) Anchor Handling Tug Supply**	**2 oil engines** reduction geared to sc. shafts driving 2 CP propellers Total Power: 3,840kW (5,220hp) 10.0kn Caterpillar 3516B-HD 2 x Vee 4 Stroke 16 Cy. 170 x 215 each-1920kW (2610bhp) Caterpillar Inc-USA AuxGen: 2 x 800kW a.c, 2 x 350kW a.c Thrusters: 1 Tunnel thruster (f); 1 Tunnel thruster (a)
9552214 *9V8670* -	**VOS ATHENA** **Offshore Support Vessels 13 Pte Ltd** Vroon Offshore Services Pte Ltd *Singapore* *Singapore* MMSI: 566374000 Official number: 396083	**1,678** 503 1,334	Class: AB	**2012-01 Fujian Southeast Shipyard — Fuzhou FJ** Yd No: DN59M-79 Loa 59.25 Br ex - Dght 4.950 Lbp 52.20 Br md 14.95 Dpth 6.10 Welded, 1 dk	**(B21B20A) Anchor Handling Tug Supply**	**2 oil engines** reduction geared to sc. shafts driving 2 CP propellers Total Power: 3,840kW (5,220hp) 10.0kn Caterpillar 3516B-HD 2 x Vee 4 Stroke 16 Cy. 170 x 215 each-1920kW (2610bhp) Caterpillar Inc-USA AuxGen: 2 x 350kW a.c, 2 x 800kW a.c Thrusters: 1 Tunnel thruster (f); 1 Tunnel thruster (a)
9609756 *ZDNE8* -	**VOS ATHOS** **Offshore Support Vessels 20 BV** Vroon Offshore Italia Srl *Gibraltar* *Gibraltar (British)* MMSI: 236111903	**1,678** 503 1,314	Class: RI (AB)	**2012-07 Fujian Southeast Shipyard — Fuzhou FJ** Yd No: DN59M-97 Loa 59.25 Br ex - Dght 4.950 Lbp 52.20 Br md 14.95 Dpth 6.10 Welded, 1 dk	**(B21B20A) Anchor Handling Tug Supply**	**2 oil engines** reduction geared to sc. shaft (s) driving 2 CP propellers Total Power: 3,840kW (5,220hp) 10.0kn Caterpillar 3516B-HD 2 x Vee 4 Stroke 16 Cy. 170 x 215 each-1920kW (2610bhp) Caterpillar Inc-USA AuxGen: 2 x 800kW a.c, 2 x 444kW a.c Thrusters: 1 Tunnel thruster (f) Fuel: 520.0
9609768 *9V9837* -	**VOS ATLANTA** **Offshore Support Vessels 14 Pte Ltd** Vroon Offshore Services Pte Ltd *Singapore* *Singapore* MMSI: 566655000 Official number: 397646	**1,678** 503 1,308	Class: AB	**2012-09 Fujian Southeast Shipyard — Fuzhou FJ** Yd No: DN59M-98 Loa 59.25 Br ex - Dght 4.950 Lbp 52.20 Br md 14.95 Dpth 6.10 Welded, 1 dk	**(B21B20A) Anchor Handling Tug Supply**	**2 oil engines** reduction geared to sc. shaft (s) driving 2 CP propellers Total Power: 3,840kW (5,220hp) 10.0kn Caterpillar 3516C-HD 2 x Vee 4 Stroke 16 Cy. 170 x 215 each-1920kW (2610bhp) Caterpillar Inc-USA AuxGen: 2 x 800kW a.c, 2 x 350kW a.c Thrusters: 1 Tunnel thruster (f); 1 Tunnel thruster (a) Fuel: 520.0
9609770 *9V9838* -	**VOS ATLAS** **Offshore Support Vessels 14 Pte Ltd** Vroon Offshore Services Pte Ltd *Singapore* *Singapore* MMSI: 566681000 Official number: 397647	**1,678** 503 1,309	Class: AB	**2012-10 Fujian Southeast Shipyard — Fuzhou FJ** Yd No: DN59M-99 Loa 59.25 Br ex - Dght 4.950 Lbp 52.20 Br md 14.95 Dpth 6.10 Welded, 1 dk	**(B21B20A) Anchor Handling Tug Supply**	**2 oil engines** reduction geared to sc. shaft (s) driving 2 CP propellers Total Power: 3,840kW (5,220hp) 10.0kn Caterpillar 3516B-HD 2 x Vee 4 Stroke 16 Cy. 170 x 215 each-1920kW (2610bhp) Caterpillar Inc-USA AuxGen: 2 x 800kW a.c, 2 x 350kW a.c Thrusters: 1 Tunnel thruster (f); 1 Tunnel thruster (a) Fuel: 520.0
9378046 *PBNJ* -	**VOS BASE** *ex* Base Express *-2013* **Base Express BV** Vroon Offshore Services BV *Breskens* *Netherlands* MMSI: 245821000 Official number: 48368	**2,534** 760 3,130	Class: LR ✠ **100A1** SS 09/2013 offshore supply ship fire fighting Ship 1 2400m3/h with water spray *IWS EP ✠ **LMC** **UMS** Eq.Ltr: T; Cable: 467.5/38.0 U3 (a)	**2008-09 Santierul Naval Damen Galati S.A. — Galati** (Hull) Yd No: 1135 **2008-09 B.V. Scheepswerf Damen — Gorinchem** Yd No: 552006 Loa 71.98 (BB) Br ex 16.04 Dght 6.100 Lbp 66.07 Br md 16.00 Dpth 7.50 Welded, 1 dk	**(B21A20S) Platform Supply Ship**	**4 diesel electric oil engines** driving 4 gen. each 1150kW 690V a.c Connecting to 2 elec. motors each (1500kW) driving 2 Azimuth electric drive units Total Power: 4,768kW (6,484hp) 12.7kn A.B.C. 6MDZC 4 x 4 Stroke 6 Cy. 256 x 310 each-1192kW (1621bhp) Anglo Belgian Corp NV (ABC)-Belgium Thrusters: 2 Thwart. FP thruster (f)

IMO / Call sign / Flag	Name, former names, owner, manager, port	Tonnage	Class	Builder / Dimensions	Type	Machinery
8115863 *8PUE* -	**VOS CLIPPER** *ex* DEA Clipper *-2011* *ex* Landry Tide *-2007* *ex* Petromar General *-1993* **Nomis Shipping Ltd** Vroon Offshore Services Ltd *Bridgetown* *Barbados* MMSI: 314248000 Official number: 733504	**713** 213 1,200	Class: AB	**1981-10 Halter Marine, Inc. — New Orleans, La** Yd No: 1042 Converted From: Offshore Tug/Supply Ship-2007 Loa 56.39 Br ex - Dght 4.267 Lbp - Br md 12.20 Dpth 4.27 Welded, 1 dk	**(B22G2OY) Standby Safety Vessel**	**2 oil engines** reverse reduction geared to sc. shafts driving 2 FP propellers Total Power: 2,238kW (3,042hp) 12.0kn EMD (Electro-Motive) 12-645-E6 2 x Vee 2 Stroke 12 Cy. 230 x 254 each-1119kW (1521bhp) (Reconditioned , Reconditioned & fitted 1981) General Motors Corp.Electro-Motive Div.-La Grange AuxGen: 2 x 99kW Thrusters: 1 Thwart. FP thruster (f) Fuel: 220.0
7404188 *MWIN6* -	**VOS COMMANDER** *ex* DEA Commander *-2008* *ex* Normand Gard *-1996* *ex* Normand Conger *-1985* *ex* Normand Vibran *-1981* *ex* Ocean Pilot *-1979* *ex* Normand Vibran *-1976* **Nomis Shipping Ltd** Vroon Offshore Services Ltd SatCom: Inmarsat Mini-M 762018415 *Aberdeen* *United Kingdom* MMSI: 234368000 Official number: 729369	**1,152** 346 790	Class: NV	**1975-07 Scheepswerf 'Friesland' BV — Lemmer** Yd No: 73 Loa 58.98 Br ex 12.02 Dght 5.130 Lbp 51.31 Br md 11.99 Dpth 6.00 Welded, 2 dks	**(B21B20A) Anchor Handling Tug Supply** Ice Capable	**2 oil engines** sr geared to sc. shafts driving 2 CP propellers Total Power: 4,532kW (6,162hp) 8.5kn Polar SF116VS-F 2 x Vee 4 Stroke 16 Cy. 250 x 300 each-2266kW (3081bhp) AB NOHAB-Sweden AuxGen: 2 x 170kW 440V 60Hz a.c, 1 x 56kW 440V 60Hz a.c Thrusters: 1 Retract. directional thruster (f); 1 Thwart. FP thruster (f) Fuel: 350.0 (d.f.) 13.0pd
7396563 *MKKU9* -	**VOS DEE** *ex* DEA Protector *-2009* *ex* Scott Protector *-2004* *ex* Normand Carrier *-1989* **Nomis Shipping Ltd** Vroon Offshore Services Ltd *Aberdeen* *United Kingdom* MMSI: 232003682 Official number: 714165	**1,104** 331 890	Class: NV	**1974-07 Nieuwe Noord Nederlandse Scheepswerven B.V. — Groningen** Yd No: 381 Converted From: Offshore Tug/Supply Ship-1991 Lengthened-1977 Loa 57.08 Br ex 11.52 Dght 3.820 Lbp 47.60 Br md 11.50 Dpth 5.50 Welded, 2 dks	**(B22G2OY) Standby Safety Vessel**	**2 oil engines** driving 2 CP propellers Total Power: 1,472kW (2,002hp) 10.0kn De Industrie 6D7HD 2 x 4 Stroke 6 Cy. 305 x 460 each-736kW (1001bhp) B.V. Motorenfabriek "De Industrie"-Alphen a/d Rijn AuxGen: 2 x 170kW 440V 60Hz a.c, 1 x 56kW 440V 60Hz a.c Thrusters: 1 Retract. directional thruster (f); 1 Thwart. FP thruster (a) Fuel: 404.8 (d.f.) 6.0pd
8211887 *MLQP5* -	**VOS DEFENDER** *ex* Viking Defender *-2009* *ex* Cam Defender *-1995* *ex* Jagima *-1988* **Offshore Support Vessels VI Ltd** Vroon Offshore Services Ltd SatCom: Inmarsat C 423265010 *Montrose* *United Kingdom* MMSI: 232650000 Official number: 709335	**680** 204 1,300	Class: NV	**1983-05 Salthammer Baatbyggeri AS — Vestnes** (Hull) **1983-05 Th Hellesoy Skipsbyggeri AS — Lofallstrand** Yd No: 107 Loa 46.82 Br ex - Dght 6.911 Lbp 42.02 Br md 11.02 Dpth 5.11 Welded, 2 dks	**(B22G2OY) Standby Safety Vessel**	**2 oil engines** driving 2 Directional propellers Total Power: 1,978kW (2,690hp) 8.5kn Deutz SBV6M628 2 x 4 Stroke 6 Cy. 240 x 280 each-989kW (1345bhp) Kloeckner Humboldt Deutz AG-West Germany AuxGen: 2 x 175kW 230V 50Hz a.c Fuel: 155.0 (d.f.)
9366031 *MRJN7* -	**VOS DISCOVERY** *ex* Viking Discovery *-2009* **Bank of Scotland Transport Finance 1 Ltd** Vroon Offshore Services Ltd *Aberdeen* *United Kingdom* MMSI: 235050631 Official number: 912691	**1,433** 429 952	Class: LR ✠ **100A1** SS 02/2012 ✠ **LMC** **UMS** Eq.Ltr: 0; Cable: 165.0/34.0 U2 (a)	**2007-02 Astilleros Zamakona SA — Santurtzi** Yd No: 642 Loa 55.20 (BB) Br ex 13.10 Dght 4.663 Lbp 48.00 Br md 12.70 Dpth 6.25 Welded, 1 dk	**(B21A20S) Platform Supply Ship**	**4 diesel electric oil engines** driving 4 gen. each 500kW 440V a.c Connecting to 2 elec. motors each (750kW) driving 2 Azimuth electric drive units contra rotating propellers Total Power: 2,404kW (3,268hp) 10.0kn Caterpillar C18 4 x 4 Stroke 6 Cy. 145 x 183 each-601kW (817bhp) Caterpillar Inc-USA Thrusters: 1 Thwart. FP thruster (f) Fuel: 293.0 (d.f.) 7.2pd
8010001 *C6KA8* -	**VOS DON** *ex* DEA Seeker *-2009* *ex* Toisa Puffin *-2003* *ex* Marsea One *-1991* **Nomis Shipping Ltd** Vroon Offshore Services Ltd SatCom: Inmarsat M 630905910 *Nassau* *Bahamas* MMSI: 309059000 Official number: 720406	**782** 234 1,200	Class: AB	**1980-09 Halter Marine, Inc. — Moss Point, Ms** Yd No: 937 Loa 55.00 Br ex 12.22 Dght 3.664 Lbp 54.87 Br md 12.20 Dpth 4.27 Welded, 1 dk	**(B21A20S) Platform Supply Ship**	**2 oil engines** reverse reduction geared to sc. shafts driving 2 FP propellers Total Power: 1,910kW (2,596hp) 10.0kn G.M. (Detroit Diesel) 16V-149-TI 2 x Vee 2 Stroke 16 Cy. 146 x 146 each-955kW (1298bhp) General Motors Detroit DieselAllison Divn-USA AuxGen: 2 x 125kW Thrusters: 1 Thwart. FP thruster (f) Fuel: 271.0
7608485 *A8RW9* -	**VOS EMPEROR** *ex* Black Watch *-2009* *ex* Kaskazi *-1991* **Nomis Shipping Ltd** Vroon Offshore Services Ltd *Monrovia* *Liberia* MMSI: 636014173 Official number: 14173	**624** 187 286	Class: GL (LR) ✠ Classed LR until 23/3/85	**1977-04 Martin Jansen GmbH & Co. KG Schiffsw. u. Masch. — Leer** Yd No: 136 Converted From: Stern Trawler-1991 Loa 39.50 Br ex 9.83 Dght 4.551 Lbp 31.20 Br md 9.80 Dpth 5.36 Welded, 1 dk	**(B22G2OY) Standby Safety Vessel**	**1 oil engine** reverse reduction geared to sc. shaft driving 1 CP propeller Total Power: 942kW (1,281hp) 12.0kn Alpha 8V23L-VO 1 x Vee 4 Stroke 8 Cy. 225 x 300 942kW (1281bhp) Alpha Diesel A/S-Denmark AuxGen: 2 x 376kW 220/380V 50Hz a.c Thrusters: 1 Thwart. FP thruster (f) Fuel: 61.0 (d.f.)
9488138 *2CVI8* -	**VOS ENDEAVOUR** **Bank of Scotland Transport Finance 1 Ltd** Vroon Offshore Services Ltd *Aberdeen* *United Kingdom* MMSI: 235076082 Official number: 916405	**1,734** 520 1,213	Class: LR ✠ **100A1** SS 02/2010 ✠ **LMC** **UMS** Eq.Ltr: 0; Cable: 165.0/34.0 U2 (a)	**2010-02 Astilleros Zamakona Pasaia SL — Pasaia** Yd No: 673 Loa 60.00 Br ex 13.10 Dght 5.000 Lbp 52.80 Br md 12.70 Dpth 6.25 Welded, 1 dk	**(B21A20S) Platform Supply Ship**	**4 diesel electric oil engines** driving 2 gen. each 550kW 440V a.c 2 gen. each 825kW 440V a.c Connecting to 2 elec. motors each (800kW) driving 2 Azimuth electric drive units Total Power: 3,138kW (4,266hp) 10.0kn Caterpillar 3508B 2 x Vee 4 Stroke 8 Cy. 170 x 190 each-968kW (1316bhp) Caterpillar Inc-USA Caterpillar C18 2 x 4 Stroke 6 Cy. 145 x 183 each-601kW (817bhp) Caterpillar Inc-USA Thrusters: 2 Directional thruster (f) Fuel: 517.0 (d.f.)
9488152 *2DTU6* -	**VOS ENDURANCE** **Bank of Scotland Transport Finance 1 Ltd** Vroon Offshore Services Ltd *Aberdeen* *United Kingdom* MMSI: 235082004 Official number: 916997	**1,734** 520 1,209	Class: LR ✠ **100A1** SS 10/2010 ✠ **LMC** **UMS** Eq.Ltr: 0; Cable: 412.5/30.0 U3 (a)	**2010-10 Astilleros Zamakona Pasaia SL — Pasaia** Yd No: 675 Loa 60.00 Br ex 13.10 Dght 5.000 Lbp 52.80 Br md 12.70 Dpth 6.25 Welded, 1 dk	**(B21A20S) Platform Supply Ship**	**4 diesel electric oil engines** driving 2 gen. each 500kW 440V a.c 2 gen. each 910kW 440V a.c Connecting to 2 elec. motors each (800kW) driving 2 Azimuth electric drive units Total Power: 3,138kW (4,266hp) 10.0kn Caterpillar 3508B 2 x Vee 4 Stroke 8 Cy. 170 x 190 each-968kW (1316bhp) Caterpillar Inc-USA Caterpillar C18 2 x 4 Stroke 6 Cy. 145 x 183 each-601kW (817bhp) Caterpillar Inc-USA Thrusters: 2 Thwart. FP thruster (f)
9488140 *2DEN4* -	**VOS ENTERPRISE** **Bank of Scotland Transport Finance 1 Ltd** Vroon Offshore Services Ltd *Aberdeen* *United Kingdom* MMSI: 235078284 Official number: 916643	**1,734** 520 1,213	Class: LR ✠ **100A1** SS 06/2010 fire-fighting Ship 1 (2400m3/h) ✠ **LMC** **UMS** Eq.Ltr: 0; Cable: 412.5/34.0 U3 (a)	**2010-06 Astilleros Zamakona Pasaia SL — Pasaia** Yd No: 674 Loa 60.00 (BB) Br ex 13.10 Dght 5.000 Lbp 52.80 Br md 12.70 Dpth 6.25 Welded, 1 dk	**(B21A20S) Platform Supply Ship**	**4 diesel electric oil engines** driving 2 gen. each 825kW 440V a.c 2 gen. each 550kW 440V a.c Connecting to 2 elec. motors each (800kW) driving 2 Azimuth electric drive units Total Power: 3,138kW (4,266hp) 10.0kn Caterpillar 3508B 2 x Vee 4 Stroke 8 Cy. 170 x 190 each-968kW (1316bhp) Caterpillar Inc-USA Caterpillar C18 2 x 4 Stroke 6 Cy. 145 x 183 each-601kW (817bhp) Caterpillar Inc-USA Thrusters: 2 Tunnel thruster (f)
9366043 *MQHL9* -	**VOS EXPLORER** *ex* Viking Explorer *-2010* **Bank of Scotland Transport Finance 1 Ltd** Vroon Offshore Services Ltd *Aberdeen* *United Kingdom* MMSI: 235052743 Official number: 912954	**1,433** 429 952	Class: LR ✠ **100A1** SS 05/2012 ✠ **LMC** **UMS** Eq.Ltr: 0; Cable: 165.0/34.0 U2 (a)	**2007-05 Astilleros Zamakona SA — Santurtzi** Yd No: 643 Loa 55.20 (BB) Br ex 13.10 Dght 4.500 Lbp 48.00 Br md 12.70 Dpth 6.25 Welded, 1 dk	**(B22G2OY) Standby Safety Vessel**	**4 diesel electric oil engines** driving 4 gen. each 500kW 440V a.c Connecting to 2 elec. motors each (750kW) driving 2 Azimuth electric drive units contra rotating propellers Total Power: 2,404kW (3,268hp) 10.0kn Caterpillar C18 4 x 4 Stroke 6 Cy. 145 x 183 each-601kW (817bhp) Caterpillar Inc-USA Thrusters: 1 Thwart. FP thruster (f) Fuel: 340.0 (d.f.) 7.2pd

IMO / Call sign	Name / Owner	Tonnage	Class	Builder / Dimensions	Type	Machinery
9647198 *2GGY6* -	**VOS FABULOUS** **Offshore Support Vessels IX Ltd** Vroon Offshore Services Ltd *Aberdeen* *United Kingdom* MMSI: 235097311 Official number: 918829	**1,600** 480 655	Class: AB	**2014-04 Nanjing East Star Shipbuilding Co Ltd — Nanjing JS** Yd No: ESS110101 Loa 50.00 Br ex - Dght 3.750 Lbp 46.62 Br md 13.20 Dpth 5.50 Welded, 1 dk	**(B22G20Y) Standby Safety Vessel**	**2 oil engines** reduction geared to sc. shafts driving 2 CP propellers Total Power: 1,640kW (2,230hp) 10.0kn Caterpillar 3508C 2 x Vee 4 Stroke 8 Cy. 170 x 190 each-820kW (1115bhp) Caterpillar Motoren (Guangdong) CoLtd-China Thrusters: 1 Tunnel thruster (f)
9064188 *MSHE2* -	**VOS GUARDIAN** *ex* Viking Guardian *-2008* *ex* Scott Guardian *-2005* **Offshore Support Vessels IV Ltd** Vroon Offshore Services Ltd SatCom: Inmarsat C 423332910 *Leith* *United Kingdom* MMSI: 233329000 Official number: 723633	**1,218** 365 1,043 T/cm 5.9	Class: LR ✠ **100A1** SS 12/2013 ✠ **LMC** Eq.Ltr: N; Cable: 413.4/34.0 U2	**1993-12 Yorkshire D.D. Co. Ltd. — Hull** Yd No: 332 Loa 55.00 Br ex 12.92 Dght 4.500 Lbp 48.00 Br md 12.70 Dpth 5.50 Welded, 1 dk	**(B22G20Y) Standby Safety Vessel**	**2 oil engines** with clutches, flexible couplings & sr geared to sc. shafts driving 2 Directional propellers Total Power: 1,432kW (1,946hp) 8.0kn Caterpillar 3508TA 2 x Vee 4 Stroke 8 Cy. 170 x 190 each-716kW (973bhp) Caterpillar Inc-USA AuxGen: 3 x 145kW 380V 50Hz a.c Thrusters: 1 Retract. directional thruster (f) Fuel: 247.6 (d.f.) 10.6pd
9552264 *IBZY* -	**VOS HADES** *launched as* SK Line 56 *-2009* **Vroon Offshore Italia Srl** - SatCom: Inmarsat C 424727813 *Ancona* *Italy* MMSI: 247278100 Official number: 8	**1,678** 503 1,386	Class: RI (AB)	**2009-09 Fujian Southeast Shipyard — Fuzhou FJ** (Hull) Yd No: SK56 **2009-09 Nam Cheong Dockyard Sdn Bhd — Miri** Yd No: (SK56) Loa 59.25 Br ex - Dght 4.950 Lbp 52.20 Br md 14.95 Dpth 6.10 Welded, 1 dk	**(B21B20A) Anchor Handling Tug Supply**	**2 oil engines** reduction geared to sc. shafts driving 2 CP propellers Total Power: 3,840kW (5,220hp) 10.0kn Caterpillar 3516B-HD 2 x Vee 4 Stroke 16 Cy. 170 x 215 each-1920kW (2610bhp) Caterpillar Inc-USA AuxGen: 3 x 320kW a.c Thrusters: 1 Tunnel thruster (f) Fuel: 520.0
9552252 *9V8433* -	**VOS HECATE** **Offshore Support Vessels 15 Pte Ltd** Vroon Offshore Services Pte Ltd SatCom: Inmarsat C 456501912 *Singapore* *Singapore* MMSI: 565019000 Official number: 395779	**1,678** 503 1,344	Class: AB	**2010-11 Fujian Southeast Shipyard — Fuzhou FJ** Yd No: SK49 Loa 59.25 Br ex - Dght 4.950 Lbp 52.20 Br md 14.95 Dpth 6.10 Welded, 1 dk	**(B21B20A) Anchor Handling Tug Supply**	**2 oil engines** reduction geared to sc. shafts driving 2 CP propellers Total Power: 3,840kW (5,220hp) 10.0kn Caterpillar 3516B-HD 2 x Vee 4 Stroke 16 Cy. 170 x 215 each-1920kW (2610bhp) Caterpillar Inc-USA AuxGen: 3 x 350kW a.c Thrusters: 1 Tunnel thruster (f) Fuel: 500.0
9529085 *9V7932* -	**VOS HELIOS** **Offshore Support Vessels 16 Pte Ltd** Vroon Offshore Services Pte Ltd SatCom: Inmarsat C 456448010 *Singapore* *Singapore* MMSI: 564480000 Official number: 395062	**1,678** 503 1,386	Class: AB	**2009-06 Fujian Southeast Shipyard — Fuzhou FJ** Yd No: SK41 Loa 59.25 Br ex - Dght 4.950 Lbp 52.20 Br md 14.95 Dpth 6.10 Welded, 1 dk	**(B21B20A) Anchor Handling Tug Supply**	**2 oil engines** reduction geared to sc. shafts driving 2 CP propellers Total Power: 3,788kW (5,150hp) 10.0kn Caterpillar 3516B-HD 2 x Vee 4 Stroke 16 Cy. 170 x 215 each-1894kW (2575bhp) Caterpillar Inc-USA AuxGen: 3 x 320kW a.c Thrusters: 1 Tunnel thruster (f)
9570709 *ICME* -	**VOS HERA** **Vroon Offshore Italia Srl** - *Ancona* *Italy* MMSI: 247280500	**1,678** 503 1,386	Class: RI (AB)	**2010-01 Fujian Southeast Shipyard — Fuzhou FJ** Yd No: SK47 Loa 59.25 Br ex - Dght 4.950 Lbp 52.20 Br md 14.95 Dpth 6.10 Welded, 1 dk	**(B21B20A) Anchor Handling Tug Supply**	**2 oil engines** reduction geared to sc. shafts driving 2 CP propellers Total Power: 3,840kW (5,220hp) 10.0kn Caterpillar 3516B-HD 2 x Vee 4 Stroke 16 Cy. 170 x 215 each-1920kW (2610bhp) Caterpillar Inc-USA AuxGen: 3 x 350kW 50Hz a.c Thrusters: 1 Tunnel thruster (f)
9401702 *9V7941* -	**VOS HERCULES** *ex* DEA Hercules *-2009* **Offshore Support Vessels 14 Pte Ltd** Vroon Offshore Services Pte Ltd *Singapore* *Singapore* MMSI: 563236000 Official number: 395073	**1,690** 507 1,360	Class: AB (BV)	**2006-12 Fujian Southeast Shipyard — Fuzhou FJ** (Hull) Yd No: H863 **2006-12 Jaya Shipbuilding & Engineering Pte Ltd — Singapore** Yd No: 863 Loa 59.25 Br ex - Dght 4.950 Lbp 52.20 Br md 14.95 Dpth 6.10 Welded, 1 dk	**(B21B20A) Anchor Handling Tug Supply**	**2 oil engines** reduction geared to sc. shafts driving 2 CP propellers Total Power: 3,838kW (5,218hp) 10.0kn Caterpillar 3516B-TA 2 x Vee 4 Stroke 16 Cy. 170 x 190 each-1919kW (2609bhp) Caterpillar Inc-USA AuxGen: 3 x 320kW 415V 50Hz a.c Thrusters: 1 Tunnel thruster (f) Fuel: 470.0
9529059 *9V7930* -	**VOS HERMES** *launched as* SK Line 38 *-2009* **Offshore Support Vessels 16 Pte Ltd** Vroon Offshore Services Pte Ltd *Singapore* *Singapore* MMSI: 563692000 Official number: 395060	**1,678** 503 1,402	Class: AB	**2009-04 Fujian Southeast Shipyard — Fuzhou FJ** Yd No: SK38 Loa 59.25 Br ex - Dght 4.950 Lbp 52.20 Br md 14.95 Dpth 6.10 Welded, 1 dk	**(B21B20A) Anchor Handling Tug Supply**	**2 oil engines** reduction geared to sc. shafts driving 2 CP propellers Total Power: 3,840kW (5,220hp) 10.0kn Caterpillar 3516B-HD 2 x Vee 4 Stroke 16 Cy. 170 x 215 each-1920kW (2610bhp) Caterpillar Inc-USA AuxGen: 3 x 315kW a.c Thrusters: 1 Tunnel thruster (f) Fuel: 530.0
9529061 *ICCD* -	**VOS HESTIA** *launched as* SK Line 39 *-2009* **Vroon Offshore Italia Srl** - SatCom: Inmarsat C 424702533 *Ancona* *Italy* MMSI: 247278800 Official number: 9	**1,678** 503 1,386	Class: RI (AB)	**2009-04 Fujian Southeast Shipyard — Fuzhou FJ** Yd No: SK39 Loa 59.25 Br ex - Dght 4.950 Lbp 52.20 Br md 14.95 Dpth 6.10 Welded, 1 dk	**(B21B20A) Anchor Handling Tug Supply**	**2 oil engines** reduction geared to sc. shafts driving 2 CP propellers Total Power: 3,788kW (5,150hp) 10.0kn Caterpillar 3516B-HD 2 x Vee 4 Stroke 16 Cy. 170 x 215 each-1894kW (2575bhp) Caterpillar Inc-USA AuxGen: 3 x 315kW 415V 50Hz a.c Thrusters: 1 Thwart. CP thruster (f)
9552240 *9V8432* -	**VOS HYPERION** **Offshore Support Vessels 15 Pte Ltd** Vroon Offshore Services Pte Ltd *Singapore* *Singapore* MMSI: 563655000 Official number: 395778	**1,678** 503 1,370	Class: AB	**2010-06 Fujian Southeast Shipyard — Fuzhou FJ** Yd No: SK48 Loa 59.25 Br ex - Dght 4.950 Lbp 52.20 Br md 14.95 Dpth 6.10 Welded, 1 dk	**(B21B20A) Anchor Handling Tug Supply** Cranes: 1x3t	**2 oil engines** reduction geared to sc. shafts driving 2 CP propellers Total Power: 3,840kW (5,220hp) 10.0kn Caterpillar 3516B-HD 2 x Vee 4 Stroke 16 Cy. 170 x 215 each-1920kW (2610bhp) Caterpillar Inc-USA AuxGen: 3 x 350kW a.c Fuel: 464.0
9366055 *MVAW6* -	**VOS INNOVATOR** **Bank of Scotland Transport Finance 1 Ltd** Vroon Offshore Services Ltd *Aberdeen* *United Kingdom* MMSI: 235056546 Official number: 913301	**1,433** 429 981	Class: LR ✠ **100A1** SS 08/2012 ✠ **LMC** **UMS** Eq.Ltr: 0; Cable: 165.0/34.0 U2 (a)	**2007-08 Astilleros Zamakona SA — Santurtzi** Yd No: 644 Loa 55.20 (BB) Br ex 13.10 Dght 5.000 Lbp 48.00 Br md 12.70 Dpth 6.25 Welded, 1 dk	**(B21A20S) Platform Supply Ship**	**4 diesel electric oil engines** driving 4 gen. each 500kW 440V a.c Connecting to 2 elec. motors each (750kW) driving 2 Azimuth electric drive units contra rotating propellers Total Power: 2,404kW (3,268hp) 10.0kn Caterpillar C18 4 x 4 Stroke 6 Cy. 145 x 183 each-601kW (817bhp) Caterpillar Inc-USA Thrusters: 1 Thwart. FP thruster (f) Fuel: 340.0
9366067 *2AFP6* -	**VOS INSPIRER** **Bank of Scotland Transport Finance 1 Ltd** Vroon Offshore Services Ltd *Aberdeen* *United Kingdom* MMSI: 235059199 Official number: 913735	**1,433** 429 981	Class: LR ✠ **100A1** SS 12/2012 ✠ **LMC** **UMS** Eq.Ltr: 0; Cable: 165.0/34.0 U2 (a)	**2007-12 Astilleros Zamakona SA — Santurtzi** Yd No: 645 Loa 55.20 (BB) Br ex 13.10 Dght 5.000 Lbp 48.00 Br md 12.70 Dpth 6.25 Welded, 1 dk	**(B21A20S) Platform Supply Ship**	**4 diesel electric oil engines** driving 4 gen. each 500kW 440V a.c Connecting to 2 elec. motors each (750kW) driving 2 Azimuth electric drive units contra rotating propellers Total Power: 2,404kW (3,268hp) 10.0kn Caterpillar C18 4 x 4 Stroke 6 Cy. 145 x 183 each-601kW (817bhp) Caterpillar Inc-USA Thrusters: 1 Thwart. FP thruster (f) Fuel: 340.0 (d.f.)

7413127 *ZQFV4* -	**VOS IONA** *ex Viking Iona -2009 ex BUE Iona -2007* *ex Coral -1999 ex Hornbeck Coral -1997* *ex Seaboard Coral -1995 ex Boa Coral -1992* *ex Ocean Coral -1990* *ex Highland Piper 1 -1987* *ex Highland Piper -1987* **Offshore Support Vessels IV Ltd** Vroon Offshore Services Ltd SatCom: Inmarsat C 423503710 *Leith* *United Kingdom* MMSI: 235037000 Official number: 903260	**1,444** 433 1,921	Class: LR (NV) **100A1** SS 02/2013 offshore supply/oil recovery ship **LMC** Eq.Ltr: 0; Cable: 412.5/34.0 U2	**1977-03 James Brown & Hamer Ltd. — Durban** Yd No: 35 Loa 61.00 Br ex 14.30 Dght 5.130 Lbp 55.68 Br md 13.80 Dpth 6.10 Welded, 1 dk	**(B21A20S) Platform Supply Ship** Passengers: unberthed: 50; berths: 20	**2 oil engines** sr geared to sc. shafts driving 2 CP propellers Total Power: 3,090kW (4,202hp) 10.0kn MaK 6M453AK 2 x 4 Stroke 6 Cy. 320 x 420 each-1545kW (2101bhp) MaK Maschinenbau GmbH-Kiel AuxGen: 3 x 136kW 440V 60Hz a.c Thrusters: 1 Tunnel thruster (f); 1 Retract. directional thruster (f) Fuel: 326.0 (d.f.) 11.7pd
8506050 *MNEU9* -	**VOS ISLAY** *ex Viking Islay -2008 ex BUE Islay -2005* *ex Searcher -1999 ex Hornbeck Searcher -1996* *ex Sunset Searcher -1995* *ex Far Searcher -1993 ex Nuna -1991* **Offshore Support Vessels IV Ltd** Vroon Offshore Services Ltd SatCom: Inmarsat C 423299210 *Aberdeen* *United Kingdom* MMSI: 232992000 Official number: 714188	**928** 278 850	Class: LR (BV) **100A1** SS 01/2011 tug/supply ship **LMC** **UMS**	**1986-12 Astilleros Luzuriaga SA — Pasaia** Yd No: 234 Loa 53.01 Br ex - Dght 4.501 Lbp 46.00 Br md 12.01 Dpth 5.21 Welded, 1 dk	**(B21B20T) Offshore Tug/Supply Ship**	**2 oil engines** reduction geared to sc. shafts driving 2 CP propellers Total Power: 2,800kW (3,806hp) 13.8kn MaK 8M20 1 x 4 Stroke 8 Cy. 200 x 300 1400kW (1903bhp) (new engine ,made 2005) MaK Motoren GmbH & Co. KG-Kiel MaK 8M20 1 x 4 Stroke 8 Cy. 200 x 300 1400kW (1903bhp) (new engine 2005) MaK Motoren GmbH & Co. KG-Kiel AuxGen: 2 x 440kW 220/380V 50Hz a.c, 2 x 158kW 220/380V 50Hz a.c Thrusters: 1 Tunnel thruster (f) Fuel: 402.0
8500393 *GFRS* -	**VOS LISMORE** *ex Viking Lismore -2007 ex BUE Lismore -2006* *ex Baronet -1999 ex Hornbeck Baronet -1996* *ex Sunset Baronet -1995 ex Far Baronet -1993* *ex Seaforth Baronet -1989* **Offshore Support Vessels IV Ltd** Vroon Offshore Services Ltd SatCom: Inmarsat C 423300710 *Aberdeen* *United Kingdom* MMSI: 233007000 Official number: 701186	**977** 293 1,011	Class: LR (BV) **100A1** SS 08/2011 supply ship **LMC**	**1986-07 Ferguson-Ailsa Ltd — Troon** Yd No: 570 Converted From: Offshore Tug/Supply Ship-1991 Loa 53.85 Br ex 12.22 Dght 4.711 Lbp 49.28 Br md 12.01 Dpth 5.21 Welded, 1 dk	**(B21A20S) Platform Supply Ship**	**2 oil engines** with clutches, flexible couplings & sr geared to sc. shafts driving 2 CP propellers Total Power: 1,488kW (2,024hp) 11.8kn Blackstone ESL6MK2 2 x 4 Stroke 6 Cy. 222 x 292 each-744kW (1012bhp) Mirrlees Blackstone (Stamford)Ltd.-Stamford AuxGen: 2 x 250kW 220/440V 60Hz a.c, 2 x 175kW 220/440V 60Hz a.c Thrusters: 1 Thwart. CP thruster (f) Fuel: 280.5 5.5pd
8204781 *IPHH* -	**VOS MAESTRALE** *ex Maestrale Secondo -2008* *ex Astro Cherne -1994* **Vremar Srl** - *Catania* *Italy* MMSI: 247224300 Official number: 28	*308* 155 376	Class: RI (AB)	**1984-10 Maclaren BA Est. e Servicos Maritimos S.A. — Rio de Janeiro** Yd No: 274 Loa 40.16 Br ex 8.87 Dght 3.150 Lbp 34.70 Br md 8.63 Dpth 3.51 Welded, 1 dk	**(B21A20S) Platform Supply Ship**	**2 oil engines** sr reverse geared to sc. shafts driving 2 FP propellers Total Power: 1,176kW (1,598hp) 10.0kn Baudouin 12P15.2SR 2 x Vee 4 Stroke 12 Cy. 150 x 150 each-588kW (799bhp) (new engine 1998) Societe des Moteurs Baudouin SA-France AuxGen: 2 x 100kW 440V 60Hz a.c Thrusters: 1 Thwart. FP thruster (f) Fuel: 116.0 (d.f.) 3.0pd
9103893 *MWCH5* -	**VOS MASTER** *ex Caledonia Master -2008 ex Artabaze -1996* **Offshore Support Vessels V Ltd** Vroon Offshore Services Ltd *Aberdeen* *United Kingdom* MMSI: 234285000 Official number: 727832	**1,607** 482 1,528	Class: BV	**1993-10 Halter Marine, Inc. — Lockport, La** Yd No: 1324 Loa 66.45 Br ex - Dght 5.200 Lbp - Br md 14.02 Dpth 6.10 Welded, 1 dk	**(B21B20A) Anchor Handling Tug Supply**	**2 oil engines** with clutches, flexible couplings & sr geared to sc. shafts driving 2 CP propellers Total Power: 5,340kW (7,260hp) 12.0kn Caterpillar 3608TA 2 x 4 Stroke 8 Cy. 280 x 300 each-2670kW (3630bhp) Caterpillar Inc-USA AuxGen: 4 x 254kW 440/120V Thrusters: 1 Thwart. FP thruster (f)
7302237 *A8FL8* -	**VOS NORTHWIND** *ex Swallow -2004 ex Hornbeck Swallow -1996* *ex Seaboard Swallow -1995 ex Aracati -1995* **Nomis Shipping Ltd** Vroon Offshore Services Ltd *Monrovia* *Liberia* MMSI: 636012442 Official number: 12442	**652** 252 498	Class: BV (AB)	**1973-07 Shimoda Dockyard Co. Ltd. — Shimoda** Yd No: 212 Converted From: Offshore Tug/Supply Ship-1990 Loa 50.35 Br ex - Dght 3.660 Lbp 45.52 Br md 11.59 Dpth 4.58 Welded, 1 dk	**(B21A20S) Platform Supply Ship**	**2 diesel electric oil engines** driving 2 gen. each 820kW a.c driving 2 FP propellers Total Power: 1,628kW (2,214hp) 12.0kn Caterpillar D399SCAC 2 x Vee 4 Stroke 16 Cy. 159 x 203 each-814kW (1107bhp) Caterpillar Tractor Co-USA AuxGen: 2 x 184kW a.c Thrusters: 1 Thwart. FP thruster (f) Fuel: 231.5 (d.f.)
8216473 *8PSV* -	**VOS OCEAN** *ex DEA Ocean -2009 ex Needham Tide -2005* **Nomis Shipping Ltd** Vroon Offshore Services Ltd *Bridgetown* *Barbados* MMSI: 314213000 Official number: 733464	**750** 225 713	Class: AB	**1983-04 McDermott Shipyards Inc — New Iberia LA** Yd No: 154 Converted From: Offshore Supply Ship-2006 Loa 54.86 Br ex - Dght 4.500 Lbp - Br md 12.20 Dpth 4.27 Welded, 1 dk	**(B22G20Y) Standby Safety Vessel**	**2 oil engines** reverse reduction geared to sc. shafts driving 2 FP propellers Total Power: 1,678kW (2,282hp) 13.0kn Caterpillar D399SCAC 2 x Vee 4 Stroke 16 Cy. 159 x 203 each-839kW (1141bhp) Caterpillar Tractor Co-USA AuxGen: 2 x 165kW Thrusters: 1 Thwart. FP thruster (f) Fuel: 225.0
9355862 *9V7942* -	**VOS OLYMPIAN** *ex DEA Olympian -2009* **Offshore Support Vessels 14 Pte Ltd** Vroon Offshore Services Pte Ltd *Singapore* *Singapore* MMSI: 563211000 Official number: 395074	**1,772** 531 1,582	Class: AB	**2006-01 P.T. Jaya Asiatic Shipyard — Batam** Yd No: 849 Loa 62.85 Br ex - Dght 5.100 Lbp 55.80 Br md 14.95 Dpth 6.10 Welded, 1 dk	**(B21B20A) Anchor Handling Tug Supply**	**2 oil engines** reduction geared to sc. shafts driving 2 CP propellers Total Power: 4,050kW (5,506hp) 11.0kn Wartsila 6L26A 2 x 4 Stroke 6 Cy. 260 x 320 each-2025kW (2753bhp) Wartsila Finland Oy-Finland AuxGen: 2 x 1375kW a.c, 2 x 370kW a.c Thrusters: 1 Tunnel thruster (f)
9366079 *2AL07* -	**VOS PATHFINDER** **Bank of Scotland Transport Finance 1 Ltd** Vroon Offshore Services Ltd *Aberdeen* *United Kingdom* MMSI: 235060799 Official number: 914146	**1,433** 429 952	Class: LR ✠ **100A1** SS 03/2013 ✠ **LMC** **UMS** Eq.Ltr: 0; Cable: 165.0/34.0 U2 (a)	**2008-03 Astilleros Zamakona SA — Santurtzi** Yd No: 646 Loa 55.20 (BB) Br ex 13.10 Dght 5.000 Lbp 48.00 Br md 12.70 Dpth 6.25 Welded, 1 dk	**(B21A20S) Platform Supply Ship** TEU 7	**4 diesel electric oil engines** driving 4 gen. each 500kW 440V a.c Connecting to 2 elec. motors each (750kW) driving 2 Azimuth electric drive units contra rotating propellers Total Power: 2,404kW (3,268hp) 10.0kn Caterpillar C18 4 x 4 Stroke 6 Cy. 145 x 183 each-601kW (817bhp) Caterpillar Inc-USA Thrusters: 1 Thwart. FP thruster (f) Fuel: 340.0 (d.f.)
8030661 *8PTV* -	**VOS PATROL** *ex DEA Patrol -2008 ex Estay Tide -2006* **Nomis Shipping Ltd** Vroon Offshore Services Ltd *Bridgetown* *Barbados* MMSI: 314240000 Official number: 733495	**804** 241 1,200	Class: AB	**1982-12 Halter Marine, Inc. — Moss Point, Ms** Yd No: 1019 Converted From: Offshore Supply Ship-2006 Loa 62.85 Br ex - Dght 3.664 Lbp 54.87 Br md 12.20 Dpth 4.27 Welded, 1 dk	**(B22G20Y) Standby Safety Vessel**	**2 oil engines** reverse reduction geared to sc. shafts driving 2 FP propellers Total Power: 1,866kW (2,538hp) 12.0kn Caterpillar D399SCAC 2 x Vee 4 Stroke 16 Cy. 159 x 203 each-933kW (1269bhp) Caterpillar Tractor Co-USA AuxGen: 2 x 135kW Thrusters: 1 Thwart. FP thruster (f) Fuel: 258.0
9366081 *2AU05* -	**VOS PIONEER** **Offshore Support Vessels VII Ltd** Vroon Offshore Services Ltd *Aberdeen* *United Kingdom* MMSI: 235063065 Official number: 914903	**1,734** 520 850	Class: LR ✠ **100A1** SS 09/2013 fire fighting Ship 1 (2400m3/h) ✠ **LMC** **UMS** Eq.Ltr: 0; Cable: 412.5/34.0 U2 (a)	**2008-09 Astilleros Zamakona SA — Santurtzi** Yd No: 647 Loa 60.00 (BB) Br ex 13.10 Dght 5.000 Lbp 52.80 Br md 12.70 Dpth 6.25 Welded, 1 dk	**(B21A20S) Platform Supply Ship**	**4 diesel electric oil engines** driving 2 gen. each 500kW 440V a.c 2 gen. each 825kW 440V a.c Connecting to 2 elec. motors each (800kW) driving 2 Azimuth electric drive units contra rotating propellers Total Power: 3,138kW (4,266hp) 10.0kn Caterpillar 3508B 2 x Vee 4 Stroke 8 Cy. 170 x 190 each-968kW (1316bhp) Caterpillar Inc-USA Caterpillar C18 2 x 4 Stroke 6 Cy. 145 x 183 each-601kW (817bhp) Caterpillar Inc-USA Thrusters: 2 Thwart. FP thruster (f) Fuel: 479.0 (d.f.) 7.2pd

IMO / Call sign	Name, ownership	Tonnage	Class	Build / Dimensions	Type	Machinery
9273911 *PHFG* -	**VOS POWER** *ex* Power Express *-2012* *ex* Vos Power *-2012* *ex* Power Express *-2011* **Power Express BV** Vroon Offshore Services BV *Breskens* *Netherlands* MMSI: 246513000 Official number: 44466	**2,810** 843 3,859	Class: BV	**2006-06 Jiangsu Zhenjiang Shipyard Co Ltd — Zhenjiang JS** Yd No: VZJ689-01 Loa 75.00 Br ex - Dght 6.400 Lbp 69.06 Br md 17.50 Dpth 7.60 Welded, 1 dk	**(B21A20S) Platform Supply Ship**	**2 oil engines** reduction geared to sc. shafts driving 2 CP propellers Total Power: 4,916kW (6,684hp) 13.5kn Wartsila 6L32 2 x 4 Stroke 6 Cy. 320 x 400 each-2458kW (3342bhp) Wartsila Finland Oy-Finland AuxGen: 2 x 407kW 440/220V 60Hz a.c, 2 x 1500kW 450V 60Hz a.c Thrusters: 2 Tunnel thruster (f); 2 Tunnel thruster (a)
9444338 *PCDF* -	**VOS PRECIOUS** **PSV Express I BV** Vroon Offshore Services BV *Breskens* *Netherlands* MMSI: 246723000 Official number: 53725	**2,177** 1,044 3,250	Class: NV	**2010-05 Cochin Shipyard Ltd — Ernakulam** Yd No: BY-73 Loa 73.60 (BB) Br ex 16.04 Dght 5.830 Lbp 68.30 Br md 16.00 Dpth 7.00 Welded, 1 dk	**(B21A20S) Platform Supply Ship** Cranes: 1x3t	**2 oil engines** reduction geared to sc. shafts driving 2 CP propellers Total Power: 3,480kW (4,732hp) 12.0kn Bergens C25: 33L6P 2 x 4 Stroke 6 Cy. 250 x 330 each-1740kW (2366bhp) Rolls Royce Marine AS-Norway Thrusters: 2 Thwart. CP thruster (f); 2 Thwart. CP thruster (a)
9444340 *PBZK* -	**VOS PRELUDE** **PSV Express II BV** Vroon Offshore Services BV *Breskens* *Netherlands* MMSI: 245969000 Official number: 53682	**2,177** 1,044 3,250	Class: NV	**2010-06 Cochin Shipyard Ltd — Ernakulam** Yd No: BY-74 Loa 73.60 (BB) Br ex 16.04 Dght 5.830 Lbp 68.30 Br md 16.00 Dpth 7.00 Welded, 1 dk	**(B21A20S) Platform Supply Ship** Cranes: 1x3t	**2 oil engines** reduction geared to sc. shafts driving 2 CP propellers Total Power: 3,480kW (4,732hp) 12.0kn Bergens C25: 33L6P 2 x 4 Stroke 6 Cy. 250 x 330 each-1740kW (2366bhp) Rolls Royce Marine AS-Norway AuxGen: 2 x a.c, 2 x a.c Thrusters: 2 Thwart. CP thruster (f); 2 Thwart. CP thruster (a)
9273870 *PHHX* -	**VOS PRODUCER** *ex* Rig Express *-2011* **Motorschip Rig Express BV** Vroon Offshore Services BV *Breskens* *Netherlands* MMSI: 246565000 Official number: 44465	**2,810** 843 3,854	Class: BV	**2006-12 Jiangsu Zhenjiang Shipyard Co Ltd — Zhenjiang JS** Yd No: VZJ689-02 Loa 75.00 Br ex 17.90 Dght 6.400 Lbp 69.79 Br md 17.50 Dpth 7.60 Welded, 1 dk	**(B21A20S) Platform Supply Ship**	**2 oil engines** geared to sc. shafts driving 2 CP propellers Total Power: 4,920kW (6,690hp) 12.5kn Wartsila 6RN32 2 x 4 Stroke 6 Cy. 320 x 350 each-2460kW (3345bhp) Wartsila Finland Oy-Finland AuxGen: 2 x 407kW 440/220V 60Hz a.c, 2 x 1500kW 450V 60Hz a.c Thrusters: 2 Tunnel thruster (f); 2 Tunnel thruster (a) Fuel: 516.0 (d.f.)
9334026 *PHIV* -	**VOS PROMINENCE** *ex* Supply Express *-2011* **Supply Express BV** Vroon Offshore Services BV *Breskens* *Netherlands* MMSI: 244145000 Official number: 44462	**2,810** 843 3,854	Class: BV	**2007-03 Jiangsu Zhenjiang Shipyard Co Ltd — Zhenjiang JS** Yd No: VZJ689-03 Loa 75.00 Br ex 17.90 Dght 6.400 Lbp 69.60 Br md 17.50 Dpth 7.60 Welded, 1 dk	**(B21A20S) Platform Supply Ship**	**2 oil engines** reduction geared to sc. shafts driving 2 CP propellers Total Power: 4,920kW (6,690hp) 12.5kn Wartsila 6L32 2 x 4 Stroke 6 Cy. 320 x 400 each-2460kW (3345bhp) Wartsila Finland Oy-Finland AuxGen: 2 x 1500kW 440/220V 60Hz a.c, 2 x 407kW 440/220V 60Hz a.c Thrusters: 2 Tunnel thruster (f); 2 Tunnel thruster (a)
9366093 *2BLV8* -	**VOS PROSPECTOR** **Offshore Support Vessels VII Ltd** Vroon Offshore Services Ltd *Aberdeen* *United Kingdom* MMSI: 235067282 Official number: 915106	**1,734** 520 850	Class: LR ✠ **100A1** SS 10/2013 fire fighting Ship 1 (2400m3/h) ✠ **LMC** **UMS** Eq.Ltr: O; Cable: 412.5/34.0 U2 (a)	**2008-10 Astilleros Zamakona SA — Santurtzi** Yd No: 648 Loa 60.00 (BB) Br ex 13.10 Dght 4.650 Lbp 52.80 Br md 12.70 Dpth 6.25 Welded, 1 dk	**(B21A20S) Platform Supply Ship**	**4 diesel electric oil engines** driving 2 gen. each 500kW 440V a.c 2 gen. each 825kW 440V a.c Connecting to 2 elec. motors each (800kW) driving 2 Azimuth electric drive units contra rotating propellers Total Power: 3,138kW (4,266hp) 10.0kn Caterpillar 3508B 2 x Vee 4 Stroke 8 Cy. 170 x 190 each-968kW (1316bhp) Caterpillar Inc-USA Caterpillar C18 2 x 4 Stroke 6 Cy. 145 x 183 each-601kW (817bhp) Caterpillar Inc-USA Thrusters: 2 Thwart. FP thruster (f) Fuel: 340.0 (d.f.) 7.2pd
8215455 *GJCT* -	**VOS PROTECTOR** *ex* Viking Protector *-2007* *ex* Cam Protector *-1995* *ex* Sentry Hemne *-1987* **Offshore Support Vessels VI Ltd** Vroon Offshore Services Ltd SatCom: Inmarsat C 423263510 *Montrose* *United Kingdom* MMSI: 232635000 Official number: 709328	**673** 202 572	Class: NV	**1983-09 Oy Hangoverken Ab — Hanko** (Hull) **1983-09 Vaagen Verft AS — Kyrksaeterora** Yd No: 54 Loa 46.82 Br ex - Dght 6.911 Lbp 42.02 Br md 11.60 Dpth 7.45 Welded, 2 dks	**(B22G20Y) Standby Safety Vessel**	**2 oil engines** geared to sc. shafts driving 2 Directional propellers Total Power: 1,838kW (2,498hp) 9.0kn Caterpillar 3512TA 2 x Vee 4 Stroke 12 Cy. 170 x 190 each-919kW (1249bhp) Caterpillar Tractor Co-USA Fuel: 160.0
9193070 *MYGV8* -	**VOS PROVIDER** *ex* Viking Provider *-2009* **Offshore Support Vessels V Ltd** Vroon Offshore Services Ltd *Montrose* *United Kingdom* MMSI: 232821000 Official number: 902010	**2,102** 631 1,830	Class: NV	**1999-05 Husumer Schiffswerft Inh. Gebr. Kroeger GmbH & Co. KG — Husum** Yd No: 1525 Loa 68.13 Br ex 14.50 Dght 5.661 Lbp 60.00 Br md 14.50 Dpth 6.50 Welded, 1 dk	**(B21A20S) Platform Supply Ship**	**2 oil engines** with clutches, flexible couplings & sr geared to sc. shafts driving 2 CP propellers Total Power: 4,800kW (6,526hp) 10.0kn MaK 8M25 2 x 4 Stroke 8 Cy. 255 x 400 each-2400kW (3263bhp) MaK Motoren GmbH & Co. KG-Kiel AuxGen: 2 x 900kW 440V 60Hz a.c, 1 x 880kW 440V 60Hz a.c Thrusters: 1 Retract. directional thruster (f); 1 Thwart. FP thruster (f) Fuel: 470.3 (d.f.)
9664213 *IBCH* -	**VOS PRUDENCE** **PSV Express VIII BV** Vroon Offshore Italia Srl *Ancona* *Italy* MMSI: 247324600 Official number: 12	**2,937** 939 3,324	Class: RI (AB)	**2013-05 Fujian Southeast Shipyard — Fuzhou FJ** Yd No: DN75M-6 Loa 75.00 (BB) Br ex - Dght 6.500 Lbp 67.85 Br md 17.25 Dpth 8.00 Welded, 1 dk	**(B21A20S) Platform Supply Ship**	**2 oil engines** reduction geared to sc. shafts driving 2 Directional propellers Total Power: 4,412kW (5,998hp) 12.0kn Niigata 8L28HX 2 x 4 Stroke 8 Cy. 280 x 370 each-2206kW (2999bhp) Niigata Engineering Co Ltd-Japan Thrusters: 2 Thwart. CP thruster (f)
9664225 *IBCU* -	**VOS PURPOSE** **PSV Express VIII BV** Vroon Offshore Italia Srl *Ancona* *Italy* MMSI: 247325200	**2,937** 939 3,320	Class: RI (AB)	**2013-06 Fujian Southeast Shipyard — Fuzhou FJ** Yd No: DN75M-7 Loa 75.00 (BB) Br ex - Dght 6.600 Lbp 67.85 Br md 17.25 Dpth 8.00 Welded, 1 dk	**(B21A20S) Platform Supply Ship**	**2 oil engines** reduction geared to sc. shafts driving 2 Directional propellers Total Power: 4,412kW (5,998hp) 10.0kn Niigata 8L28HX 2 x 4 Stroke 8 Cy. 280 x 370 each-2206kW (2999bhp) Niigata Engineering Co Ltd-Japan Thrusters: 2 Thwart. CP thruster (f)
8216021 *MWGF5* -	**VOS RAASAY** *ex* Viking Raasay *-2008* *ex* BUE Raasay *-2006* *ex* Norse Tide *-1999* *ex* Sira Supporter *-1996* *ex* Drive Supporter *-1985* **Nomis Shipping Ltd** Vroon Offshore Services Ltd *Leith* *United Kingdom* MMSI: 232003585 Official number: 727833	**1,328** 399 1,300	Class: NV	**1983-06 FEAB-Marstrandverken — Marstrand** Yd No: 165 Loa 58.53 Br ex 13.02 Dght 5.590 Lbp 50.02 Br md 13.01 Dpth 6.51 Welded, 2 dks	**(B21A20S) Platform Supply Ship** Passengers: unberthed: 52; berths: 20 Ice Capable	**2 oil engines** with clutches, flexible couplings & sr geared to sc. shafts driving 2 CP propellers Total Power: 3,118kW (4,240hp) 10.0kn Alpha 8SL28L-VO 2 x 4 Stroke 8 Cy. 280 x 320 each-1559kW (2120bhp) B&W Alpha Diesel A/S-Denmark AuxGen: 1 x 640kW 440V 60Hz a.c, 1 x 492kW 440V 60Hz a.c, 1 x 308kW 440V 60Hz a.c Thrusters: 1 Tunnel thruster (f); 1 Retract. directional thruster (f) Fuel: 595.0 (d.f.) 5.1pd
7414054 *A8AE7* -	**VOS RAMBLER** *ex* V O S Rambler *-2008* *ex* Telco Rambler *-2004* *ex* Froyur *-1997* **Offshore Support Vessels I BV** Vroon Offshore Services BV *Monrovia* *Liberia* MMSI: 636011579 Official number: 11579	**379** 125 300	Class: BV (NV)	**1975-09 Kystvaagen Slip & Baatbyggeri — Kristiansund** Yd No: 34 Converted From: Stern Trawler-1997 Loa 37.90 (BB) Br ex 8.23 Dght 3.849 Lbp 36.52 Br md 8.21 Dpth 6.13 Welded, 2 dks	**(B22G20Y) Standby Safety Vessel** Ice Capable	**1 oil engine** driving 1 CP propeller Total Power: 850kW (1,156hp) Polar SF16RS-F 1 x 4 Stroke 6 Cy. 250 x 300 850kW (1156bhp) AB Bofors NOHAB-Sweden AuxGen: 2 x 125kW 380/220V 50Hz a.c Thrusters: 1 Directional thruster (f)

IMO / Call sign	Name, former names, owner, manager, port, flag	Tonnage	Class	Builder, dimensions	Type	Machinery
8205668 *GJSQ* -	**VOS RANGER** *ex* Viking Ranger *-2010* *ex* Cam Ranger *-1995* *ex* Sentinel Cathinka *-1988* **Offshore Support Vessels VI Ltd** Vroon Offshore Services Ltd SatCom: Inmarsat C 423249010 *Montrose* *United Kingdom* MMSI: 232490000 Official number: 709336	**680** 204 572	Class: NV	**1983-03 Batservice Verft AS — Mandal** Yd No: 661 Loa 46.72 Br ex 11.61 Dght 6.920 Lbp 42.02 Br md 11.03 Dpth 7.45 Welded, 2 dks	**(B22G20Y) Standby Safety Vessel**	**2 oil engines** with clutches, flexible couplings & sr geared to sc. shafts driving 2 Directional propellers Total Power: 1,714kW (2,330hp) 9.0kn Caterpillar 3512TA 2 x Vee 4 Stroke 12 Cy. 170 x 190 each-857kW (1165bhp) Caterpillar Tractor Co-USA AuxGen: 2 x 150kW 380V 50Hz a.c Fuel: 137.0 (d.f.)
8106989 *A8AE4* -	**VOS RULER** *ex* V O S Ruler *-2004* *ex* Telco Ruler *-2004* *ex* Geertruida *-1997* **Offshore Support Vessels I BV** Vroon Offshore Services BV SatCom: Inmarsat Mini-M 761901855 *Monrovia* *Liberia* MMSI: 636011576 Official number: 11576	**300** 90 -	Class: BV	**1982-01 Scheepswerf Metz B.V. — Urk** Yd No: 57 Converted From: Trawler-1997 Loa 36.30 Br ex - Dght 4.400 Lbp 32.20 Br md 8.01 Dpth 4.42 Welded, 1 dk	**(B22G20Y) Standby Safety Vessel**	**1 oil engine** geared to sc. shaft driving 1 FP propeller Total Power: 662kW (900hp) 10.0kn Bolnes 10DNL150/600 1 x 2 Stroke 10 Cy. 190 x 350 662kW (900bhp) 'Bolnes' Motorenfabriek BV-Netherlands AuxGen: 2 x 74kW 220V 50Hz a.c Thrusters: 1 Tunnel thruster (f) Fuel: 85.0 (d.f.)
7814278 *MWJZ5* -	**VOS RUNNER** *ex* DEA Ranger *-2008* *ex* Normand Ondur *-2004* *ex* Balta Sound *-1990* *ex* Oddstein *-1986* **Nomis Shipping Ltd** Vroon Offshore Services Ltd SatCom: Inmarsat C 423430110 *Aberdeen* *United Kingdom* MMSI: 234301000 Official number: 729230	**631** 189 600	Class: NV	**1978-01 Stocznia Remontowa 'Nauta' SA — Gdynia** (Hull) Yd No: 371 **1978-01 Kopervik Slip AS — Kopervik** Converted From: Stern Trawler-1991 Converted From: Standby Safety Vessel-1987 Converted From: Stern Trawler-1981 Lengthened-1982 Loa 50.35 Br ex 8.03 Dght 4.325 Lbp 44.71 Br md 8.00 Dpth 4.70 Welded, 1 dk	**(B22G20Y) Standby Safety Vessel** Ice Capable	**1 oil engine** driving 1 CP propeller Total Power: 1,324kW (1,800hp) 10.0kn Wichmann 6AXA 1 x 2 Stroke 6 Cy. 300 x 450 1324kW (1800bhp) Wichmann Motorfabrikk AS-Norway AuxGen: 2 x 112kW 220V 50Hz a.c Thrusters: 1 Retract. directional thruster (f); 1 Thwart. FP thruster (f); 1 Tunnel thruster (a) Fuel: 110.0 (d.f.)
9352224 *PHKK*	**VOS SATISFACTION** **DSV I Express BV** Vroon Offshore Services BV *Breskens* *Netherlands* MMSI: 244626000 Official number: 50342	**2,163** 648 1,485	Class: LR ✠ **100A1** SS 08/2012 offshore supply ship, fire fighting Ship 1 (2400m3/h) *IWS ✠ **LMC** **UMS** Eq.Ltr: R; Cable: 4800.0/38.0 FSWR	**2007-08 ABG Shipyard Ltd — Surat** Yd No: 241 Loa 61.00 Br ex 16.10 Dght 4.200 Lbp 54.00 Br md 15.80 Dpth 7.00 Welded, 1 dk	**(B22A20V) Diving Support Vessel** Cranes: 1x30t	**2 oil engines** with clutches, flexible couplings & sr geared to sc. shafts driving 2 CP propellers Total Power: 3,600kW (4,894hp) 11.0kn Wartsila 9L20 2 x 4 Stroke 9 Cy. 200 x 280 each-1800kW (2447bhp) Wartsila Finland Oy-Finland AuxGen: 2 x 390kW 440V 60Hz a.c, 2 x 1000kW a.c Thrusters: 1 Thwart. FP thruster (f); 1 Thwart. FP thruster (a) Fuel: 550.0 (d.f.)
8104125 *C6JI9* -	**VOS SCOUT** *ex* DEA Scout *-2009* *ex* Toisa Teal *-2004* *ex* Canmar Teal *-1990* **Nomis Shipping Ltd** Vroon Offshore Services Ltd *Nassau* *Bahamas* MMSI: 309061000 Official number: 395517	**516** 154 405	Class: LR (AB) **100A1** SS 10/2009 for service within the sea area enclosed between parallel 62~N and 48~N, and between the meridian of 15~W and the coast of Europe **LMC** Eq.Ltr: H; Cable: 302.5/22.0 FSWR	**1981-07 Allied Shipbuilders Ltd — North Vancouver BC** Yd No: 233 Converted From: Offshore Supply Ship-1990 Loa 39.62 Br ex 8.86 Dght 3.366 Lbp 35.58 Br md 8.84 Dpth 4.12 Welded, 1 dk	**(B22G20Y) Standby Safety Vessel**	**2 oil engines** sr reverse geared to sc. shafts driving 2 FP propellers Total Power: 1,250kW (1,700hp) 8.0kn Caterpillar D398SCAC 2 x Vee 4 Stroke 12 Cy. 159 x 203 each-625kW (850bhp) Caterpillar Tractor Co-USA AuxGen: 2 x 85kW 460V 60Hz a.c Thrusters: 1 Thwart. FP thruster (f) Fuel: 156.0 (d.f.)
9411264 *2BQY8* -	**VOS SEEKER** **Bank of Scotland Transport Finance 1 Ltd** Vroon Offshore Services Ltd *Aberdeen* *United Kingdom* MMSI: 235068568 Official number: 915477	**1,734** 520 1,213	Class: LR ✠ **100A1** SS 03/2014 ✠ **LMC** **UMS** Eq.Ltr: 0; Cable: 412.5/34.0 U3 (a)	**2009-03 Astilleros Zamakona SA — Santurtzi** Yd No: 649 Loa 60.00 (BB) Br ex 13.10 Dght 5.000 Lbp 52.80 Br md 12.70 Dpth 6.25 Welded, 1 dk	**(B21A20S) Platform Supply Ship**	**4 diesel electric oil engines** driving 2 gen. each 550kW 440V a.c 2 gen. each 825kW 440V a.c Connecting to 2 elec. motors each (800kW) driving 2 Azimuth electric drive units Total Power: 3,138kW (4,266hp) 10.0kn Caterpillar 3508B 2 x 4 Stroke 8 Cy. 170 x 190 each-968kW (1316bhp) Caterpillar Inc-USA Caterpillar C18 2 x 4 Stroke 6 Cy. 145 x 183 each-601kW (817bhp) Caterpillar Inc-USA Thrusters: 2 Thwart. FP thruster (f) Fuel: 555.0 (d.f.) 7.2pd
8121410 *GJBL* -	**VOS SENTINEL** *ex* Viking Sentinel *-2009* *ex* Cam Sentinal *-1995* *ex* Sentinel Maria *-1987* **Offshore Support Vessels VI Ltd** Vroon Offshore Services Ltd SatCom: Inmarsat C 423264810 *Montrose* *United Kingdom* MMSI: 232648000 Official number: 709327	**673** 202 572	Class: NV	**1982-10 Fiskerstrand Verft AS — Fiskarstrand** Yd No: 37 Loa 46.72 Br ex - Dght 6.749 Lbp 42.50 Br md 11.02 Dpth 7.40 Welded, 2 dks	**(B22G20Y) Standby Safety Vessel**	**2 oil engines** with clutches, flexible couplings & sr geared to sc. shafts driving 2 Directional propellers Total Power: 1,654kW (2,248hp) 8.0kn Caterpillar D399SCAC 2 x Vee 4 Stroke 16 Cy. 159 x 203 each-827kW (1124bhp) Caterpillar Tractor Co-USA AuxGen: 2 x 120kW 380V 50Hz a.c Fuel: 164.0 (d.f.)
7827029 *C6KQ7* -	**VOS SERVER** *ex* DEA Server *-2009* *ex* Toisa Plover *-2004* *ex* Veesea *-1991* *ex* Kara Seal *-1991* **Nomis Shipping Ltd** Vroon Offshore Services Ltd *Nassau* *Bahamas* MMSI: 308414000 Official number: 720721	**863** 258 1,000	Class: AB	**1979-10 Zigler Shipyards Inc — Jennings LA** Yd No: 263 Converted From: Offshore Tug/Supply Ship-1995 Loa 56.39 Br ex - Dght 3.696 Lbp 50.86 Br md 11.59 Dpth 4.27 Welded, 1 dk	**(B22G20Y) Standby Safety Vessel** Passengers: unberthed: 50; berths: 20	**2 oil engines** reverse reduction geared to sc. shaft driving 1 FP propeller Total Power: 1,678kW (2,282hp) 8.0kn Caterpillar D399SCAC 2 x Vee 4 Stroke 16 Cy. 159 x 203 each-839kW (1141bhp) Caterpillar Tractor Co-USA AuxGen: 2 x 210kW a.c Thrusters: 1 Thwart. FP thruster (f) Fuel: 230.0
8224286 *PDPN*	**VOS SHELTER** *ex* Deurloo *-2005* **VOS Shelter BV** Vroon Offshore Services BV *Breskens* *Netherlands* MMSI: 246490000 Official number: 816	**691** 207 468	Class: LR ✠ **100A1** SS 03/2013 salvage vessel ✠ **LMC** Eq.Ltr: K; Cable: 440.0/32.0 U2	**1983-12 B.V. Scheepswerven v/h H.H. Bodewes — Millingen a/d Rijn** Yd No: 770 Loa 45.55 Br ex 11.76 Dght 3.322 Lbp 42.02 Br md 11.51 Dpth 3.81 Welded, 1 dk	**(B34P2QV) Salvage Ship** Cranes: 1x20t	**2 oil engines** with clutches, flexible couplings & sr reverse geared to sc. shafts driving 2 FP propellers Total Power: 912kW (1,240hp) 11.0kn Stork DR0216K 2 x 4 Stroke 6 Cy. 210 x 300 each-456kW (620bhp) Stork Werkspoor Diesel BV-Netherlands AuxGen: 2 x 150kW 440V 60Hz a.c Thrusters: 1 Thwart. FP thruster (f) Fuel: 145.0 (d.f.)
9601510 *PCNU* -	**VOS SHINE** **DSV IV Express BV** Vroon Offshore Services BV *Breskens* *Netherlands* MMSI: 246060000 Official number: 23299 Z 212	**1,794** 538 853	Class: AB	**2012-03 Fujian Southeast Shipyard — Fuzhou FJ** Yd No: DN59M-91 Loa 60.24 Br ex - Dght 4.950 Lbp 52.20 Br md 14.95 Dpth 6.10 Welded, 1 dk	**(B22A20V) Diving Support Vessel** Cranes: 1x24t,1x3t	**2 oil engines** reduction geared to sc. shafts driving 2 CP propellers Total Power: 3,840kW (5,220hp) 11.0kn Caterpillar 3516B-HD 2 x Vee 4 Stroke 16 Cy. 170 x 215 each-1920kW (2610bhp) Caterpillar Inc-USA AuxGen: 2 x 900kW a.c, 3 x 450kW a.c Thrusters: 2 Thwart. CP thruster (f); 1 Thwart. FP thruster (a) Fuel: 480.0
8030673 *8PSW* -	**VOS SIREN** *ex* DEA Siren *-2008* *ex* Cole Tide *-2005* **Nomis Shipping Ltd** Vroon Offshore Services Ltd *Bridgetown* *Barbados* MMSI: 314214000 Official number: 733465	**686** 205 1,200	Class: AB	**1982-12 Halter Marine, Inc. — Moss Point, Ms** Yd No: 1020 Converted From: Offshore Supply Ship-2006 Loa - Br ex - Dght 3.664 Lbp 54.87 Br md 12.20 Dpth 4.27 Welded, 1 dk	**(B22G20Y) Standby Safety Vessel** Passengers: 300	**2 oil engines** reverse reduction geared to sc. shafts driving 2 FP propellers Total Power: 1,866kW (2,538hp) 12.0kn Caterpillar D399SCAC 2 x Vee 4 Stroke 16 Cy. 159 x 203 each-933kW (1269bhp) Caterpillar Tractor Co-USA AuxGen: 2 x 135kW Thrusters: 1 Thwart. FP thruster (f) Fuel: 271.0 (d.f.)
8207458 *MFTN9* -	**VOS SUPPORTER** *ex* Viking Supporter *-2008* *ex* Cam Supporter *-1995* *ex* Sentinel Teresa *-1989* **Offshore Support Vessels VI Ltd** Vroon Offshore Services Ltd SatCom: Inmarsat C 423256810 *Montrose* *United Kingdom* MMSI: 232568000 Official number: 701189	**680** 204 572	Class: NV	**1983-04 Oy Hangoverken Ab — Hanko** (Hull) **1983-04 Vaagen Verft AS — Kyrksaeterora** Yd No: 53 Loa 46.72 Br ex - Dght 6.911 Lbp 42.02 Br md 11.02 Dpth 7.45 Welded, 2 dks	**(B22G20Y) Standby Safety Vessel**	**2 oil engines** with clutches, flexible couplings & sr geared to sc. shafts driving 2 Directional propellers Total Power: 1,714kW (2,330hp) 9.0kn Caterpillar 3512TA 2 x Vee 4 Stroke 12 Cy. 170 x 190 each-857kW (1165bhp) Caterpillar Tractor Co-USA AuxGen: 2 x 120kW 380V 50Hz a.c Fuel: 164.0 (d.f.)

IMO / Call sign	Name / Owner	Tonnage	Class	Build / Dimensions	Type	Machinery
9601522 *PCPE* -	**VOS SWEET** **DSV V Express BV** Vroon Offshore Services BV *Breskens* *Netherlands* MMSI: 246609000 Official number: 55368	**1,794** 538 1,276	Class: AB	**2012**-11 **Fujian Southeast Shipyard — Fuzhou FJ** Yd No: DN59M-92 Loa 60.24 Br ex - Dght 4.950 Lbp 52.20 Br md 14.95 Dpth 6.10 Welded, 1 dk	**(B22A20V) Diving Support Vessel** Cranes: 1x24t,1x3t	**2 oil engines** reduction geared to sc. shafts driving 2 CP propellers Total Power: 3,840kW (5,220hp) 11.0kn Caterpillar 3516C-HD 2 x Vee 4 Stroke 16 Cy. 170 x 215 each-1920kW (2610bhp) Caterpillar Inc-USA AuxGen: 2 x 900kW a.c, 3 x 450kW a.c Thrusters: 2 Thwart. CP thruster (f); 1 Thwart. FP thruster (a) Fuel: 480.0 (d.f.)
8107177 *PHDJ* -	**VOS SYMPATHY** *ex* Searanger *-2005* *ex* Highland Fortress *-2000* *ex* Northern Fortress *-1993* **VOS Sympathy BV** Vroon Offshore Services BV *Breskens* *Netherlands* MMSI: 246391000 Official number: 45873	**2,770** 831 3,200	Class: NV	**1982**-05 **Ulstein Hatlo AS — Ulsteinvik** Yd No: 178 Loa 77.91 Br ex - Dght 5.004 Lbp 72.70 Br md 17.51 Dpth 7.32 Welded, 2 dks	**(B21A20S) Platform Supply Ship** Cranes: 1x50t	**2 oil engines** with clutches, flexible couplings & sr geared to sc. shafts driving 2 CP propellers Total Power: 4,502kW (6,120hp) 12.0kn Normo KVMB-12 2 x Vee 4 Stroke 12 Cy. 250 x 300 each-2251kW (3060bhp) AS Bergens Mek Verksteder-Norway AuxGen: 2 x 1256kW 440V 60Hz a.c, 2 x 244kW 440V 60Hz a.c Thrusters: 2 Thwart. CP thruster (f); 2 Tunnel thruster (a) Fuel: 1328.0 (d.f.) 18.0pd
9552630 *ICNH* -	**VOS TETHYS** *ex* Vos Hippo *-2010* **Vroon Offshore Italia Srl** - *Ancona* *Italy* MMSI: 247280800	**1,678** 503 1,386	Class: RI (AB)	**2010**-01 **Fujian Southeast Shipyard — Fuzhou FJ** Yd No: RK036 Loa 59.25 Br ex - Dght 4.950 Lbp 52.20 Br md 14.95 Dpth 6.10 Welded, 1 dk	**(B21B20T) Offshore Tug/Supply Ship** Cranes: 1	**2 oil engines** reduction geared to sc. shafts driving 2 CP propellers Total Power: 3,840kW (5,220hp) 10.0kn Caterpillar 3516B-HD 2 x Vee 4 Stroke 16 Cy. 170 x 215 each-1920kW (2610bhp) Caterpillar Inc-USA AuxGen: 3 x 350kW 415V 50Hz a.c Thrusters: 1 Tunnel thruster (f) Fuel: 530.0
9606106 *ICUE* -	**VOS THALASSA** **Offshore Support Vessels II BV** Vroon Offshore Italia Srl SatCom: Inmarsat C 424703789 *Genoa* *Italy* MMSI: 247322200 Official number: 186	**1,678** 503 1,327	Class: RI (AB)	**2012**-05 **Fujian Southeast Shipyard — Fuzhou FJ** Yd No: DN59M-96 Loa 59.25 Br ex - Dght 4.950 Lbp 52.20 Br md 14.95 Dpth 6.10 Welded, 1 dk	**(B21B20A) Anchor Handling Tug Supply**	**2 oil engines** reduction geared to sc.shafts driving 2 CP propellers Total Power: 3,840kW (5,220hp) 10.0kn Caterpillar 3516B-HD 2 x Vee 4 Stroke 16 Cy. 170 x 215 each-1920kW (2610bhp) Caterpillar Inc-USA AuxGen: 3 x 350kW a.c Thrusters: 1 Tunnel thruster (f) Fuel: 520.0
9606091 *9V9436* -	**VOS THALIA** **Offshore Support Vessels 15 Pte Ltd** Vroon Offshore Services Pte Ltd *Singapore* *Singapore* MMSI: 566435000 Official number: 397081	**1,678** 503 1,323	Class: AB	**2012**-04 **Fujian Southeast Shipyard — Fuzhou FJ** Yd No: DN59M-95 Loa 59.27 Br ex - Dght 4.950 Lbp 52.16 Br md 14.95 Dpth 6.10 Welded, 1 dk	**(B21B20A) Anchor Handling Tug Supply**	**2 oil engines** reduction geared to sc.shafts driving 2 CP propellers Total Power: 3,840kW (5,220hp) 10.0kn Caterpillar 3516B-HD 2 x Vee 4 Stroke 16 Cy. 170 x 215 each-1920kW (2610bhp) Caterpillar Inc-USA AuxGen: 3 x 350kW a.c Thrusters: 1 Tunnel thruster (f); 1 Tunnel thruster (a) Fuel: 520.0
9585742 *ZDNA9* -	**VOS THEIA** **Offshore Support Vessels II BV** Vroon Offshore Italia Srl *Gibraltar* *Gibraltar (British)* MMSI: 236111872	**1,678** 503 1,356	Class: RI (AB)	**2011**-04 **Fujian Southeast Shipyard — Fuzhou FJ** Yd No: DN59M-84 Loa 59.25 Br ex - Dght 4.950 Lbp 52.20 Br md 14.95 Dpth 6.10 Welded, 1 dk	**(B21B20A) Anchor Handling Tug Supply**	**2 oil engines** reduction geared to sc.shafts driving 2 CP propellers Total Power: 3,840kW (5,220hp) 10.0kn Caterpillar 3516B-HD 1 x Vee 4 Stroke 16 Cy. 170 x 215 1920kW (2610bhp) Caterpillar Inc-USA AuxGen: 3 x 350kW a.c Thrusters: 1 Tunnel thruster (f) Fuel: 530.0
9585754 *9V8733* -	**VOS THEMIS** **Offshore Support Vessels 12 Pte Ltd** Vroon Offshore Services Pte Ltd *Singapore* *Singapore* MMSI: 566239000 Official number: 396171	**1,678** 503 1,310	Class: AB	**2011**-10 **Fujian Southeast Shipyard — Fuzhou FJ** Yd No: DN59M-85 Loa 59.25 Br ex - Dght 4.950 Lbp 52.20 Br md 14.95 Dpth 6.10 Welded, 1 dk	**(B21B20A) Anchor Handling Tug Supply**	**2 oil engines** reduction geared to sc. shafts driving 2 CP propellers Total Power: 3,372kW (4,584hp) 10.0kn Caterpillar 3516B-HD 1 x Vee 4 Stroke 16 Cy. 170 x 215 1686kW (2292bhp) Caterpillar Inc-USA AuxGen: 3 x 350kW a.c
7711294 *MLYT2* -	**VOS TIREE** *ex* Viking Tiree *-2007* *ex* BUE Tiree *-2005* *ex* Supreme *-1999* *ex* Hornbeck Supreme *-1996* *ex* Seaboard Supreme *-1995* *ex* Sapucaia *-1990* **Offshore Support Vessels IV Ltd** Vroon Offshore Services Ltd SatCom: Inmarsat C 423429910 *Aberdeen* *United Kingdom* MMSI: 234299000 Official number: 714179	**863** 258 950	Class: AB	**1981**-07 **Estaleiros Amazonia S.A. (ESTANAVE) — Manaus** Yd No: 149 Converted From: Offshore Supply Ship-1995 Converted From: Offshore Supply Ship-1990 Loa 55.66 Br ex - Dght 3.968 Lbp 50.02 Br md 11.61 Dpth 4.63 Welded, 1 dk	**(B22G20Y) Standby Safety Vessel** Passengers: unberthed: 120; berths: 20	**2 oil engines** reverse reduction geared to sc. shafts driving 2 FP propellers Total Power: 1,850kW (2,516hp) 9.0kn Alpha 8V23L-VO 2 x Vee 4 Stroke 8 Cy. 225 x 300 each-925kW (1258bhp) Equipamentos Villares SA-Brazil AuxGen: 2 x 160kW Thrusters: 1 Tunnel thruster (f) Fuel: 204.0 (d.f.)
9391907 *A8MN8* -	**VOS TRACKER** **Offshore Support Vessels III BV** Vroon Offshore Services Ltd *Monrovia* *Liberia* MMSI: 636013384 Official number: 13384	**851** 255 425	Class: LR ✠ **100A1** SS 09/2012 safety standy vessel ✠ **LMC** **UMS** Eq.Ltr: K; Cable: 357.0/28.0 U2 (a)	**2007**-09 **'Crist' Sp z oo — Gdansk** (Hull launched by) Yd No: B47/1 **2007**-09 **B.V. Scheepswerf Maaskant — Stellendam** (Hull completed by) Yd No: 593 **2007**-09 **B.V. Scheepswerf Damen — Gorinchem** Yd No: 553004 Loa 48.20 Br ex 11.25 Dght 4.250 Lbp 44.40 Br md 11.00 Dpth 5.50 Welded, 1 dk	**(B22G20Y) Standby Safety Vessel** Passengers: 125	**1 oil engine** with clutches, flexible couplings & sr geared to sc. shaft driving 1 CP propeller Total Power: 1,325kW (1,801hp) 12.0kn A.B.C. 6DZC 1 x 4 Stroke 6 Cy. 256 x 310 1325kW (1801bhp) Anglo Belgian Corp NV (ABC)-Belgium AuxGen: 2 x 440kW 230/440V 60Hz a.c Thrusters: 1 Thwart. FP thruster (f) Fuel: 230.0 (d.f.)
9391919 *D5BM9* -	**VOS TRADER** **Offshore Support Vessels III BV** Vroon Offshore Services Ltd *Monrovia* *Liberia* MMSI: 636015561 Official number: 15561	**851** 255 425	Class: LR ✠ **100A1** SS 12/2012 ✠ **LMC** **UMS** Eq.Ltr: K; Cable: 357.0/28.0 U2 (a)	**2007**-12 **'Crist' Sp z oo — Gdansk** (Hull launched by) Yd No: B47/2 **2007**-12 **B.V. Scheepswerf Maaskant — Stellendam** (Hull completed by) Yd No: 594 **2007**-12 **B.V. Scheepswerf Damen — Gorinchem** Yd No: 553005 Loa 47.60 Br ex - Dght 4.250 Lbp 44.40 Br md 11.00 Dpth 5.50 Welded, 1 dk	**(B22G20Y) Standby Safety Vessel** Passengers: unberthed: 125	**1 oil engine** with clutches, flexible couplings & sr geared to sc. shaft driving 1 FP propeller Total Power: 1,325kW (1,801hp) 12.0kn A.B.C. 6DZC 1 x 4 Stroke 6 Cy. 256 x 310 1325kW (1801bhp) Anglo Belgian Corp NV (ABC)-Belgium AuxGen: 2 x 440kW 230/440V 60Hz a.c Thrusters: 1 Thwart. FP thruster (f)
9536296 *IINK2* -	**VOS TRAMONTANA** **Vroon Offshore Italia Srl** - *Catania* *Italy* MMSI: 247233700	**199** 59 261	Class: RI	**2008**-08 **C.R.N. Cant. Nav. Ancona S.r.l. — Ancona** Yd No: 002 Loa 32.50 Br ex 8.00 Dght 2.620 Lbp 29.80 Br md 7.90 Dpth 3.50 Welded, 1 dk	**(B34G2SE) Pollution Control Vessel** Cranes: 1	**2 oil engines** reduction geared to sc. shaft driving 2 FP propellers Total Power: 1,472kW (2,002hp) Baudouin 12M26SRP 2 x Vee 4 Stroke 12 Cy. 150 x 150 each-736kW (1001bhp) Societe des Moteurs Baudouin SA-France AuxGen: 2 x 180kW a.c Thrusters: 1 Tunnel thruster (f) Fuel: 35.0 (d.f.)
9391921 *A8MO2* -	**VOS TRAPPER** **Offshore Support Vessels III BV** Vroon Offshore Services BV *Monrovia* *Liberia* MMSI: 636013386 Official number: 13386	**851** 255 425	Class: LR ✠ **100A1** SS 03/2013 ✠ **LMC** **UMS** Eq.Ltr: K; Cable: 357.0/28.0 U2 (a)	**2008**-03 **'Crist' Sp z oo — Gdansk** (Hull) Yd No: B47/3 **2008**-03 **B.V. Scheepswerf Maaskant — Stellendam** (Hull completed by) Yd No: 595 **2008**-03 **B.V. Scheepswerf Damen — Gorinchem** Yd No: 553006 Loa 48.20 Br ex 11.25 Dght 4.250 Lbp 44.40 Br md 11.00 Dpth 5.50 Welded, 1 dk	**(B22G20Y) Standby Safety Vessel** Passengers: 125	**1 oil engine** with clutches, flexible couplings & sr geared to sc. shaft driving 1 CP propeller Total Power: 1,325kW (1,801hp) 12.0kn A.B.C. 6DZC 1 x 4 Stroke 6 Cy. 256 x 310 1325kW (1801bhp) Anglo Belgian Corp NV (ABC)-Belgium AuxGen: 2 x 440kW 440/230V 60Hz a.c Thrusters: 1 Thwart. FP thruster (f) Fuel: 230.0 (d.f.)

Ship	Tonnage	Classification	Builder / Dimensions	Type	Machinery
9391933 **VOS TRAVELLER** *A8MO3* - **Breskens Scheepvaartmaatschappij BV** Vroon Offshore Services Ltd *Monrovia* *Liberia* MMSI: 636013387 Official number: 13387	**851** 255 425	Class: LR ✠ **100A1** SS 05/2013 ✠ **LMC** **UMS** Eq.Ltr: K; Cable: 357.0/28.0 U2 (a)	**2007-12 'Crist' Sp z oo — Gdansk** (Hull) Yd No: B47/4 **2007-12 B.V. Scheepswerf Maaskant — Stellendam** (Hull completed by) Yd No: 596 **2007-12 B.V. Scheepswerf Damen — Gorinchem** Yd No: 553007 Loa 48.20 Br ex 11.25 Dght 4.250 Lbp 44.40 Br md 11.00 Dpth 5.50 Welded, 1 dk	**(B22G20Y) Standby Safety Vessel** Passengers: 125	**1 oil engine** with clutches, flexible couplings & sr geared to sc. shaft driving 1 FP propeller Total Power: 1,325kW (1,801hp) 12.0kn A.B.C. 6DZC 1 x 4 Stroke 6 Cy. 256 x 310 1325kW (1801bhp) Anglo Belgian Corp NV (ABC)-Belgium AuxGen: 2 x 440kW 230/440V 60Hz a.c Thrusters: 1 Thwart. FP thruster (f)
9585766 **VOS TRITON** *9V8734* - **Offshore Support Vessels 12 Pte Ltd** Vroon Offshore Services Pte Ltd SatCom: Inmarsat C 456613610 *Singapore* *Singapore* MMSI: 566136000 Official number: 396172	**1,678** 503 1,321	Class: AB	**2011-08 Fujian Southeast Shipyard — Fuzhou FJ** Yd No: DN59M-89 Loa 59.25 Br ex - Dght 4.950 Lbp 52.20 Br md 14.95 Dpth 6.10 Welded, 1 dk	**(B21B20A) Anchor Handling Tug Supply**	**2 oil engines** reduction geared to sc.shafts driving 2 CP propellers Total Power: 3,372kW (4,584hp) 10.0kn Caterpillar 3516B-HD 1 x Vee 4 Stroke 16 Cy. 170 x 215 1686kW (2292bhp) Caterpillar Inc-USA AuxGen: 3 x 350kW a.c Thrusters: 1 Tunnel thruster (f)
9510773 **VOS VALIANT** *2EXT9* - **Banco Santander SA** Vroon Offshore Services Ltd *Aberdeen* *United Kingdom* MMSI: 235089032 Official number: 917820	**1,734** 520 850	Class: LR ✠ **100A1** SS 10/2011 *IWS ✠ **LMC** **UMS** Eq.Ltr: O; Cable: 412.5/34.0 U3 (a)	**2011-10 Astilleros Zamakona Pasaia SL — Pasaia** Yd No: 678 Loa 60.00 (BB) Br ex 13.10 Dght 5.000 Lbp 52.80 Br md 12.70 Dpth 6.25 Welded, 1 dk	**(B21A20S) Platform Supply Ship**	**4 diesel electric oil engines** driving 2 gen. each 500kW 440V a.c 2 gen. each 825kW 440V a.c Connecting to 2 elec. motors each (800kW) driving 2 Azimuth electric drive units Total Power: 3,138kW (4,266hp) 10.0kn Caterpillar 3508B 2 x Vee 4 Stroke 8 Cy. 170 x 190 each-968kW (1316bhp) Caterpillar Inc-USA Caterpillar C18 2 x 4 Stroke 6 Cy. 145 x 183 each-601kW (817bhp) Caterpillar Inc-USA Thrusters: 2 Tunnel thruster (f)
9488164 **VOS VENTURER** *2EAJ4* - **Bank of Scotland Transport Finance 1 Ltd** Vroon Offshore Services Ltd SatCom: Inmarsat C 423592557 *Aberdeen* *United Kingdom* MMSI: 235083457	**1,734** 520 850	Class: LR ✠ **100A1** SS 02/2011 ✠ **LMC** **UMS** Eq.Ltr: O; Cable: 165.0/34.0 U2 (a)	**2011-02 Astilleros Zamakona Pasaia SL — Pasaia** Yd No: 676 Loa 60.00 (BB) Br ex 13.10 Dght 5.000 Lbp 52.80 Br md 12.70 Dpth 6.25 Welded, 1 dk	**(B21A20S) Platform Supply Ship**	**4 diesel electric oil engines** driving 2 gen. each 500kW 440V a.c 2 gen. each 910kW 440V a.c Connecting to 2 elec. motors each (800kW) driving 2 Azimuth electric drive units Total Power: 3,138kW (4,266hp) 10.0kn Caterpillar 3508B 2 x Vee 4 Stroke 8 Cy. 170 x 190 each-968kW (1316bhp) Caterpillar Inc-USA Caterpillar C18 2 x 4 Stroke 6 Cy. 145 x 183 each-601kW (817bhp) Caterpillar Inc-USA Thrusters: 2 Tunnel thruster (f)
9070668 **VOS VICTORY** *MSHF2* *ex* Viking Victory *-2008* *ex* Trafalgar Guardian *-2006* - **Offshore Support Vessels IV Ltd** Vroon Offshore Services Ltd SatCom: Inmarsat C 423334610 *Leith* *United Kingdom* MMSI: 233346000 Official number: 723632	**1,218** 365 1,043	Class: LR ✠ **100A1** SS 02/2014 ✠ **LMC** Eq.Ltr: N; Cable: 414.0/34.0 U2	**1994-02 Yorkshire D.D. Co. Ltd. — Hull** Yd No: 333 Loa 55.20 Br ex 12.92 Dght 4.500 Lbp 48.00 Br md 12.70 Dpth 5.50 Welded, 1 dk	**(B22G20Y) Standby Safety Vessel**	**2 oil engines** with flexible couplings & dr gearedto sc. shafts driving 2 Directional propellers Total Power: 1,432kW (1,946hp) 9.0kn Caterpillar 3508TA 2 x Vee 4 Stroke 8 Cy. 170 x 190 each-716kW (973bhp) Caterpillar Inc-USA AuxGen: 3 x 145kW 200/400V 50Hz a.c Thrusters: 1 Retract. directional thruster (f) Fuel: 240.0 (d.f.) 9.1pd
9488176 **VOS VIGILANT** *2EID4* - **Offshore Support Vessels VII Ltd** Vroon Offshore Services Ltd *Aberdeen* *United Kingdom* MMSI: 235085344 Official number: 917510	**1,734** 520 1,213	Class: LR ✠ **100A1** SS 06/2011 *IWS ✠ **LMC** **UMS** Eq.Ltr: O; Cable: 165.0/34.0 U2 (a)	**2011-06 Astilleros Zamakona Pasaia SL — Pasaia** Yd No: 677 Loa 60.00 Br ex 13.10 Dght 5.000 Lbp 52.80 Br md 12.70 Dpth 6.25 Welded, 1 dk	**(B21A20S) Platform Supply Ship** Single Hull	**4 diesel electric oil engines** driving 2 gen. each 550kW 440V a.c 2 gen. each 825kW 440V a.c Connecting to 2 elec. motors each (800kW) driving 2 Azimuth electric drive units Total Power: 3,138kW (4,266hp) 10.0kn Caterpillar 3508B 2 x Vee 4 Stroke 8 Cy. 170 x 190 each-968kW (1316bhp) Caterpillar Inc-USA Caterpillar C18 2 x 4 Stroke 6 Cy. 145 x 183 each-601kW (817bhp) Caterpillar Inc-USA Thrusters: 2 Directional thruster (f)
9411276 **VOS VOYAGER** *2CL05* - **Bank of Scotland Transport Finance 1 Ltd** Vroon Offshore Services Ltd *Aberdeen* *United Kingdom* MMSI: 235073828 Official number: 916203	**1,734** 520 1,213	Class: LR ✠ **100A1** SS 11/2009 ✠ **LMC** **UMS** Eq.Ltr: O; Cable: 412.5/34.0 U3 (a)	**2009-11 Astilleros Zamakona SA — Santurtzi** Yd No: 650 Loa 60.00 (BB) Br ex 13.10 Dght 4.650 Lbp 52.80 Br md 12.70 Dpth 6.25 Welded, 1 dk	**(B21A20S) Platform Supply Ship**	**4 diesel electric oil engines** driving 2 gen. each 500kW 440V a.c 2 gen. each 910kW 440V a.c Connecting to 2 elec. motors each (800kW) driving 2 Azimuth electric drive units contra rotating propellers Total Power: 3,138kW (4,266hp) 10.0kn Caterpillar 3508B 2 x Vee 4 Stroke 8 Cy. 170 x 190 each-968kW (1316bhp) Caterpillar Inc-USA Caterpillar C18 2 x 4 Stroke 6 Cy. 145 x 183 each-601kW (817bhp) Caterpillar Inc-USA Thrusters: 2 Thwart. FP thruster (f) Fuel: 479.0 (d.f.) 7.2pd
7225673 **VOS WARRIOR** *A8RZ4* *ex* Britannia Warrior *-2009* *ex* Suffolk Warrior *-1990* - **Nomis Shipping Ltd** Vroon Offshore Services Ltd *Monrovia* *Liberia* MMSI: 636014179 Official number: 14179	**430** 129 -	Class: LR ✠ **100A1** SS 02/2010 for service within the sea area enclosed between the Parallels of Latitude 62~N and 48~N, the Meridian of Longitude 15~W and the coast of Europe ✠ **LMC** Eq.Ltr: (f) ; Cable: 220.0/27.0 U1	**1973-06 Cubow Ltd. — Woolwich, London** (Hull) Yd No: 672 **1973-06 Fairmile Shipyard (Berwick) Ltd. — Berwick-on-Tweed** Yd No: 672 Converted From: Stern Trawler-1977 Loa 39.81 Br ex 8.95 Dght 3.937 Lbp 34.14 Br md 8.84 Dpth 4.73 Welded, 1 dk	**(B22G20Y) Standby Safety Vessel**	**2 oil engines** dr geared to sc. shaft driving 1 CP propeller Total Power: 1,472kW (2,002hp) 13.5kn Blackstone ESL8MK2 2 x 4 Stroke 8 Cy. 222 x 292 each-736kW (1001bhp) Mirrlees Blackstone (Stamford)Ltd.-Stamford AuxGen: 2 x 120kW 415V 50Hz a.c Thrusters: 1 Thwart. FP thruster (f)
7611470 **VOS WESTWIND** *A8FM3* *ex* Gulf Pride *-2005* *ex* Barracuda *-2002* *ex* Sambro *-1996* *ex* Cape Sambro *-1994* - **Nomis Shipping Ltd** Vroon Offshore Services Ltd *Monrovia* *Liberia* MMSI: 636012445 Official number: 12445	**871** 261 -	Class: BV (LR) ✠ Classed LR until 12/5/78	**1977-02 Marystown Shipping Enterprises Ltd — Marystown NL** Yd No: 20 Converted From: Stern Trawler-1996 Lengthened-1986 Loa 52.00 Br ex 11.16 Dght 4.110 Lbp 46.05 Br md 10.98 Dpth 5.49 Welded	**(B31A2SR) Research Survey Vessel** Ice Capable	**1 oil engine** geared to sc. shaft driving 1 CP propeller Total Power: 1,545kW (2,101hp) 12.0kn Ruston 12RK3CM 1 x Vee 4 Stroke 12 Cy. 254 x 305 1545kW (2101bhp) Ruston Diesels Ltd.-Newton-le-Willows AuxGen: 1 x 124kW 220V 60Hz a.c, 1 x 148kW 220V 60Hz a.c Thrusters: 1 Tunnel thruster (f) Fuel: 226.0
9405411 **VOS ZEUS** *9V7943* *ex* DEA Zeus *-2009* - **Offshore Support Vessels 14 Pte Ltd** Vroon Offshore Services Pte Ltd *Singapore* *Singapore* MMSI: 563223000 Official number: 395075	**1,690** 507 1,364	Class: AB (BV)	**2007-10 Fujian Southeast Shipyard — Fuzhou FJ** (Hull) Yd No: H867 **2007-10 Jaya Shipbuilding & Engineering Pte Ltd — Singapore** Yd No: 867 Loa 59.25 Br ex - Dght 4.950 Lbp 52.20 Br md 14.95 Dpth 6.10 Welded, 1 dk	**(B21B20A) Anchor Handling Tug Supply**	**2 oil engines** reduction geared to sc. shafts driving 2 CP propellers Total Power: 3,840kW (5,220hp) 11.0kn Caterpillar 3516B-HD 2 x Vee 4 Stroke 16 Cy. 170 x 215 each-1920kW (2610bhp) Caterpillar Inc-USA AuxGen: 3 x 320kW 415/220V 50Hz a.c Thrusters: 1 Tunnel thruster (f)
9236896 **VOSCO SKY** *XVIP* *ex* Medi Dubai *-2010* *ex* Medi Monaco *-2005* - **Vietnam Ocean Shipping JSC (VOSCO) (Cong Ty Co Phan Van Tai Bien Viet Nam)** - *Haiphong* *Vietnam* MMSI: 574693000 Official number: VN3235VT	**29,367** 17,651 52,523 T/cm 55.0	Class: NK VR (RI)	**2001-11 Sanoyas Hishino Meisho Corp — Kurashiki OY** Yd No: 1194 Loa 189.90 (BB) Br ex 32.30 Dght 12.041 Lbp 182.00 Br md 32.26 Dpth 17.10 Welded, 1 dk	**(A21A2BC) Bulk Carrier** Double Bottom Entire Compartment Length Grain: 66,597; Bale: 64,545 Compartments: 5 Ho, ER 5 Ha: (20.3 x 16.6)4 (20.5 x 18.3)ER Cranes: 4x30t	**1 oil engine** driving 1 FP propeller Total Power: 7,723kW (10,500hp) 14.5kn Sulzer 6RTA48T-B 1 x 2 Stroke 6 Cy. 480 x 2000 7723kW (10500bhp) Diesel United Ltd.-Aioi AuxGen: 3 x 455kW 450V 50Hz a.c Fuel: 1872.2 (r.f.) 27.8pd

9202106 *XVPY* -	**VOSCO STAR** *ex* Seabee *-2008* *ex* Grace Hawk *-2003* **Vietnam Ocean Shipping JSC (VOSCO) (Cong Ty Co Phan Van Tai Bien Viet Nam)** - SatCom: Inmarsat B 357441810 *Haiphong* *Vietnam* MMSI: 574418000 Official number: VN-28TT-VT	**27,003** 15,619 46,671 T/cm 51.4	Class: NK VR	**1999-01 Mitsui Eng. & SB. Co. Ltd. — Tamano** Yd No: 1501 Loa 189.80 (BB) Br ex - Dght 11.620 Lbp 181.00 Br md 31.00 Dpth 16.50 Welded, 1 dk	**(A21A2BC) Bulk Carrier** Grain: 59,820; Bale: 57,237 Compartments: 5 Ho, ER 5 Ha: 4 (20.8 x 17.2) (17.6 x 17.2)ER Cranes: 4x30.5t	**1 oil engine** driving 1 FP propeller Total Power: 8,165kW (11,101hp) 14.0kn B&W 6S50MC 1 x 2 Stroke 6 Cy. 500 x 1910 8165kW (11101bhp) Mitsui Engineering & Shipbuilding CLtd-Japan Fuel: 1690.0
9391634 *3WJV9* -	**VOSCO SUNRISE** **Vietnam Ocean Shipping JSC (VOSCO) (Cong Ty Co Phan Van Tai Bien Viet Nam)** - *Haiphong* *Vietnam* MMSI: 574001890 Official number: VN-84.TT-VT	**31,696** 18,819 56,472 T/cm 56.9	Class: NK VR	**2013-05 Nam Trieu Shipbuilding Industry Co. Ltd. — Haiphong** Yd No: F56-NT03 Loa 190.00 (BB) Br ex 32.29 Dght 12.700 Lbp 185.00 Br md 32.26 Dpth 18.10 Welded, 1 dk	**(A21A2BC) Bulk Carrier** Grain: 70,357; Bale: 67,111 Compartments: 5 Ho, ER 5 Ha: 4 (20.9 x 18.6)ER (14.6 x 18.6) Cranes: 4x30t	**1 oil engine** driving 1 FP propeller Total Power: 8,890kW (12,087hp) 14.5kn Wartsila 6RT-flex50 1 x 2 Stroke 6 Cy. 500 x 2050 8890kW (12087bhp) Diesel United Ltd.-Aioi AuxGen: 3 x 430kW 450V a.c Fuel: 2491.0
9290983 *3WBT9* -	**VOSCO UNITY** *ex* Medi Cork *-2011* *ex* Medi Melbourne *-2007* **Vietnam Ocean Shipping JSC (VOSCO) (Cong Ty Co Phan Van Tai Bien Viet Nam)** - *Haiphong* *Vietnam* MMSI: 574682000 Official number: VN-47.TT-VT	**29,963** 18,486 53,552 T/cm 55.3	Class: LR VR (RI) (NK) **100A1** SS 11/2013 bulk carrier strengthened for heavy cargoes, Nos. 2 & 4 holds may be empty LI ESP ESN **LMC** **UMS**	**2004-02 Imabari Shipbuilding Co Ltd — Marugame KG (Marugame Shipyard)** Yd No: 1415 Loa 189.94 (BB) Br ex - Dght 12.300 Lbp 182.00 Br md 32.26 Dpth 17.30 Welded, 1 dk	**(A21A2BC) Bulk Carrier** Grain: 68,927; Bale: 65,526 Compartments: 5 Ho, ER 5 Ha: 4 (21.1 x 17.6)ER (21.1 x 17.6) Cranes: 4x30.5t	**1 oil engine** driving 1 FP propeller Total Power: 9,480kW (12,889hp) 15.0kn MAN-B&W 6S50MC-C 1 x 2 Stroke 6 Cy. 500 x 2000 9480kW (12889bhp) Mitsui Engineering & Shipbuilding CLtd-Japan AuxGen: 3 x a.c
8977704 *V4YH2* -	**VOSINE** *ex* Abs Thor *-2014* *ex* Miss Ina *-2009* **Land-Sea Energy Services Ltd** - *St Kitts & Nevis* MMSI: 341205000 Official number: SKN 1002667	**211** 63 105	Class: IR (AB) (RS)	**1990-02 Breaux Brothers Enterprises, Inc. — Loreauville, La** Yd No: 155 Loa 38.10 Br ex - Dght 1.810 Lbp 34.24 Br md 7.98 Dpth 3.44 Welded, 1 dk	**(B21A20C) Crew/Supply Vessel** Hull Material: Aluminium Alloy Passengers: 64; cabins: 4	**4 oil engines** reduction geared to sc. shafts driving 4 FP propellers Total Power: 1,500kW (2,040hp) 18.0kn G.M. (Detroit Diesel) 12V-71-TI 1 x Vee 2 Stroke 12 Cy. 108 x 127 375kW (510bhp) (made 1990) General Motors Corp-USA G.M. (Detroit Diesel) 12V-71-TI 3 x Vee 2 Stroke 12 Cy. 108 x 127 each-375kW (510bhp) (made 1990) General Motors Corp-USA AuxGen: 2 x 40kW a.c Fuel: 42.0 (d.f.) 10.0pd
8729614 *UATR* -	**VOSKHOD** **Baltika Fishing Collective (Rybolovetskiy Kolkhoz 'Baltika')** - *St Petersburg* *Russia* MMSI: 273298300 Official number: 883072	**723** 216 414	Class: (RS)	**1989-04 Zavod "Leninskaya Kuznitsa" — Kiyev** Yd No: 1608 Loa 54.82 Br ex 10.15 Dght 4.140 Lbp 50.30 Br md 9.80 Dpth 5.00 Welded, 1 dk	**(B11A2FS) Stern Trawler**	**1 oil engine** driving 1 FP propeller Total Power: 852kW (1,158hp) 12.0kn S.K.L. 8NVD48A-2U 1 x 4 Stroke 8 Cy. 320 x 480 852kW (1158bhp) VEB Schwermaschinenbau "KarlLiebknecht" (SKL)-Magdeburg
9229116 *V2ON4* -	**VOSSBORG** *ex* Morpeth *-2007* *ex* Vossborg *-2004* **Reederei Frank Dahl ms 'Vossborg' GmbH & Co KG** Reederei Frank Dahl eK *Saint John's* *Antigua & Barbuda* MMSI: 304605000	**6,154** 3,424 8,708 T/cm 18.3	Class: GL (BV)	**2000-12 Bodewes Scheepswerf "Volharding" Foxhol B.V. — Foxhol** Yd No: 355 Loa 132.20 (BB) Br ex - Dght 7.050 Lbp 123.84 Br md 15.87 Dpth 9.65 Welded, 1 dk	**(A31A2GX) General Cargo Ship** Grain: 12,813; Bale: 12,813 TEU 552 C. 552/20' incl. 25 ref C. Compartments: 2 Ho, ER 2 Ha: (39.9 x 13.2) (52.4 x 13.2)ER Ice Capable	**1 oil engine** reduction geared to sc. shaft driving 1 CP propeller Total Power: 3,960kW (5,384hp) 14.0kn Wartsila 6R38 1 x 4 Stroke 6 Cy. 380 x 475 3960kW (5384bhp) Wartsila Nederland BV-Netherlands AuxGen: 1 x 648kW 220/440V a.c, 2 x 240kW 220/440V a.c Thrusters: 1 Tunnel thruster (f) Fuel: 464.0 (r.f.)
9277307 *PBJY* -	**VOSSDIEP** **Beheermaatschappij ms Vossdiep BV** Feederlines BV *Groningen* *Netherlands* MMSI: 245313000 Official number: 41774	**4,967** 2,631 7,250	Class: GL (LR) ✠ Classed LR until 22/4/12	**2003-05 Bodewes' Scheepswerven B.V. — Hoogezand** Yd No: 618 Loa 118.55 (BB) Br ex 15.43 Dght 7.050 Lbp 111.85 Br md 15.20 Dpth 8.45 Welded, 2 dks	**(A31A2GX) General Cargo Ship** Double Hull Grain: 9,415 TEU 390 C Ho 174 TEU C Dk 216 TEU incl 20 ref C Compartments: 2 Ho, ER 2 Ha: (42.8 x 12.7)ER (39.0 x 12.7) Ice Capable	**1 oil engine** with clutches, flexible couplings & sr geared to sc. shaft driving 1 CP propeller Total Power: 3,840kW (5,221hp) 15.0kn MaK 8M32C 1 x 4 Stroke 8 Cy. 320 x 480 3840kW (5221bhp) Caterpillar Motoren GmbH & Co. KG-Germany AuxGen: 1 x 400kW 400V 50Hz a.c, 2 x 259kW 400V 50Hz a.c Boilers: TOH (ex.g.) 10.2kgf/cm² (10.0bar), TOH (o.f.) 10.2kgf/cm² (10.0bar) Thrusters: 1 Thwart. CP thruster (f) Fuel: 82.0 (d.f.) 556.0 (r.f.)
8889270 *UCUZ* -	**VOSTOCHNAYA ZVEZDA** **Parma Co Ltd (OOO 'Parma')** - *Kholmsk* *Russia* MMSI: 273421500 Official number: 921946	**864** 259 335	Class: RS	**1995-10 AO Yaroslavskiy Sudostroitelnyy Zavod — Yaroslavl** Yd No: 392 Loa 53.70 (BB) Br ex 10.72 Dght 4.200 Lbp 47.92 Br md 10.50 Dpth 6.00 Welded, 1 dk	**(B11A2FS) Stern Trawler**	**1 oil engine** driving 1 CP propeller Total Power: 970kW (1,319hp) 12.6kn S.K.L. 8NVD48A-2U 1 x 4 Stroke 8 Cy. 320 x 480 970kW (1319bhp) SKL Motoren u. Systemtechnik AG-Magdeburg AuxGen: 1 x 300kW a.c, 3 x 150kW a.c Fuel: 192.0 (d.f.)
8957297 - -	**VOSTOCHNOYE PRIMORYE** *ex* Liao Da Gan Yu 8715 *-2000* - - *Vladivostok* *Russia* Official number: 990170	**115** 39 97		**1999-05 Rongcheng Shipbuilding Industry Co Ltd — Rongcheng SD** Yd No: Y040199524 Loa 34.00 Br ex - Dght 2.100 Lbp 29.62 Br md 6.00 Dpth 2.70 Welded, 1 dk	**(B11B2FV) Fishing Vessel**	**1 oil engine** geared to sc. shaft driving 1 FP propeller Total Power: 220kW (299hp) Chinese Std. Type Z6170ZL 1 x 4 Stroke 6 Cy. 170 x 200 220kW (299bhp) Zibo Diesel Engine Factory-China
8711772 *UUZB* -	**VOSTOCHNYY** **State Enterprise 'Sevastopol Sea Fishing Port' (Derzhavne Pidpryyemstvo Sevastopolska Morskyy Rybnyy Port)** Pacific Shipmanagement Survey & Consulting Ltd *Sevastopol* *Ukraine* MMSI: 272159000	**1,896** 1,014 3,305	Class: (RS)	**1988-02 Shipbuilding & Shiprepairing Yard 'Ivan Dimitrov' — Rousse** Yd No: 461 Converted From: Bunkering Vessel-1988 Loa 77.53 Br ex 14.54 Dght 5.360 Lbp 73.20 Br md 14.00 Dpth 6.50 Welded, 1 dk	**(A12D2LV) Vegetable Oil Tanker** Liq: 3,513; Liq (Oil): 3,513 Cargo Heating Coils Compartments: 12 Ta, ER	**1 oil engine** sr geared to sc. shaft driving 1 FP propeller Total Power: 882kW (1,199hp) 10.2kn S.K.L. 8NVD48A-2U 1 x 4 Stroke 8 Cy. 320 x 480 882kW (1199bhp) VEB Schwermaschinenbau "KarlLiebknecht" (SKL)-Magdeburg AuxGen: 2 x 150kW a.c Thrusters: 1 Thwart. CP thruster (f)
8929812 - -	**VOSTOCHNYY-1** **Kamkaydo-Krab Co Ltd (OOO 'Kamkaydo-Krab')** *Petropavlovsk-Kamchatskiy* *Russia*	**180** 54 46	Class: (RS)	**1980-08 Gorokhovetskiy Sudostroitelnyy Zavod — Gorokhovets** Yd No: 391 Loa 29.30 Br ex 8.49 Dght 3.090 Lbp 27.00 Br md 8.30 Dpth 4.30 Welded, 1 dk	**(B32A2ST) Tug** Ice Capable	**2 oil engines** driving 2 CP propellers Total Power: 882kW (1,200hp) 11.4kn Russkiy 6D30/50-4-3 2 x 2 Stroke 6 Cy. 300 x 500 each-441kW (600bhp) Mashinostroitelnyy Zavod"Russkiy-Dizel"-Leningrad AuxGen: 2 x 30kW a.c Fuel: 36.0 (d.f.)
8850413 - -	**VOSTOK** *ex* Baikal *-2005* *ex* Hosho Maru No. 58 *-2004* *ex* Syoko Maru No. 8 *-1995* *ex* Yasaka Maru No. 5 *-1994* - -	**219** 73 -		**1974 Suzuki Shipyard Co. Ltd. — Yokkaichi** L reg 29.80 Br ex - Dght 2.300 Lbp - Br md 6.20 Dpth 2.60 Welded, 1 dk	**(B11B2FV) Fishing Vessel**	**1 oil engine** driving 1 FP propeller Total Power: 346kW (470hp) Sumiyoshi 1 x 4 Stroke 346kW (470bhp) Sumiyoshi Marine Diesel Co Ltd-Japan
9133159 *UCWT* -	**VOSTOK** **Vostochno-Promyslovaya Kompaniya Co Ltd** - SatCom: Inmarsat C 427320239 *Sovetskaya Gavan* *Russia* MMSI: 273420800 Official number: 930697	**765** 241 476	Class: RS	**1996-04 AO Oston — Khabarovsk** Yd No: 899 Loa 54.90 Br ex 9.49 Dght 4.460 Lbp 50.04 Br md 9.30 Dpth 5.16 Welded, 1 dk	**(B11B2FV) Fishing Vessel**	**1 oil engine** reduction geared to sc. shaft driving 1 FP propeller Total Power: 589kW (801hp) 11.3kn S.K.L. 6NVD48A-2U 1 x 4 Stroke 6 Cy. 320 x 480 589kW (801bhp) SKL Motoren u. Systemtechnik AG-Magdeburg AuxGen: 3 x 160kW a.c Fuel: 104.0 (d.f.)

IMO / Call sign	Ship name / Former names / Owner / Port / Flag	GT / NT / DWT	Class	Builder / Dimensions	Type	Machinery
7006675 *UHDD* -	**VOSTOK** *ex* MB-7024 *-2000* *ex* Flotinspektsiya-02 *-1991* **JSC 'Mol Morstroy'** *Temryuk* *Russia* MMSI: 273452930	**234** 70 92	Class: (RS)	**1970-01 VEB Schiffswerft "Edgar Andre" — Magdeburg** Yd No: 7024 Loa 34.80 Br ex 8.51 Dght 2.969 Lbp 30.41 Br md 8.21 Dpth 3.85 Welded, 1 dk	**(B32A2ST) Tug** Ice Capable	**1 oil engine** driving 1 FP propeller Total Power: 551kW (749hp) 11.1kn S.K.L. 6NVD48A-2U 1 x 4 Stroke 6 Cy. 320 x 480 551kW (749bhp) VEB Schwermaschinenbau "KarlLiebknecht" (SKL)-Magdeburg AuxGen: 2 x 44kW Fuel: 49.0 (d.f.)
8139144 *UEKP* -	**VOSTOK** **Government of The Russian Federation** Federal State Unitary Enterprise Rosmorport *Korsakov* *Russia* MMSI: 273897800 Official number: 832371	**184** 55 46	Class: RS	**1983-10 Gorokhovetskiy Sudostroitelnyy Zavod — Gorokhovets** Yd No: 422 Loa 29.30 Br ex 8.49 Dght 3.090 Lbp 27.00 Br md 8.30 Dpth 4.35 Welded, 1 dk	**(B32A2ST) Tug** Ice Capable	**2 oil engines** driving 2 CP propellers Total Power: 882kW (1,200hp) 11.4kn Russkiy 6DR30/50-4-3 2 x 2 Stroke 6 Cy. 300 x 500 each-441kW (600bhp) Mashinostroitelnyy Zavod"Russkiy-Dizel"-Leningrad AuxGen: 2 x 30kW a.c Fuel: 42.0 (d.f.)
8504791 *UBZG7* -	**VOSTOK** *ex* Gray *-2011* *ex* Kwang Myeong *-2010* *ex* Sea Favor *-2009* *ex* Oryong No. 703 *-2008* *ex* Haeng Bok No. 105 *-2004* **DV-Flot Co Ltd** - *Nevelsk* *Russia* MMSI: 273350120	**666** 290 370	Class: RS (KR)	**1986-01 Dae Sun Shipbuilding & Engineering Co Ltd — Busan** Yd No: 291 Loa 53.29 (BB) Br ex 8.72 Dght 3.400 Lbp 46.89 Br md 8.70 Dpth 3.76 Welded, 1 dk	**(B11B2FV) Fishing Vessel** Ins: 2,556	**1 oil engine** sr geared to sc. shaft driving 1 FP propeller Total Power: 736kW (1,001hp) 11.5kn Niigata 6M28AFTE 1 x 4 Stroke 6 Cy. 280 x 480 736kW (1001bhp) Ssangyong Heavy Industries Co Ltd-South Korea AuxGen: 2 x 280kW 225V a.c Fuel: 220.0 (d.f.)
9160516 *UIWU* -	**VOSTOK-1** **JSC Vostok-1** - SatCom: Inmarsat B 327323610 *Nakhodka* *Russia* MMSI: 273827030	**716** 228 335	Class: NV RS	**1997-10 Astilleros Gondan SA — Castropol** Yd No: 396 Loa 41.50 (BB) Br ex 9.52 Dght 3.750 Lbp 34.40 Br md 9.50 Dpth 4.60 Welded, 1 dk	**(B11A2FS) Stern Trawler** Ice Capable	**1 oil engine** reduction geared to sc. shaft driving 1 FP propeller Total Power: 790kW (1,074hp) 10.0kn Caterpillar 3512TA 1 x Vee 4 Stroke 12 Cy. 170 x 190 790kW (1074bhp) Caterpillar Inc-USA AuxGen: 1 x 280kW 220/380V 50Hz a.c, 2 x 280kW 220/380V 50Hz a.c Thrusters: 1 Thwart. FP thruster (f) Fuel: 186.0 (d.f.)
8707836 *UBQF2* -	**VOSTOK-2** *ex* Kifuku Maru No. 35 *-2009* **JSC Vostok-1** - SatCom: Inmarsat C 427302443 *Nakhodka* *Russia* MMSI: 273338420	*431* 194 190	Class: RS	**1987-06 Fujishin Zosen K.K. — Kamo** Yd No: 523 Loa 37.27 Br ex 7.50 Dght 3.171 Lbp 37.01 Br md - Dpth 3.15 Welded, 1 dk	**(B11B2FV) Fishing Vessel**	**1 oil engine** with clutches & sr reverse geared to sc. shaft driving 1 CP propeller Total Power: 616kW (838hp) Yanmar T240-ET 1 x 4 Stroke 6 Cy. 240 x 310 616kW (838bhp) Yanmar Diesel Engine Co Ltd-Japan
9058048 *UBVF9* -	**VOSTOK-3** *ex* Kaiyo Maru No. 8 *-2009* **JSC Vostok-1** - *Nakhodka* *Russia* MMSI: 273332330	*703* 210 421	Class: RS	**1992-12 Niigata Engineering Co Ltd — Niigata NI** Yd No: 2252 Loa 55.95 (BB) Br ex - Dght 3.440 Lbp 49.10 Br md 8.80 Dpth 3.80 Welded, 1 dk	**(B11B2FV) Fishing Vessel**	**1 oil engine** with clutches, flexible couplings & sr geared to sc. shaft driving 1 CP propeller Total Power: 699kW (950hp) 13.2kn Niigata 6M28BFT 1 x 4 Stroke 6 Cy. 280 x 480 699kW (950bhp) Niigata Engineering Co Ltd-Japan AuxGen: 2 x 308kW 225V a.c Fuel: 244.0 (d.f.) 3.0pd
8320925 *UHZK* -	**VOSTOK-3** *ex* Fukuyoshi Maru No. 23 *-1998* *ex* Keiryo Maru No. 68 *-1994* *ex* Hakuwan Maru No. 28 *-1991* **Atlantica Co Ltd** - *Kholmsk* *Russia* MMSI: 273435810 Official number: 835825	**244** 90 193	Class: RS	**1983-08 Ozuchi Zosen Tekko — Otsuchi** Yd No: 238 Loa 38.91 (BB) Br ex - Dght 2.660 Lbp 32.01 Br md 6.61 Dpth 3.00 Welded, 1 dk	**(B11B2FV) Fishing Vessel** Ins: 104 Compartments: 4 Ho, ER 10 Ha: ER	**1 oil engine** dr reversed geared to sc. shaft driving 1 FP propeller Total Power: 713kW (969hp) 10.0kn Pielstick 6PA5 1 x 4 Stroke 6 Cy. 255 x 270 713kW (969bhp) Niigata Engineering Co Ltd-Japan AuxGen: 2 x 264kW a.c Thrusters: 1 Thwart. FP thruster (f) Fuel: 71.0 (d.f.)
8821395 *UBGG2* -	**VOSTOK-4** *ex* Kaiyo Maru No. 58 *-2010* **JSC Vostok-1** - *Nakhodka* *Russia* MMSI: 273347730	*699* 209 350	Class: RS	**1989-03 Niigata Engineering Co Ltd — Niigata NI** Yd No: 2125 Loa 54.07 (BB) Br ex - Dght 3.440 Lbp 47.90 Br md 8.70 Dpth 3.80 Welded, 1 dk	**(B11B2FV) Fishing Vessel** Ins: 505	**1 oil engine** with clutches, flexible couplings & sr geared to sc. shaft driving 1 CP propeller Total Power: 699kW (950hp) 13.4kn Niigata 6M28HFT 1 x 4 Stroke 6 Cy. 280 x 480 699kW (950bhp) Niigata Engineering Co Ltd-Japan Fuel: 243.0 (d.f.)
8809294 *UBRH9* -	**VOSTOK 5** *ex* Shans 104 *-2011* *ex* Kaio Maru No. 21 *-2011* **JSC Vostok-1** - *Nakhodka* *Russia* MMSI: 273352930	**607** 247 -	Class: RS	**1988-09 Niigata Engineering Co Ltd — Niigata NI** Yd No: 2102 Loa 49.40 (BB) Br ex - Dght 3.250 Lbp 43.74 Br md 8.30 Dpth 3.60 Welded, 1 dk	**(B11B2FV) Fishing Vessel** Ins: 404	**1 oil engine** with clutches, flexible couplings & sr geared to sc. shaft driving 1 FP propeller Total Power: 699kW (950hp) Niigata 6M28BFT 1 x 4 Stroke 6 Cy. 280 x 480 699kW (950bhp) Niigata Engineering Co Ltd-Japan
8971748 *UGZB* -	**VOSTOK ADONIS** *ex* Giryong *-2002* **JSC Vostok-1** - *Nakhodka* *Russia* MMSI: 273457970 Official number: 950582	**222** 66 75	Class: (RS)	**1995-07 Youngkwang Shipbuilding Co Ltd — Tongyeong** Loa 30.90 Br ex - Dght 2.420 Lbp 23.50 Br md 6.90 Dpth 2.65 Welded, 1 dk	**(B11B2FV) Fishing Vessel**	**1 oil engine** driving 1 FP propeller Total Power: 428kW (582hp)
7426497 - -	**VOSTOK-I** *ex* Chung Yong No. 33 *-2004* *ex* Han Dok No. 8 *-1986* *ex* Clover No. 112 *-1977* **Pacific Cargo Line Ltd**	**492** 176 312	Class: (KR)	**1975-06 Minami-Nippon Zosen KK — Ichikikushikino KS** Yd No: 228 Loa 48.32 Br ex - Dght 3.474 Lbp 42.02 Br md 8.11 Dpth 3.51 Welded, 1 dk	**(B11B2FV) Fishing Vessel** Ins: 339 4 Ha: (1.6 x 1.6)3 (1.3 x 0.9)	**1 oil engine** driving 1 FP propeller Total Power: 625kW (850hp) 12.5kn Hanshin 6LUS24G 1 x 4 Stroke 6 Cy. 240 x 405 625kW (850bhp) The Hanshin Diesel Works Ltd-Japan AuxGen: 2 x 160kW
8403961 *UHYB6* -	**VOSTOK REEFER** *ex* Esteban *-2012* *ex* Bellatrix *-2010* *ex* Dubhe *-2008* *ex* Arcturus *-2007* *ex* Dal Ocean No. 12 *-2006* *ex* Pisces *-1999* *ex* Ultimate No. 1 *-1998* *ex* Eikyu Maru No. 12 *-1995* **JSC Vostok-1** - *Nakhodka* *Russia* MMSI: 273355540	**1,045** 407 960	Class: RS	**1984-05 Niigata Engineering Co Ltd — Niigata NI** Yd No: 1816 Loa 63.00 (BB) Br ex - Dght 4.411 Lbp 55.81 Br md 10.32 Dpth 6.81 Welded, 2 dks	**(A34A2GR) Refrigerated Cargo Ship** Ins: 1,521 Compartments: 5 Ho, ER	**1 oil engine** with clutches, flexible couplings & sr geared to sc. shaft driving 1 CP propeller Total Power: 1,434kW (1,950hp) 13.0kn Niigata 6M34AFT 1 x 4 Stroke 6 Cy. 340 x 620 1434kW (1950bhp) Niigata Engineering Co Ltd-Japan AuxGen: 2 x 320kW a.c Fuel: 295.0 (d.f.)
8961755 *UAPV* -	**VOSTOK SIRIUS** *ex* Myungkwang No. 2 *-2001* **JSC Vostok-1** - *Nakhodka* *Russia* Official number: 950606	**224** 67 97	Class: (RS)	**1995-07 Keosung Shipyard Co Ltd — Geoje** Loa 33.73 Br ex - Dght 2.470 Lbp 27.28 Br md 6.90 Dpth 2.65 Welded, 1 dk	**(B11B2FV) Fishing Vessel**	**1 oil engine** driving 1 FP propeller Total Power: 430kW (585hp)
8971750 *UGKV* -	**VOSTOK VEGA** *ex* Geo Moon *-2002* **JSC Vostok-1** - *Nakhodka* *Russia* MMSI: 273456970 Official number: 950597	**223** 66 68	Class: (RS)	**1995 Haedong Shipbuilding Co Ltd — Tongyeong** Loa 30.90 Br ex - Dght 2.250 Lbp 23.50 Br md 6.90 Dpth 2.65 Welded, 1 dk	**(B11B2FV) Fishing Vessel**	**1 oil engine** driving 1 FP propeller Total Power: 428kW (582hp)
8711851 *UHHM* -	**VOSTRETSOVO** **JSC 'Port Ecosystems'** LLC Transneft-Service *Novorossiysk* *Russia* MMSI: 273819060 Official number: 884060	**1,896** 1,014 3,389	Class: RS	**1989-05 Shipbuilding & Shiprepairing Yard 'Ivan Dimitrov' — Rousse** Yd No: 469 Loa 77.53 Br ex 14.34 Dght 5.401 Lbp 73.20 Br md 14.00 Dpth 6.50 Welded, 1 dk	**(A13B2TP) Products Tanker** Liq: 3,514; Liq (Oil): 3,514 Compartments: 12 Ta, ER	**1 oil engine** driving 1 FP propeller Total Power: 885kW (1,203hp) S.K.L. 8NVD48A-2U 1 x 4 Stroke 8 Cy. 320 x 480 885kW (1203bhp) VEB Schwermaschinenbau "KarlLiebknecht" (SKL)-Magdeburg Thrusters: 1 Thwart. CP thruster (f)

IMO / Call sign / Name / Owner	Tonnage	Class	Builder / Dimensions	Type	Machinery
8722147 **VOSTRETSOVO** UCXD - **Chukotryba JSC (ZAO 'Chukotryba')** - Petropavlovsk-Kamchatskiy Russia MMSI: 273846500 Official number: 861759	**843** 252 338	Class: (RS)	**1987-05 Zavod "Leninskaya Kuznitsa" — Kiyev** Yd No: 264 Loa 53.74 Br ex 10.71 Dght 4.500 Lbp 47.92 Br md - Dpth 6.00 Welded, 1 dk	**(B11A2FS) Stern Trawler** Ice Capable	**1 oil engine** driving 1 CP propeller Total Power: 971kW (1,320hp) 12.6kn S.K.L. 8NVD48A-2U 1 x 4 Stroke 8 Cy. 320 x 480 971kW (1320bhp) VEB Schwermaschinenbau "KarlLiebknecht" (SKL)-Magdeburg AuxGen: 1 x 300kW a.c, 3 x 160kW a.c
7027382 **VOUKEFALAS** HP5855 - ex Hurricane -2009 ex Hurricane H -2007 ex Margam -1997 **Poseidon Salvage & Towage Maritime Co** - Panama Panama MMSI: 355003000 Official number: 4205210	**282** 84 189	Class: (LR) ✠ Classed LR until 1/10/09	**1970-11 R. Dunston (Hessle) Ltd. — Hessle** Yd No: S873 Loa 33.91 Br ex 9.45 Dght 4.801 Lbp 30.18 Br md 9.00 Dpth 4.58 Welded, 1 dk	**(B32A2ST) Tug**	**1 oil engine** sr reverse geared to sc. shaft driving 1 FP propeller Total Power: 1,611kW (2,190hp) 13.0kn Ruston 9ATCM 1 x 4 Stroke 9 Cy. 318 x 368 1611kW (2190bhp) English Electric Diesels Ltd.-Glasgow AuxGen: 2 x 35kW 440V 50Hz a.c, 1 x 15kW 440V 50Hz a.c Fuel: 86.5 (d.f.)
9221633 **VOULA SEAS** D5DD9 - ex Destino Dos -2012 **Almina Shipping Co** Allseas Marine SA Monrovia Liberia MMSI: 636015851 Official number: 15851	**17,431** 9,829 28,495 T/cm 39.3	Class: RI (NK)	**2002-03 Kanda Zosensho K.K. — Kawajiri** Yd No: 409 Loa 170.00 Br ex - Dght 9.767 Lbp 162.00 Br md 27.00 Dpth 13.80 Welded, 1 dk	**(A21A2BC) Bulk Carrier** Grain: 37,732; Bale: 36,683 Compartments: 5 Ho, ER 5 Ha: (14.1 x 15.0)4 (19.2 x 18.0)ER Cranes: 4x30t	**1 oil engine** driving 1 FP propeller Total Power: 5,884kW (8,000hp) 14.0kn B&W 6S42MC 1 x 2 Stroke 6 Cy. 420 x 1764 5884kW (8000bhp) Mitsui Engineering & Shipbuilding CLtd-Japan Fuel: 1215.0
9313333 **VOX BAHIA** ECFF AL-2-6-03 **Vox Bahia SL** - Algeciras Spain MMSI: 224309000 Official number: 3-6/2003	**552** 165 -		**2004-03 Francisco Cardama, SA — Vigo** Yd No: 210 Loa - Br ex - Dght - Lbp 45.00 Br md 9.00 Dpth 6.50 Welded, 1 dk	**(B11B2FV) Fishing Vessel**	**1 oil engine** geared to sc. shaft driving 1 FP propeller Total Power: 1,158kW (1,574hp) Caterpillar 3512B-TA 1 x Vee 4 Stroke 12 Cy. 170 x 190 1158kW (1574bhp) Caterpillar Inc-USA
9454096 **VOX MAXIMA** PBXL - **Vox Maxima BV** Van Oord Ship Management BV Rotterdam Netherlands MMSI: 246351000 Official number: 51582	**29,920** 8,976 53,839	Class: BV	**2009-11 IHC Dredgers BV — Kinderdijk** Yd No: C01252 Loa 195.00 (BB) Br ex - Dght 12.250 Lbp 185.00 Br md 31.00 Dpth 17.50 Welded, 1 dk	**(B33B2DT) Trailing Suction Hopper Dredger** Hopper: 31,200	**2 oil engines** reduction geared to sc. shafts driving 2 CP propellers Total Power: 28,800kW (39,156hp) 17.0kn MAN-B&W 12V48/60B 2 x Vee 4 Stroke 12 Cy. 480 x 600 each-14400kW (19578bhp) MAN B&W Diesel AG-Augsburg AuxGen: 2 x 2000kW 6600V 50Hz a.c, 1 x 1900kW 50Hz a.c, 1 x 466kW 50Hz a.c Thrusters: 2 Tunnel thruster (f) Fuel: 4367.0
9505273 **VOYAGER** 2DNF9 N 905 **Voyager Fishing Co Ltd** - Newry United Kingdom MMSI: 235080461 Official number: C19762	**3,145** 944 3,000	Class: NV	**2010-08 'Crist' Sp z oo — Gdansk** (Hull) **2010-08 Karstensens Skibsvaerft A/S — Skagen** Yd No: 410 Loa 75.40 (BB) Br ex 15.64 Dght 7.200 Lbp 66.40 Br md 15.60 Dpth 10.00 Welded, 1 dk	**(B11B2FV) Fishing Vessel** Ice Capable	**1 oil engine** reduction geared to sc. shaft driving 1 CP propeller Total Power: 8,000kW (10,877hp) 17.5kn Wartsila 16V32 1 x Vee 4 Stroke 16 Cy. 320 x 400 8000kW (10877bhp) Wartsila Finland Oy-Finland AuxGen: 2 x 820kW a.c, 1 x 3000kW a.c Thrusters: 1 Tunnel thruster (f); 1 Tunnel thruster (a) Fuel: 470.0
9553256 **VOYAGER** D5AT9 - **Sea Lanes Enterprises SA** Leros Management SA Monrovia Liberia MMSI: 636015446 Official number: 15446	**32,987** 19,212 56,584 T/cm 58.8	Class: LR ✠ **100A1** SS 09/2012 bulk carrier CSR BC-A GRAB (20) Nos. 2 & 4 holds may be empty ESP **ShipRight** (CM,ACS (B)) *IWS LI ✠ **LMC** **UMS** Eq.Ltr: M†; Cable: 632.5/73.0 U3 (a)	**2012-09 COSCO (Zhoushan) Shipyard Co Ltd — Zhoushan ZJ** Yd No: N196 Loa 189.99 (BB) Br ex 32.30 Dght 12.800 Lbp 185.60 Br md 32.26 Dpth 18.00 Welded, 1 dk	**(A21A2BC) Bulk Carrier** Grain: 71,634; Bale: 68,200 Compartments: 5 Ho, ER 5 Ha: ER Cranes: 4x30t	**1 oil engine** driving 1 FP propeller Total Power: 9,480kW (12,889hp) 14.2kn MAN-B&W 6S50MC-C 1 x 2 Stroke 6 Cy. 500 x 2000 9480kW (12889bhp) Hyundai Heavy Industries Co Ltd-South Korea AuxGen: 3 x 600kW 450V 60Hz a.c Boilers: AuxB (Comp) 9.2kgf/cm² (9.0bar)
9253894 **VOYAGER** V7FJ4 - **SAG Unternehmensbeteiligungsges mt 'Voyager' mbH & Co KG** Columbia Shipmanagement (Deutschland) GmbH Majuro Marshall Islands MMSI: 538090231 Official number: 90231	**79,525** 47,345 149,991 T/cm 112.3	Class: GL (AB)	**2002-01 Sasebo Heavy Industries Co. Ltd. — Sasebo Yard, Sasebo** Yd No: 479 Loa 272.00 (BB) Br ex 45.64 Dght 17.046 Lbp 262.00 Br md 45.60 Dpth 24.00 Welded,	**(A13A2TV) Crude Oil Tanker** Double Hull (13F) Liq: 162,591; Liq (Oil): 162,591 Cargo Heating Coils Compartments: 14 Wing Ta, ER, 2 Wing Slop Ta 3 Cargo Pump (s): 3x3500m³/hr Manifold: Bow/CM: 136m	**1 oil engine** driving 1 FP propeller Total Power: 12,372kW (16,821hp) 15.0kn B&W 6S70MC 1 x 2 Stroke 6 Cy. 700 x 2674 12372kW (16821bhp) Mitsui Engineering & Shipbuilding CLtd-Japan AuxGen: 3 x 740kW 110/440V 60Hz a.c Fuel: 120.0 (d.f.) (Heating Coils) 3770.0 (r.f.) 53.0pd
6523925 **VOYAGER** YDZR - ex Cehili -2013 ex Josenfjord -1999 ex Josenfjord-Ferjen -1987 **PT Laut Salito** - Benoa Indonesia MMSI: 525015274	**354** 107 -	Class: KI (NV)	**1965 Gravdal Skipsbyggeri — Sunde i Sunnhordland** Yd No: 360 Loa 35.38 Br ex 9.50 Dght 2.661 Lbp 30.50 Br md 9.49 Dpth 3.51 Welded, 1 dk	**(A36A2PR) Passenger/Ro-Ro Ship (Vehicles)** Passengers: 200	**2 oil engines** driving 2 FP propellers Total Power: 294kW (400hp) 10.0kn Volvo Penta TMD100A 2 x 4 Stroke 6 Cy. 121 x 140 each-147kW (200bhp) AB Volvo Penta-Sweden Fuel: 10.5 (d.f.)
8421341 **VOYAGER** 9HQN5 - ex Yellow Rose -2003 ex Andhika Madonna -1997 ex Lady Madonna -1994 ex Southern Virgo -1993 **Albatross Navigation Co Ltd** Aroania Maritime SA Valletta Malta MMSI: 248072000 Official number: 5803	**19,864** 11,551 33,347 T/cm 42.3	Class: NK	**1985-08 Kanda Zosensho K.K. — Kawajiri** Yd No: 291 Loa 179.50 (BB) Br ex 27.64 Dght 10.767 Lbp 170.01 Br md 27.61 Dpth 15.02 Welded, 1 dk	**(A21A2BC) Bulk Carrier** Grain: 42,821; Bale: 41,186 Compartments: 5 Ho, ER 5 Ha: (16.8 x 12.0)4 (19.2 x 14.4)ER Cranes: 4x25t	**1 oil engine** driving 1 FP propeller Total Power: 5,685kW (7,729hp) 14.0kn Mitsubishi 6UE52LA 1 x 2 Stroke 6 Cy. 520 x 1600 5685kW (7729bhp) Akasaka Tekkosho KK (Akasaka DieselLtd)-Japan AuxGen: 3 x 370kW a.c Fuel: 1730.0 (r.f.)
7901758 **VOYAGER** - - ex Amaltal Voyager -2009 ex Otago Challenge -1984 launched as Nueva Zelanda -1979 - -	**321** 96 200	Class: (LR) (AB) Classed LR until 17/3/10	**1979-12 Construcciones Navales Santodomingo SA — Vigo** Yd No: 465 Loa 34.32 Br ex 8.33 Dght 5.000 Lbp 28.53 Br md 8.30 Dpth 5.85 Welded, 2 dks	**(B11A2FS) Stern Trawler**	**1 oil engine** sr geared to sc. shaft driving 1 CP propeller Total Power: 747kW (1,016hp) 11.0kn Alpha 7V23LU 1 x 4 Stroke 7 Cy. 225 x 300 747kW (1016bhp) Construcciones Echevarria SA-Spain AuxGen: 2 x 104kW 380V 50Hz a.c
8709573 **VOYAGER** C6WC2 - ex Alexander Von Humboldt -2012 ex Alexander von Humboldt II -2008 ex Jules Verne -2008 ex Walrus -2007 ex Nautican -1996 ex Crown Monarch -1994 **All Leisure Holidays Ltd** V Ships Leisure SAM SatCom: Inmarsat C 430969510 Nassau Bahamas MMSI: 309695000 Official number: 8001348	**15,396** 5,817 1,384	Class: NV	**1990-10 Union Naval de Levante SA (UNL) — Valencia** Yd No: 185 Loa 152.50 (BB) Br ex 20.60 Dght 5.820 Lbp 125.49 Br md 19.80 Dpth 7.10 Welded, 4 dks	**(A37A2PC) Passenger/Cruise** Passengers: cabins: 265; berths: 556 Ice Capable	**4 oil engines** with clutches & dr geared to sc. shafts driving 2 CP propellers Total Power: 13,232kW (17,992hp) 18.8kn Normo BRM-9 4 x 4 Stroke 9 Cy. 320 x 360 each-3308kW (4498bhp) Bergen Diesel AS-Norway AuxGen: 2 x 2100kW 440V 60Hz a.c, 2 x 2100kW 440V 50Hz a.c Thrusters: 2 Thwart. FP thruster (f) Fuel: 84.0 (d.f.) 750.0 (r.f.) 31.0pd
8921779 **VOYAGER** - - **Orico Corp** - South Korea	*132* - 50		**1990-07 Mitsubishi Heavy Industries Ltd. — Shimonoseki** Yd No: 943 Loa 26.50 Br ex - Dght 1.400 Lbp 23.50 Br md 9.00 Dpth 2.60 Welded, 1 dk	**(A37B2PS) Passenger Ship** Hull Material: Aluminium Alloy Passengers: unberthed: 200	**2 oil engines** with clutches & reverse reduction geared to sc. shafts driving 2 FP propellers Total Power: 1,662kW (2,260hp) 18.9kn G.M. (Detroit Diesel) 16V-92-TA 2 x Vee 2 Stroke 16 Cy. 123 x 127 each-831kW (1130bhp) General Motors Detroit DieselAllison Divn-USA

8985957 *H03191* -	**VOYAGER** *ex* Absinthe *-2010* *ex* Claire T *-2002* *ex* Lara A *-2002* *ex* Lara *-2002* *ex* Eretria III *-2002* *ex* Nefertiti *-2002* - - *Panama* *Panama* MMSI: 353270000 Official number: 3514212B	**780** 234 -	Class: IS (LR) (AB) ✠ Classed LR until 30/6/82	**1973-07 Ast. y Talleres Celaya S.A. — Bilbao** Yd No: 132 Loa 61.26 Br ex 9.46 Dght 3.200 Lbp 53.40 Br md 9.45 Dpth 4.72 Welded, 1 dk	**(X11A2YP) Yacht** Passengers: cabins: 11; berths: 21	**2 oil engines** geared to sc. shafts driving 2 Propellers Total Power: 1,654kW (2,248hp) 13.0kn Caterpillar D399 2 x Vee 4 Stroke 16 Cy. 159 x 203 each-827kW (1124bhp) Caterpillar Tractor Co-USA
8891613 *FKRE* -	**VOYAGER 1** - **Voyager I Copropriete** - *Pointe-a-Pitre* *France* Official number: 885598	**110** - -	Class: (BV)	**1994 At. & Ch. de Bordeaux — Bordeaux** Loa 23.20 Br ex - Dght 1.311 Lbp 20.55 Br md 6.20 Dpth 2.25 Welded, 1 dk	**(A37B2PS) Passenger Ship**	**2 oil engines** reduction geared to sc. shafts driving 2 FP propellers Total Power: 1,230kW (1,672hp) 23.0kn Caterpillar 3412TA 2 x Vee 4 Stroke 12 Cy. 137 x 152 each-615kW (836bhp) Caterpillar Inc-USA
9018684 *9HIX8* -	**VOYAGER A** *ex* Iver Libra *-2006* **Voyager A Maritime Ltd** Ancora Investment Trust Inc *Valletta* *Malta* MMSI: 256025000 Official number: 9855	**21,142** 11,177 31,069 T/cm 39.8	Class: NV (RS)	**1994-07 OAO Khersonskiy Sudostroitelnyy Zavod — Kherson** Yd No: 1425 Loa 178.96 (BB) Br ex - Dght 11.974 Lbp 164.71 Br md 25.30 Dpth 15.00 Welded, 1 dk	**(A12B2TR) Chemical/Products Tanker** Double Hull (13F) Liq: 36,104; Liq (Oil): 37,352 Compartments: 14 Wing Ta, 2 Wing Slop Ta, ER 14 Cargo Pump (s): 10x425m³/hr, 4x250m³/hr Manifold: Bow/CM: 89.2m Ice Capable	**1 oil engine** driving 1 FP propeller Total Power: 7,948kW (10,806hp) 14.5kn B&W 6DKRN60/195 1 x 2 Stroke 6 Cy. 600 x 1950 7948kW (10806bhp) AO Bryanskiy MashinostroitelnyyZavod (BMZ)-Bryansk AuxGen: 3 x 880kW 380V 50Hz a.c Fuel: 127.0 (d.f.) 1403.0 (r.f.)
9319052 *3FTG9* -	**VOYAGER EXPLORER** *ex* Veritas Voyager *-2011* *ex* Miclyn Explorer *-2006* **Koleth (S) Pte Ltd** SeaBird Exploration FZ LLC *Panama* *Panama* MMSI: 353481000 Official number: 42365PEXTF	**2,943** 883 1,379	Class: AB BV (Class contemplated)	**2005-12 Jiangsu Zhenjiang Shipyard Co Ltd — Zhenjiang JS** Yd No: 96-ZJS200303 Converted From: Offshore Supply Ship-2006 Loa 67.81 Br ex 16.00 Dght 5.450 Lbp 61.70 Br md 14.95 Dpth 5.50 Welded, 1 dk	**(B31A2SR) Research Survey Vessel**	**2 oil engines** reduction geared to sc. shafts driving 2 Propellers Total Power: 3,132kW (4,258hp) 10.0kn Caterpillar 3516B-TA 2 x Vee 4 Stroke 16 Cy. 170 x 190 each-1566kW (2129bhp) Caterpillar Inc-USA AuxGen: 2 x 350kW a.c, 1 x 450kW a.c, 1 x 354kW a.c Thrusters: 1 Retract. directional thruster (f) Fuel: 982.0 (d.f.)
9425681 *J8B3705* -	**VOYAGER I** *ex* Sitaram I *-2010* *ex* Topniche 9 *-2007* **First Voyager Enterprises Ltd** Gulf Maritime Shipmanagement Co *Kingstown* *St Vincent & The Grenadines* MMSI: 376395000 Official number: 10178	**274** 82 -	Class: BV (NV)	**2007-03 Bonafile Shipbuilders & Repairs Sdn Bhd — Sandakan** Yd No: 58/04 Loa 29.20 Br ex - Dght 3.840 Lbp 27.00 Br md 9.00 Dpth 4.40 Welded, 1 dk	**(B32A2ST) Tug**	**2 oil engines** reduction geared to sc. shafts driving 2 FP propellers Total Power: 1,790kW (2,434hp) 10.0kn Cummins KTA-38-M2 2 x Vee 4 Stroke 12 Cy. 159 x 159 each-895kW (1217bhp) Cummins Engine Co Ltd-United Kingdom AuxGen: 2 x 80kW 415V 50Hz a.c Fuel: 200.0
8994104 *WCY9932* -	**VOYAGER III** - **Voyager III LLC** - *Boston, MA* *United States of America* Official number: 1077034	**218** 89 -		**1999-01 Gladding-Hearn SB. Duclos Corp. — Somerset, Ma** Yd No: P-320 Loa 34.07 Br ex - Dght 1.250 Lbp 30.07 Br md 9.22 Dpth 3.00 Welded, 1 dk	**(A37B2PS) Passenger Ship** Hull Material: Aluminium Alloy Passengers: unberthed: 348	**4 oil engines** reduction geared to sc. shafts driving 4 Water jets Total Power: 3,152kW (4,284hp) M.T.U. 12V2000M70 4 x Vee 4 Stroke 12 Cy. 130 x 150 each-788kW (1071bhp) MTU Friedrichshafen GmbH-Friedrichshafen
8507535 *XUEU4* -	**VOYAGER K** *ex* Evangelos *-2012* *ex* Sifnos Bay *-2007* *ex* Nego Kim *-2002* *ex* Maersk Cypress *-1993* *ex* Teresa O *-1993* *ex* Mashu *-1988* **Voyager Ship Management & Co SA** Trans Marine Co Ltd *Phnom Penh* *Cambodia* MMSI: 515138000 Official number: 1285980	**15,832** 8,990 26,591 T/cm 37.6	Class: NK	**1985-08 The Hakodate Dock Co Ltd — Hakodate HK** (Hull) Yd No: 727 **1985-08 Kurushima Dockyard Co. Ltd. — Onishi** Yd No: 2431 Loa 167.20 (BB) Br ex 26.29 Dght 9.543 Lbp 160.00 Br md 26.00 Dpth 13.30 Welded, 1 dk	**(A21A2BC) Bulk Carrier** Grain: 33,917; Bale: 32,681 Compartments: 5 Ho, ER 5 Ha: (13.8 x 13.0)4 (19.2 x 13.0)ER Cranes: 4x30.5t	**1 oil engine** driving 1 FP propeller Total Power: 5,075kW (6,900hp) 14.0kn B&W 6L50MCE 1 x 2 Stroke 6 Cy. 500 x 1620 5075kW (6900bhp) Hitachi Zosen Corp-Japan AuxGen: 3 x 360kW 450V 60Hz a.c Fuel: 1245.0 (r.f.)
9161716 *C6SE5* -	**VOYAGER OF THE SEAS** - **Voyager of the Seas Inc** Royal Caribbean Cruises Ltd (RCCL) *Nassau* *Bahamas* MMSI: 311317000 Official number: 8000402	**137,276** 105,011 11,132	Class: NV	**1999-10 Kvaerner Masa-Yards Inc — Turku** Yd No: 1344 Loa 311.12 (BB) Br ex 39.04 Dght 8.800 Lbp 274.70 Br md 38.60 Dpth 11.70 Welded, 8 dks plus 9 Superstructure dks.	**(A37A2PC) Passenger/Cruise** Passengers: cabins: 1557; berths: 3838	**6 diesel electric oil engines** driving 6 gen. each 13300kW 11000V a.c Connecting to 3 elec. motors each (14000kW) driving 2 Azimuth electric drive units , centre unit fixed, 1 FP propeller Total Power: 75,600kW (102,786hp) 22.1kn Wartsila 12V46C 6 x Vee 4 Stroke 12 Cy. 460 x 580 each-12600kW (17131bhp) Wartsila NSD Finland Oy-Finland Thrusters: 4 Thwart. FP thruster (f) Fuel: 216.6 (d.f.) 3393.9 (r.f.)
9658082 - -	**VOYAGER SEVEN** - **Family Win Ltd** - *Yangon* *Myanmar* Official number: 6614 (A)	**1,050** 544 -		**2012-02 Family Win Dockyard — Yangon** Yd No: LCT004FW Loa 68.58 Br ex - Dght - Lbp - Br md 15.24 Dpth 3.96 Welded, 1 dk	**(A35D2RL) Landing Craft** Bow ramp (centre)	**2 oil engines** reduction geared to sc. shafts driving 2 Propellers Total Power: 894kW (1,216hp) Cummins KTA-19-M3 2 x 4 Stroke 6 Cy. 159 x 159 each-447kW (608bhp) Cummins Engine Co Inc-USA
9300570 *3EBL9* -	**VOYAGEURS** *ex* Cape Provence *-2014* **CVI Cape Provence LLC** CarVal Investors LLC SatCom: Inmarsat C 437116210 *Panama* *Panama* MMSI: 371162000 Official number: 33369PEXT1	**89,651** 59,031 177,022 T/cm 121.4	Class: NK	**2005-07 Namura Shipbuilding Co Ltd — Imari SG** Yd No: 249 Loa 288.97 (BB) Br ex - Dght 17.955 Lbp 279.00 Br md 45.00 Dpth 24.40 Welded, 1 dk	**(A21A2BC) Bulk Carrier** Grain: 198,765; Bale: 195,968 Compartments: 9 Ho, ER 9 Ha: 7 (16.3 x 20.2) (16.3 x 15.1)ER (16.3 x 16.8)	**1 oil engine** driving 1 FP propeller Total Power: 16,860kW (22,923hp) 14.1kn Mitsubishi 6UEC68LSE 1 x 2 Stroke 6 Cy. 680 x 2690 16860kW (22923bhp) Mitsubishi Heavy Industries Ltd-Japan Fuel: 215.0 (d.f.) 5374.0 (r.f.)
8724963 *UEFG* -	**VOYEVODA** - **Preobrazheniye Trawler Fleet Base (Preobrazhenskaya Baza Tralovogo Flota)** - *Nakhodka* *Russia* Official number: 881927	**127** 38 25	Class: RS	**1988-12 Stocznia 'Odra' — Szczecin** Yd No: B3981/4 Loa 27.50 Br ex 6.27 Dght 2.100 Lbp 24.59 Br md 6.20 Dpth 2.70 Welded, 1dk	**(B32A2ST) Tug** Ice Capable	**1 oil engine** driving 1 CP propeller Total Power: 927kW (1,260hp) 11.5kn Sulzer 6ASL25D 1 x 4 Stroke 6 Cy. 250 x 300 927kW (1260bhp) in Poland
8033924 *UGZC* MI-1505	**VOYKOVO** - **Murman Fishing Collective (Rybolovetskiy Kolkhoz 'Murman')** - *Murmansk* *Russia* MMSI: 273516500	**802** 221 405	Class: RS	**1982-04 Zavod "Leninskaya Kuznitsa" — Kiyev** Yd No: 1505 Loa 54.82 Br ex 9.96 Dght 4.114 Lbp 50.29 Br md 9.80 Dpth 5.01 Welded, 1 dk	**(B11A2FS) Stern Trawler** Ins: 414 Compartments: 2 Ho, ER 3 Ha: 3 (1.5 x 1.6) Derricks: 2x1.5t; Winches: 2 Ice Capable	**1 oil engine** driving 1 CP propeller Total Power: 852kW (1,158hp) 12.0kn S.K.L. 8NVD48A-2U 1 x 4 Stroke 8 Cy. 320 x 480 852kW (1158bhp) VEB Schwermaschinenbau "KarlLiebknecht" (SKL)-Magdeburg AuxGen: 4 x 160kW Fuel: 182.0 (d.f.)
9616383 *3WIA9* -	**VP ASPHALT 1** - **VP Petrochemical Transport JSC** Vietnam Petroleum Transport JSC (VIPCO) (Cong Ty Van Tai Xang Dau Duong Thuy 1) *Haiphong* *Vietnam* MMSI: 574001620 Official number: VN-72.TT-VT	**3,125** 938 3,102	Class: NV VR	**2012-08 Hong Ha Shipbuilding Co Ltd — Haiphong** Yd No: 15 Loa 98.00 Br ex 15.03 Dght 4.600 Lbp 91.03 Br md 15.00 Dpth 7.00 Welded, 1 dk	**(A13C2LA) Asphalt/Bitumen Tanker** Double Hull (13F) Liq: 2,425; Liq (Oil): 3,000; Asphalt: 3,000 Cargo Heating Coils	**1 oil engine** with clutches, flex coup & sr rev geared to sc. shafts driving 1 FP propeller Total Power: 1,950kW (2,651hp) 12.0kn Wartsila 6L26 1 x 4 Stroke 6 Cy. 260 x 320 1950kW (2651bhp) Wartsila Italia SpA-Italy AuxGen: 3 x 280kW 440V a.c Fuel: 290.0
9616395 *3WIT9* -	**VP ASPHALT 2** - **VP Petrochemical Transport JSC** Vietnam Petroleum Transport JSC (VIPCO) (Cong Ty Van Tai Xang Dau Duong Thuy 1) *Haiphong* *Vietnam* MMSI: 574001760	**3,072** - 3,095	Class: NV VR	**2013-03 Hong Ha Shipbuilding Co Ltd — Haiphong** Yd No: 16 Loa 98.00 Br ex 15.04 Dght 4.600 Lbp 90.97 Br md 15.00 Dpth 7.00 Welded, 1 dk	**(A13C2LA) Asphalt/Bitumen Tanker** Double Hull (13F) Liq: 2,425; Liq (Oil): 3,000; Asphalt: 3,000 Cargo Heating Coils	**1 oil engine** reduction geared to sc. shaft driving 1 FP propeller Total Power: 1,950kW (2,651hp) 12.0kn Wartsila 6L26 1 x 4 Stroke 6 Cy. 260 x 320 1950kW (2651bhp) Wartsila Italia SpA-Italy AuxGen: 3 x 280kW 440V a.c Fuel: 290.0

9279886 *AUDP* - **VPT FIRE FLOAT**
Visakhapatnam Port Trust
-
Visakhapatnam *India*
Official number: 3051

345 104 128 Class: IR

2003-09 **Cochin Shipyard Ltd — Ernakulam** Yd No: BY-44
Loa 32.90 Br ex 10.02 Dght 2.700
Lbp 29.60 Br md 10.00 Dpth 4.25
Welded

(B34F2SF) Fire Fighting Vessel

2 oil engines geared to sc. shafts driving 2 FP propellers
Total Power: 678kW (922hp)
Caterpillar 3408C
2 x Vee 4 Stroke 8 Cy. 137 x 152 each-339kW (461bhp)
Caterpillar Inc-USA
AuxGen: 2 x 85kW 415V 50Hz a.c
Fuel: 31.0 (r.f.)

9556351 *YJVN3* - **VRANA TIDE**
VTG Ships Ltd
Tidewater Marine International Inc
Port Vila *Vanuatu*
MMSI: 576488000
Official number: 1806

1,370 411 1,246 Class: AB

2009-09 **Yuexin Shipbuilding Co Ltd — Guangzhou GD** Yd No: 3096
Loa 51.00 Br ex - Dght 5.000
Lbp 44.40 Br md 15.00 Dpth 6.50
Welded, 1 dk

(B21B20A) Anchor Handling Tug Supply

2 oil engines gearing integral to driving 2 Directional propellers
Total Power: 5,832kW (7,930hp) 14.8kn
GE Marine 16V228
2 x Vee 4 Stroke 16 Cy. 229 x 267 each-2916kW (3965bhp)
GE Marine Engines-Cincinnati, Oh
AuxGen: 3 x 425kW a.c
Thrusters: 1 Tunnel thruster (f)
Fuel: 800.0

8203220 - - **VRIDI SIAP**
ex Vridi *-1985*
Societe Ivoirienne d'Avitaillement Portuaire
-
Abidjan *Cote d'Ivoire*

489 307 1,020 Class: (BV)

1983-06 **Ateliers et Chantiers du Sud-Ouest — Bordeaux** Yd No: 1201
Loa 49.81 Br ex 11.41 Dght 3.001
Lbp 48.01 Br md 11.00 Dpth 3.51
Welded, 1 dk

(B35E2TF) Bunkering Tanker
Liq: 1,000; Liq (Oil): 1,000
Compartments: 8 Ta, ER
3 Cargo Pump (s)

2 oil engines geared to sc. shafts driving 2 FP propellers
Total Power: 294kW (400hp) 7.0kn
Deutz F8L413F
2 x Vee 4 Stroke 8 Cy. 120 x 125 each-147kW (200bhp)
Kloeckner Humboldt Deutz AG-West Germany

9112052 *POMJ* - **VRIES VIENA**
ex Wave A *-2012* *ex* Capella *-2011*
PT Pelayaran Vries Maritim Pratama
-
Batam *Indonesia*
MMSI: 525015945

21,145 11,177 32,396 T/cm 39.9 Class: NV (RS)

1995-08 **OAO Khersonskiy Sudostroitelnyy Zavod — Kherson** Yd No: 1427
Loa 178.96 (BB) Br ex 25.30 Dght 11.368
Lbp 165.00 Br md 25.30 Dpth 15.00
Welded, 1 dk

(A13B2TP) Products Tanker
Double Hull (13F)
Liq: 36,105; Liq (Oil): 36,105
Compartments: 14 Ta, ER
16 Cargo Pump (s): 10x425m³/hr, 6x250m³/hr
Manifold: Bow/CM: 82.5m
Ice Capable

1 oil engine driving 1 FP propeller
Total Power: 7,940kW (10,795hp) 14.5kn
MAN-B&W 6L60MC
1 x 2 Stroke 6 Cy. 600 x 1944 7940kW (10795bhp)
AO Bryanskiy MashinostroitelnyyZavod (BMZ)-Bryansk
AuxGen: 3 x 824kW 400V 50Hz a.c
Fuel: 93.5 (d.f.) (Heating Coils) 1220.0 (r.f.) 30.5pd

9277321 *PHAP* - **VRIESENDIEP**
ex Onego Merchant *-2010*
launched as Vriessendiep *-2004*
Beheermaatschappij ms Vriesendiep BV
Feederlines BV
Groningen *Netherlands*
MMSI: 245124000
Official number: 41847

5,057 2,681 7,707 Class: GL (LR)
✠ Classed LR until 15/3/12

2004-04 **ATVT Sudnobudivnyi Zavod "Zaliv" — Kerch (Hull)** Yd No: (620)
2004-04 **Bodewes' Scheepswerven B.V. — Hoogezand** Yd No: 620
Loa 119.98 (BB) Br ex 15.43 Dght 7.050
Lbp 113.65 Br md 15.20 Dpth 8.44
Welded, 1 dk

(A31A2GX) General Cargo Ship
Grain: 9,415
TEU 390 C Ho 174 TEU C Dk 216 TEU
Compartments: 2 Ho, ER
Cranes: 2x40t
Ice Capable

1 oil engine reduction geared to sc. shaft driving 1 FP propeller
Total Power: 3,840kW (5,221hp) 14.7kn
MaK 8M32C
1 x 4 Stroke 8 Cy. 320 x 480 3840kW (5221bhp)
Caterpillar Motoren GmbH & Co. KG-Germany
AuxGen: 1 x 400kW 400V 50Hz a.c, 2 x 259kW 400V 50Hz a.c
Boilers: TOH (o.f.) 10.2kgf/cm² (10.0bar), TOH (ex.g.) 10.2kgf/cm² (10.0bar)
Thrusters: 1 Thwart. FP thruster (f)

8209652 *3FWF3* - **VRINDA**
ex Eberhard *-2011*
Atlantic Bluewater Services Ltd
Sterling Oil Resources Ltd
Panama *Panama*
MMSI: 356481000
Official number: 4422712

3,075 1,559 5,238 T/cm 13.0 Class: GL

1983-05 **Kroegerwerft Rendsburg GmbH — Schacht-Audorf** Yd No: 1508
Converted From: Chemical Tanker-1985
Lengthened-1985
Loa 105.75 Br ex 15.14 Dght 5.649
Lbp 100.59 Br md 15.02 Dpth 7.80
Welded, 1 dk

(A12B2TR) Chemical/Products Tanker
Liq: 6,830; Liq (Oil): 4,673
Part Cargo Heating Coils
Compartments: 10 Ta, ER
4 Cargo Pump (s): 4x275m³/hr
Ice Capable

1 oil engine with flexible couplings & sr gearedto sc. shaft driving 1 CP propeller
Total Power: 1,820kW (2,474hp) 12.3kn
MWM TBD501-6
1 x 4 Stroke 6 Cy. 360 x 450 1820kW (2474bhp)
Motoren Werke Mannheim AG (MWM)-West Germany
AuxGen: 2 x 310kW 380V 50Hz a.c, 1 x 202kW 380V 50Hz a.c

7637149 *C4AY2* - **VRONSKIY**
ex Wisteria *-2013* *ex* Duc de Normandie *-2005*
ex Prinses Beatrix *-1986*
Nizhniy Shipping Ltd
Cia Trasmediterranea SA (Acciona Trasmediterranea)
Limassol *Cyprus*
MMSI: 210030000
Official number: 7637149

13,505 5,329 1,887 Class: BV (LR)
✠ Classed LR until 14/11/86

1978-06 **Verolme Scheepswerf Heusden B.V. — Heusden** Yd No: 959
Loa 131.02 (BB) Br ex 22.56 Dght 5.169
Lbp 119.51 Br md 22.00 Dpth 13.01
Welded, 3 dks, plus movable platforms in upper 'tween deck space

(A36A2PR) Passenger/Ro-Ro Ship (Vehicles)
Passengers: unberthed: 933; cabins: 139; berths: 567
Bow door & ramp (centre)
Len: 8.30 Wid: 5.10 Swl: -
Stern door/ramp (centre)
Len: 7.00 Wid: 5.85 Swl: -
Lane-Len: 528
Lane-clr ht: 4.35
Lorries: 30, Cars: 354, Trailers: 48

4 oil engines sr geared to sc. shafts driving 2 CP propellers
Total Power: 16,184kW (22,004hp) 21.0kn
Werkspoor 8TM410
4 x 4 Stroke 8 Cy. 410 x 470 each-4046kW (5501bhp)
Stork Werkspoor Diesel BV-Netherlands
AuxGen: 4 x 800kW 450V 60Hz a.c
Thrusters: 1 Thwart. CP thruster (f)
Fuel: 131.0 (d.f.) 735.0 (r.f.)

9676084 *D5FN5* - **VSC CASTOR**
Sea Pearl Shipholding SA
Seastar Chartering Ltd
Monrovia *Liberia*
MMSI: 636016318
Official number: 16318

31,538 18,720 55,780 T/cm 56.9 Class: NK

2014-01 **Japan Marine United Corp (JMU) — Kure HS** Yd No: 3341
Loa 190.00 (BB) Br ex - Dght 12.735
Lbp 185.00 Br md 32.26 Dpth 18.10
Welded, 1 dk

(A21A2BC) Bulk Carrier
Grain: 72,111; Bale: 67,062
Compartments: 5 Ho, ER
5 Ha: 4 (20.9 x 18.6)ER (14.6 x 18.6)
Cranes: 4x35t

1 oil engine driving 1 FP propeller
Total Power: 10,470kW (14,235hp) 14.5kn
Wartsila 6RT-flex50
1 x 2 Stroke 6 Cy. 500 x 2050 10470kW (14235bhp)
Diesel United Ltd.-Aioi
Fuel: 2170.0

9692650 *D5FT2* - **VSC POLLUX**
Elysium Holding SA
Seastar Chartering Ltd
Monrovia *Liberia*
MMSI: 636016353
Official number: 16353

31,538 18,720 55,794 T/cm 56.9 Class: NK

2014-03 **Japan Marine United Corp (JMU) — Kure HS** Yd No: 3343
Loa 190.00 (BB) Br ex - Dght 12.700
Lbp 185.00 Br md 32.26 Dpth 18.10
Welded, 1 dk

(A21A2BC) Bulk Carrier
Grain: 71,800; Bale: 66,792
Compartments: 5 Ho, ER
5 Ha: 4 (20.9 x 18.6)ER (14.6 x 18.6)

1 oil engine driving 1 FP propeller
Total Power: 10,470kW (14,235hp) 14.5kn
Wartsila 6RT-flex50
1 x 2 Stroke 6 Cy. 500 x 2050 10470kW (14235bhp)
Fuel: 2170.0

9673757 *D5FC7* - **VSC POSEIDON**
ex Dst King *-2013*
Aurelia Shipholding Ltd
Seastar Chartering Ltd
Monrovia *Liberia*
MMSI: 636016227
Official number: 16227

40,357 24,925 74,957 T/cm 67.3 Class: NK (AB)

2013-09 **Sasebo Heavy Industries Co. Ltd. — Sasebo Yard, Sasebo** Yd No: 817
Loa 225.00 (BB) Br ex 32.25 Dght 14.136
Lbp 218.00 Br md 32.20 Dpth 19.80
Welded, 1 dk

(A21A2BC) Bulk Carrier
Double Hull
Grain: 90,771; Bale: 88,950
Compartments: 7 Ho, ER
7 Ha: 6 (17.0 x 14.4)ER (15.3 x 12.9)

1 oil engine driving 1 FP propeller
Total Power: 8,700kW (11,829hp) 14.5kn
MAN-B&W 7S50ME-C8
1 x 2 Stroke 7 Cy. 500 x 2000 8700kW (11829bhp)
Mitsui Engineering & Shipbuilding CLtd-Japan
Fuel: 2470.0

9593311 *D5FH4* - **VSC TRITON**
ex Dst Queen *-2013*
Nephele Seaways Inc
Seastar Chartering Ltd
Monrovia *Liberia*
MMSI: 636016266
Official number: 16266

31,540 18,765 55,848 T/cm 56.9 Class: NK

2011-09 **IHI Marine United Inc — Kure HS** Yd No: 3319
Loa 189.96 (BB) Br ex - Dght 12.735
Lbp 185.00 Br md 32.26 Dpth 18.10
Welded, 1 dk

(A21A2BC) Bulk Carrier
Grain: 72,062; Bale: 67,062
Compartments: 5 Ho, ER
5 Ha: ER
Cranes: 4x30t

1 oil engine driving 1 FP propeller
Total Power: 8,890kW (12,087hp) 14.5kn
Wartsila 6RT-flex50
1 x 2 Stroke 6 Cy. 500 x 2050 8890kW (12087bhp)
Diesel United Ltd.-Aioi
Fuel: 2490.0

7620354 - - **VSEVOLOD TIMONOV**
-
-

697 229 518 Class: (RS)

1976-05 **Khabarovskiy Sudostroitelnyy Zavod im Kirova — Khabarovsk** Yd No: 811
Converted From: Fish Carrier
Loa 55.00 Br ex 9.50 Dght 4.340
Lbp 50.04 Br md 9.30 Dpth 5.16
Welded, 1 dk

(A31A2GX) General Cargo Ship
Ins: 648
Compartments: 2 Ho, ER
2 Ha: 2 (2.9 x 2.9)ER
Derricks: 4x1.5t; Winches: 4
Ice Capable

1 oil engine driving 1 FP propeller
Total Power: 588kW (799hp) 11.5kn
S.K.L. 6NVD48A-2U
1 x 4 Stroke 6 Cy. 320 x 480 588kW (799bhp)
VEB Schwermaschinenbau "KarlLiebknecht" (SKL)-Magdeburg
AuxGen: 3 x 150kW
Fuel: 116.0 (d.f.)

9217802 *3EPB4* - **VSG DREAM**
ex Lucent Ace *-2007*
South Vietnam Container Shipping JSC (Viconship Saigon)
-
Panama *Panama*
MMSI: 357318000
Official number: 3392708A

4,724 2,812 7,748 Class: NK

2000-03 **Shin Kochi Jyuko K.K. — Kochi** Yd No: 7127
Loa 99.92 Br ex - Dght 7.241
Lbp 93.00 Br md 19.20 Dpth 8.90
Welded, 1 dk

(A31A2GX) General Cargo Ship
Grain: 9,806; Bale: 9,200
Compartments: 2 Ho, ER
2 Ha: 2 (25.2 x 10.2)ER
Derricks: 4x25t

1 oil engine driving 1 FP propeller
Total Power: 3,236kW (4,400hp) 12.6kn
B&W 5L35MC
1 x 2 Stroke 5 Cy. 350 x 1050 3236kW (4400bhp)
Makita Corp-Japan
AuxGen: 2 x 230kW a.c
Fuel: 580.0

9103025 *3FCJ4* - **VSG GLORY**
ex Apollo Dua *-2008*
South Vietnam Container Shipping JSC (Viconship Saigon)
-
SatCom: Inmarsat C 435316610
Panama *Panama*
MMSI: 353166000
Official number: 2136394D

6,290 2,484 8,192 Class: NK

1994-04 **Higaki Zosen K.K. — Imabari** Yd No: 441
Loa 100.72 (BB) Br ex 18.62 Dght 7.809
Lbp 92.80 Br md 18.60 Dpth 13.40
Welded, 2 dks

(A31A2GX) General Cargo Ship
Grain: 14,288; Bale: 12,593
Compartments: 2 Ho, ER
2 Ha: (21.0 x 12.6) (26.6 x 12.6)ER
Cranes: 2x20t; Derricks: 1x30t

1 oil engine driving 1 FP propeller
Total Power: 2,994kW (4,071hp) 13.5kn
Mitsubishi 6UEC37LA
1 x 2 Stroke 6 Cy. 370 x 880 2994kW (4071bhp)
Kobe Hatsudoki KK-Japan
Fuel: 535.0 (r.f.)

IMO / Call sign	Name / Owner	Tonnage	Class	Builder / Dimensions	Type	Machinery	
9146912 *3EPB3* -	**VSG PRIDE** *ex* Asian Energy *-2007* *ex* Brother Soko *-1997* **South Vietnam Container Shipping JSC (Viconship Saigon)** - *Panama* *Panama* MMSI: 356076000 Official number: 3392608A	**4,738** 2,196 6,238 T/cm 13.4	Class: NK	**1996-06 Sanyo Zosen K.K. — Onomichi** Yd No: 1072 Loa 96.70 (BB) Br ex - Dght 7.346 Lbp 85.78 Br md 17.40 Dpth 11.60 Welded, 1 dk	**(A31A2GX) General Cargo Ship** Grain: 10,383; Bale: 9,867 Compartments: 2 Ho, ER 2 Ha: (14.7 x 10.5) (28.7 x 10.5)ER Derricks: 3x25t	**1 oil engine** driving 1 FP propeller Total Power: 2,427kW (3,300hp) Akasaka 1 x 4 Stroke 6 Cy. 410 x 800 2427kW (3300bhp) Akasaka Tekkosho KK (Akasaka DieselLtd)-Japan Fuel: 430.0 (r.f.)	12.0kr A41
9129017 *3WTR* -	**VSICO PIONEER** *ex* Heung-A Nagoya *-2008* **VSICO Shipping JSC** - SatCom: Inmarsat C 457411710 *Haiphong* *Vietnam* MMSI: 574117008 Official number: VN-01TT-VT	**4,914** 2,452 7,040	Class: VR (KR)	**1996-11 Daedong Shipbuilding Co Ltd — Busan** Yd No: 411 Loa 112.50 (BB) Br ex - Dght 6.712 Lbp 105.30 Br md 18.20 Dpth 8.70 Welded, 1 dk	**(A33A2CC) Container Ship (Fully Cellular)** TEU 420 C Ho 151 TEU C Dk 269 TEU incl 30 ref C	**1 oil engine** driving 1 FP propeller Total Power: 3,884kW (5,281hp) B&W 1 x 2 Stroke 6 Cy. 350 x 1050 3884kW (5281bhp) Hyundai Heavy Industries Co Ltd-South Korea AuxGen: 2 x 400kW 445V a.c Thrusters: 1 Thwart. CP thruster (f) Fuel: 666.0 (r.f.)	14.5kr 6L35MC
9674220 *3WKC9* -	**VSP EXPRESS** **Song Thu Co of Region 5 of Army Command (Cong Ty Song Tha Quan Khu V)** - *Vietnam* MMSI: 574001940	**443** 132 350	Class: BV	**2013-06 Song Thu Co. — Da Nang** Yd No: 547219 Loa 53.25 Br ex 10.10 Dght 3.200 Lbp 49.92 Br md 9.20 Dpth 4.70 Welded, 1 dk	**(B21A2OC) Crew/Supply Vessel**	**4 oil engines** driving 4 FP propellers Total Power: 4,476kW (6,084hp) Caterpillar 1 x Vee 4 Stroke 12 Cy. 170 x 215 1119kW (1521bhp) Caterpillar Inc-USA Caterpillar 3 x Vee 4 Stroke 12 Cy. 170 x 215 each-1119kW (1521bhp) Caterpillar Inc-USA AuxGen: 3 x 99kW 60Hz a.c Thrusters: 2 Tunnel thruster (f) Fuel: 160.0 (d.f.)	22.0kr 3512C 3512C
7631652 - -	**VST 1** **PSA Marine Pte Ltd** -	*209* - 80	Class: (LR) ✠ Classed LR until 2/8/09	**1977-10 Pan-Asia Shipyard & Engineering Co Pte Ltd — Singapore** Yd No: PA/35 Loa 29.11 Br ex 9.38 Dght 2.636 Lbp 25.94 Br md 8.50 Dpth 3.69 Welded, 1 dk	**(B32A2ST) Tug**	**2 oil engines** gearing integral to driving 2 Voith-Schneider propellers Total Power: 1,840kW (2,502hp) Yanmar 2 x 4 Stroke 6 Cy. 220 x 300 each-920kW (1251bhp) (new engine 1999) Yanmar Diesel Engine Co Ltd-Japan AuxGen: 2 x 75kW 400V 50Hz a.c	M220-EN
7631664 - -	**VST 2** **PSA Marine Pte Ltd** -	*203* 60 80	Class: (LR) ✠ Classed LR until 22/8/09	**1977-12 Pan-Asia Shipyard & Engineering Co Pte Ltd — Singapore** Yd No: PA/36 Loa 29.11 Br ex 9.38 Dght 2.363 Lbp 25.91 Br md 8.51 Dpth 3.69 Welded, 1 dk	**(B32A2ST) Tug**	**2 oil engines** gearing integral to driving 2 Voith-Schneider propellers Total Power: 1,840kW (2,502hp) Yanmar 2 x 4 Stroke 6 Cy. 220 x 300 each-920kW (1251bhp) (new engine 1999) Yanmar Diesel Engine Co Ltd-Japan AuxGen: 2 x 75kW 400V 50Hz a.c	M220-EN
7631676 *YD4874* -	**VST 2301** *ex* Vst 3 *-2003* **PT Jaya Samudera Abadi** - *Tanjung Priok* *Indonesia*	*201* 61 80	Class: KI (LR) ✠ Classed LR until 31/12/02	**1978-01 Pan-Asia Shipyard & Engineering Co Pte Ltd — Singapore** Yd No: PA/37 Loa 28.22 Br ex 9.25 Dght - Lbp 27.00 Br md 8.50 Dpth 4.50 Welded, 1 dk	**(B32A2ST) Tug**	**2 oil engines** geared to sc. shafts driving 2 Directional propellers Deutz 2 x 4 Stroke 8 Cy. 220 x 280 Kloeckner Humboldt Deutz AG-West Germany AuxGen: 2 x 75kW 400V 50Hz a.c	SBA8M528
8136805 - -	**VSTRECHNYY** **Triton JSC (A/O 'Triton')**	**448** 134 207	Class: (RS)	**1983 Zavod 'Nikolayevsk-na-Amure' — Nikolayevsk-na-Amure** Yd No: 1218 Loa 44.89 Br ex 9.48 Dght 3.771 Lbp 39.37 Br md - Dpth 5.11 Welded, 1 dk	**(B11B2FV) Fishing Vessel** Ice Capable	**1 oil engine** driving 1 FP propeller Total Power: 588kW (799hp) S.K.L. 1 x 4 Stroke 6 Cy. 320 x 480 588kW (799bhp) VEB Schwermaschinenbau "KarlLiebknecht" (SKL)-Magdeburg AuxGen: 3 x 150kW Fuel: 109.0 (d.f.)	11.5kr 6NVD48A-2L
9023299 - -	**VT-02** **Southern Trans Construction & Trade Stock Co** - *Saigon* *Vietnam* Official number: VNSG-1648-TH	**171** 64 2	Class: VR	**1975-01 Yard N.51 — Vietnam** Loa 36.74 Br ex 7.62 Dght 1.800 Lbp 35.05 Br md 7.40 Dpth - Welded, 1 dk	**(A31A2GX) General Cargo Ship**	**1 oil engine** geared to sc. shaft driving 1 Propeller Total Power: 257kW (349hp) Caterpillar 1 x 4 Stroke 6 Cy. 137 x 165 257kW (349bhp) Caterpillar Tractor Co-USA	8.0kr 3406E
9024528 - -	**VT 023** **Maritime Safety Co II (Cong Ty Bao Dam An Toan Hang Hai II)** Maritime Safety Enterprise No 203 (Xi Nghiep Bao Dam An Toan 203) *Haiphong* *Vietnam* MMSI: 574849000	**156** 52 118	Class: VR	**2002-11 Tam Bac Shipyard — Haiphong** Loa 36.25 Br ex 6.50 Dght 2.250 Lbp 33.00 Br md 6.20 Dpth 2.80 Welded, 1 dk	**(B31A2SR) Research Survey Vessel**	**1 oil engine** reduction geared to sc. shaft driving 1 Propeller Total Power: 237kW (322hp) Caterpillar 1 x 4 Stroke 6 Cy. 137 x 165 237kW (322bhp) Caterpillar Inc-USA	8.0kr 3406C
8868616 - -	**VT-103** **Halong Fishery Complex Enterprise (Xi Nghiep Lien Hiep Thuy San Ha Long)** - *Haiphong* *Vietnam*	*163* 54 -	Class: (VR)	**1957 in the People's Republic of China** Loa 30.25 Br ex - Dght 2.600 Lbp - Br md 6.70 Dpth 3.38 Welded, 1 dk	**(B11B2FV) Fishing Vessel**	**1 oil engine** driving 1 FP propeller Total Power: 184kW (250hp) Chinese Std. Type 1 x 4 Stroke 6 Cy. 267 x 330 184kW (250bhp) in China AuxGen: 1 x 9kW d.c, 1 x 3kW d.c	10.0kr 6267
8868642 *XVTI* -	**VT-109** **Halong Fishery Complex Enterprise (Xi Nghiep Lien Hiep Thuy San Ha Long)** - *Haiphong* *Vietnam*	*163* 54 -	Class: (VR)	**1965 in the People's Republic of China** Loa 30.70 Br ex - Dght 2.600 Lbp - Br md 6.72 Dpth 3.38 Welded, 1 dk	**(B11B2FV) Fishing Vessel**	**1 oil engine** driving 1 FP propeller Total Power: 184kW (250hp) Chinese Std. Type 1 x 4 Stroke 6 Cy. 267 x 330 184kW (250bhp) in China AuxGen: 1 x 9kW d.c, 1 x 3kW d.c	10.0kr 6267
8868630 *XVTJ* -	**VT-110** **Halong Fishery Complex Enterprise (Xi Nghiep Lien Hiep Thuy San Ha Long)** - *Haiphong* *Vietnam*	*163* 54 -	Class: (VR)	**1965 in the People's Republic of China** Loa 30.70 Br ex - Dght 3.150 Lbp - Br md 6.68 Dpth 3.70 Welded, 1 dk	**(B11B2FV) Fishing Vessel**	**1 oil engine** driving 1 FP propeller Total Power: 184kW (250hp) Chinese Std. Type 1 x 4 Stroke 6 Cy. 267 x 330 184kW (250bhp) in China AuxGen: 1 x 9kW d.c, 1 x 3kW d.c	10.0kr 6267
8868692 *XVWH* -	**VT-112** **Halong Fishery Complex Enterprise (Xi Nghiep Lien Hiep Thuy San Ha Long)** - *Haiphong* *Vietnam*	*163* 54 -	Class: (VR)	**1966 in the People's Republic of China** Loa 30.70 Br ex - Dght 2.600 Lbp - Br md 6.72 Dpth 3.38 Welded, 1 dk	**(B11B2FV) Fishing Vessel**	**1 oil engine** driving 1 FP propeller Total Power: 184kW (250hp) Chinese Std. Type 1 x 4 Stroke 6 Cy. 267 x 330 184kW (250bhp) in China AuxGen: 1 x 9kW d.c, 1 x 3kW d.c	10.0kr 6267
8868680 - -	**VT-113** **Halong Fishery Complex Enterprise (Xi Nghiep Lien Hiep Thuy San Ha Long)** - *Haiphong* *Vietnam*	*163* 54 -	Class: (VR)	**1966 in the People's Republic of China** Loa 30.70 Br ex - Dght 2.625 Lbp - Br md 6.72 Dpth 3.38 Welded, 1 dk	**(B11B2FV) Fishing Vessel**	**1 oil engine** driving 1 FP propeller Total Power: 184kW (250hp) Chinese Std. Type 1 x 4 Stroke 6 Cy. 267 x 330 184kW (250bhp) in China AuxGen: 1 x 9kW d.c, 1 x 3kW d.c	10.0kr 6267
8868678 - -	**VT-114** **Halong Fishery Complex Enterprise (Xi Nghiep Lien Hiep Thuy San Ha Long)** - *Haiphong* *Vietnam*	*163* 54 -	Class: (VR)	**1965 in the People's Republic of China** Loa 30.70 Br ex - Dght 2.600 Lbp - Br md 6.70 Dpth 3.38 Welded, 1 dk	**(B11B2FV) Fishing Vessel**	**1 oil engine** driving 1 FP propeller Total Power: 184kW (250hp) Chinese Std. Type 1 x 4 Stroke 6 Cy. 267 x 330 184kW (250bhp) in China AuxGen: 1 x 9kW d.c, 1 x 3kW d.c	10.0kr 6267
8868733 - -	**VT-115** **Halong Fishery Complex Enterprise (Xi Nghiep Lien Hiep Thuy San Ha Long)** - *Haiphong* *Vietnam*	*163* 54 -	Class: (VR)	**1965 in the People's Republic of China** Loa 30.70 Br ex - Dght 2.600 Lbp - Br md 6.70 Dpth 3.38 Welded, 1 dk	**(B11B2FV) Fishing Vessel**	**1 oil engine** driving 1 FP propeller Total Power: 184kW (250hp) Chinese Std. Type 1 x 4 Stroke 6 Cy. 267 x 330 184kW (250bhp) in China AuxGen: 1 x 9kW d.c, 1 x 3kW d.c	10.0kr 6267

8868721 **VT-116**
-
- **Halong Fishery Complex Enterprise (Xi Nghiep Lien Hiep Thuy San Ha Long)**
-
Haiphong *Vietnam*

171 54 -
Class: (VR)

1966 in the People's Republic of China
Loa 36.52 Br ex - Dght 3.150
Lbp - Br md 6.68 Dpth 3.70
Welded, 1 dk

(B11B2FV) Fishing Vessel

1 oil engine driving 1 FP propeller
Total Power: 184kW (250hp) 10.0kn
Chinese Std. Type 6267
1 x 4 Stroke 6 Cy. 267 x 330 184kW (250bhp) in China
AuxGen: 1 x 9kW d.c, 1 x 3kW d.c

8868719 **VT-117**
XVTQ
- **Halong Fishery Complex Enterprise (Xi Nghiep Lien Hiep Thuy San Ha Long)**
-
Haiphong *Vietnam*

163 54 -
Class: (VR)

1966 in the People's Republic of China
Loa 30.70 Br ex - Dght 2.560
Lbp - Br md 6.72 Dpth 3.38
Welded, 1 dk

(B11B2FV) Fishing Vessel

1 oil engine driving 1 FP propeller
Total Power: 184kW (250hp) 10.0kn
Chinese Std. Type 6267
1 x 4 Stroke 6 Cy. 267 x 330 184kW (250bhp) in China
AuxGen: 1 x 9kW d.c, 1 x 3kW d.c

9026576 **VT-0311**
3WGL
- **Maritime Safety Co II (Cong Ty Bao Dam An Toan Hang Hai II)**
-
Haiphong *Vietnam*

301 90 187
Class: VR

2004-05 Saigon Shipbuilding Industry Co — Ho Chi Minh City Yd No: ST-186
Loa 31.00 Br ex 11.32 Dght 1.600
Lbp 29.16 Br md 11.00 Dpth 2.80
Welded, 1 dk

(B34Q2QB) Buoy Tender

2 oil engines reduction geared to sc. shafts driving 2 FP propellers
Total Power: 404kW (550hp) 7.0kn
Chinese Std. Type 6160A
2 x 4 Stroke 6 Cy. 160 x 225 each-202kW (275bhp)
Weifang Diesel Engine Factory-China

8113578 **VT ELAINE**
JVDT5
- *ex* Ios Elaine *-2014* *ex* Lady Elaine *-2004*
ex Far Tracer *-1989* *ex* Tender Tracer *-1986*
Petra Offshore Ltd
Intra Oil Services Bhd
Ulaanbaatar *Mongolia*
MMSI: 457813000

2,127 638 2,047
Class: (NV)

1983-03 Scheepswerf 'Friesland' BV — Lemmer (Hull)
1983-03 Amels BV — Makkum Yd No: 379
Loa 72.07 Br ex - Dght 6.240
Lbp 63.02 Br md 15.02 Dpth 7.01
Welded, 2 dks

(B21B20A) Anchor Handling Tug Supply

4 oil engines sr geared to sc. shafts driving 2 CP propellers
Total Power: 7,768kW (10,560hp) 15.5kn
Normo KVMB-12
4 x Vee 4 Stroke 12 Cy. 250 x 300 each-1942kW (2640bhp)
AS Bergens Mek Verksteder-Norway
AuxGen: 2 x 1176kW 440V 60Hz a.c, 2 x 250kW 440V 60Hz a.c
Thrusters: 2 Thwart. CP thruster (f); 1 Tunnel thruster (a)
Fuel: 517.5 (d.f.)

8207379 **VT ELECTRON**
OVUA2
- *ex* Bregninge II *-2009* *ex* Valkyrien *-2006*
VT Shipping A/S
-
Svendborg *Denmark (DIS)*
MMSI: 219886000
Official number: D2859

291 87 145
Class: RI (LR)
✠ Classed LR until 19/12/06

1984-02 Dannebrog Vaerft A/S — Aarhus Yd No: 185
Loa 32.42 Br ex 9.53 Dght 4.061
Lbp 27.89 Br md 9.01 Dpth 4.50
Welded, 1 dk

(B32B2SP) Pusher Tug
Ice Capable

1 oil engine with clutches, flexible couplings & sr geared to sc. shaft driving 1 CP propeller
Total Power: 2,730kW (3,712hp) 14.0kn
Wartsila 8R32
1 x 4 Stroke 8 Cy. 320 x 350 2730kW (3712bhp)
Oy Wartsila Ab-Finland
AuxGen: 2 x 280kW 380V 50Hz a.c
Thrusters: 1 Thwart. CP thruster (f)
Fuel: 109.0 (d.f.) 12.0pd

7928158 **VT NEUTRON**
OXJG2
- *ex* Vindeby II *-2009* *ex* Sleipner *-2006*
VT Shipping A/S
-
SatCom: Inmarsat A 1611143
Svendborg *Denmark (DIS)*
MMSI: 219938000
Official number: D2742

275 82 98
Class: RI (LR)
✠ Classed LR until 13/12/06

1981-01 Dannebrog Vaerft A/S — Aarhus Yd No: 176
Loa 32.42 Br ex 9.50 Dght 3.847
Lbp 29.11 Br md 9.01 Dpth 4.37
Welded, 1 dk

(B32A2ST) Tug
Ice Capable

1 oil engine sr geared to sc. shaft driving 1 CP propeller
Total Power: 2,339kW (3,180hp) 15.0kn
Alpha 12U28L-VO
1 x Vee 4 Stroke 12 Cy. 280 x 320 2339kW (3180bhp)
B&W Alpha Diesel A/S-Denmark
AuxGen: 2 x 258kW 380V 50Hz a.c, 1 x 41kW 380V 50Hz a.c
Thrusters: 1 Thwart. FP thruster (f)
Fuel: 98.0 (d.f.) 10.0pd

8131116 **VT PROTON**
OUWN2
- *ex* Troense II *-2009* *ex* Volund *-2006*
VT Shipping A/S
-
SatCom: Inmarsat A 1610465
Svendborg *Denmark (DIS)*
MMSI: 219939000
Official number: D2858

291 87 147
Class: RI (LR)
✠ Classed LR until 18/12/06

1983-11 Dannebrog Vaerft A/S — Aarhus Yd No: 184
Loa 32.42 Br ex 9.53 Dght 4.061
Lbp 27.89 Br md 9.01 Dpth 4.50
Welded, 1 dk

(B32B2SP) Pusher Tug
Ice Capable

1 oil engine with clutches, flexible couplings & sr geared to sc. shaft driving 1 CP propeller
Total Power: 2,730kW (3,712hp) 14.0kn
Wartsila 8R32
1 x 4 Stroke 8 Cy. 320 x 350 2730kW (3712bhp)
Oy Wartsila Ab-Finland
AuxGen: 2 x 280kW 380V 50Hz a.c
Thrusters: 1 Thwart. CP thruster (f)
Fuel: 109.0 (d.f.) 12.0pd

9143049 **VTC ACE**
XVVA
- *ex* Ammon Ace *-2009*
Vietnam Sea Transport & Chartering Co (VITRANSCHART) (Cong Ty Van Tai Bien Va Thue Tau Vietnam)
-
Saigon *Vietnam*
MMSI: 574950000
Official number: VNSG-1970-TH

15,354 8,111 24,157
Class: NK

1996-11 Kanda Zosensho K.K. — Kawajiri Yd No: 372
Loa 158.50 (BB) Br ex - Dght 9.417
Lbp 151.00 Br md 25.80 Dpth 13.30
Welded, 1 dk

(A31A2GX) General Cargo Ship
Grain: 29,463; Bale: 28,768
Compartments: 4 Ho, ER
4 Ha: (22.4 x 14.3)Tappered 3 (24.0 x 20.2)ER
Cranes: 3x30t

1 oil engine driving 1 FP propeller
Total Power: 5,384kW (7,320hp) 13.4kn
B&W 6L42MC
1 x 2 Stroke 6 Cy. 420 x 1360 5384kW (7320bhp)
Kawasaki Heavy Industries Ltd-Japan
AuxGen: 2 x 500kW 450V a.c
Fuel: 1495.0 (r.f.) 18.5pd

9335460 **VTC DRAGON**
3WSU
- **Vietnam Sea Transport & Chartering Co (VITRANSCHART) (Cong Ty Van Tai Bien Va Thue Tau Vietnam)**
-
Saigon *Vietnam*
MMSI: 574493000
Official number: VNSG-1839-TH

14,851 7,158 22,662
Class: NK VR

2007-10 Bach Dang Shipyard — Haiphong Yd No: BV-04
Loa 153.20 Br ex - Dght 9.520
Lbp 143.00 Br md 26.00 Dpth 13.75
Welded, 1 dk

(A21A2BC) Bulk Carrier
Grain: 29,157; Bale: 28,694
Compartments: 5 Ho, ER
5 Ha: (11.2 x 15.0)3 (15.0 x 15.0)ER (10.5 x 13.2)
Cranes: 4x30.7t

1 oil engine driving 1 FP propeller
Total Power: 6,230kW (8,470hp) 13.5kn
Mitsubishi 7UEC45LA
1 x 2 Stroke 7 Cy. 450 x 1350 6230kW (8470bhp)
Akasaka Tekkosho KK (Akasaka DieselLtd)-Japan
AuxGen: 3 x 426kW a.c
Fuel: 1650.0

9113886 **VTC GLOBE**
3WOZ
- *ex* Pacoda *-2007* *ex* Tequi *-2004*
Vietnam Sea Transport & Chartering Co (VITRANSCHART) (Cong Ty Van Tai Bien Va Thue Tau Vietnam)
-
Saigon *Vietnam*
MMSI: 574452000
Official number: VNSG-1802-TH

14,436 8,741 23,726 T/cm 33.5
Class: NK VR

1995-07 KK Kanasashi — Toyohashi AI Yd No: 3400
Loa 150.52 (BB) Br ex - Dght 9.566
Lbp 143.00 Br md 26.00 Dpth 13.20
Welded, 1 dk

(A21A2BC) Bulk Carrier
Grain: 31,249; Bale: 30,169
Compartments: 4 Ho, ER
4 Ha: (17.9 x 12.8)3 (19.5 x 17.8)ER
Cranes: 4x30.5t

1 oil engine driving 1 FP propeller
Total Power: 5,295kW (7,199hp) 13.9kn
Mitsubishi 6UEC45LA
1 x 2 Stroke 6 Cy. 450 x 1350 5295kW (7199bhp)
Kobe Hatsudoki KK-Japan
AuxGen: 2 x 360kW 450V 60Hz a.c
Fuel: 52.4 (d.f.) (Part Heating Coils) 859.2 (r.f.) 18.8pd

9168752 **VTC GLORY**
XVCV
- *ex* Voge Lucia *-2010* *ex* Blue Leo *-2009*
Vietnam Sea Transport & Chartering Co (VITRANSCHART) (Cong Ty Van Tai Bien Va Thue Tau Vietnam)
-
SatCom: Inmarsat C 457486110
Saigon *Vietnam*
MMSI: 574861000
Official number: VNSG-2033-TH

14,446 8,548 23,620 T/cm 33.7
Class: NK VR

1998-06 Shin Kurushima Dockyard Co. Ltd. — Onishi Yd No: 2970
Loa 150.52 (BB) Br ex - Dght 9.566
Lbp 143.00 Br md 26.00 Dpth 13.20
Welded, 1 dk

(A21A2BC) Bulk Carrier
Grain: 30,583; Bale: 29,929
Compartments: 4 Ho, ER
4 Ha: (17.9 x 12.8)3 (19.5 x 17.8)ER
Cranes: 4x30.5t

1 oil engine driving 1 FP propeller
Total Power: 5,298kW (7,203hp) 14.0kn
Mitsubishi 6UEC45LA
1 x 2 Stroke 6 Cy. 450 x 1350 5298kW (7203bhp)
Kobe Hatsudoki KK-Japan
Fuel: 990.0

9191046 **VTC OCEAN**
3WYY
- *ex* Marion Star *-2009*
Vietnam Sea Transport & Chartering Co (VITRANSCHART) (Cong Ty Van Tai Bien Va Thue Tau Vietnam)
-
Saigon *Vietnam*
MMSI: 574432000
Official number: VNSG-1933-TH

14,762 8,075 23,492 T/cm 34.2
Class: NK VR

1999-01 Tsuneishi Heavy Industries (Cebu) Inc — Balamban Yd No: SC-007
Loa 154.38 (BB) Br ex - Dght 9.518
Lbp 146.00 Br md 26.00 Dpth 13.35
Welded, 1 dk

(A21A2BC) Bulk Carrier
Grain: 30,811; Bale: 30,089
Compartments: 4 Ho, ER
4 Ha: (19.2 x 12.7)2 (20.0 x 17.5) (20.8 x 17.5)ER
Cranes: 4x30t

1 oil engine driving 1 FP propeller
Total Power: 5,186kW (7,051hp) 14.1kn
B&W 7S35MC
1 x 2 Stroke 7 Cy. 350 x 1400 5186kW (7051bhp)
Mitsui Engineering & Shipbuilding CLtd-Japan
Fuel: 66.8 (d.f.) 917.8 (r.f.) 20.4pd

9536337 **VTC PHOENIX**
3WXR
- **Vietnam Sea Transport & Chartering Co (VITRANSCHART) (Cong Ty Van Tai Bien Va Thue Tau Vietnam)**
-
Saigon *Vietnam*
MMSI: 574435000
Official number: VNSG-1939-TH

14,851 7,158 22,763
Class: NK VR

2009-02 Bach Dang Shipyard — Haiphong Yd No: BV-07
Loa 153.20 Br ex 26.04 Dght 9.517
Lbp 143.00 Br md 26.00 Dpth 13.75
Welded, 1 dk

(A21A2BC) Bulk Carrier
Double Hull
Grain: 29,157; Bale: 28,964
Compartments: 5 Ho, ER
5 Ha: 3 (15.0 x 15.0) (11.3 x 15.0)ER (10.5 x 13.2)
Cranes: 4x30.7t

1 oil engine driving 1 FP propeller
Total Power: 6,230kW (8,470hp) 13.5kn
Mitsubishi 7UEC45LA
1 x 2 Stroke 7 Cy. 450 x 1350 6230kW (8470bhp)
Akasaka Tekkosho KK (Akasaka DieselLtd)-Japan
Fuel: 1650.0

IMO / Call sign	Name / Owner / Port	Tonnage	Class	Builder / Dimensions	Type / Cargo	Machinery
9060730 *3WVU* -	**VTC PLANET** *ex* Edelweiss *-2008* **Vietnam Sea Transport & Chartering Co (VITRANSCHART) (Cong Ty Van Tai Bien Va Thue Tau Vietnam)** - *Saigon* *Vietnam* MMSI: 574138000 Official number: VNSG-1896-TH	**13,706** 7,738 22,176 T/cm 30.3	Class: NK VR	**1993**-11 **Saiki Heavy Industries Co Ltd — Saiki OT** Yd No: 1028 Loa 157.50 (BB) Br ex - Dght 9.100 Lbp 148.00 Br md 25.00 Dpth 12.70 Welded, 1 dk	**(A21A2BC) Bulk Carrier** Grain: 29,301; Bale: 28,299 Compartments: 4 Ho, ER 4 Ha: (20.0 x 11.7)Tappered 3 (20.8 x 17.5)ER Cranes: 4x30t	**1 oil engine** driving 1 FP propeller Total Power: 5,371kW (7,302hp) 13.5kn Mitsubishi 6UEC45LA 1 x 2 Stroke 6 Cy. 450 x 1350 5371kW (7302bhp) Akasaka Tekkosho KK (Akasaka DieselLtd)-Japan AuxGen: 3 x 293kW a.c Fuel: 925.0 (r.f.)
9146900 *3WMW* -	**VTC SKY** *ex* Noble Light *-2005* *ex* Malabar Light *-2003* *ex* Hinrich Oldendorff *-2000* **Vietnam Sea Transport & Chartering Co (VITRANSCHART) (Cong Ty Van Tai Bien Va Thue Tau Vietnam)** - *Saigon* *Vietnam* MMSI: 574330000 Official number: VNSG-1754-TH	**14,743** 8,258 23,581 T/cm 34.2	Class: LR VR (NK) **100A1** SS 02/2012 bulk carrier ESP **LMC** Eq.Ltr: F†; Cable: 577.5/58.0 U3	**1997**-02 **Saiki Heavy Industries Co Ltd — Saiki OT** Yd No: 1066 Loa 154.35 (BB) Br ex 26.03 Dght 9.518 Lbp 145.50 Br md 26.00 Dpth 13.35 Welded, 1 dk	**(A21A2BC) Bulk Carrier** Grain: 30,847; Bale: 30,094 Compartments: 4 Ho, ER 4 Ha: (19.2 x 12.7)2 (20.5 x 17.5) (20.8 x 17.5)ER Cranes: 4x30t	**1 oil engine** driving 1 FP propeller Total Power: 5,296kW (7,200hp) 14.3kn Mitsubishi 6UEC45LA 1 x 2 Stroke 6 Cy. 450 x 1350 5296kW (7200bhp) Kobe Hatsudoki KK-Japan AuxGen: 2 x 440kW 440V 60Hz a.c Boilers: AuxB (Comp) 7.0kgf/cm² (6.9bar) Fuel: 278.0 (d.f.) 974.0 (r.f.)
9146895 *3WRF* -	**VTC SUN** *ex* Protagonist *-2008* *ex* Borca *-2003* *ex* Gebe Oldendorff *-2001* **Vietnam Sea Transport & Chartering Co (VITRANSCHART) (Cong Ty Van Tai Bien Va Thue Tau Vietnam)** - *Saigon* *Vietnam* MMSI: 574006000 Official number: VNSG-1851-TH	**14,743** 7,920 23,581 T/cm 34.2	Class: NK	**1996**-12 **Saiki Heavy Industries Co Ltd — Saiki OT** Yd No: 1065 Loa 154.50 (BB) Br ex - Dght 9.518 Lbp 146.00 Br md 26.00 Dpth 13.35 Welded, 1 dk	**(A21A2BC) Bulk Carrier** Grain: 30,847; Bale: 30,094 Compartments: 4 Ho, ER 4 Ha: (19.2 x 12.7)2 (20.5 x 17.5) (20.8 x 17.5)ER Cranes: 4x30t	**1 oil engine** driving 1 FP propeller Total Power: 5,296kW (7,200hp) 14.3kn Mitsubishi 6UEC45LA 1 x 2 Stroke 6 Cy. 450 x 1350 5296kW (7200bhp) Kobe Hatsudoki KK-Japan AuxGen: 3 x 1100kW a.c Fuel: 278.0 (d.f.) 974.0 (r.f.)
9180009 *XVOG* -	**VTC TIGER** *ex* Ocean Beauty *-2010* **Vietnam Sea Transport & Chartering Co (VITRANSCHART) (Cong Ty Van Tai Bien Va Thue Tau Vietnam)** - *Saigon* *Vietnam* MMSI: 574274000 Official number: VNSG-2022-TH	**16,764** 10,452 28,666	Class: NK VR	**1997**-12 **Imabari Shipbuilding Co Ltd — Marugame KG (Marugame Shipyard)** Yd No: 1290 Loa 169.00 (BB) Br ex - Dght 9.760 Lbp 160.40 Br md 27.20 Dpth 13.60 Welded, 1 dk	**(A21A2BC) Bulk Carrier** Grain: 37,523; Bale: 35,762 Compartments: 5 Ho, ER 5 Ha: (13.6 x 16.0)4 (19.2 x 17.6)ER Cranes: 4x30.5t	**1 oil engine** driving 1 FP propeller Total Power: 5,848kW (7,951hp) 14.0kn B&W 6S42MC 1 x 2 Stroke 6 Cy. 420 x 1764 5848kW (7951bhp) Mitsui Engineering & Shipbuilding CLtd-Japan Fuel: 1250.0
8982747 - -	**VTN-45** - -	**710** - -	Class: (RS)	**1977**-11 **Khersonskiy Sudostroitelnyy Zavod — Kherson** Yd No: 3 Converted From: Replenishment Tanker Loa - Br ex - Dght - Lbp - Br md - Dpth - Welded, 1 dk	**(A13B2TP) Products Tanker**	**1 oil engine** driving 1 Propeller
8811649 *UBOE9* -	**VTS-1** *ex* Piligrim 3 *-2010* *ex* Tavriya-4 *-2001* *completed as* TK-4 *-1988* **OOO Deklarantskaya Firma 'Volga Trans Servis-Broker'** *Astrakhan* *Russia* MMSI: 273311680	**1,557** 467 1,849	Class: RS (RR)	**1988**-09 **VEB Elbewerften Boizenburg/Rosslau — Rosslau** Yd No: 337 Loa 81.97 Br ex 11.93 Dght 3.580 Lbp 70.11 Br md 11.58 Dpth 4.00 Welded, 2 dks	**(A31A2GX) General Cargo Ship** TEU 70 C. 70/20'	**2 oil engines** driving 2 FP propellers Total Power: 882kW (1,200hp) 11.2kn S.K.L. 8VD36/24A-1 2 x 4 Stroke 8 Cy. 240 x 360 each-441kW (600bhp) VEB Schwermaschinenbau "KarlLiebknecht" (SKL)-Magdeburg AuxGen: 2 x 100kW a.c
8956528 *YD4831* -	**VU 1** *ex* Tiong Woon Ocean 9 *-2002* *ex* Keasin 39 *-1996* **PT Varia Usaha Lintas Segara** *Cirebon* *Indonesia*	**178** 106 -	Class: KI (BV)	**1996**-06 **Tuong Aik (Sarawak) Sdn Bhd — Sibu** Yd No: 9506 Loa 23.17 Br ex - Dght - Lbp 21.96 Br md 7.00 Dpth 2.90 Welded, 1 dk	**(B32A2ST) Tug**	**2 oil engines** geared to sc. shafts driving 2 FP propellers Total Power: 780kW (1,060hp) 12.0kn Yanmar 6LAAL-DT 2 x 4 Stroke 6 Cy. 148 x 165 each-390kW (530bhp) Yanmar Diesel Engine Co Ltd-Japan
9025534 - -	**VU ANH HUNG** *ex* Song Cam *-2007* **Vu Anh Hung Co Ltd** *Saigon* *Vietnam* Official number: VNSG-1671-TD	**346** 238 728	Class: VR	**2003**-06 **An Phu Works — Ho Chi Minh City** Loa 51.58 Br ex 8.70 Dght 3.100 Lbp 48.22 Br md 8.50 Dpth 3.60 Welded, 1 dk	**(A13B2TU) Tanker (unspecified)** Double Hull (13F) Compartments: 3 Ta, ER	**1 oil engine** reduction geared to sc. shaft driving 1 FP propeller Total Power: 530kW (721hp) 8.0kn Daiya 1 x 4 Stroke 6 Cy. 200 x 240 530kW (721bhp) (made 1998) Daiya Diesels-Japan AuxGen: 1 x 25kW 220V a.c
9565297 *3WGZ* -	**VU HOANG 09** **Agriculture Leasing Co I** Vu Hoang Transport Co Ltd SatCom: Inmarsat C 457497710 *Haiphong* *Vietnam* MMSI: 574977000	**1,599** 1,032 3,127	Class: VR	**2009**-12 **Anh Viet Co Ltd / — Haiphong** Yd No: S07-002.69 Loa 78.63 Br ex 12.62 Dght 5.220 Lbp 73.60 Br md 12.60 Dpth 6.48 Welded, 1 dk	**(A21A2BC) Bulk Carrier** Grain: 3,780 Compartments: 2 Ho, ER 2 Ha: ER 2 (19.8 x 8.4)	**1 oil engine** reduction geared for sc.shaft driving 1 FP propeller Total Power: 1,104kW (1,501hp) 10.6kn Chinese Std. Type CW8200ZC 1 x 4 Stroke 8 Cy. 200 x 270 1104kW (1501bhp) Weichai Power Co Ltd-China AuxGen: 2 x 90kW 400V a.c
9026588 - -	**VU LONG 06** **Vu Long Co Ltd** *Saigon* *Vietnam* MMSI: 574733000 Official number: VNSG-1701-TH	**643** 542 1,242	Class: VR	**2004**-05 **Nha Trang Shipbuilding Industrial Co. — Nha Trang** Yd No: TB-01 Loa 60.47 Br ex 9.72 Dght 3.780 Lbp 56.00 Br md 9.70 Dpth 4.30 Welded, 1 dk	**(A31A2GX) General Cargo Ship**	**1 oil engine** geared to sc. shaft driving 1 Propeller Total Power: 441kW (600hp) 10.0kn Weifang 8170ZC 1 x 4 Stroke 8 Cy. 170 x 200 441kW (600bhp) Weifang Diesel Engine Factory-China
8817875 *WDD3432* -	**VUI-VUI** **Nick Van Pham** - *Honolulu, HI* *United States of America* MMSI: 367131270 Official number: 930207	*151* 120 -		**1988 Tan Lee — New Orleans, La** Loa - Br ex - Dght - Lbp 22.56 Br md 7.35 Dpth 3.05 Welded, 1 dk	**(B11B2FV) Fishing Vessel**	**1 oil engine** geared to sc. shaft driving 1 FP propeller Total Power: 221kW (300hp) Cummins NTA-855-M 1 x 4 Stroke 6 Cy. 140 x 152 221kW (300bhp) Cummins Engine Co Inc-USA
8941937 *WDE9678* -	**VUI VUI II** *ex* Tourane *-1997* **Nick Van Pham** - *Honolulu, HI* *United States of America* Official number: 914121	**174** 118 -		**1987 Universal Shipbuilding, Inc. — New Iberia, La** L reg 24.23 Br ex - Dght - Lbp - Br md 7.32 Dpth 3.20 Welded, 1 dk	**(B11B2FV) Fishing Vessel**	**1 oil engine** driving 1 FP propeller
8917986 - -	**VULCAN** **Brampton Fishing Co Pty Ltd** *Fremantle, WA* *Australia* Official number: 853217	*168* 50 177		**1989**-03 **EMS Holdings Pty Ltd — Fremantle WA** Yd No: 19 Loa 24.72 Br ex 7.60 Dght 3.410 Lbp 22.68 Br md 7.40 Dpth 4.15 Welded, 1 dk	**(B11A2FT) Trawler** Ins: 100	**1 oil engine** with clutches, flexible couplings & sr reverse geared to sc. shaft driving 1 FP propeller Total Power: 410kW (557hp) 10.0kn Caterpillar 3508TA 1 x Vee 4 Stroke 8 Cy. 170 x 190 410kW (557bhp) Caterpillar Inc-USA
8744597 *ZR8227* -	**VULCAN** **Copper Moon Trading 612 (Pty) Ltd** *Port Elizabeth* *South Africa* MMSI: 601122600 Official number: 40808	**125** - -		**2009**-01 **in the Republic of South Africa** Loa 19.63 Br ex - Dght - Lbp - Br md - Dpth - Bonded, 1 dk	**(B11B2FV) Fishing Vessel** Hull Material: Reinforced Plastic	**2 oil engines** reduction geared to sc. shafts driving 2 Propellers 9.0kn
7422996 *P2V4102* -	**VULCAN** *ex* Brighton *-2010* *ex* Brigand *-1997* **Pacific Towing (PNG) Pty Ltd** SatCom: Inmarsat C 450301834 *Port Moresby* *Papua New Guinea* MMSI: 553111314	*266* 52 -	Class: (LR) ✠ Classed LR until 4/8/10	**1975**-06 **Carrington Slipways Pty Ltd — Newcastle NSW** Yd No: 107 Loa 29.01 Br ex 9.96 Dght 4.001 Lbp 24.80 Br md 9.71 Dpth 4.70 Welded, 1 dk	**(B32A2ST) Tug**	**2 oil engines** reverse reduction geared to sc. shafts driving 2 FP propellers Total Power: 1,794kW (2,440hp) 12.0kn Blackstone ESL8MK2 2 x 4 Stroke 8 Cy. 222 x 292 each-897kW (1220bhp) Mirrlees Blackstone (Stamford)Ltd.-Stamford AuxGen: 2 x 50kW 415V 50Hz a.c

IMO / Call sign	Name / Owner / Flag	Tonnage	Class	Build / Dimensions	Type / Capacity	Machinery
9337779 ICLI -	**VULCANELLO M** *ex* Marida Princess *-2008* *launched as* Clipper Kamilla *-2006* **Augusta Due Srl** - *Catania* *Italy* MMSI: 247245300 Official number: CT-32	**7,687** 3,266 11,298 T/cm 20.6	Class: RI (LR) (AB) Classed LR until 3/11/08	**2006**-11 **STX Shipbuilding Co Ltd — Busan** Yd No: 5010 Loa 116.50 (BB) Br ex 20.00 Dght 8.400 Lbp 109.00 Br md 20.00 Dpth 11.70 Welded, 1 dk	**(A12B2TR) Chemical/Products Tanker** Double Hull (13F) Liq: 11,594; Liq (Oil): 11,594 Cargo Heating Coils Compartments: 10 Wing Ta, ER, 2 Wing Slop Ta 10 Cargo Pump (s): 10x300m³/hr Manifold: Bow/CM: 58.6m	**1 oil engine** driving 1 FP propeller Total Power: 4,440kW (6,037hp) 13.6kn MAN-B&W 6S35MC 1 x 2 Stroke 6 Cy. 350 x 1400 4440kW (6037bhp) STX Engine Co Ltd-South Korea AuxGen: 3 x 450kW 450V 60Hz a.c Boilers: e (ex.g.) 9.2kgf/cm² (9.0bar), AuxB (o.f.) 9.2kgf/cm² (9.0bar) Thrusters: 1 Thwart. FP thruster (f) Fuel: 79.0 (d.f.) 790.0 (r.f.)
9145516 CB5939 -	**VULCANO** - **Blumar Seafoods** - *Valparaiso* *Chile* MMSI: 725000680 Official number: 2919	**1,166** 450 1,754		**1997**-03 **Astilleros Marco Chilena Ltda. — Iquique** Yd No: 215 Loa 62.50 (BB) Br ex - Dght 6.200 Lbp 53.50 Br md 12.00 Dpth 5.00 Welded, 1 dk	**(B11B2FV) Fishing Vessel**	**1 oil engine** geared to sc. shaft driving 1 FP propeller Total Power: 2,641kW (3,591hp) 15.0kn MaK 6M32 1 x 4 Stroke 6 Cy. 320 x 480 2641kW (3591bhp) MaK Motoren GmbH & Co. KG-Kiel AuxGen: 2 x 350kW a.c, 1 x 128kW a.c Thrusters: 1 Thwart. FP thruster (f)
9251743 ECCA	**VULCANO M** - **Mednav International SL** Augusta Due Srl SatCom: Inmarsat C 422449020 *Santa Cruz de Tenerife* *Spain (CSR)* MMSI: 224490000 Official number: 01/2003	**13,740** 6,479 21,297 T/cm 32.6	Class: RI (LR) (AB) ✠ Classed LR until 5/5/08	**2004**-02 **Factorias Vulcano SA — Vigo** Yd No: 478 Loa 161.12 (BB) Br ex 23.25 Dght 9.500 Lbp 149.80 Br md 23.00 Dpth 13.40 Welded, 1 dk	**(A12B2TR) Chemical/Products Tanker** Double Hull (13F) Liq: 24,086; Liq (Oil): 24,667 Compartments: 14 Wing Ta, 2 Wing Slop Ta, ER 14 Cargo Pump (s): 14x300m³/hr Manifold: Bow/CM: 80m Ice Capable	**1 oil engine** with clutches, flexible couplings & sr reverse geared to sc. shaft driving 1 CP propeller Total Power: 8,100kW (11,013hp) 15.0kn MaK 9M43 1 x 4 Stroke 9 Cy. 430 x 610 8100kW (11013bhp) Caterpillar Motoren GmbH & Co. KG-Germany AuxGen: 1 x 1360kW 450V 60Hz a.c, 3 x 900kW 450V 60Hz a.c Boilers: TOH (o.f.) 10.2kgf/cm² (10.0bar), TOH (ex.g.) 10.2kgf/cm² (10.0bar) Thrusters: 1 Thwart. CP thruster (f)
8108004 - -	**VULCANO TIDE** *ex* Vulcano *-2007* *ex* Gulf Fleet No. 47 *-1995* **Gulf Fleet Supply Vessels LLC** Tidewater Marine LLC	**741** 222 898	Class: AB	**1982**-02 **Quality Shipyards Inc — Houma LA** Yd No: 173 Loa 57.92 Br ex - Dght 3.658 Lbp 51.72 Br md 12.20 Dpth 4.27 Welded, 1 dk	**(B21B20A) Anchor Handling Tug Supply** Passengers: berths: 12	**2 oil engines** reverse reduction geared to sc. shafts driving 2 FP propellers Total Power: 2,868kW (3,900hp) 13.0kn EMD (Electro-Motive) 16-567-BC 2 x Vee 2 Stroke 16 Cy. 216 x 254 each-1434kW (1950bhp) (Reconditioned , Reconditioned & fitted 1982) General Motors Corp.Electro-Motive Div.-La Grange AuxGen: 2 x 99kW 440V 60Hz a.c Thrusters: 1 Thwart. FP thruster (f) Fuel: 310.0 (d.f.) 14.0pd
7331408 HO4076 -	**VULCANUS** *ex* Kursant *-2005* *ex* Vostochniy *-2002* *ex* Eastern No. 801 *-1995* *ex* Chiyo Maru No. 37 *-1988* **Neptune International Lines SA** - *Panama* *Panama* MMSI: 371366000 Official number: 33555PEXT	**380** 120 296	Class: (RS)	**1973**-07 **Niigata Engineering Co Ltd — Niigata NI** Yd No: 1238 Loa 45.62 (BB) Br ex 7.93 Dght 3.150 Lbp 40.19 Br md 7.90 Dpth 3.51 Welded, 1 dk	**(B11B2FV) Fishing Vessel**	**1 oil engine** driving 1 CP propeller Total Power: 683kW (929hp) 10.0kn Niigata 6M28DHS 1 x 4 Stroke 6 Cy. 280 x 440 683kW (929bhp) Niigata Engineering Co Ltd-Japan AuxGen: 1 x 330kW a.c, 1 x 220kW a.c Fuel: 174.0 (d.f.)
5384085 JXDR -	**VULCANUS** - **Bukser og Berging AS** - *Bergen* *Norway* MMSI: 257085600	**142** 42 -	Class: (NV)	**1959 Bolsones Verft AS — Molde** Yd No: 169 Loa 27.89 Br ex 7.04 Dght - Lbp 24.49 Br md 7.01 Dpth 3.66 Welded, 1 dk	**(B32A2ST) Tug**	**1 oil engine** driving 1 FP propeller Total Power: 706kW (960hp) Alpha 498-VO 1 x 2 Stroke 8 Cy. 290 x 490 706kW (960bhp) Alpha Diesel A/S-Denmark AuxGen: 1 x 40kW 220V d.c, 2 x 22kW 220V d.c Fuel: 31.5 (d.f.) 4.5pd
7644594 UDSY -	**VULKAN** *ex* Wulkan *-2003* **OOO 'YevroTek-Universal'** - *Novorossiysk* *Russia*	**177** 53 46	Class: RS (PR)	**1976 Gorokhovetskiy Sudostroitelnyy Zavod — Gorokhovets** Loa 29.37 Br ex 8.31 Dght 3.090 Lbp 27.71 Br md - Dpth 4.30 Welded, 1 dk	**(B32A2ST) Tug** Ice Capable	**2 oil engines** driving 2 FP propellers Total Power: 882kW (1,200hp) 10.5kn Russkiy 6D30/50-4-3 2 x 2 Stroke 6 Cy. 300 x 500 each-441kW (600bhp) Mashinostroitelnyy Zavod"Russkiy-Dizel"-Leningrad AuxGen: 2 x 25kW 230V a.c Fuel: 36.0 (d.f.)
9102502 A8KM5 -	**VULKAN** *ex* Emirates Mekong *-2012* *ex* Vulkan *-2011* *ex* MOL Springbok *-2008* *ex* Vulkan *-2006* *ex* Marfret Caraibes *-2005* *ex* CMA CGM Karukera *-2004* *ex* Vulkan *-2001* *ex* CMA CGM Karukera *-2001* *ex* Vulkan *-2001* *ex* Cap York *-2000* *ex* Vulkan *-1999* *ex* CSAV Rengo *-1999* *ex* Vulkan *-1996* **ms 'Vulkan' Schiffahrtsgesellschaft mbH & Co KG** MCC Transport Singapore Pte Ltd *Monrovia* *Liberia* MMSI: 636091192 Official number: 91192	**16,800** 8,672 22,982 T/cm 37.1	Class: GL	**1996**-03 **Stocznia Szczecinska SA — Szczecin** Yd No: B170/1/4 Loa 184.00 (BB) Br ex - Dght 9.880 Lbp 171.94 Br md 25.30 Dpth 13.50 Welded, 1 dk	**(A33A2CC) Container Ship (Fully Cellular)** Grain: 29,744 TEU 1728 C Ho 634 TEU C Dk 1096 TEU incl 200 ref C. Compartments: 4 Cell Ho, ER 9 Ha: (12.5 x 13.0)8 (12.5 x 20.6)ER Cranes: 3x40t	**1 oil engine** driving 1 FP propeller Total Power: 13,320kW (18,110hp) 19.0kn Sulzer 6RTA62U 1 x 2 Stroke 6 Cy. 620 x 2150 13320kW (18110bhp) H Cegielski Poznan SA-Poland AuxGen: 3 x 1232kW Thrusters: 1 Tunnel thruster (f) Fuel: 165.0 (d.f.) 2184.0 (r.f.)
7391288 UDRR -	**VULKAN KSUDACH** *ex* Claymore Sea *-2004* *ex* Scotoil 3 *-1979* *ex* Theriot Offshore III *-1977* **JSC 'Roliz'** - SatCom: Inmarsat A 1413261 *Vostochnyy* *Russia* MMSI: 273817400 Official number: 810300	**3,072** 921 1,747	Class: RS (NV) (AB)	**1974**-09 **Todd Pacific Shipyards Corp. — Seattle, Wa** Yd No: 60 Converted From: Offshore Tug/Supply Ship-1988 Loa 72.50 Br ex 17.07 Dght 6.600 Lbp 64.08 Br md 17.07 Dpth 8.17 Welded, 1 dk	**(B11A2FG) Factory Stern Trawler** Ice Capable	**2 oil engines** driving 2 FP propellers Total Power: 4,236kW (5,760hp) Normo KVMB-12 2 x Vee 4 Stroke 12 Cy. 250 x 300 each-2118kW (2880bhp) (new engine 1988) Bergen Diesel AS-Norway AuxGen: 2 x 1200kW 440V 60Hz a.c, 2 x 257kW 440V 60Hz a.c Thrusters: 1 Thwart. FP thruster (f) Fuel: 815.0 (d.f.)
7302380 UBGS -	**VULKANNYY** *ex* Raudinupur *-1997* **Dalkrevetka Co Ltd** - SatCom: Inmarsat M 627331810 *Nevelsk* *Russia* MMSI: 273893400	**641** 192 372	Class: RS (LR) ✠ Classed LR until 24/7/97	**1973**-02 **Niigata Engineering Co Ltd — Niigata NI** Yd No: 1163 Loa 47.05 Br ex 9.66 Dght 4.566 Lbp 41.00 Br md 9.50 Dpth 6.51 Welded, 2 dks	**(B11A2FS) Stern Trawler** Ice Capable	**1 oil engine** with clutches, flexible couplings & sr geared to sc. shaft driving 1 CP propeller Total Power: 2,200kW (2,991hp) MaK 6M453AK 1 x 4 Stroke 6 Cy. 320 x 420 2200kW (2991bhp) (new engine 1993) Krupp MaK Maschinenbau GmbH-Kiel AuxGen: 1 x 400kW 380V 50Hz a.c, 1 x 200kW 380V 50Hz a.c
7642778 - -	**VULKANOLOG** - - -	**732** 219 364	Class: (RS)	**1976**-03 **Khabarovskiy Sudostroitelnyy Zavod im Kirova — Khabarovsk** Yd No: 701 Loa 55.66 Br ex 9.53 Dght 4.171 Lbp 49.94 Br md - Dpth 5.19 Welded, 1 dk	**(B31A2SR) Research Survey Vessel** Bale: 57 Compartments: 1 Ho, ER 1 Ha: (1.9 x 1.9) Derricks: 2x2.5t Ice Capable	**1 oil engine** driving 1 CP propeller Total Power: 736kW (1,001hp) 12.0kn S.K.L. 6NVD48A-2U 1 x 4 Stroke 6 Cy. 320 x 480 736kW (1001bhp) VEB Schwermaschinenbau "KarlLiebknecht" (SKL)-Magdeburg AuxGen: 3 x 150kW Fuel: 178.0 (d.f.)
9583691 HBDY	**VULLY** - **Oceana Shipping AG** Suisse-Atlantique Societe de Navigation Maritime SA *Basel* *Switzerland* MMSI: 269144000 Official number: 203	**22,697** 11,603 34,000 T/cm 48.5	Class: BV (NV)	**2011**-06 **Shinan Heavy Industries Co Ltd — Jido** Yd No: H1008 Loa 181.10 (BB) Br ex - Dght 9.800 Lbp 172.00 Br md 30.00 Dpth 14.60 Welded, 1 dk	**(A21A2BC) Bulk Carrier** Grain: 47,090; Bale: 44,435 Compartments: 5 Ho, ER 5 Ha: 4 (19.2 x 19.2)ER (16.8 x 15.0) Cranes: 4x30t	**1 oil engine** driving 1 FP propeller Total Power: 8,580kW (11,665hp) 13.9kn MAN-B&W 6S50MC 1 x 2 Stroke 6 Cy. 500 x 1910 8580kW (11665bhp) Hyundai Heavy Industries Co Ltd-South Korea AuxGen: 3 x 600kW 60Hz a.c

7407336 *C9QA* -
VUMBA
ex Ifcor I *-1978*
Bonar
-
Maputo *Mozambique*
109 74 -
Class: (AB)
1975-01 Sandock-Austral Ltd. — Durban Yd No: 62
Loa 22.89 Br ex 6.48 Dght 2.464
Lbp 20.73 Br md 6.38 Dpth 3.33
Welded, 1 dk
(B11A2FT) Trawler
1 oil engine reverse reduction geared to sc. shaft driving 1 FP propeller
Total Power: 313kW (426hp) 8.5kn
Caterpillar D353SCAC
1 x 4 Stroke 6 Cy. 159 x 203 313kW (426bhp)
Caterpillar Tractor Co-USA
AuxGen: 2 x 20kW a.c
Fuel: 26.5 (d.f.)

8111104 *ZR6878* -
VUNA ELITA
ex Harvest Elita *-2003*
launched as Eiranova Dos *-1983*
Vuna Fishing Co Pty Ltd
-
Cape Town *South Africa*
MMSI: 601671000
Official number: 350931
361 108 248
Class: (LR) (BV)
✠ Classed LR until 2/12/93
1983-01 Construcciones Navales Santodomingo SA — Vigo Yd No: 472
Loa 37.98 Br ex 8.34 Dght 3.661
Lbp 33.46 Br md 8.31 Dpth 5.85
Welded, 2 dks
(B11A2FS) Stern Trawler
Ins: 296
Compartments: 1 Ho, ER
1 Ha: ER
1 oil engine with flexible couplings & sr gearedto sc. shaft driving 1 CP propeller
Total Power: 1,200kW (1,632hp) 10.5kn
MaK 6M332AK
1 x 4 Stroke 6 Cy. 240 x 330 1200kW (1632bhp)
Krupp MaK Maschinenbau GmbH-Kiel
AuxGen: 2 x 93kW 380V 50Hz a.c
Fuel: 54.5 (d.f.) 96.5 (r.f.) 3.5pd

9024504 - -
VUNG ANG 01
-
Ha Tinh Port
-
Haiphong *Vietnam*
148 44 4
Class: VR
2002-10 Ben Thuy Shipyard — Nghi Xuan
Loa 27.10 Br ex 7.62 Dght 2.800
Lbp 24.48 Br md 7.60 Dpth -
Welded, 1 dk
(B32A2ST) Tug
2 oil engines geared to sc. shafts driving 2 Propellers
Total Power: 1,324kW (1,800hp) 10.5kn
Caterpillar 3508
2 x Vee 4 Stroke 8 Cy. 170 x 190 each-662kW (900bhp)
Caterpillar Inc-USA

8910823 *3WHA* -
VUNG TAI PETRO 09
ex Minh Phu 09 *-2012* *ex* Thanh Cong *-2007*
ex Hokai Maru No. 3 *-2007*
Vung Tau Petro JSC (Cong Ty Co Phan Dau Khi Vung Tau)
-
Saigon *Vietnam*
Official number: VNSG-138A-TH
1,005 735 1,850
Class: VR
1989-07 Murakami Hide Zosen K.K. — Imabari Yd No: 300
Converted From: Products Tanker-2006
Loa 69.98 Br ex 12.01 Dght 4.652
Lbp 66.02 Br md 11.99 Dpth 5.31
Welded, 1 dk
(A12D2LV) Vegetable Oil Tanker
Liq: 2,110; Liq (Oil): 2,110
1 oil engine geared to sc. shaft driving 1 FP propeller
Total Power: 1,030kW (1,400hp) 11.5kn
Hanshin LH28G
1 x 4 Stroke 6 Cy. 280 x 460 1030kW (1400bhp)
The Hanshin Diesel Works Ltd-Japan
AuxGen: 2 x 120kW a.c, 1 x 35kW a.c

9532862 *XVCH* -
VUNG TAU 02
ex Jaya Chancellor *-2010*
Joint Venture 'VIETSOVPETRO'
-
Saigon *Vietnam*
MMSI: 574000030
Official number: VNSG-1997-DV
2,342 702 2,586
Class: AB
2009-12 P.T. Jaya Asiatic Shipyard — Batam Yd No: H872B
Loa 70.05 Br ex - Dght 6.100
Lbp 63.00 Br md 16.00 Dpth 7.20
Welded, 1 dk
(B21B20A) Anchor Handling Tug Supply
2 oil engines reduction geared to sc. shafts driving 2 CP propellers
Total Power: 6,000kW (8,158hp) 10.0kn
Wartsila 6L32
2 x 4 Stroke 6 Cy. 320 x 400 each-3000kW (4079bhp)
Wartsila Italia SpA-Italy
AuxGen: 2 x 1800kW 440V 60Hz a.c, 2 x 370kW 440V 60Hz a.c
Thrusters: 2 Tunnel thruster (f); 1 Tunnel thruster (a)
Fuel: 965.0

9550228 *3WZU* -
VUNG TAU 03
ex Posh Vista *-2010*
Joint Venture 'VIETSOVPETRO'
-
Saigon *Vietnam*
MMSI: 574828000
Official number: VNSG-1998-DV
2,538 761 2,594
Class: AB VR
2009-11 Yuexin Shipbuilding Co Ltd — Guangzhou GD Yd No: 3095
Loa 69.90 Br ex - Dght 5.900
Lbp 61.20 Br md 16.60 Dpth 7.20
Welded, 1 dk
(B21B20T) Offshore Tug/Supply Ship
Cranes: 1x5t
2 oil engines reduction geared to sc. shafts driving 2 CP propellers
Total Power: 5,840kW (7,940hp) 12.5kn
MAN-B&W 8L27/38
2 x 4 Stroke 8 Cy. 270 x 380 each-2920kW (3970bhp)
MAN Diesel A/S-Denmark
AuxGen: 2 x 1200kW 440V 60Hz a.c, 2 x 317kW 440V 60Hz a.c
Thrusters: 2 Thwart. CP thruster (f); 1 Thwart. CP thruster (a)

9017680 *3WZQ* -
VUNGTAU 01
ex Vung Tau 01 *-2012*
Joint Venture 'VIETSOVPETRO'
-
SatCom: Inmarsat C 457407710
Saigon *Vietnam*
MMSI: 574077067
Official number: VNSG-1312H-TH
1,599 545 1,897
Class: NV (VR)
1991-09 Daedong Shipbuilding Co Ltd — Busan Yd No: 366
Loa 66.50 (BB) Br ex - Dght 6.371
Lbp 56.40 Br md 14.50 Dpth 7.40
Welded, 2 dks
(B21B20A) Anchor Handling Tug Supply
2 oil engines with flexible couplings & sr reverse geared to sc. shafts driving 2 CP propellers
Total Power: 9,834kW (13,370hp) 11.0kn
Wartsila 12V32E
2 x Vee 4 Stroke 12 Cy. 320 x 350 each-4917kW (6685bhp)
Wartsila Diesel Oy-Finland
AuxGen: 2 x 1280kW 380V 50Hz a.c, 2 x 226kW 380V 50Hz a.c
Thrusters: 2 Thwart. CP thruster (f); 1 Tunnel thruster (a)

9633692 *3DPK* -
VUNILAGI
completed as Capricorn 88 *-2014*
Government of The Republic of The Fiji Islands (Government Shipping Service - Ministry of Works, Transport & Public Utilities)
-
Suva *Fiji*
Official number: 001554
489 147 413
Class: NK
2014-04 Capricorn Central Shipbuilding Sdn Bhd — Sibu Yd No: 033
Loa 45.50 Br ex - Dght 2.412
Lbp - Br md 10.90 Dpth 3.20
Welded, 1 dk
(A35D2RL) Landing Craft
2 oil engines reduction geared to sc. shafts driving 2 Propellers

---

8330712 *UCFJ* MI-1550
VUTAN
Energiya Fishing Collective (Rybolovetskiy Kolkhoz 'Energiya')
-
Murmansk *Russia*
MMSI: 273516000
Official number: 842782
737 221 414
Class: RS
1985-01 Zavod "Leninskaya Kuznitsa" — Kiyev Yd No: 1550
Loa 54.82 Br ex 9.95 Dght 4.141
Lbp 50.30 Br md 9.80 Dpth 5.00
Welded, 1 dk
(B11A2FS) Stern Trawler
1 oil engine driving 1 CP propeller
Total Power: 852kW (1,158hp) 12.0kn
S.K.L. 8NVD48A-2U
1 x 4 Stroke 8 Cy. 320 x 480 852kW (1158bhp)
VEB Schwermaschinenbau "KarlLiebknecht" (SKL)-Magdeburg
AuxGen: 4 x 160kW a.c
Fuel: 180.0 (d.f.)

1009211 *ZME3545* -
VVS1
-
VvS1 (NZ) Ltd
-
Auckland *New Zealand*
MMSI: 512204000
Official number: 876493
281 84 -
Class: LR
✠ **100A1** SS 05/2012
SSC
Yacht, mono, G6
LMC Cable: 240.0/12.0 U2 (a)
2007-05 Alloy Yachts — Auckland Yd No: 35
Loa 34.18 (BB) Br ex 7.78 Dght 2.450
Lbp 29.03 Br md 7.72 Dpth 3.98
Welded, 1 dk
(X11A2YP) Yacht
Hull Material: Aluminium Alloy
2 oil engines with clutches, flexible couplings & reverse reduction geared to sc. shafts driving 2 FP propellers
Total Power: 708kW (962hp) 11.0kn
Caterpillar 3406E-TA
2 x 4 Stroke 6 Cy. 137 x 165 each-354kW (481bhp)
Caterpillar Inc-USA
AuxGen: 2 x 51kW 400V 50Hz a.c
Thrusters: 1 Thwart. FP thruster (f); 1 Thwart. FP thruster (a)

7337725 *UZHD* -
VYACHESLAV ILYIN
ex Nikolay Morozov *-2005*
Government of The Republic of Ukraine
SRZ Ltd
SatCom: Inmarsat C 427285510
Mariupol *Ukraine*
MMSI: 272855000
Official number: 731594
6,635 3,370 8,455
Class: UA (RS)
1973-03 Vyborgskiy Sudostroitelnyy Zavod — Vyborg Yd No: 702
Loa 136.81 (BB) Br ex 17.84 Dght 7.900
Lbp 126.59 Br md 17.73 Dpth 10.44
Welded, 2 dks
(A31A2GX) General Cargo Ship
Grain: 11,350; Bale: 10,650; Liq: 300
TEU 229 C. 229/20'
Compartments: 1 Dp Ta in Hold, 4 Ho, ER, 4 Tw Dk
4 Ha: (9.7 x 8.0)3 (18.9 x 12.8)ER
Derricks: 2x40t,2x20t; Winches: 16
Ice Capable
1 oil engine driving 1 FP propeller
Total Power: 4,928kW (6,700hp) 16.5kn
B&W 5K62EF
1 x 2 Stroke 5 Cy. 620 x 1400 4928kW (6700bhp)
Bryanskiy Mashinostroitelnyy Zavod (BMZ)-Bryansk
AuxGen: 3 x 240kW 400V 50Hz a.c
Fuel: 160.0 (d.f.) 880.0 (r.f.)

9538115 *UBSH6* -
VYACHESLAV TIKHONOV
ex Polarcus Selma *-2011*
Polarcus Selma Ltd
SCF Novoship JSC (Novorossiysk Shipping Co)
Novorossiysk *Russia*
MMSI: 273350140
4,711 1,414 2,250
Class: NV RS
2011-08 Drydocks World - Dubai LLC — Dubai Yd No: 70
Loa 84.20 Br ex - Dght 6.000
Lbp 80.81 Br md 17.00 Dpth 7.50
Welded, 1 dk
(B31A2SR) Research Survey Vessel
Cranes: 1
Ice Capable
4 diesel electric oil engines driving 4 gen. Connecting to 2 elec. motors each (4800kW) driving 2 CP propellers
Total Power: 11,400kW (15,500hp)
Wartsila 9L26
4 x 4 Stroke 9 Cy. 260 x 320 each-2850kW (3875bhp)
Wartsila Finland Oy-Finland
Thrusters: 1 Tunnel thruster (f); 1 Retract. directional thruster (f); 1 Tunnel thruster (a)
Fuel: 1029.0

8226648 - -
VYARSKA
ex Varska *-1996* *ex* Abruka *-1992*
-
-
191 86 323
Class: (RS)
1983 Svetlovskiy Sudoremontnyy Zavod — Svetlyy Yd No: 17
Loa 29.44 Br ex 8.15 Dght 3.120
Lbp 28.50 Br md 7.60 Dpth 3.61
Welded, 1 dk
(B34G2SE) Pollution Control Vessel
Ice Capable
1 oil engine geared to sc. shaft driving 1 FP propeller
Total Power: 165kW (224hp) 7.5kn
Daldizel 6CHNSP18/22
1 x 4 Stroke 6 Cy. 180 x 220 165kW (224bhp)
Daldizel-Khabarovsk
AuxGen: 1 x 50kW, 1 x 25kW
Fuel: 11.0 (d.f.)

8216411 *VTXY* -
VYAS
ex Seaspan I *-2006* *ex* Amirah *-1997*
ARC Marine Pvt Ltd
-
Mumbai *India*
MMSI: 419003500
Official number: 2612
157 47 127
Class: IR (AB)
1984-05 Halter Marine, Inc. — Chalmette, La Yd No: 1075
Loa 34.13 Br ex - Dght -
Lbp 30.48 Br md 7.62 Dpth 3.20
Welded, 1 dk
(B34J2SD) Crew Boat
4 oil engines reverse reduction geared to sc. shafts driving 4 FP propellers
Total Power: 1,472kW (2,000hp) 21.7kn
G.M. (Detroit Diesel) 12V-71
4 x Vee 2 Stroke 12 Cy. 108 x 127 each-368kW (500bhp)
General Motors Detroit DieselAllison Divn-USA
AuxGen: 2 x 20kW 440V 60Hz a.c
Fuel: 23.0 (d.f.)

9332664 *UBAG9* -	**VYATICH** **JSC 'Sovfracht-Primorsk'** *St Petersburg* *Russia* MMSI: 273434680	**272** 81 151	Class: RS	**2004-11 OAO Leningradskiy Sudostroitelnyy Zavod 'Pella' — Otradnoye** Yd No: 602 Loa 28.50 Br ex 9.50 Dght 3.500 Lbp 26.66 Br md 9.28 Dpth 4.80 Welded, 1 dk	**(B32A2ST) Tug** Ice Capable	**2 oil engines** reduction geared to sc. shafts driving 2 Z propellers Total Power: 2,610kW (3,548hp) 12.0kn Caterpillar 3512B-HD 2 x Vee 4 Stroke 12 Cy. 170 x 215 each-1305kW (1774bhp) Caterpillar Inc-USA AuxGen: 2 x 80kW a.c
7042100 *UCPF* -	**VYBORG** *ex Arm II -2000 ex Vyborg -1997* **Real Estate Management Committee of St Petersburg City Executive Board** State Unitary Enterprise Baltic Basin Emergency-Rescue Management (FGUP Baltiyskoye Basseynoye Avariyno-Spasatelnoye Upravleniye) (Baltic BASU) *St Petersburg* *Russia* Official number: 704192	**226** 68 71	Class: (RS)	**1970 VEB Schiffswerft "Edgar Andre" — Magdeburg** Yd No: 7031 Loa 34.78 Br ex 8.51 Dght 2.840 Lbp 30.41 Br md 8.21 Dpth 3.71 Welded, 1 dk	**(B32A2ST) Tug** Ice Capable	**1 oil engine** driving 1 CP propeller Total Power: 640kW (870hp) 10.5kn S.K.L. 6NVD48A-2U 1 x 4 Stroke 6 Cy. 320 x 480 640kW (870bhp) VEB Schwermaschinenbau "KarlLiebknecht" (SKL)-Magdeburg AuxGen: 2 x 55kW Fuel: 56.0 (d.f.)
8723270 *UFVQ* -	**VYBORGSKIY** **Loran Co Ltd** *St Petersburg* *Russia* MMSI: 273252100	**2,416** 724 1,194	Class: RS	**1988-10 Sudostroitelnyy Zavod "Baltiya" — Klaypeda** Yd No: 526 Loa 85.10 Br ex 13.04 Dght 4.190 Lbp 76.80 Br md - Dpth 6.50 Welded, 1 dk	**(B12A2FF) Fish Factory Ship** Ins: 1,245 Ice Capable	**1 oil engine** driving 1 FP propeller Total Power: 852kW (1,158hp) 11.3kn S.K.L. 8NVD48A-2U 1 x 4 Stroke 8 Cy. 320 x 480 852kW (1158bhp) VEB Schwermaschinenbau "KarlLiebknecht" (SKL)-Magdeburg AuxGen: 2 x 320kW a.c, 1 x 150kW a.c
9055187 *3FBA8* -	**VYG** **Baltasar Shipping SA** Orion Shipping Co *Panama* *Panama* MMSI: 370601000 Official number: 4132610	**1,598** 834 2,300	Class: RS	**1992-12 Arminius Werke GmbH — Bodenwerder** Yd No: 10523 Loa 81.34 Br ex 11.38 Dght 4.220 Lbp 77.40 Br md 11.30 Dpth 5.40 Welded, 1 dk	**(A31A2GX) General Cargo Ship** Grain: 2,823; Bale: 2,777 TEU 72 C.Ho 48/20' C.Dk 24/20' Compartments: 1 Ho, ER 1 Ha: (50.4 x 9.0)ER Ice Capable	**1 oil engine** with flexible couplings & sr reverse geared to sc. shaft driving 1 FP propeller Total Power: 1,100kW (1,496hp) 11.0kn MaK 6M332AK 1 x 4 Stroke 6 Cy. 240 x 330 1100kW (1496bhp) Krupp MaK Maschinenbau GmbH-Kiel AuxGen: 2 x 467kW 400V 50Hz a.c Thrusters: 1 Thwart. FP thruster (f) Fuel: 91.9 (d.f.) 5.4pd
6925446 *UUAO6* -	**VYKTORY** *ex Sveasund -2009 ex Jade -1993* **ChKB Trans Ochakov** - SatCom: Inmarsat C 427257710 *Ukraine* MMSI: 272577000	**151** 45 48	Class: (GL)	**1969-09 Elsflether Werft AG — Elsfleth** Yd No: 369 Loa 26.01 Br ex 7.62 Dght 3.610 Lbp 23.02 Br md 7.60 Dpth 3.65 Welded, 1 dk	**(B32A2ST) Tug** Ice Capable	**1 oil engine** reverse reduction geared to sc. shaft driving 1 FP propeller Total Power: 971kW (1,320hp) 12.0kn Deutz SBV8M545 1 x 4 Stroke 8 Cy. 320 x 450 971kW (1320bhp) Kloeckner Humboldt Deutz AG-West Germany AuxGen: 3 x 56kW 380V 50Hz a.c Fuel: 37.0 (d.f.)
8929915 - -	**VYMPEL** **Zaliv Shipyard (SSZ 'Zaliv')** - *Kerch* *Ukraine* Official number: 730271	*187* - 46	Class: (RS)	**1973 Gorokhovetskiy Sudostroitelnyy Zavod — Gorokhovets** Yd No: 309 Loa 29.30 Br ex 8.49 Dght 3.090 Lbp 27.00 Br md - Dpth 4.35 Welded, 1 dk	**(B32A2ST) Tug** Ice Capable	**2 oil engines** driving 2 CP propellers Total Power: 882kW (1,200hp) 11.4kn Russkiy 6D30/50-4-2 2 x 2 Stroke 6 Cy. 300 x 500 each-441kW (600bhp) Mashinostroitelnyy Zavod"Russkiy-Dizel"-Leningrad AuxGen: 2 x 25kW a.c Fuel: 43.0 (d.f.)
8136350 - -	**VYNOSLIVYY** **Pacific Ocean Fishing Co Ltd (OOO 'Tikhookeanskaya Rybopromyshlennaya Kompaniya')** -	**448** 134 207	Class: (RS)	**1983-06 Zavod 'Nikolayevsk-na-Amure' — Nikolayevsk-na-Amure** Yd No: 1217 Loa 44.89 Br ex 9.48 Dght 3.771 Lbp 39.37 Br md - Dpth 5.11 Welded, 1 dk	**(B11B2FV) Fishing Vessel** Ice Capable	**1 oil engine** driving 1 FP propeller Total Power: 588kW (799hp) 11.5kn S.K.L. 6NVD48A-2U 1 x 4 Stroke 6 Cy. 320 x 480 588kW (799bhp) VEB Schwermaschinenbau "KarlLiebknecht" (SKL)-Magdeburg AuxGen: 3 x 150kW Fuel: 92.0 (d.f.)
9444766 *AUPU* -	**VYPEEN** **Cochin Port Trust** - *Kochi* *India* MMSI: 419073200 Official number: 3305	**449** 135 122	Class: IR	**2009-08 Tebma Shipyards Ltd — Chengalpattu** Yd No: 126 Loa 32.00 Br ex 11.41 Dght 5.290 Lbp 29.80 Br md 10.65 Dpth - Welded, 1 dk	**(B32A2ST) Tug**	**2 oil engines** reduction geared to sc. shafts driving 2 Voith-Schneider propellers Total Power: 3,240kW (4,406hp) 13.0kn Wartsila 9L20 2 x 4 Stroke 9 Cy. 200 x 280 each-1620kW (2203bhp) Wartsila Finland Oy-Finland
9459371 *ONGJ* -	**VYRITSA** **SBM-2 Inc** Sobelmar Antwerp NV *Antwerpen* *Belgium* MMSI: 205568000 Official number: 02 00023 2010	**22,402** 12,019 35,314 T/cm 46.5	Class: BV	**2010-06 Nanjing Dongze Shipyard Co Ltd — Nanjing JS** Yd No: 06H-04 Loa 179.90 (BB) Br ex - Dght 10.800 Lbp 171.50 Br md 28.40 Dpth 15.00 Welded, 1 dk	**(A21A2BC) Bulk Carrier** Grain: 44,294 Compartments: 5 Ho, ER 5 Ha: ER Cranes: 4x30.5t	**1 oil engine** driving 1 FP propeller Total Power: 6,480kW (8,810hp) 13.7kn MAN-B&W 6S42MC 1 x 2 Stroke 6 Cy. 420 x 1764 6480kW (8810bhp) Yichang Marine Diesel Engine Co Ltd-China AuxGen: 3 x 465kW 60Hz a.c
7630581 - -	**VYSHEGORSK** **Kit Co Ltd** -	**172** 51 89	Class: (RS)	**1976-08 Sretenskiy Sudostroitelnyy Zavod — Sretensk** Yd No: 92 Loa 33.96 Br ex 7.09 Dght 2.899 Lbp 30.00 Br md - Dpth 3.69 Welded, 1 dk	**(B11B2FV) Fishing Vessel** Bale: 96 Compartments: 1 Ho, ER 1 Ha: (1.6 x 1.3) Derricks: 2x2t; Winches: 2 Ice Capable	**1 oil engine** driving 1 FP propeller Total Power: 224kW (305hp) 9.0kn S.K.L. 8NVD36-1U 1 x 4 Stroke 8 Cy. 240 x 360 224kW (305bhp) VEB Schwermaschinenbau "KarlLiebknecht" (SKL)-Magdeburg AuxGen: 1 x 86kW, 1 x 60kW, 1 x 32kW Fuel: 23.0 (d.f.)
8328771 *UGQF* -	**VYSOKOGORNYY** **OOO 'Tsentr Pribrezhnogo Rybolovstva Ostrovnoy' (LLC Center of Offshore Fisheries 'Ostrovnoy')** - *Nevelsk* *Russia* MMSI: 273896310	**677** 233 495	Class: RS	**1984 Khabarovskiy Sudostroitelnyy Zavod im Kirova — Khabarovsk** Yd No: 848 Loa 55.02 Br ex 9.53 Dght 4.341 Lbp 50.04 Br md - Dpth 5.19 Welded, 1 dk	**(B12B2FC) Fish Carrier** Ins: 632	**1 oil engine** driving 1 FP propeller Total Power: 588kW (799hp) 11.3kn S.K.L. 6NVD48A-2U 1 x 4 Stroke 6 Cy. 320 x 480 588kW (799bhp) VEB Schwermaschinenbau "KarlLiebknecht" (SKL)-Magdeburg AuxGen: 3 x 150kW Fuel: 109.0 (d.f.)
8711289 *YJRC4* -	**VYSOKOGORSK** *ex Fesco Vysokogorsk -2013* *ex Vysokogorsk -2011* **Haddon Advisers Corp** Brouns Maritime Ltd *Port Vila* *Vanuatu* MMSI: 576291000 Official number: 2041	**7,095** 2,936 7,365 T/cm 20.2	Class: (RS)	**1991-03 Ast. Reunidos del Nervion S.A. — Bilbao** Yd No: 561 Loa 132.71 Br ex 19.86 Dght 6.880 Lbp 122.06 Br md - Dpth 8.80 Welded, 1 dk	**(A31A2GX) General Cargo Ship** Grain: 10,600; Bale: 10,022 TEU 318 Compartments: 4 Ho, ER 4 Ha: (12.6 x 10.2) (19.2 x 15.4)2 (18.8 x 15.4)ER Cranes: 4x20t Ice Capable	**1 oil engine** driving 1 CP propeller Total Power: 5,119kW (6,960hp) 15.5kn B&W 6L42MC 1 x 2 Stroke 6 Cy. 420 x 1360 5119kW (6960bhp) Bryanskiy Mashinostroitelnyy Zavod (BMZ)-Bryansk AuxGen: 2 x 440kW 380V 50Hz a.c, 1 x 400kW 380V 50Hz a.c
8723567 - -	**VYUGA** **Vanino Marine Trading Port JSC (Vaninskiy Morskoy Torgovyy Port OAO)** -	**106** 32 14	Class: (RS)	**1986-10 Zavod "Krasnyy Moryak" — Rostov-na-Donu** Yd No: 24 Loa 23.15 Br ex 6.24 Dght 1.850 Lbp 20.00 Br md - Dpth 2.80 Welded, 1 dk	**(A37B2PS) Passenger Ship** Passengers: unberthed: 70 Ice Capable	**1 oil engine** geared to sc. shaft driving 1 FP propeller Total Power: 221kW (300hp) 9.6kn Daldizel 6CHNSP18/22-300 1 x 4 Stroke 6 Cy. 180 x 220 221kW (300bhp) Daldizel-Khabarovsk AuxGen: 1 x 16kW Fuel: 6.0 (d.f.)
8728969 - -	**VYUGA** **Nikolayev Clay Works (Nikolayevskiy Glinozemnyy Zavod)** - *Nikolayev* *Ukraine* Official number: 875860	**270** 81 89	Class: (RS)	**1988-12 Brodogradiliste 'Tito' — Belgrade** Yd No: 1125 Loa 35.78 Br ex 9.49 Dght 3.280 Lbp 30.23 Br md - Dpth 4.50 Welded, 1 dk	**(B32A2ST) Tug** Ice Capable	**2 oil engines** driving 1 CP propeller Total Power: 1,854kW (2,520hp) 13.5kn Sulzer 6ASL25D 2 x 4 Stroke 6 Cy. 250 x 300 each-927kW (1260bhp) in Yugoslavia AuxGen: 1 x 150kW a.c

8858180 - -	**VYUGA** - **Government of The Russian Federation** - *St Petersburg* *Russia* Official number: 702958	*187* 56 46	Class: (RS)	**1970-12 "Petrozavod" — Leningrad** Yd No: 779 Loa 29.30 Br ex 8.62 Dght 3.090 Lbp 27.00 Br md - Dpth 4.35 Welded, 1 dk	**(B32A2ST) Tug** Ice Capable	**2 oil engines** driving 2 CP propellers Total Power: 882kW (1,200hp) 11.4kn Russkiy 6DR30/50-4-2 2 x 2 Stroke 6 Cy. 300 x 500 each-441kW (600bhp) Mashinostroitelnyy Zavod"Russkiy-Dizel"-Leningrad AuxGen: 2 x 25kW a.c
8935548 - -	**VYUZHNYY** - **Nerpa Shiprepairing Yard (SRZ 'Nerpa')** - *Murmansk* *Russia* Official number: 740254	*152* 58 163	Class: (RS)	**1974 Sudoremontnyy Zavod "Krasnaya Kuznitsa" — Arkhangelsk** Yd No: 17 Loa 35.75 Br ex 7.50 Dght 1.720 Lbp 33.55 Br md - Dpth 2.40 Welded, 1 dk	**(A31C2GD) Deck Cargo Ship** Ice Capable	**1 oil engine** geared to sc. shaft driving 1 FP propeller Total Power: 165kW (224hp) 7.8kn Daldizel 6CHNSP18/22 1 x 4 Stroke 6 Cy. 180 x 220 165kW (224bhp) Daldizel-Khabarovsk AuxGen: 2 x 12kW Fuel: 5.0 (d.f.)
7733838 - -	**VZMORYE** - **Angor Joint Stock Co (A/O 'Angor')** -	**172** 51 87	Class: (RS)	**1978-07 Sretenskiy Sudostroitelnyy Zavod — Sretensk** Yd No: 101 Loa 33.97 Br ex 7.09 Dght 2.901 Lbp 29.97 Br md 7.00 Dpth 3.65 Welded, 1 dk	**(B11B2FV) Fishing Vessel** Ins: 96 Compartments: 1 Ho, ER 1 Ha: (1.6 x 1.3) Derricks: 2x2t; Winches: 2 Ice Capable	**1 oil engine** driving 1 FP propeller Total Power: 224kW (305hp) 9.0kn S.K.L. 8NVD36-1U 1 x 4 Stroke 8 Cy. 240 x 360 224kW (305bhp) VEB Schwermaschinenbau "KarlLiebknecht" (SKL)-Magdeburg
9380192 *UDMZ* -	**VZMORYE** - **OOO 'Global-Flot'** - *Kaliningrad* *Russia* MMSI: 273318770	**1,788** 536 980	Class: RS	**2007-06 Keppel Singmarine Pte Ltd — Singapore** Yd No: 307 Loa 65.00 Br ex 15.00 Dght 4.304 Lbp 62.36 Br md 15.00 Dpth 6.20 Welded, 1 dk	**(B21B20A) Anchor Handling Tug Supply** Cranes: 1x12t Ice Capable	**2 oil engines** reduction geared to sc. shafts driving 2 CP propellers Total Power: 5,280kW (7,178hp) 13.0kn MaK 8M25 2 x 4 Stroke 8 Cy. 255 x 400 each-2640kW (3589bhp) Caterpillar Motoren GmbH & Co. KG-Germany AuxGen: 2 x 850kW a.c, 2 x 356kW a.c Thrusters: 1 Thwart. FP thruster (f) Fuel: 650.0 (d.f.)
9484687 *A8UX9* -	**W-ACE** - **Laibrook Shipholding Inc** W Marine Inc SatCom: Inmarsat C 463709693 *Monrovia* *Liberia* MMSI: 636014571 Official number: 14571	**51,239** 31,173 93,015 T/cm 80.9	Class: AB	**2011-06 Taizhou CATIC Shipbuilding Heavy Industry Ltd — Taizhou JS** Yd No: TK0204 Loa 229.20 (BB) Br ex - Dght 14.900 Lbp 222.00 Br md 38.00 Dpth 20.70 Welded, 1 dk	**(A21A2BC) Bulk Carrier** Grain: 110,330 Compartments: 7 Ho, ER 7 Ha: ER	**1 oil engine** driving 1 FP propeller Total Power: 13,560kW (18,436hp) 14.1kn MAN-B&W 6S60MC-C 1 x 2 Stroke 6 Cy. 600 x 2400 13560kW (18436bhp) Hyundai Heavy Industries Co Ltd-South Korea AuxGen: 3 x 700kW a.c Fuel: 300.0 (d.f.) 3550.0 (r.f.)
9069891 - -	**W. B. KALAPANI** - **Government of The Republic of India (Andaman & Nicobar Administration)** - *Port Blair* *India*	**315** 94 421	Class: (IR)	**2001-03 The Shalimar Works (1980) Ltd — Haora** Yd No: 759 Loa 41.00 Br ex - Dght - Lbp 38.00 Br md 8.00 Dpth 3.00 Welded, 1 dk	**(A14A2LO) Water Tanker** Single Hull Compartments: 4 Wing Ta	**1 oil engine** geared to sc. shaft driving 1 Propeller Cummins KT-1150-M 1 x 4 Stroke 6 Cy. 159 x 159 Cummins India Ltd-India
9542922 *T2KB4* -	**W.BLOSSOM** *ex Mount Jiuhua -2013 ex Ievoli Wind -2011* **Lyna Shipping Co Pte Ltd** Raffles Shipmanagement Services Pte Ltd *Funafuti* *Tuvalu* MMSI: 572571210 Official number: 28691113	**6,445** 2,914 9,119 T/cm 18.0	Class: BV NK (Class contemplated)	**2011-01 Dongfang Shipbuilding Group Co Ltd — Yueqing ZJ** Yd No: DF90-6 Loa 117.60 (BB) Br ex - Dght 7.500 Lbp 109.60 Br md 19.00 Dpth 10.00 Welded, 1 dk	**(A12B2TR) Chemical/Products Tanker** Double Hull (13F) Liq: 9,520; Liq (Oil): 9,520 Compartments: 10 Wing Ta, ER 20 Cargo Pump (s): 6x100m³/hr, 14x300m³/hr Manifold: Bow/CM: 56.3m	**1 oil engine** reduction geared to sc. shaft driving 1 FP propeller Total Power: 2,970kW (4,038hp) 13.0kn MaK 9M25C 1 x 4 Stroke 9 Cy. 255 x 400 2970kW (4038bhp) Caterpillar Motoren GmbH & Co. KG-Germany AuxGen: 3 x 520kW a.c Thrusters: 1 Tunnel thruster (f) Fuel: 20.0 (d.f.) 330.0 (r.f.)
9043835 *WBO8587* -	**W. C. PARK RESPONDER** *ex Washington Responder -2000* **Marine Spill Response Corp** - *Everett, WA* *United States of America* MMSI: 303436000 Official number: 983103	**1,335** 400 -	Class: AB	**1992-12 Halter Marine, Inc. — Lockport, La** Yd No: 1293 Loa 63.55 Br ex - Dght 4.368 Lbp 58.98 Br md 13.41 Dpth 5.18 Welded	**(B34G2SE) Pollution Control Vessel**	**2 oil engines** geared to sc. shafts driving 2 FP propellers Total Power: 1,884kW (2,562hp) 12.0kn Caterpillar 3512TA 2 x Vee 4 Stroke 12 Cy. 170 x 190 each-942kW (1281bhp) Caterpillar Inc-USA Thrusters: 1 Thwart. FP thruster (f) Fuel: 109.0
7925338 *WYQ6984* -	**W. D. HADEN II** - **Bay Houston Maritime Industries Inc** Bay-Houston Towing Co *Galveston, TX* *United States of America* MMSI: 366921860 Official number: 623709	*179* 171 -	Class: (AB)	**1980-07 McDermott Shipyards Inc — Morgan City LA** Yd No: 256 Loa 28.96 Br ex 9.78 Dght 5.157 Lbp 27.44 Br md 9.76 Dpth 6.02 Welded, 1 dk	**(B32A2ST) Tug**	**1 oil engine** reverse reduction geared to sc. shaft driving 1 FP propeller Total Power: 1,898kW (2,581hp) 11.5kn EMD (Electro-Motive) 16-645-E7 1 x Vee 2 Stroke 16 Cy. 230 x 254 1898kW (2581bhp) General Motors Corp.Electro-Motive Div.-La Grange AuxGen: 2 x 99kW
6614293 *A9D2363* -	**W. D. HOYLE** - **Bahrain Enterprise Co** - *Bahrain* *Bahrain*	*1,223* 576 -	Class: (LR) (BV) ✠ Classed LR until 24/6/92	**1967-02 Blyth Dry Docks & SB. Co. Ltd. — Blyth** (Hull launched by) Yd No: 393 **1967-02 Verolme Cork Dockyard Ltd — Cobh** (Hull completed by) Converted From: Hopper-1969 Lengthened-1964 Loa 71.20 Br ex 11.84 Dght 4.192 Lbp 67.37 Br md 11.31 Dpth 5.11 Riveted\Welded, 1 dk	**(B33B2DT) Trailing Suction Hopper Dredger** Hopper: 1,024	**2 oil engines** sr reverse geared to sc. shafts driving 2 FP propellers Total Power: 1,110kW (1,510hp) 11.0kn Blackstone ETSL8 2 x 4 Stroke 8 Cy. 222 x 292 each-555kW (755bhp) Lister Blackstone Marine Ltd.-Dursley AuxGen: 2 x 100kW 440V 50Hz a.c, 1 x 30kW 440V 50Hz a.c Fuel: 122.0 (d.f.)
7809364 *CG2965* -	**W.E. RICKER** *ex Callistratus -1984* **Government of Canada (Canadian Coast Guard)** - SatCom: Inmarsat A 1560171 *Ottawa, ON* *Canada* MMSI: 316116000 Official number: 372369	*1,105* 416 -	Class: (LR) ✠ Classed LR until 6/1/98	**1978-12 Narasaki Zosen KK — Muroran HK** Yd No: 922 Converted From: Stern Trawler-1985 Loa 57.99 (BB) Br ex 9.53 Dght 3.852 Lbp 50.53 Br md 9.50 Dpth 6.23 Welded, 2 dks	**(B11A2FS) Stern Trawler**	**1 oil engine** driving 1 CP propeller Total Power: 1,839kW (2,500hp) Akasaka AH40 1 x 4 Stroke 6 Cy. 400 x 600 1839kW (2500bhp) Akasaka Tekkosho KK (Akasaka Diesel Ltd)-Japan AuxGen: 3 x 150kW 220V 60Hz a.c
9484675 *A8UX8* -	**W-EAGLE** - **Farrell Shipping Co Ltd** W Marine Inc SatCom: Inmarsat C 463709452 *Monrovia* *Liberia* MMSI: 636014570 Official number: 14570	**51,239** 31,173 92,803 T/cm 80.9	Class: AB	**2011-03 Taizhou CATIC Shipbuilding Heavy Industry Ltd — Taizhou JS** Yd No: TK0203 Loa 229.20 (BB) Br ex - Dght 14.900 Lbp 222.00 Br md 38.00 Dpth 20.70 Welded, 1 dk	**(A21A2BC) Bulk Carrier** Grain: 110,330 Compartments: 7 Ho, ER 7 Ha: ER	**1 oil engine** driving 1 FP propeller Total Power: 13,560kW (18,436hp) 14.1kn MAN-B&W 6S60MC-C 1 x 2 Stroke 6 Cy. 600 x 2400 13560kW (18436bhp) Hyundai Heavy Industries Co Ltd-South Korea AuxGen: 3 x 700kW a.c Fuel: 300.0 (d.f.) 3480.0 (r.f.)
8110681 *C6JT8* -	**W. H. BLOUNT** *ex Amir -1991 ex Al Amir -1990* **Vulica Shipping Co Ltd** Wilhelmsen Ship Management Ltd SatCom: Inmarsat B 330827110 *Nassau* *Bahamas* MMSI: 308271000 Official number: 716407	**35,904** 15,475 59,960 T/cm 63.5	Class: LR ✠ **100A1** SS 02/2011 bulk carrier strengthened for heavy cargoes, Nos. 2, 4 & 6 holds may be empty ESP LI ✠ **LMC** Eq.Ltr: N†; Cable: 660.0/76.0 U3 (a)	**1984-04 Hyundai Heavy Industries Co Ltd — Ulsan** Yd No: 202 Converted From: Bulk Carrier-1991 Loa 224.37 (BB) Br ex 32.24 Dght 12.574 Lbp 214.99 Br md 32.20 Dpth 18.01 Welded, 1 dk	**(A23A2BD) Bulk Carrier, Self-discharging** Grain: 75,142; Bale: 71,760 Compartments: 7 Ho, ER 7 Ha: (16.1 x 13.2)6 (16.0 x 13.2)ER	**1 oil engine** driving 1 FP propeller Total Power: 11,181kW (15,202hp) 14.8kn B&W 7L67GFCA 1 x 2 Stroke 7 Cy. 670 x 1700 11181kW (15202bhp) Hyundai Engine & Machinery Co Ltd-South Korea AuxGen: 1 x 500kW 450V 60Hz a.c, 2 x 540kW 450V 60Hz a.c Boilers: e 13.0kgf/cm² (12.7bar), AuxB (o.f.) 7.0kgf/cm² (6.9bar) Fuel: 249.0 (d.f.) 3282.5 (r.f.) 48.0pd
7033094 *CZ9720* -	**W.H. HORTON** - **A Frame Contracting Ltd** - *Edmonton, AB* *Canada* Official number: 344611	*107* 73 -		**1970 Vito Steel Boat & Barge Construction Ltd — Delta BC** Loa - Br ex 7.62 Dght - Lbp 17.99 Br md - Dpth - Welded, 1 dk	**(B32A2ST) Tug**	**1 oil engine** driving 1 FP propeller Total Power: 706kW (960hp) 12.0kn

7224411
-
-
W H PARR
-
Port Nelson Ltd
-
Nelson *New Zealand*
Official number: 332349
111
-
242
Class: (LR)
✠ Classed LR until 29/8/75
1972-09 Sims Engineering Ltd — Port Chalmers
Yd No: 45
Loa 20.65 Br ex 8.06 Dght 3.226
Lbp 16.59 Br md 7.97 Dpth 3.66
Welded, 1 dk
(B32A2ST) Tug
2 oil engines geared to sc. shafts driving 2 Directional propellers
Total Power: 1,424kW (1,936hp) 9.0kn
Deutz TBD616V16
2 x Vee 4 Stroke 16 Cy. 132 x 160 each-712kW (968bhp) (new engine ,made 1972)
Deutz AG-Koeln
AuxGen: 2 x 42kW 400/230V 50Hz a.c

5264819
VCFQ
-
W.I. SCOTT PURVIS
ex Guy M No. 1 *-1991* *ex* Orient Bay *-1975*
Purvis Marine Ltd
Sault Ste Marie, ON *Canada*
Official number: 171703
206
94
-
Class: (LR)
*Classed BC until 7/41
1938-10 Marine Industries Ltee (MIL) — Sorel QC
Yd No: 62
Loa 29.42 Br ex 8.08 Dght 2.007
Lbp - Br md 8.03 Dpth 2.80
Welded, 1 dk
(B32A2ST) Tug
Compartments: 1 Ho, ER
1 Ha: (2.5 x 1.9)
2 diesel electric oil engines driving 2 CP propellers
Total Power: 882kW (1,200hp) 9.5kn
Caterpillar
1 x 4 Stroke 8 Cy. 441kW (600bhp)
Caterpillar Inc-USA
Caterpillar
1 x 4 Stroke 8 Cy. 441kW (600bhp) (made 1938)
Caterpillar Tractor Co-USA
AuxGen: 2 x 35kW 220V d.c, 1 x 12kW 220V d.c
Fuel: 61.0 (d.f.)

7309833
WX9283
-
W. J. BURTON
Omega Protein Inc
-
New Orleans, LA *United States of America*
MMSI: 366986150
Official number: 503166
539
367
-
1966 Burton Shipyard Co., Inc. — Port Arthur, Tx
Yd No: 380
L reg 49.57 Br ex 10.09 Dght -
Lbp - Br md - Dpth 3.61
Welded
(B11B2FV) Fishing Vessel
1 oil engine driving 1 FP propeller
Total Power: 1,125kW (1,530hp)

5217218
VCBM
-
W.J. IVAN PURVIS
ex Dana T. Bowen *-1975* *ex* Magpie *-1966*
Purvis Marine Ltd
Sault Ste Marie, ON *Canada*
Official number: 171701
191
88
-
1938 Marine Industries Ltee (MIL) — Sorel QC
Yd No: 63
Loa 29.42 Br ex 7.80 Dght 2.667
Lbp - Br md 7.75 Dpth -
Welded, 1 dk
(B32A2ST) Tug
1 oil engine driving 1 FP propeller
Total Power: 883kW (1,201hp) 9.8kn
National Gas
1 x 2 Stroke 5 Cy. 250 x 330 883kW (1201bhp) (new engine 1977)
National Supply Co.-Springfield, Oh
AuxGen: 3 x 25kW 220V d.c
Fuel: 64.0 (d.f.)

9491551
PNMC
-
W. M. MAKASSAR
ex Greatship Rekha *-2010*
PT PSV Indonesia
PT Wintermar
Jakarta *Indonesia*
3,245
974
3,732
Class: KI LR (IR)
✠ **100A1** SS 04/2010
offshore supply ship
RD (liquid product tanks SG 2.8), low flash point liquids (methanol, 12 degree C, methanol tanks),
WDL (upper deck aft of frame 84 strengthened for load of 5 tonnes/m2)
*IWS
EP (A,B)
✠ **LMC** **UMS**
Eq.Ltr: S;
Cable: 660.0/40.0 U3 (a)
2010-04 Colombo Dockyard Ltd. — Colombo
Yd No: 215
Loa 78.00 (BB) Br ex 17.24 Dght 6.290
Lbp 71.60 Br md 17.00 Dpth 8.00
Welded, 1 dk
(B21A20S) Platform Supply Ship
2 oil engines with clutches, flexible couplings & sr geared to sc. shafts driving 2 CP propellers
Total Power: 5,280kW (7,178hp) 13.0kn
MaK 8M25C
2 x 4 Stroke 8 Cy. 255 x 400 each-2640kW (3589bhp)
Caterpillar Motoren GmbH & Co. KG-Germany
AuxGen: 2 x 1600kW 440V 60Hz a.c, 2 x 460kW 440V 60Hz a.c
Thrusters: 2 Thwart. CP thruster (f); 2 Thwart. CP thruster (a)

9280914
PNNT
-
W. M. SULAWESI
ex Greatship Diya *-2010*
ex Waveney Castle *-2007*
PT PSV Indonesia
PT Wintermar
Jakarta *Indonesia*
MMSI: 525019563
Official number: 2882/BA
2,154
647
3,343
Class: AB KI (NV) (IR)
2003-08 SC Aker Tulcea SA — Tulcea (Hull)
Yd No: 299
2003-08 Aker Aukra AS — Aukra Yd No: 110
Loa 72.00 Br ex 16.03 Dght 5.817
Lbp 65.90 Br md 16.00 Dpth 7.00
Welded, 1 dk
(B21A20S) Platform Supply Ship
2 oil engines geared to sc. shafts driving 2 CP propellers
Total Power: 4,010kW (5,452hp) 14.5kn
Bergens KRMB-9
2 x 4 Stroke 9 Cy. 250 x 300 each-2005kW (2726bhp)
Rolls Royce Marine AS-Norway
AuxGen: 2 x 260kW 440V 60Hz a.c, 2 x 1280kW 450V 60Hz a.c
Thrusters: 2 Thwart. CP thruster (f); 1 Thwart. CP thruster (a)
Fuel: 977.0 (r.f.)

5384360
VCNM
-
W.N. TWOLAN
Ontario Ltd
-
Ottawa, ON *Canada*
MMSI: 316003277
Official number: 318527
298
13
81
Class: (LR)
✠ Classed LR until 6/66
1962-08 Geo T Davie & Sons Ltd — Levis QC
Yd No: 76
Loa 32.09 Br ex 8.97 Dght 3.366
Lbp 28.15 Br md 8.68 Dpth 4.58
Welded, 1 dk
(B32A2ST) Tug
2 oil engines with fluid couplings driving 2 FP propellers
Total Power: 1,118kW (1,520hp)
Werkspoor
2 x 4 Stroke 8 Cy. 270 x 500 each-559kW (760bhp)
NV Werkspoor-Netherlands
AuxGen: 2 x 30kW 440V 60Hz a.c

9596650
D5FE8
-
W-PACIFIC
ex Jimpacific *-2013*
Dilan Co
W Marine Inc
Monrovia *Liberia*
MMSI: 636016243
Official number: 16243
44,119
27,395
81,233
T/cm
71.9
Class: LR
✠ **100A1** SS 09/2013
bulk carrier
CSR
BC-A
Nos. 2, 4 & 6 holds may be empty
GRAB (20)
ESP
ShipRight (CM,ACS (B))
LI
*IWS
✠ **LMC** **UMS**
Eq.Ltr: Q†;
Cable: 687.5/81.0 U3 (a)
2013-09 Jiangsu Hantong Ship Heavy Industry Co Ltd — Tongzhou JS Yd No: HT82-001
Loa 229.00 Br ex 32.30 Dght 14.580
Lbp 222.50 Br md 32.26 Dpth 20.05
Welded, 1 dk
(A21A2BC) Bulk Carrier
Double Hull
Grain: 97,000; Bale: 90,784
Compartments: 7 Ho, ER
7 Ha: ER
1 oil engine driving 1 FP propeller
Total Power: 11,300kW (15,363hp) 14.1kn
MAN-B&W 6S60MC-C
1 x 2 Stroke 6 Cy. 600 x 2400 11300kW (15363bhp)
Hyundai Heavy Industries Co Ltd-South Korea
AuxGen: 3 x 600kW 450V 60Hz a.c
Boilers: AuxB (Comp) 8.8kgf/cm² (8.6bar)

7392684
ERTH
-
W POWER
ex Shireen S *-2013* *ex* Kelty *-1998*
Saga Shipping & Trading Corp Ltd
-
Giurgiulesti *Moldova*
MMSI: 214182008
312
93
-
Class: DR (LR) (KC)
✠ Classed LR until 11/7/07
1976-06 Richards (Shipbuilders) Ltd — Lowestoft
Yd No: 526
Loa 38.00 Br ex 9.63 Dght 4.039
Lbp 34.02 Br md 9.21 Dpth 4.50
Welded, 1 dk
(B32A2ST) Tug
1 oil engine sr geared to sc. shaft driving 1 CP propeller
Total Power: 1,942kW (2,640hp) 14.0kn
Ruston 12RKCM
1 x Vee 4 Stroke 12 Cy. 254 x 305 1942kW (2640bhp)
Ruston Paxman Diesels Ltd.-Colchester
AuxGen: 2 x 108kW 440V 50Hz a.c, 1 x 30kW 440V 50Hz a.c

8836625
WDC2191
-
W SCOTT NOBLE
ex Harllee Branch Jr. *-2011*
Ingram Barge Co
-
Wilmington, DE *United States of America*
MMSI: 366989280
Official number: 503828
651
553
-
1966 Dravo Corp. — Pittsburgh, Pa Yd No: 4887
Loa - Br ex - Dght -
Lbp 46.02 Br md 12.19 Dpth 2.62
Welded, 1 dk
(B32A2ST) Tug
1 oil engine driving 1 FP propeller
Total Power: 3,178kW (4,321hp)

9476666
A8UX6
-
W-SKY
Corbeil Shipping SA
W Marine Inc
SatCom: Inmarsat C 463709320
Monrovia *Liberia*
MMSI: 636014568
Official number: 14568
51,239
31,173
92,929
T/cm
80.9
Class: AB
2011-01 Taizhou CATIC Shipbuilding Heavy Industry Ltd — Taizhou JS Yd No: TK0201
Loa 229.20 (BB) Br ex - Dght 14.900
Lbp 222.00 Br md 38.00 Dpth 20.70
Welded, 1 dk
(A21A2BC) Bulk Carrier
Grain: 110,884
Compartments: 7 Ho, ER
7 Ha: ER
1 oil engine driving 1 FP propeller
Total Power: 13,560kW (18,436hp) 14.1kn
MAN-B&W 6S60MC-C
1 x 2 Stroke 6 Cy. 600 x 2400 13560kW (18436bhp)
Hyundai Heavy Industries Co Ltd-South Korea
AuxGen: 3 x 700kW a.c
Fuel: 230.0 (d.f.) 3600.0 (r.f.)

9625877
D5EE3
-
W-SMASH
completed as STX Ivory *-2013*
Ukon Ltd
W Marine Inc
Monrovia *Liberia*
MMSI: 636016053
Official number: 16053
45,055
26,973
82,742
T/cm
71.9
Class: NV (KR)
2013-06 STX (Dalian) Shipbuilding Co Ltd — Wafangdian LN Yd No: D2061
Loa 229.00 (BB) Br ex - Dght 14.520
Lbp 225.60 Br md 32.24 Dpth 20.20
Welded, 1 dk
(A21A2BC) Bulk Carrier
Grain: 95,172
Compartments: 7 Ho, ER
7 Ha: ER
1 oil engine driving 1 FP propeller
Total Power: 13,560kW (18,436hp) 14.1kn
MAN-B&W 6S60MC-C
1 x 2 Stroke 6 Cy. 600 x 2400 13560kW (18436bhp)
STX (Dalian) Engine Co Ltd-China
AuxGen: 3 x 585kW a.c

8986248
WDB3916
-
W STANFORD WHITE
State of North Carolina (Ferry Division)
-
Manns Harbor, NC *United States of America*
MMSI: 366892730
Official number: 1133333
416
143
-
2003 Orange Shipbuilding, Inc. — Orange, Tx
Yd No: 355
L reg 51.11 Br ex - Dght -
Lbp - Br md 13.41 Dpth 3.35
Welded, 1 dk
(A36A2PR) Passenger/Ro-Ro Ship (Vehicles)
Vehicles: 40
1 oil engine driving 1 Propeller

Ship	Tonnage	Class	Builder / Dimensions	Type	Machinery
9476678 *A8UX7* - **W-STAR** **Hanson Marine Ltd** W Marine Inc SatCom: Inmarsat C 463710076 *Monrovia* *Liberia* MMSI: 636014569 Official number: 14569	**51,239** 31,173 92,842 T/cm 80.9	Class: AB	**2011-07 Taizhou CATIC Shipbuilding Heavy Industry Ltd — Taizhou JS** Yd No: TK0202 Loa 229.20 (BB) Br ex - Dght 14.900 Lbp 222.00 Br md 38.00 Dpth 20.70 Welded, 1 dk	**(A21A2BC) Bulk Carrier** Grain: 110,330 Compartments: 7 Ho, ER 7 Ha: ER	**1 oil engine** driving 1 FP propeller Total Power: 13,560kW (18,436hp) 14.1kr MAN-B&W 6S60MC-C 1 x 2 Stroke 6 Cy. 600 x 2400 13560kW (18436bhp) Hyundai Heavy Industries Co Ltd-South Korea AuxGen: 3 x 700kW a.c Fuel: 300.0 (d.f.) 3550.0 (r.f.)
7009172 *HSB2244* - **W. T. G. 2** *ex* Arada No. 2 *-2000* *ex* Ethylene Unakami *-1993* **Sky Bay Co Ltd** - *Bangkok* *Thailand* Official number: 362000027	**727** 235 456 T/cm 3.0		**1970-03 Ishikawajima Ship & Chemical Plant Co Ltd — Tokyo** Yd No: 385 Loa 58.43 Br ex 10.04 Dght 3.590 Lbp 52.99 Br md 10.01 Dpth 4.40 Welded, 1 dk	**(A11B2TG) LPG Tanker** Liq (Gas): 918 2 x Gas Tank (s); 2 independent (C.mn.stl) cyl horizontal 2 Cargo Pump (s): 2x100m³/hr Manifold: Bow/CM: 24m	**1 oil engine** driving 1 FP propeller Total Power: 736kW (1,001hp) 11.0kr Hanshin 6LU28 1 x 4 Stroke 6 Cy. 280 x 440 736kW (1001bhp) Hanshin Nainenki Kogyo-Japan Fuel: 37.5 (d.f.) 4.0pd
9514937 *PBZA* - **WAALDIJK** *launched as* JRS Auriga *-2010* **Beheermaatschappij ms Waaldijk BV** Navigia Shipmanagement BV *Groningen* *Netherlands* MMSI: 245726000 Official number: 50465	**2,984** 1,598 4,891	Class: GL (Class contemplated) (BV)	**2010-06 Chowgule & Co Pvt Ltd — Goa** Yd No: 190 Loa 89.95 (BB) Br ex - Dght 6.220 Lbp 84.94 Br md 14.40 Dpth 7.85 Welded, 1 dk	**(A31A2GX) General Cargo Ship** Grain: 5,818 Compartments: 1 Ho, ER 1 Ha: ER (62.3 x 11.7)	**1 oil engine** reduction geared to sc. shaft driving 1 CP propeller Total Power: 1,980kW (2,692hp) 11.5kr MaK 6M25 1 x 4 Stroke 6 Cy. 255 x 400 1980kW (2692bhp) Caterpillar Motoren GmbH & Co. KG-Germany AuxGen: 2 x 168kW 50Hz a.c, 1 x 312kW 50Hz a.c Thrusters: 1 Tunnel thruster (f)
9659103 *ONHS* - **WAASMUNSTER** **Exmar LPG BVBA** Exmar Marine NV *Antwerpen* *Belgium* MMSI: 205655000	**25,143** 7,542 37,500	Class: LR ✠ **100A1** SS 04/2014 liquefied gas carrier, Ship type 2G Anhydrous ammonia, butadiene, butane, butane-propane mixtures, butylenes, propane and propylene in independent tanks Type A, maximum SG 0.70, partial loading dimethyl ether with maximum SG 0.735, maximum vapour pressure 0.25 bar (0.45 in harbour), minimum cargo temperature minus 50 degree C **ShipRight** (SDA,CM, ACS (B)) *IWS LI ✠ **LMC UMS +Lloyd's RMC (LG)** Eq.Ltr: M†; Cable: 632.5/73.0 U3 (a)	**2014-04 Hyundai Mipo Dockyard Co Ltd — Ulsan** Yd No: 8121 Loa 174.06 (BB) Br ex 30.03 Dght 10.300 Lbp 165.00 Br md 30.00 Dpth 18.20 Welded, 1 dk	**(A11B2TG) LPG Tanker** Liq (Gas): 38,000	**1 oil engine** driving 1 FP propeller Total Power: 8,360kW (11,366hp) 16.8kr MAN-B&W 6S50ME 1 x 4 Stroke 6 Cy. 500 x 2214 8360kW (11366bhp) AuxGen: 3 x 1102kW 450V 60Hz a.c Boilers: e (ex.g.) 11.9kgf/cm² (11.7bar), WTAuxB (o.f.) 9.2kgf/cm² (9.0bar)
9047398 *D5CA3* - **WABA** *ex* Pacific Jade *-2012* *ex* Haustrum *-2006* **Corinthians Shipping Ltd** Transocean Shipping Ventures Pvt Ltd *Monrovia* *Liberia* MMSI: 636015644 Official number: 15644	**28,277** 12,696 46,801 T/cm 51.7	Class: LR (NV) **100A1** SS 02/2009 Double Hull oil tanker ESP **LMC UMS IGS** Cable: 660.0/76.0	**1994-02 Halla Engineering & Heavy Industries Ltd — Incheon** Yd No: 198 Loa 183.20 (BB) Br ex 32.23 Dght 11.855 Lbp 174.00 Br md 32.20 Dpth 18.00 Welded, 1 dk	**(A13A2TW) Crude/Oil Products Tanker** Double Hull Liq: 52,884; Liq (Oil): 52,884 Cargo Heating Coils Compartments: 8 Wing Ta, ER 8 Cargo Pump (s): 8x850m³/hr Manifold: Bow/CM: 92m Ice Capable	**1 oil engine** driving 1 FP propeller Total Power: 7,458kW (10,140hp) 14.5kr B&W 6S50MC 1 x 2 Stroke 6 Cy. 500 x 1910 7458kW (10140bhp) Hyundai Heavy Industries Co Ltd-South Korea
9583574 *ZGBB6* - **WABI-SABI** **Tanha** Yacht Logistics Inc SatCom: Inmarsat C 431918113 *George Town* *Cayman Islands (British)* MMSI: 319181000 Official number: 742957	**492** 147 135	Class: AB	**2011-03 Westport Shipyard, Inc. — Westport, Wa** Yd No: 5008 Loa 49.94 Br ex - Dght 2.190 Lbp 43.53 Br md 9.35 Dpth 4.17 Bonded, 1 dk	**(X11A2YP) Yacht** Hull Material: Reinforced Plastic	**2 oil engines** reduction geared to sc. shafts driving 2 Propellers Total Power: 5,440kW (7,396hp) 20.0kr M.T.U. 16V4000M9 2 x Vee 4 Stroke 16 Cy. 165 x 190 each-2720kW (3698bhp) MTU Friedrichshafen GmbH-Friedrichshafen AuxGen: 2 x 99kW a.c Fuel: 75.0 (d.f.)
6710073 - - **WACHIRASAMUT** *ex* Khanalak *-2000* *ex* C. P. 9 *-1986* *ex* Summit 2 *-1982* *ex* Oceanic 2 *-1982* **Cosmo Oil Co Ltd (Thailand)** - *Bangkok* *Thailand* Official number: 101001238	*399* 183 600	Class: (LR) (CR) ✠ Classed LR until 10/69	**1967-04 Usuki Iron Works Co Ltd — Usuki OT** Yd No: 627 Loa 48.05 Br ex 7.85 Dght 2.718 Lbp 44.00 Br md 7.82 Dpth 3.20 Riveted\Welded, 1 dk	**(A13B2TP) Products Tanker** Liq: 725; Liq (Oil): 725 Cargo Heating Coils Compartments: 6 Wing Ta, ER 2 Cargo Pump (s): 1x150m³/hr, 1x100m³/hr	**1 oil engine** reverse reduction geared to sc. shaft driving 1 FP propeller Total Power: 368kW (500hp) 8.0k Cummins V12-525-M 1 x Vee 4 Stroke 12 Cy. 140 x 152 368kW (500bhp) (made 1965, fitted 1967) Cummins Engine Co Inc-USA AuxGen: 2 x 20kW 230V 50Hz a.c Fuel: 12.0 (d.f.) 1.5pd
9098385 *9LB2229* - **WACO 1** *ex* Al Qlaa 145 *-2009* **Sea Life Co Ltd** Sea Rocks Shipping LLC *Freetown* *Sierra Leone* MMSI: 667203400 Official number: SL102034	*242* 73 -	Class: IS	**2003-01 UR-Dock — Basrah** Loa 33.00 Br ex 8.75 Dght - Lbp - Br md 8.65 Dpth 3.90 Welded, 1 dk	**(B32A2ST) Tug**	**1 oil engine** driving 1 Propeller Total Power: 1,471kW (2,000hp) Blackstone 1 x 4 Stroke 1471kW (2000bhp) Lister Blackstone MirrleesMarine Ltd.-Dursley
9297072 *9KDO* - **WADDAH** **Government of The State of Kuwait (Coast Guard)** - *Kuwait* *Kuwait* MMSI: 447121000	**185** 55 15	Class: (LR) ✠ Classed LR until 15/6/06	**2005-03 OCEA SA — St-Nazaire** Yd No: 316 Loa 35.20 Br ex 7.17 Dght 1.230 Lbp 29.85 Br md 6.80 Dpth 3.80 Welded, 1 dk	**(B34H2SQ) Patrol Vessel** Hull Material: Aluminium Alloy	**2 oil engines** with clutches, flexible couplings & sr reverse geared to sc. shafts driving 2 Water jets Total Power: 3,480kW (4,732hp) M.T.U. 12V4000M 2 x Vee 4 Stroke 12 Cy. 165 x 190 each-1740kW (2366bhp) MTU Friedrichshafen GmbH-Friedrichshafen AuxGen: 2 x 78kW 400V 50Hz a.c
7820588 - - **WADDAN** **Libyan Fishing Co (LIFCO)** - *Tripoli* *Libya*	*129* 33 -	Class: (LR) ✠ Classed LR until 4/2/87	**1981-02 Khalkis Shipyard S.A. — Khalkis** Yd No: 925 Loa 24.64 (BB) Br ex 7.01 Dght 2.501 Lbp 19.56 Br md 7.00 Dpth 3.51 Welded, 1 dk	**(B11A2FS) Stern Trawler**	**1 oil engine** driving 1 CP propeller Total Power: 368kW (500hp) Alpha 405-26VO 1 x 2 Stroke 5 Cy. 260 x 400 368kW (500bhp) B&W Alpha Diesel A/S-Denmark AuxGen: 2 x 32kW 380V 50Hz a.c Fuel: 21.5 (d.f.)
8317978 *LYTR* - **WADDENS** *ex* UAFL Express *-2010* *ex* Waddens *-2002* *ex* Southern Man *-2001* *ex* Capitaine Bligh *-2000* *ex* Waddens *-1999* *ex* Rangiora *-1998* *ex* Nedlloyd Trinidad *-1995* *ex* Weser Guide *-1994* *ex* Zim Kingston *-1988* *ex* Weser Guide *-1984* **mv 'Waddens' Shipping Co Ltd** JSC 'Afalita Shipping' (UAB 'Afalita Shipping') *Klaipeda* *Lithuania* MMSI: 277487000 Official number: 851	**3,784** 1,820 5,189	Class: GL	**1984-03 Heinrich Brand Schiffswerft GmbH & Co. KG — Oldenburg** Yd No: 217 Loa 99.50 (BB) Br ex 17.23 Dght 6.501 Lbp 88.19 Br md 17.21 Dpth 8.21 Welded, 2 dks	**(A31A2GX) General Cargo Ship** Grain: 6,060; Bale: 6,000 TEU 350 C Ho 116 TEU C Dk 234 TEU incl 52 ref C Compartments: 1 Ho, ER 1 Ha: (52.2 x 13.2)ER Cranes: 2x40t Ice Capable	**1 oil engine** with flexible couplings & sr gearedto sc. shaft driving 1 CP propeller Total Power: 2,499kW (3,398hp) 14.0k MaK 6M551AK 1 x 4 Stroke 6 Cy. 450 x 550 2499kW (3398bhp) Krupp MaK Maschinenbau GmbH-Kiel AuxGen: 1 x 696kW 380V 50Hz a.c, 1 x 500kW 380V 50Hz a.c, 1 x 226kW 380V 50Hz a.c Thrusters: 1 Thwart. FP thruster (f) Fuel: 60.0 (d.f.) 400.0 (r.f.) 10.0pd
8650825 *PILQ* - **WADDENZEE** **Zand-en Schelpenwinning Waddenzee BV** - *Harlingen* *Netherlands* Official number: 17633	**349** 127 -	Class: (BV)	**1964 Barkmeijer Stroobos B.V. — Stroobos** Yd No: 158 Loa 50.06 Br ex 8.06 Dght 2.500 Lbp - Br md 8.00 Dpth 2.85 Welded, 1 dk	**(B33B2DT) Trailing Suction Hopper Dredger**	**1 oil engine** driving 1 FP propeller Total Power: 400kW (544hp) Brons 1 x 400kW (544bhp) NV Appingedammer Bronsmotorenfabrie-Netherlands

IMO / Call sign	Name / Owner	Tonnage	Class	Builder / Dimensions	Type / Capacity	Machinery
9065467 *PILR* -	**WADDENZEE** **Government of The Kingdom of The Netherlands (Rijkswaterstaat Directie Noordzee)** - *Rijswijk, Noord Brabant* *Netherlands* MMSI: 244499000 Official number: 24984	**266** 79 -	Class: BV	**1994-04 Stocznia Remontowa 'Nauta' SA — Gdynia** (Hull) Yd No: NL38 **1994-04 B.V. Scheepswerf Maaskant — Stellendam** Yd No: 487 Loa 38.43 Br ex - Dght 1.500 Lbp 35.68 Br md 8.70 Dpth 2.50 Welded	**(B34Q2QB) Buoy Tender** Ice Capable	**2 oil engines** reduction geared to sc. shafts driving 2 FP propellers Total Power: 396kW (538hp) 8.0kn Volvo Penta TMD122A 2 x 4 Stroke 6 Cy. 130 x 150 each-198kW (269bhp) AB Volvo Penta-Sweden Fuel: 8.7 (d.f.)
9194787 *A6E3047* -	**WADI AL FAI** **Port of Fujairah** - *Fujairah* *United Arab Emirates* MMSI: 470889000 Official number: 5211	**198** 59 -	Class: NV (LR) ✠ Classed LR until 27/11/07	**2006-02 OAO Leningradskiy Sudostroitelnyy Zavod 'Pella' — Otradnoye** (Hull) **2006-02 B.V. Scheepswerf Damen — Gorinchem** Yd No: 510807 Loa 25.86 Br ex 9.25 Dght 3.650 Lbp 23.00 Br md 8.90 Dpth 4.30 Welded, 1 dk	**(B32A2ST) Tug**	**2 oil engines** reduction geared to sc. shafts driving 2 Directional propellers Total Power: 2,500kW (3,400hp) Caterpillar 3512B-HD 2 x Vee 4 Stroke 12 Cy. 170 x 215 each-1250kW (1700bhp) Caterpillar Inc-USA AuxGen: 2 x 84kW 400V 50Hz a.c
9107681 *SSLL* -	**WADI ALARAB** **National Navigation Co** - SatCom: Inmarsat C 462211725 *Alexandria* *Egypt* MMSI: 622121423 Official number: 4411	**37,550** 23,072 64,214 T/cm 64.5	Class: LR ✠ **100A1** SS 10/2010 bulk carrier strengthened for heavy cargoes, Nos. 2, 4 & 6 holds may be empty ESP ESN-Hold 1 Ice Class 1D ✠ **LMC** **UMS** Eq.Ltr: N†; Cable: 660.0/76.0 U3	**1995-10 Daewoo Heavy Industries Ltd — Geoje** Yd No: 1097 Loa 225.00 (BB) Br ex 32.24 Dght 12.400 Lbp 215.00 Br md 32.20 Dpth 18.50 Welded, 1 dk	**(A21A2BC) Bulk Carrier** Grain: 82,209; Bale: 78,338 Compartments: 7 Ho, ER 7 Ha: 7 (16.6 x 14.9)ER Ice Capable	**1 oil engine** driving 1 FP propeller Total Power: 8,555kW (11,631hp) 13.0kn B&W 6S50MC 1 x 2 Stroke 6 Cy. 500 x 1910 8555kW (11631bhp) Korea Heavy Industries & ConstrCo Ltd (HANJUNG)-South Korea AuxGen: 3 x 500kW 450V 60Hz a.c Boilers: e (ex.g.) 6.9kgf/cm² (6.8bar), AuxB (o.f.) 6.9kgf/cm² (6.8bar) Fuel: 190.7 (d.f.) (Heating Coils) 2238.0 (r.f.) 31.2pd
9077898 *SSHW* -	**WADI ALARISH** **National Navigation Co** - SatCom: Inmarsat C 462211894 *Alexandria* *Egypt* MMSI: 622121420 Official number: 4226	**37,550** 20,055 64,214 T/cm 65.5	Class: LR ✠ **100A1** SS 04/2009 bulk carrier strengthened for heavy cargoes, Nos. 2, 4 & 6 holds may be empty ESP ESN-Hold 1 Ice Class 1D ✠ **LMC** **UMS** Eq.Ltr: N†; Cable: 660.0/76.0 U3	**1994-04 Daewoo Shipbuilding & Heavy Machinery Ltd — Geoje** Yd No: 1067 Loa 225.00 (BB) Br ex 32.24 Dght 12.400 Lbp 215.00 Br md 32.20 Dpth 18.50 Welded, 1 dk	**(A21A2BC) Bulk Carrier** Grain: 82,210; Bale: 78,338 Compartments: 7 Ho, ER 7 Ha: 7 (16.6 x 14.9)ER Ice Capable	**1 oil engine** driving 1 FP propeller Total Power: 8,555kW (11,631hp) 13.5kn B&W 6S50MC 1 x 2 Stroke 6 Cy. 500 x 1910 8555kW (11631bhp) Korea Heavy Industries & ConstrCo Ltd (HANJUNG)-South Korea AuxGen: 3 x 500kW 450V 60Hz a.c Boilers: AuxB (o.f.) 7.0kgf/cm² (6.9bar), AuxB (ex.g.) 7.0kgf/cm² (6.9bar) Fuel: 190.7 (d.f.) 2237.8 (r.f.) 29.0pd
9460722 *6AGS* -	**WADI ALBOSTAN** **National Navigation Co** - *Alexandria* *Egypt* MMSI: 622121410 Official number: 9256	**33,234** 22,236 57,320 T/cm 57.3	Class: LR ✠ **100A1** SS 01/2011 bulk carrier CSR BC-A GRAB (20) Nos. 2 & 4 holds may be empty ESP **ShipRight** (ACS (B),CM) *IWS LI ✠ **LMC** **UMS** Eq.Ltr: N†; Cable: 659.0/76.0 U3 (a)	**2011-01 STX Offshore & Shipbuilding Co Ltd — Changwon (Jinhae Shipyard)** Yd No: 1327 Loa 190.00 (BB) Br ex 32.26 Dght 13.000 Lbp 183.30 Br md 32.26 Dpth 18.50 Welded, 1 dk	**(A21A2BC) Bulk Carrier** Grain: 71,850 Compartments: 5 Ho, ER 5 Ha: ER Cranes: 4x30t	**1 oil engine** driving 1 FP propeller Total Power: 9,480kW (12,889hp) 14.5kn MAN-B&W 6S50MC-C 1 x 2 Stroke 6 Cy. 500 x 2000 9480kW (12889bhp) STX Engine Co Ltd-South Korea AuxGen: 3 x 625kW 440V 60Hz a.c Boilers: AuxB (Comp) 9.2kgf/cm² (9.0bar)
7302952 - -	**WADI ALHIRA** *ex Maleas -1979* **Libyan-Greek Fishing Co SA** - *Benghazi* *Libya*	*108* 47 -	Class: (HR)	**1973 Th. Zervas & Sons — Ambelaki** Loa 30.56 Br ex - Dght - Lbp 26.01 Br md 6.80 Dpth 3.41 Welded, 1 dk	**(B11A2FT) Trawler** Compartments: 1 Ho, ER 1 Ha: (0.9 x 1.3)ER Winches: 1	**1 oil engine** driving 1 FP propeller Total Power: 368kW (500hp) 10.0kn Alpha 405-26VO 1 x 2 Stroke 5 Cy. 260 x 400 368kW (500bhp) Alpha Diesel A/S-Denmark
9460760 *6AGT* -	**WADI ALKARM** **National Navigation Co** - *Alexandria* *Egypt* MMSI: 622121414 Official number: 9257	**43,790** 26,673 80,533 T/cm 71.9	Class: LR ✠ **100A1** SS 02/2011 bulk carrier CSR BC-A GRAB (20) Nos. 2, 4 & 6 holds may be empty ESP **ShipRight** (ACS (B),CM) *IWS LI ✠ **LMC** **UMS** Eq.Ltr: Q†; Cable: 687.5/81.0 U3 (a)	**2011-02 STX Offshore & Shipbuilding Co Ltd — Changwon (Jinhae Shipyard)** Yd No: 4029 Loa 229.00 (BB) Br ex 32.29 Dght 14.460 Lbp 222.00 Br md 32.24 Dpth 20.10 Welded, 1 dk	**(A21A2BC) Bulk Carrier** Grain: 95,172 Compartments: 7 Ho, ER 7 Ha: ER	**1 oil engine** driving 1 FP propeller Total Power: 11,060kW (15,037hp) 14.3kn MAN-B&W 7S50MC-C 1 x 2 Stroke 7 Cy. 500 x 2000 11060kW (15037bhp) STX Engine Co Ltd-South Korea AuxGen: 3 x 625kW 450V 60Hz a.c Boilers: AuxB (Comp) 9.2kgf/cm² (9.0bar)
9127136 *SSMM* -	**WADI ALKARNAK** **National Navigation Co** - SatCom: Inmarsat C 462211891 *Alexandria* *Egypt* MMSI: 622121425 Official number: 4720	**37,550** 20,055 64,214 T/cm 64.0	Class: LR ✠ **100A1** SS 09/2011 bulk carrier strenghtened for heavy cargoes, Nos. 2, 4 & 6 holds may be empty ESP ESN-Hold 1 Ice Class 1D ✠ **LMC** **UMS** Eq.Ltr: N†; Cable: 660.0/76.0 U3	**1997-01 Daewoo Heavy Industries Ltd — Geoje** Yd No: 1112 Loa 225.00 (BB) Br ex 32.29 Dght 12.400 Lbp 215.00 Br md 32.20 Dpth 18.50 Welded, 1 dk	**(A21A2BC) Bulk Carrier** Grain: 82,209; Bale: 78,338 Compartments: 7 Ho, ER 7 Ha: 7 (16.6 x 14.9)ER Ice Capable	**1 oil engine** driving 1 FP propeller Total Power: 8,558kW (11,635hp) 13.5kn B&W 6S50MC 1 x 2 Stroke 6 Cy. 500 x 1910 8558kW (11635bhp) Korea Heavy Industries & ConstrCo Ltd (HANJUNG)-South Korea AuxGen: 3 x 500kW 450V 60Hz a.c Boilers: e (ex.g.) 7.0kgf/cm² (6.9bar), AuxB (o.f.) 7.0kgf/cm² (6.9bar)
9208875 *SSCC* -	**WADI ALRAYAN** **National Navigation Co** - SatCom: Inmarsat C 462211840 *Alexandria* *Egypt* MMSI: 622121427 Official number: 5733	**34,083** 17,492 40,301 T/cm 60.0	Class: LR ✠ **100A1** SS 06/2010 container ship certified container securing arrangements LI Ice Class 1D ✠ **LMC** **UMS** Eq.Ltr: O†; Cable: 660.0/78.0 U3 (a)	**2000-06 Daewoo Heavy Industries Ltd — Geoje** Yd No: 4068 Loa 215.00 (BB) Br ex 32.26 Dght 13.000 Lbp 200.40 Br md 32.20 Dpth 19.00 Welded, 1 dk	**(A33A2CC) Container Ship (Fully Cellular)** TEU 3013 C Ho 1215 TEU C Dk 1798 TEU incl 368 ref C. Compartments: ER, 6 Cell Ho 11 Ha: (12.6 x 13.0)Tappered ER 10 (12.6 x 28.4) Cranes: 3x45t Ice Capable	**1 oil engine** driving 1 FP propeller Total Power: 28,832kW (39,200hp) 21.6kn B&W 8K80MC-C 1 x 2 Stroke 8 Cy. 800 x 2300 28832kW (39200bhp) HSD Engine Co Ltd-South Korea AuxGen: 4 x 1750kW 450V 60Hz a.c Boilers: AuxB (o.f.) 9.2kgf/cm² (9.0bar), AuxB (ex.g.) 9.2kgf/cm² (9.0bar) Thrusters: 1 Thwart. FP thruster (f) Fuel: 35.0 (d.f.) 8217.0 (r.f.) 108.0pd
9460772 *6AGQ* -	**WADI ALYARMOUK** **National Navigation Co** - *Alexandria* *Egypt* MMSI: 622120442 Official number: 9254	**43,790** 26,673 80,384 T/cm 71.9	Class: LR ✠ **100A1** SS 11/2010 bulk carrier CSR BC-A GRAB (20) Nos. 2, 4 & 6 holds may be empty ESP **ShipRight** (ACS (B),CM) *IWS LI ✠ **LMC** **UMS** Eq.Ltr: Q†; Cable: 687.5/81.0 U3 (a)	**2010-11 STX Offshore & Shipbuilding Co Ltd — Changwon (Jinhae Shipyard)** Yd No: 4012 Loa 228.90 (BB) Br ex 32.29 Dght 14.468 Lbp 222.00 Br md 32.24 Dpth 20.10 Welded, 1 dk	**(A21A2BC) Bulk Carrier** Grain: 95,172 Compartments: 7 Ho, ER 7 Ha: ER	**1 oil engine** driving 1 FP propeller Total Power: 11,060kW (15,037hp) 14.3kn MAN-B&W 7S50MC-C 1 x 2 Stroke 7 Cy. 500 x 2000 11060kW (15037bhp) STX Engine Co Ltd-South Korea AuxGen: 3 x 625kW 450V 60Hz a.c Boilers: AuxB (Comp) 9.2kgf/cm² (9.0bar)

IMO / Call sign	Name / Owner / Port	Tonnage	Classification	Builder / Dimensions	Type / Cargo	Machinery
9460083 *6AGR* -	**WADI FERAN** **National Navigation Co** - *Alexandria* *Egypt* MMSI: 622121413 Official number: 9255	**33,234** 19,294 57,282 T/cm 57.3	Class: LR ✠ **100A1** SS 01/2011 bulk carrier CSR BC-A GRAB (20) Nos. 2 & 4 holds may be empty ESP **ShipRight** (CM,ACS (B) *IWS LI ✠ **LMC** **UMS** Eq.Ltr: N†; Cable: 659.0/76.0 U3 (a)	**2011-01 STX Offshore & Shipbuilding Co Ltd — Changwon (Jinhae Shipyard)** Yd No: 1326 Loa 190.00 (BB) Br ex 32.26 Dght 13.000 Lbp 183.30 Br md 32.26 Dpth 18.50 Welded, 1 dk	**(A21A2BC) Bulk Carrier** Grain: 71,850 Compartments: 5 Ho, ER 5 Ha: ER Cranes: 4x30t	**1 oil engine** driving 1 FP propeller Total Power: 9,480kW (12,889hp) 14.5kn MAN-B&W 6S50MC-C 1 x 2 Stroke 6 Cy. 500 x 2000 9480kW (12889bhp) STX Engine Co Ltd-South Korea AuxGen: 3 x 625kW 440V 60Hz a.c Boilers: AuxB (Comp) 9.1kgf/cm² (8.9bar)
7302938 - -	**WADI GATTARA** *ex* Costas *-1979* **National Fishing & Marketing Co (NAFIMCO)** - *Benghazi* *Libya* Official number: 232	*122* 58 -	Class: (HR)	**1972 "Naus" Shipyard Philippou Bros. S.A. — Piraeus** Loa 28.00 Br ex 6.20 Dght 2.490 Lbp 24.01 Br md 6.18 Dpth 3.31 Welded, 1 dk	**(B11A2FT) Trawler**	**1 oil engine** driving 1 CP propeller Total Power: 294kW (400hp) 12.0kn Alpha 404-26VO 1 x 2 Stroke 4 Cy. 260 x 400 294kW (400bhp) Alpha Diesel A/S-Denmark Fuel: 45.5 (d.f.)
9258777 *7OTP* -	**WADI HASSAN** **Government of The Yemeni Republic (Yemeni Ports Authority)** - *Aden* *Yemen* Official number: 0133	**313** 93 -	Class: (LR) ✠ Classed LR until 15/10/08	**2002-10 PO SevMash Predpriyatiye — Severodvinsk** (Hull) **2002-10 B.V. Scheepswerf Damen — Gorinchem** Yd No: 511708 Loa 30.82 Br ex 10.20 Dght 4.080 Lbp 28.03 Br md 9.40 Dpth 4.80 Welded, 1 dk	**(B32A2ST) Tug**	**2 oil engines** with flexible couplings & reduction geared to sc. shafts driving 2 Directional propellers Total Power: 3,600kW (4,894hp) 13.8kn Wartsila 6L26 2 x 4 Stroke 6 Cy. 260 x 320 each-1800kW (2447bhp) Wartsila Finland Oy-Finland AuxGen: 2 x 80kW 400/230V 50Hz a.c
9258789 *7OTQ* -	**WADI HATEEB** **Government of The Yemeni Republic (Yemeni Ports Authority)** - *Aden* *Yemen* Official number: 0134	**313** 93 -	Class: (LR) (NV) ✠ Classed LR until 11/8/08	**2002-12 PO SevMash Predpriyatiye — Severodvinsk** (Hull) **2002-12 B.V. Scheepswerf Damen — Gorinchem** Yd No: 511709 Loa 30.82 Br ex 10.20 Dght 4.700 Lbp 28.03 Br md 9.40 Dpth 4.80 Welded, 1 dk	**(B32A2ST) Tug**	**2 oil engines** reduction geared to sc. shafts driving 2 Directional propellers Total Power: 3,600kW (4,894hp) 12.8kn Wartsila 6L26 2 x 4 Stroke 6 Cy. 260 x 320 each-1800kW (2447bhp) Wartsila Finland Oy-Finland AuxGen: 2 x 80kW 400/230V 50Hz a.c
7350210 - -	**WADI LABRAG** *ex* Stylianos S *-1978* **National Fishing & Marketing Co (NAFIMCO)** - *Libya*	*199* 55 -	Class: (GL)	**1973 D. C. Anastassiades & A. Ch. Tsortanides — Perama** Yd No: 73 Loa 29.24 Br ex 6.68 Dght 2.998 Lbp 25.00 Br md - Dpth 3.51 Welded, 1 dk	**(B11A2FT) Trawler**	**1 oil engine** driving 1 FP propeller Total Power: 368kW (500hp) 10.0kn Alpha 405-26VO 1 x 2 Stroke 5 Cy. 260 x 400 368kW (500bhp) Alpha Diesel A/S-Denmark
9075773 *A6E2649* -	**WADI MAI** **Port of Fujairah** - *Fujairah* *United Arab Emirates* Official number: 3384F	**135** 40 66	Class: NV (LR) ✠ Classed LR until 27/11/07	**1993-10 B.V. Scheepswerf Damen Bergum — Bergum** (Hull) **1993-10 B.V. Scheepswerf Damen — Gorinchem** Yd No: 6513 Loa 22.55 Br ex 7.45 Dght 2.750 Lbp 19.82 Br md 7.20 Dpth 3.74 Welded, 1 dk	**(B32A2ST) Tug**	**2 oil engines** with clutches, flexible couplings & sr reverse geared to sc. shafts driving 2 FP propellers Total Power: 1,610kW (2,188hp) 10.6kn G.M. (Detroit Diesel) 12V-149-T 2 x Vee 2 Stroke 12 Cy. 146 x 146 each-805kW (1094bhp) General Motors Detroit DieselAllison Divn-USA AuxGen: 3 x 40kW 380/220V 50Hz a.c
7324936 - -	**WADI MJENIN** *ex* Georgios *-1979* **National Fishing & Marketing Co (NAFIMCO)** - *Benghazi* *Libya*	*124* 60 -	Class: (HR)	**1973 "Naus" Shipyard Philippou Bros. S.A. — Piraeus** Loa 28.00 Br ex 6.20 Dght 2.490 Lbp 24.01 Br md 6.19 Dpth 3.31 Welded, 1 dk	**(B11A2FT) Trawler**	**1 oil engine** driving 1 CP propeller Total Power: 294kW (400hp) 12.0kn Alpha 404-26VO 1 x 2 Stroke 4 Cy. 260 x 400 294kW (400bhp) Alpha Diesel A/S-Denmark Fuel: 45.5 (d.f.)
9185982 *A6E2691* -	**WADI SAFAD** **Port of Fujairah** - *Fujairah* *United Arab Emirates* MMSI: 470533000 Official number: 4474	**377** 113 378	Class: NV (LR) ✠ Classed LR until 15/11/07	**1999-01 Scheepsbouw Alblas B.V. — Hendrik-Ido-Ambacht** (Hull) **1999-01 B.V. Scheepswerf Damen — Gorinchem** Yd No: 4723 Loa 37.13 Br ex 9.47 Dght 3.848 Lbp 32.93 Br md 9.00 Dpth 4.75 Welded, 1 dk	**(B32A2ST) Tug**	**2 oil engines** geared to sc. shafts driving 2 CP propellers Total Power: 3,880kW (5,276hp) 13.8kn Caterpillar 3606TA 2 x 4 Stroke 6 Cy. 280 x 300 each-1940kW (2638bhp) Caterpillar Inc-USA AuxGen: 2 x 142kW 380/220V 50Hz a.c Thrusters: 1 Thwart. FP thruster (f)
9460734 *6AGP* -	**WADI SAFAGA** **National Navigation Co** - *Alexandria* *Egypt* MMSI: 622121422 Official number: 9253	**43,736** 31,183 80,443 T/cm 71.9	Class: LR ✠ **100A1** SS 07/2010 bulk carrier CSR BC-A GRAB (20) Nos. 2, 4 & 6 holds may be empty ESP **ShipRight** (ACS (B), CM) *IWS LI ✠ **LMC** **UMS** Eq.Ltr: Q†; Cable: 687.5/81.0 U3 (a)	**2010-07 STX Offshore & Shipbuilding Co Ltd — Changwon (Jinhae Shipyard)** Yd No: 4006 Loa 228.90 (BB) Br ex 32.29 Dght 14.450 Lbp 222.00 Br md 32.24 Dpth 20.10 Welded, 1 dk	**(A21A2BC) Bulk Carrier** Grain: 95,172 Compartments: 7 Ho, ER 7 Ha: ER	**1 oil engine** driving 1 FP propeller Total Power: 11,060kW (15,037hp) 14.4kn MAN-B&W 7S50MC-C 1 x 2 Stroke 7 Cy. 500 x 2000 11060kW (15037bhp) STX Engine Co Ltd-South Korea AuxGen: 3 x 625kW 450V 60Hz a.c Boilers: WTAuxB (Comp) 9.3kgf/cm² (9.1bar)
9150391 *A6E2617* -	**WADI SAHAM** **Port of Fujairah** - *Fujairah* *United Arab Emirates* Official number: 4144	**212** 63 180	Class: NV (LR) ✠ Classed LR until 15/11/07	**1997-01 Scheepswerf Made B.V. — Made** (Hull) **1997-01 B.V. Scheepswerf Damen — Gorinchem** Yd No: 3190 Loa 30.05 Br ex 8.42 Dght 3.400 Lbp 27.50 Br md 7.80 Dpth 4.05 Welded, 1 dk	**(B32A2ST) Tug**	**2 oil engines** sr reverse geared to sc. shafts driving 2 FP propellers Total Power: 2,550kW (3,466hp) 12.2kn Caterpillar 3516TA 2 x Vee 4 Stroke 16 Cy. 170 x 190 each-1275kW (1733bhp) Caterpillar Inc-USA AuxGen: 2 x 57kW 380/220V 50Hz a.c
7392505 - -	**WADI SHATT** *ex* Eleni S *-1980* **National Fishing & Marketing Co (NAFIMCO)** - *Benghazi* *Libya*	*119* 55 111	Class: (LR) (GL) Classed LR until 29/1/97	**1975-02 D. C. Anastassiades & A. Ch. Tsortanides — Perama** Yd No: 80 Loa 29.25 Br ex 6.70 Dght 2.794 Lbp 26.74 Br md 6.68 Dpth 3.50 Welded, 1 dk	**(B11A2FT) Trawler**	**1 oil engine** driving 1 CP propeller Total Power: 441kW (600hp) 10.0kn Alpha 406-26VO 1 x 2 Stroke 6 Cy. 260 x 400 441kW (600bhp) Alpha Diesel A/S-Denmark AuxGen: 2 x 72kW 380V 50Hz a.c
9194775 *A6E3046* -	**WADI SIDR** **Port of Fujairah** - *Fujairah* *United Arab Emirates* MMSI: 470888000 Official number: 5210	**198** 59 -	Class: NV (LR) ✠ Classed LR until 27/11/07	**2006-01 OAO Leningradskiy Sudostroitelnyy Zavod 'Pella' — Otradnoye** (Hull) **2006-01 B.V. Scheepswerf Damen — Gorinchem** Yd No: 510806 Loa 25.86 Br ex 9.25 Dght 3.650 Lbp 23.00 Br md 8.90 Dpth 4.30 Welded, 1 dk	**(B32A2ST) Tug**	**2 oil engines** reduction geared to sc. shafts driving 2 Directional propellers Total Power: 2,500kW (3,400hp) Caterpillar 3512B-HD 2 x Vee 4 Stroke 12 Cy. 170 x 215 each-1250kW (1700bhp) Caterpillar Inc-USA AuxGen: 2 x 84kW 400V 50Hz a.c
9077903 *SSHX* -	**WADI SUDR** **National Navigation Co** - SatCom: Inmarsat C 462211615 *Alexandria* *Egypt* MMSI: 622121421 Official number: 4227	**37,550** 20,055 64,214 T/cm 65.5	Class: LR ✠ **100A1** SS 05/2009 bulk carrier strengthened for heavy cargoes, Nos. 2, 4 & 6 holds may be empty ESP ESN-Hold 1 LI Ice Class 1D ✠ **LMC** **UMS** Eq.Ltr: N†; Cable: 660.0/76.0 U3	**1994-05 Daewoo Shipbuilding & Heavy Machinery Ltd — Geoje** Yd No: 1074 Loa 225.00 (BB) Br ex 32.24 Dght 12.400 Lbp 215.00 Br md 32.20 Dpth 18.50 Welded, 1 dk	**(A21A2BC) Bulk Carrier** Grain: 82,210; Bale: 78,338 Compartments: 7 Ho, ER 7 Ha: 6 (16.6 x 14.9) (16.6 x 14.9)ER Ice Capable	**1 oil engine** driving 1 FP propeller Total Power: 8,555kW (11,631hp) 13.5kn B&W 6S50MC 1 x 2 Stroke 6 Cy. 500 x 1910 8555kW (11631bhp) Korea Heavy Industries & ConstrCo Ltd (HANJUNG)-South Korea AuxGen: 3 x 500kW 450V 60Hz a.c Boilers: AuxB (o.f.) 7.0kgf/cm² (6.9bar), AuxB (e.g.) 7.0kgf/cm² (6.9bar) Fuel: 190.7 (d.f.) 2237.8 (r.f.) 29.0pd

IMO / Call sign	Name / Owner / Flag	Tonnage	Class	Builder / Dimensions	Type / Capacities	Machinery
9460746 6AGU -	**WADI TIBA** **National Navigation Co** - *Alexandria* *Egypt* MMSI: 622121409 Official number: 9258	**43,736** 31,183 80,469 T/cm 71.9	Class: LR ✠ **100A1** SS 04/2011 bulk carrier CSR BC-A GRAB (20) Nos. 2, 4 & 6 holds may be empty ESP **ShipRight** (ACS (B), CM) *IWS LI ✠ **LMC** **UMS** Eq.Ltr: Q†; Cable: 687.5/81.0 U3 (a)	**2011-04 STX Offshore & Shipbuilding Co Ltd — Changwon (Jinhae Shipyard)** Yd No: 4014 Loa 229.00 (BB) Br ex 32.29 Dght 14.450 Lbp 222.00 Br md 32.24 Dpth 20.10 Welded, 1 dk	**(A21A2BC) Bulk Carrier** Grain: 95,172 Compartments: 7 Ho, ER 7 Ha: ER	**1 oil engine** driving 1 FP propeller Total Power: 11,060kW (15,037hp) 14.4kn MAN-B&W 7S50MC-C 1 x 2 Stroke 7 Cy. 500 x 2000 11060kW (15037bhp) STX Engine Co Ltd-South Korea AuxGen: 3 x 625kW 450V 60Hz a.c Boilers: AuxB (Comp) 9.2kgf/cm² (9.0bar)
7350399 - -	**WADI TLAL** *ex* Bengazi *-1978* *ex* Panormitis Junior *-1976* **National Fishing & Marketing Co (NAFIMCO)** - *Benghazi* *Libya*	*142* - 71	Class: (BV)	**1974 D. Kamitsis & Co. — Piraeus** Loa 29.65 Br ex - Dght - Lbp 26.90 Br md 6.81 Dpth 3.20 Welded, 1 dk	**(B11A2FT) Trawler**	**1 oil engine** driving 1 FP propeller Total Power: 441kW (600hp) Alpha 406-26VO 1 x 2 Stroke 6 Cy. 260 x 400 441kW (600bhp) Alpha Diesel A/S-Denmark
7324998 - -	**WADI ZAMZAM** *ex* Panagiota *-1978* **National Fishing & Marketing Co (NAFIMCO)** - *Benghazi* *Libya* Official number: 4506	*142* 70 -	Class: (BV)	**1973 D. Kamitsis & Co. — Piraeus** Loa 29.55 Br ex - Dght 2.845 Lbp 26.98 Br md 6.81 Dpth 3.61 Welded, 1 dk	**(B11A2FT) Trawler** Grain: 90	**1 oil engine** driving 1 CP propeller Total Power: 368kW (500hp) 11.0kn Alpha 405-26VO 1 x 2 Stroke 5 Cy. 260 x 400 368kW (500bhp) Alpha Diesel A/S-Denmark
8406212 VNRB -	**WADJEMUP** **Sea Swift Pty Ltd** - *Cairns, Qld* *Australia* Official number: 851450	*214* 64 175		**1984-12 Elder Prince Marine Services Pty Ltd — Fremantle WA** Yd No: 25 Loa 34.45 Br ex - Dght 1.713 Lbp 30.89 Br md 8.23 Dpth 2.16 Welded, 1 dk	**(A35D2RL) Landing Craft** Bow ramp (centre) Lane-Len: 31 Liq: 240	**3 oil engines** with clutches, flexible couplings & sr reverse geared to sc. shafts driving 3 FP propellers Total Power: 522kW (711hp) 9.0kn Rolls Royce C6NFLM 1 x 4 Stroke 6 Cy. 130 x 152 174kW (237bhp) Rolls Royce Ltd.-Coventry Rolls Royce C6TFL 2 x 4 Stroke 6 Cy. 130 x 152 each-174kW (237bhp) Rolls Royce Ltd.-Coventry AuxGen: 1 x 30kW 415V 50Hz a.c
9488102 C6XW7 -	**WADOWICE II** *ex* Wadowice *-2010* **Ares Ten Shipping Ltd** Polska Zegluga Morska PP (POLSTEAM) *Nassau* *Bahamas* MMSI: 311024300 Official number: 8001662	**24,055** 12,162 38,061	Class: AB PR	**2010-03 Tianjin Xingang Shipbuilding Industry Co Ltd — Tianjin** Yd No: 345-14 Loa 189.99 (BB) Br ex - Dght 10.400 Lbp 183.70 Br md 28.50 Dpth 15.10 Welded, 1 dk	**(A21A2BC) Bulk Carrier** Double Hull Grain: 49,032; Bale: 47,849 Compartments: 5 Ho, ER 5 Ha: ER Cranes: 4x30t Ice Capable	**1 oil engine** driving 1 FP propeller Total Power: 8,730kW (11,869hp) 14.0kn Wartsila 6RTA48T 1 x 2 Stroke 6 Cy. 480 x 2000 8730kW (11869bhp) Yichang Marine Diesel Engine Co Ltd-China AuxGen: 3 x 645kW a.c Fuel: 174.0 (d.f.) 1870.0 (r.f.)
8716485 5TMK -	**WAFA 12** *ex* Peix del Mar Doce *-2001* **Eurorim Industries Sem** - *Mauritania* MMSI: 654015400 Official number: NDB 858	**364** 109 150	Class: (BV)	**1988-06 Astilleros Zamakona SA — Santurtzi** Yd No: 150 Loa 36.71 Br ex - Dght 3.401 Lbp 31.68 Br md 8.31 Dpth 5.41 Welded, 1 dk	**(B11A2FS) Stern Trawler** Ins: 277	**1 oil engine** with flexible couplings & sr geared to sc. shaft driving 1 FP propeller Total Power: 780kW (1,060hp) Caterpillar 3512TA 1 x Vee 4 Stroke 12 Cy. 170 x 190 780kW (1060bhp) Caterpillar Inc-USA
7204265 - -	**WAFA ALBARRAK 5** *ex* Mo-Een *-1990* **Fatma Ghanih Abdul Tamam Abbadian** - *Kuwait* *Kuwait* Official number: KT1128	*160* 47 -	Class: (LR) ✠ Classed LR until 11/72	**1972-03 Hayashikane Shipbuilding & Engineering Co Ltd — Yokosuka KN** Yd No: 705 Loa 28.28 Br ex 8.01 Dght 2.864 Lbp 27.01 Br md 7.80 Dpth 3.41 Welded, 1 dk	**(B32A2ST) Tug**	**2 oil engines** driving 2 Directional propellers Total Power: 1,060kW (1,442hp) MAN G6V235/330ATL 2 x 4 Stroke 6 Cy. 235 x 330 each-530kW (721bhp) Maschinenbau Augsburg Nuernberg (MAN)-Augsburg
7009964 9KYE -	**WAFA ALBARRAK 6** *ex* Mumtaz *-1990* **Fatma Ghanih Abdul Tamam Abbadian** - *Kuwait* *Kuwait* Official number: KT1056	*158* - -	Class: (LR) ✠ Classed LR until 8/71	**1970-03 Hayashikane Shipbuilding & Engineering Co Ltd — Yokosuka KN** Yd No: 681 Loa 28.28 Br ex 8.01 Dght 2.566 Lbp 27.01 Br md 7.80 Dpth 3.41 Welded, 1 dk	**(B32A2ST) Tug**	**2 oil engines** driving 2 Voith-Schneider propellers Total Power: 1,030kW (1,400hp) MAN G6V235/330ATL 2 x 4 Stroke 6 Cy. 235 x 330 each-515kW (700bhp) Maschinenbau Augsburg Nuernberg (MAN)-Augsburg
9086318 V7LG7 -	**WAFFLE RACER** *ex* African Leopard *-2006* *ex* Pacific Mattsu *-2005* **Sirocco Management SA** Narwhal Maritime Enterprises Inc *Majuro* *Marshall Islands* MMSI: 538002741 Official number: 2741	**16,041** 9,280 26,467 T/cm 37.9	Class: BV (LR) ✠ Classed LR until 5/1/05	**1996-06 Guangzhou Shipyard International Co Ltd — Guangzhou GD** Yd No: 3130011 Loa 168.68 (BB) Br ex 26.03 Dght 9.540 Lbp 160.00 Br md 26.00 Dpth 13.30 Welded, 1 dk	**(A21A2BC) Bulk Carrier** Grain: 33,858; Bale: 32,700 Compartments: 5 Ho, ER 5 Ha: (13.9 x 13.1)4 (19.3 x 13.1)ER Cranes: 4x30t	**1 oil engine** driving 1 FP propeller Total Power: 6,074kW (8,258hp) 14.0kn B&W 5L50MC 1 x 2 Stroke 5 Cy. 500 x 1620 6074kW (8258bhp) Hudong Shipyard-China AuxGen: 3 x 456kW 450V 60Hz a.c Boilers: AuxB (Comp) 6.8kgf/cm² (6.7bar) Fuel: 180.0 (d.f.) 1180.0 (r.f.) 24.0pd
9332535 C6VX6 -	**WAFRAH** **The National Shipping Company of Saudi Arabia (BAHRI)** Mideast Ship Management Ltd SatCom: Inmarsat B 330984510 *Nassau* *Bahamas* MMSI: 309845000 Official number: 8001311	**160,782** 109,346 317,788 T/cm 178.0	Class: NV	**2007-02 Hyundai Samho Heavy Industries Co Ltd — Samho** Yd No: S300 Loa 333.04 (BB) Br ex 60.05 Dght 22.522 Lbp 319.00 Br md 60.00 Dpth 30.40 Welded, 1 dk	**(A13A2TV) Crude Oil Tanker** Double Hull (13F) Liq: 336,522; Liq (Oil): 336,522 Compartments: 5 Ta, 10 Wing Ta, 2 Wing Slop Ta, ER 3 Cargo Pump (s): 3x5500m³/hr Manifold: Bow/CM: 165m	**1 oil engine** driving 1 FP propeller Total Power: 30,266kW (41,150hp) 15.5kn Sulzer 8RTA84T-D 1 x 2 Stroke 8 Cy. 840 x 3150 30266kW (41150bhp) Hyundai Heavy Industries Co Ltd-South Korea AuxGen: 3 x 1300kW 450V 60Hz a.c Fuel: 405.0 (d.f.) 8900.0 (r.f.) 120.0pd
9328170 9KEG -	**WAFRAH** **Kuwait Oil Tanker Co SAK** - SatCom: Inmarsat C 444715355 *Kuwait* *Kuwait* MMSI: 447162000 Official number: KT1732	**63,440** 34,794 113,849 T/cm 99.2	Class: LR ✠ **100A1** SS 10/2012 Double Hull oil tanker ESP *IWS LI SPM EP (Vc) **ShipRight** (SDA, FDA, CM) ✠ **LMC** **UMS IGS** Eq.Ltr: W†; Cable: 742.5/95.0 U3 (a)	**2007-10 Daewoo Shipbuilding & Marine Engineering Co Ltd — Geoje** Yd No: 5269 Loa 249.90 (BB) Br ex 44.04 Dght 14.825 Lbp 239.00 Br md 44.00 Dpth 21.00 Welded, 1 dk	**(A13A2TW) Crude/Oil Products Tanker** Double Hull (13F) Liq: 124,520; Liq (Oil): 124,519 Compartments: 12 Wing Ta, 2 Wing Slop Ta, ER 3 Cargo Pump (s): 3x3500m³/hr Manifold: Bow/CM: 125.4m	**1 oil engine** driving 1 FP propeller Total Power: 15,806kW (21,490hp) 15.5kn MAN-B&W 7S60MC-C 1 x 2 Stroke 7 Cy. 600 x 2400 15806kW (21490bhp) Doosan Engine Co Ltd-South Korea AuxGen: 3 x 1100kW 450V 60Hz a.c Boilers: e (ex.g.) 23.5kgf/cm² (23.0bar), AuxB (o.f.) 18.6kgf/cm² (18.2bar) Fuel: 221.0 (d.f.) (Heating Coils) 3845.0 (r.f.)
9029889 - -	**WAG I** *ex* Spob Wag I *-2005* **PT Samudera Andalan Suramadu** - *Surabaya* *Indonesia*	**497** 287 -	Class: KI	**2001-01 P.T. PAL Indonesia — Surabaya** Loa 33.70 Br ex - Dght - Lbp 32.50 Br md 13.45 Dpth 3.50 Welded, 1 dk	**(A13B2TU) Tanker (unspecified)** Double Hull (13F)	**2 oil engines** geared to sc. shafts driving 2 Propellers Total Power: 530kW (720hp) 6.0kn Caterpillar D343TA 2 x 4 Stroke 6 Cy. 137 x 165 each-265kW (360bhp) Caterpillar Inc-USA AuxGen: 1 x 88kW 380/220V a.c
9268825 HPLR -	**WAH SHAN** **Newton Navigation Ltd** Sincere Navigation Corp SatCom: Inmarsat C 435504810 *Panama* *Panama* MMSI: 355048000 Official number: 2945403B	**91,165** 58,753 175,980 T/cm 122.0	Class: AB	**2003-10 China Shipbuilding Corp (CSBC) — Kaohsiung** Yd No: 807 Loa 289.00 (BB) Br ex 45.06 Dght 17.809 Lbp 281.50 Br md 45.00 Dpth 24.10 Welded, 1 dk	**(A21A2BC) Bulk Carrier** Grain: 195,362; Ore: 104,430 Compartments: 9 Ho, ER 9 Ha: 7 (16.4 x 21.6) (16.4 x 21.6)ER (15.5 x 18.0)	**1 oil engine** driving 1 FP propeller Total Power: 15,000kW (20,394hp) 14.8kn B&W 6S70MC-C 1 x 2 Stroke 6 Cy. 700 x 2800 15000kW (20394bhp) Hitachi Zosen Corp-Japan AuxGen: 3 x 720kW 450/110V 60Hz a.c Fuel: 116.0 (d.f.) 3994.0 (r.f.) 53.0pd
8896821 HQXN3 -	**WAH TUNG** *ex* Bei Bu Wan 6 *-2012* *ex* Hui Bo Quan *-2008* **Wah Tung Shipping Asia Development Co** - *San Lorenzo* *Honduras* MMSI: 334800000 Official number: L-0638540	**2,758** 1,046 3,316 T/cm 10.6	Class: (CC)	**1994-05 Qingdao Lingshan Shipyard — Jiaonan SD** Loa 84.57 Br ex - Dght 5.300 Lbp 79.00 Br md 15.00 Dpth 7.30 Welded, 1 dk	**(A33A2CC) Container Ship (Fully Cellular)** Bale: 4,954 TEU 170 C Ho 88 TEU C Dk 82 TEU incl 15 ref C. Compartments: 2 Cell Ho, ER 4 Ha: ER Ice Capable	**1 oil engine** reduction geared to sc. shaft driving 1 FP propeller Total Power: 1,103kW (1,500hp) 10.3kn Guangzhou 6320ZCD 1 x 4 Stroke 6 Cy. 320 x 440 1103kW (1500bhp) Guangzhou Diesel Engine Factory CoLtd-China AuxGen: 3 x 120kW 400V a.c Fuel: 28.0 (d.f.) 160.0 5.0pd

IMO / Call sign	Name / Owner	Tonnage	Class	Build / Dimensions	Type	Machinery
9679804 *VRLZ9* -	**WAH YAU 2** **Moral Express Ltd** - *Hong Kong* *Hong Kong* MMSI: 477995284 Official number: HK-3815	**1,119** 366 1,496	Class: CC	**2013-03 Zhuhai Doumen Baijiao Xingxingli Shipyard Co Ltd — Zhuhai GD** Yd No: 011016 Loa 40.23 Br ex - Dght 4.500 Lbp 37.70 Br md 16.50 Dpth 6.50 Welded, 1 dk	**(A13B2TP) Products Tanker** Double Hull (13F) Liq: 1,496; Liq (Oil): 1,496 Compartments: 1 Ta, 3 Wing Ta, 3 Wing Ta, 1 Wing Slop Ta, 1 Wing Slop Ta, ER	**2 oil engines** reduction geared to sc. shafts driving 2 Propellers Total Power: 1,268kW (1,724hp) Caterpillar C32 2 x Vee 4 Stroke 12 Cy. 145 x 162 each-634kW (862bhp) Caterpillar Inc-USA AuxGen: 2 x 86kW 400V a.c
9320582 *J8B4878* -	**WAHA MERMAID** *ex Jaya Mermaid 2 -2010* **Waha Mermaid Ltd** Waha Marine Agency LLC *Kingstown* *St Vincent & The Grenadines* MMSI: 376967000 Official number: 11351	**1,083** 325 827	Class: AB	**2006-04 Guangdong Hope Yue Shipbuilding Industry Ltd — Guangzhou GD** Yd No: 2125 Loa 50.00 Br ex - Dght 4.800 Lbp 45.72 Br md 13.80 Dpth 6.00 Welded, 1 dk	**(B32A2ST) Tug**	**2 oil engines** geared to sc. shafts driving 2 CP propellers Total Power: 4,046kW (5,500hp) 13.0kn Wartsila 6L26A 2 x 4 Stroke 6 Cy. 260 x 320 each-2023kW (2750bhp) Wartsila Finland Oy-Finland Thrusters: 1 Tunnel thruster (f)
8653853 - -	**WAHANA 2** **PT Pelayaran Sumber Bahari** - *Batam* *Indonesia*	**291** 88 -	Class: KI	**2010-11 PT Sumber Samudra Makmur — Batam** Loa 31.00 Br ex — Dght 3.200 Lbp 28.49 Br md 9.00 Dpth 4.00 Welded, 1 dk	**(B32A2ST) Tug**	**2 oil engines** reduction geared to sc. shafts driving 2 Propellers Total Power: 2,942kW (4,000hp) 8.0kn Yanmar 6N260-EN 2 x 4 Stroke 6 Cy. 260 x 360 each-1471kW (2000bhp) Yanmar Diesel Engine Co Ltd-Japan AuxGen: 2 x 50kW 400/230V a.c
8655693 *YD3824* -	**WAHANA 3** **PT Pelayaran Sumber Bahari** - *Batam* *Indonesia*	**236** 71 -	Class: KI	**2011-04 PT Sumber Samudra Makmur — Batam** Loa 29.30 Br ex — Dght 3.140 Lbp 27.14 Br md 8.20 Dpth 4.20 Welded, 1 dk	**(B32A2ST) Tug**	**2 oil engines** reduction geared to sc. shafts driving 2 Propellers Total Power: 1,600kW (2,176hp) 10.0kn Yanmar 6N21AL-EN 2 x 4 Stroke 6 Cy. 210 x 290 each-800kW (1088bhp) Yanmar Diesel Engine Co Ltd-Japan AuxGen: 2 x 90kW 400V a.c
8957338 *YD3678* -	**WAHANA 7** *ex International No. 1 -2010* **PT Wahana Wiratama Line** - *Batam* *Indonesia*	*100* 30 -	Class: KI	**1993 Xiamen Shipyard — Xiamen FJ** Loa 23.65 Br ex - Dght - Lbp 21.88 Br md 6.80 Dpth 3.60 Welded, 1 dk	**(B32A2ST) Tug**	**1 oil engine** driving 1 FP propeller Total Power: 655kW (891hp) 11.0kn Caterpillar 3508C 1 x Vee 4 Stroke 8 Cy. 170 x 190 655kW (891bhp) Caterpillar Inc-USA AuxGen: 1 x 6kW 220V a.c, 1 x 16kW 220V a.c
6925496 *YHJJ* -	**WAHANA BAHARI** *ex Gina -2006 ex Swadaya -1994* *ex Diana -1989 ex New Spirit -1986* *ex Margarita II -1985 ex Kormoran 1 -1982* *ex Kormoran -1977 ex Kormoran Isle -1972* **PT Wahana Baruna Khatulistiwa** - *Pontianak* *Indonesia*	**1,608** 809 1,938	Class: KI (GL)	**1969-03 Gebr. Schuerenstedt KG Schiffs- u. Bootswerft — Berne** Yd No: 1350 Loa 82.10 (BB) Br ex 12.83 Dght 3.817 Lbp 77.20 Br md 12.81 Dpth 6.15 Welded, 2 dks	**(A31A2GX) General Cargo Ship** TEU 126 C Ho 50 TEU C Dk 76 TEU Compartments: 2 Ho, ER 2 Ha: ER Ice Capable	**1 oil engine** driving 1 FP propeller Total Power: 1,765kW (2,400hp) 15.0kn MaK 6MU551AK 1 x 4 Stroke 6 Cy. 450 x 550 1765kW (2400bhp) Atlas MaK Maschinenbau GmbH-Kiel AuxGen: 3 x 175kW 220/380V 50Hz a.c
8743115 *YD3660* -	**WAHANA I** **PT Wahana Mitra Bahari** - *Batam* *Indonesia* MMSI: 525011030	**159** 48 -	Class: KI	**2009-11 PT Sumber Samudra Makmur — Batam** Loa 25.00 Br ex — Dght 2.600 Lbp 23.33 Br md 7.00 Dpth 3.60 Welded, 1 dk	**(B32A2ST) Tug**	**2 oil engines** reduction geared to sc. shafts driving 2 Propellers Total Power: 1,324kW (1,800hp) 10.0kn Caterpillar D398 2 x Vee 4 Stroke 12 Cy. 159 x 203 each-662kW (900bhp) (Re-engined , Reconditioned & refitted 2009) Caterpillar Inc-USA AuxGen: 2 x 65kW 380/230V a.c
7109520 *YHFP* -	**WAHANA NUSANTARA** *ex Sin You -2002 ex Shinryu I -1992* *ex Shinryu Maru -1989* **Ali Sentosa Lie** - *Pontianak* *Indonesia*	*1,020* 573 1,500	Class: KI	**1971-03 Honda Zosen — Saiki** Yd No: 586 Loa 63.87 Br ex 11.03 Dght 4.249 Lbp 61.00 Br md 11.00 Dpth 6.20 Welded, 1 dk	**(A31A2GX) General Cargo Ship** Compartments: 1 Ho, ER 1 Ha: (32.0 x 8.6)ER	**1 oil engine** driving 1 FP propeller Total Power: 993kW (1,350hp) 12.0kn Usuki 6MRS35HC 1 x 4 Stroke 6 Cy. 350 x 500 993kW (1350bhp) Usuki Tekkosho-Usuki
9029217 - -	**WAHANA SEJAHTERA** **PT Pelayaran Taruna Kusan Jaya (Taruna Kusan Jaya Shipping Inc)** - *Balikpapan* *Indonesia*	**561** 169 -	Class: KI	**2002-07 P.T. Galangan Balikpapan Utama — Balikpapan** Loa 48.00 Br ex - Dght - Lbp 45.50 Br md 12.80 Dpth 3.45 Welded, 1 dk	**(A35D2RL) Landing Craft**	**2 oil engines** driving 2 Propellers Total Power: 706kW (960hp) Yanmar 6MA-HTS 2 x 4 Stroke 6 Cy. 200 x 240 each-353kW (480bhp) Yanmar Diesel Engine Co Ltd-Japan AuxGen: 2 x 82kW 380/220V a.c
9028005 *YFAX* -	**WAHANA UTAMA XI** *ex Daiun Maru No. 18 -1993* *ex Shunzan Maru No. 5 -1993* **PT Bandar Bahari Permai** - *Surabaya* *Indonesia*	**480** 275 531	Class: (KI)	**1970-12 K.K. Miura Zosensho — Saiki** Loa 50.00 Br ex - Dght 3.000 Lbp 45.00 Br md 9.00 Dpth 4.90 Welded, 1 dk	**(A31A2GX) General Cargo Ship** Compartments: 1 Ho, ER 1 Ha: ER	**1 oil engine** driving 1 Propeller Total Power: 552kW (750hp) 9.5kn Otsuka SODTHS628 1 x 4 Stroke 6 Cy. 280 x 400 552kW (750bhp) KK Otsuka Diesel-Japan
8853960 - -	**WAHEI MARU** *ex Jyoyo Maru No. 38 -1991* - - *South Korea*	*101* - -		**1974 Shonan Zosen — Fukuyama** Loa 22.06 Br ex - Dght - Lbp 21.80 Br md 6.10 Dpth 2.75 Welded, 1 dk	**(B32B2SP) Pusher Tug**	**1 oil engine** driving 1 FP propeller Total Power: 883kW (1,201hp) 10.5kn Hanshin 1 x 4 Stroke 883kW (1201bhp) The Hanshin Diesel Works Ltd-Japan
9690602 *JD3641* -	**WAHEI MARU** **Heian Kaiun KK** - *Japan* MMSI: 431005189	*749* 9 2,180	Class: NK (Class contemplated)	**2014-01 K.K. Miura Zosensho — Saiki** Yd No: 1508 Loa 79.80 Br ex - Dght 7.800 Lbp - Br md 14.00 Dpth - Welded, 1 dk	**(A24D2BA) Aggregates Carrier** Double Hull	**1 oil engine** reduction geared to sc. shafts driving 1 Propeller Total Power: 1,840kW (2,502hp) Yanmar 6EY26 1 x 4 Stroke 6 Cy. 260 x 385 1840kW (2502bhp) Yanmar Diesel Engine Co Ltd-Japan
8852590 *WDC4898* -	**WAHOO** *ex Frank Purky -1995* **All Coast LLC** - *New Orleans, LA* *United States of America* MMSI: 367032490 Official number: 973475	*491* 384 -		**1981-07 Promet Pte Ltd — Singapore** Yd No: 1085 Loa - Br ex - Dght - Lbp 32.77 Br md 22.28 Dpth 2.96 Welded, 1 dk	**(B22A2ZM) Offshore Construction Vessel, jack up** Cranes: 1x70t,1x8t	**4 oil engines** reduction geared to sc. shafts driving 2 FP propellers Total Power: 1,000kW (1,360hp) G.M. (Detroit Diesel) 12V-71-N 4 x Vee 2 Stroke 12 Cy. 108 x 127 each-250kW (340bhp) General Motors Detroit DieselAllison Divn-USA
9707950 *J8B4911* -	**WAHOO I** **National Port Services Co Ltd** - *Kingstown* *St Vincent & The Grenadines* MMSI: 376944000 Official number: 11461	**155** 65 -	Class: BV	**2013-10 Damen Shipyards Changde Co Ltd — Changde HN** (Hull) Yd No: (512911) **2013-10 B.V. Scheepswerf Damen — Gorinchem** Yd No: 512911 Loa 22.73 Br ex - Dght 3.400 Lbp 20.38 Br md 10.43 Dpth 4.50 Welded, 1 dk	**(B32A2ST) Tug**	**2 oil engines** reduction geared to sc. shafts driving 2 FP propellers Total Power: 2,960kW (4,024hp) Caterpillar 3512B-HD 2 x Vee 4 Stroke 12 Cy. 170 x 215 each-1480kW (2012bhp) Caterpillar Inc-USA AuxGen: 2 x 51kW 50Hz a.c Fuel: 62.0
7950785 - -	**WAHYU** *ex Central Star 2 -2000* *ex Tank Petroleum 2 -1994* *ex Shinpuku Maru -1991* *ex Takeshima Maru No. 8 -1986* **Mujur Suria Sdn Bhd** - *San Lorenzo* *Honduras* Official number: L-1327675	**307** 155 500 T/cm 2.8	Class: (GL)	**1975-03 Takeshima Zosen K.K. — Japan** Loa 46.00 Br ex - Dght 2.901 Lbp 42.02 Br md 7.51 Dpth 3.41 Welded, 1 dk	**(A13B2TU) Tanker (unspecified)** 1 Cargo Pump (s)	**1 oil engine** driving 1 FP propeller Total Power: 515kW (700hp) 12.5kn Niigata 6MG20AX 1 x 4 Stroke 6 Cy. 200 x 260 515kW (700bhp) Niigata Engineering Co Ltd-Japan
8035582 *YHDH* -	**WAHYU PANDAN ARAN** *ex Kissei Maru -2005 ex Kitsusei Maru -2001* **PT Pelayaran Pualam Emas Sejahtera** - *Semarang* *Indonesia* MMSI: 525015319	**960** 288 -	Class: KI	**1981-07 Azumi Zosen Kensetsu K.K. — Himeji** Yd No: 87 Loa 52.30 Br ex - Dght 3.250 Lbp 49.00 Br md 17.51 Dpth 3.55 Welded, 1 dk	**(B34T2QR) Work/Repair Vessel**	**1 oil engine** driving 1 FP propeller Total Power: 736kW (1,001hp) 8.0kn Yanmar MF28-HT 1 x 4 Stroke 6 Cy. 280 x 450 736kW (1001bhp) Yanmar Diesel Engine Co Ltd-Japan

IMO / Call sign	Name / Owner / Port	Tonnage	Class	Built / Dimensions	Type	Machinery
8898398 - -	**WAI KEE M61** - **Wai Shun Shipyard Ltd** - *Dongying, Shandong* China	**140** 78 90	Class: (CC)	**1995-03 Zhejiang Huzhou Shipyard — Huzhou ZJ** Loa 23.80 Br ex - Dght - Lbp 22.00 Br md 7.20 Dpth 3.40 Welded, 1 dk	**(B21A2OS) Platform Supply Ship**	**2 oil engines** geared to sc. shafts driving 2 FP propellers Total Power: 388kW (528hp) Chinese Std. Type 12V135C 2 x Vee 4 Stroke 12 Cy. 135 x 140 each-194kW (264bhp) Wuxi Antai Power Machinery Co Ltd-China
8888020 - -	**WAI LUN 3389** - - -	*255* 160 -		**1990 in the People's Republic of China** Loa 42.50 Br ex - Dght - Lbp - Br md 6.40 Dpth 3.40 Welded, 1 dk	**(A31A2GX) General Cargo Ship**	**1 oil engine** driving 1 FP propeller
8888018 - -	**WAI LUN 9018** - - -	*255* 160 -		**1990 in the People's Republic of China** Loa 42.50 Br ex - Dght - Lbp - Br md 6.40 Dpth 3.40 Welded, 1 dk	**(A31A2GX) General Cargo Ship**	**1 oil engine** driving 1 FP propeller
8105674 *PNOY* -	**WAIGEO** *ex Anesun -2011 ex Toyo Maru No. 75 -1993* **PT Ombre Lines** - *Jakarta* Indonesia	**912** 558 1,747 T/cm 6.0	Class: KI (CC)	**1981-09 Imamura Zosen — Kure** Yd No: 275 Loa 70.31 (BB) Br ex 11.21 Dght 4.652 Lbp 64.50 Br md 11.00 Dpth 5.01 Welded, 1 dk	**(A13B2TP) Products Tanker** Liq: 2,000; Liq (Oil): 2,000 Compartments: 10 Ta, ER 2 Cargo Pump (s)	**1 oil engine** driving 1 CP propeller Total Power: 1,324kW (1,800hp) Hanshin 6EL30 1 x 4 Stroke 6 Cy. 300 x 600 1324kW (1800bhp) The Hanshin Diesel Works Ltd-Japan
7327835 *ZMIN* -	**WAIHOLA** *ex Irene M -1978* **Sanford Ltd** - *Dunedin* New Zealand MMSI: 512145000 Official number: 355808	**286** 86 -	Class: (AB)	**1973-07 Dae Sun Shipbuilding & Engineering Co Ltd — Busan** Yd No: 166 L reg 32.13 Br ex - Dght - Lbp - Br md 8.63 Dpth 3.84 Welded, 1 dk	**(B11B2FV) Fishing Vessel** Compartments: 6 Ho, ER 6 Ha:	**1 oil engine** driving 1 CP propeller Total Power: 508kW (691hp) 11.0kn Callesen 6-427-FOT 1 x 4 Stroke 6 Cy. 270 x 400 508kW (691bhp) Aabenraa Motorfabrik, HeinrichCallesen A/S-Denmark AuxGen: 2 x 100kW Fuel: 45.5
8891728 *YFMO* -	**WAIKELO INDAH** *ex Waikelo -2006 ex Kiyo Maru No. 8 -1995* *ex Ebisu Maru No. 3 -1995* **PT Sumba Harapan** - *Surabaya* Indonesia	*296* 145 364	Class: (KI)	**1976-03 Hayashi Zosen — Osakikamijima** Loa 39.16 Br ex - Dght 3.250 Lbp 35.76 Br md 7.00 Dpth 4.80 Welded, 1 dk	**(A31A2GX) General Cargo Ship** Compartments: 1 Ho, ER 1 Ha: (18.0 x 5.0)ER	**1 oil engine** geared to sc. shaft driving 1 FP propeller Total Power: 294kW (400hp) 9.0kn Yanmar 6MA-HT 1 x 4 Stroke 6 Cy. 200 x 240 294kW (400bhp) Yanmar Diesel Engine Co Ltd-Japan
9048809 - -	**WAIKIKI** - **Austral Group SAA** - *Callao* Peru Official number: CO-10446-PM	*194* 75 -		**1992 Remesa Astilleros S.A. — Callao** Yd No: 026 Loa - Br ex - Dght - Lbp - Br md - Dpth - Welded, 1 dk	**(B11B2FV) Fishing Vessel**	**1 oil engine** driving 1 FP propeller M.T.U. 1 x 4 Stroke MTU Friedrichshafen GmbH-Friedrichshafen
9212072 *ZMR3175* -	**WAIPAPA** - **Ports of Auckland Ltd** - *Auckland* New Zealand Official number: 876325	**338** - -	Class: (LR) ✠ Classed LR until 22/2/10	**2000-03 North Port Engineering Ltd — Whangarei** Yd No: 130 Loa 22.20 Br ex 9.22 Dght 3.150 Lbp 20.80 Br md 9.20 Dpth 4.15 Welded, 1 dk	**(B34T2QR) Work/Repair Vessel**	**2 oil engines** with clutches, flexible couplings & reduction geared to sc. shafts driving 2 Directional propellers Total Power: 3,282kW (4,462hp) Caterpillar 3516TA 2 x Vee 4 Stroke 16 Cy. 170 x 190 each-1641kW (2231bhp) Caterpillar Inc-USA Fuel: 91.0 (d.f.)
8848214 - -	**WAIPORI** *ex Everglory No. 1 -1979* **CP Towing Ltd** Bloomfield Marine Ltd	**319** 95 -		**1973 in Chinese Taipei** Converted From: Fishing Vessel-2008 Loa 38.35 Br ex 7.50 Dght - Lbp - Br md - Dpth 3.75 Welded, 1 dk	**(B32A2ST) Tug**	**1 oil engine** driving 1 FP propeller Total Power: 894kW (1,215hp) 10.0kn Makita GSHC6275 1 x 4 Stroke 6 Cy. 275 x 450 894kW (1215bhp) Makita Tekkosho-Japan
9027817 - -	**WAISARISA** - **PT Artika Optima Inti** - *Ambon* Indonesia	**168** 100 -	Class: KI	**1995-01 P.T. Seramu Jaya Prima Dockyard — Ambon** L reg 23.40 Br ex - Dght - Lbp 22.00 Br md 7.50 Dpth 3.00 Welded, 1 dk	**(B32A2ST) Tug**	**2 oil engines** driving 2 Propellers Total Power: 736kW (1,000hp) 9.0kn Poyaud B6L85M 2 x 4 Stroke 6 Cy. 150 x 210 each-368kW (500bhp) (, fitted 1995) Poyaud S.S.C.M.-Surgeres
9316464 *VHLO* -	**WAJARRI** - **Svitzer Australia Pty Ltd (Svitzer Australasia)** - *Port Adelaide, SA* Australia MMSI: 503481000 Official number: 857556	**294** 88 -	Class: LR ✠ **100A1** SS 12/2009 tug ✠ **LMC** **UMS** Eq.Ltr: F; Cable: 275.0/19.0 U2 (a)	**2004-12 PT Nanindah Mutiara Shipyard — Batam** Yd No: T121 Loa 28.50 Br ex 10.30 Dght 5.200 Lbp 26.50 Br md 10.30 Dpth 3.80 Welded, 1 dk	**(B32A2ST) Tug**	**2 oil engines** geared to sc. shafts driving 2 Directional propellers Total Power: 2,984kW (4,058hp) 12.0kn Caterpillar 3516B 2 x Vee 4 Stroke 16 Cy. 170 x 190 each-1492kW (2029bhp) Caterpillar Inc-USA AuxGen: 2 x 160kW 415V 50Hz a.c
8423064 - -	**WAJIMA MARU No. 11** *ex Daishi Maru No. 11 -1996* **Woo Yang Fisheries Co Ltd** - South Korea	*194* - -		**1984-08 K.K. Watanabe Zosensho — Nagasaki** Yd No: 1060 L reg 36.50 Br ex - Dght 2.900 Lbp - Br md 7.30 Dpth 3.30 Welded	**(B12B2FC) Fish Carrier**	**1 oil engine** driving 1 FP propeller
8979556 *JH3451* -	**WAJIMA MARU NO. 16** - **Wajima Gyogyo Seisan Kumiai** - *Wajima, Ishikawa* Japan Official number: 135634	*199* - -		**2003-02 K.K. Watanabe Zosensho — Nagasaki** Yd No: 103 L reg 43.01 Br ex - Dght - Lbp - Br md 7.80 Dpth 3.80 Welded, 1 dk	**(B11B2FV) Fishing Vessel**	**1 oil engine** driving 1 Propeller Niigata 6MG28HX 1 x 4 Stroke 6 Cy. 280 x 370 Niigata Engineering Co Ltd-Japan
9381017 *JD2264* -	**WAJIMA MARU NO. 17** - **Wajima Gyogyo Seisan Kumiai** - *Wajima, Ishikawa* Japan Official number: 140335	*260* - -		**2006-06 K.K. Watanabe Zosensho — Nagasaki** Yd No: 132 Loa 56.94 Br ex - Dght 3.550 Lbp 47.50 Br md 8.00 Dpth 3.97 Welded, 1 dk	**(B11B2FV) Fishing Vessel**	**1 oil engine** reduction geared to sc. shaft driving 1 FP propeller Total Power: 1,082kW (1,471hp) Niigata 6MG28HX 1 x 4 Stroke 6 Cy. 280 x 370 1082kW (1471bhp) Niigata Engineering Co Ltd-Japan
8961793 *JH3450* IK1-521	**WAJIMA MARU No. 18** - **Wajima Gyosei KK** - *Wajima, Ishikawa* Japan Official number: 135633	*110* - -		**2000-09 K.K. Watanabe Zosensho — Nagasaki** Yd No: 085 Loa 41.02 Br ex - Dght - Lbp 33.00 Br md 7.50 Dpth 3.05 Welded, 1 dk	**(B11B2FV) Fishing Vessel**	**1 oil engine** reduction geared to sc. shaft driving 1 FP propeller Total Power: 691kW (939hp) 12.5kn Niigata 6MG26HLX 1 x 4 Stroke 6 Cy. 260 x 350 691kW (939bhp) Niigata Engineering Co Ltd-Japan AuxGen: 2 x 120kW 225V a.c
8022224 - -	**WAJIMA MARU No. 76** - **F & F Corp** - South Korea	*169* - -		**1980-11 K.K. Watanabe Zosensho — Nagasaki** Yd No: 851 Loa 39.00 Br ex 6.80 Dght - Lbp 34.00 Br md 6.70 Dpth 3.30 Welded, 1 dk	**(B12B2FC) Fish Carrier**	**1 oil engine** reduction geared to sc. shaft driving 1 FP propeller Total Power: 956kW (1,300hp) Yanmar T260-ST 1 x 4 Stroke 6 Cy. 260 x 330 956kW (1300bhp) Yanmar Diesel Engine Co Ltd-Japan
8870528 *JH3306* -	**WAJIMA MARU No. 88** - **Wajima Gyogyo Seisan Kumiai** - *Wajima, Ishikawa* Japan Official number: 133212	*176* - -		**1993-09 KK Toyo Zosen Tekkosho — Kamaishi IW** L reg 32.04 Br ex - Dght - Lbp - Br md 6.60 Dpth 3.30 Welded, 1 dk	**(B11B2FV) Fishing Vessel**	**1 oil engine** driving 1 FP propeller Niigata 1 x 4 Stroke Niigata Engineering Co Ltd-Japan
9212084 *ZMR6122* -	**WAKA KUME** - **Ports of Auckland Ltd** - *Auckland* New Zealand Official number: 876332	**338** - -	Class: (LR) ✠ Classed LR until 22/2/10	**2000-05 North Port Engineering Ltd — Whangarei** Yd No: 131 Loa 22.20 Br ex 9.22 Dght 3.150 Lbp 20.80 Br md 9.20 Dpth 4.15 Welded, 1 dk	**(B32A2ST) Tug**	**2 oil engines** with clutches, flexible couplings & reduction geared to sc. shafts driving 2 Directional propellers Total Power: 3,282kW (4,462hp) Caterpillar 3516TA 2 x Vee 4 Stroke 16 Cy. 170 x 190 each-1641kW (2231bhp) Caterpillar Inc-USA Fuel: 91.0 (d.f.)

9566136 **WAKA MARU** 498
JD3062 -
- **Abo Shoten Ltd** 1,314
-
Onomichi, Hiroshima *Japan*
MMSI: 431001387
Official number: 141237

2010-05 Suzuki Shipyard Co. Ltd. — Yokkaichi Yd No: 727
Loa 65.98 Br ex - Dght 4.100
Lbp 61.80 Br md 10.00 Dpth 4.50
Welded, 1 dk

(A12A2TC) Chemical Tanker
Double Hull (13F)
Liq: 1,370
Compartments: 8 Wing Ta, ER
2 Cargo Pump (s): 2x300m³/hr

1 oil engine driving 1 FP propeller
Total Power: 1,030kW (1,400hp)
Hanshin LH28G
1 x 4 Stroke 6 Cy. 280 x 460 1030kW (1400bhp)
The Hanshin Diesel Works Ltd-Japan

8884036 **WAKA MARU** 199
- *ex* Shinyo Maru No. 17 -
- **Confort Shipping SA** 650
-

1975-06 Y.K. Okajima Zosensho — Matsuyama
Loa 50.70 Br ex - Dght 3.400
Lbp 47.00 Br md 8.30 Dpth 5.00
Welded, 1 dk

(A31A2GX) General Cargo Ship
Compartments: 1 Ho, ER
1 Ha: (26.0 x 6.1)ER

1 oil engine driving 1 FP propeller
Total Power: 588kW (799hp) 10.0kn
Yanmar
1 x 4 Stroke 588kW (799bhp)
Yanmar Diesel Engine Co Ltd-Japan

9083562 **WAKA MARU** 571
JK5386 -
- **Yasuji & Kiyoshi Yamamoto** 440
Yasuji Yamamoto
Hiroshima, Hiroshima *Japan*
MMSI: 431000663
Official number: 134117

1994-01 Ishii Zosen K.K. — Futtsu Yd No: 309
Loa 51.27 (BB) Br ex - Dght 3.259
Lbp 46.00 Br md 12.00 Dpth 3.30
Welded, 1 dk

(A24D2BA) Aggregates Carrier
Grain: 798
Compartments: 1 Ho, ER
1 Ha: ER

1 oil engine driving 1 FP propeller
Total Power: 1,030kW (1,400hp)
Yanmar MF29-UT
1 x 4 Stroke 6 Cy. 290 x 520 1030kW (1400bhp)
Yanmar Diesel Engine Co Ltd-Japan
Thrusters: 1 Thwart. FP thruster (f)

9711353 **WAKA MARU NO. 12** 499 Class: FA
- -
- **Shinmatsuura Kaiun YK** 1,670
-
Japan

2013-09 Yano Zosen K.K. — Imabari Yd No: 282
Loa 76.30 Br ex - Dght 4.302
Lbp - Br md 12.00 Dpth -
Welded, 1 dk

(A31A2GX) General Cargo Ship
Double Hull
Grain: 2,703; Bale: 2,420

1 oil engine reduction geared to sc. shaft driving 1 Propeller
Total Power: 1,618kW (2,200hp)
Niigata 6M34BGT
1 x 4 Stroke 6 Cy. 340 x 620 1618kW (2200bhp)
Niigata Engineering Co Ltd-Japan

9524229 **WAKABA** **4,713** Class: KR
3FBA5 *ex* Zenith Seoul *-2012* 2,165
- **Salt Line Co SA** 7,142
SHL Maritime Co Ltd
Panama *Panama*
MMSI: 372357000
Official number: 39781PEXT2

2009-09 Yangzhou Longchuan Shipbuilding Co Ltd — Jiangdu JS Yd No: 722
Loa 107.40 Br ex - Dght 7.019
Lbp 102.20 Br md 17.00 Dpth 9.00
Welded, 1 dk

(A31A2GX) General Cargo Ship
Compartments: 2 Ho, ER
2 Ha: ER 2 (25.2 x 12.6)
Cranes: 2x30t

1 oil engine driving 1 Propeller
Total Power: 2,648kW (3,600hp) 12.5kn
Hanshin LH41LA
1 x 4 Stroke 6 Cy. 410 x 800 2648kW (3600bhp)
The Hanshin Diesel Works Ltd-Japan
Fuel: 280.0

7722932 **WAKABA** 288
- *ex* Wakaba Maru *-1993* 165
- - 800
-

1977-10 Suzuki Shipyard Co. Ltd. — Yokkaichi Yd No: 287
Loa - Br ex - Dght 3.252
Lbp 40.01 Br md 8.41 Dpth 3.46
Riveted\Welded, 1 dk

(A13B2TU) Tanker (unspecified)

1 oil engine driving 1 FP propeller
Total Power: 368kW (500hp)
Matsui MU623B
1 x 4 Stroke 6 Cy. 230 x 380 368kW (500bhp)
Matsui Iron Works Co Ltd-Japan

8980414 **WAKABA II** 573
JL6702 -
- **Nippon Shio Kaiso Co Ltd** 1,699
-
Sakaide, Kagawa *Japan*
MMSI: 431501738
Official number: 137039

2002-09 Namikata Shipbuilding Co Ltd — Imabari EH Yd No: 216
Loa 77.28 Br ex - Dght 4.140
Lbp 72.21 Br md 12.00 Dpth 7.16
Welded, 1 dk

(A31A2GX) General Cargo Ship
Grain: 2,675

1 oil engine driving 1 Propeller
Total Power: 1,470kW (1,999hp) 12.5kn
Hanshin LH34L
1 x 4 Stroke 6 Cy. 340 x 640 1470kW (1999bhp)
The Hanshin Diesel Works Ltd-Japan

8125868 **WAKABA MARU** **102,511** Class: NK
C6YH6 30,753
- **Green Wakaba SA** 69,846
Mitsui OSK Lines Ltd (MOL)
Nassau *Bahamas*
MMSI: 311032800
Official number: 8001736

1985-04 Mitsui Eng. & SB. Co. Ltd., Chiba Works — Ichihara Yd No: 1250
Loa 283.00 (BB) Br ex - Dght 11.500
Lbp 270.01 Br md 44.81 Dpth 25.02
Welded, 1 dk

(A11A2TN) LNG Tanker
Double Bottom Entire Compartment Length
Liq (Gas): 127,209
5 x Gas Tank (s); 5 independent Kvaerner-Moss (alu) sph
10 Cargo Pump (s): 10x1000m³/hr

1 Steam Turb dr geared to sc. shaft driving 1 FP propeller
Total Power: 29,420kW (39,999hp) 19.3kn
Stal-Laval
1 x steam Turb 29420kW (39999shp)
Mitsui Engineering & Shipbuilding CLtd-Japan
AuxGen: 2 x 2500kW 450V 60Hz a.c, 1 x 1200kW 450V 60Hz a.c
Thrusters: 1 Thwart. CP thruster (f)
Fuel: 8844.5 (r.f.) 225.0 (d.f.) 186.0pd

8910031 **WAKABA MARU No. 1** 135
JM5850 *ex* Myojin Maru No. 8 *-2001* -
- *ex* Katoku Maru No. 8 *-1999* -
ex Kyoei Maru No. 81 *-1993*
Wakaba Gyogyo KK
-
SatCom: Inmarsat A 1200526
Matsue, Shimane *Japan*
Official number: 130507

1989-09 K.K. Watanabe Zosensho — Nagasaki Yd No: 1163
Loa 47.77 (BB) Br ex - Dght 2.901
Lbp 38.00 Br md 8.10 Dpth 3.31
Welded, 1 dk

(B11B2FV) Fishing Vessel

1 oil engine with clutches, flexible couplings & dr reverse geared to sc. shaft driving 1 CP propeller
Total Power: 861kW (1,171hp)
Niigata 6MG28HX
1 x 4 Stroke 6 Cy. 280 x 370 861kW (1171bhp)
Niigata Engineering Co Ltd-Japan
Thrusters: 1 Thwart. FP thruster (f)

8915134 **WAKABA MARU No. 3** 349
JNBA -
- **Kyokuyo Suisan KK** -
-
SatCom: Inmarsat B 343168610
Yaizu, Shizuoka *Japan*
MMSI: 431686000
Official number: 131936

1989-11 Niigata Engineering Co Ltd — Niigata NI Yd No: 2161
Loa 63.24 (BB) Br ex 12.02 Dght 4.460
Lbp 55.00 Br md 12.00 Dpth 7.27
Welded, 2 dks

(B11B2FV) Fishing Vessel
Ins: 1,137

1 oil engine with clutches, flexible couplings & sr reverse geared to sc. shaft driving 1 FP propeller
Total Power: 2,207kW (3,001hp)
Niigata 6MG32CLX
1 x 4 Stroke 6 Cy. 320 x 420 2207kW (3001bhp)
Niigata Engineering Co Ltd-Japan
Thrusters: 1 Thwart. FP thruster (f)

9281097 **WAKABA MARU NO. 5** 349
JHRG -
- **Kyokuyo Suisan KK** -
-
Yaizu, Shizuoka *Japan*
MMSI: 432410000
Official number: 135689

2003-06 Miho Zosensho K.K. — Shimizu Yd No: 1504
Loa 63.98 Br ex - Dght 4.460
Lbp 55.65 Br md 12.00 Dpth 7.27
Welded, 1 Dk.

(B11B2FV) Fishing Vessel

1 oil engine reverse geared to sc. shaft driving 1 Propeller
Total Power: 2,942kW (4,000hp)
Akasaka A4
1 x 4 Stroke 6 Cy. 410 x 800 2942kW (4000bhp)
Akasaka Tekkosho KK (Akasaka DieselLtd)-Japan

9062635 **WAKABA MARU No. 6** 349
JFRJ -
- **Kyokuyo Suisan KK** -
-
SatCom: Inmarsat B 343169610
Yaizu, Shizuoka *Japan*
MMSI: 431696000
Official number: 133814

1992-11 Niigata Engineering Co Ltd — Niigata NI Yd No: 2251
Loa 63.24 (BB) Br ex - Dght 4.457
Lbp 55.00 Br md 12.00 Dpth 7.27
Welded, 2 dks

(B11B2FV) Fishing Vessel

1 oil engine with clutches, flexible couplings & dr reverse geared to sc. shaft driving 1 FP propeller
Total Power: 1,912kW (2,600hp)
Daihatsu 8DLM-3
1 x 4 Stroke 8 Cy. 320 x 400 1912kW (2600bhp)
Daihatsu Diesel Manufacturing Co Lt-Japan
Thrusters: 1 Thwart. FP thruster (f)

9524865 **WAKABA MARU NO. 7** 760
7JFV -
S01-1253 **Kyokuyo Suisan KK** 1,507
-
SatCom: Inmarsat C 443272610
Yaizu, Shizuoka *Japan*
MMSI: 432726000
Official number: 141083

2009-10 Miho Zosensho K.K. — Shimizu Yd No: 1536
Loa 79.60 Br ex - Dght 5.560
Lbp 70.00 Br md 14.00 Dpth 8.30
Welded, 1 dk

(B11B2FV) Fishing Vessel

1 oil engine reduction geared to sc. shaft driving 1 FP propeller
Total Power: 2,942kW (4,000hp)
Akasaka AH41A
1 x 4 Stroke 6 Cy. 410 x 640 2942kW (4000bhp)
Akasaka Tekkosho KK (Akasaka DieselLtd)-Japan

5318610 **WAKABA MARU No. 16** 199
- *ex* Seisho Maru No. 22 *-1993* 111
- *ex* Iwate Maru *-1961* -
Tosei Sangyo KK (Tosei Industries Co Ltd)
-
South Korea

1953 KK Kanasashi Zosen — Shizuoka SZ Yd No: 157
L reg 35.27 Br ex 6.71 Dght -
Lbp - Br md - Dpth -
Riveted\Welded, 1 dk

(B12D2FR) Fishery Research Vessel

1 oil engine driving 1 FP propeller
Total Power: 405kW (551hp)
Niigata
1 x 4 Stroke 6 Cy. 350 x 520 405kW (551bhp)
Niigata Tekkosho-Japan

8820781 **WAKABA MARU NO. 18** 324
JM5801 *ex* Shosei Maru No. 18 *-2012* -
- **Wakaba Gyogyo KK** -
-
Matsue, Shimane *Japan*
Official number: 130461

1989-01 K.K. Watanabe Zosensho — Nagasaki Yd No: 1152
Loa 59.55 (BB) Br ex 8.42 Dght 4.000
Lbp 49.89 Br md 8.40 Dpth 4.40
Welded, 1 dk

(B11B2FV) Fishing Vessel
Ins: 392

1 oil engine driving 1 FP propeller
Total Power: 1,155kW (1,570hp)
Niigata 8MG28H
1 x 4 Stroke 8 Cy. 280 x 370 1155kW (1570bhp)
Niigata Engineering Co Ltd-Japan

8814627 **WAKABA MARU NO. 28** 230
JK4692 *ex* Chidori Maru No. 33 *-2002* -
- **Wakaba Gyogyo KK** -
-
Matsue, Shimane *Japan*
Official number: 128047

1988-05 Watanabe Zosen KK — Imabari EH Yd No: 1132
Loa 50.90 (BB) Br ex 8.31 Dght -
Lbp 44.90 Br md 8.30 Dpth 4.08
Welded, 1 dk

(B12B2FC) Fish Carrier
Ins: 474
Compartments: 8 Ta, ER

1 oil engine sr reverse geared to sc. shaft driving 1 FP propeller
Total Power: 861kW (1,171hp)
Hanshin 6MUH28
1 x 4 Stroke 6 Cy. 280 x 340 861kW (1171bhp)
The Hanshin Diesel Works Ltd-Japan
Thrusters: 1 Thwart. FP thruster (f)

3717623 **WAKAEI MARU No. 18** *436*
- 1,140
-
-

1988-05 K.K. Murakami Zosensho — Naruto Yd No: 177
Loa 50.73 Br ex 13.03 Dght 4.822
Lbp 45.80 Br md 13.00 Dpth 6.60
Welded, 2 dks

(B33A2DG) Grab Dredger
Grain: 874; Bale: 829
Compartments: 1 Ho, ER
1 Ha: ER

1 oil engine with clutches & reverse reduction geared to sc. shaft driving 1 FP propeller
Total Power: 736kW (1,001hp)
Niigata 6M30GT
1 x 4 Stroke 6 Cy. 300 x 530 736kW (1001bhp)
Niigata Engineering Co Ltd-Japan

8948961 **WAKAEI MARU No. 25** *135*
-
-
Shine System Co Ltd -
-
South Korea

1998-12 Nagashima Zosen KK — Kihoku ME Yd No: 523
Loa 32.65 Br ex - Dght -
Lbp - Br md 9.60 Dpth 5.80
Welded, 1 dk

(B32B2SP) Pusher Tug

2 oil engines driving 1 FP propeller
Total Power: 2,942kW (4,000hp)
Niigata 6M34BLGT
2 x 4 Stroke 6 Cy. 340 x 680 each-1471kW (2000bhp)
Niigata Engineering Co Ltd-Japan

8965359 **WAKAICHI MARU** *108*
JH3023 *ex Jintoku Maru No. 11* -
- **YK Wakaichi Suisan** -

Nango, Miyazaki *Japan*
MMSI: 431601657
Official number: 127559

1984-01 Nishii Dock Co. Ltd. — Ise Yd No: 690
L reg 29.20 Br ex - Dght -
Lbp - Br md 5.55 Dpth 2.45
Bonded, 1 dk

(B11B2FV) Fishing Vessel
Hull Material: Reinforced Plastic

1 oil engine driving 1 FP propeller
Niigata
1 x 4 Stroke
Niigata Engineering Co Ltd-Japan

9473602 **WAKAMATSU MARU** *3,057* Class: NK
JD2793 -
- **Shinwa Naiko Kaiun Kaisha Ltd** 6,500
Nichitoku Kisen KK
Tokyo *Japan*
MMSI: 431000695
Official number: 140839

2008-09 Kegoya Dock K.K. — Kure Yd No: 1110
Loa 109.40 Br ex - Dght 5.877
Lbp 102.00 Br md 20.50 Dpth 11.10
Welded, 1 dk

(A31A2GX) General Cargo Ship
Grain: 12,365; Bale: 12,263

1 oil engine driving 1 FP propeller
Total Power: 3,900kW (5,302hp) 13.5kn
MAN-B&W 6L35MC
1 x 2 Stroke 6 Cy. 350 x 1050 3900kW (5302bhp)
The Hanshin Diesel Works Ltd-Japan
Fuel: 310.0

9072874 **WAKAMIYA MARU No. 61** *495*
JL6157 -
- **Wakamiya Suisan KK** -
-
Uwajima, Ehime *Japan*
MMSI: 431443000
Official number: 133020

1993-03 Shin Yamamoto Shipbuilding & Engineering Co Ltd — Kochi KC Yd No: 331
L reg 55.65 (BB) Br ex - Dght -
Lbp - Br md 9.60 Dpth 4.80
Welded, 1 dk

(B11B2FV) Fishing Vessel

1 oil engine driving 1 FP propeller
Total Power: 1,471kW (2,000hp)
Niigata 6M34AGT
1 x 4 Stroke 6 Cy. 340 x 620 1471kW (2000bhp)
Niigata Engineering Co Ltd-Japan

8825561 **WAKAMIYO No. 11** *144*
- *ex Ayabane -2000* -
- -
-
-

1972-12 Shimoda Dockyard Co. Ltd. — Shimoda Yd No: 224
Loa 32.70 Br ex 6.52 Dght 1.800
Lbp 29.70 Br md 6.50 Dpth 3.00
Welded, 1 dk

(B34Q2QB) Buoy Tender

1 oil engine driving 1 FP propeller
Total Power: 368kW (500hp) 11.5kn
Hanshin 6L24GSH
1 x 4 Stroke 6 Cy. 240 x 400 368kW (500bhp)
The Hanshin Diesel Works Ltd-Japan

8963430 **WAKAMIZU** *187*
-
- **Hang Dong Shipbuilding Co Ltd** 300
-
South Korea

1970-07 T. Abe — Nandan
Loa 32.50 Br ex - Dght 2.900
Lbp 28.57 Br md 7.00 Dpth 3.00
Welded, 1 dk

(A14A2LO) Water Tanker

1 oil engine driving 1 FP propeller
Total Power: 147kW (200hp) 8.0kn
Yanmar
1 x 4 Stroke 147kW (200bhp)
Yanmar Diesel Engine Co Ltd-Japan

7370765 **WAKAMIZU** *199*
- *ex Hiko Maru No. 3 -2002* 127
- - 403
-
South Korea

1974-02 Kyoei Zosen KK — Mihara HS Yd No: 56
Loa 42.65 Br ex 7.62 Dght 2.845
Lbp 39.02 Br md 7.60 Dpth 2.90
Welded, 1 dk

(A12A2TC) Chemical Tanker

1 oil engine driving 1 FP propeller
Total Power: 552kW (750hp)
Makita GNLH623
1 x 4 Stroke 6 Cy. 230 x 410 552kW (750bhp)
Makita Tekkosho-Japan

9457672 **WAKANAMI MARU** *499*
JD2484 -
- **Kimura Kisen KK** 1,800
-
Imabari, Ehime *Japan*
Official number: 140613

2007-09 K.K. Watanabe Zosensho — Nagasaki Yd No: 143
Loa 74.70 Br ex - Dght 4.350
Lbp 69.00 Br md 12.00 Dpth 7.38
Welded, 1 dk

(A31A2GX) General Cargo Ship
Grain: 2,630; Bale: 2,596
Compartments: 1 Ho, ER
1 Ha: ER (40.0 x 9.5)

1 oil engine driving 1 FP propeller
Total Power: 1,618kW (2,200hp)
Hanshin LH34LA
1 x 4 Stroke 6 Cy. 340 x 640 1618kW (2200bhp)
The Hanshin Diesel Works Ltd-Japan

9360362 **WAKANATSU** *10,185* Class: NK
JD2300 -
- **Ryukyu Kaiun Kaisha ('The Ryukyu Line')** 6,890
-
Naha, Okinawa *Japan*
MMSI: 431680233
Official number: 140381

2006-09 Saiki Heavy Industries Co Ltd — Saiki OT (Hull) Yd No: 1156
2006-09 Onomichi Dockyard Co Ltd — Onomichi HS Yd No: 618
Loa 168.71 (BB) Br ex - Dght 6.716
Lbp 155.00 Br md 26.00 Dpth 18.00
Welded

(A35A2RR) Ro-Ro Cargo Ship
Angled stern door/ramp (centre)
Len: - Wid: - Swl: 70
Quarter bow door/ramp (s. f.)
Len: - Wid: - Swl: 70
Lane-Len: 2020
Cars: 245

1 oil engine driving 1 FP propeller
Total Power: 13,279kW (18,054hp) 21.5kn
MAN-B&W 8S50MC-C
1 x 2 Stroke 8 Cy. 500 x 2000 13279kW (18054bhp)
Mitsui Engineering & Shipbuilding CLtd-Japan
AuxGen: 2 x 1185kW a.c
Thrusters: 1 Tunnel thruster (f); 1 Tunnel thruster (a)
Fuel: 710.0

8997314 **WAKANATSU** *498*
JD2034 -
- **Marusan Kaiun KK** 1,550
-
Osaka, Osaka *Japan*
Official number: 140070

2004-10 K.K. Matsuura Zosensho — Osakikamijima Yd No: 553
Loa 76.20 Br ex - Dght 4.240
Lbp 70.00 Br md 12.00 Dpth 7.20
Welded, 1 dk

(A31A2GX) General Cargo Ship
Grain: 2,511
1 Ha: ER (40.2 x 10.0)

1 oil engine driving 1 Propeller
Total Power: 1,471kW (2,000hp) 12.0kn
Hanshin LH34LAG
1 x 4 Stroke 6 Cy. 340 x 640 1471kW (2000bhp)
The Hanshin Diesel Works Ltd-Japan

7828114 **WAKASA** *960*
JQUL -
- **Government of Japan (Ministry of Land, Infrastructure & Transport) (The Coastguard)** -
-
Tokyo *Japan*
MMSI: 431300249
Official number: 121645

1978-11 Kawasaki Heavy Industries Ltd — Kobe HG Yd No: 1300
Loa 77.81 Br ex 9.62 Dght 3.540
Lbp 70.20 Br md 9.60 Dpth 5.30
Welded, 1 dk

(B34H2SQ) Patrol Vessel

2 oil engines driving 2 FP propellers
Total Power: 5,148kW (7,000hp) 20.0kn
Fuji 8S40B
2 x 4 Stroke 8 Cy. 400 x 580 each-2574kW (3500bhp)
Fuji Diesel Co Ltd-Japan

9204128 **WAKASA MARU** *198*
JH3435 -
- **Sanyo Kaiji Co Ltd** -
-
Nagoya, Aichi *Japan*
Official number: 135647

1998-04 Hatayama Zosen KK — Yura WK Yd No: 228
Loa 32.82 Br ex - Dght -
Lbp 26.50 Br md 9.50 Dpth 4.29
Welded, 1 dk

(B32A2ST) Tug

2 oil engines geared integral to driving 2 Z propellers
Total Power: 2,648kW (3,600hp) 13.0kn
Yanmar 6N280-UN
2 x 4 Stroke 6 Cy. 280 x 380 each-1324kW (1800bhp)
Yanmar Diesel Engine Co Ltd-Japan

9048524 **WAKASHIMA MARU No. 2** *199*
JM6042 -
- **Kyowa Sekiyu KK** 550
-
Yokohama, Kanagawa *Japan*
Official number: 132704

1992-02 Kurinoura Dockyard Co Ltd — Yawatahama EH Yd No: 298
Loa 47.94 Br ex 7.82 Dght 3.260
Lbp 44.00 Br md 7.80 Dpth 3.30
Welded, 1 dk

(A13B2TP) Products Tanker
Compartments: 6 Ta, ER

1 oil engine reverse geared to sc. shaft driving 1 FP propeller
Total Power: 625kW (850hp)
Yanmar MF26-ST
1 x 4 Stroke 6 Cy. 260 x 500 625kW (850bhp)
Yanmar Diesel Engine Co Ltd-Japan

9145827 **WAKASHIMA MARU No. 3** *499*
JM6419 -
- **Wakashima Kaiun YK** 1,135
-
Shimonoseki, Yamaguchi *Japan*
MMSI: 431400588
Official number: 134609

1996-08 Kanmon Zosen K.K. — Shimonoseki Yd No: 575
Loa 64.00 (BB) Br ex 10.22 Dght 4.000
Lbp 60.00 Br md 10.20 Dpth 4.60
Welded, 1 dk

(A13A2TW) Crude/Oil Products Tanker
Liq: 1,204; Liq (Oil): 1,204
Compartments: 8 Ta, ER

1 oil engine driving 1 FP propeller
Total Power: 736kW (1,001hp)
Hanshin LH28G
1 x 4 Stroke 6 Cy. 280 x 460 736kW (1001bhp)
The Hanshin Diesel Works Ltd-Japan

8824490 **WAKASHIO** *208*
JH3177 -
- **Green Kaiji KK** -
-
Nagoya, Aichi *Japan*
Official number: 130070

1989-04 Kanbara Zosen K.K. — Onomichi Yd No: 380
Loa 33.52 Br ex - Dght 3.100
Lbp 28.00 Br md 9.60 Dpth 4.09
Welded, 1 dk

(B32A2ST) Tug

2 oil engines geared integral to driving 2 Z propellers
Total Power: 2,574kW (3,500hp) 13.0kn
Niigata 6L28HX
2 x 4 Stroke 6 Cy. 280 x 370 each-1287kW (1750bhp)
Niigata Engineering Co Ltd-Japan

8818908 **WAKASHIO** *198*
- -
- - 28
-

1989-03 Mitsui Eng. & SB. Co. Ltd., Chiba Works — Ichihara Yd No: CH1612
Loa 33.21 Br ex - Dght 1.468
Lbp 29.26 Br md 9.00 Dpth 3.00
Welded, 1 dk

(B34H2SQ) Patrol Vessel
Hull Material: Aluminium Alloy

2 oil engines with clutches, flexible couplings & sr geared to sc. shafts driving 2 FP propellers
Total Power: 2,206kW (3,000hp) 20.0kn
Yanmar 16LAK-ST1
2 x Vee 4 Stroke 16 Cy. 150 x 165 each-1103kW (1500bhp) (made 1988)
Yanmar Diesel Engine Co Ltd-Japan

IMO / Call sign / Fishing no.	Name / Owner / Registration	Tonnage	Class	Builder / Dimensions	Type / Cargo	Machinery
9337119 *3EKF7* -	**WAKASHIO** **Okiyo Maritime Corp** Nagashiki Shipping Co Ltd (Nagashiki Kisen KK) SatCom: Inmarsat C 437271110 *Panama* *Panama* MMSI: 372711000 Official number: 3270907A	**101,932** 66,396 203,130 T/cm 138.0	Class: NK	**2007-05 Universal Shipbuilding Corp — Tsu ME** Yd No: 046 Loa 299.95 (BB) Br ex - Dght 17.910 Lbp 290.00 Br md 50.00 Dpth 24.10 Welded, 1 dk	**(A21A2BC) Bulk Carrier** Grain: 217,968 Compartments: 9 Ho, ER 9 Ha: ER 9 (15.7 x 23.4)	**1 oil engine** driving 1 FP propeller Total Power: 16,860kW (22,923hp) 14.5kn MAN-B&W 6S70MC 1 x 2 Stroke 6 Cy. 700 x 2674 16860kW (22923bhp) Mitsui Engineering & Shipbuilding CLtd-Japan AuxGen: 3 x a.c Fuel: 5270.0
8714712 - -	**WAKASHIO MARU** - -	*116* - 105		**1988-02 Wakamatsu Zosen K.K. — Kitakyushu** Yd No: 370 Loa 33.78 Br ex 6.62 Dght 2.400 Lbp 28.70 Br md 6.60 Dpth 2.80 Welded, 1 dk	**(B11B2FV) Fishing Vessel** Ins: 37	**1 oil engine** with clutches, flexible couplings & dr reverse geared to sc. shaft driving 1 FP propeller Total Power: 588kW (799hp) 11.3kn Yanmar M200L-ST 1 x 4 Stroke 6 Cy. 200 x 260 588kW (799bhp) Yanmar Diesel Engine Co Ltd-Japan AuxGen: 1 x 200kW 225V 60Hz a.c, 1 x 80kW 225V 60Hz a.c
9118953 *JFBI* -	**WAKASHIO MARU** **Toyama National College of Technology (Toyama Shosen Koto Semmon Gakko)** - SatCom: Inmarsat C 443178410 *Imizu, Toyama* *Japan* MMSI: 431784000 Official number: 131583	*231* - 270		**1995-09 Miho Zosensho K.K. — Shimizu** Yd No: 1454 Loa 53.00 Br ex - Dght 3.371 Lbp 46.00 Br md 10.00 Dpth 5.40 Welded, 1 dk	**(B11A2FS) Stern Trawler**	**1 oil engine** driving 1 CP propeller Total Power: 956kW (1,300hp) 12.5kn Niigata 6M28BET 1 x 4 Stroke 6 Cy. 280 x 480 956kW (1300bhp) Niigata Engineering Co Ltd-Japan
7804455 *9V6594* -	**WAKASHIO MARU** *ex* Yaizu Maru No. 2 *-1992* *ex* Yaizu *-1991* **Wakashio Marine Pte Ltd** GPS Data Net Inc *Singapore* *Singapore* MMSI: 564835000 Official number: 390916	**493** 147 290	Class: NK (IR)	**1978-07 KK Kanasashi Zosen — Shizuoka SZ** Yd No: 2002 Converted From: Fishing Vessel-1992 Loa 50.30 Br ex 8.30 Dght 3.352 Lbp 44.00 Br md - Dpth 3.70 Welded, 1 dk	**(B32A2ST) Tug** Cranes: 1x5t	**1 oil engine** driving 1 FP propeller Total Power: 1,177kW (1,600hp) 11.5kn Akasaka DM33 1 x 4 Stroke 6 Cy. 330 x 500 1177kW (1600bhp) Akasaka Tekkosho KK (Akasaka DieselLtd)-Japan AuxGen: 2 x 240kW a.c Thrusters: 1 Tunnel thruster (f) Fuel: 160.0 (d.f.)
9206176 *JFRV* KG1-777	**WAKASHIO MARU No. 8** **Wakashio Suisan KK** - SatCom: Inmarsat C 443144410 *Ichikikushikino, Kagoshima* *Japan* MMSI: 431444000 Official number: 136414	*499* - 650		**1999-02 KK Kanasashi — Shizuoka SZ** Yd No: 3507 L reg 54.80 Br ex - Dght - Lbp - Br md 9.40 Dpth 4.25 Welded, 1 dk	**(B11B2FV) Fishing Vessel** Ins: 736	**1 oil engine** geared to sc. shaft driving 1 FP propeller Total Power: 1,176kW (1,599hp) Hanshin LH28G 1 x 4 Stroke 6 Cy. 280 x 460 1176kW (1599bhp) The Hanshin Diesel Works Ltd-Japan
9648415 *7JLV* -	**WAKASHIO MARU NO. 8** **Nemuro Kaiyo Gyogyo Seisan Kumiai** - *Nemuro, Hokkaido* *Japan* Official number: 141662	*199* - -		**2012-07 Miho Zosensho K.K. — Shimizu** Yd No: 1551 Loa 46.20 Br ex - Dght 2.970 Lbp - Br md 7.50 Dpth 3.35 Welded, 1 dk	**(B11B2FV) Fishing Vessel**	**1 oil engine** reduction geared to sc. shaft driving 1 Propeller Total Power: 1,838kW (2,499hp) Niigata 6MG28HX 1 x 4 Stroke 6 Cy. 280 x 370 1838kW (2499bhp) Niigata Engineering Co Ltd-Japan
7206641 - -	**WAKASHIO MARU No. 22** - -	*195* 93		**1971 Uchida Zosen — Ise** Yd No: 702 Loa - Br ex 7.42 Dght - Lbp 35.77 Br md 7.40 Dpth 3.20 Riveted\Welded, 1 dk	**(B11B2FV) Fishing Vessel**	**1 oil engine** driving 1 FP propeller Total Power: 588kW (799hp) Niigata 6M26KEHS 1 x 4 Stroke 6 Cy. 260 x 400 588kW (799bhp) Niigata Engineering Co Ltd-Japan
8814952 *7KWV* KG1-9	**WAKASHIO MARU No. 58** **KK Ushio** - SatCom: Inmarsat A 1200631 *Ichikikushikino, Kagoshima* *Japan* MMSI: 431602710 Official number: 130384	*388* - -		**1988-09 KK Kanasashi Zosen — Shizuoka SZ** Yd No: 3148 Loa 54.11 (BB) Br ex 8.77 Dght 3.401 Lbp 47.50 Br md 8.70 Dpth 3.76 Welded, 1 dk	**(B11B2FV) Fishing Vessel** Ins: 468	**1 oil engine** with clutches, flexible couplings & sr reverse geared to sc.shaft driving 1 FP propeller Total Power: 736kW (1,001hp) Hanshin LH28G 1 x 4 Stroke 6 Cy. 280 x 460 736kW (1001bhp) The Hanshin Diesel Works Ltd-Japan AuxGen: 2 x 280kW a.c
8914996 *JNHP* KG1-71	**WAKASHIO MARU No. 68** **KK Ushio** - SatCom: Inmarsat A 1200264 *Ichikikushikino, Kagoshima* *Japan* MMSI: 431602342 Official number: 131276	*398* - -		**1989-09 KK Kanasashi Zosen — Shizuoka SZ** Yd No: 3201 Loa 54.11 (BB) Br ex 8.73 Dght 3.400 Lbp 47.81 Br md 8.70 Dpth 3.75 Welded, 1 dk	**(B11B2FV) Fishing Vessel** Grain: 520; Bale: 468	**1 oil engine** with clutches, flexible couplings & sr reverse geared to sc. shaft driving 1 FP propeller Total Power: 736kW (1,001hp) Hanshin LH28G 1 x 4 Stroke 6 Cy. 280 x 460 736kW (1001bhp) The Hanshin Diesel Works Ltd-Japan
8707848 - -	**WAKASHIO MARU No. 81** *ex* Yuryo Maru No. 85 *-1993* **Yun Feng SA** China National Fisheries Corp	*322* - -		**1987-09 Fujishin Zosen K.K. — Kamo** Yd No: 525 Loa 66.02 (BB) Br ex 10.27 Dght 4.001 Lbp 57.00 Br md 10.20 Dpth 6.61 Welded	**(B11B2FV) Fishing Vessel**	**1 oil engine** with clutches & reverse reduction geared to sc. shaft driving 1 FP propeller Total Power: 736kW (1,001hp) Niigata 6M28AFTE 1 x 4 Stroke 6 Cy. 280 x 480 736kW (1001bhp) Niigata Engineering Co Ltd-Japan
9037678 - -	**WAKASHIO MARU No. 81** - -	*379* - 458		**1991-09 Miho Zosensho K.K. — Shimizu** Yd No: 1392 Loa 56.04 (BB) Br ex 8.82 Dght 3.452 Lbp 49.20 Br md 8.80 Dpth 3.80 Welded, 1 dk	**(B11B2FV) Fishing Vessel** Ins: 700	**1 oil engine** with flexible couplings & sr geared to sc. shaft driving 1 FP propeller Total Power: 736kW (1,001hp) Akasaka K28SFD 1 x 4 Stroke 6 Cy. 280 x 500 736kW (1001bhp) Akasaka Tekkosho KK (Akasaka DieselLtd)-Japan
9047910 *JMOX* KG1-582	**WAKASHIO MARU No. 82** **Maruwaka Suisan KK** - SatCom: Inmarsat A 1204772 *Ichikikushikino, Kagoshima* *Japan* MMSI: 431602620 Official number: 132651	*409* - -		**1992-02 KK Kanasashi — Shizuoka SZ** Yd No: 3291 Loa 56.70 (BB) Br ex 8.83 Dght 3.450 Lbp 49.60 Br md 8.80 Dpth 3.84 Welded, 1 dk	**(B11B2FV) Fishing Vessel** Ins: 540	**1 oil engine** with clutches, flexible couplings & sr reverse geared to sc. shaft driving 1 FP propeller Total Power: 736kW (1,001hp) Hanshin LH28LG 1 x 4 Stroke 6 Cy. 280 x 530 736kW (1001bhp) The Hanshin Diesel Works Ltd-Japan
9109249 *JDMD* KG1-283	**WAKASHIO MARU No. 83** **Maruwaka Suisan KK** - SatCom: Inmarsat B 343182910 *Ichikikushikino, Kagoshima* *Japan* MMSI: 431829000 Official number: 133575	*409* - 619		**1994-08 KK Kanasashi — Shizuoka SZ** Yd No: 3347 Loa 56.00 (BB) Br ex - Dght - Lbp 49.00 Br md 8.00 Dpth 3.00 Welded, 1 dk	**(B11B2FV) Fishing Vessel** Ins: 541	**1 oil engine** with clutches, flexible couplings & sr reverse geared to sc. shaft driving 1 FP propeller Total Power: 736kW (1,001hp) 12.4kn Hanshin LH28LG 1 x 4 Stroke 6 Cy. 280 x 530 736kW (1001bhp) The Hanshin Diesel Works Ltd-Japan AuxGen: 2 x 308kW a.c Fuel: 305.0 (d.f.) 5.0pd
9167576 *JD2708* -	**WAKASHIO MARU No. 85** **Ishigaki Gyogyo KK** - *Nemuro, Hokkaido* *Japan* MMSI: 431931000 Official number: 128565	*184* - -		**1997-05 Sanuki Shipbuilding & Iron Works Co Ltd — Mitoyo KG** Yd No: 1273 Loa - Br ex - Dght 2.690 Lbp 34.00 Br md 7.00 Dpth 3.00 Welded, 1 dk	**(B11B2FV) Fishing Vessel**	**1 oil engine** driving 1 FP propeller Total Power: 736kW (1,001hp) Niigata 6MG22HX 1 x 4 Stroke 6 Cy. 220 x 280 736kW (1001bhp) Niigata Engineering Co Ltd-Japan
8804282 *JCJJ* -	**WAKASHIO MARU No. 85** *ex* Hokko Maru No. 177 *-1995* - - SatCom: Inmarsat A 1203736 *Tokyo* *Japan* MMSI: 431602670 Official number: 127105	*349* - 933		**1988-05 Yamanishi Shipbuilding Co Ltd — Ishinomaki MG** Yd No: 960 Loa 68.84 (BB) Br ex 10.62 Dght 4.606 Lbp 60.50 Br md 10.60 Dpth 6.90 Welded, 2 dks	**(B11B2FV) Fishing Vessel** Ins: 990	**1 oil engine** with clutches, flexible couplings & sr geared to sc. shaft driving 1 FP propeller Total Power: 956kW (1,300hp) Niigata 6M31AFTE 1 x 4 Stroke 6 Cy. 310 x 530 956kW (1300bhp) Niigata Engineering Co Ltd-Japan Thrusters: 1 Thwart. FP thruster (f)

3712659 *JHNL* -	**WAKASHIO MARU No. 87** *ex Nikko Maru No. 21 -2000* **KK Ushio** - SatCom: Inmarsat A 1205507 *Ichikikushikino, Kagoshima* *Japan* MMSI: 431200210 Official number: 128473	*349* - 972	**1987-10 Miho Zosensho K.K. — Shimizu** Yd No: 1314 Loa 70.19 (BB) Br ex - Dght 4.152 Lbp 60.13 Br md 10.61 Dpth 6.96 Welded	**(B11B2FV) Fishing Vessel** Ins: 1,059	**1 oil engine** with clutches, flexible couplings & sr reverse geared to sc. shaft driving 1 FP propeller Total Power: 1,324kW (1,800hp) Akasaka K31FD 1 x 4 Stroke 6 Cy. 310 x 530 1324kW (1800bhp) Akasaka Tekkosho KK (Akasaka DieselLtd)-Japan Thrusters: 1 Thwart. CP thruster (f)
8910574 *JNGV* KG1-70	**WAKASHIO MARU No. 88** - **KK Ushio** - SatCom: Inmarsat A 1200242 *Ichikikushikino, Kagoshima* *Japan* MMSI: 431602610 Official number: 131271	*379* - -	**1989-09 KK Kanasashi Zosen — Shizuoka SZ** Yd No: 3197 Loa 54.11 (BB) Br ex 8.73 Dght 3.400 Lbp 47.50 Br md 8.70 Dpth 3.75 Welded	**(B11B2FV) Fishing Vessel** Ins: 520	**1 oil engine** with clutches, flexible couplings & sr reverse geared to sc. shaft driving 1 FP propeller Total Power: 736kW (1,001hp) Hanshin LH28G 1 x 4 Stroke 6 Cy. 280 x 460 736kW (1001bhp) The Hanshin Diesel Works Ltd-Japan
9135107 *JDWA* KG1-808	**WAKASHIO MARU No. 108** - **Wakashio Suisan KK** - SatCom: Inmarsat C 443179810 *Ichikikushikino, Kagoshima* *Japan* MMSI: 431798000 Official number: 134621	*499* - -	**1995-11 KK Kanasashi — Shizuoka SZ** Yd No: 3371 Loa 61.00 (BB) Br ex - Dght 3.870 Lbp 54.00 Br md 9.00 Dpth 4.00 Welded, 1 dk	**(B11B2FV) Fishing Vessel** Ins: 762	**1 oil engine** with clutches, flexible couplings & sr reverse geared to sc. shaft driving 1 FP propeller Total Power: 736kW (1,001hp) 12.7kn Hanshin LH28LG 1 x 4 Stroke 6 Cy. 280 x 530 736kW (1001bhp) The Hanshin Diesel Works Ltd-Japan AuxGen: 2 x 400kW 450V a.c Fuel: 322.0 (d.f.) 5.0pd
9167772 *JDXC* KG1-305	**WAKASHIO MARU No. 118** - **Maruwaka Suisan KK** - SatCom: Inmarsat B 343172510 *Ichikikushikino, Kagoshima* *Japan* MMSI: 431725000 Official number: 135424	*499* - -	**1997-06 KK Kanasashi — Shizuoka SZ** Yd No: 3463 Loa 54.00 (BB) Br ex 9.00 Dght - Lbp - Br md - Dpth 4.00 Welded, 1 dk	**(B11B2FV) Fishing Vessel** Ins: 762	**1 oil engine** with clutches, flexible couplings & sr geared to sc. shaft driving 1 FP propeller Total Power: 736kW (1,001hp) Hanshin 6LC28LG 1 x 4 Stroke 6 Cy. 280 x 530 736kW (1001bhp) The Hanshin Diesel Works Ltd-Japan
9314131 *JGAY* -	**WAKASHIO MARU NO. 128** - **Maruwaka Suisan KK** - *Ichikikushikino, Kagoshima* *Japan* MMSI: 432447000 Official number: 137200	*439* - -	**2004-03 Kanasashi Heavy Industries Co Ltd — Shizuoka SZ** Yd No: 8021 Loa 56.77 Br ex - Dght 3.500 Lbp 49.50 Br md 9.00 Dpth 3.90 Welded, 1 dk	**(B11B2FV) Fishing Vessel**	**1 oil engine** geared to sc. shaft driving 1 FP propeller Total Power: 736kW (1,001hp) Hanshin LH28G 1 x 4 Stroke 6 Cy. 280 x 460 736kW (1001bhp) The Hanshin Diesel Works Ltd-Japan
9088550 *JI3562* -	**WAKASUMIYOSHI** *ex Asahi Maru No. 6 -1999* **YK Ozaki Kisen** - *Kure, Hiroshima* *Japan* MMSI: 431300158 Official number: 134161	*199* - 643	**1994-04 K.K. Saidaiji Zosensho — Okayama** Yd No: 200 Loa 57.60 Br ex - Dght - Lbp 53.80 Br md 9.50 Dpth 5.40 Welded, 1 dk	**(A31A2GX) General Cargo Ship** Grain: 1,280; Bale: 1,228 Compartments: 1 Ho 1 Ha: (30.0 x 7.5)	**1 oil engine** geared to sc. shaft driving 1 FP propeller Total Power: 662kW (900hp) 11.0kn Akasaka K26SFD 1 x 4 Stroke 6 Cy. 260 x 480 662kW (900bhp) Akasaka Tekkosho KK (Akasaka DieselLtd)-Japan
9180451 *JJ3997* -	**WAKATA MARU** - **Naikai Eisen KK** - *Kobe, Hyogo* *Japan* MMSI: 431300512 Official number: 134259	*228* - -	**1997-03 Kanbara Zosen K.K. — Onomichi** Yd No: 490 Loa 41.80 Br ex - Dght 3.300 Lbp 34.30 Br md 9.00 Dpth 4.00 Welded, 1 dk	**(B32A2ST) Tug**	**2 oil engines** geared integral to driving 1 Propeller , 1 Z propeller Total Power: 2,942kW (4,000hp) 13.0kn Niigata 6L28HX 2 x 4 Stroke 6 Cy. 280 x 370 each-1471kW (2000bhp) Niigata Engineering Co Ltd-Japan
9180633 *JL6530* -	**WAKATAKA MARU** *ex Shinsho Maru -2009 ex Hozan Maru -1999* - - *Saga, Saga* *Japan* Official number: 135569	*497* - -	**1997-02 Mategata Zosen K.K. — Namikata** Yd No: 1063 Loa 74.82 Br ex - Dght - Lbp 70.00 Br md 12.50 Dpth 6.80 Welded, 1 dk	**(A31A2GX) General Cargo Ship** Grain: 2,766; Bale: 2,482 Compartments: 1 Ho, ER 1 Ha: (40.2 x 10.0)ER	**1 oil engine** driving 1 FP propeller Total Power: 736kW (1,001hp) 11.5kn Hanshin LH30LG 1 x 4 Stroke 6 Cy. 300 x 600 736kW (1001bhp) The Hanshin Diesel Works Ltd-Japan
9113989 *JQIX* -	**WAKATAKA MARU** - **Fisheries Research Agency** - *Shiogama, Miyagi* *Japan* MMSI: 431726000 Official number: 132240	**692** 297 407	**1995-03 Mitsui Eng. & SB. Co. Ltd. — Tamano** Yd No: 1423 Loa 57.73 (BB) Br ex - Dght 4.456 Lbp 50.60 Br md 11.00 Dpth 6.85 Welded, 1 dk	**(B12D2FR) Fishery Research Vessel**	**2 oil engines** with clutches, flexible couplings & sr geared to sc. shaft driving 1 CP propeller Total Power: 1,472kW (2,002hp) 12.0kn Yanmar T240-ET2 2 x 4 Stroke 6 Cy. 240 x 310 each-736kW (1001bhp) Yanmar Diesel Engine Co Ltd-Japan AuxGen: 2 x 360kW a.c Thrusters: 1 Thwart. CP thruster (f) Fuel: 18.0 (d.f.) 7.8pd
9152428 *JLOV* HK1-500	**WAKATAKE MARU** - **Hokkaido Prefecture - Suisanbu** - SatCom: Inmarsat B 343191910 *Hakodate, Hokkaido* *Japan* MMSI: 431919000 Official number: 132891	*666* - 622	**1997-03 Narasaki Zosen KK — Muroran HK** Yd No: 1160 Loa 64.52 (BB) Br ex - Dght 4.101 Lbp 56.13 Br md 10.00 Dpth 4.20 Welded, 1 dk	**(B34K2QT) Training Ship** Ins: 59 Compartments: 1 Ho, ER 1 Ha:	**1 oil engine** reduction geared to sc. shaft driving 1 CP propeller Total Power: 1,618kW (2,200hp) 13.6kn Niigata 6M34AFT 1 x 4 Stroke 6 Cy. 340 x 620 1618kW (2200bhp) Niigata Engineering Co Ltd-Japan Thrusters: 1 Thwart. CP thruster (f)
9058012 *JL6178* -	**WAKATAKE MARU** *ex Tokuei Maru No. 18 -2008* - - *Saga, Saga* *Japan* Official number: 133921	*499* - 1,515	**1993-09 K.K. Murakami Zosensho — Naruto** Yd No: 210 Loa 75.42 (BB) Br ex - Dght 4.060 Lbp 70.00 Br md 12.00 Dpth 7.00 Welded, 2 dks	**(A31A2GX) General Cargo Ship** Grain: 2,470; Bale: 2,364 Compartments: 1 Ho, ER 1 Ha: ER	**1 oil engine** driving 1 FP propeller Total Power: 736kW (1,001hp) Hanshin LH30LG 1 x 4 Stroke 6 Cy. 300 x 600 736kW (1001bhp) The Hanshin Diesel Works Ltd-Japan
8877540 *JD2569* -	**WAKATAKE MARU No. 35** *ex Shunyo Maru No. 61 -1998* **YK Wakatake Suisan** - *Hakodate, Hokkaido* *Japan* Official number: 125605	*131* - -	**1982-05 Fukui Zosen K.K. — Japan** L reg 27.80 Br ex - Dght - Lbp - Br md 5.70 Dpth 2.30 Welded, 1 dk	**(B11B2FV) Fishing Vessel**	**1 oil engine** driving 1 FP propeller Daihatsu 1 x 4 Stroke Daihatsu Diesel Manufacturing Co Lt-Japan
9115626 *JK5371* -	**WAKATO MARU** *ex Seiyu Maru -2011* - - *Saga, Saga* *Japan* Official number: 134680	*498* - 1,600	**1994-08 Yamanaka Zosen K.K. — Imabari** Yd No: 563 Loa - Br ex - Dght 4.240 Lbp 70.00 Br md 11.50 Dpth 7.24 Welded, 1 dk	**(A31A2GX) General Cargo Ship**	**1 oil engine** driving 1 FP propeller Total Power: 1,324kW (1,800hp) Niigata 6M31BLGT 1 x 4 Stroke 6 Cy. 310 x 600 1324kW (1800bhp) Niigata Engineering Co Ltd-Japan
8020721 - -	**WAKATOKU MARU** - **Hainan Pacific Shipping Co Ltd** - *China*	*991* 634 2,383	**1980-12 Hakata Zosen K.K. — Imabari** Yd No: 250 Loa 71.63 Br ex - Dght 5.088 Lbp 71.51 Br md 12.01 Dpth 5.52 Welded, 1 dk	**(A13B2TP) Products Tanker**	**1 oil engine** driving 1 FP propeller Total Power: 1,471kW (2,000hp) Hanshin 6EL32 1 x 4 Stroke 6 Cy. 320 x 640 1471kW (2000bhp) Hanshin Nainenki Kogyo-Japan
8513534 *YHOJ* -	**WAKATORA** *ex Wakatora Maru No. 3 -2003* **Tjhin Jeffriy Soetanto** - *Surabaya* *Indonesia*	*792* Class: KI 292 900	**1986-04 Matsuura Tekko Zosen K.K. — Osakikamijima** Yd No: 321 Converted From: Grab Dredger-2004 Loa 55.53 (BB) Br ex 11.26 Dght 4.490 Lbp 50.02 Br md 11.00 Dpth 5.80 Welded, 1 dk	**(A31A2GX) General Cargo Ship** Grain: 926; Bale: 917 Compartments: 1 Ho, ER 1 Ha: (18.2 x 8.8)ER	**1 oil engine** with clutches & reverse reduction geared to sc. shaft driving 1 FP propeller Total Power: 736kW (1,001hp) 10.0kn Hanshin 6LU28G 1 x 4 Stroke 6 Cy. 280 x 440 736kW (1001bhp) The Hanshin Diesel Works Ltd-Japan AuxGen: 2 x 120kW 445V a.c Thrusters: 1 Thwart. CP thruster (f)
9146170 *JM6445* -	**WAKATORA MARU No. 5** - **Omaezaki Kaiun KK** - *Kure, Hiroshima* *Japan* Official number: 134624	*494* - 1,600	**1996-05 Shitanoe Shipbuilding Co Ltd — Usuki OT** Yd No: 1178 Loa - Br ex - Dght 4.570 Lbp 60.00 Br md 13.20 Dpth 7.50 Welded, 1 dk	**(B34A2SS) Stone Carrier**	**1 oil engine** driving 1 FP propeller Total Power: 736kW (1,001hp) Hanshin LH34LG 1 x 4 Stroke 6 Cy. 340 x 640 736kW (1001bhp) The Hanshin Diesel Works Ltd-Japan

9281059 *JFCN* -	**WAKATORI MARU** - **Tottori Prefecture** Tottori Prefectural Board of Education *Tottori, Tottori* *Japan* MMSI: 432388000 Official number: 131799	*516* - -		**2003**-03 **Miho Zosensho K.K. — Shimizu** Yd No: 1497 Loa 57.00 Br ex - Dght 3.800 Lbp 48.00 Br md 9.50 Dpth 6.25 Welded	**(B11B2FV) Fishing Vessel**	**1 oil engine** geared to sc. shaft driving 1 Propeller Total Power: 1,471kW (2,000hp) 6MX28 Hanshin 1 x 4 Stroke 6 Cy. 280 x 380 1471kW (2000bhp) The Hanshin Diesel Works Ltd-Japan
8413459 *JD3654* -	**WAKATSURU MARU** *ex* Blue Crane 2 *-2014* *ex* Kitakami Maru *-2010* **Tsurumaru Shipping Co Ltd** - *Kitakyushu, Fukuoka* *Japan* MMSI: 431005217 Official number: 142129	**4,064** 1,560 6,703	Class: NK	**1984**-12 **Kanda Zosensho K.K. — Kawajiri** Yd No: 292 Loa 113.00 (BB) Br ex 16.03 Dght 6.960 Lbp 104.02 Br md 16.01 Dpth 8.21 Welded, 1 dk	**(A24A2BT) Cement Carrier** Grain: 5,555 Compartments: 4 Ho, ER	**1 oil engine** driving 1 FP propeller Total Power: 2,648kW (3,600hp) 12.5kn Ito M506EUS 1 x 4 Stroke 6 Cy. 500 x 880 2648kW (3600bhp) Ito Tekkosho-Japan Fuel: 170.0 (r.f.)
9119127 *JG5418* -	**WAKATSURU MARU No. 6** - **Mukaishima Marina KK** - *Onomichi, Hiroshima* *Japan* MMSI: 431100187 Official number: 135201	*749* - 1,909	Class: NK	**1995**-08 **Sasaki Shipbuilding Co Ltd — Osakikamijima HS** Yd No: 597 Loa 74.83 Br ex - Dght 4.740 Lbp 70.00 Br md 11.50 Dpth 5.25 Welded, 1 dk	**(A13B2TP) Products Tanker** Liq: 2,200; Liq (Oil): 2,200	**1 oil engine** driving 1 FP propeller Total Power: 1,618kW (2,200hp) 12.4kn Hanshin LH34L 1 x 4 Stroke 6 Cy. 340 x 640 1618kW (2200bhp) The Hanshin Diesel Works Ltd-Japan Fuel: 65.0 (d.f.)
9472531 *JD2598* -	**WAKAYAMA** - **Seibu Marine Service KK** - *Sanyoonoda, Yamaguchi* *Japan* Official number: 140718	*216* - -		**2008**-03 **Kanagawa Zosen — Kobe** Yd No: 577 Loa 35.35 Br ex - Dght - Lbp - Br md 9.40 Dpth 4.18 Welded, 1 dk	**(B32A2ST) Tug**	**2 oil engines** reduction geared to sc. shafts driving 2 Propellers Total Power: 1,470kW (1,998hp) 13.5kn Niigata 6L22HX 2 x 4 Stroke 6 Cy. 220 x 280 each-735kW (999bhp) Niigata Engineering Co Ltd-Japan
9633068 *D5DS6* -	**WAKAYAMA MARU** - **Lucretia Shipping SA** Santoku Senpaku Co Ltd *Monrovia* *Liberia* MMSI: 636015960 Official number: 15960	**92,758** 60,504 181,501 T/cm 125.0	Class: NK	**2013**-03 **Koyo Dockyard Co Ltd — Mihara HS** Yd No: 2360 Loa 291.98 (BB) Br ex - Dght 18.240 Lbp 283.80 Br md 45.00 Dpth 24.70 Welded, 1 dk	**(A21A2BC) Bulk Carrier** Grain: 201,243 Compartments: 9 Ho, ER 9 Ha: ER	**1 oil engine** driving 1 FP propeller Total Power: 18,660kW (25,370hp) 14.0kn MAN-B&W 6S70MC-C 1 x 2 Stroke 6 Cy. 700 x 2800 18660kW (25370bhp) Mitsui Engineering & Shipbuilding CLtd-Japan AuxGen: 3 x a.c Fuel: 5800.0
9066887 *JM6230* -	**WAKAYOSHI MARU** - **Wakayoshi Kaiun KK** - *Saga, Saga* *Japan* Official number: 133515	*372* - 370		**1993**-06 **K.K. Izutsu Zosensho — Nagasaki** Yd No: 1026 Loa - Br ex - Dght 3.500 Lbp 51.50 Br md 9.00 Dpth 4.10 Welded, 1 dk	**(A13B2TP) Products Tanker**	**1 oil engine** reduction geared to sc. shaft driving 1 FP propeller Total Power: 736kW (1,001hp) Hanshin LH28G 1 x 4 Stroke 6 Cy. 280 x 460 736kW (1001bhp) The Hanshin Diesel Works Ltd-Japan
8870217 *JM6248* -	**WAKAYOSHI MARU** - **Wakayoshi Kaiun YK** - *Iki, Nagasaki* *Japan* Official number: 133527	*199* - 544		**1993**-05 **Y.K. Okajima Zosensho — Matsuyama** Yd No: 240 Loa 56.30 Br ex - Dght 3.340 Lbp 50.00 Br md 9.30 Dpth 5.57 Welded, 1 dk	**(A31A2GX) General Cargo Ship**	**1 oil engine** driving 1 FP propeller Total Power: 515kW (700hp) 10.0kn Niigata 6M26AGTE 1 x 4 Stroke 6 Cy. 260 x 460 515kW (700bhp) Niigata Engineering Co Ltd-Japan
8801876 - -	**WAKAYOSHI MARU** - - - *Philippines*	*199* - 600		**1988**-01 **Yamanaka Zosen K.K. — Imabari** Yd No: 361 Loa 56.55 (BB) Br ex - Dght 3.018 Lbp 52.51 Br md 9.61 Dpth 5.21 Welded, 2 dks	**(A31A2GX) General Cargo Ship** Grain: 1,330; Bale: 1,299 Compartments: 1 Ho, ER 1 Ha: ER	**1 oil engine** with clutches & reverse reduction geared to sc. shaft driving 1 FP propeller Total Power: 574kW (780hp) Hanshin 6LU26G 1 x 4 Stroke 6 Cy. 260 x 440 574kW (780bhp) The Hanshin Diesel Works Ltd-Japan
9135585 *JL6439* -	**WAKAYOSHI MARU NO. 1** *ex* Sanei Maru No. 2 *-2011* **Wakayoshi Kaiun KK** - *Saga, Saga* *Japan* Official number: 135143	*498* - 1,402		**1995**-12 **Shitanoe Shipbuilding Co Ltd — Usuki OT** Yd No: 1172 Loa 75.40 Br ex - Dght - Lbp 70.50 Br md 12.00 Dpth 7.10 Welded, 1 dk	**(A31A2GX) General Cargo Ship** Bale: 2,351 Compartments: 1 Ho, ER 1 Ha: (40.0 x 9.6)ER	**1 oil engine** driving 1 FP propeller Total Power: 736kW (1,001hp) 12.3kn Hanshin LH32LG 1 x 4 Stroke 6 Cy. 320 x 640 736kW (1001bhp) The Hanshin Diesel Works Ltd-Japan Fuel: 72.0 (d.f.) 5.0pd
9390434 *JD2262* -	**WAKAYOSHI MARU NO. 2** *ex* Kinyo Maru No. 1 *-2013* **Wakayoshi Kaiun KK** KK Kirishima Kaiun Shokai *Saga, Saga* *Japan* MMSI: 431501858 Official number: 140331	*999* - 2,296	Class: NK	**2006**-05 **Hakata Zosen K.K. — Imabari** Yd No: 673 Loa 79.90 Br ex - Dght 5.013 Lbp 76.00 Br md 12.00 Dpth 5.70 Welded, 1 dk	**(A13B2TP) Products Tanker** Double Hull (13F) Liq: 2,250; Liq (Oil): 2,250	**1 oil engine** reduction geared to sc. shaft driving 1 FP propeller Total Power: 1,618kW (2,200hp) 12.9kn Daihatsu 6DKM-26 1 x 4 Stroke 6 Cy. 260 x 380 1618kW (2200bhp) Daihatsu Diesel Manufacturing Co Lt-Japan AuxGen: 2 x a.c Fuel: 113.0 (r.f.)
9624603 *JD3359* -	**WAKAZUKI** - **Government of Japan (Ministry of Land, Infrastructure & Transport) (The Coastguard)** - *Tokyo* *Japan* Official number: 141627	*102* - -		**2012**-07 **Universal Shipbuilding Corp — Yokohama KN (Keihin Shipyard)** Yd No: 0076 Loa 32.50 Br ex - Dght 3.300 Lbp - Br md 6.50 Dpth - Welded, 1 dk	**(B34H2SQ) Patrol Vessel**	**2 oil engines** reduction geared to sc. shafts driving 2 Propellers
7940431 *WSX8109* -	**WAKEFIELD** *ex* D. E. C. O. XI *-1979* **Scallop King Inc** - *Corpus Christi, TX* *United States of America* Official number: 604051	*115* 84 -		**1979 St Augustine Trawlers, Inc. — Saint Augustine, Fl** L reg 19.76 Br ex 6.71 Dght - Lbp - Br md - Dpth 3.13 Welded, 1 dk	**(B11A2FT) Trawler**	**1 oil engine** driving 1 FP propeller Total Power: 382kW (519hp) Caterpillar 3412TA 1 x Vee 4 Stroke 12 Cy. 137 x 152 382kW (519bhp) Caterpillar Tractor Co-USA
8864957 *JM6170* -	**WAKO MARU** - **Nakamura Kaiun YK** - *Iki, Nagasaki* *Japan* Official number: 132751	*446* - 1,100		**1992**-08 **K.K. Kamishima Zosensho — Osakikamijima** Yd No: 530 Loa 64.23 (BB) Br ex - Dght 4.100 Lbp 55.00 Br md 12.00 Dpth 5.90 Welded, 1 dk	**(A24D2BA) Aggregates Carrier** Compartments: 1 Ho, ER 1 Ha: ER	**1 oil engine** sr geared to sc. shaft driving 1 FP propeller Total Power: 1,324kW (1,800hp) Hanshin LH31G 1 x 4 Stroke 6 Cy. 310 x 530 1324kW (1800bhp) The Hanshin Diesel Works Ltd-Japan Thrusters: 1 Thwart. FP thruster (f)
8925086 *JI3551* -	**WAKO MARU** - **Hikari Kisen KK** - *Tanabe, Wakayama* *Japan* Official number: 134154	*499* - 1,250		**1996**-07 **Katsuura Dockyard Co. Ltd. — Nachi-Katsuura** Yd No: 338 Loa 61.90 Br ex - Dght 4.250 Lbp 58.00 Br md 10.50 Dpth 4.70 Welded, 1 dk	**(A13B2TP) Products Tanker** 2 Cargo Pump (s): 2x600m³/hr	**1 oil engine** driving 1 FP propeller Total Power: 736kW (1,001hp) 11.5kn Niigata 6M28BFT 1 x 4 Stroke 6 Cy. 280 x 480 736kW (1001bhp) Niigata Engineering Co Ltd-Japan
9651046 *JD3389* -	**WAKO MARU NO. 2** - **Heiwa Kaiun KK** - *Kure, Hiroshima* *Japan* MMSI: 431003801 Official number: 141721	*2,018* - 3,394	Class: NK	**2012**-09 **Sasaki Shipbuilding Co Ltd — Osakikamijima HS** Yd No: 677 Loa 89.56 Br ex - Dght 5.512 Lbp 83.00 Br md 14.60 Dpth 6.70 Welded, 1 dk	**(A13B2TP) Products Tanker** Double Hull (13F) Liq: 3,577; Liq (Oil): 3,650	**1 oil engine** driving 1 FP propeller Total Power: 2,425kW (3,297hp) Akasaka A41 1 x 4 Stroke 6 Cy. 410 x 800 2425kW (3297bhp) Akasaka Tekkosho KK (Akasaka DieselLtd)-Japan Fuel: 240.0
8889696 *JM6406* -	**WAKO MARU No. 3** - **Nakamura Kaiun YK** - *Iki, Nagasaki* *Japan* Official number: 134564	*499* - 1,199		**1995**-05 **K.K. Kamishima Zosensho — Osakikamijima** Yd No: 573 Loa 69.61 Br ex - Dght 3.970 Lbp 60.00 Br md 13.00 Dpth 6.10 Welded, 1 dk	**(A24D2BA) Aggregates Carrier**	**1 oil engine** driving 1 FP propeller Total Power: 736kW (1,001hp) 10.0kn Niigata 6M34AGT 1 x 4 Stroke 6 Cy. 340 x 620 736kW (1001bhp) Niigata Engineering Co Ltd-Japan
9559729 *JD2997* -	**WAKOU MARU** - **Miyazaki Kaiun Co Ltd** - *Imabari, Ehime* *Japan* MMSI: 431001142 Official number: 141149	*3,794* - 4,999	Class: NK	**2010**-01 **Kanrei Zosen K.K. — Naruto** Yd No: 420 Loa 104.97 (BB) Br ex - Dght 6.380 Lbp 98.80 Br md 16.00 Dpth 8.30 Welded, 1 dk	**(A13B2TP) Products Tanker** Double Hull (13F) Liq: 6,173; Liq (Oil): 6,173	**1 oil engine** driving 1 FP propeller Total Power: 3,250kW (4,419hp) 13.7kn MAN-B&W 6L35MC 1 x 2 Stroke 6 Cy. 350 x 1050 3250kW (4419bhp) Hitachi Zosen Corp-Japan AuxGen: 2 x 550kW a.c Fuel: 220.0

IMO / Call sign	Name / Owner	Tonnage	Class	Builder / Dimensions	Type	Machinery
3862662 DFDR -	**WAL** **Schiffahrts-Compagnie Bremerhaven eV** - *Bremerhaven* *Germany* MMSI: 211253400	**636** 191 99	Class: GL	**1938 Stettiner Oderwerke AG — Stettin** Yd No: 800 Loa 49.96 Br ex - Dght 5.250 Lbp 42.50 Br md 11.50 Dpth 6.05 Welded, 1 dk	**(B34C2SI) Icebreaker** Ice Capable	**1 Steam Recip** driving 1 FP propeller Total Power: 365kW (496hp) 1 x Steam Recip. 365kW (496ihp) Stettiner Oderwerke AG-Stettin
3036258 DLCQ -	**WAL** **Bugsier-, Reederei- und Bergungs-Gesellschaft mbH & Co KG** - SatCom: Inmarsat C 421120710 *Bremen* *Germany* MMSI: 211207100 Official number: 4666	**368** 110 210	Class: GL	**1992-12 Peene-Werft GmbH — Wolgast** Yd No: 418 Loa 31.34 Br ex 10.00 Dght 3.502 Lbp 29.80 Br md 9.84 Dpth 4.22 Welded, 1 dk	**(B32A2ST) Tug** Ice Capable	**2 oil engines** gearing integral to driving 2 Voith-Schneider propellers Total Power: 2,900kW (3,942hp) 12.0kn MaK 8M332C 2 x 4 Stroke 8 Cy. 240 x 330 each-1450kW (1971bhp) Krupp MaK Maschinenbau GmbH-Kiel AuxGen: 2 x 85kW a.c
7609790 DPYV -	**WAL** **Taucher Knoth (Nachf) GmbH & Co KG** - *Hamburg* *Germany* MMSI: 211235160 Official number: 17644	*873* 269 -	Class: GL (DS)	**1974 Zavod im. "Ordzhonikidze" — Sevastopol** Yd No: 1511 Loa 40.67 Br ex 20.25 Dght 2.019 Lbp 40.49 Br md 20.02 Dpth 3.41 Welded, 1 dk	**(B34B2SC) Crane Vessel** Cranes: 1x100t,1x25t Ice Capable	**2 diesel electric oil engines** driving 2 gen. each 320kW 380V Connecting to 2 elec. motors driving 2 Voith-Schneider propellers Total Power: 662kW (900hp) 6.0kn Pervomaysk 6CH25/34 2 x 4 Stroke 6 Cy. 250 x 340 each-331kW (450bhp) Pervomaydizelmash (PDM)-Pervomaysk
8510893 VJWC -	**WALAN** *ex* Walana **Svitzer Australia Pty Ltd (Svitzer Australasia)** - *Sydney, NSW* *Australia* MMSI: 503112800 Official number: 852301	*356* 106 460	Class: AB	**1986-12 Tamar Shipbuilding Pty Ltd — Launceston TAS** Yd No: 43 Loa 32.30 Br ex - Dght 4.550 Lbp 29.44 Br md 10.90 Dpth 5.00 Welded, 1 dk	**(B32A2ST) Tug**	**2 oil engines** with clutches & sr geared to sc. shafts driving 2 FP propellers Total Power: 2,648kW (3,600hp) 12.0kn Daihatsu 6DSM-28 2 x 4 Stroke 6 Cy. 280 x 340 each-1324kW (1800bhp) Daihatsu Diesel Manufacturing Co Lt-Japan AuxGen: 2 x 150kW a.c
7629609 YDCM -	**WALEA** *ex* Discovery *-1982* *ex* Sea Glory III *-1982* *ex* Seiun Maru No. 7 *-1981* **PT Pelayaran Prima Jaya Samudra** - *Jakarta* *Indonesia* MMSI: 525015071	*1,114* 664 2,218	Class: KI (BV)	**1969-05 Murakami Hide Zosen K.K. — Imabari** Yd No: 61 Loa 70.36 Br ex 11.43 Dght 5.119 Lbp 65.61 Br md 11.41 Dpth 5.85 Welded, 1 dk	**(A31A2GX) General Cargo Ship** Compartments: 1 Ho, ER 1 Ha: (33.0 x 6.5)ER Derricks: 2x10t; Winches: 2	**1 oil engine** driving 1 FP propeller Total Power: 1,177kW (1,600hp) 13.0kn Makita FSHC638 1 x 4 Stroke 6 Cy. 380 x 540 1177kW (1600bhp) Makita Diesel Co Ltd-Japan AuxGen: 2 x 64kW 225V 60Hz a.c Fuel: 588.5
5313452 PLUO -	**WALET** *ex* Sanyo Maru *-1976* **PT Pelayaran Payung Samudra** - *Palembang* *Indonesia* Official number: 375933	*154* 47 -	Class: (KI) (NK)	**1961-03 Yamamoto Zosen KK — Kochi KC** Loa 27.56 Br ex 7.32 Dght 2.990 Lbp 25.38 Br md 7.29 Dpth 3.61 Welded, 1 dk	**(B32A2ST) Tug**	**2 oil engines** driving 2 FP propellers Total Power: 1,030kW (1,400hp) 8.0kn G.M. (Detroit Diesel) 16V-71 2 x Vee 2 Stroke 16 Cy. 108 x 127 each-515kW (700bhp) (new engine 1984) General Motors Detroit DieselAllison Divn-USA AuxGen: 1 x 32kW 220/390V a.c Fuel: 26.5
8961573 YD3256 -	**WALET LAUT** *ex* Kairyu Maru *-2005* *ex* Sakaiminato Maru *-2005* **PT Alfa Kencana Samudra** - *Batam* *Indonesia*	*140* 42 -	Class: KI	**1967-11 Ando Shipbuilding Co. Ltd. — Tokyo** Yd No: 193 Loa 25.00 Br ex - Dght 2.260 Lbp 22.00 Br md 7.50 Dpth 3.20 Welded, 1 dk	**(B32A2ST) Tug**	**2 oil engines** driving 2 FP propellers Total Power: 588kW (800hp) 10.0kn Yanmar 6MAL-HT 2 x 4 Stroke 6 Cy. 200 x 240 each-294kW (400bhp) Yanmar Diesel Engine Co Ltd-Japan AuxGen: 1 x 46kW 225/130V a.c, 1 x 24kW 225/130V a.c
6424428 - -	**WALID 1** *ex* Ruba *-2009* *ex* Kolthom *-1996* *ex* Lubna *-1991* *ex* Ghina II *-1990* *ex* Voline *-1973* -	**684** 326 900	Class: (GL)	**1964 J.J. Sietas Schiffswerft — Hamburg** Yd No: 544 Loa 58.43 Br ex 9.45 Dght 3.810 Lbp 53.19 Br md 9.40 Dpth 5.90 Welded, 1 dk & S dk	**(A31A2GX) General Cargo Ship** Grain: 1,707; Bale: 1,548 Compartments: 2 Ho, ER 2 Ha: (9.3 x 5.9) (17.0 x 5.9)ER Derricks: 3x2t Ice Capable	**1 oil engine** driving 1 FP propeller Total Power: 368kW (500hp) 11.0kn Deutz RBV6M545 1 x 4 Stroke 6 Cy. 320 x 450 368kW (500bhp) Kloeckner Humboldt Deutz AG-West Germany
8986822 PP5188 -	**WALKER I** *ex* Brasil III *-2004* **Trico Servicos Maritimos Ltda** Trico Marine Operators Inc *Rio de Janeiro* *Brazil* Official number: 7710777	**158** 47 -		**1977 Swiftships Inc — Morgan City LA** Yd No: 153 Loa 28.36 Br ex - Dght 2.960 Lbp - Br md 8.23 Dpth 3.20 Welded, 1 dk	**(B32A2ST) Tug**	**2 oil engines** reduction geared to sc. shafts driving 2 Propellers Total Power: 1,176kW (1,598hp) G.M. (Detroit Diesel) 12V-149 2 x Vee 2 Stroke 12 Cy. 146 x 146 each-588kW (799bhp) General Motors Corp-USA AuxGen: 2 x 40kW a.c
7233151 WYX2158 -	**WALLA WALLA** **State of Washington (Department of Transportation)** Washington State Department of Transportation (Washington State Ferries) *Seattle, WA* *United States of America* MMSI: 366710810 Official number: 546382	*3,246* 1,198 1,220	Class: (AB)	**1973-04 Todd Pacific Shipyards Corp. — Seattle, Wa** Yd No: 54 Loa 134.12 Br ex 26.52 Dght 5.182 Lbp 127.41 Br md 26.47 Dpth 7.55 Welded, 1 dk	**(A36A2PR) Passenger/Ro-Ro Ship (Vehicles)** Passengers: unberthed: 2000 Bow door/ramp (centre) Stern door/ramp (centre) Cars: 188	**4 diesel electric oil engines** driving 4 gen. each 1900kW 325V a.c Connecting to 2 elec. motors driving 2 Propellers aft, 1 fwd Total Power: 8,460kW (11,504hp) 20.0kn EMD (Electro-Motive) 16-645-E7B 4 x Vee 2 Stroke 16 Cy. 230 x 254 each-2115kW (2876bhp) General Motors Corp-USA AuxGen: 2 x 550kW 450V 60Hz a.c, 1 x 100kW 450V 60Hz a.c Fuel: 490.5
7739363 WCZ2731 -	**WALLACE B** *ex* Miss Elizabeth *-2001* **Craig A Wallis** - *Palacios, TX* *United States of America* Official number: 590442	*121* 86 -		**1977 Master Marine, Inc. — Bayou La Batre, Al** Yd No: 197 L reg 22.59 Br ex 6.71 Dght - Lbp - Br md - Dpth 3.41 Welded, 1 dk	**(B11A2FT) Trawler**	**1 oil engine** geared to sc. shaft driving 1 FP propeller Total Power: 316kW (430hp) G.M. (Detroit Diesel) 12V-71 1 x Vee 2 Stroke 12 Cy. 108 x 127 316kW (430bhp) General Motors Corp-USA
8936580 WDC3035 -	**WALLACE E** *ex* Western Comet *-2011* **SDS Lumber Co** - *Bingen, WA* *United States of America* MMSI: 367001840 Official number: 511362	*299* 203 -	Class: (AB)	**1967 Albina Engine & Machine Works, Inc. — Portland, Or** Yd No: 399 Loa 35.05 Br ex - Dght - Lbp - Br md 10.67 Dpth 2.90 Welded, 1 dk	**(B32A2ST) Tug**	**2 oil engines** driving 2 FP propellers Total Power: 2,206kW (3,000hp) EMD (Electro-Motive) 12-645-E2 2 x Vee 2 Stroke 12 Cy. 230 x 254 each-1103kW (1500bhp) General Motors Detroit DieselAllison Divn-USA
8967400 WDA4201 -	**WALLACE GLENN** **Diamond Services Corp** - *Morgan City, LA* *United States of America* MMSI: 367537460 Official number: 1105415	**350** 102 -		**2001-03 Swiftships Shipbuilders LLC — Morgan City LA** Loa 51.81 Br ex - Dght 1.820 Lbp - Br md 9.14 Dpth 3.68 Welded, 1 dk	**(B21A20C) Crew/Supply Vessel** Hull Material: Aluminium Alloy Passengers: unberthed: 80	**4 oil engines** geared to sc. shafts driving 4 Water jets Total Power: 3,972kW (5,400hp) 28.0kn Cummins KTA-38-M2 4 x Vee 4 Stroke 12 Cy. 159 x 159 each-993kW (1350bhp) Cummins Engine Co Inc-USA AuxGen: 2 x 50kW a.c Thrusters: 1 Thwart. FP thruster (f)
5393529 - -	**WALLODA** *ex* Nina Kathrine Nordfisk *-1985* *ex* Wotan *-1974* **Walloda Pacific Ltd** -	*267* 138 -	Class: (GL)	**1956 Muetzelfeldtwerft GmbH — Cuxhaven** Yd No: 143 Loa 40.06 Br ex 7.75 Dght 2.744 Lbp 38.38 Br md 7.70 Dpth 3.41 Riveted\Welded, 1 dk	**(B11B2FV) Fishing Vessel** Compartments: 2 Ho, ER 27 Ha: ER Ice Capable	**1 oil engine** driving 1 FP propeller Total Power: 441kW (600hp) Deutz RBV6M545 1 x 4 Stroke 6 Cy. 320 x 450 441kW (600bhp) Kloeckner Humboldt Deutz AG-West Germany AuxGen: 1 x 17kW 220/380V 50Hz a.c, 1 x 8kW 220/380V 50Hz a.c, 1 x 8kW 220/380V 50Hz a.c
8989238 LXWY -	**WALLY B** **Wake Maritime Sarl** - *Luxembourg* *Luxembourg* MMSI: 253214000 Official number: 5-30	**102** 30 -	Class: AB	**1999-06 Pendennis Shipyard Ltd. — Falmouth** Yd No: 30 Loa 32.72 Br ex 7.90 Dght 2.330 Lbp 28.73 Br md 7.85 Dpth 3.10 Bonded, 1 dk	**(X11A2YS) Yacht (Sailing)** Hull Material: Reinforced Plastic Passengers: cabins: 3; berths: 6	**1 oil engine** driving 1 Propeller Total Power: 257kW (349hp) 10.0kn Caterpillar 3126TA 1 x 4 Stroke 6 Cy. 110 x 127 257kW (349bhp) Caterpillar Inc-USA Thrusters: 1 Thwart. FP thruster (f); 1 Tunnel thruster (a)
9155573 NZNE -	**WALNUT** **Government of The United States of America (US Coast Guard)** - *Honolulu, HI* *United States of America* MMSI: 366953000	**1,928** 578 350	Class: (AB)	**1999-03 Marinette Marine Corp — Marinette WI** Yd No: 205 Loa 68.58 Br ex - Dght 3.960 Lbp 62.79 Br md 14.02 Dpth 5.98 Welded, 1 dk	**(B34Q2QB) Buoy Tender**	**2 oil engines** reduction geared to sc. shaft driving 1 FP propeller Total Power: 4,560kW (6,200hp) Caterpillar 3608TA 2 x 4 Stroke 8 Cy. 280 x 300 each-2280kW (3100bhp) Caterpillar Inc-USA Thrusters: 1 Thwart. FP thruster (f)

IMO / Call sign	Name / Owner / Manager / Flag	Tonnage	Class	Build	Type	Machinery
9305348 *H8DY*	**WALNUT EXPRESS** **Silver Sapphire Inc** MOL Tankship Management (Asia) Pte Ltd *Panama* *Panama* MMSI: 351145000 Official number: 2998304B	**27,972** 12,193 45,729 T/cm 49.9	Class: NK	**2004-06 Minaminippon Shipbuilding Co Ltd — Usuki OT** Yd No: 680 Loa 179.80 (BB) Br ex 32.23 Dght 12.100 Lbp 171.00 Br md 32.20 Dpth 18.80 Welded, 1 dk	**(A13B2TP) Products Tanker** Double Hull (13F) Liq: 53,068; Liq (Oil): 55,902 Cargo Heating Coils Compartments: 12 Wing Ta, ER, 2 Wing Slop Ta 4 Cargo Pump (s): 4x950m³/hr Manifold: Bow/CM: 91.9m	**1 oil engine** driving 1 FP propeller Total Power: 8,572kW (11,654hp) 14.5kr B&W 6S50MC 1 x 2 Stroke 6 Cy. 500 x 1910 8572kW (11654bhp) Mitsui Engineering & Shipbuilding CLtd-Japan Fuel: 163.0 (d.f.) 2442.0 (r.f.)
8704028 - -	**WALRUS** **L W van IJsseldijk** -	**138** 41 -		**1987-10 Gebr. Buys Scheepsbouw B.V. — Krimpen a/d IJssel** Yd No: 43 Loa 30.05 Br ex - Dght 1.650 Lbp 29.21 Br md 8.51 Dpth 2.27 Welded, 1 dk	**(B11B2FV) Fishing Vessel**	**2 oil engines** with clutches, flexible couplings & sr reverse geared to sc. shafts driving 2 FP propellers Total Power: 600kW (816hp) Caterpillar 3406TA 2 x 4 Stroke 6 Cy. 137 x 165 each-300kW (408bhp) Caterpillar Inc-USA
7917202 *PIOW* -	**WALRUS** *ex* Wilhelmina-Jeanine *-2007* **Van der Straaten Aannemingsgroep BV** Van der Straaten Beheer BV *Hansweert* *Netherlands* MMSI: 246208000 Official number: 2100	**175** 52 -	Class: GL	**1979-07 Scheepswerf A. Baars Azn. B.V. — Sliedrecht** Yd No: 687 Lengthened-1987 Loa 37.50 Br ex 9.05 Dght 1.340 Lbp 37.34 Br md 9.01 Dpth 1.81 Welded, 1 dk	**(B11B2FV) Fishing Vessel** Compartments: 1 Ho, ER Derricks: 2	**2 oil engines** reverse reduction geared to sc. shafts driving 2 FP propellers Total Power: 264kW (358hp) G.M. (Detroit Diesel) 6V-71-N 2 x Vee 2 Stroke 6 Cy. 108 x 127 each-132kW (179bhp) Detroit Diesel Corporation-Detroit, Mi
8135954 *CB4212* -	**WALRUS** *ex* Dirkje *-1989* **Marcelino Gonzalez Rivera** - *Valparaiso* *Chile* MMSI: 725002980 Official number: 2643	*140* - -		**1970 N.V. Jacht- en Scheepswerf M. Veldthuis — Groningen** Yd No: 228 Loa 28.50 Br ex - Dght - Lbp - Br md - Dpth - Welded, 1 dk	**(B11A2FT) Trawler**	**1 oil engine** driving 1 FP propeller Total Power: 588kW (799hp)
8012011 *IITZ2* -	**WALTER C.** *ex* Walcheren *-2009* *ex* Smit Frankrijk *-2000* **Eureco Srl** - *Palermo* *Italy* MMSI: 247268600	**194** 58 -	Class: RI (BV)	**1981-05 B.V. Scheepswerf Jonker & Stans — Hendrik-Ido-Ambacht** Yd No: 356 Loa 28.43 Br ex - Dght 3.310 Lbp 25.02 Br md 8.52 Dpth 4.22 Welded, 1 dk	**(B32A2ST) Tug**	**2 oil engines** reverse reduction geared to sc. shafts driving 2 CP propellers Total Power: 1,500kW (2,040hp) 12.5kr Kromhout 6FCHD240 2 x 4 Stroke 6 Cy. 240 x 260 each-750kW (1020bhp) Stork Werkspoor Diesel BV-Netherlands AuxGen: 2 x 100kW 380V 50Hz a.c Fuel: 161.5
8968155 - -	**WALTER FACHIN** **Government of The Republic of Italy (Ministero dei Trasporti e della Navigazione - Unita' Gestione Infrastrutture)** - *Italy*	*140* 50 -	Class: (RI)	**1990 C.R.N. Cant. Nav. Ancona S.r.l. — Ancona** Yd No: 104 Loa 28.60 Br ex - Dght 1.800 Lbp - Br md 6.17 Dpth 3.38 Welded, 1 dk	**(B34H2SQ) Patrol Vessel**	**4 oil engines** geared to sc. shafts driving 2 FP propellers Total Power: 2,588kW (3,520hp) 22.0kr Isotta Fraschini ID36SS8 4 x Vee 4 Stroke 8 Cy. 170 x 170 each-647kW (880bhp) Isotta Fraschini SpA-Italy
8714841 *DFVT* -	**WALTER HAMMANN** **Hammann & Prahm Reederei GmbH & Co KG ms 'Walter Hammann'** Hammann & Prahm Reederei GmbH *Wischhafen* *Germany* MMSI: 211214650 Official number: 2312	**1,156** 346 1,323	Class: GL	**1988-12 Koetter-Werft GmbH — Haren/Ems** Yd No: 82 Loa 58.75 (BB) Br ex 11.74 Dght 3.530 Lbp 55.20 Br md 11.65 Dpth 5.50 Welded, 2 dks	**(A31A2GX) General Cargo Ship** Grain: 2,217; Bale: 2,210 TEU 50 C. 50/20' Compartments: 1 Ho, ER 1 Ha: (34.7 x 9.2)ER Ice Capable	**1 oil engine** sr geared to sc. shaft driving 1 CP propeller Total Power: 720kW (979hp) 9.5kr MWM TBD440- 1 x 4 Stroke 6 Cy. 230 x 270 720kW (979bhp) Motoren Werke Mannheim AG (MWM)-West Germany AuxGen: 1 x 134kW 220/380V a.c, 1 x 67kW 220/380V a.c, 1 x 26kW 220/380V a.c Thrusters: 1 Thwart. FP thruster (f)
7514684 *WXU3434* -	**WALTER J. MCCARTHY JR.** *ex* Belle River *-1990* **Armstrong Steamship Co** American Steamship Co *Wilmington, DE* *United States of America* MMSI: 366906610 Official number: 585852	*35,652* 33,263 82,209 T/cm 95.0	Class: AB	**1977-08 Bay Shipbuilding Co — Sturgeon Bay WI** Yd No: 716 Loa 304.81 Br ex - Dght 10.383 Lbp 301.79 Br md 32.01 Dpth 17.10 Welded, 1 dk	**(A23A2BK) Bulk Carrier, Self-discharging, Laker** Grain: 78,319 Compartments: 7 Ho, ER 37 Ha: 37 (3.3 x 17.0)ER	**4 oil engines** sr geared to sc. shafts driving 2 CP propellers Total Power: 10,296kW (14,000hp) 14.0k EMD (Electro-Motive) 20-645-E7 4 x Vee 2 Stroke 20 Cy. 230 x 254 each-2574kW (3500bhp) General Motors Corp.Electro-Motive Div.-La Grange AuxGen: 2 x 600kW 480V 60Hz a.c Thrusters: 1 Thwart. FP thruster (f); 1 Tunnel thruster (a)
8990885 *WDE2905* -	**WALTER N** **Elizabeth F Inc** - *Kodiak, AK* *United States of America* MMSI: 369516000 Official number: 257365	**229** 68 -		**1949 in the United States of America** L reg 26.58 Br ex - Dght - Lbp - Br md 10.67 Dpth 3.35 Welded, 1 dk	**(B11B2FV) Fishing Vessel**	**1 oil engine** driving 1 Propeller
9048392 *DBFR* -	**WALTHER HERWIG III** **Government of The Federal Republic of Germany (Bundesanstalt fuer Landwirtschaft und Ernahrung BLE) (Federal Office for Agriculture & Food)** - SatCom: Inmarsat C 421121550 *Bremerhaven* *Germany* MMSI: 211215500	**2,131** 639 561	Class: GL	**1993-12 Detlef Hegemann Rolandwerft GmbH & Co. KG — Berne** Yd No: 167 Loa 63.18 Br ex 15.22 Dght 5.500 Lbp 55.31 Br md 14.80 Dpth 8.90 Welded, 2 dks	**(B12D2FR) Fishery Research Vessel** Ice Capable	**1 oil engine** with clutches & sr geared to sc. shaft driving 1 CP propeller Total Power: 1,800kW (2,447hp) 13.0k MaK 6M453 1 x 4 Stroke 6 Cy. 320 x 420 1800kW (2447bhp) Krupp MaK Maschinenbau GmbH-Kiel AuxGen: 1 x 1705kW 660V 50Hz a.c, 1 x 875kW 660V 50Hz a.c, 1 x 594kW 50V 50Hz a.c Thrusters: 1 Directional thruster (f) Fuel: 410.0 (d.f.) 12.0pd
7208649 *YJQG3* -	**WALVIS** *ex* Aaltje *-2007* *ex* Erika *-2000* **Walvis Shipping Ltd** Van Laar Maritime BV *Port Vila* *Vanuatu* MMSI: 576448000 Official number: 1940	*108* 32 -		**1972-04 Julius Diedrich Schiffswerft GmbH & Co KG — Moormerland** Yd No: 113 Converted From: Fishing Vessel-2007 Loa 23.85 Br ex - Dght 3.000 Lbp 22.57 Br md 6.40 Dpth 3.32 Welded, 1 dk	**(B34L2QU) Utility Vessel**	**1 oil engine** geared to sc. shaft driving 1 FP propeller Total Power: 368kW (500hp) 11.0k Deutz SBA12M81 1 x Vee 4 Stroke 12 Cy. 142 x 160 368kW (500bhp) Kloeckner Humboldt Deutz AG-West Germany AuxGen: 3 x 220/380V a.c
7000645 - -	**WALVIS** *ex* Zwaantje *-1989* *ex* Harmen Post *-1986* *ex* De Vrouw Aaltje *-1982* *ex* Geertruida *-1982* - -	**157** 55		**1969 W. Visser & Zoon N.V. Werf "De Lastdrager" — Den Helder** Yd No: 61 Loa 30.48 Br ex 7.09 Dght - Lbp 26.98 Br md 6.99 Dpth 3.48 Welded, 1 dk	**(B11A2FT) Trawler**	**1 oil engine** driving 1 FP propeller Total Power: 706kW (960hp) Bolnes 8DNL190/60 1 x 2 Stroke 8 Cy. 190 x 350 706kW (960bhp) NV Machinefabriek 'Bolnes' v/h JHvan Cappellen-Netherlands
8127490 *J8RF7* -	**WALVIS 1** *ex* Reliant Seahorse *-1996* *ex* Mar 24 *-1985* *ex* PBR/372 *-1984* **Rosewalk Enterprises Ltd** Consolidated Projects Ltd (CPL) *Kingstown* *St Vincent & The Grenadines* MMSI: 376629000 Official number: 7037	**713** 213 1,104	Class: AB	**1982-07 Hudson Shipbuilders, Inc. (HUDSHIP) — Pascagoula, Ms** Yd No: 104 Loa 53.35 Br ex - Dght 3.806 Lbp 49.76 Br md 12.20 Dpth 4.45 Welded, 1 dk	**(B21A20S) Platform Supply Ship** Passengers: berths: 17 Grain: 4,000 Compartments: 4 Ta, ER	**2 oil engines** sr reverse geared to sc. shafts driving 2 FP propellers Total Power: 2,824kW (3,840hp) Caterpillar 3516T 2 x Vee 4 Stroke 16 Cy. 170 x 190 each-1412kW (1920bhp) (new engine 1995) Caterpillar Inc-USA AuxGen: 2 x 75kW Thrusters: 1 Thwart. FP thruster (f)
7390313 *5NSJ2* -	**WALVIS 2** *ex* Atlantic Seahorse *-1996* **Jem International Ltd** West African Ventures Ltd *Nigeria* MMSI: 657508000	**929** 278 986	Class: AB	**1975-10 Burton Shipyard Co., Inc. — Port Arthur, Tx** Yd No: 511 Loa 60.94 Br ex 12.20 Dght 4.358 Lbp 56.69 Br md 12.15 Dpth 5.19 Welded, 1 dk	**(B21B20A) Anchor Handling Tug Supply** Ice Capable	**2 oil engines** reverse reduction geared to sc. shafts driving 2 FP propellers Total Power: 4,230kW (5,752hp) 15.0k EMD (Electro-Motive) 16-645-E 2 x Vee 2 Stroke 16 Cy. 230 x 254 each-2115kW (2876bhp) General Motors Corp.Electro-Motive Div.-La Grange AuxGen: 2 x 99kW Fuel: 514.0 (d.f.)

IMO / Call sign / Flag	Name / Owner / Manager / Registry	Tonnage	Class	Builder / Dimensions	Type	Machinery
7827512 *J8UC6* -	**WALVIS 5** *ex Western Narrows -1997* **Ottoman Inc** Walvis Nigeria Ltd *Kingstown* *St Vincent & The Grenadines* MMSI: 376354000 Official number: 7636	**757** 227 -	Class: AB	**1980-03 Mangone Shipbuilding Co. — Houston, Tx** Yd No: 127 Converted From: Research Vessel-1988 Loa 56.39 Br ex - Dght 4.187 Lbp 51.74 Br md 11.59 Dpth 4.88 Welded, 1 dk	**(B22A20V) Diving Support Vessel** Cranes: 1x15t; Derricks: 1x25t	**2 oil engines** reduction geared to sc. shafts driving 2 FP propellers Total Power: 2,074kW (2,820hp) 13.0kn Caterpillar 3516TA 2 x Vee 4 Stroke 16 Cy. 170 x 190 each-1037kW (1410bhp) (new engine 1998) Caterpillar Inc-USA AuxGen: 3 x 99kW a.c Thrusters: 1 Thwart. FP thruster (f) Fuel: 340.0 (d.f.)
8211033 *J8RS8* -	**WALVIS 6** *ex Zamil Abdullah -1996* **Copperleaf Holdings Ltd** Walvis International (CI) Ltd *Kingstown* *St Vincent & The Grenadines* MMSI: 376632000 Official number: 7142	**1,070** 321 1,289	Class: BV (NK)	**1982-10 Wakamatsu Zosen K.K. — Kitakyushu** Yd No: 328 Loa 60.86 Br ex 13.19 Dght 4.785 Lbp 56.44 Br md 13.15 Dpth 5.52 Welded, 1 dk	**(B21A20S) Platform Supply Ship**	**2 oil engines** with clutches, flexible couplings & sr reverse geared to sc. shafts driving 2 FP propellers Total Power: 3,090kW (4,202hp) 11.0kn Daihatsu 6DSM-32 2 x 4 Stroke 6 Cy. 320 x 380 each-1545kW (2101bhp) Daihatsu Diesel Manufacturing Co Lt-Japan AuxGen: 3 x 150kW 440V 60Hz a.c Thrusters: 1 Thwart. CP thruster (f) Fuel: 262.5 (d.f.) 15.5pd
8211021 *5NSJ5* -	**WALVIS 7** *ex Zamil Munira -1997* **Glowgold International Ltd** Walvis International (CI) Ltd *Lagos* *Nigeria* MMSI: 657511000	**1,070** 321 1,295	Class: BV (NK)	**1982-08 Wakamatsu Zosen K.K. — Kitakyushu** Yd No: 327 Loa 60.86 Br ex 13.19 Dght 4.785 Lbp 56.44 Br md 13.15 Dpth 5.52 Welded, 1 dk	**(B21A20S) Platform Supply Ship** Passengers: berths: 17	**2 oil engines** with clutches, flexible couplings & sr reverse geared to sc. shafts driving 2 FP propellers Total Power: 3,090kW (4,202hp) 11.0kn Daihatsu 6DSM-32 2 x 4 Stroke 6 Cy. 320 x 380 each-1545kW (2101bhp) Daihatsu Diesel Manufacturing Co Lt-Japan AuxGen: 3 x 150kW 440V 60Hz a.c Thrusters: 1 Thwart. CP thruster (f) Fuel: 262.5 (d.f.) 15.5pd
7343853 *J8TJ8* -	**WALVIS 8** *ex Dea Master -1997 ex Georgturm -1995* **Panfield Ltd** Walvis International (CI) Ltd *Kingstown* *St Vincent & The Grenadines* MMSI: 376271000 Official number: 7486	**1,049** 314 936	Class: AB (GL)	**1973-12 Schiffswerft Hugo Peters — Wewelsfleth** (Hull) Yd No: 551 **1973-12 JG Hitzler Schiffswerft und Masch GmbH & Co KG — Lauenburg** Yd No: 741 Loa 57.41 Br ex 11.74 Dght 4.501 Lbp 50.60 Br md 11.71 Dpth 5.62 Welded, 1 dk	**(B21B20T) Offshore Tug/Supply Ship** Ice Capable	**2 oil engines** reduction geared to sc. shafts driving 2 CP propellers Total Power: 1,692kW (2,300hp) 13.0kn MWM TBD441V16 2 x Vee 4 Stroke 16 Cy. 230 x 270 each-846kW (1150bhp) Motoren Werke Mannheim AG (MWM)-West Germany AuxGen: 3 x 285kW 380V 50Hz a.c Thrusters: 1 Thwart. FP thruster (f)
9199969 *5NXX* -	**WALVIS 12** **Vatax Ltd** Walvis Nigeria Ltd *Lagos* *Nigeria* MMSI: 657105200	**297** 89 -	Class: BV	**1998-02 Shanghai Fishing Vessel Shipyard — Shanghai** Yd No: XY-2082 Loa 31.80 Br ex - Dght 3.200 Lbp 29.34 Br md 9.60 Dpth 4.15 Welded, 1 dk	**(B32A2ST) Tug**	**2 oil engines** geared to sc. shafts driving 2 Directional propellers Total Power: 1,910kW (2,596hp) 12.5kn Caterpillar 3512TA 2 x Vee 4 Stroke 12 Cy. 170 x 190 each-955kW (1298bhp) Caterpillar Inc-USA AuxGen: 2 x 85kW 400/220V 50Hz a.c
8515518 *VLWA* -	**WAMBIRI** **Svitzer Australia Pty Ltd (Svitzer Australasia)** - *Fremantle, WA* *Australia* MMSI: 503081000 Official number: 852127	**470** 141 -	Class: LR ✠ **100A1** SS 11/2011 tug ✠ **LMC** **UMS** Eq.Ltr: H; Cable: 302.5/22.0 U2 (a)	**1986-11 Australian Shipbuilding Industries (WA) Pty Ltd — Fremantle WA** Yd No: 241 Loa 33.92 Br ex 11.43 Dght 4.923 Lbp 30.00 Br md 10.82 Dpth 5.41 Welded, 1 dk	**(B32A2ST) Tug**	**2 oil engines** driving 2 gen. each 180kW gearing integral to driving 2 Z propellers Total Power: 3,530kW (4,800hp) 14.0kn Daihatsu 8DSM-28 2 x 4 Stroke 8 Cy. 280 x 340 each-1765kW (2400bhp) Daihatsu Diesel Manufacturing Co Lt-Japan AuxGen: 2 x 150kW 415V 50Hz a.c Fuel: 217.2 (d.f.) 13.5pd
8896546 - -	**WAMO** *ex Alain-I -1995* - -	**181** 109 -		**1975 in France** Loa 25.00 Br ex - Dght - Lbp - Br md 6.70 Dpth 2.20 Welded, 1 dk	**(B11B2FV) Fishing Vessel**	**1 oil engine** geared to sc. shaft driving 1 FP propeller Total Power: 290kW (394hp) Caterpillar D353TA 1 x 4 Stroke 6 Cy. 159 x 203 290kW (394bhp) (new engine 1990) Caterpillar Inc-USA
9089786 *9WIZ5* -	**WAN 105** *ex Modalwan 1056 -2007* **Coastal Transport (Sandakan) Sdn Bhd** - *Kota Kinabalu* *Malaysia* Official number: 332214	**117** 36 -	Class: GL	**2003-10 Bonafile Shipbuilders & Repairs Sdn Bhd — Sandakan** Yd No: 20/02 Loa 23.00 Br ex - Dght 2.938 Lbp - Br md 6.80 Dpth 3.50 Welded, 1 dk	**(B32A2ST) Tug**	**2 oil engines** reverse reduction geared to sc. shafts driving 2 FP propellers Total Power: 896kW (1,218hp) Yanmar 6LAA-UTE 2 x 4 Stroke 6 Cy. 148 x 165 each-448kW (609bhp) Yanmar Diesel Engine Co Ltd-Japan
9593971 *9V9464* -	**WAN CHENG 1** **Chye Heng Marine Pte Ltd** - *Singapore* *Singapore* MMSI: 563019820 Official number: 397122	**141** 42 -	Class: RI	**2011-11 Kiong Nguong Shipbuilding Contractor Co — Sibu** Yd No: 2067 Loa 23.50 Br ex - Dght 2.540 Lbp 21.39 Br md 7.32 Dpth 3.20 Welded, 1 dk	**(B32A2ST) Tug**	**2 oil engines** reduction geared to sc. shafts driving 2 FP propellers Total Power: 894kW (1,216hp) Cummins KTA-19-M3 2 x 4 Stroke 6 Cy. 159 x 159 each-447kW (608bhp) Chongqing Cummins Engine Co Ltd-China AuxGen: 2 x 50kW 400V 50Hz a.c
8321010 *XUGY8* -	**WAN HAI** *ex Yue Xin -2009 ex Wakaba Maru -2002* **Sea Contentment Shipping Co Ltd** - SatCom: Inmarsat C 451522310 *Phnom Penh* *Cambodia* MMSI: 515223000 Official number: 0286197	**1,457** 721 1,525	Class: UM	**1987-01 Yamanaka Zosen K.K. — Imabari** Yd No: 336 Loa 73.72 (BB) Br ex - Dght 4.152 Lbp 69.02 Br md 11.71 Dpth 7.22 Welded, 2 dks	**(A31A2GX) General Cargo Ship** Grain: 3,031; Bale: 3,014 Compartments: 1 Ho, ER, 1 Tw Dk 1 Ha: ER	**1 oil engine** driving 1 FP propeller Total Power: 1,177kW (1,600hp) Hanshin 6EL30 1 x 4 Stroke 6 Cy. 300 x 600 1177kW (1600bhp) The Hanshin Diesel Works Ltd-Japan
9493298 *9V7589* -	**WAN HAI 101** **Wan Hai Lines (Singapore) Pte Ltd** Wan Hai Lines Ltd *Singapore* *Singapore* MMSI: 566590000 Official number: 394471	**9,834** 3,867 11,500	Class: CC (NV)	**2012-07 CSBC Corp, Taiwan — Keelung** Yd No: 996 Loa 144.10 (BB) Br ex - Dght 7.300 Lbp 136.10 Br md 22.50 Dpth 11.20 Welded, 1 dk	**(A33A2CC) Container Ship (Fully Cellular)** TEU 1040	**1 oil engine** driving 1 FP propeller Total Power: 9,480kW (12,889hp) 18.8kn MAN-B&W 6S50MC-C 1 x 2 Stroke 6 Cy. 500 x 2000 9480kW (12889bhp) Doosan Engine Co Ltd-South Korea AuxGen: 3 x a.c Thrusters: 1 Tunnel thruster (f)
9493303 *9V7590* -	**WAN HAI 102** **Wan Hai Lines (Singapore) Pte Ltd** Wan Hai Lines Ltd *Singapore* *Singapore* MMSI: 566653000 Official number: 394472	**9,834** 3,867 11,500	Class: CC NV	**2012-08 CSBC Corp, Taiwan — Keelung** Yd No: 997 Loa 144.10 (BB) Br ex - Dght 7.300 Lbp 136.10 Br md 22.50 Dpth 11.20 Welded, 1 dk	**(A33A2CC) Container Ship (Fully Cellular)** TEU 1040	**1 oil engine** driving 1 FP propeller Total Power: 9,480kW (12,889hp) 18.8kn MAN-B&W 6S50MC-C 1 x 2 Stroke 6 Cy. 500 x 2000 9480kW (12889bhp) Doosan Engine Co Ltd-South Korea AuxGen: 3 x a.c Thrusters: 1 Tunnel thruster (f)
9596349 *9V8967* -	**WAN HAI 103** **Wan Hai Lines (Singapore) Pte Ltd** Wan Hai Lines Ltd *Singapore* *Singapore* MMSI: 566703000 Official number: 396445	**9,834** 3,867 11,500	Class: NV	**2012-10 CSBC Corp, Taiwan — Keelung** Yd No: 998 Loa 144.10 (BB) Br ex - Dght 7.300 Lbp 136.10 Br md 22.50 Dpth 11.20 Welded, 1 dk	**(A33A2CC) Container Ship (Fully Cellular)** TEU 1040	**1 oil engine** driving 1 FP propeller Total Power: 9,480kW (12,889hp) 18.8kn MAN-B&W 6S50MC-C 1 x 2 Stroke 6 Cy. 500 x 2000 9480kW (12889bhp) Doosan Engine Co Ltd-South Korea AuxGen: 3 x a.c Thrusters: 1 Tunnel thruster (f)
9596789 *9V8968* -	**WAN HAI 105** **Wan Hai Lines (Singapore) Pte Ltd** Wan Hai Lines Ltd *Singapore* *Singapore* MMSI: 566760000 Official number: 396446	**9,834** 3,867 11,500	Class: NV	**2012-11 CSBC Corp, Taiwan — Keelung** Yd No: 999 Loa 144.10 (BB) Br ex - Dght 7.300 Lbp 136.10 Br md 22.50 Dpth 11.20 Welded, 1 dk	**(A33A2CC) Container Ship (Fully Cellular)** TEU 1040	**1 oil engine** driving 1 FP propeller Total Power: 9,480kW (12,889hp) 18.8kn MAN-B&W 6S50MC-C 1 x 2 Stroke 6 Cy. 500 x 2000 9480kW (12889bhp) Doosan Engine Co Ltd-South Korea AuxGen: 3 x a.c Thrusters: 1 Tunnel thruster (f)

9132894 *BLBB* -	**WAN HAI 161** **Wan Hai Lines Ltd** - SatCom: Inmarsat C 441625710 *Keelung* *Chinese Taipei* MMSI: 416257000 Official number: 013241	**13,246** 6,477 17,738 T/cm 31.8	Class: CR NV (NK)	**1996-08 Shin Kochi Jyuko K.K. — Kochi** Yd No: 7081 Loa 159.52 (BB) Br ex - Dght 8.717 Lbp 150.00 Br md 25.00 Dpth 12.80 Welded, 1 dk	**(A33A2CC) Container Ship (Fully Cellular)** TEU 1088 C Ho 496 TEU C Dk 592 TEU incl 100 ref C. Compartments: 5 Cell Ho, ER 15 Ha: ER	**1 oil engine** driving 1 FP propeller Total Power: 8,562kW (11,641hp) B&W 1 x 2 Stroke 6 Cy. 500 x 1910 8562kW (11641bhp) Mitsui Engineering & Shipbuilding CLtd-Japan AuxGen: 3 x 560kW 450V 60Hz a.c Thrusters: 1 Tunnel thruster (f) Fuel: 150.0 (d.f.) 1275.0 (r.f.) 35.0pd	17.6kr 6S50MC
9132909 *BLBZ* -	**WAN HAI 162** **Wan Hai Lines Ltd** - SatCom: Inmarsat C 441625811 *Keelung* *Chinese Taipei* MMSI: 416258000 Official number: 013242	**13,246** 6,477 17,697 T/cm 31.8	Class: CR NV (NK)	**1996-11 Shin Kochi Jyuko K.K. — Kochi** Yd No: 7082 Loa 159.52 (BB) Br ex - Dght 8.717 Lbp 150.00 Br md 25.00 Dpth 12.80 Welded, 1 dk	**(A33A2CC) Container Ship (Fully Cellular)** TEU 1088 C Ho 496 TEU C Dk 592 TEU incl 100 ref C. Compartments: 5 Cell Ho, ER 15 Ha: ER	**1 oil engine** driving 1 FP propeller Total Power: 8,562kW (11,641hp) B&W 1 x 2 Stroke 6 Cy. 500 x 1910 8562kW (11641bhp) Mitsui Engineering & Shipbuilding CLtd-Japan AuxGen: 3 x 560kW 450V 60Hz a.c Thrusters: 1 Tunnel thruster (f)	17.6kr 6S50MC
9158848 *S6EN6* -	**WAN HAI 163** **Wan Hai Lines (Singapore) Pte Ltd** Wan Hai Lines Ltd SatCom: Inmarsat C 456509611 *Singapore* *Singapore* MMSI: 565096000 Official number: 391969	**13,246** 6,479 17,706 T/cm 31.8	Class: CR NK	**1998-03 Shin Kochi Jyuko K.K. — Kochi** Yd No: 7102 Loa 159.52 (BB) Br ex - Dght 8.719 Lbp 150.00 Br md 25.00 Dpth 12.80 Welded, 1 dk	**(A33A2CC) Container Ship (Fully Cellular)** TEU 1088 C Ho 496 TEU C Dk 592 TEU incl 100 ref C. Compartments: 5 Cell Ho, ER 15 Ha: ER	**1 oil engine** driving 1 FP propeller Total Power: 8,562kW (11,641hp) B&W 1 x 2 Stroke 6 Cy. 500 x 1910 8562kW (11641bhp) Mitsui Engineering & Shipbuilding CLtd-Japan AuxGen: 3 x 560kW 450V 60Hz a.c Thrusters: 1 Tunnel thruster (f) Fuel: 1210.0	17.6kr 6S50MC
9158850 *S6EN7* -	**WAN HAI 165** **Wan Hai Lines (Singapore) Pte Ltd** Wan Hai Lines Ltd SatCom: Inmarsat C 456512811 *Singapore* *Singapore* MMSI: 565128000 Official number: 391970	**13,246** 6,479 17,717 T/cm 31.8	Class: CR NK	**1998-06 Shin Kochi Jyuko K.K. — Kochi** Yd No: 7103 Loa 159.52 (BB) Br ex - Dght 8.719 Lbp 150.00 Br md 25.00 Dpth 12.80 Welded, 1 dk	**(A33A2CC) Container Ship (Fully Cellular)** TEU 1088 C Ho 496 TEU C Dk 592 TEU incl 100 ref C. Compartments: 5 Cell Ho, ER 15 Ha: ER	**1 oil engine** driving 1 FP propeller Total Power: 8,562kW (11,641hp) B&W 1 x 2 Stroke 6 Cy. 500 x 1910 8562kW (11641bhp) Mitsui Engineering & Shipbuilding CLtd-Japan AuxGen: 3 x 560kW 450V 60Hz a.c Thrusters: 1 Tunnel thruster (f) Fuel: 1210.0	18.5k 6S50MC
9380257 *VRFC9* -	**WAN HAI 171** *ex Ocean Victoria -2009* **Interasia Lines (HK) Ltd** Wan Hai Lines Ltd SatCom: Inmarsat C 447700768 *Hong Kong* *Hong Kong* MMSI: 477217400 Official number: HK-2382	**16,488** 7,615 22,171	Class: AB	**2009-03 CSBC Corp, Taiwan — Keelung** Yd No: 891 Loa 172.70 (BB) Br ex - Dght 9.500 Lbp 162.10 Br md 27.30 Dpth 13.50 Welded, 1 dk	**(A33A2CC) Container Ship (Fully Cellular)** TEU 1809 incl 300 ref C	**1 oil engine** driving 1 FP propeller Total Power: 15,806kW (21,490hp) MAN-B&W 1 x 2 Stroke 7 Cy. 600 x 2400 15806kW (21490bhp) Kawasaki Heavy Industries Ltd-Japan AuxGen: 3 x 1200kW a.c Thrusters: 1 Tunnel thruster (f) Fuel: 166.0 (d.f.) 1846.0 (r.f.)	19.0k 7S60MC-
9380269 *VRFF4* -	**WAN HAI 172** **Wan Hai Lines (HK) Ltd** Wan Hai Lines Ltd SatCom: Inmarsat C 447700796 *Hong Kong* *Hong Kong* MMSI: 477225300 Official number: HK-2400	**16,488** 7,615 22,171	Class: AB (KR)	**2009-04 CSBC Corp, Taiwan — Keelung** Yd No: 892 Loa 172.70 (BB) Br ex - Dght 9.500 Lbp 162.10 Br md 27.30 Dpth 13.50 Welded, 1 dk	**(A33A2CC) Container Ship (Fully Cellular)** TEU 1809 incl 300 ref C	**1 oil engine** driving 1 FP propeller Total Power: 15,806kW (21,490hp) MAN-B&W 1 x 2 Stroke 7 Cy. 600 x 2400 15806kW (21490bhp) Kawasaki Heavy Industries Ltd-Japan AuxGen: 3 x 1200kW a.c Thrusters: 1 Tunnel thruster (f)	19.0k 7S60MC-
8901755 *BLBX* -	**WAN HAI 202** **Wan Hai Lines Ltd** - SatCom: Inmarsat C 441626010 *Keelung* *Chinese Taipei* MMSI: 416260000 Official number: 12300	**17,123** 7,246 23,692 T/cm 39.1	Class: CR (AB)	**1990-02 Naikai Shipbuilding & Engineering Co Ltd — Onomichi HS (Setoda Shipyard)** Yd No: 543 Loa 174.00 (BB) Br ex 27.03 Dght 9.850 Lbp 164.00 Br md 27.00 Dpth 14.60 Welded, 1 dk	**(A33A2CC) Container Ship (Fully Cellular)** TEU 1057 C Ho 598 TEU C Dk 459 TEU incl 70 ref C. Compartments: 5 Cell Ho, ER 9 Ha: ER Gantry cranes: 1x35t	**1 oil engine** driving 1 FP propeller Total Power: 8,974kW (12,201hp) B&W 1 x 2 Stroke 7 Cy. 500 x 1910 8974kW (12201bhp) Hitachi Zosen Corp-Japan AuxGen: 1 x 800kW a.c, 3 x 580kW a.c, 1 x 130kW a.c, 1 x 80kW a.c Thrusters: 1 Thwart. CP thruster (f) Fuel: 179.3 (d.f.) 840.3 (r.f.) 33.9pd	17.5k 7S50M
8914013 *VRMM2* -	**WAN HAI 203** **Wan Hai Lines Ltd** - *Hong Kong* *Hong Kong* MMSI: 477752700 Official number: HK-3913	**17,134** 7,246 23,729 T/cm 39.1	Class: CC CR (AB)	**1990-06 Naikai Shipbuilding & Engineering Co Ltd — Onomichi HS (Setoda Shipyard)** Yd No: 553 Loa 174.00 (BB) Br ex - Dght 9.869 Lbp 164.89 Br md 27.01 Dpth 14.61 Welded, 1 dk	**(A33A2CC) Container Ship (Fully Cellular)** TEU 1057 C Ho 598 TEU C Dk 459 TEU incl 60 ref C. Compartments: 5 Cell Ho, ER 9 Ha: ER Gantry cranes: 1x35t	**1 oil engine** driving 1 FP propeller Total Power: 8,974kW (12,201hp) B&W 1 x 2 Stroke 7 Cy. 500 x 1910 8974kW (12201bhp) Hitachi Zosen Corp-Japan AuxGen: 1 x 800kW a.c, 3 x 580kW a.c, 1 x 130kW a.c, 1 x 80kW a.c Thrusters: 1 Thwart. CP thruster (f) Fuel: 179.3 (d.f.) 840.3 (r.f.) 33.9pd	17.5k 7S50M
8914025 *S6BV5* -	**WAN HAI 205** **Wan Hai Lines (Singapore) Pte Ltd** Wan Hai Lines Ltd SatCom: Inmarsat C 456331110 *Singapore* *Singapore* MMSI: 563311000 Official number: 390914	**17,134** 7,246 23,676 T/cm 39.1	Class: CC CR (AB)	**1990-10 Naikai Shipbuilding & Engineering Co Ltd — Onomichi HS (Setoda Shipyard)** Yd No: 554 Loa 174.00 (BB) Br ex - Dght 9.869 Lbp 164.89 Br md 27.00 Dpth 14.60 Welded, 1 dk	**(A33A2CC) Container Ship (Fully Cellular)** TEU 1057 C Ho 598 TEU C Dk 459 TEU incl 70 ref C. Compartments: 5 Cell Ho, ER 9 Ha: ER Gantry cranes: 1x35t	**1 oil engine** driving 1 FP propeller Total Power: 8,974kW (12,201hp) B&W 1 x 2 Stroke 7 Cy. 500 x 1910 8974kW (12201bhp) Hitachi Zosen Corp-Japan AuxGen: 1 x 800kW a.c, 3 x 580kW a.c, 1 x 130kW a.c, 1 x 80kW a.c Thrusters: 1 Thwart. CP thruster (f) Fuel: 179.3 (d.f.) 840.3 (r.f.) 33.9pd	17.5k 7S50M
9002702 *S6EN8* -	**WAN HAI 206** **Wan Hai Lines (Singapore) Pte Ltd** Wan Hai Lines Ltd SatCom: Inmarsat C 456512910 *Singapore* *Singapore* MMSI: 565129000 Official number: 391971	**17,136** 7,247 23,724 T/cm 39.1	Class: NV (AB) (CR)	**1991-08 Naikai Shipbuilding & Engineering Co Ltd — Onomichi HS (Setoda Shipyard)** Yd No: 563 Loa 174.60 (BB) Br ex 27.03 Dght 9.869 Lbp 164.00 Br md 27.00 Dpth 14.60 Welded, 1 dk	**(A33A2CC) Container Ship (Fully Cellular)** TEU 1057 C Ho 598 TEU C Dk 459 TEU incl 70 ref C. Compartments: 5 Cell Ho, ER 9 Ha: ER Gantry cranes: 1x35t	**1 oil engine** driving 1 FP propeller Total Power: 8,974kW (12,201hp) B&W 1 x 2 Stroke 7 Cy. 500 x 1910 8974kW (12201bhp) Hitachi Zosen Corp-Japan AuxGen: 3 x 650kW a.c Thrusters: 1 Tunnel thruster (f) Fuel: 179.3 (d.f.) 840.3 (r.f.) 33.9pd	17.5k 7S50M
9039561 *9VHX* -	**WAN HAI 207** **Wan Hai Lines (Singapore) Pte Ltd** Wan Hai Lines Ltd SatCom: Inmarsat C 456427710 *Singapore* *Singapore* MMSI: 564277000 Official number: 387752	**17,136** 7,247 23,690 T/cm 39.1	Class: CC (AB)	**1992-08 Naikai Zosen Corp — Onomichi HS (Setoda Shipyard)** Yd No: 573 Loa 174.60 (BB) Br ex 27.03 Dght 9.869 Lbp 164.00 Br md 27.00 Dpth 14.60 Welded, 1 dk	**(A33A2CC) Container Ship (Fully Cellular)** TEU 1057 C Ho 598 TEU C Dk 459 TEU incl 70 ref C. Compartments: 5 Cell Ho, ER 9 Ha: ER	**1 oil engine** driving 1 FP propeller Total Power: 8,974kW (12,201hp) B&W 1 x 2 Stroke 7 Cy. 500 x 1910 8974kW (12201bhp) Hitachi Zosen Corp-Japan AuxGen: 3 x 650kW 440V 50Hz a.c Thrusters: 1 Thwart. CP thruster (f) Fuel: 142.0 (d.f.) 796.0 (r.f.) 33.2pd	17.5k 7S50M
9048574 *9VDR* -	**WAN HAI 211** *launched as* Wan Hai 208 *-1993* **Wan Hai Lines (Singapore) Pte Ltd** Wan Hai Lines Ltd SatCom: Inmarsat C 456427810 *Singapore* *Singapore* MMSI: 564278000 Official number: 387753	**17,138** 7,247 23,837 T/cm 39.1	Class: NK (AB)	**1993-02 Naikai Zosen Corp — Onomichi HS (Setoda Shipyard)** Yd No: 578 Loa 174.60 (BB) Br ex 27.03 Dght 9.869 Lbp 164.00 Br md 27.00 Dpth 14.60 Welded, 1 dk	**(A33A2CC) Container Ship (Fully Cellular)** TEU 1298 C Ho 598 TEU C Dk 700 TEU incl 70 ref C. Compartments: 5 Cell Ho, ER 9 Ha: ER	**1 oil engine** driving 1 FP propeller Total Power: 8,974kW (12,201hp) B&W 1 x 2 Stroke 7 Cy. 500 x 1910 8974kW (12201bhp) Hitachi Zosen Corp-Japan AuxGen: 3 x 650kW 440V 50Hz a.c Thrusters: 1 Thwart. CP thruster (f) Fuel: 142.0 (d.f.) 796.0 (r.f.) 33.2pd	17.5k 7S50M
9048586 *9VEJ* -	**WAN HAI 212** *launched as* Wan Hai 209 *-1993* **Wan Hai Lines (Singapore) Pte Ltd** Wan Hai Lines Ltd SatCom: Inmarsat C 456427910 *Singapore* *Singapore* MMSI: 564279000 Official number: 387754	**17,138** 7,247 23,877 T/cm 39.1	Class: CC (AB)	**1993-03 Naikai Zosen Corp — Onomichi HS (Setoda Shipyard)** Yd No: 579 Loa 174.60 (BB) Br ex 27.03 Dght 9.100 Lbp 164.00 Br md 27.00 Dpth 14.60 Welded, 1 dk	**(A33A2CC) Container Ship (Fully Cellular)** TEU 1298 C Ho 598 TEU C Dk 700 TEU incl 70 ref C. Compartments: 5 Cell Ho, ER 9 Ha: ER	**1 oil engine** driving 1 FP propeller Total Power: 8,974kW (12,201hp) B&W 1 x 2 Stroke 7 Cy. 500 x 1910 8974kW (12201bhp) Hitachi Zosen Corp-Japan AuxGen: 3 x 650kW 440V 50Hz a.c Thrusters: 1 Thwart. CP thruster (f) Fuel: 142.0 (d.f.) 796.0 (r.f.) 33.2pd	17.5k 7S50M

IMO / Call sign	Name / Owner / Flag	Tonnage	Class	Build	Type	Machinery
9059121 *S6SF* -	**WAN HAI 213** **Wan Hai Lines (Singapore) Pte Ltd** Wan Hai Lines Ltd SatCom: Inmarsat C 456449511 *Singapore* *Singapore* MMSI: 564495000 Official number: 388082	**17,138** 7,247 22,000 T/cm 39.1	Class: NV (AB)	**1993-10 Naikai Zosen Corp — Onomichi HS (Setoda Shipyard)** Yd No: 584 Loa 174.60 (BB) Br ex 27.03 Dght 9.100 Lbp 164.00 Br md 27.00 Dpth 14.60 Welded, 1 dk	**(A33A2CC) Container Ship (Fully Cellular)** TEU 1368 C Ho 598 TEU C Dk 770 TEU incl 160 ref C. Compartments: 5 Cell Ho, ER 9 Ha: ER	**1 oil engine** driving 1 FP propeller Total Power: 8,974kW (12,201hp) 17.5kn B&W 7S50MC 1 x 2 Stroke 7 Cy. 500 x 1910 8974kW (12201bhp) Hitachi Zosen Corp-Japan AuxGen: 3 x 650kW 440V 50Hz a.c Thrusters: 1 Thwart. CP thruster (f) Fuel: 142.0 (d.f.) 796.0 (r.f.) 33.2pd
9059133 *S6SG* -	**WAN HAI 215** **Wan Hai Lines (Singapore) Pte Ltd** Wan Hai Lines Ltd SatCom: Inmarsat C 456449611 *Singapore* *Singapore* MMSI: 564496000 Official number: 388083	**17,138** 7,247 23,801 T/cm 39.1	Class: NK (AB)	**1994-01 Naikai Zosen Corp — Onomichi HS (Setoda Shipyard)** Yd No: 585 Loa 174.60 (BB) Br ex 27.03 Dght 9.869 Lbp 164.00 Br md 27.00 Dpth 14.60 Welded, 1 dk	**(A33A2CC) Container Ship (Fully Cellular)** TEU 1368 C Ho 598 TEU C Dk 770 TEU incl 160 ref C. Compartments: 5 Cell Ho, ER 9 Ha: ER	**1 oil engine** driving 1 FP propeller Total Power: 8,974kW (12,201hp) 17.5kn B&W 7S50MC 1 x 2 Stroke 7 Cy. 500 x 1910 8974kW (12201bhp) Hitachi Zosen Corp-Japan AuxGen: 3 x 650kW 440V 50Hz a.c Thrusters: 1 Thwart. CP thruster (f) Fuel: 142.0 (d.f.) 796.0 (r.f.) 33.2pd
9059145 *S6SI* -	**WAN HAI 216** **Wan Hai Lines (Singapore) Pte Ltd** Wan Hai Lines Ltd SatCom: Inmarsat C 456449810 *Singapore* *Singapore* MMSI: 564498000 Official number: 388085	**17,138** 7,247 23,837 T/cm 39.1	Class: NV (AB)	**1994-02 Naikai Zosen Corp — Onomichi HS (Setoda Shipyard)** Yd No: 586 Loa 174.60 (BB) Br ex 27.03 Dght 9.869 Lbp 164.00 Br md 27.00 Dpth 14.60 Welded, 1 dk	**(A33A2CC) Container Ship (Fully Cellular)** TEU 1368 C Ho 598 TEU C Dk 770 TEU incl 160 ref C. Compartments: 5 Cell Ho, ER 9 Ha: ER	**1 oil engine** driving 1 FP propeller Total Power: 8,974kW (12,201hp) 17.5kn B&W 7S50MC 1 x 2 Stroke 7 Cy. 500 x 1910 8974kW (12201bhp) Hitachi Zosen Corp-Japan AuxGen: 3 x 650kW 440V 50Hz a.c Thrusters: 1 Thwart. CP thruster (f) Fuel: 142.0 (d.f.) 796.0 (r.f.) 33.2pd
9074432 *S6SK* -	**WAN HAI 221** **Wan Hai Lines (Singapore) Pte Ltd** Wan Hai Lines Ltd SatCom: Inmarsat C 456450011 *Singapore* *Singapore* MMSI: 564500000 Official number: 388087	**16,911** 7,238 23,802 T/cm 39.1	Class: BV (AB)	**1994-06 Naikai Zosen Corp — Onomichi HS (Setoda Shipyard)** Yd No: 592 Loa 172.15 (BB) Br ex 27.03 Dght 9.869 Lbp 164.00 Br md 27.00 Dpth 14.60 Welded, 1 dk	**(A33A2CC) Container Ship (Fully Cellular)** TEU 1368 C Ho 598 TEU C Dk 770 TEU incl 160 ref C. Compartments: 5 Cell Ho, ER 9 Ha: ER	**1 oil engine** driving 1 FP propeller Total Power: 8,974kW (12,201hp) 17.5kn B&W 7S50MC 1 x 2 Stroke 7 Cy. 500 x 1910 8974kW (12201bhp) Hitachi Zosen Corp-Japan AuxGen: 3 x 650kW 60Hz a.c Thrusters: 1 Thwart. CP thruster (f) Fuel: 1148.0
9074444 *S6SJ* -	**WAN HAI 222** **Wan Hai Lines (Singapore) Pte Ltd** Wan Hai Lines Ltd SatCom: Inmarsat C 456449910 *Singapore* *Singapore* MMSI: 564499000 Official number: 388086	**16,911** 7,238 23,429 T/cm 39.1	Class: BV (AB)	**1994-08 Naikai Zosen Corp — Onomichi HS (Setoda Shipyard)** Yd No: 593 Loa 172.15 (BB) Br ex 27.03 Dght 9.869 Lbp 164.00 Br md 27.00 Dpth 14.60 Welded, 1 dk	**(A33A2CC) Container Ship (Fully Cellular)** TEU 1368 C Ho 598 TEU C Dk 770 TEU incl 160 ref C. Compartments: 5 Cell Ho 9 Ha:	**1 oil engine** driving 1 FP propeller Total Power: 8,974kW (12,201hp) 17.5kn B&W 7S50MC 1 x 2 Stroke 7 Cy. 500 x 1910 8974kW (12201bhp) Hitachi Zosen Corp-Japan AuxGen: 3 x 650kW 60Hz a.c Thrusters: 1 Thwart. CP thruster (f) Fuel: 1148.0
9074456 *S6SH* -	**WAN HAI 223** **Wan Hai Lines (Singapore) Pte Ltd** Wan Hai Lines Ltd SatCom: Inmarsat C 456449711 *Singapore* *Singapore* MMSI: 564497000 Official number: 388084	**16,911** 7,238 23,799 T/cm 39.1	Class: NK (AB)	**1994-09 Naikai Zosen Corp — Onomichi HS (Setoda Shipyard)** Yd No: 594 Loa 172.15 (BB) Br ex 27.03 Dght 9.869 Lbp 164.00 Br md 27.00 Dpth 14.60 Welded, 1 dk	**(A33A2CC) Container Ship (Fully Cellular)** TEU 1368 C Ho 598 TEU C Dk 770 TEU incl 160 ref C. Compartments: 5 Cell Ho 9 Ha:	**1 oil engine** driving 1 FP propeller Total Power: 8,974kW (12,201hp) 17.5kn B&W 7S50MC 1 x 2 Stroke 7 Cy. 500 x 1910 8974kW (12201bhp) Hitachi Zosen Corp-Japan AuxGen: 3 x a.c Thrusters: 1 Thwart. CP thruster (f) Fuel: 1148.0 (r.f.)
9074468 *S6FX5* -	**WAN HAI 225** **Wan Hai Lines (Singapore) Pte Ltd** Wan Hai Lines Ltd SatCom: Inmarsat C 456439412 *Singapore* *Singapore* MMSI: 564394000 Official number: 389657	**16,988** 7,287 23,792 T/cm 39.1	Class: CR NK (AB)	**1994-12 Naikai Zosen Corp — Onomichi HS (Setoda Shipyard)** Yd No: 595 Loa 172.15 (BB) Br ex 27.03 Dght 9.869 Lbp 164.00 Br md 27.00 Dpth 14.60 Welded, 1 dk	**(A33A2CC) Container Ship (Fully Cellular)** TEU 1368 C Ho 598 TEU C Dk 770 TEU incl 160 ref C. Compartments: 5 Cell Ho, ER 9 Ha: ER	**1 oil engine** driving 1 FP propeller Total Power: 9,101kW (12,374hp) 17.5kn B&W 7S50MC 1 x 2 Stroke 7 Cy. 500 x 1910 9101kW (12374bhp) Hitachi Zosen Corp-Japan AuxGen: 1 x a.c Thrusters: 1 Thwart. CP thruster (f) Fuel: 1040.0 (r.f.)
9208150 *S6EN9* -	**WAN HAI 231** **Wan Hai Lines (Singapore) Pte Ltd** Wan Hai Lines Ltd *Singapore* *Singapore* MMSI: 565130000 Official number: 391972	**17,751** 6,636 21,052 T/cm 41.3	Class: CC CR (AB)	**2000-02 Naikai Zosen Corp — Onomichi HS (Setoda Shipyard)** Yd No: 652 Loa 191.50 (BB) Br ex - Dght 9.500 Lbp 180.00 Br md 28.00 Dpth 14.10 Welded, 1 dk	**(A33A2CC) Container Ship (Fully Cellular)** TEU 1660 C Ho 560 TEU C Dk 1100 TEU incl 150 ref C Compartments: 5 Cell Ho, ER 9 Ha: ER	**1 oil engine** driving 1 FP propeller Total Power: 15,807kW (21,491hp) 21.0kn B&W 7S60MC-C 1 x 2 Stroke 7 Cy. 600 x 2400 15807kW (21491bhp) Hitachi Zosen Corp-Japan AuxGen: 3 x 880kW a.c Thrusters: 1 Thwart. FP thruster (f) Fuel: 1978.0 (r.f.) 61.0pd
9208162 *S6EL2* -	**WAN HAI 232** **Wan Hai Lines (Singapore) Pte Ltd** Wan Hai Lines Ltd *Singapore* *Singapore* MMSI: 565131000 Official number: 391973	**17,751** 6,636 21,008 T/cm 41.3	Class: CC CR (AB)	**2000-04 Naikai Zosen Corp — Onomichi HS (Setoda Shipyard)** Yd No: 653 Loa 191.44 (BB) Br ex - Dght 9.520 Lbp 180.00 Br md 28.00 Dpth 14.10 Welded, 1 dk	**(A33A2CC) Container Ship (Fully Cellular)** TEU 1660 C Ho 560 TEU C Dk 1100 TEU incl 150 ref C Compartments: 5 Cell Ho, ER 9 Ha: ER	**1 oil engine** driving 1 FP propeller Total Power: 15,807kW (21,491hp) 21.0kn B&W 7S60MC-C 1 x 2 Stroke 7 Cy. 600 x 2400 15807kW (21491bhp) Hitachi Zosen Corp-Japan AuxGen: 3 x 880kW 450V 60Hz a.c Thrusters: 1 Thwart. CP thruster (f) Fuel: 70.0 (d.f.) (Heating Coils) 1779.0 (r.f.) 61.1pd
9208174 *BLBH* -	**WAN HAI 233** **Wan Hai Lines Ltd** - *Keelung* *Chinese Taipei* MMSI: 416335000 Official number: 013796	**17,751** 6,636 21,017 T/cm 41.3	Class: CR NV (AB)	**2000-06 Naikai Zosen Corp — Onomichi HS (Setoda Shipyard)** Yd No: 654 Loa 191.45 (BB) Br ex - Dght 9.520 Lbp 180.00 Br md 28.00 Dpth 14.10 Welded, 1 dk	**(A33A2CC) Container Ship (Fully Cellular)** TEU 1660 C Ho 560 TEU C Dk 1100 TEU incl 150 ref C Compartments: 5 Cell Ho, ER 9 Ha: (12.8 x 7.2) (12.8 x 16.5)Tappered 7 (12.8 x 21.6)ER	**1 oil engine** driving 1 FP propeller Total Power: 15,807kW (21,491hp) 21.0kn B&W 7S60MC-C 1 x 2 Stroke 7 Cy. 600 x 2400 15807kW (21491bhp) Hitachi Zosen Corp-Japan AuxGen: 3 x 880kW 450V 60Hz a.c Thrusters: 1 Thwart. CP thruster (f) Fuel: 1978.0 (r.f.) (Heating Coils) 59.9pd
9208186 *BLBP* -	**WAN HAI 235** **Wan Hai Lines Ltd** - *Keelung* *Chinese Taipei* MMSI: 416337000 Official number: 013797	**17,751** 6,636 21,028 T/cm 41.3	Class: CR NV (AB)	**2000-08 Naikai Zosen Corp — Onomichi HS (Setoda Shipyard)** Yd No: 655 Loa 191.45 (BB) Br ex - Dght 9.500 Lbp 180.49 Br md 28.00 Dpth 14.10 Welded, 1 dk	**(A33A2CC) Container Ship (Fully Cellular)** TEU 1660 C Ho 560 TEU C Dk 1100 TEU incl 150 ref C Compartments: 5 Cell Ho, ER 9 Ha:	**1 oil engine** driving 1 FP propeller Total Power: 15,807kW (21,491hp) 21.0kn B&W 7S60MC-C 1 x 2 Stroke 7 Cy. 600 x 2400 15807kW (21491bhp) Hitachi Zosen Corp-Japan AuxGen: 3 x 880kW a.c Thrusters: 1 Thwart. FP thruster (f) Fuel: 78.0 (d.f.) 2000.0 (r.f.) 60.0pd
9230206 *9VHZ8* -	**WAN HAI 261** *ex Freedom -2006 ex Wan Hai 261 -2005* **Wan Hai Lines (Singapore) Pte Ltd** Wan Hai Lines Ltd *Singapore* *Singapore* MMSI: 563250000 Official number: 389436	**18,872** 8,515 23,672	Class: BV	**2001-07 Shin Kurushima Dockyard Co. Ltd. — Onishi** Yd No: 5105 Loa 198.00 (BB) Br ex - Dght 9.532 Lbp 184.00 Br md 28.00 Dpth 14.00 Welded, 1 dk	**(A33A2CC) Container Ship (Fully Cellular)** TEU 1675 incl 200 ref C.	**1 oil engine** driving 1 FP propeller Total Power: 15,785kW (21,461hp) 21.0kn B&W 7S60MC-C 1 x 2 Stroke 7 Cy. 600 x 2400 15785kW (21461bhp) Mitsui Engineering & Shipbuilding CLtd-Japan AuxGen: 3 x 1360kW 440/100V 60Hz a.c Thrusters: 1 Thwart. FP thruster (f) Fuel: 2692.0 (r.f.)
9230218 *9VDB2* -	**WAN HAI 262** **Wan Hai Lines (Singapore) Pte Ltd** Wan Hai Lines Ltd *Singapore* *Singapore* MMSI: 563256000 Official number: 389437	**18,872** 8,515 21,800	Class: BV	**2001-09 Shin Kurushima Dockyard Co. Ltd. — Onishi** Yd No: 5106 Loa 198.00 (BB) Br ex - Dght 9.500 Lbp 184.00 Br md 28.00 Dpth 14.00 Welded, 1 dk	**(A33A2CC) Container Ship (Fully Cellular)** TEU 1675 incl 200 ref C.	**1 oil engine** driving 1 FP propeller Total Power: 15,785kW (21,461hp) 21.0kn B&W 7S60MC-C 1 x 2 Stroke 7 Cy. 600 x 2400 15785kW (21461bhp) Mitsui Engineering & Shipbuilding CLtd-Japan AuxGen: 3 x 1360kW 440/100V 60Hz a.c Thrusters: 1 Thwart. FP thruster (f) Fuel: 2692.0 (r.f.)
9230220 *9VDB3* -	**WAN HAI 263** **Wan Hai Lines (Singapore) Pte Ltd** Wan Hai Lines Ltd *Singapore* *Singapore* MMSI: 563412000 Official number: 389438	**18,872** 8,515 23,635	Class: BV	**2001-12 Shin Kurushima Dockyard Co. Ltd. — Onishi** Yd No: 5107 Loa 198.00 (BB) Br ex - Dght 9.532 Lbp 184.00 Br md 28.00 Dpth 14.00 Welded, 1 dk	**(A33A2CC) Container Ship (Fully Cellular)** TEU 1675 incl 200 ref C.	**1 oil engine** driving 1 FP propeller Total Power: 15,785kW (21,461hp) 21.0kn B&W 7S60MC-C 1 x 2 Stroke 7 Cy. 600 x 2400 15785kW (21461bhp) Mitsui Engineering & Shipbuilding CLtd-Japan AuxGen: 3 x 1360kW 440/100V 60Hz a.c Thrusters: 1 Thwart. FP thruster (f)

IMO / Call sign	Name / Owner	Tonnage	Class	Build / Dimensions	Type	Machinery
9230232 *9VDB4* -	**WAN HAI 265** **Wan Hai Lines (Singapore) Pte Ltd** Wan Hai Lines Ltd *Singapore* *Singapore* MMSI: 564395000 Official number: 389439	**18,872** 8,515 23,643	Class: BV	**2002-02 Shin Kurushima Dockyard Co. Ltd. — Onishi** Yd No: 5108 Loa 198.00 (BB) Br ex - Dght 9.532 Lbp 184.00 Br md 28.00 Dpth 14.00 Welded, 1 dk	**(A33A2CC) Container Ship (Fully Cellular)** TEU 1675 incl 200 ref C.	**1 oil engine** driving 1 FP propeller Total Power: 15,785kW (21,461hp) 21.0kn B&W 7S60MC-C 1 x 2 Stroke 7 Cy. 600 x 2400 15785kW (21461bhp) Mitsui Engineering & Shipbuilding CLtd-Japan AuxGen: 3 x 1360kW 440/100V 60Hz a.c Thrusters: 1 Thwart. FP thruster (f) Fuel: 2692.0
9233636 *9VDB5* -	**WAN HAI 266** **Wan Hai Lines (Singapore) Pte Ltd** Wan Hai Lines Ltd *Singapore* *Singapore* MMSI: 564489000 Official number: 389440	**18,872** 8,515 23,648	Class: CR NK	**2002-04 Shin Kurushima Dockyard Co. Ltd. — Onishi** Yd No: 5115 Loa 198.04 (BB) Br ex - Dght 9.532 Lbp 184.00 Br md 28.00 Dpth 14.00 Welded, 1 dk	**(A33A2CC) Container Ship (Fully Cellular)** TEU 1572 incl 240 ref C.	**1 oil engine** driving 1 FP propeller Total Power: 15,785kW (21,461hp) 21.0kn B&W 7S60MC-C 1 x 2 Stroke 7 Cy. 600 x 2400 15785kW (21461bhp) Mitsui Engineering & Shipbuilding CLtd-Japan AuxGen: 3 x a.c Thrusters: 1 Thwart. FP thruster (f) Fuel: 2430.0
9233648 *9VDB6* -	**WAN HAI 267** **Wan Hai Lines (Singapore) Pte Ltd** Wan Hai Lines Ltd *Singapore* *Singapore* MMSI: 564565000 Official number: 389441	**18,872** 8,515 23,623	Class: CR NK	**2002-06 Shin Kurushima Dockyard Co. Ltd. — Onishi** Yd No: 5116 Loa 198.00 (BB) Br ex - Dght 9.530 Lbp 184.00 Br md 28.00 Dpth 14.00 Welded, 1 dk	**(A33A2CC) Container Ship (Fully Cellular)** TEU 1572 incl 240 ref C.	**1 oil engine** driving 1 FP propeller Total Power: 15,806kW (21,490hp) 21.0kn B&W 7S60MC-C 1 x 2 Stroke 7 Cy. 600 x 2400 15806kW (21490bhp) Mitsui Engineering & Shipbuilding CLtd-Japan AuxGen: 3 x a.c Thrusters: 1 Thwart. FP thruster (f) Fuel: 2430.0
9493250 *9V7584* -	**WAN HAI 271** **Wan Hai Lines (Singapore) Pte Ltd** Wan Hai Lines Ltd *Singapore* *Singapore* MMSI: 566235000 Official number: 394466	**16,776** 7,348 21,650	Class: NV	**2011-10 CSBC Corp, Taiwan — Keelung** Yd No: 975 Loa 172.10 (BB) Br ex - Dght 9.500 Lbp 162.10 Br md 27.30 Dpth 13.70 Welded, 1 dk	**(A33A2CC) Container Ship (Fully Cellular)** TEU 1805 incl 300 ref C	**1 oil engine** driving 1 FP propeller Total Power: 15,806kW (21,490hp) 19.0kn MAN-B&W 7S60MC-C 1 x 2 Stroke 7 Cy. 600 x 2400 15806kW (21490bhp) Doosan Engine Co Ltd-South Korea AuxGen: 3 x 1270kW a.c Thrusters: 1 Tunnel thruster (f)
9493262 *9V7585* -	**WAN HAI 272** **Wan Hai Lines (Singapore) Pte Ltd** Wan Hai Lines Ltd *Singapore* *Singapore* MMSI: 566340000 Official number: 394467	**16,776** 7,348 21,650	Class: NV	**2011-12 CSBC Corp, Taiwan — Keelung** Yd No: 976 Loa 172.10 (BB) Br ex - Dght 9.500 Lbp 162.10 Br md 27.30 Dpth 13.70 Welded, 1 dk	**(A33A2CC) Container Ship (Fully Cellular)** TEU 1805 incl 300 ref C	**1 oil engine** driving 1 FP propeller Total Power: 15,806kW (21,490hp) 19.0kn MAN-B&W 7S60MC-C 1 x 2 Stroke 7 Cy. 600 x 2400 15806kW (21490bhp) Doosan Engine Co Ltd-South Korea AuxGen: 3 x 1270kW a.c Thrusters: 1 Tunnel thruster (f)
9493274 *9V7586* -	**WAN HAI 273** **Wan Hai Lines (Singapore) Pte Ltd** Wan Hai Lines Ltd *Singapore* *Singapore* MMSI: 566406000 Official number: 394468	**16,776** 7,348 21,650	Class: CC (NV)	**2012-02 CSBC Corp, Taiwan — Keelung** Yd No: 977 Loa 172.10 (BB) Br ex - Dght 8.500 Lbp 162.10 Br md 27.30 Dpth 13.70 Welded, 1 dk	**(A33A2CC) Container Ship (Fully Cellular)** TEU 1805 incl 300 ref C	**1 oil engine** driving 1 FP propeller Total Power: 15,820kW (21,509hp) 19.0kn MAN-B&W 7S60MC-C 1 x 2 Stroke 7 Cy. 600 x 2400 15820kW (21509bhp) Doosan Engine Co Ltd-South Korea AuxGen: 3 x 1270kW a.c Thrusters: 1 Tunnel thruster (f)
9493286 *9V7588* -	**WAN HAI 275** **Wan Hai Lines (Singapore) Pte Ltd** Wan Hai Lines Ltd *Singapore* *Singapore* MMSI: 566469000 Official number: 394470	**16,776** 7,348 21,650	Class: CC NV	**2012-04 CSBC Corp, Taiwan — Keelung** Yd No: 978 Loa 172.10 (BB) Br ex - Dght 8.500 Lbp 162.10 Br md 27.30 Dpth 13.70 Welded, 1 dk	**(A33A2CC) Container Ship (Fully Cellular)** TEU 1805 incl 300 ref C	**1 oil engine** driving 1 FP propeller Total Power: 15,806kW (21,490hp) 19.0kn MAN-B&W 7S60MC-C 1 x 2 Stroke 7 Cy. 600 x 2400 15806kW (21490bhp) Doosan Engine Co Ltd-South Korea AuxGen: 3 x 1270kW a.c Thrusters: 1 Tunnel thruster (f)
9238155 *9VDB7* -	**WAN HAI 301** **Wan Hai Lines (Singapore) Pte Ltd** Wan Hai Lines Ltd *Singapore* *Singapore* MMSI: 563513000 Official number: 389442	**26,681** 10,855 30,250	Class: BV	**2001-12 Naikai Zosen Corp — Onomichi HS (Setoda Shipyard)** Yd No: 663 Loa 199.95 (BB) Br ex - Dght 10.824 Lbp 188.00 Br md 32.20 Dpth 16.60 Welded, 1 dk	**(A33A2CC) Container Ship (Fully Cellular)** TEU 2496 incl. 320 ref C.	**1 oil engine** driving 1 FP propeller Total Power: 21,735kW (29,551hp) 22.2kn B&W 7S70MC-C 1 x 2 Stroke 7 Cy. 700 x 2800 21735kW (29551bhp) Hitachi Zosen Corp-Japan AuxGen: 3 x 1760kW 440/100V 60Hz a.c Thrusters: 1 Tunnel thruster (f) Fuel: 3281.0
9238167 *9VDB8* -	**WAN HAI 302** **Wan Hai Lines (Singapore) Pte Ltd** Wan Hai Lines Ltd *Singapore* *Singapore* MMSI: 564440000 Official number: 389443	**26,681** 10,855 30,234	Class: BV	**2002-03 Naikai Zosen Corp — Onomichi HS (Setoda Shipyard)** Yd No: 664 Loa 199.95 (BB) Br ex - Dght 10.920 Lbp 188.00 Br md 32.20 Dpth 16.60 Welded, 1 dk	**(A33A2CC) Container Ship (Fully Cellular)** TEU 2496 incl. 320 ref C.	**1 oil engine** driving 1 FP propeller Total Power: 21,735kW (29,551hp) 22.2kn B&W 7S70MC-C 1 x 2 Stroke 7 Cy. 700 x 2800 21735kW (29551bhp) Hitachi Zosen Corp-Japan AuxGen: 3 x 1760kW 440/100V 60Hz a.c Thrusters: 1 Tunnel thruster (f) Fuel: 3281.0
9238179 *S6DT5* -	**WAN HAI 303** **Wan Hai Lines (Singapore) Pte Ltd** Wan Hai Lines Ltd *Singapore* *Singapore* MMSI: 564524000 Official number: 389696	**26,681** 10,855 30,240	Class: BV	**2002-05 Naikai Zosen Corp — Onomichi HS (Setoda Shipyard)** Yd No: 665 Loa 199.95 (BB) Br ex - Dght 10.900 Lbp 188.00 Br md 32.20 Dpth 16.60 Welded, 1 dk	**(A33A2CC) Container Ship (Fully Cellular)** TEU 2496 incl. 320 ref C.	**1 oil engine** driving 1 FP propeller Total Power: 21,735kW (29,551hp) 22.2kn B&W 7S70MC-C 1 x 2 Stroke 7 Cy. 700 x 2800 21735kW (29551bhp) Hitachi Zosen Corp-Japan AuxGen: 3 x 1760kW 440/100V 60Hz a.c Thrusters: 1 Tunnel thruster (f) Fuel: 3281.0
9238181 *S6DT6* -	**WAN HAI 305** **Wan Hai Lines (Singapore) Pte Ltd** Wan Hai Lines Ltd *Singapore* *Singapore* MMSI: 564640000 Official number: 389698	**26,681** 10,855 30,246	Class: BV	**2002-07 Naikai Zosen Corp — Onomichi HS (Setoda Shipyard)** Yd No: 666 Loa 199.95 (BB) Br ex 32.20 Dght 10.924 Lbp 188.00 Br md 32.20 Dpth 16.60 Welded, 1 dk	**(A33A2CC) Container Ship (Fully Cellular)** TEU 2496 incl. 320 ref C.	**1 oil engine** driving 1 FP propeller Total Power: 21,735kW (29,551hp) 22.2kn B&W 7S70MC-C 1 x 2 Stroke 7 Cy. 700 x 2800 21735kW (29551bhp) Hitachi Zosen Corp-Japan AuxGen: 3 x 1760kW 440/100V 60Hz a.c Thrusters: 1 Tunnel thruster (f)
9237084 *S6DT7* -	**WAN HAI 306** **Wan Hai Lines (Singapore) Pte Ltd** Wan Hai Lines Ltd *Singapore* *Singapore* MMSI: 564768000 Official number: 389698	**25,836** 11,708 30,738	Class: BV	**2002-10 China Shipbuilding Corp — Keelung** Yd No: 785 Loa 195.60 (BB) Br ex - Dght 11.510 Lbp 185.50 Br md 30.20 Dpth 16.60 Welded, 1 dk	**(A33A2CC) Container Ship (Fully Cellular)** TEU 2226 C Ho 870 TEU C Dk 1346 TEU incl 400 ref C. Cranes: 3x45t	**1 oil engine** driving 1 FP propeller Total Power: 24,830kW (33,759hp) 21.5kn B&W 8S70MC-C 1 x 2 Stroke 8 Cy. 700 x 2800 24830kW (33759bhp) AuxGen: 3 x 1700kW 440/110V 60Hz a.c Thrusters: 1 Thwart. CP thruster (f)
9237096 *S6DT8* -	**WAN HAI 307** **Wan Hai Lines (Singapore) Pte Ltd** Wan Hai Lines Ltd *Singapore* *Singapore* MMSI: 564868000 Official number: 389699	**25,836** 11,708 30,738	Class: BV	**2002-12 China Shipbuilding Corp — Keelung** Yd No: 786 Loa 196.60 (BB) Br ex - Dght 11.510 Lbp 187.08 Br md 30.20 Dpth 16.60 Welded, 1 dk	**(A33A2CC) Container Ship (Fully Cellular)** TEU 2226 C Ho 870 TEU C Dk 1346 TEU incl 400 ref C. Compartments: 5 Cell Ho, ER Cranes: 3x45t	**1 oil engine** driving 1 FP propeller Total Power: 24,830kW (33,759hp) 21.5kn B&W 8S70MC-C 1 x 2 Stroke 8 Cy. 700 x 2800 24830kW (33759bhp) Hyundai Heavy Industries Co Ltd-South Korea AuxGen: 3 x 1700kW a.c Thrusters: 1 Thwart. CP thruster (f)
9248681 *S6AS5* -	**WAN HAI 311** **Wan Hai Lines (Singapore) Pte Ltd** Wan Hai Lines Ltd SatCom: Inmarsat C 456348511 *Singapore* *Singapore* MMSI: 563485000 Official number: 390799	**27,800** 12,621 32,937	Class: CC (NK)	**2005-09 Jurong Shipyard Pte Ltd — Singapore** Yd No: 1067 Loa 213.00 (BB) Br ex - Dght 11.515 Lbp 202.10 Br md 32.20 Dpth 16.50 Welded, 1 dk	**(A33A2CC) Container Ship (Fully Cellular)** Double Hull TEU 2646 incl 400 ref C. Compartments: 5 Cell Ho, ER	**1 oil engine** driving 1 FP propeller Total Power: 25,228kW (34,300hp) 22.7kn MAN-B&W 7K80MC-C 1 x 2 Stroke 7 Cy. 800 x 2300 25228kW (34300bhp) Hitachi Zosen Corp-Japan AuxGen: 1 x 1270kW a.c Thrusters: 1 Tunnel thruster (f)
9248693 *S6AS6* -	**WAN HAI 312** **Wan Hai Lines (Singapore) Pte Ltd** Wan Hai Lines Ltd *Singapore* *Singapore* MMSI: 565032000 Official number: 390800	**27,800** 12,621 33,055	Class: CC (NK)	**2006-01 Jurong Shipyard Pte Ltd — Singapore** Yd No: 1068 Loa 213.00 (BB) Br ex - Dght 11.500 Lbp 202.10 Br md 32.20 Dpth 12.50 Welded, 1 dk	**(A33A2CC) Container Ship (Fully Cellular)** TEU 2646 incl 400 ref C. Compartments: 5 Cell Ho, ER	**1 oil engine** driving 1 FP propeller Total Power: 25,228kW (34,300hp) 22.7kn MAN-B&W 7K80MC-C 1 x 2 Stroke 7 Cy. 800 x 2300 25228kW (34300bhp) Hitachi Zosen Corp-Japan Thrusters: 1 Thwart. CP thruster (f)

IMO / Call sign	Name / Owner / Manager	GT / NT / DWT	Class	Builder / Dimensions	Type	Machinery
9248708 *S6AS9*	**WAN HAI 313** **Wan Hai Lines (Singapore) Pte Ltd** Wan Hai Lines Ltd SatCom: Inmarsat C 456513210 *Singapore* *Singapore* MMSI: 565132000 Official number: 390803	**27,800** 12,621 32,937	Class: CC (NK)	**2006-04 Jurong Shipyard Pte Ltd — Singapore** Yd No: 1069 Loa 213.00 (BB) Br ex - Dght 11.500 Lbp 202.10 Br md 32.20 Dpth 16.50 Welded, 1 dk	**(A33A2CC) Container Ship (Fully Cellular)** Bale: 50,801 TEU 2646 incl 400 ref C. Compartments: 5 Cell Ho, ER	**1 oil engine** driving 1 FP propeller Total Power: 25,228kW (34,300hp) 22.7kn MAN-B&W 7K80MC-C 1 x 2 Stroke 7 Cy. 800 x 2300 25228kW (34300bhp) Hitachi Zosen Corp-Japan Thrusters: 1 Thwart. CP thruster (f)
9302695 *S6AV5*	**WAN HAI 315** **Wan Hai Lines (Singapore) Pte Ltd** Wan Hai Lines Ltd SatCom: Inmarsat C 456522010 *Singapore* *Singapore* MMSI: 565220000 Official number: 390807	**27,800** 12,621 32,937	Class: CR NK	**2006-09 Jurong Shipyard Pte Ltd — Singapore** Yd No: 1070 Loa 213.00 (BB) Br ex - Dght 11.516 Lbp 202.10 Br md 32.20 Dpth 16.50 Welded, 1 dk	**(A33A2CC) Container Ship (Fully Cellular)** Bale: 50,800 TEU 2646 incl 400 ref C.	**1 oil engine** driving 1 FP propeller Total Power: 25,270kW (34,357hp) 22.7kn MAN-B&W 7K80MC-C 1 x 2 Stroke 7 Cy. 800 x 2300 25270kW (34357bhp) Hitachi Zosen Corp-Japan AuxGen: 4 x a.c Thrusters: 1 Tunnel thruster (f) Fuel: 3360.0
9342700 *9VKB5* -	**WAN HAI 316** **Wan Hai Lines (Singapore) Pte Ltd** Wan Hai Lines Ltd SatCom: Inmarsat C 456542510 *Singapore* *Singapore* MMSI: 565425000 Official number: 391889	**27,800** 12,621 32,937	Class: NK	**2007-06 Jurong Shipyard Pte Ltd — Singapore** Yd No: 1075 Loa 213.00 (BB) Br ex - Dght 11.516 Lbp 202.10 Br md 32.20 Dpth 16.50 Welded, 1 dk	**(A33A2CC) Container Ship (Fully Cellular)** Double Hull Bale: 50,800 TEU 2646 incl 400 ref C.	**1 oil engine** driving 1 FP propeller Total Power: 25,270kW (34,357hp) 22.7kn MAN-B&W 7K80MC-C 1 x 2 Stroke 7 Cy. 800 x 2300 25270kW (34357bhp) Hitachi Zosen Corp-Japan AuxGen: 4 x a.c Thrusters: 1 Tunnel thruster (f) Fuel: 435.0 (d.f.) 3735.0 (r.f.) 103.0pd
9342712 *9VKB6* -	**WAN HAI 317** **Wan Hai Lines (Singapore) Pte Ltd** Wan Hai Lines Ltd SatCom: Inmarsat C 456577710 *Singapore* *Singapore* MMSI: 565777000 Official number: 391890	**27,800** 12,621 33,055	Class: NK (CR)	**2008-01 Jurong Shipyard Pte Ltd — Singapore** Yd No: 1076 Loa 213.00 (BB) Br ex - Dght 11.516 Lbp 202.10 Br md 32.20 Dpth 12.50 Welded, 1 dk	**(A33A2CC) Container Ship (Fully Cellular)** Double Hull Bale: 50,800 TEU 2646 incl 400 ref C.	**1 oil engine** driving 1 FP propeller Total Power: 25,270kW (34,357hp) 22.7kn MAN-B&W 7K80MC-C 1 x 2 Stroke 7 Cy. 800 x 2300 25270kW (34357bhp) Hitachi Zosen Corp-Japan AuxGen: 4 x a.c Thrusters: 1 Tunnel thruster (f) Fuel: 3760.0
9294848 *S6AS7* -	**WAN HAI 501** **Wan Hai Lines (Singapore) Pte Ltd** Wan Hai Lines Ltd SatCom: Inmarsat C 456338210 *Singapore* *Singapore* MMSI: 563382000 Official number: 390801	**42,579** 19,125 52,249	Class: NV	**2005-07 China Shipbuilding Corp (CSBC) — Kaohsiung** Yd No: 835 Loa 268.80 (BB) Br ex 32.30 Dght 12.500 Lbp 256.50 Br md 32.20 Dpth 19.20 Welded, 1 dk	**(A33A2CC) Container Ship (Fully Cellular)** TEU 4252 C Ho 2112 TEU C Dk 2140 incl 500 ref C.	**1 oil engine** driving 1 FP propeller Total Power: 36,540kW (49,680hp) 24.0kn MAN-B&W 8K90MC-C 1 x 2 Stroke 8 Cy. 900 x 2300 36540kW (49680bhp) Hyundai Heavy Industries Co Ltd-South Korea AuxGen: 3 x a.c Thrusters: 1 Tunnel thruster (f)
9294862 *S6AV2*	**WAN HAI 503** *ex India Express -2013 ex Wan Hai 503 -2011* **Wan Hai Lines (Singapore) Pte Ltd** Wan Hai Lines Ltd *Singapore* *Singapore* MMSI: 563812000 Official number: 390804	**42,579** 19,125 51,300	Class: NV	**2005-10 China Shipbuilding Corp (CSBC) — Kaohsiung** Yd No: 837 Loa 268.80 (BB) Br ex - Dght 12.500 Lbp 256.50 Br md 32.20 Dpth 19.20 Welded, 1 dk	**(A33A2CC) Container Ship (Fully Cellular)** TEU 4252 C Ho 2112 TEU C Dk 2140 incl 500 ref C.	**1 oil engine** driving 1 FP propeller Total Power: 36,540kW (49,680hp) 24.0kn B&W 8K90MC-C 1 x 2 Stroke 8 Cy. 900 x 2300 36540kW (49680bhp) Hyundai Heavy Industries Co Ltd-South Korea AuxGen: 3 x 2100kW a.c Thrusters: 1 Tunnel thruster (f)
9294874 *S6AV3* -	**WAN HAI 505** *ex MOL Dynasty -2011 ex WAN HAI 505 -2008* **Wan Hai Lines (Singapore) Pte Ltd** Wan Hai Lines Ltd SatCom: Inmarsat C 456500410 *Singapore* *Singapore* MMSI: 565004000 Official number: 390805	**42,894** 19,177 52,146	Class: NK	**2005-11 China Shipbuilding Corp (CSBC) — Kaohsiung** Yd No: 838 Loa 268.80 (BB) Br ex - Dght 12.520 Lbp 256.50 Br md 32.20 Dpth 19.20 Welded, 1 dk	**(A33A2CC) Container Ship (Fully Cellular)** TEU 4252 C Ho 2112 TEU C Dk 2140 incl 500 ref C.	**1 oil engine** driving 1 FP propeller Total Power: 36,564kW (49,712hp) 24.0kn B&W 8K90MC-C 1 x 2 Stroke 8 Cy. 900 x 2300 36564kW (49712bhp) Hyundai Heavy Industries Co Ltd-South Korea AuxGen: 3 x a.c Thrusters: 1 Thwart. CP thruster (f) Fuel: 4430.0
9294886 *S6AV4* -	**WAN HAI 506** *ex Brazil Express -2013 ex Wan Hai 506 -2011* **Wan Hai Lines (Singapore) Pte Ltd** Wan Hai Lines Ltd *Singapore* *Singapore* MMSI: 565005000 Official number: 390806	**42,894** 19,177 52,146	Class: CR NK	**2005-11 China Shipbuilding Corp (CSBC) — Kaohsiung** Yd No: 839 Loa 268.80 (BB) Br ex - Dght 12.520 Lbp 256.50 Br md 32.20 Dpth 19.20 Welded, 1 dk	**(A33A2CC) Container Ship (Fully Cellular)** TEU 4252 C Ho 2112 TEU C Dk 2140 incl 500 ref C.	**1 oil engine** driving 1 FP propeller Total Power: 36,564kW (49,712hp) 24.0kn B&W 8K90MC-C 1 x 2 Stroke 8 Cy. 900 x 2300 36564kW (49712bhp) Hyundai Heavy Industries Co Ltd-South Korea AuxGen: 4 x a.c Thrusters: 1 Thwart. CP thruster (f) Fuel: 4430.0
9326407 *9VJJ5* -	**WAN HAI 507** *ex Kota Salam -2008 ex Wan Hai 507 -2007* **Wan Hai Lines (Singapore) Pte Ltd** Wan Hai Lines Ltd *Singapore* *Singapore* MMSI: 565536000 Official number: 391881	**42,894** 19,177 52,146	Class: CC (Class contemplated) (NK)	**2007-08 CSBC Corp, Taiwan — Kaohsiung** Yd No: 857 Loa 268.80 (BB) Br ex 32.20 Dght 12.535 Lbp 256.50 Br md 32.20 Dpth 19.20 Welded, 1 dk	**(A33A2CC) Container Ship (Fully Cellular)** TEU 4252 C Ho 2112 TEU C Dk 2140 TEU incl 500 ref C.	**1 oil engine** driving 1 FP propeller Total Power: 36,540kW (49,680hp) 24.0kn MAN-B&W 8K90MC-C 1 x 2 Stroke 8 Cy. 900 x 2300 36540kW (49680bhp) Hitachi Zosen Corp-Japan AuxGen: 3 x a.c Thrusters: 1 Thwart. CP thruster (f) Fuel: 4680.0
9326419 *9VJJ6* -	**WAN HAI 508** *ex MOL Dawn -2014 ex Wan Hai 508 -2012* **Wan Hai Lines (Singapore) Pte Ltd** Wan Hai Lines Ltd SatCom: Inmarsat C 456556710 *Singapore* *Singapore* MMSI: 565567000 Official number: 391882	**42,894** 19,177 52,146	Class: CC CR (NK)	**2007-09 CSBC Corp, Taiwan — Kaohsiung** Yd No: 858 Loa 268.80 (BB) Br ex - Dght 12.535 Lbp 256.50 Br md 32.20 Dpth 19.20 Welded, 1 dk	**(A33A2CC) Container Ship (Fully Cellular)** TEU 4252 C Ho 2112 C Dk 2140 TEU incl 500 ref C.	**1 oil engine** driving 1 FP propeller Total Power: 36,540kW (49,680hp) 24.0kn MAN-B&W 8K90MC-C 1 x 2 Stroke 8 Cy. 900 x 2300 36540kW (49680bhp) Hitachi Zosen Corp-Japan AuxGen: 3 x a.c Thrusters: 1 Thwart. CP thruster (f) Fuel: 4680.0
9326433 *9VJJ8* -	**WAN HAI 510** *ex America Express -2012* *ex Wan Hai 510 -2011* **Wan Hai Lines (Singapore) Pte Ltd** Wan Hai Lines Ltd *Singapore* *Singapore* MMSI: 565741000 Official number: 391884	**42,894** 19,177 52,146	Class: CC (NK) (CR)	**2008-01 CSBC Corp, Taiwan — Kaohsiung** Yd No: 860 Loa 268.80 (BB) Br ex - Dght 12.535 Lbp 256.60 Br md 32.20 Dpth 19.20 Welded, 1 dk	**(A33A2CC) Container Ship (Fully Cellular)** TEU 4250 incl 363 ref C	**1 oil engine** driving 1 FP propeller Total Power: 36,560kW (49,707hp) 24.0kn MAN-B&W 8K90MC-C 1 x 2 Stroke 8 Cy. 900 x 2300 36560kW (49707bhp) Hitachi Zosen Corp-Japan AuxGen: 4 x a.c Thrusters: 1 Tunnel thruster (f) Fuel: 4680.0
9455296 *9V7577* -	**WAN HAI 511** *ex CCNI Antuco -2013 ex Wan Hai 511 -2012* **Wan Hai Lines (Singapore) Pte Ltd** Wan Hai Lines Ltd *Singapore* *Singapore* MMSI: 566510000 Official number: 394459	**46,854** 20,469 57,830	Class: NV	**2012-05 CSBC Corp, Taiwan — Kaohsiung** Yd No: 950 Loa 259.00 (BB) Br ex 38.20 Dght 12.800 Lbp 246.40 Br md 37.30 Dpth 19.40 Welded, 1 dk	**(A33A2CC) Container Ship (Fully Cellular)** TEU 4532 incl 400 ref C.	**1 oil engine** driving 1 FP propeller Total Power: 36,560kW (49,707hp) 23.2kn MAN-B&W 8K90MC-C 1 x 2 Stroke 8 Cy. 900 x 2300 36560kW (49707bhp) Hitachi Zosen Corp-Japan AuxGen: 3 x a.c Thrusters: 1 Tunnel thruster (f)
9457622 *9V7578* -	**WAN HAI 512** **Wan Hai Lines (Singapore) Pte Ltd** Wan Hai Lines Ltd *Singapore* *Singapore* MMSI: 566642000 Official number: 394460	**47,309** 20,964 57,830	Class: NK	**2012-08 CSBC Corp, Taiwan — Kaohsiung** Yd No: 951 Loa 259.00 (BB) Br ex - Dght 12.840 Lbp 246.40 Br md 37.30 Dpth 19.40 Welded, 1 dk	**(A33A2CC) Container Ship (Fully Cellular)** TEU 4532 incl 400 ref C.	**1 oil engine** driving 1 FP propeller Total Power: 36,560kW (49,707hp) 23.2kn MAN-B&W 8K90MC-C 1 x 2 Stroke 8 Cy. 900 x 2300 36560kW (49707bhp) Hitachi Zosen Corp-Japan Thrusters: 1 Tunnel thruster (f) Fuel: 5210.0
9457634 *9V7579* -	**WAN HAI 513** **Wan Hai Lines (Singapore) Pte Ltd** Wan Hai Lines Ltd *Singapore* *Singapore* MMSI: 566730000 Official number: 394461	**46,904** 20,469 57,830	Class: NV	**2012-11 CSBC Corp, Taiwan — Kaohsiung** Yd No: 952 Loa 259.00 (BB) Br ex - Dght 12.800 Lbp 246.40 Br md 37.30 Dpth 19.40 Welded, 1 dk	**(A33A2CC) Container Ship (Fully Cellular)** TEU 4532 incl 400 ref C.	**1 oil engine** driving 1 FP propeller Total Power: 36,560kW (49,707hp) 23.2kn MAN-B&W 8K90MC-C 1 x 2 Stroke 8 Cy. 900 x 2300 36560kW (49707bhp) Hitachi Zosen Corp-Japan AuxGen: 3 x a.c Thrusters: 1 Tunnel thruster (f)

9457646 **WAN HAI 515**
9V7581
-
Wan Hai Lines (Singapore) Pte Ltd
Wan Hai Lines Ltd
Singapore *Singapore*
MMSI: 566828000
Official number: 394463

47,259 Class: NK
20,964
57,830

2013-02 CSBC Corp, Taiwan — Kaohsiung
Yd No: 953
Loa 259.00 (BB) Br ex - Dght 12.840
Lbp 246.40 Br md 37.30 Dpth 19.40
Welded, 1 dk

(A33A2CC) Container Ship (Fully Cellular)
TEU 4532 incl 400 ref C.

1 oil engine driving 1 FP propeller
Total Power: 36,560kW (49,707hp) 23.2k
MAN-B&W 8K90MC-
1 x 2 Stroke 8 Cy. 900 x 2300 36560kW (49707bhp)
Hitachi Zosen Corp-Japan
Thrusters: 1 Tunnel thruster (f)
Fuel: 5210.0

9457658 **WAN HAI 516**
9V7582
-
Wan Hai Lines (Singapore) Pte Ltd
Wan Hai Lines Ltd
Singapore *Singapore*
MMSI: 566886000
Official number: 394464

47,250 Class: BV
20,463
57,830

2013-04 CSBC Corp, Taiwan — Kaohsiung
Yd No: 962
Loa 259.00 (BB) Br ex - Dght 12.800
Lbp 246.40 Br md 37.30 Dpth 19.40
Welded, 1 dk

(A33A2CC) Container Ship (Fully Cellular)
TEU 4532 incl 400 ref C

1 oil engine driving 1 FP propeller
Total Power: 36,560kW (49,707hp) 23.2k
MAN-B&W 8K90MC-
1 x 2 Stroke 8 Cy. 900 x 2300 36560kW (49707bhp)
Doosan Engine Co Ltd-South Korea
AuxGen: 3 x 2280kW 60Hz a.c
Fuel: 5210.0

9457660 **WAN HAI 517**
9V7583
-
Wan Hai Lines (Singapore) Pte Ltd
Wan Hai Lines Ltd
Singapore *Singapore*
MMSI: 566942000
Official number: 394465

47,250 Class: BV
20,463
57,830

2013-06 CSBC Corp, Taiwan — Kaohsiung
Yd No: 963
Loa 259.00 (BB) Br ex - Dght 11.000
Lbp 246.40 Br md 37.30 Dpth 19.40
Welded, 1 dk

(A33A2CC) Container Ship (Fully Cellular)
TEU 4532 incl 400 ref C.

1 oil engine driving 1 FP propeller
Total Power: 36,560kW (49,707hp) 23.2k
MAN-B&W 8K90MC-
1 x 2 Stroke 8 Cy. 900 x 2300 36560kW (49707bhp)
Doosan Engine Co Ltd-South Korea
AuxGen: 3 x 2280kW 60Hz a.c
Fuel: 5210.0

9327786 **WAN HAI 601**
9VJJ9
-
ex Hanjin Lyon *-2012* *ex* Wan Hai 601 *-2010*
Eastwest Trades Inc
Wan Hai Lines (Singapore) Pte Ltd
SatCom: Inmarsat C 456550810
Singapore *Singapore*
MMSI: 565508000
Official number: 391885

66,199 Class: NV
34,052
67,680

2007-07 CSBC Corp, Taiwan — Kaohsiung
Yd No: 870
Loa 276.20 (BB) Br ex - Dght 14.000
Lbp 263.80 Br md 40.00 Dpth 24.20
Welded, 1 dk

(A33A2CC) Container Ship (Fully Cellular)
TEU 5527 C Ho 2601 TEU C Dk 2926 TEU incl 500 ref C.

1 oil engine driving 1 FP propeller
Total Power: 54,942kW (74,699hp) 26.0k
Wartsila 10RTA96
1 x 2 Stroke 10 Cy. 960 x 2500 54942kW (74699bhp)
Hyundai Heavy Industries Co Ltd-South Korea
AuxGen: 4 x a.c
Thrusters: 1 Tunnel thruster (f)

9327798 **WAN HAI 602**
9VKB2
-
Eastwest Trades Inc
Wan Hai Lines (Singapore) Pte Ltd
SatCom: Inmarsat C 456558010
Singapore *Singapore*
MMSI: 565580000
Official number: 391886

66,199 Class: NV
34,052
67,797

2007-09 CSBC Corp, Taiwan — Kaohsiung
Yd No: 871
Loa 276.20 (BB) Br ex 40.10 Dght 14.000
Lbp 263.80 Br md 40.00 Dpth 20.17
Welded, 1 dk

(A33A2CC) Container Ship (Fully Cellular)
TEU 5527 C Ho 2601 TEU C Dk 2926 TEU incl 500 ref C.

1 oil engine driving 1 FP propeller
Total Power: 54,942kW (74,699hp) 26.0k
Wartsila 10RTA96
1 x 2 Stroke 10 Cy. 960 x 2500 54942kW (74699bhp)
Hyundai Heavy Industries Co Ltd-South Korea
AuxGen: 4 x a.c
Thrusters: 1 Tunnel thruster (f)

9327803 **WAN HAI 603**
9VKB3
-
Eastwest Trades Inc
Wan Hai Lines (Singapore) Pte Ltd
SatCom: Inmarsat C 456566210
Singapore *Singapore*
MMSI: 565662000
Official number: 391887

66,199 Class: NV (CR)
34,052
67,797

2007-11 CSBC Corp, Taiwan — Kaohsiung
Yd No: 872
Loa 276.20 (BB) Br ex 40.10 Dght 14.000
Lbp 263.80 Br md 40.00 Dpth 20.17
Welded, 1 dk

(A33A2CC) Container Ship (Fully Cellular)
TEU 5527 C Ho 2601 TEU C Dk 2926 TEU incl 500 ref C.

1 oil engine driving 1 FP propeller
Total Power: 57,200kW (77,769hp) 26.0k
Wartsila 10RTA96
1 x 2 Stroke 10 Cy. 960 x 2500 57200kW (77769bhp)
Hyundai Heavy Industries Co Ltd-South Korea
AuxGen: 4 x a.c
Thrusters: 1 Tunnel thruster (f)

9331165 **WAN HAI 605**
9VKB4
-
Eastwest Trades Inc
Wan Hai Lines (Singapore) Pte Ltd
SatCom: Inmarsat C 456576110
Singapore *Singapore*
MMSI: 565761000
Official number: 391888

66,199 Class: NV (CR)
34,052
67,797

2008-01 CSBC Corp, Taiwan — Kaohsiung
Yd No: 873
Loa 276.20 (BB) Br ex - Dght 14.000
Lbp 263.80 Br md 40.00 Dpth 24.20
Welded, 1 dk

(A33A2CC) Container Ship (Fully Cellular)
TEU 5527 C Ho 2601 TEU C Dk 2926 TEU incl 500 ref C.

1 oil engine driving 1 FP propeller
Total Power: 54,942kW (74,699hp) 26.0k
Wartsila 10RTA96
1 x 2 Stroke 10 Cy. 960 x 2500 54942kW (74699bhp)
Hyundai Heavy Industries Co Ltd-South Korea
AuxGen: 4 x a.c
Thrusters: 1 Tunnel thruster (f)

8116661 **WAN HE**
H8OJ
-
ex Evdoxia *-2011* *ex* Darya Ma *-2003*
King Fortune Shipping Ltd
Wan Jia International Shipping & Trading Ltd
Panama *Panama*
MMSI: 354432000
Official number: 4296311

17,770 Class: PD (LR)
10,500 ✠ Classed LR until 8/6/11
30,750
T/cm
37.6

1983-03 Sunderland Shipbuilders Ltd. — Pallion, Sunderland Yd No: 21
Loa 188.17 Br ex 23.17 Dght 10.656
Lbp 181.31 Br md 23.11 Dpth 14.51
Welded, 1 dk

(A21A2BC) Bulk Carrier
Grain: 36,849; Bale: 34,827
TEU 542
Compartments: 6 Ho, ER
6 Ha: (11.3 x 12.8)5 (14.4 x 12.8)ER
Cranes: 3x25t,2x16t

1 oil engine driving 1 FP propeller
Total Power: 8,375kW (11,387hp) 15.0k
Sulzer 5RND76
1 x 2 Stroke 5 Cy. 760 x 1550 8375kW (11387bhp)
Clark Hawthorn Ltd.-Newcastle
AuxGen: 3 x 525kW 450V 60Hz a.c
Boilers: AuxB (o.f.) 7.1kgf/cm² (7.0bar), AuxB (e.g.) 7.1kgf/cm² (7.0bar)
Fuel: 262.0 (d.f.) 1723.0 (r.f.) 37.5pd

8663999 **WAN HUA 9**
BKXW5
-
ex Qi Xing 21 *-2006*
Zhejiang Yonghua Ocean Shipping Co Ltd
Nanjing Zhonggang Shipping Co Ltd
China
Official number: 070311000573

2,256
1,253
3,056

2006-10 Zhoushan Dinghai Panzhi Shipyard — Zhoushan ZJ Yd No: LJX541C-100
Loa 91.03 Br ex - Dght -
Lbp - Br md 13.50 Dpth 6.50
Welded, 1 dk

(A12A2TC) Chemical Tanker
Double Hull

1 oil engine driving 1 Propeller

7041027 **WAN JI**
BEFW
-
ex Gerd Wesch *-1986*
Anhui Ocean Shipping Co Ltd
-
Shanghai *China*
MMSI: 412445040

3,527 Class: (CC) (GL)
2,131
5,490

1971-03 Gebr. Schuerenstedt KG Schiffs- u. Bootswerft — Berne Yd No: 1355
Loa 105.94 (BB) Br ex 16.11 Dght 6.640
Lbp 97.00 Br md 16.00 Dpth 8.30
Welded, 2 dks

(A31A2GX) General Cargo Ship
Grain: 7,872; Bale: 7,334
TEU 186 C. 186/20' (40')
Compartments: 2 Ho, ER
2 Ha: 2 (24.6 x 10.5)ER
Cranes: 1x50t,1x30t,2x8t; Winches: 4
Ice Capable

1 oil engine sr geared to sc. shaft driving 1 FP propeller
Total Power: 2,942kW (4,000hp) 15.0k
MaK 8M551A
1 x 4 Stroke 8 Cy. 450 x 550 2942kW (4000bhp)
Atlas MaK Maschinenbau GmbH-Kiel
AuxGen: 2 x 232kW 220/380V 50Hz a.c, 1 x 124kW 220/380V 50Hz a.c
Thrusters: 1 Thwart. FP thruster (f)
Fuel: 366.0 (d.f.) 15.0pd

8316479 **WAN LI**
3FBJ9
-
ex Atlantic Might *-2013* *ex* Ulcas *-2009*
ex Kelvin Resource *-1994* *ex* Bream *-1990*
Wan Li Shipping Ltd
Wan Jia International Shipping & Trading Ltd
Panama *Panama*
MMSI: 357400000
Official number: 4129110A

25,227 Class: PR (Class contemplated) (LR) (NV)
14,040 Classed LR until 1/7/13
42,244

1985-06 Mitsubishi Heavy Industries Ltd. — Nagasaki Yd No: 1945
Loa 188.89 (BB) Br ex 30.04 Dght 10.977
Lbp 181.00 Br md 30.00 Dpth 15.70
Welded, 1 dk

(A21A2BC) Bulk Carrier
Grain: 54,138; Bale: 53,231
TEU 914
Compartments: 5 Ho, ER
5 Ha: ER
Cranes: 4x24.5t

1 oil engine driving 1 FP propeller
Total Power: 8,474kW (11,521hp) 14.8k
Sulzer 6RTA5
1 x 2 Stroke 6 Cy. 580 x 1700 8474kW (11521bhp)
Mitsubishi Heavy Industries Ltd-Japan
AuxGen: 3 x 550kW 440V 60Hz a.c
Boilers: e (ex.g.) 6.0kgf/cm² (5.9bar), AuxB (o.f.) 6.0kgf/cm² (5.9bar)

8306735 **WAN LI**
BTBC
-
ex Shang Cheng *-2012*
Dalian Port Wantong Logistics Co Ltd
-
SatCom: Inmarsat A 1571271
Shanghai *China*
MMSI: 412206480

9,683 Class: (CC)
4,637
13,449

1984-11 Dalian Shipyard Co Ltd — Dalian LN
Yd No: C120/1
Converted From: Container Ship (Fully Cellular)-2008
Loa 147.50 (BB) Br ex - Dght 8.190
Lbp 138.00 Br md 22.20 Dpth 10.90
Welded, 1 dk

(A21A2BC) Bulk Carrier
Grain: 16,567; Bale: 15,999
Compartments: 4 Ho, ER
4 Ha: ER

1 oil engine driving 1 FP propeller
Total Power: 5,502kW (7,481hp) 15.0k
B&W 5L55G
1 x 2 Stroke 5 Cy. 550 x 1380 5502kW (7481bhp)
Dalian Marine Diesel Works-China

9416355 **WAN LI 8**
BLBI
-
Ningbo Merchant Refrigeration Shipping Co
-
Ningbo, Zhejiang *China*
MMSI: 413405160

2,612 Class: CC
1,472
4,071

2007-01 Taizhou Haibin Shipbuilding & Repairing Co Ltd — Sanmen County ZJ
Yd No: HBCCS-05-01
Loa 84.80 Br ex - Dght 6.000
Lbp 77.70 Br md 14.20 Dpth 7.60
Welded, 1 dk

(A31A2GX) General Cargo Ship
Grain: 5,083
Compartments: 2 Ho, ER
2 Ha: ER 2 (21.6 x 9.0)

1 oil engine reduction geared to sc. shaft driving 1 FP propeller
Total Power: 1,325kW (1,801hp) 11.0k
Guangzhou 6320ZC
1 x 4 Stroke 6 Cy. 320 x 440 1325kW (1801bhp)
Guangzhou Diesel Engine Factory CoLtd-China
AuxGen: 2 x 120kW 400V a.c

9061227 **WAN LONG HAI**
JVYX4
-
ex Hua Jin *-2011* *ex* Zhe Hai 315 *-2007*
Long Gang Shipping Co Ltd
East Grand Shipping Co Ltd
Ulaanbaatar *Mongolia*
MMSI: 457747000
Official number: 32391394

4,061 Class: (CC)
1,827
5,133

1994-03 Wuhu Shipyard — Wuhu AH
Yd No: 5100-1
Loa 98.50 Br ex - Dght 5.800
Lbp 92.00 Br md 16.80 Dpth 7.80
Welded, 1 dk

(A31A2GX) General Cargo Ship
Grain: 6,235
TEU 254 C.Ho 124/20' C.Dk 130/20'
Compartments: 2 Ho, ER
2 Ha: (19.5 x 12.6) (37.7 x 12.6)ER
Ice Capable

2 oil engines geared to sc. shafts driving 2 FP propellers
Total Power: 2,000kW (2,720hp) 12.5k
Alpha 8L23/3
2 x 4 Stroke 8 Cy. 225 x 300 each-1000kW (1360bhp)
Zhenjiang Marine Diesel Works-China
AuxGen: 3 x 90kW 400V a.c

9661871 **WAN MAY**
VRLM6
-
launched as Ocean Capital *-2012*
Zhongqiao Shipping Ltd
Foremost Maritime Corp
Hong Kong *Hong Kong*
MMSI: 477190500
Official number: HK-3708

91,387 Class: AB
58,745
176,460
T/cm
120.6

2012-11 Shanghai Waigaoqiao Shipbuilding Co Ltd — Shanghai Yd No: 1256
Loa 292.00 (BB) Br ex - Dght 18.300
Lbp 282.00 Br md 45.00 Dpth 24.80
Welded, 1 dk

(A21A2BC) Bulk Carrier
Grain: 194,179; Bale: 183,425
Compartments: 9 Ho, ER
9 Ha: ER

1 oil engine driving 1 FP propeller
Total Power: 16,860kW (22,923hp) 14.0k
MAN-B&W 6S70MC-C
1 x 2 Stroke 6 Cy. 700 x 2800 16860kW (22923bhp)
CSSC MES Diesel Co Ltd-China
AuxGen: 3 x 900kW a.c
Fuel: 380.0 (d.f.) 4780.0 (r.f.)

8300054 **WAN NIAN HONG** - - **Guangzhou Maritime Transport (Group) Co Ltd** - *Guangzhou, Guangdong* *China*	*7,669* Class: (CC) 3,847 3,019	**1984-09 Hudong Shipyard — Shanghai** Yd No: 1137 Loa 138.00 Br ex - Dght 6.001 Lbp 124.00 Br md 17.60 Dpth 8.40 Welded, 2 dks	**(A32A2GF) General Cargo/Passenger Ship**	**1 oil engine** driving 1 FP propeller Total Power: 6,620kW (9,001hp) Hudong 9ESDZ43/82B 1 x 2 Stroke 9 Cy. 430 x 820 6620kW (9001bhp) Hudong Shipyard-China
9424077 **WAN NIAN QING** *BIOY* *launched as* San Han 008 *-2007* - **Shanghai Sinochem-Stolt Shipping Ltd** - SatCom: Inmarsat C 441300026 *Shanghai* *China* MMSI: 413371050	**2,252** Class: CC 1,024 3,175	**2007-01 Zhejiang Dongpeng Shipbuilding & Repair Co Ltd — Zhoushan ZJ** Yd No: 05-05 Loa 91.03 Br ex 13.52 Dght 5.000 Lbp 84.30 Br md 13.50 Dpth 6.50 Welded, 1 dk	**(A12B2TR) Chemical/Products Tanker** Double Hull (13F) Liq: 3,741; Liq (Oil): 3,741 Compartments: 12 Wing Ta, ER	**1 oil engine** reduction geared to sc. shaft driving 1 FP propeller Total Power: 1,765kW (2,400hp) 11.5kn Chinese Std. Type G8300ZC 1 x 4 Stroke 8 Cy. 300 x 380 1765kW (2400bhp) Ningbo CSI Power & Machinery GroupCo Ltd-China AuxGen: 2 x 120kW 400V a.c
9285768 **WAN QING SHA** *BSPN* - **CCCC Guangzhou Dredging Co Ltd** - SatCom: Inmarsat C 441200631 *Guangzhou, Guangdong* *China* MMSI: 412053050	**11,030** Class: CC 3,310 15,814	**2004-07 IHC Holland NV Dredgers — Kinderdijk** Yd No: C01238 Loa 128.75 Br ex - Dght 8.750 Lbp 121.00 Br md 24.50 Dpth 10.10 Welded, 1 dk	**(B33B2DT) Trailing Suction Hopper Dredger** Hopper: 10,028	**2 oil engines** geared to sc. shafts driving 2 CP propellers Total Power: 12,000kW (16,316hp) 15.2kn Sulzer 8ZAL40S 2 x 4 Stroke 8 Cy. 400 x 560 each-6000kW (8158bhp) Wartsila Italia SpA-Italy Thrusters: 2 Thwart. FP thruster (f)
8664321 **WAN RONG 168** *T3EW2* - **PT Budi Mulia Bahtera Santosa** - *Tarawa* *Kiribati* MMSI: 529551000 Official number: K-15011293	**1,247** 698 -	**2001-09 Yueqing Huanghuagang Shipyard — Yueqing ZJ** Yd No: HHG010302 Loa 68.10 Br ex - Dght - Lbp - Br md 11.20 Dpth 5.60 Welded, 1 dk	**(A31A2GX) General Cargo Ship**	**1 oil engine** reduction geared to sc. shaft driving 1 FP propeller Total Power: 661kW (899hp) Chinese Std. Type 1 x 661kW (899bhp) Shanghai Xinzhong Power MachinePlant-China
8664204 **WAN RONG 188** *T3JN2* - **PT Budi Mulia Bahtera Santosa** - *Tarawa* *Kiribati* MMSI: 529639000 Official number: K-16111398	**2,827** 1,583 5,400	**2011-08 Yueqing Zhongrui Shipyard Co Ltd — Yueqing ZJ** Yd No: 080301 Loa 98.00 Br ex - Dght 6.000 Lbp - Br md 14.50 Dpth 7.20 Welded, 1 dk	**(A31A2GX) General Cargo Ship**	**1 oil engine** driving 1 Propeller Total Power: 1,543kW (2,098hp) Akasaka 1 x 1543kW (2098bhp) Akasaka Tekkosho KK (Akasaka DieselLtd)-Japan
8741569 **WAN RONG HAI** *BAPO* - **Dalian Wantong Ronghai Shipping Co Ltd** Dalian Shipping Group Co Ltd *Dalian, Liaoning* *China* MMSI: 412206430	**11,585** Class: CC 6,256 3,252	**2008-06 Huanghai Shipbuilding Co Ltd — Rongcheng SD** Loa 129.90 (BB) Br ex - Dght 5.000 Lbp 120.40 Br md 20.40 Dpth 12.30 Welded, 1 dk	**(A36A2PR) Passenger/Ro-Ro Ship (Vehicles)** Passengers: unberthed: 200; cabins: 164; berths: 900 Stern door/ramp (centre) Len: 8.00 Wid: 6.00 Swl: - Side door/ramp (s. f.) Len: 11.00 Wid: 5.00 Swl: - Lane-Len: 733 Lane-clr ht: 4.75 Cars: 155 Ice Capable	**2 oil engines** reduction geared to sc. shafts driving 2 CP propellers Total Power: 5,000kW (6,798hp) 15.7kn Daihatsu 8DKM-28 2 x 4 Stroke 8 Cy. 280 x 390 each-2500kW (3399bhp) Shaanxi Diesel Heavy Industry Co Lt-China AuxGen: 3 x 720kW 400V a.c Thrusters: 1 Tunnel thruster (f) Fuel: 87.0 (d.f.) 275.0 (r.f.) 21.0pd
8604357 **WAN RUN** *3ERN6* *ex* Hattie *-2013* *ex* Honor *-2007* - *ex* Marin Trader I *-1997* *ex* Maratea *-1987* **Wan Chun Shipping Ltd** Wan Jia International Shipping & Trading Ltd SatCom: Inmarsat C 437152910 *Panama* *Panama* MMSI: 371529000 Official number: 4516813	**15,847** Class: IS (NK) 8,996 26,679 T/cm 31.6	**1986-06 Kurushima Dockyard Co. Ltd. — Onishi** Yd No: 2482 Loa 167.20 (BB) Br ex - Dght 9.541 Lbp 160.03 Br md 26.01 Dpth 13.31 Welded, 1 dk	**(A21A2BC) Bulk Carrier** Grain: 33,903; Bale: 32,773 Compartments: 5 Ho, ER 5 Ha: ER Cranes: 4x30.5t	**1 oil engine** driving 1 FP propeller Total Power: 5,075kW (6,900hp) 14.0kn B&W 6L50MCE 1 x 2 Stroke 6 Cy. 500 x 1620 5075kW (6900bhp) Hitachi Zosen Corp-Japan AuxGen: 3 x 288kW a.c Fuel: 1230.0 (r.f.)
9503718 **WAN SENDARI** *9V7455* - **Bintan Resort Ferries Pte Ltd** - *Singapore* *Singapore* MMSI: 565927000 Official number: 394245	**551** Class: LR (BV) 177 **100A1** SS 03/2009 540 SSC Pasenger (A), catamaran HSC G2 **LMC** **UMS** Cable: 194.0/16.0 U3 (a)	**2009-03 Afai Southern Shipyard (Panyu Guangzhou) Ltd — Guangzhou GD** (Hull) Yd No: 012 **2009-03 B.V. Scheepswerf Damen — Gorinchem** Yd No: 538726 Loa 42.16 (BB) Br ex 11.60 Dght 1.500 Lbp 40.09 Br md 11.30 Dpth 3.80 Welded, 2 dks	**(A37B2PS) Passenger Ship** Hull Material: Aluminium Alloy Passengers: unberthed: 300	**4 oil engines** with clutches, flexible couplings & sr geared to sc. shafts driving 4 Water jets Total Power: 5,760kW (7,832hp) M.T.U. 16V2000M72 4 x Vee 4 Stroke 16 Cy. 135 x 156 each-1440kW (1958bhp) MTU Friedrichshafen GmbH-Friedrichshafen AuxGen: 2 x 65kW 60Hz a.c
9503720 **WAN SERI BENI** *9V7456* - **Bintan Resort Ferries Pte Ltd** - *Singapore* *Singapore* MMSI: 565928000 Official number: 394246	**551** Class: LR (BV) 177 **100A1** SS 03/2009 540 SSC, passenger (A), catamaran, HSC, G2 **LMC** **UMS** Cable: 173.2/16.0 U3 (a)	**2009-03 Afai Southern Shipyard (Panyu Guangzhou) Ltd — Guangzhou GD** (Hull) Yd No: 013 **2009-03 B.V. Scheepswerf Damen — Gorinchem** Yd No: 538727 Loa 42.16 Br ex 11.60 Dght 1.500 Lbp 40.09 Br md 11.30 Dpth 3.80 Welded, 1 dk	**(A37B2PS) Passenger Ship** Hull Material: Aluminium Alloy Passengers: unberthed: 300	**4 oil engines** with clutches, flexible couplings & sr geared to sc. shafts driving 4 Water jets Total Power: 4,200kW (5,712hp) M.T.U. 16V2000M70 4 x Vee 4 Stroke 16 Cy. 130 x 150 each-1050kW (1428bhp) MTU Friedrichshafen GmbH-Friedrichshafen AuxGen: 2 x 56kW 415V 50Hz a.c
8601197 **WAN SHOU SHAN** *BRUE* - **China Shipping Development Co Ltd Tramp Co** - SatCom: Inmarsat C 441272510 *Guangzhou, Guangdong* *China* MMSI: 412592000	**26,835** Class: CC 11,009 39,837	**1990-01 Dalian Shipyard Co Ltd — Dalian LN** Yd No: BJ350/3 Loa 195.00 (BB) Br ex - Dght 10.000 Lbp 185.02 Br md 32.00 Dpth 15.20 Welded, 1 dk	**(A21A2BC) Bulk Carrier** Grain: 47,114 Compartments: 6 Ho, ER 6 Ha: (15.4 x 16.0)5 (16.0 x 16.0)ER Ice Capable	**1 oil engine** driving 1 FP propeller Total Power: 8,171kW (11,109hp) 14.5kn Sulzer 6RTA52 1 x 2 Stroke 6 Cy. 520 x 1800 8171kW (11109bhp) Dalian Marine Diesel Works-China
7717793 **WAN SHUI** *BAGU* *ex* Iberian Confidence *-2002* *ex* Condor *-1996* - *ex* Lux Condor *-1989* *ex* Mar Liguria *-1989* - - *Dalian, Liaoning* *China* MMSI: 412204020	**9,265** Class: (LR) (BV) 6,222 ✠ Classed LR until 4/89 15,384 T/cm 25.0	**1983-06 Astilleros Espanoles SA (AESA) — Seville** Yd No: 249 Loa 140.46 (BB) Br ex 21.44 Dght 8.945 Lbp 134.02 Br md 21.40 Dpth 12.20 Welded, 2 dks	**(A31A2GX) General Cargo Ship** Grain: 22,191; Bale: 20,290 Compartments: 4 Ho, ER, 4 Tw Dk 4 Ha: (13.5 x 8.0) (7.5 x 12.6)2 (20.2 x 12.6)ER Derricks: 1x50t,3x25t,4x5t	**1 oil engine** driving 1 FP propeller Total Power: 5,804kW (7,891hp) 14.0kn B&W 8K45GFCA 1 x 2 Stroke 8 Cy. 450 x 900 5804kW (7891bhp) Astilleros Espanoles SA (AESA)-Spain AuxGen: 3 x 480kW 220/410V 60Hz a.c Fuel: 110.0 (d.f.) 1043.0 (r.f.)
9623594 **WAN TONG** *BTBM3* - **Dalian Port Wantong Logistics Co Ltd** - SatCom: Inmarsat C 441201068 *Dalian, Liaoning* *China* MMSI: 412203360	**21,270** Class: CC 10,278 29,070	**2012-07 Huanghai Shipbuilding Co Ltd — Rongcheng SD** Yd No: HCY-141 Loa 166.31 (BB) Br ex 27.70 Dght 10.100 Lbp 158.32 Br md 27.40 Dpth 14.20 Welded, 1 dk	**(A31A2GX) General Cargo Ship** Grain: 39,102; Bale: 39,102 TEU 1220 C Ho 702 TEU C Dk 518 TEU. Compartments: 4 Ho, ER 4 Ha: 2 (33.6 x 23.0) (24.9 x 23.0)ER (19.0 x 18.0) Cranes: 2x60t,1x40t Ice Capable	**1 oil engine** driving 1 FP propeller Total Power: 6,810kW (9,259hp) 15.2kn MAN-B&W 6S40ME-B9 1 x 2 Stroke 6 Cy. 400 x 1770 6810kW (9259bhp) STX Engine Co Ltd-South Korea AuxGen: 3 x 600kW 450V a.c
9622497 **WAN TONG HAI** *BAKA* - **Dalian Ronghai Shipping Co Ltd** Dalian Shipping Group Co Ltd *Dalian, Liaoning* *China* MMSI: 412208030	**24,105** Class: CC - 7,646	**2010-11 Huanghai Shipbuilding Co Ltd — Rongcheng SD** Loa 163.95 Br ex - Dght 5.950 Lbp 151.10 Br md 25.00 Dpth 13.40 Welded, 1 dk	**(A36A2PR) Passenger/Ro-Ro Ship (Vehicles)** Passengers: 1650 Lane-Len: 2000 Vehicles: 192 Ice Capable	**2 oil engines** reduction geared to sc. shafts driving 2 Propellers Total Power: 12,000kW (16,316hp) 18.5kn Wartsila 12V32 2 x Vee 4 Stroke 12 Cy. 320 x 400 each-6000kW (8158bhp) Wartsila Finland Oy-Finland AuxGen: 2 x 1100kW 400V a.c, 3 x 670kW 400V a.c
9095151 **WAN TONG XING 1** - *ex* Jin Bai Hai 11 *-2008* *ex* Zhehai 309 *-2006* - **Wan Tong International Shipping (HK) Ltd** -	**5,244** 3,520 -	**1984-08 Fujian Fishing Vessel Shipyard — Fuzhou FJ** Loa 127.87 Br ex - Dght 7.750 Lbp 119.00 Br md 18.30 Dpth 9.90 Welded, 1 dk	**(A31A2GX) General Cargo Ship**	**1 oil engine** driving 1 Propeller Total Power: 2,976kW (4,046hp) Mitsubishi 6UET52/90D 1 x 2 Stroke 6 Cy. 520 x 900 2976kW (4046bhp) The Hanshin Diesel Works Ltd-Japan

Identity / Owner	Tonnage	Class	Build / Dimensions	Type / Capacity	Machinery
8308941 *3FLP5* - **WAN VOYAGER** *ex* Chios Liberty *-2012* *ex* MC Aquamarine *-2009* *ex* Antares G *-2007* *ex* Norita *-2005* *ex* Anita *-1991* *ex* Neo Campanula *-1990* *ex* Sanko Campanula *-1987* **Wan Cheng Shipping Pte Ltd** Five Ocean Maritime Services Co Ltd *Panama* *Panama* MMSI: 373254000 Official number: 4389512	**22,135** 12,665 38,891 T/cm 47.2	Class: RI (NV) (NK)	**1984-06 Ishikawajima-Harima Heavy Industries Co Ltd (IHI) — Aioi HG** Yd No: 2874 Loa 180.80 (BB) Br ex 30.54 Dght 10.932 Lbp 171.00 Br md 30.51 Dpth 15.32 Welded, 1 dk	**(A21A2BC) Bulk Carrier** Grain: 46,112; Bale: 44,492 Compartments: 5 Ho, ER 5 Ha: (15.2 x 12.8)4 (19.2 x 15.2)ER Cranes: 4x25t	**1 oil engine** driving 1 FP propeller Total Power: 5,884kW (8,000hp) 14.3k Sulzer 6RTA5 1 x 2 Stroke 6 Cy. 580 x 1700 5884kW (8000bhp) Ishikawajima Harima Heavy IndustrieCo Ltd (IHI)-Japan AuxGen: 3 x 450kW 450V 60Hz a.c Fuel: 86.5 (d.f.) (Heating Coils) 1626.5 (r.f.) 23.0pd
7809027 - - **WAN XIANG** *ex* Zheng Chang *-2010* *ex* Shun Feng 168 *-2007* *ex* Dong Chang Sheng *-2003* *ex* Kiku Maru No. 27 *-1994* -	**168** 50 -	Class: (CC)	**1978-07 Nagasaki Zosen K.K. — Nagasaki** Yd No: 656 Loa 36.45 Br ex - Dght 2.401 Lbp 30.21 Br md 6.32 Dpth 2.82 Welded, 1 dk	**(B11B2FV) Fishing Vessel**	**1 oil engine** reduction geared to sc. shaft driving 1 FP propeller Total Power: 515kW (700hp) Niigata 6L25BX 1 x 4 Stroke 6 Cy. 250 x 320 515kW (700bhp) Niigata Engineering Co Ltd-Japan
7043465 *BEDH* - **WAN XIANG** *ex* Popi *-1988* *ex* Papua *-1987* *ex* Waigani Express *-1981* *ex* Bellatrix *-1978* **Anhui Ocean Shipping Co Ltd** *Shanghai* *China* MMSI: 412550040	**4,891** 3,439 7,550	Class: (CC) (GL)	**1971-04 Orenstein & Koppel AG — Luebeck** Yd No: 678 Loa 116.80 (BB) Br ex - Dght 7.511 Lbp 108.60 Br md 18.26 Dpth 9.94 Welded, 2 dks	**(A31A2GX) General Cargo Ship** Grain: 10,902; Bale: 9,967 TEU 475 C. 475/20' Compartments: 3 Ho, ER 3 Ha: (12.6 x 8.0)2 (19.5 x 12.8)ER Cranes: 2x15t,3x8t Ice Capable	**1 oil engine** reduction geared to sc. shaft driving 1 FP propeller Total Power: 4,045kW (5,500hp) 16.5kn MaK 12M551AK 1 x Vee 4 Stroke 12 Cy. 450 x 550 4045kW (5500bhp) Atlas MaK Maschinenbau GmbH-Kiel AuxGen: 3 x 304kW 380V 50Hz a.c Thrusters: 1 Thwart. FP thruster (a) Fuel: 640.0 (r.f.)
9623609 *BSAV* - **WAN XIANG** *ex* Wan He *-2012* **Dalian Port Wantong Logistics Co Ltd** *Dalian, Liaoning* *China* MMSI: 412208780	**21,270** 10,278 29,011	Class: CC	**2012-12 Huanghai Shipbuilding Co Ltd — Rongcheng SD** Yd No: HCY-142 Loa 166.31 (BB) Br ex 27.70 Dght 10.100 Lbp 158.32 Br md 27.40 Dpth 14.20 Welded, 1 dk	**(A31A2GX) General Cargo Ship** Grain: 39,102; Bale: 39,102 TEU 1220 C Ho 702 TEU C dk 518 TEU Compartments: 4 Ho, ER 4 Ha: 2 (33.6 x 23.0) (24.9 x 23.0)ER (19.0 x 18.0) Cranes: 2x60t,1x40t Ice Capable	**1 oil engine** driving 1 FP propeller Total Power: 6,810kW (9,259hp) 15.2kn MAN-B&W 6S40ME-B9 1 x 2 Stroke 6 Cy. 400 x 1770 6810kW (9259bhp) STX Engine Co Ltd-South Korea AuxGen: 3 x 600kW 450V a.c
8667309 - - **WAN XIANG 799** **Wuhu Wan Feng Shipping Co Ltd** *Wuhu, Anhui* *China* Official number: 2012G2300151	**9,994** 4,341 16,340	Class: ZC	**2012-03 Chaohu Yingjiang Shipbuilding & Repair Co Ltd — Wuwei County AH** Yd No: YJ2012001 Loa 139.80 Br ex - Dght 2.800 Lbp 132.60 Br md 22.00 Dpth 10.50 Welded, 1 dk	**(A24D2BA) Aggregates Carrier**	**2 oil engines** reduction geared to sc. shafts driving 1 Propeller Total Power: 1,618kW (2,200hp) Chinese Std. Type 1 x 809kW (1100bhp) Qingdao Zichai Boyang Diesel EngineCo Ltd-China Chinese Std. Type LC8250ZLC 1 x 4 Stroke 8 Cy. 250 x 320 809kW (1100bhp) Qingdao Zichai Boyang Diesel EngineCo Ltd-China
9092771 - - **WAN XUAN CHENG HUO 3701** **Penton Engineering Sdn Bhd** Wealthy Logistic Sdn Bhd	**590** 376 700		**2004-10 Anji Jingui Shiprepair Yard — Anji County ZJ** Yd No: H0012 Loa 58.00 Br ex - Dght - Lbp - Br md 11.00 Dpth 3.30 Welded, 1 dk	**(A31A2GX) General Cargo Ship**	**2 oil engines** driving 2 Propellers Total Power: 434kW (590hp) Chinese Std. Type 2 x 4 Stroke each-217kW (295bhp) in China
9092783 - - **WAN XUAN CHENG HUO 3702** - -	**590** 376 700		**2004-10 Anji Jingui Shiprepair Yard — Anji County ZJ** Yd No: H0032 Loa 58.00 Br ex - Dght - Lbp - Br md 11.00 Dpth 3.30 Welded, 1 dk	**(A31A2GX) General Cargo Ship**	**2 oil engines** driving 2 Propellers Total Power: 434kW (590hp) Chinese Std. Type 2 x 4 Stroke each-217kW (295bhp) in China
9092795 - - **WAN XUAN CHENG HUO 3703** **Penton Engineering Sdn Bhd** Wealthy Logistic Sdn Bhd	**495** 325 700		**2004-11 Dongtai Jianguo Shipbuilding Co Ltd — Dongtai JS** Yd No: H0072 Loa 52.00 Br ex - Dght - Lbp - Br md 10.00 Dpth 3.00 Welded, 1 dk	**(A31A2GX) General Cargo Ship**	**2 oil engines** driving 2 Propellers Total Power: 404kW (550hp) Chinese Std. Type 2 x 4 Stroke each-202kW (275bhp) in China
9664976 *BLBL* - **WAN YANG 35** **Ningbo Merchant Shipping Co Ltd** - SatCom: Inmarsat C 441301816 *Ningbo, Zhejiang* *China* MMSI: 413447290	**22,475** 11,913 35,045 T/cm 47.4	Class: CC	**2012-06 Zhejiang Jiuzhou Shipbuilding Co Ltd — Sanmen County ZJ** Yd No: JZ-001 Loa 179.88 (BB) Br ex 28.85 Dght 9.830 Lbp 172.00 Br md 28.80 Dpth 14.60 Welded, 1 dk	**(A21A2BC) Bulk Carrier** Double Sides Entire Compartment Length Grain: 45,647 Compartments: 5 Ho, ER 5 Ha: 4 (20.0 x 20.0)ER (13.6 x 15.4) Cranes: 4x30t	**1 oil engine** driving 1 FP propeller Total Power: 6,480kW (8,810hp) 14.0kn MAN-B&W 6S42MC 1 x 2 Stroke 6 Cy. 420 x 1764 6480kW (8810bhp) Hyundai Heavy Industries Co Ltd-South Korea AuxGen: 3 x 465kW 450V a.c
9638537 *BKCD* - **WAN YANG 36** **Ningbo Merchant Shipping Co Ltd** - SatCom: Inmarsat C 441369099 *Ningbo, Zhejiang* *China* MMSI: 413443260	**23,670** 13,049 38,183	Class: CC	**2011-12 Jiangsu Mingyang Shipbuilding Co Ltd — Guannan County JS** Yd No: MYSB003 Loa 183.50 Br ex - Dght 11.300 Lbp 175.00 Br md 28.60 Dpth 15.80 Welded, 1 dk	**(A21A2BC) Bulk Carrier** Double Hull Grain: 48,100 Compartments: 5 Ho, ER 5 Ha: 4 (16.3 x 20.4)ER (14.0 x 16.1) Cranes: 4x30t Ice Capable	**1 oil engine** driving 1 FP propeller Total Power: 6,480kW (8,810hp) 12.0kn MAN-B&W 6S42MC 1 x 2 Stroke 6 Cy. 420 x 1764 6480kW (8810bhp) H Cegielski Poznan SA-Poland AuxGen: 3 x 430kW 400V a.c
9349083 *VRLP4* - **WAN ZHOU XING 9** *launched as* Assopos *-2010* **Hong Kong Million Boat Shipping Ltd** Taihua Ship Management Ltd *Hong Kong* *Hong Kong* MMSI: 477319800	**8,525** 3,829 11,975 T/cm 23.3	Class: CC	**2010-07 Jiujiang Yinxing Shipbuilding Co Ltd — Xingzi County JX** Yd No: YX004 Loa 134.85 (BB) Br ex 22.02 Dght 7.580 Lbp 126.00 Br md 22.00 Dpth 10.60 Welded, 1 dk	**(A12B2TR) Chemical/Products Tanker** Double Hull (13F) Liq: 13,943; Liq (Oil): 13,897 Cargo Heating Coils Compartments: 10 Wing Ta, 1 Slop Ta, 2 Wing Slop Ta, ER 10 Cargo Pump (s): 10x300m³/hr Manifold: Bow/CM: 74m Ice Capable	**1 oil engine** reduction geared to sc. shafts driving 1 FP propeller Total Power: 4,500kW (6,118hp) 13.0kn Wartsila 9L32 1 x 4 Stroke 9 Cy. 320 x 400 4500kW (6118bhp) Wartsila Finland Oy-Finland AuxGen: 2 x 670kW 400V 60Hz a.c Thrusters: 1 Thwart. FP thruster (f) Fuel: 104.0 (d.f.) 666.0 (r.f.)
9308663 *HSB3403* - **WANA BHUM** **Regional Container Lines Pte Ltd** RCL Shipmanagement Pte Ltd *Bangkok* *Thailand* MMSI: 567317000 Official number: 490000036	**23,922** 9,737 30,832	Class: NK	**2005-06 Mitsubishi Heavy Industries Ltd. — Shimonoseki** Yd No: 1107 Loa 194.90 (BB) Br ex 30.63 Dght 11.425 Lbp 186.00 Br md 30.60 Dpth 16.80 Welded, 1 dk	**(A33A2CC) Container Ship (Fully Cellular)** TEU 2378 incl 240 ref C.	**1 oil engine** driving 1 FP propeller Total Power: 20,580kW (27,981hp) 21.5kn Mitsubishi 7UEC68LSE 1 x 2 Stroke 7 Cy. 680 x 2690 20580kW (27981bhp) Mitsubishi Heavy Industries Ltd-Japan AuxGen: 3 x 1400kW 450/230V 60Hz a.c Thrusters: 1 Tunnel thruster (f) Fuel: 2800.0
8876845 - - **WANBANG YONGYUE TUO 1** *ex* Kaisho Maru *-2007* **Zhoushan IMC-Yongyue Shipyard & Engineering Co Ltd**	*320* 96 -		**1994-03 Sanoyas Hishino Meisho Corp — Kurashiki OY** Loa 36.20 Br ex - Dght 3.200 Lbp 31.50 Br md 9.80 Dpth 4.38 Welded, 1 dk	**(B32A2ST) Tug**	**2 oil engines** driving 2 Z propellers Total Power: 2,648kW (3,600hp) 13.7kn Niigata 6L28HX 2 x 4 Stroke 6 Cy. 280 x 370 each-1324kW (1800bhp) Niigata Engineering Co Ltd-Japan
6517897 - - **WANDA** *ex* Kyokuyo Maru *-1983* **Ferry Line Public Co Ltd** - *Thailand* Official number: 261033115	*494* - 177		**1965 Kanda Zosensho K.K. — Kure** Yd No: 99 Loa 44.61 Br ex 11.10 Dght 2.490 Lbp 40.49 Br md 9.81 Dpth 3.61 Welded, 1 dk	**(A37B2PS) Passenger Ship** Passengers: unberthed: 330	**2 oil engines** driving 2 FP propellers Total Power: 956kW (1,300hp) 12.5kn Niigata 6L25BXB 2 x 4 Stroke 6 Cy. 250 x 320 each-478kW (650bhp) Niigata Engineering Co Ltd-Japan AuxGen: 2 x 40kW 225V a.c Fuel: 17.5 5.0pd
8034186 - - **WANDA** - -	*612* - 520	Class: (BV)	**1975 Estaleiros Amazonia S.A. (ESTANAVE) — Manaus** Loa 45.01 Br ex - Dght - Lbp - Br md 10.80 Dpth 3.61 Welded, 1 dk	**(A31A2GX) General Cargo Ship** Grain: 600 Compartments: 1 Ho, ER	**1 oil engine** driving 1 FP propeller Total Power: 313kW (426hp) 9.0kn Caterpillar D353SCAC 1 x 4 Stroke 6 Cy. 159 x 203 313kW (426bhp) Caterpillar Tractor Co-USA AuxGen: 1 x 40kW

IMO / Call sign	Name / Former names / Owner / Manager / Port / Flag	Tonnage	Class	Builder / Dimensions	Type	Machinery
415947 *CXE6*	**WANDA A** *ex* Vento Di Nortada *-2014* *ex* Wanda A *-2012* **Limar Liman ve Gemi Isletmeleri AS (Limar Port & Ship Operators SA)** Arkas Denizcilik ve Nakliyat AS (Arkas Shipping & Transport AS) *Izmir* *Turkey* MMSI: 271040007 Official number: 4998	**17,687** 6,700 21,990	Class: AB (GL)	**2009-08 Peene-Werft GmbH — Wolgast** Yd No: 555 Loa 184.01 (BB) Br ex - Dght 9.000 Lbp 176.00 Br md 24.50 Dpth 14.20 Welded, 1 dk	**(A33A2CC) Container Ship (Fully Cellular)** TEU 1604 incl 178 ref C. Compartments: 5 Cell Ho, ER Cranes: 3x45t Ice Capable	**1 oil engine** driving 1 CP propeller Total Power: 13,280kW (18,055hp) 20.0kn MAN-B&W 8S50MC-C 1 x 2 Stroke 8 Cy. 500 x 2000 13280kW (18055bhp) STX Engine Co Ltd-South Korea AuxGen: 1 x 910kW 450V a.c, 4 x 740kW 450V a.c Thrusters: 1 Tunnel thruster (f)
385869	**WANDA R** *ex* Prins van Oranje *-1960* **C B Wallace** - *Georgetown* *Guyana* Official number: 82945	*182* 129 -		**1908 N.V. Nederlandsche Scheepsbouw-Mij. — Amsterdam** Yd No: 87 L reg 38.71 Br ex 7.32 Dght 3.353 Lbp - Br md 7.27 Dpth - Riveted, 1 dk	**(A31A2GX) General Cargo Ship**	**1 oil engine** driving 1 FP propeller Total Power: 177kW (241hp) 9.0kn Kelvin T8 1 x 4 Stroke 8 Cy. 165 x 184 177kW (241bhp) (new engine 1960) Bergius Co. Ltd.-Glasgow Fuel: 15.0
569011 *RPW*	**WANDELAAR** **Wandelaar Invest SA** DAB Vloot *Ostend* *Belgium* MMSI: 205594000 Official number: 01 00804 2012	**2,462** 739 307	Class: GL	**2012-04 Bremerhavener Dock GmbH (BREDO) — Bremerhaven** (Hull) Yd No: 6474 **2012-04 Schiffs- u. Yachtwerft Abeking & Rasmussen GmbH & Co. — Lemwerder** Yd No: 6474 Loa 60.82 (BB) Br ex - Dght 6.500 Lbp 54.30 Br md 24.60 Dpth 11.33 Welded, 1 dk	**(B34N2QP) Pilot Vessel**	**4 diesel electric oil engines** driving 4 gen. each 685kW 400V a.c Connecting to 2 elec. motors each (1210kW) driving 2 FP propellers Total Power: 3,040kW (4,132hp) 13.2kn M.T.U. 8V4000M50 4 x Vee 4 Stroke 8 Cy. 165 x 190 each-760kW (1033bhp) MTU Friedrichshafen GmbH-Friedrichshafen Thrusters: 1 Tunnel thruster (f)
101217	**WANDERER** *ex* Caliente *-1960* **Compania de Navigation Aguadulce SA** -	*272* 185 -		**1965 Burton Shipyard Co., Inc. — Port Arthur, Tx** Yd No: 373 Loa 50.30 Br ex 11.59 Dght 2.998 Lbp 47.10 Br md - Dpth 3.66 Welded, 1 dk	**(B21A20S) Platform Supply Ship** Passengers: berths: 19	**2 oil engines** driving 2 FP propellers Total Power: 1,126kW (1,530hp) 10.0kn Caterpillar D398SCAC 2 x Vee 4 Stroke 12 Cy. 159 x 203 each-563kW (765bhp) Caterpillar Tractor Co-USA AuxGen: 2 x 60kW Fuel: 137.0 (d.f.)
188908 *8YU9*	**WANDERLUST** *ex* Furtrans Bulk *-2011* *launched as* Talon II *-2006* **Wander Navigation Ltd** Primal Shipmanagement Inc SatCom: Inmarsat C 463709658 *Monrovia* *Liberia* MMSI: 636015138 Official number: 15138	**25,312** 13,825 41,675 T/cm 48.3	Class: NK (BV)	**2006-02 Bulyard Shipbuilding Industry AD — Varna** (Hull) Yd No: 512 **2006-02 Anadolu Deniz Insaat Kizaklari San. ve Tic. Ltd. Sti. — Tuzla** Yd No: 203 Loa 186.45 (BB) Br ex - Dght 11.480 Lbp 177.00 Br md 30.00 Dpth 16.20 Welded, 1 dk	**(A21A2BC) Bulk Carrier** Double Bottom Entire Compartment Length Grain: 52,226; Bale: 51,363 Compartments: 5 Ho, ER 5 Ha: 2 (19.3 x 15.4)2 (19.3 x 15.4)ER (19.7 x 15.4) Cranes: 4x30t Ice Capable	**1 oil engine** driving 1 FP propeller Total Power: 8,340kW (11,339hp) 14.5kn B&W 8L50MC 1 x 2 Stroke 8 Cy. 500 x 1620 8340kW (11339bhp) H Cegielski Poznan SA-Poland AuxGen: 3 x 600kW 440/240V 60Hz a.c Fuel: 190.0 (d.f.) 1720.0 (r.f.) 31.0pd
039153 *JQ2155*	**WANDILLA** - - *Sydney, NSW* *Australia* MMSI: 503276300 Official number: 343938	*242* 72 -	Class: (LR) ✠ Classed LR until 1/8/12	**1971-02 Adelaide Ship Construction Pty Ltd — Port Adelaide SA** Yd No: 69 Loa 30.31 Br ex 8.67 Dght 4.407 Lbp 26.07 Br md 8.49 Dpth 4.93 Welded	**(B32A2ST) Tug**	**2 oil engines** sr geared to sc. shafts driving 2 Directional propellers Total Power: 1,398kW (1,900hp) 11.6kn Daihatsu 8PSHTCM-26 2 x 4 Stroke 8 Cy. 260 x 320 each-699kW (950bhp) Daihatsu Diesel Manufacturing Co Lt-Japan AuxGen: 2 x 60kW 415V 50Hz a.c Fuel: 38.5 (d.f.)
385948 *SD6241*	**WANDO RIVER** *ex* Wind Rush *-1960* **Wando River Corp** - *Warren, RI* *United States of America* MMSI: 366159260 Official number: 275396	*148* 122 -		**1957 Byrd Commercial Diving Inc. — Miami, Fl** Converted From: General Cargo Ship L reg 28.32 Br ex 8.51 Dght - Lbp - Br md - Dpth - Welded, 1 dk	**(B11B2FV) Fishing Vessel**	**2 oil engines** driving 2 FP propellers Total Power: 150kW (204hp) G.M. (Detroit Diesel) 6V-71-N 2 x Vee 2 Stroke 6 Cy. 108 x 127 each-75kW (102bhp) (made 1955, fitted 1959) Detroit Diesel Corporation-Detroit, Mi
219197 *TVF*	**WANDOOR** **Government of The Republic of India (Andaman & Nicobar Administration)** The Shipping Corporation of India Ltd (SCI) *Mumbai* *India* MMSI: 419029600 Official number: 2916	**449** 135 135	Class: IR	**2004-07 Hindustan Shipyard Ltd — Visakhapatnam** Yd No: 11108 Loa 40.40 Br ex 8.62 Dght 2.660 Lbp 36.50 Br md 8.40 Dpth 4.00 Welded, 1 dk	**(A37B2PS) Passenger Ship** Passengers: unberthed: 100	**2 oil engines** geared to sc. shafts driving 2 FP propellers Total Power: 1,324kW (1,800hp) 12.0kn Yanmar M200-EN 2 x 4 Stroke 6 Cy. 200 x 260 each-662kW (900bhp) Yanmar Diesel Engine Co Ltd-Japan AuxGen: 2 x 80kW 415V 50Hz a.c Fuel: 43.0 (d.f.)
38861	**WANG BONG** *ex* Wang Wigal *-1960* *ex* Wang Wige *-1960* - -	**5,798** 3,202 9,015	Class: KC	**1989-10 Wuhu Shipyard — Wuhu AH** Yd No: 08-21 Loa 116.45 Br ex - Dght 7.610 Lbp 107.00 Br md 18.60 Dpth 9.50 Welded, 1 dk	**(A31A2GX) General Cargo Ship**	**1 oil engine** driving 1 Propeller Total Power: 4,450kW (6,050hp) 14.0kn Mitsubishi 5UEC45LA 1 x 2 Stroke 5 Cy. 450 x 1350 4450kW (6050bhp) Kobe Hatsudoki KK-Japan
283526 *PCX*	**WANG CHI** **China Shipping Tanker Co Ltd** *Shanghai* *China* MMSI: 413067000	**26,955** 11,381 42,003 T/cm 51.5	Class: CC	**2004-04 Guangzhou Shipyard International Co Ltd — Guangzhou GD** Yd No: 02130002 Loa 187.80 (BB) Br ex 31.53 Dght 11.300 Lbp 178.00 Br md 31.50 Dpth 16.80 Welded, 1 dk	**(A13B2TP) Products Tanker** Double Hull (13F) Liq: 44,646; Liq (Oil): 46,831 Cargo Heating Coils Compartments: 12 Wing Ta, 2 Wing Slop Ta, ER 3 Cargo Pump (s): 3x1200m³/hr Manifold: Bow/CM: 94.6m Ice Capable	**1 oil engine** driving 1 FP propeller Total Power: 8,580kW (11,665hp) 14.5kn MAN-B&W 6S50MC 1 x 2 Stroke 6 Cy. 500 x 1910 8580kW (11665bhp) Dalian Marine Diesel Works-China AuxGen: 3 x 664kW 450V a.c Fuel: 82.0 (d.f.) 1341.0 (r.f.)
37647	**WANG JONG** *ex* Wang Chang *-2009* **Korea Kunhae Co Ltd** -	**10,058** 6,822 16,270	Class: KC	**1992-08 Nampo Shipyard — Nampo** Yd No: 920-3 Loa 149.75 Br ex - Dght 9.240 Lbp 139.30 Br md 21.00 Dpth 12.50 Welded, 1 dk	**(A31A2GX) General Cargo Ship** Grain: 22,300	**1 oil engine** reduction geared to sc. shaft driving 1 FP propeller Total Power: 6,391kW (8,689hp) 13.0kn MAN 16V40/54A 1 x Vee 4 Stroke 16 Cy. 400 x 540 6391kW (8689bhp) MAN B&W Diesel AG-Augsburg
78080	**WANG KAEW** *ex* Ferry Osumi No. 2 *-1991* **Asset Management Donsak - Samui Port Ltd** - *Bangkok* *Thailand* Official number: 341003256	*990* 467 445		**1974-09 Nakamura Shipbuilding & Engine Works Co. Ltd. — Matsue** Yd No: 120 Loa 71.23 Br ex 13.01 Dght 3.493 Lbp 65.00 Br md 12.98 Dpth 4.70 Welded, 1 dk	**(A36A2PR) Passenger/Ro-Ro Ship (Vehicles)** Passengers: unberthed: 737	**2 oil engines** driving 2 FP propellers Total Power: 4,118kW (5,598hp) 16.5kn Daihatsu 8DSM-32 2 x 4 Stroke 8 Cy. 320 x 380 each-2059kW (2799bhp) Daihatsu Diesel Manufacturing Co Lt-Japan Fuel: 103.0
20956	**WANG NAI** *ex* Konpira Maru *-1981* **Asset Management Donsak - Samui Port Ltd** - *Bangkok* *Thailand* Official number: 241028271	*794* 416 -		**1963-07 Shikoku Dockyard Co. Ltd. — Takamatsu** Yd No: 652 Loa 56.00 Br ex 11.03 Dght 2.769 Lbp 52.00 Br md 11.00 Dpth 3.99 Welded, 1 dk	**(A36A2PR) Passenger/Ro-Ro Ship (Vehicles)** Passengers: unberthed: 475	**2 oil engines** driving 2 FP propellers Total Power: 1,132kW (1,540hp) 12.5kn Nippon Hatsudoki HS6NV325 2 x 4 Stroke 6 Cy. 325 x 460 each-566kW (770bhp) Nippon Hatsudoki-Japan AuxGen: 2 x 64kW 225V a.c Fuel: 45.5 2.5pd
35145	**WANG NGERN** *ex* Kochi *-1990* **Asset Management Donsak - Samui Port Ltd** - *Thailand* Official number: 338400025	*653* 336 274		**1971-05 Nakamura Shipbuilding & Engine Works Co. Ltd. — Matsue** Yd No: 101 Loa 50.20 Br ex 11.00 Dght 2.947 Lbp 45.01 Br md 10.98 Dpth 3.79 Welded	**(A36A2PR) Passenger/Ro-Ro Ship (Vehicles)** Passengers: unberthed: 250 Trailers: 8	**1 oil engine** driving 2 FP propellers Total Power: 1,471kW (2,000hp) 14.0kn Daihatsu 1 x 4 Stroke 1471kW (2000bhp) Daihatsu Diesel Manufacturing Co Lt-Japan
33109	**WANG NOK** *ex* Dogo Maru *-1981* **Phuket Dinner Cruise Co Ltd** - *Bangkok* *Thailand* Official number: 241028263	*877* 464 263		**1964-10 Hashihama Shipbuilding Co Ltd — Imabari EH** Yd No: 172 Loa 57.00 Br ex 11.03 Dght 2.591 Lbp 52.99 Br md 10.98 Dpth 4.02 Welded, 3 dks	**(A37B2PS) Passenger Ship** Passengers: unberthed: 682	**2 oil engines** driving 2 FP propellers Total Power: 1,250kW (1,700hp) 13.0kn Hanshin 2 x 4 Stroke each-625kW (850bhp) Hanshin Nainenki Kogyo-Japan AuxGen: 1 x 88kW 225V a.c Fuel: 51.5 3.0pd

7535169 *HSJQ* - **WANG THONG** *ex* Matsuyama *-1988* **Asset Management Donsak - Samui Port Ltd** - *Bangkok* *Thailand* Official number: 311000016
638 342 -
1970-06 Nakamura Shipbuilding & Engine Works Co. Ltd. — Matsue
Loa 45.52 Br ex 12.20 Dght 3.506
Lbp 40.49 Br md 12.15 Dpth 3.71
Welded
(A37B2PS) Passenger Ship
Passengers: unberthed: 415
2 oil engines driving 2 FP propellers
Total Power: 1,472kW (2,002hp) 13.0k
Daihatsu
2 x 4 Stroke each-736kW (1001bhp)
Daihatsu Diesel Manufacturing Co Lt-Japan

8833283 *BPGM* **WANG XIN** **China Shipping Passenger Liner Co Ltd** - *Shanghai* *China*
3,858 2,006 1,110
1984 Qiuxin Shipyard — Shanghai
Loa 106.67 Br ex - Dght 3.800
Lbp 97.00 Br md 15.80 Dpth 7.70
Welded, 2 dks
(A32A2GF) General Cargo/Passenger Ship
Grain: 818
Compartments: 1 Ho, ER
1 Ha: (5.7 x 5.4)ER
Derricks: 2x3t; Winches: 2
2 oil engines driving 2 FP propellers
Total Power: 4,414kW (6,002hp) 16.0k
Hudong 6ESDZ43/82
2 x 2 Stroke 6 Cy. 430 x 820 each-2207kW (3001bhp)
Hudong Shipyard-China
AuxGen: 3 x 250kW 400V a.c

8703725 - - **WANGAN 1 GO** *ex* Tenei Maru No. 58 *-1998* **Daiei Shipping Co Ltd**
499 - 1,293
1987-08 Shinhama Dockyard Co. Ltd. — Tamano Yd No: 230
Loa - Br ex - Dght 4.130
Lbp 59.01 Br md 13.50 Dpth 6.20
Welded, 1 dk
(B33A2DG) Grab Dredger
1 oil engine driving 1 FP propeller
Total Power: 736kW (1,001hp)
Fuji 6S32
1 x 4 Stroke 6 Cy. 320 x 610 736kW (1001bhp)
Fuji Diesel Co Ltd-Japan

5385998 - - **WANGANUI** **Wanganui Harbour Board** -
252 82 288
Class: (LR) ✠
1950-01 Henry Robb Ltd. — Leith Yd No: 395
Loa 34.47 Br ex 8.69 Dght 2.744
Lbp 32.77 Br md 8.27 Dpth 2.82
Riveted\Welded, 1 dk
(B33B2DG) Grab Hopper Dredger
1 oil engine driving 1 FP propeller
Total Power: 265kW (360hp) 8.8k
Polar M44
1 x 2 Stroke 4 Cy. 250 x 420 265kW (360bhp)
British Polar Engines Ltd.-Glasgow
Fuel: 21.5

9461166 *3FPT5* - **WANGARATTA** **Oshima Shipping SA** Misuga Kaiun Co Ltd SatCom: Inmarsat C 437032510 *Panama* *Panama* MMSI: 370325000 Official number: 4259911
43,012 27,239 82,206 T/cm 70.2
Class: NK
2011-02 Tsuneishi Shipbuilding Co Ltd — Fukuyama HS Yd No: 1442
Loa 228.99 Br ex - Dght 14.430
Lbp 222.00 Br md 32.26 Dpth 20.05
Welded, 1 dk
(A21A2BC) Bulk Carrier
Grain: 97,381
Compartments: 7 Ho, ER
7 Ha: ER
1 oil engine driving 1 FP propeller
Total Power: 9,710kW (13,202hp) 14.5k
MAN-B&W 6S60MC-C
1 x 2 Stroke 6 Cy. 600 x 2400 9710kW (13202bhp)
Mitsui Engineering & Shipbuilding CLtd-Japan
Fuel: 3184.0 (r.f.)

7807304 - - **WANGARD** *ex* Martere *-1998* *ex* Lille-Tove *-1992* - -
299 172 474
Class: (BV)
1980-07 Aabenraa Vaerft A/S — Aabenraa Yd No: 32
Loa 48.34 Br ex 8.41 Dght 2.950
Lbp 44.40 Br md - Dpth 3.41
Welded, 1 dk
(A31A2GX) General Cargo Ship
Grain: 633; Bale: 577
Compartments: 1 Ho, ER
1 Ha: (22.1 x 5.4)ER
Ice Capable
1 oil engine with clutches & sr geared to sc. shaft driving 1 CP propeller
Total Power: 294kW (400hp) 10.0k
Callesen 5-427-E
1 x 4 Stroke 5 Cy. 270 x 400 294kW (400bhp)
Aabenraa Motorfabrik, HeinrichCallesen A/S-Denmark
Fuel: 35.5 (d.f.) 1.5pd

7529809 *VJCI* - **WANGARY** *ex* Corsair *-2010* **Svitzer Australia Pty Ltd & Stannard Marine Pty Ltd** Port Lincoln Tugs Pty Ltd *Port Lincoln, SA* *Australia* MMSI: 503020000 Official number: 374437
266 52 -
Class: LR ✠ **100A1** SS 04/2013 tug ✠ **LMC** **UMS** Eq.Ltr: F; Cable: U2
1976-03 Carrington Slipways Pty Ltd — Newcastle NSW Yd No: 114
Loa 29.01 Br ex 9.96 Dght 4.026
Lbp 24.80 Br md 9.71 Dpth 4.70
Welded, 1 dk
(B32A2ST) Tug
2 oil engines reverse reduction geared to sc. shafts driving 2 FP propellers
Total Power: 1,794kW (2,440hp) 12.0k
Blackstone ESL8
2 x 4 Stroke 8 Cy. 222 x 292 each-897kW (1220bhp)
Mirrlees Blackstone (Stamford)Ltd.-Stamford
AuxGen: 2 x 68kW 415V 50Hz a.c

8993887 *DBIW* - **WANGEROOG** **Government of The Federal Republic of Germany (Der Bundesminister fuer Verkehr, Bau und Stadtentwicklung)** - *Bremerhaven* *Germany* MMSI: 211113790
228 68 14
Class: GL
2004-10 Schiffs- u. Yachtwerft Abeking & Rasmussen GmbH & Co. — Lemwerder Yd No: 6468
Loa 25.65 Br ex - Dght 2.700
Lbp - Br md 13.00 Dpth 5.90
Welded, 1 dk
(B34N2QP) Pilot Vessel
Hull Material: Aluminium Alloy
2 oil engines reverse reduction geared to sc. shafts driving 2 Propellers
Total Power: 1,576kW (2,142hp)
M.T.U. 12V2000M70
2 x Vee 4 Stroke 12 Cy. 130 x 150 each-788kW (1071bhp)
MTU Friedrichshafen GmbH-Friedrichshafen

8417247 *DCRL* **WANGEROOGE** **Reederei Warrings KG** DB AutoZug GmbH SatCom: Inmarsat C 421121196 *Carolinensiel* *Germany* MMSI: 211298680 Official number: 4105
621 186 99
Class: GL
1985-05 Husumer Schiffswerft Inh. Gebr. Kroeger GmbH & Co. KG — Husum Yd No: 1496
Loa 45.30 (BB) Br ex 9.91 Dght 1.312
Lbp 42.00 Br md 9.71 Dpth 2.01
Welded, 1 dk
(A37B2PS) Passenger Ship
Passengers: unberthed: 760
Ice Capable
4 oil engines sr reverse geared to sc. shafts driving 2 Propellers , 1 fwd
Total Power: 952kW (1,296hp) 11.5kn
Volvo Penta TAMD121C
4 x 4 Stroke 6 Cy. 130 x 150 each-238kW (324bhp)
AB Volvo Penta-Sweden
AuxGen: 1 x 212kW a.c, 1 x 100kW a.c
Thrusters: 1 Thwart. FP thruster (f)
Fuel: 20.0 (d.f.) 2.5pd

9041552 *HMLM* - **WANGJAESAN 2** *ex* Fu Hai No. 10 *-2013* *ex* Asian Queen *-2003* **Korea Wangjaesan Shipping Co Ltd** - *North Korea* MMSI: 445039000
4,157 1,945 5,547
Class: KC (NK)
1991-10 Iwagi Zosen Co Ltd — Kamijima EH Yd No: 144
Loa 96.42 Br ex - Dght 5.814
Lbp 89.95 Br md 18.50 Dpth 9.20
Welded, 1 dk
(A31A2GX) General Cargo Ship
Grain: 9,435; Bale: 8,822
2 Ha: (18.2 x 10.4) (33.8 x 10.4)ER
Derricks: 1x25t,2x20t
1 oil engine driving 1 FP propeller
Total Power: 2,060kW (2,801hp) 12.0kn
Akasaka A38
1 x 4 Stroke 6 Cy. 380 x 740 2060kW (2801bhp)
Akasaka Tekkosho KK (Akasaka DieselLtd)-Japan
AuxGen: 3 x 121kW a.c
Fuel: 365.0 (r.f.)

7505906 *9WGR4* - **WANGSA MAJU** *ex* E. T. Ocean V *-2008* *ex* Pacific Ranger *-1989* **Multiara Wangsa Resources Sdn Bhd** Tiama Marine Industries Sdn Bhd *Kuching* *Malaysia* MMSI: 533000525 Official number: 330761
584 176 940
Class: (CC) (AB)
1976-06 Halter Marine, Inc. — Lockport, La Yd No: 541
Loa 53.65 Br ex 11.61 Dght 3.649
Lbp 50.45 Br md 11.59 Dpth 4.27
Welded, 1 dk
(B21A2OS) Platform Supply Ship
2 oil engines reverse reduction geared to sc. shafts driving 2 FP propellers
Total Power: 2,588kW (3,518hp) 12.0kn
Nohab F28V
2 x Vee 4 Stroke 8 Cy. 250 x 300 each-1294kW (1759bhp)
AB Bofors NOHAB-Sweden
AuxGen: 2 x 99kW a.c
Thrusters: 1 Thwart. FP thruster (f)

9120774 *3FJH7* - **WANHE** **Wanhe Shipping Inc** COSCO Container Lines Co Ltd (COSCON) SatCom: Inmarsat B 335121710 *Panama* *Panama* MMSI: 351217000 Official number: 2400297CH
65,140 36,668 69,285 T/cm 91.1
Class: LR ✠ **100A1** SS 11/2011 container ship certified container securing arrangements *IWS LI Ice Class 1D ✠ **LMC** **UMS** Eq.Ltr: W†; Cable: 749.9/95.0 U3
1997-07 Kawasaki Heavy Industries Ltd — Sakaide KG Yd No: 1462
Loa 280.00 (BB) Br ex 39.90 Dght 14.000
Lbp 267.00 Br md 39.80 Dpth 23.60
Welded, 1 dk
(A33A2CC) Container Ship (Fully Cellular)
TEU 5618 C Ho 2790 TEU C Dk 2828 TEU incl 1002 ref C
Compartments: ER, 7 Cell Ho
16 Ha: ER
Ice Capable
1 oil engine driving 1 FP propeller
Total Power: 43,100kW (58,599hp) 24.5kn
B&W 10L90MC
1 x 2 Stroke 10 Cy. 900 x 2916 43100kW (58599bhp)
Kawasaki Heavy Industries Ltd-Japan
AuxGen: 4 x 2280kW 440V 60Hz a.c
Boilers: e (ex.g.) 12.0kgf/cm² (11.8bar), AuxB (o.f.) 8.0kgf/cm² (7.8bar)
Thrusters: 1 Thwart. CP thruster (f)

8859677 *HP6533* - **WANIKIKI** *ex* Kroton *-2009* **Compania Petrolera Venezolana (COPEVEN) CA** - *Panama* *Panama* Official number: 39034PEXT1
241 155 -
1989 Constructores Navales Julio Marino — Venezuela
Loa 34.11 (BB) Br ex - Dght -
Lbp - Br md 9.00 Dpth -
Welded, 1 dk
(A31A2GX) General Cargo Ship
2 oil engines driving 2 FP propellers

9615808 *VRJX6*
WANISA
launched as Dong Chuan 47 *-2012*
Hoi Fuk Shipping Co Ltd
CS Puyuan Marine Co Ltd
Hong Kong *Hong Kong*
MMSI: 477817600
Official number: HK-3376
43,717 26,510 79,401 T/cm 71.9
Class: LR
✠ **100A1** SS 03/2012
bulk carrier
CSR
BC-A
GRAB (20)
Nos. 2, 4 & 6 holds may be empty
ESP
ShipRight (ACS (B), CM)
*IWS
LI
Ice Class 1D
Max/min draught fwd 15.400/4.176m
Max/min draught aft 15.702/6.934m
Required power 5081kw, installed power 11629kw
✠ **LMC** **UMS**
Eq.Ltr: Q†;
Cable: 687.5/81.0 U3 (a)
2012-03 Jiangsu Eastern Heavy Industry Co Ltd — Jingjiang JS Yd No: 10C-066
Loa 229.00 (BB) Br ex 32.30 Dght 14.600
Lbp 222.00 Br md 32.26 Dpth 20.25
Welded, 1 dk
(A21A2BC) Bulk Carrier
Grain: 97,000; Bale: 90,784
Compartments: 7 Ho, ER
7 Ha: ER
Ice Capable
1 oil engine driving 1 FP propeller
Total Power: 11,620kW (15,799hp) 14.0kn
Wartsila 7RT-flex50
1 x 2 Stroke 7 Cy. 500 x 2050 11620kW (15799bhp)
H Cegielski Poznan SA-Poland
AuxGen: 3 x 700kW 450V 60Hz a.c
Boilers: AuxB (Comp) 8.2kgf/cm² (8.0bar)

8028034 -
WANTED
ex Luciana M *-1993* *ex* Guido C *-1986*
ex Cristina Ciavaglia *-1984*
Alfredo Gaetani e C
-
Ancona *Italy*
Official number: 769
151 48 -
Class: (RI)
1982-06 Cant. Navalmeccanico di Senigallia S.p.A. — Senigallia Yd No: 58
Loa 29.80 (BB) Br ex 6.84 Dght 2.880
Lbp 23.91 Br md 6.71 Dpth 3.41
Welded, 1 dk
(B11A2FS) Stern Trawler
Ins: 72
Compartments: 1 Ho, ER
3 Ha:
1 oil engine with clutches, flexible couplings & sr reverse geared to sc. shaft driving 1 FP propeller
Total Power: 485kW (659hp)
S.K.L. 6NVD48-2U
1 x 4 Stroke 6 Cy. 320 x 480 485kW (659bhp)
VEB Schwermaschinenbau "KarlLiebknecht" (SKL)-Magdeburg

8964197 *5NFE* -
WAO BENUE
ex Miss Frieda *-2005*
West Africa Offshore Ltd
SEACOR Marine (West Africa) SAS
Nigeria
Official number: SR88
217 65 -
1990-07 Breaux Bay Craft, Inc. — Loreauville, La Yd No: 1641
Loa - Br ex - Dght 1.850
Lbp 34.32 Br md 7.97 Dpth 3.37
Welded, 1 dk
(B21A20C) Crew/Supply Vessel
Hull Material: Aluminium Alloy
4 oil engines reverse reduction geared to sc. shafts driving 2 FP propellers
Total Power: 1,500kW (2,040hp) 22.0kn
G.M. (Detroit Diesel) 12V-71-TI
4 x Vee 2 Stroke 12 Cy. 108 x 127 each-375kW (510bhp)
General Motors Detroit DieselAllison Divn-USA
AuxGen: 2 x 40kW a.c

8978423 *5NFEZ* -
WAO BRASS
ex Norman Mccall *-2008*
West Africa Offshore Ltd
-
Nigeria
Official number: SR1186
390 117 282
1989-01 Gulf Craft Inc — Patterson LA Yd No: 335
Loa 49.00 Br ex - Dght 2.000
Lbp 46.00 Br md 9.14 Dpth 3.20
Welded, 1 dk
(B21A20C) Crew/Supply Vessel
Hull Material: Aluminium Alloy
Passengers: 48; cabins: 4
6 oil engines geared to sc. shafts driving 6 FP propellers
Total Power: 3,000kW (4,080hp) 20.0kn
Cummins KTA-19-M2
6 x 4 Stroke 6 Cy. 159 x 159 each-500kW (680bhp)
Cummins Engine Co Inc-USA
AuxGen: 2 x 50kW 60Hz a.c
Fuel: 55.0 (d.f.) 20.0pd

7816680 *5NJS* -
WAO ETHIOPE
ex Seabulk Washington *-2007*
ex H. O. S. Deep Sun *-1994*
ex John W. Pugh *-1982*
Global West Vessel Specialist Ltd
-
Lagos *Nigeria*
MMSI: 657195000
Official number: SR523
571 171 800
Class: (AB)
1978-11 RYSCO Shipyard Inc. — Blountstown, Fl Yd No: 43
Loa 53.34 Br ex - Dght 3.390
Lbp 49.38 Br md 11.59 Dpth 3.97
Welded, 1 dk
(B21B20T) Offshore Tug/Supply Ship
2 oil engines reverse reduction geared to sc. shafts driving 2 FP propellers
Total Power: 1,654kW (2,248hp) 10.0kn
Caterpillar D399SCAC
2 x Vee 4 Stroke 16 Cy. 159 x 203 each-827kW (1124bhp)
Caterpillar Tractor Co-USA
AuxGen: 2 x 75kW
Thrusters: 1 Thwart. FP thruster (f)

8923387 *5NBCM* -
WAO-NIGER
ex Henry McCall *-2003*
West Africa Offshore Ltd
SEACOR Marine (West Africa) SAS
Lagos *Nigeria*
Official number: 377262
147 44 -
Class: (AB)
1979-01 Gulf Craft Inc — Patterson LA Yd No: 227
Loa 33.53 Br ex - Dght 1.500
Lbp 33.49 Br md 7.62 Dpth 2.60
Welded, 1 dk
(B21A20C) Crew/Supply Vessel
Hull Material: Aluminium Alloy
4 oil engines driving 4 FP propellers
Total Power: 1,528kW (2,076hp)

8113669 *5NFE3* -
WAO SAMBREIRO
ex Mako *-2008* *ex* Smit-Lloyd 26 *-2000*
West Africa Offshore Ltd
-
Lagos *Nigeria*
Official number: SR1183
1,089 326 1,082
Class: AB
1982-10 Tille Scheepsbouw B.V. — Kootstertille Yd No: 232
Loa 57.46 Br ex 12.53 Dght 4.809
Lbp 52.53 Br md 12.21 Dpth 5.82
Welded, 1 dk
(B21B20A) Anchor Handling Tug Supply
2 oil engines with flexible couplings & sr gearedto sc. shafts driving 2 CP propellers
Total Power: 3,356kW (4,562hp) 11.5kn
Kromhout 9FHD240
2 x 4 Stroke 9 Cy. 240 x 260 each-1678kW (2281bhp)
Stork Werkspoor Diesel BV-Netherlands
AuxGen: 1 x 150kW 440V 60Hz a.c, 2 x 140kW 440V 60Hz a.c
Thrusters: 1 Thwart. CP thruster (f)
Fuel: 433.0 (d.f.) 7.0pd

8625569 *JM5489* -
WAPEN VAN HOORN
Kanmon Kisen KK
-
Kitakyushu, Fukuoka *Japan*
Official number: 127865
187 - -
1986-03 Maebata Zosen Tekko K.K. — Sasebo Yd No: 169
Loa 34.02 Br ex - Dght 1.920
Lbp 27.01 Br md 6.80 Dpth 2.60
Welded, 1 dk
(A37B2PS) Passenger Ship
1 oil engine driving 1 FP propeller
Total Power: 633kW (861hp) 10.0kn
Daihatsu
1 x 4 Stroke 633kW (861bhp)
Daihatsu Diesel Manufacturing Co Lt-Japan

9378022 *2BSH6* -
WAPPEN VON AUGSBURG
Schiffahrtsgesellschaft Wappen von Augsburg mbH & Co KG
North Sea Tankers BV
London *United Kingdom*
MMSI: 235068896
Official number: 3914
5,200 2,530 8,132 T/cm 18.0
Class: GL
2009-03 Santierul Naval Damen Galati S.A. — Galati Yd No: 1118
Loa 116.90 (BB) Br ex - Dght 7.415
Lbp 110.40 Br md 18.00 Dpth 9.40
Welded, 1 dk
(A12B2TR) Chemical/Products Tanker
Double Hull (13F)
Liq: 8,575; Liq (Oil): 8,593
Cargo Heating Coils
Compartments: 14 Wing Ta, 2 Wing Slop Ta, ER
14 Cargo Pump (s): 14x200m³/hr
Manifold: Bow/CM: 60m
2 oil engines reduction geared to sc. shafts driving 2 CP propellers
Total Power: 3,600kW (4,894hp) 14.5kn
MAN-B&W 6L27/38
2 x 4 Stroke 6 Cy. 270 x 380 each-1800kW (2447bhp)
MAN Diesel A/S-Denmark
AuxGen: 2 x 378kW 400V a.c, 1 x 480kW 400V a.c
Thrusters: 1 Tunnel thruster (f)
Fuel: 109.0 (d.f.) 468.0 (r.f.)

9255828 *A8XB6* -
WAPPEN VON BAYERN
Schiffahrtsgesellschaft Wappen von Bayern mbH & Co KG
Poseidon Schiffahrt GmbH
Monrovia *Liberia*
MMSI: 636092109
Official number: 92109
5,145 2,532 8,234 T/cm 18.0
Class: GL NK
2003-07 Santierul Naval Damen Galati S.A. — Galati (Hull) Yd No: 990
2003-07 Lindenau GmbH Schiffswerft u. Maschinenfabrik — Kiel Yd No: 263
Loa 116.82 (BB) Br ex - Dght 7.415
Lbp 110.40 Br md 18.00 Dpth 9.40
Welded, 1 dk
(A12B2TR) Chemical/Products Tanker
Double Hull (13F)
Liq: 8,972; Liq (Oil): 8,562
Cargo Heating Coils
Compartments: 14 Wing Ta, 2 Wing Slop Ta, ER
16 Cargo Pump (s): 14x200m³/hr, 2x300m³/hr
Manifold: Bow/CM: 60.1m
Ice Capable
2 oil engines geared to sc. shafts driving 2 CP propellers
Total Power: 3,600kW (4,894hp) 15.0kn
MAN-B&W 6L27/38
2 x 4 Stroke 6 Cy. 270 x 380 each-1800kW (2447bhp)
MAN B&W Diesel AG-Augsburg
AuxGen: 3 x 378kW 400/230V 50Hz a.c, 2 x 420kW 400/230V 50Hz a.c
Thrusters: 1 Tunnel thruster (f)
Fuel: 109.0 (d.f.) 499.0 (r.f.)

9255804 *A8XB4* -
WAPPEN VON BERLIN
Schiffahrtsgesellschaft Wappen von Berlin mbH & Co KG
Poseidon Schiffahrt GmbH
Monrovia *Liberia*
MMSI: 636092107
Official number: 92107
5,145 2,532 8,254 T/cm 18.0
Class: NK (GL)
2003-02 Santierul Naval Damen Galati S.A. — Galati (Hull) Yd No: 988
2003-02 Lindenau GmbH Schiffswerft u. Maschinenfabrik — Kiel Yd No: 261
Loa 116.90 (BB) Br ex 18.03 Dght 7.400
Lbp 110.40 Br md 18.00 Dpth 9.40
Welded, 1 dk
(A12B2TR) Chemical/Products Tanker
Double Hull (13F)
Liq: 8,593; Liq (Oil): 8,593
Cargo Heating Coils
Compartments: 14 Wing Ta, 2 Wing Slop Ta, ER
14 Cargo Pump (s): 12x200m³/hr, 2x300m³/hr
Manifold: Bow/CM: 60.1m
Ice Capable
2 oil engines reduction geared to sc. shafts driving 2 CP propellers
Total Power: 3,600kW (4,894hp) 15.0kn
MAN-B&W 6L27/38
2 x 4 Stroke 6 Cy. 270 x 380 each-1800kW (2447bhp)
MAN B&W Diesel A/S-Denmark
AuxGen: 3 x 378kW 400/230V 50Hz a.c, 2 x 420kW 400/230V 50Hz a.c
Thrusters: 1 Tunnel thruster (f)
Fuel: 112.0 (d.f.) 473.0 (r.f.)

7525918 *DCTN* -
WAPPEN VON BORKUM
ex Princess Isabella *-1994*
ex Stadt Borkum *-1988* *ex* Hannover *-1979*
AG 'Ems'
-
Borkum *Germany*
MMSI: 211221190
Official number: 4473
287 116 32
Class: GL
1976-05 Schiffswerft Gebr Schloemer Oldersum — Moormerland Yd No: 259
Loa 42.83 Br ex 7.83 Dght 1.061
Lbp 38.82 Br md 7.22 Dpth 2.95
Welded, 1 dk
(A37B2PS) Passenger Ship
Passengers: unberthed: 371
2 oil engines reverse reduction geared to sc. shafts driving 2 FP propellers
Total Power: 560kW (762hp) 11.0kn
Volvo Penta TAMD122A
2 x 4 Stroke 6 Cy. 130 x 150 each-280kW (381bhp) (new engine 1995)
AB Volvo Penta-Sweden
AuxGen: 2 x 60kW 220/380V a.c
Thrusters: 1 Water jet (f)

IMO / Call sign	Name / Owner	Tonnage	Class	Build / Dimensions	Type / Cargo	Machinery
9260835 *A8XB7* -	**WAPPEN VON BREMEN** **Schiffahrtsgesellschaft Wappen von Bremen mbH & Co KG** Poseidon Schiffahrt GmbH *Monrovia* *Liberia* MMSI: 636092110 Official number: 92110	**5,145** 2,532 8,211 T/cm 18.0	Class: AB NK (GL)	2003-12 **Santierul Naval Damen Galati S.A. — Galati** (Hull) Yd No: 991 2003-12 **Lindenau GmbH Schiffswerft u. Maschinenfabrik — Kiel** Yd No: 264 Loa 116.87 (BB) Br ex - Dght 7.415 Lbp 110.40 Br md 18.00 Dpth 9.40 Welded, 1 dk	**(A12B2TR) Chemical/Products Tanker** Double Hull (13F) Liq: 8,564; Liq (Oil): 8,564 Compartments: 14 Wing Ta, 2 Wing Slop Ta, ER 16 Cargo Pump (s): 14x200m^3/hr, 2x300m^3/hr Manifold: Bow/CM: 60.1m Ice Capable	**2 oil engines** geared to sc. shafts driving 2 CP propellers Total Power: 3,600kW (4,894hp) 15.0k MAN-B&W 6L27/3 2 x 4 Stroke 6 Cy. 270 x 380 each-1800kW (2447bhp) MAN B&W Diesel A/S-Denmark AuxGen: 3 x 378kW 400/230V 50Hz a.c, 2 x 420kW 400/230V 50Hz a.c Thrusters: 1 Tunnel thruster (f) Fuel: 109.0 (d.f.) 499.0 (r.f.)
9365245 *A8XH9* -	**WAPPEN VON DRESDEN** **Schiffahrtsgesellschaft Wappen von Dresden mbH & Co KG** Poseidon Schiffahrt GmbH *Monrovia* *Liberia* MMSI: 636092141 Official number: 92141	**5,200** 2,530 8,211 T/cm 18.0	Class: NK (AB) (GL)	2007-08 **Santierul Naval Damen Galati S.A. — Galati** Yd No: 1109 Loa 116.89 (BB) Br ex - Dght 7.415 Lbp 110.40 Br md 18.00 Dpth 9.40 Welded, 1 dk	**(A12B2TR) Chemical/Products Tanker** Double Hull (13F) Liq: 8,564; Liq (Oil): 8,564 Cargo Heating Coils 16 Cargo Pump (s): 14x200m^3/hr, 2x300m^3/hr Ice Capable	**2 oil engines** reduction geared to sc. shafts driving 2 CP propellers Total Power: 2,648kW (3,600hp) 14.0k MAN-B&W 6L27/3 2 x 4 Stroke 6 Cy. 270 x 380 each-1324kW (1800bhp) MAN Diesel A/S-Denmark AuxGen: 2 x 492kW 400/230V a.c, 2 x 380kW 400/230V a.c Thrusters: 1 Tunnel thruster (f)
9365269 *2AXH2* -	**WAPPEN VON FLENSBURG** **Schiffahrtsgesellschaft Wappen von Flensburg mbH & Co KG** North Sea Tankers BV *London* *United Kingdom* MMSI: 235063697	**5,200** 2,530 8,154 T/cm 18.0	Class: GL NK	2008-12 **Santierul Naval Damen Galati S.A. — Galati** Yd No: 1111 Loa 116.90 (BB) Br ex - Dght 7.415 Lbp 110.40 Br md 18.00 Dpth 9.40 Welded, 1 dk	**(A12B2TR) Chemical/Products Tanker** Double Hull (13F) Liq: 8,586; Liq (Oil): 8,586 Cargo Heating Coils Compartments: 14 Wing Ta, 2 Wing Slop Ta, ER 14 Cargo Pump (s): 12x200m^3/hr, 2x300m^3/hr Manifold: Bow/CM: 60m	**2 oil engines** reduction geared to sc. shafts driving 2 CP propellers Total Power: 3,600kW (4,894hp) 15.0k MAN-B&W 6L27/3 2 x 4 Stroke 6 Cy. 270 x 380 each-1800kW (2447bhp) MAN Diesel A/S-Denmark AuxGen: 1 x 492kW 400V a.c, 2 x 378kW 400V a.c Thrusters: 1 Tunnel thruster (f) Fuel: 109.0 (d.f.) 468.0 (r.f.)
9274537 *A8XB9* -	**WAPPEN VON FRANKFURT** **Schiffahrtsgesellschaft Wappen von Frankfurt mbH & Co KG** Poseidon Schiffahrt GmbH *Monrovia* *Liberia* MMSI: 636092112 Official number: 92112	**5,145** 2,532 8,182 T/cm 18.0	Class: GL NK	2005-12 **Santierul Naval Damen Galati S.A. — Galati** Yd No: 1059 Loa 116.90 (BB) Br ex 18.20 Dght 7.415 Lbp 110.40 Br md 18.00 Dpth 9.40 Welded, 1 dk	**(A12B2TR) Chemical/Products Tanker** Double Hull (13F) Liq: 8,564; Liq (Oil): 8,564 Cargo Heating Coils Compartments: 14 Wing Ta, 2 Wing Slop Ta, ER 16 Cargo Pump (s): 2x300m^3/hr, 14x200m^3/hr Manifold: Bow/CM: 60.1m Ice Capable	**2 oil engines** reduction geared to sc. shafts driving 2 CP propellers Total Power: 4,080kW (5,548hp) 15.0k MAN-B&W 6L27/3 2 x 4 Stroke 6 Cy. 270 x 380 each-2040kW (2774bhp) MAN B&W Diesel A/S-Denmark Thrusters: 1 Tunnel thruster (f)
9255799 *A8XB3* -	**WAPPEN VON HAMBURG** **Schiffahrtsgesellschaft Wappen von Hamburg mbH & Co KG** Poseidon Schiffahrt GmbH *Monrovia* *Liberia* MMSI: 636092106 Official number: 92106	**5,145** 2,532 8,241 T/cm 18.5	Class: GL	2002-11 **Santierul Naval Damen Galati S.A. — Galati** (Hull) Yd No: 987 2002-11 **Lindenau GmbH Schiffswerft u. Maschinenfabrik — Kiel** Yd No: 260 Loa 116.90 (BB) Br ex - Dght 7.415 Lbp 110.40 Br md 18.00 Dpth 9.40 Welded, 1 Dk.	**(A12B2TR) Chemical/Products Tanker** Double Hull (13F) Liq: 8,593; Liq (Oil): 8,593 Cargo Heating Coils Compartments: 14 Wing Ta, 2 Wing Slop Ta, ER 14 Cargo Pump (s): 14x200m^3/hr Manifold: Bow/CM: 60.1m Ice Capable	**2 oil engines** geared to sc. shafts driving 2 CP propellers Total Power: 3,600kW (4,894hp) 15.0k MAN-B&W 6L27/3 2 x 4 Stroke 6 Cy. 270 x 380 each-1800kW (2447bhp) MAN B&W Diesel A/S-Denmark AuxGen: 3 x 378kW 50Hz a.c, 2 x 420kW 400/230V 50Hz a.c Thrusters: 1 Thwart. FP thruster (f) Fuel: 109.0 (d.f.) 499.0 (r.f.)
9260847 *A8XB8* -	**WAPPEN VON LEIPZIG** **Schiffahrtsgesellschaft Wappen von Leipzig mbH & Co KG** Wappen Hamburg Shipping Co Ltd *Monrovia* *Liberia* MMSI: 636092111 Official number: 92111	**5,145** 2,532 8,230 T/cm 18.0	Class: NK (GL)	2004-02 **Santierul Naval Damen Galati S.A. — Galati** (Hull) Yd No: 992 2004-02 **Lindenau GmbH Schiffswerft u. Maschinenfabrik — Kiel** Yd No: 265 Loa 116.85 (BB) Br ex - Dght 7.414 Lbp 110.40 Br md 18.00 Dpth 9.40 Welded, 1 dk	**(A12B2TR) Chemical/Products Tanker** Double Hull (13F) Liq: 8,594; Liq (Oil): 8,594 Cargo Heating Coils Compartments: 14 Wing Ta, 2 Wing Slop Ta, ER 16 Cargo Pump (s): 14x200m^3/hr, 2x300m^3/hr Manifold: Bow/CM: 60.1m Ice Capable	**2 oil engines** geared to sc. shafts driving 2 CP propellers Total Power: 3,600kW (4,894hp) 14.5k MAN-B&W 6L27/3 2 x 4 Stroke 6 Cy. 270 x 380 each-1800kW (2447bhp) MAN B&W Diesel A/S-Denmark AuxGen: 3 x 473kW 400/230V 50Hz a.c, 2 x 525kW 50Hz a.c Thrusters: 1 Tunnel thruster (f) Fuel: 109.0 (d.f.) 499.0 (r.f.)
9255816 *A8XB5* -	**WAPPEN VON MUNCHEN** **Schiffahrtsgesellschaft Wappen von Munchen mbH & Co KG** Poseidon Schiffahrt GmbH *Monrovia* *Liberia* MMSI: 636092108 Official number: 92108	**5,145** 2,732 8,266 T/cm 18.0	Class: NK (AB) (GL)	2003-05 **Santierul Naval Damen Galati S.A. — Galati** (Hull) Yd No: 989 2003-05 **Lindenau GmbH Schiffswerft u. Maschinenfabrik — Kiel** Yd No: 262 Loa 116.83 (BB) Br ex - Dght 7.415 Lbp 110.40 Br md 18.00 Dpth 9.40 Welded, 1 dk	**(A12B2TR) Chemical/Products Tanker** Double Hull (13F) Liq: 8,922; Liq (Oil): 8,564 Cargo Heating Coils Compartments: 14 Wing Ta, 2 Wing Slop Ta, ER 16 Cargo Pump (s): 14x200m^3/hr, 2x300m^3/hr Manifold: Bow/CM: 60.1m Ice Capable	**2 oil engines** geared to sc. shafts driving 2 CP propellers Total Power: 3,600kW (4,894hp) 15.0k MAN-B&W 6L27/3 2 x 4 Stroke 6 Cy. 270 x 380 each-1800kW (2447bhp) MAN B&W Diesel A/S-Denmark AuxGen: 3 x 378kW 50Hz a.c, 2 x 420kW 400/230V 50Hz a.c Thrusters: 1 Tunnel thruster (f) Fuel: 109.0 (d.f.) 499.0 (r.f.)
7935395 *DCUP* -	**WAPPEN VON NORDERNEY** *ex* Wappen von Eckernforde *-1980* *ex* Donald Duck *-1980* *launched as* Frisia XII *-1967* **AG Reederei Norden-Frisia** Cassen-Tours GmbH *Norderney* *Germany* MMSI: 211217800 Official number: 4916	**154** 64 -	Class: GL	1967 **C Cassens Schiffswerft — Emden** Yd No: 84 Widened-1980 Loa 31.12 Br ex 7.04 Dght 0.991 Lbp 28.45 Br md 7.03 Dpth 1.65 Welded, 1 dk	**(A37B2PS) Passenger Ship** Passengers: unberthed: 220 Ice Capable	**2 oil engines** reverse reduction geared to sc. shafts driving 2 FP propellers Total Power: 530kW (720hp) 12.5k Volvo Penta TAMD122 2 x 4 Stroke 6 Cy. 130 x 150 each-265kW (360bhp) (new engine 1993) AB Volvo Penta-Sweden AuxGen: 1 x 24kW 380/220V a.c
9365257 *D5DZ6* -	**WAPPEN VON NURNBERG** **Schiffahrtsgesellschaft Wappen von Nuernberg mbH & Co KG** RHL Hamburger Lloyd Tanker GmbH & Co KG *Monrovia* *Liberia* MMSI: 636092495 Official number: 92495	**5,200** 2,541 8,157 T/cm 18.0	Class: NK (AB) (GL)	2007-12 **Santierul Naval Damen Galati S.A. — Galati** Yd No: 1110 Loa 116.90 (BB) Br ex - Dght 7.430 Lbp 110.40 Br md 18.00 Dpth 9.40 Welded, 1 dk	**(A12B2TR) Chemical/Products Tanker** Double Hull (13F) Liq: 8,593; Liq (Oil): 8,593 Cargo Heating Coils Compartments: 14 Wing Ta, 2 Wing Slop Ta, Wing ER 14 Cargo Pump (s): 2x300m^3/hr, 12x200m^3/hr Manifold: Bow/CM: 60m Ice Capable	**2 oil engines** reduction geared to sc. shafts driving 2 CP propellers Total Power: 3,600kW (4,894hp) 14.0k MAN-B&W 6L27/3 2 x 4 Stroke 6 Cy. 270 x 380 each-1800kW (2447bhp) MAN Diesel A/S-Denmark AuxGen: 2 x 492kW 380/220V 50Hz a.c, 2 x 378kW 380/220V 50Hz a.c Thrusters: 1 Tunnel thruster (f) Fuel: 109.0 (d.f.) 468.0 (r.f.)
9274549 *A8XC2* -	**WAPPEN VON STUTTGART** **Schiffahrtsgesellschaft Wappen von Stuttgart mbH & Co KG** Poseidon Schiffahrt GmbH *Monrovia* *Liberia* MMSI: 636092113 Official number: 92113	**5,145** 2,532 8,184 T/cm 18.0	Class: AB (Class contemplated) GL NK	2006-05 **Santierul Naval Damen Galati S.A. — Galati** Yd No: 1060 Loa 116.89 (BB) Br ex 18.20 Dght 7.415 Lbp 110.40 Br md 18.00 Dpth 9.40 Welded, 1 dk	**(A12B2TR) Chemical/Products Tanker** Double Hull (13F) Liq: 8,564; Liq (Oil): 8,564 Cargo Heating Coils Compartments: 14 Wing Ta, 2 Wing Slop Ta, ER 14 Cargo Pump (s): 12x200m^3/hr, 2x300m^3/hr Manifold: Bow/CM: 60.1m Ice Capable	**2 oil engines** reduction geared to sc. shafts driving 2 CP propellers Total Power: 4,080kW (5,548hp) 15.0k MAN-B&W 6L27/3 2 x 4 Stroke 6 Cy. 270 x 380 each-2040kW (2774bhp) MAN B&W Diesel A/S-Denmark AuxGen: 3 x 378kW 400/230V 50Hz a.c, 2 x 428kW 400/230V 50Hz a.c Thrusters: 1 Tunnel thruster (f) Fuel: 109.0 (d.f.) 499.0 (r.f.)
9009322 *WDB7881* -	**WAR ADMIRAL** *ex* H. O. S. War Admiral *-1996* *ex* Mr. Vick *-1994* **Point Marine LLC** Tidewater Marine International Inc *Wilmington, DE* *United States of America* MMSI: 368164000 Official number: 975924	**1,105** 331 1,200	Class: AB	1991-07 **Halter Marine, Inc. — Lockport, La** Yd No: 1243 Loa 67.06 Br ex - Dght 4.110 Lbp 60.44 Br md 13.41 Dpth 4.88 Welded	**(B21A20S) Platform Supply Ship**	**2 oil engines** geared to sc. shafts driving 2 FP propellers Total Power: 2,868kW (3,900hp) 12.0k EMD (Electro-Motive) 16-645-E 2 x Vee 2 Stroke 16 Cy. 230 x 254 each-1434kW (1950bhp) General Motors Detroit DieselAllison Divn-USA
9636321 *XYUA* -	**WAR NATE ZA** **Thuriya Sandar Win Co Ltd** - *Yangon* *Myanmar* Official number: 6531A	**1,120** 824 -		2011-01 **Myanma Port Authority — Yangon (Theinphyu Dockyard)** Yd No: 32MPA Loa 65.24 Br ex 18.29 Dght - Lbp - Br md 18.00 Dpth 3.66 Welded, 1 dk	**(A35D2RL) Landing Craft** Bow ramp (centre)	**2 oil engines** reduction geared to sc. shafts driving 2 Propellers Total Power: 1,986kW (2,700hp) Nissan RH1 2 x Vee 4 Stroke 10 Cy. 135 x 125 each-993kW (1350bhp) Nissan Diesel Motor Co. Ltd.-Ageo

232266 *KCL*	**WARA** **Kuwait Oil Co KSC** - *Kuwait* *Kuwait* MMSI: 447093000 Official number: KT1665	**499** 149 319	Class: LR ✠ **100A1** SS 07/2012 oil recovery ship Kuwait Harbour service ✠ **LMC** Eq.Ltr: J; Cable: 357.5/26.0 U2 (a)	**2002-07 Kuwait Shipbuilding & Repair Yard Co. — Kuwait** Yd No: 1182 Loa 33.00 Br ex 11.42 Dght 3.550 Lbp 30.60 Br md 11.00 Dpth 5.00 Welded, 1 dk	**(B34G2SE) Pollution Control Vessel** Compartments: 2 Ta, ER	**2 oil engines** with clutches, flexible couplings & sr reverse geared to sc. shafts driving 2 CP propellers Total Power: 1,740kW (2,366hp) 10.0kn Deutz TBD620BV8 2 x Vee 4 Stroke 8 Cy. 170 x 195 each-870kW (1183bhp) Deutz AG-Koeln AuxGen: 2 x 256kW 440V 50Hz a.c Boilers: TOH (o.f.) 10.2kgf/cm² (10.0bar) Thrusters: 1 Thwart. FP thruster (f) Fuel: 91.0 (d.f.)
626642 *B5215*	**WARA MARU** *ex* Daikoku Maru *-2004* **PT Sarana Lintas Bahari** - *Surabaya* *Indonesia*	*676* 276 686	Class: KI	**1985-07 K.K. Kamishima Zosensho — Osakikamijima** Yd No: 170 Loa 55.60 Br ex - Dght 3.170 Lbp 51.00 Br md 9.40 Dpth 5.40 Welded, 1 dk	**(A31A2GX) General Cargo Ship**	**1 oil engine** driving 1 FP propeller Total Power: 368kW (500hp) 11.0kn Niigata 6M26AGT 1 x 4 Stroke 6 Cy. 260 x 460 368kW (500bhp) Niigata Engineering Co Ltd-Japan
984915 *2V5475*	**WARANGOI** *ex* Anes *-2011* *ex* Niaga Jaya IX *-2005* **East New Britain Port Services Pty Ltd** - *Port Moresby* *Papua New Guinea* MMSI: 553111637	**907** 273 263	Class: RI (KI)	**2003-01 Galangan Kapal Tunas Harapan — Samarinda** Loa 67.34 Br ex - Dght 2.780 Lbp 64.64 Br md 13.60 Dpth 3.68 Welded, 1 dk	**(A35D2RL) Landing Craft** Bow ramp (centre)	**2 oil engines** geared to sc. shafts driving 2 Propellers Total Power: 942kW (1,280hp) 7.5kn Yanmar 6LAHM-STE3 2 x 4 Stroke 6 Cy. 150 x 165 each-471kW (640bhp) (made 2000) Yanmar Diesel Engine Co Ltd-Japan
093842	**WARAO** *ex* Houston Pilot No. 3 *-2006* **Aquamar SA** -	**133** 91 -		**1970-01 Weaver Shipyards — Orange, Tx** Yd No: S160 Converted From: Pilot Vessel-2006 L reg 26.00 Br ex - Dght - Lbp - Br md 6.30 Dpth 2.80 Welded, 1 dk	**(B31A2SR) Research Survey Vessel**	**2 oil engines** geared to sc. shafts driving 2 Propellers Total Power: 1,692kW (2,300hp) 17.0kn Caterpillar 2 x 4 Stroke each-846kW (1150bhp) Caterpillar Tractor Co-USA
458729	**WARATAB** **Sea Ports Corp** - *Port Sudan* *Sudan*	**269** 80 202	Class: (LR) ✠ Classed LR until 28/7/10	**2008-09 Santierul Naval Damen Galati S.A. — Galati** (Hull) Yd No: 1141 **2008-09 B.V. Scheepswerf Damen — Gorinchem** Yd No: 511617 Loa 29.24 Br ex 8.85 Dght 3.630 Lbp 26.63 Br md 8.80 Dpth 4.60 Welded, 1 dk	**(B32A2ST) Tug**	**2 oil engines** with flexible couplings & reduction geared to sc. shafts driving 2 FP propellers Total Power: 1,920kW (2,610hp) MAN-B&W 6L23/30A 2 x 4 Stroke 6 Cy. 225 x 300 each-960kW (1305bhp) MAN Diesel A/S-Denmark AuxGen: 2 x 80kW 400V 50Hz a.c Thrusters: 1 Thwart. FP thruster (f)
119070 *UA2769*	**WARAY I** *ex* Waray *-2006* *ex* Gyokuho Maru *-1998* *ex* Ryokai Maru *-1991* *ex* Shinkashima No. 5 *-1989* **Malayan Towage & Salvage Corp (SALVTUG)** - *Manila* *Philippines* Official number: 00-0000233	*207* 122 -		**1970 Ishikawajima Ship & Chemical Plant Co Ltd — Tokyo** Yd No: 408 Loa 28.30 Br ex 8.64 Dght 2.591 Lbp 25.02 Br md 8.62 Dpth 3.48 Welded, 1 dk	**(B32A2ST) Tug**	**2 oil engines** gearing integral to driving 2 Z propellers Total Power: 810kW (1,102hp) 11.0kn Fuji 6MD27.5CH 2 x 4 Stroke 6 Cy. 275 x 320 each-405kW (551bhp) Fuji Diesel Co Ltd-Japan
579858 *6E2705*	**WARAYA** **Liwa Marine Services LLC** - *Abu Dhabi* *United Arab Emirates* MMSI: 470543000 Official number: 6208	**1,070** 576 1,527	Class: AB	**2010-07 Josefa Slipways Inc — Manila** Yd No: 009 Loa 65.60 Br ex 14.80 Dght 3.000 Lbp 61.00 Br md 14.20 Dpth 4.25 Welded, 1 dk	**(A35D2RL) Landing Craft** Bow ramp (centre)	**2 oil engines** reduction geared to sc. shafts driving 2 FP propellers Total Power: 1,066kW (1,450hp) Caterpillar C18 2 x 4 Stroke 6 Cy. 145 x 183 each-533kW (725bhp) Caterpillar Inc-USA AuxGen: 2 x 69kW a.c
334117	**WARBA** **Government of The State of Kuwait (Ministry of Interior)** - *Kuwait* *Kuwait*	**610** 183 320	Class: (LR) ✠ Classed LR until 20/2/07	**2005-11 Singapore Technologies Marine Ltd — Singapore** Yd No: 610 Loa 49.00 Br ex 12.10 Dght 1.989 Lbp 44.23 Br md 11.80 Dpth 2.80 Welded, 1 dk	**(A35D2RL) Landing Craft** Bow ramp (centre) Len: 2.40 Wid: 5.00 Swl: -	**2 oil engines** with clutches, flexible couplings & reduction geared to sc. shafts driving 2 FP propellers Total Power: 1,908kW (2,594hp) Caterpillar 3512B 2 x Vee 4 Stroke 12 Cy. 170 x 190 each-954kW (1297bhp) Caterpillar Inc-USA AuxGen: 1 x 250kW 415V 50Hz a.c, 2 x 200kW 415V 50Hz a.c Thrusters: 1 Water jet (f)
376127	**WARBABY FOX** **Government of Bermuda (Department of Marine & Ports Services)** - *Hamilton* *Bermuda (British)*	**317** 124 30	Class: LR ✠ **100A1** SS 08/2011 SSC passenger, catamaran HSC G2 Bermuda service **LMC** Cable: 10.0/12.0 U2 (a)	**2006-08 Robert E Derecktor of Connecticut LLC — Bridgeport CT** Yd No: 85025 Loa 37.80 Br ex 9.30 Dght 1.400 Lbp 35.80 Br md 9.00 Dpth 2.81 Welded, 1 dk	**(A37B2PS) Passenger Ship** Passengers: unberthed: 353	**4 oil engines** with clutches & geared to sc. shafts driving 4 Water jets Total Power: 3,152kW (4,284hp) 33.0kn M.T.U. 12V2000M70 4 x Vee 4 Stroke 12 Cy. 130 x 150 each-788kW (1071bhp) MTU Friedrichshafen GmbH-Friedrichshafen AuxGen: 2 x 65kW 208V 60Hz a.c
467201 *LF*	**WARBER** **A Visser, M Bakker & F Wink** Wijnne & Barends Cargadoors - en Agentuurkantoren BV SatCom: Inmarsat C 424524110 *Lemmer* *Netherlands* MMSI: 245241000 Official number: 52789	**2,862** 1,433 4,114	Class: BV (LR) ✠ Classed LR until 14/10/11	**2010-08 Zhejiang Hexing Shipyard — Wenling ZJ** Yd No: 06-004 Loa 94.70 Br ex 13.44 Dght 5.690 Lbp 91.35 Br md 13.40 Dpth 7.80 Welded, 1 dk	**(A31A2GX) General Cargo Ship** Grain: 5,507 TEU 60 on dk Compartments: 1 Ho, ER 1 Ha: ER (61.6 x 11.2) Ice Capable	**1 oil engine** with flexible couplings & sr geared to sc. shaft driving 1 CP propeller Total Power: 2,010kW (2,733hp) 13.0kn MaK 6M25C 1 x 4 Stroke 6 Cy. 255 x 400 2010kW (2733bhp) Caterpillar Motoren GmbH & Co. KG-Germany AuxGen: 2 x 140kW 400V 50Hz a.c, 1 x 312kW 400V 50Hz a.c Boilers: TOH (o.f.) 10.2kgf/cm² (10.0bar), TOH (ex.g.) 10.2kgf/cm² (10.0bar) Thrusters: 1 Tunnel thruster (f)
01077 *RQ2*	**WARD TIDE** *ex* SK Line 55 *-2011* **Platinum Fleet Ltd** Tidewater Marine LLC *Port Vila* *Vanuatu* MMSI: 577003000 Official number: 2073	**1,674** 502 1,343	Class: AB	**2011-10 Fujian Southeast Shipyard — Fuzhou FJ** Yd No: SK55 Loa 59.25 Br ex - Dght 4.950 Lbp 52.20 Br md 14.95 Dpth 6.10 Welded, 1 dk	**(B21B20A) Anchor Handling Tug Supply**	**2 oil engines** reduction geared to sc. shafts driving 2 CP propellers Total Power: 3,840kW (5,220hp) 11.0kn Caterpillar 3516B-HD 2 x Vee 4 Stroke 16 Cy. 170 x 215 each-1920kW (2610bhp) Caterpillar Inc-USA AuxGen: 2 x 800kW a.c, 2 x 350kW a.c Thrusters: 1 Tunnel thruster (f) Fuel: 520.0
23022	**WARDA** *ex* Sin Ching Mou No. 22 *-1978* **MAPEX** - *Casablanca* *Morocco* Official number: 6-728	*268* 144 -		**1972 Kaohsiung Shipbuilding Co. Ltd. — Kaohsiung** Loa 33.51 Br ex - Dght - Lbp - Br md 7.03 Dpth 3.03 Welded, 1 dk	**(B11B2FV) Fishing Vessel**	**1 oil engine** driving 1 FP propeller Total Power: 736kW (1,001hp)
30759 *Z2737*	**WARDAH** *ex* Marathi *-2013* *ex* Sea Rose I *-2007* *ex* Rose *-2003* *ex* Neptra Pioneer *-1995* **Med Trust Marine Ltd** National Bunkering Co Ltd *Jeddah* *Saudi Arabia* MMSI: 403211200 Official number: 36210PEXT2	**2,611** 1,576 4,674 T/cm 11.5	Class: NV (BV) (NK)	**1992-08 Atlantis Engineering & Construction Pte Ltd — Singapore** Yd No: 1007 Loa 85.76 Br ex - Dght 5.910 Lbp 81.34 Br md 15.80 Dpth 7.20 Welded, 1 dk	**(A13B2TP) Products Tanker** Single Hull Liq: 5,000; Liq (Oil): 5,000 2 Cargo Pump (s)	**1 oil engine** reverse reduction geared to sc. shaft driving 1 FP propeller Total Power: 2,060kW (2,801hp) 12.0kn Yanmar 6N330-EN 1 x 4 Stroke 6 Cy. 330 x 440 2060kW (2801bhp) Yanmar Diesel Engine Co Ltd-Japan AuxGen: 3 x 118kW a.c
08285 *OUS*	**WARDEH** *ex* Jaikur I *-2007* *ex* Tablat *-2007* **Khalifeh Shipping Line Co** - SatCom: Inmarsat C 445052210 *Beirut* *Lebanon* MMSI: 450522000 Official number: B-4330	**8,393** 1,125 3,516	Class: IS (BV)	**1978-08 Towa Zosen K.K. — Shimonoseki** Yd No: 501 Converted From: Ro-Ro Cargo Ship-2007 Loa 131.02 (BB) Br ex 18.52 Dght 6.219 Lbp 120.02 Br md 18.01 Dpth 13.49 Welded, 2 dks	**(A38A2GL) Livestock Carrier** 1 Ha: (10.5 x 5.4)ER	**2 oil engines** geared to sc. shafts driving 2 CP propellers Total Power: 8,826kW (12,000hp) 21.8kn Pielstick 12PC2-2V-400 2 x Vee 4 Stroke 12 Cy. 400 x 460 each-4413kW (6000bhp) Nippon Kokan KK (NKK Corp)-Japan Thrusters: 1 Thwart. FP thruster (f)

IMO / Call sign / Flag	Name, owner, manager, port	Tonnage	Classification	Build / Dimensions	Type	Machinery
9553921 *VJG4093* -	**WAREE** *ex* Asd 512259 *-2012* **Government of The Commonwealth of Australia (Department of Defence)** DMS Maritime Pty Ltd *Sydney, NSW* *Australia* MMSI: 503702700 Official number: 860451	**250** 75 126	Class: LR ✠ **100A1** SS 10/2012 tug *IWS **LMC** **UMS** Eq.Ltr: F; Cable: 275.0/19.0 U2 (a)	**2012-10 Song Thu Co. — Da Nang** (Hull) Yd No: (512259) **2012-10 B.V. Scheepswerf Damen — Gorinchem** Yd No: 512259 Loa 24.47 Br ex 11.33 Dght 3.600 Lbp 22.16 Br md 10.70 Dpth 4.60 Welded, 1 dk	**(B32A2ST) Tug**	**2 oil engines** gearing integral to driving 2 Z propellers Total Power: 4,200kW (5,710hp) Caterpillar 3516B-H 2 x Vee 4 Stroke 16 Cy. 170 x 215 each-2100kW (2855bhp) Caterpillar Inc-USA AuxGen: 2 x 60kW 400V 50Hz a.c
7330789 *YDHH* -	**WAREMBUNGAN** *ex* Harrier *-1985* *ex* Yufukujin Maru *-1982* **PT Citra Bintang Familindo** - *Jakarta* *Indonesia* MMSI: 525015372	**1,272** 638 2,200	Class: (KI)	**1973-09 Hakata Zosen K.K. — Imabari** Yd No: 135 Loa 77.70 Br ex 12.04 Dght 5.106 Lbp 73.97 Br md 12.02 Dpth 5.49 Riveted\Welded, 1 dk	**(A13B2TP) Products Tanker**	**1 oil engine** driving 1 FP propeller Total Power: 1,471kW (2,000hp) Hanshin 6LU3 1 x 4 Stroke 6 Cy. 380 x 580 1471kW (2000bhp) Hanshin Nainenki Kogyo-Japan
9672351 *POYG* -	**WARIH MAS** *ex* Boda 2 *-2013* - - *Indonesia* MMSI: 525019100	**6,640** 3,718 8,180	Class: (CC)	**2012-11 Ningbo Boda Shipbuilding Co Ltd — Xiangshan County ZJ** Yd No: BD1202 Loa 119.90 (BB) Br ex - Dght 5.200 Lbp 115.00 Br md 21.80 Dpth 7.30 Welded, 1 dk	**(A33A2CC) Container Ship (Fully Cellular)** TEU 537	**1 oil engine** reduction geared to sc. shaft driving 1 FP propeller Total Power: 2,060kW (2,801hp) 10.5k Thrusters: 1 Tunnel thruster (f)
8340365 - -	**WARINGIN LESTARI** *ex* Bintang 24 *-1994* **PT Pelayaran Bina Usaha Surya** - *Jakarta* *Indonesia*	*173* 80 200	Class: KI	**1976 P.T. Menara — Tegal** Loa - Br ex - Dght - Lbp 32.52 Br md 6.80 Dpth 2.49 Welded, 1 dk	**(A31A2GX) General Cargo Ship**	**1 oil engine** driving 1 FP propeller Total Power: 221kW (300hp) Deutz BF6M71 1 x Vee 4 Stroke 6 Cy. 135 x 160 221kW (300bhp) Kloeckner Humboldt Deutz AG-West Germany
9027829 *YB6037* -	**WARINGIN SURYA** *ex* Mentaren *-1993* *ex* Flobamora *-1991* **PT Pelayaran Bina Usaha Surya** - *Surabaya* *Indonesia*	**194** 115 -	Class: (KI)	**1977-01 PT Mahakam Baja Utama — Samarinda** L reg 39.00 Br ex - Dght - Lbp 37.75 Br md 7.20 Dpth 2.00 Welded, 1 dk	**(A31A2GX) General Cargo Ship**	**1 oil engine** geared to sc. shaft driving 1 Propeller Total Power: 202kW (275hp) Caterpillar 340 1 x 4 Stroke 6 Cy. 137 x 165 202kW (275bhp) Caterpillar Tractor Co-USA
9343417 *HSRW* -	**WARISA NAREE** *ex* Good Pride *-2013* **Precious Ponds Ltd** Great Circle Shipping Agency Ltd *Bangkok* *Thailand* MMSI: 567105000	**32,661** 18,210 53,840 T/cm 57.3	Class: LR (IR) (NV) **100A1** SS 04/2010 bulk carrier BC-A Nos. 2 & 4 holds or No. 3 hold may be empty with cargo in other holds of maximum density 1.35t/m3 inner bottom strengthened for regular discharge by heavy grabs ESP ESN *IWS LI **LMC** **UMS**	**2010-04 Hindustan Shipyard Ltd — Visakhapatnam** Yd No: 11136 Loa 190.02 (BB) Br ex 32.32 Dght 12.630 Lbp 183.04 Br md 32.26 Dpth 17.50 Welded, 1 dk	**(A21A2BC) Bulk Carrier** Double Hull Grain: 65,900; Bale: 64,000 Compartments: 5 Ho, ER 5 Ha: 4 (21.6 x 22.4)ER (19.2 x 20.8) Cranes: 4x36t	**1 oil engine** driving 1 FP propeller Total Power: 9,720kW (13,215hp) 14.2k Wartsila 6RT-flex5 1 x 2 Stroke 6 Cy. 500 x 2050 9720kW (13215bhp) Diesel United Ltd.-Aioi AuxGen: 3 x 645kW a.c Fuel: 200.0 (d.f.) 2000.0 (r.f.) 34.5pd
9375070 *9MFD7* -	**WARISAN ALAM** *ex* Sterlink Valiant *-2007* **Warisan Alam Enterprise Sdn Bhd** Gagasan Offshore Fleet Sdn Bhd *Port Klang* *Malaysia* MMSI: 533000155 Official number: 332365	**226** 68 -	Class: BV	**2006-04 NGV Tech Sdn Bhd — Telok Panglima Garang** Yd No: 1027 Loa 34.00 Br ex - Dght 1.800 Lbp 32.00 Br md 7.85 Dpth 3.30 Welded, 1 dk	**(B21A2OC) Crew/Supply Vessel** Hull Material: Aluminium Alloy Passengers: unberthed: 50	**3 oil engines** reduction geared to sc. shafts driving 3 FP propellers Total Power: 3,018kW (4,104hp) 18.0k Cummins KTA-38-M 3 x Vee 4 Stroke 12 Cy. 159 x 159 each-1006kW (1368bhp) Cummins Engine Co Ltd-United Kingdom AuxGen: 2 x 75kW 415/220V 50Hz a.c Thrusters: 1 Tunnel thruster (f)
9529384 *9MID8* -	**WARISAN GEMILANG** **Warisan Alam Enterprise Sdn Bhd** Malayan Energistik Solutions Sdn Bhd *Port Klang* *Malaysia* MMSI: 533983000 Official number: 333969	**226** 67 -	Class: BV	**2008-11 NGV Tech Sdn Bhd — Telok Panglima Garang** Yd No: 1119 Loa 34.00 Br ex - Dght 1.500 Lbp 31.93 Br md 7.85 Dpth 3.30 Welded, 1 dk	**(B21A2OC) Crew/Supply Vessel** Hull Material: Aluminium Alloy	**3 oil engines** reduction geared to sc. shafts driving 3 FP propellers Total Power: 3,198kW (4,347hp) 25.0k Cummins KTA-38-M 3 x Vee 4 Stroke 12 Cy. 159 x 159 each-1066kW (1449bhp) Cummins Engine Co Ltd-United Kingdom
9353668 *HSCW* -	**WARIYA NAREE** *ex* Good Precedent *-2013* **Precious Comets Ltd** Great Circle Shipping Agency Ltd *Thailand* MMSI: 567274000	**32,661** 18,210 53,840 T/cm 57.3	Class: LR (IR) (NV) **100A1** SS 02/2011 bulk carrier BC-A Nos. 2 & 4 holds may be empty or No. 3 hold may be empty with cargoes in other holds of maximum density 1.35t/m3 Inner bottom strengthened for regular discharge by heavy grabs ESP ESN *IWS LI **LMC** **UMS** Cable: 660.0/78.0 U3 (a)	**2011-02 Hindustan Shipyard Ltd — Visakhapatnam** Yd No: 11137 Loa 190.00 (BB) Br ex 32.31 Dght 12.620 Lbp 183.05 Br md 32.27 Dpth 17.52 Welded, 1 dk	**(A21A2BC) Bulk Carrier** Double Hull Grain: 65,944; Bale: 64,000 Compartments: 5 Ho, ER 5 Ha: ER Cranes: 4x36t	**1 oil engine** driving 1 FP propeller Total Power: 9,480kW (12,889hp) 14.2k Wartsila 6RT-flex5 1 x 2 Stroke 6 Cy. 500 x 2050 9480kW (12889bhp) Diesel United Ltd.-Aioi AuxGen: 3 x 645kW 450V 60Hz a.c Boilers: AuxB (Comp) 8.6kgf/cm² (8.4bar)
8519590 *CQRT* -	**WARLOCK** *ex* Maasbank *-2005* **Acamar SAS** Nuova Naviservice Srl SatCom: Inmarsat C 425599626 *Madeira* *Portugal (MAR)* MMSI: 255801360 Official number: 1292	**609** 182 358	Class: RI (AB)	**1987-05 Scheepswerf "De Waal" B.V. — Zaltbommel** Yd No: 722 Loa 37.44 Br ex - Dght 4.750 Lbp 34.07 Br md 11.02 Dpth 5.52 Welded, 1 dk	**(B21B20A) Anchor Handling Tug Supply**	**2 oil engines** sr geared to sc. shafts driving 2 CP propellers Total Power: 3,846kW (5,230hp) 14.0k Wartsila 12V2 2 x Vee 4 Stroke 12 Cy. 220 x 240 each-1923kW (2615bhp) Wartsila Diesel Oy-Finland AuxGen: 1 x 500kW a.c, 2 x 125kW a.c Thrusters: 1 Thwart. CP thruster (f)
7101360 *HQGP8* -	**WARM WIND** *ex* Tomahawk *-1989* *ex* Chevron *-1989* **Sam McCoy Shipping S de RL** - *San Lorenzo* *Honduras* Official number: L-0323437	*126* 86 -		**1956 Platzer Shipyard — Houston, Tx** Yd No: 201 Loa - Br ex 6.10 Dght - Lbp 27.08 Br md - Dpth 3.05 Welded, 1 dk	**(B34J2SD) Crew Boat**	**2 oil engines** driving 2 FP propellers Total Power: 736kW (1,000hp)
9285146 *C6TY2* -	**WARMIA** **Nero Four Shipping Ltd** Polska Zegluga Morska PP (POLSTEAM) *Nassau* *Bahamas* MMSI: 311832000 Official number: 8000882	**24,109** 12,806 38,056	Class: LR PR ✠ **100A1** SS 10/2010 bulk carrier BC-A strengthened for heavy cargoes, Nos. 2 & 4 holds may be empty ESP *IWS LI **ShipRight** (SDA, FDA, CM) Ice Class 1C FS at draught of 10.634m Max/min draughts fwd 10.634/4.19m Max/min draughts aft 10.634/6.24m Power required 3524kw, installed 7368kw ✠ **LMC** **UMS** Eq.Ltr: A†; Cable: 605.0/66.0 U3 (a)	**2005-10 Tianjin Xingang Shipyard — Tianjin** Yd No: 345-4 Loa 190.06 (BB) Br ex 28.58 Dght 10.400 Lbp 183.70 Br md 28.50 Dpth 15.10 Welded, 1 dk	**(A21A2BC) Bulk Carrier** Double Hull Grain: 49,032; Bale: 47,849 Compartments: 5 Ho, ER 5 Ha: 4 (22.4 x 18.0)ER (16.8 x 16.8) Cranes: 4x30t Ice Capable	**1 oil engine** driving 1 FP propeller Total Power: 7,368kW (10,018hp) 14.0k Sulzer 6RTA48T 1 x 2 Stroke 6 Cy. 480 x 2000 7368kW (10018bhp) Yichang Marine Diesel Engine Co Ltd-China AuxGen: 3 x 600kW 450V 60Hz a.c Boilers: WTAuxB (Comp) 9.0kgf/cm² (8.8bar)

IMO / Call sign	Name / Owner	Tonnage	Class	Builder / Dimensions	Type / Capacity	Machinery
9454838 V2DN4	**WARNOW** *ex* Blue Lion *-2013 launched as* Laga *-2009* **Roland Ship Administration GmbH & Co KG** Reederei Erwin Strahlmann eK *Saint John's* *Antigua & Barbuda* MMSI: 305264000	**4,255** 2,341 6,050	Class: GL (BV)	**2009-06 Jiangsu Changbo Shipyard Co Ltd — Jingjiang JS** (Hull) Yd No: 06-004 **2009-06 Volharding Shipyards B.V. — Foxhol** Yd No: 649 Loa 114.40 (BB) Br ex 14.50 Dght 6.040 Lbp 108.30 Br md 14.40 Dpth 8.10 Welded, 1 dk	**(A31A2GX) General Cargo Ship** Grain: 8,501 TEU 256 C Ho 144 TEU C Dk 112 TEU Compartments: 2 Ho, ER 2 Ha: (44.5 x 11.7)ER (38.2 x 11.7) Ice Capable	**1 oil engine** reduction geared to sc. shaft driving 1 CP propeller Total Power: 2,971kW (4,039hp) 12.0kn MaK 9M25C 1 x 4 Stroke 9 Cy. 255 x 400 2971kW (4039bhp) Caterpillar Motoren (Guangdong) CoLtd-China AuxGen: 2 x 188kW 380V 50Hz a.c Thrusters: 1 Tunnel thruster (f)
5386318	**WARNOW** - -	*132* 46 -	Class: (DS)	**1956 Schiffbau u. Reparaturwerft Stralsund — Stralsund** Yd No: 2009 Loa 26.45 Br ex 6.71 Dght 3.550 Lbp 23.40 Br md - Dpth 3.66 Welded, 1 dk	**(B11B2FV) Fishing Vessel** Compartments: 1 Ho, ER 1 Ha: ER Ice Capable	**1 oil engine** driving 1 FP propeller Total Power: 221kW (300hp) 8.0kn S.K.L. 1 x 4 Stroke 6 Cy. 240 x 360 221kW (300bhp) VEB Schwermaschinenbau "KarlLiebknecht" (SKL)-Magdeburg AuxGen: 2 x 14kW 110V d.c
9437127 V2DM4	**WARNOW BELUGA** *ex* Vento Di Maestrale *-2012* *ex* Warnow Beluga *-2011* **Schifffahrtskontor Warnow GmbH & Co KG ms 'Warnow Beluga'** Marlow Ship Management Deutschland GmbH & Co KG SatCom: Inmarsat C 430525810 *Saint John's* *Antigua & Barbuda* MMSI: 305258000 Official number: 4478	**15,334** 5,983 18,444	Class: GL	**2008-05 Zhejiang Ouhua Shipbuilding Co Ltd — Zhoushan ZJ** Yd No: 502 Loa 166.17 (BB) Br ex - Dght 9.500 Lbp 155.08 Br md 25.00 Dpth 14.20 Welded, 1 dk	**(A33A2CC) Container Ship (Fully Cellular)** TEU 1284 C Ho 472 TEU C Dk 812 TEU incl 390 ref C	**1 oil engine** reduction geared to sc. shaft driving 1 CP propeller Total Power: 11,120kW (15,119hp) 19.0kn MAN-B&W 8L58/64 1 x 4 Stroke 8 Cy. 580 x 640 11120kW (15119bhp) AuxGen: 3 x 1650kW a.c Thrusters: 1 Tunnel thruster (f)
9509803 5BMJ3 -	**WARNOW BOATSWAIN** **Pacific Vest Shipping Co Ltd** MCC Transport Singapore Pte Ltd SatCom: Inmarsat C 420942510 *Limassol* *Cyprus* MMSI: 209425000	**17,068** - 21,281	Class: GL	**2012-03 Zhejiang Ouhua Shipbuilding Co Ltd — Zhoushan ZJ** Yd No: 564 Loa 180.38 (BB) Br ex - Dght 9.500 Lbp 169.24 Br md 25.00 Dpth 14.20 Welded, 1 dk	**(A33A2CC) Container Ship (Fully Cellular)** TEU 1496 incl 276 ref C.	**1 oil engine** reduction geared to sc. shaft driving 1 CP propeller Total Power: 11,120kW (15,119hp) 18.5kn MAN-B&W 8L58/64CD 1 x 4 Stroke 8 Cy. 580 x 640 11120kW (15119bhp) MAN B&W Diesel AG-Augsburg AuxGen: 3 x 1665kW a.c Thrusters: 1 Tunnel thruster (f)
9437256 V2EI5	**WARNOW CARP** **Schifffahrtskontor Warnow GmbH & Co KG ms 'Warnow Carp'** COSCO Container Lines Co Ltd (COSCON) SatCom: Inmarsat C 430544010 *Saint John's* *Antigua & Barbuda* MMSI: 305440000 Official number: 4632	**9,946** 4,900 11,968	Class: GL	**2009-05 Zhejiang Ouhua Shipbuilding Co Ltd — Zhoushan ZJ** Yd No: 512 Loa 139.09 (BB) Br ex - Dght 8.800 Lbp 129.00 Br md 22.60 Dpth 11.80 Welded, 1 dk	**(A33A2CC) Container Ship (Fully Cellular)** TEU 990 incl 254 ref C.	**1 oil engine** reduction geared to sc. shaft driving 1 CP propeller Total Power: 9,600kW (13,052hp) 19.0kn MAN-B&W 8L48/60B 1 x 4 Stroke 8 Cy. 480 x 600 9600kW (13052bhp) MAN B&W Diesel AG-Augsburg AuxGen: 1 x 2000kW 450V a.c, 2 x 910kW 450V a.c Thrusters: 1 Tunnel thruster (f); 1 Tunnel thruster (f)
9449857 5BVL2 -	**WARNOW CHIEF** **Lexano Shipping Co Ltd** Marlow Navigation Co Ltd *Limassol* *Cyprus* MMSI: 209138000	**17,068** 7,036 21,191	Class: GL	**2009-10 Zhejiang Ouhua Shipbuilding Co Ltd — Zhoushan ZJ** Yd No: 524 Loa 180.36 (BB) Br ex - Dght 9.500 Lbp 169.30 Br md 25.00 Dpth 14.20 Welded, 1 dk	**(A33A2CC) Container Ship (Fully Cellular)** TEU 1496 TEU incl 276 ref C	**1 oil engine** reduction geared to sc. shaft driving 1 CP propeller Total Power: 11,202kW (15,230hp) 18.5kn MAN-B&W 8L58/64CD 1 x 4 Stroke 8 Cy. 580 x 640 11202kW (15230bhp) MAN B&W Diesel AG-Augsburg AuxGen: 3 x 1600kW 450V a.c Thrusters: 1 Tunnel thruster (f)
9395070 5BTW3 -	**WARNOW DOLPHIN** *ex* TS Kaohsiung *-2008* **Asmato Shipping Co Ltd** Marlow Ship Management Deutschland GmbH & Co KG *Limassol* *Cyprus* MMSI: 210159000 Official number: 9395070	**15,375** 5,983 18,275	Class: GL	**2007-06 Zhejiang Ouhua Shipbuilding Co Ltd — Zhoushan ZJ** Yd No: 2040 Loa 166.15 (BB) Br ex - Dght 9.500 Lbp 155.08 Br md 25.00 Dpth 14.20 Welded, 1 dk	**(A33A2CC) Container Ship (Fully Cellular)** TEU 1296 C Ho 472 C Dk 824 TEU incl 390 ref C. Cranes: 2x45t	**1 oil engine** reduction geared to sc. shaft driving 1 CP propeller Total Power: 11,200kW (15,228hp) 19.0kn MAN-B&W 8L58/64 1 x 4 Stroke 8 Cy. 580 x 640 11200kW (15228bhp) MAN B&W Diesel AG-Augsburg AuxGen: 4 x 1600kW 450/230V a.c Thrusters: 1 Tunnel thruster (f)
9594482 D5AD5 -	**WARNOW JUPITER** **Schifffahrtskontor Warnow GmbH & Co KG ms 'Warnow Jupiter'** Oriental Horizon Shipping Co Ltd *Monrovia* *Liberia* MMSI: 636092303 Official number: 92303	**22,863** 10,602 33,402	Class: GL	**2011-10 Zhejiang Ouhua Shipbuilding Co Ltd — Zhoushan ZJ** Yd No: 582 Loa 179.44 (BB) Br ex 28.23 Dght 10.800 Lbp 168.94 Br md 28.00 Dpth 15.10 Welded, 1 dk	**(A31A2GX) General Cargo Ship** Grain: 39,927; Bale: 37,490 TEU 1158 C Ho 484 TEU C Dk 674 incl 30 ref C. Compartments: 5 Ho, ER 5 Ha: 3 (25.6 x 24.4) (12.8 x 24.4)ER (12.6 x 20.4) Cranes: 4x60t	**1 oil engine** driving 1 FP propeller Total Power: 9,480kW (12,889hp) 15.0kn MAN-B&W 6S50MC-C 1 x 2 Stroke 6 Cy. 500 x 2000 9480kW (12889bhp) STX Engine Co Ltd-South Korea AuxGen: 2 x 500kW 400V 60Hz a.c, 1 x 400kW 400V 60Hz a.c Fuel: 120.0 (d.f.) 2040.0 (r.f.)
9509712 A8YQ5 -	**WARNOW MARS** **Schifffahrtskontor Warnow GmbH & Co KG ms 'Warnow Mars'** Marlow Ship Management Deutschland GmbH & Co KG *Monrovia* *Liberia* MMSI: 636092215 Official number: 92215	**22,863** 10,602 33,200	Class: GL	**2011-06 Zhejiang Ouhua Shipbuilding Co Ltd — Zhoushan ZJ** Yd No: 560 Loa 179.46 (BB) Br ex 28.23 Dght 10.800 Lbp 168.98 Br md 28.00 Dpth 15.10 Welded, 1 dk	**(A31A2GX) General Cargo Ship** Grain: 39,927; Bale: 37,490 TEU 1158 C Ho 484 TEU C Dk 674 incl 30 ref C. Compartments: 5 Ho, ER 5 Ha: 3 (25.6 x 24.4) (12.8 x 24.4)ER (12.6 x 20.4) Cranes: 4x60t	**1 oil engine** driving 1 FP propeller Total Power: 8,800kW (11,964hp) 15.0kn MAN-B&W 6S50MC-C 1 x 2 Stroke 6 Cy. 500 x 2000 8800kW (11964bhp) STX Engine Co Ltd-South Korea AuxGen: 2 x 500kW 400V 60Hz a.c, 1 x 400kW 400V 60Hz a.c Fuel: 120.0 (d.f.) 2040.0 (r.f.)
9449833 5BRD2 -	**WARNOW MASTER** **Samaria Shipping Co Ltd** MCC Transport Singapore Pte Ltd SatCom: Inmarsat C 421214510 *Limassol* *Cyprus* MMSI: 212145000 Official number: 9449833	**17,068** 7,036 21,146	Class: GL	**2009-08 Zhejiang Ouhua Shipbuilding Co Ltd — Zhoushan ZJ** Yd No: 522 Loa 180.36 (BB) Br ex - Dght 9.500 Lbp 169.30 Br md 25.00 Dpth 14.20 Welded, 1 dk	**(A33A2CC) Container Ship (Fully Cellular)** TEU 1496 incl 276 ref C.	**1 oil engine** reduction geared to sc. shaft driving 1 CP propeller Total Power: 11,120kW (15,119hp) 18.5kn MAN-B&W 8L58/64 1 x 4 Stroke 8 Cy. 580 x 640 11120kW (15119bhp) MAN B&W Diesel AG-Augsburg AuxGen: 3 x 1600kW 450V a.c Thrusters: 1 Tunnel thruster (f)
9509786 5BVK2 -	**WARNOW MATE** **Marfurie Shipping Co Ltd** MCC Transport Singapore Pte Ltd *Limassol* *Cyprus* MMSI: 209140000	**17,068** 7,036 21,200	Class: GL	**2010-01 Zhejiang Ouhua Shipbuilding Co Ltd — Zhoushan ZJ** Yd No: 562 Loa 180.36 (BB) Br ex - Dght 9.500 Lbp 169.22 Br md 25.00 Dpth 14.20 Welded, 1 dk	**(A33A2CC) Container Ship (Fully Cellular)** TEU 1496 incl 276 ref C.	**1 oil engine** reduction geared to sc. shaft driving 1 CP propeller Total Power: 11,200kW (15,228hp) 18.5kn MAN-B&W 8L58/64CD 1 x 4 Stroke 8 Cy. 580 x 640 11200kW (15228bhp) MAN B&W Diesel AG-Augsburg AuxGen: 3 x 1600kW 450V a.c Thrusters: 1 Tunnel thruster (f)
9509695 A8WI4 -	**WARNOW MERKUR** **Schifffahrtskontor Warnow GmbH & Co KG ms 'Warnow Merkur'** Marlow Ship Management Deutschland GmbH & Co KG *Monrovia* *Liberia* MMSI: 636092081 Official number: 92081	**22,863** 10,602 33,192	Class: GL	**2010-10 Zhejiang Ouhua Shipbuilding Co Ltd — Zhoushan ZJ** Yd No: 558 Loa 179.46 (BB) Br ex 28.23 Dght 10.800 Lbp 168.95 Br md 28.00 Dpth 15.10 Welded, 1 dk	**(A31A2GX) General Cargo Ship** Grain: 39,927; Bale: 37,490 TEU 1158 C Ho 484 TEU C Dk 674 incl 30 ref C. Compartments: 5 Ho, ER 5 Ha: 3 (25.6 x 24.4) (12.8 x 24.4)ER (12.6 x 20.4) Cranes: 4x60t	**1 oil engine** driving 1 FP propeller Total Power: 8,800kW (11,964hp) 15.0kn MAN-B&W 6S50MC-C 1 x 2 Stroke 6 Cy. 500 x 2000 8800kW (11964bhp) STX Engine Co Ltd-South Korea AuxGen: 2 x 500kW 400V 60Hz a.c, 1 x 400kW 400V 60Hz a.c Fuel: 120.0 (d.f.) 2040.0 (r.f.)
9509671 A8VX3 -	**WARNOW MOON** **Schifffahrtskontor Warnow GmbH & Co KG ms 'Warnow Moon'** Medstar Shipmanagement Ltd *Monrovia* *Liberia* MMSI: 636092050 Official number: 92050	**22,863** 10,602 33,299	Class: GL	**2010-07 Zhejiang Ouhua Shipbuilding Co Ltd — Zhoushan ZJ** Yd No: 556 Loa 179.42 (BB) Br ex 28.23 Dght 10.800 Lbp 168.98 Br md 28.00 Dpth 15.10 Welded, 1 dk	**(A31A2GX) General Cargo Ship** Grain: 39,927; Bale: 37,490 TEU 1158 C Ho 484 TEU C Dk 674 incl 30 ref C. Compartments: 5 Ho, ER 5 Ha: 3 (25.6 x 24.4) (12.8 x 24.4)ER (12.6 x 20.4) Cranes: 4x60t	**1 oil engine** driving 1 FP propeller Total Power: 8,800kW (11,964hp) 15.0kn MAN-B&W 6S50MC-C 1 x 2 Stroke 6 Cy. 500 x 2000 8800kW (11964bhp) STX Engine Co Ltd-South Korea AuxGen: 2 x 500kW 400V 60Hz a.c, 1 x 400kW 400V 60Hz a.c Fuel: 120.0 (d.f.) 2040.0 (r.f.)

IMO / Call sign	Name / Owner / Manager / Flag	Tonnage (GT / NT / DWT)	Class	Built / Dimensions	Type / Capacity	Machinery
9395111 *V2DD2* -	**WARNOW ORCA** *ex* APL Colima *-2012* **Schifffahrtskontor Warnow GmbH & Co KG ms 'Warnow Orca'** Marlow Ship Management Deutschland GmbH & Co KG SatCom: Inmarsat C 430517310 *Saint John's* *Antigua & Barbuda* MMSI: 305173000 Official number: 4405	**15,375** 5,983 18,270	Class: GL	**2007-11 Zhejiang Ouhua Shipbuilding Co Ltd — Zhoushan ZJ** Yd No: 2044 Loa 166.15 (BB) Br ex - Dght 9.500 Lbp 155.08 Br md 25.00 Dpth 14.20 Welded, 1 dk	**(A33A2CC) Container Ship (Fully Cellular)** TEU 1296 C Ho 472 TEU C Dk 824 TEU incl 390 ref C Cranes: 2x45t Ice Capable	**1 oil engine** reduction geared to sc. shaft driving 1 CP propeller Total Power: 11,200kW (15,228hp) 19.0k MAN-B&W 8L58/6 1 x 4 Stroke 8 Cy. 580 x 640 11200kW (15228bhp) AuxGen: 4 x 1600kW 450V 60Hz a.c Thrusters: 1 Tunnel thruster (f)
9437218 *V2DD3* -	**WARNOW PERCH** **Schifffahrtskontor Warnow GmbH & Co KG ms 'Warnow Perch'** Marlow Ship Management Deutschland GmbH & Co KG SatCom: Inmarsat C 430517410 *Saint John's* *Antigua & Barbuda* MMSI: 305174000 Official number: 4404	**9,946** 4,900 11,968	Class: GL	**2007-12 Zhejiang Ouhua Shipbuilding Co Ltd — Zhoushan ZJ** Yd No: 508 Loa 139.10 (BB) Br ex - Dght 8.800 Lbp 129.00 Br md 22.60 Dpth 11.80 Welded, 1 dk	**(A33A2CC) Container Ship (Fully Cellular)** TEU 990 incl 254 ref C.	**1 oil engine** reduction geared to sc. shaft driving 1 CP propeller Total Power: 9,600kW (13,052hp) 19.0k MAN-B&W 8L48/60 1 x 4 Stroke 8 Cy. 480 x 600 9600kW (13052bhp) MAN B&W Diesel AG-Augsburg AuxGen: 2 x 910kW 450V 60Hz a.c, 1 x 2000kW 450V 60Hz a.c Thrusters: 1 Tunnel thruster (f); 1 Tunnel thruster (f)
9437141 *V2QC8* -	**WARNOW PORPOISE** **Warnow Porpoise Shipping Co Ltd** Schifffahrtskontor Warnow GmbH & Co KG SatCom: Inmarsat C 430531310 *Saint John's* *Antigua & Barbuda* MMSI: 305313000	**15,334** 5,983 18,464	Class: GL	**2008-07 Zhejiang Ouhua Shipbuilding Co Ltd — Zhoushan ZJ** Yd No: 504 Loa 166.15 (BB) Br ex - Dght 9.500 Lbp 155.08 Br md 25.00 Dpth 14.20 Welded, 1 dk	**(A33A2CC) Container Ship (Fully Cellular)** TEU 1296 C Ho 472 TEU C Dk 824 TEU incl 390 ref C	**1 oil engine** reduction geared to sc. shaft driving 1 CP propeller Total Power: 11,200kW (15,228hp) 19.0k MAN-B&W 8L58/6 1 x 4 Stroke 8 Cy. 580 x 640 11200kW (15228bhp) MAN B&W Diesel AG-Augsburg AuxGen: 3 x 1600kW 450V a.c Thrusters: 1 Tunnel thruster (f)
9509619 *A8UH3* -	**WARNOW STAR** **Schifffahrtskontor Warnow GmbH & Co KG ms 'Warnow Star'** GB Shipping & Chartering GmbH *Monrovia* *Liberia* MMSI: 636091900 Official number: 91900	**22,863** 10,602 33,271	Class: GL	**2010-01 Zhejiang Ouhua Shipbuilding Co Ltd — Zhoushan ZJ** Yd No: 552 Loa 179.46 (BB) Br ex 28.23 Dght 10.800 Lbp 168.97 Br md 28.00 Dpth 15.10 Welded, 1 dk	**(A31A2GX) General Cargo Ship** Grain: 39,927; Bale: 37,490 TEU 1158 C Ho 484 TEU C Dk 674 incl 30 ref C. Compartments: 5 Ho, ER 5 Ha: 3 (25.6 x 24.4) (12.8 x 24.4)ER (12.6 x 20.4) Cranes: 4x60t	**1 oil engine** driving 1 FP propeller Total Power: 8,800kW (11,964hp) 15.0k MAN-B&W 6S50MC- 1 x 2 Stroke 6 Cy. 500 x 2000 8800kW (11964bhp) STX Engine Co Ltd-South Korea AuxGen: 2 x 500kW 400V 60Hz a.c, 1 x 400kW 400V 60Hz a.c Fuel: 120.0 (d.f.) 2040.0 (r.f.)
9509633 *A8VK9* -	**WARNOW SUN** **Schifffahrtskontor Warnow GmbH & Co KG ms 'Warnow Sun'** Medstar Shipmanagement Ltd *Monrovia* *Liberia* MMSI: 636092018 Official number: 92018	**22,863** 10,602 33,227	Class: GL	**2010-06 Zhejiang Ouhua Shipbuilding Co Ltd — Zhoushan ZJ** Yd No: 554 Loa 179.46 (BB) Br ex 28.23 Dght 10.800 Lbp 168.95 Br md 28.00 Dpth 15.10 Welded, 1 dk	**(A31A2GX) General Cargo Ship** Grain: 39,927; Bale: 37,490 TEU 1158 C Ho 484 TEU C Dk 674 incl 30 ref C. Compartments: 5 Ho, ER 5 Ha: 3 (25.6 x 24.4) (12.8 x 24.4)ER (12.6 x 20.4) Cranes: 4x60t	**1 oil engine** driving 1 FP propeller Total Power: 8,800kW (11,964hp) 15.0k MAN-B&W 6S50MC- 1 x 2 Stroke 6 Cy. 500 x 2000 8800kW (11964bhp) STX Engine Co Ltd-South Korea AuxGen: 2 x 500kW 400V 60Hz a.c, 1 x 400kW 400V 60Hz a.c Fuel: 120.0 (d.f.) 2040.0 (r.f.)
9437232 *V2DR5* -	**WARNOW TROUT** **Schifffahrtskontor Warnow GmbH & Co KG ms 'Warnow Trout'** Marlow Ship Management Deutschland GmbH & Co KG *Saint John's* *Antigua & Barbuda* MMSI: 305314000 Official number: 4521	**9,946** 4,900 11,983	Class: GL	**2008-07 Zhejiang Ouhua Shipbuilding Co Ltd — Zhoushan ZJ** Yd No: 510 Loa 139.10 (BB) Br ex Dght 8.800 Lbp 129.00 Br md 22.60 Dpth 11.80 Welded, 1 dk	**(A33A2CC) Container Ship (Fully Cellular)** TEU 990 incl 254 ref C	**1 oil engine** reduction geared to sc. shaft (s) driving 1 CP propeller Total Power: 9,600kW (13,052hp) 19.0k MAN-B&W 8L48/60 1 x 4 Stroke 8 Cy. 480 x 600 9600kW (13052bhp) MAN B&W Diesel AG-Augsburg AuxGen: 1 x 2000kW 450/230V a.c, 2 x 830kW 450/230V a.c Thrusters: 1 Tunnel thruster (f); 1 Tunnel thruster (f)
9437191 *V2DW9* -	**WARNOW VAQUITA** **Schifffahrtskontor Warnow GmbH & Co KG ms 'Warnow Vaquita'** Marlow Ship Management Deutschland GmbH & Co KG *Saint John's* *Antigua & Barbuda* MMSI: 305360000 Official number: 4564	**15,334** 5,983 18,343	Class: GL	**2008-10 Zhejiang Ouhua Shipbuilding Co Ltd — Zhoushan ZJ** Yd No: 506 Loa 166.15 (BB) Br ex - Dght 9.500 Lbp 155.08 Br md 25.00 Dpth 14.20 Welded, 1 dk	**(A33A2CC) Container Ship (Fully Cellular)** TEU 1284 C Ho 472 TEU C Dk 812 TEU incl 390 ref C	**1 oil engine** reduction geared to sc. shaft driving 1 CP propeller Total Power: 11,120kW (15,119hp) 19.0k MAN-B&W 8L58/6 1 x 4 Stroke 8 Cy. 580 x 640 11120kW (15119bhp) MAN B&W Diesel AG-Augsburg AuxGen: 3 x 1600kW a.c Thrusters: 1 Tunnel thruster (f)
9594509 *D5BY2* -	**WARNOW VENUS** **Hai Jiao 1303 Ltd** Marlow Ship Management Deutschland GmbH & Co KG *Monrovia* *Liberia* MMSI: 636015629 Official number: 15629	**22,863** 10,602 33,217	Class: GL	**2012-04 Zhejiang Ouhua Shipbuilding Co Ltd — Zhoushan ZJ** Yd No: 584 Loa 179.44 (BB) Br ex 28.23 Dght 10.800 Lbp 168.97 Br md 28.00 Dpth 15.10 Welded, 1 dk	**(A31A2GX) General Cargo Ship** Grain: 39,927; Bale: 37,490 TEU 1158 C Ho 484 TEU C Dk 674 incl 30 ref C. Compartments: 5 Ho, ER 5 Ha: 3 (25.6 x 24.4) (12.8 x 24.4)ER (12.6 x 20.4) Cranes: 4x60t	**1 oil engine** driving 1 FP propeller Total Power: 8,800kW (11,964hp) 15.0k MAN-B&W 6S50MC- 1 x 2 Stroke 6 Cy. 500 x 2000 8800kW (11964bhp) STX Engine Co Ltd-South Korea AuxGen: 2 x 500kW 400V 60Hz a.c, 1 x 400kW 400V 60Hz a.c Fuel: 120.0 (d.f.) 2040.0 (r.f.)
9395032 *5BXD3* -	**WARNOW WHALE** *ex* CMA CGM Corfu *-2009* *ex* Warnow Whale *-2007* **Princesia Shipping Co Ltd** GB Shipping & Chartering GmbH *Limassol* *Cyprus* MMSI: 209862000 Official number: 9395032	**15,375** 5,983 18,318	Class: GL	**2007-01 Zhejiang Ouhua Shipbuilding Co Ltd — Zhoushan ZJ** Yd No: 2036 Loa 166.15 (BB) Br ex - Dght 9.500 Lbp 155.08 Br md 25.00 Dpth 14.20 Welded, 1 dk	**(A33A2CC) Container Ship (Fully Cellular)** TEU 1296 C Ho 472 C Dk 824 TEU incl 390 ref C. Cranes: 2x40t	**1 oil engine** driving 1 FP propeller Total Power: 11,200kW (15,228hp) 19.0k MAN-B&W 8L58/6 1 x 4 Stroke 8 Cy. 580 x 640 11200kW (15228bhp) MAN B&W Diesel AG-West Germany AuxGen: 4 x 1600kW 450/220V a.c Thrusters: 1 Tunnel thruster (f)
9098505 *YB9522* -	**WAROPEN SATU** **PT Pelayaran Armada Bandar Bangun Persada** - *Palembang* *Indonesia*	**200** 77 -	Class: KI	**2007-04 P.T. Mariana Bahagia — Palembang** L reg 32.00 Br ex Dght 2.400 Lbp 27.50 Br md 8.00 Dpth 2.80 Welded, 1 dk	**(A13B2TU) Tanker (unspecified)** Double Hull (13F)	**2 oil engines** reduction geared to sc. shafts driving 2 Propellers Total Power: 376kW (512hp) Yanmar 6CH-U 2 x 4 Stroke 6 Cy. 105 x 125 each-188kW (256bhp) (made 2005) Yanmar Diesel Engine Co Ltd-Japan
9621340 *7JQT* -	**WARRAMBOO** **Mitsui OSK Lines Ltd (MOL)** MOL Ship Management Co Ltd (MOLSHIP) *Tokyo* *Japan* MMSI: 432965000 Official number: 142100	**132,512** - 250,718	Class: NK	**2014-01 Namura Shipbuilding Co Ltd — Imari SG** Yd No: 353 Loa 329.95 Br ex - Dght 18.025 Lbp 321.00 Br md 57.00 Dpth 25.10 Welded, 1 dk	**(A21B2BO) Ore Carrier** Grain: 164,768 Compartments: 5 Ho, ER 9 Ha: ER	**1 oil engine** driving 1 FP propeller Total Power: 27,160kW (36,927hp) 14.5k MAN-B&W 7S80MC- 1 x 2 Stroke 7 Cy. 800 x 3200 27160kW (36927bhp) Mitsui Engineering & Shipbuilding CLtd-Japan
7126748 *VM3869* -	**WARREN** **Svitzer Australia Pty Ltd & Stannard Marine Pty Ltd** Svitzer Australia Pty Ltd (Svitzer Australasia) *Port Lincoln, SA* *Australia* MMSI: 503401000 Official number: 355096	*170* 1 -	Class: (AB)	**1971 Adelaide Ship Construction Pty Ltd — Port Adelaide SA** Yd No: 71 Loa - Br ex - Dght 3.480 Lbp 23.75 Br md 7.32 Dpth 4.07 Welded, 1 dk	**(B32A2ST) Tug**	**2 oil engines** geared to sc. shafts driving 2 FP propellers Total Power: 1,176kW (1,598hp) 11.5k Blackstone ESL 2 x 4 Stroke 8 Cy. 222 x 292 each-588kW (799bhp) Mirrlees Blackstone (Stamford)Ltd.-Stamford AuxGen: 2 x 25kW
9399454 *WDD7841* -	**WARREN THOMAS** **Supreme Offshore Services Inc** - *Houma, LA* *United States of America* MMSI: 367192070 Official number: 1180722	**567** 197 672		**2007-06 Lockport Fabrication Inc — Lockport LA** Yd No: 002 Loa 50.59 Br ex - Dght 3.648 Lbp 49.39 Br md 10.97 Dpth 3.65 Welded, 1 dk	**(B21A2OS) Platform Supply Ship** Passengers: 18	**2 oil engines** reduction geared to sc. shafts driving 2 CP propellers Total Power: 1,268kW (1,724hp) Cummins KTA-38-M 2 x Vee 4 Stroke 12 Cy. 159 x 159 each-634kW (862bhp) Cummins Engine Co Inc-USA AuxGen: 2 x 99kW a.c Thrusters: 1 Thwart. FP thruster (f)

114218 /NRL	**WARRENDER** *ex* Riverside Cloud *-2003* *ex* Gulf Cloud *-2002* **Perkins Shipping Pty Ltd** - SatCom: Inmarsat C 450301643 *Brisbane, Qld* *Australia* MMSI: 503060000 Official number: 855251	**946** 283 1,150	Class: LR (BV) **100A1** SS 08/2010 **LMC** **UMS** Eq.Ltr: M; Cable: 385.0/32.0 U2 (a)	**1995**-08 **Marine Steel (Northland) Ltd — Whangarei** Yd No: 114 Loa 67.89 Br ex - Dght 2.950 Lbp 62.78 Br md 14.20 Dpth 4.20 Welded, 1 dk	**(A31A2GX) General Cargo Ship** TEU 62	**2 oil engines** geared to sc. shafts driving 2 FP propellers Total Power: 2,310kW (3,140hp) 11.0kn Caterpillar 3508TA 2 x Vee 4 Stroke 8 Cy. 170 x 190 each-1155kW (1570bhp) Caterpillar Inc-USA AuxGen: 2 x 230kW 415/220V 50Hz a.c
009973 I02201	**WARREN'S PRIDE** *ex* Crusader *-2006* *ex* H. O. S. Crusader *-1996* *ex* Victoria G *-1994* **G & W Transport** - *Panama* *Panama* MMSI: 372329000 Official number: 3328307B	*801* 240 1,200	Class: (AB)	**1981**-02 **Halter Marine, Inc. — Lockport, La** Yd No: 931 Loa - Br ex - Dght 3.944 Lbp 56.70 Br md 12.20 Dpth 4.58 Welded, 1 dk	**(B21A20S) Platform Supply Ship**	**2 oil engines** reverse reduction geared to sc. shafts driving 2 FP propellers Total Power: 2,206kW (3,000hp) 12.0kn EMD (Electro-Motive) 12-645-E6 2 x Vee 2 Stroke 12 Cy. 230 x 254 each-1103kW (1500bhp) General Motors Corp.Electro-Motive Div.-La Grange AuxGen: 2 x 99kW Thrusters: 1 Thwart. FP thruster (f)
508233 'JDW	**WARRINGA** **Svitzer Australia Pty Ltd (Svitzer Australasia)** - SatCom: Inmarsat C 450301624 *Sydney, NSW* *Australia* MMSI: 503076000 Official number: 374357	*235* - -	Class: LR ✠ **100A1** SS 03/2012 tug ✠ **LMC** Eq.Ltr: (F) ; Cable: U2	**1977**-02 **Tamar Shipbuilding Pty Ltd — Launceston TAS** Yd No: 22 Loa 30.18 Br ex 8.72 Dght 3.683 Lbp 27.06 Br md 8.54 Dpth 4.42 Welded, 1 dk	**(B32A2ST) Tug**	**2 oil engines** reverse reduction geared to sc. shafts driving 2 FP propellers Total Power: 1,794kW (2,440hp) 12.0kn Blackstone ESL8MK2 2 x 4 Stroke 8 Cy. 222 x 292 each-897kW (1220bhp) Mirrlees Blackstone (Stamford)Ltd.-Stamford AuxGen: 2 x 72kW 415V 50Hz a.c
390909 /BN4383	**WARRIOR** **Crowley Marine Services Inc** - *San Francisco, CA* *United States of America* MMSI: 366887190 Official number: 565291	**538** 161 -	Class: AB	**1975**-05 **McDermott Shipyards Inc — Morgan City LA** Yd No: 202 Loa 41.46 Br ex 11.13 Dght 5.160 Lbp 39.22 Br md 11.08 Dpth 5.80 Welded, 1 dk	**(B32A2ST) Tug**	**2 oil engines** reverse reduction geared to sc. shafts driving 2 FP propellers Total Power: 5,296kW (7,200hp) 14.0kn EMD (Electro-Motive) 20-645-E7B 2 x Vee 2 Stroke 20 Cy. 230 x 254 each-2648kW (3600bhp) General Motors Corp.Electro-Motive Div.-La Grange AuxGen: 2 x 90kW Fuel: 782.5 (d.f.)
111268 /DB6462	**WARRIOR** *ex* C-2 *-1994* *ex* Susan Richards *-1994* *ex* Ben F. Royal *-1994* *ex* F. F. Clain *-1980* *ex* DPC 47 *-1946* **Tug Warrior Inc** - *Charleston, SC* *United States of America* Official number: 244783	*146* 99 -	Class: (AB)	**1943 Decatur Iron & Steel Co. — Decatur, Al** Yd No: 47 Loa 25.91 Br ex 7.37 Dght - Lbp 25.00 Br md 7.32 Dpth 3.20 Welded, 1 dk	**(B32A2ST) Tug**	**1 oil engine** sr geared to sc. shaft driving 1 FP propeller Total Power: 515kW (700hp) 11.0kn EMD (Electro-Motive) 8-567 1 x Vee 2 Stroke 8 Cy. 216 x 254 515kW (700bhp) General Motors Corp-USA Fuel: 71.0 (d.f.)
948627	**WARRIOR** **Versaggi Shrimp Corp** - *Tampa, FL* *United States of America* Official number: 612939	*115* 79 -		**1979 St Augustine Trawlers, Inc. — Saint Augustine, Fl** L reg 20.61 Br ex 6.18 Dght - Lbp - Br md - Dpth 3.36 Bonded, 1 dk	**(B11B2FV) Fishing Vessel** Hull Material: Reinforced Plastic	**1 oil engine** driving 1 FP propeller Total Power: 305kW (415hp) Caterpillar 3412T 1 x Vee 4 Stroke 12 Cy. 137 x 152 305kW (415bhp) Caterpillar Tractor Co-USA
605985 /DE6633	**WARRIOR** *ex* Freedom *-1990* **Warrior Fishing Corp** - *Philadelphia, PA* *United States of America* Official number: 693641	*139* 103 -		**1985 Eastern Marine, Inc. — Panama City, Fl** Yd No: 96 Loa 29.27 Br ex - Dght - Lbp 7.62 Br md 4.20 Dpth - Welded, 1 dk	**(B11A2FS) Stern Trawler** Ins: 210	**1 oil engine** geared to sc. shaft driving 1 FP propeller Total Power: 1,118kW (1,520hp) Caterpillar 3512TA 1 x Vee 4 Stroke 12 Cy. 170 x 190 1118kW (1520bhp) Caterpillar Tractor Co-USA
964305 'DC7597	**WARRIOR** *ex* Seabulk Winn *-1990* *ex* Rapid Runner *-1990* **Crusader Marine Offshore LLC** Comar Marine LLC *Morgan City, LA* *United States of America* Official number: 976173	**219** 65 -		**1991**-06 **Breaux Bay Craft, Inc. — Loreauville, La** Yd No: 1648 Loa 40.84 Br ex - Dght - Lbp 39.62 Br md 7.99 Dpth 3.51 Welded, 1 dk	**(B21A20C) Crew/Supply Vessel** Hull Material: Aluminium Alloy	**4 oil engines** geared to sc. shafts driving 4 FP propellers Total Power: 2,248kW (3,056hp) Caterpillar 3412TA 4 x Vee 4 Stroke 12 Cy. 137 x 152 each-562kW (764bhp) Caterpillar Inc-USA
338382	**WARRIOR** *ex* Ocean Star I *-1990* *ex* Camaleon *-1990* *ex* Veracruz *-1998* - -	*127* 69 -		**1984 John E. Doak — Brunswick, Ga** L reg 20.88 Br ex - Dght - Lbp - Br md 6.25 Dpth 3.96 Welded, 1 dk	**(B11B2FV) Fishing Vessel**	**1 oil engine** driving 1 FP propeller Total Power: 368kW (500hp) 10.0kn G.M. (Detroit Diesel) 12V-71 1 x Vee 2 Stroke 12 Cy. 108 x 127 368kW (500bhp) Detroit Diesel Corporation-Detroit, Mi
605865 5YK3	**WARRIOR** **Rattray Business Inc** Enterprises Shipping & Trading SA *Nassau* *Bahamas* MMSI: 311036300 Official number: 8001748	**33,044** 19,231 57,000 T/cm 58.8	Class: BV	**2012**-05 **Jinling Shipyard — Nanjing JS** Yd No: JLZ9100406 Loa 189.99 (BB) Br ex - Dght 12.800 Lbp 185.00 Br md 32.26 Dpth 18.00 Welded, 1 dk	**(A21A2BC) Bulk Carrier** Grain: 71,634; Bale: 68,200 Compartments: 5 Ho, ER 5 Ha: 4 (21.3 x 18.3)ER (18.9 x 18.3) Cranes: 4x30t	**1 oil engine** driving 1 FP propeller Total Power: 9,480kW (12,889hp) 14.2kn MAN-B&W 6S50MC-C 1 x 2 Stroke 6 Cy. 500 x 2000 9480kW (12889bhp) Doosan Engine Co Ltd-South Korea AuxGen: 3 x 600kW 60Hz a.c Fuel: 1950.0
338195 'DD4501	**WARRIOR II** *ex* Wallys Pride *-1976* **Hunters Offshore Enterprises Inc** - *Eureka, CA* *United States of America* MMSI: 367145530 Official number: 539091	*137* 93 -		**1972 Ericson Marine — Tarpon Springs, Fl** L reg 22.16 Br ex 6.86 Dght - Lbp - Br md - Dpth 3.76 Welded, 1 dk	**(B11B2FV) Fishing Vessel**	**1 oil engine** driving 1 FP propeller Total Power: 441kW (600hp)
002726 IZW	**WARRIOR SPIRIT** *ex* Warrior Express *-2006* *ex* Malta Express *-2006* *ex* Porto Cardo *-1999* **Achieva Shipping II Ltd** FleetPro Ocean Inc *Basseterre* *St Kitts & Nevis* MMSI: 341678000	**11,457** 3,437 4,788	Class: BV (RI)	**1980**-05 **Societe Nouvelle des Ateliers et Chantiers du Havre — Le Havre** Yd No: 253 Loa 126.50 Br ex - Dght 6.320 Lbp 115.80 Br md 21.01 Dpth 7.52 Welded, 2 dks	**(A36A2PR) Passenger/Ro-Ro Ship (Vehicles)** Passengers: cabins: 48; berths: 105; driver berths: 96 Stern door & ramp Len: 5.50 Wid: 11.00 Swl: 50 Lane-Len: 1150 Lane-clr ht: 4.50 Cars: 440 Bale: 15,300 1 Ha: (15.0 x 3.0)ER	**2 oil engines** geared to sc. shafts driving 2 CP propellers Total Power: 11,032kW (15,000hp) 18.0kn Pielstick 12PC2-5V-400 2 x Vee 4 Stroke 12 Cy. 400 x 460 each-5516kW (7500bhp) Alsthom Atlantique-France AuxGen: 2 x 780kW 380/220V 50Hz a.c Thrusters: 1 Thwart. CP thruster (f) Fuel: 81.0 (d.f.) 475.0 (r.f.) 43.0pd
428279)7097	**WARRIS** **Offshore International Shipping & Trading Enterprises Ltd SA** Gulf Shipping Maritime Establishment *Panama* *Panama* MMSI: 353583000 Official number: 4030209	**696** 208 531	Class: LR ✠ **100A1** SS 03/2009 anchor handler tug, fire-fighting Ship 1 (2400m3/h) with water spray EP ✠ **LMC** Eq.Ltr: J; Cable: 660.0/26.0 U2 (a)	**2009**-03 **Santierul Naval Damen Galati S.A. — Galati** (Hull) Yd No: 1144 **2009**-03 **B.V. Scheepswerf Damen — Gorinchem** Yd No: 512007 Loa 45.10 Br ex 11.23 Dght 4.300 Lbp 39.70 Br md 11.00 Dpth 4.90 Welded, 1 dk	**(B21B20A) Anchor Handling Tug Supply**	**2 oil engines** with clutches, flexible couplings & reverse reduction geared to sc. shafts driving 2 FP propellers Total Power: 5,420kW (7,370hp) 12.7kn Caterpillar C280-8 2 x 4 Stroke 8 Cy. 280 x 300 each-2710kW (3685bhp) Caterpillar Inc-USA AuxGen: 2 x 165kW 415V 50Hz a.c, 1 x 500kW 400V 50Hz a.c Thrusters: 1 Thwart. FP thruster (f)
615389 'ZE3	**WARSAW** **Warsaw Shipping Co Ltd** SMT Shipmanagement & Transport Gdynia Ltd Sp z oo *Majuro* *Marshall Islands* MMSI: 538004802 Official number: 4802	**44,980** 27,045 81,755 T/cm 71.9	Class: AB BV	**2012**-10 **Jiangsu Newyangzi Shipbuilding Co Ltd — Jingjiang JS** Yd No: YZJ2010-967 Loa 229.00 (BB) Br ex 32.29 Dght 14.450 Lbp 225.10 Br md 32.26 Dpth 20.20 Welded, 1 dk	**(A21A2BC) Bulk Carrier** Grain: 96,472; Bale: 90,783 Compartments: 7 Ho, ER 7 Ha: ER	**1 oil engine** driving 1 FP propeller Total Power: 9,500kW (12,916hp) 13.7kn MAN-B&W 6S60MC-C 1 x 2 Stroke 6 Cy. 600 x 2400 9500kW (12916bhp) Doosan Engine Co Ltd-South Korea AuxGen: 3 x 600kW a.c Fuel: 360.0 (d.f.) 2800.0 (r.f.) 32.0pd
665849 'CA8	**WARTA** *ex* Chairman *-2013* *ex* Alim *-2010* *launched as* Iran Alim *-2009* - **Rahbaran Omid Darya Ship Management Co** *Iran* MMSI: 422040300	**31,117** 18,159 53,100	Class: (BV)	**2009**-02 **Yangzhou Dayang Shipbuilding Co Ltd — Yangzhou JS** Yd No: DY112 Loa 189.99 Br ex - Dght 12.490 Lbp 182.00 Br md 32.26 Dpth 17.20 Welded, 1 dk	**(A21A2BC) Bulk Carrier** Grain: 65,049 Compartments: 5 Ho, ER 5 Ha: ER Cranes: 4x35t	**1 oil engine** driving 1 FP propeller Total Power: 9,480kW (12,889hp) 14.7kn MAN-B&W 6S50MC-C 1 x 2 Stroke 6 Cy. 500 x 2000 9480kW (12889bhp) Doosan Engine Co Ltd-South Korea AuxGen: 3 x 720kW 60Hz a.c Fuel: 2200.0

IMO / Call sign	Name / Owner / Port	Tonnage	Class	Build / Dimensions	Type / Capacities	Machinery
5386411 *SEYW* -	**WARTENA** **Baltic Offshore Kalmar** Baltic Offshore Rederi AB *Karlskrona* Sweden MMSI: 265288000	**407** 143 460	Class: (BV)	**1958-09 NV Scheepswerf G Bijlsma & Zoon — Wartena** Yd No: 535 Converted From: General Cargo Ship Loa 48.75 Br ex 7.75 Dght 2.902 Lbp 42.98 Br md 7.70 Dpth 3.15 Riveted\Welded, 1 dk	**(B34D2SL) Cable Layer** Compartments: 1 Ho, ER 1 Ha: (21.3 x 5.0) Derricks: 2x2t; Winches: 2	**1 oil engine** driving 1 FP propeller Total Power: 276kW (375hp) 9.5k De Industrie 5D7 1 x 4 Stroke 5 Cy. 305 x 460 276kW (375bhp) NV Motorenfabriek 'De Industrie'-Netherlands AuxGen: 2 x 24kW 380V a.c, 1 x 24kW 380V a.c
8202628 - -	**WARTURM** **VTG Supply Boat Liberia Inc** Tidewater Marine International Inc	**887** 266 926	Class: AB (GL)	**1983-06 Teraoka Shipyard Co Ltd — Minamiawaji HG** Yd No: 219 Loa 57.41 Br ex 12.07 Dght 4.222 Lbp 51.80 Br md 12.01 Dpth 4.78 Welded, 1 dk	**(B21B20A) Anchor Handling Tug Supply**	**2 oil engines** reverse reduction geared to sc. shafts driving 2 FP propellers Total Power: 2,942kW (4,000hp) 12.5k Yanmar 8Z280-E 2 x 4 Stroke 8 Cy. 280 x 360 each-1471kW (2000bhp) Yanmar Diesel Engine Co Ltd-Japan Thrusters: 1 Thwart. FP thruster (f)
6829202 - -	**WARUN** *ex* Eiho Maru *-1981* **Petrol Line Co Ltd** - *Bangkok* Thailand Official number: 241027576	*984* 649 2,050		**1968 Shimoda Dockyard Co. Ltd. — Shimoda** Yd No: 159 Loa 66.99 Br ex 11.03 Dght 5.004 Lbp 62.49 Br md 11.00 Dpth 5.41 Welded, 1 dk	**(A13B2TP) Products Tanker** Liq: 2,398; Liq (Oil): 2,398 Compartments: 6 Ta, ER	**2 oil engines** driving 2 FP propellers Total Power: 956kW (1,300hp) 10.0k Daihatsu 6PSTCM-26 2 x 4 Stroke 6 Cy. 260 x 320 each-478kW (650bhp) Daihatsu Kogyo-Japan AuxGen: 1 x 20kW 115V d.c, 1 x 15kW 115V d.c Fuel: 53.0
7856197 *YD2054* -	**WARUNA I** *ex* Katsuragi Maru *-2003* **PT Waruna Nusa Sentana** - *Belawan* Indonesia	**243** 73 125	Class: KI (NK)	**1977-09 Hikari Kogyo K.K. — Yokosuka** Loa 31.72 Br ex - Dght 2.700 Lbp 26.50 Br md 8.60 Dpth 3.50 Welded, 1 dk	**(B32A2ST) Tug**	**2 oil engines** driving 2 FP propellers Total Power: 1,912kW (2,600hp) 13.0k Daihatsu 6DSM-2 2 x 4 Stroke 6 Cy. 260 x 320 each-956kW (1300bhp) Daihatsu Diesel Manufacturing Co Lt-Japan
7330947 *YD2058* -	**WARUNA II** *ex* Maju Rigel *-2003* *ex* Kansai Maru 3 *-2001* *ex* Kansai Maru No. 3 *-1999* *ex* Shonan Maru No. 8 *-1987* *ex* Masuei Maru No. 31 *-1981* **PT Waruna Nusa Sentana** - *Belawan* Indonesia	**221** 67 90	Class: KI (NK)	**1973-09 Ishikawajima Ship & Chemical Plant Co Ltd — Tokyo** Yd No: 451 Loa 31.72 Br ex 8.64 Dght 2.700 Lbp 26.50 Br md 8.62 Dpth 3.51 Welded, 1 dk	**(B32A2ST) Tug**	**2 oil engines** reduction geared to sc. shafts driving 2 Directional propellers Total Power: 1,912kW (2,600hp) 13.8k Daihatsu 6DSM-2 2 x 4 Stroke 6 Cy. 260 x 320 each-956kW (1300bhp) Daihatsu Diesel Manufacturing Co Lt-Japan AuxGen: 2 x 48kW a.c Fuel: 40.0
9356000 *YD2072* -	**WARUNA JAYA** **PT Multi Jaya Samudera** - *Belawan* Indonesia	**278** 83 -	Class: KI (BV)	**2005-06 Guangzhou Panyu Lingshan Shipyard Ltd — Guangzhou GD** Yd No: 110 Loa 28.90 Br ex - Dght 3.640 Lbp 22.50 Br md 9.00 Dpth 4.70 Welded, 1 dk	**(B32A2ST) Tug**	**2 oil engines** reduction geared to sc. shafts driving 2 Z propellers Total Power: 2,386kW (3,244hp) 12.0k Cummins KTA-50-M 2 x Vee 4 Stroke 16 Cy. 159 x 159 each-1193kW (1622bhp Cummins Engine Co Inc-USA AuxGen: 2 x 60kW 400/220V 50Hz a.c
9356012 *YD2071* -	**WARUNA MULIA** **PT Multi Jaya Samudera** - *Belawan* Indonesia	**278** 83 -	Class: KI (BV)	**2005-09 Guangzhou Panyu Lingshan Shipyard Ltd — Guangzhou GD** Yd No: 111 Loa 28.90 Br ex - Dght 3.600 Lbp 23.20 Br md 9.00 Dpth 4.70 Welded, 1 dk	**(B32A2ST) Tug**	**2 oil engines** reduction geared to sc. shafts driving 2 Z propellers Total Power: 2,384kW (3,242hp) 12.4k Cummins KTA-50-M 2 x Vee 4 Stroke 16 Cy. 159 x 159 each-1192kW (1621bhp Cummins Engine Co Inc-USA AuxGen: 2 x 60kW 420V a.c
9549865 *PNNC* -	**WARUNA SAFETY** **PT Waruna Nusa Sentana** PT Multi Jaya Samudera *Belawan* Indonesia MMSI: 525015729	**828** 248 851	Class: BV	**2010-01 Nanjing East Star Shipbuilding Co Ltd — Nanjing JS** Yd No: 08ESS-T4703 Loa 47.00 Br ex - Dght 4.000 Lbp 41.40 Br md 12.80 Dpth 4.85 Welded, 1 dk	**(B21B20A) Anchor Handling Tug Supply**	**2 oil engines** reduction geared to sc. shafts driving 2 FP propellers Total Power: 3,432kW (4,666hp) 12.0k Cummins QSK60-M 2 x Vee 4 Stroke 16 Cy. 159 x 190 each-1716kW (2333bhp Cummins Engine Co Inc-USA AuxGen: 3 x 245kW 415V 50Hz a.c Thrusters: 1 Tunnel thruster (f)
9683702 *POZJ* -	**WARUNA SUPPLY** **PT Waruna Nusa Sentana** PT Multi Jaya Samudera *Belawan* Indonesia MMSI: 525021160 Official number: 1352/Ppa	**881** 265 851		**2012-12 PT Waruna Nusa Sentana — Medan** Yd No: 015 Loa 47.00 Br ex - Dght 4.200 Lbp 41.40 Br md 12.80 Dpth 4.85 Welded, 1 dk	**(B21B20A) Anchor Handling Tug Supply**	**2 oil engines** reduction geared to sc. shafts driving 2 Propellers
6620254 *VJFW* -	**WARUNDA** **Frank Byrne Pty Ltd** - *Sydney, NSW* Australia Official number: 317903	*225* 56 155	Class: (LR) (NV) ✠ Classed LR until 20/1/89	**1966-12 Adelaide Ship Construction Pty Ltd — Port Adelaide SA** Yd No: 32 Converted From: Tug-1988 Loa 31.85 Br ex 8.56 Dght 3.658 Lbp 29.24 Br md 8.07 Dpth 4.46 Welded	**(B11A2FS) Stern Trawler**	**1 oil engine** sr geared to sc. shaft driving 1 CP propeller Total Power: 1,059kW (1,440hp) 12.0k General Motors 16-278- 1 x Vee 2 Stroke 16 Cy. 222 x 267 1059kW (1440bhp) (Re-engined ,made 1944, refitted 1966) General Motors Corp-USA AuxGen: 1 x 100kW a.c, 1 x 71kW a.c Fuel: 23.5 (d.f.)
9134359 *S6II* -	**WARWICK** **Orange Maritime Pte Ltd** Executive Ship Management Pte Ltd SatCom: Inmarsat C 456393910 *Singapore* Singapore MMSI: 563939000 Official number: 387167	**5,953** 1,786 6,996 T/cm 18.8	Class: NK	**1996-03 Shin Kochi Jyuko K.K. — Kochi** Yd No: 7076 Loa 119.02 (BB) Br ex 18.83 Dght 6.627 Lbp 112.00 Br md 18.80 Dpth 9.00 Welded, 1 dk	**(A11B2TG) LPG Tanker** Double Bottom Entire Compartment Length Liq (Gas): 6,373 3 x Gas Tank (s); 3 independent (C.mn.stl) cyl horizontal 3 Cargo Pump (s): 3x400m³/hr Manifold: Bow/CM: 67.2m	**1 oil engine** driving 1 FP propeller Total Power: 4,531kW (6,160hp) 15.0k B&W 7L35M 1 x 2 Stroke 7 Cy. 350 x 1050 4531kW (6160bhp) Hitachi Zosen Corp-Japan AuxGen: 2 x 350kW 440V 60Hz a.c Fuel: 124.0 (d.f.) 633.0 (r.f.) 16.5pd
8000226 *OJQB* -	**WASA EXPRESS** *ex* Betancuria *-2012* *ex* Thjelvar *-2011* *ex* Rostock *-2010* *ex* Thjelvar *-2007* *ex* Color Traveller *-2006* *ex* Thjelvar *-2004* *ex* Sally Star *-1997* *ex* Travemunde Link *-1988* *ex* Travemunde *-1987* **NLC Ferry Ab Oy** - *Vaasa* Finland MMSI: 230636000	**17,053** 7,729 4,150	Class: NV	**1981-06 Oy Wartsila Ab — Helsinki** Yd No: 432 Loa 137.42 (BB) Br ex 24.80 Dght 5.760 Lbp 124.53 Br md 22.31 Dpth 6.70 Welded, 5 dks	**(A36A2PR) Passenger/Ro-Ro Ship (Vehicles)** Passengers: unberthed: 1787; cabins: 80; berths: 284 Bow ramp Len: 6.50 Wid: 3.50 Swl: - Bow door & ramp Len: 5.00 Wid: 4.50 Swl: - Stern ramp (upr) Len: 6.50 Wid: 3.50 Swl: - Stern ramp Len: 5.00 Wid: 6.00 Swl: - Stern door/ramp (p) Len: 5.00 Wid: 5.54 Swl: - Stern door/ramp (s) Len: 5.00 Wid: 5.54 Swl: - Side door (p) Side door (s) Lane-Len: 1200 Cars: 450, Trailers: 54 Ice Capable	**4 oil engines** reduction geared to sc. shafts driving 2 CP propellers Total Power: 14,860kW (20,204hp) 18.5k Wartsila 12V3 4 x Vee 4 Stroke 12 Cy. 320 x 350 each-3715kW (5051bhp Oy Wartsila Ab-Finland AuxGen: 2 x 1200kW 380V 50Hz a.c, 2 x 1172kW 380V 50Hz a.c Thrusters: 2 Thwart. CP thruster (f) Fuel: 65.6 (d.f.) 529.0 (r.f.)
5148601 *SJHL* -	**WASA LEJON** *ex* Gota Lejon *-1994* *ex* Bremmenholm *-1980* *ex* Manger *-1979* *ex* Herdia *-1972* *ex* Fjordbusso *-1954* **Royal Stockholm Cruise Line AB** - *Norrkoping* Sweden MMSI: 265596640	**120** 55 -	Class: (NV)	**1946 Kristiansands Mek. Verksted AS — Kristiansand** Yd No: 181 Loa 29.62 Br ex 5.62 Dght - Lbp - Br md 5.59 Dpth 2.19 Riveted\Welded, 1 dk	**(A37B2PS) Passenger Ship** Passengers: 232	**2 oil engines** driving 2 FP propellers Total Power: 338kW (460hp) Deutz SBA8M5 2 x 4 Stroke 8 Cy. 130 x 170 each-169kW (230bhp) (new engine 1961) Kloeckner Humboldt Deutz AG-West Germany

9141625 P3TL7 -	**WASABORG** *ex* Seaboard Liberty *-2002* *ex* Wasaborg *-2001* *ex* P&O Nedlloyd Belem *-1998* *ex* Wasaborg *-1998* **Schiffahrtsgesellschaft Zachariassen & Fisser mbH & Co** KG Fisser & v Doornum GmbH & Co SatCom: Inmarsat M 621249410 *Limassol* *Cyprus* MMSI: 212494000 Official number: P510	**4,150** 2,005 5,399 T/cm 14.0	Class: GL	**1997-11 Jiangsu Jiangyang Shipyard Group Co Ltd — Yangzhou JS** Yd No: JY94008 Loa 100.62 (BB) Br ex - Dght 6.390 Lbp 94.80 Br md 16.20 Dpth 8.20 Welded, 1 dk	**(A31A2GX) General Cargo Ship** Grain: 7,264; Bale: 7,235 TEU 369 Compartments: 1 Ho, ER 2 Ha: ER Cranes: 2x40t Ice Capable	**1 oil engine** reduction geared to sc. shaft driving 1 CP propeller Total Power: 3,960kW (5,384hp) 15.5kn MaK 9M32 1 x 4 Stroke 9 Cy. 320 x 480 3960kW (5384bhp) MaK Motoren GmbH & Co. KG-Kiel AuxGen: 1 x 440kW 220/380V a.c, 3 x 340kW 220/380V a.c Thrusters: 1 Thwart. FP thruster (f) Fuel: 60.0 (d.f.) 330.0 (r.f.)
8410598 - -	**WASHIN MARU** **Transport Maritime ET Telesta** - *Madagascar*	*197* - 700		**1984-10 Maeno Zosen KK — Sanyoonoda YC** Yd No: 106 Loa 56.32 Br ex 9.20 Dght 3.152 Lbp 51.01 Br md 9.01 Dpth 5.41 Welded, 2 dks	**(A31A2GX) General Cargo Ship** Compartments: 1 Ho, ER 1 Ha: ER	**1 oil engine** geared to sc. shaft driving 1 FP propeller Total Power: 588kW (799hp) Hanshin 6LU26G 1 x 4 Stroke 6 Cy. 260 x 440 588kW (799bhp) The Hanshin Diesel Works Ltd-Japan
8207733 WAJ2544 -	**WASHINGTON** *ex* Falcon *-2012* *ex* Delta Billie *-1999* *ex* Kinsman Falcon *-1993* **Shaver Transportation Co** - *Portland, ME* *United States of America* MMSI: 366946880 Official number: 959654	**298** 89 -	Class: (AB)	**1990-02 Cameron Shipbuilders, Inc. — Brownsville, Tx** (Hull launched by) Yd No: 119 **1990-02 Tampa Shipyards Inc — Tampa FL** (Hull completed by) Loa 28.33 Br ex - Dght - Lbp 28.19 Br md 11.58 Dpth 3.81 Welded, 1 dk	**(B32A2ST) Tug**	**2 oil engines** gearing integral to driving 2 Z propellers Total Power: 2,354kW (3,200hp) 8.0kn B&W 7S28LU 2 x 2 Stroke 7 Cy. 240 x 320 each-1177kW (1600bhp) MAN B&W Diesel A/S-Denmark AuxGen: 2 x 135kW
7050846 WY5149 -	**WASHINGTON** **Huffington Ocean Trawlers Inc** - *Houston, TX* *United States of America* Official number: 516857	*141* 96 -		**1968 Bishop Shipbuilding Corp. — Aransas Pass, Tx** L reg 24.36 Br ex 6.71 Dght - Lbp - Br md - Dpth 3.69 Welded	**(B11B2FV) Fishing Vessel**	**1 oil engine** driving 1 FP propeller Total Power: 313kW (426hp)
9398216 VRFD6 -	**WASHINGTON** *ex* APL Washington *-2014* **Metropolitan Harbour Ltd** Synergy Management Ltd SatCom: Inmarsat C 447701850 *Hong Kong* *Hong Kong* MMSI: 477218500 Official number: HK-2387	**75,582** 45,153 85,760 T/cm 100.6	Class: GL	**2009-04 Hyundai Heavy Industries Co Ltd — Ulsan** Yd No: 1948 Loa 304.15 (BB) Br ex - Dght 14.500 Lbp 292.00 Br md 40.00 Dpth 24.80 Welded, 1 dk	**(A33A2CC) Container Ship (Fully Cellular)** TEU 6500 incl 600 ref C	**1 oil engine** driving 1 FP propeller Total Power: 57,100kW (77,633hp) 24.8kn MAN-B&W 10K98MC-C 1 x 2 Stroke 10 Cy. 980 x 2400 57100kW (77633bhp) Hyundai Heavy Industries Co Ltd-South Korea AuxGen: 2 x 2666kW 450V a.c, 2 x 2346kW 450V a.c Thrusters: 1 Tunnel thruster (f)
9243198 WDD3826 -	**WASHINGTON EXPRESS** *ex* CP Denali *-2006* *ex* Lykes Flyer *-2005* **Wilmington Trust Co, as Trustee** Hapag-Lloyd AG *Washington, DC* *United States of America* MMSI: 367136710 Official number: 1191634	**40,146** 18,097 40,478 T/cm 64.6	Class: AB	**2003-01 China Shipbuilding Corp (CSBC) — Kaohsiung** Yd No: 793 Loa 243.35 (BB) Br ex - Dght 11.000 Lbp 232.40 Br md 32.20 Dpth 19.50 Welded, 1 dk	**(A33A2CC) Container Ship (Fully Cellular)** TEU 3237 C Ho 1420 TEU C Dk 1817 TEU incl 400 ref C. Cranes: 4x45t	**1 oil engine** driving 1 FP propeller Total Power: 28,832kW (39,200hp) 22.5kn B&W 8K80MC-C 1 x 2 Stroke 8 Cy. 800 x 2300 28832kW (39200bhp) Doosan Engine Co Ltd-South Korea AuxGen: 3 x 2280kW a.c Thrusters: 1 Thwart. CP thruster (f) Fuel: 222.0 (d.f.) 4305.0 (r.f.) 110.0pd
9211602 DYDE -	**WASHINGTON TRADER** **Nisshin Shipping Co Ltd & Ratu Shipping Co SA** Nisshin Shipping Co Ltd (Nisshin Kaiun KK) *Manila* *Philippines* MMSI: 548543000 Official number: MNLA000520	**38,928** 24,319 74,228 T/cm 67.0	Class: BV	**2000-02 Sasebo Heavy Industries Co. Ltd. — Sasebo Yard, Sasebo** Yd No: 461 Loa 225.00 Br ex - Dght 13.820 Lbp 218.00 Br md 32.20 Dpth 19.20 Welded, 1 dk	**(A21A2BC) Bulk Carrier** Grain: 87,500 Compartments: 7 Ho, ER 7 Ha: 6 (17.0 x 14.4)ER (15.3 x 12.8)	**1 oil engine** driving 1 FP propeller Total Power: 8,827kW (12,001hp) 15.0kn B&W 6S60MC 1 x 2 Stroke 6 Cy. 600 x 2292 8827kW (12001bhp) Mitsui Engineering & Shipbuilding CLtd-Japan
8130277 JJ3306 -	**WASHU** **Government of Japan (Ministry of Land, Infrastructure & Transport - Bureau of Ports & Harbors - No 3 Harbor Construction Bureau)** - *Kobe, Hyogo* *Japan* Official number: 125206	*194* - 115		**1982-03 Mitsubishi Heavy Industries Ltd. — Kobe** Yd No: 1132 Loa 29.49 Br ex 10.83 Dght 2.201 Lbp 27.89 Br md 10.80 Dpth 3.13 Welded, 1 dk	**(B34G2SE) Pollution Control Vessel**	**2 oil engines** sr geared to sc. shafts driving 2 FP propellers Total Power: 706kW (960hp) G.M. (Detroit Diesel) 16V-71-N 2 x Vee 2 Stroke 16 Cy. 108 x 127 each-353kW (480bhp) General Motors Corp-USA
9267780 JK5636 -	**WASHU MARU** **Seagate Corp** - *Kure, Hiroshima* *Japan* Official number: 136201	*244* - -		**2002-05 Kanagawa Zosen — Kobe** Yd No: 506 Loa 37.20 Br ex - Dght - Lbp - Br md 9.80 Dpth 4.21 Welded, 1 dk	**(B32A2ST) Tug**	**2 oil engines** driving 2 FP propellers Total Power: 2,942kW (4,000hp) Yanmar 6N280-SN 2 x 4 Stroke 6 Cy. 280 x 380 each-1471kW (2000bhp) Yanmar Diesel Engine Co Ltd-Japan
7110610 YDES -	**WASIAN** *ex* Swallow *-1984* *ex* Houn Maru *-1982* *ex* Kyozan Maru No. 3 *-1982* **PT Pejaka Lines** - *Jakarta* *Indonesia*	*1,481* 922 2,507	Class: (KI)	**1971-08 Geibi Zosen Kogyo — Kure** Yd No: 230 Loa 73.18 Br ex 11.54 Dght 5.560 Lbp 68.03 Br md 11.51 Dpth 7.80 Welded, 1 dk	**(A31A2GX) General Cargo Ship** Grain: 3,425; Bale: 3,145 Compartments: 1 Ho, ER 1 Ha: (36.1 x 7.0)ER Derricks: 2x10t; Winches: 6	**1 oil engine** driving 1 FP propeller Total Power: 1,471kW (2,000hp) 12.0kn Nippon Hatsudoki 6N38T 1 x 4 Stroke 6 Cy. 380 x 580 1471kW (2000bhp) Nippon Hatsudoki-Japan AuxGen: 2 x 80kW 220V a.c Fuel: 116.0 5.5pd
9124873 JI3591 -	**WASO MARU No. 3** **Nanko Kisen KK** - *Saiki, Oita* *Japan* MMSI: 431300341 Official number: 135046	*748* - 2,100		**1996-01 Nakatani Shipyard Co. Ltd. — Etajima** Yd No: 570 Loa 86.00 (BB) Br ex - Dght 4.410 Lbp 78.00 Br md 13.00 Dpth 7.70 Welded, 1 dk	**(A31A2GX) General Cargo Ship** Bale: 3,409	**1 oil engine** with clutches & sr geared to sc. shaft driving 1 FP propeller Total Power: 1,618kW (2,200hp) Daihatsu 6DKM-28 1 x 4 Stroke 6 Cy. 280 x 390 1618kW (2200bhp) Daihatsu Diesel Manufacturing Co Lt-Japan Thrusters: 1 Thwart. CP thruster (f)
9260330 HO3096 -	**WASSAY** **Offshore International Shipping & Trading Enterprises Ltd SA** Gulf Shipping Maritime Establishment *Panama* *Panama* MMSI: 351141000 Official number: 2916503B	**625** 187 325	Class: LR ✠ **100A1** SS 03/2013 tug ✠ **LMC** Eq.Ltr: I; Cable: 550.0/24.0 U2 (a)	**2003-03 Stocznia Tczew Sp z oo — Tczew** (Hull) Yd No: (512002) **2003-03 B.V. Scheepswerf Damen — Gorinchem** Yd No: 512002 Loa 40.83 Br ex 11.20 Dght 4.750 Lbp 35.03 Br md 10.99 Dpth 4.90 Welded, 1 dk	**(B32A2ST) Tug**	**2 oil engines** with clutches, flexible couplings & sr reverse geared to sc. shafts driving 2 FP propellers Total Power: 2,864kW (3,894hp) 12.0kn Caterpillar 3516TA 2 x Vee 4 Stroke 16 Cy. 170 x 190 each-1432kW (1947bhp) Caterpillar Inc-USA AuxGen: 2 x 125kW 400V 50Hz a.c Thrusters: 1 Thwart. FP thruster (f)
8854275 WDD4294 -	**WASSILIE B** *ex* Insatiable *-2010* *ex* Lady Aleutian *-2009* *ex* Lady Alaska *-1992* **Wassilie B LLC** - *Quinhagak, AK* *United States of America* MMSI: 367142770 Official number: 640544	*196* 158 -		**1981 Hansen Boat Co. — Marysville, Wa** Loa - Br ex - Dght - Lbp 32.55 Br md 7.92 Dpth 2.65 Welded, 1 dk	**(B11B2FV) Fishing Vessel**	**1 oil engine** driving 1 FP propeller
9278179 A7MJ -	**WASSIT** **Qatar Shipping Co (Q Ship) SPC** - *Doha* *Qatar* MMSI: 466001000 Official number: 197/2004	**528** 158 280	Class: LR (AB) **100A1** SS 03/2009 tug **LMC**	**2004-03 Bharati Shipyard Ltd — Ratnagiri** Yd No: 304 Loa 38.00 Br ex - Dght 4.500 Lbp 36.50 Br md 10.70 Dpth 5.50 Welded	**(B32A2ST) Tug**	**2 oil engines** geared to sc. shafts driving 2 Propellers Total Power: 3,380kW (4,596hp) Wartsila 9L20C 2 x 4 Stroke 9 Cy. 200 x 280 each-1690kW (2298bhp) Wartsila Finland Oy-Finland
8606757 3XWS -	**WASSOU** *ex* Ozernitsa *-2009* **Murmansk Trawl Fleet Co (OAO 'Murmanskiy Tralovyy Flot')** - *Conakry* *Guinea* Official number: 001DNMM2008	**1,895** 568 678	Class: (RS)	**1986-04 VEB Volkswerft Stralsund — Stralsund** Yd No: 707 Loa 62.25 Br ex 13.82 Dght - Lbp 55.00 Br md 13.81 Dpth 9.20 Welded, 2 dks	**(B11A2FS) Stern Trawler** Ins: 580 Ice Capable	**2 oil engines** sr geared to sc. shaft driving 1 CP propeller Total Power: 1,764kW (2,398hp) 12.9kn S.K.L. 8VD26/20AL-2 2 x 4 Stroke 8 Cy. 200 x 260 each-882kW (1199bhp) VEB Schwermaschinenbau "KarlLiebknecht" (SKL)-Magdeburg AuxGen: 1 x 640kW a.c, 3 x 568kW a.c, 1 x 260kW a.c

7335466 HSB2276 -
WASUT
ex Jintana ex Chula No. 4 ex Asean Jaya -1993
ex Kyokuyo Maru -1979 ex Asozan Maru -1979
Siamgas & Petrochemicals PCL (SIAM GAS)
-
Bangkok *Thailand*
Official number: 371000042

672 357 1,111
Class: (NK)

1969 Higaki Zosen K.K. — Imabari Yd No: 92
Loa 54.31 Br ex 9.40 Dght 3.966
Lbp 49.51 Br md - Dpth 4.09
Welded, 1 dk

(A13B2TU) Tanker (unspecified)
Liq: 1,269; Liq (Oil): 1,269
Compartments: 8 Ta, ER

1 oil engine driving 1 FP propeller
Total Power: 883kW (1,201hp) 10.5kr
Hanshin 6LU32
1 x 4 Stroke 6 Cy. 320 x 510 883kW (1201bhp)
Hanshin Nainenki Kogyo-Japan
AuxGen: 2 x 20kW
Fuel: 37.5 3.5pd

8511976 VJJL -
WATAGAN
ex Shell Cove -1996
Tasmanian Ports Corporation Pty Ltd (TasPorts)
-
Sydney, NSW *Australia*
MMSI: 503083000
Official number: 852026

352 105 -
Class: LR
✠ **100A1** SS 11/2011
tug
✠ **LMC** **UMS**
Eq.Ltr: F;
Cable: 275.0/19.0 U2 (a)

1986-09 North Queensland Engineers & Agents Pty Ltd — Cairns QLD Yd No: 128
Loa 32.01 Br ex 10.95 Dght 4.271
Lbp 29.42 Br md 10.53 Dpth 5.03
Welded, 1 dk

(B32A2ST) Tug

2 oil engines with clutches, flexible couplings & dr geared to sc. shafts driving 2 Z propellers
Total Power: 2,646kW (3,598hp)
Niigata 6L28BX
2 x 4 Stroke 6 Cy. 280 x 320 each-1323kW (1799bhp)
Niigata Engineering Co Ltd-Japan
AuxGen: 2 x 90kW 415V 50Hz a.c

9460045 JD2905 -
WATATSUMI
Japan Railway Construction, Transport & Technology Agency & Uwakai Kisen KK
Uwakai Kisen KK
Seiyo, Ehime *Japan*
MMSI: 431000926
Official number: 141003

3,751 - 5,594
Class: NK

2009-05 Hakata Zosen K.K. — Imabari Yd No: 708
Loa 104.91 Br ex - Dght 6.713
Lbp 98.00 Br md 16.00 Dpth 8.50
Welded, 1 dk

(A13B2TP) Products Tanker
Double Hull (13F)
Liq: 6,223; Liq (Oil): 6,223

1 oil engine driving 1 FP propeller
Total Power: 3,309kW (4,499hp) 14.2kr
Akasaka A45
1 x 4 Stroke 6 Cy. 450 x 880 3309kW (4499bhp)
Akasaka Tekkosho KK (Akasaka DieselLtd)-Japan
Fuel: 325.0

9102253 C6OE5 -
WATBAN
ex Tl Watban -2011 ex Watban -2007
The National Shipping Company of Saudi Arabia (BAHRI)
Mideast Ship Management Ltd
SatCom: Inmarsat B 330967110
Nassau *Bahamas*
MMSI: 309671000
Official number: 728113

163,882 97,415 300,361 T/cm 171.9
Class: LR
✠ **100A1** SS 08/2011
Double Hull oil tanker
ESP
SPM
*IWS
ShipRight (SDA, FDA, CM)
✠ **LMC** **UMS IGS**
Eq.Ltr: F*;
Cable: 770.0/122.0 U3 (a)

1996-08 Mitsubishi Heavy Industries Ltd. — Nagasaki Yd No: 2095
Loa 340.00 (BB) Br ex 56.05 Dght 22.500
Lbp 328.00 Br md 56.00 Dpth 31.80
Welded, 1 dk

(A13A2TV) Crude Oil Tanker
Double Hull (13F)
Liq: 333,212; Liq (Oil): 333,212
Compartments: 5 Ta, 10 Wing Ta, ER, 2 Wing Slop Ta
4 Cargo Pump (s): 3x5000m³/hr, 1x2750m³/hr
Manifold: Bow/CM: 171m

1 oil engine driving 1 FP propeller
Total Power: 24,722kW (33,612hp) 15.0k
Mitsubishi 7UEC85LS
1 x 2 Stroke 7 Cy. 850 x 3150 24722kW (33612bhp)
Mitsubishi Heavy Industries Ltd-Japan
AuxGen: 1 x 1000kW 450V 60Hz a.c, 3 x 1050kW 450V 60Hz a.c
Boilers: 2 AuxB (o.f.) 21.9kgf/cm² (21.5bar), AuxB (ex.g.) 11.9kgf/cm² (11.7bar)
Fuel: 286.0 (d.f.) (Heating Coils) 6734.0 (r.f.) 86.0pd

8855774 WDB2625 -
WATCHMAN
ex Tracy D -2000
Doumit Fish LLC
-
Cathlamet, WA *United States of America*
MMSI: 366877950
Official number: 646135

165 49 -

1982 Giddings Boat Works, Inc. — Charleston, Or
Loa - Br ex - Dght -
Lbp 25.21 Br md 7.32 Dpth 2.32
Welded, 1 dk

(B11B2FV) Fishing Vessel

1 oil engine driving 1 FP propeller

9046435 DSLM -
WATER BIRD
ex Ck Pioneer -2012 ex Daesan Pioneer -2008
KSM Co Ltd
-
Busan *South Korea*
MMSI: 440499000
Official number: BSR-910031

1,323 698 2,181 T/cm 7.1
Class: KR

1991-02 Shinyoung Shipbuilding Industry Co Ltd — Yeosu Yd No: 155
Loa 69.75 Br ex - Dght 5.146
Lbp 64.60 Br md 12.00 Dpth 5.80
Welded, 1 dk

(A12A2TC) Chemical Tanker
Liq: 2,358
Cargo Heating Coils
Compartments: 8 Wing Ta, 2 Wing Slop Ta, ER
2 Cargo Pump (s): 2x300m³/hr
Manifold: Bow/CM: 24m

1 oil engine sr geared to sc. shaft driving 1 FP propeller
Total Power: 1,261kW (1,714hp) 11.5k
Alpha 6L28/3
1 x 4 Stroke 6 Cy. 280 x 320 1261kW (1714bhp)
Ssangyong Heavy Industries Co Ltd-South Korea
Thrusters: 1 Thwart. FP thruster (a)
Fuel: 26.0 (d.f.) 106.0 (r.f.)

9135183 DSOV3 -
WATER BREEZE
ex Chem Bridge -2011 ex Clarice -2006
KSM Co Ltd
-
Jeju *South Korea*
MMSI: 440396000
Official number: JJR-069581

5,254 2,910 8,511 T/cm 16.5
Class: KR (NK)

1996-03 Miyoshi Shipbuilding Co Ltd — Uwajima EH Yd No: 329
Loa 121.35 (BB) Br ex 17.23 Dght 7.997
Lbp 112.40 Br md 17.20 Dpth 9.80
Welded, 1 dk

(A12B2TR) Chemical/Products Tanker
Double Hull
Liq: 10,278; Liq (Oil): 10,278
Cargo Heating Coils
Compartments: 3 Ta (s.stl), 5 Ta, 12 Wing Ta, 4 Wing Ta (s.stl), ER
24 Cargo Pump (s): 5x200m³/hr, 4x150m³/hr, 15x100m³/hr
Manifold: Bow/CM: 61.3m

1 oil engine driving 1 FP propeller
Total Power: 4,531kW (6,160hp) 14.0k
B&W 7L35M
1 x 2 Stroke 7 Cy. 350 x 1050 4531kW (6160bhp)
Makita Corp-Japan
AuxGen: 3 x 360kW a.c
Thrusters: 1 Thwart. FP thruster (f)
Fuel: 93.0 (d.f.) 763.0 (r.f.)

8327375 HO6990 -
WATER IRON
ex Mizushima Maru No. 2 -1983
Ilona Trading Corp
-
Panama *Panama*
Official number: 10304KJ

193 103 380

1967 Oka Zosen Tekko K.K. — Ushimado
Loa 38.00 Br ex - Dght -
Lbp 34.02 Br md 7.31 Dpth 3.10
Welded, 1 dk

(A31A2GX) General Cargo Ship
1 Ha: (17.9 x 5.9)ER

1 oil engine driving 1 FP propeller
Total Power: 257kW (349hp) 8.0k

8621226 V3TS4 -
WATER ISLAND
ex Mizushima Maru No. 2 -2003
S Road Co Ltd (OOO S Roud)
-
Belize City *Belize*
MMSI: 312083000
Official number: 160310609

273 202 390

1983 K.K. Kamishima Zosensho — Osakikamijima Yd No: 136
Loa 39.53 Br ex - Dght 3.101
Lbp 35.01 Br md 7.31 Dpth 3.41
Welded, 1 dk

(A31A2GX) General Cargo Ship

1 oil engine driving 1 FP propeller
Total Power: 331kW (450hp) 9.8k
Matsui ML624GH
1 x 4 Stroke 6 Cy. 240 x 400 331kW (450bhp)
Matsui Iron Works Co Ltd-Japan

9620865 AVQX -
WATER LILY
completed as Sea Tetra -2012
launched as Saam Itza -2012
Polestar Maritime Ltd
-
Mumbai *India*
MMSI: 419000482
Official number: 3938

462 138 197
Class: AB IR

2012-03 Shunde Huaxing Shipyard — Foshan GD (Hull) Yd No: (HY2172)
2012-03 Bonny Fair Development Ltd — Hong Kong Yd No: HY2172
Loa 31.00 Br ex 11.30 Dght 4.300
Lbp 27.70 Br md 11.00 Dpth 5.60
Welded, 1 dk

(B32A2ST) Tug

2 oil engines reduction geared to sc. shafts driving 2 Propellers
Total Power: 3,650kW (4,962hp) 10.0k
Caterpillar 3516B-H
2 x Vee 4 Stroke 16 Cy. 170 x 215 each-1825kW (2481bhp)
Caterpillar Inc-USA
AuxGen: 1 x 155kW a.c

9615602 9WLF6 -
WATER MASTER
Woodman Water Master Sdn Bhd
-
Kuching *Malaysia*
MMSI: 533170037
Official number: 333355

2,126 638 3,214
Class: NK

2012-09 Sarawak Land Shipyard Sdn Bhd — Miri Yd No: 103
Loa 75.89 Br ex - Dght 3.976
Lbp 71.63 Br md 18.60 Dpth 5.18
Welded, 1 dk

(A35D2RL) Landing Craft
Liq: 2,686

2 oil engines reduction geared to sc. shafts driving 2 Propellers
Total Power: 1,518kW (2,064hp) 10.0k
Mitsubishi S6R2-MTK3
2 x 4 Stroke 6 Cy. 170 x 220 each-759kW (1032bhp)
Mitsubishi Heavy Industries Ltd-Japan
Fuel: 480.0

9045168 A8OE3 -
WATER PHOENIX
ex Lake Phoenix -2012 ex Amber Rose -1996
'Water Phoenix' Schiffahrtsgesellschaft mbH & Co KG
Triton Schiffahrts GmbH
Monrovia *Liberia*
MMSI: 636092422
Official number: 92422

7,303 4,812 8,075
Class: BV (NK)

1992-12 Shin Kochi Jyuko K.K. — Kochi Yd No: 7026
Loa 134.02 (BB) Br ex - Dght 7.569
Lbp 125.01 Br md 20.80 Dpth 10.17
Welded, 1 dk, 2nd & 3rd dks in holds only

(A34A2GR) Refrigerated Cargo Ship
Cars: 291
Ins: 11,137
TEU 12 incl 12 ref C
Compartments: 4 Ho, ER, 1 Tw Dk in Fo'c's'l, 7 Tw Dk
4 Ha: 4 (7.4 x 7.3)ER
Derricks: 8x5t

1 oil engine driving 1 FP propeller
Total Power: 7,061kW (9,600hp) 19.3k
Mitsubishi 8UEC45L
1 x 2 Stroke 8 Cy. 450 x 1350 7061kW (9600bhp)
Kobe Hatsudoki KK-Japan
AuxGen: 3 x 500kW 450V 60Hz a.c

8119950 HP9372 -
WATER SPIRIT
ex Southern Gulf -1987
WS Holdings Ltd
-
Panama *Panama*
MMSI: 352334000
Official number: 4262711

325 98 500
Class: (AB)

1980 Depend-A-Craft — Pierre Part, La Yd No: 47
Loa - Br ex - Dght 3.841
Lbp 47.55 Br md 11.59 Dpth 4.35
Welded, 1 dk

(B21A2OS) Platform Supply Ship

2 oil engines reverse reduction geared to sc. shafts driving 2 FP propellers
Total Power: 1,368kW (1,860hp) 11.0k
G.M. (Detroit Diesel) 16V-14
2 x Vee 2 Stroke 16 Cy. 146 x 146 each-684kW (930bhp)
General Motors Detroit DieselAllison Divn-USA
AuxGen: 2 x 90kW a.c

7309950 - -
WATER SPIRIT
Economy Shipping Co Ltd
Turks Islands *Turks & Caicos Islands (British)*
Official number: 316154

124 84 -

1970 Davis Shipbuilding Co. — Freeport, Tx
L reg 20.76 Br ex 6.71 Dght -
Lbp - Br md - Dpth 3.69
Welded, 1 dk

(B11B2FV) Fishing Vessel

1 oil engine driving 1 FP propeller
Total Power: 294kW (400hp) 12.0k
G.M. (Detroit Diesel) 8V-71-
1 x Vee 2 Stroke 8 Cy. 108 x 127 294kW (400bhp)
General Motors Corp-USA

7349091 LJAC -
WATERBJORN
ex Bugsier 4 -1997
Kristiansund Taubaatservice AS
-
Kristiansund *Norway*
MMSI: 257413900

184 55 104
Class: GL

1973-10 Schiffswerft u. Maschinenfabrik Max Sieghold — Bremerhaven Yd No: 164
Loa 26.07 Br ex 8.87 Dght 2.798
Lbp 23.80 Br md 8.81 Dpth 3.59
Welded, 1 dk

(B32A2ST) Tug
Ice Capable

2 oil engines geared to sc. shafts driving 2 Directional propellers
Total Power: 1,280kW (1,740hp)
Deutz SBA6M52
2 x 4 Stroke 6 Cy. 220 x 280 each-640kW (870bhp)
Kloeckner Humboldt Deutz AG-West Germany

IMO / Call sign	Name / Owner	Tonnage	Class	Builder / Dimensions	Type	Machinery
9476874 YJVY4 -	**WATERBUCK** **DBGP** Galliano Marine Service LLC *Port Vila* *Vanuatu* MMSI: 576008000 Official number: 1886	**2,311** 693 1,940	Class: AB	**2010-01 Stocznia Polnocna SA (Northern Shipyard) — Gdansk** (Hull) Yd No: B844/15 **2010-01 Gdanska Stocznia 'Remontowa' SA — Gdansk** Yd No: 1674/15 Loa 70.00 Br ex - Dght 5.100 Lbp 63.60 Br md 15.50 Dpth 6.60 Welded, 1 dk	**(B21B20A) Anchor Handling Tug Supply** Passengers: cabins: 13	**2 oil engines** reduction geared to sc. shafts driving 2 CP propellers Total Power: 10,120kW (13,760hp) 14.0kn Caterpillar C280-16 2 x Vee 4 Stroke 16 Cy. 280 x 300 each-5060kW (6880bhp) Caterpillar Inc-USA AuxGen: 2 x 1724kW a.c, 1 x 250kW a.c Thrusters: 2 Thwart. FP thruster (f); 1 Thwart. FP thruster (a) Fuel: 820.0
8634869 - -	**WATERCAT** *ex* Lenson - -	**113** 40 -		**1986 Teijon Telakka Oy — Teijo** Loa 25.00 Br ex - Dght 1.000 Lbp - Br md 6.40 Dpth - Welded, 1 dk	**(A37B2PS) Passenger Ship** Hull Material: Aluminium Alloy Passengers: unberthed: 100	**2 oil engines** driving 2 FP propellers Total Power: 604kW (822hp) 16.0kn
8977807 WDF4766 -	**WATEREE** *ex* Sam McCall *-2010* **Starfleet Marine Transportation Inc** *Charleston, SC* *United States of America* MMSI: 367455610 Official number: 976496	**285** 85 283		**1991-08 Gulf Craft Inc — Patterson LA** Yd No: 357 Loa 49.00 Br ex - Dght 2.000 Lbp 45.00 Br md 9.00 Dpth 3.00 Welded, 1 dk	**(B21A20C) Crew/Supply Vessel** Hull Material: Aluminium Alloy Passengers: 101; cabins: 4	**6 oil engines** reduction geared to sc. shafts driving 6 FP propellers Total Power: 3,000kW (4,080hp) 22.0kn Cummins KTA-19-M 6 x 4 Stroke 6 Cy. 159 x 159 each-500kW (680bhp) Cummins Engine Co Inc-USA AuxGen: 2 x 50kW 60Hz a.c
9174517 9V5524 -	**WATERFRONT 1** **IKM International Pte Ltd** Indo Falcon Shipping & Travel Pte Ltd *Singapore* *Singapore* MMSI: 564426000 Official number: 397955	**145** 61 40	Class: BV	**1997-11 WaveMaster International Pty Ltd — Fremantle WA** Yd No: 152 Loa 30.50 Br ex - Dght 0.950 Lbp 28.80 Br md 6.50 Dpth 3.80 Welded, 1 dk	**(A37B2PS) Passenger Ship** Passengers: unberthed: 200	**3 oil engines** geared to sc. shafts driving 3 Water jets Total Power: 1,980kW (2,691hp) 28.0kn M.T.U. 12V183TE92 3 x Vee 4 Stroke 12 Cy. 128 x 142 each-660kW (897bhp) MTU Friedrichshafen GmbH-Friedrichshafen
9174529 9V5525 -	**WATERFRONT 2** **IKM International Pte Ltd** Indo Falcon Shipping & Travel Pte Ltd *Singapore* *Singapore* MMSI: 564427000 Official number: 397956	**145** 61 40	Class: BV	**1997-11 WaveMaster International Pty Ltd — Fremantle WA** Yd No: 153 Loa 30.30 Br ex - Dght 1.000 Lbp 28.80 Br md 6.50 Dpth 3.80 Welded	**(A37B2PS) Passenger Ship** Passengers: unberthed: 200	**3 oil engines** geared to sc. shafts driving 3 Water jets Total Power: 1,980kW (2,691hp) 28.0kn M.T.U. 12V183TE92 3 x Vee 4 Stroke 12 Cy. 128 x 142 each-660kW (897bhp) MTU Friedrichshafen GmbH-Friedrichshafen
8522327 - -	**WATERGATE 1** *ex* Oh Seung No. 101 *-2013* **Watergate Petroleum & Gas Nigeria Ltd** *Lagos* *Nigeria* Official number: 377869	**477** 105 1,152	Class: (KR)	**1986 Chungmu Shipbuilding Co Inc — Tongyeong** Yd No: 111 Loa 58.50 Br ex 9.43 Dght 4.111 Lbp 52.02 Br md 9.40 Dpth 4.40 Welded, 1 dk	**(A13B2TU) Tanker (unspecified)** Liq: 1,296; Liq (Oil): 1,296	**1 oil engine** driving 1 FP propeller Total Power: 412kW (560hp) 10.5kn Hanshin 6L26BGSH 1 x 4 Stroke 6 Cy. 260 x 400 412kW (560bhp) Ssangyong Heavy Industries Co Ltd-South Korea AuxGen: 1 x 64kW 225V a.c
9110860 PIMV -	**WATERGEUS** **Wagenborg Sleepdienst BV** *Delfzijl* *Netherlands* MMSI: 246317000 Official number: 28218	**134** 40 -	Class: BV	**1995-03 Stocznia Tczew Sp z oo — Tczew** (Hull) **1995-03 B.V. Scheepswerf Damen — Gorinchem** Yd No: 6518 Loa 22.50 Br ex 7.25 Dght 2.800 Lbp 20.41 Br md 7.20 Dpth 3.70 Welded, 1 dk	**(B32A2ST) Tug** Ice Capable	**2 oil engines** geared to sc. shafts driving 2 FP propellers Total Power: 1,330kW (1,808hp) 12.0kn Wartsila UD25V12 2 x Vee 4 Stroke 12 Cy. 150 x 180 each-665kW (904bhp) Wartsila SACM Diesel SA-France AuxGen: 2 x 46kW 220/380V a.c Fuel: 35.0 (d.f.) 5.2pd
8318166 PIMU -	**WATERMAN** **Wagenborg Sleepdienst BV** *Delfzijl* *Netherlands* MMSI: 245128000 Official number: 2450	**236** 70 136	Class: LR ✠ **100A1** SS 05/2012 tug for service maximum 200 miles offshore ✠ **LMC** Eq.Ltr: F; Cable: 275.0/19.0 U2 (a)	**1987-12 Bodewes Binnenvaart B.V. — Millingen a/d Rijn** Yd No: 773 Loa 28.50 Br ex 9.15 Dght 3.250 Lbp 24.90 Br md 8.81 Dpth 4.27 Welded, 1 dk	**(B32A2ST) Tug**	**2 oil engines** with clutches, flexible couplings & sr reverse geared to sc. shafts driving 2 FP propellers Total Power: 1,800kW (2,448hp) 12.3kn MWM TBD440-6K 2 x 4 Stroke 6 Cy. 230 x 270 each-900kW (1224bhp) Motoren Werke Mannheim AG (MWM)-West Germany AuxGen: 2 x 70kW 220/380V 50Hz a.c
7349118 LJTH -	**WATERMAN** *ex* Bugsier 10 *-1999* **Kristiansund Taubaatservice AS** *Kristiansund* *Norway* MMSI: 259587000	**179** 53 -	Class: GL	**1974-08 Schiffswerft u. Maschinenfabrik Max Sieghold — Bremerhaven** Yd No: 166 Loa 26.73 Br ex 8.84 Dght 2.801 Lbp 23.80 Br md 8.80 Dpth 3.59 Welded, 1 dk	**(B32A2ST) Tug** Ice Capable	**2 oil engines** geared to sc. shafts driving 2 Directional propellers Total Power: 1,280kW (1,740hp) Deutz SBA6M528 2 x 4 Stroke 6 Cy. 220 x 280 each-640kW (870bhp) Kloeckner Humboldt Deutz AG-West Germany
7033575 - -	**WATERMAN 8** *ex* Tong Choon *-1999* *ex* Delta Power *-1993* *ex* Sunny Eagle *-1992* *ex* Sanpuku Maru *-1991* **PT Pelayaran Flora Bahari Marine Services** - *Indonesia*	**428** 129 152	Class: (GL) (NK)	**1970-02 Sanyo Zosen K.K. — Onomichi** Yd No: 577 Lengthened-1976 Loa 40.70 Br ex 9.02 Dght 3.658 Lbp 38.59 Br md 9.00 Dpth 3.99 Welded, 1 dk	**(B32B2SP) Pusher Tug**	**2 oil engines** driving 2 FP propellers Total Power: 2,354kW (3,200hp) 11.5kn Niigata 6M31X 2 x 4 Stroke 6 Cy. 310 x 460 each-1177kW (1600bhp) (new engine ,made 1973) Niigata Engineering Co Ltd-Japan AuxGen: 2 x 64kW 220/440V a.c
8982266 NWAA -	**WATERS** **Military Sealift Command (MSC)** - *United States of America* MMSI: 367851000 Official number: CG037934	**12,663** 3,798 6,446	Class: AB	**1993-05 Avondale Industries, Inc., Shipyards Div. — New Orleans, La** Yd No: 2370 Loa 137.70 Br ex - Dght 7.020 Lbp 130.60 Br md 21.03 Dpth 11.23 Welded, 2 dks	**(B31A2SR) Research Survey Vessel** Ice Capable	**5 diesel electric oil engines** driving 5 gen. each 12500kW Connecting to 2 elec. motors driving 2 Propellers Total Power: 12,500kW (16,995hp) 12.0kn EMD (Electro-Motive) 16-645-F7B 5 x Vee 2 Stroke 16 Cy. 230 x 254 each-2500kW (3399bhp) General Motors Corp.Electro-Motive Div.-La Grange Thrusters: 2 Tunnel thruster (f); 2 Tunnel thruster (a)
9428059 PCIV -	**WATERSTRAAT** **NV Shipping Co Waterstraat** Wagenborg Sleepdienst BV *Delfzijl* *Netherlands* MMSI: 246758000 Official number: 54169	**294** 88 149	Class: LR ✠ **100A1** SS 09/2013 escort tug fire fighting Ship 1 (2400m3/h) **LMC** **UMS** Eq.Ltr: F; Cable: 275.0/19.0 U2 (a)	**2008-09 Damen Shipyards Gdynia SA — Gdynia** (Hull) Yd No: (511553) **2008-09 B.V. Scheepswerf Damen — Gorinchem** Yd No: 511553 Loa 28.75 Br ex 10.43 Dght 3.600 Lbp 25.78 Br md 9.80 Dpth 4.60 Welded, 1 dk	**(B32A2ST) Tug**	**2 oil engines** reduction geared to sc. shafts driving 2 Directional propellers Total Power: 3,730kW (5,072hp) Caterpillar 3516B-HD 2 x Vee 4 Stroke 16 Cy. 170 x 215 each-1865kW (2536bhp) Caterpillar Inc-USA AuxGen: 2 x 86kW 400V 50Hz a.c
9428047 PCIW -	**WATERSTROOM** **NV Shipping Co Waterstroom** Wagenborg Sleepdienst BV *Delfzijl* *Netherlands* MMSI: 246759000 Official number: 54170	**294** - 143	Class: LR ✠ **100A1** SS 07/2013 escort tug, fire fighting Ship 1 (2400 m3/h) **LMC** **UMS** Eq.Ltr: F; Cable: 275.0/19.0 U2 (a)	**2008-07 Damen Shipyards Gdynia SA — Gdynia** (Hull) Yd No: (511552) **2008-07 B.V. Scheepswerf Damen — Gorinchem** Yd No: 511552 Loa 28.67 Br ex 10.43 Dght 3.600 Lbp 25.78 Br md 9.80 Dpth 4.60 Welded, 1 dk	**(B32A2ST) Tug**	**2 oil engines** reduction geared to sc. shafts driving 2 Directional propellers Total Power: 3,730kW (5,072hp) Caterpillar 3516B-HD 2 x Vee 4 Stroke 16 Cy. 170 x 215 each-1865kW (2536bhp) Caterpillar Inc-USA AuxGen: 2 x 86kW 400/230V a.c
9240005 5BGD2 -	**WATERWAY** **BW Marine (Cyprus) Ltd** Westminster Dredging Co Ltd *Limassol* *Cyprus* MMSI: 210407000	**5,395** 1,618 6,605	Class: BV	**2001-02 Merwede Shipyard BV — Hardinxveld** Yd No: 686 Loa 97.70 (BB) Br ex 23.02 Dght 6.580 Lbp 84.08 Br md 23.00 Dpth 7.00 Welded, 1 dk	**(B33B2DT) Trailing Suction Hopper Dredger** Hopper: 4,900 Cranes: 2	**2 oil engines** with clutches, flexible couplings & sr geared to sc. shafts driving 2 CP propellers Total Power: 5,520kW (7,504hp) 13.2kn Wartsila 6L32 2 x 4 Stroke 6 Cy. 320 x 400 each-2760kW (3752bhp) Wartsila NSD Nederland BV-Netherlands AuxGen: 1 x 1500kW 400V 50Hz a.c, 1 x 600kW 400V 50Hz a.c Thrusters: 1 Thwart. FP thruster (f) Fuel: 660.0 (d.f.) 25.0pd
9143594 J8B3859 -	**WATERWAY** *ex* Alissa *-2008* **Waterway Shipping Ltd** Baltnautic Shipping Ltd *Kingstown* *St Vincent & The Grenadines* MMSI: 376532000 Official number: 10332	**1,143** 456 1,454	Class: BV	**1996-10 Plocka Stocznia Rzeczna — Plock** (Hull) **1996-10 Schiffswerft Schloemer GmbH & Co KG — Moormerland** Yd No: 602 Loa 81.40 (BB) Br ex 9.50 Dght 3.150 Lbp 78.66 Br md 9.46 Dpth 4.65 Welded, 1 dk	**(A31A2GX) General Cargo Ship** Grain: 2,095; Bale: 2,095 TEU 50 C.Ho 50/20' Compartments: 1 Ho, ER 1 Ha: (52.2 x 7.6)ER	**1 oil engine** with clutches & reverse reduction geared to sc. shaft driving 1 FP propeller Total Power: 895kW (1,217hp) 8.0kn Cummins KTA-38-M2 1 x Vee 4 Stroke 12 Cy. 159 x 159 895kW (1217bhp) Cummins Engine Co Ltd-United Kingdom AuxGen: 2 x 48kW 220/380V 50Hz a.c Thrusters: 1 Thwart. FP thruster (f) Fuel: 52.0 (d.f.) (Part Heating Coils) 3.3pd

IMO / Call sign	Name, owner, registry	Tonnage	Class	Builder & dimensions	Type	Machinery
8104046 *P2V5561* -	**WATO** *ex* Iron Cove *-1997* **Pacific Towing (PNG) Pty Ltd** - *Port Moresby* *Papua New Guinea* MMSI: 553111692 Official number: 001426	*347* 107 730	Class: LR ✠ **100A1** SS 06/2012 tug ✠ **LMC** **UMS** Eq.Ltr: F; Cable: 275.0/19.0 U2	**1982-10 Carrington Slipways Pty Ltd — Newcastle NSW** Yd No: 151 Loa 33.30 Br ex 10.93 Dght 4.271 Lbp 29.39 Br md 10.52 Dpth 5.01 Welded, 1 dk	**(B32A2ST) Tug**	**2 oil engines** with clutches, flexible couplings & dr geared to sc. shafts driving 2 Z propellers Total Power: 2,648kW (3,600hp) 12.8kn Niigata 6L28BX 2 x 4 Stroke 6 Cy. 280 x 320 each-1324kW (1800bhp) Niigata Engineering Co Ltd-Japan AuxGen: 2 x 125kW 415V 50Hz a.c Fuel: 78.0 (d.f.) 11.0pd
9416862 *FMLK*	**WATOA** *ex* Hung Seng 043 *-2006* **Manutrans SAS** *Noumea* *France* MMSI: 540008400	**137** 42 115	Class: BV (GL)	**2006-12 Hung Seng Shipbuilding Sdn Bhd — Sibu** Yd No: 043 Loa 23.50 Br ex 7.33 Dght 2.600 Lbp 21.44 Br md 7.32 Dpth 3.10 Welded, 1 dk	**(B32A2ST) Tug**	**2 oil engines** reduction geared to sc. shafts driving 2 FP propellers Total Power: 882kW (1,200hp) Cummins KTA-19-M3 2 x 4 Stroke 6 Cy. 159 x 159 each-441kW (600bhp) Cummins Engine Co Inc-USA
8740321 - -	**WATTANA NAVEE 2** **Porncharoen Transport Ltd Partnership** *Bangkok* *Thailand* Official number: 480001593	**116** 73 -		**2005 Nava Progress Co. Ltd. — Samut Prakan** Loa 35.00 Br ex - Dght - Lbp - Br md 6.00 Dpth 2.45 Welded, 1 dk	**(A13B2TP) Products Tanker** Double Hull (13F)	**1 oil engine** reduction geared to sc. shaft driving 1 Propeller Total Power: 257kW (349hp) Cummins 1 x 4 Stroke 257kW (349bhp) Cummins Engine Co Inc-USA
8826656 *DJDB* WYK 8	**WATTENLAEUFER** **Wyk 8 Muschelfischereibetrieb GmbH** - *Wyk auf Foehr* *Germany* MMSI: 211363690 Official number: 12302	**217** 65 169		**1987-09 Husumer Schiffswerft Inh. Gebr. Kroeger GmbH & Co. KG — Husum** Yd No: 1506 Loa 35.60 Br ex - Dght - Lbp 33.18 Br md 10.00 Dpth 1.90 Welded, 1 dk	**(B11B2FV) Fishing Vessel**	**2 oil engines** dr reverse geared to sc. shafts driving 2 FP propellers Total Power: 750kW (1,020hp) Caterpillar 3412TA 2 x Vee 4 Stroke 12 Cy. 137 x 152 each-375kW (510bhp) (new engine 1998) Caterpillar Inc-USA AuxGen: 1 x 132kW 380V a.c
8803680 *VJAC* -	**WAURI** **Government of The Commonwealth of Australia (Department of Primary Industry)** - SatCom: Inmarsat C 450300465 *Cairns, Qld* *Australia* Official number: 852993	**145** 21 -		**1988-03 North Queensland Engineers & Agents Pty Ltd — Cairns QLD** Yd No: 129 Loa 25.20 Br ex 8.72 Dght 2.120 Lbp 21.49 Br md 8.60 Dpth 3.41 Welded, 1 dk	**(B12D2FP) Fishery Patrol Vessel**	**2 oil engines** with clutches, flexible couplings & sr geared to sc. shafts driving 2 FP propellers Total Power: 1,210kW (1,646hp) 17.0kn MWM TBD234V12 2 x Vee 4 Stroke 12 Cy. 128 x 140 each-605kW (823bhp) Motoren Werke Mannheim AG (MWM)-West Germany AuxGen: 2 x 30kW 415V 50Hz a.c
9313785 *PHBZ* -	**WAVE** *ex* Flinterwave *-2011* **Wave BV** Flinter Shipping BV *Heerenveen* *Netherlands* MMSI: 246264000 Official number: 42472	**2,999** 1,640 4,537	Class: BV	**2004-11 Scheepswerf Ferus Smit BV — Westerbroek** Yd No: 352 Loa 89.78 (BB) Br ex - Dght 5.950 Lbp 84.99 Br md 14.00 Dpth 7.50 Welded, 1 dk	**(A31A2GX) General Cargo Ship** Grain: 6,080 TEU 146 C Ho 102 TEU C Dk 44 TEU incl 10 ref C. Compartments: 1 Ho, ER 1 Ha: ER (61.5 x 11.5) Ice Capable	**1 oil engine** geared to sc. shaft driving 1 CP propeller Total Power: 2,640kW (3,589hp) 13.0kn MaK 8M25 1 x 4 Stroke 8 Cy. 255 x 400 2640kW (3589bhp) Caterpillar Motoren GmbH & Co. KG-Germany AuxGen: 1 x 340kW 400/230V 50Hz a.c, 1 x 244kW 400/230V 50Hz a.c Thrusters: 1 Tunnel thruster (f) Fuel: 28.5 (d.f.) 233.0 (d.f.)
9670468 - -	**WAVE - 1** **Raka Enterprise** *Chittagong* *Bangladesh* Official number: C-1851	**895** 511 1,600	Class: RI	**2013-10 FMC Dockyard Ltd — Boalkhali** Yd No: 52 Loa 74.00 Br ex - Dght 3.800 Lbp 70.20 Br md 11.00 Dpth 5.00 Welded, 1 dk	**(A13B2TP) Products Tanker** Double Hull (13F)	**2 oil engines** reduction geared to sc. shaft (s) driving 2 Propellers Total Power: 1,576kW (2,142hp) 10.0kn
5187009 *D6BJ3* -	**WAVE BABE** *ex* Courageous *-2004* *ex* Walrus Gale *-2003* *ex* Kilavuz 3 *-2002* - - *Moroni* *Union of Comoros* MMSI: 616076000 Official number: 1200106	**164** - -	Class: (TL) (GL)	**1961 Denizcilik Bankasi T.A.O. — Halic, Istanbul** Yd No: 131 Loa 31.88 Br ex 8.56 Dght 3.461 Lbp 29.01 Br md 8.11 Dpth 3.84 Welded, 1 dk	**(B32A2ST) Tug**	**1 oil engine** driving 1 FP propeller Total Power: 901kW (1,225hp) 12.0kn Fiat C367 1 x 2 Stroke 7 Cy. 360 x 650 901kW (1225bhp) SA Fiat SGM-Torino AuxGen: 2 x 60kW 220V d.c, 1 x 15kW 220V d.c
5221893 *P3VL9* -	**WAVE DANCER 1** *ex* Margarita *-2004* **Wave Dance Shipping Co Ltd** *Limassol* *Cyprus* MMSI: 210480000 Official number: 8616609	**401** 120		**1962 Sava Slipway — Keratsini** Converted From: Ferry (Passenger only)-2004 Loa 28.15 Br ex 6.63 Dght - Lbp - Br md - Dpth - Welded, 1 dk	**(A37B2PS) Passenger Ship**	**2 oil engines** geared to sc. shaft driving 1 FP propeller Total Power: 176kW (240hp)
9470313 *VRGL8*	**WAVE FRIEND** **Ocean Friend Corp Ltd** P&F Marine Co Ltd SatCom: Inmarsat C 447702368 *Hong Kong* *Hong Kong* MMSI: 477728900 Official number: HK-2663	**17,018** 10,108 28,325 T/cm 39.7	Class: NK	**2010-03 Imabari Shipbuilding Co Ltd — Imabari EH (Imabari Shipyard)** Yd No: 715 Loa 169.37 (BB) Br ex 27.24 Dght 9.819 Lbp 160.40 Br md 27.20 Dpth 13.60 Welded, 1 dk	**(A21A2BC) Bulk Carrier** Grain: 37,320; Bale: 35,742 Compartments: 5 Ho, ER 5 Ha: 4 (19.2 x 17.6)ER (13.6 x 16.0) Cranes: 4x30.5t	**1 oil engine** driving 1 FP propeller Total Power: 5,850kW (7,954hp) 14.5kn MAN-B&W 6S42MC 1 x 2 Stroke 6 Cy. 420 x 1764 5850kW (7954bhp) Makita Corp-Japan AuxGen: 3 x 440kW 60Hz a.c Fuel: 1235.0
6412645 - -	**WAVE RUNNER** *ex* Coastal Nomad *-2005* *ex* Biscayne Freeze *-1985* *ex* Omega One *-1981* *ex* Southern Isle *-1979* *ex* Blue Cloud *-1972* -	**1,002** 493 -	Class: (LR) ✠ Classed LR until 1/1/81	**1964-06 Davie Shipbuilding Ltd — Levis QC** Yd No: 646 Loa 67.06 Br ex 10.75 Dght 4.287 Lbp 61.02 Br md 10.67 Dpth 5.80 Welded, 2 dks	**(A34A2GR) Refrigerated Cargo Ship** Ins: 1,229 Compartments: 2 Ho, 6 Wing Ta, 3 Ta, ER, 2 Tw Dk 2 Ha: 2 (8.2 x 3.8)ER Derricks: 4x6t; Winches: 4 Ice Capable	**1 oil engine** driving 1 FP propeller Total Power: 971kW (1,320hp) 12.0kn Deutz RBV8M545 1 x 4 Stroke 8 Cy. 320 x 450 971kW (1320bhp) Kloeckner Humboldt Deutz AG-West Germany Fuel: 121.0 (d.f.)
9100748 *MZBC8* -	**WAVE SENTINEL** *ex* Island Commodore *-2000* **Global Cable II AS** Global Marine Systems Ltd SatCom: Inmarsat C 430930610 *London* *United Kingdom* MMSI: 232616000 Official number: 902895	**12,330** 3,700 4,552	Class: AB (NV)	**1995-06 Koninklijke Schelde Groep B.V. — Vlissingen** Yd No: 376 Converted From: Ro-Ro Cargo Ship-2000 Loa 137.50 (BB) Br ex - Dght 6.014 Lbp 118.70 Br md 21.00 Dpth 7.50 Welded	**(B34D2SL) Cable Layer** Passengers: cabins: 12; berths: 12 A-frames: 1x35t	**2 oil engines** dr geared to sc. shafts driving 2 CP propellers Total Power: 9,000kW (12,236hp) 12.0kn MaK 6M552C 2 x 4 Stroke 6 Cy. 450 x 520 each-4500kW (6118bhp) Krupp MaK Maschinenbau GmbH-Kiel AuxGen: 2 x 845kW 440V 60Hz a.c, 3 x 1456kW a.c Thrusters: 2 Thwart. CP thruster (f); 1 Tunnel thruster (f); 2 Directional thruster (a) Fuel: 112.0 (d.f.) 727.0 (r.f.) 41.0pd
8126549 *J8AF6* -	**WAVE TRADER** *ex* Vinland Saga *-2010* **Seatrader International SA** Wavecrest Shipmanagement Inc SatCom: Inmarsat C 437793410 *Kingstown* *St Vincent & The Grenadines* MMSI: 377934000	**972** 590 1,605	Class: TM (BV)	**1982-10 A/S Bogense Skibsvaerft — Bogense** Yd No: 231 Lengthened-1987 Loa 63.20 Br ex - Dght 4.500 Lbp 50.02 Br md 9.61 Dpth 5.62 Welded, 2 dks	**(A31A2GX) General Cargo Ship** Grain: 1,718; Bale: 1,548 Compartments: 2 Ho, ER 2 Ha: (19.0 x 6.2) (15.3 x 6.2)ER Derricks: 2x5t; Winches: 2 Ice Capable	**1 oil engine** driving 1 CP propeller Total Power: 725kW (986hp) 10.0kn MWM TBD440-6K 1 x 4 Stroke 6 Cy. 230 x 270 725kW (986bhp) Motoren Werke Mannheim AG (MWM)-West Germany
8027810 *MZD07* -	**WAVE VENTURE** *ex* Kraka *-2000* *ex* Mercandian Governor *-1988* *ex* Governor *-1985* *ex* Mercandian Governor *-1984* **Global Marine Systems Ltd** - *London* *United Kingdom* MMSI: 234270000 Official number: 902722	**10,076** 3,023 5,012	Class: AB (NV)	**1982-11 Frederikshavn Vaerft A/S — Frederikshavn** Yd No: 402 Converted From: Ferry (Passenger/Vehicle)-2000 Converted From: Ro-Ro Cargo Ship-1988 Loa 141.50 (BB) Br ex 19.41 Dght 6.100 Lbp 122.85 Br md 19.38 Dpth 11.61 Welded, 2 dks	**(B34D2SL) Cable Layer** Bale: 13,790 A-frames: 1x10t	**1 oil engine** with clutches, flexible couplings & sr geared to sc. shaft driving 1 CP propeller Total Power: 3,597kW (4,890hp) 12.5kn MaK 12M453AK 1 x Vee 4 Stroke 12 Cy. 320 x 420 3597kW (4890bhp) Krupp MaK Maschinenbau GmbH-Kiel AuxGen: 3 x 1530kW 440V 60Hz a.c, 3 x 1511kW 440V 60Hz a.c Thrusters: 1 Thwart. FP thruster (f); 1 Tunnel thruster (f); 1 Tunnel thruster (f); 2 Directional thruster (a) Fuel: 240.0 (d.f.) 707.0 (r.f.)

IMO / Call sign	Ship / Owner / Registry	Tonnage	Class	Build / Dimensions	Type	Machinery
9257840 *9V6134*	**WAVEMASTER 3** **Berlian Ferries Pte Ltd** - *Singapore* *Singapore* MMSI: 563002830 Official number: 389503	**253** 84 43	Class: NV	**2001-11 WaveMaster International Pty Ltd — Fremantle WA** Yd No: 201 Loa 37.60 Br ex 7.32 Dght 2.250 Lbp 31.60 Br md 7.00 Dpth 2.50 Welded	**(A37B2PS) Passenger Ship** Hull Material: Aluminium Alloy Passengers: unberthed: 170	**3 oil engines** reduction geared to sc. shafts driving 3 FP propellers Total Power: 2,463kW (3,348hp) 29.0kn Caterpillar 3412E 3 x Vee 4 Stroke 12 Cy. 137 x 152 each-821kW (1116bhp) Caterpillar Inc-USA AuxGen: 2 x 72kW a.c Fuel: 10.5 (d.f.)
9257888 *9V6136*	**WAVEMASTER 5** **Berlian Ferries Pte Ltd** - *Singapore* *Singapore* MMSI: 563002840 Official number: 389504	**253** 84 43	Class: NV	**2001-11 WaveMaster International Pty Ltd — Fremantle WA** Yd No: 202 Loa 37.60 Br ex 7.32 Dght 2.250 Lbp 31.60 Br md 7.00 Dpth 2.50 Welded	**(A37B2PS) Passenger Ship** Hull Material: Aluminium Alloy Passengers: unberthed: 200	**3 oil engines** reduction geared to sc. shafts driving 3 FP propellers Total Power: 2,463kW (3,348hp) Caterpillar 3412E 3 x Vee 4 Stroke 12 Cy. 137 x 152 each-821kW (1116bhp) Caterpillar Inc-USA
9261126 *9V6137*	**WAVEMASTER 6** **Berlian Ferries Pte Ltd** - *Singapore* *Singapore* MMSI: 563002940 Official number: 389505	**253** 84 43	Class: NV	**2001-11 WaveMaster International Pty Ltd — Fremantle WA** Yd No: 203 Loa 37.60 Br ex 7.32 Dght 1.030 Lbp 31.60 Br md 7.00 Dpth 2.50 Welded	**(A37B2PS) Passenger Ship** Hull Material: Aluminium Alloy Passengers: unberthed: 170	**3 oil engines** geared to sc. shafts driving 3 FP propellers Total Power: 2,463kW (3,348hp) 32.0kn Caterpillar 3412E 3 x Vee 4 Stroke 12 Cy. 137 x 152 each-821kW (1116bhp) Caterpillar Inc-USA
9264257 *9V6138*	**WAVEMASTER 7** **Berlian Ferries Pte Ltd** - *Singapore* *Singapore* MMSI: 564051526 Official number: 389506	**253** 84 43	Class: NV	**2002-01 WaveMaster International Pty Ltd — Fremantle WA** Yd No: 204 Loa 37.60 Br ex 7.32 Dght 1.030 Lbp 31.60 Br md 7.00 Dpth 2.50 Welded	**(A37B2PS) Passenger Ship** Hull Material: Aluminium Alloy Passengers: unberthed: 170	**3 oil engines** reduction geared to sc. shafts driving 3 FP propellers Total Power: 2,463kW (3,348hp) 32.0kn Caterpillar 3412E 3 x Vee 4 Stroke 12 Cy. 137 x 152 each-821kW (1116bhp) Caterpillar Inc-USA
9268459 *9V6139*	**WAVEMASTER 8** **Berlian Ferries Pte Ltd** - *Singapore* *Singapore* MMSI: 563003090 Official number: 389508	**253** 84 43	Class: NV	**2002-03 WaveMaster International Pty Ltd — Fremantle WA** Yd No: 205 Loa 37.60 Br ex 7.32 Dght 2.250 Lbp 31.60 Br md 7.00 Dpth 2.50 Welded, 1 dk	**(A37B2PS) Passenger Ship** Hull Material: Aluminium Alloy Passengers: unberthed: 170	**3 oil engines** reduction geared to sc. shafts driving 3 FP propellers Total Power: 2,463kW (3,348hp) 32.0kn Caterpillar 3412E 3 x Vee 4 Stroke 12 Cy. 137 x 152 each-821kW (1116bhp) Caterpillar Inc-USA
9275232 *9V6140*	**WAVEMASTER 9** **Berlian Ferries Pte Ltd** - *Singapore* *Singapore* MMSI: 563003330 Official number: 389509	**253** 84 43	Class: NV	**2002-05 WaveMaster International Pty Ltd — Fremantle WA** Yd No: 206 Loa 37.60 Br ex 7.32 Dght 2.250 Lbp 31.60 Br md 7.00 Dpth 2.50 Welded, 1 dk	**(A37B2PS) Passenger Ship** Hull Material: Aluminium Alloy Passengers: unberthed: 170	**3 oil engines** reduction geared to sc. shafts driving 3 FP propellers Total Power: 2,463kW (3,348hp) 32.0kn Caterpillar 3412E 3 x Vee 4 Stroke 12 Cy. 137 x 152 each-821kW (1116bhp) Caterpillar Inc-USA
9307906 *9V6141*	**WAVEMASTER 10** **Berlian Ferries Pte Ltd** - *Singapore* *Singapore* MMSI: 563004840 Official number: 389510	**256** 86 17	Class: BV	**2003-12 Greenbay Marine Pte Ltd — Singapore** Yd No: 135 Loa 37.20 Br ex 7.00 Dght 1.200 Lbp 33.24 Br md - Dpth 2.80 Welded, 1 dk	**(A37B2PS) Passenger Ship** Hull Material: Aluminium Alloy Passengers: unberthed: 170	**3 oil engines** geared to sc. shafts driving 2 FP propellers , 1 Water jet Total Power: 2,364kW (3,213hp) M.T.U. 12V2000M70 3 x Vee 4 Stroke 12 Cy. 130 x 150 each-788kW (1071bhp) MTU Friedrichshafen GmbH-Friedrichshafen AuxGen: 2 x 75kW a.c
5386954 *GRPM*	**WAVERLEY** **Waverley Steam Navigation Co Ltd** - *Glasgow* *United Kingdom* MMSI: 232001540 Official number: 169494	*693* 327 128		**1947-07 A. & J. Inglis Ltd. — Glasgow** Yd No: 1330 Loa 73.13 Br ex 17.45 Dght 1.918 Lbp 73.06 Br md 9.20 Dpth 2.67 Riveted, 1 dk	**(A37B2PS) Passenger Ship** Passengers: unberthed: 950	**1 Steam Recip** driving 2 Paddle wheels 14.0kn Rankin & Blackmore Ltd.-Greenock AuxGen: 1 x 15kW 110V d.c
1009871 *ZCTE7*	**WAVERUNNER** **Oakman Global Corp** - *George Town* *Cayman Islands (British)* MMSI: 319804000 Official number: 740035	**309** 92 -	✠ **100A1** SS 05/2012 HSC Yacht, mono, G6 SSC Cable: 110.0/14.0 U2 (a)	**2007-05 Palmer Johnson Yachts LLC — Sturgeon Bay WI** Yd No: 245 Loa 41.14 Br ex 8.46 Dght 1.950 Lbp 34.02 Br md 8.40 Dpth 4.14 Welded, 1 dk	**(X11A2YP) Yacht** Hull Material: Aluminium Alloy	**2 oil engines** sr geared to sc. shafts driving 2 FP propellers Total Power: 5,440kW (7,396hp) M.T.U. 16V4000M90 2 x Vee 4 Stroke 16 Cy. 165 x 190 each-2720kW (3698bhp) Detroit Diesel Corporation-Detroit, Mi AuxGen: 2 x 62kW 230V 50Hz a.c Thrusters: 1 Thwart. FP thruster (f)
9558672 *9WGE7*	**WAWASAN 3** **Jaya Coastal Transport Sdn Bhd** - *Kuching* *Malaysia* MMSI: 533000853 Official number: 333052	**495** 148 -	Class: BV	**2009-11 Kaibuok Shipyard (M) Sdn Bhd — Sibu** Yd No: 0710 Loa 47.00 Br ex - Dght 2.470 Lbp 43.21 Br md 11.00 Dpth 3.20 Welded, 1 dk	**(A35D2RL) Landing Craft**	**2 oil engines** reduction geared to sc. shafts driving 2 FP propellers Total Power: 894kW (1,216hp) 10.0kn Cummins KTA-19-M3 2 x 4 Stroke 6 Cy. 159 x 159 each-447kW (608bhp) Cummins India Ltd-India AuxGen: 2 x 80kW 50Hz a.c
9614373 *9WKQ8*	**WAWASAN 5** **Jaya Coastal Marine Logistic Sdn Bhd** - *Kuching* *Malaysia* MMSI: 533002780 Official number: 333260	**499** 149 -	Class: BV	**2010-10 Sapor Shipbuilding Industries Sdn Bhd — Sibu** Yd No: SAPOR 50 Loa 47.00 Br ex - Dght 2.500 Lbp 43.21 Br md 11.00 Dpth 3.20 Welded, 1 dk	**(A35D2RL) Landing Craft** Bow ramp (centre)	**2 oil engines** reduction geared to sc. shaft driving 2 FP propellers Total Power: 1,220kW (1,658hp) 11.0kn Yanmar 6AYM-ETE 2 x 4 Stroke 6 Cy. 155 x 180 each-610kW (829bhp) Yanmar Diesel Engine Co Ltd-Japan AuxGen: 3 x 80kW 50Hz a.c Thrusters: 1 Tunnel thruster (f)
9589231 *9WKJ6*	**WAWASAN 8** **Jaya Coastal Transport Sdn Bhd** - *Kuching* *Malaysia* MMSI: 533004270 Official number: 333218	**480** 144 438	Class: BV	**2010-09 Shin Yang Shipyard Sdn Bhd — Miri** Yd No: 339 Loa 46.00 Br ex - Dght 2.500 Lbp 42.70 Br md 10.90 Dpth 3.20 Welded, 1 dk	**(A35D2RL) Landing Craft** Bow ramp (centre)	**2 oil engines** reduction geared to sc. shafts driving 2 FP propellers Total Power: 894kW (1,216hp) 10.0kn Cummins KTA-19-M3 2 x 4 Stroke 6 Cy. 159 x 159 each-447kW (608bhp) Cummins Engine Co Inc-USA AuxGen: 2 x 80kW a.c
9600968 *9WKQ9*	**WAWASAN 9** **Jaya Coastal Transport Sdn Bhd** - *Kuching* *Malaysia* MMSI: 533000995 Official number: 333266	**490** 147 -	Class: BV	**2011-01 Shin Yang Shipyard Sdn Bhd — Miri** Yd No: 343 Loa 46.00 Br ex - Dght 2.500 Lbp 42.70 Br md 10.90 Dpth 3.20 Welded, 1 dk	**(A35D2RL) Landing Craft** Bow ramp (centre)	**2 oil engines** reduction geared to sc. shafts driving 2 FP propellers Total Power: 1,220kW (1,658hp) 10.0kn Yanmar 6AYM-ETE 2 x 4 Stroke 6 Cy. 155 x 180 each-610kW (829bhp) Yanmar Diesel Engine Co Ltd-Japan AuxGen: 2 x 80kW 50Hz a.c Fuel: 380.0
9412763 *3EWR4*	**WAWASAN EMERALD** **Yaoki Shipping SA** Aurora Tankers Management Pte Ltd SatCom: Inmarsat C 437148310 *Panama* *Panama* MMSI: 371483000 Official number: 4143110	**11,749** 6,223 19,848 T/cm 29.3	Class: NK (BV)	**2010-03 Kitanihon Zosen K.K. — Hachinohe** Yd No: 510 Loa 141.00 (BB) Br ex 24.22 Dght 9.810 Lbp 133.00 Br md 24.20 Dpth 13.20 Welded, 1 dk	**(A12B2TR) Chemical/Products Tanker** Double Hull (13F) Liq: 22,000; Liq (Oil): 22,000 Cargo Heating Coils Compartments: 20 Wing Ta, ER Manifold: Bow/CM: 69.5m	**1 oil engine** driving 1 FP propeller Total Power: 6,230kW (8,470hp) 14.5kn Mitsubishi 7UEC45LA 1 x 2 Stroke 7 Cy. 450 x 1350 6230kW (8470bhp) Akasaka Tekkosho KK (Akasaka DieselLtd)-Japan AuxGen: 3 x 480kW 60Hz a.c Thrusters: 1 Tunnel thruster (f) Fuel: 1142.0
9565613 *3EPSV*	**WAWASAN JADE** **Yaoki Shipping SA** MSI Ship Management Pte Ltd SatCom: Inmarsat C 435411510 *Panama* *Panama* MMSI: 354115000 Official number: 4173910	**11,749** 6,223 19,842 T/cm 29.3	Class: NK (BV)	**2010-07 Kitanihon Zosen K.K. — Hachinohe** Yd No: 512 Loa 141.00 (BB) Br ex - Dght 9.814 Lbp 133.00 Br md 24.20 Dpth 13.20 Welded, 1 dk	**(A12B2TR) Chemical/Products Tanker** Double Hull (13F) Liq: 22,129; Liq (Oil): 21,688 Cargo Heating Coils Compartments: 20 Wing Ta, ER 20 Cargo Pump (s): 8x200m³/hr, 12x300m³/hr Manifold: Bow/CM: 69.5m	**1 oil engine** driving 1 FP propeller Total Power: 6,230kW (8,470hp) 14.5kn Mitsubishi 7UEC45LA 1 x 2 Stroke 7 Cy. 450 x 1350 6230kW (8470bhp) Akasaka Tekkosho KK (Akasaka DieselLtd)-Japan AuxGen: 3 x 480kW 60Hz a.c Thrusters: 1 Tunnel thruster (f) Fuel: 1142.0

IMO / Call sign	Name / Owner	Tonnage	Class	Builder / Dimensions	Type / Cargo	Machinery	Speed / Model
9477517 *3EVU7* -	**WAWASAN RUBY** **Trio Happiness SA** Aurora Tankers Management Pte Ltd *Panama* — *Panama* MMSI: 355619000 Official number: 4158410	**11,568** 6,060 19,957 T/cm 28.8	Class: NK	**2010-03 Usuki Shipyard Co Ltd — Usuki OT** Yd No: 1720 Loa 145.53 (BB) Br ex - Dght 9.665 Lbp 137.00 Br md 23.70 Dpth 13.35 Welded, 1 dk	**(A12B2TR) Chemical/Products Tanker** Double Hull (13F) Liq: 22,187; Liq (Oil): 22,500 Cargo Heating Coils Compartments: 20 Wing Ta, ER 20 Cargo Pump (s): 6x150m³/hr, 14x250m³/hr Manifold: Bow/CM: 75m	**1 oil engine** driving 1 FP propeller Total Power: 6,150kW (8,362hp) MAN-B&W 1 x 2 Stroke 6 Cy. 420 x 1764 6150kW (8362bhp) Makita Corp-Japan AuxGen: 3 x 440kW a.c Thrusters: 1 Tunnel thruster (f) Fuel: 150.0 (d.f.) 911.0 (r.f.)	14.3kn 6S42MC
9508158 *VRER4* -	**WAWASAN SAPPHIRE** **Anchor Trans Inc** Aurora Tankers Management Pte Ltd *Hong Kong* — *Hong Kong* MMSI: 477177300 Official number: HK-2290	**11,572** 6,178 19,814 T/cm 29.3	Class: NK	**2008-12 Kitanihon Zosen K.K. — Hachinohe** Yd No: 390 Loa 141.00 (BB) Br ex - Dght 9.774 Lbp 133.00 Br md 24.20 Dpth 13.20 Welded, 1 dk	**(A12B2TR) Chemical/Products Tanker** Double Hull (13F) Liq: 20,492; Liq (Oil): 21,715 Cargo Heating Coils Compartments: 20 Wing Ta, 2 Wing Slop Ta, ER 20 Cargo Pump (s): 12x300m³/hr, 8x200m³/hr Manifold: Bow/CM: 69.5m	**1 oil engine** driving 1 FP propeller Total Power: 6,150kW (8,362hp) MAN-B&W 1 x 2 Stroke 6 Cy. 420 x 1764 6150kW (8362bhp) Hitachi Zosen Corp-Japan AuxGen: 3 x 450kW a.c Thrusters: 1 Tunnel thruster (f) Fuel: 190.0 (d.f.) 1145.0 (r.f.)	14.5kn 6S42MC
9398606 *9WGQ7* -	**WAWASAN SATU** **Jaya Coastal Transport Sdn Bhd** *Kuching* — *Malaysia* MMSI: 533000498 Official number: 330729	**472** 142 600	Class: BV	**2006-06 Jana Seribu Shipbuilding (M) Sdn Bhd — Sibu** Yd No: 2026 Loa 45.12 Br ex - Dght 2.400 Lbp 40.00 Br md 13.70 Dpth 3.20 Welded, 1 dk	**(A31C2GD) Deck Cargo Ship**	**2 oil engines** reduction geared to sc. shafts driving 2 FP propellers Total Power: 736kW (1,000hp) Cummins 2 x 4 Stroke 6 Cy. 159 x 159 each-368kW (500bhp) Cummins Engine Co Inc-USA	10.0kn KTA-19-M1
9565601 *3EZS5* -	**WAWASAN TOPAZ** **KT Neo Marine SA** Aurora Tankers Management Pte Ltd SatCom: Inmarsat C 435384010 *Panama* — *Panama* MMSI: 353840000 Official number: 4155210A	**11,749** 6,223 19,854 T/cm 29.3	Class: NK (BV)	**2010-05 Kitanihon Zosen K.K. — Hachinohe** Yd No: 511 Loa 141.00 (BB) Br ex - Dght 9.814 Lbp 133.00 Br md 24.20 Dpth 13.20 Welded, 1 dk	**(A12B2TR) Chemical/Products Tanker** Double Hull (13F) Liq: 21,696; Liq (Oil): 21,696 Cargo Heating Coils Compartments: 20 Wing Ta 20 Cargo Pump (s): 8x200m³/hr, 12x300m³/hr Manifold: Bow/CM: 69.5m	**1 oil engine** driving 1 FP propeller Total Power: 6,230kW (8,470hp) Mitsubishi 1 x 2 Stroke 7 Cy. 450 x 1350 6230kW (8470bhp) Akasaka Tekkosho KK (Akasaka DieselLtd)-Japan AuxGen: 3 x 480kW 60Hz a.c Thrusters: 1 Tunnel thruster (f) Fuel: 120.0 (d.f.) 910.0	14.5kn 7UEC45LA
7814462 *C6TY9* -	**WAWEL** *ex* Alkmini A *-2004* *ex* PO Canterbury *-2004* *ex* P&OSL Canterbury *-2002* *ex* Stena Fantasia *-1999* *ex* Fantasia *-1990* *ex* Fiesta *-1990* *ex* Tzarevetz *-1988* *ex* Scandinavia *-1982* **Adabar Co Ltd** Polish Baltic Shipping Co (POLFERRIES) (Polska Zegluga Baltycka SA) *Nassau* — *Bahamas* MMSI: 311852000 Official number: 8000894	**25,318** 12,889 3,501 T/cm 34.9	Class: GL (LR) (BV) (NV) Classed LR until 11/2/05	**1980-03 Kockums Varv AB — Malmo** Yd No: 569 Converted From: Ferry (Passenger/Vehicle)-1990 Loa 163.51 (BB) Br ex 27.63 Dght 6.505 Lbp 150.76 Br md 23.00 Dpth 16.01 Welded, 2 dks	**(A36A2PR) Passenger/Ro-Ro Ship (Vehicles)** Passengers: unberthed: 1800 Slewing stern door/ramp (p) Len: 22.00 Wid: 8.00 Swl: - Slewing stern door/ramp (s) Len: 22.00 Wid: 8.00 Swl: - Lane-Len: 2250 Lane-Wid: 8.00 Lane-clr ht: 6.20 Cars: 430	**2 oil engines** driving 2 CP propellers Total Power: 13,790kW (18,748hp) Sulzer 2 x 2 Stroke 7 Cy. 560 x 1150 each-6895kW (9374bhp) Sumitomo Heavy Industries Ltd-Japan AuxGen: 3 x 2400kW 440V 60Hz a.c, 3 x 880kW 440V 60Hz a.c, 1 x 840kW 440V 60Hz a.c Boilers: 2 AuxB (o.f.) Thrusters: 2 Thwart. CP thruster (f) Fuel: 117.0 (d.f.) 3028.0 (r.f.)	18.0kn 7RLA56
8218330 *SKMI* -	**WAXHOLM I** **Waxholms Angfartygs AB** - *Vaxholm* — *Sweden* MMSI: 265522500	**387** 148 25		**1983-06 Lunde Varv & Verkstads AB — Ramvik** Yd No: 218 Loa 36.02 Br ex 9.02 Dght 1.590 Lbp 35.51 Br md - Dpth - Welded, 1 dk	**(A37B2PS) Passenger Ship**	**2 oil engines** with clutches, flexible couplings & sr geared to sc. shafts driving 2 CP propellers Total Power: 294kW (400hp) Scania 2 x 4 Stroke 6 Cy. 127 x 145 each-147kW (200bhp) Saab Scania AB-Sweden	DSI1140M
8224999 *SKNW* -	**WAXHOLM II** **Waxholms Angfartygs AB** - *Vaxholm* — *Sweden* MMSI: 265522510	**387** 148 50		**1983-12 Lunde Varv & Verkstads AB — Ramvik** Yd No: 219 Loa 35.51 Br ex 9.02 Dght 1.591 Lbp 35.51 Br md - Dpth - Welded, 1 dk	**(A37B2PS) Passenger Ship**	**2 oil engines** with clutches, flexible couplings & sr geared to sc. shafts driving 2 CP propellers Total Power: 398kW (542hp) Scania 2 x 4 Stroke 6 Cy. 127 x 145 each-199kW (271bhp) Saab Scania AB-Sweden AuxGen: 2 x 60kW 380V 50Hz a.c Fuel: 6.0 (d.f.) 2.5pd	12.0kn DSI1140M
8873623 - -	**WAYABULA II** **PT Bumi Indah Permai** - *Samarinda* — *Indonesia*	**269** 81 -	Class: (KI)	**1992-05 PT Dwi Warna Shipyard — Samarinda** Loa 44.50 Br ex - Dght - Lbp 40.72 Br md 8.98 Dpth 2.62 Welded, 1 dk	**(A35D2RL) Landing Craft** Bow door/ramp (centre)	**2 oil engines** reduction geared to sc. shafts driving 2 FP propellers Total Power: 442kW (600hp) Cummins 2 x 4 Stroke 6 Cy. 140 x 152 each-221kW (300bhp) Cummins Brasil Ltda-Brazil AuxGen: 1 x 48kW 115/230V a.c	9.2kn NT-855-M
9027831 - -	**WAYABULA INDAH II** **PT Bumi Indah Permai** - *Samarinda* — *Indonesia*	**205** 62 -	Class: (KI)	**1998-09 PT Bumi Indah Permai — Samarinda** Loa 29.00 Br ex - Dght - Lbp 25.50 Br md 8.00 Dpth 3.25 Welded, 1 dk	**(B32A2ST) Tug**	**2 oil engines** geared to sc. shafts driving 2 Propellers Total Power: 1,382kW (1,878hp) Cummins 2 x Vee 4 Stroke 12 Cy. 159 x 159 each-691kW (939bhp) (made 1996) Cummins Engine Co Ltd-United Kingdom	12.0kn KTA-38-M
9027843 - -	**WAYABULA IV** **PT Bumi Indah Permai** - *Samarinda* — *Indonesia*	**135** 81 -	Class: (KI)	**1993-12 C.V. Teknik Jaya Industri — Samarinda** L reg 22.50 Br ex - Dght - Lbp 21.12 Br md 6.50 Dpth 2.78 Welded, 1 dk	**(B32A2ST) Tug**	**2 oil engines** driving 1 Propeller Total Power: 780kW (1,060hp) Yanmar 2 x 4 Stroke 6 Cy. 148 x 165 each-390kW (530bhp) (made 1993) Yanmar Diesel Engine Co Ltd-Japan	6LAA-UTE
8892514 - -	**WAYABULA VI** **PT Bumi Indah Permai** - *Samarinda* — *Indonesia*	*145* 87 -	Class: (KI)	**1995-03 C.V. Dok Swarga — Samarinda** Loa 21.75 Br ex - Dght - Lbp 19.45 Br md 6.30 Dpth 3.00 Welded, 1 dk	**(B32A2ST) Tug**	**2 oil engines** reduction geared to sc. shafts driving 2 FP propellers Total Power: 486kW (660hp) Yanmar 2 x 4 Stroke 6 Cy. 117 x 140 each-243kW (330bhp) Yanmar Diesel Engine Co Ltd-Japan	8.0kn 6GH-UTE
8897992 *YFKU* -	**WAYABULA VIII** **PT Bumi Indah Permai** - *Samarinda* — *Indonesia*	**318** 96 -	Class: KI	**1995-10 C.V. Dok Swarga — Samarinda** Loa 47.50 Br ex - Dght 2.040 Lbp 43.20 Br md 9.00 Dpth 2.75 Welded, 1 dk	**(A35D2RL) Landing Craft** Bow ramp (centre)	**2 oil engines** reduction geared to sc. shafts driving 2 FP propellers Total Power: 514kW (698hp) Cummins 2 x 4 Stroke 6 Cy. 140 x 152 each-257kW (349bhp) Cummins Engine Co Inc-USA	10.0kn NTA-855-M
8625167 - -	**WAYO MARU No. 8** - - - — *South Korea*	*236* - 552		**1987-06 Sasaki Shipbuilding Co Ltd — Osakikamijima HS** Yd No: 508 Loa 43.01 Br ex - Dght 2.690 Lbp 40.01 Br md 9.01 Dpth 3.31 Welded, 1 dk	**(A13B2TU) Tanker (unspecified)**	**1 oil engine** driving 1 FP propeller Total Power: 368kW (500hp) Matsui 1 x 4 Stroke 6 Cy. 240 x 400 368kW (500bhp) Matsui Iron Works Co Ltd-Japan	8.3kn ML624GS
9151498 *JI3622* -	**WAYU MARU** **Arita Kaiun KK** - *Osaka, Osaka* — *Japan* MMSI: 431300458 Official number: 135920	*489* - 1,500		**1996-11 K.K. Yoshida Zosen Kogyo — Arida** Yd No: 503 Loa 68.13 Br ex - Dght - Lbp 63.00 Br md 13.20 Dpth 7.20 Welded, 1 dk	**(A31A2GX) General Cargo Ship** Compartments: 1 Ho, ER 1 Ha: (25.2 x 10.2)ER Cranes: 1x24t	**1 oil engine** driving 1 FP propeller Total Power: 736kW (1,001hp) Niigata 1 x 4 Stroke 6 Cy. 340 x 620 736kW (1001bhp) Niigata Engineering Co Ltd-Japan	11.0kn 6M34BGT
7223998 - -	**WAYWARD WIND** *ex* Billy D *-1982* *ex* Olympic King *-1982* *ex* Endeavour *-1980* *ex* Olympic King *-1975* *ex* Shawn *-1974* **Alaskan Dream Ventures Inc** - *Homer, AK* — *United States of America* Official number: 534777	*131* 108 -		**1971 Lantana Boatyard, Inc. — Lake Worth, Fl** L reg 21.74 Br ex 6.71 Dght - Lbp - Br md - Dpth 3.79 Welded, 1 dk	**(B11B2FV) Fishing Vessel** Hull Material: Aluminium Alloy	**1 oil engine** driving 1 FP propeller Total Power: 268kW (364hp)	

7428782 **WAZN**
5AOA
ex Nego Loader -1981
Brega Petroleum Marketing Co
-
Tobruk Libya

485 Class: (LR) (AB)
239 Classed LR until 29/4/92
596

1976-08 Singapore Shipbuilding & Engineering Pte Ltd — Singapore Yd No: 115
Loa 49.79 Br ex 12.37 Dght 2.439
Lbp 44.89 Br md 12.20 Dpth 3.20
Welded, 1 dk

(A35D2RL) Landing Craft
Bow door/ramp
Compartments: 5 Ta, ER

2 oil engines reverse reduction geared to sc. shafts driving 2 FP propellers
Total Power: 736kW (1,000hp) 8.8kn
MWM TBD601-6
2 x 4 Stroke 6 Cy. 160 x 165 each-368kW (500bhp)
Motoren Werke Mannheim AG (MWM)-West Germany
AuxGen: 2 x 40kW 415V 50Hz a.c

8999025 **WB-39**
-
ex LCM-8515 -2005
McLean Contracting Co
-
Baltimore, MD United States of America
Official number: 1178608

122
98
-

1968-01 Marinette Marine Corp — Marinette WI
Converted From: Infantry Landing Craft-2005
Loa 22.60 Br ex - Dght 1.600
Lbp - Br md 6.40 Dpth 2.80
Welded, 1 dk

(A35D2RL) Landing Craft
Bow ramp (f)

2 oil engines driving 2 Propellers
Total Power: 442kW (600hp)
G.M. (Detroit Diesel)
2 x 2 Stroke each-221kW (300bhp)
General Motors Detroit DieselAllison Divn-USA

7391719 **WB-FORCE I**
-
ex Valiant Nader -2004 ex Avenger -1994
ex Indefatigable -1986 ex Chambon Bora -1984
ex Sea Diamond -1980
-
-

455 Class: (LR) (BV)
136 Classed LR until 1/2/05
316

1975-03 Brodogradiliste 'Tito' Beograd - Brod 'Sava' — Macvanska Mitrovica
Yd No: 922
Converted From: Offshore Tug/Supply Ship-1984
Loa 39.88 Br ex 10.11 Dght 4.611
Lbp 32.29 Br md 9.61 Dpth 5.29
Welded, 1 dk

(B32A2ST) Tug

2 oil engines sr geared to sc. shafts driving 2 CP propellers
Total Power: 3,648kW (4,960hp)
Alpha 16V23LU
2 x Vee 4 Stroke 16 Cy. 225 x 300 each-1824kW (2480bhp)
Alpha Diesel A/S-Denmark
AuxGen: 2 x 112kW 400V 50Hz a.c
Thrusters: 1 Thwart. FP thruster (f)

8888393 **WB NEVA**
UEME
ex Samur 9 -2012 ex A Can -2003
ex Netcom -2003 ex Tanya -1998
ex Boby Bojilov-14 -1998 ex ST-1316 -1994
Whitebox (Malta) Ltd
LLC 'Imflot Logistics'
Taganrog Russia
MMSI: 273443250

1,839 Class: (RS)
552
2,755

1986-07 Sudostroitelnyy Zavod im Volodarskogo — Rybinsk Yd No: 04908
Loa 88.90 Br ex - Dght 4.100
Lbp 83.75 Br md 12.30 Dpth 6.00
Welded, 1 dk

(A31A2GX) General Cargo Ship
Grain: 2,230
Compartments: 1 Ho, ER
2 Ha: 2 (19.8 x 9.0)ER
Ice Capable

2 oil engines driving 2 FP propellers
Total Power: 1,030kW (1,400hp) 10.0kn
S.K.L. 6NVDS48A-2U
2 x 4 Stroke 6 Cy. 320 x 480 each-515kW (700bhp)
VEB Schwermaschinenbau "KarlLiebknecht" (SKL)-Magdeburg

9545766 **WBI TRINITY**
3FNB4
-
Workboat International DMC CO
-
Panama Panama
MMSI: 370841000
Official number: 4026609

1,159 Class: BV (AB)
347
1,000

2008-10 Nantong MLC Tongbao Shipbuilding Co Ltd — Rugao JS Yd No: MLC5283
Loa 52.80 Br ex - Dght 4.520
Lbp 47.20 Br md 13.20 Dpth 5.20
Welded, 1 dk

(B21B20A) Anchor Handling Tug Supply

2 oil engines reduction geared to sc. shafts driving 2 FP propellers
Total Power: 4,414kW (6,002hp) 11.0kn
Yanmar 8N280M-SV
2 x 4 Stroke 8 Cy. 280 x 380 each-2207kW (3001bhp)
Yanmar Diesel Engine Co Ltd-Japan
AuxGen: 1 x 600kW a.c, 2 x 400kW a.c
Thrusters: 1 Tunnel thruster (f)
Fuel: 497.0

8123195 **WD MERSEY**
2ALU5
ex Bragadin -2008
Westminster Dredging Co Ltd
-
Liverpool United Kingdom
MMSI: 235060858
Official number: 914176

1,595 Class: BV (RI)
478
2,778

1983-01 Lucchese Achille Cantiere per Costruzioni — Venezia Yd No: 84
Loa 67.59 Br ex 13.03 Dght 5.281
Lbp 61.93 Br md 13.01 Dpth 6.30
Welded, 1 dk

(B33B2DS) Suction Hopper Dredger
Hopper: 1,826
Compartments: 1 Ho, ER
1 Ha: ER

2 oil engines with clutches, flexible couplings & sr geared to sc. shafts driving 2 FP propellers
Total Power: 1,860kW (2,528hp) 9.0kn
GMT BL230.6L
2 x 4 Stroke 6 Cy. 230 x 310 each-930kW (1264bhp)
Grandi Motori Trieste-Italy
Thrusters: 1 Thwart. FP thruster (f)

9071856 **WDT 23**
-
-
PT Tri Sukses Wanatama

112 Class: (NK)
34
91

1992-10 Yong Choo Kui Shipyard Sdn Bhd — Sibu
Yd No: 3692
Loa 23.00 Br ex - Dght 2.162
Lbp 21.80 Br md 6.70 Dpth 2.85
Welded, 1 dk

(B32A2ST) Tug

2 oil engines geared to sc. shafts driving 2 FP propellers
Total Power: 600kW (816hp) 10.0kn
Caterpillar 3408TA
2 x Vee 4 Stroke 8 Cy. 137 x 152 each-300kW (408bhp)
Caterpillar Inc-USA
AuxGen: 2 x 16kW a.c

9044188 **WEAL POS**
DSNS6
-
Keumyang Shipping Co Ltd
-
Jeju South Korea
MMSI: 440266000
Official number: JJR-049653

2,479 Class: KR
815
3,712

1992-08 Dae Sun Shipbuilding & Engineering Co Ltd — Busan Yd No: 391
Loa 94.50 Br ex - Dght 5.750
Lbp 88.01 Br md 14.00 Dpth 7.00
Welded, 1 dk

(A31A2GX) General Cargo Ship
Grain: 2,987
Compartments: 2 Ho, ER
2 Ha: 2 (25.0 x 9.5)ER

1 oil engine driving 1 FP propeller
Total Power: 2,189kW (2,976hp)
B&W 6S26MC
1 x 2 Stroke 6 Cy. 260 x 980 2189kW (2976bhp)
Ssangyong Heavy Industries Co Ltd-South Korea

8999037 **WEALTHY**
9V6923
ex Shun Hai You -2006
Wealthy Marine Pte Ltd
Shipmate Pte Ltd
Singapore Singapore
MMSI: 565270000
Official number: 392126

1,084 Class: BV
329
1,300

1997-05 Lingshan Shipyard — Guangzhou GD
Loa 70.00 Br ex - Dght 3.500
Lbp 65.00 Br md 12.00 Dpth 4.80
Welded, 1 dk

(A13B2TP) Products Tanker

2 oil engines driving 2 Propellers
Total Power: 1,102kW (1,498hp)
Chinese Std. Type 6250
2 x 4 Stroke 6 Cy. 250 x 300 each-551kW (749bhp)
Hongyan Machinery Factory-China

9044190 **WEALTHY POS**
DSNU3
-
Keumyang Shipping Co Ltd
-
Jeju South Korea
MMSI: 440310000
Official number: JJR-049760

1,767 Class: KR
612
2,643
T/cm
8.4

1992-10 Dae Sun Shipbuilding & Engineering Co Ltd — Busan Yd No: 392
Loa 84.25 Br ex - Dght 5.280
Lbp 77.81 Br md 12.70 Dpth 6.40
Welded, 1 dk

(A31A2GX) General Cargo Ship
Bale: 2,092
Compartments: 2 Ho, ER
2 Ha: ER

1 oil engine driving 1 FP propeller
Total Power: 1,324kW (1,800hp) 11.8kn
Akasaka A31
1 x 4 Stroke 6 Cy. 310 x 600 1324kW (1800bhp)
Hyundai Heavy Industries Co Ltd-South Korea
AuxGen: 2 x 220kW 445V 60Hz a.c
Fuel: 62.1 (d.f.) 227.6 (r.f.) 6.1pd

8952156 **WEATHERBIRD II**
WDE4661
ex Weatherbird -1989 ex Aunt Bea -1989
University of South Florida
-
St Petersburg, FL United States of America
MMSI: 338578000
Official number: 652213

304
91
-

1982-01 Bosarge Marine, Inc. — Bayou La Batre, Al Yd No: 1
Loa - Br ex - Dght 2.430
Lbp 35.05 Br md 8.53 Dpth 3.20
Welded, 1 dk

(B31A2SR) Research Survey Vessel

2 oil engines reduction geared to sc. shafts driving 2 FP propellers
Total Power: 736kW (1,000hp) 9.5kn
G.M. (Detroit Diesel) 16V-71
2 x Vee 2 Stroke 16 Cy. 108 x 127 each-368kW (500bhp)
General Motors Detroit DieselAllison Divn-USA
AuxGen: 2 x 75kW 110V
Thrusters: 1 Directional thruster (f)

8990433 **WEATHERLY**
WDB7383
ex Quincy Ii -2012
O'Hara Corp
-
New Bedford, MA United States of America
MMSI: 366941560
Official number: 1153437

283
64
-

2004 Rodriguez Boat Builders, Inc. — Coden, Al
Yd No: 236
L reg 28.01 Br ex - Dght -
Lbp - Br md 8.53 Dpth 4.57
Welded, 1 dk

(B11B2FV) Fishing Vessel

1 oil engine geared to sc. shaft driving 1 Propeller
Total Power: 941kW (1,279hp)
Caterpillar 3512
1 x Vee 4 Stroke 12 Cy. 170 x 190 941kW (1279bhp)
Caterpillar Inc-USA
AuxGen: 2 x 240kW

9562984 **WEAVER**
J8B4825
ex DMS Weaver -2013 ex Claire H -2012
Damen Marine Services BV
Thong Yong 2000 Marine Pte Ltd
Kingstown St Vincent & The Grenadines
MMSI: 375856000
Official number: 11298

154 Class: BV
46
250

2011-04 Damen Shipyards Kozle Sp z oo — Kedzierzyn-Kozle (Hull) Yd No: 1145
2011-04 B.V. Scheepswerf Damen Hardinxveld — Hardinxveld-Giessendam Yd No: 571596
Loa 23.33 Br ex 9.32 Dght 2.250
Lbp 21.25 Br md 9.00 Dpth 3.20
Welded, 1 dk

(B34L2QU) Utility Vessel
Cranes: 2

2 oil engines reduction geared to sc. shafts driving 2 FP propellers
Total Power: 1,302kW (1,770hp) 9.0kn
Caterpillar 3412D
2 x Vee 4 Stroke 12 Cy. 145 x 162 each-651kW (885bhp)
Caterpillar Inc-USA
AuxGen: 1 x 74kW 50Hz a.c
Fuel: 43.0 (d.f.)

9151826 **WEAVER ARROW**
C6PG5
-
Gearbulk Shipowning Ltd
Gearbulk Ltd
SatCom: Inmarsat A 1320104
Nassau Bahamas
MMSI: 309996000
Official number: 730584

36,008 Class: NV
15,797
55,402
T/cm
58.1

1998-07 Dalian New Shipbuilding Heavy Industries Co Ltd — Dalian LN
Yd No: BC460-8
Loa 199.70 (BB) Br ex - Dght 13.518
Lbp 192.00 Br md 32.20 Dpth 19.30
Welded, 1 dk

(A31A2GO) Open Hatch Cargo Ship
Double Sides Entire Compartment Length
Grain: 61,337; Bale: 61,339
TEU 1788 C Ho 1356 TEU C Dk 432 TEU
Compartments: 10 Ho, ER
10 Ha: (13.2 x 18.0)7 (13.2 x 27.4)2 (13.2 x 23.0)ER
Gantry cranes: 2x40t

1 oil engine driving 1 FP propeller
Total Power: 11,520kW (15,663hp) 14.2kn
B&W 6L60MC
1 x 2 Stroke 6 Cy. 600 x 1944 11520kW (15663bhp)
Dalian Marine Diesel Works-China
AuxGen: 3 x 910kW 220/440V 60Hz a.c
Thrusters: 1 Tunnel thruster (f)
Fuel: 225.7 (d.f.) (Heating Coils) 2540.3 (r.f.) 50.0pd

7337579 **WEBB CROSBY**
WDF8795
ex Lady Jill -2011
Crosby Marine Transportation LLC
Crosby Tugs LLC
New Orleans, LA United States of America
MMSI: 367498650
Official number: 511695

242 Class: AB
72
-

1967 Main Iron Works, Inc. — Houma, La
Yd No: 194
Loa - Br ex - Dght 3.836
Lbp 33.51 Br md 8.54 Dpth 4.22
Welded, 1 dk

(B32A2ST) Tug

2 oil engines sr reverse geared to sc. shafts driving 2 FP propellers
Total Power: 1,654kW (2,248hp)
Caterpillar D399TA
2 x Vee 4 Stroke 16 Cy. 159 x 203 each-827kW (1124bhp)
Caterpillar Tractor Co-USA
AuxGen: 2 x 40kW

8319603 *9WCZ6* -	**WEC 9** *ex* Kyokuyo *-2002* *ex* Nagato Maru *-2000* *ex* Nagato Maru No. 6 *-1996* **WEC Transport Service Sdn Bhd** Canter Singapore Pte Ltd *Kuching* *Malaysia* MMSI: 533516000 Official number: 328176	**927** 573 1,821		**1983-11 Tokushima Zosen Sangyo K.K. — Komatsushima** Yd No: 1657 Loa 74.48 Br ex - Dght 4.709 Lbp 68.00 Br md 11.00 Dpth 5.01 Welded, 1 dk	**(A12B2TR) Chemical/Products Tanker** Liq: 2,150; Liq (Oil): 2,150 Compartments: 8 Ta, ER	**1 oil engine** driving 1 FP propeller Total Power: 1,177kW (1,600hp) Akasaka DM33 1 x 4 Stroke 6 Cy. 330 x 500 1177kW (1600bhp) Akasaka Tekkosho KK (Akasaka DieselLtd)-Japan
9143972 *MCXD5* -	**WEC BRUEGHEL** *ex* K-Ocean *-2010* *ex* City of Oporto *-2008* *ex* K-Ocean *-2004* *ex* Alk *-2003* **K-Ocean Sechste RST Schiffahrtsgesellschaft mbH & Co KG** K & K Schiffahrts GmbH & Co KG (K&K) *London* *United Kingdom* MMSI: 235800000 Official number: 18521	**6,362** 3,998 7,224 T/cm 15.0	Class: GL	**1998-08 J.J. Sietas KG Schiffswerft GmbH & Co. — Hamburg** Yd No: 1148 Loa 121.76 (BB) Br ex 18.45 Dght 6.690 Lbp 114.90 Br md 18.20 Dpth 8.30 Welded, 1 dk	**(A33A2CC) Container Ship (Fully Cellular)** Double Bottom Entire Compartment Length TEU 700 C Ho 108 TEU Open/Ho 324 TEU C Dk 268 TEU incl 70 ref. Compartments: 4 Cell Ho, ER 3 Ha: (12.4 x 12.9) (12.4 x 15.6) (12.6 x 15.6)ER	**1 oil engine** with flexible couplings & sr gearedto sc. shaft driving 1 CP propeller Total Power: 5,300kW (7,206hp) 16.5kn MAN 8L40/54 1 x 4 Stroke 8 Cy. 400 x 540 5300kW (7206bhp) MAN B&W Diesel AG-Augsburg AuxGen: 1 x 556kW 220/400V 50Hz a.c, 2 x 320kW 220/400V 50Hz a.c Thrusters: 1 Thwart. FP thruster (f) Fuel: 130.0 (d.f.) (Heating Coils) 576.0 (r.f.) 25.0pd
9376050 *5BJB2* -	**WEC GOYA** *ex* Wilhelm *-2008* **ms 'Wilhelm II' Jens und Waller GmbH & Co KG** Reederei Jens & Waller GmbH & Co KG *Limassol* *Cyprus* MMSI: 212777000 Official number: 9376050	**9,981** 6,006 11,255	Class: BV (GL)	**2008-06 J.J. Sietas KG Schiffswerft GmbH & Co. — Hamburg** Yd No: 1286 Loa 134.44 (BB) Br ex - Dght 8.710 Lbp 124.41 Br md 22.50 Dpth 11.30 Welded, 1 dk	**(A33A2CC) Container Ship (Fully Cellular)** TEU 868 incl 234 ref C. Ice Capable	**1 oil engine** reduction geared to sc. shaft driving 1 CP propeller Total Power: 8,400kW (11,421hp) 18.5kn MaK 9M43 1 x 4 Stroke 9 Cy. 430 x 610 8400kW (11421bhp) Caterpillar Motoren GmbH & Co. KG-Germany AuxGen: 1 x 1488kW 400V a.c, 1 x 1112kW 400/230V a.c, 1 x 924kW 400/230V a.c Thrusters: 1 Tunnel thruster (f)
9134153 *5BSJ3* -	**WEC MAJORELLE** *ex* AFL New England *-2012* *ex* Hohesand *-2011* *ex* Hohebank *-2003* *ex* Susan Borchard *-2001* *ex* Pentland *-1997* *completed as* Hohebank *-1996* **ARA Halifax Shipping BV** ARA Ship Management BV *Limassol* *Cyprus* MMSI: 210312000	**6,362** 3,998 7,223 T/cm 15.0	Class: GL	**1996-09 J.J. Sietas KG Schiffswerft GmbH & Co. — Hamburg** Yd No: 1131 Loa 121.83 (BB) Br ex 18.45 Dght 6.690 Lbp 114.90 Br md 18.20 Dpth 8.30 Welded, 1 dk	**(A33A2CC) Container Ship (Fully Cellular)** TEU 700 C Ho 432 TEU C Dk 268 TEU incl 100 ref. Compartments: 4 Cell Ho, ER 3 Ha: (12.4 x 12.9) (12.4 x 15.6) (12.6 x 15.6)ER	**1 oil engine** with flexible couplings & sr geared to sc. shaft driving 1 CP propeller Total Power: 5,300kW (7,206hp) 16.5kn MAN 8L40/54 1 x 4 Stroke 8 Cy. 400 x 540 5300kW (7206bhp) MAN B&W Diesel AG-Augsburg AuxGen: 2 x 320kW 380/220V a.c, 1 x 556kW 380/220V a.c Thrusters: 1 Thwart. FP thruster (f)
9354416 *5BLE2* -	**WEC VELAZQUEZ** *ex* Conelbe *-2008* **ms 'Conelbe' 1240 Bereederungsges mbH & Co KG** Conmar Shipping GmbH & Co KG SatCom: Inmarsat C 421090310 *Limassol* *Cyprus* MMSI: 210903000 Official number: 9354416	**9,962** 6,006 11,433	Class: GL	**2007-08 J.J. Sietas KG Schiffswerft GmbH & Co. — Hamburg** Yd No: 1240 Loa 134.44 (BB) Br ex - Dght 8.710 Lbp 124.41 Br md 22.50 Dpth 11.30 Welded, 1 dk	**(A33A2CC) Container Ship (Fully Cellular)** TEU 868 C Ho 601 TEU C Dk 267 TEU incl 234 ref C. Compartments: 4 Cell Ho, ER Ice Capable	**1 oil engine** reduction geared to sc. shafts driving 1 CP propeller Total Power: 8,286kW (11,266hp) 18.5kn MaK 9M43C 1 x 4 Stroke 9 Cy. 430 x 610 8286kW (11266bhp) Caterpillar Motoren GmbH & Co. KG-Germany AuxGen: 1 x 1488kW 400/230V a.c, 1 x 1112kW 400/230V a.c, 1 x 924kW 400/230V a.c Thrusters: 1 Tunnel thruster (f)
7604439 *WSD7079* -	**WECOMA** **National Science Foundation** Oregon State University (College of Earth, Ocean & Atmospheric Sciences) (CEOAS) SatCom: Inmarsat C 430301410 *Newport, OR* *United States of America* MMSI: 303014000 Official number: 041525	**769** 230 -		**1975 Peterson Builders, Inc. — Sturgeon Bay, Wi** Yd No: 9250-2 Loa 53.93 Br ex - Dght 4.379 Lbp 48.16 Br md 10.06 Dpth 4.58 Welded, 1 dk	**(B31A2SR) Research Survey Vessel**	**1 oil engine** sr geared to sc. shaft driving 1 CP propeller Total Power: 2,115kW (2,876hp) 14.5kn EMD (Electro-Motive) 16-645-E7B 1 x Vee 2 Stroke 16 Cy. 230 x 254 2115kW (2876bhp) General Motors Corp.Electro-Motive Div.-La Grange AuxGen: 2 x 750kW Thrusters: 1 Thwart. FP thruster (f) Fuel: 191.0 (d.f.)
9251937 *9V5850* -	**WECOY 1** **Wecoy Lines Pte Ltd** Wecoy Services Pte Ltd *Singapore* *Singapore* MMSI: 563095000 Official number: 388754	**245** 73 -	Class: (AB)	**2001-04 Shangnan Shipyard — Shanghai** Yd No: H8045 Loa 29.00 Br ex - Dght 3.500 Lbp 27.01 Br md 8.96 Dpth 4.24 Welded, 1 dk	**(B32A2ST) Tug**	**2 oil engines** reduction geared to sc. shafts driving 2 FP propellers Total Power: 2,088kW (2,838hp) Cummins KTA-50-M2 2 x Vee 4 Stroke 16 Cy. 159 x 159 each-1044kW (1419bhp) Cummins Engine Co Inc-USA Fuel: 193.0
9267819 - -	**WECOY 3** **Wecoy Maritime Pte Ltd** Metico Shipbuilding Pte Ltd	**247** 74 -	Class: (AB)	**2002-03 Kouan Shipbuilding Industry Co — Taizhou JS** Yd No: WM29-04 Loa 29.00 Br ex - Dght 3.590 Lbp 27.02 Br md 9.00 Dpth 4.23 Welded, 1 dk	**(B32A2ST) Tug**	**2 oil engines** reduction geared to sc. shafts driving 2 FP propellers Total Power: 2,388kW (3,246hp) Caterpillar 3516TA 2 x Vee 4 Stroke 16 Cy. 170 x 190 each-1194kW (1623bhp) Caterpillar Inc-USA
9267821 *9V5987* -	**WECOY 5** **Wecoy Lines Pte Ltd** Wecoy Services Pte Ltd *Singapore* *Singapore* MMSI: 563285000 Official number: 389075	**247** 74 -	Class: AB	**2002-03 Kouan Shipbuilding Industry Co — Taizhou JS** Yd No: WM29-05 Loa 29.00 Br ex - Dght 3.590 Lbp 27.02 Br md 9.00 Dpth 4.23 Welded, 1 dk	**(B32A2ST) Tug**	**2 oil engines** reverse reduction geared to sc. shafts driving 2 FP propellers Total Power: 2,984kW (4,058hp) Cummins KTA-50-M2 2 x Vee 4 Stroke 16 Cy. 159 x 159 each-1492kW (2029bhp) Cummins Engine Co Ltd-United Kingdom AuxGen: 2 x 75kW a.c
9301213 - -	**WECOY 6** - -	**245** 73 217	Class: AB	**2003-07 Shangnan Shipyard — Shanghai** Yd No: 1 Loa 29.00 Br ex 9.00 Dght 3.500 Lbp 27.01 Br md 8.96 Dpth 4.24 Welded, 1 dk	**(B32A2ST) Tug**	**2 oil engines** geared to sc. shafts driving 2 FP propellers Total Power: 1,766kW (2,402hp) Yanmar M220-EN 2 x 4 Stroke 6 Cy. 220 x 300 each-883kW (1201bhp) Yanmar Diesel Engine Co Ltd-Japan
9301225 *YD3997* -	**WECOY 7** **PT Metico** Wecoy Services Pte Ltd *Batam* *Indonesia*	**245** 73 212	Class: KI (AB)	**2003-11 Shangnan Shipyard — Shanghai** Yd No: 2 Loa 29.00 Br ex 9.00 Dght 3.500 Lbp 27.01 Br md 9.00 Dpth 4.25 Welded, 1 dk	**(B32A2ST) Tug**	**2 oil engines** geared to sc. shafts driving 2 FP propellers Total Power: 1,766kW (2,402hp) Yanmar M220-EN 2 x 4 Stroke 6 Cy. 220 x 300 each-883kW (1201bhp) Yanmar Diesel Engine Co Ltd-Japan AuxGen: 2 x 100kW 400V a.c
8741820 *WDD6653* -	**WEDDELL SEA** *ex* Scott C *-2011* **K-Sea Operating LLC** *New York, NY* *United States of America* MMSI: 367175780 Official number: 1197377	*190* 129 -		**2007-03 Seaboats, Inc. — Fall River, Ma** Yd No: 7 L reg 31.97 Br ex - Dght 5.180 Lbp - Br md 11.52 Dpth 5.94 Welded, 1 dk	**(B32A2ST) Tug**	**2 oil engines** reduction geared to sc. shafts driving 2 Propellers Total Power: 3,372kW (4,584hp) Caterpillar 3516B-HD 2 x Vee 4 Stroke 16 Cy. 170 x 215 each-1686kW (2292bhp) Caterpillar Inc-USA
8127531 *WRB3696* -	**WEDELL FOSS** **Foss Maritime Co** - *Seattle, WA* *United States of America* MMSI: 366976920 Official number: 649840	**320** 96 -	Class: (AB)	**1982-07 Tacoma Boatbuilding Co., Inc. — Tacoma, Wa** Yd No: 437 Loa 30.48 Br ex - Dght 3.500 Lbp 29.27 Br md 10.97 Dpth 4.11 Welded, 1 dk	**(B32A2ST) Tug** Compartments: 1 Ho, ER 1 Ha:	**3 oil engines** gearing integral to driving 2 Voith-Schneider propellers , 1 Z propeller Total Power: 3,456kW (4,700hp) 12.0kn Cummins KTA-50-M2 1 x Vee 4 Stroke 16 Cy. 159 x 159 1250kW (1700bhp) (new engine 2005) Cummins Engine Co Ltd-United Kingdom EMD (Electro-Motive) 12-645-E6 2 x Vee 2 Stroke 12 Cy. 230 x 254 each-1103kW (1500bhp) General Motors Corp.Electro-Motive Div.-La Grange AuxGen: 2 x 75kW
8989862 *ZCII* -	**WEDGE TOO** **Wedge Transportation Ltd** Wedge International Holdings BV *George Town* *Cayman Islands (British)* MMSI: 319861000 Official number: 735604	**1,300** 390 1,456	Class: AB	**2002-11 de Vries Scheepsbouw B.V. — Aalsmeer** Yd No: 664 Loa 64.82 Br ex 11.40 Dght 3.350 Lbp 56.66 Br md 11.00 Dpth 5.75 Welded, 1 dk	**(X11A2YP) Yacht**	**2 oil engines** reduction geared to sc. shafts driving 2 Propellers Total Power: 2,986kW (4,060hp) 13.0kn Caterpillar 3516B-TA 2 x Vee 4 Stroke 16 Cy. 170 x 190 each-1493kW (2030bhp) Caterpillar Inc-USA AuxGen: 3 x 215kW 400V 50Hz a.c

803430 *VJN2964*
WEELA
232 – 135
Class: (LR) ✠ Classed LR until 7/10/07
Devine Marine Group Pty Ltd (Devine Marine Salvage)
-
Sydney, NSW *Australia*
MMSI: 503077000
Official number: 332003
1968-03 Adelaide Ship Construction Pty Ltd — Port Adelaide SA Yd No: 40
Loa 32.21 Br ex 8.56 Dght 4.007
Lbp 28.96 Br md 8.08 Dpth 4.47
Welded
(B32A2ST) Tug
1 oil engine sr reverse geared to sc. shaft driving 1 FP propeller
Total Power: 1,236kW (1,680hp) 11.0kn
Mirrlees KMR-6
1 x 4 Stroke 6 Cy. 381 x 457 1236kW (1680bhp)
Mirrlees National Ltd.-Stockport
AuxGen: 2 x 40kW 220V d.c
Fuel: 36.5 (d.f.)

7006950 *PD5955*
WEERT
ex Howard Barge No. 3 *-1975* *ex* B 45 *-1973*
Mijnster Zand- en Grinthandel BV
Van Oord Nederland BV
Rotterdam *Netherlands*
MMSI: 244660220
Official number: 3869
769 230 1,799
Class: (BV) (GL)
1970 Theodor Buschmann Schiffswerft GmbH & Co. — Hamburg Yd No: 126
Loa 65.03 Br ex 11.03 Dght 2.650
Lbp 60.03 Br md 10.98 Dpth 3.51
Welded, 1 dk
(B34A2SH) Hopper, Motor
Compartments: 1 Ho, ER
1 Ha: (48.0 x 8.0)ER
2 oil engines reverse reduction geared to sc. shafts driving 2 FP propellers
Total Power: 716kW (974hp) 9.0kn
Deutz SBA8M816
2 x 4 Stroke 8 Cy. 142 x 160 each-358kW (487bhp) (new engine 1979)
Kloeckner Humboldt Deutz AG-West Germany
AuxGen: 2 x 30kW 220/380V 50Hz a.c, 1 x 28kW 220/380V 50Hz a.c, 1 x 20kW 220V d.c
Thrusters: 1 Directional thruster (f)

9093062 *DUJ2118*
WEESAM EXPRESS
ex Weesam Express 1 *-1973*
SRN Fast Seacrafts Inc
Zamboanga *Philippines*
Official number: ZAM2D00436
226 50 -
1996-01 Yong Choo Kui Shipyard Sdn Bhd — Sibu
L reg 41.00 Br ex - Dght -
Lbp - Br md 5.50 Dpth 2.75
Welded, 1 dk
(A37B2PS) Passenger Ship
Passengers: unberthed: 252
2 oil engines driving 2 Propellers
Total Power: 3,310kW (4,500hp) 20.0kn
Mitsubishi S16R-MPTA
2 x Vee 4 Stroke 16 Cy. 170 x 180 each-1655kW (2250bhp)
Mitsubishi Heavy Industries Ltd-Japan

8982383 *DUJ2128*
WEESAM EXPRESS 2
ex Pintas Samudra 2 *-1998*
SRN Fast Seacrafts Inc
Zamboanga *Philippines*
Official number: ZAM2D01151
136 49 -
1998-01 Yong Choo Kui Shipyard Sdn Bhd — Sibu Yd No: 8396
Loa 40.00 Br ex 4.62 Dght 1.350
Lbp 35.48 Br md 4.52 Dpth 2.10
Welded, 1 dk
(A37B2PS) Passenger Ship
Passengers: unberthed: 165
2 oil engines geared to sc. shafts driving 2 Propellers
Total Power: 1,618kW (2,200hp)
Yanmar 12LAK (M)-STE2
2 x Vee 4 Stroke 12 Cy. 150 x 165 each-809kW (1100bhp)
Yanmar Diesel Engine Co Ltd-Japan

9093024 *DUJ2139*
WEESAM EXPRESS 3
SRN Fast Seacrafts Inc
Iloilo *Philippines*
Official number: ZAM2D00503
146 42 -
1998-01 Yong Choo Kui Shipyard Sdn Bhd — Sibu
L reg 41.00 Br ex - Dght -
Lbp - Br md 4.72 Dpth 2.50
Welded, 1 dk
(A37B2PS) Passenger Ship
Hull Material: Aluminium Alloy
Passengers: unberthed: 199
2 oil engines geared to sc. shafts driving 2 Propellers
Total Power: 1,864kW (2,534hp) 30.0kn
Caterpillar 3512TA
2 x Vee 4 Stroke 12 Cy. 170 x 190 each-932kW (1267bhp)
Caterpillar Inc-USA

8965579 *DUJ2158*
WEESAM EXPRESS 5
Sunrise Energy Sdn Bhd
SRN Fast Seacrafts Inc
Zamboanga *Philippines*
Official number: ZAM2D00536
230 63 -
1999-10 Yong Choo Kui Shipyard Sdn Bhd — Sibu Yd No: 4697
Loa 39.68 Br ex - Dght -
Lbp - Br md 5.50 Dpth 1.85
Welded, 1 dk
(A37B2PS) Passenger Ship
Passengers: unberthed: 268
2 oil engines reduction geared to sc. shafts driving 2 FP propellers
Total Power: 3,530kW (4,800hp) 32.0kn
Caterpillar 3516TA
2 x Vee 4 Stroke 16 Cy. 170 x 190 each-1765kW (2400bhp)
Caterpillar Inc-USA

9093036
WEESAM EXPRESS 6
SRN Fast Seacrafts Inc
Iloilo *Philippines*
Official number: ZAM2D00970
219 38 -
2002-01 Yong Choo Kui Shipyard Sdn Bhd — Sibu
L reg 40.61 Br ex - Dght -
Lbp - Br md 5.00 Dpth 2.50
Welded, 1 dk
(A37B2PS) Passenger Ship
Hull Material: Aluminium Alloy
Passengers: unberthed: 250
2 oil engines driving 2 Propellers
Total Power: 2,500kW (3,400hp)
Cummins
2 x Vee 4 Stroke 16 Cy. each-1250kW (1700bhp)
Cummins Engine Co Inc-USA

8666721 *DUJ2245*
WEESAM EXPRESS 7
SRN Fast Seacrafts Inc
Zamboanga *Philippines*
206 47 85
2006-01 Yong Choo Kui Shipyard Sdn Bhd — Sibu
Loa 44.00 Br ex 5.00 Dght -
Lbp - Br md - Dpth -
Welded, 1 dk
(A37B2PS) Passenger Ship
Passengers: unberthed: 190
2 oil engines reduction geared to sc. shafts driving 2 FP propellers
Total Power: 2,984kW (4,058hp)
Cummins KTA-50-M2
2 x Vee 4 Stroke 16 Cy. 159 x 159 each-1492kW (2029bhp)
Cummins Engine Co Inc-USA

9385465 *DUJ2235*
WEESAM EXPRESS 8
SRN Fast Seacrafts Inc
Zamboanga *Philippines*
MMSI: 548031400
Official number: ZAM2D01319
206 47 85
2006-06 Yong Choo Kui Shipyard Sdn Bhd — Sibu Yd No: 2489
Loa 43.47 Br ex - Dght 1.400
Lbp 39.83 Br md 4.72 Dpth 2.13
Welded, 1 dk
(A37B2PS) Passenger Ship
Passengers: unberthed: 270
2 oil engines reduction geared to sc. shafts driving 2 FP propellers
Total Power: 2,500kW (3,400hp)
Cummins KTA-50-M2
2 x Vee 4 Stroke 16 Cy. 159 x 159 each-1250kW (1700bhp)
Cummins Engine Co Inc-USA

8901054 *DBBC*
WEGA
Government of The Federal Republic of Germany (Der Bundesminister fuer Verkehr, Bau und Stadtentwicklung)
Government of The Federal Republic of Germany (Bundesamt fuer Seeschiffahrt und Hydrographie)
SatCom: Inmarsat A 1121156
Hamburg *Germany*
MMSI: 211205970
969 290 160
Class: GL
1990-11 Kroeger Werft GmbH & Co. KG — Schacht-Audorf Yd No: 1522
Loa 52.00 (BB) Br ex 11.56 Dght 3.451
Lbp 47.20 Br md 11.40 Dpth 5.25
Welded, 1 dk
(B31A2SR) Research Survey Vessel
Ice Capable
2 diesel electric oil engines driving 2 gen. each 510kW 380V a.c 1 gen. of 267kW 380V a.c Connecting to 1 elec. Motor of (559kW) driving 1 FP propeller
Total Power: 1,320kW (1,794hp) 10.0kn
M.T.U. 12V183TA51
2 x Vee 4 Stroke 12 Cy. 128 x 142 each-660kW (897bhp)
MTU Friedrichshafen GmbH-Friedrichshafen
Thrusters: 1 Water jet (f); 1 Directional thruster (a)
Fuel: 91.0 (d.f.)

9141118 *DHEW*
WEGA
ex Containerships V *-2009*
launched as Wega *-1996*
ms 'Wega' GmbH & Co KG
Wegener Bereederungsgesellschaft mbH & Co KG (Reederei H - P Wegener)
SatCom: Inmarsat C 421123588
Hamburg *Germany*
MMSI: 211235880
Official number: 17915
7,550 3,957 8,912
Class: GL
1996-05 J.J. Sietas KG Schiffswerft GmbH & Co. — Hamburg Yd No: 1132
Loa 151.14 (BB) Br ex 19.66 Dght 7.420
Lbp 141.40 Br md 19.40 Dpth 9.30
Welded, 1 dk
(A33A2CC) Container Ship (Fully Cellular)
Grain: 13,221; Bale: 12,568
TEU 749 C Ho 248 TEU C Dk 501 TEU incl 102 ref C.
Compartments: 4 Cell Ho, ER
4 Ha: ER
Ice Capable
1 oil engine with flexible couplings & sr gearedto sc. shaft driving 1 CP propeller
Total Power: 10,000kW (13,596hp) 21.5kn
MaK 8M601C
1 x 4 Stroke 8 Cy. 580 x 600 10000kW (13596bhp)
Krupp MaK Maschinenbau GmbH-Kiel
AuxGen: 1 x 1276kW 220/380V 50Hz a.c, 2 x 320kW 220/380V 50Hz a.c
Thrusters: 1 Thwart. CP thruster (f)

6801042 *DEKE*
WEGA
ex Elsfleth *-2010* *ex* Wega *-1994*
JS Jade ms 'Wega' GmbH & Co KG
Wilhelmshaven *Germany*
MMSI: 211238490
Official number: 494
155 46 66
Class: GL
1967-12 Jadewerft Wilhelmshaven GmbH — Wilhelmshaven Yd No: 112
Loa 29.49 Br ex 7.85 Dght 3.125
Lbp 27.26 Br md 7.50 Dpth 3.84
Welded, 1 dk
(B32A2ST) Tug
Ice Capable
1 oil engine reverse reduction geared to sc. shaft driving 1 FP propeller
Total Power: 883kW (1,201hp)
Deutz SBV8M545
1 x 4 Stroke 8 Cy. 320 x 450 883kW (1201bhp)
Kloeckner Humboldt Deutz AG-West Germany
AuxGen: 2 x 28kW 220/380V 50Hz a.c
Fuel: 33.5 (d.f.)

7019737 *HSPF*
WEGA 1
ex Vega 1 *-2000* *ex* Malee *-2000*
ex Sang Thai Marine *-1995*
ex Ocean Seven 1 *-1977* *ex* Taiyo Maru *-1975*
Vega Shipping & Travel Agency Co
Bangkok *Thailand*
Official number: 201018888
2,753 1,656 4,662
Class: (NK)
1970-03 Fukuoka Shipbuilding Co Ltd — Fukuoka FO Yd No: 967
Loa 95.69 Br ex 15.04 Dght 6.097
Lbp 88.50 Br md 15.02 Dpth 7.29
Welded, 1 dk
(A31A2GX) General Cargo Ship
Grain: 5,820; Bale: 5,550
Compartments: 2 Ho, ER
2 Ha: (22.1 x 8.0) (24.6 x 8.0)ER
Derricks: 1x15t,2x10t
1 oil engine driving 1 FP propeller
Total Power: 2,207kW (3,001hp) 12.0kn
Mitsubishi 6UET39/65C
1 x 2 Stroke 6 Cy. 390 x 650 2207kW (3001bhp)
Kobe Hatsudoki KK-Japan
AuxGen: 2 x 128kW 445V 60Hz a.c
Fuel: 405.5 10.0pd

8892411 *DDFX*
WEGA II
Dieter Hermann Niessen
Fedderwardersiel *Germany*
MMSI: 211232640
Official number: 1573
106 44 16
Class: GL
1986 Neptun-Werft Theodor Bartels & Co. — Bremen Yd No: 9875
L reg 18.36 Br ex - Dght 1.100
Lbp - Br md 6.00 Dpth 1.60
Welded, 1 dk
(A37B2PS) Passenger Ship
2 oil engines reduction geared to sc. shafts driving 2 FP propellers
Total Power: 220kW (300hp) 8.0kn
MAN D0266ME
2 x 4 Stroke 6 Cy. 102 x 116 each-110kW (150bhp)
MAN Nutzfahrzeuge AG-Nuernberg
AuxGen: 1 x 20kW 380V a.c

9232383 *V7DR6*
WEHR ALSTER
ex CSAV Rio Baker *-2009* *ex* CCNI Arica *-2004*
completed as Wehr Alster *-2002*
SBT Shipping Co Ltd
Oskar Wehr KG (GmbH & Co)
Majuro *Marshall Islands*
MMSI: 538001697
Official number: 1697
25,630 12,733 33,694 T/cm 45.0
Class: NV (GL)
2002-03 Volkswerft Stralsund GmbH — Stralsund Yd No: 438
Loa 207.46 (BB) Br ex - Dght 11.400
Lbp 195.40 Br md 29.80 Dpth 16.40
Welded, 1 dk
(A33A2CC) Container Ship (Fully Cellular)
TEU 2474 C Ho 992 TEU C Dk 1482 TEU incl 400 ref C.
Cranes: 3x45t
Ice Capable
1 oil engine driving 1 FP propeller
Total Power: 19,810kW (26,934hp) 21.6kn
B&W 7L70MC
1 x 2 Stroke 7 Cy. 700 x 2268 19810kW (26934bhp)
Doosan Engine Co Ltd-South Korea
AuxGen: 3 x 1520kW 440/220V a.c
Thrusters: 1 Thwart. CP thruster (f)

9232395 *V7DT6* -	**WEHR BILLE** *ex* Niledutch Singapore *-2012* *ex* Wehr Bille *-2010* *ex* NYK Estrela *-2009* *ex* CSAV Rio Cochamo *-2004* *ex* Wehr Bille *-2004* *ex* CCNI Antartico *-2003* *launched as* Wehr Bille *-2002* **SBT Bille Shipping Co Ltd** Oskar Wehr KG (GmbH & Co) *Majuro* *Marshall Islands* MMSI: 538001704 Official number: 1704	**25,630** 12,733 33,739 T/cm 45.0	Class: NV (GL)	**2002-05 Volkswerft Stralsund GmbH — Stralsund** Yd No: 439 Loa 207.40 (BB) Br ex - Dght 11.400 Lbp 195.40 Br md 29.80 Dpth 16.40 Welded, 1 dk	**(A33A2CC) Container Ship (Fully Cellular)** TEU 2474 C Ho 992 TEU C Dk 1482 TEU incl 400 ref C. Cranes: 3x45t Ice Capable	**1 oil engine** driving 1 FP propeller Total Power: 19,810kW (26,934hp) B&W 1 x 2 Stroke 7 Cy. 700 x 2268 19810kW (26934bhp) Doosan Engine Co Ltd-South Korea AuxGen: 3 x 1520kW 440V a.c Thrusters: 1 Thwart. CP thruster (f)	21.6k 7L70M
9149902 *V7CY4* -	**WEHR BLANKENESE** *ex* CSAV Montreal *-2007* *ex* Norasia Montreal *-2001* *ex* Illapel *-2000* **ms 'Wehr Blankenese' Schiffahrtsgesellschaft mbH & Co KG** MCC Transport Singapore Pte Ltd *Majuro* *Marshall Islands* MMSI: 538090032 Official number: 90032	**16,177** 8,803 23,021 T/cm 37.1	Class: GL (LR) (NV) ✠ Classed LR until 22/5/00	**1999-12 Stocznia Szczecinska Porta Holding SA — Szczecin** Yd No: B170/1/20 Loa 184.10 (BB) Br ex 25.53 Dght 9.890 Lbp 171.94 Br md 25.30 Dpth 13.50 Welded, 1 dk	**(A33A2CC) Container Ship (Fully Cellular)** Bale: 29,000 TEU 1730 C Ho 634 TEU C Dk 1096 TEU incl 200 ref C. Compartments: 4 Cell Ho, ER 9 Ha: (12.5 x 13.0)8 (12.5 x 20.6)ER Cranes: 3x45t	**1 oil engine** driving 1 FP propeller Total Power: 13,320kW (18,110hp) Sulzer 1 x 2 Stroke 6 Cy. 620 x 2150 13320kW (18110bhp) H Cegielski Poznan SA-Poland AuxGen: 3 x 1096kW 450V 60Hz a.c Thrusters: 1 Thwart. FP thruster (f) Fuel: 165.9 (d.f.) (Heating Coils) 2229.7 (r.f.) 53.2pd	19.0k 6RTA62U
9236688 *V7DH7* -	**WEHR ELBE** *ex* CSAV Callao *-2008* *launched as* Wehr Elbe *-2001* **ms 'Wehr Elbe' Schiffahrtsges mbH & Co KG** Oskar Wehr KG (GmbH & Co) *Majuro* *Marshall Islands* MMSI: 538090081 Official number: 90081	**25,703** 12,028 33,657 T/cm 52.0	Class: NV (GL)	**2001-10 Kvaerner Warnow Werft GmbH — Rostock** Yd No: 24 Loa 208.31 (BB) Br ex - Dght 11.400 Lbp 195.00 Br md 29.80 Dpth 16.40 Welded, 1 dk	**(A33A2CC) Container Ship (Fully Cellular)** TEU 2524 C Ho 960 TEU C Dk 1564 TEU incl 400 ref C. Cranes: 3x45t Ice Capable	**1 oil engine** driving 1 FP propeller Total Power: 19,810kW (26,934hp) B&W 1 x 2 Stroke 7 Cy. 700 x 2268 19810kW (26934bhp) Manises Diesel Engine Co. S.A.-Valencia AuxGen: 4 x 1300kW 440/220V 60Hz a.c Thrusters: 1 Thwart. CP thruster (f)	22.0k 7L70M
9252981 *V7DY3* -	**WEHR HAVEL** *ex* CCNI Andes *-2011* *ex* Wehr Havel *-2010* *ex* CSAV Rio Tolten *-2009* *ex* Wehr Havel *-2004* **Partenreederei ms 'Wehr Havel'** Oskar Wehr KG (GmbH & Co) *Majuro* *Marshall Islands* MMSI: 538090127 Official number: 90127	**25,703** 12,028 33,748 T/cm 52.0	Class: NV (GL)	**2002-09 Kvaerner Warnow Werft GmbH — Rostock** Yd No: 28 Loa 208.30 (BB) Br ex - Dght 11.400 Lbp 195.00 Br md 29.80 Dpth 16.40 Welded, 1 dk	**(A33A2CC) Container Ship (Fully Cellular)** Grain: 44,900 TEU 2524 C Ho 960 TEU C Dk 1564 TEU incl 481 ref C. Cranes: 3x45t Ice Capable	**1 oil engine** driving 1 FP propeller Total Power: 19,796kW (26,915hp) B&W 1 x 2 Stroke 7 Cy. 700 x 2268 19796kW (26915bhp) Manises Diesel Engine Co. S.A.-Valencia AuxGen: 4 x 1290kW a.c Thrusters: 1 Tunnel thruster (f)	21.7k 7L70M
9301330 *V7ZG9* -	**WEHR HONG KONG** *ex* Maersk Dellys *-2014* *completed as* Wehr Hong Kong *-2006* **Wehr Containercarriers GmbH & Co KG** Oskar Wehr KG (GmbH & Co) *Majuro* *Marshall Islands* MMSI: 538090450 Official number: 90450	**54,193** 31,232 68,383 T/cm 83.2	Class: GL	**2006-02 Hanjin Heavy Industries & Construction Co Ltd — Busan** Yd No: 143 Loa 294.10 (BB) Br ex - Dght 13.521 Lbp 283.00 Br md 32.20 Dpth 21.60 Welded, 1 dk	**(A33A2CC) Container Ship (Fully Cellular)** TEU 5089 incl 454 ref C.	**1 oil engine** driving 1 FP propeller Total Power: 41,130kW (55,920hp) MAN-B&W 1 x 2 Stroke 9 Cy. 900 x 2300 41130kW (55920bhp) Doosan Engine Co Ltd-South Korea AuxGen: 4 x 1790kW 450/230V a.c Thrusters: 1 Thwart. CP thruster (f)	24.3k 9K90MC-C
9144134 *V7DQ8* -	**WEHR KOBLENZ** *ex* CCNI Bilbao *-2009* *ex* Wehr Koblenz *-2008* *ex* MOL Springbok *-2006* *ex* P&O Nedlloyd Portbury *-2006* *ex* P&O Nedlloyd Calypso *-2004* *ex* Costa Rica *-2002* *ex* Wehr Koblenz *-2001* *ex* Panamerican *-2001* *ex* CSAV Rio Amazonas *-1999* *launched as* Wehr Koblenz *-1998* **ms 'Wehr Koblenz' Schiffahrtsgesellschaft mbH & Co KG** Oskar Wehr KG (GmbH & Co) *Majuro* *Marshall Islands* MMSI: 538090056 Official number: 90056	**16,801** 8,672 23,026 T/cm 37.1	Class: GL	**1998-02 Stocznia Szczecinska SA — Szczecin** Yd No: B170/1/11 Loa 183.87 (BB) Br ex - Dght 9.880 Lbp 171.94 Br md 25.30 Dpth 13.50 Welded, 1 dk	**(A33A2CC) Container Ship (Fully Cellular)** Grain: 29,744 TEU 1730 C Ho 634 TEU C Dk 1096 TEU incl 200 ref C. Compartments: 4 Cell Ho, ER 9 Ha: (12.5 x 13.0)8 (12.5 x 20.6)ER Cranes: 3x45t	**1 oil engine** driving 1 FP propeller Total Power: 13,320kW (18,110hp) Sulzer 1 x 2 Stroke 6 Cy. 620 x 2150 13320kW (18110bhp) H Cegielski Poznan SA-Poland AuxGen: 3 x 1096kW 450V 60Hz a.c Thrusters: 1 Thwart. FP thruster (f) Fuel: 155.0 (d.f.) (Heating Coils) 2211.0 (r.f.) 51.0pd	19.0k 6RTA62U
9252993 *V7DY4* -	**WEHR OSTE** *ex* CCNI Concepcion *-2011* *ex* Wehr Oste *-2010* *ex* Callao Express *-2010* *ex* P&O Nedlloyd Yarra Valley *-2006* *ex* Wehr Oste *-2003* **Partenreederei ms 'Wehr Oste'** Oskar Wehr KG (GmbH & Co) *Majuro* *Marshall Islands* MMSI: 538090128 Official number: 90128	**25,703** 12,028 33,670 T/cm 52.0	Class: NV (GL)	**2002-11 Kvaerner Warnow Werft GmbH — Rostock** Yd No: 29 Loa 208.30 (BB) Br ex 30.04 Dght 11.400 Lbp 195.00 Br md 29.80 Dpth 16.40 Welded, 1 dk	**(A33A2CC) Container Ship (Fully Cellular)** Double Bottom Entire Compartment Length TEU 2524 C Ho 960 TEU C Dk 1564 TEU incl 481 ref C. Compartments: 5 Cell Ho, ER 10 Ha: (12.6 x 20.8)8 (12.6 x 26.0)ER (12.6 x 15.7) Cranes: 3x45t Ice Capable	**1 oil engine** driving 1 FP propeller Total Power: 19,796kW (26,915hp) B&W 1 x 2 Stroke 7 Cy. 700 x 2268 19796kW (26915bhp) Manises Diesel Engine Co. S.A.-Valencia AuxGen: 4 x 1360kW a.c Thrusters: 1 Thwart. CP thruster (f) Fuel: 247.0 (d.f.) 2332.0 (r.f.) 74.0pd	21.7k 7L70M
9301328 *V7ZG7* -	**WEHR SINGAPORE** *ex* Maersk Derince *-2014* *completed as* Wehr Singapore *-2006* **Wehr Containercarriers GmbH & Co KG** Oskar Wehr KG (GmbH & Co) *Majuro* *Marshall Islands* MMSI: 538090449 Official number: 90448	**54,193** 31,232 68,483 T/cm 83.2	Class: GL	**2006-01 Hanjin Heavy Industries & Construction Co Ltd — Busan** Yd No: 142 Loa 294.10 (BB) Br ex - Dght 13.521 Lbp 283.00 Br md 32.20 Dpth 21.60 Welded, 1 dk	**(A33A2CC) Container Ship (Fully Cellular)** TEU 5089 incl 454 ref C.	**1 oil engine** driving 1 FP propeller Total Power: 41,040kW (55,798hp) MAN-B&W 1 x 2 Stroke 9 Cy. 900 x 2300 41040kW (55798bhp) Doosan Engine Co Ltd-South Korea AuxGen: 4 x 1790kW 450/230V a.c Thrusters: 1 Thwart. CP thruster (f)	24.3k 9K90MC-C
9243239 *V7DR5* -	**WEHR TRAVE** *ex* CCNI Valparaiso *-2011* *ex* Wehr Trave *-2010* *ex* CSAV Rio Puelo *-2009* *ex* CCNI Aysen *-2004* *launched as* Wehr Trave *-2002* **SBT Shipping Co Ltd** Oskar Wehr KG (GmbH & Co) *Majuro* *Marshall Islands* MMSI: 538001696 Official number: 1696	**25,703** 12,028 33,795 T/cm 52.0	Class: NV (GL)	**2002-04 Kvaerner Warnow Werft GmbH — Rostock** Yd No: 26 Loa 208.30 (BB) Br ex - Dght 11.400 Lbp 195.00 Br md 29.80 Dpth 16.40 Welded, 1 dk	**(A33A2CC) Container Ship (Fully Cellular)** TEU 2524 C Ho 960 TEU C Dk 1564 TEU incl 400 ref C. Cranes: 3x45t Ice Capable	**1 oil engine** driving 1 FP propeller Total Power: 19,810kW (26,934hp) B&W 1 x 2 Stroke 7 Cy. 700 x 2268 19810kW (26934bhp) Doosan Engine Co Ltd-South Korea AuxGen: 4 x 1290kW 440/220V 60Hz a.c Thrusters: 1 Tunnel thruster (f)	21.7k 7L70M
9243241 *V7DT7* -	**WEHR WARNOW** *ex* CCNI Constitucion *-2011* *ex* Wehr Warnow *-2010* *ex* CSAV Rio Maule *-2009* *ex* Columbus China *-2004* *ex* Wehr Warnow *-2002* **SBT Warnow Shipping Co Ltd** Oskar Wehr KG (GmbH & Co) *Majuro* *Marshall Islands* MMSI: 538001705 Official number: 1705	**25,703** 12,028 33,691 T/cm 52.0	Class: NV (GL)	**2002-06 Kvaerner Warnow Werft GmbH — Rostock** Yd No: 27 Loa 208.30 (BB) Br ex - Dght 11.400 Lbp 195.00 Br md 29.80 Dpth 16.40 Welded, 1 dk	**(A33A2CC) Container Ship (Fully Cellular)** TEU 2524 C Ho 960 TEU C Dk 1564 TEU incl 481 ref C. Cranes: 3x45t Ice Capable	**1 oil engine** driving 1 FP propeller Total Power: 19,796kW (26,915hp) B&W 1 x 2 Stroke 7 Cy. 700 x 2268 19796kW (26915bhp) H Cegielski Poznan SA-Poland AuxGen: 4 x 1300kW 440/220V 60Hz a.c Thrusters: 1 Thwart. CP thruster (f)	21.7k 7L70M
9236690 *V7DG6* -	**WEHR WESER** *ex* Libra New York *-2009* *launched as* Wehr Weser *-2001* **ms 'Wehr Weser' Schiffahrtsges mbH & Co KG** Oskar Wehr KG (GmbH & Co) *Majuro* *Marshall Islands* MMSI: 538090082 Official number: 90082	**25,703** 12,028 33,691 T/cm 52.0	Class: NV (GL)	**2001-12 Kvaerner Warnow Werft GmbH — Rostock** Yd No: 25 Loa 208.30 (BB) Br ex - Dght 11.400 Lbp 195.00 Br md 29.80 Dpth 16.40 Welded, 1 dk	**(A33A2CC) Container Ship (Fully Cellular)** TEU 2524 C Ho 960 TEU C Dk 1564 TEU incl 400 ref C. Cranes: 3x45t Ice Capable	**1 oil engine** driving 1 FP propeller Total Power: 19,810kW (26,934hp) B&W 1 x 2 Stroke 7 Cy. 700 x 2268 19810kW (26934bhp) Manises Diesel Engine Co. S.A.-Valencia AuxGen: 4 x 1290kW 440/220V 60Hz a.c Thrusters: 1 Thwart. CP thruster (f)	22.0k 7L70M

IMO / Call sign / Fishing no.	Name / Owner / Manager / Flag	GT / NT / DWT	Class	Builder / Dimensions	Type / Cargo	Machinery
9262481 *VRFD5* -	**WEI CHI** *launched as* Ruby Star *-2009* **Wei Chi Shipping SA** China Shipping Tanker Co Ltd SatCom: Inmarsat C 447701747 *Hong Kong* — *Hong Kong* MMSI: 477217800 Official number: HK-2386	**31,150** 12,072 45,854 T/cm 52.5	Class: LR ✠ **100A** SS 06/2009 Double Hull oil tanker ESP **ShipRight** (SDA, FDA, CM) LI SPM Ice Class 1B at 12.392m draught Max/min draught fwd 12.392/6.517m Max/min draught aft 12.392/6.517m Required power 10610kw, installed power 10900kw ✠ **LMC** **UMS IGS** Eq.Ltr: M†; Cable: 577.5/73.0 U3 (a)	**2009-06 China Shipping Industry (Jiangsu) Co Ltd — Jiangdu JS** Yd No: A46000-01 Loa 187.20 (BB) Br ex 32.29 Dght 12.100 Lbp 176.70 Br md 32.25 Dpth 18.90 Welded, 1 dk	**(A13A2TW) Crude/Oil Products Tanker** Double Hull (13F) Liq: 52,711; Liq (Oil): 54,850 Cargo Heating Coils Compartments: 12 Wing Ta, 2 Wing Slop Ta, ER 12 Cargo Pump (s): 12x600m³/hr Manifold: Bow/CM: 95.5m Ice Capable	**1 oil engine** driving 1 FP propeller Total Power: 10,900kW (14,820hp) 14.0kn Wartsila 5RT-flex58T 1 x 2 Stroke 5 Cy. 580 x 2416 10900kW (14820bhp) Dalian Marine Diesel Co Ltd-China AuxGen: 3 x 975kW 450V 60Hz a.c Boilers: e (ex.g.) 17.3kgf/cm² (17.0bar), AuxB (o.f.) 14.3kgf/cm² (14.0bar) Thrusters: 1 Thwart. CP thruster (f) Fuel: 280.0 (d.f.) 1795.0 (r.f.)
9181924 - -	**WEI CHING** **Wei Ching Empresa Oceano SA** -	**498** 177 -		**1997-11 Lien Ho Shipbuilding Co, Ltd — Kaohsiung** Yd No: 073 Loa - Br ex - Dght - Lbp 53.45 Br md 8.50 Dpth 3.65 Welded, 1 dk	**(B11B2FV) Fishing Vessel**	**1 oil engine** driving 1 FP propeller Total Power: 1,030kW (1,400hp) Hanshin LH28G 1 x 4 Stroke 6 Cy. 280 x 460 1030kW (1400bhp) The Hanshin Diesel Works Ltd-Japan
7425998 - -	**WEI FA** *ex* Kobe I *-1997* *ex* Stainless Maru No. 2 *-1994* - -	*497* 344 1,123		**1976-02 K.K. Matsuo Tekko Zosensho — Matsue** Yd No: 285 Loa - Br ex 9.22 Dght 4.192 Lbp 53.50 Br md 9.20 Dpth 4.50 Riveted\Welded, 1 dk	**(A12A2TC) Chemical Tanker**	**1 oil engine** driving 1 FP propeller Total Power: 883kW (1,201hp) Makita GNLH6275 1 x 4 Stroke 6 Cy. 275 x 450 883kW (1201bhp) Makita Diesel Co Ltd-Japan
9113563 *3FEV4* -	**WEI FONG** *ex* Golden Joy *-2009* *ex* Clipper Joy *-2006* *ex* China Joy *-2004* **Good Master Shipping Ltd** Wei Fong Shipping Co Ltd SatCom: Inmarsat C 435537811 *Panama* — *Panama* MMSI: 355378000 Official number: 4130810	**38,679** 24,059 70,045 T/cm 65.8	Class: NK (AB)	**1994-09 Jiangnan Shipyard — Shanghai** Yd No: 2204 Loa 225.00 (BB) Br ex - Dght 13.622 Lbp 215.00 Br md 32.20 Dpth 18.70 Welded, 1 dk	**(A21A2BC) Bulk Carrier** Grain: 85,007; Bale: 81,348 Compartments: 7 Ho, ER 7 Ha: (14.6 x 13.2)6 (14.6 x 15.0)ER	**1 oil engine** driving 1 FP propeller Total Power: 12,265kW (16,675hp) 14.5kn B&W 6S60MC 1 x 2 Stroke 6 Cy. 600 x 2292 12265kW (16675bhp) Dalian Marine Diesel Works-China AuxGen: 3 x 520kW 440V 60Hz a.c Fuel: 276.5 (d.f.) 2560.2 (r.f.) 33.7pd
9260093 *YCHL* -	**WEI GANG TUO 10** **PT Sentosa Segara Mulia Shipping** PT Wintermar *Jakarta* — *Indonesia*	**377** 113 -	Class: BV KI	**2001-04 Penglai Bohai Shipyard Co Ltd — Penglai SD** Yd No: 00-10 Loa 38.88 Br ex - Dght 3.300 Lbp 32.80 Br md 9.80 Dpth 4.40 Welded, 1 dk	**(B32A2ST) Tug**	**2 oil engines** geared to sc. shafts driving 2 FP propellers Total Power: 2,942kW (4,000hp) 13.7kn Daihatsu 6DKM-26 2 x 4 Stroke 6 Cy. 260 x 380 each-1471kW (2000bhp) Daihatsu Diesel Manufacturing Co Lt-Japan AuxGen: 2 x 93kW a.c
9601091 *VRJM8* -	**WEI HE** **Fastlink Shipping Ltd** Wei Fong Shipping Co Ltd SatCom: Inmarsat C 447704488 *Hong Kong* — *Hong Kong* MMSI: 477024200 Official number: HK-3292	**43,550** 27,579 79,440 T/cm 71.9	Class: NK	**2012-06 Jinhai Heavy Industry Co Ltd — Daishan County ZJ** Yd No: J0029 Loa 229.00 Br ex 32.30 Dght 14.640 Lbp 222.00 Br md 32.26 Dpth 20.25 Welded, 1 dk	**(A21A2BC) Bulk Carrier** Grain: 97,885; Bale: 90,784 Compartments: 7 Ho, ER 7 Ha: ER	**1 oil engine** driving 1 FP propeller Total Power: 11,900kW (16,179hp) 14.5kn MAN-B&W 5S60MC-C 1 x 2 Stroke 5 Cy. 600 x 2400 11900kW (16179bhp) Hitachi Zosen Corp-Japan Fuel: 3250.0
8715845 *BROY* -	**WEI HU LING** *ex* Xiang Hao *-2004* *ex* Wei Hu Ling *-1999* **China Shipping Container Lines Co Ltd** - SatCom: Inmarsat C 441272810 *Guangzhou, Guangdong* — *China* MMSI: 412050710	**13,253** 5,744 20,412	Class: (CC)	**1991-01 Guangzhou Shipyard — Guangzhou GD** Yd No: 81010 Converted From: Bulk Carrier-1999 Loa 164.00 Br ex - Dght 9.800 Lbp 154.00 Br md 22.00 Dpth 13.40 Welded, 1 dk	**(A31A2GX) General Cargo Ship** Grain: 25,373 TEU 996 Compartments: 5 Ho, ER 5 Ha: (12.6 x 11.2)4 (14.0 x 12.8)ER Ice Capable	**1 oil engine** driving 1 FP propeller Total Power: 5,826kW (7,921hp) 14.5kn Sulzer 6RTA48 1 x 2 Stroke 6 Cy. 480 x 1400 5826kW (7921bhp) Shanghai Diesel Engine Co Ltd-China AuxGen: 3 x 388kW 400V a.c, 1 x 90kW 400V a.c
8421523 *BKUW3* -	**WEI JIA** *ex* Ji Hua *-2006* *ex* Superway *-1995* *ex* Day Crux *-1991* **Dalian Haida Shipping Co Ltd** - *Zhoushan, Zhejiang* — *China* MMSI: 412205160	**1,389** 641 2,201	Class: (CC) (NK)	**1985-03 Sanuki Shipbuilding & Iron Works Co Ltd — Mitoyo KG** Yd No: 1138 Loa 75.95 Br ex - Dght 5.062 Lbp 69.96 Br md 12.01 Dpth 6.00 Welded, 1 dk	**(A12B2TR) Chemical/Products Tanker** Liq: 2,394; Liq (Oil): 2,394 Compartments: 8 Ta, ER	**1 oil engine** driving 1 FP propeller Total Power: 1,103kW (1,500hp) 11.0kn Akasaka A28 1 x 4 Stroke 6 Cy. 280 x 550 1103kW (1500bhp) Akasaka Tekkosho KK (Akasaka DieselLtd)-Japan AuxGen: 1 x 180kW 225V 60Hz a.c, 2 x 104kW 225V 60Hz a.c
6510150 *H3BI* -	**WEI LI** *ex* Shinryo Maru No. 18 *-1976* **Manfung Shipping SA** - *Panama* — *Panama* Official number: 06953PEXT3	*253* 129 -	Class: (CR)	**1965 Kochiken Zosen — Kochi** Yd No: 285 Loa 38.61 Br ex 7.45 Dght 3.150 Lbp 38.10 Br md 7.40 Dpth 3.41 Riveted\Welded, 1 dk	**(B11B2FV) Fishing Vessel** Ins: 289 Compartments: 4 Ho, ER 4 Ha: 2 (1.0 x 0.7)2 (1.2 x 1.3)ER	**1 oil engine** driving 1 FP propeller Total Power: 515kW (700hp) 12.5kn Fuji 6SD30 1 x 4 Stroke 6 Cy. 300 x 430 515kW (700bhp) Fuji Diesel Co Ltd-Japan AuxGen: 2 x 64kW 225V a.c
9597628 *BSBA* -	**WEI LI** *ex* Magnificent *-2012* *ex* Wei Li *-2010* **Shanghai Salvage Co** - *Shanghai* — *China* MMSI: 413046070	**25,390** 7,617 18,334	Class: AB CC	**2010-08 Shanghai Zhenhua Port Machinery Co Ltd — Shanghai** Yd No: ZPMC1206 Loa 141.00 Br ex 43.40 Dght 8.400 Lbp 137.60 Br md 40.00 Dpth 12.80 Welded, 1 dk	**(B34B2SC) Crane Vessel** Cranes: 1x3000t Ice Capable	**6 diesel electric oil engines** driving 6 gen. Connecting to 2 elec. motors each (4500kW) driving 2 Azimuth electric drive units Total Power: 27,000kW (36,708hp) 12.0kn MAN-B&W 9L32/40 1 x 4 Stroke 9 Cy. 320 x 400 4500kW (6118bhp) MAN-B&W 9L32/40 5 x 4 Stroke 9 Cy. 320 x 400 each-4500kW (6118bhp) Thrusters: 1 Tunnel thruster (f); 2 Retract. directional thruster (f) Fuel: 740.0 (d.f.) 2439.0 (r.f.)
8430081 - -	**WEI LI No. 7** **Wei Li Fishery Co Ltd** - *San Lorenzo* — *Honduras* Official number: L-1823007	**456** 311 -		**1979 Shin Tien Erh Shipbuilding Co, Ltd — Kaohsiung** L reg 45.00 Br ex - Dght - Lbp - Br md 8.32 Dpth 2.80 Welded, 1 dk	**(B11B2FV) Fishing Vessel**	**1 oil engine** driving 1 FP propeller Total Power: 809kW (1,100hp) 12.0kn
8628573 *BZFR* CT6-1051	**WEI LIEN 123** **Wei Lien Marine Products Co Ltd** - *Kaohsiung* — *Chinese Taipei* Official number: 009454	**363** 156 -		**1985-08 San Yang Shipbuilding Co., Ltd. — Kaohsiung** Loa 47.84 Br ex - Dght 3.140 Lbp 42.34 Br md 7.78 Dpth 3.50 Welded, 1 dk	**(B11B2FV) Fishing Vessel**	**1 oil engine** driving 1 FP propeller Fuji Fuji Diesel Co Ltd-Japan
8628585 *BZFS* CT6-1052	**WEI LIEN 213** **Wei Sheng Marine Products Co Ltd** - *Kaohsiung* — *Chinese Taipei* Official number: 009453	**363** 156 -		**1985-08 San Yang Shipbuilding Co., Ltd. — Kaohsiung** Loa 47.84 Br ex - Dght 3.140 Lbp 42.34 Br md 7.78 Dpth 3.50 Welded, 1 dk	**(B11B2FV) Fishing Vessel**	**1 oil engine** driving 1 FP propeller Fuji Fuji Diesel Co Ltd-Japan
8879160 *V3NT5* -	**WEI LONG** *ex* Marushin Maru *-2009* *ex* Showa Maru *-2009* **Winner Shipping Ltd** Weihai Jiayang International Shipping Management Co Ltd *Belize City* — *Belize* MMSI: 312369000 Official number: 610920005	**1,483** 835 1,600	Class: IT (NK)	**1994-09 K.K. Uno Zosensho — Imabari** Yd No: 500 Loa 75.15 Br ex - Dght 4.153 Lbp 70.50 Br md 12.00 Dpth 7.13 Welded, 1 dk	**(A31A2GX) General Cargo Ship** Grain: 2,769; Bale: 2,638 Compartments: 1 Ho, ER 1 Ha: (40.4 x 9.4)ER	**1 oil engine** driving 1 FP propeller Total Power: 1,324kW (1,800hp) 11.5kn Makita LS33L 1 x 4 Stroke 6 Cy. 330 x 640 1324kW (1800bhp) Makita Corp-Japan
8626381 - -	**WEI LONG NO. 9** *ex* Shoun Maru *-2003* *ex* Seiko Maru *-1998* - -	*488* - 812		**1984 Fujiwara Zosensho — Imabari** Loa 53.70 Br ex - Dght 3.201 Lbp 50.02 Br md 11.51 Dpth 5.01 Welded, 1 dk	**(A24D2BA) Aggregates Carrier**	**1 oil engine** driving 1 FP propeller Total Power: 699kW (950hp) 10.0kn Niigata 1 x 4 Stroke 699kW (950bhp) Niigata Engineering Co Ltd-Japan

8810346 *XUUG3* -	**WEI XIANG** *ex* Nikko Maru No. 18 *-2008* *ex* Showa Maru No. 18 *-2003* *ex* Eiyoshi Maru No. 5 *-1991* **Wei Xiang Shipping Co Ltd** Yantai Weisheng International Shipping Co Ltd *Phnom Penh* *Cambodia* MMSI: 514059000 Official number: 0888092	**1,986** 1,209 609		**1988-09 K.K. Miura Zosensho — Saiki** Yd No: 820 Loa 51.80 Br ex - Dght 3.600 Lbp 46.80 Br md 10.80 Dpth 5.40 Welded	**(A31A2GX) General Cargo Ship** Compartments: 1 Ho 1 Ha: (18.2 x 8.5)	**1 oil engine** driving 1 FP propeller Total Power: 736kW (1,001hp) 10.0kn Niigata 6M28BGT 1 x 4 Stroke 6 Cy. 280 x 480 736kW (1001bhp) Niigata Engineering Co Ltd-Japan
8801553 *XULC8* -	**WEI YUAN 8** *ex* Sanko *-2002* **Sinostep Shipping Ltd** - *Phnom Penh* *Cambodia* MMSI: 514453000 Official number: 0887922	**1,096** 355 900	Class: UM	**1987-10 Mategata Zosen K.K. — Namikata** Yd No: 1016 Loa - Br ex - Dght 3.401 Lbp 65.03 Br md 10.51 Dpth 6.08 Welded	**(A31A2GX) General Cargo Ship**	**1 oil engine** reverse geared to sc. shaft driving 1 FP propeller Total Power: 736kW (1,001hp) Akasaka K28R 1 x 4 Stroke 6 Cy. 280 x 480 736kW (1001bhp) Akasaka Tekkosho KK (Akasaka DieselLtd)-Japan
9183829 *CQLI* -	**WEICHSELSTERN** - **mt 'Weichselstern' Schifffahrtsgesellschaft mbH & Co KG** Nordic Tankers Trading A/S *Madeira* *Portugal (MAR)* MMSI: 255804960 Official number: TEMP151M	**14,400** 6,937 21,823 T/cm 38.9	Class: GL	**1999-12 Stocznia Gdynia SA — Gdynia** Yd No: 8189/2 Loa 162.16 Br ex - Dght 8.800 Lbp 155.87 Br md 27.18 Dpth 12.00 Welded, 1 dk	**(A12B2TR) Chemical/Products Tanker** Double Hull (13F) Liq: 23,970; Liq (Oil): 23,970 Cargo Heating Coils Compartments: 1 Ta, 12 Wing Ta, ER, 1 Wing Slop Ta 13 Cargo Pump (s): 6x550m³/hr, 7x350m³/hr Manifold: Bow/CM: 80m Ice Capable	**1 oil engine** driving 1 CP propeller Total Power: 7,860kW (10,686hp) 15.0kn MAN-B&W 6S46MC-C 1 x 2 Stroke 6 Cy. 460 x 1932 7860kW (10686bhp) H Cegielski Poznan SA-Poland AuxGen: 1 x 720kW 440/220V 60Hz a.c, 3 x 664kW 440/220V 60Hz a.c Thrusters: 1 Thwart. CP thruster (f) Fuel: 1276.0 (r.f.) (Heating Coils) 29.0pd
8876455 *9V5022* -	**WEIHAI 1** - **Reliance Marine Engineering Pte Ltd** - *Singapore* *Singapore* Official number: 386197	**107** 31 -	Class: GL	**1994-07 Kiong Nguong Shipbuilding Contractor Co — Sibu** Yd No: 009 Loa 20.51 Br ex - Dght 2.942 Lbp - Br md 6.10 Dpth 3.05 Welded, 1 dk	**(B32A2ST) Tug**	**2 oil engines** reduction geared to sc. shafts driving 2 FP propellers Total Power: 532kW (724hp) Cummins NTA-855-M 2 x 4 Stroke 6 Cy. 140 x 152 each-266kW (362bhp) Cummins Engine Co Inc-USA AuxGen: 2 x 12kW 220V a.c
9126546 *9V5123* -	**WEIHAI 5** - **Chye Heng Marine Pte Ltd** - *Singapore* *Singapore* MMSI: 563577000 Official number: 386510	**106** 31 -	Class: GL (BV)	**1995-03 Nga Chai Shipyard Sdn Bhd — Sibu** Yd No: 9402 Loa 23.17 Br ex - Dght 2.400 Lbp 21.03 Br md 6.70 Dpth 2.90 Welded, 1 dk	**(B32A2ST) Tug**	**2 oil engines** reverse reduction geared to sc. shafts driving 2 FP propellers Total Power: 746kW (1,014hp) Cummins KT-19-M500 2 x 4 Stroke 6 Cy. 159 x 159 each-373kW (507bhp) (made 1992) Cummins Engine Co Inc-USA AuxGen: 2 x 26kW 220/415V 50Hz a.c Fuel: 73.0 (d.f.)
9503859 *3ERE2* -	**WEILAN 1** - **Weilan Haihang Group Co Ltd** HK Guanya Shipping Ltd *Panama* *Panama* MMSI: 370019000 Official number: 37240PEXT	**5,849** 3,275 9,520	Class: (CC)	**2007-12 Fujian Fu'an Shunjiang Shipyard Co Ltd — Fu'an FJ** Loa 127.80 Br ex - Dght 6.500 Lbp 121.10 Br md 18.80 Dpth 8.60 Welded, 1 dk	**(A31A2GX) General Cargo Ship**	**1 oil engine** reduction geared to sc. shaft driving 1 Propeller Total Power: 2,500kW (3,399hp) 13.0kn Daihatsu 8DKM-28 1 x 4 Stroke 8 Cy. 280 x 390 2500kW (3399bhp) Shaanxi Diesel Heavy Industry Co Lt-China
9503861 - -	**WEILAN 2** - **Weilan Haihang Group Co Ltd** HK Guanya Shipping Ltd	**7,065** 3,418 9,520		**2008-01 in the People's Republic of China** Loa 136.80 Br ex 19.00 Dght 7.700 Lbp 126.00 Br md 10.00 Dpth - Welded, 1 dk	**(A21A2BC) Bulk Carrier** Grain: 13,600	**1 oil engine** driving 1 Propeller 11.5kn
9236119 - -	**WEILUN NO. 6** *ex* Chang Hung No. 7 *-2006* **Jiangsu Weilun Shipping Co Ltd** *China* MMSI: 413550040	**5,625** 2,136 10,000	Class: CC (BV)	**2002-03 Jiangsu Xinhua Shipyard Co Ltd — Nanjing JS** Yd No: H406 Loa 103.80 Br ex - Dght 5.600 Lbp 100.10 Br md 25.00 Dpth 7.50 Welded, 1 dk	**(A31C2GD) Deck Cargo Ship**	**2 oil engines** geared to sc. shafts driving 2 FP propellers Total Power: 3,386kW (4,604hp) 11.0kn Daihatsu 6DLM-28 2 x 4 Stroke 6 Cy. 280 x 360 each-1693kW (2302bhp) Daihatsu Diesel Manufacturing Co Lt-Japan
5187061 - -	**WEISSHAUPT** *ex* Hellas *-2003* *ex* Aghios Gerassimos *-1999* *ex* Kilgarth *-1984* *ex* Kilmore *-1969* - -	**198** 47	Class: (LR) ✠ Classed LR until 6/6/84	**1958-12 W. J. Yarwood & Sons Ltd. — Northwich** Yd No: 914 Loa 31.55 Br ex 8.46 Dght 3.595 Lbp 28.96 Br md 8.08 Dpth 3.97 Riveted\Welded, 1 dk	**(B32A2ST) Tug**	**1 oil engine** dr reverse geared to sc. shaft driving 1 FP propeller Total Power: 934kW (1,270hp) 11.5kn Ruston 7VLBXM 1 x 4 Stroke 7 Cy. 381 x 508 934kW (1270bhp) Ruston & Hornsby Ltd.-Lincoln AuxGen: 2 x 35kW 220V d.c, 1 x 10kW 220V d.c Fuel: 50.5 (d.f.)
9126974 *V2ER* -	**WEISSHORN** *ex* MSC Ghana *-2004* *ex* Weisshorn *-2002* *ex* DAL East London *-2001* *ex* Weisshorn *-2000* *ex* P&O Nedlloyd Mauritius *-1999* *ex* Weisshorn *-1998* **ms 'Weisshorn' Contal (Deutschland) GmbH & Co KG** Reederei Gebr Winter GmbH & Co KG SatCom: Inmarsat C 430401442 *Saint John's* *Antigua & Barbuda* MMSI: 304010697 Official number: 2097	**12,029** 6,171 14,643 T/cm 28.6	Class: GL	**1996-05 Volkswerft Stralsund GmbH — Stralsund** Yd No: 407 Loa 157.13 (BB) Br ex 23.74 Dght 9.300 Lbp 147.00 Br md 23.50 Dpth 12.80 Welded, 1 dk	**(A33A2CC) Container Ship (Fully Cellular)** TEU 1122 C Ho 454 TEU C Dk 668 TEU incl 150 ref C. Compartments: 4 Cell Ho, ER 7 Ha: ER Cranes: 2x45t	**1 oil engine** driving 1 CP propeller Total Power: 10,920kW (14,847hp) 19.6kn Sulzer 7RTA52U 1 x 2 Stroke 7 Cy. 520 x 1800 10920kW (14847bhp) Dieselmotorenwerk Rostock GmbH-Rostock AuxGen: 1 x 1000kW 440V 60Hz a.c, 2 x 900kW 440V 60Hz a.c Thrusters: 1 Thwart. FP thruster (f) Fuel: 173.0 (d.f.) 1350.0 (r.f.) 44.0pd
8407840 - -	**WEITEK** *ex* Allwell Perfect *-1998* *ex* Hosei Maru No. 8 *-1997* **Sentek Petroleum Trading Pte Ltd** Sentek Marine & Trading Pte Ltd	**313** 153 520	Class: GL	**1984-08 Maeno Zosen KK — Sanyoonoda YC** Yd No: 105 Loa 48.32 Br ex - Dght 3.036 Lbp 44.02 Br md 7.82 Dpth 3.46 Welded, 1 dk	**(A13B2TP) Products Tanker** Liq: 600; Liq (Oil): 600 Compartments: 6 Ta, ER	**1 oil engine** driving 1 FP propeller Total Power: 552kW (750hp) 10.0kn Hanshin 6LU26 1 x 4 Stroke 6 Cy. 260 x 440 552kW (750bhp) The Hanshin Diesel Works Ltd-Japan AuxGen: 1 x 64kW 220V a.c, 1 x 40kW 220V a.c
9244336 *9V6005* -	**WEIYUAN I** - **Reliance Marine Engineering Pte Ltd** - *Singapore* *Singapore* Official number: 389143	**142** 43 134	Class: NK	**2000-12 Yong Choo Kui Shipyard Sdn Bhd — Sibu** Yd No: 5320 Loa 23.50 Br ex - Dght 2.712 Lbp 21.07 Br md 7.32 Dpth 3.20 Welded, 1 dk	**(B32A2ST) Tug**	**2 oil engines** geared to sc. shafts driving 2 FP propellers Total Power: 894kW (1,216hp) Cummins KTA-19-M 2 x 4 Stroke 6 Cy. 159 x 159 each-447kW (608bhp) Cummins Engine Co Inc-USA Fuel: 100.0 (d.f.)
5385053 *SULK* -	**WEKAR** - **Suez Canal Authority** - *Port Said* *Egypt*	*152* 137 -	Class: (GL)	**1962 Timsah SB. Co. — Ismailia** Yd No: 104 Loa 27.23 Br ex 7.88 Dght 2.693 Lbp 25.00 Br md 7.24 Dpth 3.81 Welded, 1 dk	**(B32A2ST) Tug**	**1 oil engine** geared to sc. shaft driving 1 FP propeller Total Power: 883kW (1,201hp) 12.5kn EMD (Electro-Motive) 16-567-C 1 x Vee 2 Stroke 16 Cy. 216 x 254 883kW (1201bhp) General Motors Corp-USA
8659974 - -	**WELEZA I** - **Jindal ITF Ltd** - *Panaji* *India* Official number: PNJ 594	**1,673** 1,490 2,700	Class: IR	**2011-10 Goa Ore Carriers — Goa** Yd No: 7 Loa 75.00 Br ex 14.00 Dght 3.300 Lbp - Br md - Dpth 4.75 Welded, 1 dk	**(A31A2GX) General Cargo Ship**	**2 oil engines** driving 2 FP propellers Cummins Cummins India Ltd-India
9587465 *VRII7* -	**WELFINE** - **Everfair Shipping Ltd** Wanlong Ocean Shipping Group Ltd *Hong Kong* *Hong Kong* MMSI: 477493900 Official number: HK-3055	**51,265** 31,203 93,146 T/cm 80.8	Class: AB	**2011-06 Jiangsu Newyangzi Shipbuilding Co Ltd — Jingjiang JS** Yd No: YZJ2006-918 Loa 229.20 (BB) Br ex 38.04 Dght 14.900 Lbp 222.00 Br md 38.00 Dpth 20.70 Welded, 1 dk	**(A21A2BC) Bulk Carrier** Grain: 110,330 Compartments: 7 Ho, ER 7 Ha: 5 (17.9 x 17.0)ER 2 (15.3 x 14.6)	**1 oil engine** driving 1 FP propeller Total Power: 13,560kW (18,436hp) 14.1kn MAN-B&W 6S60MC-C 1 x 2 Stroke 6 Cy. 600 x 2400 13560kW (18436bhp) STX Engine Co Ltd-South Korea AuxGen: 3 x a.c Fuel: 233.0 (d.f.) 3563.0 (r.f.)

IMO / Call sign	Name, owner, port, flag	Tonnage	Class	Builder, dimensions	Type, capacities	Machinery
574418 'RHJ6	**WELHERO** **Carry Shipping Ltd** South Farocean Shipping Ltd *Hong Kong* *Hong Kong* MMSI: 477959600 Official number: HK-2854	**51,158** 31,267 93,328 T/cm 80.8	Class: CC (AB)	**2010-10 Jiangsu Newyangzi Shipbuilding Co Ltd — Jingjiang JS** Yd No: YZJ2006-905 Loa 229.20 (BB) Br ex 38.04 Dght 14.900 Lbp 222.00 Br md 38.00 Dpth 20.70 Welded, 1 dk	**(A21A2BC) Bulk Carrier** Grain: 110,330 Compartments: 7 Ho, ER 7 Ha: 5 (17.9 x 17.0)ER 2 (15.3 x 14.6)	**1 oil engine** driving 1 FP propeller Total Power: 13,560kW (18,436hp) 14.1kn MAN-B&W 6S60MC-C 1 x 2 Stroke 6 Cy. 600 x 2400 13560kW (18436bhp) STX Engine Co Ltd-South Korea AuxGen: 3 x a.c Fuel: 200.0 (d.f.) 3400.0 (r.f.)
112208	**WELIGOUWA** **Ceylon Fishery Harbours Corp** - *Colombo* *Sri Lanka*	**222** 66 115	Class: (LR) ✠ Classed LR until 22/3/00	**1995-09 Dunston Ship Repairers Ltd. — Hull** Yd No: H1011 Loa 40.30 Br ex 9.92 Dght 1.375 Lbp 33.00 Br md 9.70 Dpth 2.50 Welded, 1 dk	**(B33A2DC) Cutter Suction Dredger** Hopper: 75	**2 oil engines** with clutches, hydraulic couplings & reduction geared to sc. shafts, via hydraulic motors driving 2 Directional propellers retractable outboard Total Power: 640kW (870hp) 7.5kn Caterpillar 3406TA 2 x 4 Stroke 6 Cy. 137 x 165 each-320kW (435bhp) Caterpillar Inc-USA AuxGen: 1 x 50kW 415V 50Hz a.c, 1 x 36kW 415V 50Hz a.c
8616180 OWST 3 430	**WELL-BANK** *ex Sandra -2007 ex M. H. Beyer -1991* **Jens Christian Bang Andersen & Sven Aage Bang Andersen** - *Skagen* *Denmark* MMSI: 219439000 Official number: H945	*113* 33 -		**1986-02 Bruces Nya Verkstad AB — Landskrona** Yd No: 520 Loa 21.01 Br ex 6.46 Dght - Lbp 16.51 Br md 6.32 Dpth 5.16 Welded, 2 dks	**(B11B2FV) Fishing Vessel**	**1 oil engine** geared to sc. shaft driving 1 FP propeller Total Power: 299kW (407hp) Caterpillar 1 x 4 Stroke 8 Cy. 299kW (407bhp) Caterpillar Tractor Co-USA
9061564 3FDV4 -	**WELL DEEP** *ex Bet Intruder -2012 ex Tobata Max -2008* *ex Thanos F -2006 ex Peruvian Express -2005* *ex Silver Regia -2003 ex River Stream -2003* *ex Silver Star -2000* **Perpetual Goodluck Ltd** COSCO Wallem Ship Management Co Ltd *Panama* *Panama* MMSI: 373018000 Official number: 4461813	**35,874** 23,407 69,235 T/cm 64.4	Class: CC (BV) (NK)	**1993-04 Imabari Shipbuilding Co Ltd — Marugame KG (Marugame Shipyard)** Yd No: 1206 Loa 224.98 (BB) Br ex - Dght 12.000 Lbp 215.00 Br md 32.20 Dpth 18.30 Welded, 1 dk	**(A21A2BC) Bulk Carrier** Grain: 82,025 Compartments: 7 Ho, ER 7 Ha: (13.0 x 12.8)3 (17.9 x 14.4) (16.3 x 14.4) (17.3 x 14.4) (14.7 x 14.4)ER	**1 oil engine** driving 1 FP propeller Total Power: 8,827kW (12,001hp) 14.5kn Sulzer 6RTA62 1 x 2 Stroke 6 Cy. 620 x 2150 8827kW (12001bhp) Mitsubishi Heavy Industries Ltd-Japan AuxGen: 4 x 353kW a.c Fuel: 2347.0
9421996 2ARS4 -	**WELL ENHANCER** **Helix Well Ops (UK) Ltd** - SatCom: Inmarsat C 423591188 *Aberdeen* *United Kingdom* MMSI: 235062421 Official number: 915333	**9,383** 2,815 7,950	Class: NV	**2009-08 IHC Krimpen Shipyard BV — Krimpen a/d IJssel** Yd No: 7715 Loa 131.70 (BB) Br ex 22.00 Dght 6.750 Lbp 117.70 Br md 21.95 Dpth 9.50 Welded, 1 dk	**(B22F2OW) Well Stimulation Vessel**	**6 diesel electric oil engines** driving 4 gen. each 2520kW 6600V a.c 2 gen. each 1265kW 6600V a.c Connecting to 2 elec. motors each (3000kW) driving 2 Azimuth electric drive units Total Power: 15,680kW (21,318hp) 13.0kn MAN-B&W 5L27/38 2 x 4 Stroke 5 Cy. 270 x 380 each-1900kW (2583bhp) MAN Diesel A/S-Denmark MAN-B&W 9L27/38 4 x 4 Stroke 9 Cy. 270 x 380 each-2970kW (4038bhp) MAN Diesel A/S-Denmark Thrusters: 2 Tunnel thruster (f); 1 Retract. directional thruster (f)
8614223 H3HU -	**WELL FAITH** *ex Cirene Star -2010 ex Nordana Sarah -2010* *ex Cirene Star -2008 ex Fret Sologne -2002* *ex Sea Lion -1997 ex Regine -1995* **Well-Faith Shipping Co Ltd** Sanhe Marine Co Ltd *Panama* *Panama* MMSI: 355880000 Official number: 4193810	**5,755** 3,088 7,765	Class: RI (BV) (GL)	**1987-04 J.J. Sietas KG Schiffswerft GmbH & Co. — Hamburg** Yd No: 959 Loa 107.45 (BB) Br ex 19.26 Dght 7.868 Lbp 98.61 Br md 19.02 Dpth 10.70 Welded, 2 dks	**(A31A2GX) General Cargo Ship** Grain: 10,282; Bale: 10,269 TEU 461 C. 461/20' (40') incl. 30 ref C. Compartments: 1 Ho, ER, 1 Tw Dk 1 Ha: (64.0 x 15.2)ER Cranes: 2x100t Ice Capable	**1 oil engine** with flexible couplings & sr gearedto sc. shaft driving 1 CP propeller Total Power: 3,230kW (4,392hp) 13.5kn Deutz SBV8M640 1 x 4 Stroke 8 Cy. 370 x 400 3230kW (4392bhp) Kloeckner Humboldt Deutz AG-West Germany
8745230 - -	**WELLAND** **Dan Minor & Sons Inc** - *Ottawa, ON* *Canada* Official number: 197912	**100** 30 -		**1954 Russel-Hipwell Engines Ltd — Owen Sound ON** L reg 24.38 Br ex - Dght - Lbp - Br md 6.10 Dpth 3.18 Welded, 1 dk	**(B32A2ST) Tug**	**1 oil engine** reduction geared to sc. shaft driving 1 Propeller Total Power: 736kW (1,001hp)
9294537 C4EW2 -	**WELLE** *ex Nordwelle -2011* **Schiffahrtsgesellschaft ms 'Welle' mbH & Co KG** Reederei Nord Ltd *Limassol* *Cyprus* MMSI: 209597000 Official number: 9294537	**26,611** 12,679 34,740 T/cm 51.1	Class: GL (Class contemplated) (NV) (KR)	**2005-11 STX Shipbuilding Co Ltd — Changwon (Jinhae Shipyard)** Yd No: 1166 Loa 210.00 (BB) Br ex - Dght 11.500 Lbp 198.80 Br md 30.10 Dpth 16.70 Welded, 1 dk	**(A33A2CC) Container Ship (Fully Cellular)** TEU 2572 C Ho 938 TEU C Dk 1634 TEU incl 600 ref C. Compartments: 5 Cell Ho, ER 10 Ha: (12.6 x 20.4)8 (12.6 x 25.7)ER (12.6 x 15.4)	**1 oil engine** driving 1 FP propeller Total Power: 24,880kW (33,827hp) 21.5kn MAN-B&W 8S70MC-C 1 x 2 Stroke 8 Cy. 700 x 2800 24880kW (33827bhp) STX Engine Co Ltd-South Korea AuxGen: 4 x 1680kW 440V 60Hz a.c Thrusters: 1 Thwart. CP thruster (f) Fuel: 130.0 (d.f.) 4005.0 (r.f.)
1007627 - -	**WELLENREITER** **Sail Yong Ltd** - *Valletta* *Malta*	**254** 76 26	Class: LR ✠ **100A1** SS 05/2013 SSC Yacht Mono, G6 **LMC** Cable: 240.0/16.0 M4	**2003-08 Jachtwerf Jongert B.V. — Medemblik** Yd No: 409 Loa 45.00 Br ex 8.90 Dght - Lbp 34.00 Br md 8.60 Dpth 4.13 Welded, 1 dk	**(X11A2YS) Yacht (Sailing)** Hull Material: Aluminium Alloy	**1 oil engine** with clutches, flexible couplings & sr reverse geared to sc. shaft driving 1 CP propeller Total Power: 500kW (680hp) M.T.U. 8V2000M70 1 x Vee 4 Stroke 8 Cy. 130 x 150 500kW (680bhp) MTU Friedrichshafen GmbH-Friedrichshafen AuxGen: 1 x 50kW 220V 50Hz a.c, 1 x 45kW 220V 50Hz a.c Thrusters: 1 Thwart. FP thruster (f); 1 Thwart. FP thruster (a)
7734923 - -	**WELLESAND** *ex Wittesand -2005 ex Nickel -2005* **Orascom (OPTD)**	*266* 84 59	Class: (GL)	**1952 Jadewerft Wilhelmshaven GmbH — Wilhelmshaven** Yd No: 10 Loa 43.77 Br ex 7.95 Dght 2.301 Lbp 40.04 Br md 7.50 Dpth 3.00 Welded, 1 dk	**(B31A2SR) Research Survey Vessel**	**1 oil engine** driving 1 FP propeller Total Power: 268kW (364hp) 10.0kn MWM RH335SU 1 x 4 Stroke 6 Cy. 250 x 350 268kW (364bhp) Motoren Werke Mannheim AG (MWM)-West Germany
7301099 - -	**WELLESLEY** *ex N. Z. Explorer -2002 ex Proud Australia -1995* *ex Proud Sydney -1992 ex Talei-Anda -1990* **Wellesley Pacific Ltd**	**334** 180 -		**1972 The Fiji Marine Shipyard & Slipways — Suva** Loa 39.32 Br ex 7.35 Dght 1.829 Lbp 34.85 Br md 7.32 Dpth 2.90 Welded, 1 dk	**(A37A2PC) Passenger/Cruise** Passengers: cabins: 16; berths: 190	**2 oil engines** driving 2 FP propellers Total Power: 376kW (512hp) 11.0kn Rolls Royce C6TFL 2 x 4 Stroke 6 Cy. 130 x 152 each-188kW (256bhp) Rolls Royce Ltd.-Shrewsbury
7915151 GBVN -	**WELLINGTON** *ex Smit Canada -2008 ex Canada -2007* **TP Towage Co Ltd** - *Liverpool* *United Kingdom* MMSI: 232002703 Official number: 389166	**282** 84 84	Class: LR ✠ **100A1** SS 05/2013 tug Coastal Service Gibraltar, Morocco and Iberian Peninsular South of Lisbon and Valencia, including Ports of Lisbon and Valencia ✠ **LMC** Eq.Ltr: (E) C; Cable: 247.5/17.5 U2	**1980-12 McTay Marine Ltd. — Bromborough** Yd No: 38 Loa 30.21 Br ex 9.45 Dght 4.401 Lbp 28.50 Br md 9.01 Dpth 3.81 Welded, 1 dk	**(B32A2ST) Tug**	**2 oil engines** gearing integral to driving 2 Voith-Schneider propellers Total Power: 1,942kW (2,640hp) 12.0kn Ruston 6RKCM 2 x 4 Stroke 6 Cy. 254 x 305 each-971kW (1320bhp) Ruston Diesels Ltd.-Newton-le-Willows AuxGen: 2 x 78kW 440V 50Hz a.c Fuel: 60.0 (d.f.) 6.5pd
9368481 ZMFS -	**WELLINGTON** *launched as Nuship Wellington -2010* **Government of New Zealand (Royal New Zealand Navy)** - SatCom: Inmarsat C 450303276 *New Zealand* MMSI: 512159000	**2,342** 702 200	Class: LR ✠ **100A1** SS 05/2010 SSC, patrol, mono, G5 Ice Class 1C at a maximum draught of 3.828m Max/min draught fwd 3.828/3.388m Max/min draught aft 3.828/3.388m Required power 3280kw, installed power 10800kw ✠ **LMC** **UMS** Eq.Ltr: O; Cable: U3 (a)	**2010-05 BAE Systems Australia Defence Pty Ltd — Melbourne VIC** Yd No: OPV2 Loa 85.00 Br ex 14.01 Dght 3.600 Lbp 73.56 Br md 14.00 Dpth 6.65 Welded, 1 dk	**(B34H2SQ) Patrol Vessel**	**2 oil engines** with clutches, flexible couplings & sr reverse geared to sc. shafts driving 2 CP propellers Total Power: 10,800kW (14,684hp) MAN-B&W 12RK280 2 x Vee 4 Stroke 12 Cy. 280 x 330 each-5400kW (7342bhp) MAN B&W Diesel AG-Augsburg AuxGen: 3 x 500kW 440V 60Hz a.c Thrusters: 1 Thwart. CP thruster (f)

9224051 *DFCX2* -	**WELLINGTON EXPRESS** *ex* CP Tabasco *-2006* *ex* TMM Tabasco *-2005* *completed as* Silvia *-2001* **Amombi Vermietungsgesellschaft mbH** Hapag-Lloyd AG *Hamburg* *Germany* MMSI: 218087000 Official number: 21285	**23,652** 10,596 29,894	Class: AB (GL)	**2000-12 Stocznia Gdynia SA — Gdynia** Yd No: 8229/2 Loa 188.10 (BB) Br ex - Dght 11.500 Lbp 175.60 Br md 30.00 Dpth 16.75 Welded, 1 dk	**(A33A2CC) Container Ship (Fully Cellular)** TEU 2078 C Ho 850 TEU C Dk 1228 TEU incl 432 ref C. 9 Ha: ER Cranes: 3x45t Ice Capable	**1 oil engine** driving 1 FP propeller Total Power: 17,940kW (24,391hp) 21.0k Sulzer 6RTA72 1 x 2 Stroke 6 Cy. 720 x 2500 17940kW (24391bhp) H Cegielski Poznan SA-Poland AuxGen: 4 x 1192kW 220/440V a.c Thrusters: 1 Thwart. FP thruster (f) Fuel: 2814.0 (r.f.)
8917584 *C6TJ9* -	**WELLINGTON STAR** *ex* Bothnian Reefer *-2003* **Star Reefers UK Ltd** Star Reefers Poland Sp z oo *Nassau* *Bahamas* MMSI: 311668000 Official number: 8000755	**7,944** 4,632 11,103 T/cm 22.5	Class: BV NV (LR) ✠ Classed LR until 17/11/98	**1992-12 Kaldnes AS — Tonsberg** (Hull) Yd No: 004 **1992-12 Kvaerner Kleven Ulsteinvik AS — Ulsteinvik** Yd No: 248 Loa 140.50 (BB) Br ex 19.73 Dght 9.620 Lbp 130.00 Br md 19.70 Dpth 13.00 Welded, 1 dk, 2nd & 3rd dks in Nos. 1 to 4 holds, 4th dk in Nos. 2 to 4 holds	**(A34A2GR) Refrigerated Cargo Ship** Ins: 12,015 TEU 204 C Ho 108 TEU C Dk 96 TEU incl 42 ref C Compartments: 4 Ho, 4 Tw Dk, ER 4 Ha: (12.6 x 5.4)3 (12.6 x 10.6)ER Cranes: 2x36t,2x8t	**1 oil engine** with flexible couplings & sr geared to sc. shaft driving 1 CP propeller Total Power: 11,925kW (16,213hp) 21.8k MAN 9L58/6 1 x 4 Stroke 9 Cy. 580 x 640 11925kW (16213bhp) MAN B&W Diesel AG-Augsburg AuxGen: 1 x 1649kW 450V 60Hz a.c, 4 x 650kW 450V 60Hz a.c Thrusters: 1 Thwart. CP thruster (f)
9516777 *D5BG5* -	**WELLINGTON STRAIT** **ms 'Wellington Strait' GmbH & Co KG** Carsten Rehder Schiffsmakler und Reederei GmbH & Co KG *Monrovia* *Liberia* MMSI: 636092379 Official number: 92379	**18,358** 10,908 23,367 T/cm 38.0	Class: GL	**2012-04 Guangzhou Wenchong Shipyard Co Ltd — Guangzhou GD** Yd No: 391 Loa 175.49 (BB) Br ex - Dght 10.900 Lbp 165.00 Br md 27.40 Dpth 14.30 Welded, 1 dk	**(A33A2CC) Container Ship (Fully Cellular)** TEU 1740 C Ho 700 TEU C Dk 1040 TEU incl 300 ref C Compartments: 5 Cell Ho, ER Cranes: 2x40t	**1 oil engine** driving 1 FP propeller Total Power: 16,660kW (22,651hp) 19.8k MAN-B&W 7S60MC-C 1 x 2 Stroke 7 Cy. 600 x 2400 16660kW (22651bhp) Hudong Heavy Machinery Co Ltd-China AuxGen: 2 x 1710kW 450V 60Hz a.c, 1 x 1140kW 450V 60Hz a.c Thrusters: 1 Tunnel thruster (f) Fuel: 170.0 (d.f.) 1700.0 (r.f.)
8324579 *MGGL8* -	**WELLSERVICER** *ex* CSO Wellservicer *-2008* *ex* Stena Wellservicer *-1994* **Technip UK Ltd** - SatCom: Inmarsat A 1441470 *Aberdeen* *United Kingdom* MMSI: 232287000 Official number: 701195	**9,158** 2,747 4,615	Class: NV	**1989-01 North East Shipbuilders Ltd. — Pallion, Sunderland** Yd No: 25 Loa 111.40 Br ex 22.96 Dght 7.260 Lbp 100.00 Br md 22.50 Dpth 11.82 Welded	**(B22A2OV) Diving Support Vessel** Passengers: berths: 147 Cranes: 2x32.5t Ice Capable	**6 diesel electric oil engines** driving 6 gen. each 373kW Connecting to 6 elec. motors driving 3 Directional propellers Contr. pitch Total Power: 12,600kW (17,130hp) 15.0k Wartsila 12V20 6 x Vee 4 Stroke 12 Cy. 200 x 240 each-2100kW (2855bhp) (new engine 2003) Wartsila France SA-France Thrusters: 2 Thwart. CP thruster (f)
9574456 *VRIO7* -	**WELPROFIT** **Goodluck Shipping Ltd** Tuofu Shipping Management Ltd *Hong Kong* *Hong Kong* MMSI: 477276700 Official number: HK-3105	**51,265** 31,203 93,250 T/cm 80.8	Class: AB	**2011-09 Jiangsu Newyangzi Shipbuilding Co Ltd — Jingjiang JS** Yd No: YZJ2006-909 Loa 229.20 (BB) Br ex 38.04 Dght 14.900 Lbp 222.00 Br md 38.00 Dpth 20.70 Welded, 1 dk	**(A21A2BC) Bulk Carrier** Grain: 110,330 Compartments: 7 Ho, ER 7 Ha: ER	**1 oil engine** driving 1 FP propeller Total Power: 11,800kW (16,043hp) 14.1k MAN-B&W 6S60MC-C 1 x 2 Stroke 6 Cy. 600 x 2400 11800kW (16043bhp) Doosan Engine Co Ltd-South Korea AuxGen: 3 x 730kW a.c Fuel: 233.0 (d.f.) 3563.0 (r.f.) 46.0pd
8611491 *MGKA8* -	**WELSH PIPER** **British Dredging Ltd** CEMEX UK Marine Ltd *Newport, Gwent* *United Kingdom* MMSI: 232003506 Official number: 712575	**1,251** 375 1,923 T/cm 7.2	Class: LR ✠ **100A1** SS 09/2012 dredger U.K. home trade service, bottom strengthened for operating aground ✠ **LMC** Eq.Ltr: M; Cable: 412.5/36.0	**1987-09 Appledore Ferguson Shipbuilders Ltd — Bideford** Yd No: 143 Loa 69.02 Br ex 12.50 Dght 4.368 Lbp 65.00 Br md 12.41 Dpth 5.21 Welded, 1 dk	**(B33A2DS) Suction Dredger** Hopper: 750 Compartments: 1 Ho, ER 1 Ha: ER	**1 oil engine** with clutches, flexible couplings & sr reverse geared to sc. shaft driving 1 FP propeller Total Power: 1,080kW (1,468hp) 11.0k Wartsila 6L2 1 x 4 Stroke 6 Cy. 200 x 280 1080kW (1468bhp) (new engine 2005) Wartsila Finland Oy-Finland AuxGen: 1 x 668kW 415V 50Hz a.c, 1 x 550kW 415V 50Hz a.c, 1 x 156kW 415V 50Hz a.c Thrusters: 1 Thwart. FP thruster (f)
9178020 *MXNS5* -	**WELSHMAN** *ex* Kincraig *-2009* **SMS Towage Ltd** Specialist Marine Services Ltd *Hull* *United Kingdom* MMSI: 235070529 Official number: 900839	**292** 87 200	Class: LR (BV) **100A1** SS 09/2012 tug limited European trading area and North to Trondheim, South to Gibraltar **LMC** **UMS** Eq.Ltr: F; Cable: 275.0/22.0 U2	**1998-01 Matsuura Tekko Zosen K.K. — Osakikamijima** Yd No: 506 Loa 31.00 Br ex 9.80 Dght 3.500 Lbp 29.06 Br md 9.00 Dpth 4.70 Welded, 1 dk	**(B32A2ST) Tug**	**2 oil engines** gearing integral to driving 2 Z propellers Total Power: 2,648kW (3,600hp) 13.0k Niigata 6L25H 2 x 4 Stroke 6 Cy. 250 x 350 each-1324kW (1800bhp) Niigata Engineering Co Ltd-Japan AuxGen: 2 x 80kW 415V 50Hz a.c, 1 x 32kW 415V 50Hz a.c
9574391 *VRGT4* -	**WELSUCCESS** **Vita Shipping Ltd** Tuofu Shipping Management Ltd SatCom: Inmarsat C 447702567 *Hong Kong* *Hong Kong* MMSI: 477749500 Official number: HK-2723	**51,265** 31,203 93,328 T/cm 80.9	Class: AB	**2010-05 Jiangsu Newyangzi Shipbuilding Co Ltd — Jingjiang JS** Yd No: YZJ2006-903 Loa 229.20 (BB) Br ex 38.04 Dght 14.900 Lbp 222.00 Br md 38.00 Dpth 20.70 Welded, 1 dk	**(A21A2BC) Bulk Carrier** Grain: 110,300 Compartments: 7 Ho, ER 7 Ha: ER	**1 oil engine** driving 1 FP propeller Total Power: 13,560kW (18,436hp) 14.1k MAN-B&W 6S60MC-C 1 x 2 Stroke 6 Cy. 600 x 2400 13560kW (18436bhp) STX Engine Co Ltd-South Korea AuxGen: 3 x 730kW a.c Fuel: 212.0 (d.f.) 3525.0 (r.f.)
9574444 *VRHS5* -	**WELTRUST** **Hong Kong Top Express Shipping Ltd** Wanlong Ocean Shipping Group Ltd SatCom: Inmarsat C 447702957 *Hong Kong* *Hong Kong* MMSI: 477986600 Official number: HK-2925	**51,265** 31,203 93,217 T/cm 80.8	Class: AB	**2010-12 Jiangsu Newyangzi Shipbuilding Co Ltd — Jingjiang JS** Yd No: YZJ2006-908 Loa 229.20 (BB) Br ex 38.04 Dght 14.900 Lbp 222.00 Br md 38.00 Dpth 20.70 Welded, 1 dk	**(A21A2BC) Bulk Carrier** Grain: 110,330 Compartments: 7 Ho, ER 7 Ha: 5 (17.9 x 17.0)ER 2 (15.3 x 14.6)	**1 oil engine** driving 1 FP propeller Total Power: 13,560kW (18,436hp) 14.1k MAN-B&W 6S60MC-C 1 x 2 Stroke 6 Cy. 600 x 2400 13560kW (18436bhp) STX Engine Co Ltd-South Korea AuxGen: 3 x 730kW a.c Fuel: 233.0 (d.f.) 3560.0 (r.f.)
8901676 *3ETI7* -	**WELVIEW** *ex* Quasar *-2008* *ex* Freja Svea *-1997* *ex* Paola *-1989* **Hongfa Shipping Pte Ltd** Oriental Jinrong Ship Management Co Ltd *Panama* *Panama* MMSI: 370574000 Official number: 3488009	**53,891** 25,279 97,197 T/cm 89.8	Class: CC (NK)	**1989-10 Imabari Shipbuilding Co Ltd — Marugame KG (Marugame Shipyard)** Yd No: 1174 Converted From: Crude Oil Tanker-2009 Loa 246.84 (BB) Br ex 42.20 Dght 13.419 Lbp 235.00 Br md 42.00 Dpth 19.50 Welded, 1 dk	**(A21A2BC) Bulk Carrier** Double Sides Entire Compartment Length Grain: 100,070; Bale: 99,570 Compartments: 8 Ho, ER 8 Ha: 6 (13.5 x 16.9) (18.0 x 16.9)ER (13.6 x 13.5)	**1 oil engine** driving 1 FP propeller Total Power: 10,151kW (13,801hp) 11.5k B&W 6S70MC 1 x 2 Stroke 6 Cy. 700 x 2674 10151kW (13801bhp) Mitsui Engineering & Shipbuilding CLtd-Japan AuxGen: 3 x 480kW a.c Fuel: 196.0 (d.f.) 3167.0 (r.f.)
9074731 *V5WW* -	**WELWITCHIA** **Government of The Republic of Namibia (Ministry of Fisheries & Marine Resources)** - *Luderitz* *Namibia* MMSI: 659001000 Official number: 94LB001	**490** 147 283	Class: NK	**1994-01 Miho Zosensho K.K. — Shimizu** Yd No: 1427 Loa 47.28 Br ex - Dght 3.612 Lbp 41.00 Br md 8.30 Dpth 4.00 Welded, 1 dk	**(B12D2FR) Fishery Research Vessel** Ins: 61	**1 oil engine** with flexible couplings & sr geared to sc. shaft driving 1 CP propeller Total Power: 1,030kW (1,400hp) 11.5kn Yanmar T240-E 1 x 4 Stroke 6 Cy. 240 x 310 1030kW (1400bhp) Yanmar Diesel Engine Co Ltd-Japan Thrusters: 1 Thwart. FP thruster (f) Fuel: 140.0 (r.f.)
9162526 *C6XV9* -	**WELWITSCHIA** *ex* Monneron *-2009* **Welwitschia Shipping Co Ltd** Sociedad Nacional de Combustiveis de Angola (SONANGOL) SatCom: Inmarsat C 431100534 *Nassau* *Bahamas* MMSI: 311023600 Official number: 8001656	**28,322** 12,343 45,999 T/cm 51.8	Class: NV (LR) (BV) Classed LR until 4/6/10	**1998-12 Daedong Shipbuilding Co Ltd — Changwon (Jinhae Shipyard)** Yd No: 1018 Loa 182.89 (BB) Br ex 32.23 Dght 12.156 Lbp 173.90 Br md 32.20 Dpth 18.00 Welded, 1 dk	**(A12B2TR) Chemical/Products Tanker** Double Hull (13F) Liq: 48,945; Liq (Oil): 48,945 Cargo Heating Coils Compartments: 12 Wing Ta, ER, 2 Wing Slop Ta 12 Cargo Pump (s): 12x600m³/hr Manifold: Bow/CM: 92m	**1 oil engine** driving 1 FP propeller Total Power: 8,562kW (11,641hp) 14.5kn B&W 6S50MC 1 x 2 Stroke 6 Cy. 500 x 1910 8562kW (11641bhp) Hyundai Heavy Industries Co Ltd-South Korea AuxGen: 3 x 600kW 440V 60Hz a.c Boilers: e (ex.g.) 10.2kgf/cm² (10.0bar), WTAuxB (o.f.) 7.1kgf/cm² (7.0bar) Fuel: 192.2 (d.f.) (Heating Coils) 1363.2 (r.f.) 31.0pd
9200275 - -	**WELWITSCHIA** **IMASA** *Angola*	**358** - 396		**1999-04 Astilleros Armon SA — Navia** Yd No: 488 Loa 30.00 Br ex - Dght 4.400 Lbp 26.80 Br md 9.85 Dpth 5.40 Welded, 1 dk	**(B32A2ST) Tug**	**2 oil engines** reduction geared to sc. shafts driving 2 Directional propellers Total Power: 2,942kW (4,000hp) 12.0kn Caterpillar 3516TA 2 x Vee 4 Stroke 16 Cy. 170 x 190 each-1471kW (2000bhp) Caterpillar Inc-USA AuxGen: 2 x 88kW 380V 50Hz a.c

IMO / Call sign	Name / Owner / Manager / Flag	Tonnage	Class	Built / Dimensions	Type / Cargo	Machinery
8660325 V3GS2 HSFL-BZ-16	**WEN CAI 1** **Chi Hsiang Fishery Co Ltd** *Belize City* *Belize* MMSI: 312198000 Official number: 281110175	257 78 -		**2005-12 Shing Sheng Fa Boat Building Co — Kaohsiung** Loa 32.57 Br ex 6.80 Dght - Lbp 29.80 Br md - Dpth 2.90 Welded, 1 dk	**(B11B2FV) Fishing Vessel**	**1 oil engine** reduction geared to sc. shafts driving 1 Propeller Total Power: 634kW (862hp) Cummins KTA-38-M0 1 x Vee 4 Stroke 12 Cy. 159 x 159 634kW (862bhp) Cummins Diesel International Ltd-USA
8660337 - -	**WEN CAI 2** **Chi Hsiang Fishery Co Ltd** -	257 78 -		**2005-12 Shing Sheng Fa Boat Building Co — Kaohsiung** Loa 32.57 Br ex 6.80 Dght - Lbp 29.80 Br md - Dpth 2.90 Welded, 1 dk	**(B11B2FV) Fishing Vessel**	**1 oil engine** reduction geared to sc. shafts driving 1 Propeller Total Power: 634kW (862hp) Cummins KTA-38-M0 1 x Vee 4 Stroke 12 Cy. 159 x 159 634kW (862bhp) Cummins Diesel International Ltd-USA
8896819 T3NW -	**WEN CHENG** *ex Huan Hai 8 -2008* **Zheng Shun Shipping Co Ltd** DL East Shipping Co Ltd *Tarawa* *Kiribati* MMSI: 529142000 Official number: K-16941303	**2,423** 1,406 4,140	Class: IZ (CC)	**1994-12 Shanghai Fishing Vessel Shipyard — Shanghai** Lengthened & Widened & Deepened-2008 Loa 92.43 Br ex - Dght 3.820 Lbp 62.00 Br md 13.50 Dpth 7.00 Welded, 1 dk	**(A31A2GX) General Cargo Ship** Grain: 1,614 Compartments: 2 Ho, ER 2 Ha: ER	**1 oil engine** reverse geared to sc. shaft driving 1 FP propeller Total Power: 1,325kW (1,801hp) 10.0kn Akasaka A31R 1 x 4 Stroke 6 Cy. 310 x 600 1325kW (1801bhp) (new engine 2011) Akasaka Tekkosho KK (Akasaka DieselLtd)-Japan AuxGen: 2 x 64kW 400V a.c
8652196 - -	**WEN CHENG NO. 2** *ex Full Shine No. 2 -2011* *ex Jing Dan Tong No. 737 -2011* **Wen Cheng Fishery Co Ltd**	218 70 -		**1975-12 San Yang Shipbuilding Co., Ltd. — Kaohsiung** Loa - Br ex - Dght - Lbp - Br md - Dpth - Welded, 1 dk	**(B11B2FV) Fishing Vessel**	**1 oil engine** driving 1 Propeller
9642772 VRMS4 -	**WEN DE** **Fenghua Shipping SA** *Hong Kong* *Hong Kong* MMSI: 477050400 Official number: HK-3963	**44,543** 26,987 81,200 T/cm 72.3	Class: NV	**2013-12 Dalian Shipbuilding Industry Co Ltd — Dalian LN (No 2 Yard)** Yd No: BC810-7 Loa 228.93 (BB) Br ex - Dght 14.580 Lbp 225.46 Br md 32.29 Dpth 20.10 Welded, 1 dk	**(A21A2BC) Bulk Carrier** Grain: 97,000 Compartments: 6 Ho, ER 7 Ha: 6 (15.8 x 15.0)ER (15.8 x 12.0)	**1 oil engine** driving 1 FP propeller Total Power: 11,900kW (16,179hp) 14.5kn MAN-B&W 5S60ME-C8 1 x 2 Stroke 5 Cy. 600 x 2400 11900kW (16179bhp) Dalian Marine Diesel Co Ltd-China AuxGen: 3 x a.c
8662414 - -	**WEN FENG 6** **Nantong Kanghai Shipping Co Ltd** *Nantong, Jiangsu* *China* Official number: CN20022910105	**2,315** 1,296 -		**2009-01 Nantong Huigang Shipbuilding Co Ltd — Qidong JS** Yd No: 2002-07 Loa 90.37 Br ex - Dght 5.700 Lbp 84.66 Br md 13.60 Dpth 7.00 Welded, 1 dk	**(A31A2GX) General Cargo Ship**	**1 oil engine** driving 1 Propeller Total Power: 1,324kW (1,800hp) Chinese Std. Type G6300ZC 1 x 4 Stroke 6 Cy. 300 x 380 1324kW (1800bhp)
8650576 - -	**WEN MING** **Coastal Maritime Agencies Ltd** *Tanzania* Official number: 100116	493 252 -		**2005 San Yang Shipbuilding Co., Ltd. — Kaohsiung** Yd No: T22011-02 Loa 49.68 Br ex 8.60 Dght - Lbp - Br md - Dpth - Welded, 1 dk	**(B11B2FV) Fishing Vessel**	**1 oil engine** driving 1 Propeller
9029712 T3KR -	**WEN PENG** *ex Heng Feng You 188 -2007* **DL Wen Peng Shipping Co Ltd** DL East Shipping Co Ltd *Tarawa* *Kiribati* MMSI: 529065000 Official number: K-10000719	**1,550** 868 2,600	Class: IZ	**2000-08 Zhangshu Shipping Transportation Co Shipyard — Zhangshu JX** Converted From: Products Tanker-2007 Loa 70.75 (BB) Br ex 11.60 Dght 5.000 Lbp 57.00 Br md 9.60 Dpth 7.10 Welded, 1 dk	**(A31A2GX) General Cargo Ship** Compartments: 1 Ho, ER 1 Ha: ER (39.0 x 8.0)	**1 oil engine** driving 1 Propeller Total Power: 919kW (1,249hp) 10.0kn Yanmar Z280-ST3 1 x 4 Stroke 6 Cy. 260 x 280 919kW (1249bhp) Yanmar Diesel Engine Co Ltd-Japan
9311804 XUCS3 -	**WEN SHAN** **Shunfeng Shipping (International) Co Ltd** Blue Ocean Ship Management Co Ltd *Phnom Penh* *Cambodia* MMSI: 514405000 Official number: 5769008	**1,757** 1,239 2,800	Class: UB (CC)	**2004-02 Yantai Beifang Shipyard — Yantai SD** Yd No: 14-11 Loa 78.07 Br ex - Dght 5.200 Lbp 72.96 Br md 12.80 Dpth 6.45 Welded, 1 dk	**(A31A2GX) General Cargo Ship** Compartments: 2 Ho, ER 2 Ha: (21.1 x 9.8)ER (19.8 x 9.8)	**1 oil engine** driving 1 FP propeller Total Power: 1,414kW (1,922hp) 12.2kn MAN-B&W 8L23/30 1 x 4 Stroke 8 Cy. 225 x 300 1414kW (1922bhp) Zhenjiang Marine Diesel Works-China AuxGen: 2 x 75kW 400V
9102667 - -	**WEN SHENG 202** *ex Yu Feng No. 202 -1997* **Wen Sheng Fishery SA** - SatCom: Inmarsat B 341661810	489 192 250		**1994-05 Jong Shyn Shipbuilding Co., Ltd. — Kaohsiung** Yd No: 036 Loa 53.15 Br ex - Dght 3.400 Lbp 45.60 Br md 8.30 Dpth 3.65 Welded, 1 dk	**(B11B2FV) Fishing Vessel** Ins: 751	**1 oil engine** driving 1 FP propeller Total Power: 883kW (1,201hp) Niigata 6M26AGTE 1 x 4 Stroke 6 Cy. 260 x 460 883kW (1201bhp) Niigata Engineering Co Ltd-Japan
8947486 - -	**WEN SHENG No. 116** - -	*423* 168 -		**1985 Fong Kuo Shipbuilding Co Ltd — Kaohsiung** L reg 40.26 Br ex - Dght - Lbp - Br md 7.80 Dpth 3.37 Welded, 1 dk	**(B11B2FV) Fishing Vessel**	**1 oil engine** driving 1 FP propeller Total Power: 736kW (1,001hp) 11.8kn Niigata 1 x 4 Stroke 736kW (1001bhp) Niigata Engineering Co Ltd-Japan
8950354 - -	**WEN SHUN No. 601** *ex Tong Ying No. 233 -1997* **Kwo Jeng Fishery St Vincent Ltd**	*181* 54 -		**1996 Fujian Fishing Vessel Shipyard — Fuzhou FJ** Loa 27.30 Br ex - Dght - Lbp - Br md 6.00 Dpth 2.65 Welded, 1 dk	**(B11A2FT) Trawler**	**1 oil engine** driving 1 FP propeller Chinese Std. Type 1 x 4 Stroke in China
8950378 - -	**WEN SHUN No. 606** *ex Tong Ying No. 263 -1997* **Kwo Jeng Fishery St Vincent Ltd**	*181* 54 -		**1996 Fujian Fishing Vessel Shipyard — Fuzhou FJ** Loa 27.30 Br ex - Dght - Lbp - Br md 6.00 Dpth 2.65 Welded, 1 dk	**(B11A2FT) Trawler**	**1 oil engine** driving 1 FP propeller Chinese Std. Type 1 x 4 Stroke in China
8994295 XUCS7 -	**WEN TENG NO. 688** **Kee Yu Pao** -	119 57 -		**2001-01 Lien Fong Shipbuilding Co., Ltd. — Hsinyuan** L reg 25.80 Br ex - Dght - Lbp - Br md 5.30 Dpth 2.20 Bonded, 1 dk	**(B11B2FV) Fishing Vessel** Hull Material: Reinforced Plastic	**1 oil engine** driving 1 Propeller Total Power: 858kW (1,167hp) 11.5kn Mitsubishi S12A2-MPTK 1 x Vee 4 Stroke 12 Cy. 150 x 160 858kW (1167bhp) Mitsubishi Heavy Industries Ltd-Japan
8718639 3FRR4 -	**WEN XIANG** *ex Meitoku Maru No. 10 -2010* **Wen Xiang International Trading Co Ltd** DL East Shipping Co Ltd *Panama* *Panama* MMSI: 354254000 Official number: 4185610	**1,970** 1,078 981	Class: IT	**1988-05 Shitanoe Shipbuilding Co Ltd — Usuki OT** Yd No: 1082 Converted From: Bulk Aggregates Carrier-2010 Loa 57.99 (BB) Br ex 11.33 Dght 4.250 Lbp 52.02 Br md 11.31 Dpth 6.00 Welded, 1 dk	**(A31A2GX) General Cargo Ship** Grain: 767 Compartments: 1 Ho, ER 1 Ha: (17.6 x 8.6)ER	**1 oil engine** driving 1 FP propeller Total Power: 736kW (1,001hp) Makita MNL28M 1 x 4 Stroke 6 Cy. 280 x 480 736kW (1001bhp) Makita Diesel Co Ltd-Japan
8805248 - -	**WEN YUAN** *ex Syu Wa No. 18 -2005* *ex Hishi Maru No. 18 -2003* **Win Shine International Shipping Ltd** DL East Shipping Co Ltd	**1,357** 809 1,130		**1988-06 Sasaki Shipbuilding Co Ltd — Osakikamijima HS** Yd No: 518 Loa 61.74 Br ex - Dght 3.715 Lbp 57.50 Br md 9.80 Dpth 3.95 Welded, 1 dk	**(A13B2TP) Products Tanker** Liq: 1,296; Liq (Oil): 1,296 Compartments: 8 Ta, ER	**1 oil engine** with clutches, flexible couplings & reverse reduction geared to sc. shaft driving 1 FP propeller Total Power: 883kW (1,201hp) Hanshin 6LU28G 1 x 4 Stroke 6 Cy. 280 x 440 883kW (1201bhp) The Hanshin Diesel Works Ltd-Japan
9571052 VRHX6 -	**WEN ZHOU WAN** **Wealth China Shipping (HK) Ltd** COSCO Southern Asphalt Shipping Co Ltd SatCom: Inmarsat C 447702975 *Hong Kong* *Hong Kong* MMSI: 477051100 Official number: HK2967	**4,126** 1,717 5,902 T/cm 15.9	Class: BV	**2011-02 Taizhou Yuanyang Shipbuilding Co Ltd — Linhai ZJ** Yd No: CYC-109 Loa 112.10 (BB) Br ex - Dght 6.000 Lbp 105.50 Br md 16.20 Dpth 8.00 Welded, 1 dk	**(A13C2LA) Asphalt/Bitumen Tanker** Double Hull (13F) Liq: 5,522; Liq (Oil): 5,522 Cargo Heating Coils Compartments: 10 Wing Ta, ER 2 Cargo Pump (s): 2x600m³/hr Manifold: Bow/CM: 46.6m Ice Capable	**1 oil engine** reducton geared to sc. shaft driving 1 CP propeller Total Power: 2,574kW (3,500hp) 12.5kn Yanmar 6N330-EN 1 x 4 Stroke 6 Cy. 330 x 440 2574kW (3500bhp) Yanmar Diesel Engine Co Ltd-Japan AuxGen: 3 x 200kW 408V 50Hz a.c Fuel: 77.0 (d.f.) 401.0 (r.f.)
9342059 BJNB -	**WEN ZHU** **Sinochem Shipping Co Ltd (Hainan)** Aoxing Ship Management (Shanghai) Ltd SatCom: Inmarsat Mini-M 764637114 *Haikou, Hainan* *China* MMSI: 413520360	**2,635** 1,105 3,800 T/cm 11.2	Class: CC	**2007-09 Chuandong Shipyard — Chongqing** Yd No: HT0082 Loa 95.68 (BB) Br ex 15.03 Dght 5.400 Lbp 90.00 Br md 15.00 Dpth 6.90 Welded, 1 dk	**(A12B2TR) Chemical/Products Tanker** Double Hull (13F) Liq: 3,941; Liq (Oil): 3,941 Cargo Heating Coils Compartments: 4 Wing Ta, 4 Ta, 1 Slop Ta, ER 8 Cargo Pump (s): 6x120m³/hr, 2x150m³/hr Manifold: Bow/CM: 47.8m	**1 oil engine** reduction geared to sc. shaft driving 1 FP propeller Total Power: 2,574kW (3,500hp) 13.0kn Daihatsu 8DKM-28L 1 x 4 Stroke 8 Cy. 280 x 390 2574kW (3500bhp) Shaanxi Diesel Heavy Industry Co Lt-China AuxGen: 3 x 240kW 400V a.c Fuel: 111.0 (d.f.) 309.0 (r.f.)

9488475 *BOCP* -	**WEN ZHU HAI** **COSCO Bulk Carrier Co Ltd (COSCO BULK)** - *Tianjin* *China* MMSI: 413376000	**40,896** 25,825 76,611 T/cm 68.2	Class: CC	**2008-09 Jiangnan Shipyard (Group) Co Ltd — Shanghai** Yd No: H2409 Loa 225.00 Br ex - Dght 14.200 Lbp 217.00 Br md 32.26 Dpth 19.60 Welded, 1 dk	**(A21A2BC) Bulk Carrier** Grain: 90,100 Compartments: 7 Ho, ER 7 Ha: 6 (15.5 x 14.4)ER (14.6 x 13.2)	**1 oil engine** driving 1 FP propeller Total Power: 10,200kW (13,868hp) 14.5kr MAN-B&W 5S60MC 1 x 2 Stroke 5 Cy. 600 x 2292 10200kW (13868bhp) Hudong Heavy Machinery Co Ltd-China AuxGen: 3 x 560kW 450V a.c
8329799 *YBXC* -	**WENAS III** **PT Wenas Frozen Prawns Ltd** - *Surabaya* *Indonesia*	*100* 27 -	Class: (KI)	**1964 Niigata Engineering Co Ltd — Niigata NI** Loa 25.66 Br ex - Dght 2.301 Lbp - Br md 5.40 Dpth 2.57 Welded, 1 dk	**(B11B2FV) Fishing Vessel**	**1 oil engine** driving 1 FP propeller Total Power: 331kW (450hp) Niigata 6M26HS 1 x 4 Stroke 6 Cy. 260 x 400 331kW (450bhp) Niigata Engineering Co Ltd-Japan
9137351 *WCY3378* -	**WENATCHEE** **State of Washington (Department of Transportation)** Washington State Department of Transportation (Washington State Ferries) *Seattle, WA* *United States of America* MMSI: 366749710 Official number: 1061309	**12,689** 5,426 1,393		**1998-05 Todd Pacific Shipyards Corp. — Seattle, Wa** Yd No: 92 Loa 138.00 Br ex 27.00 Dght 5.334 Lbp 125.40 Br md 26.73 Dpth 7.51 Welded, 1 dk	**(A36A2PR) Passenger/Ro-Ro Ship (Vehicles)** Passengers: unberthed: 2500 Bow door/ramp (centre) Stern door/ramp (centre) Cars: 202	**4 diesel electric oil engines** driving 4 gen. each 3000kW 4160V a.c Connecting to 2 elec. motors each (4413kW) driving 2 Propellers 1 fwd and 1 aft Total Power: 10,592kW (14,400hp) 18.0kr EMD (Electro-Motive) 16-710-G7 4 x Vee 2 Stroke 16 Cy. 230 x 279 each-2648kW (3600bhp) General Motors Corp.Electro-Motive Div.-La Grange AuxGen: 2 x 455kW a.c
9236860 *WDA2273* -	**WENDY MORAN** **Moran Towing Corp** - *Wilmington, DE* *United States of America* Official number: 1102493	**232** 69 -	Class: AB	**2000-08 Washburn & Doughty Associates Inc — East Boothbay ME** Yd No: 70 Loa 28.04 Br ex - Dght 3.490 Lbp 27.50 Br md 9.75 Dpth 4.20 Welded, 1 dk	**(B32A2ST) Tug**	**2 oil engines** gearing integral to driving 2 Z propellers Total Power: 3,090kW (4,202hp) EMD (Electro-Motive) 16-645-E2 2 x Vee 2 Stroke 16 Cy. 230 x 254 each-1545kW (2101bhp) General Motors Corp.Electro-Motive Div.-La Grange AuxGen: 2 x 50kW a.c
7638466 *WCZ5698* -	**WENDY O** *ex* Moana Hele *-2011* *ex* Peter Foss *-1977* **Olson Marine Inc** - *Ketchikan, AK* *United States of America* MMSI: 367498540 Official number: 582268	*125* 85 570	Class: (AB)	**1977-05 Main Iron Works, Inc. — Houma, La** Yd No: 320 Loa 29.85 Br ex 9.78 Dght 3.880 Lbp 27.97 Br md 9.76 Dpth 4.58 Welded, 1 dk	**(B32A2ST) Tug**	**2 oil engines** reverse reduction geared to sc. shafts driving 2 FP propellers Total Power: 1,654kW (2,248hp) 10.0kn Caterpillar D399SCAC 2 x Vee 4 Stroke 16 Cy. 159 x 203 each-827kW (1124bhp) Caterpillar Tractor Co-USA AuxGen: 2 x 75kW Fuel: 217.0 (d.f.)
6418625 *WDD4689* -	**WENDY SEAA** *ex* Pennypride *-1995* **Michael R Brown** - *Anacortes, WA* *United States of America* MMSI: 367347000 Official number: 1043151	**277** 83 -	Class: (LR) (AB) Classed LR until 15/3/84	**1964-11 Ferguson Industries Ltd — Pictou NS** Yd No: 151 Converted From: Trawler-1987 Loa 36.58 Br ex 7.60 Dght 3.201 Lbp 32.39 Br md 7.51 Dpth 3.92 Welded, 1 dk	**(B11B2FV) Fishing Vessel** Compartments: 1 Ho, ER 2 Ha:	**1 oil engine** sr geared to sc. shaft driving 1 FP propeller Total Power: 485kW (659hp) Stork RHO218K 1 x 4 Stroke 8 Cy. 210 x 300 485kW (659bhp) Koninklijke Machinefabriek GebrStork & Co NV-Netherlands AuxGen: 2 x 40kW 220V 60Hz a.c Fuel: 30.5 (d.f.)
8962046 *5NQA* -	**WENETU** *ex* Calabar Carrier *-2005* *ex* Brenda G *-2005* **Riverman Nigeria Ltd** *Lagos* *Nigeria* MMSI: 657572000	**189** 56 -		**1975 Offshore Trawlers, Inc. — Bayou La Batre, Al** Yd No: 14 Loa 31.28 Br ex - Dght 2.900 Lbp 29.04 Br md 7.59 Dpth 3.53 Welded, 1 dk	**(B21A20S) Platform Supply Ship**	**1 oil engine** driving 1 FP propeller Total Power: 883kW (1,201hp)
8015207 *4SSJ* -	**WENNAPPUWA MARU** **Government of The Democratic Socialist Republic of Sri Lanka** - *Colombo* *Sri Lanka*	*190* - -		**1980-10 Uchida Zosen — Ise** Yd No: 809 Loa - Br ex - Dght 2.301 Lbp 30.03 Br md 7.01 Dpth 2.93 Welded, 1 dk	**(B11B2FV) Fishing Vessel**	**1 oil engine** geared to sc. shaft driving 1 FP propeller Total Power: 515kW (700hp) Akasaka MH23R 1 x 4 Stroke 6 Cy. 230 x 390 515kW (700bhp) Akasaka Tekkosho KK (Akasaka DieselLtd)-Japan AuxGen: 2 x 120kW 405V 50Hz a.c
8972003 - -	**WENONAH II** - **Muskoka Steamship & Historical Society** *Toronto, ON* *Canada* Official number: 823618	**447** 138 -		**2002-05 McNally Construction Inc — Belleville ON** L reg 36.20 Br ex - Dght - Lbp - Br md 8.50 Dpth 3.40 Welded	**(A37B2PS) Passenger Ship** Passengers: unberthed: 200	**2 oil engines** driving 2 Propellers Total Power: 566kW (770hp) 11.0kn Thrusters: 1 Thwart. FP thruster (f)
9549310 *3FAV6* -	**WENXIANG** **Jin Xiang Shipping Co Ltd** Weihai Weitong Marine Shipping Co Ltd SatCom: Inmarsat C 437157113 *Panama* *Panama* MMSI: 371571000 Official number: 4172710	**1,970** 1,068 2,768	Class: CC	**2010-03 Shandong Baibuting Shipbuilding Co Ltd — Rongcheng SD** Yd No: BBTBC 009 Loa 79.99 Br ex - Dght 5.200 Lbp 74.00 Br md 13.60 Dpth 7.00 Welded, 1 dk	**(A31A2GX) General Cargo Ship** Compartments: 1 Ho, ER 1 Ha: ER (38.4 x 9.0) Ice Capable	**1 oil engine** reduction geared to sc. shaft driving 1 FP propeller Total Power: 1,103kW (1,500hp) 11.7kn Chinese Std. Type LB8250ZLC 1 x 4 Stroke 8 Cy. 250 x 320 1103kW (1500bhp) Zibo Diesel Engine Factory-China AuxGen: 2 x 120kW 400V a.c
9364124 *9H8269* -	**WENZINA** **Tug Malta Ltd** - *Valletta* *Malta* MMSI: 256000113 Official number: 9948	*207* 75 150	Class: LR ✠ **100A1** SS 05/2011 tug Malta coastal service **LMC** **UMS** Eq.Ltr: F; Cable: 275.0/19.0 U2 (a)	**2006-05 Song Cam Shipyard — Haiphong** (Hull) Yd No: (512207) **2006-05 B.V. Scheepswerf Damen — Gorinchem** Yd No: 512207 Loa 24.55 Br ex 11.49 Dght 3.526 Lbp 22.16 Br md 10.70 Dpth 4.60 Welded, 1 dk	**(B32A2ST) Tug**	**2 oil engines** reduction geared to sc. shafts driving 2 Directional propellers Total Power: 4,200kW (5,710hp) Caterpillar 3516B-HD 2 x Vee 4 Stroke 16 Cy. 170 x 215 each-2100kW (2855bhp) Caterpillar Inc-USA AuxGen: 2 x 50kW 400V 50Hz a.c Fuel: 70.0 (d.f.)
7115476 *D9JF* -	**WEOL MI** *ex* Kikusei Maru *-1983* **Tong Bo Marine & Shipping Co Ltd** Dong Bo Marine & Shipping Co Ltd *Incheon* *South Korea* Official number: ICR-710118	*186* 55 94	Class: KR	**1971 Shin Yamamoto Shipbuilding & Engineering Co Ltd — Kochi KC** Yd No: 147 Loa 28.05 Br ex 8.34 Dght 2.801 Lbp 26.50 Br md 8.31 Dpth 3.61 Riveted\Welded, 1 dk	**(B32A2ST) Tug**	**2 oil engines** reduction geared to sc. shafts driving 2 FP propellers Total Power: 1,104kW (1,500hp) 10.5kn Niigata 6MG20AX 2 x 4 Stroke 6 Cy. 200 x 260 each-552kW (750bhp) Niigata Engineering Co Ltd-Japan AuxGen: 2 x 40kW 225V a.c
1009467 *ZCXE5* -	**WERE DREAMS** **Were Dreams Ltd** - *George Town* *Cayman Islands (British)* MMSI: 319331000 Official number: 740650	**642** 192 -	Class: LR ✠ **100A1** SS 03/2013 SSC Yacht, mono, G6 **LMC** **UMS** Cable: 385.0/22.0 U2 (a)	**2008-03 Damen Shipyards Gdynia SA — Gdynia** (Hull) Yd No: (453) **2008-03 Amels BV — Vlissingen** Yd No: 453 Loa 52.35 Br ex 9.04 Dght 3.250 Lbp 45.40 Br md 9.00 Dpth 4.90 Welded, 1 dk	**(X11A2YP) Yacht** Passengers: berths: 12	**2 oil engines** with clutches, flexible couplings & sr reverse geared to sc. shafts driving 2 FP propellers Total Power: 2,100kW (2,856hp) M.T.U. 16V2000M70 2 x Vee 4 Stroke 16 Cy. 130 x 150 each-1050kW (1428bhp) MTU Friedrichshafen GmbH-Friedrichshafen AuxGen: 2 x 155kW 400V 50Hz a.c Thrusters: 1 Thwart. FP thruster (f)
9524140 *DIFS2* -	**WERNER MOBIUS** **STRABAG Wasserbau GmbH** - *Hamburg* *Germany* MMSI: 218430000 Official number: 22713	**6,725** 2,185 7,445	Class: GL	**2010-10 J.J. Sietas KG Schiffswerft GmbH & Co. — Hamburg** Yd No: 1305 Loa 118.47 (BB) Br ex - Dght 5.700 Lbp 106.70 Br md 21.00 Dpth 7.70 Welded, 1 dk	**(B33B2DT) Trailing Suction Hopper Dredger** Hopper: 7,350	**4 diesel electric oil engines** driving 4 gen. each 1600kW 690V a.c Connecting to 2 elec. motors driving 2 FP propellers Total Power: 6,564kW (8,924hp) 13.5kn Caterpillar 3516B-TA 1 x Vee 4 Stroke 16 Cy. 170 x 190 1641kW (2231bhp) Caterpillar Inc-USA Caterpillar 3516B-TA 3 x Vee 4 Stroke 16 Cy. 170 x 190 each-1641kW (2231bhp) Caterpillar Inc-USA Thrusters: 1 Tunnel thruster (f)
9192636 *V2GL2* -	**WERRA** *ex* Korsika *-2013* **Roland Ship Administration GmbH & Co KG** Reederei Erwin Strahlmann eK SatCom: Inmarsat C 430421410 *Saint John's* *Antigua & Barbuda* MMSI: 304214000	**2,997** 1,741 4,443	Class: GL	**2001-05 Slovenske Lodenice a.s. — Komarno** Yd No: 3022 Loa 99.90 (BB) Br ex - Dght 5.670 Lbp 95.30 Br md 12.80 Dpth 7.55 Welded, 1 dk	**(A31A2GX) General Cargo Ship** Double Hull Grain: 5,841 TEU 297 C.Ho 129/20' C.Dk 167/20' incl.30 ref C Compartments: 1 Ho, ER 2 Ha: (38.0 x 10.2) (31.3 x 10.2)ER Ice Capable	**1 oil engine** reduction geared to sc. shaft driving 1 CP propeller Total Power: 2,550kW (3,467hp) 12.5kn MWM TBD645L6 1 x 4 Stroke 6 Cy. 330 x 450 2550kW (3467bhp) Deutz AG-Koeln AuxGen: 1 x 640kW 380/220V a.c, 2 x 168kW 380/220V a.c Thrusters: 1 Thwart. FP thruster (f) Fuel: 207.0 (d.f.)

IMO / Call sign	Name / Owner / Flag	Tonnage	Class	Builder / Dimensions	Type	Machinery
8947022 - -	**WEST AFRICA 1** *ex* Liao Yu 811 **1st International Seafood Traders LLC** - - *Uruguay*	*198* 73 -		**1982 Dalian Fishing Vessel Co — Dalian LN** L reg 38.56 Br ex - Dght - Lbp - Br md 7.60 Dpth 3.80 Welded, 1 dk	**(B11B2FV) Fishing Vessel**	**1 oil engine** geared to sc. shaft driving 1 FP propeller Total Power: 441kW (600hp) 10.0kn Chinese Std. Type 8300 1 x 4 Stroke 8 Cy. 300 x 380 441kW (600bhp) Dalian Fishing Vessel Co-China
8947046 - -	**WEST AFRICA-3** *ex* Liao Yu 827 *-1998* - -	*198* 73 -		**1983 Dalian Fishing Vessel Co — Dalian LN** L reg 38.56 Br ex - Dght - Lbp - Br md 7.60 Dpth 3.80 Welded, 1 dk	**(B11B2FV) Fishing Vessel**	**1 oil engine** geared to sc. shaft driving 1 FP propeller Total Power: 441kW (600hp) 10.0kn Chinese Std. Type 8300 1 x 4 Stroke 8 Cy. 300 x 380 441kW (600bhp) Dalian Fishing Vessel Co-China
8947058 - -	**WEST AFRICA-4** *ex* Liao Yu 828 *-1998* - -	*198* 73 -		**1983 Dalian Fishing Vessel Co — Dalian LN** L reg 38.56 Br ex - Dght - Lbp - Br md 7.60 Dpth 3.80 Welded, 1 dk	**(B11B2FV) Fishing Vessel**	**1 oil engine** geared to sc. shaft driving 1 FP propeller Total Power: 441kW (600hp) 10.0kn Chinese Std. Type 8300 1 x 4 Stroke 8 Cy. 300 x 380 441kW (600bhp) Dalian Fishing Vessel Co-China
8947060 - -	**WEST AFRICA-5** *ex* Liao Yu 831 *-1998* - -	*198* 73 -		**1983 Dalian Fishing Vessel Co — Dalian LN** L reg 38.56 Br ex - Dght - Lbp - Br md 7.60 Dpth 3.80 Welded, 1 dk	**(B11B2FV) Fishing Vessel**	**1 oil engine** geared to sc. shaft driving 1 FP propeller Total Power: 441kW (600hp) 10.0kn Chinese Std. Type 8300 1 x 4 Stroke 8 Cy. 300 x 380 441kW (600bhp) Dalian Fishing Vessel Co-China
8947072 - -	**WEST AFRICA-6** *ex* Liao Yu 832 *-1998* - -	*198* 73 -		**1982 Dalian Fishing Vessel Co — Dalian LN** L reg 38.56 Br ex - Dght - Lbp - Br md 7.60 Dpth 3.80 Welded, 1 dk	**(B11B2FV) Fishing Vessel**	**1 oil engine** geared to sc. shaft driving 1 FP propeller Total Power: 441kW (600hp) 10.0kn Chinese Std. Type 8300 1 x 4 Stroke 8 Cy. 300 x 380 441kW (600bhp) Dalian Fishing Vessel Co-China
8756576 *H03234* -	**WEST ALPHA** *ex* Dyvi Alpha *-1988* **North Atlantic Alpha Ltd** North Atlantic Management AS *Panama* *Panama* MMSI: 351651000 Official number: 2962204D	**17,193** 5,157 -	Class: NV	**1986-10 Nippon Kokan KK (NKK Corp) — Tsu ME** Yd No: SP-15 Loa 98.55 Br ex 76.31 Dght 21.500 Lbp 98.54 Br md - Dpth 34.68 Welded, 1 dk	**(Z11C3ZE) Drilling Rig, semi Submersible** Cranes: 2x55t	**6 diesel electric oil engines** driving 6 gen. Connecting to 4 elec. motors driving 4 Azimuth electric drive units Total Power: 10,812kW (14,700hp) 5.0kn Wartsila 2 x 4 Stroke each-1802kW (2450bhp) (new engine 1986) Wartsila 4 x 4 Stroke each-1802kW (2450bhp) (new engine 2009)
8768775 *3EOK7* -	**WEST AQUARIUS** **Seadrill China Operations Ltd** Seadrill Americas Inc SatCom: Inmarsat C 435669110 *Panama* *Panama* MMSI: 356691000 Official number: 3482109A	**40,731** 12,220 -	Class: NV	**2008-08 Daewoo Shipbuilding & Marine Engineering Co Ltd — Geoje** Yd No: 3020 Loa 116.60 Br ex 96.60 Dght 25.000 Lbp - Br md 78.00 Dpth 45.00 Welded, 1 dk	**(Z11C3ZE) Drilling Rig, semi Submersible** Cranes: 2x80t	**8 diesel electric oil engines** driving 8 gen. Connecting to 8 elec. motors each (3450kW) driving 7 Azimuth electric drive units Total Power: 35,120kW (47,752hp) 7.0kn Wartsila 12V32LN 1 x Vee 4 Stroke 12 Cy. 320 x 350 4390kW (5969bhp) (new engine 2008) Wartsila Finland Oy-Finland Wartsila 12V32LN 7 x Vee 4 Stroke 12 Cy. 320 x 350 each-4390kW (5969bhp) (new engine 2008) Wartsila Finland Oy-Finland AuxGen: 8 x 4708kW a.c
9609392 *3FEZ6* -	**WEST AURIGA** **Seadrill Gulf Operation Auriga LLC** Seadrill Americas Inc *Panama* *Panama* MMSI: 373287000 Official number: 4488113	**60,555** 18,166 60,554	Class: AB	**2013-04 Samsung Heavy Industries Co Ltd — Geoje** Yd No: 1911 Loa 227.82 (BB) Br ex 42.00 Dght - Lbp 219.40 Br md - Dpth 19.00 Welded, 1 dk	**(B22B20D) Drilling Ship** Cranes: 4	**6 diesel electric oil engines** driving 6 gen. each 7000kW a.c Connecting to 2 elec. motors each (4500kW) driving 2 Azimuth electric drive units Total Power: 48,000kW (65,262hp) 12.0kn MAN-B&W 16V32/40 6 x Vee 4 Stroke 16 Cy. 320 x 400 each-8000kW (10877bhp) STX Engine Co Ltd-South Korea Thrusters: 1 Directional thruster (f); 1 Directional thruster (a); 1 Directional thruster (p. f.); 1 Directional thruster (s. f.) Fuel: 6050.0 (d.f.)
9278868 *VRZP8* -	**WEST BAY** *ex* Tiara Ocean *-2010* **West Bay Shipping Ltd** Pacific Basin Shipping (HK) Ltd *Hong Kong* *Hong Kong* MMSI: 477090000 Official number: HK-1237	**30,061** 17,738 52,532 T/cm 55.5	Class: NK	**2004-02 Tsuneishi Heavy Industries (Cebu) Inc — Balamban** Yd No: SC-045 Loa 189.99 Br ex - Dght 12.022 Lbp 182.00 Br md 32.26 Dpth 17.00 Welded, 1 Dk.	**(A21A2BC) Bulk Carrier** Grain: 67,756; Bale: 65,601 Compartments: 5 Ho, ER 5 Ha: 4 (21.3 x 18.4)ER (20.4 x 18.4) Cranes: 4x30t	**1 oil engine** driving 1 FP propeller Total Power: 7,800kW (10,605hp) 14.3kn B&W 6S50MC 1 x 2 Stroke 6 Cy. 500 x 1910 7800kW (10605bhp) Mitsui Engineering & Shipbuilding CLtd-Japan Fuel: 2150.0
8853518 - -	**WEST BAY BUILDERS 1** *ex* Sprig II *-2005* **West Bay Builders Inc** *San Francisco, CA* *United States of America* Official number: 633675	*121* 97 -		**1954 Higgins Industries, Inc. — New Orleans, La** Loa - Br ex - Dght - Lbp 23.16 Br md 6.40 Dpth 2.77 Welded, 1 dk	**(B11B2FV) Fishing Vessel**	**1 oil engine** driving 1 FP propeller
7514024 *DYQH* -	**WEST BAY I** *ex* Sunny Ocean *-2002* *ex* Miyo Maru *-1996* *ex* Shonan Maru *-1987* **West Bay College Co** *Manila* *Philippines* Official number: MNLD009819	*646* - 495		**1975-10 Niigata Engineering Co Ltd — Niigata NI** Yd No: 1378 Loa 51.34 Br ex 8.72 Dght 3.506 Lbp 44.58 Br md 8.69 Dpth 3.89 Welded, 1 dk	**(B11B2FV) Fishing Vessel**	**1 oil engine** driving 1 FP propeller Total Power: 736kW (1,001hp) Niigata 6M28KEHS 1 x 4 Stroke 6 Cy. 280 x 440 736kW (1001bhp) Niigata Engineering Co Ltd-Japan
7910113 *VM6336* -	**WEST BLUFF** **Northern Bluff Fisheries Pty Ltd** *Darwin, NT* *Australia* Official number: 375252	*150* 93 65		**1978-06 Ocean Shipyards (WA) Pty Ltd — Fremantle WA** Yd No: 122 Loa 22.53 Br ex - Dght - Lbp 21.70 Br md 6.75 Dpth 3.76 Welded, 1 dk	**(B11A2FT) Trawler**	**1 oil engine** reverse reduction geared to sc. shaft driving 1 FP propeller Total Power: 268kW (364hp) Caterpillar 3408TA 1 x Vee 4 Stroke 8 Cy. 137 x 152 268kW (364bhp) Caterpillar Tractor Co-USA
9522348 *H07494* -	**WEST CALLISTO** **Seadrill Callisto Ltd** Seadrill Management AS *Panama* *Panama* Official number: 4194310C	**10,406** 3,121 4,500	Class: AB	**2010-08 Keppel FELS Ltd — Singapore** Yd No: B311 Loa 71.34 Br ex 63.41 Dght 4.880 Lbp - Br md 63.40 Dpth 7.62 Welded, 1 dk	**(Z11C4ZD) Drilling Rig, jack up** Cranes: 3x45t	**1 oil engine** driving 1 Propeller AuxGen: 5 x 1700kW 60Hz a.c
9372523 *3EOL* -	**WEST CAPELLA** **Seadrill Deepwater Drillship Ltd** Seadrill Management (S) Pte Ltd SatCom: Inmarsat C 435673611 *Panama* *Panama* MMSI: 356736000 Official number: 3476409	**59,626** 17,888 61,311	Class: AB	**2008-12 Samsung Heavy Industries Co Ltd — Geoje** Yd No: 1687 Loa 227.80 Br ex - Dght 12.050 Lbp 219.40 Br md 42.00 Dpth 19.00 Welded, 1 dk	**(B22B20D) Drilling Ship** Cranes: 4x85t	**6 diesel electric oil engines** driving 6 gen. each 4800kW 11000V a.c Connecting to 2 elec. motors driving 2 Azimuth electric drive units Total Power: 48,000kW (65,262hp) 11.5kn Wartsila 16V32 6 x Vee 4 Stroke 16 Cy. 320 x 400 each-8000kW (10877bhp) Wartsila Finland Oy-Finland Thrusters: 4 Directional thruster
8770821 *3FCB* -	**WEST CAPRICORN** *ex* Seadrill 14 *-2011* **Seabras Rig Holdco Kft** Seadrill Management (S) Pte Ltd *Panama* *Panama* MMSI: 352683000 Official number: 4405312	**30,147** 9,044 20,570	Class: AB	**2011-12 Jurong Shipyard Pte Ltd — Singapore** Yd No: 11-1095 Loa 115.70 Br ex 90.40 Dght 17.000 Lbp 98.82 Br md 78.68 Dpth 36.00 Welded, 1 dk	**(Z11C3ZE) Drilling Rig, semi Submersible** Cranes: 2	**8 diesel electric oil engines** driving 8 gen. each 5000kW a.c Connecting to 8 elec. motors each (3300kW) driving 8 Directional propellers Total Power: 40,248kW (54,720hp) 7.0kn Caterpillar C280-12 8 x Vee 4 Stroke 12 Cy. 280 x 300 each-5031kW (6840bhp) Caterpillar Inc-USA Fuel: 4360.0 (d.f.)

9017202 *C6UP7* - **WEST CARRIER**
ex Vliehors *-2005* *ex* Almenum *-2004*
Vestfrakt Shipping AS
Lighthouse Ship Management AS
Nassau *Bahamas*
MMSI: 311911000
Official number: 8001026

1,425 / 677 / 1,830

Class: LR
✠ **100A1** SS 02/2012
bottom strengthened for loading and unloading aground
✠ **LMC**
Eq.Ltr: (K) ; Cable: 357.5/30.0 U2

1992-02 **Barkmeijer Stroobos B.V. — Stroobos** Yd No: 262
Loa 74.00 Br ex 11.60 Dght 4.380
Lbp 69.10 Br md 11.50 Dpth 6.05
Welded, 1 dk

(A31A2GX) General Cargo Ship
Grain: 2,690
Compartments: 1 Ho, ER
1 Ha: ER

1 oil engine with clutches, flexible couplings & dr reverse geared to sc. shaft driving 1 FP propeller
Total Power: 1,065kW (1,448hp) 10.0kn
A.B.C. 6DZC
1 x 4 Stroke 6 Cy. 256 x 310 1065kW (1448bhp)
Anglo Belgian Corp NV (ABC)-Belgium
AuxGen: 2 x 70kW 380V 50Hz a.c
Thrusters: 1 Thwart. CP thruster (f)
Fuel: 106.2 (d.f.)

9604213 *3FCY7* - **WEST ECLIPSE**
ex Songa Eclipse *-2013*
Seadrill Eclipse Ltd
Seadrill Management AS
Panama *Panama*
MMSI: 356630000
Official number: 44219PEXT

30,923 / 9,276 / 33,000

Class: AB

2011-08 **Jurong Shipyard Pte Ltd — Singapore** Yd No: 11-1094
Loa 121.22 Br ex 90.90 Dght 8.350
Lbp - Br md - Dpth 136.67
Welded, 1 dk

(Z11C3ZE) Drilling Rig, semi Submersible

8 diesel electric oil engines driving 8 Directional propellers
Total Power: 40,248kW (54,720hp) 6.0kn
Caterpillar C280-12
8 x Vee 4 Stroke 12 Cy. 280 x 300 each-5031kW (6840bhp)
Caterpillar Inc-USA
Fuel: 3158.0

8768438 *3FUA8* - **WEST EMINENCE**
West Eminence Ltd
Seadrill Americas Inc
SatCom: Inmarsat C 437094210
Panama *Panama*
MMSI: 370942000
Official number: 4037109A

35,412 / 10,624 / 25,325

Class: NV

2009-03 **Samsung Heavy Industries Co Ltd — Geoje** Yd No: 7056
Loa 83.20 Br ex 72.72 Dght 23.500
Lbp - Br md - Dpth 36.15
Welded, 1 dk

(Z11C3ZE) Drilling Rig, semi Submersible
Cranes: 2x75t

8 diesel electric oil engines driving 8 gen. Connecting to 8 elec. motors driving 8 Azimuth electric drive units
Total Power: 41,600kW (56,560hp) 8.0kn
Caterpillar 3616
1 x Vee 4 Stroke 16 Cy. 280 x 300 5200kW (7070bhp) (new engine 2009)
Caterpillar Inc-USA
Caterpillar 3616
7 x Vee 4 Stroke 16 Cy. 280 x 300 each-5200kW (7070bhp) (new engine 2009)
Caterpillar Inc-USA
AuxGen: 8 x 4400kW a.c

9228605 - - **WEST FRONTIER**
Shinhan Shipping Co Ltd
-
Boryeong *South Korea*
MMSI: 440200128
Official number: DSR-019032

140 / - / 20

Class: KR

2001-03 **FBMA-Babcock Marine Inc — Balamban** Yd No: 1009
Loa 25.00 Br ex - Dght 1.500
Lbp 22.90 Br md 8.50 Dpth -
Welded, 1 dk

(A37B2PS) Passenger Ship
Hull Material: Aluminium Alloy
Passengers: unberthed: 180

2 oil engines reduction geared to sc. shafts driving 2 FP propellers
Total Power: 1,124kW (1,528hp) 25.0kn
Caterpillar 3412TA
2 x Vee 4 Stroke 12 Cy. 137 x 152 each-562kW (764bhp)
Caterpillar Inc-USA

9459931 *HPKD* - **WEST GEMINI**
Seadrill Gemini Ltd
Seadrill Ltd
Panama *Panama*
MMSI: 354982000
Official number: 4205310

59,626 / 17,888 / 61,122

Class: AB

2010-06 **Samsung Heavy Industries Co Ltd — Geoje** Yd No: 1769
Loa 227.80 Br ex - Dght 12.000
Lbp 219.40 Br md 42.00 Dpth 19.00
Welded, 1 dk

(B22B2OD) Drilling Ship
Cranes: 4x85t

6 diesel electric oil engines driving 6 gen. each 7000kW 11000V a.c Connecting to 2 elec. motors each (4500kW) driving 2 Azimuth electric drive units
Total Power: 48,000kW (65,262hp) 11.5kn
Wartsila 16V32
6 x Vee 4 Stroke 16 Cy. 320 x 400 each-8000kW (10877bhp)
Wartsila Finland Oy-Finland
Thrusters: 2 Directional thruster (f); 2 Directional thruster (a)
Fuel: 4629.0 (d.f.)

8768763 *3EOK9* - **WEST HERCULES**
SFL Hercules Ltd
North Atlantic Management AS
SatCom: Inmarsat C 435671110
Panama *Panama*
MMSI: 356711000
Official number: 3476709A

40,731 / 12,220 / 41,000

Class: NV

2008-10 **Daewoo Shipbuilding & Marine Engineering Co Ltd — Geoje** Yd No: 3019
Loa 116.50 Br ex 96.60 Dght 25.000
Lbp - Br md - Dpth 45.00
Welded, 1 dk

(Z11C3ZE) Drilling Rig, semi Submersible

8 diesel electric oil engines driving 8 gen. Connecting to 8 elec. motors each (3450kW) driving 8 Azimuth electric drive units
Total Power: 37,664kW (51,208hp) 7.0kn
Wartsila 12V32LN
1 x Vee 4 Stroke 12 Cy. 320 x 350 4708kW (6401bhp) (new engine 2008)
Wartsila Finland Oy-Finland
Wartsila 12V32LN
7 x Vee 4 Stroke 12 Cy. 320 x 350 each-4708kW (6401bhp) (new engine 2008)
Wartsila Finland Oy-Finland
AuxGen: 8 x 4708kW a.c

8771186 *3EXU7* - **WEST JAYA**
launched as West Berani III *-2011*
Seadrill Jaya Ltd
Seadrill Management AS
Panama *Panama*
MMSI: 370831000
Official number: 370831000

15,839 / 4,751 / 9,984

Class: AB

2011-03 **Keppel FELS Ltd — Singapore** Yd No: B313
Loa 100.58 Br ex 47.06 Dght 12.100
Lbp 93.87 Br md 45.04 Dpth 20.10
Welded, 1 dk

(Z11C3ZM) Maintenance Platform, semi Submersible
Cranes: 1x250t,1x44t

6 diesel electric oil engines driving 6 gen. each 1600kW a.c driving 2 Propellers
Total Power: 9,600kW (13,050hp)
Caterpillar 3516B-TA
6 x Vee 4 Stroke 16 Cy. 170 x 190 each-1600kW (2175bhp)
Caterpillar Inc-USA

8768749 *C6WD6* - **WEST LEO**
ex Seadragon I *-2012* *ex* Oban B *-2011*
launched as Moss Sagitarius II *-2010*
Seadrill Leo Ltd
Seadrill Ltd
Nassau *Bahamas*
Official number: 8001359

39,833 / 11,950 / 14,508

Class: NV

2012-01 **PO SevMash Predpriyatiye — Severodvinsk** (Hull launched by) Yd No: 93150
2012-01 **Jurong Shipyard Pte Ltd — Singapore** (Hull completed by) Yd No: 11-1099
Loa 118.56 Br ex - Dght 9.650
Lbp - Br md 72.72 Dpth 38.65
Welded, 1 dk

(Z11C3ZE) Drilling Rig, semi Submersible

8 diesel electric oil engines driving 4 gen. each 5210kW a.c 4 gen. each 3480kW a.c Connecting to 8 elec. motors driving 8 Azimuth electric drive units
Total Power: 36,880kW (50,140hp)
Bergens B32: 40L8P
4 x 4 Stroke 8 Cy. 320 x 400 each-3685kW (5010bhp)
Rolls Royce Marine AS-Norway
Bergens B32: 40V12P
4 x Vee 4 Stroke 12 Cy. 320 x 400 each-5535kW (7525bhp)
Rolls Royce Marine AS-Norway
Thrusters: 8 Directional thruster (wing)

8012097 *YLBL* - **WEST LYNDA**
ex Sun Trader *-2003* *ex* Solstraum *-1990*
ex Aun *-1985*
VEXOIL Bunkering Ltd
-
Riga *Latvia*
MMSI: 275110000

2,092 / 694 / 3,020 / T/cm / 9.1

Class: RS (NV) (BV)

1981-12 **Mandals Slip & Mekaniske Verksted AS — Mandal** (Hull) Yd No: 86
1981-12 **Batservice Verft AS — Mandal** Yd No: 662
Converted From: Chemical Tanker-2009
Loa 79.63 (BB) Br ex 14.03 Dght 5.551
Lbp 74.02 Br md 14.01 Dpth 6.91
Welded, 1 dk.

(A13B2TP) Products Tanker
Single Hull
Liq: 2,975; Liq (Oil): 2,975
Cargo Heating Coils
Compartments: 12 Ta, ER
12 Cargo Pump (s): 12x80m³/hr
Manifold: Bow/CM: 41m
Ice Capable

1 oil engine sr geared to sc. shaft driving 1 CP propeller
Total Power: 1,449kW (1,970hp) 12.5kn
Normo KVM-12
1 x Vee 4 Stroke 12 Cy. 250 x 300 1449kW (1970bhp)
AS Bergens Mek Verksteder-Norway
AuxGen: 3 x 198kW 440V 60Hz a.c
Thrusters: 1 Thwart. FP thruster (f)
Fuel: 43.0 (d.f.) (Part Heating Coils) 150.0 (r.f.) 9.0pd

9162100 *3ERR2* - **WEST NAVIGATOR**
ex West Navion *-2003* *ex* MST Odin *-1999*
North Atlantic Navigator Ltd
North Atlantic Management AS
Panama *Panama*
MMSI: 370144000
Official number: 3444408A

69,851 / 20,955 / 99,304

Class: NV

1998-02 **Samsung Heavy Industries Co Ltd — Geoje** Yd No: 1211
Converted From: Shuttle Tanker-2000
Loa 253.00 (BB) Br ex 42.00 Dght 15.850
Lbp 233.00 Br md 41.95 Dpth 23.20
Welded, 1 dk

(B22B2OD) Drilling Ship
Double Hull
Cranes: 2

4 diesel electric oil engines driving 4 gen. each 5600kW 6600V a.c Connecting to 2 elec. motors driving 2 FP propellers
Total Power: 17,212kW (23,400hp) 11.6kn
Wartsila 6R46
4 x 4 Stroke 6 Cy. 460 x 580 each-4303kW (5850bhp)
Wartsila NSD Finland Oy-Finland
Thrusters: 2 Thwart. FP thruster (f)

9230672 *BZTX8* - **WEST OCEAN**
ex Kiev *-2006* *ex* Darwin *-2003*
China National Fisheries Corp
SatCom: Inmarsat C 441296115
China

647 / 194 / -

2001-03 **Lien Cherng Shipbuilding Co, Ltd — Kaohsiung** Yd No: 099
Loa 54.55 Br ex - Dght 3.500
Lbp 46.50 Br md 8.50 Dpth 3.65
Welded, 1 dk

(B11B2FV) Fishing Vessel
Bale: 321; Ins: 109

1 oil engine geared to sc. shaft driving 1 FP propeller
Total Power: 883kW (1,201hp)
Akasaka K26SFD
1 x 4 Stroke 6 Cy. 260 x 480 883kW (1201bhp)
Akasaka Tekkosho KK (Akasaka DieselLtd)-Japan

7638492 *DUH2830* - **WEST OCEAN 1**
ex Lift 1 *-2010* *ex* Lift-Off *-2003*
ex Christodoulos *-2002* *ex* Alexandros III *-2000*
ex Lift-Off *-1987*
West Ocean Lines & Transport Inc
-
Cebu *Philippines*
Official number: CEB1008240

3,039 / 1,688 / 3,953

Class: (LR)
✠ Classed LR until 18/3/09

1977-12 **Batservice Verft AS — Mandal** Yd No: 651
Loa 97.06 (BB) Br ex 15.04 Dght 5.906
Lbp 88.91 Br md 15.00 Dpth 8.46
Welded, 2 dks

(A31A2GX) General Cargo Ship
Grain: 6,840; Bale: 6,215
TEU 184 C.Ho 134/20' (40') C.Dk 50/20' (40') incl. ref C.
Compartments: 2 Ho, ER, 2 Tw Dk
2 Ha: (13.0 x 10.2) (40.3 x 10.6)ER
Derricks: 1x110t,1x35t,1x25t; Winches: 3

1 oil engine sr geared to sc. shaft driving 1 CP propeller
Total Power: 2,575kW (3,501hp) 14.5kn
MaK 6M551AK
1 x 4 Stroke 6 Cy. 450 x 550 2575kW (3501bhp)
MaK Maschinenbau GmbH-Kiel
AuxGen: 3 x 148kW 440V 60Hz a.c
Fuel: 56.5 (d.f.) (Heating Coils) 304.0 (r.f.)

7036981 *DUGA8* - **WEST OCEAN 3**
ex San Sebastian *-1987* *ex* Ryusho Maru *-1980*
Key west Shipping Line Corp
-
Cebu *Philippines*
Official number: ILO3000003

2,749 / 1,910 / 4,432

Class: (AB) (NK)

1970-09 **Kurushima Dockyard Co. Ltd. — Imabari** Yd No: 708
Converted From: General Cargo Ship-1980
Loa 93.20 Br ex 15.04 Dght 6.071
Lbp 86.01 Br md 15.02 Dpth 7.22
Welded, 1 dk

(A33A2CC) Container Ship (Fully Cellular)
Bale: 5,493
TEU 397 C Ho 225 TEU C Dk 172 TEU
Compartments: 2 Cell Ho, ER
2 Ha: (24.0 x 7.4) (24.5 x 7.4)ER
Derricks: 3

1 oil engine driving 1 FP propeller
Total Power: 1,839kW (2,500hp) 11.5kn
Hanshin 6L46SH
1 x 4 Stroke 6 Cy. 460 x 680 1839kW (2500bhp)
The Hanshin Diesel Works Ltd-Japan
AuxGen: 2 x 132kW 445V a.c
Fuel: 437.0 8.0pd

IMO / Call sign	Name / Owner	Tonnage	Class	Build / Dimensions	Type	Machinery
768567 P5271	**WEST ORION** *launched as* Seadrill 13 *-2010* **Seadrill Orion Ltd** Seadrill Management AS *Panama* *Panama* MMSI: 370076000 Official number: 4172910A	**30,147** 9,044 7,000	Class: AB	**2010-04 Jurong Shipyard Pte Ltd — Singapore** Yd No: 11-1091 Loa 115.70 Br ex 90.40 Dght 17.000 Lbp 98.82 Br md 74.42 Dpth 36.00 Welded, 1 dk	**(Z11C3ZE) Drilling Rig, semi Submersible**	**8 diesel electric oil engines** driving 8 gen. Connecting to 8 elec. motors each (3350kW) driving 8 Azimuth electric drive units Total Power: 36,640kW (49,816hp) Caterpillar 3616 1 x Vee 4 Stroke 16 Cy. 280 x 300 4580kW (6227bhp) (new engine 2010) Caterpillar Inc-USA Caterpillar 3616 7 x Vee 4 Stroke 16 Cy. 280 x 300 each-4580kW (6227bhp) (new engine 2010) Caterpillar Inc-USA
770766 V9395	**WEST PEGASUS** *ex* Sea Dragon II *-2011* **Seadrill Pegasus (S) Pte Ltd** - SatCom: Inmarsat C 456601210 *Singapore* *Singapore* MMSI: 566012000 Official number: 397017	**39,833** 11,768 -	Class: NV	**2011-03 OAO Vyborgskiy Sudostroitelnyy Zavod — Vyborg** (Hull launched by) Yd No: 102 **2011-03 Jurong Shipyard Pte Ltd — Singapore** (Hull completed by) Yd No: 11-1098 Loa 118.56 Br ex - Dght 9.850 Lbp - Br md 72.69 Dpth 38.63 Welded, 1 dk	**(Z11C3ZE) Drilling Rig, semi Submersible**	**8 diesel electric oil engines** driving 4 gen. each 5210kW a.c 4 gen. each 3480kW a.c Connecting to 8 elec. motors each (3800kW) driving 8 Azimuth electric drive units Total Power: 40,000kW (54,384hp) Bergens B32: 40L8P 4 x 4 Stroke 8 Cy. 320 x 400 each-4000kW (5438bhp) Rolls Royce Marine AS-Norway Bergens B32: 40V12P 4 x Vee 4 Stroke 12 Cy. 320 x 400 each-6000kW (8158bhp) Rolls Royce Marine AS-Norway
768294 ETB9	**WEST PHOENIX** **North Atlantic Phoenix Ltd** North Atlantic Management AS SatCom: Inmarsat C 437050610 *Panama* *Panama* MMSI: 370506000 Official number: 3484909A	**35,568** 10,670 25,325	Class: NV	**2008-03 Samsung Heavy Industries Co Ltd — Geoje** Yd No: 7045 Loa 83.23 Br ex 71.65 Dght 23.500 Lbp - Br md - Dpth 36.15 Welded, 1 dk	**(Z11C3ZE) Drilling Rig, semi Submersible**	**8 diesel electric oil engines** driving 8 gen. Connecting to 8 elec. motors driving 8 Azimuth electric drive units Total Power: 36,640kW (49,816hp) 8.0kn Wartsila 12V32 1 x Vee 4 Stroke 12 Cy. 320 x 400 4580kW (6227bhp) (new engine 2008) Wartsila Finland Oy-Finland Wartsila 12V32 7 x Vee 4 Stroke 12 Cy. 320 x 400 each-4580kW (6227bhp) Wartsila Finland Oy-Finland
9372535 3EOK6	**WEST POLARIS** **SFL West Polaris Ltd** Seadrill Offshore AS SatCom: Inmarsat C 435665610 *Panama* *Panama* MMSI: 356656000 Official number: 3486309A	**59,626** 17,888 61,439	Class: AB	**2008-07 Samsung Heavy Industries Co Ltd — Geoje** Yd No: 1657 Loa 227.80 Br ex - Dght 12.050 Lbp 219.40 Br md 42.00 Dpth 19.00 Welded, 1 dk	**(B22B20D) Drilling Ship** Cranes: 4x85t	**6 diesel electric oil engines** driving 6 gen. each 4800kW 11000V a.c Connecting to 3 elec. motors each (4500kW) driving 3 Azimuth electric drive units Total Power: 48,000kW (65,262hp) 11.5kn Wartsila 16V32 6 x Vee 4 Stroke 16 Cy. 320 x 400 each-8000kW (10877bhp) Wartsila Finland Oy-Finland Thrusters: 3 Directional thruster (f) Fuel: 511.0 (d.f.) 6091.0 (r.f.)
9132703 3FTM5 -	**WEST SCENT** *ex* Eagle Strength *-2009* *ex* Angullia *-1997* *ex* Dragon Komodo *-1996* *ex* Angullia *-1996* **Nautical Trend Shipping Co Inc** Future Trend Nautical LLC SatCom: Inmarsat C 435598710 *Panama* *Panama* MMSI: 355987000 Official number: 24770PEXT9	**11,875** 6,625 15,326	Class: NK	**1995-12 Iwagi Zosen Co Ltd — Kamijima EH** Yd No: 163 Loa 145.68 (BB) Br ex - Dght 8.814 Lbp 136.00 Br md 25.00 Dpth 12.80 Welded, 1 dk	**(A33A2CC) Container Ship (Fully Cellular)** TEU 954 C Ho 428 TEU C Dk 526 TEU incl 100 ref C. Compartments: 4 Cell Ho, ER 14 Ha: ER Cranes: 2x35t	**1 oil engine** driving 1 FP propeller Total Power: 8,562kW (11,641hp) 17.3kn B&W 6S50MC 1 x 2 Stroke 6 Cy. 500 x 1910 8562kW (11641bhp) Hitachi Zosen Corp-Japan Thrusters: 1 Tunnel thruster (f) Fuel: 940.0 (r.f.)
6510590 - AFT 67	**WEST SEA** *ex* Damero *-1998* **Toiman Fishing Co Ltd** *Takoradi* *Ghana* Official number: 316932	*524* 232 660	Class: (BV)	**1965 Ast. Celaya — Bilbao** Yd No: 77 Loa 55.02 Br ex 9.05 Dght 3.925 Lbp 49.61 Br md 9.00 Dpth 4.42 Riveted\Welded, 2 dks	**(B11B2FV) Fishing Vessel** Ins: 555 Compartments: 3 Ho, ER 3 Ha: 3 (1.6 x 1.6)ER Derricks: 2x1t; Winches: 2	**1 oil engine** driving 1 FP propeller Total Power: 956kW (1,300hp) 12.8kn MAN G9V30/45ATL 1 x 4 Stroke 9 Cy. 300 x 450 956kW (1300bhp) Maschinenbau Augsburg Nuernberg (MAN)-Augsburg Fuel: 291.0 (d.f.)
8768402 3EMK6 -	**WEST SIRIUS** **Seadrill Hungary KFT** Seadrill Americas Inc SatCom: Inmarsat C 435757511 *Panama* *Panama* MMSI: 357575000 Official number: 3411108A	**30,147** 9,044 -	Class: AB	**2008-03 Jurong Shipyard Pte Ltd — Singapore** Yd No: 1085 Loa 115.70 Br ex 90.40 Dght 17.000 Lbp 98.82 Br md 78.68 Dpth 36.00 Welded, 1 dk	**(Z11C3ZE) Drilling Rig, semi Submersible**	**8 diesel electric oil engines** driving 8 gen. each 4800kW a.c Connecting to 8 elec. motors each (3350kW) driving 8 Azimuth electric drive units Total Power: 40,000kW (54,384hp) Caterpillar 3616 8 x Vee 4 Stroke 16 Cy. 280 x 300 each-5000kW (6798bhp) Caterpillar Inc-USA
7814254 C6QI4 -	**WEST STREAM** *ex* Golfstraum *-1998* **Key Shipping AS** Fjord Shipping AS *Nassau* *Bahamas* MMSI: 308241000 Official number: 732167	**1,845** 696 2,550 T/cm 8.5	Class: NV RI	**1979-11 Bolsones Verft AS — Molde** Yd No: 262 Loa 80.17 (BB) Br ex 13.03 Dght 5.850 Lbp 74.91 Br md 13.01 Dpth 7.35 Welded, 1 dk.	**(A12B2TR) Chemical/Products Tanker** Double Hull (13F) Liq: 2,666; Liq (Oil): 2,666 Cargo Heating Coils Compartments: 12 Ta, ER 12 Cargo Pump (s): 12x80m³/hr Manifold: Bow/CM: 40m Ice Capable	**1 oil engine** geared to sc. shaft driving 1 CP propeller Total Power: 1,655kW (2,250hp) 13.0kn Normo KVMB-12 1 x Vee 4 Stroke 12 Cy. 250 x 300 1655kW (2250bhp) AS Bergens Mek Verksteder-Norway AuxGen: 3 x 132kW 380V 50Hz a.c Fuel: 38.5 (d.f.) (Part Heating Coils) 122.0 (r.f.) 7.0pd
8768414 3ERV6 -	**WEST TAURUS** **SFL Deepwater Ltd** Seadrill Management (S) Pte Ltd SatCom: Inmarsat C 437017910 *Panama* *Panama* MMSI: 370179000 Official number: 4086509	**30,147** 9,044 -	Class: AB	**2008-11 Jurong Shipyard Pte Ltd — Singapore** Yd No: 1086 Loa 115.70 Br ex 90.40 Dght 17.000 Lbp 98.82 Br md 78.68 Dpth 36.00 Welded, 1 dk	**(Z11C3ZE) Drilling Rig, semi Submersible**	**8 diesel electric oil engines** driving 8 gen. each 4800kW a.c Connecting to 8 elec. motors each (3350kW) driving 8 Directional propellers Total Power: 40,000kW (54,384hp) Caterpillar 3616 8 x Vee 4 Stroke 16 Cy. 280 x 300 each-5000kW (6798bhp) Caterpillar Inc-USA
9623934 3FJI4 -	**WEST TELLUS** **Seadrill Tellus Ltd** Seadrill Ltd *Panama* *Panama* MMSI: 373289000 Official number: 43218PEXT	**60,969** 18,291 60,485	Class: AB NV	**2013-10 Samsung Heavy Industries Co Ltd — Geoje** Yd No: 2020 Loa 227.82 (BB) Br ex 44.59 Dght 12.000 Lbp 211.33 Br md 42.05 Dpth 19.00 Welded, 1 dk	**(B22B20D) Drilling Ship** Cranes: 1x165t,3x85t	**6 diesel electric oil engines** driving 6 gen. each 7000kW a.c Connecting to 2 elec. motors each (4500kW) driving 2 Azimuth electric drive units Total Power: 48,000kW (65,262hp) 12.0kn MAN-B&W 16V32/40 6 x Vee 4 Stroke 16 Cy. 320 x 400 each-8000kW (10877bhp) STX Engine Co Ltd-South Korea Thrusters: 1 Directional thruster (f); 1 Directional thruster (a); 1 Directional thruster (p. f.); 1 Directional thruster (s. f.); 1 Directional thruster (p. a.); 1 Directional thruster (s. a.)
9609407 3FNX5 -	**WEST VELA** **Seadrill Vela Hungary Kft** Seadrill Management AS *Panama* *Panama* MMSI: 373290000 Official number: 4508013	**60,555** 18,166 60,546	Class: AB	**2013-06 Samsung Heavy Industries Co Ltd — Geoje** Yd No: 1912 Loa 227.82 (BB) Br ex - Dght 12.000 Lbp 219.40 Br md 42.00 Dpth 19.00 Welded, 1 dk	**(B22B20D) Drilling Ship** Cranes: 4x85t	**6 diesel electric oil engines** driving 6 gen. each 7000kW a.c Connecting to 2 elec. motors each (4500kW) driving 2 Azimuth electric drive units Total Power: 48,000kW (65,262hp) 12.0kn MAN-B&W 16V32/40 6 x Vee 4 Stroke 16 Cy. 320 x 400 each-8000kW (10877bhp) STX Engine Co Ltd-South Korea Thrusters: 1 Directional thruster (f); 1 Directional thruster (a); 1 Directional thruster (p. f.); 1 Directional thruster (s. f.) Fuel: 6050.0 (d.f.)
8764365 3FZQ -	**WEST VENTURE** *ex* West Future *-2000* **North Atlantic Venture Ltd** North Atlantic Management AS *Panama* *Panama* MMSI: 356313000 Official number: 4352812	**31,248** 9,375 -	Class: NV	**1999-09 Hitachi Zosen Corp — Nagasu KM** Yd No: 1073 Loa 117.60 Br ex 69.70 Dght - Lbp - Br md - Dpth 23.50 Welded, 1 dk	**(Z11C3ZE) Drilling Rig, semi Submersible** Cranes: 2x60t,1x15t	**8 diesel electric oil engines** driving 8 gen. each 3800kW a.c Connecting to 8 elec. motors each (3025kW) driving 8 Azimuth electric drive units Total Power: 32,000kW (43,504hp) 8.5kn Wartsila 12V32LN 8 x Vee 4 Stroke 12 Cy. 320 x 350 each-4000kW (5438bhp) Wartsila NSD Finland Oy-Finland

8954879 *SMCY*	**WEST WIND** *ex* Shuttle II *-2007* *ex* Shuttle Karlstad *-2004* **Geodells Intressenter AB** - *Kyrkesund* Sweden MMSI: 265604750	**1,985** - 2,040	Class: (NV)	**1989-06 Scheepswerf Ravestein BV — Deest** Yd No: 262 Converted From: General Cargo/Tanker-1989 Loa 87.50 (BB) Br ex 13.06 Dght 3.630 Lbp 82.50 Br md 13.00 Dpth 5.00 Welded, 1 dk	**(A31C2GD) Deck Cargo Ship** Cranes: 1 Ice Capable	**6 diesel electric oil engines** driving 6 gen. each 360kW 440V Connecting to 2 elec. motors driving 2 Directional propellers Total Power: 2,076kW (2,820hp) Volvo Penta TAMD162 6 x 4 Stroke 6 Cy. 144 x 165 each-346kW (470bhp) AB Volvo Penta-Sweden AuxGen: 1 x 83kW 220/440V 60Hz a.c Thrusters: 1 Thwart. FP thruster (f)
8855499 - -	**WEST WIND '84** - **Sahlman Seafoods Inc** -	*101* 69 -		**1984 Steiner Shipyard, Inc. — Bayou La Batre, Al** Loa 22.86 Br ex - Dght - Lbp 20.33 Br md 6.71 Dpth 3.32 Welded, 1 dk	**(B11A2FT) Trawler**	**1 oil engine** geared to sc. shaft driving 1 FP propeller Total Power: 268kW (364hp) Cummins KT-1150-M 1 x 4 Stroke 6 Cy. 159 x 159 268kW (364bhp) Cummins Engine Co Inc-USA
7050860 - -	**WEST WIND II** - - -	*129* 88 -		**1969 Master Marine, Inc. — Bayou La Batre, Al** L reg 22.19 Br ex 6.76 Dght - Lbp - Br md - Dpth 3.56 Welded	**(B11B2FV) Fishing Vessel**	**1 oil engine** driving 1 FP propeller Total Power: 313kW (426hp)
8860858 *DGWV* HF 573	**WESTBANK** - **Kutterfisch-Westbank Fischereigesellschaft mbH** - *Sassnitz* Germany MMSI: 211390480 Official number: 16260	*107* 32 -		**1990-07 Luebbe Voss GmbH — Westerende-Kirchloog** Loa - Br ex - Dght - Lbp 19.40 Br md 6.30 Dpth 3.50 Welded, 1 dk	**(B11B2FV) Fishing Vessel**	**1 oil engine** reverse reduction geared to sc. shaft driving 1 CP propeller Total Power: 397kW (540hp) Deutz SBA12M816 1 x Vee 4 Stroke 12 Cy. 142 x 160 397kW (540bhp) (made 1989) Kloeckner Humboldt Deutz AG-West Germany AuxGen: 1 x 62kW 220/380V a.c, 1 x 38kW 220/380V a.c
8739231 *OXRG* HM 424	**WESTBANK** - **Fiskeriselskabet Westbank ApS** - *Hanstholm* Denmark MMSI: 219010989 Official number: H 1524	**127** 38 -		**2007-11 Vestvaerftet ApS — Hvide Sande** Yd No: 265 Loa 17.98 (BB) Br ex - Dght - Lbp 16.44 Br md 6.60 Dpth 5.44 Welded, 1 dk	**(B11A2FS) Stern Trawler**	**1 oil engine** driving 1 Propeller Total Power: 373kW (507hp) Thrusters: 1 Thwart. FP thruster (f)
7741976 - -	**WESTBAY** *ex* Sandvik af Styrso *-1993* *ex* Dalenni *-1991* **Pursuit Fishing Ltd** -	*162* 57 -	Class: (NV)	**1978 p/f Torshavnar Skipasmidja — Torshavn** Yd No: 23 Loa 28.30 Br ex 7.52 Dght - Lbp 23.50 Br md - Dpth 3.41 Welded, 2 dks	**(B11A2FS) Stern Trawler**	**1 oil engine** driving 1 FP propeller Total Power: 919kW (1,249hp) Caterpillar 3512TA 1 x Vee 4 Stroke 12 Cy. 170 x 190 919kW (1249bhp) (new engine 1983) Caterpillar Tractor Co-USA AuxGen: 2 x 52kW 380V 50Hz a.c
9568988 *ORPT* -	**WESTDIEP** - **Wandelaar Invest SA** DAB Vloot *Ostend* Belgium MMSI: 205591000 Official number: 01 00781 2011	**227** 67 14	Class: GL	**2011-05 Schiffs- u. Yachtwerft Abeking & Rasmussen GmbH & Co. — Lemwerder** Yd No: 6471 Loa 25.65 (BB) Br ex - Dght 2.700 Lbp 23.25 Br md 13.00 Dpth 5.90 Welded, 1 dk	**(B34N2QP) Pilot Vessel**	**2 oil engines** with clutches, flexible couplings & sr geared to sc. shafts driving 2 FP propellers Total Power: 1,576kW (2,142hp) 18.0kn M.T.U. 12V2000M70 2 x Vee 4 Stroke 12 Cy. 130 x 150 each-788kW (1071bhp) MTU Friedrichshafen GmbH-Friedrichshafen
8024454 - -	**WESTELLA** *ex* Cornelis Vrolijk Fzn. *-1988* **Pesqueros Del Pacifico SAC** Tecnologica de Alimentos SA *Callao* Peru	**2,031** 823 1,870	Class: LR ✠ **100A1** SS 11/2011 stern trawler ✠ **LMC** **UMS** Eq.Ltr: 0; Cable: 440.0/34.0 U2	**1981-10 Scheepswerf en Mfbk. Ysselwerf B.V. — Capelle a/d IJssel** Yd No: 201 Lengthened-1985 Loa 86.26 (BB) Br ex 12.76 Dght 4.973 Lbp 78.95 Br md 12.51 Dpth 8.01 Welded, 2 dks	**(B11A2FG) Factory Stern Trawler**	**1 oil engine** with flexible couplings & sr gearedto sc. shaft driving 1 CP propeller Total Power: 2,648kW (3,600hp) Deutz SBV6M540 1 x 4 Stroke 6 Cy. 370 x 400 2648kW (3600bhp) Kloeckner Humboldt Deutz AG-West Germany AuxGen: 2 x 818kW 380V 50Hz a.c, 1 x 450kW 250V d.c, 1 x 200kW 250V d.c Boilers: TOH (o.f.) 10.2kgf/cm² (10.0bar), TOH (ex.g.) (fitted: 1981) 10.2kgf/cm² (10.0bar)
9297527 *A8HD5* -	**WESTERBROOK** *ex* Maersk Dartmouth *-2010* **Westerbrook Shipping GmbH & Co KG** Hans Peterson & Soehne GmbH & Co KG *Monrovia* Liberia MMSI: 636091283 Official number: 91283	**54,592** 34,532 66,583	Class: GL	**2005-07 Hyundai Heavy Industries Co Ltd — Ulsan** Yd No: 1608 Loa 294.10 (BB) Br ex - Dght 13.650 Lbp 283.20 Br md 32.20 Dpth 21.80 Welded, 1 dk	**(A33A2CC) Container Ship (Fully Cellular)** TEU 5043 C Ho 2263 TEU C Dk 2780 TEU incl 550 ref C. Compartments: ER, 6 Cell Ho	**1 oil engine** driving 1 FP propeller Total Power: 51,480kW (69,992hp) 25.5kn Sulzer 9RTA96C 1 x 2 Stroke 9 Cy. 960 x 2500 51480kW (69992bhp) Hyundai Heavy Industries Co Ltd-South Korea AuxGen: 4 x 2280kW 450/230V a.c Thrusters: 1 Tunnel thruster (f)
9137674 *A8LH7* -	**WESTERBURG** *ex* CMA CGM Accra *-2007* *ex* Westerburg *-2007* *ex* Tuscany Bridge *-2007* *ex* Westerburg *-2003* *ex* Lykes Achiever *-2001* *ex* Westerburg *-1998* *ex* Maersk La Plata *-1998* *ex* Westerburg *-1997* **Burg Shipping Co Ltd** Hans Peterson & Soehne GmbH & Co KG *Monrovia* Liberia MMSI: 636015895 Official number: 15895	**23,896** 10,474 30,291 T/cm 47.0	Class: GL	**1997-07 Stocznia Gdynia SA — Gdynia** Yd No: 8143/2 Loa 188.02 (BB) Br ex 30.32 Dght 11.500 Lbp 175.60 Br md 30.00 Dpth 16.75 Welded, 1 dk	**(A33A2CC) Container Ship (Fully Cellular)** TEU 2072 C Ho 836 TEU C Dk 1236 incl 300 ref C. Compartments: 5 Cell Ho, ER 9 Ha: (12.8 x 15.7)Tappered (12.8 x 20.8)7 (12.8 x 26.0)ER Cranes: 3x45t	**1 oil engine** driving 1 FP propeller Total Power: 17,940kW (24,391hp) 21.0kn Sulzer 6RTA72U 1 x 2 Stroke 6 Cy. 720 x 2500 17940kW (24391bhp) H Cegielski Poznan SA-Poland AuxGen: 1 x 1200kW 450V 60Hz a.c, 2 x 1000kW 450V 60Hz a.c Thrusters: 1 Thwart. CP thruster (f) Fuel: 238.7 (d.f.) (Heating Coils) 2628.2 (r.f.) 76.0pd
9226891 *PINX* -	**WESTERDAM** - **HAL Antillen NV** Holland America Line NV SatCom: Inmarsat C 424412811 *Rotterdam* Netherlands MMSI: 244128000 Official number: 42579	**82,348** 42,635 10,965 T/cm 74.9	Class: LR (RI) ✠ **100A1** CS 04/2009 passenger ship *IWS ✠ **LMC** Eq.Ltr: U†; Cable: 722.9/90.0 U3 (a)	**2004-04 Fincantieri-Cant. Nav. Italiani S.p.A. (Breda) — Venezia** Yd No: 6077 Loa 285.24 (BB) Br ex 32.24 Dght 8.000 Lbp 253.93 Br md 32.21 Dpth 36.98 Welded	**(A37A2PC) Passenger/Cruise** Passengers: cabins: 925; berths: 2250	**5 diesel electric oil engines & 1 turbo electric Gas Turb** driving 3 gen. each 11200kW 11000V a.c 2 gen. each 8400kW 11000V a.c 1 gen. of 14000kW 11000V a.c Connecting to 2 elec. motors each (17600kW) driving 2 Azimuth electric drive units Total Power: 75,140kW (102,162hp) 22.0kn Sulzer 12ZAV40S 2 x Vee 4 Stroke 12 Cy. 400 x 560 each-8640kW (11747bhp) Wartsila Italia SpA-Italy Sulzer 16ZAV40S 3 x Vee 4 Stroke 16 Cy. 400 x 560 each-11520kW (15663bhp) Wartsila Italia SpA-Italy GE Marine LM2500 1 x Gas Turb 23300kW (31679shp) General Electric Co.-Lynn, Ma Boilers: e (ex.g.) 11.2kgf/cm² (11.0bar), e (ex.g.) 11.0kgf/cm² (10.8bar), WTAuxB (o.f.) 9.5kgf/cm² (9.3bar) Thrusters: 3 Thwart. CP thruster (f) Fuel: 588.0 (d.f.) 2315.0 (r.f.)
9316361 *A8JY5* -	**WESTERDIEK** *ex* MSC Mendoza *-2009* *ex* Westerdiek *-2007* **Westerdiek Shipping GmbH & Co KG** Hans Peterson & Soehne GmbH & Co KG *Monrovia* Liberia MMSI: 636091159 Official number: 91159	**32,060** 12,611 39,000	Class: NV	**2007-01 Stocznia Gdansk SA — Gdansk** Yd No: 8184/13 Loa 210.85 (BB) Br ex - Dght 12.000 Lbp 195.97 Br md 32.26 Dpth 19.00 Welded, 1 dk	**(A33A2CC) Container Ship (Fully Cellular)** TEU 2732 C Ho 1222 TEU C Dk 1510 TEU incl 450 ref C. Ice Capable	**1 oil engine** driving 1 FP propeller Total Power: 21,733kW (29,548hp) 22.5kn MAN-B&W 7S70MC-C 1 x 2 Stroke 7 Cy. 700 x 2800 21733kW (29548bhp) H Cegielski Poznan SA-Poland AuxGen: 4 x 1260kW 440V 60Hz a.c Thrusters: 1 Tunnel thruster (f)
8137342 *DCPO* -	**WESTEREMS** *ex* Bernhard *-2007* **Jan van Gerpen** - *Borkum* Germany Official number: 3766	*136* 81 -		**1905 JG Hitzler Schiffswerft u Masch GmbH & Co KG — Lauenburg** Loa 33.79 Br ex 6.20 Dght - Lbp 32.03 Br md 6.15 Dpth 2.49 Welded, 1 dk	**(B33A2DS) Suction Dredger** Hopper: 940	**1 oil engine** reverse reduction geared to sc. shaft driving 1 FP propeller Total Power: 147kW (200hp) Cummins NT-855-M 1 x 4 Stroke 6 Cy. 140 x 152 147kW (200bhp) (new engine 1982) Cummins Engine Co Inc-USA

No.	Ship / Owner	Tonnage	Class	Builder / Dimensions	Type / Capacity	Machinery
9137698 D5DJ7	**WESTERHAMM** *ex* Cala Paradiso *-2008* *ex* DAL Karoo *-2004* *ex* Westerhamm *-2002* *ex* Actor *-2001* *ex* Westerhamm *-1999* **Westerhamm Shipping Co Ltd** Hans Peterson & Soehne GmbH & Co KG *Monrovia* *Liberia* MMSI: 636015900 Official number: 15900	**23,896** 10,474 30,259 T/cm 47.0	Class: GL	**1998-09 Stocznia Gdynia SA — Gdynia** Yd No: 8143/3 Loa 188.02 (BB) Br ex 30.34 Dght 11.500 Lbp 175.60 Br md 30.00 Dpth 16.75 Welded, 1 dk	**(A33A2CC) Container Ship (Fully Cellular)** TEU 2072 C Ho 836 TEU C Dk 1236 TEU incl 300 ref C. Compartments: 5 Cell Ho, ER 9 Ha: (12.8 x 15.7)Tappered (12.8 x 20.8)7 (12.8 x 26.0)ER Cranes: 3x45t	**1 oil engine** driving 1 FP propeller Total Power: 17,940kW (24,391hp) 21.0kn Sulzer 6RTA72U 1 x 2 Stroke 6 Cy. 720 x 2500 17940kW (24391bhp) H Cegielski Poznan SA-Poland AuxGen: 2 x 1400kW 440/220V a.c, 1 x 1196kW 440/220V a.c Thrusters: 1 Thwart. CP thruster (f)
9202089 V2FB7 -	**WESTERHAVEN** *ex* CTE Barcelona *-2001* *ex* Westerhaven *-2000* **ms 'Westerhaven' Schiffahrts GmbH & Co KG** Reider Shipping BV *Saint John's* *Antigua & Barbuda* MMSI: 305625000	**7,541** 3,432 8,450 T/cm 22.3	Class: GL	**2000-03 Brodotrogir dd - Shipyard Trogir — Trogir** (Hull) Yd No: 246 **2000-03 Schiffswerft und Maschinenfabrik Cassens GmbH — Emden** Yd No: 222 Loa 127.00 (BB) Br ex 20.46 Dght 7.700 Lbp 119.40 Br md 20.40 Dpth 10.35 Welded, 1 dk	**(A31A2GX) General Cargo Ship** Grain: 11,830 TEU 712 C Ho 245 TEU C Dk 467 TEU incl 100 ref C. Compartments: 3 Cell Ho, ER 3 Ha: (25.4 x 13.1)2 (25.4 x 15.8)ER Cranes: 2x40t Ice Capable	**1 oil engine** with flexible couplings & sr gearedto sc. shaft driving 1 CP propeller Total Power: 6,000kW (8,158hp) 17.0kn MaK 8M552C 1 x 4 Stroke 8 Cy. 450 x 520 6000kW (8158bhp) MaK Motoren GmbH & Co. KG-Kiel AuxGen: 1 x 1032kW 220/440V 60Hz a.c, 2 x 800kW 220/440V 60Hz a.c Thrusters: 1 Thwart. FP thruster (f) Fuel: 92.1 (d.f.) (Heating Coils) 611.0 (r.f.) 25.0pd
9202091 V2FB5 -	**WESTERKADE** **ms 'Westerkade' Schiffahrts GmbH & Co KG** Reider Shipping BV *Saint John's* *Antigua & Barbuda* MMSI: 305623000	**7,541** 3,432 8,450 T/cm 22.3	Class: GL	**2000-07 Brodotrogir dd - Shipyard Trogir — Trogir** (Hull) Yd No: 247 **2000-07 Schiffswerft und Maschinenfabrik Cassens GmbH — Emden** Yd No: 223 Loa 127.00 (BB) Br ex - Dght 7.700 Lbp 119.40 Br md 20.44 Dpth 10.35 Welded, 1 dk	**(A31A2GX) General Cargo Ship** Grain: 11,835 TEU 712 C Ho 245 TEU C Dk 467 TEU incl 100 ref C. Compartments: 3 Cell Ho, ER 3 Ha: (25.4 x 13.1)2 (25.4 x 15.8)ER Cranes: 2x40t Ice Capable	**1 oil engine** with flexible couplings & sr gearedto sc. shaft driving 1 CP propeller Total Power: 6,000kW (8,158hp) 17.0kn MaK 8M552C 1 x 4 Stroke 8 Cy. 450 x 520 6000kW (8158bhp) MaK Motoren GmbH & Co. KG-Kiel AuxGen: 1 x 1032kW 220/440V 60Hz a.c, 2 x 800kW 220/440V 60Hz a.c Thrusters: 1 Thwart. FP thruster (f) Fuel: 92.1 (d.f.) (Heating Coils) 611.0 (r.f.) 25.0pd
9206669 V2AT2 -	**WESTERLAND** *ex* Marcliff *-2005* **ms 'Westerland' GmbH & Co KG** Reederei Eckhoff GmbH & Co KG *Saint John's* *Antigua & Barbuda* MMSI: 304011002 Official number: 3536	**4,028** 2,218 5,085	Class: GL (BV)	**2000-01 Jinling Shipyard — Nanjing JS** Yd No: 98-0102 Loa 100.55 (BB) Br ex - Dght 6.470 Lbp 95.40 Br md 18.50 Dpth 8.25 Welded, 1 dk	**(A31A2GX) General Cargo Ship** Grain: 7,646 TEU 506 C Ho 143 TEU C Dk 363 TEU incl 60 ref C. Compartments: 3 Ho, ER 3 Ha: ER Cranes: 2x40t Ice Capable	**1 oil engine** reduction geared to sc. shaft driving 1 CP propeller Total Power: 3,960kW (5,384hp) 16.0kn MaK 9M32 1 x 4 Stroke 9 Cy. 320 x 480 3960kW (5384bhp) MaK Motoren GmbH & Co. KG-Kiel AuxGen: 1 x 624kW 380V 50Hz a.c, 3 x 340kW 380V 50Hz a.c Thrusters: 1 Thwart. FP thruster (f)
9240328 LXWL -	**WESTERLAND** *ex* CSAV Mexico *-2011* *ex* Westerland *-2005* *ex* Alianca Hamburgo *-2003* **Westerland Shipping GmbH & Co KG** Hans Peterson & Soehne GmbH & Co KG *Luxembourg* *Luxembourg* MMSI: 253157000	**30,047** 12,671 35,768 T/cm 57.0	Class: GL	**2002-04 Stocznia Gdynia SA — Gdynia** Yd No: 8230/3 Loa 207.90 (BB) Br ex - Dght 11.500 Lbp 192.80 Br md 32.24 Dpth 16.80 Welded, 1 dk	**(A33A2CC) Container Ship (Fully Cellular)** TEU 2764 C Ho 1000 TEU C Dk 1764 TEU incl 400 ref C. Cranes: 3x45t,1x35t	**1 oil engine** driving 1 FP propeller Total Power: 24,830kW (33,759hp) 22.0kn B&W 8S70MC 1 x 2 Stroke 8 Cy. 700 x 2674 24830kW (33759bhp) H Cegielski Poznan SA-Poland AuxGen: 2 x 1000kW 440/220V 60Hz a.c, 2 x 1200kW 440/220V 60Hz a.c Thrusters: 1 Tunnel thruster (f)
7041091 3DZA -	**WESTERLAND** **Bligh Water Shipping Ltd** Suilven Shipping Ltd *Suva* *Fiji* MMSI: 520129000	**1,509** 575 356	Class: (GL) (BV)	**1971-03 Husumer Schiffswerft — Husum** Yd No: 1297 Loa 58.35 Br ex 12.40 Dght 2.502 Lbp 53.42 Br md 12.37 Dpth 3.61 Welded, 1 dk	**(A36A2PR) Passenger/Ro-Ro Ship (Vehicles)** Passengers: unberthed: 400 Ice Capable	**2 oil engines** driving 2 FP propellers Total Power: 1,740kW (2,366hp) MWM TBD604BL6 2 x 4 Stroke 6 Cy. 170 x 195 each-870kW (1183bhp) (new engine 1988) Motoren Werke Mannheim AG (MWM)-West Germany
7221548 EI2585 D 635	**WESTERLEA** *ex* Azalea *-1980* **Maramour Ltd** SA Pesca Coruna *Dublin* *Irish Republic* Official number: 402567	*292* 187 -	Class: (LR) Classed LR until 23/8/06	**1972-07 Scheepsbouw- en Constructiebedr. K. Hakvoort N.V. — Monnickendam** Yd No: 135 Lengthened-1978 Lengthened-1974 Loa 33.61 Br ex 7.42 Dght - Lbp 31.60 Br md 7.29 Dpth 3.69 Welded, 1 dk	**(B11A2FT) Trawler**	**1 oil engine** sr geared to sc. shaft driving 1 CP propeller Total Power: 736kW (1,001hp) 10.0kn Blackstone ESL8 1 x 4 Stroke 8 Cy. 222 x 292 736kW (1001bhp) (new engine 1978) Mirrlees Blackstone (Stamford)Ltd.-Stamford AuxGen: 2 x 64kW 380V a.c Thrusters: 1 Thwart. FP thruster (f); 1 Tunnel thruster (a)
8855451 WDA7098 -	**WESTERLY** *ex* Zingaro *-1980* **Westerly LLC** - *Petersburg, AK* *United States of America* MMSI: 366839630 Official number: 656740	**176** 52 -		**1983 Weldit Corp. — Bellingham, Wa** Loa - Br ex - Dght - Lbp 24.26 Br md 7.92 Dpth 2.44 Welded, 1 dk	**(B11B2FV) Fishing Vessel**	**1 oil engine** driving 1 FP propeller
9222106 A8CH2 -	**WESTERMOOR** *ex* Niledutch Springbok *-2014* *ex* Westermoor *-2012* **Westermoor Shipping GmbH & Co KG** Hans Peterson & Soehne GmbH & Co KG *Monrovia* *Liberia* MMSI: 636090646 Official number: 90646	**30,047** 12,671 35,653 T/cm 57.0	Class: GL	**2001-08 Stocznia Gdynia SA — Gdynia** Yd No: 8230/1 Loa 207.94 (BB) Br ex - Dght 11.500 Lbp 190.80 Br md 32.24 Dpth 16.80 Welded, 1 dk	**(A33A2CC) Container Ship (Fully Cellular)** TEU 2764 C Ho 1000 TEU C Dk 1764 TEU incl 400 ref C. Compartments: 5 Cell Ho, ER 10 Ha: ER Cranes: 3x45t,1x35t	**1 oil engine** driving 1 FP propeller Total Power: 24,840kW (33,772hp) 22.0kn B&W 8S70MC-C 1 x 2 Stroke 8 Cy. 700 x 2800 24840kW (33772bhp) H Cegielski Poznan SA-Poland AuxGen: 2 x 1000kW 440/220V 60Hz a.c, 2 x 1200kW 440/220V 60Hz a.c Thrusters: 1 Tunnel thruster (f)
7437616 WYT9565 -	**WESTERN** *ex* Offshore Trawler *-2012* **Uri Enterprises Inc** - *Seattle, WA* *United States of America* Official number: 548157	*146* 99 -		**1973 Offshore Trawlers, Inc. — Bayou La Batre, Al** L reg 21.92 Br ex 6.71 Dght - Lbp - Br md - Dpth 3.61 Welded, 1 dk	**(B11A2FT) Trawler**	**1 oil engine** driving 1 FP propeller Total Power: 294kW (400hp)
7028350 - -	**WESTERN 102** - **Western Shellfish International** - *Panama* *Panama*	*200* - -	Class: (AB)	**1970 Astilleros de Veracruz S.A. — Veracruz** Yd No: 52 Loa - Br ex 6.79 Dght - Lbp 24.06 Br md - Dpth 3.71 Welded, 1 dk	**(B11B2FV) Fishing Vessel** Compartments: 1 Ho, ER 1 Ha:	**1 oil engine** reverse reduction geared to sc. shaft driving 1 FP propeller Total Power: 416kW (566hp) Caterpillar D379SCAC 1 x Vee 4 Stroke 8 Cy. 159 x 203 416kW (566bhp) Caterpillar Tractor Co-USA
7031735 - -	**WESTERN 103** - **Western Shellfish International** - *Panama* *Panama*	*170* - -	Class: (AB)	**1970 Astilleros de Veracruz S.A. — Veracruz** Yd No: 53 Loa - Br ex 6.79 Dght - Lbp 24.06 Br md - Dpth 3.71 Welded, 1 dk	**(B11B2FV) Fishing Vessel** Compartments: 1 Ho, ER 1 Ha:	**1 oil engine** reverse reduction geared to sc. shaft driving 1 FP propeller Total Power: 416kW (566hp) Caterpillar D379SCAC 1 x Vee 4 Stroke 8 Cy. 159 x 203 416kW (566bhp) Caterpillar Tractor Co-USA
8136142 - -	**WESTERN ADVENTURE II** *ex* Swansea Bay *-2008* *ex* Levina Wilhelmina *-2001* **O'Sullivan McCarthy Mussel Development Ltd** - *Tralee* *Irish Republic* Official number: 404120	**132** 39 -		**1980 Stertil Stokvis-Kelley B.V. — Kootstertille** Yd No: 202 Loa 32.14 Br ex - Dght 2.000 Lbp 28.88 Br md 6.52 Dpth 2.62 Welded, 1 dk	**(B11B2FV) Fishing Vessel**	**1 oil engine** driving 1 FP propeller Total Power: 221kW (300hp) Mitsubishi 1 x 221kW (300bhp) Mitsubishi Heavy Industries Ltd-Japan
9609677 5BPY3 -	**WESTERN AIDA** **Bellum Shipping Ltd** Westlake SA *Limassol* *Cyprus* MMSI: 210263000 Official number: 9609677	**22,668** 11,856 37,000	Class: BV	**2012-05 Hyundai Mipo Dockyard Co Ltd — Ulsan** Yd No: 6107 Loa 187.00 (BB) Br ex - Dght 10.400 Lbp 178.00 Br md 28.60 Dpth 15.60 Welded, 1 dk	**(A21A2BC) Bulk Carrier** Grain: 49,729 Compartments: 5 Ho, ER 5 Ha: ER Cranes: 4	**1 oil engine** driving 1 FP propeller Total Power: 7,700kW (10,469hp) 14.3kn MAN-B&W 6S46MC-C 1 x 2 Stroke 6 Cy. 460 x 1932 7700kW (10469bhp) Hyundai Heavy Industries Co Ltd-South Korea AuxGen: 3 x 540kW 60Hz a.c Fuel: 1750.0
9289855 V7XA4 -	**WESTERN ALBERTITO** *ex* Ace Bulker *-2011* **Nevis Shipholding Ltd** Univan Ship Management Ltd *Majuro* *Marshall Islands* MMSI: 538004435 Official number: 4435	**16,966** 10,498 28,498 T/cm 39.7	Class: NK	**2003-04 Imabari Shipbuilding Co Ltd — Imabari EH (Imabari Shipyard)** Yd No: 588 Loa 169.26 (BB) Br ex - Dght 9.778 Lbp 160.40 Br md 27.20 Dpth 13.60 Welded, 1 dk	**(A21A2BC) Bulk Carrier** Grain: 37,523; Bale: 35,762 Compartments: 5 Ho, ER 5 Ha: ER 4 (19.2 x 17.6) (13.6 x 16.0) Cranes: 4x30.5t	**1 oil engine** driving 1 FP propeller Total Power: 5,854kW (7,959hp) 14.0kn MAN-B&W 6S42MC 1 x 2 Stroke 6 Cy. 420 x 1764 5854kW (7959bhp) Makita Corp-Japan AuxGen: 3 x 440kW 440/110V 60Hz a.c Fuel: 121.0 (d.f.) (Heating Coils) 1181.0 (r.f.) 21.9pd

9594535 VRJQ2 -
WESTERN AUSTRALIA
SFL Tyne Inc
Golden Ocean Management AS
Hong Kong — Hong Kong
MMSI: 477847900
Official number: HK-3316
19,998 10,444 31,905 T/cm 45.3 — Class: NV
2012-02 Guangzhou Wenchong Shipyard Co Ltd — Guangzhou GD Yd No: 409
Loa 176.50 (BB) Br ex - Dght 10.000
Lbp 171.00 Br md 27.00 Dpth 14.20
Welded, 1 dk
(A21A2BC) Bulk Carrier
Grain: 40,442; Bale: 39,882
Compartments: 5 Ho, ER
5 Ha: 4 (15.6 x 20.0)ER (15.6 x 16.5)
Cranes: 4x30t
1 oil engine driving 1 FP propeller
Total Power: 6,480kW (8,810hp) 14.3kn
MAN-B&W 6S42MC
1 x 2 Stroke 6 Cy. 420 x 1764 6480kW (8810bhp)
AuxGen: 3 x 595kW 60Hz a.c
Fuel: 113.0 (d.f.) 1260.0 (r.f.)

9609691 5BSZ3 -
WESTERN BOHEME
Jarilo Shipping Ltd
Westlake SA
Limassol — Cyprus
MMSI: 210261000
22,668 11,856 37,000 — Class: BV
2012-10 Hyundai Mipo Dockyard Co Ltd — Ulsan Yd No: 6109
Loa 187.00 (BB) Br ex - Dght 10.400
Lbp 178.00 Br md 28.60 Dpth 15.60
Welded, 1 dk
(A21A2BC) Bulk Carrier
Grain: 49,729
Compartments: 5 Ho, ER
5 Ha: ER
Cranes: 4
1 oil engine driving 1 FP propeller
Total Power: 7,700kW (10,469hp) 14.3kn
MAN-B&W 6S46MC-C
1 x 2 Stroke 6 Cy. 460 x 1932 7700kW (10469bhp)
Hyundai Heavy Industries Co Ltd-South Korea
AuxGen: 3 x 540kW 60Hz a.c
Fuel: 1750.0

9609720 5BVZ3 -
WESTERN CARMEN
Svarga Marine Ltd
Westlake SA
Limassol — Cyprus
MMSI: 210509000
Official number: 9609720
22,668 11,856 37,000 — Class: BV
2013-04 Hyundai Mipo Dockyard Co Ltd — Ulsan Yd No: 6112
Loa 187.00 (BB) Br ex - Dght 10.400
Lbp 178.00 Br md 28.60 Dpth 15.60
Welded, 1 dk
(A21A2BC) Bulk Carrier
Grain: 49,687
Compartments: 5 Ho, ER
5 Ha: ER
Cranes: 4
1 oil engine driving 1 FP propeller
Total Power: 7,700kW (10,469hp) 14.3kn
MAN-B&W 6S46MC-C
1 x 2 Stroke 6 Cy. 460 x 1932 7700kW (10469bhp)
Hyundai Heavy Industries Co Ltd-South Korea
AuxGen: 3 x 540kW 60Hz a.c

8029636 3FIZ8 -
WESTERN CHARM
ex Dora *-2011* *ex* Oak *-2002* *ex* Verdin *-1994*
ex Luntian *-1993* *ex* Verdant *-1987*
Cetrade International Ltd
Nobpac Ship Management Ltd
SatCom: Inmarsat C 435402010
Panama — Panama
MMSI: 354020000
Official number: 4301311
12,906 8,595 21,951 T/cm 30.0 — Class: (NK)
1981-11 Tohoku Shipbuilding Co Ltd — Shiogama MG Yd No: 201
Loa 155.20 (BB) Br ex 22.90 Dght 9.959
Lbp 145.70 Br md 22.86 Dpth 13.60
Welded, 1 dk
(A21A2BC) Bulk Carrier
Grain: 30,633; Bale: 26,593
Compartments: 4 Ho, ER
4 Ha: (20.0 x 10.3)3 (20.2 x 11.2)ER
Derricks: 4x25t; Winches: 4
1 oil engine driving 1 FP propeller
Total Power: 5,913kW (8,039hp) 15.0kn
B&W 6L55GFC
1 x 2 Stroke 6 Cy. 550 x 1380 5913kW (8039bhp)
Hitachi Zosen Corp-Japan
AuxGen: 2 x 400kW 450V 60Hz a.c
Fuel: 190.5 (d.f.) 1091.0 (r.f.) 25.0pd

9281982 EILQ SO 237
WESTERN CHIEFTAIN
Premier Trawlers Ltd
-
Sligo — Irish Republic
MMSI: 250105600
Official number: 403792
663 199 - — Class: NV
2004-01 Stal-Rem SA — Gdansk (Hull) Yd No: B328/1
2004-01 Karstensens Skibsvaerft A/S — Skagen Yd No: 391
Loa 45.00 Br ex 10.52 Dght 6.500
Lbp 42.00 Br md 10.50 Dpth 7.10
Welded, 1 dk
(B11A2FS) Stern Trawler
1 oil engine geared to sc. shaft driving 1 CP propeller
Total Power: 2,400kW (3,263hp) 12.0kn
MaK 8M25
1 x 4 Stroke 8 Cy. 255 x 400 2400kW (3263bhp)
Caterpillar Motoren GmbH & Co. KG-Germany
AuxGen: 1 x a.c, 1 x a.c
Thrusters: 1 Thwart. CP thruster (f); 1 Thwart. FP thruster (a)

8217166 DUL6497 -
WESTERN COAST
ex Idaho *-1997* *ex* Rishiri *-1991*
DFC Tuna Venture Corp
-
General Santos — Philippines
Official number: DAV4003977
830 260 2,131 — Class: (NK)
1983-01 Taihei Kogyo K.K. — Hashihama, Imabari Yd No: 1505
Loa 83.93 (BB) Br ex - Dght 5.020
Lbp 78.64 Br md 13.61 Dpth 5.06
Welded, 2 dks
(A34A2GR) Refrigerated Cargo Ship
Ins: 2,920
Compartments: 3 Ho, ER
3 Ha: 3 (4.9 x 4.8)ER
Derricks: 6x5t; Winches: 6
1 oil engine driving 1 FP propeller
Total Power: 1,912kW (2,600hp) 13.5kn
Akasaka A37
1 x 4 Stroke 6 Cy. 370 x 720 1912kW (2600bhp)
Akasaka Tekkosho KK (Akasaka DieselLtd)-Japan
AuxGen: 2 x 360kW a.c

9455923 VRLM7 -
WESTERN COPENHAGEN
ex Sfl Dee *-2013*
SFL Dee Inc
Golden Ocean Group Ltd (GOGL)
Hong Kong — Hong Kong
MMSI: 477016700
Official number: HK-3709
19,998 10,444 31,716 T/cm 45.3 — Class: NV
2013-03 Guangzhou Wenchong Shipyard Co Ltd — Guangzhou GD Yd No: 388
Loa 176.50 (BB) Br ex 27.04 Dght 10.000
Lbp 171.00 Br md 27.00 Dpth 14.20
Welded, 1 dk
(A21A2BC) Bulk Carrier
Grain: 40,443; Bale: 39,882
Compartments: 5 Ho, ER
5 Ha: (18.4 x 16.2)3 (19.2 x 16.2)ER (14.7 x 14.6)
Cranes: 4x30t
1 oil engine driving 1 FP propeller
Total Power: 6,480kW (8,810hp) 14.3kn
MAN-B&W 6S42MC
1 x 2 Stroke 6 Cy. 420 x 1764 6480kW (8810bhp)
AuxGen: 3 x 560kW a.c
Fuel: 136.0 (d.f.) 1312.0 (r.f.)

7515925 WSB9934 -
WESTERN DAWN
ex Arleen *-1973*
f/v Western Dawn LLC
-
Seattle, WA — United States of America
MMSI: 366264360
Official number: 524423
198 134 -
1969 Bender Welding & Machine Co Inc — Mobile AL Yd No: 242
L reg 24.36 Br ex 7.35 Dght -
Lbp - Br md - Dpth 3.43
Welded, 1 dk
(B11A2FT) Trawler
1 oil engine driving 1 FP propeller
Total Power: 530kW (721hp)

9520613 V7ZC9 -
WESTERN EHIME
Misuga SA
Misuga Kaiun Co Ltd
Majuro — Marshall Islands
MMSI: 538004793
Official number: 4793
32,309 19,458 58,105 T/cm 57.4 — Class: NK
2012-10 Tsuneishi Heavy Industries (Cebu) Inc — Balamban Yd No: SC-152
Loa 189.99 (BB) Br ex - Dght 12.826
Lbp 185.60 Br md 32.26 Dpth 18.00
Welded, 1 dk
(A21A2BC) Bulk Carrier
Grain: 72,689; Bale: 70,122
Compartments: 5 Ho, ER
5 Ha: ER
Cranes: 4x30t
1 oil engine driving 1 FP propeller
Total Power: 8,400kW (11,421hp) 14.5kn
MAN-B&W 6S50MC-C
1 x 2 Stroke 6 Cy. 500 x 2000 8400kW (11421bhp)
Mitsui Engineering & Shipbuilding CLtd-Japan
Fuel: 2380.0

8610681 EIDN D 653
WESTERN ENDEAVOUR
Western Seaboard Fishing Co Ltd
-
SatCom: Inmarsat A 1656205
Dublin — Irish Republic
MMSI: 250190000
Official number: 402489
1,988 770 1,988 — Class: NV
1987-05 AS Mjellem & Karlsen — Bergen Yd No: 138
Loa 71.02 (BB) Br ex - Dght 5.930
Lbp 64.93 Br md 12.62 Dpth 8.51
Welded, 2 dks
(B11A2FS) Stern Trawler
Grain: 432; Ins: 1,957
Ice Capable
1 oil engine geared to sc. shaft driving 1 CP propeller
Total Power: 2,998kW (4,076hp)
Wichmann WX28V10
1 x Vee 4 Stroke 10 Cy. 280 x 360 2998kW (4076bhp)
Wichmann Motorfabrikk AS-Norway
AuxGen: 1 x 1600kW 440V 60Hz a.c, 3 x 288kW 440V 60Hz a.c, 1 x 72kW 440V 60Hz a.c
Thrusters: 1 Thwart. CP thruster (f); 1 Tunnel thruster (a)

8803642 P2V4659 -
WESTERN ENDEAVOUR
Coral Trader Ltd
Coral Sea Shipping Lines Pty Ltd
Port Moresby — Papua New Guinea
MMSI: 553111184
Official number: 000418
2,754 826 3,630 — Class: AB
1988-09 Sing Koon Seng Shipbuilding & Engineering Ltd — Singapore Yd No: 680
Converted From: General Cargo Ship-1999
Lengthened & New forept-1999
Loa 88.20 Br ex - Dght 3.710
Lbp 85.20 Br md 17.50 Dpth 5.40
Welded, 1 dk
(A21B2BO) Ore Carrier
Grain: 2,283
TEU 117 C. 117/20'
Compartments: 1 Ho, ER
1 Ha: (31.8 x 8.5)ER
2 oil engines reverse reduction geared to sc. shafts driving 2 FP propellers
Total Power: 1,766kW (2,402hp) 10.0kn
Wartsila 6R22HF
2 x 4 Stroke 6 Cy. 220 x 240 each-883kW (1201bhp)
Wartsila Diesel Singapore Pte Ltd-Singapore
AuxGen: 2 x 160kW a.c
Fuel: 216.0

8016342 UDQN -
WESTERN ENTERPRISE
ex Spring Rain *-1987*
Pacific Ocean Fishing Co Ltd (OOO 'Tikhookeanskaya Rybopromyshlennaya Kompaniya')
-
Magadan — Russia
MMSI: 273417010
Official number: YU6298
780 234 1,200 — Class: RS (AB)
1980-12 Halter Marine, Inc. — Moss Point, Ms Yd No: 964
Converted From: Offshore Tug/Supply Ship-1987
Loa 54.87 Br ex - Dght 3.810
Lbp - Br md 12.20 Dpth 4.27
Welded, 1 dk
(B11B2FV) Fishing Vessel
2 oil engines reverse reduction geared to sc. shafts driving 2 FP propellers
Total Power: 1,854kW (2,520hp) 12.0kn
EMD (Electro-Motive) 12-645-E2
2 x Vee 2 Stroke 12 Cy. 230 x 254 each-927kW (1260bhp)
(Re-engined ,made 1952, Reconditioned & fitted 1980)
General Motors Detroit DieselAllison Divn-USA
Thrusters: 1 Thwart. FP thruster (f)
Fuel: 315.0 (d.f.)

9609689 5BPX3 -
WESTERN FEDORA
Heket Shipping Ltd
Westlake SA
SatCom: Inmarsat C 421023910
Limassol — Cyprus
MMSI: 210239000
Official number: 9609689
22,668 11,856 37,000 — Class: BV
2012-07 Hyundai Mipo Dockyard Co Ltd — Ulsan Yd No: 6108
Loa 187.00 (BB) Br ex - Dght 10.400
Lbp 178.00 Br md 28.60 Dpth 15.60
Welded, 1 dk
(A21A2BC) Bulk Carrier
Grain: 49,729
Compartments: 5 Ho, ER
5 Ha: ER
Cranes: 4
1 oil engine driving 1 FP propeller
Total Power: 7,700kW (10,469hp) 14.3kn
MAN-B&W 6S46MC-C
1 x 2 Stroke 6 Cy. 460 x 1932 7700kW (10469bhp)
Hyundai Heavy Industries Co Ltd-South Korea
AuxGen: 3 x 540kW 60Hz a.c
Fuel: 1750.0

5220837 VC5029 -
WESTERN FLYER
ex G. C. Marsh *-1975* *ex* G. C. Marc II *-1969*
ex Marc II *-1967*
Norson Pacific Ventures Inc
-
Vancouver, BC — Canada
Official number: 319722
137 71 - — Class: (LR) ✠ Classed LR until 6/71
1962-09 Marine Industries Ltee (MIL) — Sorel QC Yd No: 290
Loa 24.95 Br ex 6.71 Dght -
Lbp 22.48 Br md 6.56 Dpth 3.36
Welded
(B11A2FT) Trawler
1 oil engine with hydraulic coupling driving 1 CP propeller
Total Power: 250kW (340hp)
Alpha 404-24VO
1 x 2 Stroke 4 Cy. 240 x 400 250kW (340bhp)
Alpha Diesel A/S-Denmark

IMO / Call sign	Name / Owner / Port	Tonnage	Class	Builder / Dimensions	Type	Machinery
842478 2V4726	**WESTERN FLYER** **P&O Maritime Services (PNG) Ltd** - *Port Moresby* *Papua New Guinea* MMSI: 553111165 Official number: 000445	**2,782** 1,016 3,681	Class: AB	**1990-03 Sing Koon Seng Shipbuilding & Engineering Ltd — Singapore** (Aft section) Yd No: 690 **2000 Singapore Technologies Shipbuilding & Engineering Ltd. — Singapore** (Fwd section) Converted From: General Cargo Ship-2000 Lengthened & Joined Loa 88.20 Br ex - Dght 3.710 Lbp 71.40 Br md 17.50 Dpth 4.60 Welded, 1 dk	**(A21B2B0) Ore Carrier** Grain: 1,444; Liq: 2,000 Compartments: 1 Ho/Ta, ER	**2 oil engines** reverse reduction geared to sc. shafts driving 2 FP propellers Total Power: 1,856kW (2,524hp) 10.0kn Kromhout 6FGHD240 2 x 4 Stroke 6 Cy. 240 x 260 each-928kW (1262bhp) Stork Wartsila Diesel BV-Netherlands AuxGen: 2 x 160kW a.c
990902 VDD2611	**WESTERN FLYER** **Monterey Bay Aquarium Research Institute** - *San Francisco, CA* *United States of America* MMSI: 367766000 Official number: 1038571	**856** 250 -		**1996-01 SWATH Ocean Systems, LLC — Chula Vista, Ca** Yd No: 6001 Loa 35.66 Br ex - Dght 3.650 Lbp - Br md 16.15 Dpth - Welded, 1 dk	**(B31A2SR) Research Survey Vessel** Passengers: berths: 14	**5 diesel electric oil engines** driving 2 gen. each 850kW a.c 2 gen. each 350kW a.c 1 gen. of 195kW a.c Connecting to 2 elec. motors driving 2 FP propellers Total Power: 2,595kW (3,529hp) 8.0kn Caterpillar 3306B-TA 1 x 4 Stroke 6 Cy. 121 x 152 195kW (265bhp) Caterpillar Inc-USA Caterpillar 3408 2 x Vee 4 Stroke 8 Cy. 137 x 152 each-350kW (476bhp) Caterpillar Inc-USA Caterpillar 3512 2 x Vee 4 Stroke 12 Cy. 170 x 190 each-850kW (1156bhp) Caterpillar Inc-USA Thrusters: 2 Tunnel thruster (f)
650925 FAH6	**WESTERN HAKATA** **Ambitious Line SA** Shikishima Kisen KK *Panama* *Panama* MMSI: 354822000 Official number: 45678KJ	**34,815** 20,209 61,353 T/cm 61.4	Class: NK	**2014-03 Imabari Shipbuilding Co Ltd — Imabari EH (Imabari Shipyard)** Yd No: 810 Loa 199.98 (BB) Br ex - Dght 13.010 Lbp 195.00 Br md 32.24 Dpth 18.60 Welded, 1 dk	**(A21A2BC) Bulk Carrier** Grain: 77,674; Bale: 73,552 Compartments: 5 Ho, ER 5 Ha: 4 (23.5 x 19.0)ER (18.7 x 19.0) Cranes: 4x30t	**1 oil engine** driving 1 FP propeller Total Power: 9,960kW (13,542hp) 14.5kn MAN-B&W 6S50MC-C8 1 x 2 Stroke 6 Cy. 500 x 2000 9960kW (13542bhp) Mitsui Engineering & Shipbuilding CLtd-Japan
325776 EJK5	**WESTERN HIGHWAY** **Bulkstar Enterprise Co Ltd** Taiyo Nippon Kisen Co Ltd *Panama* *Panama* MMSI: 372548000 Official number: 3269907A	**39,422** 11,827 12,980	Class: NK	**2007-03 Shin Kurushima Dockyard Co. Ltd. — Onishi** Yd No: 5346 Loa 188.03 (BB) Br ex - Dght 8.524 Lbp 183.70 Br md 28.20 Dpth 19.81 Welded	**(A35B2RV) Vehicles Carrier** Double Hull Side door/ramp (s) Len: - Wid: - Swl: 35 Quarter stern door/ramp (s. a.) Len: - Wid: - Swl: 150 Cars: 3,893	**1 oil engine** driving 1 FP propeller Total Power: 11,000kW (14,956hp) 20.0kn Mitsubishi 8UEC50LSII 1 x 2 Stroke 8 Cy. 500 x 1950 11000kW (14956bhp) Kobe Hatsudoki KK-Japan Thrusters: 1 Tunnel thruster (f) Fuel: 2580.0
455911 RLH9	**WESTERN HOUSTON** *ex* Guangzhou Wenchong 375 *-2012* **SFL Clyde Inc** Golden Ocean Management AS *Hong Kong* *Hong Kong* MMSI: 477305400 Official number: HK-3671	**19,998** 10,444 31,639 T/cm 45.3	Class: NV	**2012-11 Guangzhou Wenchong Shipyard Co Ltd — Guangzhou GD** Yd No: 375 Loa 176.50 (BB) Br ex 27.03 Dght 10.000 Lbp 171.00 Br md 27.00 Dpth 14.20 Welded, 1 dk	**(A21A2BC) Bulk Carrier** Grain: 40,442; Bale: 39,882 Compartments: 5 Ho, ER 5 Ha: ER Cranes: 4x30t	**1 oil engine** driving 1 FP propeller Total Power: 6,480kW (8,810hp) 14.3kn MAN-B&W 6S42MC 1 x 2 Stroke 6 Cy. 420 x 1764 6480kW (8810bhp) AuxGen: 3 x a.c
927788 G6273	**WESTERN INVESTOR** **Jim Pattison Enterprises Ltd & K Smith Fishing Ltd** Jim Pattison Enterprises Ltd *Vancouver, BC* *Canada* MMSI: 316005771 Official number: 393512	*119* 46 125		**1980-02 Allied Shipbuilders Ltd — North Vancouver BC** Yd No: 223 Loa 24.06 Br ex 7.17 Dght 2.928 Lbp 20.53 Br md 7.01 Dpth 3.36 Welded, 1 dk	**(B11B2FV) Fishing Vessel**	**1 oil engine** geared to sc. shaft driving 1 FP propeller Total Power: 515kW (700hp) 10.8kn Caterpillar D348SCAC 1 x Vee 4 Stroke 12 Cy. 137 x 165 515kW (700bhp) Caterpillar Tractor Co-USA Thrusters: 1 Thwart. FP thruster (f)
853028 RS7787	**WESTERN ISLES** *ex* Shunpu Maru *-2001* **Transyacht Pacific Co Ltd** - SatCom: Inmarsat M 600799751 *Hong Kong* *Hong Kong* MMSI: 477991053	*366* 110 94		**1974-03 Ishikawajima-Harima Heavy Industries Co Ltd (IHI) — Tokyo** Yd No: 2420 Converted From: Research Vessel-2005 Loa 48.90 Br ex - Dght 2.920 Lbp 44.00 Br md 7.80 Dpth 3.92 Welded, 1 dk	**(X11A2YP) Yacht** Passengers: cabins: 6; berths: 12	**1 oil engine** driving 1 FP propeller Total Power: 552kW (750hp) 11.0kn Daihatsu 1 x 4 Stroke 552kW (750bhp) Daihatsu Diesel Manufacturing Co Lt-Japan Thrusters: 1 Thwart. FP thruster (f)
003242 MOW	**WESTERN KIM** *ex* South Seas *-1989* **Dongwon Industries Co Ltd** - SatCom: Inmarsat C 444039512 *Busan* *South Korea* MMSI: 440644000 Official number: 9511010-6260000	*1,201* 486 1,675	Class: KR	**1981-03 J M Martinac Shipbuilding Corp — Tacoma WA** Yd No: 224 Loa 68.13 Br ex - Dght 6.138 Lbp 59.31 Br md 12.81 Dpth 5.59 Welded, 1 dk	**(B11B2FV) Fishing Vessel** Grain: 662; Bale: 555	**1 oil engine** geared to sc. shaft driving 1 Directional propeller Total Power: 2,648kW (3,600hp) EMD (Electro-Motive) 20-645-E7 1 x Vee 2 Stroke 20 Cy. 230 x 254 2648kW (3600bhp) General Motors Corp.Electro-Motive Div.-La Grange Thrusters: 1 Thwart. FP thruster (f)
503896 Y7367	**WESTERN KING** **R A Roberts Fishing Ltd** - *Vancouver, BC* *Canada* MMSI: 316003779 Official number: 322411	*178* 88 -		**1964 Benson Bros Shipbuilding Co (1960) Ltd — Vancouver BC** L reg 24.88 Br ex 7.50 Dght - Lbp - Br md 7.45 Dpth - Welded, 1 dk	**(B11B2FV) Fishing Vessel**	**1 oil engine** driving 1 FP propeller Total Power: 496kW (674hp) Caterpillar D379SCAC 1 x Vee 4 Stroke 8 Cy. 159 x 203 496kW (674bhp) Caterpillar Tractor Co-USA
584891 7YG5	**WESTERN KOBE** **IMS Maritime SA** IMECS Co Ltd SatCom: Inmarsat C 453837540 *Majuro* *Marshall Islands* MMSI: 538004655 Official number: 4655	**33,084** 19,142 58,737 T/cm 59.5	Class: BV (NK)	**2012-07 Kawasaki Heavy Industries Ltd — Kobe HG** Yd No: 1705 Loa 197.00 (BB) Br ex - Dght 12.650 Lbp 194.00 Br md 32.26 Dpth 18.10 Welded, 1 dk	**(A21A2BC) Bulk Carrier** Grain: 73,614; Bale: 70,963 Compartments: 5 Ho, ER 5 Ha: ER Cranes: 4x30t	**1 oil engine** driving 1 FP propeller Total Power: 8,630kW (11,733hp) 14.5kn MAN-B&W 6S50MC-C 1 x 2 Stroke 6 Cy. 500 x 2000 8630kW (11733bhp) Kawasaki Heavy Industries Ltd-Japan AuxGen: 3 x 500kW 60Hz a.c Fuel: 2170.0
609706 BTA3	**WESTERN LUCREZIA** **Pheacians Shipping Ltd** Westlake SA *Limassol* *Cyprus* MMSI: 210279000	**22,668** 11,856 37,000	Class: BV	**2013-01 Hyundai Mipo Dockyard Co Ltd — Ulsan** Yd No: 6110 Loa 187.00 (BB) Br ex - Dght 10.400 Lbp 178.00 Br md 28.60 Dpth 15.60 Welded, 1 dk	**(A21A2BC) Bulk Carrier** Grain: 49,729; Bale: 47,948 Compartments: 5 Ho, ER 5 Ha: ER Cranes: 4x30t	**1 oil engine** driving 1 FP propeller Total Power: 7,700kW (10,469hp) 14.3kn MAN-B&W 6S46MC-C8 1 x 2 Stroke 6 Cy. 460 x 1932 7700kW (10469bhp) Hyundai Heavy Industries Co Ltd-South Korea AuxGen: 3 x 540kW 60Hz a.c Fuel: 244.0 (d.f.) 1487.0 (r.f.)
587154 RGU9	**WESTERN MAPLE** **Forever Shine Shipping Ltd** Maple Leaf Shipping Co Ltd *Hong Kong* *Hong Kong* MMSI: 477852900 Official number: HK-2736	**20,867** 11,821 32,493 T/cm 46.1	Class: GL (CC)	**2010-09 Taizhou Maple Leaf Shipbuilding Co Ltd — Linhai ZJ** Yd No: LBC31800-025 Loa 179.90 (BB) Br ex - Dght 10.150 Lbp 171.50 Br md 28.40 Dpth 14.10 Welded, 1 dk	**(A21A2BC) Bulk Carrier** Grain: 42,565 Compartments: 5 Ho, ER 5 Ha: ER Cranes: 4x30.5t	**1 oil engine** driving 1 FP propeller Total Power: 6,480kW (8,810hp) 13.7kn MAN-B&W 6S42MC 1 x 2 Stroke 6 Cy. 420 x 1764 6480kW (8810bhp) STX Engine Co Ltd-South Korea AuxGen: 3 x 465kW 450V a.c
577549 FVE9	**WESTERN MARINE** **Fortune Sunrise Shipping SA** Sinokor Merchant Marine Co Ltd *Panama* *Panama* MMSI: 355653000 Official number: 4345612	**63,624** 38,766 114,583 T/cm 103.6	Class: KR	**2012-01 Nantong Mingde Heavy Industry Co Ltd — Tongzhou JS** Yd No: MD128 Loa 255.00 (BB) Br ex - Dght 14.519 Lbp 248.00 Br md 43.00 Dpth 20.20 Welded, 1 dk	**(A21A2BC) Bulk Carrier** Grain: 133,000 Compartments: 7 Ho, ER 7 Ha: 5 (18.4 x 20.4)ER 2 (16.7 x 18.1)	**1 oil engine** driving 1 FP propeller Total Power: 13,570kW (18,450hp) 14.5kn MAN-B&W 6S60MC-C 1 x 2 Stroke 6 Cy. 600 x 2400 13570kW (18450bhp) Doosan Engine Co Ltd-South Korea Fuel: 6830.0
663879	**WESTERN MARINE 087** **Nurjahan Group** - *Bangladesh*	**1,000** - 1,300	Class: GL (Class contemplated)	**2013-03 Western Marine Shipyard Ltd — Chittagong** Yd No: 087 Loa 65.00 Br ex - Dght 4.000 Lbp - Br md 11.00 Dpth 5.50 Welded, 1 dk	**(A12E2LE) Edible Oil Tanker** Double Hull (13F)	**1 oil engine** driving 1 Propeller

IMO / Call sign	Name / Owner	Tonnage	Class	Construction	Type	Machinery
9663881 - -	**WESTERN MARINE 088** - **Nurjahan Group** - *Bangladesh*	**1,000** - 1,300	Class: GL (Class contemplated)	**2013-08 Western Marine Shipyard Ltd — Chittagong** Yd No: 088 Loa 65.00 Br ex - Dght 4.000 Lbp - Br md 11.00 Dpth 5.50 Welded, 1 dk	**(A12E2LE) Edible Oil Tanker** Double Hull (13F)	**1 oil engine** driving 1 Propeller
7719648 *WDB5173* -	**WESTERN MARINER** *ex* West Point **Western Mariner LLC** - *Seattle, WA* *United States of America* MMSI: 366906730 Official number: 585926	**254** 76 -		**1977-08 Marine Construction & Design Co. (MARCO) — Seattle, Wa** Yd No: 326 Loa 32.95 Br ex 8.82 Dght 3.964 Lbp 29.29 Br md 8.60 Dpth 4.45 Welded, 1 dk	**(B11B2FV) Fishing Vessel**	**1 oil engine** geared to sc. shaft driving 1 FP propeller Total Power: 625kW (850hp) Caterpillar D398SCAC 1 x Vee 4 Stroke 12 Cy. 159 x 203 625kW (850bhp) Caterpillar Tractor Co-USA
9010149 *HP6387* -	**WESTERN MONARCH** - **GECOSHIP AS** WesternGeco Fleet Management SatCom: Inmarsat C 435211110 *Panama* *Panama* MMSI: 352111000 Official number: 2000292F	**6,635** 1,991 2,926	Class: NV	**1991-09 Ulstein Verft AS — Ulsteinvik** Yd No: 231 Loa 92.50 Br ex - Dght 6.915 Lbp 81.03 Br md 20.00 Dpth 9.00 Welded, 3 dks	**(B31A2SR) Research Survey Vessel** Ice Capable	**3 diesel electric oil engines** driving 3 gen. each 3200kW 6600V a.c 1 gen. of 600kW 6600V a.c Connecting to 2 elec. motors driving 2 CP propellers Total Power: 10,110kW (13,746hp) 16.0kn Normo BRM-8 3 x 4 Stroke 8 Cy. 320 x 360 each-3370kW (4582bhp) Bergen Diesel AS-Norway Thrusters: 1 Thwart. FP thruster (f)
9603051 *LAMN7* -	**WESTERN MOSCOW** - **WA II LP** Western Bulk AS *Oslo* *Norway (NIS)* MMSI: 257014000	**32,839** 19,559 57,970 T/cm 59.2	Class: NV (BV)	**2011-10 Yangzhou Dayang Shipbuilding Co Ltd — Yangzhou JS** Yd No: DY3069 Loa 189.99 (BB) Br ex - Dght 12.950 Lbp 185.00 Br md 32.26 Dpth 18.00 Welded, 1 dk	**(A21A2BC) Bulk Carrier** Grain: 71,549; Bale: 69,760 Compartments: 5 Ho, ER 5 Ha: ER Cranes: 4x35t	**1 oil engine** driving 1 FP propeller Total Power: 8,700kW (11,829hp) 14.3kn MAN-B&W 6S50MC-C 1 x 2 Stroke 6 Cy. 500 x 2000 8700kW (11829bhp) Doosan Engine Co Ltd-South Korea AuxGen: 3 x 610kW 60Hz a.c
9032953 *WDE6616* -	**WESTERN NAVIGATOR** - **Western Towboat Co** - *Seattle, WA* *United States of America* MMSI: 303177000 Official number: 973968	**216** 64 -		**1991-05 Western Towboat Co — Seattle WA** Yd No: 8 Loa 28.65 Br ex - Dght 4.267 Lbp - Br md 8.62 Dpth 4.62 Welded, 1 dk	**(B32A2ST) Tug**	**2 oil engines** sr geared to sc. shafts driving 2 FP propellers Total Power: 2,648kW (3,600hp) 10.0kn Caterpillar 3516TA 2 x Vee 4 Stroke 16 Cy. 170 x 190 each-1324kW (1800bhp) Caterpillar Inc-USA AuxGen: 2 x 60kW 208V 60Hz a.c Fuel: 210.0 (d.f.) 8.5pd
9187514 *3FEN9* -	**WESTERN NEPTUNE** - **GECOSHIP AS** WesternGeco AS *Panama* *Panama* MMSI: 357268000 Official number: 2813501CH	**8,369** 2,511 4,538	Class: NV	**1999-11 Ulstein Verft AS — Ulsteinvik** Yd No: 242 Loa 92.50 (BB) Br ex 23.90 Dght 7.300 Lbp 80.10 Br md 23.00 Dpth 9.00 Welded, 1 dk	**(B31A2SR) Research Survey Vessel** Ice Capable	**2 oil engines** reduction geared to sc. shaft (s) driving 2 CP propellers Total Power: 7,950kW (10,808hp) 16.0kn Normo BRM-9 2 x 4 Stroke 9 Cy. 320 x 360 each-3975kW (5404bhp) Ulstein Bergen AS-Norway AuxGen: 2 x 2400kW 450V 60Hz a.c, 2 x 1440kW 450V 60Hz a.c Thrusters: 1 Tunnel thruster (f)
9374002 *LAJH7* -	**WESTERN OSLO** *ex* Gem of Madras *-2009* **Lyngholmen Shipping AS** Western Bulk AS *Oslo* *Norway (NIS)* MMSI: 257460000	**31,532** 18,767 56,548 T/cm 56.9	Class: NV (NK)	**2008-02 IHI Marine United Inc — Yokohama KN** Yd No: 3238 Loa 190.00 (BB) Br ex - Dght 12.735 Lbp 185.00 Br md 32.26 Dpth 18.10 Welded, 1 dk	**(A21A2BC) Bulk Carrier** Grain: 72,111; Bale: 67,110 Compartments: 5 Ho, ER 5 Ha: 4 (20.9 x 18.6)ER (14.6 x 18.6) Cranes: 4x35t	**1 oil engine** driving 1 FP propeller Total Power: 8,890kW (12,087hp) 14.5kn Wartsila 6RT-flex50 1 x 2 Stroke 6 Cy. 500 x 2050 8890kW (12087bhp) Diesel United Ltd.-Aioi AuxGen: 4 x 342kW a.c Fuel: 2360.0
7508893 *WDD5296* -	**WESTERN PACIFIC** *ex* Madrugador *-1980* **Western Pacific Fisheries Inc** - SatCom: Inmarsat C 433857810 *Honolulu, HI* *United States of America* MMSI: 367666000 Official number: 564010	**2,024** 1,170 -		**1975-04 Campbell Industries — San Diego, Ca** Yd No: 105 Loa 66.53 Br ex 12.20 Dght - Lbp 58.83 Br md - Dpth 5.80 Welded, 1 dk	**(B11B2FV) Fishing Vessel**	**1 oil engine** driving 1 FP propeller Total Power: 2,611kW (3,550hp) EMD (Electro-Motive) 20-645-E7 1 x Vee 2 Stroke 20 Cy. 230 x 254 2611kW (3550bhp) General Motors Corp.Electro-Motive Div.-La Grange
7050212 *WY5510* -	**WESTERN PACIFIC** *ex* Gulf Gypsy *-1980* **Wes Pac Boat Co** - *Anchorage, AK* *United States of America* Official number: 517957	*132* 90 -		**1968 Marine Builders, Inc. — Mobile, Al** L reg 22.86 Br ex 6.84 Dght - Lbp - Br md - Dpth 3.41 Welded	**(B11B2FV) Fishing Vessel**	**1 oil engine** driving 1 FP propeller Total Power: 368kW (500hp)
9050448 *HP7161* -	**WESTERN PATRIOT** - **GECOSHIP AS** WesternGeco Fleet Management SatCom: Inmarsat C 435227410 *Panama* *Panama* MMSI: 352274000 Official number: 2093293G	**3,586** 1,076 2,925	Class: NV	**1993-04 Ulstein Verft AS — Ulsteinvik** Yd No: 233 Loa 78.00 Br ex - Dght 5.915 Lbp 67.70 Br md 17.00 Dpth 7.60 Welded, 3 dks	**(B31A2SR) Research Survey Vessel** Ice Capable	**2 oil engines** with clutches, flexible couplings & sr geared to sc. shafts driving 2 CP propellers Total Power: 4,858kW (6,604hp) 15.6kn Normo BRM-6 2 x 4 Stroke 6 Cy. 320 x 360 each-2429kW (3302bhp) Ulstein Bergen AS-Norway AuxGen: 2 x 1600kW 440V 60Hz a.c, 1 x 1070kW 440V 60Hz a.c Thrusters: 1 Thwart. CP thruster (f) Fuel: 1400.0 (d.f.)
9010125 *3EYQ8* -	**WESTERN PRIDE** - **GECOSHIP AS** WesternGeco Fleet Management SatCom: Inmarsat C 435208910 *Panama* *Panama* MMSI: 352089000 Official number: 1999392F	**2,945** 883 -	Class: NV	**1991-07 Ulstein Verft AS — Ulsteinvik** Yd No: 225 Loa 71.50 Br ex - Dght 5.915 Lbp 61.20 Br md 17.00 Dpth 7.60 Welded	**(B31A2SR) Research Survey Vessel** Ice Capable	**2 oil engines** driving 2 FP propellers Total Power: 4,856kW (6,602hp) 15.0kn Normo BRM-6 2 x 4 Stroke 6 Cy. 320 x 360 each-2428kW (3301bhp) Bergen Diesel AS-Norway Thrusters: 1 Tunnel thruster (f)
5042986 *WDC5555* -	**WESTERN QUEEN** *ex* Coastal Voyager *-1980* *ex* Viceroy *-1980* *ex* Bertha Ann *-1971* *ex* Cpl. John J. Pinder, Jr. *-1971* **Western Queen Fisheries LLC** - *Seattle, WA* *United States of America* MMSI: 366665430 Official number: 284906	**803** 371 -	Class: (AB)	**1945 Ingalls SB. Corp. — Decatur, Al** Yd No: 608 Converted From: General Cargo Ship-1978 L reg 50.75 Br ex 9.76 Dght 3.061 Lbp 50.30 Br md 9.71 Dpth 4.37 Welded, 1 dk	**(B11B2FV) Fishing Vessel** Compartments: 2 Ho, ER 2 Ha: ER	**2 oil engines** driving 2 FP propellers Total Power: 832kW (1,132hp) General Motors 6-278A 2 x 2 Stroke 6 Cy. 222 x 267 each-416kW (566bhp) General Motors Corp-USA Fuel: 74.0
7437214 *WBN3008* -	**WESTERN RANGER** *ex* Oio *-1993* **Western Towboat Co** - *Seattle, WA* *United States of America* MMSI: 367579000 Official number: 516924	**328** - -	Class: (AB)	**1968 Halter Marine Services, Inc. — New Orleans, La** Yd No: 207 Loa - Br ex - Dght 4.420 Lbp 31.88 Br md 9.45 Dpth 5.01 Welded, 1 dk	**(B32A2ST) Tug**	**2 oil engines** reverse reduction geared to sc. shafts driving 2 FP propellers Total Power: 1,250kW (1,700hp) Caterpillar D398TA 2 x Vee 4 Stroke 12 Cy. 159 x 203 each-625kW (850bhp) Caterpillar Tractor Co-USA AuxGen: 2 x 60kW Fuel: 283.5 (d.f.)
7926394 *ZMNN* -	**WESTERN RANGER** - **Sanford Ltd** - *Nelson* *New Zealand* Official number: 394707	**312** 96 300		**1981-02 Whangarei Eng. & Construction Co. Ltd. — Whangarei** Yd No: 160 Loa 35.97 Br ex 9.31 Dght 3.582 Lbp 33.08 Br md 9.29 Dpth 4.14 Welded, 1 dk	**(B11B2FV) Fishing Vessel**	**1 oil engine** geared to sc. shaft driving 1 FP propeller Total Power: 827kW (1,124hp) 12.0kn Caterpillar D399SCAC 1 x Vee 4 Stroke 16 Cy. 159 x 203 827kW (1124bhp) Caterpillar Tractor Co-USA
9017757 *3ELY9* -	**WESTERN REGENT** - **GECOSHIP AS** WesternGeco AS SatCom: Inmarsat C 435262910 *Panama* *Panama* MMSI: 352629000 Official number: 2026492J	**6,398** 1,920 2,926	Class: NV	**1992-04 Ulstein Verft AS — Ulsteinvik** Yd No: 232 Loa 92.50 Br ex - Dght 7.515 Lbp 80.00 Br md 20.00 Dpth 9.00 Welded, 3 dks	**(B31A2SR) Research Survey Vessel** Ice Capable	**3 diesel electric oil engines** driving 3 gen. each 3200kW 1 gen. of 600kW Connecting to 2 elec. motors driving 2 FP propellers Total Power: 10,110kW (13,746hp) 16.0kn Normo BRM-8 3 x 4 Stroke 8 Cy. 320 x 360 each-3370kW (4582bhp) Bergen Diesel AS-Norway Thrusters: 1 Thwart. FP thruster (f)

IMO / Call sign	Name / Owner / Manager / Registry	Tonnage	Class	Builder / Dimensions	Type / Capacity	Machinery
7534713 WAX9143 -	**WESTERN SEA** **Western Sea Inc** - *Boston, MA* *United States of America* Official number: 563802	*170* 115 -		**1975 Win-Mar Construction, Inc. — New Bern, NC** L reg 23.99 Br ex 7.32 Dght - Lbp - Br md - Dpth 3.38 Welded, 1 dk	**(B11B2FV) Fishing Vessel**	**1 oil engine** driving 1 FP propeller Total Power: 331kW (450hp)
9660619 DUEQ -	**WESTERN SEATTLE** **Ratu Shipping Co SA** Nisshin Shipping Co Ltd (Nisshin Kaiun KK) *Manila* *Philippines* MMSI: 548868000	**32,350** 19,448 57,689 T/cm 57.4	Class: BV NK (Class contemplated)	**2014-01 Tsuneishi Group (Zhoushan) Shipbuilding Inc — Daishan County ZJ** Yd No: SS-136 Loa 190.00 (BB) Br ex - Dght 12.800 Lbp 185.60 Br md 32.26 Dpth 18.00 Welded, 1 dk	**(A21A2BC) Bulk Carrier** Grain: 72,360; Bale: 70,557 Compartments: 5 Ho, ER 5 Ha: ER Cranes: 4x30t	**1 oil engine** driving 1 FP propeller Total Power: 8,360kW (11,366hp) 14.5kn MAN-B&W 6S50MC-C 1 x 2 Stroke 6 Cy. 500 x 2000 8360kW (11366bhp) Mitsui Engineering & Shipbuilding CLtd-Japan
8131374 5VCK6 -	**WESTERN SHORE** **Faruck Iftikhar Chatha** m/s Canadian Sea Supplies *Lome* *Togo* MMSI: 671417000	**748** 224 350	Class: (AB)	**1982-09 Quality Shipbuilders Inc. — Moss Point, Ms** Yd No: 117 Loa 47.63 Br ex - Dght 3.744 Lbp - Br md 11.59 Dpth 3.97 Welded, 1 dk	**(B31A2SR) Research Survey Vessel**	**2 oil engines** reverse reduction geared to sc. shafts driving 2 CP propellers Total Power: 1,656kW (2,252hp) 8.0kn Caterpillar D399SCAC 2 x Vee 4 Stroke 16 Cy. 159 x 203 each-828kW (1126bhp) Caterpillar Tractor Co-USA AuxGen: 2 x 230kW a.c Thrusters: 1 Directional thruster (f)
9254501 DYKK -	**WESTERN SINGAPORE** *ex* Bright Bulker *-2008* **Ratu Shipping Co SA** Nisshin Shipping Co Ltd (Nisshin Kaiun KK) *Manila* *Philippines* MMSI: 548652000 Official number: MNLA000583	**30,011** 17,843 52,239 T/cm 55.5	Class: BV	**2003-02 Tsuneishi Heavy Industries (Cebu) Inc — Balamban** Yd No: SC-035 Loa 189.90 (BB) Br ex - Dght 12.000 Lbp 179.84 Br md 32.26 Dpth 17.00 Welded, 1 dk	**(A21A2BC) Bulk Carrier** Grain: 67,500; Bale: 65,600 Compartments: 5 Ho, ER 5 Ha: 4 (21.0 x 18.4)ER (20.4 x 18.4) Cranes: 4x30t	**1 oil engine** driving 1 FP propeller Total Power: 7,800kW (10,605hp) 14.5kn B&W 6S50MC 1 x 2 Stroke 6 Cy. 500 x 1910 7800kW (10605bhp) Mitsui Engineering & Shipbuilding CLtd-Japan AuxGen: 3 x 440kW 450/100V 60Hz a.c
9050450 3EIL5 -	**WESTERN SPIRIT** *ex* Eastern Spirit *-2006* *ex* Western Spirit *-2001* **Chouest Cyprus Marine Ltd** WesternGeco Fleet Management *Panama* *Panama* MMSI: 372293000 Official number: 35166PEXTF3	**4,447** 1,335 2,925	Class: NV	**1993-10 Ulstein Verft AS — Ulsteinvik** Yd No: 234 Loa 78.00 Br ex - Dght 5.915 Lbp 67.70 Br md 17.00 Dpth 7.60 Welded, 3 dks	**(B31A2SR) Research Survey Vessel** Ice Capable	**2 oil engines** with clutches, flexible couplings & sr geared to sc. shafts driving 2 CP propellers Total Power: 4,858kW (6,604hp) 15.6kn Normo BRM-6 2 x 4 Stroke 6 Cy. 320 x 360 each-2429kW (3302bhp) Ulstein Bergen AS-Norway AuxGen: 2 x 1600kW 440V 60Hz a.c, 1 x 1070kW 440V 60Hz a.c Thrusters: 1 Thwart. CP thruster (f) Fuel: 1400.0 (d.f.)
8842480 P2V4725 -	**WESTERN STAR** **Coral Trader Ltd** Coral Sea Shipping Lines Pty Ltd SatCom: Inmarsat C 455300056 *Port Moresby* *Papua New Guinea* MMSI: 553111164 Official number: 000446	**2,318** 1,142 2,945	Class: AB	**1990-03 Sing Koon Seng Shipbuilding & Engineering Ltd — Singapore** (Aft section) Yd No: 301 **1988 Sing Koon Seng Shipbuilding & Engineering Ltd — Singapore** (Fwd section) Yd No: 680 **2000 Singapore Technologies Shipbuilding & Engineering Ltd. — Singapore** (Joined by) Converted From: General Cargo Ship-2000 Lengthened & Joined-2000 Loa 80.40 Br ex - Dght 3.710 Lbp 71.40 Br md 17.50 Dpth 4.60 Welded, 1 dk	**(A21B2BO) Ore Carrier** Grain: 1,444; Liq: 2,172 TEU 108 C. 108/20' Compartments: 1 Ho/Ta, ER	**2 oil engines** reverse reduction geared to sc. shafts driving 2 FP propellers Total Power: 1,856kW (2,524hp) 10.0kn Kromhout 6FHD240G 2 x 4 Stroke 6 Cy. 240 x 260 each-928kW (1262bhp) Stork Wartsila Diesel BV-Netherlands AuxGen: 2 x 177kW a.c, 1 x 170kW a.c
8423806 WDE6437 -	**WESTERN STAR** **Georgia-Pacific Consumer Products LP** - *Portland, OR* *United States of America* Official number: 275206	*177* 120 -		**1957-01 Gunderson Brothers Engineering Corp — Portland OR** Yd No: 4640 Loa - Br ex - Dght - Lbp 23.78 Br md 7.93 Dpth 3.05 Welded, 1 dk	**(B32A2ST) Tug**	**1 oil engine** driving 1 FP propeller Total Power: 588kW (799hp) Enterprise DMG8 1 x 4 Stroke 8 Cy. 305 x 381 588kW (799bhp) General Metals Corp.-San Francisco, Ca
7365813 EI6645 -	**WESTERN STAR** *ex* Lilly L *-2002* *ex* Pieter Senior *-2002* *ex* Jacoba Hermina *-2001* *ex* Twee Gebroeders *-1993* *ex* Willem en Klaas *-1979* **Gary & John Brosnan, Oliver Keane & Tom Kennedy** *Wexford* *Irish Republic* Official number: 403330	**220** 66 -		**1974-10 Scheepswerf Vooruit B.V. — Zaandam** Yd No: 347 Lengthened-1986 Loa 33.81 Br ex 7.19 Dght 2.850 Lbp 30.36 Br md 7.17 Dpth 3.81 Welded, 1 dk	**(B11B2FV) Fishing Vessel**	**1 oil engine** driving 1 FP propeller Total Power: 912kW (1,240hp) 10.0kn De Industrie 8D7HD 1 x 4 Stroke 8 Cy. 305 x 460 912kW (1240bhp) B.V. Motorenfabriek "De Industrie"-Alphen a/d Rijn
9559688 LALN7 -	**WESTERN STAVANGER** *launched as* Shinyo Quality *-2010* **Western Bulk Shipowning II AS** Western Bulk AS SatCom: Inmarsat C 425900210 *Oslo* *Norway (NIS)* MMSI: 259002000	**20,846** 11,800 32,581	Class: NV (AB)	**2010-08 Jiangsu Zhenjiang Shipyard Co Ltd — Zhenjiang JS** Yd No: VZJ432-0602 Loa 179.90 (BB) Br ex 28.43 Dght 10.170 Lbp 171.50 Br md 28.40 Dpth 14.10 Welded, 1 dk	**(A21A2BC) Bulk Carrier** Grain: 43,694 Compartments: 5 Ho, ER 5 Ha: ER Cranes: 4x30.5t	**1 oil engine** driving 1 FP propeller Total Power: 7,900kW (10,741hp) 14.0kn MAN-B&W 5S50MC-C 1 x 2 Stroke 5 Cy. 500 x 2000 7900kW (10741bhp) AuxGen: 3 x 440kW a.c Fuel: 150.0 (d.f.) 1500.0 (r.f.)
9603063 LANM7 -	**WESTERN TEXAS** **WA III LP** Western Bulk AS *Oslo* *Norway (NIS)* MMSI: 257094000	**32,839** 19,559 57,970 T/cm 59.2	Class: NV (BV)	**2011-11 Yangzhou Dayang Shipbuilding Co Ltd — Yangzhou JS** Yd No: DY3070 Loa 189.99 (BB) Br ex - Dght 12.950 Lbp 185.00 Br md 32.26 Dpth 18.00 Welded, 1 dk	**(A21A2BC) Bulk Carrier** Grain: 71,549; Bale: 69,760 Compartments: 5 Ho, ER 5 Ha: ER Cranes: 4x35t	**1 oil engine** driving 1 FP propeller Total Power: 9,960kW (13,542hp) 14.3kn MAN-B&W 6S50MC-C 1 x 2 Stroke 6 Cy. 500 x 2000 9960kW (13542bhp) AuxGen: 3 x 610kW a.c
8962486 WCX4599 -	**WESTERN TITAN** **Western Towboat Co** - *Seattle, WA* *United States of America* MMSI: 338854000 Official number: 1052805	**486** 145 -		**1997 Western Towboat Co — Seattle WA** Yd No: 11 Loa 30.57 Br ex - Dght - Lbp - Br md 10.66 Dpth 6.15 Welded, 1 dk	**(B32A2ST) Tug**	**2 oil engines** gearing integral to driving 2 Z propellers Total Power: 3,132kW (4,258hp) Caterpillar 3516B 2 x Vee 4 Stroke 16 Cy. 170 x 190 each-1566kW (2129bhp) Caterpillar Inc-USA AuxGen: 2 x 135kW 60Hz a.c
9593361 HPNC -	**WESTERN TOKYO** **Solar Ace Corp** Sojitz Marine & Engineering Corp (SOMEC) SatCom: Inmarsat C 437338410 *Panama* *Panama* MMSI: 373384000 Official number: 4393812	**31,538** 18,765 55,831 T/cm 56.9	Class: NK	**2012-06 IHI Marine United Inc — Kure HS** Yd No: 3324 Loa 190.00 (BB) Br ex - Dght 12.735 Lbp 185.00 Br md 32.26 Dpth 18.10 Welded, 1 dk	**(A21A2BC) Bulk Carrier** Grain: 72,062; Bale: 67,062 Compartments: 5 Ho, ER 5 Ha: ER Cranes: 4x30t	**1 oil engine** driving 1 FP propeller Total Power: 8,890kW (12,087hp) 14.5kn Wartsila 6RT-flex50 1 x 2 Stroke 6 Cy. 500 x 2050 8890kW (12087bhp) Diesel United Ltd.-Aioi Fuel: 2490.0
9609718 5BVA3 -	**WESTERN TOSCA** **Ridgewave Shipping Ltd** Westlake SA *Limassol* *Cyprus* MMSI: 210292000	**22,668** 11,856 37,000	Class: BV	**2013-02 Hyundai Mipo Dockyard Co Ltd — Ulsan** Yd No: 6111 Loa 187.00 (BB) Br ex - Dght 10.400 Lbp 178.00 Br md 28.60 Dpth 15.60 Welded, 1 dk	**(A21A2BC) Bulk Carrier** Grain: 49,729 Compartments: 5 Ho, ER 5 Ha: ER Cranes: 4	**1 oil engine** driving 1 FP propeller Total Power: 7,700kW (10,469hp) 14.3kn MAN-B&W 6S46MC-C 1 x 2 Stroke 6 Cy. 460 x 1932 7700kW (10469bhp) Hyundai Heavy Industries Co Ltd-South Korea AuxGen: 3 x 540kW 60Hz a.c Fuel: 1750.0
9187502 3FEO9 -	**WESTERN TRIDENT** **GECOSHIP AS** WesternGeco AS SatCom: Inmarsat C 435727010 *Panama* *Panama* MMSI: 357269000 Official number: 2637699CH	**8,369** 2,511 4,568	Class: NV	**1999-03 Ulstein Verft AS — Ulsteinvik** Yd No: 241 Loa 92.50 (BB) Br ex - Dght 7.300 Lbp 80.10 Br md 23.00 Dpth 9.00 Welded, 1 dk	**(B31A2SR) Research Survey Vessel** Ice Capable	**2 oil engines** reduction geared to sc. shafts driving 2 CP propellers Total Power: 7,944kW (10,800hp) 16.0kn Normo BRM-9 2 x 4 Stroke 9 Cy. 320 x 360 each-3972kW (5400bhp) Ulstein Bergen AS-Norway AuxGen: 2 x 2400kW 220/440V 60Hz a.c, 2 x 1440kW 220/440V 60Hz a.c Thrusters: 1 Thwart. FP thruster (f)

9030761 *P2V4810* -
WESTERN TRIUMPH
P&O Maritime Services (PNG) Ltd
-
SatCom: Inmarsat C 455300057
Port Moresby *Papua New Guinea*
MMSI: 553111147
Official number: 000483

2,768 Class: AB
830
3,686

1992-04 Sing Koon Seng Shipbuilding & Engineering Ltd — Singapore Yd No: 698
Converted From: General Cargo Ship-2002
New forept & Lengthened-2002
Loa 88.20 Br ex - Dght 3.000
Lbp 85.20 Br md 17.50 Dpth 5.40
Welded, 1 dk

(A21B2BO) Ore Carrier
Grain: 1,800

2 oil engines driving 2 FP propellers
Total Power: 1,766kW (2,402hp) 10.0kn
Wartsila 6R22
2 x 4 Stroke 6 Cy. 220 x 240 each-883kW (1201bhp)
Wartsila Diesel Oy-Finland

8333348 *CFB9494* -
WESTERN TUGGER
ex Doug McKeil *-2005* *ex* Dawson B. *-1997*
ex Frankie D *-1997* *ex* Gaelic Challenge *-1995*
ex Taurus *-1989* *ex* LT-643 *-1977*
Midnight Marine Ltd
Miller Shipping Ltd
St John's, NL *Canada*
MMSI: 316002104
Official number: 820322

389 Class: (AB)
117
-

1944 Jakobson Shipyard, Inc. — Oyster Bay, NY
Yd No: 307
Loa - Br ex - Dght 4.837
Lbp 35.06 Br md 9.15 Dpth 5.49
Welded, 1 dk

(B32A2ST) Tug

1 oil engine geared to sc. shaft driving 1 FP propeller
Total Power: 1,416kW (1,925hp)
EMD (Electro-Motive) 16-645-E6
1 x Vee 2 Stroke 16 Cy. 230 x 254 1416kW (1925bhp) (new engine 1979)
General Motors Detroit DieselAllison Divn-USA

9095008 *WDD5460* -
WESTERN VENTURE
Irish Venture Inc
-
Gloucester, MA *United States of America*
MMSI: 367158720
Official number: 1194562

1,115
334
-

2006-01 Boconco, Inc. — Bayou La Batre, Al
Yd No: 125
L reg 44.59 Br ex - Dght -
Lbp - Br md 12.19 Dpth 4.26
Welded, 1 dk

(B11A2FT) Trawler

2 oil engines reduction geared to sc. shafts driving 2 Propellers
Total Power: 2,460kW (3,344hp)
Caterpillar 3512B-TA
2 x Vee 4 Stroke 12 Cy. 170 x 190 each-1230kW (1672bhp)
Caterpillar Inc-USA
AuxGen: 2 x 550kW a.c
Thrusters: 1 Tunnel thruster (f); 1 Tunnel thruster (a)

8501971 *P2V4718* -
WESTERN VENTURER
ex United Venturer *-1991*
P&O Maritime Services (PNG) Ltd
-
SatCom: Inmarsat A 1543315
Port Moresby *Papua New Guinea*
Official number: 000435

185
57
-

1985-04 Dashwood Shipyard Co. Ltd. — Hong Kong Yd No: 150
Loa 24.95 (BB) Br ex 9.02 Dght 2.032
Lbp - Br md - Dpth 2.58
Welded

(B31A2SR) Research Survey Vessel

2 oil engines geared to sc. shafts driving 2 FP propellers
9.0kn
Caterpillar
2 x 4 Stroke
Caterpillar Inc-USA

6728070 - -
WESTERN VIKING
ex Ouingondy *-1991*
Magone Marine Service Inc
-
Dutch Harbor, AK *United States of America*
Official number: 507161

199
135
-

1967 Dorchester Shipbuilding Corp. — Dorchester, NJ
Converted From: Stern Trawler-2011
Loa 30.64 Br ex - Dght 3.048
Lbp 25.61 Br md 7.36 Dpth 4.12
Welded, 3 dks

(B34L2QU) Utility Vessel

1 oil engine reduction geared to sc. shaft driving 1 FP propeller
Total Power: 625kW (850hp)
Caterpillar D398TA
1 x Vee 4 Stroke 12 Cy. 159 x 203 625kW (850bhp)
Caterpillar Tractor Co-USA

9334337 *EISZ* SO 718
WESTERN VIKING
ex Western Viking III *-2006*
F D Premier Fishing
Frank Doherty
Sligo *Irish Republic*
MMSI: 250090000
Official number: 403934

834 Class: NV
250
992

2005-09 Stal-Rem SA — Gdansk (Hull)
2005-09 Karstensens Skibsvaerft A/S — Skagen
Yd No: 396
Loa 51.00 Br ex 11.31 Dght 5.800
Lbp 45.60 Br md 11.20 Dpth 7.40
Welded, 1 dk

(B11B2FV) Fishing Vessel

1 oil engine geared to sc. shaft driving 1 CP propeller
Total Power: 2,999kW (4,077hp)
MAN-B&W 9L27/38
1 x 4 Stroke 9 Cy. 270 x 380 2999kW (4077bhp)
MAN B&W Diesel A/S-Denmark
AuxGen: 1 x a.c, 1 x a.c, 1 x a.c
Thrusters: 1 Tunnel thruster (f); 1 Tunnel thruster (a)

7604192 *WCZ7785* -
WESTERN WAVE
Sprat Inc
-
Portland, ME *United States of America*
Official number: 554607

159
108
-

1974 Barbour Boat Works Inc. — New Bern, NC
L reg 20.64 Br ex - Dght -
Lbp - Br md 7.32 Dpth 3.71
Welded

(B11B2FV) Fishing Vessel

1 oil engine driving 1 FP propeller
Total Power: 246kW (334hp)

9490820 *LAMQ7* -
WESTERN WILTON
WA I LP
Western Bulk AS
Oslo *Norway (NIS)*
MMSI: 259818000

32,839 Class: NV (BV)
19,559
57,970
T/cm
59.2

2011-04 Yangzhou Dayang Shipbuilding Co Ltd — Yangzhou JS Yd No: DY3031
Loa 189.99 (BB) Br ex - Dght 12.950
Lbp 185.00 Br md 32.26 Dpth 18.00
Welded, 1 dk

(A21A2BC) Bulk Carrier
Grain: 71,549; Bale: 69,760
Compartments: 5 Ho, ER
5 Ha: ER
Cranes: 4x35t

1 oil engine driving 1 FP propeller
Total Power: 9,960kW (13,542hp) 14.3kn
MAN-B&W 6S50MC-C
1 x 2 Stroke 6 Cy. 500 x 2000 9960kW (13542bhp)
AuxGen: 3 x 700kW a.c

9071492 *P2V4393* -
WESTERN ZENITH
P&O Maritime Services (PNG) Ltd
-
Port Moresby *Papua New Guinea*
MMSI: 553111145
Official number: 000483

2,768 Class: AB
642
3,655

1993-01 President Marine Pte Ltd — Singapore
Yd No: 137
Converted From: General Cargo Ship-1999
Lengthened & Deepened & New forept-1999
Loa 88.00 Br ex - Dght 3.712
Lbp 84.94 Br md 17.50 Dpth 4.60
Welded

(A21B2BO) Ore Carrier
Grain: 2,206
TEU 36 C. 36/20'

2 oil engines reverse reduction geared to sc. shafts driving 2 FP propellers
Total Power: 1,766kW (2,402hp) 10.0kn
Wartsila 6R22D
2 x 4 Stroke 6 Cy. 220 x 240 each-883kW (1201bhp)
Wartsila Diesel Oy-Finland
AuxGen: 2 x 108kW a.c
Fuel: 537.0

6815639 *SMZN* -
WESTERO AV HONO
ex Westero *-2011* *ex* Bentin *-2002*
ex Havset *-1986* *ex* Busen Junior *-1982*
ex Hordagutt *-1979*
Tomas Mikael Larsson
Hono *Sweden*
MMSI: 266011000

272
81
-

1968 Skaalurens Skipsbyggeri AS — Rosendal
Yd No: 213/27
Loa 30.79 Br ex 7.04 Dght -
Lbp 27.01 Br md 7.01 Dpth 3.59
Welded, 1 dk

(B11B2FV) Fishing Vessel
Compartments: 2 Ho, ER
2 Ha: (2.6 x 1.9) (1.0 x 0.9)ER
Derricks: 1x3t

1 oil engine driving 1 CP propeller
Total Power: 397kW (540hp) 11.0kn
Wichmann 5ACA
1 x 2 Stroke 5 Cy. 280 x 420 397kW (540bhp)
Wichmann Motorfabrikk AS-Norway
AuxGen: 1 x 20kW 220V 50Hz a.c, 1 x 6kW 220V 50Hz a.c
Fuel: 30.0 (d.f.)

9569009 *ORPV* -
WESTERSCHELDE
Wandelaar Invest SA
DAB Vloot
Ostend *Belgium*
MMSI: 205593000
Official number: 01 00796 2011

227 Class: GL
67
14

2011-12 Schiffs- u. Yachtwerft Abeking & Rasmussen GmbH & Co. — Lemwerder
Yd No: 6473
Loa 25.65 Br ex - Dght 2.700
Lbp 23.25 Br md 13.00 Dpth 5.90
Welded, 1 dk

(B34N2QP) Pilot Vessel
Hull Material: Aluminium Alloy

2 diesel electric oil engines driving 2 gen. each 900kW Connecting to 2 elec. motors each (900kW) driving 2 FP propellers
Total Power: 1,576kW (2,142hp) 18.0kn
M.T.U. 12V2000M70
2 x Vee 4 Stroke 12 Cy. 130 x 150 each-788kW (1071bhp)
MTU Friedrichshafen GmbH-Friedrichshafen

9316347 *A8IG9* -
WESTERTAL
ex CMA CGM Melbourne *-2008*
completed as Westertal *-2006*
Westertal Shipping GmbH & Co KG
Hans Peterson & Soehne GmbH & Co KG
Monrovia *Liberia*
MMSI: 636090975
Official number: 90975

32,060 Class: NV
12,611
38,700

2006-02 Stocznia Gdanska - Grupa Stoczni Gdynia SA — Gdansk Yd No: 8184/10
Loa 210.85 (BB) Br ex - Dght 12.000
Lbp 195.94 Br md 32.25 Dpth 19.00
Welded, 1 dk

(A33A2CC) Container Ship (Fully Cellular)
TEU 2732 C Ho 1222 TEU C Dk 1510 TEU incl 450 ref C.
Ice Capable

1 oil engine driving 1 FP propeller
Total Power: 21,733kW (29,548hp) 22.5kn
MAN-B&W 7S70MC-C
1 x 2 Stroke 7 Cy. 700 x 2800 21733kW (29548bhp)
H Cegielski Poznan SA-Poland
AuxGen: 4 x a.c
Thrusters: 1 Tunnel thruster (f)

9201970 *PBJC* -
WESTEWIND
ex Agenor *-2008* *ex* Hilja Marjan *-2005*
J L Weststrate
Wagenborg Shipping BV
245029000
Wemeldinge *Netherlands*
MMSI: 245029000
Official number: 37878

2,080 Class: BV
1,168
2,815

2003-02 Ceskoslovenska Plavba Labska a.s. (CSPL) — Decin (Hull)
2003-02 Scheepswerf Peters B.V. — Kampen
Yd No: 473
Loa 88.95 Br ex - Dght 4.350
Lbp 84.95 Br md 12.40 Dpth 5.65
Welded, 1 dk

(A31A2GX) General Cargo Ship
Grain: 3,877
Compartments: 1 Ho, ER
1 Ha: (62.4 x 10.2)ER
Ice Capable

1 oil engine reduction geared to sc. shaft driving 1 FP propeller
Total Power: 1,320kW (1,795hp) 10.5kn
Wartsila 8L20
1 x 4 Stroke 8 Cy. 200 x 280 1320kW (1795bhp)
Wartsila Nederland BV-Netherlands

6721357 *OJPJ* -
WESTFJORD
ex Vastfjord *-2012* *ex* Westfjord *-2011*
ex Vastfjord *-2006*
Hellstroms Fisk Ab
-
Kaskinen *Finland*

422 Class: (NV)
121
-

1967 Broderna Jonssons Torrdocka — Lidkoping
Yd No: 15
Loa 38.94 Br ex 7.83 Dght 2.801
Lbp 29.11 Br md 7.80 Dpth 3.87
Welded, 1 dk

(B11B2FV) Fishing Vessel
Compartments: 2 Ho, ER
5 Ha: (0.9 x 0.9) (0.9 x 1.3) (1.5 x 1.5)2 (1.2 x 1.5)ER
Derricks: 1x3.5t,1x0.5t; Winches: 1
Ice Capable

1 oil engine driving 1 FP propeller
Total Power: 883kW (1,201hp)
Jonkopings
1 x Vee 4 Stroke 10 Cy. 260 x 400 883kW (1201bhp)
AB Jonkopings Motorfabrik-Sweden

9196187 *PDBQ* -
WESTGARD
ex Sabinia *-2006*
Bore Westgard BV
Bore Ltd (Bore Oy Ab)
SatCom: Inmarsat C 424645710
Rotterdam *Netherlands*
MMSI: 246457000
Official number: 37043

2,868 Class: NV (LR) (BV)
1,613 Classed LR until 10/10/11
3,780
T/cm
11.0

2000-04 Scheepswerf Peters B.V. — Kampen
Yd No: 464
Loa 89.25 Br ex 13.40 Dght 5.670
Lbp 84.60 Br md 13.30 Dpth 7.15
Welded, 1 dk

(A31A2GX) General Cargo Ship
Grain: 5,829
TEU 208 C.Ho 112 TEU C.Dk 96 TEU
Compartments: 1 Ho, ER
1 Ha: (63.0 x 11.2)ER
Ice Capable

1 oil engine with flexible couplings & sr reverse geared to sc. shaft driving 1 CP propeller
Total Power: 1,800kW (2,447hp) 12.5kn
MaK 6M25
1 x 4 Stroke 6 Cy. 255 x 400 1800kW (2447bhp)
MaK Motoren GmbH & Co. KG-Kiel
AuxGen: 1 x 256kW 400V 50Hz a.c
Thrusters: 1 Thwart. FP thruster (f)
Fuel: 298.6 (d.f.) 8.0pd

No.	Name / Owner	Tonnage	Class	Builder / Dimensions	Type	Machinery
303642 IQDE6	**WESTGARTH** *ex Yashima -1992* **Svitzer Marine Ltd** - *Bristol* *United Kingdom* MMSI: 235029148 Official number: 720118	**266** 79 70	Class: LR **100A1** SS 04/2011 tug limited European trading area **LMC** Eq.Ltr: E; Cable: 300.0/24.0 U2	1983-05 **Hanasaki Zosensho K.K. — Yokosuka** Yd No: 190 Loa 32.11 Br ex 9.90 Dght 2.920 Lbp 30.82 Br md 8.81 Dpth 3.88 Welded, 1 dk	**(B32A2ST) Tug**	**2 oil engines** gearing integral to driving 2 Z propellers Total Power: 1,912kW (2,600hp) Niigata 6L25CXE 2 x 4 Stroke 6 Cy. 250 x 320 each-956kW (1300bhp) Niigata Engineering Co Ltd-Japan AuxGen: 2 x 64kW 220V 60Hz a.c
493224 5CN2	**WESTGATE** **Dresto Shipping Inc** Eastern Pacific Shipping Pte Ltd *Monrovia* *Liberia* MMSI: 636015739 Official number: 15739	**17,025** 10,108 28,202 T/cm 39.7	Class: NK	2011-03 **I-S Shipyard Co Ltd — Imabari EH** Yd No: S-A042 Loa 169.37 (BB) Br ex - Dght 9.819 Lbp 160.40 Br md 27.20 Dpth 13.60 Welded, 1 dk	**(A21A2BC) Bulk Carrier** Grain: 37,320; Bale: 35,742 Compartments: 5 Ho, ER 5 Ha: 4 (19.2 x 17.6)ER (13.6 x 16.0) Cranes: 4x30.5t	**1 oil engine** driving 1 FP propeller Total Power: 5,850kW (7,954hp) 14.0kn MAN-B&W 6S42MC 1 x 2 Stroke 6 Cy. 420 x 1764 5850kW (7954bhp) Makita Corp-Japan AuxGen: 3 x 440kW 60Hz a.c
837382 '03992	**WESTHINDER** **Deepsea Transport Systems Ltd** ADG Shipmanagement SIA *Panama* *Panama* Official number: 017531789PX	**462** 138 -		**1990 N.V. Scheepswerven L. de Graeve — Zeebrugge** Loa 40.68 Br ex - Dght - Lbp - Br md 9.09 Dpth - Welded, 1 dk	**(B11B2FV) Fishing Vessel**	**1 oil engine** driving 1 FP propeller Total Power: 880kW (1,196hp) MaK 1 x 4 Stroke 880kW (1196bhp) Krupp MaK Maschinenbau GmbH-Kiel
855487 /TJ8166	**WESTLING** **Harlan Dean Jr** - *Stryker, MT* *United States of America* Official number: 633577	*170* 51 -		**1981 Giddings Boat Works, Inc. — Charleston, Or** Loa - Br ex - Dght - Lbp 25.45 Br md 7.32 Dpth 2.38 Welded, 1 dk	**(B11B2FV) Fishing Vessel**	**1 oil engine** driving 1 FP propeller
520132 V7724	**WESTMINSTER** **Snow Shipping (Pte) Ltd** Komaya Shipping Co (Pte) Ltd SatCom: Inmarsat C 456635310 *Singapore* *Singapore* MMSI: 566353000 Official number: 394708	**7,222** 2,664 9,011 T/cm 20.7	Class: BV	2011-12 **K.K. Miura Zosensho — Saiki** Yd No: 1362 Loa 119.95 (BB) Br ex 19.04 Dght 7.600 Lbp 115.00 Br md 19.00 Dpth 10.00 Welded, 1 dk	**(A11B2TG) LPG Tanker** Double Bottom Entire Compartment Length Liq (Gas): 9,333 4 x Gas Tank (s); 4 independent (stl) cyl horizontal 4 Cargo Pump (s): 4x300m³/hr Manifold: Bow/CM: 55.7m	**1 oil engine** driving 1 FP propeller Total Power: 4,900kW (6,662hp) 15.0kn MAN-B&W 7S35MC 1 x 2 Stroke 7 Cy. 350 x 1400 4900kW (6662bhp) The Hanshin Diesel Works Ltd-Japan AuxGen: 2 x 480kW 450V 60Hz a.c Thrusters: 1 Tunnel thruster (f) Fuel: 397.0 (d.f.) 807.0 (r.f.)
243227 /DB5285	**WESTPAC EXPRESS** **Bali Westpac 2006 LLC** HMS Global Maritime Inc *Mobile, AL* *United States of America* MMSI: 369323000 Official number: 1145652	**8,403** 2,521 750 T/cm 6.5	Class: GL	2001-07 **Austal Ships Pty Ltd — Fremantle WA** Yd No: 130 Loa 101.00 (BB) Br ex - Dght 5.103 Lbp 86.21 Br md 26.65 Dpth 9.40 Welded	**(A36A2PR) Passenger/Ro-Ro Ship (Vehicles)** Hull Material: Aluminium Alloy Passengers: unberthed: 970 Bow door/ramp Len: 11.70 Wid: 10.00 Swl: 35 Stern door/ramp Len: 19.60 Wid: 10.80 Swl: 35 Lane-Len: 334 Cars: 96, Trailers: 16	**4 oil engines** with clutches, flexible couplings & reduction geared to sc. shafts driving 4 Water jets Total Power: 28,800kW (39,156hp) 34.0kn Caterpillar 3618TA 4 x Vee 4 Stroke 18 Cy. 280 x 300 each-7200kW (9789bhp) Caterpillar Inc-USA AuxGen: 4 x 280kW 400V 50Hz a.c Fuel: 278.0 (d.f.) 168.0pd
219408 5EN4	**WESTPHALIA** *ex Emirates Kabir -2013 ex APL Jakarta -2006* *completed as Julia -2003* *launched as Alessa -2003* **ms 'Hammonia Westphalia Nova' Schiffahrts GmbH & Co KG** Hammonia Reederei GmbH & Co KG *Monrovia* *Liberia* MMSI: 636092511 Official number: 92511	**35,824** 14,870 42,090 T/cm 62.0	Class: GL	2003-11 **Stocznia Szczecinska Nowa Sp z oo — Szczecin** Yd No: B178/I/07 Loa 220.32 (BB) Br ex 32.30 Dght 12.150 Lbp 210.20 Br md 32.24 Dpth 18.70 Welded, 1 dk	**(A33A2CC) Container Ship (Fully Cellular)** Grain: 62,500; Bale: 50,000 TEU 3091 C Ho 1408 TEU C Dk 1683 TEU incl 500 ref C. Compartments: 6 Cell Ho, ER 11 Ha: (12.6 x 18.0)10 (12.6 x 28.3)ER	**1 oil engine** driving 1 FP propeller Total Power: 25,228kW (34,300hp) 22.5kn B&W 7K80MC-C 1 x 2 Stroke 7 Cy. 800 x 2300 25228kW (34300bhp) H Cegielski Poznan SA-Poland AuxGen: 2 x 1200kW a.c, 2 x 1000kW a.c Thrusters: 1 Thwart. CP thruster (f) Fuel: 3397.0 (r.f.)
017396 /DB4299	**WESTPORT** **E & J Scallop Corp** - *New Bedford, MA* *United States of America* MMSI: 366896950 Official number: 619338	*196* 133 -		1980 **Bender Welding & Machine Co Inc — Mobile AL** Yd No: 758 L reg 26.86 Br ex 7.93 Dght - Lbp - Br md 7.62 Dpth 4.14 Welded, 1 dk	**(B11B2FV) Fishing Vessel**	**1 oil engine** geared to sc. shaft driving 1 FP propeller Total Power: 827kW (1,124hp) 11.5kn Caterpillar D399SCAC 1 x Vee 4 Stroke 16 Cy. 159 x 203 827kW (1124bhp) Caterpillar Tractor Co-USA
423249 MJW	**WESTPORT** **Holcim (New Zealand) Ltd** - *Lyttelton* *New Zealand* MMSI: 512000049 Official number: 343625	**3,091** 927 4,081	Class: LR ✠ **100A1** CS 01/2011 ✠ **LMC** **UMS** Eq.Ltr: S; Cable: U2	1976-01 **J.J. Sietas Schiffswerft — Hamburg** Yd No: 749 Loa 94.52 (BB) Br ex 14.25 Dght 5.849 Lbp 90.23 Br md 14.02 Dpth 6.25 Welded, 1 dk	**(A24A2BT) Cement Carrier** Grain: 3,007 Compartments: 2 Ho, ER Cranes: 1x3t	**2 oil engines** reduction geared to sc. shaft driving 1 CP propeller Total Power: 2,648kW (3,600hp) 13.5kn MaK 6M452AK 2 x 4 Stroke 6 Cy. 320 x 450 each-1324kW (1800bhp) MaK Maschinenbau GmbH-Kiel AuxGen: 1 x 220kW 420V 50Hz a.c Thrusters: 1 Thwart. FP thruster (f)
654921 GCW8	**WESTPORT 40M** - - *George Town* *Cayman Islands (British)* MMSI: 319465000 Official number: 743830	**333** 99 62	Class: AB	2013-01 **Westport Shipyard, Inc. — Westport, Wa** Yd No: 4009 Loa 39.60 Br ex - Dght 2.040 Lbp 34.03 Br md 7.92 Dpth 3.78 Bonded, 1 dk	**(X11A2YP) Yacht** Hull Material: Reinforced Plastic	**2 oil engines** reduction geared to sc. shafts driving 2 FP propellers Total Power: 4,320kW (5,874hp) 20.0kn M.T.U. 12V4000M73L 2 x Vee 4 Stroke 12 Cy. 165 x 190 each-2160kW (2937bhp) MTU Friedrichshafen GmbH-Friedrichshafen AuxGen: 2 x 92kW a.c Fuel: 37.0 (d.f.)
812849 /TH4325	**WESTRAC** **Western Towboat Co** - *Seattle, WA* *United States of America* MMSI: 366993010 Official number: 918736	*143* 97 -		1988-01 **Western Towboat Co — Seattle WA** Loa 23.17 Br ex 8.54 Dght 4.268 Lbp - Br md - Dpth 4.57 Welded, 1 dk	**(B32A2ST) Tug**	**2 oil engines** gearing integral to driving 2 Z propellers Total Power: 1,472kW (2,002hp) Caterpillar 3512TA 2 x Vee 4 Stroke 12 Cy. 170 x 190 each-736kW (1001bhp) Caterpillar Inc-USA AuxGen: 2 x 50kW 208V 60Hz a.c
587520 'NW6381	**WESTSEA ANNEMARIE** *ex Anne S -2010* **Westsea Marine Pty Ltd** - *Fremantle, WA* *Australia* MMSI: 503486600 Official number: 859619	**135** 40 187	Class: BV	2010-05 **Neptune Shipyards BV — Aalst (Nl)** Yd No: 381 Loa 21.50 Br ex - Dght 2.040 Lbp 20.25 Br md 9.00 Dpth 3.00 Welded, 1 dk	**(B34L2QU) Utility Vessel**	**2 oil engines** reduction geared to sc. shafts driving 2 FP propellers Total Power: 1,194kW (1,624hp) 10.0kn Cummins QSK19-M 2 x 4 Stroke 6 Cy. 159 x 159 each-597kW (812bhp) Cummins Engine Co Inc-USA AuxGen: 2 x 86kW 50Hz a.c
550905 'NW6402	**WESTSEA GAIL** *ex Hako 30 -2011* **Westsea Offshore Pte Ltd** - *Fremantle, WA* *Australia* MMSI: 503650000 Official number: 859715	**573** 172 332	Class: GL (AB)	2009-11 **Jiangsu Wuxi Shipyard Co Ltd — Wuxi JS** (Hull) Yd No: (1349) 2009-11 **Pacific Ocean Engineering & Trading Pte Ltd (POET) — Singapore** Yd No: 1349 Loa 41.80 Br ex 10.05 Dght 3.600 Lbp 37.40 Br md 10.00 Dpth 4.60 Welded, 1 dk	**(B21B20A) Anchor Handling Tug Supply**	**2 oil engines** reverse reduction geared to sc. shafts driving 2 FP propellers Total Power: 2,984kW (4,058hp) 11.0kn Mitsubishi S8U-MPTK 2 x 4 Stroke 8 Cy. 240 x 260 each-1492kW (2029bhp) Mitsubishi Heavy Industries Ltd-Japan AuxGen: 3 x 226kW 415V a.c Thrusters: 1 Tunnel thruster (f) Fuel: 225.0 (r.f.)
492658 'NW6088	**WESTSEA HAWK** *ex Westsea Jaguar -2009* **Westsea Investments Pty Ltd** - *Fremantle, WA* *Australia* MMSI: 503204800 Official number: 858481	**251** 76 137	Class: BV (NK)	2008-03 **PT Palma Progress Shipyard — Batam** Yd No: 284 Loa 29.50 Br ex - Dght 3.570 Lbp 27.00 Br md 9.00 Dpth 4.16 Welded, 1 dk	**(B32A2ST) Tug**	**2 oil engines** reduction geared to sc. shafts driving 2 FP propellers Total Power: 2,080kW (2,828hp) Mitsubishi S12R-MPTK 2 x Vee 4 Stroke 12 Cy. 170 x 180 each-1040kW (1414bhp) Mitsubishi Heavy Industries Ltd-Japan Fuel: 171.0 (d.f.)

LR/IMO No. / Call sign	Name / Owner / Manager / Port / Flag	Tonnage	Class	Builder / Dimensions	Type / Cargo	Machinery
9619658 *T2WQ3* -	**WESTSEA KESTREL** **C&D Prosper (Hong Kong) Shipping Co Ltd** Westsea Investments Pty Ltd *Funafuti* *Tuvalu* MMSI: 572300210	**646** 193 495	Class: BV	**2011-08 Yuexin Shipbuilding Co Ltd — Guangzhou GD** Yd No: 3128 Loa 45.00 Br ex - Dght 3.800 Lbp 39.40 Br md 11.80 Dpth 4.60 Welded, 1 dk	**(B21B20A) Anchor Handling Tug Supply**	**2 oil engines** reduction geared to sc. shafts driving 2 FP propellers Total Power: 3,130kW (4,256hp) Caterpillar 3516B-HD 2 x Vee 4 Stroke 16 Cy. 170 x 215 each-1565kW (2128bhp) Caterpillar Inc-USA AuxGen: 3 x 245kW 50Hz a.c Thrusters: 1 Tunnel thruster (f) Fuel: 520.0
8950873 *VJN3190* -	**WESTSEA PELICAN** *ex* Westsea Panther *-2012* *ex* Ocean Juliet *-2007* **Westsea Investments Pty Ltd** - *Fremantle, WA* *Australia* Official number: 858366	**144** 44 -	Class: GL	**1998-09 PT Nanindah Mutiara Shipyard — Batam** Yd No: T51 Loa - Br ex - Dght - Lbp 21.44 Br md 7.50 Dpth 4.15 Welded, 1 dk	**(B32A2ST) Tug**	**2 oil engines** reduction geared to sc. shafts driving 2 FP propellers Total Power: 940kW (1,278hp) 10.0kn Yanmar 6LAHM-STE 2 x 4 Stroke 6 Cy. 150 x 165 each-470kW (639bhp) Yanmar Diesel Engine Co Ltd-Japan AuxGen: 2 x 32kW 220/380V a.c
9568081 *9V2648* -	**WESTSEA PHOENIX** *ex* Mawar *-2011* *ex* Hako 32 *-2009* **Genesis Marine Pte Ltd** Westsea Offshore Pte Ltd *Singapore* *Singapore* MMSI: 564490000 Official number: 399263	**646** 193 495	Class: BV	**2009-12 Yuexin Shipbuilding Co Ltd — Guangzhou GD** Yd No: 3127 Loa 45.00 Br ex 12.00 Dght 3.800 Lbp 39.40 Br md 11.80 Dpth 4.60 Welded, 1 dk	**(B21B20A) Anchor Handling Tug Supply**	**2 oil engines** reduction geared to sc. shafts driving 2 FP propellers Total Power: 3,282kW (4,462hp) 12.0kn Caterpillar 3516B-TA 2 x Vee 4 Stroke 16 Cy. 170 x 190 each-1641kW (2231bhp) Caterpillar Inc-USA AuxGen: 3 x 245kW 50Hz a.c Fuel: 520.0 (d.f.)
9558828 *9V8423* -	**WESTSEA TITAN** *ex* Crest Titan 1 *-2013* **Genesis Marine Pte Ltd** Westsea Offshore Pte Ltd *Singapore* *Singapore* MMSI: 564247000 Official number: 395765	**1,027** 308 858	Class: AB	**2010-09 Weihai Xinghai Shipyard Co Ltd — Weihai SD** Yd No: 08MZC007 Loa 49.95 Br ex 12.62 Dght 4.500 Lbp 43.60 Br md 12.60 Dpth 5.75 Welded, 1 dk	**(B21B20A) Anchor Handling Tug Supply**	**2 oil engines** reduction geared to sc. shafts driving 2 CP propellers Total Power: 3,440kW (4,678hp) Caterpillar 3516B-HD 2 x Vee 4 Stroke 16 Cy. 170 x 215 each-1720kW (2339bhp) Caterpillar Inc-USA AuxGen: 3 x 295kW a.c
7822421 *OUJB2* -	**WESTSUND** *ex* Strathfoyle *-2002* *ex* Clausentum *-1993* **Svendborg Bugser A/S (Svendborg Towing Co Ltd)** - *Svendborg* *Denmark (DIS)* MMSI: 220124000 Official number: D3991	**366** 109 263	Class: GL (LR) ✠ Classed LR until 29/9/03	**1980-01 Richards (Shipbuilders) Ltd — Lowestoft** Yd No: 547 Loa 33.25 Br ex 10.29 Dght 4.180 Lbp 29.01 Br md 9.76 Dpth 4.91 Welded, 1 dk	**(B32A2ST) Tug**	**2 oil engines** sr geared to sc. shafts driving 2 CP propellers Total Power: 2,074kW (2,820hp) 12.5kn Ruston 6RKCM 2 x 4 Stroke 6 Cy. 254 x 305 each-1037kW (1410bhp) Ruston Diesels Ltd.-Newton-le-Willows AuxGen: 3 x 80kW 440V 50Hz a.c, 1 x 20kW 440V 50Hz a.c
9142667 - -	**WESTVOORNE** *ex* Heeresingel *-2004* *ex* Lys Rover *-2000* *completed as* Heeresingel *-1996* **Schepers Navigamus Trans GmbH & Co KG** Hartel Shipping & Chartering BV *Saint John's* *Antigua & Barbuda*	**2,035** 1,168 2,780	Class: GL (BV)	**1996-10 Tille Scheepsbouw Kootstertille B.V. — Kootstertille** Yd No: 311 Loa 90.60 (BB) Br ex - Dght 4.290 Lbp 84.95 Br md 13.75 Dpth 5.55 Welded, 1 dk	**(A31A2GX) General Cargo Ship** Bale: 3,922 TEU 205 C. 205/20' incl. 20 ref. C Compartments: 1 Ho, ER 1 Ha: (61.8 x 10.8)ER Ice Capable	**1 oil engine** geared to sc. shaft driving 1 FP propeller Total Power: 1,800kW (2,447hp) 13.5kn Stork-Wartsila 6SW28 1 x 4 Stroke 6 Cy. 280 x 300 1800kW (2447bhp) Stork Wartsila Diesel BV-Netherlands Thrusters: 1 Thwart. FP thruster (f)
7730484 *WZL8190* -	**WESTWARD** **Sea Education Association Inc** - *Boston, MA* *United States of America* MMSI: 366724490 Official number: 1144281	*125* 85	Class: (AB)	**1961 Yacht- u. Bootswerft Abeking & Rasmussen — Lemwerder** Yd No: 5619 Loa 38.10 Br ex 6.71 Dght - Lbp 25.00 Br md 6.56 Dpth 4.22 Welded, 1 dk	**(B31A2SR) Research Survey Vessel**	**1 oil engine** reverse reduction geared to sc. shaft driving 1 FP propeller Total Power: 368kW (500hp) 10.0kn Cummins KTA-19-M 1 x 4 Stroke 6 Cy. 159 x 159 368kW (500bhp) (new engine 1988) Cummins Engine Co Inc-USA AuxGen: 2 x 22kW a.c, 1 x 10kW a.c
7926473 *WSD7123* -	**WESTWARD I** *ex* Calvin L. Stinson *-1996* **Westward Ltd Partnership** - *Seattle, WA* *United States of America* MMSI: 367490000 Official number: 615165	*184* 125 275		**1980 Bellinger Shipyards, Inc. — Jacksonville, Fl** Yd No: 115 Loa 41.18 Br ex - Dght 3.661 Lbp 36.28 Br md 9.47 Dpth 5.19 Welded, 2 dks	**(B11A2FS) Stern Trawler**	**1 oil engine** geared to sc. shaft driving 1 CP propeller Total Power: 1,067kW (1,451hp) EMD (Electro-Motive) 12-645-E6 1 x Vee 2 Stroke 12 Cy. 230 x 254 1067kW (1451bhp) General Motors Corp.Electro-Motive Div.-La Grange
7431868 *EILK* G 185	**WESTWARD ISLE** *ex* Girl Stephanie *-2003* *ex* Julie Anne *-1997* **Westward Isle Fishing Ltd** - *Galway* *Irish Republic* MMSI: 250104900 Official number: 403126	*283* - -		**1975-11 Scheepswerf Vooruit B.V. — Zaandam** Yd No: 349 Lengthened L reg 31.98 Br ex 7.85 Dght - Lbp - Br md 7.80 Dpth 4.09 Welded, 1 dk	**(B11B2FV) Fishing Vessel**	**1 oil engine** reduction geared to sc. shaft driving 1 FP propeller Total Power: 700kW (952hp) 10.5kn MAN-B&W 8L23/30A 1 x 4 Stroke 8 Cy. 225 x 300 700kW (952bhp) (new engine 2001) MAN B&W Diesel A/S-Denmark Thrusters: 1 Thwart. FP thruster (f); 1 Thwart. FP thruster (a)
7743467 *WCX9055* -	**WESTWARD WIND** **Highland Light Seafoods LLC** - SatCom: Inmarsat A 1511405 *Seattle, WA* *United States of America* MMSI: 367000620 Official number: 595289	*441* 299 -		**1978 Bender Welding & Machine Co Inc — Mobile AL** Yd No: 302 Lengthened & Rebuilt-1988 Loa 48.77 Br ex 10.37 Dght - Lbp 39.62 Br md 10.36 Dpth 3.43 Welded, 1 dk	**(B11B2FV) Fishing Vessel** Ins: 113 Cranes: 1x12t	**2 oil engines** geared to sc. shafts driving 2 FP propellers Total Power: 1,176kW (1,598hp) G.M. (Detroit Diesel) 12V-149-TI 2 x Vee 2 Stroke 12 Cy. 146 x 146 each-588kW (799bhp) General Motors Detroit DieselAllison Divn-USA
6339051 *HQVO8* -	**WESTWIND** *ex* Alaskan Eight *-1994* *ex* Express *-1991* *ex* State Express *-1977* *ex* National Pride *-1963* **Cheransant Obas** - *San Lorenzo* *Honduras* MMSI: 334931000 Official number: L-0327564	**778** 233 762	Class: (AB)	**1957-04 Arnold V. Walker Shipyard, Inc. — Pascagoula, Ms** Yd No: 119 Converted From: General Cargo Ship-1977 L reg 39.84 Br ex 9.78 Dght 2.556 Lbp 39.98 Br md 9.76 Dpth 3.05 Welded, 1 dk	**(B11B2FV) Fishing Vessel**	**2 oil engines** driving 2 FP propellers Total Power: 648kW (882hp) General Motors 2 x Vee 2 Stroke 12 Cy. 127 x 142 each-324kW (441bhp) General Motors Corp-USA AuxGen: 2 x 60kW 115/208V 60Hz a.c Fuel: 95.5 (d.f.)
8943894 - -	**WESTWIND** *ex* Funny Girl II *-1998* *ex* Daphne *-1998* - -	**177** 53 -		**1961 Orlogsvaerftet (Naval Dockyard) — Copenhagen** Loa 37.00 Br ex 6.77 Dght 1.650 Lbp 34.50 Br md 6.75 Dpth 3.70 Welded, 1 dk	**(B34K2QT) Training Ship**	**2 oil engines** driving 2 FP propellers Total Power: 5,296kW (7,200hp) Maybach 2 x 4 Stroke each-2648kW (3600bhp) Maybach Motorenbau GmbH-Friedrichshafen
9160384 *DYLX* -	**WESTWIND GRACE** **Southern Isle Maritime SA** Baliwag Navigation Inc *Manila* *Philippines* MMSI: 548348000 Official number: MNLA000415	**7,463** 3,285 10,065	Class: NK	**1997-11 Honda Zosen — Saiki** Yd No: 1008 Loa 112.96 (BB) Br ex - Dght 8.365 Lbp 103.10 Br md 19.60 Dpth 13.50 Welded, 1 dk	**(A31A2GX) General Cargo Ship** Grain: 16,544; Bale: 15,130 Compartments: 2 Ho, ER 2 Ha: (21.0 x 11.2) (35.0 x 11.2)ER Cranes: 2x30.5t; Derricks: 1x30t	**1 oil engine** driving 1 FP propeller Total Power: 3,884kW (5,281hp) 13.0kn B&W 6L35MC 1 x 2 Stroke 6 Cy. 350 x 1050 3884kW (5281bhp) Makita Corp-Japan AuxGen: 2 x 280kW a.c Fuel: 130.0 (d.f.) 564.0 (r.f.) 16.3pd
9173135 *ELWZ5* -	**WESTWOOD CASCADE** *ex* Santa Fabiola *-2011* *ex* CMA CGM Nyala *-2009* *ex* Santa Fabiola *-2008* *ex* P&O Nedlloyd Singapore *-2005* **KG ms 'Santa Fabiola' Offen Reederei GmbH & Co** Reederei Claus-Peter Offen GmbH & Co KG SatCom: Inmarsat C 463678460 *Monrovia* *Liberia* MMSI: 636090329 Official number: 90329	**21,583** 11,807 30,046 T/cm 45.6	Class: GL	**1999-06 Flender Werft AG — Luebeck** Yd No: 671 Loa 183.65 (BB) Br ex - Dght 11.540 Lbp 172.71 Br md 29.80 Dpth 15.60 Welded, 1 dk	**(A33A2CC) Container Ship (Fully Cellular)** TEU 2169 C Ho 866 TEU C Dk 1303 TEU incl 420 ref C Compartments: ER, 5 Cell Ho 9 Ha: (12.7 x 15.4) (12.7 x 20.4)ER 7 (12.7 x 25.4) Cranes: 2x45t,2x35t	**1 oil engine** driving 1 FP propeller Total Power: 12,240kW (16,642hp) 20.0kn B&W 6S60MC 1 x 2 Stroke 6 Cy. 600 x 2292 12240kW (16642bhp) Hyundai Heavy Industries Co Ltd-South Korea AuxGen: 4 x 960kW a.c Thrusters: 1 Thwart. CP thruster (f) Fuel: 174.6 (d.f.) 1548.3 (r.f.)

9226047 *C6SI4* -	**WESTWOOD COLUMBIA** **SW Maritime 2 Inc** Thor Dahl Shipmanagement AS *Nassau* *Bahamas* MMSI: 311353000 Official number: 8000447	**32,551** 13,477 45,000	Class: NV	**2002**-09 **Stocznia Gdynia SA — Gdynia** Yd No: 8228/2 Loa 199.90 (BB) Br ex 31.01 Dght 12.500 Lbp 190.91 Br md 31.00 Dpth 17.75 Welded, 1 dk	**(A31A2GO) Open Hatch Cargo Ship** Grain: 52,000 TEU 2048 C Ho 1078 TEU C Dk 970 TEU incl 50 ref C. Compartments: 10 Ho, ER 11 Ha: (13.2 x 17.9) (13.2 x 20.4)9 (13.2 x 25.3)ER Gantry cranes: 2x40t	**1 oil engine** driving 1 FP propeller Total Power: 13,548kW (18,420hp) 17.0kn MAN-B&W 6S60MC-C 1 x 2 Stroke 6 Cy. 600 x 2400 13548kW (18420bhp) H Cegielski Poznan SA-Poland AuxGen: 3 x 1200kW 440/220V 60Hz a.c Thrusters: 1 Tunnel thruster (f)
9162253 *A8AJ4* -	**WESTWOOD DISCOVERY** *ex* Santa Fiorenza *-2011* *ex* CMA CGM Niger *-2009* *ex* Santa Fiorenza *-2007* *ex* P&O Nedlloyd Arica *-2002* *launched as* Santa Fiorenza *-1998* **KG ms 'Santa Fiorenza' Offen Reederei GmbH & Co** Reederei Claus-Peter Offen GmbH & Co KG *Monrovia* *Liberia* MMSI: 636090559 Official number: 90559	**21,583** 11,807 30,007 T/cm 45.5	Class: GL	**1998**-03 **Flender Werft AG — Luebeck** Yd No: 663 Loa 183.24 (BB) Br ex 29.94 Dght 11.541 Lbp 172.71 Br md 29.80 Dpth 15.60 Welded, 1 dk	**(A33A2CC) Container Ship (Fully Cellular)** TEU 2169 C Ho 866 TEU C Dk 1303 TEU incl 420 ref C Compartments: 5 Cell Ho, ER 9 Ha: (12.7 x 15.4) (12.7 x 20.4)7 (12.7 x 25.4)ER Cranes: 2x40t,1x25t,1x10t	**1 oil engine** driving 1 FP propeller Total Power: 12,240kW (16,642hp) 20.0kn B&W 6S60MC 1 x 2 Stroke 6 Cy. 600 x 2292 12240kW (16642bhp) Mitsui Engineering & Shipbuilding CLtd-Japan AuxGen: 3 x 1040kW a.c, 1 x 780kW a.c Thrusters: 1 Thwart. CP thruster (f) Fuel: 174.6 (d.f.) 1548.3 (r.f.)
9226061 *C6UB2* -	**WESTWOOD OLYMPIA** **SW Maritime 4 Inc** Thor Dahl Shipmanagement AS *Nassau* *Bahamas* MMSI: 311864000 Official number: 8000449	**32,551** 13,243 45,000	Class: NV	**2004**-11 **Stocznia Gdynia SA — Gdynia** Yd No: 8228/4 Loa 199.90 (BB) Br ex 31.07 Dght 12.500 Lbp 191.00 Br md 31.00 Dpth 17.75 Welded, 1 dk	**(A31A2GO) Open Hatch Cargo Ship** Grain: 52,000 TEU 2048 C Ho 1078 TEU C Dk 970 TEU incl 50 ref C. Gantry cranes: 2x40t	**1 oil engine** driving 1 FP propeller Total Power: 13,548kW (18,420hp) 17.0kn B&W 6S60MC-C 1 x 2 Stroke 6 Cy. 600 x 2400 13548kW (18420bhp) H Cegielski Poznan SA-Poland AuxGen: 3 x 1259kW 60Hz a.c Thrusters: 1 Tunnel thruster (f)
9162265 *DANR* -	**WESTWOOD PACIFIC** *ex* Santa Federica *-2011* *ex* P&O Nedlloyd Santiago *-2002* *launched as* Santa Fredericia *-1998* **KG ms 'Santa Federica' Offen Reederei GmbH & Co** Reederei Claus-Peter Offen GmbH & Co KG SatCom: Inmarsat C 421151710 *Hamburg* *Germany* MMSI: 211517000 Official number: 18440	**21,583** 11,807 30,007 T/cm 45.5	Class: GL	**1998**-07 **Flender Werft AG — Luebeck** Yd No: 664 Loa 183.16 (BB) Br ex 29.94 Dght 11.541 Lbp 172.71 Br md 29.80 Dpth 15.60 Welded, 1 dk	**(A33A2CC) Container Ship (Fully Cellular)** TEU 2169 C Ho 866 TEU C Dk 1303 TEU incl 420 ref C Compartments: 5 Cell Ho, ER 9 Ha: (12.7 x 15.4) (12.7 x 20.4)7 (12.7 x 25.4)ER Cranes: 2x45t,2x35t	**1 oil engine** driving 1 FP propeller Total Power: 12,240kW (16,642hp) 20.0kn B&W 6S60MC 1 x 2 Stroke 6 Cy. 600 x 2292 12240kW (16642bhp) Mitsui Engineering & Shipbuilding CLtd-Japan AuxGen: 3 x 1040kW a.c, 1 x 780kW a.c Thrusters: 1 Thwart. CP thruster (f) Fuel: 174.6 (d.f.) 1548.3 (r.f.)
9226035 *C6SI3* -	**WESTWOOD RAINIER** **SW Maritime 1 Inc** Thor Dahl Shipmanagement AS *Nassau* *Bahamas* MMSI: 311349000 Official number: 8000445	**32,551** 13,243 48,000	Class: NV	**2002**-06 **Stocznia Gdynia SA — Gdynia** Yd No: 8228/1 Loa 200.00 (BB) Br ex - Dght 11.500 Lbp 190.88 Br md 31.01 Dpth 17.74 Welded, 1 dk	**(A31A2GO) Open Hatch Cargo Ship** Grain: 52,000 TEU 2048 C Ho 1078 TEU C Dk 970 TEU incl 50 ref C. Compartments: 10 Ho 10 Ha: (13.2 x 17.9) (13.2 x 20.4)8 (13.2 x 25.3)ER Gantry cranes: 2x40t	**1 oil engine** driving 1 FP propeller Total Power: 13,548kW (18,420hp) 17.0kn MAN-B&W 6S60MC-C 1 x 2 Stroke 6 Cy. 600 x 2400 13548kW (18420bhp) H Cegielski Poznan SA-Poland AuxGen: 3 x 1259kW 440/220V 60Hz a.c Thrusters: 1 Thwart. CP thruster (f)
9226059 *C6SI6* -	**WESTWOOD VICTORIA** **SW Maritime 3 Inc** Thor Dahl Shipmanagement AS *Nassau* *Bahamas* MMSI: 311351000 Official number: 8000450	**32,551** 13,468 45,851	Class: NV	**2003**-05 **Stocznia Gdynia SA — Gdynia** Yd No: 8228/3 Loa 199.90 (BB) Br ex 31.07 Dght 12.500 Lbp 190.88 Br md 31.00 Dpth 17.75 Welded, 1 dk	**(A31A2GO) Open Hatch Cargo Ship** Double Hull Grain: 52,000 TEU 2048 C Ho 1078 TEU C Dk 970 TEU incl 50 ref C. Compartments: 10 Ho, ER 10 Ha: (13.2 x 20.4)8 (13.2 x 25.3)ER (13.2 x 17.9) Gantry cranes: 2x45t	**1 oil engine** driving 1 FP propeller Total Power: 13,548kW (18,420hp) 17.0kn B&W 6S60MC-C 1 x 2 Stroke 6 Cy. 600 x 2400 13548kW (18420bhp) H Cegielski Poznan SA-Poland AuxGen: 3 x 1259kW 440/220V 60Hz a.c Thrusters: 1 Tunnel thruster (f)
7739002 *WDC5933* -	**WET & WILD** *ex* Elliana Mae *-2010* *ex* Wet & Wild *-2009* *ex* Sandy Lee *-2009* **f/v Wet & Wild** - *Moss Landing, CA* *United States of America* MMSI: 367048690 Official number: 589969	*114* 77 -		**1978 Rodriguez Boat Builders, Inc. — Coden, Al** Yd No: 7 L reg 21.98 Br ex 6.76 Dght - Lbp - Br md - Dpth 3.38 Welded, 1 dk	**(B11B2FV) Fishing Vessel**	**1 oil engine** driving 1 FP propeller Total Power: 294kW (400hp)
9096105 - -	**WETAR** **Government of The Republic of Indonesia (Direktorat Jenderal Perhubungan Laut - Ministry of Sea Communications)** - *Ambon* *Indonesia*	**948** 285 802	Class: KI	**2006**-12 **P.T. Sanur Marindo Shipyard — Tegal** L reg 58.00 Br ex - Dght 3.190 Lbp 53.07 Br md 10.20 Dpth 4.50 Welded, 1 dk	**(A32A2GF) General Cargo/Passenger Ship**	**2 oil engines** geared to sc. shafts driving 2 Propellers Total Power: 1,204kW (1,636hp) Mitsubishi S6R2-MPTK 2 x 4 Stroke 6 Cy. 170 x 220 each-602kW (818bhp) Mitsubishi Heavy Industries Ltd-Japan
8988741 *YHDB* -	**WEWAH** *ex* Lintas Bahari 20 *-2009* *ex* Lucky Star 3 *-2009* *ex* Guo Bao 2 *-2007* *ex* Qing Man 3 *-2005* **PT Lintas Bahari Nusantara** - *Indonesia*	**1,204** 674 -	Class: KI	**1983**-10 **Zhangshu Shipping Transportation Co Shipyard — Zhangshu JX** Loa 66.58 Br ex - Dght - Lbp - Br md 11.00 Dpth 6.20 Welded, 1 dk	**(A31A2GX) General Cargo Ship**	**1 oil engine** geared to sc. shaft driving 1 Propeller Total Power: 736kW (1,001hp) Chinese Std. Type 8300ZLC 1 x 4 Stroke 8 Cy. 300 x 380 736kW (1001bhp) Zibo Diesel Engine Factory-China
8221973 - -	**WEWAH** *ex* Kowa Maru No. 5 *-1998* **PT Lintas Bahari Nusantara** - *Indonesia*	**486** 314 526		**1982**-12 **KK Ura Kyodo Zosensho — Awaji HG** Yd No: 226 Loa - Br ex - Dght 3.120 Lbp 46.00 Br md 8.01 Dpth 4.68 Welded, 1 dk	**(A31A2GX) General Cargo Ship** Compartments: 1 Ho, ER 1 Ha: ER	**1 oil engine** driving 1 FP propeller Total Power: 441kW (600hp) Matsui ML624GS 1 x 4 Stroke 6 Cy. 240 x 400 441kW (600bhp) Matsui Iron Works Co Ltd-Japan
8830841 *P2V4142* -	**WEWAK** **Kambang Holding Ltd** Lutheran Shipping (LUSHIP) *Madang* *Papua New Guinea* MMSI: 553111126 Official number: 000412	**1,128** 541 1,294	Class: AB	**1988**-07 **Guangzhou Huangpu Shipyard — Guangzhou GD** Yd No: P-8732 Loa - Br ex - Dght 3.500 Lbp 48.00 Br md 12.60 Dpth 5.00 Welded, 1 dk	**(A31A2GX) General Cargo Ship** Compartments: 1 Ho, ER 1 Ha: ER Cranes: 2	**3 oil engines** sr geared to sc. shafts driving 3 FP propellers Total Power: 684kW (930hp) 10.5kn Gardner 6LYTI 3 x 4 Stroke 6 Cy. 140 x 168 each-228kW (310bhp) L. Gardner & Sons Ltd.-Manchester AuxGen: 2 x 76kW a.c
9631606 *YJSF8* -	**WEYLAND TIDE** **Indigo Fleet Ltd** Tidewater Marine LLC *Port Vila* *Vanuatu* MMSI: 577022000 Official number: 2089	**2,605** 781 2,564	Class: AB	**2012**-09 **Guangdong Yuexin Ocean Engineering Co Ltd — Guangzhou GD** Yd No: 3137 Loa 69.90 Br ex - Dght 5.890 Lbp 61.20 Br md 16.60 Dpth 7.20 Welded, 1 dk	**(B21B20A) Anchor Handling Tug Supply**	**2 oil engines** gearing integral to driving 2 Directional propellers Total Power: 6,104kW (8,298hp) 12.5kn GE Marine 16V228 2 x Vee 4 Stroke 16 Cy. 229 x 267 each-3052kW (4149bhp) GE Marine Engines-Cincinnati, Oh AuxGen: 2 x 1264kW a.c, 2 x 425kW a.c
9191797 *J8WZ9* -	**WEZA** **SONASURF Ltd** Bourbon Offshore Greenmar SA *Kingstown* *St Vincent & The Grenadines* MMSI: 375182000 Official number: 8239	**1,734** 520 2,374	Class: BV	**1999**-07 **Chantiers Piriou — Concarneau** Yd No: 204 Loa 64.02 Br ex - Dght 5.750 Lbp 58.83 Br md 15.50 Dpth 6.80 Welded, 1 dk	**(B21B20A) Anchor Handling Tug Supply**	**2 oil engines** with clutches, flexible couplings & sr reverse geared to sc. shafts driving 2 CP propellers Total Power: 4,016kW (5,460hp) 12.0kn Normo KRMB-9 2 x 4 Stroke 9 Cy. 250 x 300 each-2008kW (2730bhp) Ulstein Bergen AS-Norway AuxGen: 2 x 1280kW 440V 60Hz a.c, 2 x 250kW 440V 60Hz a.c Thrusters: 1 Retract. directional thruster (f); 1 Thwart. FP thruster (f); 1 Tunnel thruster (a) Fuel: 990.0 (d.f.) 24.0pd
9573191 *PQ2251* -	**WEZEN** **Saveiros Camuyrano - Servicos Maritimos SA** *Rio de Janeiro* *Brazil* MMSI: 710000391 Official number: 3813881334	**250** 75 112	Class: LR ✠ **100A1** SS 07/2011 tug, Brazilian coastal service **LMC** **UMS** Eq.Ltr: F; Cable: 275.0/19.0 U2 (a)	**2011**-07 **Wilson, Sons SA — Guaruja** (Hull) Yd No: 117 **2011**-07 **B.V. Scheepswerf Damen — Gorinchem** Yd No: 512245 Loa 24.55 Br ex 11.70 Dght 5.300 Lbp 20.80 Br md 10.70 Dpth 4.60 Welded, 1 dk	**(B32A2ST) Tug**	**2 oil engines** reduction geared to sc. shafts driving 2 Directional propellers Total Power: 3,634kW (4,940hp) Caterpillar 3516B 2 x Vee 4 Stroke 16 Cy. 170 x 190 each-1817kW (2470bhp) Caterpillar Inc-USA AuxGen: 2 x 55kW 220V 60Hz a.c

Ship / Owner	Tonnage / Class	Built / Dimensions	Type	Machinery
9452969 **WG AMUNDSEN** *5BXE2* - **Esenia Shipping Co Ltd** WesternGeco Ltd *Limassol* *Cyprus* MMSI: 212835000 Official number: 28028	**6,926** Class: NV 2,078 3,700	**2010-02 Hijos de J. Barreras S.A. — Vigo** Yd No: 1659 Loa 88.80 Br ex - Dght 6.600 Lbp 82.00 Br md 19.00 Dpth 8.00 Welded, 1 dk	**(B31A2SR) Research Survey Vessel** Cranes: 1 Ice Capable	**6 diesel electric oil engines** driving 6 gen. each 1700kW 440V a.c Connecting to 2 elec. motors each (3100kW) driving 2 Azimuth electric drive units Total Power: 10,266kW (13,956hp) 15.0kn Wartsila 9L20 6 x 4 Stroke 9 Cy. 200 x 280 each-1711kW (2326bhp) Wartsila Finland Oy-Finland Thrusters: 1 Tunnel thruster (f); 1 Retract. directional thruster (f) Fuel: 1350.0
9452945 **WG COLUMBUS** *5BNS2* - **Kerisa Shipping Co Ltd** WesternGeco Ltd *Limassol* *Cyprus* MMSI: 212764000	**6,922** Class: NV 2,077 3,700	**2009-03 Hijos de J. Barreras S.A. — Vigo** Yd No: 1657 Loa 88.80 Br ex - Dght 6.600 Lbp 82.00 Br md 19.00 Dpth 8.00 Welded, 1 dk	**(B31A2SR) Research Survey Vessel**	**6 diesel electric oil engines** driving 6 gen. each 1620kW a.c Connecting to 2 elec. motors each (3000kW) driving 2 CP propellers Total Power: 10,266kW (13,956hp) 15.0kn Wartsila 9L20 6 x 4 Stroke 9 Cy. 200 x 280 each-1711kW (2326bhp) Wartsila Finland Oy-Finland Thrusters: 1 Tunnel thruster (f); 1 Retract. directional thruster (f) Fuel: 1365.0 (r.f.)
9488554 **WG COOK** *5BPC2* - **Eastern Echo Holding Ltd** WesternGeco AS *Limassol* *Cyprus* MMSI: 210624000	**6,599** Class: NV 1,980 3,800	**2010-08 Drydocks World - Dubai LLC — Dubai** Yd No: 65 Loa 88.80 Br ex - Dght 6.600 Lbp 82.00 Br md 19.00 Dpth 8.00 Welded, 1 dk	**(B31A2SR) Research Survey Vessel** Ice Capable	**6 diesel electric oil engines** driving 6 gen. each 1620kW a.c Connecting to 2 elec. motors each (3000kW) driving 2 Azimuth electric drive units Total Power: 10,266kW (13,956hp) 15.0kn Wartsila 9L20 6 x 4 Stroke 9 Cy. 200 x 280 each-1711kW (2326bhp) Wartsila Finland Oy-Finland Thrusters: 1 Tunnel thruster (f); 1 Retract. directional thruster (f) Fuel: 1310.0 (d.f.)
9452957 **WG MAGELLAN** *5BPK2* - **Pimolia Marine Co Ltd** WesternGeco Ltd SatCom: Inmarsat C 421296610 *Limassol* *Cyprus* MMSI: 212966000 Official number: 9452957	**6,922** Class: NV 2,077 3,700	**2009-07 Hijos de J. Barreras S.A. — Vigo** Yd No: 1658 Loa 88.80 Br ex - Dght 6.600 Lbp 82.00 Br md 19.00 Dpth 8.00 Welded, 1 dk	**(B31A2SR) Research Survey Vessel** Ice Capable	**6 diesel electric oil engines** driving 6 gen. Connecting to 2 elec. motors driving 2 Azimuth electric drive units Total Power: 10,266kW (13,956hp) 15.0kn Wartsila 9L20 6 x 4 Stroke 9 Cy. 200 x 280 each-1711kW (2326bhp) Wartsila Finland Oy-Finland Thrusters: 1 Tunnel thruster (f); 1 Retract. directional thruster (f)
9488542 **WG TASMAN** *5BPB2* - **Eastern Echo Holding Ltd** WesternGeco Ltd *Limassol* *Cyprus* MMSI: 212593000	**6,599** Class: NV 1,980 3,800	**2010-03 Drydocks World - Dubai LLC — Dubai** Yd No: 64 Loa 88.80 Br ex - Dght 6.600 Lbp 82.00 Br md 19.00 Dpth 8.00 Welded, 1 dk	**(B31A2SR) Research Survey Vessel** Ice Capable	**6 diesel electric oil engines** driving 6 gen. each 1620kW a.c Connecting to 2 elec. motors driving 2 Directional propellers Total Power: 9,720kW (13,218hp) 15.0kn Wartsila 9L20 6 x 4 Stroke 9 Cy. 200 x 280 each-1620kW (2203bhp) Wartsila Finland Oy-Finland Thrusters: 1 Tunnel thruster (f); 1 Retract. directional thruster (f)
9452971 **WG VESPUCCI** *5BXF2* - **Tosia Navigation Co Ltd** WesternGeco Ltd SatCom: Inmarsat C 421284320 *Limassol* *Cyprus* MMSI: 209128000 Official number: 9452971	**6,926** Class: NV 2,078 3,700	**2010-04 Hijos de J. Barreras S.A. — Vigo** Yd No: 1660 Loa 88.80 Br ex - Dght 6.600 Lbp 82.00 Br md 19.00 Dpth 8.00 Welded, 1 dk	**(B31A2SR) Research Survey Vessel** Ice Capable	**6 diesel electric oil engines** driving 6 gen. each 1700kW 440V a.c Connecting to 2 elec. motors each (3000kW) driving 2 Azimuth electric drive units Total Power: 10,266kW (13,956hp) 15.0kn Wartsila 9L20 6 x 4 Stroke 9 Cy. 200 x 280 each-1711kW (2326bhp) Wartsila Finland Oy-Finland Thrusters: 1 Tunnel thruster (f); 1 Retract. directional thruster (f)
9117870 **WHA JIN NO. 107** *DSDB8* *ex Yeo Myung No. 7 -2008* *ex Jukyeng No. 5 -2005* - **Yeo Myong Shipping Co Ltd** Hwa Jin Co Ltd *Incheon* *South Korea* MMSI: 440120500 Official number: ICR-931213	**499** Class: KR - 1,237	**1994-01 Hanpo Shipbuilding Co Ltd — Busan** Yd No: 004 Loa 60.96 Br ex - Dght 4.312 Lbp 55.91 Br md 9.80 Dpth 4.70 Welded, 1 dk	**(A13B2TP) Products Tanker**	**1 oil engine** driving 1 FP propeller Total Power: 1,030kW (1,400hp) 11.7kn Niigata 6M28AGTE 1 x 4 Stroke 6 Cy. 280 x 480 1030kW (1400bhp) Ssangyong Heavy Industries Co Ltd-South Korea AuxGen: 2 x 65kW 225V a.c
5186952 **WHA YANG No. 75** *6LJW* *ex Kikusui Maru No. 5 -1972* **Wha Yang Industrial Co Ltd** - *Busan* *South Korea* Official number: BF22023	*240* Class: (KR) 131 -	**1962 KK Kanasashi Zosen — Shizuoka SZ** Yd No: 497 Loa 40.87 Br ex 7.35 Dght 2.998 Lbp 36.58 Br md 7.29 Dpth 3.41 Welded, 1 dk	**(B11B2FV) Fishing Vessel** Ins: 151 3 Ha: 3 (1.2 x 1.3)	**1 oil engine** driving 1 FP propeller Total Power: 478kW (650hp) 10.0kn Hanshin V6 1 x 4 Stroke 6 Cy. 320 x 450 478kW (650bhp) Hanshin Nainenki Kogyo-Japan AuxGen: 2 x 48kW 225V a.c
6422585 **WHA YANG No. 78** *6LCK* *ex Genryo Maru No. 28 -1975* - **Wha Yang Industrial Co Ltd** - *Busan* *South Korea* Official number: BS-A-1806	*253* Class: (KR) 127 -	**1964 KK Kanasashi Zosen — Shizuoka SZ** Yd No: 580 Loa 43.72 Br ex 7.57 Dght 2.896 Lbp 38.54 Br md 7.50 Dpth 3.31 Welded, 1 dk	**(B11B2FV) Fishing Vessel** Ins: 279 4 Ha: 2 (4.7 x 7.9)2 (1.1 x 1.3)	**1 oil engine** driving 1 FP propeller Total Power: 515kW (700hp) 10.3kn Akasaka MK6SS 1 x 4 Stroke 6 Cy. 300 x 420 515kW (700bhp) Akasaka Tekkosho KK (Akasaka DieselLtd)-Japan AuxGen: 2 x 104kW 230V a.c
6715906 **WHA YANG No. 102** *6NFY* *ex Hatto Maru No. 82 -1974* - **Wha Yang Industrial Co Ltd** - *Busan* *South Korea* Official number: BF38152	*346* Class: (KR) 165 -	**1966 Niigata Engineering Co Ltd — Niigata NI** Yd No: 681 Loa 53.57 Br ex 8.28 Dght - Lbp 49.03 Br md 8.23 Dpth 5.82 Welded, 2 dks	**(B11A2FS) Stern Trawler** Ins: 398 4 Ha: (1.6 x 2.0) (1.6 x 2.6) (1.7 x 2.1) (1.0 x 1.5)	**1 oil engine** driving 1 FP propeller Total Power: 1,471kW (2,000hp) 12.5kn Niigata 6MG31EZ 1 x 4 Stroke 6 Cy. 310 x 380 1471kW (2000bhp) (new engine 1970) Niigata Engineering Co Ltd-Japan AuxGen: 2 x 100kW 225V a.c
7330454 **WHALE** *ex Perseus -1974* *ex Hans -1974* - - -	**179** 76 -	**1973 Chantier et Armement A. Seghers — Oostende** (Hull) Yd No: C54 **1973 Machinefabriek Zwitser B.V. — Katwijk aan Zee** Yd No: 72.118 Lengthened-1987 Loa 37.95 Br ex 7.57 Dght - Lbp 34.90 Br md 7.50 Dpth 3.26 Welded, 1 dk	**(B11A2FT) Trawler**	**1 oil engine** driving 1 FP propeller Total Power: 747kW (1,016hp) Kromhout 9F/SW240 1 x 4 Stroke 9 Cy. 240 x 260 747kW (1016bhp) Stork Werkspoor Diesel BV-Netherlands
9396268 **WHALE 01** *YDA4195* - **PT Prima Armada Samudra** - *Jakarta* *Indonesia* Official number: 2006 PST NO 4187/L	**241** Class: NK 73 239	**2006-05 Borneo Shipping & Timber Agencies Sdn Ltd — Bintulu** Yd No: 79 Loa 27.00 Br ex - Dght 3.512 Lbp 25.20 Br md 8.53 Dpth 4.12 Welded, 1 dk	**(B32A2ST) Tug**	**2 oil engines** reduction geared to sc. shafts driving 2 Propellers Total Power: 1,264kW (1,718hp) Caterpillar 3412D 2 x Vee 4 Stroke 12 Cy. 145 x 162 each-632kW (859bhp) Caterpillar Inc-USA Fuel: 135.0 (d.f.)
9451678 **WHALE 3** *YD3735* - **PT Capitol Nusantara Indonesia** ASL Offshore & Marine Pte Ltd *Tanjungpinang* *Indonesia*	**227** Class: GL KI (NK) 69 242	**2007-06 Borneo Shipping & Timber Agencies Sdn Ltd — Bintulu** Yd No: 81 Loa 27.00 Br ex 8.53 Dght 3.510 Lbp 25.20 Br md 8.53 Dpth 4.12 Welded, 1 dk	**(B32A2ST) Tug**	**2 oil engines** reduction geared to sc. shafts driving 2 Propellers Total Power: 1,264kW (1,718hp) Caterpillar 3412D 2 x Vee 4 Stroke 12 Cy. 145 x 162 each-632kW (859bhp) Caterpillar Inc-USA AuxGen: 1 x a.c Fuel: 150.0 (d.f.)
9455416 **WHALE 5** *YD3725* - **PT Capitol Nusantara Indonesia** - *Tanjungpinang* *Indonesia*	**227** Class: (GL) (NK) 69 239	**2007-07 Borneo Shipping & Timber Agencies Sdn Ltd — Bintulu** Yd No: 82 Loa 27.00 Br ex 8.53 Dght 3.512 Lbp 25.20 Br md 8.53 Dpth 4.12 Welded, 1 dk	**(B32A2ST) Tug**	**2 oil engines** reduction geared to sc. shafts driving 2 Propellers Total Power: 1,264kW (1,718hp) Caterpillar 3412D 2 x Vee 4 Stroke 12 Cy. 145 x 162 each-632kW (859bhp) Caterpillar Inc-USA AuxGen: 1 x a.c Fuel: 155.0 (d.f.)

IMO / Call sign	Name / Owner	Tonnage	Class	Built	Type	Machinery
455428 *D3726*	**WHALE 7** **PT Capitol Nusantara Indonesia** ASL Offshore & Marine Pte Ltd *Tanjungpinang* *Indonesia*	**227** 69 234	Class: GL KI (NK)	**2007-08 Borneo Shipping & Timber Agencies Sdn Ltd — Bintulu** Yd No: 85 Loa 27.00 Br ex - Dght 3.512 Lbp 24.73 Br md 8.53 Dpth 4.12 Welded, 1 dk	**(B32A2ST) Tug**	**2 oil engines** reduction geared to sc. shafts driving 2 Propellers Total Power: 1,264kW (1,718hp) Caterpillar 3412D 2 x Vee 4 Stroke 12 Cy. 145 x 162 each-632kW (859bhp) Caterpillar Inc-USA Fuel: 155.0 (d.f.)
801489	**WHALE CAY** *ex* Mitsuba Maru *-1999* *ex* Asama Maru *-1990* **Freepoint Tug & Towing Services** Svitzer (Caribbean) Ltd	**259** 77 -		**1978-01 Sagami Zosen Tekko K.K. — Yokosuka** Yd No: 192 Loa - Br ex - Dght 3.050 Lbp 27.56 Br md 8.81 Dpth 3.51 Welded	**(B32A2ST) Tug**	**2 oil engines** driving 2 FP propellers Total Power: 1,912kW (2,600hp) Niigata 6L25BX 2 x 4 Stroke 6 Cy. 250 x 320 each-956kW (1300bhp) Niigata Engineering Co Ltd-Japan
388430 *05107*	**WHALE SHARK** *ex* Joshua *-2005* **Hercules Liftboat Co LLC** - *Panama* *Panama* MMSI: 357453000 Official number: 3485809B	**1,142** 342 -	Class: LR (AB) **OU100A** SS 02/2013 self elevating unit restricted service **LMC**	**2005-04 La Force Shipyard Inc — Coden AL** Yd No: 140 Loa 39.63 Br ex 30.49 Dght - Lbp - Br md - Dpth 3.35 Welded, 1 dk	**(B22A2ZM) Offshore Construction Vessel, jack up** Cranes: 1x100t	**2 oil engines** reduction geared to sc. shafts driving 2 Propellers Total Power: 1,412kW (1,920hp) Caterpillar 3508B 2 x Vee 4 Stroke 8 Cy. 170 x 190 each-706kW (960bhp) Caterpillar Inc-USA
979908 *CFQ4*	**WHALE SONG** **Whale Song Ltd** - *George Town* *Cayman Islands (British)* Official number: 734501	**185** 55 -	Class: (AB)	**2001-05 Halter Marine, Inc. — Lockport, La** (Hull) Yd No: 1872 **2001-05 Trinity Yachts LLC — New Orleans LA** Yd No: 380 Loa 28.65 Br ex - Dght 2.130 Lbp 25.75 Br md 7.30 Dpth 3.80 Welded, 1 dk	**(X11A2YP) Yacht**	**2 oil engines** reduction geared to sc. shafts driving 2 FP propellers Total Power: 656kW (892hp) 12.0kn Caterpillar 3406TA 2 x 4 Stroke 6 Cy. 137 x 165 each-328kW (446bhp) Caterpillar Inc-USA AuxGen: 2 x 65kW a.c Thrusters: 1 Thwart. FP thruster (f)
329370 *DB8159*	**WHALING CITY EXPRESS** **Interlake Leasing IV Inc** Seastreak Martha's Vineyard LLC *New Bedford, MA* *United States of America* Official number: 1156934	**232** - 20		**2004-06 Robert E Derecktor Inc — Mamaroneck NY** Yd No: 4400 Loa 29.00 Br ex - Dght 1.400 Lbp 24.70 Br md 8.50 Dpth 3.40 Welded, 1 dk	**(A37B2PS) Passenger Ship** Hull Material: Aluminium Alloy Passengers: 149	**2 oil engines** geared to sc. shafts driving 2 FP propellers Total Power: 2,100kW (2,856hp) 29.0kn M.T.U. 16V2000M70 2 x Vee 4 Stroke 16 Cy. 130 x 150 each-1050kW (1428bhp) MTU Friedrichshafen GmbH-Friedrichshafen
633812 *EZQ4*	**WHALSA LASS** **Research Fishing Co Ltd** LHD Ltd SatCom: Inmarsat C 423592955 *Lerwick* *United Kingdom* MMSI: 235089425 Official number: 917973	**255** 76 -		**2011-10 Safe Co Ltd Sp z oo — Gdynia** (Hull) Yd No: (571661) **2011-10 B.V. Scheepswerf Damen Hardinxveld — Hardinxveld-Giessendam** Yd No: 571661 Loa 26.00 Br ex - Dght 2.250 Lbp 23.93 Br md 11.50 Dpth 3.50 Welded, 1 dk	**(B34L2QU) Utility Vessel** Cranes: 2x10t	**3 oil engines** reduction geared to sc. shafts driving 3 FP propellers Total Power: 1,953kW (2,655hp) 9.7kn Caterpillar C32 3 x Vee 4 Stroke 12 Cy. 145 x 162 each-651kW (885bhp) Caterpillar Inc-USA Thrusters: 1 Tunnel thruster (f)
600516 *RIG9*	**WHAMPOA** **Hongkong United Dockyards Ltd** The Hongkong Salvage & Towage Co Ltd *Hong Kong* *Hong Kong* MMSI: 477847300 Official number: HK-3041	**481** 144 262	Class: LR ✠ **100A1** SS 11/2011 tug ✠ **LMC** Eq.Ltr: H; Cable: 275.0/19.0 U2 (a)	**2011-11 Hin Lee (Zhuhai) Shipyard Co Ltd — Zhuhai GD** (Hull) Yd No: 230 **2011-11 Cheoy Lee Shipyards Ltd — Hong Kong** Yd No: 5020 Loa 30.25 Br ex - Dght 4.500 Lbp - Br md 11.60 Dpth 5.00 Welded, 1 dk	**(B32A2ST) Tug**	**2 oil engines** gearing integral to driving 2 Z propellers Total Power: 3,676kW (4,998hp) Niigata 6L28HX 2 x 4 Stroke 6 Cy. 280 x 370 each-1838kW (2499bhp) Niigata Engineering Co Ltd-Japan AuxGen: 2 x 80kW 380V 50Hz a.c
823184 *EQZ*	**WHEELER** **Government of The United States of America (Department of The Army - Corps of Engineers)** - SatCom: Inmarsat C 436698210 *New Orleans, LA* *United States of America* MMSI: 366982000	*10,614* 8,135 10,518	Class: (AB)	**1982-09 Avondale Shipyards Inc. — Avondale, La** Yd No: 2322 Loa 124.67 Br ex - Dght 8.992 Lbp 117.07 Br md 23.79 Dpth 11.89 Welded, 1 dk	**(B33B2DT) Trailing Suction Hopper Dredger** Hopper: 6,116 Cranes: 1x20t	**2 oil engines** sr geared to sc. shafts driving 2 CP propellers Total Power: 7,650kW (10,400hp) 14.0kn Cooper Bessemer KSV16T 2 x Vee 4 Stroke 16 Cy. 343 x 419 each-3825kW (5200bhp) Cooper Energy Services Inc-USA AuxGen: 3 x 1000kW Thrusters: 1 Tunnel thruster (f)
994075 *H6937*	**WHEELS** **Wheels Yachting Ltd** - *Valletta* *Malta* MMSI: 215243000 Official number: 7763	**267** 80 190		**2002-06 Horizon Yacht Co Ltd — Kaohsiung** Yd No: 110-007 Loa 35.50 Br ex - Dght - Lbp 30.50 Br md 7.54 Dpth 1.98 Bonded, 1 dk	**(X11A2YP) Yacht** Hull Material: Reinforced Plastic Passengers: cabins: 5; berths: 10	**2 oil engines** reduction geared to sc. shafts driving 2 Propellers Total Power: 2,686kW (3,652hp) 14.0kn M.T.U. 16V2000M90 2 x Vee 4 Stroke 16 Cy. 130 x 150 each-1343kW (1826bhp) MTU Friedrichshafen GmbH-Friedrichshafen
556923 *DE8224*	**WHEELS** **Hendrick Marine LLC** - *Charlotte, NC* *United States of America* MMSI: 367403020 Official number: 1218222	**456** 136 130	Class: AB	**2009-01 Trinity Yachts LLC — New Orleans LA** Yd No: 046 Loa 50.00 Br ex 8.54 Dght 2.320 Lbp 44.40 Br md 8.50 Dpth 4.21 Welded, 1 dk	**(X11A2YP) Yacht** Hull Material: Aluminium Alloy	**2 oil engines** reduction geared to sc. shafts driving 2 FP propellers Total Power: 3,310kW (4,500hp) Caterpillar 3512B 2 x Vee 4 Stroke 12 Cy. 170 x 190 each-1655kW (2250bhp) Caterpillar Inc-USA AuxGen: 2 x 130kW a.c
953203 *WYC* M 679	**WHISKI** *ex* I. A. Strande *-2009* **Thomsen Michael & Erik** - *Hanstholm* *Denmark* MMSI: 219618000 Official number: H261	**106** 36 -		**1960 I/S Mortensens Skibsbyggeri — Frederikshavn** Loa 28.31 Br ex - Dght - Lbp - Br md 5.80 Dpth 2.75 Welded, 1 dk	**(B11B2FV) Fishing Vessel**	**1 oil engine** driving 1 FP propeller Total Power: 390kW (530hp)
766105	**WHISKY ACHIEVEMENT** *ex* Superior Achievement *-2010* *ex* C. G. Hentze *-2010* *ex* Blue Streak 11 *-2010* **DeWayle International Ltd** - *Lagos* *Nigeria* Official number: SR1494	**274** 82 -		**1982 Blue Streak Industries, Inc. — Chalmette, La** Yd No: BLU JB 61 L reg 24.60 Br ex - Dght - Lbp - Br md 16.45 Dpth 2.43 Welded, 1 dk	**(B22A2ZM) Offshore Construction Vessel, jack up**	**2 oil engines** reduction geared to sc. shafts driving 2 Propellers G.M. (Detroit Diesel) 12V-71 2 x Vee 2 Stroke 12 Cy. 108 x 127 General Motors Detroit DieselAllison Divn-USA
115851 *WY*	**WHISKY STAR 1** *ex* Javelin Tide *-2012* *ex* Petromar Javelin *-1988* **DeWayle International Ltd** - *Nigeria*	**713** 213 1,200	Class: AB BV (Class contemplated)	**1982-03 Halter Marine, Inc. — Lockport, La** Yd No: 1041 Loa 56.50 Br ex - Dght 3.664 Lbp 56.39 Br md 12.20 Dpth 4.27 Welded, 1 dk	**(B21B20T) Offshore Tug/Supply Ship**	**2 oil engines** reverse reduction geared to sc. shafts driving 2 FP propellers Total Power: 2,206kW (3,000hp) 12.0kn EMD (Electro-Motive) 12-645-E6 2 x Vee 2 Stroke 12 Cy. 230 x 254 each-1103kW (1500bhp) (Re-engined ,made 1956, Reconditioned & fitted 1982) General Motors Corp.Electro-Motive Div.-La Grange AuxGen: 2 x 99kW a.c Thrusters: 1 Thwart. FP thruster (f)
115978	**WHISKY STAR IX** *ex* Tartan Tide *-2011* *ex* Ensco Tartan *-2003* *ex* PBR/465 *-1988* *launched as* Golden Star *-1981* **DeWayle International Ltd** - *Lagos* *Nigeria* Official number: 377808	**680** 208 931	Class: (AB)	**1981-12 Moss Point Marine, Inc. — Escatawpa, Ms** Yd No: 11 Loa - Br ex - Dght 3.671 Lbp 52.74 Br md 12.20 Dpth 4.27 Welded, 1 dk	**(B21A20S) Platform Supply Ship**	**2 oil engines** reverse reduction geared to sc. shafts driving 2 FP propellers Total Power: 2,206kW (3,000hp) 12.0kn EMD (Electro-Motive) 12-645-E6 2 x Vee 2 Stroke 12 Cy. 230 x 254 each-1103kW (1500bhp) (Reconditioned , Reconditioned & fitted 1981) General Motors Corp.Electro-Motive Div.-La Grange AuxGen: 2 x 150kW a.c Thrusters: 1 Thwart. FP thruster (f)
108028	**WHISKY STAR VI** *ex* Gulf Fleet No. 53 *-2009* **DeWayle International Ltd** - *Honduras* Official number: U-1528360	**738** 221 916	Class: BV (Class contemplated) (AB)	**1982-04 Quality Shipyards Inc — Houma LA** Yd No: 175 Loa 57.92 Br ex - Dght 3.658 Lbp 51.72 Br md 12.20 Dpth 4.27 Welded, 1 dk	**(B21B20A) Anchor Handling Tug Supply** Passengers: berths: 12	**2 oil engines** reverse reduction geared to sc. shafts driving 2 FP propellers Total Power: 2,868kW (3,900hp) 12.0kn EMD (Electro-Motive) 16-567-BC 2 x Vee 2 Stroke 16 Cy. 216 x 254 each-1434kW (1950bhp) (Reconditioned , Reconditioned & fitted 1982) General Motors Corp.Electro-Motive Div.-La Grange AuxGen: 2 x 99kW 440V 60Hz a.c Thrusters: 1 Thwart. FP thruster (f) Fuel: 310.0 (d.f.) 14.0pd

IMO / Call sign	Name / Owner	Tonnage	Class	Build / Dimensions	Type	Machinery
8767367 - -	**WHISKY STAR VII** *ex Superior Discovery -2011* *ex P. H. Holmes -2011 ex Blue Streak 9 -2011* **DeWayle International Ltd** - *Lagos* *Nigeria* Official number: SR1756	276 188 -		**1981 Blue Streak Industries, Inc. — Chalmette, La** Yd No: BLU JB 49 L reg 23.16 Br ex - Dght - Lbp - Br md 11.58 Dpth 2.43 Welded, 1 dk	**(B22A2ZM) Offshore Construction Vessel, jack up**	**2 oil engines** reduction geared to sc. shafts driving 2 Propellers Total Power: 1,060kW (1,442hp) G.M. (Detroit Diesel) 16V-92 2 x Vee 2 Stroke 16 Cy. 123 x 127 each-530kW (721bhp) General Motors Detroit DieselAllison Divn-USA
8767446 - -	**WHISKY STAR XI** *ex Superior Triumph -2011 ex Power XI -2004* *ex Mr. Don -1997* **DeWayle International Ltd** - *Lagos* *Nigeria* Official number: SR1757	245 216 -		**1982 Crown Point Industries — Marrero, La** Yd No: 104 Loa 27.43 Br ex 12.20 Dght - Lbp - Br md - Dpth 2.43 Welded, 1 dk	**(B22A2ZM) Offshore Construction Vessel, jack up** Cranes: 1x80t,1x10t	**2 oil engines** driving 2 Propellers Total Power: 574kW (780hp) 4.0kn G.M. (Detroit Diesel) 16V-71 2 x Vee 2 Stroke 16 Cy. 108 x 127 each-287kW (390bhp) Detroit Diesel Corporation-Detroit, Mi AuxGen: 2 x 99kW 60Hz a.c
8763115 - -	**WHISKY STAR XII** *ex Superior Success -2011* *ex Gulf Island IX -2011* **DeWayle International Ltd** - *Lagos* *Nigeria* Official number: SR1758	276 188 -		**1982 Superior Lift Boats — Lafayette, La** Yd No: 3 L reg 23.41 Br ex - Dght 1.830 Lbp - Br md 11.58 Dpth 2.43 Welded, 1 dk	**(B22A2ZM) Offshore Construction Vessel, jack up** Cranes: 1x70t	**2 oil engines** geared to sc. shafts driving 2 Propellers Total Power: 1,060kW (1,442hp) G.M. (Detroit Diesel) 16V-92 2 x Vee 2 Stroke 16 Cy. 123 x 127 each-530kW (721bhp) Detroit Diesel Corporation-Detroit, Mi
8757104 - -	**WHISKY STAR XIII** *ex Superior Excellence -2011* *ex Gulf Island IV -2005* **DeWayle International Ltd** - *Lagos* *Nigeria* Official number: SR1759	276 174 -		**1984 Crown Point Industries — Marrero, La** Yd No: 109 Loa 33.54 Br ex 15.24 Dght 2.033 Lbp - Br md - Dpth 3.05 Welded, 1 dk	**(B22A2ZM) Offshore Construction Vessel, jack up** Cranes: 1x75t	**2 oil engines** geared to sc. shafts driving 2 Propellers Total Power: 736kW (1,000hp) G.M. (Detroit Diesel) 16V-71 2 x Vee 2 Stroke 16 Cy. 108 x 127 each-368kW (500bhp) Detroit Diesel Corporation-Detroit, Mi
1007445 *ZCIV7*	**WHISPER** - **Whisper Yacht Ltd** Churchill Yacht Partners *George Town* *Cayman Islands (British)* MMSI: 319911000 Official number: 736844	180 54 -	Class: LR ✠ **100A1** SS 08/2013 SSC Yacht, mono, G6 **LMC** Cable: 240.0/16.0 U2	**2003-08 Holland Jachtbouw B.V. — Zaandam** Yd No: 034 Loa 35.46 Br ex 8.30 Dght 2.500 Lbp 26.24 Br md 8.10 Dpth 4.36 Welded, 1 dk	**(X11A2YS) Yacht (Sailing)** Hull Material: Aluminium Alloy	**2 oil engines** with clutches, flexible couplings & sr geared to sc. shafts driving 2 CP propellers Total Power: 448kW (610hp) 12.0kn Lugger L6108A2 2 x 4 Stroke 6 Cy. 108 x 130 each-224kW (305bhp) Alaska Diesel Electric Inc-USA AuxGen: 2 x 35kW 400V 50Hz a.c Thrusters: 1 Thwart. FP thruster (f)
9524384 *9H9365* -	**WHISPERING ANGEL** *ex Junie Ii -2012* **GMW 55 Ltd** - *Valletta* *Malta* MMSI: 249382000 Official number: 9524384	235 70 -	Class: RI	**2008-07 ISA Produzione Srl — Ancona** Yd No: 120.09 Loa 36.40 Br ex - Dght 1.500 Lbp 30.00 Br md 7.40 Dpth 3.66 Bonded, 1 dk	**(X11A2YP) Yacht** Hull Material: Reinforced Plastic	**3 oil engines** reduction geared to sc. shafts driving 3 Propellers Total Power: 5,370kW (7,302hp) M.T.U. 16V2000M93 3 x Vee 4 Stroke 16 Cy. 135 x 156 each-1790kW (2434bhp) MTU Friedrichshafen GmbH-Friedrichshafen
9358371 *5BCD3* -	**WHISTLER** - **Barbour Shipping Inc** Navarone SA SatCom: Inmarsat C 421032510 *Limassol* *Cyprus* MMSI: 210325000 Official number: RCS11959	22,790 12,130 37,272 T/cm 44.1	Class: AB	**2007-06 Tianjin Xingang Shipyard — Tianjin** Yd No: 348-2 Loa 199.90 (BB) Br ex - Dght 10.750 Lbp 192.00 Br md 23.70 Dpth 15.30 Welded, 1 dk	**(A21A2BC) Bulk Carrier** Grain: 42,779; Bale: 42,351 Compartments: 6 Ho, ER 6 Ha: ER Cranes: 4x40t Ice Capable	**1 oil engine** driving 1 FP propeller Total Power: 7,860kW (10,686hp) 14.5kn MAN-B&W 6S46MC-C 1 x 2 Stroke 6 Cy. 460 x 1932 7860kW (10686bhp) Hudong Heavy Machinery Co Ltd-China AuxGen: 3 x 825kW a.c Thrusters: 1 Tunnel thruster (f) Fuel: 104.0 (d.f.) 1617.0 (r.f.)
7627089 *V5WY*	**WHITBY** - **Tresso Trading 383 Pty Ltd** Novanam Ltd *Walvis Bay* *Namibia* Official number: 95WB019	200 60 -	Class: (LR) ✠ Classed LR until 27/5/08	**1977-07 Nagasaki Zosen K.K. — Nagasaki** Yd No: 602 Loa 30.71 (BB) Br ex 7.60 Dght 3.071 Lbp 25.79 Br md 7.52 Dpth 3.20 Welded, 1 dk	**(B11A2FS) Stern Trawler** Ins: 150 Compartments: 1 Ho, ER 1 Ha: (1.9 x 1.9)ER Derricks: 2	**1 oil engine** reverse reduction geared to sc. shaft driving 1 CP propeller Total Power: 625kW (850hp) 10.0kn Daihatsu 6DS-22 1 x 4 Stroke 6 Cy. 220 x 280 625kW (850bhp) Daihatsu Diesel Manufacturing Co Lt-Japan AuxGen: 2 x 110kW 415V 50Hz a.c
9027867 - -	**WHITBY** - **PT Alim Baharijaya Shipping** - *Samarinda* *Indonesia*	404 122 -	Class: KI	**2002-08 P.T. Kaltim Shipyard — Samarinda** L reg 42.00 Br ex - Dght 2.450 Lbp 40.00 Br md 10.00 Dpth 3.00 Welded, 1 dk	**(A35D2RL) Landing Craft** Bow ramp (centre)	**2 oil engines** geared to sc. shafts driving 2 Propellers Total Power: 698kW (950hp) 7.0kn Caterpillar 3408TA 2 x Vee 4 Stroke 8 Cy. 137 x 152 each-349kW (475bhp) Caterpillar Inc-USA
9252278 *VQAU3*	**WHITCHALLENGER** - **Whitchallenger Shipping Ltd** John H Whitaker (Tankers) Ltd *Douglas* *Isle of Man (British)* MMSI: 235007413 Official number: 734764	2,958 1,355 4,516 T/cm 11.2	Class: LR ✠ **100A1** SS 10/2012 Double Hull oil tanker ESP strengthened for loading and unloading aground ✠ **LMC** **UMS** Eq.Ltr: S; Cable: 467.5/42.0 U2 (a)	**2002-10 Tuzla Gemi Endustrisi A.S. — Tuzla** Yd No: 023 Loa 84.95 (BB) Br ex 15.30 Dght 6.300 Lbp 80.80 Br md 15.00 Dpth 8.60 Welded, 1 dk	**(A13B2TP) Products Tanker** Double Hull (13F) Liq: 5,094; Liq (Oil): 4,845 Cargo Heating Coils Compartments: 14 Wing Ta, 1 Slop Ta, ER 3 Cargo Pump (s): 1x500m³/hr, 2x250m³/hr	**1 oil engine** with flexible couplings & sr geared to sc. shaft driving 1 CP propeller Total Power: 1,850kW (2,515hp) 10.3kn MaK 6M25 1 x 4 Stroke 6 Cy. 255 x 400 1850kW (2515bhp) Caterpillar Motoren GmbH & Co. KG-Germany AuxGen: 2 x 312kW 415V 50Hz a.c Boilers: TOH (o.f.) 9.2kgf/cm² (9.0bar) Thrusters: 1 Water jet (f)
9252280 *VQPX7* -	**WHITCHAMPION** - **Whitchampion Ltd** John H Whitaker (Tankers) Ltd *Douglas* *Isle of Man (British)* MMSI: 235009956 Official number: 734765	2,965 1,355 4,513 T/cm 11.3	Class: LR ✠ **100A1** SS 06/2013 Double Hull oil tanker ESP strengthened for loading and unloading aground ✠ **LMC** **UMS** Eq.Ltr: S; Cable: 467.5/42.0 U2 (a)	**2003-06 Tuzla Gemi Endustrisi A.S. — Tuzla** Yd No: 024 Loa 84.95 Br ex 15.30 Dght 6.300 Lbp 80.80 Br md 15.00 Dpth 8.60 Welded, 1 dk	**(A13B2TP) Products Tanker** Double Hull (13F) Liq: 4,992; Liq (Oil): 4,955 Cargo Heating Coils Compartments: 14 Wing Ta, 1 Slop Ta, ER 14 Cargo Pump (s): 14x200m³/hr	**1 oil engine** with flexibel couplings & sr geared to sc. shaft driving 1 CP propeller Total Power: 1,850kW (2,515hp) 10.3kn MaK 6M25 1 x 4 Stroke 6 Cy. 255 x 400 1850kW (2515bhp) Caterpillar Motoren GmbH & Co. KG-Germany AuxGen: 2 x 312kW 415V 50Hz a.c, 1 x 80kW 415V 50Hz a.c Boilers: TOH (o.f.) 9.2kgf/cm² (9.0bar) Thrusters: 1 Thwart. FP thruster (f) Fuel: 206.9 (d.f.)
9274460 *VRMR6* -	**WHITE BAY** *ex Athos -2013* **White Bay Ltd** Pacific Basin Shipping (HK) Ltd *Hong Kong* *Hong Kong* MMSI: 477942100	30,012 17,843 52,248 T/cm 55.5	Class: NK (BV)	**2004-04 Tsuneishi Heavy Industries (Cebu) Inc — Balamban** Yd No: SC-043 Loa 190.00 (BB) Br ex - Dght 12.000 Lbp 182.87 Br md 32.26 Dpth 17.00 Welded, 1 dk	**(A21A2BC) Bulk Carrier** Grain: 67,500; Bale: 65,601 Compartments: 5 Ho, ER 5 Ha: 4 (21.2 x 18.4)ER (20.4 x 18.4) Cranes: 4x30t	**1 oil engine** driving 1 FP propeller Total Power: 7,800kW (10,605hp) 14.5kn B&W 6S50MC 1 x 2 Stroke 6 Cy. 500 x 1910 7800kW (10605bhp) Mitsui Engineering & Shipbuilding CLtd-Japan
7214492 *ERUC*	**WHITE BREAM** *ex Yucin -2013 ex Anna -2012 ex Betta -2011* *ex Aspet 1 -2007 ex Uluc Ka -2001* *ex Delta Lady -1994 ex Amalie Essberger -1987* **Andrew D Robertson & Sons International Trade & Investments LLP** Valmar Oil Ltd *Moldova* MMSI: 214182104	992 442 1,537 T/cm 5.8	Class: DR (TL) (GL)	**1972-07 JG Hitzler Schiffswerft und Masch GmbH & Co KG — Lauenburg** Yd No: 729 Loa 69.32 Br ex 10.72 Dght 4.660 Lbp 64.04 Br md 10.71 Dpth 6.35 Welded, 1 dk	**(A12B2TR) Chemical/Products Tanker** Double Bottom Entire Compartment Length Liq: 1,786; Liq (Oil): 1,786 Cargo Heating Coils Compartments: 4 Ta, 4 Ta (s.stl), ER 6 Cargo Pump (s): 2x85m³/hr, 4x77m³/hr Manifold: Bow/CM: 46m Ice Capable	**1 oil engine** geared to sc. shaft driving 1 CP propeller Total Power: 971kW (1,320hp) 12.0kn Deutz SBV8M545 1 x 4 Stroke 8 Cy. 320 x 450 971kW (1320bhp) Kloeckner Humboldt Deutz AG-West Germany AuxGen: 4 x 60kW 440V 60Hz a.c Fuel: 53.0 (d.f.) 5.0pd
9317183 *H3DQ* -	**WHITE CAMERON** - **White Panama SA** KK White Line *Panama* *Panama* MMSI: 356932000 Official number: 3046105B	7,442 3,957 11,417	Class: NK	**2005-01 Nishi Shipbuilding Co Ltd — Imabari EH** Yd No: 441 Loa 110.67 (BB) Br ex - Dght 9.214 Lbp 102.16 Br md 19.20 Dpth 13.50 Welded, 1 dk	**(A31A2GX) General Cargo Ship** Grain: 15,760; Bale: 14,681 2 Ha: (33.6 x 14.0)ER (20.3 x 14.0) Cranes: 1x60t,2x30.7t; Derricks: 1x30t	**1 oil engine** driving 1 FP propeller Total Power: 3,900kW (5,302hp) 13.3kn B&W 6L35MC 1 x 2 Stroke 6 Cy. 350 x 1050 3900kW (5302bhp) Makita Corp-Japan Fuel: 705.0
9276913 *9VAY8* -	**WHITE CATTLEYA 11** - **RJG 03 Singapore Pte Ltd** VLK Traders Singapore Pte Ltd *Singapore* *Singapore* MMSI: 563253000 Official number: 390199	2,300 1,091 3,541 T/cm 9.7	Class: NK	**2003-03 Higaki Zosen K.K. — Imabari** Yd No: 550 Loa 86.45 (BB) Br ex 13.64 Dght 5.912 Lbp 79.95 Br md 13.60 Dpth 6.90 Welded, 1 dk	**(A12B2TR) Chemical/Products Tanker** Double Bottom Entire Compartment Length Liq: 3,785; Liq (Oil): 3,785 Cargo Heating Coils Compartments: 10 Wing Ta, 2 Wing Slop Ta, ER 6 Cargo Pump (s): 6x300m³/hr Manifold: Bow/CM: 38.4m	**1 oil engine** driving 1 FP propeller Total Power: 1,618kW (2,200hp) Akasaka A34C 1 x 4 Stroke 6 Cy. 340 x 620 1618kW (2200bhp) Akasaka Tekkosho KK (Akasaka DieselLtd)-Japan AuxGen: 2 x 150kW 450V 60Hz a.c Fuel: 55.0 (d.f.) 143.0 (r.f.)

IMO / Call sign	Name / Owner	Tonnage	Class	Construction	Type	Machinery
9330135 *9VDE2* -	**WHITE CATTLEYA 12** **Cybele Singapore Pte Ltd** VLK Traders Singapore Pte Ltd *Singapore* *Singapore* MMSI: 564874000 Official number: 391197	**4,120** 1,781 6,144 T/cm 14.2	Class: NK	**2005-05 Higaki Zosen K.K. — Imabari** Yd No: 578 Loa 97.16 (BB) Br ex 18.23 Dght 6.713 Lbp 89.90 Br md 18.00 Dpth 9.15 Welded, 1 dk	**(A12B2TR) Chemical/Products Tanker** Double Hull (13F) Liq: 6,489; Liq (Oil): 6,621 Cargo Heating Coils Compartments: 8 Wing Ta, 2 Wing Slop Ta, ER 8 Cargo Pump (s): 8x300m^3/hr Manifold: Bow/CM: 46m	**1 oil engine** driving 1 FP propeller Total Power: 2,427kW (3,300hp) 13.2kn Hanshin LH41L 1 x 4 Stroke 6 Cy. 410 x 800 2427kW (3300bhp) The Hanshin Diesel Works Ltd-Japan AuxGen: 2 x 200kW 450V 60Hz a.c Fuel: 109.0 (d.f.) 257.0 (r.f.)
1002990 *ZCOE7* -	**WHITE CLOUD** *ex* New Horizon L *-2003* **Ballast Holdings Ltd** YCO SAM *George Town* *Cayman Islands (British)* MMSI: 319403000 Official number: 738137	**968** 290 770	Class: LR ✠ **100A1** SS 05/2010 Yacht ✠ **LMC** **UMS** Eq.Ltr: I;	**1983-04 Jacht- en Scheepswerf C. van Lent & Zonen B.V. — Kaag** Yd No: 745 Loa 59.96 Br ex 9.69 Dght 3.350 Lbp 54.59 Br md - Dpth 5.33 Welded, 1 dk	**(X11A2YP) Yacht**	**2 oil engines** driving 2 FP propellers Total Power: 4,414kW (6,002hp) M.T.U. 12V1163TB62 2 x Vee 4 Stroke 12 Cy. 230 x 280 each-2207kW (3001bhp) MTU Friedrichshafen GmbH-Friedrichshafen Fuel: 126.3 (d.f.)
9378826 *3FSL7* -	**WHITE CORAL** **White Reefer Line Corp** Kobe Shipmanagement Co Ltd SatCom: Inmarsat C 435376910 *Panama* *Panama* MMSI: 353769000 Official number: 4056709	**19,817** 10,953 32,115 T/cm 45.1	Class: NK	**2009-07 The Hakodate Dock Co Ltd — Hakodate HK** Yd No: 826 Loa 175.53 (BB) Br ex - Dght 9.640 Lbp 167.00 Br md 29.40 Dpth 13.70 Welded, 1 dk	**(A21A2BC) Bulk Carrier** Double Hull Grain: 42,657; Bale: 41,095 Compartments: 5 Ho, ER 5 Ha: ER Cranes: 4x30t	**1 oil engine** driving 1 FP propeller Total Power: 6,840kW (9,300hp) 14.4kn Mitsubishi 6UEC52LA 1 x 2 Stroke 6 Cy. 520 x 1600 6840kW (9300bhp) Kobe Hatsudoki KK-Japan Fuel: 1450.0
9330666 *A8LK6* -	**WHITE DIAMOND** **Seldan Shipping Inc** XT Management Ltd *Monrovia* *Liberia* MMSI: 636013215 Official number: 13215	**32,578** 18,070 53,538 T/cm 57.3	Class: NK (NV)	**2008-07 Ha Long Shipbuilding Co Ltd — Ha Long** Yd No: HR-53-HL04 Loa 190.00 (BB) Br ex - Dght 12.600 Lbp 183.25 Br md 32.26 Dpth 17.50 Welded, 1 dk	**(A21A2BC) Bulk Carrier** Double Hull Grain: 65,900; Bale: 64,000 Compartments: 5 Ho, ER 5 Ha: 4 (21.6 x 22.4)ER (19.2 x 20.8) Cranes: 4x36t	**1 oil engine** driving 1 FP propeller Total Power: 9,479kW (12,888hp) 14.2kn MAN-B&W 6S50MC-C 1 x 2 Stroke 6 Cy. 500 x 2000 9479kW (12888bhp) Dalian Marine Diesel Works-China AuxGen: 3 x 680kW 440V 60Hz a.c Fuel: 215.0 (d.f.) 2000.0 (r.f.) 34.5pd
9082594 - -	**WHITE DOLPHIN** **Government of The People's Republic of China** - *China*	*400* - 25	Class: (CC)	**1994-09 WaveMaster International Pty Ltd — Fremantle WA** Yd No: 052 Loa 24.90 Br ex - Dght 1.650 Lbp - Br md 8.00 Dpth - Welded, 1 dk	**(A37B2PS) Passenger Ship** Hull Material: Aluminium Alloy Passengers: unberthed: 218	**2 oil engines** with clutches, flexible couplings & sr reverse geared to sc. shafts driving 2 FP propellers Total Power: 1,220kW (1,658hp) 25.0kn M.T.U. 12V183TE72 2 x Vee 4 Stroke 12 Cy. 128 x 142 each-610kW (829bhp) MTU Friedrichshafen GmbH-Friedrichshafen
8807430 *3EVO6* -	**WHITE DOLPHIN** **Sun Panama Shipping SA** Hayama Senpaku KK (Hayama Shipping Ltd) SatCom: Inmarsat A 1331276 *Panama* *Panama* MMSI: 351817000 Official number: 1811989F	**5,893** 3,362 7,101	Class: NK	**1988-10 Imabari Shipbuilding Co Ltd — Imabari EH (Imabari Shipyard)** Yd No: 471 Loa 136.83 (BB) Br ex - Dght 7.615 Lbp 129.00 Br md 18.00 Dpth 10.50 Welded	**(A34A2GR) Refrigerated Cargo Ship** Ins: 9,061 TEU 16 incl 8 ref C Compartments: 4 Ho, ER 4 Ha: 4 (8.4 x 6.4)ER Derricks: 8x3.5t	**1 oil engine** driving 1 FP propeller Total Power: 4,671kW (6,351hp) 17.6kn B&W 5L50MC 1 x 2 Stroke 5 Cy. 500 x 1620 4671kW (6351bhp) Mitsui Engineering & Shipbuilding CLtd-Japan AuxGen: 4 x 370kW a.c Thrusters: 1 Tunnel thruster (f) Fuel: 60.0 (d.f.) 840.0 (r.f.) 16.0pd
8502262 - -	**WHITE DOVE TOO** **Deep Sea Ocean SA** - *Panama* *Panama* Official number: 4036209	**385** 116 -		**1984 Roanoke Island Steel & Boat Works, Inc. — Wanchese, NC** Yd No: 14 Loa 37.19 Br ex 9.94 Dght 3.841 Lbp - Br md 9.15 Dpth 4.45 Welded, 1 dk	**(B11B2FV) Fishing Vessel**	**1 oil engine** geared to sc. shaft driving 1 FP propeller Total Power: 313kW (426hp) 10.5kn Caterpillar D353SCAC 1 x 4 Stroke 6 Cy. 159 x 203 313kW (426bhp) Caterpillar Tractor Co-USA
8210376 *HP3029* -	**WHITE EAGLE** *ex* Nova Hh *-2011* *ex* UPCO 7 *-2010* *ex* U7b *-2009* *ex* Upco 1 *-2008* *ex* A. H. Star 1 *-2008* *ex* Gulfstar *-2007* *ex* Meiwa Maru No. 7 *-2007* **Amsterdam Shipping Services Inc** Al Rafedain Marine Services LLC *Panama* *Panama* MMSI: 372021000 Official number: 41861PEXT1	**998** 786 1,718		**1982-11 Kogushi Zosen K.K. — Okayama** Yd No: 237 Loa 71.00 Br ex - Dght 4.634 Lbp 66.02 Br md 11.02 Dpth 5.01 Welded, 1 dk	**(A12B2TR) Chemical/Products Tanker** Liq: 1,800; Liq (Oil): 1,800 Compartments: 8 Ta, ER	**1 oil engine** geared to sc. shaft driving 1 FP propeller Total Power: 1,177kW (1,600hp) 10.0kn Hanshin 6LU35G 1 x 4 Stroke 6 Cy. 350 x 550 1177kW (1600bhp) The Hanshin Diesel Works Ltd-Japan
8651570 *HP5788* -	**WHITE EAGLE III** *ex* White Eagle *-2012* **Compania Naviera la Mundial SA** - *Panama* *Panama* MMSI: 373441000 Official number: 43350PEXT	**165** 50 -		**1982 Camcraft, Inc. — Marrero, La** Yd No: 268 Loa 33.53 Br ex 7.92 Dght - Lbp - Br md 7.80 Dpth 3.50 Welded, 1 dk	**(B21A20S) Platform Supply Ship**	**1 oil engine** driving 1 Propeller 15.0kn
8514837 *DUA6521* -	**WHITE EGRET** *ex* Daikichi Maru No. 68 *-2008* **Royal Pacific Rim Fishing Corp** - *Manila* *Philippines* Official number: BATM007965	*492* 236 707		**1985-12 Miho Zosensho K.K. — Shimizu** Yd No: 1266 Loa 66.38 (BB) Br ex 10.24 Dght 4.001 Lbp 56.52 Br md 9.52 Dpth 4.45 Welded, 1 dk	**(B11B2FV) Fishing Vessel** Ins: 712	**1 oil engine** with clutches, flexible couplings & sr geared to sc. shaft driving 1 FP propeller Total Power: 1,471kW (2,000hp) Akasaka DM36KFD 1 x 4 Stroke 6 Cy. 360 x 540 1471kW (2000bhp) Akasaka Tekkosho KK (Akasaka DieselLtd)-Japan
9607291 *9HA2891* -	**WHITE FIN** **White Fin Shipping Ltd** Finner Ship Management Ltd *Valletta* *Malta* MMSI: 256608000 Official number: 9607291	**33,042** 18,700 56,780 T/cm 58.8	Class: BV GL	**2011-11 Yangfan Group Co Ltd — Zhoushan ZJ** Yd No: 2177 Loa 189.99 (BB) Br ex - Dght 12.800 Lbp 185.64 Br md 32.26 Dpth 18.00 Welded, 1 dk	**(A21A2BC) Bulk Carrier** Grain: 71,634; Bale: 68,200 Compartments: 5 Ho, ER 5 Ha: ER Cranes: 4x30t	**1 oil engine** driving 1 FP propeller Total Power: 9,480kW (12,889hp) 14.2kn MAN-B&W 6S50MC-C8 1 x 2 Stroke 6 Cy. 500 x 2000 9480kW (12889bhp) STX Engine Co Ltd-South Korea
9593359 *V7YD2* -	**WHITE HALO** **Prosper Sunwaito SA** Sugahara Kisen KK *Majuro* *Marshall Islands* MMSI: 538004630 Official number: 4630	**31,541** 18,765 55,830 T/cm 56.9	Class: NK	**2012-04 IHI Marine United Inc — Kure HS** Yd No: 3326 Loa 189.96 (BB) Br ex - Dght 12.735 Lbp 185.00 Br md 32.26 Dpth 18.10 Welded, 1 dk	**(A21A2BC) Bulk Carrier** Grain: 72,062; Bale: 67,062 Compartments: 5 Ho, ER 5 Ha: ER Cranes: 4x30t	**1 oil engine** driving 1 FP propeller Total Power: 8,890kW (12,087hp) 14.5kn Wartsila 6RT-flex50 1 x 2 Stroke 6 Cy. 500 x 2050 8890kW (12087bhp) Diesel United Ltd.-Aioi Fuel: 2490.0
9460394 *V7YI2* -	**WHITE HAWK** **Triton Navigation BV** - SatCom: Inmarsat C 453837562 *Majuro* *Marshall Islands* MMSI: 538004665 Official number: 4665	**34,039** 19,947 61,360 T/cm 60.0	Class: NK	**2012-04 Oshima Shipbuilding Co Ltd — Saikai NS** Yd No: 10543 Loa 199.98 (BB) Br ex - Dght 12.845 Lbp 196.00 Br md 32.26 Dpth 18.33 Welded, 1 dk	**(A21A2BC) Bulk Carrier** Grain: 76,913; Bale: 75,312 Compartments: 5 Ho, ER 5 Ha: ER Cranes: 4x30t	**1 oil engine** driving 1 FP propeller Total Power: 8,201kW (11,150hp) 14.5kn MAN-B&W 6S50MC-C 1 x 2 Stroke 6 Cy. 500 x 2000 8201kW (11150bhp) Kawasaki Heavy Industries Ltd-Japan AuxGen: 3 x a.c Fuel: 1970.0
8963222 *WDC4970* -	**WHITE HOLLY** *ex* Wagl-543 *-2008* *ex* YF-341 *-2008* **Vincent G Backen** - *San Francisco, CA* *United States of America* MMSI: 366896000 Official number: 1152166	**141** 126 -		**1944-06 Basalt Rock Co. Inc. — Napa, Ca** Converted From: Training Vessel-2005 Converted From: Hospital Vessel-2002 Converted From: Buoy Tender-1998 Converted From: General Cargo Ship-1947 Loa 40.50 Br ex - Dght 3.100 Lbp - Br md 9.14 Dpth 2.67 Welded, 1 dk	**(B31A2SR) Research Survey Vessel**	**2 oil engines** driving 2 FP propellers Total Power: 442kW (600hp) 9.0kn Caterpillar 2 x 4 Stroke each-221kW (300bhp) (new engine 1944) Caterpillar Tractor Co-USA
9670169 *3FKB5* -	**WHITE INABA** **White Panama SA** - *Panama* *Panama* MMSI: 371642000 Official number: 4465513	**9,639** 4,458 13,946 T/cm 22.0	Class: NK	**2013-03 Higaki Zosen K.K. — Imabari** Yd No: 673 Loa 127.50 (BB) Br ex - Dght 9.165 Lbp 119.50 Br md 19.60 Dpth 14.00 Welded, 1 dk	**(A31A2GX) General Cargo Ship** Grain: 18,861; Bale: 17,913 Compartments: 2 Ho, ER 2 Ha: ER Cranes: 2x30.7t	**1 oil engine** driving 1 FP propeller Total Power: 4,440kW (6,037hp) 13.5kn MAN-B&W 6S35MC7 1 x 2 Stroke 6 Cy. 350 x 1400 4440kW (6037bhp) Makita Corp-Japan Fuel: 850.0

9364875 *3EFE* -	**WHITE IYO** **White Panama SA** KK White Line *Panama* *Panama* MMSI: 353488000 Official number: 3187406A	**7,498** 3,974 11,346	Class: NK	**2006-06 Nishi Shipbuilding Co Ltd — Imabari EH** Yd No: 446 Loa 110.49 Br ex - Dght 9.214 Lbp 102.16 Br md 19.20 Dpth 13.50 Welded, 1 dk	**(A31A2GX) General Cargo Ship** Grain: 15,824; Bale: 14,713 Cranes: 1x60t,2x30t; Derricks: 1x30t	**1 oil engine** driving 1 FP propeller Total Power: 3,900kW (5,302hp) 13.3kn MAN-B&W 6L35MC 1 x 2 Stroke 6 Cy. 350 x 1050 3900kW (5302bhp) Makita Corp-Japan Fuel: 620.0
9325075 *7JCG* -	**WHITE KINGDOM** **Mitsui OSK Lines Ltd (MOL)** Magsaysay MOL Ship Management Inc *Tokyo* *Japan* MMSI: 432606000 Official number: 140547	**46,422** 14,565 53,873	Class: NK	**2007-08 Sanoyas Hishino Meisho Corp — Kurashiki OY** Yd No: 1253 Loa 203.50 Br ex - Dght 10.818 Lbp 196.00 Br md 37.20 Dpth 22.30 Welded, 1 dk	**(A24B2BW) Wood Chips Carrier** Grain: 115,686 Compartments: 6 Ho, ER 6 Ha: 2 (16.2 x 22.5)2 (15.4 x 22.5)ER 2 (14.6 x 22.5) Cranes: 3x15.5t	**1 oil engine** driving 1 FP propeller Total Power: 9,120kW (12,400hp) 14.5kn MAN-B&W 6S50MC-C 1 x 2 Stroke 6 Cy. 500 x 2000 9120kW (12400bhp) Mitsui Engineering & Shipbuilding CLtd-Japan Fuel: 3030.0
9515668 *3ETA5* -	**WHITE LILY** **White Line Co Ltd & White Panama SA** KK White Line *Panama* *Panama* MMSI: 370487000 Official number: 3437908A	**7,514** 3,974 11,354	Class: NK	**2008-09 I-S Shipyard Co Ltd — Imabari EH** Yd No: 456 Loa 110.49 Br ex - Dght 9.200 Lbp 102.16 Br md 19.20 Dpth 13.50 Welded, 1 dk	**(A31A2GX) General Cargo Ship** Grain: 15,823; Bale: 14,713 Compartments: 2 Ho, 2 Tw Dk, ER 2 Ha: ER Cranes: 1x60t,2x30.7t; Derricks: 1x30t	**1 oil engine** driving 1 FP propeller Total Power: 3,900kW (5,302hp) 13.3kn MAN-B&W 6L35MC 1 x 2 Stroke 6 Cy. 350 x 1050 3900kW (5302bhp) Makita Corp-Japan Fuel: 700.0 (r.f.)
6619061 *DUA6070* -	**WHITE MAGNOLIA 2** *ex* Pelagis 109 *-2002* *ex* Gulf Stream 7 *-2000* **Frabelle Fishing Corp** - *Manila* *Philippines* Official number: MNLD001408	*135* 63 137	Class: (NK)	**1965-07 Fukuoka Shipbuilding Co Ltd — Fukuoka FO** Loa 33.38 Br ex 6.43 Dght - Lbp 29.70 Br md 6.41 Dpth 3.00 Welded, 1 dk	**(B11B2FV) Fishing Vessel**	**1 oil engine** driving 1 FP propeller Total Power: 331kW (450hp) 10.0kn Usuki 6MRS27 1 x 4 Stroke 6 Cy. 270 x 400 331kW (450bhp) Usuki Tekkosho-Usuki Fuel: 32.5
9589994 *HOHY* -	**WHITE MARY** **YO Rising SA** Temm Maritime Co Ltd SatCom: Inmarsat C 437022011 *Panama* *Panama* MMSI: 370220000 Official number: 4225411	**7,141** 2,681 8,955	Class: NK	**2010-12 Jong Shyn Shipbuilding Co., Ltd. — Kaohsiung** Yd No: 173 Loa 110.00 (BB) Br ex 18.83 Dght 7.964 Lbp 102.00 Br md 18.80 Dpth 12.70 Welded, 1 dk	**(A31A2GX) General Cargo Ship** Grain: 13,448; Bale: 12,661 Compartments: 2 Ho, 2 Tw Dk, ER 2 Ha: ER 2 (25.5 x 13.5) Cranes: 2x30t	**1 oil engine** driving 1 Propeller Total Power: 3,309kW (4,499hp) 13.0kn Hanshin LH46LA 1 x 4 Stroke 6 Cy. 460 x 880 3309kW (4499bhp) The Hanshin Diesel Works Ltd-Japan
9347138 *3EFH3* -	**WHITE MIYABI** *ex* Clematis *-2010* **White Panama SA** KK White Line *Panama* *Panama* MMSI: 355438000 Official number: 3189306C	**9,593** 4,062 12,922	Class: NK	**2006-06 Kanasashi Heavy Industries Co Ltd — Shizuoka SZ** Yd No: 8102 Loa 119.99 (BB) Br ex 21.23 Dght 8.820 Lbp 111.50 Br md 21.20 Dpth 14.30 Welded, 1 dk	**(A31A2GX) General Cargo Ship** Grain: 20,843; Bale: 19,845 Compartments: 2 Ho, ER 2 Ha: ER 2 (29.3 x 15.0) Cranes: 2x30.7t	**1 oil engine** driving 1 FP propeller Total Power: 3,900kW (5,302hp) 12.5kn MAN-B&W 6L35MC 1 x 2 Stroke 6 Cy. 350 x 1050 3900kW (5302bhp) The Hanshin Diesel Works Ltd-Japan Fuel: 885.0
9350111 *3EEC7* -	**WHITE MIZUHO** **White Panama SA** KK White Line *Panama* *Panama* MMSI: 371773000 Official number: 3132506A	**7,444** 3,957 11,427	Class: NK	**2006-01 Nishi Shipbuilding Co Ltd — Imabari EH** Yd No: 443 Loa 110.67 Br ex - Dght 9.214 Lbp 102.16 Br md 19.20 Dpth 13.50 Welded, 1 dk	**(A31A2GX) General Cargo Ship** Grain: 15,760; Bale: 14,681 Cranes: 1x60t,2x30t; Derricks: 1x30t	**1 oil engine** driving 1 FP propeller Total Power: 3,900kW (5,302hp) 13.0kn MAN-B&W 6L35MC 1 x 2 Stroke 6 Cy. 350 x 1050 3900kW (5302bhp) (made 2006) Makita Corp-Japan Fuel: 710.0
9588158 *D5EP7* -	**WHITE MOON** *ex* Broadway *-2013* **Seetip Maritime Ltd** Zodiac Maritime Agencies Ltd *Monrovia* *Liberia* MMSI: 636016128 Official number: 16128	**83,824** 51,595 160,152 T/cm 120.0	Class: NV	**2012-07 HHIC-Phil Inc — Subic** Yd No: 060 Loa 274.00 (BB) Br ex 48.04 Dght 17.200 Lbp 264.00 Br md 48.00 Dpth 23.50 Welded, 1 dk	**(A13A2TV) Crude Oil Tanker** Double Hull (13F) Liq: 172,600; Liq (Oil): 176,500 Compartments: 12 Wing Ta, 2 Wing Slop Ta, ER 3 Cargo Pump (s): 3x4000m³/hr	**1 oil engine** driving 1 FP propeller Total Power: 18,660kW (25,370hp) 15.3kn MAN-B&W 6S70MC-C 1 x 2 Stroke 6 Cy. 700 x 2800 18660kW (25370bhp) MAN Diesel A/S-Denmark AuxGen: 3 x a.c
7818092 *STWN* -	**WHITE NILE** **Sudan Shipping Line Ltd** SatCom: Inmarsat C 466241212 *Port Sudan* *Sudan* MMSI: 662414000 Official number: 019/79	**9,874** 6,060 12,905	Class: (LR) ✠ Classed LR until 21/11/01	**1979-12 B&W Skibsvaerft A/S — Copenhagen** Yd No: 879 Loa 133.31 (BB) Br ex 20.55 Dght 9.418 Lbp 122.31 Br md 20.50 Dpth 12.22 Welded, 2 dks	**(A31A2GA) General Cargo Ship (with Ro-Ro facility)** Quarter stern door/ramp (s) Grain: 20,110; Bale: 18,970; Liq: 850 TEU 372 C Ho 200 TEU C Dk 172 TEU Compartments: 4 Ho, ER, 1 RoRo Tw Dk 4 Ha: (6.7 x 5.8)Tappered (14.1 x 10.2)2 (26.9 x 10.3)ER Cranes: 1x36t,1x35t,1x18t,2x12.5t	**1 oil engine** driving 1 FP propeller Total Power: 4,928kW (6,700hp) 15.0kn B&W 5L55GFC 1 x 2 Stroke 5 Cy. 550 x 1380 4928kW (6700bhp) B&W Diesel A/S-Denmark AuxGen: 2 x 500kW 450V 60Hz a.c, 1 x 300kW 450V 60Hz a.c Fuel: 184.0 (d.f.) 867.0 (r.f.)
8207331 *C6JD8* -	**WHITE PEARL** *ex* Siskin Arrow *-2011* *ex* Monique L D *-1990* **White Pearl Shipping Co Ltd** SMT Shipping (Cyprus) Ltd SatCom: Inmarsat A 1103307 *Nassau* *Bahamas* MMSI: 308529000 Official number: 716253	**26,130** 11,832 39,273 T/cm 47.2	Class: NV (BV)	**1985-02 Stocznia im Komuny Paryskiej — Gdynia** Yd No: B538/02 Loa 183.22 (BB) Br ex 29.09 Dght 11.800 Lbp 175.32 Br md 29.01 Dpth 16.31 Welded, 1 dk	**(A31A2GO) Open Hatch Cargo Ship** Double Sides Entire Compartment Length Grain: 43,628; Bale: 42,397 TEU 1584 Compartments: 5 Ho, ER 5 Ha: 3 (25.6 x 23.0)2 (20.8 x 20.4)ER Gantry cranes: 2x25t	**1 oil engine** driving 1 FP propeller Total Power: 8,250kW (11,217hp) 12.9kn B&W 6L67GFCA 1 x 2 Stroke 6 Cy. 670 x 1700 8250kW (11217bhp) Zaklady Przemyslu Metalowego 'HCegielski' SA-Poznan AuxGen: 3 x 720kW 450V 60Hz a.c Fuel: 31.0 (d.f.) 3035.0 (r.f.) 26.0pd
8204212 -	**WHITE PEARL** *ex* Hakuryu Maru No. 1 *-1992* - -	*204* 63 -		**1982-06 Minami-Kyushu Zosen KK — Ichikikushikino KS** Yd No: 366 Loa 35.51 (BB) Br ex 7.37 Dght 2.061 Lbp 30.48 Br md 7.07 Dpth 2.82 Welded, 1 dk	**(B11B2FV) Fishing Vessel**	**1 oil engine** reverse reduction geared to sc. shaft driving 1 FP propeller Total Power: 754kW (1,025hp) Yanmar 6Z280L-ET 1 x 4 Stroke 6 Cy. 280 x 360 754kW (1025bhp) Yanmar Diesel Engine Co Ltd-Japan
5129734 *SMOX* -	**WHITE PEARL** *ex* Natie *-1988* *ex* Kaja H *-1986* *ex* Jens N *-1981* *ex* Inger H *-1975* *ex* Gerhard Jacobs *-1971* *ex* Christoph Kleemeyer *-1962* *ex* Marieluise *-1951* **Arild Johansson** - *Helsingborg* *Sweden*	*207* 106 375	Class: (GL)	**1934 C. Luehring — Brake** Yd No: 181 Lengthened & Deepened-1951 Loa 39.02 Br ex 6.10 Dght 2.650 Lbp 35.36 Br md 6.05 Dpth 3.00 Riveted, 1 dk	**(A31A2GX) General Cargo Ship** Grain: 411 2 Ha: ER	**1 oil engine** reverse reduction geared to sc. shaft driving 1 FP propeller Total Power: 147kW (200hp) 6.5kn MWM RH330SU 1 x 4 Stroke 6 Cy. 215 x 300 147kW (200bhp) (new engine 1962) Motoren Werke Mannheim AG (MWM)-West Germany
8731992 *TCLF2* -	**WHITE PRINCE** **Fun n Sun** - *Marmaris* *Turkey* Official number: 8877	**349** 115 -		**2000-07 in Turkey** Yd No: 722 Loa 45.00 Br ex - Dght 2.000 Lbp 38.60 Br md 10.00 Dpth 3.25 Welded, 1 dk	**(A37B2PS) Passenger Ship**	**2 oil engines** driving 2 Propellers Total Power: 794kW (1,080hp) Iveco Aifo 2 x 4 Stroke each-397kW (540bhp) IVECO AIFO S.p.A.-Pregnana Milanese
7230666 *3FQT2* -	**WHITE PURL** *ex* Marygas *-2012* *ex* Iran Gaz *-2012* *ex* Norgas Master *-1991* *ex* Fernwave *-1988* **Klaxon Maritime SA** Taiyoung Shipping Co Ltd *Panama* *Panama* MMSI: 355889000 Official number: 43921PEXT	**9,496** 3,403 11,832 T/cm 22.3	Class: (BV) (NV)	**1972-12 Moss Rosenberg Verft AS (Moss Verft) — Moss** Yd No: 173 Loa 138.94 (BB) Br ex 20.55 Dght 9.208 Lbp 127.87 Br md 20.52 Dpth 11.92 Welded, 1 dk	**(A11B2TG) LPG Tanker** Liq (Gas): 12,058 4 x Gas Tank (s); 4 independent (C.mn.stl) cyl horizontal 5 Cargo Pump (s): 5x185m³/hr Manifold: Bow/CM: 49m Ice Capable	**1 oil engine** driving 1 CP propeller Total Power: 7,281kW (9,899hp) 17.5kn Sulzer 6RND68 1 x 2 Stroke 6 Cy. 680 x 1250 7281kW (9899bhp) Sulzer Bros Ltd-Switzerland AuxGen: 3 x 600kW 440V 60Hz a.c Fuel: 159.5 (d.f.) (Heating Coils) 1402.0 (r.f.) 39.5pd
1007380 *C6RJ4* -	**WHITE RABBIT** *ex* White Rabbit *-2013* **White Rabbit Ltd** *Nassau* *Bahamas* MMSI: 311055000 Official number: 8000197	**464** 139 28	Class: LR ✠ **100A1** SS 07/2010 SSC Yacht catamaran HSC G3 service area **LMC** Cable: 137.5/17.5 U2 (a)	**2000-10 Image Marine Pty Ltd — Fremantle WA** Yd No: 161 Loa 36.00 Br ex - Dght 1.600 Lbp 32.40 Br md 12.00 Dpth 3.83 Welded, 2 dks	**(X11A2YP) Yacht** Hull Material: Aluminium Alloy	**2 oil engines** with clutches & sr reverse geared to sc. shafts driving 2 FP propellers Total Power: 2,014kW (2,738hp) 20.0kn M.T.U. 12V2000M90 2 x Vee 4 Stroke 12 Cy. 130 x 150 each-1007kW (1369bhp) MTU Friedrichshafen GmbH-Friedrichshafen AuxGen: 2 x 84kW 415V 50Hz a.c Thrusters: 2 Thwart. FP thruster (f)

Ship / Owner	Tonnage / Class	Builder / Dimensions	Type / Cargo	Machinery
346495 *8Y4470* **WHITE RABBIT** **White Rabbit Echo Ltd** Doreen Tan *Kingstown* *St Vincent & The Grenadines* MMSI: 375845000 Official number: 40940	**1,178** 354 121 Class: NV	**2005-06 North West Bay Ships Pty Ltd — Margate TAS** Yd No: 4 Loa 61.45 Br ex 15.69 Dght 3.560 Lbp 55.99 Br md 15.40 Dpth 6.07 Welded, 1 dk	**(X11A2YP) Yacht** Hull Material: Aluminium Alloy	**2 oil engines** reduction geared to sc. shaft (s) driving 2 FP propellers Total Power: 3,090kW (4,202hp) 20.0kn Caterpillar 3512 2 x Vee 4 Stroke 12 Cy. 170 x 190 each-1545kW (2101bhp) Caterpillar Inc-USA AuxGen: 2 x a.c
324502 *EEW7* **WHITE ROSE** **KSF 8 International SA** Korea Line Corp SatCom: Inmarsat C 437195410 *Panama* *Panama* MMSI: 371954000 Official number: 3175706A	**89,097** 56,106 171,827 Class: KR	**2006-02 Daewoo Shipbuilding & Marine Engineering Co Ltd — Geoje** Yd No: 1162 Loa 289.00 (BB) Br ex - Dght 17.923 Lbp 276.45 Br md 45.00 Dpth 24.30 Welded, 1 dk	**(A21A2BC) Bulk Carrier** Double Hull Grain: 187,606 Compartments: 9 Ho, ER 9 Ha: 7 (14.7 x 21.0)ER 2 (14.7 x 15.3)	**1 oil engine** driving 1 FP propeller Total Power: 18,660kW (25,370hp) 14.5kn MAN-B&W 6S70MC-C 1 x 2 Stroke 6 Cy. 700 x 2800 18660kW (25370bhp) Doosan Engine Co Ltd-South Korea AuxGen: 4 x 800kW 450V a.c Fuel: 5459.6 (r.f.)
008140 *EEW5* **WHITE ROSE OF DRACHS** **Novus Yachts Ltd** Nigel Burgess Ltd (BURGESS) *London* *United Kingdom* MMSI: 235862000 Official number: 908608	*1,643* 492 269 Class: LR ✠ **100A1** SS 06/2009 SSC Yacht (P), mono, G6 ✠ **LMC** **UMS** Cable: 220.0/30.0 U3 (a)	**2004-06 Peters Schiffbau GmbH — Wewelsfleth** Yd No: 675 Loa 65.05 (BB) Br ex 12.00 Dght 4.250 Lbp 54.28 Br md 11.88 Dpth 7.41 Welded, 1 dk	**(X11A2YP) Yacht**	**2 oil engines** with clutches, flexible couplings & sr reverse geared to sc. shafts driving 2 FP propellers Total Power: 4,500kW (6,118hp) 17.0kn Deutz SBV12M628 2 x Vee 4 Stroke 12 Cy. 240 x 280 each-2250kW (3059bhp) Deutz AG-Koeln AuxGen: 2 x 320kW 400V 50Hz a.c Thrusters: 1 Thwart. FP thruster (f); 1 Water jet (a)
349655 *7ZU8* **WHITE SHARK** *ex Fairchem Scout -2014 ex Purwati -2012* **Adonis Shipping Pte Ltd** Fairfield Chemical Carriers Inc *Majuro* *Marshall Islands* MMSI: 538004919 Official number: 4919	**12,105** 6,665 20,896 T/cm 30.3 Class: NK	**2007-02 Shin Kurushima Dockyard Co. Ltd. — Akitsu** Yd No: 5411 Loa 147.83 (BB) Br ex - Dght 9.770 Lbp 141.00 Br md 24.20 Dpth 12.85 Welded, 1 dk	**(A12B2TR) Chemical/Products Tanker** Double Hull (13F) Liq: 21,502; Liq (Oil): 21,502 Cargo Heating Coils Compartments: 20 Wing Ta (s.stl), 2 Wing Slop Ta (s.stl), ER 22 Cargo Pump (s): 14x330m³/hr, 8x200m³/hr Manifold: Bow/CM: 76.6m	**1 oil engine** driving 1 FP propeller Total Power: 6,150kW (8,362hp) 15.1kn MAN-B&W 6S42MC 1 x 2 Stroke 6 Cy. 420 x 1764 6150kW (8362bhp) Makita Corp-Japan AuxGen: 3 x 450kW a.c Thrusters: 1 Tunnel thruster (f) Fuel: 98.0 (d.f.) 1003.0 (r.f.)
323663 *CNP2* **WHITE STAR** **White Star International** Fraser Worldwide SAM *George Town* *Cayman Islands (British)* MMSI: 319035000 Official number: 737357	*499* 149 - Class: AB	**2004-07 Trinity Yachts LLC — New Orleans LA** Yd No: 029 Loa 48.00 Br ex 8.53 Dght - Lbp 40.54 Br md - Dpth 4.20 Welded, 1 dk	**(X11A2YP) Yacht**	**2 oil engines** geared to sc. shafts driving 2 FP propellers Total Power: 3,000kW (4,078hp) Caterpillar 3512B 2 x Vee 4 Stroke 12 Cy. 170 x 190 each-1500kW (2039bhp) Caterpillar Inc-USA
282338 *OSU* **WHITE TOBA** **White Panama SA** KK White Line *Panama* *Panama* MMSI: 356477000 Official number: 2894103B	**7,442** 3,957 11,443 Class: NK	**2003-01 Nishi Shipbuilding Co Ltd — Imabari EH** Yd No: 435 Loa 110.67 (BB) Br ex - Dght 9.214 Lbp 102.16 Br md 19.20 Dpth 13.50 Welded, 1 dk	**(A31A2GX) General Cargo Ship** Grain: 15,760; Bale: 14,681 2 Ha: (33.6 x 14.0)ER (20.3 x 14.0) Cranes: 2x30t; Derricks: 1x30t	**1 oil engine** driving 1 FP propeller Total Power: 3,900kW (5,302hp) 13.3kn MAN-B&W 6L35MC 1 x 2 Stroke 6 Cy. 350 x 1050 3900kW (5302bhp) Makita Corp-Japan AuxGen: 3 x a.c Fuel: 710.0
445241 *ERF4* **WHITE TOKIO** **White Panama SA** KK White Line *Panama* *Panama* MMSI: 370029000 Official number: 3398308	**7,514** 3,974 11,342 Class: NK	**2008-06 I-S Shipyard Co Ltd — Imabari EH** Yd No: 454 Loa 110.49 Br ex - Dght 9.214 Lbp 102.16 Br md 19.20 Dpth 13.50 Welded, 1 dk	**(A31A2GX) General Cargo Ship** Grain: 15,824; Bale: 14,713 Cranes: 2x30.7t; Derricks: 1x30t	**1 oil engine** driving 1 FP propeller Total Power: 3,900kW (5,302hp) 13.3kn MAN-B&W 6L35MC 1 x 2 Stroke 6 Cy. 350 x 1050 3900kW (5302bhp) Makita Corp-Japan Fuel: 705.0 (r.f.)
695810 *3NP* **WHITE TOMONY** **White Panama SA** KK White Line *Panama* *Panama* MMSI: 354343000 Official number: 45645TJ	**9,658** 4,458 13,919 T/cm 22.0 Class: NK	**2014-03 Higaki Zosen K.K. — Imabari** Yd No: 675 Loa 127.50 (BB) Br ex - Dght 9.465 Lbp 119.50 Br md 19.60 Dpth 14.50 Welded, 1 dk	**(A31A2GX) General Cargo Ship** Grain: 20,000; Bale: 18,598 Compartments: 2 Ho, 2 Tw Dk, ER 2 Ha: (30.8 x 14.9)ER (31.5 x 14.9) Cranes: 2x30.8t; Derricks: 2x30t	**1 oil engine** driving 1 FP propeller 13.5kn
438617 *DC7934* **WHITE WATER** **White Water Seafood Corp** - *Marathon, FL* *United States of America* MMSI: 367079190 Official number: 1026595	**164** 49 -	**1994 La Force Shipyard Inc — Coden AL** Yd No: 56 L reg 26.03 Br ex - Dght - Lbp - Br md 7.32 Dpth 3.75 Welded, 1 dk	**(B11B2FV) Fishing Vessel**	**1 oil engine** driving 1 FP propeller
492329 *3QI3* **WHITEBOX VOLGA** *ex Citta Di Mantova -2012 ex ST-1385 -2007* **Whitebox Ltd** LLC 'Imflot Logistics' *Taganrog* *Russia* MMSI: 273351960	**1,551** 593 1,278 Class: RS (RR)	**1987-03 Brodogradiliste 'Boris Kidric' — Apatin** Yd No: 1089 Loa 85.94 Br ex 12.20 Dght 2.550 Lbp 82.34 Br md 12.00 Dpth 3.50 Welded, 1 dk	**(A31A2GX) General Cargo Ship** Ice Capable	**2 oil engines** geared to sc. shafts driving 2 Propellers Total Power: 920kW (1,250hp) Alpha 6T23LU-2 2 x 4 Stroke 6 Cy. 225 x 300 each-460kW (625bhp) Titovi Zavodi 'Litostroj'-Yugoslavia
439880 *FN6287* **WHITEFISH BAY** **The CSL Group Inc (Canada Steamship Lines)** - *Montreal, QC* *Canada* MMSI: 316023341 Official number: 836914	**24,430** 8,116 37,690 Class: LR ✠ **100A1** Lake SS 05/2013 Great Lakes bulk carrier for service on the Great Lakes and River St. Lawrence **ShipRight** ACS (B) LI ECO ✠ **LMC** **UMS** Cable: 330.0/52.0 U3 (a)	**2013-05 Chengxi Shipyard Co Ltd — Jiangyin JS** Yd No: CX9303 Loa 225.47 (BB) Br ex 23.79 Dght 10.100 Lbp 222.61 Br md 23.76 Dpth 14.75 Welded, 1 dk	**(A23A2BK) Bulk Carrier, Self-discharging, Laker** Grain: 39,000 Compartments: 5 Ho, ER 5 Ha: ER	**1 oil engine** driving 1 CP propeller Total Power: 10,680kW (14,521hp) 13.5kn MAN-B&W 6S50ME-B9 1 x 2 Stroke 6 Cy. 500 x 2214 10680kW (14521bhp) Hudong Heavy Machinery Co Ltd-China AuxGen: 2 x 1250kW 450V 60Hz a.c, 1 x 938kW 450V 60Hz a.c, 1 x 2640kW 590V 60Hz a.c Boilers: TOH (ex.g.) 10.2kgf/cm² (10.0bar), TOH (o.f.) 10.2kgf/cm² (10.0bar), TOH (ex.g.) 10.2kgf/cm² (10.0bar) Thrusters: 1 Thwart. FP thruster (f); 1 Thwart. FP thruster (a)
414780 *VZ* **WHITEHEAD SECONDA** *ex Whitehead II -1997* **Whitehead Alenia Sistemi Subacquei Spa (WASS)** - *Livorno* *Italy* Official number: 902	*174* 58 165 Class: RI	**1987-12 Cant. Nav. Picchiotti SpA — Viareggio** Yd No: 570 Loa 27.50 (BB) Br ex 6.90 Dght 2.130 Lbp 26.00 Br md - Dpth 3.90 Welded, 1 dk	**(B34L2QU) Utility Vessel**	**2 oil engines** with flexible couplings & reverse reduction geared to sc. shafts driving 2 FP propellers Total Power: 1,910kW (2,596hp) Caterpillar 3512TA 2 x Vee 4 Stroke 12 Cy. 170 x 190 each-955kW (1298bhp) Caterpillar Inc-USA
434222 *CT9* **WHITHAVEN** *ex Galp Marine -2011* **John H Whitaker (Tankers) Ltd** - *Douglas* *Isle of Man (British)* MMSI: 235084022 Official number: 742822	**1,922** 835 2,779 Class: BV	**2005-03 Bengbu Shenzhou Machinery Co Ltd — Bengbu AH** Yd No: 2650 Loa 82.98 Br ex 12.53 Dght 5.000 Lbp 79.45 Br md 12.50 Dpth 6.30 Welded, 1 dk	**(A13B2TP) Products Tanker** Double Hull (13F) Ice Capable	**2 oil engines** reduction geared to sc. shafts driving 2 Propellers Total Power: 1,492kW (2,028hp) 11.0kn Caterpillar 3508B 2 x Vee 4 Stroke 8 Cy. 170 x 190 each-746kW (1014bhp) Caterpillar Inc-USA Thrusters: 1 Tunnel thruster (f)
462390 *93852* **WHITING ANN** *ex Ocean Whiskey -2005* **Linden Shipping International** Van Oord NV *Panama* *Panama* MMSI: 351019000 Official number: 3273807B	**144** 44 - Class: GL	**2001-12 PT Nanindah Mutiara Shipyard — Batam** Yd No: T80 Loa 23.50 Br ex - Dght 2.500 Lbp 21.44 Br md 7.50 Dpth 3.10 Welded, 1 dk	**(B32A2ST) Tug**	**2 oil engines** geared to sc. shafts driving 2 FP propellers Total Power: 882kW (1,200hp) Cummins KTA-19-M 2 x 4 Stroke 6 Cy. 159 x 159 each-441kW (600bhp) Chongqing Cummins Engine Co Ltd-China
435400 *YK2* **WHITNAVIGATOR** **John H Whitaker (Tankers) Ltd** - *Douglas* *Isle of Man (British)* MMSI: 235076809 Official number: 741954	**1,350** 490 1,798 Class: BV	**2010-09 Modest Infrastructure Ltd — Bhavnagar** Yd No: 308 Loa 69.60 Br ex 12.02 Dght 4.500 Lbp 66.30 Br md 12.00 Dpth 6.00 Welded, 1 dk	**(A13B2TP) Products Tanker** Double Hull (13F) Liq: 1,728; Liq (Oil): 1,728 Compartments: 5 Wing Ta, 5 Wing Ta, 2 Wing Slop Ta, ER 3 Cargo Pump (s): 3x250m³/hr	**2 oil engines** reduction geared to sc. shafts driving 2 FP propellers Total Power: 882kW (1,200hp) 9.0kn Caterpillar C18 2 x 4 Stroke 6 Cy. 145 x 183 each-441kW (600bhp) Caterpillar Inc-USA AuxGen: 2 x 205kW 50Hz a.c Thrusters: 1 Tunnel thruster (f) Fuel: 64.0 (d.f.)

IMO / Call sign	Name / Owner	Tonnage	Class	Build	Type / Capacity	Machinery
9551337 *HOXD* -	**WHITNEY** **New Seagull Shipping SA** Koyo Kaiun Asia Pte Ltd SatCom: Inmarsat C 437300042 *Panama* *Panama* MMSI: 356876000 Official number: 38845TJ	**8,417** 4,375 14,206 T/cm 23.4	Class: NK	**2009-05 Asakawa Zosen K.K. — Imabari** Yd No: 568 Loa 134.16 (BB) Br ex 20.52 Dght 8.813 Lbp 125.00 Br md 20.50 Dpth 11.60 Welded, 1 dk	**(A12B2TR) Chemical/Products Tanker** Double Hull (13F) Liq: 16,254; Liq (Oil): 15,596 Cargo Heating Coils Compartments: 18 Wing Ta (s.stl), 1 Wing Slop Ta (s.stl), 1 Wing Slop Ta, ER 18 Cargo Pump (s): 10x300m³/hr, 8x200m³/hr Manifold: Bow/CM: 61.7m	**1 oil engine** driving 1 FP propeller Total Power: 4,440kW (6,037hp) 13.9kr MAN-B&W 6S35MC 1 x 2 Stroke 6 Cy. 350 x 1400 4440kW (6037bhp) Makita Corp-Japan AuxGen: 3 x 417kW a.c Thrusters: 1 Tunnel thruster (f) Fuel: 82.0 (d.f.) 733.0 (r.f.)
8911085 *A8KZ8* -	**WHITNEY BAY** *ex* United Cool *-2006* *ex* EW Whitney *-2002* **Whitney Bay Shipping Co BV** Seatrade Groningen BV *Monrovia* *Liberia* MMSI: 636013153 Official number: 13153	**8,739** 4,085 9,687	Class: NK	**1990-02 Shin Kurushima Dockyard Co. Ltd. — Onishi** Yd No: 2652 Loa 141.01 Br ex - Dght 8.508 Lbp 133.03 Br md 20.60 Dpth 13.00 Welded, 1 dk	**(A34A2GR) Refrigerated Cargo Ship** Ins: 12,720 Compartments: 4 Ho, ER 4 Ha: (7.4 x 6.0)3 (8.1 x 6.0)ER Derricks: 8x5t	**1 oil engine** driving 1 FP propeller Total Power: 7,945kW (10,802hp) 18.5kn Mitsubishi 6UEC52LS 1 x 2 Stroke 6 Cy. 520 x 1850 7945kW (10802bhp) Kobe Hatsudoki KK-Japan Fuel: 1265.0 (r.f.)
9342607 *MPUN5* -	**WHITONIA** **John H Whitaker (Tankers) Ltd** - *Douglas* *Isle of Man (British)* MMSI: 235040503 Official number: 737862	**4,292** 1,963 7,511	Class: LR ✠ **100A1** SS 01/2012 Double Hull oil tanker ESP for the carriage of bunker fuel FP exceeding 60 degree C LI English Channel and North European coastal service east of Land's End and between Brest and River Elbe in resonable weather ✠ **LMC** Eq.Ltr: V; Cable: 495.0/42.0 U3 (a)	**2007-01 Dubai Drydocks — Dubai** Yd No: NB41 Loa 101.08 Br ex 18.02 Dght 6.700 Lbp 95.20 Br md 18.00 Dpth 8.80 Welded, 1 dk	**(A13B2TP) Products Tanker** Double Hull (13F) Liq: 6,800; Liq (Oil): 6,800 Compartments: 10 Wing Ta, 1 Slop Ta, ER	**2 oil engines** reduction geared to sc. shafts driving 2 FP propellers Total Power: 1,472kW (2,002hp) 8.0kn Yanmar 6RY17P-GV 2 x 4 Stroke 6 Cy. 165 x 219 each-736kW (1001bhp) Yanmar Diesel Engine Co Ltd-Japan AuxGen: 1 x 245kW 380V 50Hz a.c, 2 x 500kW 380V 50Hz a.c Thrusters: 1 Thwart. FP thruster (f) Fuel: 112.0 (d.f.)
6906165 - -	**WHITSPRAY** *ex* Bristolian *-1993* - -	*899* 533 1,321	Class: (LR) ✠ Classed LR until 20/1/04	**1969-03 Bayerische Schiffbaug. mbH vorm. A. Schellenberger — Erlenbach** Yd No: 1007 Lengthened-1971 Loa 64.62 Br ex 11.10 Dght 3.391 Lbp 62.21 Br md 11.00 Dpth 3.99 Welded, 1 dk	**(A13B2TP) Products Tanker** Single Hull Liq: 1,837; Liq (Oil): 1,837 Compartments: 10 Ta, ER 2 Cargo Pump (s)	**1 oil engine** sr reverse geared to sc. shaft driving 1 FP propeller Total Power: 485kW (659hp) 10.0kn Blackstone ERS8 1 x 4 Stroke 8 Cy. 222 x 292 485kW (659bhp) Lister Blackstone Marine Ltd.-Dursley AuxGen: 2 x 23kW 400V 50Hz a.c Fuel: 16.5 (d.f.) 2.5pd
9287833 *3FL08* -	**WHITSTAR** *ex* Border Heather *-2010* **John H Whitaker (Tankers) Ltd** Maruba SCA Empresa de Navegacion Maritima *Panama* *Panama* MMSI: 357422000 Official number: 44119PEXTF2	**2,159** 824 3,185	Class: LR ✠ **100A1** SS 09/2009 Double Hull oil tanker bottom strengthened for loading and unloading aground ESP LI ✠ **LMC** **UMS** Eq.Ltr: Q; Cable: 440.0/38.0 U3 (a)	**2004-09 Santierul Naval Damen Galati S.A. — Galati** (Hull) Yd No: 1035 **2004-09 B.V. Scheepswerf Damen Bergum — Bergum** Yd No: 9357 Loa 75.10 (BB) Br ex 14.17 Dght 5.760 Lbp 70.40 Br md 14.00 Dpth 7.60 Welded, 1 dk	**(A13B2TP) Products Tanker** Double Hull (13F) Liq: 3,005; Liq (Oil): 3,005 Compartments: 2 Ta, 8 Wing Ta, 1 Slop Ta, ER 10 Cargo Pump (s): 10x200m³/hr	**1 oil engine** with flexible couplings & sr geared to sc. shaft driving 1 CP propeller Total Power: 2,400kW (3,263hp) 12.0kn MaK 8M25 1 x 4 Stroke 8 Cy. 255 x 400 2400kW (3263bhp) Caterpillar Motoren GmbH & Co. KG-Germany AuxGen: 2 x 420kW 400V 50Hz a.c, 1 x 400kW 400V 50Hz a.c Boilers: TOH (o.f.) 10.2kgf/cm² (10.0bar) Thrusters: 1 Thwart. FP thruster (f) Fuel: 90.0
8216497 *H05951* -	**WHITTIE TEUS** *ex* Whittie T *-2007* *ex* Whittie Tide *-2005* **Shipping Charters Venture Corp** Teus Maritima SAS *Panama* *Panama* MMSI: 354140000 Official number: 41989PEXT	**804** 241 713	Class: (AB)	**1983-06 McDermott Shipyards Inc — New Iberia LA** Yd No: 156 Loa 54.87 (BB) Br ex 12.48 Dght 3.728 Lbp 51.82 Br md 12.20 Dpth 4.27 Welded, 1 dk	**(B21A20S) Platform Supply Ship**	**2 oil engines** reverse reduction geared to sc. shafts driving 2 FP propellers Total Power: 1,654kW (2,248hp) 11.0kn Caterpillar D399SCAC 2 x Vee 4 Stroke 16 Cy. 159 x 203 each-827kW (1124bhp) Caterpillar Tractor Co-USA AuxGen: 2 x 135kW 480V 60Hz a.c Thrusters: 1 Thwart. FP thruster (f) Fuel: 341.5 (d.f.) 7.5pd
8957819 - -	**WHOPPER STOPPER** **Ronald Stone** - *Beaufort, NC* *United States of America* Official number: 1098250	**133** 106 -		**1999 Davis Boatworks, Inc. — Wanchese, NC** Yd No: 900 L reg 23.77 Br ex - Dght - Lbp - Br md 6.15 Dpth 3.84 Bonded, 1 dk	**(B11B2FV) Fishing Vessel** Hull Material: Reinforced Plastic	**1 oil engine** driving 1 FP propeller
9723837 - -	**WHS 2503 P** **PT WHS Global Mandiri** - *Tanjung Priok* *Indonesia*	**1,980** 1,320 -	Class: RI (Class contemplated)	**2013-11 Jiangsu Huatai Shipbuilding Co Ltd — Taixing JS** Yd No: HT-71 Loa 88.28 Br ex - Dght 4.000 Lbp 83.55 Br md 15.00 Dpth 4.80 Welded, 1 dk	**(A13B2TP) Products Tanker**	**2 oil engines** driving 2 Propellers Total Power: 1,200kW (1,632hp) Chinese Std. Type Z8170ZLC 2 x 4 Stroke 8 Cy. 170 x 200 each-600kW (816bhp) Weichai Power Co Ltd-China
8732142 *J8Y4091* -	**WHY NOT** *ex* Nobody *-2011* **Nobody Charter Ltd** Dominion Marine Corporate Services Ltd *Kingstown* *St Vincent & The Grenadines* MMSI: 377241000 Official number: 40561	**190** 57 -	Class: (AB)	**2001-05 Overmarine SpA — Viareggio** Yd No: 108/05 Loa 33.40 Br ex 7.12 Dght 1.200 Lbp 30.68 Br md 7.12 Dpth 3.40 Bonded, 1 dk	**(X11A2YP) Yacht** Hull Material: Reinforced Plastic	**2 Gas Turbs** geared to sc. shafts driving 2 Water jets Total Power: 6,860kW (9,326hp) Avco TF40 2 x Gas Turb each-3430kW (4663shp) Textron Lycoming-Stratford, Ct
9653032 *2FFX3* -	**WHY WORRY** **UniCredit Leasing SpA** Pelagos Yachts Ltd *London* *United Kingdom* MMSI: 235090917 Official number: 918216	**419** 125 105	Class: (AB)	**2012-02 Baglietto S.p.A. — Varazze** Yd No: 10207 Loa 42.75 (BB) Br ex 8.90 Dght 3.080 Lbp 37.40 Br md 8.40 Dpth 4.75 Welded, 1 dk	**(X11A2YP) Yacht**	**2 oil engines** reduction geared to sc. shafts driving 2 Propellers Total Power: 2,908kW (3,954hp) 15.5kn Caterpillar 3512B 2 x Vee 4 Stroke 12 Cy. 170 x 190 each-1454kW (1977bhp) Caterpillar Inc-USA AuxGen: 2 x 86kW a.c Fuel: 85.0 (d.f.)
8703153 - -	**WIABUNA** *ex* Eva Burrows *-1999* **Adstan Tug Charters Partnership** Svitzer Australia Pty Ltd (Svitzer Australasia) *Sydney, NSW* *Australia* Official number: 852924	**156** 46 -		**1987-12 Carrington Slipways Pty Ltd — Newcastle NSW** Yd No: 203 Loa 24.52 Br ex - Dght 3.001 Lbp 22.00 Br md 8.01 Dpth 4.02 Welded, 1 dk	**(B32A2ST) Tug**	**2 oil engines** with clutches & dr reverse geared to sc. shafts driving 2 CP propellers Total Power: 1,030kW (1,400hp) G.M. (Detroit Diesel) 12V-92 2 x Vee 2 Stroke 12 Cy. 123 x 127 each-515kW (700bhp) General Motors Detroit DieselAllison Divn-USA Thrusters: 1 Thwart. FP thruster (f)
7009483 *HSB2143* -	**WICHAI 2** *ex* Navakun 5 *-1999* *ex* Shinsho Maru *-1985* **Phairot Khongkhan** - *Bangkok* *Thailand* Official number: 291038836	*853* 458 714 T/cm 4.7	Class: (NK)	**1970-01 Taguma Zosen KK — Onomichi HS** Yd No: 80 Loa 58.32 Br ex 10.04 Dght 4.060 Lbp 52.99 Br md 10.01 Dpth 4.70 Riveted\Welded, 1 dk	**(A11B2TG) LPG Tanker** Liq (Gas): 1,063 2 x Gas Tank (s); 2 independent (C.mn.stl) sph horizontal 2 Cargo Pump (s): 2x200m³/hr Manifold: Bow/CM: 25m	**1 oil engine** driving 1 FP propeller Total Power: 515kW (700hp) 10.0kn Daihatsu 6DSM-26 1 x 4 Stroke 6 Cy. 260 x 320 515kW (700bhp) Daihatsu Kogyo-Japan Fuel: 7.5 (d.f.) 30.5 (r.f.) 3.0pd
9002166 *DYEI* -	**WICHITA BELLE** *ex* New Era *-2004* *ex* Georgia Rainbow II *-2001* **Avon Maritime Corp** Roymar Ship Management Inc *Manila* *Philippines* MMSI: 548695000 Official number: MNLA00626	**17,590** 10,303 28,843 T/cm 38.9	Class: NK	**1991-02 KK Kanasashi Zosen — Toyohashi AI** Yd No: 3240 Converted From: Bulk Carrier-2008 Loa 170.00 (BB) Br ex - Dght 10.101 Lbp 162.50 Br md 26.50 Dpth 14.20 Welded, 1 dk	**(A31A2GX) General Cargo Ship** Grain: 37,341; Bale: 36,932 Compartments: 5 Ho, ER, 5 Tw Dk 5 Ha: (12.3 x 10.1) (21.5 x 13.3)2 (21.5 x 25.2) (21.5 x 21.1)ER Cranes: 4x30.4t	**1 oil engine** driving 1 FP propeller Total Power: 5,664kW (7,701hp) 14.0kn Mitsubishi 5UEC52LS 1 x 2 Stroke 5 Cy. 520 x 1850 5664kW (7701bhp) Kobe Hatsudoki KK-Japan AuxGen: 3 x 400kW 450V 60Hz a.c Fuel: 161.8 (d.f.) 1119.7 (r.f.) 19.7pd
7234179 *YFFA* -	**WICITRA DHARMA** *ex* Sakurajima Maru No. 10 *-1997* **PT Dharma Lautan Utama** - *Surabaya* *Indonesia* MMSI: 525000010	**571** 171 360	Class: KI	**1972-10 Usuki Iron Works Co Ltd — Saiki OT** Yd No: 1163 Loa 53.25 Br ex 13.21 Dght 2.706 Lbp 49.00 Br md 12.60 Dpth 3.61 Welded, 2 dks	**(A36A2PR) Passenger/Ro-Ro Ship (Vehicles)** Passengers: unberthed: 347	**2 oil engines** geared to sc. shaft driving 1 FP propeller Total Power: 1,472kW (2,002hp) Hanshin 6LUD26G 2 x 4 Stroke 6 Cy. 260 x 440 each-736kW (1001bhp) Hanshin Nainenki Kogyo-Japan

IMO / Call sign	Name / Owner / Port	Tonnage	Class	Builder / Dimensions	Type	Machinery
8900672 *VHN4825* -	**WICKHAM** *ex* R 20 *-1994* *ex* Radhwa 20 *-1993* **Svitzer Australia Pty Ltd (Svitzer Australasia)** - *Newcastle, NSW* *Australia* MMSI: 503574000 Official number: 854875	**496** 148 -	Class: LR ✠ **100A1** SS 11/2008 tug ✠ **LMC** Eq.Ltr: H; Cable: 302.5/22.0 U2	**1990-06 Scheepswerf Jac. den Breejen & Zoon B.V. — Hardinxveld-G.** (Hull) Yd No: 2260 **1990-06 B.V. Scheepswerf Damen — Gorinchem** Yd No: 3931 Loa 37.60 Br ex 11.90 Dght 1.561 Lbp 34.75 Br md 11.50 Dpth 4.25 Welded, 1 dk	**(B32A2ST) Tug**	**2 oil engines** gearing integral to driving 2 Voith-Schneider propellers Total Power: 3,600kW (4,894hp) MAN 18V20/27 2 x Vee 4 Stroke 18 Cy. 200 x 270 each-1800kW (2447bhp) MAN B&W Diesel AG-West Germany AuxGen: 2 x 184kW 440V 60Hz a.c
9393474 *C6YL6*	**WICKO** *ex* Jagodne *-2010* **Erato Four Shipping Ltd** Polska Zegluga Morska PP (POLSTEAM) SatCom: Inmarsat C 431100842 *Nassau* *Bahamas* MMSI: 311037500 Official number: 8001759	**20,603** 9,705 29,903	Class: NV PR **100A1** 11/2010 Class contemplated	**2010-11 Nantong Mingde Heavy Industry Co Ltd — Tongzhou JS** Yd No: -30000LBC-04 Loa 190.00 (BB) Br ex 23.76 Dght 10.100 Lbp 182.60 Br md 23.60 Dpth 14.60 Welded, 1 dk	**(A21A2BC) Bulk Carrier** Double Hull Grain: 38,340 Compartments: 6 Ho, ER 6 Ha: ER Cranes: 3 Ice Capable	**1 oil engine** driving 1 CP propeller Total Power: 9,480kW (12,889hp) 14.5kn Wartsila 6RTA48T-B 1 x 2 Stroke 6 Cy. 480 x 2000 9480kW (12889bhp) AuxGen: 2 x a.c, 1 x a.c Thrusters: 1 Tunnel thruster (f)
9377444 *WDC7747* -	**WICOMICO** **Vane Line Bunkering Inc** - *Baltimore, MD* *United States of America* MMSI: 367076210 Official number: 1177830	**327** 98 364		**2005-12 Thoma-Sea Boatbuilders Inc — Houma LA** Yd No: 127 Loa 29.72 Br ex - Dght 3.960 Lbp - Br md 10.36 Dpth 4.57 Welded, 1 dk	**(B32B2SP) Pusher Tug**	**2 oil engines** reverse reduction geared to sc.shafts driving 2 FP propellers Total Power: 3,090kW (4,202hp) Caterpillar 3516B 2 x Vee 4 Stroke 16 Cy. 170 x 190 each-1545kW (2101bhp) Caterpillar Inc-USA
9456240 *A8WH7*	**WIDAR** **ms 'Widar' Reederei Tamke GmbH & Co KG** Dietrich Tamke KG SatCom: Inmarsat C 463708658 *Monrovia* *Liberia* MMSI: 636092080 Official number: 92080	**32,987** 19,250 56,859 T/cm 58.8	Class: GL (LR) ✠ Classed LR until 6/1/11	**2011-01 Jiangsu Hantong Ship Heavy Industry Co Ltd — Tongzhou JS** Yd No: 026 Loa 189.96 (BB) Br ex 32.29 Dght 12.810 Lbp 184.99 Br md 32.25 Dpth 18.00 Welded, 1 dk	**(A21A2BC) Bulk Carrier** Grain: 71,634; Bale: 68,200 Compartments: 5 Ho, ER 5 Ha: ER Cranes: 4x35t	**1 oil engine** driving 1 FP propeller Total Power: 9,480kW (12,889hp) 14.2kn MAN-B&W 6S50MC-C 1 x 2 Stroke 6 Cy. 500 x 2000 9480kW (12889bhp) STX Engine Co Ltd-South Korea AuxGen: 3 x 600kW 440V 60Hz a.c Boilers: AuxB (Comp) 7.9kgf/cm² (7.7bar)
7732585 *WBM7123*	**WIDE BAY** **Trident Seafoods Corp** - *Seattle, WA* *United States of America* MMSI: 366971220 Official number: 583100	*123* 106 -		**1977 Whitney Fidalgo Seafoods — Seattle, Wa** Yd No: 2 L reg 21.31 Br ex - Dght - Lbp - Br md 7.32 Dpth 2.21 Welded, 1 dk	**(B11B2FV) Fishing Vessel**	**1 oil engine** driving 1 FP propeller Total Power: 405kW (551hp)
9033842 *DSNM8* -	**WIDE POS** **Keumyang Shipping Co Ltd** - *Jeju* *South Korea* MMSI: 441400000 Official number: JJR-048880	**2,509** 863 3,640	Class: KR	**1992-03 ShinA Shipbuilding Co Ltd — Tongyeong** Yd No: 354 Loa 94.50 Br ex - Dght 5.657 Lbp 88.03 Br md 14.00 Dpth 7.00 Welded, 1 dk	**(A31A2GX) General Cargo Ship** Grain: 2,978; Bale: 2,822 Compartments: 2 Ho, ER 2 Ha: 2 (25.0 x 9.5)ER	**1 oil engine** reverse geared to sc. shaft driving 1 FP propeller Total Power: 1,692kW (2,300hp) 12.0kn Hanshin 6EL38 1 x 4 Stroke 6 Cy. 380 x 760 1692kW (2300bhp) The Hanshin Diesel Works Ltd-Japan AuxGen: 2 x 180kW 445V a.c
7110892 - -	**WIDE TIDE** **Naviera Buena Suerte** - *Honduras*	*197* 134 -		**1965 American Marine Corp. — New Orleans, La** Yd No: 905 Loa - Br ex 10.67 Dght 3.074 Lbp 43.39 Br md - Dpth 3.66 Welded, 1 dk	**(B21B20A) Anchor Handling Tug Supply**	**2 oil engines** driving 2 FP propellers Total Power: 1,126kW (1,530hp) Caterpillar D398SCAC 2 x Vee 4 Stroke 12 Cy. 159 x 203 each-563kW (765bhp) Caterpillar Tractor Co-USA
8954817 *YB2548* -	**WIDI 5** **PT Pelayaran Sinjori Tata Laut** Rusli *Tanjungpinang* *Indonesia* Official number: 180/PPM	**100** 30 -		**1994 Bintan Shipping Corp — Tanjungpinang** Loa 27.85 Br ex - Dght 2.000 Lbp 25.63 Br md 4.44 Dpth - Welded, 1 dk	**(A37B2PS) Passenger Ship**	**2 oil engines** geared to sc. shafts driving 2 FP propellers Total Power: 1,220kW (1,658hp) M.T.U. 12V183TE72 2 x Vee 4 Stroke 12 Cy. 128 x 142 each-610kW (829bhp) MTU Friedrichshafen GmbH-Friedrichshafen
8954829 *YB4296* -	**WIDI 8** **Arman** - *Jakarta* *Indonesia* Official number: 1590/BC	**140** 42 -	Class: (KI)	**1995-01 P.T. Asia Marine Fibrindo — Tangerang** Loa 30.90 Br ex - Dght 2.138 Lbp 27.74 Br md 5.47 Dpth 2.85 Bonded, 1 dk	**(A37B2PS) Passenger Ship** Hull Material: Reinforced Plastic	**3 oil engines** geared to sc. shafts driving 3 FP propellers Total Power: 1,830kW (2,487hp) 13.4kn M.T.U. 12V183TE72 3 x Vee 4 Stroke 12 Cy. 128 x 142 each-610kW (829bhp) MTU Friedrichshafen GmbH-Friedrichshafen
8954831 *YB3301* -	**WIDI EXPRESS 9** **PT Pelayaran Sinjori Tata Laut** Rusli *Tanjungpinang* *Indonesia* Official number: 724/GGA	**123** 37 -	Class: (KI)	**1998-01 P.T. Anggun Segara — Tanjungpinang** Loa 30.00 Br ex 5.28 Dght 1.700 Lbp 27.26 Br md 5.10 Dpth 2.90 Bonded, 1 dk	**(A37B2PS) Passenger Ship** Hull Material: Reinforced Plastic	**3 oil engines** geared to sc. shafts driving 3 FP propellers Total Power: 1,611kW (2,190hp) 26.0kn M.T.U. MB837EA500 3 x Vee 4 Stroke 8 Cy. 138 x 105 each-537kW (730bhp) (made 1976, fitted 1998) MTU Friedrichshafen GmbH-Friedrichshafen
8997003 *YB3340* -	**WIDI EXPRESS 10** **PT Pelayaran Sinjori Tata Laut** - *Tanjungpinang* *Indonesia*	**116** 35 -	Class: KI	**1997 P.T. Anggun Segara — Tanjungpinang** Loa 30.00 Br ex 5.28 Dght - Lbp 28.22 Br md 5.10 Dpth 2.50 Bonded, 1 dk	**(A37B2PS) Passenger Ship** Hull Material: Reinforced Plastic	**3 oil engines** reduction geared to sc. shafts driving 3 Propellers Total Power: 1,830kW (2,487hp) 24.0kn M.T.U. MB838 3 x Vee 4 Stroke 10 Cy. 170 x 175 each-610kW (829bhp) (made 1986, fitted 1997) MTU Friedrichshafen GmbH-Friedrichshafen
9068550 *YB3329* -	**WIDI EXPRESS 18** *ex* Merbau Gamma *-2005* **PT Pelayaran Sinjori Tata Laut** - *Indonesia* MMSI: 525023044	**160** 48 -	Class: (BV)	**1989-05 Sunbeam Trading Pte Ltd — Singapore** Yd No: 8 Loa 28.17 Br ex - Dght 1.000 Lbp 25.83 Br md 5.09 Dpth 3.50 Welded, 1 dk	**(A37B2PS) Passenger Ship** Hull Material: Aluminium Alloy	**3 oil engines** geared to sc. shafts driving 3 Propellers Total Power: 1,236kW (1,680hp) 25.0kn MAN D2840LE 3 x Vee 4 Stroke 10 Cy. 128 x 142 each-412kW (560bhp) MAN Nutzfahrzeuge AG-Nuernberg
9068562 *YB3332* -	**WIDI EXPRESS 19** *ex* Merbau Delta *-2002* **PT Pelayaran Sinjori Tata Laut** - *Indonesia* MMSI: 525023045	**160** 48 -	Class: (BV)	**1989-06 Sunbeam Trading Pte Ltd — Singapore** Yd No: 9 Loa 28.17 Br ex - Dght 1.000 Lbp 25.83 Br md 5.09 Dpth 3.50 Welded, 1 dk	**(A37B2PS) Passenger Ship** Hull Material: Aluminium Alloy	**3 oil engines** geared to sc. shafts driving 3 Propellers Total Power: 1,236kW (1,680hp) 25.0kn MAN D2840LE 3 x Vee 4 Stroke 10 Cy. 128 x 142 each-412kW (560bhp) MAN Nutzfahrzeuge AG-Nuernberg
9068421 - -	**WIDI EXPRESS 20** *ex* Merbau Alpha *-2001* **PT Pelayaran Sinjori Tata Laut** - *Batam* *Indonesia*	**160** - -	Class: (KI) (BV)	**1989-05 Sunbeam Trading Pte Ltd — Singapore** Yd No: 6 L reg 28.17 Br ex - Dght 0.800 Lbp 25.96 Br md 6.10 Dpth 3.15 Welded, 1 dk	**(A37B2PS) Passenger Ship** Hull Material: Aluminium Alloy	**3 oil engines** geared to sc. shafts driving 3 Propellers Total Power: 1,236kW (1,680hp) 25.0kn MAN D2840LE 3 x Vee 4 Stroke 10 Cy. 128 x 142 each-412kW (560bhp) MAN Nutzfahrzeuge AG-Nuernberg
9068548 *YB3331* -	**WIDI EXPRESS 21** *ex* Merbau Beta *-2002* **PT Pelayaran Sinjori Tata Laut** - *Indonesia* MMSI: 525023047	**160** 48 -	Class: (BV)	**1989-05 Sunbeam Trading Pte Ltd — Singapore** Yd No: 7 L reg 25.83 Br ex - Dght 1.000 Lbp 28.17 Br md 5.09 Dpth 3.50 Welded, 1 dk	**(A37B2PS) Passenger Ship** Hull Material: Aluminium Alloy	**3 oil engines** geared to sc. shafts driving 3 Propellers Total Power: 1,236kW (1,680hp) 25.0kn MAN D2840LE 3 x Vee 4 Stroke 10 Cy. 128 x 142 each-412kW (560bhp) MAN Nutzfahrzeuge AG-Nuernberg
9029956 - -	**WIDMARINE 1** *ex* Dillah Samudra Ix *-2002* **PT Capitalinc Finance** - *Samarinda* *Indonesia*	**191** 58 -	Class: KI	**2005-09 CV Muji Rahayu — Tenggarong** Loa 28.00 Br ex - Dght 2.490 Lbp 26.40 Br md 8.10 Dpth 3.30 Welded, 1 dk	**(B32A2ST) Tug**	**2 oil engines** geared to sc. shafts driving 2 Propellers Total Power: 1,220kW (1,658hp) Yanmar 6AYM-ETE 2 x 4 Stroke 6 Cy. 155 x 180 each-610kW (829bhp) Yanmar Diesel Engine Co Ltd-Japan AuxGen: 2 x 82kW 380/220V a.c
9689079 - -	**WIDMARINE 8** **PT Widhi Satria Jaya Lines** - *Batam* *Indonesia* Official number: 4888/PPM	**148** 46 111	Class: GL	**2013-03 PT Nongsa Jaya Buana — Batam** Yd No: 143 Loa 23.50 Br ex 7.32 Dght 2.720 Lbp 21.07 Br md 7.30 Dpth 3.20 Welded, 1 dk	**(B32A2ST) Tug**	**2 oil engines** reduction geared to sc. shafts driving 2 Propellers Total Power: 830kW (1,128hp) Mitsubishi S6B3-MPTK 2 x 4 Stroke 6 Cy. 135 x 170 each-415kW (564bhp) Mitsubishi Heavy Industries Ltd-Japan

Ship / Owner	Tonnage	Class	Builder / Dimensions	Type / Cargo	Machinery
9127930 **WIDO CAR FERRY** - - **Government of The Republic of South Korea (Ministry of Land, Transport & Maritime Affairs)** Gyerim Shipping Co Ltd *Gunsan* *South Korea* MMSI: 440502500 Official number: KSR-953767	**260** - 80	Class: (KR)	**1995**-07 **Kwangyang Shipbuilding & Engineering Co Ltd — Janghang** Yd No: 114 Loa 49.70 Br ex - Dght 1.512 Lbp 43.00 Br md 8.80 Dpth 2.75 Welded, 1 dk	**(A36A2PR) Passenger/Ro-Ro Ship (Vehicles)**	**2 oil engines** driving 2 FP propellers Total Power: 954kW (1,298hp) 15.0kn G.M. (Detroit Diesel) 8V-149-TI 2 x Vee 2 Stroke 8 Cy. 146 x 146 each-477kW (649bhp) Detroit Diesel Corporation-Detroit, Mi
9528483 **WIDOR** *5BSH2* - **ms 'Widor' Interscan Shipmanagement GmbH & Co KG** Interscan Schiffahrtsgesellschaft mbH SatCom: Inmarsat C 421242311 *Limassol* *Cyprus* MMSI: 212423000 Official number: 9528483	**2,474** 1,412 3,417	Class: BV (LR) ✠ Classed LR until 1/6/09	**2009**-06 **Marine Projects Ltd Sp z oo — Gdansk** (Hull) Yd No: (703) **2009**-06 **Bodewes' Scheepswerven B.V. — Hoogezand** Yd No: 703 Loa 82.50 (BB) Br ex 12.60 Dght 5.300 Lbp 79.54 Br md 12.50 Dpth 8.00 Welded, 1 dk	**(A31A2GX) General Cargo Ship** Grain: 5,014 TEU 34 Compartments: 1 Ho, ER 1 Ha: ER (55.0 x 10.3) Ice Capable	**1 oil engine** with flexible couplings & sr geared to sc. shaft driving 1 CP propeller Total Power: 1,850kW (2,515hp) 12.5kn MaK 6M25 1 x 4 Stroke 6 Cy. 255 x 400 1850kW (2515bhp) Caterpillar Motoren GmbH & Co. KG-Germany AuxGen: 1 x 264kW 400V 50Hz a.c, 1 x 150kW 400V 50Hz a.c Thrusters: 1 Water jet (f)
9252735 **WIDUKIND** *A8KH9* *ex* Sci Diya *-2008* *ex* Widukind *-2007* *launched as* Hera *-2006* - **ms 'Esteship' Reederei Tamke GmbH & Co KG** Transeste Schiffahrt GmbH *Monrovia* *Liberia* MMSI: 636091178 Official number: 91178	**35,881** 14,444 42,200 T/cm 62.0	Class: GL	**2006**-10 **Stocznia Szczecinska Nowa Sp z oo — Szczecin** Yd No: B178/I/18 Loa 220.31 (BB) Br ex 32.30 Dght 12.150 Lbp 210.20 Br md 32.24 Dpth 18.70 Welded, 1 dk	**(A33A2CC) Container Ship (Fully Cellular)** TEU 3091 C Ho 1408 TEU C Dk 1683 TEU incl 500 ref C. Compartments: 6 Cell Ho, ER 11 Ha: (12.6 x 18.0)10 (12.6 x 28.3)ER Cranes: 3x45t	**1 oil engine** driving 1 FP propeller Total Power: 26,270kW (35,717hp) 22.5kn MAN-B&W 7K80MC-C 1 x 2 Stroke 7 Cy. 800 x 2300 26270kW (35717bhp) H Cegielski Poznan SA-Poland AuxGen: 2 x 1200kW 440V 60Hz a.c, 2 x 1000kW 440V 60Hz a.c Thrusters: 1 Thwart. CP thruster (f) Fuel: 215.8 (d.f.) 3680.0 (r.f.) 97.5pd
9197478 **WIEBKE** *V2OD9* - **SAL Heavy Lift GmbH** *Saint John's* *Antigua & Barbuda* MMSI: 304140000 Official number: 2905	**8,397** 4,178 9,370 T/cm 25.0	Class: GL	**2000**-09 **J.J. Sietas KG Schiffswerft GmbH & Co. — Hamburg** Yd No: 1175 Loa 151.65 (BB) Br ex - Dght 7.850 Lbp 142.10 Br md 20.40 Dpth 10.50 Welded, 1 dk plus 1 hoistable tween deck	**(A31A2GX) General Cargo Ship** Double Bottom Entire Compartment Length Grain: 13,604; Bale: 13,604 Compartments: 1 Ho, ER, 1 Tw Dk 1 Ha: (84.0 x 15.8)ER Cranes: 2x320t,1x200t	**1 oil engine** with flexible couplings & sr gearedto sc. shaft driving 1 CP propeller Total Power: 9,450kW (12,848hp) 18.0kn MAN 9L48/60 1 x 4 Stroke 9 Cy. 480 x 600 9450kW (12848bhp) MAN B&W Diesel AG-Augsburg AuxGen: 3 x 304kW 230/400V 50Hz a.c, 1 x 1000kW 380/220V a.c Thrusters: 1 Thwart. CP thruster (f) Fuel: 154.0 (d.f.) (Heating Coils) 1050.0 (r.f.) 40.0pd
7924401 **WIEBKE D** *V2CN* *ex* Pandor *-1997* - **Drabert Schiffahrtsgesellschaft mbH** - *Saint John's* *Antigua & Barbuda* MMSI: 304010786	**1,441** 459 1,795	Class: GL	**1980**-04 **J.J. Sietas KG Schiffswerft GmbH & Co. — Hamburg** Yd No: 910 Converted From: General Cargo Ship-1997 Loa 80.96 (BB) Br ex 11.33 Dght 3.290 Lbp 77.78 Br md 11.31 Dpth 5.41 Welded, 2 dks	**(A31A2GX) General Cargo Ship** Grain: 2,444; Bale: 2,425 Compartments: 1 Ho, ER 1 Ha: (49.2 x 8.9)ER	**1 oil engine** reduction geared to sc. shaft driving 1 FP propeller Total Power: 243kW (330hp) 10.5kn Deutz SBA8M528 1 x 4 Stroke 8 Cy. 220 x 280 243kW (330bhp) Kloeckner Humboldt Deutz AG-West Germany Thrusters: 1 Tunnel thruster (f)
9568990 **WIELINGEN** *ORPU* - **Wandelaar Invest SA** DAB Vloot *Ostend* *Belgium* MMSI: 205592000 Official number: 01 00789 2011	**227** 67 14	Class: GL	**2011**-08 **Schiffs- u. Yachtwerft Abeking & Rasmussen GmbH & Co. — Lemwerder** Yd No: 6472 Loa 25.65 (BB) Br ex - Dght 2.700 Lbp 23.25 Br md 13.00 Dpth 5.90 Welded, 1 dk	**(B34N2QP) Pilot Vessel** Hull Material: Aluminium Alloy	**2 oil engines** with clutches, flexible couplings & sr geared to sc. shafts driving 2 FP propellers Total Power: 1,576kW (2,142hp) 18.0kn M.T.U. 12V2000M70 2 x Vee 4 Stroke 12 Cy. 130 x 150 each-788kW (1071bhp) MTU Friedrichshafen GmbH-Friedrichshafen
8821931 **WIENIAWSKI** *9HIM6* - **Wieniawski Maritime Co Ltd** Chinese-Polish JSC (Chinsko-Polskie Towarzystwo Okretowe SA) (CHIPOLBROK) *Valletta* *Malta* MMSI: 248552000 Official number: 6569	**18,278** 9,088 22,130 T/cm 38.5	Class: LR (PR) ✠ **100A1** SS 05/2012 strengthened for heavy cargoes, container cargoes in Nos. 1, 2, 3 & 4 holds also on upper and poop decks and hatch covers LI Ice Class 1C FS at draught of 9.30m Max/min draught fwd 9.158/5.012m Max/min draught aft 10.248/6.466m Required power 6403kw, installed power 9500kw ✠ **LMC** **UMS** Eq.Ltr: I†; Cable: 605.0/64.0 U3 (a)	**1992**-05 **'3 Maj' Brodogradiliste dd — Rijeka** Yd No: 658 Loa 169.75 (BB) Br ex 27.55 Dght 9.300 Lbp 162.64 Br md 27.50 Dpth 13.80 Welded, 1 dk, 2nd dk in Nos. 1 - 4 holds, 3rd dk in Nos. 2 - 4 holds	**(A31A2GX) General Cargo Ship** Grain: 36,808; Bale: 33,214 TEU 1094 C Ho 472 TEU C Dk 622 TEU incl 30 ref C. Compartments: 4 Ho, ER, 4 Tw Dk 7 Ha: (12.7 x 15.9)4 (25.5 x 10.3)2 (19.1 x 10.3)ER Cranes: 4x24.5t Ice Capable	**1 oil engine** driving 1 FP propeller Total Power: 9,500kW (12,916hp) 16.5kn Sulzer 5RTA62 1 x 2 Stroke 5 Cy. 620 x 2150 9500kW (12916bhp) '3 Maj' Motori i Dizalice dd-Croatia AuxGen: 3 x 704kW 450V 60Hz a.c Boilers: e (ex.g.) 8.2kgf/cm² (8.0bar), AuxB (o.f.) 8.2kgf/cm² (8.0bar) Fuel: 69.0 (d.f.) 1014.0 (r.f.) 39.1pd
9424156 **WIGEON** *WDH2680* *ex* Caitlyn A Callais *-2014* - **mv Wigeon LLC** Adriatic Marine LLC *New Orleans, LA* *United States of America* MMSI: 367000090 Official number: 1191498	**878** 263 1,276		**2006**-09 **Master Boat Builders, Inc. — Coden, Al** Yd No: 380 Loa 51.50 Br ex - Dght 3.800 Lbp - Br md 14.00 Dpth 4.57 Welded, 1 dk	**(B21A2OS) Platform Supply Ship**	**2 oil engines** reduction geared to sc. shafts driving 2 Propellers Total Power: 1,940kW (2,638hp) 13.5kn Caterpillar 3512B 2 x Vee 4 Stroke 12 Cy. 170 x 190 each-970kW (1319bhp) Caterpillar Inc-USA Thrusters: 2 Tunnel thruster (f); 1 Tunnel thruster (a)
9358395 **WIGEON** *5BCC3* - **Oryx Shipping Inc** Navarone SA SatCom: Inmarsat C 421019210 *Limassol* *Cyprus* MMSI: 210192000 Official number: RCS11958	**22,790** 12,130 37,238 T/cm 44.1	Class: AB	**2007**-11 **Tianjin Xingang Shipyard — Tianjin** Yd No: 348-4 Loa 199.90 (BB) Br ex - Dght 10.750 Lbp 192.00 Br md 23.70 Dpth 15.30 Welded, 1 dk	**(A21A2BC) Bulk Carrier** Grain: 42,779; Bale: 42,351 Compartments: 6 Ho, ER 6 Ha: ER Cranes: 4x40t Ice Capable	**1 oil engine** driving 1 FP propeller Total Power: 7,860kW (10,686hp) 14.5kn MAN-B&W 6S46MC-C 1 x 2 Stroke 6 Cy. 460 x 1932 7860kW (10686bhp) Hudong Heavy Machinery Co Ltd-China AuxGen: 3 x 660kW a.c Thrusters: 1 Tunnel thruster (f) Fuel: 104.0 (d.f.) 1617.0 (r.f.)
9263978 **WIGGINS TIDE** *YJUR9* *ex* DMS Conquest *-2005* - **Tidewater Assets Ltd** Tidewater Marine International Inc *Port Vila* *Vanuatu* MMSI: 576032000 Official number: 1644	**2,421** 726 1,074	Class: AB	**2002**-12 **Kouan Shipbuilding Industry Co — Taizhou JS** Yd No: 60-01 Loa 60.11 Br ex - Dght 4.100 Lbp 54.20 Br md 17.00 Dpth 5.50 Welded, 1 dk	**(B22A2OR) Offshore Support Vessel** Cranes: 1x160t	**2 oil engines** geared to sc. shafts driving 2 Directional propellers Total Power: 2,162kW (2,940hp) 10.8kn Wartsila 6L20 2 x 4 Stroke 6 Cy. 200 x 280 each-1081kW (1470bhp) Wartsila Finland Oy-Finland AuxGen: 3 x 700kW 415V 50Hz a.c, 1 x 250kW 415V 50Hz a.c Thrusters: 2 Thwart. FP thruster (f) Fuel: 420.0
9446972 **WIGHT LIGHT** *2BBX5* - **WIGHTlink Ltd (Isle of Wight Ferries)** - *London* *United Kingdom* MMSI: 235064784 Official number: 914710	**2,546** 763 348	Class: LR ✠ **100A1** CS 08/2013 passenger/vehicle ferry operating area service, inside the Isle of Wight within an area bounded by lines drawn between the Church Spire, West Wittering to Trinity Church, Bembridge to the eastward and the Needles and Hurst Point to the westward service EP *IWS ✠ **LMC** Eq.Ltr: P; Cable: 385.0/28.0 U3 (a)	**2008**-08 **Brodogradiliste Kraljevica dd — Kraljevica** Yd No: 550 Loa 62.40 (BB) Br ex 16.42 Dght 2.300 Lbp 61.00 Br md 16.00 Dpth 4.50 Welded, 4 dks	**(A36A2PR) Passenger/Ro-Ro Ship (Vehicles)** Passengers: unberthed: 360 Bow door/ramp (centre) Len: 6.00 Wid: 3.80 Swl: - Stern door/ramp (centre) Len: 6.00 Wid: 3.80 Swl: - Lane-Len: 110 Lane-clr ht: 4.90 Cars: 65	**4 oil engines** gearing integral to driving 2 Voith-Schneider propellers Total Power: 1,916kW (2,604hp) 11.0kn Volvo Penta D16MH 4 x 4 Stroke 6 Cy. 144 x 165 each-479kW (651bhp) AB Volvo Penta-Sweden AuxGen: 4 x 225kW 415V 50Hz a.c Fuel: 35.0 (d.f.) 11.0pd

IMO / Call sign	Name / Owner / Port / Flag	Tonnage	Classification	Build / Dimensions	Type	Machinery
512537 BWG5	**WIGHT RYDER I** **WIGHTlink Ltd (Isle of Wight Ferries)** - *Portsmouth* *United Kingdom* MMSI: 235069875 Official number: 915585	520 164 130	Class: LR ✠ **100A1** SS 05/2009 SSC passenger (A) catamaran HSC G3 (range to refuge 89 nautical miles - Portsmouth to Ryde & Portsmouth to Poole ferry services) ✠ **LMC** **UMS** Eq.Ltr: E; Cable: 27.0/19.0 U2 (a)	**2009-05 FBMA Marine Inc — Balamban** Yd No: 1026 Loa 40.90 Br ex 12.01 Dght 1.600 Lbp 38.40 Br md 12.00 Dpth 4.50 Welded, 1 dk	**(A37B2PS) Passenger Ship** Hull Material: Aluminium Alloy Passengers: unberthed: 260	**2 oil engines** with clutches, flexible couplings & reverse reduction geared to sc. shafts driving 2 FP propellers Total Power: 1,940kW (2,638hp) 20.0kn Caterpillar C32 2 x Vee 4 Stroke 12 Cy. 145 x 162 each-970kW (1319bhp) (new engine 2012) Caterpillar Inc-USA AuxGen: 2 x 58kW 415V 50Hz a.c Thrusters: 2 Thwart. FP thruster (f)
512549 BWG7	**WIGHT RYDER II** **WIGHTlink Ltd (Isle of Wight Ferries)** - *Portsmouth* *United Kingdom* MMSI: 235069877 Official number: 915586	520 164 130	Class: LR ✠ **100A1** SS 06/2009 SSC passenger (A) catamaran HSC G3 (range to refuge 89 nautical miles-Portsmouth to Ryde and Portsmouth to Poole ferry service) ✠ **LMC** **UMS** Eq.Ltr: E; Cable: 27.0/19.0 U2 (a)	**2009-06 FBMA Marine Inc — Balamban** Yd No: 1027 Loa 40.90 Br ex 12.01 Dght 1.600 Lbp 38.40 Br md 12.00 Dpth 4.50 Welded, 1 dk	**(A37B2PS) Passenger Ship** Hull Material: Aluminium Alloy Passengers: unberthed: 260	**2 oil engines** with clutches, flexible couplings & reverse reduction geared to sc. shafts driving 2 FP propellers Total Power: 1,940kW (2,638hp) 20.0kn Caterpillar C32 2 x Vee 4 Stroke 12 Cy. 145 x 162 each-970kW (1319bhp) (new engine 2012) Caterpillar Inc-USA AuxGen: 2 x 58kW 415V 50Hz a.c Thrusters: 2 Thwart. FP thruster (f)
056997 PQA7	**WIGHT SCENE** **Solent & Wightline Cruises Ltd** - *Cowes* *United Kingdom* MMSI: 235031588 Official number: 721359	279 134 150		**1992-06 F.L. Steelcraft — Ynyslas, Borth** Yd No: 22191 Loa 26.40 Br ex - Dght 2.000 Lbp 25.98 Br md 10.00 Dpth 3.61 Welded, 2 dks	**(A37B2PS) Passenger Ship** Passengers: unberthed: 500	**2 oil engines** sr reverse geared to sc. shafts driving 2 FP propellers Total Power: 514kW (698hp) 12.0kn Cummins NTA-855-M 2 x 4 Stroke 6 Cy. 140 x 152 each-257kW (349bhp) Cummins Engine Co Ltd-United Kingdom Thrusters: 1 Thwart. FP thruster (f)
446984 ABV8	**WIGHT SKY** **WIGHTlink Ltd (Isle of Wight Ferries)** - *London* *United Kingdom* MMSI: 235064783 Official number: 914857	2,546 763 360	Class: LR ✠ **100A** CS 09/2013 passenger/vehicle ferry operating area service, inside the isle of Wight within an area bounded by lines drawn between the Church Spire, West Wittering to Trinity Church, Bembridge to the eastward and the Needles and Hurst Point to the westward EP *IWS ✠ **LMC** Cable: 385.0/28.0 U3 (a)	**2008-09 Brodogradiliste Kraljevica dd — Kraljevica** Yd No: 551 Loa 62.40 (BB) Br ex 16.42 Dght 2.300 Lbp 60.99 Br md 16.00 Dpth 4.50 Welded, 1 dk	**(A36A2PR) Passenger/Ro-Ro Ship (Vehicles)** Passengers: unberthed: 360 Bow door/ramp (centre) Stern door/ramp (centre) Cars: 65	**4 oil engines** gearing integral to driving 2 Voith-Schneider propellers 11.0kn Volvo Penta D16MH 4 x 4 Stroke 6 Cy. 144 x 165 AB Volvo Penta-Sweden AuxGen: 4 x 225kW 415V 50Hz a.c
490416 3BW9	**WIGHT SUN** **WIGHTlink Ltd (Isle of Wight Ferries)** - *London* *United Kingdom* MMSI: 235064777 Official number: 914851	2,546 763 360	Class: LR ✠ **100A1** CS 12/2013 passenger/vehicle ferry *IWS EP operating area service - inside the Isle of Wight within an area bounded by lines drawn between the Church Spire, West Whittering to Trinity Church, Bembridge to the eastward and the Needles and Hurst Point to the westward ✠ **LMC** Cable: 385.0/28.0 U3 (a)	**2008-12 Brodogradiliste Kraljevica dd — Kraljevica** Yd No: 552 Loa 62.40 (BB) Br ex 16.42 Dght 2.300 Lbp 60.99 Br md 16.00 Dpth 4.50 Welded, 1 dk	**(A36A2PR) Passenger/Ro-Ro Ship (Vehicles)** Passengers: unberthed: 360 Bow door/ramp (centre) Stern door/ramp (centre) Cars: 65	**4 oil engines** gearing integral to driving 2 Voith-Schneider propellers Total Power: 1,912kW (2,600hp) 11.0kn Volvo Penta D16 4 x 4 Stroke 6 Cy. 144 x 165 each-478kW (650bhp) AB Volvo Penta-Sweden AuxGen: 4 x 225kW 415V 50Hz a.c
92502	**WIJAYA DUA** **PT Asia Mega Lines** - *Jakarta* *Indonesia*	*126* 75 -	Class: KI	**1994-11 P.T. Wayata Kencana Dockyard — Jakarta** Loa 23.00 Br ex - Dght 2.300 Lbp 22.40 Br md 7.00 Dpth 3.00 Welded, 1 dk	**(B32A2ST) Tug**	**2 oil engines** driving 2 FP propellers Total Power: 988kW (1,344hp) Caterpillar 3412TA 2 x Vee 4 Stroke 12 Cy. 137 x 152 each-494kW (672bhp) Caterpillar Inc-USA
29516	**WIJAYA I** **CV Wijaya Karya Abadi** - *Samarinda* *Indonesia*	118 70 -	Class: KI	**2004-01 C.V. Karya Lestari Industri — Samarinda** Loa 23.00 Br ex - Dght 1.990 Lbp 22.60 Br md 6.50 Dpth 2.80 Welded, 1 dk	**(B32A2ST) Tug**	**2 oil engines** driving 2 Propellers Total Power: 810kW (1,102hp) Volvo Penta TAMD165A 2 x 4 Stroke 6 Cy. 144 x 165 each-405kW (551bhp) AB Volvo Penta-Sweden AuxGen: 2 x 82kW 400V a.c
92288 06866	**WIJAYA II** **CV Wijaya Karya Abadi** - *Samarinda* *Indonesia*	118 65 -	Class: KI	**2004-01 C.V. Karya Lestari Industri — Samarinda** Loa 23.00 Br ex - Dght - Lbp 22.15 Br md 6.50 Dpth 2.80 Welded, 1 dk	**(B32A2ST) Tug**	**2 oil engines** geared to sc. shafts driving 2 Propellers Total Power: 846kW (1,151hp) Volvo Penta TAMD165A 2 x 4 Stroke 6 Cy. 144 x 165 each-405kW (551bhp) AB Volvo Penta-Sweden
21675	**WIJAYA KUSUMA 2** **PT Agniputra Jayakusuma** - *Samarinda* *Indonesia* MMSI: 525006046 Official number: 4483	1,422 887 -	Class: KI	**2011-03 PT Anugerah Wijaya Bersaudara — Samarinda** Yd No: 1422/34 Loa 71.00 Br ex 16.15 Dght 3.600 Lbp 68.70 Br md 16.00 Dpth 4.80 Welded, 1 dk	**(B35E2TF) Bunkering Tanker**	**2 oil engines** driving 1 Propeller Total Power: 1,220kW (1,658hp) Yanmar 6AYM-ETE 2 x 4 Stroke 6 Cy. 155 x 180 each-610kW (829bhp) Yanmar Diesel Engine Co Ltd-Japan
21687 JD	**WIJAYA KUSUMA 3** **PT Agniputra Jayakusuma** - *Samarinda* *Indonesia* MMSI: 525006047 Official number: 4484	1,775 1,174 -	Class: KI	**2011-03 PT Anugerah Wijaya Bersaudara — Samarinda** Yd No: 1775/35 Loa 80.00 Br ex 18.15 Dght 3.600 Lbp 78.00 Br md 18.00 Dpth 4.80 Welded, 1 dk	**(B35E2TF) Bunkering Tanker**	**2 oil engines** driving 2 Propellers Total Power: 1,220kW (1,658hp) Mitsubishi S6R2-MPTK 2 x 4 Stroke 6 Cy. 170 x 220 each-610kW (829bhp) Mitsubishi Heavy Industries Ltd-Japan AuxGen: 2 x 60kW a.c
92497	**WIJAYA SATU** **PT Teguh Permata Nusantara** - *Jakarta* *Indonesia*	*126* 75 -	Class: KI	**1994-08 P.T. Wayata Kencana Dockyard — Jakarta** Loa 23.00 Br ex - Dght 2.300 Lbp 22.40 Br md 7.00 Dpth 3.00 Welded, 1 dk	**(B32A2ST) Tug**	**2 oil engines** driving 2 FP propellers Total Power: 988kW (1,344hp) Caterpillar 3412TA 2 x Vee 4 Stroke 12 Cy. 137 x 152 each-494kW (672bhp) (made 1993) Caterpillar Inc-USA
27910	**WIJAYA TIGA** **PT Teguh Permata Nusantara** - *Jakarta* *Indonesia*	126 75 -	Class: KI	**1995-09 P.T. Wayata Kencana Dockyard — Jakarta** L reg 23.00 Br ex - Dght 2.300 Lbp 22.40 Br md 7.00 Dpth 3.00 Welded, 1 dk	**(B32A2ST) Tug**	**2 oil engines** geared to sc. shafts driving 2 Propellers Total Power: 988kW (1,344hp) 10.0kn Caterpillar 3412 2 x Vee 4 Stroke 12 Cy. 137 x 152 each-494kW (672bhp) (made 1993) Caterpillar Inc-USA
53682 CV	**WIKANDA NAREE** *ex Good Day -2013* **Precious Ornaments Ltd** Precious Shipping Public Co Ltd *Bangkok* *Thailand* MMSI: 567273000 Official number: 3759	32,660 18,210 53,000 T/cm 57.3	Class: LR (IR) (NV) **100A1** SS 07/2013 bulk carrier BC-A inner bottom strengthened for regular discharge by heavy grabs, Nos, 3 or 2 & 4 holds may be empty ESP *IWS LI **LMC**	**2013-07 Hindustan Shipyard Ltd — Visakhapatnam** Yd No: 11139 Loa 190.00 (BB) Br ex 32.40 Dght 12.620 Lbp 183.25 Br md 32.26 Dpth 17.50 Welded, 1 dk	**(A21A2BC) Bulk Carrier** Double Hull Grain: 65,900; Bale: 64,000 Compartments: 5 Ho, ER 5 Ha: 4 (21.6 x 22.4)ER (19.2 x 20.8) Cranes: 4x36t	**1 oil engine** driving 1 FP propeller Total Power: 9,960kW (13,542hp) 14.2kn Wartsila 6RT-flex50 1 x 2 Stroke 6 Cy. 500 x 2050 9960kW (13542bhp) Hitachi Zosen Corp-Japan AuxGen: 3 x 645kW a.c

IMO / Call sign	Name, former names, owner, port	GT / NT / DWT	Class	Builder, dimensions	Type, cargo	Machinery
6604327 *HSBM* -	**WIKORN** *ex* Oversea 9 *ex* Summit 7 *-1982* *ex* Oceanic 7 *-1976* *ex* Fuji Maru No. 11 *-1972* **Phairot Khongkhan** - *Bangkok* *Thailand* Official number: 151000957	*776* 467 1,342		**1965 Hashihama Shipbuilding Co Ltd — Imabari EH** Yd No: 190 Loa 60.79 Br ex 9.02 Dght 4.496 Lbp 56.01 Br md 9.00 Dpth 4.73 Riveted\Welded, 1 dk	**(A13B2TP) Products Tanker** Liq: 1,600; Liq (Oil): 1,600 Cargo Heating Coils Compartments: 8 Ta, ER 2 Cargo Pump (s): 2x300m³/hr	**1 oil engine** driving 1 FP propeller Total Power: 736kW (1,001hp) 10.5kr Hanshin Z68 1 x 4 Stroke 8 Cy. 260 x 330 736kW (1001bhp) Hanshin Nainenki Kogyo-Japan AuxGen: 2 x 24kW 225V a.c
9100774 *4LNY2* -	**WILA** *ex* Bah *-2014* *ex* Ubah *-2013* *ex* Tavros *-2012* *ex* Limi *-2012* *ex* Victor Dubrovskiy *-2007* **Bah Shipping Co SA** Sahara Mina LLC *Batumi* *Georgia*	**5,431** 2,319 8,055 T/cm 16.5	Class: BV (NV)	**1997-04 Admiralteyskiy Sudostroitelnyy Zavod — Sankt-Peterburg** Yd No: 02720 Loa 109.00 (BB) Br ex 18.60 Dght 7.650 Lbp 102.07 Br md 18.60 Dpth 9.50 Welded, 1 dk	**(A12B2TR) Chemical/Products Tanker** Double Hull (13F) Liq: 7,944; Liq (Oil): 7,944 Cargo Heating Coils Compartments: 10 Wing Ta, ER, 2 Wing Slop Ta 10 Cargo Pump (s): 10x200m³/hr Manifold: Bow/CM: 55.4m Ice Capable	**1 oil engine** driving 1 CP propeller Total Power: 3,884kW (5,281hp) 14.2kr B&W 6L35MC 1 x 2 Stroke 6 Cy. 350 x 1050 3884kW (5281bhp) AO Bryanskiy MashinostroitelnyyZavod (BMZ)-Bryansk AuxGen: 3 x 500kW a.c Thrusters: 1 Thwart. FP thruster (f) Fuel: 144.8 (d.f.) 369.7 (r.f.)
9268435 *YJUK2*	**WILBERT TIDE** *launched as* Seacor Rover *-2004* **Gulf Fleet Middle East Ltd** Tidex Nigeria Ltd *Port Vila* *Vanuatu* MMSI: 576955000 Official number: 1589	**1,598** 479 1,388	Class: AB	**2002-11 Jaya Shipbuilding & Engineering Pte Ltd — Singapore** Yd No: 828 Loa 61.00 Br ex - Dght 4.800 Lbp 54.00 Br md 14.95 Dpth 5.80 Welded, 1 dk	**(B21B20A) Anchor Handling Tug Supply**	**2 oil engines** geared to sc. shafts driving 2 CP propellers Total Power: 4,050kW (5,506hp) Wartsila 6L26A 2 x 4 Stroke 6 Cy. 260 x 320 each-2025kW (2753bhp) Wartsila Finland Oy-Finland AuxGen: 2 x 315kW a.c Thrusters: 2 Tunnel thruster (f) Fuel: 700.0
7614264 *5VAR3* -	**WILBUR** *ex* Wilbur R Clark *-2010* *ex* Pacific Victory *-2007* *ex* Petro Challenger *-2000* *ex* Marine Challenger *-1991* *ex* Polar Explorer *-1991* *ex* LT-789 *-1991* **Ferdinand Shipping Corp** ERES NV *Lome* *Togo* MMSI: 671132000	**574** 172 -		**1944 Marietta Manufacturing Co. — Point Pleasant, WV** Yd No: 525 Loa - Br ex 10.06 Dght 4.979 Lbp 42.98 Br md 10.01 Dpth 5.74 Welded, 1 dk	**(B32A2ST) Tug**	**2 oil engines** geared to sc. shaft driving 1 FP propeller Total Power: 2,868kW (3,900hp) EMD (Electro-Motive) 16-645-E2 2 x Vee 2 Stroke 16 Cy. 230 x 254 each-1434kW (1950bhp) (new engine 1976) General Motors Corp.Electro-Motive Div.-La Grange
8316948 *WCZ6971* -	**WILD CATCH** *ex* Capt. Bobby B *-2011* *ex* Phoenix *-2003* *ex* Makandra No. 19 *-1992* **Wild Shrimper Inc** - *Port Canaveral, FL* *United States of America* Official number: 1024993	*134* 91 -		**1983 Master Marine, Inc. — Bayou La Batre, Al** Yd No: 261 Loa 25.30 Br ex - Dght 3.000 Lbp 21.67 Br md 6.72 Dpth 3.81 Welded, 1 dk	**(B11A2FT) Trawler** Ins: 91	**1 oil engine** reduction geared to sc. shaft driving 1 FP propeller Total Power: 331kW (450hp) Caterpillar 3412T 1 x Vee 4 Stroke 12 Cy. 137 x 152 331kW (450bhp) Caterpillar Tractor Co-USA
9181132 *3FJV8* -	**WILD COSMOS** - **NYK Reefers Ltd** NYKCool AB SatCom: Inmarsat B 335569410 *Panama* *Panama* MMSI: 355694000 Official number: 2552598C	**9,859** 5,124 10,097	Class: NK	**1998-04 Iwagi Zosen Co Ltd — Kamijima EH** Yd No: 173 Loa 149.92 Br ex - Dght 8.717 Lbp 137.80 Br md 22.10 Dpth 13.00 Welded, 1 dk	**(A34A2GR) Refrigerated Cargo Ship** Ins: 14,153 TEU 160 incl 58 ref C Compartments: 4 Ho, ER 4 Ha: 4 (8.0 x 8.0)ER Cranes: 2x35t,2x8t	**1 oil engine** driving 1 FP propeller Total Power: 9,628kW (13,090hp) 20.0kn Mitsubishi 7UEC50LSII 1 x 2 Stroke 7 Cy. 500 x 1950 9628kW (13090bhp) Akasaka Tekkosho KK (Akasaka DieselLtd)-Japan Fuel: 1420.0
9181168 *3FUT8* -	**WILD LOTUS** - **NYK Reefers Ltd** NYKCool AB SatCom: Inmarsat B 335240810 *Panama* *Panama* MMSI: 352408000 Official number: 2591198C	**9,860** 5,124 10,139	Class: NK	**1998-10 Iwagi Zosen Co Ltd — Kamijima EH** Yd No: 176 Loa 149.92 (BB) Br ex - Dght 8.717 Lbp 137.80 Br md 22.10 Dpth 13.00 Welded, 1 dk	**(A34A2GR) Refrigerated Cargo Ship** Ins: 14,155 TEU 160 incl 58 ref C Compartments: 4 Ho, ER 4 Ha: 4 (8.0 x 8.0)ER Cranes: 2x35t,2x8t	**1 oil engine** driving 1 FP propeller Total Power: 9,628kW (13,090hp) 19.8kn Mitsubishi 7UEC50LSII 1 x 2 Stroke 7 Cy. 500 x 1950 9628kW (13090bhp) Akasaka Tekkosho KK (Akasaka DieselLtd)-Japan Fuel: 1325.0
8706521 - -	**WILD ORCHID** *ex* Captain Will *-2003* **Orchid Enterprise Inc** - *Brownsville, TX* *United States of America* Official number: 910028	*101* 68 -		**1987-02 Steiner Shipyard, Inc. — Bayou La Batre, Al** Yd No: 250 Loa 22.86 Br ex - Dght - Lbp - Br md 6.71 Dpth 3.36 Welded, 1 dk	**(B11A2FT) Trawler** Ins: 65	**1 oil engine** geared to sc. shaft driving 1 FP propeller Total Power: 296kW (402hp) Caterpillar 3408TA 1 x Vee 4 Stroke 8 Cy. 137 x 152 296kW (402bhp) Caterpillar Inc-USA Fuel: 47.5 (r.f.)
9191474 *3FXS8* -	**WILD PEONY** - **NYK Reefers Ltd** NYKCool AB SatCom: Inmarsat B 335704110 *Panama* *Panama* MMSI: 357041000 Official number: 2601999C	**9,859** 5,124 10,110 T/cm 24.0	Class: NK	**1998-11 Iwagi Zosen Co Ltd — Kamijima EH** Yd No: 183 Loa 149.92 (BB) Br ex - Dght 8.717 Lbp 137.80 Br md 22.10 Dpth 13.00 Welded, 4 dks	**(A34A2GR) Refrigerated Cargo Ship** Ins: 14,155 TEU 160 incl 58 ref C Compartments: 4 Ho, ER, 12 Tw Dk 4 Ha: 4 (7.4 x 7.4)ER Cranes: 2x35t,2x8t	**1 oil engine** driving 1 FP propeller Total Power: 9,628kW (13,090hp) 20.0kn Mitsubishi 7UEC50LSII 1 x 2 Stroke 7 Cy. 500 x 1950 9628kW (13090bhp) Akasaka Tekkosho KK (Akasaka DieselLtd)-Japan AuxGen: 3 x 1100kW 440V 60Hz a.c Fuel: 85.0 (d.f.) (Heating Coils) 1365.0 (r.f.) 40.8pd
9076296 *WBD6757* -	**WILDCAT** - **GJR Marine LLC** Rodi Marine LLC *Lafayette, LA* *United States of America* Official number: 981473	**309** 92 -		**1992-06 Breaux Bay Craft, Inc. — Loreauville, La** Yd No: 1655 Loa 46.32 Br ex - Dght - Lbp - Br md 9.14 Dpth 3.65 Welded, 1 dk	**(B21A20C) Crew/Supply Vessel** Hull Material: Aluminium Alloy	**2 oil engines** geared to sc. shafts driving 2 FP propellers Caterpillar 2 x 4 Stroke Caterpillar Inc-USA
8940402 - -	**WILDCAT** - **Eva doo** - *Croatia*	**118** 35 -		**1996 Ocean Marine, Inc. — Bayou La Batre, Al** Yd No: 329 L reg 22.68 Br ex - Dght - Lbp - Br md 7.01 Dpth 3.72 Welded, 1 dk	**(B11B2FV) Fishing Vessel**	**1 oil engine** driving 1 FP propeller
9203198 - -	**WILDCAT 17** - **ACG Joy Express Liner** - *Cebu* *Philippines* Official number: CEB1006221	**134** 40 15		**2001-04 ACG Joy Express Liner — Brisbane QLD** Yd No: 1028 Loa 23.80 Br ex - Dght 1.730 Lbp 23.03 Br md 7.44 Dpth 2.44 Welded	**(A37B2PS) Passenger Ship** Hull Material: Aluminium Alloy Passengers: unberthed: 150	**2 oil engines** reduction geared to sc. shafts driving 2 FP propellers Total Power: 912kW (1,240hp) 25.0kn Yanmar 6LAH-STE3 2 x 4 Stroke 6 Cy. 150 x 165 each-456kW (620bhp) Yanmar Diesel Engine Co Ltd-Japan
8744406 *ZR7086* -	**WILDEGANS II** - **Runtu Visserye (EDMS) BPK** - *Cape Town* *South Africa* MMSI: 601072900 Official number: 10735	**144** 43 -		**2007-01 Tallie Marine Pty Ltd — St Helena Bay** Loa 19.40 Br ex - Dght - Lbp - Br md 7.20 Dpth 3.60 Bonded, 1 dk	**(B11B2FV) Fishing Vessel** Hull Material: Reinforced Plastic	**1 oil engine** driving 1 Propeller
6926359 *ZR3174* SH1385	**WILDEKUS** - **Oceana Brands Ltd** - *Cape Town* *South Africa* MMSI: 601563000 Official number: 350631	*409* 122 -		**1969 Globe Engineering Works Ltd. — Cape Town** Yd No: 154 Lengthened-1975 Loa 36.10 Br ex 8.23 Dght 4.268 Lbp 34.93 Br md 8.21 Dpth 4.32 Welded, 1 dk	**(B11A2FT) Trawler** Compartments: 1 Ho, ER 1 Ha: (2.8 x 1.9)ER	**1 oil engine** driving 1 FP propeller Total Power: 625kW (850hp) Caterpillar 1 x 4 Stroke 625kW (850bhp) (new engine 1980) Caterpillar Tractor Co-USA
8859689 *WDC4580* -	**WILDERNESS DISCOVERER** *ex* Mayan Prince *-1998* **SeaLodge I LLC** - *Juneau, AK* *United States of America* MMSI: 366746920 Official number: 952722	*683* 204 -		**1992-06 Blount Marine Corp. — Warren, RI** Yd No: 280 Loa 53.34 Br ex 11.89 Dght - Lbp - Br md - Dpth - Welded, 1 dk	**(A37A2PC) Passenger/Cruise** Passengers: cabins: 47; berths: 92	**2 oil engines** with flexible couplings & sr reverse geared to sc. shafts driving 2 FP propellers Total Power: 736kW (1,000hp) Cummins KTA-19-M 2 x 4 Stroke 6 Cy. 159 x 159 each-368kW (500bhp) Cummins Engine Co Inc-USA AuxGen: 2 x 95kW a.c Thrusters: 1 Thwart. FP thruster (f)

7641413 *WDG2904*	**WILDERNESS EXPLORER** *ex* Spirit of Discovery *-2011* *ex* Columbia *-2001* *ex* Independence *-2001* **Innersea Discoveries LLC (Un-Cruise Adventures)** - *Sitka, AK* *United States of America* MMSI: 367167190 Official number: 574958	**910** 341 -		**1976**-08 **Eastern Shipbuilding Corp. — Boothbay Harbor, Me** Yd No: 1 Loa 51.85 Br ex 11.12 Dght 2.136 Lbp 44.20 Br md 10.98 Dpth 3.55 Welded, 1 dk	**(A37A2PC) Passenger/Cruise** Passengers: cabins: 43; berths: 84	**2 oil engines** reduction geared to sc. shaft driving 1 FP propeller Total Power: 730kW (992hp) 13.0kn Caterpillar D343TA 2 x 4 Stroke 6 Cy. 137 x 165 each-365kW (496bhp) Caterpillar Tractor Co-USA
8014409 *V7WU7* -	**WILENERGY** *ex* Banshu Maru *-2011* **Awilco LNG 3 AS** Awilco LNG ASA *Majuro* *Marshall Islands* MMSI: 538004395 Official number: 4395	**102,390** 30,717 67,055	Class: NK	**1983**-10 **Mitsubishi Heavy Industries Ltd. — Nagasaki** Yd No: 1870 Loa 283.00 (BB) Br ex 44.58 Dght 11.500 Lbp 273.82 Br md 44.51 Dpth 25.02 Welded, 1 dk	**(A11A2TN) LNG Tanker** Double Bottom Entire Compartment Length Liq (Gas): 125,788 5 x Gas Tank (s); 5 independent Kvaerner-Moss (alu) sph 10 Cargo Pump (s): 10x1000m^3/hr	**1 Steam Turb** dr geared to sc. shaft driving 1 FP propeller Total Power: 29,420kW (39,999hp) 19.3kn Mitsubishi 1 x steam Turb 29420kW (39999shp) Mitsubishi Heavy Industries Ltd-Japan AuxGen: 2 x 2500kW 450V 60Hz a.c, 1 x 1200kW 450V 60Hz a.c Thrusters: 1 Thwart. CP thruster (f) Fuel: 6282.0 (r.f.) 351.0 (d.f.) 181.0pd
5215789 *CFG8081* -	**WILF SEYMOUR** *ex* Salvager *-2004* *ex* M. Moran *-2000* *ex* Port Arthur *-1972* *ex* M. Moran *-1970* **McKeil Work Boats Ltd** McKeil Marine Ltd *Hamilton, ON* *Canada* MMSI: 316003878 Official number: 822429	*442* 107 -	Class: (AB)	**1961**-07 **Gulfport Shipbuilding Corp. — Port Arthur, Tx** Yd No: 547 Loa 36.58 Br ex 9.94 Dght 5.157 Lbp 34.14 Br md 9.61 Dpth 5.72 Welded, 1 dk	**(B32A2ST) Tug**	**2 oil engines** reverse reduction geared to sc. shafts driving 2 FP propellers Total Power: 4,230kW (5,752hp) EMD (Electro-Motive) 16-645-E5 2 x Vee 2 Stroke 16 Cy. 230 x 254 each-2115kW (2876bhp) (new engine 1969) General Motors Corp-USA AuxGen: 2 x 60kW, 2 x 35kW Fuel: 234.0 (d.f.)
9627954 *LARL7*	**WILFORCE** **Wilforce LLC** Awilco LNG ASA *Oslo* *Norway (NIS)* MMSI: 258702000	**102,315** 30,695 87,750	Class: NV	**2013**-09 **Daewoo Shipbuilding & Marine Engineering Co Ltd — Geoje** Yd No: 2289 Loa 290.00 (BB) Br ex 44.04 Dght 12.500 Lbp 280.96 Br md 44.00 Dpth 26.00 Welded, 1 dk	**(A11A2TN) LNG Tanker** Liq (Gas): 155,900 Ice Capable	**4 oil engines** driving 4 gen. Connecting to 2 elec. motors reduction geared to sc. shaft driving 1 FP propeller Total Power: 34,200kW (46,498hp) 19.5kn Wartsila 12V50DF 2 x Vee 4 Stroke 12 Cy. 500 x 580 each-11400kW (15499bhp) Wartsila Italia SpA-Italy Wartsila 6L50DF 2 x 4 Stroke 6 Cy. 500 x 580 each-5700kW (7750bhp) Wartsila Italia SpA-Italy Thrusters: 1 Tunnel thruster (f)
7629271 - -	**WILFRED M. COHEN** *ex* A. T. Lowmaster *-1976* **Purvis Marine Ltd** - *Sault Ste Marie, ON* *Canada* Official number: 318428	*284* 133 -		**1948**-06 **Newport News Shipbuilding — Newport News, Va** Yd No: 468 Loa 31.25 Br ex 8.56 Dght - Lbp - Br md - Dpth 4.60 Welded, 1 dk	**(B32A2ST) Tug**	**1 oil engine** reduction geared to sc. shaft driving 1 FP propeller Total Power: 1,471kW (2,000hp) 13.0kn Fairbanks, Morse 10-38D8-1/8 1 x 2 Stroke 10 Cy. 207 x 254 1471kW (2000bhp) Fairbanks Morse & Co.-New Orleans, La AuxGen: 2 x 130kW 480V 60Hz a.c
5389580 - -	**WILGA** *ex* Banbury Cross *-1955* *ex* Metinda II *-1950* *ex* Empire Nan *-1946* **World Dredging Ltd** Geylang *Panama* *Panama* Official number: 773477	*256* 168 171	Class: (LR) ✠ Classed LR until 16/12/83	**1945**-12 **Scott & Sons — Bowling** Yd No: 375 Loa 34.45 Br ex 9.17 Dght 4.134 Lbp 32.01 Br md 9.15 Dpth - Riveted\Welded, 1 dk	**(B32A2ST) Tug**	**1 oil engine** driving 1 FP propeller Total Power: 852kW (1,158hp) 11.0kn G.M. (Detroit Diesel) 16V-149 1 x Vee 2 Stroke 16 Cy. 146 x 146 852kW (1158bhp) (new engine 1975) General Motors Detroit DieselAllison Divn-USA AuxGen: 1 x 10kW 110V d.c
9018921 *VNXT* -	**WILGA** - **Svitzer Australia Pty Ltd (Svitzer Australasia)** - *Fremantle, WA* *Australia* MMSI: 503528000 Official number: 854184	*365* 109 460	Class: AB	**1991**-09 **Ocean Shipyards (WA) Pty Ltd — Fremantle WA** Yd No: 173 Loa 32.30 Br ex - Dght 4.400 Lbp 29.45 Br md 10.53 Dpth 5.00 Welded, 1 dk	**(B32A2ST) Tug**	**2 oil engines** with clutches & sr geared to sc. shafts driving 2 Directional propellers Total Power: 2,648kW (3,600hp) 12.0kn Daihatsu 6DLM-28S 2 x 4 Stroke 6 Cy. 280 x 360 each-1324kW (1800bhp) Daihatsu Diesel Manufacturing Co Lt-Japan AuxGen: 1 x 120kW 415V 50Hz a.c, 1 x 80kW 415V 50Hz a.c Fuel: 78.7 (d.f.)
8125832 *LAMR7* -	**WILGAS** *ex* Dewa Maru *-2011* **Awilco LNG 1 AS** Awilco LNG ASA *Oslo* *Norway (NIS)* MMSI: 259861000 Official number: 8125832	**102,376** 30,712 67,552	Class: NV (NK)	**1984**-07 **Mitsubishi Heavy Industries Ltd. — Nagasaki** Yd No: 1890 Loa 283.00 (BB) Br ex 44.58 Dght 11.527 Lbp 273.82 Br md 44.51 Dpth 25.02 Welded, 1 dk	**(A11A2TN) LNG Tanker** Liq (Gas): 126,975 5 x Gas Tank (s); 5 independent Kvaerner-Moss (alu) sph 10 Cargo Pump (s): 10x1000m^3/hr	**1 Steam Turb** dr geared to sc. shaft driving 1 FP propeller Total Power: 29,420kW (39,999hp) 19.3kn Mitsubishi 1 x steam Turb 29420kW (39999shp) Mitsubishi Heavy Industries Ltd-Japan AuxGen: 2 x 2500kW 450V 60Hz a.c, 1 x 1200kW 450V 60Hz a.c Thrusters: 1 Thwart. CP thruster (f) Fuel: 6282.0 (r.f.) 348.0 (d.f.) 181.0pd
7315595 - -	**WILHADITURM** - -	**859** 258 922	Class: AB (GL)	**1973**-06 **Schiffswerft Hugo Peters — Wewelsfleth** (Hull) Yd No: 550 **1973**-06 **JG Hitzler Schiffswerft und Masch GmbH & Co KG — Lauenburg** Yd No: 740 Loa 57.51 Br ex 12.02 Dght 4.502 Lbp 50.60 Br md 11.71 Dpth 5.62 Welded, 1 dk	**(B21B20T) Offshore Tug/Supply Ship** Derricks: 1x5t Ice Capable	**2 oil engines** reduction geared to sc. shafts driving 2 CP propellers Total Power: 3,384kW (4,600hp) 13.0kn MWM TBD441V16 2 x Vee 4 Stroke 16 Cy. 230 x 270 each-1692kW (2300bhp) Motoren Werke Mannheim AG (MWM)-West Germany Fuel: 142.0 (d.f.)
9112806 *A8CG3* -	**WILHELM E** *ex* YM Osaka *-2009* *ex* Independent Endeavor *-2008* *ex* Astoria D *-2000* *ex* Libra New York *-1999* *ex* Libra Valencia *-1997* *launched as* Astoria *-1995* **Siebte Beteiligungs-KG TIM Shipping mbH & Co** Norddeutsche Reederei H Schuldt GmbH & Co KG *Monrovia* *Liberia* MMSI: 636090639 Official number: 90639	**14,844** 7,613 20,406 T/cm 35.2	Class: GL	**1995**-11 **Kvaerner Warnow Werft GmbH — Rostock** Yd No: 435 Loa 167.07 (BB) Br ex - Dght 9.840 Lbp 156.71 Br md 25.00 Dpth 13.40 Welded, 1 dk	**(A33A2CC) Container Ship (Fully Cellular)** Grain: 26,111 TEU 1452 C Ho 534 TEU C Dk 918 TEU incl 150 ref C. Compartments: 6 Cell Ho, ER 8 Ha: (12.5 x 10.7)Tappered (12.5 x 15.9)6 (12.5 x 21.1)ER	**1 oil engine** driving 1 FP propeller Total Power: 11,130kW (15,132hp) 19.0kn Sulzer 7RTA58 1 x 2 Stroke 7 Cy. 580 x 1700 11130kW (15132bhp) Dieselmotorenwerk Rostock GmbH-Rostock AuxGen: 1 x 1000kW 440/220V a.c, 3 x 900kW 440/220V a.c Thrusters: 1 Thwart. CP thruster (f) Fuel: 1248.0 (r.f.)
8650124 *DD4864* -	**WILHELM KRUEGER** *ex* Hafenbaudirecktor Dr. H.C. Wilhelm Kruger *-1981* **STRABAG Wasserbau GmbH** - *Hamburg* *Germany* MMSI: 211298250	**2,994** 898 4,458		**1941** **Luebecker Maschinenbau Ges. — Luebeck** Loa 102.00 Br ex - Dght 6.200 Lbp - Br md 16.06 Dpth 7.24 Welded, 1 dk	**(B33B2DT) Trailing Suction Hopper Dredger** Hopper: 3,026	**2 diesel electric oil engines** driving 2 Propellers Total Power: 3,874kW (5,268hp)
9155626 *MXDQ7* -	**WILHELM SCHULTE** **Freya Shipping Ltd** Bernhard Schulte (Hellas) SPLLC SatCom: Inmarsat B 323209511 *Douglas* *Isle of Man (British)* MMSI: 232095000 Official number: 730491	**15,180** 4,785 18,094 T/cm 38.0	Class: GL	**1998**-08 **Jiangnan Shipyard (Group) Co Ltd — Shanghai** Yd No: H2231 Loa 154.98 (BB) Br ex 23.13 Dght 9.800 Lbp 147.00 Br md 23.10 Dpth 12.70 Welded, 1 dk	**(A11B2TG) LPG Tanker** Double Bottom Entire Compartment Length Liq (Gas): 23,912 3 x Gas Tank (s); 3 independent (stl) dcy horizontal 6 Cargo Pump (s): 6x250m^3/hr Manifold: Bow/CM: 77.6m Ice Capable	**1 oil engine** driving 1 FP propeller Total Power: 9,360kW (12,726hp) 16.0kn Sulzer 6RTA52U 1 x 2 Stroke 6 Cy. 520 x 1800 9360kW (12726bhp) Shanghai Shipyard-China AuxGen: 1 x 1080kW 220/440V 60Hz a.c, 3 x 850kW 440/220V 60Hz a.c Thrusters: 1 Tunnel thruster (f) Fuel: 255.0 (d.f.) 1665.0 (r.f.)
9021502 *MNDQ9* LT 60	**WILHELMINA** *ex* St. Matthew *-2004* **Wilhelmina BV** - *Lowestoft* *United Kingdom* MMSI: 232003050 Official number: B12216	**428** 128	Class: LR **100A1** SS 05/2011 trawler **LMC** Cable: 302.5/20.5 U2 (a)	**1991**-01 **Brodogradiliste 'Begej' — Zrenjanin** (Hull) Yd No: 227 **1991**-05 **B.V. Scheepswerf Maaskant — Stellendam** Yd No: 485 Loa 40.01 (BB) Br ex - Dght 4.001 Lbp 35.20 Br md 8.50 Dpth 4.70 Welded, 1 dk	**(B11A2FT) Trawler**	**1 oil engine** with clutches, flexible couplings & sr reverse geared to sc. shaft driving 1 FP propeller Total Power: 1,323kW (1,799hp) Caterpillar 3608 1 x 4 Stroke 8 Cy. 280 x 300 1323kW (1799bhp) (new engine 2004) Caterpillar Inc-USA AuxGen: 2 x 100kW 380V 50Hz a.c, 1 x 85kW 380V 50Hz a.c Thrusters: 1 Thwart. FP thruster (f)

IMO / Call sign	Name / Owner	Tonnage	Class	Builder / Dimensions	Type	Machinery
8718811 *OUSS* -	**WILHELMINA** - - *Esbjerg* *Denmark* Official number: H 1720	283 85 -		**1988-07 J.H. van Eijk & Zonen B.V. — Sliedrecht** Yd No: 364 Loa 40.16 Br ex - Dght 1.430 Lbp 37.75 Br md 10.00 Dpth 1.90 Welded, 1 dk	**(B11B2FV) Fishing Vessel**	**2 oil engines** with clutches, flexible couplings & sr reverse geared to sc. shafts driving 2 FP propellers Total Power: 530kW (720hp) G.M. (Detroit Diesel) 12V-71 2 x Vee 2 Stroke 12 Cy. 108 x 127 each-265kW (360bhp) General Motors Detroit DieselAllison Divn-USA
9405590 *PHHF* UK 112	**WILHELMINA** **Visserijbedrijf YE 137 BV** - *Urk* *Netherlands* MMSI: 246557000 Official number: 48289	296 88 -		**2006-12 'Crist' Sp z oo — Gdansk** (Hull) **2006-12 B.V. Scheepswerf Maaskant — Stellendam** Yd No: 592 Loa 28.30 Br ex - Dght - Lbp 24.70 Br md 8.20 Dpth 4.10 Welded, 1 dk	**(B11A2FS) Stern Trawler**	**1 oil engine** reduction geared to sc. shaft driving 1 CP propeller Total Power: 920kW (1,251hp) Cummins Wartsila 8L170 1 x 4 Stroke 8 Cy. 170 x 200 920kW (1251bhp) Cummins Engine Co Ltd-United Kingdom Thrusters: 1 Tunnel thruster (f)
9539080 *LXWH* -	**WILHELMINE** **Shiplux IX SA** EuroShip Services Ltd *Luxembourg* *Luxembourg* MMSI: 253023000	21,020 6,306 6,374	Class: BV	**2012-04 Kyokuyo Shipyard Corp — Shimonoseki YC** Yd No: 502 Loa 152.00 (BB) Br ex 25.20 Dght 5.630 Lbp 142.00 Br md 22.00 Dpth 16.20 Welded, 4 dks	**(A35A2RR) Ro-Ro Cargo Ship** Stern door/ramp (centre) Len: 14.50 Wid: 18.00 Swl: 150 Lane-Len: 2342 Lane-clr ht: 7.00	**1 oil engine** reduction geared to sc. shaft driving 1 CP propeller Total Power: 7,000kW (9,517hp) 15.8kn Wartsila 16V32 1 x Vee 4 Stroke 16 Cy. 320 x 400 7000kW (9517bhp) Wartsila Finland Oy-Finland AuxGen: 1 x 2000kW 60Hz a.c, 3 x 500kW 60Hz a.c Thrusters: 1 Tunnel thruster (f); 1 Tunnel thruster (a) Fuel: 890.0
8007133 *DGKW* -	**WILHELMINE** **Petersen & Alpers GmbH & Co KG** - *Hamburg* *Germany* MMSI: 211442010 Official number: 12930	207 62 93	Class: GL	**1980-11 Muetzelfeldtwerft GmbH — Cuxhaven** Yd No: 199 Loa 26.75 Br ex 8.84 Dght 4.400 Lbp 24.82 Br md 8.81 Dpth 3.61 Welded, 1 dk	**(B32A2ST) Tug** Ice Capable	**2 oil engines** reduction geared to sc. shafts driving 2 Z propellers Total Power: 1,262kW (1,716hp) Deutz SBA6M528 2 x 4 Stroke 6 Cy. 220 x 280 each-631kW (858bhp) Kloeckner Humboldt Deutz AG-West Germany AuxGen: 2 x 30kW 380/220V 50Hz a.c
5389774 *OIWF* -	**WILHELMINE** *ex* Wilhelmine Oltmann *-1988* **Lundstrum Torvald KB** - *Kemio* *Finland* MMSI: 230999690 Official number: 10122	355 128 550	Class: (GL)	**1953 Stader Schiffswerft GmbH — Stade** Yd No: 162 Lengthened-1961 Loa 51.24 Br ex 7.52 Dght 2.920 Lbp 46.72 Br md - Dpth 3.36 Riveted\Welded, 1 dk	**(A31A2GX) General Cargo Ship** Grain: 761; Bale: 700 Compartments: 1 Ho, ER 2 Ha: 2 (9.5 x 5.0)ER Derricks: 2x2t Ice Capable	**1 oil engine** driving 1 FP propeller Total Power: 184kW (250hp) 8.0kn Deutz RV6M545 1 x 4 Stroke 6 Cy. 320 x 450 184kW (250bhp) Kloeckner Humboldt Deutz AG-West Germany
9295440 *PCAS* -	**WILHELMINE ESSBERGER** *ex* UCT Ellis *-2011* *ex* Cape Ellis *-2008* **Wilhelmine Essb BV** John T Essberger GmbH & Co KG *Dordrecht* *Netherlands* MMSI: 244961000	5,815 2,541 8,657 T/cm 18.8	Class: GL (BV)	**2005-08 INP Heavy Industries Co Ltd — Ulsan** Yd No: 1135 Loa 115.00 (BB) Br ex 18.83 Dght 7.410 Lbp 108.00 Br md 18.80 Dpth 9.70 Welded, 1 dk	**(A12B2TR) Chemical/Products Tanker** Double Hull (13F) Liq: 8,953; Liq (Oil): 8,953 Cargo Heating Coils Compartments: 16 Wing Ta, 2 Wing Slop Ta, ER 16 Cargo Pump (s): 10x300m^3/hr, 4x200m^3/hr, 2x100m^3/hr Manifold: Bow/CM: 52.6m	**1 oil engine** driving 1 FP propeller Total Power: 4,440kW (6,037hp) 14.5kn MAN-B&W 6S35MC 1 x 2 Stroke 6 Cy. 350 x 1400 4440kW (6037bhp) Hyundai Heavy Industries Co Ltd-South Korea AuxGen: 3 x 560kW 440V 60Hz a.c Thrusters: 1 Tunnel thruster (f) Fuel: 73.0 (d.f.) 583.0 (r.f.)
9183403 *DCZI* -	**WILHELMSHAVEN** - **Unterweser Reederei GmbH (URAG Unterweser Reederei GmbH)** - *Wilhelmshaven* *Germany* MMSI: 211282710 Official number: 440	359 107 163	Class: GL	**1998-09 JG Hitzler Schiffswerft u Masch GmbH & Co KG — Lauenburg** Yd No: 813 Loa 30.60 Br ex 11.65 Dght 3.000 Lbp 27.70 Br md 11.00 Dpth 4.00 Welded, 1 dk	**(B32A2ST) Tug** Ice Capable	**2 oil engines** gearing integral to driving 2 Voith-Schneider propellers Total Power: 3,690kW (5,016hp) 10.0kn Deutz SBV9M628 2 x 4 Stroke 9 Cy. 240 x 280 each-1845kW (2508bhp) Motoren Werke Mannheim AG (MWM)-Mannheim AuxGen: 2 x 140kW 400V 50Hz a.c Fuel: 140.0 (d.f.) 13.0pd
9157210 *YFSR* -	**WILIS** - **Government of The Republic of Indonesia (Direktorat Jenderal Perhubungan Laut - Ministry of Sea Communications)** PT Pelayaran Nasional Indonesia (PELNI) *Surabaya* *Indonesia* MMSI: 525005038	2,620 786 400	Class: KI	**1999-10 P.T. PAL Indonesia — Surabaya** Yd No: 126 Loa 74.00 Br ex - Dght 2.850 Lbp 68.00 Br md 15.20 Dpth 8.50 Welded, 3 dks	**(A37B2PS) Passenger Ship** Passengers: unberthed: 510; berths: 44	**2 oil engines** reduction geared to sc. shafts driving 2 FP propellers Total Power: 2,400kW (3,264hp) 14.0kn MaK 8M20 2 x 4 Stroke 8 Cy. 200 x 300 each-1200kW (1632bhp) MaK Motoren GmbH & Co. KG-Kiel
7114161 *WDD6648* -	**WILKIN A FALGOUT** *ex* Ponce Service *-2006* *ex* Republic *-1999* *ex* Puerto Rico Sun *-1997* **W A F Marine LLC** Global Towing Service LLC *Larose, LA* *United States of America* MMSI: 367175740 Official number: 529198	278 83 -	Class: AB	**1970 Main Iron Works, Inc. — Houma, La** Yd No: 238 Loa - Br ex - Dght 3.836 Lbp 32.44 Br md 9.15 Dpth 4.42 Welded, 1 dk	**(B32A2ST) Tug**	**2 oil engines** reverse reduction geared to sc. shafts driving 2 FP propellers Total Power: 2,868kW (3,900hp) EMD (Electro-Motive) 16-645-E5 2 x Vee 2 Stroke 16 Cy. 230 x 254 each-1434kW (1950bhp) General Motors Corp-USA AuxGen: 2 x 60kW Fuel: 171.5 (d.f.)
5389841 *MBSF* -	**WILL** *ex* Will Everard *-1971* **Will Charter Ltd** - *Maldon* *United Kingdom* MMSI: 235000922 Official number: 148677	139 42 -	Class: (LR) ✠ Classed LR until 9/65	**1925-07 Fellows & Co Ltd — Great Yarmouth** Yd No: 308 Converted From: General Cargo Ship-1987 L reg 29.75 Br ex 7.04 Dght 2.636 Lbp 29.57 Br md 7.01 Dpth 2.90 Riveted, 1 dk	**(B35A2QE) Exhibition Vessel**	**1 oil engine** driving 1 FP propeller Total Power: 107kW (145hp) 6.0kn Gardner 1 x 4 Stroke 107kW (145bhp) (new engine 1993) L. Gardner & Sons Ltd.-Manchester
7225831 *E5WW* -	**WILL WATCH** *ex* Cheung Shing *-2001* *ex* Will Watch *-1997* *ex* Al-Mustafa *-1986* *ex* St. Benedict *-1984* **United Fame Investments (Cook Islands) Ltd** - *Avatiu* *Cook Islands* MMSI: 518000001 Official number: C101/1	1,587 525 1,016	Class: (LR) ✠ Classed LR until 1/5/13	**1973-03 Ferguson Bros (Port Glasgow) Ltd — Port Glasgow** Yd No: 464 Converted From: Stern Trawler-1987 L reg 69.44 Br ex 12.76 Dght 5.335 Lbp 65.44 Br md 12.66 Dpth 8.08 Welded, 1 dk, 2nd dk clear of hold	**(B11A2FG) Factory Stern Trawler** Ins: 1,005	**1 oil engine** driving 1 CP propeller Total Power: 2,104kW (2,861hp) 14.3kn Polar M68T 1 x 2 Stroke 8 Cy. 500 x 700 2104kW (2861bhp) British Polar Engines Ltd.-Glasgow AuxGen: 3 x 308kW 440V 50Hz a.c Boilers: db 6.9kgf/cm^2 (6.8bar)
8972998 - -	**WILLAMETTE** - **Shaver Transportation Co** - *Portland, OR* *United States of America* MMSI: 367513230 Official number: 1085937	325 97 -		**1999 J M Martinac Shipbuilding Corp — Tacoma WA** Yd No: 240 L reg 26.49 Br ex - Dght - Lbp - Br md 10.50 Dpth 3.29 Welded, 1 dk	**(B32A2ST) Tug**	**2 oil engines** gearing integral to driving 2 Z propellers Total Power: 2,206kW (3,000hp) 13.0kn G.M. (Detroit Diesel) 16V-149-TI 2 x Vee 2 Stroke 16 Cy. 146 x 146 each-1103kW (1500bhp) General Motors Detroit DieselAllison Divn-USA
7301518 *WDD3873* -	**WILLAMETTE CHAMPION** *ex* Lewiston *-2010* *ex* Chemical Express *-2010* **Williamette Champion LLC** Olympic Tug & Barge Inc *Portland, OR* *United States of America* MMSI: 367137380 Official number: 538759	*199* 135 -		**1972 Houma Shipbuilding Co Inc — Houma LA** Rebuilt-1990 L reg 24.08 Br ex 7.93 Dght 2.230 Lbp - Br md - Dpth 3.20 Welded	**(B32A2ST) Tug**	**2 oil engines** reduction geared to sc. shafts driving 2 FP propellers Total Power: 2,560kW (3,480hp) Caterpillar 3512 1 x 1280kW (1740bhp) (new engine 1972) Caterpillar Inc-USA AuxGen: 2 x 60Hz a.c Fuel: 130.0 (d.f.)
8203127 *VMBE* -	**WILLARA** *ex* Blackburn Cove *-1997* **Svitzer Australia Pty Ltd (Svitzer Australasia)** - *Sydney, NSW* *Australia* Official number: 850155	350 105 287	Class: LR ✠ **100A1** SS 03/2013 tug harbour service ✠ **LMC** **UMS** Eq.Ltr: F; Cable: 275.0/19.0 U2	**1983-03 Carrington Slipways Pty Ltd — Newcastle NSW** Yd No: 155 Loa 33.30 Br ex 10.93 Dght 4.271 Lbp 29.39 Br md 10.52 Dpth 5.01 Welded, 1 dk	**(B32A2ST) Tug**	**2 oil engines** gearing integral to driving 2 Z propellers Total Power: 2,648kW (3,600hp) 12.8kn Niigata 6L28BX 2 x 4 Stroke 6 Cy. 280 x 320 each-1324kW (1800bhp) Niigata Engineering Co Ltd-Japan AuxGen: 2 x 125kW 415V 50Hz a.c Fuel: 78.0 (d.f.) 11.0pd
7316472 *WX9278* -	**WILLARD P. LEBEOUF** - **Omega Protein Inc** - *Moss Point, MS* *United States of America* MMSI: 367088190 Official number: 298972	*555* 377 -		**1965 Burton Shipyard Co., Inc. — Port Arthur, Tx** Yd No: 379 L reg 51.03 Br ex 10.11 Dght - Lbp - Br md - Dpth 3.61 Welded	**(B11B2FV) Fishing Vessel**	**1 oil engine** driving 1 FP propeller Total Power: 1,125kW (1,530hp) Caterpillar D398SCAC 1 x Vee 4 Stroke 12 Cy. 159 x 203 1125kW (1530bhp) Caterpillar Tractor Co-USA

604386 DIW -95-V	**WILLASSEN** *ex* Radek *-2008* *ex* Gangstad Junior *-2006* *ex* Noragutt *-2004* *ex* Ovraboen *-2002* *ex* Liaholm *-1981* **Willassen Senior AS** - *Svolvaer* *Norway* MMSI: 257850500	**278** 83 122	Class: (NV)	**1976-06 Bolsones Verft AS — Molde** Yd No: 246 Lengthened-1984 Loa 27.44 Br ex - Dght - Lbp 23.45 Br md 6.79 Dpth - Welded, 2 dks	**(B11B2FV) Fishing Vessel** 2 Ha: ER	**1 oil engine** geared to sc. shaft driving 1 FP propeller Total Power: 578kW (786hp) Caterpillar 3508TA 1 x Vee 4 Stroke 8 Cy. 170 x 190 578kW (786bhp) (new engine 1990) Caterpillar Inc-USA AuxGen: 1 x 40kW 220V 50Hz a.c, 1 x 6kW 220V 50Hz a.c
232486 FBN	**WILLEKE** *ex* Hansa Parijs *-2006* **M M Schenkel** Wagenborg Shipping BV SatCom: Inmarsat C 424537711 *Delfzijl* *Netherlands* MMSI: 245377000 Official number: 38208	**1,435** 718 1,680	Class: BV	**2000-12 AO Pribaltiyskiy Sudostroitelnyy Zavod "Yantar" — Kaliningrad** (Hull) **2000-12 Scheepswerf Peters B.V. — Kampen** Yd No: 478 Loa 79.99 Br ex - Dght 3.400 Lbp 78.80 Br md 10.40 Dpth 4.80 Welded, 1 dk	**(A31A2GX) General Cargo Ship** Grain: 2,691 TEU 72 C.Ho 48/20' C.Dk 24/20' Compartments: 1 Ho, ER 1 Ha: (53.4 x 8.4)ER	**1 oil engine** reduction geared to sc. shaft driving 1 FP propeller Total Power: 990kW (1,346hp) 9.5kn Caterpillar 3512TA 1 x Vee 4 Stroke 12 Cy. 170 x 190 990kW (1346bhp) Caterpillar Inc-USA AuxGen: 1 x 184kW 400/220V 50Hz a.c Thrusters: 1 Thwart. FP thruster (f)
325389	**WILLEM** - -	**390** 117 -		**1984-11 Stocznia Remontowa 'Nauta' SA — Gdynia** (Hull) **1984-11 B.V. Scheepswerf Maaskant — Stellendam** Yd No: 415 Loa 40.14 Br ex - Dght 3.541 Lbp 36.50 Br md 8.01 Dpth 4.73 Welded, 1 dk	**(B11B2FV) Fishing Vessel**	**1 oil engine** with clutches, flexible couplings & sr reverse geared to sc. shaft driving 1 FP propeller Total Power: 1,665kW (2,264hp) Wartsila 6L26 1 x 4 Stroke 6 Cy. 260 x 320 1665kW (2264bhp) (new engine 1997) Stork Wartsila Diesel BV-Netherlands AuxGen: 2 x 100kW 440V 60Hz a.c Thrusters: 1 Thwart. FP thruster (f)
53383	**WILLEM BARENTSZ** *ex* Landsort *-1989* *ex* Holenweg *-1966* *ex* Johanne Becker *-1960* - -	*180* - -	Class: (GL)	**1931 Gebr. van Diepen — Waterhuizen** Yd No: 789 Converted From: General Cargo Ship-1989 Lengthened-1950 Loa 49.70 Br ex 6.10 Dght 1.600 Lbp - Br md - Dpth 2.29 Riveted, 1 dk	**(A37B2PS) Passenger Ship**	**1 oil engine** driving 1 FP propeller Total Power: 110kW (150hp) 8.5kn MWM RH235 1 x 4 Stroke 4 Cy. 250 x 350 110kW (150bhp) (new engine 1943) Motorenwerk Mannheim AG (MWM)-Germany
72820 3XT	**WILLEM BARENTSZ** *ex* Hansestar *-2008* **EVT BV** - *Netherlands* MMSI: 245401000	**250** - 50	Class: (GL)	**1997-07 Lindstols Skips- & Baatbyggeri AS — Risor** Yd No: 308 Loa 33.30 Br ex 10.30 Dght 1.590 Lbp - Br md - Dpth - Welded, 1 dk	**(A37B2PS) Passenger Ship** Hull Material: Aluminium Alloy Passengers: unberthed: 322	**2 oil engines** reduction geared to sc. shafts driving 2 Water jets Total Power: 3,000kW (4,078hp) 35.0kn M.T.U. 12V396TE74 2 x Vee 4 Stroke 12 Cy. 165 x 185 each-1500kW (2039bhp) MTU Friedrichshafen GmbH-Friedrichshafen
673074 KWI	**WILLEM DE VLAMINGH** **Willem SA** Dredging & Maritime Management SA *Luxembourg* *Luxembourg* MMSI: 253525000	**7,737** 2,321 6,500	Class: BV	**2011-09 STX Offshore & Shipbuilding Co Ltd — Busan** Yd No: 5053 Loa 115.00 (BB) Br ex - Dght 5.500 Lbp 106.75 Br md 23.00 Dpth 7.00 Welded, 1 dk	**(B34A2SS) Stone Carrier**	**2 diesel electric oil engines** driving 2 gen. each 4000kW a.c Connecting to 2 elec. motors driving 2 Azimuth electric drive units Total Power: 8,000kW (10,876hp) 13.5kn MAN-B&W 8L32/40 2 x 4 Stroke 8 Cy. 320 x 400 each-4000kW (5438bhp) MAN B&W Diesel AG-Augsburg Thrusters: 2 Tunnel thruster
19420 PM 158	**WILLEM JACOB** **Zeevisserijbedrijf A van Urk BV** - *Urk* *Netherlands* MMSI: 246161000 Official number: 24270	**161** 48 -	Class: (GL)	**1993-03 Brodogradiliste 'Tisa' — Novi Becej** (Hull) Yd No: 77 **1993-03 B.V. Scheepswerf Maaskant — Stellendam** Yd No: 495 Loa 23.97 (BB) Br ex - Dght 2.740 Lbp 22.57 Br md 7.00 Dpth 3.65 Welded	**(B11B2FV) Fishing Vessel**	**1 oil engine** geared to sc. shaft driving 1 FP propeller Total Power: 221kW (300hp) MWM TBD604BL6 1 x 4 Stroke 6 Cy. 170 x 195 221kW (300bhp) Motoren Werke Mannheim AG (MWM)-Mannheim
87306 CI CH 302	**WILLEM VAN DER ZWAN** **AZ Ocean Pelagic Fisheries BV** W van der Zwan & Zn BV *Scheveningen* *Netherlands* MMSI: 246429000 Official number: 35505	**9,494** 3,344 8,720	Class: LR ✠ **100A1** SS 09/2009 stern trawler ✠ **LMC** **UMS** Eq.Ltr: A†; Cable: 522.5/50.0 U3 (a)	**2000-05 Construcciones Navales P Freire SA — Vigo** Yd No: 405 Loa 142.30 (BB) Br ex 19.06 Dght 7.100 Lbp 129.50 Br md 18.70 Dpth 8.35 Welded, 1 dk	**(B11A2FS) Stern Trawler** Ins: 11,320; Liq: 11,320	**1 oil engine** with clutches, flexible couplings & sr geared to sc. shaft driving 1 CP propeller Total Power: 7,500kW (10,197hp) 16.0kn Wartsila 12V38 1 x Vee 4 Stroke 12 Cy. 380 x 475 7500kW (10197bhp) Wartsila NSD Nederland BV-Netherlands AuxGen: 2 x 2160kW 440V 60Hz a.c Boilers: TOH (o.f.) 10.2kgf/cm² (10.0bar), TOH (ex.g.) 10.2kgf/cm² (10.0bar) Thrusters: 1 Thwart. CP thruster (f) Fuel: 1485.0 (r.f.)
49065 VU3	**WILLEM VAN ORANJE** **Baggermaatschappij Boskalis BV** - *Limassol* *Cyprus* MMSI: 210621000	**13,917** 4,175 21,200	Class: BV	**2010-09 IHC Dredgers BV — Kinderdijk** Yd No: C01254 Loa 137.00 (BB) Br ex - Dght 8.000 Lbp 125.00 Br md 28.00 Dpth 13.50 Welded, 1 dk	**(B33B2DT) Trailing Suction Hopper Dredger** Passengers: berths: 24 Hopper: 12,000 Compartments: 2 Ho, ER	**2 oil engines** reduction geared to sc. shafts driving 2 CP propellers Total Power: 12,000kW (16,316hp) 15.4kn Wartsila 12V32 2 x Vee 4 Stroke 12 Cy. 320 x 400 each-6000kW (8158bhp) Wartsila Finland Oy-Finland AuxGen: 1 x 1520kW 50Hz a.c, 2 x 5080kW 6600V 50Hz a.c Thrusters: 2 Tunnel thruster (f) Fuel: 1500.0
92226 3997 136	**WILLEM W** **Visko Sea Products Pty Ltd** - *Cape Town* *South Africa* MMSI: 601015400 Official number: 19716	*105* - -		**1997-01 Tallie Marine Pty Ltd — St Helena Bay** L reg 19.35 Br ex - Dght 2.400 Lbp - Br md 6.65 Dpth - Bonded, 1 dk	**(B11A2FT) Trawler** Hull Material: Reinforced Plastic	**1 oil engine** driving 1 Propeller Total Power: 272kW (370hp) 9.0kn G.M. (Detroit Diesel) 1 x 272kW (370bhp) Detroit Diesel Corporation-Detroit, Mi
05826 PL 33	**WILLEMPJE HOEKSTRA** **Zeevisserij Gebroeders P en T de Boer BV** - SatCom: Inmarsat C 424529310 *Urk* *Netherlands* MMSI: 245293000 Official number: 2244	**426** 127 -		**1987-02 Scheepswerf Bodewes Gruno B.V. — Foxhol** Yd No: 261 Loa 39.38 Br ex - Dght 3.530 Lbp 35.13 Br md 8.51 Dpth 4.73 Welded, 1 dk	**(B11B2FV) Fishing Vessel**	**1 oil engine** reduction geared to sc. shaft driving 1 FP propeller Total Power: 1,700kW (2,311hp) Stork-Werkspoor 6SW280 1 x 4 Stroke 6 Cy. 280 x 300 1700kW (2311bhp) Stork Werkspoor Diesel BV-Netherlands
60413 FE8	**WILLI** *ex* Willi Rickmers *-2013* *ex* Sea Puma *-2006* *ex* Crowley Lion *-2001* *ex* CSAV Boston *-2000* *launched as* Willi Rickmers *-1998* **KG ms 'Willi Rickmers' Schiffahrtsgesellschaft mbH & Cie** Uniteam Marine Shipping GmbH *Majuro* *Marshall Islands* MMSI: 538090210 Official number: 90210	**26,125** 10,106 30,738 T/cm 49.5	Class: GL	**1998-08 China Shipbuilding Corp (CSBC) — Kaohsiung** Yd No: 667 Loa 195.57 (BB) Br ex - Dght 11.020 Lbp 185.50 Br md 30.20 Dpth 16.60 Welded, 1 dk	**(A33A2CC) Container Ship (Fully Cellular)** TEU 2226 C Ho 868 TEU C Dk 1358 TEU incl 214 ref C. Compartments: 5 Cell Ho, ER 9 Ha: (12.6 x 21.1)Tappered (12.6 x 25.7)Tappered 7 (12.6 x 26.1)ER Cranes: 3x45t	**1 oil engine** driving 1 FP propeller Total Power: 20,875kW (28,382hp) 20.0kn B&W 7S70MC 1 x 2 Stroke 7 Cy. 700 x 2674 20875kW (28382bhp) Hyundai Heavy Industries Co Ltd-South Korea AuxGen: 2 x 1200kW 450/220V 60Hz a.c, 2 x 1000kW 450/220V 60Hz a.c Thrusters: 1 Thwart. CP thruster (f) Fuel: 170.0 (d.f.) 2270.0 (r.f.) 85.0pd
68524 6584	**WILLIAM** **Heriyanto** PT Perusahaan Pelayaran Rusianto Bersaudara *Samarinda* *Indonesia* Official number: 2003 IIK NO 3199/L	**138** 82 -	Class: KI	**2003-05 PT Menumbar Kaltim — Samarinda** Yd No: 043 Loa 25.15 Br ex - Dght 2.990 Lbp 23.40 Br md 6.80 Dpth 3.60 Welded, 1 dk	**(B32A2ST) Tug**	**1 oil engine** reduction geared to sc. shaft driving 1 Propeller Total Power: 883kW (1,201hp) 10.0kn Yanmar 12LAK-ST1 1 x Vee 4 Stroke 12 Cy. 150 x 165 883kW (1201bhp) Yanmar Diesel Engine Co Ltd-Japan
29138 6049	**WILLIAM 2** **Heriyanto** PT Perusahaan Pelayaran Rusianto Bersaudara *Samarinda* *Indonesia* Official number: 2006 IIK NO 3837/L	**247** 75 -	Class: KI	**2006-02 PT Menumbar Kaltim — Samarinda** Yd No: 05042 Loa 29.00 Br ex - Dght 3.500 Lbp 26.88 Br md 9.00 Dpth 4.25 Welded, 1 dk	**(B32A2ST) Tug**	**2 oil engines** reduction geared to sc. shafts driving 2 Propellers Total Power: 1,766kW (2,402hp) Caterpillar 3512 2 x Vee 4 Stroke 12 Cy. 170 x 190 each-883kW (1201bhp) Caterpillar Inc-USA AuxGen: 2 x 82kW 380V a.c

IMO / Call sign / Flag	Name / Owner / Port	GT / NT / DWT	Class	Builder / Dimensions	Type	Machinery
9099872 *YDA6112* -	**WILLIAM 3** **Herlina Arifin** - *Samarinda* *Indonesia* Official number: 4413	**248** 75 -	Class: KI	**2007**-12 **PT Menumbar Kaltim — Samarinda** Yd No: 06002 Loa 29.00 Br ex - Dght 3.360 Lbp 28.13 Br md 9.00 Dpth 4.50 Welded, 1 dk	**(B32A2ST) Tug**	**2 oil engines** reduction geared to sc. shafts driving 2 Propellers Total Power: 1,472kW (2,002hp) Cummins KTA-38-M1 2 x Vee 4 Stroke 12 Cy. 159 x 159 each-736kW (1001bhp) Cummins Engine Co Inc-USA
8016392 *WDE3445* -	**WILLIAM BISSO** *ex* Harvey Gladiator *-2008* *ex* Craig A. Cheramie *-1988* *ex* Persistence *-1983* **Bisso Marine Co Inc** - *New Orleans, LA* *United States of America* MMSI: 366965970 Official number: 641479	**309** 92 -	Class: AB	**1981**-09 **Modern Marine Power, Inc. — Houma, La** Yd No: 39 Loa 35.05 Br ex 9.76 Dght 3.731 Lbp 32.16 Br md 9.75 Dpth 4.37 Welded, 1 dk	**(B32A2ST) Tug**	**2 oil engines** reverse reduction geared to sc. shafts driving 2 FP propellers Total Power: 2,868kW (3,900hp) 11.0kn EMD (Electro-Motive) 16-645-C 2 x Vee 2 Stroke 16 Cy. 230 x 254 each-1434kW (1950bhp) (Re-engined ,made 1976, Reconditioned & fitted 1983) General Motors Detroit DieselAllison Divn-USA AuxGen: 2 x 75kW a.c Fuel: 283.1 (r.f.)
8744822 - -	**WILLIAM BRADLEY** **Horizon Marine Inc** - *Edmonton, AB* *Canada* Official number: 810639	**338** 223 -		**1991**-01 **A Frame Contracting Ltd — Fort McMurray AB** L reg 45.63 Br ex - Dght - Lbp - Br md 10.97 Dpth 2.01 Welded, 1 dk	**(A31A2GX) General Cargo Ship**	**2 oil engines** reduction geared to sc. shafts driving 2 Propellers Total Power: 1,000kW (1,360hp)
8992340 *WDC4593* -	**WILLIAM BRECKINRIDGE** *ex* Ocean Eagle *-2005* *ex* Miss Paulene *-2005* **Savannah Marine Services Inc** - *Savannah, GA* *United States of America* MMSI: 367027150 Official number: 638901	*121* 82 -		**1981**-01 **Rodriguez Boat Builders, Inc. — Coden, Al** Yd No: 34 L reg 19.66 Br ex - Dght - Lbp - Br md 7.32 Dpth 2.74 Welded, 1 dk	**(B32A2ST) Tug**	**1 oil engine** driving 1 Propeller
5390345 *ZM2060* -	**WILLIAM C. DALDY** **The Steam Tug William C Daldy Preservation Society Inc** - *Auckland* *New Zealand* Official number: 157787	*323* 97 -	Class: (LR) ✠ Classed LR until 11/61	**1935**-11 **Lobnitz & Co. Ltd. — Renfrew** Yd No: 986 Loa 38.41 Br ex 9.78 Dght 4.160 Lbp 35.82 Br md 9.76 Dpth 4.23 Riveted	**(B32A2ST) Tug** Derricks: 1; Winches: 1	**2 Steam Recips** driving 2 FP propellers 11.0kn Lobnitz & Co. Ltd.-Renfrew AuxGen: 1 x 15kW 230V d.c Fuel: 137.0 (c)
8423818 *WDC6778* -	**WILLIAM C. GAYNOR** *ex* Captain Barnaby *-2003* *ex* William C. Gaynor *-1989* **MCM Marine Inc** - *Cleveland, OH* *United States of America* MMSI: 367061180 Official number: 272731	*187* 103 -		**1956 Defoe Shipbuilding Co. — Bay City, Mi** Yd No: 429 Loa - Br ex - Dght 3.258 Lbp 27.01 Br md 7.93 Dpth 3.59 Welded, 1 dk	**(B32A2ST) Tug**	**1 oil engine** driving 1 FP propeller Total Power: 993kW (1,350hp) General Motors 8-278A 1 x 2 Stroke 8 Cy. 222 x 267 993kW (1350bhp) General Motors Corp-USA
9258909 *YJSJ3* -	**WILLIAM C HIGHTOWER** **Tidewater Hulls Ltd** Tidewater Marine International Inc *Port Vila* *Vanuatu* MMSI: 576749000 Official number: 1389	**3,183** 954 3,955	Class: AB	**2002**-10 **Singapore Technologies Marine Ltd — Singapore** Yd No: 605 Loa 79.50 (BB) Br ex - Dght 6.300 Lbp 70.30 Br md 18.30 Dpth 7.50 Welded, 1 dk	**(B21A20S) Platform Supply Ship**	**4 diesel electric oil engines** driving 4 gen. each 1800kW Connecting to 2 elec. motors driving 2 Azimuth electric drive units Total Power: 7,504kW (10,204hp) 13.0kn Caterpillar 3516B 4 x Vee 4 Stroke 16 Cy. 170 x 190 each-1876kW (2551bhp) Caterpillar Inc-USA Thrusters: 1 Tunnel thruster (f); 1 Retract. directional thruster (f) Fuel: 1320.0
9259795 *YJSU5* -	**WILLIAM C. O'MALLEY** **Tidewater Assets Ltd** Tidewater Marine International Inc *Port Vila* *Vanuatu* MMSI: 576834000 Official number: 1471	**4,544** 1,363 3,011	Class: AB	**2004**-07 **Yantai Raffles Shipyard Co Ltd — Yantai SD** Yd No: YRF2000-120 Loa 85.50 Br ex 21.00 Dght 6.800 Lbp 73.90 Br md 21.00 Dpth 8.00 Welded, 1 dk	**(B21B20A) Anchor Handling Tug Supply**	**4 diesel electric oil engines** driving 4 gen. each 4300kW Connecting to 2 elec. motors each (3357kW) driving 2 CP propellers Total Power: 17,652kW (24,000hp) EMD (Electro-Motive) 16-265H 4 x Vee 4 Stroke 16 Cy. 265 x 300 each-4413kW (6000bhp) General Motors Corp.Electro-Motive Div.-La Grange
5322623 *WD5901* -	**WILLIAM C. SELVICK** *ex* Sherman H. Serre *-1977* **Selvick Marine Towing Corp** - *Sturgeon Bay, WI* *United States of America* Official number: 254168	*142* 97 -	Class: (AB)	**1944 Platzer Boat Works — Houston, Tx** Yd No: 128 Loa 25.91 Br ex 7.01 Dght 2.744 Lbp 24.67 Br md 6.99 Dpth 3.15 Welded, 1 dk	**(B32A2ST) Tug** Winches: 1	**1 oil engine** driving 1 FP propeller Total Power: 478kW (650hp) 12.0kn Fuel: 56.0
8992807 *WDE4795* -	**WILLIAM D** *ex* E A *-2012* *ex* E. A. Cenac *-2010* *ex* Aug V *-2009* *ex* Genie Cenac *-2005* *ex* Letha C. Edwards *-2005* **Pinnacle III LP** - *Freeport, TX* *United States of America* MMSI: 367000450 Official number: 275606	*266* 181 -		**1957**-01 **E.W. & A.P. Dupont, Inc. — Patterson, La** L reg 28.96 Br ex - Dght - Lbp - Br md 9.14 Dpth 3.00 Welded, 1 dk	**(B32A2ST) Tug**	**1 oil engine** driving 1 Propeller Total Power: 1,324kW (1,800hp)
5224053 *WDC3317* -	**WILLIAM E.** *ex* Marie J. *-2006* *ex* Marie J. Turecamo *-2006* **Donjon Marine Co Inc** - *New York, NY* *United States of America* MMSI: 367005710 Official number: 264306	*144* 98 -		**1952 Jakobson Shipyard, Inc. — Oyster Bay, NY** Yd No: 340 L reg 25.85 Br ex 7.32 Dght - Lbp - Br md - Dpth 2.93 Welded, 1 dk	**(B32A2ST) Tug**	**1 oil engine** driving 1 FP propeller Total Power: 736kW (1,001hp)
9173666 *YJSY6* -	**WILLIAM E BRIGHT** *ex* Mercury Bay *-2003* **Maroon Fleet Ltd** Tidewater Marine Australia Pty Ltd *Port Vila* *Vanuatu* MMSI: 576868000 Official number: 1504	**1,969** 845 3,122	Class: AB (NV)	**1998**-07 **Brattvaag Skipsverft AS — Brattvaag** Yd No: 71 Loa 67.00 Br ex - Dght 5.910 Lbp 61.80 Br md 16.00 Dpth 7.00 Welded, 1 dk	**(B21A20S) Platform Supply Ship**	**2 oil engines** reduction geared to sc. shafts driving 2 FP propellers Total Power: 4,010kW (5,452hp) 12.0kn Normo KRMB-9 2 x 4 Stroke 9 Cy. 250 x 300 each-2005kW (2726bhp) Ulstein Bergen AS-Norway AuxGen: 2 x 1280kW 230/440V 60Hz a.c, 2 x 248kW 230/440V 60Hz a.c Thrusters: 1 Thwart. FP thruster (f); 1 Directional thruster (f); 1 Tunnel thruster (a) Fuel: 734.0 (d.f.)
9641168 - -	**WILLIAM FRANKLAND** **Government of Canada (Ministry of Transportation for The Province of New Brunswick)** Coastal Transport Ltd *Grand Manan I, NB* *Canada* MMSI: 316020643 Official number: 835819	**245** 74 -		**2011**-08 **Chantier Naval Forillon Inc — Gaspe QC** L reg 33.13 Br ex - Dght - Lbp - Br md 10.50 Dpth 2.40 Welded, 1 dk	**(A36A2PR) Passenger/Ro-Ro Ship (Vehicles)** Bow ramp (f) Stern ramp (a) Cars: 12	**2 oil engines** reduction geared to sc. shafts driving 2 Voith-Schneider propellers Total Power: 574kW (780hp) 9.0kn Caterpillar 2 x 4 Stroke each-287kW (390bhp) Caterpillar Inc-USA
9227247 - -	**WILLIAM G BURNETT** **Texas Dept of Transportation - Port Aransas Ferry System** - *Port Aransas, TX* *United States of America* Official number: 1088381	**192** 65 -	Class: (AB)	**2000**-03 **in the United States of America** Yd No: 99-102 Loa 30.30 Br ex - Dght 2.570 Lbp 28.87 Br md 13.45 Dpth 3.54 Welded	**(A36A2PR) Passenger/Ro-Ro Ship (Vehicles)**	**2 oil engines** reverse reduction geared to sc. shafts driving 2 FP propellers 1 fwd and 1 aft Total Power: 442kW (600hp) 10.0kn G.M. (Detroit Diesel) 8V-92 2 x Vee 2 Stroke 8 Cy. 123 x 127 each-221kW (300bhp) Detroit Diesel Corporation-Detroit, Mi AuxGen: 2 x 40kW a.c Fuel: 7.0 (d.f.)

8810762 **WILLIAM HENRY II**
MKUJ5
DH 5
185 Class: (LR)
79 ✠ Classed LR until 27/5/94
\-
R Mitchelmore
\-
Dartmouth *United Kingdom*
MMSI: 235001800
Official number: B10066

1989-04 Scheepswerf 'Friesland' BV — Lemmer Yd No: 123
Loa 22.51 Br ex 6.80 Dght 3.201
Lbp 19.50 Br md 6.70 Dpth 4.00
Welded, 1 dk

(B11A2FT) Trawler

1 oil engine with clutches & dr reverse geared to sc. shaft driving 1 FP propeller
Total Power: 394kW (536hp)
Kelvin TBSC8
1 x 4 Stroke 8 Cy. 165 x 184 394kW (536bhp)
Kelvin Diesels Ltd., GECDiesels-Glasgow
AuxGen: 2 x 104kW 380V 50Hz a.c, 1 x 18kW 380V 50Hz a.c
Thrusters: 1 Thwart. FP thruster (f)

5029946 **WILLIAM HOEY**
WD5884
\-
149
64
\-
ex Carolyn Hoey *-2013* *ex* Atlas *-2013*
Gaelic Tugboat Co
\-
Detroit, MI *United States of America*
Official number: 261843

1951 Alexander Shipyards, Inc. — New Orleans, La Yd No: 479
Loa 27.01 Br ex 7.62 Dght -
Lbp - Br md - Dpth -
Welded, 1 dk

(B32A2ST) Tug

1 oil engine driving 1 FP propeller
Total Power: 662kW (900hp)
EMD (Electro-Motive) 12-567-BC
1 x Vee 2 Stroke 12 Cy. 216 x 254 662kW (900bhp)
General Motors Corp-USA

7030444 **WILLIAM J. MOORE**
VO2054
\-
564 ✠ **100A1** SS 12/2008
24 tug
435 ✠ **LMC**
Eq.Ltr: (h) ; Cable: U2
ex Alice A *-2002* *ex* Raider IV *-1988*
ex Raider *-1987* *ex* Seaspan Raider *-1987*
ex Warrawee *-1976*
K-Sea Canada Corp
\-
St John's, NL *Canada*
MMSI: 316001278
Official number: 343910

1970-12 Adelaide Ship Construction Pty Ltd — Port Adelaide SA Yd No: 55
Converted From: Tug
Loa 41.15 Br ex 10.60 Dght 5.898
Lbp 36.73 Br md 10.37 Dpth 5.87
Welded, 1 dk

(B32B2SA) Articulated Pusher Tug

2 oil engines with flexible couplings & sr reverse geared to sc. shafts driving 2 CP propellers
Total Power: 3,000kW (4,078hp) 13.5kn
EMD (Electro-Motive) 16-645
2 x Vee 2 Stroke 16 Cy. 230 x 254 each-1500kW (2039bhp) (new engine 2003)
General Motors Corp.Electro-Motive Div.-La Grange
AuxGen: 2 x 155kW 220V
Thrusters: 1 Thwart. FP thruster (f)
Fuel: 280.5 (d.f.)

7322055 **WILLIAM L. WARNER**
WDB6765
\-
492
334
\-
ex Jos. F. Bigane *-2005*
Fuel Boat Holdings LLC
Warner Petroleum Corp
Chicago, IL *United States of America*
Official number: 545832

1973 Halter Marine Services, Inc. — New Orleans, La Yd No: 368
L reg 38.81 Br ex - Dght 3.664
Lbp 38.81 Br md 12.19 Dpth 4.26
Welded, 1 dk

(A12D2LV) Vegetable Oil Tanker

1 oil engine driving 1 FP propeller

7948433 **WILLIAM & LAUREN**
WAN8365
\-
116
79
\-
ex Ella & Josie *-1990*
f/v William & Lauren Inc
\-
Barnegat Light, NJ *United States of America*
MMSI: 367059740
Official number: 615155

1979 Eastern Marine, Inc. — Panama City, Fl Yd No: 18
L reg 19.63 Br ex 6.71 Dght -
Lbp - Br md - Dpth 3.26
Welded, 1 dk

(B11B2FV) Fishing Vessel

1 oil engine driving 1 FP propeller
Total Power: 331kW (450hp)

8886383 **WILLIAM LYNN**
WDD5669
\-
157
107
\-
ex Vic-Ter-Rae *-2011*
Lynn & William Inc
\-
Portland, ME *United States of America*
MMSI: 367161740
Official number: 674825

1984 La Force Shipyard Inc — Coden AL Yd No: 19
L reg 23.37 Br ex - Dght -
Lbp - Br md 7.31 Dpth 3.60
Welded, 1 dk

(B11B2FV) Fishing Vessel

1 oil engine driving 1 FP propeller

8835140 **WILLIAM M**
WDC4110
\-
189 Class: (AB)
87
\-
ex C-Tractor 1 *-2005*
Bay-Houston Towing Co
\-
Houston, TX *United States of America*
MMSI: 367019240
Official number: 952220

1989 North American Shipbuilding Inc — Larose LA Yd No: 133
Loa - Br ex - Dght -
Lbp 29.29 Br md 11.31 Dpth 3.20
Welded, 1 dk

(B32A2ST) Tug

2 oil engines gearing integral to driving 2 Z propellers
Total Power: 3,016kW (4,100hp) 12.0kn
EMD (Electro-Motive) 16-645-E8
2 x Vee 2 Stroke 16 Cy. 230 x 254 each-1508kW (2050bhp)
General Motors Corp.Electro-Motive Div.-La Grange
AuxGen: 2 x 150kW a.c
Fuel: 160.0 (d.f.)

8944707 **WILLIAM MICHAEL 1**
DUA2649
\-
485
300
\-
William Michael Shipping Corp
\-
Cebu *Philippines*
Official number: CEB1000207

1972 in Japan
Loa - Br ex - Dght -
Lbp 55.30 Br md 10.00 Dpth 3.00
Welded, 1 dk

(A13B2TU) Tanker (unspecified)

1 oil engine driving 1 FP propeller
Total Power: 883kW (1,201hp)
Hanshin
1 x 4 Stroke 883kW (1201bhp)
The Hanshin Diesel Works Ltd-Japan

8740802 **WILLIAM OF LADRAM**
OPSJ
B.462
385
115
\-
ex Vidar *-2013*
Shannon NV
\-
Blankenberge *Belgium*
MMSI: 205345000
Official number: 01 00408 1999

2000-06 N.V. Scheepswerven L. de Graeve — Zeebrugge
Loa 37.81 Br ex - Dght -
Lbp 32.98 Br md 8.56 Dpth 4.80
Welded, 1 dk

(B11A2FT) Trawler

1 oil engine reduction geared to sc. shaft driving 1 Propeller
Total Power: 1,176kW (1,599hp)
MaK
1 x 4 Stroke 1176kW (1599bhp)
Caterpillar Motoren GmbH & Co. KG-Germany

8851077 **WILLIAM R**
WDC3249
\-
186
84
\-
ex Standard No. 4 *-2001*
Foss Maritime Co
\-
San Francisco, CA *United States of America*
MMSI: 367004680
Official number: 276863

1958 Colberg Boat Works — Stockton, Ca
Loa - Br ex - Dght -
Lbp 22.68 Br md 7.99 Dpth 3.14
Welded, 1 dk

(B32A2ST) Tug

1 oil engine driving 1 FP propeller
Total Power: 942kW (1,281hp)

9476862 **WILLIAM R CROYLE II**
YJVW5
\-
2,301 Class: AB
690
2,068
Tidewater Marine International Inc
Tidewater Marine LLC
Port Vila *Vanuatu*
MMSI: 576058000
Official number: 1871

2009-09 Stocznia Polnocna SA (Northern Shipyard) — Gdansk (Hull) Yd No: B844/14
2009-09 Gdanska Stocznia 'Remontowa' SA — Gdansk Yd No: 1674/14
Loa 70.00 Br ex - Dght 5.290
Lbp 64.60 Br md 15.50 Dpth 6.60
Welded, 1 dk

(B21B20A) Anchor Handling Tug Supply
Passengers: cabins: 13

2 oil engines reduction geared to sc. shafts driving 2 CP propellers
Total Power: 10,120kW (13,760hp) 14.0kn
Caterpillar C280-16
2 x Vee 4 Stroke 16 Cy. 280 x 300 each-5060kW (6880bhp)
Caterpillar Inc-USA
AuxGen: 2 x 1724kW a.c, 1 x 250kW a.c
Thrusters: 2 Thwart. FP thruster (f); 1 Thwart. FP thruster (a)

9670286 **WILLIAM S**
WDG4522
\-
358 Class: AB (Class contemplated)
107
240
Bisso Towboat Co Inc
\-
New Orleans, LA *United States of America*
MMSI: 367537450
Official number: 1239737

2012-07 Main Iron Works, Inc. — Houma, La
Loa 30.49 Br ex - Dght 4.150
Lbp - Br md 11.59 Dpth 5.49
Welded, 1 dk

(B32A2ST) Tug

2 oil engines reduction geared to sc. shafts driving 2 Propellers
Total Power: 2,984kW (4,058hp)
Caterpillar 3516C
1 x Vee 4 Stroke 16 Cy. 170 x 190 1492kW (2029bhp)
Caterpillar Inc-USA
Fuel: 160.0

7010365 **WILLIAM SAMPSON STEVENSON**
MATR6
PZ 191
142
42
\-
ex Deo Juvante *-1984* *ex* Aaltje Jacobus *-1974*
launched as Jaap Jacoba *-1970*
W Stevenson & Sons
\-
Penzance *United Kingdom*
MMSI: 232005830
Official number: A21655

1970-03 Holland Launch N.V. — Zaandam Yd No: 443
Loa 28.22 Br ex 6.48 Dght -
Lbp 25.53 Br md 6.39 Dpth 3.23
Welded, 1 dk

(B11B2FV) Fishing Vessel

1 oil engine driving 1 FP propeller
Total Power: 552kW (750hp)
Stork DR0218K
1 x 4 Stroke 8 Cy. 210 x 300 552kW (750bhp)
Stork Werkspoor Diesel BV-Netherlands

9303778 **WILLIAM SHAKESPEARE**
A8JZ7
\-
35,581 Class: GL
19,407
44,022
ex Emirates Kanako *-2012*
ex William Shakespeare *-2007*
ms 'WS Schlueter' GmbH & Co KG
Norddeutsche Reederei H Schuldt GmbH & Co KG
Monrovia *Liberia*
MMSI: 636091166
Official number: 91166

2007-02 Hanjin Heavy Industries & Construction Co Ltd — Busan Yd No: 151
Loa 222.53 (BB) Br ex - Dght 12.000
Lbp 212.00 Br md 32.20 Dpth 19.30
Welded, 1 dk

(A33A2CC) Container Ship (Fully Cellular)
TEU 3398 TEU incl 300 ref C

1 oil engine driving 1 FP propeller
Total Power: 28,880kW (39,265hp) 22.7kn
MAN-B&W 8K80MC-C
1 x 2 Stroke 8 Cy. 800 x 2300 28880kW (39265bhp)
Doosan Engine Co Ltd-South Korea
AuxGen: 4 x 1200kW 450V a.c
Thrusters: 1 Tunnel thruster (f)

8645064 **WILLIAM STEVENSON**
2QEF
PZ 195
104
76
\-
W Stevenson & Sons
\-
Penzance *United Kingdom*
MMSI: 232005750
Official number: A21659

1967 in the Netherlands
Loa 26.00 Br ex - Dght -
Lbp - Br md 6.50 Dpth 3.30
Welded, 1 dk

(B11A2FT) Trawler

1 oil engine driving 1 Propeller
Total Power: 559kW (760hp)
MaK
1 x 4 Stroke 559kW (760bhp)
Caterpillar Motoren GmbH & Co. KG-Germany

IMO / Call sign / Fishing no.	Name / Owner / Registry	Tonnage	Class	Builder / Dimensions	Type / Cargo	Machinery
9436068 *A8PU3* -	**WILLIAM STRAIT** *ex* Viking Hawk *-2009* **William Strait Shipping Co Ltd** Carsten Rehder Schiffsmakler und Reederei GmbH & Co KG SatCom: Inmarsat C 463704352 *Monrovia* *Liberia* MMSI: 636013833 Official number: 13833	**18,485** 10,277 23,707 T/cm 38.0	Class: GL	**2009-05 Guangzhou Wenchong Shipyard Co Ltd — Guangzhou GD** Yd No: 359 Loa 176.84 (BB) Br ex - Dght 10.900 Lbp 166.41 Br md 27.40 Dpth 14.30 Welded, 1 dk	**(A33A2CC) Container Ship (Fully Cellular)** TEU 1732 C Ho 700 TEU C Dk 1032 TEU incl 320 ref C Compartments: 5 Cell Ho, ER Cranes: 2x45t	**1 oil engine** driving 1 FP propeller Total Power: 16,660kW (22,651hp) 20.6kn MAN-B&W 7S60MC-C 1 x 2 Stroke 7 Cy. 600 x 2400 16660kW (22651bhp) Hudong Heavy Machinery Co Ltd-China AuxGen: 3 x 1520kW 450V 60Hz a.c Thrusters: 1 Tunnel thruster (f) Fuel: 170.0 (d.f.) 1700.0 (r.f.)
9177284 *NNIA* -	**WILLIAM TATE** **Government of The United States of America (US Coast Guard)** - *Philadelphia, PA* *United States of America* MMSI: 338954000	**903** 270 200	Class: (AB)	**1999-09 Marinette Marine Corp — Marinette WI** Yd No: 560 Loa 53.34 Br ex - Dght 2.410 Lbp 47.24 Br md 10.97 Dpth 4.30 Welded, 1 dk	**(B34Q2QB) Buoy Tender** Ice Capable	**2 oil engines** reduction geared to sc. shafts driving 2 Directional propellers Total Power: 750kW (1,020hp) Caterpillar 3508TA 2 x Vee 4 Stroke 8 Cy. 170 x 190 each-375kW (510bhp) Caterpillar Inc-USA Thrusters: 1 Thwart. FP thruster (f)
8213122 - -	**WILLIAM TIDE** *launched as* Petromar Titan *-1983* **Twenty Grand Marine Service LLC** Tidewater Marine International Inc	**804** 241 1,200	Class: (AB)	**1983-02 Halter Marine, Inc. — New Orleans, La** Yd No: 1078 Loa 58.53 Br ex 12.20 Dght 3.928 Lbp 52.63 Br md 12.18 Dpth 4.58 Welded, 1 dk	**(B21B20T) Offshore Tug/Supply Ship**	**2 oil engines** reverse reduction geared to sc. shafts driving 2 FP propellers Total Power: 3,390kW (4,610hp) 12.0kn EMD (Electro-Motive) 12-645-E7B 2 x Vee 2 Stroke 12 Cy. 230 x 254 each-1695kW (2305bhp) General Motors Corp.Electro-Motive Div.-La Grange AuxGen: 2 x 99kW a.c Fuel: 180.0
9152686 *EIEI3* WD 74	**WILLIE JOE** *ex* Connie Vinther *-2008* **Joseph G Whelan** - *Wexford* *Irish Republic* MMSI: 250001333 Official number: 404006	**139** 41 -		**1997-10 Stocznia Polnocna SA (Northern Shipyard) — Gdansk** (Hull launched by) Yd No: B686/2 **1997-10 Vestvaerftet ApS — Hvide Sande** (Hull completed by) Yd No: 212 **1997-10 B.V. Scheepswerf Maaskant — Stellendam** Loa 23.95 Br ex - Dght - Lbp 20.97 Br md 6.50 Dpth 3.40 Welded, 1 dk	**(B11A2FT) Trawler**	**1 oil engine** geared to sc. shaft driving 1 FP propeller Total Power: 220kW (299hp) Mitsubishi S6R2-MPTA 1 x 4 Stroke 6 Cy. 170 x 220 220kW (299bhp) Mitsubishi Heavy Industries Ltd-Japan AuxGen: 2 x 89kW a.c
7121047 - -	**WILLING BOYS** *ex* Pimar *-1981* **Vixor Ltd** -	*199* 59 -	Class: (BV)	**1972 Astilleros Gondan SA — Castropol** Yd No: 64 Loa 30.25 Br ex 7.04 Dght 2.998 Lbp 25.02 Br md 7.00 Dpth 3.70 Welded, 1 dk	**(B11A2FS) Stern Trawler**	**1 oil engine** driving 1 FP propeller Total Power: 552kW (750hp) 11.0kn M.T.M. TI629C 1 x 4 Stroke 6 Cy. 295 x 420 552kW (750bhp) La Maquinista Terrestre y Mar (MTM)-Spain Fuel: 82.0 (d.f.)
8662139 - N 102	**WILLING LAD** **Murdock L&S** - *Newry* *United Kingdom* Official number: C19587	**136** - -		**2010 in the United Kingdom** Loa - Br ex - Dght - Lbp - Br md - Dpth - Welded, 1 dk	**(B11B2FV) Fishing Vessel**	**1 oil engine** reduction geared to sc. shaft driving 1 Propeller
9155547 *NIIW* -	**WILLOW** **Government of The United States of America (US Coast Guard)** - *Newport, RI* *United States of America* MMSI: 368782000	**1,928** 578 350	Class: (AB)	**1997-11 Marinette Marine Corp — Marinette WI** Yd No: 202 Loa 68.58 Br ex - Dght 3.960 Lbp 62.79 Br md 14.02 Dpth 5.98 Welded, 1 dk	**(B34Q2QB) Buoy Tender**	**2 oil engines** geared to sc. shaft driving 1 FP propeller Total Power: 4,560kW (6,200hp) Caterpillar 3608TA 2 x 4 Stroke 8 Cy. 280 x 300 each-2280kW (3100bhp) Caterpillar Inc-USA Thrusters: 1 Thwart. FP thruster (f)
8811546 *MKVK9* -	**WILLOWGARTH** **Svitzer Marine Ltd** - SatCom: Inmarsat C 423302810 *Liverpool* *United Kingdom* MMSI: 233028000 Official number: 704497	**392** 117 -	Class: LR ✠ **100A1** SS 07/2009 tug ✠ **LMC** **UMS** Eq.Ltr: (H) ; Cable: 330.0/30.0 U2	**1989-07 Richards (Shipbuilders) Ltd — Lowestoft** Yd No: 580 Loa 31.60 Br ex 9.54 Dght 4.050 Lbp 27.10 Br md 9.50 Dpth 4.80 Welded, 1 dk	**(B32A2ST) Tug**	**2 oil engines** with clutches, flexible couplings & dr geared to sc. shafts driving 2 Directional propellers Total Power: 2,536kW (3,448hp) 12.0kn Ruston 6RK270M 2 x 4 Stroke 6 Cy. 270 x 305 each-1268kW (1724bhp) Ruston Diesels Ltd.-Newton-le-Willows AuxGen: 3 x 80kW 440V 50Hz a.c
8655033 *J8Y4292* -	**WILLPOWER** *ex* Breeze *-2010* *ex* Cayman Pearl *-2005* **Punch Holdings Pty Ltd** Mansueto Marine Srl *Kingstown* *St Vincent & The Grenadines* Official number: 40762	**161** 48 90	Class: (RI)	**2001-01 Sunseeker International Ltd — Poole** Loa 31.01 Br ex - Dght 1.980 Lbp - Br md 6.30 Dpth 2.55 Bonded, 1 dk	**(X11A2YP) Yacht** Hull Material: Reinforced Plastic	**2 oil engines** reduction geared to sc. shafts driving 2 Propellers Total Power: 2,686kW (3,652hp) 18.0kn M.T.U. 16V2000M90 2 x Vee 4 Stroke 16 Cy. 130 x 150 each-1343kW (1826bhp) MTU Friedrichshafen GmbH-Friedrichshafen
9268241 *ZDFW5* -	**WILLY** **Reederei tms 'Willy' GmbH & Co** Carl F Peters (GmbH & Co) *Gibraltar* *Gibraltar (British)* MMSI: 236213000 Official number: 110498	**4,973** 2,241 7,415 T/cm 15.0	Class: GL	**2003-08 Sedef Gemi Endustrisi A.S. — Tuzla** Yd No: 125 Converted From: Products Tanker-2009 Loa 106.13 (BB) Br ex - Dght 7.450 Lbp 101.08 Br md 16.50 Dpth 10.60 Welded, 1 dk	**(A12B2TR) Chemical/Products Tanker** Double Hull (13F) Liq: 8,987; Liq (Oil): 8,991 Cargo Heating Coils Compartments: 12 Wing Ta, 2 Wing Slop Ta, ER 14 Cargo Pump (s): 10x200m³/hr, 4x100m³/hr Manifold: Bow/CM: 56m Ice Capable	**1 oil engine** geared to sc. shaft driving 1 CP propeller Total Power: 2,880kW (3,916hp) 13.1kn MaK 6M32C 1 x 4 Stroke 6 Cy. 320 x 480 2880kW (3916bhp) Caterpillar Motoren GmbH & Co. KG-Germany AuxGen: 3 x 480kW a.c, 1 x 630kW a.c Thrusters: 1 Tunnel thruster (f) Fuel: 70.0 (d.f.) 448.0 (r.f.)
9521186 *ECOT* -	**WILLY-T** **Remolques y Servicios Maritimos SL (REYSER)** SAR Remolcadores SL *Barcelona* *Spain* MMSI: 225394000 Official number: 1-1/2008	**327** - 77	Class: LR ✠ **100A1** SS 04/2009 escort tug, fire-fighting Ship 1 (2400 m3/h) with water spray *IWS ✠ **LMC** **UMS CCS** Eq.Ltr: G; Cable: 302.5/20.5 U2 (a)	**2009-04 Astilleros Zamakona Pasaia SL — Pasaia** Yd No: 653 Loa 27.55 Br ex 16.12 Dght 1.500 Lbp 26.84 Br md 15.25 Dpth 3.30 Welded, 1 dk	**(B32A2ST) Tug**	**2 oil engines** gearing integral to driving 2 Z propellers Total Power: 3,730kW (5,072hp) 12.0kn Caterpillar 3516B-HD 2 x Vee 4 Stroke 16 Cy. 170 x 215 each-1865kW (2536bhp) Caterpillar Motoren GmbH & Co. KG-Germany AuxGen: 2 x 98kW 400V 50Hz a.c
7367794 - -	**WILMA** - -	**292** 87 -		**1974-02 Scheepswerf Metz B.V. — Urk** Yd No: 37 Lengthened-1980 Loa 39.83 Br ex 7.80 Dght 3.110 Lbp 36.06 Br md 7.70 Dpth 4.15 Welded, 1 dk	**(B11B2FV) Fishing Vessel**	**1 oil engine** driving 1 FP propeller Total Power: 1,177kW (1,600hp) MaK 8M452AK 1 x 4 Stroke 8 Cy. 320 x 450 1177kW (1600bhp) MaK Maschinenbau GmbH-Kiel
9147679 *V2AB2* -	**WILMA** **SAL Heavy Lift GmbH** - SatCom: Inmarsat A 1304657 *Saint John's* *Antigua & Barbuda* MMSI: 304080754 Official number: 2376	**8,388** 4,178 9,544	Class: GL	**1997-09 J.J. Sietas KG Schiffswerft GmbH & Co. — Hamburg** Yd No: 1099 Loa 151.65 (BB) Br ex 20.64 Dght 7.850 Lbp 142.10 Br md 20.40 Dpth 10.50 Welded, 1 dk	**(A31A2GX) General Cargo Ship** Grain: 13,614; Bale: 12,791 Compartments: 1 Ho, ER 1 Ha: (82.9 x 15.8)ER Cranes: 2x275t,1x150t	**1 oil engine** with flexible couplings & sr gearedto sc. shaft driving 1 CP propeller Total Power: 9,450kW (12,848hp) 18.0kn MAN 9L48/60 1 x 4 Stroke 9 Cy. 480 x 600 9450kW (12848bhp) MAN B&W Diesel AG-Augsburg AuxGen: 1 x 1050kW 380V 50Hz a.c, 3 x 350kW 380V 50Hz a.c Thrusters: 1 Thwart. CP thruster (f) Fuel: 155.0 (d.f.) (Heating Coils) 1051.0 (r.f.) 46.0pd
7937989 *HO5432* -	**WILMA I** *ex* Wilma *-1981* *ex* Evelyn Collins *-1978* **Planta Trust Co** - *Panama* *Panama* Official number: 1126081	*196* 133 -		**1968 Nolty J. Theriot Inc. — Golden Meadow, La** Yd No: 23 Loa - Br ex - Dght - Lbp 29.11 Br md 8.23 Dpth 3.66 Welded, 1 dk	**(B32A2ST) Tug**	**1 oil engine** driving 1 FP propeller Total Power: 2,207kW (3,001hp)

835906 PFX 154	**WILMAR** **Wilmar PVBA Rederij** - SatCom: Inmarsat C 420516510 *Ostend* *Belgium* MMSI: 205165000 Official number: 01 00165 1996	**207** 62 -		**1988 Scheepswerven Seghers N.V. — Oostende** Loa 25.94 Br ex - Dght - Lbp - Br md 7.66 Dpth - Welded, 1 dk	**(B11A2FS) Stern Trawler**	**1 oil engine** driving 1 FP propeller Total Power: 519kW (706hp) Caterpillar 1 x 4 Stroke 519kW (706bhp) Caterpillar Inc-USA
013950 7WS3	**WILPOWER** *ex* Bishu Maru *-2011* **Awilco LNG 2 AS** Awilco LNG ASA *Majuro* *Marshall Islands* MMSI: 538004379 Official number: 4379	**97,395** 29,218 69,991	Class: NK	**1983-08 Kawasaki Heavy Industries Ltd — Sakaide KG** Yd No: 1334 Loa 281.00 (BB) Br ex 44.30 Dght 11.467 Lbp 268.03 Br md 44.21 Dpth 25.02 Welded, 1 dk	**(A11A2TN) LNG Tanker** Liq (Gas): 125,929 5 x Gas Tank (s); 5 independent Kvaerner-Moss (alu) sph 10 Cargo Pump (s): 10x1000m³/hr	**1 Steam Turb** dr geared to sc. shaft driving 1 FP propeller Total Power: 29,420kW (39,999hp) 19.3kn Kawasaki UC-450 1 x steam Turb 29420kW (39999shp) Kawasaki Heavy Industries Ltd-Japan AuxGen: 2 x 2500kW 450V 60Hz a.c, 1 x 1200kW 450V 60Hz a.c Thrusters: 1 Thwart. CP thruster (f) Fuel: 7000.0 (r.f.) 280.0 (d.f.) 190.0pd
627966 ARM7	**WILPRIDE** **Wilpride LLC** Awilco LNG ASA *Oslo* *Norway (NIS)* MMSI: 258703000 Official number: 9627966	**102,315** 30,695 87,677	Class: NV	**2013-11 Daewoo Shipbuilding & Marine Engineering Co Ltd — Geoje** Yd No: 2290 Loa 290.00 (BB) Br ex 44.04 Dght 12.500 Lbp 279.00 Br md 44.00 Dpth 26.00 Welded, 1 dk	**(A11A2TN) LNG Tanker** Liq (Gas): 156,007 Ice Capable	**4 diesel electric oil engines** driving 4 gen. Connecting to 2 elec. motors driving 1 FP propeller Total Power: 34,200kW (46,498hp) 19.5kn Wartsila 12V50DF 1 x Vee 4 Stroke 12 Cy. 500 x 580 11400kW (15499bhp) Wartsila Italia SpA-Italy Wartsila 6L50DF 2 x 4 Stroke 6 Cy. 500 x 580 each-5700kW (7750bhp) Wartsila Italia SpA-Italy Thrusters: 1 Tunnel thruster
507350 HA2471	**WILSON ALGECIRAS** **Kapitan Siegfried Bojen- Schiffahrtsbetrieb eK** - *Valletta* *Malta* MMSI: 248689000 Official number: 9507350	**2,451** 1,037 3,583	Class: GL	**2010-09 Slovenske Lodenice a.s. — Komarno** Yd No: 2119 Loa 88.25 Br ex - Dght 5.139 Lbp 84.60 Br md 12.40 Dpth 6.70 Welded, 1 dk	**(A31A2GX) General Cargo Ship** Grain: 3,970 TEU 20 Compartments: 2 Ho, ER 2 Ha: (31.8 x 10.1)ER (25.2 x 10.1) Ice Capable	**1 oil engine** reverse reduction geared to sc. shaft driving 1 FP propeller Total Power: 1,200kW (1,632hp) 10.5kn Wartsila 6L20 1 x 4 Stroke 6 Cy. 200 x 280 1200kW (1632bhp) Wartsila Finland Oy-Finland AuxGen: 1 x 172kW 400V a.c, 1 x 96kW 400V a.c, 1 x 93kW 400V a.c Thrusters: 1 Tunnel thruster (f)
507374 HA2539	**WILSON ALICANTE** **Kapitan Siegfried Bojen- Schiffahrtsbetrieb eK** - SatCom: Inmarsat C 424883510 *Valletta* *Malta* MMSI: 248835000 Official number: 9507374	**2,451** 1,325 3,600	Class: GL	**2010-12 Slovenske Lodenice a.s. — Komarno** Yd No: 2121 Loa 88.24 Br ex - Dght 5.139 Lbp 84.60 Br md 12.40 Dpth 6.70 Welded, 1 dk	**(A31A2GX) General Cargo Ship** Grain: 3,970 TEU 20 Compartments: 2 Ho, ER 2 Ha: (31.8 x 10.1)ER (25.2 x 10.1) Ice Capable	**1 oil engine** reverse reduction geared to sc. shaft driving 1 FP propeller Total Power: 1,200kW (1,632hp) 10.5kn Wartsila 6L20 1 x 4 Stroke 6 Cy. 200 x 280 1200kW (1632bhp) Wartsila Finland Oy-Finland AuxGen: 1 x 93kW 400V a.c, 2 x 172kW 400V a.c, 1 x 96kW 400V a.c Thrusters: 1 Tunnel thruster (f)
507362 HA2502	**WILSON ALMERIA** **Kapitan Siegfried Bojen- Schiffahrtsbetrieb eK** - *Valletta* *Malta* MMSI: 248764000 Official number: 9507362	**2,451** 1,325 3,586	Class: GL	**2010-10 Slovenske Lodenice a.s. — Komarno** Yd No: 2120 Loa 88.23 Br ex - Dght 5.139 Lbp 84.60 Br md 12.40 Dpth 6.70 Welded, 1 dk	**(A31A2GX) General Cargo Ship** Grain: 3,970 TEU 20 Compartments: 2 Ho, ER 2 Ha: (31.8 x 10.1)ER (25.2 x 10.1) Ice Capable	**1 oil engine** reverse reduction geared to sc. shaft driving 1 FP propeller Total Power: 1,200kW (1,632hp) 10.5kn Wartsila 6L20 1 x 4 Stroke 6 Cy. 200 x 280 1200kW (1632bhp) Wartsila Finland Oy-Finland AuxGen: 1 x 93kW 400V a.c, 1 x 172kW 400V a.c, 1 x 96kW 400V a.c Thrusters: 1 Tunnel thruster (f)
313735 2EO7	**WILSON AMSTERDAM** *launched as* Tanne Kankena *-2009* **ms 'Tanne Kankena' Reederei Bojen GmbH & Co KG** Kapitan Siegfried Bojen- Schiffahrtsbetrieb eK *Saint John's* *Antigua & Barbuda* MMSI: 305497000 Official number: 4686	**2,451** 1,033 3,602	Class: GL	**2009-11 Slovenske Lodenice a.s. — Komarno** Yd No: 2114 Loa 88.25 Br ex - Dght 5.139 Lbp 84.60 Br md 12.40 Dpth 6.70 Welded, 1 dk	**(A31A2GX) General Cargo Ship** Grain: 4,512 TEU 20 on Dk Compartments: 2 Ho, ER 2 Ha: (31.8 x 10.1)ER (25.2 x 10.1) Ice Capable	**1 oil engine** reverse reduction geared to sc. shaft driving 1 FP propeller Total Power: 1,200kW (1,632hp) 10.5kn Wartsila 6L20 1 x 4 Stroke 6 Cy. 200 x 280 1200kW (1632bhp) Wartsila Finland Oy-Finland AuxGen: 1 x 93kW 400V a.c, 1 x 96kW 400V a.c, 1 x 168kW 400V a.c Thrusters: 1 Tunnel thruster (f)
313759 HA2370	**WILSON ASTAKOS** **ms 'Gata Noneka' Reederei Bojen GmbH & Co KG** Kapitan Siegfried Bojen- Schiffahrtsbetrieb eK *Valletta* *Malta* MMSI: 248448000 Official number: 9313759	**2,451** 1,033 3,597	Class: GL	**2010-07 Slovenske Lodenice a.s. — Komarno** Yd No: 2118 Loa 88.26 Br ex - Dght 5.130 Lbp 84.60 Br md 12.40 Dpth 6.70 Welded, 1 dk	**(A31A2GX) General Cargo Ship** Grain: 3,970 TEU 20 incl 6 ref C Compartments: 2 Ho, ER 2 Ha: (31.8 x 10.1)ER (25.2 x 10.1) Ice Capable	**1 oil engine** reverse reduction geared to sc. shaft driving 1 FP propeller Total Power: 1,200kW (1,632hp) 10.5kn Wartsila 6L20 1 x 4 Stroke 6 Cy. 200 x 280 1200kW (1632bhp) Wartsila Finland Oy-Finland AuxGen: 1 x 168kW 400V a.c, 1 x 92kW 400V a.c, 1 x 96kW 400V a.c Thrusters: 1 Tunnel thruster (f) Fuel: 165.0 (r.f.) 5.0pd
313709 HQT9	**WILSON AVILES** *launched as* Hero Omken *-2008* **ms 'Hero Omken' Reederei Bojen GmbH & Co KG** Kapitan Siegfried Bojen- Schiffahrtsbetrieb eK *Valletta* *Malta* MMSI: 249380000 Official number: 9313709	**2,451** 1,325 3,596 T/cm 10.5	Class: GL	**2008-10 Slovenske Lodenice a.s. — Komarno** Yd No: 2111 Loa 88.30 Br ex - Dght 5.130 Lbp 84.60 Br md 12.40 Dpth 6.70 Welded, 1 dk	**(A31A2GX) General Cargo Ship** Grain: 4,515; Bale: 4,515 TEU 20 on Dk Compartments: 2 Ho, ER 2 Ha: (31.8 x 10.1)ER (25.2 x 10.1) Ice Capable	**1 oil engine** reverse reduction geared to sc. shaft driving 1 FP propeller Total Power: 1,200kW (1,632hp) 10.3kn Wartsila 6L20 1 x 4 Stroke 6 Cy. 200 x 280 1200kW (1632bhp) Wartsila Finland Oy-Finland AuxGen: 1 x 160kW 400V a.c, 1 x 96kW 400V a.c, 1 x 93kW 400V a.c Thrusters: 1 Tunnel thruster (f)
313747 HA2335	**WILSON AVONMOUTH** **ms 'Affo Beninga' Reederei Bojen GmbH & Co KG** Kapitan Siegfried Bojen- Schiffahrtsbetrieb eK *Valletta* *Malta* MMSI: 248367000 Official number: 9313747	**2,451** 1,033 3,594	Class: GL	**2010-04 Slovenske Lodenice a.s. — Komarno** Yd No: 2117 Loa 88.24 Br ex - Dght 5.130 Lbp 84.60 Br md 12.40 Dpth 6.70 Welded, 1 dk	**(A31A2GX) General Cargo Ship** Grain: 3,970 TEU 20 Compartments: 2 Ho, ER 2 Ha: (31.8 x 10.1)ER (25.2 x 10.1) Ice Capable	**1 oil engine** reverse reduction geared to sc. shaft driving 1 FP propeller Total Power: 1,125kW (1,530hp) 10.3kn Wartsila 6L20 1 x 4 Stroke 6 Cy. 200 x 280 1125kW (1530bhp) Wartsila Finland Oy-Finland AuxGen: 1 x 110kW 400V a.c, 1 x 168kW 400V a.c, 1 x 96kW 400V a.c Thrusters: 1 Tunnel thruster (f) Fuel: 150.0 (r.f.)
310208 HWW6	**WILSON BAR** *ex* Wilson Korsnes *-2002* *ex* Korsnes *-2000* *ex* General Ricarte *-1992* *ex* Korsnes *-1986* **Wilson Shipowning AS** Wilson EuroCarriers AS SatCom: Inmarsat C 435203110 *Valletta* *Malta* MMSI: 248937000 Official number: 7173	**3,967** 2,212 6,105	Class: BV (NV)	**1979-11 AS Storviks Mek. Verksted — Kristiansund** Yd No: 90 **1983 Fosen Mek. Verksteder AS — Rissa** (Additional cargo section) Lengthened-1983 Loa 107.02 Br ex 15.04 Dght 6.485 Lbp 100.36 Br md 15.02 Dpth 8.01 Welded, 1 dk	**(A31A2GX) General Cargo Ship** Grain: 7,400; Bale: 7,310 Compartments: 3 Ho, ER 3 Ha: (14.0 x 8.0) (33.3 x 12.0) (12.8 x 8.0)ER	**1 oil engine** sr geared to sc. shaft driving 1 CP propeller Total Power: 2,942kW (4,000hp) 13.5kn Werkspoor 6TM410 1 x 4 Stroke 6 Cy. 410 x 470 2942kW (4000bhp) Stork Werkspoor Diesel BV-Netherlands AuxGen: 2 x 296kW 440V 60Hz a.c Fuel: 88.0 (d.f.) 395.0 (r.f.) 13.5pd
314705 HJX9	**WILSON BILBAO** *ex* Niklas *-2008* *ex* Padua *-1999* **Wilson Shipowning AS** Wilson EuroCarriers AS SatCom: Inmarsat C 424907710 *Valletta* *Malta* MMSI: 249077000 Official number: 9014705	**2,446** 1,369 3,735	Class: GL	**1992-07 Slovenske Lodenice a.s. — Komarno** Yd No: 2905 Loa 87.90 (BB) Br ex - Dght 5.490 Lbp 81.00 Br md 12.80 Dpth 7.10 Welded, 1 dk	**(A31A2GX) General Cargo Ship** Grain: 4,615; Bale: 4,590 TEU 176 C. 176/20' Compartments: 1 Ho, ER 1 Ha: (56.6 x 10.2)ER Ice Capable	**1 oil engine** reverse reduction geared to sc. shaft driving 1 FP propeller Total Power: 1,500kW (2,039hp) 10.6kn Deutz SBV8M628 1 x 4 Stroke 8 Cy. 240 x 280 1500kW (2039bhp) Motoren Werke Mannheim AG (MWM)-Mannheim AuxGen: 3 x 104kW 220/380V 50Hz a.c Thrusters: 1 Thwart. FP thruster (f)

9124419 *9HQP4* -	**WILSON BLYTH** *ex* Kapitan Drobinin *-2004* **Wilson Shipowning AS** Wilson EuroCarriers AS SatCom: Inmarsat C 424931110 *Valletta* *Malta* MMSI: 249311000 Official number: 4462	**2,446** 1,369 3,713 T/cm 10.0	Class: BV (NV) (GL)	**1995-06 Slovenske Lodenice a.s. — Komarno** Yd No: 2924 Loa 87.90 (BB) Br ex - Dght 5.490 Lbp 81.32 Br md 12.80 Dpth 7.10 Welded, 1 dk	**(A31A2GX) General Cargo Ship** Double Hull Grain: 4,650; Bale: 4,620 TEU 176 C.Ho 108/20' C.Dk 68/20' incl. 6 ref C. Compartments: 1 Ho, ER 1 Ha: (56.6 x 10.2)ER Ice Capable	**1 oil engine** with clutches, flexible couplings & sr reverse geared to sc. shaft driving 1 FP propeller Total Power: 1,500kW (2,039hp) 10.5kn Deutz SBV8M628 1 x 4 Stroke 8 Cy. 240 x 280 1500kW (2039bhp) Motoren Werke Mannheim AG (MWM)-Mannheim AuxGen: 3 x 104kW 220/380V 50Hz a.c Thrusters: 1 Thwart. FP thruster (f) Fuel: 33.0 (d.f.) 166.0 (d.f.) 7.7pd
9106924 *9HNO4* -	**WILSON BORG** *ex* Northern Linanes *-2002* **Wilson Shipowning AS** Wilson EuroCarriers AS SatCom: Inmarsat C 424921110 *Valletta* *Malta* MMSI: 249211000 Official number: 4307	**2,446** 1,369 3,720 T/cm 10.1	Class: BV (NV) (GL)	**1994-11 Slovenske Lodenice a.s. — Komarno** Yd No: 2922 Loa 87.90 (BB) Br ex 12.90 Dght 5.511 Lbp 83.50 Br md 12.80 Dpth 7.10 Welded, 1 dk	**(A31A2GX) General Cargo Ship** Double Hull Grain: 4,650; Bale: 4,620 TEU 176 C.Ho 108/20' C.Dk 68/20' incl. 6 ref C. Compartments: 1 Ho, ER 1 Ha: (56.6 x 10.2)ER Ice Capable	**1 oil engine** with clutches, flexible couplings & sr reverse geared to sc. shaft driving 1 FP propeller Total Power: 1,500kW (2,039hp) 10.5kn Deutz SBV8M628 1 x 4 Stroke 8 Cy. 240 x 280 1500kW (2039bhp) Motoren Werke Mannheim AG (MWM)-Mannheim AuxGen: 3 x 104kW 220/380V 50Hz a.c Thrusters: 1 Thwart. FP thruster (f) Fuel: 33.0 (d.f.) 166.0 (d.f.) 6.3pd
9150511 *9HJI5* -	**WILSON BRAKE** *ex* Northern Lindnes *-2004* **Olga Shipping Co Ltd** Wilson Ship Management AS *Valletta* *Malta* MMSI: 249879000 Official number: 5473	**2,446** 1,369 3,710 T/cm 10.1	Class: BV (GL)	**1997-05 Slovenske Lodenice a.s. — Komarno** Yd No: 2934 Loa 87.90 (BB) Br ex - Dght 5.510 Lbp 83.50 Br md 12.80 Dpth 7.10 Welded, 1 dk	**(A31A2GX) General Cargo Ship** Double Hull Grain: 4,650; Bale: 4,620 TEU 176 C. 176/20' Compartments: 1 Ho, ER 1 Ha: (56.6 x 10.2)ER Ice Capable	**1 oil engine** reduction geared to sc. shaft driving 1 FP propeller Total Power: 1,500kW (2,039hp) 10.5kn Deutz SBV8M628 1 x 4 Stroke 8 Cy. 240 x 280 1500kW (2039bhp) Motoren Werke Mannheim AG (MWM)-Mannheim AuxGen: 3 x 104kW 220/380V 50Hz a.c Thrusters: 1 Thwart. FP thruster (f) Fuel: 30.0 (d.f.) 163.0 (d.f.) 6.0pd
9014717 *9HJV9* -	**WILSON BREMEN** *ex* Helen *-2008* *ex* Pandora *-1999* **Wilson Shipowning AS** Wilson EuroCarriers AS SatCom: Inmarsat C 424907610 *Valletta* *Malta* MMSI: 249076000 Official number: 9014717	**2,446** 1,369 3,735	Class: GL	**1992-11 Slovenske Lodenice a.s. — Komarno** Yd No: 2906 Loa 87.73 (BB) Br ex - Dght 5.498 Lbp 81.00 Br md 12.80 Dpth 7.10 Welded, 2 dks	**(A31A2GX) General Cargo Ship** Grain: 4,650; Bale: 4,620 TEU 184 C.Ho 108/20' C.Dk 76/20' Compartments: 1 Ho, ER 1 Ha: (56.6 x 10.2)ER Ice Capable	**1 oil engine** reverse reduction geared to sc. shaft driving 1 FP propeller Total Power: 1,500kW (2,039hp) 10.6kn Deutz SBV8M628 1 x 4 Stroke 8 Cy. 240 x 280 1500kW (2039bhp) Kloeckner Humboldt Deutz AG-Germany AuxGen: 3 x 104kW 220/380V 50Hz a.c, 1 x 39kW a.c Thrusters: 1 Thwart. FP thruster (f)
9126900 *9HSV4* -	**WILSON BREST** *ex* Northern Lesnes *-2002* **Wilson Shipowning AS** Wilson EuroCarriers AS SatCom: Inmarsat C 424937710 *Valletta* *Malta* MMSI: 249377000 Official number: 4568	**2,446** 1,369 3,712 T/cm 10.0	Class: BV (NV) (GL)	**1995-09 Slovenske Lodenice a.s. — Komarno** Yd No: 2927 Loa 87.90 (BB) Br ex 12.89 Dght 5.498 Lbp 83.50 Br md 12.80 Dpth 7.10 Welded, 1 dk	**(A31A2GX) General Cargo Ship** Double Hull Grain: 4,650; Bale: 4,620 TEU 176 C.Ho 108/20' C.Dk 68/20' incl. 6 ref C. Compartments: 1 Ho, ER 1 Ha: (56.6 x 10.2)ER Ice Capable	**1 oil engine** with clutches, flexible couplings & sr reverse geared to sc. shaft driving 1 FP propeller Total Power: 1,500kW (2,039hp) 10.5kn Deutz SBV8M628 1 x 4 Stroke 8 Cy. 240 x 280 1500kW (2039bhp) Motoren Werke Mannheim AG (MWM)-Mannheim AuxGen: 3 x 104kW 220/380V 50Hz a.c Thrusters: 1 Thwart. FP thruster (f) Fuel: 33.0 (d.f.) 166.0 (d.f.) 6.3pd
9150494 *9HFR5* -	**WILSON BRUGGE** *ex* Northern Larsnes *-2004* **Emary Shipping Co Ltd** Wilson Ship Management AS SatCom: Inmarsat C 424977210 *Valletta* *Malta* MMSI: 249772000 Official number: 5290	**2,446** 1,369 3,694 T/cm 10.1	Class: BV (GL)	**1996-12 Slovenske Lodenice a.s. — Komarno** Yd No: 2932 Loa 87.90 (BB) Br ex - Dght 5.498 Lbp 83.50 Br md 12.80 Dpth 7.10 Welded, 1 dk	**(A31A2GX) General Cargo Ship** Double Hull Grain: 4,650; Bale: 4,620 TEU 176 C. 176/20' Compartments: 1 Ho, ER 1 Ha: (56.6 x 10.2)ER Ice Capable	**1 oil engine** reduction geared to sc. shaft driving 1 FP propeller Total Power: 1,500kW (2,039hp) 10.5kn Deutz SBV8M628 1 x 4 Stroke 8 Cy. 240 x 280 1500kW (2039bhp) Motoren Werke Mannheim AG (MWM)-Mannheim Thrusters: 1 Thwart. FP thruster (f) Fuel: 30.0 (d.f.) 163.0 (d.f.) 6.0pd
9192612 *8PSY* -	**WILSON CADIZ** *ex* Dutch Sun *-2006* **Wilson Shipowning AS** Wilson EuroCarriers AS *Bridgetown* *Barbados* MMSI: 314216000 Official number: 733467	**2,999** 1,733 4,432 T/cm 11.9	Class: GL	**2000-01 Slovenske Lodenice a.s. — Komarno** Yd No: 3010 Loa 99.90 (BB) Br ex - Dght 5.670 Lbp 95.30 Br md 12.80 Dpth 7.55 Welded, 1 dk	**(A31A2GX) General Cargo Ship** Double Hull Grain: 5,841 TEU 297 C Ho 129 TEU C Dk 168 TEU incl 30 ref C. Compartments: 1 Ho, ER 2 Ha: ER Ice Capable	**1 oil engine** reduction geared to sc. shaft driving 1 CP propeller Total Power: 2,550kW (3,467hp) 13.5kn MWM TBD645L6 1 x 4 Stroke 6 Cy. 330 x 450 2550kW (3467bhp) Deutz AG-Koeln AuxGen: 1 x 640kW 220/380V a.c, 2 x 168kW 220/380V a.c Thrusters: 1 Thwart. FP thruster (f) Fuel: 190.0 (d.f.) 9.9pd
9173290 *8PRM* -	**WILSON CAEN** *ex* Dutch Navigator *-2004* **Wilson Shipowning AS** Wilson EuroCarriers AS *Bridgetown* *Barbados* MMSI: 314179000 Official number: 733426	**2,999** 1,733 4,451 T/cm 11.9	Class: GL	**1998-04 Slovenske Lodenice a.s. — Komarno** Yd No: 3007 Loa 99.90 (BB) Br ex - Dght 5.650 Lbp 95.80 Br md 12.80 Dpth 7.25 Welded, 1 dk	**(A31A2GX) General Cargo Ship** Double Hull Grain: 5,841; Bale: 5,841 TEU 297 C.Ho 129/20' (40') C.Dk 168/20' (40') incl. 30 ref C. Compartments: 1 Ho, ER 2 Ha: (38.0 x 10.2) (31.1 x 10.2)ER Ice Capable	**1 oil engine** reduction geared to sc. shaft driving 1 CP propeller Total Power: 2,550kW (3,467hp) 12.5kn MWM TBD645L6 1 x 4 Stroke 6 Cy. 330 x 450 2550kW (3467bhp) MTU Friedrichshafen GmbH-Friedrichshafen Thrusters: 1 Thwart. FP thruster (f) Fuel: 190.0 (d.f.) 10.0pd
9156101 *8PUK* -	**WILSON CALAIS** *ex* Steffen Sibum *-2008* *ex* Schelde Star *-2005* *ex* Heinrich Wessels *-2002* **Caiano Ship AS** Wilson EuroCarriers AS *Bridgetown* *Barbados* MMSI: 314255000	**2,994** 1,733 4,450	Class: GL	**2001-10 Slovenske Lodenice a.s. — Komarno** (Hull) Yd No: 3015 **2001-10 Brodogradiliste 'Sava' — Macvanska Mitrovica** Yd No: 319 Loa 99.85 (BB) Br ex - Dght 5.680 Lbp 95.52 Br md 12.80 Dpth 7.55 Welded, 1 dk	**(A31A2GX) General Cargo Ship** Double Hull Grain: 5,890 Compartments: 2 Ho, ER Ice Capable	**1 oil engine** geared to sc. shaft driving 1 CP propeller Total Power: 2,550kW (3,467hp) 13.0kn MWM TBD645L6 1 x 4 Stroke 6 Cy. 330 x 450 2550kW (3467bhp) Deutz AG-Koeln AuxGen: 1 x 640kW 380V a.c, 2 x 160kW 380V a.c Thrusters: 1 Thwart. FP thruster (f)
9125073 *V2LA9* -	**WILSON CARDIFF** *ex* Poet *-2013* *ex* German Feeder *-2000* **ms 'German-Feeder' WESCO Shipping GmbH & Co KG** Wessels Reederei GmbH & Co KG *Saint John's* *Antigua & Barbuda* MMSI: 304010986 Official number: 3696	**2,997** 1,741 4,444	Class: GL	**1997-06 Slovenske Lodenice a.s. — Komarno** Yd No: 3004 Loa 99.88 (BB) Br ex - Dght 5.666 Lbp 95.30 Br md 12.80 Dpth 7.55 Welded, 1 dk	**(A31A2GX) General Cargo Ship** Double Hull Grain: 5,841 TEU 297 C.Ho 129/20' C.Dk 168/20' incl 30 ref C. Compartments: 1 Ho, ER 2 Ha: (38.0 x 10.2) (31.2 x 10.2)ER Ice Capable	**1 oil engine** reduction geared to sc. shaft driving 1 CP propeller Total Power: 2,550kW (3,467hp) 13.0kn MWM TBD645L6 1 x 4 Stroke 6 Cy. 330 x 450 2550kW (3467bhp) Deutz AG-Koeln AuxGen: 1 x 640kW a.c, 2 x 168kW a.c Thrusters: 1 Thwart. FP thruster (f) Fuel: 196.0 (d.f.)
9125059 *V2CA5* -	**WILSON CHATHAM** *ex* Wotan *-2013* **ms 'Wotan' Schiffahrts GmbH & Co KG** Wessels Reederei GmbH & Co KG SatCom: Inmarsat C 421124133 *Saint John's* *Antigua & Barbuda* MMSI: 304195000 Official number: 3611	**2,997** 1,741 4,454	Class: GL	**1996-10 Slovenske Lodenice a.s. — Komarno** Yd No: 3002 Loa 99.75 (BB) Br ex - Dght 5.630 Lbp 95.80 Br md 12.80 Dpth 7.55 Welded, 1 dk	**(A31A2GX) General Cargo Ship** Grain: 5,841 TEU 297 C.Ho 129/20' C.Dk 168/20' Compartments: 1 Ho, ER 2 Ha: (38.0 x 10.2) (31.2 x 10.2)ER Ice Capable	**1 oil engine** reduction geared to sc. shaft driving 1 CP propeller Total Power: 2,550kW (3,467hp) 13.5kn MWM TBD645L6 1 x 4 Stroke 6 Cy. 330 x 450 2550kW (3467bhp) Motoren Werke Mannheim AG (MWM)-Mannheim AuxGen: 1 x 640kW 220/380V a.c, 2 x 168kW 220/380V a.c Thrusters: 1 Thwart. FP thruster (f)
9178458 *8PRV* -	**WILSON CLYDE** *ex* Admiral Sun *-2004* *ex* Dutch Trader *-2001* **Wilson Shipowning AS** Wilson EuroCarriers AS *Bridgetown* *Barbados* MMSI: 314187000 Official number: 733437	**2,999** 1,733 4,438	Class: GL	**1998-05 Slovenske Lodenice a.s. — Komarno** Yd No: 3008 Loa 99.90 (BB) Br ex - Dght 5.680 Lbp 95.80 Br md 12.80 Dpth 7.55 Welded, 1 dk	**(A31A2GX) General Cargo Ship** Grain: 5,915 TEU 297 C.Ho 129/20' C.Dk 168/20' incl. 30 ref C. Compartments: 1 Ho, ER 2 Ha: (38.0 x 10.2) (31.3 x 10.2)ER Ice Capable	**1 oil engine** with flexible couplings & reductiongeared to sc. shaft driving 1 CP propeller Total Power: 2,550kW (3,467hp) 13.0kn MWM TBD645L6 1 x 4 Stroke 6 Cy. 330 x 450 2550kW (3467bhp) Motoren Werke Mannheim AG (MWM)-Mannheim AuxGen: 2 x 190kW 380V 50Hz a.c Thrusters: 1 Thwart. FP thruster (f) Fuel: 180.0 (d.f.) 9.8pd
9178460 *8PRO* -	**WILSON CORK** *ex* Dutch Express *-2004* **Wilson Shipowning AS** Wilson EuroCarriers AS *Bridgetown* *Barbados* MMSI: 314180000 Official number: 733430	**2,999** 1,733 4,444	Class: GL	**1998-09 Slovenske Lodenice a.s. — Komarno** Yd No: 3009 Loa 99.90 (BB) Br ex - Dght 5.630 Lbp 95.80 Br md 12.80 Dpth 7.55 Welded, 1 dk	**(A31A2GX) General Cargo Ship** Grain: 5,841 TEU 297 C.Ho 129/20' C.Dk 168/20' incl. 30 ref C Compartments: 1 Ho, ER 2 Ha: (38.0 x 10.2) (31.3 x 10.2)ER Ice Capable	**1 oil engine** reduction geared to sc. shafts driving 1 CP propeller Total Power: 2,550kW (3,467hp) 13.0kn MWM TBD645L6 1 x 4 Stroke 6 Cy. 330 x 450 2550kW (3467bhp) MTU Friedrichshafen GmbH-Friedrichshafen AuxGen: 1 x 640kW 220/380V 50Hz a.c, 2 x 168kW 220/380V a.c Thrusters: 1 Thwart. FP thruster (f) Fuel: 180.0 (d.f.) 9.8pd

IMO / Call sign	Name / Owner / Manager / Flag	Tonnage	Class	Builder / Dimensions	Type / Capacity	Machinery
9125085 V2NA4	**WILSON CORPACH** *ex* Faust *-2013* *ex* German Express *-1997* **Rudiger Fleig Schiffahrts KG ms 'Faust'** Wessels Reederei GmbH & Co KG SatCom: Inmarsat C 430430210 *Saint John's* *Antigua & Barbuda* MMSI: 304302000	**2,997** 1,741 4,444	Class: GL	**1997-08 Slovenske Lodenice a.s. — Komarno** Yd No: 3005 Loa 99.90 (BB) Br ex - Dght 5.666 Lbp 95.30 Br md 12.80 Dpth 7.55 Welded, 1 dk	**(A31A2GX) General Cargo Ship** Grain: 5,841; Bale: 5,841 TEU 297 C.Ho 129/20' C.Dk 168/20' Compartments: 1 Ho, ER 2 Ha: (38.0 x 10.2) (31.2 x 10.2)ER Ice Capable	**1 oil engine** reduction geared to sc. shaft driving 1 CP propeller Total Power: 2,550kW (3,467hp) 13.0kn MWM TBD645L6 1 x 4 Stroke 6 Cy. 330 x 450 2550kW (3467bhp) MTU Friedrichshafen GmbH-Friedrichshafen AuxGen: 1 x 640kW 220/380V a.c, 2 x 168kW 220/380V a.c Thrusters: 1 Thwart. FP thruster (f)
9005754 8PUH -	**WILSON DOVER** *ex* Hanseatic Spring *-2007* *ex* P&O Nedlloyd Spring *-2005* *ex* Anna J *-2005* *ex* Admiral Sky *-2001* *ex* Anna J *-2001* *ex* MF Egypt *-1999* *ex* Intermodal Egypt *-1996* *ex* Anna J *-1993* **Wilson Shipowning AS** Wilson EuroCarriers AS *Bridgetown* *Barbados* MMSI: 314251000 Official number: 733507	**2,480** 1,206 3,269	Class: GL (NV)	**1993-06 Estaleiros Navais do Mondego S.A. — Figueira da Foz** (Hull) Yd No: 223 **1993-06 Estaleiros Navais de Viana do Castelo S.A. — Viana do Castelo** Loa 87.47 (BB) Br ex 13.00 Dght 5.075 Lbp 82.25 Br md 12.98 Dpth 7.10 Welded, 1 dk	**(A31A2GX) General Cargo Ship** Grain: 4,650 TEU 202 C. 202/20' incl. 30 ref C. Compartments: 1 Ho, ER 1 Ha: (57.4 x 10.2)ER Ice Capable	**1 oil engine** with clutches & sr geared to sc. shaft driving 1 CP propeller Total Power: 1,470kW (1,999hp) 12.5kn Alpha 6L28/32A 1 x 4 Stroke 6 Cy. 280 x 320 1470kW (1999bhp) MAN B&W Diesel A/S-Denmark AuxGen: 1 x 216kW 220/380V a.c, 2 x 140kW 220/380V a.c Thrusters: 1 Thwart. FP thruster (f) Fuel: 123.0 (d.f.) 7.3pd
9005742 8PTC -	**WILSON DVINA** *ex* Hanseatic Swift *-2006* *ex* P&O Nedlloyd Swift *-2005* *ex* Heide J *-2005* *ex* Eastmed *-2002* *ex* Zim Eastmed *-2002* *ex* MF Carrier *-1999* *ex* Intermodal Carrier *-1996* *ex* Rhein Carrier *-1995* *ex* Heide J *-1993* **Wilson Shipowning AS** Wilson EuroCarriers AS *Bridgetown* *Barbados* MMSI: 314220000 Official number: 733471	**2,481** 1,206 3,269	Class: GL	**1992-09 Estaleiros Navais do Mondego S.A. — Figueira da Foz** (Hull) Yd No: 222 **1992-09 Estaleiros Navais de Viana do Castelo S.A. — Viana do Castelo** Loa 87.42 (BB) Br ex - Dght 5.075 Lbp 82.10 Br md 13.00 Dpth 7.10 Welded, 1 dk	**(A31A2GX) General Cargo Ship** Grain: 4,650 TEU 153 C.Ho 104/20' C.Dk 49/20' incl. 30 ref C. Compartments: 1 Ho, ER 1 Ha: (57.4 x 10.2)ER Ice Capable	**1 oil engine** with clutches & sr geared to sc. shaft driving 1 CP propeller Total Power: 1,470kW (1,999hp) 12.0kn Alpha 6L28/32A 1 x 4 Stroke 6 Cy. 280 x 320 1470kW (1999bhp) MAN B&W Diesel A/S-Denmark AuxGen: 1 x 216kW 220/380V a.c, 2 x 140kW 220/380V a.c Thrusters: 1 Thwart. FP thruster (f) Fuel: 123.0 (d.f.) 7.3pd
9060675 9HGK9 -	**WILSON ELBE** *ex* Johann *-2007* *ex* Heinrich Bojen *-1998* **Wilson Shipowning AS** Wilson EuroCarriers AS *Valletta* *Malta* MMSI: 256953000 Official number: 9060675	**1,589** 844 2,665	Class: GL	**1993-06 Slovenske Lodenice a.s. — Komarno** Yd No: 1301 Loa 82.37 (BB) Br ex - Dght 4.789 Lbp 79.82 Br md 11.35 Dpth 6.10 Welded, 1 dk	**(A31A2GX) General Cargo Ship** Grain: 3,144 TEU 110 C.Ho 46/20' C.Dk 64/20' Compartments: 1 Ho, ER 1 Ha: (53.4 x 9.0)ER Ice Capable	**1 oil engine** with flexible couplings & sr geared to sc. shaft driving 1 FP propeller Total Power: 1,015kW (1,380hp) 9.7kn Deutz SBV6M628 1 x 4 Stroke 6 Cy. 240 x 280 1015kW (1380bhp) Motoren Werke Mannheim AG (MWM)-Mannheim AuxGen: 2 x 68kW 380V 50Hz a.c Thrusters: 1 Thwart. FP thruster (f) Fuel: 110.0 (d.f.) 4.8pd
9117117 8PUN -	**WILSON EMS** *ex* Fundo *-2007* *ex* Preussen *-1995* **Wilson Shipowning AS** Wilson EuroCarriers AS *Bridgetown* *Barbados* MMSI: 314258000	**989** 528 1,536	Class: GL	**1995-03 Ceskoslovenska Plavba Labska a.s. (CSPL) — Chvaletice** Yd No: 101 Loa 72.53 Br ex - Dght 4.050 Lbp 69.00 Br md 9.48 Dpth 5.75 Welded, 1 dk	**(A31A2GX) General Cargo Ship** Double Bottom Entire Compartment Length Grain: 1,994 TEU 63 C. 63/20' Compartments: 1 Ho, ER 1 Ha: (44.4 x 7.6)ER Ice Capable	**1 oil engine** geared to sc. shaft driving 1 FP propeller Total Power: 930kW (1,264hp) 11.0kn Deutz SBV6M628 1 x 4 Stroke 6 Cy. 240 x 280 930kW (1264bhp) Motoren Werke Mannheim AG (MWM)-Mannheim Thrusters: 1 Water jet (f) Fuel: 76.0
8119572 8PXI -	**WILSON EXPRESS** *ex* Green Bergen *-2004* *ex* Bentago *-1998* **Wilson Shipowning II AS** Wilson EuroCarriers AS *Bridgetown* *Barbados* MMSI: 314336000	**6,182** 4,289 5,864	Class: BV (LR) (NV) Classed LR until 6/10/10	**1983-10 Fosen Mek. Verksteder AS — Rissa** (Aft section) Yd No: 34 **1983-10 FEAB-Marstrandverken — Marstrand** (Fwd section) Yd No: 159 Loa 130.83 (BB) Br ex 18.03 Dght 6.160 Lbp 117.81 Br md 18.00 Dpth 8.60 Welded, 3 dks	**(A34A2GR) Refrigerated Cargo Ship** Side door/ramp (s. f.) Side door/ramp (s. a.) Ins: 9,061 TEU 164 incl 32 ref C Compartments: 3 Ho, ER, 7 Tw Dk	**1 oil engine** with flexible couplings & sr gearedto sc. shaft driving 1 CP propeller Total Power: 7,356kW (10,001hp) 17.5kn MaK 12M552AK 1 x Vee 4 Stroke 12 Cy. 450 x 520 7356kW (10001bhp) Krupp MaK Maschinenbau GmbH-Kiel AuxGen: 2 x 840kW 540V 60Hz a.c, 1 x 520kW 450V 60Hz a.c Boilers: e (ex.g.) 9.2kgf/cm² (9.0bar), AuxB (o.f.) 9.2kgf/cm² (9.0bar) Thrusters: 1 Thwart. CP thruster (f)
9491733 8PAE7 -	**WILSON FARSUND** **Wilson Shipowning AS** Wilson Management AS *Bridgetown* *Barbados* MMSI: 314377000	**3,561** - 4,340 T/cm 12.7	Class: GL	**2012-03 Shandong Baibuting Shipbuilding Co Ltd — Rongcheng SD** Yd No: BBT001 Loa 89.94 (BB) Br ex - Dght 5.800 Lbp 84.95 Br md 15.40 Dpth 7.60 Welded, 1 dk	**(A31A2GX) General Cargo Ship** Grain: 5,776; Bale: 5,509 Compartments: 1 Ho, ER 1 Ha: ER (54.6 x 12.6) Ice Capable	**1 oil engine** reduction geared to sc. shaft driving 1 CP propeller Total Power: 2,040kW (2,774hp) 11.8kn Wartsila 6L26 1 x 4 Stroke 6 Cy. 260 x 320 2040kW (2774bhp) Wartsila Finland Oy-Finland AuxGen: 2 x 200kW 220/400V 50Hz a.c, 1 x 344kW 220/400V 50Hz a.c Thrusters: 1 Tunnel thruster (f) Fuel: 140.0
9491757 8PAH4 -	**WILSON FEDJE** **Wilson Shipowning AS** Wilson Management AS SatCom: Inmarsat C 431439710 *Bridgetown* *Barbados* MMSI: 314397000 Official number: 733660	**3,561** 1,590 4,501	Class: GL	**2012-10 Shandong Baibuting Shipbuilding Co Ltd — Rongcheng SD** Yd No: BBT003 Loa 89.93 (BB) Br ex - Dght 5.800 Lbp 84.95 Br md 15.40 Dpth 7.60 Welded, 1 dk	**(A31A2GX) General Cargo Ship** Grain: 5,776; Bale: 5,509 TEU 195 C Ho 120 TEU C Dk 75 TEU Compartments: 1 Ho, ER 1 Ha: ER (54.6 x 12.6) Ice Capable	**1 oil engine** reduction geared to sc. shaft driving 1 CP propeller Total Power: 2,040kW (2,774hp) 11.8kn Wartsila 6L26 1 x 4 Stroke 6 Cy. 260 x 320 2040kW (2774bhp) Wartsila Italia SpA-Italy AuxGen: 2 x 200kW 440V 50Hz a.c, 1 x 300kW 220/440V 50Hz a.c Thrusters: 1 Thwart. FP thruster (f)
9491769 8PAH5 -	**WILSON FINNFJORD** **Wilson Shipowning AS** Wilson Management AS *Bridgetown* *Barbados* MMSI: 314398000 Official number: 733661	**3,561** - 4,518 T/cm 12.5	Class: GL	**2012-12 Shandong Baibuting Shipbuilding Co Ltd — Rongcheng SD** Yd No: BBT004 Loa 89.95 (BB) Br ex - Dght 5.800 Lbp 84.95 Br md 15.40 Dpth 7.60 Welded, 1 dk	**(A31A2GX) General Cargo Ship** Grain: 5,684; Bale: 5,684 TEU 195 C Ho 120 TEU C Dk 75 TEU Compartments: 1 Ho, ER 1 Ha: ER (54.6 x 12.6) Ice Capable	**1 oil engine** reverse reduction geared to sc. shaft driving 1 CP propeller Total Power: 2,040kW (2,774hp) 11.8kn Wartsila 6L26 1 x 4 Stroke 6 Cy. 260 x 320 2040kW (2774bhp) Wartsila Italia SpA-Italy AuxGen: 2 x 200kW 400/220V 50Hz a.c, 1 x 300kW 400/220V 50Hz a.c Thrusters: 1 Tunnel thruster (f) Fuel: 235.0
7631042 8PPB -	**WILSON FJORD** *ex* Victoria *-2002* *ex* Continental Alpha *-1994* *ex* Commodore S *-1994* *ex* Scott Survivor *-1992* *ex* Commodore Enterprise *-1987* **Wilson Shipowning AS** Wilson EuroCarriers AS SatCom: Inmarsat C 431410610 *Bridgetown* *Barbados* MMSI: 314106000 Official number: 725468	**2,764** 1,437 3,283	Class: BV (LR) ✠ Classed LR until 1/11/09	**1977-11 Appledore Shipbuilders Ltd — Bideford** Yd No: A.S.118 Loa 95.15 (BB) Br ex 13.77 Dght 5.500 Lbp 88.80 Br md 13.61 Dpth 7.50 Welded, 2 dks	**(A31A2GX) General Cargo Ship** Grain: 5,470; Bale: 5,151 TEU 194 C.Ho 124/20' C.Dk 70/20' incl. 12 ref C. Compartments: 1 Ho, ER 2 Ha: (24.6 x 10.2) (37.1 x 10.2)ER	**1 oil engine** sr geared to sc. shaft driving 1 FP propeller Total Power: 2,400kW (3,263hp) 13.0kn Wichmann 8V28B 1 x Vee 4 Stroke 8 Cy. 280 x 360 2400kW (3263bhp) (new engine 1994) Wartsila Propulsion AS-Norway AuxGen: 1 x 260kW 415V 50Hz a.c, 1 x 120kW 415V 50Hz a.c, 2 x 108kW 415V 50Hz a.c Thrusters: 1 Thwart. CP thruster (f)
9491745 8PAH3 -	**WILSON FLUSHING** **Wilson Shipowning AS** Wilson Management AS *Bridgetown* *Barbados* MMSI: 314396000	**3,561** - 4,321 T/cm 12.7	Class: GL	**2012-08 Shandong Baibuting Shipbuilding Co Ltd — Rongcheng SD** Yd No: BBT002 Loa 89.96 (BB) Br ex - Dght 5.800 Lbp 84.95 Br md 15.40 Dpth 7.60 Welded, 1 dk	**(A31A2GX) General Cargo Ship** Grain: 5,776; Bale: 5,509 Compartments: 1 Ho, ER 1 Ha: ER (54.6 x 12.6) Ice Capable	**1 oil engine** reduction geared to sc. shaft driving 1 CP propeller Total Power: 2,040kW (2,774hp) 11.8kn Wartsila 6L26 1 x 4 Stroke 6 Cy. 260 x 320 2040kW (2774bhp) Wartsila Finland Oy-Finland AuxGen: 2 x 200kW 220/400V 50Hz a.c, 1 x 344kW 220/400V 50Hz a.c Thrusters: 1 Thwart. FP thruster (f)

IMO / Call sign	Name / Owners / Flag	Tonnage	Class	Built	Type / Capacity	Machinery
9171096 *8PTS* -	**WILSON GAETA** *ex* Hermann Sibum *-2006* *ex* Northern Lake *-2002* **Wilson Shipowning AS** Wilson EuroCarriers AS *Bridgetown* *Barbados* MMSI: 314237000 Official number: 733492	**2,446** 1,369 3,697	Class: GL	**1998-05 Slovenske Lodenice a.s. — Komarno** Yd No: 2942 Loa 87.97 (BB) Br ex 12.90 Dght 5.498 Lbp 81.00 Br md 12.80 Dpth 7.10 Welded, 1 dk	**(A31A2GX) General Cargo Ship** Double Hull Grain: 4,591; Bale: 4,561 TEU 176 C Ho 108 TEU C Dk 68 TEU incl 6 ref C Compartments: 1 Ho, ER 1 Ha: (56.5 x 10.2)ER Ice Capable	**1 oil engine** with clutches, flexible couplings & sr reverse geared to sc. shaft driving 1 FP propeller Total Power: 1,500kW (2,039hp) 10.5kn Deutz SBV8M628 1 x 4 Stroke 8 Cy. 240 x 280 1500kW (2039bhp) Motoren Werke Mannheim AG (MWM)-Mannheim AuxGen: 3 x 104kW 220/400V 50Hz a.c Thrusters: 1 Thwart. FP thruster (f) Fuel: 165.0 (d.f.) 6.0pd
9000833 *8PSO* -	**WILSON GARSTON** *ex* Hanseatic Sun *-2005* *ex* Pionier *-2003* **Wilson Shipowning AS** Wilson EuroCarriers AS *Bridgetown* *Barbados* MMSI: 314206000 Official number: 733458	**2,270** 973 2,801	Class: GL	**1989-10 Schiffs. Hugo Peters Wewelsfleth Peters & Co. GmbH — Wewelsfleth** Yd No: 631 Loa 82.51 Br ex - Dght 5.690 Lbp 78.90 Br md 12.50 Dpth 7.20 Welded, 1 dk	**(A31A2GX) General Cargo Ship** Grain: 4,392; Bale: 4,392 TEU 137 C. 137/20' Compartments: 1 Ho, ER 1 Ha: (52.2 x 10.2)ER Ice Capable	**1 oil engine** with flexible couplings & sr geared to sc. shaft driving 1 CP propeller Total Power: 1,200kW (1,632hp) 11.0kn Wichmann 6L28B 1 x 2 Stroke 6 Cy. 280 x 360 1200kW (1632bhp) Wartsila Wichmann Diesel AS-Norway AuxGen: 1 x 600kW 440V a.c, 1 x 200kW 440V a.c Thrusters: 1 Thwart. FP thruster (f)
9056026 *8PRZ* -	**WILSON GDANSK** *ex* Carrier *-2005* *ex* Seaprincess *-1998* *ex* Rugen *-1997* **Wilson Shipowning AS** Wilson EuroCarriers AS *Bridgetown* *Barbados* MMSI: 314191000 Official number: 733441	**2,506** 1,351 3,686	Class: GL	**1993-03 Slovenske Lodenice a.s. — Komarno** Yd No: 2916 Loa 87.77 (BB) Br ex 12.90 Dght 5.518 Lbp 81.00 Br md 12.80 Dpth 7.10 Welded, 1 dk	**(A31A2GX) General Cargo Ship** Grain: 4,650; Bale: 4,620 TEU 168 C.Ho 108/20' C.Dk 60/20' Compartments: 1 Ho, ER 1 Ha: (56.6 x 10.2)ER Ice Capable	**1 oil engine** reduction geared to sc. shaft driving 1 CP propeller Total Power: 1,470kW (1,999hp) 11.5kn Alpha 6L28/32A 1 x 4 Stroke 6 Cy. 280 x 320 1470kW (1999bhp) MAN B&W Diesel A/S-Denmark AuxGen: 1 x 400kW 220/380V 50Hz a.c, 2 x 212kW 220/380V 50Hz a.c Thrusters: 1 Thwart. FP thruster (f)
9056064 *8PSA* -	**WILSON GDYNIA** *ex* Dutch Sea *-2005* *ex* Gata Bay *-1998* *ex* Vilm *-1997* **Wilson Shipowning AS** Wilson EuroCarriers AS *Bridgetown* *Barbados* MMSI: 314192000	**2,506** 1,351 3,632	Class: GL	**1994-01 Slovenske Lodenice a.s. — Komarno** Yd No: 2920 Loa 87.87 (BB) Br ex - Dght 5.520 Lbp 81.60 Br md 12.80 Dpth 7.10 Welded, 1 dk	**(A31A2GX) General Cargo Ship** Double Bottom Entire Compartment Length Grain: 4,649; Bale: 4,620 TEU 168 C.Ho 108/20' C.Dk 60/20' Compartments: 1 Ho, ER 1 Ha: (56.6 x 10.2)ER Ice Capable	**1 oil engine** reduction geared to sc. shaft driving 1 CP propeller Total Power: 1,470kW (1,999hp) 11.5kn Alpha 6L28/32A 1 x 4 Stroke 6 Cy. 280 x 320 1470kW (1999bhp) MAN B&W Diesel A/S-Denmark AuxGen: 1 x 400kW 400V 50Hz a.c, 2 x 215kW 400V 50Hz a.c Thrusters: 1 Directional thruster (f) Fuel: 137.0 (d.f.) 6.5pd
9150236 *9HBK5* -	**WILSON GHENT** *ex* Northern Loknes *-2004* **Wilson Shipowning AS** Wilson EuroCarriers AS SatCom: Inmarsat C 424964710 *Valletta* *Malta* MMSI: 249647000 Official number: 5028	**2,446** 1,369 3,707 T/cm 10.1	Class: BV (GL)	**1996-08 Slovenske Lodenice a.s. — Komarno** Yd No: 2930 Loa 87.90 (BB) Br ex - Dght 5.510 Lbp 83.50 Br md 12.80 Dpth 7.10 Welded, 1 dk	**(A31A2GX) General Cargo Ship** Double Hull Grain: 4,650; Bale: 4,620 TEU 176 C. 176/20' Compartments: 1 Ho, ER 1 Ha: (56.6 x 10.2)ER Ice Capable	**1 oil engine** geared to sc. shaft driving 1 FP propeller Total Power: 1,501kW (2,041hp) 10.5kn Deutz SBV8M628 1 x 4 Stroke 8 Cy. 240 x 280 1501kW (2041bhp) Motoren Werke Mannheim AG (MWM)-Mannheim AuxGen: 3 x 130kW a.c, 1 x 49kW a.c Thrusters: 1 Thwart. FP thruster (f) Fuel: 30.0 (d.f.) 163.0 (d.f.) 6.0pd
9056038 *8PSC* -	**WILSON GIJON** *ex* Dutch Spear *-2005* *ex* MCL Fortune *-2003* *ex* Seafortune *-1998* *ex* Hiddensee *-1997* **Wilson Shipowning AS** Wilson EuroCarriers AS *Bridgetown* *Barbados* MMSI: 314194000 Official number: 733444	**2,506** 1,351 3,689	Class: GL	**1993-04 Slovenske Lodenice a.s. — Komarno** Yd No: 2917 Loa 87.75 (BB) Br ex - Dght 5.520 Lbp 81.85 Br md 12.80 Dpth 7.10 Welded, 1 dk	**(A31A2GX) General Cargo Ship** Grain: 4,650; Bale: 4,620 TEU 168 C.Ho 108/20' C.Dk 60/20' Compartments: 1 Ho, ER 1 Ha: (56.6 x 10.2)ER Ice Capable	**1 oil engine** reduction geared to sc. shaft driving 1 CP propeller Total Power: 1,470kW (1,999hp) 11.5kn Alpha 6L28/32A 1 x 4 Stroke 6 Cy. 280 x 320 1470kW (1999bhp) MAN B&W Diesel A/S-Denmark AuxGen: 1 x 400kW 220/380V 50Hz a.c, 2 x 212kW 220/380V 50Hz a.c Thrusters: 1 Thwart. FP thruster (f)
9126687 *9HSC4* -	**WILSON GOOLE** *ex* Northern Loftnes *-2002* **Wilson Shipowning AS** Wilson EuroCarriers AS SatCom: Inmarsat C 424935910 *Valletta* *Malta* MMSI: 249359000 Official number: 4531	**2,446** 1,369 3,704 T/cm 10.1	Class: BV (NV) (GL)	**1995-07 Slovenske Lodenice a.s. — Komarno** Yd No: 2926 Loa 87.97 (BB) Br ex 12.89 Dght 5.510 Lbp 82.86 Br md 12.79 Dpth 7.09 Welded, 1 dk	**(A31A2GX) General Cargo Ship** Double Hull Grain: 4,650; Bale: 4,620 TEU 176 C.Ho 108/20' C.Dk 68/20' incl. 6 ref C. Compartments: 1 Ho, ER 1 Ha: (56.6 x 10.2)ER Ice Capable	**1 oil engine** with clutches, flexible couplings & sr reverse geared to sc. shaft driving 1 FP propeller Total Power: 1,500kW (2,039hp) 10.5kn Deutz SBV8M628 1 x 4 Stroke 8 Cy. 240 x 280 1500kW (2039bhp) Motoren Werke Mannheim AG (MWM)-Mannheim AuxGen: 3 x 104kW 220/380V 50Hz a.c Thrusters: 1 Thwart. FP thruster (f) Fuel: 33.0 (d.f.) 166.0 (d.f.) 7.0pd
9056040 *8PSB* -	**WILSON GRIMSBY** *ex* Express *-2005* *ex* Seapride Spirit *-1998* *ex* Poel *-1997* **Wilson Shipowning AS** Wilson EuroCarriers AS *Bridgetown* *Barbados* MMSI: 314193000 Official number: 733443	**2,506** 1,351 3,689	Class: GL	**1993-05 Slovenske Lodenice a.s. — Komarno** Yd No: 2918 Loa 87.70 (BB) Br ex - Dght 5.520 Lbp 81.00 Br md 12.80 Dpth 7.10 Welded, 1 dk	**(A31A2GX) General Cargo Ship** Grain: 4,650; Bale: 4,620 TEU 168 C.Ho 108/20' C.Dk 60/20' Compartments: 1 Ho, ER 1 Ha: (56.6 x 10.2)ER Ice Capable	**1 oil engine** reduction geared to sc. shaft driving 1 CP propeller Total Power: 1,470kW (1,999hp) 11.5kn Alpha 6L28/32A 1 x 4 Stroke 6 Cy. 280 x 320 1470kW (1999bhp) MAN B&W Diesel A/S-Denmark AuxGen: 1 x 400kW 220/380V 50Hz a.c, 2 x 212kW 220/380V 50Hz a.c Thrusters: 1 Thwart. FP thruster (f)
9126912 *9HXV4* -	**WILSON GRIP** *ex* Northern Liftnes *-2002* **Wilson Shipowning AS** Wilson EuroCarriers AS SatCom: Inmarsat C 424952810 *Valletta* *Malta* MMSI: 249528000 Official number: 4818	**2,446** 1,369 3,680 T/cm 10.0	Class: BV (NV) (GL)	**1996-04 Slovenske Lodenice a.s. — Komarno** Yd No: 2928 Loa 87.90 (BB) Br ex 12.89 Dght 5.511 Lbp 81.32 Br md 12.80 Dpth 7.10 Welded, 1 dk	**(A31A2GX) General Cargo Ship** Double Hull Grain: 4,650; Bale: 4,620 TEU 176 C.Ho 108/20' C.Dk 68/20' incl. 6 ref C. Compartments: 1 Ho, ER 1 Ha: (56.6 x 10.2)ER Ice Capable	**1 oil engine** with clutches, flexible couplings & sr reverse geared to sc. shaft driving 1 FP propeller Total Power: 1,500kW (2,039hp) 10.5kn Deutz SBV8M628 1 x 4 Stroke 8 Cy. 240 x 280 1500kW (2039bhp) Motoren Werke Mannheim AG (MWM)-Mannheim AuxGen: 3 x 104kW 230/400V 50Hz a.c Thrusters: 1 Thwart. FP thruster (f) Fuel: 30.0 (d.f.) 163.0 (d.f.) 7.5pd
9064891 *9HJP9* -	**WILSON HARRIER** *ex* Laura Helena *-2008* **Wilson Shipowning AS** Wilson EuroCarriers AS *Valletta* *Malta* MMSI: 249066000 Official number: 9064891	**2,811** 1,688 4,206 T/cm 11.1	Class: GL	**1993-07 Scheepswerf Pattje B.V. — Waterhuizen** Yd No: 384 Loa 91.20 (BB) Br ex - Dght 5.770 Lbp 84.80 Br md 13.80 Dpth 7.15 Welded, 1 dk	**(A31A2GX) General Cargo Ship** Double Hull Grain: 5,663 TEU 190 C.Ho 112/20' C.Dk 78/20' Compartments: 1 Ho, ER 1 Ha: (62.7 x 11.2)ER Ice Capable	**1 oil engine** with flexible couplings & sr geared to sc. shaft driving 1 CP propeller Total Power: 2,200kW (2,991hp) 12.5kn MaK 6M453C 1 x 4 Stroke 6 Cy. 320 x 420 2200kW (2991bhp) Krupp MaK Maschinenbau GmbH-Kiel AuxGen: 1 x 270kW 380V 50Hz a.c, 1 x 145kW 380V 50Hz a.c Thrusters: 1 Thwart. FP thruster (f) Fuel: 60.0 (d.f.) 222.0 (r.f.) 9.0pd
9064906 *8PTD* -	**WILSON HAWK** *ex* Haugo *-2006* launched as Niels *-1994* **Wilson Shipowning AS** Wilson EuroCarriers AS *Bridgetown* *Barbados* MMSI: 314222000 Official number: 733472	**2,811** 1,688 4,284	Class: GL	**1994-03 Scheepswerf Pattje B.V. — Waterhuizen** Yd No: 385 Loa 91.20 (BB) Br ex 13.85 Dght 5.770 Lbp 84.80 Br md 13.80 Dpth 7.15 Welded, 1 dk	**(A31A2GX) General Cargo Ship** Double Hull Grain: 5,624 TEU 190 C. 190/20' Compartments: 1 Ho, ER 1 Ha: ER Ice Capable	**1 oil engine** with flexible couplings & sr reverse geared to sc. shaft driving 1 CP propeller Total Power: 2,200kW (2,991hp) 12.5kn MaK 6M453C 1 x 4 Stroke 6 Cy. 320 x 420 2200kW (2991bhp) Krupp MaK Maschinenbau GmbH-Kiel AuxGen: 1 x 220kW a.c, 1 x 145kW 380V 50Hz a.c, 1 x 80kW 380V 50Hz a.c Thrusters: 1 Thwart. FP thruster (f) Fuel: 60.0 (d.f.) 252.0 (r.f.) 5.0pd
9116022 *9HJW9* -	**WILSON HERON** *ex* Garmo *-2008* launched as Ilka *-1994* **Wilson Shipowning AS** Wilson EuroCarriers AS *Valletta* *Malta* MMSI: 249075000 Official number: 9116022	**2,901** 1,693 4,228	Class: GL	**1994-11 Scheepswerf Pattje B.V. — Waterhuizen** Yd No: 387 Loa 91.20 (BB) Br ex - Dght 5.800 Lbp 84.80 Br md 13.80 Dpth 7.15 Welded, 1 dk	**(A31A2GX) General Cargo Ship** Double Hull Grain: 5,720 TEU 242 C. 242/20' Compartments: 1 Ho, ER 1 Ha: (62.7 x 11.2)ER Ice Capable	**1 oil engine** with flexible couplings & sr reverse geared to sc. shaft driving 1 CP propeller Total Power: 2,200kW (2,991hp) 12.5kn MaK 6M453C 1 x 4 Stroke 6 Cy. 320 x 420 2200kW (2991bhp) Krupp MaK Maschinenbau GmbH-Kiel AuxGen: 1 x 216kW 220/380V a.c, 1 x 145kW 220/380V a.c Thrusters: 1 Thwart. FP thruster (f) Fuel: 70.0 (d.f.) 234.0 (r.f.) 8.0pd
9017434 *P3TW9* -	**WILSON HOOK** *ex* Lena Katharina *-2004* **mv 'Mautern' Shipping Co Ltd** Wilson Ship Management AS *Limassol* *Cyprus* MMSI: 210604000 Official number: 9017434	**2,993** 1,575 4,280 T/cm 11.7	Class: GL	**2003-11 AD Brodogradiliste 'Sava' — Macvanska Mitrovica** Yd No: 313 Loa 89.98 (BB) Br ex 15.46 Dght 5.640 Lbp 84.80 Br md 15.20 Dpth 7.10 Welded	**(A31A2GX) General Cargo Ship** Double Bottom Entire Compartment Length Grain: 5,546; Bale: 5,546 TEU 144 C. 144/20' Compartments: 1 Ho, ER 1 Ha: ER (52.7 x 12.8) Ice Capable	**1 oil engine** geared to sc. shaft driving 1 CP propeller Total Power: 2,079kW (2,827hp) 12.3kn MaK 6M453C 1 x 4 Stroke 6 Cy. 320 x 420 2079kW (2827bhp) MaK Motoren GmbH & Co. KG-Kiel AuxGen: 2 x 200kW 400/220V a.c, 1 x 440kW 400/220V a.c Thrusters: 1 Tunnel thruster (f) Fuel: 25.0 (d.f.) 190.0 (r.f.)

198604 *3DQ9*	**WILSON HULL** *ex* Joching *-2005* **mv 'Joching' Co Ltd** Oesterreichischer Lloyd Seereederei (Cyprus) Ltd *Limassol* *Cyprus* MMSI: 209972000 Official number: 9198604	**3,037** 1,503 4,247 T/cm 11.6	Class: GL	**2001-12 Rousse Shipyard JSC — Rousse** Yd No: 1001 Loa 89.87 (BB) Br ex - Dght 5.640 Lbp 84.80 Br md 15.20 Dpth 7.10 Welded, 1 dk	**(A31A2GX) General Cargo Ship** Double Hull Grain: 5,568; Bale: 5,568 TEU 325 C. 325/20 Compartments: 1 Ho, ER 1 Ha: ER (52.7 x 12.8) Ice Capable	**1 oil engine** reduction geared to sc. shaft driving 1 CP propeller Total Power: 2,400kW (3,263hp) 12.5kn MaK 8M25 1 x 4 Stroke 8 Cy. 255 x 400 2400kW (3263bhp) Caterpillar Motoren GmbH & Co. KG-Germany Thrusters: 1 Tunnel thruster (f) Fuel: 46.0 (d.f.) 217.0 (r.f.) 10.0pd
017381 *PSP*	**WILSON HUMBER** *ex* Marble Bay *-2005* *launched as* Stone *-1999* **Wilson Shipowning AS** Wilson EuroCarriers AS *Bridgetown* *Barbados* MMSI: 314207000	**3,092** 1,634 4,167	Class: BV (NV) (GL)	**1999-04 Brodogradiliste 'Begej' — Zrenjanin** (Hull launched by) Yd No: 225 **1999-04 Brodogradiliste Kladovo — Kladovo** (Hull completed by) Loa 89.90 (BB) Br ex - Dght 5.600 Lbp 84.80 Br md 15.80 Dpth 7.10 Welded, 1 dk	**(A31A2GX) General Cargo Ship** Grain: 5,546; Bale: 5,250 Compartments: 1 Ho, ER 1 Ha: (52.7 x 12.8)ER Ice Capable	**1 oil engine** reduction geared to sc. shaft driving 1 CP propeller Total Power: 2,080kW (2,828hp) 11.7kn MaK 6M453C 1 x 4 Stroke 6 Cy. 320 x 420 2080kW (2828bhp) Krupp MaK Maschinenbau GmbH-Kiel AuxGen: 1 x 440kW 380V 50Hz a.c, 2 x 208kW 380V 50Hz a.c Thrusters: 1 Thwart. FP thruster (f)
017379 *PSQ*	**WILSON HUSUM** *ex* Marble Sea *-2005* *launched as* Marble *-1998* **Wilson Shipowning AS** Wilson EuroCarriers AS *Bridgetown* *Barbados* MMSI: 314208000	**3,092** 1,634 4,119 T/cm 11.6	Class: BV (NV) (GL)	**1998-07 Brodogradiliste 'Begej' — Zrenjanin** (Hull launched by) Yd No: 224 **1998-07 Brodogradiliste Kladovo — Kladovo** (Hull completed by) Loa 89.90 (BB) Br ex - Dght 5.600 Lbp 84.80 Br md 15.20 Dpth 7.10 Welded, 1 dk	**(A24E2BL) Limestone Carrier** Grain: 5,417; Bale: 5,417 Compartments: 1 Ho, ER 1 Ha: (52.7 x 12.8)ER Gantry cranes: 1x8t Ice Capable	**1 oil engine** with clutches, flexible couplings & sr geared to sc. shaft driving 1 CP propeller Total Power: 2,079kW (2,827hp) 13.1kn MaK 6M453C 1 x 4 Stroke 6 Cy. 320 x 420 2079kW (2827bhp) MaK Motoren GmbH & Co. KG-Kiel AuxGen: 1 x 440kW 380V 50Hz a.c, 2 x 247kW 380V 50Hz a.c Thrusters: 1 Thwart. CP thruster (f) Fuel: 201.2 (d.f.) 10.5pd
198458 *PUO*	**WILSON LAHN** *ex* Moravia *-2004* **Wilson Shipowning AS** Wilson EuroCarriers AS *Bridgetown* *Barbados* MMSI: 314259000 Official number: 733516	**1,559** 815 2,500	Class: GL	**2001-03 Ceskoslovenska Plavba Labska a.s. (CSPL) — Chvaletice** Yd No: 202 Loa 83.16 (BB) Br ex 10.95 Dght 4.772 Lbp 79.20 Br md 10.90 Dpth 6.05 Welded, 1 dk	**(A31A2GX) General Cargo Ship** Double Hull Grain: 2,840 TEU 94 C.Ho 46/20' C.Dk 48/20' Compartments: 1 Ho, ER 1 Ha: (53.4 x 8.5)ER Ice Capable	**1 oil engine** geared to sc. shaft driving 1 FP propeller Total Power: 1,500kW (2,039hp) 12.0kn Deutz SBV8M628 1 x 4 Stroke 8 Cy. 240 x 280 1500kW (2039bhp) Deutz AG-Koeln AuxGen: 2 x 160kW 220/380V 50Hz a.c, 1 x 158kW 380/220V 50Hz a.c Thrusters: 1 Thwart. FP thruster (f)
582855 *9VZ8*	**WILSON LARVIK** *ex* Niklas *-2013* **ms 'Wes Orpheus' Schiffahrts GmbH & Co KG** Hermann Lohmann Bereederungen GmbH & Co KG *Monrovia* *Liberia* MMSI: 636092062 Official number: 92062	**2,452** 1,369 3,657 T/cm 10.1	Class: GL	**2010-08 Slovenske Lodenice a.s. — Komarno** Yd No: 2983 Loa 87.83 (BB) Br ex - Dght 5.490 Lbp 81.32 Br md 12.80 Dpth 7.10 Welded, 1 dk	**(A31A2GX) General Cargo Ship** Double Hull Grain: 4,588 TEU 36 Compartments: 1 Ho, ER 1 Ha: ER (56.6 x 10.0) Ice Capable	**1 oil engine** reduction geared to sc. shaft driving 1 CP propeller Total Power: 1,520kW (2,067hp) 11.7kn MaK 8M20C 1 x 4 Stroke 8 Cy. 200 x 300 1520kW (2067bhp) Caterpillar Motoren GmbH & Co. KG-Germany AuxGen: 1 x 240kW 400V a.c, 2 x 180kW 400V a.c Thrusters: 1 Tunnel thruster (f)
150482 *HEB5*	**WILSON LEER** *ex* Northern Langnes *-2002* **Wilson Shipowning AS** Wilson EuroCarriers AS SatCom: Inmarsat C 424972010 *Valletta* *Malta* MMSI: 249720000 Official number: 5199	**2,446** 1,369 3,695 T/cm 10.1	Class: BV (GL)	**1996-11 Slovenske Lodenice a.s. — Komarno** Yd No: 2931 Loa 87.90 (BB) Br ex 12.90 Dght 5.510 Lbp 83.50 Br md 12.80 Dpth 7.10 Welded, 1 dk	**(A31A2GX) General Cargo Ship** Double Hull Grain: 4,650; Bale: 4,620 TEU 176 C. 176/20' Compartments: 1 Ho, ER 1 Ha: (56.6 x 10.2)ER Ice Capable	**1 oil engine** geared to sc. shaft driving 1 FP propeller Total Power: 1,501kW (2,041hp) 10.5kn Deutz SBV8M628 1 x 4 Stroke 8 Cy. 240 x 280 1501kW (2041bhp) Motoren Werke Mannheim AG (MWM)-Mannheim Thrusters: 1 Tunnel thruster (f) Fuel: 30.0 (d.f.) 163.0 (d.f.) 6.0pd
150509 *HII5*	**WILSON LEITH** *ex* Northern Launes *-2002* **Wilson Shipowning AS** Wilson EuroCarriers AS SatCom: Inmarsat C 424984910 *Valletta* *Malta* MMSI: 249849000 Official number: 5417	**2,446** 1,369 3,695 T/cm 10.1	Class: BV (GL)	**1997-04 Slovenske Lodenice a.s. — Komarno** Yd No: 2933 Loa 87.90 (BB) Br ex - Dght 5.498 Lbp 83.50 Br md 12.80 Dpth 7.10 Welded, 1 dk	**(A31A2GX) General Cargo Ship** Double Hull Grain: 4,650; Bale: 4,620 TEU 176 C. 176/20' Compartments: 1 Ho, ER 1 Ha: (56.6 x 10.2)ER Ice Capable	**1 oil engine** reduction geared to sc. shaft driving 1 FP propeller Total Power: 1,500kW (2,039hp) 10.5kn Deutz SBV8M628 1 x 4 Stroke 8 Cy. 240 x 280 1500kW (2039bhp) Motoren Werke Mannheim AG (MWM)-Mannheim AuxGen: 3 x 104kW 220/380V a.c Thrusters: 1 Thwart. FP thruster (f) Fuel: 30.0 (d.f.) 163.0 (d.f.) 6.0pd
617337 *5NU3*	**WILSON LISBON** *ex* Marten *-2013* **Hermann Lohmann Schiffahrts GmbH & Co KG ms 'Marten'** Hermann Lohmann Bereederungen GmbH & Co KG *Limassol* *Cyprus* MMSI: 212376000 Official number: 9617337	**2,589** - 3,801	Class: GL	**2012-05 Slovenske Lodenice a.s. — Komarno** Yd No: 3804 Loa 89.86 (BB) Br ex - Dght 5.540 Lbp - Br md 12.80 Dpth 7.10 Welded, 1 dk	**(A31A2GX) General Cargo Ship** Grain: 4,750 Compartments: 1 Ho, ER 1 Ha: ER Ice Capable	**1 oil engine** reduction geared to sc. shaft driving 1 CP propeller Total Power: 1,520kW (2,067hp) MaK 8M20C 1 x 4 Stroke 8 Cy. 200 x 300 1520kW (2067bhp) Caterpillar Motoren GmbH & Co. KG-Germany Thrusters: 1 Tunnel thruster (f)
117208 *PRW*	**WILSON LISTA** *ex* Wani Venture *-2004* *ex* Venture *-2002* *ex* Sea Severn *-2001* *ex* Venture *-2000* *ex* MSC Venture *-1999* *ex* Lys Trader *-1996* **Wilson Shipowning AS** Wilson EuroCarriers AS *Bridgetown* *Barbados* MMSI: 314188000 Official number: 733438	**2,446** 1,369 3,717	Class: GL	**1994-12 Slovenske Lodenice a.s. — Komarno** Yd No: 2915 Loa 87.95 (BB) Br ex - Dght 5.498 Lbp 81.00 Br md 12.80 Dpth 7.10 Welded, 1 dk	**(A31A2GX) General Cargo Ship** Double Hull Grain: 4,649; Bale: 4,620 TEU 176 C. 176/20' Compartments: 1 Ho, ER 1 Ha: (56.5 x 10.2)ER Ice Capable	**1 oil engine** reduction geared to sc. shaft driving 1 FP propeller Total Power: 1,500kW (2,039hp) 12.0kn Deutz SBV8M628 1 x 4 Stroke 8 Cy. 240 x 280 1500kW (2039bhp) Motoren Werke Mannheim AG (MWM)-Mannheim AuxGen: 3 x 115kW a.c Thrusters: 1 Thwart. FP thruster (f) Fuel: 114.5 (d.f.) 7.0pd
617325 *5NF3*	**WILSON LIVORNO** *ex* Santa Helena I *-2013* **Hermann Lohmann Schiffahrts GmbH & Co KG ms 'Santa Helena'** Hermann Lohmann Bereederungen GmbH & Co KG *Limassol* *Cyprus* MMSI: 210075000	**2,589** - 3,800	Class: GL	**2012-03 Slovenske Lodenice a.s. — Komarno** Yd No: 3803 Loa 89.86 Br ex - Dght 5.540 Lbp - Br md 12.80 Dpth 7.10 Welded, 1 dk	**(A31A2GX) General Cargo Ship** Grain: 4,750 Compartments: 1 Ho, ER 1 Ha: ER Ice Capable	**1 oil engine** reduction geared to sc. shaft driving 1 CP propeller Total Power: 1,520kW (2,067hp) 12.0kn MaK 8M20C 1 x 4 Stroke 8 Cy. 200 x 300 1520kW (2067bhp) Caterpillar Motoren GmbH & Co. KG-Germany
582867 *2FD3*	**WILSON LUBECK** *ex* Helen Anna *-2013* **Hermann Lohmann Schiffahrts GmbH & Co KG ms 'Helen-Anna'** Hermann Lohmann Bereederungen GmbH & Co KG SatCom: Inmarsat C 430563910 *Saint John's* *Antigua & Barbuda* MMSI: 305639000	**2,452** 1,369 3,650 T/cm 10.1	Class: GL	**2010-11 Slovenske Lodenice a.s. — Komarno** Yd No: 2984 Loa 87.84 (BB) Br ex - Dght 5.490 Lbp 81.32 Br md 12.80 Dpth 7.10 Welded, 1 dk	**(A31A2GX) General Cargo Ship** Double Hull Grain: 4,600; Bale: 4,587 TEU 36 Compartments: 1 Ho, ER 1 Ha: ER (56.6 x 10.2) Ice Capable	**1 oil engine** reduction geared to sc. shaft driving 1 CP propeller Total Power: 1,520kW (2,067hp) 11.7kn MaK 8M20C 1 x 4 Stroke 8 Cy. 200 x 300 1520kW (2067bhp) Caterpillar Motoren GmbH & Co. KG-Germany AuxGen: 1 x 240kW 400V a.c, 2 x 180kW 400V a.c Thrusters: 1 Tunnel thruster (f) Fuel: 260.0
145554 *PSZ*	**WILSON MAAS** *ex* Pardubice *-2001* **Wilson Shipowning AS** Wilson EuroCarriers AS *Bridgetown* *Barbados* MMSI: 314217000	**1,169** 635 1,847	Class: GL	**1997-12 Ceskoslovenska Plavba Labska a.s. (CSPL) — Chvaletice** Yd No: 104 Loa 78.09 (BB) Br ex 9.48 Dght 4.350 Lbp 73.80 Br md 9.46 Dpth 5.75 Welded, 1 dk	**(A31A2GX) General Cargo Ship** Grain: 2,200 TEU 72 C.Ho 48/20' C.Dk 24/20' Compartments: 1 Ho, ER 1 Ha: (49.8 x 7.8)ER Ice Capable	**1 oil engine** reduction geared to sc. shaft driving 1 FP propeller Total Power: 1,125kW (1,530hp) 12.0kn Deutz SBV6M628 1 x 4 Stroke 6 Cy. 240 x 280 1125kW (1530bhp) Motoren Werke Mannheim AG (MWM)-Mannheim Thrusters: 1 Thwart. FP thruster (f)
113485 *PRQ*	**WILSON MAIN** *ex* Pola *-2004* *ex* Heinke *-1998* **Wilson Shipowning AS** Wilson EuroCarriers AS *Bridgetown* *Barbados* MMSI: 314182000 Official number: 733432	**1,690** 838 2,561	Class: GL	**1990-06 Koetter-Werft GmbH — Haren/Ems** Yd No: 85 Loa 82.50 (BB) Br ex 11.40 Dght 4.500 Lbp 79.20 Br md 11.35 Dpth 5.80 Welded, 1 dk	**(A31A2GX) General Cargo Ship** Grain: 3,369; Bale: 3,300 TEU 84 C.Ho 48/20' C.Dk 36/20' Compartments: 1 Ho, ER 1 Ha: (54.6 x 9.0)ER Ice Capable	**1 oil engine** sr reverse geared to sc. shaft driving 1 FP propeller Total Power: 600kW (816hp) 10.5kn Deutz SBV6M628 1 x 4 Stroke 6 Cy. 240 x 280 600kW (816bhp) Motoren Werke Mannheim AG (MWM)-West Germany AuxGen: 2 x 88kW 220/380V a.c, 1 x 66kW 220/380V a.c Thrusters: 1 Retract. directional thruster (f)
110210 *HUH7*	**WILSON MALM** *ex* Garnes *-2002* *ex* General Campos *-1992* *ex* Garnes *-1986* **Wilson Shipowning AS** Wilson EuroCarriers AS *Valletta* *Malta* MMSI: 215579000 Official number: 8620	**3,967** 2,212 5,995	Class: BV (NV)	**1980-06 AS Storviks Mek. Verksted — Kristiansund** Yd No: 91 **1983 Fosen Mek. Verksteder AS — Rissa** (Additional cargo section) Lengthened-1983 Loa 107.02 Br ex 15.04 Dght 6.485 Lbp 100.36 Br md 15.02 Dpth 8.01 Welded, 1 dk	**(A31A2GX) General Cargo Ship** Grain: 7,949; Bale: 7,295 Compartments: 3 Ho, ER 3 Ha: (14.0 x 8.0) (33.3 x 12.0) (12.8 x 8.0)ER	**1 oil engine** sr geared to sc. shaft driving 1 CP propeller Total Power: 2,942kW (4,000hp) 13.5kn Werkspoor 6TM410 1 x 4 Stroke 6 Cy. 410 x 470 2942kW (4000bhp) Stork Werkspoor Diesel BV-Netherlands AuxGen: 2 x 296kW 440V 60Hz a.c Fuel: 88.0 (d.f.) 395.0 (r.f.) 13.5pd

IMO / Call sign	Name / Owner / Manager / Flag	Tonnage	Class	Builder / Dimensions	Type / Cargo	Machinery	Speed / Engine
7707839 *P3ZB4* -	**WILSON MALO** *ex* Blankenes *-2005* *ex* Black Sea *-1993* **Wilson Shipowning AS** Wilson EuroCarriers AS SatCom: Inmarsat C 420900416 *Limassol* *Cyprus* MMSI: 209810000 Official number: 709888	**4,061** 2,510 6,433 T/cm 13.9	Class: GL (LR) ✠ Classed LR until 8/10/97	**1978-10 Gotaverken Solvesborg AB — Solvesborg** Yd No: 88 Loa 105.64 Br ex 14.94 Dght 6.830 Lbp 99.90 Br md 14.90 Dpth 9.00 Welded, 1 dk	**(A31A2GX) General Cargo Ship** Double Hull Grain: 8,415; Bale: 7,746 TEU 238 C.Ho 138/20' C.Dk 100/20' Compartments: 2 Ho, ER 2 Ha: (33.5 x 12.5) (32.3 x 12.5)ER Ice Capable	**1 oil engine** sr geared to sc shaft driving 1 FP propeller Total Power: 2,460kW (3,345hp) Wartsila 1 x 4 Stroke 6 Cy. 320 x 350 2460kW (3345bhp) (new engine 1988) Wartsila Diesel Oy-Finland AuxGen: 1 x 480kW 220/440V 60Hz a.c, 2 x 200kW 220/440V 60Hz a.c Thrusters: 1 Thwart. CP thruster (f) Fuel: 26.0 (d.f.) 305.0 (r.f.) 7.8pd	10.5k 6R3
7610103 *9HRL6* -	**WILSON MARIN** *ex* Fromnes *-2003* *ex* Framnes *-1998* **Wilson Shipowning AS** Wilson EuroCarriers AS SatCom: Inmarsat C 424878010 *Valletta* *Malta* MMSI: 248780000 Official number: 6881	**3,949** 2,307 5,845 T/cm 13.8	Class: GL	**1978-04 Fr. Luerssen Werft GmbH & Co. — Bremen** Yd No: 13455 Lengthened-1984 Loa 105.70 Br ex 15.42 Dght 6.890 Lbp 99.01 Br md 15.10 Dpth 8.01 Welded, 1 dk	**(A21A2BC) Bulk Carrier** Double Bottom Entire Compartment Length Grain: 6,536; Bale: 6,180 Compartments: 1 Dp Ta, 3 Ho, ER 3 Ha: (7.1 x 9.9)2 (18.9 x 9.9)ER Cranes: 2x12.5t Ice Capable	**1 oil engine** geared to sc. shaft driving 1 FP propeller Total Power: 2,942kW (4,000hp) Pielstick 1 x 4 Stroke 8 Cy. 400 x 460 2942kW (4000bhp) Blohm + Voss AG-West Germany Thrusters: 1 Tunnel thruster (f) Fuel: 68.0 (d.f.) 303.0 (r.f.) 9.3pd	11.0k 8PC2-2L-40
7810222 *P3PA6* -	**WILSON MERSIN** *ex* Ramnes *-2004* *ex* Raknes *-1995* *ex* Eemnes *-1992* *ex* Raknes *-1986* **Wilson Shipowning AS** Wilson EuroCarriers AS *Limassol* *Cyprus* MMSI: 210072000 Official number: 710590	**3,937** 2,062 6,186	Class: BV (NV)	**1981-07 AS Storviks Mek. Verksted — Kristiansund** Yd No: 92 Loa 106.86 Br ex 15.04 Dght 6.743 Lbp 100.51 Br md 15.02 Dpth 8.77 Welded, 1 dk	**(A31A2GX) General Cargo Ship** Grain: 7,430; Bale: 7,295 Compartments: 3 Ho, ER 3 Ha: (14.1 x 8.0) (33.3 x 12.0) (12.8 x 8.0)ER	**1 oil engine** geared to sc. shaft driving 1 FP propeller Total Power: 2,648kW (3,600hp) Werkspoor 1 x 4 Stroke 6 Cy. 410 x 470 2648kW (3600bhp) Stork Werkspoor Diesel BV-Netherlands AuxGen: 2 x 296kW 440V 60Hz a.c Fuel: 88.5 (d.f.) 368.0 (r.f.) 13.5pd	13.5k 6TM41
9060687 *9HGJ9* -	**WILSON MOSEL** *ex* Neermoor *-2007* **Wilson Shipowning AS** Wilson EuroCarriers AS *Valletta* *Malta* MMSI: 256951000 Official number: 9060687	**1,589** 844 2,665	Class: GL	**1993-07 Slovenske Lodenice a.s. — Komarno** Yd No: 1302 Loa 82.56 (BB) Br ex - Dght 4.789 Lbp 79.82 Br md 11.35 Dpth 6.10 Welded, 1 dk	**(A31A2GX) General Cargo Ship** Cars: 72 Grain: 3,144 TEU 118 C Ho 46 TEU C Dk 72 TEU incl 6 ref C. Compartments: 1 Ho, ER 1 Ha: (53.4 x 9.0)ER Ice Capable	**1 oil engine** with flexible couplings & sr geared to sc. shaft driving 1 FP propeller Total Power: 1,015kW (1,380hp) Deutz 1 x 4 Stroke 6 Cy. 240 x 280 1015kW (1380bhp) Motoren Werke Mannheim AG (MWM)-Mannheim AuxGen: 2 x 68kW 380V 50Hz a.c Thrusters: 1 Thwart. FP thruster (f) Fuel: 110.0 (d.f.) 4.8pd	9.7kn SBV6M628
9431018 *9HA2627* -	**WILSON NANJING** **Wilson Shipowning AS** Wilson Management AS *Valletta* *Malta* MMSI: 215061000 Official number: 9431018	**6,118** 2,966 8,333 T/cm 17.6	Class: GL	**2012-01 Yichang Shipyard — Yichang HB** Yd No: 2006-B026 Loa 123.04 (BB) Br ex 17.00 Dght 7.400 Lbp 115.50 Br md 16.50 Dpth 10.20 Welded, 1 dk	**(A31A2GX) General Cargo Ship** Double Bottom Entire Compartment Length Grain: 10,930 TEU 60 Compartments: 2 Ho, ER 2 Ha: (49.7 x 13.5)ER (25.9 x 13.5) Ice Capable	**1 oil engine** reduction geared to sc. shaft driving 1 CP propeller Total Power: 3,680kW (5,003hp) Wartsila 1 x 4 Stroke 8 Cy. 320 x 400 3680kW (5003bhp) Wartsila Finland Oy-Finland AuxGen: 1 x 500kW 400V a.c, 2 x 350kW 400V a.c Thrusters: 1 Tunnel thruster (f) Fuel: 81.0 (d.f.) 400.0 (r.f.)	12.5kn 8L32
9430973 *9HA2463* -	**WILSON NANTES** **Wilson Shipowning AS** Wilson EuroCarriers AS SatCom: Inmarsat C 424867410 *Valletta* *Malta* MMSI: 248674000 Official number: 9430973	**6,118** 2,966 8,339 T/cm 17.6	Class: GL	**2011-01 Yichang Shipyard — Yichang HB** Yd No: 2006-B022 Loa 123.13 Br ex - Dght 7.400 Lbp 115.49 Br md 16.50 Dpth 10.20 Welded, 1 dk	**(A31A2GX) General Cargo Ship** Double Bottom Entire Compartment Length Grain: 10,930 Compartments: 2 Ho, ER 2 Ha: (49.7 x 13.5)ER (25.9 x 13.5) Ice Capable	**1 oil engine** reduction geared to sc. shaft driving 1 CP propeller Total Power: 3,680kW (5,003hp) Wartsila 1 x 4 Stroke 8 Cy. 320 x 400 3680kW (5003bhp) Wartsila Finland Oy-Finland AuxGen: 1 x 500kW 400V a.c, 2 x 380kW 400V a.c Thrusters: 1 Tunnel thruster (f) Fuel: 81.0 (d.f.) 400.0 (r.f.)	12.5kn 8L32
9430961 *9HA2464* -	**WILSON NARVIK** **Wilson Shipowning AS** Wilson EuroCarriers AS SatCom: Inmarsat C 424867510 *Valletta* *Malta* MMSI: 248675000 Official number: 9430961	**6,118** 2,966 8,354 T/cm 17.6	Class: GL	**2011-01 Yichang Shipyard — Yichang HB** Yd No: 2006-B021 Loa 123.04 Br ex - Dght 7.400 Lbp 115.45 Br md 16.50 Dpth 10.20 Welded, 1 dk	**(A31A2GX) General Cargo Ship** Double Bottom Entire Compartment Length Grain: 10,930 Compartments: 2 Ho, ER 2 Ha: (49.7 x 13.5)ER (25.9 x 13.5) Ice Capable	**1 oil engine** reduction geared to sc. shaft driving 1 CP propeller Total Power: 3,680kW (5,003hp) Wartsila 1 x 4 Stroke 8 Cy. 320 x 400 3680kW (5003bhp) Wartsila Finland Oy-Finland AuxGen: 1 x 500kW 400V a.c, 2 x 380kW 400V a.c Thrusters: 1 Tunnel thruster (f) Fuel: 80.8 (d.f.) 400.0 (r.f.)	12.5kn 8L32
9431006 *9HA2628* -	**WILSON NEWCASTLE** **Wilson Shipowning AS** Wilson Management AS *Valletta* *Malta* MMSI: 215062000 Official number: 9431006	**6,118** 2,966 8,326 T/cm 17.6	Class: GL	**2011-10 Yichang Shipyard — Yichang HB** Yd No: 2006-B025 Loa 123.04 (BB) Br ex 17.00 Dght 7.400 Lbp 115.50 Br md 16.50 Dpth 10.20 Welded, 1 dk	**(A31A2GX) General Cargo Ship** Double Bottom Entire Compartment Length Grain: 10,930 Compartments: 2 Ho, ER 2 Ha: (49.7 x 13.5)ER (25.9 x 13.5) Ice Capable	**1 oil engine** reduction geared to sc. shaft driving 1 CP propeller Total Power: 3,680kW (5,003hp) Wartsila 1 x 4 Stroke 8 Cy. 320 x 400 3680kW (5003bhp) Wartsila Finland Oy-Finland Thrusters: 1 Tunnel thruster (f) Fuel: 81.0 (d.f.) 400.0 (r.f.)	12.5kn 8L32
9430985 *9HA2465* -	**WILSON NEWPORT** **Wilson Shipowning AS** Wilson EuroCarriers AS *Valletta* *Malta* MMSI: 248676000 Official number: 9430985	**6,118** 2,966 8,321 T/cm 17.6	Class: GL	**2011-04 Yichang Shipyard — Yichang HB** Yd No: 2006-B023 Loa 123.03 Br ex - Dght 7.400 Lbp 115.49 Br md 16.50 Dpth 10.20 Welded, 1 dk	**(A31A2GX) General Cargo Ship** Double Bottom Entire Compartment Length Grain: 10,930 Compartments: 2 Ho, ER 2 Ha: (49.7 x 13.5)ER (25.9 x 13.5) Ice Capable	**1 oil engine** reduction geared to sc. shaft driving 1 CP propeller Total Power: 3,680kW (5,003hp) Wartsila 1 x 4 Stroke 8 Cy. 320 x 400 3680kW (5003bhp) Wartsila Finland Oy-Finland AuxGen: 1 x 500kW 400V a.c, 2 x 380kW 400V a.c Thrusters: 1 Tunnel thruster (f) Fuel: 81.0 (d.f.) 400.0 (r.f.)	12.5kn 8L32
9430959 *9HA2385* -	**WILSON NICE** **Wilson Shipowning AS** Wilson EuroCarriers AS *Valletta* *Malta* MMSI: 248494000 Official number: 9430959	**6,118** 2,966 8,301 T/cm 17.6	Class: GL	**2010-08 Yichang Shipyard — Yichang HB** Yd No: 2006-B020 Loa 123.07 (BB) Br ex - Dght 7.400 Lbp 115.45 Br md 16.50 Dpth 10.20 Welded, 1 dk	**(A31A2GX) General Cargo Ship** Double Bottom Entire Compartment Length Grain: 10,930 Compartments: 2 Ho, ER 2 Ha: (49.7 x 13.5)ER (25.9 x 13.5) Ice Capable	**1 oil engine** reduction geared to sc. shaft driving 1 CP propeller Total Power: 3,680kW (5,003hp) Wartsila 1 x 4 Stroke 8 Cy. 320 x 400 3680kW (5003bhp) Wartsila Finland Oy-Finland AuxGen: 1 x 500kW 400V a.c, 2 x 380kW 400V a.c Thrusters: 1 Tunnel thruster (f) Fuel: 81.0 (d.f.) 400.0 (r.f.)	12.5kn 8L32
9430997 *9HA2466* -	**WILSON NORFOLK** **Wilson Shipowning AS** Wilson Management AS *Valletta* *Malta* MMSI: 248678000 Official number: 9430997	**6,118** 2,966 8,313 T/cm 17.6	Class: GL	**2011-08 Yichang Shipyard — Yichang HB** Yd No: 2006-B024 Loa 123.04 (BB) Br ex 17.00 Dght 7.400 Lbp 115.50 Br md 16.50 Dpth 10.20 Welded, 1 dk	**(A31A2GX) General Cargo Ship** Double Bottom Entire Compartment Length Grain: 10,930 Compartments: 2 Ho, ER 2 Ha: (49.7 x 13.5)ER (25.9 x 13.5) Ice Capable	**1 oil engine** reduction geared to sc. shaft driving 1 CP propeller Total Power: 3,680kW (5,003hp) Wartsila 1 x 4 Stroke 8 Cy. 320 x 400 3680kW (5003bhp) Wartsila Finland Oy-Finland AuxGen: 1 x 500kW 400V a.c, 2 x 380kW 400V a.c Thrusters: 1 Tunnel thruster (f) Fuel: 60.0 (d.f.) 400.0 (r.f.)	12.5kn 8L32
9430947 *9HA2312* -	**WILSON NORTH** **Wilson Shipowning AS** Wilson EuroCarriers AS *Valletta* *Malta* MMSI: 248313000 Official number: 9430947	**6,118** 2,966 8,334 T/cm 17.6	Class: GL	**2010-05 Yichang Shipyard — Yichang HB** Yd No: 2006-B019 Loa 123.05 (BB) Br ex - Dght 7.400 Lbp 115.47 Br md 16.50 Dpth 10.20 Welded, 1 dk	**(A31A2GX) General Cargo Ship** Double Bottom Entire Compartment Length Grain: 10,930 Compartments: 2 Ho, ER 2 Ha: (49.7 x 13.5)ER (25.9 x 13.5) Ice Capable	**1 oil engine** reduction geared to sc. shaft driving 1 CP propeller Total Power: 3,680kW (5,003hp) Wartsila 1 x 4 Stroke 8 Cy. 320 x 400 3680kW (5003bhp) Wartsila Finland Oy-Finland AuxGen: 1 x 500kW 400V a.c, 2 x 350kW 400V a.c Thrusters: 1 Tunnel thruster (f) Fuel: 81.0 (d.f.) 400.0 (r.f.)	12.5kn 8L32

7382665 *9HUY5*
WILSON REEF
ex Refsnes *-2003* *ex* Saint Brevin *-2000*
ex Refsnes *-1983*
Wilson Shipowning AS
Wilson EuroCarriers AS
SatCom: Inmarsat C 424820010
Valletta *Malta*
MMSI: 248200000
Official number: 5969

3,883 Class: BV (NV)
2,133
6,258
T/cm
13.4

1975-06 Kleven Mek Verksted AS — Ulsteinvik
Yd No: 26
Loa 103.49 (BB) Br ex 16.11 Dght 6.960
Lbp 96.68 Br md 16.01 Dpth 8.79
Welded, 1 dk

(A21A2BC) Bulk Carrier
Grain: 7,697; Bale: 6,831
Compartments: 1 Dp Ta, 2 Ho, ER
4 Ha: 2 (2.8 x 2.9)2 (24.1 x 10.0)ER

2 oil engines geared to sc. shaft driving 1 CP propeller
Total Power: 2,796kW (3,802hp) 12.0kn
Normo KVM-12
2 x Vee 4 Stroke 12 Cy. 250 x 300 each-1398kW (1901bhp)
AS Bergens Mek Verksteder-Norway
AuxGen: 1 x 160kW 440V 60Hz a.c, 2 x 149kW 440V 60Hz a.c
Fuel: 54.0 (d.f.) 599.0 (r.f.) 13.0pd

9168116 *8PUP*
WILSON RHINE
ex Lovosice *-2000*
Wilson Shipowning AS
Wilson EuroCarriers AS
Bridgetown *Barbados*
MMSI: 314260000

1,171 Class: GL
635
1,815

1998-12 Ceskoslovenska Plavba Labska a.s. (CSPL) — Chvaletice Yd No: 105
Loa 78.30 (BB) Br ex - Dght 4.350
Lbp 74.26 Br md 9.46 Dpth 5.75
Welded, 1 dk

(A31A2GX) General Cargo Ship
Grain: 2,200
TEU 72 C.Ho 48/20' C.Dk 24/20'
1 Ha: (49.1 x 7.6)
Ice Capable

1 oil engine geared to sc. shaft driving 1 FP propeller
Total Power: 1,125kW (1,530hp) 12.0kn
Deutz SBV6M628
1 x 4 Stroke 6 Cy. 240 x 280 1125kW (1530bhp)
Motoren Werke Mannheim AG (MWM)-Mannheim
Thrusters: 1 Tunnel thruster (f)

7382500 *8PQT*
WILSON RIGA
ex Risnes *-2003* *ex* General Luna *-1990*
ex Ronnes *-1985*
Wilson Ship AS
Wilson EuroCarriers AS
SatCom: Inmarsat C 431415910
Bridgetown *Barbados*
MMSI: 314159000
Official number: 733407

3,890 Class: BV (NV)
2,048
6,085
T/cm
13.2

1976-02 Georg Eides Sonner AS — Hoylandsbygd
Yd No: 101
Loa 103.56 (BB) Br ex 16.11 Dght 6.966
Lbp 96.68 Br md 16.01 Dpth 8.82
Welded, 1 dk

(A21A2BC) Bulk Carrier
Double Hull
Grain: 7,697; Bale: 6,831
Compartments: 1 Dp Ta in Hold, 2 Ho, ER
4 Ha: 2 (2.8 x 2.9)2 (24.1 x 10.0)ER

2 oil engines geared to sc. shaft driving 1 CP propeller
Total Power: 2,794kW (3,798hp) 12.0kn
Normo KVM-12
2 x Vee 4 Stroke 12 Cy. 250 x 300 each-1397kW (1899bhp)
AS Bergens Mek Verksteder-Norway
AuxGen: 2 x 300kW 440V 60Hz a.c, 1 x 160kW 440V 60Hz a.c
Fuel: 53.5 (d.f.) 599.5 (r.f.) 15.0pd

7382495 *9HCC6*
WILSON ROSS
ex Rossnes *-2004* *ex* Saint Brice *-2000*
ex Rossnes *-1982*
Wilson Shipowning AS
Wilson EuroCarriers AS
SatCom: Inmarsat C 424837910
Valletta *Malta*
MMSI: 248379000
Official number: 6283

3,883 Class: BV (NV)
2,133
6,258
T/cm
13.4

1975-06 Georg Eides Sonner AS — Hoylandsbygd
Yd No: 100
Loa 103.49 (BB) Br ex 16.11 Dght 6.960
Lbp 96.68 Br md 16.01 Dpth 8.79
Welded, 1 dk

(A21A2BC) Bulk Carrier
Grain: 7,697; Bale: 6,831
Compartments: 1 Dp Ta in Hold, 2 Ho, ER
4 Ha: 2 (2.8 x 2.9)2 (24.1 x 10.0)ER

2 oil engines geared to sc. shaft driving 1 CP propeller
Total Power: 2,796kW (3,802hp) 12.5kn
Normo KVM-12
2 x Vee 4 Stroke 12 Cy. 250 x 300 each-1398kW (1901bhp)
AS Bergens Mek Verksteder-Norway
AuxGen: 1 x 160kW 440V 60Hz a.c
Fuel: 608.5 (r.f.) 14.5pd

7414183 *8PQS*
WILSON ROUEN
ex Rafnes *-2003* *ex* General Garcia *-1989*
ex Rafnes *-1986*
Wilson Shipowning AS
Wilson EuroCarriers AS
SatCom: Inmarsat C 431415810
Bridgetown *Barbados*
MMSI: 314158000
Official number: 733406

3,885 Class: BV (NV)
2,048
6,085
T/cm
13.2

1976-10 Kleven Mek Verksted AS — Ulsteinvik
Yd No: 28
Loa 103.56 (BB) Br ex 16.01 Dght 6.960
Lbp 96.83 Br md 15.98 Dpth 8.82
Welded, 1 dk

(A21A2BC) Bulk Carrier
Double Bottom Entire Compartment Length
Grain: 7,697; Bale: 6,831
Compartments: 1 Dp Ta, 2 Ho, ER
4 Ha: 2 (2.8 x 2.9)2 (24.1 x 10.0)ER

2 oil engines geared to sc. shaft driving 1 CP propeller
Total Power: 2,794kW (3,798hp) 12.4kn
Normo KVM-12
2 x Vee 4 Stroke 12 Cy. 250 x 300 each-1397kW (1899bhp)
AS Bergens Mek Verksteder-Norway
AuxGen: 2 x 300kW 440V 60Hz a.c, 1 x 160kW 440V 60Hz a.c
Fuel: 53.5 (d.f.) 599.5 (r.f.) 15.0pd

7419200 *9HSL5*
WILSON ROUGH
ex Radnes *-2004* *ex* Lugano *-1989*
ex Radnes *-1984*
Wilson Shipowning AS
Wilson EuroCarriers AS
SatCom: Inmarsat C 424813110
Valletta *Malta*
MMSI: 248131000
Official number: 5869

3,885 Class: BV (NV)
2,048
6,085
T/cm
13.2

1976-12 Georg Eides Sonner AS — Hoylandsbygd
Yd No: 102
Loa 103.56 (BB) Br ex 16.01 Dght 6.960
Lbp 96.93 Br md 15.51 Dpth 8.82
Welded, 1 dk

(A21A2BC) Bulk Carrier
Double Bottom Entire Compartment Length
Grain: 7,697; Bale: 6,831
Compartments: 1 Dp Ta, 2 Ho, ER
4 Ha: 2 (2.8 x 2.9)2 (24.1 x 10.0)ER

2 oil engines geared to sc. shaft driving 1 CP propeller
Total Power: 2,796kW (3,802hp) 12.5kn
Normo KVM-12
2 x Vee 4 Stroke 12 Cy. 250 x 300 each-1398kW (1901bhp)
AS Bergens Mek Verksteder-Norway
AuxGen: 2 x 300kW 440V 60Hz a.c, 1 x 160kW 440V 60Hz a.c
Fuel: 53.5 (d.f.) 420.0 (r.f.) 12.5pd

9145542 *8PTA*
WILSON RUHR
ex Pilsen *-2001*
Wilson Shipowning AS
Wilson EuroCarriers AS
Bridgetown *Barbados*
MMSI: 314218000

1,169 Class: GL
635
1,831

1997-06 Ceskoslovenska Plavba Labska a.s. (CSPL) — Chvaletice Yd No: 103
Loa 78.08 (BB) Br ex 9.48 Dght 4.350
Lbp 73.80 Br md 9.46 Dpth 5.75
Welded, 1 dk

(A31A2GX) General Cargo Ship
Double Bottom Entire Compartment Length
Grain: 2,200
TEU 72 C.Ho 48/20' C.Dk 24/20'
Compartments: 1 Ho, ER
1 Ha: (49.8 x 7.8)ER
Ice Capable

1 oil engine reduction geared to sc. shaft driving 1 FP propeller
Total Power: 1,125kW (1,530hp) 12.0kn
Deutz SBV6M628
1 x 4 Stroke 6 Cy. 240 x 280 1125kW (1530bhp)
Motoren Werke Mannheim AG (MWM)-Mannheim
Thrusters: 1 Thwart. FP thruster (f)

7382677 *8PRC*
WILSON RYE
ex Lucillia *-2003* *ex* Nornes *-1997*
ex Riknes *-1994* *ex* General Papa *-1992*
ex Saint Jean *-1987* *ex* Riknes *-1983*
Wilson Shipowning AS
Wilson EuroCarriers AS
SatCom: Inmarsat C 431416810
Bridgetown *Barbados*
MMSI: 314168000
Official number: 733417

3,883 Class: BV (NV)
2,133
6,258
T/cm
13.4

1976-04 Kleven Mek Verksted AS — Ulsteinvik
Yd No: 27
Loa 103.56 (BB) Br ex 16.01 Dght 6.966
Lbp 96.83 Br md 15.98 Dpth 8.82
Welded, 1 dk

(A21A2BC) Bulk Carrier
Grain: 7,697; Bale: 6,831
Compartments: 1 Dp Ta in Hold, 2 Ho, ER
4 Ha: 2 (2.8 x 2.9)2 (24.1 x 10.0)ER

2 oil engines geared to sc. shaft driving 1 FP propeller
Total Power: 2,794kW (3,798hp) 12.5kn
Normo KVM-12
2 x Vee 4 Stroke 12 Cy. 250 x 300 each-1397kW (1899bhp)
AS Bergens Mek Verksteder-Norway
AuxGen: 1 x 191kW 440V 60Hz a.c, 1 x 128kW 440V 60Hz a.c
Fuel: 541.0 (d.f.) 12.0pd

9125841 *8PUQ*
WILSON SAAR
ex A. Wetzel *-2001*
Wilson Shipowning AS
Wilson EuroCarriers AS
Bridgetown *Barbados*
MMSI: 314261000
Official number: 733518

1,043 Class: GL
577
1,687

1996-07 Ceskoslovenska Plavba Labska a.s. (CSPL) — Chvaletice Yd No: 102
Loa 73.48 (BB) Br ex - Dght 4.350
Lbp 69.00 Br md 9.46 Dpth 5.75
Welded, 1 dk

(A31A2GX) General Cargo Ship
Grain: 1,994
TEU 63 C Ho 42 TEU C Dk 21 TEU
Compartments: 1 Ho, ER
1 Ha: (44.4 x 7.6)ER
Ice Capable

1 oil engine reduction geared to sc. shaft driving 1 FP propeller
Total Power: 930kW (1,264hp) 10.5kn
Deutz SBV6M628
1 x 4 Stroke 6 Cy. 240 x 280 930kW (1264bhp)
Motoren Mannheim AG (MWM)-Mannheim
AuxGen: 2 x 60kW 220/380V a.c
Thrusters: 1 Tunnel thruster (f)

8918461 *P3PD8*
WILSON SAGA
ex Borealnes *-2003*
Wilson Shipowning AS
Wilson EuroCarriers AS
Limassol *Cyprus*
MMSI: 212893000
Official number: 731004

4,200 Class: BV (NV)
2,144
6,489
T/cm
14.8

1998-03 Brodogradiliste Apatin — Apatin
Yd No: 1104
Loa 112.70 (BB) Br ex 15.50 Dght 6.690
Lbp 106.24 Br md 15.00 Dpth 8.60
Welded, 1 dk

(A31A2GX) General Cargo Ship
Double Hull
Grain: 7,335; Bale: 7,335
Compartments: 2 Ho, ER
2 Ha: 2 (35.0 x 12.5)ER
Ice Capable

1 oil engine with clutches, flexible couplings & sr geared to sc. shaft driving 1 CP propeller
Total Power: 2,640kW (3,589hp) 12.5kn
Alpha 12V28/32A
1 x Vee 4 Stroke 12 Cy. 280 x 320 2640kW (3589bhp)
MAN B&W Diesel A/S-Denmark
AuxGen: 1 x 763kW 220/450V 60Hz a.c, 2 x 260kW 220/450V 60Hz a.c
Thrusters: 1 Thwart. CP thruster (f)
Fuel: 58.0 (d.f.) (Heating Coils) 370.0 (r.f.) 11.3pd

8918459 *8PAK4*
WILSON SKAW
ex Elianna *-2002* *ex* Langenes *-1998*
Wilson Shipowning AS
Wilson EuroCarriers AS
Bridgetown *Barbados*
MMSI: 314420000

4,197 Class: BV (NV)
2,033
6,460
T/cm
14.8

1996-07 Brodogradiliste Apatin — Apatin
Yd No: 1103
Loa 112.70 (BB) Br ex - Dght 6.680
Lbp - Br md 15.20 Dpth 8.60
Welded, 1 dk

(A31A2GX) General Cargo Ship
Double Hull
Grain: 7,419; Bale: 7,419
Compartments: 2 Ho, ER
2 Ha: 2 (35.0 x 12.5)ER
Ice Capable

1 oil engine geared to sc. shaft driving 1 CP propeller
Total Power: 2,640kW (3,589hp) 12.5kn
Alpha 12V28/32A
1 x Vee 4 Stroke 12 Cy. 280 x 320 2640kW (3589bhp)
MAN B&W Diesel A/S-Denmark
AuxGen: 1 x 610kW 220/440V 60Hz a.c, 2 x 259kW 220/440V 60Hz a.c
Thrusters: 1 Thwart. FP thruster (f)
Fuel: 372.0 (r.f.) 58.0 (d.f.) 12.5pd

9017393 *P3VJ8*
WILSON SKY
completed as Weissenkirchen *-2001*
launched as Marble Fjord *-2001*
mv 'Weissenkirchen' Co Ltd
Wilson Ship Management AS
Limassol *Cyprus*
MMSI: 209432000
Official number: 9017393

3,037 Class: GL
1,623
4,263
T/cm
11.6

2001-04 Brodogradiliste 'Begej' — Zrenjanin (Hull)
Yd No: 229
2001-04 Rousse Shipyard JSC — Rousse
Loa 89.90 (BB) Br ex - Dght 5.640
Lbp 84.80 Br md 15.20 Dpth 7.10
Welded, 1 dk

(A31A2GX) General Cargo Ship
Double Hull
Grain: 5,568
TEU 114 C. 114/20' (40')
Compartments: 1 Ho, ER
1 Ha: (52.8 x 12.8)ER
Ice Capable

1 oil engine with flexible couplings & sr gearedto sc. shaft driving 1 FP propeller
Total Power: 2,400kW (3,263hp) 12.5kn
MaK 8M25
1 x 4 Stroke 8 Cy. 255 x 400 2400kW (3263bhp)
Krupp MaK Maschinenbau GmbH-Kiel
AuxGen: 1 x 440kW 400V 50Hz a.c, 2 x 190kW 440V 50Hz a.c
Thrusters: 1 Thwart. FP thruster (f)
Fuel: 16.0 (d.f.) 153.0 (r.f.) 9.2pd

7411375 *8PVU*
WILSON SPLIT
ex RekSnes *-2008* *ex* General Valeriano *-1992*
ex Reksnes *-1986*
Wilson Split AS
Wilson EuroCarriers AS
SatCom: Inmarsat C 431429310
Bridgetown *Barbados*
MMSI: 314293000

3,885 Class: BV (NV)
2,133
5,913
T/cm
13.2

1977-01 Brodrene Lothe AS, Flytedokken — Haugesund Yd No: 36
Loa 103.56 (BB) Br ex 16.01 Dght 6.960
Lbp 96.75 Br md 15.51 Dpth 8.82
Welded, 1 dk

(A21A2BC) Bulk Carrier
Grain: 7,697; Bale: 6,831
Compartments: 1 Dp Ta in Hold, 2 Ho, ER
4 Ha: 2 (2.8 x 2.9)2 (24.1 x 10.0)ER
Gantry cranes: 1

2 oil engines geared to sc. shaft driving 1 CP propeller
Total Power: 2,794kW (3,798hp) 12.5kn
Normo KVM-12
2 x Vee 4 Stroke 12 Cy. 250 x 300 each-1397kW (1899bhp)
AS Bergens Mek Verksteder-Norway
AuxGen: 2 x 300kW 440V 60Hz a.c, 1 x 160kW 440V 60Hz a.c
Fuel: 53.5 (d.f.) 420.0 (r.f.) 15.0pd

IMO / Call sign	Name / Owner / Manager	Tonnage	Class	Builder / Dimensions	Type	Machinery
8918485 *9HQW8* -	**WILSON STADT** *ex* Linito *-2006* **Wilson Shipowning AS** Wilson EuroCarriers AS SatCom: Inmarsat C 425631210 *Valletta* *Malta* MMSI: 256312000 Official number: 8918485	**4,200** 2,144 6,463 T/cm 14.8	Class: BV (NV)	**2000-11 Brodogradiliste Apatin — Apatin** Yd No: 1106 Loa 112.65 (BB) Br ex 15.50 Dght 6.684 Lbp 106.24 Br md 15.20 Dpth 8.61 Welded, 1 dk	**(A31A2GX) General Cargo Ship** Double Hull Grain: 7,574; Bale: 7,574 Cargo Heating Coils Compartments: 2 Ho, ER 2 Ha: 2 (35.0 x 12.5)ER Ice Capable	**1 oil engine** with clutches, flexible couplings & sr geared to sc. shaft driving 1 CP propeller Total Power: 2,648kW (3,600hp) 12.5k MAN-B&W 12V28/32 1 x Vee 4 Stroke 12 Cy. 280 x 320 2648kW (3600bhp) MAN B&W Diesel A/S-Denmark AuxGen: 2 x 262kW 220/440V 60Hz a.c Thrusters: 1 Thwart. FP thruster (f) Fuel: 56.4 (d.f.) (Heating Coils) 360.2 (r.f.) 10.8pd
8805597 *SKQJ* -	**WILSON STAR** *ex* Mini Star *-2003* **Westco AB** - SatCom: Inmarsat C 426573510 *Skarhamn* *Sweden* MMSI: 265735000	**5,593** 1,864 4,452 T/cm 15.0	Class: GL	**1988-12 J.J. Sietas KG Schiffswerft GmbH & Co. — Hamburg** Yd No: 1024 Loa 107.34 (BB) Br ex 17.20 Dght 6.054 Lbp 98.00 Br md 17.00 Dpth 9.90 Welded, 2 dks	**(A35A2RR) Ro-Ro Cargo Ship** Stern door/ramp (centre) Len: 12.50 Wid: 8.00 Swl: 250 Side door/ramp (s) Len: - Wid: - Swl: 12 Lane-Len: 375 Lane-Wid: 2.80 Lane-clr ht: 5.50 Bale: 9,765 TEU 180 Compartments: 2 Ho, ER 3 Ha: (25.5 x 14.5)Tappered (12.6 x 10.1) (25.5 x 14.5)ER Ice Capable	**1 oil engine** with flexible couplings & sr reverse geared to sc. shaft driving 1 CP propeller Total Power: 2,960kW (4,024hp) 15.3k Wartsila 8R32I 1 x 4 Stroke 8 Cy. 320 x 350 2960kW (4024bhp) Wartsila Diesel Oy-Finland AuxGen: 1 x 540kW 220/380V 50Hz a.c, 3 x 288kW 220/380V 50Hz a.c Thrusters: 1 Thwart. FP thruster (f)
8918473 *P3JD8* -	**WILSON SUND** *ex* Isnes *-2005* **Wilson Shipowning AS** Wilson EuroCarriers AS *Limassol* *Cyprus* MMSI: 212795000 Official number: 8918473	**4,200** 2,144 6,274 T/cm 14.8	Class: BV (NV)	**1999-02 Brodogradiliste Apatin — Apatin** Yd No: 1105 Loa 112.70 (BB) Br ex 15.50 Dght 6.260 Lbp 106.24 Br md 15.20 Dpth 8.60 Welded, 1 dk	**(A31A2GX) General Cargo Ship** Grain: 7,335; Bale: 7,335 Compartments: 2 Ho, ER 2 Ha: 2 (35.0 x 12.5)ER Ice Capable	**1 oil engine** with clutches, flexible couplings & sr geared to sc. shaft driving 1 CP propeller Total Power: 2,640kW (3,589hp) 12.5k Alpha 12V28/32 1 x Vee 4 Stroke 12 Cy. 280 x 320 2640kW (3589bhp) MAN B&W Diesel A/S-Denmark AuxGen: 1 x 763kW 220/440V 60Hz a.c, 2 x 260kW 220/440V 60Hz a.c Thrusters: 1 Thwart. CP thruster (f) Fuel: 58.0 (d.f.) (Heating Coils) 370.0 (r.f.) 11.3pd
7616224 *9HVN5* -	**WILSON TANA** *ex* Husnes *-2002* *ex* Hook Head *-1993* *ex* Sumburgh Head *-1990* **Wilson Shipowning AS** Wilson EuroCarriers AS SatCom: Inmarsat C 424821110 *Valletta* *Malta* MMSI: 248211000 Official number: 6000	**4,907** 2,764 7,174	Class: BV (LR) ✠ Classed LR until 5/5/11	**1977-04 Hashihama Shipbuilding Co Ltd — Imabari EH** Yd No: 624 Loa 110.55 Br ex 17.58 Dght 7.017 Lbp 101.91 Br md 17.51 Dpth 8.62 Welded, 1 dk	**(A31A2GX) General Cargo Ship** Grain: 9,422; Bale: 9,046 Compartments: 3 Ho, ER 4 Ha: (12.5 x 11.9)3 (12.5 x 13.4)ER Ice Capable	**1 oil engine** driving 1 FP propeller Total Power: 3,310kW (4,500hp) 11.5k Mitsubishi 6UET45/80 1 x 2 Stroke 6 Cy. 450 x 800 3310kW (4500bhp) Kobe Hatsudoki KK-Japan AuxGen: 3 x 200kW 445V 60Hz a.c Boilers: AuxB (Comp) 7.0kgf/cm² (6.9bar) Fuel: 61.0 (d.f.) 499.0 (r.f.) 14.0pd
9150535 *9HKQ5* -	**WILSON TEES** *ex* Northern Lurnes *-2002* **Wilson Shipowning AS** Wilson EuroCarriers AS *Valletta* *Malta* MMSI: 249910000 Official number: 5529	**2,446** 1,369 3,695 T/cm 10.1	Class: BV (GL)	**1997-06 Slovenske Lodenice a.s. — Komarno** Yd No: 2936 Loa 87.90 (BB) Br ex - Dght 5.498 Lbp 83.50 Br md 12.80 Dpth 7.10 Welded, 1 dk	**(A31A2GX) General Cargo Ship** Double Hull Grain: 4,650; Bale: 4,620 TEU 176 C. 176/20' Compartments: 1 Ho, ER 1 Ha: (56.6 x 10.2)ER Ice Capable	**1 oil engine** reduction geared to sc. shaft driving 1 FP propeller Total Power: 1,500kW (2,039hp) 10.5k Deutz SBV8M62 1 x 4 Stroke 8 Cy. 240 x 280 1500kW (2039bhp) Motoren Werke Mannheim AG (MWM)-Mannheim AuxGen: 3 x 104kW 220/380V a.c Thrusters: 1 Thwart. FP thruster (f) Fuel: 30.0 (d.f.) 163.0 (d.f.) 6.0pd
7926095 *P3LG5* -	**WILSON TRENT** *ex* Hernes *-2004* *ex* Rora Head *-1993* **Unistar Shipping Co Ltd** Wilson Ship Management AS SatCom: Inmarsat C 420900199 *Limassol* *Cyprus* MMSI: 210478000 Official number: 709980	**4,924** 2,651 7,102 T/cm 15.6	Class: GL (LR) ✠ Classed LR until 11/5/98	**1980-09 Miho Zosensho K.K. — Shimizu** Yd No: 1154 Loa 110.55 Br ex 17.56 Dght 7.016 Lbp 101.91 Br md 17.51 Dpth 8.62 Welded, 1 dk	**(A31A2GX) General Cargo Ship** Grain: 9,442; Bale: 9,065 Compartments: 3 Ho, ER 4 Ha: (12.5 x 12.0)3 (13.4 x 13.5)ER Ice Capable	**1 oil engine** driving 1 FP propeller Total Power: 3,310kW (4,500hp) 11.5k Mitsubishi 6UET45/80 1 x 2 Stroke 6 Cy. 450 x 800 3310kW (4500bhp) Kobe Hatsudoki KK-Japan AuxGen: 3 x 200kW 445V 60Hz a.c Fuel: 70.0 (d.f.) 620.0 (r.f.) 11.0pd
7915307 *9HWY5* -	**WILSON TYNE** *ex* Hordnes *-2003* *ex* Barra Head *-1996* **Wilson Shipowning AS** Wilson EuroCarriers AS *Valletta* *Malta* MMSI: 248245000 Official number: 6083	**4,913** 2,531 7,107 T/cm 15.6	Class: BV (LR) ✠ Classed LR until 8/5/11	**1980-06 Miho Zosensho K.K. — Shimizu** Yd No: 1151 Loa 110.55 Br ex 17.56 Dght 7.016 Lbp 101.91 Br md 17.51 Dpth 8.62 Welded, 1 dk	**(A31A2GX) General Cargo Ship** Grain: 9,442; Bale: 9,065 Compartments: 3 Ho, ER 4 Ha: (12.5 x 12.0)3 (12.5 x 13.4)ER Ice Capable	**1 oil engine** driving 1 FP propeller Total Power: 3,310kW (4,500hp) 11.0k Mitsubishi 6UET45/80 1 x 2 Stroke 6 Cy. 450 x 800 3310kW (4500bhp) Kobe Hatsudoki KK-Japan AuxGen: 3 x 200kW 445V 60Hz a.c Boilers: AuxB (Comp) 7.0kgf/cm² (6.9bar) Fuel: 59.0 (d.f.) 323.0 (r.f.) 11.0pd
9178446 *8PUR* -	**WILSON WAAL** *ex* Podebrady *-2002* **Wilson Shipowning AS** Wilson EuroCarriers AS *Bridgetown* *Barbados* MMSI: 314262000	**1,170** 635 1,836	Class: GL	**1999-06 Ceskoslovenska Plavba Labska a.s. (CSPL) — Chvaletice** Yd No: 106 Loa 78.16 (BB) Br ex - Dght 4.350 Lbp 73.80 Br md 9.46 Dpth 5.75 Welded, 1 dk	**(A31A2GX) General Cargo Ship** Double Bottom Entire Compartment Length Grain: 2,200 TEU 72 C.Ho 48/20' C.Dk 24/20' 1 Ha: (49.1 x 7.6)ER Ice Capable	**1 oil engine** reduction geared to sc. shaft driving 1 FP propeller Total Power: 1,125kW (1,530hp) 12.0k Deutz SBV6M62 1 x 4 Stroke 6 Cy. 240 x 280 1125kW (1530bhp) Deutz AG-Koeln AuxGen: 2 x 92kW a.c Thrusters: 1 Thwart. FP thruster (f)
8201569 *GDDC* -	**WILTON** **PD Teesport Ltd** - *Middlesbrough* *United Kingdom* MMSI: 232004109 Official number: 341887	**345** 103 84	Class: LR ✠ **100A1** SS 08/2010 Tees Bay & approaches service in an area bounded 7 miles North to 5 miles South of River Tees with occasional voyages to Whitby & the River Tyne & not more than 12 miles offshore in reasonable weather between 1st April and 31st August ✠ **LMC** Eq.Ltr: G; Cable: 302.5/20.5 U2 (a)	**1983-07 George Brown & Co. (Marine) Ltd. — Greenock** (Hull launched by) Yd No: 286 **1983-07 Tees & Hartlepool Port Authority — Greenock** (Hull completed by) Loa 40.54 Br ex 9.68 Dght 1.931 Lbp 37.01 Br md 9.25 Dpth 3.66 Welded, 1 dk	**(B34Q2QB) Buoy Tender** Cranes: 1x30t	**1 oil engine** driving 3 hydraulic pumps connected to thruster units driving 1 Directional propeller Total Power: 883kW (1,201hp) 8.5k Nohab F26 1 x 4 Stroke 6 Cy. 250 x 300 883kW (1201bhp) British Polar Engines Ltd.-Glasgow AuxGen: 1 x 150kW 415V 50Hz a.c, 1 x 42kW 415V 50Hz a.c Thrusters: 1 Directional thruster (f) Fuel: 47.0 (d.f.)
7535626 *DUA6145* -	**WILYN** *ex* Yoshiei Maru No. 36 *-1992* *ex* Tenyo Maru No. 5 *-1984* **Mega Fishing Corp** - *Manila* *Philippines* Official number: MNLD007507	*166* 96 -		**1975-04 Kidoura Shipyard Co Ltd — Kesennuma MG** Yd No: 322 Loa 37.85 Br ex 6.63 Dght 2.801 Lbp - Br md 6.61 Dpth 3.20 Welded, 1 dk	**(B11B2FV) Fishing Vessel** Ins: 172	**1 oil engine** driving 1 FP propeller Total Power: 699kW (950hp) 11.3k Akasaka AH2 1 x 4 Stroke 6 Cy. 250 x 410 699kW (950bhp) Akasaka Tekkosho KK (Akasaka DieselLtd)-Japan AuxGen: 1 x 100kW 225V a.c, 1 x 80kW 225V a.c
8919972 *9MEX5* -	**WIN 1** *ex* May 1 *-2013* *ex* STT Kingston *-2011* *ex* MMM Kingston *-2011* *ex* Rosalie *-2003* - - *Port Klang* *Malaysia* MMSI: 533752000 Official number: 330327	**4,355** 1,877 7,078 T/cm 14.9	Class: KR (LR) (NK) Classed LR until 29/10/10	**1990-06 Kurinoura Dockyard Co Ltd — Yawatahama EH** Yd No: 281 Loa 111.00 (BB) Br ex - Dght 7.274 Lbp 101.85 Br md 16.50 Dpth 8.50 Welded, 1 dk	**(A12B2TR) Chemical/Products Tanker** Double Bottom Entire Compartment Length Liq: 8,253; Liq (Oil): 8,424 Cargo Heating Coils Compartments: 8 Ta, 10 Wing Ta, 2 Slop Ta, ER 20 Cargo Pump (s): 15x100m³/hr, 5x200m³/hr Manifold: Bow/CM: 56.5m	**1 oil engine** driving 1 CP propeller Total Power: 2,831kW (3,849hp) 13.7k Mitsubishi 7UEC37 1 x 2 Stroke 7 Cy. 370 x 880 2831kW (3849bhp) Akasaka Tekkosho KK (Akasaka DieselLtd)-Japan AuxGen: 1 x 272kW 440V 60Hz a.c, 2 x 272kW 440V 60Hz a.c Boilers: e (ex.g.), AuxB (o.f.) 10.0kgf/cm² (9.8bar) Fuel: 124.0 (d.f.) 596.0 (r.f.)

Number / Call sign	Ship / Owner / Flag	Tonnage	Class	Builder / Dimensions	Type / Cargo	Machinery	Speed / Model
065132 *MLR9*	**WIN 2** *ex* May 2 *-2013* *ex* MMM Dayton *-2011* *ex* Donghwa Ace *-2004* *ex* Diamond *-2002* *ex* Nam Young No. 92 *-1994* **May Maritime Services Sdn Bhd** - *Port Klang* *Malaysia* MMSI: 533060800 Official number: 334331	**2,043** 906 3,529 T/cm 9.9	Class: KR (LR) (AB) Classed LR until 14/7/10	**1992-07 Woori Shipbuilding Co Ltd — Tongyeong** Yd No: 101 Loa 81.50 (BB) Br ex 14.22 Dght 5.781 Lbp 75.00 Br md 14.00 Dpth 6.50 Welded, 1 dk	**(A12B2TR) Chemical/Products Tanker** Liq: 3,803; Liq (Oil): 3,803 Cargo Heating Coils Compartments: 10 Wing Ta, 2 Wing Slop Ta, ER 4 Cargo Pump (s): 2x200m³/hr, 2x300m³/hr Manifold: Bow/CM: 44m	**1 oil engine** driving 1 FP propeller Total Power: 1,680kW (2,284hp) Alpha 1 x 4 Stroke 8 Cy. 280 x 320 1680kW (2284bhp) Ssangyong Heavy Industries Co Ltd-South Korea AuxGen: 2 x 184kW 445V a.c Boilers: AuxB Fuel: 45.0 (d.f.) 130.0 (r.f.)	13.8kn 8L28/32
301292 *EVL4*	**WIN BRIGHT** *ex* Hika Wi *-2002* *ex* Andhika Wijaya *-2002* **Win Bright Shipping SA** Dalian Master Well Ship Management Co Ltd *Panama* *Panama* MMSI: 357371000 Official number: 4211311	**5,464** 2,262 6,846	Class: NK (KI)	**1983-07 Higaki Zosen K.K. — Imabari** Yd No: 297 Loa 98.18 (BB) Br ex 18.01 Dght 7.544 Lbp 89.95 Br md 18.00 Dpth 13.00 Welded, 2 dks	**(A31A2GX) General Cargo Ship** Grain: 13,070; Bale: 12,097 Compartments: 2 Ho, ER, 2 Tw Dk 2 Ha: (22.2 x 9.8) (24.7 x 9.8)ER Derricks: 4x20t	**1 oil engine** driving 1 FP propeller Total Power: 2,427kW (3,300hp) Hanshin 1 x 4 Stroke 6 Cy. 400 x 800 2427kW (3300bhp) The Hanshin Diesel Works Ltd-Japan AuxGen: 3 x 280kW 440V 60Hz a.c Fuel: 82.0 (d.f.) 431.5 (r.f.) 10.5pd	13.0kn 6EL40
697399 *I2622*	**WIN FAR FU NO. 1** **Win Far Fishery Co Ltd** - *Kaohsiung* *Chinese Taipei* Official number: 015313	**999** 446 1,185	Class: CR (Class contemplated)	**2013-05 Jong Shyn Shipbuilding Co., Ltd. — Kaohsiung** Yd No: 230 Loa 74.55 Br ex - Dght 4.300 Lbp 65.80 Br md 11.00 Dpth 4.50 Welded, 1 dk	**(B11B2FV) Fishing Vessel**	**1 oil engine** reduction geared to sc. shaft driving 1 Propeller Total Power: 1,765kW (2,400hp) Akasaka 1 x 4 Stroke 6 Cy. 1765kW (2400bhp) Akasaka Tekkosho KK (Akasaka DieselLtd)-Japan	
747214 *I2485*	**WIN FAR NO. 161** **Win Jyi Fishery Co Ltd** - *Kaohsiung* *Chinese Taipei* MMSI: 416872000 Official number: 012654	**696** 303 372		**1995-07 Lin Sheng Shipbuilding Co, Ltd — Kaohsiung** Loa 56.35 (BB) Br ex - Dght 2.480 Lbp 50.00 Br md 8.90 Dpth 3.85 Welded, 1 dk	**(B11B2FV) Fishing Vessel**	**1 oil engine** driving 1 FP propeller Total Power: 1,030kW (1,400hp)	
747226 *I2487*	**WIN FAR NO. 162** **Win Chia Fishery Co Ltd** - *Kaohsiung* *Chinese Taipei* MMSI: 416874000 Official number: 012666	**696** 303 358		**1994-05 Lin Sheng Shipbuilding Co, Ltd — Kaohsiung** Loa 56.35 Br ex - Dght 2.480 Lbp 50.00 Br md 8.90 Dpth 3.85 Welded, 1 dk	**(B11B2FV) Fishing Vessel**	**1 oil engine** driving 1 FP propeller Total Power: 1,030kW (1,400hp)	
747238 *EDT*	**WIN FAR NO. 606** **Yu Fu Fishery Co Ltd** - *Kaohsiung* *Chinese Taipei* MMSI: 416899000 Official number: 012850	**1,124** 384 1,000		**1994-10 Lin Sheng Shipbuilding Co, Ltd — Kaohsiung** Loa 70.26 Br ex - Dght 4.650 Lbp 60.66 Br md 12.24 Dpth 7.25 Welded, 1 dk	**(B11B2FV) Fishing Vessel**	**1 oil engine** driving 1 FP propeller Total Power: 2,354kW (3,200hp)	
747240 *EAB*	**WIN FAR NO. 626** **Win Chang Fishery Co Ltd** - *Kaohsiung* *Chinese Taipei* MMSI: 416500000 Official number: 012129	**1,098** 338 1,000		**1991-06 Lin Sheng Shipbuilding Co, Ltd — Kaohsiung** Loa 65.70 Br ex - Dght 4.650 Lbp 58.03 Br md 12.24 Dpth 7.25 Welded, 1 dk	**(B11B2FV) Fishing Vessel**	**1 oil engine** driving 1 Propeller Total Power: 2,206kW (2,999hp) Daihatsu 1 x 4 Stroke 8 Cy. 2206kW (2999bhp) Daihatsu Diesel Manufacturing Co Lt-Japan	
747252 *L2039*	**WIN FAR NO. 636** **Win Hsiung Fishery Co Ltd** - *Kaohsiung* *Chinese Taipei* MMSI: 416898000 Official number: 012175	**1,098** 338 1,000		**1991-12 Lin Sheng Shipbuilding Co, Ltd — Kaohsiung** Loa 65.80 Br ex - Dght 4.650 Lbp 58.03 Br md 12.24 Dpth 7.25 Welded, 1 dk	**(B11B2FV) Fishing Vessel**	**1 oil engine** driving 1 Propeller Total Power: 2,206kW (2,999hp) Daihatsu 1 x 4 Stroke 8 Cy. 2206kW (2999bhp) Daihatsu Diesel Manufacturing Co Lt-Japan	
108946 *EDU* 2836	**WIN FAR NO. 666** **Yu Cherng Fishery Co Ltd** Win Far Fishery Group SatCom: Inmarsat A 1356124 *Kaohsiung* *Chinese Taipei* MMSI: 416501000 Official number: CT8-0072	**1,096** 416 1,034		**1994-12 Fong Kuo Shipbuilding Co Ltd — Kaohsiung** Yd No: 310 Loa 69.29 (BB) Br ex 12.40 Dght 4.830 Lbp 60.71 Br md 12.20 Dpth 7.20 Welded, 2 dks	**(B11B2FV) Fishing Vessel**	**1 oil engine** with flexible couplings & sr reverse geared to sc. shaft driving 1 FP propeller Total Power: 2,354kW (3,200hp) Akasaka 1 x 4 Stroke 6 Cy. 400 x 640 2354kW (3200bhp) Akasaka Tekkosho KK (Akasaka DieselLtd)-Japan Thrusters: 1 Thwart. FP thruster (f)	DM40AKFD
747288 *3335*	**WIN FAR NO. 818** **Win Shing Fishery Co Ltd** - *Kaohsiung* *Chinese Taipei* MMSI: 416047600 Official number: 013698	**496** 242 357		**1999-11 Sen Koh Shipbuilding Corp — Kaohsiung** Yd No: 117 Loa 56.00 Br ex - Dght 2.110 Lbp 47.30 Br md 8.60 Dpth 3.70 Welded, 1 dk	**(B11B2FV) Fishing Vessel**	**1 oil engine** driving 1 FP propeller Total Power: 1,030kW (1,400hp)	
219537 *2574*	**WIN FAR No. 828** **Win Ji Far Fishery Co Ltd** - *Kaohsiung* *Chinese Taipei* MMSI: 416128600 Official number: 014177	**530** 238 -		**2000-01 Jong Shyn Shipbuilding Co., Ltd. — Kaohsiung** Yd No: 079 Loa 56.00 Br ex - Dght 2.093 Lbp 47.30 Br md 8.60 Dpth 3.70 Welded, 1 dk	**(B11B2FV) Fishing Vessel**	**1 oil engine** driving 1 FP propeller Total Power: 1,030kW (1,400hp) Akasaka 1 x 4 Stroke 1030kW (1400bhp) Akasaka Tekkosho KK (Akasaka DieselLtd)-Japan	
747290 *2521*	**WIN FAR NO. 838** **Win Jin Fishery Co Ltd** - *Kaohsiung* *Chinese Taipei* MMSI: 416333000 Official number: 013704	**630** 286 405		**2000-06 Sen Koh Shipbuilding Corp — Kaohsiung** Yd No: 120 Loa 59.20 Br ex - Dght 2.060 Lbp 50.80 Br md 9.00 Dpth 3.75 Welded, 1 dk	**(B11B2FV) Fishing Vessel**	**1 oil engine** driving 1 FP propeller Total Power: 1,030kW (1,400hp)	
15945 *2568*	**WIN FAR No. 868** **Win Lung Tai Fishery Co Ltd** - *Kaohsiung* *Chinese Taipei* MMSI: 416112600 Official number: 014176	**530** 238 357		**2000-01 Jong Shyn Shipbuilding Co., Ltd. — Kaohsiung** Yd No: 073 Loa 56.00 Br ex - Dght 2.060 Lbp 47.30 Br md 8.60 Dpth 3.70 Welded, 1 dk	**(B11B2FV) Fishing Vessel**	**1 oil engine** driving 1 FP propeller Total Power: 1,030kW (1,400hp) Akasaka 1 x 4 Stroke 1030kW (1400bhp) Akasaka Tekkosho KK (Akasaka DieselLtd)-Japan	12.0kn
19549 *2572*	**WIN FAR No. 878** **Win Feng Tai Fishery Co Ltd** - *Kaohsiung* *Chinese Taipei* MMSI: 416116500 Official number: 014191	**530** 238 357		**2000-01 Jong Shyn Shipbuilding Co., Ltd. — Kaohsiung** Yd No: 078 Loa 56.00 Br ex - Dght 2.093 Lbp 47.30 Br md 8.60 Dpth 3.70 Welded, 1 dk	**(B11B2FV) Fishing Vessel**	**1 oil engine** driving 1 FP propeller Total Power: 1,030kW (1,400hp) Akasaka 1 x 4 Stroke 1030kW (1400bhp) Akasaka Tekkosho KK (Akasaka DieselLtd)-Japan	
47329 *I3337*	**WIN FAR NO. 888** **Win Ching Tai Fishery Co Ltd** - *Kaohsiung* *Chinese Taipei* MMSI: 416069500 Official number: 013705	**496** 239 357		**2000-08 Sen Koh Shipbuilding Corp — Kaohsiung** Yd No: 118 Loa 56.00 Br ex - Dght 2.120 Lbp 47.30 Br md 8.60 Dpth 3.70 Welded, 1 dk	**(B11B2FV) Fishing Vessel**	**1 oil engine** driving 1 FP propeller Total Power: 1,030kW (1,400hp)	

8747331 *BI2107* -	**WIN FAR TSAIR NO. 66** **Win Far Fishery Co Ltd** - *Kaohsiung* *Chinese Taipei* MMSI: 416712000 Official number: 010020	**861** 370 1,077		**1986-12 Lien Ho Shipbuilding Co, Ltd — Kaohsiung** Loa 63.15 Br ex - Dght 3.900 Lbp 55.00 Br md 10.00 Dpth 4.20 Welded, 1 dk	**(B11B2FV) Fishing Vessel**	**1 oil engine** driving 1 Propeller Total Power: 1,103kW (1,500hp) Daihatsu 1 x 4 Stroke 6 Cy. 1103kW (1500bhp) Daihatsu Diesel Manufacturing Co Lt-Japan
8747343 *BI2505* -	**WIN FAR TSAIR NO. 616** **Win Hand Fishery Co Ltd** - *Kaohsiung* *Chinese Taipei* MMSI: 416528000 Official number: 013356	**919** 482 734		**1997-07 Jong Shyn Shipbuilding Co., Ltd. — Kaohsiung** Yd No: 056 Loa 71.70 Br ex - Dght 4.300 Lbp 62.72 Br md 11.00 Dpth 4.60 Welded, 1 dk	**(B11B2FV) Fishing Vessel**	**1 oil engine** driving 1 FP propeller Total Power: 1,618kW (2,200hp) Daihatsu 1 x 4 Stroke 6 Cy. 1618kW (2200bhp) Daihatsu Diesel Manufacturing Co Lt-Japan
8747355 *BI2378* -	**WIN FU LAI** **Yu Ming Chuen Fishery Co Ltd** - *Kaohsiung* *Chinese Taipei* MMSI: 416527000 Official number: 011638	**993** 415 1,180		**1989-10 San Yang Shipbuilding Co., Ltd. — Kaohsiung** Loa 63.12 Br ex - Dght 4.300 Lbp 57.75 Br md 10.60 Dpth 4.72 Welded, 1 dk	**(B11B2FV) Fishing Vessel**	**1 oil engine** driving 1 CP propeller Total Power: 1,692kW (2,300hp)
7523958 - -	**WIN HANVERKY** *ex* Kachidoki Maru *-1994* **Zhangjiagang Win Hanverky Container Terminal Co Ltd**	*198* 64 72		**1976-01 Hikari Kogyo K.K. — Yokosuka** Yd No: 277 Loa 31.70 Br ex 8.64 Dght 2.718 Lbp 26.50 Br md 8.62 Dpth 3.51 Welded, 1 dk	**(B32A2ST) Tug**	**2 oil engines** driving 2 FP propellers Total Power: 956kW (1,300hp) Daihatsu 6RSNTM-26E 2 x 4 Stroke 6 Cy. 260 x 320 each-478kW (650bhp) Daihatsu Diesel Manufacturing Co Lt-Japan
9085443 *VRZL8* -	**WIN HONEY** *ex* Brother Hope *-2004* **Treasure Way Shipping Ltd** Dalian Master Well Ship Management Co Ltd *Hong Kong* *Hong Kong* MMSI: 477040400 Official number: HK-1205	**6,205** 2,873 8,177 T/cm 16.3	Class: NK	**1994-07 ShinA Shipbuilding Co Ltd — Tongyeong** Yd No: 370 Loa 100.45 (BB) Br ex 19.03 Dght 7.863 Lbp 94.50 Br md 19.00 Dpth 12.50 Welded, 2 dks	**(A31A2GX) General Cargo Ship** Grain: 14,231; Bale: 13,262 TEU 126/20' Compartments: 2 Ho, ER 2 Ha: (22.8 x 10.0) (26.7 x 12.5)ER Derricks: 4x25t	**1 oil engine** driving 1 FP propeller Total Power: 2,942kW (4,000hp) 12.0kn Hanshin 6EL44 1 x 4 Stroke 6 Cy. 440 x 880 2942kW (4000bhp) The Hanshin Diesel Works Ltd-Japan AuxGen: 3 x 488kW a.c Fuel: 480.0 (r.f.)
8747202 *BI2106* -	**WIN HONG NO. 1** *ex* Win Chuen *-2011* **Win Hong Yang Fishery Co Ltd** - *Kaohsiung* *Chinese Taipei* MMSI: 416845000 Official number: 009969	**965** 375 686		**1987-10 Shin Tien Erh Shipbuilding Co, Ltd — Kaohsiung** Loa 62.00 Br ex - Dght 3.850 Lbp 54.25 Br md 9.60 Dpth 4.35 Welded, 1 dk	**(B11B2FV) Fishing Vessel**	**1 oil engine** driving 1 FP propeller Total Power: 1,397kW (1,899hp) Daihatsu 1 x 4 Stroke 6 Cy. 1397kW (1899bhp) Daihatsu Diesel Manufacturing Co Lt-Japan
8747367 *BI2133* -	**WIN JI** **Win Deng Tai Fishery Co Ltd** - *Kaohsiung* *Chinese Taipei* MMSI: 416848000 Official number: 010523	**885** 375 1,194		**1987-10 Shin Tien Erh Shipbuilding Co, Ltd — Kaohsiung** Loa 62.00 Br ex - Dght 3.850 Lbp 54.25 Br md 9.60 Dpth 4.35 Welded, 1 dk	**(B11B2FV) Fishing Vessel**	**1 oil engine** driving 1 FP propeller Total Power: 1,397kW (1,899hp) Daihatsu 1 x 4 Stroke 6 Cy. 1397kW (1899bhp) Daihatsu Diesel Manufacturing Co Lt-Japan
8747379 *BH2954* -	**WIN LAI FAR** **Win Ji Far Fishery Co Ltd** - *Kaohsiung* *Chinese Taipei* MMSI: 416875000 Official number: 008676	**499** 212 378		**1983-11 Shin Tien Erh Shipbuilding Co, Ltd — Kaohsiung** Loa 53.80 Br ex - Dght 3.400 Lbp 47.03 Br md 8.60 Dpth 3.80 Welded, 1 dk	**(B11B2FV) Fishing Vessel**	**1 oil engine** driving 1 Propeller Total Power: 736kW (1,001hp)
9254783 *V3SP5* -	**WIN LONG** *ex* Dong Hao *-2007* **Eastern Glory Shipping Ltd** Weihai Safe Ocean Co Ltd *Belize City* *Belize* MMSI: 312467000 Official number: 030720187	**1,535** 919 2,282	Class: CC	**2001-07 Rongcheng Xixiakou Shipyard Co Ltd — Rongcheng SD** Yd No: 001 Loa 79.90 (BB) Br ex - Dght 4.700 Lbp 74.00 Br md 12.40 Dpth 5.95 Welded, 1 dk.	**(A31A2GX) General Cargo Ship** Grain: 2,937 Compartments: 2 Ho, ER 2 Ha: ER Ice Capable	**1 oil engine** reduction geared to sc. shaft. driving 1 FP propeller Total Power: 1,324kW (1,800hp) 11.0kn Chinese Std. Type LB8250ZLC 1 x 4 Stroke 8 Cy. 250 x 320 1324kW (1800bhp) Zibo Diesel Engine Factory-China AuxGen: 2 x 136kW 400V a.c
8745785 - -	**WIN PERFECT 778** *ex* Fangzhou 777 *-2011* **Win Perfect Resources Pte Ltd**	**1,485** 445 -		**2002-08 in the People's Republic of China** Loa 75.30 Br ex 15.47 Dght - Lbp 66.00 Br md 15.30 Dpth 4.00 Welded, 1 dk	**(B33A2DU) Dredger (unspecified)**	**2 oil engines** reduction geared to sc. shafts driving 2 Propellers Total Power: 3,600kW (4,894hp) 8.0kn Caterpillar 3516B 2 x Vee 4 Stroke 16 Cy. 170 x 190 each-1800kW (2447bhp) Caterpillar Inc-USA
7810571 *3FWH6* -	**WIN SHENG** *ex* Nippo *-1995* *ex* Shikishima Reefer *-1992* **Win Sheng Marine S de RL** Win Far Fishery Group SatCom: Inmarsat C 435659120 *Panama* *Panama* MMSI: 356591000 Official number: 2369697CH	**4,177** 1,883 4,360	Class: NK	**1979-01 Miyoshi Shipbuilding Co Ltd — Uwajima EH** Yd No: 243 Loa 122.47 Br ex - Dght 6.531 Lbp 114.00 Br md 16.01 Dpth 9.71 Riveted\Welded, 1 dk, 2nd & 3rd dks in cargo holds only	**(A34A2GR) Refrigerated Cargo Ship** Ins: 5,465 Compartments: 3 Ho, ER, 6 Tw Dk 3 Ha: 3 (7.2 x 6.0)ER Derricks: 6x5t	**1 oil engine** driving 1 FP propeller Total Power: 4,560kW (6,200hp) 15.0kn Mitsubishi 6UEC52/105D 1 x 2 Stroke 6 Cy. 520 x 1050 4560kW (6200bhp) Kobe Hatsudoki KK-Japan AuxGen: 3 x 400kW 450V 60Hz a.c Fuel: 193.0 (d.f.) 1000.5 (r.f.) 25.0pd
7311460 *3FWL6* -	**WIN SHING 1** *ex* Win Shing *-1996* *ex* Keiho No. 87 *-1992* *ex* Taisei Maru No. 87 *-1991* **Win Shing Marine Co Ltd** Win Far Fishery Group SatCom: Inmarsat A 1334231 *Panama* *Panama* MMSI: 354831000 Official number: 2372297CH	**3,506** 1,526 4,446	Class: (NK)	**1973-04 Hayashikane Shipbuilding & Engineering Co Ltd — Nagasaki NS** Yd No: 827 Loa 114.28 Br ex 15.85 Dght 6.717 Lbp 105.01 Br md 15.80 Dpth 8.21 Welded, 1 dk	**(A34A2GR) Refrigerated Cargo Ship** Ins: 4,954 Compartments: 3 Ho, ER 6 Ha: 2 (4.6 x 3.5)4 (4.9 x 3.5)ER Cranes: 6x1.5t; Derricks: 6x3t	**1 oil engine** driving 1 FP propeller Total Power: 5,517kW (7,501hp) 17.5kn Mitsubishi 8UET52/90D 1 x 2 Stroke 8 Cy. 520 x 900 5517kW (7501bhp) Kobe Hatsudoki Seizosho-Japan AuxGen: 2 x 508kW 445V 60Hz a.c Fuel: 958.0 (d.f.) 407.0 (r.f.) 20.5pd
7332713 *BECS* -	**WIN SHUN SHING** *ex* Dairyo Maru *-1988* **Win Shu Fishery Co Ltd** - SatCom: Inmarsat A 1350212 *Chinese Taipei* MMSI: 416778000	*2,955* 1,538 3,742	Class: CR (NK)	**1973-11 Shikoku Dockyard Co. Ltd. — Takamatsu** Yd No: 764 Loa 100.01 (BB) Br ex 15.83 Dght 6.325 Lbp 92.00 Br md 15.80 Dpth 8.41 Riveted\Welded, 1 dk, pt 2nd dk	**(A34A2GR) Refrigerated Cargo Ship** Ins: 3,547 Compartments: 3 Ho, ER, 1 Tw Dk 3 Ha: 3 (4.8 x 5.0) Derricks: 2x5t,4x3t; Winches: 6	**1 oil engine** driving 1 FP propeller Total Power: 3,972kW (5,400hp) 15.5kn Mitsubishi 6UEC52/105C 1 x 2 Stroke 6 Cy. 520 x 1050 3972kW (5400bhp) Kobe Hatsudoki Seizosho-Japan AuxGen: 2 x 360kW 445V 60Hz a.c Fuel: 157.5 (d.f.) 614.5 (r.f.) 24.0pd
9274422 *3DXG* -	**WIN STAR 1** **Ocean Harvest (Fiji) Ltd** - *Suva* *Fiji*	**113** 34 62	Class: (BV)	**2002-08 Jiangxi Jiangxin Shipyard — Hukou County JX** Yd No: 02 Loa 25.96 Br ex 6.50 Dght 2.130 Lbp 23.07 Br md 5.70 Dpth 2.40 Welded, 1 dk	**(B11B2FV) Fishing Vessel**	**1 oil engine** geared to sc. shaft driving 1 FP propeller Total Power: 237kW (322hp) 10.1kn Cummins NTA-855-M 1 x 4 Stroke 6 Cy. 140 x 152 237kW (322bhp) Chongqing Cummins Engine Co Ltd-China AuxGen: 2 x 150kW
9275000 *3DXH* -	**WIN STAR 2** **Ocean Harvest (Fiji) Ltd** - *Suva* *Fiji*	**113** 34 62	Class: (BV)	**2002-08 Jiangxi Jiangxin Shipyard — Hukou County JX** Yd No: 01 Loa 25.96 Br ex 6.50 Dght 2.130 Lbp 23.07 Br md 5.70 Dpth 2.40 Welded, 1 dk	**(B11B2FV) Fishing Vessel**	**1 oil engine** geared to sc. shaft driving 1 FP propeller Total Power: 237kW (322hp) 10.0kn Cummins NTA-855-M 1 x 4 Stroke 6 Cy. 140 x 152 237kW (322bhp) Chongqing Cummins Engine Co Ltd-China AuxGen: 2 x 150kW
7302299 *T3MY* -	**WIN UNI** *ex* Wiin Terng Far *-2006* *ex* Sun Shime *-1994* *ex* Fukuyo Maru *-1987* **Max Step Shipping Ltd** Fengrun Shipping Co Ltd *Tarawa* *Kiribati* MMSI: 529120000 Official number: K16721348	**2,910** 1,417 3,597	Class: IZ PS (CR) (NK)	**1973-03 Kurushima Dockyard Co. Ltd. — Imabari** Yd No: 738 Loa 104.96 Br ex 15.04 Dght 6.617 Lbp 95.99 Br md 15.02 Dpth 7.80 Riveted\Welded, 1 dk	**(A34A2GR) Refrigerated Cargo Ship** Ins: 3,770 Compartments: 3 Ho, ER 3 Ha: 3 (7.0 x 5.0) Derricks: 6x3t	**1 oil engine** driving 1 FP propeller Total Power: 3,310kW (4,500hp) 15.3kn Mitsubishi 6UET45/80D 1 x 2 Stroke 6 Cy. 450 x 800 3310kW (4500bhp) Kobe Hatsudoki KK-Japan AuxGen: 3 x 280kW 450V 60Hz a.c Fuel: 103.0 (d.f.) 540.0 (r.f.) 15.0pd

	Name / Owner	Tonnage	Class	Builder / Dimensions	Type	Machinery
747381 *I2379*	**WIN YU YIH** **Yu Yi Chuen Fishery Co Ltd** - *Kaohsiung* *Chinese Taipei* MMSI: 416525000 Official number: 011774	**991** 297 1,180		**1990-01 San Yang Shipbuilding Co., Ltd. — Kaohsiung** Loa 63.12 Br ex - Dght 4.300 Lbp 57.75 Br md 10.60 Dpth 7.18 Welded, 1 dk	**(B11B2FV) Fishing Vessel**	**1 oil engine** driving 1 CP propeller Total Power: 1,692kW (2,300hp)
027922	**WINBUILD SAKTI** **PT Wintermar** - *Jakarta* *Indonesia*	**201** 95 -	Class: (KI)	**1998-08 Forward Shipbuilding Enterprise Sdn Bhd — Sibu** L reg 35.18 Br ex - Dght - Lbp 30.57 Br md 8.53 Dpth 2.50 Welded, 1 dk	**(A35D2RL) Landing Craft** Bow ramp (centre)	**2 oil engines** reduction geared to sc. shafts driving 2 Propellers Total Power: 514kW (698hp) 7.0kn Cummins NTA-855-M 2 x 4 Stroke 6 Cy. 140 x 152 each-257kW (349bhp) Cummins Diesel International Ltd-USA
212462 *7BU3*	**WINCANTON** **Australia Gas AS** Bernhard Schulte Shipmanagement (Singapore) Pte Ltd *Majuro* *Marshall Islands* MMSI: 538005199 Official number: 5199	**6,738** 2,428 9,203 T/cm 16.5	Class: BV	**2000-03 Asakawa Zosen K.K. — Imabari** Yd No: 412 Loa 119.95 (BB) Br ex 17.63 Dght 8.200 Lbp 113.13 Br md 17.60 Dpth 10.10 Welded, 1 dk	**(A11B2TG) LPG Tanker** Double Sides Entire Compartment Length Liq (Gas): 8,538 2 x Gas Tank (s); 2 independent (stl) cyl horizontal 2 Cargo Pump (s): 2x450m³/hr Manifold: Bow/CM: 60.9m	**1 oil engine** driving 1 FP propeller Total Power: 4,891kW (6,650hp) 15.0kn B&W 7S35MC 1 x 2 Stroke 7 Cy. 350 x 1400 4891kW (6650bhp) Hitachi Zosen Corp-Japan AuxGen: 3 x 480kW 440/100V 60Hz a.c Thrusters: 1 Thwart. CP thruster (f) Fuel: 109.0 (d.f.) (Heating Coils) 783.0 (r.f.) 21.3pd
929911	**WINCHESTER** *ex* Lady Janice *-1982* **Ray Berkshire Ltd** - *St John's, NL* *Canada* MMSI: 316002146 Official number: 331390	**384** 115 -	Class: (LR) ✠ Classed LR until 3/74	**1970-04 Fishermen's Loan Board of Prince Edward Island — Georgetown PE** Yd No: 21 Converted From: Stern Trawler-2000 Loa 39.10 Br ex 8.64 Dght - Lbp 34.07 Br md 8.53 Dpth 5.24 Welded, 1 dk	**(A37B2PS) Passenger Ship**	**2 oil engines** sr geared to sc. shaft driving 1 CP propeller Total Power: 1,344kW (1,828hp) 10.0kn Caterpillar D398SCAC 2 x Vee 4 Stroke 12 Cy. 159 x 203 each-672kW (914bhp) Caterpillar Tractor Co-USA AuxGen: 2 x 40kW 220V 60Hz a.c
516789 *5BG4*	**WINCHESTER STRAIT** *launched as* Hansa Wolfsburg *-2012* **ms 'Winchester Strait' GmbH & Co KG** Carsten Rehder Schiffsmakler und Reederei GmbH & Co KG *Monrovia* *Liberia* MMSI: 636092378 Official number: 92378	**18,358** 10,334 23,295 T/cm 38.0	Class: GL	**2012-03 Guangzhou Wenchong Shipyard Co Ltd — Guangzhou GD** Yd No: 392 Loa 175.47 (BB) Br ex - Dght 10.900 Lbp 165.00 Br md 27.40 Dpth 14.30 Welded, 1 dk	**(A33A2CC) Container Ship (Fully Cellular)** TEU 1740 C Ho 700 TEU C Dk 1040 TEU incl 300 ref C Compartments: 5 Cell Ho, ER Cranes: 2x40t	**1 oil engine** driving 1 FP propeller Total Power: 16,660kW (22,651hp) 19.8kn MAN-B&W 7S60MC-C8 1 x 2 Stroke 7 Cy. 600 x 2400 16660kW (22651bhp) Hudong Heavy Machinery Co Ltd-China AuxGen: 3 x 1180kW 60Hz a.c Thrusters: 1 Tunnel thruster (f) Fuel: 170.0 (d.f.) 1700.0 (r.f.)
107851 *XSW2*	**WIND** **DBB Jack-Up Services A/S** - *Aarhus* *Denmark (DIS)* MMSI: 220520000 Official number: D4279	**1,501** 426 1,463	Class: NV (LR) ✠ Classed LR until 9/1/08	**1996-01 Santierul Naval Galati S.A. — Galati** (Hull) **1996-01 N.V. Scheepswerf van Rupelmonde — Rupelmonde** Yd No: 196 Loa 55.00 Br ex - Dght 2.400 Lbp - Br md 17.93 Dpth 4.00 Welded, 1 dk	**(Z11C4ZC) Crane Platform, jack up** Cranes: 1x250t	**2 diesel electric oil engines** reduction geared to sc. shafts driving 2 Directional propellers Total Power: 1,272kW (1,730hp) G.M. (Detroit Diesel) 16V-92-TA 2 x Vee 2 Stroke 16 Cy. 123 x 127 each-636kW (865bhp) (made 1980, fitted 1996) Detroit Diesel Corporation-Detroit, Mi AuxGen: 2 x 200kW 420V a.c Thrusters: 2 Directional thruster (f)
347548 *DKR8*	**WIND AMBITION** *ex* Cesme *-2010* *ex* King of Scandinavia *-2002* *ex* Venus *-1994* *ex* Scandinavica *-1990* *ex* Tarak L *-1989* *ex* Scandinavica *-1989* *ex* Stena Scandinavica *-1987* *ex* Prinsessan Birgitta *-1982* **C-bed II BV** - SatCom: Inmarsat C 423592285 *London* *United Kingdom* MMSI: 235079807 Official number: 916862	**13,336** 4,384 1,600	Class: RI (NV) (TL)	**1974-04 Oy Wartsila Ab — Turku** Yd No: 1214 Converted From: Ferry (Passenger/Vehicle)-2010 Loa 152.39 (BB) Br ex 20.05 Dght 5.620 Lbp 132.21 Br md 20.00 Dpth 12.93 Welded, 3 dks	**(B22A2ZA) Accommodation Ship** Bow door/ramp (centre) Len: 7.20 Wid: 5.90 Swl: 50 Stern door/ramp (centre) Len: 14.16 Wid: 4.43 Swl: 50 Lane-Len: 1270 Lane-Wid: 4.00 Lane-clr ht: 4.20 Lorries: 24, Cars: 200 Ice Capable	**2 oil engines** with clutches, flexible couplings & sr geared to sc. shafts driving 2 CP propellers Total Power: 15,898kW (21,614hp) 18.5kn Pielstick 18PC2-5V-400 2 x Vee 4 Stroke 18 Cy. 400 x 460 each-7949kW (10807bhp) Oy Wartsila Ab-Finland AuxGen: 4 x 912kW 380V 50Hz a.c, 1 x 192kW 380V 50Hz a.c Thrusters: 1 Thwart. CP thruster (f); 1 Tunnel thruster (a) Fuel: 181.0 (d.f.) 371.0 (r.f.) 30.5pd
214753 *B4668*	**WIND EXPRESS** *ex* Esl Express *-2012* *ex* Oil Express *-2011* *ex* Springfield *-1982* *ex* West Eagle *-1981* **Wind Express Shipping GmbH & Co KG** GRS Rohden Shipping GmbH & Co KG *Kingstown* *St Vincent & The Grenadines* MMSI: 376129000 Official number: 11141	**931** 280 812	Class: NV	**1972 B.V. Scheepswerf "Waterhuizen" J. Pattje — Waterhuizen** Yd No: 296 Converted From: Offshore Supply Ship-2012 Loa 53.17 Br ex 11.52 Dght 3.772 Lbp 49.31 Br md 11.46 Dpth 5.52 Welded, 2 dks	**(B22A20V) Diving Support Vessel** Liq: 104; Liq (Oil): 104 Compartments: 3 Ta, ER Cranes: 1x13t; Winches: 1	**2 oil engines** driving 2 CP propellers Total Power: 1,368kW (1,860hp) 12.0kn De Industrie 6D7HDN 2 x 4 Stroke 6 Cy. 305 x 460 each-684kW (930bhp) NV Motorenfabriek 'De Industrie'-Netherlands AuxGen: 2 x 170kW 440V 60Hz a.c Thrusters: 1 Thwart. FP thruster (f) Fuel: 357.5 (d.f.) 7.0pd
230410 *D2957*	**WIND FORCE** *ex* Heyang Eeho *-1998* *ex* Annie Mae Candies *-1983* **Sea Eagle Marine Services** Sea Eagles Shipping LLC *Bahrain* *Bahrain* MMSI: 408760000 Official number: BN 3040	*586* 175 561	Class: BV (KR) (AB)	**1972 Burton Shipyard Co., Inc. — Port Arthur, Tx** Yd No: 487 Loa 53.35 Br ex 11.59 Dght 3.700 Lbp 49.79 Br md - Dpth 4.27 Welded, 1 dk	**(B21B20T) Offshore Tug/Supply Ship**	**2 oil engines** reduction geared to sc. shafts driving 2 FP propellers Total Power: 3,090kW (4,202hp) 10.0kn EMD (Electro-Motive) 16-645-E2 2 x Vee 2 Stroke 16 Cy. 230 x 254 each-1545kW (2101bhp) General Motors Corp.Electro-Motive Div.-La Grange AuxGen: 2 x 67kW 220V a.c Thrusters: 1 Tunnel thruster (f) Fuel: 252.0 (d.f.)
64059 *GIB2*	**WIND FORCE I** **Frisia Offshore GmbH & Co KG** AG Reederei Norden-Frisia *Norddeich* *Germany* MMSI: 211461570 Official number: 5823	**105** 31 13	Class: GL	**2009-06 Schiffswerft Diedrich GmbH & Co KG — Moormerland** Yd No: 1001 Loa 22.00 Br ex 8.60 Dght 1.920 Lbp 19.38 Br md 8.30 Dpth 3.16 Welded, 1 dk	**(B21A20C) Crew/Supply Vessel** Hull Material: Aluminium Alloy	**2 oil engines** reverse reduction geared to sc. shafts driving 2 FP propellers Total Power: 1,620kW (2,202hp) 20.0kn Caterpillar C32 2 x Vee 4 Stroke 12 Cy. 145 x 162 each-810kW (1101bhp) Caterpillar Inc-USA AuxGen: 2 x 69kW 400V a.c Thrusters: 2 Tunnel thruster 1 (p) 1 (s)
90444 *B3459*	**WIND FORCE II** **Frisia Offshore GmbH & Co KG** AG Reederei Norden-Frisia *Valletta* *Malta* MMSI: 229480000 Official number: 9690444	**101** 31 18	Class: NV	**2013-05 Baltic Workboats AS — Kaarma** (Hull) Yd No: (90119) **2013-05 Schiffswerft Diedrich GmbH & Co KG — Moormerland** Yd No: 90119 Loa 21.55 Br ex 8.60 Dght 1.940 Lbp 19.53 Br md 7.97 Dpth 3.16 Welded, 1 dk	**(B21A20C) Crew/Supply Vessel** Hull Material: Aluminium Alloy	**2 oil engines** reduction geared to sc. shafts driving 2 Propellers Total Power: 1,800kW (2,448hp) M.T.U. 10V2000M72 2 x Vee 4 Stroke 10 Cy. 135 x 156 each-900kW (1224bhp) MTU Friedrichshafen GmbH-Friedrichshafen Thrusters: 2 Tunnel thruster (f)
23452 *KS2*	**WIND FORRADER** *ex* Beauty Song *-2011* *ex* Smara III *-2002* *ex* Bosco Polar *-1996* *ex* Reefer Badger *-1994* **Ginsor Ltd** JSC Atlantrybflot Scientific-Industrial Association (OAO Nauchno-Promyshlennoye Obyedineniye 'Atlantrybflot') *Charlestown* *St Kitts & Nevis* MMSI: 341111000 Official number: SKN 1002283	**4,128** 1,719 5,018	Class: RS (NK)	**1983-04 Kishimoto Zosen K.K. — Kinoe** Yd No: 528 Loa 107.17 (BB) Br ex - Dght 6.573 Lbp 99.83 Br md 17.11 Dpth 6.91 Welded, 3 dks	**(A34A2GR) Refrigerated Cargo Ship** Ins: 5,468 Compartments: 3 Ho, ER 3 Ha: 3 (6.6 x 5.5)ER Derricks: 6x5t	**1 oil engine** driving 1 FP propeller Total Power: 5,869kW (7,979hp) 16.8kn Mitsubishi 7UEC45HA 1 x 2 Stroke 7 Cy. 450 x 1150 5869kW (7979bhp) Akasaka Tekkosho KK (Akasaka DieselLtd)-Japan AuxGen: 2 x 680kW 445V 60Hz a.c Fuel: 1122.0 (r.f.) 27.0pd
16686 *IC*	**WIND LIFT 1** **Ocean Breeze Energy GmbH & Co KG** Wulf Seetransporte GmbH & Co KG SatCom: Inmarsat C 421831910 *Cuxhaven* *Germany* MMSI: 218319000 Official number: 1039	**7,962** 2,388 2,623	Class: GL	**2010-02 UAB Vakaru Laivu Remontas (JSC Western Shiprepair) — Klaipeda** Yd No: 34 Loa 93.86 Br ex - Dght 4.000 Lbp 85.50 Br md 36.00 Dpth 7.40 Welded, 1 dk	**(B22A2ZM) Offshore Construction Vessel, jack up** Single Hull Cranes: 1x500t	**4 diesel electric oil engines** driving 4 gen. each 1520kW a.c Connecting to 4 elec. motors each (1100kW) driving 2 Azimuth electric drive units 2 propellers aft. 2 fwd Total Power: 6,660kW (9,056hp) 8.0kn Wartsila 9L20 4 x 4 Stroke 9 Cy. 200 x 280 each-1665kW (2264bhp) Thrusters: 2 Directional thruster (f)

8020642 *2FYA5* -	**WIND PERFECTION** *ex* Julia *-2012* *ex* Christian IV *-2008* *ex* Bayard *-1990* *ex* Olau Britannia *-1990* **C-Bed III BV** - *London* *United Kingdom* MMSI: 235095204 Official number: 740495	**22,161** Class: RI (NV) (GL) 8,921 2,880	**1982-05 AG Weser Seebeckwerft — Bremerhaven** Yd No: 1031 Converted From: Ferry (Passenger/Vehicle)-2013 Loa 154.48 (BB) Br ex 24.24 Dght 5.820 Lbp 136.02 Br md 24.21 Dpth 13.60 Welded, 4 dks	**(B22A2ZA) Accommodation Ship** Passengers: berths: 150 Bow door & ramp (centre) Len: 9.95 Wid: 6.68 Swl: - Stern door/ramp (p) Len: 5.56 Wid: 6.16 Swl: - Stern door/ramp (s) Len: 5.56 Wid: 6.16 Swl: - Ice Capable	**4 oil engines** sr geared to sc. shafts driving 2 CP propellers Total Power: 15,300kW (20,800hp) 17.5kr Pielstick 8PC2-5L-40(4 x 4 Stroke 8 Cy. 400 x 460 each-3825kW (5200bhp) Blohm + Voss AG-West Germany AuxGen: 2 x 1120kW 450V 60Hz a.c, 2 x 800kW 450V 60Hz a.c, 1 x 204kW 450V 60Hz a.c Thrusters: 2 Thwart. FP thruster (f) Fuel: 220.0 (d.f.) 700.0 (r.f.) 70.0pd
6918560 *2AR07* -	**WIND SOLUTION** *ex* Palau *-2008* *ex* Commodore *-2003* *ex* Stena Prince *-1999* *ex* Lion Prince *-1998* *ex* Europafarjan I *-1987* *ex* Stena Nordica *-1985* *ex* Prinsessan Christina *-1983* *ex* Safe Christina *-1982* *ex* Prinsessan Christina *-1981* **C-bed BV** - *London* *United Kingdom* MMSI: 235062382 Official number: 914317	**8,893** Class: RI (LR) 2,667 ✠ Classed LR until 13/5/99 1,845	**1969-12 Aalborg Vaerft A/S — Aalborg** Yd No: 180 Converted From: Ferry (Passenger/Vehicle)-2008 Loa 122.71 (BB) Br ex 19.61 Dght 5.250 Lbp 109.91 Br md 19.21 Dpth 12.60 Welded, 2 dks, 3rd dk clear of mchy. space	**(B22A2ZA) Accommodation Ship** Passengers: cabins: 476; berths: 1030 Stern door (centre) Lane-Len: 420 Ice Capable	**8 oil engines** with flexible couplings & sr geared to sc. shafts driving 2 CP propellers Total Power: 10,328kW (14,040hp) 20.5kn Polar SF112VS-E 8 x Vee 4 Stroke 12 Cy. 250 x 300 each-1291kW (1755bhp) AB NOHAB-Sweden AuxGen: 3 x 736kW 380V 50Hz a.c Thrusters: 1 Thwart. CP thruster (f) Fuel: 339.5 (d.f.) 25.5pd
8603509 *C6CY9* -	**WIND SPIRIT** - **Wind Spirit Ltd** Windstar Cruises Ltd SatCom: Inmarsat C 430800417 *Nassau* *Bahamas* MMSI: 309056000 Official number: 711121	**5,736** Class: BV 1,788 847	**1988-03 Societe Nouvelle des Ateliers et Chantiers du Havre — Le Havre** Yd No: 272 Loa 134.02 Br ex 15.83 Dght 4.101 Lbp 108.46 Br md 15.80 Dpth 9.30 Welded, 3 dks	**(A37A2PC) Passenger/Cruise** Passengers: cabins: 75; berths: 148	**3 diesel electric oil engines** driving 3 gen. each 1000kW a.c Connecting to 1 elec. Motor driving 1 CP propeller Total Power: 3,150kW (4,284hp) 11.0kn Wartsila 6R32E 3 x 4 Stroke 6 Cy. 320 x 350 each-1050kW (1428bhp) Wartsila Diesel Normed SA-France Thrusters: 1 Thwart. CP thruster (f) Fuel: 202.0 (d.f.) 6.0pd
8420878 *C6CA9* -	**WIND STAR** - **Wind Star Ltd** Windstar Cruises Ltd SatCom: Inmarsat C 430916320 *Nassau* *Bahamas* MMSI: 309163000 Official number: 710711	**5,703** Class: BV 1,710 922	**1986-10 Societe Nouvelle des Ateliers et Chantiers du Havre — Le Havre** Yd No: 269 Loa 134.02 Br ex 19.61 Dght 4.111 Lbp 108.46 Br md 15.80 Dpth 6.66 Welded, 3 dks	**(A37A2PC) Passenger/Cruise** Passengers: cabins: 74; berths: 159	**3 diesel electric oil engines** driving 3 gen. each 1000kW a.c Connecting to 1 elec. Motor driving 1 CP propeller Total Power: 3,150kW (4,284hp) 11.0kn Wartsila 6R22 3 x 4 Stroke 6 Cy. 220 x 240 each-1050kW (1428bhp) Wartsila Diesel Normed SA-France Thrusters: 1 Thwart. CP thruster (f) Fuel: 202.0 (d.f.) 6.0pd
7330260 - -	**WIND STAR** *ex* Dolphin III *-1997* *ex* Dolphin *-1993* *ex* Registro *-1991* **Amber Shipping Ltd** Ben-Tech Marine & Oil Services	**464** Class: (AB) 315 929	**1973 Mangone Shipbuilding Co. — Houston, Tx** Yd No: 110 Loa 56.39 Br ex - Dght 4.192 Lbp 51.69 Br md 11.59 Dpth 4.88 Welded, 1 dk	**(B21B20T) Offshore Tug/Supply Ship**	**2 oil engines** reverse reduction geared to sc. shafts driving 2 FP propellers Total Power: 4,286kW (5,828hp) 15.0kn EMD (Electro-Motive) 16-645-E7B 2 x Vee 2 Stroke 16 Cy. 230 x 254 each-2143kW (2914bhp) General Motors Corp.Electro-Motive Div.-La Grange AuxGen: 2 x 100kW 440V 60Hz a.c Thrusters: 1 Thwart. FP thruster (f) Fuel: 335.5 (d.f.) 25.5pd
9566148 *OWBZ2* -	**WIND SUPPLIER** - **DONG Energy Power A/S** DONG Energy A/S *Esbjerg* *Denmark (DIS)* MMSI: 219014012 Official number: A530	**173** Class: (BV) 51 52	**2010-01 A/S Hvide Sande Skibs- og Baadebyggeri — Hvide Sande** Yd No: 119 Loa 32.20 Br ex - Dght 1.700 Lbp 30.00 Br md 6.90 Dpth 3.45 Welded, 1 dk	**(B21A20C) Crew/Supply Vessel** Hull Material: Aluminium Alloy Passengers: unberthed: 24	**2 oil engines** reduction geared to sc. shafts driving 2 CP propellers Total Power: 2,880kW (3,916hp) 25.0kn M.T.U. 16V2000M72 2 x Vee 4 Stroke 16 Cy. 135 x 156 each-1440kW (1958bhp) MTU Friedrichshafen GmbH-Friedrichshafen Thrusters: 2 Retract. directional thruster (f)
8700785 *C6I06* -	**WIND SURF** *ex* Club Med 1 *-1997* *launched as* La Fayette *-1989* **Degrees Ltd** Windstar Cruises Ltd *Nassau* *Bahamas* MMSI: 309242000 Official number: 731037	**14,745** Class: BV 5,056 1,654	**1989-12 Societe Nouvelle des Ateliers et Chantiers du Havre — Le Havre** Yd No: 274 Loa 187.20 Br ex 20.02 Dght 5.010 Lbp 156.00 Br md 20.00 Dpth 13.90 Welded, 2 dks	**(A37A2PC) Passenger/Cruise** Passengers: cabins: 156; berths: 312	**4 diesel electric oil engines** driving 4 gen. each 2280kW a.c Connecting to 2 elec. motors each (1840kW) driving 2 CP propellers Total Power: 9,720kW (13,216hp) 15.0kn Wartsila 6R32E 4 x 4 Stroke 6 Cy. 320 x 350 each-2430kW (3304bhp) Moteurs Duvant Crepelle-France Thrusters: 1 Thwart. CP thruster (f); 1 Thwart. CP thruster (a) Fuel: 405.0 (d.f.)
6723903 *VM3508* -	**WINDALIA** - **Elder-Prince Marine Services Pty Ltd** - *Fremantle, WA* *Australia* Official number: 196968	*283* 224 -	**1967 John Franetovich & Co — Fremantle WA** Converted From: Landing Craft Loa 27.67 Br ex 8.26 Dght 1.677 Lbp 26.45 Br md 8.23 Dpth 1.83 Welded, 1 dk	**(B31A2SR) Research Survey Vessel** Winches: 1	**4 oil engines** driving 4 FP propellers Total Power: 368kW (500hp) 8.0kn Perkins T6.3544 4 x 4 Stroke 6 Cy. 98 x 127 each-92kW (125bhp) (new engine 1973) Rolls Royce Motors of Australia PtyLtd-Australia AuxGen: 2 x 1kW 24V d.c Fuel: 20.5 (d.f.) 1.0pd
7433919 *UHPN* -	**WINDANCE** *ex* Vindans *-2007* *ex* Windance *-1993* **OOO Rybolovnaya Kompaniya 'Vostochnaya Ekspeditsiya' (Eastern Expedition Fishing Co Ltd)** - SatCom: Inmarsat M 627302310 *Petropavlovsk-Kamchatskiy* *Russia* MMSI: 273849410 Official number: 763434	**824** Class: (RS) (AB) 284 757	**1976-09 Halter Marine, Inc. — Moss Point, Ms** Yd No: 521 Converted From: Offshore Supply Ship-1988 Loa 54.10 Br ex 12.19 Dght 3.470 Lbp 51.30 Br md 12.15 Dpth 4.27 Welded, 1 dk	**(B11B2FV) Fishing Vessel** Ins: 375	**2 oil engines** reverse reduction geared to sc. shafts driving 2 FP propellers Total Power: 2,220kW (3,018hp) 12.0kn EMD (Electro-Motive) 12-645-E6 2 x Vee 2 Stroke 12 Cy. 230 x 254 each-1110kW (1509bhp) General Motors Corp.Electro-Motive Div.-La Grange AuxGen: 2 x 150kW a.c Fuel: 265.0 (d.f.)
9574913 *2ELU3* -	**WINDCAT 101** - **Windcat Workboats BV** - SatCom: Inmarsat C 424656711 *Fleetwood* *United Kingdom* Official number: 917555	**208** Class: NV 63 30	**2010-12 Bloemsma Van Breemen Shipyard — Makkum** Yd No: 142 Loa 27.86 Br ex 9.32 Dght 1.580 Lbp 22.00 Br md 9.06 Dpth 3.76 Welded, 1 dk	**(B21A20C) Crew/Supply Vessel** Passengers: unberthed: 45	**4 oil engines** reduction geared to sc. shafts driving 2 CP propellers Total Power: 2,880kW (3,916hp) M.T.U. 8V2000M72 4 x Vee 4 Stroke 8 Cy. 135 x 156 each-720kW (979bhp) MTU Friedrichshafen GmbH-Friedrichshafen AuxGen: 2 x a.c Thrusters: 2 Tunnel thruster 1 (p) 1 (s)
9707376 *DHNN2* -	**WINDEA ONE** - **Schifffahrtsgesellschaft WINDEA CTV one GmbH & Co KG** WINDEA Offshore GmbH & Co KG *Emden* *Germany* MMSI: 211624330 Official number: 6191	**170** Class: BV 60 25	**2013-09 Damen Shipyards Singapore Pte Ltd — Singapore** (Hull) Yd No: (532521) **2013-09 B.V. Scheepswerf Damen — Gorinchem** Yd No: 532521 Loa 25.75 Br ex - Dght 2.200 Lbp 23.73 Br md 10.40 Dpth 3.50 Welded, 1 dk	**(B21A20C) Crew/Supply Vessel** Hull Material: Aluminium Alloy	**2 oil engines** reduction geared to sc. shafts driving 2 FP propellers Total Power: 1,640kW (2,230hp) 20.0kn Caterpillar C32 2 x Vee 4 Stroke 12 Cy. 145 x 162 each-820kW (1115bhp) Caterpillar Inc-USA AuxGen: 2 x 23kW 50Hz a.c Thrusters: 2 Tunnel thruster 1 (p) 1 (s) Fuel: 19.0 (d.f.)
9483061 *V7SK7* -	**WINDERMERE** - **Hallin Diving Services Ltd** Hallin Marine Singapore Pte Ltd *Majuro* *Marshall Islands* MMSI: 538003672 Official number: 3672	**4,750** Class: AB 1,425 2,408	**2010-05 Drydocks World - Singapore Pte Ltd — Singapore** Yd No: 196 Loa 79.80 (BB) Br ex - Dght 5.500 Lbp 72.35 Br md 20.40 Dpth 8.00 Welded, 1 dk	**(B22A20V) Diving Support Vessel** Cranes: 1x50t	**4 diesel electric oil engines** driving 4 gen. Connecting to 2 elec. motors each (2500kW) driving 2 Voith-Schneider propellers Total Power: 7,300kW (9,924hp) 10.0kn Caterpillar 3516B-TA 4 x Vee 4 Stroke 16 Cy. 170 x 190 each-1825kW (2481bhp) Caterpillar Inc-USA AuxGen: 1 x 590kW a.c Thrusters: 3 Tunnel thruster (f) Fuel: 900.0 (d.f.)

807662 *HA3428*	**WINDFROST** *ex* Wind Frost *-2013* *ex* Amer Everest *-2008* *ex* Hokkaido Rex *-1995* **Dream Faith SA** Lavinia Corp *Valletta* *Malta* MMSI: 229587000 Official number: 8807662	**9,072** 5,838 11,438	Class: LR (AB) (NK) **100A1** SS 08/2013 refrigerated cargo ship **LMC** **Lloyd's RMC** Eq.Ltr: B†; Cable: 550.0/58.0 U2 (a)	**1989**-01 **Shin Kurushima Dockyard Co. Ltd. — Onishi** Yd No: 2605 Loa 148.50 (BB) Br ex - Dght 9.417 Lbp 140.00 Br md 20.60 Dpth 12.80 Welded, 1 dk, 2nd, 3rd & 4th dks in cargo holds only	**(A34A2GR) Refrigerated Cargo Ship** Double Bottom Entire Compartment Length Bale: 14,027; Ins: 14,027 Compartments: 4 Ho, ER, 4 Tw Dk 4 Ha: (10.0 x 7.5)3 (12.6 x 8.2)ER Derricks: 8x7t	**1 oil engine** driving 1 FP propeller Total Power: 6,863kW (9,331hp) 19.0kn Mitsubishi 6UEC52LA 1 x 2 Stroke 6 Cy. 520 x 1600 6863kW (9331bhp) Kobe Hatsudoki KK-Japan AuxGen: 3 x 560kW 440V 60Hz a.c Boilers: AuxB (Comp) 7.1kgf/cm² (7.0bar) Fuel: 108.3 (d.f.) 905.5 (r.f.) 22.4pd
948603 *VDF8688*	**WINDHAM BAY** *ex* Traci-C *-2013* - - *Petersburg, AK* *United States of America* MMSI: 367497490 Official number: 615434	*141* 98 -		**1979 Desco Marine — Saint Augustine, Fl** Yd No: 286-F L reg 20.85 Br ex 6.74 Dght - Lbp - Br md - Dpth 3.74 Bonded, 1 dk	**(B11A2FS) Stern Trawler** Hull Material: Reinforced Plastic	**1 oil engine** geared to sc. shaft driving 1 FP propeller Total Power: 268kW (364hp) Cummins KT-1150-M 1 x 4 Stroke 6 Cy. 159 x 159 268kW (364bhp) Cummins Engine Co Inc-USA
404769 *JOY*	**WINDO** *ex* Dano *-2011* **Ab Kotka Fiskeri - Kotkan Kalastus Oy** - *Kemio* *Finland* MMSI: 230012000 Official number: 12682	**526** 115 324		**1985**-11 **Kalmar Fartygsreparationer AB — Kalmar** Yd No: 465 Loa 33.66 Br ex 8.69 Dght 4.280 Lbp 30.03 Br md 8.62 Dpth 6.51 Welded, 1 dk	**(B11A2FS) Stern Trawler** Ins: 250	**1 oil engine** with flexible couplings & sr gearedto sc. shaft driving 1 CP propeller Total Power: 1,103kW (1,500hp) Deutz SBV6M628 1 x 4 Stroke 6 Cy. 240 x 280 1103kW (1500bhp) Kloeckner Humboldt Deutz AG-West Germany Thrusters: 1 Thwart. FP thruster (f)
109849 *JJY*	**WINDO** *ex* Orca *-2002* *ex* Troika *-1996* *ex* Trojka *-1986* *ex* Janne Vest *-1984* *ex* Eva Nordfisk *-1980* **Windo Fisk AB** - *Dragsfjard* *Finland*	**116** 35 -		**1960 Scheepsbouw- en Constructiebedr. K. Hakvoort N.V. — Monnickendam** (Hull) Yd No: 70 **1960 Karstensens Skibsvaerft A/S — Skagen** Loa 27.01 Br ex 6.30 Dght - Lbp - Br md 6.20 Dpth - Welded	**(B11B2FV) Fishing Vessel**	**1 oil engine** driving 1 FP propeller Total Power: 250kW (340hp) Alpha 405-FO 1 x 2 Stroke 5 Cy. 230 x 400 250kW (340bhp) Alpha Diesel A/S-Denmark
429500	**WINDROSE** *ex* Tina M *-2005* *ex* Aya *-1996* *ex* Ritena *-1993* *ex* Marine *-1991* *ex* Mariner *-1988* *ex* Windrose *-1987* *ex* Hedwig Lunstedt *-1963* - -	**428** 235 630	Class: (HR) (GL)	**1955**-01 **Schiffswerft W. Holst — Hamburg** Yd No: 196 Lengthened-1956 Loa 52.84 Br ex 8.41 Dght 3.201 Lbp 48.04 Br md 8.39 Dpth 3.54 Riveted\Welded, 1 dk	**(A31A2GX) General Cargo Ship** Grain: 911; Bale: 842 Compartments: 2 Ho, ER 2 Ha: (10.8 x 5.0) (15.0 x 5.0)ER Ice Capable	**1 oil engine** driving 1 FP propeller Total Power: 221kW (300hp) 9.0kn MaK MAU423 1 x 4 Stroke 8 Cy. 290 x 420 221kW (300bhp) Maschinenbau Kiel AG (MaK)-Kiel
986107 *VZT*	**WINDROSE OF AMSTERDAM** *ex* Windrose *-2004* **Windrose Charter BV** - *Willemstad* *Curacao* MMSI: 306753000	**139** 41 -	Class: AB	**2002**-02 **Holland Jachtbouw B.V. — Zaandam** Yd No: 023 Loa 46.31 Br ex 8.06 Dght 4.340 Lbp 29.30 Br md 8.00 Dpth 3.54 Welded, 1 dk	**(X11A2YS) Yacht (Sailing)** Hull Material: Aluminium Alloy	**1 oil engine** geared to sc. shaft driving 1 Propeller Total Power: 313kW (426hp) Lugger L6125A 1 x 4 Stroke 6 Cy. 125 x 150 313kW (426bhp) Alaska Diesel Electric Inc-USA
808334 *X6242*	**WINDRUNNER** *ex* Ruby K. II *-1978* **Windrunner Fisheries Inc** - *Coos Bay, OR* *United States of America* Official number: 504039	*147* 100 -		**1966 Rush & Bryan — Freeport, Tx** L reg 21.71 Br ex 6.86 Dght - Lbp - Br md - Dpth 3.54 Welded, 1 dk	**(B11B2FV) Fishing Vessel**	**1 oil engine** driving 1 FP propeller Total Power: 279kW (379hp)
128879 *VAW*	**WINDSOR** **Orange Maritime Pte Ltd** Executive Ship Management Pte Ltd SatCom: Inmarsat C 456388110 *Singapore* *Singapore* MMSI: 563881000 Official number: 387030	**5,953** 1,786 6,987 T/cm 18.8	Class: NK	**1996**-01 **Shin Kochi Jyuko K.K. — Kochi** Yd No: 7075 Loa 119.02 (BB) Br ex 18.83 Dght 6.627 Lbp 112.00 Br md 18.80 Dpth 9.00 Welded, 1 dk	**(A11B2TG) LPG Tanker** Double Bottom Entire Compartment Length Liq (Gas): 6,505 3 x Gas Tank (s); 3 independent cyl horizontal 3 Cargo Pump (s): 3x400m³/hr Manifold: Bow/CM: 68m	**1 oil engine** driving 1 FP propeller Total Power: 4,531kW (6,160hp) 15.0kn B&W 7L35MC 1 x 2 Stroke 7 Cy. 350 x 1050 4531kW (6160bhp) Hitachi Zosen Corp-Japan AuxGen: 3 x 363kW a.c Fuel: 124.0 (d.f.) 632.0 (r.f.)
439959 *EPT5*	**WINDSOR ADVENTURE** **Ocean Excel Shipholding SA** Fednav Ltd *Panama* *Panama* MMSI: 372454000 Official number: 3382308A	**31,247** 18,504 55,975 T/cm 55.8	Class: NV (NK)	**2008**-03 **Mitsui Eng. & SB. Co. Ltd. — Tamano** Yd No: 1666 Loa 189.99 (BB) Br ex 32.29 Dght 12.550 Lbp 182.00 Br md 32.26 Dpth 17.90 Welded, 1 dk	**(A21A2BC) Bulk Carrier** Grain: 70,811; Bale: 68,044 Compartments: 5 Ho, ER 5 Ha: 4 (21.1 x 18.9)ER (17.6 x 18.9) Cranes: 4x30.5t	**1 oil engine** driving 1 FP propeller Total Power: 9,480kW (12,889hp) 14.5kn MAN-B&W 6S50MC-C 1 x 2 Stroke 6 Cy. 500 x 2000 9480kW (12889bhp) Mitsui Engineering & Shipbuilding CLtd-Japan AuxGen: 3 x a.c
419957 *MJA*	**WINDSOR CASTLE** *ex* Fingal *-2000* **Tamahine Investments Ltd** SatCom: Inmarsat A 1440341 *London* *United Kingdom* MMSI: 235000737 Official number: 305299	**1,268** 380 619	Class: (LR) ✠ Classed LR until 12/64	**1964**-01 **Blythswood SB. Co. Ltd. — Glasgow** Yd No: 140 Loa 72.85 Br ex 12.30 Dght 4.186 Lbp 65.54 Br md 12.20 Dpth 5.64 Riveted\Welded, 1 dk, 2nd dk except in mchy. space	**(B34Q2QX) Lighthouse Tender** Compartments: 2 Ho, ER 2 Ha: (3.6 x 3.6) (3.5 x 2.4) Derricks: 1x12t,1x6t,4x3t	**2 oil engines** driving 2 FP propellers Total Power: 1,766kW (2,402hp) Polar MN16S 2 x 2 Stroke 6 Cy. 340 x 570 each-883kW (1201bhp) British Polar Engines Ltd.-Glasgow AuxGen: 3 x 90kW 220V d.c
416115 *LEE7*	**WINDSOR KNUTSEN** *launched as* Windsor *-2007* **KNOT Shuttle Tankers 18 AS** Knutsen OAS Shipping AS SatCom: Inmarsat C 425893110 *Haugesund* *Norway (NIS)* MMSI: 258931000	**88,704** 51,210 162,258 T/cm 126.6	Class: NV	**2007**-05 **Daewoo Shipbuilding & Marine Engineering Co Ltd — Geoje** Yd No: 5274 Converted From: Crude Oil/Products Tanker-2011 Loa 280.50 (BB) Br ex 50.06 Dght 16.524 Lbp 270.00 Br md 50.00 Dpth 23.00 Welded, 1 dk	**(A13A2TS) Shuttle Tanker** Double Hull (13F) Liq: 176,118; Liq (Oil): 176,118 Cargo Heating Coils Compartments: 12 Wing Ta, 2 Wing Slop Ta, Wing ER 3 Cargo Pump (s): 3x3700m³/hr Manifold: Bow/CM: 136.3m Ice Capable	**1 oil engine** driving 1 CP propeller Total Power: 21,770kW (29,598hp) 15.5kn MAN-B&W 7S70ME-C 1 x 2 Stroke 7 Cy. 700 x 2800 21770kW (29598bhp) Doosan Engine Co Ltd-South Korea AuxGen: 3 x 1040kW a.c Thrusters: 1 Tunnel thruster (f) Fuel: 255.0 (d.f.) 3950.0 (r.f.)
135545 *DHJ5*	**WINDSTAR** *ex* Don Eugenio *-2012* *ex* Shinho Maru *-1977* **Matsya Shipping Lines Corp** - *Manila* *Philippines* Official number: MNLD001966	*1,000* 683 1,533		**1969**-10 **Higaki Zosen K.K. — Imabari** Yd No: 102 Loa 60.89 Br ex 9.81 Dght 4.928 Lbp 55.78 Br md 9.78 Dpth 5.01 Welded, 2 dks	**(A31A2GX) General Cargo Ship** Grain: 2,145; Bale: 1,913 Compartments: 1 Ho, ER 1 Ha: (28.0 x 6.4)ER Derricks: 2x5t	**1 oil engine** driving 1 FP propeller Total Power: 1,030kW (1,400hp) 12.0kn Makita FSHC633 1 x 4 Stroke 6 Cy. 330 x 500 1030kW (1400bhp) Makita Tekkosho-Japan AuxGen: 2 x 56kW 225V a.c Fuel: 99.5 2.0pd
134494 *HL6*	**WINDSTAR** *ex* Athene *-2006* *ex* Wani Star *-2005* *ex* Star *-2002* *completed as* Huberna *-1991* **Torso Rederi AB** M Hannestad AS *Bergen* *Norway (NIS)* MMSI: 257943000	**2,237** 1,215 3,278	Class: RI (GL)	**1991**-12 **Schiffswerft und Maschinenfabrik Cassens GmbH — Emden** Yd No: 186 Loa 82.65 (BB) Br ex 12.62 Dght 5.285 Lbp 79.10 Br md 12.60 Dpth 6.65 Welded, 1 dk	**(A31A2GX) General Cargo Ship** Grain: 4,248 TEU 138 C.Ho 93/20' C.Dk 45/20' incl. 8 ref C. Compartments: 1 Ho, ER 1 Ha: (54.0 x 10.3)ER Ice Capable	**1 oil engine** sr reverse geared to sc. shaft driving 1 FP propeller Total Power: 1,100kW (1,496hp) 11.0kn Deutz SBV8M628 1 x 4 Stroke 8 Cy. 240 x 280 1100kW (1496bhp) Motoren Werke Mannheim AG (MWM)-Mannheim AuxGen: 2 x 128kW 220/380V a.c Thrusters: 1 Thwart. FP thruster (f) Fuel: 130.0 (d.f.) 6.0pd
162083 *MCL7*	**WINDSTAR 2** **Satun Shipping Sdn Bhd** Harbour-Link Marine Services Sdn Bhd *Port Klang* *Malaysia* Official number: 327321	**138** - -	Class: NV	**1996**-11 **Super-Light Shipbuilding Contractor — Sibu** Yd No: 24 Loa 23.80 Br ex - Dght - Lbp 21.30 Br md 7.60 Dpth 3.70 Welded, 1 dk	**(B32A2ST) Tug**	**2 oil engines** geared to sc. shafts driving 2 FP propellers Total Power: 744kW (1,012hp) 10.9kn Cummins KTA-19-M 2 x 4 Stroke 6 Cy. 159 x 159 each-372kW (506bhp) Cummins Engine Co Inc-USA AuxGen: 2 x 40kW 415V 50Hz a.c
157571 *MFJ*	**WINDU KARSA DWITYA** *ex* Ferry Senshu *-2007* **PT Windu Karsa** - *Jakarta* *Indonesia* MMSI: 525016187	**2,553** 766 400	Class: KI	**1997**-09 **K.K. Tachibana Senpaku Tekko — Anan** Yd No: 861 Loa 85.00 Br ex - Dght - Lbp 78.80 Br md 14.50 Dpth 5.70 Welded, 1 dk	**(A37B2PS) Passenger Ship**	**2 oil engines** driving 2 FP propellers Total Power: 5,884kW (8,000hp) Daihatsu 6DLM-40A 2 x 4 Stroke 6 Cy. 400 x 480 each-2942kW (4000bhp) Daihatsu Diesel Manufacturing Co Lt-Japan AuxGen: 2 x 560kW a.c

IMO / Call sign	Name / Owner	Tonnage	Classification	Build / Dimensions	Type	Machinery	Speed
8510350 *YGIO* -	**WINDU KARSA PRATAMA** *ex* Ikuho *-1999* **PT Windu Karsa** *Jakarta* *Indonesia* MMSI: 525015491	*3,123* 937 903	Class: KI	**1985**-11 **Shinhama Dockyard Co. Ltd. — Anan** Yd No: 763 Loa 89.95 Br ex - Dght 4.001 Lbp 84.31 Br md 16.62 Dpth 5.52 Welded, 2 dks	**(A36A2PR) Passenger/Ro-Ro Ship (Vehicles)** Passengers: unberthed: 760 Bow door/ramp Len: 5.10 Wid: 5.30 Swl: - Stern door/ramp Len: 4.19 Wid: 5.80 Swl: - Lane-Len: 300 Lane-clr ht: 4.45 Trailers: 30	**4 oil engines** sr reverse geared to sc. shafts driving 2 FP propellers Total Power: 5,296kW (7,200hp) Daihatsu 4 x 4 Stroke 6 Cy. 280 x 360 each-1324kW (1800bhp) Daihatsu Diesel Manufacturing Co Lt-Japan Thrusters: 1 Thwart. CP thruster (f)	17.5k 6DLM-2
7227695 - -	**WINDWARD** *ex* Windward Vf *-2009* *ex* N. R. Junction *-2009* **Cygnet Bay Sales Pty Ltd** -	*202* 136 -		**1972 Australian Shipbuilding Industries (WA) Pty Ltd — Fremantle WA** Yd No: 122 Converted From: Trawler-2013 L reg 23.32 Br ex 6.84 Dght - Lbp 23.32 Br md - Dpth 3.92 Welded, 1 dk	**(X11A2YP) Yacht**	**1 oil engine** driving 1 FP propeller Total Power: 313kW (426hp) Caterpillar 1 x 4 Stroke 6 Cy. 159 x 203 313kW (426bhp) Caterpillar Tractor Co-USA	10.0k D353SCA
7365679 *HO2459* -	**WINDWARD** *ex* Furore *-2010* *ex* Telco Torres *-2001* *ex* Deo Volente II *-1991* **Carina Offshore Ltd** *Panama* *Panama* MMSI: 372528000 Official number: 3396008A	**235** 70 -	Class: (BV)	**1974**-11 **Holland Launch B.V. — Zaandam** Yd No: 531 Converted From: Trawler-1993 Loa 34.78 Br ex 7.57 Dght 3.753 Lbp 30.87 Br md 7.50 Dpth 4.02 Welded, 1 dk	**(B22G20Y) Standby Safety Vessel**	**1 oil engine** driving 1 FP propeller Total Power: 908kW (1,235hp) Kromhout 1 x 4 Stroke 9 Cy. 240 x 260 908kW (1235bhp) Stork Werkspoor Diesel BV-Netherlands Fuel: 65.0 (d.f.)	10.0k 9F/SW24
5407502 - -	**WINDWARD** *ex* Nordfjord 1 *-1991* **Equity Chambers** -	**924** 363 -	Class: (NV)	**1963 Aukra Bruk AS — Aukra** Yd No: 17 Loa 57.31 Br ex 11.38 Dght 3.506 Lbp 50.22 Br md 11.35 Dpth 4.30 Welded, 1 dk	**(A36A2PR) Passenger/Ro-Ro Ship (Vehicles)** Passengers: unberthed: 290; berths: 60 Lane-Len: 96 Compartments: 1 Ho, ER 1 Ha: (6.4 x 2.5)ER Cranes: 1x10t,1x3t	**2 oil engines** driving 2 FP propellers Total Power: 1,472kW (2,002hp) Normo 2 x 4 Stroke 8 Cy. 250 x 300 each-736kW (1001bhp) AS Bergens Mek Verksteder-Norway AuxGen: 2 x 152kW 220V 50Hz a.c Thrusters: 1 Thwart. FP thruster (f) Fuel: 132.0 (d.f.)	13.0k LSMC-8
8856314 *WDC5268* -	**WINDWARD** *ex* Rebel *-2001* **Point Five Inc** *Warrendale, OR* *United States of America* Official number: 931898	*137* 101 -		**1988**-01 **Samish Maritime, Inc. — Edison, Wa** Yd No: 1 Loa - Br ex - Dght - Lbp 25.09 Br md 6.76 Dpth 2.04 Welded, 1 dk	**(B11B2FV) Fishing Vessel**	**1 oil engine** driving 1 FP propeller	
8953112 - -	**WINDY WEATHER** **McLaughlin Marine Services Inc** *Kingston* *Jamaica* Official number: JMF04007	*121* 97 -		**1987 Steiner Shipyard, Inc. — Bayou La Batre, Al** Yd No: 260 L reg 22.86 Br ex - Dght - Lbp - Br md 6.70 Dpth 3.35 Welded, 1 dk	**(B11B2FV) Fishing Vessel**	**1 oil engine** geared to sc. shaft driving 1 FP propeller Total Power: 268kW (364hp) Cummins 1 x 4 Stroke 6 Cy. 159 x 159 268kW (364bhp) Cummins Engine Co Inc-USA	9.0k KT-19-M
8808707 *3EYH6* -	**WINE TRADER** *ex* Duch Mate *-2012* **Rubia BV** Sicilship Srl *Panama* *Panama* MMSI: 373552000 Official number: 43450PEXTF	**4,297** 1,799 6,259 T/cm 15.0	Class: LR ✠ **100A1** SS 08/2009 Doubel Hull chemical tanker, Ship Type 2 CR (s.stl) SG 1.86, all tanks ESP LI Ice Class 1D at a maximum draught of 6.35m Max/min draughts fwd 6.6/n.a Max/min draughts aft 2.75/n.a Power required 1369kw, power installed 3375kw ✠ **LMC** **UMS** Eq.Ltr: U; Cable: 495.0/46.0 U3 (a)	**1989**-08 **Verolme Scheepswerf Heusden B.V. — Heusden** Yd No: 1016 Converted From: Chemical/Products Tanker-2012 Lengthened-1998 Loa 118.02 Br ex 17.10 Dght 6.210 Lbp 111.23 Br md 17.00 Dpth 8.70 Welded, 1 dk	**(A12A2TC) Chemical Tanker** Double Hull (13F) Liq: 6,384; Liq (Oil): 9,761 Compartments: 18 Wing Ta, 2 Wing Slop Ta, ER 18 Cargo Pump (s): 18x100m³/hr Manifold: Bow/CM: 67.2m Ice Capable	**1 oil engine** with flexible couplings & sr reverse geared to sc. shaft driving 1 CP propeller Total Power: 3,375kW (4,589hp) Wartsila 1 x 4 Stroke 9 Cy. 320 x 350 3375kW (4589bhp) Wartsila Diesel Oy-Finland AuxGen: 1 x 515kW 440V 60Hz a.c, 2 x 375kW 440V 60Hz a.c Boilers: 2 TOH (o.f.) 10.2kgf/cm² (10.0bar), TOH (ex.g.) 10.2kgf/cm² (10.0bar) Thrusters: 1 Thwart. FP thruster (f) Fuel: 64.0 (d.f.) 302.0 (r.f.)	15.0kn 9R32D
9269166 *3DWO* -	**WINFULL 6** **Wistar Fiji Ltd** *Suva* *Fiji*	**158** 47 84	Class: (BV)	**2001 Zhoushan Zhentai Shipbuilding — Zhoushan ZJ** Yd No: D02 Loa 29.77 Br ex - Dght 3.000 Lbp 26.40 Br md 6.40 Dpth 3.00 Welded, 1 dk	**(B11B2FV) Fishing Vessel**	**1 oil engine** reduction geared to sc. shaft driving 1 FP propeller Total Power: 447kW (608hp) Cummins 1 x 4 Stroke 6 Cy. 159 x 159 447kW (608bhp) Chongqing Cummins Engine Co Ltd-China AuxGen: 2 x 200kW	KTA-19-M3
9256743 *VRXD8* -	**WING DART** **World Hero International Ltd** *Hong Kong* *Hong Kong* MMSI: 477911000 Official number: HK-0723	**897** 303 1,073	Class: CC	**2001**-08 **Guangdong Jiangmen Shipyard Co Ltd — Jiangmen GD** Yd No: 015A Loa 49.96 Br ex - Dght 2.800 Lbp 48.60 Br md 13.00 Dpth 4.75 Welded, 1 dk	**(A33A2CC) Container Ship (Fully Cellular)** Grain: 4,156; Bale: 4,156 TEU 160 Compartments: 1 Cell Ho, ER 1 Ha: (37.1 x 10.2)ER	**2 oil engines** geared to sc. shafts driving 2 FP propellers Total Power: 668kW (908hp) Cummins 2 x 4 Stroke 6 Cy. 159 x 159 each-334kW (454bhp) Chongqing Cummins Engine Co Ltd-China AuxGen: 1 x 64kW 400V a.c, 1 x 50kW 400V a.c	9.2kn KTA-19-M
8953784 - -	**WING LEE 12** *ex* Chen Da 509 *-1997* - -	**1,562** 1,015 -		**1996 Nanchang Shipyard — Nanchang JX** L reg 75.80 Br ex - Dght - Lbp - Br md 13.38 Dpth 5.48 Welded, 1 dk	**(A31A2GX) General Cargo Ship**	**2 oil engines** driving 2 FP propellers Total Power: 1,102kW (1,498hp) Chinese Std. Type 2 x 4 Stroke each-551kW (749bhp) in China	15.0kn
8933394 -	**WING LEE 22** - -	**606** 218 -		**1996**-11 **Nanchang Shipyard — Nanchang JX** Loa - Br ex - Dght 2.910 Lbp 46.50 Br md 10.50 Dpth 4.30 Welded, 1 dk	**(A31A2GX) General Cargo Ship**	**2 oil engines** driving 2 FP propellers Total Power: 1,104kW (1,500hp) Chinese Std. Type 2 x 4 Stroke 6 Cy. 300 x 380 each-552kW (750bhp) Ningbo Zhonghua Dongli PowerMachinery Co Ltd -China	6300
8933382 - -	**WING LEE 128** - -	**1,562** 1,015 -		**1997 Wenzhou Zhongxing Shipyard — Wenzhou ZJ** Loa 75.80 Br ex - Dght - Lbp - Br md 13.38 Dpth 5.48 Welded, 1 dk	**(A31A2GX) General Cargo Ship**	**2 oil engines** driving 2 FP propellers Total Power: 1,102kW (1,498hp)	
9121819 - -	**WING LEE No. 21** **Wing Lee Ltd** *Zhuhai, Guangdong* *China*	**1,348** 608 2,472	Class: (CC)	**1994**-12 **Qidong Fishing Vessel Shipyard — Qidong JS** Loa 53.64 Br ex - Dght 4.040 Lbp 51.50 Br md 17.07 Dpth 4.97 Welded, 1 dk	**(A31A2GX) General Cargo Ship** Grain: 1,950 Compartments: 1 Ho, ER 1 Ha: ER	**2 oil engines** geared to sc. shafts driving 2 FP propellers Total Power: 820kW (1,114hp) Chinese Std. Type 2 x 4 Stroke 6 Cy. 200 x 225 each-410kW (557bhp) Weifang Diesel Engine Factory-China	16.0kn 6200Z
8632251 - -	**WING LUEN** **Willful Shipping Ltd**	**495** 198 -		**1988 Yuezhong Shipyard — Zhongshan GD** L reg 38.10 Br ex - Dght 2.600 Lbp - Br md 10.20 Dpth 4.08 Welded, 1 dk	**(A31A2GX) General Cargo Ship**	**1 oil engine** driving 1 FP propeller Total Power: 954kW (1,297hp) Caterpillar 1 x Vee 4 Stroke 12 Cy. 170 x 190 954kW (1297bhp) Caterpillar Inc-USA	10.5kn 3512TA
8955017 - -	**WING SANG 108** *ex* Min Yu 606 *-2002* - -	**488** 146 -		**1985 Dalian Fishing Vessel Co — Dalian LN** Loa 49.05 Br ex - Dght 3.500 Lbp 43.50 Br md 8.40 Dpth 3.85 Welded, 1 dk	**(B12B2FC) Fish Carrier**	**1 oil engine** driving 1 FP propeller Total Power: 956kW (1,300hp) Niigata 1 x 4 Stroke 956kW (1300bhp) Niigata Engineering Co Ltd-Japan	
8946781 - -	**WING SING** *ex* Yue Shan Tou 1003 *-1999* - -	**167** 80 -		**1996 Chaozhou Shipyard — Chaozhou GD** L reg 34.40 Br ex - Dght - Lbp - Br md 6.30 Dpth 3.40 Welded, 1 dk	**(A13B2TU) Tanker (unspecified)**	**2 oil engines** geared to sc. shafts driving 2 FP propellers Total Power: 220kW (300hp) Chinese Std. Type 2 x 4 Stroke 6 Cy. 135 x 140 each-110kW (150bhp) Shanghai Diesel Engine Co Ltd-China	6135

No.	Name / Owner	Tonnage	Class	Builder / Dimensions	Type / Cargo	Machinery
411888	**WINGER** *ex* Jackson 2 *-1970* *ex* Jaczon 2 *-1968* - -	*134* 41 -		**1963 NV Scheepsbouwwerf en Machinefabriek H de Haas — Maassluis** Yd No: 119 Loa 27.56 Br ex 6.33 Dght 3.048 Lbp 24.08 Br md 6.28 Dpth 3.20 Welded, 1 dk	**(B11A2FT) Trawler**	**1 oil engine** driving 1 FP propeller Total Power: 375kW (510hp) 10.0kn De Industrie 6D6 1 x 4 Stroke 6 Cy. 250 x 350 375kW (510bhp) NV Motorenfabriek 'De Industrie'-Netherlands
428702	**WINGER** *ex* Ponta Do Garajau *-2012* **Laurus Seaways Co Ltd** Prometheus Maritime Ltd	**187** 56 -	Class: RP (LR) ✠ Classed LR until 15/5/95	**1963-06 Estaleiros Navais do Mondego S.A. — Figueira da Foz** Yd No: 71 Loa 29.57 Br ex 8.11 Dght 3.353 Lbp 26.83 Br md 7.78 Dpth 3.89 Welded	**(B32A2ST) Tug**	**2 oil engines** with flexible couplings & sr geared to sc. shaft driving 1 CP propeller Total Power: 798kW (1,084hp) MWM TRH435S 2 x 4 Stroke 6 Cy. 250 x 350 each-399kW (542bhp) Motoren Werke Mannheim AG (MWM)-West Germany AuxGen: 2 x 70kW 110V
326172 *ITX* ID 210	**WINGS OF THE MORNING** **Alex McCarthy Shellfish** - *Wexford* *Irish Republic* MMSI: 250000264 Official number: 403809	**487** 146 450	Class: LR ✠ **100A1** SS 04/2010 fishing vessel **LMC** Cable: 222.4/22.0 U2 (a)	**2005-04 Stal-Rem SA — Gdansk** (Hull) Yd No: B333/2 **2005-04 Machinefabriek Padmos Stellendam B.V. — Stellendam** Yd No: 173 Loa 44.65 (BB) Br ex - Dght 2.500 Lbp 40.60 Br md 10.00 Dpth 3.10 Welded, 1 dk	**(B11B2FV) Fishing Vessel**	**2 oil engines** with clutches, flexible couplings & sr geared to sc. shafts driving 2 FP propellers Total Power: 662kW (900hp) 11.5kn Mitsubishi S6R-MPTA 2 x 4 Stroke 6 Cy. 170 x 180 each-331kW (450bhp) Mitsubishi Heavy Industries Ltd-Japan AuxGen: 1 x 590kW 400V 50Hz a.c, 1 x 64kW 400V 50Hz a.c Thrusters: 2 Thwart. FP thruster (f)
200457 *7TM8*	**WINGSAIL** *ex* Medi Trader *-2010* **Xiangfan Marine Co Ltd** COSCO Shanghai Ship Management Co Ltd (COSHIPMAN) SatCom: Inmarsat C 453834970 *Majuro* *Marshall Islands* MMSI: 538003834 Official number: 3834	**26,580** 16,450 48,220 T/cm 51.8	Class: BV	**1999-09 Oshima Shipbuilding Co Ltd — Saikai NS** Yd No: 10276 Loa 189.33 (BB) Br ex - Dght 11.730 Lbp 178.09 Br md 30.95 Dpth 16.40 Welded, 1 dk	**(A21A2BC) Bulk Carrier** Grain: 60,956; Bale: 59,778 Compartments: 5 Ho, ER 5 Ha: (17.1 x 15.6)2 (21.6 x 15.6)2 (19.8 x 15.6)ER Cranes: 4x30t	**1 oil engine** driving 1 FP propeller Total Power: 7,282kW (9,901hp) 15.0kn Mitsubishi 6UEC50LSII 1 x 2 Stroke 6 Cy. 500 x 1950 7282kW (9901bhp) Mitsubishi Heavy Industries Ltd-Japan
896455	**WINIFRED M** *ex* Jose Gregorio *-2010* *ex* Alice Austin *-2010* **Ira Matherson** -	*123* 83 -		**1975 in Venezuela** Loa 22.82 Br ex - Dght - Lbp - Br md 6.60 Dpth - Welded, 1 dk	**(A31A2GX) General Cargo Ship**	**1 oil engine** driving 1 FP propeller
650523 *WOJ3*	**WINJAYA** **Grazie Fortune Group Inc** An Nur Marine Services (M) Sdn Bhd *Kuching* *Malaysia* Official number: 334713	**295** 88 -	Class: BV	**2012-03 Sapor Shipbuilding Industries Sdn Bhd — Sibu** Yd No: SAPOR 77 Loa 30.00 Br ex - Dght 3.680 Lbp 27.62 Br md 9.00 Dpth 4.38 Welded, 1 dk	**(B32A2ST) Tug**	**2 oil engines** reduction geared to sc. shafts driving 2 FP propellers Total Power: 2,238kW (3,042hp) Cummins KTA-38-M2 2 x Vee 4 Stroke 12 Cy. 159 x 159 each-1119kW (1521bhp) Cummins Engine Co Ltd-United Kingdom AuxGen: 2 x 80kW 50Hz a.c Fuel: 300.0 (d.f.)
119488 *RBE7*	**WINLAND DALIAN** *ex* Platinum Sapphire *-2005* *ex* Izzet Incekara *-2004* *ex* Seaboard Panama *-1998* *ex* Izzet Incekara *-1998* *ex* Maersk Manila *-1998* *ex* Izzet Incekara *-1996* *ex* Emine Izzet *-1996* **Winland Dalian Shipping SA** Dalian Master Well Ship Management Co Ltd *Hong Kong* *Hong Kong* MMSI: 477998700 Official number: HK-1563	**8,944** 4,313 12,630 T/cm 22.4	Class: CC (GL) (AB)	**1996-06 Selah Makina Sanayi ve Ticaret A.S. — Tuzla, Istanbul** Yd No: 023 Loa 140.50 (BB) Br ex - Dght 8.638 Lbp 127.40 Br md 20.80 Dpth 11.70 Welded, 1 dk	**(A33A2CC) Container Ship (Fully Cellular)** Grain: 14,731; Bale: 14,731 TEU 860 C Ho 306 TEU C Dk 554 TEU incl 60 ref C. Compartments: 4 Cell Ho, ER 4 Ha: (12.6 x 12.8) (12.6 x 17.6)2 (25.2 x 17.6)ER Cranes: 2x40t,1x36t	**1 oil engine** with flexible couplings & sr gearedto sc. shaft driving 1 CP propeller Total Power: 5,430kW (7,383hp) 17.0kn Wartsila 6R46 1 x 4 Stroke 6 Cy. 460 x 580 5430kW (7383bhp) Wartsila Diesel Oy-Finland AuxGen: 1 x 480kW 380V 50Hz a.c, 3 x 360kW 380V 50Hz a.c Thrusters: 1 Thwart. FP thruster (f) Fuel: 326.0 (d.f.) 1091.0 (r.f.) 21.5pd
311479 *TPK*	**WINNER** **Chendur Sea Foods Ltd** - *Chennai* *India*	*155* 47 80	Class: (IR) (NV)	**1988-05 Australian Shipbuilding Industries (WA) Pty Ltd — Fremantle WA** Yd No: 262 Loa 24.95 Br ex 7.45 Dght 3.201 Lbp - Br md 7.42 Dpth 4.00 Welded, 1 dk	**(B11A2FT) Trawler** Ins: 110	**1 oil engine** with flexible couplings & sr gearedto sc. shaft driving 1 CP propeller Total Power: 372kW (506hp) Caterpillar 3412T 1 x Vee 4 Stroke 12 Cy. 137 x 152 372kW (506bhp) Caterpillar Inc-USA AuxGen: 2 x 50kW 415V 50Hz a.c
372305	**WINNER** *ex* Bunker *-2011* *ex* Barrier *-1990* *ex* Ulco *-1972* **SC F & M Bunkering Services Srl** - *Constanta* *Romania* Official number: 2821	**499** 222 605 T/cm 4.5	Class: (LR) ✠ Classed LR until 26/2/71	**1958-05 J. Pollock, Sons & Co. Ltd. — Faversham** Yd No: 2105 Loa 52.35 Br ex 10.42 Dght 2.530 Lbp 49.54 Br md 10.06 Dpth 3.20 Riveted\Welded, 1 dk	**(A13B2TP) Products Tanker** Liq: 671; Liq (Oil): 671 Cargo Heating Coils Compartments: 7 Ta, ER 2 Cargo Pump (s): 2x180m³/hr	**1 oil engine** driving 1 FP propeller Total Power: 368kW (500hp) 9.5kn Deutz RBV6M545 1 x 4 Stroke 6 Cy. 320 x 450 368kW (500bhp) Kloeckner Humboldt Deutz AG-West Germany Fuel: 20.5 2.0pd
138191	**WINNER** *ex* Razumnoye *-2007* - -	**649** 198 304	Class: (RS)	**1974-11 Khabarovskiy Sudostroitelnyy Zavod im Kirova — Khabarovsk** Yd No: 245 Loa 54.84 Br ex 9.38 Dght 3.810 Lbp 49.99 Br md 9.35 Dpth 4.73 Welded, 1 dk	**(B11A2FT) Trawler** Ins: 284 Compartments: 2 Ho, ER 2 Ha: 2 (1.5 x 1.6) Derricks: 1x3t Ice Capable	**1 oil engine** driving 1 FP propeller Total Power: 588kW (799hp) 11.7kn S.K.L. 8NVD48AU 1 x 4 Stroke 8 Cy. 320 x 480 588kW (799bhp) VEB Schwermaschinenbau "KarlLiebknecht" (SKL)-Magdeburg AuxGen: 3 x 100kW Fuel: 148.0 (d.f.)
140667 *VFJ6*	**WINNER** *ex* Ursula *-2013* **Golden Prime Maritime Pte Ltd** Glory Ship Management Pte Ltd *Singapore* *Singapore* MMSI: 565896000 Official number: 393426	**11,254** 4,831 16,927 T/cm 28.1	Class: LR (BV) **100A1** SS 06/2013 Double Hull oil and chemical tanker, Ship Type 2 ESP *IWS LI **LMC** **IGS**	**2008-06 Jiujiang Yinxing Shipbuilding Co Ltd — Xingzi County JX** Yd No: YX006 Loa 144.71 (BB) Br ex 23.24 Dght 8.800 Lbp 135.60 Br md 23.00 Dpth 12.52 Welded, 1 dk	**(A12B2TR) Chemical/Products Tanker** Double Hull (13F) Liq: 19,021; Liq (Oil): 18,812 Cargo Heating Coils Compartments: 12 Wing Ta, 2 Wing Slop Ta, ER 10 Cargo Pump (s): 10x500m³/hr Manifold: Bow/CM: 74.1m	**1 oil engine** driving 1 FP propeller Total Power: 4,437kW (6,033hp) 13.5kn MAN-B&W 6S35MC 1 x 2 Stroke 6 Cy. 350 x 1400 4437kW (6033bhp) (new engine 2008) STX Engine Co Ltd-South Korea AuxGen: 3 x a.c Thrusters: 1 Tunnel thruster (f) Fuel: 90.0 (d.f.) 670.0 (r.f.)
747276 *7UV* C2012_29	**WINNER 808** *ex* Win Far No. 808 *-2000* **Winner Maritime Ltd** *Victoria* *Seychelles* MMSI: 664626000 Official number: 50203	**630** 286 405		**2000-06 Sen Koh Shipbuilding Corp — Kaohsiung** Yd No: 123 Loa 59.20 Br ex - Dght 2.060 Lbp 50.80 Br md 9.00 Dpth 3.75 Welded, 1 dk	**(B11B2FV) Fishing Vessel**	**1 oil engine** driving 1 FP propeller Total Power: 1,030kW (1,400hp)
429965 *DER6*	**WINNER No. 1** **Andres Enterprises (HK) Ltd** - *San Lorenzo* *Honduras* Official number: L-1822883	*330* 175 -		**1986 Sali Shipbuilding Co., Ltd. — Province of Taiwan** L reg 37.94 Br ex - Dght 2.800 Lbp - Br md 6.50 Dpth 3.40 Welded, 1 dk	**(B11B2FV) Fishing Vessel**	**1 oil engine** driving 1 FP propeller 10.0kn
429977 *DER7*	**WINNER No. 2** *ex* Fortune Star II *-2000* **Andres Enterprises (HK) Ltd** - *San Lorenzo* *Honduras* Official number: L-1822881	*330* 174 -		**1986 Sali Shipbuilding Co., Ltd. — Province of Taiwan** L reg 37.94 Br ex - Dght 2.800 Lbp - Br md 6.50 Dpth 3.40 Welded, 1 dk	**(B11B2FV) Fishing Vessel**	**1 oil engine** driving 1 FP propeller 10.0kn
801852 *5U2601*	**WINNER S** *ex* Pomorie *-2009* **Winner Maritime Co Ltd Corp** TGS Shipping Services Ltd *Avatiu* *Cook Islands* MMSI: 518654000 Official number: 1690	**2,453** 990 3,262	Class: BR	**1983-02 Shipbuilding & Shiprepairing Yard 'Ivan Dimitrov' — Rousse** Yd No: 379 Loa 113.98 Br ex 13.21 Dght 3.790 Lbp 111.84 Br md 13.01 Dpth 5.52 Welded, 1 dk	**(A31A2GX) General Cargo Ship** Bale: 4,297 Compartments: 4 Ho, ER 4 Ha: (17.6 x 9.1)3 (18.1 x 9.1)ER Ice Capable	**2 oil engines** driving 2 FP propellers Total Power: 970kW (1,318hp) 10.8kn S.K.L. 6NVD48A-2U 2 x 4 Stroke 6 Cy. 320 x 480 each-485kW (659bhp) VEB Schwermaschinenbau "KarlLiebknecht" (SKL)-Magdeburg

Ship	Tonnage	Class	Builder / Dimensions	Type	Machinery
7356989 **WINNIE DES MASCAREIGNES** - - - -	*148* 40 41	Class: (LR) ✠ Classed LR until 25/11/77	**1976-06 Taylor Smith & Co. Ltd. — Port Louis (Mauritius)** Yd No: 18773 Loa 28.91 Br ex 8.03 Dght 2.763 Lbp 26.12 Br md 7.60 Dpth 3.43 Welded, 1 dk	**(B32A2ST) Tug**	**2 oil engines** reverse reduction geared to sc. shafts driving 2 FP propellers Total Power: 610kW (830hp) 10.0kr Kelvin TASC8 2 x 4 Stroke 8 Cy. 165 x 184 each-305kW (415bhp) GEC Diesels Ltd.Kelvin Marine Div.-Glasgow AuxGen: 2 x 40kW 400V 50Hz a.c
9617739 **WINNING ANGEL** *9V9095* - **Winning Angel Shipping Pte Ltd** Winning Alliance (S) Pte Ltd SatCom: Inmarsat C 456664910 *Singapore* *Singapore* MMSI: 566649000 Official number: 396625	**33,180** 19,294 58,799 T/cm 59.5	Class: CC	**2012-09 Nantong COSCO KHI Ship Engineering Co Ltd (NACKS) — Nantong JS** Yd No: 131 Loa 197.00 (BB) Br ex - Dght 12.650 Lbp 194.00 Br md 32.26 Dpth 18.10 Welded, 1 dk	**(A21A2BC) Bulk Carrier** Grain: 73,679; Bale: 70,963 Compartments: 5 Ho, ER 5 Ha: 4 (20.9 x 18.6)ER (18.3 x 18.6) Cranes: 4x30.5t	**1 oil engine** driving 1 FP propeller Total Power: 8,630kW (11,733hp) 14.5kr MAN-B&W 6S50MC-C8 1 x 2 Stroke 6 Cy. 500 x 2000 8630kW (11733bhp) Dalian Marine Diesel Co Ltd-China AuxGen: 3 x 500kW 450V a.c
9617741 **WINNING BRIGHT** *9V9096* - **Winning Bright Shipping Pte Ltd** Winning Alliance (S) Pte Ltd SatCom: Inmarsat C 456667710 *Singapore* *Singapore* MMSI: 566677000 Official number: 396626	**33,180** 19,294 58,756 T/cm 59.5	Class: CC	**2012-09 Nantong COSCO KHI Ship Engineering Co Ltd (NACKS) — Nantong JS** Yd No: 132 Loa 197.00 (BB) Br ex - Dght 12.650 Lbp 194.00 Br md 32.26 Dpth 18.10 Welded, 1 dk	**(A21A2BC) Bulk Carrier** Grain: 73,679; Bale: 70,963 Compartments: 5 Ho, ER 5 Ha: 4 (20.9 x 18.6)ER (18.3 x 18.6) Cranes: 4x30.5t	**1 oil engine** driving 1 FP propeller Total Power: 8,630kW (11,733hp) 14.5kr MAN-B&W 6S50MC-C8 1 x 2 Stroke 6 Cy. 500 x 2000 8630kW (11733bhp) Dalian Marine Diesel Co Ltd-China AuxGen: 3 x 500kW 450V a.c
9105322 **WINNING BROTHER** *3EZV5* *ex* Noni M *-2013* *ex* Cape Jacaranda *-2010* - **Graceful Shipping SA** Winning Shipping (HK) Co Ltd *Panama* *Panama* MMSI: 353667000 Official number: 4498613	**93,698** 61,307 185,777	Class: NK	**1995-06 Kawasaki Heavy Industries Ltd — Sakaide KG** Yd No: 1447 Loa 290.00 (BB) Br ex - Dght 18.480 Lbp 280.00 Br md 46.00 Dpth 25.00 Welded, 1 dk	**(A21A2BC) Bulk Carrier** Grain: 203,779 Compartments: 9 Ho, ER 9 Ha: (15.3 x 19.3)7 (15.3 x 21.2) (15.3 x 18.0)ER	**1 oil engine** driving 1 FP propeller Total Power: 15,373kW (20,901hp) 14.0kr B&W 7S70MC 1 x 2 Stroke 7 Cy. 700 x 2674 15373kW (20901bhp) Kawasaki Heavy Industries Ltd-Japan AuxGen: 3 x 610kW a.c Fuel: 4220.0 (r.f.)
9325001 **WINNING CONFIDENCE** *9V9664* *ex* Begonia *-2011* - **Winning Confidence Shipping Pte Ltd** Winning Shipping (HK) Co Ltd *Singapore* *Singapore* MMSI: 566311000 Official number: 397444	**90,091** 59,287 180,265 T/cm 121.0	Class: NK (KR)	**2005-02 Imabari Shipbuilding Co Ltd — Saijo EH (Saijo Shipyard)** Yd No: 8018 Loa 288.93 (BB) Br ex - Dght 18.170 Lbp 280.80 Br md 45.00 Dpth 24.70 Welded, 1 dk	**(A21A2BC) Bulk Carrier** Grain: 199,725 Compartments: 9 Ho, ER 9 Ha: 8 (15.7 x 20.8)ER (15.7 x 17.6)	**1 oil engine** driving 1 FP propeller Total Power: 18,630kW (25,329hp) 14.5kn B&W 6S70MC-C 1 x 2 Stroke 6 Cy. 700 x 2800 18630kW (25329bhp) Mitsui Engineering & Shipbuilding CLtd-Japan Fuel: 5670.0
9374088 **WINNING DILIGENCE** *9V6750* *ex* Regena N *-2012* - **Winning Diligence Shipping Pte Ltd** Winning Alliance (S) Pte Ltd *Singapore* *Singapore* MMSI: 566545000 Official number: 397912	**90,091** 59,287 180,277 T/cm 121.0	Class: NK (NV)	**2006-05 Imabari Shipbuilding Co Ltd — Saijo EH (Saijo Shipyard)** Yd No: 8054 Loa 288.93 (BB) Br ex - Dght 18.174 Lbp 280.80 Br md 45.00 Dpth 24.70 Welded, 1 dk	**(A21A2BC) Bulk Carrier** Grain: 199,725 Compartments: 9 Ho, ER 9 Ha: ER	**1 oil engine** driving 1 FP propeller Total Power: 18,630kW (25,329hp) 14.5kn MAN-B&W 6S70MC-C 1 x 2 Stroke 6 Cy. 700 x 2800 18630kW (25329bhp) Mitsui Engineering & Shipbuilding CLtd-Japan Fuel: 5670.0
9620188 **WINNING DRIVE** *WDG4948* - **Winning Way LLC** - *Fort Lauderdale, FL* *United States of America* MMSI: 367541760	**333** 99 62	Class: AB	**2012-02 Westport Shipyard, Inc. — Westport, Wa** Yd No: 4006 Loa 39.60 Br ex - Dght 1.650 Lbp 33.70 Br md 7.90 Dpth 3.75 Bonded, 1 dk	**(X11A2YP) Yacht** Hull Material: Reinforced Plastic	**2 oil engines** reduction geared to sc. shafts driving 2 FP propellers Total Power: 4,080kW (5,548hp) 20.0kn M.T.U. 12V4000M90 2 x Vee 4 Stroke 12 Cy. 165 x 190 each-2040kW (2774bhp) Detroit Diesel Corporation-Detroit, Mi AuxGen: 2 x 92kW a.c Fuel: 37.0 (d.f.)
9232058 **WINNING ENDURANCE** *9V5631* *ex* Bulk Asia *-2013* - **Winning Endurance Shipping Pte Ltd** Winning Alliance (S) Pte Ltd SatCom: Inmarsat C 456684511 *Singapore* *Singapore* MMSI: 566845000 Official number: 398448	**87,590** 56,834 170,578 T/cm 119.5	Class: NK (GL) (AB)	**2001-01 Sasebo Heavy Industries Co. Ltd. — Sasebo Yard, Sasebo** Yd No: 472 Loa 289.00 (BB) Br ex - Dght 17.976 Lbp 279.00 Br md 44.98 Dpth 24.40 Welded, 1 dk	**(A21A2BC) Bulk Carrier** Double Bottom Entire Compartment Length Grain: 190,153 Cargo Heating Coils Compartments: 9 Ho, ER 9 Ha: (17.1 x 20.2)Tappered 8 (15.4 x 21.3)ER	**1 oil engine** driving 1 FP propeller Total Power: 16,857kW (22,919hp) 14.5kn B&W 6S70MC 1 x 2 Stroke 6 Cy. 700 x 2674 16857kW (22919bhp) Mitsui Engineering & Shipbuilding CLtd-Japan AuxGen: 3 x 780kW 440V 60Hz a.c Fuel: 161.4 (d.f.) (Heating Coils) 4027.8 (r.f.) 58.0pd
9314076 **WINNING FAITH** *9V2157* *ex* Pacific Tiara *-2013* - **Winning Furtherance Shipping Pte Ltd** Winning Alliance (S) Pte Ltd *Singapore* *Singapore* MMSI: 566963000 Official number: 398682	**90,091** 59,287 180,310 T/cm 121.0	Class: NK	**2004-10 Koyo Dockyard Co Ltd — Mihara HS** Yd No: 2183 Loa 288.93 (BB) Br ex - Dght 18.170 Lbp 280.80 Br md 45.00 Dpth 24.70 Welded, 1 dk	**(A21A2BC) Bulk Carrier** Double Bottom Entire Compartment Length Grain: 199,725 Compartments: 9 Ho, ER 9 Ha: 8 (15.7 x 20.8)ER (15.7 x 17.6)	**1 oil engine** driving 1 FP propeller Total Power: 18,630kW (25,329hp) 14.5kn B&W 6S70MC-C 1 x 2 Stroke 6 Cy. 700 x 2800 18630kW (25329bhp) Mitsui Engineering & Shipbuilding CLtd-Japan AuxGen: 3 x 660kW 440/110V 60Hz a.c Fuel: 244.0 (d.f.) 4741.0 (r.f.) 44.7pd
9041215 **WINNING FRIEND** *3FQS5* *ex* Cape Europe *-2013* - **Fruitful Shipping SA** Qingdao Winning International Ships Management Co Ltd *Panama* *Panama* MMSI: 373115000 Official number: 4491013	**77,090** 47,175 152,034 T/cm 106.3	Class: CR NK (AB)	**1993-08 China Shipbuilding Corp (CSBC) — Kaohsiung** Yd No: 562 Loa 270.07 (BB) Br ex 43.40 Dght 17.575 Lbp 260.00 Br md 43.00 Dpth 23.00 Welded, 1 dk	**(A21A2BC) Bulk Carrier** Grain: 164,597; Bale: 162,730 Compartments: 9 Ho, ER 9 Ha: 9 (14.2 x 18.4)ER	**1 oil engine** driving 1 FP propeller Total Power: 12,607kW (17,140hp) 13.9kn B&W 5L80MCE 1 x 2 Stroke 5 Cy. 800 x 2592 12607kW (17140bhp) Hitachi Zosen Corp-Japan AuxGen: 2 x 700kW a.c Fuel: 3818.0
8748945 **WINNING NO. 8** *3DZK* - **Sunshine Fisheries Co Ltd** - *Suva* *Fiji* Official number: 000662	**193** 57 -		**2008-04 Huanghai Shipbuilding Co Ltd — Rongcheng SD** Loa 36.60 Br ex - Dght 2.600 Lbp - Br md 6.60 Dpth 3.30 Welded, 1 dk	**(B11B2FV) Fishing Vessel**	**1 oil engine** reduction geared to sc. shaft driving 1 Propeller Total Power: 377kW (513hp)
9677430 **WINNING PIONEER 1** *YDB4289* *ex* IM 2 *-2013* - **Winning Logistic Co Ltd** Winning Logistics Services Pte Ltd *Jakarta* *Indonesia* MMSI: 525021269	**248** 74 -	Class: BV	**2013-01 Fuzhou Cangshan Xiayang Shipyard — Fuzhou FJ** Yd No: EW2903 Loa 29.00 Br ex - Dght 3.900 Lbp 26.50 Br md 9.00 Dpth 4.25 Welded, 1 dk	**(B32A2ST) Tug**	**2 oil engines** reduction geared to sc. shafts driving 2 FP propellers Total Power: 1,768kW (2,404hp) Cummins KTA-38-M2 2 x Vee 4 Stroke 12 Cy. 159 x 159 each-884kW (1202bhp) Cummins Engine Co Ltd-United Kingdom AuxGen: 2 x 75kW 50Hz a.c Fuel: 200.0 (d.f.)
9677442 **WINNING PIONEER 2** *YDB4343* *ex* Im 3 *-2013* - **PT Winning Logistik Indonesia** Winning Logistics Services Pte Ltd *Jakarta* *Indonesia* MMSI: 525018098	**248** 74 -	Class: BV	**2013-01 Fuzhou Cangshan Xiayang Shipyard — Fuzhou FJ** Yd No: EW2904 Loa 29.00 Br ex - Dght 3.900 Lbp 26.50 Br md 9.00 Dpth 4.25 Welded, 1 dk	**(B32A2ST) Tug**	**2 oil engines** reduction geared to sc. shafts driving 2 FP propellers Total Power: 1,768kW (2,404hp) Cummins KTA-38-M2 2 x Vee 4 Stroke 12 Cy. 159 x 159 each-884kW (1202bhp) Cummins Engine Co Ltd-United Kingdom AuxGen: 2 x 75kW 50Hz a.c Fuel: 200.0 (d.f.)
9049841 **WINNY SEGARA LESTARI** - - **PT Capitol Nusantara Indonesia** - *Balikpapan* *Indonesia*	**280** 84 -	Class: KI	**2004-01 PT Segara Jaya Lestari — Balikpapan** Loa 32.00 Br ex - Dght 3.190 Lbp 29.73 Br md 9.00 Dpth 4.30 Welded, 1 dk	**(B32A2ST) Tug**	**2 oil engines** driving 2 Propellers Total Power: 2,420kW (3,290hp) Mitsubishi S12R-MPTK 2 x Vee 4 Stroke 12 Cy. 170 x 180 each-1210kW (1645bhp) Mitsubishi Heavy Industries Ltd-Japan AuxGen: 2 x 92kW 210V a.c
9255622 **WINONA** *DCHA2* *launched as* Vermontborg *-2004* - **ms 'Winona' Schiffahrts GmbH & Co Reederei KG** Intersee Schiffahrtsgesellschaft mbH & Co KG *Haren/Ems* *Germany* Official number: 5312	**6,361** 3,099 9,857 T/cm 18.3	Class: BV	**2004-02 Daewoo-Mangalia Heavy Industries S.A. — Mangalia** (Hull) Yd No: 1042 **2004-02 Bodewes Scheepswerf "Volharding" Foxhol B.V. — Foxhol** Yd No: 515 Loa 132.20 Br ex - Dght 7.750 Lbp 123.84 Br md 15.87 Dpth 11.15 Welded, 1 dk	**(A31A2GX) General Cargo Ship** Grain: 12,813 TEU 552 C. 552/20' Compartments: 2 Ho, ER 2 Ha: (52.5 x 13.2)ER (39.9 x 13.2) Ice Capable	**1 oil engine** geared to sc. shaft driving 1 CP propeller Total Power: 3,840kW (5,221hp) 15.0kn MaK 8M32C 1 x 4 Stroke 8 Cy. 320 x 480 3840kW (5221bhp) Caterpillar Motoren GmbH & Co. KG-Germany AuxGen: 2 x 285kW 450/230V 60Hz a.c, 1 x 640kW 400/230V 60Hz a.c Thrusters: 1 Thwart. CP thruster (f)

587934 OTD	**WINPOSH RAMPART** *ex* Posh Rampart *-2012* **PT Win Offshore** Posh Fleet Services Pte Ltd *Jakarta* *Indonesia* MMSI: 525003174 Official number: 571	**2,588** 776 2,448	Class: AB	**2012-05 PaxOcean Engineering (Zhuhai) Co Ltd — Zhuhai GD** Yd No: PY1005 Loa 71.50 Br ex - Dght 5.900 Lbp 61.20 Br md 16.60 Dpth 7.20 Welded, 1 dk	**(B21B20A) Anchor Handling Tug Supply**	**2 oil engines** reduction geared to sc. shafts driving 2 CP propellers Total Power: 5,884kW (8,000hp) 13.0kn MAN-B&W 8L27/38 2 x 4 Stroke 8 Cy. 270 x 380 each-2942kW (4000bhp) MAN Diesel A/S-Denmark AuxGen: 2 x 1200kW a.c, 2 x 425kW a.c Fuel: 760.0
709879 XR	**WINPOSH READY** *launched as* Posh Ready *-2014* **Starling Shipping Pte Ltd** POSH Semco Pte Ltd *Indonesia* MMSI: 525019668	**2,530** 759 2,605	Class: AB	**2014-03 PaxOcean Engineering (Zhuhai) Co Ltd — Zhuhai GD** Yd No: PX1022 Loa 70.50 Br ex - Dght 5.900 Lbp 61.20 Br md 16.60 Dpth 7.20 Welded, 1 dk	**(B21B20A) Anchor Handling Tug Supply**	**2 oil engines** reduction geared to sc. shafts driving 2 Propellers Total Power: 11,768kW (16,000hp) MaK 2 x each-5884kW (8000bhp) Caterpillar Motoren GmbH & Co. KG-Germany
650242 PT	**WINPOSH REGENT** *ex* Posh Value *-2013* **PT Win Offshore** Posh Fleet Services Pte Ltd *Jakarta* *Indonesia* MMSI: 525019656	**2,538** 761 2,591	Class: AB	**2010-07 Yuexin Shipbuilding Co Ltd — Guangzhou GD** Yd No: 3103 Loa 69.90 Br ex - Dght 4.500 Lbp 61.20 Br md 16.60 Dpth 7.20 Welded, 1 dk	**(B21B20T) Offshore Tug/Supply Ship** Cranes: 1x5t	**2 oil engines** reduction geared to sc. shafts driving 2 CP propellers Total Power: 5,844kW (7,946hp) 12.5kn MAN-B&W 8L27/38 2 x 4 Stroke 8 Cy. 270 x 380 each-2922kW (3973bhp) MAN Diesel A/S-Denmark AuxGen: 2 x 1200kW 440V 60Hz a.c, 2 x 370kW 440V 60Hz a.c Thrusters: 2 Thwart. CP thruster (f); 1 Thwart. CP thruster (a)
687946 UV	**WINPOSH RESOLVE** *ex* Posh Ranger *-2012* **PT Win Offshore** Posh Fleet Services Pte Ltd *Jakarta* *Indonesia* MMSI: 525003213 Official number: 3025	**2,588** 776 2,449	Class: AB	**2012-08 PaxOcean Engineering (Zhuhai) Co Ltd — Zhuhai GD** Yd No: PY1006 Loa 71.50 (BB) Br ex - Dght 5.900 Lbp 61.20 Br md 16.60 Dpth 7.20 Welded, 1 dk	**(B21B20A) Anchor Handling Tug Supply**	**2 oil engines** reduction geared to sc. shafts driving 2 CP propellers Total Power: 5,884kW (8,000hp) 13.0kn MAN-B&W 8L27/38 2 x 4 Stroke 8 Cy. 270 x 380 each-2942kW (4000bhp) AuxGen: 2 x 1200kW a.c, 2 x 425kW a.c Thrusters: 2 Tunnel thruster (f) Fuel: 760.0
208552 /5745	**WINSTAR CHAMPION** **TYS Marine Services Pte Ltd** Winstar Shipping Pte Ltd *Singapore* *Singapore* Official number: 388480	**161** 49 125	Class: GL	**1999-01 P.T. Wanamas Puspita Shipyard — Batam** Yd No: WPT01/97 Loa 23.38 Br ex - Dght - Lbp 22.99 Br md 7.60 Dpth 3.20 Welded, 1 dk	**(B32A2ST) Tug**	**2 oil engines** reduction geared to sc. shafts driving 2 FP propellers Total Power: 820kW (1,114hp) 11.0kn Caterpillar 3412TA 2 x Vee 4 Stroke 12 Cy. 137 x 152 each-410kW (557bhp) Caterpillar Inc-USA
992836 /6359	**WINSTAR GRACE** *ex* Bina Ocean 5 *-2007* **TYS Marine Services Pte Ltd** Winstar Shipping Pte Ltd *Singapore* *Singapore* Official number: 390195	**142** 43 120	Class: GL	**2003-08 Tuong Aik Shipyard Sdn Bhd — Sibu** Yd No: 2302 Loa 23.50 Br ex - Dght 2.661 Lbp - Br md 7.32 Dpth 3.20 Welded, 1 dk	**(B32A2ST) Tug**	**2 oil engines** geared to sc. shafts driving 2 FP propellers Total Power: 746kW (1,014hp) Cummins KT-19-M 2 x 4 Stroke 6 Cy. 159 x 159 each-373kW (507bhp) Cummins Engine Co Inc-USA
737001	**WINSTON** **PT Cahaya Bintang Borneo** - *Pontianak* *Indonesia*	**165** 50 -	Class: KI	**2008-07 CV Bina Citra — Pontianak** Loa 23.80 Br ex - Dght - Lbp 21.50 Br md 7.30 Dpth 3.60 Welded, 1 dk	**(B32A2ST) Tug**	**2 oil engines** driving 2 Propellers Total Power: 980kW (1,332hp) Mitsubishi S6A3-MPTK 2 x 4 Stroke 6 Cy. 150 x 175 each-490kW (666bhp) Mitsubishi Heavy Industries Ltd-Japan
641827 KQ	**WINSTON** **Longusta Trawling Co Pty Ltd** - *Cape Town* *South Africa* Official number: 350364	*166* 84 -		**1960 VEB Ernst Thaelmann-Werft — Brandenburg** Loa 28.48 Br ex 6.66 Dght - Lbp - Br md - Dpth 3.08 Welded, 1 dk	**(B11B2FV) Fishing Vessel**	**1 oil engine** driving 1 FP propeller
716124 YJ4	**WINTEC** *ex* Mulberry *-2002* **Suntec Maritime Ltd** Shanghai Anrita Shipping Co Ltd SatCom: Inmarsat C 447720510 *Hong Kong* *Hong Kong* MMSI: 477205000 Official number: HK-0978	**36,623** 17,395 45,673	Class: NK (LR) Classed LR until 17/8/11	**1988-10 Imabari Shipbuilding Co Ltd — Marugame KG (Marugame Shipyard)** Yd No: 1163 Loa 197.90 (BB) Br ex - Dght 11.019 Lbp 189.00 Br md 32.20 Dpth 21.60 Welded, 1 dk	**(A24B2BW) Wood Chips Carrier** Grain: 91,760 Compartments: 6 Ho, ER 6 Ha: (12.8 x 16.0)4 (14.4 x 16.0) (11.2 x 16.0)ER Cranes: 3x12t	**1 oil engine** driving 1 FP propeller Total Power: 6,804kW (9,251hp) 13.8kn Mitsubishi 6UEC52LS 1 x 2 Stroke 6 Cy. 520 x 1850 6804kW (9251bhp) Akasaka Tekkosho KK (Akasaka DieselLtd)-Japan AuxGen: 4 x 624kW a.c Fuel: 2260.0
778309 JF3	**WINTEK** *ex* C. P. 37 *-2012* *ex* Tokuei Maru No. 21 *-2004* *ex* Seiko Maru No. 1 *-2000* **Karway International Ltd** Fu Sheng Shipping Safety Management Consultant Co Ltd *Panama* *Panama* MMSI: 373062000 Official number: 4400312	**1,794** 863 2,926	Class: (BV) (NK)	**1993-11 KK Kanasashi — Shizuoka SZ** Yd No: 3327 Loa 89.21 (BB) Br ex - Dght 5.602 Lbp 82.00 Br md 13.00 Dpth 6.40 Welded, 1 dk	**(A13B2TP) Products Tanker** Double Bottom Entire Compartment Length Liq: 3,194; Liq (Oil): 3,194 Compartments: 8 Ta, ER	**1 oil engine** driving 1 CP propeller Total Power: 2,207kW (3,001hp) 14.0kn Akasaka A38 1 x 4 Stroke 6 Cy. 380 x 740 2207kW (3001bhp) Akasaka Tekkosho KK (Akasaka DieselLtd)-Japan AuxGen: 3 x 149kW a.c Thrusters: 1 Thwart. FP thruster (f)
416800 QA7	**WINTER** **Sante Shipholding Co** NGM Energy SA *Majuro* *Marshall Islands* MMSI: 538003324 Official number: 3324	**8,539** 4,117 13,052 T/cm 23.2	Class: AB	**2009-03 21st Century Shipbuilding Co Ltd — Tongyeong** Yd No: 247 Loa 128.60 (BB) Br ex - Dght 8.714 Lbp 120.40 Br md 20.40 Dpth 11.50 Welded, 1 dk	**(A12B2TR) Chemical/Products Tanker** Double Hull (13F) Liq: 14,080; Liq (Oil): 14,094 Cargo Heating Coils Compartments: 12 Wing Ta, 2 Wing Slop Ta, ER 12 Cargo Pump (s): 12x300m³/hr Manifold: Bow/CM: 60.7m	**1 oil engine** driving 1 FP propeller Total Power: 4,440kW (6,037hp) 13.5kn MAN-B&W 6S35MC 1 x 2 Stroke 6 Cy. 350 x 1400 4440kW (6037bhp) STX Engine Co Ltd-South Korea AuxGen: 3 x 480kW a.c Thrusters: 1 Tunnel thruster (f) Fuel: 65.0 (d.f.) 575.0 (r.f.)
409726 D09	**WINTERSET** *ex* Anangel Fidelity *-2001* **Labbeholmen Shipping AS** SMT Shipmanagement & Transport Gdynia Ltd Sp z oo SatCom: Inmarsat A 1554744 *Majuro* *Marshall Islands* MMSI: 538001682 Official number: 1682	**13,491** 5,301 23,570 T/cm 32.0	Class: BV (AB) (HR)	**1979-09 Ishikawajima-Harima Heavy Industries Co Ltd (IHI) — Aioi HG** Yd No: 2563 Converted From: General Cargo Ship-2008 Loa 164.34 (BB) Br ex - Dght 10.100 Lbp 155.48 Br md 22.86 Dpth 14.15 Welded, 1 dk	**(A24A2BT) Cement Carrier** Grain: 30,425; Bale: 29,569 Compartments: 5 Ho, ER 8 Ha: (12.8 x 17.3)Tappered 6 (12.8 x 17.3) (6.4 x 14.4)ER	**1 oil engine** sr geared to sc. shaft driving 1 CP propeller Total Power: 5,737kW (7,800hp) 15.0kn Pielstick 12PC2-5V-400 1 x Vee 4 Stroke 12 Cy. 400 x 460 5737kW (7800bhp) Ishikawajima Harima Heavy IndustrieCo Ltd (IHI)-Japan AuxGen: 1 x 450kW 450V 60Hz a.c, 1 x 160kW 450V 60Hz a.c Fuel: 134.0 (d.f.) (Part Heating Coils) 1097.0 (r.f.) 24.5pd
38706 7541	**WINTON R 118** *ex* Yue Ding Hu Gong 0448 *-2009* **Winton Enterprises Ltd** - *Panama* *Panama* Official number: 38772PEXT	**958** 287 -		**2007 Xijiang Shipyard — Liuzhou GX** L reg 60.80 Br ex - Dght - Lbp - Br md 14.80 Dpth 3.80 Welded, 1 dk	**(B33A2DU) Dredger (unspecified)**	**2 oil engines** geared to sc. shafts driving 2 Propellers Total Power: 472kW (642hp) 7.0kn Cummins 2 x 4 Stroke each-236kW (321bhp) Cummins Engine Co Inc-USA
21681 8238	**WINTON R18** *ex* Shun Yang Gong 38 *-2008* *ex* Yue Yun Fu Gong 0222 *-2005* **Winton Enterprises Ltd** Yangning Marine International Co Ltd *Panama* *Panama* Official number: 4148310	**711** 213 -		**2005-04 Shantang Navigation Shipyard Co Ltd — Qingyuan GD** Yd No: 0034 Loa 43.63 Br ex 14.80 Dght - Lbp 41.70 Br md 13.80 Dpth 4.20 Welded, 1 dk	**(B32A2ST) Tug**	**2 oil engines** driving 2 Propellers Total Power: 354kW (482hp) 8.0kn Chinese Std. Type 12V135C 2 x Vee 4 Stroke 12 Cy. 135 x 140 each-177kW (241bhp) Shanghai Diesel Engine Co Ltd-China
21679 8153	**WINTON T28** *ex* Yue Huizhou Hou 6968 *-2008* **Winton Enterprises Ltd** - *Panama* *Panama* Official number: 38009PEXT	**891** 267 -		**2003-11 Huizhou Tonghu Shipbuilding Corp — Huizhou GD** Yd No: 015 Loa 63.90 Br ex 14.20 Dght - Lbp 59.90 Br md 13.80 Dpth 4.08 Welded, 1 dk	**(A31A2GX) General Cargo Ship**	**2 oil engines** reduction geared to sc. shafts driving 2 FP propellers Total Power: 440kW (598hp) 9.0kn

IMO / Call sign	Name / Owner	Tonnage	Class	Builder / Dimensions	Type	Machinery
9097197 *HP8147* -	**WINTON T98** *ex* Shun Yang 132 *-2008* *ex* Fan Yun Ji 1020 *-2007* **Winton Enterprises Ltd** - *Panama* *Panama* Official number: 4063509	**1,055** 316 1,811		**1993**-11 **Guangxi Guijiang Shipyard — Wuzhou GX** Loa 66.00 Br ex - Dght 3.500 Lbp 61.40 Br md 14.50 Dpth 4.22 Welded, 1 dk	**(A24D2BA) Aggregates Carrier**	**2 oil engines** reduction geared to sc. shafts driving 2 Propellers Total Power: 516kW (702hp) 9.0 Weifang X6170Z 2 x 4 Stroke 6 Cy. 170 x 200 each-258kW (351bhp) Weifang Diesel Engine Factory-China
9097460 *HP8165* -	**WINTON T108** *ex* Yue Hong Ji 398 *-2008* **Winton Enterprises Ltd** - *Panama* *Panama* Official number: 4148110	**661** 198 1,691		**2002**-10 **Guangzhou Xintang Shipping Co Shipyard — Zengcheng GD** Loa 59.20 Br ex - Dght 2.700 Lbp 56.00 Br md 13.00 Dpth 3.30 Welded, 1 dk	**(A24D2BA) Aggregates Carrier**	**2 oil engines** reduction geared to sc. shafts driving 2 Propellers Total Power: 948kW (1,288hp) 9.0 Cummins NTA-855- 2 x 4 Stroke 6 Cy. 140 x 152 each-474kW (644bhp) Chongqing Cummins Engine Co Ltd-China
9535943 *H05935* -	**WINTON T128** *ex* Shi Tai 6368 *-2008* *ex* Pan Yun Ji 1021 *-2008* **Winton Enterprises Ltd** - *Panama* *Panama* Official number: 4156410	**1,467** 440 3,369		**2003**-03 **Guangzhou Panyu Yuefeng Shiprepair & Building Yard — Guangzhou GD** Loa 73.00 Br ex 15.40 Dght 3.860 Lbp 70.15 Br md 15.00 Dpth 4.50 Welded, 1 dk	**(A24D2BA) Aggregates Carrier**	**2 oil engines** reduction geared to sc. shafts driving 2 FP propellers Total Power: 1,080kW (1,468hp) Chinese Std. Type Z8170Z 2 x 4 Stroke 8 Cy. 170 x 200 each-540kW (734bhp) Zibo Diesel Engine Factory-China
8733421 *H06233* -	**WINTON T188** *ex* Zhengdong 363 *-2007* **Winton Enterprises Ltd** - *Panama* *Panama* Official number: 4157610	*923* 277 -		**2004**-01 **Dongguan Dongsheng Shipyard Co Ltd — Dongguan GD** Loa 60.10 Br ex 13.98 Dght 3.000 Lbp 57.00 Br md 13.58 Dpth 3.60 Welded, 1 dk	**(A24D2BA) Aggregates Carrier**	**2 oil engines** geared to sc. shafts driving 2 Propellers Total Power: 440kW (598hp) 9.0 Weifang X6170Z 2 x 4 Stroke 6 Cy. 170 x 200 each-220kW (299bhp) Weifang Diesel Engine Factory-China
8628212 *V8V2031* -	**WIRA** *ex* Armada 8 *-2002* **Emas Laut Sdn Bhd** Marine Support Services *Muara* *Brunei* Official number: 0031	**181** 54 -	Class: AB	**1987 Nam Cheong Dockyard Sdn Bhd — Miri** Yd No: 350 Loa - Br ex - Dght 2.212 Lbp 32.52 Br md 7.00 Dpth 3.41 Welded, 1 dk	**(B22G20Y) Standby Safety Vessel**	**2 oil engines** reverse reduction geared to sc. shafts driving 2 FP propellers Total Power: 1,176kW (1,598hp) 15.3 Yanmar 12LAA-D 2 x Vee 4 Stroke 12 Cy. 148 x 165 each-588kW (799bhp) Showa Precision Mchy. Co. Ltd.-Amagasaki AuxGen: 2 x 64kW a.c
8135485 - -	**WIRA 3** *ex* Hai Hin 28 *-1988* *ex* C. P. 101 *-1988* *ex* Kaiho Maru *-1988* **Kasman Marine Pte Ltd**	*102* 30 -	Class: (GL)	**1971 KK Izumi Zosensho — Kitakyushu** Loa 23.53 Br ex 7.04 Dght 2.340 Lbp 21.04 Br md 7.01 Dpth 2.80 Welded, 1 dk	**(B32A2ST) Tug**	**2 oil engines** driving 2 FP propellers Total Power: 736kW (1,000hp) 11.5 Kubota M6D20B 2 x 4 Stroke 6 Cy. 200 x 240 each-368kW (500bhp) Kubota Tekkosho-Japan
9740768 - -	**WIRA GLORY** *ex* Fu Ri Yun 918 *-2014* **PT Wira Jaya Logitama Lines** - *Freetown* *Sierra Leone*	**1,568** 878 -	Class: SL	**2013**-09 **Zhejiang Tianshi Shipbuilding Co Ltd — Wenling ZJ** Yd No: TS081 Loa 77.90 Br ex - Dght - Lbp 72.50 Br md 16.80 Dpth 4.20 Welded, 1 dk	**(A31C2GD) Deck Cargo Ship**	**2 oil engines** reduction geared to sc. shafts driving 2 Propellers Total Power: 1,200kW (1,632hp) Chinese Std. Type Z8170Z 2 x 4 Stroke 8 Cy. 170 x 200 each-600kW (816bhp) Zibo Diesel Engine Factory-China
8999178 - -	**WIRA JAYA** - **PT Adijayanti Pertiwi** - *Balikpapan* *Indonesia*	**490** 147 -	Class: (KI)	**1997**-03 **P.T. Galangan Kapal Mas Pioner — Samarinda** L reg 54.00 Br ex - Dght - Lbp 49.48 Br md 11.00 Dpth 3.06 Welded, 1 dk	**(A35D2RL) Landing Craft** Bow ramp (centre)	**2 oil engines** geared to sc. shafts driving 2 Propellers Total Power: 692kW (940hp) Caterpillar 34 2 x Vee 4 Stroke 8 Cy. 137 x 152 each-346kW (470bhp) Caterpillar Inc-USA
9027934 - -	**WIRA LAUT** - **PT Layar Lintas Jaya** - *Samarinda* *Indonesia*	**225** 68 -	Class: KI	**1996**-11 **PT Candi Pasifik — Samarinda** L reg 29.00 Br ex - Dght - Lbp 26.44 Br md 8.60 Dpth 3.99 Welded, 1 dk	**(B32A2ST) Tug**	**2 oil engines** geared to sc. shafts driving 2 Propellers Total Power: 1,654kW (2,248hp) Caterpillar D3 2 x Vee 4 Stroke 16 Cy. 159 x 203 each-827kW (1124bhp) Caterpillar Inc-USA
9028938 *YB6231* -	**WIRA LAUT** - **PT Wira Laut** - *Balikpapan* *Indonesia*	**163** 49 -	Class: KI	**2002**-07 **Bonafile Shipbuilders & Repairs Sdn Bhd — Sandakan** Loa - Br ex - Dght - Lbp 30.06 Br md 7.70 Dpth 2.44 Welded, 1 dk	**(A35D2RL) Landing Craft** Bow ramp (centre)	**2 oil engines** geared to sc. shafts driving 2 Propellers Total Power: 284kW (386hp) Cummins NT2 2 x 4 Stroke 6 Cy. each-142kW (193bhp) Cummins Engine Co Inc-USA AuxGen: 2 x 96kW 225V a.c, 1 x 46kW 225V a.c
7512870 *HSB2278* -	**WIRA ORN 2** *ex* Parinda No. 3 *-1995* *ex* Tokai Maru *-1993* **World Marine Transport Co Ltd** - *Bangkok* *Thailand* Official number: 372000011	*991* 630 1,220	Class: (NK)	**1975**-12 **Sanyo Zosen K.K. — Onomichi** Yd No: 718 Loa 67.90 Br ex 11.03 Dght 4.414 Lbp 62.01 Br md 11.00 Dpth 5.01 Riveted\Welded, 1 dk	**(A12A2TC) Chemical Tanker** Liq: 1,388	**1 oil engine** driving 1 FP propeller Total Power: 1,177kW (1,600hp) 12.8 Makita KSLH6 1 x 4 Stroke 6 Cy. 300 x 480 1177kW (1600bhp) Makita Diesel Co Ltd-Japan
9707302 *9LY2643* -	**WIRA PRIME** *completed as* Fu Ri Yun 999 *-2013* **PT Wira Jaya Logitama Lines** - *Sierra Leone* MMSI: 667003446	**1,568** 878 -	Class: ZC	**2013**-08 **Zhejiang Tianshi Shipbuilding Co Ltd — Wenling ZJ** Loa 77.90 Br ex - Dght 3.150 Lbp 72.50 Br md 16.80 Dpth 4.20 Welded, 1 dk	**(A31C2GD) Deck Cargo Ship** Bow ramp (centre)	**2 oil engines** reduction geared to sc. shafts driving 2 Propellers Total Power: 1,150kW (1,564hp) Chinese Std. Type Z8170Z 2 x 4 Stroke 8 Cy. 170 x 200 each-575kW (782bhp) Zibo Diesel Engine Factory-China
8892485 *YD6168* -	**WIRA TIMUR II** - **PT Wira Timur Segara** - *Samarinda* *Indonesia*	*108* 64 -	Class: KI	**1993**-10 **C.V. Swadaya Utama — Samarinda** Loa - Br ex - Dght 2.300 Lbp 19.25 Br md 6.10 Dpth 2.50 Welded, 1 dk	**(B32A2ST) Tug**	**2 oil engines** driving 2 FP propellers Total Power: 618kW (840hp) Caterpillar 3408PC 2 x Vee 4 Stroke 8 Cy. 137 x 152 each-309kW (420bhp) Caterpillar Inc-USA
8892473 - -	**WIRA TIMUR III** - **PT Wira Timur Segara** - *Samarinda* *Indonesia*	**129** 39 -	Class: KI	**1994**-07 **C.V. Swadaya Utama — Samarinda** Loa 22.50 Br ex - Dght - Lbp 20.88 Br md 6.50 Dpth 3.15 Welded, 1 dk	**(B32A2ST) Tug**	**2 oil engines** reduction geared to sc. shafts driving 2 FP propellers Total Power: 618kW (840hp) Caterpillar 340 2 x Vee 4 Stroke 8 Cy. 137 x 152 each-309kW (420bhp) Caterpillar Inc-USA
9027958 - -	**WIRA TIMUR IX** - **PT Grand Duta Bahari** - *Samarinda* *Indonesia*	**224** 68 -	Class: KI	**2002**-02 **C.V. Swadaya Utama — Samarinda** L reg 31.50 Br ex - Dght - Lbp 28.28 Br md 7.80 Dpth 2.90 Welded, 1 dk	**(B32A2ST) Tug**	**2 oil engines** geared to sc. shafts driving 2 Propellers Total Power: 918kW (1,248hp) Caterpillar 341 2 x Vee 4 Stroke 12 Cy. 137 x 152 each-459kW (624bhp) Caterpillar Inc-USA
8958863 *YD6417* -	**WIRA TIMUR VII** - **PT Armada Kaltim Jaya** - *Samarinda* *Indonesia*	**145** 87 -	Class: KI	**1999**-10 **C.V. Swadaya Utama — Samarinda** L reg 25.25 Br ex - Dght - Lbp 25.25 Br md 7.00 Dpth 3.20 Welded, 1 dk	**(B32A2ST) Tug**	**2 oil engines** reduction geared to sc. shafts driving 2 FP propellers Total Power: 1,508kW (2,050hp) Caterpillar D398 2 x Vee 4 Stroke 12 Cy. 159 x 203 each-754kW (1025bhp) (Re-engined ,made 1982, Reconditioned & fitted 1999) Caterpillar Tractor Co-USA
9027946 - -	**WIRA TIMUR VIII** - **PT Taurus Naksatra Abadi** - *Samarinda* *Indonesia*	**147** 45 -	Class: KI	**1999**-10 **C.V. Swadaya Utama — Samarinda** L reg 28.00 Br ex - Dght - Lbp 26.25 Br md 7.50 Dpth 3.20 Welded, 1 dk	**(B32A2ST) Tug**	**2 oil engines** geared to sc. shafts driving 2 Propellers Total Power: 1,508kW (2,050hp) Caterpillar D3 2 x Vee 4 Stroke 12 Cy. 159 x 203 each-754kW (1025bhp) Caterpillar Inc-USA
9029748 - -	**WIRA TIMUR XII** - **PT Pelayaran Niaga Baru** - *Samarinda* *Indonesia*	**145** 87 -	Class: KI	**2003**-12 **C.V. Swadaya Utama — Samarinda** Loa 25.20 Br ex - Dght 2.710 Lbp 22.70 Br md 7.00 Dpth 3.20 Welded, 1 dk	**(B32A2ST) Tug**	**2 oil engines** geared to sc. shafts driving 2 Propellers Total Power: 918kW (1,248hp) 8.0 Caterpillar 341 2 x Vee 4 Stroke 12 Cy. 137 x 152 each-459kW (624bhp) (made 1995, fitted 2003) Caterpillar Inc-USA AuxGen: 2 x 88kW 380/220V a.c

IMO / Call sign / Fishing no.	Name / Owner / Port / Flag	Tonnage	Class	Builder / Dimensions	Type	Machinery
029554 *YD6597* -	**WIRA TIMUR XVII** **PT Wira Timur Segara** - *Samarinda* Indonesia	**145** 87 -	Class: KI	**2003-01 C.V. Swadaya Utama — Samarinda** Loa 25.25 Br ex - Dght 2.590 Lbp 23.80 Br md 7.00 Dpth 3.20 Welded, 1 dk	**(B32A2ST) Tug**	**2 oil engines** geared to sc. shafts driving 1 Propeller Total Power: 920kW (1,250hp) Caterpillar 3412TA 2 x Vee 4 Stroke 12 Cy. 137 x 152 each-460kW (625bhp) Caterpillar Inc-USA AuxGen: 2 x 82kW 400V a.c
233058 *PKXU* -	**WIRABUANA I** *ex* Azusa Maru *-1974* **PT Taliabu Timber** - *Jakarta* Indonesia	*133* 64 38		**1959-12 Sanoyasu Dockyard Co Ltd — Osaka OS** Yd No: 174 Loa 31.68 Br ex 5.72 Dght 1.994 Lbp 29.01 Br md - Dpth 2.60 Welded, 1 dk	**(A32A2GF) General Cargo/Passenger Ship** Passengers: unberthed: 108 Grain: 42; Bale: 36 Compartments: 1 Ho, ER 1 Ha: (2.2 x 2.2) Derricks: 1x1t; Winches: 1	**1 oil engine** driving 1 FP propeller Total Power: 235kW (320hp) 11.5kn Nippon Hatsudoki 1 x 4 Stroke 6 Cy. 265 x 400 235kW (320bhp) Nippon Hatsudoki-Japan AuxGen: 1 x 17kW 115V d.c, 1 x 5kW 115V d.c
7031955 - -	**WIRACOCHA** - -	*285* 113 -	Class: (GL)	**1970 Ast. Picsa S.A. — Callao** Yd No: 337 L reg 30.94 Br ex 7.62 Dght - Lbp - Br md - Dpth 3.66 Welded, 1 dk	**(B11B2FV) Fishing Vessel**	**1 oil engine** driving 1 FP propeller Total Power: 588kW (799hp) 10.0kn G.M. (Detroit Diesel) 12V-149 1 x Vee 2 Stroke 12 Cy. 146 x 146 588kW (799bhp) General Motors Corp-USA
8870279 *PNBN* -	**WIRAMAS** *ex* Daifuku Maru No. 11 *-2009* **PT Pelayaran Nusantara Sri Indrapura** - *Tanjung Priok* Indonesia MMSI: 525023106	**1,299** 453 1,451	Class: KI	**1993-05 Namikata Shipbuilding Co Ltd — Imabari EH** Yd No: 181 Loa 76.00 Br ex - Dght 4.080 Lbp 72.68 Br md 12.00 Dpth 7.00 Welded, 1 dk	**(A31A2GX) General Cargo Ship**	**1 oil engine** reverse geared to sc. shaft driving 1 FP propeller Total Power: 736kW (1,001hp) 11.0kn Akasaka A31R 1 x 4 Stroke 6 Cy. 310 x 600 736kW (1001bhp) Akasaka Tekkosho KK (Akasaka DieselLtd)-Japan
9006162 *YFIG* -	**WIRAS PERMATA No. 1** *ex* Jiang Hai 2 *-1990* **Kerta Jaya CV** - *Jakarta* Indonesia	**947** 511 1,502	Class: KI (LR) (CC) Classed LR until 29/3/96	**1990 Wuhu Shipyard — Wuhu AH** Yd No: 2122/1 Loa 62.85 Br ex 11.62 Dght 4.200 Lbp 58.00 Br md 11.60 Dpth 5.00 Welded, 1 dk	**(A31A2GX) General Cargo Ship**	**1 oil engine** dr reverse geared to sc. shaft driving 1 FP propeller Total Power: 441kW (600hp) Chinese Std. Type 6300 1 x 4 Stroke 6 Cy. 300 x 380 441kW (600bhp) Ningbo Engine Factory-China AuxGen: 3 x 64kW 400V 50Hz a.c
9006174 *YFIH* -	**WIRAS PERMATA No. 2** *ex* Jiang Hai 3 *-1990* **PT Bintanindo Sentosa Daya** - *Jakarta* Indonesia MMSI: 525023105	**947** 511 1,502	Class: KI (LR) (CC) Classed LR until 29/3/96	**1990 Wuhu Shipyard — Wuhu AH** Yd No: 2122/2 Loa 62.85 Br ex 11.62 Dght 4.200 Lbp 58.00 Br md 11.60 Dpth 5.00 Welded, 1 dk	**(A31A2GX) General Cargo Ship**	**1 oil engine** dr reverse geared to sc. shaft driving 1 FP propeller Total Power: 441kW (600hp) Chinese Std. Type 6300 1 x 4 Stroke 6 Cy. 300 x 380 441kW (600bhp) Guangzhou Diesel Engine Factory CoLtd-China AuxGen: 3 x 64kW 400V 50Hz a.c
9117519 *ZNAT4* PH 110	**WIRON 1** **Interfish Wirons Ltd** Jaczon BV *Plymouth* United Kingdom MMSI: 235001239 Official number: C17275	**1,059** 388 819	Class: LR ✠ **100A1** SS 10/2010 stern trawler ✠ **LMC** **UMS** Eq.Ltr: L; Cable: 385.0/30.0 U2 (a)	**1995-10 S.A. Balenciaga — Zumaya** Yd No: 371 Loa 51.44 (BB) Br ex 11.62 Dght 5.200 Lbp 45.00 Br md 11.60 Dpth 7.90 Welded, 2 dks	**(B11A2FS) Stern Trawler**	**1 oil engine** with flexible couplings & sr geared to sc. shaft driving 1 CP propeller Total Power: 1,800kW (2,447hp) 11.0kn Stork-Werkspoor 6SW280 1 x 4 Stroke 6 Cy. 280 x 300 1800kW (2447bhp) Stork Wartsila Diesel BV-Netherlands AuxGen: 1 x 1000kW 440V 60Hz a.c, 2 x 300kW 440V 60Hz a.c Thrusters: 1 Thwart. FP thruster (f)
9117521 *ZNAT5* PH 220	**WIRON 2** **Interfish Wirons Ltd** Jaczon BV *Plymouth* United Kingdom MMSI: 235001770 Official number: C17276	**1,068** 388 819	Class: LR ✠ **100A1** SS 11/2010 stern trawler ✠ **LMC** **UMS** Eq.Ltr: L; Cable: 385.0/30.0 U2 (a)	**1996-11 S.A. Balenciaga — Zumaya** Yd No: 372 Loa 51.44 (BB) Br ex 11.74 Dght 5.200 Lbp 45.00 Br md 11.60 Dpth 7.90 Welded, 2 dks	**(B11A2FS) Stern Trawler**	**1 oil engine** with clutches, flexible couplings & sr geared to sc. shaft driving 1 CP propeller Total Power: 1,800kW (2,447hp) 11.0kn Stork-Werkspoor 6SW280 1 x 4 Stroke 6 Cy. 280 x 300 1800kW (2447bhp) Stork Wartsila Diesel BV-Netherlands AuxGen: 1 x 1000kW 440V 60Hz a.c, 2 x 300kW 440V 60Hz a.c Thrusters: 1 Thwart. CP thruster (f)
9249556 *PBGV* SCH 22	**WIRON 5** **Jaczon Visserij Maatschappij Wiron BV** Jaczon BV *Scheveningen* Netherlands MMSI: 246021000 Official number: 39671	**1,227** 368 -	Class: LR ✠ **100A1** SS 07/2012 stern trawler ✠ **LMC** **UMS** Eq.Ltr: L; Cable: 385.5/30.0 U2 (a)	**2002-07 Construcciones Navales P Freire SA — Vigo** Yd No: 501 Loa 55.60 (BB) Br ex 11.90 Dght 5.200 Lbp 49.45 Br md 11.60 Dpth 7.90 Welded, 1 dk	**(B11A2FS) Stern Trawler** Compartments: 2 Ho, ER	**1 oil engine** with clutches, flexible couplings & sr geared to sc. shaft driving 1 CP propeller Total Power: 2,760kW (3,752hp) 13.0kn Wartsila 6L32 1 x 4 Stroke 6 Cy. 320 x 400 2760kW (3752bhp) Wartsila Diesel S.A.-Bermeo AuxGen: 1 x 1200kW 440V 60Hz a.c, 2 x 600kW 440V 60Hz a.c Thrusters: 1 Thwart. CP thruster (f)
9249568 *PBGW* SCH 23	**WIRON 6** **Jaczon 'Orange Klipper' BV** Jaczon BV *Scheveningen* Netherlands MMSI: 246033000 Official number: 39672	**1,227** 368 -	Class: LR ✠ **100A1** SS 08/2012 stern trawler ✠ **LMC** **UMS** Eq.Ltr: L; Cable: 385.5/30.0 U2 (a)	**2002-08 Construcciones Navales P Freire SA — Vigo** Yd No: 502 Loa 55.60 (BB) Br ex 11.90 Dght 5.200 Lbp 49.45 Br md 11.60 Dpth 7.90 Welded, 1 dk	**(B11A2FS) Stern Trawler**	**1 oil engine** with clutches, flexible couplings & sr geared to sc. shaft driving 1 CP propeller Total Power: 2,760kW (3,752hp) 13.0kn Wartsila 6L32 1 x 4 Stroke 6 Cy. 320 x 400 2760kW (3752bhp) Wartsila Diesel S.A.-Bermeo Thrusters: 1 Thwart. CP thruster (f)
8611867 *LW9537* -	**WIRON IV** **Euro Jacob Fisheries SA** Argentina MMSI: 701000933 Official number: 01476	*296* 256 -	Class: (RI)	**1987-04 Stocznia Remontowa 'Nauta' SA — Gdynia** Yd No: 419 Loa 39.91 Br ex - Dght 4.437 Lbp 37.42 Br md 8.51 Dpth 4.68 Welded, 1 dk	**(B11A2FS) Stern Trawler**	**1 oil engine** driving 1 FP propeller Total Power: 1,103kW (1,500hp) Kromhout 8FDHD240 1 x 4 Stroke 8 Cy. 240 x 260 1103kW (1500bhp) Stork Werkspoor Diesel BV-Netherlands
8417364 *V5SR* L533	**WIRON V** **Seawork Fish Processors (Pty) Ltd** - *Luderitz* Namibia Official number: 91LB048	**441** 235 300		**1986-03 Stocznia Remontowa 'Nauta' SA — Gdynia** Yd No: 416 Loa 36.81 (BB) Br ex - Dght 3.501 Lbp 32.97 Br md 8.51 Dpth 4.68 Welded, 1 dk	**(B11A2FS) Stern Trawler** Ins: 393 Ice Capable	**1 oil engine** geared to sc. shaft driving 1 CP propeller Total Power: 883kW (1,201hp) 12.0kn Kromhout 6FHD240 1 x 4 Stroke 6 Cy. 240 x 260 883kW (1201bhp) Stork Werkspoor Diesel BV-Netherlands AuxGen: 1 x 400kW a.c, 1 x 200kW a.c, 1 x 80kW a.c Fuel: 77.5 (r.f.)
8417376 *V5TW* L534	**WIRON VI** **Blue Angra (Namibia) (Pty) Ltd** - *Luderitz* Namibia Official number: 91LB049	**444** 235 -		**1986-05 Stocznia Remontowa 'Nauta' SA — Gdynia** Yd No: 417 Loa 36.56 (BB) Br ex - Dght 3.501 Lbp 33.00 Br md 8.51 Dpth 4.65 Welded, 1 dk	**(B11A2FS) Stern Trawler** Ins: 393 Ice Capable	**1 oil engine** driving 1 FP propeller Total Power: 883kW (1,201hp) 12.0kn Kromhout 6FEHD240 1 x 4 Stroke 6 Cy. 240 x 260 883kW (1201bhp) Stork Werkspoor Diesel BV-Netherlands AuxGen: 1 x 400kW a.c, 1 x 200kW a.c, 1 x 80kW a.c Fuel: 77.5 (r.f.)
9255579 *PBGA* -	**WISAFOREST** **Beheermaatschappij ms 'Veendiep' BV** Feederlines BV *Groningen* Netherlands MMSI: 245096000 Official number: 40396	**5,052** 2,838 7,750	Class: LR ✠ **100A1** SS 05/2012 strengthened for heavy cargoes, in hold and on upper deck hatch covers Ice Class 1A (Finnish-Swedish Ice Class Rules 1985) Max draught midship 7.20m Max/min draught aft 7.197/4.367m Max/min draught fwd 7.197/1.837m Power required 2864kw, installed 3840kw ✠ **LMC** **UMS** Eq.Ltr: W; Cable: 499.3/44.0 U3 (a)	**2002-05 Bodewes' Scheepswerven B.V. — Hoogezand** Yd No: 607 Loa 118.55 (BB) Br ex 15.43 Dght 7.030 Lbp 111.85 Br md 15.20 Dpth 8.44 Welded, 2 dks	**(A31A2GX) General Cargo Ship** Grain: 9,415 TEU 390 C Ho 174 TEU C Dk 216 TEU Compartments: 2 Ho, ER 2 Ha: (39.0 x 12.7) (44.3 x 12.7)ER Cranes: 2x40t Ice Capable	**1 oil engine** with clutches, flexible couplings & sr geared to sc. shaft driving 1 CP propeller Total Power: 3,800kW (5,166hp) 12.0kn MaK 8M32C 1 x 4 Stroke 8 Cy. 320 x 480 3800kW (5166bhp) Caterpillar Motoren GmbH & Co. KG-Germany AuxGen: 1 x 400kW 400V 50Hz a.c, 4 x 264kW 400V 50Hz a.c Thrusters: 1 Tunnel thruster (f)

9426489 *LAFB7* -	**WISBY ARGAN** **Casablanca Tankers AB** Wisby Tankers AB *Oslo* *Norway (NIS)* MMSI: 259746000	**4,776** Class: NV (GL) 2,008 7,348	**2009-11 Penglai Zhongbai Jinglu Ship Industry Co Ltd — Penglai SD** Yd No: JL0001 (T) Loa 99.80 (BB) Br ex 18.25 Dght 7.000 Lbp 95.00 Br md 18.00 Dpth 9.00 Welded, 1 dk	**(A12B2TR) Chemical/Products Tanker** Double Hull (13F) Liq: 7,099; Liq (Oil): 7,099	**1 oil engine** reduction geared to sc. shaft driving 1 CP propeller Total Power: 2,925kW (3,977hp) 12.0kn Wartsila 9L26 1 x 4 Stroke 9 Cy. 260 x 320 2925kW (3977bhp) Wartsila Italia SpA-Italy AuxGen: 3 x a.c, 1 x a.c Thrusters: 1 Tunnel thruster (f)
9426491 *LAFC7* -	**WISBY CEDAR** **Casablanca Tankers AB** Wisby Tankers AB *Oslo* *Norway (NIS)* MMSI: 259747000	**4,776** Class: NV (GL) 2,008 7,348	**2010-06 Penglai Zhongbai Jinglu Ship Industry Co Ltd — Penglai SD** Yd No: JL0002 (T) Loa 99.78 (BB) Br ex 18.25 Dght 7.000 Lbp 95.00 Br md 18.00 Dpth 9.00 Welded, 1 dk	**(A12B2TR) Chemical/Products Tanker** Double Hull (13F) Liq: 7,099; Liq (Oil): 7,099	**1 oil engine** reduction geared to sc. shaft driving 1 CP propeller Total Power: 2,925kW (3,977hp) 12.0kn Wartsila 9L26 1 x 4 Stroke 9 Cy. 260 x 320 2925kW (3977bhp) Wartsila Italia SpA-Italy AuxGen: 3 x 525kW a.c, 1 x a.c Thrusters: 1 Tunnel thruster (f)
9518880 *LAHV7* -	**WISBY TEAK** **Wisby Tankers AB** - *Oslo* *Norway (NIS)* MMSI: 259944000	**4,776** Class: GL 2,008 7,374	**2011-12 Penglai Zhongbai Jinglu Ship Industry Co Ltd — Penglai SD** Yd No: JL0014 (T) Loa 99.87 (BB) Br ex 18.25 Dght 7.000 Lbp 95.00 Br md 18.00 Dpth 9.00 Welded, 1 dk	**(A12B2TR) Chemical/Products Tanker** Double Hull (13F) Liq: 7,099; Liq (Oil): 7,099	**1 oil engine** reduction geared to sc. shaft driving 1 CP propeller Total Power: 2,925kW (3,977hp) 14.0kn Wartsila 9L26 1 x 4 Stroke 9 Cy. 260 x 320 2925kW (3977bhp) Wartsila Italia SpA-Italy AuxGen: 1 x 750kW 450V a.c, 3 x 350kW 450V a.c Thrusters: 1 Tunnel thruster (f)
9283459 *PCTJ* -	**WISBY VERITY** **WT Shipping BV/Wisby Tankers AB** Wisby Tankers AB SatCom: Inmarsat C 424529110 *Zuidlaren* *Netherlands* MMSI: 245291000	**4,295** Class: BV 2,141 7,479 T/cm 15.9	**2004-07 Ferus Smit Leer GmbH — Leer** Yd No: 344 Loa 116.35 (BB) Br ex 15.11 Dght 6.750 Lbp 110.90 Br md 15.00 Dpth 9.30 Welded, 1 dk	**(A13B2TP) Products Tanker** Double Hull (13F) Liq: 8,046; Liq (Oil): 8,046 5 Cargo Pump (s): 5x300m³/hr Manifold: Bow/CM: 66m Ice Capable	**1 oil engine** geared to sc. shaft driving 1 CP propeller Total Power: 3,840kW (5,221hp) 13.0kn MaK 8M32 1 x 4 Stroke 8 Cy. 320 x 480 3840kW (5221bhp) Caterpillar Motoren GmbH & Co. KG-Germany AuxGen: 3 x 390kW 440V 60Hz a.c Thrusters: 1 Tunnel thruster (f)
9398486 *SBYU* -	**WISBY WAVE** **Wisby Tankers AB** - *Visby* *Sweden* MMSI: 266317000	**4,283** Class: BV 2,150 7,517 T/cm 15.9	**2009-10 Scheepswerf Ferus Smit BV — Westerbroek** Yd No: 390 Loa 116.35 (BB) Br ex - Dght 6.750 Lbp 110.90 Br md 15.00 Dpth 9.30 Welded, 1 dk	**(A12B2TR) Chemical/Products Tanker** Double Hull (13F) Liq: 8,198; Liq (Oil): 8,198 Ice Capable	**1 oil engine** reduction geared to sc. shaft driving 1 CP propeller Total Power: 3,480kW (4,731hp) 13.2kn MaK 8M32C 1 x 4 Stroke 8 Cy. 320 x 480 3480kW (4731bhp) Caterpillar Motoren GmbH & Co. KG-Germany AuxGen: 3 x 265kW 440V 60Hz a.c, 1 x 360kW 440V 60Hz a.c Thrusters: 1 Tunnel thruster (f) Fuel: 297.0 (r.f.)
9512460 *WDE2552* -	**WISDOM** **Nordic Fisheries Inc** - *New Bedford, MA* *United States of America* MMSI: 367326440 Official number: 1206423	**244** 73 -	**2008-01 Duckworth Steel Boats, Inc. — Tarpon Springs, Fl** Yd No: 052 L reg 25.78 Br ex - Dght - Lbp - Br md 8.53 Dpth 4.41 Welded, 1 dk	**(B11B2FV) Fishing Vessel**	**1 oil engine** geared to sc. shaft driving 1 Propeller Caterpillar 1 x 4 Stroke Caterpillar Inc-USA
9419802 *V2CK3* -	**WISDOM** *ex* Jasmine Scan *-2012* *ex* Wisdom *-2010* *ex* BBC Thailand *-2008* *completed as* Wisdom *-2006* *launched as* FCC Wisdom *-2006* **ms 'Wisdom' GmbH & Co KG** Candler Schiffahrt GmbH *Saint John's* *Antigua & Barbuda* MMSI: 305026000 Official number: 10038	**6,494** Class: GL (CC) 2,872 8,191	**2006-12 Chongqing Dongfeng Ship Industry Co — Chongqing** Yd No: K05-1008 Loa 116.23 (BB) Br ex - Dght 7.000 Lbp 110.00 Br md 18.00 Dpth 10.40 Welded, 1 dk	**(A31A2GX) General Cargo Ship** Grain: 11,705; Bale: 11,681 TEU 271 incl 10 ref C. Compartments: 2 Ho, 2 Tw Dk, ER 2 Ha: (44.8 x 15.0)ER (25.9 x 15.0) Cranes: 2x45t Ice Capable	**1 oil engine** reverse reduction geared to sc.shaft driving 1 FP propeller Total Power: 2,500kW (3,399hp) 12.0kn Daihatsu 8DKM-28 1 x 4 Stroke 8 Cy. 280 x 390 2500kW (3399bhp) Shaanxi Diesel Heavy Industry Co Lt-China AuxGen: 3 x 265kW 380V a.c
9659505 *S6LY7* -	**WISDOM** **Sino Ships Pte Ltd** United Maritime Pte Ltd *Singapore* *Singapore* MMSI: 566538000 Official number: 397855	**2,239** Class: CC 926 3,610	**2013-09 Qinhuangdao China Harbour Shbldg Industry Co Ltd — Qinhuangdao HE** Yd No: 2010/38-03 Loa 78.00 Br ex - Dght 5.000 Lbp 74.00 Br md 15.30 Dpth 6.90 Welded, 1 dk	**(A13B2TP) Products Tanker** Double Hull (13F) Liq: 3,217; Liq (Oil): 3,217 Compartments: 4 Wing Ta, 4 Wing Ta, 1 Wing Slop Ta, 1 Wing Slop Ta, ER	**2 oil engines** driving 2 Propellers Total Power: 1,342kW (1,824hp) 10.5kn Cummins KTA-38-M0 2 x Vee 4 Stroke 12 Cy. 159 x 159 each-671kW (912bhp) Chongqing Cummins Engine Co Ltd-China AuxGen: 2 x 250kW a.c
9641833 *3FGZ8* -	**WISDOM ACE** **Cypress Maritime (Panama) SA & Koyo Shosen Kaisha Ltd** Shoei Kisen Kaisha Ltd *Panama* *Panama* MMSI: 352044000 Official number: 4499613	**59,409** Class: NK 19,081 19,227	**2013-06 Imabari Shipbuilding Co Ltd — Marugame KG (Marugame Shipyard)** Yd No: 1536 Loa 199.97 (BB) Br ex - Dght 10.017 Lbp 192.00 Br md 32.26 Dpth 34.80 Welded, 10 dks plus 2 movable dks	**(A35B2RV) Vehicles Carrier** Side door/ramp (s) Quarter stern door/ramp (s. a.) Cars: 5,198	**1 oil engine** driving 1 FP propeller Total Power: 15,100kW (20,530hp) 20.7kn Mitsubishi 8UEC60LSII 1 x 2 Stroke 8 Cy. 600 x 2300 15100kW (20530bhp) Kobe Hatsudoki KK-Japan AuxGen: 3 x 1130kW a.c Thrusters: 1 Tunnel thruster (f) Fuel: 2783.0
9180047 *3FMU8* -	**WISDOM GRACE** *ex* MOL Grace *-2014* *ex* Grace Island *-2000* **TG Finance Co Ltd** Wisdom Marine Lines SA *Panama* *Panama* MMSI: 351255000 Official number: 27219PEXT4	**13,199** Class: NK 7,391 18,193 T/cm 32.0	**1998-06 Imabari Shipbuilding Co Ltd — Imabari EH (Imabari Shipyard)** Yd No: 544 Loa 161.85 (BB) Br ex - Dght 9.065 Lbp 150.00 Br md 25.60 Dpth 12.90 Welded, 1 dk	**(A33A2CC) Container Ship (Fully Cellular)** TEU 1032 C Ho 496 TEU C Dk 536 TEU incl 100 ref C Compartments: 4 Cell Ho, ER 16 Ha: 2 (12.6 x 5.6)14 (12.6 x 10.7)ER	**1 oil engine** driving 1 FP propeller Total Power: 9,989kW (13,581hp) 18.3kn B&W 7S50MC 1 x 2 Stroke 7 Cy. 500 x 1910 9989kW (13581bhp) Mitsui Engineering & Shipbuilding CLtd-Japan AuxGen: 3 x 735kW 450V 60Hz a.c Thrusters: 1 Thwart. CP thruster (f) Fuel: 170.8 (d.f.) (Heating Coils) 1216.1 (r.f.) 38.0pd
9596325 *H8BQ* -	**WISDOM OF THE SEA 1** **Benecia Marines SA** Pan Ocean Co Ltd SatCom: Inmarsat C 435667210 *Panama* *Panama* MMSI: 356672000 Official number: 4314111	**93,565** Class: KR 59,297 180,144	**2011-07 Daehan Shipbuilding Co Ltd — Hwawon (Haenam Shipyard)** Yd No: 1048 Loa 292.00 (BB) Br ex 45.06 Dght 18.220 Lbp 283.00 Br md 45.00 Dpth 24.75 Welded, 1 dk	**(A21A2BC) Bulk Carrier** Grain: 198,860 Compartments: 9 Ho, ER 9 Ha: 7 (15.8 x 20.4)ER 2 (14.9 x 15.3)	**1 oil engine** driving 1 FP propeller Total Power: 18,660kW (25,370hp) 15.4kn MAN-B&W 6S70MC-C8 1 x 2 Stroke 6 Cy. 700 x 2800 18660kW (25370bhp) Doosan Engine Co Ltd-South Korea
9596337 *3EVF2* -	**WISDOM OF THE SEA 2** **Celandine Marines SA** Pan Ocean Co Ltd SatCom: Inmarsat C 435514511 *Panama* *Panama* MMSI: 355145000 Official number: 4317211	**93,565** Class: KR 59,297 180,184	**2011-07 Daehan Shipbuilding Co Ltd — Hwawon (Haenam Shipyard)** Yd No: 1049 Loa 292.00 (BB) Br ex 45.06 Dght 18.220 Lbp 283.00 Br md 45.00 Dpth 24.75 Welded, 1 dk	**(A21A2BC) Bulk Carrier** Grain: 198,860 Compartments: 9 Ho, ER 9 Ha: 7 (15.8 x 20.4)ER 2 (14.9 x 15.3)	**1 oil engine** driving 1 FP propeller Total Power: 19,620kW (26,675hp) 15.4kn MAN-B&W 6S70MC-C8 1 x 2 Stroke 6 Cy. 700 x 2800 19620kW (26675bhp) Doosan Engine Co Ltd-South Korea
9504231 *IIJS2* -	**WISE** **Nuova CoEdMar Srl** - *Chioggia* *Italy* MMSI: 247238100 Official number: CI3625	*747* Class: RI - 750	**2008-06 in Italy** Yd No: 01/2006 Loa 49.74 Br ex - Dght 2.800 Lbp 48.00 Br md 13.98 Dpth 3.50 Welded, 1 dk	**(A31C2GD) Deck Cargo Ship**	**2 oil engines** geared to sc. shafts driving 2 Propellers Total Power: 760kW (1,034hp) Cummins KT-19-M 2 x 4 Stroke 6 Cy. 159 x 159 each-380kW (517bhp) Cummins Engine Co Inc-USA
9353644 *YD6905* -	**WISE 161** *ex* Sea Glory 10 *-2006* **PT Wahana Yasa International Shipping** PT GlobalTrans Energy International *Banjarmasin* *Indonesia*	**164** Class: RI (GL) 51 -	**2005-07 P.T. Tunas Karya Bahari Indonesia — Indonesia** Yd No: 42 Loa 25.00 Br ex - Dght 2.700 Lbp 22.89 Br md 7.32 Dpth 3.35 Welded, 1 dk	**(B32A2ST) Tug**	**2 oil engines** reduction geared to sc. shafts driving 2 Propellers Total Power: 1,202kW (1,634hp) Mitsubishi S6R2-MPTK 2 x 4 Stroke 6 Cy. 170 x 220 each-601kW (817bhp) Mitsubishi Heavy Industries Ltd-Japan

IMO / Call sign	Name / Owner	Tonnage	Class	Build / Dimensions	Type	Machinery
9506629 YDA4577 -	**WISE 162** *ex* SG 28 *-2010* **PT Wahana Yasa International Shipping** - *Jakarta* *Indonesia* MMSI: 525015655	**192** - 192	Class: RI (GL)	**2009-03 Rajang Maju Shipbuilding Sdn Bhd — Sibu** Yd No: 73 Loa 26.00 Br ex - Dght 3.000 Lbp 23.86 Br md 8.00 Dpth 3.65 Welded, 1 dk	**(B32A2ST) Tug**	**2 oil engines** reverse reduction geared to sc. shafts driving 2 FP propellers Total Power: 1,220kW (1,658hp) Yanmar 6AYM-ETE 2 x 4 Stroke 6 Cy. 155 x 180 each-610kW (829bhp) Yanmar Diesel Engine Co Ltd-Japan
9396579 YDA4177 -	**WISE 201** **PT Wahana Yasa International Shipping** PT GlobalTrans Energy International *Jakarta* *Indonesia* MMSI: 525015111	**240** 74 -	Class: RI (GL)	**2006-06 P.T. Tunas Karya Bahari Indonesia — Indonesia** Yd No: 57 Loa 29.00 Br ex - Dght 3.627 Lbp 27.00 Br md 9.00 Dpth 4.27 Welded, 1 dk	**(B32B2SP) Pusher Tug**	**2 oil engines** reverse reduction geared to sc. shafts driving 2 FP propellers Total Power: 1,518kW (2,064hp) 11.0kn Mitsubishi S6R2-MPTK3 2 x 4 Stroke 6 Cy. 170 x 220 each-759kW (1032bhp) Mitsubishi Heavy Industries Ltd-Japan AuxGen: 2 x 50kW 415/220V a.c
9396581 YDA4178 -	**WISE 202** **PT Wahana Yasa International Shipping** PT GlobalTrans Energy International *Jakarta* *Indonesia* MMSI: 525015110	**240** 74 -	Class: RI (GL)	**2006-06 P.T. Tunas Karya Bahari Indonesia — Indonesia** Yd No: 58 Loa 29.00 Br ex - Dght 3.627 Lbp 27.00 Br md 9.00 Dpth 4.27 Welded, 1 dk	**(B32B2SP) Pusher Tug**	**2 oil engines** reverse reduction geared to sc. shafts driving 2 FP propellers Total Power: 1,518kW (2,064hp) 11.0kn Mitsubishi S6R2-MPTK3 2 x 4 Stroke 6 Cy. 170 x 220 each-759kW (1032bhp) Mitsubishi Heavy Industries Ltd-Japan AuxGen: 2 x 50kW 415/220V a.c
9662007 - -	**WISE CASTLE** **Heung Hae Co Ltd** - *Incheon* *South Korea* Official number: ICR-121833	**160** - 113	Class: KR	**2012-11 DH Shipbuilding Co Ltd — Incheon** Yd No: 1103 Loa 27.50 Br ex 8.02 Dght 2.910 Lbp 25.30 Br md 8.00 Dpth 3.70 Welded, 1 dk	**(B32A2ST) Tug**	**2 oil engines** reduction geared to sc. shafts driving 2 Propellers Total Power: 1,470kW (1,998hp) Niigata 6L19HX 2 x 4 Stroke 6 Cy. 190 x 260 each-735kW (999bhp) Niigata Engineering Co Ltd-Japan Fuel: 50.0 (d.f.)
9074523 3EHZ9 -	**WISE I** *ex* Bosporus *-2013* *ex* World Place *-2003* **Wise Energy Equipment Co Ltd** East Sunrise Ship Management Ltd *Panama* *Panama* MMSI: 373683000 Official number: 44909PEXT	**77,211** 49,261 150,973 T/cm 109.7	Class: LR (NV) **100A1** SS 01/2010 bulk carrier strengthened for heavy cargoes, Nos. 2, 4, 6 & 8 holds may be empty strengthened for regular discharge by heavy grabs ESP ESN hold No. 1 LI **LMC** **UMS**	**1995-01 Daewoo Heavy Industries Ltd — Geoje** Yd No: 1092 Loa 274.00 (BB) Br ex 45.04 Dght 16.919 Lbp 264.00 Br md 45.00 Dpth 23.20 Welded, 1 dk	**(A21A2BC) Bulk Carrier** Grain: 169,379 Compartments: 9 Ho, ER 9 Ha: (13.8 x 15.3)8 (13.8 x 20.4)ER	**1 oil engine** driving 1 FP propeller Total Power: 12,137kW (16,501hp) 13.5kn B&W 5S70MC 1 x 2 Stroke 5 Cy. 700 x 2674 12137kW (16501bhp) Korea Heavy Industries & ConstrCo Ltd (HANJUNG)-South Korea AuxGen: 3 x 600kW 220/450V 60Hz a.c
9568457 3EW03 -	**WISE SW** **Wise Pescadores SA Panama** Shih Wei Navigation Co Ltd SatCom: Inmarsat C 435588711 *Panama* *Panama* MMSI: 355887000 Official number: 4147310	**8,435** 3,683 11,700 T/cm 20.0	Class: BV (CR)	**2010-03 Higaki Zosen K.K. — Imabari** Yd No: 638 Loa 116.99 (BB) Br ex - Dght 8.850 Lbp 109.01 Br md 19.60 Dpth 14.00 Welded, 1 dk	**(A31A2GX) General Cargo Ship** Grain: 17,620 Compartments: 2 Ho, 2 Tw Dk, ER 2 Ha: ER Cranes: 2x30.7t; Derricks: 1x30t	**1 oil engine** driving 1 FP propeller Total Power: 3,900kW (5,302hp) 13.4kn MAN-B&W 6L35MC 1 x 2 Stroke 6 Cy. 350 x 1050 3900kW (5302bhp) Makita Corp-Japan AuxGen: 2 x 320kW 60Hz a.c
9555278 YJVT2 -	**WISE TIDE II** **Platinum Fleet Ltd** Tidewater Marine Australia Pty Ltd SatCom: Inmarsat C 457616410 *Port Vila* *Vanuatu* MMSI: 576164000 Official number: 1844	**2,308** 852 3,230	Class: AB	**2009-07 Zhejiang Shipbuilding Co Ltd — Fenghua ZJ** Yd No: 07-170 Loa 73.21 Br ex - Dght 5.500 Lbp 70.77 Br md 16.50 Dpth 6.81 Welded, 1 dk	**(B21A20S) Platform Supply Ship**	**3 diesel electric oil engines** driving 3 gen. Connecting to 3 elec. motors driving 2 Azimuth electric drive units , 1 FP propeller Total Power: 5,148kW (6,999hp) 11.5kn Cummins QSK60-M 3 x Vee 4 Stroke 16 Cy. 159 x 190 each-1716kW (2333bhp) Chongqing Cummins Engine Co Ltd-China Thrusters: 2 Thwart. CP thruster (f)
9512898 DSBL5 -	**WISE YOUNG** **Joong Ang Shipping Co Ltd** - *Jeju* *South Korea* MMSI: 440006000 Official number: JJR-111039	**44,290** - 82,012	Class: KR	**2011-06 Daewoo Shipbuilding & Marine Engineering Co Ltd — Geoje** Yd No: 1189 Loa 229.00 (BB) Br ex - Dght 14.520 Lbp 218.25 Br md 32.26 Dpth 20.20 Welded, 1 dk	**(A21A2BC) Bulk Carrier** Grain: 96,500 Compartments: 7 Ho, ER 7 Ha: 6 (15.2 x 15.0)ER (15.2 x 13.3)	**1 oil engine** driving 1 FP propeller Total Power: 14,280kW (19,415hp) 14.5kn MAN-B&W 6S60MC-C8 1 x 2 Stroke 6 Cy. 600 x 2400 14280kW (19415bhp) Hyundai Heavy Industries Co Ltd-South Korea
9578531 3FAK2 -	**WISH WAY** **Wish Way Shipping Corp** CCCC International Shipping Corp *Panama* *Panama* MMSI: 371578000 Official number: 4247211	**16,611** 4,983 21,243	Class: CC	**2010-09 CCCC BOMESC Marine Industry Co Ltd — Tianjin** Yd No: 2008-020 Loa 156.00 (BB) Br ex - Dght 7.450 Lbp 149.40 Br md 36.00 Dpth 10.00 Welded, 1 dk	**(A38C3GH) Heavy Load Carrier, semi submersible** Ice Capable	**3 diesel electric oil engines** driving 3 gen. each 4320kW 6600V a.c Connecting to 2 elec. motors driving 2 Directional propellers Total Power: 13,200kW (17,946hp) 14.0kn MAN-B&W 9L32/40CD 3 x 4 Stroke 9 Cy. 320 x 400 each-4400kW (5982bhp) STX Engine Co Ltd-South Korea Thrusters: 2 Tunnel thruster (f)
8901585 YJZL7 -	**WISLA** *ex* Wislanes *-1999* **Rikson International Ltd** Primo-Faro Ltd *Port Vila* *Vanuatu* MMSI: 576082000	**9,815** 4,798 13,770 T/cm 25.5	Class: PR	**1992-04 Stocznia Szczecinska SA — Szczecin** Yd No: B567/01 Loa 143.70 (BB) Br ex 20.92 Dght 8.420 Lbp 132.41 Br md 20.60 Dpth 11.35 Welded, 1 dk	**(A21A2BC) Bulk Carrier** Grain: 16,659 Compartments: 5 Ho, ER 5 Ha: (9.8 x 9.0)4 (12.8 x 11.7)ER Cranes: 4x16t,1x12.5t Ice Capable	**1 oil engine** driving 1 FP propeller Total Power: 4,690kW (6,377hp) 13.5kn B&W 6L50MCE 1 x 2 Stroke 6 Cy. 500 x 1620 4690kW (6377bhp) H Cegielski Poznan SA-Poland AuxGen: 1 x 560kW 400V a.c, 3 x 470kW 400V a.c
5317226 - -	**WISMARIA** *ex* Seebad Heringsdorf *-1995* - -	**377** 113 63	Class: (DS) (GL)	**1961 VEB Schiffswerft "Edgar Andre" — Magdeburg** Yd No: 4 Loa 43.21 Br ex 7.62 Dght 2.210 Lbp 39.20 Br md - Dpth 3.38 Welded, 1 dk	**(A37B2PS) Passenger Ship** Passengers: unberthed: 243	**2 oil engines** driving 2 FP propellers Total Power: 382kW (520hp) 10.0kn S.K.L. 6NVD36-1U 2 x 4 Stroke 6 Cy. 240 x 360 each-191kW (260bhp) VEB Maschinenbau Halberstadt-Halberstadt AuxGen: 1 x 64kW 220/380V a.c
7424085 - -	**WISNU I** *launched as* Bayu I *-1979* **PT PERTAMINA (PERSERO)** - *Jakarta* *Indonesia*	*114* 34 15	Class: KI	**1979-03 P.T. Adiguna Shipbuilding & Engineering — Jakarta** Yd No: 66 Loa 27.51 Br ex - Dght 1.712 Lbp 25.02 Br md 6.51 Dpth 2.82 Welded, 1 dk	**(B32A2ST) Tug**	**2 oil engines** sr reverse geared to sc. shafts driving 2 FP propellers Total Power: 706kW (960hp) Mitsubishi S6N-MTK-2 2 x 4 Stroke 6 Cy. 160 x 180 each-353kW (480bhp) (made 1977, fitted 1979) Mitsubishi Heavy Industries Ltd-Japan
7424097 - -	**WISNU II** *launched as* Bayu II *-1979* **PT PERTAMINA (PERSERO)** - *Jakarta* *Indonesia*	*116* 35 15	Class: KI	**1979-04 P.T. Adiguna Shipbuilding & Engineering — Jakarta** Yd No: 67 Loa 27.51 Br ex - Dght 1.712 Lbp 25.02 Br md 6.51 Dpth 2.82 Welded, 1 dk	**(B32A2ST) Tug**	**2 oil engines** sr reverse geared to sc. shafts driving 2 FP propellers Total Power: 706kW (960hp) Mitsubishi S6N-MTK-2 2 x 4 Stroke 6 Cy. 160 x 180 each-353kW (480bhp) Mitsubishi Heavy Industries Ltd-Japan
7424114 - -	**WISNU IV** **PT PERTAMINA (PERSERO)** - *Jakarta* *Indonesia*	*123* 37 159	Class: KI	**1981-08 P.T. Adiguna Shipbuilding & Engineering — Jakarta** Yd No: 69 Loa 27.51 Br ex - Dght 1.712 Lbp 25.02 Br md 6.51 Dpth 2.82 Welded, 1 dk	**(B32A2ST) Tug**	**2 oil engines** sr reverse geared to sc. shafts driving 2 FP propellers Total Power: 706kW (960hp) Mitsubishi S6N-MTK-2 2 x 4 Stroke 6 Cy. 160 x 180 each-353kW (480bhp) Mitsubishi Heavy Industries Ltd-Japan
7719741 YD5039 -	**WISNU IX** *launched as* Bayu IX *-1980* **PT PERTAMINA (PERSERO)** - *Jakarta* *Indonesia* MMSI: 525080490	*114* 35 15	Class: KI	**1980-04 P.T. Adiguna Shipbuilding & Engineering — Jakarta** Yd No: 74 Loa 27.51 Br ex - Dght 1.712 Lbp 25.02 Br md 6.51 Dpth 2.82 Welded, 1 dk	**(B32A2ST) Tug**	**2 oil engines** sr reverse geared to sc. shafts driving 2 FP propellers Total Power: 706kW (960hp) Mitsubishi S6N-MTK-2 2 x 4 Stroke 6 Cy. 160 x 180 each-353kW (480bhp) Mitsubishi Heavy Industries Ltd-Japan
7523269 - -	**WISNU V** *launched as* Bayu V *-1980* **PT PERTAMINA (PERSERO)** - *Jakarta* *Indonesia*	*114* 35 15	Class: KI	**1980-01 P.T. Adiguna Shipbuilding & Engineering — Jakarta** Yd No: 70 Loa 27.51 Br ex - Dght 1.712 Lbp 25.02 Br md 6.51 Dpth 2.82 Welded, 1 dk	**(B32A2ST) Tug**	**2 oil engines** sr reverse geared to sc. shafts driving 2 FP propellers Total Power: 706kW (960hp) Mitsubishi S6N-MTK-2 2 x 4 Stroke 6 Cy. 160 x 180 each-353kW (480bhp) Mitsubishi Heavy Industries Ltd-Japan

7523271 *YDDR* -	**WISNU VI** **PT PERTAMINA (PERSERO)** - *Jakarta* *Indonesia*	*114* 35 159	Class: (KI)	**1981-06 P.T. Adiguna Shipbuilding & Engineering — Jakarta** Yd No: 71 Loa 27.51 Br ex - Dght 1.712 Lbp 25.02 Br md 6.51 Dpth 2.82 Welded, 1 dk	**(B32A2ST) Tug**	**2 oil engines** sr reverse geared to sc. shafts driving 2 FP propellers Total Power: 706kW (960hp) Mitsubishi S6N-MTK-2 2 x 4 Stroke 6 Cy. 160 x 180 each-353kW (480bhp) Mitsubishi Heavy Industries Ltd-Japan
7532064 - -	**WISNU VII** *launched as* Bayu VII *-1979* **PT PERTAMINA (PERSERO)** - *Jakarta* *Indonesia*	*114* 35 159	Class: KI	**1979-12 P.T. Adiguna Shipbuilding & Engineering — Jakarta** Yd No: 72 Loa 27.51 Br ex - Dght 1.712 Lbp 25.02 Br md 6.51 Dpth 2.82 Welded, 1 dk	**(B32A2ST) Tug**	**2 oil engines** sr reverse geared to sc. shafts driving 2 FP propellers Total Power: 706kW (960hp) Mitsubishi S6N-MTK-2 2 x 4 Stroke 6 Cy. 160 x 180 each-353kW (480bhp) Mitsubishi Heavy Industries Ltd-Japan
7532076 *YDDN* -	**WISNU VIII** **PT PERTAMINA (PERSERO)** - *Jakarta* *Indonesia*	*115* 35 159	Class: KI	**1981-08 P.T. Adiguna Shipbuilding & Engineering — Jakarta** Yd No: 73 Loa 27.51 Br ex - Dght 1.712 Lbp 25.02 Br md 6.51 Dpth 2.82 Welded, 1 dk	**(B32A2ST) Tug**	**2 oil engines** sr reverse geared to sc. shafts driving 2 FP propellers Total Power: 706kW (960hp) Mitsubishi S6N-TK 2 x 4 Stroke 6 Cy. 160 x 180 each-353kW (480bhp) Mitsubishi Heavy Industries Ltd-Japan
7811238 - -	**WISNU XI** *launched as* Bayu XI *-1980* **PT PERTAMINA (PERSERO)** - *Jakarta* *Indonesia*	*101* 31 15	Class: KI	**1980 P.T. Adiguna Shipbuilding & Engineering — Jakarta** Yd No: 76 Loa 27.51 Br ex - Dght 1.712 Lbp 25.02 Br md 6.51 Dpth 2.82 Welded, 1 dk	**(B32A2ST) Tug**	**2 oil engines** sr reverse geared to sc. shafts driving 2 FP propellers Total Power: 706kW (960hp) Mitsubishi S6N-MTK-2 2 x 4 Stroke 6 Cy. 160 x 180 each-353kW (480bhp) Mitsubishi Heavy Industries Ltd-Japan
7826386 - -	**WISNU XII** **PT PERTAMINA (PERSERO)** - *Jakarta* *Indonesia*	*114* 35 15	Class: (KI)	**1983-09 P.T. Adiguna Shipbuilding & Engineering — Jakarta** Yd No: 77 Loa 27.51 Br ex 6.63 Dght 1.712 Lbp 25.02 Br md 6.51 Dpth 5.80 Welded, 1 dk	**(B32A2ST) Tug**	**2 oil engines** sr geared to sc. shafts driving 2 FP propellers Total Power: 706kW (960hp) 12.5kn Mitsubishi S6N-MTK-2 2 x 4 Stroke 6 Cy. 160 x 180 each-353kW (480bhp) Mitsubishi Heavy Industries Ltd-Japan AuxGen: 1 x 40kW 220V 50Hz a.c Fuel: 7.5 (d.f.)
8985086 *PCIA* BRU 50	**WISSELVALLIGHEID** **H Hoogerheide Beheer BV & L de Waal Beheer BV** - *Bruinisse* *Netherlands* MMSI: 246516000 Official number: 26869	**155** 46 -		**1915-01 D. Boot — Alphen a/d Rijn** Loa 33.77 Br ex - Dght - Lbp 31.15 Br md 7.10 Dpth 2.63 Riveted, 1 dk	**(B11B2FV) Fishing Vessel**	**1 oil engine** driving 1 Propeller
8112407 *VMWT* -	**WISTARI** *ex* W. J. Trotter *-1985* **Svitzer Australia Pty Ltd (Svitzer Australasia)** - *Brisbane, Qld* *Australia* MMSI: 503035000 Official number: 850341	*396* 117 368	Class: LR ✠ **100A1** SS 11/2012 tug ✠ **LMC** **UMS** Eq.Ltr: G; Cable: 302.5/20.5 U2	**1982-12 Carrington Slipways Pty Ltd — Newcastle NSW** Yd No: 153 Loa 33.91 Br ex 11.10 Dght 4.601 Lbp 29.67 Br md 10.83 Dpth 5.41 Welded, 1 dk	**(B32A2ST) Tug**	**2 oil engines** with clutches, flexible couplings & dr geared to sc. shafts driving 2 Directional propellers Total Power: 2,648kW (3,600hp) 11.5kn Daihatsu 6DSM-28 2 x 4 Stroke 6 Cy. 280 x 340 each-1324kW (1800bhp) Daihatsu Diesel Manufacturing Co Lt-Japan AuxGen: 2 x 125kW 415V 50Hz a.c Fuel: 118.0 (d.f.) 6.5pd
9355197 *ZCTE* -	**WISTERIA ACE** **Polar Express SA** MOL Ocean Expert Co Ltd *George Town* *Cayman Islands (British)* MMSI: 319834000 Official number: 740029	**59,952** 18,543 17,325 T/cm 51.9	Class: NK	**2007-05 Toyohashi Shipbuilding Co Ltd — Toyohashi AI** Yd No: 3597 Loa 199.99 (BB) Br ex - Dght 9.725 Lbp 192.00 Br md 32.26 Dpth 14.65 Welded, 9 dks plus 2 movable dks	**(A35B2RV) Vehicles Carrier** Side door/ramp (s) Len: 17.00 Wid: 6.50 Swl: 35 Quarter stern door/ramp (s. a.) Len: 35.00 Wid: 8.00 Swl: 150 Cars: 6,287	**1 oil engine** driving 1 FP propeller Total Power: 15,090kW (20,516hp) 19.8kn Mitsubishi 8UEC60LSII 1 x 2 Stroke 8 Cy. 600 x 2300 15090kW (20516bhp) Kobe Hatsudoki KK-Japan Thrusters: 1 Tunnel thruster (f) Fuel: 2700.0
8987321 *MGAB5* -	**WISTING** **Wisting Ltd** Pelagos Yachts Ltd *Ramsey* *Isle of Man (British)* MMSI: 235055577 Official number: 735403	**162** 48 -	Class: LR **100A1** SS 08/2012 SSC Yacht, mono, G6 **LMC** Cable: 137.5/16.0 U2 (a)	**1978-01 Voldnes Skipsverft AS — Fosnavaag** Yd No: 20 Converted From: Supply Tender-2007 Loa 31.30 Br ex - Dght 2.660 Lbp 26.30 Br md 6.70 Dpth 3.55 Welded, 1 dk	**(X11A2YP) Yacht**	**2 diesel electric oil engines** driving 2 gen. each 200kW 400V a.c Connecting to 1 elec. Motor of (390kW) driving 1 FP propeller Total Power: 780kW (1,060hp) 10.5kn Caterpillar C9 2 x 4 Stroke 6 Cy. 112 x 149 each-390kW (530bhp) (new engine 2007) Caterpillar Inc-USA Thrusters: 1 Thwart. FP thruster (f)
9418781 *LASW* -	**WITH JUNIOR** **Egil Ulvan Rederi AS** Ulvan Personal AS SatCom: Inmarsat C 425912010 *Trondheim* *Norway* MMSI: 259120000	**2,362** 1,388 1,950	Class: NV	**2009-05 AS Rigas Kugu Buvetava (Riga Shipyard) — Riga** (Hull) **2009-05 Moen Slip AS — Kolvereid** Yd No: 67 Loa 66.70 (BB) Br ex - Dght 5.250 Lbp 61.70 Br md 14.60 Dpth 10.82 Welded, 1 dk	**(A31B2GP) Palletised Cargo Ship** Grain: 3,873; Ins: 1,363 TEU 59 C.Ho 6/20' C.Dk 59/20' incl 12 ref C. Cranes: 1x50t Ice Capable	**1 oil engine** reduction geared to sc. shafts driving 1 CP propeller Total Power: 1,840kW (2,502hp) 12.5kn A.B.C. 8DZC 1 x 4 Stroke 8 Cy. 256 x 310 1840kW (2502bhp) Anglo Belgian Corp NV (ABC)-Belgium AuxGen: 1 x 450kW a.c, 1 x 700kW a.c Thrusters: 1 Tunnel thruster (f); 1 Tunnel thruster (a)
5108637 - -	**WITSERVICE II** *ex* Esso Tug No. 2 *-1985* *ex* Socony 17 *-1985* *ex* S. T. Co. No. 17 *-1985* *ex* S. O. Co. No. 17 *-1985* - -	*233* 63 -		**1907 Skinner SB. & D.D. Co. — Baltimore, Md** L reg 27.44 Br ex 7.01 Dght - Lbp - Br md 6.96 Dpth - Riveted	**(B32A2ST) Tug**	**1 oil engine** driving 1 FP propeller Total Power: 662kW (900hp) EMD (Electro-Motive) 12-567-BC 1 x Vee 2 Stroke 12 Cy. 216 x 254 662kW (900bhp) (, fitted 1943) General Motors Corp-USA
9014676 *V2DA* -	**WITTENBERGEN** **ms 'Wittenbergen' Koss River Liner KG** Wessels Reederei GmbH & Co KG SatCom: Inmarsat C 430434110 *Saint John's* *Antigua & Barbuda* MMSI: 304341000	**2,381** 957 3,600	Class: GL	**1992-01 Slovenske Lodenice a.s. — Komarno** Yd No: 2902 Loa 88.70 Br ex - Dght 5.450 Lbp 81.00 Br md 12.80 Dpth 7.10 Welded, 1 dk	**(A31A2GX) General Cargo Ship** Grain: 4,650; Bale: 4,620 TEU 176 C. 176/20' Compartments: 1 Ho, ER 1 Ha: (56.6 x 10.2)ER Ice Capable	**1 oil engine** reverse reduction geared to sc. shaft driving 1 FP propeller Total Power: 1,500kW (2,039hp) 10.6kn Deutz SBV8M628 1 x 4 Stroke 8 Cy. 240 x 280 1500kW (2039bhp) Kloeckner Humboldt Deutz AG-Germany AuxGen: 3 x 104kW 220/380V 50Hz a.c Thrusters: 1 Thwart. FP thruster (f)
9104859 - -	**WITTOW** - -	*340* - 110		**1994-08 Oderwerft GmbH — Eisenhuettenstadt** Yd No: 2522 Loa 39.90 Br ex 12.39 Dght 1.300 Lbp - Br md 11.10 Dpth 2.50 Welded, 1 dk	**(A36A2PR) Passenger/Ro-Ro Ship (Vehicles)** Passengers: unberthed: 150 Bow ramp (centre) Stern ramp (centre) Cars: 25	**3 oil engines** gearing integral to driving 2 Voith-Schneider propellers 1 fwd and 1 aft Total Power: 555kW (756hp) 7.5kn MWM TBD234V6 3 x Vee 4 Stroke 6 Cy. 128 x 140 each-185kW (252bhp) Motoren Werke Mannheim AG (MWM)-Mannheim AuxGen: 1 x 30kW 220/400V 50Hz a.c Fuel: 12.0 (d.f.)
8136427 *HO6928* -	**WITTUG** *ex* Wittug I *-1983* *ex* LT-536 *-1983* **Witwater Corp** West Indies Transport Ltda SA *Panama* *Panama* MMSI: 354032000 Official number: 1840289A	**537** 161 -	Class: (AB)	**1944 Levingston SB. Co. — Orange, Tx** Yd No: 332 L reg 41.40 Br ex - Dght 4.701 Lbp 41.00 Br md 10.05 Dpth 5.11 Welded, 2 dks	**(B32A2ST) Tug**	**2 diesel electric oil engines** driving 2 FP propellers Total Power: 1,398kW (1,900hp) General Motors 12-278A 2 x Vee 2 Stroke 12 Cy. 222 x 267 each-699kW (950bhp) General Motors Corp.Electro-Motive Div.-U.S.A.
7616729 *DUA2726* -	**WIWIT** *ex* Myojin Maru No. 5 *-1996* *ex* Myojin Maru No. 25 *-1987* *ex* Yakushi Maru No. 25 *-1986* **Irma Fishing & Trading Inc** - *Manila* *Philippines* Official number: MNLD009101	*189* 99 123		**1976-10 Niigata Engineering Co Ltd — Niigata NI** Yd No: 1531 Loa 37.34 Br ex 6.94 Dght 2.667 Lbp 31.32 Br md 6.91 Dpth 2.80 Welded, 1 dk	**(B11B2FV) Fishing Vessel**	**1 oil engine** driving 1 FP propeller Total Power: 956kW (1,300hp) Niigata 6L28BX 1 x 4 Stroke 8 Cy. 280 x 320 956kW (1300bhp) Niigata Engineering Co Ltd-Japan

IMO / Call sign	Name / Owner	Tonnage	Class	Builder / Dimensions	Type	Machinery
181986 0BBN	**WIZ SKY** *ex* Hai In *-2012* *ex* Proceeder *-2008* **WIZ GLS Co Ltd** - *Jeju* *South Korea* MMSI: 441960000 Official number: JJR-121034	6,715 3,633 8,932	Class: KR (NK)	**1998**-07 **Shin Kurushima Dockyard Co. Ltd. — Hashihama, Imabari** Yd No: 2976 Loa 99.97 Br ex - Dght 8.226 Lbp 93.50 Br md 19.60 Dpth 13.60 Welded, 1 dk	**(A31A2GX) General Cargo Ship** Grain: 15,691; Bale: 14,507 Compartments: 2 Ho, ER 2 Ha: (21.0 x 12.6) (27.0 x 12.6)ER Cranes: 2x30.5t; Derricks: 1x30t	**1 oil engine** driving 1 FP propeller Total Power: 3,884kW (5,281hp) 16.0kn B&W 6L35MC 1 x 2 Stroke 6 Cy. 350 x 1050 3884kW (5281bhp) Makita Corp-Japan
8992883 WDC6082 -	**WIZARD** *ex* YO-210 *-1974* **K H Colburn Inc** - *Seattle, WA* *United States of America* MMSI: 367050980 Official number: 594470	*499* 371 -		**1945**-01 **Ira S. Bushey & Son, Inc. — New York, NY** Yd No: 581 Converted From: Replenishment Tanker-1945 Loa 45.93 Br ex - Dght - Lbp - Br md 9.17 Dpth 3.96 Welded, 1 dk	**(B11B2FV) Fishing Vessel**	**1 oil engine** driving 1 Propeller Caterpillar 1 x 4 Stroke Caterpillar Inc-USA
1003554 - -	**WIZARD** *ex* Rewind *-2012* *ex* Amphitrite Kapa *-2007* *ex* Amphitrite K *-2006* *ex* Amphitrite *-2002* *ex* Sabidan IV *-1995* **Malvern Ventures Ltd** Solent International Marine Consultants Ltd *London* *United Kingdom* Official number: 905436	207 62 -	Class: LR ✠ **100A1** SS 03/2013 Yacht ***LMC**	**1985**-10 **Scheepswerf Porsius B.V. — Zaandam** Loa 28.06 Br ex 7.32 Dght 2.250 Lbp 24.40 Br md - Dpth 4.02 Welded, 1 dk	**(X11A2YP) Yacht**	**2 oil engines** driving 2 FP propellers Total Power: 804kW (1,094hp) Daimler 2 x Vee 4 Stroke 12 Cy. each-402kW (547bhp) Daimler Benz AG-West Germany
8510104 XUEG4	**WIZARD** *ex* Kookyang Pohang *-2012* *ex* Ky Fortune *-2011* *ex* Seanet Dream *-2007* *ex* Tongli Success *-2006* *ex* Wahana *-2004* *ex* Sun Kung No. 11 *-2003* *ex* Hercules *-1996* **Atlas Pacific Shipping Co Ltd** Trans Line Co Ltd *Phnom Penh* *Cambodia* MMSI: 514342000 Official number: 1285836	5,545 2,310 6,691	Class: GM (NK)	**1985**-11 **Kochi Jyuko K.K. — Kochi** Yd No: 2456 Loa 100.17 (BB) Br ex - Dght 7.576 Lbp 89.79 Br md 18.81 Dpth 12.90 Welded, 2 dks	**(A31A2GX) General Cargo Ship** Grain: 12,952; Bale: 11,847 TEU 151 C. 151/20' Compartments: 2 Ho, ER 2 Ha: 2 (20.3 x 10.2)ER Derricks: 1x30t,3x25t	**1 oil engine** driving 1 FP propeller Total Power: 2,795kW (3,800hp) 13.0kn B&W 5L35MC 1 x 2 Stroke 5 Cy. 350 x 1050 2795kW (3800bhp) Makita Diesel Co Ltd-Japan Fuel: 525.0 (r.f.)
9231913 HP3508 -	**WJT-1201** *ex* Sea Harvest *-2010* *ex* Profit Harvest *-2006* **Woongjin Development Co Ltd** - *Panama* *Panama* Official number: 4196210	135 41 121	Class: RI (AB) (NK)	**2000**-05 **Forward Shipbuilding Enterprise Sdn Bhd — Sibu** Yd No: 68 Loa 23.15 Br ex - Dght 2.545 Lbp 21.05 Br md 7.30 Dpth 3.00 Welded, 1 dk	**(B32B2SP) Pusher Tug**	**2 oil engines** reduction geared to sc. shafts driving 2 FP propellers Total Power: 954kW (1,298hp) 12.0kn Yanmar 6LAHM-STE3 2 x 4 Stroke 6 Cy. 150 x 165 each-477kW (649bhp) Yanmar Diesel Engine Co Ltd-Japan AuxGen: 2 x 20kW a.c Fuel: 95.0 (d.f.)
9259446 HP7066 -	**WJT-1202** *ex* Valiant Seahorse *-2010* *ex* Ocean Island *-2003* **Woong Jin Development SA** Woongjin Development Co Ltd *Panama* *Panama* Official number: 4184510	136 41 102	Class: KR (AB) (NK)	**2001**-11 **Dalian Shipyard Co Ltd — Dalian LN** Yd No: TU23-1 Loa 23.15 Br ex - Dght 2.500 Lbp 21.05 Br md 7.30 Dpth 3.00 Welded, 1 dk	**(B32A2ST) Tug**	**2 oil engines** reduction geared to sc. shafts driving 2 FP propellers Total Power: 912kW (1,240hp) Yanmar 6LAHM-STE3 2 x 4 Stroke 6 Cy. 150 x 165 each-456kW (620bhp) Yanmar Diesel Engine Co Ltd-Japan AuxGen: 2 x 20kW a.c Fuel: 124.0 (d.f.)
9280342 HP5393 -	**WJT-1203** *ex* Sea Lion *-2010* *ex* Kim Heng 99 *-2006* **Woong Jin Development SA** Woongjin Development Co Ltd *Panama* *Panama* Official number: 4180710	128 39 130	Class: RI (KR) (AB) (NK)	**2002**-06 **Yong Choo Kui Shipyard Sdn Bhd — Sibu** Yd No: 6521 Loa 23.15 Br ex - Dght 2.512 Lbp 21.67 Br md 7.30 Dpth 3.00 Welded, 1 Dk.	**(B32A2ST) Tug**	**2 oil engines** reduction geared to sc. shafts driving 2 FP propellers Total Power: 882kW (1,200hp) Cummins KTA-19-M3 2 x 4 Stroke 6 Cy. 159 x 159 each-441kW (600bhp) Cummins Engine Co Inc-USA AuxGen: 2 x a.c
9277503 HP6929 -	**WJT-1204** *ex* Sea Storm *-2010* *ex* Kim Heng 77 *-2006* **Woong Jin Development SA** Woongjin Development Co Ltd *Panama* *Panama* Official number: 4182510	148 45 125	Class: RI (KR) (AB) (GL) (NK)	**2002**-07 **Tuong Aik (Sarawak) Sdn Bhd — Sibu** Yd No: 2111 Loa 23.80 Br ex - Dght 2.972 Lbp 21.85 Br md 7.60 Dpth 3.70 Welded, 1 dk	**(B32A2ST) Tug**	**2 oil engines** geared to sc. shafts driving 2 FP propellers Total Power: 918kW (1,248hp) Caterpillar 3412TA 2 x Vee 4 Stroke 12 Cy. 137 x 152 each-459kW (624bhp) Caterpillar Inc-USA Fuel: 85.0 (d.f.)
9385295 HP6996 -	**WJT-1601** *ex* Sea Glory *-2010* *ex* Sea Glory 16 *-2006* **Woongjin Development Co Ltd** - *Panama* *Panama* Official number: 4196110	192 58 217	Class: GL (NK) (NV)	**2006**-02 **Forward Marine Enterprise Sdn Bhd — Sibu** Yd No: FM-2 Loa 26.00 Br ex - Dght 3.214 Lbp 23.83 Br md 8.00 Dpth 3.65 Welded, 1 dk	**(B32A2ST) Tug**	**2 oil engines** reduction geared to sc. shafts driving 2 FP propellers Total Power: 1,220kW (1,658hp) Yanmar 6AYM-ETE 2 x 4 Stroke 6 Cy. 155 x 180 each-610kW (829bhp) Yanmar Diesel Engine Co Ltd-Japan Fuel: 115.0 (d.f.)
9045340 HP4503 -	**WJT-2401** *ex* Ecs Baran *-2013* *ex* Hercules *-2011* *ex* Ena Hercules *-2007* *ex* Trans Hercules *-1999* *ex* SSP 789 *-1992* **Woong Jin Development SA** Woongjin Development Co Ltd *Panama* *Panama* MMSI: 372586000 Official number: 44956PEXT	220 66 179	Class: BV (AB)	**1991**-05 **President Marine Pte Ltd — Singapore** Yd No: 063 L reg 27.08 Br ex - Dght - Lbp - Br md 8.72 Dpth 4.11 Welded, 1 dk	**(B32A2ST) Tug**	**2 oil engines** sr geared to sc. shafts driving 2 FP propellers Total Power: 1,766kW (2,402hp) 10.5kn Yanmar M220-EN 2 x 4 Stroke 6 Cy. 220 x 300 each-883kW (1201bhp) Yanmar Diesel Engine Co Ltd-Japan AuxGen: 2 x 40kW 415V 50Hz a.c Fuel: 125.0 (d.f.) 6.5pd
9027972 - -	**WKA OCEAN** *ex* Anggrek Indah *-2003* **PT Mitra Baruna Sarana** - *Samarinda* *Indonesia*	109 65 -	Class: KI	**2000**-07 **P.T. Karya Mulyo Teknik — Samarinda** Loa 21.00 Br ex - Dght 2.180 Lbp 18.75 Br md 6.10 Dpth 2.50 Welded, 1 dk	**(B32A2ST) Tug**	**2 oil engines** geared to sc. shafts driving 2 FP propellers Total Power: 588kW (800hp) Nissan RD10 2 x Vee 4 Stroke 10 Cy. 135 x 125 each-294kW (400bhp) Nissan Diesel Motor Co. Ltd.-Ageo AuxGen: 1 x 20kW 380/220V a.c, 1 x 18kW 380/220V a.c
8999221 - -	**WKA STAR** - **PT Mitra Baruna Sarana** - *Samarinda* *Indonesia*	169 101 -	Class: KI	**2001**-01 **P.T. Galangan Kapal Mas Pioner — Samarinda** L reg 23.00 Br ex - Dght 2.390 Lbp 21.50 Br md 6.55 Dpth 3.00 Welded, 1 dk	**(B32A2ST) Tug**	**2 oil engines** geared to sc. shafts driving 2 Propellers Total Power: 588kW (800hp) 8.0kn Mitsubishi 10DC11-1A 2 x Vee 4 Stroke 10 Cy. 141 x 152 each-294kW (400bhp) (made 1995, fitted 2001) Mitsubishi Heavy Industries Ltd-Japan
8128573 SPG3578 -	**WLA-84** *ex* En Avant *-2011* *ex* Cornelis Trijntje *-2003* **Denega Necel Sp j** - *Wladyslawowo* *Poland* Official number: RO/S-G-1272	122 36 -	Class: PR	**1982 Scheepswerf Veldthuis B.V. — Zuidbroek** Yd No: 308 Loa 25.16 Br ex 6.00 Dght 2.330 Lbp - Br md - Dpth 3.10 Welded, 1 dk	**(B11B2FV) Fishing Vessel**	**1 oil engine** driving 1 FP propeller Total Power: 271kW (368hp) Mitsubishi S6N-MPTK 1 x 4 Stroke 6 Cy. 160 x 180 271kW (368bhp) Mitsubishi Heavy Industries Ltd-Japan
7038288 - -	**WLA-109** - -	*107* 40 43	Class: (PR)	**1959 Gdynska Stocznia Remontowa — Gdynia** Yd No: B25s/198 Loa 24.62 Br ex 6.61 Dght 2.501 Lbp 21.95 Br md - Dpth 3.38 Welded, 1 dk	**(B11B2FV) Fishing Vessel**	**1 oil engine** driving 1 FP propeller Total Power: 165kW (224hp) 10.0kn Volund DM-330 1 x 4 Stroke 3 Cy. 300 x 410 165kW (224bhp) A/S Volund-Denmark AuxGen: 2 x 3kW 24V d.c, 1 x 1kW 24V d.c
7025061 - -	**WLA-120** *ex* HEL-105 *-2000* *ex* Arion I *-1992* *ex* HEL-105 *-1989* - -	107 - 42	Class: PR	**1960**-05 **Gdynska Stocznia Remontowa — Gdynia** Yd No: B25s/211 Loa 24.54 Br ex 6.58 Dght 2.361 Lbp 21.95 Br md - Dpth 3.38 Welded, 1 dk	**(B11B2FV) Fishing Vessel**	**1 oil engine** driving 1 FP propeller Total Power: 165kW (224hp) 10.0kn Volund DM-330 1 x 4 Stroke 3 Cy. 300 x 410 165kW (224bhp) A/S Volund-Denmark AuxGen: 1 x 2kW 24V d.c, 1 x 2kW 24V d.c, 1 x 1kW 24V d.c
7038305 - -	**WLA-132** - -	*107* 40 35	Class: (PR)	**1959 Gdynska Stocznia Remontowa — Gdynia** Yd No: B25s/201 Loa 24.62 Br ex 6.61 Dght 2.420 Lbp 21.95 Br md - Dpth 3.38 Welded, 1 dk	**(B11B2FV) Fishing Vessel**	**1 oil engine** driving 1 FP propeller Total Power: 165kW (224hp) 10.0kn Volund DM-330 1 x 4 Stroke 3 Cy. 300 x 410 165kW (224bhp) A/S Volund-Denmark AuxGen: 1 x 4kW 24V d.c, 1 x 1kW 24V d.c

IMO / Call sign / Flag	Name / Owner	GT / NT / DWT	Class	Builder / Dimensions	Type	Machinery	Speed
7040918 - -	**WLA-134** *ex* SWI-44 -	*107* 40 56	Class: (PR)	**1959 Gdynska Stocznia Remontowa — Gdynia** Yd No: B25s/186 Loa 24.62 Br ex 6.61 Dght - Lbp 21.95 Br md - Dpth 3.38 Welded, 1 dk	**(B11B2FV) Fishing Vessel**	**1 oil engine** driving 1 FP propeller Total Power: 165kW (224hp) Volund 1 x 4 Stroke 3 Cy. 300 x 410 165kW (224bhp) A/S Volund-Denmark AuxGen: 1 x 4kW 24V d.c, 1 x 1kW 24V d.c	10.0kr DM-33
7040956 - -	**WLA-138** - -	*107* 39 36	Class: (PR)	**1960-08 Gdynska Stocznia Remontowa — Gdynia** Yd No: B25s/214 Loa 24.55 Br ex 6.58 Dght 2.291 Lbp 21.95 Br md - Dpth 3.38 Welded, 1 dk	**(B11B2FV) Fishing Vessel**	**1 oil engine** driving 1 FP propeller Total Power: 165kW (224hp) Volund 1 x 4 Stroke 3 Cy. 300 x 410 165kW (224bhp) A/S Volund-Denmark AuxGen: 1 x 3kW 24V d.c, 1 x 1kW 24V d.c	10.0kn DM-330
7040970 - -	**WLA-146** - -	*106* 39 36	Class: (PR)	**1962-06 Gdynska Stocznia Remontowa — Gdynia** Yd No: B25s/253 Loa 24.54 Br ex 6.58 Dght 2.380 Lbp 21.95 Br md - Dpth 3.38 Welded, 1 dk	**(B11B2FV) Fishing Vessel**	**1 oil engine** driving 1 FP propeller Total Power: 165kW (224hp) Volund 1 x 4 Stroke 3 Cy. 300 x 410 165kW (224bhp) A/S Volund-Denmark AuxGen: 1 x 3kW 24V d.c, 1 x 1kW 24V d.c	10.0kn DM-330
7045853 - -	**WLA-149** - -	*106* 39 41	Class: PR	**1962-10 Gdynska Stocznia Remontowa — Gdynia** Yd No: B25s/256 Loa 24.62 Br ex 6.58 Dght 2.291 Lbp 21.95 Br md - Dpth 3.38 Welded, 1 dk	**(B11B2FV) Fishing Vessel**	**1 oil engine** driving 1 FP propeller Total Power: 165kW (224hp) Volund 1 x 4 Stroke 3 Cy. 300 x 410 165kW (224bhp) A/S Volund-Denmark AuxGen: 1 x 3kW 24V d.c, 1 x 1kW 24V d.c	9.5kn DM-330
7045891 - -	**WLA-153** - -	*107* 38 35	Class: (PR)	**1964-05 Gdynska Stocznia Remontowa — Gdynia** Yd No: B25s/263 Loa 24.58 Br ex 6.58 Dght 2.500 Lbp 21.95 Br md - Dpth 3.38 Welded, 1 dk	**(B11B2FV) Fishing Vessel**	**1 oil engine** driving 1 FP propeller Total Power: 165kW (224hp) Volund 1 x 4 Stroke 3 Cy. 300 x 410 165kW (224bhp) A/S Volund-Denmark AuxGen: 1 x 3kW 24V d.c, 1 x 2kW 24V d.c, 1 x 1kW 24V d.c	9.0kn DM-330
7321855 - -	**WLA-204** - -	*104* 37 38	Class: (PR)	**1973-05 Stocznia Ustka SA — Ustka** Yd No: B25s/A17 Loa 24.52 Br ex 6.58 Dght 2.450 Lbp 21.85 Br md 6.56 Dpth 3.36 Welded, 1 dk	**(B11B2FV) Fishing Vessel**	**1 oil engine** driving 1 CP propeller Total Power: 257kW (349hp) Wola 1 x Vee 4 Stroke 12 Cy. 135 x 155 257kW (349bhp) Zaklady Mechaniczne 'PZL Wola' im MNowotki-Poalnd AuxGen: 2 x 4kW 24V d.c	10.5kn 22H12A
7393470 - -	**WLA-208** - -	*106* 39 44	Class: (PR)	**1974-07 Stocznia Ustka SA — Ustka** Yd No: B25s/A34 Loa 24.48 Br ex 6.58 Dght 2.501 Lbp 21.85 Br md 6.56 Dpth 3.38 Welded, 1 dk	**(B11B2FV) Fishing Vessel**	**1 oil engine** driving 1 CP propeller Total Power: 257kW (349hp) Wola 1 x Vee 4 Stroke 12 Cy. 135 x 155 257kW (349bhp) Zaklady Mechaniczne 'PZL Wola' im MNowotki-Poalnd AuxGen: 2 x 4kW 30V d.c	10.0kn 22H12A
7635701 *SPG2444* WLA-288	**WLA-288** **Lech Muza** - *Wladyslawowo* *Poland* MMSI: 261007120	**142** 43 68	Class: PR	**1979-04 Stocznia Ustka SA — Ustka** Yd No: B403/15 Loa 26.24 Br ex - Dght 2.966 Lbp 22.51 Br md 7.22 Dpth 3.48 Welded, 1 dk	**(B11A2FS) Stern Trawler**	**1 oil engine** geared to sc. shaft driving 1 CP propeller Total Power: 419kW (570hp) Sulzer 1 x 4 Stroke 6 Cy. 200 x 240 419kW (570bhp) Puckie Zaklady Mechaniczne Ltd-Puck AuxGen: 1 x 32kW 400V a.c, 1 x 29kW 400V a.c	10.8kn 6AL20/24
7635799 - WLA-290	**WLA-290** *ex* Greifswalder Oie *-1978* **Leszek Sadalski** - *Wladyslawowo* *Poland*	*106* 32 58	Class: (PR)	**1978-03 Stocznia Ustka SA — Ustka** Yd No: B403/06 Loa 26.29 Br ex - Dght 2.900 Lbp 22.51 Br md 7.23 Dpth 3.48 Welded, 1 dk	**(B11A2FS) Stern Trawler**	**1 oil engine** reduction geared to sc. shaft driving 1 CP propeller Total Power: 419kW (570hp) Sulzer 1 x 4 Stroke 6 Cy. 200 x 240 419kW (570bhp) Puckie Zaklady Mechaniczne Ltd-Puck AuxGen: 1 x 37kW 400V a.c	10.8kn 6AL20/24
7635787 *SPG2441* WLA-291	**WLA-291** *launched as* Danholm *-1978* **Wiktor Bolda & Jan Kobus** - *Wladyslawowo* *Poland* MMSI: 261005270	**143** 43 58	Class: PR	**1978-04 Stocznia Ustka SA — Ustka** Yd No: B403/07 Loa 26.29 Br ex - Dght 2.900 Lbp 22.51 Br md 7.23 Dpth 3.48 Welded, 1 dk	**(B11A2FS) Stern Trawler**	**1 oil engine** reduction geared to sc. shaft driving 1 CP propeller Total Power: 419kW (570hp) Sulzer 1 x 4 Stroke 6 Cy. 200 x 240 419kW (570bhp) Puckie Zaklady Mechaniczne Ltd-Puck AuxGen: 2 x 37kW 400V a.c	10.8kn 6AL20/24
7635749 *SPG2016* WLA-295	**WLA-295** **Jaroslaw Dominik** - *Wladyslawowo* *Poland* MMSI: 261004780 Official number: ROG/S/203	**143** 43 68	Class: PR	**1978-12 Stocznia Ustka SA — Ustka** Yd No: B403/11 Loa 26.27 Br ex - Dght 2.980 Lbp 22.48 Br md 7.23 Dpth 3.48 Welded, 1 dk	**(B11A2FS) Stern Trawler**	**1 oil engine** reduction geared to sc. shaft driving 1 CP propeller Total Power: 419kW (570hp) Sulzer 1 x 4 Stroke 6 Cy. 200 x 240 419kW (570bhp) Puckie Zaklady Mechaniczne Ltd-Puck AuxGen: 1 x 32kW 400V a.c, 1 x 29kW 400V a.c	10.8kn 6AL20/24
7635725 - -	**WLA-297** - -	**143** 43 68	Class: PR	**1979-03 Stocznia Ustka SA — Ustka** Yd No: B403/13 Loa 26.29 Br ex - Dght 2.931 Lbp 22.48 Br md 7.23 Dpth 3.48 Welded, 1 dk	**(B11A2FS) Stern Trawler** Ice Capable	**1 oil engine** geared to sc. shaft driving 1 CP propeller Total Power: 419kW (570hp) Sulzer 1 x 4 Stroke 6 Cy. 200 x 240 419kW (570bhp) Puckie Zaklady Mechaniczne Ltd-Puck AuxGen: 1 x 32kW 400V a.c, 1 x 29kW 400V a.c	10.8kn 6AL20/24
7637709 -	**WLA-298** **Oman Fisheries Co SAOG** *Oman*	*114* 35 69	Class: (PR)	**1977-12 Stocznia Ustka SA — Ustka** Yd No: B410/20 Loa 25.79 Br ex - Dght 3.169 Lbp 22.48 Br md 7.26 Dpth 3.43 Welded, 1 dk	**(B11A2FT) Trawler** Grain: 90	**1 oil engine** reduction geared to sc. shaft driving 1 CP propeller Total Power: 419kW (570hp) Sulzer 1 x 4 Stroke 6 Cy. 200 x 240 419kW (570bhp) Puckie Zaklady Mechaniczne Ltd-Puck AuxGen: 1 x 32kW 400V a.c, 1 x 29kW 400V a.c	10.8kn 6AL20/24
7521302 -	**WLA-302** - -	*114* 35 58	Class: (PR)	**1976-03 Stocznia Ustka SA — Ustka** Yd No: B410/203 Loa 25.68 Br ex 7.24 Dght 2.890 Lbp 22.48 Br md 7.21 Dpth 3.51 Welded, 1 dk	**(B11A2FS) Stern Trawler** Grain: 90	**1 oil engine** reduction geared to sc. shaft driving 1 CP propeller Total Power: 419kW (570hp) Sulzer 1 x 4 Stroke 6 Cy. 200 x 240 419kW (570bhp) Puckie Zaklady Mechaniczne Ltd-Puck AuxGen: 1 x 32kW 400V a.c, 1 x 29kW 400V a.c	10.8kn 6AL20/24
7531864 - -	**WLA-303** - -	**161** 48 58	Class: PR	**1976-07 Stocznia Ustka SA — Ustka** Yd No: B410/204 Loa 25.68 Br ex 7.24 Dght 2.820 Lbp 22.48 Br md 7.21 Dpth 3.51 Welded, 1 dk	**(B11A2FS) Stern Trawler** Grain: 90	**1 oil engine** reduction geared to sc. shaft driving 1 CP propeller Total Power: 419kW (570hp) Sulzer 1 x 4 Stroke 6 Cy. 200 x 240 419kW (570bhp) Puckie Zaklady Mechaniczne Ltd-Puck AuxGen: 1 x 32kW 400V a.c, 1 x 29kW 400V a.c	10.8kn 6AL20/24
7905998 *SPG2448* WLA-305	**WLA-305** **Przedsiebiorstwo Polowow I Uslug Rybackich 'Szkuner' (Fishing & Fishery Services Enterprise)** - *Wladyslawowo* *Poland* MMSI: 261004830 Official number: ROG/S/692	**141** 42 69	Class: PR	**1980-02 Stocznia Ustka SA — Ustka** Yd No: B410/343 Loa 25.68 Br ex - Dght 2.920 Lbp 22.51 Br md 7.23 Dpth 3.48 Welded, 1 dk	**(B11A2FS) Stern Trawler**	**1 oil engine** geared to sc. shaft driving 1 CP propeller Total Power: 419kW (570hp) Sulzer 1 x 4 Stroke 6 Cy. 200 x 240 419kW (570bhp) Puckie Zaklady Mechaniczne Ltd-Puck AuxGen: 1 x 36kW 400V a.c, 1 x 32kW 400V a.c	10.8kn 6AL20/24
7906007 - -	**WLA-306** - -	**161** 48 69	Class: PR	**1980-02 Stocznia Ustka SA — Ustka** Yd No: B410/344 Loa 25.71 Br ex - Dght 2.920 Lbp 22.51 Br md 7.23 Dpth 3.48 Welded, 1 dk	**(B11A2FS) Stern Trawler**	**1 oil engine** geared to sc. shaft driving 1 CP propeller Total Power: 419kW (570hp) Sulzer 1 x 4 Stroke 6 Cy. 200 x 240 419kW (570bhp) Puckie Zaklady Mechaniczne Ltd-Puck AuxGen: 1 x 36kW 400V a.c, 1 x 36kW 400V a.c	10.8kn 6AL20/24

IMO / Call sign / Former names	Name / Owner / Manager / Port / Flag	GT / NT / DWT	Classification	Build / Dimensions	Type	Machinery
905974 *SPG2446* WLA-307	**WLA-307** **Danuta Jedrych** - *Wladyslawowo* *Poland* MMSI: 261003620	**139** 41 68	Class: PR	**1979-12 Stocznia Ustka SA — Ustka** Yd No: B410/341 Loa 25.68 Br ex - Dght 2.980 Lbp 22.51 Br md 7.23 Dpth 3.48 Welded, 1 dk	**(B11A2FS) Stern Trawler**	**1 oil engine** geared to sc. shaft driving 1 CP propeller Total Power: 419kW (570hp) 10.8kn Sulzer 6AL20/24 1 x 4 Stroke 6 Cy. 200 x 240 419kW (570bhp) Puckie Zaklady Mechaniczne Ltd-Puck AuxGen: 1 x 32kW 400V a.c, 1 x 29kW 400V a.c
8107373 - L710	**WLA-308** **Karibib Visserye Beperk (Karibib Fisheries Pty Ltd)** Tunacor Ltd *Luderitz* *Namibia* Official number: 93LB039	*132* 44 79	Class: (PR)	**1983-01 Stocznia Ustka SA — Ustka** Yd No: B410/69 Loa 25.77 Br ex - Dght 3.000 Lbp 22.03 Br md 7.21 Dpth 3.49 Welded, 1 dk	**(B11A2FS) Stern Trawler**	**1 oil engine** geared to sc. shaft driving 1 FP propeller Total Power: 419kW (570hp) Sulzer 6AL20/24 1 x 4 Stroke 6 Cy. 200 x 240 419kW (570bhp) Puckie Zaklady Mechaniczne Ltd-Puck
8600296 *SPG2117* WLA-310	**WLA-310** **Przedsiebiorstwo Polowow I Uslug Rybackich 'Szkuner' (Fishing & Fishery Services Enterprise)** - *Wladyslawowo* *Poland* MMSI: 261004850 Official number: ROG/S/77	**177** 53 126	Class: PR	**1989-04 Stocznia Ustka SA — Ustka** Yd No: B280/04 Loa 26.77 Br ex - Dght 3.200 Lbp - Br md 7.39 Dpth 3.66 Welded	**(B11A2FS) Stern Trawler**	**1 oil engine** geared to sc. shaft driving 1 FP propeller Total Power: 419kW (570hp) 10.0kn Sulzer 6AL20/24 1 x 4 Stroke 6 Cy. 200 x 240 419kW (570bhp) Zaklady Przemyslu Metalowego 'HCegielski' SA-Poznan
8600351 *SPG2273* WLA-311	**WLA-311** **Przedsiebiorstwo Polowow I Uslug Rybackich 'Szkuner' (Fishing & Fishery Services Enterprise)** - *Wladyslawowo* *Poland* MMSI: 261004860	**166** 50 126	Class: PR	**1990-06 Stocznia Ustka SA — Ustka** Yd No: B280/10 Loa 26.76 Br ex - Dght 3.200 Lbp 23.84 Br md 7.41 Dpth 3.66 Welded, 1 dk	**(B11A2FS) Stern Trawler** Ins: 140	**1 oil engine** geared to sc. shaft driving 1 FP propeller Total Power: 419kW (570hp) 10.0kn Sulzer 6AL20D 1 x 4 Stroke 6 Cy. 200 x 240 419kW (570bhp) Zaklady Przemyslu Metalowego 'HCegielski' SA-Poznan AuxGen: 1 x 50kW 400V a.c, 1 x 41kW 400V a.c
8600363 *SPG2274* WLA-312	**WLA-312** **Przedsiebiorstwo Polowow I Uslug Rybackich 'Szkuner' (Fishing & Fishery Services Enterprise)** - *Wladyslawowo* *Poland* MMSI: 261004870	**178** 53 126	Class: PR	**1990-09 Stocznia Ustka SA — Ustka** Yd No: B280/11 Loa 26.78 Br ex - Dght 3.200 Lbp 23.87 Br md 7.40 Dpth 3.66 Welded, 1dk	**(B11A2FS) Stern Trawler** Ins: 140	**1 oil engine** geared to sc. shaft driving 1 FP propeller Total Power: 419kW (570hp) 10.0kn Sulzer 6AL20/24 1 x 4 Stroke 6 Cy. 200 x 240 419kW (570bhp) Zaklady Przemyslu Metalowego 'HCegielski' SA-Poznan AuxGen: 1 x 50kW 400V a.c, 1 x 41kW 400V a.c
9271925 *P3QU9* -	**WLADYSLAW ORKAN** **Stemblar Shipping Co Ltd** Chinese-Polish JSC (Chinsko-Polskie Towarzystwo Okretowe SA) (CHIPOLBROK) *Limassol* *Cyprus* MMSI: 212280000 Official number: 9271925	**24,167** 10,714 30,435	Class: LR (GL) **100A1** SS 11/2013 container cargoes in all holds and on hatch covers *IWS LI **LMC** **UMS** Eq.Ltr: L†; Cable: 632.5/70.0 U3 (a)	**2003-10 Shanghai Shipyard — Shanghai** Yd No: 191 Loa 199.80 (BB) Br ex - Dght 11.000 Lbp 189.00 Br md 27.80 Dpth 15.50 Welded, 1 dk	**(A31A2GX) General Cargo Ship** Double Bottom Entire Compartment Length Grain: 40,143; Bale: 37,000 TEU 1904 incl 50 ref C. Cranes: 2x320t,2x50t Ice Capable	**1 oil engine** driving 1 FP propeller Total Power: 16,520kW (22,461hp) 19.2kn Sulzer 7RT-flex60C 1 x 2 Stroke 7 Cy. 600 x 2250 16520kW (22461bhp) Hyundai Heavy Industries Co Ltd-South Korea AuxGen: 3 x 960kW 440/220V a.c Boilers: e (ex.g.) 8.7kgf/cm² (8.5bar), AuxB (o.f.) 7.1kgf/cm² (7.0bar) Thrusters: 1 Tunnel thruster (f)
9395795 *9WGP8* -	**WM BENEFIT PLUS III** **Benefit Plus Sdn Bhd** Woodman Sdn Bhd *Kuching* *Malaysia* MMSI: 533000469 Official number: 330727	**269** 81 298	Class: NK	**2006-06 Berjaya Dockyard Sdn Bhd — Miri** Yd No: 29 Loa 30.20 Br ex - Dght 3.600 Lbp 27.71 Br md 8.60 Dpth 4.30 Welded, 1 dk	**(B32A2ST) Tug**	**2 oil engines** reduction geared to sc. shafts driving 2 Propellers Total Power: 1,516kW (2,062hp) 10.0kn Mitsubishi S6R2-MPTK2 2 x 4 Stroke 6 Cy. 170 x 220 each-758kW (1031bhp) Mitsubishi Heavy Industries Ltd-Japan AuxGen: 2 x a.c Fuel: 215.0 (d.f.)
9386641 *POTF* -	**WM FORTUNE I** **PT Sandi Adi Perkasa** - *Pontianak* *Indonesia* Official number: 2012 HHA NO.2953/L	**308** 93 285	Class: NK	**2006-05 Berjaya Dockyard Sdn Bhd — Miri** Yd No: 14 Loa 31.00 Br ex - Dght 3.512 Lbp 28.59 Br md 9.15 Dpth 4.30 Welded, 1 dk	**(B32A2ST) Tug**	**2 oil engines** reduction geared to sc. shafts driving 2 Propellers Total Power: 1,492kW (2,028hp) 11.0kn Caterpillar 3508 2 x Vee 4 Stroke 8 Cy. 170 x 190 each-746kW (1014bhp) Caterpillar Inc-USA AuxGen: 2 x a.c Fuel: 230.0 (d.f.)
6400575 - -	**WM. LYON MACKENZIE** **Corporation of the City of Toronto** - *Toronto, ON* *Canada* Official number: 318774	*102* 50 29	Class: (LR) ✠ Classed LR until 9/71	**1964-05 Russel Brothers Ltd — Owen Sound ON** Yd No: 1216 Loa 24.72 Br ex 6.30 Dght - Lbp 23.02 Br md 6.10 Dpth 3.05 Welded, 1 dk	**(B32A2ST) Tug** 2 Ha: (7.3 x 7.3) (9.1 x 13.7) Cranes: 1x0.5t	**2 oil engines** sr reverse geared to sc. shafts driving 2 FP propellers Total Power: 920kW (1,250hp) Cummins VT-1710-M 2 x Vee 4 Stroke 12 Cy. 140 x 152 each-460kW (625bhp) Cummins Engine Co Inc-USA AuxGen: 2 x 36kW 450V 60Hz a.c
9645530 *YDHN* -	**WM NATUNA** **PT WM Offshore** PT Wintermar Offshore Marine *Jakarta* *Indonesia* MMSI: 525021159	**3,451** 1,035 3,687	Class: AB (Class contemplated)	**2012-12 POET (China) Shipbuilding & Engineering Co Ltd — Taixing JS** (Hull) Yd No: (1509) **2012-12 Pacific Ocean Engineering & Trading Pte Ltd (POET) — Singapore** Yd No: 1509 Loa 76.00 (BB) Br ex 17.60 Dght 6.300 Lbp 68.40 Br md 17.60 Dpth 7.80 Welded, 1 dk	**(B22A2OR) Offshore Support Vessel**	**2 oil engines** reduction geared to sc. shafts driving 2 Propellers Total Power: 3,676kW (4,998hp) 12.0kn Niigata 6L28HX 2 x 4 Stroke 6 Cy. 280 x 370 each-1838kW (2499bhp) Niigata Engineering Co Ltd-Japan Thrusters: 2 Tunnel thruster (f)
9328821 *9WFR3* -	**WM OCEANLINE I** **Marsol Shin Yang (L) Bhd** Shin Yang Shipping Sdn Bhd *Kuching* *Malaysia* MMSI: 533569000 Official number: 329626	**282** 85 182	Class: BV (NK)	**2004-08 Celtug Service Shipyard Sdn Bhd — Sibu** Yd No: 307 Loa 31.00 Br ex - Dght 3.212 Lbp 28.40 Br md 8.54 Dpth 4.00 Welded, 1 dk	**(B32A2ST) Tug**	**2 oil engines** geared to sc. shafts driving 2 FP propellers Total Power: 1,472kW (2,002hp) 11.0kn Cummins KTA-38-M1 2 x Vee 4 Stroke 12 Cy. 159 x 159 each-736kW (1001bhp) Cummins Engine Co Ltd-United Kingdom Fuel: 187.0 (r.f.)
9320776 *9WFX6* -	**WM OCEANLINE III** **Woodman Oceanline Sdn Bhd** Woodman Sdn Bhd *Kuching* *Malaysia* MMSI: 533550000 Official number: 329171	**263** 79 155	Class: (NK)	**2004-05 Celtug Service Shipyard Sdn Bhd — Sibu** Yd No: 302 Loa 31.00 Br ex - Dght 3.012 Lbp 28.72 Br md 8.54 Dpth 3.80 Welded, 1 dk	**(B32A2ST) Tug**	**2 oil engines** geared to sc. shafts driving 2 FP propellers Total Power: 1,490kW (2,026hp) 12.0kn Cummins KTA-38-M1 2 x Vee 4 Stroke 12 Cy. 159 x 159 each-745kW (1013bhp) Cummins Engine Co Inc-USA AuxGen: 2 x a.c Fuel: 165.0 (d.f.)
7316563 *WYZ3045* -	**WM. P. KENNEDY III** **Charles F Turan** - *New Orleans, LA* *United States of America* Official number: 527698	*143* 101 -		**1970 at Mobile, Al** L reg 20.76 Br ex 7.01 Dght - Lbp - Br md - Dpth 3.51 Welded	**(B11B2FV) Fishing Vessel**	**1 oil engine** driving 1 FP propeller Total Power: 257kW (349hp)
9686950 *JZTO* -	**WM PACIFIC** **PT WM Offshore** - *Jakarta* *Indonesia* MMSI: 525012321	**4,223** 1,267 5,257	Class: AB	**2014-03 POET (China) Shipbuilding & Engineering Co Ltd — Taixing JS** (Hull) Yd No: 1457 **2014-03 Pacific Ocean Engineering & Trading Pte Ltd (POET) — Singapore** Yd No: 1457 Loa 83.00 Br ex - Dght - Lbp 72.00 Br md 20.00 Dpth 9.00 Welded, 1 dk	**(B21A20S) Platform Supply Ship**	**2 oil engines** reduction geared to sc. shafts driving 2 Propellers Niigata 2 x 4 Stroke Niigata Engineering Co Ltd-Japan
9376804 *9WGG5* -	**WM SOUTHERNLINE I** **Marsol Shin Yang (L) Bhd** Marsol Shin Yang LLC *Kuching* *Malaysia* MMSI: 533784000 Official number: 330645	**319** 96 287	Class: NK	**2005-12 Berjaya Dockyard Sdn Bhd — Miri** Yd No: 13 Loa 31.00 Br ex - Dght 3.512 Lbp 28.59 Br md 9.15 Dpth 4.30 Welded, 1 dk	**(B32A2ST) Tug**	**2 oil engines** reduction geared to sc. shafts driving 2 Propellers Total Power: 1,492kW (2,028hp) Caterpillar 3508B 2 x Vee 4 Stroke 8 Cy. 170 x 190 each-746kW (1014bhp) Caterpillar Inc-USA Fuel: 230.0 (d.f.)

9376579 9WGG3 -
WM WATER MASTER I
Marsol Shin Yang (L) Bhd
Marsol Shin Yang LLC
Kuching *Malaysia*
MMSI: 533000456
Official number: 330640
319 96 284 Class: NK
2005-12 Berjaya Dockyard Sdn Bhd — Miri Yd No: 04
Loa 31.00 Br ex - Dght 3.512
Lbp 28.59 Br md 9.15 Dpth 4.30
Welded, 1 dk
(B32A2ST) Tug
2 oil engines reduction geared to sc. shafts driving 2 Propellers
Total Power: 1,472kW (2,002hp)
Caterpillar 3508B-TA
2 x Vee 4 Stroke 8 Cy. 170 x 190 each-736kW (1001bhp)
Caterpillar Inc-USA
Fuel: 230.0 (d.f.)

9329576 C4BD2 -
WMS AMSTERDAM
ex SYMS Changjiang -2008
completed as WMS Amsterdam -2005
WMS Amsterdam Navigation Ltd
Navigia Shipmanagement BV
Limassol *Cyprus*
MMSI: 210068000
Official number: 9329576
7,464 3,085 8,212 T/cm 22.0 Class: GL
2005-03 Fujian Mawei Shipbuilding Ltd — Fuzhou FJ Yd No: 437-5
Loa 129.51 (BB) Br ex - Dght 7.400
Lbp 120.34 Br md 20.60 Dpth 10.80
Welded, 1 dk
(A33A2CC) Container Ship (Fully Cellular)
Double Bottom Entire Compartment Length
Passengers: berths: 4
TEU 698 C Ho 226 TEU C Dk 472 TEU incl 120 ref C.
Ice Capable
1 oil engine reduction geared to sc. shaft driving 1 CP propeller
Total Power: 7,200kW (9,789hp) 16.0kn
MaK 8M43
1 x 4 Stroke 8 Cy. 430 x 610 7200kW (9789bhp)
Caterpillar Motoren GmbH & Co. KG-Germany
AuxGen: 3 x 450kW 450/230V 60Hz a.c, 1 x 1000kW 450/230V 60Hz a.c
Thrusters: 1 Thwart. CP thruster (f)

9339038 C4NV2
WMS GRONINGEN
Mar Diamond Shipping Co Ltd
Marlow Navigation Co Ltd
Limassol *Cyprus*
MMSI: 209840000
7,545 3,165 8,173 T/cm 22.0 Class: GL
2006-11 Fujian Mawei Shipbuilding Ltd — Fuzhou FJ Yd No: 437-10
Loa 129.60 (BB) Br ex - Dght 7.400
Lbp 120.34 Br md 20.60 Dpth 10.80
Welded, 1 dk
(A33A2CC) Container Ship (Fully Cellular)
Double Bottom Entire Compartment Length
TEU 698 C Ho 226 TEU C Dk 472 TEU incl 120 ref C.
Compartments: 4 Cell Ho, ER
4 Ha: (12.5 x 15.8)2 (25.4 x 15.8)ER (6.4 x 10.7)
Ice Capable
1 oil engine reduction geared to sc. shaft driving 1 CP propeller
Total Power: 7,200kW (9,789hp) 16.0kn
MaK 8M43C
1 x 4 Stroke 8 Cy. 430 x 610 7200kW (9789bhp)
Caterpillar Motoren GmbH & Co. KG-Germany
AuxGen: 3 x 450kW 450/220V a.c, 1 x 1000kW 450/220V a.c
Thrusters: 1 Thwart. FP thruster (f)

9339040 C4RN2
WMS HARLINGEN
Mar Jade Shipping Co Ltd
Marlow Navigation Co Ltd
Limassol *Cyprus*
MMSI: 210757000
7,545 3,165 8,243 T/cm 22.0 Class: GL
2007-01 Fujian Mawei Shipbuilding Ltd — Fuzhou FJ Yd No: 437-11
Loa 129.62 (BB) Br ex - Dght 7.400
Lbp 120.34 Br md 20.60 Dpth 10.80
Welded, 1 dk
(A33A2CC) Container Ship (Fully Cellular)
Double Bottom Entire Compartment Length
TEU 698 C Ho 226 TEU C Dk 472 TEU incl 120 ref C.
Compartments: 4 Cell Ho, ER
4 Ha: ER
Ice Capable
1 oil engine reduction geared to sc. shaft driving 1 CP propeller
Total Power: 7,200kW (9,789hp) 16.0kn
MaK 8M43C
1 x 4 Stroke 8 Cy. 430 x 610 7200kW (9789bhp)
Caterpillar Motoren GmbH & Co. KG-Germany
AuxGen: 3 x 450kW 450/230V a.c, 1 x 1000kW 450/230V a.c
Thrusters: 1 Thwart. FP thruster (f)

9329588 C4CE2 -
WMS ROTTERDAM
ex SYMS Huanghe -2008
launched as WMS Rotterdam -2005
WMS Rotterdam Navigation Ltd
Navigia Shipmanagement BV
Limassol *Cyprus*
MMSI: 209248000
Official number: 9329588
7,464 3,085 8,217 T/cm 22.0 Class: GL
2005-06 Fujian Mawei Shipbuilding Ltd — Fuzhou FJ Yd No: 437-6
Loa 129.56 (BB) Br ex - Dght 7.400
Lbp 120.34 Br md 20.60 Dpth 10.80
Welded, 1 dk
(A33A2CC) Container Ship (Fully Cellular)
Double Bottom Entire Compartment Length
TEU 698 C Ho 226 TEU C Dk 472 TEU incl 120 ref C.
Ice Capable
1 oil engine reduction geared to sc. shaft driving 1 CP propeller
Total Power: 7,200kW (9,789hp) 16.0kn
MaK 8M43
1 x 4 Stroke 8 Cy. 430 x 610 7200kW (9789bhp)
Caterpillar Motoren GmbH & Co. KG-Germany
AuxGen: 3 x 450kW 450/230V a.c, 1 x 1000kW 450/230V a.c
Thrusters: 1 Tunnel thruster (f)

9329590 C4DK2 -
WMS VLISSINGEN
ex SYMS Zhujiang -2008
launched as WMS Vlissingen -2005
WMS Vlissingen Navigation Ltd
Navigia Shipmanagement BV
SatCom: Inmarsat C 421044810
Limassol *Cyprus*
MMSI: 210448000
Official number: 9329590
7,464 3,085 8,282 T/cm 22.0 Class: GL
2005-09 Fujian Mawei Shipbuilding Ltd — Fuzhou FJ Yd No: 437-7
Loa 129.58 (BB) Br ex - Dght 7.400
Lbp 120.34 Br md 20.60 Dpth 10.80
Welded, 1 dk
(A33A2CC) Container Ship (Fully Cellular)
TEU 698 C Ho 226 TEU C Dk 472 TEU incl 120 ref C.
Ice Capable
1 oil engine with flexible couplings & sr geared to sc. shaft driving 1 CP propeller
Total Power: 7,200kW (9,789hp) 16.0kn
MaK 8M43
1 x 4 Stroke 8 Cy. 430 x 610 7200kW (9789bhp)
Caterpillar Motoren GmbH & Co. KG-Germany
AuxGen: 3 x 500kW 440/220V 60Hz a.c
Thrusters: 1 Thwart. CP thruster (f)

9416783 VRHI5 -
WO LONG SONG
COSCOL (HK) Investment & Development Co Ltd
COSCO (HK) Shipping Co Ltd
SatCom: Inmarsat C 447701861
Hong Kong *Hong Kong*
MMSI: 477962500
Official number: HK-2845
20,619 11,482 27,000 Class: CC
2010-11 Taizhou Kouan Shipbuilding Co Ltd — Taizhou JS Yd No: KA604
Loa 179.50 (BB) Br ex 27.40 Dght 10.500
Lbp 169.50 Br md 27.20 Dpth 14.50
Welded, 1 dk
(A31A2GX) General Cargo Ship
Grain: 40,419; Bale: 38,088
TEU 1391 C Ho 606 TEU C Dk 785 TEU
Compartments: 5 Ho, ER
5 Ha: (9.8 x 11.1) (23.6 x 15.9)ER 3 (25.7 x 23.6)
Cranes: 1x90t,2x45t,1x40t
Ice Capable
1 oil engine driving 1 FP propeller
Total Power: 8,250kW (11,217hp) 15.1kn
Mitsubishi 6UEC50LSII
1 x 2 Stroke 6 Cy. 500 x 1950 8250kW (11217bhp)
Mitsubishi Heavy Industries Ltd-Japan
AuxGen: 3 x 700kW 450V a.c
Thrusters: 1 Tunnel thruster (f)

8648705 BH3054 LL1693
WOEN SHUENN CHANG
Woen Shuenn Chang Ocean Enterprise Co Ltd
Kaohsiung *Chinese Taipei*
Official number: CT6-1054
429 203 -
1986-07 Fong Kuo Shipbuilding Co Ltd — Kaohsiung Yd No: 237
Loa 48.80 Br ex - Dght -
Lbp - Br md 8.00 Dpth -
Welded, 1 dk
(B11B2FV) Fishing Vessel
1 oil engine driving 1 FP propeller
Total Power: 736kW (1,001hp)
Sumiyoshi S26G
1 x 4 Stroke 6 Cy. 260 x 470 736kW (1001bhp)
Sumiyoshi Marine Diesel Co Ltd-Japan

8648717 BH2942 LL1750
WOEN YU CHANG NO. 6
Yin Chou Fishery Co Ltd
Kaohsiung *Chinese Taipei*
Official number: CT6-0942
376 240 -
1983-05 Fong Kuo Shipbuilding Co Ltd — Kaohsiung Yd No: 192
Loa 45.79 Br ex 7.62 Dght -
Lbp - Br md - Dpth -
Welded, 1 dk
(B11B2FV) Fishing Vessel
1 oil engine driving 1 FP propeller

9294549 C4FF2 -
WOGE
ex Australia Express -2013 ex Nordwoge -2011
Schifffahrtsgesellschaft ms 'Woge' mbH & Co KG
Reederei Nord Ltd
Limassol *Cyprus*
MMSI: 210439000
Official number: 9294549
26,611 12,679 34,704 T/cm 51.1 Class: GL (Class contemplated) (NV) (KR)
2006-02 STX Shipbuilding Co Ltd — Changwon (Jinhae Shipyard) Yd No: 1167
Loa 210.00 (BB) Br ex - Dght 11.518
Lbp 198.80 Br md 30.10 Dpth 16.70
Welded, 1 dk
(A33A2CC) Container Ship (Fully Cellular)
TEU 2572 C Ho 938 TEU C Dk 1634 TEU incl 600 ref C.
Compartments: 5 Cell Ho, ER
10 Ha: (12.6 x 20.4)8 (12.6 x 25.7)ER (12.6 x 15.4)
1 oil engine driving 1 FP propeller
Total Power: 24,880kW (33,827hp) 21.5kn
MAN-B&W 8S70MC-C
1 x 2 Stroke 8 Cy. 700 x 2800 24880kW (33827bhp)
STX Engine Co Ltd-South Korea
AuxGen: 4 x 1680kW 440V 60Hz a.c
Thrusters: 1 Thwart. CP thruster (f)
Fuel: 130.0 (d.f.) 4005.0 (r.f.)

5184980 SPG2490 -
WOJTEK
ex Irbis -2008 ex Kemsing -1993
COMAL Sp z oo
Gdynia *Poland*
MMSI: 261200000
Official number: ROG/S/71
134 40 - Class: PR (LR)
Classed LR until 18/10/94
1960 Theodor Buschmann Schiffswerft GmbH & Co. — Hamburg Yd No: 77
Loa 28.22 Br ex 7.60 Dght 3.125
Lbp 25.81 Br md 7.00 Dpth 3.54
Welded, 1 dk
(B32A2ST) Tug
1 oil engine driving 1 CP propeller
Total Power: 736kW (1,001hp)
MAN G8V30/45ATL
1 x 4 Stroke 8 Cy. 300 x 450 736kW (1001bhp)
Maschinenbau Augsburg Nuernberg (MAN)-Augsburg
AuxGen: 1 x 35kW 230V d.c, 1 x 10kW 230V d.c
Thrusters: 1 Thwart. FP thruster (f)

7376202 - -
WOKYANG
ex Daikoku Maru No. 18 -1983
Orient Industria S de RL
Young Kwang Wonyang Fisheries Co Ltd
San Lorenzo *Honduras*
Official number: L-0200470
165 68 -
1973 Uchida Zosen — Ise Yd No: 741
Loa - Br ex 7.14 Dght -
Lbp 33.81 Br md 7.12 Dpth 2.95
Riveted\Welded, 1 dk
(B11B2FV) Fishing Vessel
1 oil engine geared to sc. shaft driving 1 FP propeller
Total Power: 478kW (650hp)
Daihatsu 6PSHTCM-26E
1 x 4 Stroke 6 Cy. 260 x 320 478kW (650bhp)
Daihatsu Diesel Manufacturing Co Lt-Japan

7236672 - -
WOKYANG 15
ex Maruroku Maru No. 25 -1987
-
-
192 95 225
1972 Miho Zosensho K.K. — Shimizu Yd No: 852
Loa 41.71 Br ex 7.55 Dght 2.921
Lbp 36.25 Br md 7.52 Dpth 3.10
Welded, 1 dk
(B11B2FV) Fishing Vessel
1 oil engine driving 1 FP propeller
Total Power: 552kW (750hp)
Niigata 6M26KCHS
1 x 4 Stroke 6 Cy. 260 x 400 552kW (750bhp)
Niigata Engineering Co Ltd-Japan

7729241 D7RZ -
WOL KWANG
Tong Yang Cement Corp
-
Busan *South Korea*
MMSI: 440374000
Official number: BSR-785966
3,185 1,869 5,229 Class: KR
1978-07 Koyo Dockyard Co Ltd — Mihara HS Yd No: IWS-5
Loa 96.04 Br ex 15.52 Dght 6.447
Lbp 89.95 Br md 15.51 Dpth 8.01
Welded, 1 dk
(A24A2BT) Cement Carrier
Grain: 4,654
1 oil engine geared to sc. shaft driving 1 FP propeller
Total Power: 2,427kW (3,300hp) 14.3kn
Makita KGS43B
1 x 4 Stroke 6 Cy. 430 x 650 2427kW (3300bhp)
Makita Tekkosho-Japan
AuxGen: 2 x 130kW 450V a.c

8875920 - -
WOL SUNG
Myung Sung Machine Industry Ltd Partnership
Tong Yang Cement Corp
Samcheonpo *South Korea*
Official number: DHR-933419
143 - 69 Class: KR
1993-08 ShinA Shipbuilding Co Ltd — Tongyeong Yd No: 363
Loa 30.00 Br ex - Dght -
Lbp 25.00 Br md 8.60 Dpth 3.60
Welded, 1 dk
(B32A2ST) Tug
2 oil engines geared to sc. shafts driving 2 FP propellers
Total Power: 1,338kW (1,820hp) 12.2kn
Alpha 6L23/30
2 x 4 Stroke 6 Cy. 225 x 300 each-669kW (910bhp)
Ssangyong Heavy Industries Co Ltd-South Korea
AuxGen: 3 x 45kW 225V a.c
Fuel: 31.0 (d.f.)

Identity	Name / Owner	Tonnage	Class	Build	Type	Machinery
305640	**WOLDSTAD** **Government of The United States of America (Alaskan Department of Public Safety)** - SatCom: Inmarsat C 436619010 *Kodiak, AK* *United States of America* Official number: 650501	*304* 207 512		**1982**-08 **Nichols Bros. Boat Builders, Inc. — Freeland, Wa** Yd No: S-64 Loa 36.89 Br ex 8.54 Dght - Lbp - Br md - Dpth 3.81 Welded, 1 dk	**(B34M2QS) Search & Rescue Vessel**	**2 oil engines** sr geared to sc. shafts driving 2 CP propellers Total Power: 1,472kW (2,002hp) G.M. (Detroit Diesel) 16V-149-TI 2 x Vee 2 Stroke 16 Cy. 146 x 146 each-736kW (1001bhp) General Motors Detroit DieselAllison Divn-USA Thrusters: 1 Directional thruster (f)
023332 *SDEM*	**WOLF** *ex* Argo *-2003* *ex* Salomo Salar *-1993* *ex* Argo *-1986* **Carl Anders Peter Ekby** - *Stockholm* *Sweden*	**174** 64 366	Class: (GL)	**1909 P. Larsson — Torrskog** Converted From: Oil Tanker Converted From: General Cargo Ship-1952 L reg 33.75 Br ex 6.74 Dght 2.744 Lbp - Br md 6.71 Dpth 3.18 Riveted, 1 dk	**(X11A2YP) Yacht**	**1 oil engine** driving 1 FP propeller Total Power: 147kW (200hp) 9.0kn Bolinders 1 x 2 Stroke 2 Cy. 380 x 410 147kW (200bhp) (new engine 1950) AB Bolinder Munktell-Sweden
036260 *DDOA*	**WOLF** *ex* Stadt Wolf *-2011* *ex* Wolf *-2010* **Bugsier-, Reederei- und Bergungs-Gesellschaft mbH & Co KG** - *Bremen* *Germany* MMSI: 218767000 Official number: 5104	**368** 110 180	Class: GL	**1993**-03 **Peene-Werft GmbH — Wolgast** Yd No: 419 Loa 31.34 Br ex 10.00 Dght 3.502 Lbp 29.80 Br md 9.84 Dpth 4.22 Welded, 1 dk	**(B32A2ST) Tug** Ice Capable	**2 oil engines** gearing integral to driving 2 Voith-Schneider propellers Total Power: 3,200kW (4,350hp) MaK 8M332C 2 x 4 Stroke 8 Cy. 240 x 330 each-1600kW (2175bhp) Krupp MaK Maschinenbau GmbH-Kiel AuxGen: 2 x 85kW 400V 50Hz a.c Fuel: 130.0 (d.f.)
9699622 *JEU2*	**WOLF** **Righetti Navi Srl** - *Ravenna* *Italy* MMSI: 247340100	**265** - 100	Class: RI	**2013**-09 **T. Mariotti SpA — Genova** Yd No: 122 Loa 38.07 Br ex - Dght 2.050 Lbp 34.41 Br md 8.20 Dpth 3.90 Welded, 1 dk	**(B21A20C) Crew/Supply Vessel** Hull Material: Aluminium Alloy	**3 oil engines** reduction geared to sc. shafts driving 3 FP propellers Total Power: 4,476kW (6,087hp) 27.0kn Cummins KTA-50-M2 3 x Vee 4 Stroke 16 Cy. 159 x 159 each-1492kW (2029bhp) Cummins Engine Co Ltd-United Kingdom Thrusters: 1 Tunnel thruster (f); 1 Tunnel thruster (a)
9638721 *HC5209*	**WOLF BUDDY** **Dimas Alfredo Bolanoa Pombosa** Divewolf Live Aboard CIA Ltd *Puerto Baquerizo Moreno* *Ecuador* MMSI: 735058877 Official number: TN0100509	**189** 145 44	Class: IS (Class contemplated)	**2011**-07 **Varadero Mariduena — Guayaquil** Yd No: 16 Loa 36.72 Br ex 8.22 Dght 1.420 Lbp 30.15 Br md 8.20 Dpth 3.09 Welded, 1 dk	**(A37A2PC) Passenger/Cruise** Passengers: cabins: 8; berths: 16	**2 oil engines** reduction geared to sc. shafts driving 2 Water jets Total Power: 1,066kW (1,450hp) 12.0kn Caterpillar C18 2 x 4 Stroke 6 Cy. 145 x 183 each-533kW (725bhp) Caterpillar Inc-USA
8887129 - -	**WOLF LARSEN** **Raoul Vincent** - *Northport, NY* *United States of America* Official number: 914297	*110* 88 -		**1988** Loa 23.00 Br ex - Dght - Lbp - Br md 6.00 Dpth 3.50 Welded, 1 dk	**(B11B2FV) Fishing Vessel**	**1 oil engine** driving 1 FP propeller
7423079 *VA3418* -	**WOLFE ISLANDER III** **Government of Canada (Ministry of Transportation & Communications for The Province of Ontario)** - *Kingston, ON* *Canada* MMSI: 316013007 Official number: 197730	**985** 667 237 T/cm 9.1		**1975**-12 **Port Arthur Shipbuilding Co — Thunder Bay ON** Yd No: 128 Loa 62.49 Br ex 20.27 Dght 2.286 Lbp 58.98 Br md 19.79 Dpth 3.48 Welded, 1 dk	**(A36A2PR) Passenger/Ro-Ro Ship (Vehicles)** Bow ramp (f) Len: 1.20 Wid: 11.00 Swl: - Stern ramp (a) Len: 1.20 Wid: 11.00 Swl: - Lane-Len: 61 Lane-Wid: 3.00 Lane-clr ht: 4.40 Cars: 55	**4 oil engines** driving 4 Propellers 2 fwd and 2 aft Total Power: 1,680kW (2,284hp) 12.0kn Caterpillar 3412E 4 x Vee 4 Stroke 12 Cy. 137 x 152 each-420kW (571bhp) (new engine 1975) Caterpillar Tractor Co-USA AuxGen: 2 x 150kW 110/600V 60Hz a.c
8758536 *WDA5238* -	**WOLFFISH** *ex* Superior Mission *-2005* *ex* L. M. Romero *-2005* *ex* C-Jack II *-2005* *ex* Hydrojack II *-1979* *ex* C-Jack II *-1977* **Hercules Liftboat Co LLC** *New Orleans, LA* *United States of America* Official number: 587423	**137** 93 -		**1977 Sun Contractors, Inc. — Harvey, La** L reg 18.74 Br ex - Dght - Lbp - Br md 9.75 Dpth 2.13 Welded, 1 dk	**(B22A2ZM) Offshore Construction Vessel, jack up**	**2 oil engines** geared to sc. shafts driving 2 Propellers G.M. (Detroit Diesel) 8V-71 2 x Vee 2 Stroke 8 Cy. 108 x 127 General Motors Detroit DieselAllison Divn-USA AuxGen: 2 x 30kW 255/450V a.c
9183817 *CQLH*	**WOLGASTERN** **mt 'Wolgastern' Schifffahrtsgesellschaft mbH & Co KG** TB Marine Shipmanagement GmbH & Co KG *Madeira* *Portugal (MAR)* MMSI: 255804950 Official number: TEMP150M	**14,400** 6,937 21,823 T/cm 38.0	Class: GL	**1999**-12 **Stocznia Gdynia SA — Gdynia** Yd No: 8189/1 Loa 162.16 Br ex 27.18 Dght 8.800 Lbp 155.00 Br md 27.18 Dpth 12.00 Welded, 1 dk	**(A12B2TR) Chemical/Products Tanker** Double Hull (13F) Liq: 23,833; Liq (Oil): 23,833 Cargo Heating Coils Compartments: 1 Ta, 12 Wing Ta, 1 Wing Slop Ta, ER 13 Cargo Pump (s): 6x550m³/hr, 7x350m³/hr Manifold: Bow/CM: 80m Ice Capable	**1 oil engine** driving 1 CP propeller Total Power: 7,860kW (10,686hp) 15.0kn B&W 6S46MC-C 1 x 2 Stroke 6 Cy. 460 x 1932 7860kW (10686bhp) H Cegielski Poznan SA-Poland AuxGen: 1 x 720kW 440/220V 60Hz a.c, 3 x 664kW 440/220V 60Hz a.c Thrusters: 1 Thwart. CP thruster (f)
8420842 *C6WN4* -	**WOLIN** *ex* Sky Wind *-2007* *ex* Oresund *-2002* **Wolin Line Ltd** Polska Zegluga Morska PP (POLSTEAM) *Nassau* *Bahamas* MMSI: 309801000 Official number: 8001414	**22,874** 6,862 5,143	Class: NV	**1986**-10 **Moss Fredrikstad Verft AS — Moss** Yd No: 204 Converted From: Ro-Ro Cargo Ship-2002 Loa 186.02 (BB) Br ex 23.70 Dght 5.900 Lbp 178.13 Br md 23.11 Dpth 8.11 Welded, 2 dks	**(A36A2PT) Passenger/Ro-Ro Ship (Vehicles/Rail)** Passengers: unberthed: 126; cabins: 69; berths: 238 Bow door & ramp (centre) Stern ramp (centre) Len: 5.30 Wid: 10.00 Swl: - Lane-Len: 1770 Lane-clr ht: 4.85 Cars: 57, Trailers: 36, Rail Wagons: 50 Ice Capable	**4 oil engines** with clutches & reduction geared to sc. shafts driving 2 CP propellers Total Power: 13,200kW (17,948hp) 18.0kn MAN 6L40/45 4 x 4 Stroke 6 Cy. 400 x 450 each-3300kW (4487bhp) MAN B&W Diesel GmbH-Augsburg AuxGen: 2 x 2256kW 380V 50Hz a.c, 2 x 1944kW 380V 50Hz a.c Thrusters: 2 Thwart. FP thruster (f); 1 Tunnel thruster (a) Fuel: 695.5 (r.f.) 54.0pd
9115925 *V2AK7* -	**WOLTHUSEN** *ex* Saar Hamburg *-1996* **W Bockstiegel GmbH & Co Reederei KG ms 'Wolthusen'** W Bockstiegel Reederei GmbH & Co KG SatCom: Inmarsat C 430401353 *Saint John's* *Antigua & Barbuda* MMSI: 304010620 Official number: 2462	**2,846** 1,584 4,372	Class: GL	**1995**-11 **Bodewes' Scheepswerven B.V. — Hoogezand** Yd No: 572 Loa 90.33 (BB) Br ex - Dght 5.858 Lbp 84.60 Br md 13.20 Dpth 7.30 Welded, 1 dk	**(A31A2GX) General Cargo Ship** Double Bottom Entire Compartment Length Grain: 5,793 TEU 234 C.Ho 114/20' C.Dk 120/20' Compartments: 1 Ho, ER 1 Ha: (65.0 x 10.6)ER Ice Capable	**1 oil engine** reduction geared to sc. shaft driving 1 CP propeller Total Power: 1,800kW (2,447hp) 11.5kn Deutz SBV9M628 1 x 4 Stroke 9 Cy. 240 x 280 1800kW (2447bhp) Motoren Werke Mannheim AG (MWM)-Mannheim AuxGen: 1 x 325kW 220/380V a.c, 2 x 136kW a.c Thrusters: 1 Thwart. FP thruster (f) Fuel: 206.0 (d.f.)
7613258 *DVRK*	**WOLVERINE** *ex* Shokei Maru *-1987* **Loadstar Shipping Co Inc** - *Manila* *Philippines* Official number: 00-0000456	*992* 578 2,877	Class: (NK)	**1976**-08 **Ube Dockyard Co. Ltd. — Ube** Yd No: 152 Loa 78.42 Br ex 12.22 Dght 5.716 Lbp 72.01 Br md 12.21 Dpth 5.82 Welded, 2 dks	**(A31A2GX) General Cargo Ship** Grain: 4,012; Bale: 3,863	**1 oil engine** driving 1 FP propeller Total Power: 1,471kW (2,000hp) 11.0kn Hanshin 6LUD35 1 x 4 Stroke 6 Cy. 350 x 550 1471kW (2000bhp) Hanshin Nainenki Kogyo-Japan
7636016 *P2V5448* -	**WOMBI** **Pacific Towing (PNG) Pty Ltd** - *Port Moresby* *Papua New Guinea* MMSI: 553111625 Official number: 001293	*265* 37 -	Class: (LR) ✠ Classed LR until 25/8/11	**1978**-09 **Carrington Slipways Pty Ltd — Newcastle NSW** Yd No: 130 Loa 30.00 Br ex 9.96 Dght 4.026 Lbp 24.80 Br md 9.71 Dpth 4.70 Welded, 1 dk	**(B32A2ST) Tug**	**2 oil engines** reverse reduction geared to sc. shafts driving 2 FP propellers Total Power: 1,794kW (2,440hp) 12.0kn Blackstone ESL8 2 x 4 Stroke 8 Cy. 222 x 292 each-897kW (1220bhp) Mirrlees Blackstone (Stamford)Ltd.-Stamford AuxGen: 2 x 68kW 415V 50Hz a.c
6716338 *6KWR* -	**WON CHANG No. 81** *ex* Sam Young No. 77 *-1984* *ex* Tae Yang No. 101 *-1984* *ex* Kook Yang No. 101 *-1984* **Heo Jeong-Won** - *Busan* *South Korea* Official number: BS-A-311	*133* 41 113	Class: (KR)	**1967 Fukuoka Shipbuilding Co Ltd — Fukuoka FO** Yd No: 882 Loa 33.56 Br ex 6.15 Dght 2.401 Lbp 28.61 Br md 6.10 Dpth 2.75 Welded, 1 dk	**(B11B2FV) Fishing Vessel** Ins: 100 4 Ha: 4 (0.9 x 1.1)	**1 oil engine** driving 1 FP propeller Total Power: 331kW (450hp) 9.0kn Hanshin Z76 1 x 4 Stroke 6 Cy. 270 x 400 331kW (450bhp) Hanshin Nainenki Kogyo-Japan AuxGen: 2 x 26kW 230V a.c

IMO / Call sign / Flag	Name / Owner / Port	Tonnage	Class	Builder / Dimensions	Type	Machinery
6716388 *6KWW* -	**WON CHANG No. 82** *ex* Sam Young No. 78 *-1984* *ex* Tae Yang No. 107 *-1984* *ex* Kook Yang No. 107 *-1984* **Heo Jeong-Won** - *Busan* *South Korea* Official number: BS-A-316	*133* 41 113	Class: (KR)	**1967 Fukuoka Shipbuilding Co Ltd — Fukuoka FO** Yd No: 885 Loa 33.56 Br ex 6.15 Dght 2.401 Lbp 28.61 Br md 6.10 Dpth 2.75 Welded, 1 dk	**(B11B2FV) Fishing Vessel** Ins: 100 4 Ha: 4 (0.9 x 1.1)	**1 oil engine** driving 1 FP propeller Total Power: 331kW (450hp) 9.0kr Hanshin Z76 1 x 4 Stroke 6 Cy. 270 x 400 331kW (450bhp) Hanshin Nainenki Kogyo-Japan AuxGen: 2 x 26kW 230V a.c
9159787 *HMY04* -	**WON SAN 2** - **Yusong Shipping Co** - *Nampho* *North Korea* MMSI: 445309000 Official number: 3800078	**2,654** 796 3,187	Class: KC	**1996-08 Wonsan Shipyard — Wonsan** Converted From: Research Vessel Loa 83.10 Br ex 14.60 Dght 5.120 Lbp 75.00 Br md - Dpth 7.15 Welded, 1 dk	**(A31A2GX) General Cargo Ship**	**1 oil engine** driving 1 FP propeller Total Power: 1,556kW (2,116hp)
8957247 - -	**WON YOUNG No. 101** - **Ban Young Keun** - *Busan* *South Korea* Official number: BSR-990079	**188** 56 -		**1999-05 Eunsung Co Ltd — Busan** Loa 35.00 Br ex - Dght 2.400 Lbp 32.64 Br md 7.00 Dpth 3.40 Welded, 1 dk	**(B32A2ST) Tug**	**1 oil engine** driving 1 FP propeller Total Power: 1,471kW (2,000hp) Hanshin LH32LG 1 x 4 Stroke 6 Cy. 320 x 640 1471kW (2000bhp) The Hanshin Diesel Works Ltd-Japan
7903809 *DUH2617* -	**WONDERFUL STARS** *ex* Ferry Agata *-2008* **Roble Shipping Lines Inc** - *Cebu* *Philippines* Official number: CEB1006936	*1,297* 389 546		**1979-07 Naikai Shipbuilding & Engineering Co Ltd — Onomichi HS (Taguma Shipyard)** Yd No: 445 Loa 71.33 Br ex 13.42 Dght 3.701 Lbp 64.01 Br md 13.40 Dpth 4.63 Welded, 2 dks	**(A36A2PR) Passenger/Ro-Ro Ship (Vehicles)** Passengers: unberthed: 478 Cars: 50	**2 oil engines** reduction geared to sc. shafts driving 2 FP propellers Total Power: 3,090kW (4,202hp) 15.5kn Niigata 6MG31EZ 2 x 4 Stroke 6 Cy. 310 x 380 each-1545kW (2101bhp) Niigata Engineering Co Ltd-Japan AuxGen: 2 x 180kW 225V a.c Fuel: 13.5 (d.f.) 56.0 (r.f.) 15.5pd
7393834 *PNBG* -	**WONG LOI** *ex* IOS Tudan *-2007* *ex* I. O. S. Tudan *-2003* *ex* CHH Mighty *-1996* *ex* Ragna Viking *-1993* *ex* Gruno Ragna *-1976* **PT Indoliziz Marine** - *Cirebon* *Indonesia* MMSI: 525016553	**1,232** 370 1,680	Class: KI (NV)	**1976-03 Aukra Bruk AS — Aukra** Yd No: 57 Loa 63.58 Br ex 13.01 Dght 5.750 Lbp 55.00 Br md 13.00 Dpth 6.66 Welded, 2 dks	**(B21B20T) Offshore Tug/Supply Ship** Ice Capable	**2 oil engines** driving 2 CP propellers Total Power: 5,884kW (8,000hp) 12.0kn MaK 12M453AK 2 x Vee 4 Stroke 12 Cy. 320 x 420 each-2942kW (4000bhp) MaK Maschinenbau GmbH-Kiel AuxGen: 1 x 140kW 440V 60Hz a.c, 1 x 135kW 440V 60Hz a.c, 1 x 104kW 440V 60Hz a.c Thrusters: 1 Thwart. FP thruster (f) Fuel: 538.5 (r.f.) 26.5pd
8116465 *VKAW* -	**WONGA** - **Svitzer Australia Pty Ltd (Svitzer Australasia)** - *Sydney, NSW* *Australia* MMSI: 503074000 Official number: 850878	*427* 129 420	Class: AB	**1983-12 Tamar Shipbuilding Pty Ltd — Launceston TAS** Yd No: 37 Loa 32.31 Br ex 10.90 Dght 4.809 Lbp 27.06 Br md 10.61 Dpth 5.36 Welded, 1 dk	**(B32A2ST) Tug**	**2 oil engines** with clutches & sr geared to sc. shafts driving 2 Directional propellers Total Power: 2,648kW (3,600hp) 13.0kn Daihatsu 6DSM-28 2 x 4 Stroke 6 Cy. 280 x 340 each-1324kW (1800bhp) Daihatsu Diesel Manufacturing Co Lt-Japan AuxGen: 2 x 125kW
9169108 - -	**WONJIN** - **Youngjin Enterprise Co Ltd** - *Incheon* *South Korea* MMSI: 440001040 Official number: ICR-972828	**211** - 105	Class: KR	**1997-06 Samkwang Shipbuilding & Engineering Co Ltd — Incheon** Yd No: 96-06 Loa 38.00 Br ex - Dght - Lbp 34.00 Br md 9.00 Dpth 3.75 Welded, 1 dk	**(B32A2ST) Tug**	**2 oil engines** driving 2 FP propellers Total Power: 3,178kW (4,320hp) 15.1kn Pielstick 8PA5L 2 x 4 Stroke 8 Cy. 255 x 270 each-1589kW (2160bhp) Ssangyong Heavy Industries Co Ltd-South Korea
9035668 - -	**WONJIN NO. 1** *ex* Izumi Maru No. 8 *-2005* **Bong Shin Co Ltd** Dawon Shipping Co Ltd *Busan* *South Korea* MMSI: 440109130 Official number: BSR-050244	*697* - 980	Class: KR (NK)	**1991-12 Sanyo Zosen K.K. — Onomichi** Yd No: 1032 Loa 67.99 Br ex 11.02 Dght 3.902 Lbp 63.00 Br md 11.00 Dpth 4.80 Welded, 1 dk	**(A11B2TG) LPG Tanker** Liq (Gas): 1,258 2 x Gas Tank (s);	**1 oil engine** driving 1 CP propeller Total Power: 1,177kW (1,600hp) 11.5kn Akasaka K28SFD 1 x 4 Stroke 6 Cy. 280 x 500 1177kW (1600bhp) Akasaka Tekkosho KK (Akasaka DieselLtd)-Japan AuxGen: 3 x 202kW a.c Thrusters: 1 Thwart. FP thruster (f)
9081148 *D9QQ* -	**WONJIN NO. 3** - **Dong Shin Shipping Co Ltd** - *Pohang* *South Korea* MMSI: 440400660 Official number: PHR-926094	**1,589** - 3,071	Class: KR	**1992-10 Hyangdo Shipbuilding Co Ltd — Pohang** Yd No: 75 Loa 72.30 Br ex - Dght 5.152 Lbp 68.75 Br md 15.50 Dpth 6.30 Welded, 1 dk	**(A31A2GX) General Cargo Ship** Grain: 3,081 Compartments: 1 Ho, ER 1 Ha: (44.8 x 10.0)ER	**1 oil engine** sr geared to sc. shaft driving 1 FP propeller Total Power: 1,030kW (1,400hp) 11.0kn Niigata 6M28AFTE 1 x 4 Stroke 6 Cy. 280 x 480 1030kW (1400bhp) Ssangyong Heavy Industries Co Ltd-South Korea AuxGen: 2 x 104kW 225V a.c
8622787 - -	**WONJIN No. 5** *ex* Eiko Maru No. 8 *-2000* **Kang Jin Shipping Corp** - *Pohang* *South Korea* Official number: PHR-996537	*975* - 1,749	Class: (KR)	**1983-10 Kinoura Zosen K.K. — Imabari** Yd No: 108 Loa 67.78 Br ex - Dght 4.613 Lbp 62.10 Br md 13.01 Dpth 6.30 Welded, 1 dk	**(B33A2DG) Grab Dredger** Bale: 1,051 Compartments: 1 Ho, ER 1 Ha: (19.5 x 10.0)ER Cranes: 1x15t	**1 oil engine** reverse geared to sc. shaft driving 1 FP propeller Total Power: 1,324kW (1,800hp) 11.9kn Akasaka A31R 1 x 4 Stroke 6 Cy. 310 x 600 1324kW (1800bhp) Akasaka Tekkosho KK (Akasaka DieselLtd)-Japan AuxGen: 2 x 240kW 225V a.c
8429434 *DTAA4* -	**WONJIN NO. 101** *ex* Nam Hae No. 101 *-2000* *ex* Jin Yang No. 101 *-1999* **Wonjin Deep Sea Ltd** - *Busan* *South Korea* Official number: 9508027-6481350	**515** 328 532	Class: (KR)	**1973 Sambo Shipbuilding Co Ltd — Sacheon** Loa 56.11 Br ex 9.05 Dght 4.050 Lbp 49.03 Br md 9.01 Dpth 4.09 Welded, 1 dk	**(B11B2FV) Fishing Vessel**	**1 oil engine** driving 1 FP propeller Total Power: 988kW (1,343hp) Akasaka 1 x 4 Stroke 6 Cy. 230 x 500 988kW (1343bhp) Akasaka Tekkosho KK (Akasaka DieselLtd)-Japan AuxGen: 2 x 492kW 400V a.c
9186522 *YD4567* -	**WONOKROMO** - **PT PERTAMINA (PERSERO)** - *Jakarta* *Indonesia*	**224** 68 -	Class: (KI) (NK)	**1998-03 P.T. Noahtu Shipyard — Panjang** Yd No: 28 Loa 28.00 Br ex - Dght 2.700 Lbp 24.85 Br md 8.60 Dpth 3.50 Welded, 1 dk	**(B32A2ST) Tug**	**2 oil engines** driving 2 FP propellers Total Power: 956kW (1,300hp) Niigata 6NSD-M 2 x 4 Stroke 6 Cy. 160 x 210 each-478kW (650bhp) Niigata Engineering Co Ltd-Japan AuxGen: 2 x 150kW a.c
8898829 - -	**WONSAN-1** - **Hongwon Fishery Station** -	**2,759** 828 1,250		**1987 Wonsan Shipyard — Wonsan** Loa 83.15 Br ex 14.60 Dght 5.240 Lbp - Br md - Dpth 9.75 Welded, 1 dk	**(B11A2FG) Factory Stern Trawler**	**1 oil engine** driving 1 FP propeller Total Power: 1,654kW (2,249hp) Sulzer 6TAD48 1 x 2 Stroke 6 Cy. 480 x 700 1654kW (2249bhp) Tvornica Dizel Motora 'Jugoturbina'-Yugoslavia
9036387 *DSEM6* -	**WOO BONG** *ex* Woo Geun *-2010* *ex* Global Eos *-1996* **Keoje Marine Co Ltd** - *Jeju* *South Korea* MMSI: 440402000 Official number: JJR-962488	**4,702** 2,118 8,057 T/cm 16.0	Class: KR (NK)	**1991-10 Higaki Zosen K.K. — Imabari** Yd No: 398 Loa 112.09 (BB) Br ex 18.62 Dght 6.944 Lbp 104.00 Br md 18.60 Dpth 8.60 Welded, 1 dk	**(A12B2TR) Chemical/Products Tanker** Double Bottom Entire Compartment Length Liq: 8,359; Liq (Oil): 8,359 Compartments: 16 Wing Ta, ER 4 Cargo Pump (s): 4x300m³/hr Manifold: Bow/CM: 56.1m	**1 oil engine** driving 1 FP propeller Total Power: 2,994kW (4,071hp) 12.7kn Mitsubishi 6UEC37LA 1 x 2 Stroke 6 Cy. 370 x 880 2994kW (4071bhp) Kobe Hatsudoki KK-Japan AuxGen: 2 x 280kW 450V a.c Fuel: 92.1 (d.f.) 612.6 (r.f.)
8629838 *6KIV* -	**WOO CHANG** - **Kim Hung-Man** - *Ulleung* *South Korea* Official number: 9504015-6479409	**106** - 133	Class: (KR)	**1984-07 Simguen Shipbuilding & Engineering Industry — Changwon** Loa 37.12 Br ex - Dght 2.648 Lbp 29.00 Br md 6.00 Dpth 2.90 Welded, 1 dk	**(B11B2FV) Fishing Vessel**	**1 oil engine** driving 1 FP propeller Total Power: 272kW (370hp) Yanmar 6ML-HT 1 x 4 Stroke 6 Cy. 200 x 240 272kW (370bhp) Ssangyong Heavy Industries Co Ltd-South Korea AuxGen: 1 x 80kW 225V a.c
7850650 *D7SX* -	**WOO CHANG** *ex* Chemicarry No. 15 *-1985* *ex* Seisui Maru No. 1 *-1976* **Shin Ho Bunkering Co** - *Busan* *South Korea* Official number: BSR-645805	*416* 158 614	Class: (KR)	**1964 Usuki Iron Works Co Ltd — Saiki OT** Yd No: 583 Loa 48.77 Br ex - Dght 3.620 Lbp 44.00 Br md 8.64 Dpth 3.92 Riveted\Welded, 1 dk	**(A12A2TC) Chemical Tanker** Liq: 589 Compartments: 6 Ta, ER	**1 oil engine** geared to sc. shaft driving 1 FP propeller Total Power: 552kW (750hp) 10.5kn Fuji 6MD27.5CH 1 x 4 Stroke 6 Cy. 275 x 320 552kW (750bhp) Fuji Diesel Co Ltd-Japan AuxGen: 1 x 30kW 230V a.c Fuel: 32.5 (d.f.) (Part Heating Coils) 2.5pd

IMO / Call sign	Name / Owner / Manager / Port	Tonnage	Class	Builder / Dimensions	Type / Capacities	Machinery
377822 DSMS2	**WOO CHOON** *completed as* Navigator *-2009* **Woolim Shipping Co Ltd** Woolim Marine Co Ltd *Jeju* *South Korea* MMSI: 441730000 Official number: JJR-094407	**3,978** 1,793 5,690 T/cm 14.5	Class: KR (AB)	**2009-12 Qingdao Hyundai Shipbuilding Co Ltd — Jiaonan SD** Yd No: 205 Loa 105.50 (BB) Br ex - Dght 6.130 Lbp 98.00 Br md 16.60 Dpth 8.60 Welded, 1 dk	**(A12B2TR) Chemical/Products Tanker** Double Hull (13F) Liq: 6,121; Liq (Oil): 6,446 Cargo Heating Coils Compartments: 10 Wing Ta, 2 Wing Slop Ta, ER 10 Cargo Pump (s): 10x200m³/hr Manifold: Bow/CM: 56.4m	**1 oil engine** reduction geared to sc. shaft driving 1 CP propeller Total Power: 3,000kW (4,079hp) 14.0kn Wartsila 6L32 1 x 4 Stroke 6 Cy. 320 x 400 3000kW (4079bhp) Wartsila Finland Oy-Finland AuxGen: 3 x 480kW a.c, 1 x 1500kW a.c Thrusters: 1 Tunnel thruster (f) Fuel: 201.0 (d.f.) 140.0 (r.f.)
411575 7BJ5	**WOO GEUN** *ex* Artemis *-2013* *ex* Celestia *-2013* **DJT Carrier SA** Woolim Marine Co Ltd *Majuro* *Marshall Islands* MMSI: 538005151 Official number: 5151	**8,473** 4,031 12,932 T/cm 22.9	Class: KR (NK)	**2007-10 Samho Shipbuilding Co Ltd — Tongyeong** Yd No: 1084 Loa 127.20 (BB) Br ex 20.43 Dght 8.714 Lbp 119.00 Br md 20.40 Dpth 11.50 Welded, 1 dk	**(A12B2TR) Chemical/Products Tanker** Double Hull (13F) Liq: 13,067; Liq (Oil): 13,067 Cargo Heating Coils Compartments: 12 Wing Ta, 2 Wing Slop Ta, ER 12 Cargo Pump (s): 12x300m³/hr Manifold: Bow/CM: 59.9m	**1 oil engine** driving 1 FP propeller Total Power: 3,569kW (4,852hp) 13.4kn MAN-B&W 6S35MC 1 x 2 Stroke 6 Cy. 350 x 1400 3569kW (4852bhp) STX Engine Co Ltd-South Korea AuxGen: 3 x 450kW a.c Thrusters: 1 Tunnel thruster (f) Fuel: 74.0 (d.f.) 677.0 (r.f.)
299226 7YC4	**WOO GUM** **DV Dragon SA** Woolim Marine Co Ltd *Majuro* *Marshall Islands* MMSI: 538004626 Official number: 4626	**2,361** 1,086 3,449 T/cm 10.1	Class: KR	**2004-05 Nokbong Shipbuilding Co Ltd — Geoje** Yd No: 392 Loa 87.31 (BB) Br ex - Dght 5.813 Lbp 79.80 Br md 14.00 Dpth 7.30 Welded, 1 dk	**(A12B2TR) Chemical/Products Tanker** Double Hull (13F) Liq: 3,743; Liq (Oil): 3,951 Cargo Heating Coils Compartments: ER, 10 Wing Ta, 2 Wing Slop Ta 10 Cargo Pump (s): 10x200m³/hr Manifold: Bow/CM: 41.9m	**1 oil engine** reduction geared to sc. shaft driving 1 CP propeller Total Power: 1,960kW (2,665hp) 13.5kn MAN-B&W 8L28/32A 1 x 4 Stroke 8 Cy. 280 x 320 1960kW (2665bhp) STX Engine Co Ltd-South Korea AuxGen: 2 x 400kW 450V a.c Fuel: 58.0 (d.f.) 136.0 (r.f.)
284427 HJL9	**WOO HWANG** **GSH1 Chem-Prod Carrier III AS** Woolim Shipping Co Ltd *Valletta* *Malta* MMSI: 249059000 Official number: 9284427	**2,361** 1,086 3,451 T/cm 10.1	Class: KR	**2003-12 Nokbong Shipbuilding Co Ltd — Geoje** Yd No: 390 Loa 87.31 (BB) Br ex - Dght 5.813 Lbp 79.99 Br md 14.00 Dpth 7.30 Welded, 1 dk	**(A12B2TR) Chemical/Products Tanker** Double Hull (13F) Liq: 3,812; Liq (Oil): 3,812 Cargo Heating Coils Compartments: 1 Ta, 8 Wing Ta, 1 Slop Ta, ER 9 Cargo Pump (s): 9x200m³/hr Manifold: Bow/CM: 42.8m	**1 oil engine** reduction geared to sc. shaft driving 1 CP propeller Total Power: 1,960kW (2,665hp) 12.3kn MAN-B&W 8L28/32A 1 x 4 Stroke 8 Cy. 280 x 320 1960kW (2665bhp) STX Corp-South Korea AuxGen: 2 x 400kW 450V a.c Fuel: 58.0 (d.f.) 155.0 (r.f.)
268667 7QT8	**WOO HYEON** **Woo Chem-Carrier AS** Woolim Marine Co Ltd *Majuro* *Marshall Islands* MMSI: 538003437 Official number: 3437	**2,362** 1,086 3,466 T/cm 10.1	Class: KR	**2003-07 Nokbong Shipbuilding Co Ltd — Geoje** Yd No: 388 Loa 87.31 (BB) Br ex 14.02 Dght 5.813 Lbp 79.80 Br md 14.00 Dpth 7.30 Welded, 1 dk	**(A12B2TR) Chemical/Products Tanker** Double Hull (13F) Liq: 3,352; Liq (Oil): 3,812 Cargo Heating Coils Compartments: 10 Wing Ta, ER 10 Cargo Pump (s): 10x200m³/hr Manifold: Bow/CM: 44.6m	**1 oil engine** reduction geared to sc. shaft driving 1 FP propeller Total Power: 1,960kW (2,665hp) 12.3kn MAN-B&W 8L28/32A 1 x 4 Stroke 8 Cy. 280 x 320 1960kW (2665bhp) STX Corp-South Korea AuxGen: 2 x 400kW 450V a.c Fuel: 58.0 (d.f.) 155.0 (r.f.)
629577 LWW	**WOO IL NO. 505** *ex* Dong Won No. 308 *-1987* **Dong Won Fisheries Co Ltd** - *Busan* *South Korea* MMSI: 440937000 Official number: 9506131-6210005	*129* - 183	Class: (KR)	**1987-09 Jinhae Ship Construction Industrial Co Ltd — Changwon** Yd No: 8762 Loa 40.49 Br ex - Dght 3.108 Lbp 34.84 Br md 7.30 Dpth - Welded, 1 dk	**(B11B2FV) Fishing Vessel**	**1 oil engine** driving 1 FP propeller Total Power: 1,177kW (1,600hp) 13.7kn Hanshin 6LUN28 1 x 4 Stroke 6 Cy. 280 x 480 1177kW (1600bhp) Ssangyong Heavy Industries Co Ltd-South Korea AuxGen: 1 x 144kW 225V a.c
865121 SFG3	**WOO JEONG** *ex* Woo Bog *-2010* *ex* Fuji Maru No. 12 *-2000* **Young Sung Global Co Ltd** - *Busan* *South Korea* MMSI: 440100730 Official number: BSR-002550	*1,579* - 3,295	Class: KR (NK)	**1992-09 Hakata Zosen K.K. — Imabari** Yd No: 526 Loa 89.00 Br ex - Dght 5.907 Lbp 82.00 Br md 13.00 Dpth 6.50 Welded, 1 dk	**(A13B2TP) Products Tanker** Liq: 3,001; Liq (Oil): 3,001 Compartments: 8 Wing Ta, ER	**1 oil engine** reverse geared to sc. shaft driving 1 FP propeller Total Power: 1,765kW (2,400hp) 12.0kn Hanshin 6EL35G 1 x 4 Stroke 6 Cy. 350 x 700 1765kW (2400bhp) The Hanshin Diesel Works Ltd-Japan AuxGen: 3 x 200kW a.c
949446	**WOO JIN No. 16** **Kim Jung-Sun** - *Tongyeong* *South Korea*	**195** 48 -		**1997-06 Hanryu Shipbuilding Co Ltd — Tongyeong** Yd No: 203 Loa 37.60 Br ex - Dght 2.470 Lbp 32.50 Br md 6.40 Dpth 2.90 Welded, 1 dk	**(B12B2FC) Fish Carrier**	**1 oil engine** driving 1 FP propeller Total Power: 494kW (672hp) Caterpillar 1 x 4 Stroke 494kW (672bhp) Caterpillar Inc-USA
320813 TBJ9	**WOO JIN No. 26** *ex* Shinko Maru No. 18 *-2002* *ex* Kaiyo Maru No. 18 *-1990* *ex* Koei Maru No. 56 *-1986* **Woojin Marine Products Co Ltd** Korean Society of Ship Inspection & Technology *Tongyeong* *South Korea* Official number: 0203002-6482200	*279* - -		**1973-03 Goriki Zosensho — Ise** Yd No: 738 Loa - Br ex 8.23 Dght 3.175 Lbp 43.11 Br md 8.21 Dpth 3.56 Riveted\Welded, 1 dk	**(B11B2FV) Fishing Vessel**	**1 oil engine** driving 1 FP propeller Total Power: 736kW (1,001hp) Niigata 6L28X 1 x 4 Stroke 6 Cy. 280 x 440 736kW (1001bhp) Niigata Engineering Co Ltd-Japan
416072 LKG	**WOO JIN No. 53** *ex* Kyeong Yang No. 1 *-1989* *ex* Yu Sung No. 108 *-1984* *ex* Tae Sun No. 1 *-1983* *ex* Sanyo Maru No. 18 *-1983* *ex* Junyo Maru No. 18 *-1976* **Kim Young-Il** - *Busan* *South Korea* Official number: BS02-A1840	*269* 133 341	Class: (KR)	**1963 Tokushima Zosen Sangyo K.K. — Komatsushima** Yd No: 150 Loa 45.55 Br ex - Dght 3.319 Lbp 39.98 Br md 7.60 Dpth 3.51 Riveted\Welded, 1 dk	**(B11B2FV) Fishing Vessel** Ins: 407 4 Ha: 2 (1.0 x 1.0)2 (1.4 x 1.4)ER	**1 oil engine** driving 1 FP propeller Total Power: 699kW (950hp) 13.3kn Makita 1 x 4 Stroke 6 Cy. 350 x 500 699kW (950bhp) Makita Tekkosho-Japan AuxGen: 2 x 80kW 230V a.c Fuel: 169.5
297280 7YC3	**WOO JONG** **DV Dragon SA** Woolim Shipping Co Ltd *Majuro* *Marshall Islands* MMSI: 538004625 Official number: 4625	**2,361** 1,086 3,449 T/cm 10.1	Class: KR	**2004-03 Nokbong Shipbuilding Co Ltd — Geoje** Yd No: 391 Loa 87.31 (BB) Br ex - Dght 5.813 Lbp 79.80 Br md 14.00 Dpth 7.30 Welded, 1 dk	**(A12B2TR) Chemical/Products Tanker** Double Hull Liq: 3,741; Liq (Oil): 3,812 Cargo Heating Coils Compartments: 1 Ta, 8 Wing Ta, 1 Slop Ta, ER 10 Cargo Pump (s): 10x200m³/hr Manifold: Bow/CM: 42.8m	**1 oil engine** geared to sc. shaft driving 1 CP propeller Total Power: 1,960kW (2,665hp) 12.3kn MAN-B&W 8L28/32A 1 x 4 Stroke 8 Cy. 280 x 320 1960kW (2665bhp) (made 2003) STX Corp-South Korea AuxGen: 2 x 400kW 450V a.c Fuel: 51.0 (d.f.) 131.0 (r.f.)
409986 7RL7	**WOO JUN** **Woo Chem Partner AS** Woolim Marine Co Ltd *Majuro* *Marshall Islands* MMSI: 538003535 Official number: 3535	**4,688** 2,172 6,790 T/cm 16.5	Class: KR	**2008-01 Mokpo Shipbuilding & Engineering Co Ltd — Mokpo** Yd No: 06-181 Loa 109.99 (BB) Br ex - Dght 6.713 Lbp 102.70 Br md 18.20 Dpth 8.50 Welded, 1 dk	**(A12B2TR) Chemical/Products Tanker** Double Hull (13F) Liq: 7,323; Liq (Oil): 7,323 Cargo Heating Coils Compartments: 12 Wing Ta, 2 Wing Slop Ta, Wing ER 12 Cargo Pump (s): 12x200m³/hr Manifold: Bow/CM: 52.1m	**1 oil engine** driving 1 FP propeller Total Power: 3,309kW (4,499hp) 13.5kn Hanshin LH46LA 1 x 4 Stroke 6 Cy. 460 x 880 3309kW (4499bhp) The Hanshin Diesel Works Ltd-Japan Thrusters: 1 Tunnel thruster (f) Fuel: 70.0 (d.f.) 330.0 (r.f.)
876326 DSAQ550	**WOO JUNG No. 1** **Friendship Marine Co Ltd** - *Yeosu* *South Korea* Official number: YSR-945230	**202** - 95	Class: (KR)	**1994 Kwangyang Shipbuilding & Engineering Co Ltd — Janghang** Loa 35.30 Br ex - Dght - Lbp 29.50 Br md 9.60 Dpth 4.20 Welded, 1 dk	**(B32A2ST) Tug**	**2 oil engines** driving 2 FP propellers Total Power: 1,156kW (1,572hp) 13.4kn Caterpillar 3516TA 2 x Vee 4 Stroke 16 Cy. 170 x 190 each-578kW (786bhp) Caterpillar Inc-USA AuxGen: 2 x 69kW 225V a.c Fuel: 53.0
701905 MMX	**WOO JUNG No. 5** *ex* Kohoku Maru No. 6 *-1972* **Sail Fisheries Co Ltd** - *Busan* *South Korea* Official number: BS-A-630	*312* 156 -	Class: (KR)	**1966 Hayashikane Shipbuilding & Engineering Co Ltd — Shimonoseki YC** Yd No: 1076 Loa 44.51 Br ex 8.23 Dght 3.404 Lbp 40.62 Br md 8.21 Dpth 3.79 Welded, 2 dks	**(B11A2FS) Stern Trawler** Ins: 340 3 Ha: 2 (1.5 x 1.7) (1.5 x 2.4)ER	**1 oil engine** driving 1 FP propeller Total Power: 883kW (1,201hp) 12.3kn MAN G6V30/42ATL 1 x 4 Stroke 6 Cy. 300 x 420 883kW (1201bhp) Mitsubishi Heavy Industries Ltd-Japan AuxGen: 2 x 80kW 225V a.c

8325949 *D9KG* -	**WOO JUNG No. 7** *ex* Hae Kup No. 7 *-1998* *ex* Dong Seung *-1986* **Woojung Shipping Co Ltd** - *Busan* *South Korea* Official number: BSR-828680	*271* 130 464	Class: (KR)	**1983-02 Sun-Il Shipbuilding Co Ltd — Geoje** Yd No: 77 Loa 33.10 Br ex 7.04 Dght 3.380 Lbp 30.03 Br md 7.01 Dpth 3.51 Welded, 1 dk	**(A13B2TU) Tanker (unspecified)** Liq: 376; Liq (Oil): 376 Compartments: 6 Ta, ER	**1 oil engine** with clutches & sr geared to sc. shaft driving 1 FP propeller Total Power: 294kW (400hp) Kubota M6D26E 1 x 4 Stroke 6 Cy. 260 x 320 294kW (400bhp) Kubota Tekkosho-Japan AuxGen: 1 x 24kW 220V a.c
8610552 - -	**WOO KYUNG** *ex* Seiko Maru *-1999* - - *Busan* *South Korea* Official number: BSR-990404	*199* - 563		**1986-12 Murakami Hide Zosen K.K. — Imabari** Yd No: 260 Loa 45.60 (BB) Br ex - Dght 3.200 Lbp 42.00 Br md 8.60 Dpth 3.40 Welded, 1 dk	**(A12A2TC) Chemical Tanker**	**1 oil engine** driving 1 FP propeller Total Power: 515kW (700hp) Yanmar MF26-HT 1 x 4 Stroke 6 Cy. 260 x 500 515kW (700bhp) Yanmar Diesel Engine Co Ltd-Japan
9414046 *DSMV2* -	**WOO LIM** *ex* Sunrise Acacia *-2010* **Woolim Shipping Co Ltd** Woolim Marine Co Ltd *Jeju* *South Korea* MMSI: 441933000 Official number: JJR-102212	**7,206** 3,884 12,489 T/cm 20.7	Class: KR (NK)	**2007-09 Miyoshi Shipbuilding Co Ltd — Uwajima EH** Yd No: 391 Loa 124.00 (BB) Br ex 20.03 Dght 8.771 Lbp 116.00 Br md 20.00 Dpth 11.20 Welded, 1 dk	**(A12B2TR) Chemical/Products Tanker** Double Hull (13F) Liq: 13,395; Liq (Oil): 13,300 Cargo Heating Coils Compartments: 14 Wing Ta, ER 14 Cargo Pump (s): 4x100m³/hr, 8x200m³/hr, 2x300m³/hr Manifold: Bow/CM: 64.5m	**1 oil engine** driving 1 FP propeller Total Power: 4,200kW (5,710hp) 13.5kn MAN-B&W 6S35MC 1 x 2 Stroke 6 Cy. 350 x 1400 4200kW (5710bhp) Makita Corp-Japan AuxGen: 3 x 400kW a.c Fuel: 88.0 (d.f.) 670.0 (r.f.)
9416317 *V7YB9* -	**WOO MIN** - **DV Dragon SA** Woolim Marine Co Ltd *Majuro* *Marshall Islands* MMSI: 538004623 Official number: 4623	**4,688** 2,172 6,814 T/cm 16.5	Class: KR	**2008-04 Mokpo Shipbuilding & Engineering Co Ltd — Mokpo** Yd No: 06-182 Loa 109.99 (BB) Br ex - Dght 6.713 Lbp 102.43 Br md 18.20 Dpth 8.50 Welded, 1 dk	**(A12B2TR) Chemical/Products Tanker** Double Hull (13F) Liq: 7,325; Liq (Oil): 7,325 Cargo Heating Coils Compartments: 12 Wing Ta, ER, 2 Wing Slop Ta 12 Cargo Pump (s): 12x200m³/hr Manifold: Bow/CM: 52.1m	**1 oil engine** driving 1 FP propeller Total Power: 3,309kW (4,499hp) 13.3kn Hanshin LH46LA 1 x 4 Stroke 6 Cy. 460 x 880 3309kW (4499bhp) The Hanshin Diesel Works Ltd-Japan AuxGen: 3 x 454kW 450V 60Hz a.c Thrusters: 1 Tunnel thruster (f) Fuel: 79.0 (d.f.) 333.0 (r.f.)
9284415 *V7QT6* -	**WOO SEOK** - **Woo Chem-Carrier AS** Woolim Shipping Co Ltd *Majuro* *Marshall Islands* MMSI: 538003435 Official number: 3435	**2,362** 1,086 3,449 T/cm 10.1	Class: KR	**2003-10 Nokbong Shipbuilding Co Ltd — Geoje** Yd No: 389 Loa 87.31 (BB) Br ex - Dght 5.813 Lbp 79.80 Br md 14.00 Dpth 7.30 Welded, 1 dk	**(A12B2TR) Chemical/Products Tanker** Double Hull (13F) Liq: 3,942; Liq (Oil): 3,942 Cargo Heating Coils Compartments: 1 Slop Ta, ER, 10 Wing Ta 10 Cargo Pump (s): 10x200m³/hr Manifold: Bow/CM: 45.3m	**1 oil engine** geared to sc. shaft driving 1 CP propeller Total Power: 1,960kW (2,665hp) 12.3kn MAN-B&W 8L28/32A 1 x 4 Stroke 8 Cy. 280 x 320 1960kW (2665bhp) (made 2003) STX Corp-South Korea AuxGen: 2 x 400kW 450V a.c Fuel: 50.0 (d.f.) 137.0 (r.f.)
9230335 *DSFN9* -	**WOO SUN** - **Keoje Marine Co Ltd** - SatCom: Inmarsat C 444036536 *Incheon* *South Korea* MMSI: 441089000 Official number: BSR-012571	**2,115** 1,117 3,415 T/cm 9.8	Class: KR	**2001-03 INP Heavy Industries Co Ltd — Ulsan** Yd No: 1113 Loa 84.40 (BB) Br ex - Dght 5.750 Lbp 79.00 Br md 14.00 Dpth 6.75 Welded, 1 dk	**(A12B2TR) Chemical/Products Tanker** Double Hull (13F) Liq: 4,078; Liq (Oil): 4,078 Cargo Heating Coils Compartments: 10 Wing Ta, 1 Slop Ta, ER 10 Cargo Pump (s): 10x200m³/hr Manifold: Bow/CM: 34.5m	**1 oil engine** reduction geared to sc. shaft driving 1 FP propeller Total Power: 1,960kW (2,665hp) 12.0kn MAN-B&W 8L28/32A 1 x 4 Stroke 8 Cy. 280 x 320 1960kW (2665bhp) (made 2000) Ssangyong Heavy Industries Co Ltd-South Korea AuxGen: 2 x 450V a.c
9416329 *V7YC2* -	**WOO SUNG** - **DV Dragon SA** Woolim Shipping Co Ltd *Majuro* *Marshall Islands* MMSI: 538004624 Official number: 4624	**4,688** 2,172 6,822 T/cm 16.5	Class: KR	**2008-09 Mokpo Shipbuilding & Engineering Co Ltd — Mokpo** Yd No: 06-184 Loa 109.99 (BB) Br ex - Dght 6.713 Lbp 102.43 Br md 18.20 Dpth 8.50 Welded, 1 dk	**(A12B2TR) Chemical/Products Tanker** Double Hull (13F) Liq: 7,322; Liq (Oil): 7,322 Cargo Heating Coils Compartments: 12 Wing Ta (s.stl), 2 Wing Slop Ta (s.stl), ER (s.stl) 12 Cargo Pump (s): 12x200m³/hr Manifold: Bow/CM: 52.1m	**1 oil engine** driving 1 FP propeller Total Power: 3,309kW (4,499hp) 13.3kn Hanshin LH46LA 1 x 4 Stroke 6 Cy. 460 x 880 3309kW (4499bhp) The Hanshin Diesel Works Ltd-Japan AuxGen: 3 x 450kW a.c Thrusters: 1 Thwart. FP thruster Fuel: 80.0 (d.f.) 330.0 (r.f.)
8608688 - -	**WOO SUNG No. 3** *ex* Futaba Maru *-1997* **Kwang Woon Shipping Co Ltd** - *Yeosu* *South Korea* MMSI: 440312260 Official number: YSR-975804	*160* - 181	Class: KR	**1986-07 Kanagawa Zosen — Kobe** Yd No: 288 Loa 31.30 Br ex - Dght 3.001 Lbp 27.01 Br md 8.81 Dpth 3.81 Welded, 1 dk	**(B32A2ST) Tug**	**2 oil engines** driving 2 FP propellers Total Power: 2,206kW (3,000hp) 13.5kn Niigata 6L25CXE 2 x 4 Stroke 6 Cy. 250 x 320 each-1103kW (1500bhp) Niigata Engineering Co Ltd-Japan
8815437 - -	**WOO SUNG No. 5** *ex* Shinsoma Maru *-1997* **Kwang Woon Shipping Co Ltd** - *Yeosu* *South Korea* Official number: YSR-975811	*162* - 181	Class: KR	**1988-12 Kanagawa Zosen — Kobe** Yd No: 320 Loa 31.30 Br ex - Dght 3.000 Lbp 27.00 Br md 8.80 Dpth 3.80 Welded, 1 dk	**(B32A2ST) Tug**	**2 oil engines** driving 2 FP propellers Total Power: 2,206kW (3,000hp) Niigata 6L25CXE 2 x 4 Stroke 6 Cy. 250 x 320 each-1103kW (1500bhp) Niigata Engineering Co Ltd-Japan
7379539 *6NQL* -	**WOO SUNG No. 71** *ex* Dong Geong No. 23 *-1986* *ex* Kwang Myung No. 170 *-1984* **Lee Mal-Hyang** - *Busan* *South Korea* Official number: BS02-A2169	*363* 186 480	Class: (KR)	**1974-02 Miho Zosensho K.K. — Shimizu** Yd No: 953 Loa 53.40 Br ex 8.82 Dght 3.405 Lbp 47.00 Br md 8.77 Dpth 3.61 Welded, 1 dk	**(B11B2FV) Fishing Vessel** Ins: 513 3 Ha: 2 (1.3 x 0.9) (1.7 x 1.7)ER	**1 oil engine** driving 1 FP propeller Total Power: 993kW (1,350hp) 11.8kn Akasaka AH28 1 x 4 Stroke 6 Cy. 280 x 440 993kW (1350bhp) Akasaka Tekkosho KK (Akasaka DieselLtd)-Japan AuxGen: 2 x 200kW 225V a.c
8629852 *HLIB* -	**WOO SUNG No. 101** - **Woo Sung Commercial Co Ltd** - *Pohang* *South Korea* Official number: KN6669-A478	*106* 45 76	Class: (KR)	**1983 Pohang Shipbuilding Co Ltd — Pohang** Yd No: 101 Loa 34.25 Br ex - Dght 2.498 Lbp 29.00 Br md 6.00 Dpth 2.75 Welded, 1 dk	**(B11B2FV) Fishing Vessel** Compartments: 1 Wing Ta	**1 oil engine** driving 1 FP propeller Total Power: 331kW (450hp) AuxGen: 2 x 160kW 225V a.c
8629864 *DTVA* -	**WOO SUNG No. 103** - **Sho Yug-Ji** - *Pohang* *South Korea* Official number: KN6669-A521	*129* 43 95	Class: (KR)	**1984 Pohang Shipbuilding Co Ltd — Pohang** Loa 34.97 Br ex - Dght 2.894 Lbp 29.00 Br md 6.00 Dpth 2.95 Welded, 1 dk	**(B11B2FV) Fishing Vessel**	**1 oil engine** driving 1 FP propeller Total Power: 331kW (450hp) Niigata 6L16XB-B 1 x 4 Stroke 6 Cy. 160 x 200 331kW (450bhp) Ssangyong Heavy Industries Co Ltd-South Korea AuxGen: 2 x 208kW 225V a.c
8629888 *DTVC* -	**WOO SUNG No. 207** - **Kim Yung-Man** - *Pohang* *South Korea* Official number: KN66.69-A600	*106* - 90	Class: (KR)	**1985-09 Pohang Shipbuilding Co Ltd — Pohang** Loa 34.97 Br ex - Dght 2.727 Lbp 29.00 Br md 6.00 Dpth 2.95 Welded, 1 dk	**(B11B2FV) Fishing Vessel**	**1 oil engine** driving 1 FP propeller Total Power: 285kW (387hp) Cummins KT-19-M 1 x 4 Stroke 6 Cy. 159 x 159 285kW (387bhp) Ssangyong Heavy Industries Co Ltd-South Korea AuxGen: 1 x 208kW 225V a.c
9258040 *9HJJ9* -	**WOO TAE** - **GSH1 Chem-Prod Carrier III AS** Woolim Marine Co Ltd *Valletta* *Malta* MMSI: 249057000 Official number: 9258040	**5,328** 2,520 7,968 T/cm 17.5	Class: KR	**2002-03 Nokbong Shipbuilding Co Ltd — Geoje** Yd No: 385 Loa 113.00 (BB) Br ex 18.23 Dght 7.313 Lbp 105.00 Br md 18.20 Dpth 9.60 Welded, 1 dk	**(A12B2TR) Chemical/Products Tanker** Double Hull (13F) Liq: 8,414; Liq (Oil): 8,971 Compartments: 10 Wing Ta, 2 Wing Slop Ta, ER 10 Cargo Pump (s): 4x300m³/hr, 6x200m³/hr Manifold: Bow/CM: 56.8m	**1 oil engine** driving 1 FP propeller Total Power: 3,884kW (5,281hp) 13.0kn MAN-B&W 6L35MC 1 x 2 Stroke 6 Cy. 350 x 1050 3884kW (5281bhp) STX Corp-South Korea AuxGen: 4 x 320kW 445V Thrusters: 1 Tunnel thruster (f) Fuel: 103.0 (d.f.) 543.0 (r.f.)
9240213 *9HJK9* -	**WOO WON** - **GSH1 Chem-Prod Carrier III AS** Woolim Shipping Co Ltd *Valletta* *Malta* MMSI: 249058000 Official number: 9240213	**2,360** 1,084 3,528 T/cm 9.8	Class: KR	**2001-06 Nokbong Shipbuilding Co Ltd — Geoje** Yd No: 383 Loa 87.28 (BB) Br ex - Dght 5.813 Lbp 79.80 Br md 14.00 Dpth 7.30 Welded, 1 dk	**(A12B2TR) Chemical/Products Tanker** Double Hull (13F) Liq: 3,870; Liq (Oil): 3,870 Cargo Heating Coils Compartments: 1 Ta, 8 Wing Ta, 1 Slop Ta, ER 9 Cargo Pump (s): 9x200m³/hr Manifold: Bow/CM: 42.8m	**1 oil engine** reduction geared to sc. shaft driving 1 FP propeller Total Power: 1,960kW (2,665hp) 12.3kn MAN-B&W 8L28/32A 1 x 4 Stroke 8 Cy. 280 x 320 1960kW (2665bhp) STX Corp-South Korea AuxGen: 2 x 400kW 450V a.c Fuel: 53.0 (d.f.) 137.0 (r.f.)

IMO / Call sign	Name / Owner	Tonnage / Class	Builder / Dimensions	Type	Machinery
015817 *DTAT*	**WOO YANG No. 77** *ex* Ryong Sung No. 77 *-1984* *ex* Sin Bul San No. 21 *-1983* **Cho Hyo-Sik** - *Busan* *South Korea* Official number: BS-A-1762	*149* Class: (KR) 29 139	**1980-02 Jinhae Ship Construction Industrial Co Ltd — Changwon** Loa 39.27 Br ex 7.32 Dght - Lbp 31.81 Br md 7.31 Dpth 2.93 Welded, 1 dk	**(B11B2FV) Fishing Vessel**	**1 oil engine** reverse geared to sc. shaft driving 1 FP propeller Total Power: 1,177kW (1,600hp) 12.5kn Niigata 6M31EX 1 x 4 Stroke 6 Cy. 310 x 460 1177kW (1600bhp) Niigata Engineering Co Ltd-Japan AuxGen: 1 x 80kW 225V a.c
629776 *6MVD*	**WOO YANG No. 105** **Woo Yang Fisheries Co Ltd** - *Busan* *South Korea* Official number: BS02-A747	*277* Class: (KR) 148 -	**1964 Miho Zosensho K.K. — Shimizu** Loa 46.00 Br ex - Dght 3.232 Lbp 40.49 Br md 7.50 Dpth 3.61 Welded, 1 dk	**(B11B2FV) Fishing Vessel** Ins: 347 3 Ha: 3 (1.5 x 1.5)	**1 oil engine** driving 1 FP propeller Total Power: 478kW (650hp) 10.8kn Ito 1 x 4 Stroke 6 Cy. 310 x 480 478kW (650bhp) Ito Tekkosho-Japan AuxGen: 2 x 64kW 230V a.c
606413 *6LBR*	**WOO YANG No. 107** *ex* Hae Bung No. 23 *-1975* **Woo Yang Fisheries Co Ltd** - *Busan* *South Korea* Official number: BS-A-503	*347* Class: (KR) 151 364	**1967 Nichiro Zosen K.K. — Ishinomaki** Loa 48.42 Br ex - Dght 3.521 Lbp 43.85 Br md 8.50 Dpth 3.76 Welded, 1 dk	**(B11A2FS) Stern Trawler** Ins: 359	**1 oil engine** driving 1 FP propeller Total Power: 1,324kW (1,800hp) 11.5kn Akasaka 6DH38SS 1 x 4 Stroke 6 Cy. 380 x 560 1324kW (1800bhp) Akasaka Tekkosho KK (Akasaka DieselLtd)-Japan AuxGen: 2 x 104kW 230V a.c
709080 *DTFT* -	**WOO YANG NO. 111** *ex* Dong A No. 111 *-2009* **Han Il Leasing Co Ltd** Dong Ah Fisheries Co Ltd *Busan* *South Korea* MMSI: 440716000 Official number: BS-A-2548	*129* Class: (KR) - 88	**1987-12 Dae Sun Shipbuilding & Engineering Co Ltd — Busan** Yd No: 323 Loa 46.41 Br ex - Dght 2.843 Lbp 37.01 Br md 7.90 Dpth 3.23 Welded, 1 dk	**(B11B2FV) Fishing Vessel**	**1 oil engine** reverse reduction geared to sc. shaft driving 1 FP propeller Total Power: 1,765kW (2,400hp) 16.8kn Pielstick 8PA5L 1 x 4 Stroke 8 Cy. 255 x 270 1765kW (2400bhp) Ssangyong Heavy Industries Co Ltd-South Korea AuxGen: 2 x 112kW 225V a.c
081796 *6LTM* -	**WOO YANG NO. 121** *ex* New Kwanghae No. 92 *-2009* **Choi In-Suk** - SatCom: Inmarsat A 1660510 *Busan* *South Korea* MMSI: 440735000 Official number: 9506015-6210006	**129** Class: (KR) - 134	**1992-11 Jinhae Ship Construction Industrial Co Ltd — Changwon** Loa 43.30 (BB) Br ex 8.02 Dght 3.286 Lbp 34.78 Br md 7.60 Dpth 3.10 Welded, 1 dk	**(B11B2FV) Fishing Vessel**	**1 oil engine** geared to sc. shaft driving 1 FP propeller Total Power: 1,765kW (2,400hp) Pielstick 8PA5L 1 x 4 Stroke 8 Cy. 255 x 270 1765kW (2400bhp) Ssangyong Heavy Industries Co Ltd-South Korea AuxGen: 2 x 212kW 225V a.c Thrusters: 1 Thwart. FP thruster (f)
9558816 *DSRN4* -	**WOO YEON** *ex* Menara Dua *-2013* **Keoje Marine Co Ltd** - *Jeju* *South Korea* MMSI: 441922000 Official number: JJR-131033	**5,036** Class: KR (BV) 2,272 7,116 T/cm 17.6	**2009-12 Zhejiang Shenzhou Shipbuilding Co Ltd — Xiangshan County ZJ** Yd No: SZ08007 Loa 118.00 (BB) Br ex - Dght 6.600 Lbp 110.00 Br md 17.60 Dpth 9.00 Welded, 1 dk	**(A13B2TP) Products Tanker** Double Hull (13F) Liq: 8,063; Liq (Oil): 8,063 Cargo Heating Coils Compartments: 10 Wing Ta, 2 Wing Slop Ta, ER 2 Cargo Pump (s): 2x750m³/hr Manifold: Bow/CM: 58.2m	**1 oil engine** reduction geared to sc. shaft driving 1 FP propeller Total Power: 2,574kW (3,500hp) 12.0kn Yanmar 6N330-EN 1 x 4 Stroke 6 Cy. 330 x 440 2574kW (3500bhp) Qingdao Zichai Boyang Diesel EngineCo Ltd-China AuxGen: 2 x 500kW 60Hz a.c Fuel: 348.0 (r.f.)
9152208 *DSRG2* -	**WOO YOUNG** *ex* Dorothea *-2011* **Woolim Shipping Co Ltd** Woolim Marine Co Ltd *Incheon* *South Korea* MMSI: 441821000 Official number: ICR-111914	**3,721** Class: KR (NK) 1,678 5,980 T/cm 13.5	**1997-02 Kurinoura Dockyard Co Ltd — Yawatahama EH** Yd No: 338 Loa 104.50 (BB) Br ex - Dght 7.044 Lbp 97.00 Br md 16.40 Dpth 8.50 Welded, 1 dk	**(A12B2TR) Chemical/Products Tanker** Double Hull (13F) Liq: 5,914; Liq (Oil): 5,914 Cargo Heating Coils Compartments: 12 Wing Ta (s.stl), ER (s.stl) 12 Cargo Pump (s): 6x200m³/hr, 6x150m³/hr Manifold: Bow/CM: 50.2m	**1 oil engine** driving 1 FP propeller Total Power: 3,236kW (4,400hp) 13.0kn MAN-B&W 5L35MC 1 x 2 Stroke 5 Cy. 350 x 1050 3236kW (4400bhp) Makita Corp-Japan AuxGen: 3 x 280kW 445V 60Hz a.c Fuel: 85.0 (d.f.) 305.0 (r.f.)
7717901 - -	**WOODCHUCK** *ex* Cattleya Ace *-1987* *ex* Izumi *-1979* - -	**3,642** Class: (NK) 2,311 5,776	**1978-02 Geibi Zosen Kogyo — Kure** Yd No: 278 Loa 98.00 Br ex 17.05 Dght 6.414 Lbp 89.90 Br md 17.01 Dpth 7.19 Welded, 1 dk	**(A31A2GX) General Cargo Ship** Grain: 8,109; Bale: 7,423 Derricks: 1x20t,2x15t	**1 oil engine** driving 1 FP propeller Total Power: 2,427kW (3,300hp) 12.3kn Makita KGS43B 1 x 4 Stroke 6 Cy. 430 x 650 2427kW (3300bhp) Makita Diesel Co Ltd-Japan AuxGen: 2 x 144kW a.c
9493236 *D5BX7* -	**WOODGATE** **Shaz Shipping Inc** Zodiac Maritime Agencies Ltd *Monrovia* *Liberia* MMSI: 636015627 Official number: 15627	**17,025** Class: NK 10,108 28,219 T/cm 39.7	**2011-05 I-S Shipyard Co Ltd — Imabari EH** Yd No: S-A043 Loa 169.37 (BB) Br ex - Dght 9.819 Lbp 160.40 Br md 27.20 Dpth 13.60 Welded, 1 dk	**(A21A2BC) Bulk Carrier** Grain: 37,320; Bale: 35,742 Compartments: 5 Ho, ER 5 Ha: 4 (19.2 x 17.6)ER (13.6 x 16.0) Cranes: 4x30.5t	**1 oil engine** driving 1 FP propeller Total Power: 5,850kW (7,954hp) 14.0kn MAN-B&W 6S42MC 1 x 2 Stroke 6 Cy. 420 x 1764 5850kW (7954bhp) Makita Corp-Japan AuxGen: 3 x 440kW 60Hz a.c
8967773 *YDA6997* -	**WOODMAN 36** **PT Sandi Adi Perkasa** - *Samarinda* *Indonesia*	*183* Class: NK 55 186	**2000-10 C E Ling Shipbuilding Sdn Bhd — Miri** Yd No: 026 Loa 25.50 Br ex 7.92 Dght 3.012 Lbp 23.87 Br md 7.80 Dpth 3.65 Welded, 1 dk	**(B32A2ST) Tug**	**2 oil engines** reduction geared to sc. shaft (s) driving 1 FP propeller Total Power: 1,060kW (1,442hp) 10.0kn Caterpillar 3412B 2 x Vee 4 Stroke 12 Cy. 137 x 152 each-530kW (721bhp) Caterpillar Inc-USA AuxGen: 2 x 41kW a.c Fuel: 130.0 (d.f.)
9257307 *9WFB8* -	**WOODMAN 38** **Woodman Sdn Bhd** - *Kuching* *Malaysia* MMSI: 533170074 Official number: 329376	**194** Class: NK 59 188	**2001-08 C E Ling Shipbuilding Sdn Bhd — Miri** Yd No: 027 Loa 26.07 Br ex - Dght 3.012 Lbp 23.88 Br md 8.23 Dpth 3.60 Welded, 1 dk	**(B32A2ST) Tug**	**2 oil engines** reduction geared to sc. shafts driving 2 FP propellers Total Power: 1,076kW (1,462hp) 11.0kn Caterpillar 3412 2 x Vee 4 Stroke 12 Cy. 137 x 152 each-538kW (731bhp) Caterpillar Inc-USA AuxGen: 2 x 33kW a.c Fuel: 175.0 (d.f.)
7111169 *DUA4025* -	**WOODROSE** *ex* Kinko Maru No. 8 *-1989* *ex* Shinsei Maru No. 30 *-1983* **Frabelle Fishing Corp** - *Manila* *Philippines* Official number: MNLD000700	*243* 153 599	**1971-03 K.K. Matsuura Zosensho — Osakikamijima** Yd No: 170 Loa 48.01 Br ex 8.03 Dght 3.214 Lbp 45.01 Br md 8.01 Dpth 3.31 Welded, 1 dk	**(A31A2GX) General Cargo Ship** Compartments: 1 Ho, ER 1 Ha: (28.9 x 6.0)	**1 oil engine** driving 1 FP propeller Total Power: 559kW (760hp) 10.5kn Mitsubishi 12DE20MT 1 x Vee 4 Stroke 12 Cy. 150 x 200 559kW (760bhp) Mitsubishi Heavy Industries Ltd-Japan AuxGen: 1 x 6kW 110V a.c Fuel: 17.0 3.5pd
9369899 *9V8262* -	**WOODSIDE DONALDSON** **Malt Singapore Pte Ltd** Teekay Shipping (Glasgow) Ltd SatCom: Inmarsat C 456462910 *Singapore* *Singapore* MMSI: 564629000 Official number: 395529	**104,169** Class: BV 32,537 82,085 T/cm 105.5	**2009-10 Samsung Heavy Industries Co Ltd — Geoje** Yd No: 1632 Loa 286.18 (BB) Br ex - Dght 12.120 Lbp 275.00 Br md 43.40 Dpth 26.60 Welded, 1 dk	**(A11A2TN) LNG Tanker** Double Bottom Entire Compartment Length Liq (Gas): 162,620 4 x Gas Tank (s); 4 membrane (s.stl) pri horizontal 8 Cargo Pump (s): 8x1750m³/hr Manifold: Bow/CM: 141.8m	**4 diesel electric oil engines** driving 3 gen. each 11000kW 6600V a.c 1 gen. of 5500kW 6600V a.c Connecting to 2 elec. motors each (13250kW) driving 1 FP propeller Total Power: 39,900kW (54,247hp) 19.5kn Wartsila 12V50DF 3 x Vee 4 Stroke 12 Cy. 500 x 580 each-11400kW (15499bhp) Wartsila France SA-France Wartsila 6L50DF 1 x 4 Stroke 6 Cy. 500 x 580 5700kW (7750bhp) Wartsila France SA-France Thrusters: 1 Tunnel thruster (f) Fuel: 1270.0 (d.f.) 4840.0 (r.f.)
9633161 *SVBU9* -	**WOODSIDE GOODE** **Armour Co Ltd** Maran Gas Maritime Inc *Piraeus* *Greece* MMSI: 241276000	**103,928** Class: NV 31,179 90,125	**2013-10 Daewoo Shipbuilding & Marine Engineering Co Ltd — Geoje** Yd No: 2295 Loa 294.20 (BB) Br ex 44.03 Dght 11.500 Lbp 283.20 Br md 44.00 Dpth 26.00 Welded, 1 dk	**(A11A2TN) LNG Tanker** Liq (Gas): 159,800	**4 diesel electric oil engines** driving 4 gen. each 7880kW Connecting to 2 elec. motors each (13260kW) driving 2 FP propellers Total Power: 34,200kW (46,500hp) 19.5kn Wartsila 9L50DF 1 x 4 Stroke 9 Cy. 500 x 580 8550kW (11625bhp) Wartsila Italia SpA-Italy Wartsila 9L50DF 3 x 4 Stroke 9 Cy. 500 x 580 each-8550kW (11625bhp) Wartsila Italia SpA-Italy Thrusters: 1 Tunnel thruster (centre)

IMO / Call sign / Flag	Name / Owner / Manager / Port	Tonnage	Class	Builder / Dimensions	Type	Machinery
8702070 - -	**WOODSIDE I** **City of Dartmouth** - *Halifax, NS* *Canada* Official number: 805165	*256* 161 15		**1986-12 Pictou Industries Ltd — Pictou NS** Yd No: 220 Loa 24.11 Br ex 9.78 Dght - Lbp 23.78 Br md 9.45 Dpth 1.53 Welded, 1 dk	**(A37B2PS) Passenger Ship**	**2 oil engines** with clutches, flexible couplings & sr geared to sc. shaft driving 2 Directional propellers aft, 1 fwd Total Power: 338kW (460hp) Caterpillar 3306T 2 x 4 Stroke 6 Cy. 121 x 152 each-169kW (230bhp) Caterpillar Inc-USA
9627485 *SVBS6* -	**WOODSIDE ROGERS** **Margie Seaway Corp** Maran Gas Maritime Inc *Piraeus* *Greece* MMSI: 241254000	**103,928** 31,179 90,327	Class: NV	**2013-07 Daewoo Shipbuilding & Marine Engineering Co Ltd — Geoje** Yd No: 2288 Loa 294.20 (BB) Br ex 44.03 Dght 11.500 Lbp 283.20 Br md 44.00 Dpth 26.00 Welded, 1 dk	**(A11A2TN) LNG Tanker** Liq (Gas): 159,800	**4 diesel electric oil engines** driving 4 gen. each 7880kW a.c Connecting to 2 elec. motors each (13260kW) driving 2 FP propellers Total Power: 34,200kW (46,500hp) 19.5kn Wartsila 9L50DF 1 x 4 Stroke 9 Cy. 500 x 580 8550kW (11625bhp) Wartsila Italia SpA-Italy Wartsila 9L50DF 3 x 4 Stroke 9 Cy. 500 x 580 each-8550kW (11625bhp) Wartsila Italia SpA-Italy Thrusters: 1 Tunnel thruster (centre)
9347918 *V7QI3* -	**WOODSTAR** **Woodstar Shipping LLC** Eagle Shipping International (USA) LLC *Majuro* *Marshall Islands* MMSI: 538003369 Official number: 3369	**31,144** 18,571 53,389 T/cm 56.4	Class: NK	**2008-10 Yangzhou Dayang Shipbuilding Co Ltd — Yangzhou JS** Yd No: DY115 Loa 189.99 (BB) Br ex - Dght 12.508 Lbp 182.00 Br md 32.26 Dpth 17.20 Welded, 1 dk	**(A21A2BC) Bulk Carrier** Double Hull Grain: 65,045; Bale: 63,654 Compartments: 5 Ho, ER 5 Ha: 4 (21.3 x 18.3)ER (18.9 x 18.3) Cranes: 4x35t	**1 oil engine** driving 1 FP propeller Total Power: 9,480kW (12,889hp) 14.7kn MAN-B&W 6S50MC-C 1 x 2 Stroke 6 Cy. 500 x 2000 9480kW (12889bhp) Doosan Engine Co Ltd-South Korea AuxGen: 3 x a.c Fuel: 2020.0
7303009 *2BUY7* -	**WOODSTOCK 1** *ex* Woodstock I *-2009* *ex* Woodstock *-1996* *ex* A. D. Due *-1995* **Seafast Marine Ltd** Caldive Ltd *Inverness* *United Kingdom* MMSI: 235069559	**256** 76 356	Class: RI	**1973-01 Cooperativa Metallurgica Ing G Tommasi Srl — Ancona** Yd No: 18 Converted From: General Cargo Ship, Inland Waterways-2009 Loa 34.14 Br ex 10.37 Dght 1.829 Lbp 32.54 Br md 10.00 Dpth 2.82 Welded, 1 dk	**(B34B2SC) Crane Vessel** Cranes: 1x200t	**2 oil engines** geared to sc. shafts driving 2 FP propellers Total Power: 380kW (516hp) 7.0kn Deutz F6M716 2 x 4 Stroke 6 Cy. 135 x 160 each-190kW (258bhp) Kloeckner Humboldt Deutz AG-West Germany
7733175 *WYG7509* -	**WOODY** **Woody Shrimp Co Inc** - *Corpus Christi, TX* *United States of America* Official number: 585717	*118* 80 -		**1977 Marine Mart, Inc. — Port Isabel, Tx** Yd No: 160 L reg 20.73 Br ex - Dght - Lbp - Br md 6.20 Dpth 3.66 Welded, 1 dk	**(B11B2FV) Fishing Vessel**	**1 oil engine** driving 1 FP propeller Total Power: 268kW (364hp) Caterpillar 1 x 4 Stroke 268kW (364bhp) Caterpillar Tractor Co-USA
8921676 *DSQK2* -	**WOOHYUN HAEMIL** *ex* Dong Ho *-2011* *ex* Thanks Twenty *-2009* **Woohyun Shipping Co Ltd** SM Leader Co Ltd *Jeju* *South Korea* MMSI: 441604000 Official number: JJR-092110	**5,144** 2,990 6,806	Class: KR (NK)	**1990-04 Hakata Zosen K.K. — Imabari** Yd No: 508 Loa 110.00 (BB) Br ex 17.42 Dght 7.264 Lbp 102.87 Br md 17.40 Dpth 10.50 Welded, 1 dk	**(A31A2GX) General Cargo Ship** Grain: 10,819; Bale: 10,079 Compartments: 2 Ho, ER 2 Ha: ER Derricks: 2x30t,2x25t	**1 oil engine** driving 1 CP propeller Total Power: 3,354kW (4,560hp) 16.1kn B&W 6L35MC 1 x 2 Stroke 6 Cy. 350 x 1050 3354kW (4560bhp) The Hanshin Diesel Works Ltd-Japan Thrusters: 1 Thwart. CP thruster (f)
8921341 *DSBG7* -	**WOOHYUN QUEEN** *ex* Inter Noble *-2010* *ex* Exceed 2 *-2002* **Woohyun Shipping Co Ltd** Boo Kwang Shipping Co Ltd *Jeju* *South Korea* MMSI: 441202000 Official number: JJR-022607	**5,914** 2,392 7,583	Class: KR (NK)	**1990-08 Murakami Hide Zosen K.K. — Imabari** Yd No: 315 Loa 106.50 (BB) Br ex - Dght 7.374 Lbp 97.00 Br md 18.20 Dpth 8.35 Welded, 1 dk	**(A31A2GX) General Cargo Ship** Grain: 8,290; Bale: 7,828 Compartments: 2 Ho, ER 2 Ha: (25.2 x 9.0) (28.0 x 9.0)ER Cranes: 2x25t; Derricks: 2x15t	**1 oil engine** driving 1 FP propeller Total Power: 2,795kW (3,800hp) 12.0kn B&W 5L35MC 1 x 2 Stroke 5 Cy. 350 x 1050 2795kW (3800bhp) Makita Diesel Co Ltd-Japan AuxGen: 3 x 144kW a.c
9272814 *DSRN3* -	**WOOJIN CHEMI** *ex* Miranda *-2013* **Woo Jin Shipping Co Ltd** - *Jeju* *South Korea* MMSI: 441921000 Official number: JJR-131025	**5,347** 2,702 8,522 T/cm 16.6	Class: KR (NK)	**2003-04 Kurinoura Dockyard Co Ltd — Yawatahama EH** Yd No: 370 Loa 119.98 (BB) Br ex 17.23 Dght 7.944 Lbp 112.40 Br md 17.20 Dpth 9.80 Welded, 1 dk	**(A12B2TR) Chemical/Products Tanker** Double Hull (13F) Liq: 9,335; Liq (Oil): 9,335 Cargo Heating Coils Compartments: 16 Wing Ta (s.stl), ER 16 Cargo Pump (s): 16x200m³/hr Manifold: Bow/CM: 57.7m	**1 oil engine** driving 1 FP propeller Total Power: 3,906kW (5,311hp) 14.5kn MAN-B&W 6L35MC 1 x 2 Stroke 6 Cy. 350 x 1050 3906kW (5311bhp) Makita Corp-Japan AuxGen: 3 x 300kW a.c Thrusters: 1 Tunnel thruster (f) Fuel: 95.0 (d.f.) 564.0 (r.f.)
9114505 *DSQL9* -	**WOOJIN EMERALD** *ex* Suzanne *-2009* **Woo Jin Shipping Co Ltd** - *Jeju* *South Korea* MMSI: 441621000 Official number: JJR-092297	**5,998** 3,562 11,533 T/cm 19.3	Class: KR (NK)	**1995-03 Hayashikane Dockyard Co Ltd — Nagasaki NS** Yd No: 1010 Loa 113.95 (BB) Br ex 20.23 Dght 8.915 Lbp 108.00 Br md 20.20 Dpth 11.35 Welded, 1 dk	**(A12B2TR) Chemical/Products Tanker** Double Hull (13F) Liq: 11,838; Liq (Oil): 11,784 Cargo Heating Coils Compartments: 24 Wing Ta, ER, 2 Wing Slop Ta 24 Cargo Pump (s): 24x200m³/hr Manifold: Bow/CM: 60.2m	**1 oil engine** driving 1 FP propeller Total Power: 3,354kW (4,560hp) 11.5kn B&W 6L35MC 1 x 2 Stroke 6 Cy. 350 x 1050 3354kW (4560bhp) Hitachi Zosen Corp-Japan AuxGen: 3 x 480kW 445V a.c Thrusters: 1 Thwart. FP thruster (f) Fuel: 99.0 (d.f.) 679.0 (r.f.)
9287027 *DSNH2* -	**WOOJIN PIONEER** **Woo Jin Shipping Co Ltd** - *Jeju* *South Korea* MMSI: 441346000 Official number: JJR-031169	**2,712** 1,102 4,050 T/cm 11.3	Class: KR	**2003-09 Nichizo Iron Works & Marine Corp — Onomichi HS** Yd No: 168 Loa 92.50 (BB) Br ex 15.02 Dght 5.812 Lbp 85.00 Br md 15.00 Dpth 7.20 Welded, 1 dk	**(A12B2TR) Chemical/Products Tanker** Double Hull (13F) Liq: 4,032; Liq (Oil): 4,032 Cargo Heating Coils Compartments: 1 Ta (s.stl), 8 Wing Ta (s.stl), ER 9 Cargo Pump (s): 9x150m³/hr Manifold: Bow/CM: 43m	**1 oil engine** driving 1 FP propeller Total Power: 2,574kW (3,500hp) 12.5kn Hanshin LH41LA 1 x 4 Stroke 6 Cy. 410 x 800 2574kW (3500bhp) The Hanshin Diesel Works Ltd-Japan AuxGen: 2 x 280kW 445V a.c Thrusters: 1 Tunnel thruster (f) Fuel: 72.0 (d.f.) 346.0 (r.f.)
6723197 *D8UB* -	**WOOJUNG No. 1** *ex* Hae Kup No. 1 *-2000* *ex* Nisshin Maru *-1973* **Woojung Shipping Co Ltd** - *Busan* *South Korea* Official number: BSR-686136	*491* 286 870	Class: (KR)	**1967 Hanasaki Zosensho K.K. — Yokosuka** Yd No: 121 Loa 50.45 Br ex 9.22 Dght 3.749 Lbp 47.00 Br md 9.20 Dpth 4.20 Welded, 1 dk	**(A13B2TU) Tanker (unspecified)** Liq: 1,115; Liq (Oil): 1,115 Compartments: 2 Ta, 2 Wing Ta, ER 4 Cargo Pump (s): 1x387m³/hr, 1x374m³/hr, 1x176m³/hr, 1x177m³/hr	**1 oil engine** driving 1 FP propeller Total Power: 441kW (600hp) 10.5kn Kanegafuchi 1 x 4 Stroke 6 Cy. 270 x 400 441kW (600bhp) Kanegafuchi Diesel-Japan AuxGen: 1 x 15kW 225V a.c
9249893 *V7QT9* -	**WOOLIM DRAGON** **Woo Chem-Carrier AS** Woomin Shipping Co Ltd *Majuro* *Marshall Islands* MMSI: 538003438 Official number: 3438	**5,331** 2,538 7,972 T/cm 17.5	Class: KR	**2002-08 Nokbong Shipbuilding Co Ltd — Geoje** Yd No: 384 Loa 113.00 (BB) Br ex 18.21 Dght 7.313 Lbp 105.40 Br md 18.20 Dpth 9.60 Welded, 1 dk	**(A12B2TR) Chemical/Products Tanker** Double Hull (13F) Liq: 8,248; Liq (Oil): 8,248 Cargo Heating Coils Compartments: 10 Wing Ta, ER, 2 Wing Slop Ta 10 Cargo Pump (s): 4x300m³/hr, 6x200m³/hr Manifold: Bow/CM: 57.7m	**1 oil engine** driving 1 FP propeller Total Power: 3,906kW (5,311hp) 13.0kn B&W 6L35MC 1 x 2 Stroke 6 Cy. 350 x 1050 3906kW (5311bhp) STX Corp-South Korea AuxGen: 4 x 320kW 445V a.c Thrusters: 1 Tunnel thruster (f) Fuel: 70.0 (d.f.) 460.0 (r.f.)
9411692 *V7YC5* -	**WOOLIM DRAGON 3** **DV Dragon SA** Woolim Marine Co Ltd *Majuro* *Marshall Islands* MMSI: 538004627 Official number: 4627	**5,598** 2,524 8,042 T/cm 17.7	Class: KR	**2008-03 Nokbong Shipbuilding Co Ltd — Geoje** Yd No: 415 Loa 113.08 (BB) Br ex - Dght 7.463 Lbp 105.00 Br md 18.20 Dpth 9.60 Welded, 1 dk	**(A12B2TR) Chemical/Products Tanker** Double Hull (13F) Liq: 8,396; Liq (Oil): 8,396 Cargo Heating Coils Compartments: 10 Wing Ta, 2 Wing Slop Ta, ER 10 Cargo Pump (s): 10x200m³/hr Manifold: Bow/CM: 60m	**1 oil engine** driving 1 CP propeller Total Power: 3,900kW (5,302hp) 13.7kn MAN-B&W 6L35MC 1 x 2 Stroke 6 Cy. 350 x 1050 3900kW (5302bhp) STX Engine Co Ltd-South Korea AuxGen: 3 x 480kW 450V a.c Thrusters: 1 Tunnel thruster (f) Fuel: 109.0 (d.f.) 537.0 (r.f.)
9412426 *DSQA2* -	**WOOLIM DRAGON 5** **Woolim Shipping Co Ltd** Woolim Marine Co Ltd *Jeju* *South Korea* MMSI: 441507000 Official number: JJR-088443	**5,589** 2,524 8,062 T/cm 17.7	Class: KR	**2008-07 Nokbong Shipbuilding Co Ltd — Geoje** Yd No: 416 Loa 113.08 (BB) Br ex - Dght 7.463 Lbp 105.00 Br md 18.20 Dpth 9.60 Welded, 1 dk	**(A12B2TR) Chemical/Products Tanker** Double Hull (13F) Liq: 8,398; Liq (Oil): 8,398 Cargo Heating Coils Compartments: 10 Wing Ta, 1 Wing Slop Ta, ER 10 Cargo Pump (s): 10x200m³/hr Manifold: Bow/CM: 60m	**1 oil engine** driving 1 FP propeller Total Power: 3,900kW (5,302hp) 13.7kn MAN-B&W 6L35MC 1 x 2 Stroke 6 Cy. 350 x 1050 3900kW (5302bhp) STX Engine Co Ltd-South Korea AuxGen: 4 x 480kW a.c Thrusters: 1 Tunnel thruster (f) Fuel: 65.0 (d.f.) 490.0 (r.f.)

435870 SQI3	**WOOLIM DRAGON 7** **Woolim Shipping Co Ltd** Woolim Marine Co Ltd SatCom: Inmarsat C 444058810 *Jeju* *South Korea* MMSI: 441588000 Official number: JJR-092134	**5,557** 2,667 8,960 T/cm 18.9	Class: KR	**2009-06 Mokpo Shipbuilding & Engineering Co Ltd — Mokpo** Yd No: 07-185 Loa 115.64 (BB) Br ex - Dght 7.600 Lbp 108.00 Br md 18.80 Dpth 10.40 Welded, 1 dk	**(A12B2TR) Chemical/Products Tanker** Double Hull (13F) Liq: 8,973; Liq (Oil): 8,973 Cargo Heating Coils Compartments: 12 Wing Ta, 2 Wing Slop Ta, ER 12 Cargo Pump (s): 12x200m³/hr Manifold: Bow/CM: 58.1m	**1 oil engine** driving 1 FP propeller Total Power: 3,900kW (5,302hp) 13.5kn MAN-B&W 6L35MC 1 x 2 Stroke 6 Cy. 350 x 1050 3900kW (5302bhp) STX Engine Co Ltd-South Korea AuxGen: 3 x 480kW 450V a.c Thrusters: 1 Tunnel thruster (f) Fuel: 82.0 (d.f.) 658.0 (r.f.)
440069 DSQM5	**WOOLIM DRAGON 9** **Woolim Shipping Co Ltd** - *Jeju* *South Korea* MMSI: 441626000 Official number: JJR-111012	**6,402** 2,667 8,964 T/cm 18.9	Class: KR	**2011-02 Mokpo Shipbuilding & Engineering Co Ltd — Mokpo** Yd No: 07-186 Loa 115.64 (BB) Br ex - Dght 7.613 Lbp 108.00 Br md 18.80 Dpth 10.40 Welded, 1 dk	**(A12B2TR) Chemical/Products Tanker** Double Hull (13F) Liq: 8,986; Liq (Oil): 9,652 Cargo Heating Coils Compartments: 12 Wing Ta, 2 Wing Slop Ta, ER 12 Cargo Pump (s): 12x200m³/hr Manifold: Bow/CM: 54.9m	**1 oil engine** driving 1 FP propeller Total Power: 3,900kW (5,302hp) 13.5kn MAN-B&W 6L35MC 1 x 2 Stroke 6 Cy. 350 x 1050 3900kW (5302bhp) STX Engine Co Ltd-South Korea AuxGen: 3 x 480kW 450V a.c Thrusters: 1 Tunnel thruster (f) Fuel: 82.0 (d.f.) 648.0 (r.f.)
3490076 DSQW6	**WOOLIM DRAGON 11** **Woolim Shipping Co Ltd** - SatCom: Inmarsat C 444000462 *Jeju* *South Korea* MMSI: 441736000 Official number: JJR-111002	**6,402** 2,667 8,947 T/cm 18.9	Class: KR	**2011-01 Mokpo Shipbuilding & Engineering Co Ltd — Mokpo** Yd No: 07-187 Loa 115.64 (BB) Br ex 18.80 Dght 7.613 Lbp 108.00 Br md 18.60 Dpth 10.40 Welded, 1 dk	**(A12B2TR) Chemical/Products Tanker** Double Hull (13F) Liq: 9,031; Liq (Oil): 9,031 Cargo Heating Coils Compartments: 12 Wing Ta, 2 Wing Slop Ta, ER 12 Cargo Pump (s): 12x200m³/hr Manifold: Bow/CM: 54.9m	**1 oil engine** driving 1 FP propeller Total Power: 3,900kW (5,302hp) 13.5kn MAN-B&W 6L35MC 1 x 2 Stroke 6 Cy. 350 x 1050 3900kW (5302bhp) STX Engine Co Ltd-South Korea AuxGen: 3 x 480kW 450V a.c Thrusters: 1 Tunnel thruster (f) Fuel: 82.0 (d.f.) 648.0 (r.f.)
9584499 9HA2901	**WOOLLOOMOOLOO** **Pergamos Owning Co Ltd** TMS Bulkers Ltd *Valletta* *Malta* MMSI: 256662000 Official number: 9584499	**41,254** 25,658 76,064 T/cm 68.6	Class: AB	**2012-02 Hudong-Zhonghua Shipbuilding (Group) Co Ltd — Shanghai** Yd No: H1637A Loa 225.00 (BB) Br ex - Dght 14.250 Lbp 217.00 Br md 32.26 Dpth 19.70 Welded, 1 dk	**(A21A2BC) Bulk Carrier** Grain: 90,540; Bale: 89,882 Compartments: 7 Ho, ER 7 Ha: ER	**1 oil engine** driving 1 FP propeller Total Power: 10,000kW (13,596hp) 14.5kn MAN-B&W 5S60MC-C8 1 x 2 Stroke 5 Cy. 600 x 2400 10000kW (13596bhp) Hudong Heavy Machinery Co Ltd-China AuxGen: 3 x 570kW a.c Fuel: 267.0 (d.f.) 2709.0 (r.f.)
5392800 DUH2655 -	**WOONA** **Sealoader Shipping Corp** - *Batangas* *Philippines* Official number: BAT5003478	**289** 177 206	Class: (LR) (NK) ✠ Classed LR until 6/7/73	**1954-01 James Lamont & Co. Ltd. — Port Glasgow** Yd No: 379 Loa 34.85 Br ex 9.17 Dght 3.937 Lbp 32.29 Br md 9.14 Dpth 4.27 Riveted, 1 dk	**(B32A2ST) Tug** Winches: 1	**1 oil engine** driving 1 FP propeller Total Power: 919kW (1,249hp) 11.3kn Fuji 6M27.5FH 1 x 4 Stroke 6 Cy. 275 x 320 919kW (1249bhp) (new engine 1974) Fuji Diesel Co Ltd-Japan Fuel: 147.5 (d.f.) 4.5pd
8302650 VJEI -	**WOONA** **Svitzer Australia Pty Ltd (Svitzer Australasia)** *Sydney, NSW* *Australia* MMSI: 503075000 Official number: 851148	*427* 129 420	Class: AB	**1984-06 Tamar Shipbuilding Pty Ltd — Launceston TAS** Yd No: 38 Loa 32.31 Br ex 10.90 Dght 4.809 Lbp 27.06 Br md 10.61 Dpth 5.36 Welded, 1 dk	**(B32A2ST) Tug**	**2 oil engines** with clutches & sr geared to sc. shafts driving 2 Directional propellers Total Power: 2,648kW (3,600hp) 13.3kn Daihatsu 6DSM-28 2 x 4 Stroke 6 Cy. 280 x 340 each-1324kW (1800bhp) Daihatsu Diesel Manufacturing Co Lt-Japan AuxGen: 2 x 125kW
9093658 HP6318 -	**WOONGJIN T-3600** *ex* Kanyo *-2009* **Woongjin Development Co Ltd** *Panama* *Panama* MMSI: 352628000 Official number: 41582PEXT	**315** 94 227	Class: KR	**2005-10 Muneta Zosen K.K. — Akashi** Yd No: 1155 Loa 31.36 Br ex - Dght 3.800 Lbp 28.00 Br md 9.00 Dpth 3.99 Welded, 1 dk	**(B32A2ST) Tug**	**1 oil engine** geared to sc. shaft driving 1 Propeller Total Power: 1,324kW (1,800hp) 13.2kn Yanmar 6N260M-SV 1 x 4 Stroke 6 Cy. 260 x 360 1324kW (1800bhp) Yanmar Diesel Engine Co Ltd-Japan
7606035 VMBC -	**WOOREE** *ex* Botany Cove *-1997* **Svitzer Australia Pty Ltd (Svitzer Australasia)** *Sydney, NSW* *Australia* MMSI: 503276400 Official number: 374356	*266* 52 -	Class: AB	**1976-06 Carrington Slipways Pty Ltd — Newcastle NSW** Yd No: 118 Loa 29.01 Br ex 9.96 Dght 4.030 Lbp 26.22 Br md 9.54 Dpth 4.70 Welded, 1 dk	**(B32A2ST) Tug**	**2 oil engines** reverse reduction geared to sc. shafts driving 2 FP propellers Total Power: 1,794kW (2,440hp) 12.0kn Blackstone EZSL8 2 x 4 Stroke 8 Cy. 222 x 292 each-897kW (1220bhp) Mirrlees Blackstone (Stamford)Ltd.-Stamford AuxGen: 2 x 68kW
8408595 HMYW9 -	**WOORY STAR** *ex* Tamnda *-2006* *ex* Polaris No. 9 *-2001* *ex* Stella Polaris *-2000* **Korea 56 Trading Co** *Nampho* *North Korea* MMSI: 445393000 Official number: 3404557	**3,154** 1,550 4,360	Class: KC (NK)	**1984-07 Kochi Jyuko (Eiho Zosen) K.K. — Kochi** Yd No: 1710 Loa 89.29 (BB) Br ex - Dght 6.273 Lbp 81.51 Br md 12.00 Dpth 9.65 Welded, 2 dks	**(A31A2GX) General Cargo Ship** Grain: 7,088; Bale: 6,879 TEU 72 C.72/20' Compartments: 2 Ho, ER 2 Ha: (14.0 x 10.2) (26.6 x 10.2)ER Derricks: 2x25t,1x20t	**1 oil engine** driving 1 FP propeller Total Power: 1,765kW (2,400hp) 11.8kn Hanshin 6EL35 1 x 4 Stroke 6 Cy. 350 x 700 1765kW (2400bhp) The Hanshin Diesel Works Ltd-Japan AuxGen: 2 x 200kW a.c Fuel: 380.0 6.0pd
8717910 3FWY8 -	**WOORY STAR 2** *ex* Busan Express *-2011* *ex* New Busan Express *-1992* **Hongkong Haian Int'l Development Ltd** Korea 56 Trading Co SatCom: Inmarsat C 437242613 *Panama* *Panama* MMSI: 372426000 Official number: 4292811	**3,671** 1,225 4,385	Class: OM (KR)	**1988-12 Dae Sun Shipbuilding & Engineering Co Ltd — Busan** Yd No: 345 Loa 101.60 Br ex - Dght 5.812 Lbp 93.00 Br md 16.00 Dpth 8.60 Welded, 1 dk	**(A31A2GX) General Cargo Ship** Grain: 5,568; Bale: 5,465 TEU 175 C.175/20' 3 Ha: (6.3 x 5.4)2 (25.4 x 10.4)ER	**1 oil engine** driving 1 FP propeller Total Power: 2,427kW (3,300hp) 13.5kn Wartsila 6R32E 1 x 4 Stroke 6 Cy. 320 x 350 2427kW (3300bhp) Ssangyong Heavy Industries Co Ltd-South Korea AuxGen: 3 x 280kW 445V a.c
9021576 3FEB -	**WOORY STAR 3** *ex* J Morning *-2013* *ex* Jh Riung *-2011* *ex* Intrans Gaon *-2008* *ex* Boo Kwang *-2006* *ex* Chang Hong *-2005* *ex* Rikuyo *-2001* *ex* Brother Light *-1997* **Shinhan Capital Co Ltd** Jewoo Marine Co Ltd *Panama* *Panama* MMSI: 351633000 Official number: 44727PEXT	**4,333** 2,752 7,136	Class: KR OM (CC) (NK)	**1991-06 Daedong Shipbuilding Co Ltd — Busan** Yd No: 365 Loa 110.29 (BB) Br ex - Dght 7.096 Lbp 101.66 Br md 16.40 Dpth 8.80 Welded, 1 dk	**(A31A2GX) General Cargo Ship** Grain: 9,692; Bale: 8,537 Compartments: 2 Ho, ER 2 Ha: (28.6 x 10.0) (30.6 x 10.0)ER Derricks: 2x22t,2x20t	**1 oil engine** driving 1 FP propeller Total Power: 2,942kW (4,000hp) 13.0kn Akasaka A45 1 x 4 Stroke 6 Cy. 450 x 880 2942kW (4000bhp) Akasaka Tekkosho KK (Akasaka DieselLtd)-Japan AuxGen: 2 x 200kW a.c
9159311 DSRF3 -	**WOOSHIN ACE** *ex* Sun Challenger *-2011* **D M Shipping Co Ltd** Kassia Shipping Co Ltd SatCom: Inmarsat C 444080910 *Busan* *South Korea* MMSI: 441809000 Official number: BSR-110107	**3,866** 2,064 6,575 T/cm 14.2	Class: KR (NK)	**1998-04 Murakami Hide Zosen K.K. — Imabari** Yd No: 393 Loa 105.00 (BB) Br ex 16.83 Dght 6.950 Lbp 97.00 Br md 16.80 Dpth 8.40 Welded, 1 dk	**(A12B2TR) Chemical/Products Tanker** Double Hull (13F) Liq: 7,072; Liq (Oil): 7,165 Cargo Heating Coils Compartments: 8 Ta, 8 Wing Ta, 2 Wing Slop Ta, ER 16 Cargo Pump (s): 9x300m³/hr, 7x200m³/hr Manifold: Bow/CM: 53.2m	**1 oil engine** driving 1 FP propeller Total Power: 3,089kW (4,200hp) 13.0kn Mitsubishi 6UEC37LA 1 x 2 Stroke 6 Cy. 370 x 880 3089kW (4200bhp) Akasaka Tekkosho KK (Akasaka DieselLtd)-Japan AuxGen: 2 x 240kW 445V a.c Fuel: 87.0 (d.f.) 492.0 (r.f.)
8878817 DSDJ6 -	**WOOSUN NO. 101** *ex* Koun No. 1 *-2007* **Choyang Shipping Co Ltd** - *Busan* *South Korea* MMSI: 441653000 Official number: BSR-940621	**208** - 91	Class: KR	**1994-06 Namsung Shipyard Co Ltd — Busan** Yd No: 9301 Loa 34.00 Br ex - Dght - Lbp 30.00 Br md 8.20 Dpth 3.40 Welded, 1 dk	**(B32A2ST) Tug**	**1 oil engine** reduction geared to sc. shaft driving 1 FP propeller Total Power: 1,192kW (1,621hp) 12.5kn Pielstick 6PA5 1 x 4 Stroke 6 Cy. 255 x 270 1192kW (1621bhp) Ssangyong Heavy Industries Co Ltd-South Korea AuxGen: 2 x 60kW 225V a.c Fuel: 66.0 (d.f.)
8957340 DSQO7 -	**WOOSUN NO. 103** *ex* Young Bin No. 101 *-2009* *ex* An Jung No. 1 *-2000* *ex* Sewon No. 7 *-2000* **Lee Yean Ju** Choyang Shipping Co Ltd *Busan* *South Korea* MMSI: 441647000 Official number: BSR-900661	**199** 59 -		**1990-07 Kyungnam Shipbuilding Co Ltd — Busan** Loa 34.70 Br ex - Dght 2.600 Lbp 30.00 Br md 7.50 Dpth 3.60 Welded, 1 dk	**(B32A2ST) Tug**	**1 oil engine** driving 1 FP propeller Total Power: 3,384kW (4,601hp) Niigata M7F43AS 1 x 4 Stroke 7 Cy. 430 x 540 3384kW (4601bhp) Niigata Engineering Co Ltd-Japan

Ship	Tonnage / Class	Construction	Type	Machinery
7522863 *DSPK7* - **WOOSUN NO. 303** *ex* SPT No. 6 *-2011* *ex* Chung Hae No. 2 *-2009* *ex* Omi No. 2 *-2007* *ex* Tonen No. 10 *-2005* *ex* Koyo Maru *-2001* **Choyang Shipping Co Ltd** - *Busan* *South Korea* MMSI: 441164000 Official number: BSR-070981	200 - -	**1976-03 Tokushima Zosen Sangyo K.K. — Komatsushima** Yd No: 507 Loa - Br ex - Dght 3.101 Lbp 29.57 Br md 9.52 Dpth 4.32 Welded, 1 dk	**(B32A2ST) Tug**	**2 oil engines** geared to sc. shafts driving 2 FP propellers Total Power: 2,354kW (3,200hp) Fuji 6L27.5 2 x 4 Stroke 6 Cy. 275 x 320 each-1177kW (1600bhp) Fuji Diesel Co Ltd-Japan
9481726 *3EOZ9* - **WOOYANG ACE** **Tiger Lines SA** Woo Yang Shipping Co Ltd *Panama* *Panama* MMSI: 354090000 Official number: 3376203A	4,825 Class: KR 3,497 7,023	**2008-03 Nanjing Wujiazui Shipbuilding Co Ltd — Nanjing JS** Yd No: WJZ018 Loa 103.26 Br ex - Dght 6.813 Lbp 100.08 Br md 18.00 Dpth 9.20 Welded, 1 dk	**(A31A2GX) General Cargo Ship** Compartments: 3 Ho, ER 3 Ha: ER 3 (24.5 x 12.6) Derricks: 2x30t,2x25t	**1 oil engine** driving 1 Propeller Total Power: 2,647kW (3,599hp) 12.3kn Hanshin LH41LA 1 x 4 Stroke 6 Cy. 410 x 800 2647kW (3599bhp) The Hanshin Diesel Works Ltd-Japan AuxGen: 2 x 320kW 450V a.c
9033830 *DSNK9* - **WOOYANG CLOVER** **Woo Yang Shipping Co Ltd** - *Jeju* *South Korea* MMSI: 441384000 Official number: JJR-048826	2,120 Class: KR 863 3,643	**1991-12 ShinA Shipbuilding Co Ltd — Tongyeong** Yd No: 353 Loa 94.50 (BB) Br ex 14.02 Dght 5.657 Lbp 88.00 Br md 14.00 Dpth 7.00 Welded, 1 dk	**(A31A2GX) General Cargo Ship** Grain: 2,978; Bale: 2,822 Compartments: 2 Ho, ER 2 Ha: 2 (25.0 x 9.5)ER	**1 oil engine** reverse geared to sc. shaft driving 1 FP propeller Total Power: 1,692kW (2,300hp) 12.0kn Hanshin 6EL38 1 x 4 Stroke 6 Cy. 380 x 760 1692kW (2300bhp) The Hanshin Diesel Works Ltd-Japan AuxGen: 2 x 180kW 445V a.c
9044243 *DSNT3* - **WOOYANG DANDY** **Woo Yang Shipping Co Ltd** - *Jeju* *South Korea* MMSI: 440279000 Official number: JJR-049738	1,831 Class: KR 592 2,594	**1992-08 ShinA Shipbuilding Co Ltd — Tongyeong** Yd No: 357 Loa 83.73 (BB) Br ex 12.72 Dght 5.262 Lbp 77.80 Br md 12.70 Dpth 6.40 Welded, 1 dk	**(A31A2GX) General Cargo Ship** Grain: 2,242 Compartments: 2 Ho, ER 2 Ha: ER	**1 oil engine** reverse geared to sc. shaft driving 1 FP propeller Total Power: 1,324kW (1,800hp) Akasaka A31F 1 x 4 Stroke 6 Cy. 310 x 600 1324kW (1800bhp) Hyundai Heavy Industries Co Ltd-South Korea
9044255 *DSNU8* - **WOOYANG ELITE** **Woo Yang Shipping Co Ltd** - *Jeju* *South Korea* MMSI: 440326000 Official number: JJR-049837	1,830 Class: KR 592 2,594	**1992-09 ShinA Shipbuilding Co Ltd — Tongyeong** Yd No: 358 Loa 83.73 (BB) Br ex 12.72 Dght 5.262 Lbp 77.80 Br md 12.70 Dpth 6.40 Welded, 1 dk	**(A31A2GX) General Cargo Ship** Grain: 2,242 Compartments: 2 Ho, ER 2 Ha: ER	**1 oil engine** reverse geared to sc. shaft driving 1 FP propeller Total Power: 1,324kW (1,800hp) Akasaka A31F 1 x 4 Stroke 6 Cy. 310 x 600 1324kW (1800bhp) Hyundai Heavy Industries Co Ltd-South Korea
9071442 *DSOM5* - **WOOYANG FRIEND** **Woo Yang Shipping Co Ltd** - *Jeju* *South Korea* MMSI: 440893000 Official number: JJR-051560	1,580 Class: KR 545 2,163	**1993-09 ShinA Shipbuilding Co Ltd — Tongyeong** Yd No: 366 Loa 79.10 (BB) Br ex 12.24 Dght 5.012 Lbp 73.52 Br md 12.00 Dpth 6.20 Welded, 1 dk	**(A31A2GX) General Cargo Ship** Grain: 1,591 Compartments: 1 Ho, ER 1 Ha: ER	**1 oil engine** with clutches, flexible couplings & sr reverse geared to sc. shaft driving 1 FP propeller Total Power: 1,261kW (1,714hp) 13.8kn Alpha 6L28/32A 1 x 4 Stroke 6 Cy. 280 x 320 1261kW (1714bhp) Ssangyong Heavy Industries Co Ltd-South Korea AuxGen: 2 x 150kW 440V 60Hz a.c Fuel: 30.0 (d.f.) 94.0 (r.f.) 10.0pd
9033854 *DSNP4* - **WOOYANG GLORY** **Woo Yang Shipping Co Ltd** - *Jeju* *South Korea* MMSI: 441420000 Official number: JJR-049431	2,498 Class: KR 863 3,643	**1992-04 ShinA Shipbuilding Co Ltd — Tongyeong** Yd No: 355 Loa 94.50 (BB) Br ex 14.02 Dght 5.657 Lbp 88.00 Br md 14.00 Dpth 7.00 Welded, 1 dk	**(A31A2GX) General Cargo Ship** Grain: 2,978; Bale: 2,822 Compartments: 2 Ho, ER 2 Ha: 2 (25.0 x 9.5)ER	**1 oil engine** reverse geared to sc. shaft driving 1 FP propeller Total Power: 1,692kW (2,300hp) 12.0kn Hanshin 6EL38 1 x 4 Stroke 6 Cy. 380 x 760 1692kW (2300bhp) The Hanshin Diesel Works Ltd-Japan AuxGen: 2 x 180kW 445V a.c
9425306 *DSPJ4* - **WOOYANG LEADER** **Woo Yang Shipping Co Ltd** - *Jeju* *South Korea* MMSI: 441125000 Official number: JJR-079846	4,825 Class: KR 3,497 7,037	**2007-08 Nanjing Wujiazui Shipbuilding Co Ltd — Nanjing JS** Yd No: WJZ007 Loa 103.26 (BB) Br ex - Dght 6.813 Lbp 100.08 Br md 18.00 Dpth 9.20 Welded, 1 dk	**(A31A2GX) General Cargo Ship** Compartments: 2 Ho, ER 2 Ha: (25.9 x 12.6)ER (24.5 x 12.6) Derricks: 2x30t,2x25t	**1 oil engine** driving 1 FP propeller Total Power: 2,648kW (3,600hp) 12.3kn Hanshin LH41LA 1 x 4 Stroke 6 Cy. 410 x 800 2648kW (3600bhp) The Hanshin Diesel Works Ltd-Japan AuxGen: 2 x 320kW 450V a.c Fuel: 415.0
9166900 *3EHU5* - **WOOYANG QUEEN** *ex* Hai Lang *-2013* *ex* Yuan Zi *-2009* *ex* Georath *-2004* *ex* Sea Magpie *-2003* **Oriental Shipholding SA** Woo Yang Shipping Co Ltd *Panama* *Panama* MMSI: 372248000 Official number: 3244907B	37,663 Class: KR (NK) 24,166 71,298 T/cm 65.1	**1997-07 Namura Shipbuilding Co Ltd — Imari SG** Yd No: 958 Loa 224.89 (BB) Br ex 32.24 Dght 13.450 Lbp 215.00 Br md 32.20 Dpth 18.60 Welded, 1 dk	**(A21A2BC) Bulk Carrier** Grain: 85,512 Compartments: 7 Ho, ER 7 Ha: (16.8 x 13.2)6 (16.8 x 14.9)ER	**1 oil engine** driving 1 FP propeller Total Power: 9,033kW (12,281hp) 14.2kn B&W 6S60MC 1 x 2 Stroke 6 Cy. 600 x 2292 9033kW (12281bhp) Hitachi Zosen Corp-Japan AuxGen: 3 x 400kW a.c Fuel: 2265.0 (r.f.)
9164823 *3EXG8* - **WOOYANG STERLING** *ex* Clipper Sterling *-2010* *ex* Changsha *-2006* *ex* Clipper Sterling *-2005* *ex* VOC Sterling *-2004* *ex* Clipper Sterling *-2000* **Zenith Star Maritime SA** Woo Yang Shipping Co Ltd *Panama* *Panama* MMSI: 352286000 Official number: 4129910	14,118 Class: KR (AB) 6,124 20,756 T/cm 30.3	**1999-09 Keppel Hitachi Zosen Pte Ltd — Singapore** Yd No: 027 Loa 157.90 (BB) Br ex - Dght 9.730 Lbp 149.49 Br md 23.10 Dpth 13.80 Welded, 1 dk	**(A31A2GX) General Cargo Ship** Grain: 23,880; Bale: 23,795 TEU 847 C Ho 390 TEU C Dk 457 TEU incl 54 ref C. Compartments: 4 Ho, ER 4 Ha: (25.6 x 18.2)3 (19.2 x 18.2)ER Cranes: 3x36t	**1 oil engine** driving 1 FP propeller Total Power: 6,157kW (8,371hp) 15.0kn B&W 6S42MC 1 x 2 Stroke 6 Cy. 420 x 1764 6157kW (8371bhp) Hitachi Zosen Corp-Japan AuxGen: 3 x 600kW 450V a.c
9520223 *3FRM8* - **WOOYANG VICTORY** *ex* Bizan *-2013* **Emerald Ocean Maritime SA** Unitra Maritime Co Ltd *Panama* *Panama* MMSI: 370855000 Official number: 38169PEXT3	4,825 Class: KR 2,315 7,321	**2008-11 Nanjing Wujiazui Shipbuilding Co Ltd — Nanjing JS** Yd No: WJZ021 Loa 108.09 Br ex - Dght 6.813 Lbp 100.08 Br md 18.00 Dpth 9.20 Welded, 1 dk	**(A31A2GX) General Cargo Ship** Compartments: 2 Ho, ER 2 Ha: ER 2 (24.5 x 12.6) Derricks: 2x30t,2x25t	**1 oil engine** driving 1 Propeller Total Power: 2,648kW (3,600hp) 12.3kn Hanshin LH41LA 1 x 4 Stroke 6 Cy. 410 x 800 2648kW (3600bhp) The Hanshin Diesel Works Ltd-Japan
9286372 - - **WOR PONGPAN** **Viroj Visetpongphan** - *Bangkok* *Thailand* Official number: 459200017	325 123 -	**2002-02 Mits Decisions Co., Ltd. — Samut Sakhon** Loa 37.00 Br ex 8.00 Dght - Lbp 34.00 Br md - Dpth 4.85 Welded, 1 dk	**(B12B2FC) Fish Carrier**	**1 oil engine** geared to sc. shaft driving 1 FP propeller Total Power: 549kW (746hp) Cummins 1 x 4 Stroke 549kW (746bhp) Cummins Engine Co Inc-USA
9251121 *H9ZH* - **WORCESTER** **Olympian Enterprises Inc** Diamantis Pateras Maritime Ltd *Panama* *Panama* MMSI: 351344000 Official number: 2839502C	5,763 Class: NK 1,999 6,621 T/cm 17.4	**2002-03 Murakami Hide Zosen K.K. — Imabari** Yd No: 521 Loa 119.29 (BB) Br ex 18.23 Dght 6.464 Lbp 112.50 Br md 18.20 Dpth 8.40 Welded, 1 dk	**(A11B2TG) LPG Tanker** Double Bottom Entire Compartment Length Liq (Gas): 7,079 2 x Gas Tank (s); 2 independent cyl horizontal 2 Cargo Pump (s): 2x450m³/hr Manifold: Bow/CM: 56.2m	**1 oil engine** driving 1 FP propeller Total Power: 4,531kW (6,160hp) 15.0kn B&W 7L35MC 1 x 2 Stroke 7 Cy. 350 x 1050 4531kW (6160bhp) Hitachi Zosen Corp-Japan AuxGen: 2 x 360kW 450V 60Hz a.c Thrusters: 1 Tunnel thruster (f) Fuel: 147.0 (d.f.) 641.0 (r.f.)
6924935 - - **WORK CHIEF** *ex* Kysten *-1991* **Kelpie Shipping Ltd** Cross Ship-Repair Ltd	291 Class: (NV) 137 417	**1969 Brattvag Skipsinnredning & J Johansen Sveiseverksted — Brattvaag** Yd No: 24 Loa 40.26 Br ex 9.02 Dght 3.562 Lbp 35.99 Br md 9.00 Dpth 3.68 Welded, 1 dk	**(A32A2GF) General Cargo/Passenger Ship** Passengers: 90 Grain: 775; Bale: 601; Ins: 105 Compartments: 2 Ho, ER 1 Ha: (3.9 x 2.5)ER Cranes: 1x8t Ice Capable	**1 oil engine** driving 1 FP propeller Total Power: 416kW (566hp) 10.0kn Caterpillar D379SCAC 1 x Vee 4 Stroke 8 Cy. 159 x 203 416kW (566bhp) Caterpillar Tractor Co-USA AuxGen: 2 x 72kW 220V 50Hz a.c Thrusters: 1 Thwart. FP thruster (f) Fuel: 16.5 (d.f.)
8026309 *HQIX2* - **WORK HORSE** *ex* Warri Seahorse *-1992* **Sycamore Services Ltd** Offshore Shipping Consultant *San Lorenzo* *Honduras* Official number: L-1324056	*407* Class: (AB) 180 350	**1981-06 B.V. Scheepswerf Damen Bergum — Bergum** (Hull) **1981-06 B.V. Scheepswerf Damen — Gorinchem** Yd No: 4601 Loa 45.01 Br ex - Dght 2.136 Lbp 43.21 Br md 10.51 Dpth 2.93 Welded, 1 dk	**(B21A2OP) Pipe Carrier**	**3 oil engines** reverse reduction geared to sc. shafts driving 3 FP propellers Total Power: 795kW (1,080hp) 9.0kn G.M. (Detroit Diesel) 12V-71 3 x Vee 2 Stroke 12 Cy. 108 x 127 each-265kW (360bhp) General Motors Corp-USA AuxGen: 2 x 75kW Thrusters: 1 Thwart. FP thruster (f)

IMO / Call sign	Name / Owner / Manager / Port / Flag	Tonnage	Class	Builder / Dimensions	Type / Cargo	Machinery
9524700 V7ZW6	**WORLD** **Miraero SG No 5 SA** Genel Denizcilik Nakliyati AS (GEDEN LINES) *Majuro* *Marshall Islands* MMSI: 538004931 Official number: 4931	**32,795** 18,550 55,340 T/cm 57.1	Class: NV	2013-01 **Hyundai-Vinashin Shipyard Co Ltd — Ninh Hoa** Yd No: S053 Loa 188.00 (BB) Br ex - Dght 12.800 Lbp 182.52 Br md 32.26 Dpth 18.30 Welded, 1 dk	**(A21A2BC) Bulk Carrier** Grain: 67,681 Compartments: 5 Ho, ER 5 Ha: ER Cranes: 4x30t	**1 oil engine** driving 1 FP propeller Total Power: 9,480kW (12,889hp) 14.5kn MAN-B&W 6S50MC-C8 1 x 2 Stroke 6 Cy. 500 x 2000 9480kW (12889bhp) Hyundai Heavy Industries Co Ltd-South Korea AuxGen: 3 x a.c
9648025 LASB7	**WORLD DIAMOND** **World Wide Supply 1 CV** Remoy Management AS *Fosnavaag* *Norway (NIS)* MMSI: 258863000	**3,832** 1,516 3,520	Class: LR ✠**100A1** SS 06/2013 offshore supply ship SG 2.8 (mud tanks) WDL (5t/m2 aft to fr. 73) EP (I,O,P) *IWS LI ✠**LMC** **UMS** Eq.Ltr: V; Cable: 495.0/42.0 U3	2013-06 **Santierul Naval Damen Galati S.A. — Galati** (Hull) Yd No: 1230 2013-06 **B.V. Scheepswerf Damen — Gorinchem** Yd No: 552022 Loa 80.03 Br ex 16.30 Dght 6.150 Lbp 75.64 Br md 16.20 Dpth 7.50 Welded, 1 dk	**(B21A20S) Platform Supply Ship**	**4 diesel electric oil engines** driving 2 gen. each 944kW 690V a.c 2 gen. each 1360kW 690V a.c Connecting to 2 elec. motors each (1500kW) driving 2 Azimuth electric drive units Total Power: 4,852kW (6,596hp) Caterpillar 3512C 2 x Vee 4 Stroke 12 Cy. 170 x 215 each-1432kW (1947bhp) Caterpillar Inc-USA Caterpillar C32 2 x Vee 4 Stroke 12 Cy. 145 x 162 each-994kW (1351bhp) Caterpillar Inc-USA Thrusters: 2 Thwart. FP thruster (f) Fuel: 300.0
9650200 LASJ7 -	**WORLD EMERALD** **World Wide Supply 4 CV** Remoy Management AS *Fosnavaag* *Norway (NIS)* MMSI: 258845000	**3,832** 1,516 3,521	Class: LR ✠**100A1** SS 10/2013 offshore supply ship SG 2.8 (mud tanks) WDL (5t/m2 aft to frame 73) EP (I,O,P) *IWS LI ✠**LMC** **UMS** Eq.Ltr: V; Cable: 495.0/42.0 U3	2013-10 **Santierul Naval Damen Galati S.A. — Galati** (Hull) Yd No: 1233 2013-10 **B.V. Scheepswerf Damen — Gorinchem** Yd No: 552025 Loa 80.03 Br ex 16.30 Dght 6.150 Lbp 75.64 Br md 16.20 Dpth 7.50 Welded, 1 dk	**(B21A20S) Platform Supply Ship**	**4 diesel electric oil engines** driving 2 gen. each 1360kW 690V a.c 2 gen. each 994kW 690V a.c Connecting to 2 elec. motors each (1500kW) driving 2 Azimuth electric drive units Total Power: 4,852kW (6,596hp) Caterpillar 3512C 2 x Vee 4 Stroke 12 Cy. 170 x 215 each-1432kW (1947bhp) Caterpillar Inc-USA Caterpillar C32 2 x Vee 4 Stroke 12 Cy. 145 x 162 each-994kW (1351bhp) Caterpillar Inc-USA Thrusters: 2 Thwart. FP thruster (f) Fuel: 300.0
7102182 BEHF -	**WORLD EXPRESS No. 1** **An Hwa Oceanic Enterprises Inc Ltd** - *Kaohsiung* *Chinese Taipei*	*252* 103 -	Class: (CR)	1971 **Fong Kuo Shipbuilding Co Ltd — Kaohsiung** Loa 36.50 Br ex 6.53 Dght - Lbp 31.98 Br md 6.51 Dpth 2.98 Welded, 1 dk	**(B11B2FV) Fishing Vessel** Compartments: 3 Ho, ER 4 Ha: 2 (1.0 x 0.4)2 (1.1 x 0.4)ER	**1 oil engine** driving 1 FP propeller Total Power: 405kW (551hp) 9.0kn Alpha 405-26VO 1 x 2 Stroke 5 Cy. 260 x 400 405kW (551bhp) Taiwan Machinery ManufacturingCorp.-Kaohsiung AuxGen: 2 x 64kW 220V a.c
7316587 - -	**WORLD FISHERIES No. 2** **World Wide Marketers Ltd** - *New York, NY* *United States of America* Official number: 509086	*101* 69 -		1967 **Rockport Yacht & Supply Co. (RYSCO) — Rockport, Tx** L reg 20.49 Br ex 6.71 Dght - Lbp - Br md - Dpth 3.31 Welded, 1 dk	**(B11B2FV) Fishing Vessel** Compartments: 1 Ho, ER 1 Ha: (1.1 x 1.6)	**1 oil engine** driving 1 FP propeller Total Power: 313kW (426hp) Caterpillar D353SCAC 1 x 4 Stroke 6 Cy. 159 x 203 313kW (426bhp) Caterpillar Tractor Co-USA
9681742 OWJP2 -	**WORLD GOLF** **World Marine Offshore A/S** - *Esbjerg* *Denmark (DIS)* MMSI: 219018008 Official number: D4598	**153** 49 39	Class: GL	2013-05 **Fjellstrand AS — Omastrand** Yd No: 1690 Loa 23.65 (BB) Br ex - Dght 2.500 Lbp 22.67 Br md 9.50 Dpth 4.60 Welded, 1 dk	**(B21A20C) Crew/Supply Vessel**	**4 oil engines** reduction geared to sc. shafts driving 2 Propellers 25.0kn Scania Scania AB-Sweden Thrusters: 1 Tunnel thruster (f)
9382970 A8WQ2 -	**WORLD HARMONY** *completed as* Sonata *-2009* **Sayers Shipping Corp** Tsakos Columbia Shipmanagement (TCM) SA *Monrovia* *Liberia* MMSI: 636014804 Official number: 14804	**41,676** 21,792 74,471 T/cm 67.2	Class: AB	2009-04 **Sungdong Shipbuilding & Marine Engineering Co Ltd — Tongyeong** Yd No: 3017 Loa 228.00 (BB) Br ex 32.56 Dght 14.317 Lbp 219.00 Br md 32.24 Dpth 20.60 Welded, 1 dk	**(A13A2TW) Crude/Oil Products Tanker** Double Hull (13F) Liq: 78,928; Liq (Oil): 83,104 Cargo Heating Coils Compartments: 12 Wing Ta, 2 Wing Slop Ta, ER 3 Cargo Pump (s): 3x2000m³/hr Manifold: Bow/CM: 113.1m	**1 oil engine** driving 1 FP propeller Total Power: 12,240kW (16,642hp) 15.3kn MAN-B&W 6S60MC 1 x 2 Stroke 6 Cy. 600 x 2292 12240kW (16642bhp) STX Engine Co Ltd-South Korea AuxGen: 3 x 680kW a.c Fuel: 122.0 (d.f.) 2138.0 (r.f.)
9120047 DSMP2 -	**WORLD HONOR** *ex* Capital Queen *-2009* **K-World Line Co Ltd** - *Jeju* *South Korea* MMSI: 441727000 Official number: JJR-093970	**6,241** 2,871 8,689	Class: KR (NK)	1995-07 **Shin Kurushima Dockyard Co. Ltd. — Hashihama, Imabari** Yd No: 2851 Loa 100.59 (BB) Br ex - Dght 8.219 Lbp 93.50 Br md 18.80 Dpth 13.00 Welded, 1 dk	**(A31A2GX) General Cargo Ship** Grain: 13,941; Bale: 13,096 Compartments: 2 Ho, ER 2 Ha: 2 (24.0 x 12.6)ER Cranes: 2x30t; Derricks: 2x25t	**1 oil engine** driving 1 FP propeller Total Power: 3,236kW (4,400hp) 12.5kn B&W 5L35MC 1 x 2 Stroke 5 Cy. 350 x 1050 3236kW (4400bhp) Makita Corp-Japan
8656996 9HZH8 -	**WORLD IS NOT ENOUGH** **Millenium Yachting Co Ltd** - *Valletta* *Malta* Official number: 10589	**373** 111 -		2004-12 **Millennium Super Yachts BV — Hardinxveld-Giessendam** Yd No: P910 Loa 36.27 Br ex - Dght 1.740 Lbp - Br md 8.25 Dpth 3.72 Welded, 1 dk	**(X11A2YP) Yacht** Hull Material: Aluminium Alloy	**4 oil engines** reduction geared to sc. shafts driving 1 Propeller
9681302 OWJT2 -	**WORLD MISTRAL** **World Marine Offshore A/S** - *Esbjerg* *Denmark* MMSI: 219018009 Official number: D4600	**153** 49 40	Class: GL	2013-09 **Fjellstrand AS — Omastrand** Yd No: 1692 Loa 23.65 (BB) Br ex - Dght 2.500 Lbp 22.67 Br md 9.50 Dpth 4.60 Welded, 1 dk	**(B21A20C) Crew/Supply Vessel** Hull Material: Aluminium Alloy	**4 oil engines** reduction geared to sc. shafts driving 2 Propellers Total Power: 1,472kW (2,000hp) 25.0kn Scania DI13 M 4 x 4 Stroke 6 Cy. 130 x 160 each-368kW (500bhp) Scania AB-Sweden Thrusters: 1 Tunnel thruster (f) Fuel: 7.7 (d.f.)
9422225 9V2133 -	**WORLD NAVIGATOR** **Trivia Shipping Pte Ltd** NYK Shipmanagement Pte Ltd *Singapore* *Singapore* MMSI: 566932000 Official number: 398654	**29,151** 12,241 46,639 T/cm 52.0	Class: AB	2010-07 **Hyundai Mipo Dockyard Co Ltd — Ulsan** Yd No: 2104 Loa 183.17 (BB) Br ex 32.23 Dght 12.318 Lbp 174.00 Br md 32.00 Dpth 18.80 Welded, 1 dk	**(A12B2TR) Chemical/Products Tanker** Double Hull (13F) Liq: 52,166; Liq (Oil): 53,372 Compartments: 12 Wing Ta, 2 Wing Slop Ta, ER 14 Cargo Pump (s): 12x600m³/hr, 2x300m³/hr	**1 oil engine** driving 1 FP propeller Total Power: 8,600kW (11,693hp) 14.8kn MAN-B&W 6S50MC-C 1 x 2 Stroke 6 Cy. 500 x 2000 8600kW (11693bhp) Hyundai Heavy Industries Co Ltd-South Korea AuxGen: 3 x 1030kW a.c Fuel: 232.0 (d.f.) 1713.0 (r.f.)
9664433 LAST7 -	**WORLD OPAL** **World Wide Supply 5 CV** Remoy Management AS *Fosnavaag* *Norway (NIS)* MMSI: 258995000	**3,832** 1,516 3,300	Class: LR (Class contemplated) **100A1** 12/2013 Class contemplated	2013-12 **Santierul Naval Damen Galati S.A. — Galati** (Hull) Yd No: 1238 2013-12 **B.V. Scheepswerf Damen — Gorinchem** Yd No: 552026 Loa 80.03 Br ex 19.13 Dght 6.150 Lbp 75.30 Br md 16.20 Dpth 7.50 Welded, 1 dk	**(B21A20S) Platform Supply Ship**	**4 oil engines** driving 2 gen. each 1352kW 690V a.c 2 gen. each 994kW 690V a.c Connecting to 2 elec. motors each (1500kW) driving 2 Azimuth electric drive units Total Power: 4,852kW (6,596hp) Caterpillar 3512C 2 x Vee 4 Stroke 12 Cy. 170 x 215 each-1432kW (1947bhp) Caterpillar Inc-USA Caterpillar C32 2 x Vee 4 Stroke 12 Cy. 145 x 162 each-994kW (1351bhp) Caterpillar Inc-USA Thrusters: 2 Thwart. FP thruster (f)
9642100 OWJS2 -	**WORLD PASSAT** **World Marine Offshore A/S** - *Esbjerg* *Denmark (DIS)* MMSI: 219018011	**153** 49 39	Class: GL	2013-07 **Fjellstrand AS — Omastrand** Yd No: 1691 Loa 23.65 (BB) Br ex - Dght 2.500 Lbp 22.67 Br md 9.50 Dpth 4.60 Welded, 1 dk	**(B21A20C) Crew/Supply Vessel**	**4 oil engines** reduction geared to sc. shafts driving 2 Propellers 25.0kn Scania Scania AB-Sweden Thrusters: 1 Tunnel thruster (f)

IMO / Call sign	Name / Owner / Flag	Tonnage	Class	Builder / Dimensions	Type	Machinery
9638123 *LASI7* -	**WORLD PEARL** World Wide Supply 3 CV Remoy Management AS *Fosnavaag* *Norway (NIS)* MMSI: 258854000	**3,832** 1,516 3,514	Class: LR ✠**100A1** SS 09/2013 offshore supply ship SG 2.8 (mud tanks), WDL (5t/m2 aft to Fr. 73) EP (I,O,P) *IWS LI ✠**LMC** **UMS** Eq.Ltr: V; Cable: 495.0/42.0 U3	**2013-09 Santierul Naval Damen Galati S.A. — Galati** (Hull) Yd No: 1232 **2013-09 B.V. Scheepswerf Damen — Gorinchem** Yd No: 552024 Loa 80.03 Br ex 16.30 Dght 6.150 Lbp 75.64 Br md 16.20 Dpth 7.50 Welded, 1 dk	**(B21A20S) Platform Supply Ship**	**4 diesel electric oil engines** driving 2 gen. each 1360kW 690V a.c 2 gen. each 994kW 690V a.c Connecting to 2 elec. motors each (1500kW) driving 2 Azimuth electric drive units Total Power: 4,852kW (6,596hp) Caterpillar 3512C 2 x Vee 4 Stroke 12 Cy. 170 x 190 each-1432kW (1947bhp) Caterpillar Inc-USA Caterpillar C32 2 x Vee 4 Stroke 12 Cy. 145 x 162 each-994kW (1351bhp) Caterpillar Inc-USA Thrusters: 2 Thwart. FP thruster (f) Fuel: 300.0
9648166 *LASH7* -	**WORLD PERIDOT** World Wide Supply 2 CV Remoy Management AS *Fosnavaag* *Norway (NIS)* MMSI: 258859000	**3,832** 1,516 3,514	Class: LR ✠**100A1** SS 08/2013 offshore supply ship SG 2.8 (mud tanks), WDL (5t/m2 aft to Fr. 73) EP (I,O,P) *IWS LI ✠**LMC** **UMS** Eq.Ltr: V; Cable: 495.0/42.0 U3	**2013-08 Santierul Naval Damen Galati S.A. — Galati** (Hull) Yd No: 1231 **2013-08 B.V. Scheepswerf Damen — Gorinchem** Yd No: 552023 Loa 80.03 Br ex 16.30 Dght 6.150 Lbp 75.64 Br md 16.20 Dpth 7.50 Welded, 1 dk	**(B21A20S) Platform Supply Ship**	**4 diesel electric oil engines** driving 2 gen. each 1360kW 690V a.c 2 gen. each 994kW 690V a.c Connecting to 2 elec. motors each (1500kW) driving 2 Azimuth electric drive units Total Power: 4,852kW (6,596hp) Caterpillar 3512C 2 x Vee 4 Stroke 12 Cy. 170 x 190 each-1432kW (1947bhp) Caterpillar Inc-USA Caterpillar C32 2 x Vee 4 Stroke 12 Cy. 145 x 162 each-994kW (1351bhp) Caterpillar Inc-USA Thrusters: 2 Thwart. FP thruster (f) Fuel: 300.0
9664445 *LASU7* -	**WORLD SAPPHIRE** World Wide Supply 6 CV Remoy Management AS *Fosnavaag* *Norway (NIS)* MMSI: 258996000	**3,832** 1,516 3,300	Class: LR (Class contemplated) **100A1** 12/2013 Class contemplated	**2013-12 Santierul Naval Damen Galati S.A. — Galati** (Hull) Yd No: 1239 **2013-12 B.V. Scheepswerf Damen — Gorinchem** Yd No: 552027 Loa 80.03 Br ex 19.13 Dght 6.150 Lbp 75.30 Br md 16.20 Dpth 7.50 Welded, 1 dk	**(B21A20S) Platform Supply Ship**	**4 oil engines** driving 2 gen. each 1352kW 690V a.c 2 gen. each 994kW 690V a.c Connecting to 2 elec. motors each (1500kW) driving 2 Azimuth electric drive units Total Power: 4,852kW (6,596hp) Caterpillar 3512C 2 x Vee 4 Stroke 12 Cy. 170 x 215 each-1432kW (1947bhp) Caterpillar Inc-USA Caterpillar C32 2 x Vee 4 Stroke 12 Cy. 145 x 162 each-994kW (1351bhp) Caterpillar Inc-USA Thrusters: 2 Thwart. FP thruster (f) Fuel: 454.0 (d.f.)
9681730 *OWJU2* -	**WORLD SCIROCCO** World Marine Offshore A/S *Esbjerg* *Denmark* MMSI: 219018007 Official number: D4601	**153** 49 40	Class: GL	**2013-09 Fjellstrand AS — Omastrand** Yd No: 1693 Loa 23.18 (BB) Br ex - Dght 2.500 Lbp 22.67 Br md 9.50 Dpth 4.60 Welded, 1 dk	**(B21A20C) Crew/Supply Vessel**	**4 oil engines** reduction geared to sc. shafts driving 2 Propellers 25.0kn Scania Scania AB-Sweden Thrusters: 1 Tunnel thruster (f)
9591064 *3FBJ3* -	**WORLD SIRIUS** World Star Shipping SA Mitsui OSK Lines Ltd (MOL) SatCom: Inmarsat C 435327310 *Panama* *Panama* MMSI: 353237000 Official number: 4284011	**17,027** 10,108 28,392 T/cm 39.7	Class: NK	**2011-06 Imabari Shipbuilding Co Ltd — Imabari EH (Imabari Shipyard)** Yd No: 753 Loa 169.37 (BB) Br ex - Dght 9.819 Lbp 160.40 Br md 27.20 Dpth 13.60 Welded, 1 dk	**(A21A2BC) Bulk Carrier** Grain: 37,320; Bale: 35,743 Compartments: 5 Ho, ER 5 Ha: ER Cranes: 4x30.7t	**1 oil engine** driving 1 FP propeller Total Power: 5,850kW (7,954hp) 14.5kn MAN-B&W 6S42MC 1 x 2 Stroke 6 Cy. 420 x 1764 5850kW (7954bhp) Makita Corp-Japan
9175925 *ELWG7* -	**WORLD SPIRIT** Transpacific Marine Inc Nissan Motor Car Carrier Co Ltd (Nissan Senyo Sen KK) SatCom: Inmarsat B 363687310 *Monrovia* *Liberia* MMSI: 636011023 Official number: 11023	**37,949** 11,385 14,101	Class: NK	**1998-10 KK Kanasashi — Toyohashi AI** Yd No: 3465 Loa 174.98 (BB) Br ex - Dght 8.519 Lbp 166.00 Br md 29.20 Dpth 11.51 Welded	**(A35B2RV) Vehicles Carrier** Side door/ramp (s) Len: 17.10 Wid: 4.50 Swl: 16 Quarter stern door/ramp (s. a.) Len: 30.00 Wid: 7.00 Swl: 80 Cars: 3,200	**1 oil engine** driving 1 FP propeller Total Power: 10,592kW (14,401hp) 19.0kn Mitsubishi 8UEC52LS 1 x 2 Stroke 8 Cy. 520 x 1850 10592kW (14401bhp) Kobe Hatsudoki KK-Japan AuxGen: 3 x 760kW 450V a.c Thrusters: 1 Thwart. FP thruster (f) Fuel: 2118.0 (r.f.) 38.0pd
8890968 - -	**WORLD STAR** The Star Ferry Co Ltd *Hong Kong* *Hong Kong* Official number: 711329	**352** 186 -		**1989-07 Wang Tak Engineering & Shipbuilding Co Ltd — Hong Kong** Loa - Br ex - Dght 2.100 Lbp 44.39 Br md 9.30 Dpth 3.60 Welded, 1 dk	**(A37B2PS) Passenger Ship** Passengers: unberthed: 755	**1 oil engine** geared to sc. shaft driving 2 Propellers 1 fwd and 1 aft Total Power: 599kW (814hp) 11.7kn MAN 6L20/27 1 x 4 Stroke 6 Cy. 200 x 270 599kW (814bhp) MAN B&W Diesel GmbH-Augsburg
9260988 *HOFB* -	**WORLD STAR** Cypress Navigation Co SA Setsuyo Kisen Co Ltd *Panama* *Panama* MMSI: 354549764 Official number: 2856902C	**9,004** 3,075 9,756	Class: NK	**2002-06 Higaki Zosen K.K. — Imabari** Yd No: 538 Loa 119.35 (BB) Br ex - Dght 7.890 Lbp 110.02 Br md 19.60 Dpth 8.60 Welded	**(A31A2GA) General Cargo Ship (with Ro-Ro facility)** Angled stern door/ramp (s. a.) Grain: 19,888; Bale: 18,877 Cranes: 2x30.7t; Derricks: 1x30t	**1 oil engine** driving 1 FP propeller Total Power: 4,457kW (6,060hp) 14.2kn B&W 6S35MC 1 x 2 Stroke 6 Cy. 350 x 1400 4457kW (6060bhp) Kawasaki Heavy Industries Ltd-Japan AuxGen: 2 x 310kW a.c Fuel: 710.0
5421053 *6NVV* -	**WORLD STAR No. 2** *ex* Koyo Maru No. 8 Sail Fisheries Co Ltd *Busan* *South Korea* Official number: BS-A-1450	*192* 100 -	Class: (KR)	**1963 Niigata Engineering Co Ltd — Niigata NI** Yd No: 531 Loa 38.94 Br ex 6.96 Dght 2.794 Lbp 34.14 Br md 6.91 Dpth 3.10 Welded, 1 dk	**(B11B2FV) Fishing Vessel** Ins: 251 3 Ha: 3 (1.2 x 1.2)	**1 oil engine** driving 1 FP propeller Total Power: 405kW (551hp) 9.8kn Niigata 6M28DHS 1 x 4 Stroke 6 Cy. 280 x 440 405kW (551bhp) Niigata Engineering Co Ltd-Japan AuxGen: 2 x 80kW 225V a.c
5422344 - -	**WORLD STAR No. 7** *ex* Sakura Maru No. 5 *-1974* Sail Fisheries Co Ltd *Busan* *South Korea* Official number: BS-A-1452	*191* 86 -	Class: (KR)	**1963 Niigata Engineering Co Ltd — Niigata NI** Yd No: 530 Loa 38.94 Br ex 6.96 Dght 2.794 Lbp 34.14 Br md 6.91 Dpth 3.10 Welded, 1 dk	**(B11B2FV) Fishing Vessel**	**1 oil engine** driving 1 FP propeller Total Power: 405kW (551hp) 9.8kn Niigata 6M28DHS 1 x 4 Stroke 6 Cy. 280 x 440 405kW (551bhp) Niigata Engineering Co Ltd-Japan
9344045 *DYOX* -	**WORLD SWAN II** Cygnet Bulk Carriers SA Magsaysay MOL Ship Management Inc *Manila* *Philippines* MMSI: 548748000 Official number: MNLA000676	**39,895** 21,193 49,603	Class: NK	**2006-11 Tsuneishi Corp — Fukuyama HS** Yd No: 1330 Loa 199.90 (BB) Br ex 32.30 Dght 11.547 Lbp 191.50 Br md 32.20 Dpth 22.75 Welded, 1 dk	**(A24B2BW) Wood Chips Carrier** Grain: 102,126 Compartments: 6 Ho, ER 6 Ha: ER Cranes: 3x14.7t	**1 oil engine** driving 1 FP propeller Total Power: 8,580kW (11,665hp) 14.0kn MAN-B&W 6S50MC 1 x 2 Stroke 6 Cy. 500 x 1910 8580kW (11665bhp) Mitsui Engineering & Shipbuilding CLtd-Japan AuxGen: 3 x a.c Fuel: 2630.0
7000724 *HP7306* -	**WORLD TUG 1** *ex* Mendexa *-2012* *ex* Edurne *-2011* *ex* Raices *-2010* *ex* Inigo Lopez Tapia *-1978* World Towage & Salvage Corp Hakvoort Sea Transport BV *Panama* *Panama* MMSI: 373678000 Official number: 4463713	**221** 66 175	Class: (GL)	**1970 S.L. Ardeag — Bilbao** Yd No: 49 Loa 31.15 Br ex 8.34 Dght 3.506 Lbp 28.00 Br md 8.34 Dpth 4.40 Welded, 1 dk	**(B32A2ST) Tug**	**1 oil engine** geared to sc. shaft driving 1 FP propeller Total Power: 1,324kW (1,800hp) 13.0kn Deutz SBV8M628 1 x 4 Stroke 8 Cy. 240 x 280 1324kW (1800bhp) (new engine 1984) Hijos de J Barreras SA-Spain
9146869 *DSQF3* -	**WORLD WINNER** *ex* OS Genesis *-2010* *ex* Bright Sky *-2009* *ex* Lion Heart *-2008* K-World Line Co Ltd Harry Shipping Co Ltd *Jeju* *South Korea* MMSI: 441554000 Official number: JJR-081883	**6,154** 3,097 8,522	Class: KR (NK)	**1996-07 Nishi Shipbuilding Co Ltd — Imabari EH** Yd No: 399 Loa 100.64 (BB) Br ex - Dght 8.190 Lbp 94.59 Br md 18.80 Dpth 13.00 Welded, 1 dk	**(A31A2GX) General Cargo Ship** Grain: 14,711; Bale: 13,536 Compartments: 2 Ho, ER 2 Ha: (21.7 x 12.8) (25.2 x 12.8)ER Cranes: 1x30.5t,2x25t	**1 oil engine** driving 1 FP propeller Total Power: 3,236kW (4,400hp) 12.5kn B&W 5L35MC 1 x 2 Stroke 5 Cy. 350 x 1050 3236kW (4400bhp) Makita Corp-Japan

IMO / Call sign	Name / Owner	Tonnage	Class	Builder / Dimensions	Type	Machinery
305992 S5ER8	**WOTAN** *ex* Weser *-1993* **Adria Tow doo** *Koper* *Slovenia* MMSI: 278037000 Official number: 133	**245** 73 -	Class: CS RI (GL)	**1973**-05 **Jadewerft Wilhelmshaven GmbH — Wilhelmshaven** Yd No: 132 Loa 29.93 Br ex 8.82 Dght 2.750 Lbp 28.50 Br md 8.79 Dpth 3.59 Welded, 1 dk	**(B32B2SP) Pusher Tug** Ice Capable	**2 oil engines** gearing integral to driving 2 Voith-Schneider propellers Total Power: 1,472kW (2,002hp) Deutz SBA8M528 2 x 4 Stroke 8 Cy. 220 x 280 each-736kW (1001bhp) Kloeckner Humboldt Deutz AG-West Germany
8010104 - D 339	**WOURI I** **Crevettes du Cameroun** - *Douala* *Cameroon*	*157* - -		**1980**-01 **Rockport Yacht & Supply Co. (RYSCO) — Rockport, Tx** Loa - Br ex - Dght - Lbp 25.33 Br md 7.01 Dpth 3.66 Welded, 1 dk	**(B11A2FS) Stern Trawler**	**1 oil engine** driving 1 FP propeller Total Power: 1,324kW (1,800hp) 11.0kn Caterpillar 3412T 1 x Vee 4 Stroke 12 Cy. 137 x 152 1324kW (1800bhp) Caterpillar Tractor Co-USA
8010116 - D 340	**WOURI II** **Crevettes du Cameroun** - *Douala* *Cameroon*	*157* - -		**1980**-01 **Rockport Yacht & Supply Co. (RYSCO) — Rockport, Tx** Loa - Br ex - Dght - Lbp 25.33 Br md 7.01 Dpth 3.66 Welded, 1 dk	**(B11A2FS) Stern Trawler**	**1 oil engine** driving 1 FP propeller Total Power: 1,324kW (1,800hp) 11.0kn Caterpillar 3412T 1 x Vee 4 Stroke 12 Cy. 137 x 152 1324kW (1800bhp) Caterpillar Tractor Co-USA
8010128 - D 341	**WOURI III** **Crevettes du Cameroun** - *Douala* *Cameroon*	*157* - -		**1980**-01 **Rockport Yacht & Supply Co. (RYSCO) — Rockport, Tx** Loa - Br ex - Dght - Lbp 25.33 Br md 7.01 Dpth 3.66 Welded, 1 dk	**(B11A2FS) Stern Trawler**	**1 oil engine** driving 1 FP propeller Total Power: 1,324kW (1,800hp) 11.0kn Caterpillar 3412T 1 x Vee 4 Stroke 12 Cy. 137 x 152 1324kW (1800bhp) Caterpillar Tractor Co-USA
8010130 - D 347	**WOURI IV** **Crevettes du Cameroun** - *Douala* *Cameroon*	*157* - -		**1980**-03 **Rockport Yacht & Supply Co. (RYSCO) — Rockport, Tx** Yd No: 483 Loa - Br ex - Dght - Lbp 25.33 Br md 7.01 Dpth 3.66 Welded, 1 dk	**(B11A2FS) Stern Trawler**	**1 oil engine** driving 1 FP propeller Total Power: 1,324kW (1,800hp) 11.0kn Caterpillar 3412T 1 x Vee 4 Stroke 12 Cy. 137 x 152 1324kW (1800bhp) Caterpillar Tractor Co-USA
8010180 - D 368	**WOURI IX** **Crevettes du Cameroun** - *Douala* *Cameroon*	*157* - -		**1980**-05 **Rockport Yacht & Supply Co. (RYSCO) — Rockport, Tx** Yd No: 488 Loa - Br ex - Dght - Lbp 25.33 Br md 7.01 Dpth 3.66 Welded, 1 dk	**(B11A2FS) Stern Trawler**	**1 oil engine** driving 1 FP propeller Total Power: 1,324kW (1,800hp) 11.0kn Caterpillar 3412T 1 x Vee 4 Stroke 12 Cy. 137 x 152 1324kW (1800bhp) Caterpillar Tractor Co-USA
7632084 - D 279	**WOURI STAR** *ex* Gudrun Safe *-1978* **Compagnie de Peche et de Mareyage (COPEMAR)** - *Douala* *Cameroon*	*149* 79 -		**1976**-07 **Soby Motorfabrik og Staalskibsvaerft A/S — Soby** (Hull launched by) Yd No: 55 **1976**-07 **Rantzausminde Baadbyggeri og Aarefabrik — Svendborg** (Hull completed by) Yd No: 1515 Loa 29.77 Br ex 6.79 Dght - Lbp - Br md - Dpth 3.18 Welded	**(B11B2FV) Fishing Vessel**	**1 oil engine** geared to sc. shaft driving 1 FP propeller Total Power: 368kW (500hp) Grenaa 6FR24TK 1 x 4 Stroke 6 Cy. 240 x 300 368kW (500bhp) A/S Grenaa Motorfabrik-Denmark
8010142 - D 348	**WOURI V** **Crevettes du Cameroun** - *Douala* *Cameroon*	*157* - -		**1980**-03 **Rockport Yacht & Supply Co. (RYSCO) — Rockport, Tx** Yd No: 484 Loa - Br ex - Dght - Lbp 25.33 Br md 7.01 Dpth 3.66 Welded, 1 dk	**(B11A2FS) Stern Trawler**	**1 oil engine** driving 1 FP propeller Total Power: 1,324kW (1,800hp) 11.0kn Caterpillar 3412T 1 x Vee 4 Stroke 12 Cy. 137 x 152 1324kW (1800bhp) Caterpillar Tractor Co-USA
8010154 - D 349	**WOURI VI** **Crevettes du Cameroun** - *Douala* *Cameroon*	*157* - -		**1980**-03 **Rockport Yacht & Supply Co. (RYSCO) — Rockport, Tx** Yd No: 485 Loa - Br ex - Dght - Lbp 25.33 Br md 7.01 Dpth 3.66 Welded, 1 dk	**(B11A2FS) Stern Trawler**	**1 oil engine** driving 1 FP propeller Total Power: 1,324kW (1,800hp) 11.0kn Caterpillar 3412T 1 x Vee 4 Stroke 12 Cy. 137 x 152 1324kW (1800bhp) Caterpillar Tractor Co-USA
8010166 - D 366	**WOURI VII** **Crevettes du Cameroun** - *Douala* *Cameroon*	*157* - -		**1980**-05 **Rockport Yacht & Supply Co. (RYSCO) — Rockport, Tx** Yd No: 486 Loa - Br ex - Dght - Lbp 25.33 Br md 7.01 Dpth 3.66 Welded, 1 dk	**(B11A2FS) Stern Trawler**	**1 oil engine** driving 1 FP propeller Total Power: 1,324kW (1,800hp) 11.0kn Caterpillar 3412T 1 x Vee 4 Stroke 12 Cy. 137 x 152 1324kW (1800bhp) Caterpillar Tractor Co-USA
8010178 - D 367	**WOURI VIII** **Crevettes du Cameroun** - *Douala* *Cameroon*	*157* - -		**1980**-05 **Rockport Yacht & Supply Co. (RYSCO) — Rockport, Tx** Yd No: 487 Loa - Br ex - Dght - Lbp 25.33 Br md 7.01 Dpth 3.66 Welded, 1 dk	**(B11A2FS) Stern Trawler**	**1 oil engine** driving 1 FP propeller Total Power: 1,324kW (1,800hp) 11.0kn Caterpillar 3412T 1 x Vee 4 Stroke 12 Cy. 137 x 152 1324kW (1800bhp) Caterpillar Tractor Co-USA
8010192 - D 369	**WOURI X** **Crevettes du Cameroun** - *Douala* *Cameroon*	*157* - -		**1980**-05 **Rockport Yacht & Supply Co. (RYSCO) — Rockport, Tx** Yd No: 489 Loa - Br ex - Dght - Lbp 25.33 Br md 7.01 Dpth 3.66 Welded, 1 dk	**(B11A2FS) Stern Trawler**	**1 oil engine** driving 1 FP propeller Total Power: 1,324kW (1,800hp) 11.0kn Caterpillar 3412T 1 x Vee 4 Stroke 12 Cy. 137 x 152 1324kW (1800bhp) Caterpillar Tractor Co-USA
9564877 *PBPE* GO 1	**WOUTER ADRIAANTJE** **VOF Visserijbedrijf W Melissant en Zonen** - *Goedereede* *Netherlands* MMSI: 246233000 Official number: 38602	**215** 64 -		**2009**-03 **'Crist' Sp z oo — Gdansk** (Hull) Yd No: B2469 **2009**-03 **B.V. Scheepswerf Maaskant — Stellendam** Yd No: 573 Loa 26.99 (BB) Br ex - Dght - Lbp 24.33 Br md 6.90 Dpth 3.80 Welded, 1 dk	**(B11A2FS) Stern Trawler**	**1 oil engine** reverse reduction geared to sc. shaft driving 1 CP propeller Total Power: 820kW (1,115hp) 10.0kn Caterpillar C32 1 x Vee 4 Stroke 12 Cy. 145 x 162 820kW (1115bhp) Caterpillar Inc-USA Thrusters: 1 Tunnel thruster (f)
7520683 *WDD6285* -	**WRANGLER** **M/V Wrangler Inc** - *Astoria, OR* *United States of America* Official number: 552616	*112* 76 -		**1973 Kristi, Inc. — Freeport, Tx** L reg 21.98 Br ex 6.81 Dght - Lbp - Br md - Dpth 3.08 Welded, 1 dk	**(B11B2FV) Fishing Vessel**	**1 oil engine** driving 1 FP propeller Total Power: 246kW (334hp)
9690690 *ESKB* -	**WRANGO** **Government of The Republic of Estonia (Estonian Maritime Administration) (Eesti Veeteede Amet)** - *Estonia* MMSI: 276810000 Official number: 0E1202	**135** 41 27		**2013**-10 **Reval Shipbuilding OU — Tallinn** Yd No: 701 Loa 24.70 Br ex 7.06 Dght 1.900 Lbp 21.50 Br md 6.00 Dpth 3.00 Welded, 1 dk	**(A36A2PR) Passenger/Ro-Ro Ship (Vehicles)** Passengers: unberthed: 74	**2 oil engines** driving 2 FP propellers Total Power: 764kW (1,038hp) 10.0kn Iveco Aifo 1 x 4 Stroke 382kW (519bhp)
9347906 *V7PI7* -	**WREN** **Wren Shipping LLC** Eagle Shipping International (USA) LLC *Majuro* *Marshall Islands* MMSI: 538003236 Official number: 3236	**31,144** 18,571 53,348 T/cm 56.4	Class: NK	**2008**-06 **Yangzhou Dayang Shipbuilding Co Ltd — Yangzhou JS** Yd No: DY121 Loa 189.99 (BB) Br ex - Dght 12.508 Lbp 182.00 Br md 32.26 Dpth 17.20 Welded, 1 dk	**(A21A2BC) Bulk Carrier** Double Hull Grain: 65,049; Bale: 63,654 Compartments: 5 Ho, ER 5 Ha: 4 (21.3 x 18.3)ER (18.9 x 18.3) Cranes: 4x35t	**1 oil engine** driving 1 FP propeller Total Power: 9,480kW (12,889hp) 14.7kn MAN-B&W 6S50MC-C 1 x 2 Stroke 6 Cy. 500 x 2000 9480kW (12889bhp) Doosan Engine Co Ltd-South Korea AuxGen: 3 x 480kW a.c Fuel: 2020.0 (Heating Coils)
9565716 *A8WT3* -	**WRESTLER** **Wrestle Navigation Ltd** International Maritime Advisors & Management Corp *Monrovia* *Liberia* MMSI: 636092095 Official number: 92095	**18,493** 10,335 29,229	Class: NK	**2010**-01 **Nantong Nikka Shipbuilding Co Ltd — Nantong JS** Yd No: 005 Loa 169.99 (BB) Br ex - Dght 10.060 Lbp 163.60 Br md 27.00 Dpth 14.20 Welded, 1 dk	**(A21A2BC) Bulk Carrier** Grain: 39,988; Bale: 39,296 Compartments: 5 Ho, ER 5 Ha: 4 (20.1 x 17.7)ER (12.1 x 16.0) Cranes: 4x30t	**1 oil engine** driving 1 FP propeller Total Power: 5,730kW (7,791hp) 14.2kn MAN-B&W 5S50MC 1 x 2 Stroke 5 Cy. 500 x 1910 5730kW (7791bhp) Hitachi Zosen Corp-Japan Fuel: 1383.0 (r.f.)
9679141 *PQ9899* -	**WS PHOENIX** **Saveiros Camuyrano - Servicos Maritimos SA** - *Brazil* MMSI: 710016210	**250** 75 150	Class: LR (Class contemplated) **100A1** 03/2014	**2014**-03 **Wilson, Sons SA — Guaruja** (Hull) Yd No: 138 **2014**-03 **B.V. Scheepswerf Damen — Gorinchem** Yd No: 512271 Loa 24.47 Br ex 11.50 Dght 5.150 Lbp 22.16 Br md 10.70 Dpth 4.60 Welded, 1 dk	**(B32A2ST) Tug**	**2 oil engines** reduction geared to sc. shafts driving 2 Propellers Total Power: 2,984kW (4,058hp) Caterpillar 3516C 2 x Vee 4 Stroke 16 Cy. 170 x 190 each-1492kW (2029bhp) Caterpillar Inc-USA

IMO / Call sign	Name / Owner / Port	Tonnage	Class	Builder / Dimensions	Type / Cargo	Machinery
9160267 *BORB* -	**WU CHANG HAI** **COSCO Bulk Carrier Co Ltd (COSCO BULK)** - *Tianjin* *China* MMSI: 412216000	**16,677** 8,739 27,635 T/cm 38.0	Class: CC	**1998-10 Guangzhou Shipyard International Co Ltd — Guangzhou GD** Yd No: 6130003 Loa 168.76 (BB) Br ex - Dght 9.820 Lbp 160.00 Br md 26.00 Dpth 13.70 Welded, 1 dk	**(A21A2BC) Bulk Carrier** Grain: 35,133; Bale: 33,930 Compartments: 5 Ho, ER 5 Ha: (13.9 x 13.1)4 (19.3 x 13.1)ER Cranes: 4x30t	**1 oil engine** driving 1 FP propeller Total Power: 4,468kW (6,075hp) 14.0kn Sulzer 6RTA48 1 x 2 Stroke 6 Cy. 480 x 1400 4468kW (6075bhp) Yichang Marine Diesel Engine Co Ltd-China AuxGen: 3 x 502kW 440V 60Hz a.c Fuel: 176.9 (d.f.) (Heating Coils) 1071.4 (r.f.) 23.3pd
8877265 - -	**WU CHIANG** **Government of Taiwan (Port Inspection Department of Kinmen County)** - *Kaohsiung* *Chinese Taipei* Official number: 124748	*124* 49 23	Class: CR	**1994 Fong Kuo Shipbuilding Co Ltd — Kaohsiung** Loa 23.80 Br ex 6.40 Dght 1.400 Lbp 20.40 Br md 6.00 Dpth 2.20 Welded, 1 dk	**(A37B2PS) Passenger Ship**	**2 oil engines** driving 2 FP propellers Total Power: 148kW (202hp) Yamaha ME580 2 x 4 Stroke 6 Cy. 104 x 113 each-74kW (101bhp) Yamaha Motor Co. Ltd.-Iwata
8401793 *3FTJ6* -	**WU FENG** *ex* Mallika Naree *-2009* *ex* Keyera *-1995* *ex* Ocean Aya *-1995* *ex* Puff *-1990* *ex* Koryu Maru *-1989* **Wufeng Shipping SA** Dalian Chain Star Ship Management Co Ltd *Panama* *Panama* MMSI: 370887000 Official number: 4045709	**13,880** 8,046 23,386	Class: (NK)	**1984-04 K.K. Uwajima Zosensho — Uwajima** Yd No: 2288 Loa 158.00 (BB) Br ex - Dght 9.972 Lbp 148.00 Br md 24.60 Dpth 13.60 Welded, 1 dk	**(A21A2BC) Bulk Carrier** Grain: 29,208; Bale: 28,308 Compartments: 4 Ho, ER 4 Ha: (19.2 x 11.2)2 (24.8 x 12.8) (24.0 x 12.8)ER Cranes: 2x25.9t,2x25.4t	**1 oil engine** driving 1 FP propeller Total Power: 4,413kW (6,000hp) 13.8kn Mitsubishi 6UEC52HA 1 x 2 Stroke 6 Cy. 520 x 1250 4413kW (6000bhp) Kobe Hatsudoki KK-Japan AuxGen: 2 x 400kW 450V 60Hz a.c Fuel: 1035.0 (r.f.)
9506332 - -	**WU GEN FU** **International Fongyuen Shipping Ltd** - *China*	**23,000** - 35,000 T/cm 47.4		**2010-08 Zhejiang Hexing Shipyard — Wenling ZJ** Yd No: HX-V07 Loa 179.88 (BB) Br ex - Dght 10.300 Lbp 172.00 Br md 28.80 Dpth 14.60 Welded, 1 dk	**(A21A2BC) Bulk Carrier** Grain: 45,645 Compartments: 5 Ho, ER 5 Ha: ER Cranes: 4x30t	**1 oil engine** driving 1 FP propeller Total Power: 6,480kW (8,810hp) 14.0kn MAN-B&W 6S42MC 1 x 2 Stroke 6 Cy. 420 x 1764 6480kW (8810bhp) STX Engine Co Ltd-South Korea
9632313 *VRLP6* -	**WU GUI SHAN** **Yin Ge Shipping Co Ltd** China Shipping International Shipmanagement Co Ltd *Hong Kong* *Hong Kong* MMSI: 477222100 Official number: HK-3732	**32,962** 19,142 56,625 T/cm 58.8	Class: CC	**2013-11 China Shipping Industry (Jiangsu) Co Ltd — Jiangdu JS** Yd No: CIS57000-08 Loa 189.99 (BB) Br ex 32.30 Dght 12.800 Lbp 185.00 Br md 32.26 Dpth 18.00 Welded, 1 dk	**(A21A2BC) Bulk Carrier** Grain: 71,634; Bale: 68,200 Compartments: 5 Ho, ER 5 Ha: 4 (21.3 x 18.3)ER (18.9 x 18.3) Cranes: 4x30t	**1 oil engine** driving 1 FP propeller Total Power: 9,480kW (12,889hp) 14.2kn MAN-B&W 6S50MC-C 1 x 2 Stroke 6 Cy. 500 x 2000 9480kW (12889bhp) Dalian Marine Diesel Co Ltd-China AuxGen: 3 x 600kW 450V a.c
9108910 *BRQS* -	**WU LING SHAN** *ex* Silver Shing *-2008* *ex* Wu Ling Shan *-1996* **China Shipping Tanker Co Ltd** - *Shanghai* *China* MMSI: 412790000	**27,117** 11,380 40,181	Class: CC (BV)	**1996-11 Shanghai Shipyard — Shanghai** Yd No: 157 Loa 195.00 (BB) Br ex 32.00 Dght 10.000 Lbp 185.00 Br md - Dpth 15.20 Welded, 1 dk	**(A21A2BC) Bulk Carrier** Grain: 48,968 Compartments: 6 Ho, ER 6 Ha: (15.3 x 16.0)5 (16.0 x 16.0)ER Ice Capable	**1 oil engine** driving 1 FP propeller Total Power: 5,951kW (8,091hp) 14.3kn Sulzer 6RTA52 1 x 2 Stroke 6 Cy. 520 x 1800 5951kW (8091bhp) Shanghai Diesel Engine Co Ltd-China AuxGen: 3 x 440kW 220/400V 50Hz a.c
9578139 *BTJY* -	**WU LIU XIAN FENG** **Shanghai International Port Group Logistics Co Ltd** - *Shanghai* *China* MMSI: 413375860	**5,201** 1,560 8,776	Class: CC	**2009-12 Guangzhou Panyu Shenghai Shipyard Co Ltd — Guangzhou GD** Yd No: SH200808 Loa 108.30 Br ex - Dght 5.450 Lbp 99.50 Br md 26.00 Dpth 7.38 Welded, 1 dk	**(A38B2GB) Barge Carrier** Ice Capable	**2 oil engines** driving 2 FP propellers Total Power: 4,120kW (5,602hp) 13.0kn Guangzhou 8320ZC 2 x 4 Stroke 8 Cy. 320 x 440 each-2060kW (2801bhp) Guangzhou Diesel Engine Factory CoLtd-China AuxGen: 3 x 250kW 400V a.c
9534004 *9VNH2* -	**WU TAI SAN** **Nan Tao Maritime (Pte) Ltd** Nova Tankers A/S 773210104 *Singapore* *Singapore* MMSI: 563359000 Official number: 393031	**164,580** 108,314 318,663 T/cm 181.2	Class: LR ✠ **100A1** SS 04/2011 Double Hull oil tanker CSR ESP **ShipRight** (CM, ACS (B)) *IWS LI SPM ✠ **LMC** **UMS IGS** Eq.Ltr: E*; Cable: 770.0/117.0 U3 (a)	**2011-04 Shanghai Waigaoqiao Shipbuilding Co Ltd — Shanghai** Yd No: 1191 Loa 332.89 (BB) Br ex 60.03 Dght 22.662 Lbp 319.90 Br md 60.00 Dpth 30.51 Welded, 1 dk	**(A13A2TV) Crude Oil Tanker** Double Hull (13F) Liq: 336,271; Liq (Oil): 334,950 Cargo Heating Coils Compartments: 5 Ta, 10 Wing Ta, 2 Wing Slop Ta, ER 3 Cargo Pump (s): 3x5000m³/hr Manifold: Bow/CM: 167.2m	**1 oil engine** driving 1 FP propeller Total Power: 29,400kW (39,972hp) 16.1kn Wartsila 7RT-flex84T 1 x 2 Stroke 7 Cy. 840 x 3150 29400kW (39972bhp) Wartsila Hyundai Engine Co Ltd-South Korea AuxGen: 3 x 1270kW 450V 60Hz a.c Boilers: e (ex.g.) 22.4kgf/cm² (22.0bar), WTAuxB (o.f.) 18.0kgf/cm² (17.7bar) Fuel: 550.0 (d.f.) 9370.0 (r.f.)
8705371 - -	**WU TONG SHAN** *ex* Xi Que *-2005* - - *Shanghai* *China*	*7,160* 3,723 2,500		**1987-11 Tianjin Xingang Shipyard — Tianjin** Yd No: 250 Loa 120.00 Br ex - Dght 5.201 Lbp 108.00 Br md 18.80 Dpth 9.60 Welded	**(A32A2GF) General Cargo/Passenger Ship**	**2 oil engines** driving 2 FP propellers Total Power: 5,002kW (6,800hp) B&W 5L35MC 2 x 2 Stroke 5 Cy. 350 x 1050 each-2501kW (3400bhp) Hudong Shipyard-China
9604598 *BDNB9* -	**WU XING 5** **Qinhuangdao Wuxing Shipping Co Ltd** - *Qinhuangdao, Hebei* *China* MMSI: 414050000	**32,965** 19,224 56,892 T/cm 58.8	Class: CC	**2012-05 COSCO (Guangdong) Shipyard Co Ltd — Dongguan GD** Yd No: N277 Loa 189.99 (BB) Br ex - Dght 12.800 Lbp 185.00 Br md 32.26 Dpth 18.00 Welded, 1 dk	**(A21A2BC) Bulk Carrier** Grain: 71,634; Bale: 68,200 Compartments: 5 Ho, ER 5 Ha: 4 (21.3 x 18.3)ER (18.9 x 18.3) Cranes: 4x30t	**1 oil engine** driving 1 FP propeller Total Power: 9,480kW (12,889hp) 14.2kn MAN-B&W 6S50MC-C 1 x 2 Stroke 6 Cy. 500 x 2000 9480kW (12889bhp) Dalian Marine Diesel Co Ltd-China AuxGen: 3 x 600kW 450V a.c
9601182 *BDPI* -	**WU XING 6** **Qinhuangdao Wuxing Shipping Co Ltd** - *Qinhuangdao, Hebei* *China* MMSI: 413271420	**32,965** 19,224 56,816 T/cm 58.8	Class: CC	**2011-05 COSCO (Guangdong) Shipyard Co Ltd — Dongguan GD** Yd No: N231 Loa 189.99 (BB) Br ex - Dght 12.800 Lbp 185.00 Br md 32.26 Dpth 18.00 Welded, 1 dk	**(A21A2BC) Bulk Carrier** Grain: 71,634; Bale: 68,200 Compartments: 5 Ho, ER 5 Ha: 4 (21.3 x 18.3)ER (18.9 x 18.3) Cranes: 4x30t	**1 oil engine** driving 1 FP propeller Total Power: 9,480kW (12,889hp) 14.2kn MAN-B&W 6S50MC-C 1 x 2 Stroke 6 Cy. 500 x 2000 9480kW (12889bhp) Dalian Marine Diesel Co Ltd-China AuxGen: 3 x 600kW 450V a.c
9488217 *BQCF* -	**WU YI HAI** **COSCO Bulk Carrier Co Ltd (COSCO BULK)** - *Tianjin* *China* MMSI: 413360000	**32,460** 17,889 53,393 T/cm 57.3	Class: CC	**2008-06 Chengxi Shipyard Co Ltd — Jiangyin JS** Yd No: CX4244 Loa 190.00 (BB) Br ex - Dght 12.540 Lbp 183.05 Br md 32.26 Dpth 17.50 Welded, 1 dk	**(A21A2BC) Bulk Carrier** Grain: 65,748; Bale: 64,000 Compartments: 5 Ho, ER 5 Ha: 4 (21.6 x 22.4)ER (19.2 x 20.8) Cranes: 4x36t	**1 oil engine** driving 1 FP propeller Total Power: 9,480kW (12,889hp) 14.2kn MAN-B&W 6S50MC-C 1 x 2 Stroke 6 Cy. 500 x 2000 9480kW (12889bhp) Hudong Heavy Machinery Co Ltd-China AuxGen: 3 x 680kW 450V Fuel: 215.0 (d.f.) 2000.0 (r.f.) 34.5pd
9039315 *BXIA* -	**WU YI HU** **Government of The People's Republic of China (The Joint Passenger Transportation Company of Jiangmen & Hongkong Macau)** - *Jiangmen, Guangdong* *China* MMSI: 412462040	*458* 137 43	Class: CC	**1991-12 WaveMaster International Pty Ltd — Fremantle WA** Yd No: 028 Loa 38.70 Br ex - Dght 1.000 Lbp 33.60 Br md 11.00 Dpth 3.70 Welded, 1 dk	**(A37B2PS) Passenger Ship** Passengers: unberthed: 354	**2 oil engines** geared to sc. shafts driving 2 Water jets Total Power: 3,160kW (4,296hp) 30.0kn M.T.U. 16V396TE74 2 x Vee 4 Stroke 16 Cy. 165 x 185 each-1580kW (2148bhp) MTU Friedrichshafen GmbH-Friedrichshafen AuxGen: 2 x 108kW 220/380V a.c Fuel: 7.7 (d.f.) 17.9pd
9629366 *9VCF6* -	**WU YI SAN** **Nan Zhou Maritime (Pte) Ltd** Nova Tankers A/S SatCom: Inmarsat C 456655110 *Singapore* *Singapore* MMSI: 566551000 Official number: 393027	**164,169** 108,429 318,445 T/cm 181.2	Class: AB	**2012-10 Shanghai Jiangnan Changxing Shipbuilding Co Ltd — Shanghai** Yd No: H1252 Loa 333.04 (BB) Br ex 60.04 Dght 22.622 Lbp 319.03 Br md 60.00 Dpth 30.50 Welded, 1 dk	**(A13A2TV) Crude Oil Tanker** Double Hull (13F) Liq: 335,807; Liq (Oil): 325,000 Compartments: 5 Ta, 10 Wing Ta, 2 Wing Slop Ta, ER 3 Cargo Pump (s): 3x5000m³/hr Manifold: Bow/CM: 165.2m	**1 oil engine** driving 1 FP propeller Total Power: 29,400kW (39,972hp) 15.8kn Wartsila 7RT-flex84T 1 x 2 Stroke 7 Cy. 840 x 3150 29400kW (39972bhp) Hyundai Heavy Industries Co Ltd-South Korea AuxGen: 3 x 1270kW a.c
9040247 *BVBR8* -	**WU YUAN** *ex* Shuang Zi Xing *-2006* *ex* Cocoaisland *-1996* *ex* Royal Vancouver *-1996* **Xiamen Ocean Shipping Co (COSCO XIAMEN)** - *Xiamen, Fujian* *China* MMSI: 413273000	**476** 238 39	Class: CC (NV)	**1991-10 Kvaerner Fjellstrand AS — Omastrand** Yd No: 1607 Loa 40.00 Br ex 10.10 Dght 1.640 Lbp 37.30 Br md 10.10 Dpth 3.93 Welded	**(A37B2PS) Passenger Ship** Hull Material: Aluminium Alloy Passengers: unberthed: 302	**2 oil engines** geared to sc. shafts driving 2 Water jets Total Power: 3,998kW (5,436hp) 35.0kn M.T.U. 16V396TE74L 2 x Vee 4 Stroke 16 Cy. 165 x 185 each-1999kW (2718bhp) MTU Friedrichshafen GmbH-Friedrichshafen AuxGen: 2 x 68kW 380V 50Hz a.c

9734458 - -	**WU ZHI SHAN** **Hainan Strait Shipping Co Ltd** - *Haikou, Hainan* *China* MMSI: 413523180	**10,940** 5,907 2,073		**2013-12 Taizhou Kouan Shipbuilding Co Ltd — Taizhou JS** Yd No: TK0412 Loa 123.90 Br ex - Dght 4.200 Lbp 116.50 Br md 20.50 Dpth 6.30 Welded, 1 dk	**(A36A2PR) Passenger/Ro-Ro Ship (Vehicles)**	**1 oil engine** driving 1 Propeller Total Power: 2,060kW (2,801hp)
8711112 *BRWW* -	**WU ZHOU 2** *ex* Vassilios *-2006* *ex* Marinicki *-2005* *ex* Mariniki *-1999* *ex* Caribbean Sky *-1999* *ex* Polar Star *-1989* **Chaozhou Xingwang Shipping Co Ltd** China Shipping International Shipmanagement Co Ltd *Chaozhou, Guangdong* *China* MMSI: 413460620	**36,042** 23,043 64,282 T/cm 67.0	Class: CC (AB)	**1989-07 Hyundai Heavy Industries Co Ltd — Ulsan** Yd No: 619 Loa 225.00 (BB) Br ex 32.24 Dght 13.122 Lbp 215.64 Br md 32.20 Dpth 18.00 Welded, 1 dk	**(A21A2BC) Bulk Carrier** Grain: 80,250; Bale: 76,407 Compartments: 7 Ho, ER 7 Ha: 7 (14.3 x 14.9)ER	**1 oil engine** driving 1 FP propeller Total Power: 8,569kW (11,650hp) 14.5kn B&W 6S60MCE 1 x 2 Stroke 6 Cy. 600 x 2292 8569kW (11650bhp) Hyundai Heavy Industries Co Ltd-South Korea AuxGen: 3 x 540kW a.c
9662758 *BRWC* -	**WU ZHOU 6** **Chaozhou Xingwang Shipping Co Ltd** China Shipping International Shipmanagement Co Ltd SatCom: Inmarsat C 441289813 *Chaozhou, Guangdong* *China* MMSI: 412898000 Official number: 090013000017	**41,303** 26,050 75,981 T/cm 68.6	Class: CC	**2013-03 Hudong-Zhonghua Shipbuilding (Group) Co Ltd — Shanghai** Yd No: H1655A Loa 225.00 (BB) Br ex - Dght 14.267 Lbp 217.00 Br md 32.26 Dpth 19.70 Welded, 1 dk	**(A21A2BC) Bulk Carrier** Grain: 90,540; Bale: 89,882 Compartments: 7 Ho, ER 7 Ha: 6 (14.6 x 15.0)ER (14.6 x 13.2)	**1 oil engine** driving 1 FP propeller Total Power: 10,000kW (13,596hp) 14.5kn MAN-B&W 5S60MC-C8 1 x 2 Stroke 5 Cy. 600 x 2400 10000kW (13596bhp) Hudong Heavy Machinery Co Ltd-China AuxGen: 3 x 570kW 450V a.c Fuel: 164.0 (d.f.) 2709.0 (r.f.)
9662760 *BRWG* -	**WU ZHOU 8** **Chaozhou Xingwang Shipping Co Ltd** China Shipping International Shipmanagement Co Ltd *Chaozhou, Guangdong* *China* MMSI: 412072000 Official number: CN20126010746	**41,303** 26,050 76,005 T/cm 68.6	Class: CC	**2013-05 Hudong-Zhonghua Shipbuilding (Group) Co Ltd — Shanghai** Yd No: H1656A Loa 225.00 (BB) Br ex - Dght 14.267 Lbp 217.00 Br md 32.26 Dpth 19.70 Welded, 1 dk	**(A21A2BC) Bulk Carrier** Grain: 90,540; Bale: 89,521 Compartments: 7 Ho, ER 7 Ha: 6 (14.6 x 15.0)ER (14.6 x 13.2)	**1 oil engine** driving 1 FP propeller Total Power: 10,000kW (13,596hp) 14.5kn MAN-B&W 5S60MC-C8 1 x 2 Stroke 5 Cy. 600 x 2400 10000kW (13596bhp) Hudong Heavy Machinery Co Ltd-China AuxGen: 3 x 570kW 450V a.c Fuel: 260.0 (d.f.) 2700.0 (r.f.)
8412091 *BRWV* -	**WU ZHOU YI HAO** *ex* Oinoussian Father *-2005* **Chaozhou Xingwang Shipping Co Ltd** China Shipping International Shipmanagement Co Ltd *Chaozhou, Guangdong* *China* MMSI: 413044000	**35,911** 22,557 64,313 T/cm 64.8	Class: CC (LR) (KR) ✠ Classed LR until 2/1/05	**1987-03 Hyundai Heavy Industries Co Ltd — Ulsan** Yd No: 389 Loa 225.03 (BB) Br ex 32.26 Dght 13.124 Lbp 215.65 Br md 32.20 Dpth 18.01 Welded, 1 dk	**(A21A2BC) Bulk Carrier** Grain: 79,769; Bale: 75,780 Compartments: 7 Ho, ER 7 Ha: 7 (14.4 x 15.0)ER	**1 oil engine** driving 1 FP propeller Total Power: 7,899kW (10,739hp) 15.0kn B&W 5L70MCE 1 x 2 Stroke 5 Cy. 700 x 2268 7899kW (10739bhp) Hyundai Engine & Machinery Co Ltd-South Korea AuxGen: 3 x 570kW 450V 60Hz a.c Boilers: e 11.0kgf/cm² (10.8bar), AuxB (o.f.) 7.9kgf/cm² (7.7bar) Fuel: 284.0 (d.f.) 1990.0 (r.f.) 30.0pd
9494371 *BOCM* -	**WU ZHU HAI** **COSCO Bulk Carrier Co Ltd (COSCO BULK)** - *Tianjin* *China* MMSI: 412032000	**40,896** 25,825 76,428 T/cm 68.2	Class: CC	**2008-12 Jiangnan Shipyard (Group) Co Ltd — Shanghai** Yd No: H2410 Loa 225.00 (BB) Br ex - Dght 14.200 Lbp 217.00 Br md 32.26 Dpth 19.60 Welded, 1 dk	**(A21A2BC) Bulk Carrier** Grain: 90,100 Compartments: 7 Ho, ER 7 Ha: 6 (15.5 x 14.4)ER (14.6 x 13.2)	**1 oil engine** driving 1 FP propeller Total Power: 10,200kW (13,868hp) 14.5kn MAN-B&W 5S60MC 1 x 2 Stroke 5 Cy. 600 x 2292 10200kW (13868bhp) Hudong Heavy Machinery Co Ltd-China AuxGen: 3 x 560kW 450V a.c
9657844 *9VBK8* -	**WUCHANG** **The China Navigation Co Pte Ltd** - *Singapore* *Singapore* MMSI: 563579000 Official number: 398085	**24,785** 12,537 39,128	Class: LR ✠ **100A1** SS 10/2013 bulk carrier CSR BC-A GRAB (25) Nos. 2 & 4 holds may be empty ESP **ShipRight** (CM,ACS (B)) *IWS LI ✠ **LMC** **UMS** Eq.Ltr: k†; Cable: 634.7/68.0 U3 (a)	**2013-10 Chengxi Shipyard Co Ltd — Jiangyin JS** Yd No: CX0341 Loa 179.99 (BB) Br ex 30.03 Dght 10.500 Lbp 176.65 Br md 30.00 Dpth 15.00 Welded, 1 dk	**(A21A2BC) Bulk Carrier** Double Hull Grain: 48,500 Compartments: 5 Ho, ER 5 Ha: ER Cranes: 4x30t	**1 oil engine** driving 1 FP propeller Total Power: 6,050kW (8,226hp) 14.7kn Wartsila 5RT-flex50 1 x 2 Stroke 5 Cy. 500 x 2050 6050kW (8226bhp) Hudong Heavy Machinery Co Ltd-China AuxGen: 3 x 740kW 450V 60Hz a.c Boilers: AuxB (Comp) 9.2kgf/cm² (9.0bar)
9657856 *9VBK9* -	**WUCHOW** **The China Navigation Co Pte Ltd** - *Singapore* *Singapore* MMSI: 563650000 Official number: 398086	**24,785** 12,543 39,090	Class: LR ✠ **100A1** SS 12/2013 bulk carrier CSR BC-A GRAB (25) Nos. 2 & 4 holds may be empty ESP **ShipRight** (CM,ACS (B)) *IWS LI ✠ **LMC** **UMS** Eq.Ltr: k†; Cable: 634.7/68.0 U3 (a)	**2013-12 Chengxi Shipyard Co Ltd — Jiangyin JS** Yd No: CX0342 Loa 179.99 (BB) Br ex 30.03 Dght 10.500 Lbp 176.65 Br md 30.00 Dpth 15.00 Welded, 1 dk	**(A21A2BC) Bulk Carrier** Double Hull Grain: 48,500 Compartments: 5 Ho, ER 5 Ha: ER Cranes: 4x30t	**1 oil engine** driving 1 FP propeller Total Power: 6,050kW (8,226hp) 14.7kn Wartsila 5RT-flex50 1 x 2 Stroke 5 Cy. 500 x 2050 6050kW (8226bhp) Hudong Heavy Machinery Co Ltd-China AuxGen: 3 x 740kW 450V 60Hz a.c Boilers: AuxB (Comp) 9.2kgf/cm² (9.0bar)
9008691 *A8PE2* -	**WUGANG ASIA** *ex* Asian Jewel *-2008* *ex* Helios Breeze *-2004* **Lambar Maritime (No 2) Inc** Zodiac Maritime Agencies Ltd SatCom: Inmarsat C 463702139 *Monrovia* *Liberia* MMSI: 636013758 Official number: 13758	**152,020** 74,317 264,484	Class: LR (NK) **100A1** SS 01/2009 ore carrier ESP LI **LMC** **UMS** Eq.Ltr: C*; Cable: 770.0/111.0 U3 (a)	**1992-01 Nippon Kokan KK (NKK Corp) — Tsu ME** Yd No: 130 Converted From: Crude Oil Tanker-2009 Loa 332.00 (BB) Br ex - Dght 19.525 Lbp 318.00 Br md 58.00 Dpth 29.50 Welded, 1 dk	**(A21B2BO) Ore Carrier** Grain: 142,556 Compartments: 7 Ho, ER 7 Ha: 3 (29.9 x 16.2)3 (17.9 x 16.2)ER (15.5 x 13.8)	**1 oil engine** driving 1 FP propeller Total Power: 19,748kW (26,849hp) 15.2kn Sulzer 7RTA84M 1 x 2 Stroke 7 Cy. 840 x 2900 19748kW (26849bhp) Diesel United Ltd.-Aioi AuxGen: 2 x 680kW 450V 60Hz a.c, 1 x 1068kW 450V 60Hz a.c Boilers: AuxB (ex.g.) 5.5kgf/cm² (5.4bar) 5.0kgf/cm² (4.9bar), AuxB (o.f.) 24.5kgf/cm² (24.0bar) Fuel: 266.0 (d.f.) 5370.0 (r.f.)
9085352 *A8PT4* -	**WUGANG ATLANTIC** *ex* Atlantic Jewel *-2008* *ex* C. Trust *-2007* *ex* C. Achiever *-2003* *ex* Yukong Achiever *-1997* **Spert Shipping Inc** Zodiac Maritime Agencies Ltd SatCom: Inmarsat C 463702442 *Monrovia* *Liberia* MMSI: 636013827 Official number: 13827	**156,281** 46,884 281,226 T/cm 167.6	Class: LR (KR) (NV) **100A1** SS 04/2009 ore carrier ESP LI holds designed for loading/unloading by grabs having a max. specific weight of up to 25 tonnes **LMC** **UMS** Eq.Ltr: F*; Cable: 770.0/122.0 U3 (a)	**1995-12 Daewoo Heavy Industries Ltd — Geoje** Yd No: 5089 Converted From: Crude Oil Tanker-2009 Loa 327.50 (BB) Br ex - Dght 20.820 Lbp 310.90 Br md 57.20 Dpth 30.40 Welded, 1 dk	**(A21B2BO) Ore Carrier** Grain: 156,451 Compartments: 8 Ho, ER 8 Ha: ER	**1 oil engine** driving 1 FP propeller Total Power: 24,119kW (32,792hp) 14.5kn B&W 7S80MC 1 x 2 Stroke 7 Cy. 800 x 3056 24119kW (32792bhp) Korea Heavy Industries & ConstrCo Ltd (HANJUNG)-South Korea AuxGen: 3 x 940kW 220/440V 60Hz a.c Boilers: e (ex.g.), AuxB (o.f.)
9510486 *D5BQ7* -	**WUGANG CAIFU** **Barcas Shipping (No 2) Inc** Zodiac Maritime Agencies Ltd SatCom: Inmarsat C 463712450 *Monrovia* *Liberia* MMSI: 636015585 Official number: 15585	**153,604** 51,860 299,382 T/cm 172.9	Class: LR ✠ **100A1** SS 05/2012 ore carrier ESP **ShipRight** (SDA, FDA, CM) *IWS LI ✠ **LMC** **UMS** Eq.Ltr: F*; Cable: 770.0/122.0 U3 (a)	**2012-05 STX Offshore & Shipbuilding Co Ltd — Changwon (Jinhae Shipyard)** Yd No: 1353 Loa 327.00 (BB) Br ex 55.04 Dght 21.400 Lbp 321.50 Br md 55.00 Dpth 29.00 Welded, 1 dk	**(A21B2BO) Ore Carrier** Grain: 186,500 Compartments: 7 Ho, ER 7 Ha: ER	**1 oil engine** driving 1 FP propeller Total Power: 25,080kW (34,099hp) 14.6kn MAN-B&W 6S80MC-C 1 x 2 Stroke 6 Cy. 800 x 3200 25080kW (34099bhp) STX Engine Co Ltd-South Korea AuxGen: 3 x 1250kW 450V 60Hz a.c Boilers: AuxB (Comp) 9.2kgf/cm² (9.0bar)

IMO / Call sign	Name / Owner / Manager	Tonnage	Classification	Builder / Dimensions	Type / Cargo	Machinery
9510474 *2FBQ4* -	**WUGANG HAOYUN** **Tocir Shipping Inc** Zodiac Maritime Agencies Ltd SatCom: Inmarsat C 423592999 *London* *United Kingdom* MMSI: 235089901 Official number: 917929	**153,604** 51,860 297,980 T/cm 172.9	Class: LR ✠ **100A1** SS 11/2011 ore carrier ESP **ShipRight** (SDA,FDA,CM) *IWS LI ✠ **LMC** **UMS** Eq.Ltr: F*; Cable: 770.0/122.0 U3 (a)	**2011-11 STX Offshore & Shipbuilding Co Ltd — Changwon (Jinhae Shipyard)** Yd No: 1308 Loa 327.00 (BB) Br ex 55.04 Dght 21.400 Lbp 321.50 Br md 55.00 Dpth 29.00 Welded, 1 dk	**(A21B2BO) Ore Carrier** Grain: 186,500 Compartments: 7 Ho, ER 7 Ha: ER	**1 oil engine** driving 1 FP propeller Total Power: 25,080kW (34,099hp) 14.6kn MAN-B&W 6S80MC-C 1 x 2 Stroke 6 Cy. 800 x 3200 25080kW (34099bhp) STX Engine Co Ltd-South Korea AuxGen: 3 x 1250kW 450V 60Hz a.c Boilers: AuxB (Comp) 9.2kgf/cm² (9.0bar)
9437268 *7JJX* -	**WUGANG INNOVATION** **Nippon Yusen Kabushiki Kaisha (NYK Line)** - SatCom: Inmarsat C 443283010 *Tokyo* *Japan* MMSI: 432830000 Official number: 141511	**132,466** 45,971 250,868	Class: NK	**2011-10 Namura Shipbuilding Co Ltd — Imari SG** Yd No: 321 Loa 329.95 (BB) Br ex - Dght 18.030 Lbp 321.00 Br md 57.00 Dpth 25.10 Welded, 1 dk	**(A21B2BO) Ore Carrier** Grain: 164,768 Compartments: 5 Ho, ER 9 Ha: ER	**1 oil engine** driving 1 FP propeller Total Power: 21,910kW (29,789hp) 14.5kn MAN-B&W 7S80MC-C 1 x 2 Stroke 7 Cy. 800 x 3200 21910kW (29789bhp) Mitsui Engineering & Shipbuilding CLtd-Japan Fuel: 8390.0
9002685 *A8DG3* -	**WUGANG ORIENT** *ex* Orient Jewel *-2007* *ex* Nichiyo *-2003* *ex* Goho *-1994* *launched as* Sea Duchess *-1991* **Powys Shipping SA** Zodiac Maritime Agencies Ltd SatCom: Inmarsat C 463694930 *Monrovia* *Liberia* MMSI: 636012067 Official number: 12067	**146,548** 44,546 267,710 T/cm 166.0	Class: LR (NK) (NV) **100A1** SS 08/2013 ore carrier ESP LI **LMC** **UMS**	**1991-09 Hitachi Zosen Corp — Nagasu KM** Yd No: 4853 Converted From: Crude Oil Tanker-2008 Loa 326.19 (BB) Br ex - Dght 20.277 Lbp 313.00 Br md 56.60 Dpth 28.60 Welded, 1 dk	**(A21B2BO) Ore Carrier** Grain: 156,261 Compartments: 10 Ho, ER 10 Ha: ER	**1 oil engine** driving 1 FP propeller Total Power: 17,618kW (23,953hp) 13.0kn B&W 6S80MC 1 x 2 Stroke 6 Cy. 800 x 3056 17618kW (23953bhp) Hitachi Zosen Corp-Japan AuxGen: 3 x 750kW 450V 60Hz a.c Boilers: e (ex.g.) 35.7kgf/cm² (35.0bar), AuxB (o.f.) 30.1kgf/cm² (29.5bar) Fuel: 413.0 (d.f.) 3834.1 (r.f.) 68.0pd
9657868 *9VCM9* -	**WUHU** *ex* Chengxi 0343 *-2014* **The China Navigation Co Pte Ltd** - *Singapore* *Singapore* MMSI: 563992000	**24,785** 12,545 39,500	Class: LR (Class contemplated) **100A1** 03/2014	**2014-03 Chengxi Shipyard Co Ltd — Jiangyin JS** Yd No: CX0343 Loa 179.99 (BB) Br ex - Dght 10.500 Lbp 176.65 Br md 30.00 Dpth 15.00 Welded, 1 dk	**(A21A2BC) Bulk Carrier** Double Hull Grain: 48,500 Compartments: 5 Ho, ER 5 Ha: ER Cranes: 4x30t	**1 oil engine** driving 1 FP propeller Total Power: 6,050kW (8,226hp) 14.0kn Wartsila 5RT-flex50 1 x 2 Stroke 5 Cy. 500 x 2050 6050kW (8226bhp)
9645700 *VRLH5* -	**WUI LUNG** *ex* Tong Mao 201 *-2012* **Yonghang Shipping (HK) Ltd** Zhejiang Yonghang Shipping Co Ltd *Hong Kong* *Hong Kong* MMSI: 477001500 Official number: HK-3667	**8,896** 5,397 13,600	Class: CC	**2012-06 Zhejiang Haifeng Shipbuilding Co Ltd — Linhai ZJ** Yd No: HF1015 Loa 140.70 Br ex - Dght 7.950 Lbp 131.80 Br md 20.00 Dpth 10.80 Welded, 1 dk	**(A31A2GX) General Cargo Ship** Grain: 18,648 Compartments: 3 Ho, ER 3 Ha: ER 3 (23.8 x 11.8) Cranes: 2x30t Ice Capable	**1 oil engine** reduction geared to sc. shaft driving 1 FP propeller Total Power: 3,552kW (4,829hp) 12.0kn Guangzhou 8G32 1 x 4 Stroke 8 Cy. 320 x 480 3552kW (4829bhp) Guangzhou Diesel Engine Factory CoLtd-China AuxGen: 3 x 350kW 400V a.c
8665375 *9LY2654* -	**WULAN 1** *ex* Yue Jian Hang 03 *-2013* **PT GPI Shipping Indonesia** - *Freetown* *Sierra Leone* MMSI: 667042000 Official number: SL103457	**1,183** 662 1,997	Class: ZC	**2007-10 Qingyuan Fucheng Baimiao Shipyard — Qingyuan GD** Yd No: BM-0702 Loa 67.80 Br ex 14.84 Dght 3.330 Lbp 64.80 Br md 14.60 Dpth 3.98 Welded, 1 dk	**(A24D2BA) Aggregates Carrier**	**2 oil engines** reduction geared to sc. shafts driving 2 Propellers Total Power: 1,356kW (1,844hp) Cummins 2 x each-678kW (922bhp) Chongqing Cummins Engine Co Ltd-China
9183075 *DFJP* -	**WULF 7** *ex* Uran *-2011* *ex* Danegarth *-2004* *ex* Uran *-2003* **Otto Wulf GmbH & Co KG** - *Cuxhaven* *Germany* MMSI: 211626110 Official number: 1055	**360** 108 285	Class: RI	**1998-10 Astilleros Armon SA — Navia** Yd No: 427 Loa 30.00 Br ex - Dght 4.700 Lbp 26.80 Br md 9.85 Dpth 5.40 Welded, 1 dk	**(B32A2ST) Tug**	**2 oil engines** reduction geared to sc. shafts driving 2 Directional propellers Total Power: 3,000kW (4,078hp) MaK 9M20 2 x 4 Stroke 9 Cy. 200 x 300 each-1500kW (2039bhp) MaK Motoren GmbH & Co. KG-Kiel AuxGen: 2 x 180kW 380V 50Hz a.c
8714243 *DFLW* -	**WULF 9** *ex* Siri *-2014* *ex* SV Siri *-2012* *ex* Siri *-2011* *ex* Velox *-2002* **Otto Wulf GmbH & Co KG** Wulf Seetransporte GmbH & Co KG *Cuxhaven* *Germany* MMSI: 211629290	**429** 128 375	Class: RI (Class contemplated) (LR) (NV) Classed LR until 1/6/13	**1988-05 Batservice Verft AS — Mandal** Yd No: 673 Loa 33.30 Br ex - Dght 5.020 Lbp 29.95 Br md 10.00 Dpth 5.60 Welded, 1 dk	**(B32A2ST) Tug**	**2 oil engines** with clutches, flexible couplings & reduction geared to sc. shafts driving 2 Z propellers Total Power: 3,200kW (4,350hp) 13.3kn MaK 8M332AK 2 x 4 Stroke 8 Cy. 240 x 330 each-1600kW (2175bhp) (made 1987, fitted 1988) Krupp MaK Maschinenbau GmbH-Kiel AuxGen: 2 x 160kW 380V 50Hz a.c Thrusters: 2 Thwart. FP thruster (f) Fuel: 98.5 (d.f.) 6.0pd
9559535 - -	**WULIAO 18** **Zhongqing Shipping Marine** - *Zhoushan, Zhejiang* *China* Official number: 00800048	**3,000** 1,500 5,000		**2009-09 ...** Yd No: 07008 Loa 75.00 Br ex - Dght 8.000 Lbp - Br md 16.00 Dpth 12.00 Welded, 1 dk	**(A31A2GX) General Cargo Ship**	**1 oil engine** reduction geared to sc. shaft driving 1 Propeller Total Power: 1,765kW (2,400hp) 11.0kn Chinese Std. Type 8320ZC 1 x 4 Stroke 8 Cy. 320 x 440 1765kW (2400bhp) Guangzhou Diesel Engine Factory CoLtd-China
9657870 *9V6816* -	**WULIN** *ex* Chengxi 0344 *-2014* **The China Navigation Co Pte Ltd** - *Singapore* *Singapore* MMSI: 564349000 Official number: 398088	**24,785** 12,538 39,500	Class: LR (Class contemplated) **100A1** 03/2014	**2014-03 Chengxi Shipyard Co Ltd — Jiangyin JS** Yd No: CX0344 Loa 179.99 (BB) Br ex - Dght 10.500 Lbp 176.65 Br md 30.00 Dpth 15.00 Welded, 1 dk	**(A21A2BC) Bulk Carrier** Double Hull Grain: 48,500 Compartments: 5 Ho, ER 5 Ha: ER Cranes: 4x30t	**1 oil engine** driving 1 FP propeller Total Power: 6,050kW (8,226hp) 14.0kn Wartsila 5RT-flex50 1 x 2 Stroke 5 Cy. 500 x 2050 6050kW (8226bhp) AuxGen: 3 x a.c
9196929 *VHN9140* -	**WUNMA** **Investment Co Pty Ltd** P&O Maritime Services Pty Ltd *Karumba, Qld* *Australia* MMSI: 503092000 Official number: 856959	**4,868** 1,619 5,140	Class: LR ✠ **100A1** SS 09/2009 strengthened for heavy cargoes coastal service in the Gulf of Carpentaria *IWS ✠ **LMC** **UMS** Eq.Ltr: V; Cable: 495.0/48.0 U2	**1999-08 Jiangsu Yangzijiang Shipbuilding Co Ltd — Jiangyin JS** Yd No: YZJ98-571E4 Loa 113.50 (BB) Br ex 22.08 Dght 3.800 Lbp 104.85 Br md 21.00 Dpth 7.85 Welded, 1 dk	**(A23A2BD) Bulk Carrier, Self-discharging** Grain: 5,100	**3 oil engines** with clutches, flexible couplings & sr reverse geared to sc. shafts driving 3 FP propellers Total Power: 2,400kW (3,264hp) 9.0kn Yanmar 6N21A-EN 3 x 4 Stroke 6 Cy. 210 x 290 each-800kW (1088bhp) Yanmar Diesel Engine Co Ltd-Japan AuxGen: 3 x 720kW 400V 50Hz a.c, 1 x 400kW 400V 50Hz a.c Thrusters: 1 Thwart. CP thruster (f); 1 Water jet (f)
6600149 *D6BS3* -	**WWM 1** *ex* Hafentor *-1984* *ex* NVG 3 *-1969* **Kazem Hamdavi** Humaid Badir Marine Shipping Establishment *Moroni* *Union of Comoros* MMSI: 616146000 Official number: 1200185	**580** 174 795	Class: (BV) (GL)	**1965 JG Hitzler Schiffswerft und Masch GmbH & Co KG — Lauenburg** Yd No: 686 Loa 52.71 Br ex 11.26 Dght 3.372 Lbp 51.31 Br md 11.00 Dpth 3.97 Welded, 1 dk	**(B21B20T) Offshore Tug/Supply Ship** Ice Capable	**2 oil engines** driving 2 FP propellers Total Power: 1,398kW (1,900hp) 12.5kn MWM TB12RS18/22 2 x Vee 4 Stroke 12 Cy. 180 x 220 each-699kW (950bhp) Motoren Werke Mannheim AG (MWM)-West Germany
7614551 *VNBQ* -	**WYAMBI** **South Sea Towage Ltd** - *Mackay, Qld* *Australia* MMSI: 503036000 Official number: 374394	*266* 52 -	Class: (AB)	**1976-11 Carrington Slipways Pty Ltd — Newcastle NSW** Yd No: 121 Loa 29.01 Br ex 9.96 Dght 4.001 Lbp 26.22 Br md 9.54 Dpth 4.73 Welded, 1 dk	**(B32A2ST) Tug**	**2 oil engines** reverse reduction geared to sc. shafts driving 2 FP propellers Total Power: 1,838kW (2,498hp) 12.0kn Blackstone EZSL8 2 x 4 Stroke 8 Cy. 222 x 292 each-919kW (1249bhp) Mirrlees Blackstone (Stamford)Ltd.-Stamford AuxGen: 2 x 68kW a.c
9620097 *WDG5079* -	**WYATT CANDIES** **Otto Candies LLC** - *New Orleans, LA* *United States of America* MMSI: 367543070 Official number: 1242012	**4,770** 1,431 2,700	Class: NV	**2013-02 Candies Shipbuilders LLC — Houma LA** Yd No: 152 Converted From: Maintenance Vessel, Offshore-2013 Loa 88.85 Br ex - Dght 5.000 Lbp - Br md 18.00 Dpth 7.40 Welded, 1 dk	**(B22A20V) Diving Support Vessel**	**4 diesel electric oil engines** driving 4 gen. Connecting to 2 elec. motors driving 2 Azimuth electric drive units Total Power: 7,060kW (9,600hp) Caterpillar 3512C-HD 4 x Vee 4 Stroke 12 Cy. 170 x 215 each-1765kW (2400bhp) Caterpillar Inc-USA Thrusters: 2 Tunnel thruster (f)

IMO / Call sign	Name / Owner	Tonnage / Class	Builder / Dimensions	Type	Machinery
769523 WDD9502 -	**WYATT LEE** **Wyatt Lee LLC** Offshore Marine Contractors Inc *New Orleans, LA* *United States of America* MMSI: 367312360 Official number: 1203042	**450** 135 290	**2007-11 Conrad Industries, Inc. — Morgan City, La** Yd No: 763 Loa 34.44 Br ex 21.34 Dght 2.057 Lbp 29.20 Br md 19.66 Dpth 2.75 Welded, 1 dk	**(B22A2ZM) Offshore Construction Vessel, jack up** Cranes: 1x110t,1x30t	**2 oil engines** reduction geared to sc. shafts driving 2 Propellers Total Power: 794kW (1,080hp) Caterpillar 3412 2 x Vee 4 Stroke 12 Cy. 137 x 152 each-397kW (540bhp) Caterpillar Inc-USA AuxGen: 2 x 99kW a.c
3974178 - -	**WYATT M** *ex* Progress *-2006* *ex* Thomas A. Payette *-1996* *ex* Michael D. Misner *-1993* *ex* P. J. Murer *-1986* **McKeil Work Boats Ltd** McKeil Marine Ltd *Nanticoke, ON* *Canada* Official number: 179211	**109** 32 -	**1948 Russel Brothers Ltd — Owen Sound ON** L reg 24.50 Br ex - Dght - Lbp - Br md 6.10 Dpth 3.00 Welded, 1 dk	**(B32A2ST) Tug**	**2 oil engines** driving 2 FP propellers Total Power: 1,472kW (2,002hp) 12.0kn G.M. (Detroit Diesel) 12V-149-TI 2 x Vee 2 Stroke 12 Cy. 146 x 146 each-736kW (1001bhp) General Motors of Canada Ltd-Canada
5266958 VDJT -	**WYATT MCKEIL** *ex* Otis Wack *-1997* **Heddle Marine Service Inc** McKeil Marine Ltd *Hamilton, ON* *Canada* Official number: 150639	*237* 118 -	Class: (LR) ✠ Classed LR until 17/12/97 **1950-12 Davie Shipbuilding & Repairing Co Ltd — Levis QC** Loa 31.25 Br ex 7.95 Dght 3.398 Lbp 28.76 Br md 7.93 Dpth 4.12 Welded, 1 dk	**(B32A2ST) Tug**	**1 oil engine** sr geared to sc. shaft driving 1 FP propeller Total Power: 883kW (1,201hp) 12.0kn General Motors 12-278A 1 x Vee 2 Stroke 12 Cy. 222 x 267 883kW (1201bhp) General Motors Corp-USA Fuel: 84.5
9386976 ZDIN2 -	**WYBELSUM** **Briese Schiffahrts GmbH & Co KG ms 'Wybelsum'** Briese Schiffahrts GmbH & Co KG *Gibraltar* *Gibraltar (British)* MMSI: 236465000	**15,597** 6,717 17,083	Class: GL **2008-06 Shandong Weihai Shipyard — Weihai SD** Yd No: CZ048 Loa 161.09 (BB) Br ex - Dght 9.900 Lbp 151.00 Br md 25.00 Dpth 13.90 Welded, 1 dk	**(A33A2CC) Container Ship (Fully Cellular)** TEU 1402 C Ho 492 TEU C Dk 910 TEU incl 250 ref C. Ice Capable	**1 oil engine** driving 1 FP propeller Total Power: 13,560kW (18,436hp) 19.0kn MAN-B&W 6S60MC-C 1 x 2 Stroke 6 Cy. 600 x 2400 13560kW (18436bhp) (new engine 2008) Hudong Heavy Machinery Co Ltd-China AuxGen: 3 x 752kW 440/220V a.c Thrusters: 1 Tunnel thruster (f)
6718465 - -	**WYBIA** **L D Shipping Pty Ltd** - *Launceston, Tas* *Australia* Official number: 315385	*216* - 155	Class: (LR) ✠ Classed LR until 14/9/01 **1967-09 Adelaide Ship Construction Pty Ltd — Port Adelaide SA** Yd No: 35 Loa 30.10 Br ex 8.49 Dght 4.230 Lbp 27.21 Br md 8.08 Dpth 4.55 Welded, 1 dk	**(B32A2ST) Tug** 1 Ha: (1.0 x 1.3)	**1 oil engine** dr reverse geared to sc. shaft driving 1 FP propeller Total Power: 930kW (1,264hp) 10.5kn Ruston 8RKCM 1 x Vee 4 Stroke 8 Cy. 254 x 305 930kW (1264bhp) English Electric Co. Ltd.-Stafford AuxGen: 2 x 30kW 220V d.c Fuel: 26.5 (d.f.)
9512379 WDE3583 -	**WYE RIVER** **Vane Line Bunkering Inc** - *Baltimore, MD* *United States of America* MMSI: 367341190 Official number: 1208437	**327** 98 364	**2008-07 Thoma-Sea Boatbuilders Inc — Houma La** Yd No: 134 Loa 30.49 Br ex - Dght - Lbp 30.26 Br md 10.37 Dpth 4.57 Welded, 1 dk	**(B32B2SP) Pusher Tug**	**2 oil engines** reverse reduction geared to sc. shafts driving 2 FP propellers Total Power: 3,282kW (4,462hp) Caterpillar 3516 2 x Vee 4 Stroke 16 Cy. 170 x 190 each-1641kW (2231bhp) Caterpillar Inc-USA
9193068 MHGJ4 -	**WYESTORM** *ex* SD Atlas *-2010* *ex* Atlas *-2009* *ex* Yenikale *-2005* **Itchen Marine (Towage) Ltd** - *London* *United Kingdom* MMSI: 235024715 Official number: 4490	**168** 97 57	Class: (LR) (AB) Classed LR until 31/10/10 **1999-07 Dearsan Gemi Insaat ve Sanayii Koll. Sti. — Tuzla** Yd No: 11 Loa 21.30 Br ex 7.37 Dght 2.400 Lbp 18.90 Br md 7.80 Dpth 3.30 Welded, 1 dk	**(B32A2ST) Tug**	**2 oil engines** with flexible couplings & reverse reduction geared to sc. shafts driving 2 FP propellers Total Power: 1,566kW (2,130hp) Caterpillar 3508TA 2 x Vee 4 Stroke 8 Cy. 170 x 190 each-783kW (1065bhp) Caterpillar Inc-USA AuxGen: 2 x 50kW 380V 50Hz a.c
7929229 MDMR4 -	**WYKE CASTLE** *ex* Pullman *-2004* *ex* Kiso Maru *-2004* **Portland Port Ltd** - *Hull* *United Kingdom* Official number: 908408	*192* 57 40	Class: (LR) Classed LR until 25/3/09 **1980-03 Hikari Kogyo K.K. — Yokosuka** Yd No: 305 Loa 26.92 Br ex 9.30 Dght 2.291 Lbp 25.24 Br md 8.30 Dpth 3.50 Welded, 1 dk	**(B32A2ST) Tug**	**2 oil engines** dr geared to sc. shafts driving 2 Directional propellers Total Power: 1,176kW (1,598hp) Yanmar 6GL-DT 2 x 4 Stroke 6 Cy. 240 x 290 each-588kW (799bhp) Yanmar Diesel Engine Co Ltd-Japan AuxGen: 2 x 60kW 445V 60Hz a.c
5126718 PIWS -	**WYLDE SWAN** *ex* Jemo *-2009* *ex* Gaupoy *-1974* *ex* Are *-1960* *ex* Harriet *-1949* *ex* Ursula *-1939* *ex* Bromberg *-1939* **Vof 'Swan Fan Makkum'** Rood Boven Groen *Makkum* *Netherlands* MMSI: 244074000 Official number: 51760	**269** 85 355	Class: (NV) **1920-01 Deutsche Werke Kiel AG — Kiel** Yd No: 52 Converted From: General Cargo Ship-2010 Lengthened-1940 Lengthened-1925 Loa 52.00 Br ex 7.37 Dght 3.899 Lbp - Br md 7.32 Dpth 4.07 Riveted, 1 dk	**(X11B2QN) Sail Training Ship** Grain: 538 Compartments: 1 Ho, ER 1 Ha: ER Derricks: 1; Winches: 2	**2 oil engines** reduction geared to sc. shafts driving 2 Propellers Total Power: 506kW (688hp) Caterpillar C12 2 x 4 Stroke 6 Cy. 130 x 150 each-253kW (344bhp) (new engine 2010) Caterpillar Inc-USA
7738632 NWEQ -	**WYMAN** **Military Sealift Command (MSC)** - *United States of America*	*2,617* 835 706	Class: (AB) **1971-07 Defoe Shipbuilding Co. — Bay City, Mi** Yd No: 445 Loa 87.36 Br ex - Dght 4.890 Lbp 79.66 Br md 14.64 Dpth 7.17 Welded, 1 dk	**(B31A2SR) Research Survey Vessel** Ice Capable	**2 diesel electric oil engines** driving 1 FP propeller Total Power: 2,648kW (3,600hp) 15.5kn Alco 12V251E 2 x Vee 4 Stroke 12 Cy. 229 x 267 each-1324kW (1800bhp) Alco Products Inc-USA AuxGen: 3 x 300kW 450V 60Hz a.c Thrusters: 1 Thwart. FP thruster (f)
8968753 WBT4608 -	**WYNEMA SPIRIT** **Wheelhouse Holdings LLC** Brusco Tug & Barge Inc *Seattle, WA* *United States of America* MMSI: 367566980 Official number: 1101425	**198** 158 -	**2000-05 Diversified Marine, Inc. — Portland, Or** Yd No: 12 Loa 23.80 Br ex - Dght - Lbp - Br md 9.30 Dpth 3.40 Welded, 1 dk	**(B32A2ST) Tug**	**2 oil engines** gearing integral to driving 2 Z propellers Total Power: 2,648kW (3,600hp) M.T.U. 12V4000M60 2 x Vee 4 Stroke 12 Cy. 165 x 190 each-1324kW (1800bhp) Detroit Diesel Corporation-Detroit, Mi Fuel: 22.0 (d.f.)
7431777 VM5945 -	**WYOLA** *ex* Pirate *-1976* **Global Marine & Engineering Pty Ltd** - *Melbourne, Vic* *Australia* MMSI: 503123400 Official number: 355785	*266* 52 -	Class: (LR) ✠ Classed LR until 2/4/12 **1975-12 Carrington Slipways Pty Ltd — Newcastle NSW** Yd No: 113 Loa 29.01 Br ex 9.96 Dght 3.988 Lbp 24.80 Br md 9.71 Dpth 4.70 Welded, 1 dk	**(B32A2ST) Tug**	**2 oil engines** reverse reduction geared to sc. shafts driving 2 FP propellers Total Power: 1,794kW (2,440hp) 12.0kn Blackstone ESL8MK2 2 x 4 Stroke 8 Cy. 222 x 292 each-897kW (1220bhp) Mirrlees Blackstone (Stamford)Ltd.-Stamford AuxGen: 2 x 68kW 415V 50Hz a.c
9018945 VNXL -	**WYONG** **Svitzer Australia Pty Ltd & Stannard Marine Pty Ltd** Svitzer Australia Pty Ltd (Svitzer Australasia) *Darwin, NT* *Australia* MMSI: 503590000 Official number: 854115	*365* 109 251	Class: AB **1992-03 Ocean Shipyards (WA) Pty Ltd — Fremantle WA** Yd No: 175 Loa 32.00 Br ex - Dght 4.550 Lbp 29.45 Br md 10.53 Dpth 5.00 Welded, 1 dk	**(B32A2ST) Tug**	**2 oil engines** driving 2 gen. each 95kW a.c gearing integral to driving 2 Z propellers Total Power: 2,650kW (3,602hp) 12.0kn Daihatsu 6DLM-28S 2 x 4 Stroke 6 Cy. 280 x 360 each-1325kW (1801bhp) Daihatsu Diesel Manufacturing Co Lt-Japan AuxGen: 1 x 120kW 415V 50Hz a.c, 1 x 80kW 415V 50Hz a.c Fuel: 78.7 (d.f.)
5393907 ZCXD7 -	**WYUNA** **Classic Wyuna Ltd** - *George Town* *Cayman Islands (British)* Official number: 740643	*1,313* 312 655	Class: (LR) ✠ Classed LR until 26/6/81 **1953-08 Ferguson Bros (Port Glasgow) Ltd — Port Glasgow** Yd No: 404 Converted From: Pilot Vessel-1981 Loa 63.58 Br ex 11.92 Dght 4.585 Lbp 56.77 Br md 11.89 Dpth 6.86 Riveted\Welded, 2 dks	**(B34K2QT) Training Ship**	**3 diesel electric oil engines** driving 3 gen. each 380kW 400V d.c Connecting to 2 elec. motors driving 2 FP propellers Total Power: 1,428kW (1,941hp) English Electric 8RKCM 3 x Vee 4 Stroke 8 Cy. 254 x 305 each-476kW (647bhp) English Electric Co. Ltd.-Stafford AuxGen: 2 x 150kW 220V d.c, 3 x 60kW 220V d.c, 1 x 50kW 220V d.c
1003736 2EVU7 -	**X CHIOS** *ex* Xi *-2011* *ex* X *-2009* *ex* Time For Us *-2009* *ex* Sea Jewel *-2007* *ex* Anticipation *-1999* *ex* Cristal A *-1999* *ex* Sea Jewel *-1999* **Harbourbase Ltd** Exantas EPE *London* *United Kingdom* MMSI: 235088564 Official number: 917753	**429** 128 -	Class: LR ✠ **100A1** SS 03/2012 Yacht ✠ **LMC** **1987-10 de Vries Scheepsbouw B.V. — Aalsmeer** Yd No: 636 Loa 42.60 Br ex 8.20 Dght 2.800 Lbp 40.35 Br md - Dpth 4.75 Welded, 1 dk	**(X11A2YP) Yacht**	**2 oil engines** geared to sc. shafts driving 2 FP propellers Total Power: 1,156kW (1,572hp) Caterpillar 3508TA 2 x Vee 4 Stroke 8 Cy. 170 x 190 each-578kW (786bhp) Caterpillar Inc-USA

8711485 *A6E2984* -
X-PRESS 27
ex Abeer Fourteen *-2007*
Barwil Dubai LLC
Miclyn Express Offshore Pte Ltd
Dubai *United Arab Emirates*
MMSI: 470820000
Official number: 5009
172 51 -
Class: BV (AB)
1987 Aluminum Boats, Inc. — Marrero, La
Yd No: 304
Loa - Br ex - Dght 1.893
Lbp 33.53 Br md 7.93 Dpth 3.66
Welded, 1 dk
(B21A20C) Crew/Supply Vessel
Hull Material: Aluminium Alloy
4 oil engines reverse reduction geared to sc. shafts driving 4 FP propellers
Total Power: 1,500kW (2,040hp) 20.0kn
G.M. (Detroit Diesel) 12V-71
4 x Vee 2 Stroke 12 Cy. 108 x 127 each-375kW (510bhp)
General Motors Detroit DieselAllison Divn-USA
AuxGen: 2 x 40kW a.c

9152911 *9V2269* -
X-PRESS BRAHMAPUTRA
ex Lilly Rickmers *-2013*
ex CMA CGM St Martin *-2013*
ex CGM Basse-Terre *-2001*
ex Lilly Rickmers *-1998*
Telok Ayer Pte Ltd
Sea Consortium Pte Ltd (X-Press Feeders)
Singapore *Singapore*
MMSI: 563191000
Official number: 398824
10,752 5,478 14,070 T/cm 29.3
Class: GL
1998-06 Stocznia Szczecinska SA — Szczecin
Yd No: B183/2/30
Loa 162.86 (BB) Br ex 22.62 Dght 8.110
Lbp 153.41 Br md 22.30 Dpth 11.10
Welded, 1 dk
(A33A2CC) Container Ship (Fully Cellular)
Grain: 19,215
TEU 1162 C Ho 390 TEU C Dk 782 TEU incl 110 ref C.
Compartments: 4 Cell Ho, ER
8 Ha: ER
Cranes: 3x40t
1 oil engine driving 1 CP propeller
Total Power: 6,930kW (9,422hp) 17.0kn
B&W 6L50MC
1 x 2 Stroke 6 Cy. 500 x 1620 6930kW (9422bhp)
H Cegielski Poznan SA-Poland
AuxGen: 1 x 1000kW 220/380V 50Hz a.c, 3 x 504kW 220/380V 50Hz a.c
Thrusters: 1 Thwart. CP thruster (f)
Fuel: 148.4 (d.f.) (Heating Coils) 1231.6 (r.f.) 30.5pd

9311737 *9V2036* -
X-PRESS EUPHRATES
ex Jenaz *-2013* *ex* Maersk Jenaz *-2012*
X-Press Euphrates Pte Ltd
Wilhelmsen Ship Management Singapore Pte Ltd
Singapore *Singapore*
MMSI: 566836000
Official number: 398447
28,911 15,023 39,228 T/cm 56.7
Class: GL
2006-09 Hyundai Mipo Dockyard Co Ltd — Ulsan
Yd No: 0390
Loa 222.16 (BB) Br ex - Dght 12.000
Lbp 210.00 Br md 30.00 Dpth 16.80
Welded, 1 dk
(A33A2CC) Container Ship (Fully Cellular)
TEU 2824 C Ho 1026 TEU C Dk 1798 TEU incl 586 ref C.
1 oil engine driving 1 FP propeller
Total Power: 25,270kW (34,357hp) 22.5kn
MAN-B&W 7K80MC-C
1 x 2 Stroke 7 Cy. 800 x 2300 25270kW (34357bhp)
Hyundai Heavy Industries Co Ltd-South Korea
AuxGen: 4 x 1600kW 440/230V 60Hz a.c
Thrusters: 1 Tunnel thruster (f)
Fuel: 183.0 (d.f.) 3209.0 (r.f.)

9301093 *A8ZB4* -
X-PRESS GANGES
ex Beluga Majesty *-2011*
ex Delta St. Petersburg *-2009*
launched as Beluga Majesty *-2006*
Vega Beteiligungsgesellschaft Delta mbH & Co KG
Vega-Reederei Friedrich Dauber GmbH & Co KG
Monrovia *Liberia*
MMSI: 636092239
Official number: 92239
8,971 4,776 10,744 T/cm 27.3
Class: GL
2006-03 OAO Damen Shipyards Okean — Nikolayev (Hull) Yd No: 9115
2006-03 Volharding Shipyards B.V. — Foxhol
Yd No: 567
Loa 154.85 (BB) Br ex - Dght 6.974
Lbp 144.80 Br md 21.50 Dpth 9.30
Welded, 1 dk
(A33A2CC) Container Ship (Fully Cellular)
Double Bottom Entire Compartment Length
TEU 917 C Ho 267 TEU C Dk 650 TEU incl 200 ref C
Compartments: 4 Cell Ho, ER
4 Ha: 2 (25.5 x 18.5) (12.6 x 18.5)ER (25.9 x 18.5)
Ice Capable
1 oil engine sr geared to sc. shaft driving 1 CP propeller
Total Power: 7,999kW (10,875hp) 14.0kn
MaK 8M43C
1 x 4 Stroke 8 Cy. 430 x 610 7999kW (10875bhp)
Caterpillar Motoren GmbH & Co. KG-Germany
AuxGen: 1 x 1150kW a.c, 2 x 416kW a.c
Thrusters: 1 Thwart. CP thruster (f)
Fuel: 93.5 (d.f.) 703.0 (r.f.)

9301201 *A8ZB5* -
X-PRESS HOOGLY
ex Beluga Mastery *-2011*
ex Delta Rotterdam *-2008*
completed as Beluga Mastery *-2006*
ms 'Hammonia Mastery' Schiffahrts GmbH & Co KG
Hammonia Reederei GmbH & Co KG
Monrovia *Liberia*
MMSI: 636092240
Official number: 92240
8,971 4,776 10,744 T/cm 27.3
Class: GL
2006-01 OAO Damen Shipyards Okean — Nikolayev (Hull) Yd No: 9114
2006-01 Volharding Shipyards B.V. — Foxhol
Yd No: 566
Loa 154.85 (BB) Br ex - Dght 6.974
Lbp 144.80 Br md 21.50 Dpth 9.30
Welded, 1 dk
(A33A2CC) Container Ship (Fully Cellular)
Double Bottom Entire Compartment Length
TEU 917 C Ho 267 TEU C Dk 650 TEU incl 200 ref C
Compartments: 4 Cell Ho, ER
4 Ha: 2 (25.3 x 18.5) (12.6 x 18.5)ER (25.5 x 18.5)
Ice Capable
1 oil engine geared to sc. shaft driving 1 CP propeller
Total Power: 7,999kW (10,875hp) 14.0kn
MaK 8M43
1 x 4 Stroke 8 Cy. 430 x 610 7999kW (10875bhp)
Caterpillar Motoren GmbH & Co. KG-Germany
AuxGen: 2 x 432kW a.c, 1 x 1150kW a.c
Thrusters: 1 Thwart. CP thruster (f)
Fuel: 93.5 (d.f.) 703.0 (r.f.)

9159646 *9VAX9* -
X-PRESS INDUS
ex Bunga Teratai 3 *-2012*
ex Bunga Teratai Tiga *-2003*
ex Bunga Teratai 3 *-2003*
X-Press Indus Pte Ltd
Bibby Ship Management (Singapore) Pte Ltd
Singapore *Singapore*
MMSI: 566577000
Official number: 397960
21,339 8,940 24,554 T/cm 42.9
Class: LR
✠ **100A1** SS 07/2013
container ship
*IWS
LI
✠ **LMC** **UMS**
Eq.Ltr: K†;
Cable: 632.5/68.0 U3 (a)
1998-07 Daewoo Heavy Industries Ltd — Geoje
Yd No: 4066
Loa 184.07 (BB) Br ex 27.45 Dght 10.200
Lbp 174.02 Br md 27.40 Dpth 15.85
Welded, 1 dk
(A33A2CC) Container Ship (Fully Cellular)
TEU 1725 C Ho 778 TEU C Dk 947 TEU incl 242 ref C.
Compartments: 5 Cell Ho, ER
9 Ha: (12.6 x 13.1) (12.6 x 18.3)7 (12.6 x 23.4)ER
1 oil engine driving 1 FP propeller
Total Power: 12,260kW (16,669hp) 19.0kn
B&W 6S60MC
1 x 2 Stroke 6 Cy. 600 x 2292 12260kW (16669bhp)
Korea Heavy Industries & ConstrCo Ltd (HANJUNG)-South Korea
AuxGen: 3 x 1400kW 450V 60Hz a.c
Boilers: AuxB (Comp) 8.0kgf/cm² (7.8bar)
Thrusters: 1 Thwart. CP thruster (f)

9348912 *9V2443* -
X-PRESS KAILASH
ex STX Mumbai *-2013*
launched as King Anton *-2008*
Prince Edward Pte Ltd
Sea Consortium Pte Ltd (X-Press Feeders)
Singapore *Singapore*
MMSI: 563839000
Official number: 399024
28,007 13,574 37,901 T/cm 56.8
Class: GL (Class contemplated) (KR)
2008-04 Aker MTW Werft GmbH — Wismar
Yd No: 152
2008-04 Aker Warnemuende Operations GmbH — Rostock (Fwd & pt cargo sections)
Loa 221.73 (BB) Br ex - Dght 11.400
Lbp 209.62 Br md 29.81 Dpth 16.40
Welded, 1 dk
(A33A2CC) Container Ship (Fully Cellular)
TEU 2742 C Ho 1112 TEU C Dk 1630 TEU incl 400 ref C
Compartments: 5 Cell Ho, ER
5 Ha: (- x 25.4)3 (26.9 x 25.4)ER (26.9 x 20.4)
Ice Capable
1 oil engine driving 1 FP propeller
Total Power: 21,769kW (29,597hp) 21.0kn
MAN-B&W 7L70MC-C
1 x 2 Stroke 7 Cy. 700 x 2360 21769kW (29597bhp)
H Cegielski Poznan SA-Poland
AuxGen: 5 x 1302kW 450V a.c
Thrusters: 1 Tunnel thruster (f)
Fuel: 175.0 (d.f.) 2608.0 (r.f.)

9348924 *9V2444* -
X-PRESS KARAKORAM
ex STX Melbourne *-2013*
Tras Link Pte Ltd
Sea Consortium Pte Ltd (X-Press Feeders)
Singapore *Singapore*
MMSI: 563842000
Official number: 399025
28,007 13,574 37,934 T/cm 56.8
Class: GL (KR)
2008-07 Aker MTW Werft GmbH — Wismar
Yd No: 157
2008-07 Aker Warnemuende Operations GmbH — Rostock (Fwd & pt cargo sections)
Loa 221.73 (BB) Br ex - Dght 11.390
Lbp 209.62 Br md 29.82 Dpth 16.40
Welded, 1 dk
(A33A2CC) Container Ship (Fully Cellular)
TEU 2742 C Ho 1112 TEU C Dk 1630 TEU incl 400 ref C
Compartments: 5 Cell Ho, ER
1 oil engine driving 1 FP propeller
Total Power: 21,769kW (29,597hp) 21.0kn
MAN-B&W 7L70MC-C
1 x 2 Stroke 7 Cy. 700 x 2360 21769kW (29597bhp)
H Cegielski Poznan SA-Poland
AuxGen: 5 x 1302kW 450V a.c
Thrusters: 1 Tunnel thruster (f)

9327683 *9V2365* -
X-PRESS MAKALU
ex Arelia *-2013* *ex* Maruba Victory *-2010*
completed as Arelia *-2008*
Cantonment Close Pte Ltd
Wilhelmsen Ship Management Singapore Pte Ltd
Singapore *Singapore*
MMSI: 564032000
Official number: 398944
32,161 12,604 39,000
Class: NV
2008-03 Stocznia Gdansk SA — Gdansk (Hull)
Yd No: 8184/18
2008-03 Stocznia Gdynia SA — Gdynia
Yd No: 8184/18
Loa 210.91 (BB) Br ex - Dght 12.000
Lbp 195.95 Br md 32.25 Dpth 19.00
Welded, 1 dk
(A33A2CC) Container Ship (Fully Cellular)
TEU 2714 incl 500 ref C.
Cranes: 3x45t
1 oil engine driving 1 FP propeller
Total Power: 21,733kW (29,548hp) 22.5kn
MAN-B&W 7S70MC-C
1 x 2 Stroke 7 Cy. 700 x 2800 21733kW (29548bhp)
H Cegielski Poznan SA-Poland
AuxGen: 4 x a.c
Thrusters: 1 Tunnel thruster (f)

9276341 *9HA3446* -
X-PRESS MONTE BIANCO
ex Tetuan *-2013* *ex* Varmland *-2009*
ex Tetuan *-2005* *ex* Columba J *-2004*
Wallich Pte Ltd
Norbulk Shipping UK Ltd
Valletta *Malta*
MMSI: 229610000
Official number: 9276341
6,434 3,218 8,496
Class: GL
2003-06 Detlef Hegemann Rolandwerft GmbH & Co. KG — Berne Yd No: 199
Loa 133.58 (BB) Br ex - Dght 7.357
Lbp 126.80 Br md 19.40 Dpth 9.45
Welded, 1 dk
(A33A2CC) Container Ship (Fully Cellular)
Double Bottom Entire Compartment Length
TEU 707 C Ho 204 TEU C Dk 503 TEU incl 150 ref C.
Ice Capable
1 oil engine geared to sc. shaft driving 1 CP propeller
Total Power: 7,195kW (9,782hp) 17.9kn
MaK 8M43
1 x 4 Stroke 8 Cy. 430 x 610 7195kW (9782bhp)
Caterpillar Motoren GmbH & Co. KG-Germany
AuxGen: 2 x 400kW 440/220V a.c, 1 x 1200kW 440/220V a.c
Thrusters: 1 Thwart. FP thruster (f)
Fuel: 100.0 (d.f.) 570.0 (r.f.)

9365960 *9V2320* -
X-PRESS MULHACEN
ex Flintercarrier *-2013*
ex Judith Borchard *-2013*
ex Flintercarrier *-2012*
launched as Fresena Sailor *-2008*
Chulia Pte Ltd
Norbulk Shipping Pte Ltd
Singapore *Singapore*
MMSI: 563445000
Official number: 398882
7,702 3,614 9,620
Class: BV (GL)
2008-07 Nantong Mingde Heavy Industry Co Ltd — Tongzhou JS (Hull)
2008-07 All Ships Outfitting & Repairs — Krimpen a/d Lek Yd No: 253
Loa 141.60 (BB) Br ex 20.95 Dght 7.300
Lbp 132.30 Br md 20.60 Dpth 9.50
Welded, 1 dk
(A33A2CC) Container Ship (Fully Cellular)
TEU 809 C Ho 238 TEU C Dk 571 TEU incl 200 ref C
Compartments: 3 Cell Ho, ER
3 Ha: ER
Ice Capable
1 oil engine reduction geared to sc. shaft driving 1 CP propeller
Total Power: 9,240kW (12,563hp) 18.5kn
Wartsila 8L46D
1 x 4 Stroke 8 Cy. 460 x 580 9240kW (12563bhp)
Wartsila Finland Oy-Finland
Thrusters: 1 Tunnel thruster (f)

9152583 *A8DP7* -
X-PRESS PADMA
ex Hansa Caledonia *-2013*
ex Maersk Malaga *-2007*
ex Hansa Caledonia *-2003*
ex CSAV Suape *-1998*
ex Hansa Caledonia *-1998*
Marchant Maritime Co
Shanghai Costamare Ship Management Co Ltd
Monrovia *Liberia*
MMSI: 636016105
Official number: 16105
16,915 7,595 21,563 T/cm 38.4
Class: GL
1998-04 Hanjin Heavy Industries Co Ltd — Ulsan
Yd No: 636
Loa 168.02 (BB) Br ex - Dght 9.200
Lbp 158.00 Br md 27.20 Dpth 13.80
Welded, 1 dk
(A33A2CC) Container Ship (Fully Cellular)
TEU 1645 C Ho 606 TEU C Dk 1039 TEU incl 128 ref C.
8 Ha:
Cranes: 2x40t,1x10t
1 oil engine driving 1 FP propeller
Total Power: 11,950kW (16,247hp) 19.3kn
B&W 6S60MC
1 x 2 Stroke 6 Cy. 600 x 2292 11950kW (16247bhp)
Hyundai Heavy Industries Co Ltd-South Korea
AuxGen: 3 x 600kW a.c
Thrusters: 1 Thwart. CP thruster (f)

7810545 - -
X-PRESS SINGAPORE
ex Jaya Moon *-2000* *ex* Eagle Moon *-1998*
ex Benvalla *-1993* *ex* Tiger Star *-1992*
ex Maersk Asia Quarto *-1992*
ex Maersk Rando *-1991* *ex* Benvalla *-1986*
Fujian Ocean Shipping Co Ltd (FOSCO)
Fuzhou Minlun Shipping Co Ltd
7,179 2,550 8,050
Class: (LR)
✠ Classed LR until 16/6/04
1979-03 Mitsubishi Heavy Industries Ltd. — Kobe
Yd No: 1101
Loa 120.30 (BB) Br ex 20.55 Dght 6.914
Lbp 111.99 Br md 20.50 Dpth 11.00
Welded, 1 dk
(A33A2CC) Container Ship (Fully Cellular)
TEU 454 C Ho 216 TEU C Dk 238 incl 20 ref C
Compartments: 3 Cell Ho, ER
10 Ha: 2 (12.8 x 5.3)8 (12.8 x 8.0)ER
1 oil engine driving 1 FP propeller
Total Power: 4,413kW (6,000hp) 14.0kn
Mitsubishi 6UET52/90D
1 x 2 Stroke 6 Cy. 520 x 900 4413kW (6000bhp)
Akasaka Tekkosho KK (Akasaka DieselLtd)-Japan
AuxGen: 3 x 320kW 450V 60Hz a.c
Boilers: AuxB (Comp) 7.0kgf/cm² (6.9bar)
Fuel: 105.5 (d.f.) 474.0 (r.f.)

Ship	Tonnage	Class	Builder / Dimensions	Type	Machinery
9412476 **X-PRESS TAJUMULCO** *9V2362* *ex* Friesedijk *-2013* - *launched as* E. R. Helsinki *-2010* **Upper Cross Pte Ltd** Norbulk Shipping Pte Ltd *Singapore* *Singapore* MMSI: 564050000 Official number: 398940	**9,994** 5,198 12,306	Class: GL (NV)	**2010-07 Fujian Mawei Shipbuilding Ltd — Fuzhou FJ** Yd No: 431-11 Loa 140.68 (BB) Br ex - Dght 8.700 Lbp 130.55 Br md 23.19 Dpth 11.50 Welded, 1 dk	**(A33A2CC) Container Ship (Fully Cellular)** TEU 880 C Ho 325 TEU C Dk 555 TEU incl 231 ref C Compartments: 3 Cell Ho, ER 3 Ha: ER Cranes: 2 Ice Capable	**1 oil engine** reduction geared to sc. shaft driving 1 CP propeller Total Power: 9,240kW (12,563hp) 18.3kn Wartsila 8L46F 1 x 4 Stroke 8 Cy. 460 x 580 9240kW (12563bhp) Wartsila Finland Oy-Finland AuxGen: 1 x 1500kW 450V a.c, 2 x 1370kW 450V a.c Thrusters: 1 Tunnel thruster (f); 1 Tunnel thruster (a)
9159658 **X-PRESS TIGRIS** *9VDT4* *ex* Bunga Teratai 4 *-2012* - *ex* Bunga Teratai Empat *-2005* *ex* Bunga Teratai 4 *-2003* **X-Press Tigris Pte Ltd** Bibby Ship Management (Singapore) Pte Ltd *Singapore* *Singapore* MMSI: 566576000 Official number: 397961	**21,339** 8,940 24,561 T/cm 42.9	Class: LR ✠ **100A1** SS 10/2013 container ship *IWS LI ✠ **LMC** **UMS** Eq.Ltr: K†; Cable: 632.5/68.0 U3 (a)	**1998-10 Daewoo Heavy Industries Ltd — Geoje** Yd No: 4067 Loa 184.07 (BB) Br ex 27.45 Dght 10.200 Lbp 174.02 Br md 27.02 Dpth 15.80 Welded, 1 dk	**(A33A2CC) Container Ship (Fully Cellular)** TEU 1725 C Ho 778 TEU C Dk 947 TEU incl 242 ref C. Compartments: 5 Cell Ho, ER 9 Ha: (12.6 x 13.1) (12.6 x 18.3)7 (12.6 x 23.4)ER	**1 oil engine** driving 1 FP propeller Total Power: 12,260kW (16,669hp) 19.0kn B&W 6S60MC 1 x 2 Stroke 6 Cy. 600 x 2292 12260kW (16669bhp) Korea Heavy Industries & ConstrCo Ltd (HANJUNG)-South Korea AuxGen: 3 x 1400kW 450V 60Hz a.c Boilers: AuxB (Comp) 8.1kgf/cm² (7.9bar) Thrusters: 1 Thwart. CP thruster (f)
9152909 **X-PRESS YAMUNA** *9V9867* *ex* Laurita Rickmers *-2013* - *ex* CMA CGM St Laurent *-2010* *ex* Laurita *-2002* *ex* Melbridge Pearl *-1999* *ex* Laurita Rickmers *-1998* **Kreta Ayer Pte Ltd** Sea Consortium Pte Ltd (X-Press Feeders) *Singapore* *Singapore* MMSI: 563070000 Official number: 398768	**10,752** 5,478 14,086 T/cm 29.3	Class: GL	**1998-05 Stocznia Szczecinska SA — Szczecin** Yd No: B183/2/29 Loa 162.89 (BB) Br ex - Dght 8.100 Lbp 153.40 Br md 22.30 Dpth 11.10 Welded, 1 dk	**(A33A2CC) Container Ship (Fully Cellular)** Grain: 19,450 TEU 1162 C Ho 390 TEU C Dk 782 TEU incl 100 ref C. Compartments: 4 Cell Ho, ER 8 Ha: ER Cranes: 3x40t	**1 oil engine** driving 1 CP propeller Total Power: 7,988kW (10,860hp) 17.0kn B&W 6L50MC 1 x 2 Stroke 6 Cy. 500 x 1620 7988kW (10860bhp) H Cegielski Poznan SA-Poland AuxGen: 1 x 1000kW 220/380V 50Hz a.c, 3 x 504kW 220/380V 50Hz a.c Thrusters: 1 Thwart. CP thruster (f) Fuel: 148.4 (d.f.) (Heating Coils) 1231.6 (r.f.) 27.0pd
9412488 **X-PRESS YERUPAJA** *9V2351* *ex* Flevodijk *-2013* *ex* CCL Yokohama *-2011* - *ex* E. R. Visby *-2010* **Nankin Pte Ltd** Norbulk Shipping Pte Ltd *Singapore* *Singapore* MMSI: 563587000 Official number: 398926	**9,994** 5,198 11,863	Class: GL	**2010-03 Fujian Mawei Shipbuilding Ltd — Fuzhou FJ** Yd No: 431-12 Loa 140.71 (BB) Br ex - Dght 8.700 Lbp 130.55 Br md 23.19 Dpth 11.50 Welded, 1 dk	**(A33A2CC) Container Ship (Fully Cellular)** TEU 877 C Ho 322 TEU C Dk 555 TEU incl 231 ref C Compartments: 3 Cell Ho, ER 3 Ha: ER Cranes: 2x45t Ice Capable	**1 oil engine** reduction geared to sc. shaft driving 1 CP propeller Total Power: 9,240kW (12,563hp) 18.3kn Wartsila 8L46F 1 x 4 Stroke 8 Cy. 460 x 580 9240kW (12563bhp) Wartsila Diesel S.A.-Bermeo AuxGen: 1 x 1500kW 450V a.c, 2 x 1370kW 450V a.c Thrusters: 1 Tunnel thruster (f); 1 Tunnel thruster (a)
7720207 **XALOC** *EHSK* - **Botamavi Servicios Generales Maritimos SL** *Tarragona* *Spain* Official number: 1-1/1995	*102* 36 40	Class: (AB)	**1978-12 Ast. de Tarragona — Tarragona** Yd No: 199 Loa 20.02 Br ex - Dght 2.601 Lbp 17.48 Br md 7.00 Dpth 3.69 Welded, 1 dk	**(B32A2ST) Tug**	**1 oil engine** reverse reduction geared to sc. shaft driving 1 FP propeller Total Power: 853kW (1,160hp) 11.0kn Deutz SBA8M528 1 x 4 Stroke 8 Cy. 220 x 280 853kW (1160bhp) Hijos de J Barreras SA-Spain AuxGen: 2 x 32kW
7625380 **XAMAR 2** - - **Somali Ports Authority (Wakaaladda Dekedaha Soomaliyeed)** - *Mogadiscio* *Somalia*	*157* - 60	Class: (BV)	**1977-05 Scheepswerf Jac. den Breejen & Zoon B.V. — Hardinxveld-G.** (Hull) **1977-05 B.V. Scheepswerf Damen — Gorinchem** Yd No: 789 Loa 22.15 Br ex 6.61 Dght 3.420 Lbp - Br md - Dpth - Welded, 1 dk	**(B32B2SP) Pusher Tug**	**2 oil engines** geared to sc. shafts driving 2 FP propellers Total Power: 842kW (1,144hp) Caterpillar D379TA 2 x Vee 4 Stroke 8 Cy. 159 x 203 each-421kW (572bhp) Caterpillar Tractor Co-USA
7909322 **XANADU I** - - **Binding Nominees Pty Ltd** - *Fremantle, WA* *Australia* Official number: 375137	*121* 80 -		**1978 K Shipyard Construction Co — Fremantle WA** Loa 22.81 Br ex 6.53 Dght 3.101 Lbp 21.42 Br md 6.41 Dpth 3.51 Welded, 1 dk	**(B11A2FT) Trawler**	**1 oil engine** reduction geared to sc. shaft driving 1 FP propeller Total Power: 331kW (450hp) 10.0kn Caterpillar 3412T 1 x Vee 4 Stroke 12 Cy. 137 x 152 331kW (450bhp) Caterpillar Tractor Co-USA
9248980 **XANGONGO** *D3N2059* - **Government of The People's Republic of Angola (Missao de Estudos Bioceanologicos e de Pesca de Angola)** Inter-Burgo SA *Luanda* *Angola*	**222** - 334	Class: (KR)	**2001-04 Yongsung Shipbuilding Co Ltd — Geoje** Yd No: 171 Loa 45.61 Br ex - Dght - Lbp 37.50 Br md 7.20 Dpth 4.20 Welded, 1 dk	**(B11B2FV) Fishing Vessel** Ins: 360	**1 oil engine** geared to sc. shaft driving 1 FP propeller Total Power: 883kW (1,201hp) Yanmar M220-EN 1 x 4 Stroke 6 Cy. 220 x 300 883kW (1201bhp) Yanmar Diesel Engine Co Ltd-Japan
9246152 **XANTHIA** *LAUR5* - **Utkilen Shipinvest KS** Utkilen AS *Bergen* *Norway (NIS)* MMSI: 257970000	**10,578** 5,364 17,031 T/cm 28.5	Class: NV	**2003-02 Aker Aukra AS — Aukra** Yd No: 108 Loa 147.30 (BB) Br ex 22.44 Dght 8.750 Lbp 138.60 Br md 22.00 Dpth 11.50 Welded, 1 dk	**(A12B2TR) Chemical/Products Tanker** Double Hull (13F) Liq: 18,456; Liq (Oil): 17,520 Cargo Heating Coils Compartments: 20 Wing Ta (s.stl), ER 20 Cargo Pump (s): 20x300m³/hr Manifold: Bow/CM: 75.4m Ice Capable	**1 oil engine** reduction geared to sc. shaft driving 1 CP propeller Total Power: 7,200kW (9,789hp) 16.0kn MaK 8M43 1 x 4 Stroke 8 Cy. 430 x 610 7200kW (9789bhp) Caterpillar Motoren GmbH & Co. KG-Germany AuxGen: 4 x 400kW a.c, 1 x 1360kW a.c Thrusters: 1 Tunnel thruster (f) Fuel: 157.0 (d.f.) 724.0 (r.f.)
9289178 **XANTHOS** *A8FJ4* - **Vivian Marine Inc** Pleiades Shipping Agents SA *Monrovia* *Liberia* MMSI: 636012425 Official number: 12425	**35,711** 16,707 61,369 T/cm 64.5	Class: LR ✠ **100A1** SS 02/2010 Double Hull oil tanker ESP *IWS LI **ShipRight** (SDA, FDA, CM) ✠ **LMC** **UMS IGS** Eq.Ltr: N†; Cable: 665.0/76.0 U3 (a)	**2005-02 Sumitomo Heavy Industries Marine & Engineering Co., Ltd. — Yokosuka** Yd No: 1305 Loa 213.36 (BB) Br ex 32.29 Dght 12.280 Lbp 206.56 Br md 32.26 Dpth 18.50 Welded, 1 dk	**(A13A2TV) Crude Oil Tanker** Double Hull (13F) Liq: 64,006; Liq (Oil): 64,006 Cargo Heating Coils Compartments: 10 Wing Ta, 2 Wing Slop Ta, ER 3 Cargo Pump (s): 3x2000m³/hr Manifold: Bow/CM: 102.9m	**1 oil engine** driving 1 FP propeller Total Power: 10,010kW (13,610hp) 15.0kn B&W 7S50MC 1 x 2 Stroke 7 Cy. 500 x 1910 10010kW (13610bhp) Mitsui Engineering & Shipbuilding CLtd-Japan AuxGen: 3 x 560kW 450/220V 60Hz a.c Boilers: e (ex.g.) 22.0kgf/cm² (21.6bar), WTAuxB (o.f.) 18.4kgf/cm² (18.0bar) Fuel: 235.0 (d.f.) 2153.0 (r.f.) 41.0pd
8979013 **XAVIER III** *HC2117* *ex* Lobo De Mar III *-2010* - **Medina Alejandro Antonio Panchana** - *Puerto Baquerizo Moreno* *Ecuador* Official number: TN-01-0986	*162* 51 -		**1996 Carlos Burgos Sabando — Ecuador** L reg 25.50 Br ex - Dght - Lbp - Br md 7.40 Dpth - Welded, 1 dk	**(A37B2PS) Passenger Ship** Passengers: cabins: 8; berths: 16	**2 oil engines** driving 2 Propellers
8816297 **XEFINA** - *ex* Sha Tin *-2003* - **Maputo Port Development Co Sarl (MPDC)** P&O Maritime Mozambique SA *Maputo* *Mozambique*	*188* 55 281	Class: (BV)	**1989-03 Imamura Zosen — Kure** Yd No: 333 Loa 24.60 Br ex 9.15 Dght 3.501 Lbp 22.39 Br md 8.51 Dpth 4.73 Welded, 1 dk	**(B32A2ST) Tug**	**2 oil engines** with clutches, flexible couplings & reduction geared to sc. shafts driving 2 Z propellers Total Power: 2,428kW (3,302hp) 12.3kn Niigata 6L25CXE 2 x 4 Stroke 6 Cy. 250 x 320 each-1214kW (1651bhp) (made 1988) Niigata Engineering Co Ltd-Japan AuxGen: 2 x 64kW 380V 50Hz a.c
7385344 **XEITOSINO** *LW9130* - **Pesuar SA** - *San Antonio Oeste* *Argentina* MMSI: 701006071 Official number: 0403	**444** 173 -	Class: (BV)	**1975-09 Ast. de Mallorca S.A. — Palma de Mallorca** Yd No: 211 Lengthened-1982 Loa 53.22 Br ex - Dght 4.090 Lbp 46.06 Br md 9.50 Dpth 6.48 Welded, 2 dks	**(B11A2FT) Trawler**	**1 oil engine** driving 1 CP propeller Total Power: 1,030kW (1,400hp) 12.5kn Deutz RBV8M545 1 x 4 Stroke 8 Cy. 320 x 450 1030kW (1400bhp) (made 1972, fitted 1975) Kloeckner Humboldt Deutz AG-West Germany
7811276 **XEL-HA** - *ex* Alijumbo Secondo *-1982* - **Government of Mexico (Ministry of Tourism)** - *Cancun* *Mexico*	*208* 132 40	Class: (RI)	**1980-07 Navaltecnica — San Benedetto del Tronto** Yd No: 203 Loa 30.97 Br ex 12.60 Dght 3.691 Lbp 26.70 Br md 5.49 Dpth 3.46 Welded, 1 dk	**(A37B2PS) Passenger Ship** Hull Material: Aluminium Alloy Passengers: unberthed: 151	**2 oil engines** reverse reduction geared to sc. shafts driving 2 FP propellers Total Power: 772kW (1,050hp) M.T.U. 12V331TC82 2 x Vee 4 Stroke 12 Cy. 165 x 155 each-386kW (525bhp) MTU Friedrichshafen GmbH-Friedrichshafen

9360958 *3EIU8* -	**XENA** *ex* Southern Eagle *-2010* *ex* Shamrock Eagle *-2009* **New Glory Shipping SA** Bernhard Schulte Shipmanagement (Singapore) Pte Ltd SatCom: Inmarsat C 437240510 *Panama* *Panama* MMSI: 372405000 Official number: 35274PEXT	**11,733** 6,321 19,980 T/cm 29.8	Class: NK	**2007-02 Fukuoka Shipbuilding Co Ltd — Nagasaki NS** Yd No: 2010 Loa 144.09 (BB) Br ex 24.23 Dght 9.652 Lbp 136.00 Br md 24.19 Dpth 12.90 Welded, 1 dk	**(A12B2TR) Chemical/Products Tanker** Double Hull (13F) Liq: 20,526; Liq (Oil): 21,600 Cargo Heating Coils Compartments: 18 Wing Ta (s.stl), 2 Wing Slop Ta (s.stl), ER 18 Cargo Pump (s): 12x300m³/hr, 6x200m³/hr Manifold: Bow/CM: 74.1m	**1 oil engine** driving 1 FP propeller Total Power: 6,150kW (8,362hp) 14.5kn MAN-B&W 6S42MC 1 x 2 Stroke 6 Cy. 420 x 1764 6150kW (8362bhp) Imex Co Ltd-Japan AuxGen: 3 x 400kW a.c Thrusters: 1 Tunnel thruster (f) Fuel: 126.0 (d.f.) 894.0 (r.f.)
9344318 *IZZQ* -	**XENIA** **Bunkeroil Srl** B & A Engineering Srl SatCom: Inmarsat C 424703256 *Livorno* *Italy* MMSI: 247157300	**1,304** 500 1,710	Class: BV RI	**2006-04 Sahin Celik Sanayi A.S. — Tuzla** Yd No: 37 Loa 67.65 Br ex - Dght 4.300 Lbp 64.40 Br md 12.00 Dpth 5.50 Welded, 1 dk	**(A12B2TR) Chemical/Products Tanker** Double Hull (13F)	**2 oil engines** reduction geared to sc. shafts driving 2 FP propellers Total Power: 1,472kW (2,002hp) Yanmar 2 x 4 Stroke each-736kW (1001bhp) Yanmar Diesel Engine Co Ltd-Japan
9317834 *5BXG3* -	**XENIA** *ex* Brilliant Sunrise *-2013* **Vasstwo Shipping Corp** Safety Management Overseas SA *Limassol* *Cyprus* MMSI: 209889000 Official number: 9317834	**47,051** 27,005 87,144 T/cm 79.7	Class: LR (NK) **100A1** SS 08/2011 bulk carrier BC-A strengthened for heavy cargoes, Nos. 2, 4 & 6 holds may be empty ESP ESN *IWS LI **LMC** **UMS**	**2006-08 IHI Marine United Inc — Yokohama KN** Yd No: 3211 Loa 229.00 (BB) Br ex 36.54 Dght 14.100 Lbp 219.90 Br md 36.50 Dpth 19.90 Welded, 1 dk	**(A21A2BC) Bulk Carrier** Double Hull Grain: 98,961; Bale: 94,844 Compartments: 7 Ho, ER 7 Ha: (14.3 x 16.8)2 (17.1 x 16.8)3 (17.1 x 16.8)ER (16.2 x 15.1)	**1 oil engine** driving 1 FP propeller Total Power: 10,300kW (14,004hp) 14.5kn Sulzer 6RTA58T 1 x 2 Stroke 6 Cy. 580 x 2416 10300kW (14004bhp) Diesel United Ltd.-Aioi AuxGen: 3 x 520kW 450V 60Hz a.c Fuel: 279.0 (d.f.) 3048.0 (r.f.)
9217163 *V2OI4* -	**XENIA** **ms 'Xenia' Schiffahrts GmbH & Co Reederei KG** Intersee Schiffahrtsgesellschaft mbH & Co KG *Saint John's* *Antigua & Barbuda* MMSI: 304443000 Official number: 3790	**7,406** 3,859 10,610 T/cm 21.0	Class: GL (LR) ✠ Classed LR until 18/12/10	**2002-12 B.V. Scheepswerf Damen Hoogezand — Foxhol** Yd No: 818 **2002-12 Damen Shipyards Yichang Co Ltd — Yichang HB** (Hull) Loa 142.69 (BB) Br ex 18.35 Dght 7.330 Lbp 136.18 Br md 18.25 Dpth 10.15 Welded, 1 dk	**(A31A2GX) General Cargo Ship** Grain: 14,695 TEU 668 C Ho 291 TEU C Dk 377 TEU incl 60 ref C. Compartments: 2 Ho, ER 2 Ha: ER Cranes: 2x60t	**1 oil engine** with flexible couplings & sr geared to sc. shaft driving 1 CP propeller Total Power: 4,320kW (5,873hp) 14.8kn MaK 9M32 1 x 4 Stroke 9 Cy. 320 x 480 4320kW (5873bhp) MaK Motoren GmbH & Co. KG-Kiel AuxGen: 1 x 452kW 400V 50Hz a.c, 3 x 260kW 400V 50Hz a.c Boilers: TOH (ex.g.) 10.2kgf/cm² (10.0bar), TOH (o.f.) 10.2kgf/cm² (10.0bar) Thrusters: 1 Thwart. CP thruster (f) Fuel: 50.0 (d.f.) 587.0 (r.f.)
7806831 - -	**XENIA** *ex* Fierbinti *-1998* -	*5,983* 3,531 8,750	Class: (RN)	**1978-06 Santierul Naval Galati S.A. — Galati** Yd No: 677 Loa 130.77 (BB) Br ex - Dght 8.102 Lbp 121.05 Br md 17.70 Dpth 10.20 Welded, 1 dk & S dk	**(A31A2GX) General Cargo Ship** Grain: 11,980; Bale: 11,067 Compartments: 4 Ho, ER 4 Ha: (11.9 x 5.9)3 (13.6 x 9.9)ER Cranes: 4x5t Ice Capable	**1 oil engine** driving 1 FP propeller Total Power: 4,487kW (6,101hp) 15.0kn Sulzer 5RD68 1 x 2 Stroke 5 Cy. 680 x 1250 4487kW (6101bhp) Zaklady Przemyslu Metalowego 'HCegielski' SA-Poznan AuxGen: 3 x 200kW 400V 50Hz a.c Fuel: 1146.0
8810839 *EHUE* -	**XEOS** **Pesquerias Xeos SL** - *Viveiro* *Spain* Official number: 3-2994/	**230** 69 160	Class: (BV)	**1989-03 Construcciones Navales P Freire SA — Vigo** Yd No: 336 Loa 29.99 Br ex - Dght 3.450 Lbp 25.00 Br md 7.50 Dpth 5.60 Welded, 2 dks	**(B11A2FS) Stern Trawler** Ins: 115	**1 oil engine** with flexible couplings & sr geared to sc. shaft driving 1 FP propeller Total Power: 515kW (700hp) 10.3kn Caterpillar 3508TA 1 x Vee 4 Stroke 8 Cy. 170 x 190 515kW (700bhp) Caterpillar Inc-USA AuxGen: 3 x 96kW 220V a.c
9046411 *9V8477* -	**XETHA BHUM** **Regional Container Lines Public Co Ltd** RCL Shipmanagement Pte Ltd *Singapore* *Singapore* MMSI: 565303000 Official number: 395839	**11,086** 5,045 15,302 T/cm 30.2	Class: GL	**1993-06 Hanjin Heavy Industries Co Ltd — Ulsan** Yd No: 618 Loa 145.65 (BB) Br ex 25.04 Dght 8.140 Lbp 135.00 Br md 25.00 Dpth 11.50 Welded, 1 dk	**(A33A2CC) Container Ship (Fully Cellular)** TEU 1288 incl 60 ref C. Compartments: 2 Cell Ho, ER 12 Ha: 4 (12.6 x 10.4)8 (12.5 x 10.4)ER Cranes: 2x40t	**1 oil engine** driving 1 FP propeller Total Power: 10,415kW (14,160hp) 17.0kn B&W 6L60MC 1 x 2 Stroke 6 Cy. 600 x 1944 10415kW (14160bhp) Hyundai Heavy Industries Co Ltd-South Korea AuxGen: 3 x 560kW 220/440V 60Hz a.c Thrusters: 1 Thwart. CP thruster (f) Fuel: 66.1 (d.f.) (Heating Coils) 1075.0 (r.f.) 42.0pd
9127942 *BQBF* -	**XI CHANG HAI** *ex* Xichanghai *-2009* *launched as* COS Diamond *-1997* **Quanzhou Ocean Shipping Co (COSCO QUANZHOU)** COSCO Far-Reaching Shipping Co Ltd *Shanghai* *China* MMSI: 413361000	**18,070** 9,485 27,000 T/cm 38.9	Class: CC (AB)	**1997-08 Hudong Shipbuilding Group — Shanghai** Yd No: H1231A Loa 175.00 (BB) Br ex - Dght 9.820 Lbp 165.00 Br md 26.00 Dpth 13.90 Welded, 1 dk	**(A21A2BC) Bulk Carrier** Grain: 36,840; Bale: 35,736 Compartments: 5 Ho, ER 5 Ha: (14.2 x 12.8)4 (19.2 x 14.4)ER Cranes: 4x30t	**1 oil engine** driving 1 FP propeller Total Power: 5,763kW (7,835hp) 14.0kn B&W 5L50MC 1 x 2 Stroke 5 Cy. 500 x 1620 5763kW (7835bhp) Hudong Shipyard-China AuxGen: 3 x 440kW a.c
8505173 *BTDR*	**XI GING KAN 1** **Government of The People's Republic of China (China National Technical Import Corp)** - *Shijiugang, Shandong* *China*	*210* - 178		**1985-08 Minami-Kyushu Zosen KK — Ichikikushikino KS** Yd No: 506 Loa 29.47 Br ex 8.13 Dght 2.601 Lbp 26.60 Br md 7.92 Dpth 3.61 Welded, 1 dk	**(B32A2ST) Tug**	**2 oil engines** with clutches & sr geared to sc. shafts driving 2 FP propellers Total Power: 500kW (680hp) Yanmar 6M-HT 2 x 4 Stroke 6 Cy. 200 x 240 each-250kW (340bhp) Yanmar Diesel Engine Co Ltd-Japan
8997182 - -	**XI WANG 68** *ex* Hati Baik I *-2011* *ex* Xi Wang 68 *-2007* **Beihai Fumao Logistics Co Ltd** Beihai Jiajie Warehousing & Stevedoring Co Ltd *Beihai, Guangxi* *China* MMSI: 412502750 Official number: 100210000042	**2,996** 1,667 3,600		**1984-04 Guangdong New China Shipyard Co Ltd — Dongguan GD** Loa - Br ex - Dght 6.200 Lbp 92.00 Br md 13.80 Dpth 7.82 Welded, 1 dk	**(A31A2GX) General Cargo Ship**	**1 oil engine** reduction geared to sc. shaft driving 1 Propeller Total Power: 1,800kW (2,447hp) Blackstone ESL16WDS 1 x Vee 4 Stroke 16 Cy. 222 x 292 1800kW (2447bhp) (, fitted 1984) Mirrlees Blackstone (Stamford)Ltd.-Stamford
9187540 - -	**XI YANG 12 HAO** **Changjiang Wuhan Waterway Engineering Bureau** - *Wuhan, Hubei* *China* MMSI: 412592270	**1,626** 487 561	Class: CC	**1998-02 Wuchang Shipyard — Wuhan HB** Yd No: A979 Loa 93.12 Br ex - Dght 2.560 Lbp 72.60 Br md 16.00 Dpth 4.60 Welded, 1 dk	**(B33A2DC) Cutter Suction Dredger**	**1 oil engine** driving 1 FP propeller
9208320 *BTYY* -	**XI YANG SHI WU HAO** *ex* Xi Yang 15 Hao *-2005* **Nanjing Changjiang Waterway Engineering Bureau** - *Nanjing, Jiangsu* *China* MMSI: 413355190 Official number: 99H1008	**1,555** 466 450	Class: CC	**1999-03 Wuchang Shipyard — Wuhan HB** Yd No: A015L Loa 89.15 Br ex - Dght 2.600 Lbp 65.40 Br md 16.00 Dpth 4.60 Welded, 1 dk	**(B33A2DC) Cutter Suction Dredger**	**1 oil engine** driving 1 FP propeller Total Power: 680kW (925hp) S.K.L. 8VD18/16AL-3 1 x 4 Stroke 6 Cy. 160 x 180 680kW (925bhp) SKL Motoren u. Systemtechnik AG-Magdeburg
8833087 - -	**XIA SHUI YUN 23** **Xiamen Water Transport Corp** - *Xiamen, Fujian* *China*	*265* 138 300		**1985 Dalian Shengli Dockyard — Dalian LN** Loa 38.66 Br ex - Dght 3.000 Lbp 35.00 Br md 7.40 Dpth 3.50 Welded, 1 dk	**(A31A2GX) General Cargo Ship**	**1 oil engine** geared to sc. shaft driving 1 FP propeller Total Power: 257kW (349hp) Chinese Std. Type 6160A 1 x 4 Stroke 6 Cy. 160 x 225 257kW (349bhp) Weifang Diesel Engine Factory-China AuxGen: 1 x 24kW 400V a.c
9639452 *BKQC5* -	**XIA ZHI YUAN 6** **Zhejiang Share-Ever Business Co Ltd** - SatCom: Inmarsat C 441410110 *Zhoushan, Zhejiang* *China* MMSI: 414101000	**32,793** 9,838 37,904	Class: CC	**2012-06 Zhejiang Peninsula Ship Industry Co Ltd — Zhoushan ZJ** Yd No: GP10C069 Loa 195.20 Br ex - Dght 8.600 Lbp 185.20 Br md 41.50 Dpth 12.00 Welded, 1 dk	**(A38C3GH) Heavy Load Carrier, semi submersible** Ice Capable	**3 diesel electric oil engines** driving 3 gen. each 5000kW 6600V a.c Connecting to 2 elec. motors each (5000kW) driving 2 FP propellers Total Power: 13,035kW (17,721hp) 13.5kn Wartsila 1 x 4345kW (5907bhp) Wartsila 2 x each-4345kW (5907bhp) Thrusters: 2 Tunnel thruster (f)

577824 KPR5	**XIA ZHI YUAN 7** *launched as* Shun Hang 203 *-2010* **Zhejiang Share-Ever Business Co Ltd** - *Zhoushan, Zhejiang* *China* MMSI: 412763250	**17,888** 9,713 27,000	Class: CC	**2010-07 No 4807 Shipyard of PLA — Fu'an FJ** Yd No: 20073903 Loa 169.37 (BB) Br ex - Dght 10.200 Lbp 159.80 Br md 25.00 Dpth 14.30 Welded, 1 dk	**(A21A2BC) Bulk Carrier** Double Sides Entire Compartment Length Grain: 34,930 Compartments: 4 Ho, ER 4 Ha: 2 (22.5 x 15.0) (23.3 x 15.0)ER (20.8 x 13.0) Cranes: 3x30t Ice Capable	**1 oil engine** driving 1 FP propeller Total Power: 5,222kW (7,100hp) 13.5kn MAN-B&W 6S40ME-B9 1 x 2 Stroke 6 Cy. 400 x 1770 5222kW (7100bhp) Yichang Marine Diesel Engine Co Ltd-China AuxGen: 3 x 540kW 400V a.c
329203 CFH -VI-51-04	**XIADAS DOUS** - **Xiadas da Guarda SA** - *La Guardia* *Spain* MMSI: 224267000 Official number: 3-1/2004	**331** 99 -		**2004-06 Montajes Cies S.L. — Vigo** Yd No: 113 Loa - Br ex - Dght - Lbp 26.00 Br md 7.50 Dpth 3.50 Welded, 1 dk	**(B11A2FS) Stern Trawler**	**1 oil engine** geared to sc. shaft driving 1 FP propeller Total Power: 435kW (591hp) A.B.C. 6MDXS 1 x 4 Stroke 6 Cy. 242 x 320 435kW (591bhp) Anglo Belgian Corp NV (ABC)-Belgium
920854 FI02	**XIAMEN JINGTAI** *ex* Valiant *-2011* *ex* Sanko Pageant *-1999* **Jingtai Shipping Co Ltd** - *Panama* *Panama* MMSI: 353920000 Official number: 4248911	**56,943** 24,017 91,834 T/cm 88.5	Class: RI (LR) (NK) Classed LR until 8/6/10	**1992-08 Namura Shipbuilding Co Ltd — Imari SG** Yd No: 916 Converted From: Crude Oil/Products Tanker-2011 Loa 241.80 (BB) Br ex 42.04 Dght 13.500 Lbp 232.84 Br md 42.00 Dpth 20.40 Welded, 1 dk	**(A21A2BC) Bulk Carrier** Grain: 100,711 Compartments: 5 Ho, ER 5 Ha: ER	**1 oil engine** driving 1 FP propeller Total Power: 10,150kW (13,800hp) 13.5kn B&W 7S60MC 1 x 2 Stroke 7 Cy. 600 x 2292 10150kW (13800bhp) Hitachi Zosen Corp-Japan AuxGen: 3 x 500kW 440V 60Hz a.c, 1 x 72kW 440V 60Hz a.c Boilers: e (ex.g.) 22.0kgf/cm² (21.6bar), AuxB (o.f.) 18.1kgf/cm² (17.8bar) Fuel: 140.8 (d.f.) (Heating Coils) 2093.7 (r.f.)
588586 5DV7	**XIAN** *ex* Christine Star *-2013* **Xian Shipping Ltd** International Maritime Advisors & Management Corp *Monrovia* *Liberia* MMSI: 636015983 Official number: 15983	**32,983** 19,191 56,854 T/cm 58.8	Class: NK	**2011-01 COSCO (Dalian) Shipyard Co Ltd — Dalian LN** Yd No: N222 Loa 189.99 (BB) Br ex - Dght 12.818 Lbp 185.00 Br md 32.26 Dpth 18.00 Welded, 1 dk	**(A21A2BC) Bulk Carrier** Grain: 71,634; Bale: 68,200 Compartments: 5 Ho, ER 5 Ha: ER Cranes: 4x36t	**1 oil engine** driving 1 FP propeller Total Power: 9,480kW (12,889hp) 14.5kn MAN-B&W 6S50MC-C 1 x 2 Stroke 6 Cy. 500 x 2000 9480kW (12889bhp) Mitsui Engineering & Shipbuilding CLtd-Japan Fuel: 2405.0 (r.f.)
404381 OVC	**XIAN HU** *ex* Oriental Beauty *-2002* *ex* Coral Queen *-1999* **Shenzhen Shekou Shipping Transportation Co Ltd** - SatCom: Inmarsat A 1335260 *Shenzhen, Guangdong* *China* MMSI: 412465120	**5,235** 3,297 8,415	Class: CC (NK)	**1984-10 Daedong Shipbuilding Co Ltd — Busan** Yd No: 273 Loa 117.86 Br ex 18.04 Dght 7.208 Lbp 110.01 Br md 18.01 Dpth 9.12 Welded, 1 dk	**(A31A2GX) General Cargo Ship** Grain: 12,357; Bale: 10,495 Compartments: 2 Ho, ER 2 Ha: (30.7 x 9.0) (33.6 x 9.0)ER Derricks: 4x15t	**1 oil engine** driving 1 FP propeller Total Power: 2,868kW (3,899hp) 12.0kn Mitsubishi 6UEC37H-II 1 x 2 Stroke 6 Cy. 370 x 880 2868kW (3899bhp) Kobe Hatsudoki KK-Japan AuxGen: 2 x 160kW a.c
259214	**XIAN LI 1** - **Zhuhai Tongda Shipping Co Ltd** - *Zhuhai, Guangdong* *China*	**193** 57 -	Class: CC	**2002-08 Hin Lee (Zhuhai) Shipyard Co Ltd — Zhuhai GD** Yd No: 009 Loa 25.00 Br ex - Dght 3.100 Lbp 22.65 Br md 8.00 Dpth 3.90 Welded, 1 dk	**(B32A2ST) Tug**	**2 oil engines** reduction geared to sc. shafts driving 2 FP propellers Total Power: 760kW (1,034hp) Cummins KTA-19-M500 2 x 4 Stroke 6 Cy. 159 x 159 each-380kW (517bhp) Chongqing Cummins Engine Co Ltd-China AuxGen: 2 x 40kW 400V a.c
914157 JUS	**XIAN PING No. 3** *ex* Kyokushin No. 1 *-1996* *ex* Kyokushin Maru *-1995* **Hainan International Energy Shipping Co Ltd** - *Haikou, Hainan* *China* MMSI: 412520350	**2,697** 1,208 3,749 T/cm 10.6	Class: (CC) (NK)	**1979-11 Ube Dockyard Co. Ltd. — Ube** Yd No: 158 Loa 91.55 Br ex 14.23 Dght 5.910 Lbp 85.22 Br md 14.20 Dpth 7.12 Welded, 1 dk	**(A13B2TP) Products Tanker** Liq: 4,232; Liq (Oil): 4,232 Compartments: 8 Ta, ER 2 Cargo Pump (s): 2x1200m³/hr Manifold: Bow/CM: 43m	**1 oil engine** reduction geared to sc. shaft driving 1 FP propeller Total Power: 2,501kW (3,400hp) 13.5kn MaK 9M453AK 1 x 4 Stroke 9 Cy. 320 x 420 2501kW (3400bhp) Ube Industries Ltd-Japan AuxGen: 2 x 200kW 445V 60Hz a.c Fuel: 64.0 (d.f.) (Heating Coils) 275.0 (r.f.) 13.5pd
913397	**XIAN YI** *ex* Xian Fu *-1995* *ex* Shun Tai *-2003* *ex* Sun Fortune *-1995* *ex* Kokai Maru *-1993* - SatCom: Inmarsat C 441294510 *Shekou, Guangdong* *China* Official number: 16000283	**4,239** 2,543 6,657	Class: (CC) (NK)	**1980-02 Murakami Hide Zosen K.K. — Imabari** Yd No: 176 Loa 105.01 Br ex - Dght 7.071 Lbp 98.02 Br md 16.80 Dpth 8.62 Welded, 1 dk	**(A31A2GX) General Cargo Ship** Grain: 8,624; Bale: 8,072 Compartments: 2 Ho, ER 2 Ha: (25.2 x 8.9) (27.9 x 8.9)ER Derricks: 4x15t	**1 oil engine** driving 1 FP propeller Total Power: 2,795kW (3,800hp) 12.3kn Mitsubishi 6UET45/75C 1 x 2 Stroke 6 Cy. 450 x 750 2795kW (3800bhp) Kobe Hatsudoki KK-Japan AuxGen: 2 x 144kW 445V 60Hz a.c Fuel: 89.0 (d.f.) 505.0 (r.f.) 12.5pd
279903 AMF	**XIAN YU 2** - **Dalian Fu Cheng Aquatic Co Ltd** - SatCom: Inmarsat C 441236715 *Dalian, Liaoning* *China* MMSI: 412203940	**497** 149 564	Class: CC	**2002-10 Huanghai Shipbuilding Co Ltd — Rongcheng SD** Yd No: 407 Loa 54.20 Br ex - Dght 3.700 Lbp 48.00 Br md 8.80 Dpth 4.30 Welded	**(B12C2FL) Live Fish Carrier (Well Boat)**	**1 oil engine** reduction geared to sc. shaft driving 1 Propeller Total Power: 882kW (1,199hp) 12.0kn Chinese Std. Type LB6250ZLC 1 x 4 Stroke 6 Cy. 250 x 320 882kW (1199bhp) Zibo Diesel Engine Factory-China AuxGen: 2 x 150kW 400V a.c
232008 ANF	**XIAN YU NO. 1** - **Dandong Daludao Haixing Enterprise (Group) Co Ltd** - *Dalian, Liaoning* *China* MMSI: 412203020 Official number: 030001000031	**287** 93 212	Class: CC	**2000-05 Huanghai Shipbuilding Co Ltd — Rongcheng SD** Yd No: A402-2 Loa 49.95 Br ex - Dght 2.800 Lbp 46.00 Br md 7.40 Dpth 3.70 Welded, 1 dk	**(A34A2GR) Refrigerated Cargo Ship** Ins: 338 Compartments: 3 Ho, ER 3 Ha: ER 3 (2.1 x 1.9)	**1 oil engine** reduction geared to sc. shaft driving 1 FP propeller Total Power: 1,324kW (1,800hp) 15.0kn Chinese Std. Type LB8250ZLC 1 x 4 Stroke 8 Cy. 250 x 320 1324kW (1800bhp) Zibo Diesel Engine Factory-China AuxGen: 2 x 64kW 400V a.c
296535 3KNJ4	**XIAN ZHOU 5** - **Zhejiang Daishan County Penglai Passenger Shipping Co Ltd** - *Zhoushan, Zhejiang* *China* MMSI: 412412750	**348** 180 45	Class: CC	**2003-06 Wuhan Nanhua High Speed Ship Engineering Co Ltd — Wuhan HB** Yd No: 465-2 Loa 48.00 Br ex - Dght 1.290 Lbp 43.00 Br md 6.40 Dpth 3.30 Welded, 1 dk	**(A37B2PS) Passenger Ship**	**2 oil engines** geared to sc. shafts driving 2 FP propellers Total Power: 3,284kW (4,464hp) 28.0kn Caterpillar 3516B-TA 2 x Vee 4 Stroke 16 Cy. 170 x 190 each-1642kW (2232bhp) (made 2003) Caterpillar Inc-USA AuxGen: 2 x 75kW 400V a.c
741571 3KPE2	**XIAN ZHOU 6** - **Zhejiang Daishan County Penglai Passenger Shipping Co Ltd** - *Zhoushan, Zhejiang* *China* MMSI: 412422520	**383** 191 36	Class: CC	**2004-09 Wuhan Nanhua High Speed Ship Engineering Co Ltd — Wuhan HB** Loa 48.30 Br ex - Dght 1.500 Lbp 43.00 Br md 7.20 Dpth 3.30 Welded, 1 dk	**(A37B2PS) Passenger Ship**	**2 oil engines** reduction geared to sc. shafts driving 2 Propellers Total Power: 3,372kW (4,584hp) 31.0kn Caterpillar 3516B-HD 2 x Vee 4 Stroke 16 Cy. 170 x 215 each-1686kW (2292bhp) Caterpillar Inc-USA AuxGen: 2 x 75kW 400V a.c
689885 YDB4389	**XIANG** - **PT J & Y Transhipment** - *Jakarta* *Indonesia*	**284** 85 290	Class: BV	**2013-09 Nantong Yahua Shipbuilding Co Ltd — Nantong JS** Yd No: YH139 Loa 30.00 Br ex - Dght 3.600 Lbp 27.70 Br md 8.60 Dpth 4.12 Welded, 1 dk	**(B32A2ST) Tug**	**2 oil engines** reduction geared to sc. shafts driving 2 FP propellers Total Power: 1,492kW (2,028hp) Caterpillar C32 ACERT 2 x Vee 4 Stroke 12 Cy. 145 x 162 each-746kW (1014bhp) Caterpillar Inc-USA Fuel: 210.0
316431 3EGW3	**XIANG AN CHENG** *ex* Kota Singa *-2006* **Xiamen Ocean Shipping Co (COSCO XIAMEN)** - *Panama* *Panama* MMSI: 371471000 Official number: 3218306B	**12,725** 7,918 20,621 T/cm 30.1	Class: CC (LR) ✠ Classed LR until 12/2/08	**1985-01 Mitsubishi Heavy Industries Ltd. — Kobe** Yd No: 1146 Converted From: Container Ship (Fully Cellular)-2006 Converted From: General Cargo Ship-2003 Loa 146.51 (BB) Br ex 25.05 Dght 9.802 Lbp 140.01 Br md 25.00 Dpth 13.59 Welded, 1 dk, 2nd dk in way of Nos. 2, 3 & 4 holds (max. load on TwD hatch covers 3T/sq metre)	**(A31A2GX) General Cargo Ship** Grain: 28,722; Bale: 26,718 TEU 716 C Ho 314 TEU C Dk 402 TEU incl 40 ref C. Compartments: 4 Ho, ER, 4 Tw Dk 7 Ha: 4 (25.6 x 8.0)3 (12.8 x 8.0)ER Cranes: 4x25t	**1 oil engine** driving 1 FP propeller Total Power: 4,888kW (6,646hp) 15.0kn Mitsubishi 5UEC52HA 1 x 2 Stroke 5 Cy. 520 x 1250 4888kW (6646bhp) Mitsubishi Heavy Industries Ltd-Japan AuxGen: 3 x 550kW 450V 60Hz a.c Boilers: e 10.9kgf/cm² (10.7bar), AuxB (o.f.) 6.9kgf/cm² (6.8bar) Fuel: 203.0 (d.f.) 992.5 (r.f.) 20.5pd

9017501 *BPMP* -	**XIANG BIN** *ex* Zhen Fen 16 *-1999* **China Shipping Container Lines Co Ltd** SatCom: Inmarsat B 341250010 *Shanghai* *China* MMSI: 412500000	**13,253** 5,744 20,297	Class: CC	**1992**-12 **Shanghai Shipyard — Shanghai** Yd No: 147 Converted From: Bulk Carrier-1999 Loa 164.00 (BB) Br ex - Dght 9.840 Lbp 154.00 Br md 22.00 Dpth 13.40 Welded, 1 dk	**(A33A2CC) Container Ship (Fully Cellular)** TEU 1004 C Ho 460 TEU C Dk 544 TEU incl 100 ref C. Compartments: 5 Cell Ho, ER 9 Ha: ER Ice Capable	**1 oil engine** driving 1 FP propeller Total Power: 5,649kW (7,680hp) Sulzer 1 x 2 Stroke 6 Cy. 480 x 1400 5649kW (7680bhp) Shanghai Diesel Engine Co Ltd-China AuxGen: 3 x 440kW 400V a.c Fuel: 261.6 (d.f.) 810.9 (r.f.)	15.0kr 6RTA48
9050539 *BRQM* -	**XIANG CANG** *ex* Xian Xia Ling *-1999* **Guangzhou Maritime Transport (Group) Co Ltd** China Shipping Container Lines Co Ltd *Guangzhou, Guangdong* *China* MMSI: 412582000	*13,253* 7,157 20,156	Class: (CC)	**1993**-04 **Shanghai Shipyard — Shanghai** Yd No: 148 Converted From: Bulk Carrier-1993 Loa 164.00 (BB) Br ex - Dght 9.860 Lbp 152.00 Br md 22.00 Dpth 13.50 Welded, 1 dk	**(A33A2CC) Container Ship (Fully Cellular)** TEU 1004 C Ho 460 TEU C Dk 544 TEU incl 100 ref C. Compartments: 5 Ho, ER 5 Ha: (11.2 x 11.2)4 (13.3 x 12.8)ER Ice Capable	**1 oil engine** driving 1 FP propeller Total Power: 5,649kW (7,680hp) Sulzer 1 x 2 Stroke 6 Cy. 480 x 1400 5649kW (7680bhp) Shanghai Diesel Engine Co Ltd-China	15.0kr 6RTA48
7816757 - -	**XIANG CHUN** *ex* Hong Qi 189 *-1999* **Guangzhou Maritime Transport (Group) Co Ltd** *Guangzhou, Guangdong* *China*	**3,921** 1,623 4,887	Class: (CC)	**1980**-12 **Brodogradiliste Split (Brodosplit) — Split** Yd No: 302 Loa 107.00 Br ex 15.24 Dght 6.420 Lbp 98.90 Br md 15.20 Dpth 8.00 Welded, 1 dk	**(A31A2GX) General Cargo Ship** Grain: 6,294 Compartments: 4 Ho, ER 4 Ha: 4 (9.0 x 8.3)ER Derricks: 8x10t; Winches: 8 Ice Capable	**1 oil engine** driving 1 FP propeller Total Power: 2,207kW (3,001hp) Sulzer 1 x 2 Stroke 6 Cy. 440 x 760 2207kW (3001bhp) Tvornica Dizel Motora 'Jugoturbina'-Yugoslavia AuxGen: 3 x 232kW 400V 50Hz a.c	12.8kn 6RD44
7724904 - -	**XIANG DA 757** *ex* Daiko Maru No. 1 *-1998* *ex* Akashi Maru No. 18 *-1985* **Xiang Da Shipping Co Ltd** *Quanzhou, Fujian* *China* MMSI: 412445340 Official number: 080402000330	**967** 541 1,040		**1978**-12 **K.K. Miura Zosensho — Saiki** Yd No: 553 Loa - Br ex - Dght 3.571 Lbp 61.00 Br md 10.50 Dpth 5.34 Welded	**(A31A2GX) General Cargo Ship**	**1 oil engine** driving 1 FP propeller Total Power: 1,030kW (1,400hp) Hanshin 1 x 4 Stroke 6 Cy. 280 x 480 1030kW (1400bhp) Hanshin Nainenki Kogyo-Japan	6LUN28A
8414908 *BPCE* -	**XIANG DAN** *ex* Xin Cheng *-1998* **China Shipping Tanker Co Ltd** China Shipping Container Lines Co Ltd SatCom: Inmarsat C 441243310 *Shanghai* *China* MMSI: 412521000 Official number: 040100915	*4,967* 2,421 6,700	Class: (CC)	**1987**-02 **Zhonghua Shipyard — Shanghai** Yd No: 325 Loa 109.90 Br ex - Dght 7.000 Lbp 99.00 Br md 17.60 Dpth 9.00 Welded, 1 dk	**(A31A2GX) General Cargo Ship**	**1 oil engine** driving 1 FP propeller Total Power: 3,400kW (4,623hp) Sulzer 1 x 2 Stroke 5 Cy. 380 x 1100 3400kW (4623bhp) Sulzer Bros Ltd-Switzerland	12.0kn 5RTA38
7816733 - -	**XIANG DONG** *ex* Hong Qi 187 *-1998* **China Shipping Container Lines Co Ltd** *Guangzhou, Guangdong* *China*	**3,921** 1,623 4,887	Class: (CC)	**1980**-09 **Brodogradiliste Split (Brodosplit) — Split** Yd No: 300 Loa 107.00 Br ex 15.24 Dght 6.420 Lbp 98.90 Br md 15.20 Dpth 8.00 Welded, 1 dk	**(A31A2GX) General Cargo Ship** Grain: 6,294 Compartments: 4 Ho, ER 4 Ha: 4 (9.0 x 8.3)ER Derricks: 8x10t; Winches: 8	**1 oil engine** driving 1 FP propeller Total Power: 2,207kW (3,001hp) Sulzer 1 x 2 Stroke 6 Cy. 440 x 760 2207kW (3001bhp) Tvornica Dizel Motora 'Jugoturbina'-Yugoslavia AuxGen: 3 x 232kW 400V 50Hz a.c	12.8kn 6RD44
8828886 - -	**XIANG FENG** *ex* Hong Qi 154 *-1999* **Shanghai Puhai Shipping Co Ltd** *Shanghai* *China*	**4,119** 1,796 5,205	Class: (CC)	**1985**-07 **Mawei Shipyard — Fuzhou FJ** Loa 105.32 Br ex - Dght 6.500 Lbp 99.00 Br md 16.00 Dpth 9.00 Welded, 2 dks	**(A31A2GX) General Cargo Ship** Grain: 7,654; Bale: 7,041 3 Ha: (10.5 x 8.0) (16.8 x 8.0) (12.6 x 8.0)ER Cranes: 1x10t; Derricks: 3x5t	**1 oil engine** driving 1 FP propeller Total Power: 2,207kW (3,001hp) Hudong 1 x 2 Stroke 6 Cy. 430 x 820 2207kW (3001bhp) Hudong Shipyard-China AuxGen: 3 x 250kW 400V a.c	13.0kn 6ESDZ43/82B
8832564 *BRVV* -	**XIANG FU** *ex* Shi Bao *-1999* **Shanghai Puhai Shipping Co Ltd** *Shanghai* *China* MMSI: 412600000	**4,119** 1,796 5,224	Class: (CC)	**1986 Wuhu Shipyard — Wuhu AH** Loa 105.31 Br ex - Dght 6.520 Lbp 99.00 Br md 16.00 Dpth 9.00 Welded, 2 dks	**(A31A2GX) General Cargo Ship** Grain: 7,654; Bale: 7,041 Compartments: 3 Ho, ER 3 Ha: (10.5 x 8.0) (16.8 x 8.0) (12.6 x 8.0)ER Derricks: 1x10t,3x5t	**1 oil engine** driving 1 FP propeller Total Power: 2,207kW (3,001hp) Hudong 1 x 2 Stroke 6 Cy. 430 x 820 2207kW (3001bhp) Hudong Shipyard-China AuxGen: 3 x 250kW 400V a.c	13.0kn 6ESDZ43/82C
9575371 *XUAL4*	**XIANG HAN 8** **Chan Fong Transport Co Ltd** Zhoushan Yueda Shipping Co Ltd SatCom: Inmarsat C 451434910 *Phnom Penh* *Cambodia* MMSI: 514349000 Official number: 0909398	**2,991** 1,675 5,000	Class: UB (CC)	**2010**-01 **Zhoushan Xintai Shipbuilding & Repair Co Ltd — Zhoushan ZJ** Yd No: 805 Loa 96.90 (BB) Br ex - Dght 5.850 Lbp 89.90 Br md 15.80 Dpth 7.40 Welded, 1 dk	**(A31A2GX) General Cargo Ship** Grain: 6,800; Bale: 6,500	**1 oil engine** reduction geared to sc. shaft driving 1 Propeller Total Power: 1,765kW (2,400hp) Chinese Std. Type 1 x 4 Stroke 8 Cy. 300 x 380 1765kW (2400bhp) Ningbo CSI Power & Machinery GroupCo Ltd-China	11.0kn G8300ZC
8666252 - -	**XIANG HAN SHOU FU 0399** **Wu Liang Qing** *China*	**385** 216 -		**2010**-11 **Taoyuan Dewei Shipbuilding Co Ltd — Taoyuan County HN** Loa 52.00 Br ex - Dght - Lbp - Br md 9.00 Dpth 4.00 Welded, 1 dk	**(B34R2QY) Supply Tender**	**1 oil engine** reduction geared to sc. shaft driving 1 Propeller Total Power: 441kW (600hp) Chinese Std. Type 1 x 441kW (600bhp) Zibo Diesel Engine Factory-China	
8828850 *BRVW* -	**XIANG HENG** *ex* Hong Qi 176 *-1999* **Shanghai Puhai Shipping Co Ltd** *Shanghai* *China* MMSI: 412051080	**4,105** 1,806 5,206	Class: (CC)	**1985 Wuchang Shipyard — Wuhan HB** Loa 105.20 Br ex - Dght 6.500 Lbp 98.90 Br md 16.00 Dpth 9.00 Welded, 2 dks	**(A31A2GX) General Cargo Ship** Grain: 7,655; Bale: 7,041 Compartments: 3 Ho, ER 3 Ha: (10.5 x 8.0) (16.8 x 8.0) (12.6 x 8.0)ER Derricks: 1x10t,3x5t	**1 oil engine** driving 1 FP propeller Total Power: 2,207kW (3,001hp) Hudong 1 x 2 Stroke 6 Cy. 430 x 820 2207kW (3001bhp) Hudong Shipyard-China AuxGen: 3 x 250kW 400V a.c	13.0kn 6ESDZ43/82B
9109873 *BAHO* -	**XIANG HUA** *ex* Tian Du Feng *-2010* *ex* Southern Jaguar *-1998* **Dalian Surui Shipping Co Ltd** Xinao Engery Shipping Co Ltd (Dalian) *Dalian, Liaoning* *China* MMSI: 412207890	**2,075** 965 3,191 T/cm 9.6	Class: (CC) (NK)	**1994**-11 **Fukuoka Shipbuilding Co Ltd — Fukuoka FO** Yd No: 1182 Loa 88.60 (BB) Br ex - Dght 5.500 Lbp 82.00 Br md 13.60 Dpth 6.50 Welded, 1 dk	**(A12B2TR) Chemical/Products Tanker** Liq: 3,351; Liq (Oil): 3,537 Cargo Heating Coils Compartments: 4 Ta, 8 Wing Ta, ER, 2 Wing Slop Ta 9 Cargo Pump (s): 4x100m³/hr, 5x150m³/hr Manifold: Bow/CM: 45.8m	**1 oil engine** driving 1 FP propeller Total Power: 2,405kW (3,270hp) B&W 1 x 2 Stroke 6 Cy. 260 x 980 2405kW (3270bhp) Makita Corp-Japan	13.2kn 6S26MC
9017496 *BPMO* -	**XIANG JI** *ex* Zhen Fen 15 *-1999* **China Shipping Container Lines Co Ltd** SatCom: Inmarsat B 341272910 *Shanghai* *China* MMSI: 412729000	**13,253** 5,744 18,274	Class: CC	**1992**-09 **Shanghai Shipyard — Shanghai** Yd No: 146 Converted From: Bulk Carrier-1999 Loa 164.00 (BB) Br ex - Dght 9.590 Lbp 152.00 Br md 22.00 Dpth 13.40 Welded, 1 dk	**(A33A2CC) Container Ship (Fully Cellular)** Grain: 24,648 TEU 1004 C Ho 460 TEU C Dk 544 TEU incl 100 ref C. Compartments: 5 Ho, ER 5 Ha: (11.2 x 11.2)4 (13.3 x 12.8)ER Ice Capable	**1 oil engine** driving 1 FP propeller Total Power: 5,649kW (7,680hp) Sulzer 1 x 2 Stroke 6 Cy. 480 x 1400 5649kW (7680bhp) Shanghai Diesel Engine Co Ltd-China	15.0kn 6RTA48
8884402 *BPMU* -	**XIANG JIN** *ex* Zhen Fen 21 *-1999* **China Shipping Container Lines Co Ltd** *Shanghai* *China* MMSI: 412503000	**13,253** 5,744 18,274	Class: CC	**1993**-07 **Shanghai Shipyard — Shanghai** Converted From: Bulk Carrier-1999 Loa 164.00 (BB) Br ex - Dght 9.860 Lbp 154.00 Br md 22.00 Dpth 13.40 Welded, 1 dk	**(A33A2CC) Container Ship (Fully Cellular)** TEU 1004 C Ho 460 TEU C Dk 544 TEU incl 100 ref C. Compartments: 5 Cell Ho, ER 9 Ha: ER Ice Capable	**1 oil engine** driving 1 FP propeller Total Power: 4,566kW (6,208hp) Sulzer 1 x 2 Stroke 6 Cy. 480 x 1400 4566kW (6208bhp) Shanghai Shipyard-China AuxGen: 3 x 440kW 400V a.c Fuel: 250.0 (d.f.) 762.0 (r.f.)	14.0kn 6RTA48
8607543 - -	**XIANG JU** *ex* Xing Bao *-1998* **Guangzhou Maritime Transport (Group) Co Ltd** China Shipping Container Lines Co Ltd SatCom: Inmarsat B 341216710 *Guangzhou, Guangdong* *China*	*3,995* 1,918 5,036	Class: (CC) (RN)	**1991**-12 **Santierul Naval Galati S.A. — Galati** Yd No: 817 Loa 101.50 (BB) Br ex - Dght 6.800 Lbp 91.13 Br md 16.40 Dpth 8.60 Welded, 2 dks	**(A31A2GX) General Cargo Ship** Grain: 6,680; Bale: 6,135 TEU 92 C.Ho 68/20' C.Dk 24/20' Compartments: 3 Ho, ER 3 Ha: (7.0 x 13.2)2 (12.7 x 13.2)ER Derricks: 6x5t	**1 oil engine** with flexible couplings & dr reverse geared to sc. shaft driving 1 FP propeller Total Power: 2,758kW (3,750hp) MAN 1 x 4 Stroke 6 Cy. 400 x 540 2758kW (3750bhp) U.C.M. Resita S.A.-Resita	14.0kn 6L40/54A
8414879 *BPCB*	**XIANG LIAN** *ex* Xin Ping *-1998* **China Shipping Tanker Co Ltd** China Shipping Container Lines Co Ltd *Shanghai* *China* MMSI: 412519000 Official number: 040100914	**4,966** 2,464 6,700	Class: (CC)	**1985**-11 **Zhonghua Shipyard — Shanghai** Yd No: 322 Loa 106.90 Br ex - Dght 7.000 Lbp 99.00 Br md 17.60 Dpth 9.00 Welded, 2 dks	**(A31A2GX) General Cargo Ship** TEU 253 C Ho 103 TEU C Dk 150 TEU incl 60 ref C. Compartments: 2 Ho, ER Ice Capable	**1 oil engine** driving 1 FP propeller Total Power: 3,400kW (4,623hp) Sulzer 1 x 2 Stroke 5 Cy. 380 x 1100 3400kW (4623bhp) Sulzer Bros Ltd-Switzerland Fuel: 60.0 (d.f.) 200.0 (r.f.)	5RTA38

8315853 *BRVT* -	**XIANG LING** *ex* Hong Qi 173 *-1999* **Shanghai Puhai Shipping Co Ltd** *Shanghai* *China* MMSI: 412051060	**4,119** 1,769 5,276	Class: (CC)	**1981-04 Guangzhou Wenchong Shipyard — Guangzhou GD** Converted From: General Cargo Ship-1999 Loa 105.27 Br ex - Dght 6.500 Lbp 99.48 Br md 16.00 Dpth 9.00 Welded, 1 dk	**(A33A2CC) Container Ship (Fully Cellular)** TEU 210 C Ho 110 TEU C Dk 100 TEU incl 30 ref C. 10 Ha: ER	**1 oil engine** geared to sc. shaft driving 1 FP propeller Total Power: 3,000kW (4,079hp) 15.5kn Hudong 6ESDZ43/82B 1 x 2 Stroke 6 Cy. 430 x 820 3000kW (4079bhp) Hudong Shipyard-China Fuel: 120.0 (d.f.) 213.0 (r.f.)
8607555 - -	**XIANG LIU** *ex* Liu Bao *-1998* **Guangzhou Maritime Transport (Group) Co Ltd** China Shipping Container Lines Co Ltd *Guangzhou, Guangdong* *China* MMSI: 412550000	*3,995* 1,918 4,870	Class: (CC)	**1986-10 Santierul Naval Braila — Braila** Yd No: 1302 Loa 101.52 Br ex - Dght 6.800 Lbp 94.13 Br md 16.40 Dpth 8.60 Welded	**(A31A2GX) General Cargo Ship**	**1 oil engine** geared to sc. shaft driving 1 FP propeller Total Power: 2,758kW (3,750hp) 14.0kn MAN 6L40/54A 1 x 4 Stroke 6 Cy. 400 x 540 2758kW (3750bhp) U.C.M. Resita S.A.-Resita AuxGen: 3 x 264kW 390V a.c
8864933 *XUBW2* -	**XIANG LONG** *ex* Sankatsura *-2010* **FS Shipping Ltd SA** East Way Marine Co Ltd SatCom: Inmarsat C 451538110 *Phnom Penh* *Cambodia* MMSI: 515381000 Official number: 1092640	**1,541** 817 1,600	Class: UB	**1992-08 Watanabe Zosen KK — Imabari EH** Yd No: 265 Loa 75.20 (BB) Br ex - Dght 4.110 Lbp 70.50 Br md 12.00 Dpth 7.05 Welded, 2 dks	**(A31A2GX) General Cargo Ship** Compartments: 1 Ho, ER	**1 oil engine** reverse geared to sc. shaft driving 1 FP propeller Total Power: 736kW (1,001hp) Niigata 6M31AFTE 1 x 4 Stroke 6 Cy. 310 x 530 736kW (1001bhp) Niigata Engineering Co Ltd-Japan Thrusters: 1 Thwart. FP thruster (f)
9147057 *V3TS8* -	**XIANG LONG NO. 2** *ex* Kisho Maru *-2013* **FS Shipping Ltd SA** East Way Marine Co Ltd *Belize City* *Belize* MMSI: 312738000 Official number: 611320043	**1,481** 629 1,600	Class: IT	**1996-05 Yamanaka Zosen K.K. — Imabari** Yd No: 587 Loa 74.90 (BB) Br ex - Dght 4.080 Lbp 70.00 Br md 12.00 Dpth 7.01 Welded, 1 dk	**(A31A2GX) General Cargo Ship** Grain: 2,852; Bale: 2,791 Compartments: 1 Ho, ER 1 Ha: ER	**1 oil engine** reverse geared to sc. shaft driving 1 FP propeller Total Power: 1,324kW (1,800hp) 11.5kn Hanshin LH30LG 1 x 4 Stroke 6 Cy. 300 x 600 1324kW (1800bhp) The Hanshin Diesel Works Ltd-Japan Thrusters: 1 Thwart. FP thruster (f)
9114799 *BPPE* -	**XIANG MING** - **Yangshan E Shipping Co Ltd** China Shipping Container Lines Co Ltd *Yangshan, Zhejiang* *China* MMSI: 414763000 Official number: CN19947675271	**7,864** 3,802 8,634	Class: CC	**1997-07 SC Santierul Naval SA Braila — Braila** Yd No: 1339 Loa 139.00 (BB) Br ex - Dght 6.700 Lbp 129.70 Br md 20.80 Dpth 8.70 Welded, 1 dk	**(A31A2GX) General Cargo Ship** Grain: 13,882 TEU 514 C Ho 234 TEU C Dk 280 TEU incl 70 ref C. Compartments: 4 Ho, ER 4 Ha: ER	**1 oil engine** driving 1 FP propeller Total Power: 5,670kW (7,709hp) 15.0kn MAN-B&W 6L42MC 1 x 2 Stroke 6 Cy. 420 x 1360 5670kW (7709bhp) U.C.M. Resita S.A.-Resita
9073969 *BPMV* -	**XIANG NING** *ex* Zhen Fen 22 *-1999* **China Shipping Container Lines Co Ltd** - *Shanghai* *China* MMSI: 412504000	**13,396** 5,744 18,274	Class: (CC)	**1995-03 Shanghai Shipyard — Shanghai** Yd No: 153 Converted From: Bulk Carrier-1999 Loa 164.00 (BB) Br ex - Dght 9.590 Lbp 154.00 Br md 22.00 Dpth 13.40 Welded, 1 dk	**(A33A2CC) Container Ship (Fully Cellular)** TEU 1004 C Ho 460 TEU C Dk 544 TEU incl 100 ref C. Compartments: 5 Cell Ho, ER 9 Ha: ER Ice Capable	**1 oil engine** driving 1 FP propeller Total Power: 7,920kW (10,768hp) 15.0kn Sulzer 6RTA48 1 x 2 Stroke 6 Cy. 480 x 1400 7920kW (10768bhp) Shanghai Shipyard-China AuxGen: 3 x 440kW 400V a.c Fuel: 269.8 (d.f.) 798.1 (r.f.)
9073971 *BPMW* -	**XIANG PING** *ex* Zhen Fen 23 *-1999* **China Shipping Container Lines Co Ltd** - SatCom: Inmarsat C 441215210 *Shanghai* *China* MMSI: 412785000	**13,396** 5,744 18,274	Class: CC	**1995-07 Shanghai Shipyard — Shanghai** Yd No: 154 Converted From: Bulk Carrier-1999 Loa 164.00 (BB) Br ex - Dght 9.590 Lbp 154.00 Br md 22.00 Dpth 13.40 Welded, 1 dk	**(A33A2CC) Container Ship (Fully Cellular)** TEU 1004 C Ho 460 TEU C Dk 544 TEU incl 100 ref C. Compartments: 5 Cell Ho, ER 9 Ha: ER Ice Capable	**1 oil engine** driving 1 FP propeller Total Power: 7,920kW (10,768hp) 15.0kn Sulzer 6RTA48 1 x 2 Stroke 6 Cy. 480 x 1400 7920kW (10768bhp) Shanghai Shipyard-China AuxGen: 3 x 440kW 400V a.c Fuel: 269.8 (d.f.) 798.1 (r.f.)
9483102 *BOON* -	**XIANG RUI KOU** *launched as* Xiang An Kou *-2011* **COSCO Shipping Co Ltd (COSCOL)** - *Guangzhou, Guangdong* *China* MMSI: 414017000	**35,568** 10,670 48,293	Class: CC (NV)	**2011-07 Guangzhou Huangpu Shipbuilding Co Ltd — Guangzhou GD** (Hull) Yd No: 3012 **2011-07 Guangzhou Shipyard International Co Ltd — Guangzhou GD** Yd No: 07130002 Loa 216.70 (BB) Br ex 43.10 Dght 9.680 Lbp 212.13 Br md 43.00 Dpth 13.00 Welded, 1 dk	**(A38C3GH) Heavy Load Carrier, semi submersible** Cranes: 2x35t Ice Capable	**4 diesel electric oil engines** driving 4 gen. each 3689kW 6600V a.c Connecting to 2 elec. motors each (5250kW) driving 2 FP propellers Total Power: 15,360kW (20,884hp) 14.0kn Wartsila 8L32 4 x 4 Stroke 8 Cy. 320 x 400 each-3840kW (5221bhp) Thrusters: 2 Tunnel thruster (f)
8712491 *3FRL6* -	**XIANG RUI MEN** *ex* Xiang Gui Men *-2013* *ex* Thor Nexus *-2011* *ex* Seaboard Valparaiso *-2003* *ex* Bellavia *-2002* *ex* Tasman Navigator *-2000* *ex* T.A. Navigator *-1999* *ex* Bellavia *-1993* *ex* Westgate Bridge *-1993* *ex* Bellavia *-1991* **NYB Shipping Inc** Nanjing Ocean Shipping Co Ltd (NASCO) *Panama* *Panama* MMSI: 354654000 Official number: 42015PEXT1	**15,520** 7,689 20,377 T/cm 34.6	Class: BV (GL)	**1989-02 VEB Warnowwerft Warnemuende — Rostock** Yd No: 286 Lengthened-1989 Loa 181.51 (BB) Br ex - Dght 10.072 Lbp 168.41 Br md 23.06 Dpth 13.42 Welded, 2 dks	**(A31A2GX) General Cargo Ship** Passengers: berths: 10 Grain: 27,200; Bale: 25,400 TEU 1128 C Ho 420 TEU C Dk 708 TEU incl 136 ref C Compartments: 4 Ho, ER, 4 Tw Dk 9 Ha: (12.7 x 13.0)2 (12.8 x 7.8)4 (25.3 x 7.8)2 (19.2 x 7.8)ER Cranes: 1x40t,3x25t; Derricks: 1x12.5t Ice Capable	**1 oil engine** driving 1 CP propeller Total Power: 7,950kW (10,809hp) 14.0kn Sulzer 5RTA58 1 x 2 Stroke 5 Cy. 580 x 1700 7950kW (10809bhp) VEB Dieselmotorenwerk Rostock-Rostock AuxGen: 1 x 1000kW 220/380V 50Hz a.c, 3 x 744kW 220/380V 50Hz a.c Thrusters: 1 Thwart. FP thruster (f) Fuel: 315.0 (d.f.) 1106.2 (r.f.) 35.5pd
9657272 *BVGJ8* -	**XIANG RUN 66** - **Xiamen Zhongxiangrun Shipping Service Co Ltd** - *Xiamen, Fujian* *China* MMSI: 413696870	**2,835** 850 2,640	Class: CC	**2012-05 Fujian Changxing Shipbuilding Co Ltd — Fu'an FJ** Yd No: CX10-001TL Loa 73.60 Br ex 18.02 Dght 6.200 Lbp 65.50 Br md 17.20 Dpth 7.50 Welded, 1 dk	**(B21B20T) Offshore Tug/Supply Ship** Ice Capable	**4 oil engines** reduction geared to sc. shafts driving 4 CP propellers Total Power: 7,764kW (10,556hp) 14.3kn Chinese Std. Type 8320ZC 4 x 4 Stroke 8 Cy. 320 x 440 each-1941kW (2639bhp) Guangzhou Diesel Engine Factory CoLtd-China AuxGen: 2 x 1400kW 400V a.c, 2 x 350kW 400V a.c
9523897 *BLAU3* -	**XIANG SHAN 5** - **Xiangshan County Shipping Co Ltd** - SatCom: Inmarsat C 441301578 *Ningbo, Zhejiang* *China* MMSI: 413439970	**4,133** 1,644 5,914	Class: CC	**2012-06 Sanmen Jiantiaogang Shiprepair & Building Co Ltd — Sanmen County ZJ** Yd No: JTG-001 Loa 112.10 Br ex - Dght 6.000 Lbp 105.50 Br md 16.20 Dpth 8.00 Welded, 1 dk	**(A13C2LA) Asphalt/Bitumen Tanker** Double Hull (13F) Liq: 5,521; Liq (Oil): 5,521 Compartments: 5 Wing Ta, 5 Wing Ta, 1 Wing Slop Ta, 1 Wing Slop Ta, ER Ice Capable	**1 oil engine** reduction geared to sc. shaft driving 1 Propeller Total Power: 2,574kW (3,500hp) 12.6kn Yanmar 6N330-EN 1 x 4 Stroke 6 Cy. 330 x 440 2574kW (3500bhp) Qingdao Zichai Boyang Diesel EngineCo Ltd-China AuxGen: 3 x 200kW 400V a.c
8415873 *XUQC8* -	**XIANG SHENG** *ex* Everbloom *-2008* *ex* Zhou Shan 15 *-2001* *ex* Shin Chang 3 *-2000* *ex* Houn Maru *-1999* **Dragon Win Shipping Co Ltd** Shanghai Xiangda Shipping Co Ltd *Phnom Penh* *Cambodia* MMSI: 515321000 Official number: 0884209	**1,209** 588 1,700	Class: UB (GM)	**1984-12 K.K. Matsuura Zosensho — Osakikamijima** Yd No: 317 Loa 71.79 Br ex 11.54 Dght 4.500 Lbp 67.01 Br md 11.51 Dpth 6.41 Welded, 2 dks	**(A31A2GX) General Cargo Ship** Grain: 2,055; Bale: 2,030 Compartments: 1 Ho, ER 1 Ha: ER	**1 oil engine** with clutches, flexible couplings & sr geared to sc. shaft driving 1 CP propeller Total Power: 956kW (1,300hp) Hanshin 6LUN28A 1 x 4 Stroke 6 Cy. 280 x 480 956kW (1300bhp) The Hanshin Diesel Works Ltd-Japan
9057472 *BJRB* -	**XIANG SHUI WAN** *ex* Maritim Frankfurt *-2010* *ex* MSC Boston *-2010* *ex* Norasia Fribourg *-1997* - *Yangpu, Hainan* *China* MMSI: 413014000	**42,323** 17,675 44,510	Class: (CC) (GL)	**1993-12 Howaldtswerke-Deutsche Werft AG (HDW) — Kiel** Yd No: 286 Loa 242.00 (BB) Br ex - Dght 12.460 Lbp 229.50 Br md 32.24 Dpth 23.00 Welded, 1 dk	**(A33A2CC) Container Ship (Fully Cellular)** TEU 3469 incl 198 ref C Compartments: 8 Cell Ho, ER 3 Ha: ER	**1 oil engine** driving 1 FP propeller Total Power: 27,290kW (37,103hp) 22.5kn Mitsubishi 7UEC85LSC 1 x 2 Stroke 7 Cy. 850 x 2360 27290kW (37103bhp) Mitsubishi Heavy Industries Ltd-Japan AuxGen: 1 x 1500kW 400V 60Hz a.c, 2 x 1450kW 400V 60Hz a.c Thrusters: 1 Thwart. CP thruster (f) Fuel: 207.5 (d.f.) 3984.0 (r.f.)
8991138 - -	**XIANG SHUN** *ex* Kang Far *-2008* *ex* Xie Chang 53 *-2005* - - *China*	**1,505** 959 -		**1986 Zhoushan Putuo Yaofeng Shipbuilding Co Ltd — Zhoushan ZJ** Loa 76.00 Br ex - Dght 4.950 Lbp 70.00 Br md 12.00 Dpth 6.00 Welded, 1 dk	**(A31A2GX) General Cargo Ship**	**1 oil engine** driving 1 Propeller Total Power: 883kW (1,201hp) Hanshin 6LU28 1 x 4 Stroke 6 Cy. 280 x 440 883kW (1201bhp) The Hanshin Diesel Works Ltd-Japan
8812837 *BUSJ* -	**XIANG SHUN** *ex* Arevalo *-1996* *ex* Lourdes Giralt *-1996* **Nanjing Changjiang LPG Transportation & Trade Co Ltd** Nanjing Tanker Corp SatCom: Inmarsat C 441294015 *Nanjing, Jiangsu* *China* MMSI: 412077230	**1,970** 591 1,257	Class: CC (GL)	**1990-11 SA Juliana Constructora Gijonesa — Gijon** Yd No: 327 Loa 79.80 (BB) Br ex - Dght 4.100 Lbp 72.80 Br md 12.95 Dpth 5.50 Welded, 1 dk	**(A11B2TG) LPG Tanker** Liq (Gas): 1,600 2 x Gas Tank (s); 2 cyl horizontal 2 Cargo Pump (s): 2x100m³/hr	**1 oil engine** driving 1 FP propeller Total Power: 1,677kW (2,280hp) 13.0kn B&W 5S26MC 1 x 2 Stroke 5 Cy. 260 x 980 1677kW (2280bhp) Astilleros Espanoles SA (AESA)-Spain AuxGen: 3 x 250kW 220/440V a.c

IMO / Call sign	Name / Owner	Tonnage / Class	Builder / Dimensions	Type	Machinery
8607622 - - -	**XIANG SONG** *ex You Yi 22 -1998* **China Shipping Tanker Co Ltd** China Shipping Container Lines Co Ltd *Shanghai* *China*	**3,995** Class: (CC) 1,918 5,060	**1992-10 SC Santierul Naval SA Braila — Braila** Yd No: 1307 Loa 101.50 Br ex - Dght 6.970 Lbp 94.13 Br md 16.60 Dpth 8.60 Welded, 1 dk	**(A31A2GX) General Cargo Ship** Grain: 6,681; Bale: 6,135	**1 oil engine** geared to sc. shaft driving 1 FP propeller Total Power: 2,758kW (3,750hp) 14.0kn MAN 6L40/54A 1 x 4 Stroke 6 Cy. 400 x 540 2758kW (3750bhp) U.C.M. Resita S.A.-Resita
8626551 - - -	**XIANG TONG** *ex Yayoi Maru -2001 ex Yayoi -1996* - -	**1,233** Class: UB 800 1,566	**1985 Yamanaka Zosen K.K. — Imabari** Loa 70.95 Br ex - Dght 4.201 Lbp 65.99 Br md 11.51 Dpth 6.71 Welded, 1 dk	**(A31A2GX) General Cargo Ship** Grain: 2,602; Bale: 2,508	**1 oil engine** driving 1 FP propeller Total Power: 883kW (1,201hp) 10.5kn Hanshin 6LUN28 1 x 4 Stroke 6 Cy. 280 x 480 883kW (1201bhp) The Hanshin Diesel Works Ltd-Japan
9522439 - -	**XIANG TONG 8** - **Weihai City Xiangtong Shipping Co Ltd** - *China*	**2,797** 1,628 4,380	**2008-11 Zhejiang Shipbuilding Co Ltd — Ningbo ZJ** Yd No: 07-086 Loa 95.00 Br ex - Dght 5.900 Lbp 88.00 Br md 13.80 Dpth 7.66 Welded, 1 dk	**(A31A2GX) General Cargo Ship**	**1 oil engine** reduction geared to sc. shaft driving 1 FP propeller Total Power: 1,325kW (1,801hp) Guangzhou 6320ZCD 1 x 4 Stroke 6 Cy. 320 x 440 1325kW (1801bhp) Guangzhou Diesel Engine Factory CoLtd-China
9532123 *XUFH3*	**XIANG TONG 9** - **Yantai Fuhai Shipping Co Ltd** - SatCom: Inmarsat C 451426910 *Phnom Penh* *Cambodia* MMSI: 514269000 Official number: 0909338	**2,797** Class: (CC) 1,628 -	**2009-08 Zhejiang Shipbuilding Co Ltd — Ningbo ZJ** Yd No: HJ0801 Loa 95.00 Br ex Dght - Lbp 88.00 Br md 13.80 Dpth 7.66 Welded, 1 dk	**(A31A2GX) General Cargo Ship**	**1 oil engine** reduction geared to sc. shaft driving 1 FP propeller Total Power: 1,325kW (1,801hp) Guangzhou 6320ZCD 1 x 4 Stroke 6 Cy. 320 x 440 1325kW (1801bhp) Guangzhou Diesel Engine Factory CoLtd-China
9106352 *3FOM5* -	**XIANG WANG** - **PH Xiang Wang Shipping SA** Shanghai Puhai Shipping Co Ltd SatCom: Inmarsat C 435571910 *Panama* *Panama* MMSI: 355719000 Official number: 2248495G	**4,960** Class: CC (LR) 2,665 ✠ Classed LR until 13/3/09 7,069 T/cm 16.6	**1995-10 Daedong Shipbuilding Co Ltd — Busan** Yd No: 399 Loa 112.50 (BB) Br ex 18.23 Dght 6.712 Lbp 105.00 Br md 18.20 Dpth 8.70 Welded, 1 dk	**(A33A2CC) Container Ship (Fully Cellular)** TEU 392 C Ho 151 TEU C Dk 241 TEU Compartments: 6 Ho, ER 6 Ha: ER Ice Capable	**1 oil engine** driving 1 FP propeller Total Power: 3,352kW (4,557hp) 14.0kn B&W 6L35MC 1 x 2 Stroke 6 Cy. 350 x 1050 3352kW (4557bhp) Ssangyong Heavy Industries Co Ltd-South Korea AuxGen: 2 x 400kW 445V 60Hz a.c Boilers: AuxB (Comp) 9.1kgf/cm² (8.9bar)
8664527 - -	**XIANG WANG CAI 9** - **Zhoushan Xiangwang Shiqiao Zhuangyun Gongcheng Co** - *Zhoushan, Zhejiang* *China* MMSI: 412760340 Official number: 2002C2301184	**997** Class: ZC 299 -	**2002-06 Anhui Dangtu Jianghai Shipbuilding Co Ltd — Dangtu County AH** Loa 74.00 Br ex - Dght 1.751 Lbp 69.56 Br md 10.80 Dpth 3.10 Welded, 1 dk	**(B33A2DS) Suction Dredger**	**2 oil engines** driving 2 Propellers Total Power: 662kW (900hp) Chinese Std. Type 2 x each-331kW (450bhp) in China
9106364 *BPPF* -	**XIANG XING** - **Shanghai Puhai Shipping Co Ltd** - *Yangshan, Zhejiang* *China* MMSI: 414765000	**4,960** Class: CC (LR) 2,665 ✠ Classed LR until 6/3/09 7,069 T/cm 16.6	**1995-09 Daedong Shipbuilding Co Ltd — Busan** Yd No: 398 Loa 112.50 (BB) Br ex 18.23 Dght 6.712 Lbp 105.00 Br md 18.20 Dpth 8.70 Welded, 1 dk	**(A33A2CC) Container Ship (Fully Cellular)** TEU 392 C Ho 151 TEU C Dk 241 TEU Compartments: 6 Ho, ER 6 Ha: ER Ice Capable	**1 oil engine** driving 1 FP propeller Total Power: 3,352kW (4,557hp) 14.0kn B&W 6L35MC 1 x 2 Stroke 6 Cy. 350 x 1050 3352kW (4557bhp) Ssangyong Heavy Industries Co Ltd-South Korea AuxGen: 2 x 400kW 445V 60Hz a.c Boilers: AuxB (Comp) 9.1kgf/cm² (8.9bar)
9079822 *3FXY3* -	**XIANG XIU** *ex Dolphin Bravery -1997 ex Xiang Xiu -1996* **Shanghai Puhai Shipping (Hong Kong) Co Ltd** Shanghai Puhai Shipping Co Ltd SatCom: Inmarsat C 435297710 *Panama* *Panama* MMSI: 352977000 Official number: 2130294I	**4,018** Class: CC (NK) 2,007 5,658	**1994-03 Daedong Shipbuilding Co Ltd — Busan** Yd No: 387 Loa 107.77 (BB) Br ex - Dght 6.513 Lbp 99.30 Br md 15.85 Dpth 8.50 Welded, 1 dk	**(A33A2CC) Container Ship (Fully Cellular)** TEU 316 C Ho 138 TEU C Dk 178 TEU incl 50 ref C Compartments: 5 Cell Ho, ER 5 Ha: 5 (12.6 x 12.8)ER	**1 oil engine** driving 1 FP propeller Total Power: 3,354kW (4,560hp) 15.4kn B&W 6L35MC 1 x 2 Stroke 6 Cy. 350 x 1050 3354kW (4560bhp) Ssangyong Heavy Industries Co Ltd-South Korea
9086904 *3FII6* -	**XIANG XUE LAN** - **Common Freesia Chartering SA** China Shipping International Shipmanagement Co Ltd SatCom: Inmarsat A 1360262 *Panama* *Panama* MMSI: 356552000 Official number: 2319596D	**16,071** Class: CC (GL) 5,295 6,512	**1996-03 MTW Schiffswerft GmbH — Wismar** Yd No: 162 Loa 150.54 (BB) Br ex - Dght 7.150 Lbp 137.50 Br md 24.00 Dpth 13.20 Welded, 1 dk	**(A33B2CP) Passenger/Container Ship** Passengers: cabins: 122; berths: 392 TEU 293 incl 30 ref C. Compartments: 3 Ho, ER 3 Ha: 3 (12.8 x 18.2)ER Cranes: 1x36t	**2 oil engines** with clutches & sr geared to sc. shaft driving 1 CP propeller Total Power: 15,000kW (20,394hp) 20.0kn MaK 6M601C 2 x 4 Stroke 6 Cy. 580 x 600 each-7500kW (10197bhp) Krupp MaK Maschinenbau GmbH-Kiel Thrusters: 1 Thwart. CP thruster (f)
9618604 *BTJL* -	**XIANG YANG 8 HAO** - **SIPG Logistics Co Ltd** - *Shanghai* *China*	**4,086** Class: CC 2,288 -	**2011-12 Wison (Nantong) Heavy Industry Co Ltd — Nantong JS** Yd No: M013 Loa 70.80 Br ex - Dght 3.992 Lbp 70.00 Br md 29.60 Dpth 5.50 Welded, 1 dk	**(B34B2SC) Crane Vessel** Cranes: 1	**2 oil engines** reduction geared to sc. shafts driving 2 Propellers Total Power: 1,800kW (2,448hp)
8875011 *BBML* -	**XIANG YANG HONG 06** *ex Hao Li -2012 ex Kai Fu -2007* **Government of The People's Republic of China (North Sea Branch of State Oceanic Administration)** Qingdao Foto International Shipping Management Co Ltd SatCom: Inmarsat A 1572157 *Qingdao, Shandong* *China* MMSI: 413320530	**2,867** Class: CC 1,037 3,421	**1993-03 Donghai Shipyard — Shanghai** Loa 91.00 Br ex - Dght 5.170 Lbp 84.00 Br md 14.70 Dpth 7.60 Welded, 1 dk	**(A31A2GX) General Cargo Ship** Grain: 4,933 TEU 90 C.Ho 90/20' Compartments: 2 Ho, ER 2 Ha: (2.8 x 2.8) (53.2 x 10.4)ER Ice Capable	**1 oil engine** driving 1 FP propeller Total Power: 2,464kW (3,350hp) 13.6kn B&W 4L35MC 1 x 2 Stroke 4 Cy. 350 x 1050 2464kW (3350bhp) Kobe Hatsudoki KK-Japan AuxGen: 3 x 200kW 400V a.c
8425074 *BNPC* -	**XIANG YANG HONG 09** - **Government of The People's Republic of China (North Sea Branch of State Oceanic Administration)** - SatCom: Inmarsat A 1570246 *Qingdao, Shandong* *China* MMSI: 412917000	**3,536** Class: CC 1,060 1,626	**1978 Hudong Shipyard — Shanghai** Loa 112.05 Br ex - Dght 5.514 Lbp 97.50 Br md 15.20 Dpth 8.20 Welded, 2 dks	**(B31A2SR) Research Survey Vessel**	**2 oil engines** driving 2 FP propellers Total Power: 6,620kW (9,000hp) 18.0kn Hudong 9ESDZ43/82B 2 x 2 Stroke 9 Cy. 430 x 820 each-3310kW (4500bhp) Hudong Shipyard-China AuxGen: 4 x 400kW 400V 50Hz a.c
9696199 *BKLS* -	**XIANG YANG HONG 10** - **Zhejiang Tehe Shipping Co Ltd** - *Wenzhou, Zhejiang* *China* MMSI: 413452850	**4,502** Class: CC 1,350 -	**2014-01 Wenzhou Zhongou Shipbuilding Co Ltd — Yueqing ZJ** Yd No: Z01105 Loa 93.00 Br ex - Dght 5.500 Lbp 82.80 Br md 17.40 Dpth 8.80 Welded, 1 dk	**(B31A2SR) Research Survey Vessel**	**2 oil engines** driving 2 gen. each 1500kW 690V Connecting to 2 elec. motors each (1500kW) reduction geared to sc. shafts driving 2 Propellers Total Power: 3,800kW (5,166hp) Chinese Std. Type 2 x 4 Stroke each-1900kW (2583bhp)
8425000 *BNTB* -	**XIANG YANG HONG 14** - **Government of The People's Republic of China (South Sea Branch of the State Oceanic Administration)** - SatCom: Inmarsat C 441292111 *Guangzhou, Guangdong* *China* MMSI: 412921000	**3,141** Class: CC 942 1,739	**1981 Hudong Shipyard — Shanghai** Loa 110.99 Br ex - Dght 5.510 Lbp 97.55 Br md 15.20 Dpth 8.20 Welded, 1 dk	**(B31A2SR) Research Survey Vessel**	**2 oil engines** driving 1 FP propeller Total Power: 13,240kW (18,002hp) 18.8kn Hudong 9ESDZ43/82B 2 x 2 Stroke 9 Cy. 430 x 820 each-6620kW (9001bhp) Hudong Shipyard-China AuxGen: 3 x 400kW 400V 50Hz a.c
8414867 *BPCA* -	**XIANG YING** *ex Xin He -1998* **China Shipping Tanker Co Ltd** - SatCom: Inmarsat C 441249410 *Shanghai* *China* MMSI: 412041040	**4,966** Class: (CC) 2,464 6,700	**1985-09 Zhonghua Shipyard — Shanghai** Yd No: 319 Loa 106.90 Br ex - Dght 8.860 Lbp 99.00 Br md 17.60 Dpth 9.00 Welded, 2 dks	**(A31A2GX) General Cargo Ship** TEU 253 C Ho 103 TEU C Dk 150 TEU incl 60 ref C. Compartments: 2 Ho, ER Ice Capable	**1 oil engine** driving 1 FP propeller Total Power: 3,400kW (4,623hp) Sulzer 5RTA38 1 x 2 Stroke 5 Cy. 380 x 1100 3400kW (4623bhp) Sulzer Bros Ltd-Switzerland Fuel: 77.0 (d.f.) 220.0 (r.f.)

IMO / Call sign	Name / Owner	Tonnage / Class	Builder / Dimensions	Type / Capacity	Machinery
689550 XUGJ4	**XIANG YUAN** **Mr Wang Yiwen** Dana Shipping Co Ltd *Phnom Penh* *Cambodia* MMSI: 515593000	**2,998** Class: UB ZC (Class contemplated) 1,678 5,326	**2013-06 Wenling Yuanyang Shiprepair & Building Co Ltd — Wenling ZJ** Yd No: YY-2012-18 Loa 98.00 Br ex - Dght 5.900 Lbp 91.50 Br md 15.80 Dpth 7.40 Welded, 1 dk	**(A21A2BC) Bulk Carrier** Grain: 6,700	**1 oil engine** reduction geared to sc. shaft driving 1 FP propeller Total Power: 1,765kW (2,400hp) 14.0kn Chinese Std. Type 8320ZC 1 x 4 Stroke 8 Cy. 320 x 440 1765kW (2400bhp) Guangzhou Diesel Engine Factory CoLtd-China
693159 -	**XIANG YUAN JIANG JI 0123** **Lay Shop Lda** - *Freetown* *Sierra Leone* MMSI: 667003421	**1,040** 364 1,600	**2013-01 Yuanjiang Wudaozhou Orient Red Shipbuilding Co Ltd — Yuanjiang HN** Yd No: OR-68 L reg 66.80 Br ex - Dght 2.350 Lbp - Br md 12.45 Dpth 3.00 Welded, 1 dk	**(A31A2GX) General Cargo Ship**	**2 oil engines** reduction geared to sc. shafts driving 2 Propellers Total Power: 550kW (748hp) Chinese Std. Type G128ZLC 2 x 4 Stroke each-275kW (374bhp) Shanghai Diesel Engine Co Ltd-China
3037358 3OJH	**XIANG YUN** **Guangzhou Ocean Shipping Co (COSCOGZ)** - *Tianjin* *China* MMSI: 412239000	**6,241** Class: (CC) 2,838 7,228	**1980-07 Tianjin Xingang Shipyard — Tianjin** Loa 124.00 Br ex - Dght 7.351 Lbp 115.00 Br md 18.00 Dpth 10.40 Welded, 2 dks	**(A31A2GX) General Cargo Ship** Grain: 11,062; Bale: 9,651 Compartments: 4 Ho, ER 4 Ha: 2 (13.3 x 9.0)2 (11.2 x 6.0) Derricks: 1x30t,12x5t; Winches: 12	**1 oil engine** driving 1 FP propeller Total Power: 4,413kW (6,000hp) 15.5kn MAN K6Z52/90N 1 x 2 Stroke 6 Cy. 520 x 900 4413kW (6000bhp) Kawasaki Heavy Industries Ltd-Japan AuxGen: 1 x 340kW 390V 50Hz a.c, 2 x 250kW 390V 50Hz a.c
8113724 XUAD6	**XIANG YUN HAI** *ex* Atalanta 1 *-2009* *ex* Atalanta *-2006* *ex* Jinli *-1998* *ex* Nippo Maru No. 85 *-1996* **Xiang Yun Hai Shipping Pte Ltd** Yantai Dahai Shipping Co Ltd *Phnom Penh* *Cambodia* MMSI: 514308000 Official number: 0982442	**3,663** Class: UB (GL) (NK) 1,958 4,999	**1982-10 Fukuoka Shipbuilding Co Ltd — Fukuoka FO** Yd No: 1100 Loa 106.18 (BB) Br ex 15.52 Dght 6.380 Lbp 98.02 Br md 15.51 Dpth 7.73 Welded, 1 dk	**(A13B2TP) Products Tanker** Liq: 5,550; Liq (Oil): 5,550 Compartments: 8 Ta, ER	**1 oil engine** driving 1 FP propeller Total Power: 2,868kW (3,899hp) 13.5kn Mitsubishi 6UEC37LA 1 x 2 Stroke 6 Cy. 370 x 880 2868kW (3899bhp) Kobe Hatsudoki KK-Japan AuxGen: 2 x 200kW 445V 60Hz a.c Thrusters: 1 Thwart. CP thruster (f) Fuel: 58.5 (d.f.) 281.5 (r.f.) 12.5pd
9483097 BQCW -	**XIANG YUN KOU** **COSCO Shipping Co Ltd (COSCOL)** - SatCom: Inmarsat C 441301575 *Guangzhou, Guangdong* *China* MMSI: 413055620	**35,568** Class: CC (NV) 10,670 48,231	**2011-01 Guangzhou Huangpu Shipbuilding Co Ltd — Guangzhou GD** (Hull) Yd No: 3011 **2011-01 Guangzhou Shipyard International Co Ltd — Guangzhou GD** Yd No: 07130001 Loa 216.70 (BB) Br ex 43.10 Dght 9.680 Lbp 212.13 Br md 43.00 Dpth 13.00 Welded, 1 dk	**(A38C3GH) Heavy Load Carrier, semi submersible** Cranes: 2x35t Ice Capable	**4 diesel electric oil engines** driving 4 gen. each 3689kW 6600V a.c Connecting to 2 elec. motors each (5250kW) driving 2 FP propellers Total Power: 15,360kW (20,884hp) 14.0kn Wartsila 8L32 4 x 4 Stroke 8 Cy. 320 x 400 each-3840kW (5221bhp) AuxGen: 4 x 3689kW 6600V a.c Thrusters: 2 Tunnel thruster (f)
8830542 BRNZ -	**XIANG ZHONG** *ex* Tai Bao *-1999* **Shanghai Puhai Shipping Co Ltd** *Shanghai* *China* MMSI: 412553000	**4,119** Class: (CC) 1,769 5,206	**1986-07 Wuchang Shipyard — Wuhan HB** Loa 105.32 Br ex - Dght 6.500 Lbp 99.00 Br md 16.00 Dpth 9.00 Welded, 2 dks	**(A31A2GX) General Cargo Ship** Grain: 7,654; Bale: 7,041 TEU 150 C.Ho 150/20' (40') Compartments: 3 Ho, ER 3 Ha: (10.5 x 8.0) (16.8 x 8.0) (12.6 x 8.0)ER Derricks: 1x10t,3x5t	**1 oil engine** driving 1 FP propeller Total Power: 2,207kW (3,001hp) 13.0kn Hudong 6ESDZ43/82C 1 x 2 Stroke 6 Cy. 430 x 820 2207kW (3001bhp) Hudong Shipyard-China AuxGen: 3 x 250kW 400V a.c
8747147 T3YR -	**XIANG ZHOU** *ex* Golden Star *-2011* *ex* Wan Mu Chun 18 *-2011* **Feng Xing Guo** Ningbo Shanglun Ship Management Co Ltd *Tarawa* *Kiribati* MMSI: 529378000 Official number: K-13091189	**2,971** Class: IZ 1,663 6,033	**2009-03 Linhai Hangchang Shipbuilding Co Ltd — Linhai ZJ** Yd No: 0902 Loa 96.90 Br ex - Dght - Lbp - Br md 15.80 Dpth 7.40 Welded, 1 dk	**(A31A2GX) General Cargo Ship**	**1 oil engine** reduction geared to sc. shaft driving 1 FP propeller Total Power: 1,766kW (2,401hp) 11.0kn Chinese Std. Type G8300ZC 1 x 4 Stroke 8 Cy. 300 x 380 1766kW (2401bhp) Ningbo CSI Power & Machinery GroupCo Ltd-China
9050541 BRQN -	**XIANG ZHOU** *ex* Feng Xiang Ling *-1999* **Guangzhou Maritime Transport (Group) Co Ltd** China Shipping Container Lines Co Ltd *Guangzhou, Guangdong* *China* MMSI: 412583000	**13,253** Class: (CC) 5,744 20,156	**1993-08 Shanghai Shipyard — Shanghai** Yd No: 149 Converted From: Bulk Carrier-1999 Loa 164.00 (BB) Br ex - Dght 9.840 Lbp 154.00 Br md 22.00 Dpth 13.40 Welded, 1 dk	**(A33A2CC) Container Ship (Fully Cellular)** TEU 1004 C Ho 460 TEU C Dk 544 TEU incl 100 ref C. Compartments: 5 Cell Ho, ER 9 Ha: ER Ice Capable	**1 oil engine** driving 1 FP propeller Total Power: 5,649kW (7,680hp) 14.0kn Sulzer 6RTA48 1 x 2 Stroke 6 Cy. 480 x 1400 5649kW (7680bhp) Shanghai Diesel Engine Co Ltd-China Fuel: 270.0 (d.f.) 797.0 (r.f.)
9114804 BPPC -	**XIANG ZHU** **China Shipping (Group) Co** China Shipping Container Lines Co Ltd *China* MMSI: 414759000	**7,864** Class: CC 3,802 8,634	**1998-04 SC Santierul Naval SA Braila — Braila** Yd No: 1340 Loa 139.40 (BB) Br ex - Dght 6.250 Lbp 129.62 Br md 20.80 Dpth 8.70 Welded, 1 dk	**(A33A2CC) Container Ship (Fully Cellular)** TEU 514 C Ho 234 TEU C Dk 280 TEU incl 70 ref C. Compartments: 4 Cell Ho, ER 4 Ha: (13.3 x 10.8)3 (27.3 x 16.5)ER Ice Capable	**1 oil engine** driving 1 FP propeller Total Power: 5,630kW (7,655hp) 15.0kn MAN-B&W 6L42MC 1 x 2 Stroke 6 Cy. 420 x 1360 5630kW (7655bhp) U.C.M. Resita S.A.-Resita AuxGen: 3 x 440kW a.c
7811111 - -	**XIANGHUA** *ex* Vision *-1998* *ex* Planeta *-1996* *ex* Incotrans Progress *-1985* *ex* Planeta *-1984* *ex* Seaway Dispatch *-1980* **China Shipping Container Lines Co Ltd** - *Haikou, Hainan* *China*	**9,690** Class: (GL) 5,006 13,140	**1979-03 Gebr. Schuerenstedt KG Schiffswerft GmbH & Co. — Berne** Yd No: 1372 Converted From: Container Ship (Fully Cellular)-2005 Loa 145.12 (BB) Br ex 22.08 Dght 8.442 Lbp 134.83 Br md 22.01 Dpth 11.10 Welded, 1 dk	**(B33B2DT) Trailing Suction Hopper Dredger** Grain: 16,314; Bale: 15,253 TEU 602 C Ho 314 TEU C Dk 288 TEU incl 35 ref C. Compartments: 4 Cell Ho, ER 13 Ha: ER Ice Capable	**2 oil engines** reduction geared to sc. shaft driving 1 CP propeller Total Power: 10,004kW (13,602hp) 18.3kn MaK 9M552AK 2 x 4 Stroke 9 Cy. 450 x 520 each-5002kW (6801bhp) MaK Maschinenbau GmbH-Kiel AuxGen: 2 x 480kW 380V 50Hz a.c, 1 x 350kW 380V 50Hz a.c
8662933 3EYZ8 -	**XIANGJING EXPRESS** *ex* Xiang Jing 838 *-2013* *ex* Hua Shun 838 *-2013* *ex* Tong Da 838 *-2010* **Qingdao Shengjing Marine Shipping Co Ltd** Hongkong Xiangjing Shipping Co Ltd *Panama* *Panama* MMSI: 371506000 Official number: 45080PEXTF	**1,904** Class: ZC 1,200 -	**2001-09 Zhejiang Yueqing Qiligang Ship Industry Co Ltd — Yueqing ZJ** Loa 83.90 Br ex - Dght - Lbp - Br md 12.60 Dpth 6.50 Welded, 1 dk	**(A31A2GX) General Cargo Ship**	**1 oil engine** driving 1 FP propeller Total Power: 735kW (999hp) 10.0kn Chinese Std. Type 1 x 735kW (999bhp) Ningbo CSI Power & Machinery GroupCo Ltd-China
8603640 BJLV -	**XIANGZHI** *ex* Patriot *-2007* *ex* Yohfu *-2001* *launched as* Orange Bay *-1987* **Yang Pu Zhe Hai Shipping Co Ltd** *Yangpu, Hainan* *China* MMSI: 413457000	**15,941** Class: (NK) 8,926 26,712 T/cm 37.6	**1987-03 The Hakodate Dock Co Ltd — Hakodate HK** (Hull) Yd No: 732 **1987-03 Kurushima Dockyard Co. Ltd. — Onishi** Yd No: 2437 Loa 167.21 (BB) Br ex 26.29 Dght 9.543 Lbp 160.00 Br md 26.01 Dpth 13.31 Welded, 1 dk	**(A21A2BC) Bulk Carrier** Grain: 33,917; Bale: 32,681 Compartments: 4 Ho, ER 4 Ha: (20.8 x 13.1)3 (23.1 x 13.1)ER Cranes: 4x30.5t	**1 oil engine** driving 1 FP propeller Total Power: 5,074kW (6,899hp) 14.0kn B&W 6L50MCE 1 x 2 Stroke 6 Cy. 500 x 1620 5074kW (6899bhp) Hitachi Zosen Corp-Japan AuxGen: 3 x 360kW 450V 60Hz a.c
9401269 BVBI7 -	**XIAO JIANG** **Fujian Huarong Marine Shipping Group Corp** - *Fuzhou, Fujian* *China* MMSI: 413690160	**4,713** Class: CC 2,526 6,009	**2006-09 Haidong Shipyard — Taizhou ZJ** Yd No: HD2004-03 Loa 116.50 (BB) Br ex - Dght 6.160 Lbp 108.10 Br md 15.90 Dpth 8.20 Welded, 1 dk	**(A33A2CC) Container Ship (Fully Cellular)** TEU 451 C Ho 181 TEU C Dk 270 TEU incl 40 ref C	**1 oil engine** reduction geared to sc. shaft driving 1 FP propeller Total Power: 2,970kW (4,038hp) 14.0kn MaK 9M25 1 x 4 Stroke 9 Cy. 255 x 400 2970kW (4038bhp) Caterpillar Motoren GmbH & Co. KG-Germany AuxGen: 3 x 250kW 400V a.c
9592044 VRJN2 -	**XIAO YU** **Hai Kuo Shipping 1226 Ltd** Shandong Shipping Corp *Hong Kong* *Hong Kong* MMSI: 477091200 Official number: HK-3294	**41,260** Class: AB 25,658 76,116 T/cm 68.6	**2012-01 Hudong-Zhonghua Shipbuilding (Group) Co Ltd — Shanghai** Yd No: H1642A Loa 225.00 (BB) Br ex - Dght 14.250 Lbp 217.00 Br md 32.26 Dpth 19.70 Welded, 1 dk	**(A21A2BC) Bulk Carrier** Grain: 90,540; Bale: 89,882 Compartments: 7 Ho, ER 7 Ha: ER	**1 oil engine** driving 1 FP propeller Total Power: 10,000kW (13,596hp) 14.5kn MAN-B&W 5S60MC-C 1 x 2 Stroke 5 Cy. 600 x 2400 10000kW (13596bhp) Hudong Heavy Machinery Co Ltd-China AuxGen: 3 x 570kW a.c Fuel: 267.0 (d.f.) 2709.0 (r.f.)
9141601 BIPD -	**XIAO YUN** *ex* Blue Clouds *-2008* *ex* Su Yue *-2006* *ex* Yue Da 18 *-1997* **Shanghai Hai Hua Shipping Co Ltd (HASCO)** - *Shanghai* *China* MMSI: 413371280	**3,805** Class: CC 1,480 4,340	**1996-10 Chengxi Shipyard — Jiangyin JS** Yd No: 9501-2 Loa 93.00 Br ex - Dght 5.660 Lbp 84.80 Br md 17.60 Dpth 7.80 Welded, 1 dk	**(A31A2GX) General Cargo Ship** Grain: 5,425; Bale: 5,425 TEU 300 C. 300/20' Compartments: 2 Ho, ER 2 Ha: (25.4 x 12.6)ER (18.9 x 12.6)Tappered Ice Capable	**1 oil engine** driving 1 FP propeller Total Power: 3,360kW (4,568hp) 14.0kn B&W 6L35MC 1 x 2 Stroke 6 Cy. 350 x 1050 3360kW (4568bhp) Yichang Marine Diesel Engine Co Ltd-China AuxGen: 2 x 292kW 400V a.c

Identity	Name / Owner	Tonnage	Class	Builder / Dimensions	Type / Capacity	Machinery
9610509 *2ER09* -	**XIAOYI C** **Medina 8000 Ltd** Carisbrooke Shipping Ltd *Douglas* *Isle of Man (British)* MMSI: 235087579 Official number: 742874	**5,629** 2,877 8,053 T/cm 17.8	Class: LR (GL) **100A1** SS 09/2011 strengthened for heavy cargoes LI **LMC** **UMS** Cable: 385.0/46.0 U3 (a)	**2011-09 Jiangsu Yangzijiang Shipbuilding Co Ltd — Jiangyin JS** Yd No: 2008-828 Loa 108.20 (BB) Br ex 18.48 Dght 7.057 Lbp 103.90 Br md 18.20 Dpth 9.00 Welded, 1 dk	**(A31A2GX) General Cargo Ship** Grain: 10,255; Bale: 10,255 Compartments: 3 Ho, ER 3 Ha: 2 (25.9 x 15.2)ER (17.5 x 15.2) Cranes: 2x25t Ice Capable	**1 oil engine** with flexible couplings & dr geared to sc. shaft driving 1 CP propeller Total Power: 3,000kW (4,079hp) 12.4kr MaK 6M32C 1 x 4 Stroke 6 Cy. 320 x 480 3000kW (4079bhp) Caterpillar Motoren GmbH & Co. KG-Germany AuxGen: 1 x 360kW 60Hz a.c, 2 x 500kW 440V 60Hz a.c Boilers: AuxB (o.f.) 7.2kgf/cm² (7.1bar) Thrusters: 1 Thwart. FP thruster (f)
9139048 *BORY* -	**XIBOHE** **Shanghai Panasia Shipping Co Ltd** COSCO Container Lines Co Ltd (COSCON) *Shanghai* *China* MMSI: 412110000	**36,772** 21,268 44,911 T/cm 64.6	Class: CC (LR) ✠ Classed LR until 7/12/12	**1997-12 Samsung Heavy Industries Co Ltd — Geoje** Yd No: 1200 Loa 242.85 (BB) Br ex 32.28 Dght 12.023 Lbp 226.70 Br md 32.20 Dpth 19.00 Welded, 1 dk	**(A33A2CC) Container Ship (Fully Cellular)** TEU 3400 C Ho 1460 TEU C Dk 1940 TEU incl 300 ref C. Compartments: ER, 7 Cell Ho 13 Ha: ER	**1 oil engine** driving 1 FP propeller Total Power: 20,595kW (28,001hp) 21.0kn B&W 6L80MC 1 x 2 Stroke 6 Cy. 800 x 2592 20595kW (28001bhp) Samsung Heavy Industries Co Ltd-South Korea AuxGen: 3 x 1470kW 450V 60Hz a.c Boilers: e (ex.g.) 11.7kgf/cm² (11.5bar), AuxB (o.f.) 6.9kgf/cm² (6.8bar) Thrusters: 1 Thwart. FP thruster (f)
9357157 *XCHW7* -	**XICALANGO** *completed as* Bourbon Himalia *-2007* **Naviera Bourbon Tamaulipas SA de CV** SatCom: Inmarsat C 434501010 *Tampico* *Mexico* MMSI: 345010043	**2,542** 762 3,230	Class: GL (BV)	**2007-01 Zhejiang Shipbuilding Co Ltd — Ningbo ZJ** Yd No: 05-134 Loa 73.20 Br ex - Dght 5.630 Lbp 70.76 Br md 16.50 Dpth 6.80 Welded, 1 dk	**(B21A2OS) Platform Supply Ship**	**3 diesel electric oil engines** driving 3 gen. each 1825kW 440V a.c Connecting to 2 elec. motors each (1920kW) driving 2 Z propellers Total Power: 5,475kW (7,443hp) 11.5kn Cummins QSK60-M 3 x Vee 4 Stroke 16 Cy. 159 x 190 each-1825kW (2481bhp) Chongqing Cummins Engine Co Ltd-China Thrusters: 2 Thwart. CP thruster (f) Fuel: 1736.6 (r.f.)
7815105 - -	**XIE CHENG** *ex* Hyupsung G-3 *-2004* *ex* Shoun Maru *-2004* - -	*496* 206 -		**1978-08 Kochi Jyuko K.K. — Kochi** Yd No: 1277 Loa - Br ex - Dght 2.852 Lbp 43.01 Br md 16.01 Dpth 3.41 Riveted\Welded, 1 dk	**(B34B2SC) Crane Vessel** Cranes: 1x120t	**2 oil engines** driving 1 FP propeller Total Power: 882kW (1,200hp) Yanmar 6MAL-DHT 2 x 4 Stroke 6 Cy. 200 x 240 each-441kW (600bhp) Yanmar Diesel Engine Co Ltd-Japan
8891352 - -	**XIE HANG 228** *ex* Hai Lung No. 2 *-2003* **Guangdong Xiehang Transportation Co Ltd** - *China*	**1,391** 547 2,337	Class: (CC)	**1995 Qidong Fishing Vessel Shipyard — Qidong JS** Yd No: 4 Loa 59.30 Br ex - Dght 4.183 Lbp 51.88 Br md 17.07 Dpth 4.97 Welded, 1 dk	**(A31A2GX) General Cargo Ship**	**2 oil engines** geared to sc. shafts driving 2 FP propellers Total Power: 764kW (1,038hp) Chinese Std. Type 6200Z 2 x 4 Stroke 6 Cy. 200 x 225 each-382kW (519bhp) Weifang Diesel Engine Factory-China
8891340 - -	**XIE HANG 238** *ex* Wan Lung *-2003* **Guangdong Xiehang Transportation Co Ltd** - *China*	**1,391** 547 2,337	Class: (CC)	**1995-07 Qidong Fishing Vessel Shipyard — Qidong JS** Yd No: 3 Loa 59.30 Br ex - Dght 4.183 Lbp 51.88 Br md 17.07 Dpth 4.97 Welded, 1 dk	**(A31A2GX) General Cargo Ship**	**2 oil engines** geared to sc. shafts driving 2 FP propellers Total Power: 764kW (1,038hp) Chinese Std. Type 6200Z 2 x 4 Stroke 6 Cy. 200 x 225 each-382kW (519bhp) Weifang Diesel Engine Factory-China
9071155 *BNCY* -	**XIE RONG 11** *ex* Timber Trader XII *-2007* **Glory Navigation Co Ltd** - *Keelung* *Chinese Taipei* MMSI: 416424000 Official number: 014813	**5,543** 2,393 6,993	Class: CR NK	**1994-04 Nishi Shipbuilding Co Ltd — Imabari EH** (Hull) Yd No: 381 **1994-04 Imabari Shipbuilding Co Ltd — Imabari EH (Imabari Shipyard)** Loa 97.55 (BB) Br ex - Dght 7.422 Lbp 89.95 Br md 18.80 Dpth 12.90 Welded, 1 dk	**(A31A2GX) General Cargo Ship** Grain: 13,539; Bale: 12,319 Compartments: 2 Ho, ER 2 Ha: (22.4 x 10.2) (25.2 x 10.2)ER Cranes: 2x25t,2x15t	**1 oil engine** driving 1 FP propeller Total Power: 3,236kW (4,400hp) 10.5kn Mitsubishi 6UEC33LSII 1 x 2 Stroke 6 Cy. 330 x 1050 3236kW (4400bhp) Akasaka Tekkosho KK (Akasaka DieselLtd)-Japan AuxGen: 2 x 220kW 440V 60Hz a.c Fuel: 53.5 (d.f.) 250.3 (r.f.) 13.0pd
9473389 *BPAF* -	**XIN AN YANG** **China Shipping Tanker Co Ltd** *Shanghai* *China* MMSI: 413157000 Official number: 010007000257	**152,740** 97,129 297,491 T/cm 177.9	Class: CC	**2007-11 Dalian Shipbuilding Industry Co Ltd — Dalian LN (No 2 Yard)** Yd No: T2980-3 Loa 330.00 (BB) Br ex 60.05 Dght 21.502 Lbp 316.00 Br md 60.00 Dpth 29.70 Welded, 1 dk	**(A13A2TV) Crude Oil Tanker** Double Hull (13F) Liq: 324,601; Liq (Oil): 324,601 Compartments: 5 Ta, 10 Wing Ta, 2 Wing Slop Ta, ER 3 Cargo Pump (s): 3x5500m³/hr Manifold: Bow/CM: 162.5m	**1 oil engine** driving 1 FP propeller Total Power: 25,480kW (34,643hp) 15.8kn MAN-B&W 7S80MC 1 x 2 Stroke 7 Cy. 800 x 3056 25480kW (34643bhp) Dalian Marine Diesel Works-China AuxGen: 3 x 950kW 450V 60Hz a.c Fuel: 429.6 (d.f.) 7117.3 (r.f.)
9590553 *BLMJ* -	**XIN AO TAI 1** **Yueqin City Lida Ocean Shipping Co Ltd** *Wenzhou, Zhejiang* *China* MMSI: 413438570	**11,258** 5,188 16,774	Class: CC	**2010-07 Zhejiang Aotai Shipbuilding Co Ltd — Yueqing ZJ** Yd No: AT0615 Loa 145.50 Br ex - Dght 8.800 Lbp 136.20 Br md 23.00 Dpth 12.50 Welded, 1 dk	**(A12B2TR) Chemical/Products Tanker** Double Hull (13F) Liq: 19,160; Liq (Oil): 19,160 Compartments: 6 Wing Ta, 6 Wing Ta, 1 Wing Slop Ta, 1 Wing Slop Ta, ER Ice Capable	**1 oil engine** driving 1 FP propeller Total Power: 3,810kW (5,180hp) 14.0kn MAN-B&W 7S35MC 1 x 2 Stroke 7 Cy. 350 x 1400 3810kW (5180bhp) STX Engine Co Ltd-South Korea AuxGen: 3 x 560kW 450V a.c
8905933 *BPAK* -	**XIN BEI HAI** *ex* Marmara *-2010* *ex* MSC Marmara *-2010* *ex* Marmara Sea *-2008* *ex* Zim Dalian *-2005* *ex* Choyang Victory *-1998* **China Shipping Container Lines Co Ltd** - *China* MMSI: 413174000	**36,584** 15,135 44,025 T/cm 64.4	Class: (LR) (KR) (AB) Classed LR until 12/6/10	**1990-10 Daewoo Shipbuilding & Heavy Machinery Ltd — Geoje** Yd No: 4022 Loa 240.00 (BB) Br ex - Dght 11.717 Lbp 224.09 Br md 32.21 Dpth 19.00 Welded, 1 dk	**(A33A2CC) Container Ship (Fully Cellular)** Double Bottom Entire Compartment Length TEU 2797 C Ho 1350 TEU C Dk 1447 TEU incl 99 ref C. Compartments: ER, 7 Cell Ho 14 Ha: 24 Wing Ha:	**1 oil engine** driving 1 FP propeller Total Power: 24,455kW (33,249hp) 22.0kn Sulzer 7RTA84 1 x 2 Stroke 7 Cy. 840 x 2400 24455kW (33249bhp) Hyundai Heavy Industries Co Ltd-South Korea AuxGen: 3 x 1000kW 440V 60Hz a.c Thrusters: 1 Thwart. CP thruster (f) Fuel: 253.9 (d.f.) 3801.1 (r.f.) 90.4pd
9309966 *BPBR* -	**XIN BEI LUN** **China Shipping Container Lines Co Ltd** *Shanghai* *China* MMSI: 413145000	**41,482** 24,001 52,223	Class: CC	**2005-10 Dalian New Shipbuilding Heavy Industries Co Ltd — Dalian LN** Yd No: C4250-4 Loa 263.23 (BB) Br ex 32.30 Dght 12.800 Lbp 251.88 Br md 32.25 Dpth 19.30 Welded, 1 dk	**(A33A2CC) Container Ship (Fully Cellular)** TEU 4250 C Ho 1586 TEU C Dk 2664 TEU incl 400 ref C. Ice Capable	**1 oil engine** driving 1 FP propeller Total Power: 36,480kW (49,598hp) 24.2kn MAN-B&W 8K90MC-C 1 x 2 Stroke 8 Cy. 900 x 2300 36480kW (49598bhp) Mitsui Engineering & Shipbuilding CLtd-Japan AuxGen: 3 x 1960kW 450V 60Hz a.c Thrusters: 1 Thwart. CP thruster (f)
9314246 *VRCS5* -	**XIN BEIJING** **Yangshan D Shipping Co Ltd** China International Ship Management Co Ltd (CISM) SatCom: Inmarsat C 447700661 *Hong Kong* *Hong Kong* MMSI: 477768100 Official number: HK-1882	**108,069** 57,365 111,571	Class: LR ✠ **100A1** SS 04/2012 container ship **ShipRight** (SDA, FDA, CM) *IWS LI EP ✠ **LMC** **UMS** Eq.Ltr: c*; Cable: 759.0/111.0 U3 (a)	**2007-04 Samsung Heavy Industries Co Ltd — Geoje** Yd No: 1567 Loa 336.70 (BB) Br ex 45.64 Dght 15.030 Lbp 321.97 Br md 45.60 Dpth 27.20 Welded, 1 dk	**(A33A2CC) Container Ship (Fully Cellular)** TEU 9572 C Ho 4666 TEU C Dk 4906 TEU incl 700 ref C. Compartments: 9 Cell Ho, ER	**1 oil engine** driving 1 FP propeller Total Power: 68,520kW (93,160hp) 25.2kn MAN-B&W 12K98MC-C 1 x 2 Stroke 12 Cy. 980 x 2400 68520kW (93160bhp) Doosan Engine Co Ltd-South Korea AuxGen: 4 x 2750kW 6600V 60Hz a.c Boilers: e (ex.g.) 8.2kgf/cm² (8.0bar), WTAuxB (o.f.) 8.2kgf/cm² (8.0bar) Thrusters: 1 Thwart. CP thruster (f)
8661276 - -	**XIN BI HAI 1** *ex* Jin Shan Quan 1 *-2007* **PT Majukarsa Perdana Jaya Line** -	**1,706** 955 -	Class: IZ	**2002-08 Yueqing Donggang Shipbuilding Co Ltd — Yueqing ZJ** Loa 81.50 Br ex - Dght 5.400 Lbp 75.50 Br md 12.00 Dpth 6.50 Welded, 1 dk	**(A31A2GX) General Cargo Ship**	**1 oil engine** reduction geared to sc. shaft driving 1 FP propeller Total Power: 735kW (999hp) Chinese Std. Type 6300ZC 1 x 4 Stroke 6 Cy. 300 x 380 735kW (999bhp) Ningbo CSI Power & Machinery GroupCo Ltd-China
8306773 *BVFB5* -	**XIN BIN CHENG** *ex* Bin Cheng *-2009* **Fujian Changan Shipping Co Ltd** - SatCom: Inmarsat A 1570743 *Quanzhou, Fujian* *China* MMSI: 412187000	**9,683** 4,637 13,508	Class: (CC)	**1985 Dalian Shipyard Co Ltd — Dalian LN** Yd No: C120/5 Converted From: Container Ship (Fully Cellular)-2009 Loa 147.50 (BB) Br ex - Dght 8.000 Lbp 138.00 Br md 22.20 Dpth 10.90 Welded, 1 dk	**(A21A2BC) Bulk Carrier** Grain: 16,567; Bale: 15,999 Compartments: 3 Ho, ER 3 Ha: ER Ice Capable	**1 oil engine** driving 1 FP propeller Total Power: 5,502kW (7,481hp) 14.0kn B&W 5L55GB 1 x 2 Stroke 5 Cy. 550 x 1380 5502kW (7481bhp) Dalian Marine Diesel Works-China Thrusters: 1 Tunnel thruster (f)

IMO / Call sign	Name / Owner / Registry	Tonnage	Class	Builder / Dimensions	Type / Cargo	Machinery
9492098 3EYB5	**XIN BIN HAI** **China Neptune Shipping Inc** Vision Ship Management Ltd SatCom: Inmarsat C 435320411 *Panama* *Panama* MMSI: 353204000 Official number: 4151810	**94,863** 59,660 180,086 T/cm 124.3	Class: LR ✠ **100A1** SS 03/2010 bulk carrier CSR BC-A GRAB (25) Nos. 2, 4, 6 & 8 holds may be empty ESP **ShipRight** (CM) *IWS LI ✠ **LMC** **UMS** Eq.Ltr: B*; Cable: 742.5/107.0 U3 (a)	**2010**-03 **Dalian Shipbuilding Industry Co Ltd — Dalian LN (No 2 Yard)** Yd No: BC1800-27 Loa 294.47 (BB) Br ex 46.12 Dght 18.100 Lbp 284.81 Br md 46.00 Dpth 24.79 Welded, 1 dk	**(A21A2BC) Bulk Carrier** Grain: 201,953 Compartments: 9 Ho, ER 9 Ha: 7 (15.5 x 20.0)ER 2 (15.5 x 16.5)	**1 oil engine** driving 1 FP propeller Total Power: 18,660kW (25,370hp) 14.5kn MAN-B&W 6S70MC-C 1 x 2 Stroke 6 Cy. 700 x 2800 18660kW (25370bhp) Dalian Marine Diesel Co Ltd-China AuxGen: 3 x 900kW 450V 60Hz a.c Boilers: AuxB (Comp) 8.9kgf/cm^2 (8.7bar)
9051222 BVJW5 -	**XIN BIN JIANG** *ex* Da Xin Hua Lian Yun Gang *-2014* *ex* Conti Germany *-2010* *ex* MSC Victoria *-2001* *ex* Contship Germany *-1998* **Fujian Changan Shipping Co Ltd** - *Quanzhou, Fujian* *China* MMSI: 413699440	**16,236** 9,475 23,596 T/cm 36.1	Class: CC (GL)	**1992**-11 **Bremer Vulkan AG Schiffbau u. Maschinenfabrik — Bremen** Yd No: 105 Loa 164.05 (BB) Br ex - Dght 10.661 Lbp 153.70 Br md 27.50 Dpth 14.30 Welded, 1 dk	**(A33A2CC) Container Ship (Fully Cellular)** Passengers: berths: 7 Grain: 32,650; Bale: 32,025 TEU 1599 C Ho 618 TEU C Dk 981 TEU incl 70 ref C. Compartments: 3 Cell Ho, ER 8 Ha: 8 (12.5 x 23.1)ER Cranes: 3x40t Ice Capable	**1 oil engine** driving 1 FP propeller Total Power: 10,440kW (14,194hp) 18.0kn B&W 6L60MC 1 x 2 Stroke 6 Cy. 600 x 1944 10440kW (14194bhp) Bremer Vulkan AG Schiffbau u.Maschinenfabrik-Bremen AuxGen: 1 x 800kW 230/450V a.c, 2 x 785kW 230/450V a.c, 1 x 524kW 230/450V a.c Thrusters: 1 Thwart. FP thruster (f) Fuel: 185.1 (d.f.) 1928.1 (r.f.) 48.3pd
9579444 BVGL5 -	**XIN BO LIN 3** **Mintai Shipping Co Ltd** - SatCom: Inmarsat C 441301698 *Quanzhou, Fujian* *China* MMSI: 413695970	**21,744** 10,954 32,650	Class: CC	**2011**-03 **Linhai Hongsheng Shipbuilding Co Ltd — Linhai ZJ** Yd No: 2007-22 Loa 179.90 (BB) Br ex 28.64 Dght 10.000 Lbp 172.00 Br md 28.60 Dpth 14.60 Welded, 1 dk	**(A21A2BC) Bulk Carrier** Grain: 41,625 Compartments: 5 Ho, ER 5 Ha: ER 5 (16.8 x 16.8) Cranes: 4x30t Ice Capable	**1 oil engine** driving 1 FP propeller Total Power: 6,480kW (8,810hp) 13.5kn MAN-B&W 6S42MC 1 x 2 Stroke 6 Cy. 420 x 1764 6480kW (8810bhp) Yichang Marine Diesel Engine Co Ltd-China AuxGen: 3 x 500kW 400V a.c
9523093 BPKL -	**XIN CANG ZHOU** **China Shipping Container Lines Co Ltd** - *Shanghai* *China* MMSI: 414758000	**47,917** 24,185 67,001	Class: CC	**2013**-05 **Shanghai Jiangnan Changxing Heavy Industry Co Ltd — Shanghai** Yd No: H1056A Loa 255.10 (BB) Br ex - Dght 13.000 Lbp 242.00 Br md 37.30 Dpth 19.60 Welded, 1 dk	**(A33A2CC) Container Ship (Fully Cellular)** TEU 4738 C Ho 1826 TEU C Dk 2912 TEU incl 300 ref C	**1 oil engine** driving 1 FP propeller Total Power: 21,910kW (29,789hp) 18.0kn Wartsila 7RT-flex68 1 x 2 Stroke 7 Cy. 680 x 2720 21910kW (29789bhp) Doosan Engine Co Ltd-South Korea
9312559 BPBS -	**XIN CHANG SHA** **China Shipping Container Lines Co Ltd** - *Shanghai* *China* MMSI: 413146000	**41,482** 24,001 52,214	Class: CC	**2005**-11 **Dalian New Shipbuilding Heavy Industries Co Ltd — Dalian LN** Yd No: C4250-5 Loa 263.23 (BB) Br ex 32.30 Dght 12.800 Lbp 251.88 Br md 32.25 Dpth 19.30 Welded, 1 dk	**(A33A2CC) Container Ship (Fully Cellular)** TEU 4250 C Ho 1586 TEU C Dk 2664 TEU incl 400 ref C. Compartments: 7 Cell Ho, ER Ice Capable	**1 oil engine** driving 1 FP propeller Total Power: 36,480kW (49,598hp) 24.2kn MAN-B&W 8K90MC-C 1 x 2 Stroke 8 Cy. 900 x 2300 36480kW (49598bhp) Mitsui Engineering & Shipbuilding CLtd-Japan AuxGen: 3 x 1960kW 450V 60Hz a.c Thrusters: 1 Tunnel thruster (f)
9304813 BPBG -	**XIN CHANG SHU** **China Shipping Container Lines Co Ltd** - SatCom: Inmarsat C 441313310 *Shanghai* *China* MMSI: 413133000	**66,452** 37,567 69,229	Class: CC	**2005**-07 **Hudong-Zhonghua Shipbuilding (Group) Co Ltd — Shanghai** Yd No: H1355A Loa 279.90 (BB) Br ex - Dght 14.000 Lbp 265.80 Br md 40.30 Dpth 24.10 Welded, 1 dk	**(A33A2CC) Container Ship (Fully Cellular)** TEU 5668 C Ho 2586 TEU C Dk 3082 TEU incl 610 ref C.	**1 oil engine** driving 1 FP propeller Total Power: 54,720kW (74,397hp) 25.7kn MAN-B&W 12K90MC-C 1 x 2 Stroke 12 Cy. 900 x 2300 54720kW (74397bhp) Mitsui Engineering & Shipbuilding CLtd-Japan AuxGen: 4 x 2320kW 450/230V 60Hz a.c Thrusters: 1 Tunnel thruster (f)
8222678 - -	**XIN CHAO** *ex* Man Chiu *-2002* - -	**1,439** 558 439		**1983**-04 **Taiwan Machinery Manufacturing Corp. — Kaohsiung** Yd No: 721 Loa 63.53 Br ex 13.42 Dght 3.150 Lbp - Br md - Dpth 4.45 Welded, 1 dk	**(A36A2PR) Passenger/Ro-Ro Ship (Vehicles)** Passengers: unberthed: 1728	**2 oil engines** with clutches, flexible couplings & dr reverse geared to sc. shafts driving 2 Directional propellers Total Power: 2,200kW (2,992hp) MAN 12V20/27 2 x Vee 4 Stroke 12 Cy. 200 x 270 each-1100kW (1496bhp) Maschinenbau Augsburg Nuernberg (MAN)-Augsburg
8321711 BVKJ7 -	**XIN CHAO HE** *ex* Chao He *-2012* **Shanghai PanAsia Shipping Co Ltd** - SatCom: Inmarsat C 441240610 *Fuzhou, Fujian* *China* MMSI: 412173000	**19,835** 9,455 25,545	Class: (CC) (GL)	**1985**-02 **Seebeckwerft AG — Bremerhaven** Yd No: 1046 Loa 170.02 (BB) Br ex 28.61 Dght 10.702 Lbp 158.20 Br md 28.40 Dpth 15.45 Welded, 1 dk	**(A33A2CC) Container Ship (Fully Cellular)** TEU 1328 C Ho 676 TEU C Dk 652 TEU incl 54 ref C. Compartments: 5 Cell Ho, ER 8 Ha: 8 (12.9 x 5.4)ER 16 Wing Ha: 2 (12.9 x 2.8)14 (12.9 x 8.1) Ice Capable	**1 oil engine** driving 1 FP propeller Total Power: 10,797kW (14,680hp) 17.0kn B&W 6L70MCE 1 x 2 Stroke 6 Cy. 700 x 2268 10797kW (14680bhp) Kawasaki Heavy Industries Ltd-Japan AuxGen: 1 x 1100kW 450V 60Hz a.c, 2 x 800kW 450V 60Hz a.c, 1 x 440kW 450V 60Hz a.c Thrusters: 1 Thwart. FP thruster (f)
9304772 BPBC -	**XIN CHI WAN** **China Shipping Container Lines Co Ltd** - SatCom: Inmarsat C 441307210 *Shanghai* *China* MMSI: 413072000 Official number: 010004000089	**66,452** 37,567 69,271	Class: CC	**2004**-06 **Hudong-Zhonghua Shipbuilding (Group) Co Ltd — Shanghai** Yd No: H1351A Loa 279.60 (BB) Br ex - Dght 14.000 Lbp 265.80 Br md 40.30 Dpth 24.10 Welded, 1 dk	**(A33A2CC) Container Ship (Fully Cellular)** TEU 5668 C Ho 2586 TEU C Dk 3082 TEU incl 610 ref C. Compartments: 7 Cell Ho, ER	**1 oil engine** driving 1 FP propeller Total Power: 54,809kW (74,518hp) 25.7kn MAN-B&W 12K90MC-C 1 x 2 Stroke 12 Cy. 900 x 2300 54809kW (74518bhp) Mitsui Engineering & Shipbuilding CLtd-Japan AuxGen: 4 x 2320kW 450/230V 60Hz a.c Thrusters: 1 Tunnel thruster (f)
9262118 BPBH -	**XIN CHONG QING** **China Shipping Container Lines Co Ltd** - SatCom: Inmarsat C 441305510 *Shanghai* *China* MMSI: 413055000	**41,482** 24,001 50,188	Class: CC (AB)	**2003**-08 **Hudong-Zhonghua Shipbuilding (Group) Co Ltd — Shanghai** Yd No: H1293A Loa 263.23 (BB) Br ex - Dght 12.820 Lbp 251.40 Br md 32.20 Dpth 19.30 Welded, 1 dk	**(A33A2CC) Container Ship (Fully Cellular)** TEU 4051 C Ho 1586 TEU C Dk 2465 TEU incl 400 ref C. Compartments: 7 Cell Ho, ER Ice Capable	**1 oil engine** driving 1 FP propeller Total Power: 36,543kW (49,684hp) 24.2kn MAN-B&W 8K90MC-C 1 x 2 Stroke 8 Cy. 900 x 2300 36543kW (49684bhp) Mitsui Engineering & Shipbuilding CLtd-Japan AuxGen: 3 x 1960kW 450/230V 60Hz a.c Thrusters: 1 Tunnel thruster (f)
8666068 9LY2668 -	**XIN CHUAN 6** **PT Pelayaran Rimba Megah Armada** - *Freetown* *Sierra Leone* Official number: SL103471	**2,672** 1,496 3,500		**2004**-05 **Zhejiang Yueqing Qiligang Ship Industry Co Ltd — Yueqing ZJ** Loa 95.15 Br ex - Dght - Lbp - Br md 14.50 Dpth 6.40 Welded, 1 dk	**(A31A2GX) General Cargo Ship**	**1 oil engine** driving 1 FP propeller Total Power: 1,103kW (1,500hp) Chinese Std. Type 6320ZCD 1 x 4 Stroke 6 Cy. 320 x 440 1103kW (1500bhp) Guangzhou Diesel Engine Factory CoLtd-China
8321709 BVMR7 -	**XIN CHUN HE** *ex* Chun He *-2013* **Shanghai PanAsia Shipping Co Ltd** - SatCom: Inmarsat C 441241010 *Shanghai* *China* MMSI: 412172000	**19,835** 9,455 25,545	Class: (CC) (GL)	**1984**-11 **Seebeckwerft AG — Bremerhaven** Yd No: 1045 Loa 170.02 (BB) Br ex 28.61 Dght 10.720 Lbp 158.20 Br md 28.40 Dpth 15.45 Welded, 1 dk	**(A33A2CC) Container Ship (Fully Cellular)** TEU 1328 C Ho 676 TEU C Dk 652 TEU incl 54 ref C. Compartments: 5 Cell Ho, ER 8 Ha: 8 (12.9 x 5.4)ER 16 Wing Ha: 2 (12.9 x 2.8)14 (12.9 x 8.1) Ice Capable	**1 oil engine** driving 1 FP propeller Total Power: 10,797kW (14,680hp) 17.0kn B&W 6L70MCE 1 x 2 Stroke 6 Cy. 700 x 2268 10797kW (14680bhp) Kawasaki Heavy Industries Ltd-Japan AuxGen: 1 x 1100kW 450V 60Hz a.c, 2 x 800kW 450V 60Hz a.c, 1 x 440kW 450V 60Hz a.c Thrusters: 1 Thwart. FP thruster (f)
9661833 VRKQ9 -	**XIN DA 1** **Asia Shipping Development Ltd** Taihua Ship Management Ltd *Hong Kong* *Hong Kong* MMSI: 477978600	**2,990** 1,191 4,000	Class: BV	**2012**-03 **Zhejiang Nangang Shipyard Co Ltd — Rui'an ZJ** Yd No: NG011 Loa 94.40 Br ex - Dght 5.850 Lbp 88.00 Br md 15.40 Dpth 7.60 Welded, 1 dk	**(A13B2TP) Products Tanker** Double Hull (13F) Liq: 3,995; Liq (Oil): 3,995 Cargo Heating Coils Compartments: 4 Wing Ta, 4 Wing Ta, ER 2 Cargo Pump (s): 2x500m^3/hr	**1 oil engine** reduction geared to sc. shaft driving 1 FP propeller Total Power: 2,207kW (3,001hp) 12.9kn Yanmar 6N330-UN 1 x 4 Stroke 6 Cy. 330 x 440 2207kW (3001bhp) Qingdao Zichai Boyang Diesel EngineCo Ltd-China AuxGen: 3 x 320kW 60Hz a.c Fuel: 280.0
9661845 VRKR2 -	**XIN DA 2** **Asia Shipping Development Ltd** Taihua Ship Management Ltd *Hong Kong* *Hong Kong* MMSI: 477978500 Official number: HK-3533	**2,990** 1,191 4,000	Class: BV	**2012**-06 **Zhejiang Nangang Shipyard Co Ltd — Rui'an ZJ** Yd No: NG012 Loa 94.40 Br ex - Dght 5.850 Lbp 88.00 Br md 15.40 Dpth 7.61 Welded, 1 dk	**(A13B2TP) Products Tanker** Double Hull (13F) Liq: 3,993; Liq (Oil): 3,993 Compartments: 4 Wing Ta, 4 Wing Ta, ER 2 Cargo Pump (s): 2x500m^3/hr	**1 oil engine** reduction geared to sc. shaft driving 1 FP propeller Total Power: 2,207kW (3,001hp) 12.9kn Yanmar 6N330-UN 1 x 4 Stroke 6 Cy. 330 x 440 2207kW (3001bhp) Qingdao Zichai Boyang Diesel EngineCo Ltd-China AuxGen: 3 x 320kW 60Hz a.c Fuel: 285.0

8308783 *BRNS* -	**XIN DA JIANG** *ex* Okyroe *-2003* *ex* Ma Long Hai *-1999* **Guangdong Haidian Shipping Co Ltd** - SatCom: Inmarsat C 441232715 *Guangzhou, Guangdong* *China* MMSI: 412838000	**26,736** 12,122 41,634	Class: (CC)	**1984-06 Hayashikane Shipbuilding & Engineering Co Ltd — Shimonoseki YC** Yd No: 1268 Loa 189.00 (BB) Br ex 31.25 Dght 10.918 Lbp 180.00 Br md 31.20 Dpth 16.70 Welded, 1 dk	**(A21A2BC) Bulk Carrier** Grain: 54,388; Bale: 52,293 Compartments: 5 Ho, ER 5 Ha: (16.9 x 11.2)4 (16.9 x 14.0)ER Cranes: 4 Ice Capable	**1 oil engine** driving 1 FP propeller Total Power: 7,392kW (10,050hp) 13.5kn B&W 6L60MC 1 x 2 Stroke 6 Cy. 600 x 1944 7392kW (10050bhp) Mitsui Engineering & Shipbuilding CLtd-Japan
9234331 *BPAO* -	**XIN DA LIAN** **China Shipping Container Lines Co Ltd** - SatCom: Inmarsat C 441305010 *Shanghai* *China* MMSI: 413050000	**66,433** 37,567 69,023	Class: CC	**2003-02 Dalian New Shipbuilding Heavy Industries Co Ltd — Dalian LN** Yd No: C5600-1 Loa 279.60 (BB) Br ex - Dght 14.000 Lbp 265.80 Br md 40.30 Dpth 24.10 Welded, 1 dk	**(A33A2CC) Container Ship (Fully Cellular)** TEU 5668 C Ho 2586 TEU C Dk 3082 TEU incl 610 ref C. Compartments: ER, 7 Cell Ho 15 Ha: ER Ice Capable	**1 oil engine** driving 1 FP propeller Total Power: 54,720kW (74,397hp) 25.7kn MAN-B&W 12K90MC-C 1 x 2 Stroke 12 Cy. 900 x 2300 54720kW (74397bhp) Mitsui Engineering & Shipbuilding CLtd-Japan AuxGen: 4 x 2320kW 450/230V 60Hz a.c Thrusters: 1 Tunnel thruster (f) Fuel: 370.0 (d.f.) 6533.0 (r.f.)
9337949 *BPKE* -	**XIN DA YANG ZHOU** **China Shipping Container Lines Co Ltd** - SatCom: Inmarsat C 441317310 *Shanghai* *China* MMSI: 413173000	**90,757** 57,364 102,418	Class: CC GL	**2009-04 Hudong-Zhonghua Shipbuilding (Group) Co Ltd — Shanghai** Yd No: H1385A Loa 335.06 (BB) Br ex 42.84 Dght 14.650 Lbp 320.06 Br md 42.80 Dpth 24.80 Welded, 1 dk	**(A33A2CC) Container Ship (Fully Cellular)** TEU 8528 C Ho 3874 TEU C Dk 4554 TEU incl 700 ref C. Compartments: 9 Cell Ho, ER	**1 oil engine** driving 1 FP propeller Total Power: 68,520kW (93,160hp) 25.0kn MAN-B&W 12K98MC-C 1 x 2 Stroke 12 Cy. 980 x 2400 68520kW (93160bhp) Mitsui Engineering & Shipbuilding CLtd-Japan AuxGen: 4 x 2760kW 6600V a.c Thrusters: 1 Tunnel thruster (f)
9312597 *BPBY* -	**XIN DAN DONG** **China Shipping Container Lines Co Ltd** - *Shanghai* *China* MMSI: 413153000	**41,482** 24,001 52,210	Class: CC	**2006-04 Dalian Shipbuilding Industry Co Ltd — Dalian LN (No 2 Yard)** Yd No: C4250-19 Loa 263.23 (BB) Br ex 32.30 Dght 12.800 Lbp 251.88 Br md 32.25 Dpth 19.30 Welded, 1 dk	**(A33A2CC) Container Ship (Fully Cellular)** TEU 4250 C Ho 1586 TEU C Dk 2664 TEU incl 400 ref C. Compartments: 7 Cell Ho, ER Ice Capable	**1 oil engine** driving 1 FP propeller Total Power: 36,480kW (49,598hp) 24.2kn MAN-B&W 8K90MC-C 1 x 2 Stroke 8 Cy. 900 x 2300 36480kW (49598bhp) Doosan Engine Co Ltd-South Korea AuxGen: 3 x 1960kW 450V 60Hz a.c Thrusters: 1 Tunnel thruster (f)
9614048 *VRMR4* -	**XIN DAN YANG** **Xin Dan Yang Shipping SA** China Shipping Tanker Co Ltd *Hong Kong* *Hong Kong* MMSI: 477219800 Official number: HK-3955	**164,492** 108,061 322,829	Class: CC NV	**2013-11 Dalian Shipbuilding Industry Co Ltd — Dalian LN (No 2 Yard)** Yd No: T3000-54 Loa 333.00 (BB) Br ex 60.04 Dght 22.600 Lbp 320.00 Br md 60.00 Dpth 30.50 Welded, 1 dk	**(A13A2TV) Crude Oil Tanker** Double Hull (13F) Liq: 336,988; Liq (Oil): 300,000 Compartments: 6 Wing Ta, 5 Ta, 4 Wing Ta, 1 Wing Slop Ta, 1 Wing Slop Ta, ER 3 Cargo Pump (s): 3x5000m³/hr	**1 oil engine** driving 1 FP propeller Total Power: 29,260kW (39,782hp) 15.0kn MAN-B&W 7S80ME-C8 1 x 2 Stroke 7 Cy. 800 x 3200 29260kW (39782bhp) Dalian Marine Diesel Co Ltd-China AuxGen: 3 x 1050kW 450V a.c
9342578 *BBDE* -	**XIN DE** **Yantai Quanzhou Ocean Transportation Co** - *Yantai, Shandong* *China* MMSI: 412326230	**1,970** 1,068 2,835	Class: CC	**2005-01 Rongcheng Haida Shipbuilding Co Ltd — Rongcheng SD** Yd No: HDBC002 Loa 79.99 Br ex - Dght 5.200 Lbp 74.00 Br md 13.60 Dpth 7.00 Welded, 1 dk	**(A21A2BC) Bulk Carrier** Grain: 4,127; Bale: 3,893 Compartments: 1 Ho, ER 1 Ha: ER (38.4 x 9.0) Ice Capable	**1 oil engine** geared to sc. shaft driving 1 FP propeller Total Power: 1,080kW (1,468hp) 11.7kn MAN-B&W 8L23/30 1 x 4 Stroke 8 Cy. 225 x 300 1080kW (1468bhp) Zhenjiang Marine Diesel Works-China AuxGen: 2 x 100kW 400V a.c
7007631 *HP8256* -	**XIN DE** *ex* Vismin *-1993* *ex* Trans Bay *-1990* *ex* Knardal *-1986* **Zheng Yang Shipping Inc** - *Panama* *Panama* Official number: 24297PEXT	**1,395** 419 1,016	Class: (NV)	**1970-04 Batservice Verft AS — Arendal** Yd No: 590 Loa 71.18 Br ex 13.24 Dght 2.998 Lbp 66.02 Br md 13.21 Dpth 5.85 Welded, 2 dks	**(A31A2GX) General Cargo Ship** Grain: 1,961; Bale: 1,720 Compartments: 1 Ho, ER 2 Ha: 2 (10.8 x 7.2)ER Ice Capable	**1 oil engine** driving 1 FP propeller Total Power: 883kW (1,201hp) 12.0kn MaK 1 x 4 Stroke 6 Cy. 320 x 450 883kW (1201bhp) Atlas MaK Maschinenbau GmbH-Kiel AuxGen: 2 x 47kW 220V 50Hz a.c Fuel: 48.5 (d.f.) 4.0pd
9597044 *BRTO* -	**XIN DONG GUAN 1** **Dongguan Haichang Shipping Co Ltd** - SatCom: Inmarsat C 441277813 *Dongguan, Guangdong* *China* MMSI: 412778000	**39,500** - 70,871	Class: CC (Class contemplated)	**2011-01 Zhejiang Zhenghe Shipbuilding Co Ltd — Zhoushan ZJ** Yd No: ZH7031 Loa 221.70 (BB) Br ex - Dght 14.000 Lbp - Br md 32.26 Dpth 19.60 Welded, 1 dk	**(A21A2BC) Bulk Carrier** Grain: 86,990 Compartments: 6 Ho, ER 6 Ha: ER	**1 oil engine** driving 1 FP propeller Total Power: 11,300kW (15,363hp) 13.0kn MAN-B&W 5S60MC-C 1 x 2 Stroke 5 Cy. 600 x 2400 11300kW (15363bhp)
8711100 *BRTN* -	**XIN DONG GUAN 2** *ex* Corato *-2006* *ex* Meridian Sky *-1999* **Dongguan Haichang Shipping Co Ltd** - SatCom: Inmarsat C 441202519 *Dongguan, Guangdong* *China* MMSI: 412469750	**36,042** 23,043 64,282 T/cm 67.0	Class: CC (AB)	**1989-06 Hyundai Heavy Industries Co Ltd — Ulsan** Yd No: 618 Loa 225.00 (BB) Br ex 32.24 Dght 13.122 Lbp 215.64 Br md 32.20 Dpth 18.00 Welded, 1 dk	**(A21A2BC) Bulk Carrier** Grain: 80,250; Bale: 76,407 Compartments: 7 Ho, ER 7 Ha: (14.3 x 14.9)6 (14.3 x 14.9)ER	**1 oil engine** driving 1 FP propeller Total Power: 8,569kW (11,650hp) 12.0kn B&W 6S60MCE 1 x 2 Stroke 6 Cy. 600 x 2292 8569kW (11650bhp) Hyundai Heavy Industries Co Ltd-South Korea AuxGen: 3 x 540kW a.c
9132961 *BRTM* -	**XIN DONG GUAN 3** *ex* Serene Star *-2007* *ex* Singa Star *-2000* **Dongguan Haichang Shipping Co Ltd** - *Dongguan, Guangdong* *China* MMSI: 413320000	**36,561** 23,007 69,512 T/cm 65.6	Class: CC (NK)	**1996-01 Tsuneishi Shipbuilding Co Ltd — Fukuyama HS** Yd No: 1093 Loa 225.00 (BB) Br ex 32.24 Dght 13.252 Lbp 215.00 Br md 32.20 Dpth 18.30 Welded, 1 dk	**(A21A2BC) Bulk Carrier** Grain: 81,809 Compartments: 7 Ho, ER 7 Ha: (14.3 x 12.8)6 (16.8 x 14.4)ER	**1 oil engine** driving 1 FP propeller Total Power: 8,915kW (12,121hp) 13.5kn B&W 6S60MC 1 x 2 Stroke 6 Cy. 600 x 2292 8915kW (12121bhp) Mitsui Engineering & Shipbuilding CLtd-Japan AuxGen: 3 x 440kW 450V a.c
9660633 *BRRO* -	**XIN DONG GUAN 4** **Dongguan Haichang Shipping Co Ltd** - SatCom: Inmarsat C 441406410 *Dongguan, Guangdong* *China* MMSI: 414064000	**39,500** - 70,776	Class: CC (Class contemplated)	**2011-11 Zhejiang Zhenghe Shipbuilding Co Ltd — Zhoushan ZJ** Loa 221.63 (BB) Br ex - Dght 14.000 Lbp - Br md 32.26 Dpth 19.60 Welded, 1 dk	**(A21A2BC) Bulk Carrier** Grain: 86,990 Compartments: 7 Ho, ER 7 Ha: ER	**1 oil engine** driving 1 FP propeller Total Power: 11,300kW (15,363hp) 13.0kn MAN-B&W 5S60MC-C 1 x 2 Stroke 5 Cy. 600 x 2400 11300kW (15363bhp)
9660645 *BRRK* -	**XIN DONG GUAN 5** **Dongguan Haichang Shipping Co Ltd** - *Dongguan, Guangdong* *China* MMSI: 412453000 Official number: 090212000037	**38,861** 21,762 70,707	Class: CC	**2012-05 Zhejiang Zhenghe Shipbuilding Co Ltd — Zhoushan ZJ** Yd No: ZH7051 Loa 221.59 (BB) Br ex - Dght 14.000 Lbp 216.16 Br md 32.26 Dpth 18.00 Welded, 1 dk	**(A21A2BC) Bulk Carrier** Grain: 82,000 Compartments: 6 Ho, ER 6 Ha: ER	**1 oil engine** driving 1 FP propeller Total Power: 11,300kW (15,363hp) 13.0kn MAN-B&W 5S60MC-C 1 x 2 Stroke 5 Cy. 600 x 2400 11300kW (15363bhp)
9597056 *BRTG* -	**XIN DONG GUAN 7** **Dongguan Haichang Shipping Co Ltd** - SatCom: Inmarsat C 441291313 *Dongguan, Guangdong* *China* MMSI: 412913000	**39,500** - 70,807	Class: CC (Class contemplated)	**2011-03 Zhejiang Zhenghe Shipbuilding Co Ltd — Zhoushan ZJ** Yd No: ZH7032 Loa 221.64 (BB) Br ex - Dght 14.000 Lbp - Br md 32.26 Dpth 19.60 Welded, 1 dk	**(A21A2BC) Bulk Carrier** Grain: 86,990 Compartments: 6 Ho, ER 6 Ha: ER	**1 oil engine** driving 1 FP propeller Total Power: 11,300kW (15,363hp) 13.0kn MAN-B&W 5S60MC-C 1 x 2 Stroke 5 Cy. 600 x 2400 11300kW (15363bhp)
9597068 *BRTH* -	**XIN DONG GUAN 8** **Dongguan Haichang Shipping Co Ltd** - SatCom: Inmarsat C 441219762 *Dongguan, Guangdong* *China* MMSI: 412541000	**39,500** - 70,767	Class: CC (Class contemplated)	**2011-05 Zhejiang Zhenghe Shipbuilding Co Ltd — Zhoushan ZJ** Yd No: ZH7033 Loa 221.64 (BB) Br ex - Dght 14.000 Lbp - Br md 32.26 Dpth 19.60 Welded, 1 dk	**(A21A2BC) Bulk Carrier** Grain: 86,990 Compartments: 6 Ho, ER 3 Ha: ER	**1 oil engine** driving 1 FP propeller Total Power: 11,300kW (15,363hp) 13.0kn MAN-B&W 5S60MC-C 1 x 2 Stroke 5 Cy. 600 x 2400 11300kW (15363bhp)
9597070 *BRTP* -	**XIN DONG GUAN 9** **Dongguan Haichang Shipping Co Ltd** - SatCom: Inmarsat C 441219829 *Dongguan, Guangdong* *China* MMSI: 412028000	**39,500** - 70,785	Class: CC (Class contemplated)	**2011-07 Zhejiang Zhenghe Shipbuilding Co Ltd — Zhoushan ZJ** Yd No: ZH7034 Loa 221.62 (BB) Br ex - Dght 14.000 Lbp - Br md 32.26 Dpth 19.60 Welded, 1 dk	**(A21A2BC) Bulk Carrier** Grain: 86,990 Compartments: 6 Ho, ER 6 Ha: ER	**1 oil engine** driving 1 FP propeller Total Power: 11,300kW (15,363hp) 13.0kn MAN-B&W 5S60MC-C 1 x 2 Stroke 5 Cy. 600 x 2400 11300kW (15363bhp)
9597082 *BRRN* -	**XIN DONG GUAN 10** **Dongguan Haichang Shipping Co Ltd** - SatCom: Inmarsat C 441214213 *Dongguan, Guangdong* *China* MMSI: 412142000	**39,500** - 70,773	Class: CC (Class contemplated)	**2011-09 Zhejiang Zhenghe Shipbuilding Co Ltd — Zhoushan ZJ** Yd No: ZH7035 Loa 221.62 (BB) Br ex - Dght 14.000 Lbp - Br md 32.26 Dpth 19.60 Welded, 1 dk	**(A21A2BC) Bulk Carrier** Grain: 86,990 Compartments: 1 Ho	**1 oil engine** driving 1 FP propeller Total Power: 11,300kW (15,363hp) 13.0kn MAN-B&W 5S60MC-C 1 x 2 Stroke 5 Cy. 600 x 2400 11300kW (15363bhp)

	Name / Owner	Tonnage	Class	Built	Type	Machinery
959075 LLM	**XIN FA** **Oujiang Shipping Co Ltd** - *Wenzhou, Zhejiang* *China*	*190* 47 176	Class: (CC)	**1985 Yuhuan Xuangang Shipyard — Yuhuan County ZJ** Loa 36.50 Br ex - Dght 3.400 Lbp 31.00 Br md 6.60 Dpth 3.92 Welded, 1 dk	**(B12B2FC) Fish Carrier** Ins: 44 Compartments: 2 Ho	**1 oil engine** geared to sc. shaft driving 1 FP propeller 12.0kn Chinese Std. Type 6200Z 1 x 4 Stroke 6 Cy. 200 x 225 Weifang Diesel Engine Factory-China AuxGen: 2 x 24kW 400V a.c
225852	**XIN FA** *ex* Man Fat *-2002* - -	*777* 369 -		**1981 Hong Kong Shipyard Ltd. — Hong Kong** Loa 57.61 Br ex 10.52 Dght - Lbp - Br md - Dpth 3.56 Welded, 3 dks	**(A37B2PS) Passenger Ship**	**1 oil engine** reverse reduction geared to sc. shaft driving 1 FP propeller Total Power: 1,242kW (1,689hp) 15.0kn MAN G7V30/45ATL 1 x 4 Stroke 7 Cy. 300 x 450 1242kW (1689bhp) Maschinenbau Augsburg Nuernberg (MAN)-Augsburg
309930 PBN	**XIN FANG CHENG** **China Shipping Container Lines Co Ltd** - *Shanghai* *China* MMSI: 413138000	**41,482** 24,001 52,106	Class: CC	**2005-07 Dalian New Shipbuilding Heavy Industries Co Ltd — Dalian LN** Yd No: C4250-1 Loa 262.23 (BB) Br ex 32.30 Dght 12.800 Lbp 251.88 Br md 32.25 Dpth 19.30 Welded, 1 dk	**(A33A2CC) Container Ship (Fully Cellular)** TEU 4250 C Ho 1586 TEU C Dk 2664 TEU incl 400 ref C. Ice Capable	**1 oil engine** driving 1 FP propeller Total Power: 36,480kW (49,598hp) 24.2kn MAN-B&W 8K90MC-C 1 x 2 Stroke 8 Cy. 900 x 2300 36480kW (49598bhp) Doosan Engine Co Ltd-South Korea AuxGen: 3 x 1960kW 450V 60Hz a.c Thrusters: 1 Tunnel thruster (f)
705905	**XIN FEI** *ex* Man Fee *-2002* - -	**1,510** 602 746		**1987-06 Hong Kong Shipyard Ltd. — Hong Kong** Loa 65.00 Br ex 11.89 Dght 2.671 Lbp 61.98 Br md 11.59 Dpth 4.27 Welded, 1 dk	**(A37B2PS) Passenger Ship**	**1 oil engine** driving 1 FP propeller Total Power: 1,100kW (1,496hp) MAN 12V20/27 1 x Vee 4 Stroke 12 Cy. 200 x 270 1100kW (1496bhp) MAN B&W Diesel GmbH-Augsburg
337937 PKD	**XIN FEI ZHOU** **China Shipping Container Lines Co Ltd** - SatCom: Inmarsat C 441317110 *Shanghai* *China* MMSI: 413171000 Official number: 010008000198	**90,757** 57,364 102,379	Class: CC GL	**2008-12 Hudong-Zhonghua Shipbuilding (Group) Co Ltd — Shanghai** Yd No: H1384A Loa 335.06 (BB) Br ex 42.84 Dght 14.650 Lbp 320.06 Br md 42.79 Dpth 24.80 Welded, 1 dk	**(A33A2CC) Container Ship (Fully Cellular)** TEU 8528 C Ho 3874 TEU C Dk 4554 TEU incl 700 ref C. Ice Capable	**1 oil engine** driving 1 FP propeller Total Power: 68,520kW (93,160hp) 25.0kn MAN-B&W 12K98MC-C 1 x 2 Stroke 12 Cy. 980 x 2400 68520kW (93160bhp) Mitsui Engineering & Shipbuilding CLtd-Japan AuxGen: 4 x 2760kW 6600/450V a.c Thrusters: 1 Tunnel thruster (f)
131204 AKE	**XIN FENG FU ZHOU** *ex* Paraking *-2013* *ex* Anna Rickmers *-2012* *ex* CCNI Chagres *-2007* *launched as* Anna Rickmers *-1998* **Dalian Trawind Marine Co Ltd** Dalian Trawind International Ship Management Co Ltd *Dalian, Liaoning* *China* MMSI: 412209240	**28,148** 13,514 44,572 T/cm 52.1	Class: CC RI (GL)	**1998-02 Stocznia Szczecinska SA — Szczecin** Yd No: B577/1/2 Loa 184.97 (BB) Br ex - Dght 12.050 Lbp 175.60 Br md 32.20 Dpth 16.95 Welded, 1 dk	**(A31A2GX) General Cargo Ship** Grain: 51,096; Bale: 49,966 TEU 1830 C Ho 922 TEU C Dk 908 TEU incl 110 ref C Compartments: 4 Ho, 4 Cell Ho, ER 8 Ha: (12.6 x 12.8)7 (12.6 x 28.0)ER Cranes: 3x40t	**1 oil engine** driving 1 FP propeller Total Power: 12,000kW (16,315hp) 15.5kn Sulzer 6RTA58T 1 x 2 Stroke 6 Cy. 580 x 2416 12000kW (16315bhp) H Cegielski Poznan SA-Poland AuxGen: 3 x 937kW 450V 60Hz a.c Fuel: 300.0 (d.f.) 3755.0 (r.f.) 50.0pd
077288 AKS	**XIN FENG GUANG ZHOU** *ex* Hobart *-2013* *ex* MSC Hobart *-2013* *ex* E. R. Hobart *-2007* *ex* MSC Hobart *-2007* *ex* E. R. Hobart *-2004* *ex* Mosel *-2002* *ex* Zim Koper *-1998* *ex* Hyundai Longview *-1996* - - *China* MMSI: 412209130	**22,738** 11,881 33,523 T/cm 44.4	Class: (GL) (AB)	**1994-04 Halla Engineering & Heavy Industries Ltd — Incheon** Yd No: 201 Loa 187.54 (BB) Br ex 28.44 Dght 11.113 Lbp 178.00 Br md 28.40 Dpth 15.60 Welded, 1 dk	**(A33A2CC) Container Ship (Fully Cellular)** Grain: 42,759 TEU 2004 C Ho 914 TEU C Dk 1090 TEU incl 115 ref C. Compartments: ER, 5 Cell Ho 10 Ha: ER	**1 oil engine** driving 1 FP propeller Total Power: 15,710kW (21,359hp) 18.0kn B&W 6L70MC 1 x 2 Stroke 6 Cy. 700 x 2268 15710kW (21359bhp) Hyundai Heavy Industries Co Ltd-South Korea AuxGen: 3 x 925kW 60Hz a.c Thrusters: 1 Thwart. FP thruster (f)
348042 FYN5	**XIN FENG HAI** **Li Jiuliang, Zhang Xinxiang & Qiu Zhiguo** Shanghai Haizheng Ship Management Co Ltd SatCom: Inmarsat C 435109613 *Panama* *Panama* MMSI: 351096000 Official number: 42393PEXTF1	**2,915** 1,701 4,980	Class: OM PD ZC (Class contemplated)	**2010-07 in the People's Republic of China** Loa 98.00 (BB) Br ex - Dght 3.495 Lbp 89.85 Br md 15.80 Dpth 7.35 Welded, 1 dk	**(A31A2GX) General Cargo Ship** Grain: 6,825; Bale: 6,279 Compartments: 2 Ho, ER 2 Ha: (27.1 x 12.9)ER (25.8 x 12.9)	**1 oil engine** reduction geared to sc. shaft driving 1 FP propeller Total Power: 2,000kW (2,719hp) 10.0kn Chinese Std. Type 8300ZC 1 x 4 Stroke 8 Cy. 300 x 380 2000kW (2719bhp) Wuxi Antai Power Machinery Co Ltd-China AuxGen: 2 x 130kW a.c Fuel: 139.0 (d.f.)
070163 LEJ	**XIN FENG NINGBO** *ex* Sima Singapore *-2013* *ex* Ocean Promoter *-2011* *ex* MSC Greece *-2009* *ex* Trade Maple *-2002* *ex* MSC Hamburg *-2001* *ex* Trade Maple *-2001* **Dalian Trawind Marine Co Ltd** Dalian Trawind International Ship Management Co Ltd *Ningbo, Zhejiang* *China* MMSI: 413452480	**29,195** 17,589 35,551 T/cm 51.7	Class: CC (LR) ✠ Classed LR until 14/8/13	**1995-03 Hyundai Heavy Industries Co Ltd — Ulsan** Yd No: 870 Loa 196.36 (BB) Br ex 32.30 Dght 11.517 Lbp 184.00 Br md 32.25 Dpth 18.80 Welded, 1 dk	**(A33A2CC) Container Ship (Fully Cellular)** TEU 2227 C Ho 1164 TEU C Dk 1063 TEU incl 99 ref C. Compartments: ER, 6 Cell Ho 10 Ha: ER	**1 oil engine** driving 1 FP propeller Total Power: 19,257kW (26,182hp) 20.0kn B&W 7S70MC 1 x 2 Stroke 7 Cy. 700 x 2674 19257kW (26182bhp) Hyundai Heavy Industries Co Ltd-South Korea AuxGen: 3 x 800kW 440/220V 60Hz a.c Boilers: AuxB (Comp) 6.9kgf/cm² (6.8bar) Thrusters: 1 Thwart. CP thruster (f) Fuel: 214.0 (d.f.) 2626.0 (r.f.)
147576 FQW4	**XIN FU XING** *ex* Xi Feng Shan *-2012* **Fuzhou Haisheng Shipping Co Ltd** - *Panama* *Panama* MMSI: 373769000 Official number: 43641PEXTF1	**2,772** 1,161 3,393	Class: CC	**1996-09 Donghai Shipyard — Shanghai** Yd No: 93321 Loa 84.57 Br ex - Dght 5.500 Lbp 79.00 Br md 14.76 Dpth 7.30 Welded, 1 dk	**(A33A2CC) Container Ship (Fully Cellular)** TEU 170 Compartments: 2 Cell Ho, ER 2 Ha: ER Ice Capable	**1 oil engine** geared to sc. shaft driving 1 FP propeller Total Power: 1,300kW (1,767hp) 12.0kn Alpha 6L28/32 1 x 4 Stroke 6 Cy. 280 x 320 1300kW (1767bhp) Zhenjiang Marine Diesel Works-China AuxGen: 3 x 120kW 400V a.c
304796 PBE	**XIN FU ZHOU** **China Shipping Container Lines Co Ltd** - SatCom: Inmarsat C 441307610 *Shanghai* *China* MMSI: 413076000	**66,452** 37,567 69,235	Class: CC	**2004-09 Hudong-Zhonghua Shipbuilding (Group) Co Ltd — Shanghai** Yd No: H1353A Loa 279.90 (BB) Br ex - Dght 14.000 Lbp 265.80 Br md 40.30 Dpth 24.10 Welded, 1 dk	**(A33A2CC) Container Ship (Fully Cellular)** TEU 5668 C Ho 2586 TEU C Dk 3082 TEU incl 610 ref C. Compartments: 7 Cell Ho, ER	**1 oil engine** driving 1 FP propeller Total Power: 54,719kW (74,396hp) 26.0kn MAN-B&W 12K90MC-C 1 x 2 Stroke 12 Cy. 900 x 2300 54719kW (74396bhp) Mitsui Engineering & Shipbuilding CLtd-Japan AuxGen: 4 x 2320kW 450/230V 60Hz a.c Thrusters: 1 Tunnel thruster (f)
222680	**XIN GUANG** *ex* Man Kwong *-2002* - -	**1,415** 567 439		**1983-05 Taiwan Machinery Manufacturing Corp. — Kaohsiung** Yd No: 722 Loa 65.00 Br ex 12.45 Dght 3.000 Lbp 58.58 Br md 11.59 Dpth 4.27 Welded, 1 dk	**(A37B2PS) Passenger Ship** Passengers: unberthed: 1520	**2 oil engines** with flexible couplings & sr reverse geared to sc. shafts driving 2 Directional propellers Total Power: 2,170kW (2,950hp) 15.2kn MAN 12V20/27 2 x Vee 4 Stroke 12 Cy. 200 x 270 each-1085kW (1475bhp) Maschinenbau Augsburg Nuernberg (MAN)-Augsburg AuxGen: 3 x 160kW a.c Fuel: 28.5 1.9pd
108573 RNA	**XIN GUANG ZHOU** *ex* Uniringgitt *-2000* *ex* Mare Baltico *-1999* *ex* St-Cergue *-1989* *ex* Bridgeworth *-1985* **Guangdong Haidian Shipping Co Ltd** - *Guangzhou, Guangdong* *China* MMSI: 412463420	**35,707** 22,348 64,310 T/cm 63.8	Class: (LR) (CC) (RI) ✠ Classed LR until 1/1/95	**1983-05 B&W Skibsvaerft A/S — Copenhagen** Yd No: 874 Loa 225.03 (BB) Br ex 32.31 Dght 13.060 Lbp 213.72 Br md 32.25 Dpth 18.01 Welded, 1 dk	**(A21A2BC) Bulk Carrier** Grain: 78,790; Bale: 75,490 TEU 891 Compartments: 7 Ho, ER 7 Ha: 7 (14.4 x 15.0)ER Cranes: 1x35t,3x25t	**1 oil engine** driving 1 FP propeller Total Power: 9,268kW (12,601hp) 15.0kn B&W 5L80GFCA 1 x 2 Stroke 5 Cy. 800 x 1950 9268kW (12601bhp) B&W Diesel A/S-Denmark AuxGen: 3 x 500kW 440V 60Hz a.c Fuel: 330.0 (d.f.) (Heating Coils) 2810.0 (r.f.) 40.5pd
222707	**XIN GUO** *ex* Man Kwok *-2002* - -	**1,510** 602 439		**1983-06 Taiwan Machinery Manufacturing Corp. — Kaohsiung** Yd No: 727 Loa 65.00 Br ex 12.45 Dght 3.150 Lbp 58.58 Br md 11.59 Dpth 4.45 Welded, 1 dk	**(A37B2PS) Passenger Ship** Passengers: 1520	**2 oil engines** with flexible couplings & sr reverse geared to sc. shafts driving 2 Directional propellers Total Power: 2,200kW (2,992hp) MAN 12V20/27 2 x Vee 4 Stroke 12 Cy. 200 x 270 each-1100kW (1496bhp) Maschinenbau Augsburg Nuernberg (MAN)-Augsburg
291925 NZ5	**XIN HAI** *ex* Jin An *-2010* **Xin Hai Shipping Corp Ltd** Yantai New Ocean International Shipping Co Ltd *Belize City* *Belize* MMSI: 312151000 Official number: 611020007	**1,997** 1,088 2,863	Class: CC	**2003-06 Qingdao Lingshan Ship Engineering Co Ltd — Jiaonan SD** Yd No: 97 Loa 79.99 Br ex - Dght 5.200 Lbp 74.00 Br md 13.60 Dpth 7.00 Welded, 1 dk	**(A21A2BC) Bulk Carrier** Grain: 4,127; Bale: 3,893 Compartments: 1 Ho, ER 1 Ha: ER (38.4 x 10.0) Ice Capable	**1 oil engine** geared to sc. shaft driving 1 CP propeller Total Power: 1,080kW (1,468hp) 11.6kn MAN-B&W 8L23/30 1 x 4 Stroke 8 Cy. 225 x 300 1080kW (1468bhp) Zhenjiang Marine Diesel Works-China

IMO / Call sign	Name / Owner / Manager / Flag	Tonnage	Class	Builder / Dimensions	Type / Capacity	Machinery
8660040 *V3TC8* -	**XIN HAI 18** *ex* Hong Jia 18 *-2011* **Liang De Lu** Weihai Xinhai Shipping Co Ltd *Belize City* *Belize* MMSI: 312235000 Official number: 611320041	**2,989** 1,730 -	Class: IT	**2004-12 Wenling Yongfa Shiprepair & Building Co Ltd — Wenling ZJ** Loa 96.90 Br ex - Dght 5.750 Lbp 89.80 Br md 16.20 Dpth 7.15 Welded, 1 dk	**(A31A2GX) General Cargo Ship**	**1 oil engine** driving 1 Propeller Total Power: 2,000kW (2,719hp) 11.0k Chinese Std. Type G8300Z 1 x 4 Stroke 8 Cy. 300 x 380 2000kW (2719bhp) Wuxi Antai Power Machinery Co Ltd-China
9167667 *3FVC4* -	**XIN HAI 68** *ex* Little Bear *-2010* *ex* Great Bear *-2003* **Xinhai Ocean Shipping Ltd** Weihai Xinhai Shipping Co Ltd SatCom: Inmarsat C 435510710 *Panama* *Panama* MMSI: 355107000 Official number: 4231011A	**4,732** 2,011 6,277 T/cm 13.4	Class: IT (NK)	**1997-08 Sanyo Zosen K.K. — Onomichi** Yd No: 1080 Loa 96.70 Br ex - Dght 7.346 Lbp 85.80 Br md 17.40 Dpth 11.60 Welded, 1 dk	**(A31A2GX) General Cargo Ship** Grain: 9,821; Bale: 9,574 Compartments: 2 Ho, ER 2 Ha: (16.1 x 12.6) (31.5 x 12.6)ER Cranes: 3x25t	**1 oil engine** driving 1 FP propeller Total Power: 2,427kW (3,300hp) 12.0k Akasaka A41 1 x 4 Stroke 6 Cy. 410 x 800 2427kW (3300bhp) Akasaka Tekkosho KK (Akasaka DieselLtd)-Japan Fuel: 445.0
8660052 - -	**XIN HAI 88** *ex* Wan Lun Da 68 *-2012* **Lv Yi Qiang** Weihai Xinhai Shipping Co Ltd *Belize City* *Belize* Official number: 611320038	**2,998** 1,697 -	Class: IT	**2010-09 Jiaojiang Qiansuo Shipyard — Taizhou ZJ** Loa 99.80 Br ex - Dght 5.600 Lbp 93.42 Br md 16.00 Dpth 7.10 Welded, 1 dk	**(A31A2GX) General Cargo Ship**	**1 oil engine** reduction geared to sc. shaft driving 1 FP propeller Total Power: 1,912kW (2,600hp) 11.0k Chinese Std. Type LC9250ZLC 1 x 4 Stroke 9 Cy. 250 x 320 1912kW (2600bhp) Qingdao Zichai Boyang Diesel EngineCo Ltd-China
8657574 *V3QX8* -	**XIN HAI 98** *ex* Hong Jia 85 *-2012* **Rong Fengjing** Weihai Xinhai Shipping Co Ltd *Belize City* *Belize* MMSI: 312040000 Official number: 611220031	**2,998** 1,990 5,044	Class: IZ (Class contemplated)	**2009-12 in the People's Republic of China** Loa 96.50 Br ex - Dght 5.950 Lbp 90.80 Br md 15.80 Dpth 7.40 Welded, 1 dk	**(A31A2GX) General Cargo Ship**	**1 oil engine** reduction geared to sc. shaft driving 1 Propeller Total Power: 2,000kW (2,719hp) 11.0k Chinese Std. Type 8300ZC 1 x 4 Stroke 8 Cy. 300 x 380 2000kW (2719bhp) Ningbo CSI Power & Machinery GroupCo Ltd-China
9485605 *BQDK* -	**XIN HAI FENG** - **CHEC Dredging Co Ltd** CCCC Shanghai Dredging Co Ltd *Shanghai* *China* MMSI: 412375290	**17,089** 5,126 16,513	Class: CC	**2008-11 Guangzhou Wenchong Shipyard Co Ltd — Guangzhou GD** Yd No: 349 Loa 160.90 (BB) Br ex - Dght 8.000 Lbp 151.40 Br md 27.00 Dpth 11.80 Welded, 1 dk	**(B33B2DT) Trailing Suction Hopper Dredger** Hopper: 16,888	**2 oil engines** geared to sc. shafts driving 2 Propellers Total Power: 23,200kW (31,542hp) 16.0k Wartsila 16V38 2 x Vee 4 Stroke 16 Cy. 380 x 475 each-11600kW (15771bhp) Wartsila Italia SpA-Italy AuxGen: 1 x 1300kW 690/400V a.c, 2 x 3200kW 690/400V a.c Thrusters: 2 Tunnel thruster (f)
8217336 *XUCT3* -	**XIN HAI HAO** *ex* Pacificsound *-2008* *ex* Harukaze *-2000* **New Chang An International Shipping Co Ltd** Tianjin Marine Shipping Co Ltd *Phnom Penh* *Cambodia* MMSI: 514081000 Official number: 0883148	**9,971** 6,276 18,592 T/cm 29.0	Class: UB (NK)	**1984-03 Minaminippon Shipbuilding Co Ltd — Usuki OT** Yd No: 562 Converted From: Chemical/Products Tanker-2009 Loa 151.30 (BB) Br ex 22.84 Dght 9.216 Lbp 140.11 Br md 22.80 Dpth 11.99 Welded, 1 dk	**(A31A2GX) General Cargo Ship** Double Bottom Entire Compartment Length Grain: 21,000 Compartments: 4 Ho, ER 4 Ha: ER Cranes: 3	**1 oil engine** driving 1 FP propeller Total Power: 5,001kW (6,799hp) 13.7k Mitsubishi 6UEC52/125H 1 x 2 Stroke 6 Cy. 520 x 1250 5001kW (6799bhp) Akasaka Tekkosho KK (Akasaka DieselLtd)-Japan
9582635 *VRHE6*	**XIN HAI HE** - **Xinzhou International Shipping Co Ltd** Dalian Shenghua Ship Management Co Ltd *Hong Kong* *Hong Kong* MMSI: 477550200 Official number: HK-2813	**5,188** 2,247 7,446	Class: RI	**2011-05 Zhoushan Haichen Marine Service & Engineering Co Ltd — Zhoushan ZJ** Yd No: HC09-03 Loa 99.90 Br ex - Dght 7.000 Lbp 93.00 Br md 19.00 Dpth 10.50 Welded, 1 dk	**(A31A2GX) General Cargo Ship**	**1 oil engine** reduction geared to sc. shaft driving 1 FP propeller Total Power: 2,574kW (3,500hp) 12.0k Yanmar 6N330-EN 1 x 4 Stroke 6 Cy. 330 x 440 2574kW (3500bhp) Qingdao Zichai Boyang Diesel EngineCo Ltd-China AuxGen: 2 x 320kW 450V 60Hz a.c
9121039 *BIAI3* -	**XIN HAI HONG** *ex* Xin Hai Li *-2011* *ex* ACX Aki *-2002* *ex* Xin Hai Li *-2001* *ex* OOCL Hiroshima *-2000* *ex* Xin Hai Li *-1999* **Orient International Logistics Holding Shanghai Newseas Navigation Co Ltd** - *Shanghai* *China* MMSI: 413376350	**4,090** 2,030 5,945	Class: CC (NK)	**1995-11 ShinA Shipbuilding Co Ltd — Tongyeong** Yd No: 381 Loa 107.55 (BB) Br ex 17.24 Dght 6.513 Lbp 98.00 Br md 17.20 Dpth 8.30 Welded, 1 dk	**(A33A2CC) Container Ship (Fully Cellular)** Bale: 6,668 TEU 342 C Ho 132 TEU C Dk 210 TEU incl 50 ref C. Compartments: 5 Ho, ER 5 Ha: (12.5 x 8.0)4 (12.5 x 13.2)ER	**1 oil engine** driving 1 FP propeller Total Power: 3,354kW (4,560hp) 16.0k B&W 6L35MC 1 x 2 Stroke 6 Cy. 350 x 1050 3354kW (4560bhp) Ssangyong Heavy Industries Co Ltd-South Korea Fuel: 340.0 (r.f.)
9367061 *BQDH* -	**XIN HAI HU** - **CHEC Dredging Co Ltd** CCCC Shanghai Dredging Co Ltd *Shanghai* *China* MMSI: 413040020	**15,163** 4,548 15,921	Class: CC	**2007-05 Guangzhou Wenchong Shipyard Co Ltd — Guangzhou GD** Yd No: 343 Loa 150.70 (BB) Br ex - Dght 8.000 Lbp 141.60 Br md 27.00 Dpth 11.00 Welded, 1 dk	**(B33B2DT) Trailing Suction Hopper Dredger** Hopper: 13,500 Cranes: 1x30t,1x22.5t	**2 oil engines** reduction geared to sc. shafts driving 2 Propellers Total Power: 18,000kW (24,472hp) 15.5k Sulzer 12ZAV40S 2 x Vee 4 Stroke 12 Cy. 400 x 560 each-9000kW (12236bhp) Wartsila Finland Oy-Finland AuxGen: 1 x 950kW 400V a.c, 1 x 730kW 400V a.c, 2 x 3040kW 690V Thrusters: 2 Tunnel thruster (f)
9609201 *BSAK* -	**XIN HAI HU 4** - **CHEC Dredging Co Ltd** - *Shanghai* *China* MMSI: 412043810	**13,323** 3,997 13,204	Class: CC	**2011-09 Guangzhou Wenchong Shipyard Co Ltd — Guangzhou GD** Yd No: 411 Loa 135.00 (BB) Br ex - Dght 7.400 Lbp 125.60 Br md 27.00 Dpth 10.10 Welded, 1 dk	**(B33B2DT) Trailing Suction Hopper Dredger** Hopper: 11,876 Compartments: 1 Ho, ER 1 Ha: ER (56.0 x 18.5)	**2 oil engines** reduction geared to sc. shafts driving 2 Propellers Total Power: 15,000kW (20,394hp) 15.0k MAN-B&W 16V32/4 2 x Vee 4 Stroke 16 Cy. 320 x 400 each-7500kW (10197bhp) MAN B&W Diesel AG-Augsburg AuxGen: 2 x 2600kW 690V a.c, 1 x 800kW 400V a.c Thrusters: 2 Tunnel thruster (f)
9609213 *BSII* -	**XIN HAI HU 5** - **CHEC Dredging Co Ltd** - SatCom: Inmarsat C 441219858 *Shanghai* *China* MMSI: 412379030	**13,323** 3,997 13,162	Class: CC	**2011-12 Guangzhou Wenchong Shipyard Co Ltd — Guangzhou GD** Yd No: 412 Loa 135.60 Br ex - Dght 7.400 Lbp 125.60 Br md 27.00 Dpth 10.10 Welded, 1 dk	**(B33B2DT) Trailing Suction Hopper Dredger** Liq (Gas): 11,876 Compartments: 1 Ho, ER 1 Ha: ER (56.0 x 18.5)	**2 oil engines** reduction geared to sc. shafts driving 2 Propellers Total Power: 16,000kW (21,754hp) 15.0k MAN-B&W 16V32/4 2 x Vee 4 Stroke 16 Cy. 320 x 400 each-8000kW (10877bhp) MAN B&W Diesel AG-Augsburg AuxGen: 2 x 2600kW 690V a.c
9659244 *BSIR* -	**XIN HAI HU 8** - **CCCC Shanghai Dredging Co Ltd** - *Shanghai* *China* MMSI: 412379490	**11,313** 3,412 12,750	Class: CC	**2012-12 Shanghai Zhenhua Industries Co Ltd — Nantong JS** Yd No: ZPMC1038 Loa 130.30 Br ex 26.00 Dght 6.800 Lbp 115.00 Br md 25.60 Dpth 9.20 Welded, 1 dk	**(B33B2DT) Trailing Suction Hopper Dredger** Hopper: 10,000 Compartments: 1 Ho, ER 1 Ha: ER (52.5 x 16.8)	**2 diesel electric oil engines** driving 2 gen. each 5760kW 6600V a.c Connecting to 2 elec. motors driving 2 Propellers Total Power: 12,000kW (16,316hp) 15.0k MAN-B&W 12V32/40C 2 x Vee 4 Stroke 12 Cy. 320 x 400 each-6000kW (8158bhp) MAN B&W Diesel AG-Augsburg
9631709 *BSJB* -	**XIN HAI HU 9** *ex* Hang Jun 9003 *-2012* **SDC Waterway Construction Co Ltd** - *Ningbo, Zhejiang* *China* MMSI: 412765420	**11,373** 3,412 13,725	Class: CC	**2012-06 Guangzhou Wenchong Shipyard Co Ltd — Guangzhou GD** Yd No: 431 Loa 130.30 (BB) Br ex - Dght 6.800 Lbp 115.00 Br md 25.60 Dpth 9.20 Welded, 1 dk	**(B33B2DT) Trailing Suction Hopper Dredger** Hopper: 10,000 Compartments: 1 Ho, ER 1 Ha: ER (52.5 x 16.8)	**2 oil engines** reduction geared to sc. shaft (s) driving 2 Propellers Total Power: 12,000kW (16,316hp) 15.0k MAN-B&W 12V32/40C 2 x Vee 4 Stroke 12 Cy. 320 x 400 each-6000kW (8158bhp AuxGen: 2 x 5760kW 6600V a.c, 1 x 1200kW 400V a.c Thrusters: 2 Tunnel thruster (f)
7433048 *BSNB* -	**XIN HAI JING** *ex* World Lapis *-2002* *ex* Epta *-1998* *ex* Kalapati *-1988* *ex* Port Royal *-1986* *ex* Cape Trafalgar *-1984* **CHEC Dredging Co Ltd** CCCC Shanghai Dredging Co Ltd SatCom: Inmarsat C 441237415 *Shanghai* *China* MMSI: 412045170	**15,907** 4,772 13,679 T/cm 38.8	Class: CC (LR) ✠ Classed LR until 1/8/02	**1981-09 Cia Comercio e Navegacao (CCN) — Niteroi (Estaleiro Maua)** Yd No: 136 Converted From: Bulk Carrier-2002 Loa 173.16 (BB) Br ex 26.67 Dght 8.800 Lbp 162.01 Br md 26.61 Dpth 13.52 Welded, 1 dk	**(B33B2DT) Trailing Suction Hopper Dredger** Hopper: 13,000 Cranes: 1	**1 oil engine** driving 1 FP propeller Total Power: 9,782kW (13,300hp) 15.0k MAN K7SZ70/125 1 x 2 Stroke 7 Cy. 700 x 1250 9782kW (13300bhp) Mecanica Pesada SA-Brazil AuxGen: 3 x 520kW 450V 60Hz a.c Boilers: AuxB (o.f.) 7.0kgf/cm² (6.9bar), AuxB (ex.g.) 7.0kgf/cm² (6.9bar) Thrusters: 1 Tunnel thruster (f) Fuel: 255.0 (d.f.) 1949.0 (r.f.) 34.5pd

IMO / Call sign	Name / Owner	Tonnage	Class	Builder / Dimensions	Type	Machinery
9309954 BPBQ	**XIN HAI KOU** **China Shipping Container Lines Co Ltd** - *Shanghai* *China* MMSI: 413144000	**41,482** 24,001 52,212	Class: CC	**2005-09 Dalian New Shipbuilding Heavy Industries Co Ltd — Dalian LN** Yd No: C4250-3 Loa 263.23 (BB) Br ex 32.30 Dght 12.800 Lbp 251.88 Br md 32.25 Dpth 19.30 Welded, 1 dk	**(A33A2CC) Container Ship (Fully Cellular)** TEU 4250 C Ho 1586 TEU C Dk 2664 TEU incl 400 ref C. Compartments: 7 Cell Ho, ER Ice Capable	**1 oil engine** driving 1 FP propeller Total Power: 36,480kW (49,598hp) 24.2kn MAN-B&W 8K90MC-C 1 x 2 Stroke 8 Cy. 900 x 2300 36480kW (49598bhp) Mitsui Engineering & Shipbuilding CLtd-Japan AuxGen: 3 x 1960kW 450V 60Hz a.c Thrusters: 1 Tunnel thruster (f)
9247845 BSNS	**XIN HAI LONG** **CHEC Dredging Co Ltd** CCCC Shanghai Dredging Co Ltd *Shanghai* *China* MMSI: 412678000	**14,091** 4,227 14,864	Class: CC	**2003-03 IHC Holland NV Dredgers — Kinderdijk** Yd No: C01225 Loa 152.71 Br ex - Dght 9.000 Lbp 140.00 Br md 27.00 Dpth 10.40 Welded, 1 dk	**(B33B2DT) Trailing Suction Hopper Dredger** Hopper: 12,888 Compartments: 1 Ho, ER 1 Ha: ER (51.0 x 8.8)	**2 oil engines** geared to sc. shafts driving 2 CP propellers Total Power: 18,000kW (24,472hp) 16.3kn Sulzer 12ZAV40S 2 x Vee 4 Stroke 12 Cy. 400 x 560 each-9000kW (12236bhp) Wartsila Nederland BV-Netherlands Thrusters: 2 Tunnel thruster (f)
9562489 BQDM	**XIN HAI MA** **CHEC Dredging Co Ltd** - *Shanghai* *China* MMSI: 413375380	**11,701** 3,510 14,835	Class: CC	**2010-02 Guangzhou Wenchong Shipyard Co Ltd — Guangzhou GD** Yd No: 378 Loa 134.40 Br ex - Dght 7.400 Lbp 125.60 Br md 25.32 Dpth 10.00 Welded, 1 dk	**(B33B2DT) Trailing Suction Hopper Dredger** Hopper: 9,590	**2 oil engines** reduction geared to sc. shafts driving 2 Propellers Total Power: 17,400kW (23,658hp) 15.0kn Wartsila 12V38 2 x Vee 4 Stroke 12 Cy. 380 x 475 each-8700kW (11829bhp) Wartsila Italia SpA-Italy AuxGen: 1 x 950kW 400V a.c, 2 x 2500kW 690V a.c Thrusters: 2 Tunnel thruster (f)
9557642 BQDN -	**XIN HAI NIU** **CHEC Dredging Co Ltd** CCCC Shanghai Dredging Co Ltd *Shanghai* *China* MMSI: 413375390	**11,701** 3,510 15,403	Class: CC	**2009-11 Guangzhou Wenchong Shipyard Co Ltd — Guangzhou GD** Yd No: 370 Loa 134.40 (BB) Br ex - Dght 7.400 Lbp 125.60 Br md 25.32 Dpth 10.00 Welded, 1 dk	**(B33B2DT) Trailing Suction Hopper Dredger** Hopper: 10,000	**2 oil engines** geared to sc. safts driving 2 FP propellers Total Power: 16,800kW (22,842hp) 15.0kn Wartsila 12V38B 2 x Vee 4 Stroke 12 Cy. 380 x 475 each-8400kW (11421bhp) Wartsila Finland Oy-Finland Thrusters: 2 Tunnel thruster (f)
7900443 - -	**XIN HAI NO. 3** *ex* Hai Xin No. 1 *-2000* *ex* Shinkurashiki Maru *-1988* - - *China*	**1,448** 752 490		**1979-02 Kanda Zosensho K.K. — Japan** Yd No: 236 Loa 57.99 Br ex 14.51 Dght 3.050 Lbp 53.22 Br md 12.06 Dpth 4.02 Welded, 1 dk	**(A37B2PS) Passenger Ship**	**2 oil engines** reduction geared to sc. shafts driving 2 FP propellers Total Power: 1,912kW (2,600hp) Daihatsu 6DSM-26 2 x 4 Stroke 6 Cy. 260 x 320 each-956kW (1300bhp) Daihatsu Diesel Manufacturing Co Lt-Japan
7927104 - -	**XIN HAI NO. 4** *ex* Hai Xin No. 2 *-2000* *ex* Shin Marugame Maru *-1999* - *China*	**1,448** 752 493		**1979-12 Kanda Zosensho K.K. — Kawajiri** Yd No: 252 Loa 57.99 Br ex - Dght 3.090 Lbp 53.22 Br md 14.51 Dpth 4.02 Welded, 1 dk	**(A36A2PR) Passenger/Ro-Ro Ship (Vehicles)** Passengers: unberthed: 700	**2 oil engines** geared to sc. shafts driving 2 FP propellers Total Power: 1,912kW (2,600hp) Daihatsu 6DSM-26 2 x 4 Stroke 6 Cy. 260 x 320 each-956kW (1300bhp) Daihatsu Diesel Manufacturing Co Lt-Japan
7429592 - -	**XIN HAI No. 8** *ex* Iyo *-1993* **Ocean Cheer Shipping Inc** Mitsui Warehouse Co Ltd (Mitsui-Soko Co Ltd)	*698* 295 241		**1975-09 Imamura Zosen — Kure** Yd No: 202 Loa 55.76 Br ex 13.11 Dght 2.642 Lbp 52.51 Br md 11.10 Dpth 3.81 Welded, 1 dk	**(A36A2PR) Passenger/Ro-Ro Ship (Vehicles)** Passengers: unberthed: 490 Trailers: 19	**2 oil engines** driving 2 FP propellers Total Power: 956kW (1,300hp) 14.0kn Daihatsu 6DSM-26 2 x 4 Stroke 6 Cy. 260 x 320 each-478kW (650bhp) Daihatsu Diesel Manufacturing Co Lt-Japan
9099078 - -	**XIN HAI NO. 9** **Hainan Strait Shipping Co Ltd** *Haikou, Hainan* *China* MMSI: 412523110	**626** 325 1,000		**1992-10 Guangdong New China Shipyard Co Ltd — Dongguan GD** Loa - Br ex - Dght 3.800 Lbp 58.83 Br md 11.60 Dpth - Welded, 1 dk	**(A31A2GX) General Cargo Ship**	**1 oil engine** driving 1 Propeller Total Power: 720kW (979hp) Chinese Std. Type 1 x 4 Stroke 720kW (979bhp) Guangzhou Diesel Engine Factory CoLtd-China
9405980 XUNS8 -	**XIN HAI RONG** **Sea Otter Merchant Shipping Co Ltd** Ever Maru Shipping SA SatCom: Inmarsat C 451477620 *Phnom Penh* *Cambodia* MMSI: 514776000 Official number: 0606396	**4,327** 2,423 6,500	Class: UB	**2006-07 Zhoushan Longtai Shipbuilding Co Ltd — Zhoushan ZJ** Loa 116.66 (BB) Br ex - Dght 6.300 Lbp 108.00 Br md 16.20 Dpth 8.20 Welded, 1 dk	**(A31A2GX) General Cargo Ship** Grain: 9,298; Bale: 8,545 Compartments: 3 Ho, ER 3 Ha: ER	**1 oil engine** reduction geared to sc. shaft driving 1 FP propeller Total Power: 2,060kW (2,801hp) 11.5kn Chinese Std. Type 8320ZCD 1 x 4 Stroke 2060kW (2801bhp) Guangzhou Diesel Engine Factory CoLtd-China AuxGen: 3 x 160kW a.c Fuel: 76.0 (d.f.) 278.0 (r.f.)
9587001 3EWH6 -	**XIN HAI SHENG 17** *ex* Zhen Wei 17 *-2013* **Yan Song Jun & Others** *Panama* *Panama* MMSI: 372154000 Official number: 44712PEXTF	**9,268** 5,371 14,763	Class: IB	**2010-01 Zhoushan Haitian Shipyard Co Ltd — Daishan County ZJ** Yd No: HT0810 Loa 144.58 (BB) Br ex - Dght 8.000 Lbp 136.00 Br md 21.00 Dpth 10.80 Welded, 1 dk	**(A31A2GX) General Cargo Ship** Grain: 20,800	**1 oil engine** reduction geared to sc. shaft driving 1 FP propeller Total Power: 1,765kW (2,400hp) 12.0kn Chinese Std. Type 8320ZC 1 x 4 Stroke 8 Cy. 320 x 440 1765kW (2400bhp) Ningbo CSI Power & Machinery GroupCo Ltd-China
9617076 BVLM7 -	**XIN HAI TONG 1** **Fuzhou Highton Shipping Co Ltd** - *Fuzhou, Fujian* *China*	**31,638** 17,717 51,038	Class: ZC (CC)	**2013-01 Taizhou Sanfu Ship Engineering Co Ltd — Taizhou JS** Yd No: SF100115 Loa 199.95 (BB) Br ex - Dght 12.100 Lbp 195.00 Br md 32.26 Dpth 16.50 Welded, 1 dk	**(A21A2BC) Bulk Carrier** Grain: 59,100 Compartments: 5 Ho, ER 5 Ha: ER Cranes: 4x30t Ice Capable	**1 oil engine** driving 1 FP propeller Total Power: 5,640kW (7,668hp) 14.0kn MAN-B&W 6S46MC-C 1 x 2 Stroke 6 Cy. 460 x 1932 5640kW (7668bhp)
9617088 BVNO7 -	**XIN HAI TONG 2** **Fuzhou Highton Shipping Co Ltd** - *Fuzhou, Fujian* *China*	**31,663** 17,731 50,958	Class: CC	**2013-07 Taizhou Sanfu Ship Engineering Co Ltd — Taizhou JS** Yd No: SF100116 Loa 199.95 (BB) Br ex - Dght 12.100 Lbp 195.00 Br md 32.26 Dpth 16.50 Welded, 1 dk	**(A21A2BC) Bulk Carrier** Grain: 59,100 Compartments: 5 Ho, ER 5 Ha: ER Cranes: 4x30t Ice Capable	**1 oil engine** driving 1 FP propeller Total Power: 5,640kW (7,668hp) 14.0kn MAN-B&W 6S46MC-C 1 x 2 Stroke 6 Cy. 460 x 1932 5640kW (7668bhp) Hudong Heavy Machinery Co Ltd-China
9734501 BVOK7 -	**XIN HAI TONG 3** **Fuzhou Highton Shipping Co Ltd** - *Fuzhou, Fujian* *China* MMSI: 413987000	**31,663** 17,731 48,891		**2013-10 Taizhou Sanfu Ship Engineering Co Ltd — Taizhou JS** Yd No: SF100117 Loa 199.95 Br ex - Dght 12.100 Lbp 195.00 Br md 32.26 Dpth 16.50 Welded, 1 dk	**(A21A2BC) Bulk Carrier**	**1 oil engine** driving 1 Propeller
9701803 BVON7 -	**XIN HAI TONG 5** *ex* Lan Hai Da Sao *-2014* **Fuzhou Highton Shipping Co Ltd** - *China* MMSI: 414181000	**31,000** - 51,000		**2014-01 Taizhou CATIC Shipbuilding Heavy Industry Ltd — Taizhou JS** Yd No: TC0301 Loa 199.95 (BB) Br ex - Dght 10.800 Lbp - Br md 32.26 Dpth 16.50 Welded, 1 dk	**(A21A2BC) Bulk Carrier** Grain: 59,100 Compartments: 5 Ho, ER 5 Ha: ER Cranes: 4x30t	**1 oil engine** driving 1 FP propeller 15.0kn
9701815 - -	**XIN HAI TONG 6** *ex* Lan Hai Xiang Qin *-2014* **Fuzhou Highton Shipping Co Ltd** - *China*	**31,000** - 51,000		**2014-02 Taizhou CATIC Shipbuilding Heavy Industry Ltd — Taizhou JS** Yd No: TC0302 Loa 199.95 (BB) Br ex - Dght 10.800 Lbp - Br md 32.26 Dpth 16.50 Welded, 1 dk	**(A21A2BC) Bulk Carrier** Grain: 59,100 Compartments: 5 Ho, ER 5 Ha: ER Cranes: 4x30t	**1 oil engine** driving 1 FP propeller 15.0kn
9701827 BVOM7 -	**XIN HAI TONG 7** *ex* Lan Hai Hao You *-2014* **Fuzhou Highton Shipping Co Ltd** - *China* MMSI: 414183000	**31,000** - 51,000	Class: CC (Class contemplated)	**2014-02 Taizhou CATIC Shipbuilding Heavy Industry Ltd — Taizhou JS** Yd No: TC0305 Loa 199.95 (BB) Br ex - Dght 10.800 Lbp - Br md 32.26 Dpth 16.50 Welded, 1 dk	**(A21A2BC) Bulk Carrier** Grain: 59,100 Compartments: 5 Ho, ER 5 Ha: ER Cranes: 4x30t	**1 oil engine** driving 1 FP propeller 15.0kn
9431484 BIRW -	**XIN HAI XIU** *ex* Dong Fang 29 *-2008* **Shanghai Zhonggu Xinliang Shipping Co Ltd** - *Shanghai* *China* MMSI: 412373880	**6,680** 3,190 9,500	Class: CC	**2007-09 Ningbo Dongfang Shipyard Co Ltd — Ningbo ZJ** Yd No: C05-004 Loa 131.55 Br ex - Dght 6.900 Lbp 122.00 Br md 18.80 Dpth 9.40 Welded, 1 dk	**(A31A2GX) General Cargo Ship** Grain: 10,973; Bale: 10,973 TEU 529 C Ho 216 TEU C Dk 313 TEU. Compartments: 3 Ho, ER 3 Ha: (31.5 x 15.0)ER 2 (25.2 x 15.0) Ice Capable	**1 oil engine** reduction geared to sc. shafts driving 1 FP propeller Total Power: 2,944kW (4,003hp) 14.3kn Pielstick 8PC2-5L 1 x 4 Stroke 8 Cy. 400 x 460 2944kW (4003bhp) Shaanxi Diesel Heavy Industry Co Lt-China

IMO / Call sign	Name / Owner / Manager	Tonnage	Class	Builder / Dimensions	Type / Capacity	Machinery
8909903 - -	**XIN HAI ZHOU** *ex* Kakogawa Maru *-2007* **Ever Maru Shipping Co Ltd** Ever Maru Shipping SA	*5,410* 2,025 8,500	Class: UB (NK)	**1989-10 Shin Kurushima Dockyard Co. Ltd. — Akitsu** Yd No: 2636 Loa 128.02 (BB) Br ex - Dght 6.245 Lbp 119.50 Br md 18.80 Dpth 7.95 Welded, 1 dk	**(A24E2BL) Limestone Carrier** Grain: 7,076 Compartments: 3 Ho, ER 3 Ha: 2 (16.8 x 11.2) (22.4 x 11.2)ER	**1 oil engine** driving 1 FP propeller Total Power: 2,939kW (3,996hp) 14.5kn Hanshin 6LF50 1 x 4 Stroke 6 Cy. 500 x 800 2939kW (3996bhp) The Hanshin Diesel Works Ltd-Japan AuxGen: 2 x 200kW a.c Thrusters: 1 Thwart. CP thruster (f)
8656609 *3FZA3* -	**XIN HAI ZHOU 26** **Ningbo Haizhou Shipping Co Ltd** YKJ Shipping Co Ltd *Panama* *Panama* MMSI: 373958000 Official number: 43821PEXTF	**14,095** 7,829 21,902	Class: OM (ZC)	**2009-07 Zhejiang Richland Shipbuilding Co Ltd — Zhoushan ZJ** Yd No: 200831470836 Loa 160.91 Br ex - Dght 9.500 Lbp 149.80 Br md 23.80 Dpth 13.00 Welded, 1 dk	**(A21A2BC) Bulk Carrier** Grain: 27,600	**1 oil engine** driving 1 FP propeller Total Power: 4,051kW (5,508hp) 11.0kn
9592082 *VRLW8* -	**XIN HAN** **Great Fame Enterprise Ltd** Global Marine Ship Management Co Ltd *Hong Kong* *Hong Kong* MMSI: 477631800 Official number: HK-3790	**44,543** 26,982 82,297 T/cm 72.3	Class: CC NV	**2013-06 Dalian Shipbuilding Industry Co Ltd — Dalian LN (No 2 Yard)** Yd No: BC810-4 Loa 229.00 (BB) Br ex 32.30 Dght 14.450 Lbp 225.42 Br md 32.26 Dpth 20.10 Welded, 1 dk	**(A21A2BC) Bulk Carrier** Grain: 97,138 Compartments: 7 Ho, ER 7 Ha: 6 (15.8 x 15.0)ER (15.8 x 12.0)	**1 oil engine** driving 1 FP propeller Total Power: 9,800kW (13,324hp) 14.5kn MAN-B&W 5S60ME-C8 1 x 2 Stroke 5 Cy. 600 x 2400 9800kW (13324bhp) Dalian Marine Diesel Co Ltd-China AuxGen: 3 x 600kW 450V a.c
9389784 *VRGB4* -	**XIN HAN YANG** **Xin Han Yang Shipping SA** China Shipping Tanker Co Ltd SatCom: Inmarsat C 447702297 *Hong Kong* *Hong Kong* MMSI: 477639800 Official number: HK-2576	**152,727** 98,415 297,293 T/cm 177.9	Class: CC	**2009-12 Dalian Shipbuilding Industry Co Ltd — Dalian LN (No 2 Yard)** Yd No: T3000-21 Loa 330.00 (BB) Br ex 60.05 Dght 21.500 Lbp 316.00 Br md 60.00 Dpth 29.70 Welded, 1 dk	**(A13A2TV) Crude Oil Tanker** Double Hull (13F) Liq: 324,600; Liq (Oil): 324,600 Compartments: 5 Ta, 10 Wing Ta, 2 Wing Slop Ta, ER 3 Cargo Pump (s): 3x5500m³/hr Manifold: Bow/CM: 162.5m	**1 oil engine** driving 1 FP propeller Total Power: 25,480kW (34,643hp) 15.8kn MAN-B&W 7S80MC 1 x 2 Stroke 7 Cy. 800 x 3056 25480kW (34643bhp) Doosan Engine Co Ltd-South Korea AuxGen: 3 x 975kW 450V a.c Fuel: 429.6 (d.f.) 7117.3 (r.f.)
9523017 *BPKG* -	**XIN HANG ZHOU** **China Shipping Container Lines Co Ltd** - SatCom: Inmarsat C 441471310 *Shanghai* *China* MMSI: 414713000 Official number: 0012000103	**47,917** 24,185 67,040	Class: CC	**2012-05 Shanghai Jiangnan Changxing Heavy Industry Co Ltd — Shanghai** Yd No: H1051A Loa 255.10 (BB) Br ex - Dght 13.500 Lbp 242.00 Br md 37.30 Dpth 19.60 Welded, 1 dk	**(A33A2CC) Container Ship (Fully Cellular)** TEU 4738 C Ho 1826 TEU C Dk 2912 TEU incl 300 ref C Ice Capable	**1 oil engine** driving 1 FP propeller Total Power: 21,910kW (29,789hp) 18.0kn Wartsila 7RT-flex68 1 x 2 Stroke 7 Cy. 680 x 2720 21910kW (29789bhp) Doosan Engine Co Ltd-South Korea AuxGen: 1 x 1240kW 450V a.c, 2 x 1650kW 450V a.c Thrusters: 1 Tunnel thruster (f)
9367891 *3FTD2* -	**XIN HE DA** **Zhoushan Hefeng Shipping Co Ltd** Peace Ocean Shipping SA *Panama* *Panama* MMSI: 352004000 Official number: 43864PEXTF1	**7,808** 4,372 10,800	Class: IB	**2005-11 Zhoushan Zhaobao Shipbuilding & Repair Co Ltd — Zhoushan ZJ** Loa 135.30 (BB) Br ex - Dght 7.670 Lbp 125.60 Br md 20.80 Dpth 10.50 Welded, 1 dk	**(A33A2CC) Container Ship (Fully Cellular)** TEU 716 C Ho 330 TEU C Dk 386 TEU incl 40 ref C. Compartments: 4 Cell Ho, ER 4 Ha: ER	**1 oil engine** driving 1 FP propeller Total Power: 5,882kW (7,997hp) 14.5kn MAN-B&W 6L42MC 1 x 2 Stroke 6 Cy. 420 x 1360 5882kW (7997bhp) Hudong Heavy Machinery Co Ltd-China AuxGen: 2 x 600kW a.c
9101089 *BXDA* -	**XIN HE SHAN** **He Gang Passenger Transportation Co Ltd** Yuet Hing Marine Supplies Co Ltd *Jiangmen, Guangdong* *China* MMSI: 412460960	**467** 156 37	Class: CC	**1994-07 Austal Ships Pty Ltd — Fremantle WA** Yd No: 111 Loa 40.10 Br ex 10.31 Dght 1.275 Lbp 35.00 Br md 10.00 Dpth 3.80 Welded, 1 dk	**(A37B2PS) Passenger Ship** Hull Material: Aluminium Alloy Passengers: unberthed: 300	**2 oil engines** with clutches, flexible couplings & sr geared to sc. shafts driving 2 Water jets Total Power: 3,920kW (5,330hp) M.T.U. 16V396TE74L 2 x Vee 4 Stroke 16 Cy. 165 x 185 each-1960kW (2665bhp) MTU Friedrichshafen GmbH-Friedrichshafen
9651084 *BKXZ5* -	**XIN HENG SHUN 8** **Zhejiang Hengshun Shipping Co Ltd** *Zhoushan, Zhejiang* *China* MMSI: 413445460	**2,984** 1,427 4,389	Class: CC	**2012-05 Taizhou Zhongzhou Shipbuilding Co Ltd — Sanmen County ZJ** Yd No: ZZSY-06 Loa 96.17 (BB) Br ex 15.22 Dght 5.600 Lbp 89.80 Br md 15.20 Dpth 7.00 Welded, 1 dk	**(A12B2TR) Chemical/Products Tanker** Double Hull (13F) Liq: 4,784; Liq (Oil): 4,784 Cargo Heating Coils Compartments: 5 Wing Ta, 5 Wing Ta, 1 Wing Slop Ta, 1 Wing Slop Ta, ER Manifold: Bow/CM: 56.5m Ice Capable	**1 oil engine** reduction geared to sc. shaft driving 1 FP propeller Total Power: 2,000kW (2,719hp) 11.5kn Chinese Std. Type G8300ZC 1 x 4 Stroke 8 Cy. 300 x 380 2000kW (2719bhp) Ningbo CSI Power & Machinery GroupCo Ltd-China AuxGen: 2 x 200kW 400V a.c
9642796 *VRMG9* -	**XIN HONG** **Max Ocean Shipping Ltd** South Ocean Shipping Co Ltd *Hong Kong* *Hong Kong* MMSI: 477519300 Official number: HK-3872	**44,543** 26,987 82,226 T/cm 72.3	Class: CC NV	**2013-10 Dalian Shipbuilding Industry Co Ltd — Dalian LN (No 2 Yard)** Yd No: BC810-9 Loa 229.00 (BB) Br ex - Dght 14.580 Lbp 225.50 Br md 32.26 Dpth 20.25 Welded, 1 dk	**(A21A2BC) Bulk Carrier** Grain: 97,138 Compartments: 7 Ho, ER 7 Ha: 6 (15.8 x 15.0)ER (15.8 x 12.0)	**1 oil engine** driving 1 FP propeller Total Power: 9,800kW (13,324hp) 14.5kn MAN-B&W 5S60ME-C8 1 x 2 Stroke 5 Cy. 600 x 2400 9800kW (13324bhp) Dalian Marine Diesel Co Ltd-China AuxGen: 3 x 600kW 450V a.c
9562295 *BVEB8* -	**XIN HONG BAO SHI** **Fujian Xiamen Shipping Corp** - SatCom: Inmarsat C 441386010 *Xiamen, Fujian* *China* MMSI: 413860000	**32,911** 19,156 57,122 T/cm 58.8	Class: CC	**2009-09 Yangzhou Guoyu Shipbuilding Co Ltd — Yangzhou JS** Yd No: GY440 Loa 189.99 (BB) Br ex - Dght 12.800 Lbp 185.00 Br md 32.26 Dpth 18.00 Welded, 1 dk	**(A21A2BC) Bulk Carrier** Grain: 71,634; Bale: 68,200 Compartments: 5 Ho, ER 5 Ha: 4 (21.3 x 18.3)ER (18.9 x 18.3) Cranes: 4x36t	**1 oil engine** driving 1 FP propeller Total Power: 9,720kW (13,215hp) 14.2kn Wartsila 6RT-flex50 1 x 2 Stroke 6 Cy. 500 x 2050 9720kW (13215bhp) Diesel United Ltd.-Aioi AuxGen: 3 x 600kW 450V a.c
9086930 *BRNE* -	**XIN HONG HAI** *ex* Alabanda *-2011* *ex* Wilrider *-2003* *ex* Abidin Pak *-2002* *ex* Channel Prosperity *-1997* **Guangdong Haidian Shipping Co Ltd** - SatCom: Inmarsat C 441280410 *Guangzhou, Guangdong* *China* MMSI: 412804000	**38,433** 24,680 74,044 T/cm 66.1	Class: CC (NK) (TL) (NV) (BV)	**1995-05 Hashihama Shipbuilding Co Ltd — Tadotsu KG** (Hull) Yd No: 1061 **1995-05 Tsuneishi Shipbuilding Co Ltd — Fukuyama HS** Yd No: 1061 Loa 225.00 (BB) Br ex - Dght 13.870 Lbp 216.00 Br md 32.26 Dpth 19.10 Welded, 1 dk	**(A21A2BC) Bulk Carrier** Grain: 88,332 Compartments: 7 Ho, ER 7 Ha: (15.3 x 12.8)6 (17.0 x 15.4)ER	**1 oil engine** driving 1 FP propeller Total Power: 8,899kW (12,099hp) 14.5kn B&W 6S60MC 1 x 2 Stroke 6 Cy. 600 x 2292 8899kW (12099bhp) Mitsui Engineering & Shipbuilding CLtd-Japan AuxGen: 3 x 400kW 450V 60Hz a.c Fuel: 2070.0 (r.f.)
9314222 *VRCH5* -	**XIN HONG KONG** **Yangshan C Shipping Co Ltd** China International Ship Management Co Ltd (CISM) SatCom: Inmarsat C 447759360 *Hong Kong* *Hong Kong* MMSI: 477593600 Official number: HK-1794	**108,069** 57,365 111,746	Class: LR ✠ **100A1** SS 02/2012 container ship **ShipRight** (SDA, FDA, CM) *IWS LI EP ✠ **LMC** **UMS** Eq.Ltr: c*; Cable: 759.0/111.0 U3 (a)	**2007-02 Samsung Heavy Industries Co Ltd — Geoje** Yd No: 1565 Loa 336.70 (BB) Br ex 45.64 Dght 15.030 Lbp 321.00 Br md 45.60 Dpth 27.20 Welded, 1 dk	**(A33A2CC) Container Ship (Fully Cellular)** TEU 9572 C Ho 4666 TEU C Dk 4906 TEU incl 700 ref C. Compartments: 9 Cell Ho, ER	**1 oil engine** driving 1 FP propeller Total Power: 68,520kW (93,160hp) 25.2kn MAN-B&W 12K98MC-C 1 x 2 Stroke 12 Cy. 980 x 2400 68520kW (93160bhp) Doosan Engine Co Ltd-South Korea AuxGen: 4 x 2750kW 6600V 60Hz a.c Boilers: e (ex.g.) 8.2kgf/cm² (8.0bar), WTAuxB (o.f.) 8.2kgf/cm² (8.0bar) Thrusters: 1 Thwart. CP thruster (f)
9008615 *BPAY* -	**XIN HU ZHOU** *ex* MSC Basel *-2012* *ex* Shanghai Senator *-2004* *ex* DSR Atlantic *-1997* **China Shipping Container Lines Co Ltd** - *China* MMSI: 414717000	**34,231** 16,058 45,696 T/cm 58.5	Class: (GL)	**1992-08 Thyssen Nordseewerke GmbH — Emden** Yd No: 499 Loa 216.19 (BB) Br ex - Dght 12.520 Lbp 206.15 Br md 32.20 Dpth 19.40 Welded, 1 dk	**(A33A2CC) Container Ship (Fully Cellular)** Grain: 70,903 TEU 2680 C Ho 1406 TEU C Dk 1274 TEU incl 150 ref C. Compartments: 6 Cell Ho, ER 11 Ha: (12.6 x 15.4) (12.6 x 23.0)9 (12.6 x 28.1)ER Ice Capable	**1 oil engine** driving 1 FP propeller Total Power: 16,440kW (22,352hp) 19.0kn Sulzer 6RTA72 1 x 2 Stroke 6 Cy. 720 x 2500 16440kW (22352bhp) Bremer Vulkan AG Schiffbau u.Maschinenfabrik-Bremen AuxGen: 2 x 900kW 220/440V a.c, 1 x 560kW 220/440V a.c, 1 x 118kW 220/440V a.c Thrusters: 1 Thwart. FP thruster (f) Fuel: 105.0 (d.f.) 3590.0 (r.f.) 63.0pd
9407172 - -	**XIN HUA** *ex* Zhen Hua 69 *-2011* **Dandong Xinhua Shipping Co Ltd** Yantai Xiaochuan Shipping Co Ltd *Wenzhou, Zhejiang* *China*	**2,986** 1,809 5,294	Class: UB	**2006-06 Duchang Shipbuilding General Yard — Duchang County JX** Loa 97.80 Br ex - Dght 5.850 Lbp 91.50 Br md 15.80 Dpth 7.40 Welded, 1 dk	**(A31A2GX) General Cargo Ship**	**1 oil engine** reduction geared to sc. shaft driving 1 FP propeller Total Power: 2,060kW (2,801hp) 11.0kn Guangzhou 8320ZC 1 x 4 Stroke 8 Cy. 320 x 440 2060kW (2801bhp) Guangzhou Diesel Engine Factory CoLtd-China
9592068 *VRKM5* -	**XIN HUA** **Well Fame Shipping Ltd** South Ocean Shipping Co Ltd *Hong Kong* *Hong Kong* MMSI: 477098200 Official number: HK-3496	**44,543** 26,958 82,269 T/cm 72.5	Class: CC NV	**2012-11 Dalian Shipbuilding Industry Co Ltd — Dalian LN (No 2 Yard)** Yd No: BC810-2 Loa 228.97 (BB) Br ex 32.30 Dght 14.450 Lbp 225.40 Br md 32.26 Dpth 20.10 Welded, 1 dk	**(A21A2BC) Bulk Carrier** Grain: 97,138 Compartments: 7 Ho, ER 7 Ha: 6 (15.8 x 15.0)ER (15.8 x 12.0)	**1 oil engine** driving 1 FP propeller Total Power: 9,800kW (13,324hp) 14.5kn MAN-B&W 5S60ME-C8 1 x 2 Stroke 5 Cy. 600 x 2400 9800kW (13324bhp) Dalian Marine Diesel Co Ltd-China AuxGen: 3 x 600kW 450V a.c Fuel: 173.0 (d.f.) 2529.0 (r.f.)

IMO / Call sign	Name / Owner	Tonnage	Class	Build	Type	Machinery
032803	**XIN HUA 7** **China Shipping Tanker Co Ltd** - *Shanghai* *China* MMSI: 412712000	**2,720** 1,462 3,881	Class: (CC)	**1981**-07 **Zhonghua Shipyard — Shanghai** Loa 101.15 Br ex - Dght 6.171 Lbp 92.30 Br md 13.80 Dpth 7.70 Welded, 2 dks	**(A31A2GX) General Cargo Ship** Bale: 4,641 Compartments: 3 Ho, ER, 3 Tw Dk 3 Ha: (9.7 x 7.0)2 (11.0 x 7.0)ER Derricks: 6x5t	**1 oil engine** driving 1 FP propeller Total Power: 2,207kW (3,001hp) 14.0kn Hudong 6ESDZ43/82B 1 x 2 Stroke 6 Cy. 430 x 820 2207kW (3001bhp) Hudong Shipyard-China AuxGen: 2 x 250kW 400V 50Hz a.c Fuel: 45.5 (d.f.) 86.5 (r.f.)
222965	**XIN HUA 8** - - *Shanghai* *China*	**2,720** 1,462 3,881	Class: (CC)	**1981**-12 **Zhonghua Shipyard — Shanghai** Loa 101.15 Br ex - Dght 6.171 Lbp 92.05 Br md 13.80 Dpth 7.70 Welded, 2 dks	**(A31A2GX) General Cargo Ship** Bale: 4,641 Compartments: 3 Ho, ER, 3 Tw Dk 3 Ha: (9.7 x 7.0)2 (11.0 x 7.0)ER Derricks: 6x5t	**1 oil engine** driving 1 FP propeller Total Power: 2,207kW (3,001hp) 14.0kn Hudong 6ESDZ43/82B 1 x 2 Stroke 6 Cy. 430 x 820 2207kW (3001bhp) Hudong Shipyard-China AuxGen: 2 x 250kW 400V 50Hz a.c Fuel: 45.5 (d.f.) 86.5 (r.f.)
310044 *3PBP*	**XIN HUANG PU** **China Shipping Container Lines Co Ltd** - *Shanghai* *China* MMSI: 413142000	**41,482** 24,001 52,216	Class: CC	**2005**-08 **Hudong-Zhonghua Shipbuilding (Group) Co Ltd — Shanghai** Yd No: H1358A Loa 263.23 (BB) Br ex - Dght 12.820 Lbp 251.40 Br md 32.20 Dpth 19.30 Welded, 1 dk	**(A33A2CC) Container Ship (Fully Cellular)** TEU 4250 C Ho 1586 TEU C Dk 2664 TEU incl 500 ref C. Compartments: 7 Cell Ho, ER Ice Capable	**1 oil engine** driving 1 FP propeller Total Power: 36,480kW (49,598hp) 24.2kn MAN-B&W 8K90MC-C 1 x 2 Stroke 8 Cy. 900 x 2300 36480kW (49598bhp) Mitsui Engineering & Shipbuilding CLtd-Japan AuxGen: 3 x 1960kW 450V a.c Thrusters: 1 Tunnel thruster (f)
9141182 *3FJI6* -	**XIN HUI HE** **Xinhuihe Maritime Inc** COSCO Container Lines Co Ltd (COSCON) SatCom: Inmarsat B 335660410 *Panama* *Panama* MMSI: 356604000 Official number: 2317096D	**12,122** 5,598 15,673	Class: AB	**1996**-07 **KK Kanasashi — Shizuoka SZ** Yd No: 3387 Loa 144.73 (BB) Br ex - Dght 8.617 Lbp 135.63 Br md 25.00 Dpth 12.77 Welded, 1 dk	**(A33A2CC) Container Ship (Fully Cellular)** TEU 836 incl 100 ref C. Compartments: 4 Cell Ho, ER 14 Ha: ER	**1 oil engine** driving 1 FP propeller Total Power: 7,988kW (10,860hp) 17.0kn B&W 6L50MC 1 x 2 Stroke 6 Cy. 500 x 1620 7988kW (10860bhp) Kawasaki Heavy Industries Ltd-Japan AuxGen: 3 x 560kW a.c Thrusters: 1 Thwart. FP thruster (f) Fuel: 1138.0 (r.f.) 31.2pd
9523108 *3PKM*	**XIN HUI ZHOU** **China Shipping Container Lines Co Ltd** - *Shanghai* *China* MMSI: 414760000	**47,917** 24,185 66,967	Class: CC	**2013**-07 **Shanghai Jiangnan Changxing Heavy Industry Co Ltd — Shanghai** Yd No: H1057A Loa 255.10 (BB) Br ex - Dght 13.500 Lbp 242.00 Br md 37.30 Dpth 19.60 Welded, 1 dk	**(A33A2CC) Container Ship (Fully Cellular)** TEU 4738 C Ho 1826 TEU C Dk 2912 TEU incl 300 ref C Ice Capable	**1 oil engine** driving 1 FP propeller Total Power: 21,910kW (29,789hp) 18.0kn Wartsila 7RT-flex68 1 x 2 Stroke 7 Cy. 680 x 2720 21910kW (29789bhp) Doosan Engine Co Ltd-South Korea AuxGen: 1 x 1240kW 450V a.c, 2 x 1650kW 450V a.c
9277113 *3VIF*	**XIN JI MEI** **Xiamen United Shipping & Enterprises Ltd** Xiamen Ocean Shipping Co (COSCO XIAMEN) *Xiamen, Fujian* *China* MMSI: 412443620	**575** 316 88	Class: CC	**2002**-06 **Wuhan Nanhua High Speed Ship Engineering Co Ltd — Wuhan HB** Yd No: 449 Loa 49.98 Br ex 9.88 Dght 1.950 Lbp 43.50 Br md 9.00 Dpth 3.60 Welded	**(A37B2PS) Passenger Ship**	**2 oil engines** reduction geared to sc. shafts driving 2 FP propellers Total Power: 1,576kW (2,142hp) 17.0kn M.T.U. 12V2000M70 2 x Vee 4 Stroke 12 Cy. 130 x 150 each-788kW (1071bhp) (made 2001) MTU Friedrichshafen GmbH-Friedrichshafen AuxGen: 2 x 75kW 400V a.c
9065376 *BOAL*	**XIN JIAN ZHEN** **China-Japan International Ferry Co Ltd** - SatCom: Inmarsat A 1572302 *Shanghai* *China* MMSI: 412104000 Official number: HU-04000456	**14,543** 4,595 4,321	Class: CC	**1994**-04 **Onomichi Dockyard Co Ltd — Onomichi HS** Yd No: 372 Loa 156.67 (BB) Br ex 23.03 Dght 6.273 Lbp 143.00 Br md 23.00 Dpth 14.80 Welded, 2 dks	**(A36A2PR) Passenger/Ro-Ro Ship (Vehicles)** Passengers: 355 Quarter stern door/ramp (s) Len: 21.00 Wid: 7.50 Swl: 60 TEU 218 C. 218/20' incl. 60 Ref C.	**2 oil engines** with flexible couplings & sr geared to sc. shafts driving 2 CP propellers Total Power: 15,446kW (21,000hp) 21.0kn Pielstick 14PC2-6V-400 2 x Vee 4 Stroke 14 Cy. 400 x 460 each-7723kW (10500bhp) Nippon Kokan KK (NKK Corp)-Japan AuxGen: 3 x 800kW 450V a.c Thrusters: 1 Thwart. CP thruster (f) Fuel: 623.0 (d.f.) 58.6pd
9005716 *BLAF* -	**XIN JIANG SHA 2** *ex Shogen Maru -2003* **Ningbo Haiguang Shipping Co Ltd** *Ningbo, Zhejiang* *China* MMSI: 412408810	**1,368** 766 1,311	Class: CC (NK) (ZC)	**1991**-03 **Shirahama Zosen K.K. — Honai** Yd No: 150 Loa 70.60 (BB) Br ex - Dght 4.480 Lbp 65.00 Br md 12.00 Dpth 5.50 Welded, 1 dk	**(A11B2TG) LPG Tanker** Liq (Gas): 1,720 3 x Gas Tank (s); , ER	**1 oil engine** driving 1 FP propeller Total Power: 1,765kW (2,400hp) 12.0kn Hanshin 6EL35 1 x 4 Stroke 6 Cy. 350 x 700 1765kW (2400bhp) The Hanshin Diesel Works Ltd-Japan AuxGen: 2 x 200kW a.c
8989070 *XUGT2* -	**XIN JIE** **Harvestech International Ltd** East Maritime Services Co Ltd *Phnom Penh* *Cambodia* MMSI: 515379000 Official number: 1304090	**2,995** 1,999 5,300	Class: IB	**2004**-10 **Zhejiang Shunhang Ship Manufacturing Co Ltd — Yueqing ZJ** Loa 106.20 Br ex - Dght 5.500 Lbp - Br md 16.20 Dpth 6.80 Welded, 1 dk	**(A31A2GX) General Cargo Ship**	**1 oil engine** geared to sc. shaft driving 1 Propeller Total Power: 1,765kW (2,400hp) 11.5kn Chinese Std. Type 1 x 4 Stroke 1765kW (2400bhp) Wuxi Antai Power Machinery Co Ltd-China
8328537 - - -	**XIN JIE** *ex Man Kit -2001* - -	*233* 95 -		**1982**-01 **Hong Kong Shipyard Ltd. — Hong Kong** L reg 42.34 Br ex 8.26 Dght - Lbp - Br md - Dpth 2.44 Welded, 2 dks	**(A37B2PS) Passenger Ship**	**2 oil engines** driving 2 FP propellers Total Power: 376kW (512hp) 13.0kn M.T.U. 2 x 4 Stroke 6 Cy. 155 x 165 each-188kW (256bhp) MTU Friedrichshafen GmbH-Friedrichshafen
8660002 *3FEY5* -	**XIN JIN** *ex Guan Quan -2013 ex Bo Zhen 2 -2013* *ex Ming Hai Tong 2 -2008* **Shantou Bozhen Marine Co Ltd** Guangdong Tongcheng Shipping Co Ltd *Panama* *Panama* MMSI: 353582000 Official number: 44429PEXTF2	**3,763** 1,956 6,417	Class: ZC	**2004**-06 **Haidong Shipyard — Taizhou ZJ** Yd No: HD03-011 Loa 104.84 Br ex - Dght 6.200 Lbp 98.20 Br md 16.50 Dpth 7.90 Welded, 1 dk	**(A31A2GX) General Cargo Ship**	**1 oil engine** driving 1 FP propeller Total Power: 1,765kW (2,400hp) 11.0kn Guangzhou 8320ZCD 1 x 4 Stroke 8 Cy. 320 x 440 1765kW (2400bhp) Guangzhou Diesel Engine Factory CoLtd-China
9482677 *3FEQ2* -	**XIN JIN HAI** **China Sun Shipping Inc** Vision Ship Management Ltd SatCom: Inmarsat C 435630313 *Panama* *Panama* MMSI: 356303000 Official number: 4101810	**94,863** 59,641 180,406 T/cm 124.3	Class: LR ✠ **100A1** SS 11/2009 bulk carrier CSR BC-A GRAB (25) Nos. 2, 4, 6 & 8 holds may be empty ESP **ShipRight** (CM) *IWS LI ✠ **LMC** **UMS** Eq.Ltr: B*; Cable: 738.9/107.0 U3 (a)	**2009**-11 **Dalian Shipbuilding Industry Co Ltd — Dalian LN (No 2 Yard)** Yd No: BC1800-23 Loa 294.91 (BB) Br ex 46.05 Dght 18.100 Lbp 285.00 Br md 46.00 Dpth 24.80 Welded, 1 dk	**(A21A2BC) Bulk Carrier** Grain: 201,953 Compartments: 9 Ho, ER 9 Ha: ER	**1 oil engine** driving 1 FP propeller Total Power: 18,660kW (25,370hp) 14.5kn MAN-B&W 6S70MC-C 1 x 2 Stroke 6 Cy. 700 x 2800 18660kW (25370bhp) Dalian Marine Diesel Co Ltd-China AuxGen: 3 x 900kW 450V 60Hz a.c Boilers: AuxB (Comp) 8.9kgf/cm² (8.7bar)
9294068 *BPAD* -	**XIN JIN YANG** **China Shipping Tanker Co Ltd** - SatCom: Inmarsat C 441312110 *Shanghai* *China* MMSI: 413121000	**152,740** 97,129 297,376 T/cm 177.9	Class: CC NV	**2004**-11 **Dalian New Shipbuilding Heavy Industries Co Ltd — Dalian LN** Yd No: T2980-1 Loa 330.00 (BB) Br ex - Dght 21.500 Lbp 316.00 Br md 60.00 Dpth 29.70 Welded, 1 dk	**(A13A2TV) Crude Oil Tanker** Double Hull (13F) Liq: 324,631; Liq (Oil): 333,307 Compartments: 5 Ta, 10 Wing Ta, ER, 2 Wing Slop Ta 3 Cargo Pump (s): 3x5500m³/hr Manifold: Bow/CM: 162m	**1 oil engine** driving 1 FP propeller Total Power: 27,158kW (36,924hp) 15.8kn Sulzer 7RTA84T-B 1 x 2 Stroke 7 Cy. 840 x 3150 27158kW (36924bhp) Doosan Engine Co Ltd-South Korea AuxGen: 3 x 950kW 450V a.c Fuel: 429.6 (d.f.) 7117.3 (r.f.)
8026074 *BPAM*	**XIN JIN ZHOU** *ex Maple River -2002 ex Tor Bay -1993* **China Shipping Container Lines Co Ltd** - *Shanghai* *China* MMSI: 412546000	**33,267** 17,480 34,477	Class: CC (LR) ✠ Classed LR until 15/5/02	**1982**-07 **Thyssen Nordseewerke GmbH — Emden** Yd No: 472 Loa 216.08 (BB) Br ex 32.31 Dght 11.019 Lbp 205.87 Br md 32.26 Dpth 18.80 Welded, 1 dk	**(A33A2CC) Container Ship (Fully Cellular)** Double Sides Entire Compartment Length Bale: 60,743 TEU 2159 C Ho 1116 TEU C Dk 1043 TEU incl 121 ref C. Compartments: ER, 6 Cell Ho 21 Ha: (13.2 x 11.4)2 (13.2 x 8.1)2 (13.2 x 10.8)ER 16 (13.2 x 13.4)	**1 oil engine** driving 1 FP propeller Total Power: 14,501kW (19,716hp) 18.0kn B&W 5L90GFCA 1 x 2 Stroke 5 Cy. 900 x 2180 14501kW (19716bhp) B&W Diesel A/S-Denmark AuxGen: 3 x 960kW 450V 60Hz a.c, 1 x 720kW 450V 60Hz a.c Thrusters: 1 Thwart. CP thruster (f) Fuel: 75.0 (d.f.) 2200.0 (r.f.) 70.0pd

IMO / Call sign	Name / Owner	Tonnage	Class	Builder / Dimensions	Type / Capacity	Machinery
8716332 *BRNC* -	**XIN JING HAI** *ex* Athinagoras *-2006* *ex* Maritsa N. P. *-2005* *ex* Co-Op Harvest *-2003* **Guangdong Haidian Shipping Co Ltd** - *Guangzhou, Guangdong* *China* MMSI: 413249000	**36,983** 22,940 68,377 T/cm 65.2	Class: CC (LR) (NK) Classed LR until 26/7/06	**1988-07 Namura Shipbuilding Co Ltd — Imari SG** Yd No: 893 Loa 224.94 (BB) Br ex 32.26 Dght 13.222 Lbp 217.00 Br md 32.20 Dpth 18.20 Welded, 1 dk	**(A21A2BC) Bulk Carrier** Grain: 80,605 Compartments: 7 Ho, ER 7 Ha: (16.6 x 13.2) (16.6 x 14.9)5 (16.6 x 14.9)ER	**1 oil engine** driving 1 FP propeller Total Power: 9,635kW (13,100hp) 14.7k Sulzer 6RTA62 1 x 2 Stroke 6 Cy. 620 x 2150 9635kW (13100bhp) Mitsubishi Heavy Industries Ltd-Japan AuxGen: 2 x 560kW 450V a.c, 1 x 440kW 450V a.c, 1 x 100kW 450V a.c
8905945 *BPAL* -	**XIN JIU ZHOU** *ex* Black Sea *-2010* *ex* MSC Black Sea *-2010* *ex* Black Sea *-2008* *ex* Zim Ravenna I *-2005* *ex* Choyang Glory *-1998* **China Shipping Container Lines Co Ltd** - *China* MMSI: 413175000	**36,584** 15,135 44,014 T/cm 64.4	Class: (LR) (CC) (KR) (AB) Classed LR until 1/6/10	**1990-09 Daewoo Shipbuilding & Heavy Machinery Ltd — Geoje** Yd No: 4023 Loa 240.00 (BB) Br ex - Dght 11.717 Lbp 224.00 Br md 32.21 Dpth 19.00 Welded, 1 dk	**(A33A2CC) Container Ship (Fully Cellular)** TEU 2797 C Ho 1350 TEU C Dk 1447 TEU incl 99 ref C. Compartments: 7 Ho, ER 14 Ha: 24 Wing Ha:	**1 oil engine** driving 1 FP propeller Total Power: 24,455kW (33,249hp) 22.0kn Sulzer 7RTA84 1 x 2 Stroke 7 Cy. 840 x 2400 24455kW (33249bhp) Hyundai Heavy Industries Co Ltd-South Korea AuxGen: 3 x 1000kW 440V 60Hz a.c Thrusters: 1 Thwart. CP thruster (f) Fuel: 253.9 (d.f.) 3801.1 (r.f.) 90.4pd
8901872 *BLAN8* -	**XIN KAI YUAN 5** *ex* Jolly Platino *-2010* *ex* European Senator *-1997* **Zhejiang Guoyuan Shipping Co Ltd** - *Ningbo, Zhejiang* *China* MMSI: 413439580	**24,305** 10,391 31,584 T/cm 47.5	Class: CC (LR) (RI) (GL) ✠	**1990-10 Hyundai Heavy Industries Co Ltd — Ulsan** Yd No: 675 Loa 181.62 (BB) Br ex - Dght 10.300 Lbp 174.20 Br md 31.41 Dpth 16.01 Welded, 1 dk	**(A33A2CC) Container Ship (Fully Cellular)** TEU 2026 Ho 928 TEU C Dk 1098 TEU incl 100 ref C. Compartments: 4 Cell Ho, ER 18 Ha: 2 (12.8 x 5.3)16 (12.8 x 13.1)ER	**1 oil engine** driving 1 FP propeller Total Power: 13,138kW (17,862hp) 18.0kn B&W 7S60MC 1 x 2 Stroke 7 Cy. 600 x 2292 13138kW (17862bhp) Hyundai Heavy Industries Co Ltd-South Korea AuxGen: 2 x 720kW 220/440V 60Hz a.c, 1 x 500kW 220/440V 60Hz a.c Fuel: 298.0 (d.f.) 2284.0 (r.f.) 53.0pd
9523031 *BPKI* -	**XIN LAN ZHOU** - **China Shipping Container Lines Co Ltd** - SatCom: Inmarsat C 441472110 *Shanghai* *China* MMSI: 414721000	**47,917** 24,185 67,061	Class: CC	**2012-06 Shanghai Jiangnan Changxing Heavy Industry Co Ltd — Shanghai** Yd No: H1053A Loa 255.10 (BB) Br ex - Dght 13.500 Lbp 242.00 Br md 37.30 Dpth 19.60 Welded, 1 dk	**(A33A2CC) Container Ship (Fully Cellular)** TEU 4738 C Ho 1826 TEU C Dk 2912 incl 300 ref C Ice Capable	**1 oil engine** driving 1 FP propeller Total Power: 21,910kW (29,789hp) 18.0kn Wartsila 7RT-flex68 1 x 2 Stroke 7 Cy. 680 x 2720 21910kW (29789bhp) Doosan Engine Co Ltd-South Korea AuxGen: 1 x 1240kW 450V a.c, 2 x 1650kW 450V a.c Thrusters: 1 Tunnel thruster (f)
9614050 *VRMT7* -	**XIN LIAN YANG** - **Xin Lian Yang Shipping SA** China Shipping Tanker Co Ltd *Hong Kong* *Hong Kong* MMSI: 477257200 Official number: HK-3974	**164,106** 108,061 322,861	Class: CC NV	**2014-01 Dalian Shipbuilding Industry Co Ltd — Dalian LN (No 2 Yard)** Yd No: T3000-55 Loa 333.00 (BB) Br ex 60.04 Dght 22.600 Lbp 320.00 Br md 60.00 Dpth 30.50 Welded, 1 dk	**(A13A2TV) Crude Oil Tanker** Double Hull (13F) Liq: 300,000; Liq (Oil): 300,000 Compartments: 5 Wing Ta, 5 Ta, 5 Wing Ta, 1 Wing Slop Ta, 1 Wing Slop Ta, ER 3 Cargo Pump (s): 3x5000m³/hr	**1 oil engine** driving 1 FP propeller Total Power: 29,260kW (39,782hp) 15.0kn MAN-B&W 7S80ME-C8 1 x 2 Stroke 7 Cy. 800 x 3200 29260kW (39782bhp) AuxGen: 3 x 1120kW a.c
9234355 *BPAT* -	**XIN LIAN YUN GANG** - **China Shipping Container Lines Co Ltd** - SatCom: Inmarsat C 441305810 *Shanghai* *China* MMSI: 413058000	**66,433** 37,567 68,944	Class: CC	**2003-09 Dalian New Shipbuilding Heavy Industries Co Ltd — Dalian LN** Yd No: C5600-3 Loa 279.60 (BB) Br ex - Dght 14.000 Lbp 265.80 Br md 40.30 Dpth 24.10 Welded, 1 dk	**(A33A2CC) Container Ship (Fully Cellular)** TEU 5668 C Ho 2586 TEU C Dk 3082 TEU incl 610 ref C. Compartments: 7 Cell Ho, ER Ice Capable	**1 oil engine** driving 1 FP propeller Total Power: 54,809kW (74,518hp) 25.7kn MAN-B&W 12K90MC-C 1 x 2 Stroke 12 Cy. 900 x 2300 54809kW (74518bhp) Mitsui Engineering & Shipbuilding CLtd-Japan AuxGen: 4 x 2320kW 450/230V 60Hz a.c Thrusters: 1 Tunnel thruster (f)
9209726 *BJYP* -	**XIN LIANG** - **Xinliang Shipping Co Ltd of China Grains & Logistics Corp** - SatCom: Inmarsat C 441204312 *Yangpu, Hainan* *China* MMSI: 412521060 Official number: 110003000037	**3,580** 1,323 4,039 T/cm 12.7	Class: CC	**1999-04 Jiangdu Yuehai Shipbuilding Co Ltd — Jiangdu JS** Yd No: J3001 Loa 93.00 (BB) Br ex 16.21 Dght 4.950 Lbp 84.80 Br md 16.20 Dpth 7.20 Welded, 1 dk	**(A31A2GX) General Cargo Ship** Grain: 5,200; Bale: 5,050 TEU 231 C Ho 117 TEU C Dk 114 TEU incl 12 ref C. Compartments: 2 Cell Ho, ER 2 Ha: 2 (25.2 x 12.6)ER	**2 oil engines** with clutches, flexible couplings & sr reverse geared to sc. shafts driving 2 FP propellers Total Power: 1,800kW (2,448hp) 12.6kn Wartsila 6L20 2 x 4 Stroke 6 Cy. 200 x 280 each-900kW (1224bhp) Wartsila NSD Finland Oy-Finland AuxGen: 3 x 160kW 400V 50Hz a.c
8864622 *XUAX6* -	**XIN LONG** *ex* Yuki Maru No. 18 *-2010* **CI Marine Hongkong Co Ltd** East Way Marine Co Ltd *Phnom Penh* *Cambodia* MMSI: 514430000 Official number: 1092516	**1,483** 835 1,581		**1992-04 K.K. Uno Zosensho — Imabari** Yd No: 225 Loa 75.00 Br ex - Dght 4.150 Lbp 70.50 Br md 12.00 Dpth 7.12 Welded, 1 dk	**(A31A2GX) General Cargo Ship** Grain: 2,951; Bale: 2,780	**1 oil engine** geared to sc. shaft driving 1 FP propeller Total Power: 736kW (1,001hp) 12.0kn Hanshin LH31G 1 x 4 Stroke 6 Cy. 310 x 530 736kW (1001bhp) The Hanshin Diesel Works Ltd-Japan
7706392 *BOYU* -	**XIN LONG** *ex* Shoei Maru No. 5 *-1995* *ex* Sewa Maru No. 2 *-1989* **Shenzhen Southern China LPG Shipping Co Ltd** - *Shenzhen, Guangdong* *China* MMSI: 412461530	**763** 318 770	Class: (CC) (NK)	**1977-08 Shirahama Zosen K.K. — Honai** Yd No: 83 Loa 61.20 Br ex - Dght 4.002 Lbp 55.50 Br md 10.00 Dpth 4.60 Welded, 1 dk	**(A11B2TG) LPG Tanker** Liq (Gas): 1,180 2 x Gas Tank (s);	**1 oil engine** driving 1 FP propeller Total Power: 1,177kW (1,600hp) Akasaka DM33 1 x 4 Stroke 6 Cy. 330 x 500 1177kW (1600bhp) Akasaka Tekkosho KK (Akasaka DieselLtd)-Japan AuxGen: 2 x 120kW a.c
9307217 *VRBX6* -	**XIN LOS ANGELES** - **Yangshan A Shipping Co Ltd** China International Ship Management Co Ltd (CISM) SatCom: Inmarsat C 447715870 *Hong Kong* *Hong Kong* MMSI: 477158700 Official number: HK-1715	**108,069** 57,365 111,889	Class: LR ✠ **100A1** SS 06/2011 container ship *IWS LI EP **ShipRight** (SDA, FDA, CM) ✠ **LMC** **UMS** Eq.Ltr: A†; Cable: 759.0/111.0 U3 (a)	**2006-06 Samsung Heavy Industries Co Ltd — Geoje** Yd No: 1558 Loa 336.70 (BB) Br ex 45.64 Dght 15.030 Lbp 321.00 Br md 45.60 Dpth 27.20 Welded, 1 dk	**(A33A2CC) Container Ship (Fully Cellular)** TEU 9572 C Ho 4666 TEU C Dk 4906 TEU incl 700 ref C. Compartments: 9 Cell Ho, ER 9 Ha: ER	**1 oil engine** driving 1 FP propeller Total Power: 68,520kW (93,160hp) 25.2kn MAN-B&W 12K98MC-C 1 x 2 Stroke 12 Cy. 980 x 2400 68520kW (93160bhp) Doosan Engine Co Ltd-South Korea AuxGen: 4 x 2750kW 6600V 60Hz a.c Boilers: e (ex.g.) 8.3kgf/cm² (8.1bar), WTAuxB (o.f.) 8.2kgf/cm² (8.0bar) Thrusters: 1 Thwart. CP thruster (f)
9142007 *BVEO8* -	**XIN LU BAO SHI** *ex* Morning Sky *-2010* **Fujian Xiamen Shipping Corp** - SatCom: Inmarsat C 441393510 *Xiamen, Fujian* *China* MMSI: 413935000	**26,018** 15,520 45,888 T/cm 50.5	Class: CC (NK)	**1996-07 Imabari Shipbuilding Co Ltd — Marugame KG (Marugame Shipyard)** Yd No: 1255 Loa 189.83 (BB) Br ex - Dght 11.660 Lbp 180.60 Br md 31.00 Dpth 16.50 Welded, 1 dk	**(A21A2BC) Bulk Carrier** Grain: 58,881; Bale: 56,201 Compartments: 5 Ho, ER 5 Ha: (20.0 x 16.0)4 (20.8 x 17.6)ER Cranes: 4x30.5t	**1 oil engine** driving 1 FP propeller Total Power: 8,562kW (11,641hp) 14.5kn B&W 6S50MC 1 x 2 Stroke 6 Cy. 500 x 1910 8562kW (11641bhp) Mitsui Engineering & Shipbuilding CLtd-Japan AuxGen: 3 x 400kW 450V 60Hz a.c Fuel: 153.0 (d.f.) (Heating Coils) 1892.0 (r.f.) 28.5pd
8734920 *BVCW8* -	**XIN LU SHENG 3** - **Xiamen Lusheng Shipping Co Ltd** - *Xiamen, Fujian* *China* MMSI: 413693120 Official number: 180008000013	**10,740** 6,014 17,087	Class: (CC)	**2008-01 Ninghai Shipbuilding & Repair Co Ltd — Ninghai County ZJ** Yd No: NH-0701 Loa 149.18 Br ex - Dght 8.650 Lbp 140.88 Br md 21.00 Dpth 11.70 Welded, 1 dk	**(A21A2BC) Bulk Carrier** Grain: 24,000 Compartments: 4 Ho, ER 4 Ha: ER	**1 oil engine** reduction geared to sc. shaft driving 1 FP propeller Total Power: 2,942kW (4,000hp) 12.0kn Yanmar 8N330-UN 1 x 4 Stroke 8 Cy. 330 x 440 2942kW (4000bhp) Qingdao Zichai Boyang Diesel EngineCo Ltd-China
8736356 *BVAH8* -	**XIN LU SHENG 8** - **Xiamen Lusheng Shipping Co Ltd** - *Xiamen, Fujian* *China* MMSI: 413498000 Official number: 2008XM0872	**10,740** 6,014 17,045	Class: (CC)	**2008-10 Zhejiang Yueqing Qiligang Ship Industry Co Ltd — Yueqing ZJ** Yd No: QLG-0706 Loa 149.18 Br ex - Dght 8.660 Lbp 143.48 Br md 21.00 Dpth 11.70 Welded, 1 dk	**(A21A2BC) Bulk Carrier** Grain: 24,000 Compartments: 4 Ho, ER 4 Ha: ER	**1 oil engine** reduction geared to sc. shaft driving 1 FP propeller Total Power: 2,942kW (4,000hp) 12.0kn Yanmar 8N330-UN 1 x 4 Stroke 8 Cy. 330 x 440 2942kW (4000bhp) Qingdao Zichai Boyang Diesel EngineCo Ltd-China
9337925 *BPKC* -	**XIN MEI ZHOU** - **China Shipping Container Lines Co Ltd** - *Shanghai* *China* MMSI: 413165000 Official number: 008000045	**90,757** 57,364 102,453	Class: CC GL	**2008-04 Hudong-Zhonghua Shipbuilding (Group) Co Ltd — Shanghai** Yd No: H1383A Loa 335.00 (BB) Br ex 42.84 Dght 14.650 Lbp 320.06 Br md 42.80 Dpth 24.80 Welded, 1 dk	**(A33A2CC) Container Ship (Fully Cellular)** TEU 8528 C Ho 3874 TEU C Dk 4554 TEU incl 700 ref C.	**1 oil engine** driving 1 FP propeller Total Power: 68,520kW (93,160hp) 25.4kn MAN-B&W 12K98MC-C 1 x 2 Stroke 12 Cy. 980 x 2400 68520kW (93160bhp) Mitsui Engineering & Shipbuilding CLtd-Japan AuxGen: 4 x 2760kW 6600V a.c Thrusters: 1 Tunnel thruster (f)
8880054 *BBQB* -	**XIN MING** *ex* Jin He Leng 1 *-2005* *ex* Lu Shui 107 *-2003* **Dalian Hualong Enterprise Group Import & Products Head Co** - *Qingdao, Shandong* *China*	**232** 69 -	Class: (CC)	**1986 Qingdao Shipyard — Qingdao SD** Loa 43.70 Br ex - Dght 2.750 Lbp 39.00 Br md 7.60 Dpth 3.50 Welded, 1 dk	**(A34A2GR) Refrigerated Cargo Ship** Ins: 438	**1 oil engine** geared to sc. shaft driving 1 FP propeller Total Power: 400kW (544hp) 12.0kn Chinese Std. Type 6300 1 x 4 Stroke 6 Cy. 300 x 380 400kW (544bhp) Ningbo Engine Factory-China AuxGen: 2 x 40kW 400V a.c

021256	**XIN MING DA** *ex* Fuxiang *-2004* *ex* Fengzhou *-2004* *ex* Tirta Niaga VII *-2002* *ex* Patricia *-2002* *ex* Louisa *-1999* *ex* Rosa *-1997* *ex* Continental Rose *-1995* *ex* Sunny Crane *-1988* **HK Sun Tai Wah Shipping Co** Nanjing Yongzheng Marine Co Ltd	**3,667** 1,927 6,155 T/cm 14.1	Class: (KI) (NK) (IR)	**1981-04 Murakami Hide Zosen K.K. — Imabari** Yd No: 198 Loa 105.01 Br ex - Dght 6.708 Lbp 98.41 Br md 15.51 Dpth 7.80 Welded, 1 dk	**(A12B2TR) Chemical/Products Tanker** Liq: 6,748; Liq (Oil): 6,748 Cargo Heating Coils 5 Cargo Pump (s)	**1 oil engine** driving 1 FP propeller Total Power: 2,869kW (3,901hp) 12.5kn Mitsubishi 6UEC37/88H 1 x 2 Stroke 6 Cy. 370 x 880 2869kW (3901bhp) Kobe Hatsudoki KK-Japan AuxGen: 2 x 160kW 445V 60Hz a.c
621663 *KOG6*	**XIN MING DA 28** **Zhejiang Xinmingda Shipping Co Ltd** - SatCom: Inmarsat C 441369266 *Zhoushan, Zhejiang* *China* MMSI: 413446430	**8,344** 4,043 12,637	Class: CC	**2012-06 Ningbo Dongfang Shipyard Co Ltd — Ningbo ZJ** Yd No: DFC10-118 Loa 131.60 Br ex 20.83 Dght 8.200 Lbp 123.00 Br md 20.80 Dpth 11.20 Welded, 1 dk	**(A13B2TP) Products Tanker** Double Hull (13F) Liq: 13,770; Liq (Oil): 13,770 Compartments: 5 Wing Ta, 5 Wing Ta, 1 Wing Slop Ta, 1 Wing Slop Ta, ER Ice Capable	**1 oil engine** reduction geared to sc. shaft driving 1 FP propeller Total Power: 3,552kW (4,829hp) 12.5kn Guangzhou 8G32 1 x 4 Stroke 8 Cy. 320 x 480 3552kW (4829bhp) Guangzhou Diesel Engine Factory CoLtd-China AuxGen: 3 x 300kW 400V a.c
196450 *RRG*	**XIN MING LONG** *ex* Yu Tian 9 *-2010* *ex* Gas Eternity *-2007* **Zhuhai Changhang Shipping Co Ltd** - *Zhuhai, Guangdong* *China* MMSI: 413461720	**3,549** 1,064 2,998 T/cm 12.6	Class: CC (BV)	**1998-12 Watanabe Zosen KK — Imabari EH** Yd No: 311 Loa 95.50 Br ex - Dght 4.500 Lbp 88.50 Br md 16.60 Dpth 7.10 Welded, 1 dk	**(A11B2TG) LPG Tanker** Liq (Gas): 3,500 2 x Gas Tank (s); 2 independent cyl 2 Cargo Pump (s): 2x300m³/hr	**1 oil engine** driving 1 FP propeller Total Power: 2,405kW (3,270hp) 13.0kn B&W 6S26MC 1 x 2 Stroke 6 Cy. 260 x 980 2405kW (3270bhp) Makita Corp-Japan Fuel: 423.0 (r.f.)
656307 *LBA9*	**XIN MING ZHOU 18** **Ningbo United Container Marine Co Ltd** - *Ningbo, Zhejiang* *China* MMSI: 413453640	**9,653** 4,636 12,543	Class: CC	**2014-03 Yangfan Group Co Ltd — Zhoushan ZJ** Yd No: 2267 Loa 143.20 (BB) Br ex - Dght 8.300 Lbp 133.40 Br md 22.60 Dpth 11.30 Welded, 1 dk	**(A33A2CC) Container Ship (Fully Cellular)** TEU 1100	**1 oil engine** driving 1 FP propeller Total Power: 8,730kW (11,869hp) 17.0kn Wartsila 6RT-flex48T 1 x 2 Stroke 6 Cy. 480 x 2000 8730kW (11869bhp) Hudong Heavy Machinery Co Ltd-China
991841 *MPM*	**XIN NAN FANG 96** **Qinzhou South Shipping Co Ltd** - *Qinzhou, Guangxi* *China* MMSI: 412500980 Official number: 440600691	**2,800** 1,568 3,000		**1990-02 Yueqing Shipyard Co Ltd — Yueqing ZJ** Loa 98.20 Br ex - Dght 6.000 Lbp 89.50 Br md 13.86 Dpth 7.60 Welded, 1 dk	**(A31A2GX) General Cargo Ship**	**1 oil engine** driving 1 FP propeller Total Power: 735kW (999hp) Makita 1 x 4 Stroke 735kW (999bhp) Makita Tekkosho-Japan
310056 *PBT*	**XIN NAN SHA** **China Shipping Container Lines Co Ltd** - *Shanghai* *China* MMSI: 413147000 Official number: 010005003	**41,482** 24,001 52,191	Class: CC	**2005-10 Hudong-Zhonghua Shipbuilding (Group) Co Ltd — Shanghai** Yd No: H1359A Loa 263.20 (BB) Br ex - Dght 12.800 Lbp 251.80 Br md 32.20 Dpth 19.30 Welded, 1 dk	**(A33A2CC) Container Ship (Fully Cellular)** TEU 4250 C Ho 1586 TEU C Dk 2664 TEU incl 500 ref C. Compartments: 7 Cell Ho, ER Ice Capable	**1 oil engine** driving 1 FP propeller Total Power: 36,560kW (49,707hp) 24.2kn MAN-B&W 8K90MC-C 1 x 2 Stroke 8 Cy. 900 x 2300 36560kW (49707bhp) Mitsui Engineering & Shipbuilding CLtd-Japan AuxGen: 3 x 1960kW 450V a.c Thrusters: 1 Tunnel thruster (f)
262132 *PBJ*	**XIN NAN TONG** **China Shipping Container Lines Co Ltd** - SatCom: Inmarsat C 441306310 *Shanghai* *China* MMSI: 413063000	**41,482** 24,001 50,151	Class: CC (AB)	**2003-11 Hudong-Zhonghua Shipbuilding (Group) Co Ltd — Shanghai** Yd No: H1295A Loa 263.20 (BB) Br ex - Dght 12.800 Lbp 251.88 Br md 32.20 Dpth 19.30 Welded, 1 dk	**(A33A2CC) Container Ship (Fully Cellular)** TEU 4051 C Ho 1586 TEU C Dk 2465 TEU incl 400 ref C. Compartments: ER, 7 Cell Ho 14 Ha: ER	**1 oil engine** driving 1 FP propeller Total Power: 36,543kW (49,684hp) 24.2kn MAN-B&W 8K90MC-C 1 x 2 Stroke 8 Cy. 900 x 2300 36543kW (49684bhp) Mitsui Engineering & Shipbuilding CLtd-Japan AuxGen: 3 x 1960kW 450/230V 60Hz a.c Thrusters: 1 Tunnel thruster (f)
717386 *KPV*	**XIN NING** **Government of The People's Republic of China (Taishan County Guanghai Port Ltd)** - *Guanghai, Guangdong* *China* MMSI: 413370380	**512** 164 37	Class: (NV) (CC)	**1988-07 Precision Marine Holding Pty Ltd — Fremantle WA** Yd No: 863 Loa 39.70 (BB) Br ex - Dght 1.040 Lbp 35.70 Br md 12.90 Dpth 3.70 Welded, 1 dk	**(A37B2PS) Passenger Ship** Hull Material: Aluminium Alloy Passengers: unberthed: 352	**2 oil engines** with flexible couplings & sr gearedto sc. shafts driving 2 Water jets Total Power: 3,358kW (4,566hp) 33.0kn MWM TBD604BV16 2 x Vee 4 Stroke 16 Cy. 170 x 195 each-1679kW (2283bhp) Motoren Werke Mannheim AG (MWM)-West Germany
270464 *PAS*	**XIN NING BO** **China Shipping Container Lines Co Ltd** - SatCom: Inmarsat C 441305710 *Shanghai* *China* MMSI: 413057000	**66,433** 37,567 69,303	Class: CC	**2003-10 Hudong-Zhonghua Shipbuilding (Group) Co Ltd — Shanghai** Yd No: H1265A Loa 279.60 (BB) Br ex - Dght 14.000 Lbp 265.80 Br md 40.30 Dpth 24.10 Welded	**(A33A2CC) Container Ship (Fully Cellular)** TEU 5668 C Ho 2586 TEU C Dk 3082 TEU incl 610 ref C. Compartments: 7 Cell Ho, ER Ice Capable	**1 oil engine** driving 1 FP propeller Total Power: 54,720kW (74,397hp) 25.7kn MAN-B&W 12K90MC-C 1 x 2 Stroke 12 Cy. 900 x 2300 54720kW (74397bhp) Mitsui Engineering & Shipbuilding CLtd-Japan AuxGen: 4 x 2320kW 450/230V 60Hz a.c Thrusters: 1 Tunnel thruster (f)
408545 *RNB*	**XIN NING JIANG** *ex* Yellow Stone *-2003* *ex* GTS Aurora *-1998* *ex* New Glory *-1996* **Guangdong Haidian Shipping Co Ltd** - SatCom: Inmarsat A 126162446 *Guangzhou, Guangdong* *China* MMSI: 412464970	**26,951** 15,848 46,056	Class: (CC) (BV) (NK)	**1985-06 Imabari Shipbuilding Co Ltd — Marugame KG (Marugame Shipyard)** Yd No: 1136 Loa 189.95 (BB) Br ex - Dght 11.891 Lbp 180.02 Br md 32.21 Dpth 16.51 Welded, 1 dk	**(A21A2BC) Bulk Carrier** Grain: 58,033; Bale: 55,740 TEU 176 Compartments: 5 Ho, ER 5 Ha: 4 (20.8 x 16.0) (18.4 x 16.0)ER Cranes: 4x25t	**1 oil engine** driving 1 FP propeller Total Power: 6,178kW (8,400hp) 13.3kn B&W 6L60MCE 1 x 2 Stroke 6 Cy. 600 x 1944 6178kW (8400bhp) Hitachi Zosen Corp-Japan
295024 *PAE*	**XIN NING YANG** **China Shipping Tanker Co Ltd** - SatCom: Inmarsat C 441312810 *Shanghai* *China* MMSI: 413128000	**152,740** 97,129 297,439 T/cm 177.9	Class: CC NV	**2005-04 Dalian New Shipbuilding Heavy Industries Co Ltd — Dalian LN** Yd No: T2980-2 Loa 329.96 Br ex - Dght 21.500 Lbp 315.92 Br md 59.98 Dpth 29.70 Welded, 1 dk	**(A13A2TV) Crude Oil Tanker** Double Hull (13F) Liq: 333,307; Liq (Oil): 333,307 Compartments: 10 Wing Ta, ER 3 Cargo Pump (s): 3x5500m³/hr Manifold: Bow/CM: 162m	**1 oil engine** driving 1 FP propeller Total Power: 27,158kW (36,924hp) 17.4kn Sulzer 7RTA84T-B 1 x 2 Stroke 7 Cy. 840 x 3150 27158kW (36924bhp) (made 2004) Doosan Engine Co Ltd-South Korea AuxGen: 3 x 950kW 450V a.c
437913 *PKB*	**XIN OU ZHOU** **China Shipping Container Lines Co Ltd** - SatCom: Inmarsat C 441315910 *Shanghai* *China* MMSI: 413159000 Official number: 0007000258	**90,757** 57,364 102,460	Class: CC GL	**2007-11 Hudong-Zhonghua Shipbuilding (Group) Co Ltd — Shanghai** Yd No: H1382A Loa 335.00 (BB) Br ex 42.84 Dght 14.650 Lbp 320.06 Br md 42.80 Dpth 24.80 Welded, 1 dk	**(A33A2CC) Container Ship (Fully Cellular)** TEU 8528 C Ho 3874 TEU C Dk 4554 TEU incl 700 ref C.	**1 oil engine** driving 1 FP propeller Total Power: 68,520kW (93,160hp) 26.4kn MAN-B&W 12K98MC-C 1 x 2 Stroke 12 Cy. 980 x 2400 68520kW (93160bhp) Mitsui Engineering & Shipbuilding CLtd-Japan AuxGen: 4 x 2760kW 6600V a.c Thrusters: 1 Tunnel thruster (f)
408965 *FP*	**XIN PENG** *ex* Angel Pearl *-2011* *ex* Surmene 4 *-2010* *ex* Neo Chrysanthemum *-1995* *ex* Sanko Chrysanthemum *-1987* **Hong Kong Xinwang Shipping Ltd** Zhonghang Maritime Service Co Ltd *Panama* *Panama* MMSI: 355430000 Official number: 4306211	**22,143** 12,665 38,888 T/cm 47.2	Class: (NK)	**1984-09 Ishikawajima-Harima Heavy Industries Co Ltd (IHI) — Aioi HG** Yd No: 2876 Loa 179.90 (BB) Br ex 30.54 Dght 10.932 Lbp 171.00 Br md 30.51 Dpth 15.32 Welded, 1 dk	**(A21A2BC) Bulk Carrier** Grain: 46,112; Bale: 44,492 Compartments: 5 Ho, ER 5 Ha: (15.2 x 12.8)4 (19.2 x 15.2)ER Cranes: 4x25t	**1 oil engine** driving 1 FP propeller Total Power: 5,884kW (8,000hp) 15.0kn Sulzer 6RTA58 1 x 2 Stroke 6 Cy. 580 x 1700 5884kW (8000bhp) Ishikawajima Harima Heavy IndustrieCo Ltd (IHI)-Japan AuxGen: 3 x 450kW 450V 60Hz a.c Fuel: 86.5 (d.f.) (Heating Coils) 1626.5 (r.f.) 23.0pd
837360 *XID*	**XIN PENG** *ex* Yu Hua *-1998* **Shenzhen Luxiang Marine Co Ltd** - *Shenzhen, Guangdong* *China*	**2,686** 1,396 3,864	Class: (CC)	**1979-09 Zhonghua Shipyard — Shanghai** Loa 101.15 Br ex - Dght 6.000 Lbp 92.30 Br md 13.80 Dpth 7.70 Welded, 2 dks	**(A31A2GX) General Cargo Ship** Grain: 5,140; Bale: 4,625 Compartments: 3 Ho, ER 3 Ha: (9.6 x 6.8) (10.8 x 6.8) (10.9 x 6.8)ER Derricks: 6x5t; Winches: 6	**1 oil engine** driving 1 FP propeller Total Power: 2,207kW (3,001hp) 16.0kn Hudong 6ESDZ43/82C 1 x 2 Stroke 6 Cy. 430 x 820 2207kW (3001bhp) Weifang Diesel Engine Factory-China AuxGen: 2 x 250kW 400V 50Hz a.c
972161 *RND*	**XIN PING HAI** *ex* Energy Phoenix *-2009* **Guangdong Haidian Shipping Co Ltd** - *Guangzhou, Guangdong* *China* MMSI: 413891000	**36,074** 23,452 68,636 T/cm 64.2	Class: CC (NK)	**1994-08 Sasebo Heavy Industries Co. Ltd. — Sasebo Yard, Sasebo** Yd No: 393 Loa 224.00 (BB) Br ex - Dght 13.289 Lbp 215.00 Br md 32.20 Dpth 18.20 Welded, 1 dk	**(A21A2BC) Bulk Carrier** Grain: 81,337 Compartments: 7 Ho, ER 7 Ha: (14.4 x 12.8)6 (17.6 x 14.4)ER	**1 oil engine** driving 1 FP propeller Total Power: 10,224kW (13,901hp) 14.0kn B&W 5S60MC 1 x 2 Stroke 5 Cy. 600 x 2292 10224kW (13901bhp) Mitsui Engineering & Shipbuilding CLtd-Japan AuxGen: 3 x 450kW 450V 60Hz a.c Fuel: 86.3 (d.f.) 1785.5 (r.f.) 27.2pd

9198329 *VRBV2* -
XIN PING YANG
ex Formosapetro Discovery *-2006*
Xin Ping Yang Shipping SA
China Shipping Tanker Co Ltd
SatCom: Inmarsat C 447710990
Hong Kong *Hong Kong*
MMSI: 477109900
Official number: HK-1695
149,274 / 90,656 / 281,434 / T/cm 170.1
Class: AB
2001-09 Ishikawajima-Harima Heavy Industries Co Ltd (IHI) — Kure Yd No: 3128
Loa 330.00 (BB) Br ex - Dght 20.428
Lbp 316.60 Br md 60.00 Dpth 28.90
Welded, 1 dk
(A13A2TV) Crude Oil Tanker
Double Hull (13F)
Liq: 321,889; Liq (Oil): 321,889
Compartments: 5 Ta, 10 Wing Ta, ER
3 Cargo Pump (s): 3x5000m³/hr
Manifold: Bow/CM: 155m
1 oil engine driving 1 FP propeller
Total Power: 22,354kW (30,392hp) 15.4k
Sulzer 7RTA84T
1 x 2 Stroke 7 Cy. 840 x 3150 22354kW (30392bhp)
Diesel United Ltd.-Aioi
AuxGen: 3 x 930kW 450V 60Hz a.c
Fuel: 360.6 (d.f.) (Heating Coils) 6100.4 (r.f.) 79.0pd

9270440 *BPAP* -
XIN PU DONG
China Shipping Container Lines Co Ltd
-
SatCom: Inmarsat C 441306010
Shanghai *China*
MMSI: 413060000
66,433 / 37,567 / 69,303
Class: CC
2003-02 Hudong-Zhonghua Shipbuilding (Group) Co Ltd — Shanghai Yd No: H1263A
Loa 279.60 (BB) Br ex - Dght 14.000
Lbp 265.80 Br md 40.30 Dpth 24.10
Welded, 1 dk
(A33A2CC) Container Ship (Fully Cellular)
Bale: 132,790
TEU 5668 C Ho 2586 TEU C Dk 3082 TEU incl 610 ref C.
Compartments: 7 Cell Ho, ER
7 Ha: (28.5 x 36.0)4 (29.4 x 36.0) (45.4 x 24.2)ER (28.4 x 36.0)
Ice Capable
1 oil engine driving 1 FP propeller
Total Power: 54,720kW (74,397hp) 25.7kn
MAN-B&W 12K90MC-C
1 x 2 Stroke 12 Cy. 900 x 2300 54720kW (74397bhp)
Mitsui Engineering & Shipbuilding CLtd-Japan
AuxGen: 4 x 2320kW 450/230V 60Hz a.c
Thrusters: 1 Tunnel thruster (f)

9416628 *BPFA* -
XIN PU YANG
China Shipping Tanker Co Ltd
-
Shanghai *China*
MMSI: 413176000
Official number: 09F0211
161,488 / 104,666 / 309,362 / T/cm 182.2
Class: CC NV
2010-01 Guangzhou Longxue Shipbuilding Co Ltd — Guangzhou GD Yd No: L0001
Loa 332.95 (BB) Br ex 60.04 Dght 21.800
Lbp 319.90 Br md 60.00 Dpth 29.79
Welded, 1 dk
(A13A2TV) Crude Oil Tanker
Double Hull (13F)
Liq: 334,494; Liq (Oil): 334,494
Compartments: 5 Ta, 10 Wing Ta, 2 Wing Slop Ta, ER
3 Cargo Pump (s): 3x5500m³/hr
Manifold: Bow/CM: 167m
1 oil engine driving 1 FP propeller
Total Power: 29,400kW (39,972hp) 15.7kn
Wartsila 7RTA84T
1 x 2 Stroke 7 Cy. 840 x 3150 29400kW (39972bhp)
Wartsila Switzerland Ltd-Switzerland
AuxGen: 3 x 1050kW 450V 50Hz a.c
Fuel: 420.0 (d.f.) 6600.0 (r.f.)

8656910 *BHSD* -
XIN QIAN JIN 2
Jiangdu Qianjin Shipping & Trading Co Ltd
-
Yangzhou, Jiangsu *China*
Official number: 060706000010
1,195 / 669 / 1,406
Class: CC
2006-02 Yangzhou Kejin Shipyard Co Ltd — Jiangdu JS Yd No: 05003
Loa 71.20 Br ex - Dght 3.850
Lbp 64.90 Br md 11.20 Dpth 5.00
Welded, 1 dk
(A12B2TR) Chemical/Products Tanker
Double Hull (13F)
2 oil engines reduction geared to sc. shafts driving 2 Propellers
Chinese Std. Type CW6200ZC
2 x 4 Stroke 6 Cy. 200 x 270
Weichai Power Co Ltd-China

9144500 *VRVQ6* -
XIN QIANG
Kingswill Shipping Ltd
COSCO (HK) Shipping Co Ltd
SatCom: Inmarsat B 347761010
Hong Kong *Hong Kong*
MMSI: 477610000
Official number: HK-0400
26,062 / 14,872 / 45,732 / T/cm 49.8
Class: NK
1998-06 Tsuneishi Shipbuilding Co Ltd — Fukuyama HS Yd No: 1122
Loa 186.00 (BB) Br ex - Dght 11.620
Lbp 177.00 Br md 30.40 Dpth 16.50
Welded, 1 dk
(A21A2BC) Bulk Carrier
Grain: 57,208; Bale: 55,564
Compartments: 5 Ho, ER
5 Ha: (20.0 x 15.3)4 (20.8 x 15.3)ER
Cranes: 4x25t
1 oil engine driving 1 FP propeller
Total Power: 7,172kW (9,751hp) 14.0kn
B&W 6S50MC
1 x 2 Stroke 6 Cy. 500 x 1910 7172kW (9751bhp)
Mitsui Engineering & Shipbuilding CLtd-Japan
Fuel: 1535.0 (r.f.)

9304784 *BPBD* -
XIN QIN HUANG DAO
China Shipping Container Lines Co Ltd
-
SatCom: Inmarsat C 441307310
Shanghai *China*
MMSI: 413073000
66,452 / 37,567 / 69,303
Class: CC
2004-07 Hudong-Zhonghua Shipbuilding (Group) Co Ltd — Shanghai Yd No: H1352A
Loa 279.60 (BB) Br ex - Dght 14.000
Lbp 265.80 Br md 40.30 Dpth 24.10
Welded, 1 dk
(A33A2CC) Container Ship (Fully Cellular)
TEU 5668 C Ho 2586 TEU C Dk 3082 TEU incl 610 ref C.
Compartments: 7 Cell Ho, ER
1 oil engine driving 1 FP propeller
Total Power: 54,719kW (74,396hp) 26.0kn
MAN-B&W 12K90MC-C
1 x 2 Stroke 12 Cy. 900 x 2300 54719kW (74396bhp)
Mitsui Engineering & Shipbuilding CLtd-Japan
AuxGen: 4 x 2320kW 450/230V 60Hz a.c
Thrusters: 1 Tunnel thruster (f)

9523005 *BPKF* -
XIN QIN ZHOU
China Shipping Container Lines Co Ltd
-
SatCom: Inmarsat C 441470010
Shanghai *China*
MMSI: 414700000
47,917 / 24,165 / 66,904
Class: CC
2012-03 Shanghai Jiangnan Changxing Heavy Industry Co Ltd — Shanghai Yd No: H1050A
Loa 255.10 (BB) Br ex - Dght 13.500
Lbp 242.00 Br md 37.30 Dpth 19.60
Welded, 1 dk
(A33A2CC) Container Ship (Fully Cellular)
TEU 4738 C Ho 1826 TEU C Dk 2912 incl 300 ref C
Compartments: 7 Cell Ho, ER
Ice Capable
1 oil engine driving 1 FP propeller
Total Power: 21,910kW (29,789hp) 18.0kn
Wartsila 7RT-flex68
1 x 2 Stroke 7 Cy. 680 x 2720 21910kW (29789bhp)
Doosan Engine Co Ltd-South Korea
AuxGen: 2 x 1650kW 450V a.c, 1 x 1240kW 450V a.c
Thrusters: 1 Tunnel thruster (f)

9270452 *BPAR* -
XIN QING DAO
China Shipping Container Lines Co Ltd
-
SatCom: Inmarsat C 441305410
Shanghai *China*
MMSI: 413054000
66,433 / 37,567 / 69,423
Class: CC
2003-05 Hudong-Zhonghua Shipbuilding (Group) Co Ltd — Shanghai Yd No: H1264A
Loa 279.90 (BB) Br ex 40.30 Dght 14.000
Lbp 265.80 Br md 40.00 Dpth 24.10
Welded
(A33A2CC) Container Ship (Fully Cellular)
TEU 5668 C Ho 2586 TEU C Dk 3082 TEU incl 610 ref C.
Compartments: 7 Cell Ho, ER
1 oil engine driving 1 FP propeller
Total Power: 54,720kW (74,397hp) 25.7kn
B&W 12K90MC-C
1 x 2 Stroke 12 Cy. 900 x 2300 54720kW (74397bhp)
Mitsui Engineering & Shipbuilding CLtd-Japan
AuxGen: 4 x 2320kW 450/230V 60Hz a.c
Thrusters: 1 Tunnel thruster (f)

8318001 *BVJS7* -
XIN QIU HE
ex Qiu He *-2012*
Shanghai PanAsia Shipping Co Ltd
-
SatCom: Inmarsat B 341216610
Shanghai *China*
MMSI: 413697220
19,732 / 8,377 / 25,808
Class: (CC) (AB)
1984-12 Flensburger Schiffbau-Ges. mbH — Flensburg Yd No: 2018
Loa 171.00 (BB) Br ex 28.68 Dght 10.902
Lbp 160.00 Br md 28.40 Dpth 15.60
Welded, 1 dk
(A33A2CC) Container Ship (Fully Cellular)
TEU 1328 C Ho 676 TEU C Dk 652 TEU incl 54 ref C.
Compartments: 4 Cell Ho, ER
15 Ha: (13.7 x 11.4)14 (13.0 x 10.7)ER
1 oil engine driving 1 FP propeller
Total Power: 10,054kW (13,669hp) 17.5kn
B&W 6L70MCE
1 x 2 Stroke 6 Cy. 700 x 2268 10054kW (13669bhp)
B&W Diesel A/S-Denmark
AuxGen: 1 x 1072kW a.c, 2 x 800kW a.c, 1 x 352kW a.c
Thrusters: 1 Thwart. FP thruster (f)

8738768 *3FCY6* -
XIN QUAN
Lv Yi Qiang
Weihai Xinhai Shipping Co Ltd
Panama *Panama*
MMSI: 371272000
Official number: 39631PEXTF2
2,982 / 1,750 / 5,176
Class: IT
2008-12 Wenling Yuanyang Shiprepair & Building Co Ltd — Wenling ZJ
Loa 98.23 Br ex - Dght 5.550
Lbp 91.00 Br md 16.20 Dpth 6.95
Welded, 1 dk
(A21A2BC) Bulk Carrier
1 oil engine reduction geared to sc. shaft driving 1 Propeller
Total Power: 2,000kW (2,719hp) 11.5kn
Chinese Std. Type
1 x 4 Stroke 2000kW (2719bhp)
Wuxi Antai Power Machinery Co Ltd-China

9310032 *BPBM* -
XIN QUAN ZHOU
China Shipping Container Lines Co Ltd
-
Shanghai *China*
MMSI: 413132000
41,482 / 24,001 / 52,216
Class: CC
2005-05 Hudong-Zhonghua Shipbuilding (Group) Co Ltd — Shanghai Yd No: H1357A
Loa 263.20 (BB) Br ex - Dght 12.800
Lbp 251.80 Br md 32.20 Dpth 19.30
Welded, 1 dk
(A33A2CC) Container Ship (Fully Cellular)
TEU 4250 C Ho 1586 TEU C Dk 2664 TEU incl 500 ref C.
Compartments: 7 Cell Ho, ER
Ice Capable
1 oil engine driving 1 FP propeller
Total Power: 36,480kW (49,598hp) 24.2kn
MAN-B&W 8K90MC-C
1 x 2 Stroke 8 Cy. 900 x 2300 36480kW (49598bhp)
Mitsui Engineering & Shipbuilding CLtd-Japan
AuxGen: 3 x 1960kW 450V a.c
Thrusters: 1 Tunnel thruster (f)

9361067 *BKON4* -
XIN QUN DAO
Zhoushan Hefeng Shipping Co Ltd
Peace Ocean Shipping SA
China
MMSI: 412429910
7,808 / 4,372 / 10,800
Class: IB
2005-03 Zhoushan Zhaobao Shipbuilding & Repair Co Ltd — Zhoushan ZJ
Loa 135.30 (BB) Br ex - Dght 7.670
Lbp 125.60 Br md 20.80 Dpth 10.50
Welded, 1 dk
(A33A2CC) Container Ship (Fully Cellular)
TEU 716 C Ho 330 TEU C Dk 386 TEU incl 40 ref C.
1 oil engine driving 1 FP propeller
Total Power: 5,882kW (7,997hp) 14.5kn
B&W 6L42MC
1 x 2 Stroke 6 Cy. 420 x 1360 5882kW (7997bhp)
Hudong Heavy Machinery Co Ltd-China
AuxGen: 2 x 600kW 440/220V 60Hz a.c

9312561 *BPBU* -
XIN RI ZHAO
China Shipping Container Lines Co Ltd
-
Shanghai *China*
MMSI: 413148000
41,482 / 24,001 / 52,191
Class: CC
2005-11 Dalian New Shipbuilding Heavy Industries Co Ltd — Dalian LN Yd No: C4250-6
Loa 263.23 (BB) Br ex 32.30 Dght 12.820
Lbp 251.88 Br md 32.25 Dpth 19.30
Welded, 1 dk
(A33A2CC) Container Ship (Fully Cellular)
TEU 4250 C Ho 1586 TEU C Dk 2664 TEU incl 400 ref C.
Compartments: 7 Cell Ho, ER
Ice Capable
1 oil engine driving 1 FP propeller
Total Power: 36,480kW (49,598hp) 24.2kn
MAN-B&W 8K90MC-C
1 x 2 Stroke 8 Cy. 900 x 2300 36480kW (49598bhp)
Doosan Engine Co Ltd-South Korea
AuxGen: 3 x 1960kW 450V 60Hz a.c
Thrusters: 1 Tunnel thruster (f)

8889464 *BEFL* -
XIN RONG
ex Tong Guan Shan *-2007*
Anhui Ocean Shipping Co Ltd
-
SatCom: Inmarsat C 441200211
Nanjing, Jiangsu *China*
MMSI: 413492000
1,490 / 863 / 2,146
Class: (CC)
1991-07 Shandong Weihai Shipyard — Weihai SD
Loa 71.82 Br ex - Dght 4.800
Lbp 66.00 Br md 12.80 Dpth 6.20
Welded, 1 dk
(A31A2GX) General Cargo Ship
1 oil engine driving 1 FP propeller
Total Power: 662kW (900hp) 10.0kn
Chinese Std. Type 6350ZC
1 x 4 Stroke 6 Cy. 350 x 500 662kW (900bhp)
Yichang Marine Diesel Engine Co Ltd-China
AuxGen: 2 x 90kW 400V a.c

9065534 *T3HC2* -
XIN RUI
ex Fong Kuo No. 807 *-2013*
Soar Long Ltd
-
Tarawa *Kiribati*
MMSI: 529605000
Official number: K17921340
2,839 / 945 / 2,695
Class: IZ IS (CR) (NK)
1992-08 Fong Kuo Shipbuilding Co Ltd — Kaohsiung Yd No: 300
Loa 97.40 (BB) Br ex - Dght 5.200
Lbp 89.87 Br md 15.40 Dpth 8.80
Welded, 2 dks
(A34A2GR) Refrigerated Cargo Ship
Ins: 3,606
Compartments: 3 Ho, ER
3 Ha: 3 (4.8 x 4.8)ER
Derricks: 6x5t
1 oil engine with clutches, flexible couplings & sr geared to sc. shaft driving 1 CP propeller
Total Power: 2,207kW (3,001hp) 14.7kn
Daihatsu 8DLM-32
1 x 4 Stroke 8 Cy. 320 x 400 2207kW (3001bhp)
Daihatsu Diesel Manufacturing Co Lt-Japan
AuxGen: 3 x 400kW a.c

8661408 *BKDT* -
XIN RUI 1
ex Chang Xin 62 *-2010*
Ningbo Lixin Logistics Co Ltd
New United (Dalian) Marine Service Co Ltd
Ningbo, Zhejiang *China*
Official number: 070109000079
2,996 / 1,667 / 5,200
Class: ZC
2008-12 Wenling Xingyuan Shipbuilding & Repair Co Ltd — Wenling ZJ
Loa 96.50 Br ex - Dght 5.950
Lbp 90.80 Br md 15.80 Dpth 7.40
Welded, 1 dk
(A31A2GX) General Cargo Ship
1 oil engine reduction geared to sc. shafts driving 1 FP propeller
Total Power: 1,765kW (2,400hp)
Chinese Std. Type
1 x 1765kW (2400bhp)
Guangzhou Diesel Engine Factory CoLtd-China

559420 *EXI7*	**XIN RUI 2** **Dalian Trawind Shipping Co Ltd** Dalian Trawind International Ship Management Co Ltd SatCom: Inmarsat C 437083410 *Panama* *Panama* MMSI: 370834000 Official number: 39123PEXTF2	**2,993** 1,816 5,380	Class: IT	**2009-06 Wenling Xingyuan Shipbuilding & Repair Co Ltd — Wenling ZJ** Loa 99.98 (BB) Br ex - Dght 6.060 Lbp 92.40 Br md 15.80 Dpth 7.60 Welded, 1 dk	**(A31A2GX) General Cargo Ship**	**1 oil engine** reduction geared to sc. shaft driving 1 Propeller Total Power: 2,059kW (2,799hp) 12.2kn Chinese Std. Type 8320ZC 1 x 4 Stroke 8 Cy. 320 x 440 2059kW (2799bhp) Guangzhou Diesel Engine Factory CoLtd-China
904604 *UUG9*	**XIN RUI 6** *ex* Eastern Sun *-2009* *ex* Rui Feng *-2008* *ex* Great Sea *-2003* *ex* Hosei Maru No. 56 *-2003* **Xinrui Shipping Co Ltd** Huawei Shipping Co Ltd *Phnom Penh* *Cambodia* MMSI: 515055000 Official number: 0889064	**1,492** 836 1,352	Class: UB	**1989-07 Honda Zosen — Saiki** Yd No: 801 Loa 72.60 (BB) Br ex - Dght 4.271 Lbp 67.00 Br md 12.20 Dpth 7.00 Welded, 1 dk	**(A31A2GX) General Cargo Ship** Compartments: 2 Ho, ER 2 Ha: ER	**1 oil engine** geared to sc. shaft driving 1 CP propeller Total Power: 1,177kW (1,600hp) Hanshin 6LU35G 1 x 4 Stroke 6 Cy. 350 x 550 1177kW (1600bhp) The Hanshin Diesel Works Ltd-Japan Thrusters: 1 Tunnel thruster (f)
566423 *FIZ7*	**XIN RUI HAI** **Sedon (Hong Kong) Ltd** - *Panama* *Panama* MMSI: 373913000 Official number: 4429512	**31,754** 18,653 56,092 T/cm 55.8	Class: NK	**2012-10 Mitsui Eng. & SB. Co. Ltd., Chiba Works — Ichihara** Yd No: 1834 Loa 189.99 (BB) Br ex - Dght 12.730 Lbp 182.00 Br md 32.25 Dpth 18.10 Welded, 1 dk	**(A21A2BC) Bulk Carrier** Grain: 70,811; Bale: 68,000 Compartments: 5 Ho, ER 5 Ha: ER Cranes: 4x30t	**1 oil engine** driving 1 FP propeller Total Power: 9,070kW (12,332hp) 14.5kn MAN-B&W 6S50MC-C 1 x 2 Stroke 6 Cy. 500 x 2000 9070kW (12332bhp) Mitsui Engineering & Shipbuilding CLtd-Japan Fuel: 2310.0
137636 *RGR9*	**XIN RUN** *ex* Bulk Fern *-2010* *ex* Red Fern *-2005* *launched as* Halla Pride *-1998* **Chinese Port Shipping Ltd** Xin Run Yang (HK) Shipping Co Ltd *Hong Kong* *Hong Kong* MMSI: 477744400 Official number: HK-2712	**38,995** 24,436 73,326 T/cm 67.8	Class: NV (LR) (AB) (KR) (RI) ✠ Classed LR until 31/8/01	**1998-04 Halla Engineering & Heavy Industries, Ltd. — Samho** Yd No: 1031 Loa 225.00 (BB) Br ex 32.29 Dght 13.765 Lbp 217.00 Br md 32.25 Dpth 19.00 Welded, 1 dk	**(A21A2BC) Bulk Carrier** Grain: 86,082; Bale: 81,778 Compartments: 7 Ho, ER 7 Ha: (15.1 x 12.0)6 (15.1 x 15.0)ER	**1 oil engine** driving 1 FP propeller Total Power: 8,230kW (11,190hp) 14.0kn B&W 5S60MC 1 x 2 Stroke 5 Cy. 600 x 2292 8230kW (11190bhp) Hyundai Heavy Industries Co Ltd-South Korea AuxGen: 3 x 490kW 450V 60Hz a.c
710098 *KST6*	**XIN RUN 3** **Zhejiang Xinrun Shipping Co Ltd** - *Zhoushan, Zhejiang* *China* MMSI: 413452990	**2,571** 771 2,973	Class: CC	**2014-01 Yangfan Group Co Ltd — Zhoushan ZJ** Yd No: 2398 Loa 73.30 Br ex - Dght 6.000 Lbp 65.00 Br md 17.00 Dpth 7.20 Welded, 1 dk	**(B21B20T) Offshore Tug/Supply Ship**	**2 oil engines** reduction geared to sc. shafts driving 2 Propellers Total Power: 5,884kW (8,000hp) Daihatsu 8DKM-28 2 x 4 Stroke 8 Cy. 280 x 390 each-2942kW (4000bhp)
601352 *KSC5*	**XIN RUN 5** **Zhejiang Xinrun Shipping Co Ltd** Zhoushan Huacheng Shipping Co Ltd SatCom: Inmarsat C 441301673 *Zhoushan, Zhejiang* *China* MMSI: 413440190	**2,469** 740 -	Class: CC	**2011-03 Zhejiang Fangyuan Ship Industry Co Ltd — Linhai ZJ** Yd No: FY2009023 Loa 71.90 Br ex 17.35 Dght 5.300 Lbp 64.10 Br md 17.00 Dpth 7.00 Welded, 1 dk	**(B21B20T) Offshore Tug/Supply Ship** Ice Capable	**2 oil engines** reduction geared to sc. shafts driving 2 Propellers Total Power: 6,120kW (8,320hp) 13.0kn MAN-B&W 9L27/38 2 x 4 Stroke 9 Cy. 270 x 380 each-3060kW (4160bhp) Zhenjiang Marine Diesel Works-China AuxGen: 2 x 1100kW 400V a.c, 2 x 350kW 400V a.c
590412 *KNW6*	**XIN RUN 8** *ex* Xinghang Youfu 4 *-2012* **Zhejiang Xinrun Shipping Co Ltd** - SatCom: Inmarsat C 441301644 *Zhoushan, Zhejiang* *China* MMSI: 413446530	**828** 281 -	Class: CC	**2010-11 Jiujiang Yinxing Shipbuilding Co Ltd — Xingzi County JX** Yd No: YT36-04 Loa 53.00 Br ex - Dght 4.100 Lbp 48.00 Br md 12.00 Dpth 5.20 Welded, 1 dk	**(B21B20T) Offshore Tug/Supply Ship** Ice Capable	**2 oil engines** reduction geared to sc. shafts driving 2 Propellers Total Power: 2,206kW (3,000hp) 12.0kn Chinese Std. Type 6320ZC 2 x 4 Stroke 6 Cy. 320 x 440 each-1103kW (1500bhp) Guangzhou Diesel Engine Factory CoLtd-China AuxGen: 3 x 300kW 400V a.c
480148 *BCY9*	**XIN RUN 17** *ex* Qian Li Shan 7 *-2011* **Fujian Congrong Shipping Co Ltd** - *Fuzhou, Fujian* *China* MMSI: 413327010	**2,993** 1,809 4,980	Class: (CC)	**2008-03 Mindong Congmao Ship Industry Co Ltd — Fu'an FJ** Yd No: 07 Loa 98.80 Br ex 15.10 Dght 6.000 Lbp 91.60 Br md 15.00 Dpth 7.40 Welded, 1 dk	**(A13B2TP) Products Tanker** Double Hull (13F) Liq: 6,142; Liq (Oil): 6,142 Compartments: 10 Wing Ta, 2 Wing Slop Ta, ER	**1 oil engine** reduction geared to sc. shaft driving 1 FP propeller Total Power: 1,325kW (1,801hp) 11.0kn Guangzhou 6320ZCD 1 x 4 Stroke 6 Cy. 320 x 440 1325kW (1801bhp) Guangzhou Diesel Engine Factory CoLtd-China AuxGen: 3 x 180kW 400V a.c
389760 *RFN2*	**XIN RUN YANG** **Xin Run Yang Shipping SA** China Shipping Tanker Co Ltd SatCom: Inmarsat C 447702118 *Hong Kong* *Hong Kong* MMSI: 477541700 Official number: HK-2461	**152,727** 98,415 297,134 T/cm 177.9	Class: CC	**2009-07 Dalian Shipbuilding Industry Co Ltd — Dalian LN (No 2 Yard)** Yd No: T3000-19 Loa 330.00 (BB) Br ex 60.05 Dght 21.522 Lbp 316.00 Br md 60.00 Dpth 29.70 Welded, 1 dk	**(A13A2TV) Crude Oil Tanker** Double Hull (13F) Liq: 324,296; Liq (Oil): 324,296 Compartments: 5 Ta, 10 Wing Ta, 2 Wing Slop Ta, ER 3 Cargo Pump (s): 3x5500m³/hr Manifold: Bow/CM: 163.6m	**1 oil engine** driving 1 FP propeller Total Power: 25,480kW (34,643hp) 15.8kn MAN-B&W 7S80MC 1 x 2 Stroke 7 Cy. 800 x 3056 25480kW (34643bhp) Doosan Engine Co Ltd-South Korea AuxGen: 3 x 975kW 450V a.c Fuel: 429.6 (d.f.) 7117.3 (r.f.)
309942 *PBO*	**XIN SHAN TOU** **China Shipping Container Lines Co Ltd** - *Shanghai* *China* MMSI: 413141000	**41,482** 24,001 52,157	Class: CC	**2005-09 Dalian New Shipbuilding Heavy Industries Co Ltd — Dalian LN** Yd No: C4250-2 Loa 262.23 (BB) Br ex 32.30 Dght 12.800 Lbp 251.88 Br md 32.25 Dpth 19.30 Welded, 1 dk	**(A33A2CC) Container Ship (Fully Cellular)** TEU 4250 C Ho 1586 TEU C Dk 2664 TEU incl 400 ref C.	**1 oil engine** driving 1 FP propeller Total Power: 36,480kW (49,598hp) 24.2kn MAN-B&W 8K90MC-C 1 x 2 Stroke 8 Cy. 900 x 2300 36480kW (49598bhp) Doosan Engine Co Ltd-South Korea AuxGen: 3 x 1960kW 450V 60Hz a.c Thrusters: 1 Tunnel thruster (f)
307777 *EWY8*	**XIN SHANG** *ex* Ks Grace *-2012* *ex* Lady *-2011* *ex* Siswala *-2002* *ex* Spring Swallow *-1998* *ex* Sanko Swallow *-1986* **Hongkong Xinda Shipping Ltd** Hong Kong Shun Xin Marine Ltd SatCom: Inmarsat C 435749810 *Panama* *Panama* MMSI: 357498000 Official number: 4305611A	**24,111** 13,019 41,090 T/cm 48.1	Class: BV (NV) (NK)	**1985-04 Oshima Shipbuilding Co Ltd — Saikai NS** Yd No: 10079 Loa 185.20 (BB) Br ex - Dght 11.102 Lbp 176.03 Br md 29.50 Dpth 15.83 Welded, 1 dk	**(A21A2BC) Bulk Carrier** Grain: 50,416; Bale: 49,443 Compartments: 5 Ho, ER 5 Ha: (14.4 x 15.0)4 (19.2 x 15.0)ER Cranes: 4x25t	**1 oil engine** driving 1 FP propeller Total Power: 6,377kW (8,670hp) 13.9kn Sulzer 6RTA58 1 x 2 Stroke 6 Cy. 580 x 1700 6377kW (8670bhp) Sumitomo Heavy Industries Ltd-Japan AuxGen: 3 x 420kW 450V 60Hz a.c Fuel: 216.0 (d.f.) (Heating Coils) 1651.0 (r.f.) 24.5pd
431962 *PGL*	**XIN SHANG HAI YOU LUN** *ex* Zhan Xin *-1998* **Shanghai Marine (Group) Co** China Shipping Passenger Liner Co Ltd *Shanghai* *China*	**3,857** 2,006 2,894	Class: (CC)	**1983 Qiuxin Shipyard — Shanghai** Loa 106.67 Br ex - Dght 3.800 Lbp 97.00 Br md 15.80 Dpth 7.70 Welded, 2 dks	**(A32A2GF) General Cargo/Passenger Ship** Grain: 818 Compartments: 1 Ho, ER 1 Ha: (5.7 x 5.4)ER	**2 oil engines** reduction geared to sc. shafts driving 2 FP propellers Total Power: 4,414kW (6,002hp) 18.0kn Hudong 6ESDZ43/82B 2 x 2 Stroke 6 Cy. 430 x 820 each-2207kW (3001bhp) Hudong Shipyard-China AuxGen: 3 x 250kW 400V a.c
407231 *CC6*	**XIN SHANGHAI** **Yangshan B Shipping Co Ltd** China International Ship Management Co Ltd (CISM) SatCom: Inmarsat C 447728290 *Hong Kong* *Hong Kong* MMSI: 477282900 Official number: HK-1755	**108,069** 57,365 111,737	Class: LR ✠ **100A1** SS 10/2011 container ship **ShipRight** (SDA, FDA, CM) *IWS LI EP ✠ **LMC** **UMS** Eq.Ltr: A†; Cable: 759.0/111.0 U3 (a)	**2006-10 Samsung Heavy Industries Co Ltd — Geoje** Yd No: 1560 Loa 336.70 (BB) Br ex 45.64 Dght 15.030 Lbp 321.00 Br md 45.60 Dpth 27.20 Welded, 1 dk	**(A33A2CC) Container Ship (Fully Cellular)** TEU 9574 C Ho 4668 TEU C Dk 4906 TEU incl 700 ref C. Compartments: 9 Cell Ho, ER 9 Ha: ER	**1 oil engine** driving 1 FP propeller Total Power: 68,520kW (93,160hp) 25.2kn MAN-B&W 12K98MC-C 1 x 2 Stroke 12 Cy. 980 x 2400 68520kW (93160bhp) Doosan Engine Co Ltd-South Korea AuxGen: 4 x 2750kW 6600V 60Hz a.c Boilers: e (ex.g.) 8.3kgf/cm² (8.1bar), WTAuxB (o.f.) 8.3kgf/cm² (8.1bar) Thrusters: 1 Thwart. CP thruster (f)
647772 *FX3*	**XIN SHEN TONG 188** *launched as* New Shentong 188 *-2012* **Taizhou Shentong Shipping Co Ltd** - *Taizhou, Zhejiang* *China* MMSI: 413445950	**2,930** 1,255 4,600	Class: CC	**2012-06 Yangzhou Haichuan Shipyard — Yangzhou JS** Yd No: HCR25 Loa 96.08 (BB) Br ex 15.20 Dght 5.650 Lbp 91.54 Br md - Dpth 7.20 Welded, 1 dk	**(A12A2TC) Chemical Tanker** Double Hull (13F)	**1 oil engine** reduction geared to sc. shaft driving 1 Propeller Total Power: 2,060kW (2,801hp) 12.0kn Daihatsu 8DKM-28 1 x 4 Stroke 8 Cy. 280 x 390 2060kW (2801bhp) Shaanxi Diesel Heavy Industry Co Lt-China

IMO / Call sign	Ship / Owner	Tonnage	Class	Built / Dimensions	Type	Machinery	
9416654 *BPAH* -	**XIN SHEN YANG** **China Shipping Tanker Co Ltd** - *Shanghai* *China* MMSI: 413183000	**161,488** 104,666 309,189 T/cm 182.2	Class: CC NV	2010-12 **Guangzhou Longxue Shipbuilding Co Ltd — Guangzhou GD** Yd No: L0004 Loa 332.95 (BB) Br ex 60.04 Dght 21.800 Lbp 320.00 Br md 60.00 Dpth 29.80 Welded, 1 dk	**(A13A2TV) Crude Oil Tanker** Double Hull (13F) Liq: 334,500; Liq (Oil): 334,500 Compartments: 5 Ta, 10 Wing Ta, 2 Wing Slop Ta, ER 3 Cargo Pump (s): 3x5500m³/hr Manifold: Bow/CM: 167m	**1 oil engine** driving 1 FP propeller Total Power: 29,400kW (39,972hp) Wartsila 1 x 2 Stroke 7 Cy. 840 x 3150 29400kW (39972bhp) Wartsila Switzerland Ltd-Switzerland AuxGen: 3 x 1050kW 450V a.c Fuel: 420.0 (d.f.) 6600.0 (r.f.)	15.7k 7RTA84
8307882 *3FVJ4* -	**XIN SHENG** *ex* Dina G *-2012* *ex* Giorgis Milas *-2009* *ex* Nota A *-2005* *ex* Hanei Pearl *-1999* *ex* Sanko Pearl *-1985* **Hongkong Haoxin Shipping Ltd** Hong Kong Shun Xin Marine Ltd SatCom: Inmarsat C 435152110 *Panama* *Panama* MMSI: 351521000 Official number: 4030909B	**22,009** 12,589 37,725 T/cm 45.9	Class: (NK)	1984-03 **Sasebo Heavy Industries Co. Ltd. — Sasebo Yard, Sasebo** Yd No: 328 Loa 188.00 (BB) Br ex 28.28 Dght 10.861 Lbp 180.01 Br md 28.01 Dpth 15.40 Welded, 1 dk	**(A21A2BC) Bulk Carrier** Grain: 47,588; Bale: 45,961 Compartments: 5 Ho, ER 5 Ha: 5 (19.2 x 14.9)ER Cranes: 4x25t	**1 oil engine** driving 1 FP propeller Total Power: 5,101kW (6,935hp) Sulzer 1 x 2 Stroke 6 Cy. 580 x 1700 5101kW (6935bhp) Hitachi Zosen Corp-Japan AuxGen: 3 x 400kW 450V 60Hz a.c Fuel: 122.5 (d.f.) (Heating Coils) 1435.5 (r.f.) 22.5pd	14.0kr 6RTA58
8519526 *XUEH3* -	**XIN SHENG** *ex* Treasure *-2007* *ex* Chun Fu *-2004* *ex* Miyashin *-1999* *ex* Miyashin Maru *-1999* **Xin Sheng Shipping Ltd** V-Sky Shipping Ltd SatCom: Inmarsat C 451433310 *Phnom Penh* *Cambodia* MMSI: 514333000 Official number: 9985139	**1,289** 551 1,590	Class: GM (UM)	1986-01 **Yamanaka Zosen K.K. — Imabari** Yd No: 320 Loa 72.73 Br ex - Dght 4.333 Lbp 68.00 Br md 11.51 Dpth 6.71 Welded	**(A31A2GX) General Cargo Ship** Grain: 2,731; Bale: 2,290 Compartments: 1 Ho, ER 1 Ha: ER	**1 oil engine** with clutches, flexible couplings & sr reverse geared to sc. shaft driving 1 FP propeller Total Power: 1,030kW (1,400hp) Hanshin 1 x 4 Stroke 6 Cy. 280 x 460 1030kW (1400bhp) The Hanshin Diesel Works Ltd-Japan	11.5kn LH28G
9598907 *3FTQ9* -	**XIN SHENG 68** **Xi Ai Xin** Weihai Yongsheng International Ship Management Co Ltd SatCom: Inmarsat C 437103613 *Panama* *Panama* MMSI: 371036000 Official number: 41069PEXTF1	**2,990** 1,962 6,546	Class: IT	2010-10 **Linhai Jianghai Shipbuilding Co Ltd — Linhai ZJ** Yd No: ZXS4896 II Loa 98.22 Br ex - Dght - Lbp 91.00 Br md 16.20 Dpth 6.90 Welded, 1 dk	**(A31A2GX) General Cargo Ship**	**1 oil engine** reduction geared to sc. shaft driving 1 FP propeller Total Power: 1,765kW (2,400hp) Chinese Std. Type 1 x 4 Stroke 8 Cy. 300 x 380 1765kW (2400bhp) Wuxi Antai Power Machinery Co Ltd-China	10.0kn G8300ZC
8703505 - -	**XIN SHI DAI NO. 28** *ex* Choko Maru No. 28 *-2003* **Muelle Ocho SA** - *Argentina* Official number: 02165	*509* - 912		1987-09 **Kitanihon Zosen K.K. — Hachinohe** Yd No: 218 Loa 67.87 (BB) Br ex - Dght 4.257 Lbp 57.00 Br md 10.22 Dpth 6.61 Welded, 2 dks	**(B11B2FV) Fishing Vessel**	**1 oil engine** driving 1 FP propeller Total Power: 1,000kW (1,360hp) Akasaka 1 x 4 Stroke 6 Cy. 280 x 500 1000kW (1360bhp) Akasaka Tekkosho KK (Akasaka DieselLtd)-Japan AuxGen: 2 x 400kW 225V 60Hz a.c Thrusters: 1 Thwart. CP thruster (f) Fuel: 287.5 (d.f.) 8.5pd	12.5kn K28S
8963052 - -	**XIN SHI JI** *ex* Rui Feng 8 *-2004* *ex* Jian Guo *-2001* *ex* Zhe Zhou Yu Leng 226 *-2001* *ex* Heng Sheng Xing 658 *-2001* **Wan Zhou (Panama) Marine Co Ltd** Nanjing Yongzheng Marine Co Ltd	**689** 317 780		1979-08 **Hong Kong YuanXing Shipyard — Hong Kong** Loa - Br ex - Dght 4.900 Lbp 58.60 Br md 9.60 Dpth 5.60 Welded, 1 dk	**(A34A2GR) Refrigerated Cargo Ship**	**1 oil engine** geared to sc. shaft driving 1 FP propeller Total Power: 294kW (400hp) Chinese Std. Type 1 x 4 Stroke 6 Cy. 300 x 380 294kW (400bhp) Guangzhou Diesel Engine Factory CoLtd-China	6300
8653463 *BZUY8* -	**XIN SHI JI 37** **Zhejiang Ocean Family Co Ltd** - *Zhoushan, Zhejiang* *China* Official number: Z07-100721	**497** 228 -		2001-07 **Zhejiang Yangfan Ship Group Co Ltd — Zhoushan ZJ** Loa 48.60 Br ex 8.70 Dght - Lbp - Br md - Dpth 3.75 Welded, 1 dk	**(B11B2FV) Fishing Vessel**	**1 oil engine** driving 1 Propeller Total Power: 882kW (1,199hp)	
8615007 *BZ1UU* -	**XIN SHI JI 68** *ex* Hoyo Maru No. 68 *-2009* *ex* Toyama Maru No. 1 *-2004* **Zhejiang Ocean Family Co Ltd** - *Zhoushan, Zhejiang* *China* Official number: Z07-100722	**596** 215 492		1986-12 **Niigata Engineering Co Ltd — Niigata NI** Yd No: 2026 Loa 54.11 (BB) Br ex - Dght 3.441 Lbp 44.29 Br md 8.70 Dpth 3.81 Welded, 1 dk	**(B11B2FV) Fishing Vessel** Ins: 502	**1 oil engine** with clutches, flexible couplings & sr geared to sc. shaft driving 1 CP propeller Total Power: 699kW (950hp) Niigata 1 x 4 Stroke 6 Cy. 280 x 480 699kW (950bhp) Niigata Engineering Co Ltd-Japan	6M28AFTE
8909812 *BZ2UU* -	**XIN SHI JI 69** *ex* Hoyo Maru No. 18 *-2009* *ex* Kintoku Maru No. 12 *-2003* **Zhejiang Ocean Family Co Ltd** - *Zhoushan, Zhejiang* *China* Official number: Z07-100723	**516** 180 -		1989-09 **Niigata Engineering Co Ltd — Niigata NI** Yd No: 2132 Loa 49.42 (BB) Br ex - Dght 3.249 Lbp 43.75 Br md 8.30 Dpth 3.60 Welded	**(B11B2FV) Fishing Vessel** Ins: 409	**1 oil engine** with clutches, flexible couplings & sr reverse geared to sc. shaft driving 1 FP propeller Total Power: 699kW (950hp) Niigata 1 x 4 Stroke 6 Cy. 280 x 480 699kW (950bhp) Niigata Engineering Co Ltd-Japan	6M28BFT
8653475 *BZVY9* -	**XIN SHI JI 70** **Zhejiang Ocean Family Co Ltd** - *Zhoushan, Zhejiang* *China* Official number: Z07-100724	**634** 208 -		2005-01 **Zhejiang Yangfan Ship Group Co Ltd — Zhoushan ZJ** Loa 48.70 Br ex 8.50 Dght - Lbp - Br md - Dpth 3.65 Welded, 1 dk	**(B11B2FV) Fishing Vessel**	**1 oil engine** driving 1 Propeller Total Power: 735kW (999hp)	
8653487 *BZVZ2* -	**XIN SHI JI 71** **Zhejiang Ocean Family Co Ltd** - *Zhoushan, Zhejiang* *China* Official number: Z07-100725	**634** 208 -		2005-01 **Zhejiang Yangfan Ship Group Co Ltd — Zhoushan ZJ** Loa 48.70 Br ex 8.50 Dght - Lbp - Br md - Dpth 3.65 Welded, 1 dk	**(B11B2FV) Fishing Vessel**	**1 oil engine** driving 1 Propeller Total Power: 735kW (999hp)	
8649462 *BZVZ4* -	**XIN SHI JI 73** **Zhejiang Ocean Family Co Ltd** - *Zhoushan, Zhejiang* *China* Official number: Z07-100727	**634** 208 -		2005-05 **Zhejiang Yangfan Ship Group Co Ltd — Zhoushan ZJ** Yd No: 05207 Loa 48.70 Br ex - Dght - Lbp - Br md 8.50 Dpth 3.65 Welded, 1 dk	**(B11B2FV) Fishing Vessel**	**1 oil engine** driving 1 Propeller	
8649474 *BZVZ5* -	**XIN SHI JI 75** **Zhejiang Ocean Family Co Ltd** - *Zhoushan, Zhejiang* *China* Official number: Z07-100728	**634** 208 -		2005-05 **Zhejiang Yangfan Ship Group Co Ltd — Zhoushan ZJ** Yd No: 05208 Loa 48.70 Br ex - Dght - Lbp - Br md 8.50 Dpth 3.65 Welded, 1 dk	**(B11B2FV) Fishing Vessel**	**1 oil engine** driving 1 Propeller	
8653504 *BZVZ6* -	**XIN SHI JI 76** **Zhejiang Ocean Family Co Ltd** - *Zhoushan, Zhejiang* *China* Official number: Z07-100729	**634** 208 -		2005-05 **Zhejiang Yangfan Ship Group Co Ltd — Zhoushan ZJ** Loa 48.70 Br ex 8.50 Dght - Lbp - Br md - Dpth 3.65 Welded, 1 dk	**(B11B2FV) Fishing Vessel**	**1 oil engine** driving 1 Propeller Total Power: 735kW (999hp)	
8653516 *BZVZ7* -	**XIN SHI JI 77** **Zhejiang Ocean Family Co Ltd** - *Zhoushan, Zhejiang* *China* Official number: Z07-100730	**634** 208 -		2005-05 **Zhejiang Yangfan Ship Group Co Ltd — Zhoushan ZJ** Loa 48.70 Br ex 8.50 Dght - Lbp - Br md - Dpth 3.65 Welded, 1 dk	**(B11B2FV) Fishing Vessel**	**1 oil engine** driving 1 Propeller Total Power: 735kW (999hp)	
8653528 *BZVZ8* -	**XIN SHI JI 78** **Zhejiang Ocean Family Co Ltd** - *Zhoushan, Zhejiang* *China* Official number: Z07-100731	**634** 208 -		2005-03 **Zhoushan Dinghai Panzhi Shipyard — Zhoushan ZJ** Loa 48.70 Br ex 8.50 Dght - Lbp - Br md - Dpth 3.65 Welded, 1 dk	**(B11B2FV) Fishing Vessel**	**1 oil engine** driving 1 Propeller Total Power: 735kW (999hp)	

653530 **XIN SHI JI 79** 634 / 208 / -
ZVZ9
Zhejiang Ocean Family Co Ltd
-
Zhoushan, Zhejiang *China*
Official number: Z07-100732

2005-03 **Zhoushan Dinghai Panzhi Shipyard — Zhoushan ZJ**
Loa 48.70 Br ex 8.50 Dght -
Lbp - Br md - Dpth 3.65
Welded, 1 dk

(B11B2FV) Fishing Vessel

1 oil engine driving 1 Propeller
Total Power: 735kW (999hp)

8653542 **XIN SHI JI 82** 634 / 208 / -
ZVY5
Zhejiang Ocean Family Co Ltd
-
Zhoushan, Zhejiang *China*
Official number: Z07-100735

2004-09 **Zhejiang Yangfan Ship Group Co Ltd — Zhoushan ZJ**
Loa 48.70 Br ex 8.50 Dght -
Lbp - Br md - Dpth 3.65
Welded, 1 dk

(B11B2FV) Fishing Vessel

1 oil engine driving 1 Propeller
Total Power: 735kW (999hp)

8653554 **XIN SHI JI 85** 634 / 208 / -
BZVY7
Zhejiang Ocean Family Co Ltd
-
Zhoushan, Zhejiang *China*
Official number: Z07-100737

2004-10 **Zhoushan Dinghai Panzhi Shipyard — Zhoushan ZJ**
Loa 48.70 Br ex 8.50 Dght -
Lbp - Br md - Dpth 3.65
Welded, 1 dk

(B11B2FV) Fishing Vessel

1 oil engine driving 1 Propeller
Total Power: 735kW (999hp)

8653566 **XIN SHI JI 86** 634 / 208 / -
BZVY8
Zhejiang Ocean Family Co Ltd
-
Zhoushan, Zhejiang *China*
Official number: Z07-100738

2004-10 **Zhoushan Dinghai Panzhi Shipyard — Zhoushan ZJ**
Loa 48.70 Br ex 8.50 Dght -
Lbp - Br md - Dpth 3.65
Welded, 1 dk

(B11B2FV) Fishing Vessel

1 oil engine driving 1 Propeller
Total Power: 735kW (999hp)

8748775 **XIN SHI JI 101** 996 / 313 / -
BZ4UB
-
Zhejiang Ocean Family Co Ltd
-
Zhoushan, Zhejiang *China*

1990 Lin Sheng Shipbuilding Co, Ltd — Kaohsiung
Loa 56.94 Br ex - Dght -
Lbp - Br md 12.24 Dpth 7.25
Welded, 1 dk

(B11B2FV) Fishing Vessel

1 oil engine driving 1 Propeller
Total Power: 2,206kW (2,999hp)
Daihatsu
1 x 4 Stroke 2206kW (2999bhp)
Daihatsu Diesel Manufacturing Co Lt-Japan

8748787 **XIN SHI JI 102** 996 / 313 / -
BZ5UB
Zhejiang Ocean Family Co Ltd
-
Zhoushan, Zhejiang *China*

1990 Lin Sheng Shipbuilding Co, Ltd — Kaohsiung
Loa 56.94 Br ex - Dght -
Lbp - Br md 12.24 Dpth 7.25
Welded, 1 dk

(B11B2FV) Fishing Vessel

1 oil engine driving 1 Propeller
Total Power: 2,206kW (2,999hp)
Daihatsu
1 x 4 Stroke 2206kW (2999bhp)
Daihatsu Diesel Manufacturing Co Lt-Japan

9493432 **XIN SHI JI 128** 33,511 / 18,766 / 57,000 Class: ZC
BRSK
Shenhuazhonghai Shipping Co Ltd
-
SatCom: Inmarsat C 441256310
Shanghai *China*
MMSI: 412563000
Official number: 060709990182

2009-09 **China Shipping Industry (Jiangsu) Co Ltd — Jiangdu JS**
Loa 199.99 (BB) Br ex - Dght 12.500
Lbp 192.00 Br md 32.26 Dpth 18.00
Welded, 1 dk

(A21A2BC) Bulk Carrier
Grain: 71,634
Compartments: 5 Ho, ER
5 Ha: ER

1 oil engine driving 1 FP propeller
Total Power: 9,960kW (13,542hp) 14.2kn
MAN-B&W 6S50MC-C
1 x 2 Stroke 6 Cy. 500 x 2000 9960kW (13542bhp)

9493482 **XIN SHI JI 168** 33,511 / 18,766 / 57,000 Class: ZC
BRSJ
-
Shenhuazhonghai Shipping Co Ltd
-
SatCom: Inmarsat C 441256810
Shanghai *China*
MMSI: 412568000
Official number: 090310000013

2010-03 **China Shipping Industry (Jiangsu) Co Ltd — Jiangdu JS**
Loa 199.99 (BB) Br ex - Dght 12.500
Lbp 192.00 Br md 32.26 Dpth 18.00
Welded, 1 dk

(A21A2BC) Bulk Carrier
Grain: 71,634
Compartments: 5 Ho, ER
5 Ha: ER

1 oil engine driving 1 FP propeller
Total Power: 9,960kW (13,542hp) 14.2kn
MAN-B&W 6S50MC-C
1 x 2 Stroke 6 Cy. 500 x 2000 9960kW (13542bhp)

9663570 **XIN SHI JI 201** 396 / 154 / -
BZ1VS
-
Zhejiang Ocean Fisheries Group Co Ltd
-
Zhoushan, Zhejiang *China*
MMSI: 412420792

2012-03 **Taizhou Hongtai Ship Industry Co Ltd — Taizhou ZJ**
L reg 40.13 Br ex - Dght -
Lbp - Br md 7.00 Dpth 3.80
Welded, 1 dk

(B11B2FV) Fishing Vessel

1 oil engine driving 1 Propeller
Total Power: 660kW (897hp)
Chinese Std. Type CW6200
1 x 4 Stroke 6 Cy. 200 x 270 660kW (897bhp)
in China

9663582 **XIN SHI JI 202** 396 / 154 / -
BZ2VS
-
Zhejiang Ocean Fisheries Group Co Ltd
-
Zhoushan, Zhejiang *China*
MMSI: 412420793

2012-03 **Taizhou Hongtai Ship Industry Co Ltd — Taizhou ZJ**
L reg 40.13 Br ex - Dght -
Lbp - Br md 7.00 Dpth 3.80
Welded, 1 dk

(B11B2FV) Fishing Vessel

1 oil engine driving 1 Propeller
Total Power: 660kW (897hp)
Chinese Std. Type CW6200
1 x 4 Stroke 6 Cy. 200 x 270 660kW (897bhp)
in China

9663594 **XIN SHI JI 203** 396 / 154 / -
BZ3VS
-
Zhejiang Ocean Fisheries Group Co Ltd
-
Zhoushan, Zhejiang *China*
MMSI: 412420794

2012-03 **Taizhou Hongtai Ship Industry Co Ltd — Taizhou ZJ**
L reg 40.13 Br ex - Dght -
Lbp - Br md 7.00 Dpth 3.80
Welded, 1 dk

(B11B2FV) Fishing Vessel

1 oil engine driving 1 Propeller
Total Power: 660kW (897hp)
Chinese Std. Type CW6200
1 x 4 Stroke 6 Cy. 200 x 270 660kW (897bhp)
in China

9663609 **XIN SHI JI 205** 396 / 154 / -
BZ4VS
-
Zhejiang Ocean Fisheries Group Co Ltd
-
Zhoushan, Zhejiang *China*
MMSI: 412420795

2012-03 **Taizhou Hongtai Ship Industry Co Ltd — Taizhou ZJ**
L reg 40.13 Br ex - Dght -
Lbp - Br md 7.00 Dpth 3.80
Welded, 1 dk

(B11B2FV) Fishing Vessel

1 oil engine driving 1 Propeller
Total Power: 660kW (897hp)
Chinese Std. Type CW6200
1 x 4 Stroke 6 Cy. 200 x 270 660kW (897bhp)
in China

9663611 **XIN SHI JI 206** 396 / 154 / -
BV5VS
-
Zhejiang Ocean Fisheries Group Co Ltd
-
Zhoushan, Zhejiang *China*
MMSI: 412420796

2012-03 **Taizhou Hongtai Ship Industry Co Ltd — Taizhou ZJ**
L reg 40.13 Br ex - Dght -
Lbp - Br md 7.00 Dpth 3.80
Welded, 1 dk

(B11B2FV) Fishing Vessel

1 oil engine driving 1 Propeller
Total Power: 660kW (897hp)
Chinese Std. Type CW6200
1 x 4 Stroke 6 Cy. 200 x 270 660kW (897bhp)
in China

9727481 **XIN SHI JI 215** 462 / 147 / -
BZ2VX
-
Zhejiang Ocean Fisheries Group Co Ltd
-
Zhoushan, Zhejiang *China*
MMSI: 412420891
Official number: 3301002013090001

2013-09 **Zhoushan Hetai Shipbuilding & Repair Co Ltd — Daishan County ZJ**
Loa 44.00 Br ex - Dght -
Lbp - Br md 7.60 Dpth 3.80
Welded, 1 dk

(B11B2FV) Fishing Vessel

1 oil engine driving 1 Propeller
Total Power: 660kW (897hp)
Chinese Std. Type CW6200
1 x 4 Stroke 6 Cy. 200 x 270 660kW (897bhp)
in China

9079224 **XIN SHI JI HAO** 478 / 159 / 50 Class: (CC) (NV)
-
-
ex Xin Shi Ji -2005
Shanghai Chongming Assets Management Co Ltd
Shanghai Yatong Co Ltd
Yantai, Shandong *China*

1993-05 **Kvaerner Fjellstrand AS — Omastrand**
Yd No: 1612
Loa 40.00 Br ex - Dght -
Lbp 36.00 Br md 10.00 Dpth 3.96
Welded

(A37B2PS) Passenger Ship
Hull Material: Aluminium Alloy
Passengers: unberthed: 324

2 oil engines geared to sc. shafts driving 2 Water jets
Total Power: 4,002kW (5,442hp) 34.0kn
M.T.U. 16V396TE74
2 x Vee 4 Stroke 16 Cy. 165 x 185 each-2001kW (2721bhp)
MTU Friedrichshafen GmbH-Friedrichshafen
AuxGen: 2 x 76kW 380V 50Hz a.c
Fuel: 10.4 (d.f.)

8430574 **XIN SHI JI No. 6** *621* / 190 / -
-
-
ex Benny No. 87 -2005 ex Daniel No. 5 -2005
-
-

1990 Lien Ho Shipbuilding Co, Ltd — Kaohsiung
Loa 49.15 Br ex - Dght -
Lbp - Br md 8.90 Dpth 3.75
Welded, 1 dk

(B11B2FV) Fishing Vessel

1 oil engine driving 1 FP propeller
Total Power: 1,030kW (1,400hp) 12.0kn
Akasaka
1 x 4 Stroke 1030kW (1400bhp)
Akasaka Tekkosho KK (Akasaka DieselLtd)-Japan

8651233 **XIN SHI JI NO. 7** 497 / 228 / -
BZUS5
001423
Zhejiang Ocean Fisheries Group Co Ltd
-
Zhoushan, Zhejiang *China*
MMSI: 412985000
Official number: Z07-010254

2001-01 **Zhejiang Yangfan Ship Group Co Ltd — Zhoushan ZJ**
Loa 48.60 Br ex 8.70 Dght -
Lbp - Br md - Dpth 3.75
Welded, 1 dk

(B11B2FV) Fishing Vessel

1 oil engine driving 1 Propeller
Total Power: 882kW (1,199hp)

IMO / Call sign / Official no.	Name, ex-names, owner, manager, port, flag	Tonnage	Class	Builder, dimensions	Type, capacities	Machinery
9036337 *BZUU2* 004752	**XIN SHI JI NO. 10** *ex* Jeffrey No. 816 *-2008* *ex* Katco 7 *-1997* *ex* Shotoku Maru No. 83 *-1997* **Zhejiang Ocean Fisheries Group Co Ltd** - *Zhoushan, Zhejiang* *China* MMSI: 412674190 Official number: Z07-000189	**576** 250 -		**1991-09 Fujishin Zosen K.K. — Kamo** Yd No: 571 Loa 56.56 Br ex - Dght 3.400 Lbp 48.95 Br md 8.90 Dpth 3.80 Welded, 1 dk	**(B11B2FV) Fishing Vessel**	**1 oil engine** with clutches & sr reverse geared to sc. shaft driving 1 CP propeller Total Power: 1,029kW (1,399hp) Matsui M31M3 1 x 4 Stroke 6 Cy. 310 x 550 1029kW (1399bhp) Matsui Iron Works Co Ltd-Japan
8021153 *BZUS9* 001418	**XIN SHI JI NO. 12** *ex* Shoei Maru No. 7 *-2008* **Zhejiang Ocean Fisheries Group Co Ltd** - *Zhoushan, Zhejiang* *China* MMSI: 412679180 Official number: Z07-010259	**628** 205 417		**1980-12 Miho Zosensho K.K. — Shimizu** Yd No: 1188 Loa 52.41 Br ex 8.82 Dght 3.390 Lbp 46.00 Br md 8.81 Dpth 3.76 Welded, 1 dk	**(B11B2FV) Fishing Vessel**	**1 oil engine** reduction geared to sc. shaft driving 1 FP propeller Total Power: 956kW (1,300hp) Akasaka DM28AFD 1 x 4 Stroke 6 Cy. 280 x 460 956kW (1300bhp) Akasaka Tekkosho KK (Akasaka DieselLtd)-Japan
8651269 *BZUT4* -	**XIN SHI JI NO. 17** **Zhejiang Ocean Fisheries Group Co Ltd** - *Zhoushan, Zhejiang* *China* MMSI: 412679210 Official number: Z07-010261	**497** 228 -		**2001-04 Zhejiang Yangfan Ship Group Co Ltd — Zhoushan ZJ** Loa 48.60 Br ex 8.70 Dght - Lbp - Br md - Dpth 3.75 Welded, 1 dk	**(B11B2FV) Fishing Vessel**	**1 oil engine** driving 1 Propeller Total Power: 883kW (1,201hp)
8653499 *BZVZ3* -	**XIN SHI JI NO. 72** **Zhejiang Ocean Family Co Ltd** - *Zhoushan, Zhejiang* *China* MMSI: 412695570 Official number: Z07-100726	**634** 208 -		**2005-01 Zhejiang Yangfan Ship Group Co Ltd — Zhoushan ZJ** Loa 56.50 Br ex 8.50 Dght 3.300 Lbp 48.70 Br md - Dpth 3.65 Welded, 1 dk	**(B11B2FV) Fishing Vessel**	**1 oil engine** driving 1 FP propeller Total Power: 882kW (1,199hp) Niigata 6M26AFTE 1 x 4 Stroke 6 Cy. 260 x 460 882kW (1199bhp) Niigata Engineering Co Ltd-Japan
8651271 *BZUZ5* 001422	**XIN SHI JI NO. 87** **Zhejiang Ocean Fisheries Group Co Ltd** - *Zhoushan, Zhejiang* *China* MMSI: 412993000 Official number: Z07-010285	**497** 228 -		**2001-11 Zhejiang Yangfan Ship Group Co Ltd — Zhoushan ZJ** Loa 48.60 Br ex 8.70 Dght - Lbp - Br md - Dpth 3.75 Welded, 1 dk	**(B11B2FV) Fishing Vessel**	**1 oil engine** driving 1 Propeller Total Power: 735kW (999hp)
9252199 *VRGZ2* -	**XIN SHUN** *ex* Orange Tiara *-2010* **Speedway Transportation Ltd** Xin Shun Yang (HK) Shipping Co Ltd SatCom: Inmarsat C 447702856 *Hong Kong* *Hong Kong* MMSI: 477786200 Official number: HK-2769	**38,871** 25,208 75,846 T/cm 65.8	Class: NK	**2002-11 Sanoyas Hishino Meisho Corp — Kurashiki OY** Yd No: 1202 Loa 225.00 (BB) Br ex 32.30 Dght 13.994 Lbp 217.00 Br md 32.26 Dpth 19.30 Welded, 1 dk	**(A21A2BC) Bulk Carrier** Double Bottom Entire Compartment Length Grain: 89,250 Compartments: 7 Ho, ER 7 Ha: (16.3 x 13.4)6 (17.1 x 15.0)ER	**1 oil engine** driving 1 FP propeller Total Power: 8,973kW (12,200hp) 14.0kn B&W 7S50MC-C 1 x 2 Stroke 7 Cy. 500 x 2000 8973kW (12200bhp) Mitsui Engineering & Shipbuilding CLtd-Japan AuxGen: 3 x 400kW 450V 60Hz a.c Fuel: 151.0 (d.f.) (Heating Coils) 2691.0 (r.f.) 30.5pd
9262144 *BPBK* -	**XIN SU ZHOU** **China Shipping Container Lines Co Ltd** - *Shanghai* *China* MMSI: 413068000	**41,482** 24,001 50,137	Class: CC	**2004-02 Hudong-Zhonghua Shipbuilding (Group) Co Ltd — Shanghai** Yd No: H1296A Loa 263.20 (BB) Br ex - Dght 12.800 Lbp 251.40 Br md 32.20 Dpth 19.30 Welded, 1 dk	**(A33A2CC) Container Ship (Fully Cellular)** TEU 4051 C Ho 1586 TEU C Dk 2465 TEU incl 400 ref C. Compartments: 7 Cell Ho, ER	**1 oil engine** driving 1 FP propeller Total Power: 36,543kW (49,684hp) 24.2kn B&W 8K90MC-C 1 x 2 Stroke 8 Cy. 900 x 2300 36543kW (49684bhp) Mitsui Engineering & Shipbuilding CLtd-Japan AuxGen: 3 x 1960kW 450/230V 60Hz a.c Thrusters: 1 Tunnel thruster (f)
9320465 *BPNA* -	**XIN TAI CANG** **China Shipping Container Lines Co Ltd** - *Shanghai* *China* MMSI: 413166000	**41,482** 24,001 52,245	Class: CC	**2008-07 Dalian Shipbuilding Industry Co Ltd — Dalian LN (No 2 Yard)** Yd No: C4250-26 Loa 263.23 (BB) Br ex 32.30 Dght 12.800 Lbp 251.88 Br md 32.25 Dpth 19.30 Welded, 1 dk	**(A33A2CC) Container Ship (Fully Cellular)** Bale: 79,953 TEU 4250 C Ho 1586 TEU C Dk 2664 TEU incl 400 ref cont. Compartments: 7 Cell Ho, ER Ice Capable	**1 oil engine** driving 1 FP propeller Total Power: 36,560kW (49,707hp) 24.2kn MAN-B&W 8K90MC-C 1 x 2 Stroke 8 Cy. 900 x 2300 36560kW (49707bhp) Doosan Engine Co Ltd-South Korea AuxGen: 3 x 1960kW 450V a.c Thrusters: 1 Tunnel thruster (f)
9578622 *3EW07* -	**XIN TAI HAI** **China Earth Shipping Inc** Vision Ship Management Ltd *Panama* *Panama* MMSI: 353912000 Official number: 4301611	**94,710** 59,527 180,346 T/cm 124.3	Class: CC	**2011-05 Dalian Shipbuilding Industry Co Ltd — Dalian LN (No 2 Yard)** Yd No: BC1800-33 Loa 295.00 (BB) Br ex - Dght 18.100 Lbp 285.00 Br md 46.00 Dpth 24.80 Welded, 1 dk	**(A21A2BC) Bulk Carrier** Grain: 201,953 9 Ha: 8 (15.5 x 20.0)ER (15.5 x 16.5)	**1 oil engine** driving 1 FP propeller Total Power: 18,660kW (25,370hp) 14.5kn MAN-B&W 6S70MC-C 1 x 2 Stroke 6 Cy. 700 x 2800 18660kW (25370bhp) Hyundai Heavy Industries Co Ltd-South Korea AuxGen: 3 x 900kW 450V a.c
9111797 - -	**XIN TAI SHUN 2** *ex* Xiang Rong *-2007* **Shanghai Xinou Shipping Co Ltd** *Shanghai* *China*	**2,752** 1,192 3,337	Class: (CC)	**1994-06 Huanghai Shipbuilding Co Ltd — Rongcheng SD** Yd No: 12 Loa 84.57 Br ex - Dght 5.500 Lbp 79.00 Br md 15.00 Dpth 7.30 Welded, 1 dk	**(A33A2CC) Container Ship (Fully Cellular)** TEU 170	**1 oil engine** reduction geared to sc. shaft driving 1 FP propeller Total Power: 1,456kW (1,980hp) 12.0kn Chinese Std. Type 6300ZC 1 x 4 Stroke 6 Cy. 300 x 380 1456kW (1980bhp) Guangzhou Diesel Engine Factory CoLtd-China AuxGen: 3 x 120kW 400V a.c
9655822 *BDNF5* -	**XIN TANG SHAN HAI 1** **Tang Shan Hua Xing Shipping Co Ltd** Shanghai Yuhai Shipping Co *Tangshan, Hebei* *China* MMSI: 414152000	**44,725** 27,509 81,870 T/cm 71.9	Class: CC	**2013-04 COSCO (Dalian) Shipyard Co Ltd — Dalian LN** Yd No: N358 Loa 229.00 (BB) Br ex - Dght 14.500 Lbp 225.50 Br md 32.26 Dpth 20.25 Welded, 1 dk	**(A21A2BC) Bulk Carrier** Grain: 98,456; Bale: 90,784 Compartments: 7 Ho, ER 7 Ha: 5 (15.7 x 15.0) (13.1 x 15.0)ER (13.1 x 13.2)	**1 oil engine** driving 1 FP propeller Total Power: 11,900kW (16,179hp) 14.1kn MAN-B&W 5S60ME-C8 1 x 2 Stroke 5 Cy. 600 x 2400 11900kW (16179bhp) STX Engine Co Ltd-South Korea AuxGen: 3 x 650kW a.c
9234343 *BPAQ* -	**XIN TIAN JIN** **China Shipping Container Lines Co Ltd** - SatCom: Inmarsat C 441305310 *Shanghai* *China* MMSI: 413053000	**66,433** 37,567 69,403	Class: CC	**2003-06 Dalian New Shipbuilding Heavy Industries Co Ltd — Dalian LN** Yd No: C5600-2 Loa 279.60 (BB) Br ex - Dght 14.000 Lbp 265.80 Br md 40.30 Dpth 24.10 Welded, 1 dk	**(A33A2CC) Container Ship (Fully Cellular)** Bale: 227,522 TEU 5668 C Ho 2586 TEU C Dk 3082 TEU incl 610 ref C. Compartments: 5 Cell Ho, ER Ice Capable	**1 oil engine** driving 1 FP propeller Total Power: 54,809kW (74,518hp) 25.7kn MAN-B&W 12K90MC-C 1 x 2 Stroke 12 Cy. 900 x 2300 54809kW (74518bhp) Mitsui Engineering & Shipbuilding CLtd-Japan AuxGen: 4 x 2320kW 450/230V 60Hz a.c Thrusters: 1 Tunnel thruster (f)
9389758 *VREQ3* -	**XIN TONG YANG** **Xin Tong Yang Shipping SA** China Shipping Tanker Co Ltd SatCom: Inmarsat C 447701396 *Hong Kong* *Hong Kong* MMSI: 477173200 Official number: HK-2281	**152,740** 97,129 297,183 T/cm 177.9	Class: CC	**2009-01 Dalian Shipbuilding Industry Co Ltd — Dalian LN (No 2 Yard)** Yd No: T3000-18 Loa 330.00 (BB) Br ex 60.05 Dght 21.500 Lbp 316.00 Br md 60.00 Dpth 29.70 Welded, 1 dk	**(A13A2TV) Crude Oil Tanker** Double Hull (13F) Liq: 324,599; Liq (Oil): 333,305 Compartments: 5 Ta, 10 Wing Ta, 2 Wing Slop Ta, ER 3 Cargo Pump (s): 3x5500m³/hr Manifold: Bow/CM: 162.5m	**1 oil engine** driving 1 FP propeller Total Power: 25,480kW (34,643hp) 15.8kn MAN-B&W 7S80MC 1 x 2 Stroke 7 Cy. 800 x 3056 25480kW (34643bhp) Doosan Engine Co Ltd-South Korea AuxGen: 3 x 975kW 450V a.c Fuel: 429.6 (d.f.) 7117.3 (r.f.)
9036973 *BJPI* -	**XIN TONG YANG** *ex* An Qing *-2007* *ex* Good Hope *-2005* *ex* Hope *-1999* *ex* Panagia *-1996* *ex* Sea Giant *-1996* *completed as* J. P. C. Koruna *-1996* *launched as* Moreni *-1996* **Hainan Tongli Shipping Co Ltd** Fujian Shipping Co (FUSCO) *Shekou, Guangdong* *China* MMSI: 412523160	**50,552** 31,114 89,090 T/cm 86.8	Class: (CC) (GL)	**1996-02 Santierul Naval "2 Mai" Mangalia S.A. — Mangalia** Yd No: 853 Loa 228.50 Br ex - Dght 14.000 Lbp 220.50 Br md 43.00 Dpth 19.00 Welded, 1 dk	**(A13A2TV) Crude Oil Tanker** Single Hull Liq: 107,343; Liq (Oil): 107,343 Cargo Heating Coils Compartments: 11 Ta, ER	**1 oil engine** driving 1 FP propeller Total Power: 11,181kW (15,202hp) 13.0kn MAN K8SZ70/150CL 1 x 2 Stroke 8 Cy. 700 x 1500 11181kW (15202bhp) U.C.M. Resita S.A.-Resita AuxGen: 1 x 1000kW 220/380V a.c, 2 x 760kW 220/380V a.c Fuel: 2308.0 (r.f.)
9297448 *BJLN* -	**XIN TONG ZHOU** *ex* Fidelity *-2011* **Hainan Tongli Shipping Co Ltd** Fujian Shipping Co (FUSCO) SatCom: Inmarsat C 441301772 *Haikou, Hainan* *China* MMSI: 413521690	**38,842** 21,249 71,049 T/cm 66.9	Class: CC (BV)	**2005-09 Onomichi Dockyard Co Ltd — Onomichi HS** Yd No: 512 Loa 228.56 (BB) Br ex 32.23 Dght 13.700 Lbp 218.00 Br md 32.20 Dpth 19.60 Welded, 1 dk	**(A13A2TV) Crude Oil Tanker** Double Hull (13F) Liq: 77,932; Liq (Oil): 80,370 Cargo Heating Coils Compartments: 12 Wing Ta, ER, 2 Wing Slop Ta 3 Cargo Pump (s): 3x2000m³/hr Manifold: Bow/CM: 115.5m	**1 oil engine** driving 1 FP propeller Total Power: 12,240kW (16,642hp) 15.9kn B&W 6S60MC 1 x 2 Stroke 6 Cy. 600 x 2292 12240kW (16642bhp) Mitsui Engineering & Shipbuilding CLtd-Japan

312573 *PBV*	**XIN WEI HAI** **China Shipping Container Lines Co Ltd** - *Shanghai* *China* MMSI: 413149000	**41,482** 24,001 52,219	Class: CC	**2006-01 Dalian Shipbuilding Industry Co Ltd — Dalian LN (No 2 Yard)** Yd No: C4250-7 Loa 263.23 (BB) Br ex 32.30 Dght 12.800 Lbp 251.88 Br md 32.25 Dpth 19.30 Welded, 1 dk	**(A33A2CC) Container Ship (Fully Cellular)** TEU 4250 C Ho 1586 TEU C Dk 2664 TEU incl 400 ref C. Compartments: 7 Cell Ho, ER Ice Capable	**1 oil engine** driving 1 FP propeller Total Power: 36,480kW (49,598hp) 24.2kn MAN-B&W 8K90MC-C 1 x 2 Stroke 8 Cy. 900 x 2300 36480kW (49598bhp) Doosan Engine Co Ltd-South Korea AuxGen: 3 x 1960kW 450V 60Hz a.c Thrusters: 1 Tunnel thruster (f)
523043 *PKJ*	**XIN WEN ZHOU** **China Shipping Container Lines Co Ltd** - *Shanghai* *China* MMSI: 414736000	**47,917** 24,185 67,052	Class: CC	**2013-03 Shanghai Jiangnan Changxing Heavy Industry Co Ltd — Shanghai** Yd No: H1054A Loa 255.10 (BB) Br ex - Dght 13.500 Lbp 242.00 Br md 37.30 Dpth 19.60 Welded, 1 dk	**(A33A2CC) Container Ship (Fully Cellular)** TEU 4738 C Ho 1826 TEU C Dk 2912 incl 300 ref C Ice Capable	**1 oil engine** driving 1 FP propeller Total Power: 21,910kW (29,789hp) 18.0kn Wartsila 7RT-flex68 1 x 2 Stroke 7 Cy. 680 x 2720 21910kW (29789bhp) Doosan Engine Co Ltd-South Korea AuxGen: 1 x 1240kW 450V a.c, 2 x 1650kW 450V a.c Thrusters: 1 Tunnel thruster (f)
328596 *PND*	**XIN WU HAN** **China Shipping Container Lines Co Ltd** - *Shanghai* *China* MMSI: 413169000	**41,482** 24,001 52,233	Class: CC	**2008-10 Dalian Shipbuilding Industry Co Ltd — Dalian LN (No 2 Yard)** Yd No: C4250-28 Loa 263.23 (BB) Br ex 32.30 Dght 12.800 Lbp 251.88 Br md 32.25 Dpth 19.30 Welded, 1 dk	**(A33A2CC) Container Ship (Fully Cellular)** TEU 4250 C Ho 1586 TEU C Dk 2664 TEU incl 400 ref C. Ice Capable	**1 oil engine** driving 1 FP propeller Total Power: 36,560kW (49,707hp) 24.2kn MAN-B&W 8K90MC-C 1 x 2 Stroke 8 Cy. 900 x 2300 36560kW (49707bhp) Doosan Engine Co Ltd-South Korea AuxGen: 3 x 1960kW 450V a.c Thrusters: 1 Tunnel thruster (f)
270476 *PBB*	**XIN XIA MEN** **China Shipping Container Lines Co Ltd** - SatCom: Inmarsat C 441306510 *Shanghai* *China* MMSI: 413065000	**66,433** 37,567 69,259	Class: CC	**2004-03 Hudong-Zhonghua Shipbuilding (Group) Co Ltd — Shanghai** Yd No: H1266A Loa 279.90 (BB) Br ex - Dght 14.000 Lbp 265.80 Br md 40.30 Dpth 24.10 Welded	**(A33A2CC) Container Ship (Fully Cellular)** TEU 5668 C Ho 2586 TEU C Dk 3082 TEU incl 610 ref C. Compartments: 7 Cell Ho, ER	**1 oil engine** driving 1 FP propeller Total Power: 54,809kW (74,518hp) 25.7kn MAN-B&W 12K90MC-C 1 x 2 Stroke 12 Cy. 900 x 2300 54809kW (74518bhp) Mitsui Engineering & Shipbuilding CLtd-Japan AuxGen: 4 x 2320kW 450/230V 60Hz a.c Thrusters: 1 Tunnel thruster (f)
416630 *PAI*	**XIN XIA YANG** **China Shipping Tanker Co Ltd** - *Shanghai* *China* MMSI: 413188000	**161,488** 104,666 309,140 T/cm 182.2	Class: CC NV	**2011-02 Guangzhou Longxue Shipbuilding Co Ltd — Guangzhou GD** Yd No: L0002 Loa 332.95 (BB) Br ex 60.04 Dght 21.800 Lbp 319.86 Br md 60.00 Dpth 29.79 Welded, 1 dk	**(A13A2TV) Crude Oil Tanker** Double Hull (13F) Liq: 334,500; Liq (Oil): 334,500 Compartments: 5 Ta, 10 Wing Ta, 2 Wing Slop Ta, ER 3 Cargo Pump (s): 3x5500m³/hr Manifold: Bow/CM: 167m	**1 oil engine** driving 1 FP propeller Total Power: 26,460kW (35,975hp) 15.7kn Wartsila 7RTA84T 1 x 2 Stroke 7 Cy. 840 x 3150 26460kW (35975bhp) Wartsila Switzerland Ltd-Switzerland AuxGen: 3 x 1050kW 450V a.c Fuel: 420.0 (d.f.) 6600.0 (r.f.)
328525	**XIN XIAN** *ex Man Heen -2002* - -	*233* 95 -		**1982 Hong Kong Shipyard Ltd. — Hong Kong** L reg 42.34 Br ex 8.26 Dght - Lbp - Br md - Dpth 2.44 Welded, 2 dks	**(A37B2PS) Passenger Ship**	**2 oil engines** driving 1 FP propeller Total Power: 750kW (1,020hp) 13.0kn M.T.U. 6V331TC82 2 x Vee 4 Stroke 6 Cy. 165 x 155 each-375kW (510bhp) MTU Friedrichshafen GmbH-Friedrichshafen
032692 *IOQ*	**XIN XIANG AN** *ex Lucy Oldendorff -2009* **Shanghai Yang Pu Zhe Hai Shipping Co Ltd** - *Shanghai* *China* MMSI: 413905000	**13,696** 7,791 22,160 T/cm 32.8	Class: CC (LR) (AB) Classed LR until 27/9/09	**1992-05 Saiki Heavy Industries Co Ltd — Saiki OT** Yd No: 1018 Loa 157.00 (BB) Br ex 25.04 Dght 9.115 Lbp 148.00 Br md 25.00 Dpth 12.70 Welded, 1 dk	**(A21A2BC) Bulk Carrier** Grain: 29,301; Bale: 28,299 Compartments: 4 Ho, ER 4 Ha: (20.0 x 11.7)Tappered 3 (20.8 x 17.5)ER Cranes: 4x30t	**1 oil engine** driving 1 FP propeller Total Power: 5,295kW (7,199hp) 14.0kn Mitsubishi 6UEC45LA 1 x 2 Stroke 6 Cy. 450 x 1350 5295kW (7199bhp) Akasaka Tekkosho KK (Akasaka DieselLtd)-Japan AuxGen: 2 x 480kW 440V 60Hz a.c Fuel: 240.9 (d.f.) (Part Heating Coils) 710.1 (r.f.) 21.9pd
566411 *FGS*	**XIN XIANG HAI** **NCN Corp** COSCO Bulk Carrier Co Ltd (COSCO BULK) SatCom: Inmarsat C 437366510 *Panama* *Panama* MMSI: 373665000 Official number: 43545TJ	**31,754** 18,653 56,111 T/cm 55.8	Class: NK	**2012-07 Mitsui Eng. & SB. Co. Ltd., Chiba Works — Ichihara** Yd No: 1833 Loa 189.99 (BB) Br ex - Dght 12.720 Lbp 182.00 Br md 32.25 Dpth 18.10 Welded, 1 dk	**(A21A2BC) Bulk Carrier** Grain: 71,345; Bale: 68,733 Compartments: 5 Ho, ER 5 Ha: ER Cranes: 4x30t	**1 oil engine** driving 1 FP propeller Total Power: 9,070kW (12,332hp) 14.5kn MAN-B&W 6S50MC-C 1 x 2 Stroke 6 Cy. 500 x 2000 9070kW (12332bhp) Mitsui Engineering & Shipbuilding CLtd-Japan Fuel: 2310.0
524972	**XIN XIANG HE** *ex Jin Hai Tong -2007 ex Su Da -2003* *ex Verdi -1990 ex Alange -1990* **Tianjin New Legend Shipping Co Ltd** Tianjin Xinhai International Ship Management Co Ltd (New Legend Group) *Tianjin* *China* MMSI: 413300320	**6,806** 3,659 6,829	Class: (CC) (GL)	**1978-12 Ast. del Cadagua W. E. Gonzalez S.A. — Bilbao** Yd No: 105 Loa 133.23 (BB) Br ex 19.05 Dght 8.033 Lbp 121.32 Br md 19.02 Dpth 10.62 Welded, 2 dks	**(A31A2GX) General Cargo Ship** Passengers: berths: 6 Grain: 12,967; Bale: 11,414; Ins: 1,224; Liq: 500 TEU 288 C. Ho 244/20' (40') C.Dk 44/20' (40') incl. 24 ref. C. Compartments: 3 Ho, ER, 3 Tw Dk 3 Ha: (14.0 x 10.0) (38.2 x 12.8) (14.2 x 12.8)ER Derricks: 2x50t,8x6t; Winches: 14 Ice Capable	**1 oil engine** driving 1 FP propeller Total Power: 5,186kW (7,051hp) 15.0kn B&W 8K45GFCA 1 x 2 Stroke 8 Cy. 450 x 900 5186kW (7051bhp) Astilleros Espanoles SA (AESA)-Spain AuxGen: 3 x 360kW 220/380V 50Hz a.c Fuel: 261.0 (d.f.) 943.5 (r.f.) 19.5pd
411413 *PQW*	**XIN XIANG NING** *ex Alexandra -2011 ex Virginia -2003* *ex Blue Vega -2002 ex Young Sato -1994* *ex Perenne -1989 ex Sun Grace -1987* **Yang Pu Zhe Hai Shipping Co Ltd** - *Yangpu, Hainan* *China* MMSI: 413520120	**14,158** 7,928 23,675	Class: (NK)	**1985-09 Usuki Iron Works Co Ltd — Saiki OT** Yd No: 1320 Loa 160.00 (BB) Br ex 24.44 Dght 9.920 Lbp 150.00 Br md 24.40 Dpth 13.60 Welded, 1 dk	**(A21A2BC) Bulk Carrier** Grain: 30,707; Bale: 29,378 Compartments: 4 Ho, ER 4 Ha: (18.6 x 11.2)2 (20.8 x 12.8) (21.6 x 12.8)ER Cranes: 1x30t,3x25t	**1 oil engine** driving 1 FP propeller Total Power: 5,281kW (7,180hp) 14.0kn Mitsubishi 6UEC52LA 1 x 2 Stroke 6 Cy. 520 x 1600 5281kW (7180bhp) Kobe Hatsudoki KK-Japan AuxGen: 3 x 274kW a.c Fuel: 1514.0
032707 *NK*	**XIN XIANG RUI** *ex Elisabeth Oldendorff -2010* **Yang Pu Zhe Hai Shipping Co Ltd** - *Shanghai* *China* MMSI: 412513000	**13,696** 7,791 22,154 T/cm 32.8	Class: CC (LR) (AB) Classed LR until 3/9/09	**1992-07 Saiki Heavy Industries Co Ltd — Saiki OT** Yd No: 1020 Loa 157.50 (BB) Br ex 25.04 Dght 9.115 Lbp 148.00 Br md 25.00 Dpth 12.70 Welded, 1 dk	**(A21A2BC) Bulk Carrier** Grain: 29,301; Bale: 28,299 Compartments: 4 Ho, ER 4 Ha: (20.0 x 11.7)Tappered 3 (20.8 x 17.5)ER Cranes: 4x30t	**1 oil engine** driving 1 FP propeller Total Power: 5,295kW (7,199hp) 14.0kn Mitsubishi 6UEC45LA 1 x 2 Stroke 6 Cy. 450 x 1350 5295kW (7199bhp) Akasaka Tekkosho KK (Akasaka DieselLtd)-Japan AuxGen: 2 x 480kW 440V 60Hz a.c Boilers: AuxB (o.f.) 7.1kgf/cm² (7.0bar) Fuel: 240.9 (d.f.) (Part Heating Coils) 710.1 (r.f.) 21.9pd
225864	**XIN XING** *ex Man Hing -2002* - -	*777* 369 -		**1981 Hong Kong Shipyard Ltd. — Hong Kong** Loa 57.61 Br ex 10.52 Dght - Lbp - Br md - Dpth 3.56 Welded, 3 dks	**(A37B2PS) Passenger Ship**	**1 oil engine** reverse reduction geared to sc. shaft driving 1 FP propeller Total Power: 1,242kW (1,689hp) 15.0kn MAN G7V30/45ATL 1 x 4 Stroke 7 Cy. 300 x 450 1242kW (1689bhp) Maschinenbau Augsburg Nuernberg (MAN)-Augsburg
518742 *JAT8*	**XIN XING** *ex Sea Eagle -2008 ex Midas 2 -2004* *ex Kifune Maru -1999* **Golden Coast Shipping Ltd** V-Sky Shipping Ltd *Phnom Penh* *Cambodia* MMSI: 514032000 Official number: 0885991	**1,261** 555 1,580	Class: GM (KR)	**1986-01 Kishigami Zosen K.K. — Akitsu** Yd No: 1858 Loa 68.00 (BB) Br ex - Dght 4.411 Lbp 66.02 Br md 11.51 Dpth 6.71 Welded, 1 dk	**(A31A2GX) General Cargo Ship** Compartments: 1 Ho, ER 1 Ha: ER	**1 oil engine** with flexible couplings & sr gearedto sc. shaft driving 1 FP propeller Total Power: 883kW (1,201hp) Akasaka DM28AKFD 1 x 4 Stroke 6 Cy. 280 x 460 883kW (1201bhp) Akasaka Tekkosho KK (Akasaka DieselLtd)-Japan
818049 *VKI7*	**XIN XING HE** *ex Xing He -2012* **Pingtan Jinyuan Shipping Co Ltd** - *Fuzhou, Fujian* *China* MMSI: 412070000	**19,283** 10,798 25,925	Class: ZC (CC) (GL)	**1985-02 Howaldtswerke-Deutsche Werft AG (HDW) — Kiel** Yd No: 205 Loa 172.00 (BB) Br ex 28.71 Dght 10.702 Lbp 160.00 Br md 28.40 Dpth 15.50 Welded, 1 dk	**(A33A2CC) Container Ship (Fully Cellular)** TEU 1328 C Ho 676 TEU C Dk 652 TEU incl 54 ref C. Compartments: 4 Cell Ho, ER 16 Ha: 2 (12.5 x -)14 (12.5 x 10.3)ER Ice Capable	**1 oil engine** driving 1 FP propeller Total Power: 10,150kW (13,800hp) 17.0kn B&W 6L70MCE 1 x 2 Stroke 6 Cy. 700 x 2268 10150kW (13800bhp) Mitsui Engineering & Shipbuilding CLtd-Japan AuxGen: 1 x 1000kW 450V 60Hz a.c, 2 x 850kW 450V 60Hz a.c, 1 x 350kW 450V 60Hz a.c Thrusters: 1 Thwart. FP thruster (f)
717714 *EV*	**XIN XING No. 1** **China Xinxing Shipping Co** - *Shanghai* *China*	*680* 239 600	Class: (CC)	**1988-08 Teraoka Shipyard Co Ltd — Minamiawaji HG** Yd No: 267 Loa 58.00 Br ex - Dght 3.650 Lbp 54.00 Br md 9.50 Dpth 4.30 Welded, 1 dk	**(A13B2TP) Products Tanker** Liq: 873; Liq (Oil): 873 Compartments: 6 Ta, ER	**1 oil engine** driving 1 FP propeller Total Power: 736kW (1,001hp) Yanmar M220-UN 1 x 4 Stroke 6 Cy. 220 x 300 736kW (1001bhp) Yanmar Diesel Engine Co Ltd-Japan

Ship	Tonnage / Class	Builder / Dimensions	Type / Cargo	Machinery
9523081 **XIN XU ZHOU** *BPKK* - **China Shipping Container Lines Co Ltd** - *Shanghai* *China* MMSI: 414752000	**47,917** Class: CC 24,185 66,926	**2013-03 Shanghai Jiangnan Changxing Heavy Industry Co Ltd — Shanghai** Yd No: H1055A Loa 255.10 (BB) Br ex - Dght 13.000 Lbp 242.00 Br md 37.30 Dpth 19.60 Welded, 1 dk	**(A33A2CC) Container Ship (Fully Cellular)** TEU 4738 C Ho 1826 TEU C Dk 2912 TEU incl 300 ref C Ice Capable	**1 oil engine** driving 1 FP propeller Total Power: 21,910kW (29,789hp) 18.0k Wartsila 7RT-flex6 1 x 2 Stroke 7 Cy. 680 x 2720 21910kW (29789bhp) Doosan Engine Co Ltd-South Korea AuxGen: 1 x 1240kW 450V a.c, 2 x 1650kW 450V a.c Thrusters: 1 Tunnel thruster (f)
8656221 **XIN YA NO. 6** *BZXH3* - **Shenzhen Szap Overseas Fisheries Co Ltd** - *Shenzhen, Guangdong* *China* Official number: YQ000004	**190** 76 -	**1995-12 Jiangxi Jiangxin Shipyard — Hukou County JX** Loa 29.70 Br ex 6.80 Dght - Lbp - Br md - Dpth 3.70 Welded, 1 dk	**(B11B2FV) Fishing Vessel**	**1 oil engine** driving 1 Propeller
8656233 **XIN YA NO. 7** *BZXH4* - **Shenzhen Szap Overseas Fisheries Co Ltd** - *Shenzhen, Guangdong* *China* Official number: YQ000005	**190** 76 -	**1995-12 Jiangxi Jiangxin Shipyard — Hukou County JX** Loa 29.70 Br ex 6.80 Dght - Lbp - Br md - Dpth 3.70 Welded, 1 dk	**(B11B2FV) Fishing Vessel**	**1 oil engine** driving 1 Propeller
9334935 **XIN YA ZHOU** *BPKA* - **China Shipping Container Lines Co Ltd** - SatCom: Inmarsat C 441316110 *Shanghai* *China* MMSI: 413161000 Official number: 0007000222	**90,757** Class: CC GL 57,364 102,395	**2007-08 Hudong-Zhonghua Shipbuilding (Group) Co Ltd — Shanghai** Yd No: H1381A Loa 335.00 (BB) Br ex - Dght 14.650 Lbp 320.06 Br md 42.80 Dpth 24.80 Welded, 1 dk	**(A33A2CC) Container Ship (Fully Cellular)** TEU 8528 C Ho 3874 TEU C Dk 4554 TEU incl 700 ref C. Compartments: 9 Cell Ho, ER	**1 oil engine** driving 1 FP propeller Total Power: 68,520kW (93,160hp) 26.4k MAN-B&W 12K98MC- 1 x 2 Stroke 12 Cy. 980 x 2400 68520kW (93160bhp) Mitsui Engineering & Shipbuilding CLtd-Japan AuxGen: 4 x 2760kW 6600V a.c Thrusters: 1 Tunnel thruster (f)
9304801 **XIN YAN TAI** *BPBF* - **China Shipping Container Lines Co Ltd** - SatCom: Inmarsat C 441312510 *Shanghai* *China* MMSI: 413125000 Official number: 05M1002	**66,452** Class: CC 37,567 69,225	**2005-01 Hudong-Zhonghua Shipbuilding (Group) Co Ltd — Shanghai** Yd No: H1354A Loa 279.90 (BB) Br ex - Dght 14.021 Lbp 265.80 Br md 40.30 Dpth 24.10 Welded, 1 dk	**(A33A2CC) Container Ship (Fully Cellular)** TEU 5668 C Ho 2586 TEU C Dk 3082 TEU incl 610 ref C. Compartments: 7 Cell Ho, ER Ice Capable	**1 oil engine** driving 1 FP propeller Total Power: 54,809kW (74,518hp) 25.7k MAN-B&W 12K90MC- 1 x 2 Stroke 12 Cy. 900 x 2300 54809kW (74518bhp) Mitsui Engineering & Shipbuilding CLtd-Japan AuxGen: 4 x 2320kW 450/230V 60Hz a.c Thrusters: 1 Thwart. CP thruster (f)
9234367 **XIN YAN TIAN** *BPBA* - **China Shipping Container Lines Co Ltd** - SatCom: Inmarsat C 441306410 *Shanghai* *China* MMSI: 413064000	**66,433** Class: CC 37,567 68,023	**2004-01 Dalian New Shipbuilding Heavy Industries Co Ltd — Dalian LN** Yd No: C5600-4 Loa 279.60 (BB) Br ex - Dght 14.000 Lbp 265.80 Br md 40.30 Dpth 24.10 Welded, 1 dk	**(A33A2CC) Container Ship (Fully Cellular)** TEU 5668 C Ho 2586 TEU C Dk 3082 TEU incl 610 ref C. Compartments: 7 Cell Ho, ER	**1 oil engine** driving 1 FP propeller Total Power: 54,809kW (74,518hp) 25.7k MAN-B&W 12K90MC- 1 x 2 Stroke 12 Cy. 900 x 2300 54809kW (74518bhp) Mitsui Engineering & Shipbuilding CLtd-Japan AuxGen: 4 x 2320kW 450V/230V 60Hz a.c Thrusters: 1 Tunnel thruster (f)
9333498 **XIN YANG** *V3EO* - **Xin Yang Shipping Co Ltd** Yantai New Ocean International Shipping Co Ltd *Belize City* *Belize* MMSI: 312225000 Official number: 060420693	**1,997** Class: CC 1,106 2,846 T/cm 8.7	**2004-12 Qingdao Lingshan Ship Engineering Co Ltd — Jiaonan SD** Yd No: 113 Loa 79.99 Br ex - Dght 5.200 Lbp 74.00 Br md 13.60 Dpth 7.00 Welded, 1 dk	**(A21A2BC) Bulk Carrier** Double Bottom Entire Compartment Length Grain: 4,127; Bale: 3,893 Compartments: 1 Ho, ER 1 Ha: ER (38.4 x 10.0) Ice Capable	**1 oil engine** reduction geared to sc. shaft driving 1 FP propeller Total Power: 1,080kW (1,468hp) 11.7k MAN-B&W 8L23/3 1 x 4 Stroke 8 Cy. 225 x 300 1080kW (1468bhp) Zhenjiang Marine Diesel Works-China AuxGen: 3 x 90kW 380/220V 50Hz a.c Fuel: 62.0 (d.f.) 121.0 (r.f.) 5.0pd
8415990 **XIN YANG 9** *9LA2110* - *ex* Fengshun 16 *-2010* *ex* Tokuyama Maru *-2001* **Integrity Ocean Co Ltd** *Freetown* *Sierra Leone* MMSI: 667401100 Official number: SL104011	**1,258** Class: OM 557 1,600	**1984-12 K.K. Miura Zosensho — Saiki** Yd No: 718 Loa 70.70 Br ex 11.50 Dght 4.421 Lbp 66.02 Br md 11.50 Dpth 6.70 Welded	**(A31A2GX) General Cargo Ship** Single Hull	**1 oil engine** driving 1 FP propeller Total Power: 883kW (1,201hp) 11.0k Niigata 6M28AFT 1 x 4 Stroke 6 Cy. 280 x 480 883kW (1201bhp) Niigata Engineering Co Ltd-Japan
8657809 **XIN YANG 688** *V3QE9* - *ex* Xin He Xie 8 *-2012* **Xiu Jun Tan** Huaxin Shipping (Hongkong) Ltd *Belize City* *Belize* MMSI: 312078000 Official number: 611220032	**2,988** Class: IT 1,755 -	**2011-06 Viva Vessel Group Co Ltd — Yueqing ZJ** Loa 97.00 Br ex - Dght 5.950 Lbp 89.80 Br md 15.80 Dpth 7.40 Welded, 1 dk	**(A31A2GX) General Cargo Ship**	**1 oil engine** reduction geared to sc. shaft driving 1 Propeller Total Power: 2,000kW (2,719hp) 11.0k Chinese Std. Type 8300Z 1 x 4 Stroke 8 Cy. 300 x 380 2000kW (2719bhp) Wuxi Antai Power Machinery Co Ltd-China
9320477 **XIN YANG PU** *BPNC* - **China Shipping Container Lines Co Ltd** - *Shanghai* *China* MMSI: 413167000	**41,482** Class: CC 24,001 52,200	**2008-07 Dalian Shipbuilding Industry Co Ltd — Dalian LN (No 2 Yard)** Yd No: C4250-27 Loa 263.23 (BB) Br ex 32.30 Dght 12.800 Lbp 251.88 Br md 32.25 Dpth 19.30 Welded, 1 dk	**(A33A2CC) Container Ship (Fully Cellular)** Bale: 79,953 TEU 4250 C Ho 1586 TEU C Dk 2664 TEU incl 400 ref C. Compartments: 7 Cell Ho, ER Ice Capable	**1 oil engine** driving 1 FP propeller Total Power: 36,560kW (49,707hp) 24.2k MAN-B&W 8K90MC- 1 x 2 Stroke 8 Cy. 900 x 2300 36560kW (49707bhp) Doosan Engine Co Ltd-South Korea AuxGen: 3 x 1960kW 450V a.c Thrusters: 1 Tunnel thruster (f)
9310020 **XIN YANG SHAN** *BPBL* - **China Shipping Container Lines Co Ltd** - *Shanghai* *China* MMSI: 413131000	**41,482** Class: CC 24,001 52,242	**2005-04 Hudong-Zhonghua Shipbuilding (Group) Co Ltd — Shanghai** Yd No: H1356A Loa 263.20 (BB) Br ex - Dght 12.800 Lbp 251.40 Br md 32.20 Dpth 19.30 Welded, 1 dk	**(A33A2CC) Container Ship (Fully Cellular)** TEU 4250 C Ho 1586 TEU C Dk 2664 TEU incl 500 ref C. Compartments: 7 Cell Ho, ER Ice Capable	**1 oil engine** driving 1 FP propeller Total Power: 36,480kW (49,598hp) 24.2k MAN-B&W 8K90MC- 1 x 2 Stroke 8 Cy. 900 x 2300 36480kW (49598bhp) Mitsui Engineering & Shipbuilding CLtd-Japan AuxGen: 3 x 1960kW 450V a.c Thrusters: 1 Tunnel thruster (f)
9262120 **XIN YANG ZHOU** *BPBI* - **China Shipping Container Lines Co Ltd** - *Shanghai* *China* MMSI: 413059000	**41,482** Class: CC 24,001 50,137	**2004-03 Hudong-Zhonghua Shipbuilding (Group) Co Ltd — Shanghai** Yd No: H1294A Loa 263.20 (BB) Br ex - Dght 12.800 Lbp 251.40 Br md 32.20 Dpth 19.30 Welded, 1 dk	**(A33A2CC) Container Ship (Fully Cellular)** TEU 4051 C Ho 1586 TEU C Dk 2465 TEU incl 400 ref C. Compartments: 7 Cell Ho, ER	**1 oil engine** driving 1 FP propeller Total Power: 36,543kW (49,684hp) 24.2k MAN-B&W 8K90MC- 1 x 2 Stroke 8 Cy. 900 x 2300 36543kW (49684bhp) Mitsui Engineering & Shipbuilding CLtd-Japan AuxGen: 3 x 1960kW 450/230V 60Hz a.c Thrusters: 1 Tunnel thruster (f)
9615664 **XIN YI HAI 16** *BKSM6* - *ex* Yuan Xun 7 *-2013* *launched as* Yuan Sheng 56 *-2011* **Zhejiang Zhoushan Yi Hai Shipping Co Ltd** Seacon Ships Management Co Ltd SatCom: Inmarsat C 441369055 *Zhoushan, Zhejiang* *China* MMSI: 413452370	**32,964** Class: CC 19,142 56,806 T/cm 58.8	**2011-06 Zhejiang Zhenghe Shipbuilding Co Ltd — Zhoushan ZJ** Yd No: 1036 Loa 189.99 (BB) Br ex - Dght 12.800 Lbp 185.00 Br md 32.26 Dpth 18.00 Welded, 1 dk	**(A21A2BC) Bulk Carrier** Grain: 71,634; Bale: 68,200 Compartments: 5 Ho, ER 5 Ha: 4 (21.3 x 18.3)ER (18.9 x 18.3) Cranes: 4x36t	**1 oil engine** driving 1 FP propeller Total Power: 9,480kW (12,889hp) 14.2k MAN-B&W 6S50MC- 1 x 2 Stroke 6 Cy. 500 x 2000 9480kW (12889bhp) STX Engine Co Ltd-South Korea AuxGen: 3 x 600kW 450V a.c
9608269 **XIN YI HAI 26** *BKRY5* - *ex* Hua Jie 17 *-2013* **Zhejiang Zhoushan Yi Hai Shipping Co Ltd** - SatCom: Inmarsat C 441301675 *Zhoushan, Zhejiang* *China* MMSI: 413440820	**3,927** Class: CC 1,861 5,667 T/cm 9.4	**2011-01 Zhejiang Dongpeng Shipbuilding & Repair Co Ltd — Zhoushan ZJ** Yd No: 07-018 Loa 110.25 (BB) Br ex 15.83 Dght 6.000 Lbp 103.65 Br md 15.80 Dpth 7.40 Welded, 1 dk	**(A12A2TC) Chemical Tanker** Double Hull (13F) Liq: 6,302 Cargo Heating Coils Compartments: 1 Ta, 12 Wing Ta, 1 Slop Ta, ER 13 Cargo Pump (s): 13x200m³/hr Manifold: Bow/CM: 68m Ice Capable	**1 oil engine** reduction geared to sc. shaft driving 1 FP propeller Total Power: 2,574kW (3,500hp) 12.0k Yanmar 6N330-E 1 x 4 Stroke 6 Cy. 330 x 440 2574kW (3500bhp) Qingdao Zichai Boyang Diesel EngineCo Ltd-China AuxGen: 3 x 280kW 400V a.c Fuel: 35.0 (d.f.) 418.0 (r.f.)
8318037 **XIN YIN HE** *BVJY7* - *ex* Yin He *-2013* **Shanghai PanAsia Shipping Co Ltd** - SatCom: Inmarsat B 341207110 *Shanghai* *China* MMSI: 412071000	**19,237** Class: (CC) (GL) 8,922 25,925	**1984-12 Howaldtswerke-Deutsche Werft AG (HDW) — Kiel** Yd No: 204 Loa 172.00 (BB) Br ex 28.71 Dght 10.680 Lbp 160.00 Br md 28.40 Dpth 15.50 Welded, 1 dk	**(A33A2CC) Container Ship (Fully Cellular)** TEU 1328 C Ho 676 TEU C Dk 652 TEU incl 54 ref C. Compartments: 4 Cell Ho, ER 16 Ha: 2 (12.5 x -)14 (12.5 x 10.3)ER Ice Capable	**1 oil engine** driving 1 FP propeller Total Power: 10,150kW (13,800hp) 17.0k B&W 6L70MC 1 x 2 Stroke 6 Cy. 700 x 2268 10150kW (13800bhp) Mitsui Engineering & Shipbuilding CLtd-Japan AuxGen: 1 x 1000kW 450V 60Hz a.c, 2 x 850kW 450V 60Hz a.c, 1 x 350kW 450V 60Hz a.c Thrusters: 1 Thwart. FP thruster (f)

IMO / Call sign	Name / Owner / Port	Tonnage	Class	Builder / Dimensions	Type	Machinery
3219865 - -	**XIN YING** *ex* Man Ying *-2002* - -	*483* 97 71		**1982-05 Hong Kong Shipyard Ltd. — Hong Kong** Loa 44.20 Br ex 8.72 Dght 1.955 Lbp 39.20 Br md 8.23 Dpth 3.36 Welded, 2 dks	**(A37B2PS) Passenger Ship** Compartments: 2 Ho, ER	**2 oil engines** with flexible couplings & sr reverse geared to sc. shafts driving 2 FP propellers Total Power: 750kW (1,020hp) M.T.U. 6V331TC70 2 x Vee 4 Stroke 6 Cy. 165 x 155 each-375kW (510bhp) MTU Friedrichshafen GmbH-Friedrichshafen
9312585 BPBX -	**XIN YING KOU** **China Shipping Container Lines Co Ltd** - *Shanghai* *China* MMSI: 413151000	**41,482** 24,001 52,186	Class: CC	**2006-03 Dalian Shipbuilding Industry Co Ltd — Dalian LN (No 2 Yard)** Yd No: C4250-18 Loa 263.23 (BB) Br ex 32.30 Dght 12.800 Lbp 251.88 Br md 32.25 Dpth 19.30 Welded, 1 dk	**(A33A2CC) Container Ship (Fully Cellular)** Bale: 79,653 TEU 4250 C Ho 1586 TEU C Dk 2664 TEU incl 400 ref C. Compartments: 7 Cell Ho, ER Ice Capable	**1 oil engine** driving 1 FP propeller Total Power: 36,480kW (49,598hp) 24.2kn MAN-B&W 8K90MC-C 1 x 2 Stroke 8 Cy. 900 x 2300 36480kW (49598bhp) Doosan Engine Co Ltd-South Korea AuxGen: 3 x 1960kW 450V 60Hz a.c Thrusters: 1 Tunnel thruster (f)
8814524 BJTO -	**XIN YING WAN** *ex* MSC Seine *-2010* *ex* CMA CGM Seine *-2008* *ex* Hanjin Hamburg *-2003* *launched as* Hanjin Vancouver *-1990* - - *Yangpu, Hainan* *China* MMSI: 413968000	**37,193** 15,205 44,044 T/cm 64.4	Class: CC (LR) (KR) (AB) Classed LR until 1/2/10	**1990-06 Samsung Shipbuilding & Heavy Industries Co Ltd — Geoje** Yd No: 1072 Loa 242.87 (BB) Br ex 32.27 Dght 11.717 Lbp 226.73 Br md 32.22 Dpth 19.03 Welded, 1 dk	**(A33A2CC) Container Ship (Fully Cellular)** TEU 2932 C Ho 1348 TEU C Dk 1584 TEU incl 153 ref C. Compartments: ER, 7 Cell Ho 14 Ha: 2 (13.0 x 8.1)2 (13.0 x 10.5)ER 10 (12.6 x 10.5) 24 Wing Ha: 2 (12.6 x 5.4)5 (13.0 x 8.0)17 (12.6 x 8.0)	**1 oil engine** driving 1 FP propeller Total Power: 23,170kW (31,502hp) 21.7kn Sulzer 7RTA84 1 x 2 Stroke 7 Cy. 840 x 2400 23170kW (31502bhp) Korea Heavy Industries & ConstrCo Ltd (HANJUNG)-South Korea AuxGen: 3 x 1000kW 450V 60Hz a.c Boilers: e (ex.g.) 7.0kgf/cm² (6.9bar), AuxB (o.f.) 9.0kgf/cm² (8.8bar) Thrusters: 1 Thwart. CP thruster (f)
9416642 BPAG -	**XIN YONG YANG** **China Shipping Tanker Co Ltd** - *Shanghai* *China* MMSI: 413180000	**161,488** 104,666 309,266 T/cm 182.2	Class: CC NV	**2010-07 Guangzhou Longxue Shipbuilding Co Ltd — Guangzhou GD** Yd No: L0003 Loa 332.95 (BB) Br ex 60.04 Dght 21.800 Lbp 319.90 Br md 60.00 Dpth 29.79 Welded, 1 dk	**(A13A2TV) Crude Oil Tanker** Double Hull (13F) Liq: 334,500; Liq (Oil): 334,500 Compartments: 5 Ta, 10 Wing Ta, 2 Wing Slop Ta, ER 3 Cargo Pump (s): 3x5500m³/hr Manifold: Bow/CM: 167m	**1 oil engine** driving 1 FP propeller Total Power: 26,460kW (35,975hp) 15.7kn Wartsila 7RTA84T 1 x 2 Stroke 7 Cy. 840 x 3150 26460kW (35975bhp) Wartsila Switzerland Ltd-Switzerland AuxGen: 3 x 1050kW 450V 50Hz a.c Fuel: 420.0 (d.f.) 6600.0 (r.f.)
8833673 BLAA5 -	**XIN YU 5** *ex* Zhou Yu Leng No. 2 *-2009* **Ningbo Xiangshan Fishery Trade Development Co Ltd** - SatCom: Inmarsat C 441300098 *Ningbo, Zhejiang* *China* MMSI: 413416130	**490** 153 250	Class: CC	**1987 Guangzhou Fishing Vessel Shipyard — Guangzhou GD** Loa 54.17 Br ex - Dght 2.870 Lbp 48.00 Br md 9.00 Dpth 4.30 Welded, 1 dk	**(A34A2GR) Refrigerated Cargo Ship** Ins: 541 Compartments: 2 Ho, ER Derricks: 2x1t	**1 oil engine** geared to sc. shaft driving 1 FP propeller Total Power: 294kW (400hp) 11.5kn Chinese Std. Type 6300 1 x 4 Stroke 6 Cy. 300 x 380 294kW (400bhp) Guangzhou Fishing Vessel Shipyard-China AuxGen: 2 x 90kW 400V a.c
9110810 BDRD -	**XIN YU JIN XIANG** *ex* Yu Jin Xiang *-2008* **Qinhuangdao Economic & Technological Development Zone Chuangyuan Shipping Co Ltd** - SatCom: Inmarsat C 441216410 *Qinhuangdao, Hebei* *China* MMSI: 413353000	**12,304** 4,046 5,700	Class: CC	**1995-11 Merwede Shipyard BV — Hardinxveld** Yd No: 667 Loa 148.20 Br ex - Dght 6.100 Lbp 135.70 Br md 22.70 Dpth 10.00 Welded, 1 dk	**(A32A2GF) General Cargo/Passenger Ship** Passengers: cabins: 95; berths: 348 TEU 224 Cranes: 2x20t	**2 oil engines** with flexible couplings & sr gearedto sc. shafts driving 2 CP propellers Total Power: 12,976kW (17,642hp) 20.0kn Sulzer 9ZAL40S 2 x 4 Stroke 9 Cy. 400 x 560 each-6488kW (8821bhp) Zaklady Urzadzen Technicznych'Zgoda' SA-Poland AuxGen: 3 x 800kW 220/380V 50Hz a.c Fuel: 155.0 (d.f.) 415.0 (r.f.)
8721234 BZZO6 -	**XIN YU NO. 1** *ex* Gloucester *-2006* *ex* Gorbenko *-1997* *ex* Yefim Gorbenko *-1996* **China National Fisheries Corp** - *Qinhuangdao, Hebei* *China* MMSI: 412270038	**4,407** 1,322 1,810	Class: (LR) (RS) Classed LR until 1/1/06	**1988-07 GP Chernomorskiy Sudostroitelnyy Zavod — Nikolayev** Yd No: 570 Loa 104.50 Br ex 16.03 Dght 5.900 Lbp 96.40 Br md - Dpth 10.20 Welded, 2 dks	**(B11A2FG) Factory Stern Trawler** Ice Capable	**2 oil engines** reduction geared to sc. shaft driving 1 CP propeller Total Power: 5,148kW (7,000hp) 16.1kn Russkiy 6CHN40/46 2 x 4 Stroke 6 Cy. 400 x 460 each-2574kW (3500bhp) Mashinostroitelnyy Zavod"Russkiy-Dizel"-Leningrad AuxGen: 2 x 1600kW 220/380V 50Hz a.c, 3 x 344kW 220/380V 50Hz a.c Boilers: 2 e (ex.g.) 8.2kgf/cm² (8.0bar), AuxB (o.f.) 8.2kgf/cm² (8.0bar) Fuel: 1226.0 (d.f.) 23.0pd
9430595 BVBZ7 -	**XIN YUAN 16** **Fujian Yuanyuan Shipping Co Ltd** *Fuzhou, Fujian* *China* MMSI: 413692370	**2,970** 1,579 4,142	Class: CC	**2007-05 Fuzhou Cangshan Xiayang Shipyard — Fuzhou FJ** Yd No: 06-016 Loa 94.80 Br ex - Dght 6.000 Lbp 87.30 Br md 15.20 Dpth 7.80 Welded, 1 dk	**(A31A2GX) General Cargo Ship** Grain: 5,679; Bale: 5,679 TEU 274 C Ho 124 TEU C Dk 150 TEU. Compartments: 2 Ho, ER 2 Ha: (32.4 x 12.5)ER (25.8 x 12.5)	**1 oil engine** reduction geared to sc. shaft driving 1 FP propeller Total Power: 2,059kW (2,799hp) 12.5kn Guangzhou 8320ZC 1 x 4 Stroke 8 Cy. 320 x 440 2059kW (2799bhp) Guangzhou Diesel Engine Factory CoLtd-China AuxGen: 3 x 150kW 400V a.c
8656714 BVBJ7 -	**XIN YUAN 19** **Fujian Shunyuan Shipping Co Ltd** *Fuzhou, Fujian* *China* MMSI: 413690460 Official number: 080108000058	**1,981** 1,109 2,910	Class: CC (Class contemplated)	**2006-08 Fujian Hanhai Shipbuilding Co Ltd — Lianjiang County FJ** Yd No: 200501 Loa 88.67 Br ex - Dght 4.800 Lbp 83.25 Br md 13.20 Dpth 6.00 Welded, 1 dk	**(A31A2GX) General Cargo Ship**	**1 oil engine** reduction geared to sc. shaft driving 1 Propeller Total Power: 735kW (999hp) Chinese Std. Type LB8250ZLC 1 x 4 Stroke 8 Cy. 250 x 320 735kW (999bhp) Zibo Diesel Engine Factory-China
8656958 BVGX2 -	**XIN YUAN 66** *ex* Fu Feng *-2004* **Yong Chuan Chen** Fujian Yuanyuan Shipping Co Ltd *Fuzhou, Fujian* *China* MMSI: 412453590 Official number: 370100113	**1,584** 887 1,508	Class: CC	**1995-07 Chongqing Shipyard — Chongqing** Loa 81.27 Br ex - Dght - Lbp 75.80 Br md 13.00 Dpth 5.20 Welded, 1 dk	**(A33A2CC) Container Ship (Fully Cellular)**	**1 oil engine** reduction geared to sc. shaft driving 1 Propeller Total Power: 1,456kW (1,980hp) Guangzhou 6320ZCD 1 x 4 Stroke 6 Cy. 320 x 440 1456kW (1980bhp) Guangzhou Diesel Engine Factory CoLtd-China
9365714 3ETY -	**XIN YUAN 68** *ex* Hua Haida 15 *-2008* *ex* Eastern Paris 2 *-2006* *ex* Ming Yang Zhou 2 *-2005* **Weihai Xinhai Shipping Co Ltd** - *Panama* *Panama* MMSI: 371002000 Official number: 41035PEXTF	**1,989** 1,179 3,331	Class: IT	**2005-08 Wenling Hexing Shipbuilding & Repair Yard — Wenling ZJ** Yd No: WL2005-12 Loa 88.00 Br ex - Dght 5.000 Lbp 81.70 Br md 13.20 Dpth 6.20 Welded, 1 dk	**(A31A2GX) General Cargo Ship**	**1 oil engine** reduction geared to sc. shaft driving 1 FP propeller Total Power: 736kW (1,001hp) 9.5kn Chinese Std. Type 8300ZLC 1 x 4 Stroke 8 Cy. 300 x 380 736kW (1001bhp) Zibo Diesel Engine Factory-China
8811065 - -	**XIN YUE** *ex* Kaio Maru *-2003* - -	*468* - 1,380		**1988-11 Imamura Zosen — Kure** Yd No: 332 Loa 59.50 (BB) Br ex 12.22 Dght 4.438 Lbp 54.00 Br md 12.20 Dpth 6.30 Welded	**(A24D2BA) Aggregates Carrier** Grain: 942	**1 oil engine** with clutches, flexible couplings & reduction geared to sc. shaft driving 1 FP propeller Total Power: 736kW (1,001hp) Niigata 6M31AGTE 1 x 4 Stroke 6 Cy. 310 x 530 736kW (1001bhp) Niigata Engineering Co Ltd-Japan Thrusters: 1 Thwart. FP thruster (f)
9637600 BRTR -	**XIN YUE SHUN** **Guangzhou Zhenxing Shipping Co Ltd** Guangzhou Maritime Transport (Group) Co Ltd SatCom: Inmarsat C 441203514 *China* MMSI: 412035000	**32,300** 18,700 57,000 T/cm 58.8	Class: ZC	**2011-08 China Shipping Industry (Jiangsu) Co Ltd — Jiangdu JS** Yd No: IS57300/A-09 Loa 189.99 (BB) Br ex 32.30 Dght 12.800 Lbp 185.00 Br md 32.26 Dpth 18.00 Welded, 1 dk	**(A21A2BC) Bulk Carrier** Grain: 71,634; Bale: 68,200 Compartments: 5 Ho, ER 5 Ha: ER Cranes: 4x30t	**1 oil engine** driving 1 FP propeller Total Power: 9,480kW (12,889hp) 14.2kn MAN-B&W 6S50MC-C 1 x 2 Stroke 6 Cy. 500 x 2000 9480kW (12889bhp)
9389772 VRFR6 -	**XIN YUE YANG** **Xin Yue Yang Shipping SA** China Shipping Tanker Co Ltd SatCom: Inmarsat C 447702143 *Hong Kong* *Hong Kong* MMSI: 477595500 Official number: HK-2497	**152,727** 98,415 297,232 T/cm 177.9	Class: CC	**2009-09 Dalian Shipbuilding Industry Co Ltd — Dalian LN (No 2 Yard)** Yd No: T3000-20 Loa 330.00 (BB) Br ex 60.04 Dght 21.500 Lbp 316.00 Br md 60.00 Dpth 29.70 Welded, 1 dk	**(A13A2TV) Crude Oil Tanker** Double Hull (13F) Liq: 324,279; Liq (Oil): 324,279 Compartments: 5 Ta, 10 Wing Ta, 2 Wing Slop Ta 3 Cargo Pump (s): 3x5500m³/hr Manifold: Bow/CM: 162.5m	**1 oil engine** driving 1 FP propeller Total Power: 25,480kW (34,643hp) 15.8kn MAN-B&W 7S80MC 1 x 2 Stroke 7 Cy. 800 x 3056 25480kW (34643bhp) Doosan Engine Co Ltd-South Korea AuxGen: 3 x 975kW 450V a.c Fuel: 429.6 (d.f.) 7117.3 (r.f.)

IMO / Call sign	Name / Owner	Tonnage	Class	Builder / Dimensions	Type	Machinery
9361940 *BAOZ* -	**XIN YUN FENG** **Dalian Golden Fortune Container Shipping Co Ltd** - SatCom: Inmarsat C 441200217 *China* MMSI: 412205920	**2,994** 1,585 5,130	Class: (CC)	**2005-12 Wenling Xingyuan Shipbuilding & Repair Co Ltd — Wenling ZJ** Loa 98.00 Br ex - Dght 5.700 Lbp 91.05 Br md 15.80 Dpth 7.40 Welded, 1 dk	**(A31A2GX) General Cargo Ship** Grain: 6,825; Bale: 6,279	**1 oil engine** reduction geared to sc. shaft driving 1 FP propeller Total Power: 1,765kW (2,400hp) 12.2kr Chinese Std. Type 1 x 4 Stroke 1765kW (2400bhp) Wuxi Antai Power Machinery Co Ltd-China
9378814 *BPBW* -	**XIN ZHAN JIANG** **China Shipping Container Lines Co Ltd** - *Shanghai* *China* MMSI: 413150000	**41,482** 24,001 52,279	Class: CC	**2006-02 Hudong-Zhonghua Shipbuilding (Group) Co Ltd — Shanghai** Yd No: H1360A Loa 263.23 (BB) Br ex - Dght 12.800 Lbp 251.40 Br md 32.20 Dpth 19.30 Welded, 1 dk	**(A33A2CC) Container Ship (Fully Cellular)** Bale: 79,653 TEU 4250 C Ho 1586 TEU C Dk 2664 TEU incl 500 ref C. Compartments: 7 Cell Ho, ER 14 Ha: 2 (12.6 x 23.1)11 (12.6 x 28.2)ER (12.6 x 13.0) Ice Capable	**1 oil engine** driving 1 FP propeller Total Power: 36,480kW (49,598hp) 24.2kn MAN-B&W 8K90MC-C 1 x 2 Stroke 8 Cy. 900 x 2300 36480kW (49598bhp) Mitsui Engineering & Shipbuilding CLtd-Japan AuxGen: 3 x 1960kW 450V a.c Thrusters: 1 Thwart. CP thruster (f)
9328601 *BPNF* -	**XIN ZHANG ZHOU** **China Shipping Container Lines Co Ltd** - *Shanghai* *China* MMSI: 413170000	**41,482** 24,001 52,216	Class: CC	**2008-11 Dalian Shipbuilding Industry Co Ltd — Dalian LN (No 2 Yard)** Yd No: C4250-29 Loa 263.23 (BB) Br ex 32.30 Dght 12.800 Lbp 251.88 Br md 32.25 Dpth 19.30 Welded, 1 dk	**(A33A2CC) Container Ship (Fully Cellular)** TEU 4250 C Ho 1586 TEU C Dk 2664 TEU incl 400 ref C. Ice Capable	**1 oil engine** driving 1 FP propeller Total Power: 36,560kW (49,707hp) 24.2kn MAN-B&W 8K90MC-C 1 x 2 Stroke 8 Cy. 900 x 2300 36560kW (49707bhp) Doosan Engine Co Ltd-South Korea AuxGen: 3 x 1960kW 450V a.c Thrusters: 1 Tunnel thruster (f)
9523029 *BPKH* -	**XIN ZHENG ZHOU** **China Shipping Container Lines Co Ltd** - SatCom: Inmarsat C 441471410 *Shanghai* *China* MMSI: 414714000	**47,917** 24,185 67,041	Class: CC	**2012-06 Shanghai Jiangnan Changxing Heavy Industry Co Ltd — Shanghai** Yd No: H1052A Loa 255.10 (BB) Br ex - Dght 13.500 Lbp 242.00 Br md 37.30 Dpth 19.60 Welded, 1 dk	**(A33A2CC) Container Ship (Fully Cellular)** TEU 4738 C Ho 1826 TEU C Dk 2912 TEU incl 300 ref C Ice Capable	**1 oil engine** driving 1 FP propeller Total Power: 21,910kW (29,789hp) 18.0kn Wartsila 7RT-flex68 1 x 2 Stroke 7 Cy. 680 x 2720 21910kW (29789bhp) Doosan Engine Co Ltd-South Korea AuxGen: 2 x 1650kW 450V a.c, 1 x 1240kW 450V a.c Thrusters: 1 Tunnel thruster (f)
8214425 - -	**XIN ZHONG** *ex Man Chung -2002* - -	*234* 99 72		**1982 Hong Kong Shipyard Ltd. — Hong Kong** Loa 44.20 Br ex 8.72 Dght 1.956 Lbp 39.20 Br md 8.23 Dpth 3.36 Welded, 2 dks	**(A37B2PS) Passenger Ship** Compartments: 2 Ho, ER	**2 oil engines** with flexible couplings & sr reverse geared to sc. shafts driving 2 FP propellers Total Power: 750kW (1,020hp) 12.5kn M.T.U. 6V331TC71 2 x Vee 4 Stroke 6 Cy. 165 x 155 each-375kW (510bhp) MTU Friedrichshafen GmbH-Friedrichshafen AuxGen: 2 x 120kW 380V 50Hz a.c Fuel: 14.5 (d.f.)
9021150 *XUBL4* -	**XIN ZHOU** *ex Koei Maru No. 51 -2010* **Xin Zhou Shipping Co Ltd** Dana Shipping Co Ltd *Phnom Penh* *Cambodia* MMSI: 514498000 Official number: 1091621	**1,450** 441 1,600	Class: UB	**1991-04 Honda Zosen — Saiki** Yd No: 827 Loa 76.59 Br ex - Dght 4.200 Lbp 70.01 Br md 12.01 Dpth 7.01 Welded, 1 dk	**(A31A2GX) General Cargo Ship** Compartments: 1 Ho, 1 Tw Dk, ER 1 Ha: (40.2 x 9.5)ER	**1 oil engine** driving 1 FP propeller Total Power: 1,177kW (1,600hp) 11.0kn Niigata 6M28HFT 1 x 4 Stroke 6 Cy. 280 x 480 1177kW (1600bhp) Niigata Engineering Co Ltd-Japan
8652823 *HMVY3* -	**XIN ZHOU 2** **Ningbo Liping Shipping Co Ltd** Tae Dong Gang Shipping Co *Nampho* *North Korea* MMSI: 445708000 Official number: 5305267	**3,390** 1,898 5,300	Class: KC	**2003-04 Zhejiang Dongfang Shipbuilding Co Ltd — Yueqing ZJ** Yd No: DF0207 Loa 98.00 (BB) Br ex - Dght 5.900 Lbp - Br md 15.80 Dpth 7.40 Welded, 1 dk	**(A31A2GX) General Cargo Ship** Grain: 6,825; Bale: 6,279 Compartments: 2 Ho, ER 2 Ha: (27.1 x 12.9)ER (25.8 x 12.9)	**1 oil engine** reduction geared to sc. shafts driving 1 FP propeller Total Power: 2,000kW (2,719hp) Chinese Std. Type G8300ZC 1 x 4 Stroke 8 Cy. 300 x 380 2000kW (2719bhp) AuxGen: 2 x 130kW a.c Fuel: 139.0 (d.f.)
9577575 *3EZE4* -	**XIN ZHOU 6** **YKJ Shipping Co Ltd** Ningbo FTZ Cosnavi International Shipping Management Co Ltd *Panama* *Panama* MMSI: 373285000 Official number: 43210PEXTF	**9,244** 5,265 14,690	Class: OM	**2009-03 Ningbo Dongfang Shipyard Co Ltd — Ningbo ZJ** Yd No: DFC08-067 Loa 144.58 (BB) Br ex - Dght 8.000 Lbp 136.00 Br md 21.00 Dpth 10.80 Welded, 1 dk	**(A21A2BC) Bulk Carrier** Grain: 18,905	**1 oil engine** driving 1 FP propeller Total Power: 2,970kW (4,038hp) 13.5kn
8656611 *BAKC9* -	**XIN ZHOU 9** **Ningbo Liping Shipping Co Ltd** YKJ Shipping Co Ltd *Ningbo, Zhejiang* *China* MMSI: 413409690 Official number: 070109000055	**9,113** 5,103 14,738	Class: ZC (Class contemplated)	**2007-06 Ningbo Dongfang Shipyard Co Ltd — Ningbo ZJ** Yd No: DFC06-034 Loa 144.60 Br ex - Dght 8.000 Lbp 136.00 Br md 21.00 Dpth 10.80 Welded, 1 dk	**(A31A2GX) General Cargo Ship** Grain: 21,200	**1 oil engine** driving 1 FP propeller Total Power: 2,665kW (3,623hp) Guangzhou 1 x 2665kW (3623bhp) Guangzhou Diesel Engine Factory CoLtd-China
9635559 *BLTI5* -	**XIN ZHOU 18** **Ningbo Liping Shipping Co Ltd** Tae Dong Gang Shipping Co *Hangzhou, Zhejiang* *China*	**29,189** 16,345 46,620	Class: CC	**2012-09 Ningbo Dongfang Shipyard Co Ltd — Ningbo ZJ** Yd No: DFC10-116 Loa 189.90 Br ex - Dght 11.000 Lbp 182.00 Br md 33.60 Dpth 15.50 Welded, 1 dk	**(A21A2BC) Bulk Carrier** Grain: 59,500 Compartments: 5 Ho, ER 5 Ha: ER	**1 oil engine** driving 1 FP propeller Total Power: 6,480kW (8,810hp) 14.5kn MAN-B&W 6S42MC7 1 x 2 Stroke 6 Cy. 420 x 1764 6480kW (8810bhp) in China
8655722 *3FLB6* -	**XIN ZHOU HAI** **Gu Saiwen, Li Jiulang & Qiu Zhiguo** Shanghai Hope Ship Management Co Ltd *Panama* *Panama* MMSI: 373876000 Official number: 43738PEXTF1	**2,959** 1,859 -	Class: PD	**2005-03 Zhoushan Zhaobao Shipbuilding & Repair Co Ltd — Zhoushan ZJ** Yd No: 06 Loa 98.00 Br ex - Dght - Lbp 90.50 Br md 15.80 Dpth 7.40 Welded, 1 dk	**(A31A2GX) General Cargo Ship**	**1 oil engine** reduction geared to sc. shaft driving 1 Propeller Total Power: 2,000kW (2,719hp) 10.0kn Chinese Std. Type 8300ZC 1 x 4 Stroke 8 Cy. 300 x 380 2000kW (2719bhp) Wuxi Antai Power Machinery Co Ltd-China
9255024 *BOCD* -	**XINFA HAI** **COSCO Bulk Carrier Co Ltd (COSCO BULK)** - SatCom: Inmarsat C 441301710 *Tianjin* *China* MMSI: 413017000 Official number: 04R1001	**88,856** 58,333 174,766 T/cm 119.0	Class: CC	**2004-02 Shanghai Waigaoqiao Shipbuilding Co Ltd — Shanghai** Yd No: 002 Loa 289.00 (BB) Br ex 45.05 Dght 18.120 Lbp 279.00 Br md 45.00 Dpth 24.50 Welded, 1 dk	**(A21A2BC) Bulk Carrier** Double Bottom Entire Compartment Length Grain: 193,030; Bale: 183,425 Compartments: 9 Ho, ER 9 Ha: 7 (15.5 x 20.0)2 (15.5 x 16.5)ER	**1 oil engine** driving 1 FP propeller Total Power: 16,858kW (22,920hp) 14.5kn MAN-B&W 6S70MC 1 x 2 Stroke 6 Cy. 700 x 2674 16858kW (22920bhp) Hudong Heavy Machinery Co Ltd-China AuxGen: 3 x 750kW 450V 60Hz a.c Fuel: 370.0 (d.f.) 5079.0 (r.f.)
8307507 *3FVA4* -	**XING AN DA** *ex Sifnos Pride -2009 ex SJN Orcas -2007* *ex Angelina F -2005 ex Aurora Opal -2004* *ex Sanko Heart -1994* **Xing An Da Shipping Ltd** Hong Sheng Da Shipmanagement Pte Ltd SatCom: Inmarsat C 437300041 *Panama* *Panama* MMSI: 353505000 Official number: 4061009A	**19,340** 12,311 33,024 T/cm 41.1	Class: PS (NK)	**1984-11 Mitsubishi Heavy Industries Ltd. — Shimonoseki** Yd No: 863 Loa 174.70 (BB) Br ex 27.03 Dght 10.630 Lbp 167.01 Br md 27.01 Dpth 14.81 Welded, 1 dk	**(A21A2BC) Bulk Carrier** Grain: 45,071; Bale: 39,476 TEU 140 Compartments: 5 Ho, ER 5 Ha: (12.8 x 12.8)4 (19.2 x 12.8)ER Cranes: 4x25t	**1 oil engine** driving 1 FP propeller Total Power: 4,832kW (6,570hp) 14.0kn Mitsubishi 6UE52LA 1 x 2 Stroke 6 Cy. 520 x 1600 4832kW (6570bhp) Mitsubishi Heavy Industries Ltd-Japan AuxGen: 3 x 450kW 450V 60Hz a.c Fuel: 184.0 (d.f.) (Heating Coils) 1459.0 (r.f.) 22.0pd
9602837 *V3QY7* -	**XING CHANG 16** **Zhoushan Xinhua Shipping Co Ltd** *Belize City* *Belize* MMSI: 312115000 Official number: 611230026	**7,332** 3,299 8,219	Class: CC	**2012-02 Zhoushan Haitian Shipyard Co Ltd — Daishan County ZJ** Yd No: HT0811 Loa 123.00 (BB) Br ex 20.82 Dght 7.200 Lbp 114.50 Br md 20.80 Dpth 9.80 Welded, 1 dk	**(A31A2GX) General Cargo Ship** Grain: 11,263 TEU 626 C Ho 191 TEU C Dk 435 TEU. Compartments: 3 Ho, 3 Tw Dk, ER 3 Ha: ER Cranes: 2x35t Ice Capable	**1 oil engine** reduction geared to sc. shaft driving 1 Propeller Total Power: 3,310kW (4,500hp) 13.0kn Yanmar 8N330-EN 1 x 4 Stroke 8 Cy. 330 x 440 3310kW (4500bhp) Qingdao Zichai Boyang Diesel EngineCo Ltd-China AuxGen: 3 x 350kW 450V a.c Thrusters: 1 Tunnel thruster (f)
9377767 *V3IT* -	**XING CHANG NO. 6** **Zhoushan Xinhua Shipping Co Ltd** *Belize City* *Belize* MMSI: 312731000 Official number: 160520738	**1,998** 1,305 4,133 T/cm 10.2	Class: IT	**2005-11 Zhejiang Fusen Ship Co Ltd — Daishan County ZJ** Loa 87.80 (BB) Br ex - Dght 5.900 Lbp 79.95 Br md 13.80 Dpth 7.45 Welded, 1 dk	**(A31A2GX) General Cargo Ship**	**1 oil engine** reduction geared to sc. shaft driving 1 FP propeller Total Power: 1,325kW (1,801hp) 10.0kn Guangzhou 6320ZCD 1 x 4 Stroke 6 Cy. 320 x 440 1325kW (1801bhp) Guangzhou Diesel Engine Factory CoLtd-China AuxGen: 2 x 152kW 400V 60Hz a.c Fuel: 39.0 (d.f.) (Heating Coils) 104.0 (r.f.) 5.1pd

IMO / Call sign	Name / Owner / Manager	Tonnage	Class	Builder / Dimensions	Type / Cargo	Machinery
9283514 3PCW -	**XING CHI** **China Shipping Tanker Co Ltd** - *Shanghai* *China* MMSI: 413066000	**26,955** 11,381 42,017 T/cm 51.5	Class: CC	**2004-03 Guangzhou Shipyard International Co Ltd — Guangzhou GD** Yd No: 02130001 Loa 187.80 (BB) Br ex 31.53 Dght 11.300 Lbp 178.00 Br md 31.50 Dpth 16.80 Welded, 1 dk	**(A13B2TP) Products Tanker** Double Hull (13F) Liq: 44,692; Liq (Oil): 44,692 Cargo Heating Coils Compartments: 12 Wing Ta, 2 Wing Slop Ta, ER 3 Cargo Pump (s): 3x1200m³/hr Manifold: Bow/CM: 95m Ice Capable	**1 oil engine** driving 1 FP propeller Total Power: 8,580kW (11,665hp) 14.5kn MAN-B&W 6S50MC 1 x 2 Stroke 6 Cy. 500 x 1910 8580kW (11665bhp) Dalian Marine Diesel Works-China AuxGen: 3 x 664kW 450V a.c Fuel: 82.0 (d.f.) 1341.0 (r.f.)
3978734 - -	**XING DA** *ex* Zhe Tai Yu Leng 618 *-2005* *ex* Victory *-2005* *ex* Zhe Pu Leng 1 *-2004* *ex* Hai Fa Yun 7 *-2004* **Haihong Shipping Ltd** Rong Da International Shipping Management Ltd	**741** 215 -		**1982-07 Shanghai Fishing Vessel Shipyard — Shanghai** Loa 61.90 Br ex - Dght 4.150 Lbp 56.50 Br md 9.80 Dpth 4.90 Welded, 1 dk	**(B12B2FC) Fish Carrier**	**1 oil engine** geared to sc. shaft driving 1 Propeller Total Power: 441kW (600hp) Chinese Std. Type 6230ZC 1 x 4 Stroke 6 Cy. 230 x 300 441kW (600bhp) Shanghai Fishing Vessel Shipyard-China
3402448 3FQL3 356649000	**XING FU DA** *ex* Nan Shan *-2011* *ex* Ocean Trader *-2001* *ex* Ocean Trade *-1999* *ex* Balsa 31 *-1996* **Xing Fu Da Shipping Ltd** Hong Sheng Da Shipmanagement Pte Ltd SatCom: Inmarsat C 435664913 *Panama* *Panama* MMSI: 356649000 Official number: 42019PEXT	**4,010** 2,428 6,266	Class: (CC) (NK)	**1984-04 Taihei Kogyo K.K. — Hashihama, Imabari** Yd No: 1672 Loa 106.48 Br ex - Dght 6.701 Lbp 97.95 Br md 16.41 Dpth 8.16 Welded, 1 dk	**(A31A2GX) General Cargo Ship** Grain: 8,346; Bale: 7,653 Compartments: 2 Ho, ER 2 Ha: (28.4 x 8.4) (28.6 x 8.4)ER Derricks: 4x15t	**1 oil engine** driving 1 FP propeller Total Power: 2,869kW (3,901hp) 12.8kn Mitsubishi 6UEC37H-II 1 x 2 Stroke 6 Cy. 370 x 880 2869kW (3901bhp) Akasaka Tekkosho KK (Akasaka DieselLtd)-Japan
9608958 BOEI -	**XING FU SONG** **China Ocean Shipping (Group) Co (COSCO)** COSCO Shipping Co Ltd (COSCOL) *Guangzhou, Guangdong* *China* MMSI: 413471960	**20,684** 11,468 27,292	Class: CC	**2012-09 Guangzhou Huangpu Shipbuilding Co Ltd — Guangzhou GD** Yd No: 2320 Loa 179.50 (BB) Br ex 27.60 Dght 10.200 Lbp 169.50 Br md 27.20 Dpth 14.50 Welded, 1 dk	**(A31A2GX) General Cargo Ship** Grain: 40,419; Bale: 37,590 TEU 1371 C Ho 606 TEU C Dk 765 TEU Compartments: 5 Ho, ER 5 Ha: ER Cranes: 1x90t,2x45t,1x40t Ice Capable	**1 oil engine** driving 1 FP propeller Total Power: 8,250kW (11,217hp) 15.1kn MAN-B&W 6S50ME-C8 1 x 2 Stroke 6 Cy. 500 x 2000 8250kW (11217bhp) Hudong Heavy Machinery Co Ltd-China AuxGen: 3 x 700kW 450V a.c
8667828 - -	**XING GANG 11** **Cangnan Xinggang Shipping Co Ltd** - *Wenzhou, Zhejiang* *China*	**499** 279 -	Class: ZC	**2005-01 Zhejiang Jiaoshan Shiprepair & Building Yard — Wenling ZJ** Loa 52.80 Br ex - Dght - Lbp - Br md 8.80 Dpth 4.15 Welded, 1 dk	**(A31A2GX) General Cargo Ship**	**1 oil engine** driving 1 Propeller Total Power: 218kW (296hp) Chinese Std. Type 1 x 218kW (296bhp) Zibo Diesel Engine Factory-China
8659326 3EXY5 -	**XING GUANG** **Xingzi County TongHai Vessel Co Ltd** - *Panama* *Panama* MMSI: 355396000 Official number: 44290PEXTF1	**2,965** 1,771 -	Class: OM	**2004-01 Duchang Shipbuilding General Yard — Duchang County JX** Loa 93.70 Br ex - Dght - Lbp - Br md 15.60 Dpth 7.50 Welded, 1 dk	**(A31A2GX) General Cargo Ship**	**1 oil engine** reduction geared to sc. shaft driving 1 Propeller Total Power: 1,765kW (2,400hp) 10.0kn Chinese Std. Type 8320ZC 1 x 4 Stroke 8 Cy. 320 x 440 1765kW (2400bhp) (new engine 2004) Guangzhou Diesel Engine Factory CoLtd-China
7414509 - -	**XING GUANG** *ex* Chang Long *-1999* *ex* Aslina *-1988* *ex* Toa Ace *-1987* *ex* Leah *-1986* *ex* Srikandi *-1982* *ex* Musashi *-1980* - - *China*	**3,632** 2,154 6,099	Class: (CC) (NK)	**1975-07 Shinhama Dockyard Co. Ltd. — Anan** Yd No: 698 Loa 106.47 Br ex - Dght 6.600 Lbp 98.00 Br md 16.03 Dpth 8.20 Riveted\Welded, 1 dk	**(A31A2GX) General Cargo Ship** Grain: 7,522; Bale: 7,034 2 Ha: (26.1 x 8.3) (28.7 x 8.3)ER Derricks: 4x15t	**1 oil engine** driving 1 FP propeller Total Power: 2,795kW (3,800hp) 12.5kn Mitsubishi 6UET45/75C 1 x 2 Stroke 6 Cy. 450 x 750 2795kW (3800bhp) Kobe Hatsudoki KK-Japan AuxGen: 2 x 144kW Fuel: 574.0 12.0pd
9367126 T3NU -	**XING GUANG 5** **Wu Qinian** Gold Glory International Ship Management Ltd *Tarawa* *Kiribati* MMSI: 529140000 Official number: K-11050801	**2,398** 1,342 4,241	Class: IZ	**2005-08 Zhoushan Putuo Luomen Shiprepair & Building Co Ltd — Zhoushan ZJ** Loa 87.00 Br ex - Dght 6.000 Lbp 79.95 Br md 13.80 Dpth 7.35 Welded, 1 dk	**(A31A2GX) General Cargo Ship**	**1 oil engine** driving 1 FP propeller Total Power: 736kW (1,001hp) Chinese Std. Type G6300ZCA 1 x 4 Stroke 6 Cy. 300 x 380 736kW (1001bhp) Ningbo CSI Power & Machinery GroupCo Ltd-China
9530620 3EWT2 -	**XING GUANG 18** **Zhoushan Putuo Yonghai Shipping Ltd** Xingguang Int'l Marine Management Ltd SatCom: Inmarsat C 437272010 *Panama* *Panama* MMSI: 372720000 Official number: 39915PEXTF2	**8,850** 4,414 -	Class: IS	**2009-11 Yuanfan Shipbuilding Co Ltd — Yueqing ZJ** Yd No: CP-3 Loa 139.70 Br ex - Dght 7.800 Lbp 130.70 Br md 20.00 Dpth 10.80 Welded, 1 dk	**(A31A2GX) General Cargo Ship**	**1 oil engine** reduction geared to sc. shaft driving 1 FP propeller Total Power: 2,795kW (3,800hp) Chinese Std. Type GN8320ZC 1 x 4 Stroke 8 Cy. 320 x 380 2795kW (3800bhp) Ningbo CSI Power & Machinery GroupCo Ltd-China
9367281 - -	**XING HAI** *completed as* Lian Hui *-2005* - -	**2,974** 1,665 5,147		**2005-06 Jiaojiang Qiansuo Shipyard — Taizhou ZJ** Loa 96.90 Br ex - Dght 5.820 Lbp 89.80 Br md 15.80 Dpth 7.40 Welded, 1 dk	**(A31A2GX) General Cargo Ship** Grain: 6,398; Bale: 6,398	**1 oil engine** driving 1 FP propeller Total Power: 1,471kW (2,000hp) 12.0kn Chinese Std. Type LB8250ZLC 1 x 4 Stroke 8 Cy. 250 x 320 1471kW (2000bhp) Zibo Diesel Engine Factory-China
9635494 BLFZ4 -	**XING HAI CHU YUN 7** **Zhongrong Logistics Co Ltd** - *China* MMSI: 413442220	**5,028** - 8,200	Class: CC (Class contemplated)	**2011-07 Ningbo Dongfang Shipyard Co Ltd — Ningbo ZJ** Yd No: DFC09-096 Loa 119.95 Br ex - Dght 7.300 Lbp - Br md 16.70 Dpth - Welded, 1 dk	**(A13B2TP) Products Tanker** Double Hull (13F)	**1 oil engine** reduction geared to sc. shaft driving 1 FP propeller Total Power: 2,206kW (2,999hp) 14.0kn Guangzhou 8320ZC 1 x 4 Stroke 8 Cy. 320 x 440 2206kW (2999bhp) Guangzhou Diesel Engine Factory CoLtd-China
8990330 BBLX7 -	**XING HAI FENG** **Weihai Qiangyu Shipping Co Ltd** Sea Star Global Shipping Co Ltd *Weihai, Shandong* *China* MMSI: 412326370	**2,980** 1,668 5,500	Class: ZC	**2004-12 Yueqing Huanghuagang Shipyard — Yueqing ZJ** Loa 104.20 Br ex - Dght 5.700 Lbp 95.80 Br md 15.80 Dpth 7.20 Welded, 1 dk	**(A31A2GX) General Cargo Ship**	**1 oil engine** reduction geared to sc. shaft driving 1 Propeller Total Power: 1,765kW (2,400hp) 11.0kn Chinese Std. Type G8300ZC 1 x 4 Stroke 8 Cy. 300 x 380 1765kW (2400bhp) Wuxi Antai Power Machinery Co Ltd-China
9563500 BLGK7 -	**XING HAI HUA 728** *ex* Xing Long Zhou 728 *-2011* **Wenling Yinhua Shipping Co Ltd** Guangxi Yuhang Shipping Co Ltd SatCom: Inmarsat C 441219129 *Taizhou, Zhejiang* *China* MMSI: 412760920	**11,656** 5,109 17,204	Class: CC	**2009-09 Zhejiang Zhenxing Shiprepair & Building Co Ltd — Wenling ZJ** Yd No: ZX011 Loa 150.00 Br ex 23.24 Dght 8.800 Lbp 140.40 Br md 23.00 Dpth 12.50 Welded, 1 dk	**(A13B2TP) Products Tanker** Double Hull (13F) Liq: 18,710; Liq (Oil): 18,710 Compartments: 12 Wing Ta, 2 Wing Slop Ta, ER Ice Capable	**1 oil engine** reduction geared to sc. shaft driving 1 FP propeller Total Power: 4,400kW (5,982hp) 13.0kn Pielstick 8PC2-6 1 x 4 Stroke 8 Cy. 400 x 460 4400kW (5982bhp) Shaanxi Diesel Heavy Industry Co Lt-China AuxGen: 3 x 450kW 400V a.c
9570113 HP5831 -	**XING HAI WAN** **Xinghaiwan Maritime Co Ltd** COSCO Southern Asphalt Shipping Co Ltd SatCom: Inmarsat C 4437173711 *Panama* *Panama* MMSI: 371737000 Official number: 4166210B	**5,565** 1,669 6,123 T/cm 16.6	Class: CC	**2009-12 Guangzhou Huangpu Shipbuilding Co Ltd — Guangzhou GD** Yd No: 2288 Loa 106.99 (BB) Br ex 17.62 Dght 6.500 Lbp 101.50 Br md 17.60 Dpth 10.10 Welded, 1 dk	**(A13C2LA) Asphalt/Bitumen Tanker** Double Hull (13F) Asphalt: 5,726 Cargo Heating Coils Compartments: 8 Wing Ta, ER 2 Cargo Pump (s): 2x400m³/hr Manifold: Bow/CM: 50.5m	**1 oil engine** reduction geared to sc. shaft driving 1 CP propeller Total Power: 2,925kW (3,977hp) 13.0kn Wartsila 9L26 1 x 4 Stroke 9 Cy. 260 x 320 2925kW (3977bhp) Wartsila Finland Oy-Finland AuxGen: 2 x 400kW 450V 60Hz a.c, 1 x 400kW 450V a.c Thrusters: 1 Tunnel thruster (f) Fuel: 62.0 (d.f.) 476.0 (r.f.)
8715481 3FLD -	**XING HENG DA** *ex* Chios Joy *-2012* *ex* Grace T *-2005* *ex* Maersk Teluk *-2000* *ex* Neptunus *-1990* *ex* Knight Kim *-1989* **Xing Heng Da Shipping Ltd** Hong Sheng Da Shipmanagement Pte Ltd *Panama* *Panama* MMSI: 373451000 Official number: 4421312	**37,086** 22,646 68,762 T/cm 67.1	Class: CC (LR) ✠ Classed LR until 11/5/07	**1989-07 Hyundai Heavy Industries Co Ltd — Ulsan** Yd No: 626 Loa 224.36 (BB) Br ex 32.24 Dght 13.200 Lbp 215.02 Br md 32.20 Dpth 18.30 Welded, 1 dk	**(A21A2BC) Bulk Carrier** Grain: 80,428; Bale: 76,407 Compartments: 7 Ho, ER 7 Ha: (14.4 x 12.0)6 (14.4 x 15.0)ER Cranes: 4x25t	**1 oil engine** driving 1 FP propeller Total Power: 7,502kW (10,200hp) 14.0kn B&W 5S60MCE 1 x 2 Stroke 5 Cy. 600 x 2292 7502kW (10200bhp) Hyundai Heavy Industries Co Ltd-South Korea AuxGen: 3 x 460kW 450V 60Hz a.c Boilers: e New 11.9kgf/cm² (11.7bar), AuxB New (o.f.) 6.9kgf/cm² (6.8bar)

7526168 *3EYC4* -
XING HUA
ex Ilena *-2002* *ex* Spirit *-1993*
ex Norman Spirit *-1991* *ex* John G *-1988*
ex John Gregos *-1984*
Sheen Venture Shipping Ltd
Fujian Huarong Marine Shipping Group Corp
SatCom: Inmarsat C 437226910
Panama *Panama*
MMSI: 372269000
Official number: 4128610
16,699 8,251 27,476 T/cm 38.6
Class: PS (NV) (AB)
1977-03 **Oshima Shipbuilding Co Ltd — Saikai NS** Yd No: 014
Loa 169.55 (BB) Br ex 26.34 Dght 9.613
Lbp 163.02 Br md 26.31 Dpth 13.62
Welded, 1 dk
(A21A2BC) Bulk Carrier
Grain: 35,714; Bale: 31,369
Compartments: 5 Ho, ER
5 Ha: (12.5 x 11.9)2 (14.4 x 11.9)2 (12.8 x 11.9)ER
Cranes: 5x15t
1 oil engine driving 1 FP propeller
Total Power: 8,496kW (11,551hp) 13.0kr
Sulzer 7RND68
1 x 2 Stroke 7 Cy. 680 x 1250 8496kW (11551bhp)
Sumitomo Heavy Industries Ltd-Japan
AuxGen: 3 x 450kW 440V 60Hz a.c
Fuel: 179.0 (d.f.) (Heating Coils) 1653.5 (r.f.) 40.0pd

8954635 - -
XING HUA HAI 1
ex Jin Gui *-2005* *ex* Xiong Fa Cheng *-2000*
Huahai Shipping Holding (HK) Co Ltd
Nanjing Huahai Shipping Co Ltd
2,967 1,608 5,384
1988-02 **Wuchang Shipyard — Wuhan HB**
Loa 102.20 (BB) Br ex - Dght 5.000
Lbp 91.25 Br md 16.00 Dpth 8.60
Welded, 1 dk
(A33A2CC) Container Ship (Fully Cellular)
TEU 420
1 oil engine driving 1 FP propeller
Total Power: 2,339kW (3,180hp)
Alpha 12U28L-VO
1 x Vee 4 Stroke 12 Cy. 280 x 320 2339kW (3180bhp)
MAN B&W Diesel A/S-Denmark

8208323 *XUGZ2* -
XING JI DA
ex Miltiades *-2011* *ex* Toro *-2007*
ex Ulloa *-2000* *ex* Astart *-1993*
ex Liberty *-1988* *ex* La Liberte *-1987*
Xing Ji Da Shipping Ltd
Shenghao Marine (Hong Kong) Ltd
Phnom Penh *Cambodia*
MMSI: 514236000
Official number: 1383161
16,887 10,311 28,126
Class: IS (AB)
1983-03 **Naikai Shipbuilding & Engineering Co Ltd — Onomichi HS (Setoda Shipyard)** Yd No: 481
Loa 178.21 (BB) Br ex 23.14 Dght 10.610
Lbp 167.21 Br md 23.11 Dpth 14.76
Welded, 1 dk
(A21A2BC) Bulk Carrier
Grain: 38,539; Bale: 33,607
Compartments: 5 Ho, ER
5 Ha: (12.0 x 11.5)3 (19.2 x 11.5) (17.6 x 11.5)ER
Cranes: 4x25t
1 oil engine driving 1 FP propeller
Total Power: 7,723kW (10,500hp) 16.8kn
B&W 7L55GFCA
1 x 2 Stroke 7 Cy. 550 x 1380 7723kW (10500bhp)
Hitachi Zosen Corp-Japan
AuxGen: 3 x 440kW

8518522 *JVWZ4* -
XING JIA
ex Jin Hai You 10 *-2012* *ex* Jian She 10 *-2011*
Petro-Century Holdings Ltd
Vanguard Shipping Safety Management Consultant Co Ltd
Ulaanbaatar *Mongolia*
MMSI: 457644000
Official number: 31561286
3,335 1,748 5,214
Class: IS (Class contemplated) (CC)
1987-12 **Shanghai Shipyard — Shanghai** Yd No: 702
Loa 107.42 Br ex - Dght 6.401
Lbp 98.00 Br md 15.00 Dpth 7.49
Welded, 1 dk
(A13B2TP) Products Tanker
Single Hull
1 oil engine driving 1 FP propeller
Total Power: 3,420kW (4,650hp) 13.5kn
Sulzer 5RTA38
1 x 2 Stroke 5 Cy. 380 x 1100 3420kW (4650bhp)
Shanghai Diesel Engine Co Ltd-China

9030785 *BVQR* -
XING LIN
Xiamen Special Economic Zone Shipping Co Ltd
Xiamen, Fujian *China*
1,782 734 2,100
Class: (CC)
1993-03 **Chengxi Shipyard — Jiangyin JS** Yd No: 9101-1
Loa 79.55 Br ex - Dght 4.300
Lbp 73.00 Br md 13.60 Dpth 5.60
Welded, 1 dk
(A31A2GX) General Cargo Ship
TEU 118 C.Ho 48/20' C.Dk 70/20'
Compartments: 1 Ho, ER
1 Ha: (38.4 x 10.3)ER
1 oil engine geared to sc. shaft driving 1 FP propeller
Total Power: 595kW (809hp)
Daihatsu 6DSM-22
1 x 4 Stroke 6 Cy. 220 x 280 595kW (809bhp)
Shaanxi Diesel Engine Factory-China

9655286 *BLFE9* -
XING LONG ZHOU 569
Xing Long Zhou Marine Group Co Ltd
Taizhou, Jiangsu *China*
MMSI: 413446520
4,576 2,562 6,678
Class: CC
2012-07 **Linhai Hongsheng Shipbuilding Co Ltd — Linhai ZJ** Yd No: 2011-35
Loa 117.18 (BB) Br ex - Dght 6.394
Lbp 110.72 Br md 16.30 Dpth 8.30
Welded, 1 dk
(A13B2TP) Products Tanker
Double Hull (13F)
Ice Capable
1 oil engine reduction geared to sc. shaft driving 1 FP propeller
Total Power: 2,206kW (2,999hp) 13.0kn
Chinese Std. Type 8320ZC
1 x 4 Stroke 8 Cy. 320 x 440 2206kW (2999bhp)

9673032 *3EUI9* -
XING LONG ZHOU 665
Xing Long Zhou Shipping Group Co Ltd & Shanghai Gehai Shipping Co Ltd
Innovative Vision International Ltd
Panama *Panama*
MMSI: 357367000
Official number: 44027PEXTF1
9,265 4,223 13,600
Class: OM
2012-08 **Zhejiang Huaxia Shipbuilding Co Ltd — Yueqing ZJ** Yd No: CHX010-1
Loa 146.63 Br ex - Dght 8.000
Lbp 137.00 Br md 21.00 Dpth 11.20
Welded, 1 dk
(A12B2TR) Chemical/Products Tanker
Double Hull (13F)
1 oil engine driving 1 Propeller
Total Power: 2,970kW (4,038hp) 11.0kn

8901107 *3EAJ4* -
XING MIN DA
ex Theareston *-2013* *ex* Torm Marina *-2006*
Min Jian Shipping Ltd
Hong Sheng Da Shipmanagement Pte Ltd
Panama *Panama*
MMSI: 354889000
Official number: 3232607B
36,573 22,893 69,637 T/cm 65.6
Class: NV
1990-03 **Hashihama Shipbuilding Co Ltd — Tadotsu KG** (Hull) Yd No: 869
1990-03 **Tsuneishi Shipbuilding Co Ltd — Fukuyama HS** Yd No: 631
Loa 225.00 (BB) Br ex 32.24 Dght 13.223
Lbp 215.00 Br md 32.20 Dpth 18.30
Welded, 1 dk
(A21A2BC) Bulk Carrier
Grain: 81,839
Compartments: 7 Ho, ER
7 Ha: (14.2 x 12.8)6 (16.8 x 14.4)ER
Cranes: 4x25t
1 oil engine driving 1 FP propeller
Total Power: 8,905kW (12,107hp) 14.0kn
B&W 6S60MC
1 x 2 Stroke 6 Cy. 600 x 2292 8905kW (12107bhp)
Kawasaki Heavy Industries Ltd-Japan
AuxGen: 3 x 400kW 440V 60Hz a.c
Fuel: 187.0 (d.f.) 2335.0 (r.f.) 30.0pd

8220163 *3FVC9* -
XING PENG DA
ex Sun *-2011* *ex* Pima *-2000* *ex* Bel Air *-1991*
ex Ryozan Maru *-1989*
Xing Peng Da Shipping Ltd
Hong Sheng Da Shipmanagement Pte Ltd
SatCom: Inmarsat C 437165811
Panama *Panama*
MMSI: 371658000
Official number: 4261011A
36,526 21,783 66,894
Class: IT (NK) (AB)
1983-11 **Mitsubishi Heavy Industries Ltd. — Nagasaki** Yd No: 1913
Loa 224.99 (BB) Br ex 32.26 Dght 12.227
Lbp 216.00 Br md 32.20 Dpth 17.70
Welded, 1 dk
(A21A2BC) Bulk Carrier
Grain: 77,776
Compartments: 7 Ho, ER
7 Ha: (16.0 x 11.6)6 (16.0 x 13.2)ER
1 oil engine reduction geared to sc. shaft driving 1 FP propeller
Total Power: 7,760kW (10,550hp) 14.0kn
MAN 10V52/55A
1 x Vee 4 Stroke 10 Cy. 520 x 550 7760kW (10550bhp)
Mitsubishi Heavy Industries Ltd-Japan
AuxGen: 3 x 480kW 450V 60Hz a.c
Fuel: 154.0 (d.f.) 2073.0 (r.f.) 28.5pd

9524396 *VREG9* -
XING PING
Blue Ocean Navigation Ltd
Dandong Marine Shipping Co Ltd
Hong Kong *Hong Kong*
MMSI: 477110900
Official number: HK-2207
5,275 2,309 7,991
Class: CC
2008-07 **Huanghai Shipbuilding Co Ltd — Rongcheng SD** Yd No: HCY-84
Loa 117.00 Br ex - Dght 6.400
Lbp 110.00 Br md 19.70 Dpth 8.50
Welded, 1 dk
(A31A2GX) General Cargo Ship
Grain: 9,608; Bale: 9,608
TEU 629 C Ho 200 TEU C Dk 429 TEU.
Compartments: 3 Ho, ER
3 Ha: (25.4 x 15.0) (31.9 x 15.0)ER (19.5 x 15.0)
Ice Capable
2 oil engines reduction geared to sc. shafts driving 2 FP propellers
Total Power: 5,000kW (6,798hp) 13.8kn
Daihatsu 8DKM-28
2 x 4 Stroke 8 Cy. 280 x 390 each-2500kW (3399bhp)
Shaanxi Diesel Heavy Industry Co Lt-China
AuxGen: 3 x 250kW 400V a.c

7108928 *HQOT2* -
XING PU YI HAO
ex Rama *-1989* *ex* Neufeld *-1994*
ex Rhein *-1988*
Pine River Shipping
San Lorenzo *Honduras*
999 718 1,985
Class: (CC) (GL)
1971-06 **J.J. Sietas Schiffswerft — Hamburg** Yd No: 684
Loa 74.00 Br ex 10.83 Dght 5.071
Lbp 68.36 Br md 10.81 Dpth 6.02
Welded, 2 dks
(A31A2GX) General Cargo Ship
Grain: 2,432; Bale: 2,169
TEU 87 C. 87/20'
Compartments: 1 Ho, ER
1 Ha: (40.2 x 7.6)ER
Ice Capable
1 oil engine driving 1 FP propeller
Total Power: 971kW (1,320hp) 12.5kn
Deutz RBV8M545
1 x 4 Stroke 8 Cy. 320 x 450 971kW (1320bhp)
Kloeckner Humboldt Deutz AG-West Germany

8842076 *BWRX* -
XING QUAN
Fujian Quanzhou Shipping Affairs Co
-
Fuzhou, Fujian *China*
MMSI: 412445810
1,004 506 1,568
Class: (CC)
1989 **Wuchang Shipyard — Wuhan HB**
Loa 63.93 Br ex - Dght -
Lbp 59.00 Br md 11.50 Dpth 5.50
Welded, 1 dk
(A31A2GX) General Cargo Ship
1 oil engine driving 1 FP propeller
Total Power: 662kW (900hp) 12.2kn
Chinese Std. Type 6350
1 x 4 Stroke 6 Cy. 350 x 500 662kW (900bhp)
Shanghai Diesel Engine Co Ltd-China
AuxGen: 2 x 75kW 400V a.c, 1 x 24kW 400V a.c

8926377 *BAZC* -
XING SHENG
ex Rui Feng *-1988*
-
-
Dalian, Liaoning *China*
996 622 1,561
1995-05 **Wenzhou Dongfang Shipyard — Yueqing ZJ**
Loa 67.00 Br ex - Dght -
Lbp 59.80 Br md 10.50 Dpth 5.00
Welded, 1 dk
(A31A2GX) General Cargo Ship
1 oil engine geared to sc. shaft driving 1 FP propeller
Total Power: 552kW (750hp)
Chinese Std. Type 6300
1 x 4 Stroke 6 Cy. 300 x 380 552kW (750bhp)
Ningbo Zhonghua Dongli PowerMachinery Co Ltd -China

8896900 *BTQB* -
XING SHUN
Zhanjiang Harbour Shipping Co
Zhanjiang, Guangdong *China*
124 62 15
Class: (CC)
1995 **Wuhan Nanhua High Speed Ship Engineering Co Ltd — Wuhan HB**
Loa 38.00 Br ex - Dght 1.260
Lbp 33.12 Br md 4.40 Dpth 2.30
Welded, 1 dk
(A37B2PS) Passenger Ship
2 oil engines driving 2 FP propellers
Total Power: 1,410kW (1,918hp) 28.0kn
Dorman SEAKING-8
2 x 4 Stroke 8 Cy. 160 x 190 each-705kW (959bhp)
Perkins Engines Ltd.-Peterborough

8662488 *BVIS5* -
XING TONG 9
Quanzhou Quangang Xingtong Shipping Co Ltd
Quanzhou, Fujian *China*
MMSI: 413697790
Official number: 080413000001
2,995 1,677 4,683
Class: CC (Class contemplated)
2012-12 **Zhejiang Hangchang Shipbuilding Co Ltd — Linhai ZJ** Yd No: HCB11-096
Loa 98.98 Br ex 15.63 Dght 5.750
Lbp 90.60 Br md 15.60 Dpth 7.40
Welded, 1 dk
(A13B2TP) Products Tanker
Double Hull (13F)
1 oil engine reduction geared to sc. shafts driving 2 Propellers
Total Power: 1,914kW (2,602hp)
Daihatsu 6DKM-28
1 x 4 Stroke 6 Cy. 280 x 390 1914kW (2602bhp)
Shaanxi Diesel Heavy Industry Co Lt-China

9702974 *BVIT5* -
XING TONG 10
Quanzhou Quangang Xingtong Shipping Co Ltd
-
Quanzhou, Fujian *China*
MMSI: 413697810
Official number: 080413000005
2,995 1,677 4,709
Class: CC (Class contemplated)
2013-01 **Zhejiang Hangchang Shipbuilding Co Ltd — Linhai ZJ** Yd No: HCB12-097
Loa 98.98 Br ex 15.63 Dght 5.750
Lbp 90.60 Br md 15.60 Dpth 7.40
Welded, 1 dk
(A13B2TP) Products Tanker
Double Hull (13F)
1 oil engine driving 1 FP propeller
Total Power: 1,912kW (2,600hp)
Chinese Std. Type 8320ZC
1 x 4 Stroke 8 Cy. 320 x 440 1912kW (2600bhp)
Shaanxi Diesel Heavy Industry Co Lt-China

IMO / Call sign	Name / Owners / Manager	GT / NT / DWT	Class	Built / Dimensions	Type / Cargo	Machinery
592939 BVGE5	**XING TONG 89** **Quanzhou Quangang Xingtong Shipping Co Ltd** - *Quanzhou, Fujian* *China* MMSI: 413695640	**5,035** 2,272 7,000	Class: (BV)	**2010-09 Jiujiang Donghai Shipbuilding Co Ltd — Jiujiang JX** Yd No: DH001 Loa 118.00 Br ex - Dght 6.600 Lbp 110.00 Br md 17.60 Dpth 9.00 Welded, 1 dk	**(A12B2TR) Chemical/Products Tanker** Double Hull (13F) Liq: 8,048; Liq (Oil): 8,048 Compartments: 5 Wing Ta, 5 Wing Ta, ER	**1 oil engine** reduction geared to sc. shaft driving 1 FP propeller Total Power: 2,574kW (3,500hp) 12.5kn Yanmar 6N330-EN 1 x 4 Stroke 6 Cy. 330 x 440 2574kW (3500bhp) Qingdao Zichai Boyang Diesel EngineCo Ltd-China AuxGen: 2 x 312kW 60Hz a.c
596143 BVGY5	**XING TONG 99** **Quanzhou Quangang Xingtong Shipping Co Ltd** - *Quanzhou, Fujian* *China* MMSI: 413696210	**5,683** 2,815 9,002	Class: CC	**2011-07 Zhejiang Hangchang Shipbuilding Co Ltd — Linhai ZJ** Yd No: HCB09-090 Loa 125.70 Br ex - Dght 7.100 Lbp 117.70 Br md 17.60 Dpth 9.40 Welded, 1 dk	**(A12B2TR) Chemical/Products Tanker** Double Hull (13F) Liq: 9,491; Liq (Oil): 9,491 Compartments: 6 Wing Ta, 6 Wing Ta, 1 Wing Slop Ta, 1 Wing Slop Ta, ER Ice Capable	**1 oil engine** reduction geared to sc. shaft driving 1 Propeller Total Power: 2,500kW (3,399hp) 12.5kn Daihatsu 8DKM-28 1 x 4 Stroke 8 Cy. 280 x 390 2500kW (3399bhp) Shaanxi Diesel Heavy Industry Co Lt-China AuxGen: 3 x 200kW 400V a.c
647174 -	**XING YANG 7** *ex* Xing Xiang 7 *-2013* **Zhang Jinhui & Yang Xuejun** HongKong XingXiang Co Ltd	**3,518** 1,970 5,633	Class: IZ RI	**2011-11 Ningbo Daxie Development Zone Shipyard Co Ltd — Ningbo ZJ** Yd No: S4083-100-03 Loa 97.28 Br ex - Dght 6.200 Lbp 89.80 Br md 15.80 Dpth 7.70 Welded, 1 dk	**(A21A2BC) Bulk Carrier**	**1 oil engine** reduction geared to sc. shaft driving 1 FP propeller Total Power: 2,060kW (2,801hp) 12.0kn Guangzhou 1 x 2060kW (2801bhp) Guangzhou Diesel Engine Factory CoLtd-China AuxGen: 3 x 105kW a.c
7620756 BXHL	**XING YE** *ex* Izumi Maru No. 51 *-1996* **Xing Ye Shipping Co Ltd** Shantou Navigation Corp *Shantou, Guangdong* *China* MMSI: 412462960	*998* 628 1,141	Class: (CC) (NK)	**1976-11 Hashihama Shipbuilding Co Ltd — Imabari EH** Yd No: 636 Loa 67.52 Br ex 11.23 Dght 4.301 Lbp 62.01 Br md 11.21 Dpth 5.11 Welded, 1 dk	**(A11B2TG) LPG Tanker** Liq (Gas): 1,512 2 x Gas Tank (s);	**1 oil engine** driving 1 FP propeller Total Power: 1,839kW (2,500hp) 12.5kn Akasaka AH40 1 x 4 Stroke 6 Cy. 400 x 600 1839kW (2500bhp) Akasaka Tekkosho KK (Akasaka DieselLtd)-Japan AuxGen: 3 x 328kW
7703766 BPYU -	**XING YE 1** *ex* Princess Sarah *-1990* *ex* Estella *-1987* *ex* Ocean Constructor *-1983* **Qianxi Shipping Development Co Ltd** - SatCom: Inmarsat C 441299410 *Ningbo, Zhejiang* *China* MMSI: 412461000	**3,239** 2,355 6,543	Class: (CC) (NK) (CR)	**1979-02 China Shipbuilding Corp (CSBC) — Kaohsiung** Yd No: 16 Loa 108.51 Br ex 16.24 Dght 6.655 Lbp 100.01 Br md 16.21 Dpth 8.11 Welded, 1 dk	**(A31A2GX) General Cargo Ship** Grain: 8,492; Bale: 7,996 Compartments: 2 Ho, ER 2 Ha: (27.2 x 8.3) (28.1 x 8.3)ER Derricks: 2x20t,2x15t; Winches: 6	**1 oil engine** driving 1 FP propeller Total Power: 2,795kW (3,800hp) 15.0kn Mitsubishi 6UET45/75C 1 x 2 Stroke 6 Cy. 450 x 750 2795kW (3800bhp) Akasaka Tekkosho KK (Akasaka DieselLtd)-Japan AuxGen: 2 x 160kW 450V 60Hz a.c Fuel: 557.0 (r.f.)
8924422 BJWQ -	**XING YE 515** - - *Haikou, Hainan* *China*	*380* 188 -		**1996-04 Chongqing Shipyard — Chongqing** Loa 49.80 Br ex - Dght 2.600 Lbp - Br md 10.20 Dpth 3.60 Welded, 1 dk	**(A31A2GX) General Cargo Ship**	**2 oil engines** geared to sc. shafts driving 2 FP propellers Total Power: 368kW (500hp) Chinese Std. Type 6160A 2 x 4 Stroke 6 Cy. 160 x 225 each-184kW (250bhp) Weifang Diesel Engine Factory-China
9073311 XUAA4 -	**XING YUAN** *ex* Hau Tong *-2011* *ex* Myoriki No. 53 *-2004* **Hongkong Longhai Shipping Co Ltd** Yun Xing Shipping Co Ltd SatCom: Inmarsat C 451528110 *Phnom Penh* *Cambodia* MMSI: 515569000	**3,015** 1,993 5,369	Class: UB	**1993-06 Honda Zosen — Saiki** Yd No: 849 Loa 94.90 Br ex - Dght 6.500 Lbp 89.40 Br md 14.80 Dpth 8.90 Welded	**(A24D2BA) Aggregates Carrier** Grain: 7,085; Bale: 6,700 Compartments: 2 Ho, ER 2 Ha: ER 2 (24.6 x 10.8)	**1 oil engine** driving 1 FP propeller Total Power: 1,471kW (2,000hp) 10.0kn Hanshin LH36LAG 1 x 4 Stroke 6 Cy. 360 x 670 1471kW (2000bhp) The Hanshin Diesel Works Ltd-Japan
9663219 BHNZ3 -	**XING YUN YANG** **Nanjing Sumec Shipping Co Ltd** Jiangsu Fanzhou Shipping Co Ltd *Nanjing, Jiangsu* *China* MMSI: 413361990 Official number: CN20127554128	**2,831** 849 2,598	Class: CC	**2013-03 Jiangsu Zhenjiang Shipyard Co Ltd — Zhenjiang JS** Yd No: VZJ6215-1001 Loa 75.00 (BB) Br ex 17.72 Dght 6.400 Lbp 66.00 Br md 16.80 Dpth 7.80 Welded, 1 dk	**(B21A20S) Platform Supply Ship** Ice Capable	**2 oil engines** reduction geared to sc. shafts driving 2 Propellers Total Power: 10,080kW (13,704hp) 15.6kn MAN-B&W 9L32/44CR 2 x 4 Stroke 9 Cy. 320 x 440 each-5040kW (6852bhp) in China AuxGen: 2 x 2000kW 400V a.c, 2 x 450kW 400V a.c Thrusters: 2 Tunnel thruster (f)
9067453 BXOZ -	**XING ZHONG** *ex* Hui Yang *-2004* **Zhongshan Hong Kong Passenger Shipping Co-op Co Ltd** Chu Kong Shipping Enterprises (Holdings) Co Ltd *Zhongshan, Guangdong* *China* MMSI: 412884000	**560** 188 42	Class: CC	**1993-06 Austal Ships Pty Ltd — Fremantle WA** Yd No: 100 Loa 39.90 (BB) Br ex 13.21 Dght 1.350 Lbp 35.00 Br md 12.90 Dpth 3.80 Welded, 1 dk	**(A37B2PS) Passenger Ship** Hull Material: Aluminium Alloy Passengers: unberthed: 368	**2 oil engines** with clutches, flexible couplings & dr geared to sc. shafts driving 2 Water jets Total Power: 3,840kW (5,220hp) 32.5kn M.T.U. 16V396TE74L 2 x Vee 4 Stroke 16 Cy. 165 x 185 each-1920kW (2610bhp) MTU Friedrichshafen GmbH-Friedrichshafen AuxGen: 2 x 108kW 380V a.c
9118214 - -	**XINGANG 287** **Tianjin Harbour Construction & Development Co** - *China*	**300** - 600		**1994-12 Tianjin Xingang Shipyard — Tianjin** Yd No: 287 Loa 49.90 Br ex - Dght 3.800 Lbp 47.00 Br md 9.80 Dpth 4.60 Welded, 1 dk	**(B21A20S) Platform Supply Ship**	**1 oil engine** geared to sc. shaft driving 1 FP propeller Chinese Std. Type 1 x 4 Stroke Anqing Marine Diesel Engine Works-China
9590400 BANC -	**XINGHANG YOUFU 3** **Dalian Transquare-line International Ship Management Co Ltd** - SatCom: Inmarsat C 441301643 *Dalian, Liaoning* *China* MMSI: 413202380	**828** 281 -	Class: CC	**2010-11 Jiujiang Yinxing Shipbuilding Co Ltd — Xingzi County JX** Yd No: YT36-03 Loa 53.00 Br ex - Dght 4.100 Lbp 48.00 Br md 12.00 Dpth 5.20 Welded, 1 dk	**(B21B20T) Offshore Tug/Supply Ship** Ice Capable	**2 oil engines** reduction geared to sc. shafts driving 2 Propellers Total Power: 2,206kW (3,000hp) 12.0kn Chinese Std. Type 6320ZC 2 x 4 Stroke 6 Cy. 320 x 440 each-1103kW (1500bhp) Guangzhou Diesel Engine Factory CoLtd-China AuxGen: 3 x 400kW 400V a.c
9478509 BLGS8 -	**XINGLONGZHOU 172** *ex* Nautilus Explorer *-2010* **Taizhou Xinglongzhou Shipping Co Ltd** - *China* MMSI: 413444250	**5,036** 2,272 7,000	Class: (BV)	**2009-10 Zhejiang Hexing Shipyard — Wenling ZJ** Yd No: HQ1003 Loa 118.00 Br ex - Dght 6.600 Lbp 110.67 Br md 17.60 Dpth 10.50 Welded, 1 dk	**(A13B2TP) Products Tanker** Double Hull (13F)	**1 oil engine** reduction geared to sc. shaft driving 1 CP propeller Total Power: 2,970kW (4,038hp) 12.0kn MaK 9M25 1 x 4 Stroke 9 Cy. 255 x 400 2970kW (4038bhp) Caterpillar Motoren GmbH & Co. KG-Germany
9064011 - -	**XINHE TIANJIN** - - *China*	*2,205* - 3,200		**1991-12 Tianjin Xinhe Shipyard — Tianjin** Loa 81.15 Br ex - Dght 4.200 Lbp 78.40 Br md 15.00 Dpth 6.80 Welded	**(A31A2GX) General Cargo Ship** TEU 100 C. 100/20'	**1 oil engine** reduction geared to sc. shaft driving 1 FP propeller Total Power: 969kW (1,317hp) Chinese Std. Type 6320ZCD 1 x 4 Stroke 6 Cy. 320 x 440 969kW (1317bhp) in China
8652902 - -	**XINHONG 18** **Centurypeak Investment Ltd** - *China* MMSI: 413464650	**2,099** 1,175 -		**2009-11 Zhejiang Jiaoshan Shiprepair & Building Yard — Wenling ZJ** Loa 75.00 Br ex - Dght - Lbp 72.00 Br md 16.80 Dpth 4.20 Welded, 1 dk	**(A31A2GX) General Cargo Ship**	**2 oil engines** driving 2 Propellers 12.5kn Chinese Std. Type Weichai Power Co Ltd-China
8652914 - -	**XINHONG 28** *ex* Wan Xiang 145 *-2010* **Centurypeak Investment Ltd** - *China* MMSI: 413464660	**2,099** 1,175 -		**2009-11 Zhejiang Jiaoshan Shiprepair & Building Yard — Wenling ZJ** Loa 75.00 Br ex - Dght - Lbp 72.00 Br md 16.80 Dpth 4.20 Welded, 1 dk	**(A31A2GX) General Cargo Ship**	**2 oil engines** driving 2 Propellers 12.5kn Chinese Std. Type Weichai Power Co Ltd-China
9497373 VRMW3 -	**XINHUI EXPRESS** **Xinhui Express Ltd** Nova Shipping & Logistics Pte Ltd *Hong Kong* *Hong Kong* MMSI: 477686500 Official number: HK-3994	**54,693** 20,576 70,060	Class: AB	**2014-02 Nantong Mingde Heavy Industry Co Ltd — Tongzhou JS** Yd No: .7M CF CC-02 Loa 215.40 (BB) Br ex - Dght 12.800 Lbp 210.60 Br md 37.00 Dpth 23.95 Welded, 1 dk	**(A24B2BW) Wood Chips Carrier** Grain: 133,243	**1 oil engine** driving 1 FP propeller Total Power: 10,470kW (14,235hp) 14.5kn Wartsila 6RT-flex50 1 x 2 Stroke 6 Cy. 500 x 2050 10470kW (14235bhp) Hefei Rong'an Power Machinery Co Lt-China
9535046 H9AD	**XINOU 1** **Xinou (Hong Kong) Shipping Ltd** Sea & Har Shipping Co Ltd *Panama* *Panama* Official number: 38346PEXT	**4,967** 2,108 6,462		**2008-07 Zhejiang Yueqing Qiligang Ship Industry Co Ltd — Yueqing ZJ** Yd No: DFQ07-J413 Loa 118.45 Br ex - Dght 5.800 Lbp 109.00 Br md 17.00 Dpth 8.00 Welded, 1 dk	**(A31A2GX) General Cargo Ship**	**1 oil engine** reduction geared to sc. shaft driving 1 FP propeller Total Power: 2,060kW (2,801hp) 12.0kn Guangzhou 8320ZC 1 x 4 Stroke 8 Cy. 320 x 440 2060kW (2801bhp) Guangzhou Diesel Engine Factory CoLtd-China

8647660 - -	**XINTAYLOR** *ex* Wan Xiang 166 *-2011* *ex* Star Dredging 9 *-2011* *ex* Wan Xiang 166 *-2011* **Xintaylor Ltd** Star Dredging Pte Ltd	**2,752** 1,541 -		**2009-04 Anhui Ma'anshan Meihua Shipbuilding Co Ltd — Dangtu County AH** Yd No: 2009W2300184 Loa 88.80 Br ex - Dght - Lbp 84.00 Br md 15.80 Dpth 5.80 Welded, 1 dk	**(A24D2BA) Aggregates Carrier**	**2 oil engines** reduction geared to sc. shafts driving 2 Propellers Total Power: 1,320kW (1,794hp) 10.0kr Chinese Std. Type CW6200ZC 2 x 4 Stroke 6 Cy. 200 x 270 each-660kW (897bhp) Weichai Power Co Ltd-China
7739612 - -	**XINWANG** *ex* Victory Oil 02 *-1999* *ex* Golden Dragon 168 *-1998* *ex* Fil Tanker *-1995* *ex* Bintang Laut 5 *-1988* - -	**575** 264 851	Class: (NK)	**1978 Asian Welding Machinery Pte Ltd — Singapore** Loa 54.97 Br ex 10.62 Dght 2.731 Lbp 51.95 Br md 10.60 Dpth 3.40 Welded, 1 dk	**(A13B2TU) Tanker (unspecified)** Liq: 972; Liq (Oil): 972	**2 oil engines** geared to sc. shafts driving 2 FP propellers Total Power: 912kW (1,240hp) 10.0kr Cummins VT-28-M2 2 x Vee 4 Stroke 12 Cy. 140 x 152 each-456kW (620bhp) Cummins Engine Co Inc-USA AuxGen: 2 x 38kW a.c
9255012 *BORA* -	**XINWANG HAI** - **COSCO Bulk Carrier Co Ltd (COSCO BULK)** - SatCom: Inmarsat C 441301210 *Tianjin* *China* MMSI: 413012000	**88,856** 58,333 174,732 T/cm 119.0	Class: CC	**2003-11 Shanghai Waigaoqiao Shipbuilding Co Ltd — Shanghai** Yd No: 001 Loa 289.00 (BB) Br ex 45.05 Dght 18.120 Lbp 279.00 Br md 45.00 Dpth 24.50 Welded, 1 dk	**(A21A2BC) Bulk Carrier** Double Bottom Entire Compartment Length Grain: 193,008; Bale: 183,425 Compartments: 9 Ho, ER 9 Ha: 7 (15.5 x 20.0)2 (15.5 x 16.5)ER	**1 oil engine** driving 1 FP propeller Total Power: 16,858kW (22,920hp) 14.5kn MAN-B&W 6S70MC 1 x 2 Stroke 6 Cy. 700 x 2674 16858kW (22920bhp) Hudong Heavy Machinery Co Ltd-China AuxGen: 3 x 800kW 450V 60Hz a.c Fuel: 372.0 (d.f.) 5082.0 (r.f.)
8663808 *3FBP7* -	**XIONG HAI** *ex* Fu Tong *-2013* **Shantou Sun Rising Shipping Co Ltd** Sun Rising Shipmanagement Co Ltd *Panama* *Panama* MMSI: 372183000 Official number: 45286PEXTF	**2,982** 1,969 5,020	Class: CC (Class contemplated)	**2009-07 Jiangdu Jianghai Shiprepair Yard — Yangzhou JS** Loa 96.50 Br ex - Dght 5.950 Lbp 93.22 Br md 15.80 Dpth 7.40 Welded, 1 dk	**(A31A2GX) General Cargo Ship**	**1 oil engine** driving 1 Propeller Total Power: 2,000kW (2,719hp) 11.6kn Chinese Std. Type 8300ZC 1 x 4 Stroke 8 Cy. 300 x 380 2000kW (2719bhp) Wuxi Antai Power Machinery Co Ltd-China
9042001 - -	**XIONGNU BARU 33** *ex* Draco I *-2010* *ex* Liberty *-2008* *ex* Tonka *-2008* *ex* Chilbo San No. 33 *-2008* *ex* Hammer *-2006* *ex* Carran *-2005* *ex* Seo Yang No. 88 *-2004* *ex* Dong Bang No. 139 *-1993* - -	**1,047** 314 652	Class: (BV) (KR)	**1990-12 Dae Sun Shipbuilding & Engineering Co Ltd — Busan** Yd No: 377 Loa 61.72 (BB) Br ex 9.52 Dght 4.171 Lbp 53.20 Br md 9.50 Dpth 4.15 Welded, 1 dk	**(B11B2FV) Fishing Vessel** Ins: 938	**1 oil engine** sr geared to sc. shaft driving 1 FP propeller Total Power: 1,177kW (1,600hp) 12.5kn Hanshin LH28LG 1 x 4 Stroke 6 Cy. 280 x 530 1177kW (1600bhp) The Hanshin Diesel Works Ltd-Japan AuxGen: 3 x 400kW 225V a.c
7825021 *XCZM* -	**XITLE** *ex* Panay *-1988* *ex* Douglas Fir *-1981* **Naviera Armamex SA de CV** - *Ciudad del Carmen* *Mexico* MMSI: 345070014	*4,237* 1,896 7,948	Class: GL (NK)	**1979-07 K.K. Uwajima Zosensho — Uwajima** Yd No: 2096 Loa 117.51 Br ex 20.83 Dght 5.495 Lbp 112.02 Br md 20.81 Dpth 7.52 Welded, 1 dk	**(A13B2TP) Products Tanker** Double Bottom Entire Compartment Length Liq: 7,298; Liq (Oil): 7,298 Compartments: 10 Ta, ER	**1 oil engine** sr geared to sc. shaft driving 1 FP propeller Total Power: 2,868kW (3,899hp) 11.5kn Pielstick 6PC2-5L-400 1 x 4 Stroke 6 Cy. 400 x 460 2868kW (3899bhp) Ishikawajima Harima Heavy IndustrieCo Ltd (IHI)-Japan AuxGen: 3 x 160kW 220/440V a.c
9611668 *BPGG* -	**XIU CHI** - **China Shipping Tanker Co Ltd** - *Shanghai* *China* MMSI: 414734000	**30,325** 12,886 48,781	Class: CC	**2012-11 Guangzhou Shipyard International Co Ltd — Guangzhou GD** Yd No: 10130017 Loa 184.88 (BB) Br ex 32.23 Dght 12.400 Lbp 176.00 Br md 32.20 Dpth 18.60 Welded, 1 dk	**(A13A2TW) Crude/Oil Products Tanker** Double Hull (13F) Liq: 50,760; Liq (Oil): 50,760 Compartments: 6 Wing Ta, 6 Wing Ta, 1 Wing Slop Ta, 1 Wing Slop Ta, ER Ice Capable	**1 oil engine** driving 1 FP propeller Total Power: 9,960kW (13,542hp) 14.5kn MAN-B&W 6S50ME-C8 1 x 2 Stroke 6 Cy. 500 x 2000 9960kW (13542bhp)
8313348 *BUWR* -	**XIU HAI** *ex* Gang Hai 676 *-2005* *ex* Siri Phatra *-2002* *ex* Belgallantry *-2002* *ex* Western Gallantry *-1996* *launched as* Pacific Gallantry *-1987* **China Changhang Freight Co** - SatCom: Inmarsat C 441285215 *China* MMSI: 412079290	**25,865** 13,129 43,467 T/cm 50.1	Class: (NV)	**1987-09 Tsuneishi Shipbuilding Co Ltd — Fukuyama HS** Yd No: 549 Converted From: Bulk/Oil Carrier (OBO)-2004 Converted From: Bulk Carrier-1987 Loa 185.83 (BB) Br ex 30.43 Dght 11.319 Lbp 177.02 Br md 30.41 Dpth 16.21 Welded, 1 dk	**(A21A2BC) Bulk Carrier** Grain: 48,166 Compartments: 7 Ho, ER 7 Ha: 7 (12.8 x 15.3)ER Cranes: 4x25t	**1 oil engine** driving 1 FP propeller Total Power: 7,120kW (9,680hp) 14.5kn B&W 6L60MCE 1 x 2 Stroke 6 Cy. 600 x 1944 7120kW (9680bhp) Mitsui Engineering & Shipbuilding CLtd-Japan AuxGen: 2 x 660kW 220/440V 60Hz a.c, 1 x 80kW 220/440V 60Hz a.c Fuel: 1208.0 (r.f.)
9043005 *BOBZ* -	**XIU HE** *ex* Pretty River *-2009* **COSCO Container Lines Co Ltd (COSCON)** - *Shanghai* *China* MMSI: 413451000	**22,746** 11,964 33,548 T/cm 44.4	Class: CC (NV) (AB)	**1993-01 Halla Engineering & Heavy Industries Ltd — Incheon** Yd No: 195 Loa 187.60 (BB) Br ex 28.43 Dght 11.113 Lbp 179.34 Br md 28.40 Dpth 15.60 Welded, 1 dk	**(A33A2CC) Container Ship (Fully Cellular)** Grain: 53,324 TEU 1923 C Ho 914 TEU C Dk 1009 TEU incl 60 ref C. Compartments: ER, 5 Cell Ho 5 Ha: ER	**1 oil engine** driving 1 FP propeller Total Power: 15,712kW (21,362hp) 18.0kn B&W 6L70MC 1 x 2 Stroke 6 Cy. 700 x 2268 15712kW (21362bhp) Hyundai Heavy Industries Co Ltd-South Korea AuxGen: 3 x 825kW a.c Thrusters: 1 Thwart. CP thruster (f)
9633862 *V3QR8* -	**XIU SHAN** *ex* Shun Tong *-2012* *completed as* Eastern Topaz *-2012* **Yidong Shipping Ltd** Blue Ocean Ship Management Co Ltd *Belize City* *Belize* MMSI: 312828000 Official number: 611220030	**4,559** 2,497 6,650	Class: BV	**2012-06 Weihai Donghai Shipyard Co Ltd — Weihai SD** Yd No: DHZ-10-40 Loa 104.20 (BB) Br ex - Dght 6.600 Lbp 97.50 Br md 17.20 Dpth 8.50 Welded, 1 dk	**(A31A2GX) General Cargo Ship** Grain: 8,732 Compartments: 2 Ho, ER 2 Ha: ER 2 (26.6 x 12.0) Cranes: 2x30t Ice Capable	**1 oil engine** reduction geared to sc. shaft driving 1 FP propeller Total Power: 2,720kW (3,698hp) 12.8kn MAN-B&W 8L27/38 1 x 4 Stroke 8 Cy. 270 x 380 2720kW (3698bhp) ZGPT Diesel Heavy Industry Co Ltd-China AuxGen: 3 x 280kW 50Hz a.c Fuel: 590.0
9138264 *DSRJ5* -	**XIUMEI SHANGHAI** *ex* Fabian Schulte *-2012* *ex* CMA CGM Iroko *-2009* *ex* Fabian Schulte *-2007* *ex* Maersk Cabello *-1998* *ex* Fabian Schulte *-1997* **Sinokor Merchant Marine Co Ltd** Korea Shipmanagers Co Ltd *Jeju* *South Korea* MMSI: 441883000 Official number: JJR-121069	**15,906** 9,227 22,264	Class: KR (GL)	**1997-09 MTW Schiffswerft GmbH — Wismar** Yd No: 302 Loa 167.84 (BB) Br ex - Dght 10.810 Lbp 156.92 Br md 26.70 Dpth 14.40 Welded, 1 dk	**(A33A2CC) Container Ship (Fully Cellular)** TEU 1608 C Ho 595 TEU C Dk 1013 TEU incl 200 ref C. 8 Ha: Cranes: 3x45t Ice Capable	**1 oil engine** driving 1 FP propeller Total Power: 15,540kW (21,128hp) 20.1kn Sulzer 7RTA62U 1 x 2 Stroke 7 Cy. 620 x 2150 15540kW (21128bhp) Dieselmotorenwerk Vulkan GmbH-Rostock AuxGen: 1 x 1440kW 220/440V a.c, 3 x 880kW 220/440V a.c Thrusters: 1 Thwart. CP thruster (f)
9138252 *DSRK5* -	**XIUMEI TIANJIN** *ex* Antje Schulte *-2012* *ex* Alianca Rotterdam *-2001* *ex* Antje Schulte *-2000* *ex* CGM Mascareignes *-1999* *ex* CGM Santos Dumont II *-1999* *ex* Alianca America *-1998* *ex* CSAV Reloncav *-1998* *ex* Antje Schulte *-1997* **Sinokor Merchant Marine Co Ltd** - *Jeju* *South Korea* MMSI: 441892000 Official number: JJR-131006	**15,906** 9,227 22,264	Class: KR (GL)	**1997-05 MTW Schiffswerft GmbH — Wismar** Yd No: 301 Loa 167.97 (BB) Br ex - Dght 10.820 Lbp 156.92 Br md 26.70 Dpth 14.40 Welded, 1 dk	**(A33A2CC) Container Ship (Fully Cellular)** TEU 1608 C Ho 595 TEU C Dk 1013 TEU incl 200 ref C. 8 Ha: Cranes: 3x40t Ice Capable	**1 oil engine** driving 1 FP propeller Total Power: 15,540kW (21,128hp) 21.0kn Sulzer 7RTA62U 1 x 2 Stroke 7 Cy. 620 x 2150 15540kW (21128bhp) Dieselmotorenwerk Vulkan GmbH-Rostock AuxGen: 1 x 1440kW 440V a.c, 3 x 880kW 440/220V a.c Thrusters: 1 Thwart. CP thruster (f)
8035207 *UDFN* -	**XIX SYEZD VLKSM** *ex* Shantar *-1998* *ex* XIX Syezd VLKSM *-1998* **Marlin Co Ltd (OOO 'Marlin')** - *Kholmsk* *Russia* MMSI: 273890600	**780** 234 332	Class: (RS)	**1982-05 Volgogradskiy Sudostroitelnyy Zavod — Volgograd** Yd No: 202 Loa 53.75 Br ex 10.72 Dght 4.290 Lbp 47.92 Br md 10.50 Dpth 6.00 Welded, 1 dk	**(B11A2FS) Stern Trawler** Ins: 218 Compartments: 1 Ho, ER 1 Ha: (1.6 x 1.6) Derricks: 2x1.5t Ice Capable	**1 oil engine** driving 1 FP propeller Total Power: 971kW (1,320hp) 12.8kn S.K.L. 8NVD48A-2U 1 x 4 Stroke 8 Cy. 320 x 480 971kW (1320bhp) VEB Schwermaschinenbau "KarlLiebknecht" (SKL)-Magdeburg Fuel: 182.0 (d.f.)
7413828 *6KCB5* -	**XIXILI** *ex* Saint Martin *-1996* *ex* Anzika *-1995* **Dongwon Industries Co Ltd** - *Busan* *South Korea* MMSI: 441865000 Official number: 7413828	**2,201** 660 3,944	Class: KR (BV) (RI)	**1978-02 Soc. Esercizio Cant. S.p.A. — Viareggio** Yd No: 620 Loa 78.80 Br ex 13.75 Dght 5.716 Lbp 71.60 Br md 13.72 Dpth 6.66 Welded, 2 dks	**(B11B2FV) Fishing Vessel**	**2 oil engines** geared to sc. shaft driving 1 CP propeller Total Power: 4,414kW (6,002hp) 16.0kn Nohab F216V 2 x Vee 4 Stroke 16 Cy. 250 x 300 each-2207kW (3001bhp) AB Bofors NOHAB-Sweden

IMO / Call sign	Name / Owners / Flag	Tonnage	Class	Builder / Dimensions	Type / Capacities	Machinery
847959 HA625	**XMUN** *ex* Riems *-1992* **Ocean Way Co Ltd** - *Valletta* *Malta* Official number: 3922	*115* 51 200		**1959 VEB Peene-Werft — Wolgast** Shortened-1997 Loa 32.25 Br ex 9.00 Dght 2.650 Lbp 26.89 Br md - Dpth 3.90 Welded, 1 dk	**(A13B2TU) Tanker (unspecified)**	**2 oil engines** driving 2 FP propellers Total Power: 588kW (800hp) S.K.L. 8NVD26A-2 2 x 4 Stroke 8 Cy. 180 x 260 each-294kW (400bhp) VEB Schwermaschinenbau "KarlLiebknecht" (SKL)-Magdeburg
146601 HA2838	**XO LION** *ex* Tina A *-2014* *ex* Ljubljana *-2012* *ex* Star Sea Bird *-2005* **XO Lion ApS** Action Maritime SA *Valletta* *Malta* MMSI: 256301000 Official number: 9146601	**24,953** 13,547 42,717 T/cm 48.8	Class: BV (NK)	**1997-03 Ishikawajima-Harima Heavy Industries Co Ltd (IHI) — Tokyo** Yd No: 3073 Loa 181.50 (BB) Br ex 30.53 Dght 11.373 Lbp 172.00 Br md 30.50 Dpth 16.40 Welded, 1 dk	**(A21A2BC) Bulk Carrier** Grain: 52,680; Bale: 52,379 Compartments: 5 Ho, ER 5 Ha: (15.2 x 12.8)4 (19.2 x 15.2)ER Cranes: 4x30t	**1 oil engine** driving 1 FP propeller Total Power: 6,988kW (9,501hp) 14.5kn Sulzer 6RTA48T 1 x 2 Stroke 6 Cy. 480 x 2000 6988kW (9501bhp) Diesel United Ltd.-Aioi
142215 EAY8	**XO TIGER** *ex* Nesrin Aksoy *-2014* *ex* Flores *-2007* *ex* Primax *-1999* **XO Tiger ApS** Action Maritime SA *Panama* *Panama* MMSI: 370234000 Official number: 45579PEXT	**27,011** 16,011 46,609 T/cm 51.4	Class: NK	**1997-01 Mitsui Eng. & SB. Co. Ltd. — Tamano** Yd No: 1433 Loa 189.80 (BB) Br ex - Dght 11.620 Lbp 181.00 Br md 31.00 Dpth 16.50 Welded, 1 dk	**(A21A2BC) Bulk Carrier** Grain: 59,820; Bale: 57,237 Compartments: 5 Ho, ER 5 Ha: 4 (20.8 x 17.2) (17.2 x 17.2)ER Cranes: 4x30t	**1 oil engine** driving 1 FP propeller Total Power: 8,562kW (11,641hp) 14.5kn B&W 6S50MC 1 x 2 Stroke 6 Cy. 500 x 1910 8562kW (11641bhp) Mitsui Engineering & Shipbuilding CLtd-Japan Fuel: 1855.0 (r.f.)
374888 -	**XOH PAEK** *ex* So Baek *-2003* *ex* Dae Hung Ho *-1999* *ex* Denpasar II *-1983* *ex* Hsing Chan No. 1 *-1974* - -	*3,597* 2,094 6,066	Class: KC (NK)	**1974-07 Nishi Shipbuilding Co Ltd — Imabari EH** Yd No: 158 Loa 102.62 Br ex 16.24 Dght 6.700 Lbp 95.99 Br md 16.20 Dpth 8.21 Welded, 1 dk	**(A31A2GX) General Cargo Ship** Grain: 7,722; Bale: 7,078 Compartments: 2 Ho, ER 2 Ha: (25.9 x 8.3) (28.6 x 8.3)ER Derricks: 4x15t; Winches: 4	**1 oil engine** driving 1 FP propeller Total Power: 2,795kW (3,800hp) 12.8kn Mitsubishi 6UET45/75C 1 x 2 Stroke 6 Cy. 450 x 750 2795kW (3800bhp) Akasaka Tekkosho KK (Akasaka DieselLtd)-Japan AuxGen: 2 x 136kW Fuel: 514.0 (r.f.) 12.0pd
130186 -	**XOLOESCUINTLE** *ex* Marflota IV *-1974* *ex* Tiburon IV *-1974* **Promotora de Productos del Mar SA de CV** - *La Paz* *Mexico*	*423* 127 276	Class: (NK)	**1982-03 Miho Zosensho K.K. — Shimizu** Yd No: 1206 Loa 44.46 Br ex 8.03 Dght 3.095 Lbp 38.31 Br md 8.01 Dpth 3.20 Welded, 1 dk	**(B11B2FV) Fishing Vessel** Ins: 299 Compartments: 2 Ho, ER 2 Ha: 2 (1.6 x 1.6)ER	**1 oil engine** with clutches, flexible couplings & sr geared to sc. shaft driving 1 CP propeller Total Power: 662kW (900hp) 10.5kn Niigata 6MG25BX 1 x 4 Stroke 6 Cy. 250 x 320 662kW (900bhp) Niigata Engineering Co Ltd-Japan AuxGen: 2 x 122kW
9228368 HC2083 -	**XPEDITION** *ex* Sun Bay *-2004* **Islas Galapagos Turismo y Vapores CA** Royal Caribbean Cruises Ltd (RCCL) *Guayaquil* *Ecuador* MMSI: 735023483 Official number: TN-00-0459	**2,842** 864 570	Class: LR (GL) **100A1** CS 06/2011 passenger ship **LMC** **UMS**	**2001-03 Schiffswerft und Maschinenfabrik Cassens GmbH — Emden** Yd No: 228 Loa 88.50 (BB) Br ex - Dght 3.600 Lbp 78.00 Br md 14.00 Dpth 5.85 Welded, 5 dks	**(A37A2PC) Passenger/Cruise** Double Bottom Entire Compartment Length Passengers: cabins: 46; berths: 96	**1 oil engine** with clutches & reduction geared to sc. shaft driving 1 CP propeller Total Power: 1,850kW (2,515hp) 13.5kn MaK 6M25 1 x 4 Stroke 6 Cy. 255 x 400 1850kW (2515bhp) MaK Motoren GmbH & Co. KG-Kiel AuxGen: 1 x 800kW 400V 50Hz a.c, 2 x 760kW 400V 50Hz a.c Thrusters: 1 Thwart. FP thruster (f) Fuel: 97.0 (d.f.) 8.0pd
9083031 JYB114	**XPRESS** *ex* Lucky-3 *-2008* *ex* Elos *-2002* *ex* Redhawk *-2001* *ex* Nordblitz *-1998* **Sindbad For Marine Transport** - *Aqaba* *Jordan* Official number: 9	**121** 45 15	Class: IM (GL)	**1994-08 Henze Werft GmbH — Bremerhaven** Yd No: 1121 Loa 22.40 Br ex - Dght 1.352 Lbp 19.10 Br md 7.43 Dpth 2.40 Welded, 1 dk	**(A37B2PS) Passenger Ship** Passengers: unberthed: 114	**2 oil engines** reduction geared to sc. shafts driving 2 CP propellers Total Power: 1,464kW (1,990hp) 27.0kn MAN D2842LE 2 x Vee 4 Stroke 12 Cy. 128 x 142 each-732kW (995bhp) MAN Nutzfahrzeuge AG-Nuernberg AuxGen: 1 x 18kW a.c
9563316 3WEE9 -	**XUAN HIEU GROUP 19** - **Xuan Hieu Group JSC** - *Haiphong* *Vietnam* MMSI: 574916000	**1,599** 952 2,870	Class: VR	**2012-12 Minh Tuan Transport & Trading JSC — Truc Ninh** Yd No: TKT140-X1 Loa 79.57 Br ex 12.62 Dght 5.140 Lbp 75.37 Br md 12.60 Dpth 6.20 Welded, 1 dk	**(A21A2BC) Bulk Carrier** Grain: 3,512; Bale: 3,164 Compartments: 2 Ho, ER 2 Ha: (18.2 x 8.0)ER (19.3 x 8.0)	**1 oil engine** reduction geared to sc. shaft driving 1 FP propeller Total Power: 1,103kW (1,500hp) 10.0kn Chinese Std. Type 8300ZLC 1 x 4 Stroke 8 Cy. 300 x 380 1103kW (1500bhp) Zibo Diesel Engine Factory-China AuxGen: 2 x 84kW 380V a.c Fuel: 69.0 (d.f.)
9571791 3WJQ9 -	**XUAN HIEU GROUP 76** - **Agriculture Leasing Co I** Xuan Hieu Group JSC *Haiphong* *Vietnam* MMSI: 574001860	**1,599** 952 2,902	Class: VR	**2013-05 Minh Tuan Transport & Trading JSC — Truc Ninh** Yd No: TKT140-X3 Loa 79.57 Br ex 12.62 Dght 5.140 Lbp 75.37 Br md 12.60 Dpth 6.20 Welded, 1 dk	**(A31A2GX) General Cargo Ship** Grain: 3,512; Bale: 3,164 Compartments: 2 Ho, ER 2 Ha: (18.2 x 8.0)ER (19.3 x 8.0)	**1 oil engine** reduction geared to sc. shaft driving 1 FP propeller Total Power: 1,103kW (1,500hp) 10.0kn Chinese Std. Type 8300ZLC 1 x 4 Stroke 8 Cy. 300 x 380 1103kW (1500bhp) Zibo Diesel Engine Factory-China AuxGen: 2 x 80kW 400V a.c Fuel: 70.0
9548029 BIBD8 -	**XUAN JING** *ex* Ding Heng 12 *-2013* *ex* Yun Men Feng *-2010* **Shanghai Sanhan Shipping Co Ltd** - *Shanghai* *China* MMSI: 412380030	**1,956** 713 3,881 T/cm 12.3	Class: CC	**2009-09 Yangzhou Haichuan Shipyard — Yangzhou JS** Yd No: HC20 Loa 85.60 (BB) Br ex 12.62 Dght 5.400 Lbp 78.50 Br md 12.60 Dpth 6.60 Welded, 1 dk	**(A12B2TR) Chemical/Products Tanker** Double Hull (13F) Liq: 4,052; Liq (Oil): 2,621 Cargo Heating Coils Compartments: 8 Wing Ta (s.stl), 1 Slop Ta (s.stl), ER (s.stl) 8 Cargo Pump (s): 8x300m³/hr Manifold: Bow/CM: 40.2m Ice Capable	**1 oil engine** reduction geared to sc. shaft driving 1 FP propeller Total Power: 1,545kW (2,101hp) Chinese Std. Type 6320ZC 1 x 4 Stroke 6 Cy. 320 x 440 1545kW (2101bhp) Guangzhou Diesel Engine Factory CoLtd-China AuxGen: 3 x 150kW 400V a.c Fuel: 50.0 (d.f.) 140.0 (r.f.)
9634775 3WDI9 -	**XUAN LAM 10** - **Xuan Lam Co Ltd** - *Haiphong* *Vietnam*	**1,599** 1,014 3,190	Class: VR	**2011-06 Nguyen Phuc JSC — Xuan Truong** Yd No: HT-158.B3 Loa 79.99 Br ex 12.62 Dght 5.440 Lbp 74.80 Br md 12.60 Dpth 6.48 Welded, 1 dk	**(A31A2GX) General Cargo Ship** Grain: 3,735; Bale: 3,366 Compartments: 2 Ho, ER 2 Ha: ER 2 (18.6 x 7.6)	**1 oil engine** reduction geared to sc. shaft driving 1 FP propeller Total Power: 720kW (979hp) 11.0kn Chinese Std. Type CW8200ZC 1 x 4 Stroke 8 Cy. 200 x 270 720kW (979bhp) Weichai Power Co Ltd-China AuxGen: 2 x 75kW 380V a.c Fuel: 35.0
7515511 WCK7746 -	**XUAN LOC** *ex* Aquila *-2001* **Andy Dung Thien Le** - *Houston, TX* *United States of America* Official number: 551936	*117* 80 -		**1973 Superior Fabricators, Inc. — Bayou La Batre, Al** Yd No: 16 L reg 20.58 Br ex 6.71 Dght - Lbp - Br md - Dpth 3.56 Welded, 1 dk	**(B11A2FT) Trawler**	**1 oil engine** driving 1 FP propeller Total Power: 588kW (799hp) G.M. (Detroit Diesel) 12V-149 1 x Vee 2 Stroke 12 Cy. 146 x 146 588kW (799bhp) General Motors Detroit DieselAllison Divn-USA
9324021 ECIZ 3-GI-63-04	**XUAN MONCHO** - **Pesquerias Pixuetinas SL** - *Aviles* *Spain* MMSI: 224152340 Official number: 3-3/2004	**309** 149 -		**2005-06 Astilleros Ria de Aviles SL — Nieva** Yd No: 109 Loa 32.00 Br ex - Dght - Lbp 26.00 Br md 7.60 Dpth 3.60 Welded, 1 dk	**(B11B2FV) Fishing Vessel**	**1 oil engine** geared to sc. shaft driving 1 FP propeller Total Power: 552kW (750hp) 10.0kn GUASCOR F360TA-SP 1 x Vee 4 Stroke 12 Cy. 152 x 165 552kW (750bhp) Gutierrez Ascunce Corp (GUASCOR)-Spain
9349095 BIAD3 -	**XUAN NING** *ex* Akadimos *-2010* **Shanghai Sanhan Shipping Co Ltd** Shanghai Xuanrun Shipping Co Ltd *Shanghai* *China* MMSI: 413376120	**8,525** 3,829 11,974 T/cm 23.3	Class: CC	**2010-07 Jiujiang Yinxing Shipbuilding Co Ltd — Xingzi County JX** Yd No: YX005 Loa 134.85 (BB) Br ex 22.03 Dght 7.580 Lbp 126.00 Br md 22.00 Dpth 10.60 Welded, 1 dk	**(A12B2TR) Chemical/Products Tanker** Double Hull (13F) Liq: 13,897; Liq (Oil): 13,897 Cargo Heating Coils Compartments: 10 Wing Ta, ER, 2 Wing Slop Ta 10 Cargo Pump (s): 10x300m³/hr Manifold: Bow/CM: 74m Ice Capable	**1 oil engine** reduction geared to sc. shaft driving 1 FP propeller Total Power: 4,500kW (6,118hp) 13.0kn Wartsila 9L32 1 x 4 Stroke 9 Cy. 320 x 400 4500kW (6118bhp) Wartsila Finland Oy-Finland AuxGen: 2 x 670kW 400V 60Hz a.c Thrusters: 1 Thwart. FP thruster (f) Fuel: 104.0 (d.f.) 666.0 (r.f.)

8869103 *3WAF* -
XUAN PHU
ex Song Hong *-2012* *ex* Song Hong 01 *-2001*
Ahn Sang Co Ltd (Cong Ty Tnhh Anh Sang)
-
Haiphong *Vietnam*
MMSI: 574999537
Official number: VN-1206-VT

980 564 1,754 Class: VR

1991 Hanoi Shipyard — Hanoi
Rebuilt-2003
Loa 63.90 Br ex 10.97 Dght 4.600
Lbp 59.75 Br md 10.80 Dpth 5.60
Welded, 1 dk

(A31A2GX) General Cargo Ship
Grain: 1,006
Compartments: 2 Ho, ER
Cranes: 1x50t

1 oil engine driving 1 FP propeller
Total Power: 425kW (578hp) 10.0k
S.K.L. 8NVD36-1
1 x 4 Stroke 8 Cy. 240 x 360 425kW (578bhp)
SKL Motoren u. Systemtechnik AG-Magdeburg

8869115 *3WDE* -
XUAN PHU
ex Dong Hai 27 *-2012* *ex* Tam Phat 27 *-2005*
ex Song Hoa 01 *-2003*
Dong Hai JSC (Cong Ty Co Phan Thuong Mai Van Tai Bien Dong Hai)
-
Haiphong *Vietnam*
Official number: VN-1610-VT

238 158 499 Class: VR

1990 Kien An Shipbuilding Works — Haiphong
Loa 45.00 Br ex 7.42 Dght 2.700
Lbp 42.00 Br md 7.20 Dpth 3.25
Welded, 1 dk

(A31A2GX) General Cargo Ship
Grain: 311
Compartments: 2 Ho, ER
2 Ha: 2 (7.0 x 4.0)ER

1 oil engine reduction geared to sc. shaft driving 1 FP propeller
Total Power: 147kW (200hp) 8.0kn
Chinese Std. Type 6160A
1 x 4 Stroke 6 Cy. 160 x 225 147kW (200bhp) (new engine 2004)
Weifang Diesel Engine Factory-China
AuxGen: 1 x 7kW a.c
Fuel: 7.0

9588548 *XVID* -
XUAN THANH 18
Xuan Thanh Transport JSC
-
SatCom: Inmarsat C 457499928
Haiphong *Vietnam*
MMSI: 574000520

1,599 1,032 3,102 Class: VR

2010-08 Trung Bo Co Ltd — Giao Thuy
Yd No: VNB02-14
Loa 79.80 Br ex 12.62 Dght 5.300
Lbp 74.80 Br md 12.60 Dpth 6.48
Welded, 1 dk

(A21A2BC) Bulk Carrier
Grain: 3,799; Bale: 3,423
Compartments: 2 Ho, ER
2 Ha: ER 2 (18.6 x 7.6)

1 oil engine reduction geared to sc. shafts driving 1 FP propeller
Total Power: 735kW (999hp) 10.0kn
Chinese Std. Type LB6250ZLC
1 x 4 Stroke 6 Cy. 250 x 320 735kW (999bhp) (made 2008)
Zibo Diesel Engine Factory-China
AuxGen: 2 x 85kW 400V 50Hz a.c
Fuel: 50.0 (d.f.)

9215127 *BOEZ* -
XUAN WU HU
Dalian Ocean Shipping Co (COSCO DALIAN)
-
SatCom: Inmarsat B 341237210
Dalian, Liaoning *China*
MMSI: 412372000
Official number: 00Y4001

38,999 20,758 68,429 T/cm 66.0 Class: CC

2000-10 Dalian New Shipbuilding Heavy Industries Co Ltd — Dalian LN
Yd No: T680-1
Loa 229.00 (BB) Br ex - Dght 13.700
Lbp 219.00 Br md 32.20 Dpth 19.20
Welded, 1 dk

(A13A2TW) Crude/Oil Products Tanker
Double Hull (13F)
Liq: 71,443; Liq (Oil): 71,443
Cargo Heating Coils
Compartments: 1 Ta, ER, 10 Wing Ta, 2 Wing Slop Ta
3 Cargo Pump (s): 3x2000m³/hr
Manifold: Bow/CM: 111.4m
Ice Capable

1 oil engine driving 1 FP propeller
Total Power: 9,500kW (12,916hp) 14.6kn
MAN-B&W 5S60MC
1 x 2 Stroke 5 Cy. 600 x 2292 9500kW (12916bhp)
Dalian Marine Diesel Works-China
AuxGen: 3 x 720kW 450V 50Hz a.c
Fuel: 177.0 (d.f.) (Heating Coils) 1967.0 (r.f.)

9158379 *3FVC6* -
XUCHANGHAI
Xuchanghai Shipping Inc
COSCO Bulk Carrier Co Ltd (COSCO BULK)
SatCom: Inmarsat B 335422810
Panama *Panama*
MMSI: 354228000
Official number: 2356897CH

18,074 9,485 27,110 T/cm 38.9 Class: CC (AB)

1997-01 Hudong Shipbuilding Group — Shanghai
Yd No: H1228A
Loa 175.00 (BB) Br ex 26.48 Dght 9.816
Lbp 165.00 Br md 26.00 Dpth 13.90
Welded, 1 dk

(A21A2BC) Bulk Carrier
Grain: 37,996; Bale: 37,218
Compartments: 5 Ho, ER
5 Ha: (14.2 x 12.8)4 (19.2 x 14.4)ER
Cranes: 4x30t

1 oil engine driving 1 FP propeller
Total Power: 5,848kW (7,951hp) 14.0kn
B&W 5L50MC
1 x 2 Stroke 5 Cy. 500 x 1620 5848kW (7951bhp)
Hudong Shipyard-China

9183128 *EAQY* 3-VILL-11-
XUDEMIL
Pesquera Anpajo
-
Santa Eugenia de Ribeira *Spain*
MMSI: 224157780
Official number: 3-1/1998

222 - 122

1998-04 Astilleros Armon Burela SA — Burela
Yd No: 78
Loa - Br ex - Dght 3.200
Lbp 23.00 Br md 7.50 Dpth 3.50
Welded, 1 dk

(B11A2FS) Stern Trawler
Bale: 134

1 oil engine geared to sc. shaft driving 1 FP propeller
Total Power: 368kW (500hp) 9.5kn
Caterpillar
1 x 4 Stroke 368kW (500bhp)
Caterpillar Inc-USA

7525451 *BOWY* -
XUE HAI
Qingdao Ocean Shipping Co Ltd (COSCO QINGDAO)
-
SatCom: Inmarsat C 441255810
Qingdao, Shandong *China*
MMSI: 412179000

29,286 15,619 46,585 Class: (CC) (BV)

1977-11 Brodogradiliste '3 Maj' — Rijeka
Yd No: 580
Loa 212.86 (BB) Br ex - Dght 12.161
Lbp 199.86 Br md 28.00 Dpth 17.40
Welded, 1 dk

(A21A2BC) Bulk Carrier
Grain: 59,096
Compartments: 7 Ho, ER
7 Ha: 7 (12.6 x 14.2)
Cranes: 4x15t
Ice Capable

1 oil engine driving 1 FP propeller
Total Power: 10,297kW (14,000hp) 14.0kn
Sulzer 7RND76
1 x 2 Stroke 7 Cy. 760 x 1550 10297kW (14000bhp)
Tvornica Dizel Motora '3 Maj'-Yugoslavia
AuxGen: 3 x 416kW 400V 50Hz a.c

8203816 *3FVB3* -
XUE LIN
ex Snowmass *-2010* *ex* Keifu Maru *-1993*
HongKong Runsheng Shipping Co Ltd
Shandong Jinghai Industrial Group Co Ltd
SatCom: Inmarsat C 435276911
Panama *Panama*
MMSI: 354461000
Official number: 41939PEXT

4,677 2,726 5,539 Class: PD (NK)

1982-06 Fukuoka Shipbuilding Co Ltd — Fukuoka FO Yd No: 1095
Loa 108.61 (BB) Br ex 17.22 Dght 7.814
Lbp 99.00 Br md 17.20 Dpth 10.00
Welded, 2 dks

(A34A2GR) Refrigerated Cargo Ship
Ins: 2,452
Compartments: 3 Ho, ER
3 Ha: 3 (6.8 x 6.1)ER
Derricks: 8x5t

1 oil engine driving 1 FP propeller
Total Power: 5,149kW (7,001hp) 15.0kn
Mitsubishi 7UEC45/115H
1 x 2 Stroke 7 Cy. 450 x 1150 5149kW (7001bhp)
Kobe Hatsudoki KK-Japan
AuxGen: 3 x 400kW 445V 60Hz a.c
Fuel: 102.5 (d.f.) 967.5 (r.f.) 24.5pd

8877899 *BNSK* -
XUE LONG
ex Snow Dragon *-1995*
Government of The People's Republic of China (Polar Research Institute of China)
-
SatCom: Inmarsat C 441286310
Shanghai *China*
MMSI: 412863000

14,997 4,499 8,759 Class: CC (RS)

1993-06 OAO Khersonskiy Sudostroitelnyy Zavod — Kherson Yd No: 6003
Loa 166.43 Br ex 22.96 Dght 8.710
Lbp 156.44 Br md 22.60 Dpth 13.50
Welded, 2 dks

(B34C2SZ) Icebreaker/Research
Passengers: 128
Side door & ramp (s. a.)
Grain: 16,900; Bale: 15,060; Ins: 330
TEU 325 incl 20 ref C.
Compartments: 4 Ho, ER, 3 Tw Dk
6 Ha: 2 (25.6 x 7.8)4 (12.5 x 7.8)ER
Cranes: 4x25t
Ice Capable

1 oil engine driving 1 FP propeller
Total Power: 13,200kW (17,947hp) 16.5kn
B&W 8DKRN60/195
1 x 2 Stroke 8 Cy. 600 x 1950 13200kW (17947bhp)
AO Bryanskiy MashinostroitelnyyZavod (BMZ)-Bryansk

9482079 *BJZK* -
XUE SONG
Sinochem Shipping Co Ltd (Hainan)
Aoxing Ship Management (Shanghai) Ltd
Haikou, Hainan *China*
MMSI: 413332000

8,551 4,044 12,645 T/cm 22.7 Class: CC

2008-05 Zhejiang Changhong Shipbuilding Co Ltd — Wenling ZJ Yd No: 0601
Loa 134.85 (BB) Br ex 22.03 Dght 7.806
Lbp 126.83 Br md 22.00 Dpth 10.60
Welded, 1 dk

(A12B2TR) Chemical/Products Tanker
Double Hull (13F)
Liq: 14,403; Liq (Oil): 13,896
Cargo Heating Coils
Compartments: 10 Wing Ta, 2 Wing Slop Ta, ER
12 Cargo Pump (s): 2x100m³/hr, 10x300m³/hr
Manifold: Bow/CM: 62.8m
Ice Capable

1 oil engine driving 1 FP propeller
Total Power: 3,824kW (5,199hp) 13.0kn
Pielstick 8PC2-5L
1 x 4 Stroke 8 Cy. 400 x 460 3824kW (5199bhp)
Guangzhou Diesel Engine Factory CoLtd-China
AuxGen: 3 x 300kW 400V a.c
Thrusters: 1 Tunnel thruster (f)
Fuel: 189.0 (d.f.) 1058.0 (r.f.)

9411159 *BXYS* -
XUN LONG 4
Shenzhen Xunlong Passenger Shipping Ltd
-
Shenzhen, Guangdong *China*
MMSI: 413462220

438 139 25 Class: CC

2007-12 Wang Tak Engineering & Shipbuilding Co Ltd — Hong Kong Yd No: Y2602
Loa 33.00 Br ex - Dght 1.030
Lbp 30.59 Br md 8.81 Dpth 2.70
Welded, 1 dk

(A37B2PS) Passenger Ship
Passengers: unberthed: 232

2 oil engines reduction geared to sc. shafts driving 2 Water jets
Total Power: 2,686kW (3,652hp) 26.0kn
M.T.U. 16V2000M70
2 x Vee 4 Stroke 16 Cy. 130 x 150 each-1343kW (1826bhp)
MTU Friedrichshafen GmbH-Friedrichshafen
AuxGen: 2 x 75kW 400V a.c

9658587 *BYGW* -
XUN LONG 5
Shenzhen Xunlong Passenger Shipping Ltd
-
Shenzhen, Guangdong *China*

282 94 40 Class: CC

2012-03 Afai Southern Shipyard (Panyu Guangzhou) Ltd — Guangzhou GD
Yd No: 028
Loa 34.00 Br ex - Dght 1.350
Lbp 32.15 Br md 8.50 Dpth 3.05
Welded, 1 dk

(A37B2PS) Passenger Ship
Hull Material: Aluminium Alloy
Passengers: unberthed: 188

2 oil engines reduction geared to sc. shafts driving 2 Water jets
Total Power: 2,100kW (2,856hp) 28.0kn
M.T.U. 16V2000M70
2 x Vee 4 Stroke 16 Cy. 130 x 150 each-1050kW (1428bhp)
MTU Friedrichshafen GmbH-Friedrichshafen
AuxGen: 2 x 86kW 400V a.c

9658599 *BYIC* -
XUN LONG 6
Shenzhen Xunlong Passenger Shipping Ltd
-
Shenzhen, Guangdong *China*

282 94 40 Class: CC

2012-04 Afai Southern Shipyard (Panyu Guangzhou) Ltd — Guangzhou GD
Yd No: 029
Loa 34.00 (BB) Br ex - Dght 1.350
Lbp 32.15 Br md 8.50 Dpth 3.05
Welded, 1 dk

(A37B2PS) Passenger Ship
Hull Material: Aluminium Alloy
Passengers: unberthed: 188

2 oil engines reduction geared to sc. shafts driving 2 Water jets
Total Power: 2,100kW (2,856hp) 28.0kn
M.T.U. 16V2000M70
2 x Vee 4 Stroke 16 Cy. 130 x 150 each-1050kW (1428bhp)
MTU Friedrichshafen GmbH-Friedrichshafen
AuxGen: 2 x 86kW 400V a.c

9119347 *BXBL* -
XUN LONG No. 1
ex Xunlong *-1995*
Shenzhen Xunlong Passenger Shipping Ltd
-
Shenzhen, Guangdong *China*
MMSI: 412469240

505 172 37 Class: CC (NV)

1995-09 Rosendal Verft AS — Rosendal
Yd No: 266
Loa 36.68 Br ex - Dght 1.520
Lbp 31.60 Br md 9.60 Dpth 3.67
Welded, 1 dk

(A37B2PS) Passenger Ship
Hull Material: Aluminium Alloy
Passengers: unberthed: 308

4 oil engines geared to sc. shafts driving 2 CP propellers
Total Power: 2,688kW (3,656hp) 35.0kn
M.T.U. 12V183TE92
4 x Vee 4 Stroke 12 Cy. 128 x 142 each-672kW (914bhp)
MTU Friedrichshafen GmbH-Friedrichshafen

185097 XEZ	**XUN LONG No. 2** **Shenzhen Xunlong Passenger Shipping Ltd** - *Shenzhen, Guangdong* *China* MMSI: 412469250	**531** 159 33	Class: CC	**1998-08 Batservice Holding AS — Mandal** Yd No: 18 Loa 38.00 Br ex - Dght 1.920 Lbp 34.75 Br md 11.20 Dpth 3.90 Welded	**(A37B2PS) Passenger Ship** Hull Material: Aluminium Alloy Passengers: unberthed: 354	**4 oil engines** geared to sc. shafts driving 2 CP propellers Total Power: 3,120kW (4,240hp) 33.0kn M.T.U. 12V2000M70 4 x Vee 4 Stroke 12 Cy. 130 x 150 each-780kW (1060bhp) MTU Friedrichshafen GmbH-Friedrichshafen AuxGen: 2 x 97kW a.c
411147 XZA	**XUNLONG 3** **Shenzhen Xunlong Passenger Shipping Ltd** - *Shenzhen, Guangdong* *China* MMSI: 413461990	**438** 139 25	Class: CC	**2007-08 Wang Tak Engineering & Shipbuilding Co Ltd — Hong Kong** Yd No: Y2601 Loa 33.00 Br ex - Dght 1.030 Lbp 30.59 Br md 8.81 Dpth 2.70 Welded, 1 dk	**(A37B2PS) Passenger Ship** Passengers: unberthed: 232	**2 oil engines** reduction geared to sc. shafts driving 2 Water jets Total Power: 2,686kW (3,652hp) 26.0kn M.T.U. 16V2000M70 2 x Vee 4 Stroke 16 Cy. 130 x 150 each-1343kW (1826bhp) MTU Friedrichshafen GmbH-Friedrichshafen AuxGen: 2 x 75kW 400V a.c
308675 SB3402	**XUTRA BHUM** **Regional Container Lines Public Co Ltd** RCL Shipmanagement Pte Ltd *Bangkok* *Thailand* MMSI: 567318000 Official number: 490000159	**23,922** 9,737 30,832	Class: NK	**2005-08 Mitsubishi Heavy Industries Ltd. — Shimonoseki** Yd No: 1108 Loa 194.90 (BB) Br ex 30.63 Dght 11.425 Lbp 186.00 Br md 30.60 Dpth 16.80 Welded, 1 dk	**(A33A2CC) Container Ship (Fully Cellular)** TEU 2378 incl 240 ref C.	**1 oil engine** driving 1 FP propeller Total Power: 20,580kW (27,981hp) 21.5kn Mitsubishi 7UEC68LSE 1 x 2 Stroke 7 Cy. 680 x 2690 20580kW (27981bhp) Mitsubishi Heavy Industries Ltd-Japan AuxGen: 3 x 1400kW 450/230V 60Hz a.c Thrusters: 1 Tunnel thruster (f) Fuel: 2810.0
329071 CHX -VI-720-0	**XUXO** **Pesquera Alba SL** - *Vigo* *Spain* MMSI: 224578000 Official number: 3-20/2004	**238** 71 -		**2005-02 Astilleros Armon Vigo SA — Vigo** Yd No: 46 Loa 29.78 Br ex - Dght 3.100 Lbp 23.00 Br md 7.50 Dpth 3.50 Welded, 1 dk	**(B11B2FV) Fishing Vessel** Grain: 105	**1 oil engine** geared to sc. shaft driving 1 FP propeller Total Power: 456kW (620hp) 11.5kn Caterpillar 3508TA 1 x Vee 4 Stroke 8 Cy. 170 x 190 456kW (620bhp) Caterpillar Inc-USA
589243 VUN	**XUYEN A 18** **Xuyen A Co Ltd** - SatCom: Inmarsat C 457499918 *Haiphong* *Vietnam* MMSI: 574012592	**1,599** 1,027 3,101	Class: VR	**2010-06 Nguyen Phuc JSC — Xuan Truong** Yd No: HT-159-02 Loa 79.20 Br ex 12.62 Dght 5.300 Lbp 74.80 Br md 12.60 Dpth 6.48 Welded, 1 dk	**(A21A2BC) Bulk Carrier** Grain: 3,780; Bale: 3,406 Compartments: 2 Ho, ER 2 Ha: ER 2 (18.6 x 7.6)	**1 oil engine** reduction geared to sc. shaft driving 1 FP propeller Total Power: 1,103kW (1,500hp) 10.0kn Chinese Std. Type 8300ZLC 1 x 4 Stroke 8 Cy. 300 x 380 1103kW (1500bhp) Zibo Diesel Engine Factory-China AuxGen: 2 x 75kW 400V 50Hz a.c Fuel: 100.0 (d.f.)
721052 GAZ -0559	**XX SYEZD VLKSM** **Okeanrybflot JSC (A/O 'Okeanrybflot')** - *Petropavlovsk-Kamchatskiy* *Russia* MMSI: 273843020 Official number: 851851	**4,407** 1,322 1,810	Class: RS	**1987-05 GP Chernomorskiy Sudostroitelnyy Zavod — Nikolayev** Yd No: 559 Loa 104.50 Br ex 16.03 Dght 5.900 Lbp 96.40 Br md 16.00 Dpth 10.20 Welded, 2 dks	**(B11A2FG) Factory Stern Trawler** Bale: 420; Ins: 2,219 Ice Capable	**2 oil engines** geared to sc. shaft driving 1 CP propeller Total Power: 5,148kW (7,000hp) 16.1kn Russkiy 6CHN40/46 2 x 4 Stroke 6 Cy. 400 x 460 each-2574kW (3500bhp) Mashinostroitelnyy Zavod"Russkiy-Dizel"-Leningrad AuxGen: 2 x 1600kW 220/380V 50Hz a.c, 3 x 200kW 220/380V 50Hz a.c Fuel: 1226.0 (d.f.)
721040 GPK	**XXVII SYEZD KPSS** **Okeanrybflot JSC (A/O 'Okeanrybflot')** - *Petropavlovsk-Kamchatskiy* *Russia* MMSI: 273841020 Official number: 841686	**4,407** 1,322 1,810	Class: RS	**1985-11 GP Chernomorskiy Sudostroitelnyy Zavod — Nikolayev** Yd No: 550 Loa 104.50 Br ex 16.03 Dght 5.900 Lbp 96.40 Br md 16.00 Dpth 10.20 Welded, 2 dks	**(B11A2FG) Factory Stern Trawler** Bale: 420; Ins: 2,219 Ice Capable	**2 oil engines** reduction geared to sc. shaft driving 1 CP propeller Total Power: 5,148kW (7,000hp) 16.1kn Russkiy 6CHN40/46 2 x 4 Stroke 6 Cy. 400 x 460 each-2574kW (3500bhp) Mashinostroitelnyy Zavod"Russkiy-Dizel"-Leningrad AuxGen: 2 x 1600kW 220/380V 50Hz a.c, 3 x 200kW 220/380V 50Hz a.c Fuel: 1227.0 (d.f.)
555930 JGT6	**XZIBER** *ex* Laurana *-2013* *ex* Maralisa *-2002* *ex* Nedlloyd 80 *-1990* *ex* Aldabi *-1977* *ex* Hendrick *-1976* **Mayfly Corp** - *Phnom Penh* *Cambodia* MMSI: 515089000 Official number: 1371093	**1,370** 558 2,094		**1971 N.V. Scheepswerf en Machinefabriek "Vahali" — Gendt** Yd No: 438 Loa 95.00 Br ex - Dght 3.370 Lbp - Br md 9.55 Dpth 6.05 Welded, 1 dk	**(A13B2TP) Products Tanker**	**1 oil engine** driving 1 Propeller Total Power: 853kW (1,160hp) MaK 1 x 853kW (1160bhp) MaK Maschinenbau GmbH-Kiel
106953 TDZ	**Y. S. F. 101** **Yamuna Shipping Ltd** - *Mumbai* *India* Official number: 1950	*115* 51 -	Class: (IR)	**1981-12 Machinefabriek D.E. Gorter B.V. — Hoogezand** (Hull) Yd No: 81-7006 **1981-12 B.V. Scheepswerf Damen — Gorinchem** Yd No: 4103 Loa 23.50 Br ex 6.53 Dght 2.501 Lbp 21.01 Br md 6.51 Dpth 3.36 Welded, 1 dk	**(B11A2FT) Trawler**	**1 oil engine** geared to sc. shaft driving 1 FP propeller Total Power: 268kW (364hp) Caterpillar 3408TA 1 x Vee 4 Stroke 8 Cy. 137 x 152 268kW (364bhp) Caterpillar Tractor Co-USA
106965 TFB	**Y. S. F. 102** **Yamuna Shipping Ltd** - *Mumbai* *India* Official number: 1951	*115* 51 -	Class: (IR)	**1981-12 Machinefabriek D.E. Gorter B.V. — Hoogezand** (Hull) Yd No: 81-7007 **1981-12 B.V. Scheepswerf Damen — Gorinchem** Yd No: 4104 Loa 23.50 Br ex 6.53 Dght 2.501 Lbp 21.01 Br md 6.51 Dpth 3.36 Welded	**(B11A2FT) Trawler**	**1 oil engine** geared to sc. shaft driving 1 FP propeller Total Power: 268kW (364hp) Caterpillar 3408TA 1 x Vee 4 Stroke 8 Cy. 137 x 152 268kW (364bhp) Caterpillar Tractor Co-USA
108638 5M	**YA CHUKLI BOLONG** **Government of The Republic of Gambia (Ministry of Agriculture & Natural Resourses)** - *Banjul* *Gambia* Official number: 100014	*128* 35 106	Class: (LR) ✠ Classed LR until 2/3/84	**1982-04 Carl B Hoffmanns Maskinfabrik A/S — Esbjerg** (Hull) Yd No: 43 **1982-04 Soren Larsen & Sonners Skibsvaerft A/S — Nykobing Mors** Yd No: 150 Loa 24.62 Br ex 6.76 Dght 3.055 Lbp 21.21 Br md 6.71 Dpth 3.31 Welded, 1 dk	**(B11A2FS) Stern Trawler** Ins: 72 Compartments: 1 Ho, ER 1 Ha:	**1 oil engine** reverse reduction geared to sc. shaft driving 1 CP propeller Total Power: 405kW (551hp) Alpha 405-26VO 1 x 2 Stroke 5 Cy. 260 x 400 405kW (551bhp) B&W Alpha Diesel A/S-Denmark AuxGen: 2 x 36kW 380V 50Hz a.c
223115 03971	**YA HAYDAR** *ex* Ya Ali *-2005* *ex* Marc Trader *-2003* *ex* Marc L *-1996* **Badran Shipping Services Ltd** Seas Ark SA *Panama* *Panama* MMSI: 371150000 Official number: 3263407A	**1,301** 446 1,501	Class: PM (GL)	**1983-11 Hermann Suerken GmbH & Co. KG — Papenburg** Yd No: 319 Loa 74.88 (BB) Br ex 10.60 Dght 3.366 Lbp 70.52 Br md 10.51 Dpth 5.70 Welded, 2 dks	**(A31A2GX) General Cargo Ship** Grain: 2,351; Bale: 2,310 Compartments: 1 Ho, ER 1 Ha: (46.8 x 8.2)ER	**1 oil engine** with clutches, flexible couplings & sr reverse geared to sc. shaft driving 1 FP propeller Total Power: 441kW (600hp) 10.3kn Deutz RBA6M528 1 x 4 Stroke 6 Cy. 220 x 280 441kW (600bhp) Kloeckner Humboldt Deutz AG-West Germany AuxGen: 3 x 93kW 380V 50Hz a.c Thrusters: 1 Thwart. FP thruster (f)
043017 0BY	**YA HE** *ex* Dainty River *-2008* **COSCO Container Lines Co Ltd (COSCON)** - *Shanghai* *China* MMSI: 413450000	**22,746** 11,964 33,577 T/cm 44.4	Class: CC (NV) (AB)	**1993-04 Halla Engineering & Heavy Industries Ltd — Incheon** Yd No: 196 Loa 187.60 (BB) Br ex 28.43 Dght 11.217 Lbp 178.00 Br md 28.40 Dpth 15.60 Welded, 1 dk	**(A33A2CC) Container Ship (Fully Cellular)** Grain: 42,776 TEU 1923 C Ho 914 TEU C Dk 1009 TEU incl 60 ref C. Compartments: ER, 5 Cell Ho 5 Ha: ER	**1 oil engine** driving 1 FP propeller Total Power: 15,712kW (21,362hp) 18.0kn B&W 6L70MC 1 x 2 Stroke 6 Cy. 700 x 2268 15712kW (21362bhp) Hyundai Heavy Industries Co Ltd-South Korea AuxGen: 3 x 960kW 220/440V 60Hz a.c Thrusters: 1 Thwart. CP thruster (f)
627969	**YA HOSSEIN** *ex* Sanwa Maru *-2011* **Hadi Khedri**	*199* - 621		**1986-07 YK Furumoto Tekko Zosensho — Osakikamijima** Loa 56.74 Br ex - Dght 2.820 Lbp 52.00 Br md 9.80 Dpth 4.95 Welded, 1 dk	**(A31A2GX) General Cargo Ship** Bale: 1,240	**1 oil engine** geared to sc. shaft driving 1 FP propeller Total Power: 588kW (799hp) 11.0kn Hanshin 6LU26G 1 x 4 Stroke 6 Cy. 260 x 440 588kW (799bhp) The Hanshin Diesel Works Ltd-Japan
150242 KY	**YA LONG JIANG** *ex* Far Eastern Express *-2010* **SDIC Far East Shipping Co Ltd** - *Yangpu, Hainan* *China* MMSI: 413867000	**35,874** 23,407 69,310 T/cm 64.4	Class: ZC (NK) (CR)	**1992-12 Imabari Shipbuilding Co Ltd — Marugame KG (Marugame Shipyard)** Yd No: 1204 Loa 224.98 (BB) Br ex - Dght 13.278 Lbp 215.00 Br md 32.20 Dpth 18.30 Welded, 1 dk	**(A21A2BC) Bulk Carrier** Grain: 82,025 Compartments: 7 Ho, ER 7 Ha: (13.0 x 12.8)4 (17.9 x 14.4) (16.3 x 14.4) (14.7 x 14.4)ER	**1 oil engine** driving 1 FP propeller Total Power: 8,827kW (12,001hp) 14.2kn Sulzer 6RTA62 1 x 2 Stroke 6 Cy. 620 x 2150 8827kW (12001bhp) Mitsubishi Heavy Industries Ltd-Japan AuxGen: 2 x 480kW 450V 60Hz a.c Fuel: 2120.0 (r.f.)

IMO / Call sign	Name / Owner / Manager	Tonnage	Class	Builder / Dimensions	Type / Cargo	Machinery
9360398 *VRCK5* -	**YA LONG WAN** **Yalongwan Maritime Co Ltd** COSCO Southern Asphalt Shipping Co Ltd *Hong Kong* *Hong Kong* MMSI: 477633800 Official number: HK-1818	**5,530** 1,659 6,012	Class: LR ✠ **100A1** SS 01/2012 Double Hull oil and asphalt tanker, carriage of oils with a FP exceeding 60 degree C, cargo temp. 200 degree C, in independent tanks, SG 1.04 t/m3, PV+0.21 bar gauge, ESP LI ✠ **LMC** **UMS** Eq.Ltr: X; Cable: 490.4/46.0 U3 (a)	**2007-01 Zhejiang Shipbuilding Co Ltd — Ningbo ZJ** Yd No: 05-135 Loa 106.84 (BB) Br ex 17.60 Dght 6.450 Lbp 101.50 Br md 17.60 Dpth 10.10 Welded, 1 dk	**(A13A2TV) Crude Oil Tanker** Double Hull (13F) Liq: 5,680; Liq (Oil): 5,680; Asphalt: 5,880 Cargo Heating Coils Compartments: 8 Wing Ta, ER	**1 oil engine** driving 1 FP propeller Total Power: 4,440kW (6,037hp) 13.5k MAN-B&W 6S35M 1 x 2 Stroke 6 Cy. 350 x 1400 4440kW (6037bhp) Yichang Marine Diesel Engine Co Ltd-China AuxGen: 3 x 360kW 450V 60Hz a.c Boilers: TOH (ex.g.) 10.2kgf/cm² (10.0bar), TOH (o.f.) 10.2kgf/cm² (10.0bar) Fuel: 76.0 (d.f.) 422.0 (r.f.)
9272591 *BATI* -	**YA LU JIANG** **Dandong Jifa Shipping Co Ltd** Dandong Marine Shipping Co Ltd *Dalian, Liaoning* *China* MMSI: 412204480 Official number: 04U1004	**5,250** 2,976 7,436	Class: CC	**2004-02 Huanghai Shipbuilding Co Ltd — Rongcheng SD** Yd No: Y-19 Loa 110.00 Br ex - Dght 6.500 Lbp 103.30 Br md 19.70 Dpth 8.50 Welded, 1 dk	**(A31A2GX) General Cargo Ship** Grain: 8,767 TEU 538 C Ho 181 TEU C Dk 357 TEU. Compartments: 3 Ho, ER 3 Ha: 2 (25.4 x 15.0)ER (19.5 x 15.0) Ice Capable	**2 oil engines** reduction geared to sc. shafts driving 2 FP propellers Total Power: 2,940kW (3,998hp) 12.5k Chinese Std. Type LB8250ZL 2 x 4 Stroke 8 Cy. 250 x 320 each-1470kW (1999bhp) Zibo Diesel Engine Factory-China AuxGen: 3 x 150kW 400V a.c
7823762 *BXGA* -	**YA PING** *ex Shinshu Maru -2005* **Tianjin Southwest Maritime Ltd** - *Fangchenggang, Guangxi* *China*	**734** 411 750 T/cm 4.7	Class: (CC) (NK)	**1979-02 Sanyo Zosen K.K. — Onomichi** Yd No: 773 Loa 61.80 Br ex - Dght 3.901 Lbp 56.22 Br md 10.00 Dpth 4.40 Riveted\Welded, 1 dk	**(A11B2TG) LPG Tanker** Liq (Gas): 1,157 2 x Gas Tank (s); 2 independent (C.mn.stl) sph horizontal 2 Cargo Pump (s): 2x300m³/hr Manifold: Bow/CM: 27m	**1 oil engine** driving 1 FP propeller Total Power: 1,177kW (1,600hp) 12.3k Akasaka DM3 1 x 4 Stroke 6 Cy. 330 x 500 1177kW (1600bhp) Akasaka Tekkosho KK (Akasaka DieselLtd)-Japan Fuel: 14.5 (d.f.) 61.0 (r.f.) 5.0pd
9086978 *BRWU* -	**YA TAI 1** *ex Paragon -2009 ex Oceanic Enterprise -2004* **Chaozhou Yatai Shipping Co Ltd** China Shipping International Shipmanagement Co Ltd *Chaozhou, Guangdong* *China* MMSI: 413684000	**38,205** 24,113 71,259 T/cm 42.2	Class: CC (NK)	**1995-01 Namura Shipbuilding Co Ltd — Imari SG** Yd No: 927 Loa 225.00 (BB) Br ex - Dght 13.652 Lbp 217.00 Br md 32.20 Dpth 18.80 Welded, 1 dk	**(A21A2BC) Bulk Carrier** Grain: 85,011 Compartments: 7 Ho, ER 7 Ha: (16.6 x 13.2)6 (16.6 x 14.9)ER	**1 oil engine** driving 1 FP propeller Total Power: 7,503kW (10,201hp) 13.8k Sulzer 6RTA6 1 x 2 Stroke 6 Cy. 620 x 2150 7503kW (10201bhp) Mitsubishi Heavy Industries Ltd-Japan
9568160 *BRWA* -	**YA TAI 2** **Chaozhou Yatai Shipping Co Ltd** China Shipping International Shipmanagement Co Ltd SatCom: Inmarsat C 441205713 *Chaozhou, Guangdong* *China* MMSI: 412057000	**41,303** 26,050 76,022 T/cm 68.6	Class: CC	**2012-02 Hudong-Zhonghua Shipbuilding (Group) Co Ltd — Shanghai** Yd No: H1611A Loa 225.00 (BB) Br ex - Dght 14.200 Lbp 217.00 Br md 32.26 Dpth 19.70 Welded, 1 dk	**(A21A2BC) Bulk Carrier** Grain: 90,540; Bale: 89,882 Compartments: 7 Ho, ER 7 Ha: 6 (14.6 x 15.0)ER (14.6 x 13.2)	**1 oil engine** driving 1 FP propeller Total Power: 10,000kW (13,596hp) 14.5k MAN-B&W 5S60MC-C 1 x 2 Stroke 5 Cy. 600 x 2400 10000kW (13596bhp) Hudong Heavy Machinery Co Ltd-China AuxGen: 3 x 570kW 450V a.c
9580481 *BRWB* -	**YA TAI 3** **Chaozhou Yatai Shipping Co Ltd** China Shipping International Shipmanagement Co Ltd SatCom: Inmarsat C 441227411 *Chaozhou, Guangdong* *China* MMSI: 412274000	**41,303** 26,050 76,037 T/cm 68.6	Class: CC	**2012-05 Hudong-Zhonghua Shipbuilding (Group) Co Ltd — Shanghai** Yd No: H1612A Loa 225.00 (BB) Br ex - Dght 14.267 Lbp 217.00 Br md 32.26 Dpth 19.70 Welded, 1 dk	**(A21A2BC) Bulk Carrier** Grain: 90,540; Bale: 89,882 Compartments: 7 Ho, ER 7 Ha: 6 (14.6 x 15.0)ER (14.6 x 13.2)	**1 oil engine** driving 1 FP propeller Total Power: 10,000kW (13,596hp) 14.5k MAN-B&W 5S60MC-C 1 x 2 Stroke 5 Cy. 600 x 2400 10000kW (13596bhp) Hudong Heavy Machinery Co Ltd-China AuxGen: 3 x 570kW 450V a.c Fuel: 164.0 (d.f.) 2709.0 (r.f.)
7907697 *C6QB6* -	**YA TOIVO** *ex Challenger -2000* **Sea View Shipping Ltd** ARGO Ship Management & Services Srl SatCom: Inmarsat C 430897110 *Nassau* *Bahamas* MMSI: 308971000 Official number: 731052	**9,111** 2,733 2,124	Class: RI (LR) ✠	**1984-07 Scott Lithgow Ltd. — Greenock** Yd No: 753 Converted From: Diving Tender-2000 Lengthened & Widened Loa 148.00 (BB) Br ex - Dght 5.671 Lbp 128.50 Br md 24.00 Dpth 10.88 Welded, 3 dks	**(B35C2SM) Mining Vessel**	**5 diesel electric oil engines** driving 5 gen. each 2500kW 3300V a.c Connecting to 2 elec. motors each (1250kW) driving 2 Voith-Schneider propellers Total Power: 13,120kW (17,840hp) 15.0k Ruston 16RKC 5 x Vee 4 Stroke 16 Cy. 254 x 305 each-2624kW (3568bhp Ruston Diesels Ltd.-Newton-le-Willows AuxGen: 2 x 750kW 440V 60Hz a.c Thrusters: 3 Thwart. CP thruster (f)
9203992 *BURC* -	**YA ZHOU XIONG SHI** *ex Asia Lion -2009* **Nanjing Tanker Corp** - *Shanghai* *China* MMSI: 413804000	**23,357** 10,497 33,499 T/cm 50.6	Class: CC (BV)	**1999-05 Bohai Shipyard — Huludao LN** Yd No: 505-2 Loa 180.44 (BB) Br ex - Dght 9.415 Lbp 171.20 Br md 32.20 Dpth 14.60 Welded, 1 dk	**(A13B2TP) Products Tanker** Double Hull (13F) Liq: 38,549; Liq (Oil): 38,549 Compartments: 9 Ta, ER 2 Cargo Pump (s): 2x1650m³/hr Manifold: Bow/CM: 92m Ice Capable	**1 oil engine** driving 1 FP propeller Total Power: 7,355kW (10,000hp) 14.0k Sulzer 6RTA5 1 x 2 Stroke 6 Cy. 520 x 1800 7355kW (10000bhp) Yichang Marine Diesel Engine Co Ltd-China
1000291 *ZCPK8* -	**YAAKUN** *ex Al Menwar -2006* **Aspin Holdings Ltd** *George Town* *Cayman Islands (British)* MMSI: 319007000 Official number: 739164	**986** 295 555	Class: LR ✠ **100A1** SS 06/2012 Yacht ✠ **LMC**	**1987-11 Cantiere Navale Nicolini S.r.l. — Ancona** Yd No: 1871 Loa 61.78 Br ex 9.77 Dght 4.280 Lbp 56.28 Br md - Dpth 5.85 Welded, 1 dk	**(X11A2YP) Yacht**	**2 oil engines** driving 2 FP propellers Total Power: 5,580kW (7,586hp) M.T.U. 16V95 2 x Vee 4 Stroke 16 Cy. 230 x 230 each-2790kW (3793bhp MTU Friedrichshafen GmbH-Friedrichshafen Fuel: 120.0 (d.f.)
9015797 *XYMT* -	**YAAN BYAE** *ex Ocean Brave -2011* **Star Fleet Management SA** Far-East Transport Co Ltd *Yangon* *Myanmar* MMSI: 506105000	**5,484** 2,135 6,950	Class: BV	**1991-03 Hakata Zosen K.K. — Imabari** Yd No: 515 Loa 97.95 Br ex - Dght 7.490 Lbp 89.97 Br md 18.22 Dpth 13.01 Welded, 2 dks	**(A31A2GX) General Cargo Ship** Grain: 12,850; Bale: 11,640 Compartments: 2 Ho, ER, 2 Tw Dk 2 Ha: 2 (24.5 x 11.0)ER Cranes: 1x52t; Derricks: 2x20t	**1 oil engine** driving 1 FP propeller Total Power: 2,427kW (3,300hp) 14.6k Hanshin 6EL4 1 x 4 Stroke 6 Cy. 400 x 800 2427kW (3300bhp) The Hanshin Diesel Works Ltd-Japan AuxGen: 3 x 520kW 100/440V 60Hz a.c
8960751 *4RBY* -	**YAANIK** *ex Penguin Pride -2011* *ex Merlimau Pride -2011* **GAC Marine Services Pvt Ltd** GAC Shipping Ltd *Colombo* *Sri Lanka* MMSI: 417222338	**111** 33 -	Class: BV IR (Class contemplated)	**1994 Seaspray Boats Pty Ltd — Fremantle WA** Yd No: E100 Loa 21.46 Br ex - Dght 1.600 Lbp - Br md 6.44 Dpth 2.43 Welded, 1 dk	**(A37B2PS) Passenger Ship** Hull Material: Aluminium Alloy	**2 oil engines** geared to sc. shafts driving 2 FP propellers Total Power: 1,220kW (1,658hp) M.T.U. 12V183TE7 2 x Vee 4 Stroke 12 Cy. 128 x 142 each-610kW (829bhp) MTU Friedrichshafen GmbH-Friedrichshafen
7828774 - -	**YABLONOVSKIY** **Vostokshipsupport Co Ltd** -	**739** 221 350	Class: (RS)	**1979-09 Yaroslavskiy Sudostroitelnyy Zavod — Yaroslavl** Yd No: 339 Loa 53.75 (BB) Br ex 10.72 Dght 4.290 Lbp 47.92 Br md - Dpth 6.00 Welded, 1 dk	**(B11A2FS) Stern Trawler** Ins: 218 Compartments: 1 Ho, ER 2 Ha: 2 (1.6 x 1.6) Derricks: 2x3.3t	**1 oil engine** driving 1 CP propeller Total Power: 971kW (1,320hp) 12.8k S.K.L. 8NVD48A-2 1 x 4 Stroke 8 Cy. 320 x 480 971kW (1320bhp) VEB Schwermaschinenbau "KarlLiebknecht" (SKL)-Magdeburg Thrusters: 1 Thwart. FP thruster (f); 1 Tunnel thruster (a)
8660478 *XCRZ9* -	**YACATECUTLI** **Arrendadora Ve Por Mas SA de CV** Naviera Magna SA de CV *Puerto Juarez* *Mexico* MMSI: 345110011 Official number: 2301487021-6	**299** 91 -		**2010-06 Midship Marine, Inc. — New Orleans, La** Yd No: 303 Loa 37.98 Br ex 7.92 Dght 1.370 Lbp 35.20 Br md 7.62 Dpth 3.20 Welded, 1 dk	**(A37B2PS) Passenger Ship** Hull Material: Aluminium Alloy Passengers: unberthed: 450	**4 oil engines** reduction geared to sc. shafts driving 4 Propellers Total Power: 1,796kW (2,440hp) Caterpillar 341 4 x Vee 4 Stroke 12 Cy. 137 x 152 each-449kW (610bhp) Caterpillar Inc-USA
9552587 *JD3186* -	**YACHIHO MARU** **Techno Chubu Co Ltd** - *Nagoya, Aichi* *Japan* Official number: 141432	*199* - -		**2011-07 Niigata Shipbuilding & Repair Inc — Niigata NI** Yd No: 0046 Loa 33.61 Br ex - Dght 2.950 Lbp 29.00 Br md 9.70 Dpth 3.93 Welded, 1 dk	**(B32A2ST) Tug**	**2 oil engines** reduction geared to sc. shafts driving 2 Propellers Total Power: 3,676kW (4,998hp) Niigata 6L28H 2 x 4 Stroke 6 Cy. 280 x 370 each-1838kW (2499bhp) Niigata Engineering Co Ltd-Japan
9459802 *JD2508* -	**YACHIYO MARU** **Itsuwa Kaiun YK** - *Amakusa, Kumamoto* *Japan* Official number: 140643	*373* - 852		**2007-12 Koa Sangyo KK — Marugame KG** Yd No: 635 Loa 55.91 Br ex - Dght 3.870 Lbp 51.00 Br md 9.20 Dpth 4.00 Welded, 1 dk	**(A12A2TC) Chemical Tanker** Double Hull (13F)	**1 oil engine** reduction geared to sc. shaft driving 1 FP propeller Total Power: 882kW (1,199hp) 10.0k Hanshin LH26 1 x 4 Stroke 6 Cy. 260 x 440 882kW (1199bhp) The Hanshin Diesel Works Ltd-Japan

ID	Name / Owner	Tonnage	Class	Builder / Dimensions	Type	Machinery
088603 *L6323*	**YACHIYO MARU** **Kokoku Kisen YK** - *Kure, Hiroshima* *Japan* Official number: 134898	*145* - 1,200		**1994-12 Shinhama Dockyard Co. Ltd. — Tamano** Yd No: 263 Loa 39.21 Br ex - Dght - Lbp - Br md 7.00 Dpth 3.00 Welded, 1 dk	**(A13B2TP) Products Tanker**	**1 oil engine** driving 1 FP propeller Total Power: 294kW (400hp) 9.5kn Yanmar 6M-HTS 1 x 4 Stroke 6 Cy. 200 x 240 294kW (400bhp) Yanmar Diesel Engine Co Ltd-Japan
101704 *6E2832*	**YACHT 1 VETTATH** *ex* Borcos 14 *-2008* **Yacht International Co LLC** Yacht International Shipping Agency & Trading Co LLC *Sharjah* *United Arab Emirates* MMSI: 470638000 Official number: 5877	**106** 31 66	Class: RI (AB)	**1994-04 Sarawak Slipways Sdn Bhd — Miri** Yd No: 177 Loa 22.00 Br ex - Dght 1.990 Lbp 21.00 Br md 6.00 Dpth 2.90 Welded, 1 dk	**(B34S2QM) Mooring Vessel** Passengers: unberthed: 12	**2 oil engines** geared to sc. shafts driving 2 FP propellers Total Power: 442kW (600hp) 10.0kn Caterpillar 3406T 2 x 4 Stroke 6 Cy. 137 x 165 each-221kW (300bhp) Caterpillar Inc-USA AuxGen: 2 x 25kW 380V 50Hz a.c
346029 *JVV*	**YACHT EXPRESS** **Express Shipping NV** Spliethoff Transport BV *Willemstad* *Curacao* MMSI: 306814000 Official number: 2007-C-1918	**17,951** 5,386 12,500	Class: NV	**2007-10 Yantai Raffles Shipyard Co Ltd — Yantai SD** Yd No: YRF2004-178 Loa 208.89 (BB) Br ex 32.23 Dght 5.800 Lbp 205.34 Br md 32.20 Dpth 8.50 Welded, 1 dk	**(A38C3GY) Yacht Carrier, semi submersible**	**2 diesel electric oil engines** driving 2 gen. Connecting to 2 elec. motors each (5100kW) driving 2 Azimuth electric drive units Total Power: 17,400kW (23,658hp) 18.0kn Wartsila 12V38 1 x Vee 4 Stroke 12 Cy. 380 x 475 8700kW (11829bhp) Wartsila Finland Oy-Finland Wartsila 12V38B 1 x Vee 4 Stroke 12 Cy. 380 x 475 8700kW (11829bhp) Wartsila Finland Oy-Finland AuxGen: 2 x 1020kW 440V 60Hz a.c Thrusters: 1 Tunnel thruster (f)
013830 *WDS*	**YACOUB** *ex* Jakob *-1994* **Societe Cherifienne de Remorquage et d'Assistance** - *Casablanca* *Morocco* Official number: 6-853	**140** - -	Class: BV	**1990-09 B.V. Scheepswerf Damen — Gorinchem** Yd No: 6502 Loa 22.33 Br ex - Dght 3.500 Lbp 20.36 Br md 7.20 Dpth 3.75 Welded, 1 dk	**(B32A2ST) Tug**	**1 oil engine** geared to sc. shaft driving 1 FP propeller Total Power: 530kW (721hp) Caterpillar 3412TA 1 x Vee 4 Stroke 12 Cy. 137 x 152 530kW (721bhp) Caterpillar Inc-USA
161170 *7CD8*	**YACU KALLPA** *ex* Marcomanche *-2013* *ex* Niledutch Antwerp *-2009* *ex* Lydia Oldendorff *-2009* **PAL RMI Inc** Naviera Yacu Taski SA *Majuro* *Marshall Islands* MMSI: 538005247 Official number: 5247	**13,066** 6,914 20,526	Class: GL	**1998-04 Flensburger Schiffbau-Ges. mbH & Co. KG — Flensburg** Yd No: 697 Loa 153.22 Br ex - Dght 9.727 Lbp 145.75 Br md 23.60 Dpth 13.50 Welded, 1 dk	**(A31A2GX) General Cargo Ship** Grain: 24,982; Bale: 24,365 TEU 1291 C Ho 546 TEU C Dk 745 TEU incl 63 ref C. Compartments: 5 Ho, ER 5 Ha: (14.0 x 8.0)Tappered (12.5 x 15.6)3 (25.0 x 20.6)ER Cranes: 2x60t	**1 oil engine** driving 1 FP propeller Total Power: 8,253kW (11,221hp) 16.0kn Mitsubishi 6UEC50LSII 1 x 2 Stroke 6 Cy. 500 x 1950 8253kW (11221bhp) Mitsubishi Heavy Industries Ltd-Japan AuxGen: 2 x 660kW 220/440V a.c Fuel: 84.0 (d.f.) 828.0 (r.f.) 29.4pd
209327 *PCK*	**YACYRETA** **Emparex Srl** - *Asuncion* *Paraguay* Official number: 1916	*391* 323 492	Class: (NK)	**1982-09 Kambara Uruguay S.A. — Montevideo** Yd No: P-3 Loa 44.20 Br ex 11.03 Dght 2.109 Lbp 43.01 Br md 11.00 Dpth 3.00 Welded, 1 dk	**(A12D2LV) Vegetable Oil Tanker** Liq: 709	**2 oil engines** geared to sc. shafts driving 2 FP propellers Total Power: 442kW (600hp) 7.0kn Niigata 6L13CX 2 x 4 Stroke 6 Cy. 130 x 160 each-221kW (300bhp) Niigata Engineering Co Ltd-Japan AuxGen: 1 x 24kW
198202	**YADANA THEINKHA** **Government of The Union of Myanmar (Myanmar Ports Corp)** - *Myanmar*	**1,669** 501 2,040	Class: (NK)	**1998-11 Kumamoto Dock K.K. — Yatsushiro** (Hull) Yd No: 1239 **1998-11 Mitsubishi Heavy Industries Ltd. — Kobe** Yd No: 1239 Loa 68.32 Br ex - Dght 4.019 Lbp 65.20 Br md 14.60 Dpth 5.15 Welded, 1 dk	**(B33A2DU) Dredger (unspecified)** Hopper: 1,000	**2 oil engines** reduction geared to sc. shafts driving 2 FP propellers Total Power: 2,206kW (3,000hp) 10.0kn Mitsubishi S6U-MTK 2 x 4 Stroke 6 Cy. 240 x 260 each-1103kW (1500bhp) Mitsubishi Heavy Industries Ltd-Japan
147020 *TQ*	**YADANAR PAN TAUNG** **Thuriya Sandar Win Co Ltd** - *Yangon* *Myanmar* Official number: 6313 (A)	**1,620** 741 -		**2010-07 Myanma Port Authority — Yangon (Theinphyu Dockyard)** Yd No: 30MPA Loa 71.93 Br ex 20.12 Dght - Lbp - Br md 19.18 Dpth 4.57 Welded, 1 dk	**(A35D2RL) Landing Craft**	**4 oil engines** reduction geared to sc. shafts driving 4 Propellers Total Power: 1,528kW (2,076hp) Nissan RH10 4 x Vee 4 Stroke 10 Cy. 135 x 125 each-382kW (519bhp) Nissan Diesel Motor Co. Ltd.-Ageo
607647 *BRC*	**YADEGAR 2** **Government of The Islamic Republic of Iran (Ports & Maritime Organisation)** - *Chabahar* *Iran* MMSI: 422754000	**416** 125 240	Class: (BV)	**2009-10 Penglai Bohai Shipyard Co Ltd — Penglai SD** Yd No: PBZ07-83 Loa 31.00 Br ex 11.66 Dght 3.800 Lbp 27.70 Br md 11.00 Dpth 4.70 Welded, 1 dk	**(B32A2ST) Tug**	**2 oil engines** reduction geared to sc. shafts driving 2 Propellers Total Power: 3,236kW (4,400hp) Wartsila 9L20 2 x 4 Stroke 9 Cy. 200 x 280 each-1618kW (2200bhp) Wartsila Finland Oy-Finland
520765	**YADRAN** - -	*153* 46 183	Class: (BV)	**1965 AG Weser, Werk Seebeck — Bremerhaven** Yd No: 892 Loa 25.46 Br ex 7.24 Dght - Lbp 21.26 Br md 7.01 Dpth 3.51 Welded, 1 dk	**(B11B2FV) Fishing Vessel**	**1 oil engine** driving 1 FP propeller Total Power: 399kW (542hp) Caterpillar D353SCAC 1 x 4 Stroke 6 Cy. 159 x 203 399kW (542bhp) Caterpillar Tractor Co-USA
219692 *E3164*	**YAE MARU No. 21** **YK Yaemaru Gyogyo** - *Hachinohe, Aomori* *Japan* MMSI: 431704480 Official number: 136270	*178* - -		**1999-06 K.K. Yoshida Zosen Tekko — Kesennuma** Yd No: 515 L reg 34.30 Br ex - Dght - Lbp - Br md 7.00 Dpth 3.00 Welded, 1 dk	**(B11B2FV) Fishing Vessel**	**1 oil engine** driving 1 FP propeller
848501	**YAE MARU No. 31** - -	*166* - -		**1977-05 K.K. Otsuchi Kogyo — Otsuchi** L reg 30.30 Br ex - Dght - Lbp - Br md 6.30 Dpth 2.80 Welded, 1 dk	**(B11B2FV) Fishing Vessel**	**1 oil engine** driving 1 FP propeller Total Power: 346kW (470hp) Niigata 1 x 4 Stroke 346kW (470bhp) Niigata Engineering Co Ltd-Japan
561962 *JOQ*	**YAE MARU NO. 71** **Hachinohe Kisen Gyogyo KK** - *Kesennuma, Miyagi* *Japan* Official number: 141893	*184* - 163	Class: FA	**2013-06 K.K. Yoshida Zosen Tekko — Kesennuma** Yd No: 560 Loa 41.33 Br ex - Dght 2.700 Lbp - Br md 7.00 Dpth - Welded, 1 dk	**(B11B2FV) Fishing Vessel**	**1 oil engine** reduction geared to sc. shaft driving 1 Propeller Total Power: 882kW (1,199hp) Niigata 6MG26AFTE 1 x 4 Stroke 6 Cy. 260 x 460 882kW (1199bhp) Niigata Engineering Co Ltd-Japan
736605 *J2486*	**YAEGUMO** **Government of Japan (Ministry of Land, Infrastructure & Transport) (The Coastguard)** - *Tokyo* *Japan* Official number: 140615	*101* - -		**2008-03 Niigata Shipbuilding & Repair Inc — Niigata NI** Yd No: 0030 Loa 32.00 Br ex - Dght - Lbp - Br md 6.50 Dpth 3.30 Welded, 1 dk	**(B34H2SQ) Patrol Vessel** Hull Material: Aluminium Alloy	**2 oil engines** geared to sc. shafts driving 2 Propellers 36.0kn
818290	**YAEI MARU No. 2** - -	*226* 110 289		**1970 Tokushima Zosen Sangyo K.K. — Komatsushima** Yd No: 305 Loa 39.63 Br ex 7.04 Dght 2.845 Lbp 35.01 Br md 7.01 Dpth 3.15 Riveted\Welded, 1 dk	**(A31A2GX) General Cargo Ship** Compartments: 1 Ho, ER 1 Ha: (13.2 x 4.5)ER Derricks: 1x5t,1x2.5t	**1 oil engine** driving 1 FP propeller Total Power: 368kW (500hp) 9.5kn Niigata 6MG20X 1 x 4 Stroke 6 Cy. 200 x 260 368kW (500bhp) Niigata Engineering Co Ltd-Japan
81766 *C5447*	**YAESHIMA No. 12** **Akitsu Ferry KK** - *Higashihiroshima, Hiroshima* *Japan* Official number: 135281	*336* - 150		**1998-01 Naikai Zosen Corp — Onomichi HS (Setoda Shipyard)** Yd No: 637 Loa 49.90 Br ex - Dght 2.650 Lbp 38.90 Br md 11.00 Dpth 3.58 Welded, 1 dk	**(A36A2PR) Passenger/Ro-Ro Ship (Vehicles)** Passengers: 280 Bow door/ramp Stern door/ramp Lorries: 4, Cars: 10	**1 oil engine** reduction geared to sc. shafts driving 2 Propellers 1 fwd and 1 aft Total Power: 1,177kW (1,600hp) 11.5kn Daihatsu 6DLM-26FSL 1 x 4 Stroke 6 Cy. 260 x 340 1177kW (1600bhp) Daihatsu Diesel Manufacturing Co Lt-Japan

IMO / Call sign	Name / Owner	Tonnage	Class	Builder / Dimensions	Type	Machinery
8841137 *JK5082* -	**YAESHIMA No. 15** *ex* Seto No. 2 *-2000* *ex* Shuttle No. 1 *-1996* **Seiun Shoji YK** - *Higashihiroshima, Hiroshima* *Japan* Official number: 131819	*372* - -		**1990-06 Kanbara Zosen K.K. — Onomichi** Yd No: 400 Loa 49.00 Br ex - Dght 2.700 Lbp 37.70 Br md 9.50 Dpth 3.60 Welded, 1 dk	**(A36A2PR) Passenger/Ro-Ro Ship (Vehicles)** Passengers: unberthed: 250 Bow door (centre) Stern ramp (centre)	**1 oil engine** geared to sc. shaft driving 1 FP propeller Total Power: 1,177kW (1,600hp) 11.7k Daihatsu 6DLM-26F 1 x 4 Stroke 6 Cy. 260 x 340 1177kW (1600bhp) Daihatsu Diesel Manufacturing Co Lt-Japan
8013663 *JG4128* -	**YAEZUKI** - **Government of Japan (Ministry of Land, Infrastructure & Transport) (The Coastguard)** - *Tokyo* *Japan* MMSI: 431680098 Official number: 123719	*125* - -		**1981-03 Hitachi Zosen Corp — Kawasaki KN** Yd No: 117081 Loa 31.00 Br ex 6.32 Dght 1.150 Lbp 28.50 Br md 6.30 Dpth 3.30 Welded, 1 dk	**(B34H2SQ) Patrol Vessel** Hull Material: Aluminium Alloy	**2 oil engines** geared to sc. shafts driving 2 FP propellers Total Power: 1,780kW (2,420hp) 30.0k M.T.U. 16V652TB7 2 x Vee 4 Stroke 16 Cy. 190 x 230 each-890kW (1210bhp) Ikegai Tekkosho-Japan
7414200 *CB4823* -	**YAGAN** *ex* Tuna West *-1991* *ex* Balmenach *-1988* *ex* Lador *-1986* *ex* Linda Bassau *-1981* *ex* Fishing Future *-1980* *ex* Umanaq *-1978* **Compania Pesquera Camanchaca SA** - *Valparaiso* *Chile* MMSI: 725000420 Official number: 2777	**1,450** 473 1,700	Class: NV	**1976-12 Flekkefjord Slipp & Maskinfabrikk AS AS — Flekkefjord** Yd No: 119 Converted From: Research Vessel-1989 Converted From: Stern Trawler-1982 Lengthened-1993 Loa 72.87 (BB) Br ex 12.01 Dght 5.600 Lbp 67.00 Br md 11.99 Dpth 7.60 Welded, 2 dks	**(B11A2FT) Trawler** Ice Capable	**1 oil engine** reduction geared to sc. shaft driving 1 CP propeller Total Power: 2,589kW (3,520hp) 15.0k Nohab F216 1 x Vee 4 Stroke 16 Cy. 250 x 300 2589kW (3520bhp) AB Bofors NOHAB-Sweden AuxGen: 1 x 1456kW 440V 60Hz a.c, 3 x 256kW 440V 60Hz a.c Thrusters: 1 Thwart. FP thruster (f); 1 Tunnel thruster (a)
9343235 *LW3402* -	**YAGAN** *ex* Smit Antigua *-2011* **Antares Naviera SA** - *Buenos Aires* *Argentina* MMSI: 701006100 Official number: 02546	*274* 88 151	Class: LR ✠ **100A1** SS 08/2011 tug **LMC** **UMS** Eq.Ltr: F; Cable: 275.0/19.0 U2 (a)	**2006-08 Santierul Naval Damen Galati S.A. — Galati** (Hull) Yd No: 1076 **2006-08 B.V. Scheepswerf Damen — Gorinchem** Yd No: 511512 Loa 28.75 Br ex 10.43 Dght 3.608 Lbp 25.78 Br md 9.80 Dpth 4.60 Welded, 1 dk	**(B32A2ST) Tug**	**2 oil engines** reduction geared to sc. shafts driving 2 Directional propellers Total Power: 3,728kW (5,068hp) 12.9k Caterpillar 3516B-H 2 x Vee 4 Stroke 16 Cy. 170 x 215 each-1864kW (2534bhp) Caterpillar Inc-USA AuxGen: 2 x 80kW 230/400V 50Hz a.c
9604627 *CA3617* -	**YAGHAN** - **Transbordadora Austral Broom SA** - *Valparaiso* *Chile* MMSI: 725000875 Official number: 3276	**777** 205 400		**2011-12 Astilleros y Servicios Navales S.A. (ASENAV) — Valdivia** Yd No: 165 Loa 70.60 Br ex 16.12 Dght 1.900 Lbp 57.63 Br md 15.80 Dpth 2.80 Welded, 1 dk	**(A36A2PR) Passenger/Ro-Ro Ship (Vehicles)** Passengers: 250 Bow ramp (centre) Stern ramp (centre)	**4 oil engines** reduction geared to sc. shafts driving 4 FP propellers Total Power: 1,712kW (2,328hp) 11.0k Caterpillar 4 x 4 Stroke each-428kW (582bhp) Caterpillar Inc-USA
7373028 *J8UI3* -	**YAGHOOT** *ex* Permina Supply No. 11 *-1998* **Acorn Shipping & Trading Ltd** Whitesea Shipping & Supply (LLC) *Kingstown* *St Vincent & The Grenadines* MMSI: 376583000 Official number: 7681	**712** 214 934	Class: GL (KI) (AB)	**1974-06 Kanrei Zosen K.K. — Tokushima** Yd No: 185 Loa 49.99 Br ex 11.66 Dght 4.201 Lbp 45.47 Br md 11.59 Dpth 4.88 Welded, 1 dk	**(B21B20A) Anchor Handling Tug Supply** Cranes: 1x5t	**2 oil engines** reverse reduction geared to sc. shafts driving 2 FP propellers Total Power: 2,206kW (3,000hp) 10.0k Niigata 8MG25B 2 x 4 Stroke 8 Cy. 250 x 320 each-1103kW (1500bhp) Niigata Engineering Co Ltd-Japan AuxGen: 2 x 160kW 450V 60Hz a.c Thrusters: 1 Thwart. FP thruster (f) Fuel: 341.5
8316168 *EQOE* -	**YAGHOUB** - **NITC** - *Bushehr* *Iran* MMSI: 422150000 Official number: 5/63	**1,019** 305 950	Class: AS (LR) ✠ Classed LR until 31/10/00	**1984-05 Kanrei Zosen K.K. — Naruto** (Hull) Yd No: 301 **1984-05 Mitsui Ocean Development & Eng. Co. Ltd. — Japan** Yd No: 177 Loa 61.12 Br ex 12.76 Dght 4.230 Lbp 55.50 Br md 12.21 Dpth 5.01 Welded, 1 dk	**(B21A20S) Platform Supply Ship**	**2 oil engines** with clutches, flexible couplings & sr reverse geared to sc. shaft driving 2 FP propellers Total Power: 2,722kW (3,700hp) 13.0k Deutz SBV8M62 2 x 4 Stroke 8 Cy. 240 x 280 each-1361kW (1850bhp) Kloeckner Humboldt Deutz AG-West Germany AuxGen: 2 x 240kW 385V 50Hz a.c Thrusters: 1 Thwart. CP thruster (f) Fuel: 510.5 (d.f.)
8740905 *TC9240* -	**YAGMUR DENIZ** - **Cag-Gun Denizcilik Nakliyat ve Ticaret Ltd Sti** - *Istanbul* *Turkey* Official number: 21763	**169** 82 249		**1998-10 Gisan Gemi Ins. San — Istanbul** Loa 37.50 Br ex - Dght 2.390 Lbp 33.95 Br md 6.00 Dpth 2.80 Welded, 1 dk	**(A13B2TP) Products Tanker**	**2 oil engines** driving 2 Propellers MAN 2 x 4 Stroke MAN Nutzfahrzeuge AG-Nuernberg
7713929 - -	**YAGNASRI** - **Kakinada Port Authority** - *Kakinada* *India*	*240* - 250	Class: IR	**1975-11 Bharati Shipyard Ltd — Kakinada** Loa 35.11 Br ex 8.67 Dght 1.531 Lbp 33.02 Br md 8.41 Dpth 2.42 Welded, 1 dk	**(A13B2TP) Products Tanker**	**2 oil engines** geared to sc. shafts driving 2 FP propellers Total Power: 200kW (272hp) Torpedo-Rijeka T534 2 x 4 Stroke 4 Cy. 112 x 140 each-100kW (136bhp) Tvornica Motora 'Torpedo'-Yugoslavia
9130092 - -	**YAGODA 8** - **Pesquera Velebit SA** - *Peru* Official number: CE-15261-PM	**520** - -		**1996-12 SIMA Serv. Ind. de la Marina Chimbote (SIMACH) — Chimbote** Yd No: 479 Loa - Br ex - Dght - Lbp - Br md - Dpth - Welded, 1 dk	**(B11B2FV) Fishing Vessel**	**1 oil engine** geared to sc. shaft driving 1 FP propeller Total Power: 1,080kW (1,468hp) Alpha 8L23/3 1 x 4 Stroke 8 Cy. 225 x 300 1080kW (1468bhp) MAN B&W Diesel A/S-Denmark
7645483 *UEZD* -	**YAGODNOYE** - **Kamchatryboprodukt Co Ltd** - *Petropavlovsk-Kamchatskiy* *Russia* MMSI: 273423160 Official number: 771229	**172** 51 88	Class: (RS)	**1977-08 Zavod 'Nikolayevsk-na-Amure' — Nikolayevsk-na-Amure** Yd No: 156 Loa 33.96 Br ex 7.09 Dght 2.901 Lbp 30.00 Br md 7.00 Dpth 3.69 Welded, 1 dk	**(B11B2FV) Fishing Vessel** Ins: 115 Compartments: 1 Ho, ER 1 Ha: (1.7 x 1.3) Derricks: 2x2t; Winches: 2 Ice Capable	**1 oil engine** driving 1 CP propeller Total Power: 224kW (305hp) 9.5k S.K.L. 8NVD36-1 1 x 4 Stroke 8 Cy. 240 x 360 224kW (305bhp) VEB Schwermaschinenbau "KarlLiebknecht" (SKL)-Magdeburg Fuel: 20.0 (d.f.)
8953497 *UGUM* -	**YAGRY** - **JSC Grumant Flot** - *Murmansk* *Russia* MMSI: 273550600 Official number: 960194	**601** 180 332	Class: RS	**1998 FGUP Mashinostroitelnoye Predp 'Zvyozdochka' — Severodvinsk** (Hull launched by) Yd No: 03103 **1998 Kvaerner Kimek AS — Kirkenes** (Hull completed by) Loa 38.50 Br ex 10.20 Dght 4.230 Lbp 34.80 Br md - Dpth 6.70 Welded, 1 dk	**(B11A2FS) Stern Trawler** Ins: 410 Compartments: 2 Ho 2 Ha: 2 (1.5 x 2.1) Derricks: 2x1t Ice Capable	**1 oil engine** geared to sc. shaft driving 1 CP propeller Total Power: 1,000kW (1,360hp) 11.0k Wartsila 6L2 1 x 4 Stroke 6 Cy. 200 x 280 1000kW (1360bhp) Wartsila NSD Finland Oy-Finland AuxGen: 1 x 400kW a.c, 1 x 216kW a.c Fuel: 178.0 (d.f.)
7729980 - -	**YAGUAR** *ex* Marshal Yakubovskiy *-2003* **Haskell Shipping Inc** - *Union of Comoros*	**5,640** 1,692 3,169	Class: (RS)	**1978-07 Sudostroitelnyy Zavod 'Okean' — Nikolayev** Yd No: 56 Loa 111.41 (BB) Br ex 17.33 Dght 6.519 Lbp 100.01 Br md - Dpth 11.00 Welded, 2 dks	**(B11A2FG) Factory Stern Trawler** Ins: 3,806 Compartments: 4 Ho, ER 4 Ha: 3 (3.5 x 2.9) (2.2 x 1.9) Derricks: 6x3t; Winches: 6 Ice Capable	**2 oil engines** geared to sc. shaft driving 1 CP propeller Total Power: 5,148kW (7,000hp) 15.0k Skoda 6L525II 2 x 4 Stroke 6 Cy. 525 x 720 each-2574kW (3500bhp) CKD Praha-Praha
8010049 *UOV* -	**YAGUAR** *ex* Jaguar *-2005* *ex* Marsea Five *-1994* **MML Merchant BV** Enka Insaat ve Sanayi AS *Aqtau* *Kazakhstan* MMSI: 436000048	**719** 215 1,500	Class: RS (AB)	**1980-11 Halter Marine, Inc. — Moss Point, Ms** Yd No: 941 Converted From: Offshore Supply Ship-1994 Loa 54.86 Br ex 12.22 Dght 3.664 Lbp 50.70 Br md 12.19 Dpth 4.27 Welded, 1 dk	**(B21A20S) Platform Supply Ship**	**2 oil engines** reverse reduction geared to sc. shafts driving 2 FP propellers Total Power: 1,882kW (2,558hp) 9.0k G.M. (Detroit Diesel) 16V-149- 2 x Vee 2 Stroke 16 Cy. 146 x 146 each-941kW (1279bhp) General Motors Detroit DieselAllison Divn-USA AuxGen: 2 x 125kW Thrusters: 1 Thwart. FP thruster (f) Fuel: 160.0 (d.f.)
9564774 *UALH8* -	**YAGUAR** - **LLC Transneft-Service** - *Novorossiysk* *Russia* MMSI: 273353070	**395** 118 134	Class: RS	**2010-06 DP Craneship — Kerch** Yd No: 60-602 Loa 30.87 Br ex 11.50 Dght 3.900 Lbp 27.80 Br md 11.20 Dpth 5.45 Welded, 1 dk	**(B32A2ST) Tug**	**2 oil engines** reduction geared to sc. shafts driving 2 Directional propellers Total Power: 3,728kW (5,068hp) 14.0k Caterpillar 3516 2 x Vee 4 Stroke 16 Cy. 170 x 190 each-1864kW (2534bhp) Caterpillar Inc-USA AuxGen: 2 x 86kW a.c Fuel: 132.0 (d.f.)

718838 *K3966*	**YAGUMO MARU** **Kumagaya Kaiji Kogyo KK** - *Shunan, Yamaguchi* *Japan* Official number: 120423	*195* 69 83	**1978-01 Towa Zosen K.K. — Shimonoseki** Yd No: 506 Loa 30.61 Br ex 8.82 Dght 3.001 Lbp 27.01 Br md 8.81 Dpth 3.51 Welded, 1 dk	**(B32A2ST) Tug**	**2 oil engines** driving 2 FP propellers Total Power: 1,912kW (2,600hp) Niigata 6L25BX 2 x 4 Stroke 6 Cy. 250 x 320 each-956kW (1300bhp) Niigata Engineering Co Ltd-Japan
877186 *QJS3*	**YAHATA** *ex* Yahata Maru No. 1 *-1992* **Nautilus Shipping Co SA** *San Lorenzo* *Honduras* Official number: L-0324267	*139* 57 186	**1974-06 K.K. Morimoto Zosensho — Kamo** Loa 33.20 Br ex - Dght 2.630 Lbp 30.00 Br md 6.40 Dpth 2.80 Welded, 1 dk	**(B12B2FC) Fish Carrier**	**1 oil engine** driving 1 FP propeller Total Power: 588kW (799hp) 10.0kn
926444 *L6477*	**YAHATA MARU** **Shinono Kaiun KK** - *Anan, Tokushima* *Japan* MMSI: 431400594 Official number: 135512	*160* - 280	**1996-10 Hongawara Zosen K.K. — Fukuyama** Yd No: 460 Loa 33.25 Br ex - Dght - Lbp 30.50 Br md 10.00 Dpth 6.20 Welded, 1 dk	**(B32A2ST) Tug**	**2 oil engines** driving 2 FP propellers Total Power: 2,942kW (4,000hp) 10.0kn Niigata 6M34BLGT 2 x 4 Stroke 6 Cy. 340 x 680 each-1471kW (2000bhp) Niigata Engineering Co Ltd-Japan
142124 *L6274*	**YAHATA MARU** **Ishikawa Kaiun YK** - *Shikokuchuo, Ehime* *Japan* Official number: 134859	*199* - 540	**1996-06 Koa Sangyo KK — Takamatsu KG** Yd No: 593 Loa 49.60 Br ex - Dght - Lbp 45.00 Br md 7.80 Dpth 3.40 Welded, 1 dk	**(A13B2TP) Products Tanker**	**1 oil engine** driving 1 FP propeller Total Power: 736kW (1,001hp) 11.0kn Hanshin LH26G 1 x 4 Stroke 6 Cy. 260 x 440 736kW (1001bhp) The Hanshin Diesel Works Ltd-Japan
403246	**YAHATA MARU** **Orient Star Lingyun SA** Marukichi Commerce Co Ltd	*497* - 1,600	**1984-05 Shinhama Dockyard Co. Ltd. — Anan** Yd No: 753 Loa 71.79 Br ex - Dght 4.211 Lbp 67.01 Br md 11.51 Dpth 6.41 Welded, 1 dk	**(A31A2GX) General Cargo Ship** Grain: 2,140; Bale: 1,900 Compartments: 1 Ho, ER 1 Ha: ER	**1 oil engine** sr geared to sc. shaft driving 1 CP propeller Total Power: 956kW (1,300hp) Hanshin 6LUN28AG 1 x 4 Stroke 6 Cy. 280 x 480 956kW (1300bhp) The Hanshin Diesel Works Ltd-Japan
566019 *D3008*	**YAHATA MARU** **Yahata Senpaku Kyogyo Kumiai** - *Kitakyushu, Fukuoka* *Japan* MMSI: 431001106 Official number: 141161	*499* - 1,855	**2009-11 Yamanaka Zosen K.K. — Imabari** Yd No: 782 Loa 74.24 Br ex - Dght 4.360 Lbp 68.00 Br md 12.00 Dpth 7.37 Welded, 1 dk	**(A31A2GX) General Cargo Ship** Grain: 2,921	**1 oil engine** reduction geared to sc. shaft driving 1 FP propeller Total Power: 1,618kW (2,200hp) Hanshin LH34LAG 1 x 4 Stroke 6 Cy. 340 x 640 1618kW (2200bhp) The Hanshin Diesel Works Ltd-Japan
281217 *J5683*	**YAHATA MARU NO. 1** **Yahatamaru Gyogyo Unyu KK** - *Tokyo* *Japan* Official number: 137138	*199* - 750	**2002-05 K.K. Watanabe Zosensho — Nagasaki** Yd No: 100 Loa - Br ex - Dght - Lbp 41.20 Br md 8.00 Dpth 3.50 Welded	**(A31A2GX) General Cargo Ship**	**1 oil engine** driving 1 FP propeller Sumiyoshi S26G 1 x 4 Stroke 6 Cy. 260 x 470 Sumiyoshi Marine Diesel Co Ltd-Japan
125475 *M6518*	**YAHATA MARU NO. 1** **Nishi Nippon Kaiun KK** - *Kitakyushu, Fukuoka* *Japan* Official number: 134637	*198* - -	**1995-12 K.K. Odo Zosen Tekko — Shimonoseki** Yd No: 533 Loa 35.35 Br ex 9.22 Dght 3.100 Lbp 29.00 Br md 9.20 Dpth 4.16 Welded, 1 dk	**(B32A2ST) Tug**	**2 oil engines** geared integral to driving 2 Z propellers Total Power: 2,648kW (3,600hp) Niigata 6L28HX 2 x 4 Stroke 6 Cy. 280 x 370 each-1324kW (1800bhp) Niigata Engineering Co Ltd-Japan
515746 *J3439*	**YAHATA MARU No. 2** **Arai Kaiun YK** - *Himeji, Hyogo* *Japan* Official number: 125382	*377* - 1,067	**1987-01 Matsuura Tekko Zosen K.K. — Osakikamijima** Yd No: 327 Loa 55.20 (BB) Br ex 11.59 Dght 4.222 Lbp 50.02 Br md 11.51 Dpth 5.62 Welded, 1 dk	**(B33A2DG) Grab Dredger** Grain: 625 Compartments: 1 Ho, ER 1 Ha: (13.8 x 8.6)ER Cranes: 1	**1 oil engine** with clutches & reverse reduction geared to sc. shaft driving 1 FP propeller Total Power: 736kW (1,001hp) Hanshin 6LU32G 1 x 4 Stroke 6 Cy. 320 x 510 736kW (1001bhp) The Hanshin Diesel Works Ltd-Japan
864115 *J5101*	**YAHATA MARU NO. 3** **Yawata Maru Gyogyo Unyu KK** - *Tokyo* *Japan* Official number: 133134	*197* - 419	**1992-03 Takao Zosen Kogyo K.K. — Tateyama** Yd No: 115 Loa 44.00 Br ex - Dght 3.100 Lbp 40.00 Br md 8.00 Dpth 3.50 Welded, 1 dk	**(A31A2GX) General Cargo Ship**	**1 oil engine** geared to sc. shaft driving 1 FP propeller Total Power: 736kW (1,001hp) 9.5kn Sumiyoshi S26G 1 x 4 Stroke 6 Cy. 260 x 470 736kW (1001bhp) Sumiyoshi Marine Diesel Co Ltd-Japan
804220 *J3604*	**YAHATA MARU No. 5** **Seto Kaiun YK** - *Himeji, Hyogo* *Japan* Official number: 130819	*448* - 624	**1988-07 K.K. Saidaiji Zosensho — Okayama** Yd No: 153 Loa 50.50 Br ex - Dght 3.220 Lbp 46.00 Br md 10.50 Dpth 5.40 Welded, 1 dk	**(A24D2BA) Aggregates Carrier**	**1 oil engine** driving 1 FP propeller Total Power: 552kW (750hp) Hanshin 6LUN28 1 x 4 Stroke 6 Cy. 280 x 480 552kW (750bhp) The Hanshin Diesel Works Ltd-Japan
658549 *JMJ*	**YAHATA MARU NO. 5** **Kesennuma Enyo Gyogyo Seisau Kumiai (Kesennuma Pelagic Fishery Cooperative)** KK Yahata Suisan *Kesennuma, Miyagi* *Japan* MMSI: 432878000 Official number: 141714	*439* - -	**2012-09 Niigata Shipbuilding & Repair Inc — Niigata NI** Yd No: 0061 Loa 57.10 Br ex - Dght 3.500 Lbp - Br md 9.00 Dpth - Welded, 1 dk	**(B11B2FV) Fishing Vessel**	**1 oil engine** reduction geared to sc. shaft driving 1 Propeller Total Power: 1,029kW (1,399hp) Niigata 6M28BFT 1 x 4 Stroke 6 Cy. 280 x 480 1029kW (1399bhp) Niigata Engineering Co Ltd-Japan
072989 *M6227*	**YAHATA MARU No. 8** **Yamasa Kaiun KK** - *Nagasaki, Nagasaki* *Japan* Official number: 133514	*199* - 700	**1993-05 K.K. Watanabe Zosensho — Nagasaki** Yd No: 001 Loa - Br ex - Dght 3.210 Lbp 54.50 Br md 9.50 Dpth 5.45 Welded, 1 dk	**(A31A2GX) General Cargo Ship**	**1 oil engine** geared to sc. shaft driving 1 FP propeller Total Power: 736kW (1,001hp) Hanshin LH26G 1 x 4 Stroke 6 Cy. 260 x 440 736kW (1001bhp) The Hanshin Diesel Works Ltd-Japan
123055	**YAHATA MARU No. 8** - -	*149* - 165	**1979-06 K.K. Morimoto Zosensho — Kamo** Loa 37.14 (BB) Br ex 6.86 Dght 2.701 Lbp 32.01 Br md 6.71 Dpth 3.00 Welded, 1 dk	**(B12B2FC) Fish Carrier**	**1 oil engine** driving 1 FP propeller Total Power: 625kW (850hp) Niigata 6M26ZG 1 x 4 Stroke 6 Cy. 260 x 400 625kW (850bhp) Niigata Engineering Co Ltd-Japan
124036	**YAHATA MARU No. 11** *ex* Hanei Maru No. 8 *-1995* *ex* Daiun Maru *-1989* - - *Philippines*	*497* - 1,100	**1984-03 K.K. Miura Zosensho — Saiki** Yd No: 705 Loa 71.00 Br ex - Dght - Lbp 65.99 Br md 11.51 Dpth 6.51 Welded, 1 dk	**(A31A2GX) General Cargo Ship**	**1 oil engine** driving 1 FP propeller Total Power: 883kW (1,201hp) Akasaka DM28AFD 1 x 4 Stroke 6 Cy. 280 x 460 883kW (1201bhp) Akasaka Tekkosho KK (Akasaka DieselLtd)-Japan
157941 *F3113* G1-1858	**YAHATA MARU No. 11** **KK Yahata Suisan** - *Kesennuma, Miyagi* *Japan* MMSI: 432619000 Official number: 133300	*119* - 214	**1992-10 Kidoura Shipyard Co Ltd — Kesennuma MG** Yd No: 581 Loa 37.44 (BB) Br ex 6.42 Dght 2.500 Lbp - Br md 6.40 Dpth 2.80 Welded, 1 dk	**(B11B2FV) Fishing Vessel**	**1 oil engine** driving 1 CP propeller Total Power: 805kW (1,094hp) Niigata 6M26CFT 1 x 4 Stroke 6 Cy. 260 x 460 805kW (1094bhp) Niigata Engineering Co Ltd-Japan
233961 *K5554*	**YAHATA MARU No. 11** **Tokai Shosen KK** Shinwa Naiko Kaiun Kaisha Ltd *Kure, Hiroshima* *Japan* Official number: 136124	*499* - 1,570	**2001-03 K.K. Matsuura Zosensho — Osakikamijima** Yd No: 538 Loa 78.15 Br ex 12.02 Dght - Lbp 71.50 Br md 12.00 Dpth 4.10 Welded, 1 dk	**(A31A2GX) General Cargo Ship** Grain: 2,592; Bale: 2,592 Compartments: 1 Ho, ER 1 Ha: ER	**1 oil engine** driving 1 FP propeller Total Power: 1,471kW (2,000hp) 12.1kn Hanshin LH32LG 1 x 4 Stroke 6 Cy. 320 x 640 1471kW (2000bhp) The Hanshin Diesel Works Ltd-Japan AuxGen: 1 x 39kW 440V 60Hz a.c Thrusters: 1 Thwart. FP thruster (f) Fuel: 25.0 (d.f.) 73.0 (r.f.) 6.0pd

9041681 JM6112 -
YAHATA MARU NO. 12 402 - 900
ex Meiji Maru *-2010*
YK Meiji Kaiun
-
Saiki, Oita *Japan*
Official number: 132681
1991-12 **K.K. Miura Zosensho — Saiki** Yd No: 1026
Loa 65.00 Br ex - Dght 3.820
Lbp 60.00 Br md 10.50 Dpth 6.00
Welded
(A31A2GX) General Cargo Ship
1 oil engine reverse geared to sc. shaft driving 1 FP propeller
Total Power: 736kW (1,001hp)
Akasaka K28
1 x 4 Stroke 6 Cy. 280 x 480 736kW (1001bhp)
Akasaka Tekkosho KK (Akasaka DieselLtd)-Japan

8858908 - -
YAHATA MARU No. 15 499 - 1,509
-
-
-
1991-05 **K.K. Yoshida Zosen Kogyo — Arida**
Loa 74.92 Br ex - Dght 4.200
Lbp 69.50 Br md 11.70 Dpth 7.10
Welded, 1 dk
(A31A2GX) General Cargo Ship
Grain: 2,428; Bale: 2,415
1 Ha: (40.2 x 8.0)ER
1 oil engine geared to sc. shaft driving 1 FP propeller
Total Power: 736kW (1,001hp) 11.0k
Hanshin LH31
1 x 4 Stroke 6 Cy. 310 x 530 736kW (1001bhp)
The Hanshin Diesel Works Ltd-Japan

8304177 JD2595 HK1-870
YAHATA MARU No. 15 160 - 144
ex Chiyoko Maru No. 85 *-1998*
Hamaki Gyogyo KK
-
Kushiro, Hokkaido *Japan*
Official number: 125629
1983-05 **Narasaki Zosen KK — Muroran HK**
Yd No: 1052
Loa 38.13 Br ex 7.42 Dght 2.820
Lbp 33.15 Br md 7.41 Dpth 4.63
Welded, 1 dk
(B11A2FS) Stern Trawler
Ins: 120
Compartments: 1 Ho, ER
1 Ha: ER
1 oil engine with clutches, flexible couplings & dr geared to sc. shaft driving 1 CP propeller
Total Power: 861kW (1,171hp)
Fuji 6M2
1 x 4 Stroke 6 Cy. 280 x 350 861kW (1171bhp)
Fuji Diesel Co Ltd-Japan
AuxGen: 2 x 128kW 225V a.c, 1 x 24kW 225V a.c

8814976 JFWU MG1-1665
YAHATA MARU No. 18 409 - -
ex Kiei Maru No. 38 *-1999*
KK Yahata Suisan
-
SatCom: Inmarsat A 1202324
Kesennuma, Miyagi *Japan*
MMSI: 432012000
Official number: 130712
1988-10 **KK Kanasashi Zosen — Shizuoka SZ**
Yd No: 3176
Loa 54.11 Br ex 8.72 Dght 3.400
Lbp 47.50 Br md 8.70 Dpth 3.75
Welded, 1 dk
(B11B2FV) Fishing Vessel
Ins: 507
1 oil engine with clutches & sr reverse geared to sc. shaft driving 1 FP propeller
Total Power: 736kW (1,001hp)
Niigata 6M28BF
1 x 4 Stroke 6 Cy. 280 x 480 736kW (1001bhp)
Niigata Engineering Co Ltd-Japan

9004566 - -
YAHATA MARU No. 35 420 - -
ex Yoshi Maru No. 70 *-1999*
Hamaki Gyogyo KK
-
1990-08 **Niigata Engineering Co Ltd — Niigata NI**
Yd No: 2176
Loa 54.55 (BB) Br ex - Dght 3.440
Lbp 47.90 Br md 8.70 Dpth 3.80
Welded
(B11B2FV) Fishing Vessel
Ins: 502
1 oil engine with clutches, flexible couplings & sr geared to sc. shaft driving 1 CP propeller
Total Power: 699kW (950hp)
Niigata 6M28HF
1 x 4 Stroke 6 Cy. 280 x 480 699kW (950bhp)
Niigata Engineering Co Ltd-Japan

9661948 - -
YAHATA MARU NO. 68 184 - 163 Class: FA
-
Yahatamaru Gyogyo Seisan Kumiai
-
Kesennuma, Miyagi *Japan*
2013-08 **K.K. Yoshida Zosen Tekko — Kesennuma**
Yd No: 562
Loa 41.33 Br ex - Dght 2.700
Lbp - Br md 7.00 Dpth -
Welded, 1 dk
(B11B2FV) Fishing Vessel
1 oil engine reduction geared to sc. shaft driving 1 Propeller
Total Power: 882kW (1,199hp)
Niigata 6MG26AF
1 x 4 Stroke 6 Cy. 260 x 460 882kW (1199bhp)
Niigata Engineering Co Ltd-Japan

8423703 JGIE -
YAHATA MARU NO. 78 177 - -
ex Kaiko Maru No. 36 *-2010*
ex Hoyo Maru No. 21 *-1997*
-
-
Hachinohe, Aomori *Japan*
Official number: 128152
1985-04 **Miyagi-ken Zosen Tekko K.K. — Kesennuma** Yd No: 101
L reg 34.70 Br ex - Dght 2.000
Lbp - Br md 6.40 Dpth 3.00
Welded
(B11B2FV) Fishing Vessel
1 oil engine driving 1 FP propeller

8849141 JH2859 -
YAHATA MARU NO. 88 170 - -
ex Kongo Maru No. 68 *-2003*
ex Hakuun Maru No. 38 *-1991*
-
-
Hachinohe, Aomori *Japan*
Official number: 123842
1980-01 **KK Toyo Zosen Tekkosho — Kamaishi IW**
L reg 29.70 Br ex - Dght -
Lbp - Br md 6.30 Dpth 2.50
Welded, 1 dk
(B11B2FV) Fishing Vessel
1 oil engine driving 1 FP propeller
Total Power: 331kW (450hp)
Yanmar
1 x 4 Stroke 331kW (450bhp)
Yanmar Diesel Engine Co Ltd-Japan

9138472 JGTW -
YAHIKO 1,380 - -
ex Satsuma *-1999*
Government of Japan (Ministry of Land, Infrastructure & Transport) (The Coastguard)
-
Tokyo *Japan*
MMSI: 431771000
Official number: 135191
1995-10 **Sumitomo Heavy Industries Ltd. — Oppama Shipyard, Yokosuka** Yd No: 1200
Loa 93.47 Br ex - Dght 4.100
Lbp 87.00 Br md 11.50 Dpth 6.40
Welded, 1 dk
(B34H2SQ) Patrol Vessel
2 oil engines with flexible couplings & sr geared to sc. shaft driving 2 CP propellers
Total Power: 5,148kW (7,000hp) 19.0k
Niigata 8MG32CL
2 x 4 Stroke 8 Cy. 320 x 420 each-2574kW (3500bhp)
Niigata Engineering Co Ltd-Japan

7853509 - -
YAHO MARU No. 5 471 - 1,409
-
Nam Yang Navigation Corp
1977 **Mategata Zosen K.K. — Namikata**
Loa 67.01 Br ex - Dght 4.120
Lbp 62.51 Br md 11.51 Dpth 6.10
Welded, 1 dk
(A31A2GX) General Cargo Ship
1 oil engine driving 1 FP propeller
Total Power: 1,177kW (1,600hp) 11.5k
Makita
1 x 4 Stroke 1177kW (1600bhp)
Makita Diesel Co Ltd-Japan

8730869 YB9523 -
YAHUKIMO SATU **200** 77 - Class: (KI)
PT Pelayaran Armada Bandar Bangun Persada
-
Jayapura *Indonesia*
2007-04 **P.T. Mariana Bahagia — Palembang**
L reg 32.00 Br ex - Dght 2.400
Lbp 27.50 Br md 8.00 Dpth 2.80
Welded, 1 dk
(A13B2TU) Tanker (unspecified)
Double Hull (13F)
2 oil engines reduction geared to sc. shafts driving 2 Propellers
Total Power: 376kW (512hp)
Yanmar 6CH-UT
2 x 4 Stroke 6 Cy. 105 x 125 each-188kW (256bhp)
Yanmar Diesel Engine Co Ltd-Japan

7333200 V3DM3 -
YAIZA **1,125** 337 816 Class: NV (LR)
✠ Classed LR until 5/3/10
ex Sjoli *-2007* *ex* Videy *-1998* *ex* Hronn *-1979*
Charter Maritimo Archipelago Canario SL
-
Belize City *Belize*
MMSI: 312606000
Official number: 230520032
1974-03 **Stocznia im Komuny Paryskiej — Gdynia**
Yd No: B425/202
Converted From: Stern Trawler-2005
Lengthened-1982
Loa 70.01 Br ex 11.38 Dght 4.960
Lbp 61.40 Br md 11.31 Dpth 7.32
Welded, 2 dks
(A31A2GX) General Cargo Ship
Ice Capable
1 oil engine sr geared to sc. shaft driving 1 CP propeller
Total Power: 3,200kW (4,351hp) 11.5
Sulzer 6ZL40/
1 x 4 Stroke 6 Cy. 400 x 480 3200kW (4351bhp)
Zaklady Urzadzen Technicznych'Zgoda' SA-Poland
AuxGen: 1 x 288kW 400V 50Hz a.c, 1 x 200kW 305V d.c

9524877 7JEW S01-1270
YAIZU 559 - 505
Shizuoka Prefectural Office
-
SatCom: Inmarsat C 443270610
Shizuoka, Shizuoka *Japan*
MMSI: 432706000
Official number: 140976
2009-06 **Miho Zosensho K.K. — Shimizu**
Yd No: 1537
Loa 65.00 Br ex - Dght 3.650
Lbp - Br md 16.00 Dpth -
Welded, 1 dk
(B11B2FV) Fishing Vessel
1 oil engine reduction geared to sc. shaft driving 1 FP propeller
Total Power: 1,618kW (2,200hp)
Akasaka E28B
1 x 4 Stroke 6 Cy. 280 x 480 1618kW (2200bhp)
Akasaka Tekkosho KK (Akasaka DieselLtd)-Japan

7398597 - -
YAK **721** 216 1,106 Class: IS (AB)
-
Adamac Marine Services Ltd (Adamac Group)
-
Lagos *Nigeria*
1973-04 **Halter Marine Fabricators, Inc. — Moss Point, Ms** Yd No: 351
Loa 56.08 Br ex - Dght 3.480
Lbp 54.92 Br md 12.20 Dpth 4.27
Welded, 1 dk
(B21A2OS) Platform Supply Ship
2 oil engines driving 2 FP propellers
Total Power: 1,104kW (1,500hp) 12.0k
Kromhout 9FBHD24
2 x 4 Stroke 9 Cy. 240 x 260 each-552kW (750bhp)
Stork Werkspoor Diesel BV-Netherlands

5400205 - DAK 528
YAKAAR 147 49 - Class: (BV)
ex Aigue Marine *-1979*
Societe Africaine de Peche de l'Atlantique (SAPA)
-
Dakar *Senegal*
1963 **Ch. Nav. Franco-Belges — Villeneuve-la-Garenne** Yd No: 501-1
L reg 30.00 Br ex 6.91 Dght 3.501
Lbp 25.46 Br md 6.86 Dpth 3.66
Welded, 1 dk
(B11A2FT) Trawler
2 Ha: 2 (1.1 x 1.0)
Derricks: 1x1t; Winches: 1
1 oil engine driving 1 CP propeller
Total Power: 441kW (600hp) 11.8k
Baudouin DVX1
1 x Vee 4 Stroke 12 Cy. 185 x 200 441kW (600bhp)
Societe des Moteurs Baudouin SA-France
Fuel: 306.5 (d.f.)

5055323 TCBB3 -
YAKAMOZ-5 **498** 267 602 Class: (LR) (TL)
✠ Classed LR until 12/12/89
ex Antwone *-2007* *ex* Honurrinare *-2003*
ex Nur Pinar *-2002* *ex* Burak Reis *-2000*
Saroz Gemicilik ve Armatorluk Sanayi ve Ticaret Ltd Sti
-
Istanbul *Turkey*
MMSI: 271002386
1961-11 **Celiktrans Deniz Insaat Kizaklari Ltd. Sti — Tuzla,Ist** Yd No: 13
Loa 52.15 Br ex - Dght 3.120
Lbp 47.50 Br md 8.40 Dpth 3.61
Welded, 1 dk
(A13B2TU) Tanker (unspecified)
Liq: 829; Liq (Oil): 829
Compartments: 8 Ta, ER
1 oil engine with fluid couplings & reverse geared to sc. sha driving 1 FP propeller
Total Power: 375kW (510hp) 9.0k
Alpha 406-24V
1 x 2 Stroke 6 Cy. 240 x 400 375kW (510bhp)
Alpha Diesel A/S-Denmark
Fuel: 35.0 (d.f.)

8929862 - -
YAKHONT 187 - 46 Class: RS
ex Kotlin *-2000*
OOO 'Kontur-SPB'
-
St Petersburg *Russia*
Official number: 810620
1982 **Gorokhovetskiy Sudostroitelnyy Zavod — Gorokhovets** Yd No: 411
Loa 29.30 Br ex 8.49 Dght 3.090
Lbp 27.00 Br md - Dpth 4.35
Welded, 1 dk
(B32A2ST) Tug
Ice Capable
2 oil engines driving 2 CP propellers
Total Power: 882kW (1,200hp) 11.4k
Russkiy 6D30/50-4
2 x 2 Stroke 6 Cy. 300 x 500 each-441kW (600bhp)
Mashinostroitelnyy Zavod"Russkiy-Dizel"-Leningrad
AuxGen: 2 x 30kW a.c
Fuel: 30.0 (d.f.)

IMO / Call sign	Name / Owner / Manager / Flag	Tonnage	Class	Builder / Dimensions	Type / Capacity	Machinery
835360 */CD7863*	**YAKIMA** **State of Washington (Department of Transportation)** Washington State Department of Transportation (Washington State Ferries) *Seattle, WA* *United States of America* MMSI: 366772750 Official number: 511823	*2,705* 1,115 800	Class: (AB)	**1968-03 National Steel & Shipbuilding Co. (NASSCO) — San Diego, Ca** Yd No: 355 Loa 116.43 Br ex - Dght 5.500 Lbp 108.81 Br md 22.25 Dpth 7.39 Welded, 1 dk	**(A36A2PR) Passenger/Ro-Ro Ship (Vehicles)** Passengers: unberthed: 2500 Bow door/ramp (centre) Stern door/ramp (centre) Cars: 144	**4 diesel electric oil engines** driving 2 FP propellers Total Power: 6,592kW (8,964hp) 17.0kn EMD (Electro-Motive) 16-567-BC 4 x Vee 2 Stroke 16 Cy. 216 x 254 each-1648kW (2241bhp) General Motors Corp-USA AuxGen: 2 x 300kW a.c
309675 */X7735*	**YAKIMA** *ex* J. P. Moore *-2009* *ex* Valley King *-2001* - - *Port Isabel, TX* *United States of America* Official number: 506456	*116* 79 -		**1966 Border Marine Ways, Inc. — Brownsville, Tx** Yd No: 2 L reg 22.77 Br ex - Dght - Lbp - Br md 6.25 Dpth 3.56 Welded, 1 dk	**(B11B2FV) Fishing Vessel**	**1 oil engine** driving 1 FP propeller Total Power: 279kW (379hp)
915225 *YSZ*	**YAKIMA PRINCESS** *ex* Yakima *-2007* *ex* Med Trust *-2003* *ex* Iloilo I *-2002* *ex* Iloilo *-2001* *ex* K-Christina *-1998* **Montrose Maritime Corp** Roymar Ship Management Inc *Manila* *Philippines* MMSI: 548771000 Official number: MNLA000695	**23,515** 14,132 42,475	Class: LR (BV) (AB) (NK) **100A1** SS 07/2010 bulk carrier strengthened for heavy cargoes, Nos. 2 & 4 holds may be empty ESN-Hold No. 1 ESP **LMC** Eq.Ltr: J†; Cable: 605.0/66.0 U3 (a)	**1990-06 Oshima Shipbuilding Co Ltd — Saikai NS** Yd No: 10126 Loa 181.80 (BB) Br ex - Dght 11.150 Lbp 173.60 Br md 30.50 Dpth 15.80 Welded, 1 dk	**(A21A2BC) Bulk Carrier** Grain: 52,734; Bale: 51,715 Compartments: 5 Ho, ER 5 Ha: (14.4 x 15.3)4 (19.2 x 15.3)ER Cranes: 4x25t	**1 oil engine** driving 1 FP propeller Total Power: 8,470kW (11,516hp) 14.0kn Sulzer 6RTA52 1 x 2 Stroke 6 Cy. 520 x 1800 8470kW (11516bhp) Diesel United Ltd.-Aioi AuxGen: 3 x 410kW 450V 60Hz a.c Boilers: AuxB (Comp) 7.0kgf/cm² (6.9bar) Fuel: 106.0 (d.f.) 1422.0 (r.f.) 24.2pd
421779 *CBV2*	**YAKIT II** **Istanbul Buyuksehir Belediye Baskanligi** Istanbul Deniz Otobusleri Sanayi ve Ticaret AS (IDO) *Istanbul* *Turkey* MMSI: 271002376 Official number: 5709	**843** 379 1,266	Class: (TL)	**1989-02 Turkiye Gemi Sanayii A.S. — Camialti, Istanbul** Yd No: 230 Loa 65.51 Br ex - Dght 3.850 Lbp 58.90 Br md 10.70 Dpth 4.67 Welded, 1 dk	**(B35E2TF) Bunkering Tanker**	**2 oil engines** driving 2 FP propellers Total Power: 1,148kW (1,560hp) 11.5kn Sulzer 6AL20/24 2 x 4 Stroke 6 Cy. 200 x 240 each-574kW (780bhp) (, fitted 1988) Sulzer Bros Ltd-Switzerland
143790 *FQB3*	**YAKOOT** *ex* Tim *-2011* *ex* Sea Explorer *-2011* *ex* Tim *-2001* *ex* Cagema St. Vincent *-1999* *launched as* Tim *-1997* **Callier Seaways Inc** White Line Shipping & Cargo LLC *Panama* *Panama* MMSI: 352965000 Official number: 4331811	**3,850** 1,980 4,766	Class: BV (GL)	**1997-06 Estaleiros Navais de Viana do Castelo S.A. — Viana do Castelo** Yd No: 200 Loa 100.60 (BB) Br ex - Dght 5.898 Lbp 93.37 Br md 16.50 Dpth 7.50 Welded, 1 dk	**(A31A2GX) General Cargo Ship** Grain: 6,634 TEU 387 C.Ho 127/20' (40') C.Dk 260/20' (40') incl. 50 ref C. Compartments: 2 Ho, ER 2 Ha: (25.6 x 13.2) (32.0 x 13.2)ER Cranes: 2x40t Ice Capable	**1 oil engine** with flexible couplings & sr gearedto sc. shaft driving 1 CP propeller Total Power: 3,523kW (4,790hp) 15.5kn MaK 8M32 1 x 4 Stroke 8 Cy. 320 x 480 3523kW (4790bhp) MaK Motoren GmbH & Co. KG-Kiel AuxGen: 1 x 700kW 220/380V a.c, 3 x 257kW 220/380V a.c Thrusters: 1 Thwart. FP thruster (f) Fuel: 70.0 (d.f.) 280.0 (r.f.) 15.0pd
741495	**YAKOV BUTAKOV** **Trading House Mortrans Co Ltd** Mortrans Co Ltd *Vladivostok* *Russia* MMSI: 273443150	*245* 103 51	Class: RS	**1978-12 Nakhodkinskiy Sudoremontnyy Zavod — Nakhodka** Yd No: 10 Loa 38.41 Br ex 6.71 Dght 2.201 Lbp 34.50 Br md 6.70 Dpth 2.90 Welded, 1 dk	**(A37B2PS) Passenger Ship** Passengers: unberthed: 180 Ice Capable	**2 oil engines** geared to sc. shafts driving 2 FP propellers Total Power: 464kW (630hp) 12.7kn Daldizel 8CHNSP18/22 2 x 4 Stroke 8 Cy. 180 x 220 each-232kW (315bhp) Daldizel-Khabarovsk Fuel: 20.0 (d.f.)
137492 *BZH* M-0470	**YAKOV GUNIN** **Murmansk Trawl Fleet Co (OAO 'Murmanskiy Tralovyy Flot')** - *Murmansk* *Russia* MMSI: 273550400 Official number: 950421	**837** 262 1,010	Class: RS (NV)	**1997-07 Peene-Werft GmbH — Wolgast** Yd No: 470 Loa 40.80 (BB) Br ex - Dght 5.300 Lbp 34.80 Br md 11.00 Dpth 7.25 Welded, 1 dk	**(B11A2FG) Factory Stern Trawler** Ins: 440 Compartments: 1 Ho 1 Ha: (2.3 x 2.3) Ice Capable	**1 oil engine** with clutches, flexible couplings & sr geared to sc. shaft driving 1 CP propeller Total Power: 1,920kW (2,610hp) 12.0kn Alpha 12V23/30A 1 x Vee 4 Stroke 12 Cy. 225 x 300 1920kW (2610bhp) MAN B&W Diesel A/S-Denmark AuxGen: 1 x 1000kW 220/380V 50Hz a.c, 1 x 540kW 220/380V 50Hz a.c, 1 x 356kW 220/380V 50Hz a.c Fuel: 200.0 (d.f.) 8.0pd
725852 *EXN* -0233	**YAKOV PAVLOV** **Akros 1 JSC** Akros Fishing Co Ltd (A/O Akros) SatCom: Inmarsat C 427320840 *Petropavlovsk-Kamchatskiy* *Russia* MMSI: 273843610 Official number: 840772	**784** 235 338	Class: RS	**1985-05 Volgogradskiy Sudostroitelnyy Zavod — Volgograd** Yd No: 223 Loa 53.74 Br ex 10.71 Dght 4.330 Lbp 47.92 Br md 10.50 Dpth 6.00 Welded, 1 dk	**(B11A2FS) Stern Trawler** Ice Capable	**1 oil engine** driving 1 CP propeller Total Power: 970kW (1,319hp) 12.7kn S.K.L. 8NVD48A-2U 1 x 4 Stroke 8 Cy. 320 x 480 970kW (1319bhp) VEB Schwermaschinenbau "KarlLiebknecht" (SKL)-Magdeburg AuxGen: 1 x 300kW a.c, 3 x 160kW a.c, 2 x 135kW a.c
423299 *CYM*	**YAKOV SMIRNITSKIY** **Government of The Russian Federation** Government of The Russian Federation (Federal State Unitary Hydrographic Department of Ministry of Transport of Russian Federation) SatCom: Inmarsat C 427300995 *Arkhangelsk* *Russia* MMSI: 273917000	**1,267** 380 590	Class: RS	**1977-11 Oy Laivateollisuus Ab — Turku** Yd No: 317 Loa 68.46 Br ex 12.43 Dght 4.160 Lbp 60.20 Br md 12.40 Dpth 6.02 Welded, 2 dks	**(B31A2SR) Research Survey Vessel** Bale: 481 Compartments: 2 Ho, ER 2 Ha: (1.9 x 1.0) (4.8 x 3.2)ER Cranes: 1x5t,1x2t Ice Capable	**1 oil engine** geared to sc. shaft driving 1 CP propeller Total Power: 1,471kW (2,000hp) 13.5kn Deutz RBV6M358 1 x 4 Stroke 6 Cy. 400 x 580 1471kW (2000bhp) Kloeckner Humboldt Deutz AG-West Germany Thrusters: 1 Thwart. FP thruster (f) Fuel: 281.0 (d.f.)
906048	**YAKSAN** *ex* Iide *-1999* *ex* Iide Maru *-1998* *ex* Seto Reefer *-1991* *ex* Chinuya Maru *-1988* - -	**757** 288 504	Class: KC	**1980-05 K.K. Yoshida Zosen Kogyo — Arida** Yd No: 333 Loa 60.04 Br ex - Dght 3.050 Lbp 56.00 Br md 9.20 Dpth 4.90 Welded, 1 dk	**(A34A2GR) Refrigerated Cargo Ship**	**1 oil engine** driving 1 FP propeller Total Power: 736kW (1,001hp) Makita GSLH6275 1 x 4 Stroke 6 Cy. 275 x 450 736kW (1001bhp) Makita Diesel Co Ltd-Japan
915570 *V8733*	**YAKTEMI** *ex* Ansgariturm *-1979* **Emepa SA** - *Buenos Aires* *Argentina* MMSI: 701000676 Official number: 02166	*446* 274 725	Class: RI (GL)	**1969 JG Hitzler Schiffswerft und Masch GmbH & Co KG — Lauenburg** Yd No: 711 Loa 53.67 Br ex 11.03 Dght 3.366 Lbp 49.20 Br md 11.00 Dpth 3.94 Welded, 1 dk	**(B21A20S) Platform Supply Ship** Derricks: 1x5t Ice Capable	**2 oil engines** driving 2 FP propellers Total Power: 1,398kW (1,900hp) 12.0kn MWM TB12RS18/22 2 x Vee 4 Stroke 12 Cy. 180 x 220 each-699kW (950bhp) Motoren Werke Mannheim AG (MWM)-West Germany AuxGen: 1 x 336kW 380/220V 50Hz a.c Thrusters: 1 Thwart. FP thruster (f) Fuel: 279.5 (d.f.)
362877 *7QS7*	**YAKUMOSAN** **Star Express Inc** Nova Tankers A/S SatCom: Inmarsat C 453833334 *Majuro* *Marshall Islands* MMSI: 538003428 Official number: 3428	**159,943** 97,999 302,165 T/cm 182.6	Class: NK	**2008-11 IHI Marine United Inc — Kure HS** Yd No: 3223 Loa 333.00 (BB) Br ex 60.04 Dght 20.635 Lbp 324.00 Br md 60.00 Dpth 29.00 Welded, 1 dk	**(A13A2TV) Crude Oil Tanker** Double Hull (13F) Liq: 333,700; Liq (Oil): 340,000 Compartments: 10 Wing Ta, 5 Ta, 2 Wing Slop Ta, ER 3 Cargo Pump (s): 3x5500m³/hr Manifold: Bow/CM: 163.6m	**1 oil engine** driving 1 FP propeller Total Power: 27,160kW (36,927hp) 15.5kn Wartsila 7RT-flex84T 1 x 2 Stroke 7 Cy. 840 x 3150 27160kW (36927bhp) Diesel United Ltd.-Aioi AuxGen: 3 x 1100kW 450V a.c Fuel: 7335.0 (r.f.)
21288 *TG6*	**YAKUP AGA** *ex* My Ship 2 *-2008* *ex* Penyez *-2006* *ex* Electron *-2004* **Buse Denizcilik ve Ticaret Ltd Sti** Ayden Deniz Tasimaciligi Ve Ticaret AS *Istanbul* *Turkey* MMSI: 271002612	**1,923** 1,074 3,145	Class: TL (BR) (BV)	**1983-10 Bodewes' Scheepswerven B.V. — Hoogezand** Yd No: 546 Loa 80.58 (BB) Br ex 13.62 Dght 5.720 Lbp 73.51 Br md 13.42 Dpth 6.84 Welded, 2 dks	**(A31A2GX) General Cargo Ship** Grain: 3,922; Bale: 3,777 Compartments: 2 Ho, ER 2 Ha: 2 (21.5 x 9.5)ER	**1 oil engine** with flexible couplings & sr gearedto sc. shaft driving 1 FP propeller Total Power: 1,125kW (1,530hp) 12.0kn MaK 6M452AK 1 x 4 Stroke 6 Cy. 320 x 450 1125kW (1530bhp) Krupp MaK Maschinenbau GmbH-Kiel
24831	**YAKUSHI MARU No. 21** - -	*349* 189 -		**1971 Yamanishi Shipbuilding Co Ltd — Ishinomaki MG** Yd No: 681 Loa 54.39 Br ex 9.02 Dght 3.328 Lbp 48.42 Br md 9.00 Dpth 5.87 Welded, 2 dks	**(B11A2FT) Trawler**	**1 oil engine** driving 1 FP propeller Total Power: 1,839kW (2,500hp) Akasaka AH40 1 x 4 Stroke 6 Cy. 400 x 600 1839kW (2500bhp) Akasaka Tekkosho KK (Akasaka DieselLtd)-Japan

IMO / Call sign	Name / Owner / Manager	Tonnage	Class	Builder / Dimensions	Type	Machinery
7509603 *UDRI* -	**YAKUTIA** *ex* Ivan Strod *-2012* **Holding Yakutsky Rechnoy Port Co Ltd** Shipping Co 'Vega' Co Ltd SatCom: Inmarsat C 427300745 *Tiksi* *Russia* MMSI: 273194200 Official number: 742550	**3,736** 1,527 4,000	Class: RS	**1975-03 Navashinskiy Sudostroitelnyy Zavod 'Oka' — Navashino** Yd No: 1077 Loa 123.50 Br ex 15.02 Dght 4.500 Lbp 117.00 Br md 14.99 Dpth 6.51 Welded, 1 dk	**(A31A2GX) General Cargo Ship** Grain: 6,070; Bale: 5,800 Compartments: 4 Ho, ER 4 Ha: 2 (12.0 x 8.3)2 (13.7 x 8.3)ER Cranes: 2x8t Ice Capable	**2 oil engines** driving 2 FP propellers Total Power: 1,472kW (2,002hp) 11.3k Russkiy 8DR30/50- 2 x 2 Stroke 8 Cy. 300 x 500 each-736kW (1001bhp) Mashinostroitelnyy Zavod"Russkiy-Dizel"-Leningrad Fuel: 219.0 (d.f.)
7008788 *EQTS* -	**YAL** *ex* Dafi *-1993* *ex* Smit Noordzee *-1988* *ex* Noordzee *-1986* **M Yavariyan** - SatCom: Inmarsat A 1104246 *Bushehr* *Iran* MMSI: 422176000 Official number: 659	**1,371** 411 965	Class: AS (LR) ✠ Classed LR until 1/5/98	**1970-06 NV Scheepswerf & Mfbk 'De Merwede' v/h van Vliet & Co — Hardinxveld** Yd No: 599 Loa 68.51 Br ex 12.60 Dght 5.696 Lbp 62.08 Br md 12.10 Dpth 6.41 Welded	**(B32A2ST) Tug**	**1 oil engine** sr geared to sc. shaft driving 1 CP propeller Total Power: 2,574kW (3,500hp) 15.0k Werkspoor 6TM41 1 x 4 Stroke 6 Cy. 410 x 470 2574kW (3500bhp) Stork Werkspoor Diesel BV-Netherlands AuxGen: 3 x 272kW 380V 50Hz a.c Thrusters: 1 Thwart. FP thruster (f) Fuel: 874.0 (r.f.)
9154488 *TC7866* -	**YALCIN 2** - **OMH Denizcilik Petrol Urunleri Nakliye ve Pazarlama Ithalat Ihracat Sanayi ve Ticaret Ltd Sti** - *Istanbul* *Turkey* MMSI: 271010209 Official number: TUGS 627	**290** 212 550	Class: (TL)	**1996-05 Rota Denizcilik Ticaret A.S. — Tuzla, Istanbul** Loa 50.65 Br ex - Dght 3.080 Lbp 46.40 Br md 7.20 Dpth 3.50 Welded, 1 dk	**(A12A2TC) Chemical Tanker** Liq: 835 Compartments: 14 Ta, ER	**1 oil engine** with clutches, flexible couplings & sr geared to sc. shaft driving 1 FP propeller Total Power: 375kW (510hp) Volvo Penta TAMD16 1 x 4 Stroke 6 Cy. 144 x 165 375kW (510bhp) AB Volvo Penta-Sweden
7121528 *EPBA* -	**YALDA** *ex* Wanda *-1998* *ex* Vicki *-1998* **Manoochehr Jamshidi & Partners** - *Bandar Abbas* *Iran* Official number: 504	**261** 78 244	Class: AS (HR) (AB)	**1970 Corpus Christi Marine Service — Corpus Christi, Tx** Yd No: 112 Loa - Br ex 7.93 Dght 3.077 Lbp 33.48 Br md 7.92 Dpth 3.74 Welded, 1 dk	**(B21A20S) Platform Supply Ship**	**2 oil engines** reverse reduction geared to sc. shafts driving 2 FP propellers Total Power: 1,132kW (1,540hp) 12.0k G.M. (Detroit Diesel) 12V-149-N 2 x Vee 2 Stroke 12 Cy. 146 x 146 each-566kW (770bhp) General Motors Detroit DieselAllison Divn-USA AuxGen: 2 x 75kW
8328654 - -	**YALE** - **Benino-Arabe Libyenne de Peche Maritime** - *Cotonou* *Benin*	*154* 43 -	Class: (BV)	**1983 Soc. Esercizio Cant. S.p.A. — Viareggio** Yd No: 665 Loa 25.81 Br ex - Dght 2.750 Lbp 20.40 Br md 7.03 Dpth 3.41 Welded, 1 dk	**(B11A2FS) Stern Trawler**	**1 oil engine** driving 1 FP propeller Total Power: 500kW (680hp) 11.5k Baudouin 12P15.2S 1 x Vee 4 Stroke 12 Cy. 150 x 150 500kW (680bhp) Societe des Moteurs Baudouin SA-France
8926913 *V4TY* -	**YALKER** *ex* Leslie *-2007* *ex* Pollux *-2005* *ex* Kiev *-2005* *ex* Kiyev *-2004* **Steep Shipping & Trading SA** Midland Shipping Co Ltd *Charlestown* *St Kitts & Nevis* MMSI: 341517000 Official number: SKN 1001517	**2,463** 979 3,157	Class: RS (RR)	**1980-01 Santierul Naval Oltenita S.A. — Oltenita** Yd No: 119 Loa 108.40 Br ex 14.80 Dght 3.260 Lbp 105.00 Br md 14.80 Dpth 5.00 Welded, 1 dk	**(A31A2GX) General Cargo Ship** Ice Capable	**2 oil engines** driving 2 FP propellers Total Power: 1,030kW (1,400hp) 10.0k S.K.L. 6NVD48A-2 2 x 4 Stroke 6 Cy. 320 x 480 each-515kW (700bhp) VEB Schwermaschinenbau "KarlLiebknecht" (SKL)-Magdeburg AuxGen: 3 x 50kW a.c
1008011 *ZCNO6* -	**YALLA** - **Crystal Clear Ltd** - *George Town* *Cayman Islands (British)* MMSI: 319002000 Official number: 737352	**498** 149 113	Class: NV	**2004-07 Heesen Shipyards B.V. — Oss** Yd No: 12246 Loa 46.70 Br ex 8.52 Dght 2.620 Lbp 40.00 Br md 8.50 Dpth 4.30 Welded, 1 dk	**(X11A2YP) Yacht**	**2 oil engines** reduction geared to sc. shafts driving 2 FP propellers Total Power: 2,320kW (3,154hp) M.T.U. 8V4000M7 1 x Vee 4 Stroke 8 Cy. 165 x 190 1160kW (1577bhp) MTU Friedrichshafen GmbH-Friedrichshafen AuxGen: 2 x a.c, 1 x a.c
8615382 *TC6113* -	**YALOVA-I** *ex* Yalova 3 *-2001* *ex* Kumburgaz *-2001* **Izmir Buyuksehir Belediye Baskanligi** Izmir Deniz Isletmeciligi Nakliye ve Turizm Ticaret AS (Izdeniz AS) *Izmir* *Turkey* MMSI: 271001242 Official number: 1795	*307* 79 100	Class: TL	**1988-04 Turkiye Gemi Sanayii A.S. — Alaybey, Izmir** Yd No: 77 Loa 49.15 Br ex - Dght - Lbp 47.32 Br md 8.97 Dpth 2.53 Welded, 1 dk	**(A37B2PS) Passenger Ship**	**2 oil engines** driving 2 FP propellers Total Power: 936kW (1,272hp) 14.0k Sulzer 6AL20/2 2 x 4 Stroke 6 Cy. 200 x 240 each-468kW (636bhp) Turkiye Gemi Sanayii AS-Turkey
9617014 *VRJW8* -	**YAM O** - **Hongkong United Dockyards Ltd** The Hongkong Salvage & Towage Co Ltd *Hong Kong* *Hong Kong* MMSI: 477947200	**481** 144 295	Class: LR ✠ **100A1** SS 06/2012 tug ✠ **LMC** Eq.Ltr: H; Cable: 275.0/22.0 U2 (a)	**2012-06 Hin Lee (Zhuhai) Shipyard Co Ltd — Zhuhai GD** (Hull) Yd No: 234 **2012-06 Cheoy Lee Shipyards Ltd — Hong Kong** Yd No: 5023 Loa 29.98 Br ex 11.86 Dght 4.200 Lbp - Br md 11.56 Dpth 5.39 Welded, 1 dk	**(B32A2ST) Tug**	**2 oil engines** gearing integral to driving 2 Z propellers Total Power: 3,676kW (4,998hp) Niigata 6L28H 2 x 4 Stroke 6 Cy. 280 x 370 each-1838kW (2499bhp) Niigata Engineering Co Ltd-Japan AuxGen: 2 x 80kW 380V 50Hz a.c
7804704 - -	**YAMA MARU No. 5** *ex* Inari Maru No. 21 *-1987* - -	*179* - -		**1978-04 Minami-Kyushu Zosen KK — Ichikikushikino KS** Yd No: 285 Loa 38.61 Br ex - Dght 2.650 Lbp 32.11 Br md 7.05 Dpth 2.98 Welded, 1 dk	**(B11B2FV) Fishing Vessel**	**1 oil engine** driving 1 FP propeller Total Power: 662kW (900hp) Niigata 6L25B 1 x 4 Stroke 6 Cy. 250 x 320 662kW (900bhp) Niigata Engineering Co Ltd-Japan
8621109 - IG1-567	**YAMA MARU No. 7** - **Damalerio Fishing Enterprise** - *Philippines*	*135* - -		**1983 K.K. Watanabe Zosensho — Nagasaki** Yd No: 1033 Loa - Br ex - Dght - Lbp 34.12 Br md 7.51 Dpth 3.00 Welded, 1 dk	**(B12B2FC) Fish Carrier**	**1 oil engine** driving 1 FP propeller
7937056 - -	**YAMA MARU No. 27** - **Kazuko Fukuchi**	*116* 33 -		**1975-02 Nichiro Zosen K.K. — Ishinomaki** Yd No: 355 Loa 36.35 Br ex - Dght - Lbp 29.98 Br md 7.00 Dpth 2.85 Welded, 1 dk	**(B11B2FV) Fishing Vessel**	**1 oil engine** driving 1 FP propeller Total Power: 956kW (1,300hp) Niigata 6L28B 1 x 4 Stroke 6 Cy. 280 x 320 956kW (1300bhp) Niigata Engineering Co Ltd-Japan
9554456 *JD2897* -	**YAMABISHI MARU NO. 11** - **Yamane Shipping Co Ltd (Yamane Kaiun KK)** - *Tokyo* *Japan* Official number: 140993	*498* - 1,230		**2009-04 Hongawara Zosen K.K. — Fukuyama** Yd No: 625 Loa 64.80 Br ex 10.22 Dght 4.200 Lbp 61.00 Br md 10.20 Dpth 4.50 Welded, 1 dk	**(A12B2TR) Chemical/Products Tanker** Double Hull (13F)	**1 oil engine** driving 1 Propeller Total Power: 1,176kW (1,599hp) Akasaka K28 1 x 4 Stroke 6 Cy. 280 x 500 1176kW (1599bhp) Akasaka Tekkosho KK (Akasaka DieselLtd)-Japan
9078270 *JG5267* -	**YAMABISHI MARU No. 16** - **Yamane Shipping Co Ltd (Yamane Kaiun KK)** - *Tokyo* *Japan* MMSI: 431400222 Official number: 134297	*566* - 1,350		**1993-10 Imamura Zosen — Kure** Yd No: 371 Loa 65.38 (BB) Br ex - Dght 4.250 Lbp 63.88 Br md 10.40 Dpth 4.60 Welded, 1 dk	**(A12A2TC) Chemical Tanker** Compartments: 8 Ta, ER 2 Cargo Pump (s): 2x300m³/hr	**1 oil engine** driving 1 FP propeller Total Power: 1,177kW (1,600hp) Hanshin LH28 1 x 4 Stroke 6 Cy. 280 x 530 1177kW (1600bhp) The Hanshin Diesel Works Ltd-Japan
9415698 *VRGG9* -	**YAMABUKI** - **Heroic Draco Inc** Phoenix Tankers Pte Ltd SatCom: Inmarsat C 447702575 *Hong Kong* *Hong Kong* MMSI: 477691300 Official number: HK-2622	**47,005** 17,449 58,811 T/cm 71.2	Class: KR (AB)	**2010-03 Hyundai Heavy Industries Co Ltd — Ulsan** Yd No: 2019 Loa 225.28 (BB) Br ex 36.63 Dght 12.574 Lbp 215.00 Br md 36.60 Dpth 22.00 Welded, 1 dk	**(A11B2TG) LPG Tanker** Double Bottom Entire Compartment Length Liq (Gas): 80,793 4 x Gas Tank (s); 4 independent (C.mn.stl) pri horizontal 8 Cargo Pump (s): 8x600m³/hr Manifold: Bow/CM: 109.3m	**1 oil engine** driving 1 FP propeller Total Power: 13,560kW (18,436hp) 16.8k MAN-B&W 6S60MC- 1 x 2 Stroke 6 Cy. 600 x 2400 13560kW (18436bhp) Hyundai Heavy Industries Co Ltd-South Korea AuxGen: 3 x 1280kW a.c Fuel: 194.0 (d.f.) 2809.0 (r.f.)
9089279 *JM6473* -	**YAMADA MARU NO. 1** - **Yamada Suisan KK** - *Nagasaki, Nagasaki* *Japan* Official number: 135482	*113* - -		**1997-11 Nagasaki Zosen K.K. — Nagasaki** Loa 33.61 Br ex - Dght 2.450 Lbp - Br md 6.85 Dpth 3.09 Welded, 1 dk	**(B11B2FV) Fishing Vessel**	**1 oil engine** driving 1 Propeller Total Power: 1,029kW (1,399hp) 8.2k Niigata 6MG22H 1 x 4 Stroke 6 Cy. 220 x 280 1029kW (1399bhp) Niigata Engineering Co Ltd-Japan

IMO / Call sign / Fishing no.	Name / Former names / Owner / Registry	Tonnage	Class	Builder / Dimensions	Type / Cargo	Machinery
038115 *NTP* S1-1082	**YAMADA MARU No. 3** *ex* Kiku Maru No. 1 *-2000* **Yamada Suisan KK** - *Nagasaki, Nagasaki* *Japan* Official number: 132710	*162* - -		**1991**-10 **Nagasaki Zosen K.K. — Nagasaki** Yd No: 1087 Loa 39.80 (BB) Br ex - Dght 3.050 Lbp 33.00 Br md 7.50 Dpth 3.50 Welded	**(B11B2FV) Fishing Vessel**	**1 oil engine** driving 1 FP propeller Total Power: 699kW (950hp) Niigata 6M26AFTE 1 x 4 Stroke 6 Cy. 260 x 460 699kW (950bhp) Niigata Engineering Co Ltd-Japan
038127 *JM6061*	**YAMADA MARU No. 5** *ex* Kiku Maru No. 2 *-2000* **Yamada Suisan KK** - *Nagasaki, Nagasaki* *Japan* Official number: 132711	*162* - -		**1991**-10 **Nagasaki Zosen K.K. — Nagasaki** Yd No: 1088 Loa - Br ex - Dght 3.050 Lbp 33.50 Br md 7.50 Dpth 3.50 Welded	**(B11B2FV) Fishing Vessel**	**1 oil engine** driving 1 FP propeller Total Power: 699kW (950hp) Niigata 6M26AFTE 1 x 4 Stroke 6 Cy. 260 x 460 699kW (950bhp) Niigata Engineering Co Ltd-Japan
8114560 -	**YAMADA MARU No. 6** - - *China*	*144* - -		**1981**-06 **Nagasaki Zosen K.K. — Nagasaki** Yd No: 773 Loa - Br ex - Dght - Lbp 32.69 Br md 6.51 Dpth 3.00 Welded, 1 dk	**(B11A2FS) Stern Trawler**	**1 oil engine** reduction geared to sc. shaft driving 1 FP propeller Total Power: 758kW (1,031hp) Niigata 6MG25CX 1 x 4 Stroke 6 Cy. 250 x 320 758kW (1031bhp) Niigata Engineering Co Ltd-Japan
8114572 -	**YAMADA MARU No. 7** - - *China*	*144* - -		**1981**-06 **Nagasaki Zosen K.K. — Nagasaki** Yd No: 775 Loa - Br ex - Dght - Lbp 32.69 Br md 6.51 Dpth 3.00 Welded, 1 dk	**(B11A2FS) Stern Trawler**	**1 oil engine** reduction geared to sc. shaft driving 1 CP propeller Total Power: 758kW (1,031hp) 20.0kn Niigata 6MG25CX 1 x 4 Stroke 6 Cy. 250 x 320 758kW (1031bhp) Niigata Engineering Co Ltd-Japan AuxGen: 2 x 840kW 440V 60Hz a.c, 1 x 520kW 440V 60Hz a.c Thrusters: 1 Thwart. CP thruster (f)
8114584 -	**YAMADA MARU No. 12** - -	*144* - -		**1981**-07 **Nagasaki Zosen K.K. — Nagasaki** Yd No: 776 Loa - Br ex - Dght 2.661 Lbp 32.92 Br md 6.51 Dpth 3.03 Welded, 1 dk	**(B11B2FV) Fishing Vessel**	**1 oil engine** driving 1 FP propeller Total Power: 758kW (1,031hp) Niigata 6MG25CX 1 x 4 Stroke 6 Cy. 250 x 320 758kW (1031bhp) Niigata Engineering Co Ltd-Japan
8114596 -	**YAMADA MARU No. 13** - -	*144* - -		**1981**-07 **Nagasaki Zosen K.K. — Nagasaki** Yd No: 777 Loa - Br ex - Dght 2.661 Lbp 32.92 Br md 6.51 Dpth 3.03 Welded, 1 dk	**(B11B2FV) Fishing Vessel**	**1 oil engine** driving 1 FP propeller Total Power: 758kW (1,031hp) Niigata 6MG25CX 1 x 4 Stroke 6 Cy. 250 x 320 758kW (1031bhp) Niigata Engineering Co Ltd-Japan
8312928 *JMFD* NS1-945	**YAMADA MARU No. 15** **Yamada Suisan KK** *Nagasaki, Nagasaki* *Japan* Official number: 126975	*152* - 199		**1983**-09 **Nagasaki Zosen K.K. — Nagasaki** Yd No: 852 Loa 40.04 Br ex - Dght 2.739 Lbp 33.71 Br md 6.71 Dpth 3.13 Welded, 1 dk	**(B11A2FS) Stern Trawler** Ins: 150 Compartments: 4 Ho, ER 5 Ha: ER	**1 oil engine** with clutches, flexible couplings & dr reverse geared to sc. shaft driving 1 FP propeller Total Power: 699kW (950hp) Niigata 6M28AFTE 1 x 4 Stroke 6 Cy. 280 x 480 699kW (950bhp) Niigata Engineering Co Ltd-Japan
9038139 *JM6062* -	**YAMADA MARU No. 21** **Yamada Suisan KK** *Nagasaki, Nagasaki* *Japan* Official number: 132712	*164* - -		**1991**-11 **Nagasaki Zosen K.K. — Nagasaki** Yd No: 1100 Loa - Br ex - Dght 3.050 Lbp 34.00 Br md 7.50 Dpth 3.50 Welded	**(B11B2FV) Fishing Vessel**	**1 oil engine** driving 1 FP propeller Total Power: 699kW (950hp) Niigata 6M26AFTE 1 x 4 Stroke 6 Cy. 260 x 460 699kW (950bhp) Niigata Engineering Co Ltd-Japan
9038141 *JM6063* -	**YAMADA MARU No. 22** **Yamada Suisan KK** - *Nagasaki, Nagasaki* *Japan* Official number: 132713	*164* - -		**1991**-11 **Nagasaki Zosen K.K. — Nagasaki** Yd No: 1101 Loa - Br ex - Dght 3.050 Lbp 34.00 Br md 7.50 Dpth 3.50 Welded	**(B11B2FV) Fishing Vessel**	**1 oil engine** driving 1 FP propeller Total Power: 699kW (950hp) Niigata 6M26AFTE 1 x 4 Stroke 6 Cy. 260 x 460 699kW (950bhp) Niigata Engineering Co Ltd-Japan
9660982 *JD3403* -	**YAMAGATA MARU** **Wing Maritime Service Corp** *Yokohama, Kanagawa* *Japan* Official number: 141750	*190* - 80		**2012**-10 **Keihin Dock Co Ltd — Yokohama** Yd No: 303 Loa 32.80 Br ex - Dght 2.700 Lbp - Br md 8.80 Dpth - Welded, 1 dk	**(B32A2ST) Tug**	**2 oil engines** gearing integral to driving 2 Z propellers Total Power: 2,942kW (4,000hp) Niigata 6L26HLX 2 x 4 Stroke 6 Cy. 260 x 350 each-1471kW (2000bhp) Niigata Engineering Co Ltd-Japan
8308769 *9LD2417* -	**YAMAK JUNIOR** *ex* Stevns Pearl *-2012* *ex* Diana Scan *-2009* *ex* Stevns Pearl *-2005* *ex* CPC Holandia *-1995* *ex* Conti Holandia *-1987* **Eman Shipping Ltd** Kalesya Shipping Ltd SatCom: Inmarsat C 466700512 *Freetown* *Sierra Leone* MMSI: 667005117 Official number: SL105117	**4,366** 2,451 5,900	Class: DR (GL)	**1984**-03 **J.J. Sietas KG Schiffswerft GmbH & Co. — Hamburg** Yd No: 952 Loa 99.90 (BB) Br ex 17.89 Dght 6.940 Lbp 93.86 Br md 17.81 Dpth 9.00 Welded, 2 dks	**(A31A2GX) General Cargo Ship** Grain: 7,826; Bale: 7,411 TEU 323 C.Ho 129/20' (40') C.Dk 194/20' (40') incl. 20 ref C. Compartments: 1 Ho, ER 1 Ha: (63.7 x 12.7)ER Cranes: 2x80t Ice Capable	**1 oil engine** with flexible couplings & sr gearedto sc. shaft driving 1 CP propeller Total Power: 1,471kW (2,000hp) 13.8kn MaK 6M551AK 1 x 4 Stroke 6 Cy. 450 x 550 1471kW (2000bhp) Krupp MaK Maschinenbau GmbH-Kiel AuxGen: 1 x 400kW 380V 50Hz a.c, 3 x 264kW 380V 50Hz a.c Thrusters: 1 Thwart. FP thruster (f) Fuel: 112.0 (d.f.) 461.0 (r.f.) 13.0pd
9427811 *7JEI* -	**YAMAKUNI** **Government of Japan (Ministry of Land, Infrastructure & Transport) (The Coastguard)** *Tokyo* *Japan* Official number: 140879	*358* - -		**2009**-06 **Universal Shipbuilding Corp — Yokohama KN (Keihin Shipyard)** Yd No: 0047 Loa 56.00 Br ex - Dght - Lbp - Br md 8.50 Dpth 4.52 Welded, 1 dk	**(B34H2SQ) Patrol Vessel** Hull Material: Aluminium Alloy	**3 oil engines** reduction geared to sc. shafts driving 3 Water jets
9077549 *UCJT* -	**YAMAL** **Government of The Russian Federation** Federal State Unitary Enterprise 'Atomflot' SatCom: Inmarsat A 1404137 *Murmansk* *Russia* MMSI: 273132400 Official number: 863420	**20,646** 6,194 2,750	Class: RS	**1992**-10 **AO Baltiyskiy Zavod — Sankt-Peterburg** Yd No: 704 Converted From: Icebreaker-2007 Loa 150.00 Br ex 30.00 Dght 11.080 Lbp 130.56 Br md 28.00 Dpth 17.20 Welded, 4 dks	**(A37A2PC) Passenger/Cruise** Double Hull Passengers: cabins: 50; berths: 100 Cranes: 3x16t,2x10t Ice Capable	**2 turbo electric Steam Turbs** driving 6 gen. each 9000kW 780V a.c Connecting to 6 elec. motors each (8800kW) driving 3 FP propellers Total Power: 55,200kW (75,050hp) 19.5kn Russkiy TGG-27.50M5 2 x steam Turb each-27600kW (37525shp), made: 1988 in the U.S.S.R. Boilers: NRMain Boiler Type: Nuclear Steam
8887296 *UBEB* -	**YAMAL** *ex* Sabit Orudzhev *-2004* **Vega Azov Trans Co Ltd** Marine Shipping Co Ltd (OOO 'Morskaya Sudokhodnaya Kompaniya') SatCom: Inmarsat C 427300950 *Temryuk* *Russia* MMSI: 273455500 Official number: 940171	**4,110** 1,358 4,916	Class: RS	**1994**-07 **Sudostroitelnyy Zavod "Krasnoye Sormovo" — Nizhniy Novgorod** Yd No: 19611/33 Loa 117.50 Br ex 16.56 Dght 4.770 Lbp 111.40 Br md - Dpth 6.70 Welded, 1 dk	**(A31A2GX) General Cargo Ship** Grain: 5,087; Bale: 5,087 TEU 104 C. 104/20' Compartments: 3 Ho, ER 3 Ha: 3 (18.7 x 11.8)ER Ice Capable	**2 oil engines** driving 2 FP propellers Total Power: 1,940kW (2,638hp) 11.0kn S.K.L. 8NVD48A-3U 2 x 4 Stroke 8 Cy. 320 x 480 each-970kW (1319bhp) SKL Motoren u. Systemtechnik AG-Magdeburg AuxGen: 3 x 150kW a.c Thrusters: 2 Tunnel thruster (f) Fuel: 417.0 (d.f.)
8128250 *A7D6035* -	**YAMAMA** **Qatar Petroleum** - *Doha* *Qatar* Official number: 065/83	*144* 43 -	Class: (LR) ✠ Classed LR until 1/7/07	**1982**-09 **Fritimco B.V. — Bergum** (Hull) **1982**-09 **B.V. Scheepswerf Damen — Gorinchem** Yd No: 4619 Loa 30.89 Br ex 6.74 Dght 2.107 Lbp 27.64 Br md 6.53 Dpth 3.56 Welded, 1 dk	**(B21A2OC) Crew/Supply Vessel** Passengers: unberthed: 12	**2 oil engines** with clutches, flexible couplings & sr reverse geared to sc. shafts driving 2 FP propellers Total Power: 2,088kW (2,838hp) 22.0kn M.T.U. 12V396TB83 2 x Vee 4 Stroke 12 Cy. 165 x 185 each-1044kW (1419bhp) MTU Friedrichshafen GmbH-Friedrichshafen AuxGen: 2 x 60kW 415V 50Hz a.c Fuel: 14.0 (d.f.) 6.0pd
9085041 *JM6371* -	**YAMAMIYA MARU** **Yosuke Yamamiya** - *Ube, Yamaguchi* *Japan* Official number: 134461	*199* - 700		**1994**-07 **Taiyo Shipbuilding Co Ltd — Sanyoonoda YC** Yd No: 253 Loa 55.92 Br ex - Dght 3.130 Lbp 52.85 Br md 9.50 Dpth 5.30 Welded, 1 dk	**(A31A2GX) General Cargo Ship** Bale: 1,176 Compartments: 1 Ho, ER 1 Ha: ER	**1 oil engine** driving 1 FP propeller Total Power: 735kW (999hp) Hanshin LH28G 1 x 4 Stroke 6 Cy. 280 x 460 735kW (999bhp) The Hanshin Diesel Works Ltd-Japan Thrusters: 1 Thwart. FP thruster (f)

IMO / Call sign	Name / Owner / Manager / Port / Flag	Tonnage (GT / NT / DWT)	Class	Builder / Dimensions	Type	Machinery	
9620877 *CA3620* -	**YAMAN** **CPT Empresas Maritimas SA** - *Valparaiso* *Chile* MMSI: 725000878 Official number: 3286	**463** 138 -	Class: AB	**2011-08 Shunde Huaxing Shipyard — Foshan GD** (Hull) Yd No: (HY2173) **2011-08 Bonny Fair Development Ltd — Hong Kong** Yd No: HY2173 Loa 31.00 Br ex 11.30 Dght 4.300 Lbp 27.70 Br md 11.00 Dpth 5.60 Welded, 1 dk	**(B32A2ST) Tug**	**2 oil engines** reduction geared to sc. shafts driving 2 Propellers Total Power: 3,282kW (4,462hp) Caterpillar 2 x Vee 4 Stroke 16 Cy. 170 x 190 each-1641kW (2231bhp) Caterpillar Inc-USA Thrusters: 1 Tunnel thruster (f)	3516E
5083514 - -	**YAMANA** *ex* Dieter A *ex* Czajka *-1973* **Establecimiento Dafer Imageny Compania Srl**	**149** 106 100	Class: (PR)	**1952 Stocznia Polnocna (Northern Shipyard) — Gdansk** Yd No: B11/S192 Loa 32.57 Br ex 6.76 Dght 3.039 Lbp - Br md - Dpth 3.38 Riveted\Welded, 1 dk	**(B11A2FT) Trawler**	**1 oil engine** driving 1 FP propeller Total Power: 294kW (400hp) S.K.L. 1 x 4 Stroke 8 Cy. 240 x 360 294kW (400bhp) (new engine 1960) VEB Schwermaschinenbau "KarlLiebknecht" (SKL)-Magdeburg AuxGen: 1 x 66kW 330V d.c, 1 x 18kW 110V d.c, 1 x 12kW 110V d.c, 1 x 6kW 110V d.c	9.0kn
9572537 *JD3052* -	**YAMANAKA** **Japan Railway Construction, Transport & Technology Agency & Yamanaka Zosen** Yamanaka Zousen KK (Yamanaka Shipbuilding Corp) *Imabari, Ehime* *Japan* MMSI: 431001305 Official number: 141225	*748* - 2,330		**2010-03 Yamanaka Zosen K.K. — Imabari** Yd No: 787 Loa 83.13 Br ex - Dght 4.660 Lbp 77.50 Br md 13.00 Dpth 8.10 Welded, 1 dk	**(A31A2GX) General Cargo Ship** Grain: 3,978; Bale: 3,877 1 Ha: ER (44.2 x 10.2)	**1 oil engine** driving 1 FP propeller Total Power: 1,618kW (2,200hp) Hanshin 1 x 4 Stroke 6 Cy. 320 x 680 1618kW (2200bhp) The Hanshin Diesel Works Ltd-Japan	12.4kn LA32G
9100499 *J8B3776* -	**YAMANAKAKO** *ex* Yusho Ocean *-2008* **Yamanakako Shipping Co Ltd** Qingdao Harmony Shipping Co Ltd *Kingstown* *St Vincent & The Grenadines* MMSI: 375772000 Official number: 10249	**2,524** 1,296 3,372	Class: NK	**1994-04 Sanyo Zosen K.K. — Onomichi** Yd No: 1061 Loa 82.55 (BB) Br ex - Dght 5.847 Lbp 75.00 Br md 13.80 Dpth 8.00 Welded, 2 dks	**(A31A2GX) General Cargo Ship** Grain: 5,209; Bale: 4,943 Compartments: 2 Ho, ER 2 Ha: (12.6 x 9.5) (23.8 x 9.5)ER Cranes: 3x20t	**1 oil engine** driving 1 FP propeller Total Power: 1,471kW (2,000hp) Akasaka 1 x 4 Stroke 6 Cy. 380 x 740 1471kW (2000bhp) Akasaka Tekkosho KK (Akasaka DieselLtd)-Japan Thrusters: 1 Thwart. FP thruster (f) Fuel: 235.0 (r.f.)	A38
8849787 *TC4892* -	**YAMANLAR** **Turkiye Denizcilik Isletmeleri AS (Turkey Maritime Organization Inc)** - *Istanbul* *Turkey* MMSI: 271010780 Official number: 9763	*119* 88 -	Class: (TL)	**1985-07 Turkiye Gemi Sanayii A.S. — Alaybey, Izmir** Loa 26.15 Br ex - Dght 3.620 Lbp 26.15 Br md 6.70 Dpth 4.75 Welded, 1 dk	**(B32A2ST) Tug**	**1 oil engine** driving 1 FP propeller Total Power: 736kW (1,001hp) Normo 1 x 4 Stroke 6 Cy. 250 x 300 736kW (1001bhp) AS Bergens Mek Verksteder-Norway	LDMB-6
9634816 *JD3440* -	**YAMASAKURA** **Kawasaki Kinkai Kisen KK (Kawasaki Kinkai Kisen Kaisha Ltd)** Shuntoku Kisen Co Ltd *Tokyo* *Japan* MMSI: 431004122 Official number: 141806	**17,658** - 15,200	Class: NK	**2013-01 K.K. Miura Zosensho — Saiki** Yd No: 1380 Loa 149.50 Br ex - Dght 6.500 Lbp 146.00 Br md 27.20 Dpth 14.20 Welded, 1 dk	**(A23A2BD) Bulk Carrier, Self-discharging** Grain: 18,179	**1 oil engine** driving 1 FP propeller Total Power: 5,180kW (7,043hp) MAN-B&W 1 x 2 Stroke 7 Cy. 350 x 1400 5180kW (7043bhp) The Hanshin Diesel Works Ltd-Japan Fuel: 330.0	14.0kn 7S35MC
8932405 - -	**YAMASAN MARU No. 2** *ex* Koun Maru *-2008*	*137* - -		**1973-09 K.K. Izutsu Zosensho — Nagasaki** L reg 31.50 Br ex - Dght - Lbp - Br md 6.90 Dpth 2.70 Welded, 1 dk	**(B11B2FV) Fishing Vessel**	**1 oil engine** driving 1 FP propeller	
8304191 *JDRB* HK1-886	**YAMASAN MARU No. 5** *ex* Taiki Maru No. 18 *-1987* **Namima Gyogyo KK** *Wakkanai, Hokkaido* *Japan* Official number: 127081	*160* - -		**1983-08 Narasaki Zosen KK — Muroran HK** Yd No: 1055 Loa 38.00 (BB) Br ex - Dght 2.910 Lbp 33.02 Br md 7.41 Dpth 4.63 Welded, 1 dk	**(B11A2FS) Stern Trawler** Compartments: 1 Ho, ER 1 Ha: ER	**1 oil engine** with clutches, flexible couplings & sr geared to sc. shaft driving 1 CP propeller Total Power: 861kW (1,171hp) Fuji 1 x 4 Stroke 6 Cy. 280 x 350 861kW (1171bhp) Fuji Diesel Co Ltd-Japan	6M28
8410639 - -	**YAMASEN MARU** *ex* Yamasen Maru No. 61 *-2004* -	**241** 72 182		**1984-07 K.K. Murakami Zosensho — Ishinomaki** Yd No: 1173 Loa 39.40 (BB) Br ex - Dght 2.556 Lbp 31.91 Br md 6.61 Dpth 2.90 Welded, 1 dk	**(B11A2FS) Stern Trawler** Ins: 135	**1 oil engine** driving 1 FP propeller Total Power: 673kW (915hp) Daihatsu 1 x 4 Stroke 6 Cy. 240 x 320 673kW (915bhp) Daihatsu Diesel Manufacturing Co Lt-Japan	6DLM-24FS
9047960 *JG5009* -	**YAMASEN MARU NO. 35** *ex* Ohama Maru No. 38 *-2005* **YK Yamasen Maru Gyogyo** *Choshi, Chiba* *Japan* Official number: 133438	*292* - 500		**1992-03 Niigata Engineering Co Ltd — Niigata NI** Yd No: 2231 Loa 58.62 (BB) Br ex - Dght 3.730 Lbp 52.00 Br md 8.90 Dpth 4.20 Welded, 1 dk	**(B12B2FC) Fish Carrier** Ins: 460	**1 oil engine** with clutches, flexible couplings & sr reverse geared to sc. shaft driving 1 FP propeller Total Power: 853kW (1,160hp) Niigata 1 x 4 Stroke 6 Cy. 280 x 370 853kW (1160bhp) Niigata Engineering Co Ltd-Japan Thrusters: 1 Thwart. FP thruster (f)	6MG28HX
9701865 - -	**YAMASEN MARU NO. 78** **YK Yamasen Maru Gyogyo** *Japan*	*300* - -	Class: FA	**2014-03 Nagasaki Zosen K.K. — Nagasaki** Yd No: 1238 Loa 56.50 (BB) Br ex - Dght 3.300 Lbp - Br md 10.50 Dpth - Welded, 1 dk	**(B11B2FV) Fishing Vessel**	**1 oil engine** reduction geared to sc. shaft driving 1 Propeller Total Power: 2,560kW (3,481hp) Yanmar 1 x 4 Stroke 8 Cy. 260 x 385 2560kW (3481bhp) Yanmar Diesel Engine Co Ltd-Japan	8EY26
9638379 *JD3274* -	**YAMASHIRO MARU** **Yamashiro Kisen KK** *Kure, Hiroshima* *Japan* MMSI: 431003028 Official number: 141562	*199* - 770		**2011-12 Y.K. Okajima Zosensho — Matsuyama** Yd No: 268 Loa 57.64 Br ex - Dght 3.290 Lbp 51.00 Br md 9.50 Dpth 5.50 Welded, 1 dk	**(A31A2GX) General Cargo Ship**	**1 oil engine** geared to s. shaft driving 1 Propeller Total Power: 736kW (1,001hp) Hanshin 1 x 4 Stroke 6 Cy. 260 x 440 736kW (1001bhp) The Hanshin Diesel Works Ltd-Japan	11.5kn LH26G
9027996 *YB9502* -	**YAMASI JAYA** **PT Anugerah Bina Sukses** - *Jayapura* *Indonesia*	**254** 77 -	Class: KI	**1996-07 Disnav Kapal Bengkel & Galangan — Jayapura** L reg 39.00 Br ex - Dght 1.800 Lbp 36.00 Br md 9.00 Dpth 2.32 Welded, 1 dk	**(A35D2RL) Landing Craft** Bow ramp (centre)	**2 oil engines** geared to sc. shafts driving 2 Propellers Total Power: 442kW (600hp) Caterpillar 2 x 4 Stroke 6 Cy. 137 x 165 each-221kW (300bhp) Caterpillar Inc-USA	3406C-TA
9567714 *3FLW7* -	**YAMATAI** **FGL Sunrise Panama SA** Hachiuma Steamship Co Ltd (Hachiuma Kisen KK) SatCom: Inmarsat C 435783311 *Panama* *Panama* MMSI: 357833000 Official number: 4152110	**14,538** 4,362 19,818	Class: NK	**2010-03 Mitsubishi Heavy Industries Ltd. — Nagasaki** Yd No: 2271 Loa 162.00 (BB) Br ex - Dght 6.370 Lbp 152.62 Br md 38.00 Dpth 9.00 Welded, 1 dk	**(A38C2GH) Heavy Load Carrier** Cranes: 2x10t	**2 oil engines** reduction geared to sc. shafts driving 2 CP propellers Total Power: 6,618kW (8,998hp) Daihatsu 2 x 4 Stroke 6 Cy. 360 x 480 each-3309kW (4499bhp) Daihatsu Diesel Manufacturing Co Lt-Japan AuxGen: 3 x a.c Thrusters: 1 Tunnel thruster (f) Fuel: 2880.0 (r.f.)	13.9kn 6DKM-36
9567726 *3FHX* -	**YAMATO** **FPG Shipholding Panama 2 SA** Hachiuma Steamship Co Ltd (Hachiuma Kisen KK) SatCom: Inmarsat C 437137810 *Panama* *Panama* MMSI: 371378000 Official number: 4218011	**14,538** 4,362 19,812	Class: NK	**2010-11 Mitsubishi Heavy Industries Ltd. — Nagasaki** Yd No: 2272 Loa 162.00 (BB) Br ex - Dght 6.370 Lbp 152.62 Br md 38.00 Dpth 9.00 Welded, 1 dk	**(A38C2GH) Heavy Load Carrier** Cranes: 2x10t	**2 oil engines** reduction geared to sc. shafts driving 2 CP propellers Total Power: 6,436kW (8,750hp) Daihatsu 2 x 4 Stroke 6 Cy. 360 x 480 each-3218kW (4375bhp) Daihatsu Diesel Manufacturing Co Lt-Japan Thrusters: 1 Tunnel thruster (f) Fuel: 2880.0 (r.f.)	13.9kn 6DKM-36
9380867 *7JBC* -	**YAMATO** **Taishu Co Ltd** - *Hirado, Nagasaki* *Japan* MMSI: 432542000 Official number: 140252	**499** - -		**2006-01 Nagasaki Zosen K.K. — Nagasaki** Yd No: 1206 Loa 65.27 Br ex 9.49 Dght 4.000 Lbp 58.30 Br md 9.40 Dpth 4.30 Welded, 1 dk	**(B12D2FP) Fishery Patrol Vessel**	**1 oil engine** driving 1 FP propeller Total Power: 1,838kW (2,499hp) Niigata 1 x 4 Stroke 6 Cy. 280 x 370 1838kW (2499bhp) Niigata Engineering Co Ltd-Japan	6L28HX

IMO / Call sign	Name / Owner	Tonnage	Class	Built	Type	Machinery
263150 *J4049*	**YAMATO** **Hankyu Ferry Co Ltd** - *Kobe, Hyogo* *Japan* MMSI: 431301674 Official number: 135997	*13,353* - 5,560		**2003-03 Mitsubishi Heavy Industries Ltd. — Shimonoseki** Yd No: 1090 Loa 195.00 (BB) Br ex - Dght 6.700 Lbp 180.00 Br md 26.40 Dpth 15.25 Welded	**(A36A2PR) Passenger/Ro-Ro Ship (Vehicles)** Passengers: unberthed: 667 Lane-Len: 780 Cars: 128, Trailers: 229	**2 oil engines** geared to sc. shafts driving 2 FP propellers Total Power: 20,152kW (27,398hp) 23.5kn Wartsila 16V38B 2 x Vee 4 Stroke 16 Cy. 380 x 475 each-10076kW (13699bhp) Wartsila Finland Oy-Finland Thrusters: 2 Tunnel thruster (f); 1 Tunnel thruster (a)
9013309 *JBAI7* -	**YAMATO** *ex* Genyo Maru *-2010* **Antey Co Ltd (TOO 'Antey')** - *Sovetskaya Gavan* *Russia* MMSI: 273351740	*760* - 467	Class: RS	**1991-03 Wakamatsu Zosen K.K. — Kitakyushu** Yd No: 382 Loa - Br ex - Dght 3.701 Lbp 50.02 Br md 9.01 Dpth 6.13 Welded	**(B34K2QT) Training Ship**	**1 oil engine** with clutches, flexible couplings & sr geared to sc. shaft driving 1 CP propeller Total Power: 1,324kW (1,800hp) Niigata 6M31AFTE 1 x 4 Stroke 6 Cy. 310 x 530 1324kW (1800bhp) Niigata Engineering Co Ltd-Japan Thrusters: 1 Thwart. CP thruster (f)
9091600 *JD2252* -	**YAMATO** **KK Daito Corp** - *Tokyo* *Japan* Official number: 140324	*181* - -		**2006-05 Hanasaki Zosensho K.K. — Yokosuka** Yd No: 278 Loa 32.25 Br ex - Dght 2.710 Lbp 27.80 Br md 8.80 Dpth 3.90 Welded, 1 dk	**(B32A2ST) Tug**	**2 oil engines** gearing integral to driving 2 Z propellers Total Power: 2,648kW (3,600hp) Yanmar 6N260M-SV 2 x 4 Stroke 6 Cy. 260 x 360 each-1324kW (1800bhp) Yanmar Diesel Engine Co Ltd-Japan
8823264 - -	**YAMATO** *ex* Yamato Maru No. 3 *-2003* - -	*401* - 1,023		**1989-01 K.K. Yoshida Zosen Kogyo — Arida** Loa 72.30 Br ex - Dght 3.420 Lbp 66.00 Br md 11.00 Dpth 6.20 Welded, 1 dk	**(A31A2GX) General Cargo Ship**	**1 oil engine** reduction geared to sc. shaft driving 1 FP propeller Total Power: 736kW (1,001hp) Hanshin LH28G 1 x 4 Stroke 6 Cy. 280 x 460 736kW (1001bhp) The Hanshin Diesel Works Ltd-Japan
9185243 *JL6400* -	**YAMATO MARU** **Osaka Kisen KK** - *Sukumo, Kochi* *Japan* Official number: 136493	*101* - -		**1998-06 Suzuki Shipyard Co. Ltd. — Yokkaichi** Yd No: 651 Loa 25.50 Br ex - Dght - Lbp 24.00 Br md 9.50 Dpth 5.45 Welded, 1 dk	**(B32B2SP) Pusher Tug**	**2 oil engines** driving 2 FP propellers Total Power: 1,472kW (2,002hp) 10.5kn Matsui ML627GSC 2 x 4 Stroke 6 Cy. 270 x 480 each-736kW (1001bhp) Matsui Iron Works Co Ltd-Japan
8965074 *JH3480* -	**YAMATO MARU** **Sanyo Kaiji Co Ltd** - *Nagoya, Aichi* *Japan* Official number: 135677	*198* - -		**2000-10 Hatayama Zosen KK — Yura WK** Yd No: 235 Loa 32.82 Br ex - Dght - Lbp 26.50 Br md 9.50 Dpth 4.29 Welded, 1 dk	**(B32A2ST) Tug**	**2 oil engines** geared integral to driving 2 Z propellers Total Power: 2,574kW (3,500hp) 14.5kn Yanmar 6N260-SN 2 x 4 Stroke 6 Cy. 260 x 360 each-1287kW (1750bhp) Yanmar Diesel Engine Co Ltd-Japan
9067960 - -	**YAMATO MARU** - -	*149* - 400		**1993-10 Mikami Zosen K.K. — Japan** Yd No: 326 L reg 36.20 Br ex - Dght - Lbp - Br md 7.30 Dpth 3.10 Welded, 1 dk	**(A13B2TU) Tanker (unspecified)**	**1 oil engine** driving 1 FP propeller Total Power: 441kW (600hp) Yanmar MF24-HT 1 x 4 Stroke 6 Cy. 240 x 420 441kW (600bhp) Yanmar Diesel Engine Co Ltd-Japan
8020238 *JG4149* -	**YAMATO MARU** **Aki Marine KK** - *Hiroshima, Hiroshima* *Japan* Official number: 121842	*168* - -		**1980-12 Kanagawa Zosen — Kobe** Yd No: 215 Loa 30.82 Br ex 8.62 Dght - Lbp 27.01 Br md 8.60 Dpth 3.80 Welded, 1 dk	**(B32A2ST) Tug**	**2 oil engines** geared integral to driving 2 Z propellers Total Power: 1,912kW (2,600hp) 12.5kn Niigata 6L25BX 2 x 4 Stroke 6 Cy. 250 x 320 each-956kW (1300bhp) Niigata Engineering Co Ltd-Japan
9424742 *JD2408* -	**YAMATO MARU** **YK Shiba Kaiun** - *Komatsushima, Tokushima* *Japan* MMSI: 431000080 Official number: 140534	*747* - 1,957		**2007-05 Imura Zosen K.K. — Komatsushima** Yd No: 320 Loa 72.20 Br ex - Dght 4.720 Lbp 67.20 Br md 12.00 Dpth 5.20 Welded, 1 dk	**(A13B2TP) Products Tanker** Double Hull (13F) Liq: 2,200; Liq (Oil): 2,200	**1 oil engine** driving 1 FP propeller Total Power: 1,471kW (2,000hp) 12.8kn Hanshin LH34LG 1 x 4 Stroke 6 Cy. 340 x 640 1471kW (2000bhp) The Hanshin Diesel Works Ltd-Japan
9652648 *JD3412* -	**YAMATO MARU** **Yamashita Kaiun YK** - *Nagasaki, Nagasaki* *Japan* Official number: 141764	*199* - 430		**2012-10 Hakata Zosen K.K. — Imabari** Yd No: 753 Loa 46.95 (BB) Br ex - Dght 3.050 Lbp - Br md 8.00 Dpth - Welded, 1 dk	**(A13B2TP) Products Tanker** Double Hull (13F) Liq: 443; Liq (Oil): 443	**1 oil engine** reduction geared to sc. shaft driving 1 Propeller Total Power: 882kW (1,199hp) Hanshin LH26G 1 x 4 Stroke 6 Cy. 260 x 440 882kW (1199bhp) The Hanshin Diesel Works Ltd-Japan
8815372 *JL5777* -	**YAMATO MARU No. 8** - - *Ieshima, Hyogo* *Japan* Official number: 130596	*499* - 600		**1989-03 Imura Zosen K.K. — Komatsushima** Yd No: 231 L reg 51.77 Br ex - Dght 4.500 Lbp - Br md 10.60 Dpth 5.30 Welded	**(A31A2GX) General Cargo Ship**	**1 oil engine** reverse geared to sc. shaft driving 1 FP propeller Total Power: 588kW (799hp) Akasaka K26SR 1 x 4 Stroke 6 Cy. 260 x 480 588kW (799bhp) Akasaka Tekkosho KK (Akasaka DieselLtd)-Japan
9053555 *JE3111* MG1-1870	**YAMATO MARU No. 36** **Daiichi Gyogyo YK** - *Kesennuma, Miyagi* *Japan* Official number: 133297	*119* - 214		**1992-09 Kidoura Shipyard Co Ltd — Kesennuma MG** Yd No: 580 Loa 37.44 (BB) Br ex 6.42 Dght 2.500 Lbp - Br md 6.40 Dpth 2.80 Welded, 1 dk	**(B11B2FV) Fishing Vessel**	**1 oil engine** with clutches, flexible couplings & dr geared to sc. shaft driving 1 CP propeller Total Power: 592kW (805hp) Niigata 6M26AFTE 1 x 4 Stroke 6 Cy. 260 x 460 592kW (805bhp) Niigata Engineering Co Ltd-Japan
8850499 - -	**YAMATO MARU No. 38** *ex* Yahata Maru No. 28 *-1996* - - -	*138* - -		**1972 Nichiro Zosen K.K. — Ishinomaki** L reg 28.60 Br ex - Dght - Lbp - Br md 6.20 Dpth 2.60 Welded, 1 dk	**(B11B2FV) Fishing Vessel**	**1 oil engine** driving 1 FP propeller Total Power: 346kW (470hp) Niigata 1 x 4 Stroke 346kW (470bhp) Niigata Engineering Co Ltd-Japan
9313137 *3EIJ9* -	**YAMATOGAWA** **KAW1572 Shipping SA** Kawasaki Kisen Kaisha Ltd (Kawasaki Kisen KK) ('K' Line) SatCom: Inmarsat C 437224310 *Panama* *Panama* MMSI: 372243000 Official number: 3253807A	**160,231** 96,933 315,000 T/cm 184.7	Class: AB	**2006-12 Kawasaki Shipbuilding Corp — Sakaide KG** Yd No: 1572 Loa 333.00 (BB) Br ex 60.04 Dght 21.080 Lbp 324.00 Br md 60.00 Dpth 29.30 Welded, 1 dk	**(A13A2TV) Crude Oil Tanker** Double Hull (13F) Liq: 337,225; Liq (Oil): 337,225 Cargo Heating Coils Compartments: 5 Ta, 10 Wing Ta, 2 Wing Slop Ta, ER 3 Cargo Pump (s): 3x5500m³/hr Manifold: Bow/CM: 166.5m	**1 oil engine** driving 1 FP propeller Total Power: 27,160kW (36,927hp) 15.6kn MAN-B&W 7S80MC-C 1 x 2 Stroke 7 Cy. 800 x 3200 27160kW (36927bhp) Kawasaki Heavy Industries Ltd-Japan AuxGen: 3 x 1325kW a.c Fuel: 608.0 (d.f.) 7206.0 (r.f.)
9307853 *JG5708* -	**YAMAYURI** **Japan Railway Construction, Transport & Technology Agency & Naigai Kaiun KK & Bingo Kyodo Kisen KK** Bingo Kyodo Kisen KK *Tokyo* *Japan* MMSI: 431401967 Official number: 137187	*15,128* - 12,588	Class: NK	**2003-12 Imabari Shipbuilding Co Ltd — Imabari EH (Imabari Shipyard)** Yd No: 589 Loa 139.92 (BB) Br ex - Dght 6.499 Lbp 134.00 Br md 26.00 Dpth 13.60 Welded, 1 dk	**(A21A2BC) Bulk Carrier** Grain: 16,651	**1 oil engine** driving 1 FP propeller Total Power: 4,600kW (6,254hp) 14.5kn Mitsubishi 7UEC37LSII 1 x 2 Stroke 7 Cy. 370 x 1290 4600kW (6254bhp) Akasaka Tekkosho KK (Akasaka DieselLtd)-Japan AuxGen: 3 x 600kW a.c Thrusters: 1 Tunnel thruster (f) Fuel: 270.0
9653290 *JD3436* -	**YAMAYURI** **Japan Railway Construction, Transport & Technology Agency & Daiko Senpaku Co Ltd** Daiko Senpaku KK *Osaka, Osaka* *Japan* MMSI: 431004027 Official number: 141800	*498* - 1,178	Class: NK	**2012-12 KK Ura Kyodo Zosensho — Awaji HG** Yd No: 348 Loa 64.80 (BB) Br ex - Dght 4.182 Lbp 61.80 Br md 10.00 Dpth 4.50 Welded, 1 dk	**(A12B2TR) Chemical/Products Tanker** Double Hull (13F) Liq: 1,206; Liq (Oil): 1,206	**2 oil engines** driving 2 gen. each 370kW Connecting to 2 elec. motors each (370kW) driving 1 Propeller Total Power: 740kW (1,006hp) 11.5kn Fuel: 53.0
7300021 - -	**YAMAZUMI MARU No. 3** - -	*105* 26 -		**1971 Asahi Zosen K.K. — Sumoto** Yd No: 112 Loa - Br ex - Dght - Lbp - Br md - Dpth - Welded, 1 dk	**(B32A2ST) Tug**	**1 oil engine** driving 1 FP propeller

7601061 - -	**YAMBURG** *ex* Alk *-2004* *ex* Talea *-2000* *ex* Anna H *-1994* *ex* Parnass *-1988* - -	**1,801** 943 2,793	Class: (RS) (GL)	**1977-03 J.J. Sietas Schiffswerft — Hamburg** Yd No: 808 Lengthened-1978 Loa 81.18 Br ex 11.84 Dght 5.310 Lbp 76.12 Br md 11.80 Dpth 6.81 Welded, 2 dks	**(A31A2GX) General Cargo Ship** Grain: 3,768; Bale: 3,653 TEU 91 C. 91/20' Compartments: 1 Ho, ER 2 Ha: 2 (22.8 x 9.3)ER Ice Capable	**1 oil engine** driving 1 CP propeller Total Power: 1,066kW (1,449hp) 11.0k MWM TBD484- 1 x 4 Stroke 8 Cy. 320 x 480 1066kW (1449bhp) Motoren Werke Mannheim AG (MWM)-West Germany Fuel: 154.0 (d.f.)
7935199 *YFGB* -	**YAMDENA** *ex* Arado Maru No. 2 *-1994* **Go John Santiago** - *Surabaya* *Indonesia*	*640* 304 1,000	Class: KI	**1979-10 Namikata Shipbuilding Co Ltd — Imabari EH** Yd No: 100 Loa 56.30 Br ex - Dght 3.550 Lbp 52.20 Br md 9.50 Dpth 4.81 Welded, 2 dks	**(A31A2GX) General Cargo Ship**	**1 oil engine** reduction geared to sc. shaft driving 1 FP propeller Total Power: 588kW (799hp) Makita 6NLH627 1 x 4 Stroke 6 Cy. 275 x 450 588kW (799bhp) Makita Diesel Co Ltd-Japan
9361172 *A6E2300* -	**YAMEELA** *ex* Sea Scape 1 *-2010* **Government of Abu Dhabi Department of Transport** - *Abu Dhabi* *United Arab Emirates* MMSI: 470431000 Official number: 6332	**492** 183 230	Class: IR IS	**2007-03 FBMA Marine Inc — Balamban** Yd No: 1023 Loa 50.80 Br ex - Dght 1.800 Lbp 49.90 Br md 16.50 Dpth 3.50 Welded, 1 dk	**(A36A2PR) Passenger/Ro-Ro Ship (Vehicles)** Hull Material: Aluminium Alloy Passengers: unberthed: 350 Bow ramp (f) Stern ramp (a) Cars: 65	**4 oil engines** geared to sc. shafts driving 4 FP propellers Total Power: 1,764kW (2,400hp) 18.0k Cummins KTA-19-M 4 x 4 Stroke 6 Cy. 159 x 159 each-441kW (600bhp) Cummins Engine Co Inc-USA
8014291 - -	**YAMEI** *ex* Manyoshi Maru *-1994* **Mazuda International Inc** Ehara Industries Ltd	*199* 126 530		**1980-08 Maeno Zosen KK — Sanyoonoda YC** Yd No: 61 Loa 46.61 Br ex 7.68 Dght 3.245 Lbp 42.50 Br md 7.60 Dpth 3.36 Welded, 1 dk	**(A13B2TU) Tanker (unspecified)**	**1 oil engine** driving 1 FP propeller Total Power: 552kW (750hp) Hanshin 6L26BGS 1 x 4 Stroke 6 Cy. 260 x 400 552kW (750bhp) The Hanshin Diesel Works Ltd-Japan
9487263 *A8XN9*	**YAMILAH - III** **Yamilah III Shipping Co Inc** Abu Dhabi National Tanker Co (ADNATCO) *Monrovia* *Liberia* MMSI: 636014944 Official number: 14944	**42,538** 21,710 74,866 T/cm 68.0	Class: LR ✠ **100A1** SS 06/2011 Double Hull oil tanker CSR ESP **ShipRight** (ACS (B), CM) *IWS LI SPM ✠ **LMC** **UMS IGS** Eq.Ltr: P†; Cable: 659.2/78.0 U3 (a)	**2011-06 STX Offshore & Shipbuilding Co Ltd — Changwon (Jinhae Shipyard)** Yd No: 4015 Loa 228.00 (BB) Br ex 32.27 Dght 14.300 Lbp 219.00 Br md 32.24 Dpth 20.65 Welded, 1 dk	**(A13A2TW) Crude/Oil Products Tanker** Double Hull (13F) Liq: 82,925; Liq (Oil): 82,925 Compartments: 6 Wing Ta, 6 Wing Ta, 1 Wing Slop Ta, 1 Wing Slop Ta, ER	**1 oil engine** driving 1 FP propeller Total Power: 11,060kW (15,037hp) 15.0k MAN-B&W 7S50MC- 1 x 2 Stroke 7 Cy. 500 x 2000 11060kW (15037bhp) STX Engine Co Ltd-South Korea AuxGen: 3 x 900kW 450V 60Hz a.c Boilers: e (ex.g.) 22.4kgf/cm² (22.0bar), WTAuxB (o.f.) 18.4kgf/cm² (18.0bar)
8848410 *JG4865* -	**YAMIZO** **Kashima Futo KK** - *Kamisu, Ibaraki* *Japan* Official number: 131208	*162* - -		**1991-02 Keihin Dock Co Ltd — Yokohama** Yd No: 221 Loa 30.00 Br ex - Dght 2.800 Lbp 27.40 Br md 8.80 Dpth 3.57 Welded, 1 dk	**(B32A2ST) Tug**	**2 oil engines** geared integral to driving 2 Z propellers Total Power: 2,206kW (3,000hp) Pielstick 6PA 2 x 4 Stroke 6 Cy. 255 x 270 each-1103kW (1500bhp) Niigata Engineering Co Ltd-Japan
7019220 *D6CH8* -	**YAMM** *ex* Destiny *-1994* *ex* Peliner *-2004* *ex* Rhodri Mawr *-1990* **Fairline Maritime SA** Safety Management-ISM Srl SatCom: Inmarsat C 461626110 *Moroni* *Union of Comoros* MMSI: 616261000 Official number: 1200309	**4,079** 1,457 4,945	Class: IV (LR) (HR) ✠ Classed LR until 11/3/04	**1970-12 Verolme Cork Dockyard Ltd — Cobh** Yd No: 810 Loa 107.02 Br ex 17.40 Dght 4.101 Lbp 100.13 Br md 16.77 Dpth 7.93 Welded, 1 dk	**(A33A2CC) Container Ship (Fully Cellular)** TEU 182 C Ho 134 TEU C Dk 48 incl 40 ref C Compartments: 2 Cell Ho, ER 7 Ha: ER	**2 oil engines** sr reverse geared to sc. shafts driving 2 FP propellers Total Power: 3,090kW (4,202hp) 14.0k Mirrlees KLSSGMR 2 x 4 Stroke 6 Cy. 381 x 508 each-1545kW (2101bhp) Mirrlees Blackstone (Stockport)Ltd.-Stockport AuxGen: 3 x 160kW 415V 50Hz a.c Thrusters: 1 Thwart. FP thruster (f) Fuel: 96.5 (d.f.)
6818473 *VJDY* -	**YAMPI SOUND** *ex* Fourcroy 2 *-2008* *ex* Fourcroy *-2004* **Colonial Marine Consultants Pty Ltd (CMC Barging)** - *Dampier, WA* *Australia* Official number: 316169	**402** 133 374	Class: (LR) Classed LR until 6/7/00	**1968 Carrington Slipways Pty Ltd — Newcastle NSW** (Aft section) Yd No: 43 **1977 L'Nor Marine Services Inc. — Mandaue** (Fwd section) Lengthened & New forept-1977 Loa 51.21 Br ex 10.70 Dght 1.886 Lbp 46.84 Br md 10.37 Dpth 2.49 Welded, 1 dk	**(A35D2RL) Landing Craft** Bow door/ramp Len: - Wid: 5.10 Swl: - Liq: 338 18 TEU C. 18/20' incl 6 ref C	**2 oil engines** reverse reduction geared to sc. shaft driving 2 FP propellers Total Power: 544kW (740hp) 9.5k Cummins KT-1150- 2 x 4 Stroke 6 Cy. 159 x 159 each-272kW (370bhp) (new engine ,made 1981, fitted 1983) Cummins Charleston Inc-USA AuxGen: 2 x 112kW 220/440V 50Hz a.c Fuel: 41.6 (d.f.) 3.0pd
8729602 - -	**YAMSK** *ex* Vera Belik *-2002* **OOO 'Region'**	**738** 221 332	Class: (RS)	**1989-05 Volgogradskiy Sudostroitelnyy Zavod — Volgograd** Yd No: 252 Loa 53.75 Br ex - Dght 4.401 Lbp 47.93 Br md 10.72 Dpth 6.02 Welded, 1 dk	**(B11A2FS) Stern Trawler** Ice Capable	**1 oil engine** driving 1 FP propeller Total Power: 970kW (1,319hp) 12.8k S.K.L. 8NVD48A-2 1 x 4 Stroke 8 Cy. 320 x 480 970kW (1319bhp) VEB Schwermaschinenbau "KarlLiebknecht" (SKL)-Magdeburg
6512392 - -	**YAMUNA** **Andaman & Nicobar Islands (Marine Engineer)** - *Port Blair* *India*	*215* 95 110	Class: IR	**1965 AFCO Ltd. — Mumbai** Loa 33.53 Br ex 7.35 Dght 2.134 Lbp 30.48 Br md 7.01 Dpth 3.05 Welded, 1 dk	**(A31A2GX) General Cargo Ship**	**1 oil engine** driving 1 FP propeller MAN W6V175/22 1 x 4 Stroke 6 Cy. 175 x 220 Maschinenbau Augsburg Nuernberg (MAN)-Augsburg
9360556 *V2EB9* -	**YAMUNA** *ex* X-Press Yamuna *-2013* *ex* Beluga Mobilisation *-2011* **Beluga M-Serie Erste Beteiligungs GmbH** Reedereiverwaltung Heino Winter GmbH & Co KG *Saint John's* *Antigua & Barbuda* MMSI: 305380000	**8,971** 4,776 10,600 T/cm 27.3	Class: BV	**2009-02 Sainty Shipbuilding (Yangzhou) Corp Ltd — Yizheng JS** (Hull) Yd No: 07STIG003 **2009-02 Volharding Shipyards B.V. — Foxhol** Yd No: 624 Loa 154.85 (BB) Br ex - Dght 6.970 Lbp 144.90 Br md 21.50 Dpth 9.30 Welded, 1 dk	**(A33A2CC) Container Ship (Fully Cellular)** Double Bottom Entire Compartment Length TEU 917 C Ho 267 TEU C Dk 650 TEU incl 200 ref C Compartments: 4 Cell Ho, ER 4 Ha: 2 (29.3 x 18.5) (12.6 x 18.5)ER (25.5 x 18.5) Ice Capable	**1 oil engine** reduction geared to sc. shaft driving 1 CP propeller Total Power: 8,000kW (10,877hp) 18.0k MaK 8M43 1 x 4 Stroke 8 Cy. 430 x 610 8000kW (10877bhp) Caterpillar Motoren GmbH & Co. KG-Germany AuxGen: 2 x 470kW a.c, 1 x 1150kW a.c Thrusters: 1 Tunnel thruster (f)
9230505 *C6WJ6*	**YAMUNA SPIRIT** *ex* Dakota *-2007* **Yamuna Spirit LLC** Teekay Marine (Singapore) Pte Ltd SatCom: Inmarsat B 330904210 *Nassau* *Bahamas* MMSI: 309042000 Official number: 9000225	**81,270** 52,045 159,435 T/cm 118.2	Class: NV	**2002-09 Hyundai Heavy Industries Co Ltd — Ulsan** Yd No: 1373 Loa 274.20 (BB) Br ex 48.04 Dght 17.071 Lbp 264.00 Br md 48.00 Dpth 23.10 Welded, 1 dk	**(A13A2TV) Crude Oil Tanker** Double Hull (13F) Liq: 167,531; Liq (Oil): 167,531 Cargo Heating Coils Compartments: 12 Wing Ta, ER, 2 Wing Slop Ta 3 Cargo Pump (s): 3x4000m³/hr Manifold: Bow/CM: 137.9m	**1 oil engine** driving 1 FP propeller Total Power: 18,623kW (25,320hp) 15.7k B&W 6S70MC- 1 x 2 Stroke 6 Cy. 700 x 2800 18623kW (25320bhp) Hyundai Heavy Industries Co Ltd-South Korea AuxGen: 3 x 730kW 450V a.c Fuel: 200.0 (d.f.) 4500.0 (r.f.)
9488229 *BOCN*	**YAN DANG HAI** **COSCO Bulk Carrier Co Ltd (COSCO BULK)** *Tianjin* *China* MMSI: 412034000	**32,460** 17,889 53,393 T/cm 57.3	Class: CC	**2008-11 Chengxi Shipyard Co Ltd — Jiangyin JS** Yd No: CX4245 Loa 190.00 (BB) Br ex - Dght 12.540 Lbp 183.05 Br md 32.26 Dpth 17.50 Welded, 1 dk	**(A21A2BC) Bulk Carrier** Grain: 65,752; Bale: 64,000 Compartments: 5 Ho, ER 5 Ha: 4 (21.6 x 22.4)ER (19.2 x 22.4) Cranes: 4x36t	**1 oil engine** driving 1 FP propeller Total Power: 9,480kW (12,889hp) 14.2k MAN-B&W 6S50MC- 1 x 2 Stroke 6 Cy. 500 x 2000 9480kW (12889bhp) Hudong Heavy Machinery Co Ltd-China AuxGen: 3 x 680kW 450V a.c Fuel: 215.0 (d.f.) 2000.0 (r.f.) 34.5pd
8833130 - -	**YAN GANG GONG SHUI 1** **Government of The People's Republic of China (Yantai Port Affairs Administration)** - *Yantai, Shandong* *China*	*662* 400 -		**1983 Yingkou Shipyard — Yingkou LN** Loa 40.33 Br ex - Dght 3.500 Lbp 36.90 Br md 8.00 Dpth 4.20 Welded, 1 dk	**(B32A2ST) Tug**	**1 oil engine** driving 1 FP propeller Total Power: 315kW (428hp) 9.0k S.K.L. 6NVD36A-1 1 x 4 Stroke 6 Cy. 240 x 360 315kW (428bhp) VEB Schwermaschinenbau "KarlLiebknecht" (SKL)-Magdeburg AuxGen: 2 x 52kW 220V a.c
8024222 *BTHA* -	**YAN GANG TUO 1** **Government of The People's Republic of China (Yantai Port Affairs Administration)** - *Yantai, Shandong* *China*	*292* - 152	Class: (NK)	**1981-07 Ishikawajima Ship & Chemical Plant Co Ltd — Tokyo** Yd No: 524 Loa 32.83 Br ex 9.53 Dght 3.301 Lbp 26.50 Br md 9.50 Dpth 4.30 Welded, 1 dk	**(B32A2ST) Tug**	**2 oil engines** reduction geared to sc. shafts driving 2 FP propellers Total Power: 2,354kW (3,200hp) Daihatsu 8DSM-2 2 x 4 Stroke 8 Cy. 260 x 320 each-1177kW (1600bhp) Daihatsu Diesel Manufacturing Co Lt-Japan

9418274 YAN GANG TUO 11 — 400 / - / -
Shenzhen Yantian Port
-
China
2008-04 Jiangsu Zhenjiang Shipyard Co Ltd — Zhenjiang JS Yd No: 27-ZJS200601
Loa 33.00 Br ex - Dght 4.990
Lbp - Br md 11.60 Dpth 5.36
Welded, 1 dk
(B32A2ST) Tug
2 oil engines reduction geared to sc. shafts driving 2 Z propellers
Total Power: 3,676kW (4,998hp)
Niigata 6L28HX
2 x 4 Stroke 6 Cy. 280 x 370 each-1838kW (2499bhp)
Niigata Engineering Co Ltd-Japan

9418262 YAN GANG TUO 12 — 400 / - / -
Shenzhen Yantian Port
-
China
2007-05 Jiangsu Zhenjiang Shipyard Co Ltd — Zhenjiang JS Yd No: 28-ZJS200601
Loa 33.00 Br ex - Dght 4.990
Lbp - Br md 11.60 Dpth 5.36
Welded, 1 dk
(B32A2ST) Tug
2 oil engines reduction geared to sc. shafts driving 2 Z propellers
Total Power: 3,676kW (4,998hp)
Niigata 6L28HX
2 x 4 Stroke 6 Cy. 280 x 370 each-1838kW (2499bhp)
Niigata Engineering Co Ltd-Japan

8875073 *BTHG* YAN GANG TUO 17 — 298 / 89 / 145 — Class: (CC)
Yan Xing Shipping SA
Lailon Enterprises Ltd
Yantai, Shandong China
1991 Yantai Shipyard — Yantai SD
Loa 34.46 Br ex - Dght 3.200
Lbp 31.00 Br md 9.00 Dpth 4.35
Welded, 1 dk
(B32A2ST) Tug
1 oil engine driving 1 FP propeller
Total Power: 1,080kW (1,468hp) 12.0kn
Alpha 8L23/30
1 x 4 Stroke 8 Cy. 225 x 300 1080kW (1468bhp)
Zhenjiang Marine Diesel Works-China
AuxGen: 2 x 50kW 400V a.c

8955304 *BTHP* YAN GANG TUO 19 — 296 / 88 / 85 — Class: CC
Yantai Harbour Tug & Barge Co
Yantai, Shandong China
1996-09 Donghai Shipyard — Shanghai
Loa 32.83 Br ex - Dght -
Lbp 26.50 Br md 9.50 Dpth 4.30
Welded, 1 dk
(B32A2ST) Tug
2 oil engines geared to sc. shafts driving 2 FP propellers
Total Power: 2,796kW (3,802hp) 12.0kn
Daihatsu 6DLM-28
2 x 4 Stroke 6 Cy. 280 x 360 each-1398kW (1901bhp)
Daihatsu Diesel Manufacturing Co Lt-Japan
AuxGen: 2 x 75kW 400V a.c

8425024 *BSHM* YAN JIU 13 — 953 / 286 / - — Class: (CC)
China Yantai Salvage
-
SatCom: Inmarsat C 441207812
Yantai, Shandong China
MMSI: 412629000
1979-07 Wuhu Shipyard — Wuhu AH
Loa 60.22 Br ex - Dght 4.441
Lbp 54.00 Br md 11.60 Dpth 5.70
Welded, 1 dk
(B32A2ST) Tug
2 oil engines driving 2 FP propellers
Total Power: 1,942kW (2,640hp) 14.0kn
S.K.L. 8NVD48A-2U
2 x 4 Stroke 8 Cy. 320 x 480 each-971kW (1320bhp)
VEB Schwermaschinenbau "KarlLiebknecht" (SKL)-Magdeburg
AuxGen: 3 x 90kW 400V 50Hz a.c

8427022 *BSHO* YAN JIU 15 — 980 / 236 / - — Class: (CC)
China Yantai Salvage
-
Yantai, Shandong China
MMSI: 412631000
1978-07 Wuhu Shipyard — Wuhu AH
Loa 59.53 Br ex - Dght 4.441
Lbp 54.00 Br md 11.60 Dpth 5.70
Welded, 1 dk
(B32A2ST) Tug
2 oil engines driving 2 FP propellers
Total Power: 1,942kW (2,640hp) 13.8kn
S.K.L. 8NVD48A-2U
2 x 4 Stroke 8 Cy. 320 x 480 each-971kW (1320bhp)
VEB Schwermaschinenbau "KarlLiebknecht" (SKL)-Magdeburg
AuxGen: 3 x 90kW 400V 50Hz a.c

8917015 *BSHW* YAN JIU SHENG 1 — *399* / 119 / 73 — Class: (CC)
China Yantai Salvage
-
Yantai, Shandong China
1990-12 Singmarine Dockyard & Engineering Pte Ltd — Singapore Yd No: 175
Loa 49.88 Br ex - Dght 2.030
Lbp 45.58 Br md 8.00 Dpth 4.60
Welded
(B34M2QS) Search & Rescue Vessel
3 oil engines geared to sc. shafts driving 3 FP propellers
Total Power: 3,840kW (5,220hp) 28.0kn
M.T.U. 16V396TE84
3 x Vee 4 Stroke 16 Cy. 165 x 185 each-1280kW (1740bhp)
MTU Friedrichshafen GmbH-Friedrichshafen
AuxGen: 2 x 100kW 380V a.c

8833166 *BSIW* YAN JIU YOU 1 — *819* / 336 / 1,000
China Yantai Salvage
-
Yantai, Shandong China
MMSI: 412021040
1980 Mawei Shipyard — Fuzhou FJ
Loa 67.42 Br ex - Dght 3.900
Lbp 60.00 Br md 10.00 Dpth 4.50
Welded, 1 dk
(A13B2TU) Tanker (unspecified)
Liq: 2,739; Liq (Oil): 2,739
Compartments: 6 Ta, ER
1 oil engine driving 1 FP propeller
Total Power: 721kW (980hp) 10.0kn
Skoda 6L350IIPN
1 x 4 Stroke 6 Cy. 350 x 500 721kW (980bhp)
Skoda-Praha
AuxGen: 2 x 90kW 500V a.c

8833178 *BSZX* YAN JIU YOU 2 — *789* / 335 / 1,000
China Yantai Salvage
-
Yantai, Shandong China
1980 Guangdong New China Shipyard Co Ltd — Dongguan GD
Loa 67.42 Br ex - Dght 4.070
Lbp 60.00 Br md 10.00 Dpth 4.50
Welded, 1 dk
(A13B2TU) Tanker (unspecified)
Liq: 2,739; Liq (Oil): 2,739
Compartments: 6 Ta, ER
1 oil engine driving 1 FP propeller
Total Power: 596kW (810hp) 10.0kn
Chinese Std. Type 6350ZC
1 x 4 Stroke 6 Cy. 350 x 500 596kW (810bhp)
Shanghai Diesel Engine Co Ltd-China
AuxGen: 2 x 90kW 400V a.c

8956009 YAN MING 6819 — 160 / 48 / -
-
-
1999 Dalian Fishing Vessel Co — Dalian LN
L reg 36.30 Br ex - Dght -
Lbp - Br md 6.40 Dpth 3.10
Welded, 1 dk
(B11A2FS) Stern Trawler
1 oil engine driving 1 FP propeller
Total Power: 294kW (400hp) 10.0kn

8956011 YAN MING 6820 — 160 / 48 / -
-
-
1999 Dalian Fishing Vessel Co — Dalian LN
L reg 36.30 Br ex - Dght -
Lbp - Br md 6.40 Dpth 3.10
Welded, 1 dk
(B11A2FS) Stern Trawler
1 oil engine driving 1 FP propeller
Total Power: 294kW (400hp) 10.0kn

8956023 YAN MING 6825 — 160 / 48 / -
-
-
1999 Dalian Fishing Vessel Co — Dalian LN
L reg 36.30 Br ex - Dght -
Lbp - Br md 6.40 Dpth 3.10
Welded, 1 dk
(B11A2FS) Stern Trawler
1 oil engine driving 1 FP propeller
Total Power: 294kW (400hp) 10.0kn

8956035 YAN MING 6826 — 160 / 48 / -
-
-
1999 Dalian Fishing Vessel Co — Dalian LN
L reg 36.30 Br ex - Dght -
Lbp - Br md 6.40 Dpth 3.10
Welded, 1 dk
(B11A2FS) Stern Trawler
1 oil engine driving 1 FP propeller
Total Power: 294kW (400hp) 10.0kn

8801656 *PMQD* YAN NO. 1 — 961 / 515 / 1,613 — Class: KI (NK)
ex Sado Maru *-2008*
PT Bahana Line
-
Tanjung Priok Indonesia
1988-02 Murakami Hide Zosen K.K. — Imabari Yd No: 267
Converted From: Chemical Tanker-2011
Loa 70.00 Br ex 11.03 Dght 4.352
Lbp 65.00 Br md 11.00 Dpth 4.80
Welded, 1 dk
(A13B2TP) Products Tanker
Liq: 1,341; Liq (Oil): 1,341
1 oil engine driving 1 FP propeller
Total Power: 1,177kW (1,600hp)
Hanshin 6LUN30AG
1 x 4 Stroke 6 Cy. 300 x 480 1177kW (1600bhp)
The Hanshin Diesel Works Ltd-Japan
AuxGen: 2 x 96kW 415V a.c

8849622 *BBFI* YAN SHUI LENG No. 8 — *837* / 251 / 621 — Class: (CC)
Yantai Aquatic Products Supplying & Marketing Co
-
Yantai, Shandong China
MMSI: 412916000
1990 Guangzhou Fishing Vessel Shipyard — Guangzhou GD
Loa 60.80 Br ex - Dght 3.400
Lbp 54.00 Br md 9.98 Dpth 5.70
Welded, 1 dk
(B12B2FC) Fish Carrier
Ins: 1,038
1 oil engine geared to sc. shaft driving 1 FP propeller
Total Power: 541kW (736hp) 11.5kn
Chinese Std. Type 8300
1 x 4 Stroke 8 Cy. 300 x 380 541kW (736bhp)
Zibo Diesel Engine Factory-China
AuxGen: 3 x 90kW 400V a.c

9677612 *BUSQ* YAN SHUN — 7,638 / 2,292 / 4,400 — Class: BV CC
Shanghai Changshi Shipping Co Ltd
Nanjing Changjiang LPG Transportation & Trade Co Ltd
Shanghai China
MMSI: 412380190
2013-05 Jiangnan Shipyard (Group) Co Ltd — Shanghai Yd No: H2504
Loa 112.00 (BB) Br ex 19.90 Dght 5.900
Lbp 106.13 Br md 19.00 Dpth 10.60
Welded, 1 dk
(A11B2TG) LPG Tanker
Liq (Gas): 6,503
2 x Gas Tank (s); 2 horizontal
1 oil engine driving 1 FP propeller
Total Power: 4,440kW (6,037hp) 14.5kn
MAN-B&W 6S35MC7
1 x 2 Stroke 6 Cy. 350 x 1400 4440kW (6037bhp)
Jiangsu Antai Power Machinery Co Lt-China
AuxGen: 3 x 724kW 60Hz a.c, 1 x 600kW 60Hz a.c
Fuel: 610.0

7813834 YAN TONG — 6,256 / 3,296 / 8,497 — Class: (GL)
ex OOCL Ningbo *-1998* *ex* Yan Tong *-1998*
ex Lucie Schulte *-1995*
ex ScanDutch Iberia *-1991* *ex* Holsatic *-1988*
ex Independent Carrier *-1987*
ex Mediterranean Star *-1986* *ex* Holsatic *-1985*
ex Atrevida *-1985* *ex* Holsatic *-1984*
ex Zim Busan *-1983* *ex* Holsatic *-1983*
Yan Tong Shipping SA
Grand China Shipping (Yantai) Co Ltd
1981-01 China Shipbuilding Corp — Keelung Yd No: 103
Loa 118.65 (BB) Br ex 18.24 Dght 8.011
Lbp 106.51 Br md 18.22 Dpth 10.32
Welded, 2 dks
(A31A2GX) General Cargo Ship
Grain: 11,162; Bale: 10,700
TEU 443 C Ho 190 TEU C Dk 253 incl 50 ref C
Compartments: 2 Ho, ER
2 Ha: (25.2 x 13.2) (37.8 x 13.2)ER
Ice Capable
1 oil engine driving 1 CP propeller
Total Power: 5,432kW (7,385hp) 15.8kn
MAN 7L52/55
1 x 4 Stroke 7 Cy. 520 x 550 5432kW (7385bhp)
Kawasaki Heavy Industries Ltd-Japan
AuxGen: 2 x 440kW, 1 x 440kW a.c
Thrusters: 1 Thwart. FP thruster (f)

8833221 YAN YU 617 — *274* / 85 / - — Class: (CC)
China Yantai Marine Fisheries Corp
-
Yantai, Shandong China
1984 Dalian Fishing Vessel Co — Dalian LN
Loa 43.50 Br ex - Dght -
Lbp 37.00 Br md 7.60 Dpth 3.80
Welded
(B11B2FV) Fishing Vessel
1 oil engine geared to sc. shaft driving 1 FP propeller
Total Power: 441kW (600hp)
Chinese Std. Type 8300
1 x 4 Stroke 8 Cy. 300 x 380 441kW (600bhp)
Dalian Fishing Vessel Co-China
AuxGen: 2 x 90kW 400V a.c

8833271 - -	**YAN YU 618** **China Yantai Marine Fisheries Corp** - *Yantai, Shandong* *China*	274 85 -	Class: (CC)	**1984 Dalian Fishing Vessel Co — Dalian LN** Loa 43.50 Br ex - Dght - Lbp 37.00 Br md 7.60 Dpth 3.80 Welded	**(B11B2FV) Fishing Vessel**	**1 oil engine** geared to sc. shaft driving 1 FP propeller Total Power: 441kW (600hp) Chinese Std. Type 830 1 x 4 Stroke 8 Cy. 300 x 380 441kW (600bhp) Dalian Fishing Vessel Co-China AuxGen: 2 x 90kW 400V a.c
8833336 - -	**YAN YU 619** **China Yantai Marine Fisheries Corp** - *Yantai, Shandong* *China*	199 85 -	Class: (CC)	**1984 Dalian Fishing Vessel Co — Dalian LN** Loa 43.50 Br ex - Dght - Lbp 37.00 Br md 7.60 Dpth 3.80 Welded	**(B11B2FV) Fishing Vessel**	**1 oil engine** geared to sc. shaft driving 1 FP propeller Total Power: 441kW (600hp) Chinese Std. Type 8300 1 x 4 Stroke 8 Cy. 300 x 380 441kW (600bhp) Dalian Fishing Vessel Co-China AuxGen: 2 x 51kW 400V a.c
8833348 - -	**YAN YU 620** **China Yantai Marine Fisheries Corp** - *Yantai, Shandong* *China*	199 85 -	Class: (CC)	**1984 Dalian Fishing Vessel Co — Dalian LN** Loa 43.50 Br ex - Dght - Lbp 37.00 Br md 7.60 Dpth 3.80 Welded	**(B11B2FV) Fishing Vessel**	**1 oil engine** geared to sc. shaft driving 1 FP propeller Total Power: 441kW (600hp) Chinese Std. Type 8300 1 x 4 Stroke 8 Cy. 300 x 380 441kW (600bhp) Dalian Fishing Vessel Co-China AuxGen: 2 x 51kW 400V a.c
8833350 - -	**YAN YU 621** **China Yantai Marine Fisheries Corp** - *Yantai, Shandong* *China*	199 85 -	Class: (CC)	**1985 Dalian Fishing Vessel Co — Dalian LN** Loa 43.50 Br ex - Dght - Lbp 37.00 Br md 7.60 Dpth 3.80 Welded	**(B11B2FV) Fishing Vessel**	**1 oil engine** geared to sc. shaft driving 1 FP propeller Total Power: 441kW (600hp) Chinese Std. Type 8300 1 x 4 Stroke 8 Cy. 300 x 380 441kW (600bhp) Dalian Fishing Vessel Co-China AuxGen: 2 x 51kW 400V a.c
8833362 - -	**YAN YU 622** **China Yantai Marine Fisheries Corp** - *Yantai, Shandong* *China*	199 85 -	Class: (CC)	**1985 Dalian Fishing Vessel Co — Dalian LN** Loa 43.50 Br ex - Dght - Lbp 37.00 Br md 7.60 Dpth 3.80 Welded	**(B11B2FV) Fishing Vessel**	**1 oil engine** geared to sc. shaft driving 1 FP propeller Total Power: 441kW (600hp) Chinese Std. Type 8300 1 x 4 Stroke 8 Cy. 300 x 380 441kW (600bhp) Dalian Fishing Vessel Co-China AuxGen: 2 x 51kW 400V a.c
8833295 - -	**YAN YU 625** **China Yantai Marine Fisheries Corp** - *Yantai, Shandong* *China*	274 85 -	Class: (CC)	**1986 Yantai Fishing Vessel Shipyard — Yantai SD** Loa 43.50 Br ex - Dght - Lbp 37.00 Br md 7.60 Dpth 3.80 Welded	**(B11B2FV) Fishing Vessel**	**1 oil engine** geared to sc. shaft driving 1 FP propeller Total Power: 441kW (600hp) Chinese Std. Type 8300 1 x 4 Stroke 8 Cy. 300 x 380 441kW (600bhp) Zibo Diesel Engine Factory-China AuxGen: 2 x 64kW 400V a.c
8833324 - -	**YAN YU 626** **China Yantai Marine Fisheries Corp** - *Yantai, Shandong* *China*	274 85 -	Class: (CC)	**1986 Yantai Fishing Vessel Shipyard — Yantai SD** Loa 43.50 Br ex - Dght - Lbp 37.00 Br md 7.60 Dpth 3.80 Welded	**(B11B2FV) Fishing Vessel**	**1 oil engine** geared to sc. shaft driving 1 FP propeller Total Power: 441kW (600hp) Chinese Std. Type 8300 1 x 4 Stroke 8 Cy. 300 x 380 441kW (600bhp) Zibo Diesel Engine Factory-China AuxGen: 2 x 64kW 400V a.c
8833300 - -	**YAN YU 627** **China Yantai Marine Fisheries Corp** - *Yantai, Shandong* *China*	274 85 -	Class: (CC)	**1987 Yantai Fishing Vessel Shipyard — Yantai SD** Loa 43.50 Br ex - Dght - Lbp 37.00 Br md 7.60 Dpth 3.80 Welded	**(B11B2FV) Fishing Vessel**	**1 oil engine** geared to sc. shaft driving 1 FP propeller Total Power: 441kW (600hp) Chinese Std. Type 8300 1 x 4 Stroke 8 Cy. 300 x 380 441kW (600bhp) Zibo Diesel Engine Factory-China AuxGen: 2 x 64kW 400V a.c
8833312 - -	**YAN YU 628** **China Yantai Marine Fisheries Corp** - *Yantai, Shandong* *China*	274 85 -	Class: (CC)	**1987 Yantai Fishing Vessel Shipyard — Yantai SD** Loa 43.50 Br ex - Dght - Lbp 37.00 Br md 7.60 Dpth 3.80 Welded	**(B11B2FV) Fishing Vessel**	**1 oil engine** geared to sc. shaft driving 1 FP propeller Total Power: 441kW (600hp) Chinese Std. Type 8300 1 x 4 Stroke 8 Cy. 300 x 380 441kW (600bhp) Zibo Diesel Engine Factory-China AuxGen: 2 x 64kW 400V a.c
8833245 *BBEA7* -	**YAN YU 629** **China Yantai Marine Fisheries Corp** - *Yantai, Shandong* *China*	274 82 -	Class: (CC)	**1988 Yantai Fishing Vessel Shipyard — Yantai SD** Loa 43.50 Br ex - Dght 2.800 Lbp 37.00 Br md 7.60 Dpth 3.80 Welded, 1 dk	**(B11B2FV) Fishing Vessel**	**1 oil engine** driving 1 FP propeller Total Power: 324kW (441hp) 12.0kn Chinese Std. Type 8300 1 x 4 Stroke 8 Cy. 300 x 380 324kW (441bhp) Zibo Diesel Engine Factory-China AuxGen: 2 x 64kW 400V a.c
8833257 *BBEA8* -	**YAN YU 630** **China Yantai Marine Fisheries Corp** - *Yantai, Shandong* *China*	272 82 -	Class: (CC)	**1988 Yantai Fishing Vessel Shipyard — Yantai SD** Loa 43.50 Br ex - Dght 2.800 Lbp 37.00 Br md 7.60 Dpth 3.80 Welded, 1 dk	**(B11B2FV) Fishing Vessel**	**1 oil engine** driving 1 FP propeller Total Power: 324kW (441hp) 12.0kn Chinese Std. Type 8300 1 x 4 Stroke 8 Cy. 300 x 380 324kW (441bhp) Zibo Diesel Engine Factory-China AuxGen: 2 x 64kW 400V a.c
8827258 - -	**YAN YU 801** **China Yantai Marine Fisheries Corp** - *Yantai, Shandong* *China*	303 90 -	Class: (LR) (CC) Classed LR until 12/9/91	**1990-01 Dalian Fishing Vessel Co — Dalian LN** Yd No: 9012041 Loa 44.38 Br ex 7.62 Dght - Lbp 38.00 Br md 7.60 Dpth 3.75 Welded, 1 dk	**(B11A2FS) Stern Trawler**	**1 oil engine** dr reverse geared to sc. shaft driving 1 FP propeller Total Power: 733kW (997hp) Chinese Std. Type 8300 1 x 4 Stroke 8 Cy. 300 x 380 733kW (997bhp) Dalian Fishing Vessel Co-China AuxGen: 2 x 120kW 400V 50Hz a.c
8827260 - -	**YAN YU 802** **China Yantai Marine Fisheries Corp** - *Yantai, Shandong* *China*	303 90 -	Class: (LR) (CC) Classed LR until 12/9/91	**1990-01 Dalian Fishing Vessel Co — Dalian LN** Yd No: 9012042 Loa 44.38 Br ex 7.62 Dght 2.852 Lbp 38.00 Br md 7.60 Dpth 3.75 Welded, 1 dk	**(B11A2FS) Stern Trawler**	**1 oil engine** dr reverse geared to sc. shaft driving 1 FP propeller Total Power: 733kW (997hp) Chinese Std. Type 8300 1 x 4 Stroke 8 Cy. 300 x 380 733kW (997bhp) Dalian Fishing Vessel Co-China AuxGen: 2 x 120kW 400V 50Hz a.c
8880030 *BBFY* -	**YAN YU LENG No. 2** **China Yantai Marine Fisheries Corp** - SatCom: Inmarsat C 441206212 *Yantai, Shandong* *China* MMSI: 412321320	**837** 251 621	Class: (CC)	**1987 Guangzhou Fishing Vessel Shipyard — Guangzhou GD** Loa 60.80 Br ex - Dght 3.400 Lbp 54.00 Br md 9.90 Dpth 5.70 Welded, 2 dks	**(A34A2GR) Refrigerated Cargo Ship** Grain: 539; Ins: 1,038 Compartments: 1 Ho, ER 1 Ha: (4.6 x 2.5)ER Cranes: 2x2t	**1 oil engine** geared to sc. shaft driving 1 FP propeller Total Power: 809kW (1,100hp) 11.5kn Chinese Std. Type 8300 1 x 4 Stroke 8 Cy. 300 x 380 809kW (1100bhp) Dalian Fishing Vessel Co-China AuxGen: 3 x 90kW 400V a.c
8727642 - -	**YANA** - - *Turkey*	**1,178** 353 391	Class: (RS)	**1987-07 Yaroslavskiy Sudostroitelnyy Zavod — Yaroslavl** Yd No: 231 Loa 58.55 Br ex 12.67 Dght 4.760 Lbp 51.60 Br md - Dpth 5.90 Welded, 1 dk	**(B32A2ST) Tug** Ice Capable	**2 diesel electric oil engines** driving 2 gen. each 1100kW Connecting to 1 elec. Motor of (1900kW) driving 1 FP propeller Total Power: 2,200kW (2,992hp) 13.5kn Kolomna 6CHN1A30/38 2 x 4 Stroke 6 Cy. 300 x 380 each-1100kW (1496bhp) Kolomenskiy Zavod-Kolomna AuxGen: 2 x 300kW, 2 x 160kW Fuel: 331.0 (d.f.)
8622153 - -	**YANASE** *ex* Yanase 101 *-2008* *ex* Sumiwaka Maru No. 7 *-2004* *ex* Shoei Maru No. 18 *-1995* *ex* Myoriki Maru No. 8 *-1992* **PT Karya Cemerlang** -	**971** 291 1,099		**1983 K.K. Murakami Zosensho — Naruto** Yd No: 151 Loa 59.52 Br ex - Dght 4.201 Lbp 55.00 Br md 12.01 Dpth 5.80 Welded, 1 dk	**(B33A2DG) Grab Dredger**	**1 oil engine** reduction geared to sc. shaft driving 1 FP propeller Total Power: 883kW (1,201hp) 12.0kn Hanshin 6LU28RG 1 x 4 Stroke 6 Cy. 280 x 440 883kW (1201bhp) The Hanshin Diesel Works Ltd-Japan
7715185 -	**YANBU 1** **Government of The Kingdom of Saudi Arabia (Ports Authority)** Yanbu Port Management - YPM *Jeddah* *Saudi Arabia* Official number: 101-78	103 - -	Class: (LR) ✠ Classed LR until 13/8/97	**1978-01 Yokohama Yacht Co Ltd — Yokohama KN** Yd No: 738-2 Loa 23.04 Br ex 6.89 Dght 3.074 Lbp 21.01 Br md 6.71 Dpth 2.82 Welded, 1 dk	**(B32A2ST) Tug**	**2 oil engines** reverse reduction geared to sc. shafts driving 2 Directional propellers Total Power: 736kW (1,000hp) 8.5kn M.T.U. 6V396TC61 2 x Vee 4 Stroke 6 Cy. 165 x 185 each-368kW (500bhp) MTU Friedrichshafen GmbH-Friedrichshafen AuxGen: 2 x 64kW 445V 60Hz a.c

IMO / Call sign	Ship / Owner	Tonnage	Class	Builder / Dimensions	Type	Machinery
7715214 - -	**YANBU 2** **Government of The Kingdom of Saudi Arabia (Ports Authority)** Yanbu Port Management - YPM *Jeddah* *Saudi Arabia* Official number: 102-78	*103* - -	Class: (LR) ✠ Classed LR until 14/1/98	**1978-02 Yokohama Yacht Co Ltd — Yokohama KN** Yd No: 738-5 Loa 23.04 Br ex 6.89 Dght 3.074 Lbp 21.01 Br md 6.71 Dpth 2.82 Welded, 1 dk	**(B32A2ST) Tug**	**2 oil engines** reverse reduction geared to sc. shafts driving 2 Directional propellers Total Power: 736kW (1,000hp) 10.3kn M.T.U. 6V396TC61 2 x Vee 4 Stroke 6 Cy. 165 x 185 each-368kW (500bhp) MTU Friedrichshafen GmbH-Friedrichshafen AuxGen: 2 x 64kW 445V 60Hz a.c
7713759 - -	**YANBU 3** **Government of The Kingdom of Saudi Arabia (Ports Authority)** Red Sea Marine Services *Jeddah* *Saudi Arabia* Official number: 103-78	*160* - -	Class: BV (LR) ✠ Classed LR until 31/1/01	**1978-05 Hayashikane Shipbuilding & Engineering Co Ltd — Yokosuka KN** Yd No: 737 Loa 28.28 Br ex 8.01 Dght 3.798 Lbp 26.90 Br md 7.80 Dpth 3.41 Welded, 1 dk	**(B32A2ST) Tug**	**2 oil engines** geared to sc. shafts driving 2 Directional propellers Total Power: 978kW (1,330hp) 10.0kn M.T.U. 8V396TC61 2 x Vee 4 Stroke 8 Cy. 165 x 185 each-489kW (665bhp) MTU Friedrichshafen GmbH-Friedrichshafen AuxGen: 2 x 80kW 450V 60Hz a.c
8121317 *HZEZ* -	**YANBU 21** **Government of The Kingdom of Saudi Arabia (Ports Authority)** Red Sea Marine Services *Jeddah* *Saudi Arabia* Official number: SA1468	**407** 122 268	Class: BV (LR) ✠ Classed LR until 21/6/00	**1983-01 Scheepswerf Bijlsma BV — Wartena** Yd No: 617 Loa 34.02 Br ex 11.28 Dght 3.376 Lbp 32.47 Br md 11.00 Dpth 3.97 Welded, 1 dk	**(B32A2ST) Tug**	**2 oil engines** gearing integral to driving 2 Voith-Schneider propellers Total Power: 2,180kW (2,964hp) Deutz SBV6M628 2 x 4 Stroke 6 Cy. 240 x 280 each-1090kW (1482bhp) Kloeckner Humboldt Deutz AG-West Germany AuxGen: 2 x 120kW 440/220V 60Hz a.c Fuel: 120.5 (d.f.)
8224195 *HZAQ* -	**YANBU 22** **Government of The Kingdom of Saudi Arabia (Ports Authority)** Red Sea Marine Services *Jeddah* *Saudi Arabia* Official number: SA1468	**402** 120 308	Class: BV (LR) ✠ Classed LR until 12/11/97	**1984-03 Korea Shipbuilding & Engineering Corp — Busan** Yd No: 302 Loa 33.81 Br ex 11.26 Dght 5.344 Lbp 31.60 Br md 11.00 Dpth 4.02 Welded, 1 dk	**(B32A2ST) Tug**	**2 oil engines** sr geared to sc. shafts driving 2 Voith-Schneider propellers Total Power: 1,940kW (2,638hp) 12.3kn M.T.U. 12V396TC62 2 x Vee 4 Stroke 12 Cy. 165 x 185 each-970kW (1319bhp) MTU Friedrichshafen GmbH-Friedrichshafen AuxGen: 2 x 120kW 440/220V 60Hz a.c Fuel: 128.5 (d.f.)
8304713 - -	**YANBU 55** **Government of The Kingdom of Saudi Arabia (Ports Authority)** Yanbu Port Management - YPM *Yenbo* *Saudi Arabia*	**170** 51 -	Class: (LR) ✠ Classed LR until 7/1/98	**1984-01 Machinefabriek en Scheepswerf van P. Smit Jr. B.V. — Rotterdam** (Hull) **1984-01 B.V. Scheepswerf Damen — Gorinchem** Yd No: 3912 Loa 22.03 Br ex 8.72 Dght 2.417 Lbp 20.93 Br md 8.51 Dpth 3.28 Welded, 1 dk	**(B34G2SE) Pollution Control Vessel**	**2 oil engines** with clutches, flexible couplings & dr geared to sc. shafts driving 2 Directional propellers Total Power: 642kW (872hp) M.T.U. 6V396TC62 2 x Vee 4 Stroke 6 Cy. 165 x 185 each-321kW (436bhp) MTU Friedrichshafen GmbH-Friedrichshafen AuxGen: 2 x 48kW 440V 60Hz a.c Fuel: 11.0 (d.f.)
7527863 - -	**YANBU I** *ex* Jeddah *-1984* **Government of The Kingdom of Saudi Arabia (Ministry of Communications - Jeddah Port Administration)** A A Turki Corp Trading & Contracting (ATCO) *Jeddah* *Saudi Arabia*	*1,443* 1,101 -	Class: NV (GL)	**1977-04 Gutehoffnungshuette Sterkrade AG Rheinwerft Walsum — Duisburg** Yd No: 1127 Loa 52.02 Br ex 24.39 Dght 2.601 Lbp 51.62 Br md 24.01 Dpth 4.02 Welded, 1 dk	**(B34B2SC) Crane Vessel**	**2 oil engines** reverse reduction geared to sc. shafts driving 2 Voith-Schneider propellers Total Power: 964kW (1,310hp) 7.0kn M.T.U. 8V396TC61 2 x Vee 4 Stroke 8 Cy. 165 x 185 each-482kW (655bhp) MTU Friedrichshafen GmbH-Friedrichshafen AuxGen: 1 x a.c, 1 x a.c
9487134 *VNW6113* -	**YANDEYARRA** **BHP Billiton Minerals Pty Ltd (BHP Minerals) (Payroll Cannington) (BHP Minerals Perth)** Teekay Shipping (Australia) Pty Ltd *Port Hedland, WA* *Australia* MMSI: 503563000 Official number: 858650	**327** 98 -	Class: LR ✠ **100A1** SS 06/2013 tug ✠ **LMC** **UMS** Eq.Ltr: G; Cable: 312.5/20.5 U2 (a)	**2008-06 Hin Lee (Zhuhai) Shipyard Co Ltd — Zhuhai GD** (Hull) Yd No: 178 **2008-06 Cheoy Lee Shipyards Ltd — Hong Kong** Yd No: 4914 Loa 27.40 Br ex 12.10 Dght 5.200 Lbp 25.20 Br md 11.50 Dpth 5.00 Welded, 1 dk	**(B32A2ST) Tug**	**2 oil engines** gearing integral to driving 2 Z propellers Total Power: 3,730kW (5,072hp) 12.0kn Caterpillar 3516B 2 x Vee 4 Stroke 16 Cy. 170 x 215 each-1865kW (2536bhp) Caterpillar Inc-USA AuxGen: 2 x 112kW 415V 50Hz a.c
8712269 *HSB2890* -	**YANEE** *ex* Seiho Maru No. 2 *-2002* **AMA Marine Co Ltd** - *Bangkok* *Thailand* MMSI: 567037800 Official number: 451000625	**1,894** 824 3,021 T/cm 8.8	Class: (NK)	**1987-09 Higaki Zosen K.K. — Imabari** Yd No: 351 Loa 84.92 (BB) Br ex - Dght 5.789 Lbp 79.51 Br md 13.01 Dpth 6.61 Welded, 1 dk	**(A13B2TP) Products Tanker** Double Bottom Entire Compartment Length Liq: 3,419; Liq (Oil): 3,419 Compartments: 10 Ta, ER 2 Cargo Pump (s): 2x750m³/hr Manifold: Bow/CM: 42.7m	**1 oil engine** with clutches & reduction geared to sc. shaft driving 1 CP propeller Total Power: 2,059kW (2,799hp) Hanshin 6EL38 1 x 4 Stroke 6 Cy. 380 x 760 2059kW (2799bhp) The Hanshin Diesel Works Ltd-Japan AuxGen: 4 x 121kW a.c Thrusters: 1 Thwart. CP thruster (f) Fuel: 73.0 (r.f.)
9540326 *DUDC* -	**YANG A** *ex* Naftocement XVIII *-2011* *ex* Selah 54 *-2009* **Lester Maritime Inc** Nova Marine Carriers SA SatCom: Inmarsat C 454884210 *Cagayan de Oro* *Philippines* MMSI: 548842000 Official number: 10-0000699	**10,055** 4,001 15,500	Class: BV (RI)	**2009-12 Selah Makina Sanayi ve Ticaret A.S. — Tuzla, Istanbul** Yd No: 54 Loa 156.52 Br ex - Dght 8.050 Lbp 145.30 Br md 20.60 Dpth 10.70 Welded, 1 dk	**(A24A2BT) Cement Carrier** Double Hull Grain: 14,350	**1 oil engine** reduction geared to sc. shaft driving 1 FP propeller Total Power: 5,041kW (6,854hp) 14.0kn MAN-B&W 9L32/44CR 1 x 4 Stroke 9 Cy. 320 x 440 5041kW (6854bhp) MAN B&W Diesel AG-Augsburg AuxGen: 1 x 1300kW a.c, 3 x 1050kW a.c Thrusters: 1 Tunnel thruster (f) Fuel: 116.0 (d.f.) 705.0 (r.f.)
8414295 *BAWE* -	**YANG FENG** *ex* Tian Hai Shan *-2006* *ex* Suah *-2004* **Dalian Yang Feng International Shipping Business Co Ltd** Fujian Minfeng Shipping Co Ltd *Dalian, Liaoning* *China* MMSI: 412440004	**2,958** 1,371 3,421	Class: (CC) (KR) (NK)	**1984-12 Kochi Jyuko (Eiho Zosen) K.K. — Kochi** Yd No: 1751 Loa 84.64 (BB) Br ex - Dght 6.617 Lbp 78.01 Br md 16.21 Dpth 9.81 Welded, 3 dks	**(A34A2GR) Refrigerated Cargo Ship** Ins: 3,903 Compartments: 3 Ho, ER 3 Ha: 3 (5.0 x 5.0)ER Derricks: 6x5t	**1 oil engine** driving 1 FP propeller Total Power: 2,868kW (3,899hp) 14.5kn Mitsubishi 6UEC37/88H 1 x 2 Stroke 6 Cy. 370 x 880 2868kW (3899bhp) Akasaka Tekkosho KK (Akasaka DieselLtd)-Japan AuxGen: 2 x 480kW a.c
6401828 - - -	**YANG GAK DO** *ex* Takuyo Maru No. 38 *-1976* *ex* Hinode Maru No. 38 *-1976* **Korea Rungrado Shipping Co** -	*324* - -		**1963 KK Kanasashi Zosen — Shizuoka SZ** Yd No: 537 Loa 45.37 Br ex 7.57 Dght 3.300 Lbp 40.11 Br md 7.50 Dpth 3.31 Welded, 1 dk	**(B11B2FV) Fishing Vessel**	**1 oil engine** driving 1 FP propeller Total Power: 515kW (700hp) 10.5kn Akasaka MK6SS 1 x 4 Stroke 6 Cy. 300 x 420 515kW (700bhp) Akasaka Tekkosho KK (Akasaka DieselLtd)-Japan Fuel: 151.5
8832227 *HMYZ4*	**YANG GAK DO 7** *ex* Hong Hu 8 *-2006* *ex* Zhong Guo Hai Jian 13 *-1995* **Korea Yang Gak Do Shipping Co** - *Haeju* *North Korea* Official number: 2904452	**189** 56 139	Class: (CC)	**1978 Guangxi Guijiang Shipyard — Wuzhou GX** Loa 36.18 Br ex - Dght 3.120 Lbp 31.00 Br md 6.60 Dpth 3.90 Welded, 2 dks	**(B31A2SR) Research Survey Vessel**	**1 oil engine** geared to sc. shaft driving 1 FP propeller Total Power: 294kW (400hp) 11.0kn Chinese Std. Type 6300 1 x 4 Stroke 6 Cy. 300 x 380 294kW (400bhp) Guangzhou Diesel Engine Factory CoLtd-China AuxGen: 2 x 26kW 220V d.c
8323537 *HMKQ* -	**YANG GAK DO 9** *ex* Golden River *-2013* *ex* Rose River *-2002* *ex* Moon River *-1999* *ex* Shunyo Maru *-1999* **Korea Yang Gak Do Shipping Co** - *Nampho* *North Korea* MMSI: 445037000 Official number: 3405164	**1,577** 912 2,098	Class: (NK)	**1984-05 Kishimoto Zosen K.K. — Kinoe** Yd No: 538 Loa 76.87 Br ex 12.02 Dght 5.020 Lbp 72.01 Br md 12.01 Dpth 7.29 Welded, 2 dks	**(A31A2GX) General Cargo Ship** Grain: 3,350; Bale: 3,100 Compartments: 1 Ho, ER 1 Ha: ER	**1 oil engine** sr geared to sc. shaft driving 1 FP propeller Total Power: 1,000kW (1,360hp) 10.5kn Niigata 6M31AFTE 1 x 4 Stroke 6 Cy. 310 x 530 1000kW (1360bhp) Niigata Engineering Co Ltd-Japan AuxGen: 1 x 96kW 225V 60Hz a.c, 1 x 80kW 225V 60Hz a.c Fuel: 82.5 (d.f.) 5.0pd
9162447 *BOHQ* -	**YANG HAI** **COSCO Bulk Carrier Co Ltd (COSCO BULK)** - *Tianjin* *China* MMSI: 412254000	**27,585** 14,848 47,077 T/cm 53.0	Class: CC	**1998-12 Hudong Shipbuilding Group — Shanghai** Yd No: H1249A Loa 189.94 (BB) Br ex - Dght 11.718 Lbp 180.00 Br md 32.20 Dpth 16.60 Welded, 1 dk	**(A21A2BC) Bulk Carrier** Double Bottom Entire Compartment Length Grain: 57,104; Bale: 55,962 Compartments: 5 Ho, ER 5 Ha: (16.0 x 15.0)4 (17.6 x 15.0)ER Cranes: 4x30t Ice Capable	**1 oil engine** driving 1 FP propeller Total Power: 7,330kW (9,966hp) 13.8kn B&W 6L50MC 1 x 2 Stroke 6 Cy. 500 x 1620 7330kW (9966bhp) Hudong Shipyard-China AuxGen: 3 x 536kW 450V 60Hz a.c Fuel: 159.6 (d.f.) (Heating Coils) 1751.3 (r.f.)
7702621 - -	**YANG HE** *ex* Kai Chang *-2002* *ex* Washo Maru *-1994* - -	**985** 589 1,957	Class: (CC)	**1977-03 Sasaki Shipbuilding Co Ltd — Osakikamijima HS** Yd No: 257 Loa 71.50 Br ex 11.02 Dght 4.930 Lbp 65.00 Br md 11.00 Dpth 6.70 Welded, 2 dks	**(A31A2GX) General Cargo Ship** Grain: 2,761; Bale: 2,582	**1 oil engine** driving 1 FP propeller Total Power: 1,545kW (2,101hp) Akasaka DM38A 1 x 4 Stroke 6 Cy. 380 x 600 1545kW (2101bhp) Akasaka Tekkosho KK (Akasaka DieselLtd)-Japan

8942553 - -	**YANG HOON NO. 6** *ex Yang Hung No. 6 -2004* *ex Kyuei Maru No. 63 -2000* *ex Kiyo Maru No. 63 -2000* *ex Kyoho Maru No. 3 -2000* - -	*138* - -		1977-04 Iisaku Zosen K.K. — Nishi-Izu L reg 29.99 Br ex - Dght - Lbp - Br md 6.18 Dpth 2.55 Welded, 1 dk	(B11B2FV) Fishing Vessel	1 oil engine driving 1 FP propeller
9146704 *3FXA6* -	**YANG JIANG HE** - Yangjianghe Maritime Inc COSCO Container Lines Co Ltd (COSCON) SatCom: Inmarsat B 335508610 *Panama* *Panama* MMSI: 355086000 Official number: 2361897CH	12,122 5,598 15,418	Class: AB	1997-01 KK Kanasashi — Shizuoka SZ Yd No: 3392 Loa 144.73 (BB) Br ex - Dght 8.617 Lbp 135.50 Br md 25.00 Dpth 12.80 Welded, 1 dk	(A33A2CC) Container Ship (Fully Cellular) TEU 836 incl 100 ref C. Compartments: 4 Cell Ho, ER 14 Ha: ER	1 oil engine driving 1 FP propeller Total Power: 7,988kW (10,860hp) 17.0kn B&W 6L50MC 1 x 2 Stroke 6 Cy. 500 x 1620 7988kW (10860bhp) Kawasaki Heavy Industries Ltd-Japan Thrusters: 1 Thwart. FP thruster (f)
9417177 *BOGE* -	**YANG LI HU** - Dalian Ocean Shipping Co (COSCO DALIAN) - SatCom: Inmarsat Mini-M 764938830 *Dalian, Liaoning* *China* MMSI: 413975000	61,630 32,584 109,892 T/cm 92.0	Class: CC	2010-05 Dalian Shipbuilding Industry Co Ltd — Dalian LN (No 2 Yard) Yd No: PC1100-35 Loa 244.60 (BB) Br ex 42.03 Dght 15.500 Lbp 233.00 Br md 42.00 Dpth 22.20 Welded, 1 dk	(A13B2TP) Products Tanker Double Hull (13F) Liq: 117,936; Liq (Oil): 117,936 Compartments: 12 Wing Ta, ER, 2 Wing Slop Ta 3 Cargo Pump (s): 3x3300m^3/hr Manifold: Bow/CM: 121.8m	1 oil engine driving 1 FP propeller Total Power: 15,260kW (20,747hp) 15.6kn Wartsila 7RT-flex58T 1 x 2 Stroke 7 Cy. 580 x 2416 15260kW (20747bhp) Dalian Marine Diesel Co Ltd-China AuxGen: 3 x 780kW 450V a.c Fuel: 321.2 (d.f.) 3521.3 (r.f.)
9283265 *BPAB* -	**YANG LIN WAN** - China Shipping Tanker Co Ltd - SatCom: Inmarsat B 341307410 *Shanghai* *China* MMSI: 413074000	61,713 32,458 109,181 T/cm 91.9	Class: CC	2004-09 Dalian New Shipbuilding Heavy Industries Co Ltd — Dalian LN Yd No: PC1100-14 Loa 244.60 (BB) Br ex 42.03 Dght 15.470 Lbp 233.00 Br md 42.00 Dpth 22.20 Welded, 1 dk	(A13A2TW) Crude/Oil Products Tanker Double Hull (13F) Liq: 117,921; Liq (Oil): 117,921 Compartments: 12 Wing Ta, ER, 2 Wing Slop Ta 3 Cargo Pump (s): 3x3000m^3/hr Manifold: Bow/CM: 121.8m	1 oil engine driving 1 FP propeller Total Power: 15,995kW (21,747hp) 15.3kn Sulzer 7RTA62U 1 x 2 Stroke 7 Cy. 620 x 2150 15995kW (21747bhp) Dalian Marine Diesel Works-China Fuel: 174.6 (d.f.) 3381.7 (r.f.)
9417165 *BQCG* -	**YANG MEI HU** - Dalian Ocean Shipping Co (COSCO DALIAN) - SatCom: Inmarsat C 441385810 *Dalian, Liaoning* *China* MMSI: 413858000	61,630 32,584 109,855 T/cm 92.0	Class: CC	2010-02 Dalian Shipbuilding Industry Co Ltd — Dalian LN (No 2 Yard) Yd No: PC1100-34 Loa 244.60 (BB) Br ex 42.03 Dght 15.450 Lbp 233.00 Br md 42.00 Dpth 22.20 Welded, 1 dk	(A13B2TP) Products Tanker Double Hull (13F) Liq: 117,937; Liq (Oil): 117,937 Cargo Heating Coils Compartments: 12 Wing Ta, 2 Wing Slop Ta, ER 3 Cargo Pump (s): 2x3000m^3/hr, 1x3300m^3/hr Manifold: Bow/CM: 121.8m	1 oil engine driving 1 FP propeller Total Power: 14,875kW (20,224hp) 15.3kn Wartsila 7RT-flex58T 1 x 2 Stroke 7 Cy. 580 x 2416 14875kW (20224bhp) Dalian Marine Diesel Co Ltd-China AuxGen: 3 x 780kW 450V a.c Fuel: 200.0 (d.f.) 3204.0 (r.f.)
9397755 *BOGD* -	**YANG NING HU** - Dalian Ocean Shipping Co (COSCO DALIAN) - SatCom: Inmarsat C 441377010 *Dalian, Liaoning* *China* MMSI: 413770000	61,630 32,584 109,815 T/cm 92.0	Class: CC	2009-07 Dalian Shipbuilding Industry Co Ltd — Dalian LN (No 2 Yard) Yd No: PC1100-33 Loa 244.60 (BB) Br ex 42.03 Dght 15.500 Lbp 233.00 Br md 42.00 Dpth 22.20 Welded, 1 dk	(A13B2TP) Products Tanker Double Hull (13F) Liq: 117,937; Liq (Oil): 108,715 Cargo Heating Coils Compartments: 12 Wing Ta, 2 Wing Slop Ta, ER 3 Cargo Pump (s): 3x3000m^3/hr Manifold: Bow/CM: 121.8m	1 oil engine driving 1 FP propeller Total Power: 14,875kW (20,224hp) 15.3kn Wartsila 7RT-flex58T 1 x 2 Stroke 7 Cy. 580 x 2416 14875kW (20224bhp) Dalian Marine Diesel Co Ltd-China AuxGen: 3 x 780kW 450V a.c Fuel: 2713.0 (r.f.)
8005214 *3FOM8* -	**YANG PU** *ex Hakko Ace -1992 ex Mio Blanca -1984* *ex Ivy -1983* Goujing Shipping Inc - SatCom: Inmarsat C 435356910 *Panama* *Panama* MMSI: 353569000 Official number: 2575398	3,512 1,683 6,000	Class: (CC) (NK)	1980-12 Murakami Hide Zosen K.K. — Imabari Yd No: 186 Loa 102.80 Br ex - Dght 6.766 Lbp 95.03 Br md 16.01 Dpth 8.01 Welded, 1 dk	(A12B2TR) Chemical/Products Tanker Liq: 5,979; Liq (Oil): 5,979	1 oil engine driving 1 FP propeller Total Power: 2,648kW (3,600hp) 12.3kn Hanshin 6LU46A 1 x 4 Stroke 6 Cy. 460 x 740 2648kW (3600bhp) The Hanshin Diesel Works Ltd-Japan AuxGen: 2 x 132kW
7620988 *3FIR6* -	**YANG QUAN** *ex Alfa Perla -2005 ex Hermes II -2005* *ex Velimahi -1996 ex Nopal Cherry -1991* *ex Pacific Lover -1989 ex Atropos Island -1987* Yang Chun Ocean Shipping Co Ltd Perseas Shipping SA SatCom: Inmarsat C 435663110 *Panama* *Panama* MMSI: 356631000 Official number: 2333796CH	11,042 6,822 18,863 T/cm 27.7	Class: (CR) (RS) (BV) (NV) (NK)	1977-04 K.K. Uwajima Zosensho — Uwajima Yd No: 953 Loa 146.08 Br ex 22.89 Dght 9.311 Lbp 137.01 Br md 22.86 Dpth 12.60 Welded, 1 dk	(A21A2BC) Bulk Carrier Grain: 23,755; Bale: 22,707 Compartments: 4 Ho, ER 4 Ha: (16.0 x 9.6)3 (19.2 x 11.2)ER Derricks: 4x25t	1 oil engine driving 1 FP propeller Total Power: 5,884kW (8,000hp) 14.0kn Mitsubishi 6UEC52/105E 1 x 2 Stroke 6 Cy. 520 x 1050 5884kW (8000bhp) Akasaka Tekkosho KK (Akasaka DieselLtd)-Japan AuxGen: 2 x 316kW 440V 60Hz a.c Fuel: 1761.0 (r.f.)
5229405 *H04269* -	**YANG SHANG** *ex Hak Yang -1987 ex Horangy -1985* *ex Wha Yang No. 77 -1985* *ex Shosei Maru No. 25 -1985* *ex Matsusei Maru No. 25 -1976* The Towers Inc - *Panama* *Panama* Official number: 10881PEXT3	*297* 157 -	Class: (KR)	1962 KK Kanasashi Zosen — Shizuoka SZ Yd No: 491 Loa 48.52 Br ex 7.62 Dght - Lbp 42.55 Br md 7.60 Dpth 3.71 Welded, 1 dk	(B11B2FV) Fishing Vessel Ins: 479	1 oil engine driving 1 FP propeller Total Power: 736kW (1,001hp) 10.5kn Akasaka SR6SS 1 x 4 Stroke 6 Cy. 350 x 500 736kW (1001bhp) Akasaka Tekkosho KK (Akasaka DieselLtd)-Japan AuxGen: 2 x 80kW 230V a.c
8629242 *BI2526* -	**YANG SHUN NO. 6** - Yang Shun Fishery Co Ltd - *Kaohsiung* *Chinese Taipei*	503 252 -		2000-07 San Yang Shipbuilding Co., Ltd. — Kaohsiung Yd No: 804 Loa 49.68 Br ex - Dght 3.289 Lbp 48.60 Br md 8.60 Dpth 3.75 Welded, 1 dk	(B11B2FV) Fishing Vessel	1 oil engine driving 1 FP propeller Total Power: 1,103kW (1,500hp) Matsui MA29GSC-3 1 x 4 Stroke 6 Cy. 290 x 540 1103kW (1500bhp) Matsui Iron Works Co Ltd-Japan
8629254 *BH3368* -	**YANG SHUN NO. 8** - Yang Shun Fishery Co Ltd - *Kaohsiung* *Chinese Taipei*	363 109 -		2003-08 Yiti Shipbuilding Industrial Corp. — Tainan Loa 41.00 Br ex - Dght 2.509 Lbp - Br md 7.70 Dpth 2.90 Bonded, 1 dk	(B11B2FV) Fishing Vessel Hull Material: Reinforced Plastic	1 oil engine driving 1 FP propeller Total Power: 1,103kW (1,500hp) Matsui MA29GSC-3 1 x 4 Stroke 6 Cy. 290 x 540 1103kW (1500bhp) Matsui Iron Works Co Ltd-Japan
9140528 *VRNA4* -	**YANG TAI** *ex Super Adventure -2014* *ex IVS Super Adventure -2002* *ex Super Adventure -2001* Fancy State Corp Ltd - *Hong Kong* *Hong Kong* Official number: HK-4027	17,977 9,871 28,630	Class: NK	1996-09 Tsuneishi Shipbuilding Co Ltd — Fukuyama HS Yd No: 1082 Loa 172.00 (BB) Br ex - Dght 9.568 Lbp 165.00 Br md 27.00 Dpth 13.60 Welded, 1 dk	(A21A2BC) Bulk Carrier Grain: 38,472; Bale: 37,446 Compartments: 5 Ho, ER 5 Ha: (12.9 x 16.0)4 (19.8 x 17.6)ER Cranes: 4x30.5t	1 oil engine driving 1 FP propeller Total Power: 7,135kW (9,701hp) 14.0kn B&W 5S50MC 1 x 2 Stroke 5 Cy. 500 x 1910 7135kW (9701bhp) Kawasaki Heavy Industries Ltd-Japan Fuel: 1370.0 (r.f.)
8995275 - -	**YANG VITI I** *ex Blue Whale Xi -2001 ex Andatu VI -2007* PT Kurnia Tunggal Nugraha - *Jakarta* *Indonesia*	141 43 -	Class: KI	1991-04 P.T. Noahtu Shipyard — Panjang L reg 23.00 Br ex - Dght - Lbp 22.00 Br md 7.50 Dpth 3.10 Welded, 1 dk	(B32A2ST) Tug	2 oil engines geared to sc. shafts driving 2 Propellers Total Power: 912kW (1,240hp) 12.0kn Caterpillar 3412TA 2 x Vee 4 Stroke 12 Cy. 137 x 152 each-456kW (620bhp) Caterpillar Inc-USA
7714973 - -	**YANG ZHOU No. 3** *ex Towa Maru -1995* *ex Prince Maru No. 3 -1995* *ex Bridgestone Maru No. 303 -1986* Zhuhai Navigational Development Co - *Zhuhai, Guangdong* *China* Official number: 24115-PEXT1	770 285 695 T/cm 3.8	Class: (CC) (NK)	1978-04 K.K. Taihei Kogyo — Akitsu Yd No: 328 Loa 57.97 Br ex - Dght 3.891 Lbp 53.50 Br md 10.51 Dpth 4.30 Welded, 1 dk	(A11B2TG) LPG Tanker Liq (Gas): 1,093 2 x Gas Tank (s); 2 independent (C.mn.stl) cyl horizontal 2 Cargo Pump (s): 2x200m^3/hr Manifold: Bow/CM: 23m	1 oil engine reduction geared to sc. shaft driving 1 FP propeller Total Power: 1,030kW (1,400hp) 11.3kn Hanshin 6LUN28G 1 x 4 Stroke 6 Cy. 280 x 480 1030kW (1400bhp) Hanshin Nainenki Kogyo-Japan AuxGen: 3 x 100kW a.c Fuel: 18.5 (r.f.) 4.0pd
7939195 - -	**YANG ZI JIANG 2** *ex Xin Hua 5 -1982* China Yangtze River Shipping Co Ltd - *Wuhan, Hubei* *China* MMSI: 412083020	2,755 1,601 3,440	Class: (CC)	1977 Zhonghua Shipyard — Shanghai Loa 101.15 Br ex - Dght 6.000 Lbp 92.30 Br md 13.80 Dpth 7.70 Welded, 2 dks	(A31A2GX) General Cargo Ship Grain: 5,158; Bale: 4,769 Compartments: 3 Ho, ER, 3 Tw Dk 3 Ha: (9.7 x 7.0)2 (11.0 x 7.0)ER Derricks: 6x5t; Winches: 6	1 oil engine driving 1 FP propeller Total Power: 2,207kW (3,001hp) 14.0kn Hudong 6ESDZ43/82B 1 x 2 Stroke 6 Cy. 430 x 820 2207kW (3001bhp) Hudong Shipyard-China AuxGen: 2 x 250kW 400V 50Hz a.c Fuel: 45.5 (d.f.) 86.5 (r.f.)

359416 **YANGANG TUOBA** **420**
ex Bonny Fair *-2004* -
Shenzhen Yantian Port 140
-
China

2004-10 **Bonny Fair Development Ltd — Hong Kong**
Loa 36.80 Br ex - Dght 3.400
Lbp 32.30 Br md 10.00 Dpth 4.40
Welded, 1 dk

(B32A2ST) Tug

2 oil engines geared to sc. shafts driving 2 Z propellers
Total Power: 2,942kW (4,000hp) 13.5kn
Niigata 6L26HLX
2 x 4 Stroke 6 Cy. 260 x 350 each-1471kW (2000bhp)
Niigata Engineering Co Ltd-Japan
Fuel: 60.0 (d.f.)

910093 **YANGON STAR** **9,606** Class: GL
ELRN6 *ex* Hansa Rostock *-2013* 4,889
Golden Prosperity Pte Ltd 12,594
Alfa Ship Managers Pte Ltd T/cm
Monrovia *Liberia* 26.6
MMSI: 636016215
Official number: 16215

1994-10 **Stocznia Szczecinska SA — Szczecin**
Yd No: B183/304
Loa 149.55 (BB) Br ex 22.62 Dght 8.225
Lbp 140.14 Br md 22.30 Dpth 11.10
Welded, 1 dk

(A33A2CC) Container Ship (Fully Cellular)
Grain: 16,624; Bale: 16,500
TEU 1016 C Ho 334 C Dk 682 TEU incl 90 ref C.
Compartments: 4 Cell Ho, ER
7 Ha: (12.5 x 10.4)6 (12.5 x 18.0)ER
Cranes: 2x40t

1 oil engine driving 1 CP propeller
Total Power: 6,930kW (9,422hp) 17.5kn
B&W 6L50MC
1 x 2 Stroke 6 Cy. 500 x 1620 6930kW (9422bhp)
H Cegielski Poznan SA-Poland
AuxGen: 1 x 1000kW 400V a.c, 3 x 504kW 400/220V a.c
Thrusters: 1 Thwart. FP thruster (f)
Fuel: 151.0 (d.f.) 1274.0 (r.f.)

583847 **YANGTZE AMBITION** **20,969** Class: LR
VRIK9 11,811 ✠**100A1** SS 04/2011
Tianjin CMB Sea Passion Shipping Co Ltd 32,688 bulk carrier
Yangtze Navigation (Hong Kong) Co Ltd T/cm CSR
Hong Kong *Hong Kong* 46.0 BC-A
MMSI: 477514500 GRAB (25)
Official number: HK-3073 Nos. 2 & 4 holds may be empty
ESP
timber deck cargoes
*IWS
LI
✠**LMC** **UMS**
Eq.Ltr: I†;
Cable: 605.0/64.0 U3 (a)

2011-04 **Jiangmen Nanyang Ship Engineering Co Ltd — Jiangmen GD** Yd No: 601
Loa 179.90 (BB) Br ex 28.44 Dght 10.150
Lbp 171.50 Br md 28.40 Dpth 14.10
Welded, 1 dk

(A21A2BC) Bulk Carrier
Grain: 42,565; Bale: 40,558
Compartments: 5 Ho, ER
5 Ha: ER
Cranes: 4x30.5t

1 oil engine driving 1 FP propeller
Total Power: 6,480kW (8,810hp) 13.6kn
MAN-B&W 6S42MC
1 x 2 Stroke 6 Cy. 420 x 1764 6480kW (8810bhp)
Yichang Marine Diesel Engine Co Ltd-China
AuxGen: 3 x 470kW 450V 60Hz a.c
Boilers: WTAuxB (Comp) 7.5kgf/cm² (7.4bar)

9486544 **YANGTZE BRAVERY** **157,053** Class: NV
VRHK4 99,083
- **Nanjing D Two Shipping Inc** 296,951
Nanjing Tanker Corp T/cm
SatCom: Inmarsat C 447702942 177.9
Hong Kong *Hong Kong*
MMSI: 477932700
Official number: HK-2860

2011-01 **Dalian Shipbuilding Industry Co Ltd — Dalian LN (No 2 Yard)** Yd No: T3000-33
Loa 329.95 (BB) Br ex - Dght 21.500
Lbp 317.40 Br md 60.00 Dpth 29.70
Welded, 1 dk

(A13A2TV) Crude Oil Tanker
Double Hull (13F)
Liq: 324,600; Liq (Oil): 324,600
Compartments: 5 Wing Ta, 5 Ta, 5 Wing Ta, 1 Wing Slop Ta, 1 Wing Slop Ta, ER
3 Cargo Pump (s): 3x5500m³/hr

1 oil engine driving 1 FP propeller
Total Power: 25,480kW (34,643hp) 15.5kn
MAN-B&W 7S80MC
1 x 2 Stroke 7 Cy. 800 x 3056 25480kW (34643bhp)
AuxGen: 3 x 1080kW 50Hz a.c
Fuel: 440.0 (d.f.) 6000.0 (r.f.)

9584190 **YANGTZE BRILLIANCE** **20,969** Class: LR
VRJK2 11,798 ✠**100A1** SS 10/2011
- **Marina Angelite Shipping Ltd** 32,323 bulk carrier
Yangtze Navigation (Hong Kong) Co Ltd T/cm CSR
Hong Kong *Hong Kong* 46.0 BC-A
MMSI: 477328900 Hold Nos. 2 & 4 be may be empty
Official number: HK-3270 GRAB (20)
ESP
LI
*IWS
timber deck cargoes
✠**LMC** **UMS**
Eq.Ltr: I†;
Cable: 605.0/64.0 U3 (a)

2011-10 **Jiangmen Nanyang Ship Engineering Co Ltd — Jiangmen GD** Yd No: 605
Loa 179.90 (BB) Br ex 28.44 Dght 10.150
Lbp 171.50 Br md 28.40 Dpth 14.10
Welded, 1 dk

(A21A2BC) Bulk Carrier
Grain: 43,483; Bale: 40,558
Compartments: 5 Ho, ER
5 Ha: ER
Cranes: 4x30.5t

1 oil engine driving 1 FP propeller
Total Power: 6,480kW (8,810hp) 13.6kn
MAN-B&W 6S42MC
1 x 2 Stroke 6 Cy. 420 x 1764 6480kW (8810bhp)
STX (Dalian) Engine Co Ltd-China
AuxGen: 3 x 470kW 450V 60Hz a.c
Boilers: AuxB (Comp) 7.5kgf/cm² (7.4bar)
Fuel: 114.0 (d.f.) 1077.0 (r.f.) 27.0pd

9584205 **YANGTZE CLASSIC** **20,969** Class: LR
VRJW4 11,795 ✠**100A1** SS 02/2012
- **Marina Beryl Shipping Ltd** 32,503 bulk carrier
Yangtze Navigation (Hong Kong) Co Ltd T/cm CSR
Hong Kong *Hong Kong* 46.0 BC-A
MMSI: 477739600 GRAB (20)
Official number: HK-3366 Nos. 2 & 4 holds may be empty
ESP
timber deck cargoes
*IWS
LI
✠**LMC** **UMS**
Eq.Ltr: I†;
Cable: 605.0/64.0 U3 (a)

2012-02 **Jiangmen Nanyang Ship Engineering Co Ltd — Jiangmen GD** Yd No: 607
Loa 179.90 (BB) Br ex 28.44 Dght 10.150
Lbp 171.50 Br md 28.40 Dpth 14.10
Welded, 1 dk

(A21A2BC) Bulk Carrier
Grain: 42,565; Bale: 40,558
Compartments: 5 Ho, ER
5 Ha: ER
Cranes: 4x30.5t

1 oil engine driving 1 FP propeller
Total Power: 6,480kW (8,810hp) 13.6kn
MAN-B&W 6S42MC
1 x 2 Stroke 6 Cy. 420 x 1764 6480kW (8810bhp)
Yichang Marine Diesel Engine Co Ltd-China
AuxGen: 3 x 470kW 450V 60Hz a.c
Boilers: WTAuxB (Comp) 7.5kgf/cm² (7.4bar)

9486506 **YANGTZE CROWN** **164,680** Class: LR
VRJC8 108,053 ✠**100A1** SS 09/2011
- **Napoleon Shipping Inc** 317,960 Double Hull oil tanker
Nanjing Tanker Corp T/cm CSR
Hong Kong *Hong Kong* 181.2 ESP
MMSI: 477095600 **ShipRight** (CM)
Official number: HK-3212 *IWS
LI
SPM
✠**LMC** **UMS IGS**
Eq.Ltr: E*;
Cable: 770.0/117.0 U3 (a)

2011-09 **Shanghai Waigaoqiao Shipbuilding Co Ltd — Shanghai** Yd No: 1183
Loa 333.00 (BB) Br ex 60.05 Dght 22.640
Lbp 320.00 Br md 60.00 Dpth 30.50
Welded, 1 dk

(A13A2TV) Crude Oil Tanker
Double Hull (13F)
Liq: 334,900; Liq (Oil): 334,900
Cargo Heating Coils
Compartments: 5 Ta, 10 Wing Ta, 2 Wing Slop Ta, ER
3 Cargo Pump (s): 3x5500m³/hr
Manifold: Bow/CM: 165.2m

1 oil engine driving 1 FP propeller
Total Power: 29,340kW (39,891hp) 16.1kn
MAN-B&W 6S90MC-C
1 x 2 Stroke 6 Cy. 900 x 3188 29340kW (39891bhp)
Hudong Heavy Machinery Co Ltd-China
AuxGen: 3 x 1270kW 450V 60Hz a.c
Boilers: e (ex.g.) 21.4kgf/cm² (21.0bar), WTAuxB (o.f.) 18.4kgf/cm² (18.0bar)
Fuel: 480.0 (d.f.) 8440.0 (r.f.)

9486520 **YANGTZE DIAMOND** **164,680** Class: LR
VRKM3 108,053 ✠**100A1** SS 05/2012
- **Nanjing W Two Shipping Inc** 318,227 Double Hull oil tanker
CSC Oil Transportation (S) Pte Ltd T/cm CSR
Hong Kong *Hong Kong* 181.2 ESP
MMSI: 477174100 **ShipRight** CM
Official number: HK-3494 *IWS
LI
SPM
✠**LMC** **UMS IGS**
Eq.Ltr: E*;
Cable: 770.0/117.0 U3 (a)

2012-05 **Shanghai Waigaoqiao Shipbuilding Co Ltd — Shanghai** Yd No: 1185
Loa 333.00 (BB) Br ex 60.05 Dght 22.640
Lbp 320.00 Br md 60.00 Dpth 30.50
Welded, 1 dk

(A13A2TV) Crude Oil Tanker
Double Hull (13F)
Liq: 334,900; Liq (Oil): 334,900
Cargo Heating Coils
Compartments: 5 Ta, 10 Wing Ta, ER, 2 Wing Slop Ta
3 Cargo Pump (s): 3x5500m³/hr
Manifold: Bow/CM: 165.2m

1 oil engine driving 1 FP propeller
Total Power: 29,340kW (39,891hp) 16.1kn
MAN-B&W 6S90MC-C
1 x 2 Stroke 6 Cy. 900 x 3188 29340kW (39891bhp)
Hudong Heavy Machinery Co Ltd-China
AuxGen: 3 x 1270kW 450V 60Hz a.c
Boilers: e (ex.g.) 21.4kgf/cm² (21.0bar), WTAuxB (o.f.) 18.3kgf/cm² (17.9bar)
Fuel: 480.0 (d.f.) 8440.0 (r.f.)

9584217 **YANGTZE DIGNITY** **20,969** Class: LR
VRJW5 11,791 ✠**100A1** SS 01/2012
- **Marina Emerald Shipping Ltd** 32,414 bulk carrier
Yangtze Navigation (Hong Kong) Co Ltd T/cm CSR
Hong Kong *Hong Kong* 46.0 BC-A
MMSI: 477340200 GRAB (20)
Official number: HK-3367 Nos. 2 & 4 holds may be empty
ESP
timber deck cargoes
*IWS
LI
✠**LMC** **UMS**
Eq.Ltr: I†;
Cable: 605.0/64.0 U3 (a)

2012-01 **Jiangmen Nanyang Ship Engineering Co Ltd — Jiangmen GD** Yd No: 123
Loa 179.90 (BB) Br ex 28.44 Dght 10.150
Lbp 171.50 Br md 28.39 Dpth 14.10
Welded, 1 dk

(A21A2BC) Bulk Carrier
Grain: 42,565; Bale: 40,558
Compartments: 5 Ho, ER
5 Ha: ER
Cranes: 4x30.5t

1 oil engine driving 1 FP propeller
Total Power: 6,480kW (8,810hp) 13.6kn
MAN-B&W 6S42MC
1 x 2 Stroke 6 Cy. 420 x 1764 6480kW (8810bhp)
STX Engine Co Ltd-South Korea
AuxGen: 3 x 465kW 450V 60Hz a.c
Boilers: WTAuxB (Comp) 7.5kgf/cm² (7.4bar)

IMO / Call sign	Name / Owner / Manager	Tonnage	Classification	Builder / Dimensions	Type / Capacity	Machinery	
9584188 *VRIT8* -	**YANGTZE ETERNAL** **Peace Sea Co Ltd** Yangtze Navigation (Hong Kong) Co Ltd *Hong Kong* *Hong Kong* MMSI: 477899100 Official number: HK-3147	**20,969** 11,798 32,573 T/cm 46.0	Class: LR ✠**100A1** SS 07/2011 bulk carrier CSR BC-A Nos. 2 & 4 holds may be empty GRAB (25) ESP LI *IWS timber deck cargoes ✠**LMC** **UMS** Eq.Ltr: I†; Cable: 605.0/64.0 U3 (a)	**2011**-07 **Jiangmen Nanyang Ship Engineering Co Ltd — Jiangmen GD** Yd No: 604 Loa 179.90 (BB) Br ex 28.44 Dght 10.150 Lbp 171.50 Br md 28.40 Dpth 14.10 Welded, 1 dk	**(A21A2BC) Bulk Carrier** Grain: 42,565; Bale: 40,558 Compartments: 5 Ho, ER 5 Ha: ER Cranes: 4x30.5t	**1 oil engine** driving 1 FP propeller Total Power: 6,480kW (8,810hp) MAN-B&W 1 x 2 Stroke 6 Cy. 420 x 1764 6480kW (8810bhp) Yichang Marine Diesel Engine Co Ltd-China AuxGen: 3 x 470kW 450V 60Hz a.c Boilers: WTAuxB (Comp) 7.5kgf/cm² (7.4bar)	13.6k 6S42M
9584229 *VRKF3* -	**YANGTZE FLOURISH** **Marina Iridot Shipping Ltd** Yangtze Navigation (Hong Kong) Co Ltd *Hong Kong* *Hong Kong* MMSI: 477700900 Official number: HK-3437	**20,969** 11,820 32,503 T/cm 46.0	Class: LR ✠**100A1** SS 05/2012 bulk carrier CSR BC-A GRAB (20) Nos 2 and 4 holds may be empty ESP timber deck cargoes *IWS LI ✠**LMC** **UMS** Eq.Ltr: I†; Cable: 605.0/64.0 U3 (a)	**2012**-05 **Jiangmen Nanyang Ship Engineering Co Ltd — Jiangmen GD** Yd No: 124 Loa 179.90 (BB) Br ex 28.44 Dght 10.150 Lbp 171.50 Br md 28.40 Dpth 14.10 Welded, 1 dk	**(A21A2BC) Bulk Carrier** Grain: 42,565; Bale: 40,558 Compartments: 5 Ho, ER 5 Ha: ER Cranes: 4x30.5t	**1 oil engine** driving 1 FP propeller Total Power: 6,480kW (8,810hp) MAN-B&W 1 x 2 Stroke 6 Cy. 420 x 1764 6480kW (8810bhp) STX Engine Co Ltd-South Korea AuxGen: 3 x 470kW 450V 60Hz a.c Boilers: WTAuxB (Comp) 7.5kgf/cm² (7.4bar)	13.6k 6S42M
9381720 *VRGC4* -	**YANGTZE FOUNTAIN** **Betelgeuse Shipping Ltd** Nanjing Tanker Corp SatCom: Inmarsat C 447702243 *Hong Kong* *Hong Kong* MMSI: 477641400 Official number: HK-2584	**156,702** 98,937 297,580 T/cm 177.9	Class: AB CC	**2010**-01 **Shanghai Jiangnan Changxing Shipbuilding Co Ltd — Shanghai** Yd No: H2395 Loa 330.00 (BB) Br ex 60.04 Dght 21.500 Lbp 316.00 Br md 60.00 Dpth 29.70 Welded, 1 dk	**(A13A2TV) Crude Oil Tanker** Double Hull (13F) Liq: 324,572; Liq (Oil): 340,112 Compartments: 5 Ta, 10 Wing Ta, 2 Wing Slop Ta, ER 3 Cargo Pump (s): 3x5500m³/hr Manifold: Bow/CM: 162.2m	**1 oil engine** driving 1 FP propeller Total Power: 25,480kW (34,643hp) MAN-B&W 1 x 2 Stroke 7 Cy. 800 x 3056 25480kW (34643bhp) CSSC MES Diesel Co Ltd-China AuxGen: 3 x 1050kW 450V a.c Fuel: 400.0 (d.f.) 6900.0 (r.f.)	15.8k 7S80M
9405227 *VRDQ9* -	**YANGTZE FRIENDSHIP** *ex* Grand Sea *-2011* **Grand Sea Shipping Ltd** China National Foreign Trade Transportation Corp (SINOTRANS) SatCom: Inmarsat Mini-M 764839697 *Hong Kong* *Hong Kong* MMSI: 477049600 Official number: HK-2079	**160,218** 103,527 310,444 T/cm 183.7	Class: CC (NK)	**2008**-03 **Mitsui Eng. & SB. Co. Ltd., Chiba Works — Ichihara** Yd No: 1680 Loa 333.00 (BB) Br ex 60.04 Dght 20.943 Lbp 324.00 Br md 60.00 Dpth 28.80 Welded, 1 dk	**(A13A2TV) Crude Oil Tanker** Double Hull (13F) Liq: 339,586; Liq (Oil): 346,457 Compartments: 10 Wing Ta, 5 Ta, 1 Slop Ta, ER 4 Cargo Pump (s): 3x5000m³/hr, 1x2000m³/hr Manifold: Bow/CM: 167.3m	**1 oil engine** driving 1 FP propeller Total Power: 27,160kW (36,927hp) MAN-B&W 1 x 2 Stroke 7 Cy. 800 x 3200 27160kW (36927bhp) Mitsui Engineering & Shipbuilding CLtd-Japan AuxGen: 3 x 1050kW 440V 60Hz a.c Fuel: 433.0 (d.f.) 7736.0 (r.f.)	15.8k 7S80MC-
9584231 *VRKU3* -	**YANGTZE GRACE** **Marina Sapphire Shipping Ltd** Yangtze Navigation (Hong Kong) Co Ltd *Hong Kong* *Hong Kong* MMSI: 477813300 Official number: HK-3558	**20,969** 11,793 32,503 T/cm 46.0	Class: LR ✠**100A1** SS 06/2012 bulk carrier CSR BC-A GRAB (20) Nos. 2 & 4 holds may be empty ESP **ShipRight** ACS (B,D) timber deck cargoes *IWS LI ✠**LMC** **UMS** Eq.Ltr: I†; Cable: 605.0/64.0 U3 (a)	**2012**-06 **Jiangmen Nanyang Ship Engineering Co Ltd — Jiangmen GD** Yd No: 125 Loa 179.90 (BB) Br ex 28.42 Dght 10.150 Lbp 171.50 Br md 28.38 Dpth 14.10 Welded, 1 dk	**(A21A2BC) Bulk Carrier** Grain: 42,565; Bale: 40,558 Compartments: 5 Ho, ER 5 Ha: ER Cranes: 4x30.5t	**1 oil engine** driving 1 FP propeller Total Power: 6,480kW (8,810hp) MAN-B&W 1 x 2 Stroke 6 Cy. 420 x 1764 6480kW (8810bhp) Yichang Marine Diesel Engine Co Ltd-China AuxGen: 3 x 470kW 450V 60Hz a.c Boilers: WTAuxB (Comp) 7.6kgf/cm² (7.5bar)	13.6k 6S42M
9584243 *VRLA7* -	**YANGTZE HAPPINESS** **Marina Tourmaline Shipping Ltd** Yangtze Navigation (Hong Kong) Co Ltd *Hong Kong* *Hong Kong* MMSI: 477211700 Official number: HK-3612	**20,969** 11,791 32,377 T/cm 46.0	Class: LR ✠**100A1** SS 08/2012 bulk carrier CSR BC-A GRAB (20) Nos. 2 & 4 holds may be empty ESP timber deck cargoes *IWS LI **ShipRight** ACS (B,D) ✠**LMC** **UMS** Eq.Ltr: I†; Cable: 605.0/64.0 U3 (a)	**2012**-08 **Jiangmen Nanyang Ship Engineering Co Ltd — Jiangmen GD** Yd No: 126 Loa 179.90 (BB) Br ex 28.44 Dght 10.150 Lbp 171.50 Br md 28.40 Dpth 14.10 Welded, 1 dk	**(A21A2BC) Bulk Carrier** Grain: 42,565; Bale: 40,558 Compartments: 5 Ho, ER 5 Ha: ER Cranes: 4x30.5t	**1 oil engine** driving 1 FP propeller Total Power: 6,480kW (8,810hp) MAN-B&W 1 x 2 Stroke 6 Cy. 420 x 1764 6480kW (8810bhp) Yichang Marine Diesel Engine Co Ltd-China AuxGen: 3 x 465kW 450V 60Hz a.c Boilers: AuxB (Comp) 7.5kgf/cm² (7.4bar)	13.6k 6S42M
9618630 *V7AL2* -	**YANGTZE NOVA** **Yangtze Nova Pte Ltd** New Yangtze Navigation (Singapore) Pte Ltd *Majuro* *Marshall Islands* MMSI: 538005019 Official number: 5019	**29,235** 15,731 47,180	Class: CC	**2013**-01 **Jiangsu Eastern Heavy Industry Co Ltd — Jingjiang JS** Yd No: JEHIC10-811 Loa 189.99 (BB) Br ex - Dght 10.500 Lbp 185.00 Br md 32.26 Dpth 15.50 Welded, 1 dk	**(A21A2BC) Bulk Carrier** Grain: 60,276 Compartments: 5 Ho, ER 5 Ha: 4 (21.3 x 18.3)ER (18.9 x 18.3) Cranes: 4x30t Ice Capable	**1 oil engine** driving 1 FP propeller Total Power: 8,280kW (11,257hp) MAN-B&W 1 x 2 Stroke 6 Cy. 460 x 1932 8280kW (11257bhp) Doosan Engine Co Ltd-South Korea AuxGen: 3 x 535kW 400V a.c	14.2k 6S46MC-
9461972 *V7AL3* -	**YANGTZE OASIS** **New Yangtze Navigation (HongKong) Co Ltd** New Yangtze Navigation (Singapore) Pte Ltd *Majuro* *Marshall Islands* MMSI: 538005020 Official number: 5020	**23,148** 11,475 34,306	Class: BV	**2013**-04 **Nantong Huigang Shipbuilding Co Ltd — Qidong JS** (Hull launched by) Yd No: BC340-01 **2013**-04 **Lixin Shipyard — Shanghai** (Hull completed by) Yd No: LX12Z9-02 Loa 179.80 Br ex - Dght 10.200 Lbp 172.00 Br md 29.10 Dpth 14.80 Welded, 1 dk	**(A21A2BC) Bulk Carrier** Grain: 46,102 Compartments: 5 Ho, ER 5 Ha: ER Cranes: 4	**1 oil engine** driving 1 FP propeller Total Power: 7,860kW (10,686hp) MAN-B&W 1 x 2 Stroke 6 Cy. 460 x 1932 7860kW (10686bhp) STX Engine Co Ltd-South Korea AuxGen: 3 x 500kW 60Hz a.c	14.0k 6S46MC-
9371608 *VREJ5* -	**YANGTZE PEARL** **Agate Shipping Inc** Nanjing Tanker Corp SatCom: Inmarsat C 447701257 *Hong Kong* *Hong Kong* MMSI: 477114700 Official number: HK-2227	**156,702** 98,937 297,395 T/cm 178.0	Class: AB CC	**2008**-10 **Shanghai Jiangnan Changxing Shipbuilding Co Ltd — Shanghai** Yd No: H2388 Loa 330.00 (BB) Br ex 60.04 Dght 21.500 Lbp 316.00 Br md 60.00 Dpth 29.70 Welded, 1 dk	**(A13A2TV) Crude Oil Tanker** Double Hull (13F) Liq: 324,800; Liq (Oil): 333,293 Compartments: 5 Ta, 10 Wing Ta, 2 Wing Slop Ta, ER 3 Cargo Pump (s): 3x5500m³/hr Manifold: Bow/CM: 161m	**1 oil engine** driving 1 FP propeller Total Power: 25,480kW (34,643hp) MAN-B&W 1 x 2 Stroke 7 Cy. 800 x 3056 25480kW (34643bhp) Hudong Heavy Machinery Co Ltd-China AuxGen: 3 x 1050kW 450V a.c Fuel: 420.0 (d.f.) 7082.0 (r.f.)	15.8k 7S80M
9543249 *9V9147* -	**YANGTZE PIONEER** *ex* Nord London *-2011* *ex* Nord Manila *-2010* **Yangtze Pioneer Pte Ltd** New Yangtze Navigation (Singapore) Pte Ltd SatCom: Inmarsat C 456525511 *Singapore* *Singapore* MMSI: 565255000	**20,924** 11,786 32,613 T/cm 46.0	Class: LR (BV) **100A1** SS 01/2011 bulk carrier CSR BC-A GRAB (25) Nos. 2 & 4 holds may be empty ESP *IWS LI **LMC** **UMS**	**2011**-01 **Jiangmen Nanyang Ship Engineering Co Ltd — Jiangmen GD** Yd No: 119 Loa 179.90 (BB) Br ex - Dght 10.150 Lbp 171.50 Br md 28.40 Dpth 14.10 Welded, 1 dk	**(A21A2BC) Bulk Carrier** Grain: 42,565; Bale: 40,558 Compartments: 5 Ho, ER 5 Ha: 3 (20.0 x 19.2) (18.4 x 19.2)ER (14.4 x 17.6) Cranes: 4x30t	**1 oil engine** driving 1 FP propeller Total Power: 6,480kW (8,810hp) MAN-B&W 1 x 2 Stroke 6 Cy. 420 x 1764 6480kW (8810bhp) STX Engine Co Ltd-South Korea	13.7k 6S42M

IMO / Call sign	Name / Owner	Tonnage	Class	Builder / Dimensions	Type / Capacities	Machinery
486518 RJU3	**YANGTZE RAINBOW** **Nanjing W One Shipping Inc** CSC Oil Transportation (S) Pte Ltd *Hong Kong* *Hong Kong* MMSI: 477462300 Official number: HK-3349	**164,680** 108,046 318,506 T/cm 181.2	Class: LR **✠100A1** SS 01/2012 Double Hull oil tanker CSR ESP **ShipRight** CM *IWS LI SPM **✠LMC** **UMS IGS** Eq.Ltr: E*; Cable: 770.0/117.0 U3 (a)	**2012-01** **Shanghai Waigaoqiao Shipbuilding Co Ltd — Shanghai** Yd No: 1184 Loa 333.00 (BB) Br ex 60.05 Dght 22.660 Lbp 320.00 Br md 60.00 Dpth 30.50 Welded, 1 dk	**(A13A2TV) Crude Oil Tanker** Double Hull (13F) Liq: 334,900; Liq (Oil): 334,900 Cargo Heating Coils Compartments: 5 Ta, 10 Wing Ta, ER, 2 Wing Slop Ta 3 Cargo Pump (s): 3x5500m³/hr Manifold: Bow/CM: 165.2m	**1 oil engine** driving 1 FP propeller Total Power: 29,340kW (39,891hp) 16.1kn MAN-B&W 6S90MC-C 1 x 2 Stroke 6 Cy. 900 x 3188 29340kW (39891bhp) Hudong Heavy Machinery Co Ltd-China AuxGen: 3 x 1270kW 450V 60Hz a.c Boilers: e (ex.g.) 21.4kgf/cm² (21.0bar), WTAuxB (o.f.) 18.4kgf/cm² (18.0bar) Fuel: 480.0 (d.f.) 8440.0 (r.f.)
376751 RFD8 -	**YANGTZE RHYME** **Aldebaran Shipping Ltd** Nanjing Tanker Corp SatCom: Inmarsat C 447701781 *Hong Kong* *Hong Kong* MMSI: 477217900 Official number: HK-2389	**156,702** 98,937 297,188 T/cm 178.0	Class: AB CC	**2009-05** **Shanghai Jiangnan Changxing Shipbuilding Co Ltd — Shanghai** Yd No: H2394 Loa 330.00 (BB) Br ex 60.04 Dght 21.480 Lbp 316.00 Br md 60.00 Dpth 29.70 Welded, 1 dk	**(A13A2TV) Crude Oil Tanker** Double Hull (13F) Liq: 324,347; Liq (Oil): 340,112 Compartments: 5 Ta, 10 Wing Ta, 2 Wing Slop Ta, ER 3 Cargo Pump (s): 3x5500m³/hr Manifold: Bow/CM: 161m	**1 oil engine** driving 1 FP propeller Total Power: 25,480kW (34,643hp) 15.8kn MAN-B&W 7S80MC 1 x 2 Stroke 7 Cy. 800 x 3056 25480kW (34643bhp) CSSC MES Diesel Co Ltd-China AuxGen: 3 x 1312kW a.c Fuel: 420.0 (d.f.) 7082.0 (r.f.)
9330862 5BBJ2 -	**YANGTZE RIVER** *ex* Mell Senoko *-2011* *ex* Yangtze River *-2010* *ex* Australia Star *-2010* *completed as* Yangtze River *-2008* **ms 'Yangtze River' CV** Universal Shipping BV *Limassol* *Cyprus* MMSI: 212397000	**9,940** 5,020 13,749 T/cm 28.0	Class: GL	**2008-01** **Qingshan Shipyard — Wuhan HB** Yd No: 20040317 Loa 147.84 (BB) Br ex 23.45 Dght 8.510 Lbp 140.30 Br md 23.25 Dpth 11.50 Welded, 1 dk	**(A33A2CC) Container Ship (Fully Cellular)** Grain: 16,000; Bale: 16,000 TEU 1118 C Ho 334 TEU C Dk 784 TEU incl 220 ref C Compartments: 5 Cell Ho, ER Cranes: 1x45t,1x40t	**1 oil engine** reduction geared to sc. shaft driving 1 CP propeller Total Power: 9,730kW (13,229hp) 19.6kn MAN-B&W 7L58/64 1 x 4 Stroke 7 Cy. 580 x 640 9730kW (13229bhp) MAN B&W Diesel AG-Augsburg AuxGen: 3 x 570kW 60Hz a.c, 1 x 2000kW 60Hz a.c Thrusters: 1 Thwart. FP thruster (v) Fuel: 200.0 (d.f.) 1200.0 (r.f.)
9619749 VRJV4 -	**YANGTZE SPIRIT** **Oriental Elite Shipping Ltd** OSL Shipping Ltd *Hong Kong* *Hong Kong* MMSI: 477462700 Official number: HK-3358	**22,402** 12,019 35,169 T/cm 46.5	Class: BV	**2012-01** **Nanjing Dongze Shipyard Co Ltd — Nanjing JS** Yd No: 06H-92 Loa 179.90 (BB) Br ex - Dght 10.845 Lbp 171.50 Br md 28.40 Dpth 15.00 Welded, 1 dk	**(A21A2BC) Bulk Carrier** Grain: 44,321; Bale: 42,105 Compartments: 5 Ho, ER 5 Ha: 3 (20.4 x 19.5) (18.8 x 19.5)ER (14.8 x 17.9) Cranes: 4x30t	**1 oil engine** driving 1 FP propeller Total Power: 6,480kW (8,810hp) 13.7kn MAN-B&W 6S42MC 1 x 2 Stroke 6 Cy. 420 x 1764 6480kW (8810bhp) Yichang Marine Diesel Engine Co Ltd-China AuxGen: 3 x 465kW 60Hz a.c Fuel: 1895.0
9486532 VRHK3 -	**YANGTZE SPLENDOR** **Nanjing D One Shipping Inc** Nanjing Tanker Corp SatCom: Inmarsat C 447702940 *Hong Kong* *Hong Kong* MMSI: 477932600	**157,052** 99,070 297,058 T/cm 177.9	Class: NV	**2010-11** **Dalian Shipbuilding Industry Co Ltd — Dalian LN (No 2 Yard)** Yd No: T3000-32 Loa 330.05 (BB) Br ex 60.02 Dght 21.500 Lbp 317.40 Br md 60.00 Dpth 29.70 Welded, 1 dk	**(A13A2TV) Crude Oil Tanker** Double Hull (13F) Liq: 324,600; Liq (Oil): 324,600 Compartments: 5 Ta, 10 Wing Ta, 2 Wing Slop Ta, ER 3 Cargo Pump (s): 3x5500m³/hr Manifold: Bow/CM: 162.5m	**1 oil engine** driving 1 FP propeller Total Power: 25,480kW (34,643hp) 15.8kn MAN-B&W 7S80MC 1 x 2 Stroke 7 Cy. 800 x 3056 25480kW (34643bhp) AuxGen: 3 x 975kW 450V a.c
9376749 VREU6 -	**YANGTZE SPRING** **Crystal Shipping Inc** Nanjing Tanker Corp SatCom: Inmarsat C 447701520 *Hong Kong* *Hong Kong* MMSI: 477177700 Official number: HK-2315	**156,702** 98,937 297,395 T/cm 178.0	Class: AB CC	**2009-01** **Shanghai Jiangnan Changxing Shipbuilding Co Ltd — Shanghai** Yd No: H2389 Loa 330.00 (BB) Br ex 60.04 Dght 21.500 Lbp 316.00 Br md 60.00 Dpth 29.70 Welded, 1 dk	**(A13A2TV) Crude Oil Tanker** Double Hull (13F) Liq: 324,800; Liq (Oil): 333,293 Compartments: 5 Ta, 10 Wing Ta, 2 Wing Slop Ta, ER 3 Cargo Pump (s): 3x5500m³/hr Manifold: Bow/CM: 161m	**1 oil engine** driving 1 FP propeller Total Power: 25,480kW (34,643hp) 15.8kn MAN-B&W 7S80MC 1 x 2 Stroke 7 Cy. 800 x 3056 25480kW (34643bhp) Hudong Heavy Machinery Co Ltd-China AuxGen: 3 x 1050kW 450V a.c Fuel: 420.0 (d.f.) 7082.0 (r.f.)
9486491 VRIO2 -	**YANGTZE STAR** **Nappa Shipping Inc** Nanjing Tanker Corp *Hong Kong* *Hong Kong* MMSI: 477013900 Official number: HK-3100	**164,680** 108,095 318,218 T/cm 181.2	Class: LR **✠100A1** SS 06/2011 Double Hull oil tanker CSR ESP **ShipRight** (CM) *IWS LI SPM **✠LMC** **UMS IGS** Eq.Ltr: E*; Cable: 770.0/117.0 U3 (a)	**2011-06** **Shanghai Waigaoqiao Shipbuilding Co Ltd — Shanghai** Yd No: 1182 Loa 333.00 (BB) Br ex 60.05 Dght 22.660 Lbp 320.00 Br md 60.00 Dpth 30.50 Welded, 1 dk	**(A13A2TV) Crude Oil Tanker** Double Hull (13F) Liq: 334,900; Liq (Oil): 334,900 Compartments: 5 Ta, 10 Wing Ta, 2 Wing Slop Ta, ER 3 Cargo Pump (s): 3x5500m³/hr Manifold: Bow/CM: 165.2m	**1 oil engine** driving 1 FP propeller Total Power: 29,340kW (39,891hp) 16.1kn MAN-B&W 6S90MC-C 1 x 2 Stroke 6 Cy. 900 x 3188 29340kW (39891bhp) Hudong Heavy Machinery Co Ltd-China AuxGen: 3 x 1270kW 450V 60Hz a.c Boilers: e (ex.g.) 21.4kgf/cm² (21.0bar), WTAuxB (o.f.) 18.4kgf/cm² (18.0bar) Fuel: 480.0 (d.f.) 8440.0 (r.f.)
9056117 J7BB4 -	**YANGTZE STAR** *ex* Falcon *-2005* *ex* Tamba *-2003* *ex* Diamond Grace *-2000* **Platon Shipping Corp** New Shipping Ltd SatCom: Inmarsat C 432533110 *Portsmouth* *Dominica* MMSI: 325331000 Official number: 50331	**147,012** 90,794 277,095 T/cm 165.4	Class: NK	**1994-08** **Mitsubishi Heavy Industries Ltd. — Nagasaki** Yd No: 2076 Conv to DH-2010 Loa 321.95 Br ex 58.00 Dght 21.122 Lbp 310.00 Br md 58.00 Dpth 29.50 Welded, 1 dk	**(A13A2TV) Crude Oil Tanker** Double Hull (13F) Liq: 305,216; Liq (Oil): 305,216 Compartments: 6 Wing Ta, 6 Ta, ER, 2 Wing Slop Ta 4 Cargo Pump (s): 3x5000m³/hr, 1x2750m³/hr Manifold: Bow/CM: 150m	**1 oil engine** driving 1 FP propeller Total Power: 21,920kW (29,802hp) 15.5kn Mitsubishi 6UEC85LSII 1 x 2 Stroke 6 Cy. 850 x 3150 21920kW (29802bhp) Mitsubishi Heavy Industries Ltd-Japan AuxGen: 2 x 1050kW 450V a.c, 1 x 900kW 450V a.c Fuel: 365.3 (d.f.) 4773.2 (r.f.) 76.0pd
9593751 VRKI5 -	**YANGTZE XING HUA** **Minhua Shipping Co Ltd** Yangtze Navigation (Hong Kong) Co Ltd *Hong Kong* *Hong Kong* MMSI: 477598200 Official number: HK-3463	**45,271** 26,966 81,678 T/cm 72.2	Class: AB	**2012-05** **Guangzhou Longxue Shipbuilding Co Ltd — Guangzhou GD** Yd No: L0024 Loa 229.00 (BB) Br ex - Dght 14.500 Lbp 223.50 Br md 32.26 Dpth 20.20 Welded, 1 dk	**(A21A2BC) Bulk Carrier** Grain: 97,115 Compartments: 7 Ho, ER 7 Ha: ER	**1 oil engine** driving 1 FP propeller Total Power: 10,260kW (13,949hp) 14.5kn MAN-B&W 5S60MC-C 1 x 2 Stroke 5 Cy. 600 x 2400 10260kW (13949bhp) Hudong Heavy Machinery Co Ltd-China AuxGen: 3 x 620kW a.c Fuel: 210.0 (d.f.) 2930.0 (r.f.)
9593763 VRLG5 -	**YANGTZE XING JIN** **Minjin Shipping Co Ltd** Yangtze Navigation (Hong Kong) Co Ltd *Hong Kong* *Hong Kong* MMSI: 477444900 Official number: HK-3659	**45,271** 26,966 81,649 T/cm 72.2	Class: AB	**2012-11** **Guangzhou Longxue Shipbuilding Co Ltd — Guangzhou GD** Yd No: L0028 Loa 229.00 (BB) Br ex - Dght 14.500 Lbp 223.50 Br md 32.26 Dpth 20.20 Welded, 1 dk	**(A21A2BC) Bulk Carrier** Grain: 97,115 Compartments: 7 Ho, ER 7 Ha: ER	**1 oil engine** driving 1 FP propeller Total Power: 10,260kW (13,949hp) 14.5kn MAN-B&W 5S60MC-C8 1 x 2 Stroke 5 Cy. 600 x 2400 10260kW (13949bhp) Hudong Heavy Machinery Co Ltd-China AuxGen: 3 x 620kW a.c Fuel: 212.0 (d.f.) 2932.0 (r.f.)
9593775 VRLG4 -	**YANGTZE XING XIU** **Xingxiu Shipping Ltd** Yangtze Navigation (Hong Kong) Co Ltd *Hong Kong* *Hong Kong* MMSI: 477224500 Official number: HK-3658	**45,271** 26,966 82,000 T/cm 72.2	Class: AB	**2013-05** **Guangzhou Longxue Shipbuilding Co Ltd — Guangzhou GD** Yd No: L0029 Loa 229.00 (BB) Br ex - Dght 14.500 Lbp 223.50 Br md 32.26 Dpth 20.20 Welded, 1 dk	**(A21A2BC) Bulk Carrier** Grain: 97,000 Compartments: 7 Ho, ER 7 Ha: ER	**1 oil engine** driving 1 FP propeller Total Power: 10,260kW (13,949hp) 14.5kn MAN-B&W 5S60MC-C8 1 x 2 Stroke 5 Cy. 600 x 2400 10260kW (13949bhp) Hudong Heavy Machinery Co Ltd-China AuxGen: 3 x 620kW a.c Fuel: 212.0 (d.f.) 2932.0 (r.f.)
9593749 VRJR4 -	**YANGTZE XING ZHONG** **Minzhong Shipping Co Ltd** Yangtze Navigation (Hong Kong) Co Ltd *Hong Kong* *Hong Kong* MMSI: 477167400 Official number: HK-3326	**45,271** 26,966 81,622 T/cm 72.2	Class: AB	**2012-01** **Guangzhou Longxue Shipbuilding Co Ltd — Guangzhou GD** Yd No: L0022 Loa 229.00 (BB) Br ex - Dght 14.500 Lbp 223.50 Br md 32.26 Dpth 20.20 Welded, 1 dk	**(A21A2BC) Bulk Carrier** Grain: 97,115 Compartments: 7 Ho, ER 7 Ha: ER	**1 oil engine** driving 1 FP propeller Total Power: 10,260kW (13,949hp) 14.5kn MAN-B&W 5S60MC-C 1 x 2 Stroke 5 Cy. 600 x 2400 10260kW (13949bhp) Hudong Heavy Machinery Co Ltd-China AuxGen: 3 x 620kW a.c Fuel: 212.0 (d.f.) 2932.0 (r.f.)
9574420 V7BP9 -	**YANGZE NAVIGATION** *ex* Peace Voyage *-2013* **Perseus Shipping Pte Ltd** Yangzijiang Shipping Pte Ltd *Majuro* *Marshall Islands* MMSI: 538005184 Official number: 5184	**51,265** 31,203 93,236 T/cm 80.9	Class: AB	**2010-11** **Jiangsu Newyangzi Shipbuilding Co Ltd — Jingjiang JS** Yd No: YZJ2006-906 Loa 229.20 (BB) Br ex 38.04 Dght 14.900 Lbp 222.00 Br md 38.00 Dpth 20.70 Welded, 1 dk	**(A21A2BC) Bulk Carrier** Grain: 110,330; Bale: 88,904 Compartments: 7 Ho, ER 7 Ha: 5 (17.9 x 17.0)ER 2 (15.3 x 14.6)	**1 oil engine** driving 1 FP propeller Total Power: 13,560kW (18,436hp) 14.1kn MAN-B&W 6S60MC-C 1 x 2 Stroke 6 Cy. 600 x 2400 13560kW (18436bhp) Doosan Engine Co Ltd-South Korea AuxGen: 3 x 730kW a.c Fuel: 233.0 (d.f.) 3869.0 (r.f.)
9319856 - - -	**YANGZI HUA 44** *ex* Trosky *-2013* *ex* Paloma V *-2009* **Eastern Holdings Ltd**	**1,016** 305 641	Class: (BV)	**2004-06** **Astilleros Armon SA — Navia** Yd No: 607 Loa 55.00 Br ex - Dght 4.050 Lbp 46.95 Br md 10.20 Dpth 4.10 Welded, 1 dk	**(B11B2FV) Fishing Vessel** Bale: 530	**1 oil engine** geared to sc. shaft driving 1 Propeller Total Power: 1,379kW (1,875hp) 13.0kn Caterpillar 3516 1 x Vee 4 Stroke 16 Cy. 170 x 190 1379kW (1875bhp) Caterpillar Inc-USA

IMO / Call sign / Flag	Name / Owner	Tonnage	Class	Built / Dimensions	Type	Machinery	
8726727 - -	**YANINA** *ex Tavrida -1989* **Yevpatoriya Marine Trading Port** *Yevpatoriya* *Ukraine* Official number: 860102	**176** 53 31	Class: (RS)	**1987-03 Ilyichyovskiy Sudoremontnyy Zavod im. "50-letiya SSSR" — Ilyichyovsk** Yd No: 8 Loa 38.10 Br ex 7.21 Dght 1.620 Lbp 32.64 Br md - Dpth 2.90 Welded, 1 dk	**(A37B2PS) Passenger Ship** Passengers: unberthed: 294	**3 oil engines** reduction geared to sc. shafts driving 3 FP propellers Total Power: 955kW (1,299hp) Barnaultransmash 2 x 4 Stroke 6 Cy. 150 x 180 each-110kW (150bhp) Barnaultransmash-Barnaul Zvezda 1 x Vee 4 Stroke 12 Cy. 180 x 200 735kW (999bhp) "Zvezda"-Leningrad AuxGen: 2 x 16kW Fuel: 6.0 (d.f.)	17.0k 3D6 M41
5409811 *CYJT*	**YANKCANUCK** **Purvis Marine Ltd** - SatCom: Inmarsat C 431699690 *Sault Ste Marie, ON* *Canada* MMSI: 316002237 Official number: 318683	*3,280* 1,898 4,753	Class: (AB)	**1963-07 Collingwood Shipyards Ltd — Collingwood ON** Yd No: 178 Loa 98.89 Br ex 15.04 Dght 6.419 Lbp 91.75 Br md 14.94 Dpth 7.93 Riveted\Welded, 1 dk	**(A31A2GX) General Cargo Ship** Grain: 6,021 Compartments: 2 Ho, ER 2 Ha: 2 (26.8 x 10.9)ER Cranes: 1x35t	**1 oil engine** driving 1 FP propeller Total Power: 1,368kW (1,860hp) Cooper Bessemer 1 x 4 Stroke 8 Cy. 394 x 559 1368kW (1860bhp) Cooper Bessemer of Canada-Canada AuxGen: 2 x 200kW 550V 60Hz a.c Fuel: 134.0 (d.f.) 5.0pd	10.0k
7417305 *WDG9779* -	**YANKEE** *ex Loretta J -1993 ex Pye Theriot -1980* **Donjon Marine Co Inc** *New York, NY* *United States of America* MMSI: 366910810 Official number: 571215	**957** 287 -	Class: AB	**1976-03 Equitable Equipment Co. — New Orleans, La** Yd No: 1661 Widened-1981 Loa 46.72 Br ex - Dght 6.147 Lbp 43.26 Br md 14.03 Dpth 6.71 Welded, 1 dk	**(B32B2SA) Articulated Pusher Tug** Ice Capable	**2 oil engines** sr reverse geared to sc. shafts driving 2 FP propellers Total Power: 6,252kW (8,500hp) EMD (Electro-Motive) 2 x Vee 2 Stroke 20 Cy. 230 x 254 each-3126kW (4250bhp) General Motors Corp.Electro-Motive Div.-La Grange AuxGen: 2 x 99kW 220V 50Hz a.c Fuel: 738.5 (d.f.) 30.0pd	13.0k 20-645-E
7203120 *WDC3923* -	**YANKEE CLIPPER** *ex Lucil -1974* **m/v Yankee Clipper Inc** *Seattle, WA* *United States of America* Official number: 524422	*154* 105 -		**1969 Bender Welding & Machine Co Inc — Mobile AL** L reg 24.36 Br ex - Dght - Lbp - Br md 7.36 Dpth 3.46 Welded, 1 dk	**(B11B2FV) Fishing Vessel**	**1 oil engine** driving 1 FP propeller Total Power: 530kW (721hp)	
8845872 - -	**YANKEE CLIPPER** *ex Yankee Clipper I -1996 ex Pioneer -1992* *ex Crimper -1992 ex Cressida -1992* **Yankee Clipper Ltd** -	*327* 198 -		**1927-03 Fried. Krupp Germaniawerft AG — Kiel** Converted From: Yacht-1927 Loa 60.04 Br ex 9.14 Dght 5.181 Lbp - Br md 8.59 Dpth - Welded, 2 dks	**(A37A2PC) Passenger/Cruise** Passengers: cabins: 32; berths: 64	**1 oil engine** driving 1 FP propeller MAN Maschinenbau Augsburg Nuernberg (MAN)-Augsburg	
9677715 *WDG5226* -	**YANKEE FREEDOM III** **Yankee Freedom III LLC** - *Key West, FL* *United States of America* MMSI: 367544620 Official number: 1239855	**296** 27		**2012-10 Gladding-Hearn SB. Duclos Corp. — Somerset, Ma** Yd No: P-389 Loa 33.50 (BB) Br ex - Dght 2.000 Lbp - Br md 9.66 Dpth 3.81 Welded, 1 dk	**(A37B2PS) Passenger Ship** Hull Material: Aluminium Alloy Passengers: unberthed: 254	**2 oil engines** reduction geared to sc. shafts driving 2 Propellers Total Power: 3,530kW (4,800hp) Caterpillar 2 x Vee 4 Stroke 12 Cy. 170 x 215 each-1765kW (2400bhp) Caterpillar Inc-USA	28.0k 3512
8885509 *WDC7584* -	**YANKEE PRIDE** **Yankee Pride Fisheries Inc** - *Point Judith, RI* *United States of America* MMSI: 367073650 Official number: 944788	*160* 128 -		**1989 Main Iron Works, Inc. — Houma, La** Yd No: 384 L reg 23.90 Br ex - Dght - Lbp - Br md 7.02 Dpth 3.94 Welded, 1 dk	**(B11B2FV) Fishing Vessel**	**1 oil engine** driving 1 FP propeller	
9423293 *9HA2088* -	**YANNIS GORGIAS** **Aegean Anthem Shipping Co Ltd** Iolcos Hellenic Maritime Enterprises Co Ltd SatCom: Inmarsat C 424994410 *Valletta* *Malta* MMSI: 249944000 Official number: 9423293	**47,984** 27,675 87,375	Class: LR ✠ **100A1** SS 01/2010 bulk carrier CSR BC-A GRAB (20) Nos. 2, 4 & 6 holds may be empty ESP **ShipRight** (CM) *IWS LI ✠ **LMC** **UMS** Eq.Ltr: R†; Cable: 687.7/84.0 U3 (a)	**2010-01 Hudong-Zhonghua Shipbuilding (Group) Co Ltd — Shanghai** Yd No: H1538A Loa 229.00 (BB) Br ex 36.84 Dght 14.200 Lbp 221.00 Br md 36.80 Dpth 19.90 Welded, 1 dk	**(A21A2BC) Bulk Carrier** Double Hull Grain: 100,097 Compartments: 7 Ho, ER 7 Ha: ER	**1 oil engine** driving 1 FP propeller Total Power: 10,500kW (14,276hp) Wartsila 1 x 2 Stroke 6 Cy. 580 x 2416 10500kW (14276bhp) Hudong Heavy Machinery Co Ltd-China AuxGen: 3 x 600kW 440V 60Hz a.c Boilers: e (ex.g.) 12.2kgf/cm² (12.0bar), AuxB (o.f.) 9.2kgf/cm² (9.0bar)	14.5k 6RTA58T-E
9411343 *A8UB8* -	**YANNIS P.** **Dalvan Marine Inc** Marine Trust Ltd SatCom: Inmarsat C 463706887 *Monrovia* *Liberia* MMSI: 636014470 Official number: 14470	**81,347** 52,393 158,149 T/cm 118.4	Class: LR ✠ **100A1** SS 01/2010 Double Hull oil tanker CSR ESP **ShipRight** (CM) LI *IWS SPM ✠ **LMC** **UMS IGS** Eq.Ltr: Y†; Cable: 742.5/97.0 U3 (a)	**2010-01 Hyundai Samho Heavy Industries Co Ltd — Samho** Yd No: S366 Loa 274.34 (BB) Br ex 48.04 Dght 17.171 Lbp 264.00 Br md 48.00 Dpth 23.10 Welded, 1 dk	**(A13A2TV) Crude Oil Tanker** Double Hull (13F) Liq: 167,539; Liq (Oil): 167,539 Cargo Heating Coils Compartments: 12 Wing Ta, 2 Wing Slop Ta, ER 3 Cargo Pump (s): 3x4000m³/hr Manifold: Bow/CM: 137.2m	**1 oil engine** driving 1 FP propeller Total Power: 18,660kW (25,370hp) MAN-B&W 1 x 2 Stroke 6 Cy. 700 x 2800 18660kW (25370bhp) Hyundai Heavy Industries Co Ltd-South Korea AuxGen: 3 x 860kW 450V 60Hz a.c Boilers: e (ex.g.) 21.0kgf/cm² (20.6bar), WTAuxB (o.f.) 18.4kgf/cm² (18.0bar) Fuel: 200.0 (d.f.) 3650.0 (r.f.)	15.8k 6S70MC-(
9262845 *UBSR* -	**YANTAR** *ex Jackson -2003* **JSC 'Dalrybprom'** *Vladivostok* *Russia* MMSI: 273445310	**1,136** 377 650	Class: RS (NV)	**2002-06 Lien Cherng Shipbuilding Co, Ltd — Kaohsiung** Yd No: LC-110 Loa 63.15 Br ex - Dght 3.900 Lbp 55.00 Br md 10.00 Dpth 4.20 Welded, 1 dk	**(B11B2FV) Fishing Vessel** Ice Capable	**1 oil engine** driving 1 FP propeller Total Power: 1,177kW (1,600hp) Akasaka 1 x 4 Stroke 1177kW (1600bhp) Akasaka Tekkosho KK (Akasaka DieselLtd)-Japan	
8897277 *UFES* -	**YANTAR** **JSC 'Intraros' (ZAO 'Intraros')** - *Vladivostok* *Russia* Official number: 922012	**112** 33 30	Class: RS	**1995 Sretenskiy Sudostroitelnyy Zavod — Sretensk** Yd No: 307 Loa 25.45 Br ex 6.80 Dght 2.390 Lbp 23.06 Br md 6.80 Dpth 3.30 Welded, 1 dk	**(B11A2FS) Stern Trawler** Ins: 64 Ice Capable	**1 oil engine** driving 1 FP propeller Total Power: 272kW (370hp) S.K.L. 1 x 4 Stroke 6 Cy. 180 x 260 272kW (370bhp) SKL Motoren u. Systemtechnik AG-Magdeburg AuxGen: 2 x 16kW Fuel: 15.0 (d.f.)	10.0k 6NVD26A-3
8861931 *UBUE* -	**YANTAR** **Status Fish Co Ltd** - *Murmansk* *Russia*	**117** 35 30	Class: RS	**1992-02 Sosnovskiy Sudostroitelnyy Zavod — Sosnovka** Yd No: 791 Loa 25.50 Br ex 7.00 Dght 2.390 Lbp 22.00 Br md 6.80 Dpth 3.30 Welded, 1 dk	**(B11A2FS) Stern Trawler** Grain: 64 Ice Capable	**1 oil engine** driving 1 FP propeller Total Power: 220kW (299hp) S.K.L. 1 x 4 Stroke 6 Cy. 180 x 260 220kW (299bhp) SKL Motoren u. Systemtechnik AG-Magdeburg AuxGen: 2 x 14kW Fuel: 15.0 (d.f.)	9.5k 6NVD26A-2
7524419 - -	**YANTAR** **SSC FSUGE Yuzhmorgeologiya** -	**175** 52 36	Class: (RS)	**1975-07 Sretenskiy Sudostroitelnyy Zavod — Sretensk** Yd No: 77 Loa 33.96 Br ex 7.09 Dght 2.631 Lbp 30.00 Br md - Dpth 3.69 Welded, 1 dk	**(B31A2SR) Research Survey Vessel** Ice Capable	**1 oil engine** driving 1 FP propeller Total Power: 224kW (305hp) S.K.L. 1 x 4 Stroke 8 Cy. 240 x 360 224kW (305bhp) VEB Schwermaschinenbau "KarlLiebknecht" (SKL)-Magdeburg AuxGen: 1 x 86kW, 1 x 60kW Fuel: 19.0 (d.f.)	9.0k 8NVD36-1U
8226507 - -	**YANTAR** **Yantar Shipyard JSC (AO Pribaltiyskiy SSZ 'Yantar')** - *Kaliningrad* *Russia*	**182** 54 69	Class: RS	**1983 Pribaltiyskiy Sudostroitelnyy Zavod "Yantar" — Kaliningrad** Yd No: 801 Loa 29.30 Br ex 8.58 Dght 3.400 Lbp 27.00 Br md 8.30 Dpth 4.30 Welded, 1 dk	**(B32A2ST) Tug** Ice Capable	**2 oil engines** driving 2 CP propellers Total Power: 1,180kW (1,604hp) Pervomaysk 2 x 4 Stroke 8 Cy. 250 x 340 each-590kW (802bhp) Pervomaydizelmash (PDM)-Pervomaysk AuxGen: 2 x 50kW a.c	11.3k 8CHNP25/34

IMO / Call sign	Name / Owner	Tonnage	Class	Build / Dimensions	Type	Machinery
234193 JFCJ	**YANTAR-1** *ex* Oryong No. 505 *-2003* *ex* Salvia *-1994* **Orion Co Ltd** - *Sovetskaya Gavan* *Russia* MMSI: 273448750 Official number: E-0137	**2,146** 934 1,876	Class: RS (KR)	**1972-11 Uchida Zosen — Ise** Yd No: 714 Loa 84.00 Br ex - Dght 5.340 Lbp 73.80 Br md 13.01 Dpth 8.26 Welded, 2 dks	**(B11A2FS) Stern Trawler** Grain: 334; Bale: 300; Ins: 1,988 3 Ha: 2 (2.9 x 2.9) (2.5 x 1.4) Derricks: 2x5t,2x3t	**1 oil engine** driving 1 FP propeller Total Power: 2,354kW (3,200hp) 14.9kn Hanshin 6LU46 1 x 4 Stroke 6 Cy. 460 x 740 2354kW (3200bhp) Hanshin Nainenki Kogyo-Japan AuxGen: 2 x 500kW 445V a.c Fuel: 721.0 (d.f.)
8916803 UBWE5	**YANTAR-31** *ex* Oryong No. 336 *-2008* *ex* Pine 701 *-1995* **Orion Co Ltd** - *Sovetskaya Gavan* *Russia* MMSI: 273341320	**788** 327 461	Class: RS (KR)	**1990-03 Daedong Shipbuilding Co Ltd — Busan** Yd No: 357 Loa 56.07 (BB) Br ex - Dght 3.750 Lbp 49.60 Br md 8.80 Dpth 3.84 Welded	**(B11B2FV) Fishing Vessel** Ins: 608	**1 oil engine** sr reverse geared to sc. shaft driving 1 FP propeller Total Power: 883kW (1,201hp) 12.1kn Niigata 6M28AFTE 1 x 4 Stroke 6 Cy. 280 x 480 883kW (1201bhp) Ssangyong Heavy Industries Co Ltd-South Korea AuxGen: 2 x 304kW 225V a.c
8868032 UGTH -	**YANTAR-33** *ex* Mekhanik Noskov *-2011* *ex* Odeso *-2002* *ex* Mekhanik Noskov *-1999* **Orion Co Ltd** - SatCom: Inmarsat A 1407543 *Sovetskaya Gavan* *Russia* MMSI: 273842400 Official number: 922099	**812** 243 414	Class: RS	**1993-09 ATVT Zavod "Leninska Kuznya" — Kyyiv** Yd No: 1671 Loa 54.80 Br ex 10.15 Dght 4.140 Lbp 50.30 Br md 9.80 Dpth 5.00 Welded, 1 dk	**(B11A2FS) Stern Trawler** Ins: 412 Ice Capable	**1 oil engine** driving 1 CP propeller Total Power: 852kW (1,158hp) 12.0kn S.K.L. 8NVD48A-2U 1 x 4 Stroke 8 Cy. 320 x 480 852kW (1158bhp) SKL Motoren u. Systemtechnik AG-Magdeburg AuxGen: 4 x 160kW Fuel: 155.0 (d.f.)
9261504 UBHI8 -	**YANTAR-35** *ex* Ming Man No. 2 *-2012* *ex* Ming Shun No. 6 *-2003* **Orion Co Ltd** - *Sovetskaya Gavan* *Russia* MMSI: 273350850	**868** 260 473	Class: RS	**2001-11 San Yang Shipbuilding Co., Ltd. — Kaohsiung** Yd No: 8886 Loa 58.20 Br ex 9.00 Dght 3.600 Lbp 51.90 Br md 9.00 Dpth 3.95 Welded, 2 dks	**(B11B2FV) Fishing Vessel** Ins: 450	**1 oil engine** driving 1 FP propeller 12.0kn
8924800 UFSB -	**YANTARNYY** *ex* MRTK NM-3214 *-2003* *ex* MRTK-3214 *-2000* **Hermes Co Ltd-Kola (OOO 'Germes')** - *Murmansk* *Russia* Official number: 744289	**117** 35 36	Class: RS	**1974-06 Sosnovskiy Sudostroitelnyy Zavod — Sosnovka** Yd No: 3214 Loa 25.50 Br ex 7.00 Dght 2.500 Lbp 22.00 Br md 6.80 Dpth 3.30 Welded, 1 dk	**(B11B2FV) Fishing Vessel** Ins: 64	**1 oil engine** driving 1 FP propeller Total Power: 220kW (299hp) 9.5kn S.K.L. 6NVD26A-2 1 x 4 Stroke 6 Cy. 180 x 260 220kW (299bhp) VEB Schwermaschinenbau "KarlLiebknecht" (SKL)-Magdeburg AuxGen: 2 x 12kW a.c Fuel: 15.0 (d.f.)
8607232 UDYN M-0005	**YANTARNYY** *ex* Maksim Starostin *-2013* **Soglasie LLC** - SatCom: Inmarsat C 427300453 *Murmansk* *Russia* MMSI: 273523400	**7,765** 2,329 4,067	Class: RS	**1989-05 VEB Volkswerft Stralsund — Stralsund** Yd No: 814 Loa 120.70 Br ex 19.03 Dght 6.632 Lbp 108.12 Br md 19.00 Dpth 12.21 Welded, 1 dk	**(B11A2FG) Factory Stern Trawler** Grain: 496; Ins: 4,555	**2 oil engines** with clutches, flexible couplings & reduction geared to sc. shaft driving 1 CP propeller Total Power: 5,298kW (7,204hp) 15.5kn S.K.L. 6VDS48/42AL-2 2 x 4 Stroke 6 Cy. 420 x 480 each-2649kW (3602bhp) VEB Schwermaschinenbau "KarlLiebknecht" (SKL)-Magdeburg AuxGen: 2 x 1500kW a.c, 2 x 760kW a.c
9229831 DPCK -	**YANTIAN EXPRESS** *ex* Shanghai Express *-2012* *launched as* Berlin Express *-2002* **Hapag-Lloyd AG** - SatCom: Inmarsat C 421136746 *Hamburg* *Germany* MMSI: 211367460 Official number: 19330	**88,493** 36,175 100,003	Class: GL	**2002-04 Hyundai Heavy Industries Co Ltd — Ulsan** Yd No: 1364 Loa 320.58 (BB) Br ex 42.88 Dght 14.500 Lbp 304.00 Br md 42.80 Dpth 24.50 Welded, 1 dk	**(A33A2CC) Container Ship (Fully Cellular)** TEU 7506 C Ho 3748 TEU C Dk 3758 TEU incl 700 ref C. Compartments: ER, 8 Cell Ho 19 Ha: ER	**1 oil engine** driving 1 FP propeller Total Power: 68,640kW (93,323hp) 25.0kn MAN-B&W 12K98MC 1 x 2 Stroke 12 Cy. 980 x 2660 68640kW (93323bhp) Hyundai Heavy Industries Co Ltd-South Korea AuxGen: 1 x 4500kW 440V 60Hz a.c, 2 x 4000kW 440V 60Hz a.c, 1 x 2300kW 440V 60Hz a.c, 1 x 1750kW 440V 60Hz a.c Thrusters: 1 Thwart. FP thruster (f) Fuel: 498.8 (d.f.) (Heating Coils) 10074.0 (r.f.) 231.0pd
9046423 9V8478 -	**YANTRA BHUM** - **Regional Container Lines Public Co Ltd** RCL Shipmanagement Pte Ltd *Singapore* *Singapore* MMSI: 565304000 Official number: 395840	**11,086** 5,045 15,346 T/cm 30.2	Class: GL	**1993-09 Hanjin Heavy Industries Co Ltd — Ulsan** Yd No: 619 Loa 145.65 (BB) Br ex 25.04 Dght 8.149 Lbp 134.81 Br md 25.00 Dpth 11.50 Welded, 1 dk	**(A33A2CC) Container Ship (Fully Cellular)** TEU 1288 incl 60 ref C, Compartments: 2 Cell Ho, ER 12 Ha: 4 (12.6 x 10.4)8 (12.5 x 10.4)ER Cranes: 2x40t	**1 oil engine** driving 1 FP propeller Total Power: 10,415kW (14,160hp) 17.0kn B&W 6L60MC 1 x 2 Stroke 6 Cy. 600 x 1944 10415kW (14160bhp) Hyundai Heavy Industries Co Ltd-South Korea AuxGen: 3 x 560kW 440V 60Hz a.c Thrusters: 1 Thwart. CP thruster (f) Fuel: 76.5 (d.f.) 1156.8 (r.f.)
8202745 - -	**YANYAN** - **Federal Military Government of Nigeria (Department of Fisheries - Federal Ministry of Agriculture)** - *Lagos* *Nigeria*	*110* 16 -	Class: (LR) ✠	**1983-09 ShinA Shipbuilding Co Ltd — Tongyeong** Yd No: 264 Loa 34.02 Br ex 6.25 Dght 1.291 Lbp 31.55 Br md 6.00 Dpth 3.00 Welded, 1 dk	**(B12D2FP) Fishery Patrol Vessel**	**2 oil engines** with clutches & sr reverse geared to sc. shafts driving 2 FP propellers Total Power: 1,800kW (2,448hp) M.T.U. 12V396TC62 2 x Vee 4 Stroke 12 Cy. 165 x 185 each-900kW (1224bhp) MTU Friedrichshafen GmbH-Friedrichshafen AuxGen: 2 x 42kW 220V 50Hz a.c Fuel: 12.5 (d.f.)
8515037 3EYV4 -	**YAO FU** *ex* Tan Binh 34 *-2013* *ex* Pacific Bangbin *-2009* *ex* Wise King *-2007* *ex* Royal Venture *-1997* *ex* White Coral *-1993* **Yao Fu Ltd** Guangzhou Seaway International Ship Management Co Ltd *Panama* *Panama* MMSI: 371198000 Official number: 4471213A	**12,283** 7,621 21,649	Class: IT (Class contemplated) VR (NK)	**1986-01 Shin Yamamoto Shipbuilding & Engineering Co Ltd — Kochi KC** Yd No: 280 Loa 151.94 (BB) Br ex 24.03 Dght 9.689 Lbp 142.02 Br md 24.01 Dpth 13.21 Welded, 1 dk	**(A21A2BC) Bulk Carrier** Grain: 26,802; Bale: 25,730 Compartments: 4 Ho, ER 4 Ha: (17.6 x 11.2)3 (20.0 x 12.7)ER Cranes: 3x30.5t; Derricks: 1x25t	**1 oil engine** driving 1 FP propeller Total Power: 4,670kW (6,349hp) 13.0kn B&W 5L50MC 1 x 2 Stroke 5 Cy. 500 x 1620 4670kW (6349bhp) Kawasaki Heavy Industries Ltd-Japan AuxGen: 3 x 256kW a.c
8515697 BUWP -	**YAO HAI** *ex* Kamba *-2005* *ex* Angeliki D II *-1999* *ex* Yugala *-1997* *ex* Daiten *-1997* *ex* Daiten Maru *-1990* **Changjian Shipping Group Phoenix Co Ltd (CSGPC)** Shanghai Changhang Shipping Co Ltd *Wuhan, Hubei* *China* MMSI: 412079270	**36,544** 23,020 69,497 T/cm 65.5	Class: (CC) (NK)	**1986-11 Hashihama Shipbuilding Co Ltd — Tadotsu KG** Yd No: 850 Loa 225.00 (BB) Br ex 32.24 Dght 13.257 Lbp 215.02 Br md 32.21 Dpth 18.32 Welded, 1 dk	**(A21A2BC) Bulk Carrier** Grain: 81,803; Bale: 78,000 Compartments: 7 Ho, ER 7 Ha: (14.2 x 12.8)6 (16.8 x 14.4)ER	**1 oil engine** driving 1 FP propeller Total Power: 8,356kW (11,361hp) 14.0kn B&W 5L70MC 1 x 2 Stroke 5 Cy. 700 x 2268 8356kW (11361bhp) Mitsui Engineering & Shipbuilding CLtd-Japan AuxGen: 3 x 440kW 440V 60Hz a.c Fuel: 186.0 (d.f.) 2556.5 (r.f.) 32.5pd
8741210 - -	**YAO ZHOU** *ex* Nan Fang 1 *-2010* **Yao Zhou Shipping Co Ltd**	**884** 459 -	Class: UB	**1998-09 Guancheng Navigation Co Shipyard — Dongguan GD** Loa 40.80 Br ex - Dght - Lbp - Br md 13.00 Dpth 4.00 Welded, 1 dk	**(A31A2GX) General Cargo Ship**	**1 oil engine** reduction geared to sc. shaft driving 1 Propeller Total Power: 672kW (914hp) Cummins 1 x 4 Stroke 672kW (914bhp) Cummins Engine Co Inc-USA
8659235 XUGE4 -	**YAO ZHOU 66** *ex* Chuantong 666 *-2012* *ex* Jianghang 888 *-2012* **Yaozhou Marine Pte Ltd** Dana Shipping Co Ltd *Phnom Penh* *Cambodia* MMSI: 514966000	**2,943** 1,531 1,410	Class: ZC	**2004-01 Yidu Jiangnan Shipping Co Ltd** Loa 98.66 Br ex 19.16 Dght 0.860 Lbp 95.00 Br md 15.50 Dpth 3.50 Welded, 1 dk	**(A36A2PR) Passenger/Ro-Ro Ship (Vehicles)**	**2 oil engines** reduction geared to sc. shafts driving 2 Propellers Total Power: 1,150kW (1,564hp) Chinese Std. Type Z8170ZLC 2 x 4 Stroke 8 Cy. 170 x 200 each-575kW (782bhp) Zibo Diesel Engine Factory-China
9617894 JD3220 -	**YAOKI** - **Yamamoto Kaiun YK** - *Iki, Nagasaki* *Japan* MMSI: 431002703 Official number: 141480	*239* - 780		**2011-06 Tokuoka Zosen K.K. — Naruto** L reg 55.83 Br ex - Dght 3.420 Lbp 53.00 Br md 9.80 Dpth 5.65 Welded, 1 dk	**(A31A2GX) General Cargo Ship**	**1 oil engine** driving 1 Propeller Total Power: 736kW (1,001hp)

8743244 *JD2883* -	**YAOKI MARU NO. 5** **Yaoki Maru Kaiun YK** *Iki, Nagasaki* *Japan* Official number: 140949	*236* - 779	**2009-01 Tokuoka Zosen K.K. — Naruto** Loa 59.61 Br ex - Dght 3.400 Lbp 53.00 Br md 9.80 Dpth 5.65 Welded, 1 dk	**(A31A2GX) General Cargo Ship**	**1 oil engine** driving 1 Propeller Total Power: 1,029kW (1,399hp) 12.0k Akasaka K28B 1 x 4 Stroke 6 Cy. 280 x 480 1029kW (1399bhp) Akasaka Tekkosho KK (Akasaka DieselLtd)-Japan
8841046 *JM5972* -	**YAOKI MARU NO. 7** *ex* Yaoki Maru No. 5 *-2009* **Okayama Kaiun KK** *Kurashiki, Okayama* *Japan* Official number: 131361	*199* - 630	**1990-04 Y.K. Takasago Zosensho — Naruto** Yd No: 173 Loa 56.03 Br ex - Dght 3.310 Lbp 50.00 Br md 9.30 Dpth 5.45 Welded, 1 dk	**(A31A2GX) General Cargo Ship**	**1 oil engine** reverse geared to sc. shaft driving 1 FP propeller Total Power: 588kW (799hp) Akasaka T26SF 1 x 4 Stroke 6 Cy. 260 x 440 588kW (799bhp) Akasaka Tekkosho KK (Akasaka DieselLtd)-Japan
8886711 *WDE4824* -	**YAOZAA** *ex* Natalie Rose *-2007* **Ecofisherman Inc** *Honolulu, HI* *United States of America* Official number: 659760	*106* 53 -	**1983 Valhalla Yachts — Los Angeles, Ca** L reg 21.33 Br ex - Dght - Lbp - Br md 6.28 Dpth 3.45 Bonded, 1 dk	**(B11B2FV) Fishing Vessel** Hull Material: Reinforced Plastic	**1 oil engine** driving 1 FP propeller
9068251 *YD6422* -	**YAPEN II** **PT Lintas Samudra Borneo Line** *Banjarmasin* *Indonesia*	**116** Class: KI 69 -	**1997-01 PT Ady Rahmat Kamil — Banjarmasin** Loa - Br ex - Dght - Lbp 20.00 Br md 6.45 Dpth 2.70 Welded, 1 dk	**(B32A2ST) Tug**	**2 oil engines** geared to sc. shafts driving 2 Propellers Total Power: 692kW (940hp) Caterpillar 3408B 2 x Vee 4 Stroke 8 Cy. 137 x 152 each-346kW (470bhp) (made 1992, fitted 1997) Caterpillar Inc-USA
9040285 *TCBP9* -	**YAPRACIK** **BOTAS Boru Hatlari Ile Petrol Tasima AS (Botas Petroleum Pipeline Corp)** *Istanbul* *Turkey* MMSI: 271002334 Official number: 6189	**331** Class: TL (AB) 99 -	**1992-05 Gemak Sanayi ve Ticaret Koll. Sti. — Tuzla** Yd No: 10 Loa 30.50 Br ex - Dght 4.160 Lbp 29.26 Br md 10.72 Dpth 4.16 Welded, 1 dk	**(B32A2ST) Tug**	**2 oil engines** gearing integral to driving 2 Voith-Schneider propellers Total Power: 2,466kW (3,352hp) 12.0kn Caterpillar 3606TA 2 x 4 Stroke 6 Cy. 280 x 300 each-1233kW (1676bhp) Caterpillar Inc-USA
9379492 *YDCR* -	**YAPWAIRON** **Kabupaten Biak Numfor** *Jayapura* *Indonesia*	**502** Class: KI 151 210	**2005-12 P.T. Mariana Bahagia — Palembang** Yd No: 045 Loa 45.00 Br ex - Dght 2.400 Lbp 41.75 Br md 8.60 Dpth 5.20 Welded, 1 dk	**(A36A2PR) Passenger/Ro-Ro Ship (Vehicles)**	**2 oil engines** reduction geared to sc. shafts driving 2 FP propellers Total Power: 912kW (1,240hp) Yanmar 6LAH-STE3 2 x 4 Stroke 6 Cy. 150 x 165 each-456kW (620bhp) Yanmar Diesel Engine Co Ltd-Japan AuxGen: 2 x 95kW 380V a.c
7944279 - -	**YAQUI 1** **Pesquera Sisibari SA de CV** *Guaymas* *Mexico*	*104* Class: (AB) 53 -	**1977 Astilleros Monarca S.A. — Guaymas** Yd No: 595 Loa - Br ex - Dght - Lbp 20.93 Br md 6.05 Dpth 3.10 Welded, 1 dk	**(B11A2FT) Trawler**	**1 oil engine** reverse reduction geared to sc. shaft driving 1 FP propeller Total Power: 283kW (385hp) 9.0kn Waukesha F2896DM 1 x 4 Stroke 6 Cy. 216 x 216 283kW (385bhp) Waukesha Engine Div. DresserIndustries Inc.-Waukesha, Wi AuxGen: 1 x 3kW a.c, 1 x 1kW a.c
7923445 *AEPD* -	**YAQUINA** **Government of The United States of America (Department of The Army - Corps of Engineers)** *Portland, OR* *United States of America* MMSI: 366971000	*1,960* Class: (AB) 1,027 2,943	**1980-12 Norfolk SB. & D.D. Corp. — Norfolk, Va** Yd No: 178 Loa 60.97 Br ex - Dght 3.660 Lbp 58.83 Br md 17.68 Dpth 5.19 Welded, 1 dk	**(B33B2DT) Trailing Suction Hopper Dredger** Hopper: 798	**2 oil engines** sr geared to sc. shafts driving 2 CP propellers Total Power: 1,654kW (2,248hp) 10.5kn Caterpillar D399SCAC 2 x Vee 4 Stroke 16 Cy. 159 x 203 each-827kW (1124bhp) Caterpillar Tractor Co-USA AuxGen: 2 x 400kW Thrusters: 1 Thwart. FP thruster (f)
9070955 *5IM359* -	**YAR ZAR MIN T1** *ex* Asahi Maru No. 28 *-2013* *ex* Koki Maru No. 28 *-2002* **Yar Zar Min Industry Co Ltd** Golden Arrow Marine SA *Zanzibar* *Tanzania* MMSI: 677025900 Official number: 300114	**802** 470 1,950	**1993-03 Higaki Zosen K.K. — Imabari** Yd No: 417 Loa 69.90 Br ex 12.02 Dght 4.875 Lbp 66.10 Br md 12.00 Dpth 5.35 Welded, 1 dk	**(A13B2TP) Products Tanker** Compartments: 10 Ta, ER	**1 oil engine** driving 1 FP propeller Total Power: 1,471kW (2,000hp) Niigata 6M34AGT 1 x 4 Stroke 6 Cy. 340 x 620 1471kW (2000bhp) Niigata Engineering Co Ltd-Japan
8904197 *HO2789* -	**YARA** *ex* Hoyo Maru No. 21 *-2007* **RHMS Corp SA** *Panama* *Panama* Official number: 35620PEXT2	*379* - -	**1989-06 Niigata Engineering Co Ltd — Niigata NI** Yd No: 2152 Loa 54.58 (BB) Br ex - Dght 3.440 Lbp 47.90 Br md 8.70 Dpth 3.80 Welded	**(B11B2FV) Fishing Vessel**	**1 oil engine** with clutches, flexible couplings & dr geared to sc. shaft driving 1 FP propeller Total Power: 699kW (950hp) Niigata 6M28HFT 1 x 4 Stroke 6 Cy. 280 x 480 699kW (950bhp) Niigata Engineering Co Ltd-Japan
7350569 *5IM257* -	**YARA 1** *ex* Leily *-2011* *ex* Poseidon *-2006* *ex* Neptune *-1980* **Zad Al Bahar Maritime Co** Zad Fuel Co *Zanzibar* *Tanzania (Zanzibar)* MMSI: 677015700 Official number: 300021	*471* 141 -	**1974-05 Salamis Shipyards S.A. — Salamis** Yd No: 108 Loa 60.00 Br ex 12.40 Dght 1.677 Lbp 55.00 Br md 10.90 Dpth 2.29 Welded, 1 dk	**(A36A2PR) Passenger/Ro-Ro Ship (Vehicles)** Bow ramp (centre)	**2 oil engines** driving 2 FP propellers Total Power: 854kW (1,162hp) S.K.L. 2 x 4 Stroke 8 Cy. each-427kW (581bhp) VEB Schwermaschinenbau "KarlLiebknecht" (SKL)-Magdeburg
9279446 *LANT7* -	**YARA EMBLA** *ex* Norrsken *-2011* *ex* Flinterbelt *-2011* **Yara Gas Ship AS** Larvik Shipping AS SatCom: Inmarsat C 425708210 *Oslo* *Norway (NIS)* MMSI: 257082000	**2,506** Class: NV (LR) (BV) 752 ✠ Classed LR until 5/1/10 3,480	**2005-01 Marine Projects Ltd Sp z oo — Gdansk** (Hull) Yd No: (638) **2005-01 Bodewes' Scheepswerven B.V. — Hoogezand** Yd No: 638 Converted From: General Cargo Ship-2013 Loa 82.50 (BB) Br ex 12.60 Dght 5.300 Lbp 79.40 Br md 12.50 Dpth 8.00 Welded, 1 dk	**(A11C2LC) CO2 Tanker** Ice Capable	**1 oil engine** with flexible couplings & sr geared to sc. shaft driving 1 CP propeller Total Power: 1,850kW (2,515hp) 12.5kn MaK 6M25 1 x 4 Stroke 6 Cy. 255 x 400 1850kW (2515bhp) Caterpillar Motoren GmbH & Co. KG-Germany AuxGen: 1 x 145kW 400V 50Hz a.c, 1 x 264kW 400V 50Hz a.c Thrusters: 1 Water jet (f)
9345350 *LANS7* -	**YARA FROYA** *ex* Boreas *-2011* *ex* Flinterboreas *-2011* **Yara Gas Ship AS** Larvik Shipping AS SatCom: Inmarsat C 425708110 *Oslo* *Norway (NIS)* MMSI: 257081000	**2,506** Class: NV (LR) (BV) 1,464 ✠ Classed LR until 8/10/09 3,486	**2005-09 Marine Projects Ltd Sp z oo — Gdansk** (Hull) Yd No: (639) **2005-09 Bodewes' Scheepswerven B.V. — Hoogezand** Yd No: 639 Converted From: General Cargo Ship-2013 Loa 82.50 (BB) Br ex 12.60 Dght 5.300 Lbp 79.40 Br md 12.50 Dpth 8.00 Welded, 1 dk	**(A11C2LC) CO2 Tanker** Ice Capable	**1 oil engine** with flexible couplings & sr geared to sc. shaft driving 1 CP propeller Total Power: 1,850kW (2,515hp) 12.5kn MaK 6M25 1 x 4 Stroke 6 Cy. 255 x 400 1850kW (2515bhp) Caterpillar Motoren GmbH & Co. KG-Germany AuxGen: 1 x 236kW 400V 50Hz a.c, 1 x 145kW 400V 50Hz a.c Thrusters: 1 Water jet (f)
7431698 *LAZB4* -	**YARA GAS III** *ex* Hydrogas III *-2004* *ex* Coburg *-1996* *ex* Nautilus *-1988* *ex* American Cherokee *-1979* *launched as* Nautilus *-1975* **Yara Gas Ship AS** Larvik Shipping AS *Oslo* *Norway (NIS)* MMSI: 259759000	**2,198** Class: NV (GL) 660 2,645	**1975-06 KG Norderwerft GmbH & Co. — Hamburg** (Hull) **1975-06 J.J. Sietas Schiffswerft — Hamburg** Yd No: 747 Converted From: General Cargo Ship-1996 Loa 81.51 (BB) Br ex 13.42 Dght 5.039 Lbp 74.00 Br md 13.39 Dpth 5.19 Welded, 1 dk.	**(A11C2LC) CO2 Tanker** Double Hull (13F) Liq (Gas): 1,220 2 x Gas Tank (s); 2 independent (C.mn.stl) cyl horizontal 2 Cargo Pump (s): 2x250m³/hr Manifold: Bow/CM: 28m Ice Capable	**1 oil engine** reduction geared to sc. shaft driving 1 FP propeller Total Power: 1,990kW (2,706hp) 13.5kn MaK 8M453AK 1 x 4 Stroke 8 Cy. 320 x 420 1990kW (2706bhp) MaK Maschinenbau GmbH-Kiel AuxGen: 1 x 204kW 220/380V 50Hz a.c, 1 x 144kW 220/380V 50Hz a.c Thrusters: 1 Thwart. FP thruster (f) Fuel: 198.0 (d.f.)
9279410 *LATH7* -	**YARA GERDA** *ex* Flinterbaltica *-2014* **Yara Gas Ship AS** Larvik Shipping AS *Oslo* *Norway (NIS)* MMSI: 257206000	**2,474** Class: NV (LR) (BV) 1,464 ✠ Classed LR until 17/3/10 3,480	**2004-02 Marine Projects Ltd Sp z oo — Gdansk** (Hull) **2004-02 Bodewes' Scheepswerven B.V. — Hoogezand** Yd No: 635 Loa 82.50 (BB) Br ex 12.60 Dght 5.300 Lbp 79.40 Br md 12.50 Dpth 8.00 Welded, 1 dk	**(A31A2GX) General Cargo Ship** Grain: 5,323 TEU 136 C Ho 102 TEU C Dk 34 TEU Compartments: 1 Ho, ER 1 Ha: ER Ice Capable	**1 oil engine** with flexible couplings & sr geared to sc. shaft driving 1 CP propeller Total Power: 1,850kW (2,515hp) 12.5kn MaK 6M25 1 x 4 Stroke 6 Cy. 255 x 400 1850kW (2515bhp) Caterpillar Motoren GmbH & Co. KG-Germany AuxGen: 1 x 264kW 400V 50Hz a.c, 1 x 145kW 400V 50Hz a.c Thrusters: 1 Water jet (f)

IMO / Call sign	Name / Owner	Tonnage	Class	Builder / Dimensions	Type	Machinery
8023802 *VKV7155* -	**YARABAH** *ex* Nico Jebel Ali *-2008* *ex* Petromar Atlas *-1992* **Gippsland Maritime Holdings Pty Ltd** Tek-Ocean Energy Services SatCom: Inmarsat C 450303857 *Melbourne, Vic* *Australia* MMSI: 503567000 Official number: 858637	**789** 236 1,200	Class: NV (AB)	**1981-05 Halter Marine, Inc. — Moss Point, Ms** Yd No: 952 Loa - Br ex - Dght 3.928 Lbp 58.70 Br md 12.20 Dpth 4.58 Welded, 1 dk	**(B21B20T) Offshore Tug/Supply Ship**	**2 oil engines** reverse reduction geared to sc. shafts driving 2 FP propellers Total Power: 3,390kW (4,610hp) 12.0kn EMD (Electro-Motive) 12-645-E7B 2 x Vee 2 Stroke 12 Cy. 230 x 254 each-1695kW (2305bhp) General Motors Corp.Electro-Motive Div.-La Grange AuxGen: 2 x 125kW 450V 60Hz a.c Thrusters: 1 Thwart. FP thruster (f)
9420370 *EPBF9* -	**YARAN** *ex* Samin 1 *-2012* **Valfajre Shipping Co** - *Qeshm Island* *Iran* MMSI: 422021500	**9,957** 5,032 13,739 T/cm 28.0	Class: (GL)	**2009-03 Jinling Shipyard — Nanjing JS** Yd No: 04-0429 Loa 147.87 (BB) Br ex - Dght 8.500 Lbp 140.30 Br md 23.25 Dpth 11.50 Welded, 1 dk	**(A33A2CC) Container Ship (Fully Cellular)** Grain: 16,000; Bale: 16,000 TEU 1118 C Ho 334 TEU C Dk 784 incl 240 ref C Cranes: 2x45t Ice Capable	**1 oil engine** reduction geared to sc. shafts driving 1 CP propeller Total Power: 9,730kW (13,229hp) 19.6kn MAN-B&W 7L58/64 1 x 4 Stroke 7 Cy. 580 x 640 9730kW (13229bhp) (made 2009) Hudong Heavy Machinery Co Ltd-China AuxGen: 1 x 1400kW 450V a.c, 3 x 570kW 450V a.c Thrusters: 1 Tunnel thruster (f)
7710537 *VHW4443* -	**YARDIE CREEK** *ex* Inng Hua 2 *-2012* *ex* Yardie Creek *-2008* *ex* Miclyn Wave *-2000* *ex* Yardie Creek *-1993* **Arrow Pearl Co Pty Ltd** - *Fremantle, WA* *Australia* MMSI: 503636400 Official number: 850117	**546** 366 -	Class: (AB)	**1978-01 Marine Builders Pte Ltd — Singapore** Yd No: 1015 Converted From: Tug-1987 Loa 33.99 Br ex - Dght 3.112 Lbp 32.31 Br md 8.50 Dpth 3.51 Welded, 1 dk	**(B31A2SR) Research Survey Vessel**	**2 oil engines** reverse reduction geared to sc. shaft driving 1 FP propeller Total Power: 706kW (960hp) 10.0kn G.M. (Detroit Diesel) 16V-71-N 2 x Vee 2 Stroke 16 Cy. 108 x 127 each-353kW (480bhp) General Motors Detroit DieselAllison Divn-USA AuxGen: 2 x 80kW
9543500 *YYMA* -	**YARE** *ex* Guaicaipuro *-2011* **Panavenflot Corp** PDV Marina SA SatCom: Inmarsat C 477509020 *Las Piedras* *Venezuela* MMSI: 775090000 Official number: AMMT-2849	**56,326** 29,819 104,579 T/cm 88.9	Class: LR ✠ **100A1** SS 03/2011 Double Hull oil tanker CSR ESP **ShipRight** (CM,ACS (B)) *IWS LI DSPM4 ✠ **LMC** **UMS IGS** Eq.Ltr: T†; Cable: 715.0/87.0 U3 (a)	**2011-03 Sumitomo Heavy Industries Marine & Engineering Co., Ltd. — Yokosuka** Yd No: 1369 Loa 228.60 (BB) Br ex 42.04 Dght 14.800 Lbp 217.80 Br md 42.00 Dpth 21.50 Welded, 1 dk	**(A13A2TV) Crude Oil Tanker** Double Hull (13F) Liq: 98,700; Liq (Oil): 98,700 Cargo Heating Coils Compartments: 10 Wing Ta, 2 Wing Slop Ta, ER 3 Cargo Pump (s): 3x2500m³/hr Manifold: Bow/CM: 116.6m	**1 oil engine** driving 1 FP propeller Total Power: 12,350kW (16,791hp) 14.8kn MAN-B&W 6S60MC-C 1 x 2 Stroke 6 Cy. 600 x 2400 12350kW (16791bhp) Mitsui Engineering & Shipbuilding CLtd-Japan AuxGen: 3 x 640kW 450V 60Hz a.c Boilers: e (ex.g.) 21.4kgf/cm² (21.0bar), WTAuxB (o.f.) 18.4kgf/cm² (18.0bar) Fuel: 250.0 (d.f.) 2170.0 (r.f.)
8119053 *4JJU* -	**YARENGA** **Specialized Sea Oil Fleet Organisation, Caspian Sea Oil Fleet, State Oil Co of the Republic of Azerbaijan** BUE Caspian Ltd SatCom: Inmarsat C 427310038 *Baku* *Azerbaijan* MMSI: 423073100 Official number: DGR-0085	**1,585** 475 1,394	Class: RS	**1984-11 Valmetin Laivateollisuus Oy — Turku** Yd No: 352 Loa 67.32 Br ex 13.90 Dght 5.201 Lbp 58.20 Br md 13.81 Dpth 7.32 Welded, 1 dk	**(B21B20A) Anchor Handling Tug Supply** Passengers: berths: 24 Derricks: 1x10t	**4 oil engines** with clutches, flexible couplings & sr geared to sc. shafts driving 2 CP propellers Total Power: 5,330kW (7,246hp) 15.5kn Wartsila 12V22 2 x Vee 4 Stroke 12 Cy. 220 x 240 each-1780kW (2420bhp) Oy Wartsila Ab-Finland Wartsila 6R22 2 x 4 Stroke 6 Cy. 220 x 240 each-885kW (1203bhp) Oy Wartsila Ab-Finland AuxGen: 2 x 440kW 400V 50Hz a.c Thrusters: 1 Thwart. CP thruster (f) Fuel: 860.0 (d.f.)
7740726 - -	**YARKIY** - -	*163* 39 88	Class: (RS)	**1978 Astrakhanskaya Sudoverf im. "Kirova" — Astrakhan** Yd No: 111 Loa 34.02 Br ex 7.09 Dght 2.898 Lbp 30.00 Br md - Dpth 3.66 Welded, 1 dk	**(B11B2FV) Fishing Vessel** Bale: 78 Compartments: 1 Ho, ER 1 Ha: (1.6 x 1.3) Derricks: 2x2t; Winches: 2 Ice Capable	**1 oil engine** driving 1 FP propeller Total Power: 224kW (305hp) 9.0kn S.K.L. 8NVD36-1U 1 x 4 Stroke 8 Cy. 240 x 360 224kW (305bhp) VEB Schwermaschinenbau "KarlLiebknecht" (SKL)-Magdeburg
8815140 *SSDK* -	**YARMOUK** **Government of The Arab Republic of Egypt (Ministry of Agriculture- Agriculture Guidance Project Code 8004)** Government of The Arab Republic of Egypt (Ministry of Scientific Research National Institute of Oceanography & Fisheries) *Alexandria* *Egypt* MMSI: 622122238 Official number: 3208	**193** 58 168	Class: NK	**1989-01 Niigata Engineering Co Ltd — Niigata NI** Yd No: 2111 Loa 30.71 Br ex - Dght 2.700 Lbp 26.00 Br md 7.41 Dpth 3.15 Welded, 1 dk	**(B12D2FR) Fishery Research Vessel** Ins: 50	**1 oil engine** with clutches, flexible couplings & dr reverse geared to sc. shaft driving 1 FP propeller Total Power: 662kW (900hp) 10.0kn Niigata 6NSC-M 1 x 4 Stroke 6 Cy. 190 x 260 662kW (900bhp) Niigata Engineering Co Ltd-Japan AuxGen: 2 x 80kW a.c Fuel: 78.0
9046576 *UBUI5* -	**YAROSLAV MYDRYY** *ex* Ledastern *-2012* **Opair International Corp** Morskoy Standart Co Ltd SatCom: Inmarsat C 427305597 *Petropavlovsk-Kamchatskiy* *Russia* MMSI: 273352470 Official number: 4428312	**6,262** 3,130 10,463 T/cm 19.6	Class: GL RS	**1993-06 MTW Schiffswerft GmbH — Wismar** Yd No: 126 Converted From: Chemical/Products Tanker-2012 Loa 123.72 (BB) Br ex 17.92 Dght 8.360 Lbp 117.60 Br md 17.70 Dpth 10.60 Welded, 1 dk	**(A13B2TP) Products Tanker** Double Hull (13F) Liq: 10,599; Liq (Oil): 10,673 Compartments: 12 Wing Ta, 2 Wing Slop Ta, ER 12 Cargo Pump (s): 12x220m³/hr Manifold: Bow/CM: 70m Ice Capable	**1 oil engine** driving 1 CP propeller Total Power: 3,700kW (5,031hp) 12.5kn B&W 6L35MC 1 x 2 Stroke 6 Cy. 350 x 1050 3700kW (5031bhp) MAN B&W Diesel A/S-Denmark AuxGen: 1 x 500kW 220/440V 60Hz a.c, 3 x 540kW 220/440V 60Hz a.c Thrusters: 1 Thwart. FP thruster (f)
6902640 *UBPH* -	**YAROSLAVL** **Umar L Dasaev** - *Astrakhan* *Russia*	*863* 218 353	Class: (RS) (RR)	**1966 Zelenodolskiy Sudostroitelnyy Zavod im. "Gorkogo" — Zelenodolsk** Yd No: 8/921 Loa 55.12 Br ex 9.50 Dght 3.110 Lbp 48.40 Br md 9.43 Dpth 4.50 Welded	**(B12B2FC) Fish Carrier** Ins: 360 Compartments: 1 Ho, ER 1 Ha: (1.9 x 1.9)ER Cranes: 1x2.5t Ice Capable	**2 diesel electric oil engines** driving 2 gen. Connecting to 1 elec. Motor driving 1 FP propeller Total Power: 690kW (938hp) 10.0kn Pervomaysk 6CHN25/34 2 x 4 Stroke 6 Cy. 250 x 340 each-345kW (469bhp) (new engine 1982) Pervomaydizelmash (PDM)-Pervomaysk AuxGen: 1 x 475kW a.c, 1 x 100kW a.c Fuel: 157.0 (d.f.)
9300348 *UBYS* -	**YAROSLAVL** **Armator Co Ltd** Navigator LLC *St Petersburg* *Russia* MMSI: 273444390 Official number: 030237	**4,378** 1,313 5,600 T/cm 22.0	Class: RS	**2004-09 Sudostroitelnyy Zavod "Krasnoye Sormovo" — Nizhniy Novgorod** Yd No: 19614/6 Loa 141.00 Br ex 16.90 Dght 3.740 Lbp 134.88 Br md 16.80 Dpth 6.10 Welded, 1 dk	**(A13B2TP) Products Tanker** Double Hull (13F) Liq: 6,587; Liq (Oil): 6,721 Cargo Heating Coils Compartments: 12 Wing Ta, 1 Slop Ta, ER 2 Cargo Pump (s): 2x250m³/hr Manifold: Bow/CM: 70m Ice Capable	**2 oil engines** reduction geared to sc. shafts driving 2 FP propellers Total Power: 1,860kW (2,528hp) 10.0kn Wartsila 6L20 2 x 4 Stroke 6 Cy. 200 x 280 each-930kW (1264bhp) Wartsila Finland Oy-Finland Thrusters: 1 Tunnel thruster (f)
9139452 *VKV7103* -	**YARRA** *ex* Pb Yarra *-2012* *ex* Yarra *-2010* *ex* Lam Tong *-2002* **Broome Marine & Tug Pty Ltd** - *Melbourne, Vic* *Australia* MMSI: 503185400 Official number: 858472	*195* 22 127	Class: LR (BV) **100A1** SS 11/2010 tug coastal service **LMC** Cable: 302.5/22.0	**1995-11 Imamura Zosen — Kure** Yd No: 385 Loa 25.40 Br ex 8.52 Dght 3.750 Lbp 19.80 Br md 8.50 Dpth 4.70 Welded, 1 dk	**(B32A2ST) Tug**	**2 oil engines** gearing integral to driving 2 Z propellers Total Power: 2,354kW (3,200hp) 12.5kn Niigata 6L25HX 2 x 4 Stroke 6 Cy. 250 x 350 each-1177kW (1600bhp) Niigata Engineering Co Ltd-Japan AuxGen: 2 x 64kW 380V 50Hz a.c Fuel: 61.0 (d.f.) 8.2pd
9370771 *3ERJ5* -	**YARRAWONGA** **Elleair Shipping SA** Maine-Tech Shipmanagement Co Inc *Panama* *Panama* MMSI: 370067000 Official number: 3385808A	**43,152** 27,291 82,624 T/cm 70.2	Class: NK	**2008-05 Tsuneishi Holdings Corp Tsuneishi Shipbuilding Co — Fukuyama HS** Yd No: 1367 Loa 228.99 Br ex - Dght 14.429 Lbp 222.00 Br md 32.26 Dpth 20.03 Welded, 1 dk	**(A21A2BC) Bulk Carrier** Grain: 97,186 Compartments: 7 Ho, ER 7 Ha: ER	**1 oil engine** driving 1 FP propeller Total Power: 9,800kW (13,324hp) 14.5kn MAN-B&W 7S50MC-C 1 x 2 Stroke 7 Cy. 500 x 2000 9800kW (13324bhp) Mitsui Engineering & Shipbuilding CLtd-Japan AuxGen: 3 x a.c Fuel: 2764.0
8330619 - -	**YARUS** *ex* Mya-7042 *-2003* *ex* SCHS-7042 *-1999* **OOO 'Ruspromsiti'** -	**122** 36 61	Class: (RS)	**1984 Azovskaya Sudoverf — Azov** Yd No: 7042 Loa 26.50 Br ex 6.59 Dght 2.340 Lbp 22.90 Br md - Dpth 3.05 Welded, 1 dk	**(B11B2FV) Fishing Vessel**	**1 oil engine** geared to sc. shaft driving 1 FP propeller Total Power: 165kW (224hp) 9.3kn Daldizel 6CHNSP18/22 1 x 4 Stroke 6 Cy. 180 x 220 165kW (224bhp) Daldizel-Khabarovsk AuxGen: 2 x 30kW a.c Fuel: 10.0 (d.f.)

9043500 *A6E2359* -	**YARYOUR** **Abu Dhabi Petroleum Ports Operating Co (IRSHAD)** - *Abu Dhabi* *United Arab Emirates* MMSI: 470706000 Official number: 2920	**857** 257 827	Class: LR ✠**100A1** SS 12/2012 tug Arabian Gulf service firefighting ship 1 (2400m3/h) with waterspray ✠**LMC** Eq.Ltr: (L) ; Cable: 385.0/26.0 U2	**1992-12 B.V. Scheepswerf Damen Bergum — Bergum** (Hull) **1992-12 B.V. Scheepswerf Damen — Gorinchem** Yd No: 6732 Loa 45.00 Br ex 13.30 Dght 4.875 Lbp 39.33 Br md 13.00 Dpth 6.00 Welded, 1 dk	**(B21B20A) Anchor Handling Tug Supply**	**2 oil engines** with clutches, flexible couplings & sr geared to sc. shafts driving 2 CP propellers Total Power: 4,480kW (6,092hp) 13.8k Caterpillar 3608T 2 x 4 Stroke 8 Cy. 280 x 300 each-2240kW (3046bhp) Caterpillar Inc-USA AuxGen: 3 x 200kW 380V 50Hz a.c Thrusters: 1 Thwart. FP thruster (f)
8657512 *XYTV* -	**YARZA HLANTAN** **Thuriya Sandar Win Co Ltd** - *Yangon* *Myanmar* Official number: 6278 (A)	**226** 68 -		**2009-08 Myanma Port Authority — Yangon (Theinphyu Dockyard)** Yd No: MPA 35 Loa 27.43 Br ex 8.54 Dght - Lbp - Br md - Dpth 3.66 Welded, 1 dk	**(B32A2ST) Tug**	**3 oil engines** reduction geared to sc. shafts driving 3 Propellers Total Power: 1,146kW (1,557hp) Nissan RH1 3 x Vee 4 Stroke 10 Cy. 135 x 125 each-382kW (519bhp) Nissan Diesel Motor Co. Ltd.-Ageo
8919154 *3EZM8* -	**YAS** *ex* Kamari I *-2013* *ex* Kamari *-2012* *ex* Genmar Gulf *-2011* *ex* Crudegulf *-2003* *ex* Landsort *-1997* **Crown Shipping Inc** - *Panama* *Panama* MMSI: 373148000 Official number: 43084PEXT1	**81,135** 44,754 163,038 T/cm 117.6	Class: (NV)	**1991-11 Daewoo Shipbuilding & Heavy Machinery Ltd — Geoje** Yd No: 5049 Loa 274.00 (BB) Br ex 48.04 Dght 15.220 Lbp 264.00 Br md 48.00 Dpth 23.00 Welded, 1 dk	**(A13A2TW) Crude/Oil Products Tanker** Double Hull (13F) Liq: 166,747; Liq (Oil): 166,747 Compartments: 10 Wing Ta, 2 Wing Slop Ta, ER 9 Cargo Pump (s): 9x1560m³/hr Manifold: Bow/CM: 134.5m	**1 oil engine** driving 1 FP propeller Total Power: 15,420kW (20,965hp) 14.7k B&W 6S70M 1 x 2 Stroke 6 Cy. 700 x 2674 15420kW (20965bhp) Korea Heavy Industries & ConstrCo Ltd (HANJUNG)-South Korea AuxGen: 1 x 1200kW 440V 60Hz a.c, 2 x 900kW 440V 60Hz a.c Fuel: 285.2 (d.f.) (Heating Coils) 4255.5 (r.f.)
9414369 *A6E3109* -	**YAS** **Abu Dhabi National Oil Co (ADNOC)** - *Abu Dhabi* *United Arab Emirates* MMSI: 470951000 Official number: 5584	**120** - 31	Class: (LR) ✠ Classed LR until 25/3/09	**2007-12 Grandweld — Dubai** Yd No: H029/06 Loa 19.80 Br ex 8.00 Dght 2.500 Lbp 19.10 Br md 8.00 Dpth 3.50 Welded, 1 dk	**(B32A2ST) Tug**	**2 oil engines** gearing integral to driving 2 Z propellers Total Power: 1,760kW (2,392hp) M.T.U. 8V4000M6 2 x Vee 4 Stroke 8 Cy. 165 x 190 each-880kW (1196bhp) MTU Friedrichshafen GmbH-Friedrichshafen AuxGen: 2 x 51kW 400V 50Hz a.c
9678989 *D5DN6* -	**YAS** **Yas Shipping Co Inc** Abu Dhabi National Tanker Co (ADNATCO) *Monrovia* *Liberia* MMSI: 636015927 Official number: 15927	**9,289** 2,787 10,077	Class: NV	**2014-02 STX Offshore & Shipbuilding Co Ltd — Busan** Yd No: 5060 Loa 120.40 (BB) Br ex 19.82 Dght 8.800 Lbp 112.40 Br md 19.80 Dpth 11.20 Welded, 1 dk	**(A11B2TG) LPG Tanker** Liq (Gas): 9,000	**1 oil engine** driving 1 FP propeller Total Power: 4,900kW (6,662hp) MAN-B&W 7S35M 1 x 2 Stroke 7 Cy. 350 x 1400 4900kW (6662bhp) STX Engine Co Ltd-South Korea AuxGen: 3 x a.c
8727692 - -	**YAS-3206** **Lenin Fishing Collective (Rybolovetskiy Kolkhoz imeni Lenina)** -	**104** 31 58	Class: (RS)	**1988-10 Rybinskaya Sudoverf — Rybinsk** Yd No: 6 Loa 26.50 Br ex 6.50 Dght 2.320 Lbp 23.61 Br md - Dpth 3.05 Welded, 1 dk	**(B11A2FS) Stern Trawler**	**1 oil engine** driving 1 FP propeller Total Power: 220kW (299hp) 9.5k S.K.L. 6NVD26A- 1 x 4 Stroke 6 Cy. 180 x 260 220kW (299bhp) VEB Schwermaschinenbau "KarlLiebknecht" (SKL)-Magdeburg
9300532 *V7LH9* -	**YASA AYSEN** **Oceanstar Maritime Co** Ya Sa Shipping Industry & Trading SA (Ya Sa Denizcilik Sanayi ve Ticaret AS) *Majuro* *Marshall Islands* MMSI: 538002749 Official number: 2749	**31,255** 18,504 56,042 T/cm 55.8	Class: NK	**2007-03 Mitsui Eng. & SB. Co. Ltd. — Tamano** Yd No: 1621 Loa 189.99 (BB) Br ex - Dght 12.573 Lbp 182.00 Br md 32.26 Dpth 17.90 Welded, 1 dk	**(A21A2BC) Bulk Carrier** Grain: 70,811; Bale: 68,084 Compartments: 5 Ho, ER 5 Ha: 4 (21.1 x 18.9)ER (17.6 x 18.9) Cranes: 4x30t	**1 oil engine** driving 1 FP propeller Total Power: 9,480kW (12,889hp) 14.5k MAN-B&W 6S50MC- 1 x 2 Stroke 6 Cy. 500 x 2000 9480kW (12889bhp) Mitsui Engineering & Shipbuilding CLtd-Japan AuxGen: 3 x 420kW a.c Fuel: 2190.0
9324461 *V7QA2* -	**YASA DREAM** **Real Shipping Corp** Ya-Sa Gemi Isletmeciligi ve Ticaret AS (Ya-Sa Shipmanagement & Trading SA) SatCom: Inmarsat C 453832895 *Majuro* *Marshall Islands* MMSI: 538003320 Official number: 3320	**106,405** 64,038 207,805	Class: NK	**2008-10 Universal Shipbuilding Corp — Tsu ME** Yd No: 072 Loa 299.70 (BB) Br ex - Dght 18.230 Lbp 291.75 Br md 50.00 Dpth 25.00 Welded, 1 dk	**(A21A2BC) Bulk Carrier** Double Hull Grain: 218,790 Compartments: 9 Ho, ER 9 Ha: ER	**1 oil engine** driving 1 FP propeller Total Power: 16,610kW (22,583hp) 14.0k MAN-B&W 6S70MC- 1 x 2 Stroke 6 Cy. 700 x 2800 16610kW (22583bhp) Mitsui Engineering & Shipbuilding CLtd-Japan AuxGen: 4 x 455kW a.c Fuel: 500.0 (d.f.) 5000.0 (r.f.)
9619529 *V7XL3* -	**YASA EAGLE** **Yasa Eagle Shipping Ltd** Ya Sa Shipping Industry & Trading SA (Ya Sa Denizcilik Sanayi ve Ticaret AS) *Majuro* *Marshall Islands* MMSI: 538004507 Official number: 4507	**44,557** 27,170 81,525	Class: NK (KR)	**2012-01 SPP Shipbuilding Co Ltd — Sacheon** Yd No: S5097 Loa 229.00 (BB) Br ex - Dght 14.517 Lbp 223.52 Br md 32.26 Dpth 20.20 Welded, 1 dk	**(A21A2BC) Bulk Carrier** Grain: 97,215; Bale: 92,534 Compartments: 2 Ho, 5 Ho, ER 7 Ha: 6 (15.7 x 15.2)ER (14.8 x 15.2)	**1 oil engine** driving 1 FP propeller Total Power: 10,170kW (13,827hp) 14.5k MAN-B&W 6S60MC- 1 x 2 Stroke 6 Cy. 600 x 2400 10170kW (13827bhp) STX Engine Co Ltd-South Korea Fuel: 2510.0
9454503 *V7OC3* -	**YASA EMIRHAN** **Flame Shipmanagement Corp** Ya Sa Shipping Industry & Trading SA (Ya Sa Denizcilik Sanayi ve Ticaret AS) *Majuro* *Marshall Islands* MMSI: 538003057 Official number: 3057	**31,282** 18,506 55,545 T/cm 55.8	Class: NK	**2008-03 Mitsui Eng. & SB. Co. Ltd., Chiba Works — Ichihara** Yd No: 1718 Loa 189.99 Br ex - Dght 12.570 Lbp 182.00 Br md 32.26 Dpth 17.90 Welded, 1 dk	**(A21A2BC) Bulk Carrier** Grain: 70,816; Bale: 68,083 Compartments: 5 Ho, ER 5 Ha: ER Cranes: 4x30t	**1 oil engine** driving 1 FP propeller Total Power: 9,480kW (12,889hp) 14.5k MAN-B&W 6S50MC- 1 x 2 Stroke 6 Cy. 500 x 2000 9480kW (12889bhp) Mitsui Engineering & Shipbuilding CLtd-Japan AuxGen: 3 x 500kW a.c Fuel: 85.0 (d.f.) 1980.0 (r.f.)
9597123 *V7XR5* -	**YASA FALCON** **Yasa Falcon Shipping Ltd** Ya-Sa Gemi Isletmeciligi ve Ticaret AS (Ya-Sa Shipmanagement & Trading SA) *Majuro* *Marshall Islands* MMSI: 538004552 Official number: 4552	**44,557** 27,170 81,488	Class: NK (KR)	**2012-03 SPP Shipbuilding Co Ltd — Sacheon** Yd No: S5099 Loa 229.00 (BB) Br ex - Dght 14.517 Lbp 223.00 Br md 32.26 Dpth 20.20 Welded, 1 dk	**(A21A2BC) Bulk Carrier** Grain: 95,414; Bale: 91,164 Compartments: 7 Ho, ER 7 Ha: 6 (15.7 x 15.2)ER (14.8 x 15.2)	**1 oil engine** driving 1 FP propeller Total Power: 10,170kW (13,827hp) 14.4k MAN-B&W 6S60MC- 1 x 2 Stroke 6 Cy. 600 x 2400 10170kW (13827bhp) STX Engine Co Ltd-South Korea AuxGen: 3 x a.c Fuel: 2550.0
9286580 *V7JS3* -	**YASA FORTUNE** **Orion Shipmanagement Co** Ya Sa Shipping Industry & Trading SA (Ya Sa Denizcilik Sanayi ve Ticaret AS) *Majuro* *Marshall Islands* MMSI: 538002565 Official number: 2565	**42,895** 27,547 82,849 T/cm 69.4	Class: NK	**2006-05 Tsuneishi Corp — Fukuyama HS** Yd No: 1296 Loa 228.99 Br ex - Dght 14.429 Lbp 222.00 Br md 32.26 Dpth 19.90 Welded, 1 dk	**(A21A2BC) Bulk Carrier** Grain: 97,233 Compartments: 7 Ho, ER 7 Ha: 6 (17.8 x 15.4)ER (16.0 x 13.8)	**1 oil engine** driving 1 FP propeller Total Power: 9,800kW (13,324hp) 14.5k MAN-B&W 7S50MC- 1 x 2 Stroke 7 Cy. 500 x 2000 9800kW (13324bhp) Mitsui Engineering & Shipbuilding CLtd-Japan AuxGen: 3 x 455kW a.c Fuel: 2590.0
9334038 *V7KQ8* -	**YASA GOLDEN BOSPHORUS** **Ice Pearl Navigation Corp** Ya-Sa Tanker Isletmeciligi AS SatCom: Inmarsat C 453831226 *Majuro* *Marshall Islands* MMSI: 538002662 Official number: 2662	**61,342** 35,396 115,867 T/cm 99.0	Class: NK (NV)	**2007-01 Samsung Heavy Industries Co Ltd — Geoje** Yd No: 1603 Loa 248.93 (BB) Br ex 43.84 Dght 14.925 Lbp 239.00 Br md 43.80 Dpth 21.00 Welded, 1 dk	**(A13A2TV) Crude Oil Tanker** Double Hull (13F) Liq: 123,643; Liq (Oil): 123,643 Cargo Heating Coils Compartments: 12 Wing Ta, 2 Wing Slop Ta, ER 3 Cargo Pump (s): 3x2800m³/hr Manifold: Bow/CM: 125m	**1 oil engine** driving 1 FP propeller Total Power: 13,560kW (18,436hp) 15.0k MAN-B&W 6S60MC- 1 x 2 Stroke 6 Cy. 600 x 2400 13560kW (18436bhp) Doosan Engine Co Ltd-South Korea AuxGen: 3 x 660kW a.c Fuel: 306.0 (d.f.) 3481.8 (r.f.)
9339985 *V7ME9* -	**YASA GOLDEN DARDANELLES** **Tower Navigation Inc** Ya-Sa Tanker Isletmeciligi AS SatCom: Inmarsat C 453832893 *Majuro* *Marshall Islands* MMSI: 538002845 Official number: 2845	**59,745** 33,382 110,828 T/cm 93.0	Class: NK (LR) ✠ Classed LR until 24/6/08	**2008-06 Mitsui Eng. & SB. Co. Ltd., Chiba Works — Ichihara** Yd No: 1673 Loa 245.50 (BB) Br ex - Dght 14.980 Lbp 234.00 Br md 42.00 Dpth 21.50 Welded, 1 dk	**(A13A2TV) Crude Oil Tanker** Double Hull (13F) Liq: 123,431; Liq (Oil): 123,431 Cargo Heating Coils Compartments: 12 Wing Ta, 2 Wing Slop Ta, ER 3 Cargo Pump (s): 3x2800m³/hr Manifold: Bow/CM: 125m	**1 oil engine** driving 1 FP propeller Total Power: 14,280kW (19,415hp) 14.9k MAN-B&W 7S60MC 1 x 2 Stroke 7 Cy. 600 x 2292 14280kW (19415bhp) Mitsui Engineering & Shipbuilding CLtd-Japan AuxGen: 3 x 640kW 450V 60Hz a.c Boilers: e (ex.g.) 22.0kgf/cm² (21.6bar), WTAuxB (o.f.) 18.4kgf/cm² (18.0bar) Fuel: 287.3 (d.f.) 3543.5 (r.f.)

IMO / Call sign	Ship name / Owner / Manager / Port / MMSI	Tonnage	Class	Builder / Dimensions	Type / Cargo	Machinery
334040 7KQ9	**YASA GOLDEN HORN** **Progress Navigation Inc** Ya-Sa Tanker Isletmeciligi AS SatCom: Inmarsat C 453831227 *Majuro* *Marshall Islands* MMSI: 538002663 Official number: 2663	**61,342** 35,396 116,095 T/cm 99.0	Class: NK (NV)	**2007-06 Samsung Heavy Industries Co Ltd — Geoje** Yd No: 1604 Loa 248.96 (BB) Br ex 43.84 Dght 14.925 Lbp 239.00 Br md 43.80 Dpth 21.00 Welded, 1 dk	**(A13A2TV) Crude Oil Tanker** Double Hull (13F) Liq: 123,643; Liq (Oil): 123,643 Cargo Heating Coils Compartments: 12 Wing Ta, 2 Wing Slop Ta, ER 3 Cargo Pump (s): 3x2800m³/hr Manifold: Bow/CM: 125m	**1 oil engine** driving 1 FP propeller Total Power: 13,560kW (18,436hp) 15.0kn MAN-B&W 6S60MC-C 1 x 2 Stroke 6 Cy. 600 x 2400 13560kW (18436bhp) Doosan Engine Co Ltd-South Korea AuxGen: 3 x a.c Fuel: 306.0 (d.f.) 3481.0 (r.f.)
337341 7ME8	**YASA GOLDEN MARMARA** **Jolly Shipping Inc** Ya-Sa Tankercilik ve Tasimacilik AS (Yasa Tanker & Transportation SA) *Majuro* *Marshall Islands* MMSI: 538002844 Official number: 2844	**59,745** 33,382 110,769 T/cm 92.6	Class: NK (LR) ✠ Classed LR until 25/1/08	**2008-01 Mitsui Eng. & SB. Co. Ltd., Chiba Works — Ichihara** Yd No: 1672 Loa 245.50 (BB) Br ex 42.03 Dght 14.980 Lbp 234.00 Br md 42.00 Dpth 21.50 Welded, 1 dk	**(A13A2TV) Crude Oil Tanker** Double Hull (13F) Liq: 123,332; Liq (Oil): 123,332 Compartments: 12 Wing Ta, 2 Wing Slop Ta, ER 3 Cargo Pump (s): 3x2800m³/hr Manifold: Bow/CM: 123.1m	**1 oil engine** driving 1 FP propeller Total Power: 14,280kW (19,415hp) 14.9kn MAN-B&W 7S60MC 1 x 2 Stroke 7 Cy. 600 x 2292 14280kW (19415bhp) Mitsui Engineering & Shipbuilding CLtd-Japan AuxGen: 3 x 640kW 450V 60Hz a.c Boilers: e (ex.g.) 22.0kgf/cm² (21.6bar), WTAuxB (o.f.) 18.4kgf/cm² (18.0bar) Fuel: 255.0 (d.f.) 3102.0 (r.f.)
300506 7JA8	**YASA GULTEN** **Seaways Maritime SA** Ya Sa Shipping Industry & Trading SA (Ya Sa Denizcilik Sanayi ve Ticaret AS) *Majuro* *Marshall Islands* MMSI: 538002484 Official number: 2484	**31,251** 18,504 55,953 T/cm 55.8	Class: NK	**2005-11 Mitsui Eng. & SB. Co. Ltd. — Tamano** Yd No: 1598 Loa 189.99 (BB) Br ex - Dght 12.575 Lbp 182.00 Br md 32.26 Dpth 17.90 Welded, 1 dk	**(A21A2BC) Bulk Carrier** Grain: 70,811; Bale: 68,044 Compartments: 5 Ho, ER 5 Ha: 4 (21.1 x 18.9)ER (17.6 x 18.9) Cranes: 4x30t	**1 oil engine** driving 1 FP propeller Total Power: 9,480kW (12,889hp) 14.5kn MAN-B&W 6S50MC-C 1 x 2 Stroke 6 Cy. 500 x 2000 9480kW (12889bhp) Mitsui Engineering & Shipbuilding CLtd-Japan Fuel: 2190.0
342500 CMT2	**YASA H. MEHMET** **Ya Sa Shipping Industry & Trading SA (Ya Sa Denizcilik Sanayi ve Ticaret AS)** Ya-Sa Gemi Isletmeciligi ve Ticaret AS (Ya-Sa Shipmanagement & Trading SA) SatCom: Inmarsat C 427101231 *Istanbul* *Turkey* MMSI: 271042805 Official number: 2072	**44,367** 27,213 83,482 T/cm 71.0	Class: NK	**2011-09 Sanoyas Hishino Meisho Corp — Kurashiki OY** Yd No: 1297 Loa 229.00 (BB) Br ex - Dght 14.570 Lbp 224.00 Br md 32.24 Dpth 20.20 Welded, 1 dk	**(A21A2BC) Bulk Carrier** Grain: 96,121 Compartments: 7 Ho, ER 7 Ha: ER	**1 oil engine** driving 1 FP propeller Total Power: 10,740kW (14,602hp) 14.0kn MAN-B&W 6S60MC-C 1 x 2 Stroke 6 Cy. 600 x 2400 10740kW (14602bhp) Mitsui Engineering & Shipbuilding CLtd-Japan Fuel: 263.0 (d.f.) 2938.0 (r.f.)
342512 CMY4	**YASA H. MULLA** **Ya Sa Shipping Industry & Trading SA (Ya Sa Denizcilik Sanayi ve Ticaret AS)** Ya-Sa Gemi Isletmeciligi ve Ticaret AS (Ya-Sa Shipmanagement & Trading SA) SatCom: Inmarsat C 427101258 *Istanbul* *Turkey* MMSI: 271042868 Official number: 2073	**44,367** 27,213 83,482 T/cm 71.0	Class: NK	**2011-10 Sanoyas Hishino Meisho Corp — Kurashiki OY** Yd No: 1298 Loa 229.00 (BB) Br ex - Dght 14.570 Lbp 224.00 Br md 32.24 Dpth 20.20 Welded, 1 dk	**(A21A2BC) Bulk Carrier** Grain: 96,121 Compartments: 7 Ho, ER 7 Ha: ER	**1 oil engine** driving 1 FP propeller Total Power: 10,740kW (14,602hp) 14.0kn MAN-B&W 6S60MC-C 1 x 2 Stroke 6 Cy. 600 x 2400 10740kW (14602bhp) Mitsui Engineering & Shipbuilding CLtd-Japan Fuel: 3200.0
396218 7LI2	**YASA ILHAN** **Forza Shipping SA** Ya-Sa Gemi Isletmeciligi ve Ticaret AS (Ya-Sa Shipmanagement & Trading SA) *Majuro* *Marshall Islands* MMSI: 538002750 Official number: 2750	**31,255** 18,516 55,518 T/cm 55.8	Class: NK	**2007-03 Mitsui Eng. & SB. Co. Ltd. — Tamano** Yd No: 1691 Loa 189.99 (BB) Br ex - Dght 12.550 Lbp 182.00 Br md 32.26 Dpth 17.90 Welded, 1 dk	**(A21A2BC) Bulk Carrier** Grain: 70,855; Bale: 68,117 Compartments: 5 Ho, ER 5 Ha: 4 (21.1 x 18.9)ER (17.6 x 18.9) Cranes: 4x30t	**1 oil engine** driving 1 FP propeller Total Power: 9,480kW (12,889hp) 14.5kn MAN-B&W 6S50MC-C 1 x 2 Stroke 6 Cy. 500 x 2000 9480kW (12889bhp) Mitsui Engineering & Shipbuilding CLtd-Japan Fuel: 2390.0
514341 CXQ6	**YASA KAPTAN ERBIL** **Ya Sa Shipping Industry & Trading SA (Ya Sa Denizcilik Sanayi ve Ticaret AS)** - *Istanbul* *Turkey* MMSI: 271040311	**31,756** 18,651 56,169 T/cm 55.8	Class: NK	**2010-02 Mitsui Eng. & SB. Co. Ltd. — Tamano** Yd No: 1774 Loa 189.99 (BB) Br ex - Dght 12.715 Lbp 182.00 Br md 32.25 Dpth 18.10 Welded, 1 dk	**(A21A2BC) Bulk Carrier** Grain: 71,345; Bale: 68,733 Compartments: 5 Ho, ER 5 Ha: ER Cranes: 4x30t	**1 oil engine** driving 1 FP propeller Total Power: 9,070kW (12,332hp) 14.5kn MAN-B&W 6S50MC-C 1 x 2 Stroke 6 Cy. 500 x 2000 9070kW (12332bhp) Mitsui Engineering & Shipbuilding CLtd-Japan AuxGen: 3 x 480kW a.c Fuel: 2080.0
286566 7IV8	**YASA NESLIHAN** **Nouvelle Shipmanagement Co** Ya Sa Shipping Industry & Trading SA (Ya Sa Denizcilik Sanayi ve Ticaret AS) *Majuro* *Marshall Islands* MMSI: 538002459 Official number: 2459	**42,895** 27,547 82,849 T/cm 69.4	Class: NK	**2005-10 Tsuneishi Corp — Fukuyama HS** Yd No: 1294 Loa 228.99 Br ex - Dght 14.429 Lbp 222.00 Br md 32.26 Dpth 19.90 Welded, 1 dk	**(A21A2BC) Bulk Carrier** Grain: 97,233 Compartments: 7 Ho, ER 7 Ha: 6 (17.8 x 15.4)ER (16.0 x 13.8)	**1 oil engine** driving 1 FP propeller Total Power: 9,800kW (13,324hp) 14.5kn B&W 7S50MC-C 1 x 2 Stroke 7 Cy. 500 x 2000 9800kW (13324bhp) Mitsui Engineering & Shipbuilding CLtd-Japan AuxGen: 3 x 455kW a.c Fuel: 2590.0
462926 7XI5	**YASA ORION** **Seanote Navigation SA** Ya-Sa Tankercilik ve Tasimacilik AS (Yasa Tanker & Transportation SA) *Majuro* *Marshall Islands* MMSI: 538004487 Official number: 4487	**81,493** 51,283 158,475 T/cm 119.6	Class: NK (LR) ✠ Classed LR until 4/1/12	**2012-01 Samsung Heavy Industries Co Ltd — Geoje** Yd No: 1802 Loa 274.39 (BB) Br ex 48.04 Dght 17.025 Lbp 264.00 Br md 48.00 Dpth 23.20 Welded, 1 dk	**(A13A2TV) Crude Oil Tanker** Double Hull (13F) Liq: 167,400; Liq (Oil): 167,400 Cargo Heating Coils Compartments: 12 Wing Ta, 2 Wing Slop Ta, ER 3 Cargo Pump (s): 3x4000m³/hr Manifold: Bow/CM: 137m	**1 oil engine** driving 1 FP propeller Total Power: 18,660kW (25,370hp) 15.5kn MAN-B&W 6S70MC-C 1 x 2 Stroke 6 Cy. 700 x 2800 18660kW (25370bhp) Doosan Engine Co Ltd-South Korea AuxGen: 3 x 538kW 450V 60Hz a.c Boilers: e (ex.g.) 22.4kgf/cm² (22.0bar), WTAuxB (o.f.) 18.4kgf/cm² (18.0bar) Fuel: 130.0 (d.f.) 3400.0 (r.f.)
300518 7JI7	**YASA OZCAN** **Sea Breezer Shipping SA** Ya Sa Shipping Industry & Trading SA (Ya Sa Denizcilik Sanayi ve Ticaret AS) *Majuro* *Marshall Islands* MMSI: 538002527 Official number: 2527	**31,251** 18,504 55,924 T/cm 55.8	Class: NK	**2006-01 Mitsui Eng. & SB. Co. Ltd. — Tamano** Yd No: 1599 Loa 189.99 (BB) Br ex - Dght 12.550 Lbp 182.00 Br md 32.26 Dpth 17.90 Welded, 1 dk	**(A21A2BC) Bulk Carrier** Grain: 70,811; Bale: 68,044 Compartments: 5 Ho, ER 5 Ha: 4 (21.1 x 18.9)ER (17.6 x 18.9) Cranes: 4x30t	**1 oil engine** driving 1 FP propeller Total Power: 9,480kW (12,889hp) 14.5kn MAN-B&W 6S50MC-C 1 x 2 Stroke 6 Cy. 500 x 2000 9480kW (12889bhp) Mitsui Engineering & Shipbuilding CLtd-Japan Fuel: 2190.0
300520 7LI3	**YASA PEMBE** **Pacific Runner SA** Ya Sa Shipping Industry & Trading SA (Ya Sa Denizcilik Sanayi ve Ticaret AS) SatCom: Inmarsat C 453831224 *Majuro* *Marshall Islands* MMSI: 538002751 Official number: 2751	**31,255** 18,504 55,912 T/cm 55.8	Class: NK	**2007-01 Mitsui Eng. & SB. Co. Ltd. — Tamano** Yd No: 1620 Loa 189.99 (BB) Br ex 32.26 Dght 12.573 Lbp 182.00 Br md 32.26 Dpth 17.90 Welded, 1 dk	**(A21A2BC) Bulk Carrier** Grain: 70,811; Bale: 68,044 Compartments: 5 Ho, ER 5 Ha: 4 (21.1 x 18.9)ER (17.6 x 18.9) Cranes: 4x30t	**1 oil engine** driving 1 FP propeller Total Power: 9,480kW (12,889hp) 14.5kn MAN-B&W 6S50MC-C 1 x 2 Stroke 6 Cy. 500 x 2000 9480kW (12889bhp) Mitsui Engineering & Shipbuilding CLtd-Japan AuxGen: 3 x a.c Fuel: 2190.0
286578 7JJ3	**YASA PIONEER** **Tristar Shipping Co SA** Ya Sa Shipping Industry & Trading SA (Ya Sa Denizcilik Sanayi ve Ticaret AS) *Majuro* *Marshall Islands* MMSI: 538002531 Official number: 2531	**42,895** 27,547 82,849 T/cm 70.2	Class: NK	**2006-02 Tsuneishi Corp — Fukuyama HS** Yd No: 1295 Loa 228.99 Br ex - Dght 14.429 Lbp 222.00 Br md 32.26 Dpth 19.90 Welded, 1 dk	**(A21A2BC) Bulk Carrier** Grain: 97,233 Compartments: 7 Ho, ER 7 Ha: 6 (17.8 x 15.4)ER (16.0 x 13.8)	**1 oil engine** driving 1 FP propeller Total Power: 9,800kW (13,324hp) 14.5kn MAN-B&W 7S50MC-C 1 x 2 Stroke 7 Cy. 500 x 2000 9800kW (13324bhp) Mitsui Engineering & Shipbuilding CLtd-Japan Fuel: 2590.0
438406 7RY4	**YASA POLARIS** **Diver Shipmanagement SA** Ya-Sa Tanker Isletmeciligi AS SatCom: Inmarsat C 453834584 *Majuro* *Marshall Islands* MMSI: 538003601 Official number: 3601	**81,493** 51,283 158,475 T/cm 119.6	Class: NK (LR) ✠ Classed LR until 25/8/09	**2009-08 Samsung Heavy Industries Co Ltd — Geoje** Yd No: 1764 Loa 274.00 (BB) Br ex 48.04 Dght 17.030 Lbp 264.00 Br md 48.00 Dpth 23.20 Welded, 1 dk	**(A13A2TV) Crude Oil Tanker** Double Hull (13F) Liq: 167,363; Liq (Oil): 167,363 Cargo Heating Coils Compartments: 12 Wing Ta, 2 Wing Slop Ta, ER 3 Cargo Pump (s): 3x4000m³/hr Manifold: Bow/CM: 137.6m	**1 oil engine** driving 1 FP propeller Total Power: 18,660kW (25,370hp) 15.5kn MAN-B&W 6S70ME-C 1 x 2 Stroke 6 Cy. 700 x 2800 18660kW (25370bhp) Doosan Engine Co Ltd-South Korea AuxGen: 3 x 538kW 450V 60Hz a.c Boilers: e (ex.g.) 22.4kgf/cm² (22.0bar), WTAuxB (o.f.) 18.4kgf/cm² (18.0bar) Fuel: 155.0 (d.f.) 3030.0 (r.f.)

9436446 **YASA SCORPION**
V7TQ7
-
Wayfarer Navigation Ltd
Ya Sa Shipping Industry & Trading SA (Ya Sa Denizcilik Sanayi ve Ticaret AS)
SatCom: Inmarsat C 453834987
Majuro *Marshall Islands*
MMSI: 538003862
Official number: 3862

81,493 / 51,283 / 158,555 / T/cm / 119.6
Class: NK (LR) / ✠ 13/5/10

2010-05 Samsung Heavy Industries Co Ltd — Geoje Yd No: 1770
Loa 274.00 (BB) Br ex 48.04 Dght 17.025
Lbp 264.00 Br md 48.00 Dpth 23.20
Welded, 1 dk

(A13A2TV) Crude Oil Tanker
Double Hull (13F)
Liq: 167,363; Liq (Oil): 167,363
Cargo Heating Coils
Compartments: 12 Wing Ta, 2 Wing Slop Ta, ER
3 Cargo Pump (s): 3x4000m³/hr
Manifold: Bow/CM: 137.6m

1 oil engine driving 1 FP propeller
Total Power: 18,660kW (25,370hp) 15.5
MAN-B&W 6S70MC
1 x 2 Stroke 6 Cy. 700 x 2800 18660kW (25370bhp)
Doosan Engine Co Ltd-South Korea
AuxGen: 3 x 910kW 450V 60Hz a.c
Boilers: e (ex.g.) 22.4kgf/cm² (22.0bar), WTAuxB (o.f.) 17.8kgf/cm² (17.5bar)
Fuel: 155.0 (d.f.) 3030.0 (r.f.)

9438418 **YASA SOUTHERN CROSS**
V7SS7
-
Montara Navigation SA
Ya-Sa Tanker Isletmeciligi AS
SatCom: Inmarsat C 453834630
Majuro *Marshall Islands*
MMSI: 538003713
Official number: 3713

81,493 / 51,283 / 158,525 / T/cm / 119.6
Class: NK (LR) / ✠ 6/1/10

2010-01 Samsung Heavy Industries Co Ltd — Geoje Yd No: 1765
Loa 274.39 (BB) Br ex 48.04 Dght 17.025
Lbp 263.99 Br md 48.00 Dpth 23.20
Welded, 1 dk

(A13A2TV) Crude Oil Tanker
Double Hull (13F)
Liq: 167,363; Liq (Oil): 167,363
Cargo Heating Coils
Compartments: 12 Wing Ta, 2 Wing Slop Ta, ER
3 Cargo Pump (s): 3x4000m³/hr
Manifold: Bow/CM: 137.6m

1 oil engine driving 1 FP propeller
Total Power: 18,660kW (25,370hp) 15.5
MAN-B&W 6S70ME
1 x 2 Stroke 6 Cy. 700 x 2800 18660kW (25370bhp)
Doosan Engine Co Ltd-South Korea
AuxGen: 3 x 450V 60Hz a.c
Boilers: e (ex.g.) 22.4kgf/cm² (22.0bar), WTAuxB (o.f.) 18.2kgf/cm² (17.8bar)
Fuel: 155.0 (d.f.) 3300.0 (r.f.)

9296250 **YASA TEAM**
V7JI8
-
Clyde Maritime SA
Ya Sa Shipping Industry & Trading SA (Ya Sa Denizcilik Sanayi ve Ticaret AS)
Majuro *Marshall Islands*
MMSI: 538002528
Official number: 2528

38,895 / 25,194 / 75,621 / T/cm / 66.5
Class: NK

2006-02 Sanoyas Hishino Meisho Corp — Kurashiki OY Yd No: 1233
Loa 225.00 (BB) Br ex 32.26 Dght 13.995
Lbp 217.00 Br md 32.26 Dpth 19.30
Welded, 1 dk

(A21A2BC) Bulk Carrier
Grain: 89,201
Compartments: 7 Ho, ER
7 Ha: 6 (17.1 x 15.0)ER (16.3 x 13.4)

1 oil engine driving 1 FP propeller
Total Power: 8,973kW (12,200hp) 14.5
MAN-B&W 7S50MC
1 x 2 Stroke 7 Cy. 500 x 2000 8973kW (12200bhp)
Mitsui Engineering & Shipbuilding CLtd-Japan
AuxGen: 3 x 455kW 440V 60Hz a.c
Fuel: 175.0 (d.f.) 2925.0 (r.f.) 34.0pd

9296262 **YASA UNITY**
V7JN6
-
Tiffany Navigation SA
Ya-Sa Gemi Isletmeciligi ve Ticaret AS (Ya-Sa Shipmanagement & Trading SA)
Majuro *Marshall Islands*
MMSI: 538002548
Official number: 2548

38,895 / 25,194 / 75,580 / T/cm / 66.5
Class: NK

2006-04 Sanoyas Hishino Meisho Corp — Kurashiki OY Yd No: 1234
Loa 225.00 (BB) Br ex 32.26 Dght 13.995
Lbp 217.00 Br md 32.26 Dpth 19.30
Welded, 1 dk

(A21A2BC) Bulk Carrier
Grain: 89,201
Compartments: 7 Ho, ER
7 Ha: 6 (17.1 x 15.0)ER (16.3 x 13.4)

1 oil engine driving 1 FP propeller
Total Power: 8,973kW (12,200hp) 14.0
MAN-B&W 7S50MC
1 x 2 Stroke 7 Cy. 500 x 2000 8973kW (12200bhp)
Mitsui Engineering & Shipbuilding CLtd-Japan
AuxGen: 3 x 445kW 440/230V 60Hz a.c
Fuel: 175.0 (d.f.) 2625.0 (r.f.)

9396206 **YASA UNSAL SUNAR**
V7LH8
-
Seascape Navigation Inc
Ya Sa Shipping Industry & Trading SA (Ya Sa Denizcilik Sanayi ve Ticaret AS)
Majuro *Marshall Islands*
MMSI: 538002748
Official number: 2748

31,255 / 18,516 / 55,526 / T/cm / 55.8
Class: NK

2007-01 Mitsui Eng. & SB. Co. Ltd. — Tamano Yd No: 1690
Loa 189.99 (BB) Br ex 32.26 Dght 12.573
Lbp 182.00 Br md 32.26 Dpth 17.90
Welded, 1 dk

(A21A2BC) Bulk Carrier
Grain: 70,855; Bale: 68,117
Compartments: 5 Ho, ER
5 Ha: 4 (21.1 x 18.9)ER (17.6 x 18.9)
Cranes: 4x30t

1 oil engine driving 1 FP propeller
Total Power: 9,480kW (12,889hp) 14.5
MAN-B&W 6S50MC
1 x 2 Stroke 6 Cy. 500 x 2000 9480kW (12889bhp)
Mitsui Engineering & Shipbuilding CLtd-Japan
AuxGen: 3 x a.c
Fuel: 2190.0

8889995 **YASAKA**
JK5417
-
ex Sanei Maru *-2007*
-
-
Kobe, Hyogo *Japan*
Official number: 134715

199 / - / -

1995-09 K.K. Kamishima Zosensho — Osakikamijima Yd No: 580
Loa 56.98 Br ex - Dght -
Lbp 51.00 Br md 9.40 Dpth 5.40
Welded, 1 dk

(A31A2GX) General Cargo Ship

1 oil engine driving 1 FP propeller
Total Power: 736kW (1,001hp) 12.5
Matsui ML627GS
1 x 4 Stroke 6 Cy. 270 x 480 736kW (1001bhp)
Matsui Iron Works Co Ltd-Japan

8122244 **YASAKA MARU No. 3**
4DET3
-
ex Kinsei Maru *-2000*
DBP Leasing Corp
-
Philippines

105 / - / -

1981-12 Kanagawa Zosen — Kobe Yd No: 232
Loa 23.10 Br ex - Dght 2.100
Lbp 20.00 Br md 6.70 Dpth 2.99
Welded, 1 dk

(B32A2ST) Tug

2 oil engines geared integral to driving 2 Z propellers
Total Power: 662kW (900hp) 10.5
Yanmar S165L-S
2 x 4 Stroke 6 Cy. 165 x 210 each-331kW (450bhp)
Yanmar Diesel Engine Co Ltd-Japan

8131142 **YASAM ROSE**
2GPT9
-
ex Boisterous *-2013* *ex* Boisterence *-2001*
Thames Shipping Ltd
-
London *United Kingdom*
MMSI: 235099481
Official number: 918989

664 / 399 / 1,020
Class: (LR) / ✠ Classed LR until 13/1/12

1983-11 A/S Nordsovaerftet — Ringkobing Yd No: 165
Lengthened-1994
Loa 58.30 Br ex 9.28 Dght 3.230
Lbp 57.33 Br md 9.20 Dpth 4.01
Welded, 1 dk

(A31A2GX) General Cargo Ship
Grain: 1,313; Bale: 1,310
Compartments: 1 Ho, ER
1 Ha: (39.9 x 7.0)ER

1 oil engine driving 1 CP propeller
Total Power: 344kW (468hp) 10.0
Callesen 5-427-EO
1 x 4 Stroke 5 Cy. 270 x 400 344kW (468bhp)
Aabenraa Motorfabrik, HeinrichCallesen A/S-Denmark
AuxGen: 2 x 55kW 415V 50Hz a.c, 1 x 32kW 415V 50Hz a.c
Fuel: 26.0 (d.f.) 2.0pd

7522071 **YASAR DOGU-I**
TCAG6
-
ex Simonsturm *-1986*
STFA Deniz Insaati Insaat Sanayi ve Ticaret AS
-
Istanbul *Turkey*
MMSI: 271002101
Official number: 5500

699 / 210 / 954
Class: TL (GL)

1977-06 JG Hitzler Schiffswerft und Masch GmbH & Co KG — Lauenburg Yd No: 758
Loa 53.35 Br ex 11.94 Dght 4.036
Lbp 47.58 Br md 11.61 Dpth 4.63
Welded, 1 dk

(B21B20A) Anchor Handling Tug Supply

2 oil engines driving 2 FP propellers
Total Power: 2,206kW (3,000hp) 12.5
MWM TBD441V1
2 x Vee 4 Stroke 12 Cy. 230 x 270 each-1103kW (1500bhp)
Motoren Werke Mannheim AG (MWM)-West Germany
AuxGen: 2 x 160kW 380V 50Hz a.c
Thrusters: 1 Thwart. FP thruster (f)
Fuel: 566.0 (d.f.) 13.5pd

8732922 **YASARREIS-3**
TC5977
3422G760
-
-
Istanbul *Turkey*
Official number: 6404

340 / 102 / -

1993-01 at Karadeniz Eregli
Loa 42.50 Br ex - Dght -
Lbp - Br md 12.50 Dpth 3.20
Welded, 1 dk

(B11B2FV) Fishing Vessel

3 oil engines geared to sc. shafts driving 3 Propellers
Total Power: 1,199kW (1,630hp)
Caterpillar 341
1 x Vee 4 Stroke 12 Cy. 137 x 152 449kW (610bhp)
Caterpillar Inc-USA
Volvo Penta TAMD162
2 x 4 Stroke 6 Cy. 144 x 165 each-375kW (510bhp)
AB Volvo Penta-Sweden

8908014 **YASAWA LEGEND**
4DEX4
-
ex Nanuya Princess *-2013*
Discovery Fleet Corp
-
Manila *Philippines*
MMSI: 548028500
Official number: P000488

394 / 167 / 50
Class: (AB)

1988-06 The Fiji Marine Shipyard & Slipways — Suva Yd No: 84
Loa 47.00 Br ex - Dght 2.000
Lbp 42.63 Br md 8.51 Dpth 3.71
Welded, 1 dk

(A37A2PC) Passenger/Cruise
Passengers: cabins: 26; berths: 135

2 oil engines with clutches, flexible couplings & sr reverse geared to sc. shafts driving 2 FP propellers
Total Power: 592kW (804hp) 11.0
MWM TBD234V
2 x Vee 4 Stroke 8 Cy. 128 x 140 each-296kW (402bhp)
Motoren Werke Mannheim AG (MWM)-West Germany

8325638 **YASAWA PRINCESS**
-
-
-
-
Male *Maldives*

917 / 366 / 241
Class: (AB)

1985-04 The Fiji Marine Shipyard & Slipways — Suva Yd No: 81
Loa 54.89 Br ex 11.33 Dght 2.496
Lbp 47.15 Br md 11.00 Dpth 4.32
Welded, 1 dk

(A37A2PC) Passenger/Cruise
Passengers: cabins: 33; berths: 96

2 oil engines with clutches, flexible couplings & sr reverse geared to sc. shafts driving 2 FP propellers
Total Power: 1,120kW (1,522hp)
MWM TBD601-
2 x 4 Stroke 6 Cy. 160 x 165 each-560kW (761bhp)
Motoren Werke Mannheim AG (MWM)-West Germany

9136838 **YASEMIN**
9HA2114
-
ex Balsa 51 *-2009*
Dainty Shipping Co Ltd
Ist Denizcilik Ltd Sti (Ist Shipping)
Valletta *Malta*
MMSI: 249988000
Official number: 9136838

4,355 / 2,504 / 6,830
Class: NK

1996-01 Sasebo Heavy Industries Co. Ltd. — Sasebo Yard, Sasebo Yd No: 408
Loa 105.50 (BB) Br ex 16.83 Dght 6.916
Lbp 99.00 Br md 16.80 Dpth 8.80
Welded, 1 dk

(A31A2GX) General Cargo Ship
Grain: 8,878; Bale: 8,226
Compartments: 3 Ho, ER
3 Ha: (15.4 x 8.4)2 (17.5 x 9.8)ER
Cranes: 2x15t

1 oil engine driving 1 FP propeller
Total Power: 2,795kW (3,800hp) 12.5
B&W 5L35M
1 x 2 Stroke 5 Cy. 350 x 1050 2795kW (3800bhp)
Mitsui Engineering & Shipbuilding CLtd-Japan
Fuel: 420.0 (r.f.)

7425871 **YASER**
EQQA
-
ex Ramin *-1980*
Government of The Islamic Republic of Iran (Ministry of Finance)
-
Khorramshahr *Iran*

167 / 48 / 70
Class: (LR) / ✠ Classed LR until 19/11/82

1976-01 Towa Zosen K.K. — Shimonoseki Yd No: 485
Loa 27.92 Br ex 7.35 Dght 2.750
Lbp 25.10 Br md 7.00 Dpth 3.51
Welded, 1 dk

(B32A2ST) Tug

1 oil engine reverse reduction geared to sc. shaft driving 1 F propeller
Total Power: 853kW (1,160hp)
Blackstone ESL8MK
1 x 4 Stroke 8 Cy. 222 x 292 853kW (1160bhp)
Mirrlees Blackstone (Stamford)Ltd.-Stamford
AuxGen: 2 x 52kW 225V 50Hz a.c

9082697 **YASH I**
VTTF
-
Ganga Kaveri Sea Foods Ltd
-
Mormugao *India*
Official number: F-MRH-009

144 / 51 / 64
Class: (IR)

1993-02 Chowgule & Co Pvt Ltd — Goa Yd No: 107
Loa 24.01 Br ex - Dght 2.600
Lbp 21.00 Br md 7.20 Dpth 3.40
Welded, 1dk

(B11B2FV) Fishing Vessel

1 oil engine geared to sc. shaft driving 1 FP propeller
Total Power: 352kW (479hp) 9.0
Caterpillar
1 x 4 Stroke 352kW (479bhp)
Caterpillar Inc-USA

IMO / Call sign	Name / Owner / Flag	Tonnage	Class	Builder / Dimensions	Type / Cargo	Machinery
082702 *TTG*	**YASH II** **Ganga Kaveri Sea Foods Ltd** - *Mormugao* *India* Official number: F-MRH-010	*144* 51 64	Class: (IR)	**1993-02 Chowgule & Co Pvt Ltd — Goa** Yd No: 108 Loa 24.01 Br ex - Dght 2.600 Lbp 21.00 Br md 7.20 Dpth 3.40 Welded, 1 dk	**(B11B2FV) Fishing Vessel**	**1 oil engine** geared to sc. shaft driving 1 FP propeller Total Power: 352kW (479hp) 9.0kn Caterpillar 1 x 4 Stroke 352kW (479bhp) Caterpillar Inc-USA
313781	**YASHIMA** - - *South Korea*	*263* - 85		**1973-05 Ishikawajima Ship & Chemical Plant Co Ltd — Tokyo** Yd No: 446 Loa 31.30 Br ex 8.64 Dght 2.794 Lbp 28.00 Br md 8.62 Dpth 3.71 Welded, 1 dk	**(B32A2ST) Tug**	**2 oil engines** geared to sc. shafts driving 2 FP propellers Total Power: 1,912kW (2,600hp) Fuji 6M27.5FH 2 x 4 Stroke 6 Cy. 275 x 320 each-956kW (1300bhp) Fuji Diesel Co Ltd-Japan
618724 *PDX*	**YASHIMA** **Government of Japan (Ministry of Land, Infrastructure & Transport) (The Coastguard)** - *Tokyo* *Japan* MMSI: 431297000 Official number: 130214	*5,204* - -		**1988-12 Nippon Kokan KK (NKK Corp) — Yokohama KN (Tsurumi Shipyard)** Yd No: 1040 Loa 130.00 Br ex 15.55 Dght 5.250 Lbp 118.30 Br md 15.50 Dpth 8.80 Welded	**(B34H2SQ) Patrol Vessel**	**2 oil engines** with flexible couplings & sr geared to sc. shafts driving 2 CP propellers Total Power: 13,240kW (18,002hp) Pielstick 12PC2-6V-400 2 x Vee 4 Stroke 12 Cy. 400 x 460 each-6620kW (9001bhp) Ishikawajima Harima Heavy IndustrieCo Ltd (IHI)-Japan Thrusters: 1 Thwart. CP thruster (f)
115547 *M6356*	**YASHIMA MARU** **YK Yashima** - *Saikai, Nagasaki* *Japan* Official number: 133638	*199* - 645		**1995-05 Taiyo Shipbuilding Co Ltd — Sanyoonoda YC** Yd No: 256 Loa 56.00 (BB) Br ex - Dght 3.180 Lbp 51.00 Br md 9.50 Dpth 5.30 Welded, 1 dk	**(A31A2GX) General Cargo Ship** Bale: 1,152 Compartments: 1 Ho, ER 1 Ha: ER	**1 oil engine** driving 1 FP propeller Total Power: 735kW (999hp) Hanshin LH26G 1 x 4 Stroke 6 Cy. 260 x 440 735kW (999bhp) The Hanshin Diesel Works Ltd-Japan
145657 *L6471*	**YASHIMA MARU** *ex* Yoshino *-2005* **Takahashi Kaiun YK** - *Higashikagawa, Kagawa* *Japan* Official number: 135506	*199* - 700		**1996-07 Hamamoto Zosensho K.K. — Tokushima** Yd No: 810 Loa 57.01 (BB) Br ex - Dght 3.270 Lbp 52.00 Br md 9.50 Dpth 5.50 Welded, 1 dk	**(A31A2GX) General Cargo Ship** Grain: 1,332; Bale: 1,218 Compartments: 1 Ho, ER 1 Ha: ER	**1 oil engine** driving 1 FP propeller Total Power: 736kW (1,001hp) Niigata 6M26AGTE 1 x 4 Stroke 6 Cy. 260 x 460 736kW (1001bhp) Niigata Engineering Co Ltd-Japan
718495	**YASHIMA MARU No. 27** - - *China*	*299* - 628		**1988-05 K.K. Miura Zosensho — Saiki** Yd No: 812 Loa 51.50 (BB) Br ex 9.02 Dght 3.200 Lbp 47.50 Br md 9.00 Dpth 3.65 Welded, 1 dk	**(A24A2BT) Cement Carrier** Compartments: 6 Ho, ER	**1 oil engine** dr geared to sc. shaft driving 1 FP propeller Total Power: 662kW (900hp) Niigata 6NSC-M 1 x 4 Stroke 6 Cy. 190 x 260 662kW (900bhp) Niigata Engineering Co Ltd-Japan
856472	**YASHIO MARU** *ex* Kongo Maru *-1991* **PT Karya Cemerlang** - *Indonesia*	*199* - -		**1975-07 Seiko Dock K.K. — Shimizu** Loa 28.05 Br ex - Dght 2.640 Lbp 24.01 Br md 8.21 Dpth 3.61 Welded, 1 dk	**(B32B2SA) Articulated Pusher Tug**	**2 oil engines** geared integral to driving 2 Z propellers Total Power: 1,222kW (1,662hp) 10.5kn Niigata 6L20AX 2 x 4 Stroke 6 Cy. 200 x 260 each-611kW (831bhp) Niigata Engineering Co Ltd-Japan
555357 *EJO*	**YASHMA** *launched as* Yashima *-2012* **GTLK Malta Ltd** JSC Volga Shipping (OAO Sudokhodnaya Kompaniya 'Volzhskoye Parokhodstvo') *St Petersburg* *Russia* MMSI: 273353680	**3,505** 1,832 5,025	Class: RS	**2012-12 Qingdao Hyundai Shipbuilding Co Ltd — Jiaonan SD** Yd No: 310 Loa 89.96 (BB) Br ex 14.58 Dght 6.405 Lbp 84.72 Br md 14.50 Dpth 7.20 Welded, 1 dk	**(A31A2GX) General Cargo Ship** Double Hull Grain: 6,230 TEU 178 incl. 15 ref C. Compartments: 1 Ho, ER 1 Ha: ER (56.4 x 11.5) Ice Capable	**1 oil engine** reduction geared to sc. shaft driving 1 CP propeller Total Power: 2,640kW (3,589hp) 12.0kn MaK 8M25C 1 x 4 Stroke 8 Cy. 255 x 400 2640kW (3589bhp) Caterpillar Motoren GmbH & Co. KG-Germany AuxGen: 1 x 292kW a.c, 2 x 175kW a.c Thrusters: 1 Tunnel thruster (f)
721847 *LD2498*	**YASIIN** *ex* Kirazli Yali *-2013* *ex* Kaptan Veysel *-2007* **Nehir Gemicilik ve Denizcilik Isletmeleri Ticaret Ltd Sti** Tema Shipping SA *Freetown* *Sierra Leone* MMSI: 667006198	**694** 438 1,235	Class: (TL) (AB)	**1978-10 Hidrodinamik A.S. — Kavak, Istanbul** Yd No: 15 Loa 62.90 Br ex 9.43 Dght 3.633 Lbp 59.50 Br md 9.40 Dpth 4.25 Welded, 1 dk	**(A12D2LV) Vegetable Oil Tanker** Liq: 829 Compartments: 8 Ta, ER	**1 oil engine** driving 1 FP propeller Total Power: 721kW (980hp) 12.5kn Skoda 6L350PN 1 x 4 Stroke 6 Cy. 350 x 500 721kW (980bhp) CKD Praha-Praha AuxGen: 2 x 70kW a.c, 1 x 13kW a.c Fuel: 40.0
312951 *BCB*	**YASIN** **Government of The Islamic Republic of Iran (Ports & Maritime Organisation)** - *Bandar Anzali* *Iran* MMSI: 422357000	**1,752** 525 1,802	Class: (LR) ✠ Classed LR until 4/12/11	**2004-09 IHC Holland NV Dredgers — Kinderdijk** Yd No: C01240 Loa 70.30 Br ex 14.02 Dght 4.000 Lbp 63.00 Br md 14.00 Dpth 4.80 Welded, 1 dk	**(B33B2DS) Suction Hopper Dredger** Hopper: 1,000	**2 oil engines** with clutches, flexible couplings & sr geared to sc. shafts driving 2 CP propellers Total Power: 1,600kW (2,176hp) 11.3kn Deutz TBD620V8 2 x Vee 4 Stroke 8 Cy. 170 x 195 each-800kW (1088bhp) Deutz AG-Koeln AuxGen: 3 x 232kW 400V 50Hz a.c Thrusters: 1 Thwart. FP thruster (f) Fuel: 145.0 (d.f.)
408636 *SB3824*	**YASITANG** *ex* Ace 1 *-2008* *ex* Global No. 1 *-2003* *ex* Bunga Kiara *-2001* *ex* Oriental Leo *-1992* *ex* Shoun Leo *-1988* **Raum-Mitr Marine Oil Co Ltd** - *Bangkok* *Thailand* MMSI: 567342000 Official number: 510081728	**4,421** 2,127 6,769 T/cm 16.8	Class: (KR) (NV) (NK)	**1985-01 Kochi Jyuko K.K. — Kochi** Yd No: 2383 Loa 113.32 (BB) Br ex - Dght 6.318 Lbp 104.00 Br md 18.00 Dpth 8.00 Welded, 1 dk	**(A12B2TR) Chemical/Products Tanker** Double Bottom Entire Compartment Length Liq: 7,264; Liq (Oil): 7,264 Cargo Heating Coils Compartments: 15 Ta, ER 4 Cargo Pump (s)	**1 oil engine** driving 1 FP propeller Total Power: 2,992kW (4,068hp) 13.2kn B&W 6L35MC 1 x 2 Stroke 6 Cy. 350 x 1050 2992kW (4068bhp) Hitachi Zosen Corp-Japan AuxGen: 2 x 240kW 450V 60Hz a.c Fuel: 139.3 (d.f.) 583.0 (r.f.) 13.5pd
019942	**YASMIN** *ex* Ljubica C *-2008* **Australian Tuna Fisheries Pty Ltd** - *Port Adelaide, SA* *Australia* Official number: 396257	*203* 167 -	Class: (NV)	**1981-12 Colan Shipbuilders Pty Ltd — Port Adelaide SA** Yd No: 40 Loa 28.20 Br ex - Dght - Lbp 27.77 Br md 7.51 Dpth 3.92 Welded, 1 dk	**(B11B2FV) Fishing Vessel** Ins: 90; Liq: 110 Compartments: 8 Ho, ER 8 Ha:	**1 oil engine** with clutches & sr reverse geared to sc. shaft driving 1 FP propeller Total Power: 625kW (850hp) 11.0kn Caterpillar D398SCAC 1 x Vee 4 Stroke 12 Cy. 159 x 203 625kW (850bhp) Caterpillar Tractor Co-USA AuxGen: 1 x 125kW 415V 50Hz a.c, 1 x 80kW 415V 50Hz a.c
337353 *XYE*	**YASMINE** **Conway SA** Cobelfret Ferries NV SatCom: Inmarsat C 425331810 *Luxembourg* *Luxembourg* MMSI: 253318000	**49,166** 14,750 17,023	Class: NV	**2007-04 Flensburger Schiffbau-Ges. mbH & Co. KG — Flensburg** Yd No: 732 Loa 203.00 (BB) Br ex 32.90 Dght 7.800 Lbp 190.42 Br md 31.00 Dpth 18.60 Welded, 5 dks	**(A35A2RR) Ro-Ro Cargo Ship** Passengers: driver berths: 12 Stern door/ramp (p. a.) Len: 16.30 Wid: 7.50 Swl: - Stern door/ramp (s. a.) Len: 12.00 Wid: 14.50 Swl: - Lane-Len: 4600 Trailers: 305 TEU 848	**2 oil engines** geared to sc. shafts driving 2 CP propellers Total Power: 21,600kW (29,368hp) 21.7kn MaK 12M43 2 x Vee 4 Stroke 12 Cy. 430 x 610 each-10800kW (14684bhp) Caterpillar Motoren GmbH & Co. KG-Germany AuxGen: 2 x 1190kW, 1 x 761kW a.c, 2 x 2400kW a.c Thrusters: 2 Thwart. CP thruster (f)
136817 *HVD*	**YASNOMORSKIY** **AOZT 'Vostoktransservis' Marine Shipping Co** SatCom: Inmarsat C 427320797 *Vladivostok* *Russia* MMSI: 273893210 Official number: 821841	**677** 233 495	Class: (RS)	**1983 Khabarovskiy Sudostroitelnyy Zavod im Kirova — Khabarovsk** Yd No: 840 Loa 55.01 Br ex 9.52 Dght 4.340 Lbp 50.04 Br md 9.30 Dpth 5.18 Welded, 1 dk	**(B12B2FC) Fish Carrier** Ice Capable	**1 oil engine** driving 1 FP propeller Total Power: 588kW (799hp) 11.3kn S.K.L. 6NVD48A-2U 1 x 4 Stroke 6 Cy. 320 x 480 588kW (799bhp) VEB Schwermaschinenbau "KarlLiebknecht" (SKL)-Magdeburg AuxGen: 3 x 150kW Fuel: 109.0 (d.f.)
862064 *GBO*	**YASNOYE** **'Rybak' Fishing Collective (Rybolovetskiy Kolkhoz 'Rybak')** - *Khasanskiy* *Russia*	**726** 217 414	Class: (RS)	**1991-09 Zavod "Leninskaya Kuznitsa" — Kiyev** Yd No: 1642 Loa 54.82 Br ex 10.15 Dght 4.140 Lbp 50.30 Br md - Dpth 5.00 Welded, 1 dk	**(B11A2FS) Stern Trawler** Ice Capable	**1 oil engine** driving 1 FP propeller Total Power: 852kW (1,158hp) 12.0kn S.K.L. 8NVD48A-2U 1 x 4 Stroke 8 Cy. 320 x 480 852kW (1158bhp) SKL Motoren u. Systemtechnik AG-Magdeburg
933813	**YASNYY** **RN-Nakhodkanefteprodukt LLC** JSC Rosnefteflot *Nakhodka* *Russia* Official number: 822308	**235** 120 440	Class: RS	**1982-12 Bakinskiy Sudostroitelnyy Zavod im Vano Sturua — Baku** Yd No: 358 Converted From: Pollution Control Vessel-2008 Loa 35.17 Br ex 8.01 Dght 3.120 Lbp 33.25 Br md 7.58 Dpth 3.60 Welded, 1 dk	**(A13B2TP) Products Tanker** Liq: 468; Liq (Oil): 468 Compartments: 10 Ta Ice Capable	**1 oil engine** geared to sc. shaft driving 1 FP propeller Total Power: 165kW (224hp) 8.1kn Daldizel 6CHNSP18/22 1 x 4 Stroke 6 Cy. 180 x 220 165kW (224bhp) Daldizel-Khabarovsk AuxGen: 1 x 50kW a.c, 1 x 30kW a.c Fuel: 12.0 (d.f.)

IMO / Call sign	Name / Owner	Tonnage	Class	Builder / Dimensions	Type / Capacity	Machinery
8953502 - -	**YASNYY** - **Rybolovetskiy Kolkhoz 'Narody Severa'** -	**117** 35 37	Class: (RS)	**1999-10 Sretenskiy Sudostroitelnyy Zavod — Sretensk** Yd No: 315 Loa 25.45 Br ex 6.80 Dght 2.390 Lbp 22.00 Br md - Dpth 3.30 Welded, 1 dk	**(B11A2FS) Stern Trawler** Grain: 64 Compartments: 1 Ho 1 Ha: (1.5 x 1.3) Ice Capable	**1 oil engine** driving 1 FP propeller Total Power: 220kW (299hp) 10.0k S.K.L. 6NVD26A- 1 x 4 Stroke 6 Cy. 180 x 260 220kW (299bhp) SKL Motoren u. Systemtechnik AG-Magdeburg
8422242 *UGNB*	**YASNYY** *completed as* Neftegaz-20 *-1985* **State Unitary Enterprise Baltic Basin Emergency-Rescue Management (FGUP Baltiyskoye Basseynoye Avariyno-Spasatelnoye Upravleniye) (Baltic BASU)** - SatCom: Inmarsat C 427300778 *St Petersburg* *Russia* MMSI: 273428510 Official number: 850346	**2,737** 821 1,329	Class: RS	**1985-12 Stocznia im Komuny Paryskiej — Gdynia** Yd No: B92/20 Loa 81.16 Br ex 16.30 Dght 4.900 Lbp 71.46 Br md 15.97 Dpth 7.22 Welded, 2 dks	**(B21B20A) Anchor Handling Tug Supply** Derricks: 1x12.5t Ice Capable	**2 oil engines** reduction geared to sc. shafts driving 2 CP propellers Total Power: 5,296kW (7,200hp) 15.3k Sulzer 6ZL40/4 2 x 4 Stroke 6 Cy. 400 x 480 each-2648kW (3600bhp) Zaklady Przemyslu Metalowego 'HCegielski' SA-Poznan AuxGen: 3 x 384kW 400V 50Hz a.c Thrusters: 1 Thwart. FP thruster (f) Fuel: 399.0
8317265 *UCXV* -	**YASNYY** *ex* Daitoku Maru No. 7 *-2000* *ex* Seitoku Maru No. 7 *-1999* *ex* Tomi Maru No. 81 *-1992* **JSC 'Kurilskiy Rybak'** - *Nevelsk* *Russia* MMSI: 273420030 Official number: 835952	**817** 291 361	Class: RS	**1983-12 Niigata Engineering Co Ltd — Niigata NI** Yd No: 1787 Loa 57.82 (BB) Br ex - Dght 3.980 Lbp 50.22 Br md 9.91 Dpth 6.13 Welded, 1 dk	**(B11A2FS) Stern Trawler** Ins: 461 Compartments: 8 Ho, ER 12 Ha: ER	**1 oil engine** with clutches, flexible couplings & sr geared to sc. shaft driving 1 CP propeller Total Power: 1,912kW (2,600hp) Niigata 6MG40CXE 1 x 4 Stroke 6 Cy. 400 x 520 1912kW (2600bhp) Niigata Engineering Co Ltd-Japan
7740738	**YASNYY** - - -	*163* 39 88	Class: (RS)	**1978 Astrakhanskaya Sudoverf im. "Kirova" — Astrakhan** Yd No: 110 Loa 34.02 Br ex 7.09 Dght 2.896 Lbp 30.00 Br md - Dpth 3.66 Welded, 1 dk	**(B11B2FV) Fishing Vessel** Bale: 78 Compartments: 1 Ho, ER 1 Ha: (1.6 x 1.3) Derricks: 2x2t; Winches: 2 Ice Capable	**1 oil engine** driving 1 FP propeller Total Power: 224kW (305hp) 9.0kn S.K.L. 8NVD36-1U 1 x 4 Stroke 8 Cy. 240 x 360 224kW (305bhp) VEB Schwermaschinenbau "KarlLiebknecht" (SKL)-Magdeburg
6601052 -	**YASSEMIN** *ex* Thiessow *-1981* **Biscay Navigation Co Ltd** -	**299** 171 615	Class: (LR) (DS) ✠ Classed LR until 10/67	**1966-02 N.V. Scheepsbouwbedrijf v/h Th.J. Fikkers — Foxhol** Yd No: 106 Loa 47.96 Br ex 9.17 Dght 3.380 Lbp 45.37 Br md 9.15 Dpth 3.46 Welded, 1 dk	**(A31A2GX) General Cargo Ship** Grain: 1,022; Bale: 955 Compartments: 2 Ho, ER 2 Ha: 2 (8.7 x 4.9)ER Cranes: 2x3t Ice Capable	**1 oil engine** driving 1 FP propeller Total Power: 397kW (540hp) 10.0kn S.K.L. 6NVD48/32 1 x 4 Stroke 6 Cy. 320 x 480 397kW (540bhp) VEB Schwermaschinenbau "KarlLiebknecht" (SKL)-Magdeburg AuxGen: 2 x 42kW 390V 50Hz a.c Fuel: 40.0 (d.f.)
6811970 - -	**YASSINE** *ex* Balboa No. 2 *-1981* *ex* Ryuho Maru No. 11 *-1981* **Kew Espana** - *Nouadhibou* *Mauritania*	*349* 161 -	Class: (RI)	**1967 Yamanishi Shipbuilding Co Ltd — Ishinomaki MG** Yd No: 568 Loa 50.60 Br ex 8.82 Dght 3.328 Lbp 44.61 Br md 8.79 Dpth 3.79 Welded, 2 dks	**(B11A2FT) Trawler**	**1 oil engine** driving 1 FP propeller Total Power: 1,250kW (1,700hp) Akasaka 6DH38SS 1 x 4 Stroke 6 Cy. 380 x 560 1250kW (1700bhp) Akasaka Tekkosho KK (Akasaka DieselLtd)-Japan
8921236 - -	**YASU MARU No. 28** - - -	*433* - 479		**1990-04 Miho Zosensho K.K. — Shimizu** Yd No: 1375 Loa 55.45 (BB) Br ex 8.72 Dght 3.499 Lbp 49.00 Br md 8.70 Dpth 3.85 Welded, 1 dk	**(B11B2FV) Fishing Vessel** Ins: 521	**1 oil engine** with clutches & sr reverse geared to sc. shaft driving 1 FP propeller Total Power: 1,177kW (1,600hp) Akasaka K31FD 1 x 4 Stroke 6 Cy. 310 x 530 1177kW (1600bhp) Akasaka Tekkosho KK (Akasaka DieselLtd)-Japan
8707173 - -	**YASUEI MARU No. 8** - **Century Product Inc** - *Indonesia*	*199* - 670		**1987-04 Yamanaka Zosen K.K. — Imabari** Yd No: 350 Loa 55.45 (BB) Br ex 9.02 Dght 3.382 Lbp 51.52 Br md 9.01 Dpth 5.52 Welded	**(A31A2GX) General Cargo Ship**	**1 oil engine** with clutches, flexible couplings & reduction geared to sc. shaft driving 1 FP propeller Total Power: 588kW (799hp) Hanshin 6LU26G 1 x 4 Stroke 6 Cy. 260 x 440 588kW (799bhp) The Hanshin Diesel Works Ltd-Japan
8890516 *JH3405* -	**YASUICHI MARU** - **YK Yasuichi Maru** - *Shima, Mie* *Japan* MMSI: 431200140 Official number: 134405	*120* - -		**1995-12 Higashi Kyushu Shipbuilding Co Ltd — Usuki OT** L reg 29.70 Br ex - Dght - Lbp - Br md 5.60 Dpth 2.40 Bonded, 1 dk	**(B11B2FV) Fishing Vessel** Hull Material: Reinforced Plastic	**1 oil engine** driving 1 FP propeller
9209764 *HC5179* -	**YASUNI** *ex* Nomade *-2011* *ex* Vasiliy Strizh *-2010* *completed as* Ponoy *-2004* **Japina SA** - *Guayaquil* *Ecuador* Official number: R-00-00514	**161** 48 113	Class: LR (RS) ✠ **100A1** SS 09/2009 tug **LMC** Eq.Ltr: D; Cable: 247.5/17.5 U3 (a)	**2004-09 FGUP Mashinostroitelnoye Predp 'Zvyozdochka' — Severodvinsk** (Hull) Yd No: 7004 **2004-09 B.V. Scheepswerf Damen — Gorinchem** Yd No: 509810 Loa 26.09 Br ex 7.94 Dght 3.443 Lbp 23.98 Br md 7.90 Dpth 4.05 Welded, 1 dk	**(B32A2ST) Tug**	**2 oil engines** with clutches, flexible couplings & sr reverse geared to sc. shafts driving 2 FP propellers Total Power: 2,612kW (3,552hp) 12.3kn Caterpillar 3512B-HD 2 x Vee 4 Stroke 12 Cy. 170 x 215 each-1306kW (1776bhp) Caterpillar Inc-USA AuxGen: 2 x 85kW 400V 50Hz a.c
8743141 *JD2854* -	**YASUTAKA** - **Japan Railway Construction, Transport & Technology Agency & Heian Kaiun KK** Shinwa Naiko Kaiun Kaisha Ltd *Tanabe, Wakayama* *Japan* MMSI: 431000872 Official number: 140916	*749* - 2,219		**2009-04 Fukushima Zosen Ltd. — Matsue** Yd No: 360 Loa 81.50 Br ex - Dght 4.650 Lbp 74.40 Br md 13.80 Dpth 7.84 Welded, 1 dk	**(A24A2BT) Cement Carrier**	**1 oil engine** reductiom geared to sc.shaft driving 1 FP propeller Total Power: 745kW (1,013hp) 11.0kn Yanmar 6N21L-SV 1 x 4 Stroke 6 Cy. 210 x 290 745kW (1013bhp) Yanmar Diesel Engine Co Ltd-Japan
5323665 - -	**YAT TUNG** *ex* Chin I No. 17 *-2002* *ex* Kuoai No. 12 *-2002* *ex* Shinpo Maru No. 15 *-2002* **Yat Tung Fishery Co SA** -	*305* 218 -		**1962 Uchida Zosen — Ise** Yd No: 556 Loa - Br ex - Dght 2.998 Lbp 38.82 Br md 7.19 Dpth 3.48 Riveted\Welded, 1 dk	**(B11B2FV) Fishing Vessel**	**1 oil engine** driving 1 FP propeller Hanshin V6 1 x 4 Stroke 6 Cy. 320 x 450 Hanshin Nainenki Kogyo-Japan
9067726 *HZZI* -	**YATHREB 1** *ex* Jaya Opal *-1998* **Bakri Navigation Co Ltd** Red Sea Marine Services *Dammam* *Saudi Arabia* Official number: 117	**275** 82 118	Class: BV (LR) ✠ Classed LR until 22/5/00	**1994-02 Siong Huat Shipyard Pte Ltd — Singapore** Yd No: 268 Loa 29.40 Br ex 10.60 Dght 3.500 Lbp 24.57 Br md 9.60 Dpth 4.26 Welded, 1 dk	**(B32A2ST) Tug**	**2 oil engines** with clutches, flexible couplings & reduction geared to sc. shafts driving 2 Directional propellers Total Power: 1,764kW (2,398hp) 11.0kn Yanmar M220-EN 2 x 4 Stroke 6 Cy. 220 x 300 each-882kW (1199bhp) Yanmar Diesel Engine Co Ltd-Japan AuxGen: 2 x 85kW 415V 50Hz a.c Fuel: 95.0 (d.f.) 9.3pd
9067702 *HZZJ* -	**YATHREB 2** *ex* Jaya Pearl *-1998* **Bakri Navigation Co Ltd** Red Sea Marine Services *Dammam* *Saudi Arabia* Official number: 119	**275** 82 106	Class: BV (LR) ✠ Classed LR until 23/5/00	**1993-12 Siong Huat Shipyard Pte Ltd — Singapore** Yd No: 266 Loa 29.40 Br ex 10.60 Dght 3.500 Lbp 24.57 Br md 9.60 Dpth 4.26 Welded, 1 dk	**(B32A2ST) Tug**	**2 oil engines** with clutches, flexible couplings & reduction geared to sc. shafts driving 2 Directional propellers Total Power: 1,764kW (2,398hp) 11.0kn Yanmar M220-EN 2 x 4 Stroke 6 Cy. 220 x 300 each-882kW (1199bhp) Yanmar Diesel Engine Co Ltd-Japan AuxGen: 2 x 85kW 415V 50Hz a.c Fuel: 95.0 (d.f.) 9.3pd
9131319 *HZZO* -	**YATHREB III** *ex* Jaya Jade *-1998* **Bakri Navigation Co Ltd** Red Sea Marine Services *Dammam* *Saudi Arabia*	**285** 85 151	Class: BV (NV) (AB)	**1996-05 Jaya Shipbuilding & Engineering Pte Ltd — Singapore** Yd No: 808 Loa 28.00 Br ex - Dght 3.350 Lbp 26.26 Br md 9.60 Dpth 4.49 Welded, 1 dk	**(B32A2ST) Tug**	**2 oil engines** with flexible couplings & reductiongeared to sc. shafts driving 2 FP propellers Total Power: 1,884kW (2,562hp) 8.5kn G.M. (Detroit Diesel) 16V-149-T 2 x Vee 2 Stroke 16 Cy. 146 x 146 each-942kW (1281bhp) Detroit Diesel Corporation-Detroit, Mi AuxGen: 2 x 90kW 415V 50Hz a.c Fuel: 137.0 (d.f.) 6.2pd

IMO / Call sign	Name, ex-names, owner, manager, port, flag	Tonnage	Class	Builder, dimensions	Type	Machinery
875499 ZZP	**YATHREB IV** *ex* Javaria Ace *-1998* **Bakri Navigation Co Ltd** Red Sea Marine Services *Dammam* *Saudi Arabia* Official number: 7778	**216** 64 -	Class: BV HR (AB)	**1994 Jaya Shipbuilding & Engineering Pte Ltd — Singapore** Yd No: 805 Loa 26.00 Br ex - Dght 3.060 Lbp 24.41 Br md 9.10 Dpth 4.00 Welded, 1 dk	**(B32A2ST) Tug**	**2 oil engines** geared to sc. shafts driving 2 FP propellers Total Power: 1,258kW (1,710hp) 10.0kn Wartsila UD25V12M5D 2 x Vee 4 Stroke 12 Cy. 150 x 180 each-629kW (855bhp) SACM Diesel SA-France AuxGen: 2 x 90kW a.c Fuel: 58.0 (d.f.)
067714 ZZR	**YATHREB V** *ex* Jaya Ruby *-1998* **Bakri Navigation Co Ltd** Red Sea Marine Services *Dammam* *Saudi Arabia* Official number: 125	**275** 82 106	Class: BV (LR) ✠ Classed LR until 18/12/00	**1994-01 Siong Huat Shipyard Pte Ltd — Singapore** Yd No: 267 Loa 29.40 Br ex 10.60 Dght 3.230 Lbp 24.57 Br md 9.60 Dpth 4.26 Welded, 1 dk	**(B32A2ST) Tug**	**2 oil engines** with clutches, flexible couplings & reduction geared to sc. shafts driving 2 Directional propellers Total Power: 1,764kW (2,398hp) 11.0kn Yanmar M220-EN 2 x 4 Stroke 6 Cy. 220 x 300 each-882kW (1199bhp) Yanmar Diesel Engine Co Ltd-Japan AuxGen: 2 x 85kW 415V 50Hz a.c Fuel: 95.0 (d.f.) 9.3pd
711198 HP7201	**YATHRIB 1** *ex* Eiron *-1993* *ex* Erala *-1988* **Kaybee Co SA** - *Panama* *Panama* Official number: 22369BE	**416** 125 304	Class: (BV)	**1988-04 S.A. Balenciaga — Zumaya** Yd No: 327 Loa 39.63 Br ex - Dght 3.801 Lbp 32.62 Br md 8.81 Dpth 5.87 Welded, 2 dks	**(B11A2FS) Stern Trawler** Ins: 320	**1 oil engine** driving 1 CP propeller Total Power: 736kW (1,001hp) 11.2kn M.T.M. TI829C 1 x 4 Stroke 8 Cy. 295 x 420 736kW (1001bhp) (made 1976, fitted 1988) La Maquinista Terrestre y Mar (MTM)-Spain AuxGen: 3 x 480kW 380V a.c
8932510 JJ2947	**YATSUWA MARU** *ex* Itsuwa Maru *-2012* *ex* Taiho Maru No. 30 *-1997* **Seiwa Kaiun KK** - *Kobe, Hyogo* *Japan* MMSI: 431500851 Official number: 115946	*198* - 550		**1974-02 K.K. Kanmasu Zosensho — Imabari** Loa 46.00 Br ex - Dght 3.370 Lbp 42.00 Br md 7.50 Dpth 3.50 Welded, 1 dk	**(A12A2TC) Chemical Tanker** Liq: 342 Compartments: 3 Ta, ER 1 Cargo Pump (s): 1x150m³/hr	**1 oil engine** driving 1 FP propeller Total Power: 441kW (600hp) 10.5kn Hanshin 6L26AGS 1 x 4 Stroke 6 Cy. 260 x 400 441kW (600bhp) The Hanshin Diesel Works Ltd-Japan
7236505 9LY2310 -	**YAU LI NO. 1** *ex* Wing Sang 68 *-2010* *ex* Golden Taurus *-2006* *ex* Wing Sang No. 68 *-2004* *ex* Taka Maru No. 17 *-2004* *ex* Matsuei Maru No. 11 *-1984* **Yau Li Number One Ltd** - *Freetown* *Sierra Leone* MMSI: 667003113 Official number: SL103113	**280** 84 214		**1972 Miho Zosensho K.K. — Shimizu** Yd No: 831 Converted From: Fishing Vessel-2010 Loa 41.71 Br ex 7.52 Dght 2.921 Lbp 36.00 Br md 7.50 Dpth 3.10 Welded, 1 dk	**(A31A2GX) General Cargo Ship**	**1 oil engine** driving 1 FP propeller Total Power: 552kW (750hp) Niigata 6M26KCHS 1 x 4 Stroke 6 Cy. 260 x 400 552kW (750bhp) Niigata Engineering Co Ltd-Japan
8934623 - -	**YAU SHENG** *ex* Yin Yue *-1984* - -	**860** 482 -		**1990 Fujian Province Shiprepair Co — Fujian Province** L reg 67.20 Br ex - Dght - Lbp - Br md 10.00 Dpth 5.75 Welded, 1 dk	**(A31A2GX) General Cargo Ship**	**1 oil engine** driving 1 FP propeller
7616808 - -	**YAUBULA** - - *Nuku'alofa* *Tonga*	*343* 230 400		**1977-09 The Fiji Marine Shipyard & Slipways — Suva** Yd No: 40 Loa 42.52 Br ex 9.12 Dght 1.601 Lbp 41.03 Br md 9.11 Dpth 2.19 Welded, 2 dks	**(A36B2PL) Passenger/Landing Craft** Bow door/ramp	**2 oil engines** geared to sc. shafts driving 2 FP propellers Total Power: 772kW (1,050hp) 8.0kn G.M. (Detroit Diesel) 12V-71-TI 2 x Vee 2 Stroke 12 Cy. 108 x 127 each-386kW (525bhp) General Motors Detroit DieselAllison Divn-USA
8123626 YYBD	**YAVIRE** - **PDV Marina SA** - SatCom: Inmarsat C 477501810 *Las Piedras* *Venezuela* MMSI: 775018000 Official number: AMMT-1309	**11,979** 3,593 11,800	Class: LR ✠ **100A1** SS 08/2008 liquefied gas carrier for the carriage of Propane, iso butane, butane & anhydrous ammonia in independent tanks with a max. density of 0.68T/cub.M at 0.35bar at a min. temp of minus 48~C max. allowable tank vapour pressure is 4bar ✠ **LMC** **UMS** Eq.Ltr: (F†) ; Cable: 577.5/71.0 U2	**1983-06 Oy Wartsila Ab — Turku** Yd No: 1263 Loa 146.01 (BB) Br ex 22.53 Dght 8.316 Lbp 136.00 Br md 22.51 Dpth 14.05 Welded, 1 dk	**(A11B2TG) LPG Tanker** Double Bottom Entire Compartment Length Liq (Gas): 14,155 4 x Gas Tank (s); 1 independent (36% Ni.stl) dcc horizontal, 3 independent (36% Ni.stl) dcy horizontal 8 Cargo Pump (s): 8x150m³/hr	**1 oil engine** driving 1 FP propeller Total Power: 6,180kW (8,402hp) 16.3kn Sulzer 6RLB56 1 x 2 Stroke 6 Cy. 560 x 1150 6180kW (8402bhp) Oy Wartsila Ab-Finland AuxGen: 3 x 720kW 440V 60Hz a.c Boilers: AuxB (Comp) 7.1kgf/cm² (7.0bar) Fuel: 213.0 (d.f.) 835.0 (r.f.) 28.0pd
8732855 TC7735 -	**YAVUZ NAZ** *ex* Selcuk 2 *-2009* **Ali Isik** - *Bandirma* *Turkey* MMSI: 271001176 Official number: 2017	**495** - -		**1993-01 Taskinlar Gemi Sanayi ve Ticaret SA — Sinop** Converted From: Fishing Vessel-1993 Loa 29.90 Br ex - Dght - Lbp - Br md 9.30 Dpth - Welded, 1 dk	**(A37B2PS) Passenger Ship**	**1 oil engine** geared to sc. shaft driving 1 Propeller Total Power: 294kW (400hp) Volvo Penta TAMD122A 1 x 4 Stroke 6 Cy. 130 x 150 294kW (400bhp) AB Volvo Penta-Sweden
9428750 TCST3 -	**YAVUZ SULTAN SELIM-1** **Istanbul Deniz Otobusleri Sanayi ve Ticaret AS (IDO)** - *Istanbul* *Turkey* MMSI: 271000975 Official number: 1644	**2,284** 685 280	Class: TL (BV)	**2008-08 Afai Southern Shipyard (Panyu Guangzhou) Ltd — Guangzhou GD** (Hull) Yd No: 007 **2008-08 B.V. Scheepswerf Damen — Gorinchem** Yd No: 539301 Loa 85.00 Br ex 21.45 Dght 3.150 Lbp 82.27 Br md 21.04 Dpth 6.50 Welded, 1 dk	**(A36A2PR) Passenger/Ro-Ro Ship (Vehicles)** Hull Material: Aluminium Alloy Passengers: unberthed: 602; cabins: 6 Bow door (centre) Stern door (centre) Cars: 112	**4 oil engines** reduction geared to sc. shafts driving 4 Z propellers Total Power: 6,744kW (9,168hp) 22.0kn Caterpillar 3516B-HD 4 x Vee 4 Stroke 16 Cy. 170 x 215 each-1686kW (2292bhp) Caterpillar Inc-USA AuxGen: 3 x 200kW 50Hz a.c Fuel: 30.0 (d.f.)
7946423 TC4500 -	**YAVUZSULTAN** *ex* Saribas-2 *-2009* **Saribaslar Kollektif Sti** - *Istanbul* *Turkey* Official number: 4034	*299* 157 500		**1970 Gemi Insaat Kollektif Sirketi — Balat, Istanbul** Loa 48.16 Br ex - Dght 2.880 Lbp 43.21 Br md 7.00 Dpth 3.26 Welded, 1 dk	**(A31A2GX) General Cargo Ship**	**1 oil engine** driving 1 FP propeller Total Power: 588kW (799hp) 8.0kn MWM 1 x 4 Stroke 588kW (799bhp) Motoren Werke Mannheim AG (MWM)-West Germany
8853855 HP5894 -	**YAWAN No. 1** *ex* Yalaone *-1990* **PT Yala Jaya Adikerta Inc** - *Panama* *Panama* Official number: 1979191	**147** 63 -		**1990 Shing Sheng Fa Boat Building Co — Kaohsiung** L reg 23.94 Br ex - Dght - Lbp - Br md 5.60 Dpth 2.30 Welded, 1 dk	**(B11B2FV) Fishing Vessel**	**1 oil engine** driving 1 FP propeller Total Power: 588kW (799hp) 10.0kn Yanmar 1 x 4 Stroke 588kW (799bhp) Yanmar Diesel Engine Co Ltd-Japan
9217709 JG5592 -	**YAWATA** - **Yawatahama Kisen YK (Yawatahama Kisen Co Ltd)** - *Tokyo* *Japan* MMSI: 431100843 Official number: 136745	*243* - -		**1999-09 Kanagawa Zosen — Kobe** Yd No: 477 Loa 37.20 Br ex - Dght - Lbp 32.70 Br md 9.80 Dpth 4.20 Welded, 1 dk	**(B32A2ST) Tug**	**2 oil engines** gearing integral to driving 2 Z propellers Total Power: 2,648kW (3,600hp) 14.6kn Yanmar 6N280-UN 2 x 4 Stroke 6 Cy. 280 x 380 each-1324kW (1800bhp) Yanmar Diesel Engine Co Ltd-Japan AuxGen: 2 x 104kW 225V 60Hz a.c Fuel: 48.0 (d.f.) 11.0pd
6725951 - -	**YAWATA MARU No. 3** - **Alex Shipping Co Ltd**	*177* - -		**1967-09 Taguma Zosen KK — Onomichi HS** Yd No: 55 Loa 32.52 Br ex 8.23 Dght 2.998 Lbp 29.90 Br md 8.21 Dpth 3.69 Riveted\Welded, 1 dk	**(B32A2ST) Tug**	**2 oil engines** geared to sc. shafts driving 2 FP propellers Total Power: 1,472kW (2,002hp) 12.0kn Fuji 6MD32H 2 x 4 Stroke 6 Cy. 320 x 380 each-736kW (1001bhp) Fuji Diesel Co Ltd-Japan
8734580 VSPX4	**YAWEN** *ex* Mimi *-2002* **Balandro Marine Ltd** Sarnia Yachts Ltd *Guernsey* *Guernsey* MMSI: 235008700 Official number: 735118	**145** 96 -		**2001 Moonen Shipyards B.V. — 's-Hertogenbosch** Yd No: 174 L reg 24.68 Br ex - Dght 1.820 Lbp - Br md 6.10 Dpth - Welded, 1 dk	**(X11A2YP) Yacht**	**2 oil engines** geared to sc. shafts driving 2 Propellers Caterpillar 2 x 4 Stroke Caterpillar Inc-USA

8733964 *EA3681* 3-AT-24-98	**YAYO CAMPANARES** - **Jalok y Sul SL** - *Santa Pola* *Spain* Official number: 3-4/1998	**103** - -		**1998 Astilleros Pineiro, S.L. — Moana** Loa 22.00 Br ex - Dght - Lbp 18.00 Br md 6.30 Dpth 2.85 Welded, 1 dk	**(B11A2FS) Stern Trawler**	**1 oil engine** driving 1 Propeller Total Power: 195kW (265hp)
8204690 *DTAI9* -	**YAYOI** *ex* Yayoi Maru *-1993* **Daebum Marine Co Ltd** - *Busan* *South Korea* Official number: 9608003-6260004	**1,232** 392 1,175	Class: (KR) (NK)	**1982-06 Uchida Zosen — Ise** Yd No: 822 Loa 69.70 (BB) Br ex - Dght 4.022 Lbp 64.50 Br md 11.00 Dpth 4.04 Welded, 2 dks	**(A34A2GR) Refrigerated Cargo Ship** Grain: 1,420; Bale: 1,379; Ins: 1,379 Compartments: 4 Ho, ER 2 Ha: ER	**1 oil engine** driving 1 FP propeller Total Power: 1,324kW (1,800hp) Makita GSLH63 1 x 4 Stroke 6 Cy. 330 x 530 1324kW (1800bhp) Makita Diesel Co Ltd-Japan
9333242 *3EEK2* -	**YAYOI EXPRESS** - **Paean Shipping SA** MOL Tankship Management (Asia) Pte Ltd *Panama* *Panama* MMSI: 371924000 Official number: 3180606A	**28,844** 12,962 47,999 T/cm 51.8	Class: NK	**2006-02 Iwagi Zosen Co Ltd — Kamijima EH** Yd No: 233 Loa 179.90 Br ex 32.23 Dght 12.489 Lbp 172.00 Br md 32.20 Dpth 19.05 Welded, 1 dk	**(A13B2TP) Products Tanker** Double Hull (13F) Liq: 56,275; Liq (Oil): 56,275 Cargo Heating Coils Compartments: 17 Wing Ta, 1 Wing Slop Ta, ER 4 Cargo Pump (s): 4x1250m³/hr Manifold: Bow/CM: 92.4m	**1 oil engine** driving 1 FP propeller Total Power: 9,480kW (12,889hp) 15.1k MAN-B&W 6S50MC 1 x 2 Stroke 6 Cy. 500 x 2000 9480kW (12889bhp) Mitsui Engineering & Shipbuilding CLtd-Japan Fuel: 2200.0
5425956 - -	**YAYOI MARU** - - -	*131* - -		**1963 Shimoda Dockyard Co. Ltd. — Shimoda** Yd No: 132 Loa 26.06 Br ex 7.78 Dght 2.300 Lbp 23.00 Br md 7.40 Dpth 3.19 Welded, 1 dk	**(B32A2ST) Tug**	**2 oil engines** driving 2 FP propellers Total Power: 736kW (1,000hp) 14.5k Hanshin DE 2 x 4 Stroke 6 Cy. 290 x 410 each-368kW (500bhp) Hanshin Nainenki Kogyo-Japan
8632835 *JE2827* -	**YAYOI MARU NO. 32** *ex* Yoshi Maru No. 38 *-2009* *ex* Yuryo Maru No. 67 *-1995* **YK Hokuyo Suisan** - *Sakaiminato, Tottori* *Japan* Official number: 126573	*122* - -		**1983-03 Kidoura Shipyard Co Ltd — Kesennuma MG** Yd No: 513 L reg 28.20 Br ex - Dght 2.300 Lbp - Br md 5.90 Dpth 2.80 Welded, 1 dk	**(B11B2FV) Fishing Vessel**	**1 oil engine** driving 1 FP propeller Total Power: 272kW (370hp) Niigata 6M24F 1 x 4 Stroke 6 Cy. 240 x 410 272kW (370bhp) Niigata Engineering Co Ltd-Japan
7924322 *9LD2306* -	**YAZ** *ex* Ranyus I *-2013* *ex* Ranyus A *-2010* *ex* Olga *-2010* *ex* Veronika *-2005* *ex* Veronika Gokoti *-2005* *ex* Boxter *-2004* *ex* Baltic Bridge *-1997* *ex* Eliza Heeren *-1995* *ex* Akak Success *-1986* *ex* Eliza Heeren *-1986* **Farah Shipping Ltd** - *Freetown* *Sierra Leone* MMSI: 667005006 Official number: SL105006	**2,023** 1,116 2,840	Class: DR (PR) (GL)	**1981-02 Heinrich Brand Schiffswerft GmbH & Co. KG — Oldenburg** Yd No: 206 Loa 79.71 (BB) Br ex 13.03 Dght 5.675 Lbp 70.69 Br md 13.01 Dpth 7.10 Welded, 3 dks	**(A31A2GX) General Cargo Ship** Grain: 3,925; Bale: 3,880 TEU 144 C.Ho 82/20' (40') C.Dk 62/20' (40') Compartments: 1 Ho, ER 1 Ha: (43.8 x 10.2)ER Ice Capable	**1 oil engine** reduction geared to sc. shaft driving 1 CP propeller Total Power: 1,302kW (1,770hp) 12.0k MaK 8M332A 1 x 4 Stroke 8 Cy. 240 x 330 1302kW (1770bhp) Krupp MaK Maschinenbau GmbH-Kiel AuxGen: 2 x 205kW 50Hz a.c, 2 x 57kW 50Hz a.c Thrusters: 1 Thwart. FP thruster (f)
7117175 *EQUI* -	**YAZD** *ex* Supplier VI *-1995* *ex* Canmar Supplier VI *-1994* *ex* Bay Shore *-1977* **Darya Dasht Fars Co** - *Bushehr* *Iran* MMSI: 422177000 Official number: 16582	*694* 232 766	Class: AS (LR) ✠ Classed LR until 17/9/03	**1971-11 J. Bolson & Son Ltd. — Poole** Yd No: 572 Loa 56.16 Br ex 11.69 Dght 4.185 Lbp 48.82 Br md 11.43 Dpth 4.73 Welded, 1 dk	**(B21A2OS) Platform Supply Ship** Derricks: 1x5t Ice Capable	**2 oil engines** driving 2 FP propellers Total Power: 3,884kW (5,280hp) 13.3k Ruston 12RKC 2 x Vee 4 Stroke 12 Cy. 254 x 305 each-1942kW (2640bhp) Ruston Paxman Diesels Ltd.-Colchester AuxGen: 1 x 200kW 440V 60Hz a.c, 2 x 150kW 440V 60Hz a. Thrusters: 1 Water jet (f) Fuel: 497.0 (d.f.)
9555864 - -	**YAZE 1** - **Government of Dubai (Dubai Police)** - *Dubai* *United Arab Emirates*	**140** 42 25	Class: (RI)	**2009-09 Dubai Shipbuilding & Engineering LLC — Dubai** Yd No: 449 Loa 33.41 Br ex 10.40 Dght 1.500 Lbp - Br md 10.00 Dpth 2.50 Welded, 1 dk	**(B34G2SE) Pollution Control Vessel**	**2 oil engines** reduction geared to sc. shafts driving 2 FP propellers Total Power: 1,074kW (1,460hp) 12.0k Caterpillar 341 2 x Vee 4 Stroke 12 Cy. 137 x 152 each-537kW (730bhp) Caterpillar Inc-USA AuxGen: 2 x 38kW 380V 50Hz a.c
8666915 *TC9848* -	**YAZICI-IV** - - - *Istanbul* *Turkey* Official number: 1423102	**259** 163 -		**2000-05 Rota Denizcilik Ticaret A.S. — Tuzla, Istanbul** Yd No: 111 Loa 40.00 Br ex - Dght 1.300 Lbp 39.10 Br md 9.00 Dpth 2.65 Welded, 1 dk	**(A37B2PS) Passenger Ship**	**2 oil engines** reduction geared to sc. shafts driving 2 Propellers Total Power: 1,250kW (1,700hp) Iveco Aifo 8291 SRM8 2 x Vee 4 Stroke 12 Cy. 145 x 130 each-625kW (850bhp) Iveco Pegaso-Madrid
8939001 *WDD3058* -	**YAZMOND** *ex* Janice *-2013* *ex* Alliance *-2006* **Yaznak Inc** - *Winchester Bay, OR* *United States of America* MMSI: 367123290 Official number: 1029958	**175** 52 -		**1995 Johnson Shipbuilding & Repair — Bayou La Batre, Al** Yd No: 127 L reg 26.98 Br ex - Dght - Lbp - Br md 7.32 Dpth 3.66 Welded, 1 dk	**(B11B2FV) Fishing Vessel**	**1 oil engine** driving 1 FP propeller
7642106 *WDC3253* -	**YBOR CITY** *ex* Donald Bollinger *-2006* **Mobro Marine Inc** - *Jacksonville, FL* *United States of America* MMSI: 367004750 Official number: 504524	*147* 100 -		**1966 Bollinger Machine Shop & Shipyard, Inc. — Lockport, La** Yd No: 57 Loa - Br ex 7.40 Dght - Lbp 21.49 Br md 7.35 Dpth 3.48 Welded, 1 dk	**(B32A2ST) Tug**	**2 oil engines** driving 2 FP propellers Total Power: 1,066kW (1,450hp) 12.0k Caterpillar 2 x 4 Stroke each-533kW (725bhp) Caterpillar Tractor Co-USA AuxGen: 2 x 40kW 120V 60Hz a.c
9404912 *DSPP7* -	**YC ACACIA** *ex* Samho Topaz *-2012* **Bogo Shipping Co Ltd** Young Chang Enterprise Co Ltd *Jeju* *South Korea* MMSI: 441379000 Official number: JJR-072154	**4,060** 1,821 5,631 T/cm 14.5	Class: KR	**2008-01 Samho Shipbuilding Co Ltd — Tongyeong** Yd No: 1087 Loa 105.60 (BB) Br ex - Dght 6.613 Lbp 98.00 Br md 16.60 Dpth 8.60 Welded, 1 dk	**(A12B2TR) Chemical/Products Tanker** Double Hull (13F) Liq: 6,132; Liq (Oil): 6,200 Cargo Heating Coils Compartments: 10 Wing Ta, 2 Wing Slop Ta, ER 10 Cargo Pump (s): 10x200m³/hr Manifold: Bow/CM: 55.8m	**1 oil engine** driving 1 FP propeller Total Power: 2,942kW (4,000hp) 13.0k Hanshin LH46 1 x 4 Stroke 6 Cy. 460 x 880 2942kW (4000bhp) The Hanshin Diesel Works Ltd-Japan AuxGen: 3 x 480kW 445V a.c Thrusters: 1 Tunnel thruster (f) Fuel: 50.0 (d.f.) 243.0 (r.f.)
9478078 *3ESP5* -	**YC CLOVER** - **Macos Shipping SA** Young Chang Enterprise Co Ltd *Panama* *Panama* MMSI: 370388000 Official number: 3476309	**5,667** 2,743 8,981 T/cm 18.2	Class: KR	**2008-07 Kwangsung Shipbuilding Co Ltd — Mokpo** Yd No: 102 Loa 114.40 (BB) Br ex - Dght 7.813 Lbp 105.00 Br md 18.20 Dpth 10.00 Welded, 1 dk	**(A12B2TR) Chemical/Products Tanker** Double Hull (13F) Liq: 9,149; Liq (Oil): 9,149 Cargo Heating Coils Compartments: 10 Wing Ta, 2 Wing Slop Ta, ER 10 Cargo Pump (s): 6x200m³/hr, 4x300m³/hr Manifold: Bow/CM: 57.2m	**1 oil engine** driving 1 FP propeller Total Power: 4,440kW (6,037hp) 13.5k MAN-B&W 6S35M 1 x 2 Stroke 6 Cy. 350 x 1400 4440kW (6037bhp) STX Engine Co Ltd-South Korea AuxGen: 3 x 400kW 450V a.c Thrusters: 1 Tunnel thruster (f) Fuel: 82.0 (d.f.) 538.0 (r.f.)
9409364 *DSRJ2* -	**YC COSMOS** *ex* Samho Amber *-2012* **Young Chang Enterprise Co Ltd** - *Jeju* *South Korea* MMSI: 441456000 Official number: JJR-089355	**4,060** 1,821 5,631 T/cm 14.5	Class: KR	**2008-04 Samho Shipbuilding Co Ltd — Tongyeong** Yd No: 1088 Loa 105.60 (BB) Br ex - Dght 6.613 Lbp 98.00 Br md 16.60 Dpth 8.60 Welded, 1 dk	**(A12B2TR) Chemical/Products Tanker** Double Hull (13F) Liq: 6,132; Liq (Oil): 6,200 Cargo Heating Coils Compartments: 10 Wing Ta, 2 Wing Slop Ta, ER 10 Cargo Pump (s): 10x200m³/hr Manifold: Bow/CM: 55.8m	**1 oil engine** driving 1 FP propeller Total Power: 2,942kW (4,000hp) 13.0k Hanshin LH4 1 x 4 Stroke 6 Cy. 460 x 880 2942kW (4000bhp) The Hanshin Diesel Works Ltd-Japan AuxGen: 3 x 480kW 450V a.c Thrusters: 1 Tunnel thruster (f) Fuel: 50.0 (d.f.) 243.0 (r.f.)
9410105 *DSPU5* -	**YC KALMIA** - **Shinhan Capital Co Ltd** Wonnam Shipping Co Ltd *Jeju* *South Korea* MMSI: 441454000 Official number: JJR-089592	**4,688** 2,172 6,757 T/cm 16.5	Class: KR	**2008-06 Mokpo Shipbuilding & Engineering Co Ltd — Mokpo** Yd No: 06-183 Loa 109.99 (BB) Br ex - Dght 6.713 Lbp 102.43 Br md 18.20 Dpth 8.50 Welded, 1 dk	**(A12B2TR) Chemical/Products Tanker** Double Hull (13F) Liq: 7,322; Liq (Oil): 7,322 Cargo Heating Coils Compartments: 12 Wing Ta, 2 Wing Slop Ta, ER 14 Cargo Pump (s): 12x200m³/hr, 2x100m³/hr Manifold: Bow/CM: 52.1m	**1 oil engine** driving 1 FP propeller Total Power: 3,309kW (4,499hp) 13.3k Hanshin LH46L 1 x 4 Stroke 6 Cy. 460 x 880 3309kW (4499bhp) The Hanshin Diesel Works Ltd-Japan AuxGen: 4 x 625kW 450V Thrusters: 1 Tunnel thruster (f) Fuel: 70.0 (d.f.) 330.0 (r.f.)

IMO / Call sign	Name / Owner	Tonnage	Class	Builder / Dimensions	Type / Cargo	Machinery
9166948 DSQ09	**YC LILAC** *ex* OSM General *-2010* *ex* Sun Lavender *-2009* *ex* Sun Diamond *-2006* **Shinhan Capital Co Ltd** Ocean Success Maritime Co Ltd *Jeju* *South Korea* MMSI: 441227000 Official number: JJR-069311	**5,340** 2,644 8,697 T/cm 17.6	Class: KR (NK)	**1998**-03 **Usuki Shipyard Co Ltd — Usuki OT** Yd No: 1652 Loa 112.00 (BB) Br ex 19.03 Dght 7.514 Lbp 105.90 Br md 19.00 Dpth 10.00 Welded, 1 dk	**(A12B2TR) Chemical/Products Tanker** Double Hull (13F) Liq: 9,233; Liq (Oil): 9,234 Cargo Heating Coils Compartments: 12 Wing Ta, ER 12 Cargo Pump (s): 12x300m³/hr Manifold: Bow/CM: 52m	**1 oil engine** driving 1 FP propeller Total Power: 3,089kW (4,200hp) 13.3kn Mitsubishi 6UEC37LA 1 x 2 Stroke 6 Cy. 370 x 880 3089kW (4200bhp) Akasaka Tekkosho KK (Akasaka DieselLtd)-Japan AuxGen: 3 x 400kW 450V 60Hz a.c Thrusters: 1 Tunnel thruster (f) Fuel: 114.0 (d.f.) (Heating Coils) 617.0 (r.f.) 13.0pd
9262493 VRFV6 -	**YE CHI** - **Ye Chi Shipping SA** China Shipping Tanker Co Ltd *Hong Kong* *Hong Kong* MMSI: 477621300 Official number: HK-2529	**31,150** 12,076 45,740 T/cm 53.6	Class: LR ✠ **100A1** SS 11/2009 Double Hull oil tanker ESP **ShipRight** (SDA, FDA, CM) LI SPM Ice Class 1B at a draught of 12.392m Max/min draughts fwd 12.392/6.517m Max/min draughts aft 12.392/6.517m Power required 10610kw, power installed 10900kw ✠ **LMC** **UMS IGS** Eq.Ltr: M†; Cable: 577.5/73.0 U3 (a)	**2009**-11 **China Shipping Industry (Jiangsu) Co Ltd — Jiangdu JS** Yd No: A46000-02 Loa 187.22 (BB) Br ex 32.29 Dght 12.100 Lbp 176.70 Br md 32.25 Dpth 18.90 Welded, 1 dk	**(A13A2TW) Crude/Oil Products Tanker** Double Hull (13F) Liq: 52,722; Liq (Oil): 54,850 Cargo Heating Coils Compartments: 12 Wing Ta, 2 Wing Slop Ta, ER 12 Cargo Pump (s): 12x600m³/hr Manifold: Bow/CM: 95.5m Ice Capable	**1 oil engine** driving 1 FP propeller Total Power: 10,900kW (14,820hp) 14.0kn Wartsila 5RT-flex58T 1 x 2 Stroke 5 Cy. 580 x 2416 10900kW (14820bhp) Dalian Marine Diesel Co Ltd-China AuxGen: 3 x 975kW 450V 60Hz a.c Boilers: e (ex.g.) 17.3kgf/cm² (17.0bar), AuxB (o.f.) 14.3kgf/cm² (14.0bar) Thrusters: 1 Thwart. CP thruster (f) Fuel: 230.0 (d.f.) 1750.0 (r.f.)
8631013 XUCW6 -	**YE DA** *ex* Shige Maru No. 26 *-2003* **Yantai Development Zone Fengyuan Shipping Co Ltd** - *Phnom Penh* *Cambodia* MMSI: 515526000 Official number: 1187687	**1,994** 1,116 3,500	Class: UB	**1987**-06 **Sanyo Zosen K.K. — Onomichi** Converted From: Grab Dredger-2004 Lengthened-2004 Loa 89.15 Br ex 13.02 Dght 5.500 Lbp 84.00 Br md 13.00 Dpth 6.80 Welded, 1 dk	**(A31A2GX) General Cargo Ship**	**1 oil engine** driving 1 FP propeller Total Power: 1,324kW (1,800hp) 11.0kn Fuji 6S32G2 1 x 4 Stroke 6 Cy. 320 x 610 1324kW (1800bhp) Fuji Diesel Co Ltd-Japan
8628846 H04215 -	**YE JONG** *ex* Dae Dong No. 9 *-2006* **S K Lines SA** Sekyeong Shipping Co Ltd *Panama* *Panama* Official number: 3192106	**134** 107 -	Class: (KR)	**1996**-03 **Kyeong-In Engineering & Shipbuilding Co Ltd — Incheon** Yd No: 547 Loa 25.50 Br ex - Dght - Lbp - Br md 7.60 Dpth 3.20 Welded, 1 dk	**(B32A2ST) Tug**	**2 oil engines** reduction geared to sc. shafts driving 2 Propellers Total Power: 1,060kW (1,442hp) 13.3kn G.M. (Detroit Diesel) 16V-92 2 x Vee 2 Stroke 16 Cy. 123 x 127 each-530kW (721bhp) Detroit Diesel Corporation-Detroit, Mi
9469493 VRIR6 -	**YE SHAN** - **Unite Shipping Ltd** Ye Shan Shipping Ltd *Hong Kong* *Hong Kong* MMSI: 477434400 Official number: HK-3129	**43,717** 26,389 79,754	Class: LR ✠ **100A1** SS 08/2011 bulk carrier BC-A strengthened for heavy cargos, Nos. 2, 4 & 6 holds may be empty ESP **ShipRight** (SDA,FDA,CM) ESN *IWS LI Ice Class 1D at a draught of 14.934m Max/min draughts fwd 14.745/4.714m Max/min draughts aft 15.605/6.934m Required power 11620kw, installed power 11620kw ✠ **LMC** **UMS** Eq.Ltr: Q†; Cable: 687.5/81.0 U3 (a)	**2011**-08 **Fujian Crown Ocean Shipbuilding Industry Co Ltd — Lianjiang County FJ** Yd No: GH402A Loa 229.00 (BB) Br ex 32.31 Dght 14.580 Lbp 222.00 Br md 32.26 Dpth 20.25 Welded, 1 dk	**(A21A2BC) Bulk Carrier** Double Hull Grain: 97,000 Compartments: 7 Ho, ER 7 Ha: ER Ice Capable	**1 oil engine** driving 1 FP propeller Total Power: 11,620kW (15,799hp) 14.0kn Wartsila 7RT-flex50 1 x 2 Stroke 7 Cy. 500 x 2050 11620kW (15799bhp) Yichang Marine Diesel Engine Co Ltd-China AuxGen: 3 x 700kW 450V 60Hz a.c Boilers: AuxB (Comp) 7.6kgf/cm² (7.5bar)
8602036 BTSJ -	**YE XIANG GONG ZHU** *ex* Queen Coral No. 7 *-1999* **Hainan Strait Shipping Co Ltd** - SatCom: Inmarsat C 441244012 *Haikou, Hainan* *China* MMSI: 412521560 Official number: 110103000132	*4,973* - 2,700		**1986**-10 **Hayashikane Shipbuilding & Engineering Co Ltd — Shimonoseki YC** Yd No: 1295 Loa - Br ex - Dght 5.901 Lbp 126.02 Br md 20.41 Dpth 14.18 Welded	**(A36A2PR) Passenger/Ro-Ro Ship (Vehicles)** Passengers: unberthed: 500 Lane-Len: 240 Lorries: 24, Cars: 76	**2 oil engines** geared to sc. shafts driving 2 FP propellers Total Power: 8,826kW (12,000hp) Pielstick 8PC2-6L-400 2 x 4 Stroke 8 Cy. 400 x 460 each-4413kW (6000bhp) Ishikawajima Harima Heavy IndustrieCo Ltd (IHI)-Japan
8607878 TCBG4 -	**YEDITEPE-I** *ex* Yeditepe *-1990* **Istanbul Deniz Otobusleri Sanayi ve Ticaret AS (IDO)** - *Istanbul* *Turkey* MMSI: 271002471 Official number: 5576	**431** 166 125	Class: TL (NV)	**1987**-05 **Fjellstrand AS — Omastrand** Yd No: 1579 Loa 38.82 Br ex 9.71 Dght 2.500 Lbp 36.41 Br md 9.47 Dpth 3.92 Welded, 1 dk	**(A37B2PS) Passenger Ship** Hull Material: Aluminium Alloy Passengers: unberthed: 449	**2 oil engines** geared to sc. shafts driving 2 FP propellers Total Power: 2,000kW (2,720hp) 25.0kn M.T.U. 12V396TB93 2 x Vee 4 Stroke 12 Cy. 165 x 185 each-1000kW (1360bhp) MTU Friedrichshafen GmbH-Friedrichshafen AuxGen: 2 x 56kW 380V 50Hz a.c
8611051 - -	**YEDUGURI-1** - **Yeduguri Sea Foods Ltd** - *Mumbai* *India* Official number: 2242	**180** 57 138	Class: (IR) (AB)	**1988**-02 **Bharati Shipyard Ltd — Ratnagiri** Yd No: 202 Loa 27.00 (BB) Br ex 7.83 Dght 3.000 Lbp 23.50 Br md 7.50 Dpth 3.50 Welded, 1 dk	**(B11A2FS) Stern Trawler** Ins: 100	**1 oil engine** with clutches & sr reverse geared to sc. shaft driving 1 FP propeller Total Power: 405kW (551hp) Yanmar S165L-ST 1 x 4 Stroke 6 Cy. 165 x 210 405kW (551bhp) Yanmar Diesel Engine Co Ltd-Japan
8611063 - -	**YEDUGURI-2** - **Yeduguri Sea Foods Ltd** - *Mumbai* *India* Official number: 2243	**180** 57 138	Class: (IR) (AB)	**1988**-02 **Bharati Shipyard Ltd — Ratnagiri** Yd No: 203 Loa 27.00 (BB) Br ex 7.83 Dght 3.000 Lbp 23.50 Br md 7.50 Dpth 3.50 Welded, 1 dk	**(B11A2FS) Stern Trawler**	**1 oil engine** with clutches & sr reverse geared to sc. shaft driving 1 FP propeller Total Power: 405kW (551hp) Yanmar S165L-ST 1 x 4 Stroke 6 Cy. 165 x 210 405kW (551bhp) Yanmar Diesel Engine Co Ltd-Japan
8611075 - -	**YEDUGURI-3** - **Yeduguri Sea Foods Ltd** - *Mumbai* *India* Official number: 2244	**180** 57 138	Class: (IR) (AB)	**1988**-09 **Bharati Shipyard Ltd — Ratnagiri** Yd No: 204 Loa 27.00 (BB) Br ex 7.83 Dght 3.000 Lbp 23.50 Br md 7.50 Dpth 3.50 Welded, 1 dk	**(B11A2FS) Stern Trawler** Ins: 100	**1 oil engine** with clutches & sr reverse geared to sc. shaft driving 1 FP propeller Total Power: 405kW (551hp) Yanmar S165L-ST 1 x 4 Stroke 6 Cy. 165 x 210 405kW (551bhp) Yanmar Diesel Engine Co Ltd-Japan
8611087 - -	**YEDUGURI-4** - **Yeduguri Sea Foods Ltd** - *Mumbai* *India* Official number: 2245	**180** 57 138	Class: (IR) (AB)	**1988**-09 **Bharati Shipyard Ltd — Ratnagiri** Yd No: 205 Loa 27.00 (BB) Br ex 7.83 Dght 3.000 Lbp 23.50 Br md 7.50 Dpth 3.50 Welded, 1 dk	**(B11A2FS) Stern Trawler** Ins: 100	**1 oil engine** with clutches & sr reverse geared to sc. shaft driving 1 FP propeller Total Power: 405kW (551hp) Yanmar S165L-ST 1 x 4 Stroke 6 Cy. 165 x 210 405kW (551bhp) Yanmar Diesel Engine Co Ltd-Japan
6815495 - -	**YEE CHANG No. 3** - **Yee Chang Fishery Co Ltd** - *Kaohsiung* *Chinese Taipei*	*282* 189 107	Class: (CR)	**1968** **Taiwan Machinery Manufacturing Corp. — Kaohsiung** Yd No: 1432 Loa 40.19 Br ex 7.12 Dght 2.693 Lbp 35.03 Br md 7.09 Dpth 3.18 Welded, 1 dk	**(B11B2FV) Fishing Vessel** Ins: 240 Compartments: 3 Ho, ER 3 Ha: (1.9 x 1.6)2 (1.3 x 0.9)ER Derricks: 2x1t; Winches: 2	**1 oil engine** driving 1 FP propeller Total Power: 456kW (620hp) 10.5kn Akasaka MA6SS 1 x 4 Stroke 6 Cy. 270 x 400 456kW (620bhp) Akasaka Tekkosho KK (Akasaka DieselLtd)-Japan AuxGen: 2 x 64kW 225V a.c

IMO / Call sign / Flag	Name / Owner / Manager / Port	Tonnage	Class	Builder / Dimensions	Type / Capacities	Machinery
7740740 - -	**YEFREMOV** - -	**638** 191 291	Class: (RS)	**1978**-09 **Khabarovskiy Sudostroitelnyy Zavod im Kirova — Khabarovsk** Yd No: 267 Loa 54.84 Br ex 9.38 Dght 3.730 Lbp 48.94 Br md - Dpth 4.73 Welded, 1 dk	**(B11A2FT) Trawler** Ins: 284 Compartments: 2 Ho, ER 2 Ha: 2 (1.5 x 1.6) Derricks: 1x3t; Winches: 1 Ice Capable	**1 oil engine** driving 1 CP propeller Total Power: 588kW (799hp) 11.5k S.K.L. 8NVD48-2 1 x 4 Stroke 8 Cy. 320 x 480 588kW (799bhp) VEB Schwermaschinenbau "KarlLiebknecht" (SKL)-Magdeburg AuxGen: 3 x 88kW
8006024 *YB5169* -	**YEFTAS** *ex* Kinsen Maru *-1995* **PT Maroci Line** - *Surabaya* *Indonesia*	*596* 351 400	Class: (KI)	**1980**-03 **K.K. Yoshida Zosen Kogyo — Arida** Yd No: 331 Loa 54.40 Br ex - Dght 3.101 Lbp 50.02 Br md 9.40 Dpth 4.81 Welded, 1 dk	**(A31A2GX) General Cargo Ship**	**1 oil engine** driving 1 FP propeller Total Power: 588kW (799hp) Makita 6SLH627 1 x 4 Stroke 6 Cy. 275 x 450 588kW (799bhp) Makita Diesel Co Ltd-Japan
8951920 - -	**YEGOR KLIMANOV** - **Trawl Co (OOO Firma 'Tral')** -	**127** 49 9	Class: (RS)	**1974**-06 **Bakinskiy Sudostroitelnyy Zavod im Vano Sturua — Baku** Yd No: 299 Loa 34.65 Br ex 5.70 Dght 1.520 Lbp 30.00 Br md 5.30 Dpth 2.55 Welded, 1 dk	**(A37B2PS) Passenger Ship**	**2 oil engines** geared to sc. shafts driving 2 FP propellers Total Power: 464kW (630hp) 14.5k Barnaultransmash 3D12A 2 x Vee 4 Stroke 12 Cy. 150 x 180 each-232kW (315bhp) Barnaultransmash-Barnaul Fuel: 3.0 (d.f.)
9073567 *EPBG8* -	**YEKTA 110** *ex* Yekta *-2012* *ex* Kyoshin Maru No. 12 *-2011* **Abbas Daryanavard** - *Iran* MMSI: 422022400	*199* 100 629		**1993**-04 **Yamakawa Zosen Tekko K.K. — Kagoshima** Yd No: 715 Loa 58.87 Br ex 9.82 Dght 3.210 Lbp 56.76 Br md 9.80 Dpth 5.50 Welded, 1 dk	**(A31A2GX) General Cargo Ship** Grain: 1,241	**1 oil engine** driving 1 FP propeller Total Power: 625kW (850hp) Hanshin LH26G 1 x 4 Stroke 6 Cy. 260 x 440 625kW (850bhp) The Hanshin Diesel Works Ltd-Japan
9111785 *CB5536* -	**YELCHO I** - **Blumar Seafoods** - *Valparaiso* *Chile* MMSI: 725000311 Official number: 2867	**1,196** 388 1,590 T/cm 6.2		**1995**-06 **Astilleros Marco Chilena Ltda. — Iquique** Yd No: 210 Loa 64.00 (BB) Br ex 12.00 Dght 5.675 Lbp 59.00 Br md 11.80 Dpth 7.30 Welded, 2 dks	**(B11B2FV) Fishing Vessel**	**1 oil engine** with clutches & sr geared to sc. shaft driving 1 CP propeller Total Power: 2,470kW (3,358hp) 15.0kn Deutz SBV12M628 1 x Vee 4 Stroke 12 Cy. 240 x 280 2470kW (3358bhp) Motoren Werke Mannheim AG (MWM)-Mannheim Thrusters: 1 Thwart. FP thruster (f); 1 Tunnel thruster (a) Fuel: 127.0 (d.f.)
9613616 *3FV06* -	**YELENA** - **New Glory Shipping SA** Koyo Kaiun Asia Pte Ltd SatCom: Inmarsat C 437081310 *Panama* *Panama* MMSI: 370813000 Official number: 4276211	**7,271** 3,740 12,101 T/cm 21.2	Class: NK	**2011**-06 **Asakawa Zosen K.K. — Imabari** Yd No: 581 Loa 123.52 (BB) Br ex 20.22 Dght 8.464 Lbp 116.00 Br md 20.20 Dpth 10.85 Welded, 1 dk	**(A12B2TR) Chemical/Products Tanker** Double Hull (13F) Liq: 12,151; Liq (Oil): 12,151 Cargo Heating Coils Compartments: 18 Wing Ta, 2 Wing Slop Ta, ER 20 Cargo Pump (s): 14x200m³/hr, 6x300m³/hr Manifold: Bow/CM: 68.8m	**1 oil engine** driving 1 FP propeller Total Power: 4,440kW (6,037hp) 14.5kn MAN-B&W 6S35MC 1 x 2 Stroke 6 Cy. 350 x 1400 4440kW (6037bhp) Makita Corp-Japan AuxGen: 3 x a.c Thrusters: 1 Tunnel thruster (f) Fuel: 118.0 (d.f.) 631.0 (r.f.)
6928577 *HC4054* -	**YELISAVA** *ex* Sea Hunter *-1990* *ex* Anne M *-1990* **Pesquera Yelisava SA** Pesdel Compania Ltda SatCom: Inmarsat M 673509537 *Guayaquil* *Ecuador* Official number: P-00-0809	**606** 302 -	Class: (HR)	**1969 J M Martinac Shipbuilding Corp — Tacoma WA** Yd No: 178 Shortened-1980 Loa 50.40 Br ex 10.67 Dght 4.650 Lbp - Br md 10.37 Dpth 4.17 Welded, 2 dks	**(B11B2FV) Fishing Vessel** Ins: 855	**1 oil engine** reverse reduction geared to sc. shaft driving 1 FP propeller Total Power: 2,059kW (2,799hp) 14.0kn EMD (Electro-Motive) 16-645 1 x Vee 2 Stroke 16 Cy. 230 x 254 2059kW (2799bhp) General Motors Corp-USA Fuel: 158.5
8832100 *UEAT* -	**YELIZOVO** - **OOO 'Galis'** - *Petropavlovsk-Kamchatskiy* *Russia* MMSI: 273840400	**690** 234 207	Class: RS	**1990**-06 **Zavod 'Nikolayevsk-na-Amure' — Nikolayevsk-na-Amure** Yd No: 1273 Loa 52.58 Br ex 9.48 Dght 3.830 Lbp 46.69 Br md 9.30 Dpth 5.18 Welded	**(B11A2FS) Stern Trawler** Ins: 210	**1 oil engine** driving 1 FP propeller Total Power: 588kW (799hp) 11.5kn S.K.L. 6NVD48A-2U 1 x 4 Stroke 6 Cy. 320 x 480 588kW (799bhp) VEB Schwermaschinenbau "KarlLiebknecht" (SKL)-Magdeburg AuxGen: 3 x 150kW a.c Fuel: 136.0 (d.f.)
7828310 *DUA6358* -	**YELLOW BELL 2** *ex* Fukuichi Maru No. 1 *-1993* *ex* Hofuku Maru No. 31 *-1984* **Frabelle Fishing Corp** - *Manila* *Philippines* Official number: MNLD000921	*147* 97 -		**1979**-05 **Minami-Kyushu Zosen KK — Ichikikushikino KS** Yd No: 320 L reg 31.90 Br ex - Dght 2.390 Lbp 31.09 Br md 7.00 Dpth 2.80 Welded, 1 dk	**(B11B2FV) Fishing Vessel**	**1 oil engine** reverse geared to sc. shaft driving 1 FP propeller Total Power: 1,295kW (1,761hp) Akasaka AH30R 1 x 4 Stroke 6 Cy. 300 x 480 1295kW (1761bhp) Akasaka Tekkosho KK (Akasaka DieselLtd)-Japan
8428557 - -	**YELLOW BIRD** - **United Cruise Ltd** - *Nassau* *Bahamas* Official number: 384565	*189* 185 -		**1978 Caribbean Boats Ltd. — St. George's** Loa - Br ex 9.78 Dght - Lbp 19.66 Br md 9.76 Dpth - Welded, 3 dks	**(A37B2PS) Passenger Ship**	**2 oil engines** driving 2 FP propellers Total Power: 118kW (160hp) 7.0kn Perkins 2 x 4 Stroke 4 Cy. 106 x 152 each-59kW (80bhp) Perkins Engines Ltd.-Peterborough
8814495 - -	**YELLOW FIN** - **Government of The Republic of India (Director of Fishery & Survey of India)** - *Mumbai* *India* Official number: 2378	**310** 93 164	Class: IR (NK)	**1989**-02 **Niigata Engineering Co Ltd — Niigata NI** Yd No: 2115 Loa 35.76 (BB) Br ex - Dght 2.854 Lbp 31.39 Br md 7.60 Dpth 3.10 Welded, 1 dk	**(B12D2FR) Fishery Research Vessel** Ins: 117	**1 oil engine** with clutches, flexible couplings & sr reverse geared to sc. shaft driving 1 FP propeller Total Power: 588kW (799hp) 10.5kn Niigata 6NSC-M 1 x 4 Stroke 6 Cy. 190 x 260 588kW (799bhp) Niigata Engineering Co Ltd-Japan AuxGen: 2 x 208kW a.c
9607289 *9HA2801* -	**YELLOW FIN** - **Yellow Fin Shipping Ltd** Finner Ship Management Ltd SatCom: Inmarsat C 421588710 *Valletta* *Malta* MMSI: 215887000 Official number: 9607289	**33,042** 19,132 56,780 T/cm 58.8	Class: BV GL	**2011**-09 **Yangfan Group Co Ltd — Zhoushan ZJ** Yd No: 2176 Loa 189.98 Br ex - Dght 12.800 Lbp 185.64 Br md 32.26 Dpth 18.00 Welded, 1 dk	**(A21A2BC) Bulk Carrier** Grain: 71,634; Bale: 68,200 Compartments: 5 Ho, ER 5 Ha: ER Cranes: 4x30t	**1 oil engine** driving 1 FP propeller Total Power: 9,480kW (12,889hp) 14.2kn MAN-B&W 6S50MC-C 1 x 2 Stroke 6 Cy. 500 x 2000 9480kW (12889bhp) STX (Dalian) Engine Co Ltd-China
7313171 *DUWA4* -	**YELLOW GOLD** *ex* Zao Maru *-1992* *ex* Koei Maru No. 32 *-1988* *ex* Tenyo Maru No. 37 *-1986* *ex* Otori Maru No. 28 *-1982* **Zamboanga Universal Fishing Co** - *Zamboanga* *Philippines* Official number: ZAM2F00708	*339* 131 -		**1973**-03 **Kochiken Zosen — Kochi** Yd No: 435 Loa - Br ex 8.23 Dght 3.048 Lbp 44.00 Br md 8.21 Dpth 3.75 Riveted\Welded, 1 dk	**(B11B2FV) Fishing Vessel**	**1 oil engine** driving 1 FP propeller Total Power: 883kW (1,201hp) Hanshin 6LU32G 1 x 4 Stroke 6 Cy. 320 x 510 883kW (1201bhp) Hanshin Nainenki Kogyo-Japan
9499010 *V2QE8* -	**YELLOW MOON** *ex* Yingchow *-2013* *ex* Yellow Moon *-2012* *ex* Genius *-2010* **Yellow Moon Shipping Ltd** Reederei Gebr Winter GmbH & Co KG *Saint John's* *Antigua & Barbuda* MMSI: 305646000 Official number: 3074	**9,954** 5,117 13,777 T/cm 28.0	Class: NK (GL)	**2008**-06 **Jiangsu Eastern Heavy Industry Co Ltd — Jingjiang JS** Yd No: 02C-031 Loa 147.79 (BB) Br ex - Dght 8.510 Lbp 140.30 Br md 23.25 Dpth 11.50 Welded, 1 dk	**(A33A2CC) Container Ship (Fully Cellular)** Grain: 16,405; Bale: 16,084 TEU 1022 C Ho 334 TEU C Dk 688 TEU incl 220 ref C Cranes: 2x45t	**1 oil engine** driving 1 CP propeller Total Power: 9,480kW (12,889hp) 19.6kn MAN-B&W 6S50MC-C 1 x 2 Stroke 6 Cy. 500 x 2000 9480kW (12889bhp) (new engine 2008) Yichang Marine Diesel Engine Co Ltd-China AuxGen: 3 x 910kW 450V a.c Thrusters: 1 Tunnel thruster (f) Fuel: 1310.0
9276250 *D5EX9* -	**YELLOW RAY** *ex* Belsize Park *-2014* **Lombard Corporate Finance (December 3) Ltd** Eastern Pacific Shipping Pte Ltd *Monrovia* *Liberia* MMSI: 636016192 Official number: 16192	**11,590** 6,119 19,937 T/cm 28.8	Class: NK	**2003**-06 **Usuki Shipyard Co Ltd — Usuki OT** Yd No: 1681 Loa 145.53 (BB) Br ex - Dght 9.715 Lbp 137.00 Br md 23.70 Dpth 13.35 Welded, 1 dk	**(A12B2TR) Chemical/Products Tanker** Double Hull (13F) Liq: 22,175; Liq (Oil): 22,075 Cargo Heating Coils Compartments: 22 Wing Ta, 2 Wing Slop Ta, ER 22 Cargo Pump (s): 16x310m³/hr, 6x200m³/hr Manifold: Bow/CM: 74.3m	**1 oil engine** driving 1 FP propeller Total Power: 6,487kW (8,820hp) 14.6kn B&W 6S42MC 1 x 2 Stroke 6 Cy. 420 x 1764 6487kW (8820bhp) Kawasaki Heavy Industries Ltd-Japan AuxGen: 3 x 440kW a.c Thrusters: 1 Thwart. FP thruster (f) Fuel: 95.0 (d.f.) 976.0 (r.f.)

330850 *4RL2*	**YELLOW RIVER** *ex* Qatar Swift *-2009* *ex* Emirates Meru *-2008* *ex* Yellow River *-2007* **Beheermaatschappij ms Marnestroom BV** Universal Shipping BV SatCom: Inmarsat C 421034410 *Limassol* *Cyprus* MMSI: 210344000	**9,940** 5,020 13,702 T/cm 28.0	Class: GL	**2007-06 Qingshan Shipyard — Wuhan HB** Yd No: 20040316 Loa 147.87 (BB) Br ex 23.45 Dght 8.510 Lbp 140.30 Br md 23.25 Dpth 11.50 Welded, 1 dk	**(A33A2CC) Container Ship (Fully Cellular)** Grain: 16,000; Bale: 16,000 TEU 1114 C Ho 334 TEU C Dk 780 incl 220 ref C Compartments: 5 Cell Ho, ER Cranes: 2x45t	**1 oil engine** reduction geared to sc. shaft driving 1 CP propeller Total Power: 9,730kW (13,229hp) 19.6kn MAN-B&W 7L58/64 1 x 4 Stroke 7 Cy. 580 x 640 9730kW (13229bhp) MAN B&W Diesel AG-Augsburg AuxGen: 3 x 570kW 60Hz a.c, 1 x 2000kW 60Hz a.c Thrusters: 1 Tunnel thruster (f) Fuel: 235.0 (d.f.) 1375.0 (r.f.)
665097	**YELLOW SEA 1** **Yellow Sea Marine Petroleum Services** - *Alexandria* *Egypt* Official number: 8586	**159** 96 -	Class: IS (Class contemplated)	**2012-04 Nour Aleslam — Rashid** Yd No: 22 Loa 28.00 Br ex - Dght 3.000 Lbp 26.80 Br md 7.00 Dpth 3.50 Welded, 1 dk	**(B21A20C) Crew/Supply Vessel**	**2 oil engines** reduction geared to sc. shafts driving 2 Propellers G.M. (Detroit Diesel) 12V-71 2 x Vee 2 Stroke 12 Cy. 108 x 127 General Motors Corp-USA
423279 *CRR1*	**YELLOWFIN** *ex* Jackson Yellowfin *-2011* *ex* Rigdon Yellowfin *-2007* **Unifin Financiera SAPI de CV SOFOM ENR** Marinsa de Mexico SA de CV *Isla del Carmen* *Mexico* MMSI: 345070291 Official number: 04001347427-2	**320** 96 321	Class: AB	**2007-04** Yd No: 83 Loa 47.24 Br ex - Dght 3.270 Lbp 42.67 Br md 8.84 Dpth 4.26 Welded, 1 dk	**(B21A20C) Crew/Supply Vessel** Hull Material: Aluminium Alloy	**4 oil engines** reduction geared to sc. shafts driving 4 FP propellers Total Power: 5,296kW (7,200hp) Cummins KTA-50-M2 4 x Vee 4 Stroke 16 Cy. 159 x 159 each-1324kW (1800bhp) Cummins Engine Co Inc-USA AuxGen: 2 x 75kW 60Hz a.c Thrusters: 1 Tunnel thruster (f) Fuel: 124.0 (d.f.)
565584 *VDE9245*	**YELLOWFIN** **Penn Maritime Inc** - *Philadelphia, PA* *United States of America* MMSI: 367415160 Official number: 1219391	**499** 149 428	Class: AB	**2009-10 Thoma-Sea Shipbuilders LLC — Lockport LA** Yd No: 109 Loa 35.35 Br ex - Dght 4.320 Lbp 34.29 Br md 10.97 Dpth 5.12 Welded, 1 dk	**(B32B2SA) Articulated Pusher Tug**	**2 oil engines** reduction geared to sc. shafts driving 2 Propellers Total Power: 2,984kW (4,058hp) 12.0kn Cummins QSK60-M 2 x Vee 4 Stroke 16 Cy. 159 x 190 each-1492kW (2029bhp) Cummins Engine Co Inc-USA AuxGen: 3 x 99kW a.c Fuel: 343.0 (d.f.)
230898 *VCW2778*	**YELLOWFIN** *ex* Easy Rider *-2007* *ex* Lawaia *-1974* **State of California** - *Long Beach, CA* *United States of America* Official number: 537119	*109* 74 -		**1971 Lewis B. Maurer — Costa Mesa, Ca** L reg 21.16 Br ex - Dght - Lbp - Br md 7.29 Dpth 2.65 Welded, 1 dk	**(B11B2FV) Fishing Vessel** Hull Material: Aluminium Alloy	**1 oil engine** driving 1 FP propeller Total Power: 640kW (870hp)
220348 *GHB*	**YELLU I** *ex* Hassho Maru No. 21 *-2002* *ex* Shotoku Maru No. 15 *-1982* *ex* Katsu Maru No. 11 *-1982* **PT Yellu Mutiara** - *Surabaya* *Indonesia*	*397* 123 370	Class: KI	**1972-05 Miho Zosensho K.K. — Shimizu** Yd No: 819 Loa 50.40 Br ex 8.22 Dght 3.120 Lbp 44.00 Br md 8.20 Dpth 3.60 Welded, 1 dk	**(B11B2FV) Fishing Vessel**	**1 oil engine** driving 1 FP propeller Total Power: 736kW (1,001hp) Hanshin 6LU28 1 x 4 Stroke 6 Cy. 280 x 440 736kW (1001bhp) Hanshin Nainenki Kogyo-Japan
050670 *4GI2*	**YEMA** *ex* Rudderman *-2010* **Societe Congolaise des Industries de Raffinage (SOCIR)** - *Basseterre* *St Kitts & Nevis* MMSI: 341824000 Official number: SKN 1002160	**4,842** 1,773 6,417 T/cm 15.2	Class: AB (LR) ✠ Classed LR until 20/8/11	**1994-01 Malaysia Shipyard & Engineering Sdn Bhd — Pasir Gudang** Yd No: 058 Loa 101.60 (BB) Br ex 17.52 Dght 6.850 Lbp 95.64 Br md 17.50 Dpth 10.30 Welded, 1 dk	**(A13B2TP) Products Tanker** Double Hull (13F) Liq: 8,322; Liq (Oil): 8,322 Compartments: 10 Wing Ta, ER, 2 Wing Slop Ta 10 Cargo Pump (s): 10x350m³/hr Manifold: Bow/CM: 42.6m	**1 oil engine** with clutches, flexible couplings & sr reverse geared to sc. shaft driving 1 CP propeller Total Power: 2,700kW (3,671hp) 12.5kn Blackstone ESL16MK2 1 x Vee 4 Stroke 16 Cy. 222 x 292 2700kW (3671bhp) Mirrlees Blackstone (Stockport)Ltd.-Stockport AuxGen: 1 x 400kW 400V 50Hz a.c, 3 x 400kW 400V 50Hz a.c Boilers: AuxB (Comp) 9.2kgf/cm² (9.0bar), AuxB (o.f.) 9.2kgf/cm² (9.0bar) Thrusters: 1 Thwart. FP thruster (f) Fuel: 90.0 (d.f.) 421.0 (r.f.) 13.0pd
723074	**YEMANJA** *ex* Susin *-2009* *ex* Yori *-2009* *ex* Kotikovo *-2001* **JR Shipping Co Ltd** DMB International Co Ltd	**448** 134 207	Class: (RS)	**1986-06 Zavod 'Nikolayevsk-na-Amure' — Nikolayevsk-na-Amure** Yd No: 1241 Loa 44.88 Br ex 9.47 Dght 3.770 Lbp 39.37 Br md - Dpth 5.15 Welded, 1 dk	**(B11A2FS) Stern Trawler** Ice Capable	**1 oil engine** driving 1 FP propeller Total Power: 588kW (799hp) 11.5kn S.K.L. 6NVD48A-2U 1 x 4 Stroke 6 Cy. 320 x 480 588kW (799bhp) VEB Schwermaschinenbau "KarlLiebknecht" (SKL)-Magdeburg AuxGen: 3 x 150kW a.c
859964	**YEMELYAN PUGACHYOV** **Belgorod-Dnestrovskiy Sea Port Authority** - *Belgorod-Dnestrovskiy* *Ukraine* Official number: 903127	**182** 54 57	Class: (RS)	**1991-09 Gorokhovetskiy Sudostroitelnyy Zavod — Gorokhovets** Yd No: 254 Loa 29.30 Br ex - Dght 3.400 Lbp 27.00 Br md 8.60 Dpth 4.30 Welded, 1 dk	**(B32A2ST) Tug** Ice Capable	**2 oil engines** driving 2 FP propellers Total Power: 1,180kW (1,604hp) 11.5kn Pervomaysk 8CHNP25/34 2 x 4 Stroke 8 Cy. 250 x 340 each-590kW (802bhp) Pervomaydizelmash (PDM)-Pervomaysk
606832	**YEMIN** **Government of The Union of Myanmar (Ministry of Transport - Inland Water Transport Corp)** *Yangon* *Myanmar*	*160* - 20	Class: (BV)	**1965 Yokohama Zosen — Chiba** Yd No: 1049 Loa 30.48 Br ex 9.35 Dght 1.347 Lbp 28.30 Br md 9.15 Dpth 2.29 Welded, 1 dk	**(B34P2QV) Salvage Ship** 2 Ha: (0.9 x 0.9) (1.1 x 1.1)	**2 oil engines** driving 2 FP propellers Total Power: 440kW (598hp) 9.0kn Akasaka KA6BSS 2 x 4 Stroke 6 Cy. 230 x 360 each-220kW (299bhp) Akasaka Tekkosho KK (Akasaka DieselLtd)-Japan
089475 *VDD2918*	**YEMITZIS** *ex* Philadelphia *-1989* **Henry Marine Service Inc** - *New York, NY* *United States of America* MMSI: 367121540 Official number: 268826	*272* 81 -		**1954-01 R.T.C. Shipbuilding Corp. — Camden, NJ** Yd No: 227 Converted From: Tug-1992 Loa - Br ex - Dght 4.310 Lbp 31.49 Br md 8.29 Dpth 4.21 Welded, 1 dk	**(X11A2YP) Yacht**	**1 oil engine** reduction geared to sc. shaft driving 1 Propeller Total Power: 1,324kW (1,800hp) Fairbanks, Morse 10-38D8-1/8 1 x 2 Stroke 10 Cy. 207 x 254 1324kW (1800bhp) Fairbanks Morse & Co.-New Orleans, La
928720	**YEMOJA** **Federal Military Government of Nigeria (Federal Ministry of Science & Technology)** SatCom: Inmarsat B 331007618 *Lagos* *Nigeria*	*280* 100 263	Class: (LR) ✠ Classed LR until 25/1/89	**1981-02 Schiffswerft Gebr Schloemer Oldersum — Moormerland** Yd No: 177 Loa 36.23 (BB) Br ex 9.30 Dght 3.752 Lbp 32.47 Br md 9.20 Dpth 4.09 Welded	**(B11A2FS) Stern Trawler** Ins: 66	**1 oil engine** sr geared to sc. shaft driving 1 CP propeller Total Power: 941kW (1,279hp) Deutz SBA8M528 1 x 4 Stroke 8 Cy. 220 x 280 941kW (1279bhp) Kloeckner Humboldt Deutz AG-West Germany AuxGen: 1 x 400kW 400V 50Hz a.c, 1 x 240kW 400V 50Hz a.c Thrusters: 1 Thwart. FP thruster
817318 *UFZ5*	**YEN DE** *ex* Hamanako *-2013* *ex* Toko Maru *-2004* *ex* Kocho Maru *-1995* **Hongkong Yinde Shipping Co Ltd** Boyu International Ship Management Co Ltd *Phnom Penh* *Cambodia* MMSI: 514122000	*1,475* 800 1,585		**1988-11 Shin Kurushima Dockyard Co. Ltd. — Hashihama, Imabari** Yd No: 2611 Loa 74.72 (BB) Br ex - Dght 4.091 Lbp 70.00 Br md 12.00 Dpth 7.10 Welded	**(A31A2GX) General Cargo Ship** Grain: 3,288; Bale: 3,136 Compartments: 1 Ta, ER	**1 oil engine** sr reverse geared to sc. shaft driving 1 FP propeller Total Power: 1,324kW (1,800hp) Hanshin LH31G 1 x 4 Stroke 6 Cy. 310 x 530 1324kW (1800bhp) The Hanshin Diesel Works Ltd-Japan
342500 *ESW*	**YENEGOA OCEAN** *ex* Nico Shindagha *-2008* *ex* Spartan Tide *-1991* **ESL Integrated Services Ltd** - *Panama* *Panama* Official number: 37696DI	**1,080** 457 1,173	Class: (LR) (NV) ✠ Classed LR until 21/4/91	**1975-07 Hall, Russell & Co. Ltd. — Aberdeen** Yd No: 967 Loa 58.32 Br ex 13.09 Dght 4.762 Lbp 52.68 Br md 12.81 Dpth 5.95 Welded, 1 dk	**(B21B20T) Offshore Tug/Supply Ship**	**2 oil engines** geared to sc. shafts driving 2 CP propellers Total Power: 4,230kW (5,752hp) 13.0kn EMD (Electro-Motive) 16-645-E5 2 x Vee 2 Stroke 16 Cy. 230 x 254 each-2115kW (2876bhp) General Motors Corp-USA AuxGen: 3 x 240kW 415V 60Hz a.c Thrusters: 1 Thwart. FP thruster (f) Fuel: 293.5 (d.f.)
545522 *CTE7*	**YENER-C** *ex* Balaban Kardesler 1 *-2008* **Ciner Teksil Petrol Madencilik ve Nakliyat Insaat Taah Ltd Sti** - *Istanbul* *Turkey* MMSI: 271002690 Official number: TUGS1606	**2,501** 947 2,755	Class: TL	**2008-10 in Turkey** Yd No: 1 Loa 80.00 Br ex - Dght 3.453 Lbp 70.20 Br md 15.93 Dpth 4.50 Welded, 1 dk	**(A36A2PR) Passenger/Ro-Ro Ship (Vehicles)** Stern door/ramp (centre)	**2 oil engines** reduction geared to sc. shafts driving 2 Propellers Total Power: 2,750kW (3,738hp) Mitsubishi S16R-MPTK 2 x Vee 4 Stroke 16 Cy. 170 x 180 each-1375kW (1869bhp) Mitsubishi Heavy Industries Ltd-Japan

8658152 *TC9325* -	**YENI AKSU** **Ercan Kara Adi Ortakligi** - *Istanbul* *Turkey* Official number: TUGS1136	**197** 59 -		**1998-12 Gursan — Tuzla** Yd No: 005 Loa 36.90 Br ex - Dght 1.600 Lbp 34.85 Br md 7.20 Dpth 2.55 Welded, 1 dk	**(A37B2PS) Passenger Ship**	**2 oil engines** reduction geared to sc. shafts driving 2 Propellers Total Power: 1,118kW (1,520hp) MAN 2 x each-559kW (760bhp) MAN Nutzfahrzeuge AG-Nuernberg
9089188 *TC9068* -	**YENI MENDERES** **Abdullah ve Yasin Inandi** S S Turizm ve Yolcu Deniz Tasiyicilar Kooperatifi (TURYOL) *Istanbul* *Turkey* MMSI: 271010271	**252** 76 -		**1997-01 at Karadeniz Eregli** Loa 37.70 Br ex - Dght 1.560 Lbp - Br md 7.50 Dpth 2.56 Welded, 1 dk	**(A37B2PS) Passenger Ship** Passengers: unberthed: 500	**2 oil engines** driving 2 Propellers Total Power: 736kW (1,000hp) 14.0k Iveco Aifo 2 x 4 Stroke each-368kW (500bhp) IVECO AIFO S.p.A.-Pregnana Milanese
6720200 *TCAP2* -	**YENIGUL KARDESLER-II** *ex* Alipasa-4 *ex* Haldun **Mehmet ve Celal Gul Abdullah** - *Istanbul* *Turkey* MMSI: 271002357 Official number: 3774	**386** 206 668		**1967 Denizcilik Anonim Sirketi Beykoz Tersanesi — Beykoz** Yd No: 11 Loa 50.65 Br ex 7.17 Dght 2.601 Lbp 46.46 Br md 7.15 Dpth 3.13 Welded, 1 dk	**(A31A2GX) General Cargo Ship**	**1 oil engine** driving 1 FP propeller Total Power: 221kW (300hp) S.K.L. 6NVD3 1 x 4 Stroke 6 Cy. 240 x 360 221kW (300bhp) VEB Schwermaschinenbau "KarlLiebknecht" (SKL)-Magdeburg
5395589 *TC5887* -	**YENIKOY** **TDI Sehir Hatlari Isletmesi** - *Istanbul* *Turkey* Official number: 55	*483* 264 -	Class: (TL) (GL)	**1952-05 Verschure & Co's Scheepswerf & Machinefabriek NV — Amsterdam** Yd No: C0160 Loa 49.00 Br ex 9.83 Dght 2.001 Lbp 46.98 Br md 8.21 Dpth 3.12 Welded, 1 dk	**(A37B2PS) Passenger Ship**	**2 oil engines** driving 2 FP propellers Total Power: 662kW (900hp) 12.0k Sulzer 5TD2 2 x 2 Stroke 5 Cy. 290 x 500 each-331kW (450bhp) NV Koninklijke Mij 'De Schelde-Netherlands
9629586 *V7AU8* -	**YENISEI RIVER** **Navajo Marine Ltd** Dynagas Ltd *Majuro* *Marshall Islands* MMSI: 538005072 Official number: 5072	**100,236** 33,759 84,604	Class: LR ✠ **100A1** SS 07/2013 liquefied gas tanker Ship Type 2G, methane (LNG) in membrane tanks, maximum vapour pressure 0.25 bar, minimum temperature minus 163 degree C, Shipright (SDA,FDA Plus (40,NA),FDA ICE,CM,ACS (B)), *IWS LI ECO (IHM) Winterisation H (-30), D (-30) Ice Class 1A FS at draught of 12.90m Max/min draught fwd 12.90/8.90m Max/min draught aft 13.20/8.90m Required power 18751kw, installed power 24900kw ✠ **LMC** **UMS** Eq.Ltr: A*; Cable: 809.5/107.0 U3 (a)	**2013-07 Hyundai Heavy Industries Co Ltd — Ulsan** Yd No: 2556 Loa 288.10 (BB) Br ex 44.23 Dght 12.500 Lbp 275.00 Br md 44.20 Dpth 26.00 Welded, 1 dk	**(A11A2TN) LNG Tanker** Double Hull Liq (Gas): 154,880 4 x Gas Tank (s); 4 membrane Gas Transport horizontal Ice Capable	**4 diesel electric oil engines** driving 2 gen. each 11290kW 6600V a.c 2 gen. each 5650kW 6600V a.c Connecting to 2 elec. motors each (12450kW) driving 1 FP propeller Total Power: 34,280kW (46,608hp) 19.5k Wartsila 12V50D 1 x Vee 4 Stroke 12 Cy. 500 x 580 11290kW (15350bhp) Wartsila Hyundai Engine Co Ltd-South Korea Wartsila 6L50D 2 x 4 Stroke 6 Cy. 500 x 580 each-5850kW (7954bhp) Wartsila Hyundai Engine Co Ltd-South Korea Boilers: e (ex.g.) 15.6kgf/cm² (15.3bar), AuxB (o.f.) 12.3kgf/cm² (12.1bar) Thrusters: 1 Thwart. FP thruster (f)
7101944 - -	**YENISEY** - -	*1,361* 473 526	Class: (RS)	**1970-07 Zelenodolskiy Sudostroitelnyy Zavod im. "Gorkogo" — Zelenodolsk** Yd No: 510 Loa 72.09 Br ex 10.83 Dght 3.620 Lbp 64.80 Br md - Dpth 5.72 Welded	**(B11A2FT) Trawler** Grain: 677 Compartments: 2 Ho, ER 2 Ha: 2 (2.5 x 2.5) Derricks: 4x3t; Winches: 4 Ice Capable	**1 oil engine** driving 1 FP propeller Total Power: 736kW (1,001hp) 12.3k S.K.L. 8NVD48A 1 x 4 Stroke 8 Cy. 320 x 480 736kW (1001bhp) VEB Schwermaschinenbau "KarlLiebknecht" (SKL)-Magdeburg AuxGen: 2 x 300kW, 1 x 50kW Fuel: 113.0 (d.f.)
8311168 *V7MF3* -	**YENISEY** *ex* Fesco Yenisey *-2013* *ex* Yenisey *-2007* *ex* Yenisei *-2003* *ex* C. A. Margaronis *-1988* **Yenisey Maritime Ltd** Far-Eastern Shipping Co (FESCO) (Dalnevostochnoye Morskoye Parokhodstvo) *Majuro* *Marshall Islands* MMSI: 538002847 Official number: 2847	**22,629** 14,005 37,178 T/cm 45.7	Class: RS (LR) ✠ Classed LR until 11/11/03	**1985-01 Hyundai Heavy Industries Co Ltd — Ulsan** Yd No: 299 Loa 186.70 (BB) Br ex 28.45 Dght 11.046 Lbp 178.42 Br md 28.40 Dpth 15.60 Welded, 1 dk	**(A21A2BC) Bulk Carrier** Grain: 52,131; Bale: 46,092 TEU 874 Compartments: 5 Ho, ER 5 Ha: 5 (19.0 x 14.4)ER Cranes: 4x25t Ice Capable	**1 oil engine** driving 1 FP propeller Total Power: 7,950kW (10,809hp) 13.0k Sulzer 5RTA5 1 x 2 Stroke 5 Cy. 580 x 1700 7950kW (10809bhp) Hyundai Engine & Machinery Co Ltd-South Korea AuxGen: 3 x 540kW 450V 60Hz a.c Boilers: AuxB (o.f.) 8.3kgf/cm² (8.1bar), AuxB (ex.g.) 8.3kgf/cm² (8.1bar) Fuel: 1725.0 (r.f.)
7417848 *6MVX* -	**YEO RAE 33** *ex* O Yang No. 52 *-1997* *ex* Kwang Myung No. 86 *-1983* **Yeo Rae Fisheries Co Ltd** - *Busan* *South Korea* Official number: 9512145-6260006	*433* 222 514	Class: (KR)	**1974-07 Dae Sun Shipbuilding & Engineering Co Ltd — Busan** Yd No: 164 Loa 55.50 Br ex 9.02 Dght 3.598 Lbp 49.05 Br md 9.00 Dpth 3.94 Riveted\Welded, 1 dk	**(B11B2FV) Fishing Vessel** Ins: 323 3 Ha: 2 (1.3 x 0.9) (1.8 x 1.8)	**1 oil engine** driving 1 FP propeller Total Power: 1,177kW (1,600hp) 13.0k Niigata 6LA3 1 x 4 Stroke 6 Cy. 310 x 460 1177kW (1600bhp) Niigata Engineering Co Ltd-Japan AuxGen: 2 x 200kW 225V a.c
8881008 *DSDG8* -	**YEO SAN** *ex* Chun Ryong *-1998* **Shinsung Shipping Co Ltd** - *Jeju* *South Korea* MMSI: 440394000 Official number: JJR-940553	**1,975** 868 2,878	Class: KR	**1994-07 Shinyoung Shipbuilding Industry Co Ltd — Yeosu** Yd No: 173 Loa 85.50 Br ex - Dght 5.147 Lbp 78.00 Br md 13.40 Dpth 6.20 Welded, 1 dk	**(A31A2GX) General Cargo Ship** Grain: 3,064; Bale: 2,933 2 Ha: ER 2 (20.4 x 10.1)	**1 oil engine** reduction geared to sc. shaft driving 1 FP propeller Total Power: 1,261kW (1,714hp) 11.0k Alpha 6L28/3 1 x 4 Stroke 6 Cy. 280 x 320 1261kW (1714bhp) Ssangyong Heavy Industries Co Ltd-South Korea
9300647 *YJUM6* -	**YEO TIDE** **Tidewater Marine International Inc** Tidewater Marine International Inc *Port Vila* *Vanuatu* MMSI: 576976000 Official number: 1609	**1,868** 588 1,948	Class: AB	**2005-01 Pan-United Marine Ltd — Singapore** Yd No: 151 Loa 64.80 Br ex - Dght 4.200 Lbp 63.00 Br md 16.00 Dpth 5.80 Welded, 1 dk	**(B21B20A) Anchor Handling Tug Supply**	**2 oil engines** geared to sc. shafts driving 2 CP propellers Total Power: 5,208kW (7,080hp) 13.0k MaK 8M2 1 x 4 Stroke 8 Cy. 255 x 400 2604kW (3540bhp) Caterpillar Motoren GmbH & Co. KG-Germany MaK 8M2 1 x 4 Stroke 8 Cy. 255 x 400 2604kW (3540bhp) (made 2004) Caterpillar Motoren GmbH & Co. KG-Germany AuxGen: 2 x 800kW a.c, 2 x 370kW a.c Thrusters: 1 Tunnel thruster (f) Fuel: 510.0
8310059 *HQWR7* -	**YEOCOMICO** *ex* Trans Cargo I *-1998* *ex* Masirah Two *-1993* **Y II Shipping Co Ltd** - *San Lorenzo* *Honduras* MMSI: 334366000 Official number: L-0728081	**913** 320 1,299	Class: (AB)	**1983-04 Mickon Marine Industries Pte Ltd — Singapore** Yd No: 232 Loa - Br ex - Dght 2.879 Lbp 57.92 Br md 13.73 Dpth 3.69 Welded, 1 dk	**(A35D2RL) Landing Craft** Bow door/ramp Len: 6.71 Wid: 6.71 Swl: 50 Lane-Wid: 2.75 Cars: 55 TEU 54 C. 54/20' (40')	**2 oil engines** reverse reduction geared to sc. shafts driving 2 FP propellers Total Power: 764kW (1,038hp) 10.5k Caterpillar 3412PC 2 x Vee 4 Stroke 12 Cy. 137 x 152 each-382kW (519bhp) Caterpillar Tractor Co-USA AuxGen: 3 x 80kW Thrusters: 1 Thwart. FP thruster (f)
8816326 - -	**YEOMAN** *ex* Tolo *-1989* **SMS Towage Ltd** Specialist Marine Services Ltd *Hull* *United Kingdom*	*188* 55 100	Class: LR (BV) **100A1** SS 07/2012 tug United Kingdom coastal waters, within 60 miles from a safe haven **LMC**	**1989-04 Imamura Zosen — Kure** Yd No: 337 Loa 24.60 Br ex 9.15 Dght 3.501 Lbp 19.00 Br md 8.50 Dpth 4.70 Welded, 1 dk	**(B32A2ST) Tug**	**2 oil engines** with clutches, flexible couplings & reduction geared to sc. shafts driving 2 FP propellers Total Power: 2,206kW (3,000hp) 12.2k Niigata 6L25CX 2 x 4 Stroke 6 Cy. 250 x 320 each-1103kW (1500bhp) Niigata Engineering Co Ltd-Japan AuxGen: 2 x 128kW 380V a.c

7422881 **YEOMAN BANK** *ELOG5* *ex* Salmonpool *-1990* - **Holmin Ltd** Aggregate Industries Ltd SatCom: Inmarsat A 1245550 *Monrovia* *Liberia* MMSI: 636009548 Official number: 9548	**24,870** Class: NV (LR) 15,182 ✠ Classed LR until 9/90 38,997 T/cm 50.8	**1982-05 Eleusis Shipyards S.A. — Eleusis** Yd No: 10011 Converted From: Bulk Carrier-1991 Loa 204.96 (BB) Br ex 27.26 Dght 11.372 Lbp 195.46 Br md 27.21 Dpth 16.01 Welded, 1 dk	**(A23A2BD) Bulk Carrier, Self-discharging** Grain: 54,688; Bale: 45,802 Compartments: 7 Ho, ER 7 Ha: (9.0 x 12.6)6 (9.6 x 12.6)ER	**1 oil engine** driving 1 FP propeller Total Power: 10,445kW (14,201hp) 15.5kn Sulzer 6RD90 1 x 2 Stroke 6 Cy. 900 x 1550 10445kW (14201bhp) Sumitomo Heavy Industries Ltd-Japan AuxGen: 2 x 715kW 440V 60Hz a.c, 3 x 450kW 440V 60Hz a.c Thrusters: 1 Tunnel thruster (f) Fuel: 254.0 (d.f.) (Heating Coils) 2142.0 (r.f.) 54.0pd
8912297 **YEOMAN BONTRUP** *C6JQ9* *ex* Western Bridge *-2002* - **Western Bridge (Shipping) Ltd** Aggregate Industries UK Ltd SatCom: Inmarsat C 430800378 *Nassau* *Bahamas* MMSI: 308918000 Official number: 716338	**55,695** Class: LR 26,186 ✠ **100A1** SS 01/2011 96,725 bulk carrier T/cm ESP 84.6 ✠ **LMC** **UMS** Eq.Ltr: T†; Cable: 715.0/87.0 U3	**1991-01 Hashihama Shipbuilding Co Ltd — Tadotsu KG** (Hull) Yd No: 871 **1991-01 Tsuneishi Shipbuilding Co Ltd — Fukuyama HS** Yd No: 643 Loa 249.90 (BB) Br ex 38.07 Dght 15.019 Lbp 239.00 Br md 38.00 Dpth 21.50 Welded, 1 dk	**(A23A2BD) Bulk Carrier, Self-discharging** Grain: 89,896 Compartments: 5 Ho, ER 10 Ha: 10 (9.4 x 26.4)ER	**1 oil engine** driving 1 FP propeller Total Power: 15,402kW (20,941hp) 15.0kn B&W 6S70MC 1 x 2 Stroke 6 Cy. 700 x 2674 15402kW (20941bhp) Kawasaki Heavy Industries Ltd-Japan AuxGen: 2 x 1500kW 450V 60Hz a.c, 2 x 800kW 450V 60Hz a.c Boilers: AuxB (Comp) 7.0kgf/cm² (6.9bar), AuxB (o.f.) 7.0kgf/cm² (6.9bar) Thrusters: 1 Thwart. CP thruster (f); 1 Tunnel thruster (a) Fuel: 118.0 (d.f.) 3158.0 (r.f.)
8912302 **YEOMAN BRIDGE** *C6JY9* *ex* Eastern Bridge *-2000* - **Holmin Ltd** Aggregate Industries Ltd SatCom: Inmarsat A 1103652 *Nassau* *Bahamas* MMSI: 308919000 Official number: 716435	**55,695** Class: LR 26,186 ✠ **100A1** SS 05/2010 96,772 bulk carrier T/cm ESP 84.6 ✠ **LMC** **UMS** Eq.Ltr: T†; Cable: 715.0/87.0 U3	**1991-04 Hashihama Shipbuilding Co Ltd — Tadotsu KG** (Hull) Yd No: 872 **1991-02 Tsuneishi Shipbuilding Co Ltd — Fukuyama HS** Yd No: 644 Loa 249.90 (BB) Br ex 38.07 Dght 15.019 Lbp 239.00 Br md 38.00 Dpth 21.50 Welded, 1 dk	**(A23A2BD) Bulk Carrier, Self-discharging** Grain: 89,896 Compartments: 5 Ho, ER 10 Ha: 10 (9.4 x 26.4)ER	**1 oil engine** driving 1 FP propeller Total Power: 15,402kW (20,941hp) 15.0kn B&W 6S70MC 1 x 2 Stroke 6 Cy. 700 x 2674 15402kW (20941bhp) Kawasaki Heavy Industries Ltd-Japan AuxGen: 2 x 1500kW 450V 60Hz a.c, 2 x 800kW 450V 60Hz a.c Boilers: AuxB (Comp) 7.0kgf/cm² (6.9bar), AuxB (o.f.) 7.0kgf/cm² (6.9bar) Thrusters: 1 Thwart. CP thruster (f) Fuel: 118.0 (d.f.) 3166.0 (r.f.) 56.2pd
9167679 **YEON AM** *DSNY3* *ex* Trust Busan *-2007* *ex* Asia Harmony *-2004* - **Han Kook Capital Co Ltd** Shinsung Shipping Co Ltd *Jeju* *South Korea* MMSI: 440416000 Official number: JJR-042113	**4,690** Class: KR (NK) 2,069 6,175 T/cm 13.4	**1997-10 Sanyo Zosen K.K. — Onomichi** Yd No: 1081 Loa 96.70 Br ex - Dght 7.346 Lbp 85.80 Br md 17.40 Dpth 11.60 Welded, 1 dk	**(A31A2GX) General Cargo Ship** Grain: 10,412; Bale: 9,680 Compartments: 2 Ho, ER 2 Ha: (14.7 x 12.6) (28.0 x 12.6)ER Cranes: 2x31t; Derricks: 1x30t	**1 oil engine** driving 1 FP propeller Total Power: 2,427kW (3,300hp) 12.0kn Hanshin LH41L 1 x 4 Stroke 6 Cy. 410 x 800 2427kW (3300bhp) The Hanshin Diesel Works Ltd-Japan
7405302 **YEON JIN** *D900* *ex* Riyo Maru *-1984* - **O Yang Shipping Co Ltd** *Yeosu* *South Korea* Official number: YSR-746617	**154** Class: KR - 53	**1974-06 Shin Yamamoto Shipbuilding & Engineering Co Ltd — Kochi KC** Yd No: 181 Loa 27.06 Br ex 8.03 Dght 2.591 Lbp 23.50 Br md 8.01 Dpth 3.61 Riveted\Welded, 1 dk	**(B32A2ST) Tug**	**2 oil engines** driving 2 FP propellers Total Power: 986kW (1,340hp) 9.8kn Niigata 6MG20AX 2 x 4 Stroke 6 Cy. 200 x 260 each-493kW (670bhp) Niigata Engineering Co Ltd-Japan AuxGen: 2 x 80kW 225V a.c
7647027 **YEON KWANG** - - **Ocean Fishery Development Administration** *Kaohsiung* *Chinese Taipei* Official number: 1895	*424* Class: (CR) 214 -	**1959 KK Kanasashi Zosen — Shizuoka SZ** Loa 45.98 Br ex 7.98 Dght 3.410 Lbp 45.22 Br md 7.80 Dpth 3.81 Welded, 1 dk	**(B11B2FV) Fishing Vessel** Ins: 481 Compartments: 5 Ho, ER 5 Ha: 5 (1.8 x 1.5)ER	**1 oil engine** driving 1 FP propeller Total Power: 809kW (1,100hp) 10.0kn Akasaka YM6SS 1 x 4 Stroke 6 Cy. 370 x 520 809kW (1100bhp) Akasaka Tekkosho KK (Akasaka DieselLtd)-Japan AuxGen: 1 x 200kW 220V a.c, 2 x 80kW 220V a.c
6827096 **YEONG JIN No. 88** *D9DK* *ex* Sam Hae No. 107 *-1989* *ex* Han Dong *-1986* - *ex* Kozan Maru *-1981* *ex* Kasei Maru *-1981* **Jung Hwan-Kyong & Besides One** - *Busan* *South Korea* Official number: BSR-690071	*350* Class: (KR) - 630	**1968 Sanyo Zosen K.K. — Onomichi** Yd No: 382 Loa 55.86 Br ex 8.72 Dght 3.412 Lbp 46.11 Br md 8.69 Dpth 3.79 Welded, 1 dk	**(A11B2TG) LPG Tanker** Liq (Gas): 450 2 x Gas Tank (s);	**1 oil engine** driving 1 FP propeller Total Power: 662kW (900hp) 11.0kn Nippon Hatsudoki HS6NV325 1 x 4 Stroke 6 Cy. 325 x 460 662kW (900bhp) Nippon Hatsudoki-Japan AuxGen: 2 x 24kW 220V d.c Fuel: 51.0 3.0pd
8629943 **YEONG LIM** - - **Yeong Lin Marine Works Co Ltd** *Busan* *South Korea*	*250* Class: (KR) - -	**1978 Suzuki Zosen — Ishinomaki** L reg 22.00 Br ex - Dght - Lbp - Br md 8.00 Dpth 2.00 Welded, 1 dk	**(B33A2DU) Dredger (unspecified)**	**1 oil engine** driving 1 FP propeller Total Power: 441kW (600hp) Yanmar 6U-ST 1 x 4 Stroke 6 Cy. 200 x 240 441kW (600bhp) Yanmar Diesel Engine Co Ltd-Japan AuxGen: 2 x 240kW 220V a.c
9688714 **YEONGJONG NO. 1** - - **Kogas Marine Co Ltd** *Incheon* *South Korea* Official number: ICR-131831	**277** Class: KR (Class contemplated) 130 166	**2013-10 DH Shipbuilding Co Ltd — Incheon** Yd No: 1301 Loa 36.50 Br ex 10.90 Dght 3.412 Lbp 31.15 Br md 10.00 Dpth 4.50 Welded, 1 dk	**(B32A2ST) Tug**	**2 oil engines** reduction geared to sc. shafts driving 2 Propellers Total Power: 3,680kW (5,004hp) 15.7kn Yanmar 6EY26 2 x 4 Stroke 6 Cy. 260 x 385 each-1840kW (2502bhp) Yanmar Diesel Engine Co Ltd-Japan Fuel: 64.0
9551870 **YEONPYEONG NO. 2** - - **Kogas Marine Co Ltd** *Incheon* *South Korea* MMSI: 440009190 Official number: ICR-092721	**273** Class: KR - 167	**2009-05 Samkwang Shipbuilding & Engineering Co Ltd — Incheon** Yd No: SKSB-180 Loa 36.50 Br ex 10.02 Dght 3.312 Lbp 32.49 Br md 10.00 Dpth 4.50 Welded, 1 dk	**(B32A2ST) Tug**	**2 oil engines** reduction geared to sc. shafts driving 2 Propellers Total Power: 3,308kW (4,498hp) Niigata 6L28HX 2 x 4 Stroke 6 Cy. 280 x 370 each-1654kW (2249bhp) Niigata Engineering Co Ltd-Japan AuxGen: 2 x 84kW 220V a.c
8827519 **YEONWHA** *D7ID* *ex* Chun Il No. 82 *-2000* *ex* Sam Hwa *-1989* - **Ha Jeong Im** - *Busan* *South Korea* Official number: ICR-696002	*155* Class: (KR) 52 182	**1969 Kyungnam Shipbuilding Co Ltd — Busan** Loa 33.21 Br ex - Dght - Lbp 30.95 Br md 6.40 Dpth 2.50 Welded, 1 dk	**(B32A2ST) Tug**	**1 oil engine** driving 1 FP propeller Total Power: 235kW (320hp) 12.0kn Makita 1 x 4 Stroke 6 Cy. 380 x 540 235kW (320bhp) Makita Diesel Co Ltd-Japan AuxGen: 2 x 62kW 225V d.c
9231066 **YEOSU PIONEER** *3FRR2* - **Parchem AS** HAS Management Co Ltd *Panama* *Panama* MMSI: 370680000 Official number: 4015209	**887** Class: KR 382 1,238 T/cm 5.5	**2000-06 Sasaki Shipbuilding Co Ltd — Osakikamijima HS** Yd No: 627 Loa 68.80 (BB) Br ex 10.82 Dght 3.957 Lbp 64.00 Br md 10.60 Dpth 4.60 Welded, 1 dk	**(A12B2TR) Chemical/Products Tanker** Double Hull (13F) Liq: 1,388; Liq (Oil): 1,388 Cargo Heating Coils Compartments: 8 Wing Ta (s.stl), 2 Wing Slop Ta (s.stl), ER 8 Cargo Pump (s): 8x100m³/hr Manifold: Bow/CM: 34.4m	**1 oil engine** reverse geared to sc. shaft driving 1 FP propeller Total Power: 1,177kW (1,600hp) 12.4kn Akasaka A28S 1 x 4 Stroke 6 Cy. 280 x 550 1177kW (1600bhp) Akasaka Tekkosho KK (Akasaka DieselLtd)-Japan AuxGen: 2 x 144kW 225V a.c Fuel: 12.3 (d.f.) 53.6 (r.f.)
6400587 **YEREWA** *VWRY* - **Government of The Republic of India (Ministry of Home Affairs)** The Shipping Corporation of India Ltd (SCI) *Mumbai* *India* MMSI: 419313000 Official number: 1059	*1,427* Class: (LR) (IR) 428 ✠ Classed LR until 12/10/84 370	**1965-01 Mazagon Dock Ltd. — Mumbai** Yd No: 198 Loa 68.28 Br ex 11.61 Dght 2.902 Lbp 61.27 Br md 11.59 Dpth 4.65 Riveted\Welded, 1 dk	**(A32A2GF) General Cargo/Passenger Ship** Grain: 736; Bale: 651 Compartments: 2 Ho, ER 2 Ha: 2 (3.6 x 3.0)ER Derricks: 4x2t; Winches: 4	**2 oil engines** driving 2 FP propellers Total Power: 764kW (1,038hp) 12.0kn MAN G6V30/45ATL 2 x 4 Stroke 6 Cy. 300 x 450 each-382kW (519bhp) (made 1962, fitted 1965) Maschinenbau Augsburg Nuernberg (MAN)-Augsburg AuxGen: 3 x 70kW 400V 50Hz a.c, 1 x 11kW 400V 50Hz a.c Fuel: 46.5 (r.f.)
8714621 **YEROFEY KHABAROV** *UBMH5* *ex* Thor Inger *-2011* - *ex* Southern Havannah *-1997* *ex* Thor Inger *-1995* *ex* Inger Riis *-1994* **Midglen Logistics Sakhalin LLC** - SatCom: Inmarsat C 427305016 *Korsakov* *Russia* MMSI: 273357430	**1,172** Class: RS (LR) (BV) 356 Classed LR until 1/9/11 1,210	**1988-02 Svendborg Vaerft A/S — Svendborg** Yd No: 193 Loa 67.42 (BB) Br ex - Dght 3.503 Lbp 61.78 Br md 11.42 Dpth 5.51 Welded, 1 dk & portable tween dk	**(A31A2GX) General Cargo Ship** Grain: 1,869 TEU 83 C. 83/20' incl. 12 ref C. Compartments: 1 Ho, ER 1 Ha: (38.3 x 7.8)ER Cranes: 2x20t Ice Capable	**1 oil engine** with flexible couplings & sr gearedto sc. shaft driving 1 CP propeller Total Power: 599kW (814hp) 11.0kn MWM TBD440-6 1 x 4 Stroke 6 Cy. 230 x 270 599kW (814bhp) Motoren Werke Mannheim AG (MWM)-West Germany AuxGen: 2 x 230kW 380V 50Hz a.c, 1 x 135kW 380V 50Hz a.c Thrusters: 1 Thwart. FP thruster (f)

IMO No / Call sign	Name / Former names / Owner / Port / Flag	Tonnage	Class	Builder / Dimensions	Type / Details	Machinery
8867387 *XUTR7* -	**YERUSLAN** *ex* Vasiliy Ponomarchuk *-1998* *ex* Yeruslan *-1993* **Claner Shipping Ltd** - *Phnom Penh* *Cambodia* MMSI: 514197000 Official number: 9867125	**1,232** 551 1,285	Class: (RS)	**1967**-01 **Angyalfold Shipyard, Hungarian Ship & Crane Works — Budapest** Yd No: 2125 Loa 74.53 Br ex 11.30 Dght 3.980 Lbp 67.28 Br md - Dpth 5.31 Welded, 1 dk	**(A31A2GX) General Cargo Ship** Ice Capable	**2 oil engines** driving 2 FP propellers Total Power: 1,470kW (1,998hp) 11.5k Lang 8LD315R 2 x 4 Stroke 8 Cy. 315 x 450 each-735kW (999bhp) Lang Gepgyar-Budapest
7045114 - -	**YERUSLAN** - **GPO 'Balkanbalyk'** - *Turkmenbashy* *Turkmenistan*	*1,361* 473 527	Class: (RS)	**1969 Zelenodolskiy Sudostroitelnyy Zavod im. "Gorkogo" — Zelenodolsk** Yd No: 501 Loa 72.09 Br ex 10.83 Dght 3.541 Lbp 64.80 Br md - Dpth 5.72 Welded	**(B11A2FT) Trawler** Ins: 677 Compartments: 2 Ho, ER 2 Ha: 2 (2.5 x 2.5) Derricks: 4x3t; Winches: 4 Ice Capable	**1 oil engine** driving 1 FP propeller Total Power: 736kW (1,001hp) 12.3k S.K.L. 8NVD48AL 1 x 4 Stroke 8 Cy. 320 x 480 736kW (1001bhp) VEB Schwermaschinenbau "KarlLiebknecht" (SKL)-Magdeburg AuxGen: 2 x 300kW, 1 x 50kW Fuel: 122.0 (d.f.)
8230259 *UFJL* -	**YESAUL** *ex* Esaul *-2008* *ex* Hilda *-2006* *ex* Khilda *-2006* *ex* Hilda *-2000* *ex* Volgo-Balt 174 *-2000* **Navigator Shipping Co Ltd (A/O 'Navigator')** - *Taganrog* *Russia* MMSI: 273422010	**2,516** 1,196 2,863	Class: (RS) (RR)	**1973**-07 **Zavody Tazkeho Strojarstva (ZTS) — Komarno** Yd No: 1902 Loa 114.00 Br ex 13.20 Dght 3.340 Lbp 110.00 Br md 13.00 Dpth 5.50 Welded, 1 dk	**(A31A2GX) General Cargo Ship** Grain: 4,720 Compartments: 4 Ho, ER 4 Ha: (18.6 x 11.2)2 (18.8 x 11.2) (20.3 x 11.2)ER	**2 oil engines** driving 2 FP propellers Total Power: 1,030kW (1,400hp) Skoda 6L275A2 2 x 4 Stroke 6 Cy. 275 x 350 each-515kW (700bhp) CKD Praha-Praha Fuel: 111.0 (d.f.)
7739600 - LA 293	**YESHAYHU** *ex* N. R. Darwin *-1985* **Even-Ezra Agrofishing Co Ltd** - *Lagos* *Nigeria*	*158* 95 -		**1978 Australian Shipbuilding Industries (WA) Pty Ltd — Fremantle WA** Yd No: 154 Loa - Br ex - Dght - Lbp 22.69 Br md 6.86 Dpth 2.44 Welded, 1 dk	**(B11B2FV) Fishing Vessel**	**1 oil engine** driving 1 FP propeller Total Power: 313kW (426hp) 9.3kn Caterpillar D353SCAC 1 x 4 Stroke 6 Cy. 159 x 203 313kW (426bhp) Caterpillar Tractor Co-USA
9292694 *TC3046* -	**YESIL MARMARIS** - **Tugay Turizm Seyahat ve Ticaret AS (Tugay Tourism Travel & Trade Inc)** - *Izmir* *Turkey* MMSI: 271015001 Official number: 31	**196** 59 20		**2003**-04 **Yesil Marmaris Inc. — Marmaris** Loa 28.90 Br ex 7.20 Dght 1.800 Lbp 26.00 Br md 7.10 Dpth 2.85 Welded, 1 dk	**(A36A2PR) Passenger/Ro-Ro Ship (Vehicles)** Stern ramp (centre)	**2 oil engines** geared to sc. shafts driving 2 FP propellers Total Power: 736kW (1,000hp) 14.0kn Cummins 2 x 4 Stroke each-368kW (500bhp) Cummins Engine Co Inc-USA
7723572 - -	**YET KIEU** *ex* Keppel Lima *-1986* **Port Service & Coal Co (Cong Ty Cang Va Kinh Doanh Than)** - *Haiphong* *Vietnam* Official number: VN-1321-TK	**271** 81 -	Class: VR (LR) (AB) Classed LR until 11/3/87	**1978**-01 **Singmarine Shipyard Pte Ltd — Singapore** Yd No: 019 Loa 32.42 Br ex 9.61 Dght 3.750 Lbp 30.24 Br md 9.31 Dpth 4.55 Welded, 1 dk	**(B32A2ST) Tug**	**2 oil engines** with clutches, flexible couplings & sr reverse geared to sc. shafts driving 2 FP propellers Total Power: 2,800kW (3,806hp) 12.0kn MaK 8M332AK 2 x 4 Stroke 8 Cy. 240 x 330 each-1400kW (1903bhp) MaK Maschinenbau GmbH-Kiel AuxGen: 2 x 80kW 415V 50Hz a.c
6826353 *TC3440* -	**YETIM OSMAN** *ex* Umran *-1986* *ex* Capanoglu *-1986* **Cevahir Milletlerarasi Deniz Kara Nakliyat ve Ticaret AS** - *Istanbul* *Turkey* MMSI: 271010744 Official number: 3924	**275** 124 490	Class: (BV)	**1969 Deniz Insaat Kizaklari — Fener** Yd No: 114 Lengthened-1970 Loa 42.80 Br ex 7.27 Dght 3.101 Lbp - Br md 7.26 Dpth 3.43 Welded, 1 dk	**(A31A2GX) General Cargo Ship** Grain: 463; Bale: 448 Compartments: 1 Ho, ER 2 Ha: (8.1 x 4.2) (8.6 x 4.2)ER Derricks: 2x1.5t	**1 oil engine** driving 1 FP propeller Total Power: 250kW (340hp) 8.0kn Alpha 404-24VO 1 x 2 Stroke 4 Cy. 240 x 400 250kW (340bhp) A/S Burmeister & Wain's Maskin ogSkibsbyggeri-Denmark
9142796 *BR2175* -	**YEUAM SHIAN PRNCESS** *ex* La Chanteuse *-2005* *ex* Stella Maris *-2005* **Yeuam Shian Shipping Ltd** - *Kaohsiung* *Chinese Taipei*	**482** 166 75	Class: (NV)	**1995**-12 **Kvaerner Fjellstrand (S) Pte Ltd — Singapore** Yd No: 017 Loa 40.00 Br ex - Dght 1.700 Lbp - Br md 10.10 Dpth 3.94 Welded, 1 dk	**(A37B2PS) Passenger Ship** Hull Material: Aluminium Alloy Passengers: unberthed: 346	**2 oil engines** geared to sc. shafts driving 2 Water jets Total Power: 4,000kW (5,438hp) 34.0kn M.T.U. 16V396TE74L 2 x Vee 4 Stroke 16 Cy. 165 x 185 each-2000kW (2719bhp) MTU Friedrichshafen GmbH-Friedrichshafen
8649802 *BI2533* CT7-0533	**YEUN HORNG NO. 2** - **Yeun Sheng Fishery Co Ltd** - *Kaohsiung* *Chinese Taipei* Official number: 013972	**556** 273 -		**2001**-09 **Fong Kuo Shipbuilding Co Ltd — Kaohsiung** Loa 56.49 Br ex - Dght - Lbp 48.62 Br md 8.70 Dpth 3.65 Welded, 1 dk	**(B11B2FV) Fishing Vessel**	**1 oil engine** driving 1 FP propeller Niigata Niigata Engineering Co Ltd-Japan
9277242 *VRYG3* -	**YEUNG CHAU** - **Hongkong United Dockyards Ltd** The Hongkong Salvage & Towage Co Ltd *Hong Kong* *Hong Kong* MMSI: 477128000 Official number: HK-0953	**295** 88 171	Class: LR ✠ **100A1** SS 03/2013 tug ✠ **LMC** Eq.Ltr: F; Cable: 302.5/22.0 U2 (a)	**2003**-03 **Kegoya Dock K.K. — Kure** Yd No: 1078 Loa 29.00 Br ex 10.12 Dght 3.500 Lbp 23.50 Br md 9.50 Dpth 4.70 Welded, 1 dk	**(B32A2ST) Tug**	**2 oil engines** driving 2 gen. each 115kW gearing integral to driving 2 Z propellers Total Power: 2,942kW (4,000hp) 11.5kn Yanmar 6N260-EN 2 x 4 Stroke 6 Cy. 260 x 360 each-1471kW (2000bhp) Yanmar Diesel Engine Co Ltd-Japan AuxGen: 2 x 80kW 385V 50Hz a.c
9253686 - -	**YEVGENIY KOCHESHKOV** *ex* Saturn *-2007* **JSC 'Port Fleet Ltd' (ZAO 'Portovyy Flot')** - *St Petersburg* *Russia* Official number: 000138	**188** 56 119	Class: RS (LR) ✠ Classed LR until 22/11/02	**2001**-09 **OAO Leningradskiy Sudostroitelnyy Zavod 'Pella' — Otradnoye** (Hull) **2001**-09 **B.V. Scheepswerf Damen — Gorinchem** Yd No: 510802 Loa 25.86 Br ex 8.94 Dght 3.390 Lbp 23.03 Br md 8.90 Dpth 4.30 Welded, 1 dk	**(B32A2ST) Tug** Ice Capable	**2 oil engines** reduction geared to sc. shafts driving 2 Directional propellers Total Power: 2,028kW (2,758hp) 12.1kn Caterpillar 3512B-HD 2 x Vee 4 Stroke 12 Cy. 170 x 215 each-1014kW (1379bhp) Caterpillar Inc-USA AuxGen: 2 x 85kW 380V 50Hz a.c
8724092 *UFIZ* -	**YEVGENIY YEGOROV** - **JSC P/O 'Sevmash' (Production Association North Machine Building Enterprise JSC)** - *Arkhangelsk* *Russia* MMSI: 273411020 Official number: 852905	**1,178** 353 404	Class: RS	**1986**-06 **Yaroslavskiy Sudostroitelnyy Zavod — Yaroslavl** Yd No: 228 Loa 58.55 Br ex 12.67 Dght 4.690 Lbp 51.60 Br md 12.64 Dpth 5.90 Welded, 1 dk	**(B32A2ST) Tug** Derricks: 1x5t Ice Capable	**2 diesel electric oil engines** driving 2 gen. each 1100kW Connecting to 1 elec. Motor of (1900kW) driving 1 FP propeller Total Power: 2,200kW (2,992hp) 13.2kn Kolomna 6CHN30/38 2 x 4 Stroke 6 Cy. 300 x 380 each-1100kW (1496bhp) Kolomenskiy Zavod-Kolomna AuxGen: 2 x 300kW, 2 x 160kW Fuel: 331.0 (d.f.)
9076595 *UDDF* -	**YEVGENIY ZOTOV** - **Sail Co Ltd (OOO 'Seil')** - SatCom: Inmarsat C 427320854 *Nakhodka* *Russia* MMSI: 273817200	**683** 233 529	Class: RS	**1992**-10 **Khabarovskiy Sudostroitelnyy Zavod im Kirova — Khabarovsk** Yd No: 889 Loa 54.99 Br ex 9.49 Dght 4.460 Lbp 50.04 Br md 9.30 Dpth 5.16 Welded, 1 dk	**(B12B2FC) Fish Carrier** Ice Capable	**1 oil engine** driving 1 FP propeller Total Power: 588kW (799hp) 11.3kn S.K.L. 6NVD48A-2U 1 x 4 Stroke 6 Cy. 320 x 480 588kW (799bhp) SKL Motoren u. Systemtechnik AG-Magdeburg
9174311 *9V5415* -	**YEW CHOON 1** *ex* Namhai I *-2005* **Yew Choon Pte Ltd** - *Singapore* *Singapore* Official number: 387656	**125** 38 -	Class: BV	**1997**-05 **Tuong Aik (Sarawak) Sdn Bhd — Sibu** Yd No: 9610 Loa 23.15 Br ex - Dght 2.500 Lbp 21.69 Br md 7.30 Dpth 3.00 Welded, 1 dk	**(B32A2ST) Tug**	**2 oil engines** geared to sc. shafts driving 2 FP propellers Total Power: 804kW (1,094hp) 11.0kn Caterpillar 3412TA 2 x Vee 4 Stroke 12 Cy. 137 x 152 each-402kW (547bhp) Caterpillar Inc-USA
9293222 *9V6460* -	**YEW CHOON 2** *ex* Namhai II *-2006* *ex* Modalwan 2466 *-2004* **Yew Choon Pte Ltd** - *Singapore* *Singapore* Official number: 390539	**255** 76 107	Class: BV	**2003**-10 **Nanjing Tongkah Shipbuilding Co Ltd — Nanjing JS** Yd No: 2002-2902 Loa 29.20 Br ex - Dght 3.710 Lbp 27.36 Br md 9.00 Dpth 4.40 Welded, 1 dk	**(B32A2ST) Tug**	**2 oil engines** geared to sc. shafts driving 2 FP propellers Total Power: 1,788kW (2,430hp) 11.0kn Cummins KTA-38-M2 2 x Vee 4 Stroke 12 Cy. 159 x 159 each-894kW (1215bhp) Cummins Engine Co Ltd-United Kingdom AuxGen: 2 x 150kW 400/220V 50Hz a.c
9390850 *9V6876* -	**YEW CHOON 3** - **Yew Choon Pte Ltd** - *Singapore* *Singapore* Official number: 391924	**131** 40 104	Class: GL (NK)	**2006**-05 **Tuong Aik Shipyard Sdn Bhd — Sibu** Yd No: 2523 Loa 23.50 Br ex - Dght 2.412 Lbp 21.85 Br md 7.32 Dpth 3.00 Welded, 1 dk	**(B32A2ST) Tug**	**2 oil engines** reduction geared to sc. shafts driving 2 FP propellers Total Power: 896kW (1,218hp) Caterpillar 3412B 2 x Vee 4 Stroke 12 Cy. 137 x 152 each-448kW (609bhp) Caterpillar Inc-USA

IMO / Call sign	Name / Owner / Port	GT / NT / DWT	Class	Builder / Dimensions	Type	Machinery
462055 *V7144*	**YEW CHOON 5** **Yew Choon Pte Ltd** - *Singapore* *Singapore* MMSI: 563009660 Official number: 393052	262 79 314	Class: NK	**2007-07 Forward Marine Enterprise Sdn Bhd — Sibu** Yd No: FM-16 Loa 30.00 Br ex 8.61 Dght 3.510 Lbp 27.73 Br md 8.60 Dpth 4.12 Welded, 1 dk	**(B32A2ST) Tug**	**2 oil engines** reduction geared to sc. shafts driving 2 FP propellers Total Power: 1,518kW (2,064hp) Mitsubishi S6R2-MTK3L 2 x 4 Stroke 6 Cy. 170 x 220 each-759kW (1032bhp) Mitsubishi Heavy Industries Ltd-Japan Fuel: 190.0 (d.f.)
465681 *V7169*	**YEW CHOON 6** *ex* Whale 6 *-2008* **Yew Choon Pte Ltd** - *Singapore* *Singapore* Official number: 393125	227 69 235	Class: NK	**2007-10 Borneo Shipping & Timber Agencies Sdn Ltd — Bintulu** Yd No: 83 Loa 27.00 Br ex - Dght 3.513 Lbp 25.10 Br md 8.53 Dpth 4.12 Welded, 1 dk	**(B32A2ST) Tug**	**2 oil engines** reduction geared to sc. shafts driving 2 Propellers Total Power: 1,264kW (1,718hp) Caterpillar 3412D 2 x Vee 4 Stroke 12 Cy. 145 x 162 each-632kW (859bhp) Caterpillar Inc-USA Fuel: 150.0 (d.f.)
436757 *V7398*	**YEW CHOON 7** **Yew Choon Pte Ltd** - *Singapore* *Singapore* Official number: 394051	298 90 337	Class: GL	**2008-08 Forward Marine Enterprise Sdn Bhd — Sibu** Yd No: FM-28 Loa 31.10 Br ex - Dght 3.570 Lbp 28.72 Br md 9.50 Dpth 4.20 Welded, 1 dk	**(B32A2ST) Tug**	**2 oil engines** reduction geared to sc. shafts driving 2 Propellers Total Power: 2,238kW (3,042hp) Cummins KTA-38-M2 2 x Vee 4 Stroke 12 Cy. 159 x 159 each-1119kW (1521bhp) Cummins Engine Co Inc-USA
501992 *V7511*	**YEW CHOON 8** **Yew Choon Pte Ltd** - *Singapore* *Singapore* MMSI: 563629000 Official number: 394373	298 90 320	Class: GL	**2009-04 Forward Marine Enterprise Sdn Bhd — Sibu** Yd No: FM-47 Loa 31.10 Br ex - Dght 3.570 Lbp 28.72 Br md 9.50 Dpth 4.20 Welded, 1 dk	**(B32A2ST) Tug**	**2 oil engines** reverse reduction geared to sc. shafts driving 2 FP propellers Total Power: 2,386kW (3,244hp) Cummins KTA-50-M2 2 x Vee 4 Stroke 16 Cy. 159 x 159 each-1193kW (1622bhp) Cummins Engine Co Inc-USA AuxGen: 2 x 80kW 400V a.c
614828 *8B4813*	**YEWANDE** *ex* Forsa 201 *-2013* **Directed Services Ltd** - *Kingstown* *St Vincent & The Grenadines* MMSI: 375831000 Official number: 11286	128 38 135	Class: IV RI	**2013-10 Kocatepe Gemi Cekek ve Insaat Sanayi Ltd Sti — Altinova** Yd No: 14 Loa 19.95 Br ex - Dght 2.000 Lbp 17.72 Br md 7.00 Dpth 3.20 Welded, 1 dk	**(B32A2ST) Tug**	**2 oil engines** reduction geared to sc. shafts driving 2 FP propellers Total Power: 894kW (1,216hp) Caterpillar C18 ACERT 2 x 4 Stroke 6 Cy. 145 x 183 each-447kW (608bhp) Caterpillar Inc-USA AuxGen: 2 x 45kW 60Hz a.c
724248	**YEYCHANIN** *ex* PTR-50 No. 53 *-1988* -	190 57 70	Class: RR (RS)	**1988-10 Astrakhanskaya Sudoverf im. "Kirova" — Astrakhan** Yd No: 53 Loa 31.85 Br ex 7.08 Dght 2.100 Lbp 27.80 Br md - Dpth 3.15 Welded	**(B12B2FC) Fish Carrier** Ins: 100	**1 oil engine** geared to sc. shaft driving 1 FP propeller Total Power: 221kW (300hp) 10.2kn Daldizel 6CHNSP18/22-300 1 x 4 Stroke 6 Cy. 180 x 220 221kW (300bhp) Daldizel-Khabarovsk AuxGen: 2 x 25kW Fuel: 14.0 (d.f.)
725565 *'OTA*	**YEYSK** **SSC Kerch Sea Ferry** - *Kerch* *Ukraine* MMSI: 272009000 Official number: 872612	1,028 308 254	Class: UA (RS)	**1988-12 Rizhskiy Sudoremontnyy Zavod — Riga** Yd No: 505 Loa 49.72 Br ex 12.78 Dght 3.100 Lbp 42.97 Br md - Dpth 4.80 Welded, 1dk	**(A36A2PR) Passenger/Ro-Ro Ship (Vehicles)** Ice Capable	**3 diesel electric oil engines** driving 1 gen. of 88kW Connecting to 2 elec. motors each (710kW) driving 2 FP propellers Total Power: 1,986kW (2,700hp) 12.5kn S.K.L. 6VD26/20AL-2 3 x 4 Stroke 6 Cy. 200 x 260 each-662kW (900bhp) VEB Schwermaschinenbau "KarlLiebknecht" (SKL)-Magdeburg AuxGen: 1 x 88kW a.c Fuel: 69.0 (d.f.)
931724	**YG-58** *ex* STR No. 58 *-1999* **Specialized Sea Oil Fleet Organisation, Caspian Sea Oil Fleet, State Oil Co of the Republic of Azerbaijan** -	*134* 42 81	Class: (RS)	**1966-12 Astrakhan. SSZ im 10-iy God Oktyabrskoy Revolyutsii — Astrakhan** Yd No: 1 Loa 28.20 Br ex 7.30 Dght 2.770 Lbp 26.00 Br md 7.01 Dpth 3.75 Welded, 1 dk	**(B21B20T) Offshore Tug/Supply Ship** Liq: 74 Compartments: 4 Ta Ice Capable	**2 oil engines** driving 2 FP propellers Total Power: 442kW (600hp) 10.2kn Pervomaysk 6CHRP25/34 2 x 4 Stroke 6 Cy. 250 x 340 each-221kW (300bhp) (new engine 1980) Pervomaydizelmash (PDM)-Pervomaysk AuxGen: 2 x 60kW a.c Fuel: 10.0 (d.f.)
931736	**YG-62** *ex* STR No. 62 *-2001* **Specialized Sea Oil Fleet Organisation, Caspian Sea Oil Fleet, State Oil Co of the Republic of Azerbaijan** -	*154* 42 83	Class: (RS)	**1964-06 Bakinskiy Sudostroitelnyy Zavod im Vano Sturua — Baku** Yd No: 62 Loa 28.20 Br ex 7.30 Dght 2.770 Lbp 26.00 Br md 7.00 Dpth 3.50 Welded, 1 dk	**(B21B20T) Offshore Tug/Supply Ship** Ice Capable	**2 oil engines** driving 2 FP propellers Total Power: 442kW (600hp) 10.3kn Pervomaysk 6CHRP25/34 2 x 4 Stroke 6 Cy. 250 x 340 each-221kW (300bhp) (new engine 1979) Pervomaydizelmash (PDM)-Pervomaysk AuxGen: 2 x 57kW Fuel: 12.0 (d.f.)
631474 *'RKL5*	**YI CHUN 15** **Jiangsu Yichun Shipping Co Ltd** - SatCom: Inmarsat C 447704268 *Hong Kong* *Hong Kong* MMSI: 477098100 Official number: HK-3488	32,975 19,142 56,735 T/cm 58.8	Class: CC	**2012-04 Nanjing Wujiazui Shipbuilding Co Ltd — Nanjing JS** Yd No: YC020 Loa 189.99 (BB) Br ex - Dght 12.800 Lbp 185.00 Br md 32.26 Dpth 18.00 Welded, 1 dk	**(A21A2BC) Bulk Carrier** Grain: 71,634; Bale: 68,200 Compartments: 5 Ho, ER 5 Ha: 4 (21.3 x 18.3)ER (18.9 x 18.3) Cranes: 4x30t	**1 oil engine** driving 1 FP propeller Total Power: 9,480kW (12,889hp) 14.2kn MAN-B&W 6S50MC-C8 1 x 2 Stroke 6 Cy. 500 x 2000 9480kW (12889bhp) STX (Dalian) Engine Co Ltd-China AuxGen: 3 x 600kW 450V a.c
220768 *BI2571* L964928	**YI CHUN NO. 232** *ex* Apolo Ii *-2010* *ex* Yi Chun No. 232 *-2000* **Yih Shuen Horng Marine Products Co Ltd** - *Kaohsiung* *Chinese Taipei* Official number: CT7-0571	635 314 -		**2000-05 Jong Shyn Shipbuilding Co., Ltd. — Kaohsiung** Yd No: 093 Loa 59.20 Br ex - Dght 3.600 Lbp 50.80 Br md 9.00 Dpth 3.75 Welded, 1 dk	**(B11B2FV) Fishing Vessel**	**1 oil engine** driving 1 FP propeller Total Power: 883kW (1,201hp) 12.0kn Akasaka 1 x 4 Stroke 883kW (1201bhp) Akasaka Tekkosho KK (Akasaka DieselLtd)-Japan
431252 *'RHP9*	**YI DA** **Yi Da Shipping SA** Hong Kong Hai Bao Shipping Co Ltd SatCom: Inmarsat C 447703066 *Hong Kong* *Hong Kong* MMSI: 477963200 Official number: HK-2905	116,396 46,519 228,850 T/cm 156.4	Class: CC	**2010-11 Guangzhou Longxue Shipbuilding Co Ltd — Guangzhou GD** Yd No: L0008 Loa 324.99 (BB) Br ex - Dght 18.126 Lbp 314.60 Br md 52.50 Dpth 24.30 Welded, 1 dk	**(A21B2BO) Ore Carrier** Grain: 153,315 Compartments: 5 Ho, ER 9 Ha: 7 (16.7 x 16.5) (16.7 x 16.5)ER (16.7 x 13.6)	**1 oil engine** reduction geared to sc. shaft driving 1 FP propeller Total Power: 23,280kW (31,651hp) 15.0kn MAN-B&W 6S80MC-C 1 x 2 Stroke 6 Cy. 800 x 3200 23280kW (31651bhp) CSSC MES Diesel Co Ltd-China AuxGen: 3 x 960kW 450V a.c
996073	**YI FA** - -	818 366 -		**2004-01 San Yang Shipbuilding Co., Ltd. — Kaohsiung** Yd No: 822 Loa - Br ex - Dght - Lbp - Br md - Dpth - Welded, 1 dk	**(B11B2FV) Fishing Vessel**	**1 oil engine** driving 1 Propeller
655306	**YI FAN 10** **Zhangjiajie Lijun Shipping Co Ltd** - *Zhangjiajie, Hunan* *China*	3,105 1,615 4,000	Class: ZC	**2003-10 Yichang Jianghua Shiprepair & Building Co Ltd — Yichang HB** Loa 98.60 Br ex - Dght - Lbp - Br md 15.50 Dpth 3.50 Welded, 1 dk	**(A31A2GX) General Cargo Ship**	**3 oil engines** reduction geared to sc. shafts driving 3 Directional propellers Total Power: 660kW (897hp) Chinese Std. Type 3 x each-220kW (299bhp) in China
655318	**YI FAN 12** **Zhangjiajie Lijun Shipping Co Ltd** - *China*	2,812 1,462 3,500	Class: ZC	**2003-01 Yichang Fazhong Shipping Co Ltd — Yichang HB** Loa 98.38 Br ex - Dght - Lbp - Br md 15.50 Dpth 3.50 Welded, 1 dk	**(A31A2GX) General Cargo Ship**	**3 oil engines** reduction geared to sc. shafts driving 3 Directional propellers Total Power: 774kW (1,053hp) Chinese Std. Type 3 x each-258kW (351bhp) Weifang Diesel Engine Factory-China
664656 *BH3196* .T6-1196	**YI FU** *ex* Hui Hsing No. 1 *-2012* **Yuan Hung Fishery Co Ltd** - *Kaohsiung* *Chinese Taipei* Official number: 011574	496 197 -		**1989-08 Teh-I Shipbuilding Co, Ltd — Kaohsiung** L reg 44.95 Br ex - Dght - Lbp - Br md 8.20 Dpth 3.60 Welded, 1 dk	**(B11B2FV) Fishing Vessel**	**1 oil engine** reduction geared to sc. shaft driving 1 CP propeller Hanshin The Hanshin Diesel Works Ltd-Japan

8663389 *BIPP* -	**YI HAI 9** *ex* Hailian 16 *-2011* - - *Jiujiang, Jiangxi* *China* Official number: CN20043359821	**2,001** 1,120 -		**2005-09 Taizhou Haibin Shipbuilding & Repairing Co Ltd — Sanmen County ZJ** Loa 88.00 Br ex - Dght - Lbp - Br md 13.20 Dpth 6.00 Welded, 1 dk	**(A31A2GX) General Cargo Ship**	**1 oil engine** driving 1 FP propeller Total Power: 735kW (999hp) Chinese Std. Type 1 x 735kW (999bhp) Zibo Diesel Engine Factory-China
8510037 *BOFK* -	**YI JIA** *ex* Yick Jia *-2004* *ex* Lydia V *-1991* *launched as* Sakura *-1986* **Shenzhen Ocean Shipping Co (COSCO SHENZHEN)** COSCO (HK) Shipping Co Ltd *Shenzhen, Guangdong* *China* MMSI: 413019000	**35,247** 22,140 67,395 T/cm 63.2	Class: (CC) (NK)	**1986-11 Kawasaki Heavy Industries Ltd — Kobe HG** Yd No: 1396 Loa 220.20 (BB) Br ex - Dght 13.240 Lbp 212.02 Br md 32.21 Dpth 18.22 Welded, 1 dk	**(A21A2BC) Bulk Carrier** Grain: 77,311 Compartments: 7 Ho, ER 7 Ha: (14.7 x 12.0)5 (16.4 x 14.0) (14.7 x 14.0)ER	**1 oil engine** driving 1 FP propeller Total Power: 7,002kW (9,520hp) 13.8k B&W 6L60M 1 x 2 Stroke 6 Cy. 600 x 1944 7002kW (9520bhp) Kawasaki Heavy Industries Ltd-Japan AuxGen: 3 x 400kW 450V 60Hz a.c Fuel: 220.0 (d.f.) 2473.0 (r.f.) 31.0pd
8648327 *BI2520* LL964886	**YI LONG NO. 202** **Yih Shuen Marine Products Co Ltd** - *Kaohsiung* *Chinese Taipei* Official number: CT7-0520	**516** 242 -		**1999-09 Jong Shyn Shipbuilding Co., Ltd. — Kaohsiung** Loa 47.30 Br ex 8.60 Dght - Lbp - Br md - Dpth - Welded, 1 dk	**(B11B2FV) Fishing Vessel**	**1 oil engine** driving 1 Propeller
9632284 *VRJW2* -	**YI LONG SHAN** *ex* Hong Yuan *-2013* *launched as* Yi Long Shan *-2013* **Yin Guan Shipping Co Ltd** China Shipping International Shipmanagement Co Ltd *Hong Kong* *Hong Kong* MMSI: 477902500	**32,962** 19,142 57,000 T/cm 58.8	Class: CC	**2013-09 China Shipping Industry (Jiangsu) Co Ltd — Jiangdu JS** Yd No: CIS57000-05 Loa 189.99 (BB) Br ex 32.30 Dght 12.800 Lbp 185.00 Br md 32.26 Dpth 18.00 Welded, 1 dk	**(A21A2BC) Bulk Carrier** Grain: 71,634; Bale: 68,200 Compartments: 5 Ho, ER 5 Ha: 4 (21.3 x 18.3)ER (18.9 x 18.3) Cranes: 4x30t	**1 oil engine** driving 1 FP propeller Total Power: 9,480kW (12,889hp) 14.2k MAN-B&W 6S50MC- 1 x 2 Stroke 6 Cy. 500 x 2000 9480kW (12889bhp)
7803932 *BOCZ* -	**YI MEN** **Guangzhou Ocean Shipping Co (COSCOGZ)** SatCom: Inmarsat C 441277410 *Tianjin* *China* MMSI: 412219000	**10,173** 5,838 13,780	Class: (CC) (BV)	**1978-04 VEB Warnowwerft Warnemuende — Rostock** Yd No: 398 Loa 152.75 (BB) Br ex 20.35 Dght 9.321 Lbp 140.73 Br md 20.30 Dpth 11.90 Welded, 2 dks	**(A31A2GX) General Cargo Ship** Grain: 18,818; Bale: 17,403 Compartments: ER, 5 Ho 5 Ha: (8.9 x 5.8)2 (10.5 x 10.9) (18.9 x 10.9)ER (10.2 x 9.9) Derricks: 1x70t,16x10t; Winches: 16 Ice Capable	**1 oil engine** driving 1 FP propeller Total Power: 8,238kW (11,200hp) 18.0k MAN K8Z70/12C 1 x 2 Stroke 8 Cy. 700 x 1200 8238kW (11200bhp) VEB Dieselmotorenwerk Rostock-Rostock AuxGen: 3 x 400kW 380V 50Hz a.c Fuel: 1517.0 (r.f.)
8601264 *BRUF* -	**YI MENG SHAN** **Guangzhou Maritime Transport (Group) Co Ltd** China Shipping Development Co Ltd Tramp Co SatCom: Inmarsat C 441225910 *Guangzhou, Guangdong* *China* MMSI: 412593000	**26,835** 11,009 39,837	Class: (CC)	**1990-08 Dalian Shipyard Co Ltd — Dalian LN** Yd No: BJ350/5 Loa 195.00 (BB) Br ex - Dght 9.980 Lbp 185.00 Br md 32.00 Dpth 15.20 Welded, 1 dk	**(A21A2BC) Bulk Carrier** Grain: 49,019 Compartments: 6 Ho, ER 6 Ha: (15.4 x 16.0)5 (16.0 x 16.0)ER Ice Capable	**1 oil engine** driving 1 FP propeller Total Power: 7,606kW (10,341hp) 14.5k Sulzer 6RTA5 1 x 2 Stroke 6 Cy. 520 x 1800 7606kW (10341bhp) Dalian Marine Diesel Works-China AuxGen: 3 x 485kW 400V a.c
9130999 *BIAP8* -	**YI SHENG** *ex* Jin Sheng *-2011* **Jin Sheng Shipping Ltd** Lufeng Shipping Co Ltd *Shanghai* *China* MMSI: 413376690	**4,822** 2,476 6,816 T/cm 16.5	Class: CC	**1996-08 Dae Sun Shipbuilding & Engineering Co Ltd — Busan** Yd No: 422 Loa 113.00 (BB) Br ex - Dght 6.500 Lbp 103.00 Br md 19.00 Dpth 8.50 Welded, 1 dk	**(A33A2CC) Container Ship (Fully Cellular)** TEU 385 Compartments: 5 Cell Ho, ER 5 Ha: (12.6 x 13.0)Tappered 4 (12.6 x 13.0)ER	**1 oil engine** driving 1 FP propeller Total Power: 3,884kW (5,281hp) 14.0k B&W 6L35M 1 x 2 Stroke 6 Cy. 350 x 1050 3884kW (5281bhp) Ssangyong Heavy Industries Co Ltd-South Korea AuxGen: 2 x 400kW 445V a.c
8664826 *BI2555* -	**YI SHUN** *ex* Hau Shen No. 212 *-2011* **Wen Li Chen** - *Kaohsiung* *Chinese Taipei* Official number: 014063	**627** 314 -		**1999-03 Jong Shyn Shipbuilding Co., Ltd. — Kaohsiung** Yd No: 094 Loa 50.80 Br ex - Dght - Lbp - Br md 9.00 Dpth 3.75 Welded, 1 dk	**(B11B2FV) Fishing Vessel**	**1 oil engine** driving 1 Propeller
8110473 *HO3958* -	**YI TAI** *ex* Ji Hang 11 *-2005* *ex* Rong Ning 21 *-2002* *ex* Kamishima Maru *-1999* **Jin Yun Shipping Co Ltd** Dalian East Ocean Maritime Consulting Services Co Ltd *Panama* *Panama* Official number: 33301PEXT1	**1,208** 762 1,594		**1981-07 Yamanaka Zosen K.K. — Imabari** Yd No: 225 Loa 68.71 Br ex 11.54 Dght 4.252 Lbp 64.01 Br md 11.51 Dpth 6.13 Welded, 2 dks	**(A31A2GX) General Cargo Ship** Grain: 2,698; Bale: 2,427 Compartments: 1 Ho, ER 1 Ha: ER	**1 oil engine** with clutches & reverse reduction geared to sc. shaft driving 1 FP propeller Total Power: 883kW (1,201hp) Hanshin 6LUN28A 1 x 4 Stroke 6 Cy. 280 x 480 883kW (1201bhp) The Hanshin Diesel Works Ltd-Japan
8631283 - -	**YI TONG** *ex* Tenjin Maru *-2000* - -	**1,031** 443 1,050		**1987-03 K.K. Yoshida Zosen Kogyo — Arida** Loa 68.70 Br ex 10.42 Dght 3.670 Lbp 63.75 Br md 10.40 Dpth 6.00 Welded, 1 dk	**(A31A2GX) General Cargo Ship**	**1 oil engine** driving 1 FP propeller Total Power: 736kW (1,001hp) Niigata 6M26AF 1 x 4 Stroke 6 Cy. 260 x 460 736kW (1001bhp) Niigata Engineering Co Ltd-Japan
8662294 *XUGQ2* -	**YI WEI DA** *ex* Yi Wei Da 8 *-2013* *ex* Yong Tai You 6 *-2009* **Bayabas Shipping Co Ltd** Bansda Shipping Co Ltd *Phnom Penh* *Cambodia* MMSI: 514034000 Official number: 1300194	**997** 662 2,635	Class: ZC	**2000-11 Duchang Shipbuilding General Yard — Duchang County JX** Loa 78.00 Br ex - Dght 4.700 Lbp 70.60 Br md 11.20 Dpth 5.30 Welded, 1 dk	**(A13B2TP) Products Tanker**	**1 oil engine** reduction geared to sc. shaft driving 1 Propeller Total Power: 735kW (999hp)
9080455 *BXAR* -	**YI XIAN HU** **Zhongshan Hong Kong Passenger Shipping Co-op Co Ltd** Chu Kong Shipping Enterprises (Holdings) Co Ltd *Zhongshan, Guangdong* *China* MMSI: 412869000	**484** 168 48	Class: CC	**1994-03 Austal Ships Pty Ltd — Fremantle WA** Yd No: 108 Loa 40.10 (BB) Br ex 11.81 Dght 1.250 Lbp 38.00 Br md 11.50 Dpth 3.80 Welded, 1 dk	**(A37B2PS) Passenger Ship** Hull Material: Aluminium Alloy Passengers: unberthed: 354	**2 oil engines** reduction geared to sc. shafts driving 2 Water jets Total Power: 4,000kW (5,438hp) 39.5k M.T.U. 16V396TE74 2 x Vee 4 Stroke 16 Cy. 165 x 185 each-2000kW (2719bhp) (new engine 2003) MTU Friedrichshafen GmbH-Friedrichshafen AuxGen: 2 x 100kW 380V a.c
9025261 *BBIT7* -	**YI XIN 7** *ex* Lu Rong Yu 1411 *-2006* **Rongcheng Yixin Aquatic Products Co Ltd** - SatCom: Inmarsat C 441208819 *Shidao, Shandong* *China*	**138** 53 -	Class: CC	**2001-10 Rongcheng Shipbuilding Industry Co Ltd — Rongcheng SD** Loa 36.00 Br ex - Dght 2.200 Lbp 29.00 Br md 6.20 Dpth 2.90 Welded, 1 dk	**(B12C2FL) Live Fish Carrier (Well Boat)**	**1 oil engine** geared to sc. shaft driving 1 Propeller Total Power: 330kW (449hp) Chinese Std. Type G6190ZL 1 x 4 Stroke 6 Cy. 190 x 210 330kW (449bhp) Jinan Diesel Engine Co Ltd-China
9025259 *BBIT8* -	**YI XIN 8** *ex* Lu Rong Yu Shui 255 *-2006* **Rongcheng Yixin Aquatic Products Co Ltd** - *Shidao, Shandong* *China*	**170** 66 -	Class: CC	**2000-12 Rongcheng Shipbuilding Industry Co Ltd — Rongcheng SD** Loa 38.00 Br ex - Dght 2.400 Lbp 31.00 Br md 6.60 Dpth 3.10 Welded, 1 dk	**(B12C2FL) Live Fish Carrier (Well Boat)**	**1 oil engine** geared to sc. shaft driving 1 Propeller Total Power: 400kW (544hp) Chinese Std. Type G6190ZL 1 x 4 Stroke 6 Cy. 190 x 210 400kW (544bhp) Jinan Diesel Engine Co Ltd-China
9025120 *BBIT9* -	**YI XIN 9** *ex* Lu Rong Yu Shui 218 *-2006* **Rongcheng Yixin Aquatic Products Co Ltd** - SatCom: Inmarsat C 441208919 *Shidao, Shandong* *China*	**130** 53 -	Class: (CC)	**1999-09 Huanghai Shipbuilding Co Ltd — Rongcheng SD** Loa 35.00 Br ex - Dght 2.250 Lbp 29.00 Br md 6.20 Dpth 2.85 Welded, 1 dk	**(B12C2FL) Live Fish Carrier (Well Boat)**	**1 oil engine** geared to sc. shaft driving 1 Propeller Total Power: 330kW (449hp) Chinese Std. Type G6190ZL 1 x 4 Stroke 6 Cy. 190 x 210 330kW (449bhp) Jinan Diesel Engine Co Ltd-China
7802976 *BKEV* -	**YI YANG 1** *ex* Fude *-2007* *ex* Jordan II *-2005* *ex* Blue Horizon *-1995* *ex* Horizon *-1994* *ex* Far Star *-1992* *ex* Tucurui *-1989* **Fude Maritime Ltd** Shanghai Deqin Beautiful Ocean Ship Management Co Ltd *China* MMSI: 413405540	**8,203** 6,190 14,600	Class: (LR) (CC) (NV) ✠ Classed LR until 25/7/05	**1988-06 Cia Comercio e Navegacao (CCN) — Niteroi (Estaleiro Maua)** Yd No: 160 Loa 140.97 Br ex 20.46 Dght 8.850 Lbp 134.16 Br md 20.42 Dpth 11.73 Welded, 2 dks	**(A31A2GX) General Cargo Ship** Grain: 20,179; Bale: 18,261; Liq: 1,534 TEU 188 Compartments: ER, 5 Ho, 5 Tw Dk 5 Ha: (11.5 x 6.7) (12.4 x 10.2)2 (12.9 x 10.2)ER (11.4 x 6.3) Derricks: 1x40t,8x10t,2x5t	**1 oil engine** driving 1 FP propeller Total Power: 6,179kW (8,401hp) 15.0k MAN K6Z70/12C 1 x 2 Stroke 6 Cy. 700 x 1200 6179kW (8401bhp) Mecanica Pesada SA-Brazil AuxGen: 3 x 340kW 450V 60Hz a.c Fuel: 115.0 (d.f.) 1287.5 (r.f.) 28.0pd

IMO / Call sign	Name / Owner / Flag	Tonnage	Class	Builder / Dimensions	Type / Cargo	Machinery
9317224 *BICY* -	**YI YI** *ex* Regina Sapphire *-2013* **Chien Yang Shipping Co Ltd** - *Keelung* *Chinese Taipei* MMSI: 416479000	**4,754** 2,819 7,733	Class: (NK)	**2006-06 Shin Kurushima Dockyard Co. Ltd. — Hashihama, Imabari** Yd No: 5416 Loa 99.93 Br ex - Dght 7.241 Lbp 93.00 Br md 19.20 Dpth 8.90 Welded, 1 dk	**(A31A2GX) General Cargo Ship** Grain: 9,807; Bale: 9,198 Cranes: 1x30t; Derricks: 2x30t	**1 oil engine** driving 1 FP propeller Total Power: 3,250kW (4,419hp) 13.3kn MAN-B&W 5L35MC 1 x 2 Stroke 5 Cy. 350 x 1050 3250kW (4419bhp) Makita Corp-Japan Fuel: 590.0
9094808 - -	**YI YUAN BO 203** *ex* Xu Yun 203 *-2005* **Chen Zicheng** - *China*	**810** 421 361		**1984-12 Guangdong New China Shipyard Co Ltd — Dongguan GD** Loa 67.08 Br ex - Dght - Lbp - Br md 11.60 Dpth 3.80 Welded, 1 dk	**(A31A2GX) General Cargo Ship**	**2 oil engines** geared to sc. shafts driving 2 FP propellers Total Power: 880kW (1,196hp) Chinese Std. Type 6300 2 x 4 Stroke 6 Cy. 300 x 380 each-440kW (598bhp) Guangzhou Diesel Engine Factory CoLtd-China
9130987 *BIIV* -	**YI YUN** *ex* Jin Rong *-2008* **Sinotrans Container Lines Co Ltd** - *Shanghai* *China* MMSI: 413605000	**4,822** 2,476 6,816 T/cm 16.5	Class: CC	**1996-05 Dae Sun Shipbuilding & Engineering Co Ltd — Busan** Yd No: 421 Loa 113.00 (BB) Br ex - Dght 6.500 Lbp 103.00 Br md 19.00 Dpth 8.50 Welded, 1 dk	**(A33A2CC) Container Ship (Fully Cellular)** TEU 385 Compartments: 6 Cell Ho, ER 6 Ha: ER	**1 oil engine** driving 1 FP propeller Total Power: 3,354kW (4,560hp) 14.0kn B&W 6L35MC 1 x 2 Stroke 6 Cy. 350 x 1050 3354kW (4560bhp) Ssangyong Heavy Industries Co Ltd-South Korea
9635573 *BKOF6* -	**YI ZHOU 2** - **Zhejiang Yizhou Shipping Co Ltd** - *Zhoushan, Zhejiang* *China*	**5,766** 3,228 8,507	Class: CC	**2012-06 Ningbo Dongfang Shipyard Co Ltd — Ningbo ZJ** Yd No: DFC11-119 Loa 121.93 Br ex - Dght 7.285 Lbp 113.50 Br md 18.00 Dpth 9.00 Welded, 1 dk	**(A13B2TP) Products Tanker** Double Hull (13F) Ice Capable	**1 oil engine** reduction geared to sc. shaft driving 1 FP propeller Total Power: 2,501kW (3,400hp) 14.0kn Chinese Std. Type GN8320ZC 1 x 4 Stroke 8 Cy. 320 x 380 2501kW (3400bhp) Ningbo CSI Power & Machinery GroupCo Ltd-China
8920062 *3EWX8* -	**YIALIA** *ex* Newlead Esmeralda *-2012* *ex* Grand Esmeralda *-2010* *ex* Santa Esmeralda *-2007* *ex* Oceanic Ensign *-2005* *ex* Oceanic Esprit *-2004* *ex* Merchant Pride *-1998* **Lyon Shipping & Trading Co Ltd** Karlog Shipping Co Ltd *Panama* *Panama* MMSI: 373111000 Official number: 4388112	**36,725** 23,310 69,458 T/cm 67.0	Class: BV (LR) (NK) ✠ Classed LR until 28/11/00	**1990-07 Nippon Kokan KK (NKK Corp) — Tsu ME** Yd No: 121 Loa 225.00 (BB) Br ex 32.28 Dght 13.267 Lbp 216.00 Br md 32.24 Dpth 18.30 Welded, 1 dk	**(A21A2BC) Bulk Carrier** Grain: 81,855 TEU 988 Compartments: 7 Ho, ER 7 Ha: (14.8 x 11.2)6 (16.8 x 14.4)ER	**1 oil engine** driving 1 FP propeller Total Power: 8,096kW (11,007hp) 13.5kn Sulzer 6RTA62 1 x 2 Stroke 6 Cy. 620 x 2150 8096kW (11007bhp) Diesel United Ltd.-Aioi AuxGen: 3 x 480kW 450V 60Hz a.c Fuel: 206.0 (d.f.) 2485.0 (r.f.) 31.6pd
9414931 *9HA3033* -	**YIANGOS** - **Unified Investments Inc Ltd** Dynacom Tankers Management Ltd *Valletta* *Malta* MMSI: 229059000 Official number: 9414931	**156,651** 98,944 296,800 T/cm 177.4	Class: AB	**2010-08 Shanghai Jiangnan Changxing Shipbuilding Co Ltd — Shanghai** Yd No: H2415 Loa 330.00 (BB) Br ex 60.04 Dght 21.500 Lbp 316.00 Br md 60.00 Dpth 29.70 Welded, 1 dk	**(A13A2TV) Crude Oil Tanker** Double Hull (13F) Liq: 324,800; Liq (Oil): 324,800 Cargo Heating Coils Compartments: 5 Ta, 10 Wing Ta, 2 Wing Slop Ta, ER 3 Cargo Pump (s): 3x5500m³/hr Manifold: Bow/CM: 162m	**1 oil engine** driving 1 FP propeller Total Power: 22,932kW (31,178hp) 15.8kn MAN-B&W 7S80MC 1 x 2 Stroke 7 Cy. 800 x 3056 22932kW (31178bhp) CSSC MES Diesel Co Ltd-China AuxGen: 3 x 1050kW a.c Fuel: 430.0 (d.f.) 7200.0 (r.f.)
9394765 *A8OK9* -	**YIANNIS B** - **Ray Sea Shipping SA** Tsakos Columbia Shipmanagement (TCM) SA *Monrovia* *Liberia* MMSI: 636013646 Official number: 13646	**43,158** 27,291 82,562 T/cm 70.2	Class: BV CC (NK)	**2008-06 Tsuneishi Group (Zhoushan) Shipbuilding Inc — Daishan County ZJ** Yd No: SS-032 Loa 228.99 Br ex - Dght 14.430 Lbp 222.00 Br md 32.26 Dpth 20.03 Welded, 1 dk	**(A21A2BC) Bulk Carrier** Grain: 97,186 Compartments: 7 Ho, ER 7 Ha: ER	**1 oil engine** driving 1 FP propeller Total Power: 9,800kW (13,324hp) 14.5kn MAN-B&W 7S50MC-C 1 x 2 Stroke 7 Cy. 500 x 2000 9800kW (13324bhp) Mitsui Engineering & Shipbuilding CLtd-Japan AuxGen: 4 x 320kW a.c Fuel: 2870.0
5023643 *HP7240* -	**YICEL** *ex* Sea Caribbean *-2008* *ex* El Cacique *-2006* *ex* El Cacique I *-2000* *ex* El Cacique *-1981* *ex* Birgit B *-1981* *ex* Rewi *-1975* *ex* Ariadne *-1971* **Yicel Maritime Inc** - *Panama* *Panama* Official number: 45337PEXT	*195* 121 378	Class: (GL)	**1961 J.J. Sietas Schiffswerft — Hamburg** Yd No: 493 Loa 41.31 Br ex 7.29 Dght 2.515 Lbp 38.00 Br md 7.27 Dpth 3.10 Welded, 1 dk	**(A31A2GX) General Cargo Ship** Grain: 481; Bale: 453 Compartments: 1 Ho, ER 1 Ha: (18.9 x 4.7)ER Derricks: 2x2t; Winches: 2 Ice Capable	**1 oil engine** geared to sc. shaft driving 1 FP propeller Total Power: 382kW (519hp) 10.0kn Caterpillar 3412 1 x Vee 4 Stroke 12 Cy. 137 x 152 382kW (519bhp) (new engine 2013) AuxGen: 1 x 1kW 24V d.c, 1 x 1kW 24V d.c Fuel: 9.5
9158393 *3FHI7* -	**YICHANGHAI** - **Yichanghai Shipping Inc** COSCO (Cayman) Fortune Holding Co Ltd SatCom: Inmarsat B 335111910 *Panama* *Panama* MMSI: 351119000 Official number: 2379497CH	**18,074** 9,485 26,748 T/cm 38.9	Class: CC (AB)	**1997-05 Hudong Shipbuilding Group — Shanghai** Yd No: H1230A Loa 175.00 (BB) Br ex - Dght 9.800 Lbp 165.00 Br md 26.00 Dpth 13.90 Welded, 1 dk	**(A21A2BC) Bulk Carrier** Grain: 37,996; Bale: 35,742 Compartments: 5 Ho, ER 5 Ha: (14.2 x 12.8)4 (19.2 x 14.4)ER Cranes: 4x30t	**1 oil engine** driving 1 FP propeller Total Power: 5,848kW (7,951hp) 14.0kn B&W 5L50MC 1 x 2 Stroke 5 Cy. 500 x 1620 5848kW (7951bhp) Hudong Shipyard-China
7531022 - -	**YIDONG** *ex* Bama *-1998* *ex* Erminia *-1997* *ex* Kenyo Maru No. 2 *-1989* -	**922** 468 1,335	Class: (NK)	**1976-07 Sasaki Shipbuilding Co Ltd — Osakikamijima HS** Yd No: 304 Loa 56.04 Br ex 10.04 Dght 4.293 Lbp 55.28 Br md 10.01 Dpth 6.23 Welded, 2 dks	**(A31A2GX) General Cargo Ship** 1 Ha: (30.3 x 7.0)ER	**1 oil engine** driving 1 FP propeller Total Power: 1,177kW (1,600hp) Akasaka DM33 1 x 4 Stroke 6 Cy. 330 x 500 1177kW (1600bhp) Akasaka Tekkosho KK (Akasaka DieselLtd)-Japan
9187411 *9V5604* -	**YIEW SOON No. 2** - **Intone Pte Ltd** DP Marine Pte Ltd *Singapore* *Singapore* MMSI: 564567000 Official number: 388184	**196** 59 202	Class: NK	**1998-02 Yii Brothers Shipbuilding Contractor Co — Sibu** Yd No: 3397 Loa 26.50 Br ex - Dght 2.848 Lbp 24.75 Br md 8.00 Dpth 3.66 Welded, 1 dk	**(B32A2ST) Tug**	**2 oil engines** reduction geared to sc. shafts driving 2 FP propellers Total Power: 1,412kW (1,920hp) 11.0kn Caterpillar 3508TA 2 x Vee 4 Stroke 8 Cy. 170 x 190 each-706kW (960bhp) Caterpillar Inc-USA AuxGen: 2 x 50kW a.c Fuel: 147.0 (d.f.)
9007104 *9HUZ9* -	**YIGIT** *ex* Sichem Castel *-2011* *ex* Pointe Du Castel *-2008* **Transchem Shipping Ltd** Hicri Ercili Deniz Nakliyat Sanayi ve Ticaret Ltd Sti *Valletta* *Malta* MMSI: 249569000 Official number: 9007104	**3,222** 1,417 4,216 T/cm 11.0	Class: BV	**1992-06 Aukra Industrier AS — Aukra** Yd No: 83 Loa 87.50 (BB) Br ex 15.20 Dght 6.160 Lbp 82.20 Br md 15.20 Dpth 8.80 Welded, 1 dk	**(A12B2TR) Chemical/Products Tanker** Double Hull Liq: 5,038; Liq (Oil): 4,897 Cargo Heating Coils Compartments: 16 Ta, ER, 1 Wing Slop Ta 16 Cargo Pump (s): 16x175m³/hr Manifold: Bow/CM: 44.2m	**1 oil engine** sr geared to sc. shaft driving 1 CP propeller Total Power: 2,940kW (3,997hp) 14.1kn Wartsila 8R32D 1 x 4 Stroke 8 Cy. 320 x 350 2940kW (3997bhp) Wartsila Diesel Oy-Finland AuxGen: 3 x 326kW 440V 60Hz a.c Thrusters: 1 Thwart. FP thruster (f) Fuel: 52.0 (d.f.) (Part Heating Coils) 262.0 (r.f.) 17.0pd
9238076 *TCTP* -	**YIGITCAN A** *ex* Vento di Aliseo *-2005* *ex* Yigitcan A *-2001* **Limar Liman ve Gemi Isletmeleri AS (Limar Port & Ship Operators SA)** Arkas Denizcilik ve Nakliyat AS (Arkas Shipping & Transport AS) *Izmir* *Turkey* MMSI: 271000654 Official number: 3212	**14,193** 4,960 17,264 T/cm 32.8	Class: BV (GL)	**2001-10 Peene-Werft GmbH — Wolgast** Yd No: 433 Loa 154.53 (BB) Br ex - Dght 9.000 Lbp 146.70 Br md 24.50 Dpth 14.20 Welded, 1 dk	**(A33A2CC) Container Ship (Fully Cellular)** Double Bottom Entire Compartment Length TEU 1208 C Ho 476 TEU C Dk 732 TEU incl 178 ref C. Compartments: 4 Cell Ho, ER 7 Ha: ER Ice Capable	**1 oil engine** driving 1 CP propeller Total Power: 11,060kW (15,037hp) 19.3kn MAN-B&W 7S50MC-C 1 x 2 Stroke 7 Cy. 500 x 2000 11060kW (15037bhp) MAN B&W Diesel A/S-Denmark AuxGen: 3 x 782kW 440/220V 60Hz a.c, 1 x 900kW 440/220V 60Hz a.c Thrusters: 1 Thwart. FP thruster (f) Fuel: 244.1 (d.f.) (Heating Coils) 1166.0 (r.f.) 48.0pd
7947104 *TCBW2* -	**YIGITHAN** *ex* Filiz I *-2009* *ex* Enis Kose *-1992* *ex* Ali Kalyoncu *-1992* **Arda Denizcilik Nurdan** - *Istanbul* *Turkey* MMSI: 271002701 Official number: 4368	**563** 286 840		**1975 Desan Tersanesi — Tuzla, Istanbul** Loa 60.90 Br ex - Dght 3.540 Lbp 58.63 Br md 8.02 Dpth 3.71 Welded, 1 dk	**(A31A2GX) General Cargo Ship**	**1 oil engine** driving 1 FP propeller Total Power: 368kW (500hp) 8.0kn S.K.L. 6NVD36-1U 1 x 4 Stroke 6 Cy. 240 x 360 368kW (500bhp) VEB Schwermaschinenbau "KarlLiebknecht" (SKL)-Magdeburg
8626977 - -	**YIH CHUEN No. 1** - **Yih Chuen Fishery Co Ltd** - *Kaohsiung* *Chinese Taipei* Official number: CT5-0490	*205* 61 -		**1968 San Yang Shipbuilding Co., Ltd. — Kaohsiung** Loa - Br ex - Dght - Lbp - Br md - Dpth - Welded	**(B11B2FV) Fishing Vessel**	**1 oil engine** driving 1 FP propeller

No.	Name / Owner	Tonnage	Class	Construction	Type	Machinery
7236543 - -	**YIH CHYUN No. 315** *ex* Seishu Maru No. 35 *-1981* **Y C F Fishery Co Ltd** - *Kaohsiung* *Chinese Taipei*	*430* 215 524		**1972-07 Miho Zosensho K.K. — Shimizu** Yd No: 835 Loa 57.46 Br ex 9.02 Dght 3.849 Lbp 49.00 Br md 9.00 Dpth 4.12 Welded, 1 dk	**(B11B2FV) Fishing Vessel**	**1 oil engine** driving 1 FP propeller Total Power: 1,324kW (1,800hp) Hanshin 6LUD35 1 x 4 Stroke 6 Cy. 350 x 550 1324kW (1800bhp) Hanshin Nainenki Kogyo-Japan
8648315 *BI2428* LL0844	**YIH LONG NO. 101** *ex* Pai Lung No. 6 *-2011* **Yih Long Fishery Co Ltd** - *Kaohsiung* *Chinese Taipei* Official number: CT7-0428	**722** 284 -		**1990-03 Sen Koh Shipbuilding Corp — Kaohsiung** Loa 50.60 Br ex 8.90 Dght - Lbp - Br md - Dpth - Welded, 1 dk	**(B11B2FV) Fishing Vessel**	**1 oil engine** driving 1 Propeller
9176345 *BH3353* LL2290	**YIH SHUEN No. 212** **Yih Shuen Fishery SA** - *Kaohsiung* *Chinese Taipei* Official number: CT6-1353	**483** 202 -		**1997 Sen Koh Shipbuilding Corp — Kaohsiung** Loa 45.60 Br ex - Dght - Lbp - Br md 8.30 Dpth 3.30 Welded, 1 dk	**(B11B2FV) Fishing Vessel**	**1 oil engine** driving 1 FP propeller Total Power: 883kW (1,201hp) Niigata 6M26AFTE 1 x 4 Stroke 6 Cy. 260 x 460 883kW (1201bhp) Niigata Engineering Co Ltd-Japan
9086667 *TCPB4* -	**YILDIRIM BEYAZID** *ex* San Marco *-2013* *ex* Flying Viking II *-2007* *ex* Sapphire Express *-2007* *ex* Bridge 1 *-2004* *ex* Universal Mk V *-1995* **Burulas-Bursa Ulasim Toplu Tasim Isletmeciligi Sanayi ve Ticaret AS** - *Istanbul* *Turkey* MMSI: 271043572 Official number: 26722	**480** 144 75	Class: TL (NV)	**1993-12 Kvaerner Fjellstrand (S) Pte Ltd — Singapore** Yd No: 006 Loa 40.00 Br ex - Dght 3.970 Lbp 37.04 Br md 10.10 Dpth 3.97 Welded, 1 dk	**(A37B2PS) Passenger Ship** Passengers: unberthed: 266	**2 oil engines** geared to sc. shafts driving 2 Water jets Total Power: 3,785kW (5,146hp) 30.0kn M.T.U. 16V396TE74 2 x Vee 4 Stroke 16 Cy. 165 x 185 each-1814kW (2466bhp) MTU Friedrichshafen GmbH-Friedrichshafen
8031407 - -	**YILDIRIMLAR-1** *ex* Aras 10 *-2008* *ex* Odisk *-2007* *ex* Modisk 6 *-2005* *ex* Om *-2003* - -	**1,696** 715 2,187	Class: (RS)	**1980-03 VEB Elbewerften Boizenburg/Rosslau — Rosslau** Yd No: 3430 Loa 82.02 Br ex 11.80 Dght 3.900 Lbp 78.11 Br md 11.61 Dpth 4.00 Welded, 1 dk	**(A31A2GX) General Cargo Ship** TEU 70 C.Ho 34/20' C.Dk 36/20' Compartments: 2 Ho, ER 2 Ha: ER	**2 oil engines** driving 2 FP propellers Total Power: 882kW (1,200hp) S.K.L. 8VD36/24A-1 2 x 4 Stroke 8 Cy. 240 x 360 each-441kW (600bhp) VEB Schwermaschinenbau "KarlLiebknecht" (SKL)-Magdeburg Fuel: 73.0 (d.f.)
9592484 *TCZJ2* -	**YILDIZBURNU** **Arkas Petrol Urunleri ve Ticaret AS (Arkas Bunkering & Trading SA)** *Izmir* *Turkey* MMSI: 271042475	**989** 428 1,770	Class: BV	**2011-03 Celiktrans Deniz Insaat Kizaklari Ltd. Sti — Tuzla,Ist** Yd No: CS41 Loa 61.25 (BB) Br ex - Dght 4.312 Lbp 58.00 Br md 11.00 Dpth 5.10 Welded, 1 dk	**(A13B2TP) Products Tanker** Double Hull (13F) Liq: 1,604; Liq (Oil): 1,604 Compartments: 6 Wing Ta, 6 Wing Ta, ER 3 Cargo Pump (s): 2x250m³/hr, 1x120m³/hr	**2 oil engines** reduction geared to sc. shafts driving 2 FP propellers Total Power: 736kW (1,000hp) 10.5kn Cummins KTA-19-M1 2 x 4 Stroke 6 Cy. 159 x 159 each-368kW (500bhp) Cummins Engine Co Inc-USA AuxGen: 2 x 220kW 50Hz a.c Thrusters: 1 Tunnel thruster (f) Fuel: 44.9
9002544 *TCME6* -	**YILDIZLAR** *ex* Soul Of Luck *-2011* *ex* Forest King *-2009* **Yildiz Tarimsal Urunler ve Gubre Sanayi AS** Pasifik Lojistik Grubu ve Denizcilik AS SatCom: Inmarsat C 427101164 *Istanbul* *Turkey* MMSI: 271042625	**38,716** 19,368 46,826	Class: NK	**1991-02 Shin Kurushima Dockyard Co. Ltd. — Onishi** Yd No: 2696 Loa 199.98 (BB) Br ex - Dght 11.027 Lbp 191.50 Br md 32.20 Dpth 22.35 Welded, 1 dk	**(A24B2BW) Wood Chips Carrier** Grain: 99,839 Compartments: 6 Ho, ER 6 Ha: 5 (14.4 x 17.6) (12.8 x 17.6)ER Cranes: 3x14.5t	**1 oil engine** driving 1 FP propeller Total Power: 7,356kW (10,001hp) 13.0kn Mitsubishi 6UEC52LS 1 x 2 Stroke 6 Cy. 520 x 1850 7356kW (10001bhp) Kobe Hatsudoki KK-Japan AuxGen: 4 x 530kW a.c Fuel: 2080.0 (r.f.)
9145695 *TCUU4* -	**YILDIZLAR 2** *ex* Forest Creator *-2012* **Yildizlar Deniz Isletmeciligi AS** Pasifik Lojistik Grubu ve Denizcilik AS SatCom: Inmarsat C 427101363 *Istanbul* *Turkey* MMSI: 271043213	**40,328** 18,403 49,865 T/cm 57.0	Class: NK	**1996-09 Imabari Shipbuilding Co Ltd — Marugame KG (Marugame Shipyard)** Yd No: 1264 Loa 199.91 (BB) Br ex 32.24 Dght 11.547 Lbp 193.00 Br md 32.20 Dpth 22.65 Welded, 1 dk	**(A24B2BW) Wood Chips Carrier** Grain: 102,307 Compartments: 6 Ho, ER 6 Ha: 6 (14.4 x 19.2)ER Cranes: 3x14.5t	**1 oil engine** driving 1 FP propeller Total Power: 8,952kW (12,171hp) 14.7kn Mitsubishi 7UEC50LSII 1 x 2 Stroke 7 Cy. 500 x 1950 8952kW (12171bhp) Akasaka Tekkosho KK (Akasaka DieselLtd)-Japan AuxGen: 3 x 680kW 450V 60Hz a.c Fuel: 273.0 (d.f.) (Heating Coils) 2807.0 (r.f.) 35.0pd
9166510 *TCYN* -	**YILMAZ AYANOGLU** **Ayanoglu Denizcilik ve Ticaret AS** *Istanbul* *Turkey* MMSI: 271000575 Official number: 7491	**2,950** 1,807 4,600	Class: BV (TL)	**1999-05 Gisa — Tuzla** Yd No: 21 Loa 93.72 Br ex - Dght 6.080 Lbp 84.50 Br md 14.85 Dpth 7.50 Welded, 1 dk	**(A31A2GX) General Cargo Ship** Grain: 6,523; Bale: 5,741 Compartments: 2 Ho, ER	**1 diesel electric oil engine** reduction geared to sc. shaft driving 1 CP propeller Total Power: 1,999kW (2,718hp) 13.0kn MaK 6M32 1 x 4 Stroke 6 Cy. 320 x 480 1999kW (2718bhp) MaK Motoren GmbH & Co. KG-Kiel
8132598 *TCAU2* -	**YILMAZ KAPTAN** *ex* Kaptan Ahmat Paksoy *-2001* **Doganbey Denizcilik Isletmeleri Sanayi ve Ticaret Ltd Sti** - *Istanbul* *Turkey* MMSI: 271002143 Official number: 203	**942** 481 1,479	Class: TL (BV)	**1979-05 Cemalettin Oyar — Istanbul** Lengthened-1995 Loa 73.05 Br ex - Dght 3.550 Lbp 66.80 Br md 9.11 Dpth 4.14 Welded, 1 dk	**(A31A2GX) General Cargo Ship** Grain: 1,048; Bale: 1,027 Compartments: 2 Ho, ER 2 Ha: (14.8 x 6.0) (11.9 x 6.0)ER Derricks: 4x2t	**1 oil engine** reduction geared to sc. shaft driving 1 FP propeller Total Power: 625kW (850hp) 10.0kn S.K.L. 6NVD48-2U 1 x 4 Stroke 6 Cy. 320 x 480 625kW (850bhp) VEB Schwermaschinenbau "KarlLiebknecht" (SKL)-Magdeburg AuxGen: 2 x 16kW 220/380V a.c
9113575 *BPJV* -	**YIN BAO** *ex* Orpheus Island *-2007* *ex* VOC Orchid *-2006* *ex* Grand Orchid *-2004* **Shanghai Time Shipping Co Ltd** Taihua Ship Management (Shanghai) Ltd *Shanghai* *China* MMSI: 413268000	**27,610** 15,244 45,513 T/cm 51.6	Class: (LR) (CC) (AB) Classed LR until 21/1/07	**1996-03 Jiangnan Shipyard (Group) Co Ltd — Shanghai** Yd No: H2212 Loa 190.00 (BB) Br ex - Dght 11.649 Lbp 180.00 Br md 31.00 Dpth 16.50 Welded, 1 dk	**(A21A2BC) Bulk Carrier** Grain: 57,999; Bale: 56,320 Compartments: 5 Ho, ER 5 Ha: (20.0 x 16.1)4 (20.8 x 17.7)ER Cranes: 4x30t	**1 oil engine** driving 1 FP propeller Total Power: 8,520kW (11,584hp) 14.5kn Sulzer 6RTA52 1 x 2 Stroke 6 Cy. 520 x 1800 8520kW (11584bhp) Shanghai Shipyard-China AuxGen: 3 x 510kW 450V 60Hz a.c Boilers: e (ex.g.), WTAuxB (o.f.) Fuel: 102.9 (d.f.) (Heating Coils) 2012.2 (r.f.) 31.8pd
9636199 *BPOJ* -	**YIN CAI** **Shanghai Time Shipping Co Ltd** - *Shanghai* *China* MMSI: 414737000	**30,472** 15,077 48,929	Class: CC	**2012-12 Chengxi Shipyard Co Ltd — Jiangyin JS** Yd No: CX0418 Loa 189.99 (BB) Br ex - Dght 10.500 Lbp 187.00 Br md 32.26 Dpth 16.50 Welded, 1 dk	**(A21A2BC) Bulk Carrier** Grain: 62,112 Compartments: 5 Ho, ER 5 Ha: 4 (20.2 x 18.3)ER (17.6 x 18.3) Cranes: 4x30t	**1 oil engine** driving 1 FP propeller Total Power: 8,280kW (11,257hp) 14.2kn Wartsila 6RT-flex48T 1 x 2 Stroke 6 Cy. 480 x 2000 8280kW (11257bhp) Hudong Heavy Machinery Co Ltd-China AuxGen: 3 x 625kW 450V a.c
8625959 - -	**YIN DE** *ex* Cheng Gong 69 *-2007* *ex* Seiwa *-1998* **Hongkong Hangliang Shipping Co Ltd** Yantai Hangcheng International Shipping Management Co Ltd	**1,390** 630 1,588	Class: (NK)	**1985-10 Kinoura Zosen K.K. — Imabari** Loa 73.51 Br ex - Dght 4.341 Lbp 68.00 Br md 11.60 Dpth 7.29 Welded, 1 dk	**(A31A2GX) General Cargo Ship** Grain: 2,660; Bale: 2,545 1 Ha: (37.8 x 9.0)ER	**1 oil engine** driving 1 FP propeller Total Power: 956kW (1,300hp) 11.5kn Daihatsu 6DLM-28S 1 x 4 Stroke 6 Cy. 280 x 360 956kW (1300bhp) Daihatsu Diesel Manufacturing Co Lt-Japan
9077381 *BPJS* -	**YIN DONG** *ex* Dimitris C *-2007* *ex* Aditya Gopal *-2002* *ex* Skausund *-1994* **Shanghai Time Shipping Co Ltd** China Shipping International Shipmanagement Co Ltd *Shanghai* *China* MMSI: 413266000	**26,824** 13,885 43,815 T/cm 51.6	Class: (CC) (NV) (IR)	**1994-05 Daewoo Shipbuilding & Heavy Machinery Ltd — Geoje** Yd No: 1072 Loa 190.00 (BB) Br ex 30.54 Dght 11.221 Lbp 181.00 Br md 30.50 Dpth 16.60 Welded, 1 dk	**(A21A2BC) Bulk Carrier** Grain: 56,670; Bale: 54,930 Compartments: 5 Ho, ER 5 Ha: 5 (18.9 x 16.0)ER Cranes: 4x25t	**1 oil engine** driving 1 FP propeller Total Power: 8,290kW (11,271hp) 14.0kn B&W 6S50MC 1 x 2 Stroke 6 Cy. 500 x 1910 8290kW (11271bhp) Korea Heavy Industries & ConstrCo Ltd (HANJUNG)-South Korea AuxGen: 3 x 500kW 220/450V 60Hz a.c Fuel: 129.0 (d.f.) 1627.0 (r.f.)
9636163 *BPOG* -	**YIN FU** **Shanghai Time Shipping Co Ltd** - *Shanghai* *China* MMSI: 414702000	**30,472** 15,083 48,909	Class: CC	**2012-05 Chengxi Shipyard Co Ltd — Jiangyin JS** Yd No: CX0415 Loa 190.00 (BB) Br ex - Dght 10.500 Lbp 187.00 Br md 32.26 Dpth 16.50 Welded, 1 dk	**(A21A2BC) Bulk Carrier** Grain: 62,112 Compartments: 5 Ho, ER 5 Ha: 4 (20.2 x 18.3)ER (17.6 x 18.3) Cranes: 4x30t	**1 oil engine** driving 1 FP propeller Total Power: 8,280kW (11,257hp) 14.2kn Wartsila 6RT-flex48T 1 x 2 Stroke 6 Cy. 480 x 2000 8280kW (11257bhp) Hudong Heavy Machinery Co Ltd-China AuxGen: 3 x 625kW 450V a.c

484314 **YIN GUI**
JZL
Sinochem Shipping Co Ltd (Hainan)
Aoxing Ship Management (Shanghai) Ltd
SatCom: Inmarsat Mini-M 764825015
Haikou, Hainan *China*
MMSI: 413333000

8,551 Class: CC
4,044
12,710
T/cm
22.6

2008-04 **Zhejiang Changhong Shipbuilding Co Ltd — Wenling ZJ** Yd No: 0602
Loa 134.85 (BB) Br ex 22.03 Dght 7.806
Lbp 126.83 Br md 22.00 Dpth 10.60
Welded, 1 dk

(A12B2TR) Chemical/Products Tanker
Double Hull (13F)
Liq: 14,148; Liq (Oil): 14,148
Compartments: 10 Wing Ta, 2 Wing Slop Ta, ER
10 Cargo Pump (s): 10x300m³/hr
Manifold: Bow/CM: 62.8m

1 oil engine reduction geared to sc. shaft driving 1 FP propeller
Total Power: 3,824kW (5,199hp) 13.0kn
Pielstick 8PC2-5L
1 x 4 Stroke 8 Cy. 400 x 460 3824kW (5199bhp)
Guangzhou Diesel Engine Factory CoLtd-China
AuxGen: 3 x 300kW a.c
Thrusters: 1 Tunnel thruster (f)
Fuel: 189.0 (d.f.) 1058.0 (r.f.)

022121 **YIN HAI**
-
-
ex Da Kai *-2006* *ex* Min Fortune *-2003*
ex Laksana II *-1993* *ex* Balsa II *-1989*
China Bright Shipping Ltd
Xin Yin Hai Shipping Ltd
Panama *Panama*

3,994 Class: (NK)
2,424
6,246

1980-12 **K.K. Taihei Kogyo — Akitsu** Yd No: 1412
Loa 106.43 Br ex 16.44 Dght 6.702
Lbp 97.95 Br md 16.41 Dpth 8.16
Welded, 1 dk

(A31A2GX) General Cargo Ship
Grain: 8,346; Bale: 7,653
Compartments: 2 Ho, ER
2 Ha: (28.4 x 8.3) (28.5 x 8.3)ER
Derricks: 4x15t

1 oil engine driving 1 FP propeller
Total Power: 2,795kW (3,800hp) 15.6kn
Mitsubishi 6UET45/75C
1 x 2 Stroke 6 Cy. 450 x 750 2795kW (3800bhp)
Akasaka Tekkosho KK (Akasaka DieselLtd)-Japan
AuxGen: 2 x 160kW

636187 **YIN HAO**
BPOI
-
Shanghai Time Shipping Co Ltd
Fujian Shipping Co (FUSCO)
Shanghai *China*
MMSI: 414730000

30,472 Class: CC
15,077
48,905

2012-10 **Chengxi Shipyard Co Ltd — Jiangyin JS** Yd No: CX0417
Loa 189.99 Br ex - Dght 10.500
Lbp 187.00 Br md 32.26 Dpth 16.50
Welded, 1 dk

(A21A2BC) Bulk Carrier
Grain: 62,089
Compartments: 5 Ho, ER
5 Ha: 4 (20.2 x 18.3)ER (17.6 x 18.3)
Cranes: 4x30t

1 oil engine driving 1 FP propeller
Total Power: 8,280kW (11,257hp) 14.2kn
Wartsila 6RT-flex48T
1 x 2 Stroke 6 Cy. 480 x 2000 8280kW (11257bhp)
Hudong Heavy Machinery Co Ltd-China
AuxGen: 3 x 625kW 450V a.c

9654206 **YIN HE**
BPOM
-
Shanghai Time Shipping Co Ltd
-
Shanghai *China*
MMSI: 414768000

29,644 Class: CC
14,134
44,952

2014-01 **Qingdao Wuchuan Heavy Industry Co Ltd — Qingdao SD** Yd No: A226L
Loa 189.98 (BB) Br ex - Dght 10.500
Lbp 186.50 Br md 32.26 Dpth 16.00
Welded, 1 dk

(A21A2BC) Bulk Carrier
Grain: 60,200
Cranes: 4x30t

1 oil engine driving 1 FP propeller
Total Power: 9,480kW (12,889hp) 14.5kn
MAN-B&W 6S50MC-C
1 x 2 Stroke 6 Cy. 500 x 2000 9480kW (12889bhp)
Yichang Marine Diesel Engine Co Ltd-China

8126355 **YIN HE 7**
BHXW
-
ex Xi Rui 503 *-2012* *ex* Run Tong *-2011*
ex An Da Hai *-2009* *ex* Xi Rui 503 *-2008*
ex Ganghai 636 *-2008* *ex* Atlantic *-2002*
ex Atlantico *-1996*
Nanjing Laizhou Shipping Co Ltd
Nanjing Zhongda Shipping Transportation Co Ltd
Nanjing, Jiangsu *China*
MMSI: 413362440
Official number: CN19834221242

16,200 Class: ZC (IB) (BV) (AB)
9,072
26,702

1984-12 **Cia Comercio e Navegacao (CCN) — Niteroi (Estaleiro Maua)** Yd No: 164
Loa 173.16 (BB) Br ex - Dght 9.721
Lbp 162.01 Br md 26.61 Dpth 13.52
Welded, 1 dk

(A21A2BC) Bulk Carrier
Grain: 36,775; Bale: 32,095
TEU 549 C Ho 375 TEU C Dk 174 TEU
Compartments: 5 Ho, ER
5 Ha: (12.5 x 11.4) (19.6 x 16.5) (12.4 x 16.5)2 (19.8 x 16.5)ER

1 oil engine driving 1 FP propeller
Total Power: 5,502kW (7,481hp) 13.7kn
B&W 5L55GFCA
1 x 2 Stroke 5 Cy. 550 x 1380 5502kW (7481bhp)
Mecanica Pesada SA-Brazil
AuxGen: 3 x 296kW 450V 60Hz a.c

8307375 **YIN HUA**
BPDQ
-
ex Sea Fortune *-2004* *ex* Sky Hope *-2002*
ex Cebu Sampaguita *-1994*
ex Diamond Wisteria *-1989*
ex Sanko Wisteria *-1987*
Shanghai Time Shipping Co Ltd
China Shipping Guangzhou Ship Management Co Ltd
Shanghai *China*
MMSI: 412371770

24,942 Class: (CC) (NK)
14,148
42,838
T/cm
50.8

1985-01 **Mitsubishi Heavy Industries Ltd. — Nagasaki** Yd No: 1934
Loa 189.50 (BB) Br ex 30.03 Dght 10.994
Lbp 181.00 Br md 30.00 Dpth 15.70
Welded, 1 dk

(A21A2BC) Bulk Carrier
Grain: 54,070; Bale: 53,164
TEU 180
Compartments: 5 Ho, ER
5 Ha: 5 (19.2 x 15.0)ER
Cranes: 4x25t

1 oil engine driving 1 FP propeller
Total Power: 6,892kW (9,370hp) 14.2kn
Sulzer 6RTA58
1 x 2 Stroke 6 Cy. 580 x 1700 6892kW (9370bhp)
Mitsubishi Heavy Industries Ltd-Japan
AuxGen: 3 x 450kW 450V 60Hz a.c
Fuel: 183.0 (d.f.) (Heating Coils) 1370.0 (r.f.) 27.0pd

9673501 **YIN HUA 1**
BPOD
-
Shanghai Yinhua Shipping Co Ltd
China Shipping Bulk Carrier Co Ltd
Shanghai *China*
MMSI: 414767000

29,092 Class: CC
15,729
47,304

2013-11 **Jiangsu Newyangzi Shipbuilding Co Ltd — Jingjiang JS** Yd No: YZJ2012-1022
Loa 189.99 (BB) Br ex - Dght 10.500
Lbp 185.00 Br md 32.26 Dpth 15.50
Welded, 1 dk

(A21A2BC) Bulk Carrier
Grain: 60,276; Bale: 59,762
5 Ha: 4 (21.3 x 18.3)ER (18.9 x 18.3)
Ice Capable

1 oil engine driving 1 FP propeller
Total Power: 8,280kW (11,257hp) 14.3kn
MAN-B&W 6S46MC-C8
1 x 2 Stroke 6 Cy. 460 x 1932 8280kW (11257bhp)
Dalian Marine Diesel Co Ltd-China
AuxGen: 3 x 630kW 400V a.c

9348144 **YIN LI**
V3CU3
-
Belize Yin Li Shipping SA
Yantai Golden Ocean Shipping Co Ltd
Belize City *Belize*
MMSI: 312762000
Official number: 470520007

1,997 Class: CC
1,106
2,846

2005-05 **Qingdao Lingshan Ship Engineering Co Ltd — Jiaonan SD** Yd No: 118
Loa 79.99 (BB) Br ex - Dght 5.200
Lbp 74.00 Br md 13.60 Dpth 7.00
Welded, 1 dk

(A21A2BC) Bulk Carrier
Grain: 4,127; Bale: 3,893
Compartments: 1 Ho, ER
1 Ha: ER (38.4 x 10.0)
Ice Capable

1 oil engine geared to sc. shaft driving 1 FP propeller
Total Power: 1,080kW (1,468hp) 11.7kn
MAN-B&W 8L23/30
1 x 4 Stroke 8 Cy. 225 x 300 1080kW (1468bhp)
Zhenjiang Marine Diesel Works-China
AuxGen: 3 x 90kW 400V a.c

9493456 **YIN LIAN**
BPJX
-
Shanghai Time Shipping Co Ltd
China
MMSI: 413956000

33,511 Class: CC
19,142
57,000

2010-01 **China Shipping Industry (Jiangsu) Co Ltd — Jiangdu JS**
Loa 199.99 (BB) Br ex - Dght 12.500
Lbp 192.00 Br md 32.26 Dpth 18.00
Welded, 1 dk

(A21A2BC) Bulk Carrier
Grain: 71,634
Compartments: 5 Ho, ER
5 Ha: ER

1 oil engine driving 1 FP propeller
Total Power: 9,960kW (13,542hp) 14.2kn
MAN-B&W 6S50MC-C
1 x 2 Stroke 6 Cy. 500 x 2000 9960kW (13542bhp)

9012161 **YIN LONG**
XUJF7
-
ex Hosei Maru No. 58 *-2005*
Xin Yang Shipping Co Ltd
Yuan Da Shipping Co Ltd
Phnom Penh *Cambodia*
MMSI: 515851000
Official number: 0590125

1,594 Class: UB
1,075
1,517

1990-10 **Honda Zosen — Saiki** Yd No: 818
Loa 72.76 (BB) Br ex - Dght 4.360
Lbp 68.96 Br md 12.20 Dpth 7.00
Welded, 1 dk

(A31A2GX) General Cargo Ship

1 oil engine driving 1 CP propeller
Total Power: 1,177kW (1,600hp) 11.5kn
Hanshin 6LU35
1 x 4 Stroke 6 Cy. 350 x 550 1177kW (1600bhp)
The Hanshin Diesel Works Ltd-Japan
AuxGen: 1 x 120kW 225V 60Hz a.c, 1 x 100kW 225V 60Hz a.c

8971786 **YIN LONG**
-
-
Cheng Da Shipping Agency Co Ltd
-
Guangzhou, Guangdong *China*
Official number: 37038937

2,585
1,255
3,650

1983-11 **Zhonghua Shipyard — Shanghai** Yd No: 83017
Loa 101.15 Br ex - Dght -
Lbp 93.23 Br md 13.80 Dpth 7.70
Welded, 1 dk

(A31A2GX) General Cargo Ship

1 oil engine driving 1 FP propeller
Total Power: 1,910kW (2,597hp)
Hudong 6ESDZ43/82B
1 x 2 Stroke 6 Cy. 430 x 820 1910kW (2597bhp)
Hudong Shipyard-China

9636175 **YIN LU**
BPOH
-
Shanghai Time Shipping Co Ltd
JOSCO Yuansheng Shipping Management Co Ltd
Shanghai *China*
MMSI: 414703000

30,472 Class: CC
15,083
48,886

2012-06 **Chengxi Shipyard Co Ltd — Jiangyin JS** Yd No: CX0416
Loa 190.00 Br ex - Dght 10.500
Lbp 187.00 Br md 32.26 Dpth 16.50
Welded, 1 dk

(A21A2BC) Bulk Carrier
Grain: 62,112
Compartments: 5 Ho, ER
5 Ha: 4 (20.2 x 18.3)ER (17.6 x 18.3)
Cranes: 4x30t

1 oil engine driving 1 FP propeller
Total Power: 8,280kW (11,257hp) 14.2kn
Wartsila 6RT-flex48T
1 x 2 Stroke 6 Cy. 480 x 2000 8280kW (11257bhp)
Hudong Heavy Machinery Co Ltd-China
AuxGen: 3 x 625kW 450V a.c

9397705 **YIN NENG**
BPJQ
-
ex Yin Xiong *-2010* *ex* Yin He *-2010*
Shanghai Time Shipping Co Ltd
-
Shanghai *China*
MMSI: 413338000

32,460 Class: CC
17,889
53,478
T/cm
57.3

2010-06 **Chengxi Shipyard Co Ltd — Jiangyin JS** Yd No: CX4232
Loa 190.00 (BB) Br ex - Dght 12.540
Lbp 183.05 Br md 32.26 Dpth 17.50
Welded, 1 dk

(A21A2BC) Bulk Carrier
Grain: 65,752; Bale: 64,000
Compartments: 5 Ho, ER
5 Ha: 4 (21.6 x 22.4)ER (19.2 x 20.4)
Cranes: 4x36t

1 oil engine driving 1 FP propeller
Total Power: 9,480kW (12,889hp) 14.2kn
MAN-B&W 6S50MC-C
1 x 2 Stroke 6 Cy. 500 x 2000 9480kW (12889bhp)
Hudong Heavy Machinery Co Ltd-China
AuxGen: 3 x 680kW 450V 50Hz a.c
Fuel: 215.0 (d.f.) 2000.0 (r.f.) 34.5pd

9654218 **YIN NIAN**
BPON
-
Shanghai Time Shipping Co Ltd
-
Shanghai *China*
MMSI: 414769000

29,644 Class: CC
14,134
44,926

2013-11 **Qingdao Wuchuan Heavy Industry Co Ltd — Qingdao SD** Yd No: A227L
Loa 189.98 (BB) Br ex - Dght 10.500
Lbp 186.50 Br md 32.26 Dpth 16.00
Welded, 1 dk

(A21A2BC) Bulk Carrier
Grain: 61,674
Compartments: 5 Ho, ER
5 Ha: 4 (21.3 x 18.3)ER (18.9 x 18.3)
Cranes: 4x30t

1 oil engine driving 1 FP propeller
Total Power: 7,600kW (10,333hp) 13.8kn
MAN-B&W 6S50MC-C
1 x 2 Stroke 6 Cy. 500 x 2000 7600kW (10333bhp)
Yichang Marine Diesel Engine Co Ltd-China
AuxGen: 3 x 600kW 450V a.c

9396892 **YIN NING**
BPJO
-
Shanghai Time Shipping Co Ltd
-
Shanghai *China*
MMSI: 413336000

32,460 Class: CC
17,889
53,393
T/cm
57.3

2008-01 **Chengxi Shipyard Co Ltd — Jiangyin JS** Yd No: CX4229
Loa 190.00 (BB) Br ex - Dght 12.540
Lbp 183.05 Br md 32.26 Dpth 17.50
Welded, 1 dk

(A21A2BC) Bulk Carrier
Double Sides Entire Compartment Length
Grain: 65,900; Bale: 64,000
Compartments: 5 Ho, ER
5 Ha: 4 (21.6 x 22.4)ER (19.2 x 20.8)
Cranes: 4x36t

1 oil engine driving 1 FP propeller
Total Power: 8,580kW (11,665hp) 14.2kn
MAN-B&W 6S50MC
1 x 2 Stroke 6 Cy. 500 x 1910 8580kW (11665bhp)
Dalian Marine Diesel Works-China
AuxGen: 3 x 680kW 450V 60Hz a.c
Fuel: 215.0 (d.f.) 2000.0 (r.f.) 34.5pd

8901781 **YIN PENG**
BPDR
-
ex English Eminence *-2004* *ex* Schwyz *-2003*
ex Aztlan *-1995* *ex* Orient River *-1991*
Shanghai Time Shipping Co Ltd
China Shipping Guangzhou Ship Management Co Ltd
Shanghai *China*
MMSI: 412372320

25,891 Class: (CC) (NK)
13,673
43,665
T/cm
49.0

1989-06 **Tsuneishi Shipbuilding Co Ltd — Fukuyama HS** Yd No: 621
Loa 185.84 (BB) Br ex 30.44 Dght 11.300
Lbp 177.00 Br md 30.40 Dpth 16.20
Welded, 1 dk

(A21A2BC) Bulk Carrier
Grain: 53,594; Bale: 52,280
TEU 1082 C Ho 516 TEU C Dk 566 TEU
Compartments: 5 Ho, ER
5 Ha: (19.2 x 15.3)4 (20.8 x 15.3)ER
Cranes: 4x30t

1 oil engine driving 1 FP propeller
Total Power: 7,120kW (9,680hp) 14.0kn
B&W 6L60MCE
1 x 2 Stroke 6 Cy. 600 x 1944 7120kW (9680bhp)
Mitsui Engineering & Shipbuilding CLtd-Japan
AuxGen: 3 x 330kW 440V 60Hz a.c
Fuel: 276.0 (d.f.) 1574.0 (r.f.) 27.0pd

IMO / Call sign / Flag	Name / Former names / Owner / Manager / Port / MMSI	Tonnage	Class	Built / Builder / Dimensions	Type / Cargo	Machinery
9397690 *BPJP* -	**YIN PING** **Shanghai Time Shipping Co Ltd** - *Shanghai* *China* MMSI: 413980000	**32,460** 17,889 53,484 T/cm 57.3	Class: CC	**2010-05 Chengxi Shipyard Co Ltd — Jiangyin JS** Yd No: CX4231 Loa 190.00 (BB) Br ex - Dght 12.540 Lbp 183.05 Br md 32.26 Dpth 17.50 Welded, 1 dk	**(A21A2BC) Bulk Carrier** Grain: 65,752; Bale: 64,000 Compartments: 5 Ho, ER 5 Ha: 4 (21.6 x 22.4)ER (19.2 x 20.4) Cranes: 4x36t	**1 oil engine** driving 1 FP propeller Total Power: 9,480kW (12,889hp) 14.2k MAN-B&W 6S50MC- 1 x 2 Stroke 6 Cy. 500 x 2000 9480kW (12889bhp) Hudong Heavy Machinery Co Ltd-China AuxGen: 3 x 680kW 450V 50Hz a.c Fuel: 215.0 (d.f.) 2000.0 (r.f.) 34.5pd
9161053 *BPJR* -	**YIN PU** *ex* Roche Harbour *-2006* *ex* Ocean Galaxy *-2006* **Shanghai Time Shipping Co Ltd** China Shipping International Shipmanagement Co Ltd *Shanghai* *China* MMSI: 413265000	**27,011** 16,011 46,663 T/cm 51.4	Class: CC (NK)	**1997-09 Mitsui Eng. & SB. Co. Ltd. — Tamano** Yd No: 1447 Loa 189.90 (BB) Br ex - Dght 11.620 Lbp 181.00 Br md 31.00 Dpth 16.50 Welded, 1 dk	**(A21A2BC) Bulk Carrier** Grain: 59,820; Bale: 57,237 Compartments: 5 Ho, ER 5 Ha: 4 (20.8 x 17.2) (17.6 x 17.2)ER Cranes: 4x30t	**1 oil engine** driving 1 FP propeller Total Power: 8,165kW (11,101hp) 14.5k B&W 6S50M 1 x 2 Stroke 6 Cy. 500 x 1910 8165kW (11101bhp) Mitsui Engineering & Shipbuilding CLtd-Japan
9654189 *BPOK* -	**YIN RUI** **Shanghai Time Shipping Co Ltd** - *Shanghai* *China* MMSI: 414738000	**29,644** 14,134 44,945	Class: CC	**2012-12 Qingdao Wuchuan Heavy Industry Co Ltd — Qingdao SD** Yd No: A224L Loa 189.98 (BB) Br ex - Dght 10.500 Lbp 186.50 Br md 32.26 Dpth 16.00 Welded, 1 dk	**(A21A2BC) Bulk Carrier** Grain: 61,675 Compartments: 5 Ho, ER 5 Ha: 4 (21.3 x 18.3)ER (18.9 x 18.3) Cranes: 4x30t	**1 oil engine** driving 1 FP propeller Total Power: 7,600kW (10,333hp) 13.8k MAN-B&W 6S50MC- 1 x 2 Stroke 6 Cy. 500 x 2000 7600kW (10333bhp) Yichang Marine Diesel Engine Co Ltd-China AuxGen: 3 x 600kW 450V a.c
8905775 *BXOV* -	**YIN SHAN HU** **Sanfod Passenger & Cargo Transport Association** Yuet Hing Marine Supplies Co Ltd *Kaiping, Guangdong* *China*	**290** 37 35	Class: (CC)	**1989-07 WaveMaster International Pty Ltd — Fremantle WA** Yd No: 020 Loa 32.00 Br ex 9.50 Dght 1.250 Lbp 28.90 Br md 9.00 Dpth 3.55 Welded, 1 dk	**(A37B2PS) Passenger Ship** Hull Material: Aluminium Alloy Passengers: unberthed: 252	**2 oil engines** with clutches, flexible couplings & sr geared to sc. shafts driving 2 FP propellers Total Power: 2,178kW (2,962hp) 28.0k M.T.U. 12V396TB8 2 x Vee 4 Stroke 12 Cy. 165 x 185 each-1089kW (1481bhp) MTU Friedrichshafen GmbH-Friedrichshafen
9103166 *BPJT* -	**YIN SHI** *ex* Maria C *-2007* *ex* May Star *-2002* **Shanghai Time Shipping Co Ltd** - *Shanghai* *China* MMSI: 413267000	**26,093** 14,868 45,205 T/cm 51.0	Class: CC (NK)	**1994-07 Shin Kurushima Dockyard Co. Ltd. — Onishi** Yd No: 2802 Loa 188.33 (BB) Br ex - Dght 11.373 Lbp 179.50 Br md 31.00 Dpth 16.30 Welded, 1 dk	**(A21A2BC) Bulk Carrier** Grain: 58,148; Bale: 56,250 Compartments: 5 Ho, ER 5 Ha: (16.8 x 16.0)4 (20.0 x 16.0)ER Cranes: 4x25t	**1 oil engine** driving 1 FP propeller Total Power: 7,060kW (9,599hp) 14.3k Mitsubishi 6UEC52L 1 x 2 Stroke 6 Cy. 520 x 1850 7060kW (9599bhp) Kobe Hatsudoki KK-Japan AuxGen: 3 x 400kW 450V 60Hz a.c Fuel: 209.6 (d.f.) 1591.1 (r.f.) 29.9pd
9397688 *BPJN* -	**YIN SHUN** **Shanghai Time Shipping Co Ltd** - *Shanghai* *China* MMSI: 413337000	**32,460** 17,889 53,496 T/cm 57.3	Class: CC	**2009-04 Chengxi Shipyard Co Ltd — Jiangyin JS** Yd No: CX4230 Loa 190.00 (BB) Br ex - Dght 12.540 Lbp 183.05 Br md 32.26 Dpth 17.50 Welded, 1 dk	**(A21A2BC) Bulk Carrier** Double Sides Entire Compartment Length Grain: 65,900; Bale: 64,000 Compartments: 5 Ho, ER 5 Ha: 4 (21.6 x 22.4)ER (19.2 x 20.8) Cranes: 4x36t	**1 oil engine** driving 1 FP propeller Total Power: 8,580kW (11,665hp) 14.2k MAN-B&W 6S50M 1 x 2 Stroke 6 Cy. 500 x 1910 8580kW (11665bhp) Dalian Marine Diesel Co Ltd-China AuxGen: 3 x 680kW 450V 60Hz a.c Fuel: 215.0 (d.f.) 2000.0 (r.f.) 34.5pd
9106716 *BPJU* -	**YIN TAI** *ex* Roberto C *-2007* *ex* Azusa *-2002* **Shanghai Time Shipping Co Ltd** - *Shanghai* *China* MMSI: 413269000	**26,057** 14,870 45,210 T/cm 51.0	Class: CC (NK)	**1994-09 KK Kanasashi — Toyohashi AI** Yd No: 3340 Loa 188.33 (BB) Br ex - Dght 11.373 Lbp 179.50 Br md 31.00 Dpth 16.30 Welded, 1 dk	**(A21A2BC) Bulk Carrier** Grain: 58,148; Bale: 56,250 Compartments: 5 Ho, ER 5 Ha: (16.8 x 16.0)4 (20.0 x 16.0)ER Cranes: 4x25.4t	**1 oil engine** driving 1 FP propeller Total Power: 7,060kW (9,599hp) 14.6k Mitsubishi 6UEC52L 1 x 2 Stroke 6 Cy. 520 x 1850 7060kW (9599bhp) Kobe Hatsudoki KK-Japan
8422149 *BRZN* -	**YIN XING** *ex* Yi Xian Hu *-1993* **Shenzhen Pengxing Shipping Co Ltd** *Shenzhen, Guangdong* *China* MMSI: 412470030	*299* 112 100	Class: (CC) (NV)	**1985-03 Fjellstrand AS — Omastrand** Yd No: 1566 Loa 31.50 Br ex - Dght 1.671 Lbp 29.15 Br md 9.40 Dpth 3.50 Welded, 1 dk	**(A37B2PS) Passenger Ship** Hull Material: Aluminium Alloy Passengers: unberthed: 290	**2 oil engines** geared to sc. shafts driving 2 FP propellers Total Power: 2,942kW (4,000hp) 28.0k M.T.U. 16V396TB8 2 x Vee 4 Stroke 16 Cy. 165 x 185 each-1471kW (2000bhp) MTU Friedrichshafen GmbH-Friedrichshafen AuxGen: 2 x 20kW 230V 50Hz a.c
9113898 *BPDS* -	**YIN XIU** *ex* Stewart Island *-2005* *ex* Golden Duke *-2003* **Foreview (HK) Ltd** Taihua Ship Management (Shanghai) Ltd *Shanghai* *China* MMSI: 413143000	**17,380** 10,133 28,730 T/cm 36.6	Class: (CC) (NK)	**1995-08 KK Kanasashi — Toyohashi AI** Yd No: 3401 Loa 176.62 (BB) Br ex - Dght 9.632 Lbp 169.40 Br md 26.00 Dpth 13.60 Welded, 1 dk	**(A21A2BC) Bulk Carrier** Double Bottom Entire Compartment Length Grain: 39,037; Bale: 38,043 Compartments: 5 Ho, ER 5 Ha: (20.0 x 15.0)4 (20.8 x 18.3)ER Cranes: 4x30t	**1 oil engine** driving 1 FP propeller Total Power: 5,884kW (8,000hp) 13.0k Mitsubishi 5UEC52L 1 x 2 Stroke 5 Cy. 520 x 1600 5884kW (8000bhp) Akasaka Tekkosho KK (Akasaka DieselLtd)-Japan AuxGen: 2 x 440kW 450V 60Hz a.c Fuel: 98.0 (d.f.) (Heating Coils) 900.0 (r.f.) 23.5pd
9654191 *BPOL* -	**YIN XUE** **Shanghai Time Shipping Co Ltd** - *Shanghai* *China* MMSI: 414739000	**29,644** 14,134 45,010	Class: CC	**2013-01 Qingdao Wuchuan Heavy Industry Co Ltd — Qingdao SD** Yd No: A225L Loa 189.98 (BB) Br ex - Dght 10.500 Lbp 186.50 Br md 32.26 Dpth 16.00 Welded, 1 dk	**(A21A2BC) Bulk Carrier** Grain: 60,200 Compartments: 5 Ho, ER 5 Ha: 4 (21.3 x 18.3)ER (18.9 x 18.3) Cranes: 4x30t	**1 oil engine** driving 1 FP propeller Total Power: 9,480kW (12,889hp) 14.5k MAN-B&W 6S50MC- 1 x 2 Stroke 6 Cy. 500 x 2000 9480kW (12889bhp) Yichang Marine Diesel Engine Co Ltd-China
8805078 *XUSB3* -	**YIN YUAN** *ex* Shinei Maru No. 6 *-2007* **Yinyuan Shipping Ltd** Sea Plain Shipping Co Ltd *Phnom Penh* *Cambodia* MMSI: 514526000 Official number: 0788746	**1,995** 1,100 3,425	Class: UB	**1988-06 Matsuura Tekko Zosen K.K. — Osakikamijima** Yd No: 342 Converted From: Suction Dredger-2007 Loa 79.70 (BB) Br ex 13.37 Dght 5.600 Lbp - Br md 13.20 Dpth 7.20 Welded, 1 dk	**(A31A2GX) General Cargo Ship** Grain: 816 Compartments: 1 Ho, ER 1 Ha: (39.0 x 9.0)ER	**1 oil engine** with clutches & reverse reduction geared to sc. shaft driving 1 FP propeller Total Power: 736kW (1,001hp) 11.0k Hanshin 6LU35 1 x 4 Stroke 6 Cy. 350 x 550 736kW (1001bhp) The Hanshin Diesel Works Ltd-Japan Thrusters: 1 Thwart. CP thruster (f) Fuel: 3.1 (r.f.)
9493418 *BPJW* -	**YIN ZHI** **Shanghai Time Shipping Co Ltd** - *China* MMSI: 413893000	**33,511** 19,142 57,000	Class: CC	**2009-07 China Shipping Industry (Jiangsu) Co Ltd — Jiangdu JS** Loa 199.99 (BB) Br ex - Dght 12.500 Lbp 192.00 Br md 32.26 Dpth 18.00 Welded, 1 dk	**(A21A2BC) Bulk Carrier** Grain: 71,634 Compartments: 5 Ho, ER 5 Ha: ER	**1 oil engine** driving 1 FP propeller Total Power: 9,960kW (13,542hp) 14.2k MAN-B&W 6S50MC- 1 x 2 Stroke 6 Cy. 500 x 2000 9960kW (13542bhp)
8211215 - -	**YIN ZHOU HU** **Government of The People's Republic of China (Zhejiang Province Shipping Co - Zhou Shan Branch)** - *Zhoushan, Zhejiang* *China*	*134* 70 50	Class: (CC)	**1982-03 Afai Engineers & Shiprepairers Ltd — Hong Kong** Yd No: 93 Loa 22.06 Br ex - Dght 1.645 Lbp 19.35 Br md 8.70 Dpth 2.71 Welded, 1 dk	**(A37B2PS) Passenger Ship** Hull Material: Aluminium Alloy	**2 oil engines** with clutches, flexible couplings & sr reverse geared to sc. shafts driving 2 FP propellers Total Power: 1,294kW (1,760hp) Isotta Fraschini ID36SS8 2 x Vee 4 Stroke 8 Cy. 170 x 170 each-647kW (880bhp) Isotta Fraschini SpA-Italy AuxGen: 2 x 32kW 380V 50Hz a.c
9494395 *BOJT* -	**YIN ZHU HAI** **COSCO Bulk Carrier Co Ltd (COSCO BULK)** - SatCom: Inmarsat C 441368710 *Tianjin* *China* MMSI: 413687000	**40,896** 25,825 76,463 T/cm 68.2	Class: CC	**2009-06 Jiangnan Shipyard (Group) Co Ltd — Shanghai** Yd No: H2412 Loa 225.00 (BB) Br ex - Dght 14.200 Lbp 217.00 Br md 32.26 Dpth 19.60 Welded, 1 dk	**(A21A2BC) Bulk Carrier** Grain: 90,725 Compartments: 7 Ho, ER 7 Ha: 6 (15.5 x 14.4)ER (14.6 x 13.2)	**1 oil engine** driving 1 FP propeller Total Power: 10,200kW (13,868hp) 14.5k MAN-B&W 5S60M 1 x 2 Stroke 5 Cy. 600 x 2292 10200kW (13868bhp) Hudong Heavy Machinery Co Ltd-China AuxGen: 3 x 560kW 450V a.c
8987838 - -	**YINBAO 1** *ex* Yinbao *-2006* *ex* Zhe Hai 107 *-2005* - -	**3,001** 1,680 5,700		**1981-11 Ningbo Daxie Dockyard — Ningbo ZJ** Loa 101.10 Br ex - Dght 6.830 Lbp 94.00 Br md 16.00 Dpth 8.20 Welded, 1 dk	**(A31A2GX) General Cargo Ship**	**1 oil engine** driving 1 Propeller Total Power: 2,797kW (3,803hp) 11.0k
7126774 *5VAV6*	**YINCHUAN** *ex* Forthright *-2011* *ex* Blameless *-2010* *ex* Marta *-2009* *ex* Arta *-1999* *ex* Shetland Tramp *-1997* *ex* Shetland Trader *-1997* *ex* Parkesgate *-1979* **Aquamaster Navigation SA** Bosmar Ltd *Lome* *Togo* MMSI: 671154000	**847** 466 1,133	Class: (LR) (CS) ✠ Classed LR until 31/12/97	**1972-01 J. Bolson & Son Ltd. — Poole** Yd No: 573 Loa 60.91 Br ex 10.19 Dght 3.899 Lbp 57.56 Br md 10.11 Dpth 4.88 Welded, 1 dk	**(A31A2GX) General Cargo Ship** Grain: 1,689; Bale: 1,562 TEU 36 C.Ho 24/20' (40') C.Dk 12/20' (40') Compartments: 1 Ho, ER 1 Ha: (27.0 x 7.7)ER Ice Capable	**2 oil engines** reverse reduction geared to sc. shaft driving 1 FP propeller Total Power: 970kW (1,318hp) 12.0k Blackstone ERS 2 x 4 Stroke 8 Cy. 222 x 292 each-485kW (659bhp) Lister Blackstone Marine Ltd.-Dursley AuxGen: 2 x 18kW 415V 50Hz a.c Fuel: 40.5 (d.f.)

8832186 - -	**YING AN** **Government of The People's Republic of China (Qinhuangdao Harbour Administration)** - *Qinhuangdao, Hebei* *China* MMSI: 412011350	*587* 176 -	**1986 Universal Dockyard Ltd. — Hong Kong** Loa 46.96 Br ex - Dght 3.510 Lbp 44.51 Br md 10.40 Dpth 4.20 Welded, 1 dk	**(B33A2DG) Grab Dredger**	**2 oil engines** driving 2 FP propellers Total Power: 810kW (1,102hp) 10.1kn Yanmar S185L-ST 2 x 4 Stroke 6 Cy. 185 x 230 each-405kW (551bhp) Yanmar Diesel Engine Co Ltd-Japan AuxGen: 2 x 64kW 400V a.c
8884426 - -	**YING BIN 5** **Shenzhen Xunlong Passenger Shipping Ltd** - *Shenzhen, Guangdong* *China*	*193* Class: (CC) 58 19	**1993** Loa 24.50 Br ex - Dght 1.170 Lbp - Br md 8.38 Dpth 2.85 Welded, 1 dk	**(A37B2PS) Passenger Ship**	**2 oil engines** driving 2 FP propellers Total Power: 1,404kW (1,908hp) 30.0kn G.M. (Detroit Diesel) 16V-92-TA 2 x Vee 2 Stroke 16 Cy. 123 x 127 each-702kW (954bhp) Detroit Diesel Corporation-Detroit, Mi AuxGen: 2 x 40kW 220V a.c
9010058 *HOYC* -	**YING BRIDGE** *ex J. Real -2013 ex Asian Success -2003* **Ying Bridge Shipping Co Ltd** Union Rich Shipping Co Ltd *Panama* *Panama* MMSI: 352938000 Official number: 4503313	**7,090** Class: NK 3,308 10,058	**1991-05 Shin Kurushima Dockyard Co. Ltd. — Hashihama, Imabari** Yd No: 2708 Loa 110.02 (BB) Br ex - Dght 8.224 Lbp 102.00 Br md 19.20 Dpth 9.30 Welded, 2 dks	**(A31A2GX) General Cargo Ship** Grain: 17,831; Bale: 16,728 Compartments: 2 Ho, ER 2 Ha: 2 (25.2 x 10.2)ER Derricks: 4x20t	**1 oil engine** driving 1 FP propeller Total Power: 2,575kW (3,501hp) 12.4kn Mitsubishi 5UEC37LA 1 x 2 Stroke 5 Cy. 370 x 880 2575kW (3501bhp) Kobe Hatsudoki KK-Japan Fuel: 375.0 (r.f.)
9230828 *BI2564* LL2294	**YING CHIN HSIANG No. 101** **Ying Sheng Hsiang Fishery Co Ltd** - *Kaohsiung* *Chinese Taipei* Official number: CT7-0564	**599** 262 -	**2000-09 TMMC Shipyard Co, Ltd — Kaohsiung** Yd No: 101264 Loa 56.57 Br ex - Dght 3.500 Lbp 49.50 Br md 8.70 Dpth 3.80 Welded, 1 dk	**(B11B2FV) Fishing Vessel**	**1 oil engine** driving 1 FP propeller Total Power: 1,030kW (1,400hp) Niigata 1 x 4 Stroke 1030kW (1400bhp) Niigata Engineering Co Ltd-Japan
7826518 *BIAE3* -	**YING CHUN HAI** *ex An Shan -2010* **Shanghai Di Fan Shipping Co Ltd** Shanghai Zhengdong Shipping Co Ltd SatCom: Inmarsat A 1571767 *Shanghai* *China* MMSI: 412258000	**9,445** Class: (LR) (CC) 6,084 ✠ Classed LR until 3/82 15,265 T/cm 25.0	**1981-10 Astilleros Espanoles SA (AESA) — Bilbao** Yd No: 325 Loa 144.00 Br ex 21.44 Dght 8.950 Lbp 134.00 Br md 21.40 Dpth 12.20 Welded, 2 dks	**(A31A2GX) General Cargo Ship** Grain: 22,191; Bale: 20,229 Compartments: 4 Ho, ER, 4 Tw Dk 4 Ha: (13.4 x 8.0) (7.4 x 12.6)2 (20.2 x 12.6)ER Cranes: 4x12.5t	**1 oil engine** driving 1 FP propeller Total Power: 5,185kW (7,050hp) 14.0kn B&W 8K45GF 1 x 2 Stroke 8 Cy. 450 x 900 5185kW (7050bhp) Astilleros Espanoles SA (AESA)-Spain AuxGen: 3 x 376kW 450V 60Hz a.c Fuel: 221.0 (d.f.) 932.0 (r.f.)
8661484 *BI2588* CT7-0588	**YING FA HSIANG** **Ying Fa Hsiang Fishery Co Ltd** - *Kaohsiung* *Chinese Taipei* Official number: 014429	**531** 241 -	**2004-08 Fong Kuo Shipbuilding Co Ltd — Kaohsiung** Loa 48.70 Br ex - Dght - Lbp - Br md 8.50 Dpth 3.65 Welded, 1 dk	**(B11B2FV) Fishing Vessel**	**1 oil engine** driving 1 FP propeller Hanshin The Hanshin Diesel Works Ltd-Japan
9734460 *BJRG* -	**YING GE LING** **Hainan Strait Shipping Co Ltd** - *Haikou, Hainan* *China* MMSI: 413523240	**10,940** 5,907 2,073	**2014-01 Taizhou Kouan Shipbuilding Co Ltd — Taizhou JS** Yd No: TK0413 Loa 123.90 Br ex - Dght 4.200 Lbp 116.50 Br md 20.50 Dpth 6.30 Welded, 1 dk	**(A36A2PR) Passenger/Ro-Ro Ship (Vehicles)**	**1 oil engine** driving 1 Propeller Total Power: 2,400kW (3,263hp) Guangzhou 1 x 2400kW (3263bhp) CSSC MES Diesel Co Ltd-China
9063172 - -	**YING HAI** **Changhui Shipping Co** - *China*	*1,500* 919 2,300	**1994-01 Jiangxi Jiangzhou Shipyard — Ruichang JX** Yd No: A428 Loa 83.10 Br ex - Dght 4.500 Lbp 76.30 Br md 12.80 Dpth 5.90 Welded, 1 dk	**(A31A2GX) General Cargo Ship** Grain: 3,392	**1 oil engine** driving 1 FP propeller Total Power: 662kW (900hp) Chinese Std. Type 6350 1 x 4 Stroke 6 Cy. 350 x 500 662kW (900bhp) Shaanxi Diesel Engine Factory-China
8817057 - -	**YING HUA** *ex Ohkoh Maru -1999* **Shandong Bohai Ferry Co Ltd** - *China*	*4,575* Class: (NK) - 5,132	**1988-11 Imabari Shipbuilding Co Ltd — Imabari EH (Imabari Shipyard)** Yd No: 473 Loa 135.74 (BB) Br ex - Dght 6.166 Lbp 126.00 Br md 20.00 Dpth 8.80 Welded	**(A35A2RR) Ro-Ro Cargo Ship** Quarter bow door/ramp (p) Len: 23.50 Wid: 5.00 Swl: 50 Quarter stern door/ramp (p) Len: 23.50 Wid: 6.00 Swl: 50 Lane-Len: 940 Trailers: 62 TEU 58	**1 oil engine** driving 1 CP propeller Total Power: 7,981kW (10,851hp) 18.0kn B&W 7L50MC 1 x 2 Stroke 7 Cy. 500 x 1620 7981kW (10851bhp) Mitsui Engineering & Shipbuilding CLtd-Japan AuxGen: 4 x 480kW a.c
8822741 - -	**YING HUI HSIANG** - -	**705** 268 -	**1989 Fong Kuo Shipbuilding Co Ltd — Kaohsiung** Loa 54.85 Br ex 8.92 Dght 3.582 Lbp - Br md 8.90 Dpth 3.85 Welded, 1 dk	**(B11B2FV) Fishing Vessel**	**1 oil engine** geared to sc. shaft driving 1 FP propeller Total Power: 1,103kW (1,500hp) Daihatsu 6DLM-26S 1 x 4 Stroke 6 Cy. 260 x 340 1103kW (1500bhp) Daihatsu Diesel Manufacturing Co Lt-Japan
8935809 - 0000001032	**YING JEN NO. 366** *ex Chung 1 No. 201 -2011 ex Columbus -2000* *ex Ying Jen No. 366 -1997* **Ying Gian Marine Enterprise Co Ltd** - *Kaohsiung* *Chinese Taipei* MMSI: 416697000 Official number: 011109	**730** 308 352	**1988 Chung Yi Shipbuilding Corp. — Kaohsiung** Loa 55.26 Br ex - Dght 2.118 Lbp 48.36 Br md 8.70 Dpth 3.94 Welded, 1 dk	**(B11B2FV) Fishing Vessel**	**1 oil engine** driving 1 FP propeller Total Power: 883kW (1,201hp) 11.0kn Niigata 1 x 4 Stroke 883kW (1201bhp) Niigata Engineering Co Ltd-Japan
8651491 *BI2252* CT7-0252	**YING JEN NO. 636** **Ying Gian Marine Enterprise Co Ltd** - *Kaohsiung* *Chinese Taipei* Official number: 010917	**705** 268 351	**1988-06 Chung Yi Shipbuilding Corp. — Kaohsiung** Loa 54.00 Br ex - Dght 2.242 Lbp 47.26 Br md 8.51 Dpth 4.08 Welded, 1 dk	**(B11B2FV) Fishing Vessel**	**1 oil engine** driving 1 FP propeller Total Power: 883kW (1,201hp)
9092094 - -	**YING JIANG YOU 2** *ex Hua Jiang You 2 -2007* - -	*992* 550 1,968	**1997-03 Chongqing Shipyard — Chongqing** Loa 69.15 Br ex - Dght 4.550 Lbp 64.00 Br md 10.70 Dpth 5.25 Welded, 1 dk	**(A13B2TP) Products Tanker** Double Hull	**1 oil engine** driving 1 Propeller Total Power: 735kW (999hp) Chinese Std. Type 1 x 4 Stroke 735kW (999bhp) Guangzhou Diesel Engine Factory CoLtd-China
8746832 *BI2282* 0000002038	**YING MAN NO. 1** *ex Yang Jen No. 168 -2011* *ex Ying Jen No. 393 -2000* **Ying Guan Marine Enterprise Co Ltd** - *Kaohsiung* *Chinese Taipei* MMSI: 416698000 Official number: 011203	**730** 308 351	**1988-01 Chung Yi Shipbuilding Corp. — Kaohsiung** Loa 55.26 Br ex - Dght 2.200 Lbp 48.36 Br md 8.70 Dpth 3.94 Welded, 1 dk	**(B11B2FV) Fishing Vessel**	**1 oil engine** reduction geared to sc. shafts driving 1 FP propeller Total Power: 895kW (1,217hp) Niigata 1 x 895kW (1217bhp) Niigata Engineering Co Ltd-Japan
9169811 *VRLM8* -	**YING RICH** *ex Zia Belle -2012 ex CEC Cardigan -2008* *ex Maersk Charleston -1999* *ex Industrial Confidence -1998* *ex Clipper Cardigan -1997* **Ying Rich Shipping Co Ltd** JOSCO Yuansheng Shipping Management Co Ltd *Hong Kong* *Hong Kong* MMSI: 477017100 Official number: HK-3710	**6,714** Class: BV (LR) (NV) 2,888 Classed LR until 28/12/12 8,708 T/cm 18.5	**1997-09 Zhonghua Shipyard — Shanghai** Yd No: 392 Loa 100.48 (BB) Br ex - Dght 8.203 Lbp 96.07 Br md 20.41 Dpth 11.10 Welded, 2 dks	**(A31A2GX) General Cargo Ship** Grain: 10,530; Bale: 10,300 TEU 650 C Ho 220 TEU C Dk 430 TEU incl 106 ref C. Compartments: 1 Ho, ER 1 Ha: (64.4 x 15.3)ER Cranes: 2x150t Ice Capable	**1 oil engine** with flexible couplings & sr gearedto sc. shaft driving 1 CP propeller Total Power: 7,800kW (10,605hp) 16.0kn Wartsila 8R46 1 x 4 Stroke 8 Cy. 460 x 580 7800kW (10605bhp) Wartsila NSD Finland Oy-Finland AuxGen: 1 x 1072kW 450V 60Hz a.c, 3 x 530kW 450V 60Hz a.c Thrusters: 1 Thwart. CP thruster (f) Fuel: 96.5 (d.f.) (Heating Coils) 864.4 (r.f.) 28.0pd
9386835 - 0000002256	**YING RONG NO. 638** *ex Ying Rong 638 -2011* **Ying Rong Fishery Co Ltd** - *Kaohsiung* *Chinese Taipei* MMSI: 416176700 Official number: 014330	**562** 230 -	**2005-05 Fong Kuo Shipbuilding Co Ltd — Kaohsiung** Yd No: 403 Loa 56.10 Br ex - Dght 2.080 Lbp 48.60 Br md 8.70 Dpth 3.75 Welded, 1 dk	**(B11B2FV) Fishing Vessel**	**1 oil engine** reduction geared to sc. shafts driving 1 FP propeller Total Power: 1,029kW (1,399hp) Niigata 1 x 1029kW (1399bhp) Niigata Engineering Co Ltd-Japan

Ship / Owner	Tonnage	Class	Builder / Dimensions	Type	Machinery	
9611565 **YING SHUN** *3FYV3* **Hao Shun Shipping SA** HT Shipping Pte Ltd *Panama* *Panama* MMSI: 352614000 Official number: 4494113	**43,990** 27,662 82,000 T/cm 71.9	Class: BV	2013-02 **New Times Shipbuilding Co Ltd — Jingjiang JS** Yd No: 0108213 Loa 229.00 (BB) Br ex 32.29 Dght 14.450 Lbp 224.79 Br md 32.26 Dpth 20.05 Welded, 1 dk	**(A21A2BC) Bulk Carrier** Grain: 97,883; Bale: 90,784 Compartments: 7 Ho, ER 7 Ha: ER	**1 oil engine** driving 1 FP propeller Total Power: 9,800kW (13,324hp) MAN-B&W 1 x 2 Stroke 5 Cy. 600 x 2400 9800kW (13324bhp) Jiangsu Antai Power Machinery Co Lt-China AuxGen: 3 x 710kW 60Hz a.c Fuel: 3260.0	14.0k 5S60MC-C8
8896912 **YING SHUN** *BTQA* - **Zhanjiang Harbour Shipping Co** - *Zhanjiang, Guangdong* *China*	**124** 62 15	Class: CC	1995 **Wuhan Nanhua High Speed Ship Engineering Co Ltd — Wuhan HB** Loa 38.00 Br ex - Dght 1.260 Lbp 33.12 Br md 4.40 Dpth 2.30 Welded, 1 dk	**(A37B2PS) Passenger Ship**	**2 oil engines** driving 2 FP propellers Total Power: 1,410kW (1,918hp) Dorman 2 x 4 Stroke 8 Cy. 160 x 190 each-705kW (959bhp) Perkins Engines Ltd.-Peterborough	28.0kn SEAKING-8
8651506 **YING SHUN NO. 368** *BI2550* CT7-0550 **Kao Yang Fishery Co Ltd** - *Kaohsiung* *Chinese Taipei* Official number: 014112	**625** 296 564		2003-11 **Jong Shyn Shipbuilding Co., Ltd. — Kaohsiung** Loa 59.20 (BB) Br ex - Dght 2.060 Lbp 50.80 Br md 9.00 Dpth 3.75 Welded, 1 dk	**(B11B2FV) Fishing Vessel**	**1 oil engine** driving 1 FP propeller Total Power: 1,177kW (1,600hp)	
8308745 **YING STAR** *XUDV7* *ex* Vencedor *-2009* *ex* Amber *-2008* *ex* Hao Shun *-2006* *ex* Lara S *-2006* *ex* Lara B *-2004* *ex* Sable Island *-2003* *ex* Almania *-2003* *ex* CPC America *-1992* *ex* Conti Almania *-1992* **Hongzhou International Marine Repair Project Ltd** - SatCom: Inmarsat C 451561910 *Phnom Penh* *Cambodia* MMSI: 515619000 Official number: 0483115	**4,366** 2,450 5,902	Class: UB (GL)	1983-12 **J.J. Sietas KG Schiffswerft GmbH & Co. — Hamburg** Yd No: 936 Loa 99.90 (BB) Br ex 17.84 Dght 6.936 Lbp 93.86 Br md 17.81 Dpth 9.02 Welded, 2 dks	**(A31A2GX) General Cargo Ship** Grain: 7,826; Bale: 7,411 TEU 323 C.Ho 129/20' (40') C.Dk 194/20' (40') incl. 20 ref C. Compartments: 1 Ho, ER 1 Ha: (63.7 x 12.7)ER Cranes: 2x80t Ice Capable	**1 oil engine** with flexible couplings & sr gearedto sc. shaft driving 1 CP propeller Total Power: 1,471kW (2,000hp) MaK 1 x 4 Stroke 6 Cy. 450 x 550 1471kW (2000bhp) Krupp MaK Maschinenbau GmbH-Kiel AuxGen: 1 x 400kW 380V 50Hz a.c, 3 x 264kW 380V 50Hz a.c Thrusters: 1 Thwart. FP thruster (f) Fuel: 112.0 (d.f.) 461.0 (r.f.) 13.0pd	13.8kn 6M551AK
9167722 **YING XIANG** *XUHH9* *ex* Yun Hai *-2012* *ex* Taisho Maru No. 23 *-2005* **Hong Xiang Shipping Ltd** Yantai Weisheng International Shipping Co Ltd *Phnom Penh* *Cambodia* MMSI: 515803000 Official number: 0597056	**1,998** 1,330 -	Class: UB	1997-09 **Kanmon Zosen K.K. — Shimonoseki** Yd No: 580 Lengthened-2006 Loa 90.00 Br ex - Dght - Lbp 84.93 Br md 13.40 Dpth 7.20 Welded, 1 dk	**(A31A2GX) General Cargo Ship** Compartments: 1 Ho, ER 1 Ha: (22.2 x 10.0)ER	**1 oil engine** driving 1 FP propeller Total Power: 1,471kW (2,000hp) Hanshin 1 x 4 Stroke 6 Cy. 360 x 670 1471kW (2000bhp) The Hanshin Diesel Works Ltd-Japan	12.0kn LH36LAG
9028639 **YING XIN** *XUPR7* *ex* Tian Li No. 1 *-2006* **Hong Kong Gloria Shipping Co Ltd** Fu'an Yuchang Shipping Co Ltd *Phnom Penh* *Cambodia* MMSI: 514580000 Official number: 0904461	**2,970** 1,669 -	Class: UB	2004-11 **Jinglun Yunye Shipyard — Jingzhou HB** Loa 97.43 Br ex - Dght - Lbp 90.30 Br md 15.00 Dpth 7.70 Welded, 1 dk	**(A31A2GX) General Cargo Ship**	**1 oil engine** driving 1 Propeller Total Power: 1,765kW (2,400hp) Chinese Std. Type 1 x 4 Stroke 1765kW (2400bhp) in China	
8430897 **YING YUAN NO. 8** *ex* Hsin Cheng Shiang No. 101 *-2011* 0000001232 **Ying Shiun Fishery Co Ltd** - *Kaohsiung* *Chinese Taipei* MMSI: 416719000 Official number: 011028	*711* 278 620		1988 **Sen Koh Shipbuilding Corp — Kaohsiung** Loa 54.85 Br ex - Dght 2.251 Lbp 47.80 Br md 8.90 Dpth 3.85 Welded, 1 dk	**(B11B2FV) Fishing Vessel**	**1 oil engine** reduction geared to sc. shafts driving 1 FP propeller Total Power: 1,044kW (1,419hp) Hanshin 1 x 4 Stroke 6 Cy. 1044kW (1419bhp) The Hanshin Diesel Works Ltd-Japan	12.0kn
8811089 **YINHE NO. 1** *XUCX8* *ex* Shinei Maru *-2003* **Zhaoyang Shipping Co Ltd** Yuan Da Shipping Co Ltd *Phnom Penh* *Cambodia* MMSI: 515568000 Official number: 0488056	**1,592** 757 2,500	Class: UB	1988-08 **Matsuura Tekko Zosen K.K. — Osakikamijima** Yd No: 345 Converted From: Bulk Aggregates Carrier-2003 Lengthened-2003 Loa 80.50 (BB) Br ex 12.58 Dght 4.372 Lbp 77.50 Br md 12.50 Dpth 6.30 Welded, 1 dk	**(A31A2GX) General Cargo Ship** Grain: 699	**1 oil engine** driving 1 FP propeller Total Power: 1,177kW (1,600hp) Niigata 1 x 4 Stroke 6 Cy. 300 x 530 1177kW (1600bhp) Niigata Engineering Co Ltd-Japan	6M30GT
8420830 **YINHUI 3001** *BTBL* *ex* Xinmanyang I *-2010* *ex* Cheng Hang 168 *-2005* *ex* Cinta *-1995* *ex* Halim Thea *-1990* **Dalian Yinhui Shipping Co Ltd** - *Dalian, Liaoning* *China* MMSI: 412206680	**2,063** 1,214 3,418 T/cm 14.3	Class: CC (AB)	1986-08 **Malaysia Shipyard & Engineering Sdn Bhd — Pasir Gudang** Yd No: 031 Converted From: Oil Tanker-2004 Loa 85.81 Br ex 18.27 Dght 3.860 Lbp 80.60 Br md 18.20 Dpth 5.21 Welded, 1 dk	**(A31C2GD) Deck Cargo Ship** Liq: 4,000; Liq (Oil): 4,000 Compartments: 8 Ta, ER 2 Cargo Pump (s)	**2 oil engines** with clutches, flexible couplings & sr geared to sc. shafts driving 2 CP propellers Total Power: 1,766kW (2,402hp) Wartsila 2 x 4 Stroke 6 Cy. 220 x 240 each-883kW (1201bhp) Oy Wartsila Ab-Finland AuxGen: 2 x 296kW a.c Thrusters: 1 Thwart. CP thruster (f)	8.0kn 6R22
9010539 **YINKA FOLAWIYO 1** - - *Nigeria*	*150* - -		1989-10 **Master Marine, Inc. — Bayou La Batre, Al** Loa - Br ex - Dght - Lbp 25.91 Br md 7.32 Dpth - Welded	**(B11A2FS) Stern Trawler**	**1 oil engine** geared to sc. shaft driving 1 FP propeller Total Power: 530kW (721hp) Caterpillar 1 x Vee 4 Stroke 12 Cy. 137 x 152 530kW (721bhp) Caterpillar Inc-USA	3412TA
9010541 **YINKA FOLAWIYO 2** - - *Nigeria*	*150* - -		1989-10 **Master Marine, Inc. — Bayou La Batre, Al** Loa - Br ex - Dght - Lbp 25.91 Br md 7.32 Dpth - Welded	**(B11A2FS) Stern Trawler**	**1 oil engine** geared to sc. shaft driving 1 FP propeller Total Power: 530kW (721hp) Caterpillar 1 x Vee 4 Stroke 12 Cy. 137 x 152 530kW (721bhp) Caterpillar Inc-USA	3412TA
9010553 **YINKA FOLAWIYO 3** - - *Nigeria*	*150* - -		1989-11 **Master Marine, Inc. — Bayou La Batre, Al** Loa - Br ex - Dght - Lbp 23.47 Br md 7.01 Dpth - Welded	**(B11A2FS) Stern Trawler**	**1 oil engine** geared to sc. shaft driving 1 FP propeller Total Power: 530kW (721hp) Caterpillar 1 x Vee 4 Stroke 12 Cy. 137 x 152 530kW (721bhp) Caterpillar Inc-USA	3412TA
9010565 **YINKA FOLAWIYO 4** - - *Nigeria*	*150* - -		1989-11 **Master Marine, Inc. — Bayou La Batre, Al** Loa - Br ex - Dght - Lbp 23.47 Br md 7.01 Dpth - Welded	**(B11A2FS) Stern Trawler**	**1 oil engine** geared to sc. shaft driving 1 FP propeller Total Power: 530kW (721hp) Caterpillar 1 x Vee 4 Stroke 12 Cy. 137 x 152 530kW (721bhp) Caterpillar Inc-USA	3412TA
8731605 **YINSON POWER 2** *ex* Sunny No. 18 *-2008* **Yinson Power Marine Sdn Bhd** -	**140** 94		1992-01 **Qingshan Shipyard — Wuhan HB** Loa 23.75 Br ex - Dght - Lbp - Br md 6.83 Dpth 3.35 Welded, 1 dk	**(B32A2ST) Tug**	**1 oil engine** geared to sc. shaft driving 1 Propeller Total Power: 634kW (862hp) Cummins 1 x Vee 4 Stroke 12 Cy. 159 x 159 634kW (862bhp) Cummins Engine Co Inc-USA	KTA-38-M0
8731629 **YINSON POWER 5** *ex* Sun Wui Tung No. 21 *-2008* **Yinson Power Marine Sdn Bhd** -	**469** 154		1997-01 **Zhongshan Shipyard — Zhongshan GD** Loa 40.40 Br ex - Dght - Lbp - Br md 10.20 Dpth 4.16 Welded, 1 dk	**(A31A2GX) General Cargo Ship**	**2 oil engines** geared to sc. shafts driving 2 Propellers Total Power: 600kW (816hp) Caterpillar 2 x Vee 4 Stroke 8 Cy. 137 x 152 each-300kW (408bhp) Caterpillar Inc-USA	3408TA
8736655 **YINSON POWER 19** *T2XY2* *ex* Twin Power 19 *-2008* *ex* S. Yoolim 555 *-2008* **Yinson Power Marine Sdn Bhd** - *Funafuti* *Tuvalu* MMSI: 572551000 Official number: 19450308	*182* 40 77		2003 **Sang Charoen Shipping Industry Co Ltd — Bangkok** Loa 27.00 Br ex - Dght 2.800 Lbp 24.00 Br md 8.20 Dpth 4.01 Welded, 1 dk	**(B32A2ST) Tug**	**1 oil engine** geared to sc. shaft driving 1 Propeller Total Power: 1,287kW (1,750hp) MaK 1 x 4 Stroke 8 Cy. 240 x 280 1287kW (1750bhp) Caterpillar Motoren GmbH & Co. KG-Germany	8M282AK

IMO / Call sign	Name / Owner	Tonnage	Class	Build	Type	Machinery
810085 /JD2210	**YIRUMBA** **Groote Eylandt Mining Co Pty Ltd (Gemco)** BHP Billiton Petroleum Pty Ltd *Darwin, NT* *Australia* Official number: 852087	*190* 57 -	Class: (NV)	**1989-04 Ocean Shipyards (WA) Pty Ltd — Fremantle WA** Yd No: 171 Loa 23.95 Br ex - Dght 4.700 Lbp 21.60 Br md 8.00 Dpth 5.27 Welded, 1 dk	**(B32A2ST) Tug**	**2 oil engines** with clutches, flexible couplings & reduction geared to sc. shafts driving 2 Directional propellers Total Power: 1,938kW (2,634hp) 10.0kn Caterpillar 3512TA 2 x Vee 4 Stroke 12 Cy. 170 x 190 each-969kW (1317bhp) Caterpillar Inc-USA AuxGen: 2 x 100kW 240/480V 60Hz a.c Thrusters: 2 Directional thruster (f) Fuel: 30.0 (d.f.) 7.5pd
089449 -	**YIU LIAN NO. 6** **Yiu Lian Dockyards Ltd** *Shenzhen, Guangdong* *China*	**416** 124 74	Class: CC	**2004-11 Guangdong Hope Yue Shipbuilding Industry Ltd — Guangzhou GD** Loa 36.80 Br ex - Dght 3.400 Lbp 32.30 Br md 10.00 Dpth 4.40 Welded, 1 dk	**(B32A2ST) Tug**	**2 oil engines** driving 2 Propellers Total Power: 2,942kW (4,000hp) Niigata 6L26HLX 2 x 4 Stroke 6 Cy. 260 x 350 each-1471kW (2000bhp) Niigata Engineering Co Ltd-Japan AuxGen: 2 x 100kW 400V a.c
9089451 BXXR -	**YIU LIAN NO. 8** **Yiu Lian Dockyards (Skekou) Ltd** *Shenzhen, Guangdong* *China* MMSI: 412470590 Official number: 140008000002	**416** 124 74	Class: (CC)	**2006-01 Yiu Lian Dockyards (Zhangzhou) Ltd — Zhangzhou FJ** Loa 36.80 Br ex - Dght 3.400 Lbp 32.30 Br md 10.00 Dpth 4.40 Welded, 1 dk	**(B32A2ST) Tug**	**2 oil engines** Geared to sc. shafts driving 2 Propellers Total Power: 2,942kW (4,000hp) Niigata 6L26HLX 2 x 4 Stroke 6 Cy. 260 x 350 each-1471kW (2000bhp) (made 2005) Niigata Engineering Co Ltd-Japan AuxGen: 2 x 100kW 400V a.c
7734480 - -	**YIU LIAN No. 15** **Yiu Lian Dockyards Ltd** -	*254* 172 -	Class: (LR) Classed LR until 29/2/80	**1975 Yiu Lian Machinery Repairing Works Ltd — Hong Kong** Yd No: 19 Loa 32.77 Br ex 9.05 Dght 3.309 Lbp 28.20 Br md 8.39 Dpth 3.89 Welded, 1 dk	**(B32A2ST) Tug**	**2 oil engines** reverse reduction geared to sc. shafts driving 2 FP propellers Total Power: 1,104kW (1,500hp) Makita GNLH624 2 x 4 Stroke 6 Cy. 240 x 410 each-552kW (750bhp) Makita Diesel Co Ltd-Japan AuxGen: 1 x 50kW 380V 50Hz a.c, 1 x 48kW 380V 50Hz a.c
7734478 - -	**YIU LIAN No. 18** **Yiu Lian Dockyards Ltd** -	*314* 200 -	Class: (LR) ✠ Classed LR until 22/2/80	**1976 Yiu Lian Machinery Repairing Works Ltd — Hong Kong** Yd No: 28 Loa 32.85 Br ex 9.76 Dght - Lbp 26.50 Br md 9.50 Dpth 4.32 Welded, 1 dk	**(B32A2ST) Tug**	**2 oil engines** sr geared to sc. shafts driving 2 Directional propellers Total Power: 2,354kW (3,200hp) Daihatsu 8DSM-26 2 x 4 Stroke 8 Cy. 260 x 320 each-1177kW (1600bhp) Daihatsu Diesel Manufacturing Co Lt-Japan
8736215 BXZC	**YIU LIAN TUO 2** *ex* You Lian Tuo 2 *-2008* **Yiu Lian Dockyards Ltd** - *Shenzhen, Guangdong* *China*	**432** 130 -	Class: CC	**2008-11 Yiu Lian Dockyards (Zhangzhou) Ltd — Zhangzhou FJ** Loa 36.80 Br ex - Dght 3.600 Lbp 32.30 Br md 10.00 Dpth 4.60 Welded, 1 dk	**(B32A2ST) Tug**	**2 oil engines** geared to sc. shafts driving 2 Propellers Total Power: 2,942kW (4,000hp) 13.5kn Niigata 6L26HLX 2 x 4 Stroke 6 Cy. 260 x 350 each-1471kW (2000bhp) Niigata Engineering Co Ltd-Japan AuxGen: 2 x 100kW 400V a.c
9038816 DSPZ2 -	**YK SOVEREIGN** **SK Shipping Co Ltd** *Seogwipo* *South Korea* MMSI: 441498000 Official number: SGR-089561	**103,764** 31,129 72,020	Class: KR NV	**1994-12 Hyundai Heavy Industries Co Ltd — Ulsan** Yd No: 761 Loa 274.00 (BB) Br ex - Dght 11.770 Lbp 260.00 Br md 47.20 Dpth 26.50 Welded, 1 dk	**(A11A2TN) LNG Tanker** Double Bottom Entire Compartment Length Liq (Gas): 124,582 4 x Gas Tank (s); 4 independent Kvaerner-Moss (alu) sph 8 Cargo Pump (s): 8x1400m³/hr	**1 Steam Turb** reduction geared to sc. shaft driving 1 FP propeller Total Power: 19,639kW (26,701hp) 18.5kn Mitsubishi MS28-2 1 x steam Turb 19639kW (26701shp) Mitsubishi Heavy Industries Ltd-Japan AuxGen: 1 x 2700kW 220/440V 60Hz a.c, 2 x 2700kW 220/440V 60Hz a.c Thrusters: 1 Thwart. CP thruster (f)
8904305 SBCJ -	**YLVA** **A/B Goteborg-Styrso Skargardstrafik** *Gothenburg* *Sweden* MMSI: 265547230	**315** 137 50		**1989-12 AB Nya Oskarshamns Varv — Oskarshamn** Yd No: 518 Loa 34.15 Br ex - Dght - Lbp 31.50 Br md 7.55 Dpth 3.43 Welded	**(A37B2PS) Passenger Ship** Passengers: unberthed: 450	**1 oil engine** with clutches, flexible couplings & sr geared to sc. shaft driving 1 FP propeller Total Power: 638kW (867hp) Caterpillar 3508TA 1 x Vee 4 Stroke 8 Cy. 170 x 190 638kW (867bhp) Caterpillar Inc-USA Thrusters: 1 Thwart. FP thruster (f)
9622758 9HA3431 -	**YM AMAZON** **Marmara Tersanesi AS** Yilmar Denizcilik Nakliyat ve Ticaret Ltd Sti (Yilmar Shipping & Trading Ltd) *Valletta* *Malta* MMSI: 229594000 Official number: 9622758	**7,370** 3,984 11,500	Class: BV	**2013-10 Marmara Tersanesi — Yarimca** Yd No: 89 Loa 131.20 Br ex - Dght 7.850 Lbp - Br md 19.00 Dpth 7.85 Welded, 1 dk	**(A31A2GX) General Cargo Ship** Double Hull Grain: 16,300; Bale: 15,800 Ice Capable	**1 oil engine** reduction geared to sc. shaft driving 1 CP propeller Total Power: 3,360kW (4,568hp) 12.0kn MAN-B&W 6L32/44CR 1 x 4 Stroke 6 Cy. 320 x 440 3360kW (4568bhp) MAN B&W Diesel AG-Augsburg AuxGen: 3 x 350kW 60Hz a.c
9443580 VRET5 -	**YM ANTWERP** **Able Challenger Ltd** Yang Ming Marine Transport Corp *Hong Kong* *Hong Kong* MMSI: 477177100 Official number: HK-2307	**40,030** 24,450 50,500 T/cm 70.4	Class: NV	**2008-12 Samsung Heavy Industries Co Ltd — Geoje** Yd No: 1771 Loa 259.80 (BB) Br ex 32.30 Dght 12.600 Lbp 244.80 Br md 32.25 Dpth 19.30 Welded, 1 dk	**(A33A2CC) Container Ship (Fully Cellular)** TEU 4253 C. Ho 1584 C. Dk 2669 incl 400 ref C.	**1 oil engine** driving 1 FP propeller Total Power: 36,560kW (49,707hp) 23.3kn MAN-B&W 8K90MC-C 1 x 2 Stroke 8 Cy. 900 x 2300 36560kW (49707bhp) Doosan Engine Co Ltd-South Korea AuxGen: 4 x 1700kW a.c Thrusters: 1 Tunnel thruster (f)
9203629 A8AG2 -	**YM BAMBOO** *ex* Bamboo Bridge *-2006* *ex* Jupiter Bridge *-2005* *ex* Ming Bamboo *-2002* **Yang Ming (Liberia) Corp** Yang Ming Marine Transport Corp SatCom: Inmarsat C 463790279 *Monrovia* *Liberia* MMSI: 636011587 Official number: 11587	**64,005** 34,700 68,615	Class: AB	**2001-03 China Shipbuilding Corp (CSBC) — Kaohsiung** Yd No: 756 Loa 274.70 (BB) Br ex - Dght 14.000 Lbp 263.00 Br md 40.00 Dpth 24.20 Welded, 1 dk	**(A33A2CC) Container Ship (Fully Cellular)** TEU 5548 C Ho 2564 TEU C Ho 2984 TEU incl 400 ref C. Compartments: ER, 7 Cell Ho 15 Ha: ER	**1 oil engine** driving 1 FP propeller Total Power: 54,946kW (74,705hp) 26.0kn Sulzer 10RTA96C 1 x 2 Stroke 10 Cy. 960 x 2500 54946kW (74705bhp) Hyundai Heavy Industries Co Ltd-South Korea AuxGen: 4 x 1900kW 110/440V 60Hz a.c Thrusters: 1 Thwart. CP thruster (f) Fuel: 343.3 (d.f.) (Heating Coils) 7340.5 (r.f.) 197.8pd
9450571 VREX8 -	**YM BUSAN** **Magic Peninsula Ltd** Yang Ming Marine Transport Corp *Hong Kong* *Hong Kong* MMSI: 477189600 Official number: HK-2341	**40,030** 24,450 50,500 T/cm 70.4	Class: NV	**2009-01 Samsung Heavy Industries Co Ltd — Geoje** Yd No: 1772 Loa 260.00 (BB) Br ex 32.30 Dght 12.600 Lbp 244.80 Br md 32.25 Dpth 16.40 Welded, 1 dk	**(A33A2CC) Container Ship (Fully Cellular)** TEU 4253 C Ho 1584 C Dk 2669 incl 400 ref C. Compartments: 7 Cell Ho, ER	**1 oil engine** driving 1 FP propeller Total Power: 36,559kW (49,706hp) 23.3kn MAN-B&W 8K90MC-C 1 x 2 Stroke 8 Cy. 900 x 2300 36559kW (49706bhp) Doosan Engine Co Ltd-South Korea AuxGen: 4 x 1700kW a.c Thrusters: 1 Tunnel thruster (f)
9198288 H3XY -	**YM COSMOS** *ex* Ming Cosmos *-2005* **Hill Samuel Finance Ltd** Yang Ming Marine Transport Corp SatCom: Inmarsat C 435110310 *Panama* *Panama* MMSI: 351103000 Official number: 2777801C	**64,254** 35,137 68,413 T/cm 89.6	Class: NV	**2001-03 Hyundai Heavy Industries Co Ltd — Ulsan** Yd No: 1224 Loa 274.69 (BB) Br ex - Dght 14.000 Lbp 263.00 Br md 40.00 Dpth 24.20 Welded, 1 dk	**(A33A2CC) Container Ship (Fully Cellular)** TEU 5512 C Ho 2564 TEU C Dk 2948 TEU incl 400 ref C. Compartments: ER, 7 Cell Ho 15 Ha: ER	**1 oil engine** driving 1 FP propeller Total Power: 54,926kW (74,677hp) 25.9kn Sulzer 10RTA96C 1 x 2 Stroke 10 Cy. 960 x 2500 54926kW (74677bhp) Hyundai Heavy Industries Co Ltd-South Korea AuxGen: 4 x 1900kW 110/440V 60Hz a.c Thrusters: 1 Thwart. CP thruster (f) Fuel: 343.3 (d.f.) (Heating Coils) 7340.5 (r.f.) 197.8pd
9224489 A8HD4	**YM CYPRESS** *ex* Cypress Bridge *-2006* *ex* Mercury Bridge *-2005* *ex* Ming Cypress *-2002* **All Oceans Transportation Inc** Yang Ming Marine Transport Corp *Monrovia* *Liberia* MMSI: 636012707 Official number: 12707	**64,254** 35,137 68,303 T/cm 89.6	Class: BV	**2001-04 Hyundai Heavy Industries Co Ltd — Ulsan** Yd No: 1339 Loa 275.00 (BB) Br ex - Dght 14.000 Lbp 263.00 Br md 40.00 Dpth 24.20 Welded, 1 dk	**(A33A2CC) Container Ship (Fully Cellular)** TEU 5512 C Ho 2564 TEU C Dk 2948 TEU incl 400 ref C. Compartments: ER, 7 Cell Ho 15 Ha: ER	**1 oil engine** driving 1 FP propeller Total Power: 54,946kW (74,705hp) 26.0kn Sulzer 10RTA96C 1 x 2 Stroke 10 Cy. 960 x 2500 54946kW (74705bhp) Hyundai Heavy Industries Co Ltd-South Korea AuxGen: 4 x 1900kW 110/440V 60Hz a.c Thrusters: 1 Thwart. CP thruster (f) Fuel: 343.3 (d.f.) (Heating Coils) 7340.5 (r.f.) 197.8pd

IMO / Name / Owner	Tonnage	Class	Build / Dimensions	Type	Machinery
9322633 **YM EARTH** *9HFT8* - **YM Earth Tankers Ltd** Yilmar Denizcilik Nakliyat ve Ticaret Ltd Sti (Yilmar Shipping & Trading Ltd) *Valletta* *Malta* MMSI: 215937000 Official number: 9722	**4,022** 1,819 5,738 T/cm 15.0	Class: BV	**2005-08 Marmara Tersanesi — Yarimca** Yd No: 67 Loa 105.50 (BB) Br ex 16.84 Dght 6.290 Lbp 98.41 Br md 16.80 Dpth 7.40 Welded, 1 dk	**(A12B2TR) Chemical/Products Tanker** Double Hull (13F) Liq: 6,301; Liq (Oil): 6,301 Cargo Heating Coils Compartments: 10 Wing Ta, 2 Wing Slop Ta, ER 2 x Gas Tank (s); 2 cyl horizontal 10 Cargo Pump (s): 10x200m³/hr Manifold: Bow/CM: 46m Ice Capable	**1 oil engine** geared to sc. shaft driving 1 CP propeller Total Power: 2,720kW (3,698hp) 13.0k MAN-B&W 8L27/3 1 x 4 Stroke 8 Cy. 270 x 380 2720kW (3698bhp) MAN B&W Diesel A/S-Denmark AuxGen: 3 x 370kW a.c Thrusters: 1 Thwart. CP thruster (f) Fuel: 63.0 (d.f.) 257.0 (r.f.) 10.0pd
9353280 **YM EFFICIENCY** *A8OS5* - **All Oceans Transportation Inc** Yang Ming Marine Transport Corp *Monrovia* *Liberia* MMSI: 636013698 Official number: 13698	**42,741** 19,338 52,773	Class: AB (CR)	**2009-01 CSBC Corp, Taiwan — Kaohsiung** Yd No: 889 Loa 268.80 (BB) Br ex 32.30 Dght 12.500 Lbp 256.60 Br md 32.20 Dpth 19.10 Welded, 1 dk	**(A33A2CC) Container Ship (Fully Cellular)** TEU 4252 C Ho 2112 C Dk 2140 TEU incl 500 ref C. Compartments: 7 Cell Ho, ER	**1 oil engine** driving 1 FP propeller Total Power: 40,040kW (54,438hp) 24.8k Wartsila 7RT-flex96C 1 x 2 Stroke 7 Cy. 960 x 2500 40040kW (54438bhp) Diesel United Ltd.-Aioi AuxGen: 3 x 2280kW 450V 60Hz a.c Thrusters: 1 Thwart. FP thruster (f)
9353266 **YM ELIXIR** *A8OS2* - **FSL-21 Inc** Yang Ming Marine Transport Corp *Monrovia* *Liberia* MMSI: 636013695 Official number: 13695	**42,741** 19,338 51,870	Class: LR (CR) ✠ **100A1** SS 06/2013 container ship **ShipRight** (SDA, FDA, CM) *IWS LI EP ✠ **LMC** **UMS** Eq.Ltr: R†; Cable: 687.5/84.0 U3 (a)	**2008-06 CSBC Corp, Taiwan — Kaohsiung** Yd No: 887 Loa 268.80 (BB) Br ex 32.30 Dght 12.500 Lbp 256.50 Br md 32.20 Dpth 19.10 Welded, 1 dk	**(A33A2CC) Container Ship (Fully Cellular)** TEU 4252 C Ho 2112 TEU C Dk 2140 TEU incl 500 ref C. Compartments: 7 Cell Ho, ER	**1 oil engine** driving 1 FP propeller Total Power: 40,040kW (54,438hp) 24.8k Wartsila 7RT-flex96C 1 x 2 Stroke 7 Cy. 960 x 2500 40040kW (54438bhp) Diesel United Ltd.-Aioi AuxGen: 3 x 2280kW 450V 60Hz a.c Boilers: e (ex.g.) 12.2kgf/cm² (12.0bar), WTAuxB (o.f.) 9.2kgf/cm² (9.0bar) Thrusters: 1 Thwart. CP thruster (f)
9353254 **YM EMINENCE** *A8OR9* - **FSL-20 Inc** Yang Ming Marine Transport Corp *Monrovia* *Liberia* MMSI: 636013694 Official number: 13694	**42,741** 19,338 52,773	Class: LR ✠ **100A1** SS 04/2013 container ship **ShipRight** (SDA, FDA, CM) *IWS LI ✠ **LMC** **UMS** Eq.Ltr: R†; Cable: 687.5/84.0 U3 (a)	**2008-04 CSBC Corp, Taiwan — Kaohsiung** Yd No: 886 Loa 268.80 (BB) Br ex 32.30 Dght 12.500 Lbp 256.50 Br md 32.20 Dpth 19.10 Welded, 1 dk	**(A33A2CC) Container Ship (Fully Cellular)** TEU 4252 C Ho 2112 TEU C Dk 2140 TEU incl 500 ref C. Compartments: ER, 7 Cell Ho 14 Ha: (12.6 x 18.0) (12.6 x 23.1)ER 11 (12.6 x 28.3) (6.5 x 12.9)	**1 oil engine** driving 1 FP propeller Total Power: 40,040kW (54,438hp) 24.8kn Wartsila 7RT-flex96C 1 x 2 Stroke 7 Cy. 960 x 2500 40040kW (54438bhp) Diesel United Ltd.-Aioi AuxGen: 3 x 2280kW 450V 60Hz a.c Boilers: e (ex.g.) 12.2kgf/cm² (12.0bar), WTAuxB (o.f.) 9.2kgf/cm² (9.0bar) Thrusters: 1 Thwart. CP thruster (f) Fuel: 304.0 (d.f.) 4456.0 (r.f.)
9461362 **YM ENDEAVOUR** *VRIG6* - *ex* RBD Mediterraneo *-2012* **Ocean Transit Carrier SA** Yamamaru Kisen KK (Yamamaru Kisen Co Ltd) *Hong Kong* *Hong Kong* MMSI: 477802500 Official number: HK-3038	**43,012** 27,239 82,205 T/cm 70.2	Class: NK	**2011-05 Tsuneishi Shipbuilding Co Ltd — Fukuyama HS** Yd No: 1456 Loa 228.99 Br ex - Dght 14.430 Lbp 222.00 Br md 32.26 Dpth 20.05 Welded, 1 dk	**(A21A2BC) Bulk Carrier** Grain: 97,381 Compartments: 7 Ho, ER 7 Ha: ER	**1 oil engine** driving 1 FP propeller Total Power: 9,710kW (13,202hp) 14.5kn MAN-B&W 6S60MC-C 1 x 2 Stroke 6 Cy. 600 x 2400 9710kW (13202bhp) Mitsui Engineering & Shipbuilding CLtd-Japan Fuel: 3184.0 (r.f.)
9353278 **YM ENHANCER** *A8OS4* - **FSL-22 Inc** Yang Ming Marine Transport Corp *Monrovia* *Liberia* MMSI: 636013697 Official number: 13697	**42,741** 19,338 52,773	Class: AB	**2008-10 CSBC Corp, Taiwan — Kaohsiung** Yd No: 888 Loa 268.80 (BB) Br ex 32.30 Dght 13.020 Lbp 256.50 Br md 32.20 Dpth 19.10 Welded, 1 dk	**(A33A2CC) Container Ship (Fully Cellular)** TEU 4252 C Ho 2112 C Dk 2140 TEU incl 500 ref C. Compartments: 7 Cell Ho, ER	**1 oil engine** driving 1 FP propeller Total Power: 40,040kW (54,438hp) 24.8kn Wartsila 7RT-flex96C 1 x 2 Stroke 7 Cy. 960 x 2500 40040kW (54438bhp) Diesel United Ltd.-Aioi AuxGen: 3 x 2280kW a.c Thrusters: 1 Thwart. FP thruster (f)
9353292 **YM ETERNITY** *A8OS6* - **All Oceans Transportation Inc** Yang Ming Marine Transport Corp *Monrovia* *Liberia* MMSI: 636013699 Official number: 13699	**42,741** 19,338 52,773	Class: AB	**2009-03 CSBC Corp, Taiwan — Kaohsiung** Yd No: 890 Loa 268.80 (BB) Br ex - Dght 12.500 Lbp 256.60 Br md 32.20 Dpth 19.10 Welded, 1 dk	**(A33A2CC) Container Ship (Fully Cellular)** TEU 4252 C Ho 2112 C Dk 2140 TEU incl 500 ref C.	**1 oil engine** driving 1 FP propeller Total Power: 40,040kW (54,438hp) 24.8kn Wartsila 7RT-flex96C 1 x 2 Stroke 7 Cy. 960 x 2500 40040kW (54438bhp) AuxGen: 3 x 2280kW a.c Thrusters: 1 Tunnel thruster (f) Fuel: 5023.0 (r.f.)
9278090 **YM FOUNTAIN** *A8EI5* - **Yang Ming (Liberia) Corp** Yang Ming Marine Transport Corp SatCom: Inmarsat C 463696043 *Monrovia* *Liberia* MMSI: 636012253 Official number: 12253	**64,254** 35,137 68,280	Class: AB	**2004-05 China Shipbuilding Corp (CSBC) — Kaohsiung** Yd No: 802 Loa 275.00 (BB) Br ex - Dght 14.000 Lbp 263.00 Br md 40.00 Dpth 24.20 Welded	**(A33A2CC) Container Ship (Fully Cellular)** TEU 5548 C Ho 2564 TEU C Ho 2984 TEU incl 400 ref C.	**1 oil engine** driving 1 FP propeller Total Power: 54,900kW (74,642hp) 26.0kn Sulzer 10RTA96C 1 x 2 Stroke 10 Cy. 960 x 2500 54900kW (74642bhp) Hyundai Heavy Industries Co Ltd-South Korea AuxGen: 4 x 1900kW a.c Thrusters: 1 Thwart. CP thruster (f)
9267156 **YM GREAT** *H3GY* - *launched as* Ming Great *-2004* **Luster Maritime SA** SMTECH Ship Management Co Ltd SatCom: Inmarsat C 435745820 *Panama* *Panama* MMSI: 357458000 Official number: 2994504B	**66,332** 25,247 67,270	Class: NK	**2004-04 Koyo Dockyard Co Ltd — Mihara HS** Yd No: 2171 Loa 278.94 (BB) Br ex 40.10 Dght 14.021 Lbp 262.00 Br md 40.00 Dpth 24.00 Welded, 1 dk	**(A33A2CC) Container Ship (Fully Cellular)** TEU 5576 incl 500 ref C.	**1 oil engine** driving 1 FP propeller Total Power: 57,205kW (77,776hp) 25.0kn MAN-B&W 10K98MC 1 x 2 Stroke 10 Cy. 980 x 2660 57205kW (77776bhp) Mitsui Engineering & Shipbuilding CLtd-Japan AuxGen: 4 x a.c Thrusters: 1 Tunnel thruster (f) Fuel: 10430.0
9224491 **YM GREEN** *ELXZ3* - *ex* Ming Green *-2005* **All Oceans Transportation Inc** Yang Ming Marine Transport Corp SatCom: Inmarsat C 463694185 *Monrovia* *Liberia* MMSI: 636011275 Official number: 11275	**64,254** 35,137 68,413 T/cm 89.6	Class: AB	**2001-07 Hyundai Heavy Industries Co Ltd — Ulsan** Yd No: 1340 Loa 274.70 (BB) Br ex - Dght 14.000 Lbp 263.00 Br md 40.00 Dpth 24.20 Welded, 1 dk	**(A33A2CC) Container Ship (Fully Cellular)** TEU 5512 C Ho 2564 TEU C Dk 2948 TEU incl 400 ref C.	**1 oil engine** driving 1 FP propeller Total Power: 54,946kW (74,705hp) 25.9kn Sulzer 10RTA96C 1 x 2 Stroke 10 Cy. 960 x 2500 54946kW (74705bhp) Hyundai Heavy Industries Co Ltd-South Korea AuxGen: 4 x 1900kW a.c Thrusters: 1 Thwart. CP thruster (f)
9157648 **YM HAMBURG** *9V2197* - *ex* Ville de Virgo *-2004* **Sornop Marine SA** Eastern Pacific Shipping Pte Ltd *Singapore* *Singapore* MMSI: 563115000 Official number: 398728	**40,268** 23,501 49,225 T/cm 70.9	Class: LR (BV) (GL) **100A1** SS 02/2012 container ship LI **LMC** **UMS** Eq.Ltr: R†; Cable: 687.5/84.0 U3 (a)	**1997-10 Daewoo Heavy Industries Ltd — Geoje** Yd No: 4059 Loa 259.00 (BB) Br ex - Dght 12.020 Lbp 244.00 Br md 32.20 Dpth 19.00 Welded, 1 dk	**(A33A2CC) Container Ship (Fully Cellular)** TEU 3961 C Ho 1621 TEU C Dk 2340 TEU incl 150 ref C. Compartments: ER, 8 Cell Ho 8 Ha: ER	**1 oil engine** driving 1 FP propeller Total Power: 32,400kW (44,051hp) 23.7kn Sulzer 8RTA84C 1 x 2 Stroke 8 Cy. 840 x 2400 32400kW (44051bhp) Korea Heavy Industries & ConstrCo Ltd (HANJUNG)-South Korea AuxGen: 3 x 850kW 440V 60Hz a.c, 1 x 360kW 440V 60Hz a.c Boilers: AuxB (Comp) (fitted: 1997) 7.0kgf/cm² (6.9bar) Thrusters: 1 Thwart. FP thruster (f)
9299329 **YM HARMONY** *BLIG* - **Yang Ming Marine Transport Corp** - *Keelung* *Chinese Taipei* MMSI: 416427000 Official number: 014852	**15,167** 6,667 19,104	Class: AB CR	**2005-03 China Shipbuilding Corp — Keelung** Yd No: 843 Loa 168.80 (BB) Br ex - Dght 8.600 Lbp 158.00 Br md 27.30 Dpth 13.50 Welded, 1 dk	**(A33A2CC) Container Ship (Fully Cellular)** TEU 1500 C Ho 564 TEU C Dk 936 TEU incl 150 ref C.	**1 oil engine** driving 1 FP propeller Total Power: 12,651kW (17,200hp) 19.6kn MAN-B&W 8S50MC-C 1 x 2 Stroke 8 Cy. 500 x 2000 12651kW (17200bhp) Mitsui Engineering & Shipbuilding CLtd-Japan AuxGen: 3 x 900kW a.c Thrusters: 1 Tunnel thruster (f) Fuel: 142.0 (d.f.) 1928.0 (r.f.)
9299317 **YM HAWK** *BLIF* - **Yang Ming Marine Transport Corp** - *Keelung* *Chinese Taipei* MMSI: 416429000 Official number: 014850	**15,167** 6,667 19,104	Class: AB CR	**2005-01 China Shipbuilding Corp — Keelung** Yd No: 842 Loa 168.80 (BB) Br ex - Dght 8.600 Lbp 158.00 Br md 27.30 Dpth 13.50 Welded, 1 dk	**(A33A2CC) Container Ship (Fully Cellular)** TEU 1500 C Ho 564 TEU C Dk 936 TEU incl 150 ref C.	**1 oil engine** driving 1 FP propeller Total Power: 12,651kW (17,200hp) 19.4kn B&W 8S50MC-C 1 x 2 Stroke 8 Cy. 500 x 2000 12651kW (17200bhp) Mitsui Engineering & Shipbuilding CLtd-Japan AuxGen: 3 x 1125kW 440/220V 60Hz a.c Thrusters: 1 Tunnel thruster (f) Fuel: 127.9 (d.f.) 1984.0 (r.f.)
9301275 **YM HEIGHTS** *BLII* - **Yang Ming Marine Transport Corp** - *Keelung* *Chinese Taipei* MMSI: 416426000 Official number: 024851	**15,167** 6,667 19,104	Class: AB CR	**2005-07 China Shipbuilding Corp — Keelung** Yd No: 846 Loa 168.80 (BB) Br ex - Dght 8.600 Lbp 158.00 Br md 27.30 Dpth 13.50 Welded, 1 dk	**(A33A2CC) Container Ship (Fully Cellular)** TEU 1500 C Ho 564 TEU C Dk 936 TEU incl 150 ref C.	**1 oil engine** driving 1 FP propeller Total Power: 12,651kW (17,200hp) 19.4kn B&W 8S50MC-C 1 x 2 Stroke 8 Cy. 500 x 2000 12651kW (17200bhp) Mitsui Engineering & Shipbuilding CLtd-Japan AuxGen: 3 x 900kW a.c Thrusters: 1 Tunnel thruster (f)

IMO / Call sign	Name / Owner / Flag	Tonnage	Class	Build / Dimensions	Type / Cargo	Machinery
9301263 *BLIH* -	**YM HORIZON** **Yang Ming Marine Transport Corp** - *Keelung* *Chinese Taipei* MMSI: 416428000	**15,167** 6,667 19,104	Class: AB CR	**2005-06 China Shipbuilding Corp — Keelung** Yd No: 845 Loa 168.80 (BB) Br ex - Dght 8.600 Lbp 158.00 Br md 27.30 Dpth 13.50 Welded, 1 dk	**(A33A2CC) Container Ship (Fully Cellular)** TEU 1500 C Ho 564 TEU C Dk 936 TEU incl 150 ref C.	**1 oil engine** driving 1 FP propeller Total Power: 12,651kW (17,200hp) 19.4kn MAN-B&W 8S50MC-C 1 x 2 Stroke 8 Cy. 500 x 2000 12651kW (17200bhp) Mitsui Engineering & Shipbuilding CLtd-Japan AuxGen: 3 x 900kW a.c Thrusters: 1 Tunnel thruster (f)
9319129 *BLHF* -	**YM IDEALS** **Yang Ming Marine Transport Corp** - *Keelung* *Chinese Taipei* MMSI: 416488000	**16,488** 7,615 22,027	Class: BV	**2006-04 China Shipbuilding Corp — Keelung** Yd No: 850 Loa 171.90 (BB) Br ex - Dght 9.500 Lbp 162.10 Br md 27.30 Dpth 13.50 Welded, 1 dk	**(A33A2CC) Container Ship (Fully Cellular)** TEU 1799 incl 300 ref C.	**1 oil engine** driving 1 FP propeller Total Power: 15,806kW (21,490hp) 19.6kn MAN-B&W 7S60MC-C 1 x 2 Stroke 7 Cy. 600 x 2400 15806kW (21490bhp) Mitsui Engineering & Shipbuilding CLtd-Japan AuxGen: 3 x 1200kW 440/220V 60Hz a.c Thrusters: 1 Thwart. CP thruster (f) Fuel: 166.5 (d.f.) 1847.4 (r.f.)
9319088 *A8HX3* -	**YM IMAGE** **All Oceans Transportation Inc** Yang Ming Marine Transport Corp *Monrovia* *Liberia* MMSI: 636012796 Official number: 12796	**16,488** 7,615 22,027	Class: AB	**2006-10 China Shipbuilding Corp (CSBC) — Kaohsiung** Yd No: 854 Loa 172.70 (BB) Br ex - Dght 9.500 Lbp 162.10 Br md 27.30 Dpth 13.50 Welded, 1 dk	**(A33A2CC) Container Ship (Fully Cellular)** TEU 1799 incl 300 ref C	**1 oil engine** driving 1 FP propeller Total Power: 15,806kW (21,490hp) 19.6kn MAN-B&W 7S60MC-C 1 x 2 Stroke 7 Cy. 600 x 2400 15806kW (21490bhp) Mitsui Engineering & Shipbuilding CLtd-Japan AuxGen: 3 x 1200kW a.c Thrusters: 1 Tunnel thruster (f)
9319131 *A8HW8* -	**YM IMMENSE** **All Oceans Transportation Inc** Yang Ming Marine Transport Corp *Monrovia* *Liberia* MMSI: 636012793 Official number: 12793	**16,488** 7,615 21,700	Class: BV	**2006-06 China Shipbuilding Corp — Keelung** Yd No: 851 Loa 171.90 (BB) Br ex - Dght 9.500 Lbp 162.10 Br md 27.30 Dpth 13.50 Welded, 1 dk	**(A33A2CC) Container Ship (Fully Cellular)** TEU 1799 incl 300 ref C.	**1 oil engine** driving 1 FP propeller Total Power: 15,806kW (21,490hp) 19.6kn MAN-B&W 7S60MC-C 1 x 2 Stroke 7 Cy. 600 x 2400 15806kW (21490bhp) Mitsui Engineering & Shipbuilding CLtd-Japan AuxGen: 3 x 1200kW 440/220V 60Hz a.c Thrusters: 1 Thwart. CP thruster (f) Fuel: 1884.0
9334014 *A8KS9* -	**YM IMPROVEMENT** **All Oceans Transportation Inc** Yang Ming Marine Transport Corp *Monrovia* *Liberia* MMSI: 636013121 Official number: 13121	**16,472** 7,615 22,072	Class: LR ✠ **100A1** SS 11/2012 container ship **ShipRight** (SDA, CM) *IWS LI ✠ **LMC** **UMS** Eq.Ltr: J†; Cable: 605.0/66.0 U3 (a)	**2007-11 CSBC Corp, Taiwan — Keelung** Yd No: 864 Loa 172.70 (BB) Br ex 27.30 Dght 9.500 Lbp 162.10 Br md 27.30 Dpth 13.50 Welded, 1 dk	**(A33A2CC) Container Ship (Fully Cellular)** TEU 1803 incl 300 ref C. Compartments: 4 Cell Ho, ER 8 Ha: (12.6 x 18.0)6 (12.6 x 23.2)ER (12.6 x 12.9)	**1 oil engine** driving 1 FP propeller Total Power: 15,806kW (21,490hp) 19.6kn MAN-B&W 7S60MC-C 1 x 2 Stroke 7 Cy. 600 x 2400 15806kW (21490bhp) Mitsui Engineering & Shipbuilding CLtd-Japan AuxGen: 3 x 1200kW 450V 60Hz a.c Boilers: AuxB (Comp) 8.0kgf/cm² (7.8bar) Thrusters: 1 Thwart. CP thruster (f) Fuel: 105.0 (d.f.) 1563.0 (r.f.)
9334002 *BLHE* -	**YM INAUGURATION** **Yang Ming Marine Transport Corp** - *Keelung* *Chinese Taipei* MMSI: 416487000	**16,488** 7,615 22,027	Class: CR LR ✠ **100A1** SS 08/2012 container ship *IWS LI **ShipRight** (SDA, CM) ✠ **LMC** **UMS** Eq.Ltr: J†; Cable: 605.0/66.0 U3 (a)	**2007-08 CSBC Corp, Taiwan — Keelung** Yd No: 863 Loa 172.70 (BB) Br ex 27.30 Dght 9.500 Lbp 162.10 Br md 27.30 Dpth 13.50 Welded, 1 dk	**(A33A2CC) Container Ship (Fully Cellular)** TEU 1803 incl 300 ref C. Compartments: 4 Cell Ho, ER 8 Ha: (12.6 x 18.0)6 (12.6 x 23.2)ER (12.6 x 12.9)	**1 oil engine** driving 1 FP propeller Total Power: 15,820kW (21,509hp) 19.9kn MAN-B&W 7S60MC-C 1 x 2 Stroke 7 Cy. 600 x 2400 15820kW (21509bhp) Mitsui Engineering & Shipbuilding CLtd-Japan AuxGen: 3 x 1200kW 450V 60Hz a.c Boilers: AuxB (Comp) 8.0kgf/cm² (7.8bar) Thrusters: 1 Thwart. CP thruster (f) Fuel: 105.0 (d.f.) 1563.0 (r.f.)
9319155 *A8HX2* -	**YM INCEPTION** **All Oceans Transportation Inc** Yang Ming Marine Transport Corp *Monrovia* *Liberia* MMSI: 636012795 Official number: 12795	**16,488** 7,615 22,027	Class: NV	**2006-10 China Shipbuilding Corp — Keelung** Yd No: 853 Loa 172.70 (BB) Br ex 27.35 Dght 9.500 Lbp 162.10 Br md 27.30 Dpth 13.50 Welded, 1 dk	**(A33A2CC) Container Ship (Fully Cellular)** TEU 1799 incl 300 ref C.	**1 oil engine** driving 1 FP propeller Total Power: 15,806kW (21,490hp) 19.6kn MAN-B&W 7S60MC-C 1 x 2 Stroke 7 Cy. 600 x 2400 15806kW (21490bhp) Mitsui Engineering & Shipbuilding CLtd-Japan AuxGen: 3 x 1200kW 450V 60Hz a.c Thrusters: 1 Thwart. CP thruster (f) Fuel: 166.5 (d.f.) 1847.4 (r.f.)
9319143 *A8HW9* -	**YM INCREMENT** **All Oceans Transportation Inc** Yang Ming Marine Transport Corp *Monrovia* *Liberia* MMSI: 636012794 Official number: 12794	**16,488** 7,615 22,027	Class: NV	**2006-08 China Shipbuilding Corp — Keelung** Yd No: 852 Loa 172.70 (BB) Br ex 27.35 Dght 9.500 Lbp 162.10 Br md 27.30 Dpth 13.50 Welded, 1 dk	**(A33A2CC) Container Ship (Fully Cellular)** TEU 1799 incl 300 ref C.	**1 oil engine** driving 1 FP propeller Total Power: 15,806kW (21,490hp) 19.6kn MAN-B&W 7S60MC-C 1 x 2 Stroke 7 Cy. 600 x 2400 15806kW (21490bhp) Mitsui Engineering & Shipbuilding CLtd-Japan AuxGen: 3 x 1200kW 450V 60Hz a.c Thrusters: 1 Thwart. CP thruster (f)
9319090 *A8HX4* -	**YM INITIATIVE** **All Oceans Transportation Inc** Yang Ming Marine Transport Corp *Monrovia* *Liberia* MMSI: 636012797 Official number: 12797	**16,488** 7,615 22,027	Class: AB	**2007-01 China Shipbuilding Corp (CSBC) — Kaohsiung** Yd No: 855 Loa 171.90 (BB) Br ex - Dght 9.500 Lbp 162.10 Br md 27.30 Dpth 13.50 Welded, 1 dk	**(A33A2CC) Container Ship (Fully Cellular)** TEU 1799 incl 300 ref C	**1 oil engine** driving 1 FP propeller Total Power: 15,806kW (21,490hp) 19.6kn MAN-B&W 7S60MC-C 1 x 2 Stroke 7 Cy. 600 x 2400 15806kW (21490bhp) Mitsui Engineering & Shipbuilding CLtd-Japan AuxGen: 3 x 1200kW a.c Thrusters: 1 Tunnel thruster (f)
9331086 *A8KS6* -	**YM INSTRUCTION** **All Oceans Transportation Inc** Yang Ming Marine Transport Corp *Monrovia* *Liberia* MMSI: 636013118 Official number: 13118	**16,488** 7,615 22,027	Class: AB	**2007-05 CSBC Corp, Taiwan — Keelung** Yd No: 861 Loa 171.90 (BB) Br ex - Dght 9.500 Lbp 162.10 Br md 27.30 Dpth 13.50 Welded, 1 dk	**(A33A2CC) Container Ship (Fully Cellular)** TEU 1803 incl 300 ref C.	**1 oil engine** driving 1 FP propeller Total Power: 15,806kW (21,490hp) 19.6kn MAN-B&W 7S60MC-C 1 x 2 Stroke 7 Cy. 600 x 2400 15806kW (21490bhp) Mitsui Engineering & Shipbuilding CLtd-Japan AuxGen: 3 x 1200kW 450V 60Hz a.c Thrusters: 1 Thwart. CP thruster (f) Fuel: 157.2 (d.f.) 1847.4 (r.f.)
9319117 *BLHD* -	**YM INTELLIGENT** **Yang Ming Marine Transport Corp** - *Keelung* *Chinese Taipei* MMSI: 416486000 Official number: 015477	**16,488** 7,615 22,027	Class: AB (NV)	**2006-01 China Shipbuilding Corp — Keelung** Yd No: 849 Loa 172.70 (BB) Br ex - Dght 9.500 Lbp 162.10 Br md 27.30 Dpth 13.50 Welded, 1 dk	**(A33A2CC) Container Ship (Fully Cellular)** TEU 1799 incl 300 ref C.	**1 oil engine** driving 1 FP propeller Total Power: 15,806kW (21,490hp) 19.6kn MAN-B&W 7S60MC-C 1 x 2 Stroke 7 Cy. 600 x 2400 15806kW (21490bhp) Mitsui Engineering & Shipbuilding CLtd-Japan AuxGen: 3 x 1200kW 450V 60Hz a.c Thrusters: 1 Thwart. CP thruster (f) Fuel: 166.5 (d.f.) 1847.4 (r.f.)
9333993 *A8KS7* -	**YM INTERACTION** **All Oceans Transportation Inc** Yang Ming Marine Transport Corp *Monrovia* *Liberia* MMSI: 636013119 Official number: 13119	**16,488** 7,615 22,027	Class: AB	**2007-07 CSBC Corp, Taiwan — Keelung** Yd No: 862 Loa 171.90 (BB) Br ex - Dght 9.500 Lbp 162.10 Br md 27.30 Dpth 13.50 Welded, 1 dk	**(A33A2CC) Container Ship (Fully Cellular)** TEU 1803 incl 300 ref C.	**1 oil engine** driving 1 FP propeller Total Power: 15,806kW (21,490hp) 19.6kn MAN-B&W 7S60MC-C 1 x 2 Stroke 7 Cy. 600 x 2400 15806kW (21490bhp) Mitsui Engineering & Shipbuilding CLtd-Japan AuxGen: 3 x 1200kW 450V 60Hz a.c Thrusters: 1 Thwart. CP thruster (f) Fuel: 157.2 (d.f.) 1847.4 (r.f.)
9319105 *A8HX5* -	**YM INVENTIVE** **All Oceans Transportation Inc** Yang Ming Marine Transport Corp *Monrovia* *Liberia* MMSI: 636012798 Official number: 12798	**16,488** 7,615 22,027	Class: AB	**2007-03 CSBC Corp, Taiwan — Kaohsiung** Yd No: 856 Loa 171.90 (BB) Br ex - Dght 9.500 Lbp 162.10 Br md 27.30 Dpth 13.50 Welded, 1 dk	**(A33A2CC) Container Ship (Fully Cellular)** TEU 1799 incl 300 ref C	**1 oil engine** driving 1 FP propeller Total Power: 15,806kW (21,490hp) 19.6kn MAN-B&W 7S60MC-C 1 x 2 Stroke 7 Cy. 600 x 2400 15806kW (21490bhp) Mitsui Engineering & Shipbuilding CLtd-Japan AuxGen: 3 x 1200kW a.c Thrusters: 1 Tunnel thruster (f) Fuel: 166.0 (d.f.) 1847.0 (r.f.)
9291597 *9HTF8* -	**YM JUPITER** *launched as Zeycan Ana -2007* **YM Mercury Tankers Ltd** Uni-Chartering *Valletta* *Malta* MMSI: 256398000 Official number: 9291597	**10,917** 5,260 15,995 T/cm 27.1	Class: BV	**2007-01 Marmara Tersanesi — Yarimca** Yd No: 69 Loa 148.00 (BB) Br ex 21.63 Dght 8.600 Lbp 139.50 Br md 21.60 Dpth 11.30 Welded, 1 dk	**(A12B2TR) Chemical/Products Tanker** Double Hull (13F) Liq: 17,697; Liq (Oil): 17,697 Cargo Heating Coils Compartments: 12 Wing Ta, 2 Wing Slop Ta, ER 2 x Gas Tank (s); 2 cyl horizontal 12 Cargo Pump (s): 12x300m³/hr Manifold: Bow/CM: 76.6m Ice Capable	**1 oil engine** reduction geared to sc. shaft driving 1 CP propeller Total Power: 5,400kW (7,342hp) 14.0kn MaK 6M43 1 x 4 Stroke 6 Cy. 430 x 610 5400kW (7342bhp) Caterpillar Motoren GmbH & Co. KG-Germany AuxGen: 3 x 590kW 450V 60Hz a.c, 1 x 1078kW 450V 60Hz a.c Thrusters: 1 Tunnel thruster (f) Fuel: 114.0 (d.f.) 719.0 (r.f.) 20.0pd

IMO / Call sign	Name / Owner	Tonnage	Class	Builder / Dimensions	Type	Machinery
9143166 *MCGF6* -	**YM KAOHSIUNG** *ex Ville de Tanya -2004* **Ritton Maritime Inc** Zodiac Maritime Agencies Ltd *London* *United Kingdom* MMSI: 235767000 Official number: 907921	**40,068** 16,944 50,059 T/cm 70.1	Class: LR (BV) **100A1** SS 01/2013 container ship LI **LMC** **UMS** Cable: 687.5/84.0 U3 (a)	**1998-01 Halla Engineering & Heavy Industries, Ltd. — Samho** Yd No: 1033 Loa 259.50 (BB) Br ex 32.30 Dght 12.160 Lbp 245.32 Br md 32.20 Dpth 19.00 Welded, 1 dk	**(A33A2CC) Container Ship (Fully Cellular)** TEU 4031 C Ho 1653 TEU C Dk 2378 TEU incl 200 ref C. Compartments: ER, 7 Cell Ho 7 Ha: ER	**1 oil engine** driving 1 FP propeller Total Power: 36,480kW (49,598hp) 24.0k B&W 8K90MC- 1 x 2 Stroke 8 Cy. 900 x 2300 36480kW (49598bhp) Hyundai Heavy Industries Co Ltd-South Korea AuxGen: 3 x 1150kW 450V 60Hz a.c, 1 x 250kW 450V 60Hz a.c Boilers: e (ex.g.), AuxB (o.f.) Thrusters: 1 Thwart. FP thruster (f)
9450595 *VRFI2* -	**YM KEELUNG** **Superior Integrity Ltd** Univan Ship Management Ltd SatCom: Inmarsat C 447702070 *Hong Kong* *Hong Kong* MMSI: 477261800 Official number: HK-2422	**40,030** 24,450 50,500 T/cm 70.4	Class: NV	**2009-06 Samsung Heavy Industries Co Ltd — Geoje** Yd No: 1774 Loa 259.80 (BB) Br ex - Dght 12.600 Lbp 244.80 Br md 32.25 Dpth 19.30 Welded, 1 dk	**(A33A2CC) Container Ship (Fully Cellular)** TEU 4253 C Ho 1584 C Dk 2669 incl 400 ref C. Compartments: 7 Cell Ho, ER	**1 oil engine** driving 1 FP propeller Total Power: 36,560kW (49,707hp) 23.3k MAN-B&W 8K90MC- 1 x 2 Stroke 8 Cy. 900 x 2300 36560kW (49707bhp) Doosan Engine Co Ltd-South Korea AuxGen: 4 x 1700kW a.c Thrusters: 1 Tunnel thruster (f)
9387102 *3EHQ6* -	**YM LOS ANGELES** **Almirante Shipping SA** Shoei Kisen Kaisha Ltd *Panama* *Panama* MMSI: 372205000 Official number: 3234107A	**54,828** 24,104 65,123	Class: NK	**2006-12 Koyo Dockyard Co Ltd — Mihara HS** Yd No: 2222 Loa 294.03 (BB) Br ex 32.20 Dght 13.521 Lbp 283.00 Br md 32.20 Dpth 16.90 Welded, 1 dk	**(A33A2CC) Container Ship (Fully Cellular)** TEU 4923 C Ho 2142 TEU C Dk 2781 TEU incl 421 ref C	**1 oil engine** driving 1 FP propeller Total Power: 45,760kW (62,215hp) 23.8k MAN-B&W 8K98M 1 x 2 Stroke 8 Cy. 980 x 2660 45760kW (62215bhp) Mitsui Engineering & Shipbuilding CLtd-Japan AuxGen: 4 x a.c Thrusters: 1 Tunnel thruster (f) Fuel: 7785.0
9438523 *A8UU7* -	**YM MANDATE** **Expresscarrier (No 1) Corp** Danaos Shipping Co Ltd SatCom: Inmarsat C 463707772 *Monrovia* *Liberia* MMSI: 636014557 Official number: 14557	**73,675** 40,754 83,200	Class: NV	**2010-05 Hanjin Heavy Industries & Construction Co Ltd — Busan** Yd No: 214 Loa 300.00 (BB) Br ex 40.12 Dght 14.500 Lbp 286.70 Br md 40.00 Dpth 24.60 Welded, 1 dk	**(A33A2CC) Container Ship (Fully Cellular)** Double Hull TEU 6572 incl 500 ref C	**1 oil engine** driving 1 FP propeller Total Power: 57,199kW (77,768hp) 24.0k MAN-B&W 10K98ME-(1 x 2 Stroke 10 Cy. 980 x 2400 57199kW (77768bhp) Doosan Engine Co Ltd-South Korea AuxGen: 4 x 2100kW 450V a.c Thrusters: 1 Tunnel thruster (f)
9298997 *H3NC* -	**YM MARCH** *launched as Ming March -2004* **Catalina Shipping SA** Bernhard Schulte Shipmanagement (China) Co Ltd SatCom: Inmarsat C 435559010 *Panama* *Panama* MMSI: 355590000 Official number: 2990204B	**66,332** 25,247 67,270	Class: NK	**2004-05 Koyo Dockyard Co Ltd — Mihara HS** Yd No: 2172 Loa 278.94 (BB) Br ex 40.10 Dght 14.021 Lbp 262.00 Br md 40.00 Dpth 24.00 Welded, 1 dk	**(A33A2CC) Container Ship (Fully Cellular)** TEU 5576 incl 500 ref C.	**1 oil engine** driving 1 FP propeller Total Power: 57,201kW (77,770hp) 25.0k MAN-B&W 10K98M 1 x 2 Stroke 10 Cy. 980 x 2660 57201kW (77770bhp) Mitsui Engineering & Shipbuilding CLtd-Japan AuxGen: 4 x a.c Thrusters: 1 Tunnel thruster (f) Fuel: 10430.0
9551806 *9HA2678* -	**YM MARS** **YM Pluto Tankers Ltd** CSM Denizcilik Ltd Sti (Chemfleet) SatCom: Inmarsat C 421523410 *Valletta* *Malta* MMSI: 215234000 Official number: 9551806	**4,242** 1,992 6,472 T/cm 15.7	Class: BV	**2011-03 Marmara Tersanesi — Yarimca** Yd No: 83 Loa 109.00 (BB) Br ex - Dght 6.650 Lbp 101.60 Br md 15.80 Dpth 8.30 Welded, 1 dk	**(A12B2TR) Chemical/Products Tanker** Double Hull (13F) Liq: 6,883; Liq (Oil): 6,883 Cargo Heating Coils Compartments: 10 Wing Ta, 2 Wing Slop Ta, ER 10 Cargo Pump (s): 10x200m³/hr Manifold: Bow/CM: 48.9m Ice Capable	**1 oil engine** reduction geared to sc. shaft driving 1 CP propeller Total Power: 2,720kW (3,698hp) 12.0k MAN-B&W 8L27/3 1 x 4 Stroke 8 Cy. 270 x 380 2720kW (3698bhp) MAN Diesel A/S-Denmark AuxGen: 3 x 485kW a.c, 1 x 900kW a.c Thrusters: 1 Tunnel thruster (f) Fuel: 42.0 (d.f.) 317.0 (r.f.)
9485007 *A8ZD2* -	**YM MASCULINITY** **All Oceans Transportation Inc** Yang Ming Marine Transport Corp *Monrovia* *Liberia* MMSI: 636015183 Official number: 15183	**76,787** 41,396 81,145	Class: AB (CR)	**2012-04 CSBC Corp, Taiwan — Kaohsiung** Yd No: 970 Loa 305.60 (BB) Br ex - Dght 12.000 Lbp 293.16 Br md 40.00 Dpth 24.20 Welded, 1 dk	**(A33A2CC) Container Ship (Fully Cellular)** TEU 6589 incl 500 ref C	**1 oil engine** driving 1 FP propeller Total Power: 57,222kW (77,799hp) 25.3k MAN-B&W 10K98M 1 x 2 Stroke 10 Cy. 980 x 2660 57222kW (77799bhp) Mitsui Engineering & Shipbuilding CLtd-Japan AuxGen: 1 x 2200kW a.c, 4 x 2200kW a.c Thrusters: 1 Tunnel thruster (f) Fuel: 484.0 (d.f.) 8475.0 (r.f.)
9438535 *A8UU8* -	**YM MATURITY** **Expresscarrier (No 2) Corp** Danaos Shipping Co Ltd *Monrovia* *Liberia* MMSI: 636014558 Official number: 14558	**73,675** 40,754 83,200	Class: NV	**2010-07 Hanjin Heavy Industries & Construction Co Ltd — Busan** Yd No: 215 Loa 299.20 (BB) Br ex 40.12 Dght 14.500 Lbp 286.70 Br md 40.00 Dpth 24.60 Welded, 1 dk	**(A33A2CC) Container Ship (Fully Cellular)** Double Hull TEU 6572 incl 500 ref C. Compartments: 8 Cell Ho, ER 16 Ha: ER	**1 oil engine** driving 1 FP propeller Total Power: 57,199kW (77,768hp) 24.0k MAN-B&W 10K98ME- 1 x 2 Stroke 10 Cy. 980 x 2400 57199kW (77768bhp) Doosan Engine Co Ltd-South Korea AuxGen: 4 x 2210kW a.c Thrusters: 1 Tunnel thruster (f)
9452775 *9HA2392* -	**YM MERCURY** **Jasper Maritime Ltd** CSM Denizcilik Ltd Sti (Chemfleet) SatCom: Inmarsat C 424850710 *Valletta* *Malta* MMSI: 248507000 Official number: 9452775	**4,242** 1,992 6,482 T/cm 15.7	Class: BV	**2010-04 Marmara Tersanesi — Yarimca** Yd No: 82 Loa 109.00 (BB) Br ex - Dght 6.650 Lbp 102.30 Br md 16.80 Dpth 8.30 Welded, 1 dk	**(A12B2TR) Chemical/Products Tanker** Double Hull (13F) Liq: 6,883; Liq (Oil): 6,883 Cargo Heating Coils Compartments: 10 Wing Ta, 2 Wing Slop Ta, ER 10 Cargo Pump (s): 10x200m³/hr Manifold: Bow/CM: 48.9m Ice Capable	**1 oil engine** reduction geared to sc. shaft driving 1 CP propeller Total Power: 2,720kW (3,698hp) 14.0k MAN-B&W 8L27/3 1 x 4 Stroke 8 Cy. 270 x 380 2720kW (3698bhp) MAN Diesel A/S-Denmark AuxGen: 3 x 515kW a.c, 1 x 900kW a.c Thrusters: 1 Tunnel thruster (f) Fuel: 32.0 (d.f.) 280.0 (r.f.)
9484998 *A8ZC9* -	**YM MILESTONE** **All Oceans Transportation Inc** Yang Ming Marine Transport Corp SatCom: Inmarsat C 463710885 *Monrovia* *Liberia* MMSI: 636015182 Official number: 15182	**76,787** 41,396 81,145	Class: AB (CR)	**2011-10 CSBC Corp, Taiwan — Kaohsiung** Yd No: 969 Loa 305.60 (BB) Br ex - Dght 12.000 Lbp 293.16 Br md 40.00 Dpth 24.20 Welded, 1 dk	**(A33A2CC) Container Ship (Fully Cellular)** TEU 6589 incl 500 ref C	**1 oil engine** driving 1 FP propeller Total Power: 57,222kW (77,799hp) 25.3k MAN-B&W 10K98M 1 x 2 Stroke 10 Cy. 980 x 2660 57222kW (77799bhp) Mitsui Engineering & Shipbuilding CLtd-Japan AuxGen: 4 x 2200kW a.c, 2 x 2200kW a.c Thrusters: 1 Tunnel thruster (f) Fuel: 480.0 (d.f.) 8470.0 (r.f.)
9554755 *9HA3277* -	**YM MIRANDA** **YM Miranda Tankers Ltd** Yilmar Denizcilik Nakliyat ve Ticaret Ltd Sti (Yilmar Shipping & Trading Ltd) *Valletta* *Malta* MMSI: 229370000 Official number: 9554755	**8,975** 4,174 12,933 T/cm 27.1	Class: BV	**2013-01 Marmara Tersanesi — Yarimca** Yd No: 80 Loa 135.60 (BB) Br ex - Dght 8.500 Lbp 127.65 Br md 20.60 Dpth 11.00 Welded, 1 dk	**(A12B2TR) Chemical/Products Tanker** Double Hull (13F) Liq: 14,140; Liq (Oil): 14,428 Compartments: 6 Wing Ta, 6 Wing Ta, 2 Wing Slop Ta, ER 12 Cargo Pump (s): 12x300m³/hr Manifold: Bow/CM: 67m Ice Capable	**1 oil engine** reduction geared to sc. shaft driving 1 CP propeller Total Power: 4,480kW (6,091hp) 14.8k MAN-B&W 8L32/44C 1 x 4 Stroke 8 Cy. 320 x 440 4480kW (6091bhp) AuxGen: 3 x 580kW 60Hz a.c Thrusters: 1 Tunnel thruster (f) Fuel: 103.0 (d.f.) 614.0 (r.f.)
9457737 *A8XY6* -	**YM MOBILITY** **All Oceans Transportation Inc** Yang Ming Marine Transport Corp *Monrovia* *Liberia* MMSI: 636014997 Official number: 14997	**76,787** 41,396 81,145	Class: AB (CR)	**2011-05 CSBC Corp, Taiwan — Kaohsiung** Yd No: 956 Loa 305.60 (BB) Br ex - Dght 14.000 Lbp 293.16 Br md 40.00 Dpth 24.20 Welded, 1 dk	**(A33A2CC) Container Ship (Fully Cellular)** TEU 6589 incl 500 ref C	**1 oil engine** driving 1 FP propeller Total Power: 57,222kW (77,799hp) 25.3k MAN-B&W 10K98M 1 x 2 Stroke 10 Cy. 980 x 2660 57222kW (77799bhp) Mitsui Engineering & Shipbuilding CLtd-Japan AuxGen: 1 x 2200kW a.c, 4 x 2200kW a.c Thrusters: 1 Tunnel thruster (f) Fuel: 484.0 (d.f.) 8420.0 (r.f.)
9664897 *H9EW* -	**YM MODERATION** **Los Halillos Shipping Co SA** Shoei Kisen Kaisha Ltd *Panama* *Panama* MMSI: 371633000 Official number: 45663TJ	**71,821** 24,571 72,370 T/cm 95.3	Class: NK	**2014-03 Imabari Shipbuilding Co Ltd — Mihara HS (Hiroshima Shipyard)** Yd No: 2312 Loa 293.18 (BB) Br ex - Dght 14.021 Lbp 276.00 Br md 40.00 Dpth 24.30 Welded, 1 dk	**(A33A2CC) Container Ship (Fully Cellular)** TEU 6350 C Ho 2912 TEU C Dk 3438 TEU incl 500 ref C.	**1 oil engine** driving 1 FP propeller Total Power: 68,530kW (93,173hp) 25.0k MAN-B&W 11K98M 1 x 2 Stroke 11 Cy. 980 x 2660 68530kW (93173bhp) Mitsui Engineering & Shipbuilding CLtd-Japan
9664885 *D5FE7* -	**YM MODESTY** **Ben More Shipping Inc** Zodiac Maritime Agencies Ltd *Monrovia* *Liberia* MMSI: 636016242 Official number: 16242	**71,821** 24,571 72,370 T/cm 95.3	Class: NK	**2013-11 Koyo Dockyard Co Ltd — Mihara HS** Yd No: 2311 Loa 293.18 (BB) Br ex - Dght 14.021 Lbp 276.00 Br md 40.00 Dpth 24.30 Welded, 1 dk	**(A33A2CC) Container Ship (Fully Cellular)** TEU 6350 C Ho 2912 TEU C Dk 3438 TEU incl 500 ref C.	**1 oil engine** driving 1 FP propeller Total Power: 53,000kW (72,059hp) 25.0k MAN-B&W 10K98M 1 x 2 Stroke 10 Cy. 980 x 2660 53000kW (72059bhp) Mitsui Engineering & Shipbuilding CLtd-Japan Thrusters: 1 Tunnel thruster (f) Fuel: 9300.0

660011
FVL4

YM MOVEMENT
Shoei Kisen Kaisha Ltd & Paraiso Shipping SA
Shoei Kisen Kaisha Ltd
Panama *Panama*
MMSI: 357770000
Official number: 4510913

71,821 Class: NK
24,571
72,370
T/cm
95.3

2013-07 Koyo Dockyard Co Ltd — Mihara HS
Yd No: 2310
Loa 293.18 (BB) Br ex - Dght 14.021
Lbp 276.00 Br md 40.00 Dpth 24.30
Welded, 1 dk

(A33A2CC) Container Ship (Fully Cellular)
TEU 6350 C Ho 2912 TEU C Dk 3438 TEU incl 500 ref C.

1 oil engine driving 1 FP propeller
Total Power: 53,000kW (72,059hp) 25.0kn
MAN-B&W 10K98MC
1 x 2 Stroke 10 Cy. 980 x 2660 53000kW (72059bhp)
Mitsui Engineering & Shipbuilding CLtd-Japan
AuxGen: 4 x 2200kW a.c
Thrusters: 1 Tunnel thruster (f)
Fuel: 9360.0

455870
A8XY5

YM MUTUALITY
All Oceans Transportation Inc
Yang Ming Marine Transport Corp
Monrovia *Liberia*
MMSI: 636014996
Official number: 14996

76,787 Class: AB (CR)
41,396
81,145

2011-04 CSBC Corp, Taiwan — Kaohsiung
Yd No: 955
Loa 305.60 (BB) Br ex - Dght 14.000
Lbp 293.16 Br md 40.00 Dpth 24.20
Welded, 1 dk

(A33A2CC) Container Ship (Fully Cellular)
TEU 6589 incl 500 ref C

1 oil engine driving 1 FP propeller
Total Power: 57,222kW (77,799hp) 25.3kn
MAN-B&W 10K98MC
1 x 2 Stroke 10 Cy. 980 x 2660 57222kW (77799bhp)
Mitsui Engineering & Shipbuilding CLtd-Japan
AuxGen: 1 x 2200kW a.c, 4 x 2200kW a.c
Thrusters: 1 Tunnel thruster (f)
Fuel: 480.0 (d.f.) 8470.0 (r.f.)

464106
9HA2017
-

YM NEPTUNE
YM Neptune Tankers Ltd
CSM Denizcilik Ltd Sti (Chemfleet)
Valletta *Malta*
MMSI: 249813000
Official number: 9464106

4,829 Class: BV
2,297
6,970
T/cm
16.8

2009-04 Marmara Tersanesi — Yarimca Yd No: 78
Loa 119.10 (BB) Br ex - Dght 6.800
Lbp 111.60 Br md 16.90 Dpth 8.40
Welded, 1 dk

(A12B2TR) Chemical/Products Tanker
Double Hull (13F)
Liq: 7,918; Liq (Oil): 7,918
Cargo Heating Coils
Compartments: 12 Wing Ta, 2 Wing Slop Ta, ER
Manifold: Bow/CM: 59.2m

1 oil engine driving 1 CP propeller
Total Power: 3,000kW (4,079hp) 14.0kn
MAN-B&W 6L32/40CD
1 x 4 Stroke 6 Cy. 320 x 400 3000kW (4079bhp)
STX Engine Co Ltd-South Korea
Thrusters: 1 Tunnel thruster (f)
Fuel: 39.0 (d.f.) 383.0 (r.f.)

9387097
3EID8
-

YM NEW JERSEY
Shoei Kisen Kaisha Ltd & Paraiso Shipping SA
SMTECH Ship Management Co Ltd
Panama *Panama*
MMSI: 372118000
Official number: 3231107B

54,828 Class: NK
24,104
65,123

2006-11 Koyo Dockyard Co Ltd — Mihara HS
Yd No: 2221
Loa 294.03 (BB) Br ex - Dght 13.521
Lbp 283.00 Br md 32.20 Dpth 21.50
Welded, 1 dk

(A33A2CC) Container Ship (Fully Cellular)
TEU 4923 C Ho 2142 TEU C Dk 2781 TEU incl 421 ref C
Compartments: 8 Cell Ho, ER

1 oil engine driving 1 FP propeller
Total Power: 45,760kW (62,215hp) 23.8kn
MAN-B&W 8K98MC
1 x 2 Stroke 8 Cy. 980 x 2660 45760kW (62215bhp)
Mitsui Engineering & Shipbuilding CLtd-Japan
AuxGen: 4 x a.c
Thrusters: 1 Tunnel thruster (f)
Fuel: 7785.0

9295206
V7FW7
-

YM NINGBO
ex Cherokee Bridge *-2007*
'Clivia' Schiffahrts GmbH & Co KG
Herm Dauelsberg GmbH & Co KG
Majuro *Marshall Islands*
MMSI: 538090117
Official number: 90117

40,952 Class: GL
25,095
55,490
T/cm
71.6

2004-06 Hyundai Heavy Industries Co Ltd — Ulsan Yd No: 1550
Loa 260.88 (BB) Br ex - Dght 13.000
Lbp 249.71 Br md 32.25 Dpth 19.30
Welded, 1 dk

(A33A2CC) Container Ship (Fully Cellular)
TEU 4132 C Ho 1617 C Dk 2515 TEU incl 500 ref C.

1 oil engine driving 1 FP propeller
Total Power: 36,445kW (49,551hp) 24.3kn
Sulzer 9RTA84C
1 x 2 Stroke 9 Cy. 840 x 2400 36445kW (49551bhp)
Hyundai Heavy Industries Co Ltd-South Korea
AuxGen: 2 x 1995kW 450/230V 60Hz a.c, 2 x 1350kW 450/230V 60Hz a.c
Thrusters: 1 Thwart. CP thruster (f)

9001215
BLIR
-

YM NORTH
ex Ming North *-2005*
Yang Ming Marine Transport Corp
-
Keelung *Chinese Taipei*
MMSI: 416251000
Official number: 014978

46,697 Class: AB CR
21,375
45,995
T/cm
73.0

1995-10 China Shipbuilding Corp (CSBC) — Kaohsiung Yd No: 534
Loa 275.70 (BB) Br ex 32.28 Dght 12.020
Lbp 259.20 Br md 32.20 Dpth 21.20
Welded, 1 dk

(A33A2CC) Container Ship (Fully Cellular)
TEU 3725 C Ho 1814 TEU C DK 1911 TEU incl 200 ref C.
Compartments: ER, 7 Cell Ho
15 Ha: ER 30 Wing Ha:

1 oil engine driving 1 FP propeller
Total Power: 30,967kW (42,103hp) 22.5kn
B&W 10L80MC
1 x 2 Stroke 10 Cy. 800 x 2592 30967kW (42103bhp)
Mitsui Engineering & Shipbuilding CLtd-Japan
AuxGen: 3 x 1300kW 450V 60Hz a.c
Thrusters: 1 Thwart. CP thruster (f)

9450583
VREZ5
-

YM OAKLAND
Metropolitan Vitality Ltd
Univan Ship Management Ltd
Hong Kong *Hong Kong*
MMSI: 477192900
Official number: HK-2354

40,030 Class: NV
24,450
50,500
T/cm
70.4

2009-02 Samsung Heavy Industries Co Ltd — Geoje Yd No: 1773
Loa 259.80 (BB) Br ex 32.30 Dght 12.600
Lbp 248.80 Br md 32.25 Dpth 19.30
Welded, 1 dk

(A33A2CC) Container Ship (Fully Cellular)
TEU 4253 C. Ho 1584 C. Dk 2669 incl 400 ref C.
Compartments: 7 Cell Ho, ER

1 oil engine driving 1 FP propeller
Total Power: 36,560kW (49,707hp) 23.3kn
MAN-B&W 8K90MC-C
1 x 2 Stroke 8 Cy. 900 x 2300 36560kW (49707bhp)
Doosan Engine Co Ltd-South Korea
AuxGen: 4 x 1700kW a.c
Thrusters: 1 Tunnel thruster (f)

9198276
H3TM
-

YM ORCHID
ex Ming Orchid *-2005*
Hill Samuel Finance Ltd
Yang Ming Marine Transport Corp
SatCom: Inmarsat C 435304611
Panama *Panama*
MMSI: 353046000
Official number: 2766501C

64,254 Class: AB
35,137
68,303
T/cm
89.6

2000-12 Hyundai Heavy Industries Co Ltd — Ulsan Yd No: 1223
Loa 274.70 (BB) Br ex - Dght 14.000
Lbp 263.00 Br md 40.00 Dpth 24.20
Welded, 1 dk

(A33A2CC) Container Ship (Fully Cellular)
TEU 5551 C Ho 2564 TEU C Dk 2987 TEU incl 400 ref C.
Compartments: ER, 7 Cell Ho
15 Ha: ER

1 oil engine driving 1 FP propeller
Total Power: 54,946kW (74,705hp) 25.9kn
Sulzer 10RTA96C
1 x 2 Stroke 10 Cy. 960 x 2500 54946kW (74705bhp)
Hyundai Heavy Industries Co Ltd-South Korea
AuxGen: 4 x 1900kW 110/440V 60Hz a.c
Thrusters: 1 Thwart. CP thruster (f)
Fuel: 343.3 (d.f.) (Heating Coils) 7340.5 (r.f.) 197.8pd

9203631
A8HD3
-

YM PINE
ex Pine Bridge *-2006* *ex* Venus Bridge *-2005*
ex Ming Pine *-2002*
Yang Ming (Liberia) Corp
Yang Ming Marine Transport Corp
Monrovia *Liberia*
MMSI: 636012706
Official number: 12706

64,005 Class: AB (CR)
34,700
68,615

2001-04 China Shipbuilding Corp (CSBC) — Kaohsiung Yd No: 757
Loa 274.70 (BB) Br ex - Dght 14.000
Lbp 263.00 Br md 40.00 Dpth 24.20
Welded, 1 dk

(A33A2CC) Container Ship (Fully Cellular)
TEU 5548 C Ho 2564 TEU C Ho 2984 TEU incl 400 ref C.
Compartments: ER, 7 Cell Ho
15 Ha: ER

1 oil engine driving 1 FP propeller
Total Power: 54,946kW (74,705hp) 26.0kn
Sulzer 10RTA96C
1 x 2 Stroke 10 Cy. 960 x 2500 54946kW (74705bhp)
Hyundai Heavy Industries Co Ltd-South Korea
AuxGen: 4 x 1900kW 450V 60Hz a.c
Thrusters: 1 Thwart. CP thruster (f)
Fuel: 343.3 (d.f.) (Heating Coils) 7340.5 (r.f.) 197.8pd

9198264
H3NM
-

YM PLUM
ex Ming Plum *-2005*
Hill Samuel Finance Ltd
Yang Ming Marine Transport Corp
SatCom: Inmarsat C 435585610
Panama *Panama*
MMSI: 355856000
Official number: 2728000C

64,254 Class: AB
35,137
68,413
T/cm
89.6

2000-09 Hyundai Heavy Industries Co Ltd — Ulsan Yd No: 1222
Loa 274.69 (BB) Br ex - Dght 14.000
Lbp 263.00 Br md 40.00 Dpth 24.20
Welded, 1 dk

(A33A2CC) Container Ship (Fully Cellular)
TEU 5551 C Ho 2564 TEU C Dk 2987 TEU incl 400 ref C.
Compartments: ER, 7 Cell Ho
15 Ha: ER

1 oil engine driving 1 FP propeller
Total Power: 54,946kW (74,705hp) 25.9kn
Sulzer 10RTA96C
1 x 2 Stroke 10 Cy. 960 x 2500 54946kW (74705bhp)
Hyundai Heavy Industries Co Ltd-South Korea
AuxGen: 4 x 1900kW 110/440V 60Hz a.c
Thrusters: 1 Thwart. CP thruster (f)
Fuel: 343.3 (d.f.) (Heating Coils) 7340.5 (r.f.) 197.8pd

9464118
9HA2098
-

YM PLUTO
Can Maritime Ltd
MAS Shipping & Trading Inc
SatCom: Inmarsat C 424995710
Valletta *Malta*
MMSI: 249957000
Official number: 9464118

4,829 Class: BV
2,297
6,970
T/cm
16.8

2009-09 Marmara Tersanesi — Yarimca Yd No: 79
Loa 119.60 (BB) Br ex - Dght 6.743
Lbp 111.60 Br md 16.90 Dpth 8.40
Welded, 1 dk

(A12B2TR) Chemical/Products Tanker
Double Hull (13F)
Liq: 7,918; Liq (Oil): 7,918
Cargo Heating Coils
Compartments: 12 Wing Ta, 2 Wing Slop Ta, ER
12 Cargo Pump (s): 12x200m³/hr
Manifold: Bow/CM: 59.2m
Ice Capable

1 oil engine reduction geared to sc. shafts driving 1 CP propeller
Total Power: 3,000kW (4,079hp) 14.0kn
MAN-B&W 6L32/40CD
1 x 4 Stroke 6 Cy. 320 x 400 3000kW (4079bhp)
STX Engine Co Ltd-South Korea
AuxGen: 1 x 1250kW a.c, 3 x 515kW 440V a.c
Thrusters: 1 Tunnel thruster (f)
Fuel: 45.0 (d.f.) 421.0 (r.f.)

9236535
A8XT4
-

YM PORTLAND
ex Norasia Enterprise *-2007*
completed as Amaranta *-2002*
Oceanus Shipping AS
SinOceanic Shipping ASA
Monrovia *Liberia*
MMSI: 636014968
Official number: 14968

51,364 Class: NV (GL)
27,298
58,254
T/cm
77.9

2003-12 Stocznia Gdynia SA — Gdynia
Yd No: 8234/02
Loa 286.27 (BB) Br ex 32.27 Dght 13.210
Lbp 271.20 Br md 32.20 Dpth 21.80
Welded, 1 dk

(A33A2CC) Container Ship (Fully Cellular)
Double Bottom Entire Compartment Length
TEU 4444 C Ho 2051 TEU C Dk 2393 TEU incl 450 ref C.
Compartments: ER, 8 Cell Ho
16 Ha: (12.8 x 17.9) (12.8 x 23.2)ER 14 (12.8 x 28.3)
Ice Capable

1 oil engine driving 1 FP propeller
Total Power: 43,920kW (59,714hp) 25.0kn
Sulzer 8RTA96C
1 x 2 Stroke 8 Cy. 960 x 2500 43920kW (59714bhp)
H Cegielski Poznan SA-Poland
AuxGen: 2 x 1800kW 440V 60Hz a.c, 2 x 1600kW 440V 60Hz a.c
Thrusters: 1 Thwart. CP thruster (f)
Fuel: 258.9 (d.f.) 5704.0 (r.f.) 166.0pd

9287780
A8EY9
-

YM RIGHTNESS
Kuang Ming (Liberia) Corp
Kuang Ming Shipping Corp
Monrovia *Liberia*
MMSI: 636012350
Official number: 12350

41,205 Class: AB
26,189
77,684

2004-11 China Shipbuilding Corp (CSBC) — Kaohsiung Yd No: 820
Loa 224.79 (BB) Br ex - Dght 14.150
Lbp 217.00 Br md 32.26 Dpth 19.50
Welded, 1 dk

(A21A2BC) Bulk Carrier
Grain: 92,151
Compartments: 7 Ho, ER
7 Ha: 6 (17.1 x 15.0)ER (17.1 x 13.4)

1 oil engine driving 1 FP propeller
Total Power: 10,002kW (13,599hp) 14.6kn
B&W 6S60MC
1 x 2 Stroke 6 Cy. 600 x 2292 10002kW (13599bhp)
Mitsui Engineering & Shipbuilding CLtd-Japan
AuxGen: 3 x 440kW a.c
Fuel: 144.0 (d.f.) 2548.0 (r.f.)

9362138
9HFW9
-

YM SATURN
YM Mars Tankers Ltd
Yilmar Denizcilik Nakliyat ve Ticaret Ltd Sti (Yilmar Shipping & Trading Ltd)
Valletta *Malta*
MMSI: 256929000
Official number: 9362138

10,917 Class: BV
5,260
15,988
T/cm
28.4

2007-11 Marmara Tersanesi — Yarimca Yd No: 70
Loa 148.00 (BB) Br ex - Dght 8.600
Lbp 138.00 Br md 21.60 Dpth 11.30
Welded, 1 dk

(A12B2TR) Chemical/Products Tanker
Double Hull (13F)
Liq: 17,343; Liq (Oil): 17,343
Compartments: 12 Wing Ta, 2 Wing Slop Ta, ER
12 Cargo Pump (s): 12x300m³/hr
Manifold: Bow/CM: 76.6m
Ice Capable

1 oil engine reduction geared to sc. shaft driving 1 CP propeller
Total Power: 5,326kW (7,241hp) 14.5kn
MaK 6M43
1 x 4 Stroke 6 Cy. 430 x 610 5326kW (7241bhp)
Caterpillar Motoren GmbH & Co. KG-Germany
AuxGen: 3 x 620kW a.c
Thrusters: 1 Tunnel thruster (f)
Fuel: 114.0 (d.f.) (Heating Coils) 719.0 (r.f.) 23.0pd

9360910 *C4XC2* -	**YM SEATTLE** *ex* Taiwan Express *-2012* *ex* YM Seattle *-2011* **Seacarriers Services Inc** Danaos Shipping Co Ltd *Limassol* *Cyprus* MMSI: 212276000	**40,030** 24,450 50,813 T/cm 70.4	Class: NV	2007-09 **Samsung Heavy Industries Co Ltd — Geoje** Yd No: 1639 Loa 259.80 (BB) Br ex - Dght 12.600 Lbp 244.80 Br md 32.25 Dpth 19.30 Welded, 1 dk	**(A33A2CC) Container Ship (Fully Cellular)** TEU 4253 TEU incl 400 ref C. Compartments: ER, 7 Cell Ho	**1 oil engine** driving 1 FP propeller Total Power: 36,540kW (49,680hp) 23.3k MAN-B&W 8K90MC- 1 x 2 Stroke 8 Cy. 900 x 2300 36540kW (49680bhp) Doosan Engine Co Ltd-South Korea AuxGen: 4 x 1700kW a.c Thrusters: 1 Tunnel thruster (f)
9157650 *MBXZ4* -	**YM SHANGHAI** *ex* Ville d'Antares *-2004* **Nylo Maritime Inc** Zodiac Maritime Agencies Ltd *London* *United Kingdom* MMSI: 235756000 Official number: 907818	**40,268** 23,501 49,200 T/cm 70.9	Class: LR (BV) **100A1** SS 12/2012 container ship LI **LMC** **UMS** Eq.Ltr: R†; Cable: 687.5/84.0 U3 (a)	1997-12 **Daewoo Heavy Industries Ltd — Geoje** Yd No: 4060 Loa 259.00 (BB) Br ex - Dght 12.020 Lbp 244.00 Br md 32.20 Dpth 19.00 Welded, 1 dk	**(A33A2CC) Container Ship (Fully Cellular)** TEU 3961 C Ho 1621 TEU C Dk 2340 TEU incl 150 ref C Compartments: ER, 8 Cell Ho 8 Ha: (12.6 x 23.3)4 (12.6 x 28.4)ER (12.6 x 13.0)	**1 oil engine** driving 1 FP propeller Total Power: 28,338kW (38,528hp) 23.7k Sulzer 8RTA84 1 x 2 Stroke 8 Cy. 840 x 2400 28338kW (38528bhp) Korea Heavy Industries & ConstrCo Ltd (HANJUNG)-South Korea AuxGen: 3 x 850kW 440V 60Hz a.c, 1 x 360kW 440V 60Hz a.c Boilers: AuxB (Comp) 8.0kgf/cm² (7.8bar) Thrusters: 1 Thwart. FP thruster (f) Fuel: 4827.0 (r.f.)
9256224 *A8NN9* -	**YM SINGAPORE** *ex* Norasia Atria *-2008* *completed as* E. R. Wellington *-2004* **Wellington Marine Inc** Danaos Shipping Co Ltd *Monrovia* *Liberia* MMSI: 636013530 Official number: 13530	**41,855** 25,310 53,611 T/cm 71.6	Class: GL	2004-09 **Hyundai Samho Heavy Industries Co Ltd — Samho** Yd No: S179 Loa 264.21 (BB) Br ex - Dght 12.750 Lbp 249.00 Br md 32.20 Dpth 19.50 Welded, 1 dk	**(A33A2CC) Container Ship (Fully Cellular)** TEU 4300 C Ho 1610 TEU C Dk 2690 TEU incl 520 ref C. Compartments: ER, 7 Cell Ho	**1 oil engine** driving 1 FP propeller Total Power: 36,540kW (49,680hp) 24.1k MAN-B&W 8K90MC- 1 x 2 Stroke 8 Cy. 900 x 2300 36540kW (49680bhp) Hyundai Heavy Industries Co Ltd-South Korea AuxGen: 2 x 2280kW 450/230V 60Hz a.c, 2 x 1710kW 450/230V 60Hz a.c Thrusters: 1 Thwart. CP thruster (f) Fuel: 369.6 (d.f.) 4855.1 (r.f.)
9294800 *A8EI6* -	**YM SUCCESS** **Yang Ming (Liberia) Corp** Yang Ming Marine Transport Corp SatCom: Inmarsat C 463699843 *Monrovia* *Liberia* MMSI: 636012254 Official number: 12254	**64,254** 35,137 68,615	Class: AB	2004-07 **China Shipbuilding Corp (CSBC) — Kaohsiung** Yd No: 803 Loa 275.00 (BB) Br ex - Dght 14.000 Lbp 263.00 Br md 40.00 Dpth 24.20 Welded, 1 dk	**(A33A2CC) Container Ship (Fully Cellular)** TEU 5548 C Ho 2564 TEU C Ho 2984 TEU incl 400 ref C.	**1 oil engine** driving 1 FP propeller Total Power: 54,900kW (74,642hp) 26.5k Sulzer 10RTA96 1 x 2 Stroke 10 Cy. 960 x 2500 54900kW (74642bhp) Hyundai Heavy Industries Co Ltd-South Korea AuxGen: 4 x 1900kW a.c Thrusters: 1 Thwart. CP thruster (f) Fuel: 391.0 (d.f.) 7821.0 (r.f.)
9280811 *V7FW8* -	**YM TAICHUNG** *ex* Chesapeake Bay Bridge *-2007* *launched as* Silvia *-2004* **'Silvia' Schiffahrts GmbH & Co KG** Herm Dauelsberg GmbH & Co KG *Majuro* *Marshall Islands* MMSI: 538090118 Official number: 90118	**40,952** 25,095 55,497 T/cm 70.3	Class: GL	2004-05 **Hyundai Heavy Industries Co Ltd — Ulsan** Yd No: 1524 Loa 260.87 (BB) Br ex - Dght 13.000 Lbp 248.70 Br md 32.25 Dpth 19.30 Welded, 1 Dk.	**(A33A2CC) Container Ship (Fully Cellular)** TEU 4132 C Ho 1617 TEU C Dk 2515 TEU incl 500 ref C.	**1 oil engine** driving 1 FP propeller Total Power: 36,445kW (49,551hp) 24.0k Sulzer 9RTA84 1 x 2 Stroke 9 Cy. 840 x 2400 36445kW (49551bhp) Hyundai Heavy Industries Co Ltd-South Korea AuxGen: 2 x 1995kW 450/230V 60Hz a.c, 2 x 1350kW 450/230V 60Hz a.c Thrusters: 1 Thwart. CP thruster (f)
9337444 *A8OR4* -	**YM UBERTY** **Leasing Co Vessel Holdings 2008-A Ltd** Yang Ming Marine Transport Corp SatCom: Inmarsat C 463702194 *Monrovia* *Liberia* MMSI: 636013689 Official number: 13689	**90,507** 55,413 103,614	Class: AB	2008-05 **CSBC Corp, Taiwan — Kaohsiung** Yd No: 875 Loa 333.20 (BB) Br ex - Dght 14.500 Lbp 318.20 Br md 42.80 Dpth 24.50 Welded, 1 dk	**(A33A2CC) Container Ship (Fully Cellular)** TEU 8241 incl 700 ref C.	**1 oil engine** driving 1 FP propeller Total Power: 68,666kW (93,358hp) 25.6k MAN-B&W 12K98M 1 x 2 Stroke 12 Cy. 980 x 2660 68666kW (93358bhp) Mitsui Engineering & Shipbuilding CLtd-Japan AuxGen: 4 x 3000kW a.c Thrusters: 1 Tunnel thruster (f)
9462706 *BLHM* -	**YM UBIQUITY** **All Oceans Transportation Inc** Yang Ming Marine Transport Corp *Keelung* *Chinese Taipei* MMSI: 416467000 Official number: 015301	**90,532** 55,413 103,235	Class: AB CR (Class contemplated)	2012-08 **CSBC Corp, Taiwan — Kaohsiung** Yd No: 958 Loa 333.20 (BB) Br ex - Dght 13.000 Lbp 318.20 Br md 42.80 Dpth 24.50 Welded, 1 dk	**(A33A2CC) Container Ship (Fully Cellular)** TEU 8626 incl 700 ref C	**1 oil engine** driving 1 FP propeller Total Power: 68,666kW (93,358hp) 25.6k MAN-B&W 12K98M 1 x 2 Stroke 12 Cy. 980 x 2660 68666kW (93358bhp) Mitsui Engineering & Shipbuilding CLtd-Japan AuxGen: 4 x 3000kW a.c Thrusters: 1 Tunnel thruster (f) Fuel: 940.0 (d.f.) 11120.0 (r.f.)
9302645 *A8HZ7* -	**YM ULTIMATE** **Yang Ming (Liberia) Corp** Yang Ming Marine Transport Corp SatCom: Inmarsat C 463792317 *Monrovia* *Liberia* MMSI: 636012810 Official number: 12810	**90,389** 55,275 101,500	Class: NV	2007-01 **Hyundai Heavy Industries Co Ltd — Ulsan** Yd No: 1676 Loa 335.00 (BB) Br ex - Dght 14.500 Lbp 319.00 Br md 42.80 Dpth 24.60 Welded, 1 dk	**(A33A2CC) Container Ship (Fully Cellular)** TEU 8208 incl 700 ref C.	**1 oil engine** driving 1 FP propeller Total Power: 68,666kW (93,358hp) 25.6k MAN-B&W 12K98M 1 x 2 Stroke 12 Cy. 980 x 2660 68666kW (93358bhp) Hyundai Heavy Industries Co Ltd-South Korea AuxGen: 4 x 3050kW a.c Thrusters: 1 Tunnel thruster (f) Fuel: 747.9 (d.f.) 11320.9 (d.f.)
9462718 *BLHL* -	**YM UNANIMITY** **Yang Ming Marine Transport Corp** - *Keelung* *Chinese Taipei* MMSI: 416466000 Official number: 015300	**90,532** 55,413 103,235	Class: AB	2012-10 **CSBC Corp, Taiwan — Kaohsiung** Yd No: 959 Loa 333.20 (BB) Br ex - Dght 13.000 Lbp 318.20 Br md 42.80 Dpth 24.50 Welded, 1 dk	**(A33A2CC) Container Ship (Fully Cellular)** TEU 8626 incl 700 ref C	**1 oil engine** driving 1 FP propeller Total Power: 68,666kW (93,358hp) 25.6k MAN-B&W 12K98M 1 x 2 Stroke 12 Cy. 980 x 2660 68666kW (93358bhp) Mitsui Engineering & Shipbuilding CLtd-Japan AuxGen: 4 x 3000kW a.c Thrusters: 1 Tunnel thruster (f) Fuel: 940.0 (d.f.) 11120.0 (r.f.)
9462732 *BLHI* -	**YM UNICORN** **All Oceans Transportation Inc** Yang Ming Marine Transport Corp *Keelung* *Chinese Taipei* MMSI: 416464000 Official number: 015298	**90,532** 55,413 103,235	Class: AB	2013-05 **CSBC Corp, Taiwan — Kaohsiung** Yd No: 961 Loa 333.20 (BB) Br ex - Dght 13.000 Lbp 318.20 Br md 42.80 Dpth 24.50 Welded, 1 dk	**(A33A2CC) Container Ship (Fully Cellular)** TEU 8626 incl 700 ref C	**1 oil engine** driving 1 FP propeller Total Power: 68,640kW (93,323hp) 25.6k MAN-B&W 12K98M 1 x 2 Stroke 12 Cy. 980 x 2660 68640kW (93323bhp) Mitsui Engineering & Shipbuilding CLtd-Japan AuxGen: 4 x 3000kW a.c Thrusters: 1 Tunnel thruster (f) Fuel: 940.0 (d.f.) 11120.0 (r.f.)
9337482 *A8OR8* -	**YM UNIFORM** **Yang Ming (Liberia) Corp** Yang Ming Marine Transport Corp SatCom: Inmarsat C 463704390 *Monrovia* *Liberia* MMSI: 636013693 Official number: 13693	**90,507** 55,413 103,614	Class: AB	2009-03 **CSBC Corp, Taiwan — Kaohsiung** Yd No: 879 Loa 333.20 (BB) Br ex - Dght 14.500 Lbp 318.20 Br md 42.80 Dpth 24.50 Welded, 1 dk	**(A33A2CC) Container Ship (Fully Cellular)** TEU 8241 incl 700 ref C. Compartments: 9 Cell Ho, ER	**1 oil engine** driving 1 FP propeller Total Power: 68,666kW (93,358hp) 25.6k MAN-B&W 12K98M 1 x 2 Stroke 12 Cy. 980 x 2660 68666kW (93358bhp) Mitsui Engineering & Shipbuilding CLtd-Japan AuxGen: 4 x 3000kW a.c Thrusters: 1 Tunnel thruster (f)
9462691 *BLHQ* 015302	**YM UNIFORMITY** **All Oceans Transportation Inc** Yang Ming Marine Transport Corp *Keelung* *Chinese Taipei* MMSI: 416468000 Official number: 015302	**90,532** 55,413 103,235	Class: AB CR (Class contemplated)	2012-06 **CSBC Corp, Taiwan — Kaohsiung** Yd No: 957 Loa 333.20 (BB) Br ex - Dght 13.000 Lbp 318.20 Br md 42.80 Dpth 24.50 Welded, 1 dk	**(A33A2CC) Container Ship (Fully Cellular)** TEU 8626 incl 700 ref C	**1 oil engine** driving 1 FP propeller Total Power: 68,666kW (93,358hp) 25.6k MAN-B&W 12K98M 1 x 2 Stroke 12 Cy. 980 x 2660 68666kW (93358bhp) Mitsui Engineering & Shipbuilding CLtd-Japan AuxGen: 4 x 3000kW a.c Thrusters: 1 Tunnel thruster (f) Fuel: 940.0 (d.f.) 11120.0 (r.f.)
9302633 *A8HZ6* -	**YM UNISON** **Yang Ming (Liberia) Corp** Yang Ming Marine Transport Corp SatCom: Inmarsat C 463791998 *Monrovia* *Liberia* MMSI: 636012809 Official number: 12809	**90,389** 55,275 101,411	Class: BV	2006-11 **Hyundai Heavy Industries Co Ltd — Ulsan** Yd No: 1675 Loa 335.69 (BB) Br ex - Dght 14.520 Lbp 314.96 Br md 42.80 Dpth 24.50 Welded, 1 dk	**(A33A2CC) Container Ship (Fully Cellular)** TEU 8208 incl 700 ref C.	**1 oil engine** driving 1 FP propeller Total Power: 68,640kW (93,323hp) 25.6k MAN-B&W 12K98M 1 x 2 Stroke 12 Cy. 980 x 2660 68640kW (93323bhp) Hyundai Heavy Industries Co Ltd-South Korea AuxGen: 4 x 3253kW 440/110V a.c Thrusters: 1 Tunnel thruster (f) Fuel: 11304.0
9302619 *A8HZ4* -	**YM UNITY** **Yang Ming (Liberia) Corp** Yang Ming Marine Transport Corp SatCom: Inmarsat C 463791627 *Monrovia* *Liberia* MMSI: 636012807 Official number: 12807	**90,389** 55,275 101,411	Class: AB	2006-08 **Hyundai Heavy Industries Co Ltd — Ulsan** Yd No: 1673 Loa 335.00 (BB) Br ex - Dght 14.480 Lbp 319.00 Br md 42.80 Dpth 24.50 Welded, 1 dk	**(A33A2CC) Container Ship (Fully Cellular)** TEU 8208 incl 700 ref C.	**1 oil engine** driving 1 FP propeller Total Power: 68,666kW (93,358hp) 25.6k MAN-B&W 12K98M 1 x 2 Stroke 12 Cy. 980 x 2660 68666kW (93358bhp) Hyundai Heavy Industries Co Ltd-South Korea AuxGen: 4 x 3050kW a.c Thrusters: 1 Tunnel thruster (f) Fuel: 747.9 (d.f.) 11320.9 (r.f.)

IMO / Call sign	Name / Owner / Manager / Port / Flag	Tonnage	Class	Builder	Type / Capacity	Machinery
9462720 *BLHJ* -	**YM UPSURGENCE** **All Oceans Transportation Inc** Yang Ming Marine Transport Corp *Keelung* *Chinese Taipei* MMSI: 416465000 Official number: 015299	**90,532** 55,413 103,235	Class: AB	**2012-12 CSBC Corp, Taiwan — Kaohsiung** Yd No: 960 Loa 333.20 (BB) Br ex - Dght 13.000 Lbp 318.20 Br md 42.80 Dpth 24.50 Welded, 1 dk	**(A33A2CC) Container Ship (Fully Cellular)** TEU 8626 incl 700 ref C	**1 oil engine** driving 1 FP propeller Total Power: 68,666kW (93,358hp) 25.6kn MAN-B&W 12K98ME 1 x 2 Stroke 12 Cy. 980 x 2660 68666kW (93358bhp) Mitsui Engineering & Shipbuilding CLtd-Japan AuxGen: 4 x 3000kW a.c Thrusters: 1 Tunnel thruster (f) Fuel: 940.0 (d.f.) 11120.0 (r.f.)
9337468 *A8OR6* -	**YM UPWARD** **Yang Ming (Liberia) Corp** Yang Ming Marine Transport Corp SatCom: Inmarsat C 463702950 *Monrovia* *Liberia* MMSI: 636013691 Official number: 13691	**90,507** 55,413 103,607	Class: LR ✠ **100A1** SS 09/2013 container ship **ShipRight** (SDA, FDA, CM) *IWS LI EP ✠ **LMC** **UMS** Eq.Ltr: B*; Cable: 742.5/107.0 U3 (a)	**2008-09 CSBC Corp, Taiwan — Kaohsiung** Yd No: 877 Loa 333.20 (BB) Br ex 42.84 Dght 14.500 Lbp 318.20 Br md 42.80 Dpth 24.50 Welded, 1 dk	**(A33A2CC) Container Ship (Fully Cellular)** TEU 8241 incl 700 ref C. Compartments: ER, 9 Cell Ho 9 Ha: ER	**1 oil engine** driving 1 FP propeller Total Power: 68,666kW (93,358hp) 25.6kn MAN-B&W 12K98MC 1 x 2 Stroke 12 Cy. 980 x 2660 68666kW (93358bhp) Mitsui Engineering & Shipbuilding CLtd-Japan AuxGen: 4 x 3000kW 6600V 60Hz a.c Boilers: e (ex.g.) 12.2kgf/cm² (12.0bar), WTAuxB (o.f.) 8.0kgf/cm² (7.8bar) Thrusters: 1 Thwart. CP thruster (f)
9452763 *9HSQ9* -	**YM URANUS** **YM Uranus Tankers Ltd** Uni-Chartering SatCom: Inmarsat C 424946210 *Valletta* *Malta* MMSI: 249462000 Official number: 9452763	**4,829** 2,297 6,970 T/cm 16.9	Class: BV	**2008-11 Marmara Tersanesi — Yarimca** Yd No: 77 Loa 119.60 (BB) Br ex - Dght 6.743 Lbp 111.60 Br md 16.89 Dpth 8.40 Welded, 1 dk	**(A12B2TR) Chemical/Products Tanker** Double Hull (13F) Liq: 7,918; Liq (Oil): 7,900 Cargo Heating Coils Compartments: 12 Wing Ta, 2 Wing Slop Ta, ER 10 Cargo Pump (s): 10x200m³/hr Manifold: Bow/CM: 59.2m Ice Capable	**1 oil engine** reduction geared to sc. shaft driving 1 CP propeller Total Power: 3,000kW (4,079hp) 14.0kn MAN-B&W 6L32/40CD 1 x 4 Stroke 6 Cy. 320 x 400 3000kW (4079bhp) STX Engine Co Ltd-South Korea AuxGen: 1 x 1012kW 440V a.c, 3 x 485kW 440V 60Hz a.c Thrusters: 1 Tunnel thruster (f) Fuel: 45.0 (d.f.) 421.0 (r.f.)
9337470 *A8OR7* -	**YM UTILITY** **Yang Ming (Liberia) Corp** Yang Ming Marine Transport Corp SatCom: Inmarsat C 463703555 *Monrovia* *Liberia* MMSI: 636013692 Official number: 13692	**90,507** 55,413 103,614	Class: AB	**2009-01 CSBC Corp, Taiwan — Kaohsiung** Yd No: 878 Loa 333.20 (BB) Br ex - Dght 14.500 Lbp 318.20 Br md 42.80 Dpth 24.50 Welded, 1 dk	**(A33A2CC) Container Ship (Fully Cellular)** TEU 8241 incl 700 ref C.	**1 oil engine** driving 1 FP propeller Total Power: 68,640kW (93,323hp) 25.6kn MAN-B&W 12K98MC 1 x 2 Stroke 12 Cy. 980 x 2660 68640kW (93323bhp) Mitsui Engineering & Shipbuilding CLtd-Japan AuxGen: 4 x 3000kW a.c Thrusters: 1 Tunnel thruster (f)
9302621 *A8HZ5* -	**YM UTMOST** **Yang Ming (Liberia) Corp** Yang Ming Marine Transport Corp SatCom: Inmarsat C 463791758 *Monrovia* *Liberia* MMSI: 636012808 Official number: 12808	**90,389** 55,275 101,597	Class: AB	**2006-10 Hyundai Heavy Industries Co Ltd — Ulsan** Yd No: 1674 Loa 335.00 (BB) Br ex - Dght 14.500 Lbp 319.00 Br md 42.80 Dpth 24.50 Welded, 1 dk	**(A33A2CC) Container Ship (Fully Cellular)** TEU 8208 incl 700 ref C.	**1 oil engine** driving 1 FP propeller Total Power: 68,666kW (93,358hp) 25.6kn MAN-B&W 12K98MC 1 x 2 Stroke 12 Cy. 980 x 2660 68666kW (93358bhp) Hyundai Heavy Industries Co Ltd-South Korea AuxGen: 4 x 3050kW a.c Thrusters: 1 Tunnel thruster (f) Fuel: 747.9 (d.f.) 11320.9 (r.f.)
9337456 *A8OR5* -	**YM UTOPIA** **Morning Star Ltd Corp** Yang Ming Marine Transport Corp SatCom: Inmarsat C 463702539 *Monrovia* *Liberia* MMSI: 636013690 Official number: 13690	**90,507** 55,413 103,614	Class: AB	**2008-06 CSBC Corp, Taiwan — Kaohsiung** Yd No: 876 Loa 333.20 (BB) Br ex - Dght 14.500 Lbp 318.20 Br md 42.80 Dpth 24.50 Welded, 1 dk	**(A33A2CC) Container Ship (Fully Cellular)** TEU 8241 incl 700 ref C.	**1 oil engine** driving 1 FP propeller Total Power: 68,666kW (93,358hp) 25.6kn MAN-B&W 12K98MC 1 x 2 Stroke 12 Cy. 980 x 2660 68666kW (93358bhp) Mitsui Engineering & Shipbuilding CLtd-Japan AuxGen: 4 x 3000kW a.c Thrusters: 1 Tunnel thruster (f) Fuel: 849.3 (d.f.) 11016.8 (r.f.)
9363364 *C4ZL2* -	**YM VANCOUVER** **Seacarriers Lines Inc** Danaos Shipping Co Ltd *Limassol* *Cyprus* MMSI: 212714000	**40,030** 24,450 50,632 T/cm 70.4	Class: NV	**2007-11 Samsung Heavy Industries Co Ltd — Geoje** Yd No: 1640 Loa 260.04 (BB) Br ex 32.30 Dght 12.600 Lbp 244.78 Br md 32.25 Dpth 19.30 Welded, 1 dk	**(A33A2CC) Container Ship (Fully Cellular)** TEU 4253 incl 400 ref C. Compartments: ER, 7 Cell Ho	**1 oil engine** driving 1 FP propeller Total Power: 36,559kW (49,706hp) 23.3kn MAN-B&W 8K90MC-C 1 x 2 Stroke 8 Cy. 900 x 2300 36559kW (49706bhp) Doosan Engine Co Ltd-South Korea AuxGen: 4 x 1700kW a.c Thrusters: 1 Tunnel thruster (f)
9291585 *9HCB8* -	**YM VENUS** *ex* Yilyak 1 *-2005* **YM Venus Tankers Ltd** CSM Denizcilik Ltd Sti (Chemfleet) *Valletta* *Malta* MMSI: 215826000 Official number: 9453	**3,906** 1,820 5,846 T/cm 15.0	Class: BV	**2005-01 Marmara Tersanesi — Yarimca** Yd No: 62 Loa 105.50 (BB) Br ex 16.84 Dght 6.200 Lbp 99.35 Br md 16.80 Dpth 7.40 Welded, 1 dk	**(A12B2TR) Chemical/Products Tanker** Double Hull (13F) Liq: 6,292; Liq (Oil): 6,293 Cargo Heating Coils Compartments: 10 Wing Ta, 2 Wing Slop Ta, ER 2 x Gas Tank (s); 2 cyl horizontal 10 Cargo Pump (s): 10x200m³/hr Manifold: Bow/CM: 46m Ice Capable	**1 oil engine** reduction geared to sc. shaft driving 1 CP propeller Total Power: 2,880kW (3,916hp) 13.0kn MaK 6M32C 1 x 4 Stroke 6 Cy. 320 x 480 2880kW (3916bhp) Caterpillar Motoren GmbH & Co. KG-Germany AuxGen: 3 x 400kW 400V 60Hz a.c, 1 x 760kW 400V a.c Thrusters: 1 Tunnel thruster (f) Fuel: 99.0 (d.f.) 259.0 (r.f.)
9267601 *A8BR6* -	**YM VIRTUE** *ex* Ming Virtue *-2005* **Kuang Ming (Liberia) Corp** Kuang Ming Shipping Corp *Monrovia* *Liberia* MMSI: 636011842 Official number: 11842	**39,749** 25,768 76,610 T/cm 66.6	Class: AB	**2003-02 Imabari Shipbuilding Co Ltd — Marugame KG (Marugame Shipyard)** Yd No: 1359 Loa 224.94 (BB) Br ex - Dght 14.139 Lbp 217.00 Br md 32.26 Dpth 19.50 Welded, 1 dk	**(A21A2BC) Bulk Carrier** Grain: 90,740 Compartments: 7 Ho, ER 7 Ha: 6 (17.1 x 15.6)ER (17.1 x 12.8)	**1 oil engine** driving 1 FP propeller Total Power: 10,320kW (14,031hp) 15.3kn B&W 6S60MC 1 x 2 Stroke 6 Cy. 600 x 2292 10320kW (14031bhp) Mitsui Engineering & Shipbuilding CLtd-Japan AuxGen: 3 x 500kW a.c
9278088 *A8EI4* -	**YM WEALTH** **Yang Ming (Liberia) Corp** Yang Ming Marine Transport Corp SatCom: Inmarsat C 463695867 *Monrovia* *Liberia* MMSI: 636012252 Official number: 12252	**64,254** 35,137 68,280	Class: AB	**2004-03 China Shipbuilding Corp (CSBC) — Kaohsiung** Yd No: 801 Loa 275.00 (BB) Br ex - Dght 14.000 Lbp 264.95 Br md 40.00 Dpth 24.20 Welded, 1 dk	**(A33A2CC) Container Ship (Fully Cellular)** TEU 5551 C Ho 2564 TEU C Dk 2987 TEU incl 400 ref C.	**1 oil engine** driving 1 FP propeller Total Power: 54,900kW (74,642hp) 26.0kn Sulzer 10RTA96C 1 x 2 Stroke 10 Cy. 960 x 2500 54900kW (74642bhp) Hyundai Heavy Industries Co Ltd-South Korea AuxGen: 4 x 1900kW a.c Thrusters: 1 Thwart. CP thruster (f)
9121649 *A8OF9* -	**YM XIAMEN** *ex* Kuangming Kaohsiung *-2004* *ex* Jin Quan *-1999* **All Oceans Transportation Inc** Yang Ming Marine Transport Corp *Monrovia* *Liberia* MMSI: 636013617 Official number: 13617	**3,994** 2,017 5,955	Class: AB (NK)	**1995-01 Dae Sun Shipbuilding & Engineering Co Ltd — Busan** Yd No: 413 Loa 107.00 (BB) Br ex - Dght 6.543 Lbp 97.50 Br md 17.20 Dpth 8.30 Welded, 1 dk	**(A33A2CC) Container Ship (Fully Cellular)** Bale: 6,801 TEU 338 C Ho 132 TEU C Dk 206 TEU incl 25 ref C. Compartments: 5 Cell Ho, ER 5 Ha: (12.5 x 8.0)4 (12.5 x 13.2)ER	**1 oil engine** driving 1 FP propeller Total Power: 3,913kW (5,320hp) 14.5kn B&W 7L35MC 1 x 2 Stroke 7 Cy. 350 x 1050 3913kW (5320bhp) Ssangyong Heavy Industries Co Ltd-South Korea AuxGen: 2 x 360kW a.c
7505346 *SDIA* -	**YMER** **Government of The Kingdom of Sweden (Rederiet Sjofartsverket) Swedish Maritime Administration** Rederi AB Transatlantic *Norrkoping* *Sweden* MMSI: 265066000	**7,470** 2,241 2,600		**1977-10 Oy Wartsila Ab — Helsinki** Yd No: 413 Loa 104.70 Br ex 23.86 Dght 7.081 Lbp 96.02 Br md 22.52 Dpth 12.12 Welded, 2 dks	**(B34C2SI) Icebreaker** Ice Capable	**5 diesel electric oil engines** driving 5 gen. Connecting to 4 elec. motors driving 4 CP propellers 2 fwd and 2 aft Total Power: 17,100kW (23,250hp) 19.0kn Pielstick 12PC2-2V-400 5 x Vee 4 Stroke 12 Cy. 400 x 460 each-3420kW (4650bhp) Oy Wartsila Ab-Finland
8709822 *UEHO* -	**YMIR** **Luntos Co Ltd** - *Petropavlovsk-Kamchatskiy* *Russia* MMSI: 273446920	**1,225** 367 529	Class: RS (LR) ✠ Classed LR until 30/4/10	**1988-05 Simek, Sigbjorn Iversen AS — Flekkefjord** Yd No: 72 Loa 53.00 (BB) Br ex 12.55 Dght 4.952 Lbp 50.60 Br md 12.10 Dpth 7.50 Welded, 2 dks	**(B11A2FS) Stern Trawler** Ins: 525 Ice Capable	**1 oil engine** with clutches, flexible couplings & sr geared to sc. shaft driving 1 CP propeller Total Power: 2,005kW (2,726hp) Wartsila 6R32 1 x 4 Stroke 6 Cy. 320 x 350 2005kW (2726bhp) Wartsila Diesel Oy-Finland AuxGen: 1 x 1200kW 380V 50Hz a.c, 1 x 253kW 380V 50Hz a.c, 1 x 113kW 380V 50Hz a.c Thrusters: 1 Thwart. CP thruster (f) Fuel: 176.9 (r.f.)

9372341 DSPP3 -
YN OCEAN
Y-Entec Co Ltd
Fortune Marine Co Ltd
SatCom: Inmarsat Mini-M 764820174
Jeju *South Korea*
MMSI: 441361000
Official number: JJR-089514
4,960 Class: KR
2,161
6,561
T/cm
16.7
2008-05 Pha Rung Shipyard Co. — Haiphong
Yd No: FM-02
Loa 110.95 (BB) Br ex 18.20 Dght 6.713
Lbp 102.00 Br md 18.00 Dpth 8.75
Welded, 1 dk
(A12B2TR) Chemical/Products Tanker
Double Hull (13F)
Liq: 7,569; Liq (Oil): 7,569
Cargo Heating Coils
Compartments: 12 Wing Ta, 2 Wing Slop Ta, ER
12 Cargo Pump (s): 12x200m³/hr
Manifold: Bow/CM: 56.1m
1 oil engine driving 1 FP propeller
Total Power: 2,942kW (4,000hp) 13.0kr
Hanshin LH46l
1 x 4 Stroke 6 Cy. 460 x 880 2942kW (4000bhp)
The Hanshin Diesel Works Ltd-Japan
AuxGen: 3 x 400kW 450V a.c
Thrusters: 1 Tunnel thruster (f)
Fuel: 113.0 (d.f.) 354.0 (r.f.)

7933086 - -
YOBYO No. 53
-
-
174
-
-
1979-06 Toa Tekko K.K. — Yokohama Yd No: 5
Loa 27.01 Br ex - Dght 1.801
Lbp 25.51 Br md 9.01 Dpth 2.70
Welded, 1 dk
(B34X2QA) Anchor Handling Vessel
2 oil engines reduction geared to sc. shafts driving 2 FP propellers
Total Power: 354kW (482hp)
Yanmar 6MA
2 x 4 Stroke 6 Cy. 200 x 240 each-177kW (241bhp)
Yanmar Diesel Engine Co Ltd-Japan

7629570 - -
YOBYO No. 201
ex Otori Maru No. 8 *-1997*
Capitol Offshore Pte Ltd
ASL Offshore & Marine Pte Ltd
160 Class: (NK)
48
80
1970 Ishibashi Kogyo — Kitakyushu
Loa 27.21 Br ex 9.02 Dght 1.702
Lbp 24.01 Br md 9.00 Dpth 2.52
Welded
(B34X2QA) Anchor Handling Vessel
2 oil engines driving 2 FP propellers
Total Power: 338kW (460hp) 6.8kn
Yanmar 6MA
2 x 4 Stroke 6 Cy. 200 x 240 each-169kW (230bhp)
Yanmar Diesel Engine Co Ltd-Japan
AuxGen: 1 x 24kW

9251729 HQVX4 -
YOBYO No. 203
Marina Estrella S de RL
-
San Lorenzo *Honduras*
Official number: L-3727696
178
-
-
2001-05 Sagami Zosen Tekko K.K. — Yokosuka
Yd No: 272
Loa 25.00 Br ex - Dght -
Lbp - Br md 9.00 Dpth 2.80
Welded, 1 dk
(B34X2QA) Anchor Handling Vessel
2 oil engines driving 2 FP propellers
Total Power: 810kW (1,102hp) 10.0kn
Yanmar
2 x 4 Stroke each-405kW (551bhp)
Yanmar Diesel Engine Co Ltd-Japan

8984616 - -
YOBYO NO. 205
ex Riki Maru No. 2 *-2005*
-
San Lorenzo *Honduras*
Official number: L-3728389
155
46
-
1987 Hiroshi Ishii — Yokohama
Loa - Br ex - Dght -
Lbp 22.62 Br md 9.00 Dpth 2.59
Welded, 1 dk
(B34X2QA) Anchor Handling Vessel
2 oil engines driving 2 Propellers
Total Power: 810kW (1,102hp)
Yanmar
2 x 4 Stroke each-405kW (551bhp)
Yanmar Diesel Engine Co Ltd-Japan

8731772 - -
YOBYO NO. 206
ex Shinsei *-2008*
Marina Estrella S de RL
-
San Lorenzo *Honduras*
Official number: L-3728284
134
40
-
1995-10 K.K. Imai Seisakusho — Kamijima
L reg 22.16 Br ex - Dght -
Lbp 22.00 Br md 9.00 Dpth 2.60
Welded, 1 dk
(B34X2QA) Anchor Handling Vessel
1 oil engine driving 1 Propeller

8132380 - -
YOBYO NO. 300
ex Riki Maru *-2005*
Marina Estrella S de RL
-
San Lorenzo *Honduras*
Official number: L-3728118
127
38
-
1981 Shinhama Dockyard Co. Ltd. — Tamano
Yd No: 205
Loa 23.50 Br ex - Dght 1.800
Lbp 22.58 Br md 9.00 Dpth 2.70
Welded, 1 dk
(B34X2QA) Anchor Handling Vessel
1 oil engine driving 1 FP propeller

8731760 - -
YOBYO NO. 700
Marina Estrella S de RL
-
San Lorenzo *Honduras*
Official number: L-3728280
162
-
-
1986-04 Toa Tekko K.K. — Yokohama
L reg 23.51 Br ex - Dght 1.700
Lbp - Br md 8.70 Dpth 2.80
Welded, 1 dk
(B34X2QA) Anchor Handling Vessel
1 oil engine driving 1 Propeller
Total Power: 559kW (760hp)
Yanmar
1 x 4 Stroke 559kW (760bhp)
Yanmar Diesel Engine Co Ltd-Japan

9249154 JG5651
YODO
Government of Japan (Ministry of Land, Infrastructure & Transport) (The Coastguard)
-
Tokyo *Japan*
MMSI: 431100142
Official number: 137108
128
-
-
2002-03 Sumidagawa Zosen K.K. — Tokyo
Yd No: N12-61
Loa 37.00 Br ex - Dght 1.500
Lbp 35.00 Br md 6.70 Dpth 3.45
Welded, 1 dk
(B34H2SQ) Patrol Vessel
2 oil engines reduction geared to sc. shafts driving 2 FP propellers
Total Power: 4,798kW (6,524hp) 25.0kn
M.T.U. 16V4000M90
2 x Vee 4 Stroke 16 Cy. 165 x 190 each-2399kW (3262bhp)
MTU Friedrichshafen GmbH-Friedrichshafen

8922113 JI3416 -
YODO MARU
Osaka-shi Kowan Kyoku (Port & Harbour Bureau)
-
Miyazaki, Miyazaki *Japan*
Official number: 131671
153
-
-
1990-03 Kanagawa Zosen — Kobe Yd No: 337
Loa 30.20 Br ex 9.50 Dght 2.700
Lbp 25.50 Br md 8.60 Dpth 3.77
Welded, 1 dk
(B32A2ST) Tug
2 oil engines with flexible couplings & sr geared to sc. shafts driving 2 FP propellers
Total Power: 1,912kW (2,600hp) 13.2kn
Niigata 6L25CXE
2 x 4 Stroke 6 Cy. 250 x 320 each-956kW (1300bhp)
Niigata Engineering Co Ltd-Japan
AuxGen: 2 x 64kW 225V 60Hz a.c
Fuel: 27.5 (d.f.)

8974881 - -
YODOGAWA MARU NO. 18
-
-
-
102
-
-
2001-12 Y.K. Kondou — Nandan Yd No: 131
Loa 28.65 Br ex - Dght 2.500
Lbp 25.00 Br md 6.80 Dpth 3.18
Welded, 1 dk
(B32A2ST) Tug
2 oil engines driving 2 Propellers
Total Power: 588kW (800hp)
Yanmar 6N165-EN
2 x 4 Stroke 6 Cy. 165 x 232 each-294kW (400bhp)
Yanmar Diesel Engine Co Ltd-Japan

8961080 - -
YODRUK 1
Nabis Nava-Aiemvilai
-
Bangkok *Thailand*
Official number: 437401231
202
137
-
2000-11 Homchan Phaisombun — Samut Sakhon
Loa 24.10 Br ex - Dght -
Lbp - Br md 8.00 Dpth 3.50
Welded, 1 dk
(A34A2GR) Refrigerated Cargo Ship
1 oil engine driving 1 FP propeller
Total Power: 783kW (1,065hp)
Cummins
1 x 4 Stroke 783kW (1065bhp)
Cummins Engine Co Inc-USA

5302611 - -
YOFAIRA
ex El Junior *-1997* *ex* Sand Boy *-1997*
ex Rutland 1 *-1976* *ex* Jimmy *-1956*
-
-
298 Class: (NV)
145
539
1948 Seutelvens Verksted — Fredrikstad
Yd No: 38
Loa 44.68 Br ex 7.50 Dght 3.607
Lbp 40.95 Br md 7.45 Dpth 3.92
Welded, 1 dk
(A31A2GX) General Cargo Ship
Grain: 595; Bale: 566
Compartments: 1 Ho, ER
1 Ha: (17.6 x 3.9)
Derricks: 1x5t; Winches: 2
1 oil engine driving 1 FP propeller
Total Power: 441kW (600hp) 10.5kn
Wichmann 6ACA
1 x 2 Stroke 6 Cy. 280 x 420 441kW (600bhp) (new engine 1963)
Wichmann Motorfabrikk AS-Norway
AuxGen: 1 x 15kW 100V d.c, 1 x 8kW 100V d.c
Fuel: 50.5 (d.f.)

5258119 6VIR DAK 254
YOFF
ex Notre Dame de Bonne Nouvelle *-1956*
Armement Sueur
-
Dakar *Senegal*
122
43
72
1957 At. & Ch. du Nord-Ouest — Dieppe
L reg 26.61 Br ex 6.23 Dght 3.125
Lbp - Br md 6.18 Dpth 3.51
Welded, 1 dk
(B11A2FT) Trawler
2 Ha: 2 (1.0 x 1.0)
Derricks: 1x1.5t
1 oil engine driving 1 FP propeller
Total Power: 302kW (411hp) 10.0kn
Crepelle 7PS
1 x 4 Stroke 7 Cy. 230 x 300 302kW (411bhp)
Crepelle et Cie-France
Fuel: 28.5 (d.f.)

9088031 9LY2550 -
YOGASAKI MARU
Chun Chao Shipping & Trading Pte Ltd
-
Freetown *Sierra Leone*
MMSI: 667003353
2,879 Class: (NK)
-
4,799
1994-04 Murakami Hide Zosen K.K. — Imabari
Yd No: 357
Loa 96.99 Br ex - Dght 6.456
Lbp 89.00 Br md 15.50 Dpth 7.80
Welded, 1 dk
(A31A2GX) General Cargo Ship
Grain: 5,992
Compartments: 2 Ho, ER
2 Ha: (22.4 x 9.1) (25.9 x 9.1)ER
1 oil engine driving 1 FP propeller
Total Power: 2,060kW (2,801hp)
Hanshin 6EL38
1 x 4 Stroke 6 Cy. 380 x 760 2060kW (2801bhp)
The Hanshin Diesel Works Ltd-Japan
Fuel: 240.0 (r.f.)

9479785 PBMZ -
YOGI
MC Yogi BV
Yogi Exploitatie BV
Zwijndrecht *Netherlands*
MMSI: 245594000
Official number: 51711
255 Class: BV
76
-
2008-05 B.V. Scheepswerf Damen Hardinxveld — Hardinxveld-Giessendam Yd No: 1593
Loa 26.00 Br ex - Dght 2.250
Lbp 23.92 Br md 11.50 Dpth 3.50
Welded, 1 dk
(B34L2QU) Utility Vessel
Cranes: 2
3 oil engines reduction geared to sc. shafts driving 3 FP propellers
Total Power: 1,341kW (1,824hp) 9.7kn
Caterpillar 3412
3 x Vee 4 Stroke 12 Cy. 137 x 152 each-447kW (608bhp)
Caterpillar Inc-USA
AuxGen: 2 x 78kW 380/220V 50Hz a.c
Thrusters: 1 Water jet (f)

IMO / Call sign	Name / Owner	Tonnage	Builder / Dimensions	Type	Machinery
7812880 E3AA	**YOHANA** *ex* Sloman Ranger *-1996* **Yohana Shipping Co Ltd** Eritrean Shipping Lines SatCom: Inmarsat A 1215101 *Massawa* *Eritrea* MMSI: 625011000 Official number: M0001	**3,922** Class: IS (GL) 1,176 2,570	**1979-03 Howaldtswerke-Deutsche Werft AG (HDW) — Kiel** Yd No: 146 Loa 91.95 (BB) Br ex 18.14 Dght 4.210 Lbp 79.20 Br md 18.01 Dpth 7.90 Welded, 2 dks	**(A35A2RR) Ro-Ro Cargo Ship** Stern door/ramp (centre) Len: 10.00 Wid: 8.74 Swl: 192 Lane-Len: 344 Lane-Wid: 7.65 Lane-clr ht: 5.50 Trailers: 30 Bale: 6,182; Liq: 904 TEU 319 C.Ho 132/20' C.Dk 187/20' incl. 20 ref C. Compartments: 1 Ho, ER 1 Ha: (68.2 x 15.0) Cranes: 2x25t Ice Capable	**2 oil engines** sr reverse geared to sc. shafts driving 2 FP propellers Total Power: 2,354kW (3,200hp) 12.5kn Deutz SBA12M528 2 x Vee 4 Stroke 12 Cy. 220 x 280 each-1177kW (1600bhp) Kloeckner Humboldt Deutz AG-West Germany AuxGen: 3 x 184kW 440V 60Hz a.c Thrusters: 1 Thwart. FP thruster (f) Fuel: 90.5 (d.f.) 356.0 (r.f.) 12.0pd
8965086 JJ4028	**YOKA MARU** **Masuda Kaiun YK** *Awaji, Hyogo* *Japan* Official number: 135972	*349* - -	**2000-10 Tokuoka Zosen K.K. — Naruto** Yd No: 260 Loa 69.17 Br ex - Dght - Lbp 62.00 Br md 10.80 Dpth 6.20 Welded, 1 dk	**(A31A2GX) General Cargo Ship**	**1 oil engine** driving 1 FP propeller Total Power: 736kW (1,001hp) 10.7kn Hanshin LH28LG 1 x 4 Stroke 6 Cy. 280 x 530 736kW (1001bhp) The Hanshin Diesel Works Ltd-Japan Fuel: 36.0 (d.f.)
9223502 JM6686 -	**YOKO** - - *Amakusa, Kumamoto* *Japan* Official number: 136434	*196* - -	**1999-11 Kanagawa Zosen — Kobe** Yd No: 478 Loa 33.90 Br ex - Dght - Lbp 29.50 Br md 9.40 Dpth 4.00 Welded, 1 dk	**(B32A2ST) Tug**	**2 oil engines** driving 2 FP propellers Total Power: 2,942kW (4,000hp) 14.5kn Yanmar 6N280-SN 2 x 4 Stroke 6 Cy. 280 x 380 each-1471kW (2000bhp) Yanmar Diesel Engine Co Ltd-Japan AuxGen: 2 x 96kW 225V 60Hz a.c
9566863 7JHB -	**YOKO MARU** **Fisheries Research Agency** *Nagasaki, Nagasaki* *Japan* MMSI: 432787000 Official number: 141224	*692* - -	**2010-11 Niigata Shipbuilding & Repair Inc — Niigata NI** Yd No: 0047 Loa 58.60 Br ex 11.00 Dght 4.560 Lbp 52.30 Br md 10.80 Dpth 6.85 Welded, 1 dk	**(B12D2FR) Fishery Research Vessel**	**1 oil engine** reduction geared to sc. shaft driving 1 CP propeller Total Power: 1,838kW (2,499hp) Niigata 6MG28HX 1 x 4 Stroke 6 Cy. 280 x 370 1838kW (2499bhp) Niigata Engineering Co Ltd-Japan
9057903 JG5177 -	**YOKO MARU** **Tokyo Kinkai Yuso KK & Nippon Marine Service & Engineering Co Ltd (Nippon Kaiji Kogyo KK)** Nippon Marine Service & Engineering Co Ltd (Nippon Kaiji Kogyo KK) *Tokyo* *Japan* Official number: 133822	*194* - -	**1992-11 Kanagawa Zosen — Kobe** Yd No: 381 Loa 34.70 Br ex - Dght - Lbp 30.00 Br md 9.00 Dpth 4.00 Welded, 1 dk	**(B32A2ST) Tug**	**2 oil engines** geared integral to driving 2 Z propellers Total Power: 2,500kW (3,400hp) 12.5kn Niigata 6L25HX 2 x 4 Stroke 6 Cy. 250 x 350 each-1250kW (1700bhp) Niigata Engineering Co Ltd-Japan AuxGen: 2 x 96kW 225V 50Hz a.c Fuel: 62.8 (r.f.)
9159256 JL6518 -	**YOKO MARU** **Nakamura Kisen YK** *Imabari, Ehime* *Japan* Official number: 135545	*499* - 1,235	**1996-11 Mukaishima Zoki Co. Ltd. — Onomichi** Yd No: 310 Loa - Br ex - Dght 4.150 Lbp 61.80 Br md 10.00 Dpth 4.50 Welded, 1 dk	**(A12A2TC) Chemical Tanker** Compartments: 8 Wing Ta, ER 2 Cargo Pump (s): 2x300m³/hr	**1 oil engine** driving 1 FP propeller Total Power: 736kW (1,001hp) Niigata 6M31BGT 1 x 4 Stroke 6 Cy. 310 x 530 736kW (1001bhp) Niigata Engineering Co Ltd-Japan
8519394 JM5485 -	**YOKO MARU** **Sasebo Jyukogyo KK** - *Sasebo, Nagasaki* *Japan* Official number: 127860	*183* - -	**1986-02 Tokushima Zosen Sangyo K.K. — Komatsushima** Yd No: 1843 Loa - Br ex - Dght 3.001 Lbp 28.02 Br md 9.21 Dpth 4.12 Welded, 1 dk	**(B32A2ST) Tug**	**2 oil engines** driving 2 CP propellers Total Power: 2,354kW (3,200hp) Yanmar 6Z280-ST 2 x 4 Stroke 6 Cy. 280 x 360 each-1177kW (1600bhp) Yanmar Diesel Engine Co Ltd-Japan
8609668 LW4739 -	**YOKO MARU** *ex* Kiku Maru No. 58 *-2006* **Empesur SA** - *Argentina* MMSI: 701006139 Official number: 02575	*900* 295 -	**1986-09 Fujishin Zosen K.K. — Kamo** Yd No: 517 Loa 66.02 (BB) Br ex 10.24 Dght 3.901 Lbp 57.00 Br md 10.20 Dpth 6.61 Welded, 2 dks	**(B11B2FV) Fishing Vessel**	**1 oil engine** driving 1 FP propeller Total Power: 1,177kW (1,600hp) Niigata 6M31AFTE 1 x 4 Stroke 6 Cy. 310 x 530 1177kW (1600bhp) Niigata Engineering Co Ltd-Japan
8616049 V5YT L701	**YOKO-TANI** **Foodcon (Pty) Ltd** - *Luderitz* *Namibia* Official number: 93LB041	**268** Class: (NV) 80 343	**1986-01 Esbjerg Oilfield Services A/S — Esbjerg** Yd No: 52 Loa 32.01 Br ex - Dght 3.701 Lbp 27.01 Br md 7.31 Dpth - Welded, 1 dk	**(B11A2FS) Stern Trawler** Ice Capable	**1 oil engine** geared to sc. shaft driving 1 FP propeller Total Power: 662kW (900hp) 12.0kn Caterpillar 3512TA 1 x Vee 4 Stroke 12 Cy. 170 x 190 662kW (900bhp) Caterpillar Tractor Co-USA AuxGen: 2 x 80kW 380V 50Hz a.c Thrusters: 1 Thwart. FP thruster (f)
8015439 - -	**YOKOHAMA** **PT Pelayaran Nasional 'Sinar Pagoda'** *Indonesia*	*159* - -	**1981-02 Yokohama Yacht Co Ltd — Yokohama KN** Yd No: 778 Loa 30.99 Br ex 7.60 Dght 2.155 Lbp 27.51 Br md 7.21 Dpth 3.00 Welded, 1 dk	**(B34F2SF) Fire Fighting Vessel**	**3 oil engines** reduction geared to sc. shafts driving 3 FP propellers Total Power: 3,906kW (5,310hp) M.T.U. 12V652TB51 3 x Vee 4 Stroke 12 Cy. 190 x 230 each-1302kW (1770bhp) Ikegai Tekkosho-Japan
8974805 JG5560	**YOKOHAMA** **Yokohama Municipal Office** - *Yokohama, Kanagawa* *Japan* Official number: 136957	*120* - -	**2002-03 Yokohama Yacht Co Ltd — Yokohama KN** Yd No: 9670 Loa 32.20 Br ex - Dght 2.000 Lbp 27.00 Br md 7.30 Dpth 3.49 Welded, 1 dk	**(B34F2SF) Fire Fighting Vessel**	**2 oil engines** geared to sc. shafts driving 2 CP propellers Total Power: 2,942kW (4,000hp) 14.7kn M.T.U. 12V4000M70 2 x Vee 4 Stroke 12 Cy. 165 x 190 each-1471kW (2000bhp) MTU Friedrichshafen GmbH-Friedrichshafen
8711019 JCOY -	**YOKOSUKA** **Independent Administrative Institution Japan Agency for Marine-Earth Science & Technology (JAMSTEC)** Nippon Marine Enterprises Ltd *Yokosuka, Kanagawa* *Japan* MMSI: 431460000 Official number: 130301	**4,439** Class: NK 1,331 1,368	**1990-04 Kawasaki Heavy Industries Ltd — Kobe HG** Yd No: 1411 Loa 105.22 (BB) Br ex 16.02 Dght 4.671 Lbp 95.00 Br md 16.00 Dpth 7.30 Welded	**(B31A2SR) Research Survey Vessel**	**2 oil engines** geared to sc. shafts driving 2 CP propellers Total Power: 4,414kW (6,002hp) 16.0kn Daihatsu 8DLM-32 2 x 4 Stroke 8 Cy. 320 x 400 each-2207kW (3001bhp) Daihatsu Diesel Manufacturing Co Lt-Japan Thrusters: 1 Thwart. CP thruster (f) Fuel: 620.0 (r.f.)
8864854 JG5124	**YOKOSUKA MARU NO. 2** **KK Musashino Marine** - *Kawasaki, Kanagawa* *Japan* MMSI: 431100005 Official number: 133454	*553* - 1,200	**1992-09 Takao Zosen Kogyo K.K. — Tateyama** Yd No: 116 L reg 59.20 Br ex - Dght 4.100 Lbp - Br md 10.00 Dpth 4.60 Welded, 1 dk	**(B34E2SW) Waste Disposal Vessel**	**1 oil engine** driving 1 FP propeller Total Power: 1,030kW (1,400hp) Yanmar MF29-UT 1 x 4 Stroke 6 Cy. 290 x 520 1030kW (1400bhp) Yanmar Diesel Engine Co Ltd-Japan
7127534 HP2798 -	**YOLANDA I** *ex* Sea Moon *-1999* *ex* Stevns Supplier *-1997* *ex* Maersk Supplier *-1987* **Offshore Express LLC** - SatCom: Inmarsat C 437093610 *Panama* *Panama* Official number: 37992PEXT4	**574** Class: (LR) (BV) 172 ✠ Classed LR until 1/12/87 769	**1972-01 Aarhus Flydedok A/S — Aarhus** Yd No: 148 Loa 53.35 Br ex 11.23 Dght 3.455 Lbp 51.19 Br md 11.00 Dpth 4.02 Welded, 1 dk	**(B21B20T) Offshore Tug/Supply Ship** Liq: 612 Compartments: 8 Ta, 1 Ho, ER Derricks: 1x3t; Winches: 1 Ice Capable	**2 oil engines** driving 2 FP propellers Total Power: 2,794kW (3,798hp) 13.0kn MaK 8M451AK 2 x 4 Stroke 8 Cy. 320 x 450 each-1397kW (1899bhp) MaK Maschinenbau GmbH-Kiel AuxGen: 3 x 128kW 380V 50Hz a.c Thrusters: 1 Thwart. CP thruster (f) Fuel: 280.0 (d.f.)
7407958 HC4066 -	**YOLANDA L** *ex* Jeanette *-1997* *ex* Bold Fleet *-1994* *ex* Olivia *-1982* **Industria Frigorificos Pesca CA** - *Guayaquil* *Ecuador* Official number: P-00-0805	**1,375** 412 -	**1974-06 Campbell Industries — San Diego, Ca** Yd No: 99 Loa 66.43 Br ex - Dght 5.766 Lbp - Br md 12.17 Dpth 5.79 Welded	**(B11B2FV) Fishing Vessel** Ins: 1,168	**1 oil engine** driving 1 FP propeller Total Power: 2,574kW (3,500hp) General Motors 1 x 2 Stroke 2574kW (3500bhp) General Motors Corp-USA

9546291 *HC4936* -	**YOLITA II** **Mariana Torres** - *Puerto Ayora* *Ecuador* MMSI: 735058239 Official number: TN-01-00241	**250** 83 190	**2008-07 in Ecuador** Yd No: 223 Loa 31.80 Br ex - Dght 2.400 Lbp 31.10 Br md 8.00 Dpth 3.15 Welded, 1 dk	**(A37A2PC) Passenger/Cruise** Passengers: cabins: 10; berths: 16	**2 oil engines** reduction geared to sc. shafts driving 2 FP propellers Total Power: 354kW (482hp) G.M. (Detroit Diesel) 2 x each-177kW (241bhp) Detroit Diesel Corporation-Detroit, Mi
9564889 *ZGAU9* -	**YOLO** *ex* Pure White *-2010* *ex* I'm No Lady *-2008* *ex* Arno 34/08 *-2008* - - - *Cayman Islands (British)* MMSI: 319220000	**184** 55 -	**2006-10 Cantiere Navale Arno Srl — Pisa** Yd No: 34/08 Loa 34.11 Br ex - Dght 1.200 Lbp 29.37 Br md 7.35 Dpth 3.75 Bonded, 1 dk	**(X11A2YP) Yacht** Hull Material: Reinforced Plastic	**3 oil engines** reduction geared to sc. shafts driving 3 Water jets Total Power: 5,370kW (7,302hp) M.T.U. 16V2000M93 3 x Vee 4 Stroke 16 Cy. 135 x 156 each-1790kW (2434bhp) MTU Friedrichshafen GmbH-Friedrichshafen
8633645 - -	**YOMN** - **Mahoney Shipping & Marine Services** - *Alexandria* *Egypt*	*220* Class: (LR) (RS) - Classed LR until 10/7/96 -	**1971 "Petrozavod" — Leningrad** Loa 29.62 Br ex 8.32 Dght 3.200 Lbp 24.60 Br md 8.30 Dpth 4.30 Welded, 1 dk	**(B32A2ST) Tug**	**2 oil engines** driving 2 CP propellers Total Power: 882kW (1,200hp) Russkiy 6D30/50-4-2 2 x 2 Stroke 6 Cy. 300 x 500 each-441kW (600bhp) Mashinostroitelnyy Zavod"Russkiy-Dizel"-Leningrad AuxGen: 1 x 40kW 380V 50Hz a.c, 1 x 32kW 380V 50Hz a.c, 1 x 32kW 380V 50Hz a.c
7238462 - - -	**YON DAE BONG 1** *ex* Dong Chang Fa *-2002* *ex* Kyoyo Maru 78 *-1993* *ex* Myojin Maru No. 78 *-1993* *ex* Kyoyo Maru No. 11 *-1980* - -	**398** Class: KC (CC) 135 120	**1972 Miho Zosensho K.K. — Shimizu** Yd No: 850 Loa 51.05 Br ex 8.03 Dght 3.400 Lbp 43.00 Br md 8.01 Dpth 3.71 Welded, 1 dk	**(B11B2FV) Fishing Vessel** Ins: 348	**1 oil engine** driving 1 FP propeller Total Power: 1,103kW (1,500hp) 11.5kn Niigata 6M31X 1 x 4 Stroke 6 Cy. 310 x 460 1103kW (1500bhp) Niigata Engineering Co Ltd-Japan AuxGen: 2 x 200kW 220V a.c
8324256 *HMPZ*	**YON HA** *ex* Akasia Princess *-2013* *ex* Tong Xing Hai *-2012* *ex* Yuan Tong *-2005* *ex* Bigswan *-2004* *ex* White Fuji *-1997* **Songyong Shipping Co** - *North Korea* MMSI: 445044000	**2,353** Class: (NK) 1,364 3,132	**1984-07 Shirahama Zosen K.K. — Honai** Yd No: 117 Loa 84.36 (BB) Br ex 13.42 Dght 5.552 Lbp 78.01 Br md 13.40 Dpth 8.01 Welded, 2 dks	**(A31A2GX) General Cargo Ship** Grain: 4,978; Bale: 4,828 Compartments: 1 Ho, ER 1 Ha: (37.8 x 9.0)ER Derricks: 1x25t,1x15t	**1 oil engine** driving 1 FP propeller Total Power: 1,471kW (2,000hp) 11.5kn Makita LS35L 1 x 4 Stroke 6 Cy. 350 x 680 1471kW (2000bhp) Makita Diesel Co Ltd-Japan AuxGen: 2 x 120kW a.c
8742446 *7JEC* -	**YONAKUNI** **Government of Japan (Ministry of Land, Infrastructure & Transport) (The Coastguard)** - *Tokyo* *Japan* MMSI: 432675000 Official number: 140846	*1,349* - -	**2009-02 Mitsui Eng. & SB. Co. Ltd. — Tamano** Yd No: 1751 Loa 89.00 Br ex - Dght - Lbp - Br md 11.00 Dpth 5.00 Welded, 1 dk	**(B34H2SQ) Patrol Vessel**	**4 oil engines** reduction geared to sc. shafts driving 4 Water jets Total Power: 14,760kW (20,068hp)
9601807 *JD3229* -	**YONE MARU** **Japan Railway Construction, Transport & Technology Agency & Nansei Kaiun KK** Nansei Kaiun KK *Naha, Okinawa* *Japan* Official number: 141495	*749* Class: NK - 1,650	**2011-07 K.K. Miura Zosensho — Saiki** Yd No: 1356 Loa 96.37 Br ex - Dght 3.970 Lbp 86.50 Br md 13.40 Dpth 7.28 Welded, 1 dk	**(A31A2GX) General Cargo Ship** Bale: 2,961 TEU 128 incl 42 ref C	**1 oil engine** driving 1 Propeller Total Power: 3,900kW (5,302hp) 12.0kn MAN-B&W 6L35MC 1 x 2 Stroke 6 Cy. 350 x 1050 3900kW (5302bhp) The Hanshin Diesel Works Ltd-Japan Fuel: 170.0
9227730 *JF2175* -	**YONESHIRO** **Tohoku Port Service KK** - *Noshiro, Akita* *Japan* MMSI: 431700548 Official number: 120130	*196* - -	**2000-06 Kanagawa Zosen — Kobe** Yd No: 484 Loa 33.30 Br ex - Dght - Lbp 29.00 Br md 9.20 Dpth 4.18 Welded, 1 dk	**(B32A2ST) Tug**	**2 oil engines** gearing integral to driving 2 Z propellers Total Power: 2,648kW (3,600hp) 14.0kn Niigata 6L28HX 2 x 4 Stroke 6 Cy. 280 x 370 each-1324kW (1800bhp) Niigata Engineering Co Ltd-Japan AuxGen: 2 x 104kW 225V 60Hz a.c Fuel: 47.0 (d.f.)
9109706 - -	**YONG AN 1** **Purple Gold Mountain Shipping SA** China Shipping (Hong Kong) Marine Co Ltd *China* MMSI: 414704000	**26,737** Class: (CC) (BV) 12,352 44,072 T/cm 51.4	**1995-09 Hanjin Heavy Industries Co Ltd — Busan** Yd No: 025 Loa 190.00 (BB) Br ex 30.54 Dght 11.221 Lbp 181.00 Br md 30.50 Dpth 16.60 Welded, 1 dk	**(A21A2BC) Bulk Carrier** Grain: 56,675; Bale: 54,975 Compartments: 5 Ho, ER 5 Ha: 5 (18.9 x 16.0)ER Cranes: 4x30t	**1 oil engine** driving 1 FP propeller Total Power: 8,290kW (11,271hp) 14.5kn MAN-B&W 6S50MC 1 x 2 Stroke 6 Cy. 500 x 1910 8290kW (11271bhp) Korea Heavy Industries & ConstrCo Ltd (HANJUNG)-South Korea AuxGen: 3 x 500kW 450V 60Hz a.c
8919532 *BVID* -	**YONG AN CHENG** **Xiamen Ocean Shipping Co (COSCO XIAMEN)** *Xiamen, Fujian* *China* MMSI: 412442850	**16,703** Class: CC 8,748 22,814 T/cm 36.0	**1992-08 Guangzhou Shipyard — Guangzhou GD** Yd No: 01002 Loa 174.00 (BB) Br ex - Dght 10.000 Lbp 161.57 Br md 25.60 Dpth 14.20 Welded, 2 dks	**(A31A2GX) General Cargo Ship** Grain: 32,973 Compartments: 4 Ho, ER 1 Ha: ER (18.9 x 10.4) 6 Wing Ha: 4 (25.6 x 7.9)2 (19.2 x 7.9) Cranes: 2x25t,2x20t Ice Capable	**1 oil engine** driving 1 FP propeller Total Power: 8,050kW (10,945hp) 16.5kn B&W 6L60MCE 1 x 2 Stroke 6 Cy. 600 x 1944 8050kW (10945bhp) Hudong Shipyard-China AuxGen: 3 x 616kW 450V a.c
8122359 - - -	**YONG AN HO** *ex* Sea Bird *-2006* *ex* Dae Sung *-2005* *ex* Munakata Maru No. 8 *-1996* **Yongan Shipping Co Ltd** - *Busan* *South Korea* MMSI: 440103270 Official number: BSR-960290	**1,470** Class: (KR) (NK) - 3,207	**1982-04 Kishimoto Zosen K.K. — Kinoe** Yd No: 523 Loa 86.70 Br ex - Dght 5.608 Lbp 80.02 Br md 12.70 Dpth 6.23 Welded, 1 dk	**(A13B2TP) Products Tanker** Liq: 2,899; Liq (Oil): 2,899 Compartments: 10 Ta, ER	**1 oil engine** driving 1 CP propeller Total Power: 1,471kW (2,000hp) 11.8kn Hanshin 6EL32 1 x 4 Stroke 6 Cy. 320 x 640 1471kW (2000bhp) The Hanshin Diesel Works Ltd-Japan AuxGen: 1 x 200kW 445V 60Hz a.c, 1 x 128kW 445V 60Hz a.c Fuel: 40.5 (d.f.) 116.5 (r.f.) 5.5pd
9595553 - -	**YONG BAO LI 17** **Yongji Wenling Shipping Co Ltd** - *Taizhou, Zhejiang* *China*	**12,900** Class: (CC) 6,585 19,800	**2010-10 Zhejiang Zhenxing Shiprepair & Building Co Ltd — Wenling ZJ** Yd No: ZX018 Loa 155.90 Br ex - Dght 9.000 Lbp 146.80 Br md 22.60 Dpth 12.60 Welded, 1 dk	**(A21A2BC) Bulk Carrier** Grain: 25,700 Cranes: 3x30t	**1 oil engine** reduction geared to sc. shaft driving 1 FP propeller Total Power: 4,400kW (5,982hp) 12.5kn Pielstick 8PC2-6 1 x 4 Stroke 8 Cy. 400 x 460 4400kW (5982bhp) Shaanxi Diesel Heavy Industry Co Lt-China
9089114 *HMYJ5* -	**YONG BONG** **Korea Kumbyol Trading Co** - *Nampho* *North Korea* MMSI: 445213000 Official number: 2902019	**1,830** Class: KC 1,201 2,977	**1979-04 Nampo Shipyard — Nampo** Loa 81.62 Br ex - Dght 5.800 Lbp 77.00 Br md 12.50 Dpth 7.60 Welded, 1 dk	**(A31A2GX) General Cargo Ship**	**1 oil engine** driving 1 Propeller Total Power: 1,471kW (2,000hp) Makita ESHC640 1 x 4 Stroke 6 Cy. 400 x 600 1471kW (2000bhp) Makita Diesel Co Ltd-Japan
9473016 - -	**YONG CHENG 15** *ex* Tong Zhou 66 *-2007* **Zhoushan Shi Yong Cheng Shipping Co Ltd** Prime Cosmos Ltd	**4,499** 2,567 9,863	**2007-03 Zhejiang Xifeng Shipbuilding Co Ltd — Fenghua ZJ** Yd No: 01 Loa 117.40 Br ex - Dght 6.900 Lbp 108.00 Br md 16.50 Dpth 8.31 Welded, 1 dk	**(A12B2TR) Chemical/Products Tanker** Double Hull (13F)	**1 oil engine** driving 1 Propeller Total Power: 2,060kW (2,801hp) 13.6kn Chinese Std. Type 8320ZC 1 x 4 Stroke 8 Cy. 320 x 440 2060kW (2801bhp) Guangzhou Diesel Engine Factory CoLtd-China
9432373 *BKXM3*	**YONG CHENG 17** **Zhoushan Yongcheng Marine Co Ltd** - *Zhoushan, Zhejiang* *China* MMSI: 413434360 Official number: 070307000034	**3,422** Class: ZC 1,505 4,885	**2007-01 Zhoushan Putuo Luomen Shiprepair & Building Co Ltd — Zhoushan ZJ** Loa 101.50 Br ex - Dght 6.350 Lbp - Br md 15.40 Dpth 8.00 Welded, 1 dk	**(A12B2TR) Chemical/Products Tanker** Double Hull (13F)	**1 oil engine** geared to sc. shaft driving 1 FP propeller Total Power: 2,000kW (2,719hp) 11.0kn Chinese Std. Type G8300ZC 1 x 4 Stroke 6 Cy. 300 x 380 2000kW (2719bhp) Wuxi Antai Power Machinery Co Ltd-China
9649316 *BKTD5* -	**YONG CHENG 58** **Zhoushan Yongcheng Shipping Co Ltd** - *Zhoushan, Zhejiang* *China* MMSI: 413445990	**3,877** Class: CC 1,811 5,717 T/cm 16.0	**2012-06 Zhoushan Qifan Shiprepair & Building Co Ltd — Zhoushan ZJ** Yd No: QF5500-1 Loa 101.28 (BB) Br ex - Dght 6.950 Lbp 95.00 Br md 15.60 Dpth 8.50 Welded, 1 dk	**(A12B2TR) Chemical/Products Tanker** Double Hull (13F) Liq: 6,175; Liq (Oil): 6,175 Compartments: 5 Wing Ta, 5 Wing Ta, 1 Wing Slop Ta, 1 Wing Slop Ta, ER Manifold: Bow/CM: 49.7m Ice Capable	**1 oil engine** reduction geared to sc. shaft driving 1 Propeller Total Power: 2,207kW (3,001hp) 12.0kn Yanmar 6N330-UN 1 x 4 Stroke 6 Cy. 330 x 440 2207kW (3001bhp) Qingdao Zichai Boyang Diesel EngineCo Ltd-China AuxGen: 3 x 250kW 400V a.c Thrusters: 1 Tunnel thruster (f) Fuel: 120.0 (d.f.) 270.0 (r.f.)

IMO / Call sign / Flag	Name / Owner / Manager	Tonnage	Class	Builder / Dimensions	Type	Machinery
9585156 *BKPI5* -	**YONG CHENG 8012** **Zhoushan Yongcheng Shipping Co Ltd** Zhoushan Huacheng Shipping Co Ltd *Zhoushan, Zhejiang* *China* MMSI: 413439220	**2,488** 746 -	Class: CC	**2010-09 Zhejiang Fangyuan Ship Industry Co Ltd — Linhai ZJ** Yd No: FY200815 Loa 71.90 Br ex 17.35 Dght 5.300 Lbp 64.10 Br md 17.00 Dpth 7.00 Welded, 1 dk	**(B21B20T) Offshore Tug/Supply Ship** Ice Capable	**4 oil engines** reduction geared to sc. shafts driving 2 Propellers Total Power: 5,884kW (8,000hp) 13.0kn Chinese Std. Type G6300ZC 4 x 4 Stroke 6 Cy. 300 x 380 each-1471kW (2000bhp) Ningbo CSI Power & Machinery GroupCo Ltd-China AuxGen: 2 x 1100kW 400V a.c, 2 x 350kW 400V a.c
7925120 *BLEQ* -	**YONG DA** *ex* Manger *-1995* **Ningbo Huagang HSC Co Ltd** *Ningbo, Zhejiang* *China*	**200** 60 50	Class: (NV)	**1979-07 AS Fjellstrand Aluminium Yachts — Omastrand** Yd No: 1526 Loa 25.68 Br ex 9.28 Dght 1.201 Lbp - Br md - Dpth 3.51 Welded, 1 dk	**(A37B2PS) Passenger Ship** Hull Material: Aluminium Alloy Passengers: unberthed: 189	**2 oil engines** reverse reduction geared to sc. shafts driving 2 FP propellers Total Power: 1,766kW (2,402hp) M.T.U. 12V396TC62 2 x Vee 4 Stroke 12 Cy. 165 x 185 each-883kW (1201bhp) MTU Friedrichshafen GmbH-Friedrichshafen
7506144 *D8ZW* -	**YONG DUCK** *ex* Daio *-1986* **Yong Ho Shipping Co Ltd** - *Busan* *South Korea* MMSI: 440110200 Official number: BSR-866023	*274* 101 94	Class: KR	**1975-08 Hanasaki Zosensho K.K. — Yokosuka** Yd No: 165 Loa 36.28 Br ex 10.04 Dght 3.963 Lbp 32.69 Br md 10.01 Dpth 4.40 Welded, 1 dk	**(B32A2ST) Tug**	**2 oil engines** driving 2 FP propellers Total Power: 2,354kW (3,200hp) 13.5kn Niigata 6L28BX 2 x 4 Stroke 6 Cy. 280 x 320 each-1177kW (1600bhp) Niigata Engineering Co Ltd-Japan AuxGen: 2 x 64kW 225V 50Hz a.c
8300913 *H9XF* -	**YONG FA MEN** *ex* Texas Gal *-2006* *ex* Eckert Oldendorff *-2006* *ex* Texas Gal *-2004* *ex* Eckert Oldendorff *-2003* *ex* Global Asia *-2000* *ex* Eckert Oldendorff *-1999* *ex* Captain Padon *-1991* *ex* Hyundai No. 22 *-1989* **Deyuan Shipping Co Ltd** Nanjing Ocean Shipping Co Ltd (NASCO) *Panama* *Panama* MMSI: 357092000 Official number: 45655PEXT	**18,220** 10,921 29,338 T/cm 37.2	Class: LR (KR) (AB) **100A1** SS 07/2006 LI **LMC** Eq.Ltr: I†; Cable: 605.0/64.0 U3 (a)	**1983-12 Hyundai Heavy Industries Co Ltd — Ulsan** Yd No: 273 Loa 161.78 (BB) Br ex 26.04 Dght 11.550 Lbp 153.42 Br md 26.01 Dpth 16.11 Welded, 1 dk	**(A31A2GX) General Cargo Ship** Grain: 39,733; Bale: 37,746 TEU 1069 C Ho 548 TEU C Dk 521 TEU Compartments: 4 Ho, ER, 4 Tw Dk 4 Ha: (12.8 x 10.1)3 (25.6 x 17.5)ER Cranes: 4x25t	**1 oil engine** driving 1 FP propeller Total Power: 5,633kW (7,659hp) 13.7kn B&W 5L67GBE 1 x 2 Stroke 5 Cy. 670 x 1700 5633kW (7659bhp) Hyundai Engine & Machinery Co Ltd-South Korea AuxGen: 1 x 500kW 450V 60Hz a.c, 1 x 625kW 450V 60Hz a.c Boilers: AuxB (ex.g.), WTAuxB (o.f.)
9216418 *VRWR6* -	**YONG FENG** **Eastar Shipping Ltd** COSCO (HK) Shipping Co Ltd *Hong Kong* *Hong Kong* MMSI: 477819000 Official number: HK-0624	**39,873** 25,899 74,099 T/cm 64.0	Class: CC (BV) (AB)	**2000-10 Jiangnan Shipyard (Group) Co Ltd — Shanghai** Yd No: H2256 Loa 225.00 (BB) Br ex 32.45 Dght 14.022 Lbp 217.00 Br md 32.26 Dpth 19.20 Welded, 1 dk	**(A21A2BC) Bulk Carrier** Grain: 90,870; Bale: 86,173 Compartments: 7 Ho, ER 7 Ha: (15.5 x 13.2)6 (15.5 x 15.0)ER	**1 oil engine** driving 1 FP propeller Total Power: 8,662kW (11,777hp) 14.4kn MAN-B&W 5S60MC 1 x 2 Stroke 5 Cy. 600 x 2292 8662kW (11777bhp) HHM Shangchuan Diesel Co Ltd-China AuxGen: 3 x 500kW 450V a.c Fuel: 2674.0 (r.f.)
9181807 *3FEB8* -	**YONG FU** *ex* Cocoa Heart *-2011* *ex* Brave Heart *-2005* **Yongfu International Shipping Co Ltd** Fortune Sea International Ship Management Co Ltd SatCom: Inmarsat C 435205910 *Panama* *Panama* MMSI: 352059000 Official number: 2540598CH	**6,178** 3,057 8,555	Class: NK	**1998-02 Nishi Shipbuilding Co Ltd — Imabari EH** Yd No: 408 Loa 100.64 Br ex - Dght 8.189 Lbp 92.75 Br md 18.80 Dpth 13.00 Welded, 1 dk	**(A31A2GX) General Cargo Ship** Grain: 14,711; Bale: 13,536 Compartments: 2 Ho, ER 2 Ha: (21.7 x 12.8) (25.2 x 12.8)ER Cranes: 1x30.5t; Derricks: 2x25t	**1 oil engine** driving 1 FP propeller Total Power: 3,236kW (4,400hp) 12.5kn B&W 5L35MC 1 x 2 Stroke 5 Cy. 350 x 1050 3236kW (4400bhp) Makita Corp-Japan Fuel: 550.0
8746985 - -	**YONG FU** - **Zhen De Zhang**	**395** 250 -		**1995-06 Kaohsiung Shipbuilding Co. Ltd. — Kaohsiung** Yd No: JH1070 Loa 56.00 Br ex - Dght - Lbp - Br md 8.50 Dpth 3.80 Welded, 1 dk	**(A31A2GX) General Cargo Ship**	**1 oil engine** driving 1 FP propeller Total Power: 883kW (1,201hp) Cummins 1 x 4 Stroke 883kW (1201bhp) Cummins Diesel International Ltd-USA
8955354 - -	**YONG GANG HUAN ZHI** **Ningbo Pilot Station** *Ningbo, Zhejiang* *China*	**137** 41 15	Class: CC	**1998-12 No 4806 Shipyard of PLA — Zhoushan ZJ** Loa 33.40 Br ex - Dght - Lbp 31.00 Br md 6.24 Dpth 3.15 Welded, 1 dk	**(A37B2PS) Passenger Ship** Hull Material: Aluminium Alloy	**2 oil engines** geared to sc. shafts driving 2 FP propellers Total Power: 1,298kW (1,764hp) 19.0kn Cummins KTA-38-M2 2 x Vee 4 Stroke 12 Cy. 159 x 159 each-649kW (882bhp) Cummins Engine Co Inc-USA AuxGen: 2 x 75kW 400V a.c
8029301 *BTND* -	**YONG GANG TUO 6** **Government of The People's Republic of China (Ningbo Port Administration Bureau - Ministry of Communications)** - *Ningbo, Zhejiang* *China*	*331* 85 524	Class: (NK)	**1981-03 K.K. Odo Zosen Tekko — Shimonoseki** Yd No: 273 Loa 35.50 Br ex 9.83 Dght 3.440 Lbp 31.00 Br md 9.80 Dpth 4.30 Welded, 1 dk	**(B32A2ST) Tug**	**2 oil engines** sr geared to sc. shafts driving 2 FP propellers Total Power: 2,354kW (3,200hp) 14.0kn Niigata 6L25CX 2 x 4 Stroke 6 Cy. 250 x 320 each-1177kW (1600bhp) Niigata Engineering Co Ltd-Japan AuxGen: 2 x 80kW
8029313 *BTNE* -	**YONG GANG TUO 7** **Government of The People's Republic of China (Ningbo Port Administration Bureau - Ministry of Communications)** - *Ningbo, Zhejiang* *China*	*331* 85 524	Class: (NK)	**1981-03 K.K. Odo Zosen Tekko — Shimonoseki** Yd No: 274 Loa 35.50 Br ex 9.83 Dght 3.440 Lbp 31.00 Br md 9.80 Dpth 4.30 Welded, 1 dk	**(B32A2ST) Tug**	**2 oil engines** sr geared to sc. shafts driving 2 FP propellers Total Power: 2,354kW (3,200hp) 14.0kn Niigata 6L25CX 2 x 4 Stroke 6 Cy. 250 x 320 each-1177kW (1600bhp) Niigata Engineering Co Ltd-Japan AuxGen: 2 x 80kW
8029325 *BTNF* -	**YONG GANG TUO 8** **Government of The People's Republic of China (Ningbo Port Administration Bureau - Ministry of Communications)** - *Ningbo, Zhejiang* *China*	*331* 85 524	Class: (NK)	**1981-05 K.K. Odo Zosen Tekko — Shimonoseki** Yd No: 275 Loa 35.80 Br ex 9.83 Dght 3.600 Lbp 31.00 Br md 9.80 Dpth 4.34 Welded, 1 dk	**(B32A2ST) Tug**	**2 oil engines** sr geared to sc. shafts driving 2 FP propellers Total Power: 2,354kW (3,200hp) 14.0kn Niigata 6L25CX 2 x 4 Stroke 6 Cy. 250 x 320 each-1177kW (1600bhp) Niigata Engineering Co Ltd-Japan AuxGen: 2 x 80kW
8832344 *BLBV* -	**YONG GANG TUO 9** **Government of The People's Republic of China (Ningbo Port Administration Bureau - Ministry of Communications)** - *Ningbo, Zhejiang* *China*	*388* 116 143		**1988 Tianjin Xinhe Shipyard — Tianjin** Loa 35.52 Br ex - Dght 3.140 Lbp 31.00 Br md 9.80 Dpth 4.30 Welded, 1 dk	**(B32A2ST) Tug**	**2 oil engines** reduction geared to sc. shafts driving 2 FP propellers Total Power: 2,354kW (3,200hp) 13.0kn Niigata 8L25BX 2 x 4 Stroke 8 Cy. 250 x 320 each-1177kW (1600bhp) Niigata Engineering Co Ltd-Japan AuxGen: 2 x 90kW 400V a.c
9650640 - -	**YONG GANG TUO 29** *ex* Jiangsu Zhenjiang *-2011* **Government of The People's Republic of China (Ningbo Port Administration Bureau - Ministry of Communications)** -	**450** - -	Class: CC (Class contemplated)	**2011-12 Jiangsu Zhenjiang Shipyard Co Ltd — Zhenjiang JS** Loa 33.00 Br ex - Dght 5.400 Lbp - Br md 11.60 Dpth 5.36 Welded, 1 dk	**(B32A2ST) Tug**	**2 oil engines** reduction geared to sc. shaft (s) driving 2 Z propellers Total Power: 4,412kW (5,998hp) Niigata 8L28HX 2 x 4 Stroke 8 Cy. 280 x 370 each-2206kW (2999bhp) AuxGen: 2 x 100kW a.c Fuel: 93.0
8603303 *H02893* -	**YONG HE 7** *ex* Toyo No. 7 *-2002* **Yong He Shipping Lines Inc** Dalian All Profit Ship Management Co Ltd *Panama* *Panama* MMSI: 354572000 Official number: 2940303B	**1,483** 528 1,758	Class: IT (NK)	**1986-03 Tokushima Zosen Sangyo K.K. — Komatsushima** Yd No: 1890 Loa 71.62 (BB) Br ex - Dght 4.391 Lbp 65.99 Br md 11.80 Dpth 7.38 Welded, 1 dk	**(A31A2GX) General Cargo Ship** Grain: 2,913; Bale: 2,824 TEU 18 C. 18/20'	**1 oil engine** geared to sc. shaft driving 1 CP propeller Total Power: 1,324kW (1,800hp) 11.9kn Hanshin 6EL30G 1 x 4 Stroke 6 Cy. 300 x 600 1324kW (1800bhp) The Hanshin Diesel Works Ltd-Japan
8745606 - -	**YONG HE CAI 338** **Hsien Chen Chien-Jung** -	**493** 291 -		**2006-09 in the People's Republic of China** Loa 52.58 Br ex - Dght - Lbp 48.00 Br md 8.20 Dpth 4.10 Welded, 1 dk	**(A31A2GX) General Cargo Ship**	**1 oil engine** reduction geared to sc. shaft driving 1 FP propeller Total Power: 218kW (296hp) Chinese Std. Type 6190ZLC 1 x 4 Stroke 6 Cy. 190 x 210 218kW (296bhp) Jinan Diesel Engine Co Ltd-China

7028130 - -	**YONG HO I** *ex* Sir Thomas Hiley *-2001* **Yongho Industrial & Development Co Ltd** - *South Korea*	*4,006* 1,300 4,172	Class: (LR) ✠ Classed LR until 8/11/01	**1971-03 Walkers Ltd — Maryborough QLD** Yd No: 59 Loa 102.88 Br ex 16.59 Dght 5.665 Lbp 96.07 Br md 16.46 Dpth 7.24 Welded, 1 dk	**(B33B2DT) Trailing Suction Hopper Dredger** Hopper: 2,301 Compartments: 1 Ho, ER 1 Ha: (3.1 x 2.9)ER Derricks: 2x6t,2x5t	**3 diesel electric oil engines** driving 3 gen. each 1300kW 750V d.c Connecting to 2 elec. motors driving 2 FP propellers Total Power: 5,427kW (7,380hp) 12.0kn Ruston 9ATCM 3 x 4 Stroke 9 Cy. 318 x 368 each-1809kW (2460bhp) Ruston & Hornsby Ltd.-Lincoln AuxGen: 3 x 275kW 415V 50Hz a.c Thrusters: 1 Thwart. FP thruster (f) Fuel: 437.0 (r.f.)
6713764 - -	**YONG HO II** *ex* Geopotes IX *-2002* **Yongho Industrial & Development Co Ltd** - *South Korea*	**7,411** 2,223 8,189	Class: (BV)	**1967-02 NV Werf Gusto v/h Fa A F Smulders — Schiedam** Yd No: C0553 Loa 131.96 Br ex 21.06 Dght 6.800 Lbp 115.02 Br md 21.00 Dpth 10.32 Welded, 1 dk	**(B33B2DT) Trailing Suction Hopper Dredger** Hopper: 6,400 Cranes: 2x10t,1x6t	**2 oil engines** driving 2 FP propellers Total Power: 4,002kW (5,442hp) 12.0kn Smit-Bolnes V316HDK 2 x Vee 2 Stroke 16 Cy. 300 x 550 each-2001kW (2721bhp) Motorenfabriek Smit & Bolnes NV-Netherlands AuxGen: 2 x 570kW 380V 50Hz a.c Thrusters: 1 Thwart. FP thruster (f) Fuel: 792.5 (d.f.)
9571337 *XUGE9* -	**YONG HONG 9** **Shandong Yonghong Shipping Co Ltd** Weihai Huayang International Ship Management Co Ltd SatCom: Inmarsat C 451524610 *Phnom Penh* *Cambodia* MMSI: 515246000	**2,976** 1,924 5,300	Class: UB	**2009-07 Viva Vessel Group Co Ltd — Yueqing ZJ** Loa 97.00 (BB) Br ex - Dght 5.900 Lbp - Br md 15.80 Dpth 7.40 Welded, 1 dk	**(A31A2GX) General Cargo Ship** Compartments: 2 Ho, ER 2 Ha: ER	**1 oil engine** reduction geared to sc. shaft driving 1 FP propeller Total Power: 1,765kW (2,400hp) 11.0kn Guangzhou 8320ZC 1 x 4 Stroke 8 Cy. 320 x 440 1765kW (2400bhp) Guangzhou Diesel Engine Factory CoLtd-China
9016272 *XUBJ5* -	**YONG HONG 10** *ex* Sakura Maru *-2010* **Run Xiang Shipping Co Ltd** Weihai Huayang International Ship Management Co Ltd *Phnom Penh* *Cambodia* MMSI: 514488000 Official number: 1090615	**1,958** 1,057 1,952	Class: UB	**1990-09 Kegoya Dock K.K. — Kure** Yd No: 913 Loa 80.77 (BB) Br ex 13.82 Dght 4.241 Lbp 75.00 Br md 13.80 Dpth 7.35 Welded	**(A31A2GX) General Cargo Ship** Compartments: 1 Ho, ER	**1 oil engine** reverse geared to sc. shaft driving 1 FP propeller Total Power: 1,471kW (2,000hp) Niigata 6M34AGT 1 x 4 Stroke 6 Cy. 340 x 620 1471kW (2000bhp) Niigata Engineering Co Ltd-Japan Thrusters: 1 Thwart. FP thruster (f)
9635597 *BKWB5* -	**YONG HONG 168** **Zhoushan Yonghong Shipping Co Ltd** - SatCom: Inmarsat C 441369254 *Zhoushan, Zhejiang* *China* MMSI: 413445940	**7,647** 3,649 11,996	Class: CC	**2012-06 Ningbo Dongfang Shipyard Co Ltd — Ningbo ZJ** Yd No: DFC11-121 Loa 119.90 Br ex - Dght 8.430 Lbp 112.80 Br md 20.00 Dpth 11.50 Welded, 1 dk	**(A13B2TP) Products Tanker** Double Hull (13F) Liq: 12,632; Liq (Oil): 12,632 Compartments: 5 Wing Ta, 5 Wing Ta, 1 Wing Slop Ta, 1 Wing Slop Ta, ER Ice Capable	**1 oil engine** reduction geared to sc. shaft driving 1 FP propeller Total Power: 3,310kW (4,500hp) 11.5kn Yanmar 8N330-EN 1 x 4 Stroke 8 Cy. 330 x 440 3310kW (4500bhp) Qingdao Zichai Boyang Diesel EngineCo Ltd-China AuxGen: 3 x 600kW 400V a.c
7737913 *BVUP* -	**YONG HSIN** **Ocean Fishery Development Administration** - *Kaohsiung* *Chinese Taipei* Official number: 2826	*205* 98 -	Class: (CR)	**1968 Taiwan Machinery Manufacturing Corp. — Kaohsiung** Loa 34.60 Br ex 6.35 Dght 2.642 Lbp 30.48 Br md 6.20 Dpth 3.00 Welded, 1 dk	**(B11B2FV) Fishing Vessel** Compartments: 3 Ho, ER 3 Ha: 3 (1.0 x 1.0)	**1 oil engine** driving 1 FP propeller Total Power: 405kW (551hp) Alpha 405-26VO 1 x 2 Stroke 5 Cy. 260 x 400 405kW (551bhp) Taiwan Machinery ManufacturingCorp.-Kaohsiung AuxGen: 1 x 64kW 220V a.c, 1 x 40kW 220V a.c
7642118 *9WAL7* -	**YONG HUA** *ex* Salviking *-1990* **Tang Tiew Yong** - *Labuan* *Malaysia* MMSI: 533405000 Official number: 325677	**1,178** 807 861	Class: (NK)	**1975 Selco Shipyard Pte Ltd — Singapore** Converted From: Salvage Vessel-2000 Converted From: Crane Ship-1984 Lengthened & Widened-1990 Loa 71.30 Br ex - Dght 3.262 Lbp 66.80 Br md 17.22 Dpth 3.97 Welded, 1 dk	**(A31A2GX) General Cargo Ship** Cranes: 1x200t; Derricks: 1x15t	**2 oil engines** geared to sc. shafts driving 2 FP propellers Total Power: 1,228kW (1,670hp) 10.0kn Caterpillar D398 2 x Vee 4 Stroke 12 Cy. 159 x 203 each-614kW (835bhp) (new engine 1975) Caterpillar Tractor Co-USA
8947929 *9WDN7* -	**YONG HUA 2** **Yong Hua Marine Sdn Bhd** - *Kuching* *Malaysia* MMSI: 533404000 Official number: 329001	**2,359** 707 -	Class: (BV)	**1994 Yong Hing Shipyard Co — Sibu** Loa 85.37 Br ex - Dght 3.474 Lbp - Br md 21.34 Dpth 4.80 Welded, 1 dk	**(A31A2GX) General Cargo Ship**	**3 oil engines** geared to sc. shafts driving 3 FP propellers Total Power: 1,902kW (2,586hp) Caterpillar D398TA 3 x Vee 4 Stroke 12 Cy. 159 x 203 each-634kW (862bhp) Caterpillar Inc-USA
9236169 *VRWS2* -	**YONG HUAN** **Well Crown Shipping Ltd** COSCO (HK) Shipping Co Ltd *Hong Kong* *Hong Kong* MMSI: 477820000 Official number: HK-0628	**40,437** 25,855 74,823 T/cm 67.0	Class: CC	**2000-10 Hudong Shipbuilding Group — Shanghai** Yd No: H1281A Loa 225.00 (BB) Br ex - Dght 14.250 Lbp 217.00 Br md 32.26 Dpth 19.60 Welded, 1 dk	**(A21A2BC) Bulk Carrier** Grain: 91,718; Bale: 89,882 Compartments: 7 Ho, ER 7 Ha: (14.6 x 13.2)6 (14.6 x 15.0)ER	**1 oil engine** driving 1 FP propeller Total Power: 10,200kW (13,868hp) 14.5kn MAN-B&W 5S60MC 1 x 2 Stroke 5 Cy. 600 x 2292 10200kW (13868bhp) Hudong Heavy Machinery Co Ltd-China AuxGen: 3 x 530kW 450V a.c
8982204 *HO3589* -	**YONG HUI** *ex* Fu Yuan Yu F69 *-2004* *ex* Xing Hai 218 *-2004* **Yong Hui Shipping (Hong Kong) Ltd** - *Panama* *Panama* MMSI: 351598000 Official number: 32260PEXT	**436** 144 -		**1984 Fuzhou Highseas Ship Engineering Co Ltd — Fuzhou FJ** Loa 52.00 Br ex - Dght 3.200 Lbp 45.50 Br md 7.80 Dpth 3.80 Welded, 1 dk	**(B12C2FL) Live Fish Carrier (Well Boat)**	**1 oil engine** driving 1 Propeller Total Power: 405kW (551hp) Daihatsu 6DSM-26FS 1 x 4 Stroke 6 Cy. 260 x 320 405kW (551bhp) Daihatsu Diesel Manufacturing Co Lt-Japan
9701073 *BKSV6* -	**YONG JI 58** **Zhoushan Yong Ji Shipping Co Ltd** - *Zhoushan, Zhejiang* *China* MMSI: 413452950 Official number: CN20104685479	**4,406** 2,007 6,700	Class: CC	**2014-02 Ningbo Dacheng Shengli Shipyard — Ninghai County ZJ** Yd No: NDC2010-05 Loa 103.09 Br ex - Dght 7.100 Lbp 96.50 Br md 16.00 Dpth 8.80 Welded, 1 dk	**(A12B2TR) Chemical/Products Tanker** Double Hull (13F)	**1 oil engine** reduction geared to sc. shaft driving 1 FP propeller Total Power: 2,720kW (3,698hp) MAN-B&W 8L27/38 1 x 4 Stroke 8 Cy. 270 x 380 2720kW (3698bhp) ZGPT Diesel Heavy Industry Co Ltd-China
9236183 *VRWY3* -	**YONG JIA** **Silvercord Shipping Ltd** COSCO (HK) Shipping Co Ltd *Hong Kong* *Hong Kong* MMSI: 477872000 Official number: HK-0677	**40,437** 25,855 74,870 T/cm 67.0	Class: CC	**2001-03 Hudong Shipbuilding Group — Shanghai** Yd No: H1283A Loa 225.00 (BB) Br ex - Dght 14.250 Lbp 217.00 Br md 32.26 Dpth 19.60 Welded, 1 dk	**(A21A2BC) Bulk Carrier** Grain: 91,718; Bale: 89,882 Compartments: 7 Ho, ER 7 Ha: (14.6 x 13.2)6 (14.6 x 15.0)ER	**1 oil engine** driving 1 FP propeller Total Power: 10,224kW (13,901hp) 14.5kn MAN-B&W 5S60MC 1 x 2 Stroke 5 Cy. 600 x 2292 10224kW (13901bhp) Hudong Heavy Machinery Co Ltd-China AuxGen: 3 x 530kW 450V a.c
8300937 *3EOB5* -	**YONG JIA MEN** *ex* Nordana Rebecca *-2008* *ex* Eibe Oldendorff *-2006* *ex* Georgia Gal *-2005* *ex* Eibe Oldendorff *-2004* *ex* Global America *-2000* *ex* Eibe Oldendorff *-1999* *ex* Captain Bougainville *-1991* *ex* Hyundai No. 23 *-1989* **NYC Shipping Inc** Nanjing Ocean Shipping Co Ltd (NASCO) *Panama* *Panama* MMSI: 356535000 Official number: 45627PEXT	**18,220** 10,921 29,499 T/cm 37.2	Class: KR (AB)	**1983-12 Hyundai Heavy Industries Co Ltd — Ulsan** Yd No: 283 Loa 161.80 (BB) Br ex 26.04 Dght 11.515 Lbp 153.42 Br md 26.01 Dpth 16.11 Welded, 1 dk	**(A31A2GX) General Cargo Ship** Grain: 39,733; Bale: 37,746 TEU 1069 C Ho 548 TEU C Dk 521 TEU Compartments: 4 Ho, ER, 4 Tw Dk 4 Ha: (12.8 x 10.1)3 (25.6 x 17.5)ER Cranes: 4x25t	**1 oil engine** driving 1 FP propeller Total Power: 5,634kW (7,660hp) 13.7kn B&W 5L67GBE 1 x 2 Stroke 5 Cy. 670 x 1700 5634kW (7660bhp) Hyundai Engine & Machinery Co Ltd-South Korea AuxGen: 2 x 500kW 450V a.c
9586394 *9LY2244* -	**YONG JUN** **Zhejiang Yong Jun Shipping Co Ltd** Hong Kong Yongli Shipping Co Ltd *Freetown* *Sierra Leone* MMSI: 667003047 Official number: SL103047	**2,960** 1,741 3,500	Class: SL	**2010-02 Taizhou Yuanyang Shipbuilding Co Ltd — Linhai ZJ** Yd No: CYC08-07 Loa 98.22 Br ex - Dght 5.540 Lbp 91.00 Br md 16.20 Dpth 6.95 Welded, 1 dk	**(A21A2BC) Bulk Carrier**	**1 oil engine** reduction geared to sc. shaft driving 1 Propeller Total Power: 1,100kW (1,496hp) Chinese Std. Type G8300ZC 1 x 4 Stroke 8 Cy. 300 x 380 1100kW (1496bhp) in China

IMO / Call sign	Name, owner, registry	Tonnage	Class	Build, builder, dimensions	Type, cargo	Machinery
743749 *LY2294*	**YONG JUN 17** *ex* Yong Jun 7 *-2010* *ex* Tai Ping Shan 28 *-2010* **Zhejiang Yong Jun Shipping Co Ltd** Hong Kong Yongli Shipping Co Ltd *Freetown* *Sierra Leone* MMSI: 667003097 Official number: SL103097	**2,967** 1,782 5,346	Class: SL	**2009-05 Linhai Hangchang Shipbuilding Co Ltd — Linhai ZJ** Yd No: HC0906 Loa 96.90 Br ex - Dght 5.850 Lbp 89.80 Br md 15.80 Dpth 7.40 Welded, 1 dk	**(A34A2GR) Refrigerated Cargo Ship**	**1 oil engine** reduction geared to sc. shaft driving 1 FP propeller Total Power: 1,765kW (2,400hp) 11.0kn Chinese Std. Type 1 x 4 Stroke 1765kW (2400bhp) Wuxi Antai Power Machinery Co Ltd-China
640360 *KNF6*	**YONG JUN 101** *ex* Zhou Hang 1 *-2013* **Zhejiang Yongjun Marine Shipping Co Ltd** Zhejiang Huale Ocean Shipping Co Ltd SatCom: Inmarsat C 441369260 *Zhoushan, Zhejiang* *China* MMSI: 413446370 Official number: CN20115769553	**4,675** 2,486 6,667	Class: CC	**2012-06 Ningbo Jintao Shipbuilding Co Ltd — Ningbo ZJ** Yd No: JT1001 Loa 112.11 Br ex 16.43 Dght 6.350 Lbp 105.00 Br md 16.40 Dpth 8.40 Welded, 1 dk	**(A31A2GX) General Cargo Ship** Grain: 8,353 Compartments: 2 Ho, ER 2 Ha: ER 2 (30.7 x 9.8) Ice Capable	**1 oil engine** reduction geared to sc. shaft driving 1 FP propeller Total Power: 2,206kW (2,999hp) 11.8kn Guangzhou 8320ZC 1 x 4 Stroke 8 Cy. 320 x 440 2206kW (2999bhp) Guangzhou Diesel Engine Factory CoLtd-China AuxGen: 2 x 150kW 400V a.c
149586	**YONG KWANG** **Yong Ho Shipping Co Ltd** - *Busan* *South Korea* MMSI: 440100697 Official number: BSR-960466	**104** - -	Class: KR	**1996-05 Kyeong-In Engineering & Shipbuilding Co Ltd — Incheon** Yd No: 549 Loa 25.80 Br ex - Dght - Lbp 23.70 Br md 8.00 Dpth 3.60 Welded, 1 dk	**(B32A2ST) Tug**	**2 oil engines** with clutches, flexible couplings & dr geared to sc. shafts driving 2 FP propellers Total Power: 1,538kW (2,092hp) Cummins KTA-38-M 2 x Vee 4 Stroke 12 Cy. 159 x 159 each-769kW (1046bhp) Cummins Engine Co Ltd-United Kingdom
625210 *EFL9*	**YONG LI** *ex* Fu Yuan Yu F63 *-2006* *ex* Tenyo Maru No. 35 *-2003* **Feida International Marine Co Ltd** - *Panama* *Panama* MMSI: 354596000 Official number: 34627PEXT1	**1,594** 802 -		**1987-05 K.K. Yoshida Zosen Kogyo — Arida** Lengthened-2006 L reg 82.80 Br ex - Dght 4.200 Lbp 78.32 Br md 12.20 Dpth 6.51 Welded, 1 dk	**(B33A2DG) Grab Dredger**	**2 oil engines** driving 1 FP propeller Total Power: 2,648kW (3,600hp) 10.0kn Yanmar MF33-UT 2 x 4 Stroke 6 Cy. 330 x 620 each-1324kW (1800bhp) Yanmar Diesel Engine Co Ltd-Japan
228007 *RXD6*	**YONG LI** **Evergold Transportation Ltd** COSCO (HK) Shipping Co Ltd *Hong Kong* *Hong Kong* MMSI: 477912000 Official number: HK-0721	**38,641** 25,939 74,382	Class: CC (AB)	**2001-06 Oshima Shipbuilding Co Ltd — Saikai NS** Yd No: 10285 Loa 225.00 (BB) Br ex - Dght 13.920 Lbp 216.00 Br md 32.26 Dpth 18.90 Welded, 1 dk	**(A21A2BC) Bulk Carrier** Grain: 86,421; Bale: 84,851 Compartments: 7 Ho, ER 7 Ha: ER	**1 oil engine** driving 1 FP propeller Total Power: 8,290kW (11,271hp) 14.0kn B&W 7S50MC-C 1 x 2 Stroke 7 Cy. 500 x 2000 8290kW (11271bhp) Kawasaki Heavy Industries Ltd-Japan
469429 *MK*	**YONG LONG** - **Shanghai Shenglong Shipping Co Ltd** - *Shanghai* *China* MMSI: 412376020 Official number: CN20077828873	**13,774** 7,713 21,230		**2009-02 China Shipping Industry (Jiangsu) Co Ltd — Jiangdu JS** Loa 159.25 (BB) Br ex - Dght 9.400 Lbp 149.60 Br md 24.00 Dpth 13.00 Welded, 1 dk	**(A21A2BC) Bulk Carrier** Grain: 71,634 Compartments: 4 Ho, ER 4 Ha: ER Cranes: 3x25t	**1 oil engine** reduction geared to sc. shaft driving 1 FP propeller Total Power: 4,400kW (5,982hp) 14.2kn Pielstick 8PC2-6 1 x 4 Stroke 8 Cy. 400 x 460 4400kW (5982bhp) in China AuxGen: 3 x 350kW 400V a.c
124307 *JZM*	**YONG LONG FA** *ex* Yorkgate *-2001* **Yangpu Chang Long Marine Co** - SatCom: Inmarsat C 441213415 *Yangpu, Hainan* *China* MMSI: 412522920	**23,604** 14,095 38,377 T/cm 46.1	Class: (LR) (NV) ✠ Classed LR until 9/12/87	**1984-03 'Georgi Dimitrov' Shipyard — Varna** Yd No: 072 Loa 198.61 (BB) Br ex 27.87 Dght 11.189 Lbp 187.71 Br md 27.81 Dpth 15.60 Welded, 1 dk	**(A21A2BC) Bulk Carrier** Grain: 46,066; Bale: 42,481 Compartments: 7 Ho, ER 7 Ha: (12.8 x 11.2)6 (12.8 x 12.5)ER Cranes: 5x25t Ice Capable	**1 oil engine** driving 1 FP propeller Total Power: 8,500kW (11,557hp) 14.5kn Sulzer 6RND68 1 x 2 Stroke 6 Cy. 680 x 1250 8500kW (11557bhp) Zaklady Przemyslu Metalowego 'HCegielski' SA-Poznan AuxGen: 3 x 504kW 400V 50Hz a.c Fuel: 350.0 (d.f.) (Part Heating Coils) 1749.5 (r.f.)
124319 *JZN*	**YONG LONG JIU** *ex* Cape Cornwall *-2001* *ex* Bristol Lake *-1995* *ex* Montego Bay *-1988* *ex* Jonathan J *-1988* **Yangpu Chang Long Marine Co** - SatCom: Inmarsat C 441213615 *Yangpu, Hainan* *China* MMSI: 412522930	**23,609** 14,104 38,450 T/cm 46.1	Class: (LR) (NV) ✠ Classed LR until 17/12/87	**1984-08 'Georgi Dimitrov' Shipyard — Varna** Yd No: 073 Loa 198.61 (BB) Br ex 27.87 Dght 11.199 Lbp 187.71 Br md 27.81 Dpth 15.60 Welded, 1 dk	**(A21A2BC) Bulk Carrier** Grain: 46,066; Bale: 42,481 Compartments: 7 Ho, ER 7 Ha: (12.8 x 11.2)6 (12.8 x 12.5)ER Cranes: 4x25t Ice Capable	**1 oil engine** driving 1 FP propeller Total Power: 8,500kW (11,557hp) 14.5kn Sulzer 6RND68 1 x 2 Stroke 6 Cy. 680 x 1250 8500kW (11557bhp) Zaklady Przemyslu Metalowego 'HCegielski' SA-Poznan AuxGen: 3 x 520kW 380V 50Hz a.c, 1 x 32kW 380V 50Hz a.c Fuel: 350.0 (d.f.) (Part Heating Coils) 1749.5 (r.f.)
657088	**YONG MA NO. 1** **Yong Ma Shipping Co Ltd** - *Changwon* *South Korea* MMSI: 440151580 Official number: MSR-123508	*266* 153 153	Class: KR	**2012-05 Samkwang Shipbuilding & Engineering Co Ltd — Incheon** Yd No: SKSB-203 Loa 36.50 Br ex 10.02 Dght 3.312 Lbp 31.15 Br md 10.00 Dpth 4.50 Welded, 1 dk	**(B32A2ST) Tug**	**2 oil engines** reduction geared to sc. shafts driving 2 FP propellers Total Power: 3,308kW (4,498hp) Niigata 6L28HX 2 x 4 Stroke 6 Cy. 280 x 370 each-1654kW (2249bhp) Niigata Engineering Co Ltd-Japan
238163 *8GJ*	**YONG MA No. 3** *ex* Asakaze Maru *-1983* **Yong Ma Shipping Co Ltd** - *Masan* *South Korea* MMSI: 440101206 Official number: MSR-724050	*214* 73 70	Class: KR	**1972 Hanasaki Zosensho K.K. — Yokosuka** Yd No: 152 Loa 32.11 Br ex 8.82 Dght 3.302 Lbp 30.82 Br md 8.79 Dpth 3.89 Welded, 1 dk	**(B32A2ST) Tug**	**2 oil engines** driving 2 FP propellers Total Power: 1,912kW (2,600hp) 12.0kn Niigata 6L25BX 2 x 4 Stroke 6 Cy. 250 x 320 each-956kW (1300bhp) Niigata Engineering Co Ltd-Japan AuxGen: 1 x 88kW 225V a.c Fuel: 32.0 3.0pd
415756 *SDR350*	**YONG MA No. 5** *ex* Ran Maru *-1994* *ex* Suzuran Maru *-1990* **Yong Ma Shipping Co Ltd** - *Masan* *South Korea* Official number: MSR-946647	**148** - 61	Class: KR	**1984-11 Hikari Kogyo K.K. — Yokosuka** Yd No: 337 Loa 30.99 Br ex 8.82 Dght 2.540 Lbp 27.01 Br md 8.81 Dpth 3.51 Welded, 1 dk	**(B32A2ST) Tug**	**2 oil engines** driving 2 FP propellers Total Power: 2,206kW (3,000hp) 12.4kn Yanmar 6T260L-ET 2 x 4 Stroke 6 Cy. 260 x 330 each-1103kW (1500bhp) Yanmar Diesel Engine Co Ltd-Japan AuxGen: 2 x 56kW 225V a.c
429201 *8GE*	**YONG MA No. 7** *ex* Sakata Maru *-1980* *ex* Teizan Maru *-1980* **Yong Ma Shipping Co Ltd** - *Masan* *South Korea* MMSI: 440122830 Official number: MSR-634026	*120* 36 14	Class: (KR)	**1963 Tohoku Shipbuilding Co Ltd — Shiogama MG** Yd No: 41 Loa 24.69 Br ex 7.73 Dght 2.286 Lbp 22.00 Br md 7.31 Dpth 3.20 Welded, 1 dk	**(B32A2ST) Tug**	**2 oil engines** driving 2 FP propellers Total Power: 1,176kW (1,598hp) 11.8kn Matsui 2 x 4 Stroke 6 Cy. 270 x 400 each-588kW (799bhp) Matsui Iron Works Co Ltd-Japan AuxGen: 2 x 16kW 205V a.c
803874	**YONG MA No. 11** *ex* Hokuto *-1996* **Yong Ma Shipping Co Ltd** - *Masan* *South Korea* MMSI: 440116940 Official number: MRS-966528	**172** - 77	Class: KR	**1988-03 Hanasaki Zosensho K.K. — Yokosuka** Yd No: 205 Loa 32.26 Br ex 9.02 Dght 3.001 Lbp 29.01 Br md 8.81 Dpth 3.81 Welded, 1 dk	**(B32A2ST) Tug**	**2 oil engines** with clutches, flexible couplings & reduction geared to sc. shafts driving 2 FP propellers Total Power: 2,160kW (2,936hp) 13.5kn Pielstick 6PA5L255 2 x 4 Stroke 6 Cy. 255 x 270 each-1080kW (1468bhp) Niigata Engineering Co Ltd-Japan AuxGen: 2 x 80kW 220V 60Hz a.c
009542	**YONG MA NO. 17** *ex* Wakaba *-2005* **Yong Ma Shipping Co Ltd** - *Masan* *South Korea* MMSI: 440101871 Official number: MSR-017042	*232* - -	Class: KR	**1990-09 Hanasaki Zosensho K.K. — Yokosuka** Yd No: 218 Loa 36.30 Br ex 10.22 Dght 3.180 Lbp 30.80 Br md 10.00 Dpth 4.40 Welded, 1 dk	**(B32A2ST) Tug**	**2 oil engines** with clutches, flexible couplings & reduction geared to sc. shafts driving 2 FP propellers Total Power: 2,648kW (3,600hp) 14.2kn Niigata 6L28HX 2 x 4 Stroke 6 Cy. 280 x 370 each-1324kW (1800bhp) Niigata Engineering Co Ltd-Japan
741387	**YONG MA NO. 21** **Yong Ma Shipping Co Ltd** - *Masan* *South Korea* Official number: MSR-085368	*189* - 120	Class: KR	**2008-11 Samkwang Shipbuilding & Engineering Co Ltd — Incheon** Yd No: 07-10 Loa 33.50 Br ex - Dght 3.062 Lbp 28.00 Br md 9.20 Dpth 4.00 Welded, 1 dk	**(B32A2ST) Tug**	**2 oil engines** reduction geared to sc. shafts driving 2 Propellers Total Power: 1,946kW (2,646hp) 13.7kn Niigata 6MG26HLX 2 x 4 Stroke 6 Cy. 260 x 350 each-973kW (1323bhp) Niigata Engineering Co Ltd-Japan
619701	**YONG MA NO. 25** **Yong Ma Shipping Co Ltd** Yong Ma Shipping Co Ltd (Seoul) *Changwon* *South Korea* Official number: MSR-113514	**269** - 181	Class: KR	**2011-05 Samkwang Shipbuilding & Engineering Co Ltd — Incheon** Yd No: SKSB-193 Loa 36.50 Br ex 10.02 Dght 3.312 Lbp 31.00 Br md 10.00 Dpth 4.50 Welded, 1 dk	**(B32A2ST) Tug**	**2 oil engines** reduction geared to sc. shafts driving 2 Propellers Total Power: 3,676kW (4,998hp) Niigata 6L28HX 2 x 4 Stroke 6 Cy. 280 x 370 each-1838kW (2499bhp) Niigata Engineering Co Ltd-Japan

8504624 *DSBC750* -	**YONG NAM No. 1** *ex* Koho Maru *-1996* **SNC Co Ltd** - *Busan* *South Korea* Official number: BSR962226	**193** - 89	Class: KR	**1985-04 K.K. Odo Zosen Tekko — Shimonoseki** Yd No: 312 Loa 34.02 Br ex 9.45 Dght 3.101 Lbp 29.01 Br md 9.20 Dpth 4.02 Welded, 1 dk	**(B32A2ST) Tug**	**2 oil engines** with clutches, flexible couplings & dr geared to sc. shafts driving 2 FP propellers Total Power: 2,500kW (3,400hp) Fuji 6L27.5 2 x 4 Stroke 6 Cy. 275 x 320 each-1250kW (1700bhp) Fuji Diesel Co Ltd-Japan
8718457 *XUAZ3* -	**YONG PING** *ex* Jin Yang *-2007* *ex* Daifuku Maru No. 8 *-1999* **All Profit Shipping Co Ltd** Dalian All Profit Ship Management Co Ltd SatCom: Inmarsat C 451426210 *Phnom Penh* *Cambodia* MMSI: 514262000 Official number: 9988044	**1,336** 564 1,600		**1988-05 K.K. Matsuura Zosensho — Osakikamijima** Yd No: 355 Loa 73.82 Br ex 11.54 Dght 4.361 Lbp 68.00 Br md 11.50 Dpth 7.00 Welded, 2 dks	**(A31A2GX) General Cargo Ship** Grain: 2,894; Bale: 2,527 Compartments: 1 Ho, ER 1 Ha: ER	**1 oil engine** with clutches, flexible couplings & sr reverse geared to sc. shaft driving 1 FP propeller Total Power: 1,030kW (1,400hp) Hanshin LH28 1 x 4 Stroke 6 Cy. 280 x 460 1030kW (1400bhp) The Hanshin Diesel Works Ltd-Japan
8316376 *3EBW4* -	**YONG PING 5** *ex* Virginia *-2010* *ex* Tokyo Commander *-1991* *launched as* Sanko Walnut *-1985* **Safe-Forever Shipping Co** Yang Pu Zhe Hai Shipping (Hong Kong) Co Ltd SatCom: Inmarsat A 1332113 *Panama* *Panama* MMSI: 353180000 Official number: 1525185H	**15,786** 9,209 26,523 T/cm 37.6	Class: NK	**1985-09 KK Kanasashi Zosen — Toyohashi AI** Yd No: 3065 Loa 167.20 (BB) Br ex - Dght 9.541 Lbp 160.00 Br md 26.00 Dpth 13.30 Welded, 1 dk	**(A21A2BC) Bulk Carrier** Grain: 33,867; Bale: 32,650 Compartments: 5 Ho, ER 5 Ha: (13.8 x 13.0)4 (19.2 x 13.0)ER Cranes: 4x25.4t	**1 oil engine** driving 1 FP propeller Total Power: 5,075kW (6,900hp) 14.0k B&W 6L50MC 1 x 2 Stroke 6 Cy. 500 x 1620 5075kW (6900bhp) Mitsui Engineering & Shipbuilding CLtd-Japan AuxGen: 3 x 360kW 450V 60Hz a.c Fuel: 127.0 (d.f.) (Heating Coils) 1254.5 (r.f.) 20.0pd
9238894 - -	**YONG SEONG** - **Heung Hae Co Ltd** - *Incheon* *South Korea* Official number: ICR-002701	**157** - -	Class: KR	**2000-10 DH Shipbuilding Co Ltd — Incheon** Yd No: 001 Loa 31.50 Br ex - Dght - Lbp 26.80 Br md 8.60 Dpth 3.60 Welded, 1 dk	**(B32A2ST) Tug**	**2 oil engines** geared to sc. shafts driving 2 FP propellers Total Power: 1,912kW (2,600hp) 11.8k Niigata 6MG22H 2 x 4 Stroke 6 Cy. 220 x 280 each-956kW (1300bhp) Niigata Engineering Co Ltd-Japan
9401087 - -	**YONG SEONG** - **Yong Ho Shipping Co Ltd** - *Busan* *South Korea* Official number: BSR-060648	**221** - -	Class: KR	**2006-06 Samkwang Shipbuilding & Engineering Co Ltd — Incheon** Yd No: 05-12 Loa 37.50 Br ex 9.68 Dght 3.500 Lbp 32.20 Br md 9.50 Dpth 4.50 Welded, 1 dk	**(B32A2ST) Tug**	**2 oil engines** reduction geared to sc. shafts driving 2 Propellers Total Power: 3,310kW (4,500hp) Niigata 6L28H 2 x 4 Stroke 6 Cy. 280 x 370 each-1655kW (2250bhp) Niigata Engineering Co Ltd-Japan
9651670 - -	**YONG SEONG 3** - **Yong Ho Shipping Co Ltd** - *Busan* *South Korea* Official number: BSR-120009	**407** - 219	Class: KR	**2012-02 Samkwang Shipbuilding & Engineering Co Ltd — Incheon** Yd No: SKSB-200 Loa 39.85 Br ex 10.52 Dght 3.662 Lbp 34.50 Br md 10.50 Dpth 4.70 Welded, 1 dk	**(B32A2ST) Tug**	**2 oil engines** reduction geared to sc. shafts driving 2 Propellers Total Power: 4,264kW (5,798hp) Niigata 8MG28H 2 x 4 Stroke 8 Cy. 280 x 370 each-2132kW (2899bhp) Niigata Engineering Co Ltd-Japan Fuel: 75.0 (d.f.)
9243813 *VRCA4* -	**YONG SHENG** *ex* Greta-C *-2006* *launched as* Dina-C *-2002* **COSCOL (HK) Investment & Development Co Ltd** COSCO Shipping Co Ltd (COSCOL) *Hong Kong* *Hong Kong* MMSI: 477265600 Official number: HK-1737	**14,357** 6,985 19,150 T/cm 35.3	Class: LR ✠ **100A1** SS 09/2012 strengthened for heavy cargoes, containers in holds and on upper deck hatch covers LI Finnish-Swedish Ice Class 1A at draught of 8.61m Max/min draught forward 8.69/3.55m Max/min draught aft 8.69/5.70m ✠ **LMC** **UMS** Eq.Ltr: G†; Cable: 588.0/60.0 U3 (a)	**2002-09 B.V. Scheepswerf Damen Hoogezand — Foxhol** Yd No: 823 **2002-09 Santierul Naval Damen Galati S.A. — Galati** (Hull) Yd No: 995 Loa 159.99 (BB) Br ex 23.78 Dght 8.443 Lbp 152.34 Br md 23.70 Dpth 11.95 Welded, 1 dk	**(A31A2GX) General Cargo Ship** Double Bottom Entire Compartment Length Grain: 26,836 TEU 1226 C Ho 530 TEU C Dk 696 TEU incl 110 ref C. Compartments: 2 Ho, ER Cranes: 3x45t Ice Capable	**1 oil engine** driving 1 CP propeller Total Power: 7,860kW (10,686hp) 14.9k B&W 6S46MC- 1 x 2 Stroke 6 Cy. 460 x 1932 7860kW (10686bhp) MAN B&W Diesel A/S-Denmark AuxGen: 1 x 1500kW 400V 50Hz a.c, 2 x 625kW 400V 50Hz a.c Boilers: TOH (o.f.) 10.2kgf/cm² (10.0bar), TOH (ex.g.) 10.2kgf/cm² (10.0bar) Thrusters: 1 Thwart. CP thruster (f)
8400220 *3FWP* -	**YONG SHENG** *ex* Wan Fu *-2014* *ex* Barcelona *-2012* *ex* Brothers *-2007* *ex* Tulip Islands *-1993* *ex* Sanko Pinnacle *-1986* **Win Shipping Ltd** Wan Jia International Shipping & Trading Ltd *Panama* *Panama* MMSI: 373793000 Official number: 43661PEXT1	**16,605** 9,208 27,573 T/cm 37.4	Class: (BV) (NK)	**1984-12 Mitsui Eng. & SB. Co. Ltd. — Tamano** Yd No: 1310 Loa 168.31 (BB) Br ex - Dght 9.765 Lbp 158.60 Br md 26.01 Dpth 13.64 Welded, 1 dk	**(A21A2BC) Bulk Carrier** Grain: 34,666; Bale: 33,417 Compartments: 5 Ho, ER 5 Ha: (9.5 x 13.3)4 (18.9 x 13.3)ER Cranes: 4x25t	**1 oil engine** driving 1 FP propeller Total Power: 4,685kW (6,370hp) 13.0k B&W 6L50MC 1 x 2 Stroke 6 Cy. 500 x 1620 4685kW (6370bhp) Mitsui Engineering & Shipbuilding CLtd-Japan AuxGen: 3 x 400kW 450V 60Hz a.c Fuel: 102.0 (d.f.) (Heating Coils) 1360.0 (r.f.) 21.5pd
9456082 - -	**YONG SHENG 36** - - - *China*	**4,575** 2,417 7,677		**2007-03 Zhejiang Dongfang Shipbuilding Co Ltd — Yueqing ZJ** Yd No: DF18 Loa 117.00 Br ex - Dght 6.300 Lbp 108.00 Br md 16.80 Dpth 8.60 Welded, 1 dk	**(A13B2TP) Products Tanker** Double Hull (13F) Liq: 8,436; Liq (Oil): 8,436 Compartments: 10 Wing Ta, ER, 2 Wing Slop Ta 2 Cargo Pump (s): 2x500m³/hr	**1 oil engine** reduction geared to sc. shaft driving 1 FP propeller Total Power: 2,060kW (2,801hp) 12.0k Guangzhou 8320Z 1 x 4 Stroke 8 Cy. 320 x 440 2060kW (2801bhp) Guangzhou Diesel Engine Factory CoLtd-China
9398589 *BKQB4* -	**YONG SHENG HUA 3** *ex* Song Tai Shan 18 *-2009* **Zhoushan Yongsheng Shipping Co Ltd** - *Zhoushan, Zhejiang* *China* MMSI: 412435010	**887** 497 1,234	Class: (CC)	**2006-02 Zhejiang Dongpeng Shipbuilding & Repair Co Ltd — Zhoushan ZJ** Loa 62.66 Br ex - Dght 3.950 Lbp 56.60 Br md 10.20 Dpth 4.90 Welded, 1 dk	**(A12B2TR) Chemical/Products Tanker** Double Hull (13F) Liq: 1,239; Liq (Oil): 1,239 Compartments: 8 Wing Ta, ER	**1 oil engine** geared to sc. shaft driving 1 FP propeller Total Power: 551kW (749hp) 9.6k Chinese Std. Type 6300ZL 1 x 4 Stroke 6 Cy. 300 x 380 551kW (749bhp) Zibo Diesel Engine Factory-China
9592161 *BKRX5* -	**YONG SHENG HUA 7** - **Zhoushan Yongsheng Shipping Co Ltd** - SatCom: Inmarsat C 441301628 *Zhoushan, Zhejiang* *China* MMSI: 413439740	**5,233** 2,416 7,849 T/cm 17.9	Class: CC	**2011-03 Taizhou Hongda Shipbuilding Co Ltd — Linhai ZJ** Yd No: 2007-01 Loa 117.28 (BB) Br ex 18.03 Dght 7.000 Lbp 108.00 Br md 18.00 Dpth 9.00 Welded, 1 dk	**(A12B2TR) Chemical/Products Tanker** Double Hull (13F) Liq: 8,495; Liq (Oil): 8,495 Cargo Heating Coils Compartments: 6 Wing Ta, 6 Wing Ta, 1 Wing Slop Ta, 1 Wing Slop Ta, Wing ER 3 Cargo Pump (s): 3x400m³/hr Manifold: Bow/CM: 61.6m Ice Capable	**1 oil engine** reduction geared to sc. shaft driving 1 FP propeller Total Power: 2,574kW (3,500hp) 14.0k Yanmar 6N330-E 1 x 4 Stroke 6 Cy. 330 x 440 2574kW (3500bhp) Qingdao Zichai Boyang Diesel EngineCo Ltd-China AuxGen: 3 x 350kW 400V a.c Thrusters: 1 Tunnel thruster (f) Fuel: 45.0 (d.f.) 330.0 (r.f.)
9600097 *BKSS5* -	**YONG SHENG HUA 8** - **Zhoushan Yongsheng Marine Co Ltd** - SatCom: Inmarsat C 441301735 *Zhoushan, Zhejiang* *China* MMSI: 413441180	**2,994** 1,180 4,107 T/cm 12.5	Class: CC	**2011-08 Ningbo Beilun Lantian Shipbuilding Co Ltd — Ningbo ZJ** Yd No: LT1002 Loa 96.60 (BB) Br ex 15.02 Dght 5.600 Lbp 90.00 Br md 15.00 Dpth 7.40 Welded, 1 dk	**(A12B2TR) Chemical/Products Tanker** Double Hull (13F) Liq: 4,134; Liq (Oil): 4,134 Cargo Heating Coils Compartments: 8 Wing Ta, 1 Slop Ta, ER 8 Cargo Pump (s): 8x125m³/hr Manifold: Bow/CM: 49.2m Ice Capable	**1 oil engine** reduction geared to sc. shaft driving 1 FP propeller Total Power: 2,060kW (2,801hp) 12.5k Guangzhou 8320Z 1 x 4 Stroke 8 Cy. 320 x 440 2060kW (2801bhp) Guangzhou Diesel Engine Factory CoLtd-China AuxGen: 3 x 200kW 450V 60Hz a.c Fuel: 60.0 (d.f.) 176.0 (r.f.)
9578220 *3FGM9* -	**YONG SHENG VII** - **Xue Ji Xing** Weihai Yongsheng International Ship Management Co Ltd *Panama* *Panama* MMSI: 357196000 Official number: 40712PEXTF1	**2,982** 2,010 6,606	Class: IT	**2010-05 Anhui Zhongrun Heavy Industry Co Ltd — Wuhu AH** Loa 98.22 Br ex - Dght - Lbp 93.27 Br md 16.20 Dpth 6.95 Welded, 1 dk	**(A31A2GX) General Cargo Ship**	**1 oil engine** reduction geared to sc. shaft driving 1 Propeller Total Power: 2,000kW (2,719hp) Chinese Std. Type G8300Z 1 x 4 Stroke 8 Cy. 300 x 380 2000kW (2719bhp) Wuxi Antai Power Machinery Co Ltd-China
8892291 - -	**YONG SHI** *ex* Vityaz *-1996* **Hualong Shipping (Panama) Inc** Wah Tak Marine Engineering Co Ltd *Panama* *Panama* Official number: 25181HK	**3,915** 863 2,150	Class: (RS)	**1977 Sevastopolskiy Morskoy Zavod — Sevastopol** Loa 83.62 Br ex 25.40 Dght 2.250 Lbp 80.40 Br md - Dpth 7.79 Welded, 1 dk	**(B34B2SC) Crane Vessel**	**4 diesel electric oil engines** driving 4 gen. Connecting to 4 elec. motors each (500kW) driving 3 Voith-Schneider propellers Total Power: 4,000kW (5,440hp) 9.0k Kolomna 6CHN30/3 4 x 4 Stroke 6 Cy. 300 x 380 each-1000kW (1360bhp) Kolomenskiy Zavod-Kolomna AuxGen: 1 x 160kW a.c Fuel: 350.0 (d.f.)

515788 *UDC7*	**YONG SHUN** *ex* Ai Bo *-2004* *ex* Ryuzan Maru *-2000* **Feng Yuan Shipping Co Ltd** Fortune Sea International Ship Management Co Ltd *Phnom Penh* *Cambodia* MMSI: 515579000 Official number: 0486070	**1,256** 806 1,538	Class: GM	**1986**-01 **K.K. Miura Zosensho — Saiki** Yd No: 752 Loa 73.00 Br ex - Dght - Lbp 68.92 Br md 11.51 Dpth 6.81 Welded, 1 dk	**(A31A2GX) General Cargo Ship**	**1 oil engine** reduction geared to sc. shaft driving 1 FP propeller Total Power: 1,177kW (1,600hp) Hanshin 6LU32RG 1 x 4 Stroke 6 Cy. 320 x 510 1177kW (1600bhp) The Hanshin Diesel Works Ltd-Japan
506429 *P6247*	**YONG SOON** *ex* Taiyo No. 23 *-1992* *ex* Taiyo Maru No. 23 *-1991* *ex* Wakao Maru *-1989* **Lung Soon Shipping Corp** - *Panama* *Panama* Official number: 2018492	*498* 316 1,550		**1975**-06 **K.K. Matsuura Zosensho — Osakikamijima** Yd No: 227 Loa 69.65 Br ex 11.51 Dght 4.268 Lbp 65.00 Br md 11.49 Dpth 6.30 Welded, 2 dks	**(A31A2GX) General Cargo Ship**	**1 oil engine** driving 1 FP propeller Total Power: 1,177kW (1,600hp) Hanshin 6LU32 1 x 4 Stroke 6 Cy. 320 x 510 1177kW (1600bhp) Hanshin Nainenki Kogyo-Japan
624981 *EBV8*	**YONG SOON 6** *ex* Zhe Zhou Ling You *-2005* *ex* Tokuyoshi Maru No. 8 *-1998* **Kwan Kie Energy Development Co Ltd** Nanjing Yongzheng Marine Co Ltd *Panama* *Panama* MMSI: 371239000 Official number: 3146506B	*991* 550 2,417	Class: (NK)	**1985** **Sasaki Shipbuilding Co Ltd — Osakikamijima HS** Loa 81.69 Br ex - Dght 5.060 Lbp 76.00 Br md 12.01 Dpth 5.52 Welded, 1 dk	**(A13B2TP) Products Tanker** Liq: 2,499; Liq (Oil): 2,499	**1 oil engine** driving 1 FP propeller Total Power: 1,545kW (2,101hp) 11.5kn Akasaka A34 1 x 4 Stroke 6 Cy. 340 x 660 1545kW (2101bhp) Akasaka Tekkosho KK (Akasaka DieselLtd)-Japan
651913	**YONG SU** *ex* Blue Sea *-2010* *ex* Yong Su *-2003* *ex* Laurels *-2003* *ex* Ceres *-2001* *ex* Phumi *-1998* *ex* Yuen Fat *-1997* *ex* Tong Chin *-1997* *ex* Setouchi Maru No. 2 *-1990* *ex* Kyoritsu Maru No. 1 *-1975* **Sungjin Global Shipping Co Ltd** - *Busan* *South Korea* Official number: BSR-000089	**591** 382 1,415		**1973**-01 **Sasaki Shipbuilding Co Ltd — Osakikamijima HS** Loa 52.00 Br ex - Dght 3.800 Lbp 48.00 Br md 10.00 Dpth 5.50 Welded, 1 dk	**(A24D2BA) Aggregates Carrier**	**1 oil engine** driving 1 FP propeller Total Power: 662kW (900hp) 10.3kn Akasaka 1 x 4 Stroke 662kW (900bhp) Akasaka Tekkosho KK (Akasaka DieselLtd)-Japan
216420 *RWU4*	**YONG TAI** **Smart Transportation Ltd** COSCO (HK) Shipping Co Ltd *Hong Kong* *Hong Kong* MMSI: 477841000 Official number: HK-0646	**39,873** 25,899 74,061 T/cm 64.0	Class: LR (BV) (AB) **100A1** SS 01/2011 bulk carrier Nos. 1, 3, 5 & 7 holds strengthened for heavy cargoes, Nos. 2, 4 & 6 holds may be empty ESP ESN LI **LMC** **UMS** Eq.Ltr: 0†; Cable: 660.0/78.0 U3 (a)	**2001**-01 **Jiangnan Shipyard (Group) Co Ltd — Shanghai** Yd No: H2257 Loa 225.00 (BB) Br ex 32.30 Dght 14.000 Lbp 217.00 Br md 32.26 Dpth 19.20 Welded, 1 dk	**(A21A2BC) Bulk Carrier** Grain: 90,000; Bale: 86,173 Compartments: 7 Ho, ER 7 Ha: (14.6 x 13.2)6 (14.6 x 15.0)ER	**1 oil engine** driving 1 FP propeller Total Power: 8,662kW (11,777hp) 14.4kn B&W 5S60MC 1 x 2 Stroke 5 Cy. 600 x 2292 8662kW (11777bhp) HHM Shangchuan Diesel Co Ltd-China AuxGen: 3 x 500kW 450V 60Hz a.c Boilers: e (ex.g.) 6.8kgf/cm² (6.7bar), AuxB (o.f.) 6.8kgf/cm² (6.7bar)
228019 *RXH9*	**YONG TONG** **Richson Shipping Ltd** COSCO (HK) Shipping Co Ltd SatCom: Inmarsat C 447794410 *Hong Kong* *Hong Kong* MMSI: 477944000 Official number: HK-0755	**38,641** 25,939 74,382	Class: CC (AB)	**2001**-09 **Oshima Shipbuilding Co Ltd — Saikai NS** Yd No: 10286 Loa 225.00 (BB) Br ex - Dght 13.920 Lbp 216.00 Br md 32.26 Dpth 18.90 Welded, 1 dk	**(A21A2BC) Bulk Carrier** Grain: 86,421; Bale: 84,851 Compartments: 7 Ho, ER 7 Ha: ER	**1 oil engine** driving 1 FP propeller Total Power: 8,290kW (11,271hp) 14.0kn B&W 7S50MC-C 1 x 2 Stroke 7 Cy. 500 x 2000 8290kW (11271bhp) Kawasaki Heavy Industries Ltd-Japan
028981	**YONG TONG** *ex* Nikkan No. 1 *-1999* *ex* Toku Maru No. 21 *-1999* **Yong Tong Shipping Co Ltd** - *China*	**1,473** 793 2,100		**1981**-04 **K.K. Matsuura Zosensho — Osakikamijima** Yd No: 283 Loa 74.00 Br ex - Dght 4.901 Lbp 69.02 Br md 12.01 Dpth 6.86 Welded, 1 dk	**(A31A2GX) General Cargo Ship** Grain: 2,948; Bale: 2,815 Compartments: 1 Ho, ER 1 Ha: ER	**1 oil engine** driving 1 FP propeller Total Power: 1,324kW (1,800hp) Akasaka DM36 1 x 4 Stroke 6 Cy. 360 x 540 1324kW (1800bhp) Akasaka Tekkosho KK (Akasaka DieselLtd)-Japan
041837 *RHH4*	**YONG TONG 1** *ex* OS Phoenix *-2010* *ex* World Dynasty *-2009* *ex* Stolt Ntombi *-2006* *ex* Ntombi *-1997* *ex* May Fair I *-1997* **Yongtong Shipping (Hong Kong) Co Ltd** Shanghai Huitong Shipping Co Ltd SatCom: Inmarsat C 447701515 *Hong Kong* *Hong Kong* MMSI: 477881500 Official number: HK-2835	**7,916** 4,736 13,946 T/cm 22.8	Class: KR (AB)	**1991**-11 **Shin Kurushima Dockyard Co. Ltd. — Akitsu** Yd No: 2722 Loa 132.00 (BB) Br ex 20.42 Dght 8.799 Lbp 124.00 Br md 20.40 Dpth 11.20 Welded, 1 dk	**(A12A2TC) Chemical Tanker** Double Bottom Entire Compartment Length Liq: 16,539 Cargo Heating Coils Compartments: 10 Ta (s.stl), 14 Wing Ta, ER, 2 Wing Slop Ta 24 Cargo Pump (s): 14x125m³/hr, 6x300m³/hr, 4x200m³/hr Manifold: Bow/CM: 64m	**1 oil engine** driving 1 FP propeller Total Power: 3,420kW (4,650hp) 13.5kn B&W 6L35MC 1 x 2 Stroke 6 Cy. 350 x 1050 3420kW (4650bhp) Makita Corp-Japan Fuel: 153.0 (d.f.) 711.0 (r.f.) 13.0pd
101329	**YONG WANG** *ex* Lygra *-1995* **Ningbo Huagang HSC Co Ltd** - *Ningbo, Zhejiang* *China*	**282** 106 50	Class: (NV)	**1981**-11 **AS Fjellstrand Aluminium Yachts — Omastrand** Yd No: 1544 Loa 31.30 Br ex - Dght - Lbp 29.16 Br md 9.42 Dpth 3.51 Welded, 1 dk	**(A37B2PS) Passenger Ship** Hull Material: Aluminium Alloy Passengers: unberthed: 292	**2 oil engines** sr geared to sc. shafts driving 2 FP propellers Total Power: 1,956kW (2,660hp) 24.0kn M.T.U. 16V396TB83 2 x Vee 4 Stroke 16 Cy. 165 x 185 each-978kW (1330bhp) (new engine 1983) MTU Friedrichshafen GmbH-Friedrichshafen AuxGen: 2 x 24kW 220V 50Hz a.c Fuel: 9.0 (d.f.)
334486 *VSW4*	**YONG WIN 8** *ex* Bintanco *-2013* *ex* Bintang *-2012* *ex* Ocean Ruby *-2006* *ex* Nippo Maru No. 76 *-1983* **Zhongshan Yueliang Economy & Trade Import & Export Co** - *Ulaanbaatar* *Mongolia* MMSI: 457509000	**1,776** 906 2,951 T/cm 8.8	Class: (NK)	**1973**-09 **Kyokuyo Shipbuilding & Iron Works Co Ltd — Shimonoseki YC** Yd No: 256 Loa 84.71 Br ex 12.83 Dght 5.646 Lbp 78.01 Br md 12.81 Dpth 6.35 Welded, 1 dk	**(A13B2TP) Products Tanker** Liq: 3,306; Liq (Oil): 3,306 2 Cargo Pump (s)	**2 oil engines** geared to sc. shaft driving 1 FP propeller Total Power: 1,912kW (2,600hp) 12.3kn Daihatsu 12VSHTB-26D 2 x Vee 4 Stroke 12 Cy. 260 x 320 each-956kW (1300bhp) Daihatsu Diesel Manufacturing Co Lt-Japan AuxGen: 2 x 104kW 445V 60Hz a.c Fuel: 120.0 12.0pd
821714 *VAB5*	**YONG WIN 18** *ex* A1 *-2013* *ex* Ali *-2012* *ex* Bali *-2010* *ex* Sea Princess B *-2001* *ex* Sea Princess *-1999* *ex* Archon *-1994* *ex* Tenryo *-1987* *ex* Tenryo Maru *-1983* - - *Ulaanbaatar* *Mongolia* MMSI: 457749000 Official number: 32441378	**3,796** 1,921 6,598 T/cm 14.4	Class: IZ (NK)	**1979**-04 **Miyoshi Shipbuilding Co Ltd — Uwajima EH** Yd No: 246 Loa 106.84 Br ex - Dght 6.940 Lbp 98.61 Br md 16.51 Dpth 8.21 Welded, 1 dk	**(A12B2TR) Chemical/Products Tanker** Double Bottom Entire Compartment Length Liq: 7,645; Liq (Oil): 7,645 Cargo Heating Coils 4 Cargo Pump (s) Manifold: Bow/CM: 55m	**1 oil engine** driving 1 FP propeller Total Power: 2,942kW (4,000hp) 13.5kn Hanshin 6LU50A 1 x 4 Stroke 6 Cy. 500 x 800 2942kW (4000bhp) The Hanshin Diesel Works Ltd-Japan AuxGen: 2 x 160kW 445V 60Hz a.c Fuel: 112.0 (d.f.) 508.5 (r.f.) 13.5pd
806840 *EOC3*	**YONG XIA** *ex* New Golden Bridge VI *-2009* *ex* NGB 6 *-2008* *ex* Shuttle Yokosuka *-2007* *ex* Ferry Cosmo 5 *-2004* *ex* Sun Flower Erimo *-2002* *ex* Erimo Maru *-1991* **Vision Sea SA** Rong Cheng Great Dragon Shipping Co Ltd *Panama* *Panama* MMSI: 354769000 Official number: 3430108B	**25,151** 7,545 5,435	Class: CC KR	**1989**-03 **Ishikawajima-Harima Heavy Industries Co Ltd (IHI) — Tokyo** Yd No: 2979 Loa 178.00 (BB) Br ex 26.70 Dght 6.520 Lbp 166.75 Br md 25.00 Dpth 9.50 Welded	**(A36A2PR) Passenger/Ro-Ro Ship (Vehicles)** Passengers: 634 Bow door & ramp Len: 7.90 Wid: 4.66 Swl: - Quarter stern door/ramp (p) Len: 18.50 Wid: 5.00 Swl: - Lane-Len: 1488 Lane-Wid: 2.50 Lane-clr ht: 4.30 Cars: 105, Trailers: 175	**2 oil engines** dr geared to sc. shafts driving 2 CP propellers Total Power: 21,844kW (29,700hp) 23.0kn Pielstick 9PC40L570 2 x 4 Stroke 9 Cy. 570 x 750 each-10922kW (14850bhp) Ishikawajima Harima Heavy IndustrieCo Ltd (IHI)-Japan AuxGen: 4 x 1240kW 450V 60Hz a.c Thrusters: 1 Thwart. CP thruster (f); 1 Thwart. CP thruster (a) Fuel: 102.5 (d.f.) 739.5 (r.f.) 75.2pd

9604665 *BKNN6* -	**YONG XIANG 3** **Minsheng Financial Leasing Co Ltd** Zhoushan Yongxiang Shipping Co Ltd SatCom: Inmarsat C 441301823 *Tianjin* *China* MMSI: 413303550	**29,108** 15,731 47,525	Class: CC	**2012-08 Jiangsu Eastern Heavy Industry Co Ltd — Jingjiang JS** Yd No: JEHIC10-805 Loa 189.99 (BB) Br ex - Dght 10.500 Lbp 185.00 Br md 32.26 Dpth 15.50 Welded, 1 dk	**(A21A2BC) Bulk Carrier** Grain: 60,276 Compartments: 5 Ho, ER 5 Ha: 4 (21.3 x 18.3)ER (18.9 x 18.3) Cranes: 4x30t Ice Capable	**1 oil engine** driving 1 FP propeller Total Power: 8,280kW (11,257hp) 14.2k MAN-B&W 6S46MC- 1 x 2 Stroke 6 Cy. 460 x 1932 8280kW (11257bhp) Doosan Engine Co Ltd-South Korea AuxGen: 3 x 535kW 400V a.c
8668157 - -	**YONG XIANG 8** **Huang Chun You and Niu Jing Qing** *China* Official number: CN20097723680	**1,351** 756 -		**2009-07 Guanyun Tongda Shiprepair & Building Yard — Guanyun County JS** Yd No: GY200908 Loa 78.00 Br ex - Dght 2.600 Lbp - Br md 15.00 Dpth 3.80 Welded, 1 dk	**(A31C2GD) Deck Cargo Ship**	**2 oil engines** reduction geared to sc. shafts driving 2 Propellers Total Power: 800kW (1,088hp) Chinese Std. Type 6190ZL 2 x 4 Stroke 6 Cy. 190 x 210 each-400kW (544bhp) Jinan Diesel Engine Co Ltd-China
8609280 *XUCX2* -	**YONG XIANG 8** *ex* Wealth Reefer *-2011* *ex* Kedarnath *-2008* *ex* Virginia Universal *-2005* *ex* Wealth Reefer *-1996* **Yongxiang Hong Kong Co Ltd** Yu Ji Ship Management Co Ltd *Phnom Penh* *Cambodia* MMSI: 515183000 Official number: 1186688	**7,286** 3,691 7,337	Class: UB (LR) (GL) (NK) Classed LR until 1/8/11	**1986-11 K.K. Uwajima Zosensho — Uwajima** Yd No: 2498 Loa 144.50 (BB) Br ex 19.84 Dght 7.027 Lbp 136.28 Br md 19.80 Dpth 10.22 Welded, 3 dks	**(A34A2GR) Refrigerated Cargo Ship** Ins: 9,345 Compartments: 4 Ho, ER, 4 Tw Dk 4 Ha: (7.2 x 6.0)3 (8.0 x 6.0)ER Derricks: 8x5t	**1 oil engine** driving 1 FP propeller Total Power: 6,140kW (8,348hp) 19.3k B&W 6L50M 1 x 2 Stroke 6 Cy. 500 x 1620 6140kW (8348bhp) Hitachi Zosen Corp-Japan AuxGen: 3 x 480kW 440V 60Hz a.c Boilers: AuxB (Comp) 6.0kgf/cm² (5.9bar)
8739061 *BKQ13* -	**YONG XIANG 15** **Zhoushan Yongxiang Shipping Co Ltd** Shanghai Xuanrun Shipping Co Ltd *Zhoushan, Zhejiang* *China* MMSI: 412437830 Official number: 070306000138	**1,574** 881 2,197	Class: ZC	**2006-07 Zhoushan Xintai Shipbuilding & Repair Co Ltd — Zhoushan ZJ** Yd No: ZCJ05123 Loa 81.65 (BB) Br ex 12.00 Dght 4.600 Lbp 75.70 Br md 11.50 Dpth 6.50 Welded, 1 dk	**(A12A2TC) Chemical Tanker** Double Hull (13F) Liq: 2,545	**1 oil engine** reduction geared to sc. shaft driving 1 Propeller Total Power: 1,545kW (2,101hp) Guangzhou 1 x 4 Stroke 1545kW (2101bhp) Guangzhou Diesel Engine Factory CoLtd-China
8744107 *BKQJ3* -	**YONG XIANG 29** **Zhoushan Yongxiang Shipping Co Ltd** Shanghai Xuanrun Shipping Co Ltd *Zhoushan, Zhejiang* *China* MMSI: 412437840 Official number: 2006T3101106	**1,398** 782 1,620 T/cm 7.2	Class: ZC	**2006-05 Zhoushan Xintai Shipbuilding & Repair Co Ltd — Zhoushan ZJ** Loa 73.50 (BB) Br ex 11.50 Dght 3.790 Lbp 67.24 Br md 10.50 Dpth 5.61 Welded, 1 dk	**(A12A2TC) Chemical Tanker** Double Hull (13F) Cargo Heating Coils Compartments: 5 Ta, ER 2 Cargo Pump (s): 2x250m³/hr Manifold: Bow/CM: 29.9m	**1 oil engine** reduction geared to sc. shaft driving 1 FP propeller Total Power: 735kW (999hp)
9545493 *T3SA* -	**YONG XIANG 32** **Xie Lin Na** Gold Glory International Ship Management Ltd *Tarawa* *Kiribati* MMSI: 529218000 Official number: K-11090987	**4,519** 2,554 6,825	Class: IZ	**2009-03 Daishan Choujiamen Shipbuilding — Daishan County ZJ** Yd No: ZCJ0706501 Loa 110.30 Br ex - Dght 6.260 Lbp 102.70 Br md 17.20 Dpth 8.50 Welded, 1 dk	**(A31A2GX) General Cargo Ship**	**1 oil engine** reduction geared to sc. shaft driving 1 CP propeller Total Power: 2,059kW (2,799hp) 11.0k Chinese Std. Type 8320Z 1 x 4 Stroke 8 Cy. 320 x 440 2059kW (2799bhp) Guangzhou Diesel Engine Factory CoLtd-China
9099339 - -	**YONG XIANG 68** *ex* Shen Ju *-2011* - Yu Ji Ship Management Co Ltd *China* MMSI: 412420396	**1,439** 806 2,178	Class: UB	**1991-11 Zhejiang Shipyard — Ningbo ZJ** Loa 71.80 Br ex - Dght 4.800 Lbp 66.00 Br md 12.80 Dpth 6.20 Welded, 1 dk	**(A31A2GX) General Cargo Ship**	**1 oil engine** driving 1 Propeller Total Power: 662kW (900hp) 10.0k Chinese Std. Type 6350Z 1 x 4 Stroke 6 Cy. 350 x 500 662kW (900bhp) Shanghai Diesel Engine Co Ltd-China
9549267 *VRJX8* -	**YONG XIN 201** **Smart Talent (China) Ltd** Changning Shipping Co Ltd *Hong Kong* *Hong Kong* MMSI: 477817100 Official number: HK-3378	**14,244** 7,939 22,185	Class: CC	**2009-07 Ningbo Dongfang Shipyard Co Ltd — Ningbo ZJ** Yd No: C07-041 Loa 166.50 Br ex - Dght 9.200 Lbp 158.00 Br md 23.00 Dpth 13.20 Welded, 1 dk	**(A21A2BC) Bulk Carrier** Grain: 28,432 Compartments: 4 Ho, ER 4 Ha: 3 (21.0 x 13.8)ER (16.5 x 13.8) Cranes: 3x25t Ice Capable	**1 oil engine** driving 1 FP propeller Total Power: 4,457kW (6,060hp) 12.5k MAN-B&W 6S35M 1 x 2 Stroke 6 Cy. 350 x 1400 4457kW (6060bhp) (made 2009) Yichang Marine Diesel Engine Co Ltd-China AuxGen: 3 x 465kW 400V a.c
8511407 *BLVF* -	**YONG XING** **Ningbo Huagang HSC Co Ltd** *Ningbo, Zhejiang*	*399* 140 125	Class: (NV)	**1985-11 Fjellstrand AS — Omastrand** Yd No: 1570 Loa 38.80 Br ex - Dght 2.400 Lbp 36.00 Br md 9.45 Dpth 3.93 Welded, 1 dk	**(A37B2PS) Passenger Ship** Hull Material: Aluminium Alloy Passengers: unberthed: 326	**2 oil engines** geared to sc. shafts driving 2 FP propellers Total Power: 2,942kW (4,000hp) M.T.U. 16V396TB8 2 x Vee 4 Stroke 16 Cy. 165 x 185 each-1471kW (2000bhp) MTU Friedrichshafen GmbH-Friedrichshafen AuxGen: 2 x 56kW 380V 50Hz a.c
8749963 *3DYB* -	**YONG XING 1** **Zhongda Co Ltd** - *Suva* *Fiji* Official number: 000391	**136** 40 -		**2003-04 Huanghai Shipbuilding Co Ltd — Rongcheng SD** Loa 30.45 Br ex 6.20 Dght - Lbp - Br md - Dpth 2.05 Welded, 1 dk	**(B11B2FV) Fishing Vessel**	**1 oil engine** reduction geared to sc. shaft driving 1 FP propeller
8749987 *3DYC* -	**YONG XING 2** **Zhongda Co Ltd** - *Suva* *Fiji* Official number: 000392	**136** 40 -		**2003-04 Huanghai Shipbuilding Co Ltd — Rongcheng SD** Loa 30.45 Br ex 6.20 Dght - Lbp - Br md - Dpth - Welded, 1 dk	**(B11B2FV) Fishing Vessel**	**1 oil engine** reduction geared to sc. shaft driving 1 FP propeller
8749676 *3DXZ* -	**YONG XING 3** *ex* Zhong Da 1 *-2003* **Zhongda Co Ltd** - *Suva* *Fiji* Official number: 000393	**136** 40 -		**2003-04 Huanghai Shipbuilding Co Ltd — Rongcheng SD** Loa 30.45 Br ex - Dght - Lbp - Br md 6.20 Dpth - Welded, 1 dk	**(B11B2FV) Fishing Vessel**	**1 oil engine** reduction geared to sc. shaft driving 1 FP propeller Chinese Std. Type 1 x 4 Stroke Weifang Diesel Engine Factory-China
9649172 *BKDJ* -	**YONG XING 5** **Ningbo Yongzheng Shipping Co Ltd** - SatCom: Inmarsat C 441411610 *Ningbo, Zhejiang* *China* MMSI: 414116000 Official number: CN20109311780	**32,363** 17,244 52,803	Class: CC	**2012-06 Zhejiang Donghong Shipbuilding Co Ltd — Xiangshan County ZJ** Yd No: DH52000-2 Loa 195.76 (BB) Br ex - Dght 12.200 Lbp 186.10 Br md 32.26 Dpth 17.80 Welded, 1 dk	**(A21A2BC) Bulk Carrier** Grain: 69,528; Bale: 68,138 Compartments: 5 Ho, ER 5 Ha: 4 (22.1 x 16.0)ER (16.4 x 16.0) Ice Capable	**1 oil engine** driving 1 FP propeller Total Power: 7,980kW (10,850hp) 13.5k MAN-B&W 6S50MC-C 1 x 2 Stroke 6 Cy. 500 x 2000 7980kW (10850bhp) Wuxi Antai Power Machinery Co Ltd-China AuxGen: 3 x 500kW 400V a.c
9095448 - -	**YONG XING 6** - - *Ningbo, Zhejiang* *China*	**7,230** 4,048 10,000		**2005-10 Zhejiang Donghong Shipbuilding Co Ltd — Xiangshan County ZJ** Loa 118.00 (BB) Br ex - Dght - Lbp - Br md 18.60 Dpth 10.10 Welded, 1 dk	**(A31A2GX) General Cargo Ship** Grain: 13,500	**1 oil engine** driving 1 Propeller 11.5k
9517329 *BPYB* -	**YONG XING DAO** **China Shipping Gang Lian Maritime Co Ltd** China Shipping Passenger Liner Co Ltd SatCom: Inmarsat C 441209111 *Dalian, Liaoning* *China* MMSI: 412091000	**24,572** 13,269 7,662	Class: CC	**2011-03 Guangzhou Shipyard International Co Ltd — Guangzhou GD** Yd No: 08130002 Loa 167.50 (BB) Br ex - Dght 5.950 Lbp 155.00 Br md 25.20 Dpth 13.40 Welded, 1 dk	**(A36A2PR) Passenger/Ro-Ro Ship (Vehicles)** Passengers: 1400 Lane-Len: 2000 Cars: 600 Ice Capable	**2 oil engines** reduction geared to sc. shafts driving 2 CP propellers Total Power: 12,000kW (16,316hp) 18.5k Wartsila 12V3 2 x Vee 4 Stroke 12 Cy. 320 x 400 each-6000kW (8158bhp) Wartsila Finland Oy-Finland AuxGen: 2 x 1350kW 400V a.c, 2 x 1200kW 400V a.c Thrusters: 1 Tunnel thruster (f)
9295074 *BUQK* -	**YONG XING ZHOU** **Nanjing Tanker Corp** - *Nanjing, Jiangsu* *China* MMSI: 413203000	**43,062** 21,289 74,090 T/cm 67.7	Class: CC	**2005-06 Dalian Shipyard Co Ltd — Dalian LN** Yd No: PC700-2 Loa 228.60 (BB) Br ex - Dght 14.700 Lbp 217.00 Br md 32.26 Dpth 21.00 Welded, 1 dk	**(A13B2TP) Products Tanker** Double Hull (13F) Liq: 79,547; Liq (Oil): 79,547 Cargo Heating Coils Compartments: 12 Wing Ta, 2 Wing Slop Ta, ER 3 Cargo Pump (s): 3x2000m³/hr Manifold: Bow/CM: 114m Ice Capable	**1 oil engine** driving 1 FP propeller Total Power: 12,240kW (16,642hp) 14.7k MAN-B&W 6S60M 1 x 2 Stroke 6 Cy. 600 x 2292 12240kW (16642bhp) Dalian Marine Diesel Works-China AuxGen: 3 x 740kW 450V a.c Fuel: 183.0 (d.f.) 2242.0 (r.f.)

715302 *FA19*
YONG XU HAI
ex CHANG MING HAI *-2010* *ex* Bright City *-2005*
ex Bright Field *-1998* *ex* Oceanus *-1990*
Tianjin Younysun Shipping Group Co Ltd
-
Tianjin *China*
Official number: 020010000068

36,120 / 23,035 / 68,200 / T/cm / 64.7
Class: (NV)

1988-11 Sasebo Heavy Industries Co. Ltd. — Sasebo Yard, Sasebo Yd No: 368
Loa 224.00 (BB) Br ex - Dght 13.292
Lbp 215.00 Br md 32.20 Dpth 18.20
Welded, 1 dk

(A21A2BC) Bulk Carrier
Grain: 81,337
Compartments: 7 Ho, ER
7 Ha: (14.4 x 12.8)6 (17.6 x 14.4)ER

1 oil engine driving 1 FP propeller
Total Power: 7,205kW (9,796hp) 14.0kn
Sulzer 5RTA62
1 x 2 Stroke 5 Cy. 620 x 2150 7205kW (9796bhp)
Ishikawajima Harima Heavy IndustrieCo Ltd (IHI)-Japan
AuxGen: 3 x 450kW 440V 60Hz a.c
Fuel: 84.0 (d.f.) 1868.0 (r.f.) 27.0pd

420136 *KPG4*
YONG YUE 7
Zhejiang Yongyue Ocean Shipping Group Co Ltd
Zhoushan Yongyue Shipmanagement Co Ltd
Zhoushan, Zhejiang *China*
MMSI: 413415730

6,813 / 3,450 / 8,710 / T/cm / 20.7
Class: CC

2007-09 Zhoushan Longtai Shipbuilding Co Ltd — Zhoushan ZJ Yd No: 2005-1
Loa 132.60 (BB) Br ex - Dght 7.200
Lbp 123.40 Br md 19.20 Dpth 9.20
Welded, 1 dk

(A33A2CC) Container Ship (Fully Cellular)
TEU 679 C Ho 228 TEU C Dk 451 TEU incl 116 ref C.

1 oil engine reduction geared to sc. shaft driving 1 FP propeller
Total Power: 6,313kW (8,583hp) 17.0kn
MaK 7M43
1 x 4 Stroke 7 Cy. 430 x 610 6313kW (8583bhp)
Caterpillar Motoren GmbH & Co. KG-Germany
AuxGen: 2 x 350kW 400V a.c, 1 x 1160kW 400V a.c
Thrusters: 1 Tunnel thruster (f)

741026 *KOM4*
YONG YUE 11
Zhejiang Yongyue Ocean Shipping Group Co Ltd
Zhoushan Yongyue Shipmanagement Co Ltd
Zhoushan, Zhejiang *China*
MMSI: 413414930

7,221 / 4,043 / 9,750
Class: ZC

2007-06 Zhejiang Yunhai Shipbuilding & Repair Co Ltd — Zhoushan ZJ
Loa 132.60 (BB) Br ex - Dght 8.000
Lbp 123.40 Br md 19.20 Dpth 10.20
Welded, 1 dk

(A33A2CC) Container Ship (Fully Cellular)
TEU 655

1 oil engine reduction geared to sc. shaft driving 1 Propeller
Total Power: 3,824kW (5,199hp) 17.0kn
Pielstick 8PC2-5L
1 x 4 Stroke 8 Cy. 400 x 460 3824kW (5199bhp)
Shaanxi Diesel Heavy Industry Co Lt-China

741038 *KVW3*
YONG YUE 17
Zhoushan Hongfu Shipping
Zhoushan Yongyue Shipmanagement Co Ltd
Zhoushan, Zhejiang *China*
MMSI: 413402430

1,993 / 1,116 / 3,158

2006-09 Zhoushan Longtai Shipbuilding Co Ltd — Zhoushan ZJ
Loa 88.02 (BB) Br ex - Dght 5.200
Lbp 79.98 Br md 13.50 Dpth 6.00
Welded, 1 dk

(A13B2TP) Products Tanker

1 oil engine driving 1 Propeller
Total Power: 735kW (999hp) 11.0kn
Chinese Std. Type G6300ZCA
1 x 4 Stroke 6 Cy. 300 x 380 735kW (999bhp)
Ningbo CSI Power & Machinery GroupCo Ltd-China

741040 *KVX3*
YONG YUE 18
Zhoushan Hongfu Shipping
Zhoushan Yongyue Shipmanagement Co Ltd
Zhoushan, Zhejiang *China*
MMSI: 413402440

1,993 / 1,116 / 3,158
Class: ZC

2006-09 Zhoushan Longtai Shipbuilding Co Ltd — Zhoushan ZJ
Loa 88.02 (BB) Br ex - Dght 5.200
Lbp 79.98 Br md 13.50 Dpth 6.00
Welded, 1 dk

(A13B2TP) Products Tanker

1 oil engine reduction geared to sc. shaft driving 1 Propeller
Total Power: 735kW (999hp) 11.0kn
Chinese Std. Type G6300ZCA
1 x 4 Stroke 6 Cy. 300 x 380 735kW (999bhp)
Ningbo CSI Power & Machinery GroupCo Ltd-China

741052 *KRS4*
YONG YUE 20
Zhoushan Hongfu Shipping
Zhoushan Yongyue Shipmanagement Co Ltd
Zhoushan, Zhejiang *China*
MMSI: 412437050

2,090 / 1,170 / 3,350

2003-10 Zhejiang Hongguan Ship Industry Co Ltd — Linhai ZJ
Loa 87.96 (BB) Br ex - Dght 5.200
Lbp - Br md 13.50 Dpth 6.00
Welded, 1 dk

(A13B2TP) Products Tanker

1 oil engine driving 1 Propeller
Total Power: 1,324kW (1,800hp)
Chinese Std. Type G6300ZC
1 x 4 Stroke 6 Cy. 300 x 380 1324kW (1800bhp)
Ningbo CSI Power & Machinery GroupCo Ltd-China

625671
YONG ZHONG YOU 9
Ningbo Zhonghai Marine Bunker Co Ltd
-
China

499 / - / 1,000
Class: CC (Class contemplated)

2012-03 Zhejiang Chengzhou Shipbuilding Co Ltd — Sanmen County ZJ Yd No: CZ1009
Loa 53.20 Br ex - Dght 4.100
Lbp - Br md 9.20 Dpth -
Welded, 1 dk

(A13B2TP) Products Tanker
Double Hull (13F)

1 oil engine driving 1 FP propeller

422631 *FTI6*
YONGDINGHE
ex Kota Benar *-2002* *ex* Yongdinghe *-2001*
Yongdinghe Shipping Inc
COSCO Container Lines Co Ltd (COSCON)
Panama *Panama*
MMSI: 352956000
Official number: 2348797CH

9,471 / 5,188 / 12,668 / T/cm / 25.4
Class: NK

1996-11 Kyokuyo Shipyard Corp — Shimonoseki YC Yd No: 402
Loa 144.83 (BB) Br ex 22.45 Dght 8.215
Lbp 134.00 Br md 22.40 Dpth 11.00
Welded, 1 dk

(A33A2CC) Container Ship (Fully Cellular)
TEU 764 C Ho 318 TEU C Dk 446 TEU incl 60 ref C.
Compartments: 7 Cell Ho, ER
7 Ha: (12.6 x 13.5)6 (12.6 x 18.9)ER

1 oil engine driving 1 FP propeller
Total Power: 7,988kW (10,860hp) 17.0kn
B&W 6L50MC
1 x 2 Stroke 6 Cy. 500 x 1620 7988kW (10860bhp)
Kawasaki Heavy Industries Ltd-Japan
Fuel: 1070.0 (r.f.)

801826
YONGHO77
ex Arista 2 *-2014* *ex* Geo Ryang No. 2 *-2013*
ex Dong Soo *-2009* *ex* Toyo Maru No. 77 *-2003*
-
-
South Korea
MMSI: 440107810

954 / 491 / 1,998
Class: (KR)

1987-10 Shin Kurushima Dockyard Co. Ltd. — Akitsu Yd No: 1982
Loa 71.99 (BB) Br ex - Dght 5.000
Lbp 68.20 Br md 12.01 Dpth 5.31
Welded, 1 dk

(A13A2TV) Crude Oil Tanker
Liq: 2,249; Liq (Oil): 2,249
Compartments: 10 Ta, ER

1 oil engine with clutches & reduction geared to sc. shaft driving 1 CP propeller
Total Power: 1,324kW (1,800hp)
Hanshin 6EL30
1 x 4 Stroke 6 Cy. 300 x 600 1324kW (1800bhp)
The Hanshin Diesel Works Ltd-Japan

551882
YONGHUNG NO. 2
Kogas Marine Co Ltd
-
Incheon *South Korea*
MMSI: 440009470
Official number: ICR-093113

273 / - / 167
Class: KR

2009-07 Samkwang Shipbuilding & Engineering Co Ltd — Incheon Yd No: SKSB-181
Loa 36.50 Br ex 10.02 Dght 3.312
Lbp 32.49 Br md 10.00 Dpth 4.50
Welded, 1 dk

(B32A2ST) Tug

2 oil engines reduction geared to sc. shafts driving 2 Propellers
Total Power: 3,308kW (4,498hp)
Niigata 6L28HX
2 x 4 Stroke 6 Cy. 280 x 370 each-1654kW (2249bhp)
Niigata Engineering Co Ltd-Japan

202584 *3BL*
YONGJI
ex Shirane *-2014*
Yongji Shipping Ltd
Luhai Ship Management Ltd
Panama *Panama*
MMSI: 351769000
Official number: 28722PEXT3

43,376 / 23,540 / 77,672 / T/cm / 75.2
Class: NK

2000-03 Mitsui Eng. & SB. Co. Ltd. — Tamano Yd No: 1486
Loa 229.00 (BB) Br ex - Dght 12.820
Lbp 218.00 Br md 36.50 Dpth 18.50
Welded, 1 dk

(A21A2BC) Bulk Carrier
Grain: 90,493
Compartments: 5 Ho, ER
5 Ha: (24.3 x 16.0)Tappered 4 (27.5 x 16.0)ER

1 oil engine driving 1 FP propeller
Total Power: 10,223kW (13,899hp) 14.5kn
B&W 5S60MC
1 x 2 Stroke 5 Cy. 600 x 2292 10223kW (13899bhp)
Mitsui Engineering & Shipbuilding CLtd-Japan
AuxGen: 3 x 460kW 450V a.c
Fuel: 2775.0 (r.f.) 38.0pd

810861
YONGJIN
ex Haedong *-2003* *ex* Hoei Maru No. 25 *-2002*
Lee Mae-Jong & Partner
-
Busan *South Korea*
MMSI: 440105560
Official number: BSR-020624

699 / - / 2,070
Class: (KR)

1989-11 Murakami Hide Zosen K.K. — Imabari Yd No: 310
Loa - Br ex - Dght 4.901
Lbp 70.72 Br md 11.21 Dpth 5.52
Welded, 1 dk

(A13B2TP) Products Tanker

1 oil engine reverse geared to sc. shaft driving 1 FP propeller
Total Power: 1,324kW (1,800hp)
Akasaka K31R
1 x 4 Stroke 6 Cy. 310 x 530 1324kW (1800bhp)
Akasaka Tekkosho KK (Akasaka DieselLtd)-Japan

871417
YONGJOO No. 3
Ryu Bok-Soo
-
Incheon *South Korea*
Official number: ICR-902505

383 / - / 365
Class: (KR)

1990-09 Seohae Shipbuilding & Engineering Co Ltd — Incheon Yd No: 90-01
Loa 60.40 Br ex - Dght 2.162
Lbp 54.19 Br md 14.00 Dpth 3.50
Welded, 1 dk

(A36A2PR) Passenger/Ro-Ro Ship (Vehicles)

2 oil engines reduction geared to sc. shaft driving 1 FP propeller
Total Power: 326kW (444hp) 11.3kn
Scania DSI1440M
2 x Vee 4 Stroke 8 Cy. 127 x 140 each-163kW (222bhp) (made 1989)
Saab Scania AB-Sweden

102394
YONGJOO No. 5
Ryu Bok-Soo
-
Incheon *South Korea*
Official number: ICR-932072

978 / - / 328
Class: (KR)

1993-04 Seohae Shipbuilding & Engineering Co Ltd — Incheon Yd No: 92-03
Loa 79.75 Br ex - Dght 2.012
Lbp 65.00 Br md 18.00 Dpth 3.75
Welded, 1 dk

(A36A2PR) Passenger/Ro-Ro Ship (Vehicles)

2 oil engines geared to sc. shafts driving 2 FP propellers
Total Power: 1,000kW (1,360hp) 7.0kn
Caterpillar 3412TA
2 x Vee 4 Stroke 12 Cy. 137 x 152 each-500kW (680bhp)
Caterpillar Inc-USA
AuxGen: 2 x 216kW 440V a.c

150303 *RYZ5*
YONGXING
Yongxing Maritime Co Ltd
Chinese-Polish JSC (Chinsko-Polskie Towarzystwo Okretowe SA) (CHIPOLBROK)
SatCom: Inmarsat C 447745010
Hong Kong *Hong Kong*
MMSI: 477450000
Official number: HK-1107

18,207 / 9,209 / 22,309 / T/cm / 38.4
Class: CC (LR)
✠ Classed LR until 3/11/99

1998-08 '3 Maj' Brodogradiliste dd — Rijeka Yd No: 672
Loa 169.82 (BB) Br ex 27.55 Dght 9.320
Lbp 160.83 Br md 27.50 Dpth 13.80
Welded, 1 dk, 2nd dk in holds 1 2 3 & 4 3rd dk in holds 2 3 & 4 only

(A31A2GX) General Cargo Ship
Grain: 37,339; Bale: 33,606
TEU 1094 C Ho 472 TEU C Dk 622 TEU incl 30 ref C.
Compartments: 4 Ho, ER, 7 Tw Dk
7 Ha: (12.8 x 11.2)Tappered 4 (25.6 x 10.4)2 (19.2 x 10.4)ER
Cranes: 2x35t,2x25t

1 oil engine driving 1 FP propeller
Total Power: 9,500kW (12,916hp) 16.5kn
Sulzer 5RTA62
1 x 2 Stroke 5 Cy. 620 x 2150 9500kW (12916bhp)
'3 Maj' Motori i Dizalice dd-Croatia
AuxGen: 3 x 704kW 450V 60Hz a.c
Fuel: 70.7 (d.f.) 1126.9 (r.f.) 32.7pd

702193
YONSO
ex Willy *-1981*
Continental African Maritime Co Ltd
-
Takoradi *Ghana*
Official number: 316663

349 / 159 / -

1966 Fa. S. Seijmonsbergen, Scheepswerf "Concordia" — Amsterdam Yd No: 652
Loa 48.19 Br ex - Dght -
Lbp 41.79 Br md 8.51 Dpth 4.25
Welded

(B11A2FT) Trawler

1 oil engine driving 1 FP propeller
Total Power: 883kW (1,201hp) 14.0kn
Deutz RBV8M545
1 x 4 Stroke 8 Cy. 320 x 450 883kW (1201bhp)
Kloeckner Humboldt Deutz AG-West Germany

8011158 *DSEF* -	**YOO SUNG No. 1** *ex* Navio *-1996* *ex* Shinwa Maru No. 28 *-1995* *ex* Shinyu Maru No. 28 *-1987* **SJ Co Ltd** Yoo Sung Ltd *Changwon* *South Korea* MMSI: 440108600 Official number: MSR-957821	**943** - 2,110	Class: (KR)	**1980-10 K.K. Matsuura Zosensho — Osakikamijima** Yd No: 280 Loa 75.20 Br ex - Dght 4.770 Lbp 70.00 Br md 12.00 Dpth 5.50 Welded, 1 dk	**(B34E2SW) Waste Disposal Vessel**	**1 oil engine** driving 1 FP propeller Total Power: 1,545kW (2,101hp) Akasaka DM38 1 x 4 Stroke 6 Cy. 380 x 600 1545kW (2101bhp) Akasaka Tekkosho KK (Akasaka DieselLtd)-Japan
9611448 - -	**YOONS' NO. 1** - **Yoons' Marine Co Ltd** - *Gunsan* *South Korea* Official number: KSR-104241	**265** - 250	Class: KR	**2010-07 Yeunsoo Shipbuilding Co Ltd — Janghang** Yd No: 140 Loa 37.30 Br ex - Dght 3.637 Lbp 31.15 Br md 10.00 Dpth 4.50 Welded, 1 dk	**(B32A2ST) Tug**	**2 oil engines** reduction geared to sc. shafts driving 2 Propellers Total Power: 3,480kW (4,732hp) 13.9k Hyundai Himsen 6H25/33 2 x 4 Stroke 6 Cy. 250 x 330 each-1740kW (2366bhp) Hyundai Heavy Industries Co Ltd-South Korea
8741222 - -	**YOONS NO 5** *ex* Haeryong No. 11 *-2013* **Korea Tug Boat Co Ltd** - *Yeosu* *South Korea* Official number: YSR065738	**274** - -	Class: KR	**2006-06 Namyang Shipbuilding Co Ltd — Yeosu** Loa 37.30 Br ex - Dght - Lbp 31.50 Br md 10.00 Dpth 4.50 Welded, 1 dk	**(B32A2ST) Tug**	**2 oil engines** reduction geared to sc. shafts driving 2 Propellers Total Power: 3,308kW (4,498hp) Niigata 6L28H 2 x 4 Stroke 6 Cy. 280 x 370 each-1654kW (2249bhp) Niigata Engineering Co Ltd-Japan
8935392 *UFMQ* -	**YORK** *ex* Askold 1 *-2006* *ex* Leningrad *-2004* **Vermant Group Ltd** Shipmar Co Ltd *St Petersburg* *Russia* MMSI: 273340110	**2,454** 823 3,201	Class: RS (RR)	**1978-12 Santierul Naval Oltenita S.A. — Oltenita** Yd No: 111 Loa 108.40 Br ex 14.80 Dght 3.260 Lbp 101.80 Br md 14.80 Dpth 5.00 Welded, 1 dk	**(A31A2GX) General Cargo Ship** Bale: 4,385 TEU 100 C. 100/20' Compartments: 4 Ho 4 Ha: 4 (15.6 x 10.9)	**2 oil engines** driving 2 FP propellers Total Power: 1,030kW (1,400hp) 10.0k S.K.L. 6NVD48A-2 2 x 4 Stroke 6 Cy. 320 x 480 each-515kW (700bhp) VEB Schwermaschinenbau "KarlLiebknecht" (SKL)-Magdeburg AuxGen: 3 x 50kW a.c Fuel: 70.0 (d.f.)
9220421 *9VED8* -	**YORK** - **York Maritime Co Pte Ltd** Interunity Management Corp SA *Singapore* *Singapore* MMSI: 565525000 Official number: 393313	**4,807** 1,723 5,076 T/cm 15.5	Class: NK	**2000-06 Higaki Zosen K.K. — Imabari** Yd No: 517 Loa 99.93 (BB) Br ex 19.63 Dght 5.750 Lbp 94.90 Br md 19.60 Dpth 7.70 Welded, 1 dk	**(A11B2TG) LPG Tanker** Double Bottom Entire Compartment Length Liq (Gas): 6,185 2 x Gas Tank (s); 2 independent (stl) cyl horizontal 2 Cargo Pump (s): 2x400m³/hr Manifold: Bow/CM: 46.7m	**1 oil engine** driving 1 FP propeller Total Power: 3,900kW (5,302hp) 14.0k MAN-B&W 6L35M 1 x 2 Stroke 6 Cy. 350 x 1050 3900kW (5302bhp) The Hanshin Diesel Works Ltd-Japan AuxGen: 3 x 200kW 440/110V 60Hz a.c Thrusters: 1 Thwart. CP thruster (f) Fuel: 128.0 (d.f.) (Heating Coils) 571.0 (r.f.) 16.6pd
8844244 *VJT5694* -	**YORK COVE** *ex* Seven Star *-1998* *ex* Hokuyo Maru No. 2 *-1997* **Tasmanian Ports Corporation Pty Ltd (TasPorts)** - *Hobart, Tas* *Australia* Official number: 856048	*216* 65 58	Class: LR (NV) (KR) **100A1** SS 12/2011 tug coastal service **LMC**	**1990 Ryochu Kairiku Unyu K.K. — Japan** Loa 28.10 Br ex - Dght 2.700 Lbp 24.28 Br md 8.20 Dpth 3.48 Welded, 1 dk	**(B32A2ST) Tug**	**2 oil engines** driving 2 Directional propellers Total Power: 1,912kW (2,600hp) Niigata 6L22H 2 x 4 Stroke 6 Cy. 220 x 280 each-956kW (1300bhp) Niigata Engineering Co Ltd-Japan
8953174 - -	**YORK I** *ex* Ruth *-1998* - -	*179* 143 -		**1985 Rae Shipyard, Inc. — Lockport, La** Yd No: 008 L reg 22.86 Br ex - Dght - Lbp - Br md 10.97 Dpth 2.44 Welded, 1 dk	**(B21A20S) Platform Supply Ship**	**2 oil engines** geared to sc. shafts driving 2 FP propellers Total Power: 736kW (1,000hp) 7.0k G.M. (Detroit Diesel) 12V-7 2 x Vee 2 Stroke 12 Cy. 108 x 127 each-368kW (500bhp) General Motors Detroit DieselAllison Divn-USA
5396090 - -	**YORK SYME** - **Coastal Dredging & Construction Ltd** -	**149** 44 -	Class: (LR) ✠ Classed LR until 2/9/77	**1961-07 Adelaide Ship Construction Pty Ltd — Port Adelaide SA** Yd No: 8 Loa 28.96 Br ex 7.57 Dght 3.163 Lbp 26.78 Br md 7.17 Dpth 3.66 Welded, 1 dk	**(B32A2ST) Tug**	**1 oil engine** with hydraulic couplings & sr reverse geared to sc. shaft driving 1 FP propeller Total Power: 809kW (1,100hp) 11.5k Ruston 6ATC 1 x 4 Stroke 6 Cy. 318 x 368 809kW (1100bhp) Ruston & Hornsby Ltd.-Lincoln AuxGen: 2 x 35kW 220V d.c Fuel: 19.5 (d.f.)
8739310 *EIHR7* -	**YORKSHIRE LADY** *ex* LCM 24 Auster *-1989* *ex* L 783 *-1986* **Aimsiu Tracht Na hOileain Teoranta (ATNO)** - *Galway* *Irish Republic* MMSI: 250001815 Official number: 404110	**107** 32 -		**1967-01 Rheinwerft GmbH — Mainz** Loa 29.00 Br ex - Dght 1.500 Lbp - Br md 7.00 Dpth 2.20 Welded, 1 dk	**(A35D2RL) Landing Craft**	**2 oil engines** reduction geared to sc. shafts driving 2 Propellers Total Power: 324kW (440hp) 9.0k MWM 2 x each-162kW (220bhp) Motorenwerk Mannheim AG (MWM)-Germany
9655884 *2HEI6* -	**YORKSHIREMAN** *ex* Ulupinar Xiii *-2014* **SMS Towage Ltd** - *Hull* *United Kingdom* MMSI: 235102971 Official number: 919657	**144** 136 97	Class: RI	**2012-04 Sanmar Denizcilik Makina ve Ticaret — Istanbul** Yd No: 05 Loa 24.39 Br ex - Dght 3.000 Lbp 19.10 Br md 9.15 Dpth 4.04 Welded, 1 dk	**(B32A2ST) Tug**	**2 oil engines** reduction geared to sc. shafts driving 2 Directional propellers Total Power: 2,462kW (3,348hp) Caterpillar 3512 2 x Vee 4 Stroke 12 Cy. 170 x 190 each-1231kW (1674bhp) Caterpillar Inc-USA AuxGen: 2 x 67kW 380V 50Hz a.c
8949472 *WDG3446* -	**YORKTOWN** *ex* Spirit of Yorktown *-2011* *ex* Yorktown Clipper *-2007* **Explorer Maritime Cruises LLC** - *New York, NY* *United States of America* MMSI: 368373000 Official number: 928931	**2,354** 801 -	Class: (AB)	**1988-04 First Coast Shipbuilding, Inc. — Green Cove Springs, Fl** Yd No: 1 Loa 78.30 Br ex - Dght 2.600 Lbp 68.27 Br md 12.19 Dpth 3.78 Welded, 1 dk	**(A37B2PS) Passenger Ship** Passengers: berths: 138	**2 oil engines** reduction geared to sc. shafts driving 2 FP propellers Total Power: 1,332kW (1,810hp) 12.0k Caterpillar 3508T 2 x Vee 4 Stroke 8 Cy. 170 x 190 each-666kW (905bhp) Caterpillar Inc-USA AuxGen: 3 x 320kW a.c Fuel: 149.0 (d.f.)
9243174 *WDD6127* -	**YORKTOWN EXPRESS** *ex* CP Shenandoah *-2007* *ex* TMM Colima *-2005* *ex* Contship Tenacity *-2002* **Hapag-Lloyd USA LLC** Hapag-Lloyd AG *Yorktown, VA* *United States of America* MMSI: 367168650 Official number: 1195522	**40,146** 18,097 40,478 T/cm 64.6	Class: AB	**2002-10 China Shipbuilding Corp (CSBC) — Kaohsiung** Yd No: 791 Loa 243.00 (BB) Br ex - Dght 11.020 Lbp 232.40 Br md 32.20 Dpth 19.50 Welded, 1 dk	**(A33A2CC) Container Ship (Fully Cellular)** TEU 3237 C Ho 1420 TEU C Dk 1817 TEU incl 400 ref C. Cranes: 4x45t	**1 oil engine** driving 1 FP propeller Total Power: 28,832kW (39,200hp) 21.6k MAN-B&W 8K80MC- 1 x 2 Stroke 8 Cy. 800 x 2300 28832kW (39200bhp) Doosan Engine Co Ltd-South Korea AuxGen: 3 x 2280kW a.c Thrusters: 1 Thwart. CP thruster (f) Fuel: 191.9 (d.f.) 3654.5 (r.f.) 110.0pd
9078622 *JH3320* -	**YORYU MARU** *ex* Koryo Maru *-2004* *ex* Yoryu Maru *-1998* **Sanyo Bussan KK** - *Nagoya, Aichi* *Japan* Official number: 133228	*499* - 1,200		**1993-07 K.K. Miura Zosensho — Saiki** Yd No: 1068 Loa 65.00 Br ex - Dght 4.150 Lbp 60.00 Br md 10.00 Dpth 4.40 Welded, 1 dk	**(A13B2TP) Products Tanker** Liq: 1,244; Liq (Oil): 1,244 2 Cargo Pump (s): 2x600m³/hr	**1 oil engine** driving 1 FP propeller Total Power: 1,177kW (1,600hp) 11.5k Niigata 6M28HC 1 x 4 Stroke 6 Cy. 280 x 480 1177kW (1600bhp) Niigata Engineering Co Ltd-Japan Fuel: 56.0 (d.f.) 4.0pd
7938828 - -	**YOSHI III** *ex* Way Hua 3 *-1990* *ex* Bintang Jaya *-1988* *ex* Good Services *-1986* *ex* Daiei Maru No. 6 *-1980* *ex* Kyokuto Maru No. 32 *-1980* *ex* Yusei Maru No. 5 *-1980* *ex* Daiko Maru No. 2 *-1980* -	**180** 97 288	Class: (NK)	**1966 YK Furumoto Tekko Zosensho — Osakikamijima** Yd No: 180 Loa 33.69 Br ex - Dght 3.003 Lbp 29.40 Br md 6.40 Dpth 3.30 Welded, 1 dk	**(A13B2TP) Products Tanker** Liq: 384; Liq (Oil): 384	**1 oil engine** driving 1 FP propeller Total Power: 221kW (300hp) 8.0k Hanshin RZ 1 x 4 Stroke 6 Cy. 210 x 330 221kW (300bhp) The Hanshin Diesel Works Ltd-Japan
6809214 - -	**YOSHI MARU No. 1** - **Nansei Enyo Gyogyo** - *South Korea*	*113* 42 -		**1967 Tokushima Zosen K.K. — Fukuoka** Yd No: 721 Loa 34.22 Br ex 5.64 Dght 2.591 Lbp 29.39 Br md 5.62 Dpth 3.00 Welded, 1 dk	**(B11B2FV) Fishing Vessel**	**1 oil engine** driving 1 FP propeller Total Power: 552kW (750hp) Akasaka 6DH27S 1 x 4 Stroke 6 Cy. 270 x 420 552kW (750bhp) Akasaka Tekkosho KK (Akasaka DieselLtd)-Japan
8708919 - -	**YOSHI MARU No. 1** - **Seaford Shipping Lines Inc** - *Philippines*	*198* - 680		**1987-09 K.K. Miura Zosensho — Saiki** Yd No: 785 Loa 53.01 Br ex - Dght 3.282 Lbp 48.01 Br md 9.31 Dpth 5.57 Welded	**(A31A2GX) General Cargo Ship**	**1 oil engine** geared to sc. shaft driving 1 FP propeller Total Power: 625kW (850hp) Hanshin 6LU26 1 x 4 Stroke 6 Cy. 260 x 440 625kW (850bhp) The Hanshin Diesel Works Ltd-Japan

809226	**YOSHI MARU No. 2** **Nansei Enyo Gyogyo** - *South Korea*	*114* 42 -	**1967 Tokushima Zosen K.K. — Fukuoka** Yd No: 722 Loa 34.22 Br ex 5.64 Dght 2.591 Lbp 29.39 Br md 5.62 Dpth 3.00 Welded, 1 dk	**(B11B2FV) Fishing Vessel**	**1 oil engine** driving 1 FP propeller Total Power: 552kW (750hp) Akasaka 6DH27SS 1 x 4 Stroke 6 Cy. 270 x 420 552kW (750bhp) Akasaka Tekkosho KK (Akasaka DieselLtd)-Japan
621082 *E2866*	**YOSHI MARU No. 2** *ex* Chitose Maru No. 68 *-1996* *ex* Chitose Maru No. 3 *-1993* **KK Fukuei** - *Sakaiminato, Tottori* *Japan* Official number: 128211	*164* - -	**1986-11 K.K. Yoshida Zosen Tekko — Kesennuma** Yd No: 336 Loa - Br ex - Dght - Lbp 30.99 Br md 6.61 Dpth 2.65 Welded, 1 dk	**(B11B2FV) Fishing Vessel**	**1 oil engine** driving 1 FP propeller Total Power: 272kW (370hp) Hanshin 6LU24G 1 x 4 Stroke 6 Cy. 240 x 410 272kW (370bhp) The Hanshin Diesel Works Ltd-Japan
925191 *K5465*	**YOSHI MARU No. 8** **Taisei Kaiun YK** - *Kasaoka, Okayama* *Japan* Official number: 135301	*299* - -	**1996-07 Kimura Zosen K.K. — Kure** L reg 59.71 Br ex - Dght - Lbp 58.00 Br md 10.50 Dpth 6.10 Welded, 1 dk	**(A31A2GX) General Cargo Ship**	**1 oil engine** driving 1 FP propeller Total Power: 736kW (1,001hp) Hanshin LH28LG 1 x 4 Stroke 6 Cy. 280 x 530 736kW (1001bhp) The Hanshin Diesel Works Ltd-Japan
879392	**YOSHI MARU No. 18** - - - *Tonga*	*117* - -	**1982 Tonoura Dock Co. Ltd. — Miyazaki** L reg 27.30 Br ex - Dght - Lbp - Br md 6.20 Dpth 2.40 Welded, 1 dk	**(B11B2FV) Fishing Vessel**	**1 oil engine** driving 1 FP propeller Otsuka 1 x 4 Stroke KK Otsuka Diesel-Japan
819477	**YOSHI MARU No. 22** **Entreposto Frigorifico de Pesca de Mocambique Ltda** - *Quelimane* *Mozambique*	*346* 185 -	**1968 Yamanishi Shipbuilding Co Ltd — Ishinomaki MG** Yd No: 571 Loa 47.99 Br ex 8.41 Dght 3.302 Lbp 42.02 Br md 8.39 Dpth 3.76 Welded, 2 dks	**(B11A2FT) Trawler**	**1 oil engine** driving 1 FP propeller Total Power: 919kW (1,249hp) Akasaka 6DH35SS 1 x 4 Stroke 6 Cy. 350 x 520 919kW (1249bhp) Akasaka Tekkosho KK (Akasaka DieselLtd)-Japan
809238	**YOSHI MARU No. 36** **Nansei Enyo Gyogyo** - *South Korea*	*114* 42 -	**1967-12 Hakata Dock K.K. — Fukuoka** Yd No: 101 Loa 32.52 Br ex 5.74 Dght - Lbp 29.49 Br md 5.72 Dpth 2.70 Welded, 1 dk	**(B11B2FV) Fishing Vessel**	**1 oil engine** driving 1 FP propeller Total Power: 552kW (750hp) Akasaka 6DH27SS 1 x 4 Stroke 6 Cy. 270 x 420 552kW (750bhp) Akasaka Tekkosho KK (Akasaka DieselLtd)-Japan
809240	**YOSHI MARU No. 38** **Nansei Enyo Gyogyo** - *South Korea*	*114* 42 -	**1967 Hakata Dock K.K. — Fukuoka** Yd No: 102 Loa 32.52 Br ex 5.74 Dght - Lbp 29.49 Br md 5.72 Dpth 2.70 Welded, 1 dk	**(B11B2FV) Fishing Vessel**	**1 oil engine** driving 1 FP propeller Total Power: 552kW (750hp) Akasaka 6DH27SS 1 x 4 Stroke 6 Cy. 270 x 420 552kW (750bhp) Akasaka Tekkosho KK (Akasaka DieselLtd)-Japan
743294 *D2898*	**YOSHI MARU NO. 55** **YK Hiyoshi Suisan** - *Sakaiminato, Tottori* *Japan* Official number: 140995	*122* - -	**2009-06 K.K. Yoshida Zosen Tekko — Kesennuma** Loa 29.80 Br ex - Dght - Lbp 29.80 Br md 6.40 Dpth - Welded, 1 dk	**(B11B2FV) Fishing Vessel**	**1 oil engine** reduction geared to sc. shaft driving 1 Propeller Total Power: 662kW (900hp) Matsui ML624GSC-5 1 x 4 Stroke 6 Cy. 240 x 400 662kW (900bhp) Matsui Iron Works Co Ltd-Japan
954520 *M6657*	**YOSHI MARU No. 81** **YK Yoshi Maru Suisan** - *Nango, Miyazaki* *Japan* MMSI: 431295000 Official number: 135467	*158* - -	**1999-12 Higashi Kyushu Shipbuilding Co Ltd — Usuki OT** Yd No: 835 L reg 34.28 Br ex - Dght - Lbp - Br md 6.01 Dpth 2.80 Bonded, 1 dk	**(B11B2FV) Fishing Vessel** Hull Material: Reinforced Plastic	**1 oil engine** driving 1 FP propeller Niigata 6MG28HLX 1 x 4 Stroke 6 Cy. 280 x 400 Niigata Engineering Co Ltd-Japan
621006 *KNT*	**YOSHI MARU NO. 88** *ex* Seiun Maru No. 38 *-2002* **KK Fukuei** - *Sakaiminato, Tottori* *Japan* Official number: 128179	*166* - -	**1985-11 Kesennuma Tekko — Kesennuma** Yd No: 260 Loa - Br ex - Dght - Lbp 31.42 Br md 6.48 Dpth 2.90 Welded, 1 dk	**(B11B2FV) Fishing Vessel**	**1 oil engine** driving 1 FP propeller Daihatsu 1 x 4 Stroke Daihatsu Diesel Manufacturing Co Lt-Japan
633281	**YOSHIE MARU No. 28** - -	*103* - -	**1978-11 in Japan** L reg 29.80 Br ex - Dght 2.100 Lbp - Br md 5.80 Dpth 2.60 Welded, 1 dk	**(A31A2GX) General Cargo Ship**	**1 oil engine** driving 1 FP propeller
870657 *K5258*	**YOSHIEI MARU** **Yoshimatsu Furunaka** - *Kure, Hiroshima* *Japan* Official number: 134063	*199* - 600	**1993-09 Y.K. Okajima Zosensho — Matsuyama** Yd No: 241 Loa 58.01 Br ex - Dght - Lbp 52.00 Br md 9.50 Dpth 5.40 Welded, 1 dk	**(A31A2GX) General Cargo Ship** Bale: 1,069 Compartments: 1 Ho 1 Ha: (29.0 x 7.2)	**1 oil engine** driving 1 FP propeller Total Power: 736kW (1,001hp) 11.0kn Yanmar MF26-ST 1 x 4 Stroke 6 Cy. 260 x 500 736kW (1001bhp) Yanmar Diesel Engine Co Ltd-Japan
850097	**YOSHIEI MARU No. 36** **Yoshimi Hamaii**	*137* - -	**1973-05 Suzuki Shipyard Co. Ltd. — Yokkaichi** L reg 29.50 Br ex - Dght - Lbp - Br md 6.20 Dpth 2.60 Welded, 1 dk	**(B11B2FV) Fishing Vessel**	**1 oil engine** driving 1 FP propeller Total Power: 346kW (470hp)
926468 *L6481*	**YOSHIFUKUZEN MARU** **Kotobuki Kaiun YK** - *Naruto, Tokushima* *Japan* Official number: 135516	*374* - -	**1996-12 K.K. Kamishima Zosensho — Osakikamijima** Yd No: 605 Loa 60.00 Br ex - Dght - Lbp 52.50 Br md 12.00 Dpth 6.20 Welded, 1 dk	**(A24D2BA) Aggregates Carrier**	**1 oil engine** driving 1 FP propeller Total Power: 736kW (1,001hp) 10.5kn Hanshin LH31G 1 x 4 Stroke 6 Cy. 310 x 530 736kW (1001bhp) The Hanshin Diesel Works Ltd-Japan
854081 *M6057*	**YOSHIGA MARU NO. 8** *ex* Kasuga Maru No. 8 *-2000* **Yoshiga Kaiun KK** - SatCom: Inmarsat A 1206135 *Kitakyushu, Fukuoka* *Japan* Official number: 132618	*199* - 649	**1991-05 YK Furumoto Tekko Zosensho — Osakikamijima** Loa 55.11 Br ex - Dght 3.610 Lbp 49.00 Br md 9.20 Dpth 5.93 Welded, 1 dk	**(A31A2GX) General Cargo Ship** Grain: 1,217; Bale: 1,197 1 Ha: (30.0 x 7.2)ER	**1 oil engine** driving 1 FP propeller Total Power: 588kW (799hp) 11.0kn Yanmar MF28-UT 1 x 4 Stroke 6 Cy. 280 x 450 588kW (799bhp) Yanmar Diesel Engine Co Ltd-Japan
646508 *D3299*	**YOSHIHIRO MARU NO. 28** **Yamamatsu Hamamoto Suisan KK** - *Monbetsu, Hokkaido* *Japan* Official number: 141595	*160* - -	**2012-04 The Hakodate Dock Co Ltd — Muroran HK** Yd No: W3211 Loa 38.38 Br ex - Dght 3.350 Lbp - Br md 7.80 Dpth 4.61 Welded, 1 dk	**(B11A2FT) Trawler**	**1 oil engine** reduction geared to sc. shaft driving 1 Propeller Total Power: 1,471kW (2,000hp) Niigata 6MG26HLX 1 x 4 Stroke 6 Cy. 260 x 350 1471kW (2000bhp) Niigata Engineering Co Ltd-Japan
940645 *L6309*	**YOSHIHO MARU** **YK Oda Suisan** - SatCom: Inmarsat C 443183410 *Uwajima, Ehime* *Japan* MMSI: 431834000 Official number: 134886	*321* 202 -	**1996-02 K.K. Watanabe Zosensho — Nagasaki** Yd No: 038 Loa - Br ex - Dght 3.750 Lbp 49.50 Br md 8.50 Dpth 4.20 Welded, 1 dk	**(B12C2FL) Live Fish Carrier (Well Boat)**	**1 oil engine** geared to sc. shaft driving 1 FP propeller Total Power: 691kW (939hp) Yanmar 1 x 4 Stroke 691kW (939bhp) Yanmar Diesel Engine Co Ltd-Japan
246889 *L6672*	**YOSHIHO MARU No. 3** **YK Oda Suisan** - *Uwajima, Ehime* *Japan* MMSI: 431303000 Official number: 136515	*324* - -	**2001-02 K.K. Watanabe Zosensho — Nagasaki** Yd No: 086 Loa 57.70 Br ex - Dght - Lbp 50.00 Br md 8.50 Dpth 4.25 Welded, 1 dk	**(B11B2FV) Fishing Vessel**	**1 oil engine** geared to sc. shaft driving 1 FP propeller Total Power: 736kW (1,001hp) Yanmar 6N260-EN 1 x 4 Stroke 6 Cy. 260 x 360 736kW (1001bhp) Yanmar Diesel Engine Co Ltd-Japan

IMO / Call sign / Flag	Name / Owner / Port	Tonnage	Class	Build / Dimensions	Type	Machinery
7722645 *JM4292* -	**YOSHIKATSU MARU No. 65** *ex* Genpuku Maru No. 65 *-1991* **YK Yoshikatsu Gyogyo** *Hamada, Shimane* *Japan* Official number: 120677	*188* - -		**1978-04 Nagasaki Zosen K.K. — Nagasaki** Yd No: 623 Loa 43.79 Br ex 7.50 Dght 2.901 Lbp 38.03 Br md 7.21 Dpth 3.26 Welded	**(B12B2FC) Fish Carrier**	**1 oil engine** reduction geared to sc. shaft driving 1 FP propeller Total Power: 956kW (1,300hp) Niigata 6L28B 1 x 4 Stroke 6 Cy. 280 x 320 956kW (1300bhp) Niigata Engineering Co Ltd-Japan
8967369 *JI3690* -	**YOSHINO** **Kansai Kowan Service KK** *Sakai, Osaka* *Japan* Official number: 137074	*278* - -		**2001-05 Hatayama Zosen KK — Yura WK** Yd No: 236 Loa 38.00 Br ex - Dght - Lbp 32.00 Br md 9.60 Dpth 4.49 Welded, 1 dk	**(B32A2ST) Tug**	**2 oil engines** geared integral to driving 2 Z propellers Total Power: 3,236kW (4,400hp) 14.5k Niigata 6L28H 2 x 4 Stroke 6 Cy. 280 x 370 each-1618kW (2200bhp) Niigata Engineering Co Ltd-Japan
9427794 *7JDX* -	**YOSHINO** **Government of Japan (Ministry of Land, Infrastructure & Transport) (The Coastguard)** - *Tokyo* *Japan* Official number: 140831	*358* - -		**2009-03 Universal Shipbuilding Corp — Yokohama KN (Keihin Shipyard)** Yd No: 0045 Loa 56.00 Br ex - Dght - Lbp - Br md 8.50 Dpth 4.52 Welded, 1 dk	**(B34H2SQ) Patrol Vessel** Hull Material: Aluminium Alloy	**3 oil engines** reduction geared to sc. shafts driving 3 Water jets
9660970 *JD3379* -	**YOSHINO MARU** **Wing Maritime Service Corp** - *Yokohama, Kanagawa* *Japan* Official number: 141706	*190* - 80		**2012-07 Keihin Dock Co Ltd — Yokohama** Yd No: 302 Loa 32.80 Br ex - Dght 2.700 Lbp - Br md 8.80 Dpth - Welded, 1 dk	**(B32A2ST) Tug**	**2 oil engines** reduction geared to sc. shafts driving 2 Propellers Total Power: 2,942kW (4,000hp) Niigata 6L26HL 2 x 4 Stroke 6 Cy. 260 x 350 each-1471kW (2000bhp) Niigata Engineering Co Ltd-Japan
6809252 - -	**YOSHINO MARU** - -	*188* - -		**1967 Ishikawajima Ship & Chemical Plant Co Ltd — Tokyo** Yd No: 367 Loa 29.04 Br ex 8.39 Dght 2.794 Lbp 28.02 Br md 8.21 Dpth 3.89 Welded, 1 dk	**(B32A2ST) Tug**	**2 oil engines** geared to sc. shafts driving 2 FP propellers Total Power: 736kW (1,000hp) 12.5k Fuji 6MD32 2 x 4 Stroke 6 Cy. 320 x 380 each-368kW (500bhp) Fuji Diesel Co Ltd-Japan AuxGen: 1 x 30kW 225V a.c Fuel: 34.5
8879017 *JJ3818* -	**YOSHISHIGE MARU No. 38** **Nippon Kidou Kensetsu KK** *Himeji, Hyogo* *Japan* Official number: 132320	*488* - -		**1994-07 Nagashima Zosen KK — Kihoku ME** Yd No: 366 Loa 70.98 Br ex - Dght - Lbp 65.00 Br md 13.50 Dpth 6.94 Welded, 1 dk	**(A24D2BA) Aggregates Carrier** Cranes: 1	**1 oil engine** driving 1 FP propeller Total Power: 1,471kW (2,000hp) 13.0k Akasaka A3 1 x 4 Stroke 6 Cy. 370 x 720 1471kW (2000bhp) Akasaka Tekkosho KK (Akasaka DieselLtd)-Japan
8319574 - -	**YOSHITAKA MARU No. 31** - - *China*	*478* - 1,278		**1984-01 Suzuki Shipyard Co. Ltd. — Yokkaichi** Yd No: 500 Loa 62.90 Br ex - Dght 4.309 Lbp 57.99 Br md 9.50 Dpth 4.50 Welded, 1 dk	**(A12B2TR) Chemical/Products Tanker** Liq: 1,349; Liq (Oil): 1,349 Compartments: 8 Ta, ER	**1 oil engine** driving 1 FP propeller Total Power: 883kW (1,201hp) Hanshin 6LUD2 1 x 4 Stroke 6 Cy. 260 x 440 883kW (1201bhp) The Hanshin Diesel Works Ltd-Japan
9117765 - -	**YOSHITAKA MARU No. 51** - -	*749* - 1,941	Class: (NK)	**1994-10 Murakami Hide Zosen K.K. — Imabari** Yd No: 366 Loa 76.93 Br ex - Dght 4.748 Lbp 72.00 Br md 11.50 Dpth 5.25 Welded, 1 dk	**(A13B2TP) Products Tanker** Liq: 2,202; Liq (Oil): 2,202	**1 oil engine** driving 1 FP propeller Total Power: 1,471kW (2,000hp) 12.9k Yanmar MF33-E 1 x 4 Stroke 6 Cy. 330 x 620 1471kW (2000bhp) Yanmar Diesel Engine Co Ltd-Japan Fuel: 70.0 (d.f.)
9671266 *JD3513* -	**YOSHITAKA MARU NO. 93** **Ikeda Shoji KK** *Katsuura, Chiba* *Japan* MMSI: 431004506 Official number: 141920	*998* - 2,414	Class: NK	**2013-05 Murakami Hide Zosen K.K. — Imabari** Yd No: 595 Loa 79.92 Br ex - Dght 5.160 Lbp 76.10 Br md 12.20 Dpth 5.75 Welded, 1 dk	**(A13B2TP) Products Tanker** Double Hull (13F) Liq: 2,516; Liq (Oil): 2,516	**1 oil engine** reduction geared to sc. shaft driving 1 Propeller Total Power: 1,618kW (2,200hp) Daihatsu 6DKM-2 1 x 4 Stroke 6 Cy. 260 x 380 1618kW (2200bhp) Daihatsu Diesel Manufacturing Co Lt-Japan Fuel: 122.0
8115162 - -	**YOSHIUMI** **Ocean Rail Transport Ltd**	*198* - 653		**1981-08 Yano Zosen K.K. — Imabari** Yd No: 105 Loa 56.01 Br ex 9.40 Dght 3.182 Lbp 53.32 Br md 9.19 Dpth 5.01 Welded, 2 dks	**(A31A2GX) General Cargo Ship**	**1 oil engine** driving 1 FP propeller Total Power: 625kW (850hp) Niigata 6M28AG 1 x 4 Stroke 6 Cy. 280 x 480 625kW (850bhp) Niigata Engineering Co Ltd-Japan
9574274 *JD3048* -	**YOSHO MARU** **Japan Railway Construction, Transport & Technology Agency & Kyokuyo Tanker KK** Ryusei Kisen YK *Tokyo* *Japan* Official number: 141220	*499* - 1,284		**2010-05 Imura Zosen K.K. — Komatsushima** Yd No: 331 Loa 65.19 Br ex - Dght 4.220 Lbp 59.98 Br md 10.40 Dpth 4.50 Welded, 1 dk	**(A13B2TP) Products Tanker** Double Hull (13F) Liq: 1,235; Liq (Oil): 1,235	**1 oil engine** reduction geared to sc. shaft driving 1 FP propeller Total Power: 1,030kW (1,400hp) Hanshin LH28 1 x 4 Stroke 6 Cy. 280 x 460 1030kW (1400bhp) The Hanshin Diesel Works Ltd-Japan
9263148 *JH3502* -	**YOSHO MARU** **Fujitrans Corp** Kagoshima Senpaku Kaisha Ltd *Nagoya, Aichi* *Japan* MMSI: 431200632 Official number: 135683	*14,790* - 6,950	Class: NK	**2003-01 Mitsubishi Heavy Industries Ltd. — Shimonoseki** Yd No: 1089 Loa 167.00 (BB) Br ex - Dght 7.500 Lbp 158.00 Br md 30.20 Dpth 28.75 Welded, 1 dk	**(A35B2RV) Vehicles Carrier** Quarter stern door/ramp (p. a.) Len: 25.00 Wid: 7.00 Swl: 65 Quarter stern door/ramp (s. a.) Len: 25.00 Wid: 7.00 Swl: 65 Cars: 750	**1 oil engine** driving 1 CP propeller Total Power: 19,123kW (26,000hp) 23.5k Mitsubishi 12UEC52LS 1 x 2 Stroke 12 Cy. 520 x 2000 19123kW (26000bhp) Mitsubishi Heavy Industries Ltd-Japan AuxGen: 2 x 1600kW 60Hz a.c, 1 x 1600kW 60Hz a.c Thrusters: 1 Tunnel thruster (f); 2 Tunnel thruster (a) Fuel: 2698.0
8716538 *JG4805* -	**YOSHU MARU No. 1** **Nippon Kaiun KK (Nippon Shipping Co Ltd)** SatCom: Inmarsat C 443275610 *Tokyo* *Japan* MMSI: 432756000 Official number: 131129	*7,521* 2,642 11,784	Class: NK	**1988-10 Kanda Zosensho K.K. — Kawajiri** Yd No: 314 Loa 135.00 (BB) Br ex 20.63 Dght 7.991 Lbp 126.60 Br md 20.00 Dpth 9.80 Welded, 1 dk	**(A24A2BT) Cement Carrier** Grain: 9,696 Compartments: 4 Ho, ER	**1 oil engine** driving 1 CP propeller Total Power: 4,855kW (6,601hp) 14.2k Mitsubishi 6UEC45L 1 x 2 Stroke 6 Cy. 450 x 1350 4855kW (6601bhp) Akasaka Tekkosho KK (Akasaka DieselLtd)-Japan AuxGen: 2 x 920kW a.c, 1 x 320kW a.c, 1 x 110kW a.c Thrusters: 1 Thwart. FP thruster (f); 1 Thwart. FP thruster (a) Fuel: 300.0 (r.f.)
8816352 *JK4840* -	**YOSHU MARU No. 2** **Kanda Shipbuilding Co Ltd (Kanda Zosensho KK Kawajiri)** *Kure, Hiroshima* *Japan* MMSI: 431401272 Official number: 130974	*2,012* - 3,399	Class: NK	**1988-11 Kanda Zosensho K.K. — Kawajiri** Yd No: 321 Loa 86.00 (BB) Br ex 14.52 Dght 5.313 Lbp 80.00 Br md 14.50 Dpth 6.50 Welded, 1 dk	**(A24A2BT) Cement Carrier** Grain: 2,792 Compartments: 3 Ho, ER	**1 oil engine** with clutches, flexible couplings & sr geared to sc. shaft driving 1 CP propeller Total Power: 1,618kW (2,200hp) 11.7k Niigata 6M34AF 1 x 4 Stroke 6 Cy. 340 x 620 1618kW (2200bhp) Niigata Engineering Co Ltd-Japan AuxGen: 2 x 240kW 445V 60Hz a.c Thrusters: 1 Thwart. CP thruster (f) Fuel: 125.0 (r.f.)
9167643 *JG5510* -	**YOSHU MARU No. 5** **Nippon Kaiun KK (Nippon Shipping Co Ltd)** *Tokyo* *Japan* MMSI: 431400833 Official number: 135890	*4,387* - 6,506	Class: NK	**1997-09 Kanda Zosensho K.K. — Kawajiri** Yd No: 388 Loa 110.00 (BB) Br ex - Dght 6.714 Lbp 105.00 Br md 16.80 Dpth 8.50 Welded, 1 dk	**(A24A2BT) Cement Carrier** Grain: 5,580 Compartments: 3 Ho, ER	**1 oil engine** driving 1 CP propeller Total Power: 3,604kW (4,900hp) 13.3k Mitsubishi 7UEC37L 1 x 2 Stroke 7 Cy. 370 x 880 3604kW (4900bhp) Akasaka Tekkosho KK (Akasaka DieselLtd)-Japan AuxGen: 2 x 450kW a.c Thrusters: 1 Thwart. FP thruster (f) Fuel: 184.0 (r.f.) 12.9pd
8626733 - -	**YOSHU MARU No. 8** - -	*426* - 1,300		**1985-04 K.K. Murakami Zosensho — Naruto** Loa 53.01 Br ex - Dght 4.871 Lbp 47.60 Br md 12.01 Dpth 6.38 Welded, 1 dk	**(B33A2DG) Grab Dredger** Grain: 1,940	**1 oil engine** driving 1 FP propeller Total Power: 883kW (1,201hp) 10.0k Hanshin 6LUN28A 1 x 4 Stroke 6 Cy. 280 x 480 883kW (1201bhp) The Hanshin Diesel Works Ltd-Japan
9180528 *JL6501* -	**YOSHU MARU No. 11** **KK Yoshu Kogyo** - *Shikokuchuo, Ehime* *Japan* Official number: 135124	*499* - -		**1997-02 Kegoya Dock K.K. — Kure** Yd No: 995 Loa 66.50 Br ex - Dght - Lbp 61.00 Br md 13.20 Dpth 7.40 Welded, 1 dk	**(A31A2GX) General Cargo Ship** Compartments: 1 Ho, ER 1 Ha: (18.0 x 9.4)ER	**1 oil engine** driving 1 FP propeller Total Power: 1,854kW (2,521hp) 13.6k Caterpillar 3606T 1 x 4 Stroke 6 Cy. 280 x 300 1854kW (2521bhp) Caterpillar Inc-USA

IMO / Call sign	Name / Owner	Tonnage	Class	Builder / Dimensions	Type	Machinery
62477 NI	**YOSOA** *ex* Wi No. 1 *-2011* *ex* Kaiei Maru No. 1 *-2011* **PT Duamitra Oil** *Jakarta* *Indonesia*	**1,049** 642 1,950	Class: KI	**1993-03 Matsuura Tekko Zosen K.K. — Osakikamijima** Yd No: 374 Loa 74.00 (BB) Br ex - Dght 4.700 Lbp 70.00 Br md 11.70 Dpth 5.25 Welded, 1 dk	**(A13B2TP) Products Tanker** Compartments: 10 Wing Ta, ER	**1 oil engine** reverse geared to sc. shaft driving 1 FP propeller Total Power: 1,324kW (1,800hp) Hanshin 6LU32G 1 x 4 Stroke 6 Cy. 320 x 510 1324kW (1800bhp) The Hanshin Diesel Works Ltd-Japan
819113 EXD9	**YOSOR** *ex* Gracia Del Mar *-2012* **Camel Shipping Co Ltd** - *Panama* *Panama* MMSI: 354760000 Official number: 4360212A	**12,299** 6,994 8,594	Class: (RS) (GL)	**1981-06 Enrique Lorenzo y Cia SA — Vigo** Yd No: 399 Converted From: Container Ship (Fully Cellular with Ro-Ro Facility)-2011 Loa 122.71 (BB) Br ex 19.44 Dght 8.151 Lbp 108.01 Br md 19.41 Dpth 12.32 Welded, 2 dks	**(A38A2GL) Livestock Carrier** Quarter stern door/ramp (s)	**1 oil engine** geared to sc. shaft driving 1 FP propeller Total Power: 4,413kW (6,000hp) 12.0kn Deutz SBV12M540 1 x Vee 4 Stroke 12 Cy. 370 x 400 4413kW (6000bhp) Hijos de J Barreras SA-Spain
224896 NOL	**YOSRA** **Societe Atlantique d'Exploitation Maritime (SAETMA)** - SatCom: Inmarsat C 424241310 *Agadir* *Morocco*	**324** 142 337	Class: BV	**1984-06 Construcciones Navales Santodomingo SA — Vigo** Yd No: 497 Loa 38.31 Br ex 8.59 Dght 3.650 Lbp 34.78 Br md 8.51 Dpth 6.15 Welded, 1 dk	**(B11A2FS) Stern Trawler** Ins: 402 Compartments: 1 Ho, ER 2 Ha: ER	**1 oil engine** with clutches, flexible couplings & sr geared to sc. shaft driving 1 FP propeller Total Power: 853kW (1,160hp) 12.3kn Deutz SBA8M528 1 x 4 Stroke 8 Cy. 220 x 280 853kW (1160bhp) Hijos de J Barreras SA-Spain AuxGen: 2 x 140kW 380V 50Hz a.c
072525 VCU4	**YOSSA BHUM** *ex* Blue Link *-2005* *ex* Konlink *-2003* *ex* Ascot *-2001* *ex* Ratana Priya *-1998* *ex* Ratha Bhum *-1997* *ex* Ascot *-1994* **Regional Container Lines Pte Ltd** RCL Shipmanagement Pte Ltd *Singapore* *Singapore* MMSI: 565008000 Official number: 391736	**11,788** 6,625 15,414 T/cm 28.1	Class: NK	**1994-03 Iwagi Zosen Co Ltd — Kamijima EH** Yd No: 155 Loa 145.68 (BB) Br ex - Dght 8.814 Lbp 136.00 Br md 25.00 Dpth 12.80 Welded, 1 dk	**(A33A2CC) Container Ship (Fully Cellular)** TEU 818 C Ho 428 TEU C Dk 390 TEU incl 100 ref C. Compartments: 4 Cell Ho, ER 14 Ha: 12 (12.8 x 10.6)2 (12.8 x 8.0)ER Cranes: 2x35t	**1 oil engine** driving 1 FP propeller Total Power: 8,561kW (11,640hp) 17.1kn B&W 6S50MC 1 x 2 Stroke 6 Cy. 500 x 1910 8561kW (11640bhp) Mitsui Engineering & Shipbuilding CLtd-Japan Thrusters: 1 Tunnel thruster (f) Fuel: 935.0 (r.f.)
016739 SFE2	**YOSU GAS** **GS-Caltex Corp** Sangji Shipping Co Ltd SatCom: Inmarsat B 335614310 *Yeosu* *South Korea* MMSI: 440831000 Official number: YSR-995749	**3,866** 1,159 3,782 T/cm 13.7	Class: KR (NK)	**1990-11 Shin Kurushima Dockyard Co. Ltd. — Akitsu** Yd No: 2692 Loa 105.92 (BB) Br ex - Dght 5.123 Lbp 99.90 Br md 16.20 Dpth 8.00 Welded, 1 dk	**(A11B2TG) LPG Tanker** Single Hull Liq (Gas): 4,013 3 x Gas Tank (s); 3 independent (C.mn.stl) cyl horizontal 3 Cargo Pump (s): 3x350m³/hr Manifold: Bow/CM: 60.1m	**1 oil engine** driving 1 FP propeller Total Power: 2,346kW (3,190hp) 15.1kn Mitsubishi 6UEC37LA 1 x 2 Stroke 6 Cy. 370 x 880 2346kW (3190bhp) Kobe Motor Manufacturing Co.-Kobe AuxGen: 2 x 240kW 450V 60Hz a.c Fuel: 77.0 (d.f.) 446.0 (r.f.) 9.0pd
851290 D2110	**YOTEI** **Toyako Kisen KK** - *Toyako, Hokkaido* *Japan* Official number: 102605	*346* - -		**1971-06 Kushiro Senpaku Tekko K.K. — Kushiro** Loa 34.40 Br ex - Dght 2.001 Lbp 29.80 Br md 7.21 Dpth 2.49 Welded, 1 dk	**(A37B2PS) Passenger Ship** Passengers: unberthed: 554	**1 oil engine** driving 1 FP propeller Total Power: 191kW (260hp) 10.0kn Niigata 6MG16S 1 x 4 Stroke 6 Cy. 160 x 200 191kW (260bhp) Niigata Engineering Co Ltd-Japan
510075	**YOTOKU MARU No. 2** *ex* Kyokuho Maru No. 15 *-1993* - - *South Korea*	*499* - 1,180		**1985-09 Kishimoto Zosen K.K. — Kinoe** Yd No: 551 Loa 64.30 Br ex - Dght 4.050 Lbp 60.00 Br md 10.00 Dpth 4.50 Welded, 1 dk	**(A13B2TP) Products Tanker**	**1 oil engine** reverse geared to sc. shaft driving 1 FP propeller Total Power: 809kW (1,100hp) Akasaka A28R 1 x 4 Stroke 6 Cy. 280 x 550 809kW (1100bhp) Akasaka Tekkosho KK (Akasaka DieselLtd)-Japan
8876857	**YOTOKU MARU No. 61** *ex* Mito Maru No. 52 *-1993* **Amparo Shipping Corp** - *Philippines*	*108* - -		**1981 in Japan** L reg 27.40 Br ex - Dght - Lbp - Br md 5.60 Dpth 2.20 Welded, 1 dk	**(B11B2FV) Fishing Vessel**	**1 oil engine** driving 1 FP propeller
8744157 -	**YOU BANG 6** **Youbang Shipping Co Ltd** - *Ningbo, Zhejiang* *China* Official number: 070109000194	*2,972* 1,664 5,230		**2009-09 Zhejiang Xifeng Shipbuilding Co Ltd — Fenghua ZJ** Loa 96.90 Br ex - Dght 5.850 Lbp 89.80 Br md 15.80 Dpth 7.40 Welded, 1 dk	**(A31A2GX) General Cargo Ship** Grain: 6,800; Bale: 6,500	**1 oil engine** reduction geared to sc. shaft driving 1 Propeller Total Power: 2,000kW (2,719hp) 11.0kn Chinese Std. Type G8300ZC 1 x 4 Stroke 8 Cy. 300 x 380 2000kW (2719bhp) Ningbo CSI Power & Machinery GroupCo Ltd-China
8890217 VRS4253	**YOU DA** **Yiu Lian Dockyards Ltd** - *Hong Kong* *Hong Kong* Official number: HK-0197	*391* 117 168	Class: CC (BV)	**1994-07 Yantai Shipyard — Yantai SD** Loa 36.20 Br ex - Dght 3.400 Lbp 33.67 Br md 9.80 Dpth 4.36 Welded, 1 dk	**(B32A2ST) Tug**	**2 oil engines** driving 2 FP propellers Total Power: 2,400kW (3,264hp) 13.0kn Pielstick 6PA5L255 2 x 4 Stroke 6 Cy. 255 x 270 each-1200kW (1632bhp) Niigata Engineering Co Ltd-Japan AuxGen: 3 x 72kW 220/380V 50Hz a.c
8869517 VRS4254	**YOU FA** **Yiu Lian Dockyards Ltd** - *Hong Kong* *Hong Kong* Official number: HK-0164	*391* 117 168	Class: CC (BV)	**1993 Yantai Shipyard — Yantai SD** Yd No: H45 Loa 36.20 Br ex - Dght 3.400 Lbp 33.67 Br md 9.80 Dpth 4.36 Welded, 1 dk	**(B32A2ST) Tug**	**2 oil engines** reduction geared to sc. shafts driving 2 FP propellers Total Power: 2,400kW (3,264hp) Pielstick 6PA5L255 2 x 4 Stroke 6 Cy. 255 x 270 each-1200kW (1632bhp) Niigata Engineering Co Ltd-Japan AuxGen: 3 x 72kW 220/380V 50Hz a.c
9604536 BPHW -	**YOU HAO 1** **China Shipping Tanker Co Ltd** - *Shanghai* *China*	**30,334** 16,987 47,310	Class: CC	**2012-05 China Shipping Industry (Jiangsu) Co Ltd — Jiangdu JS** Yd No: IS47500/A-03 Loa 199.99 (BB) Br ex - Dght 10.700 Lbp 192.00 Br md 32.26 Dpth 16.20 Welded, 1 dk	**(A21A2BC) Bulk Carrier** Grain: 57,200 Compartments: 5 Ho, ER 5 Ha: ER Ice Capable	**1 oil engine** driving 1 FP propeller Total Power: 6,450kW (8,769hp) 13.0kn MAN-B&W 6S46MC-C 1 x 2 Stroke 6 Cy. 460 x 1932 6450kW (8769bhp) STX (Dalian) Engine Co Ltd-China
9604500 BPHX -	**YOU HAO 2** **China Shipping Tanker Co Ltd** - *Shanghai* *China*	**30,334** 16,987 47,664	Class: CC	**2012-08 China Shipping Industry (Jiangsu) Co Ltd — Jiangdu JS** Yd No: IS47500/A-02 Loa 199.99 (BB) Br ex - Dght 10.700 Lbp 192.00 Br md 32.26 Dpth 16.20 Welded, 1 dk	**(A21A2BC) Bulk Carrier** Grain: 57,200 Compartments: 5 Ho, ER 5 Ha: ER	**1 oil engine** driving 1 FP propeller Total Power: 6,450kW (8,769hp) 13.0kn MAN-B&W 6S46MC-C 1 x 2 Stroke 6 Cy. 460 x 1932 6450kW (8769bhp)
9605085 HOHX -	**YOU & ISLAND** *ex* You Island *-2011* **Ambitious Line SA** Shikishima Kisen KK *Panama* *Panama* MMSI: 372742000 Official number: 4325511	**23,264** 12,134 38,309 T/cm 48.6	Class: NK	**2011-11 Shimanami Shipyard Co Ltd — Imabari EH** Yd No: 553 Loa 179.97 (BB) Br ex - Dght 10.540 Lbp 173.00 Br md 29.80 Dpth 15.00 Welded, 1 dk	**(A21A2BC) Bulk Carrier** Grain: 47,125; Bale: 45,369 Compartments: 5 Ho, ER 5 Ha: ER Cranes: 4x30.5t	**1 oil engine** driving 1 FP propeller Total Power: 7,860kW (10,686hp) 14.7kn MAN-B&W 6S46MC-C 1 x 2 Stroke 6 Cy. 460 x 1932 7860kW (10686bhp) Makita Corp-Japan Fuel: 1940.0
6716390 6KWX -	**YOU JIN No. 21** *ex* Tae Yang No. 108 *-1985* *ex* Kook Yang No. 108 *-1985* **Kim Jum-Ork** - *Busan* *South Korea* Official number: BS-A-317	*133* 41 113	Class: (KR)	**1967 Fukuoka Shipbuilding Co Ltd — Fukuoka FO** Yd No: 886 Loa 33.56 Br ex 6.15 Dght 2.401 Lbp 28.61 Br md 6.10 Dpth 2.75 Welded, 1 dk	**(B11B2FV) Fishing Vessel** Ins: 100 4 Ha: 4 (0.9 x 1.1)	**1 oil engine** driving 1 FP propeller Total Power: 331kW (450hp) 9.0kn Hanshin Z76 1 x 4 Stroke 6 Cy. 270 x 400 331kW (450bhp) Hanshin Nainenki Kogyo-Japan AuxGen: 2 x 26kW 230V a.c
6716417 6KWZ -	**YOU JIN No. 22** *ex* Tae Yang No. 110 *-1984* *ex* Kook Yang No. 111 *-1984* **Kim Jum-Ork** - *Busan* *South Korea* Official number: BS-A-319	*133* 41 113	Class: (KR)	**1967 Fukuoka Shipbuilding Co Ltd — Fukuoka FO** Yd No: 892 Loa 33.56 Br ex 6.15 Dght 2.401 Lbp 28.61 Br md 6.10 Dpth 2.75 Welded, 1 dk	**(B11B2FV) Fishing Vessel** Ins: 100 4 Ha: 4 (0.9 x 1.1)	**1 oil engine** driving 1 FP propeller Total Power: 331kW (450hp) 9.0kn Hanshin Z76 1 x 4 Stroke 6 Cy. 270 x 400 331kW (450bhp) Hanshin Nainenki Kogyo-Japan AuxGen: 2 x 26kW 230V a.c
8913198 BQAX -	**YOU LIANG** **Shenzhen Ocean Shipping Co (COSCO SHENZHEN)** - *Shenzhen, Guangdong* *China* MMSI: 413573000	**23,303** 13,622 42,066 T/cm 47.5	Class: (CC) (NK)	**1991-02 Oshima Shipbuilding Co Ltd — Saikai NS** Yd No: 10130 Loa 180.70 (BB) Br ex - Dght 11.196 Lbp 172.00 Br md 30.50 Dpth 15.80 Welded, 1 dk	**(A21A2BC) Bulk Carrier** Grain: 51,813; Bale: 50,813 Compartments: 5 Ho, ER 5 Ha: (14.4 x 15.3)4 (19.2 x 15.3)ER Cranes: 4x25t	**1 oil engine** driving 1 FP propeller Total Power: 6,230kW (8,470hp) 14.6kn Sulzer 6RTA52 1 x 2 Stroke 6 Cy. 520 x 1800 6230kW (8470bhp) Diesel United Ltd.-Aioi AuxGen: 3 x 410kW 450V 60Hz a.c Fuel: 106.0 (d.f.) 1422.0 (r.f.) 24.2pd

IMO / Call sign	Name / Owner	Tonnage	Class	Builder / Dimensions	Type / Cargo	Machinery	
8913203 *BQAY* -	**YOU MEI** **Shenzhen Ocean Shipping Co (COSCO SHENZHEN)** - *Shenzhen, Guangdong* *China* MMSI: 413840000	**23,303** 13,622 42,035 T/cm 47.5	Class: CC (NK)	**1991-05 Oshima Shipbuilding Co Ltd — Saikai NS** Yd No: 10131 Loa 180.70 (BB) Br ex - Dght 11.196 Lbp 172.00 Br md 30.50 Dpth 15.80 Welded, 1 dk	**(A21A2BC) Bulk Carrier** Grain: 51,813; Bale: 50,813 Compartments: 5 Ho, ER 5 Ha: (14.4 x 15.3)4 (19.2 x 15.3)ER Cranes: 4x25t	**1 oil engine** driving 1 FP propeller Total Power: 6,230kW (8,470hp) Sulzer 1 x 2 Stroke 6 Cy. 520 x 1800 6230kW (8470bhp) Diesel United Ltd.-Aioi AuxGen: 3 x 410kW 450V 60Hz a.c Fuel: 106.0 (d.f.) 1422.0 (r.f.) 24.2pd	14.6 6RTA5
9478042 *BIQC* -	**YOU SHEN 1** **Shanghai Dongzhan Oil Transportation Co Ltd** - *Zhoushan, Zhejiang* *China* MMSI: 413373690	**5,163** 2,563 8,284 T/cm 19.7	Class: CC	**2007-12 Zhejiang Richland Shipbuilding Co Ltd — Zhoushan ZJ** Yd No: 6001 Loa 115.19 (BB) Br ex - Dght 6.800 Lbp 108.00 Br md 18.00 Dpth 8.90 Welded, 1 dk	**(A12B2TR) Chemical/Products Tanker** Double Hull (13F) Liq: 8,513; Liq (Oil): 8,513 Cargo Heating Coils Compartments: 10 Wing Ta, 2 Wing Slop Ta, ER 6 Cargo Pump (s): 6x400m³/hr Manifold: Bow/CM: 61.4m	**1 oil engine** reduction geared to sc. shaft driving 1 FP propeller Total Power: 2,574kW (3,500hp) Yanmar 1 x 4 Stroke 6 Cy. 330 x 440 2574kW (3500bhp) Zibo Diesel Engine Factory-China AuxGen: 2 x 350kW 400V a.c Thrusters: 1 Tunnel thruster (f) Fuel: 200.0	12.5 6N330-E
9596454 *BIAF2* -	**YOU SHEN 2** **Shanghai Dongzhan Shipping Co Ltd** - *Shanghai* *China* MMSI: 413376430	**4,608** 2,175 7,030 T/cm 15.0	Class: CC	**2011-07 Zhejiang Chenye Shipbuilding Co Ltd — Daishan County ZJ** Yd No: CY0802 Loa 103.00 (BB) Br ex - Dght 7.400 Lbp 96.50 Br md 16.00 Dpth 8.80 Welded, 1 dk	**(A12B2TR) Chemical/Products Tanker** Double Hull (13F) Liq: 7,621; Liq (Oil): 7,621 Cargo Heating Coils Compartments: 12 Wing Ta, ER 12 Cargo Pump (s): 12x180m³/hr Manifold: Bow/CM: 52.1m Ice Capable	**1 oil engine** reduction geared to sc. shaft driving 1 FP propeller Total Power: 2,574kW (3,500hp) Yanmar 1 x 4 Stroke 6 Cy. 330 x 440 2574kW (3500bhp) Qingdao Zichai Boyang Diesel EngineCo Ltd-China AuxGen: 3 x 293kW 400V 60Hz a.c Thrusters: 1 Tunnel thruster (f) Fuel: 103.0 (d.f.) 333.0 (r.f.)	12.5 6N330-E
9596466 *BIAF3* -	**YOU SHEN 3** **Shanghai Dongzhan Shipping Co Ltd** - *Shanghai* *China* MMSI: 413376440	**4,608** 2,175 7,052 T/cm 15.0	Class: CC	**2011-11 Zhejiang Chenye Shipbuilding Co Ltd — Daishan County ZJ** Yd No: CY0803 Loa 103.09 (BB) Br ex - Dght 7.400 Lbp 96.50 Br md 16.00 Dpth 8.80 Welded, 1 dk	**(A12B2TR) Chemical/Products Tanker** Double Hull (13F) Liq: 7,621; Liq (Oil): 7,621 Cargo Heating Coils Compartments: 12 Wing Ta, ER 12 Cargo Pump (s): 12x180m³/hr Manifold: Bow/CM: 52.1m Ice Capable	**1 oil engine** reduction geared to sc. shaft driving 1 FP propeller Total Power: 2,574kW (3,500hp) Yanmar 1 x 4 Stroke 6 Cy. 330 x 440 2574kW (3500bhp) Qingdao Zichai Boyang Diesel EngineCo Ltd-China AuxGen: 3 x 293kW 400V 60Hz a.c Thrusters: 1 Tunnel thruster (f) Fuel: 103.0 (d.f.) 333.0 (r.f.)	12.5 6N330-E
9507556 *BIQZ* -	**YOU SHEN 6** *ex* Bao Hai Bao *-2010* **Shanghai Dongzhan Shipping Co Ltd** - SatCom: Inmarsat C 441301290 *Shanghai* *China* MMSI: 413375480	**5,205** 2,609 8,246	Class: CC	**2010-01 Zhoushan Penglai Shiprepairing & Building Co Ltd — Daishan County ZJ** Yd No: PL0701 Loa 115.19 (BB) Br ex 18.02 Dght 6.800 Lbp 108.00 Br md 18.00 Dpth 8.90 Welded, 1 dk	**(A12B2TR) Chemical/Products Tanker** Double Hull (13F) Liq: 8,424; Liq (Oil): 8,430 Cargo Heating Coils Compartments: 10 Wing Ta, 2 Wing Slop Ta, ER 10 Cargo Pump (s): 10x200m³/hr Manifold: Bow/CM: 62.4m	**1 oil engine** driving 1 FP propeller Total Power: 2,574kW (3,500hp) Yanmar 1 x 4 Stroke 6 Cy. 330 x 440 2574kW (3500bhp) Qingdao Zichai Boyang Diesel EngineCo Ltd-China AuxGen: 3 x 350kW 400V a.c Thrusters: 1 Tunnel thruster (f) Fuel: 350.0 (d.f.) 100.0 (r.f.)	12.5 6N330-E
9318682 *9V2480* -	**YOU SHEN 8** *ex* Spring Auster *-2013* **Dongzhan Shipping (Singapore) Pte Ltd** Shanghai Dongzhan Shipping Co Ltd *Singapore* *Singapore* MMSI: 564146000 Official number: 399067	**4,160** 2,106 6,576 T/cm 15.0	Class: BV (NK)	**2004-07 Hakata Zosen K.K. — Imabari** Yd No: 662 Loa 105.94 (BB) Br ex - Dght 6.864 Lbp 99.80 Br md 16.80 Dpth 8.20 Welded, 1 dk	**(A12B2TR) Chemical/Products Tanker** Double Hull (13F) Liq: 7,352; Liq (Oil): 7,353 Cargo Heating Coils Compartments: 14 Wing Ta, 2 Wing Slop Ta, ER 14 Cargo Pump (s): 14x200m³/hr Manifold: Bow/CM: 56m	**1 oil engine** driving 1 FP propeller Total Power: 3,398kW (4,620hp) Mitsubishi 1 x 2 Stroke 6 Cy. 330 x 1050 3398kW (4620bhp) Akasaka Tekkosho KK (Akasaka DieselLtd)-Japan AuxGen: 2 x 400kW a.c Thrusters: 1 Tunnel thruster (f) Fuel: 80.0 (d.f.) 333.0 (r.f.)	13.0 6UEC33L
9425069 *9V2523* -	**YOU SHEN 9** *ex* Rui Xiang *-2014* *launched as* Crystal Hainan *-2012* **Dongzhan Shipping (Singapore) Pte Ltd** Shanghai Dongzhan Shipping Co Ltd *Singapore* *Singapore*	**6,111** 2,730 9,046 T/cm 18.4	Class: BV (AB)	**2012-03 Chongqing Chuandong Shipbuilding Industry Co Ltd — Chongqing** Yd No: HT0108 Loa 115.75 (BB) Br ex - Dght 7.800 Lbp 108.00 Br md 18.60 Dpth 10.00 Welded, 1 dk	**(A12B2TR) Chemical/Products Tanker** Double Hull (13F) Liq: 9,506; Liq (Oil): 9,700 Cargo Heating Coils Compartments: 5 Wing Ta, 5 Wing Ta, 1 Wing Slop Ta, 1 Wing Slop Ta, ER 10 Cargo Pump (s): 6x250m³/hr, 4x150m³/hr Manifold: Bow/CM: 57.7m	**1 oil engine** reduction geared to sc. shaft driving 1 CP propeller Total Power: 4,000kW (5,438hp) Wartsila 1 x 4 Stroke 8 Cy. 320 x 400 4000kW (5438bhp) Wartsila Finland Oy-Finland AuxGen: 1 x 600kW a.c, 3 x 500kW a.c Thrusters: 1 Tunnel thruster (f) Fuel: 79.0 (d.f.) 388.0 (r.f.)	13.1 8L
9425057 *9V2522* -	**YOU SHEN 10** *ex* Run Ze *-2014* *launched as* Crystal Sichuan *-2011* **Dongzhan Shipping (Singapore) Pte Ltd** Shanghai Dongzhan Shipping Co Ltd *Singapore* *Singapore*	**6,111** 2,730 9,016 T/cm 18.4	Class: BV (AB)	**2011-12 Chongqing Chuandong Shipbuilding Industry Co Ltd — Chongqing** Yd No: HT0107 Loa 115.75 (BB) Br ex - Dght 7.800 Lbp 108.00 Br md 18.60 Dpth 10.00 Welded, 1 dk	**(A12B2TR) Chemical/Products Tanker** Double Hull (13F) Liq: 9,514; Liq (Oil): 8,564 Cargo Heating Coils Compartments: 6 Wing Ta, 6 Wing Ta, 2 Wing Slop Ta, ER 12 Cargo Pump (s): 6x150m³/hr, 6x250m³/hr Manifold: Bow/CM: 57.7m	**1 oil engine** reduction geared to sc. shaft driving 1 CP propeller Total Power: 4,000kW (5,438hp) Wartsila 1 x 4 Stroke 8 Cy. 320 x 400 4000kW (5438bhp) Wartsila Finland Oy-Finland AuxGen: 1 x 600kW a.c, 3 x 500kW a.c Thrusters: 1 Tunnel thruster (f) Fuel: 81.0 (d.f.) 386.0 (r.f.)	13.1 8L
9023598 *XUNP7* -	**YOU SHUN 9** **Youshun Shipping Co Ltd** Sea Joy Shipping Ltd SatCom: Inmarsat C 451486120 *Phnom Penh* *Cambodia* MMSI: 514861000 Official number: 0605473	**1,999** 1,187 3,247	Class: UB	**2005-11 Linhai Jianghai Shipbuilding Co Ltd — Linhai ZJ** Loa 88.00 Br ex 13.23 Dght 2.927 Lbp 81.70 Br md 13.20 Dpth 3.20 Welded, 1 dk	**(A31A2GX) General Cargo Ship**	**1 oil engine** geared to sc. shaft driving 1 Propeller Total Power: 735kW (999hp) Chinese Std. Type 1 x 4 Stroke 6 Cy. 250 x 320 735kW (999bhp) Zibo Diesel Engine Factory-China	11.0 LB8250ZL
8914714 - -	**YOU YA** **Shenzhen Ocean Shipping Co (COSCO SHENZHEN)** COSCO (HK) Shipping Co Ltd *Shenzhen, Guangdong* *China* MMSI: 413574000	**17,066** 9,904 27,879 T/cm 39.5	Class: (CC) (NK)	**1990-07 KK Kanasashi Zosen — Toyohashi AI** Yd No: 3225 Loa 176.60 (BB) Br ex - Dght 9.414 Lbp 169.40 Br md 26.00 Dpth 13.30 Welded, 1 dk	**(A21A2BC) Bulk Carrier** Grain: 38,239; Bale: 37,313 Compartments: 5 Ho, ER 5 Ha: (17.9 x 12.8)4 (19.5 x 17.8)ER Cranes: 4x30.5t	**1 oil engine** driving 1 FP propeller Total Power: 5,150kW (7,002hp) Mitsubishi 1 x 2 Stroke 5 Cy. 520 x 1600 5150kW (7002bhp) Kobe Hatsudoki KK-Japan AuxGen: 3 x 400kW 450V a.c, 4 x 286kW a.c, 1 x 64kW 450V a.c	14.0 5UEC52
7820045 *BJTL* -	**YOU YI 9** **China Shipping Haisheng Co Ltd** - *Haikou, Hainan* *China*	**4,118** 1,788 4,927	Class: (CC)	**1980-09 Brodogradiliste '3 Maj' — Rijeka** Yd No: 599 Loa 107.00 Br ex 15.22 Dght 6.510 Lbp 98.96 Br md 15.20 Dpth 8.00 Welded, 1 dk	**(A31A2GX) General Cargo Ship** Grain: 6,294 Compartments: 4 Ho, ER 4 Ha: 4 (16.6 x 6.1)ER Derricks: 8x5t; Winches: 8	**1 oil engine** driving 1 FP propeller Total Power: 2,207kW (3,001hp) Sulzer 1 x 2 Stroke 6 Cy. 440 x 760 2207kW (3001bhp) Tvornica Dizel Motora 'Jugoturbina'-Yugoslavia AuxGen: 3 x 232kW 400V 50Hz a.c	12.8 6RD4
7910929 - -	**YOU YI 11** **Government of The People's Republic of China** - *Guangzhou, Guangdong* *China*	*446* 140 395		**1979-07 Yuen Hing Shipyard Ltd. — Hong Kong** Yd No: 211 Loa 63.86 Br ex 9.61 Dght 3.453 Lbp 57.99 Br md - Dpth 5.59 Welded, 2 dks	**(A31A2GX) General Cargo Ship**	**1 oil engine** driving 1 FP propeller Total Power: 2,721kW (3,699hp) MaK 1 x 4 Stroke 9 Cy. 320 x 420 2721kW (3699bhp) MaK Maschinenbau GmbH-Kiel	9M453A
7910931 - -	**YOU YI 12** **China National Cereals, Oils & Foodstuffs Import & Export Corp** - *Guangzhou, Guangdong* *China* MMSI: 412516000	*422* 147 395		**1979-12 Yuen Hing Shipyard Ltd. — Hong Kong** Yd No: 212 Loa 59.30 Br ex 9.63 Dght 3.453 Lbp 58.02 Br md 9.61 Dpth 4.56 Welded	**(A31A2GX) General Cargo Ship**	**1 oil engine** driving 1 FP propeller Total Power: 2,501kW (3,400hp) MaK 1 x 4 Stroke 2501kW (3400bhp) MaK Maschinenbau GmbH-Kiel	
8833465 *BXIW* -	**YOU YI 13** **China National Cereals, Oils & Foodstuffs Import & Export Corp** - *Guangzhou, Guangdong* *China*	*492* 157 300		**1979 Guangzhou Shipyard — Guangzhou GD** Loa 67.95 Br ex - Dght 3.100 Lbp 60.00 Br md 10.00 Dpth 4.89 Welded, 2 dks	**(A31A2GX) General Cargo Ship** Compartments: 4 Ho, ER 4 Ha: ER Cranes: 2x3t,2x2.5t	**1 oil engine** driving 1 FP propeller Total Power: 2,354kW (3,200hp) MaK 1 x 4 Stroke 9 Cy. 320 x 420 2354kW (3200bhp) MaK Maschinenbau GmbH-Kiel AuxGen: 2 x 150kW 400V a.c	16.0 9M453A
8833453 *BXIV* -	**YOU YI 14** **China National Cereals, Oils & Foodstuffs Import & Export Corp** - *Guangzhou, Guangdong* *China*	*492* 157 300		**1979 Guangzhou Shipyard — Guangzhou GD** Loa 67.95 Br ex - Dght 3.110 Lbp 60.00 Br md 10.00 Dpth 5.61 Welded, 2 dks	**(A31A2GX) General Cargo Ship** Compartments: 4 Ho, ER 4 Ha: ER Cranes: 2x3t,2x2.5t	**1 oil engine** driving 1 FP propeller Total Power: 2,354kW (3,200hp) MaK 1 x 4 Stroke 9 Cy. 320 x 420 2354kW (3200bhp) MaK Maschinenbau GmbH-Kiel AuxGen: 2 x 150kW 400V a.c	16.0 9M453A

10803 *PAJ*	**YOU YI 20** **China Shipping Bulk Carrier Co Ltd** - SatCom: Inmarsat B 341251410 *Shanghai* *China* MMSI: 412514000	**13,792** 6,759 20,457	Class: (CC)	**1992-05 Karachi Shipyard & Engineering Works Ltd. — Karachi** Yd No: 211 Loa 162.00 Br ex 22.54 Dght 9.490 Lbp 152.00 Br md 22.50 Dpth 13.30 Welded, 1 dk	**(A21A2BC) Bulk Carrier** Grain: 24,547; Bale: 23,205 Compartments: 5 Ho, ER 5 Ha: ER Ice Capable	**1 oil engine** driving 1 FP propeller Total Power: 5,119kW (6,960hp) 13.8kn B&W 6L42MC 1 x 2 Stroke 6 Cy. 420 x 1360 5119kW (6960bhp) Hitachi Zosen Corp-Japan
84152 *3568*	**YOUHOUMARU** *ex* Ryusho Maru No. 15 *-1995* **Kyokuyo Tanker KK** - *Tokyo* *Japan* Official number: 134144	*199* - 600		**1994-03 Katsuura Dockyard Co. Ltd. — Nachi-Katsuura** Yd No: 328 Loa - Br ex - Dght 3.260 Lbp 44.10 Br md 8.00 Dpth 3.40 Welded, 1 dk	**(A31A2GX) General Cargo Ship**	**1 oil engine** reverse geared to sc. shaft driving 1 FP propeller Total Power: 625kW (850hp) Hanshin 6LC26G 1 x 4 Stroke 6 Cy. 260 x 440 625kW (850bhp) The Hanshin Diesel Works Ltd-Japan
68445 *D2995*	**YOUKOUMARU** **Kyokuyo Tanker KK** Fukamizu Kaiun YK *Tokyo* *Japan* MMSI: 431001125 Official number: 141148	*498* - 1,308		**2010-01 Imura Zosen K.K. — Komatsushima** Yd No: 330 Loa 65.23 Br ex - Dght 4.200 Lbp 59.98 Br md 10.40 Dpth 4.50 Welded, 1 dk	**(A13B2TP) Products Tanker** Double Hull (13F) Liq: 1,300; Liq (Oil): 1,300	**1 oil engine** geared to sc. shaft driving 1 Propeller Total Power: 1,030kW (1,400hp) Hanshin LH28G 1 x 4 Stroke 6 Cy. 280 x 460 1030kW (1400bhp) The Hanshin Diesel Works Ltd-Japan
17567 *B3869*	**YOULIAN 2** *ex* Hai Tai *-2008* **Sealantic Co FZC** - *Kingstown* *St Vincent & The Grenadines* MMSI: 377297000 Official number: 10342	**397** 119 187	Class: (CC)	**2006-12 Yiu Lian Dockyards (Zhangzhou) Ltd — Zhangzhou FJ** Yd No: 5-05-T/HK Loa 36.80 Br ex - Dght 3.400 Lbp 32.30 Br md 10.00 Dpth 4.40 Welded, 1 dk	**(B32A2ST) Tug**	**2 oil engines** reduction geared to sc. shafts driving 2 Z propellers Total Power: 2,942kW (4,000hp) Niigata 6L26HLX 2 x 4 Stroke 6 Cy. 260 x 350 each-1471kW (2000bhp) Niigata Engineering Co Ltd-Japan AuxGen: 2 x 100kW 400V a.c
17555 *B3870*	**YOULIAN 3** *ex* Hai An *-2008* **Sealantic Co FZC** - *Kingstown* *St Vincent & The Grenadines* MMSI: 377318000 Official number: 10343	**397** 119 187	Class: BV (Class contemplated) CC	**2006-12 Yiu Lian Dockyards (Zhangzhou) Ltd — Zhangzhou FJ** Yd No: 05-03-T/HK Loa 36.80 Br ex - Dght 3.400 Lbp 34.43 Br md 10.00 Dpth 4.40 Welded, 1 dk	**(B32A2ST) Tug**	**2 oil engines** reduction geared to sc. shafts driving 2 Propellers Total Power: 2,942kW (4,000hp) Niigata 6L26HLX 2 x 4 Stroke 6 Cy. 260 x 350 each-1471kW (2000bhp) Niigata Engineering Co Ltd-Japan AuxGen: 2 x 100kW 400V a.c
89477 *DPJ*	**YOUNARA GLORY** *completed as* Delos *-2004* **DS-Rendite-Fonds Nr 127 VLCC 'Younara Glory' GmbH & Co Tankschiff KG** DS Tankers GmbH & Co KG SatCom: Inmarsat C 435430210 *Panama* *Panama* MMSI: 354302000 Official number: 36511PEXTF2	**161,235** 111,798 320,051 T/cm 178.7	Class: NV (AB)	**2004-11 Daewoo Shipbuilding & Marine Engineering Co Ltd — Geoje** Yd No: 5260 Loa 333.02 (BB) Br ex 60.04 Dght 22.470 Lbp 320.00 Br md 60.00 Dpth 30.50 Welded, 1 dk	**(A13A2TV) Crude Oil Tanker** Double Hull (13F) Liq: 340,584; Liq (Oil): 340,584 Compartments: 5 Ta, 10 Wing Ta, 2 Wing Slop Ta, ER 4 Cargo Pump (s): 3x5500m³/hr, 1x3500m³/hr Manifold: Bow/CM: 156.6m	**1 oil engine** driving 1 FP propeller Total Power: 29,412kW (39,989hp) 15.3kn MAN-B&W 6S90MC-C 1 x 2 Stroke 6 Cy. 900 x 3188 29412kW (39989bhp) Hyundai Heavy Industries Co Ltd-South Korea AuxGen: 3 x 1270kW 440/220V 60Hz a.c Fuel: 349.5 (d.f.) 8255.5 (r.f.)
12465 *QYY*	**YOUNES** *ex* Sultan Express *-2011* **NITC** - *Bushehr* *Iran* MMSI: 422100000	*213* 16 500	Class: AS (AB)	**1982-10 Master Boat Builders, Inc. — Coden, Al** Yd No: 58 Loa - Br ex 7.95 Dght 2.917 Lbp 33.53 Br md 7.93 Dpth 3.20 Welded, 1 dk	**(B21A20S) Platform Supply Ship**	**2 oil engines** reverse reduction geared to sc. shafts driving 2 FP propellers Total Power: 670kW (910hp) 12.0kn G.M. (Detroit Diesel) 16V-71-N 2 x Vee 2 Stroke 16 Cy. 108 x 127 each-335kW (455bhp) General Motors Detroit DieselAllison Divn-USA AuxGen: 2 x 50kW
19755 *BTP*	**YOUNES 6** **Kamal Marei** Kamal & Adel Sea Cargo (LLC) *Bandar Abbas* *Iran*	**191** 58 145	Class: (BV) (NK)	**2008-09 Tuong Aik Shipyard Sdn Bhd — Sibu** Yd No: 2805 Loa 26.00 Br ex - Dght 3.012 Lbp 24.29 Br md 8.00 Dpth 3.65 Welded, 1 dk	**(B32A2ST) Tug**	**2 oil engines** reduction geared to sc. shafts driving 2 Propellers Total Power: 1,518kW (2,064hp) Mitsubishi S6R2-MPTK3 2 x 4 Stroke 6 Cy. 170 x 220 each-759kW (1032bhp) Mitsubishi Heavy Industries Ltd-Japan Fuel: 130.0
09523 *A4031*	**YOUNES 10** *ex* Doce de Octubre *-1999* **Gamarsa Sarl** - *Tangier* *Morocco*	**403** 121 -	Class: BV	**1988-05 Ast. de Huelva S.A. — Huelva** Yd No: 388 Loa 36.60 Br ex - Dght 3.601 Lbp 31.02 Br md 8.41 Dpth 5.77 Welded, 2 dks	**(B11A2FS) Stern Trawler** Ins: 260	**1 oil engine** with clutches & sr reverse geared to sc. shaft driving 1 FP propeller Total Power: 780kW (1,060hp) Caterpillar 3512TA 1 x Vee 4 Stroke 12 Cy. 170 x 190 780kW (1060bhp) Caterpillar Inc-USA
04934 *VRD*	**YOUNESS NAJIB** *ex* Dae Won No. 11 *-1981* **Este Fisheries Co Ltd** - *Agadir* *Morocco* Official number: 8-545	*325* 134 411	Class: (KR)	**1967 Nichiro Zosen K.K. — Ishinomaki** Loa 48.39 Br ex - Dght 3.518 Lbp 43.01 Br md 8.50 Dpth 3.76 Welded, 1 dk	**(B11B2FV) Fishing Vessel** Ins: 486 3 Ha: 3 (1.9 x 1.9) Derricks: 8x2t	**1 oil engine** driving 1 FP propeller Total Power: 1,177kW (1,600hp) 11.5kn Fuji 6S37C 1 x 4 Stroke 6 Cy. 370 x 550 1177kW (1600bhp) Fuji Diesel Co Ltd-Japan
73967	**YOUNG 1** **WCT Engineering Bhd** - *Qatar*	**253** 76 273	Class: BV (Class contemplated) (NK)	**2005-11 Berjaya Dockyard Sdn Bhd — Miri** Yd No: 11 Loa 28.09 Br ex - Dght 3.612 Lbp 25.97 Br md 8.54 Dpth 4.30 Welded, 1 dk	**(B32A2ST) Tug**	**2 oil engines** reduction geared to sc. shafts driving 2 FP propellers Total Power: 1,516kW (2,062hp) Mitsubishi S6R2-MPTK2 2 x 4 Stroke 6 Cy. 170 x 220 each-758kW (1031bhp) Mitsubishi Heavy Industries Ltd-Japan
85582	**YOUNG 2** **WCT Engineering Bhd** - *Qatar*	**197** 60 180	Class: BV (GL)	**2006-03 Forward Marine Enterprise Sdn Bhd — Sibu** Yd No: FM-9 Loa 26.00 Br ex 8.02 Dght 3.000 Lbp 24.26 Br md 8.00 Dpth 3.65 Welded, 1 dk	**(B32A2ST) Tug**	**2 oil engines** reverse reduction geared to sc. shafts driving 2 FP propellers Total Power: 1,516kW (2,062hp) Mitsubishi S6R2-MPTK2 2 x 4 Stroke 6 Cy. 170 x 220 each-758kW (1031bhp) Mitsubishi Heavy Industries Ltd-Japan AuxGen: 2 x 78kW 415/230V a.c
42497 *GQF*	**YOUNG BOK** *ex* Fong Seong 718 *-1981* *ex* Alpine Pink *-1981* *ex* Aquarius *-1990* **Afko Fisheries Co Ltd** - *Takoradi* *Ghana* MMSI: 627013000 Official number: GSR 0013	*1,020* 306 -		**1971-02 J M Martinac Shipbuilding Corp — Tacoma WA** Yd No: 184 Shortened-1976 Loa 56.08 Br ex 11.43 Dght - Lbp - Br md 10.94 Dpth 4.63 Welded, 2 dks	**(B11B2FV) Fishing Vessel**	**1 oil engine** driving 1 FP propeller Total Power: 2,648kW (3,600hp) EMD (Electro-Motive) 20-645-E5 1 x Vee 2 Stroke 20 Cy. 230 x 254 2648kW (3600bhp) General Motors Corp-USA
29317 *KR*	**YOUNG DONG No. 7** **Kum Jung Shipping Co Ltd** - *Yeosu* *South Korea* MMSI: 440530000 Official number: YSR-853209	**468** - 920 T/cm 4.2	Class: (KR)	**1985-08 Banguhjin Engineering & Shipbuilding Co Ltd — Ulsan** Yd No: 58 Loa 57.21 Br ex 9.15 Dght 4.390 Lbp 51.52 Br md 9.12 Dpth 4.65 Welded, 1 dk	**(A13B2TU) Tanker (unspecified)** Liq: 1,143; Liq (Oil): 1,143 2 Cargo Pump (s)	**1 oil engine** driving 1 FP propeller Total Power: 552kW (750hp) 10.5kn Hanshin 6L26BGSH 1 x 4 Stroke 6 Cy. 260 x 400 552kW (750bhp) Ssangyong Heavy Industries Co Ltd-South Korea AuxGen: 2 x 60kW 225V a.c
71164 *MGW*	**YOUNG ENDEAVOUR** **Government of The Commonwealth of Australia** Government of The Commonwealth of Australia (Mine Counter Defences Systems Program Offices) (MCDSPO) *Sydney, NSW* *Australia* MMSI: 503071000	**173** 51 -	Class: LR ✠ **100A1** SS 10/2012 NS3 sail training ship SA1, SEQ, POL ✠ **LMC** Cable: 330.0/19.0 U2 (a)	**1987-07 Brooke Yachts International — Lowestoft** Yd No: 803 Loa 35.00 Br ex - Dght 4.000 Lbp 28.30 Br md 7.80 Dpth 5.65 Welded, 1 dk	**(X11B2QN) Sail Training Ship**	**2 oil engines** sr reverse geared to sc. shafts driving 2 FP propellers Total Power: 300kW (408hp) 10.0kn Perkins 2 x 4 Stroke 6 Cy. 100 x 127 each-150kW (204bhp) Detroit Diesel Eng. Co.-Detroit, Mi AuxGen: 2 x 42kW 415V 50Hz a.c
29694 *IX*	**YOUNG HEUNG No. 1** *ex* Jin Yang No. 301 *-1990* **Sam Ah Shipping Co Ltd** - *Busan* *South Korea* Official number: BS0200-A3147	*131* 52 111	Class: (KR)	**1983 Banguhjin Engineering & Shipbuilding Co Ltd — Ulsan** Loa 34.28 Br ex - Dght 2.659 Lbp 28.50 Br md 6.00 Dpth 2.75 Welded, 1 dk	**(B11B2FV) Fishing Vessel**	**1 oil engine** driving 1 FP propeller Total Power: 441kW (600hp) 10.2kn Niigata 6MG18CX 1 x 4 Stroke 6 Cy. 180 x 240 441kW (600bhp) Ssangyong Heavy Industries Co Ltd-South Korea AuxGen: 2 x 96kW 225V a.c

8629876 *6KIG* -	**YOUNG HEUNG No. 3** *ex* Korei No. 163 *-1990* **Sam Ah Shipping Co Ltd** - *Busan* *South Korea* Official number: BS0200-A3148	**108** - 142	Class: (KR)	**1984-07 Pohang Shipbuilding Co Ltd — Pohang** Loa 38.30 Br ex - Dght 2.811 Lbp 31.00 Br md 6.00 Dpth 2.98 Welded, 1 dk	**(B11B2FV) Fishing Vessel**	**1 oil engine** driving 1 FP propeller Total Power: 441kW (600hp) Niigata 6MG18C 1 x 4 Stroke 6 Cy. 180 x 240 441kW (600bhp) Ssangyong Heavy Industries Co Ltd-South Korea AuxGen: 3 x 75kW 225V a.c
8824153 *6NGF* -	**YOUNG HEUNG No. 5** *ex* Samik No. 1 *-1991* **Young-Heung Fisheries Co Ltd** - *Busan* *South Korea* Official number: BS02-A2188	*128* - 138	Class: (KR)	**1984-08 Kyungnam Shipbuilding Co Ltd — Busan** Loa 41.76 Br ex - Dght 2.879 Lbp 34.00 Br md 6.20 Dpth 2.90 Welded, 1 dk	**(B11B2FV) Fishing Vessel**	**1 oil engine** reduction geared to sc. shaft driving 1 FP propeller Total Power: 239kW (325hp) 10.0k Cummins NTA-855- 1 x 4 Stroke 6 Cy. 140 x 152 239kW (325bhp) Ssangyong Heavy Industries Co Ltd-South Korea AuxGen: 3 x 332kW 225V a.c
7417771 *6MPA* -	**YOUNG HWA No. 11** *ex* Young Heung No. 11 *-1996* *ex* O Dae Yang No. 305 *-1992* **Young Hwa Fisheries Co Ltd** - *Busan* *South Korea* Official number: 9509009-6260008	*433* 216 429	Class: (KR)	**1974-08 Daedong Shipbuilding Co Ltd — Busan** Yd No: 130 Loa 55.94 Br ex - Dght 3.650 Lbp 49.51 Br md 8.60 Dpth 4.09 Welded, 1 dk	**(B11B2FV) Fishing Vessel** Ins: 475 3 Ha: 2 (1.9 x 1.9) (1.3 x 0.9)ER	**1 oil engine** driving 1 FP propeller Total Power: 993kW (1,350hp) 12.2k Akasaka AH2 1 x 4 Stroke 6 Cy. 280 x 440 993kW (1350bhp) Akasaka Tekkosho KK (Akasaka DieselLtd)-Japan AuxGen: 2 x 200kW 225V a.c
7405352 *6KQU* -	**YOUNG HWA No. 33** *ex* Young Heung No. 33 *-1996* *ex* Dong Won No. 909 *-1991* **Young Hwa Fisheries Co Ltd** - SatCom: Inmarsat M 644073110 *Busan* *South Korea* Official number: 9508033-6260000	*451* 221 510	Class: (KR)	**1974-08 Mie Shipyard Co. Ltd. — Yokkaichi** Yd No: 122 Loa 55.66 Br ex - Dght 3.690 Lbp 49.00 Br md 9.00 Dpth 3.99 Welded, 1 dk	**(B11B2FV) Fishing Vessel** 3 Ha: 2 (1.3 x 1.0) (1.6 x 1.6)	**1 oil engine** driving 1 FP propeller Total Power: 1,103kW (1,500hp) 12.8k Akasaka AH3 1 x 4 Stroke 6 Cy. 300 x 480 1103kW (1500bhp) Akasaka Tekkosho KK (Akasaka DieselLtd)-Japan AuxGen: 2 x 200kW
7418062 *6NBT* -	**YOUNG HWA No. 99** *ex* Doo Yang No. 101 *-1995* *ex* Dong Yung No. 101 *-1990* *ex* Yung Eun No. 155 *-1988* *ex* Kwang Myung No. 155 *-1984* **Young Hwa Fisheries Co Ltd** - *Busan* *South Korea* Official number: 9507101-6260009	*329* 146 327	Class: (KR)	**1975-06 Busan Shipbuilding Co Ltd — Busan** Yd No: 135 Loa 52.25 Br ex - Dght 3.380 Lbp 45.65 Br md 8.50 Dpth 3.46 Welded, 1 dk	**(B11B2FV) Fishing Vessel** Ins: 451 3 Ha: 2 (1.3 x 0.9) (1.6 x 1.6)	**1 oil engine** driving 1 FP propeller Total Power: 736kW (1,001hp) 13.4k Niigata 6M28KH 1 x 4 Stroke 6 Cy. 280 x 440 736kW (1001bhp) Niigata Engineering Co Ltd-Japan AuxGen: 2 x 200kW 225V a.c
8709468 *DSFJ4* -	**YOUNG JIN** - **Myung Sung Machine Industry Ltd Partnership** Tong Yang Cement Corp *Busan* *South Korea* MMSI: 440267000 Official number: DHR-000768	**4,783** 2,030 8,071	Class: KR	**1988-06 ShinA Shipbuilding Co Ltd — Tongyeong** Yd No: 327 Loa 112.50 Br ex - Dght 7.057 Lbp 106.00 Br md 17.81 Dpth 9.10 Welded, 1 dk	**(A24A2BT) Cement Carrier** Grain: 7,208 Compartments: 2 Ho, ER	**1 oil engine** driving 1 FP propeller Total Power: 3,350kW (4,555hp) 15.1k B&W 6L35M 1 x 2 Stroke 6 Cy. 350 x 1050 3350kW (4555bhp) Ssangyong Heavy Industries Co Ltd-South Korea
8906004 - -	**YOUNG JIN** - - -	**4,573** 1,550 6,829	Class: (KR)	**1989-11 ShinA Shipbuilding Co Ltd — Tongyeong** Yd No: 339 Loa 115.67 (BB) Br ex 18.03 Dght 5.764 Lbp 110.08 Br md 18.00 Dpth 7.50 Welded, 1 dk	**(A24E2BL) Limestone Carrier** Grain: 5,636 Compartments: 2 Ho, ER 1 Ha: ER	**1 oil engine** driving 1 FP propeller Total Power: 2,184kW (2,969hp) 12.5k B&W 6S26M 1 x 2 Stroke 6 Cy. 260 x 980 2184kW (2969bhp) Ssangyong Heavy Industries Co Ltd-South Korea Thrusters: 1 Thwart. CP thruster (f)
9131682 *DSEA5* -	**YOUNG JIN** *ex* Green Chemist *-2010* **Young Sung Global Co Ltd** - SatCom: Inmarsat C 444006298 *Busan* *South Korea* MMSI: 440064000 Official number: BSR-951165	**2,023** 1,024 3,235 T/cm 9.4	Class: KR	**1995-08 Ilheung Shipbuilding & Engineering Co Ltd — Mokpo** Yd No: 93-46 Loa 79.50 (BB) Br ex 14.02 Dght 5.614 Lbp 73.20 Br md 14.00 Dpth 6.50 Welded, 1 dk	**(A12A2TC) Chemical Tanker** Double Bottom Entire Compartment Length Liq: 3,506 Cargo Heating Coils Compartments: 10 Wing Ta, 2 Wing Slop Ta, ER 2 Cargo Pump (s): 2x400m³/hr Manifold: Bow/CM: 40.5m	**1 oil engine** sr geared to sc. shaft driving 1 FP propeller Total Power: 1,714kW (2,330hp) 11.8k Alpha 7L28/32 1 x 4 Stroke 7 Cy. 280 x 320 1714kW (2330bhp) Ssangyong Heavy Industries Co Ltd-South Korea AuxGen: 2 x 184kW 445V a.c Thrusters: 1 Tunnel thruster (a) Fuel: 44.0 (d.f.) 141.3 (r.f.)
8313659 *D9KU* -	**YOUNG JIN No. 1** *ex* Hee Young No. 7 *-1999* *ex* Seo Bong *-1997* *ex* Woo Sung No. 209 *-1987* **Young Jin Shipping Co Ltd** - *Jeju* *South Korea* MMSI: 440114310 Official number: JJR-848613	**913** - 2,261	Class: (KR)	**1984-03 Pohang Shipbuilding Co Ltd — Pohang** Yd No: 7 Loa 70.49 Br ex 12.02 Dght 4.768 Lbp 65.00 Br md 12.01 Dpth 5.41 Welded, 1 dk	**(A31A2GX) General Cargo Ship** Grain: 1,189 Compartments: 1 Ho, ER 1 Ha: (37.1 x 7.2)ER	**1 oil engine** driving 1 FP propeller Total Power: 956kW (1,300hp) 11.6k Niigata 6M28AF 1 x 4 Stroke 6 Cy. 280 x 480 956kW (1300bhp) Ssangyong Heavy Industries Co Ltd-South Korea AuxGen: 1 x 132kW 225V a.c
8957871 *UDER* -	**YOUNG JIN No. 97** *ex* Woo Il No. 87 *-1994* *ex* Samsung No. 87 *-1992* **Suloy Joint Stock Co (A/O 'Suloy')** - *Petropavlovsk-Kamchatskiy* *Russia*	**224** 85 150	Class: (RS)	**1986-12 Kirim Shipbuilding Co Ltd — Koje** Loa 39.12 Br ex - Dght 2.760 Lbp 33.00 Br md 6.30 Dpth 2.93 Welded, 1 dk	**(B11A2FT) Trawler** Ice Capable	**1 oil engine** driving 1 FP propeller Total Power: 552kW (750hp) Hanshin 6L26BGS 1 x 4 Stroke 6 Cy. 260 x 400 552kW (750bhp) The Hanshin Diesel Works Ltd-Japan
7215109 *6MGC* -	**YOUNG JIN No. 105** *ex* Dong Bang No. 95 *-1993* *ex* Pais del Este No. 95 *-1982* *ex* Ryuho Maru No. 51 *-1982* **Jinbo Fisheries Co Ltd** - *Busan* *South Korea* Official number: 9512439-6260001	*641* 133 508	Class: (KR)	**1971 Niigata Engineering Co Ltd — Niigata NI** Yd No: 1076 Loa 54.75 Br ex 8.84 Dght 3.456 Lbp 49.66 Br md 8.80 Dpth 5.66 Welded, 1 dk	**(B11B2FV) Fishing Vessel** Ins: 442	**1 oil engine** driving 1 FP propeller Total Power: 1,471kW (2,000hp) 11.5k Niigata 6M37 1 x 4 Stroke 6 Cy. 370 x 540 1471kW (2000bhp) Niigata Engineering Co Ltd-Japan AuxGen: 2 x 245kW 225V a.c
6420599 *6MPL* -	**YOUNG JIN No. 207** *ex* Dae Wang No. 106 *-1987* *ex* World Star No. 1 *-1981* *ex* Kaiho Maru No. 23 *-1973* **Choi Yun-Sig** - *Busan* *South Korea* Official number: BS-A-1303	*236* 110 304	Class: (KR)	**1964 Miho Zosensho K.K. — Shimizu** Yd No: 514 Loa 44.12 Br ex 7.52 Dght 3.149 Lbp 38.64 Br md 7.50 Dpth 3.36 Welded, 1 dk	**(B11B2FV) Fishing Vessel** Ins: 294 Compartments: 2 Ho, ER 3 Ha: (1.3 x 0.9)2 (1.5 x 1.3)ER	**1 oil engine** driving 1 CP propeller Total Power: 515kW (700hp) 10.5k Akasaka MK6S 1 x 4 Stroke 6 Cy. 300 x 420 515kW (700bhp) Akasaka Tekkosho KK (Akasaka DieselLtd)-Japan AuxGen: 1 x 80kW 225V 60Hz a.c, 2 x 64kW 225V 60Hz a.c
7416519 - -	**YOUNG KEE** *ex* Tonan Maru *-1996* - -	*216* 69 153		**1975-01 Miho Zosensho K.K. — Shimizu** Yd No: 1007 Loa 42.25 Br ex 8.13 Dght 2.947 Lbp 34.90 Br md 6.81 Dpth 3.20 Welded, 1 dk	**(B12D2FR) Fishery Research Vessel**	**1 oil engine** driving 1 FP propeller Total Power: 736kW (1,001hp) Niigata 6L25E 1 x 4 Stroke 6 Cy. 250 x 320 736kW (1001bhp) Niigata Engineering Co Ltd-Japan
8413552 *HLIV* -	**YOUNG KIL No. 36** - **Kim Sang-Kee** - *Guryongpo* *South Korea* Official number: KN6865-A1472	*120* 42 -		**1983-06 Chungmu Shipbuilding Co Inc — Tongyeong** Yd No: 122 Loa 35.51 (BB) Br ex 6.91 Dght 2.301 Lbp 29.77 Br md 5.91 Dpth 2.82 Welded, 1 dk	**(B11B2FV) Fishing Vessel** Ins: 93	**1 oil engine** with clutches, flexible couplings & sr reverse geared to sc. shaft driving 1 FP propeller Total Power: 331kW (450hp) Niigata 6L16XB- 1 x 4 Stroke 6 Cy. 160 x 200 331kW (450bhp) Ssangyong Heavy Industries Co Ltd-South Korea
8969563 *WDC5811* -	**YOUNG KING** *ex* Master Tony *-2010* *ex* Family Dang *-2005* *ex* Dang Brothers *-2001* **Kim Dung Phung** - *Fort Worth, TX* *United States of America* MMSI: 367046750 Official number: 1118506	**178** 53 -		**2001** Yd No: 205 L reg 26.94 Br ex - Dght - Lbp - Br md 7.92 Dpth 3.81 Welded, 1 dk	**(B11B2FV) Fishing Vessel**	**1 oil engine** driving 1 FP propeller

IMO / Call sign	Name / Owner	Tonnage / Class	Builder / Dimensions	Type / Capacity	Machinery
16573 CEZ	**YOUNG KWANG** *ex* Kifuku Maru *-2005* **Portbunkerservice Co Ltd** - *Nakhodka* *Russia*	**186** Class: RS 91 300	**1976-08 Takebe Zosen — Takamatsu** Yd No: 65 Converted From: Oil Tanker-2007 Loa 37.70 Br ex 6.63 Dght 2.700 Lbp 34.02 Br md 6.61 Dpth 2.93 Welded, 1 dk	**(B34E2SW) Waste Disposal Vessel** Liq: 360; Liq (Oil): 360	**1 oil engine** driving 1 FP propeller Total Power: 272kW (370hp) 9.5kn Yanmar 6ML-HT 1 x 4 Stroke 6 Cy. 200 x 240 272kW (370bhp) Yanmar Diesel Engine Co Ltd-Japan Fuel: 7.0 (d.f.)
426200	**YOUNG LADY** **Grace Shipping Lines** - *Cebu* *Philippines* Official number: Y0001	*230* 121 400	**1979 at Manila** Loa - Br ex 7.04 Dght - Lbp 36.71 Br md 7.01 Dpth 2.80 Welded, 1 dk	**(A32A2GF) General Cargo/Passenger Ship** Passengers: 146	**1 oil engine** driving 1 FP propeller Total Power: 405kW (551hp)
933244 SAE6	**YOUNG NAM No. 2** *ex* MSC Sun *-1993* *ex* Nissho Maru No. 5 *-1992* *ex* Kisaragi Maru No. 5 *-1990* **Jin Yang Co Ltd** - *Ulsan* *South Korea* Official number: USR-937742	**492** Class: (KR) - 1,123 T/cm 5.0	**1979 Watanabe Zosen KK — Imabari EH** Yd No: 201 Loa 60.50 Br ex - Dght 3.904 Lbp 56.00 Br md 10.50 Dpth 4.40 Welded, 1 dk	**(B34E2SY) Effluent carrier** Liq: 1,232 Compartments: 8 Ta, ER 2 Cargo Pump (s): 2x400m³/hr Manifold: Bow/CM: 23m	**1 oil engine** driving 1 FP propeller Total Power: 883kW (1,201hp) 10.5kn Makita GSLH6275 1 x 4 Stroke 6 Cy. 275 x 450 883kW (1201bhp) Makita Diesel Co Ltd-Japan AuxGen: 2 x 60kW 225V a.c Fuel: 9.5 (d.f.) (Part Heating Coils) 49.5 (r.f.) 3.5pd
003283	**YOUNG No. VII** *ex* Yuryo Maru No. 28 *-1990* *ex* Yuryo Maru No. 58 *-1989* *ex* Seiwa Maru No. 28 *-1978* *ex* Chokyu Maru No. 15 *-1978* **Fine Corp Co Ltd** - *Busan* *South Korea* Official number: 9407009-6210004	*374* Class: (KR) 200 377	**1969 KK Kanasashi Zosen — Shizuoka SZ** Yd No: 927 Loa 53.14 Br ex 8.44 Dght 3.550 Lbp 47.15 Br md 8.41 Dpth 3.92 Welded, 1 dk	**(B11B2FV) Fishing Vessel**	**1 oil engine** driving 1 FP propeller Total Power: 956kW (1,300hp) 11.0kn Hanshin 6LU32 1 x 4 Stroke 6 Cy. 320 x 510 956kW (1300bhp) The Hanshin Diesel Works Ltd-Japan AuxGen: 3 x 218kW 220V a.c
405578	**YOUNG POONG No. 5** *ex* Jinam No. 5 *-1979* **Young Poong Deep Sea Fisheries Co Ltd** - *Yeosu* *South Korea* Official number: YF39009	*135* Class: (KR) 54 -	**1963 Tokushima Zosen Sangyo K.K. — Komatsushima** Yd No: 130 Loa 30.41 Br ex 5.85 Dght 2.388 Lbp 26.52 Br md 5.80 Dpth 2.70 Riveted\Welded, 1 dk	**(B11B2FV) Fishing Vessel** Ins: 64	**1 oil engine** driving 1 FP propeller Total Power: 243kW (330hp) 9.0kn Makita 1 x 4 Stroke 6 Cy. 240 x 400 243kW (330bhp) Makita Tekkosho-Japan AuxGen: 2 x 9kW 110V d.c
984977 JDUZ	**YOUNG SHIN 501** *ex* Young Ching 17 *-2002* **Biocomplex Co Ltd (OOO 'Biokompleks')** - *Nevelsk* *Russia* MMSI: 273449640 Official number: 846622	**148** Class: (RS) 55 67	**1984-05 Hyangdo Shipbuilding Co Ltd — Pohang** Yd No: 641 Loa 34.25 Br ex - Dght 2.340 Lbp 29.86 Br md 6.00 Dpth 2.76 Welded, 1 dk	**(B11B2FV) Fishing Vessel**	**1 oil engine** driving 1 Propeller Total Power: 447kW (608hp) 8.0kn Cummins 1 x 4 Stroke 447kW (608bhp) Cummins Engine Co Inc-USA Fuel: 27.0 (d.f.)
427813 SMOH	**YOUNG SHIN No. 33** *ex* Woo Jung No. 12 *-1984* *ex* Kyoshin Maru No. 1 *-1973* *ex* Kotobuki Maru No. 20 *-1973* **Choi Chan-Geu** - *Donghae, Gangwon-do* *South Korea* Official number: KW2029-A737	*171* Class: (KR) 71 -	**1963 Niigata Engineering Co Ltd — Niigata NI** Yd No: 553 Loa 38.94 Br ex 6.96 Dght 2.794 Lbp 34.65 Br md 6.91 Dpth 3.10 Welded, 1 dk	**(B11B2FV) Fishing Vessel** Ins: 392 3 Ha: 3 (1.2 x 1.2)ER	**1 oil engine** driving 1 FP propeller Total Power: 405kW (551hp) 9.8kn Niigata 6M28DHS 1 x 4 Stroke 6 Cy. 280 x 440 405kW (551bhp) Niigata Engineering Co Ltd-Japan AuxGen: 2 x 80kW 225V a.c
9317779 YJUT5 -	**YOUNG SPIRIT** **Stevens Line Co Ltd** Sato Steamship Co Ltd (Sato Kisen KK) *Port Vila* *Vanuatu* MMSI: 576115000 Official number: 1656	**19,781** Class: NK 10,786 31,894 T/cm 45.1	**2005-10 The Hakodate Dock Co Ltd — Hakodate HK** Yd No: 803 Loa 175.53 (BB) Br ex - Dght 9.569 Lbp 167.00 Br md 29.40 Dpth 13.70 Welded, 1 dk	**(A21A2BC) Bulk Carrier** Double Bottom Entire, Double Sides Partial Grain: 42,620; Bale: 40,445 Compartments: 5 Ho, ER 5 Ha: 4 (19.6 x 19.6)ER (12.8 x 15.0) Cranes: 4x30t	**1 oil engine** driving 1 FP propeller Total Power: 6,840kW (9,300hp) 14.4kn Mitsubishi 6UEC52LA 1 x 2 Stroke 6 Cy. 520 x 1600 6840kW (9300bhp) Akasaka Tekkosho KK (Akasaka DieselLtd)-Japan Fuel: 1260.0
7379474 - -	**YOUNG STAR No. 82** *ex* Young Star No. 101 *-1991* *ex* Koyo Maru No. 10 *-1988* **Young Star Fisheries S de RL** - *San Lorenzo* *Honduras* Official number: L-1823209	*299* 149 389	**1974-04 Miho Zosensho K.K. — Shimizu** Yd No: 939 Loa 50.60 (BB) Br ex 8.51 Dght 3.125 Lbp 44.10 Br md 8.49 Dpth 3.48 Welded, 1 dk	**(B11B2FV) Fishing Vessel**	**1 oil engine** driving 1 FP propeller Total Power: 809kW (1,100hp) Akasaka AH27 1 x 4 Stroke 6 Cy. 270 x 420 809kW (1100bhp) Akasaka Tekkosho KK (Akasaka DieselLtd)-Japan
8629931 6KIW -	**YOUNG SUNG** **Choi Dae-Hyeon** - *Ulleung* *South Korea* Official number: 9504016-6479408	**109** Class: (KR) - 133	**1984-07 Sungkwang Shipbuilding Co Ltd — Tongyeong** Yd No: 124 Loa 37.12 Br ex - Dght 2.776 Lbp 29.00 Br md 6.00 Dpth 2.90 Welded, 1 dk	**(B11B2FV) Fishing Vessel**	**1 oil engine** driving 1 FP propeller Total Power: 272kW (370hp) AuxGen: 1 x 64kW 225V a.c
7829455 D8AR -	**YOUNG WON No. 7** *ex* Elite Pusan *-1993* *ex* Dong Jin No. 1 *-1986* **Kim Hung-Jun** - *Busan* *South Korea* Official number: BSR-789419	*424* Class: (KR) 300 1,008	**1979-01 ShinA Shipbuilding Co Ltd — Tongyeong** Loa 60.72 Br ex - Dght 3.089 Lbp 52.00 Br md 9.11 Dpth 4.51 Welded, 1 dk	**(A31A2GX) General Cargo Ship** Grain: 1,051; Bale: 1,023 1 Ha: (27.5 x 6.1)ER Cranes: 2x3t	**1 oil engine** driving 1 FP propeller Total Power: 552kW (750hp) 11.7kn Otsuka SODHS6S25 1 x 4 Stroke 6 Cy. 250 x 410 552kW (750bhp) KK Otsuka Diesel-Japan AuxGen: 2 x 16kW 225V a.c
9034066 - -	**YOUNGA** **Compagnie des Transport par Pipe-Lines au Sahara (TRAPSA)** - *Sfax* *Tunisia*	**277** Class: BV - -	**1992-09 Scheepswerf A. Baars Azn. B.V. — Sliedrecht** (Hull) Yd No: 738 **1992-09 Delta Shipyard Sliedrecht BV — Sliedrecht** Yd No: 951 Loa 30.50 Br ex - Dght 3.840 Lbp 30.00 Br md 8.75 Dpth 4.75 Welded	**(B32A2ST) Tug**	**2 oil engines** reduction geared to sc. shafts driving 2 FP propellers Total Power: 2,000kW (2,720hp) 12.0kn Caterpillar 3512TA 2 x Vee 4 Stroke 12 Cy. 170 x 190 each-1000kW (1360bhp) Caterpillar Inc-USA
7916296 DTBI6 -	**YOUNGDUCK NO. 3** *ex* Kyung Il No. 7 *-2004* *ex* P. S. *-2003* *ex* Lilac *-1994* *ex* Fuyo Maru *-1992* **Youngduck Shipping Co Ltd** - *Busan* *South Korea* MMSI: 441160000 Official number: 0112012-6260003	**1,191** Class: (KR) (NK) 414 1,183	**1980-02 Kochi Jyuko (Kaisei Zosen) K.K. — Kochi** Yd No: 1352 Loa 65.87 Br ex - Dght 4.352 Lbp 60.48 Br md 12.21 Dpth 7.00 Welded, 2 dks	**(A34A2GR) Refrigerated Cargo Ship** Ins: 1,503 2 Ha: 2 (4.4 x 4.5)ER Derricks: 4x5t	**1 oil engine** driving 1 FP propeller Total Power: 1,324kW (1,800hp) 12.3kn Hanshin 6LU35 1 x 4 Stroke 6 Cy. 350 x 550 1324kW (1800bhp) The Hanshin Diesel Works Ltd-Japan AuxGen: 3 x 468kW
7355844 6MVW -	**YOUNGIN NO. 33** *ex* Kyung Yang No. 33 *-2004* *ex* Kwang Yang No. 107 *-1999* *ex* Jai Won No. 33 *-1991* *ex* Kwang Myung No. 85 *-1986* **Daeil Fisheries Co Ltd** - *Busan* *South Korea* Official number: 9512136-6260007	*430* Class: (KR) 233 460	**1974-03 Dae Sun Shipbuilding & Engineering Co Ltd — Busan** Yd No: 163 Loa 55.50 Br ex 9.02 Dght 3.608 Lbp 49.05 Br md 9.00 Dpth 3.97 Riveted\Welded, 1 dk	**(B11B2FV) Fishing Vessel** Ins: 338 3 Ha: 2 (1.3 x 0.9) (1.8 x 1.8)	**1 oil engine** driving 1 FP propeller Total Power: 1,177kW (1,600hp) 13.0kn Niigata 6LA31X 1 x 4 Stroke 6 Cy. 310 x 460 1177kW (1600bhp) Niigata Engineering Co Ltd-Japan AuxGen: 2 x 200kW 225V a.c
9005168 DSRN9 -	**YOUNGSAN GAS** *ex* Izumi Maru No. 2 *-2013* **Youngsan Marine Co Ltd** - *Busan* *South Korea* MMSI: 441928000 Official number: BSR-130070	*1,356* Class: KR (NK) 465 1,196 T/cm 6.5	**1990-10 Shin Yamamoto Shipbuilding & Engineering Co Ltd — Kochi KC** Yd No: 328 Loa 72.00 (BB) Br ex - Dght 4.313 Lbp 66.80 Br md 12.50 Dpth 5.60 Welded, 1 dk	**(A11B2TG) LPG Tanker** Double Bottom Entire Compartment Length Liq (Gas): 1,726 Cargo Heating Coils 2 x Gas Tank (s); 2 cyl horizontal 2 Cargo Pump (s): 2x500m³/hr Manifold: Bow/CM: 29m	**1 oil engine** driving 1 FP propeller Total Power: 1,765kW (2,400hp) 12.5kn Akasaka A37 1 x 4 Stroke 6 Cy. 370 x 720 1765kW (2400bhp) Akasaka Tekkosho KK (Akasaka DieselLtd)-Japan AuxGen: 3 x 198kW a.c Fuel: 11.0 (d.f.) 169.0 (r.f.) 7.6pd
7810997 - -	**YOUNIS** **Alexandria Port Authority** - *Alexandria* *Egypt*	*700* Class: (GL) - -	**1980-09 Timsah SB. Co. — Ismailia** Yd No: 416 L reg 36.00 Br ex - Dght 1.701 Lbp - Br md 17.61 Dpth 3.20 Welded, 1 dk	**(B34B2SC) Crane Vessel** Cranes: 1x35t	**2 oil engines** reduction geared to sc. shafts driving 2 FP propellers Total Power: 618kW (840hp) 8.0kn MAN D2542MTE 2 x Vee 4 Stroke 12 Cy. 125 x 142 each-309kW (420bhp) Maschinenbau Augsburg Nuernberg (MAN)-Augsburg

IMO / Call sign	Name / Owner	Tonnage	Class	Builder / Dimensions	Type	Machinery
7711957 *TJAV* -	**YOUPWE** **L'Office National des Ports du Cameroon (ONPC)** - *Douala* *Cameroon*	*1,808* 994 2,770	Class: (BV)	**1978-09 Davie Shipbuilding Ltd — Levis QC** Yd No: 695 Loa 76.31 Br ex - Dght 5.401 Lbp 68.61 Br md 11.82 Dpth 6.51 Welded, 1 dk	**(B33B2DT) Trailing Suction Hopper Dredger** Hopper: 1,800	**2 oil engines** reduction geared to sc. shafts driving 2 FP propellers Total Power: 2,412kW (3,280hp) 12.0k Alco 8V251 2 x Vee 4 Stroke 8 Cy. 229 x 267 each-1206kW (1640bhp) Montreal Locomotive Works-Canada
8618803 *JG4654* -	**YOUR TOWN** **Tokyoto Kanko Kisen KK** - *Tokyo* *Japan* Official number: 129850	*143* - 42		**1987-03 Sumidagawa Zosen K.K. — Tokyo** Yd No: N61-14 Loa 30.61 Br ex Dght 1.501 Lbp 29.04 Br md 7.71 Dpth 2.37 Welded	**(A37B2PS) Passenger Ship** Passengers: unberthed: 550	**1 oil engine** driving 1 FP propeller Total Power: 368kW (500hp) 11.9k Yanmar 6LAAK-U 1 x 4 Stroke 6 Cy. 148 x 165 368kW (500bhp) Yanmar Diesel Engine Co Ltd-Japan
8316106 *EQOG* -	**YOUSEF** **NITC** - *Bushehr* *Iran* MMSI: 422144000 Official number: 8/63	**584** 175 1,050	Class: AS (LR) ✠ Classed LR until 31/10/00	**1984-06 K.K. Imai Seisakusho — Kamijima** (Hull) Yd No: 240 **1984-06 Mitsui Ocean Development & Eng. Co. Ltd. — Japan** Yd No: 179 Loa 48.14 Br ex 10.24 Dght 3.960 Lbp 43.03 Br md 10.01 Dpth 4.40 Welded, 1 dk	**(B21B20T) Offshore Tug/Supply Ship**	**2 oil engines** with clutches, flexible couplings & sr reverse geared to sc. shafts driving 2 FP propellers Total Power: 2,040kW (2,774hp) Deutz SBV6M62 2 x 4 Stroke 6 Cy. 240 x 280 each-1020kW (1387bhp) Kloeckner Humboldt Deutz AG-West Germany AuxGen: 2 x 128kW 380V 50Hz a.c Thrusters: 1 Thwart. CP thruster (f) Fuel: 283.5 (d.f.)
8936499 *JG5519* -	**YOUSHINMARU** **KK Kyoshin Kaiun** - *Kainan, Wakayama* *Japan* Official number: 135900	*246* - -		**1997-11 Hongawara Zosen K.K. — Fukuyama** Yd No: 478 Loa 49.97 Br ex - Dght - Lbp - Br md 8.00 Dpth 3.50 Welded, 1 dk	**(A13B2TU) Tanker (unspecified)**	**1 oil engine** driving 1 FP propeller Total Power: 736kW (1,001hp) 11.0k Yanmar DY26-S 1 x 4 Stroke 6 Cy. 260 x 440 736kW (1001bhp) Yanmar Diesel Engine Co Ltd-Japan
7425780 - -	**YOUSIFAN** - -	*662* - 386	Class: (LR) ✠ Classed LR until 29/1/92	**1975-06 Towa Zosen K.K. — Shimonoseki** Yd No: 476 Loa 45.70 Br ex 11.03 Dght 4.611 Lbp 41.23 Br md 11.00 Dpth 5.41 Welded, 1 dk	**(B32A2ST) Tug**	**1 oil engine** driving 1 CP propeller Total Power: 3,236kW (4,400hp) Hanshin 6LU5 1 x 4 Stroke 6 Cy. 540 x 860 3236kW (4400bhp) The Hanshin Diesel Works Ltd-Japan Thrusters: 1 Thwart. FP thruster (a)
9121493 *CNLQ* -	**YOUSSEF** **Towage & Salvage Co** Societe Cherifienne de Remorquage et d'Assistance *Casablanca* *Morocco* Official number: 6-864	*119* 36 -	Class: BV (LR) ✠ Classed LR until 9/3/12	**1996-07 Stocznia Tczew Sp z oo — Tczew** (Hull) **1996-07 B.V. Scheepswerf Damen — Gorinchem** Yd No: 6523 Loa 22.55 Br ex 7.45 Dght 3.180 Lbp 19.82 Br md 7.25 Dpth 3.74 Welded, 1 dk	**(B32A2ST) Tug**	**2 oil engines** with clutches, flexible couplings & sr reverse geared to sc. shafts driving 2 FP propellers Total Power: 1,350kW (1,836hp) 11.8k Caterpillar 3508T 2 x Vee 4 Stroke 8 Cy. 170 x 190 each-675kW (918bhp) Caterpillar Inc-USA AuxGen: 2 x 50kW 380V 50Hz a.c Fuel: 30.0 (d.f.)
8919623 - -	**YOUSSEF ELSERAFY** - - *Egypt*	**150** - -	Class: (GL)	**1997-06 Alexandria Shipyard — Alexandria** Yd No: 10120 Loa - Br ex - Dght - Lbp 24.70 Br md 6.50 Dpth - Welded, 1 dk	**(B34F2SF) Fire Fighting Vessel**	**1 oil engine** driving 1 FP propeller
7611547 *5VCD3* -	**YOUZARSIF-H** *ex* Uni K *-2013* *ex* Vima Alfa *-2006* *ex* Lem Alfa *-2003* *ex* Duke *-1997* *ex* Dana Iberia *-1991* *ex* Commodore Clipper *-1990* *ex* Hamburg *-1988* *ex* Jan Kahrs *-1986* **La Mer Shipping SA** Nejem Co Marine Services *Lome* *Togo* MMSI: 671371000	**2,334** 1,309 2,103	Class: GM IO (GL)	**1977-01 KG Norderwerft GmbH & Co. — Hamburg** (Hull) **1977-01 J.J. Sietas Schiffswerft — Hamburg** Yd No: 750 Converted From: General Cargo Ship-2013 Loa 81.36 (BB) Br ex 13.44 Dght 5.900 Lbp 74.17 Br md 13.42 Dpth 5.19 Welded, 5 dks	**(A38A2GL) Livestock Carrier** Ice Capable	**1 oil engine** driving 1 FP propeller Total Power: 1,949kW (2,650hp) 13.5k MaK 8M453A 1 x 4 Stroke 8 Cy. 320 x 420 1949kW (2650bhp) MaK Maschinenbau GmbH-Kiel Thrusters: 1 Thwart. FP thruster (f)
8934116 *JI3635* -	**YOWA MARU** **Seiwa Kaiun KK** - *Osaka, Osaka* *Japan* Official number: 135935	*199* - -		**1997-08 Hongawara Zosen K.K. — Fukuyama** Yd No: 476 Loa 49.71 Br ex - Dght - Lbp 45.00 Br md 7.80 Dpth 3.30 Welded, 1 dk	**(A12A2TC) Chemical Tanker** 1 Cargo Pump (s): 1x150m³/hr	**1 oil engine** driving 1 FP propeller Total Power: 588kW (799hp) 10.0k Yanmar M200-S 1 x 4 Stroke 6 Cy. 200 x 260 588kW (799bhp) Yanmar Diesel Engine Co Ltd-Japan
9066473 *JG5200* -	**YOWA MARU** **Uyeno Transtech Co Ltd** - *Yokohama, Kanagawa* *Japan* MMSI: 431100033 Official number: 133850	*2,998* - 4,943	Class: NK	**1993-04 Shin Kurushima Dockyard Co. Ltd. — Hashihama, Imabari** Yd No: 2753 Loa 104.81 (BB) Br ex - Dght 6.280 Lbp 97.50 Br md 15.20 Dpth 7.60 Welded, 1 dk	**(A13B2TP) Products Tanker** Double Bottom Entire Compartment Length Liq: 5,027; Liq (Oil): 5,027 Compartments: 9 Ta, ER 2 Cargo Pump (s): 2x1200m³/hr	**1 oil engine** driving 1 CP propeller Total Power: 2,942kW (4,000hp) 13.3k Akasaka A4 1 x 4 Stroke 6 Cy. 450 x 880 2942kW (4000bhp) Akasaka Tekkosho KK (Akasaka DieselLtd)-Japan Thrusters: 1 Thwart. CP thruster (f) Fuel: 275.0 (r.f.)
9624483 *JD3306* -	**YOYU MARU** **Kyokuyo Tanker KK** - *Tokyo* *Japan* Official number: 141603	*499* - 1,247		**2011-12 K.K. Miura Zosensho — Saiki** Yd No: 1375 Loa 64.50 Br ex - Dght 4.240 Lbp 60.00 Br md 10.00 Dpth 4.43 Welded, 1 dk	**(A12B2TR) Chemical/Products Tanker** Double Hull (13F)	**1 oil engine** reverse reduction geared to sc. shaft driving 1 Propeller Total Power: 1,029kW (1,399hp) 11.0k Akasaka K28B 1 x 4 Stroke 6 Cy. 280 x 480 1029kW (1399bhp) Akasaka Tekkosho KK (Akasaka DieselLtd)-Japan
8899914 *JBRC* -	**YOZAN** **Higashi Nippon Senpaku KK** - SatCom: Inmarsat A 1205706 *Kesennuma, Miyagi* *Japan* MMSI: 431842000 Official number: 133341	*486* - -		**1996-03 Miyagi-ken Zosen Tekko K.K. — Kesennuma** Loa 57.53 Br ex - Dght 3.800 Lbp 48.80 Br md 8.40 Dpth 4.19 Welded, 1 dk	**(B12D2FP) Fishery Patrol Vessel**	**1 oil engine** driving 1 FP propeller Total Power: 1,471kW (2,000hp) 15.1k Yanmar 6N280-E 1 x 4 Stroke 6 Cy. 280 x 380 1471kW (2000bhp) Yanmar Diesel Engine Co Ltd-Japan
8808020 *YYV2924* -	**YRIS** *ex* Smit Barbados *-2005* *ex* King Star *-2000* *ex* Genkai *-2000* **PDV Marina SA** - *Puerto la Cruz* *Venezuela* Official number: AGSP-2779	**354** 106	Class: (LR) (BV) Classed LR until 7/11/11	**1988-08 Hanasaki Zosensho K.K. — Yokosuka** Yd No: 207 Loa 36.28 Br ex 11.31 Dght 3.301 Lbp 30.82 Br md 10.01 Dpth 4.40 Welded, 1 dk	**(B32A2ST) Tug**	**2 oil engines** with clutches, flexible couplings & reduction geared to sc. shafts driving 2 FP propellers Total Power: 2,736kW (3,720hp) 14.3k Niigata 6L28BX 2 x 4 Stroke 6 Cy. 280 x 350 each-1368kW (1860bhp) Niigata Engineering Co Ltd-Japan AuxGen: 2 x 96kW 220V 60Hz a.c Fuel: 55.0 (d.f.)
7618818 *JVAN5* -	**YTC HOPPER 7** *ex* Ham 586 *-2013* **Yeng Tong Construction Pte Ltd** - *Ulaanbaatar* *Mongolia* MMSI: 457760000	**774** 232 1,300	Class: (BV)	**1976-02 A. Vuijk & Zonen's Scheepswerven B.V. — Capelle a/d IJssel** Yd No: 875 Loa - Br ex - Dght 3.352 Lbp 60.03 Br md 11.02 Dpth 4.17 Welded, 1 dk	**(B34A2SH) Hopper, Motor** Grain: 766 Compartments: 1 Ho, ER 1 Ha: (31.2 x 7.4)ER	**2 oil engines** geared to sc. shaft driving 1 FP propeller Total Power: 802kW (1,090hp) 9.3k Deutz BF12M71 2 x Vee 4 Stroke 12 Cy. 135 x 160 each-401kW (545bhp) Kloeckner Humboldt Deutz AG-West Germany
9138537 *9V5188* -	**YTC TUG 12** *ex* LM Venture *-2009* **YTC Marine Services Pte Ltd** - *Singapore* *Singapore* MMSI: 563795000 Official number: 386766	**105** 32 89	Class: NK	**1995-08 Fong Syn Shipyard Sdn Bhd — Sibu** Yd No: 8394 Loa 21.38 Br ex - Dght 2.442 Lbp 19.88 Br md 6.40 Dpth 2.75 Welded, 1 dk	**(B32A2ST) Tug**	**2 oil engines** reduction geared to sc. shafts driving 2 FP propellers Total Power: 560kW (762hp) 9.5k Caterpillar 3406 2 x 4 Stroke 6 Cy. 137 x 165 each-280kW (381bhp) Caterpillar Inc-USA Fuel: 55.0 (d.f.)
9046069 *9V3602* -	**YTC TUG 24** *ex* Winstar Reliance *-2013* *ex* Alpha Coast *-2001* **Yeng Tong Construction Pte Ltd** - *Singapore* *Singapore* MMSI: 564265000 Official number: 383914	**220** 66 -	Class: AB	**1991-09 President Marine Pte Ltd — Singapore** Yd No: 065 Loa 29.00 Br ex - Dght 3.936 Lbp 27.08 Br md 8.60 Dpth 4.11 Welded, 1 dk	**(B32A2ST) Tug**	**2 oil engines** reverse reduction geared to sc. shafts driving 2 FP propellers Total Power: 1,176kW (1,598hp) 11.5k Yanmar 6N165-EN 2 x 4 Stroke 6 Cy. 165 x 232 each-588kW (799bhp) Yanmar Diesel Engine Co Ltd-Japan AuxGen: 2 x 60kW a.c

IMO / Call sign	Name / Owner	Tonnage	Class	Builder / Dimensions	Type	Machinery
88661 /2403	**YTC TUG 25** *ex* Apollo *-2013* **YTC Marine Services Pte Ltd** Rover Maritime Services Pte Ltd *Singapore* *Singapore* Official number: 398982	125 38 -	Class: RI (BV)	**1998-03 Kiong Nguong Shipbuilding Contractor Co — Sibu** Yd No: 97/775 Loa 23.15 Br ex - Dght 2.500 Lbp 21.69 Br md 7.30 Dpth 3.00 Welded, 1 dk	**(B32A2ST) Tug**	**2 oil engines** driving 2 FP propellers Total Power: 924kW (1,256hp) 10.8kn Yanmar 6LAHK-ST1 2 x 4 Stroke 6 Cy. 150 x 165 each-462kW (628bhp) Yanmar Diesel Engine Co Ltd-Japan AuxGen: 2 x 20kW a.c
253167 /6029	**YTC TUG 26** *ex* Ocean 2001 *-2013* **Yeng Tong Construction Pte Ltd** - *Singapore* *Singapore* Official number: 389219	249 75 219	Class: NK	**2001-07 Dalian Shipyard Co Ltd — Dalian LN** Yd No: TU28-1 Loa 28.00 Br ex - Dght 3.423 Lbp 26.10 Br md 8.80 Dpth 4.00 Welded, 1 dk	**(B32B2SP) Pusher Tug**	**2 oil engines** driving 2 FP propellers Total Power: 1,176kW (1,598hp) Yanmar 2 x 4 Stroke each-588kW (799bhp) Yanmar Diesel Engine Co Ltd-Japan AuxGen: 1 x 100kW a.c Fuel: 150.0 (d.f.)
371531 NXL	**YTTEROYNINGEN** **Norled AS** - *Trondheim* *Norway* MMSI: 258323000	632 189 343	Class: (NV)	**2006-11 UAB Vakaru Laivu Remontas (JSC Western Shiprepair) — Klaipeda** (Hull) Yd No: (53) **2006-11 Fiskerstrand Verft AS — Fiskarstrand** Yd No: 53 Loa 49.80 Br ex - Dght 3.400 Lbp 49.13 Br md 13.70 Dpth 4.80 Welded, 1 dk	**(A36A2PR) Passenger/Ro-Ro Ship (Vehicles)** Passengers: unberthed: 160 Bow ramp (centre) Stern ramp (centre) Cars: 38	**4 oil engines** reduction geared to sc. shafts driving 2 Directional propellers 2 propellers fwd, 2 aft Total Power: 1,764kW (2,400hp) 11.0kn Scania DI16 43M 4 x Vee 4 Stroke 8 Cy. 127 x 154 each-441kW (600bhp) Scania AB-Sweden
581928 FNS2	**YU AN** **Yu Lin Shipping Co Ltd** Yantai Pingyang Shipping Co Ltd SatCom: Inmarsat C 435113110 *Panama* *Panama* MMSI: 351131000 Official number: 4244411	2,690 1,435 3,586	Class: CC	**2010-12 Yantai Yu'an Shipyard Co Ltd — Changdao County SD** Yd No: YTYA0801 Loa 87.33 Br ex - Dght 6.000 Lbp 80.00 Br md 14.00 Dpth 8.50 Welded, 1 dk	**(A31A2GX) General Cargo Ship** Grain: 5,520; Bale: 4,347 Compartments: 2 Ho, ER 2 Ha: (21.0 x 9.6)ER (19.9 x 9.6) Ice Capable	**1 oil engine** reduction geared to sc. shaft driving 1 Propeller Total Power: 1,324kW (1,800hp) 10.9kn Chinese Std. Type 6320ZC 1 x 4 Stroke 6 Cy. 320 x 440 1324kW (1800bhp) Guangzhou Diesel Engine Factory CoLtd-China AuxGen: 2 x 150kW 400V a.c
814958 ECY	**YU AU** **Ocean Fishery Development Administration** - SatCom: Inmarsat A 1356142 *Kaohsiung* *Chinese Taipei* Official number: 948	*368* 256 -		**1956 Taiwan Shipbuilding Corp — Keelung** Loa 46.72 Br ex 7.22 Dght 3.099 Lbp 41.81 Br md 7.19 Dpth 3.61 Welded, 1 dk	**(B11B2FV) Fishing Vessel** Compartments: 4 Ho, ER 4 Ha: ER Derricks: 1x2t; Winches: 1	**1 oil engine** driving 1 FP propeller Total Power: 552kW (750hp) 10.5kn Niigata M6DR 1 x 4 Stroke 6 Cy. 370 x 520 552kW (750bhp) Niigata Engineering Co Ltd-Japan AuxGen: 1 x 96kW 230V 60Hz a.c, 1 x 32kW 230V 60Hz a.c
749585 H3294	**YU CHAN HSIANG** **Yu Chan Hsiang Fishery Co Ltd** - *Kaohsiung* *Chinese Taipei* Official number: 013017	489 192 -		**1995-09 Kaohsiung Shipbuilding Co. Ltd. — Kaohsiung** Loa 45.60 Br ex - Dght 3.650 Lbp - Br md 8.30 Dpth - Welded, 1 dk	**(B11B2FV) Fishing Vessel**	**1 oil engine** driving 1 Propeller
651362 2531	**YU CHEN HSIANG NO. 16** **Chung Chen Shu Hui** - *Kaohsiung* *Chinese Taipei* Official number: 013891	630 286 400		**2000-12 Sen Koh Shipbuilding Corp — Kaohsiung** Loa 59.20 Br ex - Dght 3.600 Lbp - Br md 9.00 Dpth 3.75 Welded, 1 dk	**(B11B2FV) Fishing Vessel**	**1 oil engine** driving 1 FP propeller
116200	**YU CHYUAN No. 2** **Yu Chan Fishery Co Ltd** - *Kaohsiung* *Chinese Taipei*	*250* 99 -		**1971 Fong Kuo Shipbuilding Co Ltd — Kaohsiung** Yd No: S01070 Loa 39.22 Br ex 6.94 Dght - Lbp 33.99 Br md 6.91 Dpth 3.15 Welded, 1 dk	**(B11B2FV) Fishing Vessel**	**1 oil engine** driving 1 FP propeller Total Power: 478kW (650hp) Matsue 1 x 4 Stroke 478kW (650bhp) Matsue Diesel KK-Japan
811874 VBL	**YU CHYUAN No. 6** **Yu Chyuan Ocean Developing Co Ltd** - *Kaohsiung* *Chinese Taipei*	*280* 194 -	Class: (CR)	**1972 Taiwan Machinery Manufacturing Corp. — Kaohsiung** Loa 40.21 Br ex 7.12 Dght 2.814 Lbp 35.01 Br md 7.09 Dpth 3.00 Welded, 1 dk	**(B11B2FV) Fishing Vessel** Compartments: 3 Ho, ER 4 Ha: (1.3 x 1.3)2 (0.9 x 1.0) (0.9 x 0.9)ER	**1 oil engine** driving 1 FP propeller Total Power: 566kW (770hp) 10.0kn Alpha 407-26VO 1 x 2 Stroke 7 Cy. 260 x 400 566kW (770bhp) Taiwan Machinery ManufacturingCorp.-Kaohsiung AuxGen: 2 x 100kW 230V a.c
011574	**YU DA** *ex* Mian Yuan Hao *-2001* *ex* Mean Font *-1999* *ex* Mian Yuan Hao *-1999* *ex* Hai Heng Chang *-1999* *ex* Fukuyo Maru *-1999* **Shantou Desheng Shipping Co Ltd**	963 539 1,600		**1980-06 Yamanaka Zosen K.K. — Imabari** Yd No: 227 L reg 70.62 Br ex - Dght 4.252 Lbp 66.02 Br md 11.02 Dpth 6.13 Welded, 1 dk	**(A31A2GX) General Cargo Ship**	**1 oil engine** driving 1 FP propeller Total Power: 1,324kW (1,800hp) 11.0kn Nippon Hatsudoki 1 x 4 Stroke 1324kW (1800bhp) Nippon Kokan KK (NKK Corp)-Japan
10614 3QD	**YU DAL** *ex* Camcot *-1983* *ex* Eikyo Maru *-1973* **Mokpo Merchant Marine Junior College** - SatCom: Inmarsat B 344042810 *Mokpo* *South Korea*	*2,615* 1,687 4,429	Class: (NK)	**1970-06 Kurushima Dockyard Co. Ltd. — Imabari** Yd No: 621 Loa 93.22 Br ex 15.04 Dght 6.046 Lbp 86.01 Br md 15.02 Dpth 7.22 Riveted\Welded, 1 dk	**(A31A2GX) General Cargo Ship** Grain: 5,818; Bale: 5,503 Compartments: 2 Ho, ER 2 Ha: (24.0 x 7.3) (24.4 x 7.3)ER Derricks: 2x15t,2x10t; Winches: 12	**1 oil engine** driving 1 FP propeller Total Power: 1,839kW (2,500hp) 11.8kn Hanshin 6L46 1 x 4 Stroke 6 Cy. 460 x 680 1839kW (2500bhp) Hanshin Nainenki Kogyo-Japan AuxGen: 2 x 132kW 445V a.c Fuel: 437.0
322038 PQX	**YU FENG** **Shanghai Yuhai Shipping Co** - SatCom: Inmarsat C 441202510 *Shanghai* *China* MMSI: 412049010	*9,305* 3,616 10,134	Class: CC	**1992-03 Guangzhou Wenchong Shipyard — Guangzhou GD** Yd No: 256 Loa 139.80 Br ex - Dght 8.200 Lbp 126.00 Br md 20.80 Dpth 11.40 Welded	**(B34K2QT) Training Ship**	**1 oil engine** driving 1 FP propeller Total Power: 3,480kW (4,731hp) 16.2kn B&W 6L50MCE 1 x 2 Stroke 6 Cy. 500 x 1620 3480kW (4731bhp) Shanghai Diesel Engine Co Ltd-China
528691 ETF8	**YU FENG** **Jolly Shipping Ltd** Shanghai Marukichi Ship Management Co Ltd *Panama* *Panama* MMSI: 370546000 Official number: 3464309B	2,956 1,872 5,000	Class: OM	**2008-04 Qiyang Baishui Shipbuilding Co Ltd — Qiyang County HN** Loa 99.56 Br ex - Dght 6.000 Lbp 92.71 Br md 15.60 Dpth 7.70 Welded, 1 dk	**(A31A2GX) General Cargo Ship**	**1 oil engine** geared to sc. shaft driving 1 Propeller Total Power: 1,765kW (2,400hp) 11.0kn Chinese Std. Type 8320ZC 1 x 4 Stroke 8 Cy. 320 x 440 1765kW (2400bhp) Guangzhou Diesel Engine Factory CoLtd-China
431023	**YU FENG No. 68** **Hung Chang Fishery Co Ltd** - *San Lorenzo* *Honduras* Official number: L-1822988	*719* 285 -		**1989 Sen Koh Shipbuilding Corp — Kaohsiung** L reg 50.60 Br ex - Dght 3.500 Lbp - Br md 8.90 Dpth 3.85 Welded, 1 dk	**(B11B2FV) Fishing Vessel**	**1 oil engine** driving 1 FP propeller Total Power: 1,030kW (1,400hp) 13.0kn
430512	**YU FENG No. 116** **Yung Chang Fishery Co Ltd** - SatCom: Inmarsat A 1356652 *San Lorenzo* *Honduras* Official number: L-1822976	*719* 285 -		**1989 Fong Kuo Shipbuilding Co Ltd — Kaohsiung** Loa 50.60 Br ex - Dght 3.500 Lbp - Br md 8.90 Dpth 3.85 Welded, 1 dk	**(B11B2FV) Fishing Vessel**	**1 oil engine** driving 1 FP propeller Total Power: 1,030kW (1,400hp) 13.0kn
431164 QHG6	**YU FONG 310** - - *San Lorenzo* *Honduras* Official number: L-1823598	*217* 84 -		**1980 Suao Shipbuilding Co., Ltd. — Suao** L reg 34.93 Br ex - Dght 2.800 Lbp - Br md 6.30 Dpth 3.10 Welded, 1 dk	**(B11B2FV) Fishing Vessel**	**1 oil engine** driving 1 FP propeller Total Power: 809kW (1,100hp) 10.0kn

IMO / Call sign	Name / Owner / Manager / Port	Tonnage	Class	Builder / Dimensions	Type / Cargo	Machinery	Speed / Engine
8517035 *VRGD8* -	**YU FU** *ex* Zaral *-2010 ex* Aral Wind *-2009* *ex* St. Mary *-2005 ex* Uznadze *-2000* *ex* Akademik Uznadze *-1994* **Target Shipping Ltd** RTBS Consultants Pte Ltd *Hong Kong* — *Hong Kong* MMSI: 477726300	**10,985** 5,140 17,430 T/cm 27.9	Class: NV (RS)	**1988-07 Brodogradiliste Split (Brodosplit) — Split** Yd No: 354 Converted From: Products Tanker-2007 Conv to DH-2007 Loa 151.30 (BB) Br ex 22.43 Dght 9.470 Lbp 142.94 Br md 22.40 Dpth 12.15 Welded, 1 dk	**(A12B2TR) Chemical/Products Tanker** Double Hull (13F) Liq: 17,178; Liq (Oil): 20,502 Cargo Heating Coils Compartments: 10 Wing Ta, 6 Ta, 2 Wing Slop Ta, ER 16 Cargo Pump (s): 16x250m³/hr Manifold: Bow/CM: 73.7m Ice Capable	**1 oil engine** with clutches, flexible couplings & reduction geared to sc. shaft driving 1 CP propeller Total Power: 5,701kW (7,751hp) B&W 1 x 2 Stroke 5 Cy. 500 x 1620 5701kW (7751bhp) Brodogradiliste Split (Brodosplit)-Yugoslavia AuxGen: 1 x 900kW a.c, 2 x 700kW Thrusters: 1 Thwart. FP thruster (f)	15.1k 5L50M
8992041 *XUSD9* -	**YU HAI 1** *ex* Eastern Paris 1 *-2008* *ex* Xin Jin Run 18 *-2005 ex* Lu Ping 6 *-2003* **Aoyu Shipping Co Ltd** Yilong Shipping Co Ltd *Phnom Penh* — *Cambodia* MMSI: 515029000 Official number: 0886949	**1,318** 751 2,000	Class: UB	**1986-10 Zhejiang Shipyard — Ningbo ZJ** Loa 70.70 Br ex - Dght 4.800 Lbp 65.00 Br md 12.00 Dpth 6.40 Welded, 1 dk	**(A31A2GX) General Cargo Ship**	**1 oil engine** driving 1 Propeller Total Power: 736kW (1,001hp) Niigata 1 x 4 Stroke 736kW (1001bhp) Niigata Engineering Co Ltd-Japan	
9166895 *BOEL* -	**YU HENG XIAN FENG** *ex* Alioth Leader *-2013* **NYKCOS Car Carrier Co Ltd** - *Guangzhou, Guangdong* — *China* MMSI: 412163000	**53,240** 15,972 13,418 T/cm 46.3	Class: CC (NK)	**1998-01 Mitsubishi Heavy Industries Ltd. — Nagasaki** Yd No: 2114 Loa 180.00 (BB) Br ex - Dght 9.224 Lbp 170.00 Br md 32.26 Dpth 21.67 Welded, 12 dks, Nos. 5,7,9 hoistable	**(A35B2RV) Vehicles Carrier** Side door/ramp (p) Len: 16.80 Wid: 4.20 Swl: 15 Side door/ramp (s) Len: 16.80 Wid: 4.20 Swl: 15 Quarter stern door/ramp (s. a.) Len: 31.40 Wid: 9.00 Swl: 80 Cars: 4,305	**1 oil engine** driving 1 FP propeller Total Power: 11,916kW (16,201hp) Mitsubishi 1 x 2 Stroke 7 Cy. 600 x 2200 11916kW (16201bhp) Mitsubishi Heavy Industries Ltd-Japan AuxGen: 3 x 1030kW 450V 60Hz a.c Thrusters: 1 Thwart. CP thruster (f) Fuel: 268.8 (d.f.) (Heating Coils) 2442.0 (r.f.) 45.5pd	19.0kn 7UEC60LS
9646209 *H8ER*	**YU HONG** **Rui Tong Shipping SA** Qingdao Da Tong International Shipping Management Co Ltd *Panama* — *Panama* MMSI: 372854000 Official number: 4495813	**43,974** 27,688 82,000 T/cm 71.9	Class: BV	**2013-04 Jiangsu Jinling Ships Co Ltd — Yizheng JS** Yd No: JLZ8110410 Loa 229.00 (BB) Br ex - Dght 14.450 Lbp 225.50 Br md 32.26 Dpth 20.05 Welded, 1 dk	**(A21A2BC) Bulk Carrier** Grain: 98,091; Bale: 90,784 Compartments: 7 Ho, ER 7 Ha: 5 (18.3 x 15.0) (15.7 x 15.1)ER (13.1 x 13.2)	**1 oil engine** driving 1 FP propeller Total Power: 9,800kW (13,324hp) MAN-B&W 1 x 2 Stroke 5 Cy. 600 x 2400 9800kW (13324bhp) Hyundai Heavy Industries Co Ltd-South Korea AuxGen: 3 x 710kW 60Hz a.c	14.1kn 5S60MC-C8
9306043 *BR3441*	**YU HONG** *ex* Odae Ho *-2010* - - *China*	**215** - -	Class: (KR)	**2003-10 Yeunsoo Shipbuilding Co Ltd — Janghang** Yd No: 13 Loa 34.10 Br ex - Dght 3.100 Lbp 28.60 Br md 9.50 Dpth 4.00 Welded, 1 dk	**(B32A2ST) Tug**	**2 oil engines** geared to sc. shafts driving 2 CP propellers Total Power: 3,184kW (4,328hp) M.T.U. 2 x Vee 4 Stroke 16 Cy. 165 x 190 each-1592kW (2164bhp) MTU Friedrichshafen GmbH-Friedrichshafen	12.0kn 16V4000M60
8985270 *9WH2322* -	**YU HONG NO. 1** **Yu Hong Shipping** - *Kuching* — *Malaysia* MMSI: 533000227 Official number: 326338	**581** 175 1,000		**1993-07 Forward Shipbuilding Enterprise Sdn Bhd — Sibu** Yd No: 15 Loa 43.33 Br ex 14.62 Dght - Lbp - Br md - Dpth 2.62 Welded, 1 dk	**(A35D2RL) Landing Craft** Bow ramp (f)	**2 oil engines** driving 2 Propellers Total Power: 348kW (474hp) Cummins 2 x 4 Stroke each-174kW (237bhp) Cummins Engine Co Inc-USA	
8203933 *3FV02* -	**YU HORNG** *ex* Sang Thai Quartz *-2011 ex* Sea Arrow *-1994* **Yu Horng International Co Ltd** - SatCom: Inmarsat C 435601510 *Panama* — *Panama* MMSI: 356015000 Official number: 4341612	**2,875** 1,638 4,848	Class: OM (NK)	**1981-12 K.K. Imai Seisakusho — Kamijima** Yd No: 220 Loa 90.51 (BB) Br ex 15.24 Dght 6.450 Lbp 83.30 Br md 15.21 Dpth 7.60 Welded, 1 dk	**(A31A2GX) General Cargo Ship** Grain: 5,755; Bale: 5,075 Compartments: 2 Ho, ER 2 Ha: (15.1 x 8.5) (26.0 x 8.5)ER Derricks: 3x15t	**1 oil engine** reverse reduction geared to sc. shaft driving 1 FP propeller Total Power: 1,692kW (2,300hp) Akasaka 1 x 4 Stroke 6 Cy. 380 x 600 1692kW (2300bhp) Akasaka Tekkosho KK (Akasaka DieselLtd)-Japan Fuel: 340.0 (r.f.)	11.0kn DM38AK
9172909 *YJQE3* -	**YU HSIANG MARU** **Yu I Hsiang Marine SA** Atlas Ship Management Co Ltd *Port Vila* — *Vanuatu* MMSI: 576395000 Official number: 1924	**2,713** 1,152 3,046	Class: NK	**1997-09 KK Kanasashi — Shizuoka SZ** Yd No: 3461 Loa 91.29 (BB) Br ex 14.50 Dght 5.518 Lbp 84.98 Br md - Dpth 8.60 Welded, 1 dk	**(A34A2GR) Refrigerated Cargo Ship** Bale: 880; Ins: 4,281 Compartments: 3 Ho, ER 3 Ha: 3 (3.3 x 3.2)ER Derricks: 6x4t	**1 oil engine** driving 1 FP propeller Total Power: 2,405kW (3,270hp) B&W 1 x 2 Stroke 6 Cy. 260 x 980 2405kW (3270bhp) The Hanshin Diesel Works Ltd-Japan Fuel: 810.0	14.0kn 6S26MC
8430378 *HQHO2* -	**YU HSIANG No. 216** **Lubmain International SA** - *San Lorenzo* — *Honduras* Official number: L-1923673	**435** 198 -		**1986 Fong Kuo Shipbuilding Co Ltd — Kaohsiung** L reg 41.95 Br ex - Dght 2.620 Lbp - Br md 8.00 Dpth 3.50 Welded, 1 dk	**(B11B2FV) Fishing Vessel**	**1 oil engine** driving 1 FP propeller Total Power: 736kW (1,001hp)	12.0kn
8647385 *BI2477* -	**YU HSING HSIANG NO. 126** **Yu Pae Hsiang Fishery Co Ltd** - *Kaohsiung* — *Chinese Taipei* Official number: 12023	**538** 223 -		**1991-01 Lin Sheng Shipbuilding Co, Ltd — Kaohsiung** Loa 46.50 Br ex 8.50 Dght - Lbp - Br md - Dpth 3.65 Welded, 1 dk	**(B11B2FV) Fishing Vessel**	**1 oil engine** driving 1 Propeller Sumiyoshi 1 x 4 Stroke Sumiyoshi Marine Diesel Co Ltd-Japan	
7325069 *BESK* -	**YU HSUN No. 1** **Government of Taiwan (Deep Sea Fishing Training Centre of Ministry of Economic Affairs)** *Kaohsiung* — *Chinese Taipei*	*517* 256	Class: (CR)	**1972 Taiwan Machinery Manufacturing Corp. — Kaohsiung** Loa 45.62 Br ex 8.84 Dght 3.404 Lbp 41.00 Br md 8.82 Dpth 4.02 Welded, 1 dk	**(B11B2FV) Fishing Vessel** Ins: 207 Compartments: 1 Ho, ER 1 Ha: (1.6 x 1.6)ER Derricks: 2x2t,2x1t; Winches: 4	**1 oil engine** driving 1 FP propeller Total Power: 883kW (1,201hp) Niigata 1 x 4 Stroke 6 Cy. 250 x 320 883kW (1201bhp) Niigata Engineering Co Ltd-Japan AuxGen: 2 x 104kW 130V a.c	11.0kn 6MG25BX
8849440 *BZNU* -	**YU HSUN NO. 2** *ex* Yu Shiun No. 2 *-2004* **Government of Taiwan (Deep Sea Fishing Training Centre of Ministry of Economic Affairs)** - *Kaohsiung* — *Chinese Taipei* MMSI: 416951000 Official number: 12018	**1,211** 370	Class: CR	**1990-12 Taiwan Machinery Manufacturing Corp. — Kaohsiung** Loa 64.40 Br ex - Dght 4.300 Lbp 56.80 Br md 11.40 Dpth 7.10 Welded, 2 dks	**(B11B2FV) Fishing Vessel**	**1 oil engine** driving 1 FP propeller Total Power: 1,618kW (2,200hp) Niigata 1 x 4 Stroke 6 Cy. 310 x 380 1618kW (2200bhp) Niigata Engineering Co Ltd-Japan	6MG31FZE
9375771 *3FBY2* -	**YU HUA HAI** **Yu Hua Hai Maritime SA** Qingdao Ocean Shipping Co Ltd (COSCO QINGDAO) SatCom: Inmarsat C 437162010 *Panama* — *Panama* MMSI: 371620000 Official number: 4169310	**152,148** 55,953 297,846	Class: CC	**2010-04 Nantong COSCO KHI Ship Engineering Co Ltd (NACKS) — Nantong JS** Yd No: 075 Loa 327.00 (BB) Br ex 55.05 Dght 21.400 Lbp 321.50 Br md 55.00 Dpth 29.00 Welded, 1 dk	**(A21B2BO) Ore Carrier** Grain: 184,102 Compartments: 6 Ho, ER 6 Ha: ER 6 (32.1 x 16.1)	**1 oil engine** driving 1 FP propeller Total Power: 23,280kW (31,651hp) MAN-B&W 1 x 2 Stroke 6 Cy. 800 x 3200 23280kW (31651bhp) CSSC MES Diesel Co Ltd-China AuxGen: 3 x 750kW 450V a.c	14.5kn 6S80MC-C
7204904 *D8MD* -	**YU HWA** *ex* Yu Wha Ho *-2004 ex* Yuka Maru *-1986* *ex* Caribbean Maid *-1985* *ex* Propane Maru No. 10 *-1981* - - *Busan* — *South Korea* MMSI: 440607000 Official number: BSR-766279	*1,419* 790 1,450 T/cm 7.0	Class: (KR) (NK)	**1971-12 Tokushima Zosen Sangyo K.K. — Komatsushima** Yd No: 323 Loa 73.74 Br ex 12.25 Dght 4.603 Lbp 67.49 Br md 12.20 Dpth 5.49 Riveted\Welded, 1 dk	**(A11B2TG) LPG Tanker** Liq (Gas): 1,810 2 x Gas Tank (s); 2 independent (C.mn.stl) cyl horizontal 2 Cargo Pump (s): 2x300m³/hr Manifold: Bow/CM: 30m	**1 oil engine** driving 1 FP propeller Total Power: 1,839kW (2,500hp) Akasaka 1 x 4 Stroke 6 Cy. 400 x 600 1839kW (2500bhp) Akasaka Tekkosho KK (Akasaka DieselLtd)-Japan AuxGen: 2 x 104kW 445V a.c Fuel: 64.5 (d.f.) (Heating Coils) 144.5 (r.f.) 6.0pd	13.0kn AH40
8647414 *BI2493* -	**YU I HSIANG NO. 8** *ex* Yu I Hsiang No. 666 *-1995* **Yu Ho Fishery Co Ltd** - *Kaohsiung* — *Chinese Taipei* Official number: 013014	**535** 249 -		**1995-09 Lin Sheng Shipbuilding Co, Ltd — Kaohsiung** Loa 48.70 Br ex 8.50 Dght - Lbp - Br md - Dpth 3.65 Welded, 1 dk	**(B11B2FV) Fishing Vessel**	**1 oil engine** driving 1 Propeller Sumiyoshi 1 x 4 Stroke Sumiyoshi Marine Diesel Co Ltd-Japan	

	Name / Owner	Tonnage	Class	Build / Dimensions	Type	Machinery
664620 ZJU T7-0291	**YU I HSIANG NO. 121** *ex* Ho Feng No. 121 *-2001* **Yu Kin Fishery Co Ltd** - *Kaohsiung* *Chinese Taipei* Official number: 011291	**708** 247 -		**1989**-01 **Fong Kuo Shipbuilding Co Ltd — Kaohsiung** L reg 47.80 Br ex - Dght - Lbp - Br md 8.90 Dpth 3.85 Welded, 1 dk	**(B11B2FV) Fishing Vessel**	**1 oil engine** driving 1 FP propeller
430859	**YU I HSIANG No. 131** - -	*370* 128 -		**1987 Sen Koh Shipbuilding Corp — Kaohsiung** Loa 41.80 Br ex - Dght 3.380 Lbp - Br md 8.00 Dpth 3.50 Welded, 1 dk	**(B11B2FV) Fishing Vessel**	**1 oil engine** driving 1 FP propeller Total Power: 736kW (1,001hp) 12.0kn
431360	**YU I HSIANG No. 132** **Yu Hung Fishery Co Ltd** - *San Lorenzo* *Honduras* Official number: L-1822723	*708* 247 -		**1987 Fong Kuo Shipbuilding Co Ltd — Kaohsiung** Loa 47.80 Br ex - Dght - Lbp - Br md 8.90 Dpth 3.85 Welded, 1 dk	**(B11B2FV) Fishing Vessel**	**1 oil engine** driving 1 FP propeller Total Power: 809kW (1,100hp) 12.0kn
431114	**YU I HSIANG No. 137** - -	*347* 245 -		**1988 Sen Koh Shipbuilding Corp — Kaohsiung** L reg 47.80 Br ex - Dght 2.100 Lbp - Br md 8.90 Dpth 3.85 Welded, 1 dk	**(B11B2FV) Fishing Vessel**	**1 oil engine** driving 1 FP propeller Total Power: 809kW (1,100hp) 13.0kn
430847	**YU I HSIANG No. 211** - -	*364* 128 -		**1987 Sen Koh Shipbuilding Corp — Kaohsiung** L reg 41.80 Br ex - Dght 3.260 Lbp - Br md 8.00 Dpth 3.50 Welded	**(B11B2FV) Fishing Vessel**	**1 oil engine** driving 1 FP propeller Total Power: 736kW (1,001hp) 13.0kn
647397 ZLH	**YU I HSIANG NO. 217** **Yu Sheng Fishery Co Ltd** - *Kaohsiung* *Chinese Taipei* Official number: 011591	**708** 247 -		**1989**-08 **Fong Kuo Shipbuilding Co Ltd — Kaohsiung** Loa 47.80 Br ex 8.90 Dght - Lbp - Br md - Dpth 3.85 Welded, 1 dk	**(B11B2FV) Fishing Vessel**	**1 oil engine** driving 1 Propeller Sumiyoshi 1 x 4 Stroke Sumiyoshi Marine Diesel Co Ltd-Japan
429874 J2370	**YU I HSIANG No. 221** **Yu Wei Fishery Co Ltd** - *Kaohsiung* *Chinese Taipei* Official number: 11738	**713** 248 -		**1989 Lin Sheng Shipbuilding Co, Ltd — Kaohsiung** Loa 47.80 Br ex - Dght 3.750 Lbp - Br md 8.90 Dpth 3.85 Welded, 1 dk	**(B11B2FV) Fishing Vessel**	**1 oil engine** driving 1 FP propeller Total Power: 883kW (1,201hp)
430483	**YU I HSIANG No. 227** **Yu Hung Fishery Co Ltd** - *San Lorenzo* *Honduras* Official number: L-1822720	*708* 248 -		**1988 Fong Kuo Shipbuilding Co Ltd — Kaohsiung** L reg 47.80 Br ex - Dght - Lbp - Br md 8.90 Dpth 3.85 Welded	**(B11B2FV) Fishing Vessel**	**1 oil engine** driving 1 FP propeller Total Power: 736kW (1,001hp) 13.0kn
429903 J2449	**YU I HSIANG No. 617** **Lung Feng Ocean Enterprise Co Ltd** - *Kaohsiung* *Chinese Taipei* Official number: 11943	*708* 248 -		**1990**-09 **Lin Sheng Shipbuilding Co, Ltd — Kaohsiung** L reg 47.80 Br ex - Dght 3.750 Lbp - Br md 8.90 Dpth 3.85 Welded, 1 dk	**(B11B2FV) Fishing Vessel**	**1 oil engine** driving 1 FP propeller Total Power: 883kW (1,201hp) 12.0kn Sumiyoshi 1 x 4 Stroke 6 Cy. 883kW (1201bhp) Sumiyoshi Marine Diesel Co Ltd-Japan
647402 J2448	**YU I HSIANG NO. 627** **Yu Shih Hsiang Fishery Co Ltd** - *Kaohsiung* *Chinese Taipei* Official number: 11872	**708** 247 -		**1990**-06 **Lin Sheng Shipbuilding Co, Ltd — Kaohsiung** Loa 47.80 Br ex 8.90 Dght - Lbp - Br md - Dpth 3.85 Welded, 1 dk	**(B11B2FV) Fishing Vessel**	**1 oil engine** driving 1 Propeller Sumiyoshi 1 x 4 Stroke Sumiyoshi Marine Diesel Co Ltd-Japan
647426 J2478	**YU I HSIANG NO. 701** **Yu Der Hsiang Fishery Co Ltd** - *Kaohsiung* *Chinese Taipei* Official number: 12062	**538** 223 -		**1991**-04 **Lin Sheng Shipbuilding Co, Ltd — Kaohsiung** Loa 46.50 Br ex 8.50 Dght - Lbp - Br md - Dpth 3.65 Welded, 1 dk	**(B11B2FV) Fishing Vessel**	**1 oil engine** driving 1 Propeller Sumiyoshi 1 x 4 Stroke Sumiyoshi Marine Diesel Co Ltd-Japan
394639 LGF3	**YU JI** *ex* Yong Hong 158 *-2014* *ex* Zhong Ran 52 *-2012* *ex* Yuan Chang *-2005* **Maple Leaf Shipping Co Ltd** - *Taizhou, Zhejiang* *China* MMSI: 413097000	**3,772** 1,778 5,722 T/cm 13.8	Class: CC	**1995**-10 **Jinling Shipyard — Nanjing JS** Yd No: 93-7009 Conv to DH-2009 Loa 104.65 Br ex - Dght 6.500 Lbp 98.00 Br md 16.40 Dpth 8.15 Welded, 1 dk	**(A13B2TP) Products Tanker** Double Hull (13F) Liq: 4,735; Liq (Oil): 5,218 Compartments: 4 Ta, 1 Slop Ta, ER 2 Cargo Pump (s) Ice Capable	**1 oil engine** driving 1 FP propeller Total Power: 1,650kW (2,243hp) 12.8kn Hudong 6E34/82SDZC 1 x 2 Stroke 6 Cy. 340 x 820 1650kW (2243bhp) Hudong Shipyard-China AuxGen: 2 x 312kW 400V a.c
349464	**YU JIAN No. 2** **Taiwan Fisheries Bureau** - *Keelung* *Chinese Taipei*	*275* 82 -	Class: (CR)	**1989**-11 **Taiwan Machinery Manufacturing Corp. — Kaohsiung** Loa 40.50 Br ex 7.40 Dght - Lbp 36.50 Br md 7.00 Dpth 3.50 Welded, 1 dk	**(B12D2FP) Fishery Patrol Vessel**	**2 oil engines** sr reverse geared to sc. shafts driving 2 FP propellers Total Power: 1,618kW (2,200hp) Yanmar M220-SN 2 x 4 Stroke 6 Cy. 220 x 300 each-809kW (1100bhp) Yanmar Diesel Engine Co Ltd-Japan AuxGen: 2 x 80kW 225V a.c
604383 FLJ5	**YU JIE** *ex* Spirit Of Rio *-2012* *ex* Yuba *-2008* *ex* Taisetsusan *-2005* *ex* Taisei Maru *-2002* **Jade International Shipping Inc** Ocean Sentinels Shipmanagement Pte Ltd *Panama* *Panama* MMSI: 373540000 Official number: 43980PEXT	**38,576** 22,628 72,578	Class: NK	**1987**-03 **Mitsui Eng. & SB. Co. Ltd., Chiba Works — Ichihara** Yd No: 1341 Loa 229.98 (BB) Br ex - Dght 12.270 Lbp 220.00 Br md 36.42 Dpth 16.92 Welded, 1 dk	**(A21A2BC) Bulk Carrier** Grain: 79,664 Compartments: 7 Ho, ER 7 Ha: (13.3 x 12.8)3 (18.2 x 16.0)3 (13.3 x 16.0)ER	**1 oil engine** driving 1 FP propeller Total Power: 7,502kW (10,200hp) 13.5kn B&W 6S60MCE 1 x 2 Stroke 6 Cy. 600 x 2292 7502kW (10200bhp) Mitsui Engineering & Shipbuilding CLtd-Japan AuxGen: 3 x 400kW 450V 60Hz a.c Fuel: 203.5 (d.f.) 2286.5 (r.f.)
585120 SQX8	**YU JIN ACE** - **Shinhan Capital Co Ltd** Soosung Corp Ltd *Jeju* *South Korea* MMSI: 441750000 Official number: JJR-106249	**11,481** 5,850 17,556	Class: KR	**2010**-08 **Nantong Tongshun Shiprepair & Building Co Ltd — Nantong JS** Yd No: TS070621 Loa 131.90 Br ex 22.04 Dght 10.015 Lbp 123.00 Br md 22.00 Dpth 14.50 Welded, 1 dk	**(A31A2GX) General Cargo Ship** Grain: 23,110; Bale: 21,346 Compartments: 3 Ho, ER 3 Ha: (30.8 x 14.0) (21.0 x 14.0)ER (15.0 x 12.0) Cranes: 3x30t	**1 oil engine** driving 1 FP propeller Total Power: 4,440kW (6,037hp) 14.2kn MAN-B&W 6S35MC 1 x 2 Stroke 6 Cy. 350 x 1400 4440kW (6037bhp) STX Engine Co Ltd-South Korea
318435 LLM	**YU JIN No. 87** *ex* Il Kwang No. 3 *-1987* *ex* Zenrin Maru No. 11 *-1979* **Sin Mun-Sik** - *Busan* *South Korea* Official number: BS0201-A1582	*113* 46 -	Class: (KR)	**1968 Tokushima Zosen K.K. — Fukuoka** Yd No: 733 Loa 34.75 Br ex 6.13 Dght 2.464 Lbp 29.01 Br md 6.10 Dpth 2.85 Welded, 1 dk	**(B11B2FV) Fishing Vessel** Ins: 140 5 Ha: 5 (0.9 x 1.2)	**1 oil engine** driving 1 FP propeller Total Power: 478kW (650hp) 11.5kn Hanshin Z76 1 x 4 Stroke 6 Cy. 270 x 400 478kW (650bhp) Hanshin Nainenki Kogyo-Japan AuxGen: 2 x 24kW 230V a.c
405311 MYC3	**YU JONG 1** *ex* Dae Hung 6 *-2007* *ex* Tesshin Maru *-1997* **Korea Yujong Shipping Co Ltd** - SatCom: Inmarsat C 444518410 *Wonsan* *North Korea* MMSI: 445184000 Official number: 3401406	**1,038** 357 1,665	Class: KC (NK)	**1984**-04 **Sanyo Zosen K.K. — Onomichi** Yd No: 876 Loa 70.31 Br ex - Dght 4.000 Lbp 65.56 Br md 11.02 Dpth 5.11 Welded, 1 dk	**(A13A2TV) Crude Oil Tanker** Compartments: 8 Ta, ER	**1 oil engine** driving 1 CP propeller Total Power: 1,103kW (1,500hp) Akasaka A28 1 x 4 Stroke 6 Cy. 280 x 550 1103kW (1500bhp) Akasaka Tekkosho KK (Akasaka DieselLtd)-Japan
604917 MYC6	**YU JONG 2** *ex* Dae Hung 12 *-2007* *ex* Ryoko *-2001* *ex* Ryoko Maru No. 8 *-2001* **Korea Yujong Shipping Co Ltd** - *Wonsan* *North Korea* MMSI: 445190000 Official number: 3601077	**748** 329 1,206	Class: KC	**1986**-03 **Kegoya Dock K.K. — Kure** Yd No: 856 Converted From: Chemical Tanker-2009 Loa 62.80 Br ex - Dght 4.201 Lbp 58.02 Br md 10.01 Dpth 4.63 Welded, 1 dk	**(A13B2TP) Products Tanker**	**1 oil engine** driving 1 FP propeller Total Power: 883kW (1,201hp) Hanshin LH28G 1 x 4 Stroke 6 Cy. 280 x 460 883kW (1201bhp) The Hanshin Diesel Works Ltd-Japan

IMO / Call sign	Name / Owner	Tonnage	Class	Builder / Dimensions	Type	Machinery	Speed
9378137 *BQHZ* -	**YU KUN** **Dalian Maritime University** Dalian Haida International Fleet Management Co Ltd *Dalian, Liaoning* *China* MMSI: 412701000 Official number: 030008000021	**6,106** 1,831 2,250	Class: CC	**2008-04 Wuchang Shipyard — Wuhan HB** Yd No: A156L Loa 116.00 (BB) Br ex - Dght 5.400 Lbp 105.00 Br md 18.00 Dpth 8.35 Welded	**(B34K2QT) Training Ship**	**1 oil engine** driving 1 CP propeller Total Power: 4,440kW (6,037hp) MAN-B&W 1 x 2 Stroke 6 Cy. 350 x 1400 4440kW (6037bhp) MAN Diesel A/S-Denmark AuxGen: 1 x 650kW 400V a.c, 3 x 520kW 400V a.c	16.7k 6S35M
9342023 *BJRM* -	**YU LAN** *launched as* Ying Chun *-2006* **Sinochem Shipping Co Ltd (Hainan)** Aoxing Ship Management (Shanghai) Ltd SatCom: Inmarsat C 441352017 *Haikou, Hainan* *China* MMSI: 413520060	**2,783** 1,061 3,452 T/cm 11.2	Class: CC	**2006-09 Chuandong Shipyard — Chongqing** Yd No: HT0079 Loa 91.22 (BB) Br ex - Dght 5.450 Lbp 85.70 Br md 15.00 Dpth 7.40 Welded, 1 dk	**(A12B2TR) Chemical/Products Tanker** Double Hull (13F) Liq: 3,934; Liq (Oil): 3,934 Cargo Heating Coils Compartments: 10 Wing Ta, 1 Slop Ta, ER 10 Cargo Pump (s): 10x120m³/hr Manifold: Bow/CM: 46.2m	**1 oil engine** geared to sc. shaft driving 1 FP propeller Total Power: 1,839kW (2,500hp) Daihatsu 1 x 4 Stroke 8 Cy. 280 x 390 1839kW (2500bhp) Shaanxi Diesel Heavy Industry Co Lt-China AuxGen: 3 x 240kW 400V a.c Fuel: 34.0 (d.f.) 128.0 (r.f.)	13.0k 8DKM-28
8807210 *BQCB* -	**YU LAN HAI** *ex* Sea Magnolia *-2008* *ex* Moshill *-1992* *ex* Beskydy *-1991* **COSCO Bulk Carrier Co Ltd (COSCO BULK)** *Tianjin* *China* MMSI: 413356000	**35,350** 21,472 62,873 T/cm 64.4	Class: CC (LR) (NV) ✠ Classed LR until 23/9/91	**1991-09 Daewoo Shipbuilding & Heavy Machinery Ltd — Geoje** Yd No: 1051 Loa 225.00 (BB) Br ex 32.24 Dght 12.900 Lbp 215.00 Br md 32.20 Dpth 17.80 Welded, 1 dk	**(A21A2BC) Bulk Carrier** Grain: 75,750 Compartments: 7 Ho, ER 7 Ha: ER Ice Capable	**1 oil engine** driving 1 FP propeller Total Power: 7,856kW (10,681hp) B&W 1 x 2 Stroke 6 Cy. 500 x 1910 7856kW (10681bhp) Hyundai Heavy Industries Co Ltd-South Korea AuxGen: 3 x 500kW 390V 50Hz a.c	13.8k 6S50MC
8957558 *9WDS5* -	**YU LEE 26** **Hock Seng Lee Bhd** *Kuching* *Malaysia* Official number: 328817	*123* 37 -	Class: (BV)	**1999-06 Huten Marine Sdn Bhd — Kuching** Yd No: 05/97 Loa 23.26 Br ex - Dght 2.220 Lbp 21.96 Br md 7.00 Dpth 2.90 Welded, 1 dk	**(B32A2ST) Tug**	**2 oil engines** reduction geared to sc. shafts driving 2 FP propellers Total Power: 740kW (1,006hp) Cummins 2 x 4 Stroke each-370kW (503bhp) Cummins Engine Co Inc-USA AuxGen: 2 x 20kW 220/415V 50Hz a.c	
9500950 *BRRU* -	**YU LIN HAI** **Guangdong Ocean Shipping Co Ltd (COSCO GUANGDONG)** SatCom: Inmarsat C 441208611 *Guangzhou, Guangdong* *China* MMSI: 412086000	**40,931** 25,963 75,380	Class: CC	**2012-03 Guangzhou Huangpu Shipbuilding Co Ltd — Guangzhou GD** Yd No: 3014 Loa 225.00 (BB) Br ex - Dght 14.200 Lbp 217.00 Br md 32.26 Dpth 19.60 Welded, 1 dk	**(A21A2BC) Bulk Carrier** Grain: 90,067; Bale: 90,066 Compartments: 7 Ho, ER 7 Ha: 6 (15.5 x 14.4)ER (15.5 x 13.2)	**1 oil engine** driving 1 FP propeller Total Power: 8,833kW (12,009hp) MAN-B&W 1 x 2 Stroke 5 Cy. 600 x 2292 8833kW (12009bhp) Hudong Heavy Machinery Co Ltd-China AuxGen: 3 x 560kW 450V a.c	14.5k 5S60MC
9283277 *BPAC* -	**YU LIN WAN** **China Shipping Tanker Co Ltd** SatCom: Inmarsat C 441312010 *Shanghai* *China* MMSI: 413120000	**61,713** 32,458 109,181 T/cm 91.9	Class: CC	**2004-12 Dalian New Shipbuilding Heavy Industries Co Ltd — Dalian LN** Yd No: PC1100-15 Loa 244.60 (BB) Br ex 42.03 Dght 15.470 Lbp 233.00 Br md 42.00 Dpth 22.20 Welded, 1 dk	**(A13B2TP) Products Tanker** Double Hull (13F) Liq: 117,921; Liq (Oil): 117,921 Compartments: 12 Wing Ta, ER, 2 Wing Slop Ta 3 Cargo Pump (s): 3x3000m³/hr Manifold: Bow/CM: 121.8m	**1 oil engine** driving 1 FP propeller Total Power: 15,540kW (21,128hp) Sulzer 1 x 2 Stroke 7 Cy. 620 x 2150 15540kW (21128bhp) Dalian Marine Diesel Works-China Fuel: 174.6 (d.f.) 3381.7 (r.f.)	15.3k 7RTA62U
8839770 *HO2947* -	**YU LING** *ex* Seiei Maru No. 26 *-2002* *ex* Yoshishige Maru No. 26 *-2000* **YS Trading Co** Jang-Ho Shipping Co Ltd SatCom: Inmarsat C 435606320 *Panama* *Panama* MMSI: 356063000 Official number: 3002904B	**1,597** 886 1,127	Class: IB	**1989-10 Nagashima Zosen KK — Kihoku ME** Loa 63.00 Br ex - Dght 4.000 Lbp 57.50 Br md 13.20 Dpth 6.00 Welded, 1 dk	**(A24D2BA) Aggregates Carrier**	**1 oil engine** reverse geared to sc. shaft driving 1 FP propeller Akasaka 1 x 4 Stroke 6 Cy. 330 x 500 Akasaka Tekkosho KK (Akasaka DieselLtd)-Japan	DM33
8702886 *BTBM* -	**YU LONG** **Dalian Maritime University** Dalian Linghai Shipping Co Ltd SatCom: Inmarsat C 441213012 *Dalian, Liaoning* *China* MMSI: 412001810	*9,091* 3,566 9,860	Class: CC	**1988-12 Guangzhou Wenchong Shipyard — Guangzhou GD** Yd No: 231 Loa 139.80 Br ex - Dght 8.000 Lbp 126.00 Br md 20.80 Dpth 11.40 Welded	**(B34K2QT) Training Ship**	**1 oil engine** geared to sc. shaft driving 1 FP propeller Total Power: 6,531kW (8,880hp) Sulzer 1 x 2 Stroke 6 Cy. 480 x 1400 6531kW (8880bhp) Shanghai Diesel Engine Co Ltd-China	16.2k 6RTA48
9257151 *V3NM8* -	**YU LONG** **Wang Ming-Fa** *Belize City* *Belize* MMSI: 312166000 Official number: 280110071	**125** 49 -		**2001 Jin Jianh Lih Shipbuilding Co., Ltd. — Hsinyuan** Loa - Br ex - Dght - Lbp 25.80 Br md 5.50 Dpth 2.15 Bonded, 1 dk	**(B11B2FV) Fishing Vessel** Hull Material: Reinforced Plastic	**1 oil engine** driving 1 FP propeller Cummins 1 x 4 Stroke Cummins Diesel International Ltd-USA	11.5k
8995445 *V3TT9* -	**YU LONG 125** **Pesca Tuna SA** *Belize City* *Belize* MMSI: 312880000 Official number: 280210129	**125** 49 -		**2002-01 Jin Jianh Lih Shipbuilding Co., Ltd. — Hsinyuan** Loa 25.80 Br ex - Dght - Lbp - Br md 5.50 Dpth 2.15 Bonded, 1 dk	**(B11B2FV) Fishing Vessel** Hull Material: Reinforced Plastic	**1 oil engine** driving 1 Propeller Total Power: 559kW (760hp) Cummins 1 x 4 Stroke 6 Cy. 559kW (760bhp) Cummins Engine Co Inc-USA	10.5k
9505431 *BRNV* -	**YU LONG LING** **China Shipping Haisheng Co Ltd** *Haikou, Hainan* *China* MMSI: 412523890	**19,995** 11,046 32,005	Class: CC	**2011-04 Guangzhou Huangpu Shipbuilding Co Ltd — Guangzhou GD** Yd No: 2298 Loa 177.50 (BB) Br ex 28.60 Dght 10.000 Lbp 168.00 Br md 28.20 Dpth 14.20 Welded, 1 dk	**(A21A2BC) Bulk Carrier** Grain: 42,006; Bale: 39,486 Compartments: 5 Ho, ER 5 Ha: 4 (19.2 x 16.8)ER (14.4 x 15.2) Cranes: 4x30t Ice Capable	**1 oil engine** driving 1 FP propeller Total Power: 6,480kW (8,810hp) MAN-B&W 1 x 2 Stroke 6 Cy. 420 x 1764 6480kW (8810bhp) Yichang Marine Diesel Engine Co Ltd-China AuxGen: 3 x 500kW 450V a.c	13.9k 6S42MC
9257175 - -	**YU LONG No. 2** **Yu Long Fishery Co Ltd** -	**125** 49 -		**2001 Jin Jianh Lih Shipbuilding Co., Ltd. — Hsinyuan** Loa - Br ex - Dght - Lbp 25.80 Br md 5.50 Dpth 2.15 Bonded, 1 dk	**(B11B2FV) Fishing Vessel** Hull Material: Reinforced Plastic	**1 oil engine** reduction geared to sc. shaft driving 1 FP propeller Cummins 1 x 4 Stroke Cummins Diesel International Ltd-USA	11.5k
9265550 *V3VK6* -	**YU LONG No. 6** **Wang Hungcheng** *Belize City* *Belize* MMSI: 312422000 Official number: 280210105	**125** 49 -		**2002-01 Jin Jianh Lih Shipbuilding Co., Ltd. — Hsinyuan** Loa - Br ex - Dght - Lbp 25.80 Br md 5.50 Dpth 2.15 Welded, 1 dk	**(B11B2FV) Fishing Vessel**	**1 oil engine** driving 1 FP propeller Cummins 1 x 4 Stroke Cummins Diesel International Ltd-USA	10.5k
9265562 - -	**YU LONG No. 10** **Yu Long Fishery Co Ltd** -	**125** 49 -		**2002-01 Jin Jianh Lih Shipbuilding Co., Ltd. — Hsinyuan** Loa - Br ex - Dght - Lbp 25.80 Br md 5.50 Dpth 2.15 Welded, 1 dk	**(B11B2FV) Fishing Vessel**	**1 oil engine** driving 1 FP propeller Cummins 1 x 4 Stroke Cummins Diesel International Ltd-USA	10.5k
9613886 *BPHA* -	**YU MING** **Shanghai Maritime University** China Shipping Bulk Carrier Co Ltd *Shanghai* *China* MMSI: 414726000 Official number: NJ11NB00024	**31,000** 15,000 45,800	Class: CC	**2012-12 China Shipping Industry (Jiangsu) Co Ltd — Jiangdu JS** Yd No: IS48000JX-01 Loa 189.90 Br ex - Dght 11.200 Lbp - Br md 32.26 Dpth 15.70 Welded, 1 dk	**(B34K2QT) Training Ship**	**1 oil engine** driving 1 Propeller Total Power: 9,960kW (13,542hp) MAN-B&W 1 x 2 Stroke 6 Cy. 500 x 2000 9960kW (13542bhp)	6S50ME-C8
8859213 *POJG*	**YU NO. 2** *ex* Taisei Maru *-2012* *ex* Koyo Maru *-1996* - - *Indonesia* MMSI: 525022134	*494* - 1,242		**1991-10 Tokuoka Zosen K.K. — Naruto** Loa 69.70 Br ex - Dght 4.250 Lbp 62.00 Br md 12.50 Dpth 6.50 Welded, 1 dk	**(B33A2DG) Grab Dredger** 1 Ha: (15.6 x 9.5)ER Cranes: 1x3.5t	**1 oil engine** geared to sc. shaft driving 1 FP propeller Total Power: 736kW (1,001hp) Hanshin 1 x 4 Stroke 6 Cy. 350 x 550 736kW (1001bhp) The Hanshin Diesel Works Ltd-Japan	12.5k 6LU35G

	Name / Owner	Tonnage	Class	Build / Dimensions	Type / Cargo	Machinery
840949	**YU NO. 3** *ex* Nissho Maru *-2011* - - *Indonesia*	*499* - 1,231		**1990-07 Namikata Shipbuilding Co Ltd — Imabari EH** Yd No: 166 Loa 74.91 Br ex - Dght 3.820 Lbp 70.00 Br md 11.80 Dpth 6.75 Welded, 1 dk	**(A31A2GX) General Cargo Ship**	**1 oil engine** driving 1 FP propeller Total Power: 1,177kW (1,600hp) 11.5kn Hanshin LH31G 1 x 4 Stroke 6 Cy. 310 x 530 1177kW (1600bhp) The Hanshin Diesel Works Ltd-Japan AuxGen: 2 x 200kW 445V 60Hz a.c Fuel: 30.6 (d.f.) 5.3pd
500948 RTD	**YU PENG HAI** **Guangdong Ocean Shipping Co Ltd (COSCO GUANGDONG)** - SatCom: Inmarsat C 441219410 *Guangzhou, Guangdong* *China* MMSI: 412914000	**40,913** 25,963 75,486	Class: CC	**2010-11 Guangzhou Huangpu Shipbuilding Co Ltd — Guangzhou GD** Yd No: 3013 Loa 225.00 (BB) Br ex 32.66 Dght 14.200 Lbp 217.00 Br md 32.26 Dpth 19.60 Welded, 1 dk	**(A21A2BC) Bulk Carrier** Grain: 90,100; Bale: 90,066 Compartments: 7 Ho, ER 7 Ha: 6 (15.5 x 14.4)ER (14.6 x 13.2)	**1 oil engine** driving 1 FP propeller Total Power: 10,200kW (13,868hp) 14.5kn MAN-B&W 5S60MC 1 x 2 Stroke 5 Cy. 600 x 2292 10200kW (13868bhp) Hudong Heavy Machinery Co Ltd-China AuxGen: 3 x 560kW 450V a.c
000563 OKH	**YU QI HAI** *ex* Western Trade *-1999* *ex* Western Trader *-1988* *ex* Platon *-1987* *ex* Kyriaki *-1986* **Guangdong Ocean Shipping Co Ltd (COSCO GUANGDONG)** - SatCom: Inmarsat C 441215712 *Guangzhou, Guangdong* *China* MMSI: 412157000	**35,160** 21,218 65,083	Class: CC (LR) (RI) (AB) ✠ Classed LR until 1/91	**1981-09 Nippon Kokan KK (NKK Corp) — Yokohama KN (Tsurumi Shipyard)** Yd No: 983 Loa 224.54 (BB) Br ex 32.26 Dght 12.860 Lbp 214.03 Br md 32.21 Dpth 17.71 Welded, 1 dk	**(A21A2BC) Bulk Carrier** Grain: 74,823 Compartments: 7 Ho, ER 7 Ha: (14.2 x 10.4)6 (14.7 x 14.4)ER	**1 oil engine** driving 1 FP propeller Total Power: 10,140kW (13,786hp) 15.8kn Sulzer 6RND76M 1 x 2 Stroke 6 Cy. 760 x 1550 10140kW (13786bhp) Sumitomo Heavy Industries Ltd-Japan AuxGen: 3 x 500kW 450V 60Hz a.c Fuel: 241.0 (d.f.) 3477.0 (r.f.)
607526 LFZ7	**YU RU** **Kunlun Financial Leasing Co Ltd** Maple Leaf Shipping Co Ltd *Taizhou, Jiangsu* *China* MMSI: 413442210	**11,125** 5,275 16,718 T/cm 28.6	Class: CC	**2011-06 Taizhou Maple Leaf Shipbuilding Co Ltd — Linhai ZJ** Yd No: 17000-007 Loa 150.53 Br ex 21.62 Dght 9.000 Lbp 142.00 Br md 21.60 Dpth 12.50 Welded, 1 dk	**(A12B2TR) Chemical/Products Tanker** Double Hull (13F) Liq: 18,349; Liq (Oil): 18,349 Compartments: 7 Wing Ta, 7 Wing Ta, 1 Wing Slop Ta, 1 Wing Slop Ta, ER Ice Capable	**1 oil engine** driving 1 FP propeller Total Power: 4,440kW (6,037hp) 13.5kn MAN-B&W 6S35MC 1 x 2 Stroke 6 Cy. 350 x 1400 4440kW (6037bhp) STX Engine Co Ltd-South Korea AuxGen: 3 x 550kW 450V a.c
150605	**YU SHAN 1** *ex* Nomi-B *-2006* *ex* Kyusui Maru No. 5 *-2003* *ex* Eijo Maru *-2000* **Gao Shoushan** KY Line	*198* - 400		**1971 Kato Zosensho — Yatsushiro** Yd No: 51 Loa 38.46 Br ex - Dght 3.250 Lbp 34.02 Br md 7.51 Dpth 3.31 Welded, 1 dk	**(A31A2GX) General Cargo Ship**	**1 oil engine** driving 1 FP propeller Total Power: 441kW (600hp) 9.0kn Mitsubishi 4SGAC-1 1 x 4 Stroke 4 Cy. 220 x 240 441kW (600bhp) Mitsubishi Heavy Industries Ltd-Japan
651350 I2417	**YU SHIN NO. 1** **Cheng Tsung Kun** - *Kaohsiung* *Chinese Taipei* Official number: 11801	**720** 301 -		**1980-03 Sheng Harng Shipbuilding Co. — Kaohsiung** L reg 56.90 Br ex - Dght - Lbp - Br md 8.70 Dpth 3.85 Welded, 1 dk	**(B11B2FV) Fishing Vessel**	**1 oil engine** driving 1 Propeller
632076 EXI3	**YU SHUN** **Lin Tai Shipping Co Ltd** Yantai Pingyang Shipping Co Ltd *Panama* *Panama* MMSI: 373446000 Official number: 4367512XT	**2,690** 1,435 3,595	Class: CC	**2012-01 Yantai Yu'an Shipyard Co Ltd — Changdao County SD** Yd No: YTYA0802 Loa 87.33 Br ex - Dght 6.000 Lbp 80.00 Br md 14.00 Dpth 8.50 Welded, 1 dk	**(A31A2GX) General Cargo Ship** Bale: 4,347 Compartments: 2 Ho, ER 2 Ha: (21.0 x 9.6)ER (19.6 x 9.6) Ice Capable	**1 oil engine** reduction geared to sc. shaft driving 1 Propeller Total Power: 1,324kW (1,800hp) 10.9kn Chinese Std. Type 6320ZC 1 x 4 Stroke 6 Cy. 320 x 440 1324kW (1800bhp) Guangzhou Diesel Engine Factory CoLtd-China AuxGen: 2 x 150kW 400V a.c
400854 MYD5	**YU SONG 7** *ex* Aoyang He Xie *-2010* *ex* Jiang Pu Guan *-2009* **Yusong Shipping Co** - SatCom: Inmarsat C 444528010 *Nampho* *North Korea* MMSI: 445280000 Official number: 3404961	**4,107** 2,059 5,593	Class: KC (CC)	**1984-11 Hayashikane Shipbuilding & Engineering Co Ltd — Nagasaki NS** Yd No: 926 Loa 103.50 Br ex - Dght 6.760 Lbp 95.00 Br md 16.40 Dpth 8.50 Welded, 1 dk	**(A31A2GX) General Cargo Ship** Grain: 7,281 Derricks: 4	**1 oil engine** driving 1 FP propeller Total Power: 3,354kW (4,560hp) 15.7kn B&W 6L35MC 1 x 2 Stroke 6 Cy. 350 x 1050 3354kW (4560bhp) Hitachi Zosen Corp-Japan
096791 MYT6	**YU SONG 12** *ex* Sun Lily *-2011* *ex* An Shun *-2010* *ex* Yu Chang *-2008* *ex* Hai Chang *-2000* **Double Win Co Ltd** Yusong Shipping Co *Nampho* *North Korea* MMSI: 445458000 Official number: 3805997	**1,121** 784 2,000	Class: KC	**1988-10 Shayang Shipyard — Shayang County HB** Loa 72.09 Br ex - Dght 4.400 Lbp 66.80 Br md 11.00 Dpth 5.73 Welded, 1 dk	**(A31A2GX) General Cargo Ship**	**1 oil engine** driving 1 Propeller Total Power: 624kW (848hp) Niigata 1 x 4 Stroke 624kW (848bhp) Niigata Engineering Co Ltd-Japan
330727	**YU SUNG 32** *ex* Dokai Maru *-1996* *ex* Wakashio No. 2 *-1994* **Sam Hyeup Construction Co Ltd** - *Busan* *South Korea* Official number: BSR-960533	**311** 93 -		**1973-09 Ando Shipbuilding Co. Ltd. — Tokyo** Yd No: 225 Loa 32.42 Br ex 10.04 Dght 3.201 Lbp 28.50 Br md 10.01 Dpth 4.25 Welded, 1 dk	**(B32A2ST) Tug**	**2 oil engines** driving 2 FP propellers Total Power: 2,354kW (3,200hp) Niigata 8MG25BX 2 x 4 Stroke 8 Cy. 250 x 320 each-1177kW (1600bhp) Niigata Engineering Co Ltd-Japan
832579 7WJ	**YU SUNG No. 1** *ex* Hae Kyung No. 1 *-1994* *ex* Nam Yang No. 1 *-1994* **Shin Kyung Man** - *Busan* *South Korea* Official number: BSR-618026	*499* 273 828	Class: (KR)	**1961-10 KK Kanasashi Zosen — Shizuoka SZ** L reg 49.75 Br ex - Dght 3.776 Lbp 49.41 Br md 7.51 Dpth 4.20 Welded, 1 dk	**(A13B2TU) Tanker (unspecified)** Liq: 1,000; Liq (Oil): 1,000	**1 oil engine** driving 1 FP propeller Total Power: 515kW (700hp) 13.0kn Niigata M6F31HS 1 x 4 Stroke 6 Cy. 310 x 440 515kW (700bhp) Niigata Engineering Co Ltd-Japan AuxGen: 2 x 42kW 230V a.c
523303 KJS	**YU SUNG No. 307** *ex* Hyundai No. 307 *-1987* *ex* Nam Hae No. 223 *-1983* **Yoo Sung San Up Co** - *Busan* *South Korea* Official number: BS-A-2074	*152* 85 130	Class: (KR)	**1965 Ateliers et Chantiers du Havre — Le Havre** Yd No: B21 Loa 35.29 Br ex 6.53 Dght 2.515 Lbp 30.00 Br md 6.51 Dpth 3.10 Welded, 1 dk	**(B11B2FV) Fishing Vessel** Ins: 119 3 Ha: 3 (0.8 x 0.8)ER	**1 oil engine** driving 1 FP propeller Total Power: 338kW (460hp) 9.0kn Fiat L230.8S 1 x 4 Stroke 8 Cy. 230 x 350 338kW (460bhp) SA Fiat SGM-Torino AuxGen: 2 x 25kW 220V d.c Fuel: 70.0 (d.f.)
430067	**YU TA No. 62** **Pai Hsing Fishery Co Ltd** - *San Lorenzo* *Honduras* Official number: L-1824339	**737** 350 -		**1989 Kaohsiung Shipbuilding Co. Ltd. — Kaohsiung** L reg 51.15 Br ex - Dght 2.870 Lbp - Br md 9.00 Dpth 4.30 Welded, 1 dk	**(B11B2FV) Fishing Vessel**	**1 oil engine** driving 1 FP propeller Total Power: 1,103kW (1,500hp) 13.0kn
430342 QHN9	**YU TER HSIANG No. 711** **Lubmain International SA** - *San Lorenzo* *Honduras* Official number: L-1923670	**420** 134 -		**1985 Fong Kuo Shipbuilding Co Ltd — Kaohsiung** L reg 41.80 Br ex - Dght 2.620 Lbp - Br md 8.00 Dpth 3.50 Welded, 1 dk	**(B11B2FV) Fishing Vessel**	**1 oil engine** driving 1 FP propeller Total Power: 736kW (1,001hp) 12.0kn
808877 XFO	**YU TIAN NO. 1** *ex* Ruo Han *-1983* *ex* Konko Maru No. 75 *-2000* **Wang Tong Shipping Co Ltd** Hai Sheng Shipping (HK) Co Ltd *Zhuhai, Guangdong* *China* MMSI: 412465850 Official number: 090302000183	*1,092* 611 2,000		**1978-06 Kochi Jyuko K.K. — Kochi** Yd No: 1261 L reg 68.12 Br ex - Dght 4.301 Lbp 62.01 Br md 11.20 Dpth 5.00 Riveted\Welded, 1 dk	**(A12A2TC) Chemical Tanker**	**1 oil engine** driving 1 FP propeller Total Power: 1,471kW (2,000hp) 12.8kn Niigata 6M34EX 1 x 4 Stroke 6 Cy. 340 x 520 1471kW (2000bhp) Niigata Engineering Co Ltd-Japan
810569	**YU TIAN No. 3** *ex* Izumi Maru No. 53 *-1998* **Zhuhai Wang Tong Shipping Co Ltd** - *Zhuhai, Guangdong* *China* MMSI: 412469770	**795** 308 714	Class: (CC) (NK)	**1978-11 Miyoshi Shipbuilding Co Ltd — Uwajima EH** Yd No: 242 Loa 61.07 Br ex - Dght 3.963 Lbp 55.53 Br md 10.01 Dpth 4.63 Riveted\Welded, 1 dk	**(A11B2TG) LPG Tanker** Liq (Gas): 1,183 2 x Gas Tank (s);	**1 oil engine** driving 1 FP propeller Total Power: 1,324kW (1,800hp) 11.5kn Akasaka DM36 1 x 4 Stroke 6 Cy. 360 x 540 1324kW (1800bhp) Akasaka Tekkosho KK (Akasaka DieselLtd)-Japan AuxGen: 2 x 416kW Fuel: 117.5 6.5pd

IMO / Call sign	Name / Owner / Port	Tonnage	Class	Builder / Dimensions	Type / Cargo	Machinery	Speed / Engine
9072757 *BXTA* -	**YU TIAN NO. 6** *ex* Nittan Maru No. 16 *-2004* **Wang Tong Shipping Co Ltd** *Zhuhai, Guangdong* *China* MMSI: 412467710	**1,377** 771 1,252	Class: CC (NK)	**1993-10 Naikai Zosen Corp — Onomichi HS (Setoda Shipyard)** Yd No: 588 Loa 70.00 (BB) Br ex - Dght 4.600 Lbp 64.00 Br md 11.70 Dpth 5.50 Welded, 1 dk	**(A11B2TG) LPG Tanker** Liq (Gas): 1,732 2 x Gas Tank (s); 2 independent cyl horizontal 2 Cargo Pump (s): 2x350m³/hr	**1 oil engine** driving 1 FP propeller Total Power: 1,618kW (2,200hp) Hanshin 1 x 4 Stroke 6 Cy. 340 x 640 1618kW (2200bhp) The Hanshin Diesel Works Ltd-Japan AuxGen: 3 x 178kW a.c	12.3k LH34
9688178 *BXSN* -	**YU TIAN NO. 7** **Zhuhai Wang Tong Shipping Co Ltd** - *Zhuhai, Guangdong* *China* MMSI: 413475640	**2,981** 975 3,042	Class: CC	**2013-07 Zhejiang Dongpeng Shipbuilding & Repair Co Ltd — Zhoushan ZJ** Yd No: 10-042 Loa 99.96 Br ex - Dght 5.100 Lbp 93.00 Br md 15.20 Dpth 6.90 Welded, 1 dk	**(A11B2TG) LPG Tanker** Double Hull Liq (Gas): 3,500	**1 oil engine** driving 1 Propeller	
9176280 *BXYQ* -	**YU TIAN NO. 8** *ex* Hokusei Maru *-2008* **Wang Tong Shipping Co Ltd** *Zhuhai, Guangdong* *China* MMSI: 412470530	**1,355** 759 1,368	Class: CC (NK)	**1997-11 Sasaki Shipbuilding Co Ltd — Osakikamijima HS** Yd No: 615 Loa 71.97 Br ex - Dght 4.350 Lbp 67.00 Br md 12.20 Dpth 5.50 Welded, 1 dk	**(A11B2TG) LPG Tanker** Liq (Gas): 1,811 2 x Gas Tank (s);	**1 oil engine** driving 1 FP propeller Total Power: 1,912kW (2,600hp) Akasaka 1 x 4 Stroke 6 Cy. 380 x 740 1912kW (2600bhp) Akasaka Tekkosho KK (Akasaka DieselLtd)-Japan AuxGen: 2 x 240kW 445V a.c	13.0kr A38
8748567 *BZJM* -	**YU WEN NO. 101** **Yu Wen Fishery Co Ltd** - *Kaohsiung* *Chinese Taipei* Official number: 011529	**995** 298 -		**1989-07 San Yang Shipbuilding Co., Ltd. — Kaohsiung** Yd No: 786 Loa 56.20 Br ex - Dght - Lbp - Br md 12.36 Dpth 7.20 Welded, 1 dk	**(B11B2FV) Fishing Vessel**	**1 oil engine** driving 1 Propeller Total Power: 2,206kW (2,999hp) Daihatsu 1 x 4 Stroke 8 Cy. 2206kW (2999bhp) Daihatsu Diesel Manufacturing Co Lt-Japan	
8748579 *BEBG* -	**YU WEN NO. 301** **Yue Sung Fishery Co Ltd** - *Kaohsiung* *Chinese Taipei* Official number: 011987	**1,089** 401 -		**1991-10 Fong Kuo Shipbuilding Co Ltd — Kaohsiung** Yd No: 298 Loa 60.70 Br ex - Dght - Lbp - Br md 12.20 Dpth 7.20 Welded, 1 dk	**(B11B2FV) Fishing Vessel**	**1 oil engine** driving 1 Propeller Total Power: 2,206kW (2,999hp) Daihatsu 1 x 4 Stroke 8 Cy. 320 x 400 2206kW (2999bhp) Daihatsu Diesel Manufacturing Co Lt-Japan	8DLM-32
9620554 *3FRS6* -	**YU XIANG HAI** **Yuxianghai Shipping Inc** COSCO Bulk Carrier Co Ltd (COSCO BULK) *Panama* *Panama* MMSI: 357203000 Official number: 44548PEXT	**64,654** 37,347 115,088	Class: CC	**2014-03 Shanghai Jiangnan Changxing Heavy Industry Co Ltd — Shanghai** Yd No: H1006A Loa 254.00 (BB) Br ex - Dght 14.500 Lbp 249.80 Br md 43.00 Dpth 20.80 Welded, 1 dk	**(A21A2BC) Bulk Carrier** Grain: 132,246	**1 oil engine** driving 1 FP propeller Total Power: 13,560kW (18,436hp) Wartsila 1 x 2 Stroke 6 Cy. 580 x 2416 13560kW (18436bhp) Doosan Engine Co Ltd-South Korea	14.5kn 6RT-flex58T
9606431 *BRPL* -	**YU XIAO FENG** **China Shipping Tanker Co Ltd** - *Shanghai* *China* MMSI: 414742000	**40,913** 25,963 76,000 T/cm 68.2	Class: CC	**2012-12 Jiangnan Shipyard (Group) Co Ltd — Shanghai** Yd No: H2497 Loa 225.00 (BB) Br ex 32.31 Dght 14.200 Lbp 217.00 Br md 32.26 Dpth 19.60 Welded, 1 dk	**(A21A2BC) Bulk Carrier** Grain: 90,725 Compartments: 7 Ho, ER 7 Ha: 6 (15.5 x 14.4)ER (14.6 x 13.2)	**1 oil engine** driving 1 FP propeller Total Power: 11,900kW (16,179hp) MAN-B&W 1 x 2 Stroke 5 Cy. 600 x 2400 11900kW (16179bhp)	14.5kn 5S60ME-C
8950342 - -	**YU YAO No. 202** **Yu-Ri Marine Ltd**	*103* 31 -		**1996 Shing Sheng Fa Boat Building Co — Kaohsiung** Loa - Br ex - Dght - Lbp 23.80 Br md 5.40 Dpth 2.00 Welded, 1 dk	**(B11A2FT) Trawler**	**1 oil engine** driving 1 FP propeller Total Power: 331kW (450hp) Yanmar 1 x 4 Stroke 331kW (450bhp) Yanmar Diesel Engine Co Ltd-Japan	
9675925 *BLFF9* -	**YU YI** **Maple Leaf Shipping Co Ltd** - *Taizhou, Zhejiang* *China* MMSI: 413450820	**11,553** 5,653 17,975	Class: CC	**2013-03 Taizhou Maple Leaf Shipbuilding Co Ltd — Linhai ZJ** Yd No: 18000-008 Loa 150.59 (BB) Br ex - Dght 9.100 Lbp 142.00 Br md 22.60 Dpth 12.50 Welded, 1 dk	**(A13B2TP) Products Tanker** Double Hull (13F) Liq: 19,256; Liq (Oil): 19,256 Compartments: 6 Wing Ta, 6 Wing Ta, 1 Wing Slop Ta, 1 Wing Slop Ta, ER Ice Capable	**1 oil engine** driving 1 FP propeller Total Power: 4,440kW (6,037hp) MAN-B&W 1 x 2 Stroke 6 Cy. 350 x 1400 4440kW (6037bhp) STX (Dalian) Engine Co Ltd-China AuxGen: 3 x 560kW 450V a.c	12.5kn 6S35MC7
8032956 *BDBA* -	**YU YING** **Government of Taiwan (Education Department)** - SatCom: Inmarsat A 1350465 *Keelung* *Chinese Taipei* Official number: 7882	*635* 265 320	Class: CR	**1981 Taiwan Machinery Manufacturing Corp. — Kaohsiung** Loa 49.00 Br ex 9.89 Dght 3.539 Lbp 43.01 Br md 9.81 Dpth 5.69 Welded, 2 dks	**(B11B2FV) Fishing Vessel** Ins: 92 Compartments: 1 Ho, ER 1 Ha: (1.6 x 1.6) Derricks: 1x3.3t,1x1t; Winches: 5	**1 oil engine** driving 1 CP propeller Total Power: 1,295kW (1,761hp) Akasaka 1 x 4 Stroke 6 Cy. 300 x 480 1295kW (1761bhp) Akasaka Tekkosho KK (Akasaka DieselLtd)-Japan AuxGen: 2 x 140kW 230V 60Hz a.c Thrusters: 1 Thwart. FP thruster (f)	12.3kn AH30
9108934 *BHBU* -	**YU-YING No. 2** **Taiwan Provincial Keelung Senior Marine Vocational School** - SatCom: Inmarsat B 341692510 *Keelung* *Chinese Taipei* MMSI: 416925000 Official number: 12840	**1,846** 553 1,109	Class: CR	**1995-03 China Shipbuilding Corp — Keelung** Yd No: 600 Loa 72.85 Br ex 12.62 Dght 5.000 Lbp 66.00 Br md 12.60 Dpth 5.70 Welded, 1 dk	**(B34K2QT) Training Ship** Bale: 55	**1 oil engine** driving 1 CP propeller Total Power: 3,016kW (4,101hp) B&W 1 x 2 Stroke 8 Cy. 260 x 980 3016kW (4101bhp) Mitsui Engineering & Shipbuilding CLtd-Japan Thrusters: 1 Thwart. FP thruster (f)	8S26MC
8320810 *9LY2205* -	**YU YOU** *ex* Woo Kwang *-2010* *ex* Shin Bong *-2002* *ex* Tenryugawa Maru *-1996* **Urban Light Co Ltd** Gold Advance Corp *Freetown* *Sierra Leone* MMSI: 667003008 Official number: SL103008	*1,341* 808 3,003	Class: (KR) (NK)	**1984-10 Kurinoura Dockyard Co Ltd — Yawatahama EH** Yd No: 193 Loa 86.21 Br ex 12.02 Dght 5.764 Lbp 80.02 Br md 12.01 Dpth 6.33 Welded, 1 dk	**(A13B2TP) Products Tanker** Liq: 3,000; Liq (Oil): 3,000 Compartments: 10 Ta, ER	**1 oil engine** driving 1 CP propeller Total Power: 1,618kW (2,200hp) Akasaka 1 x 4 Stroke 6 Cy. 340 x 660 1618kW (2200bhp) Akasaka Tekkosho KK (Akasaka DieselLtd)-Japan AuxGen: 3 x 120kW 446V a.c	13.0kn A34
9290024 *BR3427* -	**YU YUAN NO. 101** *ex* Sang Myung No. 1 *-2010* *ex* Jupiter *-2008* - - *China*	*196* - -	Class: (KR)	**2003-03 Samkwang Shipbuilding & Engineering Co Ltd — Incheon** Yd No: 02-07 Loa 33.50 Br ex 9.22 Dght 3.050 Lbp 28.00 Br md 9.20 Dpth 4.00 Welded, 1 dk	**(B32A2ST) Tug**	**2 oil engines** geared to sc. shafts driving 2 Propellers Total Power: 2,648kW (3,600hp) Niigata 2 x 4 Stroke 6 Cy. 220 x 300 each-1324kW (1800bhp) Niigata Engineering Co Ltd-Japan	6L22HLX
9375769 *H3BT* -	**YU ZHONG HAI** **Yu Zhong Hai Maritime SA** Qingdao Ocean Shipping Co Ltd (COSCO QINGDAO) SatCom: Inmarsat C 437279410 *Panama* *Panama* MMSI: 372794000 Official number: 4136010	**152,148** 55,953 297,959	Class: CC	**2010-02 Nantong COSCO KHI Ship Engineering Co Ltd (NACKS) — Nantong JS** Yd No: 074 Loa 327.00 (BB) Br ex 55.05 Dght 21.400 Lbp 321.50 Br md 55.00 Dpth 29.00 Welded, 1 dk	**(A21B2BO) Ore Carrier** Grain: 184,102 Compartments: 6 Ho, ER 6 Ha: ER 6 (32.1 x 16.1)	**1 oil engine** driving 1 FP propeller Total Power: 23,280kW (31,651hp) MAN-B&W 1 x 2 Stroke 6 Cy. 800 x 3200 23280kW (31651bhp) CSSC MES Diesel Co Ltd-China AuxGen: 3 x 750kW 450V a.c Fuel: 7650.0	14.5kn 6S80MC-C
8667969 *T3NC2* -	**YU ZHOU YING GANG 398** **Jiangsu Haisheng Municipal Engineering Construction Co Ltd** - *Tarawa* *Kiribati* Official number: K-18991406	**285** 86 -		**1999-10 Jiangdu Fengle Shiprepair & Building Yard — Yangzhou JS** Loa 43.20 Br ex - Dght - Lbp 41.70 Br md 8.30 Dpth 3.00 Welded, 1 dk	**(A31A2GX) General Cargo Ship**	**1 oil engine** driving 1 Propeller Total Power: 184kW (250hp) Chinese Std. Type 1 x 184kW (250bhp) Shanghai Diesel Engine Co Ltd-China	
9523160 *BRPD* -	**YU ZHU FENG** **China Shipping Tanker Co Ltd** - SatCom: Inmarsat C 441318710 *Shanghai* *China* MMSI: 413187000	**40,913** 25,963 75,519 T/cm 68.2	Class: CC	**2011-01 Jiangnan Shipyard (Group) Co Ltd — Shanghai** Yd No: H2468 Loa 225.00 (BB) Br ex - Dght 14.200 Lbp 217.00 Br md 32.26 Dpth 19.60 Welded, 1 dk	**(A21A2BC) Bulk Carrier** Grain: 90,725 Compartments: 7 Ho, ER 7 Ha: 6 (15.5 x 14.4)ER (15.5 x 13.2)	**1 oil engine** driving 1 FP propeller Total Power: 11,900kW (16,179hp) MAN-B&W 1 x 2 Stroke 5 Cy. 600 x 2400 11900kW (16179bhp) Hudong Heavy Machinery Co Ltd-China AuxGen: 3 x 560kW 450V a.c	14.5kn 5S60ME-C
7324962 *BVAK* -	**YU ZONG No. 3** **Yu Zong Marine Products Co Ltd** - *Kaohsiung* *Chinese Taipei*	*262* - -	Class: (CR)	**1971 Suao Shipbuilding Co., Ltd. — Suao** Loa 38.54 Br ex 6.94 Dght 2.858 Lbp 33.00 Br md 6.91 Dpth 3.15 Welded, 1 dk	**(B11B2FV) Fishing Vessel** Ins: 231 Compartments: 3 Ho, ER 3 Ha: 3 (1.0 x 1.1)ER	**1 oil engine** driving 1 FP propeller Total Power: 478kW (650hp) Hanshin 1 x 4 Stroke 6 Cy. 260 x 400 478kW (650bhp) Hanshin Nainenki Kogyo-Japan AuxGen: 2 x 80kW 230V a.c	10.5kn 6L26AGSH

IMO / Call sign	Name / Owner	Tonnage	Class	Builder / Dimensions	Type	Machinery
958966	**YUAN AN 77** *ex* San Tong 1 *-2009* *ex* Zhe Zhou Yu Leng 233 *-2001* **Yu Ji Ship Management Co Ltd** - *China* MMSI: 413442800	**1,235** 724 2,110		**1984-12 Yueqing Huanghuagang Shipyard — Yueqing ZJ** Loa - Br ex - Dght 5.450 Lbp 66.90 Br md 10.20 Dpth 6.30 Welded, 1 dk	**(A34A2GR) Refrigerated Cargo Ship**	**1 oil engine** driving 1 FP propeller Total Power: 735kW (999hp) MaK 1 x 4 Stroke 735kW (999bhp) Krupp MaK Maschinenbau GmbH-Kiel
446128 RFP03	**YUAN AN HAI** **Yuan An Hai Maritime SA** Qingdao Ocean Shipping Co Ltd (COSCO QINGDAO) SatCom: Inmarsat C 437093910 *Panama* *Panama* MMSI: 370939000 Official number: 4107610A	**32,957** 19,231 56,957 T/cm 58.8	Class: BV	**2009-12 COSCO (Zhoushan) Shipyard Co Ltd — Zhoushan ZJ** Yd No: ZS07001 Loa 189.99 (BB) Br ex 32.30 Dght 12.800 Lbp 185.00 Br md 32.26 Dpth 18.00 Welded, 1 dk	**(A21A2BC) Bulk Carrier** Grain: 71,634; Bale: 68,200 Compartments: 5 Ho, ER 5 Ha: ER Cranes: 4x30t	**1 oil engine** driving 1 FP propeller Total Power: 9,480kW (12,889hp) 14.2kn MAN-B&W 6S50MC-C 1 x 2 Stroke 6 Cy. 500 x 2000 9480kW (12889bhp) STX Engine Co Ltd-South Korea AuxGen: 3 x 600kW 60Hz a.c Fuel: 2189.0
661202 3I2540 CT7-00540	**YUAN BAO NO. 888** **Chin Fun Wen Fishery Co Ltd** Ocean Treasure Seafood Co Ltd *Kaohsiung* *Chinese Taipei* MMSI: 416097500 Official number: 014114	**696** 310 -		**1997-09 Fong Kuo Shipbuilding Co Ltd — Kaohsiung** L reg 50.12 Br ex - Dght - Lbp - Br md 8.90 Dpth - Welded, 1 dk	**(B11B2FV) Fishing Vessel**	**1 oil engine** reduction geared to sc. shaft driving 1 Propeller
3709016 XUAX8 -	**YUAN DA** *ex* Cheng Gong 62 *-2007* *ex* Xin Hua Xia 888 *-2007* *ex* Taiko Maru No. 18 *-1995* **Faith State Shipping Ltd** Topwin Shipping Co Ltd *Phnom Penh* *Cambodia* MMSI: 514869000 Official number: 787761	**1,685** 1,081 1,000	Class: UB	**1987-06 Shitanoe Shipbuilding Co Ltd — Usuki OT** Yd No: 1070 Converted From: Grab Dredger-2007 Lengthened-2007 Loa 73.60 (BB) Br ex 12.02 Dght 3.650 Lbp 67.60 Br md 12.01 Dpth 6.80 Welded, 1 dk	**(A31A2GX) General Cargo Ship** Grain: 582 Compartments: 1 Ho, ER 1 Ha: (15.6 x 9.0)ER Cranes: 1	**1 oil engine** driving 1 FP propeller Total Power: 1,030kW (1,400hp) Hanshin 6LU26 1 x 4 Stroke 6 Cy. 260 x 440 1030kW (1400bhp) The Hanshin Diesel Works Ltd-Japan
8916231 XUSJ7 -	**YUAN DA NO. 9** *ex* Mitsukawa Maru *-2007* **Shunhai Shipping Co Ltd** Yuan Da Shipping Co Ltd *Phnom Penh* *Cambodia* MMSI: 515654000 Official number: 0790777	**2,497** 1,409 4,640	Class: UB (NK)	**1990-03 Shin Kochi Jyuko K.K. — Kochi** Yd No: 7003 Loa 90.52 Br ex - Dght 6.640 Lbp 83.00 Br md 15.00 Dpth 8.00 Welded, 1 dk	**(A24E2BL) Limestone Carrier** Grain: 4,122; Bale: 4,086 1 Ha: (43.4 x 7.8)ER	**1 oil engine** driving 1 FP propeller Total Power: 2,060kW (2,801hp) Niigata 6M38HET 1 x 4 Stroke 6 Cy. 380 x 700 2060kW (2801bhp) Niigata Engineering Co Ltd-Japan
7338743 BYCP -	**YUAN DOA No. 11** **Yuan Doa Sea Food Co Ltd** - *Kaohsiung* *Chinese Taipei*	*395* 249 -	Class: (CR)	**1973 Chung Yi Shipbuilding Corp. — Kaohsiung** Loa 44.81 Br ex 8.21 Dght 3.252 Lbp 38.10 Br md 8.18 Dpth 3.76 Welded, 1 dk	**(B11B2FV) Fishing Vessel** Compartments: 3 Ho, ER 5 Ha: 4 (1.2 x 1.2) (0.9 x 1.2)ER	**1 oil engine** driving 1 FP propeller Total Power: 919kW (1,249hp) 12.0kn Niigata 6L28X 1 x 4 Stroke 6 Cy. 280 x 440 919kW (1249bhp) Niigata Engineering Co Ltd-Japan
7338755 - -	**YUAN DOA No. 12** **Yuan Doa Sea Food Co Ltd** - *Kaohsiung* *Chinese Taipei*	*395* 249 -	Class: (CR)	**1974 Chung Yi Shipbuilding Corp. — Kaohsiung** Loa 44.81 Br ex 8.21 Dght 3.252 Lbp 38.10 Br md 8.18 Dpth 3.76 Welded, 1 dk	**(B11B2FV) Fishing Vessel** Compartments: 3 Ho, ER 5 Ha: 4 (1.2 x 1.2) (0.9 x 1.2)ER	**1 oil engine** driving 1 FP propeller Total Power: 919kW (1,249hp) 12.0kn Niigata 6M28X 1 x 4 Stroke 6 Cy. 280 x 440 919kW (1249bhp) Niigata Engineering Co Ltd-Japan
8626094 - -	**YUAN DONG 1 HAO** *ex* Shoei Maru No. 8 *-1999* *ex* Tamayoshi Maru No. 18 *-1989* - -	*498* - 1,240		**1984 Kimura Zosen K.K. — Kure** Loa 65.51 Br ex - Dght 4.301 Lbp 60.00 Br md 13.20 Dpth 7.12 Welded, 1 dk	**(B33A2DG) Grab Dredger** Compartments: 1 Ho, ER 1 Ha: (11.7 x 10.0)ER	**1 oil engine** driving 1 FP propeller Total Power: 1,103kW (1,500hp) 12.0kn Hanshin 6LU32G 1 x 4 Stroke 6 Cy. 320 x 510 1103kW (1500bhp) The Hanshin Diesel Works Ltd-Japan
8879902 BLOM2 -	**YUAN FA** *ex* Jin Shui Leng 1 *-1998* **Zhoushan Ocean Fishery-going Group Refrigeration Shipping Co** - *Ningbo, Zhejiang* *China*	**1,091** 327 1,100	Class: (CC)	**1983 Tianjin Shipyard — Tianjin** Loa 66.80 Br ex - Dght 3.750 Lbp 60.00 Br md 11.50 Dpth 6.00 Welded, 2 dks	**(A34A2GR) Refrigerated Cargo Ship** Ins: 1,348 Compartments: 4 Ho, ER 4 Ha: ER Cranes: 2x2.5t	**1 oil engine** driving 1 FP propeller Total Power: 971kW (1,320hp) 12.0kn S.K.L. 8NVD48A-2U 1 x 4 Stroke 8 Cy. 320 x 480 971kW (1320bhp) VEB Schwermaschinenbau "KarlLiebknecht" (SKL)-Magdeburg AuxGen: 3 x 120kW 400V a.c
8108896 BROK -	**YUAN FENG ER** *ex* Yang Cheng Hu *-2010* **Yuanfeng Investment Co Ltd** Yuanfeng Shipping Co Ltd *Qingyuan, Guangdong* *China* MMSI: 412367000	**12,708** 7,116 19,989 T/cm 24.6	Class: ZC (CC)	**1982-05 Hayashikane Shipbuilding & Engineering Co Ltd — Shimonoseki YC** Yd No: 1252 Loa 158.00 (BB) Br ex 22.08 Dght 9.200 Lbp 149.00 Br md 22.00 Dpth 12.20 Welded, 1 dk	**(A13B2TP) Products Tanker** Single Hull Liq: 20,285; Liq (Oil): 20,285 Cargo Heating Coils Compartments: 15 Ta, ER 3 Cargo Pump (s) Manifold: Bow/CM: 65m	**1 oil engine** driving 1 FP propeller Total Power: 5,582kW (7,589hp) 14.0kn Sulzer 6RLA56 1 x 2 Stroke 6 Cy. 560 x 1150 5582kW (7589bhp) Ishikawajima Harima Heavy IndustrieCo Ltd (IHI)-Japan AuxGen: 3 x 500kW 450V 60Hz a.c
8021828 BROE -	**YUAN FENG HAI** *ex* Wu Chang Hu *-2009* *ex* Egret *-2003* *ex* Golden Dove *-1995* *ex* Wu Chang Hu *-1992* **Yuanfeng Investment Co Ltd** Yuanfeng Shipping Co Ltd SatCom: Inmarsat C 441300710 *Qingyuan, Guangdong* *China* MMSI: 413007000	*38,563* 16,648 60,678	Class: ZC (CC) (NK)	**1983-01 Hitachi Zosen Corp — Nagasu KM** Yd No: 4694 Converted From: Crude Oil Tanker-2009 Loa 228.50 (BB) Br ex 32.24 Dght 12.190 Lbp 219.00 Br md 32.20 Dpth 19.00 Welded, 1 dk	**(A21A2BC) Bulk Carrier** Grain: 72,300 Compartments: 7 Ho, ER 7 Ha: ER	**1 oil engine** driving 1 FP propeller Total Power: 9,194kW (12,500hp) 13.0kn B&W 7L67GFCA 1 x 2 Stroke 7 Cy. 670 x 1700 9194kW (12500bhp) Hitachi Zosen Corp-Japan AuxGen: 3 x 600kW 450V 60Hz a.c
6815500 - -	**YUAN HAI** **Yuan Hai Fishery Co Ltd** - *Kaohsiung* *Chinese Taipei*	*280* 189 107	Class: (CR)	**1968 Taiwan Machinery Manufacturing Corp. — Kaohsiung** Yd No: 1433 Loa 40.19 Br ex 7.12 Dght 2.693 Lbp 35.03 Br md 7.09 Dpth 3.18 Welded, 1 dk	**(B11B2FV) Fishing Vessel** Ins: 240 Compartments: 3 Ho, ER 3 Ha: (1.9 x 1.6)2 (1.3 x 0.9)ER Derricks: 2x1t; Winches: 2	**1 oil engine** driving 1 FP propeller Total Power: 456kW (620hp) 10.5kn Akasaka MA6SS 1 x 4 Stroke 6 Cy. 270 x 400 456kW (620bhp) Akasaka Tekkosho KK (Akasaka DieselLtd)-Japan AuxGen: 2 x 64kW 225V a.c
9131216 3EVT9 -	**YUAN HAI** *ex* Valbella *-2013* *ex* CCNI Atacama *-2008* *launched as* Valbella *-1998* **Yuanhai Shipping Co Ltd** Hongyuan Marine Co Ltd *Panama* *Panama* MMSI: 353275000 Official number: 4483013	**28,148** 13,514 44,593 T/cm 52.1	Class: RI (LR) (GL) ✠ Classed LR until 24/1/10	**1998-08 Stocznia Szczecinska SA — Szczecin** Yd No: B577/1/5 Loa 185.00 (BB) Br ex 32.25 Dght 12.054 Lbp 175.97 Br md 32.20 Dpth 16.95 Welded, 1 dk	**(A31A2GX) General Cargo Ship** Grain: 51,096; Bale: 49,966 TEU 1830 C Ho 922 TEU C Dk 908 TEU incl 110 ref C Compartments: 4 Ho, 4 Cell Ho, ER 8 Ha: (12.6 x 12.8)7 (12.6 x 28.0)ER Cranes: 3x40t	**1 oil engine** driving 1 FP propeller Total Power: 12,000kW (16,315hp) 15.5kn Sulzer 6RTA58T 1 x 2 Stroke 6 Cy. 580 x 2416 12000kW (16315bhp) H Cegielski Poznan SA-Poland AuxGen: 3 x 904kW 450V 60Hz a.c Boilers: e (ex.g.) 9.2kgf/cm² (9.0bar), AuxB (o.f.) 9.2kgf/cm² (9.0bar) Fuel: 340.0 (d.f.) 4043.0 (r.f.)
9131242 3FIA7 -	**YUAN HANG** *ex* Valparaiso *-2013* *ex* CCNI Ancud *-2012* *ex* CSAV Valencia *-2006* *ex* CCNI Ancud *-2006* *ex* CSAV Valencia *-2003* *ex* CCNI Ancud *-2001* **Yuanhang Shipping Co Ltd** Hongyuan Marine Co Ltd *Panama* *Panama* MMSI: 354350000 Official number: 4484913	**28,148** 13,514 44,596 T/cm 52.1	Class: RI (LR) (GL) ✠ Classed LR until 16/1/10	**1998-06 Stocznia Szczecinska SA — Szczecin** Yd No: B577/1/4 Loa 185.00 (BB) Br ex 32.25 Dght 12.054 Lbp 175.97 Br md 32.20 Dpth 16.95 Welded, 1 dk	**(A31A2GX) General Cargo Ship** Grain: 51,096; Bale: 49,966 TEU 1830 C Ho 922 TEU C Dk 908 TEU incl 110 ref C Compartments: 4 Ho, 4 Cell Ho, ER 8 Ha: (12.6 x 12.8)7 (12.6 x 28.0)ER Cranes: 3x40t	**1 oil engine** driving 1 FP propeller Total Power: 12,000kW (16,315hp) 15.5kn Sulzer 6RTA58T 1 x 2 Stroke 6 Cy. 580 x 2416 12000kW (16315bhp) H Cegielski Poznan SA-Poland AuxGen: 3 x 904kW 450V 60Hz a.c Boilers: e (ex.g.) 9.2kgf/cm² (9.0bar), AuxB (o.f.) 9.2kgf/cm² (9.0bar)
8662206 - -	**YUAN HANG 78** **Wenzhou Yuanhang Shipping** - *Wenzhou, Zhejiang* *China* Official number: 2005B3100575	**499** 279 -	Class: ZC	**2005-03 Wenling New Shiprepair & Building Yard — Wenling ZJ** Loa 52.80 Br ex - Dght 3.430 Lbp 48.00 Br md 8.80 Dpth 4.10 Welded, 1 dk	**(A31A2GX) General Cargo Ship**	**1 oil engine** reduction geared to sc. shaft driving 1 Propeller Total Power: 218kW (296hp) Chinese Std. Type Z6170ZL 1 x 4 Stroke 6 Cy. 170 x 200 218kW (296bhp) Zibo Diesel Engine Factory-China
8664515 BLLO -	**YUAN HANG 156** **Wenzhou Yuanhang Marine Co Ltd** - *Wenzhou, Zhejiang* *China*	**2,813** 1,575 -		**2006-07 Yuhuan Damaiyu Harbour Shiprepair & Building Yard — Yuhuan County ZJ** Yd No: H131009 Loa 95.90 Br ex - Dght - Lbp 89.00 Br md 13.80 Dpth 7.40 Welded, 1 dk	**(A31A2GX) General Cargo Ship**	**1 oil engine** reduction geared to sc. shaft driving 1 FP propeller Total Power: 1,324kW (1,800hp) Chinese Std. Type G6300ZC18B 1 x 4 Stroke 6 Cy. 300 x 380 1324kW (1800bhp)

9131254 *3FHU7* -	**YUAN HE** *ex* Anakena *-2013* *ex* CCNI Anakena *-2008* *ex* CSAV Valencia *-2005* *ex* CCNI Anakena *-2004* *launched as* Valdemosa *-1998* **Yuanhe Shipping Co Ltd** Hongyuan Marine Co Ltd *Panama* *Panama* MMSI: 354995000 Official number: 44433PEXT	**28,148** 13,514 44,583 T/cm 52.1	Class: RI (LR) (GL) ✠ Classed LR until 29/12/09	**1998-09 Stocznia Szczecinska SA — Szczecin** Yd No: B577/1/6 Loa 184.85 (BB) Br ex 32.25 Dght 12.054 Lbp 175.97 Br md 32.20 Dpth 16.95 Welded, 1 dk	**(A31A2GX) General Cargo Ship** Grain: 51,096; Bale: 49,966 TEU 1830 C Ho 922 TEU C Dk 908 TEU incl 110 ref C Compartments: 4 Ho, 4 Cell Ho, ER 8 Ha: (12.6 x 12.8)7 (12.6 x 28.0)ER Cranes: 3x40t	**1 oil engine** driving 1 FP propeller Total Power: 12,000kW (16,315hp) 15.5k Sulzer 6RTA58 1 x 2 Stroke 6 Cy. 580 x 2416 12000kW (16315bhp) H Cegielski Poznan SA-Poland AuxGen: 3 x 904kW 220/440V 60Hz a.c Boilers: e (ex.g.) 9.2kgf/cm^2 (9.0bar), AuxB (o.f.) 9.2kgf/cm^2 (9.0bar)
8217790 - -	**YUAN HENG** *ex* Helios *-2001* *ex* Kie Maru *-1998* **Faith State Shipping Ltd** Topwin Shipping Co Ltd	**1,329** 485 1,598	Class: (KR)	**1983-01 K.K. Uno Zosensho — Imabari** Yd No: 163 Loa 72.88 Br ex 11.54 Dght 4.361 Lbp 68.00 Br md 11.51 Dpth 7.01 Welded, 2 dks	**(A31A2GX) General Cargo Ship** Grain: 3,028; Bale: 2,863 Compartments: 1 Ho, ER 1 Ha: ER	**1 oil engine** with clutches, flexible couplings & sr reverse geared to sc. shaft driving 1 FP propeller Total Power: 956kW (1,300hp) Hanshin 6LUN28A 1 x 4 Stroke 6 Cy. 280 x 480 956kW (1300bhp) The Hanshin Diesel Works Ltd-Japan
8307844 *3ETL8* -	**YUAN HENG** *ex* Heiyo *-2009* *ex* Sunny Ocean *-1995* *ex* Hirado Maru *-1991* *ex* Cosmo Ocean *-1990* *ex* C. C. Oakland *-1984* **Ju Bao Men Shipping Co Ltd** Hongyuan Marine Co Ltd SatCom: Inmarsat C 435516410 *Panama* *Panama* MMSI: 355164000 Official number: 1957791F	**17,150** 9,913 26,268	Class: NK (BV)	**1984-02 Sanoyasu Dockyard Co Ltd — Kurashiki OY** Yd No: 1065 Loa 166.40 (BB) Br ex 27.67 Dght 9.682 Lbp 158.00 Br md 27.60 Dpth 13.40 Welded, 2 dks	**(A31A2GX) General Cargo Ship** Grain: 32,983; Bale: 34,202 TEU 1022 incl 98 ref C. Compartments: 5 Ho, ER, 5 Tw Dk 9 Ha: (12.9 x 10.8)6 (20.3 x 10.8)2 (13.5 x 10.8)ER Cranes: 1x35t,3x25t	**1 oil engine** driving 1 FP propeller Total Power: 7,503kW (10,201hp) 15.0k Mitsubishi 6UEC60H 1 x 2 Stroke 6 Cy. 600 x 1500 7503kW (10201bhp) Kobe Hatsudoki KK-Japan AuxGen: 3 x 450kW 450V 60Hz a.c Fuel: 232.5 (d.f.) (Heating Coils) 1840.0 (r.f.) 30.5pd
9374870 *3EDP7* -	**YUAN HONG** *ex* PWL Wuhan *-2012* *ex* Bm1 *-2010* **Four Seasons Co Ltd** - *Panama* *Panama* MMSI: 371646000 Official number: 3146106CH	**1,972** 1,395 3,432	Class: CC	**2005-12 Qingdao Heshun Shipyard Co Ltd — Qingdao SD** Yd No: HDZ-007 Loa 81.00 Br ex - Dght - Lbp 76.00 Br md 13.60 Dpth 6.80 Welded, 1 dk	**(A31A2GX) General Cargo Ship** Bale: 5,089 Compartments: 2 Ho, ER 2 Ha: ER 2 (18.6 x 9.0) Ice Capable	**1 oil engine** reduction geared to sc. shaft driving 1 FP propeller Total Power: 1,324kW (1,800hp) 8.0k Chinese Std. Type G6300Z 1 x 4 Stroke 6 Cy. 300 x 380 1324kW (1800bhp) Wuxi Antai Power Machinery Co Ltd-China AuxGen: 2 x 120kW 400V 50Hz a.c Fuel: 18.0 (d.f.) (Heating Coils) 100.0 (r.f.) 6.1pd
9295189 *BOCE* -	**YUAN HUI HAI** **COSCO Bulk Carrier Co Ltd (COSCO BULK)** - *Tianjin* *China* MMSI: 413119000	**40,473** 26,208 74,259 T/cm 67.0	Class: CC	**2006-04 Hudong-Zhonghua Shipbuilding (Group) Co Ltd — Shanghai** Yd No: H1342A Loa 225.00 (BB) Br ex - Dght 14.250 Lbp 217.00 Br md 32.26 Dpth 19.60 Welded, 1 dk	**(A21A2BC) Bulk Carrier** Grain: 91,717; Bale: 89,882 Compartments: 7 Ho, ER 7 Ha: 6 (14.6 x 15.0)ER (14.6 x 13.2)	**1 oil engine** driving 1 FP propeller Total Power: 8,990kW (12,223hp) 13.8k MAN-B&W 5S60MC-● 1 x 2 Stroke 5 Cy. 600 x 2400 8990kW (12223bhp) Hudong Heavy Machinery Co Ltd-China AuxGen: 3 x 530kW 450V a.c
9452567 *BOYN* -	**YUAN JIAN** *ex* Zhi Xian 1 *-2007* **COSCO Logistics (Guangzhou) Heavy Transportation Co Ltd** - *Guangzhou, Guangdong* *China* MMSI: 413323000	**5,113** 1,534 3,500	Class: CC	**2007-07 Zhejiang Tenglong Shipyard — Wenling ZJ** Yd No: 0618 Loa 130.00 Br ex - Dght 4.500 Lbp 123.00 Br md 23.00 Dpth 6.80 Welded, 1 dk	**(A38B2GB) Barge Carrier** Ice Capable	**2 oil engines** reduction geared to sc. shafts driving 2 FP propellers Total Power: 4,120kW (5,602hp) 11.0k Guangzhou 8320Z 2 x 4 Stroke 8 Cy. 320 x 440 each-2060kW (2801bhp) Guangzhou Diesel Engine Factory CoLtd-China AuxGen: 3 x 150kW 400V a.c
9557563 *BQCX* -	**YUAN JING** **COSCO Logistics (Guangzhou) Heavy Transportation Co Ltd** - SatCom: Inmarsat C 441204810 *Guangzhou, Guangdong* *China* MMSI: 412048000	**10,177** 3,053 12,625	Class: CC	**2009-07 Huajie Shipbuilding Co Ltd — Linhai ZJ** Yd No: 08-02-C Loa 142.80 Br ex 32.24 Dght 5.200 Lbp 134.50 Br md 32.20 Dpth 8.00 Welded, 1 dk	**(A38B2GB) Barge Carrier** Ice Capable	**2 diesel electric oil engines** driving 2 gen. each 4400kW a.c Connecting to 2 elec. motors each (2200kW) driving 2 Propellers 11.5k AuxGen: 3 x 2000kW 690V a.c
7507526 - -	**YUAN LEE** *ex* Emerald *-2007* *ex* Atila No. 101 *-1996* *ex* Han Bo No. 3 *-1994* **Yuan Lee Fishery Co Ltd**	**486** 145 451	Class: (KR)	**1974 Korea Shipbuilding & Engineering Corp — Busan** Yd No: 178 Loa 52.63 Br ex 8.44 Dght 3.496 Lbp 47.27 Br md 8.41 Dpth 3.81 Welded, 1 dk	**(B11B2FV) Fishing Vessel** Ins: 542 3 Ha: (1.0 x 0.9)2 (1.6 x 1.6)	**1 oil engine** driving 1 FP propeller Total Power: 736kW (1,001hp) 12.0k Hanshin 6LUD2 1 x 4 Stroke 6 Cy. 260 x 440 736kW (1001bhp) Hanshin Nainenki Kogyo-Japan AuxGen: 2 x 200kW 230V a.c
7211050 - -	**YUAN MAO No. 1** **Yuan Mao Fishing Co Ltd** *Kaohsiung* *Chinese Taipei*	*150* 105 81		**1971 Taiwan Machinery Manufacturing Corp. — Kaohsiung** Yd No: 503 Loa 33.91 Br ex 5.85 Dght 2.413 Lbp 29.72 Br md 5.82 Dpth 2.82 Welded, 1 dk	**(B11B2FV) Fishing Vessel**	**1 oil engine** driving 1 FP propeller Total Power: 405kW (551hp) Alpha 405-26V 1 x 2 Stroke 5 Cy. 260 x 400 405kW (551bhp) Taiwan Machinery ManufacturingCorp.-Kaohsiung
7425144 - -	**YUAN PAO** *ex* Shinryu Maru *-1997* *ex* Wakatori Maru *-1988* - -	**487** 146 426		**1975-03 Hayashikane Shipbuilding & Engineering Co Ltd — Yokosuka KN** Yd No: 727 Loa 49.38 Br ex 8.44 Dght 3.683 Lbp 42.98 Br md 8.41 Dpth 3.89 Welded, 1 dk	**(B34K2QT) Training Ship**	**1 oil engine** driving 1 FP propeller Total Power: 956kW (1,300hp) 12.0k Niigata 6MG25B 1 x 4 Stroke 6 Cy. 250 x 320 956kW (1300bhp) Niigata Engineering Co Ltd-Japan AuxGen: 2 x 200kW 225V a.c
9415313 *XUPX8* -	**YUAN QIAO** *ex* Zheng Yuan 3 *-2006* **Song Delin** Star View International Shipping Ltd SatCom: Inmarsat C 451420110 *Phnom Penh* *Cambodia* MMSI: 514201000 Official number: 0706751	**2,959** 1,657 5,265	Class: UM	**2006-08 Daishan Zhenghua Shiprepair & Building Co Ltd — Daishan County ZJ** Yd No: 050120 Loa 98.00 Br ex - Dght 5.900 Lbp 90.50 Br md 15.80 Dpth 7.40 Welded, 1 dk	**(A31A2GX) General Cargo Ship** Grain: 6,825; Bale: 6,279	**1 oil engine** reduction geared to sc. shaft driving 1 FP propeller Total Power: 1,765kW (2,400hp) 11.0k Chinese Std. Type G8300Z● 1 x 4 Stroke 8 Cy. 300 x 380 1765kW (2400bhp) Ningbo CSI Power & Machinery GroupCo Ltd-China
9417189 *BOGF* -	**YUAN SHAN HU** **Dalian Ocean Shipping Co (COSCO DALIAN)** - SatCom: Inmarsat Mini-M 764938835 *Dalian, Liaoning* *China* MMSI: 413976000 Official number: 10D0053	**152,727** 98,415 297,136 T/cm 177.9	Class: CC	**2010-04 Dalian Shipbuilding Industry Co Ltd — Dalian LN (No 2 Yard)** Yd No: T3000-23 Loa 330.00 (BB) Br ex 60.05 Dght 21.500 Lbp 316.00 Br md 60.00 Dpth 29.70 Welded, 1 dk	**(A13A2TV) Crude Oil Tanker** Double Hull (13F) Liq: 324,599; Liq (Oil): 324,599 Compartments: 5 Ta, 10 Wing Ta, 2 Wing Slop Ta, ER 3 Cargo Pump (s): 3x5500m^3/hr Manifold: Bow/CM: 162.5m	**1 oil engine** driving 1 FP propeller Total Power: 25,480kW (34,643hp) 15.8k MAN-B&W 7S80M 1 x 2 Stroke 7 Cy. 800 x 3056 25480kW (34643bhp) Dalian Marine Diesel Co Ltd-China AuxGen: 3 x 975kW 450V a.c Fuel: 457.4 (d.f.) 6246.8 (r.f.)
8703634 *XUDR3* -	**YUAN SHENG** *ex* Feng Shun 15 *-2008* *ex* Ao Peng *-2008* *ex* Zhu Ruo *-2005* *ex* Sumiwaka Maru No. 2 *-2003* **Topgold Shipping Co Ltd** Topwin Shipping Co Ltd *Phnom Penh* *Cambodia* MMSI: 514115000 Official number: 0887205	**1,937** 1,112 -		**1987-12 K.K. Murakami Zosensho — Naruto** Yd No: 175 Lengthened-2003 L reg 81.73 (BB) Br ex - Dght - Lbp - Br md 12.50 Dpth 7.00 Welded, 2 dks	**(B33A2DG) Grab Dredger** Bale: 895	**1 oil engine** reverse reduction geared to sc. shaft driving 1 FP propeller Total Power: 1,103kW (1,500hp) Niigata 6M30G 1 x 4 Stroke 6 Cy. 300 x 530 1103kW (1500bhp) Niigata Engineering Co Ltd-Japan
9564956 *BLAS6* -	**YUAN SHENG 36** *ex* Xing Long Zhou 388 *-2010* **Ningbo Joyson Grand Sea Transportation Co Ltd** - SatCom: Inmarsat C 441301440 *Ningbo, Zhejiang* *China* MMSI: 413436580	**22,491** 11,913 35,411 T/cm 47.4	Class: CC (BV)	**2010-03 Zhejiang Hexing Shipyard — Wenling ZJ** Yd No: HX-V10 Loa 179.88 (BB) Br ex - Dght 10.270 Lbp 172.00 Br md 28.80 Dpth 14.60 Welded, 1 dk	**(A21A2BC) Bulk Carrier** Double Sides Entire Compartment Length Grain: 45,418 Compartments: 5 Ho, ER 5 Ha: 4 (20.0 x 20.0)ER (13.6 x 15.4)	**1 oil engine** driving 1 FP propeller Total Power: 6,480kW (8,810hp) 14.0k● MAN-B&W 6S42M● 1 x 2 Stroke 6 Cy. 420 x 1764 6480kW (8810bhp) STX Engine Co Ltd-South Korea AuxGen: 3 x 465kW 450V a.c
9628673 *BKEN* -	**YUAN SHENG 56** **Ningbo Joyson Grand Sea Transportation Co Ltd** - *Ningbo, Zhejiang* *China* MMSI: 414055000	**32,987** 19,233 56,756 T/cm 58.8	Class: CC	**2011-11 Zhejiang Zhenghe Shipbuilding Co Ltd — Zhoushan ZJ** Yd No: 1041 Loa 189.99 (BB) Br ex - Dght 12.800 Lbp 185.00 Br md 32.26 Dpth 18.00 Welded, 1 dk	**(A21A2BC) Bulk Carrier** Grain: 71,634; Bale: 68,200 Compartments: 5 Ho, ER 5 Ha: 4 (21.3 x 18.3)ER (18.9 x 18.3) Cranes: 4x36t	**1 oil engine** driving 1 FP propeller Total Power: 9,480kW (12,889hp) 14.2k MAN-B&W 6S50MC-● 1 x 2 Stroke 6 Cy. 500 x 2000 9480kW (12889bhp) Hyundai Heavy Industries Co Ltd-South Korea AuxGen: 3 x 600kW 450V a.c

446130 FZ02	**YUAN SHUN HAI** **Yuan Shun Hai Maritime SA** Qingdao Ocean Shipping Co Ltd (COSCO QINGDAO) SatCom: Inmarsat C 435386310 *Panama* *Panama* MMSI: 353863000 Official number: 4079309A	**32,957** 19,231 57,000 T/cm 58.8	Class: BV	**2009**-08 **COSCO (Zhoushan) Shipyard Co Ltd — Zhoushan ZJ** Yd No: ZS07002 Loa 189.99 (BB) Br ex - Dght 12.800 Lbp 185.00 Br md 32.26 Dpth 18.00 Welded, 1 dk	**(A21A2BC) Bulk Carrier** Grain: 71,634; Bale: 68,200 Compartments: 5 Ho, ER 5 Ha: ER Cranes: 4x30t	**1 oil engine** driving 1 FP propeller Total Power: 9,480kW (12,889hp) 14.2kn MAN-B&W 6S50MC-C 1 x 2 Stroke 6 Cy. 500 x 2000 9480kW (12889bhp) STX Engine Co Ltd-South Korea AuxGen: 3 x 600kW 60Hz a.c
647983 H3115 L1705	**YUAN TAI** *ex* Chien Jia 113 **Yuan Tai Marine Products Co Ltd** - *Kaohsiung* *Chinese Taipei* Official number: CT6-1115	**453** 194 -		**1987**-12 **Sen Koh Shipbuilding Corp — Kaohsiung** Yd No: 017 Loa 49.80 Br ex 8.00 Dght - Lbp - Br md - Dpth - Welded, 1 dk	**(B11B2FV) Fishing Vessel**	**1 oil engine** driving 1 Propeller
650679 I2267 L1233	**YUAN TAI NO. 216** *ex* Yu Chen Hsiang *-2013* **Tai Hsiang Hao Fishery Co Ltd** - *Kaohsiung* *Chinese Taipei* MMSI: 416005500 Official number: CT7-0267	**748** 283 -		**1988**-08 **Sen Koh Shipbuilding Corp — Kaohsiung** Loa 57.05 Br ex 8.90 Dght - Lbp 50.00 Br md - Dpth 3.85 Welded, 1 dk	**(B11B2FV) Fishing Vessel**	**1 oil engine** driving 1 Propeller Sumiyoshi Sumiyoshi Marine Diesel Co Ltd-Japan
900663 ZIR	**YUAN TAI NO. 806** *ex* Chun Ying No. 806 *-2013* *ex* Jih Yu No. 706 *-2006* *ex* Kunashiri *-1989* *ex* Takashiro Maru No. 51 *-1982* - - SatCom: Inmarsat A 1350243 *Chinese Taipei* MMSI: 416001900	*993* 525 1,983	Class: (CR) (NK)	**1979**-05 **Minaminippon Shipbuilding Co Ltd — Usuki OT** Yd No: 528 Loa 83.01 Br ex 13.21 Dght 5.001 Lbp 76.99 Br md 13.20 Dpth 7.88 Welded, 2 dks	**(A34A2GR) Refrigerated Cargo Ship** Ins: 2,782 Compartments: 3 Ho, ER 3 Ha: 3 (6.6 x 4.5) Derricks: 6x4t	**1 oil engine** driving 1 FP propeller Total Power: 2,207kW (3,001hp) 14.0kn Akasaka AH40 1 x 4 Stroke 6 Cy. 400 x 600 2207kW (3001bhp) Akasaka Tekkosho KK (Akasaka DieselLtd)-Japan AuxGen: 2 x 350kW a.c
603368	**YUAN TONG YOU No. 1** *ex* Hanshin Maru No. 3 *-2000* *ex* Puerto No. 12 *-1988* *ex* Ariake Maru *-1988* -	**680** 271 1,097		**1976**-03 **Wakamatsu Zosen K.K. — Kitakyushu** Yd No: 263 Loa 58.83 Br ex 9.22 Dght 4.001 Lbp 54.01 Br md 9.21 Dpth 4.63 Welded, 1 dk	**(A24D2BA) Aggregates Carrier**	**1 oil engine** driving 1 FP propeller Total Power: 1,030kW (1,400hp) Hanshin 6LU32G 1 x 4 Stroke 6 Cy. 320 x 510 1030kW (1400bhp) Hanshin Nainenki Kogyo-Japan
887935 IHG	**YUAN WANG 3** **China Satellite Launch & Tracking Control General Maritime Tracking & Control Dept** - SatCom: Inmarsat C 441237612 *Shanghai* *China* MMSI: 412962000	**14,128** 4,238 7,396	Class: CC	**1995**-10 **Jiangnan Shipyard — Shanghai** Yd No: 2203 Loa 179.92 Br ex - Dght 8.000 Lbp 156.40 Br md 22.20 Dpth 11.60 Welded, 1 dk	**(B31A2SR) Research Survey Vessel** Ice Capable	**2 oil engines** driving 2 FP propellers Total Power: 13,646kW (18,554hp) 19.4kn B&W 8L42MC 2 x 2 Stroke 8 Cy. 420 x 1360 each-6823kW (9277bhp) Mitsui Engineering & Shipbuilding CLtd-Japan AuxGen: 4 x 900kW 400V a.c
413054 IPK	**YUAN WANG 5** **China Satellite Launch & Tracking Control General Maritime Tracking & Control Dept** - SatCom: Inmarsat C 441300051 *Shanghai* *China* MMSI: 413289000	**22,686** 6,806 11,000	Class: CC	**2007**-09 **Jiangnan Shipyard (Group) Co Ltd — Shanghai** Yd No: H2325 Loa 222.00 (BB) Br ex 26.00 Dght 8.200 Lbp 199.60 Br md 25.20 Dpth 11.70 Welded, 1 dk	**(B31A2SR) Research Survey Vessel** Ice Capable	**2 oil engines** reduction geared to sc. shafts driving 2 Propellers Total Power: 22,858kW (31,078hp) 20.0kn Wartsila 8L46C 2 x 4 Stroke 8 Cy. 460 x 580 each-11429kW (15539bhp) Wartsila Finland Oy-Finland AuxGen: 5 x 770kW 400V a.c Thrusters: 1 Tunnel thruster (f)
439527 IQK	**YUAN WANG 6** **China Satellite Launch & Tracking Control General Maritime Tracking & Control Dept** - SatCom: Inmarsat C 441332613 *Shanghai* *China* MMSI: 413326000	**22,686** 6,806 11,000	Class: CC	**2008**-04 **Jiangnan Shipyard (Group) Co Ltd — Shanghai** Yd No: H2376 Loa 222.00 (BB) Br ex 26.00 Dght 8.200 Lbp 199.60 Br md 25.20 Dpth 11.70 Welded, 1 dk	**(B31A2SR) Research Survey Vessel** Ice Capable	**2 oil engines** reduction geared to sc. shafts driving 2 Propellers Total Power: 22,858kW (31,078hp) 20.0kn Wartsila 8L46C 2 x 4 Stroke 8 Cy. 460 x 580 each-11429kW (15539bhp) Wartsila Finland Oy-Finland AuxGen: 5 x 770kW 400V a.c Thrusters: 1 Tunnel thruster (f)
516519 FTK4	**YUAN WANG HAI** **Yuanwanghai Shipping Inc** COSCO Bulk Carrier Co Ltd (COSCO BULK) SatCom: Inmarsat C 435380110 *Panama* *Panama* MMSI: 353801000 Official number: 4284811	**105,936** 67,880 207,906 T/cm 140.5	Class: CC (AB)	**2011**-06 **Nantong COSCO KHI Ship Engineering Co Ltd (NACKS) — Nantong JS** Yd No: 092 Loa 300.00 (BB) Br ex 50.06 Dght 18.225 Lbp 295.00 Br md 50.00 Dpth 24.70 Welded, 1 dk	**(A21A2BC) Bulk Carrier** Double Hull Grain: 224,873 Compartments: 9 Ho, ER 9 Ha: ER	**1 oil engine** driving 1 FP propeller Total Power: 17,950kW (24,405hp) 14.8kn MAN-B&W 6S70MC-C 1 x 2 Stroke 6 Cy. 700 x 2800 17950kW (24405bhp) CSSC MES Diesel Co Ltd-China AuxGen: 3 x 800kW 450V 60Hz a.c Fuel: 465.0 (d.f.) 5895.0 (r.f.) 68.0pd
609192 ETB8	**YUAN XIANG** *ex* Dong Hua Men *-2009* *ex* Chelsea Bridge *-2002* *ex* Apache Belle *-1996* *ex* Chelsea Bridge *-1995* *ex* Manchinchi Bridge *-1992* *ex* Tacna III *-1990* *ex* Kamateri *-1989* **Hongan Shipping Co Ltd** Hongyuan Marine Co Ltd SatCom: Inmarsat C 437050510 *Panama* *Panama* MMSI: 370505000 Official number: 3469309A	**14,538** 8,482 22,356	Class: IS (LR) ✠ Classed LR until 25/8/08	**1978**-04 **Mitsubishi Heavy Industries Ltd. — Shimonoseki** Yd No: 781 Loa 167.52 (BB) Br ex 22.94 Dght 10.434 Lbp 154.01 Br md 22.86 Dpth 14.00 Welded, 2 dks	**(A31A2GX) General Cargo Ship** Grain: 29,874; Bale: 26,922 TEU 378 C Ho 210 TEU C Dk 168 TEU Compartments: 4 Ho, ER, 3 Tw Dk 7 Ha: (13.2 x 8.9)6 (19.9 x 6.7)ER Cranes: 4x20t; Derricks: 1x120t; Winches: 4	**1 oil engine** driving 1 FP propeller Total Power: 8,496kW (11,551hp) 13.5kn Sulzer 7RND68 1 x 2 Stroke 7 Cy. 680 x 1250 8496kW (11551bhp) Mitsubishi Heavy Industries Ltd-Japan AuxGen: 3 x 550kW 450V 60Hz a.c Boilers: AuxB (Comp) 8.0kgf/cm² (7.8bar) Fuel: 170.0 (d.f.) (Heating Coils) 1204.0 (r.f.) 26.5pd
131230 EUW	**YUAN XIN** *ex* Austin Angol *-2013* *ex* CCNI Angol *-2008* *launched as* Valdivia *-1998* **Yuanxin Shipping Co Ltd** Hongyuan Marine Co Ltd *Panama* *Panama* MMSI: 371490000 Official number: 4483413	**28,148** 13,514 46,376 T/cm 52.1	Class: RI (LR) (GL) ✠ Classed LR until 19/1/10	**1998**-04 **Stocznia Szczecinska SA — Szczecin** Yd No: B577/1/3 Loa 185.00 (BB) Br ex 32.25 Dght 12.054 Lbp 175.97 Br md 32.20 Dpth 16.95 Welded, 1 dk	**(A31A2GX) General Cargo Ship** Grain: 51,096; Bale: 49,966 TEU 1830 C Ho 922 TEU C Dk 908 TEU incl 110 ref C Compartments: 4 Ho, 4 Cell Ho, ER 8 Ha: (12.6 x 12.8)7 (12.6 x 28.0)ER Cranes: 3x40t	**1 oil engine** driving 1 FP propeller Total Power: 12,000kW (16,315hp) 15.5kn Sulzer 6RTA58T 1 x 2 Stroke 6 Cy. 580 x 2416 12000kW (16315bhp) H Cegielski Poznan SA-Poland AuxGen: 3 x 904kW 450V 60Hz a.c Boilers: e (ex.g.) 9.2kgf/cm² (9.0bar), AuxB (o.f.) 9.2kgf/cm² (9.0bar)
558086 QAW	**YUAN XIN HAI** **COSCO Bulk Carrier Co Ltd (COSCO BULK)** - SatCom: Inmarsat M 600653823 *Tianjin* *China* MMSI: 413828000	**91,205** 59,001 178,076 T/cm 120.6	Class: CC	**2009**-08 **Shanghai Waigaoqiao Shipbuilding Co Ltd — Shanghai** Yd No: 1098 Loa 291.95 (BB) Br ex - Dght 18.300 Lbp 282.00 Br md 45.00 Dpth 24.80 Welded, 1 dk	**(A21A2BC) Bulk Carrier** Grain: 194,179; Bale: 183,425 Compartments: 9 Ho, ER 9 Ha: 7 (15.5 x 20.0)ER 2 (15.5 x 16.5)	**1 oil engine** driving 1 FP propeller Total Power: 16,860kW (22,923hp) 14.0kn MAN-B&W 6S70MC 1 x 2 Stroke 6 Cy. 700 x 2674 16860kW (22923bhp) Dalian Marine Diesel Co Ltd-China AuxGen: 3 x 900kW 450V a.c
098737	**YUAN XING** **Yuanxing Shipping Co Ltd** - *Fuzhou, Fujian* *China*	**4,918** 2,754 7,000		**1996**-02 **Fu'an Huanao Shipbuilding Co Ltd — Fu'an FJ** Loa 110.72 Br ex 17.00 Dght 7.400 Lbp 108.42 Br md 16.35 Dpth 9.40 Welded, 1 dk	**(A31A2GX) General Cargo Ship**	**1 oil engine** driving 1 Propeller Total Power: 2,055kW (2,794hp) 11.0kn Hanshin 6LU46 1 x 4 Stroke 6 Cy. 460 x 740 2055kW (2794bhp) The Hanshin Diesel Works Ltd-Japan
928266 VTT	**YUAN YANG** **Yuan Hai Fishery Co Ltd** - *Keelung* *Chinese Taipei*	*265* 161 -	Class: (CR)	**1969 Suao Shipbuilding Co., Ltd. — Suao** Loa 38.38 Br ex 6.94 Dght 2.642 Lbp 33.00 Br md 6.91 Dpth 3.15 Welded, 1 dk	**(B11B2FV) Fishing Vessel** Compartments: 3 Ho, ER 3 Ha: 2 (1.0 x 0.7) (0.9 x 1.2)	**1 oil engine** driving 1 FP propeller Total Power: 441kW (600hp) 10.5kn Hanshin 6L26AMSH 1 x 4 Stroke 6 Cy. 260 x 400 441kW (600bhp) Hanshin Nainenki Kogyo-Japan AuxGen: 2 x 64kW 220V a.c
398943 QCH	**YUAN YANG HU** **Dalian Ocean Shipping Co (COSCO DALIAN)** - SatCom: Inmarsat Mini-M 763682072 *Dalian, Liaoning* *China* MMSI: 413880000 Official number: BJ07NB00268	**152,727** 98,415 297,305 T/cm 177.9	Class: CC	**2010**-01 **Dalian Shipbuilding Industry Co Ltd — Dalian LN (No 2 Yard)** Yd No: T3000-22 Loa 330.00 (BB) Br ex 60.05 Dght 21.500 Lbp 316.00 Br md 60.00 Dpth 29.70 Welded, 1 dk	**(A13A2TV) Crude Oil Tanker** Double Hull (13F) Liq: 324,601; Liq (Oil): 324,601 Compartments: 5 Ta, 10 Wing Ta, 2 Wing Slop Ta, ER 3 Cargo Pump (s): 3x5500m³/hr Manifold: Bow/CM: 162.5m	**1 oil engine** driving 1 FP propeller Total Power: 25,480kW (34,643hp) 15.8kn MAN-B&W 7S80MC 1 x 2 Stroke 7 Cy. 800 x 3056 25480kW (34643bhp) Dalian Marine Diesel Co Ltd-China AuxGen: 3 x 975kW 450V a.c Fuel: 395.0 (d.f.) 5685.0 (r.f.)

LR/IMO No. / Call sign / Flag	Ship name / Owner / Port	Tonnage	Classification	Builder / Dimensions	Type	Machinery	Speed / Model
8833374 - -	**YUAN YU 1** **Zhanjiang Marine Fisheries Co** - *Zhanjiang, Guangdong* China	199 69 -	Class: (CC)	**1984 Guangzhou Fishing Vessel Shipyard — Guangzhou GD** Loa 44.66 Br ex - Dght - Lbp 39.00 Br md 7.60 Dpth 4.00 Welded	**(B11B2FV) Fishing Vessel**	**1 oil engine** geared to sc. shaft driving 1 FP propeller Total Power: 441kW (600hp) Chinese Std. Type 1 x 4 Stroke 8 Cy. 300 x 380 441kW (600bhp) Zibo Diesel Engine Factory-China AuxGen: 2 x 90kW 400V a.c	830
8833386 - -	**YUAN YU 2** **Zhanjiang Marine Fisheries Co** - *Zhanjiang, Guangdong* China	199 69 -	Class: (CC)	**1984 Guangzhou Fishing Vessel Shipyard — Guangzhou GD** Loa 44.66 Br ex - Dght - Lbp 39.00 Br md 7.60 Dpth 4.00 Welded	**(B11B2FV) Fishing Vessel**	**1 oil engine** geared to sc. shaft driving 1 FP propeller Total Power: 441kW (600hp) Chinese Std. Type 1 x 4 Stroke 8 Cy. 300 x 380 441kW (600bhp) Zibo Diesel Engine Factory-China AuxGen: 2 x 90kW 400V a.c	14.0k 830
8833398 - -	**YUAN YU 3** **Zhanjiang Marine Fisheries Co** - *Zhanjiang, Guangdong* China	270 72 -	Class: (CC)	**1981 Guangzhou Fishing Vessel Shipyard — Guangzhou GD** Loa 44.86 Br ex - Dght - Lbp 38.00 Br md 7.60 Dpth 4.00 Welded	**(B11B2FV) Fishing Vessel**	**1 oil engine** geared to sc. shaft driving 1 FP propeller Total Power: 441kW (600hp) Chinese Std. Type 1 x 4 Stroke 8 Cy. 300 x 380 441kW (600bhp) Zibo Diesel Engine Factory-China AuxGen: 2 x 64kW 400V a.c	8300
8833403 - -	**YUAN YU 4** **Zhanjiang Marine Fisheries Co** - *Zhanjiang, Guangdong* China	270 81 -	Class: (CC)	**1982 Guangzhou Fishing Vessel Shipyard — Guangzhou GD** Loa 44.86 Br ex - Dght - Lbp 38.00 Br md 7.60 Dpth 4.00 Welded	**(B11B2FV) Fishing Vessel**	**1 oil engine** geared to sc. shaft driving 1 FP propeller Total Power: 809kW (1,100hp) Chinese Std. Type 1 x 4 Stroke 8 Cy. 300 x 380 809kW (1100bhp) Dalian Fishing Vessel Co-China AuxGen: 2 x 90kW 400V a.c	8300
8833415 - -	**YUAN YU 5** **Zhanjiang Marine Fisheries Co** - *Zhanjiang, Guangdong* China	270 72 -	Class: (CC)	**1980 Guangzhou Fishing Vessel Shipyard — Guangzhou GD** Loa 44.96 Br ex - Dght - Lbp 38.00 Br md 7.60 Dpth 4.00 Welded	**(B11B2FV) Fishing Vessel**	**1 oil engine** geared to sc. shaft driving 1 FP propeller Total Power: 809kW (1,100hp) Chinese Std. Type 1 x 4 Stroke 8 Cy. 300 x 380 809kW (1100bhp) Dalian Fishing Vessel Co-China AuxGen: 2 x 90kW 400V a.c	8300
8833427 - -	**YUAN YU 6** **Zhanjiang Marine Fisheries Co** - *Zhanjiang, Guangdong* China	270 72 -	Class: (CC)	**1980 Guangzhou Fishing Vessel Shipyard — Guangzhou GD** Loa 44.86 Br ex - Dght - Lbp 38.00 Br md 7.60 Dpth 4.00 Welded	**(B11B2FV) Fishing Vessel**	**1 oil engine** geared to sc. shaft driving 1 FP propeller Total Power: 809kW (1,100hp) Chinese Std. Type 1 x 4 Stroke 8 Cy. 300 x 380 809kW (1100bhp) Dalian Fishing Vessel Co-China AuxGen: 2 x 90kW 400V a.c	8300
8833439 *BYXB7* -	**YUAN YU 9** **Zhanjiang Marine Fisheries Co** - *Zhanjiang, Guangdong* China	286 85 -	Class: (CC)	**1989 Guangzhou Fishing Vessel Shipyard — Guangzhou GD** Loa 44.86 Br ex - Dght - Lbp 38.00 Br md 7.60 Dpth 4.00 Welded	**(B11B2FV) Fishing Vessel**	**1 oil engine** geared to sc. shaft driving 1 FP propeller Total Power: 541kW (736hp) Chinese Std. Type 1 x 4 Stroke 8 Cy. 300 x 380 541kW (736bhp) Guangzhou Diesel Engine Factory CoLtd-China AuxGen: 2 x 90kW 400V a.c	8300
8833441 *BYXB8* -	**YUAN YU 10** **Zhanjiang Marine Fisheries Co** - *Zhanjiang, Guangdong* China	286 85 -	Class: (CC)	**1989 Guangzhou Fishing Vessel Shipyard — Guangzhou GD** Loa 44.86 Br ex - Dght - Lbp 38.00 Br md 7.60 Dpth 4.00 Welded	**(B11B2FV) Fishing Vessel**	**1 oil engine** geared to sc. shaft driving 1 FP propeller Total Power: 541kW (736hp) Chinese Std. Type 1 x 4 Stroke 8 Cy. 300 x 380 541kW (736bhp) Guangzhou Diesel Engine Factory CoLtd-China AuxGen: 2 x 90kW 400V a.c	8300
8863795 *BYZB3* -	**YUAN YU 15** **Zhanjiang Marine Fisheries Co** - *Zhanjiang, Guangdong* China	304 91 -	Class: (CC)	**1992 Guangzhou Fishing Vessel Shipyard — Guangzhou GD** Loa 44.86 Br ex - Dght 3.030 Lbp 38.00 Br md 7.60 Dpth 4.00 Welded, 1 dk	**(B11B2FV) Fishing Vessel**	**1 oil engine** geared to sc. shaft driving 1 FP propeller Total Power: 541kW (736hp) Chinese Std. Type 1 x 4 Stroke 8 Cy. 300 x 380 541kW (736bhp) (made 1991) Zibo Diesel Engine Factory-China AuxGen: 2 x 90kW 400V a.c	12.0kn 8300
8863800 *BYZB2* -	**YUAN YU 16** **Zhanjiang Marine Fisheries Co** - *Zhanjiang, Guangdong* China	304 91 -	Class: (CC)	**1992 Guangzhou Fishing Vessel Shipyard — Guangzhou GD** Loa 44.86 Br ex - Dght 3.030 Lbp 38.00 Br md 7.60 Dpth 4.00 Welded, 1 dk	**(B11B2FV) Fishing Vessel**	**1 oil engine** geared to sc. shaft driving 1 FP propeller Total Power: 541kW (736hp) Chinese Std. Type 1 x 4 Stroke 8 Cy. 300 x 380 541kW (736bhp) (made 1991) Zibo Diesel Engine Factory-China AuxGen: 2 x 90kW 400V a.c	12.0kn 8300
8863812 *BYYB9* -	**YUAN YU 17** **Zhanjiang Marine Fisheries Co** - *Zhanjiang, Guangdong* China	304 91 -	Class: (CC)	**1992 Guangzhou Fishing Vessel Shipyard — Guangzhou GD** Loa 44.86 Br ex - Dght 3.030 Lbp 38.00 Br md 7.60 Dpth 4.00 Welded, 1 dk	**(B11B2FV) Fishing Vessel**	**1 oil engine** geared to sc. shaft driving 1 FP propeller Total Power: 541kW (736hp) Chinese Std. Type 1 x 4 Stroke 8 Cy. 300 x 380 541kW (736bhp) (made 1991) Zibo Diesel Engine Factory-China AuxGen: 2 x 90kW 400V a.c	12.0kn 8300
8843563 *BYNB4* -	**YUAN YU 627** **Zhanjiang Marine Fisheries Co** - *Zhanjiang, Guangdong* China	286 86 140	Class: (CC)	**1979 Guangzhou Fishing Vessel Shipyard — Guangzhou GD** Loa 44.86 Br ex - Dght 3.270 Lbp 38.00 Br md 7.60 Dpth 4.00 Welded, 1 dk	**(B11B2FV) Fishing Vessel** Ins: 194	**1 oil engine** geared to sc. shaft driving 1 FP propeller Total Power: 441kW (600hp) Chinese Std. Type 1 x 4 Stroke 8 Cy. 300 x 380 441kW (600bhp) Zibo Diesel Engine Factory-China AuxGen: 2 x 90kW 400V a.c	12.0kn 8300
8843575 *BYNB5* -	**YUAN YU 628** **Zhanjiang Marine Fisheries Co** - *Zhanjiang, Guangdong* China	286 86 140	Class: (CC)	**1979 Guangzhou Fishing Vessel Shipyard — Guangzhou GD** Loa 44.86 Br ex - Dght 3.270 Lbp 38.00 Br md 7.60 Dpth 4.00 Welded, 1 dk	**(B11B2FV) Fishing Vessel** Ins: 194	**1 oil engine** geared to sc. shaft driving 1 FP propeller Total Power: 441kW (600hp) Chinese Std. Type 1 x 4 Stroke 8 Cy. 300 x 380 441kW (600bhp) Zibo Diesel Engine Factory-China AuxGen: 2 x 90kW 400V a.c	12.0kn 8300
8843587 *BYNB6* -	**YUAN YU 629** **Zhanjiang Marine Fisheries Co** - *Zhanjiang, Guangdong* China	286 86 140	Class: (CC)	**1979 Guangzhou Fishing Vessel Shipyard — Guangzhou GD** Loa 44.38 Br ex - Dght 3.270 Lbp 38.00 Br md 7.60 Dpth 4.00 Welded, 1 dk	**(B11B2FV) Fishing Vessel** Ins: 194	**1 oil engine** geared to sc. shaft driving 1 FP propeller Total Power: 441kW (600hp) Chinese Std. Type 1 x 4 Stroke 8 Cy. 300 x 380 441kW (600bhp) Zibo Diesel Engine Factory-China AuxGen: 2 x 90kW 400V a.c	12.0kn 8300
8843599 *BYNB7* -	**YUAN YU 630** **Zhanjiang Marine Fisheries Co** - *Zhanjiang, Guangdong* China	286 86 140	Class: (CC)	**1979 Guangzhou Fishing Vessel Shipyard — Guangzhou GD** Loa 44.86 Br ex - Dght 3.270 Lbp 38.00 Br md 7.60 Dpth 4.00 Welded, 1 dk	**(B11B2FV) Fishing Vessel** Ins: 194	**1 oil engine** geared to sc. shaft driving 1 FP propeller Total Power: 441kW (600hp) Chinese Std. Type 1 x 4 Stroke 8 Cy. 300 x 380 441kW (600bhp) Zibo Diesel Engine Factory-China AuxGen: 2 x 90kW 400V a.c	12.0kn 8300
9051129 *BYTB7* -	**YUAN YU 635** **Zhanjiang Marine Fisheries Co** - *Zhanjiang, Guangdong* China	238 71 123	Class: (CC)	**1991 Dalian Fishing Vessel Co — Dalian LN** Loa 38.70 Br ex - Dght 2.800 Lbp 33.00 Br md 7.40 Dpth 3.70 Welded	**(B11B2FV) Fishing Vessel**	**1 oil engine** geared to sc. shaft driving 1 FP propeller Total Power: 324kW (441hp) Chinese Std. Type 1 x 4 Stroke 6 Cy. 300 x 380 324kW (441bhp) Dalian Fishing Vessel Co-China AuxGen: 2 x 50kW 400V a.c	12.0kn 6300
8116075 *BQAQ* -	**YUAN ZHI** *ex Em. Xanthos -1996 ex Filipinas -1994* **Xiamen Ocean Shipping Co (COSCO XIAMEN)** - SatCom: Inmarsat C 441235111 *Xiamen, Fujian* China MMSI: 412422000	21,392 10,288 29,932 T/cm 39.5	Class: (LR) (CC) (BV) ✠ Classed LR until 30/5/94	**1983-06 Aalborg Vaerft A/S — Aalborg** Yd No: 243 Loa 173.64 (BB) Br ex 26.50 Dght 10.621 Lbp 160.03 Br md 26.01 Dpth 14.23 Welded, 1 dk	**(A21A2BC) Bulk Carrier** Grain: 35,068 Compartments: 6 Ho, ER 6 Ha: (11.3 x 10.2)5 (12.7 x 10.2)ER Cranes: 2x20t,3x10t	**1 oil engine** driving 1 FP propeller Total Power: 9,600kW (13,052hp) B&W 1 x 2 Stroke 6 Cy. 670 x 1700 9600kW (13052bhp) Helsingor Vaerft A/S-Denmark AuxGen: 3 x 800kW 450V 60Hz a.c Fuel: 299.0 (d.f.) 1913.0 (r.f.)	13.3kn 6L67GFCA
9295191 *BOCC* -	**YUAN ZHI HAI** **COSCO Bulk Carrier Co Ltd (COSCO BULK)** - *Tianjin* China MMSI: 413115000	40,473 26,208 74,272 T/cm 67.0	Class: CC	**2005-10 Hudong-Zhonghua Shipbuilding (Group) Co Ltd — Shanghai** Yd No: H1341A Loa 225.00 (BB) Br ex - Dght 14.250 Lbp 217.00 Br md 32.26 Dpth 19.60 Welded, 1 dk	**(A21A2BC) Bulk Carrier** Grain: 91,717; Bale: 89,882 Compartments: 7 Ho, ER 7 Ha: 6 (14.6 x 15.0)ER (14.6 x 13.2)	**1 oil engine** driving 1 FP propeller Total Power: 11,300kW (15,363hp) MAN-B&W 1 x 2 Stroke 5 Cy. 600 x 2400 11300kW (15363bhp) Hudong Heavy Machinery Co Ltd-China AuxGen: 3 x 530kW 450V a.c	13.8kn 5S60MC-C

530981 ET04	**YUANDONG 007** **Far East Drilling & Blasting Ltd** Geo Sea NV SatCom: Inmarsat C 437062310 *Panama* Panama MMSI: 370623000 Official number: 3494309A	3,693 1,107 2,701	Class: BV (Class contemplated) IS	**2009-01 Ningbo Daxie Development Zone Shipyard Co Ltd — Ningbo ZJ** Yd No: NDX08-004 Loa 100.86 Br ex - Dght 3.900 Lbp 96.00 Br md 17.60 Dpth 6.50 Welded, 1 dk	**(B34T2QR) Work/Repair Vessel**	**2 oil engines** reduction geared to sc. shafts driving 2 Propellers Total Power: 2,646kW (3,598hp) 13.0kn Chinese Std. Type G6300ZC 2 x 4 Stroke 6 Cy. 300 x 380 each-1323kW (1799bhp) Ningbo CSI Power & Machinery GroupCo Ltd-China
282388 3FX	**YUANNING SEA** **Yuan Ning Hai Shipping Co Ltd** Qingdao Ocean Shipping Co Ltd (COSCO QINGDAO) *Panama* Panama MMSI: 357672000 Official number: 2978704C	30,881 18,188 55,500 T/cm 56.3	Class: CC (LR) ✠ Classed LR until 5/7/13	**2004-03 Nantong COSCO KHI Ship Engineering Co Ltd (NACKS) — Nantong JS** Yd No: 018 Loa 189.90 (BB) Br ex 32.31 Dght 12.500 Lbp 185.00 Br md 32.26 Dpth 17.80 Welded, 1 dk	**(A21A2BC) Bulk Carrier** Grain: 69,452; Bale: 66,966 Compartments: 5 Ho, ER 5 Ha: 4 (20.0 x 18.6)ER (18.0 x 18.6) Cranes: 4x30t	**1 oil engine** driving 1 FP propeller Total Power: 8,200kW (11,149hp) 14.6kn B&W 6S50MC-C 1 x 2 Stroke 6 Cy. 500 x 2000 8200kW (11149bhp) Hudong Heavy Machinery Co Ltd-China AuxGen: 3 x 525kW 450V 60Hz a.c Boilers: AuxB (Comp) 7.7kgf/cm² (7.6bar) Fuel: 146.5 (d.f.) 1712.8 (r.f.)
282390 3SA	**YUANPING SEA** **Yuan Ping Hai Shipping Co Ltd** Qingdao Ocean Shipping Co Ltd (COSCO QINGDAO) *Panama* Panama MMSI: 354405000 Official number: 2995104C	30,881 18,188 55,500 T/cm 56.3	Class: CC (LR) ✠ Classed LR until 31/7/13	**2004-03 Nantong COSCO KHI Ship Engineering Co Ltd (NACKS) — Nantong JS** Yd No: 019 Loa 189.90 (BB) Br ex 32.31 Dght 12.500 Lbp 185.00 Br md 32.26 Dpth 17.80 Welded, 1 dk	**(A21A2BC) Bulk Carrier** Grain: 69,452; Bale: 66,966 Compartments: 5 Ho, ER 5 Ha: 4 (20.0 x 18.6)ER (18.0 x 18.6) Cranes: 4x30t	**1 oil engine** driving 1 FP propeller Total Power: 8,200kW (11,149hp) 14.6kn B&W 6S50MC-C 1 x 2 Stroke 6 Cy. 500 x 2000 8200kW (11149bhp) Hudong Heavy Machinery Co Ltd-China AuxGen: 3 x 525kW 450V 60Hz a.c Boilers: AuxB (Comp) 7.7kgf/cm² (7.6bar) Fuel: 146.5 (d.f.) 1712.0 (r.f.)
514447 ESB	**YUBARI** **Government of Japan (Ministry of Land, Infrastructure & Transport) (The Coastguard)** - *Tokyo* Japan MMSI: 431800066 Official number: 127696	*329* - -		**1985-11 Usuki Iron Works Co Ltd — Usuki OT** Yd No: 1547 Loa 67.80 Br ex 7.92 Dght 2.800 Lbp 63.00 Br md 7.90 Dpth 4.40 Welded, 1 dk	**(B34H2SQ) Patrol Vessel**	**2 oil engines** driving 2 CP propellers Total Power: 2,206kW (3,000hp) Niigata 6M31AFTE 2 x 4 Stroke 6 Cy. 310 x 530 each-1103kW (1500bhp) Niigata Engineering Co Ltd-Japan
232042 HKR	**YUBILEYNYY** **Ust-Khayryuzovskiy Fish Cannery Plant (Ust-Khayryuzovskiy Rybokonservnyy Zavod)** - *Petropavlovsk-Kamchatskiy* Russia	172 51 94	Class: RS	**1972 Zavod 'Nikolayevsk-na-Amure' — Nikolayevsk-na-Amure** Yd No: 68 Loa 33.96 Br ex 7.09 Dght 2.899 Lbp 29.97 Br md - Dpth 3.69 Welded, 1 dk	**(B11B2FV) Fishing Vessel** Bale: 115 Compartments: 1 Ho, ER 1 Ha: (1.6 x 1.3) Derricks: 2x2t Ice Capable	**1 oil engine** driving 1 FP propeller Total Power: 224kW (305hp) 9.5kn S.K.L. 8NVD36-1U 1 x 4 Stroke 8 Cy. 240 x 360 224kW (305bhp) VEB Schwermaschinenbau "KarlLiebknecht" (SKL)-Magdeburg AuxGen: 1 x 75kW, 1 x 50kW, 1 x 28kW Fuel: 24.0 (d.f.)
727654	**YUBILEYNYY** **Nikolayev Commercial Sea Port** - *Nikolayev* Ukraine Official number: 872355	106 31 14	Class: (RS)	**1988-01 Zavod "Krasnyy Moryak" — Rostov-na-Donu** Yd No: 30 Loa 23.15 Br ex 6.24 Dght 1.850 Lbp 20.00 Br md - Dpth 2.80 Welded, 1 dk	**(A37B2PS) Passenger Ship** Passengers: unberthed: 70 Ice Capable	**1 oil engine** geared to sc. shaft driving 1 FP propeller Total Power: 221kW (300hp) 9.0kn Daldizel 6CHNSP18/22 1 x 4 Stroke 6 Cy. 180 x 220 221kW (300bhp) Daldizel-Khabarovsk AuxGen: 1 x 16kW Fuel: 6.0 (d.f.)
412296	**YUCATA SPIRIT** *ex* Comox Argus *-2007* *ex* Weldwood Spirit *-1994* *ex* Lady Theresa *-1974* **Pacific Cachalot Ltd** - *Vancouver, BC* Canada Official number: 304783	*143* 38 -	Class: (LR) ✠ Classed LR until 22/11/74	**1963-03 Cook, Welton & Gemmell Ltd. — Beverley** Yd No: 984 Loa 28.61 Br ex 7.52 Dght 3.347 Lbp 25.91 Br md 7.32 Dpth 3.81 Welded, 1 dk	**(B32A2ST) Tug**	**1 oil engine** sr reverse geared to sc. shaft driving 1 FP propeller Total Power: 677kW (920hp) 11.0kn Ruston 7VEBCZM 1 x 4 Stroke 7 Cy. 260 x 368 677kW (920bhp) Ruston & Hornsby Ltd.-Lincoln Fuel: 20.5
069774 C6625	**YUCE STAR** *ex* Yeni Akdeniz *-1996* **Yuceer Tasimacilik Trz Sanayi Ticaret Ltd Sti** - *Mersin* Turkey Official number: 340	178 53 -		**1994-07 in Turkey** Loa 25.93 Br ex - Dght 2.360 Lbp - Br md 6.50 Dpth - Welded, 1 dk	**(A37B2PS) Passenger Ship**	**1 oil engine** driving 1 Propeller Total Power: 1,044kW (1,419hp) Cummins 1 x 4 Stroke 1044kW (1419bhp) Cummins Engine Co Inc-USA
659273	**YUDA** **PT Yuda Shipping** - *Samarinda* Indonesia	242 73 -	Class: KI	**2011-07 PT Mangkupalas Mitra Makmur — Samarinda** Loa 29.50 Br ex - Dght 2.800 Lbp 27.98 Br md 8.50 Dpth 3.75 Welded, 1 dk	**(B32A2ST) Tug**	**2 oil engines** reduction geared to sc. shafts driving 2 FP propellers AuxGen: 1 x 57kW 380V a.c
659223	**YUDA 01** **PT Yuda Shipping** - *Samarinda* Indonesia	116 35 -	Class: KI	**2011-08 PT Mangkupalas Mitra Makmur — Samarinda** Loa 21.75 Br ex - Dght 2.090 Lbp 20.44 Br md 6.50 Dpth 2.80 Welded, 1 dk	**(B32A2ST) Tug**	**2 oil engines** reduction geared to sc. shafts driving 2 FP propellers AuxGen: 2 x 35kW 380V a.c
658891	**YUDA 03** **PT Yuda Shipping** - *Samarinda* Indonesia	242 73 -	Class: KI	**2011-07 PT Mangkupalas Mitra Makmur — Samarinda** Loa 29.50 Br ex - Dght 2.800 Lbp 27.93 Br md 8.50 Dpth 3.75 Welded, 1 dk	**(B32A2ST) Tug**	**2 oil engines** reduction geared to sc. shafts driving 2 FP propellers AuxGen: 2 x 41kW 380V a.c
865339 K5191	**YUDAI MARU** - - *Fukuyama, Hiroshima* Japan MMSI: 431400049 Official number: 133048	*199* - 650		**1992-01 Sokooshi Zosen K.K. — Osakikamijima** Yd No: 315 L reg 54.10 Br ex - Dght 4.600 Lbp - Br md 9.30 Dpth 5.50 Welded, 1 dk	**(A31A2GX) General Cargo Ship**	**1 oil engine** driving 1 FP propeller Total Power: 736kW (1,001hp) Yanmar MF26-ST 1 x 4 Stroke 6 Cy. 260 x 500 736kW (1001bhp) Yanmar Diesel Engine Co Ltd-Japan
657017	**YUDDY 01** **PT Barokah Gemilang Perkasa** - *Samarinda* Indonesia Official number: 4384/lik	236 71 -	Class: KI	**2010-06 PT Bunga Nusa Mahakam — Samarinda** Yd No: 011 Loa 28.64 Br ex 8.20 Dght 3.050 Lbp 26.40 Br md - Dpth 3.60 Welded, 1 dk	**(B32A2ST) Tug**	**2 oil engines** reduction geared to sc. shafts driving 2 FP propellers Total Power: 1,220kW (1,658hp) Yanmar 6AYM-ETE 2 x 4 Stroke 6 Cy. 155 x 180 each-610kW (829bhp) Yanmar Diesel Engine Co Ltd-Japan AuxGen: 2 x 41kW 380V a.c
519540 TVW	**YUE CHAO 5** *ex* Daiho Maru *-1996* *ex* Ruo Xing *-2003* *ex* Daiho Maru *-2001* *ex* Asaka Maru *-1998* **Raoping Zhishan Aquiculture Co Ltd** - SatCom: Inmarsat C 441219376 *Shantou, Guangdong* China	*496* 150 685	Class: CC	**1986-03 Yamanaka Zosen K.K. — Imabari** Yd No: 322 Converted From: Chemical Tanker-2002 Loa 52.63 (BB) Br ex - Dght 3.898 Lbp 47.60 Br md 9.01 Dpth 4.22 Welded, 1 dk	**(B12B2FC) Fish Carrier**	**1 oil engine** with clutches, flexible couplings & sr reverse geared to sc. shaft driving 1 FP propeller Total Power: 588kW (799hp) Daihatsu 6DLM-20S 1 x 4 Stroke 6 Cy. 200 x 260 588kW (799bhp) Daihatsu Diesel Manufacturing Co Lt-Japan
905347	**YUE CHENG** *ex* Tokujin Maru No. 3 *-2003* - - -	1,489 812 1,500	Class: UB	**1989-09 K.K. Matsuura Zosensho — Osakikamijima** Yd No: 366 Loa 75.97 (BB) Br ex 12.02 Dght 4.160 Lbp 70.00 Br md 12.00 Dpth 7.20 Welded, 2 dks	**(A31A2GX) General Cargo Ship** Grain: 2,617 Compartments: 1 Ho, ER 1 Ha: ER	**1 oil engine** geared to sc. shaft driving 1 FP propeller Total Power: 736kW (1,001hp) Hanshin 6EL30G 1 x 4 Stroke 6 Cy. 300 x 600 736kW (1001bhp) The Hanshin Diesel Works Ltd-Japan Thrusters: 1 Thwart. FP thruster (f)
322451 RBS2	**YUE CHI** **Yue Chi Shipping SA** China Shipping Tanker Co Ltd *Hong Kong* Hong Kong MMSI: 477105700 Official number: HK-1670	26,967 11,381 42,053 T/cm 51.4	Class: CC	**2006-03 Guangzhou Shipyard International Co Ltd — Guangzhou GD** Yd No: 04130006 Loa 187.80 (BB) Br ex 31.53 Dght 11.540 Lbp 178.00 Br md 31.50 Dpth 16.80 Welded, 1 dk	**(A13B2TP) Products Tanker** Double Hull (13F) Liq: 44,646; Liq (Oil): 79,213 Cargo Heating Coils Compartments: 12 Wing Ta, 2 Wing Slop Ta, ER 3 Cargo Pump (s): 3x1200m³/hr Manifold: Bow/CM: 94.6m Ice Capable	**1 oil engine** driving 1 FP propeller Total Power: 8,580kW (11,665hp) 14.5kn MAN-B&W 6S50MC 1 x 2 Stroke 6 Cy. 500 x 1910 8580kW (11665bhp) (made 2005) Dalian Marine Diesel Works-China Fuel: 94.0 (d.f.) 1412.0 (r.f.)

IMO / Call sign	Name / Owner	Tonnage	Class	Builder / Dimensions	Type / Cargo	Machinery
9277931 *BXHM* -	**YUE DAO JUN 1** **Guangdong Waterway Bureau** - *Guangzhou, Guangdong* *China* MMSI: 412465470	**2,270** 681 2,074	Class: CC	**2002-08 Guangzhou Wenchong Shipyard Co Ltd — Guangzhou GD** Yd No: 302 Loa 79.30 Br ex - Dght 4.300 Lbp 70.00 Br md 14.00 Dpth 5.30 Welded, 1 dk	**(B33B2DT) Trailing Suction Hopper Dredger** Hopper: 1,400 Compartments: 1 Ho, ER 1 Ha: ER (24.5 x 8.8)	**2 oil engines** geared to sc. shafts driving 2 Propellers Total Power: 2,400kW (3,264hp) 11.0k S.K.L. 6VD29/24AL- 2 x 4 Stroke 6 Cy. 240 x 290 each-1200kW (1632bhp) SKL Motoren u. Systemtechnik AG-Magdeburg AuxGen: 2 x 296kW 400V a.c, 1 x 640kW 400V a.c Thrusters: 1 Tunnel thruster (f)
8808367 *BRZD* -	**YUE DIAN 1** *ex* Markman *-2005* *ex* Maersk Tapah *-2000* *ex* Lago Bentene *-1990* *launched as* Lake Towada *-1989* **Guangdong Yudean Shipping Co Ltd** - *Shenzhen, Guangdong* *China* MMSI: 413225000	**36,858** 22,944 68,429 T/cm 65.2	Class: (CC) (BV) (NK)	**1989-03 Namura Shipbuilding Co Ltd — Imari SG** Yd No: 899 Loa 225.78 (BB) Br ex 32.24 Dght 13.202 Lbp 217.00 Br md 32.20 Dpth 18.20 Welded, 1 dk	**(A21A2BC) Bulk Carrier** Grain: 78,492 Compartments: 7 Ho, ER 7 Ha: (16.6 x 13.2) (16.6 x 14.9)5 (16.6 x 14.9)ER Cranes: 4x25t	**1 oil engine** driving 1 FP propeller Total Power: 10,200kW (13,868hp) 14.0k Sulzer 6RTA6 1 x 2 Stroke 6 Cy. 620 x 2150 10200kW (13868bhp) Mitsubishi Heavy Industries Ltd-Japan AuxGen: 3 x 460kW 450V 60Hz a.c Fuel: 182.2 (d.f.) 2113.3 (r.f.) 26.2pd
9077240 *BRWL* -	**YUE DIAN 2** *ex* Esperis P *-2007* *ex* Pacific Nova *-1997* **Guangdong Yudean Shipping Co Ltd** - *Shenzhen, Guangdong* *China* MMSI: 413461340	**36,559** 23,279 70,182 T/cm 65.0	Class: CC (NK)	**1994-07 Sumitomo Heavy Industries Ltd. — Oppama Shipyard, Yokosuka** Yd No: 1194 Loa 225.00 (BB) Br ex - Dght 13.268 Lbp 218.00 Br md 32.26 Dpth 18.30 Welded, 1 dk	**(A21A2BC) Bulk Carrier** Grain: 81,839; Bale: 78,529 Compartments: 7 Ho, ER 7 Ha: (16.7 x 13.4)6 (16.7 x 15.0)ER	**1 oil engine** driving 1 FP propeller Total Power: 8,827kW (12,001hp) 14.0kr Sulzer 6RTA62 1 x 2 Stroke 6 Cy. 620 x 2150 8827kW (12001bhp) Diesel United Ltd.-Aioi AuxGen: 4 x 335kW a.c
8900488 *BTPT* -	**YUE DIAN 3** *ex* Ourania Hope *-2007* *ex* Imperial *-2005* *ex* Santa Margarita *-1994* *ex* Opal *-1991* **Guangdong Yudean Shipping Co Ltd** TOSCO KEYMAX International Ship Management Co Ltd *Shenzhen, Guangdong* *China* MMSI: 413308000	**36,120** 23,035 68,676 T/cm 64.2	Class: CS (CC) (NV)	**1989-10 Sasebo Heavy Industries Co. Ltd. — Sasebo Yard, Sasebo** Yd No: 374 Loa 224.00 (BB) Br ex 32.24 Dght 13.292 Lbp 215.02 Br md 32.21 Dpth 18.22 Welded, 1 dk	**(A21A2BC) Bulk Carrier** Grain: 81,337 Compartments: 7 Ho, ER 7 Ha: (14.4 x 12.8)6 (17.6 x 14.4)ER	**1 oil engine** driving 1 FP propeller Total Power: 7,200kW (9,789hp) 14.5kr Sulzer 5RTA62 1 x 2 Stroke 5 Cy. 620 x 2150 7200kW (9789bhp) Diesel United Ltd.-Aioi AuxGen: 3 x 450kW 440V 60Hz a.c
9061576 *BRWN* -	**YUE DIAN 4** *ex* Yerotsakos *-2008* *ex* White Diamond *-2006* *ex* Sea Diamond *-2002* **Guangdong Yudean Shipping Co Ltd** - *Shenzhen, Guangdong* *China* MMSI: 413335000	**35,874** 23,407 69,220 T/cm 64.4	Class: (CC) (NK)	**1993-07 Imabari Shipbuilding Co Ltd — Marugame KG (Marugame Shipyard)** Yd No: 1209 Loa 224.98 (BB) Br ex - Dght 13.278 Lbp 215.00 Br md 32.20 Dpth 18.30 Welded, 1 dk	**(A21A2BC) Bulk Carrier** Grain: 82,025 Compartments: 7 Ho, ER 7 Ha: (13.0 x 12.8)3 (17.9 x 14.4) (16.3 x 14.4) (17.3 x 14.4) (14.7 x 14.4)ER	**1 oil engine** driving 1 FP propeller Total Power: 8,827kW (12,001hp) 14.5kn Sulzer 6RTA62 1 x 2 Stroke 6 Cy. 620 x 2150 8827kW (12001bhp) Mitsubishi Heavy Industries Ltd-Japan
9086045 *BRWO* -	**YUE DIAN 6** *ex* Waikiki *-2008* *ex* Giuseppe d'Amato *-2005* **Guangdong Yudean Shipping Co Ltd** - *Shenzhen, Guangdong* *China* MMSI: 413375000	**39,385** 24,519 75,473 T/cm 67.8	Class: CC (BV) (RI)	**1995-04 Fincantieri-Cant. Nav. Italiani S.p.A. (Breda) — Venezia** Yd No: 5946 Loa 225.00 Br ex 32.60 Dght 14.332 Lbp 221.00 Br md 32.24 Dpth 19.70 Welded, 1 dk	**(A21A2BC) Bulk Carrier** Grain: 85,158 Compartments: 7 Ho, ER 7 Ha: (16.2 x 11.6)6 (16.2 x 14.6)ER	**1 oil engine** driving 1 FP propeller Total Power: 11,000kW (14,956hp) 15.0kn Sulzer 5RTA62U 1 x 2 Stroke 5 Cy. 620 x 2150 11000kW (14956bhp) Fincantieri Cantieri NavaliItaliani SpA-Italy AuxGen: 1 x 650kW 440V 60Hz a.c, 2 x 650kW 440V 60Hz a.c Fuel: 230.0 (d.f.) 2160.0 (r.f.) 32.0pd
9084580 *BRWI* -	**YUE DIAN 7** *ex* Solana *-2008* *ex* Linda Oldendorff *-2006* **Guangdong Yudean Shipping Co Ltd** - *Shenzhen, Guangdong* *China* MMSI: 412470870	**39,279** 24,360 75,275 T/cm 67.8	Class: (LR) (CC) (BV) (NV) ✠ Classed LR until 10/3/08	**1995-07 B&W Skibsvaerft A/S — Copenhagen** Yd No: 953 Loa 225.00 Br ex - Dght 14.310 Lbp 221.00 Br md 32.24 Dpth 19.70 Welded, 1 dk	**(A21A2BC) Bulk Carrier** Grain: 85,158 Compartments: 7 Ho, ER 7 Ha: (16.2 x 11.2)6 (16.2 x 14.6)ER	**1 oil engine** driving 1 FP propeller Total Power: 11,100kW (15,092hp) 14.0kn Sulzer 5RTA62U 1 x 2 Stroke 5 Cy. 620 x 2150 11100kW (15092bhp) Korea Heavy Industries & ConstrCo Ltd (HANJUNG)-South Korea AuxGen: 3 x 560kW 440V 60Hz a.c Fuel: 396.0 (d.f.) 2007.0 (r.f.) 35.9pd
9154098 *BYAO* -	**YUE DIAN 8** *ex* Etoile *-2009* *ex* Brave NV *-2009* *ex* Denak-A *-2006* *ex* Ohshima *-2002* *ex* Ohshima Maru *-1998* **Guangdong Yudean Shipping Co Ltd** - *Shenzhen, Guangdong* *China* MMSI: 412543000	**37,881** 23,528 72,424 T/cm 66.9	Class: CC (BV) (NK)	**1997-04 Sasebo Heavy Industries Co. Ltd. — Sasebo Yard, Sasebo** Yd No: 422 Loa 225.00 Br ex - Dght 13.521 Lbp 218.70 Br md 32.20 Dpth 18.70 Welded, 1 dk	**(A21A2BC) Bulk Carrier** Grain: 84,790 Compartments: 7 Ho, ER 7 Ha: (15.3 x 12.8)6 (17.0 x 14.4)ER	**1 oil engine** driving 1 FP propeller Total Power: 8,827kW (12,001hp) 14.5kn B&W 6S60MC 1 x 2 Stroke 6 Cy. 600 x 2292 8827kW (12001bhp) Mitsui Engineering & Shipbuilding CLtd-Japan AuxGen: 3 x 400kW 450V a.c Fuel: 75.0 (d.f.) 2341.0 (r.f.) 31.6pd
9082922 *BOLF* -	**YUE DIAN 9** *ex* Eastern Queen *-2012* **Guangdong Yudean Shipping Co Ltd** - *Shenjiamen, Zhejiang* *China* MMSI: 412569000	**37,550** 23,075 70,196 T/cm 65.5	Class: CC (LR) (KR) ✠ Classed LR until 2/8/05	**1994-07 Daewoo Shipbuilding & Heavy Machinery Ltd — Geoje** Yd No: 1089 Loa 225.00 (BB) Br ex 32.24 Dght 13.318 Lbp 215.00 Br md 32.20 Dpth 18.50 Welded, 1 dk	**(A21A2BC) Bulk Carrier** Grain: 82,210; Bale: 78,338 Compartments: 7 Ho, ER 7 Ha: 7 (16.6 x 14.9)ER Ice Capable	**1 oil engine** driving 1 FP propeller Total Power: 8,561kW (11,640hp) 13.8kn B&W 6S50MC 1 x 2 Stroke 6 Cy. 500 x 1910 8561kW (11640bhp) Hyundai Heavy Industries Co Ltd-South Korea AuxGen: 3 x 500kW 450V a.c Boilers: e (ex.g.) 10.0kgf/cm² (9.8bar), AuxB (o.f.) 7.0kgf/cm² (6.9bar)
9475521 *BYAU* -	**YUE DIAN 51** **Guangdong Yudean Shipping Co Ltd** - *Shenzhen, Guangdong* *China* MMSI: 412565000	**32,911** 19,156 57,020 T/cm 58.8	Class: CC	**2010-02 Jinling Shipyard — Nanjing JS** Yd No: JLZ070450 Loa 189.99 (BB) Br ex - Dght 12.800 Lbp 185.00 Br md 32.26 Dpth 18.00 Welded, 1 dk	**(A21A2BC) Bulk Carrier** Grain: 71,634; Bale: 68,200 Compartments: 5 Ho, ER 5 Ha: 4 (21.3 x 21.6)ER (18.9 x 19.2) Cranes: 4x30t	**1 oil engine** driving 1 FP propeller Total Power: 9,480kW (12,889hp) 14.2kn MAN-B&W 6S50MC-C 1 x 2 Stroke 6 Cy. 500 x 2000 9480kW (12889bhp) STX (Dalian) Engine Co Ltd-China AuxGen: 3 x 600kW 450V a.c
9475533 *BYDA* -	**YUE DIAN 52** **Guangdong Yudean Shipping Co Ltd** - *Shenzhen, Guangdong* *China* MMSI: 412607000	**32,911** 19,156 57,009 T/cm 58.8	Class: CC	**2010-03 Jinling Shipyard — Nanjing JS** Yd No: JLZ070451 Loa 189.99 (BB) Br ex - Dght 12.800 Lbp 185.00 Br md 32.26 Dpth 18.00 Welded, 1 dk	**(A21A2BC) Bulk Carrier** Grain: 71,634; Bale: 68,200 Compartments: 5 Ho, ER 5 Ha: 4 (21.3 x 21.6)ER (18.9 x 19.2) Cranes: 4x30t	**1 oil engine** driving 1 FP propeller Total Power: 9,480kW (12,889hp) 14.2kn MAN-B&W 6S50MC-C 1 x 2 Stroke 6 Cy. 500 x 2000 9480kW (12889bhp) STX (Dalian) Engine Co Ltd-China AuxGen: 3 x 600kW 450V a.c
9475545 *BYDU* -	**YUE DIAN 53** **Guangdong Yudean Shipping Co Ltd** - SatCom: Inmarsat C 441260211 *Shenzhen, Guangdong* *China* MMSI: 412602000	**32,911** 19,156 56,970 T/cm 58.8	Class: CC	**2010-04 Jinling Shipyard — Nanjing JS** Yd No: JLZ070452 Loa 189.99 (BB) Br ex - Dght 12.800 Lbp 185.00 Br md 32.26 Dpth 18.00 Welded, 1 dk	**(A21A2BC) Bulk Carrier** Grain: 71,634; Bale: 68,200 Compartments: 5 Ho, ER 5 Ha: 4 (21.3 x 18.3)ER (18.9 x 18.3) Cranes: 4x30t	**1 oil engine** driving 1 FP propeller Total Power: 9,320kW (12,671hp) 14.2kn MAN-B&W 6S50MC-C 1 x 2 Stroke 6 Cy. 500 x 2000 9320kW (12671bhp) STX (Dalian) Engine Co Ltd-China AuxGen: 3 x 600kW 450V a.c
9475557 *BYDV* -	**YUE DIAN 54** **Guangdong Yudean Shipping Co Ltd** - SatCom: Inmarsat C 441275510 *Shenzhen, Guangdong* *China* MMSI: 412755000	**32,911** 19,156 56,932 T/cm 58.8	Class: CC	**2010-06 Jinling Shipyard — Nanjing JS** Yd No: JLZ070453 Loa 189.99 (BB) Br ex - Dght 12.800 Lbp 185.00 Br md 32.26 Dpth 18.00 Welded, 1 dk	**(A21A2BC) Bulk Carrier** Grain: 71,634; Bale: 68,200 Compartments: 5 Ho, ER 5 Ha: 4 (21.3 x 21.6)ER (18.9 x 19.2) Cranes: 4x30t	**1 oil engine** driving 1 FP propeller Total Power: 9,480kW (12,889hp) 14.2kn MAN-B&W 6S50MC-C 1 x 2 Stroke 6 Cy. 500 x 2000 9480kW (12889bhp) STX (Dalian) Engine Co Ltd-China AuxGen: 3 x 600kW 450V a.c
9475569 *BYDP* -	**YUE DIAN 55** **Guangdong Yudean Shipping Co Ltd** - *Shenzhen, Guangdong* *China* MMSI: 413465310	**32,884** 19,156 57,037 T/cm 58.8	Class: CC	**2010-07 Jinling Shipyard — Nanjing JS** Yd No: JLZ070454 Loa 189.99 (BB) Br ex - Dght 12.800 Lbp 185.00 Br md 32.26 Dpth 18.00 Welded, 1 dk	**(A21A2BC) Bulk Carrier** Grain: 71,634; Bale: 68,200 Compartments: 5 Ho, ER 5 Ha: 4 (21.3 x 18.3)ER (18.9 x 18.3)	**1 oil engine** driving 1 FP propeller Total Power: 9,480kW (12,889hp) 14.2kn MAN-B&W 6S50MC-C 1 x 2 Stroke 6 Cy. 500 x 2000 9480kW (12889bhp) STX (Dalian) Engine Co Ltd-China AuxGen: 3 x 600kW 450V a.c
9475571 *BYFD* -	**YUE DIAN 56** **Guangdong Yudean Shipping Co Ltd** - *Shenzhen, Guangdong* *China* MMSI: 413465580	**32,884** 19,156 56,987 T/cm 58.8	Class: CC	**2010-09 Jinling Shipyard — Nanjing JS** Yd No: JLZ070455 Loa 189.99 (BB) Br ex - Dght 12.800 Lbp 185.00 Br md 32.26 Dpth 18.00 Welded, 1 dk	**(A21A2BC) Bulk Carrier** Grain: 71,634; Bale: 68,200 Compartments: 5 Ho, ER 5 Ha: 4 (21.3 x 21.6)ER (18.9 x 19.2)	**1 oil engine** driving 1 FP propeller Total Power: 9,480kW (12,889hp) 14.2kn MAN-B&W 6S50MC-C 1 x 2 Stroke 6 Cy. 500 x 2000 9480kW (12889bhp) STX (Dalian) Engine Co Ltd-China AuxGen: 3 x 600kW 450V a.c
9475583 *BYFG* -	**YUE DIAN 57** **Guangdong Yudean Shipping Co Ltd** - SatCom: Inmarsat C 441301649 *Shenzhen, Guangdong* *China* MMSI: 413466390	**32,969** 19,156 56,692 T/cm 58.8	Class: CC	**2011-01 Jinling Shipyard — Nanjing JS** Yd No: JLZ070456 Loa 189.99 (BB) Br ex - Dght 12.800 Lbp 185.00 Br md 32.26 Dpth 18.00 Welded, 1 dk	**(A21A2BC) Bulk Carrier** Grain: 71,634; Bale: 68,200 Compartments: 5 Ho, ER 5 Ha: 4 (21.3 x 21.6)ER (18.9 x 19.2) Cranes: 4x30t	**1 oil engine** driving 1 FP propeller Total Power: 9,480kW (12,889hp) 14.2kn MAN-B&W 6S50MC-C 1 x 2 Stroke 6 Cy. 500 x 2000 9480kW (12889bhp) STX (Dalian) Engine Co Ltd-China AuxGen: 3 x 600kW 450V a.c Fuel: 2400.0

IMO / Call sign	Name / Owner	Tonnage	Class	Builder / Dimensions	Type / Capacity	Machinery
475595 YFE	**YUE DIAN 58** **Guangdong Yudean Shipping Co Ltd** - SatCom: Inmarsat C 441400810 *Shenzhen, Guangdong* *China* MMSI: 414008000	**32,969** 19,156 56,711 T/cm 58.8	Class: CC	**2011-01 Jinling Shipyard — Nanjing JS** Yd No: JLZ070457 Loa 189.99 (BB) Br ex - Dght 12.800 Lbp 185.00 Br md 32.26 Dpth 18.00 Welded, 1 dk	**(A21A2BC) Bulk Carrier** Grain: 71,634; Bale: 68,200 Compartments: 5 Ho, ER 5 Ha: 4 (21.3 x 21.6)ER (18.9 x 19.2) Cranes: 4x30t	**1 oil engine** driving 1 FP propeller Total Power: 9,320kW (12,671hp) 14.2kn MAN-B&W 6S50MC-C 1 x 2 Stroke 6 Cy. 500 x 2000 9320kW (12671bhp) STX (Dalian) Engine Co Ltd-China AuxGen: 3 x 600kW 450V a.c Fuel: 2400.0
592874 BYFT	**YUE DIAN 59** **Guangdong Yudean Shipping Co Ltd** - *Shenzhen, Guangdong* *China* MMSI: 413466860	**32,969** 19,156 56,689 T/cm 58.8	Class: CC	**2011-05 Jinling Shipyard — Nanjing JS** Yd No: JLZ9100407 Loa 189.99 (BB) Br ex - Dght 12.800 Lbp 185.00 Br md 32.26 Dpth 18.00 Welded, 1 dk	**(A21A2BC) Bulk Carrier** Grain: 71,634; Bale: 68,200 Compartments: 5 Ho, ER 5 Ha: 4 (21.3 x 21.6)ER (18.9 x 19.2) Cranes: 4x30t	**1 oil engine** driving 1 FP propeller Total Power: 9,320kW (12,671hp) 14.2kn MAN-B&W 6S50MC-C 1 x 2 Stroke 6 Cy. 500 x 2000 9320kW (12671bhp) Yichang Marine Diesel Engine Co Ltd-China AuxGen: 3 x 600kW 450V a.c
9161041 VRDP6 -	**YUE DIAN 81** *ex* Yue Dian 5 *-2009* *ex* Captain D. Gregos *-2008* *ex* Ocean Argus *-2006* *ex* Global Fortune *-2004* **UHI Oriental Energy Transportation Ltd** - SatCom: Inmarsat C 447701158 *Hong Kong* *Hong Kong* MMSI: 477047300 Official number: HK-2068	**35,905** 23,407 69,091 T/cm 64.4	Class: CC (BV) (NK)	**1997-02 Koyo Dockyard Co Ltd — Mihara HS** Yd No: 2077 Loa 224.98 (BB) Br ex - Dght 13.298 Lbp 215.00 Br md 32.20 Dpth 18.30 Welded, 1 dk	**(A21A2BC) Bulk Carrier** Grain: 82,025 Compartments: 7 Ho, ER 7 Ha: 4 (17.9 x 14.4) (13.0 x 12.8) (16.3 x 14.4) (14.7 x 14.4)ER	**1 oil engine** driving 1 FP propeller Total Power: 11,400kW (15,499hp) 14.8kn Sulzer 6RTA62 1 x 2 Stroke 6 Cy. 620 x 2150 11400kW (15499bhp) Diesel United Ltd.-Aioi
9085936 V7NZ4 -	**YUE DIAN 82** *ex* Richmond *-2009* *ex* Giovanni Bottiglieri *-2007* **UHI Ocean Transportation Ltd** TOSCO KEYMAX International Ship Management Co Ltd *Majuro* *Marshall Islands* MMSI: 538003042 Official number: 3042	**39,385** 24,519 75,473 T/cm 68.4	Class: LR (RI) (BV) **100A1** SS 05/2010 bulk carrier strengthened for heavy cargoes, Nos. 2, 4 & 6 holds may be empty ESP ESN Hold No. 1 LI **LMC**	**1995-05 B&W Skibsvaerft A/S — Copenhagen** Yd No: 952 Loa 225.00 Br ex 32.50 Dght 14.330 Lbp 221.00 Br md 32.24 Dpth 19.70 Welded, 1 dk	**(A21A2BC) Bulk Carrier** Grain: 85,158 Compartments: 7 Ho, ER 7 Ha: (16.2 x 11.2)6 (16.2 x 14.6)ER	**1 oil engine** driving 1 FP propeller Total Power: 10,813kW (14,701hp) 14.5kn Sulzer 5RTA62U 1 x 2 Stroke 5 Cy. 620 x 2150 10813kW (14701bhp) Korea Heavy Industries & ConstrCo Ltd (HANJUNG)-South Korea AuxGen: 3 x 600kW 440/220V 60Hz a.c
9553775 VRHN8 -	**YUE DIAN 83** **UHI Energy Transportation Ltd** - SatCom: Inmarsat C 447701860 *Hong Kong* *Hong Kong* MMSI: 477962600 Official number: HK-2888	**47,984** 27,675 87,329	Class: LR ✠ **100A1** SS 11/2010 bulk carrier CSR BC-A GRAB (20) Nos. 2, 4 & 6 holds may be empty ESP **ShipRight** (CM) *IWS LI ✠ **LMC** **UMS** Eq.Ltr: E; Cable: 687.7/84.0 U3 (a)	**2010-11 Hudong-Zhonghua Shipbuilding (Group) Co Ltd — Shanghai** Yd No: H1550A Loa 229.00 (BB) Br ex 36.84 Dght 14.200 Lbp 221.00 Br md 36.80 Dpth 19.00 Welded, 1 dk	**(A21A2BC) Bulk Carrier** Grain: 100,097 Compartments: 7 Ho, ER 7 Ha: ER	**1 oil engine** driving 1 FP propeller Total Power: 10,500kW (14,276hp) 14.5kn Wartsila 6RT-flex58T 1 x 2 Stroke 6 Cy. 580 x 2416 10500kW (14276bhp) Hudong Heavy Machinery Co Ltd-China AuxGen: 3 x 600kW 440V 60Hz a.c Boilers: e (ex.g.) 12.2kgf/cm² (12.0bar), AuxB (o.f.) 9.2kgf/cm² (9.0bar)
9553787 VRHW8 -	**YUE DIAN 85** **UHI Marco Ocean Transportation Ltd** - SatCom: Inmarsat C 447701918 *Hong Kong* *Hong Kong* MMSI: 477387200 Official number: HK2961	**47,984** 27,675 87,000	Class: LR ✠ **100A1** SS 01/2011 bulk carrier CSR BC-A GRAB (20) Nos. 2, 4 & 6 holds may be empty ESP **ShipRight** (CM) *IWS LI ✠ **LMC** **UMS** Eq.Ltr: E; Cable: 687.7/84.0 U3 (a)	**2011-01 Hudong-Zhonghua Shipbuilding (Group) Co Ltd — Shanghai** Yd No: H1551A Loa 229.00 (BB) Br ex 36.84 Dght 14.200 Lbp 221.00 Br md 36.80 Dpth 19.90 Welded, 1 dk	**(A21A2BC) Bulk Carrier** Grain: 100,097 Compartments: 7 Ho, ER 7 Ha: ER	**1 oil engine** driving 1 FP propeller Total Power: 10,500kW (14,276hp) 14.5kn Wartsila 6RT-flex58T 1 x 2 Stroke 6 Cy. 580 x 2416 10500kW (14276bhp) Hudong Heavy Machinery Co Ltd-China AuxGen: 3 x 600kW 440V 60Hz a.c Boilers: AuxB (ex.g.) 12.2kgf/cm² (12.0bar), AuxB (o.f.) 9.2kgf/cm² (9.0bar)
9493597 BRNT -	**YUE DIAN 101** **Guangdong Yudean Shipping Co Ltd** - SatCom: Inmarsat C 441371710 *Shenzhen, Guangdong* *China* MMSI: 413717000	**51,158** 31,286 93,302 T/cm 80.9	Class: CC (AB)	**2009-05 Jiangsu Newyangzi Shipbuilding Co Ltd — Jingjiang JS** Yd No: YZJ2006-856 Loa 229.20 Br ex - Dght 14.900 Lbp 222.00 Br md 38.00 Dpth 20.70 Welded, 1 dk	**(A21A2BC) Bulk Carrier** Grain: 110,300 Compartments: 7 Ho, ER 7 Ha: 5 (17.9 x 17.0)ER 2 (15.3 x 14.6)	**1 oil engine** driving 1 FP propeller Total Power: 13,560kW (18,436hp) 14.1kn MAN-B&W 6S60MC-C 1 x 2 Stroke 6 Cy. 600 x 2400 13560kW (18436bhp) Doosan Engine Co Ltd-South Korea AuxGen: 3 x 730kW a.c
9615121 BOKC -	**YUE DIAN 102** **Guangdong Yudean Shipping Co Ltd** - *Shenzhen, Guangdong* *China* MMSI: 414043000	**64,654** 37,347 115,169	Class: CC	**2012-02 Shanghai Jiangnan Changxing Heavy Industry Co Ltd — Shanghai** Yd No: H1023A Loa 254.00 (BB) Br ex 43.06 Dght 14.500 Lbp 249.80 Br md 43.00 Dpth 20.80 Welded, 1 dk	**(A21A2BC) Bulk Carrier** Grain: 132,246 Compartments: 7 Ho, ER 7 Ha: (18.3 x 21.0)4 (19.2 x 21.0) (16.5 x 21.0)ER (14.6 x 18.0)	**1 oil engine** driving 1 FP propeller Total Power: 13,560kW (18,436hp) 14.3kn MAN-B&W 6S60MC-C8 1 x 2 Stroke 6 Cy. 600 x 2400 13560kW (18436bhp) Hudong Heavy Machinery Co Ltd-China
9615133 BOKE -	**YUE DIAN 103** **Bank of Communications Finance Leasing Co Ltd** Guangdong Yudean Shipping Co Ltd SatCom: Inmarsat C 441404410 *Shenzhen, Guangdong* *China* MMSI: 414044000	**64,654** 37,347 115,066	Class: CC	**2012-05 Shanghai Jiangnan Changxing Heavy Industry Co Ltd — Shanghai** Yd No: H1024A Loa 254.00 (BB) Br ex 43.06 Dght 14.500 Lbp 249.80 Br md 43.00 Dpth 20.80 Welded, 1 dk	**(A21A2BC) Bulk Carrier** Grain: 137,792; Bale: 132,246 Compartments: 7 Ho, ER 7 Ha: (18.3 x 21.0)4 (19.2 x 21.0) (16.5 x 21.0)ER (14.6 x 18.0)	**1 oil engine** driving 1 FP propeller Total Power: 13,560kW (18,436hp) 14.3kn MAN-B&W 6S60MC-C8 1 x 2 Stroke 6 Cy. 600 x 2400 13560kW (18436bhp) Hudong Heavy Machinery Co Ltd-China AuxGen: 3 x 720kW 450V a.c
8661355 - -	**YUE DONG GUAN CHUI 0102** **Qingyuan Tianli Transportation Co Ltd** - *Freetown* *Sierra Leone*	**624** 187 -		**1999-01 Qingyuan Qingcheng Yongli Shipyard — Qingyuan GD** Loa 38.30 Br ex 13.30 Dght - Lbp 34.20 Br md 12.80 Dpth 4.10 Welded, 1 dk	**(B33A2DU) Dredger (unspecified)**	**3 oil engines** reduction geared to sc. shafts driving 3 Propellers Total Power: 729kW (991hp) Cummins 1 x 4 Stroke 6 Cy. 140 x 152 133kW (181bhp) Chongqing Cummins Engine Co Ltd-China Cummins NTA-855-M 2 x 4 Stroke 6 Cy. 140 x 152 each-298kW (405bhp) Chongqing Cummins Engine Co Ltd-China
9093921 - -	**YUE DONG GUAN CHUI 0123** **Ye Jinquan & 2 Partners** Fuzhou Hailing Shipping Co Ltd *Dongguan, Guangdong* *China* Official number: 090204000051	**1,202** 673 -		**2004-03 in the People's Republic of China** Loa 66.80 Br ex - Dght - Lbp - Br md 14.00 Dpth 3.50 Welded, 1 dk	**(B34T2QR) Work/Repair Vessel**	**2 oil engines** geared to sc. shafts driving 2 Propellers Total Power: 1,356kW (1,844hp) Cummins KTA-19-M500 2 x 4 Stroke 6 Cy. 159 x 159 each-678kW (922bhp) Chongqing Cummins Engine Co Ltd-China
8661862 - -	**YUE DONG JIANG 678** **Hexin International Shipping Ltd** - *Dongguan, Guangdong* *China* Official number: 2009P5100174	**1,567** 877 -		**2009-04 Huizhou Tonghu Zhifa Industrial Co Ltd — Huizhou GD** Yd No: 118N Loa 68.80 Br ex - Dght - Lbp - Br md 16.00 Dpth 4.20 Welded, 1 dk	**(A24D2BA) Aggregates Carrier**	**1 oil engine** reduction geared to sc. shafts driving 1 FP propeller Total Power: 1,508kW (2,050hp) Cummins 1 x 1508kW (2050bhp) Cummins Engine Co Inc-USA
8967864 BWJQ -	**YUE GANG 168** **Fujian Longhai Second Shipping Co Ltd** - *Xiamen, Fujian* *China* Official number: 370210091	**562** 315 950		**1994-12 Dongfa Shipyard — Zhejiang Province** Loa 60.00 Br ex - Dght - Lbp 50.00 Br md 8.60 Dpth 4.50 Welded, 1 dk	**(A31A2GX) General Cargo Ship**	**1 oil engine** driving 1 FP propeller Total Power: 600kW (816hp)

IMO / Call sign / Flag	Name / Owner / Port	Tonnage	Class	Builder / Dimensions	Type / Cargo	Machinery
9202986 *BSZR* -	**YUE GONG TUO 38** *ex Big Fair 303 -2010* **The Second Engineering Company of CCCC Fourth Harbor Engineering Co Ltd** - *Guangzhou, Guangdong* *China*	**231** 69 498	Class: CC (BV)	**1999-04 Mawei Shipyard — Fuzhou FJ** Yd No: 139 Loa 28.80 Br ex 8.70 Dght 3.000 Lbp 26.10 Br md 8.40 Dpth 3.81 Welded, 1 dk	**(B32A2ST) Tug**	**2 oil engines** with clutches, flexible couplings & sr reverse geared to sc. shafts driving 2 FP propellers Total Power: 1,472kW (2,002hp) Cummins KTA-38-M 2 x Vee 4 Stroke 12 Cy. 159 x 159 each-736kW (1001bhp) (made 1997) Cummins Engine Co Ltd-United Kingdom AuxGen: 2 x 65kW 400V 50Hz a.c
9406245 *BSYZ* -	**YUE GONG TUO 68** **CCCC Fourth Harbor Engineering Co Ltd** - SatCom: Inmarsat C 441212719 *Guangzhou, Guangdong* *China* MMSI: 413053520	**1,435** 430 707	Class: CC	**2006-12 Guangzhou Hangtong Shipbuilding & Shipping Co Ltd — Jiangmen GD** Yd No: 052006 Loa 52.70 Br ex - Dght 4.500 Lbp 47.90 Br md 14.00 Dpth 6.20 Welded, 1 dk	**(B32A2ST) Tug**	**2 oil engines** reduction geared to sc. shafts driving 2 Propellers Total Power: 5,148kW (7,000hp) Yanmar 6N330-EN 2 x 4 Stroke 6 Cy. 330 x 440 each-2574kW (3500bhp) Qingdao Zichai Boyang Diesel EngineCo Ltd-China AuxGen: 3 x 400kW 400V a.c
9523158 *BRPC* -	**YUE GUAN FENG** **China Shipping Tanker Co Ltd** - *Shanghai* *China* MMSI: 412859000 Official number: 0010000221	**40,913** 25,963 75,566 T/cm 68.2	Class: CC	**2010-09 Jiangnan Shipyard (Group) Co Ltd — Shanghai** Yd No: H2467 Loa 225.00 (BB) Br ex - Dght 14.200 Lbp 217.00 Br md 32.26 Dpth 19.60 Welded, 1 dk	**(A21A2BC) Bulk Carrier** Grain: 90,068 Compartments: 7 Ho, ER 7 Ha: 6 (15.5 x 14.4)ER (15.5 x 13.2) Ice Capable	**1 oil engine** driving 1 FP propeller Total Power: 11,900kW (16,179hp) 14.5kn MAN-B&W 5S60ME-C 1 x 2 Stroke 5 Cy. 600 x 2400 11900kW (16179bhp) Hudong Heavy Machinery Co Ltd-China Fuel: 74.0 (d.f.) 1910.0 (r.f.)
8832203 *BLQK* -	**YUE HAI** **Zhoushan Tairong International Marine Co Ltd** - *Nanjing, Jiangsu* *China*	*299* 95 236	Class: (CC)	**1987 Wang Tak Engineering & Shipbuilding Co Ltd — Hong Kong** Loa 42.75 Br ex - Dght 2.850 Lbp 38.50 Br md 7.80 Dpth 3.60 Welded, 1 dk	**(A34A2GR) Refrigerated Cargo Ship** Ins: 244 Compartments: 2 Ho, ER 2 Ha: 2 (2.3 x 2.3)ER	**1 oil engine** driving 1 FP propeller Total Power: 588kW (799hp) 12.0kn Niigata 6MG20CX 1 x 4 Stroke 6 Cy. 200 x 260 588kW (799bhp) Niigata Engineering Co Ltd-Japan AuxGen: 3 x 80kW 380V a.c
8847351 - -	**YUE HAI 510** **Government of The People's Republic of China** - *China*	*607* 340 -		**1992 in the People's Republic of China** Loa - Br ex - Dght - Lbp - Br md - Dpth - Welded, 1 dk	**(A31A2GX) General Cargo Ship**	**1 oil engine** driving 1 FP propeller
8832198 - -	**YUE HAI CHUN** **Shenzhen Pengxing Shipping Co Ltd** - *Shekou, Guangdong* *China*	*134* 70 20	Class: (CC)	**1984 Afai Engineers & Shiprepairers Ltd — Hong Kong** Loa 22.07 Br ex - Dght - Lbp 19.34 Br md 8.73 Dpth 2.72 Welded, 1 dk	**(A37B2PS) Passenger Ship**	**2 oil engines** driving 2 FP propellers Total Power: 1,294kW (1,760hp) 25.0kn Isotta Fraschini ID36SS8V 2 x Vee 4 Stroke 8 Cy. 170 x 170 each-647kW (880bhp) Isotta Fraschini SpA-Italy AuxGen: 2 x 40kW 380V a.c
9255866 *BJSC* -	**YUE HAI TIE 1 HAO** **Yuehai Railway Co Ltd** - *Haikou, Hainan* *China* MMSI: 412522250	**14,381** 3,527 5,689	Class: CC	**2003-01 Jiangnan Shipyard (Group) Co Ltd — Shanghai** Yd No: H2279 Loa 165.40 (BB) Br ex - Dght 5.600 Lbp 156.00 Br md 22.60 Dpth 15.00 Welded	**(A36A2PT) Passenger/Ro-Ro Ship (Vehicles/Rail)** Passengers: unberthed: 1230; cabins: 18 Stern door (centre) Cars: 40, Trailers: 50, Rail Wagons: 40	**2 oil engines** geared to sc. shafts driving 2 CP propellers Total Power: 5,760kW (7,832hp) 15.2kn Wartsila 6L32 2 x 4 Stroke 6 Cy. 320 x 400 each-2880kW (3916bhp) Wartsila Finland Oy-Finland AuxGen: 2 x 1280kW a.c, 3 x 770kW 50Hz a.c Thrusters: 2 Thwart. CP thruster (f); 1 Thwart. CP thruster (a) Fuel: 165.0 (d.f.)
9274692 *BJSD* -	**YUE HAI TIE 2 HAO** **Yuehai Railway Co Ltd** - *Haikou, Hainan* *China* MMSI: 412522260	**14,381** 7,478 5,689	Class: CC	**2003-06 Jiangnan Shipyard (Group) Co Ltd — Shanghai** Yd No: H2280 Loa 165.40 (BB) Br ex - Dght 5.600 Lbp 156.00 Br md 22.60 Dpth 15.00 Welded	**(A36A2PT) Passenger/Ro-Ro Ship (Vehicles/Rail)** Passengers: unberthed: 1230; cabins: 18 Stern door (centre) Cars: 40, Trailers: 50, Rail Wagons: 40	**2 oil engines** geared to sc. shafts driving 2 CP propellers Total Power: 5,760kW (7,832hp) 15.2kn Wartsila 6L32 2 x 4 Stroke 6 Cy. 320 x 400 each-2880kW (3916bhp) Wartsila Finland Oy-Finland AuxGen: 2 x 1280kW a.c, 3 x 770kW 50Hz a.c Thrusters: 2 Thwart. CP thruster (f); 1 Thwart. CP thruster (a) Fuel: 165.0 (d.f.)
9633111 *BJSA* -	**YUE HAI TIE 3 HAO** **Yuehai Railway Co Ltd** - *Haikou, Hainan* *China* MMSI: 413521610	**23,217** - 6,557	Class: CC	**2011-01 Tianjin Xingang Shipbuilding Industry Co Ltd — Tianjin** Loa 188.00 (BB) Br ex - Dght 5.600 Lbp 178.00 Br md 23.00 Dpth 9.30 Welded, 1 dk	**(A36A2PT) Passenger/Ro-Ro Ship (Vehicles/Rail)** Passengers: 1508 Rail Wagons: 44	**2 oil engines** reduction geared to sc. shafts driving 2 CP propellers Total Power: 7,104kW (9,658hp) 17.0kn Guangzhou 8G32 1 x 4 Stroke 8 Cy. 320 x 480 3552kW (4829bhp) Guangzhou Diesel Engine Factory CoLtd-China AuxGen: 2 x 2300kW 400V a.c, 3 x 960kW 400V a.c Thrusters: 2 Tunnel thruster (f)
9647538 *BJSB* -	**YUE HAI TIE 4 HAO** **Yuehai Railway Co Ltd** - *Haikou, Hainan* *China* MMSI: 413521620	**23,217** - 6,525	Class: CC	**2011-05 Tianjin Xingang Shipbuilding Industry Co Ltd — Tianjin** Loa 188.00 (BB) Br ex - Dght 5.600 Lbp 178.00 Br md 23.00 Dpth 9.30 Welded, 1 dk	**(A36A2PT) Passenger/Ro-Ro Ship (Vehicles/Rail)** Passengers: 1508 Rail Wagons: 44	**2 oil engines** reduction geared to sc. shafts driving 2 CP propellers Total Power: 7,104kW (9,658hp) 17.0kn Guangzhou 8G32 2 x 4 Stroke 8 Cy. 320 x 480 each-3552kW (4829bhp) Guangzhou Diesel Engine Factory CoLtd-China AuxGen: 2 x 2300kW 400V a.c, 2 x 960kW 400V a.c Thrusters: 2 Tunnel thruster (f)
9268617 *BRSG* -	**YUE HUA** **Shenhuazhonghai Shipping Co Ltd** - *Zhuhai, Guangdong* *China* MMSI: 412377180	**6,785** 3,799 10,926	Class: (CC)	**2002-12 Jiangsu Yangzijiang Shipbuilding Co Ltd — Jiangyin JS** Yd No: 2000-629E24 Loa 118.60 Br ex - Dght 6.596 Lbp 112.60 Br md 22.60 Dpth 9.60 Welded, 1 dk	**(A21A2BC) Bulk Carrier** Grain: 13,140 Compartments: 4 Ho, ER 4 Ha: ER 4 (11.2 x 11.2) Ice Capable	**2 oil engines** geared to sc. shafts driving 2 FP propellers Total Power: 2,206kW (3,000hp) 11.5kn Daihatsu 6DLM-26S 2 x 4 Stroke 6 Cy. 260 x 340 each-1103kW (1500bhp) Shaanxi Diesel Engine Factory-China AuxGen: 3 x 150kW 400V a.c
8972132 - -	**YUE HUA YI HAO** **Yueyang Petroleum Chemical Works** - *Chenglingji, Hunan* *China*	**1,595** 893 1,062	Class: (CC)	**2000-09 Changde Shipyard — Changde HN** Loa 84.90 Br ex - Dght 2.520 Lbp 80.00 Br md 13.60 Dpth 3.80 Welded, 1 dk	**(A11B2TG) LPG Tanker** Liq (Gas): 1,902 2 x Gas Tank (s);	**2 oil engines** geared to sc. shaft driving 1 FP propeller Total Power: 1,350kW (1,836hp) 12.0kn Chinese Std. Type 6250 2 x 4 Stroke 6 Cy. 250 x 300 each-675kW (918bhp) Hongyan Machinery Factory-China AuxGen: 2 x 90kW 400V a.c
8738031 - -	**YUE HUI ZHOU HUO 9398** **Boluo Water Transportation HK & Macao Barance** - *Huizhou, Guangdong* *China*	**1,839** 1,029 -		**2005-11 in the People's Republic of China** Yd No: 1 Loa 74.38 Br ex - Dght - Lbp - Br md 16.80 Dpth 5.00 Welded, 1 dk	**(A24D2BA) Aggregates Carrier**	**2 oil engines** geared to sc. shafts driving 2 Propellers Total Power: 1,086kW (1,476hp) Cummins 2 x 4 Stroke each-543kW (738bhp) Chongqing Cummins Engine Co Ltd-China
8665387 - -	**YUE JIAN HANG 05** **Qingxin Jianhang Shipping Co Ltd** - *Qingyuan, Guangdong* *China* Official number: 091308000147	**1,361** 762 1,997	Class: ZC	**2008-04 Qingyuan Fucheng Baimiao Shipyard — Qingyuan GD** Yd No: BM-0715 Loa 67.80 Br ex 14.92 Dght 3.330 Lbp 64.80 Br md 14.60 Dpth 3.98 Welded, 1 dk	**(A24D2BA) Aggregates Carrier**	**2 oil engines** reduction geared to sc. shafts driving 2 Propellers Total Power: 1,356kW (1,844hp) Cummins 2 x each-678kW (922bhp) Chongqing Cummins Engine Co Ltd-China
9159816 *VRCG7* -	**YUE LIANG WAN** *ex Libro Doro -2006 ex Saloma -2004* *ex Rainbow Jade -1999* **Yueliangwan Maritime Co Ltd** COSCO Southern Asphalt Shipping Co Ltd SatCom: Inmarsat C 447700496 *Hong Kong* *Hong Kong* MMSI: 477607500 Official number: HK-1788	**9,020** 2,706 11,047 T/cm 22.7	Class: CC (NK)	**1999-06 Jingjiang Shipyard — Jingjiang JS** Yd No: JS96-002 Converted From: Bulk Carrier-2007 Loa 135.48 (BB) Br ex 21.44 Dght 8.100 Lbp 126.00 Br md 21.40 Dpth 11.80 Welded, 1 dk	**(A13B2TP) Products Tanker** Double Hull (13F) Liq: 9,794; Liq (Oil): 9,794; Asphalt: 9,794 Cargo Heating Coils Compartments: 8 Wing Ta, ER 3 Ha: (15.0 x 14.0) (25.5 x 16.2) (15.0 x 16.2)ER Derricks: 4x30t 2 Cargo Pump (s): 2x400m³/hr Manifold: Bow/CM: 70.4m	**1 oil engine** driving 1 FP propeller Total Power: 4,200kW (5,710hp) 13.2kn B&W 6S35MC 1 x 2 Stroke 6 Cy. 350 x 1400 4200kW (5710bhp) Yichang Marine Diesel Engine Co Ltd-China AuxGen: 3 x 450kW 440V 60Hz a.c Fuel: 241.5 (d.f.) (Heating Coils) 970.9 (r.f.) 18.4pd
9492206 *VRII2* -	**YUE MAY** **Yue Maritime LLC** Foremost Maritime Corp *Hong Kong* *Hong Kong* MMSI: 477861100 Official number: HK-3050	**91,412** 57,770 176,000 T/cm 120.6	Class: BV	**2011-07 Shanghai Waigaoqiao Shipbuilding Co Ltd — Shanghai** Yd No: 1136 Loa 292.00 (BB) Br ex 45.05 Dght 18.300 Lbp 277.94 Br md 45.00 Dpth 24.80 Welded, 1 dk	**(A21A2BC) Bulk Carrier** Grain: 193,247; Bale: 183,425 Compartments: 9 Ho, ER 9 Ha: ER	**1 oil engine** driving 1 FP propeller Total Power: 16,860kW (22,923hp) 14.0kn MAN-B&W 6S70MC 1 x 2 Stroke 6 Cy. 700 x 2674 16860kW (22923bhp) CSSC MES Diesel Co Ltd-China AuxGen: 3 x 900kW 60Hz a.c Fuel: 5100.0

IMO / Call sign	Name / Owner / Port	Tonnage	Class	Built / Dimensions	Type	Machinery
667543 *ZXL62*	**YUE NAN YU 178** **China Southern Fishery Co Ltd** - *Shekou, Guangdong* *China* MMSI: 412677430	123 36 -		**1994-04 Shunde Leliu Sanjiang Shipyard — Foshan GD** L reg 26.80 Br ex - Dght - Lbp - Br md 6.00 Dpth - Welded, 1 dk	**(B11B2FV) Fishing Vessel** Hull Material: Ferro Concrete	**2 oil engines** reduction geared to sc. shaft driving 2 Propellers Total Power: 636kW (864hp) Cummins KTA-19-M470 1 x 4 Stroke 6 Cy. 159 x 159 318kW (432bhp) Chongqing Cummins Engine Co Ltd-China
667555 *ZXL63*	**YUE NAN YU 179** **China Southern Fishery Co Ltd** - *Shekou, Guangdong* *China* MMSI: 412677420	123 36 -		**1994-04 Shunde Leliu Sanjiang Shipyard — Foshan GD** Loa 26.80 Br ex - Dght - Lbp - Br md 6.00 Dpth - Welded, 1 dk	**(B11B2FV) Fishing Vessel** Hull Material: Ferro Concrete	**2 oil engines** reduction geared to sc. shaft driving 2 Propellers Total Power: 636kW (864hp) Cummins KTA-19-M470 1 x 4 Stroke 6 Cy. 159 x 159 318kW (432bhp) Chongqing Cummins Engine Co Ltd-China
667567 *ZXL65*	**YUE NAN YU 182** **China Southern Fishery Co Ltd** - *Shekou, Guangdong* *China*	125 37 -		**1994-06 Zhanjiang Fishing Vessel Shipyard — Zhanjiang GD** L reg 26.40 Br ex - Dght - Lbp - Br md 6.00 Dpth - Welded, 1 dk	**(B11B2FV) Fishing Vessel** Hull Material: Ferro Concrete	**2 oil engines** reduction geared to sc. shaft driving 2 Propellers Total Power: 636kW (864hp) Cummins KTA-19-M470 1 x 4 Stroke 6 Cy. 159 x 159 318kW (432bhp) Chongqing Cummins Engine Co Ltd-China
547910 *RFG5*	**YUE SHAN** **Poseidon Marine Ltd** Oak Maritime (Canada) Inc SatCom: Inmarsat C 447702083 *Hong Kong* *Hong Kong* MMSI: 477264400 Official number: HK-2409	91,373 58,745 177,799 T/cm 120.6	Class: AB	**2009-09 Shanghai Waigaoqiao Shipbuilding Co Ltd — Shanghai** Yd No: 1131 Loa 292.00 (BB) Br ex - Dght 18.300 Lbp 282.00 Br md 45.00 Dpth 24.80 Welded, 1 dk	**(A21A2BC) Bulk Carrier** Grain: 194,179; Bale: 183,425 Compartments: 9 Ho, ER 9 Ha: ER	**1 oil engine** driving 1 FP propeller Total Power: 16,860kW (22,923hp) 14.0kn MAN-B&W 6S70MC 1 x 2 Stroke 6 Cy. 700 x 2674 16860kW (22923bhp) Dalian Marine Diesel Co Ltd-China AuxGen: 3 x 900kW a.c Fuel: 337.0 (d.f.) 4690.0 (r.f.)
623958 *YGA*	**YUE SHEN ZHOU 5** **Guangzhou Shenzhou Shipping Co Ltd** - *Guangzhou, Guangdong* *China* MMSI: 413467210	9,611 2,883 12,388	Class: CC	**2011-12 Zhejiang Tenglong Shipyard — Wenling ZJ** Yd No: 0910 Loa 139.50 Br ex 32.06 Dght 5.400 Lbp 131.40 Br md 32.00 Dpth 8.00 Welded, 1 dk	**(A38B2GB) Barge Carrier** Ice Capable	**2 oil engines** reduction geared to sc. shafts driving 2 Propellers Total Power: 5,330kW (7,246hp) 12.5kn Guangzhou 6G32 2 x 4 Stroke 6 Cy. 320 x 480 each-2665kW (3623bhp) Guangzhou Diesel Engine Factory CoLtd-China AuxGen: 3 x 360kW 400V a.c
628432 *DZP*	**YUE SHENG YU 302** *ex* Yu Sheng Yu 302 *-2009* **Soleil Ltd** - *Suva* *Fiji* Official number: 000748	121 36 -		**2009-03 Zhejiang Yueqing Changhong Shipbuilding Co Ltd — Yueqing ZJ** Yd No: 960301 Loa 28.50 Br ex 6.20 Dght - Lbp - Br md - Dpth 3.00 Welded, 1 dk	**(B11B2FV) Fishing Vessel**	**1 oil engine** reduction geared to sc. shaft driving 1 FP propeller Total Power: 448kW (609hp) Cummins KTA-19-M3 1 x 4 Stroke 6 Cy. 159 x 159 448kW (609bhp) Cummins Engine Co Inc-USA
667490	**YUE SHENZHEN 11188** **Shenzhen Shuiwan Pelagic Fisheries Co Ltd** - *Shekou, Guangdong* *China* Official number: 440301104683899	113 39 -		**1993-12 Zhanjiang Fishing Vessel Shipyard — Zhanjiang GD** Loa 27.33 Br ex - Dght - Lbp - Br md 5.80 Dpth 2.95 Welded, 1 dk	**(B11A2FT) Trawler** Hull Material: Ferro Concrete	**2 oil engines** reduction geared to sc. shafts driving 2 Propellers Total Power: 636kW (864hp) Cummins KTA-19-M470 2 x 4 Stroke 6 Cy. 159 x 159 each-318kW (432bhp) Weichai Power Co Ltd-China
667505	**YUE SHENZHEN 11189** **Shenzhen Shuiwan Pelagic Fisheries Co Ltd** - *Shekou, Guangdong* *China* Official number: 440301104683899	113 39 -		**1993-12 Zhanjiang Fishing Vessel Shipyard — Zhanjiang GD** Loa 27.33 Br ex - Dght - Lbp - Br md 5.80 Dpth 2.95 Welded, 1 dk	**(B11A2FT) Trawler** Hull Material: Ferro Concrete	**2 oil engines** reduction geared to sc. shafts driving 2 Propellers Total Power: 636kW (864hp) Cummins KTA-19-M470 2 x 4 Stroke 6 Cy. 159 x 159 each-318kW (432bhp) Weichai Power Co Ltd-China
649199 *DZV*	**YUE SUI XI 31016** **Soleil Ltd** - *Suva* *Fiji* Official number: 000749	128 38 -		**1994-12 in the People's Republic of China** Yd No: 9441 Loa 24.00 Br ex - Dght - Lbp - Br md 6.00 Dpth 2.00 Welded, 1 dk	**(B11B2FV) Fishing Vessel**	**1 oil engine** driving 1 Propeller
666379	**YUE TAI** **Wing Wah Oil Ship Co** - *Hong Kong* *Hong Kong* Official number: BM21693Y	362 191 484		**2002-12 Taizhou Wuzhou Shipbuilding Industry Co Ltd — Taizhou ZJ** Loa 26.70 Br ex - Dght 4.500 Lbp 23.90 Br md 10.00 Dpth 5.50 Welded, 1 dk	**(B35E2TF) Bunkering Tanker** Single Hull	**2 oil engines** reduction geared to sc. shafts driving 2 Propellers Total Power: 1,176kW (1,598hp) Cummins 2 x each-588kW (799bhp) Cummins Engine Co Inc-USA
875009 *LJI*	**YUE XING** *ex* Zhe Hai 106 *-1993* **Wenzhou Marine Shipping Co** - *Wenzhou, Zhejiang* *China*	995 495 1,381	Class: (CC)	**1986-06 Zhejiang Shipyard — Ningbo ZJ** Loa 59.23 Br ex - Dght 4.500 Lbp 54.96 Br md 10.80 Dpth 5.35 Welded, 1 dk	**(A31A2GX) General Cargo Ship** Grain: 1,687; Bale: 1,586 Compartments: 2 Ho, ER 2 Ha: 2 (10.2 x 5.8)ER	**1 oil engine** geared to sc. shaft driving 1 FP propeller Total Power: 552kW (750hp) 10.7kn Chinese Std. Type 6300 1 x 4 Stroke 6 Cy. 300 x 380 552kW (750bhp) Guangzhou Diesel Engine Factory CoLtd-China AuxGen: 2 x 75kW 400V a.c
309907 *RRD*	**YUE XIU HAI** *ex* Wadi al Kamar *-2003* **Guangzhou Pan-Ocean Shipping Co Ltd (POSCO)** - SatCom: Inmarsat C 441253715 *Guangzhou, Guangdong* *China* MMSI: 412466170	27,589 15,110 45,105 T/cm 54.3	Class: (LR) (CC) ✠ Classed LR until 16/4/03	**1985-04 Hyundai Heavy Industries Co Ltd — Ulsan** Yd No: 310 Loa 195.41 (BB) Br ex 32.29 Dght 11.419 Lbp 184.99 Br md 32.25 Dpth 16.51 Welded, 1 dk	**(A21A2BC) Bulk Carrier** Grain: 58,130 Compartments: 5 Ho, ER 5 Ha: 5 (19.2 x 15.2)ER Cranes: 4x15t Ice Capable	**1 oil engine** driving 1 FP propeller Total Power: 9,540kW (12,971hp) 13.0kn Sulzer 6RTA58 1 x 2 Stroke 6 Cy. 580 x 1700 9540kW (12971bhp) Hyundai Engine & Machinery Co Ltd-South Korea AuxGen: 3 x 450kW 450V 60Hz a.c Boilers: AuxB (o.f.) 8.9kgf/cm² (8.7bar), AuxB (ex.g.) 8.9kgf/cm² (8.7bar) Fuel: 298.5 (d.f.) 2471.0 (r.f.) 26.5pd
832423 *XBB*	**YUE YOU 102** - - *Guangzhou, Guangdong* *China*	*788* 334 1,093		**1978 Guangdong New China Shipyard Co Ltd — Dongguan GD** Loa 67.42 Br ex - Dght 4.000 Lbp 60.00 Br md 10.00 Dpth 4.50 Welded, 1 dk	**(A13B2TU) Tanker (unspecified)** Compartments: 3 Ta, ER	**1 oil engine** driving 1 FP propeller Total Power: 596kW (810hp) 10.5kn Chinese Std. Type 6350 1 x 4 Stroke 6 Cy. 350 x 500 596kW (810bhp) Shanghai Diesel Engine Co Ltd-China AuxGen: 2 x 90kW 400V a.c
017399 *XBH*	**YUE YOU 104** *ex* Yoshu Maru *-2003* - - *Guangzhou, Guangdong* *China*	*992* 623 1,922	Class: (NK)	**1969 Watanabe Zosen KK — Imabari EH** Yd No: 96 Loa 71.12 Br ex 10.83 Dght 4.820 Lbp 65.00 Br md 10.82 Dpth 5.50 Welded, 1 dk	**(A13B2TP) Products Tanker** Liq: 2,413; Liq (Oil): 2,413 Compartments: 4 Ta, ER	**2 oil engines** geared to sc. shaft driving 1 FP propeller Total Power: 1,104kW (1,500hp) 11.5kn Daihatsu 6PSHTCM-26D 2 x 4 Stroke 6 Cy. 260 x 320 each-552kW (750bhp) Daihatsu Kogyo-Japan AuxGen: 2 x 80kW 445V a.c Fuel: 216.5 5.5pd
010879 *XBC*	**YUE YOU 129** *ex* Nippo Maru *-1994* *ex* Shin Aitoku Maru *-1990* **Shenzhen Shenyue Marine Co** - *Shekou, Guangdong* *China* MMSI: 412460220	924 421 1,475	Class: (CC) (NK)	**1980-09 Imamura Zosen — Kure** Yd No: 270 Loa 72.00 Br ex 10.62 Dght 4.773 Lbp 66.00 Br md 10.60 Dpth 5.20 Welded, 1 dk	**(A13B2TP) Products Tanker** Liq: 1,300; Liq (Oil): 1,300 Compartments: 10 Ta, ER	**1 oil engine** driving 1 CP propeller Total Power: 1,177kW (1,600hp) 11.0kn Hanshin 6EL32 1 x 4 Stroke 6 Cy. 320 x 640 1177kW (1600bhp) The Hanshin Diesel Works Ltd-Japan AuxGen: 3 x 56kW a.c
929827 *XAT*	**YUE YOU 203** *ex* Kokusho Maru No. 8 *-1987* - - *Guangzhou, Guangdong* *China*	998 584 1,888	Class: (CC)	**1980-08 Mukaishima Zoki Co. Ltd. — Onomichi** Yd No: 171 Loa 70.90 Br ex 11.64 Dght 4.680 Lbp 66.00 Br md 11.60 Dpth 5.45 Welded, 1 dk	**(A13B2TP) Products Tanker**	**1 oil engine** reduction geared to sc. shaft driving 1 FP propeller Total Power: 1,177kW (1,600hp) Yanmar 6ZL-UT 1 x 4 Stroke 6 Cy. 280 x 340 1177kW (1600bhp) Yanmar Diesel Engine Co Ltd-Japan
810430 *XAV*	**YUE YOU 801** *ex* Atlantic Glory *-1993* *ex* Alberta Glory *-1983* - - *Guangzhou, Guangdong* *China* MMSI: 412460170	*4,407* 1,906 8,461	Class: (CC) (NK)	**1979-01 Kurinoura Dockyard Co Ltd — Yawatahama EH** Yd No: 135 Loa 117.10 Br ex - Dght 7.351 Lbp 108.21 Br md 17.01 Dpth 8.62 Welded, 1 dk	**(A12B2TR) Chemical/Products Tanker** Liq: 9,733; Liq (Oil): 9,733	**1 oil engine** driving 1 FP propeller Total Power: 3,310kW (4,500hp) 12.5kn Mitsubishi 6UET45/80D 1 x 2 Stroke 6 Cy. 450 x 800 3310kW (4500bhp) Akasaka Tekkosho KK (Akasaka DieselLtd)-Japan AuxGen: 1 x 200kW 445V 60Hz a.c, 2 x 160kW 445V 60Hz a.c

9175092 *VRWI8* -	**YUE YOU 901** *ex* Marine Champion *-2006* **Zhu Cheng Shipping Co Ltd** GNG Ocean Shipping Co Ltd SatCom: Inmarsat C 447701760 *Hong Kong* *Hong Kong* MMSI: 477756000 Official number: HK-0550	**6,663** 3,447 10,400 T/cm 18.3	Class: CC (BV)	**1998-08 Daedong Shipbuilding Co Ltd — Changwon (Jinhae Shipyard)** Yd No: 1017 Loa 115.00 (BB) Br ex - Dght 8.464 Lbp 107.00 Br md 18.20 Dpth 10.70 Welded, 1 dk	**(A12A2TC) Chemical Tanker** Double Hull (13F) Liq: 11,925 Compartments: 17 Ta, ER 17 Cargo Pump (s): 13x200m^3/hr, 4x100m^3/hr Manifold: Bow/CM: 57.1m	**1 oil engine** driving 1 FP propeller Total Power: 3,773kW (5,130hp) 13.5k B&W 6S35M 1 x 2 Stroke 6 Cy. 350 x 1400 3773kW (5130bhp) Hyundai Heavy Industries Co Ltd-South Korea Thrusters: 1 Tunnel thruster (f) Fuel: 655.0 (r.f.)
9175107 *VRWI7* -	**YUE YOU 902** *ex* Marine Pioneer *-2006* **Jiang Xin Shipping Co Ltd** GNG Ocean Shipping Co Ltd SatCom: Inmarsat B 363685910 *Hong Kong* *Hong Kong* MMSI: 477755000 Official number: HK-0549	**6,663** 3,447 10,400 T/cm 18.3	Class: CC (BV)	**1998-11 Daedong Shipbuilding Co Ltd — Changwon (Jinhae Shipyard)** Yd No: 1019 Loa 115.00 (BB) Br ex - Dght 8.464 Lbp 107.39 Br md 18.20 Dpth 10.70 Welded, 1 dk	**(A12A2TC) Chemical Tanker** Double Hull (13F) Liq: 11,922 Compartments: 17 Ta, ER 17 Cargo Pump (s) Manifold: Bow/CM: 57.1m	**1 oil engine** driving 1 FP propeller Total Power: 4,193kW (5,701hp) 13.5k B&W 6S35M 1 x 2 Stroke 6 Cy. 350 x 1400 4193kW (5701bhp) Hyundai Heavy Industries Co Ltd-South Korea Fuel: 632.0 (r.f.)
8896924 *BVQC* -	**YUE YOU 928** - **Xiamen Luda Shipping Co Ltd** - *Xiamen, Fujian* *China* MMSI: 412460230	**1,113** 623 677	Class: (CC)	**1993 Qianjiang Shipyard — Hangzhou ZJ** Yd No: 92-2 Loa 66.70 Br ex - Dght 2.980 Lbp 60.90 Br md 11.40 Dpth 5.00 Welded, 1 dk	**(A33A2CC) Container Ship (Fully Cellular)** Compartments: 2 Cell Ho, ER 2 Ha: ER	**2 oil engines** geared to sc. shafts driving 2 FP propellers Total Power: 588kW (800hp) 10.2k Chinese Std. Type 630 2 x 4 Stroke 6 Cy. 300 x 380 each-294kW (400bhp) Guangzhou Diesel Engine Factory CoLtd-China AuxGen: 2 x 75kW 400V a.c
8843616 *BXAG2* -	**YUE YUAN YU 1** - **Guangzhou Pelagic Fisheries Intergrated (China) Co** - *Guangzhou, Guangdong* *China*	*286* 85 115	Class: (CC)	**1990 Guangzhou Fishing Vessel Shipyard — Guangzhou GD** Loa 44.86 Br ex - Dght 3.000 Lbp 38.00 Br md 7.60 Dpth 4.00 Welded, 1 dk	**(B11B2FV) Fishing Vessel** Ins: 224	**1 oil engine** geared to sc. shaft driving 1 FP propeller Total Power: 85kW (116hp) 12.0k Yanmar 5KD 1 x 4 Stroke 5 Cy. 145 x 170 85kW (116bhp) Zibo Diesel Engine Factory-China AuxGen: 2 x 90kW 400V a.c
8843604 *BXAG3* -	**YUE YUAN YU 2** - **Guangzhou Pelagic Fisheries Intergrated (China) Co** - *Guangzhou, Guangdong* *China*	*286* 85 115	Class: (CC)	**1990 Guangzhou Fishing Vessel Shipyard — Guangzhou GD** Loa 44.86 Br ex - Dght 3.000 Lbp 38.00 Br md 7.60 Dpth 4.00 Welded, 1 dk	**(B11B2FV) Fishing Vessel** Ins: 224	**1 oil engine** geared to sc. shaft driving 1 FP propeller Total Power: 85kW (116hp) 12.0k Yanmar 5KD 1 x 4 Stroke 5 Cy. 145 x 170 85kW (116bhp) Zibo Diesel Engine Factory-China AuxGen: 2 x 90kW 400V a.c
9058347 *BXAF6* -	**YUE YUAN YU 7** - **Guangzhou Pelagic Fisheries Intergrated (China) Co** - *Guangzhou, Guangdong* *China*	*290* 87 487	Class: (CC)	**1993 Guangzhou Fishing Vessel Shipyard — Guangzhou GD** Loa 44.86 Br ex - Dght - Lbp 38.00 Br md 7.60 Dpth 4.00 Welded	**(B11B2FV) Fishing Vessel**	**1 oil engine** geared to sc. shaft driving 1 FP propeller Total Power: 735kW (999hp) 12.0k Chinese Std. Type 830 1 x 4 Stroke 8 Cy. 300 x 380 735kW (999bhp) Zibo Diesel Engine Factory-China AuxGen: 2 x 120kW 400V a.c
9058359 *BXAF7* -	**YUE YUAN YU 8** - **Guangzhou Pelagic Fisheries Intergrated (China) Co** - *Guangzhou, Guangdong* *China*	*290* 87 487	Class: (CC)	**1993 Guangzhou Fishing Vessel Shipyard — Guangzhou GD** Loa 44.86 Br ex - Dght - Lbp 38.00 Br md 7.60 Dpth 4.00 Welded	**(B11B2FV) Fishing Vessel**	**1 oil engine** geared to sc. shaft driving 1 FP propeller Total Power: 735kW (999hp) 12.0k Chinese Std. Type 830 1 x 4 Stroke 8 Cy. 300 x 380 735kW (999bhp) Zibo Diesel Engine Factory-China AuxGen: 2 x 120kW 400V a.c
8667517 *BZXL2* -	**YUE YUAN YU 168** - **China Southern Fishery Co Ltd** - *Shekou, Guangdong* *China* MMSI: 412696010	**125** 44 -		**1994-04 Zhanjiang Fishing Vessel Shipyard — Zhanjiang GD** L reg 25.68 Br ex - Dght - Lbp - Br md 6.00 Dpth - Welded, 1 dk	**(B11B2FV) Fishing Vessel** Hull Material: Ferro Concrete	**2 oil engines** reduction geared to sc. shaft driving 2 Propelle Total Power: 636kW (864hp) Cummins KTA-19-M47 1 x 4 Stroke 6 Cy. 159 x 159 318kW (432bhp) Chongqing Cummins Engine Co Ltd-China
8667529 *BZXL6* -	**YUE YUAN YU 169** - **China Southern Fishery Co Ltd** - *Shekou, Guangdong* *China* MMSI: 412696020	**125** 44 -		**1994-04 Zhanjiang Fishing Vessel Shipyard — Zhanjiang GD** L reg 25.68 Br ex - Dght - Lbp - Br md 6.00 Dpth - Welded, 1 dk	**(B11B2FV) Fishing Vessel** Hull Material: Ferro Concrete	**2 oil engines** reduction geared to sc. shaft driving 2 Propelle Total Power: 636kW (864hp) Cummins KTA-19-M47 1 x 4 Stroke 6 Cy. 159 x 159 318kW (432bhp) Chongqing Cummins Engine Co Ltd-China
8648470 *3DYO* -	**YUE YUAN YU NO. 139** - **Services Marine Ltd** - *Suva* *Fiji* Official number: YD000129	**121** 36 -		**1996-09 Zhejiang Yueqing Changhong Shipbuilding Co Ltd — Yueqing ZJ** Loa 28.50 Br ex 6.20 Dght - Lbp - Br md - Dpth 3.00 Welded, 1 dk	**(B11B2FV) Fishing Vessel**	**1 oil engine** driving 1 Propeller Cummins 1 x 4 Stroke Chongqing Cummins Engine Co Ltd-China
9046588 - -	**YUEDE** *ex* Seiun Maru *-2002* **PT Armada Contener Nusantara** -	**1,433** 432 1,580	Class: (BV) (NK)	**1992-03 Hakata Zosen K.K. — Imabari** Yd No: 525 Loa 74.10 Br ex - Dght 4.021 Lbp 69.00 Br md 12.00 Dpth 6.90 Welded	**(A31A2GX) General Cargo Ship** Bale: 2,198 Compartments: 1 Ho 1 Ha: (40.2 x 8.5)	**1 oil engine** driving 1 FP propeller Total Power: 736kW (1,001hp) 10.5k Hanshin LH28L 1 x 4 Stroke 6 Cy. 280 x 530 736kW (1001bhp) The Hanshin Diesel Works Ltd-Japan
9109926 *3FJG6* -	**YUEHAI** - **Yuehai Shipping Inc** COSCO (Cayman) Fortune Holding Co Ltd SatCom: Inmarsat A 1360313 *Panama* *Panama* MMSI: 356599000 Official number: 2316996CH	**26,063** 14,924 45,632 T/cm 49.8	Class: NV	**1996-07 Tsuneishi Shipbuilding Co Ltd — Fukuyama HS** Yd No: 1073 Loa 185.74 (BB) Br ex - Dght 11.620 Lbp 177.00 Br md 30.40 Dpth 16.50 Welded, 1 dk	**(A21A2BC) Bulk Carrier** Grain: 57,208; Bale: 55,564 Compartments: 5 Ho, ER 5 Ha: (20.0 x 15.3)4 (20.8 x 15.3)ER Cranes: 4x25t	**1 oil engine** driving 1 FP propeller Total Power: 7,167kW (9,744hp) 14.0k B&W 6S50M 1 x 2 Stroke 6 Cy. 500 x 1910 7167kW (9744bhp) Mitsui Engineering & Shipbuilding CLtd-Japan AuxGen: 3 x 480kW 450V 60Hz a.c Fuel: 1647.0 (r.f.) 26.4pd
9120750 *3FAT7* -	**YUEHE** - **Yuehe Shipping Inc** COSCO Container Lines Co Ltd (COSCON) SatCom: Inmarsat C 435621910 *Panama* *Panama* MMSI: 356219000 Official number: 2364897CH	**65,140** 36,668 69,285 T/cm 91.1	Class: LR ✠ **100A1** SS 02/2012 container ship *IWS certified container securing arrangements Ice Class 1D ✠ **LMC** **UMS** Eq.Ltr: W†; Cable: 747.5/95.0 U3	**1997-02 Kawasaki Heavy Industries Ltd — Sakaide KG** Yd No: 1460 Loa 280.00 (BB) Br ex 39.90 Dght 14.000 Lbp 267.00 Br md 39.80 Dpth 23.60 Welded, 1 dk	**(A33A2CC) Container Ship (Fully Cellular)** TEU 5618 C Ho 2790 TEU C Dk 2828 TEU incl 1002 ref C Compartments: ER, 7 Cell Ho 16 Ha: ER Ice Capable	**1 oil engine** driving 1 FP propeller Total Power: 43,100kW (58,599hp) 24.5k B&W 10L90M 1 x 2 Stroke 10 Cy. 900 x 2916 43100kW (58599bhp) Kawasaki Heavy Industries Ltd-Japan AuxGen: 4 x 2280kW 440V 60Hz a.c Boilers: e (ex.g.) 11.9kgf/cm^2 (11.7bar), AuxB (o.f.) 8.0kgf/cm^2 (7.8bar) Thrusters: 1 Thwart. CP thruster (f)
9323754 *VRAP4* -	**YUEN KOK** - **Hongkong United Dockyards Ltd** The Hongkong Salvage & Towage Co Ltd *Hong Kong* *Hong Kong* MMSI: 477991700 Official number: HK-1440	**297** 89 170	Class: LR ✠ **100A1** SS 08/2010 tug ✠ **LMC** Eq.Ltr: F; Cable: 302.5/22.0 U2 (a)	**2005-08 Hin Lee (Zhuhai) Shipyard Co Ltd — Zhuhai GD (Hull)** Yd No: 081 **2005-08 Cheoy Lee Shipyards Ltd — Hong Kong** Yd No: 4849 Loa 29.00 Br ex 10.12 Dght 3.900 Lbp 23.50 Br md 9.50 Dpth 4.70 Welded, 1 dk	**(B32A2ST) Tug**	**2 oil engines** gearing integral to driving 2 Z propellers Total Power: 2,942kW (4,000hp) 11.5k Yanmar 6N260L-E 2 x 4 Stroke 6 Cy. 260 x 360 each-1471kW (2000bhp) Yanmar Diesel Engine Co Ltd-Japan AuxGen: 2 x 80kW 385V 50Hz a.c
6709490 *HQPF* -	**YUFENG** *ex* Kwang Il No. 31 *-1983* *ex* Nikko Maru No. 35 *-1975* *ex* Seita Maru No. 15 *-1975* **Compania Naviera Jinshen S de RL** - *San Lorenzo* *Honduras* Official number: L-0200461	*232* 113 -	Class: (KR)	**1966 Miho Zosensho K.K. — Shimizu** Yd No: 596 Loa 43.59 Br ex 7.55 Dght - Lbp 38.10 Br md 7.52 Dpth 3.33 Welded, 1 dk	**(B11B2FV) Fishing Vessel** Ins: 282 3 Ha: (1.3 x 0.9)2 (1.3 x 1.4)	**1 oil engine** driving 1 FP propeller Total Power: 607kW (825hp) 11.0k Niigata 1 x 4 Stroke 6 Cy. 280 x 440 607kW (825bhp) Niigata Engineering Co Ltd-Japan AuxGen: 2 x 104kW
9588718 *VRGY5* -	**YUFENG 6** - **Million Star Corp Ltd** Grandfame Ship Management Ltd *Hong Kong* *Hong Kong* MMSI: 477812100 Official number: HK-2764	**5,031** 1,681 6,401 T/cm 16.0	Class: AB	**2010-05 Zhejiang Antai Shipyard Co Ltd — Dongtou County ZJ** Yd No: AT005 Loa 99.60 (BB) Br ex 18.22 Dght 6.500 Lbp 94.00 Br md 18.00 Dpth 9.60 Welded, 1 dk	**(A12B2TR) Chemical/Products Tanker** Double Hull (13F) Liq: 7,253; Liq (Oil): 7,253 Compartments: 10 Wing Ta, 2 Wing Slop Ta, ER 10 Cargo Pump (s): 10x300m^3/hr Manifold: Bow/CM: 49.7m	**1 oil engine** driving 1 FP propeller Total Power: 2,574kW (3,500hp) 13.5k Yanmar 6N330-E 1 x 4 Stroke 6 Cy. 330 x 440 2574kW (3500bhp) Qingdao Zichai Boyang Diesel EngineCo Ltd-China AuxGen: 3 x 500kW a.c Thrusters: 1 Tunnel thruster (f) Fuel: 115.0 (d.f.) 265.0 (r.f.)

IMO / Call sign	Name, owner, manager, port	Tonnage	Class	Builder / Dimensions	Type / Cargo	Machinery
608001 D3146	**YUFUKU** **Mochizuki Kaiun KK** - *Himeji, Hyogo* *Japan* Official number: 141374	*236* - 850		**2010-12 K.K. Murakami Zosensho — Naruto** L reg 55.77 Br ex - Dght 3.510 Lbp 54.50 Br md 9.50 Dpth 5.90 Welded, 1 dk	**(A31A2GX) General Cargo Ship** Grain: 1,485; Bale: 1,327	**1 oil engine** reduction geared to sc. shaft driving 1 Propeller Total Power: 1,029kW (1,399hp) 11.5kn Niigata 6M28BGT 1 x 4 Stroke 6 Cy. 280 x 480 1029kW (1399bhp) Niigata Engineering Co Ltd-Japan
424704 D2485	**YUFUKUJIN MARU** **Mitsuru Kisen YK & Kimoto Kisen KK** Kimoto Kisen KK *Imabari, Ehime* *Japan* MMSI: 431000332 Official number: 140614	*3,547* - 5,470	Class: NK	**2007-10 Hakata Zosen K.K. — Imabari** Yd No: 703 Loa 104.80 Br ex - Dght 6.613 Lbp 99.00 Br md 16.00 Dpth 8.20 Welded, 1 dk	**(A13B2TP) Products Tanker** Double Hull (13F) Liq: 5,600; Liq (Oil): 5,600	**1 oil engine** driving 1 FP propeller Total Power: 3,310kW (4,500hp) 14.2kn Hanshin LH46L 1 x 4 Stroke 6 Cy. 460 x 880 3310kW (4500bhp) The Hanshin Diesel Works Ltd-Japan AuxGen: 2 x a.c Fuel: 345.0
294329 EDJ9	**YUFUSAN** **Infinity Shipping Navigation SA** MOL Tankship Management (Asia) Pte Ltd SatCom: Inmarsat C 437159510 *Panama* *Panama* MMSI: 371595000 Official number: 3123106A	**160,216** 103,527 311,389 T/cm 183.9	Class: NK	**2005-11 Mitsui Eng. & SB. Co. Ltd., Chiba Works — Ichihara** Yd No: 1601 Loa 333.00 (BB) Br ex 60.04 Dght 20.943 Lbp 324.00 Br md 60.00 Dpth 28.80 Welded, 1 dk	**(A13A2TV) Crude Oil Tanker** Double Hull (13F) Liq: 339,541; Liq (Oil): 354,689 Compartments: 5 Ta, 10 Wing Ta, 2 Wing Slop Ta, ER 4 Cargo Pump (s): 3x5500m³/hr, 1x2300m³/hr Manifold: Bow/CM: 167.3m	**1 oil engine** driving 1 FP propeller Total Power: 27,160kW (36,927hp) 15.9kn MAN-B&W 7S80MC-C 1 x 2 Stroke 7 Cy. 800 x 3200 27160kW (36927bhp) Mitsui Engineering & Shipbuilding CLtd-Japan AuxGen: 3 x 1050kW 440V 60Hz a.c Fuel: 420.0 (d.f.) 7900.0 (r.f.)
861967	**YUG-06** **Sevastopol State Corp Atlantika (Gosudarstvennoye Predpriyatiye 'Atlantika')** -	**104** 31 58	Class: (RS)	**1992-06 Rybinskaya Sudoverf — Rybinsk** Yd No: 21 Loa 26.50 Br ex 6.50 Dght 2.320 Lbp 23.61 Br md - Dpth 3.05 Welded, 1 dk	**(B11A2FS) Stern Trawler**	**1 oil engine** driving 1 FP propeller Total Power: 220kW (299hp) 9.5kn S.K.L. 6NVD26A-2 1 x 4 Stroke 6 Cy. 180 x 260 220kW (299bhp) SKL Motoren u. Systemtechnik AG-Magdeburg
861979	**YUG-07** **Sevastopol State Corp Atlantika (Gosudarstvennoye Predpriyatiye 'Atlantika')** -	**104** 31 58	Class: (RS)	**1992-07 Rybinskaya Sudoverf — Rybinsk** Yd No: 22 Loa 26.50 Br ex 6.50 Dght 2.320 Lbp 23.61 Br md - Dpth 3.05 Welded, 1 dk	**(B11A2FS) Stern Trawler**	**1 oil engine** driving 1 FP propeller Total Power: 220kW (299hp) 9.5kn S.K.L. 6NVD26A-2 1 x 4 Stroke 6 Cy. 180 x 260 220kW (299bhp) SKL Motoren u. Systemtechnik AG-Magdeburg
861981	**YUG-11** - - *Abidjan* *Cote d'Ivoire*	**104** 31 58	Class: (RS)	**1991-12 Azovskaya Sudoverf — Azov** Yd No: 1053 Loa 26.50 Br ex 6.59 Dght 2.360 Lbp 22.90 Br md - Dpth 3.05 Welded, 1 dk	**(B11A2FS) Stern Trawler** Ins: 48	**1 oil engine** geared to sc. shaft driving 1 FP propeller Total Power: 165kW (224hp) 9.3kn Daldizel 6CHNSP18/22 1 x 4 Stroke 6 Cy. 180 x 220 165kW (224bhp) Daldizel-Khabarovsk AuxGen: 2 x 30kW Fuel: 9.0 (d.f.)
861993 MSJ	**YUG-12** **Kerch Fishing Combine (A/O 'Kerchenskiy Rybokombinat')** - *Kerch* *Ukraine* MMSI: 272001400 Official number: 911126	**104** 31 58	Class: (RS)	**1991-12 Azovskaya Sudoverf — Azov** Yd No: 1054 Loa 26.50 Br ex 6.59 Dght 2.360 Lbp 22.90 Br md - Dpth 3.05 Welded, 1 dk	**(B11A2FS) Stern Trawler**	**1 oil engine** geared to sc. shaft driving 1 FP propeller Total Power: 165kW (224hp) 9.3kn Daldizel 6CHNSP18/22 1 x 4 Stroke 6 Cy. 180 x 220 165kW (224bhp) Daldizel-Khabarovsk AuxGen: 2 x 30kW Fuel: 9.0 (d.f.)
328716 ECR4	**YUGAWASAN** **New Grace Maritime SA** NS United Kaiun Kaisha Ltd SatCom: Inmarsat C 437144110 *Panama* *Panama* MMSI: 371441000 Official number: 3107605A	**159,860** 97,658 302,481 T/cm 181.9	Class: NK	**2005-08 Mitsubishi Heavy Industries Ltd. — Nagasaki** Yd No: 2211 Loa 333.00 (BB) Br ex - Dght 20.638 Lbp 324.00 Br md 60.00 Dpth 29.10 Welded, 1 dk	**(A13A2TV) Crude Oil Tanker** Double Hull (13F) Liq: 340,102; Liq (Oil): 350,102 Compartments: 5 Ta, 10 Wing Ta, ER, 2 Wing Slop Ta 3 Cargo Pump (s): 3x5000m³/hr Manifold: Bow/CM: 167m	**1 oil engine** driving 1 FP propeller Total Power: 27,300kW (37,117hp) 15.5kn Mitsubishi 7UEC85LSII 1 x 2 Stroke 7 Cy. 850 x 3150 27300kW (37117bhp) Mitsubishi Heavy Industries Ltd-Japan AuxGen: 2 x 1100kW a.c, 1 x 1200kW a.c Fuel: 7100.0
087958 L6247	**YUGE MARU** **Yuge Nautical College (Yuge Shosen Koto Semmon Gakko)** - *Kamijima, Ehime* *Japan* MMSI: 431500203 Official number: 134820	*240* - -		**1994-03 Mitsui Eng. & SB. Co. Ltd. — Tamano** Yd No: 1408 Loa - Br ex - Dght 2.800 Lbp 35.00 Br md 8.00 Dpth 3.30 Welded	**(B34K2QT) Training Ship**	**1 oil engine** driving 1 CP propeller Total Power: 956kW (1,300hp) 13.0kn Daihatsu 6DLM-24S 1 x 4 Stroke 6 Cy. 240 x 320 956kW (1300bhp) Daihatsu Diesel Manufacturing Co Lt-Japan AuxGen: 2 x 150kW a.c
001971 IIJ	**YUGO VOSTOK** *ex* Yugo-Vostock *-2002* *ex* Taharaki *-2002* *ex* Ibuki Maru *-1995* **OOO 'Polluks' (Polluks Co Ltd)** - *Sovetskaya Gavan* *Russia* MMSI: 273440610	**3,099** 1,004 3,635	Class: RS (NK)	**1981-03 Naikai Shipbuilding & Engineering Co Ltd — Onomichi HS (Taguma Shipyard)** Yd No: 464 Loa 91.39 Br ex - Dght 6.414 Lbp 84.03 Br md 15.02 Dpth 9.20 Welded, 2 dks	**(B11A2FS) Stern Trawler** Ins: 2,663 4 Ha: 2 (1.5 x 2.1)2 (2.4 x 2.4) Derricks: 6x5t	**1 oil engine** driving 1 FP propeller Total Power: 3,236kW (4,400hp) 14.0kn B&W 5K45GFC 1 x 2 Stroke 5 Cy. 450 x 900 3236kW (4400bhp) Hitachi Zosen Corp-Japan AuxGen: 3 x 630kW 450V 60Hz a.c Fuel: 1067.0 (d.f.) 16.0pd
509870 GIQ	**YUGO-VOSTOK 3** *ex* Yugo Vostock No. 3 *-1995* *ex* Matsufuku Maru No. 38 *-2003* **OOO 'Polluks' (Polluks Co Ltd)** - *Sovetskaya Gavan* *Russia* MMSI: 273442270 Official number: E-0139	**708** 246 446	Class: RS (KR)	**1985-07 Fujishin Zosen K.K. — Kamo** Yd No: 510 Loa 47.71 Br ex 8.72 Dght 3.560 Lbp 47.45 Br md 8.70 Dpth 6.25 Welded, 1 dk	**(B11B2FV) Fishing Vessel**	**1 oil engine** geared to sc. shaft driving 1 FP propeller Total Power: 735kW (999hp) Akasaka DM28AKFD 1 x 4 Stroke 6 Cy. 280 x 460 735kW (999bhp) Akasaka Tekkosho KK (Akasaka DieselLtd)-Japan
133381 HLR	**YUGO-VOSTOK 5** *ex* Kasmina-1 *-2005* *ex* Jasmine No. 9 *-1999* **OOO 'Polluks' (Polluks Co Ltd)** Dong Nam Co Ltd *Sovetskaya Gavan* *Russia* MMSI: 273312510 Official number: E-0144	**743** 274 508	Class: RS (KR)	**1995-09 Koje Shipbuilding Co Ltd — Geoje** Yd No: 371 Loa 57.60 Br ex - Dght 3.400 Lbp 50.61 Br md 9.00 Dpth 5.94 Welded, 1 dk	**(B11B2FV) Fishing Vessel** Bale: 563	**1 oil engine** driving 1 FP propeller Total Power: 1,030kW (1,400hp) 13.1kn Niigata 6M28ATE 1 x 4 Stroke 6 Cy. 280 x 480 1030kW (1400bhp) Ssangyong Heavy Industries Co Ltd-South Korea
001969 EKL	**YUGO VOSTOK NO. 1** *ex* Pakura *-2002* *ex* Akagi Maru *-1994* **Morrybprom Co Ltd** - *Sovetskaya Gavan* *Russia* MMSI: 273442820 Official number: 804719	**3,097** 1,001 3,645	Class: RS (LR) (NK) Classed BC until 26/11/02	**1980-12 Naikai Shipbuilding & Engineering Co Ltd — Onomichi HS (Taguma Shipyard)** (Hull) Yd No: 463 **1980-12 Hitachi Zosen Corp — Japan** Loa 91.39 Br ex 15.00 Dght 6.414 Lbp 85.24 Br md 15.00 Dpth 6.70 Welded, 1 dk	**(B11A2FG) Factory Stern Trawler** Grain: 2,835; Bale: 2,649 4 Ha: ER Derricks: 4x5t	**1 oil engine** driving 1 FP propeller Total Power: 3,236kW (4,400hp) 14.0kn B&W 5K45GFC 1 x 2 Stroke 5 Cy. 450 x 900 3236kW (4400bhp) Hitachi Zosen Corp-Japan AuxGen: 3 x 630kW 450V 60Hz a.c Boilers: AuxB (Comp) 7.0kgf/cm² (6.9bar) Fuel: 71.5 (d.f.) 993.5 (r.f.) 16.0pd
139050 OSL	**YUGUHE** **Shanghai Panasia Shipping Co Ltd** COSCO Container Lines Co Ltd (COSCON) *Shanghai* *China* MMSI: 412087000	**36,772** 21,268 44,772 T/cm 64.6	Class: CC	**1997-12 Samsung Heavy Industries Co Ltd — Geoje** Yd No: 1201 Loa 243.00 (BB) Br ex - Dght 12.000 Lbp 226.70 Br md 32.20 Dpth 19.00 Welded, 1 dk	**(A33A2CC) Container Ship (Fully Cellular)** TEU 3400 C Ho 1460 TEU C Dk 1940 TEU incl 300 ref C. Compartments: ER, 7 Cell Ho 13 Ha: ER	**1 oil engine** driving 1 FP propeller Total Power: 20,623kW (28,039hp) 21.0kn B&W 6L80MC 1 x 2 Stroke 6 Cy. 800 x 2592 20623kW (28039bhp) Samsung Heavy Industries Co Ltd-South Korea AuxGen: 3 x 1470kW 60Hz a.c Thrusters: 1 Thwart. CP thruster (f)
815038 JQJ9	**YUH FA NO. 1** *ex* Aliikai 1 *-2011* *ex* Green Star I *-2008* *ex* Green Tree *-2002* *ex* New Star No. 1 *-1999* *ex* Shinsei Maru No. 1 *-1990* *ex* Kiho Maru No. 11 *-1989* *ex* Kamo Maru No. 78 *-1983* **Yuh Fa Fisheries (Vanuatu) Co Ltd** - *Port Vila* *Vanuatu* Official number: 2099	**499** 218 655		**1978-11 KK Kanasashi Zosen — Shizuoka SZ** Yd No: 2008 Loa 49.18 Br ex - Dght 3.252 Lbp 43.36 Br md 8.41 Dpth 3.59 Welded, 1 dk	**(B11B2FV) Fishing Vessel**	**1 oil engine** driving 1 FP propeller Total Power: 736kW (1,001hp) Hanshin 6LU28G 1 x 4 Stroke 6 Cy. 280 x 440 736kW (1001bhp) The Hanshin Diesel Works Ltd-Japan

IMO / Call sign / Flag	Name / Owner	Tonnage	Class	Build / Dimensions	Type	Machinery	
8520032 *YJTA2* -	**YUH FA NO. 201** *ex* Eisei Maru No. 7 *-2003* *ex* Kantetsu Maru No. 8 *-1993* **Yuh Fa Fisheries (Vanuatu) Co Ltd** - *Port Vila* *Vanuatu* MMSI: 576881000 Official number: 1516	**531** 159 -		**1986-01 KK Kanasashi Zosen — Shizuoka SZ** Yd No: 3091 Loa 54.89 (BB) Br ex 8.54 Dght 3.550 Lbp 46.00 Br md 8.50 Dpth 3.92 Welded, 1 dk	**(B11B2FV) Fishing Vessel** Ins: 436	**1 oil engine** with flexible couplings & sr reverse geared to sc. shaft driving 1 FP propeller Total Power: 736kW (1,001hp) Sumiyoshi 1 x 4 Stroke 6 Cy. 270 x 480 736kW (1001bhp) Sumiyoshi Marine Diesel Co Ltd-Japan	S27
8327210 - -	**YUH FUH No. 1** - -	*336* 175 -	Class: (CR)	**1983 San Yang Shipbuilding Co., Ltd. — Kaohsiung** Loa 46.66 Br ex - Dght 3.271 Lbp 41.08 Br md 7.80 Dpth 3.66 Welded, 1 dk	**(B11B2FV) Fishing Vessel** Compartments: 3 Ho, ER	**1 oil engine** driving 1 FP propeller Total Power: 883kW (1,201hp) Hanshin 1 x 4 Stroke 6 Cy. 280 x 440 883kW (1201bhp) The Hanshin Diesel Works Ltd-Japan AuxGen: 2 x 128kW 120/225V a.c	6LU28
8327234 - -	**YUH FUH No. 2** - -	*336* 175 -	Class: (CR)	**1983 San Yang Shipbuilding Co., Ltd. — Kaohsiung** Loa 46.66 Br ex - Dght 3.271 Lbp 41.08 Br md 7.80 Dpth 3.66 Welded, 1 dk	**(B11B2FV) Fishing Vessel** Compartments: 3 Ho, ER	**1 oil engine** driving 1 FP propeller Total Power: 883kW (1,201hp) Hanshin 1 x 4 Stroke 6 Cy. 280 x 440 883kW (1201bhp) The Hanshin Diesel Works Ltd-Japan AuxGen: 2 x 128kW 120/225V a.c	6LU28
8926224 - -	**YUH HUNG 212** - -	**526** 249 -		**1995 Lin Sheng Shipbuilding Co, Ltd — Kaohsiung** L reg 48.70 Br ex - Dght - Lbp - Br md 8.50 Dpth 3.65 Welded, 1 dk	**(B11B2FV) Fishing Vessel**	**1 oil engine** driving 1 FP propeller Total Power: 883kW (1,201hp) Niigata 1 x 4 Stroke 6 Cy. 883kW (1201bhp) Niigata Engineering Co Ltd-Japan	12.0k
8327222 - -	**YUH LIH No. 1** - **Bankers Equity Ltd** Myko Fisheries Ltd	*336* 175 -	Class: CR	**1983 San Yang Shipbuilding Co., Ltd. — Kaohsiung** Loa 46.66 Br ex - Dght 3.271 Lbp 41.08 Br md 7.80 Dpth 3.66 Welded, 1 dk	**(B11B2FV) Fishing Vessel** Compartments: 3 Ho, ER	**1 oil engine** driving 1 FP propeller Total Power: 883kW (1,201hp) Hanshin 1 x 4 Stroke 6 Cy. 280 x 440 883kW (1201bhp) The Hanshin Diesel Works Ltd-Japan AuxGen: 2 x 128kW 120/225V a.c	6LU28
8222616 *BDCM* -	**YUH SHAN** - **Bes Engineers Corp** - *Hualien* *Chinese Taipei*	*176* 42 67	Class: (CR)	**1982-02 China Shipbuilding Corp (CSBC) — Kaohsiung** Loa 28.38 Br ex 8.84 Dght 2.601 Lbp 25.00 Br md 8.60 Dpth 3.51 Welded, 1 dk	**(B32A2ST) Tug**	**2 oil engines** with clutches & sr geared to sc. shafts driving 2 Directional propellers Total Power: 1,176kW (1,598hp) Yanmar 2 x 4 Stroke 6 Cy. 240 x 290 each-588kW (799bhp) Yanmar Diesel Engine Co Ltd-Japan	11.0kn 6GL-DT
8649682 *BI2158* CT7-0158	**YUH YEOU NO. 31** **Unifishery Enterprise Co Ltd** - *Kaohsiung* *Chinese Taipei* Official number: 11336	**725** 286 -		**1989-02 Taiwan Machinery Manufacturing Corp. — Kaohsiung** Loa 56.50 Br ex - Dght 3.658 Lbp 49.50 Br md 8.90 Dpth 3.85 Welded, 1 dk	**(B11B2FV) Fishing Vessel**	**1 oil engine** driving 1 Propeller	
8649668 *BI2429* CT7-0429	**YUH YEOU NO. 66** **Unifishery Enterprise Co Ltd** - *Kaohsiung* *Chinese Taipei* Official number: 11814	**705** 211 -		**1990-04 Fong Kuo Shipbuilding Co Ltd — Kaohsiung** Yd No: 287 Loa 54.80 Br ex - Dght 3.582 Lbp 47.80 Br md 7.80 Dpth 3.85 Welded, 1 dk	**(B11B2FV) Fishing Vessel**	**1 oil engine** driving 1 Propeller	
8649644 *BZJQ* CT7-0295	**YUH YEOU NO. 236** **Unifishery Enterprise Co Ltd** - *Kaohsiung* *Chinese Taipei* Official number: 11205	**718** 287 -		**1988-12 Kaohsiung Shipbuilding Co. Ltd. — Kaohsiung** Yd No: 041 Loa 56.30 (BB) Br ex - Dght 3.792 Lbp 50.60 Br md 8.90 Dpth 3.85 Welded, 1 dk	**(B11B2FV) Fishing Vessel**	**1 oil engine** driving 1 Propeller	
8629280 *BG3658* -	**YUH YIH FA NO. 168** *ex* Chen Chien No. 6 *-2005* **Zeng Sen Min** - *Chinese Taipei* Official number: 014522	**212** 78 -		**2005-05 in Chinese Taipei** Loa 29.80 Br ex 6.60 Dght - Lbp - Br md - Dpth 2.80 Welded, 1 dk	**(B11B2FV) Fishing Vessel**	**1 oil engine** driving 1 Propeller Yanmar 1 x 4 Stroke 6 Cy. Yanmar Diesel Engine Co Ltd-Japan	
8430380 - -	**YUH YOW No. 1** - - SatCom: Inmarsat A 1356256	*413* 203 -		**1986 Fong Kuo Shipbuilding Co Ltd — Kaohsiung** L reg 41.80 Br ex - Dght 3.250 Lbp - Br md 8.00 Dpth 3.50 Welded, 1 dk	**(B11B2FV) Fishing Vessel**	**1 oil engine** driving 1 FP propeller Total Power: 809kW (1,100hp) Sumiyoshi 1 x 4 Stroke 809kW (1100bhp) Sumiyoshi Marine Diesel Co Ltd-Japan	9.0kn
8430392 - -	**YUH YOW No. 2** - -	*413* 203 -		**1986 Fong Kuo Shipbuilding Co Ltd — Kaohsiung** L reg 41.90 Br ex - Dght 3.250 Lbp - Br md 8.00 Dpth 3.50 Welded, 1 dk	**(B11B2FV) Fishing Vessel**	**1 oil engine** driving 1 FP propeller Total Power: 736kW (1,001hp)	11.0kn
8430914 - -	**YUH YOW No. 6** *ex* Wini No. 5 *-2005* - SatCom: Inmarsat M 641661710	*424* 151 -		**1988 Sen Koh Shipbuilding Corp — Kaohsiung** L reg 42.88 Br ex - Dght - Lbp - Br md 8.00 Dpth 3.50 Welded, 1 dk	**(B11B2FV) Fishing Vessel**	**1 oil engine** driving 1 FP propeller Total Power: 809kW (1,100hp) Akasaka 1 x 4 Stroke 809kW (1100bhp) Akasaka Tekkosho KK (Akasaka DieselLtd)-Japan	12.0kn
8430926 - -	**YUH YOW No. 8** **Yu Pao Fishery Co Ltd** - SatCom: Inmarsat B 341674710 *San Lorenzo* *Honduras* Official number: L-1924431	*424* 151 -		**1988 Sen Koh Shipbuilding Corp — Kaohsiung** L reg 42.88 Br ex - Dght 3.250 Lbp - Br md 8.00 Dpth 3.50 Welded, 1 dk	**(B11B2FV) Fishing Vessel**	**1 oil engine** driving 1 FP propeller Total Power: 809kW (1,100hp) Akasaka 1 x 4 Stroke 809kW (1100bhp) Akasaka Tekkosho KK (Akasaka DieselLtd)-Japan	9.0kn
8431035 - -	**YUH YOW No. 101** - - SatCom: Inmarsat B 341662710	**706** 282 -		**1989 Sen Koh Shipbuilding Corp — Kaohsiung** L reg 50.00 Br ex - Dght - Lbp - Br md 8.90 Dpth 3.85 Welded, 1 dk	**(B11B2FV) Fishing Vessel**	**1 oil engine** driving 1 FP propeller Total Power: 883kW (1,201hp)	12.0kn
8822753 - -	**YUH YOW No. 102** **Yu Chang Marine Products Co Ltd** - SatCom: Inmarsat B 341662810 *San Lorenzo* *Honduras* Official number: L-1824032	**719** 256 -		**1989 Sen Koh Shipbuilding Corp — Kaohsiung** Loa 57.29 Br ex 8.92 Dght 3.792 Lbp - Br md 8.90 Dpth 3.85 Welded, 1 dk	**(B11B2FV) Fishing Vessel**	**1 oil engine** geared to sc. shaft driving 1 FP propeller Total Power: 736kW (1,001hp) Akasaka 1 x 4 Stroke 6 Cy. 280 x 480 736kW (1001bhp) Akasaka Tekkosho KK (Akasaka DieselLtd)-Japan	K28FD
8431126 *V6P1102* 36129	**YUH YOW No. 127** **City Pro Management Ltd** - *Kolonia, Pohnpei* *Micronesia* MMSI: 510048000 Official number: VR0118	*729* 256 -		**1990 Sen Koh Shipbuilding Corp — Kaohsiung** Yd No: 085 Loa 54.15 Br ex - Dght - Lbp 47.80 Br md 8.90 Dpth 3.85 Welded, 1 dk	**(B11B2FV) Fishing Vessel**	**1 oil engine** reduction geared to sc. shaft driving 1 FP propeller Total Power: 883kW (1,201hp) Akasaka 1 x 4 Stroke 6 Cy. 883kW (1201bhp) Akasaka Tekkosho KK (Akasaka DieselLtd)-Japan	11.0kn
8648145 *BI2539* LL2281	**YUH YOW NO. 137** **Yu Pao Fishery Co Ltd** - *Kaohsiung* *Chinese Taipei* Official number: CT7-0539	**572** 228 -		**2002-06 Fong Kuo Shipbuilding Co Ltd — Kaohsiung** Yd No: 390 Loa 55.75 Br ex 8.70 Dght - Lbp - Br md - Dpth - Welded, 1 dk	**(B11B2FV) Fishing Vessel**	**1 oil engine** driving 1 Propeller	

No.	Ship / Owner / Registry	Tonnage	Builder / Dimensions	Type	Machinery
431138	**YUH YOW No. 201** **Yuh Yih Fishery Co Ltd** - *San Lorenzo* *Honduras* Official number: L-1924243	*717* 256 -	**1990 Sen Koh Shipbuilding Corp — Kaohsiung** L reg 50.00 Br ex - Dght 3.800 Lbp - Br md 8.90 Dpth 3.85 Welded, 1 dk	**(B11B2FV) Fishing Vessel**	**1 oil engine** driving 1 FP propeller Total Power: 883kW (1,201hp) 10.0kn
431140	**YUH YOW No. 202** **Yu Tsang Fishery Co Ltd** - SatCom: Inmarsat A 1355532 *San Lorenzo* *Honduras* Official number: L-1924031	*719* 256 -	**1990 Sen Koh Shipbuilding Corp — Kaohsiung** L reg 50.00 Br ex - Dght - Lbp - Br md 8.90 Dpth 3.85 Welded, 1 dk	**(B11B2FV) Fishing Vessel**	**1 oil engine** driving 1 FP propeller Total Power: 1,030kW (1,400hp) 11.0kn
648157 *2519* .2218	**YUH YOW NO. 227** **Yu Chang Marine Products Co Ltd** - *Kaohsiung* *Chinese Taipei* Official number: CT7-0519	**520** 221 -	**2000-03 Fong Kuo Shipbuilding Co Ltd — Kaohsiung** Yd No: 365 Loa 55.75 Br ex 8.70 Dght - Lbp - Br md - Dpth - Welded, 1 dk	**(B11B2FV) Fishing Vessel**	**1 oil engine** driving 1 Propeller
648169 *2518* .2226	**YUH YOW NO. 609** **Yu Tsang Fishery Co Ltd** - *Kaohsiung* *Chinese Taipei* Official number: CT7-0518	**520** 221 -	**2000-07 Fong Kuo Shipbuilding Co Ltd — Kaohsiung** Yd No: 369 Loa 55.75 Br ex 8.70 Dght - Lbp - Br md - Dpth - Welded, 1 dk	**(B11B2FV) Fishing Vessel**	**1 oil engine** driving 1 Propeller
648171 *2516* .2239	**YUH YOW NO. 703** **Yuh Yih Fishery Co Ltd** - *Kaohsiung* *Chinese Taipei* Official number: CT7-0516	**520** 221 -	**2000-08 Fong Kuo Shipbuilding Co Ltd — Kaohsiung** Yd No: 370 Loa 55.75 Br ex 8.70 Dght - Lbp - Br md - Dpth - Welded, 1 dk	**(B11B2FV) Fishing Vessel**	**1 oil engine** driving 1 Propeller
888989	**YUH YUEAN NO. 1** *ex* Koryo Maru No. 38 *-2003* *ex* Sumiyoshi Maru No. 5 *-2003* - -	*187* 56 -	**1981 Nishii Dock Co. Ltd. — Ise** L reg 28.00 Br ex - Dght - Lbp - Br md 5.80 Dpth 2.50 Bonded, 1 dk	**(B11B2FV) Fishing Vessel** Hull Material: Reinforced Plastic	**1 oil engine** driving 1 FP propeller Yanmar 1 x 4 Stroke Yanmar Diesel Engine Co Ltd-Japan
838001	**YUH YUEAN NO. 2** *ex* Fukutoku Maru No. 38 *-2003* *ex* Bishamon Maru No. 33 *-1995* - -	*109* 35 -	**1982 Nishii Dock Co. Ltd. — Ise** L reg 29.90 Br ex - Dght 2.100 Lbp - Br md 5.90 Dpth 2.60 Bonded, 1 dk	**(B11B2FV) Fishing Vessel** Hull Material: Reinforced Plastic	**1 oil engine** driving 1 FP propeller Total Power: 360kW (489hp) Niigata 1 x 4 Stroke 360kW (489bhp) Niigata Engineering Co Ltd-Japan
848765 *JSZ8*	**YUH YUEAN NO. 3** *ex* Jintoku Maru No. 1 *-2003* *ex* Fukuei Maru No. 11 *-2003* **Yuh Fa Fisheries (Vanuatu) Co Ltd** - *Port Vila* *Vanuatu* MMSI: 576878000 Official number: 1514	*167* 50 -	**1984-01 Nishii Dock Co. Ltd. — Ise** Yd No: 691 L reg 29.20 Br ex - Dght - Lbp - Br md 5.55 Dpth 2.45 Bonded, 1 dk	**(B11B2FV) Fishing Vessel** Hull Material: Reinforced Plastic	**1 oil engine** driving 1 FP propeller Yanmar 1 x 4 Stroke Yanmar Diesel Engine Co Ltd-Japan
898037 *D6218*	**YUHETI JAYA I** *ex* Rimba Raya I *-1995* **PT Trimanunggal Nugraha** - *Samarinda* *Indonesia*	**197** Class: KI 118 -	**1995-12 C.V. Swadaya Utama — Samarinda** Loa 25.00 Br ex - Dght 2.590 Lbp 23.00 Br md 7.50 Dpth 3.10 Welded, 1 dk	**(B32A2ST) Tug**	**2 oil engines** reduction geared to sc. shafts driving 2 FP propellers Total Power: 882kW (1,200hp) Cummins KTA-19-M3 2 x 4 Stroke 6 Cy. 159 x 159 each-441kW (600bhp) (new engine 1996) Cummins Engine Co Ltd-United Kingdom
738172 *D2643*	**YUHI MARU** **Oita Rinkai Kogyo KK** - *Oita, Oita* *Japan* Official number: 140747	*196* - -	**2008-04 K.K. Odo Zosen Tekko — Shimonoseki** Yd No: 602 Loa 35.35 Br ex - Dght 3.100 Lbp 29.00 Br md 9.20 Dpth 4.15 Welded, 1 dk	**(B32A2ST) Tug**	**2 oil engines** reduction geared to sc. shafts driving 2 Propellers Total Power: 3,676kW (4,998hp) Niigata 6L28HX 2 x 4 Stroke 6 Cy. 280 x 370 each-1838kW (2499bhp) Niigata Engineering Co Ltd-Japan
001816	**YUHO** *ex* Yuho Maru *-1998* - -	*697* Class: (NK) 425 1,485	**1980-10 K.K. Miura Zosensho — Saiki** Yd No: 600 Loa 65.77 Br ex - Dght 4.440 Lbp 60.13 Br md 10.51 Dpth 4.81 Welded, 1 dk	**(A24A2BT) Cement Carrier** Grain: 1,156	**1 oil engine** driving 1 FP propeller Total Power: 956kW (1,300hp) 11.0kn Daihatsu 6DSM-26 1 x 4 Stroke 6 Cy. 260 x 320 956kW (1300bhp) Daihatsu Diesel Manufacturing Co Lt-Japan AuxGen: 3 x 56kW a.c
603268 *QGF7*	**YUHO** *ex* Yuho Maru *-1990* *ex* Goho Maru *-1979* **Good Year Maritime Co Inc** - *San Lorenzo* *Honduras* Official number: L-1722783	*161* 56 -	**1965 Osaka Shipbuilding Co Ltd — Osaka OS** Yd No: 252 Loa - Br ex 7.65 Dght 2.388 Lbp 28.50 Br md 7.60 Dpth 3.56 Riveted\Welded, 1 dk	**(B32A2ST) Tug**	**2 oil engines** driving 2 FP propellers Total Power: 1,104kW (1,500hp) Fuji 8MD27.5H 2 x 4 Stroke 8 Cy. 275 x 320 each-552kW (750bhp) Fuji Diesel Co Ltd-Japan AuxGen: 1 x 24kW a.c, 1 x 8kW a.c Fuel: 26.5 6.0pd
424716 *D2567*	**YUHO** **Nissei Kaiun YK** - *Imabari, Ehime* *Japan* MMSI: 431000399 Official number: 140695	*749* Class: NK - 1,935	**2008-01 Hakata Zosen K.K. — Imabari** Yd No: 706 Loa 73.25 Br ex - Dght 4.703 Lbp 69.00 Br md 11.80 Dpth 5.25 Welded, 1 dk	**(A13B2TP) Products Tanker** Double Hull (13F) Liq: 2,200; Liq (Oil): 2,200	**1 oil engine** driving 1 FP propeller Total Power: 1,618kW (2,200hp) Hanshin LH34LG 1 x 4 Stroke 6 Cy. 340 x 640 1618kW (2200bhp) The Hanshin Diesel Works Ltd-Japan Fuel: 89.0 (d.f.)
597965 *D3208*	**YUHO MARU** - **Japan Railway Construction, Transport & Technology Agency & Shinpo Kaiun KK** Shinpo Kaiun KK *Matsuyama, Ehime* *Japan* MMSI: 431002508 Official number: 141457	*749* Class: NK - 1,081	**2011-04 K.K. Miura Zosensho — Saiki** Yd No: 1367 Loa 67.80 Br ex - Dght 4.165 Lbp 63.50 Br md 11.50 Dpth 4.75 Welded, 1 dk	**(A11B2TG) LPG Tanker** Liq (Gas): 1,449 2 x Gas Tank (s); 2 independent cyl horizontal	**1 oil engine** reduction geared to sc. shaft driving 1 Propeller Total Power: 1,323kW (1,799hp) 12.5kn Hanshin LA28G 1 x 4 Stroke 6 Cy. 280 x 590 1323kW (1799bhp) The Hanshin Diesel Works Ltd-Japan Fuel: 142.0
635298 *D3338*	**YUHO MARU** **Kanehiro Kisen YK** - *Imabari, Ehime* *Japan* MMSI: 431003404 Official number: 141649	**3,555** Class: NK - 5,486	**2012-05 Hakata Zosen K.K. — Imabari** Yd No: 738 Loa 104.80 (BB) Br ex - Dght 6.663 Lbp 99.00 Br md 16.00 Dpth 8.20 Welded, 1 dk	**(A13B2TP) Products Tanker** Double Hull (13F) Liq: 5,488; Liq (Oil): 5,600	**1 oil engine** driving 1 FP propeller Total Power: 3,309kW (4,499hp) 13.5kn Hanshin LH46LA 1 x 4 Stroke 6 Cy. 460 x 880 3309kW (4499bhp) The Hanshin Diesel Works Ltd-Japan Thrusters: 1 Thwart. FP thruster (f) Fuel: 370.0
824812	**YUHO MARU** *ex* Ebisu Maru No. 33 *-1993* - -	*154* 56 185	**1968 Fukuoka Shipbuilding Co Ltd — Fukuoka FO** Yd No: 922 Loa 31.68 Br ex 6.53 Dght 2.439 Lbp 26.70 Br md 6.51 Dpth 3.05 Welded, 1 dk	**(B11B2FV) Fishing Vessel**	**1 oil engine** driving 1 FP propeller Total Power: 588kW (799hp) Hanshin 6L28ASH 1 x 4 Stroke 6 Cy. 280 x 430 588kW (799bhp) Hanshin Nainenki Kogyo-Japan
805183 *M5669*	**YUHO MARU** *ex* Yuhi Maru *-2003* **Oita Rinkai Kogyo KK** - *Oita, Oita* *Japan* Official number: 130318	*198* Class: (NK) - -	**1988-06 K.K. Odo Zosen Tekko — Shimonoseki** Yd No: 355 Loa 34.02 Br ex 9.40 Dght 3.101 Lbp 29.01 Br md 9.20 Dpth 4.10 Welded, 1 dk	**(B32A2ST) Tug**	**2 oil engines** geared integral to driving 2 Z propellers Total Power: 2,500kW (3,400hp) Niigata 6L28BXF 2 x 4 Stroke 6 Cy. 280 x 350 each-1250kW (1700bhp) Niigata Engineering Co Ltd-Japan

8910782 **YUHO MARU** *498*
9MPL6 - -
- - 1,257
Port Klang *Malaysia*
MMSI: 533064300
Official number: 334390

1989-12 Mukaishima Zoki Co. Ltd. — Onomichi Yd No: 261
Loa 65.99 Br ex - Dght 4.162
Lbp 61.80 Br md 10.00 Dpth 4.50
Welded, 1 dk

(A13B2TP) Products Tanker
Liq: 1,299; Liq (Oil): 1,299
Compartments: 8 Ta, ER

1 oil engine with clutches & sr reverse geared to sc. shaft driving 1 FP propeller
Total Power: 736kW (1,001hp)
Niigata 6M28BF
1 x 4 Stroke 6 Cy. 280 x 480 736kW (1001bhp)
Niigata Engineering Co Ltd-Japan

9066136 **YUHO MARU No. 2** *434*
JK5281 -
- **KK Showa Kisen** 990
Bizen, Okayama *Japan*
MMSI: 431400168
Official number: 133696

1993-06 Hitachi Zosen Mukaishima Marine Co Ltd — Onomichi HS Yd No: 71
Loa 59.22 Br ex - Dght 3.710
Lbp 54.50 Br md 9.60 Dpth 4.30
Welded, 1 dk

(A12A2TC) Chemical Tanker
2 Cargo Pump (s): 2x400m³/hr

1 oil engine driving 1 FP propeller
Total Power: 736kW (1,001hp)
Niigata 6M26BGT
1 x 4 Stroke 6 Cy. 260 x 460 736kW (1001bhp)
Niigata Engineering Co Ltd-Japan

9482380 **YUHO MARU NO. 3** *499*
JD2491 -
- **KK Showa Kisen** 1,197
Bizen, Okayama *Japan*
MMSI: 431000336
Official number: 140622

2007-10 Hongawara Zosen K.K. — Fukuyama Yd No: 600
Loa 64.95 (BB) Br ex 10.02 Dght 3.964
Lbp 62.00 Br md 10.00 Dpth 4.50
Welded, 1 dk

(A12B2TR) Chemical/Products Tanker
Double Hull (13F)

1 oil engine driving 1 FP propeller
Total Power: 1,177kW (1,600hp)
Niigata 6M28NT
1 x 4 Stroke 6 Cy. 280 x 480 1177kW (1600bhp)
Niigata Engineering Co Ltd-Japan

9608142 **YUHO MARU NO. 5** *1,061* Class: NK
JD3225 496
- **Japan Railway Construction, Transport & Technology Agency & Myoei Kisen Co Ltd** 1,658
Seiho Kaiun Co Ltd
Bizen, Okayama *Japan*
MMSI: 432825000
Official number: 141490

2011-09 Maebata Zosen Tekko K.K. — Sasebo Yd No: 301
Loa 72.89 (BB) Br ex - Dght 4.634
Lbp 68.00 Br md 11.50 Dpth 5.35
Welded, 1 dk

(A12B2TR) Chemical/Products Tanker
Double Hull (13F)
Liq: 1,781; Liq (Oil): 1,815

1 oil engine reverse geared to sc. shaft driving 1 Propeller
Total Power: 1,323kW (1,799hp)
Akasaka AX31R
1 x 4 Stroke 6 Cy. 310 x 620 1323kW (1799bhp)
Akasaka Tekkosho KK (Akasaka DieselLtd)-Japan
Fuel: 90.0

9473614 **YUHO MARU NO. 32** *749* Class: NK
JD2768 -
- **Japan Railway Construction, Transport & Technology Agency & Showa Kisen Co Ltd & Seiwa Kaiun Co Ltd** 999
KK Showa Kisen
Bizen, Okayama *Japan*
MMSI: 431000687
Official number: 140807

2008-09 Kegoya Dock K.K. — Kure Yd No: 1121
Loa 67.90 Br ex - Dght 4.115
Lbp 63.00 Br md 11.50 Dpth 4.90
Welded, 1 dk

(A11B2TG) LPG Tanker
Liq (Gas): 1,459

1 oil engine reverse geared to sc. shaft driving 1 FP propeller
Total Power: 1,323kW (1,799hp)
Akasaka A31R
1 x 4 Stroke 6 Cy. 310 x 600 1323kW (1799bhp)
Akasaka Tekkosho KK (Akasaka DieselLtd)-Japan
Fuel: 90.0

9238272 **YUHSAN** **45,965** Class: NK
H9TE 13,790
- **Pacific Gas Transports SA** 49,999
BW Gas AS T/cm
Panama *Panama* 70.3
MMSI: 353812000
Official number: 2835502B

2002-01 Mitsubishi Heavy Industries Ltd. — Nagasaki Yd No: 2174
Loa 230.00 (BB) Br ex 36.63 Dght 10.783
Lbp 219.00 Br md 36.60 Dpth 20.80
Welded, 1 dk

(A11B2TG) LPG Tanker
Double Bottom Entire Compartment Length
Liq (Gas): 77,351
4 x Gas Tank (s); 4 independent (stl) pri horizontal
8 Cargo Pump (s): 8x550m³/hr
Manifold: Bow/CM: 112.5m

1 oil engine driving 1 FP propeller
Total Power: 11,122kW (15,121hp) 16.7kn
Mitsubishi 7UEC60LS
1 x 2 Stroke 7 Cy. 600 x 2200 11122kW (15121bhp)
Mitsubishi Heavy Industries Ltd-Japan
AuxGen: 3 x 850kW 450V 60Hz a.c
Fuel: 379.0 (d.f.) 2775.0 (r.f.)

9172739 **YUHSHO** **44,694** Class: NK
3FBH9 13,409
- **Bull Transports Inc** 49,723
Wilhelmsen Ship Management Sdn Bhd T/cm
SatCom: Inmarsat B 335716210 69.4
Panama *Panama*
MMSI: 357162000
Official number: 2625899C

1999-02 Mitsubishi Heavy Industries Ltd. — Nagasaki Yd No: 2149
Loa 230.00 (BB) Br ex 36.63 Dght 10.836
Lbp 219.00 Br md 36.60 Dpth 20.40
Welded, 1 dk

(A11B2TG) LPG Tanker
Double Bottom Entire Compartment Length
Liq (Gas): 76,929
4 x Gas Tank (s); 4 independent (C.mn.stl) pri horizontal
8 Cargo Pump (s): 8x550m³/hr
Manifold: Bow/CM: 113.1m

1 oil engine driving 1 FP propeller
Total Power: 12,357kW (16,801hp) 16.7kn
Mitsubishi 7UEC60LS
1 x 2 Stroke 7 Cy. 600 x 2200 12357kW (16801bhp)
Mitsubishi Heavy Industries Ltd-Japan
AuxGen: 3 x 880kW 450V a.c
Fuel: 126.3 (d.f.) (Heating Coils) 2483.8 (r.f.) 49.0pd

7728039 **YUHUM** *195*
DUQ2000 *ex Himeshima Maru No. 2 -1992* 86
- **Philstone Shipping Corp** 92
Cagayan de Oro *Philippines*
Official number: 10-0000153

1978-01 Usuki Iron Works Co Ltd — Usuki OT Yd No: 982
Loa 37.22 Br ex 8.84 Dght 2.050
Lbp 32.01 Br md 8.81 Dpth 2.82
Welded, 1 dk

(A37B2PS) Passenger Ship
Passengers: 141

1 oil engine reduction geared to sc. shaft driving 1 FP propeller
Total Power: 559kW (760hp)
Yanmar 6UA-UT
1 x 4 Stroke 6 Cy. 200 x 240 559kW (760bhp)
Yanmar Diesel Engine Co Ltd-Japan

9691254 **YUIHO MARU** *225* Class: FA (Class contemplated)
JD3615 -
- **Nishitaki Kaiun KK** 180
Japan
MMSI: 431005095

2013-12 Kanrei Zosen K.K. — Naruto Yd No: 433
Loa 29.50 Br ex - Dght 3.400
Lbp - Br md 9.20 Dpth -
Welded, 1 dk

(B32B2SP) Pusher Tug

2 oil engines reduction geared to sc. shafts driving 2 Propellers
Total Power: 2,646kW (3,598hp)
Hanshin LA28G
2 x 4 Stroke 6 Cy. 280 x 590 each-1323kW (1799bhp)
The Hanshin Diesel Works Ltd-Japan

9599236 **YUIMARU** *499*
JD3138 -
- **Marusan Kaiun KK** 1,640
Osaka, Osaka *Japan*
Official number: 141362

2010-12 K.K. Matsuura Zosensho — Osakikamijima Yd No: 575
L reg 72.12 (BB) Br ex - Dght 4.070
Lbp 70.00 Br md 12.50 Dpth 7.00
Welded, 1 dk

(A31A2GX) General Cargo Ship
Grain: 2,518
1 Ha: ER (40.2 x 10.0)

1 oil engine reduction geared to sc. shaft driving 1 Propeller
Total Power: 1,471kW (2,000hp) 11.5kn
Hanshin LA34G
1 x 4 Stroke 6 Cy. 340 x 720 1471kW (2000bhp)
The Hanshin Diesel Works Ltd-Japan

8630409 **YUJIN MARU NO. 53** *124*
- *ex Shinpo Maru No. 8 -2004* -
- - -
-

1983-06 Yamanishi Shipbuilding Co Ltd — Ishinomaki MG
Loa 28.70 Br ex - Dght 2.500
Lbp - Br md 6.60 Dpth 3.00
Welded, 1 dk

(B11B2FV) Fishing Vessel

1 oil engine driving 1 FP propeller
Total Power: 324kW (441hp)
Akasaka
1 x 4 Stroke 324kW (441bhp)
Akasaka Tekkosho KK (Akasaka DieselLtd)-Japan

8736772 **YUJIN MARU NO. 81** *125*
JD2527 -
HK1-1374 **Nomura Gyogyo KK** -
Hiroo, Hokkaido *Japan*
Official number: 140659

2008-03 Kidoura Shipyard Co Ltd — Kesennuma MG Yd No: 618
L reg 28.12 Br ex - Dght -
Lbp - Br md 7.40 Dpth 3.20
Welded, 1 dk

(B11B2FV) Fishing Vessel

1 oil engine driving 1 Propeller

8414453 **YUJIN NO. 1** *499*
- *ex Shosei Maru No. 1 -2014* -
- - 1,188
-
South Korea
MMSI: 440104040

1984-10 Uchida Zosen — Ise Yd No: 833
Loa 61.12 Br ex - Dght 4.328
Lbp 56.01 Br md 9.81 Dpth 4.63
Welded, 1 dk

(A13B2TU) Tanker (unspecified)
Liq: 1,150; Liq (Oil): 1,150
Compartments: 4 Ta, ER

1 oil engine driving 1 FP propeller
Total Power: 736kW (1,001hp)
Hanshin 6LUN28ARG
1 x 4 Stroke 6 Cy. 280 x 480 736kW (1001bhp)
The Hanshin Diesel Works Ltd-Japan

9094664 **YUKA** *499*
JD2254 -
- **Fudo Kaiun YK** 1,600
Kagoshima, Kagoshima *Japan*
Official number: 140327

2006-04 Koike Zosen Kaiun KK — Osakikamijima Yd No: 303
Loa 76.20 Br ex - Dght 3.900
Lbp 70.00 Br md 12.50 Dpth 6.75
Welded, 1 dk

(A31A2GX) General Cargo Ship
Grain: 2,545; Bale: 2,545

1 oil engine driving 1 Propeller
Total Power: 1,471kW (2,000hp) 12.8kn
Niigata 6M34NT-G
1 x 4 Stroke 6 Cy. 340 x 620 1471kW (2000bhp)
Niigata Engineering Co Ltd-Japan

8609034 **YUKAI MARU** *3,413* Class: (NK)
JG4636 -
- **Mitsui Muromachi Shipping Co Ltd (Mitsui Muromachi Kaiun KK)** 5,999
Tokyo *Japan*
MMSI: 431100701
Official number: 129805

1986-10 Nishi Shipbuilding Co Ltd — Imabari EH Yd No: 344
Loa 104.79 Br ex - Dght 6.809
Lbp 98.02 Br md 15.51 Dpth 8.46
Welded, 1 dk

(A31A2GX) General Cargo Ship
Grain: 7,302; Bale: 7,041
2 Ha: (30.1 x 8.4) (29.3 x 8.4)ER

1 oil engine driving 1 CP propeller
Total Power: 2,427kW (3,300hp) 11.5kn
Hanshin 6EL44
1 x 4 Stroke 6 Cy. 440 x 880 2427kW (3300bhp)
The Hanshin Diesel Works Ltd-Japan
Fuel: 120.0 (r.f.)

9674866 **YUKAI MARU** *4,383* Class: NK
JD3539 -
- **Mitsui Muromachi Shipping Co Ltd (Mitsui Muromachi Kaiun KK)** 6,299
-
Tokyo *Japan*
MMSI: 431004661
Official number: 141951

2013-07 Kegoya Dock K.K. — Kure Yd No: 1150
Loa 113.50 (BB) Br ex - Dght 6.484
Lbp 105.00 Br md 17.00 Dpth 8.20
Welded, 1 dk

(A31A2GX) General Cargo Ship
Grain: 7,867; Bale: 7,665

1 oil engine geared to sc. shaft driving 1 FP propeller
Total Power: 2,647kW (3,599hp) 14.0kn
Hanshin LH41LA
1 x 4 Stroke 6 Cy. 410 x 800 2647kW (3599bhp)
The Hanshin Diesel Works Ltd-Japan
AuxGen: 2 x 550kW a.c
Fuel: 266.0

No.	Name / Owner	Tonnage	Class	Builder / Dimensions	Type	Machinery
04366 55324	**YUKI MARU** **Corporation for Advanced Transport & Technology & Enomoto Kaisoten Co Ltd** JFE Logistics Corp *Tokyo* *Japan* MMSI: 431100131 Official number: 134963	*617* - 1,600	Class: (NK)	**1994-05 Nakatani Shipyard Co. Ltd. — Etajima** Yd No: 560 Loa 77.38 (BB) Br ex - Dght 4.220 Lbp 72.00 Br md 12.00 Dpth 7.10 Welded, 2 dks	**(A31A2GX) General Cargo Ship** Compartments: 1 Ho, ER	**1 oil engine** driving 1 FP propeller Total Power: 1,471kW (2,000hp) Hanshin LH34LAG 1 x 4 Stroke 6 Cy. 340 x 640 1471kW (2000bhp) The Hanshin Diesel Works Ltd-Japan
79220 .6571	**YUKI MARU** **Kamezaki Kaiun YK** - *Anan, Tokushima* *Japan* Official number: 135592	*498* - 1,250		**1998-12 K.K. Murakami Zosensho — Naruto** Yd No: 228 Loa 75.64 Br ex - Dght - Lbp 70.00 Br md 11.50 Dpth 7.20 Welded, 1 dk	**(A31A2GX) General Cargo Ship** Compartments: 1 Ho, ER 1 Ha: (40.2 x 9.2)ER	**1 oil engine** driving 1 FP propeller Total Power: 736kW (1,001hp) 11.5kn Hanshin LH30LG 1 x 4 Stroke 6 Cy. 300 x 600 736kW (1001bhp) The Hanshin Diesel Works Ltd-Japan
068067 K5170	**YUKI MARU** - - *Hofu, Yamaguchi* *Japan* Official number: 134080	*331* - 1,000		**1993-11 K.K. Kamishima Zosensho — Osakikamijima** Yd No: 552 Loa 65.84 Br ex - Dght 3.750 Lbp 58.00 Br md 10.50 Dpth 6.20 Welded, 1 dk	**(A31A2GX) General Cargo Ship** Bale: 1,633	**1 oil engine** reverse geared to sc. shaft driving 1 FP propeller Total Power: 736kW (1,001hp) Akasaka A28S 1 x 4 Stroke 6 Cy. 280 x 550 736kW (1001bhp) Akasaka Tekkosho KK (Akasaka DieselLtd)-Japan
803894	**YUKI MARU No. 1** *ex* Kazuei Maru No. 18 **Shinyo Suisan** - *South Korea*	*192* 83 -		**1967 KK Kanasashi Zosen — Shizuoka SZ** Yd No: 805 Loa 41.53 Br ex 6.61 Dght 2.794 Lbp 34.50 Br md 6.58 Dpth 3.20 Welded, 1 dk	**(B11B2FV) Fishing Vessel**	**1 oil engine** driving 1 FP propeller Total Power: 552kW (750hp) Niigata 1 x 4 Stroke 6 Cy. 280 x 440 552kW (750bhp) Niigata Engineering Co Ltd-Japan
736538 02477	**YUKI MARU NO. 8** **Kamezaki Kaiun YK** - *Anan, Tokushima* *Japan* Official number: 140607	*499* - 1,790		**2007-09 K.K. Murakami Zosensho — Naruto** Yd No: 262 Loa 74.50 Br ex - Dght 4.320 Lbp 69.60 Br md 12.00 Dpth 7.37 Welded, 1 dk	**(A31A2GX) General Cargo Ship** Grain: 2,852 Compartments: 1 Ho, ER 1 Ha: ER (40.0 x 9.5)	**1 oil engine** driving 1 Propeller Total Power: 1,323kW (1,799hp) 13.0kn Niigata 6M31BFT 1 x 4 Stroke 6 Cy. 310 x 530 1323kW (1799bhp) Niigata Engineering Co Ltd-Japan
094212 02141	**YUKI MARU NO. 12** **Kamezaki Kaiun YK** - *Anan, Tokushima* *Japan* MMSI: 431501827 Official number: 140199	*499* - 1,753		**2005-07 K.K. Murakami Zosensho — Naruto** Yd No: 255 Loa 70.70 Br ex - Dght 4.330 Lbp 68.00 Br md 12.30 Dpth 7.33 Welded, 1 dk	**(A31A2GX) General Cargo Ship** 1 Ha: ER (40.0 x 10.0)	**1 oil engine** driving 1 Propeller Total Power: 1,618kW (2,200hp) 11.8kn Niigata 6M34BGT 1 x 4 Stroke 6 Cy. 340 x 620 1618kW (2200bhp) Niigata Engineering Co Ltd-Japan
497701 03108	**YUKI MARU NO. 17** **YK Marukita Shoten** - SatCom: Inmarsat C 443277610 *Kesennuma, Miyagi* *Japan* MMSI: 432776000 Official number: 141311	*119* - 139		**2010-08 K.K. Yoshida Zosen Tekko — Kesennuma** Yd No: 550 Loa 36.70 (BB) Br ex - Dght 2.500 Lbp - Br md 6.40 Dpth - Welded, 1 dk	**(B11B2FV) Fishing Vessel** Ins: 152	**1 oil engine** reduction geared to sc. shafts driving 1 Propeller Total Power: 625kW (850hp) Hanshin LH26G 1 x 4 Stroke 6 Cy. 260 x 440 625kW (850bhp) The Hanshin Diesel Works Ltd-Japan
048079 E3102	**YUKI MARU NO. 77** *ex* Seifuku Maru No. 8 *-2005* **YK Marukita Shoten** - SatCom: Inmarsat M 643165910 *Kesennuma, Miyagi* *Japan* Official number: 132230	*119* - 153		**1992-06 K.K. Yoshida Zosen Tekko — Kesennuma** Yd No: 377 Loa 38.25 (BB) Br ex - Dght 2.650 Lbp 31.25 Br md 6.40 Dpth 2.80 Welded, 1 dk	**(B11B2FV) Fishing Vessel**	**1 oil engine** with clutches, flexible couplings & sr geared to sc. shaft driving 1 CP propeller Total Power: 588kW (799hp) Hanshin LH26G 1 x 4 Stroke 6 Cy. 260 x 440 588kW (799bhp) The Hanshin Diesel Works Ltd-Japan
526807 03116	**YUKIGUMO** **Government of Japan (Ministry of Land, Infrastructure & Transport) (The Coastguard)** - *Tokyo* *Japan* Official number: 141274	*101* - -		**2011-03 Niigata Shipbuilding & Repair Inc — Niigata NI** Yd No: 0048 Loa 32.00 Br ex - Dght - Lbp - Br md 6.50 Dpth 3.37 Welded, 1 dk	**(B34H2SQ) Patrol Vessel** Hull Material: Aluminium Alloy	**2 oil engines** reduction geared to sc. shafts driving 2 Water jets 36.0kn
253949	**YUKIYU MARU No. 28** *ex* Junyo Maru No. 5 *-2005* *ex* Nitto Maru No. 71 *-2005* **Tosei Sangyo KK (Tosei Industries Co Ltd)** - *South Korea*	*135* 78 -		**1953 Niigata Engineering Co Ltd — Niigata NI** Yd No: 222 L reg 29.84 Br ex 5.92 Dght - Lbp - Br md - Dpth - Riveted\Welded	**(B11A2FT) Trawler**	**1 oil engine** driving 1 FP propeller Total Power: 221kW (300hp) Niigata 1 x 4 Stroke 5 Cy. 280 x 420 221kW (300bhp) Niigata Tekkosho-Japan Fuel: 37.5
387618 C7891	**YUKMAR 1** **Yukmar Yuksel Marmara Petrol Nakliyat Sanayi ve Ticaret AS** - *Istanbul* *Turkey* MMSI: 271010172 Official number: 6941	**198** **135** **341**		**1996 Gisan Gemi Ins. San — Istanbul** Yd No: 17 Loa 42.50 Br ex - Dght 2.800 Lbp 38.90 Br md 7.00 Dpth 3.00 Welded, 1 dk	**(A13B2TU) Tanker (unspecified)** Single Hull Liq: 440; Liq (Oil): 440 Part Cargo Heating Coils Compartments: 12 Wing Ta, ER 4 Cargo Pump (s): 4x30m³/hr	**1 oil engine** geared to sc. shaft driving 1 FP propeller Total Power: 294kW (400hp) 10.0kn Volvo Penta TAMD122A 1 x 4 Stroke 6 Cy. 130 x 150 294kW (400bhp) AB Volvo Penta-Sweden AuxGen: 1 x 115kW 380/220V 50Hz a.c, 1 x 85kW 380/220V 50Hz a.c, 1 x 65kW 380/220V 50Hz a.c Fuel: 9.4 (d.f.) (Heating Coils) 2.2pd
061617 35137	**YUKO MARU** *ex* Nikko Maru *-2005* **Kyodo Kisen Co Ltd & Nissen Kisen Co Ltd** Nissen Kisen KK *Onomichi, Hiroshima* *Japan* MMSI: 431100588 Official number: 133791	*499* - 1,285	Class: NK	**1992-07 Yamanaka Zosen K.K. — Imabari** Yd No: 526 Loa 65.20 (BB) Br ex 10.02 Dght 4.290 Lbp 61.00 Br md 10.00 Dpth 4.65 Welded, 1 dk	**(A12B2TR) Chemical/Products Tanker** Liq: 1,150; Liq (Oil): 1,150 Cargo Heating Coils Compartments: 8 Wing Ta, ER 2 Cargo Pump (s): 2x400m³/hr Manifold: Bow/CM: 29m	**1 oil engine** reverse geared to sc. shaft driving 1 FP propeller Total Power: 1,030kW (1,400hp) 11.4kn Akasaka K28R 1 x 4 Stroke 6 Cy. 280 x 480 1030kW (1400bhp) Akasaka Tekkosho KK (Akasaka DieselLtd)-Japan Fuel: 14.0 (d.f.) (Part Heating Coils) 46.0 (r.f.) 4.7pd
073294 K5282	**YUKO MARU** *ex* Eiwa *-2012* *ex* Sho *-1999* **Sugahara Jeneralist Co Ltd** - *Marugame, Kagawa* *Japan* Official number: 133697	*355* - 800		**1993-07 Hitachi Zosen Mukaishima Marine Co Ltd — Onomichi HS** Yd No: 72 Loa 52.50 Br ex - Dght - Lbp 48.00 Br md 9.00 Dpth 3.90 Welded, 1 dk	**(A12A2TC) Chemical Tanker** 2 Cargo Pump (s): 2x200m³/hr	**1 oil engine** geared to sc. shaft driving 1 FP propeller Total Power: 736kW (1,001hp) 11.0kn Hanshin LH26G 1 x 4 Stroke 6 Cy. 260 x 440 736kW (1001bhp) The Hanshin Diesel Works Ltd-Japan
133006 M6429	**YUKO MARU** **Yuko YK** - *Nango, Miyazaki* *Japan* Official number: 134523	*199* - 696		**1995-07 KK Ura Kyodo Zosensho — Awaji HG** Yd No: 305 Loa 55.77 Br ex - Dght 3.340 Lbp 52.30 Br md 9.50 Dpth 5.61 Welded, 1 dk	**(A31A2GX) General Cargo Ship** Grain: 1,405; Bale: 1,383 Compartments: 1 Ho 1 Ha: (32.3 x 7.5)	**1 oil engine** driving 1 FP propeller Total Power: 736kW (1,001hp) 11.9kn Yanmar MF26-HT 1 x 4 Stroke 6 Cy. 260 x 500 736kW (1001bhp) Yanmar Diesel Engine Co Ltd-Japan
805473	**YUKO MARU** - - *China*	*399* - 680		**1978-07 Sasaki Shipbuilding Co Ltd — Osakikamijima HS** Yd No: 323 Loa 48.39 Br ex - Dght 3.760 Lbp 48.01 Br md 8.21 Dpth 3.81 Welded, 1 dk	**(A13B2TU) Tanker (unspecified)**	**1 oil engine** driving 1 FP propeller Total Power: 736kW (1,001hp) Niigata 6L28X 1 x 4 Stroke 6 Cy. 280 x 440 736kW (1001bhp) Niigata Engineering Co Ltd-Japan
614883	**YUKO MARU No. 10** **Ceymarine Enterprise** -	*312* - 888		**1986-11 Kitanihon Zosen K.K. — Hachinohe** Yd No: 213 Loa 67.75 (BB) Br ex 10.22 Dght 4.257 Lbp 57.00 Br md 10.00 Dpth 6.66 Welded, 2 dks	**(B11B2FV) Fishing Vessel** Ins: 913	**1 oil engine** driving 1 FP propeller Total Power: 1,600kW (2,175hp) Akasaka DM33 1 x 4 Stroke 6 Cy. 330 x 500 1600kW (2175bhp) Akasaka Tekkosho KK (Akasaka DieselLtd)-Japan
614617	**YUKO MARU No. 88** **Mekong Holding** -	*303* - -		**1985-11 Fujishin Zosen K.K. — Kamo** Yd No: 511 Loa 66.20 (BB) Br ex 10.24 Dght - Lbp 57.00 Br md 10.20 Dpth 6.61 Welded, 2 dks	**(B11B2FV) Fishing Vessel**	**1 oil engine** driving 1 FP propeller Total Power: 1,177kW (1,600hp) Niigata 6M31AFTE 1 x 4 Stroke 6 Cy. 310 x 530 1177kW (1600bhp) Niigata Engineering Co Ltd-Japan

ID / Call sign / Flag	Name / Owner / Port	Tonnage	Class	Build / Dimensions	Type / Cargo	Machinery
8826917 *YYP4983* -	**YUKO MARU No. 88** **Eduardo Suarez Muria** *Venezuela*	192 74 -		**1986-01 Higashi Kyushu Shipbuilding Co Ltd — Usuki OT** L reg 28.10 Br ex - Dght 2.000 Lbp - Br md 6.17 Dpth 2.40 Bonded, 1 dk	**(B11B2FV) Fishing Vessel** Hull Material: Reinforced Plastic	**1 oil engine** driving 1 FP propeller Daihatsu 1 x 4 Stroke Daihatsu Diesel Manufacturing Co Lt-Japan
9200885 *WDF4123* -	**YUKON QUEEN II** **Royal Hyway Tours Inc** *Anchorage, AK* *United States of America* MMSI: 367027520 Official number: 1077566	237 73 91	Class: (AB)	**1999-03 SBF Shipbuilders (1977) Pty Ltd — Fremantle WA** Yd No: 981 Loa 31.70 Br ex 9.60 Dght 1.006 Lbp 28.74 Br md 9.30 Dpth 2.50 Welded, 1 dk	**(A37B2PS) Passenger Ship** Hull Material: Aluminium Alloy Passengers: unberthed: 149	**4 oil engines** geared to sc. shafts driving 4 Water jets Total Power: 3,532kW (4,804hp) 35.0k M.T.U. 12V2000M7 4 x Vee 4 Stroke 12 Cy. 130 x 150 each-883kW (1201bhp) MTU Friedrichshafen GmbH-Friedrichshafen AuxGen: 2 x 52kW a.c
9411991 *2BWW6* -	**YUKON STAR** **Rigel Reederei GmbH & Co KG mt 'Yukon Star'** Rigel Schiffahrts GmbH & Co KG *Douglas* *Isle of Man (British)* MMSI: 235070031 Official number: DR0166	23,312 9,972 37,873 T/cm 45.2	Class: LR ✠ **100A1** SS 04/2014 Double Hull oil and chemical tanker, Ship Type 3 CSR ESP *IWS LI ✠ **LMC** **UMS IGS** Eq.Ltr: J†; Cable: 605.0/66.0 U3 (a)	**2009-04 Hyundai Mipo Dockyard Co Ltd — Ulsan** Yd No: 2096 Loa 184.00 (BB) Br ex 27.40 Dght 11.515 Lbp 176.00 Br md 27.40 Dpth 17.20 Welded, 1 dk	**(A12B2TR) Chemical/Products Tanker** Double Hull (13F) Liq: 40,758; Liq (Oil): 42,630 Compartments: 12 Wing Ta, 2 Wing Slop Ta, ER 12 Cargo Pump (s): 10x500m³/hr, 2x300m³/hr Manifold: Bow/CM: 92.2m	**1 oil engine** driving 1 FP propeller Total Power: 7,860kW (10,686hp) 14.5k MAN-B&W 6S46MC- 1 x 2 Stroke 6 Cy. 460 x 1932 7860kW (10686bhp) Hyundai Heavy Industries Co Ltd-South Korea AuxGen: 3 x 730kW 450V 60Hz a.c Boilers: e (ex.g.) 9.2kgf/cm² (9.0bar), WTAuxB (o.f.) 9.2kgf/cm (9.0bar) Fuel: 155.0 (d.f.) 950.0 (r.f.)
9067049 *JK5294* -	**YUKOU MARU NO. 5** *ex* Teruho Maru No. 5 *-1994* **Hopefull Marine YK** Kaisei Tsusho KK (Kaisei Tsusho Co Ltd) *Bizen, Okayama* *Japan* MMSI: 431400235 Official number: 134050	*497* - 1,214		**1993-11 Narasaki Zosen KK — Muroran HK** Yd No: 1139 Loa 64.00 (BB) Br ex - Dght 4.196 Lbp 60.15 Br md 10.00 Dpth 4.50 Welded, 1 dk	**(A13B2TP) Products Tanker** Liq: 1,123; Liq (Oil): 1,123 Compartments: 8 Ta, ER	**1 oil engine** with clutches, flexible couplings & reverse geare to sc. shaft driving 1 FP propeller Total Power: 736kW (1,001hp) Akasaka K28 1 x 4 Stroke 6 Cy. 280 x 480 736kW (1001bhp) Akasaka Tekkosho KK (Akasaka DieselLtd)-Japan
7702425 *TCYH* -	**YUKSEL IMAMOGLU** *ex* Timur Islamoglu *-1994* *ex* Tolga *-1985* **Imamoglu Denizcilik ve Kara Nakliyat Ticaret AS** - SatCom: Inmarsat C 427111520 *Istanbul* *Turkey* MMSI: 271002160 Official number: 4797	1,923 1,164 3,150	Class: TL (AB)	**1980-06 Atilim Gemi Insaat Sanayii ve Ticaret A.S. — Istanbul** Yd No: 1 Loa 82.50 Br ex 13.77 Dght 5.510 Lbp 74.66 Br md 13.76 Dpth 6.61 Welded, 2 dks	**(A31A2GX) General Cargo Ship** Grain: 4,077; Bale: 3,822 Compartments: 2 Ho, ER 2 Ha: ER Derricks: 4x5t	**1 oil engine** reverse reduction geared to sc. shaft driving 1 F propeller Total Power: 970kW (1,319hp) S.K.L. 8NVD48A-2 1 x 4 Stroke 8 Cy. 320 x 480 970kW (1319bhp) (new engin 1980) SKL Motoren u. Systemtechnik AG-Magdeburg AuxGen: 2 x 80kW a.c, 1 x 40kW a.c
7733864 *UGVO* MS-0105	**YUKSPORIT** **Industrial Commercial Firm Bussol (OOO Proizvodstvenno-Kommercheskaya Firma 'Bussol')** - *Murmansk* *Russia* Official number: 770654	174 52 98	Class: (RS)	**1978-06 Astrakhanskaya Sudoverf im. "Kirova" — Astrakhan** Yd No: 105 Loa 34.01 Br ex 7.10 Dght 2.900 Lbp 29.98 Br md 7.00 Dpth 3.66 Welded, 1 dk	**(B11B2FV) Fishing Vessel** Bale: 78 Compartments: 1 Ho, ER 1 Ha: (1.6 x 1.3) Derricks: 2x2t; Winches: 2 Ice Capable	**1 oil engine** driving 1 FP propeller Total Power: 294kW (400hp) 9.0k Iveco Aifo 8210 SRM4 1 x 4 Stroke 6 Cy. 137 x 156 294kW (400bhp) (new engine 2005) IVECO AIFO S.p.A.-Pregnana Milanese Fuel: 20.0 (d.f.)
8717130 *JCHW* -	**YUKYU MARU No. 3** *ex* Fukuho Maru No. 3 *-1998* *ex* Hakuryu Maru No. 85 *-1992* *ex* Daito Maru No. 88 *-1991* **Yukyu Gyogyo Seisan Kumiai** - *Karatsu, Saga* *Japan* Official number: 128534	*135* - 114		**1988-03 K.K. Murakami Zosensho — Ishinomaki** Yd No: 1217 Loa 46.00 (BB) Br ex 7.93 Dght 2.801 Lbp 37.01 Br md 7.90 Dpth 3.20 Welded, 1 dk	**(B11B2FV) Fishing Vessel**	**1 oil engine** with clutches, flexible couplings & sr geared to sc. shaft driving 1 CP propeller Total Power: 861kW (1,171hp) Hanshin 6MUH28 1 x 4 Stroke 6 Cy. 280 x 340 861kW (1171bhp) The Hanshin Diesel Works Ltd-Japan
7830260 -	**YUKYU MARU No. 38** *ex* Seizan Maru No. 1 *-1988* **Tong Young Industries Co Ltd** - *South Korea*	*273* - -		**1977 K.K. Izutsu Zosensho — Nagasaki** Yd No: 765 Loa 50.50 Br ex 8.21 Dght - Lbp 43.01 Br md 7.60 Dpth 3.61 Welded, 1 dk	**(B12B2FC) Fish Carrier**	**1 oil engine** reduction geared to sc. shaft driving 1 FP propeller Total Power: 824kW (1,120hp) Yanmar 6ZL-U 1 x 4 Stroke 6 Cy. 280 x 340 824kW (1120bhp) Yanmar Diesel Engine Co Ltd-Japan
8317198 - -	**YUKYU MARU NO. 72** *ex* Genpuku Maru No. 72 *-2005* - -	*287* - 454		**1983-07 Nagasaki Zosen K.K. — Nagasaki** Yd No: 837 Loa 53.70 (BB) Br ex - Dght 3.401 Lbp 46.41 Br md 7.85 Dpth 3.71 Welded, 1 dk	**(B12B2FC) Fish Carrier** Ins: 407 Compartments: 7 Ho, ER 7 Ha: ER	**1 oil engine** with clutches, flexible couplings & sr reverse geared to sc. shaft driving 1 FP propeller Total Power: 861kW (1,171hp) Niigata 6L28BX 1 x 4 Stroke 6 Cy. 280 x 320 861kW (1171bhp) Niigata Engineering Co Ltd-Japan Thrusters: 1 Thwart. FP thruster (f)
8106202 - -	**YUKYU MARU NO. 88** *ex* Yuryo Maru No. 20 *-1991* - - *South Korea*	*279* - -		**1981-04 Nagasaki Zosen K.K. — Nagasaki** Yd No: 762 Loa 44.30 Br ex - Dght 2.752 Lbp 38.21 Br md 7.41 Dpth 3.15 Welded, 1 dk	**(B11B2FV) Fishing Vessel**	**1 oil engine** reduction geared to sc. shaft driving 1 FP propeller Total Power: 956kW (1,300hp) Daihatsu 6DSM-26F 1 x 4 Stroke 6 Cy. 260 x 320 956kW (1300bhp) Daihatsu Diesel Manufacturing Co Lt-Japan
9459967 *A8ZJ3* -	**YULIA** *launched as* Harlequin *-2011* **Reederei ms 'Yulia' GmbH & Co KG** MST Mineralien Schiffahrt Spedition und Transport GmbH *Monrovia* *Liberia* MMSI: 636092253 Official number: 92253	19,814 10,208 30,878	Class: GL	**2011-05 AVIC Weihai Shipyard Co Ltd — Weihai SD** Yd No: SN321 Loa 184.90 (BB) Br ex - Dght 10.400 Lbp 178.00 Br md 23.70 Dpth 14.60 Welded, 1 dk	**(A21A2BC) Bulk Carrier** Grain: 38,635; Bale: 37,476 Compartments: 6 Ho, ER 6 Ha: (16.0 x 17.4)3 (19.2 x 17.4) (13.6 x 17.4)ER (10.4 x 13.2) Cranes: 3x30t Ice Capable	**1 oil engine** driving 1 FP propeller Total Power: 7,200kW (9,789hp) 13.5k MAN-B&W 6S46MC- 1 x 2 Stroke 6 Cy. 460 x 1932 7200kW (9789bhp) STX Engine Co Ltd-South Korea AuxGen: 3 x 680kW 450/230V 60Hz a.c Fuel: 350.0 (d.f.) 1300.0 (r.f.)
9612923 *UBJI2* -	**YULIY MAKARENKOV** **Gaztechleasing Ltd** MRP Tanker *St Petersburg* *Russia* MMSI: 273351260 Official number: 30-0132	4,541 1,929 6,707	Class: RS RR (Class contemplated)	**2013-05 OOO Verf Bratyev Nobel — Rybinsk** Yd No: 25003 Loa 139.99 Br ex - Dght 4.170 Lbp 134.10 Br md 16.60 Dpth 5.50 Welded, 1 dk	**(A13A2TW) Crude/Oil Products Tanker** Double Hull (13F) Liq: 6,870; Liq (Oil): 6,990 Compartments: 6 Ta, ER 6 Cargo Pump (s): 6x150m³/hr Ice Capable	**2 oil engines** reduction geared to sc. shafts driving 2 CP propellers Total Power: 2,400kW (3,264hp) 10.5k Wartsila 6L2 2 x 4 Stroke 6 Cy. 200 x 280 each-1200kW (1632bhp) Wartsila Finland Oy-Finland AuxGen: 3 x 292kW a.c Thrusters: 1 Thwart. FP thruster (f) Fuel: 250.0 (d.f.)
8965919 - - -	**YUMBELL** - -	*194* - -		**1972 Astilleros Marco Chilena Ltda. — Iquique** L reg 30.05 Br ex - Dght - Lbp - Br md 7.65 Dpth 3.66 Welded, 1 dk	**(B11B2FV) Fishing Vessel**	**1 oil engine** driving 1 FP propeller
9047661 *JI3482* -	**YUMESAKI** - - *Osaka, Osaka* *Japan* Official number: 133394	*187* - 50		**1992-03 Mitsui Eng. & SB. Co. Ltd. — Tamano** Yd No: TH1621 Loa 34.00 Br ex - Dght - Lbp 29.00 Br md 8.00 Dpth 3.20 Welded, 1 dk	**(A37B2PS) Passenger Ship** Hull Material: Aluminium Alloy Passengers: unberthed: 83	**2 oil engines** sr geared to sc. shafts driving 2 FP propellers Total Power: 2,912kW (3,960hp) 30.0k G.M. (Detroit Diesel) 16V-149-T 2 x Vee 2 Stroke 16 Cy. 146 x 146 each-1456kW (1980bhp) General Motors Detroit DieselAllison Divn-USA AuxGen: 2 x 50kW 225V 60Hz a.c
6713697 - -	**YUMESHIMA MARU** *ex* Kasuga Maru No. 1 *-2002* *ex* Yumeshima Maru *-2002* *ex* Take Maru No. 13 *-2000* *ex* Zuiho Maru No. 1 *-1998* *ex* Takechiyo Maru *-1983* - - -	*183* - -		**1967-02 Osaka Shipbuilding Co Ltd — Osaka OS** Yd No: 261 Loa 30.76 Br ex 7.50 Dght 2.363 Lbp 29.95 Br md 7.47 Dpth 3.36 Riveted\Welded, 1 dk	**(B32A2ST) Tug**	**2 oil engines** driving 2 FP propellers Total Power: 1,104kW (1,500hp) Daihatsu 8PSHTCM-26 2 x 4 Stroke 8 Cy. 260 x 320 each-552kW (750bhp) Daihatsu Kogyo-Japan AuxGen: 1 x 48kW

567972 *FHC9* — **YUMETAMOU**
Power Shipping SA
Doun Kisen KK (Doun Kisen Co Ltd)
SatCom: Inmarsat C 437311810
Panama — *Panama*
MMSI: 373118000
Official number: 43062KJ
92,752 60,504 181,407 T/cm 125.0 — Class: NK
2012-03 Koyo Dockyard Co Ltd — Mihara HS Yd No: 2308
Loa 291.98 (BB) Br ex - Dght 18.237
Lbp 283.80 Br md 45.00 Dpth 24.70
Welded, 1 dk
(A21A2BC) Bulk Carrier
Grain: 201,243
Compartments: 9 Ho, ER
9 Ha: ER
1 oil engine driving 1 FP propeller
Total Power: 18,660kW (25,370hp) 14.0kn
MAN-B&W 6S70MC-C
1 x 2 Stroke 6 Cy. 700 x 2800 18660kW (25370bhp)
Mitsui Engineering & Shipbuilding CLtd-Japan
AuxGen: 3 x 600kW a.c
Fuel: 5830.0

915201 *G4875* — **YUMI MARU**
Ajinomoto Butsuryu KK
-
Tokyo — *Japan*
MMSI: 431100305
Official number: 131119
193 - 460
1990-03 K.K. Odo Zosen Tekko — Shimonoseki Yd No: 368
Loa 44.50 (BB) Br ex - Dght 3.340
Lbp 40.01 Br md 7.20 Dpth 3.50
Welded, 1 dk
(A12D2LV) Vegetable Oil Tanker
Liq: 450
Compartments: 6 Ta, ER
1 oil engine geared to sc. shaft driving 1 FP propeller
Total Power: 736kW (1,001hp)
Hanshin 6LU26G
1 x 4 Stroke 6 Cy. 260 x 440 736kW (1001bhp)
The Hanshin Diesel Works Ltd-Japan
Thrusters: 1 Thwart. FP thruster (f)

954582 *G5381* — **YUMI MARU No. 2**
Ajinomoto Butsuryu KK
-
Tokyo — *Japan*
Official number: 136753
199 - -
1999-10 Iisaku Zosen K.K. — Nishi-Izu Yd No: 99188
Loa 44.60 Br ex - Dght -
Lbp 40.10 Br md 7.20 Dpth 3.50
Welded, 1 dk
(A12A2TC) Chemical Tanker
Liq: 460
2 Cargo Pump (s): 2x150m³/hr
1 oil engine driving 1 FP propeller
Total Power: 736kW (1,001hp) 10.5kn
Hanshin LH26G
1 x 4 Stroke 6 Cy. 260 x 440 736kW (1001bhp)
The Hanshin Diesel Works Ltd-Japan
Fuel: 27.0 (d.f.)

979788 *G5704* — **YUMIHARI**
KK Daito Corp
-
Tokyo — *Japan*
Official number: 137178
245 - -
2003-06 Hanasaki Zosensho K.K. — Yokosuka Yd No: 271
Loa 36.26 Br ex - Dght 3.300
Lbp - Br md 10.00 Dpth 4.39
Welded, 1 dk
(B32A2ST) Tug
2 oil engines driving 2 Z propellers
Total Power: 2,646kW (3,598hp)
Yanmar 6N280M-UV
2 x 4 Stroke 6 Cy. 280 x 380 each-1323kW (1799bhp)
Yanmar Diesel Engine Co Ltd-Japan

510711 *JD2635* — **YUMIHARI MARU**
Sasebo Heavy Industries Co Ltd
-
Sasebo, Nagasaki — *Japan*
MMSI: 432646000
Official number: 140740
195 - -
2008-04 Keihin Dock Co Ltd — Yokohama Yd No: 282
Loa 33.30 Br ex 9.20 Dght 3.100
Lbp 28.50 Br md 9.02 Dpth 3.88
Welded, 1 dk
(B32A2ST) Tug
2 oil engines geared to sc. shafts driving 2 Z propellers
Total Power: 3,676kW (4,998hp)
Niigata 6L28HX
2 x 4 Stroke 6 Cy. 280 x 370 each-1838kW (2499bhp)
Niigata Engineering Co Ltd-Japan

221213 *D7NL* — **YUMO No. 5**
Oh Yong Jin
-
Busan — *South Korea*
Official number: UM29007
356 223 610 — Class: (KR)
1964 Korea Shipbuilding & Engineering Corp — Busan
Loa - Br ex 7.29 Dght -
Lbp 40.01 Br md 7.26 Dpth 3.71
Welded, 1 dk
(A13B2TU) Tanker (unspecified)
Liq: 692; Liq (Oil): 692
1 oil engine driving 1 FP propeller
Total Power: 313kW (426hp) 9.5kn
Alpha 405-24VO
1 x 2 Stroke 5 Cy. 240 x 400 313kW (426bhp)
A/S Burmeister & Wain's Maskin ogSkibsbyggeri-Denmark

7531761 *TCBK9* — **YUMURTALIK**
-
-
Istanbul — *Turkey*
MMSI: 271002336
Official number: TUGS 441
368 135 - — Class: (TL)
1976-12 Sedef Gemi Endustrisi A.S. — Gebze Yd No: 14
Loa 36.76 Br ex 9.50 Dght 4.061
Lbp 32.80 Br md 9.10 Dpth 4.81
Welded, 1 dk
(B32A2ST) Tug
1 oil engine driving 1 FP propeller
Total Power: 1,912kW (2,600hp)
Niigata 8L31EZ
1 x 4 Stroke 8 Cy. 310 x 380 1912kW (2600bhp)
Niigata Engineering Co Ltd-Japan

8810097 — **YUN AN I**
CPC Corp Taiwan
Taiwan Navigation Co Ltd
Kaohsiung — *Chinese Taipei*
Official number: 11151
404 121 158 — Class: CR
1989-08 China Shipbuilding Corp — Keelung Yd No: 359
Loa 31.70 Br ex 11.02 Dght 4.200
Lbp 29.70 Br md 11.00 Dpth 4.70
Welded, 1 dk
(B32A2ST) Tug
2 oil engines gearing integral to driving 2 Voith-Schneider propellers
Total Power: 2,504kW (3,404hp)
Kromhout 8FHD240
2 x 4 Stroke 8 Cy. 240 x 260 each-1252kW (1702bhp)
Stork Werkspoor Diesel BV-Netherlands

8810102 *BHDF* — **YUN AN II**
CPC Corp Taiwan
Taiwan Navigation Co Ltd
Kaohsiung — *Chinese Taipei*
Official number: 11152
404 121 158 — Class: CR
1989-06 China Shipbuilding Corp — Keelung Yd No: 360
Loa 31.70 Br ex 11.02 Dght 4.200
Lbp 29.70 Br md 11.00 Dpth 4.70
Welded, 1 dk
(B32A2ST) Tug
2 oil engines gearing integral to driving 2 Voith-Schneider propellers
Total Power: 2,504kW (3,404hp)
Kromhout 8FHD240
2 x 4 Stroke 8 Cy. 240 x 260 each-1252kW (1702bhp)
Stork Werkspoor Diesel BV-Netherlands
AuxGen: 1 x 160kW 440V a.c, 1 x 160kW 254V a.c

8849452 — **YUN AN No. 3**
CPC Corp Taiwan
Taiwan Navigation Co Ltd
Kaohsiung — *Chinese Taipei*
Official number: 11501
404 121 146 — Class: CR
1990-02 Taiwan Machinery Manufacturing Corp. — Kaohsiung
Loa 31.50 Br ex 11.40 Dght -
Lbp - Br md 11.00 Dpth 4.20
Welded, 1 dk
(B32A2ST) Tug
2 oil engines driving 2 FP propellers
Total Power: 2,784kW (3,786hp)
Kromhout 8FGHD240
2 x 4 Stroke 8 Cy. 240 x 260 each-1392kW (1893bhp)
Stork Wartsila Diesel BV-Netherlands
AuxGen: 2 x 160kW 450V a.c

8849438 — **YUN AN No. 5**
CPC Corp Taiwan
Taiwan Navigation Co Ltd
Kaohsiung — *Chinese Taipei*
Official number: 11502
404 121 146 — Class: CR
1990-02 Taiwan Machinery Manufacturing Corp. — Kaohsiung
Loa 31.50 Br ex 11.40 Dght -
Lbp - Br md 11.00 Dpth 4.20
Welded, 1 dk
(B32A2ST) Tug
2 oil engines driving 2 FP propellers
Total Power: 2,784kW (3,786hp)
Kromhout 8FGHD240
2 x 4 Stroke 8 Cy. 240 x 260 each-1392kW (1893bhp)
Stork Wartsila Diesel BV-Netherlands

8966420 *BR3121* — **YUN AN NO. 6**
CPC Corp Taiwan
Kaohsiung — *Chinese Taipei*
Official number: 13447
411 123 209 — Class: CR
1999-03 Lien Ho Shipbuilding Co, Ltd — Kaohsiung
Loa 32.50 Br ex 11.72 Dght 3.000
Lbp - Br md 11.00 Dpth 4.20
Welded, 1 dk
(B32A2ST) Tug
2 oil engines reduction geared to sc. shafts driving 2 FP propellers
Total Power: 2,648kW (3,600hp) 10.7kn
Yanmar 8N21A-EV
2 x 4 Stroke 8 Cy. 210 x 290 each-1324kW (1800bhp)
Yanmar Diesel Engine Co Ltd-Japan
AuxGen: 2 x 160kW 450V a.c

8888226 *BVCA* — **YUN BAO**
Fujian Luoyuan Shipping Co
Fuzhou, Fujian — *China*
1,247 635 1,311 — Class: (CC)
1995-07 Qingshan Shipyard — Wuhan HB
Loa 73.90 Br ex - Dght 3.980
Lbp 68.40 Br md 11.20 Dpth 5.20
Welded, 1 dk
(A31A2GX) General Cargo Ship
1 oil engine driving 1 FP propeller
Total Power: 622kW (846hp)
Alpha 6T23LU
1 x 4 Stroke 6 Cy. 225 x 300 622kW (846bhp)
Guangzhou Diesel Engine Factory CoLtd-China

9019999 *H3EY* — **YUN DA**
ex Shun Yang *-2011* *ex* Marine Seoul *-2004*
ex Southern Clipper *-2002*
An Yang Shipping Co Ltd
Yantai Pingyang Shipping Co Ltd
Panama — *Panama*
MMSI: 357565000
Official number: 3007904B
2,651 1,332 3,670 — Class: CC (KR) (NK)
1991-02 Higaki Zosen K.K. — Imabari Yd No: 393
Loa 86.01 (BB) Br ex 14.52 Dght 5.724
Lbp 79.99 Br md 14.50 Dpth 8.50
Welded, 1 dk
(A31A2GX) General Cargo Ship
Grain: 5,934; Bale: 5,724
Compartments: 2 Ho, ER
2 Ha: (15.6 x 8.0) (26.0 x 8.0)ER
Derricks: 1x15t,2x10t
1 oil engine driving 1 FP propeller
Total Power: 1,470kW (1,999hp) 11.0kn
Hanshin 6EL32
1 x 4 Stroke 6 Cy. 320 x 640 1470kW (1999bhp)
Hanshin Nainenki Kogyo-Japan
AuxGen: 2 x 120kW 450V 60Hz a.c
Fuel: 57.5 (d.f.) 273.3 (r.f.) 6.5pd

8832485 *BTGH* — **YUN GANG 4**
Government of The People's Republic of China (Lianyungang Harbour Administration)
-
Lianyungang, Jiangsu — *China*
276 82 96 — Class: (CC)
1989 Hong Kong Dredging Ltd — Hong Kong
Loa - Br ex - Dght 3.030
Lbp 27.65 Br md 8.80 Dpth 3.90
Welded, 1 dk
(B32A2ST) Tug
2 oil engines driving 2 FP propellers
Total Power: 1,912kW (2,600hp) 13.0kn
Niigata 6L25CXE
2 x 4 Stroke 6 Cy. 250 x 320 each-956kW (1300bhp)
Niigata Engineering Co Ltd-Japan
AuxGen: 2 x 80kW 380V a.c

8024210 *BTGM* — **YUN GANG 8**
Government of The People's Republic of China (Lianyungang Harbour Administration)
-
Lianyungang, Jiangsu — *China*
293 - 152
1981-05 Ishikawajima Ship & Chemical Plant Co Ltd — Tokyo Yd No: 523
Loa 32.83 Br ex 9.53 Dght -
Lbp 29.55 Br md 9.52 Dpth 3.19
Welded, 1 dk
(B32A2ST) Tug
2 oil engines geared to sc. shafts driving 2 FP propellers
Total Power: 2,354kW (3,200hp)
Daihatsu 8DSM-26
2 x 4 Stroke 8 Cy. 260 x 320 each-1177kW (1600bhp)
Daihatsu Diesel Manufacturing Co Lt-Japan

8817241 *BTGN* — **YUN GANG 10**
Government of The People's Republic of China (Lianyungang Harbour Administration)
-
Lianyungang, Jiangsu — *China*
MMSI: 412031140
350 105 113
1988-07 Oshima Shipbuilding Co Ltd — Saikai NS Yd No: 10106
Loa 34.20 Br ex 9.73 Dght 3.180
Lbp 29.00 Br md 9.50 Dpth 4.40
Welded, 1 dk
(B32A2ST) Tug
2 oil engines geared to sc. shafts driving 2 Directional propellers
Total Power: 2,354kW (3,200hp)
Daihatsu 6DLM-26S
2 x 4 Stroke 6 Cy. 260 x 340 each-1177kW (1600bhp)
Daihatsu Diesel Manufacturing Co Lt-Japan

8817253 *BTGO* -	**YUN GANG 11** **Government of The People's Republic of China (Lianyungang Harbour Administration)** *Lianyungang, Jiangsu* *China* MMSI: 412031150	**350** 105 113		**1988-07 Oshima Shipbuilding Co Ltd — Saikai NS** Yd No: 10107 Loa 34.20 Br ex 9.73 Dght 3.190 Lbp 29.00 Br md 9.50 Dpth 4.40 Welded, 1 dk	**(B32A2ST) Tug**	**2 oil engines** geared to sc. shafts driving 2 Directional propellers Total Power: 2,354kW (3,200hp) Daihatsu 6DLM-2 2 x 4 Stroke 6 Cy. 260 x 340 each-1177kW (1600bhp) Daihatsu Diesel Manufacturing Co Lt-Japan
7905936 *BAZT* -	**YUN HAI** *ex* Al Kahla *-1987* **Liaoning Province Dalian Ocean Fishery Group Corp** - SatCom: Inmarsat A 1570273 *Dalian, Liaoning* *China*	*2,404* 993 1,585	Class: (CC) (NV)	**1980-04 Stocznia im Komuny Paryskiej — Gdynia** Yd No: B417/215 Loa 90.00 Br ex - Dght 5.401 Lbp 81.60 Br md 15.00 Dpth 9.40 Welded, 2 dks	**(B11A2FG) Factory Stern Trawler** Ins: 1,561 Ice Capable	**1 oil engine** sr geared to sc. shaft driving 1 CP propeller Total Power: 2,648kW (3,600hp) 15.3k Sulzer 6ZL40/4 1 x 4 Stroke 6 Cy. 400 x 480 2648kW (3600bhp) Zaklady Urzadzen Technicznych'Zgoda' SA-Poland AuxGen: 2 x 560kW 380V 50Hz a.c, 2 x 504kW 380V 50Hz a.c
8632354 *BDBS* -	**YUN HSING** **Government of Taiwan (Inspectorate General of Customs)** - *Kaohsiung* *Chinese Taipei*	*694* 289 -	Class: (CR)	**1987 China Shipbuilding Corp — Keelung** Loa 65.00 Br ex 10.01 Dght 2.950 Lbp 60.85 Br md 10.00 Dpth 5.25 Welded, 1 dk	**(B34H2SQ) Patrol Vessel**	**2 oil engines** geared to sc. shafts driving 2 FP propellers Total Power: 4,732kW (6,434hp) 19.2k MAN 12V25/3 2 x Vee 4 Stroke 12 Cy. 250 x 300 each-2366kW (3217bhp) Taiwan Machinery ManufacturingCorp.-Kaohsiung AuxGen: 2 x 200kW 450V a.c
9380283 *BTGY* -	**YUN JUN 1 HAO** **Government of The People's Republic of China (Lianyungang Harbour Administration)** *Lianyungang, Jiangsu* *China* MMSI: 413031030	**5,926** 1,777 4,500	Class: (CC)	**2007 Guangzhou Wenchong Shipyard Co Ltd — Guangzhou GD** Loa 109.00 Br ex - Dght 6.000 Lbp 102.80 Br md 18.80 Dpth 8.10 Welded, 1 dk	**(B33B2DT) Trailing Suction Hopper Dredger** Hopper: 5,000	**2 oil engines** reduction geared to sc. shafts driving 2 Propellers Total Power: 5,000kW (6,798hp) 11.8k Daihatsu 8DKM-2 2 x 4 Stroke 8 Cy. 280 x 390 each-2500kW (3399bhp) Daihatsu Diesel Manufacturing Co Lt-Japan AuxGen: 3 x 500kW 400V a.c
9523201 *BRPH* -	**YUN LONG FENG** **China Shipping Tanker Co Ltd** - *Shanghai* *China* MMSI: 413985000	**40,913** 25,963 75,394 T/cm 68.2	Class: CC	**2012-01 Jiangnan Shipyard (Group) Co Ltd — Shanghai** Yd No: H2472 Loa 225.00 (BB) Br ex - Dght 14.200 Lbp 217.00 Br md 32.26 Dpth 19.60 Welded, 1 dk	**(A21A2BC) Bulk Carrier** Grain: 90,725 Compartments: 7 Ho, ER 7 Ha: 6 (15.5 x 14.4)ER (15.5 x 13.2)	**1 oil engine** driving 1 FP propeller Total Power: 8,833kW (12,009hp) 14.5k MAN-B&W 5S60ME- 1 x 2 Stroke 5 Cy. 600 x 2400 8833kW (12009bhp) Hudong Heavy Machinery Co Ltd-China AuxGen: 3 x 560kW 450V a.c
9523196 *BRPG* -	**YUN MI FENG** **China Shipping Tanker Co Ltd** - SatCom: Inmarsat C 441319810 *Shanghai* *China* MMSI: 413198000	**40,913** 25,963 75,421 T/cm 68.2	Class: CC	**2011-11 Jiangnan Shipyard (Group) Co Ltd — Shanghai** Yd No: H2471 Loa 225.00 (BB) Br ex - Dght 14.200 Lbp 217.00 Br md 32.26 Dpth 19.60 Welded, 1 dk	**(A21A2BC) Bulk Carrier** Grain: 90,165 Compartments: 7 Ho, ER 7 Ha: 6 (15.5 x 14.4)ER (15.5 x 13.2)	**1 oil engine** driving 1 FP propeller Total Power: 8,833kW (12,009hp) 14.5k MAN-B&W 5S60ME- 1 x 2 Stroke 5 Cy. 600 x 2400 8833kW (12009bhp) Hudong Heavy Machinery Co Ltd-China AuxGen: 3 x 560kW 450V a.c
9003756 *T3FN2* -	**YUN RUN** *ex* New Hayatsuki *-2013* **Fengrun Shipping Co Ltd** - *Tarawa* *Kiribati* MMSI: 529567000	**4,287** 2,026 5,181	Class: (NK)	**1990-03 Miyoshi Shipbuilding Co Ltd — Uwajima EH** Yd No: 277 Loa 116.20 (BB) Br ex - Dght 6.864 Lbp 105.00 Br md 16.20 Dpth 9.75 Welded	**(A34A2GR) Refrigerated Cargo Ship** Ins: 5,449 Compartments: 3 Ho, ER 3 Ha: ER Derricks: 6x5t	**1 oil engine** driving 1 FP propeller Total Power: 4,472kW (6,080hp) 14.5k B&W 8L35M 1 x 2 Stroke 8 Cy. 350 x 1050 4472kW (6080bhp) Makita Corp-Japan Thrusters: 1 Thwart. CP thruster (f) Fuel: 810.0 (r.f.)
9161613 *T3FZ2* -	**YUN RUN 3** *ex* Satsuma *-2013* *ex* Satsuma 1 *-2010* **Fengrun Shipping Co Ltd** - *Tarawa* *Kiribati* MMSI: 529578000 Official number: K-16971322	**2,713** 1,152 3,051	Class: (NK)	**1997-04 KK Kanasashi — Shizuoka SZ** Yd No: 3446 Loa 91.29 (BB) Br ex - Dght 5.518 Lbp 84.98 Br md 14.00 Dpth 8.00 Welded, 1 dk	**(A34A2GR) Refrigerated Cargo Ship** Bale: 151; Ins: 4,281 Compartments: 3 Ho, ER 3 Ha: 3 (3.3 x 3.2)ER Derricks: 6x5t	**1 oil engine** driving 1 FP propeller Total Power: 1,471kW (2,000hp) 12.6k B&W 6S26M 1 x 2 Stroke 6 Cy. 260 x 980 1471kW (2000bhp) Kawasaki Heavy Industries Ltd-Japan Fuel: 830.0
9288564 *BJRN* -	**YUN SHAN** *ex* SC Wuhan *-2010* *ex* Southern York *-2010* **Sinochem Shipping Co Ltd (Hainan)** - SatCom: Inmarsat C 441301384 *Hankou, Hubei* *China* MMSI: 413521370	**4,199** 2,031 6,545 T/cm 15.0	Class: CC (NK)	**2003-08 Shitanoe Shipbuilding Co Ltd — Usuki OT** Yd No: 1230 Loa 107.54 (BB) Br ex 16.82 Dght 6.814 Lbp 100.00 Br md 16.80 Dpth 8.80 Welded, 1 dk	**(A12B2TR) Chemical/Products Tanker** Double Hull (13F) Liq: 7,162; Liq (Oil): 6,667 Cargo Heating Coils Compartments: 12 Wing Ta (s.stl), 1 Wing Slop Ta, 1 Wing Slop Ta (s.stl), ER (s.stl) 12 Cargo Pump (s): 12x200m³/hr Manifold: Bow/CM: 50.8m	**1 oil engine** driving 1 FP propeller Total Power: 3,120kW (4,242hp) 13.5k Mitsubishi 6UEC37L 1 x 2 Stroke 6 Cy. 370 x 880 3120kW (4242bhp) Akasaka Tekkosho KK (Akasaka DieselLtd)-Japan AuxGen: 3 x 400kW 450V 60Hz a.c Thrusters: 1 Thwart. CP thruster (f) Fuel: 89.0 (d.f.) (Heating Coils) 364.0 (r.f.) 14.0pd
9517020 *XURY9* -	**YUN SHENG** **Chun Wei Shipping Co Ltd** - *Phnom Penh* *Cambodia* MMSI: 514025000 Official number: 0808952	**5,702** 3,193 8,700	Class: IS UB	**2008-04 Zhoushan Honglisheng Ship Engineering Co Ltd — Zhoushan ZJ** Loa 120.00 Br ex - Dght - Lbp - Br md 18.80 Dpth 9.00 Welded, 1 dk	**(A31A2GX) General Cargo Ship**	**1 oil engine** reduction geared to sc. shaft driving 1 Propeller Total Power: 2,795kW (3,800hp) 13.0k Chinese Std. Type GN8320Z 1 x 4 Stroke 8 Cy. 320 x 380 2795kW (3800bhp) Ningbo CSI Power & Machinery GroupCo Ltd-China
8963868 *BVBS* -	**YUN SHENG** - - *Fuzhou, Fujian* *China* MMSI: 412442410 Official number: 080002000062	*764* - -		**1980 Sandu Xinli Shipyard — Ningde FJ** Loa - Br ex - Dght - Lbp - Br md - Dpth - Welded, 1 dk	**(A33A2CC) Container Ship (Fully Cellular)**	**1 oil engine** driving 1 FP propeller Niigata 1 x 4 Stroke Niigata Engineering Co Ltd-Japan
8631702 *9LY2604* -	**YUN SHIN** *ex* Bae Feng *-2011* *ex* Hon Yuin *-2010* *ex* Daiei Maru No. 5 *-1997* **Virtuous International Enterprise Inc** Billion Star Marine Services Ltd *Freetown* *Sierra Leone* MMSI: 667003407	**694** 228 594	Class: CR	**1988-02 K.K. Saidaiji Zosensho — Okayama** Yd No: 150 Converted From: Grab Dredger-2010 Loa 51.34 Br ex 10.52 Dght 4.439 Lbp 46.40 Br md 10.50 Dpth 5.40 Welded, 1 dk	**(A31A2GX) General Cargo Ship**	**1 oil engine** driving 1 FP propeller Total Power: 552kW (750hp) 11.0k Hanshin 6LUN28A 1 x 4 Stroke 6 Cy. 280 x 480 552kW (750bhp) The Hanshin Diesel Works Ltd-Japan
8920830 *BKQK4* -	**YUN TONG 17** *ex* Hai Xia *-2008* *ex* Fong Hsiung No. 1 *-2004* *ex* Hakuei Maru No. 5 *-2003* **Yuntong (HK) International Shipping Co Ltd** Zhoushan Yuntong Shipping Co Ltd *Zhoushan, Zhejiang* *China* MMSI: 413423680	**399** 119 -	Class: CC	**1990-07 Kanmon Zosen K.K. — Shimonoseki** Yd No: 520 Lengthened-2004 Loa 37.00 Br ex 8.72 Dght 3.600 Lbp 32.07 Br md 8.70 Dpth 4.50 Welded, 1 dk	**(B32B2SP) Pusher Tug**	**2 oil engines** with clutches & reverse geared to sc. shaft driving 1 FP propeller Total Power: 2,206kW (3,000hp) Hanshin LH28L 2 x 4 Stroke 6 Cy. 280 x 530 each-1103kW (1500bhp) The Hanshin Diesel Works Ltd-Japan
9702821 *BKR06* -	**YUN TONG 301** **Zhoushan Yuntong Shipping Co Ltd** Zhoushan Yongyue Shipmanagement Co Ltd *Zhoushan, Zhejiang* *China* MMSI: 413451590	**1,111** 333 742	Class: CC	**2013-10 Taizhou Haibin Shipbuilding & Repairing Co Ltd — Sanmen County ZJ** Yd No: HBCCS-13-01 Loa 53.50 Br ex 12.27 Dght 4.300 Lbp 45.70 Br md 12.00 Dpth 5.80 Welded, 1 dk	**(B32A2ST) Tug** Ice Capable	**2 oil engines** reduction geared to sc. shafts driving 2 Propellers Total Power: 2,648kW (3,600hp) Guangzhou 6320ZC 2 x 4 Stroke 6 Cy. 320 x 440 each-1324kW (1800bhp) Guangzhou Diesel Engine Factory CoLtd-China AuxGen: 2 x 200kW 400V a.c
9634141 *BKTL5* -	**YUN TONG 501** **Zhoushan Yuntong Shipping Co Ltd** - *Zhoushan, Zhejiang* *China* MMSI: 413443060	**1,689** 506 1,650	Class: CC	**2011-11 in the People's Republic of China** Yd No: 40006 Loa 62.80 Br ex 14.00 Dght 5.300 Lbp 56.80 Br md 14.00 Dpth 6.60 Welded, 1 dk	**(B21B20T) Offshore Tug/Supply Ship** Ice Capable	**2 oil engines** driving 2 Propellers Total Power: 3,646kW (4,958hp) 13.0k Niigata 6M34BLG 2 x 4 Stroke 6 Cy. 340 x 680 each-1823kW (2479bhp) Niigata Engineering Co Ltd-Japan AuxGen: 2 x 250kW 400V a.c, 1 x 830kW 400V a.c
9138501 *BFAY6* -	**YUN TONG HAI** *ex* Ming May *-2013* **Tianjin Yuntong Shipping Co Ltd** Tianjin Younysun Shipping Group Co Ltd *Tianjin* *China* MMSI: 412095000	**38,338** 24,681 74,009	Class: CC (BV)	**1997-10 Tsuneishi Shipbuilding Co Ltd — Fukuyama HS** Yd No: 1101 Loa 225.00 (BB) Br ex - Dght 13.850 Lbp 216.00 Br md 32.26 Dpth 19.10 Welded, 1 dk	**(A21A2BC) Bulk Carrier** Grain: 88,331 Compartments: 7 Ho, ER 7 Ha: (15.3 x 12.6)6 (17.0 x 15.4)ER	**1 oil engine** driving 1 FP propeller Total Power: 8,900kW (12,100hp) 14.5k B&W 6S60M 1 x 2 Stroke 6 Cy. 600 x 2292 8900kW (12100bhp) Mitsui Engineering & Shipbuilding CLtd-Japan

ID	Name / Owner	Tonnage	Class	Build / Dimensions	Type	Machinery
651060 XXY5	**YUN XIANG 9** **Zhejiang Yunxiang Shipping Co Ltd** - *Zhoushan, Zhejiang* *China* MMSI: 413444950	**2,984** 1,427 4,395	Class: CC	**2012-05** **Taizhou Zhongzhou Shipbuilding Co Ltd — Sanmen County ZJ** Yd No: ZZSY-05 Loa 96.17 (BB) Br ex 15.22 Dght 5.600 Lbp 89.80 Br md 15.20 Dpth 7.00 Welded, 1 dk	**(A12B2TR) Chemical/Products Tanker** Double Hull (13F) Liq: 4,781; Liq (Oil): 4,983 Compartments: 10 Wing Ta, 2 Wing Slop Ta, ER Manifold: Bow/CM: 52.5m Ice Capable	**1 oil engine** reduction geared to sc. shaft driving 1 FP propeller Total Power: 2,000kW (2,719hp) 11.5kn Chinese Std. Type G8300ZC 1 x 4 Stroke 8 Cy. 300 x 380 2000kW (2719bhp) Ningbo CSI Power & Machinery GroupCo Ltd-China AuxGen: 2 x 200kW 400V a.c
426925 AHU	**YUN XING 1** *ex* Shun Ji *ex* Zhou Shan 28 *-1999* *ex* Shun Ji *-1998* *ex* Zhe Leng 4 *-1998* *ex* Bo Leng Yi Hao *-1986* **Dalian Mingfa Fishery Shipping Co Ltd** - *Dalian, Liaoning* *China* MMSI: 412204290	**986** 306 500	Class: (CC)	**1979** **Bohai Shipyard — Huludao LN** Loa 66.75 Br ex - Dght 3.950 Lbp 61.50 Br md 11.50 Dpth 6.00 Welded, 1 dk	**(A34A2GR) Refrigerated Cargo Ship** Ins: 1,665 Compartments: 4 Ho, ER 4 Ha: 3 (2.2 x 3.3) (1.2 x 1.9) Cranes: 2x2t	**1 oil engine** driving 1 FP propeller Total Power: 971kW (1,320hp) 13.0kn S.K.L. 8NVD48A-2U 1 x 4 Stroke 8 Cy. 320 x 480 971kW (1320bhp) VEB Schwermaschinenbau "KarlLiebknecht" (SKL)-Magdeburg AuxGen: 3 x 120kW 400V 50Hz a.c
831912 TGV	**YUN YANG** *ex* Zi Yun *-2006* **Lianyungang Shipping Corp** - SatCom: Inmarsat B 341224310 *Lianyungang, Jiangsu* *China* MMSI: 413264000	**6,241** 2,838 6,024	Class: (CC)	**1984** **Tianjin Xingang Shipyard — Tianjin** Loa 124.00 Br ex - Dght 7.350 Lbp 115.00 Br md 18.00 Dpth 10.40 Welded, 1 dk	**(A31A2GX) General Cargo Ship** Grain: 11,062; Bale: 9,651 Compartments: 4 Ho, ER 4 Ha: ER Derricks: 12x8t Ice Capable	**1 oil engine** driving 1 FP propeller Total Power: 4,413kW (6,000hp) 14.4kn MAN K6Z52/90N 1 x 2 Stroke 6 Cy. 520 x 900 4413kW (6000bhp) Kawasaki Heavy Industries Ltd-Japan AuxGen: 3 x 280kW 390V a.c
833269 TGC	**YUN YOU 3** **China Marine Bunker Supply Co (Lianyungang Branch)** - SatCom: Inmarsat C 441214912 *Lianyungang, Jiangsu* *China* MMSI: 412031010	*1,124* 542 1,459	Class: (CC)	**1988-10** **Kumamoto Dock K.K. — Yatsushiro** Loa 68.81 Br ex - Dght 3.990 Lbp 64.00 Br md 11.40 Dpth 4.80 Welded, 1 dk	**(B35E2TF) Bunkering Tanker** Liq: 3,204; Liq (Oil): 3,204 Compartments: 6 Wing Ta, ER	**1 oil engine** driving 1 FP propeller Total Power: 883kW (1,201hp) 12.0kn Daihatsu 6DLM-22 1 x 4 Stroke 6 Cy. 220 x 300 883kW (1201bhp) (made 1980) Daihatsu Diesel Manufacturing Co Lt-Japan AuxGen: 3 x 100kW 385V a.c
017712 TGD	**YUN YOU 5** *ex* Daiei Maru No. 8 *-1994* **China Marine Bunker Supply Co (Lianyungang Branch)** - *Lianyungang, Jiangsu* *China*	**1,283** 644 2,078	Class: (CC)	**1980-11** **Kurinoura Dockyard Co Ltd — Yawatahama EH** Yd No: 160 Loa 78.26 Br ex - Dght 4.700 Lbp 72.62 Br md 12.01 Dpth 5.52 Welded, 1 dk	**(B35E2TF) Bunkering Tanker**	**1 oil engine** driving 1 FP propeller Total Power: 1,618kW (2,200hp) Hanshin 6LU38 1 x 4 Stroke 6 Cy. 380 x 580 1618kW (2200bhp) The Hanshin Diesel Works Ltd-Japan
848393 HTA	**YUN YOU 6** *ex* Hai Gong You 27 *-2010* **China Marine Bunker Supply Co (Lianyungang Branch)** - *Lianyungang, Jiangsu* *China* MMSI: 412047120	**889** 494 1,833	Class: (CC)	**1991-01** **Zhenjiang Shipyard — Zhenjiang JS** Loa 67.50 Br ex - Dght 4.100 Lbp 62.00 Br md 10.60 Dpth 4.70 Welded, 1 dk	**(B35E2TF) Bunkering Tanker**	**1 oil engine** geared to sc. shaft driving 1 FP propeller Total Power: 809kW (1,100hp) 11.0kn Daihatsu 6DSM-22 1 x 4 Stroke 6 Cy. 220 x 280 809kW (1100bhp) Shaanxi Diesel Engine Factory-China AuxGen: 2 x 90kW 400V
827650 ZBQ	**YUNG AN** **Ocean Fishery Development Administration** - *Kaohsiung* *Chinese Taipei*	*352* 240 -	Class: (CR)	**1983** **Fong Kuo Shipbuilding Co Ltd — Kaohsiung** Loa 45.65 Br ex 7.68 Dght 2.901 Lbp 39.20 Br md 7.60 Dpth 3.38 Welded, 1 dk	**(B11B2FV) Fishing Vessel** Ins: 345	**1 oil engine** driving 1 FP propeller Total Power: 588kW (799hp) 10.8kn Akasaka 6MH25SSR 1 x 4 Stroke 6 Cy. 250 x 400 588kW (799bhp) Akasaka Tekkosho KK (Akasaka DieselLtd)-Japan AuxGen: 1 x 240kW 220V a.c, 1 x 128kW 220V a.c
222630 YZH	**YUNG CHIEN** **Ocean Fishery Development Administration** - *Kaohsiung* *Chinese Taipei*	*350* 228 263	Class: (CR)	**1982-03** **Fong Kuo Shipbuilding Co Ltd — Kaohsiung** Loa 45.70 (BB) Br ex 7.70 Dght 2.901 Lbp 39.20 Br md 7.61 Dpth 3.38 Welded, 1 dk	**(B11B2FV) Fishing Vessel** Ins: 434 Compartments: 3 Ho, ER 4 Ha: ER	**1 oil engine** reverse reduction geared to sc. shaft driving 1 FP propeller Total Power: 588kW (799hp) Akasaka 6MH25SSR 1 x 4 Stroke 6 Cy. 250 x 400 588kW (799bhp) Akasaka Tekkosho KK (Akasaka DieselLtd)-Japan AuxGen: 2 x 128kW 220V 50Hz a.c
213761 WWF	**YUNG CHIH** **Rester Enterprise Corp Ltd** - *Kaohsiung* *Chinese Taipei*	*321* 217 274	Class: (CR)	**1969** **Korea Shipbuilding & Engineering Corp — Busan** Loa 43.59 Br ex 7.52 Dght 2.896 Lbp 38.61 Br md 7.50 Dpth 3.36 Welded, 1 dk	**(B11B2FV) Fishing Vessel** Ins: 385 Compartments: 3 Ho, ER 4 Ha: 2 (1.0 x 1.0)2 (1.5 x 1.5)ER Derricks: 4x1t; Winches: 4	**1 oil engine** driving 1 FP propeller Total Power: 552kW (750hp) 11.5kn Niigata 1 x 4 Stroke 6 Cy. 280 x 440 552kW (750bhp) Niigata Engineering Co Ltd-Japan AuxGen: 2 x 80kW 230V 60Hz a.c
649735 H2383 T7-0383	**YUNG CHIN NO. 101** **Yung Chin Fishery Co Ltd** - *Kaohsiung* *Chinese Taipei* Official number: 11863	**727** 285 -		**1990-05** **Taiwan Machinery Manufacturing Corp. — Kaohsiung** Loa 56.40 Br ex - Dght - Lbp - Br md 8.90 Dpth 3.85 Welded, 1 dk	**(B11B2FV) Fishing Vessel**	**1 oil engine** driving 1 FP propeller Total Power: 1,030kW (1,400hp) Niigata 1 x 1030kW (1400bhp) Niigata Engineering Co Ltd-Japan
032994 YXY	**YUNG CHOW** **Ocean Fishery Development Administration** - *Kaohsiung* *Chinese Taipei*	*352* 237 -	Class: (CR)	**1981** **Fong Kuo Shipbuilding Co Ltd — Kaohsiung** Loa 43.64 Br ex 7.68 Dght 2.901 Lbp 38.10 Br md 7.60 Dpth 3.38 Welded, 1 dk	**(B11B2FV) Fishing Vessel**	**1 oil engine** driving 1 FP propeller Total Power: 588kW (799hp) 10.8kn Niigata 6M24EGT 1 x 4 Stroke 6 Cy. 240 x 410 588kW (799bhp) Niigata Engineering Co Ltd-Japan AuxGen: 2 x 96kW 220V a.c
947137	**YUNG CHUN No. 17** **Yong Chun Fishery Co Ltd** -	*736* 312 -		**1987** **Lien Ho Shipbuilding Co, Ltd — Kaohsiung** L reg 50.80 Br ex - Dght - Lbp - Br md 9.40 Dpth 4.50 Welded, 1 dk	**(B11B2FV) Fishing Vessel**	**1 oil engine** driving 1 FP propeller Total Power: 809kW (1,100hp) 11.0kn Fuji 1 x 4 Stroke 6 Cy. 809kW (1100bhp) Fuji Diesel Co Ltd-Japan
508840 3NL	**YUNG DA FA 101** *ex* Kin Ping Hai *-2008* *ex* Yohtei Maru *-1999* *ex* Yohtei *-1999* *ex* Yohtei Maru *-1991* **Yung Tai Fa Fishery** Trilight Transport Services *Tarawa* *Kiribati* MMSI: 529132000 Official number: K-10850788	**2,436** 934 2,468	Class: CR (NK)	**1985-02** **Tokushima Zosen Sangyo K.K. — Komatsushima** Yd No: 1778 Loa 88.32 (BB) Br ex - Dght 5.074 Lbp 82.02 Br md 14.51 Dpth 8.03 Welded, 2 dks	**(A34A2GR) Refrigerated Cargo Ship** Ins: 3,455 Compartments: 3 Ho, ER 3 Ha: ER	**1 oil engine** driving 1 FP propeller Total Power: 1,626kW (2,211hp) 13.5kn Akasaka A37 1 x 4 Stroke 6 Cy. 370 x 720 1626kW (2211bhp) Akasaka Tekkosho KK (Akasaka DieselLtd)-Japan AuxGen: 2 x 400kW 450V 60Hz a.c Fuel: 108.0 (d.f.) 520.0 (r.f.) 9.5pd
823599 FEJ5	**YUNG DA FA 102** *ex* Ishikari *-2009* *ex* Ishikari Maru *-1995* **Trendy Star International Ltd** Yung Da Far Fishery Co Ltd SatCom: Inmarsat A 1354125 *Panama* *Panama* MMSI: 355141000 Official number: 2233195E	**2,829** 1,626 3,984	Class: NK	**1984-01** **Kochi Jyuko (Eiho Zosen) K.K. — Kochi** Yd No: 1636 Loa 93.88 Br ex - Dght 6.116 Lbp 86.50 Br md 16.01 Dpth 8.26 Welded, 2 dks	**(A34A2GR) Refrigerated Cargo Ship** Ins: 3,963 Compartments: 3 Ho, ER 3 Ha: 3 (7.1 x 6.0)ER Derricks: 6x5t	**1 oil engine** driving 1 FP propeller Total Power: 2,438kW (3,315hp) 16.3kn Mitsubishi 6UEC37H 1 x 2 Stroke 6 Cy. 370 x 880 2438kW (3315bhp) Kobe Hatsudoki KK-Japan AuxGen: 2 x 500kW 450V 60Hz a.c Fuel: 167.0 (d.f.) 677.5 (r.f.) 11.0pd
016076 EAX9	**YUNG DA FA 108** *ex* Spica *-2010* **Yung Wang Fa Fishery Co Ltd** - SatCom: Inmarsat A 1335520 *Panama* *Panama* MMSI: 355513000 Official number: 1987791D	**5,024** 2,893 7,000	Class: NK	**1991-09** **Fukuoka Shipbuilding Co Ltd — Fukuoka FO** Yd No: 1163 Loa 117.82 (BB) Br ex - Dght 7.605 Lbp 109.70 Br md 17.80 Dpth 10.02 Welded, 2 dks	**(A34A2GR) Refrigerated Cargo Ship** Grain: 16,850; Bale: 15,881; Ins: 7,665 4 Ha: (9.0 x 6.0)3 (9.0 x 7.5)ER Derricks: 8x5t	**1 oil engine** driving 1 FP propeller Total Power: 5,296kW (7,200hp) 16.2kn Mitsubishi 6UEC45LA 1 x 2 Stroke 6 Cy. 450 x 1350 5296kW (7200bhp) Kobe Hatsudoki KK-Japan AuxGen: 2 x 800kW 450V 60Hz a.c Fuel: 1200.0 (r.f.)
649747 H3304 T6-1304	**YUNG FENG NO. 101** **Yung Feng Fishery Co Ltd** - *Kaohsiung* *Chinese Taipei* Official number: 12747	**493** 192 -		**1995-11** **Kaohsiung Shipbuilding Co. Ltd. — Kaohsiung** Loa 53.00 Br ex - Dght - Lbp - Br md 8.30 Dpth 3.65 Welded, 1 dk	**(B11B2FV) Fishing Vessel**	**1 oil engine** driving 1 FP propeller Total Power: 883kW (1,201hp)

8024246 **YUNG GANG 16** *292*
-
- **Government of The People's Republic of China** 100
-
China
1981-09 **Ishikawajima Ship & Chemical Plant Co Ltd — Tokyo** Yd No: 526
Loa 32.85 Br ex 9.53 Dght 3.301
Lbp 26.55 Br md 9.50 Dpth 4.42
Welded, 1 dk
(B32A2ST) Tug
2 oil engines geared to sc. shafts driving 2 FP propellers
Total Power: 2,354kW (3,200hp) 8DSM-2
Daihatsu
2 x 4 Stroke 8 Cy. 260 x 320 each-1177kW (1600bhp)
Daihatsu Diesel Manufacturing Co Lt-Japan

8429240 **YUNG HAI** *492* Class: (CR)
BZGA 217
- **Ocean Fishery Development Administration** -
-
Kaohsiung *Chinese Taipei*
1985-01 **Fong Kuo Shipbuilding Co Ltd — Kaohsiung**
Loa 49.92 Br ex - Dght 3.301
Lbp 44.00 Br md 8.60 Dpth 3.69
Welded, 1 dk
(B11B2FV) Fishing Vessel
Ins: 580
Compartments: 2 Ho, ER
4 Ha:
1 oil engine driving 1 FP propeller
Total Power: 736kW (1,001hp) A245F
Akasaka
1 x 4 Stroke 6 Cy. 245 x 450 736kW (1001bhp)
Akasaka Tekkosho KK (Akasaka DieselLtd)-Japan
AuxGen: 2 x 280kW 220V a.c

8649759 **YUNG HAN NO. 101** **486**
BH3284 192
CT6-1284 **Yung Han Fishery Co Ltd** -
-
Kaohsiung *Chinese Taipei*
Official number: 12807
1994-11 **Kaohsiung Shipbuilding Co. Ltd. — Kaohsiung**
Loa 53.00 Br ex - Dght -
Lbp - Br md 8.30 Dpth 3.65
Welded, 1 dk
(B11B2FV) Fishing Vessel
1 oil engine driving 1 FP propeller
Total Power: 883kW (1,201hp)

8429238 **YUNG HANG** *492* Class: (CR)
BZGB *ex Yung Yang -2011* 217
LL1964 **China Sea-Products Development Corp** -
-
Kaohsiung *Chinese Taipei*
MMSI: 416113600
Official number: CT6-1050
1985-11 **Fong Kuo Shipbuilding Co Ltd — Kaohsiung** Yd No: 225
Loa 49.92 Br ex - Dght 3.301
Lbp 44.00 Br md 8.60 Dpth 3.69
Welded, 1 dk
(B11B2FV) Fishing Vessel
Ins: 580
Compartments: 2 Ho, ER
4 Ha:
1 oil engine driving 1 FP propeller
Total Power: 736kW (1,001hp) A245F
Akasaka
1 x 4 Stroke 6 Cy. 245 x 450 736kW (1001bhp)
Akasaka Tekkosho KK (Akasaka DieselLtd)-Japan
AuxGen: 2 x 280kW 220V a.c

8748543 **YUNG HSING FA NO. 168** **1,416**
BL2096 424
- **Yung Hsing Fa Co Ltd** -
-
Kaohsiung *Chinese Taipei*
Official number: 015010
2009-12 **Ching Fu Shipbuilding Co Ltd — Kaohsiung** Yd No: 077
Loa 71.79 Br ex - Dght 4.750
Lbp 61.85 Br md 12.20 Dpth 7.20
Welded, 1 dk
(B11B2FV) Fishing Vessel
1 oil engine reduction geared to sc. shaft driving 1 Propeller
Total Power: 2,354kW (3,200hp) 8DLM-32
Daihatsu
1 x 4 Stroke 8 Cy. 320 x 400 2354kW (3200bhp)
Daihatsu Diesel Manufacturing Co Lt-Japan

9680164 **YUNG HSING FA NO. 688** **1,428**
BL2108 428
CT8 0108 **Yung Shen Fa Fishery Co Ltd** -
-
Kaohsiung *Chinese Taipei*
MMSI: 416240900
Official number: 015289
2012-12 **Ching Fu Shipbuilding Co Ltd — Kaohsiung** Yd No: 098
Loa 63.50 Br ex - Dght -
Lbp - Br md 12.20 Dpth -
Welded, 1 dk
(B11B2FV) Fishing Vessel
1 oil engine driving 1 Propeller

8431152 **YUNG HSU No. 101** *717*
- 231
- **Yung Hsu Fishery Co Ltd** -
-
SatCom: Inmarsat A 1356152
San Lorenzo *Honduras*
Official number: L-1923538
1990 **Sen Koh Shipbuilding Corp — Kaohsiung**
L reg 48.95 Br ex - Dght -
Lbp - Br md 8.90 Dpth 3.85
Welded, 1 dk
(B11B2FV) Fishing Vessel
1 oil engine driving 1 FP propeller
Total Power: 1,030kW (1,400hp) 12.0kn
Sumiyoshi S27G
1 x 4 Stroke 6 Cy. 270 x 480 1030kW (1400bhp)
Sumiyoshi Tekkosho-Japan

8632366 **YUNG HSUAN** **452** Class: (CR)
- 196
- - 643
-
1987-12 **Fong Kuo Shipbuilding Co Ltd — Kaohsiung**
Loa 59.30 Br ex - Dght 3.800
Lbp 52.40 Br md 9.50 Dpth 4.20
Welded, 1 dk
(B11B2FV) Fishing Vessel
1 oil engine driving 1 FP propeller
Total Power: 1,030kW (1,400hp)
Niigata 6M28BFT
1 x 4 Stroke 6 Cy. 280 x 480 1030kW (1400bhp)
Niigata Engineering Co Ltd-Japan
AuxGen: 2 x 360kW 220V a.c, 1 x 200kW 220V a.c

8827698 **YUNG KAI** *796* Class: (CR)
- 252
- **Taipesar SA** 643
-
1987-11 **Fong Kuo Shipbuilding Co Ltd — Kaohsiung**
Loa 59.30 (BB) Br ex - Dght 3.800
Lbp 52.40 Br md 9.50 Dpth 4.20
Welded, 1 dk
(B11B2FV) Fishing Vessel
1 oil engine driving 1 FP propeller
Total Power: 1,030kW (1,400hp)
Niigata 6M28BFT
1 x 4 Stroke 6 Cy. 280 x 480 1030kW (1400bhp)
Niigata Tekkosho-Japan
AuxGen: 2 x 360kW 220V a.c, 1 x 200kW 220V a.c

7027590 **YUNG LI.** *252* Class: (CR)
BVWX 174
- **Ocean Fishery Development Administration** -
Kaohsiung *Chinese Taipei*
1970 **Taiwan Machinery Manufacturing Corp. — Kaohsiung**
Loa 37.70 Br ex 6.84 Dght 2.744
Lbp 35.62 Br md 6.81 Dpth 3.15
Welded, 1 dk
(B11B2FV) Fishing Vessel
Ins: 210
Compartments: 3 Ho, ER
4 Ha: 2 (1.0 x 1.1)2 (1.2 x 1.2)ER
1 oil engine driving 1 FP propeller
Total Power: 441kW (600hp) 11.0kn
Alpha 406-26VO
1 x 2 Stroke 6 Cy. 260 x 400 441kW (600bhp)
Taiwan Machinery ManufacturingCorp.-Kaohsiung
AuxGen: 2 x 64kW

6905147 **YUNG LIEN No. 1** *288* Class: (CR)
- 150
- **Yung Lien Fishery Co Ltd** 97
Kaohsiung *Chinese Taipei*
1968 **Taiwan Machinery Manufacturing Corp. — Kaohsiung** Yd No: 6177
Loa 40.19 Br ex 7.12 Dght 2.693
Lbp 35.01 Br md 7.09 Dpth 3.18
Welded, 1 dk
(B11B2FV) Fishing Vessel
Ins: 240
Compartments: 3 Ho, ER
3 Ha: (1.9 x 1.0)2 (1.3 x 1.3)ER
Derricks: 2x1t; Winches: 2
1 oil engine driving 1 FP propeller
Total Power: 456kW (620hp) 11.0kn
Akasaka MA6SS
1 x 4 Stroke 6 Cy. 270 x 400 456kW (620bhp)
Akasaka Tekkosho KK (Akasaka DieselLtd)-Japan
AuxGen: 2 x 64kW 220V 60Hz a.c

8947149 **YUNG MAN CHUN** **875**
- 356
- **Yong Chun Fishery SA** -
-
1988 **Lien Ho Shipbuilding Co, Ltd — Kaohsiung**
Loa 57.20 Br ex - Dght -
Lbp - Br md 9.40 Dpth 4.05
Welded, 1 dk
(B11B2FV) Fishing Vessel
1 oil engine driving 1 FP propeller
Total Power: 809kW (1,100hp) 13.0kn
Fuji
1 x 4 Stroke 809kW (1100bhp)
Fuji Diesel Co Ltd-Japan

8327662 **YUNG PANG** *352* Class: (CR)
BZBP 240
- **Ocean Fishery Development Administration** -
Kaohsiung *Chinese Taipei*
1983 **Fong Kuo Shipbuilding Co Ltd — Kaohsiung**
Loa 45.65 Br ex 7.68 Dght 2.901
Lbp 39.20 Br md 7.60 Dpth 3.38
Welded, 1 dk
(B11B2FV) Fishing Vessel
Ins: 345
1 oil engine driving 1 FP propeller
Total Power: 588kW (799hp) 10.8kn
Akasaka 6MH25SSR
1 x 4 Stroke 6 Cy. 250 x 400 588kW (799bhp)
Akasaka Tekkosho KK (Akasaka DieselLtd)-Japan
AuxGen: 1 x 240kW 220V a.c, 1 x 128kW 220V a.c

9395812 **YUNG PANG NO. 1** **530** Class: (CR)
BI2594 *ex Fong Kuo 405 -2006* 240
LL2276 **China Sea-Products Development Corp** 350
-
Kaohsiung *Chinese Taipei*
MMSI: 416180800
Official number: CT7-0594
2006-01 **Fong Kuo Shipbuilding Co Ltd — Kaohsiung** Yd No: 405
Loa 48.69 Br ex 8.50 Dght -
Lbp - Br md - Dpth -
Welded, 1 dk
(B11B2FV) Fishing Vessel
1 oil engine driving 1 Propeller

7515107 **YUNG SHIN No. 31** *375* Class: (CR)
- *ex Hua Won No. 101 -1977* 257
- **Yung Shin Fishery Co Ltd**
-
Kaohsiung *Chinese Taipei*
1974 **Kaohsiung Prov. Junior College of Marine Tech. SY — Kaohsiung**
Loa 43.67 Br ex 7.65 Dght -
Lbp 38.10 Br md 7.62 Dpth 2.93
Welded
(B11B2FV) Fishing Vessel
Compartments: 3 Ho, ER
3 Ha: 3 (1.0 x 1.0)
1 oil engine driving 1 FP propeller
Total Power: 883kW (1,201hp) 11.0kn
Makita GNLH6275
1 x 4 Stroke 6 Cy. 275 x 450 883kW (1201bhp)
Makita Tekkosho-Japan

7515119 **YUNG SHIN No. 32** *375* Class: (CR)
- *ex Hua Won No. 102 -1977* 257
- **Yung Shin Fishery Co Ltd**
-
Kaohsiung *Chinese Taipei*
1974 **Kaohsiung Prov. Junior College of Marine Tech. SY — Kaohsiung**
Loa 43.67 Br ex 7.65 Dght -
Lbp 38.10 Br md 7.62 Dpth 2.93
Welded
(B11B2FV) Fishing Vessel
Compartments: 3 Ho, ER
3 Ha: 3 (1.0 x 1.0)
1 oil engine driving 1 FP propeller
Total Power: 883kW (1,201hp) 11.0kn
Makita GNLH6275
1 x 4 Stroke 6 Cy. 275 x 450 883kW (1201bhp)
Makita Tekkosho-Japan

9167239 **YUNG SHUE WAN** **796** Class: LR
VRS4269 238 ✠ **100A1** SS 03/2013
- **Swire Waste Management Ltd** 659 deck cargo ship
The Hongkong Salvage & Towage Co Ltd Hong Kong coastal waters service
Hong Kong *Hong Kong* Non-perishable deck cargoes and containers
Official number: HK-0378 ✠ **LMC** Cable: 412.5/32.0 U2 (a)
1998-03 **Guangdong Jiangmen Shipyard Co Ltd — Jiangmen GD** (Hull)
1998-03 **Cheoy Lee Shipyards Ltd — Hong Kong** Yd No: 4710
Loa 45.40 Br ex 15.82 Dght 2.400
Lbp 42.15 Br md 15.00 Dpth 3.50
Welded, 1 dk
(A31C2GD) Deck Cargo Ship
TEU 29 C. 29/20'
Cranes: 1x25t
2 oil engines with clutches, flexible couplings & sr geared to sc. shafts driving 2 Directional propellers
Total Power: 970kW (1,318hp) 8.5kn
Caterpillar 3412TA
2 x Vee 4 Stroke 12 Cy. 137 x 152 each-485kW (659bhp)
Caterpillar Inc-USA
AuxGen: 2 x 160kW 400V 50Hz a.c
Thrusters: 1 Water jet (f)
Fuel: 46.3 (d.f.)

8032968 **YUNG WEI** *351* Class: (CR)
BYXA 238
- **Ocean Fishery Development Administration** -
Kaohsiung *Chinese Taipei*
1980 **Fong Kuo Shipbuilding Co Ltd — Kaohsiung**
Loa 43.64 Br ex 7.68 Dght 2.901
Lbp 38.10 Br md 7.60 Dpth 3.38
Welded, 1 dk
(B11B2FV) Fishing Vessel
1 oil engine driving 1 FP propeller
Total Power: 588kW (799hp) 10.8kn
Niigata 6M24EGT
1 x 4 Stroke 6 Cy. 240 x 410 588kW (799bhp)
Niigata Engineering Co Ltd-Japan
AuxGen: 2 x 176kW 220V a.c

032970 **YUNG WU** *351* Class: (CR)
YXB 238
Ocean Fishery Development Administration
-
Kaohsiung *Chinese Taipei*

1980 Fong Kuo Shipbuilding Co Ltd — Kaohsiung
Loa 43.64 Br ex 7.68 Dght 2.901
Lbp 38.10 Br md 7.60 Dpth 3.38
Welded, 1 dk

(B11B2FV) Fishing Vessel

1 oil engine driving 1 FP propeller
Total Power: 588kW (799hp) 10.8kn
Niigata 6M24EGT
1 x 4 Stroke 6 Cy. 240 x 410 588kW (799bhp)
Niigata Engineering Co Ltd-Japan
AuxGen: 2 x 176kW 220V a.c

121956 **YUNG YUAN** *992* Class: (CR)
ZEU *ex* Kenta Maru *-1984* *ex* Seiwa Maru *-1981* 665
ex Kotoshiro Maru No. 5 *-1981* -
Ocean Fishery Development Administration
-
Kaohsiung *Chinese Taipei*

1969 KK Kanasashi Zosen — Shizuoka SZ
Yd No: 915
Loa 70.34 Br ex 11.23 Dght 4.592
Lbp 63.48 Br md 11.21 Dpth 5.11
Welded, 1 dk

(B11B2FV) Fishing Vessel
Ins: 1,713

1 oil engine driving 1 FP propeller
Total Power: 1,324kW (1,800hp) 12.0kn
Akasaka 6DH38SS
1 x 4 Stroke 6 Cy. 380 x 560 1324kW (1800bhp)
Akasaka Tekkosho KK (Akasaka DieselLtd)-Japan

213785 **YUNG YUNG** *321* Class: (CR)
WWH 217
274
Rester Enterprise Corp Ltd
-
Kaohsiung *Chinese Taipei*

1969 Korea Shipbuilding & Engineering Corp — Busan
Loa 43.59 Br ex 7.52 Dght 2.896
Lbp 38.61 Br md 7.50 Dpth 3.36
Welded, 1 dk

(B11B2FV) Fishing Vessel
Ins: 385
Compartments: 3 Ho, ER
4 Ha: 2 (1.0 x 1.0)2 (1.5 x 1.5)ER
Derricks: 4x1t; Winches: 4

1 oil engine driving 1 FP propeller
Total Power: 552kW (750hp) 11.5kn
Niigata
1 x 4 Stroke 6 Cy. 280 x 440 552kW (750bhp)
Niigata Engineering Co Ltd-Japan
AuxGen: 2 x 80kW 230V 60Hz a.c

414917 **YUNGA** **29,104** Class: NK
RGZ5 15,527
New MF SA 50,806
Fair Field Shipping Co Ltd (Fair Field Shipping KK)
Hong Kong *Hong Kong*
MMSI: 477786900
Official number: HK-2772

2010-06 Oshima Shipbuilding Co Ltd — Saikai NS
Yd No: 10569
Loa 182.98 (BB) Br ex - Dght 12.149
Lbp 179.30 Br md 32.26 Dpth 17.15
Welded, 1 dk

(A21A2BC) Bulk Carrier
Double Hull
Grain: 59,117; Bale: 58,700
Compartments: 5 Ho, ER
5 Ha: 4 (20.5 x 25.8)ER (14.8 x 19.8)
Cranes: 4x30t

1 oil engine driving 1 FP propeller
Total Power: 7,760kW (10,550hp) 14.5kn
MAN-B&W 6S50MC-C
1 x 2 Stroke 6 Cy. 500 x 2000 7760kW (10550bhp)
Mitsui Engineering & Shipbuilding CLtd-Japan
AuxGen: 3 x 450kW a.c
Fuel: 2330.0 (r.f.)

965921 **YUNGAY** *194*
-
-
-
-

1972 Astilleros Marco Chilena Ltda. — Iquique
L reg 30.05 Br ex - Dght -
Lbp - Br md 7.65 Dpth 3.68
Welded, 1 dk

(B11B2FV) Fishing Vessel

1 oil engine driving 1 FP propeller

875748 **YUNICEE** **922** Class: KI (KR)
OBF *ex* Golden Jindo *-2011* 517
ex Wando Car Ferry No. 3 *-2001* 93
PT Surya Timur Lines
-
Surabaya *Indonesia*
MMSI: 525022043

1992 Mokpo Shipbuilding & Engineering Co Ltd — Mokpo Yd No: 92-088
Loa 56.50 Br ex - Dght 1.709
Lbp 50.00 Br md 8.60 Dpth 2.30
Welded, 1 dk

(A36A2PR) Passenger/Ro-Ro Ship (Vehicles)

3 oil engines geared to sc. shafts driving 3 FP propellers
Total Power: 1,236kW (1,680hp) 14.9kn
M.T.U. 12V183
3 x Vee 4 Stroke 12 Cy. 128 x 142 each-412kW (560bhp)
Daewoo Heavy Industries Ltd-South Korea
AuxGen: 1 x 82kW 225V a.c, 1 x 72kW 225V a.c
Fuel: 10.0 (d.f.)

257242 **YUNITA** **1,893** Class: AB
V5792 726
Britoil Offshore Services Pte Ltd 2,514
-
Singapore *Singapore*
MMSI: 564964000
Official number: 388575

2004-03 Jiangsu Wuxi Shipyard Co Ltd — Wuxi JS Yd No: H8036
Loa 86.30 (BB) Br ex - Dght 4.500
Lbp 80.00 Br md 13.50 Dpth 6.00
Welded, 1 dk

(A13B2TP) Products Tanker
Double Bottom Entire Compartment Length
Liq: 2,876; Liq (Oil): 2,876
Compartments: 12 Ta, ER
4 Cargo Pump (s): 2x500m³/hr, 2x100m³/hr

1 oil engine geared to sc. shaft driving 1 FP propeller
Total Power: 2,398kW (3,260hp) 13.0kn
MaK 8M25
1 x 4 Stroke 8 Cy. 255 x 400 2398kW (3260bhp)
Caterpillar Motoren GmbH & Co. KG-Germany
AuxGen: 3 x 300kW 380V 50Hz a.c
Thrusters: 1 Tunnel thruster (f)
Fuel: 180.0

972376 **YUNTONG 8** **394**
ex Zhe Zhou Yu Leng 206 *-2002* 189
Wang Zhongning -
He Ting

1977 Yingkou Fishing Vessel Shipyard — Yingkou LN
Loa 51.50 Br ex - Dght 3.400
Lbp 49.17 Br md 7.60 Dpth 4.20
Welded, 1 dk

(B12B2FC) Fish Carrier

1 oil engine driving 1 FP propeller
Total Power: 294kW (400hp)
Chinese Std. Type 6300
1 x 4 Stroke 6 Cy. 300 x 380 294kW (400bhp)
Guangzhou Diesel Engine Factory CoLtd-China

988882 **YUNTONG 88** **161**
ex Seven Star *-2005* *ex* Hae Song 101 *-2005* 48
- 63

1991 Daewon Shipbuilding — Busan
Loa - Br ex - Dght 2.700
Lbp 32.13 Br md 7.00 Dpth 3.50
Welded, 1 dk

(B32A2ST) Tug

1 oil engine driving 1 Propeller
Total Power: 1,471kW (2,000hp)
Niigata
1 x 4 Stroke 1471kW (2000bhp)
Niigata Engineering Co Ltd-Japan

301010 **YUNTONG 201** **354** Class: RI (NK) (AB)
2VU3 *ex* Kaisho *-2010* *ex* Adeko No. 1 *-2006* -
ex Koshi No. 1 *-1994* *ex* Yukon Ranger *-1987* 338
Yuntong (HK) International Shipping Co Ltd
Zhoushan Yuntong Shipping Co Ltd
Funafuti *Tuvalu*
MMSI: 572256210

1983-11 Labroy Marine Pte Ltd — Singapore
Yd No: T14
Converted From: Fishing Vessel
Converted From: Utility Vessel
Loa 40.00 Br ex - Dght 3.792
Lbp 35.69 Br md 9.52 Dpth 3.81
Welded, 1 dk

(B34L2QU) Utility Vessel

2 oil engines reverse reduction geared to sc. shafts driving 2 FP propellers
Total Power: 1,472kW (2,002hp) 10.0kn
Yanmar T220-ET
2 x 4 Stroke 6 Cy. 220 x 280 each-736kW (1001bhp)
Yanmar Diesel Engine Co Ltd-Japan
AuxGen: 2 x 48kW a.c

605076 **YUNTONG 202** **319** Class: (NK)
ex Aso Maru No. 11 *-2010* 93
Wendel Vega Marine Carriers Corp 197
-

1986-04 K.K. Mukai Zosensho — Nagasaki
Yd No: 563
Loa 36.30 Br ex - Dght 3.135
Lbp 33.46 Br md 8.21 Dpth 3.64
Welded, 1 dk

(B32A2ST) Tug

2 oil engines with clutches & reverse reduction geared to sc. shafts driving 2 CP propellers
Total Power: 1,472kW (2,002hp) 10.0kn
Akasaka DM26KFD
2 x 4 Stroke 6 Cy. 260 x 440 each-736kW (1001bhp)
Akasaka Tekkosho KK (Akasaka DieselLtd)-Japan
Thrusters: 1 Thwart. FP thruster (f)
Fuel: 135.0 (d.f.)

741272 **YUNUS** **394**
119
- -
-

2002-12 UR-Dock — Basrah
L reg 38.20 Br ex - Dght -
Lbp - Br md 9.00 Dpth 4.15
Welded, 1 dk

(B21B20T) Offshore Tug/Supply Ship

2 oil engines reduction geared to sc. shafts driving 2 Propellers
Total Power: 882kW (1,200hp)
Caterpillar
2 x 4 Stroke each-441kW (600bhp)
Caterpillar Inc-USA

905983 **YUNUS N** **1,998** Class: BV (KR)
CTI9 *ex* St Star *-2008* *ex* Sea Apex *-2006* 1,160
Negmar Denizcilik Yatirim AS (Negmar Shipping Investment AS) 3,052
-
Istanbul *Turkey*
MMSI: 271002644

1989-12 ShinA Shipbuilding Co Ltd — Tongyeong
Yd No: 335
Loa 88.64 (BB) Br ex 13.02 Dght 5.299
Lbp 81.50 Br md 13.00 Dpth 6.50
Welded, 1 dk

(A31A2GX) General Cargo Ship
Grain: 4,265; Bale: 3,620
TEU 78 C. 78/20' (40')
Compartments: 2 Ho, ER
3 Ha: (6.6 x 5.0) (12.6 x 10.0) (25.8 x 10.0)ER
Derricks: 1x25t,1x20t,1x15t

1 oil engine driving 1 FP propeller
Total Power: 1,765kW (2,400hp) 11.0kn
B&W 6S26MC
1 x 2 Stroke 6 Cy. 260 x 980 1765kW (2400bhp)
Ssangyong Heavy Industries Co Ltd-South Korea
AuxGen: 2 x 160kW 445V a.c
Fuel: 240.0 (d.f.)

973382 **YUNUS-S** **202** Class: (TL)
C7750 *ex* Yunus *-2009* 61
Istanbul Universitesi - Su Urunleri Fakultesi -
-
Istanbul *Turkey*
MMSI: 271043664
Official number: 499

1994-01 Anadolu Deniz Insaat Kizaklari San. ve Tic. Ltd. Sti. — Tuzla Yd No: 170a
Loa 24.00 Br ex - Dght 2.500
Lbp 20.00 Br md 6.80 Dpth 3.30
Welded, 1 dk

(B31A2SR) Research Survey Vessel

1 oil engine geared to sc. shaft driving 1 FP propeller
Total Power: 375kW (510hp) 10.0kn
Cummins KT-19-M
1 x 4 Stroke 6 Cy. 159 x 159 375kW (510bhp)
Cummins Engine Co Inc-USA
AuxGen: 2 x 105kW

827038 **YUNYY BALTIETS** **441** Class: RS
FWT 132
69
Real Estate Management Committee of St Petersburg City Executive Board
State Committee for Education (Dvorets Tvorchestra Yuniz)
St Petersburg *Russia*
MMSI: 273414310

1989-06 Baltiyskiy Zavod — Leningrad
Yd No: 00921
Loa 42.53 Br ex 8.40 Dght 3.001
Lbp 35.55 Br md - Dpth 6.05
Welded

(X11B2QN) Sail Training Ship

1 oil engine driving 1 FP propeller
Total Power: 299kW (407hp) 9.5kn
S.K.L. 8NVD36-1U
1 x 4 Stroke 8 Cy. 240 x 360 299kW (407bhp)
VEB Schwermaschinenbau "KarlLiebknecht" (SKL)-Magdeburg
AuxGen: 2 x 50kW a.c

251054 **YUO MARU** *9,348* Class: NK
D2773 -
Kawasaki Kinkai Kisen KK & Asahi Kisen KK 5,335
Shuntoku Kisen Co Ltd
Tomakomai, Hokkaido *Japan*
MMSI: 431501692
Official number: 132900

2001-06 Iwagi Zosen Co Ltd — Kamijima EH
Yd No: 195
Loa 149.40 (BB) Br ex - Dght 7.015
Lbp 138.00 Br md 24.00 Dpth 11.15
Welded

(A35A2RR) Ro-Ro Cargo Ship
Passengers: driver berths: 12
Quarter bow door/ramp (p)
Quarter stern door/ramp (p)
Lane-Len: 1260
Lane-clr ht: 4.30
Cars: 53, Trailers: 105

1 oil engine driving 1 FP propeller
Total Power: 12,640kW (17,185hp) 20.7kn
B&W 8S50MC-C
1 x 2 Stroke 8 Cy. 500 x 2000 12640kW (17185bhp)
Kawasaki Heavy Industries Ltd-Japan
AuxGen: 3 x 1020kW 450V 60Hz a.c
Thrusters: 1 Thwart. FP thruster (f); 1 Tunnel thruster (a)
Fuel: 710.0

934568 **YUPITER** **104** Class: (RS)
31
Suvorov Fishing Collective (Rybolovetskiy Kolkhoz im Suvorova) 58
-
Novorossiysk *Russia*
Official number: 921537

1994-07 AO Azovskaya Sudoverf — Azov
Yd No: 1066
Loa 26.50 Br ex 6.59 Dght 2.360
Lbp 22.90 Br md - Dpth 3.05
Welded, 1 dk

(A34A2GR) Refrigerated Cargo Ship
Ins: 48
Compartments: 1 Ho, ER
1 Ha: (1.2 x 0.8)
Cranes: 1x1t

1 oil engine geared to sc. shaft driving 1 FP propeller
Total Power: 165kW (224hp) 9.3kn
Daldizel 6CHNSP18/22
1 x 4 Stroke 6 Cy. 180 x 220 165kW (224bhp)
Daldizel-Khabarovsk
AuxGen: 2 x 30kW
Fuel: 9.0 (d.f.)

8027157 **YUPITER** **728** Class: (RS) 218 245
PJSC 'Fleet of Novorossiysk Commercial Sea Port'
LLC Shipping & Towing Co Novofleet
Odessa *Ukraine*
MMSI: 272592000
1982-11 Hollming Oy — Rauma Yd No: 243
Loa 39.90 Br ex 12.50 Dght 4.901
Lbp 36.48 Br md 12.01 Dpth 7.01
Welded, 1 dk
(B32A2ST) Tug
Ice Capable
2 oil engines dr geared to sc. shafts driving 2 CP propellers
Total Power: 3,706kW (5,038hp) 14.3k
Wartsila 6R3
2 x 4 Stroke 6 Cy. 320 x 350 each-1853kW (2519bhp)
Oy Wartsila Ab-Finland
AuxGen: 2 x 200kW, 1 x 42kW
Fuel: 224.0 (r.f.)

8033364 **YUPITER** *149* Class: (RS) 101 20
Sevastopol Port Authority
Sevastopol *Ukraine*
Official number: 811055
1981 Ilyichyovskiy Sudoremontnyy Zavod im. "50-letiya SSSR" — Ilyichyovsk Yd No: 12
Loa 28.70 Br ex 6.35 Dght 1.480
Lbp 27.00 Br md - Dpth 2.50
Welded, 1 dk
(A37B2PS) Passenger Ship
Passengers: unberthed: 250
2 oil engines driving 2 FP propellers
Total Power: 220kW (300hp) 10.4k
Barnaultransmash 3D6
2 x 2 Stroke 6 Cy. 150 x 180 each-110kW (150bhp) (new engine 1984)
Barnaultransmash-Barnaul
AuxGen: 2 x 1kW
Fuel: 2.0 (d.f.)

7741500 *UZEC* **YUPITER** *163* Class: (RS) 39 88
Shmidta Fishing Collective (Rybkolkhoz imeni P P Shmidta)
Illichevsk *Ukraine*
Official number: 780506
1979 Astrakhanskaya Sudoverf im. "Kirova" — Astrakhan Yd No: 115
Loa 34.02 Br ex 7.12 Dght 2.901
Lbp 29.98 Br md - Dpth 3.66
Welded, 1 dk
(B11B2FV) Fishing Vessel
Bale: 88
Compartments: 1 Ho, ER
1 Ha: (1.6 x 1.3)
Derricks: 2x2t; Winches: 2
Ice Capable
1 oil engine driving 1 FP propeller
Total Power: 224kW (305hp) 9.0k
S.K.L. 8VD36/24A-1
1 x 4 Stroke 8 Cy. 240 x 360 224kW (305bhp)
VEB Schwermaschinenbau "KarlLiebknecht" (SKL)-Magdeburg
AuxGen: 2 x 75kW, 1 x 28kW
Fuel: 20.0 (d.f.)

7391680 **YUPITER** **275** Class: (RS) 82 83
Government of The Russian Federation
SatCom: Inmarsat C 427302250
St Petersburg *Russia*
1975-05 Brodogradiliste 'Tito' Beograd - Brod 'Tito' — Belgrade Yd No: 919
Loa 35.43 Br ex 9.21 Dght 3.150
Lbp 30.00 Br md 9.00 Dpth 4.52
Welded, 1 dk
(B32A2ST) Tug
Ice Capable
2 oil engines geared to sc. shaft driving 1 CP propeller
Total Power: 1,700kW (2,312hp) 13.0k
B&W 7-26MTBF-40
2 x 4 Stroke 7 Cy. 260 x 400 each-850kW (1156bhp)
Titovi Zavodi 'Litostroj'-Yugoslavia
AuxGen: 2 x 100kW
Fuel: 66.0 (d.f.)

9459694 *JD2505* **YURA MARU** *744* - 1,600
Yura Kaiun KK & Yura Kisen KK
Yura Senpaku KK
Nagoya, Aichi *Japan*
MMSI: 431000389
Official number: 140638
2007-11 Sanuki Shipbuilding & Iron Works Co Ltd — Mitoyo KG Yd No: 1323
Loa 85.68 Br ex - Dght 4.010
Lbp 80.00 Br md 13.00 Dpth 7.40
Welded, 1 dk
(A31A2GX) General Cargo Ship
Grain: 4,455
Compartments: 1 Ho, ER
1 Ha: ER (48.6 x 10.0)
1 oil engine driving 1 FP propeller
Total Power: 1,910kW (2,597hp)
Akasaka A37
1 x 4 Stroke 6 Cy. 370 x 720 1910kW (2597bhp)
Akasaka Tekkosho KK (Akasaka DieselLtd)-Japan

9168362 *JH3430* **YURA MARU No. 1** *640* - 1,635
Yura Kisen KK
Nagoya, Aichi *Japan*
MMSI: 431200187
Official number: 134442
1997-04 Nakatani Shipyard Co. Ltd. — Etajima Yd No: 578
Loa 75.55 (BB) Br ex - Dght 4.160
Lbp 70.00 Br md 12.70 Dpth 7.70
Welded, 1 dk
(A31A2GX) General Cargo Ship
Grain: 3,789; Bale: 3,404
Compartments: 1 Ho, ER
1 Ha: ER
1 oil engine driving 1 CP propeller
Total Power: 1,471kW (2,000hp) 12.0kn
Akasaka
1 x 4 Stroke 6 Cy. 1471kW (2000bhp)
Akasaka Tekkosho KK (Akasaka DieselLtd)-Japan
AuxGen: 1 x 160kW 225V a.c, 1 x 120kW 225V a.c
Thrusters: 1 Thwart. FP thruster (f)
Fuel: 89.0 (d.f.)

8877071 **YURA MARU No. 18** *292* - 865
ex Eiwa Maru *-1991*
Jehan Shipping Corp
Philippines
1977 K.K. Saidaiji Zosensho — Okayama
Loa 59.70 Br ex - Dght 3.520
Lbp 55.00 Br md 9.20 Dpth 5.30
Welded, 1 dk
(A31A2GX) General Cargo Ship
Compartments: 1 Ho, ER
1 Ha: (30.8 x 7.0)ER
1 oil engine driving 1 FP propeller
Total Power: 956kW (1,300hp)
Fuji 6S30B
1 x 4 Stroke 6 Cy. 300 x 450 956kW (1300bhp)
Fuji Diesel Co Ltd-Japan

9178484 *JG5529* **YURI MARU** *469* - 650
Izushoto Kaihatsu KK
Tokyo *Japan*
Official number: 136581
1998-02 Kanmon Zosen K.K. — Shimonoseki Yd No: 581
Loa 62.00 (BB) Br ex 11.09 Dght 3.724
Lbp 57.00 Br md 11.08 Dpth 5.20
Welded, 1 dk
(A32A2GF) General Cargo/Passenger Ship
Bale: 930
1 oil engine driving 1 FP propeller
Total Power: 1,471kW (2,000hp)
Niigata 6M34BGT
1 x 4 Stroke 6 Cy. 340 x 620 1471kW (2000bhp)
Niigata Engineering Co Ltd-Japan
Thrusters: 1 Thwart. CP thruster (f)

9104304 *JM6369* **YURI MARU** *499* Class: NK - 1,200
YK Hyakumoto Kaiun
Shimonoseki, Yamaguchi *Japan*
Official number: 133656
1994-07 K.K. Miura Zosensho — Saiki Yd No: 1106
Loa 65.00 Br ex - Dght 4.211
Lbp 60.00 Br md 10.00 Dpth 4.40
Welded, 1 dk
(A13B2TP) Products Tanker
Liq: 1,213; Liq (Oil): 1,213
1 oil engine driving 1 FP propeller
Total Power: 736kW (1,001hp) 10.0kn
Yanmar MF29-ST
1 x 4 Stroke 6 Cy. 290 x 520 736kW (1001bhp)
Yanmar Diesel Engine Co Ltd-Japan
AuxGen: 3 x 93kW a.c
Fuel: 45.0 (d.f.)

9301419 *C4UL2* **YURI SENKEVICH** **60,434** Class: NV 28,502 100,869 T/cm 93.0
Comitana Investments Ltd
SCF Unicom Singapore Pte Ltd
SatCom: Inmarsat C 420922510
Limassol *Cyprus*
MMSI: 209225000
Official number: 9301419
2005-11 Hyundai Heavy Industries Co Ltd — Ulsan Yd No: 1602
Loa 246.88 (BB) Br ex 42.04 Dght 14.520
Lbp 234.00 Br md 42.00 Dpth 21.60
Welded, 1 dk
(A13A2TV) Crude Oil Tanker
Double Hull (13F)
Liq: 112,824; Liq (Oil): 122,823
Cargo Heating Coils
Compartments: 12 Wing Ta, 2 Wing Slop Ta, ER
3 Cargo Pump (s): 3x2500m³/hr
Manifold: Bow/CM: 123.5m
Ice Capable
1 oil engine driving 1 FP propeller
Total Power: 16,402kW (22,300hp) 15.2kn
MAN-B&W 7S60ME-C
1 x 2 Stroke 7 Cy. 600 x 2400 16402kW (22300bhp)
Hyundai Heavy Industries Co Ltd-South Korea
AuxGen: 3 x 1045kW 440/220V 60Hz a.c
Fuel: 311.0 (d.f.) (Heating Coils) 2935.0 (r.f.) 69.0pd

7900194 *PMRF* **YURICO** **3,780** Class: KI (NK) 1,521 6,217
ex T Young *-2008* *ex* Kaiyo Maru *-2004*
PT Pelayaran Andalas Bahtera Baruna
Jakarta *Indonesia*
MMSI: 525015397
1979-09 Tohoku Shipbuilding Co Ltd — Shiogama MG Yd No: 186
Loa 106.05 Br ex 16.34 Dght 6.530
Lbp 100.01 Br md 16.31 Dpth 8.11
Welded, 1 dk
(A24A2BT) Cement Carrier
Grain: 5,431
1 oil engine driving 1 FP propeller
Total Power: 2,795kW (3,800hp) 12.0kn
Akasaka DM47
1 x 4 Stroke 6 Cy. 470 x 760 2795kW (3800bhp)
Akasaka Tekkosho KK (Akasaka DieselLtd)-Japan
AuxGen: 3 x 264kW 450V 60Hz a.c
Fuel: 37.5 (d.f.) 114.0 (r.f.) 13.5pd

9423322 *3FIC7* **YURICOSMOS** **46,025** Class: NK 13,808 49,999 T/cm 70.2
Mi-Das Line SA
Doun Kisen KK (Doun Kisen Co Ltd)
Panama *Panama*
MMSI: 354494000
Official number: 4181410
2010-07 Mitsubishi Heavy Industries Ltd. — Nagasaki Yd No: 2246
Loa 230.00 Br ex - Dght 10.800
Lbp 219.00 Br md 36.60 Dpth 20.80
Welded, 1 dk
(A11B2TG) LPG Tanker
Liq (Gas): 78,907
4 x Gas Tank (s); 4 independent (stl) pri horizontal
8 Cargo Pump (s): 8x550m³/hr
1 oil engine driving 1 FP propeller
Total Power: 12,360kW (16,805hp) 16.4kn
Mitsubishi 7UEC60LSII
1 x 2 Stroke 7 Cy. 600 x 2300 12360kW (16805bhp)
Mitsubishi Heavy Industries Ltd-Japan
Fuel: 3156.0 (r.f.)

9363998 *UUAM2* **YURII MAKAROV** **5,197** Class: RS 2,796 6,355
Bug-7 Shipping Ltd
'Ukrrichflot' Joint Stock Shipping Co
Kherson *Ukraine*
MMSI: 272542000
2007-04 OAO Damen Shipyards Okean — Nikolayev Yd No: 9125
Loa 127.30 Br ex 16.82 Dght 4.860
Lbp 121.10 Br md 16.60 Dpth 6.70
Welded, 1 dk
(A31A2GX) General Cargo Ship
Grain: 9,980
Compartments: 3 Ho, ER
3 Ha: (32.6 x 13.0)ER 2 (25.6 x 13.0)
Ice Capable
1 oil engine reduction geared to sc. shaft driving 1 CP propeller
Total Power: 1,935kW (2,631hp) 11.2kn
MAN-B&W 9L21/31
1 x 4 Stroke 9 Cy. 210 x 310 1935kW (2631bhp)
MAN Diesel A/S-Denmark
AuxGen: 2 x 236kW 380V 50Hz a.c, 1 x 312kW 380V 50Hz a.c
Thrusters: 1 Thwart. FP thruster (f)
Fuel: 228.0 (d.f.) 10.0pd

7725958 **YURIMAYUAS** *135* - -
1977-04 SIMA Serv. Ind. de la Marina Callao (SIMAC) — Callao Yd No: 510
Loa - Br ex - Dght -
Lbp 13.34 Br md 8.83 Dpth 2.32
Welded, 1 dk
(B32A2ST) Tug
2 oil engines geared to sc. shafts driving 2 FP propellers
Total Power: 500kW (680hp)
G.M. (Detroit Diesel) 12V-71
2 x Vee 2 Stroke 12 Cy. 108 x 127 each-250kW (340bhp)
General Motors Corp-USA

9374076 *3EI08* **YURITAMOU** **90,091** Class: NK 59,287 180,184 T/cm 121.0
Mi-Das Line SA
Alfa Ship Managers Pte Ltd
SatCom: Inmarsat C 437235010
Panama *Panama*
MMSI: 372350000
Official number: 3235107A
2007-01 Imabari Shipbuilding Co Ltd — Saijo EH (Saijo Shipyard) Yd No: 8048
Loa 288.93 (BB) Br ex 45.00 Dght 18.174
Lbp 280.80 Br md 45.00 Dpth 24.70
Welded, 1 dk
(A21A2BC) Bulk Carrier
Grain: 199,725
Compartments: 9 Ho, ER
9 Ha: ER
1 oil engine driving 1 FP propeller
Total Power: 18,630kW (25,329hp) 14.5kn
MAN-B&W 6S70MC-C
1 x 2 Stroke 6 Cy. 700 x 2800 18630kW (25329bhp)
Mitsui Engineering & Shipbuilding CLtd-Japan
AuxGen: 3 x a.c
Fuel: 5390.0 (r.f.)

329558 **YURIWANG No. 5**
7EX *ex* Won Jin No. 1 *-1981*
Ongjin Shipping Co
Han Yum Forwarding Co Ltd
Incheon *South Korea*
Official number: ICR-780158

296 Class: (KR)
160
455

1979 Cheunggu Marine Industry Co Ltd — Ulsan
Loa 42.02 Br ex - Dght 2.791
Lbp 38.00 Br md 7.80 Dpth 3.20
Welded, 1 dk

(A31A2GX) General Cargo Ship
Bale: 455
1 Ha: (5.5 x 1.6)
Derricks: 1x1t

1 oil engine driving 1 FP propeller
Total Power: 250kW (340hp) 11.0kn
Sumiyoshi S6UCTE
1 x 4 Stroke 6 Cy. 260 x 400 250kW (340bhp)
Sumiyoshi Marine Diesel Co Ltd-Japan
AuxGen: 1 x 5kW 100V a.c

737652 **YURIWANG No. 7**
7BC
Han Yum Forwarding Co Ltd
-
Incheon *South Korea*
Official number: ICR-770299

290 Class: (KR)
141
363

1977 Inchon Engineering & Shipbuilding Corp — Incheon
Loa 41.99 Br ex - Dght 2.591
Lbp 38.03 Br md 7.01 Dpth 2.98
Welded, 1dk

(A31A2GX) General Cargo Ship
Grain: 415; Bale: 386
Derricks: 1x2t

1 oil engine driving 1 FP propeller
Total Power: 250kW (340hp) 10.0kn
Yanmar S165L-ST
1 x 4 Stroke 6 Cy. 165 x 210 250kW (340bhp)
Yanmar Diesel Engine Co Ltd-Japan

406705 **YURIY ARSHENEVSKIY**
*CJR
Murmansk Shipping Co (MSC)
-
SatCom: Inmarsat C 427300185
Murmansk *Russia*
MMSI: 273130400
Official number: 851156

18,574 Class: RS
7,442
22,910

1986-09 Valmet Oy — Helsinki Yd No: 320
Loa 176.65 Br ex 24.57 Dght 11.350
Lbp 164.10 Br md 24.50 Dpth 15.19
Welded, 2 dks

(A31A2GA) General Cargo Ship (with Ro-Ro facility)
Side door & ramp (s. a.)
Len: 17.50 Wid: 5.00 Swl: 56
Lane-Len: 570
Lane-Wid: 3.00
Lane-clr ht: 4.20
Cars: 140, Trailers: 36
Grain: 29,633; Bale: 27,245; Liq: 902
TEU 576 C Ho 402 TEU C Dk 174 TEU incl 50 ref C.
Compartments: 4 Ho, ER, 2 Wing Dp Ta in Hold, 6 Tw Dk
8 Ha: (12.8 x 13.0)2 (25.6 x 8.0)4 (19.2 x 8.0)ER (6.4 x 10.4)
Cranes: 3x40t,2x20t
Ice Capable

2 oil engines reduction geared to sc. shaft driving 1 CP propeller
Total Power: 15,446kW (21,000hp) 17.9kn
Sulzer 14ZV40/48
2 x Vee 2 Stroke 14 Cy. 400 x 480 each-7723kW (10500bhp)
Oy Wartsila Ab-Finland
AuxGen: 4 x 800kW 400V 50Hz a.c
Fuel: 675.5 (d.f.) 3227.5 (r.f.) 76.0pd

3827040 **YURIY GARNAYEV**
UREP
Feodosiya Port
-
Theodosia *Ukraine*
Official number: 893430

245 Class: (RS)
74
34

1989-12 Ilyichyovskiy Sudoremontnyy Zavod im. "50-letiya SSSR" — Ilyichyovsk Yd No: 21
Loa 37.60 Br ex 7.21 Dght 1.690
Lbp 34.01 Br md - Dpth 2.90
Welded, 1 dk

(A37B2PS) Passenger Ship
Passengers: unberthed: 250

3 oil engines reduction geared to sc. shafts driving 3 FP propellers
Total Power: 960kW (1,306hp) 16.5kn
Barnaultransmash 3D6C
2 x 4 Stroke 6 Cy. 150 x 180 each-110kW (150bhp)
Barnaultransmash-Barnaul
Zvezda M412
1 x Vee 4 Stroke 12 Cy. 180 x 200 740kW (1006bhp)
"Zvezda"-Leningrad
AuxGen: 2 x 16kW
Fuel: 5.0 (d.f.)

7741512 **YURIY KRYMOV**
ENUL
-
Ukrainian Danube Shipping Co
-
SatCom: Inmarsat C 427291410
Izmail *Ukraine*
MMSI: 272914000
Official number: 782830

4,517 Class: (RS)
1,927
6,100

1978 Navashinskiy Sudostroitelnyy Zavod 'Oka' — Navashino Yd No: 1202
Loa 124.42 Br ex 16.41 Dght 5.850
Lbp 117.02 Br md 15.82 Dpth 7.52
Welded, 1 dk

(A31A2GX) General Cargo Ship
Grain: 6,800; Bale: 5,800
TEU 165 C. 165/20'
Compartments: 4 Ho, ER
4 Ha: (13.2 x 10.5)3 (13.2 x 12.8)ER
Cranes: 4x8t
Ice Capable

2 oil engines driving 2 FP propellers
Total Power: 2,206kW (3,000hp) 13.0kn
Dvigatel Revolyutsii 6CHRNP36/45
2 x 4 Stroke 6 Cy. 360 x 450 each-1103kW (1500bhp)
Zavod "Dvigatel Revolyutsii"-Gorkiy
AuxGen: 3 x 180kW a.c
Fuel: 435.0 (d.f.) 2560.0 (r.f.)

6521850 **YURIY LISYANSKIY**
UIRX *ex* Ledokol 9 *-1966*
- **Federal State Unitary Enterprise Rosmorport**
St Petersburg *Russia*
MMSI: 273426110

2,255 Class: RS
676
1,092

1965-03 Admiralteyskiy Sudostroitelnyy Zavod — Leningrad Yd No: 772
Loa 67.70 Br ex 18.29 Dght 6.060
Lbp 62.01 Br md 17.51 Dpth 8.34
Welded, 2 dks

(B34C2SI) Icebreaker
Grain: 250
Compartments: 1 Ho, ER
1 Ha: (2.3 x 1.6)
Derricks: 2x1.5t; Winches: 2
Ice Capable

3 diesel electric oil engines driving 3 gen. Connecting to 1 elec. Motor of (1180kW) 2 elec. motors each (1760kW) driving 2 Propellers 2 aft and 1 fwd
Total Power: 3,972kW (5,400hp) 14.0kn
Fairbanks, Morse 10-38D8-1/8
3 x 2 Stroke 10 Cy. 207 x 254 each-1324kW (1800bhp) in the U.S.S.R.
AuxGen: 3 x 220kW, 1 x 100kW
Fuel: 617.0 (d.f.)

9130846 **YURIY OREL**
UCEQ
-
JSC Dalryba (A/O 'Dalryba')
-
SatCom: Inmarsat C 427320131
Vladivostok *Russia*
MMSI: 273813100
Official number: 940167

726 Class: RS
217
414

1995-10 ATVT Zavod "Leninska Kuznya" — Kyyiv Yd No: 1688
Loa 54.82 Br ex 10.15 Dght 4.140
Lbp 50.30 Br md 9.80 Dpth 5.00
Welded, 1 dk

(B11A2FS) Stern Trawler
Ice Capable

1 oil engine driving 1 CP propeller
Total Power: 852kW (1,158hp) 12.0kn
S.K.L. 8NVD48A-2U
1 x 4 Stroke 8 Cy. 320 x 480 852kW (1158bhp)
SKL Motoren u. Systemtechnik AG-Magdeburg
AuxGen: 3 x 200kW a.c
Fuel: 155.0 (d.f.)

7611171 **YURIY ORLENKO**
UDCY *ex* Primernyy *-2002*
- **Federal State Financed Institution 'Far-Eastern Expeditionary Division of Emergency & Rescue Operations'**
-
Vladivostok *Russia*
MMSI: 273816100
Official number: 751371

1,163 Class: RS
348
447

1976-01 Sudostroitelnyy Zavod "Zaliv" — Kerch Yd No: 600
Loa 58.55 Br ex 12.96 Dght 4.671
Lbp 51.62 Br md 12.30 Dpth 5.90
Welded, 1 dk

(B32A2ST) Tug
Ice Capable

2 diesel electric oil engines driving 2 gen. Connecting to 2 elec. motors each (950kW) driving 1 FP propeller
Total Power: 2,200kW (2,992hp) 13.5kn
Kolomna 6CHN30/38
2 x 4 Stroke 6 Cy. 300 x 380 each-1100kW (1496bhp)
Kolomenskiy Zavod-Kolomna
AuxGen: 2 x 300kW, 2 x 160kW
Fuel: 349.0 (d.f.)

8986389 **YURIY POLTORATSKIY**
UHNF *ex* Volzhskiy-21 *-2005*
- **India Shipping Co Ltd**
Sailtrade Denizcilik ve Ticaret Ltd Sti
Taganrog *Russia*
MMSI: 273312150

5,216 Class: RS (RR)
2,915
6,125

1987-09 Navashinskiy Sudostroitelnyy Zavod 'Oka' — Navashino Yd No: 1023
Loa 139.00 Br ex 16.70 Dght 4.100
Lbp 135.00 Br md 16.50 Dpth 5.50
Welded, 1 dk

(A31A2GX) General Cargo Ship
Grain: 9,648

2 oil engines driving 2 FP propellers
Total Power: 1,766kW (2,402hp) 10.0kn
Dvigatel Revolyutsii 6CHRN36/45
2 x 4 Stroke 6 Cy. 360 x 450 each-883kW (1201bhp)
Zavod "Dvigatel Revolyutsii"-Gorkiy

8723579 **YURIY SAVIN**
- *ex* Vympel *-1991*
- **Federal State Unitary Enterprise Rosmorport**
Vladivostok *Russia*
MMSI: 273136700
Official number: 873263

106 Class: (RS)
31
14

1988-05 Zavod "Krasnyy Moryak" — Rostov-na-Donu Yd No: 31
Loa 23.15 Br ex 6.24 Dght 1.850
Lbp 20.00 Br md 5.60 Dpth 2.80
Welded, 1 dk

(A37B2PS) Passenger Ship
Passengers: unberthed: 70
Ice Capable

1 oil engine geared to sc. shaft driving 1 FP propeller
Total Power: 221kW (300hp) 9.0kn
Daldizel 6CHNSP18/22-300
1 x 4 Stroke 6 Cy. 180 x 220 221kW (300bhp)
Daldizel-Khabarovsk
AuxGen: 1 x 16kW
Fuel: 6.0 (d.f.)

8603353 **YURIY TARAPUROV**
UBIZ *ex* Albatros S *-2010* *ex* Albatros *-2005*
ex Otoma *-2002* *ex* Teodor Nette *-1999*
Flot Co Ltd
Transport-Forwarding Company JSC Kamchatka Lines
Petropavlovsk-Kamchatskiy *Russia*
MMSI: 273359800

6,395 Class: RS (BV)
2,864
7,075

1988-09 Stocznia Gdanska im Lenina — Gdansk Yd No: B352/02
Loa 131.60 Br ex 19.30 Dght 7.000
Lbp 122.00 Br md - Dpth 8.80
Welded, 1 dk

(A31A2GX) General Cargo Ship
Grain: 10,076; Bale: 9,570
TEU 302
Compartments: 4 Ho, ER
4 Ha: (12.6 x 10.3) (12.6 x 15.3)2 (18.9 x 15.3)ER
Cranes: 4x12.5t
Ice Capable

1 oil engine driving 1 FP propeller
Total Power: 4,690kW (6,377hp) 14.9kn
B&W 7L45GBE
1 x 2 Stroke 7 Cy. 450 x 1200 4690kW (6377bhp)
Zaklady Przemyslu Metalowego 'HCegielski' SA-Poznan
AuxGen: 3 x 400kW a.c
Fuel: 150.0 (d.f.) 660.0 (r.f.)

8933801 **YURKIY**
-
- **Vladivostok Sea Fishing Port (OAO 'Vladivostokskiy Morskoy Rybnyy Port')**
Vladivostok *Russia*
Official number: 732686

187 Class: RS
-
46

1974 Gorokhovetskiy Sudostroitelnyy Zavod — Gorokhovets Yd No: 316
Loa 29.30 Br ex 8.49 Dght 3.090
Lbp 27.00 Br md 8.30 Dpth 4.30
Welded, 1 dk

(B32A2ST) Tug
Ice Capable

2 oil engines driving 2 CP propellers
Total Power: 882kW (1,200hp) 11.4kn
Russkiy 6D30/50-4-2
2 x 2 Stroke 6 Cy. 300 x 500 each-441kW (600bhp)
Mashinostroitelnyy Zavod"Russkiy-Dizel"-Leningrad
AuxGen: 2 x 25kW a.c
Fuel: 36.0 (d.f.)

9338230 **YURY TOPCHEV**
UFYE
- **Gazprom JSC & Gazprom Neft Shelf**
OOO Gazflot
Murmansk *Russia*
MMSI: 273319940

5,871 Class: RS (NV)
1,762
3,949

2006-11 DP Sudnobudivnyi Zavod im. "61 Kommunara" — Mykolayiv (Hull) Yd No: 3311
2006-11 Havyard Leirvik AS — Leirvik i Sogn Yd No: 083
Loa 99.30 Br ex - Dght 8.000
Lbp 84.39 Br md 19.00 Dpth 10.50
Welded, 1 dk

(B32A2ST) Tug
Double Bottom Entire Compartment Length

4 diesel electric oil engines driving 2 gen. each 6000kW a.c 2 gen. each 4000kW a.c Connecting to 2 elec. motors driving 2 Azimuth electric drive units
Total Power: 19,990kW (27,180hp) 15.0kn
Wartsila 12V32
2 x Vee 4 Stroke 12 Cy. 320 x 400 each-6000kW (8158bhp)
Wartsila Finland Oy-Finland
Wartsila 8L32
2 x 4 Stroke 8 Cy. 320 x 400 each-3995kW (5432bhp)
Wartsila Finland Oy-Finland
Thrusters: 2 Tunnel thruster (f)

7825320 - -	**YURYO MARU** *ex* Yuryo Maru No. 21 *-1989* - - *Chinese Taipei*	*116* - -		**1979-03 Nagasaki Zosen K.K. — Nagasaki** Yd No: 681 Loa 37.60 Br ex 7.70 Dght 2.371 Lbp 30.97 Br md 7.01 Dpth 2.80 Welded, 1 dk	**(B11B2FV) Fishing Vessel**	**1 oil engine** geared to sc. shaft driving 1 FP propeller Total Power: 861kW (1,171hp) Daihatsu 6DSM-2 1 x 4 Stroke 6 Cy. 280 x 340 861kW (1171bhp) Daihatsu Diesel Manufacturing Co Lt-Japan
7941605 - -	**YURYO MARU No. 38** - **El Marfenra Co Inc** - *Philippines*	*259* - -		**1980-12 K.K. Otsuchi Kogyo — Otsuchi** Yd No: 206 Loa 37.22 Br ex 7.62 Dght 3.031 Lbp - Br md - Dpth - Welded, 1 dk	**(B11B2FV) Fishing Vessel**	**1 oil engine** driving 1 FP propeller Daihatsu 1 x 4 Stroke Daihatsu Diesel Manufacturing Co Lt-Japan
8613645 *HP9986* -	**YUSEI** *ex* Yusei Maru No. 8 *-2000* **Yusei Line SA** Mitsui Warehouse Co Ltd (Mitsui-Soko Co Ltd) *Panama* *Panama* MMSI: 352118000 Official number: 2718700	**527** 199 860	Class: (BV)	**1986-07 Sasaki Shipbuilding Co Ltd — Osakikamijima HS** Yd No: 502 Loa 53.98 Br ex - Dght 3.640 Lbp 49.81 Br md 9.01 Dpth 4.12 Welded, 1 dk	**(A12A2TC) Chemical Tanker** Liq: 709 Compartments: 6 Ta, ER	**1 oil engine** with clutches, flexible couplings & reverse reduction geared to sc. shaft driving 1 FP propeller Total Power: 625kW (850hp) 10.0k Niigata 6M26BG 1 x 4 Stroke 6 Cy. 260 x 460 625kW (850bhp) Niigata Engineering Co Ltd-Japan AuxGen: 2 x 80kW 100/445V 60Hz a.c
8911592 *JM5962* -	**YUSEI MARU** - **Fuyo Kaiun KK** - *Kagoshima, Kagoshima* *Japan* MMSI: 431601042 Official number: 131318	*699* - 1,615	Class: NK	**1990-02 Kanmon Zosen K.K. — Shimonoseki** Yd No: 516 Loa 69.51 (BB) Br ex - Dght 4.313 Lbp 65.00 Br md 11.50 Dpth 5.00 Welded, 1 dk	**(A24A2BT) Cement Carrier** Grain: 1,363; Bale: 1,363 Compartments: 6 Ho, ER 6 Ha: ER	**1 oil engine** with clutches, hydraulic couplings & sr geared to sc. shaft driving 1 FP propeller Total Power: 1,177kW (1,600hp) Niigata 6M31AFT 1 x 4 Stroke 6 Cy. 310 x 530 1177kW (1600bhp) Niigata Engineering Co Ltd-Japan Fuel: 75.0 (d.f.)
8909953 - -	**YUSEI MARU** - - -	*430* - 998		**1989-10 Teraoka Shipyard Co Ltd — Minamiawaji HG** Yd No: 283 Loa - Br ex - Dght 4.201 Lbp 56.52 Br md 9.01 Dpth 4.53 Welded, 1 dk	**(A12A2TC) Chemical Tanker** Liq: 680 Compartments: 3 Ta, ER 2 Cargo Pump (s): 2x200m³/hr	**1 oil engine** driving 1 FP propeller Total Power: 736kW (1,001hp) Hanshin 6LUD2 1 x 4 Stroke 6 Cy. 260 x 440 736kW (1001bhp) The Hanshin Diesel Works Ltd-Japan
9675432 *JD3516* -	**YUSEI MARU** - **Arouzu Kaiun KK & Japan Railway Construction, Transport & Technology Agency** Arouzu Kaiun KK *Imabari, Ehime* *Japan* MMSI: 431004377 Official number: 141923	*998* - 2,306	Class: NK	**2013-05 Hakata Zosen K.K. — Imabari** Yd No: 761 Loa 72.90 (BB) Br ex - Dght 5.013 Lbp 68.50 Br md 13.50 Dpth 5.50 Welded, 1 dk	**(A13B2TP) Products Tanker** Double Hull (13F) Liq: 2,205; Liq (Oil): 2,205	**1 oil engine** geared to sc. shaft driving 1 Propeller Total Power: 1,765kW (2,400hp) Hanshin LA34 1 x 4 Stroke 6 Cy. 340 x 720 1765kW (2400bhp) The Hanshin Diesel Works Ltd-Japan Fuel: 130.0
9695808 *JD3502* -	**YUSEI MARU** - **YK Masuda Kaiun** - *Uki, Kumamoto* *Japan* Official number: 141903	*499* - 1,700		**2013-04 K.K. Matsuura Zosensho — Osakikamijima** Yd No: 582 Loa 76.20 (BB) Br ex - Dght 4.390 Lbp - Br md 12.00 Dpth 7.35 Welded, 1 dk	**(A31A2GX) General Cargo Ship** Grain: 2,495 Compartments: 1 Ho, ER 1 Ha: ER (40.0 x 9.5)	**1 oil engine** reduction geared to sc. shaft driving 1 Propeller Total Power: 1,618kW (2,200hp) Niigata 6M34BGT 1 x 4 Stroke 6 Cy. 340 x 620 1618kW (2200bhp) Niigata Engineering Co Ltd-Japan
8620973 *JH3070* -	**YUSEI MARU NO. 2** *ex* Kosei Maru No. 2 *-2005* *ex* Fukuichi Maru No. 2 *-1993* **Yusei Suisan YK** - *Okinoshima, Shimane* *Japan* Official number: 128411	*170* - -		**1985-10 K.K. Watanabe Zosensho — Nagasaki** Yd No: 1085 Loa - (BB) Br ex - Dght - Lbp 36.58 Br md 7.41 Dpth 3.71 Welded, 1 dk	**(B12B2FC) Fish Carrier**	**1 oil engine** driving 1 FP propeller Total Power: 713kW (969hp) Pielstick 6PA5 1 x 4 Stroke 6 Cy. 255 x 270 713kW (969bhp) Niigata Engineering Co Ltd-Japan
8823501 - -	**YUSEI MARU No. 30** - **PT Armada Contener Nusantara** -	*460* - 446		**1988-09 Takao Zosen Kogyo K.K. — Tateyama** Yd No: 87 Loa 47.74 Br ex - Dght 3.070 Lbp 42.00 Br md 10.60 Dpth 3.10 Welded, 1 dk	**(A24D2BA) Aggregates Carrier**	**1 oil engine** driving 1 FP propeller Total Power: 588kW (799hp) Niigata 6M26AGTE 1 x 4 Stroke 6 Cy. 260 x 460 588kW (799bhp) Niigata Engineering Co Ltd-Japan
8013819 - -	**YUSEI MARU No. 78** *ex* Daikichi Maru No. 58 *-1990* **NFH Fishing Enterprises** - *Philippines*	*153* - 210		**1980-11 K.K. Izutsu Zosensho — Nagasaki** Yd No: 826 Loa 38.99 Br ex - Dght 2.509 Lbp 32.80 Br md 6.61 Dpth 2.87 Welded, 1 dk	**(B11B2FV) Fishing Vessel**	**1 oil engine** reduction geared to sc. shaft driving 1 FP propeller Total Power: 758kW (1,031hp) Niigata 6MG25BX 1 x 4 Stroke 6 Cy. 250 x 320 758kW (1031bhp) Niigata Engineering Co Ltd-Japan
9565871 *3FDY7* -	**YUSHAN BLOSSOM** - **Trio Happiness SA** Toda Kisen KK *Panama* *Panama* MMSI: 353195000 Official number: 4210410	**7,057** 2,534 8,788	Class: NK	**2010-10 Jong Shyn Shipbuilding Co., Ltd. — Kaohsiung** Yd No: 188 Loa 110.00 (BB) Br ex 18.83 Dght 7.900 Lbp 102.00 Br md 18.80 Dpth 12.70 Welded, 1 dk	**(A31A2GX) General Cargo Ship** Grain: 12,696; Bale: 11,737 Compartments: 2 Ho, 2 Tw Dk, ER 2 Ha: ER 2 (25.5 x 13.5) Cranes: 2x30.7t	**1 oil engine** driving 1 FP propeller Total Power: 3,250kW (4,419hp) 13.0kn MAN-B&W 5L35MC 1 x 2 Stroke 5 Cy. 350 x 1050 3250kW (4419bhp) Makita Corp-Japan
9197181 *JLZS* -	**YUSHIN MARU** - **Kyodo Senpaku Kaisha Ltd** - *Tokyo* *Japan* MMSI: 431439000 Official number: 136641	*724* - 645	Class: NK	**1998-10 Naikai Zosen Corp — Onomichi HS (Setoda Shipyard)** Yd No: 638 Loa 69.61 Br ex - Dght 4.718 Lbp 62.69 Br md 10.40 Dpth 5.30 Welded, 1 dk	**(B12D2FR) Fishery Research Vessel**	**1 oil engine** driving 1 CP propeller Total Power: 3,884kW (5,281hp) 17.0kn B&W 6L35MC 1 x 2 Stroke 6 Cy. 350 x 1050 3884kW (5281bhp) The Hanshin Diesel Works Ltd-Japan AuxGen: 3 x 300kW a.c Fuel: 397.0 (d.f.) 16.0pd
9239678 *JL6604* -	**YUSHIN MARU** - **Arouzu Kaiun KK** - *Imabari, Ehime* *Japan* MMSI: 431501663 Official number: 136528	*749* - 1,933	Class: NK	**2000-11 Hakata Zosen K.K. — Imabari** Yd No: 627 Loa 69.93 Br ex - Dght 5.022 Lbp 66.00 Br md 11.50 Dpth 5.60 Welded, 1 dk	**(A13B2TP) Products Tanker** Liq: 2,240; Liq (Oil): 2,240	**1 oil engine** driving 1 FP propeller Total Power: 1,618kW (2,200hp) 12.0kn Hanshin LH34LG 1 x 4 Stroke 6 Cy. 340 x 640 1618kW (2200bhp) The Hanshin Diesel Works Ltd-Japan Fuel: 65.0
8879146 *JK5393* -	**YUSHIN MARU** - - - *Hiroshima, Hiroshima* *Japan* Official number: 134746	*496* - 489		**1994-07 Kimura Zosen K.K. — Kure** Yd No: 127 Loa 49.81 Br ex - Dght 2.970 Lbp 43.00 Br md 12.00 Dpth 5.30 Welded, 1 dk	**(A31A2GX) General Cargo Ship**	**1 oil engine** driving 1 FP propeller Total Power: 736kW (1,001hp) 10.5kn Niigata 6M28BGT 1 x 4 Stroke 6 Cy. 280 x 480 736kW (1001bhp) Niigata Engineering Co Ltd-Japan
9145906 *JL6531* -	**YUSHIN MARU** *ex* Tone Maru No. 2 *-2004* **Yushin Kaiun KK** - *Saiki, Oita* *Japan* Official number: 134888	*499* - 1,545		**1996-05 K.K. Miura Zosensho — Saiki** Yd No: 1162 Loa - Br ex - Dght 4.020 Lbp 70.00 Br md 12.30 Dpth 6.87 Welded, 1 dk	**(A31A2GX) General Cargo Ship**	**1 oil engine** driving 1 FP propeller Total Power: 736kW (1,001hp) 12.4kn Akasaka A34C 1 x 4 Stroke 6 Cy. 340 x 620 736kW (1001bhp) Akasaka Tekkosho KK (Akasaka DieselLtd)-Japan
9278040 *JPPV* -	**YUSHIN MARU NO. 2** - **Kyodo Senpaku Kaisha Ltd** - *Tokyo* *Japan* MMSI: 432364000 Official number: 137139	**1,059** 317 732	Class: NK	**2002-09 Naikai Zosen Corp — Onomichi HS (Setoda Shipyard)** Yd No: 675 Loa 69.61 Br ex - Dght 4.718 Lbp 62.69 Br md 10.80 Dpth 5.30 Welded	**(B12D2FR) Fishery Research Vessel**	**1 oil engine** driving 1 FP propeller Total Power: 3,883kW (5,279hp) B&W 6L35MC 1 x 2 Stroke 6 Cy. 350 x 1050 3883kW (5279bhp) Kawasaki Heavy Industries Ltd-Japan AuxGen: 2 x 400kW a.c Fuel: 425.0
9414096 *7JCH* -	**YUSHIN MARU NO. 3** - **Kyodo Senpaku Kaisha Ltd** - *Tokyo* *Japan* MMSI: 432621000 Official number: 140548	*742* - 726	Class: NK	**2007-10 Naikai Zosen Corp — Onomichi HS (Setoda Shipyard)** Yd No: 723 Loa 69.61 Br ex - Dght 4.560 Lbp 62.50 Br md 10.80 Dpth 5.30 Welded, 1 dk	**(B12D2FR) Fishery Research Vessel**	**1 oil engine** reduction geared to sc. shaft driving 1 CP propeller Total Power: 3,900kW (5,302hp) MAN-B&W 6L35MC 1 x 2 Stroke 6 Cy. 350 x 1050 3900kW (5302bhp) The Hanshin Diesel Works Ltd-Japan Fuel: 430.0

IMO / Call sign	Name / Owner	Tonnage	Class	Builder / Dimensions	Type / Cargo	Machinery
923844	**YUSHIN MARU No. 5** - -	488 - 1,241		**1996-05 Amakusa Zosen K.K. — Amakusa** Yd No: 113 Loa 69.20 Br ex - Dght 4.060 Lbp 64.00 Br md 13.00 Dpth 7.10 Welded, 1 dk	**(A24D2BA) Aggregates Carrier**	**1 oil engine** driving 1 FP propeller Total Power: 736kW (1,001hp) 11.0kn Niigata 6M34BGT 1 x 4 Stroke 6 Cy. 340 x 620 736kW (1001bhp) Niigata Engineering Co Ltd-Japan
720606	**YUSHIN MARU No. 8** - - Philippines	491 - 1,456		**1988-05 Kimura Zosen K.K. — Kure** Loa 68.00 Br ex 13.22 Dght 4.170 Lbp 63.00 Br md 13.20 Dpth 6.95 Welded, 1 dk	**(A24D2BA) Aggregates Carrier**	**1 oil engine** driving 1 FP propeller Total Power: 1,324kW (1,800hp) 12.9kn Niigata 6M34AGT 1 x 4 Stroke 6 Cy. 340 x 620 1324kW (1800bhp) Niigata Engineering Co Ltd-Japan
135339 L6433	**YUSHIN MARU NO. 8** ex Senyo Maru -2003 **Yushin Kaiun KK** - Saiki, Oita Japan Official number: 135138	499 - 1,500		**1995-11 K.K. Miura Zosensho — Saiki** Yd No: 1150 Loa 75.50 Br ex - Dght 3.980 Lbp 70.00 Br md 12.30 Dpth 6.87 Welded, 1 dk	**(A31A2GX) General Cargo Ship** Bale: 2,427 Compartments: 1 Ho 1 Ha: (40.2 x 9.5)	**1 oil engine** driving 1 FP propeller Total Power: 736kW (1,001hp) 11.0kn Hanshin LH34LAG 1 x 4 Stroke 6 Cy. 340 x 640 736kW (1001bhp) The Hanshin Diesel Works Ltd-Japan Fuel: 83.7 (d.f.)
238648 P3400	**YUSHO ANGEL II** ex Daito Maru -2010 ex Seiko Maru -2009 **Toua Line SA** Busan Shipping Co Ltd Panama Panama MMSI: 352898000 Official number: 4196610	1,512 855 2,768	Class: KR	**2000-11 K.K. Yoshida Zosen Kogyo — Arida** Yd No: 520 Loa 75.01 Br ex - Dght 5.513 Lbp 70.00 Br md 12.20 Dpth 7.00 Welded, 1 dk	**(A31A2GX) General Cargo Ship** Compartments: 1 Ho, ER 1 Ha: (40.3 x 10.0)ER	**1 oil engine** driving 1 FP propeller Total Power: 1,471kW (2,000hp) 11.9kn Akasaka A34C 1 x 4 Stroke 6 Cy. 340 x 620 1471kW (2000bhp) Akasaka Tekkosho KK (Akasaka DieselLtd)-Japan Fuel: 67.0 (d.f.)
597288 FXB4	**YUSHO APRICOT** **Apricot Line SA** Daito Kaiun Sangyo KK SatCom: Inmarsat C 437029810 Panama Panama MMSI: 370298000 Official number: 4258711	2,927 1,410 3,866	Class: NK	**2011-03 Kumamoto Dock K.K. — Yatsushiro** Yd No: 456 Loa 84.99 (BB) Br ex - Dght 6.150 Lbp 78.00 Br md 14.80 Dpth 9.00 Welded, 1 dk	**(A31A2GX) General Cargo Ship** Grain: 5,934; Bale: 5,666 Cranes: 2x25t	**1 oil engine** driving 1 Propeller Total Power: 1,912kW (2,600hp) Akasaka A37 1 x 4 Stroke 6 Cy. 370 x 720 1912kW (2600bhp) Akasaka Tekkosho KK (Akasaka DieselLtd)-Japan Fuel: 238.0
412971 ELM7	**YUSHO CHERRY** **Pine Forest Carriers SA** Grow-Will Inc Panama Panama MMSI: 372991000 Official number: 3301607A	7,513 3,974 11,330	Class: NK	**2007-08 Nishi Shipbuilding Co Ltd — Imabari EH** Yd No: 450 Loa 110.49 (BB) Br ex - Dght 9.200 Lbp 102.16 Br md 19.20 Dpth 13.50 Welded, 1 dk	**(A31A2GX) General Cargo Ship** Grain: 15,824; Bale: 14,713 Compartments: 2 Ho, 2 Tw Dk, ER 2 Ha: (33.6 x 14.0)ER (20.3 x 14.0) Cranes: 2x30.7t; Derricks: 1x30t	**1 oil engine** driving 1 FP propeller Total Power: 3,900kW (5,302hp) 13.3kn MAN-B&W 6L35MC 1 x 2 Stroke 6 Cy. 350 x 1050 3900kW (5302bhp) Makita Corp-Japan AuxGen: 2 x a.c Fuel: 711.0
470038 EOJ2	**YUSHO EIGHT** **TH Shipping Panama SA** Grow-Will Inc Panama Panama MMSI: 356293000 Official number: 3352908A	2,905 1,305 3,816	Class: NK	**2008-01 Kotobuki Kogyo KK — Ichikikushikino KS** Yd No: 128 Loa 84.86 (BB) Br ex 14.80 Dght 5.936 Lbp 78.00 Br md 14.80 Dpth 9.00 Welded, 1 dk	**(A31A2GX) General Cargo Ship** Grain: 5,934; Bale: 5,660 Compartments: 2 Ho, ER 2 Ha: (19.5 x 11.0)ER (18.9 x 11.0) Cranes: 2x25t	**1 oil engine** driving 1 FP propeller Total Power: 1,910kW (2,597hp) Akasaka A37 1 x 4 Stroke 6 Cy. 370 x 720 1910kW (2597bhp) Akasaka Tekkosho KK (Akasaka DieselLtd)-Japan AuxGen: 2 x a.c Thrusters: 1 Tunnel thruster (f) Fuel: 215.0
319258 8TU	**YUSHO HARUNA** **Kotobuki Shipping Corp SA** SeoYang Shipping Co Ltd Panama Panama MMSI: 354587000 Official number: 3010304C	2,956 1,279 3,825	Class: NK	**2004-07 Yamanaka Zosen K.K. — Imabari** Yd No: 700 Loa 83.90 (BB) Br ex - Dght 5.993 Lbp 78.70 Br md 14.80 Dpth 9.10 Welded, 1 dk	**(A31A2GX) General Cargo Ship** Grain: 5,901; Bale: 5,615 Compartments: 2 Ho, ER 2 Ha: ER 2 (19.6 x 10.2) Cranes: 1x50t,2x25t	**1 oil engine** driving 1 FP propeller Total Power: 1,912kW (2,600hp) 12.0kn Hanshin LH36LA 1 x 4 Stroke 6 Cy. 360 x 670 1912kW (2600bhp) The Hanshin Diesel Works Ltd-Japan Thrusters: 1 Tunnel thruster (f) Fuel: 215.0
350109 ECJ3	**YUSHO LILY** **Pine Forest Transport SA** Grow-Will Inc Panama Panama MMSI: 371375000 Official number: 3103405B	6,004 3,182 9,506	Class: NK	**2005-09 Nishi Shipbuilding Co Ltd — Imabari EH** Yd No: 442 Loa 97.61 (BB) Br ex - Dght 9.201 Lbp 89.95 Br md 18.80 Dpth 13.00 Welded, 1 dk	**(A31A2GX) General Cargo Ship** Grain: 12,141; Bale: 11,432 Compartments: 2 Ho, ER 2 Ha: (23.1 x 12.6)ER (22.4 x 12.6) Cranes: 2x30t	**1 oil engine** driving 1 FP propeller Total Power: 3,400kW (4,623hp) 13.3kn Mitsubishi 6UEC33LSII 1 x 2 Stroke 6 Cy. 330 x 1050 3400kW (4623bhp) Akasaka Tekkosho KK (Akasaka DieselLtd)-Japan Thrusters: 1 Tunnel thruster (f) Fuel: 635.0
207467 M6557	**YUSHO MARU** ex Yuhi Maru -2008 **Oita Rinkai Kogyo KK** - Oita, Oita Japan Official number: 136362	198 - -		**1998-10 K.K. Watanabe Zosensho — Nagasaki** Yd No: 068 Loa 34.47 Br ex - Dght 3.100 Lbp 29.50 Br md 8.96 Dpth 4.20 Welded, 1 dk	**(B32A2ST) Tug**	**2 oil engines** geared integral to driving 2 Z propellers Total Power: 2,648kW (3,600hp) 13.5kn Niigata 6L28HX 2 x 4 Stroke 6 Cy. 280 x 370 each-1324kW (1800bhp) Niigata Engineering Co Ltd-Japan
094183 D2138	**YUSHO MARU** **Fuyo Kaiun KK** - Kagoshima, Kagoshima Japan Official number: 140197	499 - 1,550		**2005-07 K.K. Watanabe Zosensho — Nagasaki** Loa 76.15 Br ex - Dght 4.030 Lbp 70.20 Br md 12.30 Dpth 7.00 Welded, 1 dk	**(A31A2GX) General Cargo Ship**	**1 oil engine** driving 1 Propeller Total Power: 1,618kW (2,200hp) 12.0kn Niigata 6M34BGT 1 x 4 Stroke 6 Cy. 340 x 620 1618kW (2200bhp) Niigata Engineering Co Ltd-Japan
096698 D2374	**YUSHO MARU** **Matsuda Marine KK** Matsuda Kisen KK Osaka, Osaka Japan Official number: 140484	364 - 865		**2007-03 Hongawara Zosen K.K. — Fukuyama** Yd No: 593 Loa 53.33 Br ex 9.22 Dght 3.860 Lbp 48.50 Br md 9.20 Dpth 4.10 Welded, 1 dk	**(A12A2TC) Chemical Tanker** Double Hull (13F) Liq: 865	**1 oil engine** driving 1 Propeller Total Power: 882kW (1,199hp) 11.0kn Niigata 6M26AGTE 1 x 4 Stroke 6 Cy. 260 x 460 882kW (1199bhp) Niigata Engineering Co Ltd-Japan
016143 J3699	**YUSHO MARU** **Hashimoto Kaiun YK** - Takasago, Hyogo Japan Official number: 132341	150 - 400		**1991-07 Imura Zosen K.K. — Komatsushima** Yd No: 255 Loa 50.96 (BB) Br ex - Dght 3.100 Lbp 45.00 Br md 8.20 Dpth 5.20 Welded	**(A31A2GX) General Cargo Ship** Bale: 760 Compartments: 1 Ho, ER 1 Ha: ER	**1 oil engine** geared to sc. shaft driving 1 FP propeller Total Power: 368kW (500hp) Hanshin 6LC26G 1 x 4 Stroke 6 Cy. 260 x 440 368kW (500bhp) The Hanshin Diesel Works Ltd-Japan
062491 K5214	**YUSHO MARU** **Yoshinoya Kaiun KK** - Hakodate, Hokkaido Japan MMSI: 431400118 Official number: 133688	999 - 2,375		**1993-02 K.K. Matsuura Zosensho — Osakikamijima** Yd No: 388 Loa 80.00 (BB) Br ex 11.82 Dght 5.210 Lbp 74.00 Br md 11.80 Dpth 5.75 Welded, 1 dk	**(A13B2TP) Products Tanker** Liq: 2,402; Liq (Oil): 2,402 Compartments: 10 Ta, ER	**1 oil engine** with clutches & reverse geared to sc. shaft driving 1 FP propeller Total Power: 1,765kW (2,400hp) Hanshin 6EL35G 1 x 4 Stroke 6 Cy. 350 x 700 1765kW (2400bhp) The Hanshin Diesel Works Ltd-Japan
736722 D2519	**YUSHO MARU** - - Yakushima, Kagoshima Japan Official number: 140651	499 - 1,600		**2007-12 Shinosaki Zosen — Kumamoto** Yd No: 125 Loa 75.46 Br ex - Dght 3.980 Lbp 69.80 Br md 12.50 Dpth 6.80 Welded, 1 dk	**(A31A2GX) General Cargo Ship** Bale: 2,395 Compartments: 1 Ho, ER 1 Ha: ER (40.0 x 10.0)	**1 oil engine** reverse geared to sc. shaft driving 1 FP propeller Total Power: 1,618kW (2,200hp) 12.5kn Akasaka AX33 1 x 4 Stroke 6 Cy. 330 x 620 1618kW (2200bhp) Akasaka Tekkosho KK (Akasaka DieselLtd)-Japan
877801 L6285	**YUSHO MARU** **Asuka Kisen YK (Asuka Kisen Co Ltd)** - Imabari, Ehime Japan MMSI: 431500212 Official number: 134829	586 - 1,570		**1994-05 K.K. Uno Zosensho — Imabari** Yd No: 233 Loa 76.55 Br ex - Dght 4.070 Lbp 71.90 Br md 12.00 Dpth 7.13 Welded, 1 dk	**(A31A2GX) General Cargo Ship** Grain: 3,136; Bale: 2,986 Compartments: 1 Ho, ER 1 Ha: (42.4 x 9.5)ER	**1 oil engine** driving 1 FP propeller Total Power: 1,324kW (1,800hp) 12.0kn Hanshin LH30LG 1 x 4 Stroke 6 Cy. 300 x 600 1324kW (1800bhp) The Hanshin Diesel Works Ltd-Japan
743256 D2884	**YUSHO MARU NO. 2** **Matsuki Senpaku YK** - Yakushima, Kagoshima Japan Official number: 140950	498 - 1,600		**2009-01 Shinosaki Zosen — Kumamoto** Yd No: 127 Loa 75.47 (BB) Br ex - Dght 3.970 Lbp 69.80 Br md 12.50 Dpth 6.80 Welded, 1 dk	**(A31A2GX) General Cargo Ship** Bale: 2,396 Compartments: 1 Ho, ER 1 Ha: ER (39.8 x 10.2)	**1 oil engine** driving 1 FP propeller Total Power: 1,471kW (2,000hp) 13.5kn Akasaka AX33 1 x 4 Stroke 6 Cy. 330 x 620 1471kW (2000bhp) Akasaka Tekkosho KK (Akasaka DieselLtd)-Japan Thrusters: 1 Tunnel thruster (f)

IMO / Call sign	Name / Owner / Flag	Tonnage	Class	Builder / Dimensions	Type	Machinery	Speed / Model
9004449 - - -	**YUSHO MARU NO. 7** *ex* Seio Maru No. 1 *-2004* - -	*379* - 455		**1990-05 Miho Zosensho K.K. — Shimizu** Yd No: 1377 Loa 54.74 (BB) Br ex 8.62 Dght 3.407 Lbp 48.00 Br md 8.60 Dpth 3.75 Welded, 1 dk	**(B11B2FV) Fishing Vessel** Ins: 487	**1 oil engine** with clutches & sr reverse geared to sc. shaft driving 1 FP propeller Total Power: 736kW (1,001hp) Hanshin 1 x 4 Stroke 6 Cy. 280 x 460 736kW (1001bhp) The Hanshin Diesel Works Ltd-Japan	LH28
8713421 - - -	**YUSHO MARU NO. 8** *ex* Tokuju Maru No. 85 *-2005* - -	*409* - 504		**1987-11 Niigata Engineering Co Ltd — Niigata NI** Yd No: 2071 Loa 55.81 (BB) Br ex 8.92 Dght 3.480 Lbp 49.15 Br md 8.91 Dpth 3.87 Welded, 1 dk	**(B11B2FV) Fishing Vessel** Ins: 573	**1 oil engine** with clutches, flexible couplings & sr geared to sc. shaft driving 1 CP propeller Total Power: 699kW (950hp) Niigata 1 x 4 Stroke 6 Cy. 280 x 480 699kW (950bhp) Niigata Engineering Co Ltd-Japan	6M28BF
9125425 *JM6385* -	**YUSHO MARU No. 10** **YK Yusho Kisen** *Kitakyushu, Fukuoka* *Japan* Official number: 134554	*199* - 530		**1995-10 Koa Sangyo KK — Takamatsu KG** Yd No: 587 Loa - Br ex - Dght 3.100 Lbp 45.00 Br md 7.80 Dpth 3.30 Welded, 1 dk	**(A12A2TC) Chemical Tanker** Compartments: 6 Wing Ta, ER 2 Cargo Pump (s): 2x200m³/hr	**1 oil engine** driving 1 FP propeller Total Power: 736kW (1,001hp) Hanshin 1 x 4 Stroke 6 Cy. 260 x 440 736kW (1001bhp) The Hanshin Diesel Works Ltd-Japan	10.5kn LH26
9041904 *HO2780* -	**YUSHO MERMAID** *ex* Nichiwa Maru *-2002* **TH Shipping Panama SA** Busan Shipping Co Ltd *Panama* *Panama* MMSI: 353225000 Official number: 2849902B	**1,876** 590 2,138	Class: BV (NK)	**1991-12 Yamanaka Zosen K.K. — Imabari** Yd No: 518 Loa 79.85 (BB) Br ex - Dght 4.722 Lbp 74.90 Br md 13.00 Dpth 7.80 Welded	**(A31A2GX) General Cargo Ship** Grain: 3,051 Compartments: 1 Ho, ER 1 Ha: (41.3 x 10.0)ER	**1 oil engine** driving 1 FP propeller Total Power: 1,471kW (2,000hp) Hanshin 1 x 4 Stroke 6 Cy. 350 x 550 1471kW (2000bhp) The Hanshin Diesel Works Ltd-Japan	12.0kn 6LU35
9520247 *3ESQ2* -	**YUSHO MERMAID II** **Mermaid Line SA** Busan Shipping Co Ltd *Panama* *Panama* MMSI: 370391000 Official number: 3437108A	**2,386** 824 2,467	Class: NK	**2008-09 Shinosaki Zosen — Kumamoto** Yd No: 126 Loa 82.42 (BB) Br ex - Dght 4.812 Lbp 75.84 Br md 13.50 Dpth 7.60 Welded, 1 dk	**(A31A2GX) General Cargo Ship** Bale: 4,085 Compartments: 1 Ho, ER 1 Ha: ER (40.2 x 10.2)	**1 oil engine** driving 1 Propeller Total Power: 1,471kW (2,000hp) Akasaka 1 x 4 Stroke 6 Cy. 330 x 620 1471kW (2000bhp) Akasaka Tekkosho KK (Akasaka DieselLtd)-Japan Fuel: 150.0	AX33
9492866 *3EPS7* -	**YUSHO PRINCESS II** **Stony Brook Maritime SA** Grow-Will Inc *Panama* *Panama* MMSI: 351355000 Official number: 3369208A	**7,516** 3,974 11,353	Class: NK	**2008-03 Nishi Shipbuilding Co Ltd — Imabari EH** Yd No: 457 Loa 110.49 (BB) Br ex 19.20 Dght 9.214 Lbp 102.16 Br md 19.20 Dpth 13.50 Welded, 1 dk	**(A31A2GX) General Cargo Ship** Grain: 15,824; Bale: 14,713 Compartments: 2 Ho, ER 2 Ha: (33.6 x 14.0)ER (20.3 x 14.0) Cranes: 2x30.7t; Derricks: 1x30t	**1 oil engine** driving 1 FP propeller Total Power: 3,900kW (5,302hp) MAN-B&W 1 x 2 Stroke 6 Cy. 350 x 1050 3900kW (5302bhp) Makita Corp-Japan AuxGen: 3 x 230kW a.c Fuel: 700.0	13.3kn 6L35MC
9258569 *H9PK* -	**YUSHO SEVEN** **Pine Forest Navigation SA** Grow-Will Inc *Panama* *Panama* MMSI: 352504000 Official number: 2833102C	**2,972** 1,308 3,863	Class: NK	**2001-11 Sasaki Shipbuilding Co Ltd — Osakikamijima HS** Yd No: 638 Loa 83.90 (BB) Br ex 14.82 Dght 5.993 Lbp 78.00 Br md 14.80 Dpth 9.00 Welded, 1 dk	**(A31A2GX) General Cargo Ship** Grain: 5,853; Bale: 5,530 Compartments: 2 Ho, ER 2 Ha: (18.9 x 10.7) (19.6 x 10.7)ER Cranes: 2x25t	**1 oil engine** driving 1 FP propeller Total Power: 1,912kW (2,600hp) Akasaka 1 x 4 Stroke 6 Cy. 370 x 720 1912kW (2600bhp) Akasaka Tekkosho KK (Akasaka DieselLtd)-Japan Thrusters: 1 Tunnel thruster (f) Fuel: 220.0	12.0kn A37
9342853 *3EFH5* -	**YUSHO SPICA** **Maple Island Maritime SA** Kobe Shipping Co Ltd *Panama* *Panama* MMSI: 355554000 Official number: 3186806A	**39,736** 25,724 76,598 T/cm 66.6	Class: NK	**2006-06 Imabari Shipbuilding Co Ltd — Marugame KG (Marugame Shipyard)** Yd No: 1419 Loa 224.94 (BB) Br ex 32.26 Dght 14.139 Lbp 217.00 Br md 32.26 Dpth 19.50 Welded, 1 dk	**(A21A2BC) Bulk Carrier** Grain: 90,644 Compartments: 7 Ho, ER 7 Ha: 6 (17.1 x 15.6)ER (17.1 x 12.8)	**1 oil engine** driving 1 FP propeller Total Power: 10,320kW (14,031hp) MAN-B&W 1 x 2 Stroke 6 Cy. 600 x 2292 10320kW (14031bhp) Kawasaki Heavy Industries Ltd-Japan Fuel: 2770.0	15.2kn 6S60MC
9364863 *3EEX3* -	**YUSHO STELLA** **Lunar Shore Maritime SA** Grow-Will Inc *Panama* *Panama* MMSI: 371959000 Official number: 3148206A	**6,004** 3,182 9,477	Class: NK	**2006-03 Nishi Shipbuilding Co Ltd — Imabari EH** Yd No: 445 Loa 97.61 (BB) Br ex - Dght 9.200 Lbp 89.95 Br md 18.80 Dpth 13.00 Welded, 1 dk	**(A31A2GX) General Cargo Ship** Grain: 12,141; Bale: 11,432 Compartments: 2 Ho, ER 2 Ha: (21.7 x 12.6)ER (20.3 x 12.6) Cranes: 2x30t	**1 oil engine** driving 1 FP propeller Total Power: 3,400kW (4,623hp) Mitsubishi 1 x 2 Stroke 6 Cy. 330 x 1050 3400kW (4623bhp) Akasaka Tekkosho KK (Akasaka DieselLtd)-Japan Thrusters: 1 Tunnel thruster (f) Fuel: 640.0	13.3kn 6UEC33LSII
8858702 *UGFC* -	**YUSRA** *ex* Island of Arkos *-2000* *ex* Knyaginya Mariya *-1994* *ex* Volzhskiy-52 *-1994* **Grove Maritime SA** River Med Trading Ltd *Taganrog* *Russia* MMSI: 273422360	**4,997** 2,361 5,449	Class: RS	**1992-10 OAO Navashinskiy Sudostroitelnyy Zavod 'Oka' — Navashino** Loa 138.30 Br ex 16.70 Dght 3.800 Lbp 132.25 Br md 16.50 Dpth 5.50 Welded, 1 dk	**(A31A2GX) General Cargo Ship** Grain: 6,440	**2 oil engines** driving 2 FP propellers Total Power: 1,766kW (2,402hp) Dvigatel Revolyutsii 2 x 4 Stroke 6 Cy. 360 x 450 each-883kW (1201bhp) Zavod "Dvigatel Revolyutsii"-Nizhniy Novgorod	8.0kn 6CHRNP36/45
9217577 *TCCH4* -	**YUSUF ASLAN** **Selmar Denizcilik Sanayi ve Ticaret AS** - *Istanbul* *Turkey* MMSI: 271002396	**1,233** 777 2,340	Class: BV	**2000-11 Selahattin Aslan Tersanesi — Tuzla** Yd No: 5 Loa 75.75 (BB) Br ex - Dght 5.130 Lbp 68.05 Br md 11.00 Dpth 6.00 Welded, 1 dk	**(A31A2GX) General Cargo Ship** Compartments: 2 Ho, ER 2 Ha: ER Derricks: 2	**1 oil engine** driving 1 FP propeller Total Power: 853kW (1,160hp) S.K.L. 1 x 4 Stroke 8 Cy. 320 x 480 853kW (1160bhp) SKL Motoren u. Systemtechnik AG-Magdeburg AuxGen: 2 x 91kW 380/220V 50Hz a.c, 1 x 40kW 380/220V 50Hz a.c	12.0kn 8NVD48A-1U
9119646 *TCYI8* -	**YUSUF CEPNIOGLU** *ex* Northsea Trader *-2010* *ex* MSC Krasnodar *-2001* *ex* Northsea Trader *-2000* *ex* Gracechurch Comet *-1999* *ex* Northsea Trader *-1997* *ex* Texel Bay *-1996* *ex* Northsea Trader *-1995* **Furkan Denizcilik Sanayi ve Ticaret Ltd Sti** - SatCom: Inmarsat C 427101019 *Istanbul* *Turkey* MMSI: 271041411	**4,984** 2,103 6,928	Class: AB (GL)	**1995-03 Schiffs. Hugo Peters Wewelsfleth Peters & Co. GmbH — Wewelsfleth** Yd No: 647 Loa 116.40 (BB) Br ex 19.50 Dght 7.060 Lbp 107.80 Br md 19.20 Dpth 9.20 Welded, 1 dk	**(A33A2CC) Container Ship (Fully Cellular)** Double Bottom Entire Compartment Length TEU 547 C Ho 134 TEU C Dk 413 TEU incl 40 ref C. Compartments: 2 Cell Ho, ER 2 Ha: ER Ice Capable	**1 oil engine** with flexible couplings & sr geared to sc. shaft driving 1 CP propeller Total Power: 3,960kW (5,384hp) MAN 1 x 4 Stroke 9 Cy. 320 x 400 3960kW (5384bhp) MAN B&W Diesel AG-Augsburg AuxGen: 1 x 608kW 400V 50Hz a.c, 1 x 198kW 400V 50Hz a.c Thrusters: 1 Thwart. CP thruster (f) Fuel: 102.0 (d.f.) 550.0 (r.f.) 16.1pd	16.0kn 9L32/40
7200635 *A6EF* -	**YUSUF KANOO** *ex* Jackson Creek *-1970* **Fernson Shipping & Trading** - *Sharjah* *United Arab Emirates*	*145* - -		**1957 Mobile Ship Repair, Inc. — Mobile, Al** L reg 25.00 Br ex 6.71 Dght - Lbp - Br md - Dpth - Welded	**(B31A2SR) Research Survey Vessel**	**1 oil engine** driving 1 FP propeller Total Power: 405kW (551hp)	
7819266 - -	**YUSUF KOWNEYN** **Government of The Democratic Republic of Somalia** - *Mogadiscio* *Somalia*	*121* 62 103		**1979-12 Brodogradiliste Greben — Vela Luka** Yd No: 810 Loa 23.19 Br ex 7.07 Dght 3.571 Lbp 21.21 Br md 6.85 Dpth 3.71 Bonded, 1 dk	**(B11A2FS) Stern Trawler** Hull Material: Reinforced Plastic	**1 oil engine** with clutches, flexible couplings & sr reverse geared to sc. shaft driving 1 FP propeller Total Power: 265kW (360hp) Caterpillar 1 x Vee 4 Stroke 8 Cy. 137 x 152 265kW (360bhp) Caterpillar Tractor Co-USA AuxGen: 1 x 20kW 231/400V 50Hz a.c	3408PCTA
8860274 *TCAB4* -	**YUSUF NACI KARAKURT** *ex* Kibar Kaptan *-2011* *ex* Sinan Atasoy *-1996* **Yakup Gungor ve Ortaklari** - *Istanbul* *Turkey* MMSI: 271002292 Official number: TUGS 746	*489* 263 922		**1968 Gesan Gemi Sanayii Sti — Sutluce, Istanbul** Loa 55.65 Br ex - Dght 3.690 Lbp 50.10 Br md 8.46 Dpth 4.30 Welded, 1 dk	**(A31A2GX) General Cargo Ship** Compartments: 1 Ho, ER 1 Ha: (11.5 x 4.2)ER Cranes: 2x2t	**1 oil engine** driving 1 FP propeller Total Power: 224kW (305hp) S.K.L. 1 x 4 Stroke 6 Cy. 240 x 360 224kW (305bhp) VEB Schwermaschinenbau "KarlLiebknecht" (SKL)-Magdeburg	7.0kn 6NVD36
8973394 *TC2923* -	**YUSUF REIS** **Bahri Ticaret Ltd Sti** - *Istanbul* *Turkey* MMSI: 271010192 Official number: 5141	**257** 149 500		**1983 Bayraktar — Istanbul** Yd No: 18 Loa 44.86 Br ex - Dght 2.550 Lbp - Br md 7.00 Dpth 3.00 Welded, 1 dk	**(A14A2LO) Water Tanker** Liq: 500 Compartments: 8 Ta, ER	**1 oil engine** geared to sc. shaft driving 1 FP propeller Total Power: 405kW (551hp) Volvo Penta 1 x 4 Stroke 405kW (551bhp) AB Volvo Penta-Sweden AuxGen: 1 x a.c Fuel: 16.0 (d.f.)	11.0kn

IMO / Call sign	Name / Owner	Tonnage	Class	Builder / Dimensions	Type	Machinery
312945 CQT	**YUSUF ZIYA ONIS** *ex* Dr. Adnan Biren *-1982* **Cenk Gemi Isletmeciligi AS** Marmara Denizcilik AS SatCom: Inmarsat C 427115050 *Istanbul* *Turkey* MMSI: 271000130 Official number: 4719	**8,485** 2,252 3,295	Class: RI TL (NV)	**1979**-07 **Ankerlokken Verft Forde AS — Forde** Yd No: 12 Converted From: Ro-Ro Cargo Ship-2008 Loa 113.39 Br ex - Dght 4.865 Lbp 99.35 Br md 22.20 Dpth 13.57 Welded, 2 dks	**(A36A2PR) Passenger/Ro-Ro Ship (Vehicles)** Passengers: driver berths: 12 Stern door/ramp (centre) Len: 10.15 Wid: 9.15 Swl: 80 Lane-Len: 955 Trailers: 75 TEU 318 C RoRo dk 170 TEU C Dk 148 TEU	**2 oil engines** sr reverse geared to sc. shaft driving 2 CP propellers Total Power: 2,942kW (4,000hp) 11.0kn Normo KVMB-12 2 x Vee 4 Stroke 12 Cy. 250 x 300 each-1471kW (2000bhp) AS Bergens Mek Verksteder-Norway AuxGen: 2 x 472kW 440V 60Hz a.c, 1 x 58kW 440V 60Hz a.c Thrusters: 1 Thwart. FP thruster (f) Fuel: 223.5 (d.f.) (Heating Coils) 470.1 (r.f.) 15.0pd
326160 REK5	**YUTAI AMBITIONS** **Yuship Co Ltd** Nippon Yusen Kabushiki Kaisha (NYK Line) *Hong Kong* *Hong Kong* MMSI: 477136300 Official number: HK-2235	**39,999** 25,747 77,283 T/cm 67.1	Class: NK	**2008**-11 **Oshima Shipbuilding Co Ltd — Saikai NS** Yd No: 10458 Loa 225.00 (BB) Br ex - Dght 14.190 Lbp 220.00 Br md 32.26 Dpth 19.39 Welded, 1 dk	**(A21A2BC) Bulk Carrier** Double Hull Grain: 90,588; Bale: 88,984 Compartments: 7 Ho, ER 7 Ha: ER	**1 oil engine** driving 1 FP propeller Total Power: 9,319kW (12,670hp) 14.5kn MAN-B&W 5S60MC-C 1 x 2 Stroke 5 Cy. 600 x 2400 9319kW (12670bhp) Kawasaki Heavy Industries Ltd-Japan AuxGen: 3 x a.c Fuel: 2125.0
541631 FDS4	**YUTAI BREEZE** **Pimex Holdings Ltd** Taiship Co Ltd *Panama* *Panama* MMSI: 355654000 Official number: 4123810	**30,962** 18,171 55,088 T/cm 56.3	Class: NK	**2010**-01 **Nantong COSCO KHI Ship Engineering Co Ltd (NACKS) — Nantong JS** Yd No: 106 Loa 189.90 (BB) Br ex 32.31 Dght 12.500 Lbp 185.00 Br md 32.26 Dpth 17.80 Welded, 1 dk	**(A21A2BC) Bulk Carrier** Grain: 69,452; Bale: 66,966 Compartments: 5 Ho, ER 5 Ha: 4 (20.5 x 18.6)ER (17.8 x 18.6) Cranes: 4x30.5t	**1 oil engine** driving 1 FP propeller Total Power: 8,200kW (11,149hp) 14.6kn MAN-B&W 6S50MC-C 1 x 2 Stroke 6 Cy. 500 x 2000 8200kW (11149bhp) Mitsui Engineering & Shipbuilding CLtd-Japan Fuel: 1970.0
304795 SOU3	**YUTAKA** *ex* Taiyo Maru No. 6 *-2006* **Yu Jin Shipping Co Ltd** - *Jeju* *South Korea* MMSI: 440341000 Official number: JJR-069566	**1,517** 805 1,560	Class: KR	**1989**-09 **K.K. Miura Zosensho — Saiki** Yd No: 857 Loa 76.50 (BB) Br ex 12.32 Dght 3.848 Lbp 70.00 Br md 12.30 Dpth 6.70 Welded, 2 dks	**(A31A2GX) General Cargo Ship** Bale: 2,624 Compartments: 1 Ho, ER 1 Ha: ER	**1 oil engine** driving 1 CP propeller Total Power: 1,324kW (1,800hp) 13.7kn Hanshin 6EL30 1 x 4 Stroke 6 Cy. 300 x 600 1324kW (1800bhp) The Hanshin Diesel Works Ltd-Japan
078529 .6195	**YUTAKA MARU** **Otaka Kaiun KK** - *Matsuyama, Ehime* *Japan* MMSI: 431500199 Official number: 133972	*699* - 1,925		**1994**-03 **Matsuura Tekko Zosen K.K. — Osakikamijima** Yd No: 380 Loa 70.95 (BB) Br ex - Dght 4.690 Lbp 67.20 Br md 12.00 Dpth 5.20 Welded, 1 dk	**(A13B2TP) Products Tanker** Compartments: 10 Ta, ER	**1 oil engine** reverse geared to sc. shaft driving 1 FP propeller Total Power: 735kW (999hp) Hanshin LH34LAG 1 x 4 Stroke 6 Cy. 340 x 640 735kW (999bhp) The Hanshin Diesel Works Ltd-Japan
304965 .5788	**YUTAKA MARU No. 1** **Corporation for Advanced Transport & Technology & Toyomasu Kaisou KK** Toyomasu Kaiso KK *Anan, Tokushima* *Japan* MMSI: 431501271 Official number: 130607	*2,343* - 4,438	Class: NK	**1989**-11 **Shinhama Dockyard Co. Ltd. — Anan** Yd No: 800 Loa 97.05 (BB) Br ex - Dght 5.940 Lbp 89.95 Br md 15.00 Dpth 6.80 Welded, 1 dk	**(A24A2BT) Cement Carrier** Grain: 3,622	**1 oil engine** driving 1 FP propeller Total Power: 1,839kW (2,500hp) 11.5kn Akasaka A37 1 x 4 Stroke 6 Cy. 370 x 720 1839kW (2500bhp) Akasaka Tekkosho KK (Akasaka DieselLtd)-Japan AuxGen: 3 x 181kW a.c Fuel: 100.0 (r.f.)
041679 M6154	**YUTAKA MARU No. 2** **Yamashita Kisen YK** - *Iki, Nagasaki* *Japan* Official number: 132729	*299* - 880		**1991**-11 **K.K. Miura Zosensho — Saiki** Yd No: 1023 Loa - Br ex - Dght 3.770 Lbp 58.00 Br md 10.80 Dpth 6.35 Welded	**(A31A2GX) General Cargo Ship**	**1 oil engine** driving 1 FP propeller Total Power: 736kW (1,001hp) Matsui M31M29 1 x 4 Stroke 6 Cy. 310 x 550 736kW (1001bhp) Matsui Iron Works Co Ltd-Japan
010084 .5931	**YUTAKA MARU No. 2** **Kosei Kisen KK** - *Anan, Tokushima* *Japan* MMSI: 431501293 Official number: 131460	*698* - 1,851		**1990**-09 **Wakamatsu Zosen K.K. — Kitakyushu** Yd No: 381 Loa 70.00 (BB) Br ex - Dght 4.590 Lbp 65.00 Br md 11.50 Dpth 5.10 Welded, 1 dk	**(A24A2BT) Cement Carrier** Grain: 1,524 Compartments: 8 Ho, ER	**1 oil engine** with clutches, flexible couplings & sr reverse geared to sc. shaft driving 1 FP propeller Total Power: 736kW (1,001hp) Akasaka K28SFD 1 x 4 Stroke 6 Cy. 280 x 500 736kW (1001bhp) Akasaka Tekkosho KK (Akasaka DieselLtd)-Japan
037707 M6151	**YUTAKA MARU No. 3** **MOL Naiko Ltd** - *Karatsu, Saga* *Japan* MMSI: 431601577 Official number: 132726	*697* - 1,846		**1991**-11 **Wakamatsu Zosen K.K. — Kitakyushu** Yd No: 383 Loa 70.00 (BB) Br ex 11.52 Dght 4.590 Lbp 65.00 Br md 11.50 Dpth 5.10 Welded, 1 dk	**(A24A2BT) Cement Carrier** Grain: 1,524 Compartments: 8 Ho, ER	**1 oil engine** with clutches, flexible couplings & sr geared to sc. shaft driving 1 FP propeller Total Power: 1,177kW (1,600hp) Akasaka K28SFD 1 x 4 Stroke 6 Cy. 280 x 500 1177kW (1600bhp) Akasaka Tekkosho KK (Akasaka DieselLtd)-Japan
057563 L6106	**YUTAKA MARU No. 5** **Chuo Kaiun KK** - *Anan, Tokushima* *Japan* MMSI: 431500007 Official number: 132160	*698* - 1,500		**1992**-09 **K.K. Miura Zosensho — Saiki** Yd No: 1050 L reg 61.20 Br ex - Dght 4.510 Lbp 61.00 Br md 11.00 Dpth 5.00 Welded, 1 dk	**(A24A2BT) Cement Carrier**	**1 oil engine** reverse geared to sc. shaft driving 1 FP propeller Total Power: 736kW (1,001hp) Akasaka K28R 1 x 4 Stroke 6 Cy. 280 x 480 736kW (1001bhp) Akasaka Tekkosho KK (Akasaka DieselLtd)-Japan
115327 L6349	**YUTAKA MARU No. 7** **Toho Kisen KK** - *Imabari, Ehime* *Japan* MMSI: 431500304 Official number: 134919	*699* - 1,653		**1995**-02 **K.K. Miura Zosensho — Saiki** Yd No: 1115 Loa 70.00 (BB) Br ex - Dght 4.482 Lbp 65.00 Br md 11.50 Dpth 5.00 Welded, 1 dk	**(A24A2BT) Cement Carrier** Grain: 1,390	**1 oil engine** reverse geared to sc. shaft driving 1 FP propeller Total Power: 736kW (1,001hp) 10.0kn Akasaka A31R 1 x 4 Stroke 6 Cy. 310 x 600 736kW (1001bhp) Akasaka Tekkosho KK (Akasaka DieselLtd)-Japan AuxGen: 2 x a.c Fuel: 43.0 3.5pd
032381 M6092	**YUTAKA MARU No. 8** **Yamashita Kisen YK** - *Iki, Nagasaki* *Japan* Official number: 132659	*199* - 630		**1991**-08 **Yamakawa Zosen Tekko K.K. — Kagoshima** Yd No: 703 Loa - Br ex - Dght 3.170 Lbp 52.40 Br md 9.60 Dpth 5.40 Welded, 1 dk	**(A31A2GX) General Cargo Ship**	**1 oil engine** driving 1 FP propeller Total Power: 588kW (799hp) Matsui ML627GSC 1 x 4 Stroke 6 Cy. 270 x 480 588kW (799bhp) Matsui Iron Works Co Ltd-Japan
674622 D3487	**YUTAKA MARU NO. 8** **Toyotsuru Kaiun KK** - *Kitakyushu, Fukuoka* *Japan* MMSI: 431004346 Official number: 141875	*2,947* - 4,445	Class: NK	**2013**-03 **Kyokuyo Shipyard Corp — Shimonoseki YC** Yd No: 510 Loa 97.03 (BB) Br ex - Dght 5.810 Lbp 91.50 Br md 16.00 Dpth 7.10 Welded, 1 dk	**(A24A2BT) Cement Carrier** Grain: 3,698	**1 oil engine** driving 1 FP propeller Total Power: 2,206kW (2,999hp) 13.0kn Akasaka A38S 1 x 4 Stroke 6 Cy. 380 x 740 2206kW (2999bhp) Akasaka Tekkosho KK (Akasaka DieselLtd)-Japan Fuel: 160.0
976322	**YUTAKA MARU NO. 27** **L Reid & M Gopie** - *Georgetown* *Guyana* Official number: 708509	*104* 50 -		**1974**-12 **Rockport Yacht & Supply Co. (RYSCO) — Rockport, Tx** L reg 19.80 Br ex - Dght - Lbp - Br md 6.00 Dpth 3.10 Welded, 1 dk	**(B11A2FT) Trawler**	**1 oil engine** driving 1 FP propeller Cummins 1 x 4 Stroke Cummins Engine Co Inc-USA
976310	**YUTAKA MARU NO. 28** *ex* Yutaka Maru No. 22 *-2006* **Yutaka Fisheries Co Ltd** - *Georgetown* *Guyana* Official number: 708510	*104* 50 -		**1973**-12 **Rockport Yacht & Supply Co. (RYSCO) — Rockport, Tx** L reg 19.80 Br ex - Dght - Lbp - Br md 6.00 Dpth 3.10 Welded, 1 dk	**(B11A2FT) Trawler**	**1 oil engine** driving 1 FP propeller Cummins 1 x 4 Stroke Cummins Engine Co Inc-USA

IMO / Call sign	Name / Owner / Flag	Tonnage	Class	Builder / Dimensions	Type / Capacity	Machinery
6905501 - -	**YUTAKA MARU No. 38** *ex* Kojin Maru No. 68 *-1996* *ex* Shiragami Maru *-1990* - *South Korea*	*162* - -		**1969-01 Nichiro Zosen K.K. — Hakodate** Yd No: 275 Loa 25.51 Br ex 8.03 Dght 2.693 Lbp 23.02 Br md 8.01 Dpth 3.79 Welded, 1 dk	**(B32A2ST) Tug**	**2 oil engines** driving 2 FP propellers 10.5 Fuji 6S27.5CH. 1 x 4 Stroke 6 Cy. 275 x 410 Fuji Diesel Co Ltd-Japan Fuji 6SD27. 1 x 4 Stroke 6 Cy. 275 x 410 Fuji Diesel Co Ltd-Japan AuxGen: 1 x 34kW 225V a.c Fuel: 19.5
8150306 - -	**YUTOKU** *ex* Yutoku Maru No. 2 *-1992* **Reiko Kaiun Co SA** Nippon Chuo Shoji Co	*192* - 420		**1968 Sanuki Shipbuilding & Iron Works Co Ltd — Mitoyo KG** Loa 37.01 Br ex - Dght 3.201 Lbp 35.72 Br md 7.00 Dpth 4.70 Welded, 1 dk	**(A31A2GX) General Cargo Ship**	**1 oil engine** driving 1 FP propeller Total Power: 331kW (450hp) 9.5 Makita 1 x 4 Stroke 331kW (450bhp) Makita Diesel Co Ltd-Japan
8035491 - -	**YUTOKU MARU** - -	*459* - 1,120		**1981 K.K. Murakami Zosensho — Naruto** Yd No: 128 Loa 60.33 Br ex - Dght 4.171 Lbp 55.00 Br md 10.51 Dpth 6.00 Welded, 1 dk	**(A31A2GX) General Cargo Ship**	**1 oil engine** driving 1 FP propeller 11.0 Akasaka 1 x 4 Stroke Akasaka Tekkosho KK (Akasaka DieselLtd)-Japan
9058000 *JL6124* -	**YUTOKU MARU** **YK Hosho Kaiun** *Anan, Tokushima* *Japan* Official number: 132997	*498* - 1,515		**1993-04 K.K. Murakami Zosensho — Naruto** Yd No: 208 Loa 75.42 (BB) Br ex - Dght 4.060 Lbp 70.00 Br md 12.00 Dpth 7.00 Welded, 2 dks	**(A31A2GX) General Cargo Ship** Grain: 2,469; Bale: 2,363 Compartments: 1 Ho, ER 1 Ha: ER	**1 oil engine** reverse geared to sc. shaft driving 1 FP propelle Total Power: 736kW (1,001hp) Akasaka A31 1 x 4 Stroke 6 Cy. 310 x 600 736kW (1001bhp) Akasaka Tekkosho KK (Akasaka DieselLtd)-Japan
9058830 *JK5144* -	**YUTOKU MARU** **Tahara Kisen KK** *Bizen, Okayama* *Japan* MMSI: 431400046 Official number: 132550	*998* - 1,390	Class: NK	**1992-11 Narasaki Zosen KK — Muroran HK** Yd No: 1123 Loa 71.98 (BB) Br ex 12.53 Dght 4.368 Lbp 67.00 Br md 12.50 Dpth 5.60 Welded, 1 dk	**(A11B2TG) LPG Tanker** Liq (Gas): 1,727 2 x Gas Tank (s); 2 independent cyl horizontal 2 Cargo Pump (s): 2x460m³/hr	**1 oil engine** driving 1 FP propeller Total Power: 1,471kW (2,000hp) 11.5 Akasaka A3 1 x 4 Stroke 6 Cy. 340 x 660 1471kW (2000bhp) Akasaka Tekkosho KK (Akasaka DieselLtd)-Japan AuxGen: 4 x 230kW a.c Fuel: 155.0 (r.f.)
8870138 - -	**YUTOKU MARU** *ex* Ishida Maru No. 3 *-2005* *ex* Ito Maru No. 3 *-2003* *ex* Ishida Maru No. 3 *-2002* - -	*101* - -		**1985-07 K.K. Izutsu Zosensho — Nagasaki** L reg 31.80 Br ex - Dght - Lbp - Br md 6.70 Dpth 3.20 Welded, 1 dk	**(B11B2FV) Fishing Vessel**	**1 oil engine** driving 1 FP propeller Yanmar 1 x 4 Stroke Yanmar Diesel Engine Co Ltd-Japan
9124134 *JL6466* -	**YUTOKU MARU No. 3** **KK Yutoku Kisen** Nippon Marine Co Ltd (Nippon Marine KK) *Matsushige, Tokushima* *Japan* Official number: 135501	*403* - 1,007		**1996-05 K.K. Murakami Zosensho — Naruto** Yd No: 221 Loa 68.61 (BB) Br ex - Dght 3.315 Lbp 63.60 Br md 11.00 Dpth 6.30 Welded, 2 dks	**(A31A2GX) General Cargo Ship** Grain: 1,797 Compartments: 1 Ho, ER 1 Ha: ER	**1 oil engine** reverse geared to sc. shaft driving 1 FP propelle Total Power: 736kW (1,001hp) Akasaka A2 1 x 4 Stroke 6 Cy. 280 x 550 736kW (1001bhp) Akasaka Tekkosho KK (Akasaka DieselLtd)-Japan
9105425 *JL6266* -	**YUTOKU MARU No. 8** - *Onomichi, Hiroshima* *Japan* Official number: 134845	*199* - 699		**1994-10 K.K. Murakami Zosensho — Naruto** Yd No: 215 Loa 57.79 (BB) Br ex 9.52 Dght 3.170 Lbp 53.00 Br md 9.50 Dpth 5.38 Welded, 1 dk	**(A31A2GX) General Cargo Ship** Grain: 1,097 Compartments: 1 Ho, ER 1 Ha: ER	**1 oil engine** reverse geared to sc. shaft driving 1 FP propelle Total Power: 736kW (1,001hp) Akasaka T26 1 x 4 Stroke 6 Cy. 260 x 440 736kW (1001bhp) Akasaka Tekkosho KK (Akasaka DieselLtd)-Japan
8421432 - -	**YUTOKU MARU No. 11** - - - *South Korea*	*241* - -		**1985-03 Minami-Kyushu Zosen KK — Ichikikushikino KS** Yd No: 502 Loa 46.69 Br ex 7.80 Dght - Lbp 39.81 Br md - Dpth 3.54 Welded, 1 dk	**(B11B2FV) Fishing Vessel**	**1 oil engine** geared to sc. shaft driving 1 FP propeller Total Power: 743kW (1,010hp) Daihatsu 6DLM-26 1 x 4 Stroke 6 Cy. 260 x 340 743kW (1010bhp) Daihatsu Diesel Manufacturing Co Lt-Japan
8821319 *S7WA* -	**YUTUNA 212** *ex* Tenryu Maru No. 1 *-2008* **Yutuna Fisheries Ltd** - *Victoria* *Seychelles* MMSI: 664513000 Official number: 50185	**577** 245 447		**1989-04 Miho Zosensho K.K. — Shimizu** Yd No: 1353 Loa 54.80 (BB) Br ex 8.62 Dght 3.390 Lbp 48.00 Br md 8.60 Dpth 3.75 Welded	**(B11B2FV) Fishing Vessel** Ins: 659	**1 oil engine** with clutches, flexible couplings & sr reverse geared to sc. shaft driving 1 FP propeller Total Power: 736kW (1,001hp) Akasaka K28 1 x 4 Stroke 6 Cy. 280 x 480 736kW (1001bhp) Akasaka Tekkosho KK (Akasaka DieselLtd)-Japan
9257436 *JRJN* -	**YUUKARI** **Shin-Nihonkai Ferry Co Ltd** *Otaru, Hokkaido* *Japan* MMSI: 432341000 Official number: 135344	*18,229* - 7,725		**2002-03 Ishikawajima-Harima Heavy Industries Co Ltd (IHI) — Yokohama KN** Yd No: 3146 Loa 199.90 (BB) Br ex - Dght 6.930 Lbp 188.00 Br md 26.50 Dpth 14.50 Welded	**(A36A2PR) Passenger/Ro-Ro Ship (Vehicles)** Passengers: 892 Lane-Len: 1460 Cars: 58, Trailers: 146	**2 oil engines** reduction geared to sc. shafts driving 2 FP propellers Total Power: 21,200kW (28,824hp) 22.7 Pielstick 8PC40L57 2 x 4 Stroke 8 Cy. 570 x 750 each-10600kW (14412bhp) Diesel United Ltd.-Aioi Thrusters: 2 Tunnel thruster (f); 1 Tunnel thruster (a)
7708302 *ZCDP7* -	**YUUM K'AK' NAAB** *ex* BW Enterprise *-2006* *ex* Folk Moon *-2005* *ex* Berge Enterprise *-2005* **Bergesen Worldwide Ltd** BW Offshore Norway AS *Hamilton* *Bermuda (British)* MMSI: 310489000 Official number: 733783	**189,863** 123,888 360,700 T/cm 197.6	Class: NV	**1981-09 Mitsui Eng. & SB. Co. Ltd., Chiba Works — Ichihara** Yd No: 1112 Converted From: Crude Oil Tanker-2006 Loa 340.52 (BB) Br ex 65.05 Dght 23.232 Lbp 326.68 Br md 65.00 Dpth 31.53 Welded, 1 dk	**(B22E2OF) FPSO, Oil** Single Hull Liq: 416,178; Liq (Oil): 416,178 Compartments: 6 Ta, 12 Wing Ta, ER, 2 Wing Slop Ta 4 Cargo Pump (s): 4x4500m³/hr Manifold: Bow/CM: 169m	**1 oil engine** driving 1 FP propeller Total Power: 30,082kW (40,899hp) 15.3 B&W 12L90GF 1 x 2 Stroke 12 Cy. 900 x 2180 30082kW (40899bhp) Mitsui Engineering & Shipbuilding CLtd-Japan AuxGen: 3 x 1400kW 440V 60Hz a.c Fuel: 800.0 (d.f.) 10874.0 (r.f.) 110.0pd
9653379 *JD3373* -	**YUUSHUN** **YK Mitsumo Kisen** - *Kamiamakusa, Kumamoto* *Japan* Official number: 141693	*273* - 840		**2012-07 Yano Zosen K.K. — Imabari** Yd No: 258 Loa 61.00 (BB) Br ex - Dght 3.513 Lbp - Br md 9.80 Dpth 6.00 Welded, 1 dk	**(A31A2GX) General Cargo Ship** Double Hull Grain: 1,394; Bale: 1,328	**1 oil engine** reduction geared to sc. shafts driving 1 Propelle Total Power: 1,029kW (1,399hp) 9.6 Niigata 6M28B 1 x 4 Stroke 6 Cy. 280 x 480 1029kW (1399bhp) Niigata Engineering Co Ltd-Japan Thrusters: 1 Thwart. FP thruster (f)
9369174 *3EIG3* -	**YUUZAN** **Growing Maritime SA** Setsuyo Kisen Co Ltd *Panama* *Panama* MMSI: 372153000 Official number: 3221706A	**8,626** 3,900 12,243	Class: NK	**2006-11 Higaki Zosen K.K. — Imabari** Yd No: 612 Loa 116.99 (BB) Br ex - Dght 9.115 Lbp 109.04 Br md 19.60 Dpth 14.00 Welded, 1 dk	**(A31A2GX) General Cargo Ship** Grain: 17,507; Bale: 16,362 Compartments: 2 Ho, 2 Tw Dk, ER 2 Ha: ER Cranes: 2x30t	**1 oil engine** driving 1 FP propeller Total Power: 4,200kW (5,710hp) 13.8 MAN-B&W 6S35M 1 x 2 Stroke 6 Cy. 350 x 1400 4200kW (5710bhp) Makita Corp-Japan Thrusters: 1 Tunnel thruster (f) Fuel: 943.0 (r.f.)
6402274 - -	**YUVAN No. 5** *ex* Ryofuku Maru No. 8 *-1973* - -	*192* 97 -	Class: (KR)	**1963 Yamanishi Shipbuilding Co Ltd — Ishinomaki MG** Yd No: 435 Loa 38.51 Br ex 6.96 Dght 2.769 Lbp 33.69 Br md 6.91 Dpth 3.15 Riveted\Welded, 1 dk	**(B11B2FV) Fishing Vessel** Ins: 262 3 Ha: 3 (11.9 x 11.9)ER	**1 oil engine** driving 1 FP propeller Total Power: 405kW (551hp) 10.8 Niigata 6M28DH 1 x 4 Stroke 6 Cy. 280 x 440 405kW (551bhp) Niigata Engineering Co Ltd-Japan AuxGen: 2 x 56kW 225V a.c
7741469 *UBGJ* -	**YUVENTA** *ex* Niassa *-2002* *ex* Viktor Yarmola *-1980* **Koryakskaya Fishery Co (ZAO 'Koryakskaya Rybopromyshlennaya Kompaniya')** - *Petropavlovsk-Kamchatskiy* *Russia* MMSI: 273846100	**747** 224 414	Class: (RS)	**1979-03 Zavod "Leninskaya Kuznitsa" — Kiyev** Yd No: 1459 Loa 54.82 Br ex 9.96 Dght 4.141 Lbp 50.30 Br md - Dpth 5.01 Welded, 1 dk	**(B11A2FS) Stern Trawler** Ins: 414 Compartments: 2 Ho, ER 3 Ha: 3 (1.5 x 1.6) Derricks: 2x1.5t; Winches: 2 Ice Capable	**1 oil engine** driving 1 CP propeller Total Power: 852kW (1,158hp) 12.0 S.K.L. 8NVD48A-2 1 x 4 Stroke 8 Cy. 320 x 480 852kW (1158bhp) VEB Schwermaschinenbau "KarlLiebknecht" (SKL)-Magdeburg AuxGen: 2 x 160kW a.c, 2 x 100kW a.c Fuel: 155.0 (d.f.)
9136656 *JG5442* -	**YUWA MARU** **Shinsei Kaiun YK** - *Kure, Hiroshima* *Japan* Official number: 135227	*498* - 1,250		**1996-01 Kyoei Zosen KK — Mihara HS** Yd No: 272 Loa - Br ex - Dght 4.280 Lbp 60.30 Br md 10.00 Dpth 4.50 Welded, 1 dk	**(A12A2TC) Chemical Tanker** Compartments: 8 Wing Ta, ER 2 Cargo Pump (s): 2x300m³/hr	**1 oil engine** reverse geared to sc. shaft driving 1 FP propeller Total Power: 1,030kW (1,400hp) Akasaka K28B 1 x 4 Stroke 6 Cy. 280 x 480 1030kW (1400bhp) Akasaka Tekkosho KK (Akasaka DieselLtd)-Japan

Ship	Tonnage / Class	Builder & dimensions	Type & cargo	Machinery
9281205 **YUWA MARU** *JI3700* - **Taiho Unyu KK (Taiho Shipping Co Ltd)** - *Osaka, Osaka* *Japan* Official number: 137087	*359* - 1,000	**2002-04 Hongawara Zosen K.K. — Fukuyama** Yd No: 542 Loa - Br ex - Dght - Lbp 48.50 Br md 9.20 Dpth 4.10 Welded, 1 dk	**(A12A2TC) Chemical Tanker**	**1 oil engine** driving 1 FP propeller Total Power: 736kW (1,001hp) Yanmar DY26-SN 1 x 4 Stroke 6 Cy. 260 x 440 736kW (1001bhp) Yanmar Diesel Engine Co Ltd-Japan
9322657 **YUYO** *3EPY4* - **Sunny Gas Transportation SA** Wilhelmsen Ship Management Sdn Bhd *Panama* *Panama* MMSI: 371230000 Official number: 3374408A	**45,966** Class: NK 13,790 49,999 T/cm 70.2	**2008-03 Mitsubishi Heavy Industries Ltd. — Nagasaki** Yd No: 2231 Loa 230.00 (BB) Br ex 36.63 Dght 10.785 Lbp 219.00 Br md 36.60 Dpth 20.80 Welded, 1 dk	**(A11B2TG) LPG Tanker** Double Bottom Entire Compartment Length Liq (Gas): 77,338 5 x Gas Tank (s); 4 independent (C.mn.stl) pri horizontal, ER 8 Cargo Pump (s): 8x550m³/hr Manifold: Bow/CM: 113.9m	**1 oil engine** driving 1 FP propeller Total Power: 12,360kW (16,805hp) 16.7kn Mitsubishi 7UEC60LSII 1 x 2 Stroke 7 Cy. 600 x 2300 12360kW (16805bhp) Mitsubishi Heavy Industries Ltd-Japan AuxGen: 3 x 900kW 450V a.c Fuel: 379.0 (d.f.) 2819.0 (r.f.)
9621297 **YUYO** *D5FB5* - **Erica Navigation SA** Toyo Sangyo Co Ltd (Toyo Sangyo KK) *Monrovia* *Liberia* MMSI: 636016222 Official number: 16222	**50,927** Class: NK 29,489 92,307	**2013-10 Namura Shipbuilding Co Ltd — Imari SG** Yd No: 347 Loa 234.88 (BB) Br ex - Dght 14.228 Lbp 226.00 Br md 38.00 Dpth 20.00 Welded, 1 dk	**(A21A2BC) Bulk Carrier** Double Hull Grain: 109,236 Compartments: 6 Ho, ER 6 Ha: ER	**1 oil engine** driving 1 FP propeller Total Power: 11,040kW (15,010hp) 14.7kn MAN-B&W 6S60MC-C 1 x 2 Stroke 6 Cy. 600 x 2400 11040kW (15010bhp) Mitsui Engineering & Shipbuilding CLtd-Japan AuxGen: 3 x 520kW a.c Fuel: 3620.0
9514872 **YUYO MARU** *JD2701* - **Japan Railway Construction, Transport & Technology Agency & Nissen Kisen Co Ltd** Nissen Kisen KK *Onomichi, Hiroshima* *Japan* MMSI: 431000613 Official number: 140783	*526* Class: NK - 1,202	**2008-05 Hongawara Zosen K.K. — Fukuyama** Yd No: 610 Loa 64.80 Br ex 10.22 Dght 4.200 Lbp 61.00 Br md 10.20 Dpth 4.50 Welded, 1 dk	**(A12B2TR) Chemical/Products Tanker** Double Hull (13F) Liq: 1,273; Liq (Oil): 1,273	**1 oil engine** driving 1 FP propeller Total Power: 1,176kW (1,599hp) Niigata 6M28NT 1 x 4 Stroke 6 Cy. 280 x 480 1176kW (1599bhp) Niigata Engineering Co Ltd-Japan Fuel: 55.0
9266803 **YUYO MARU** *JL6694* - **Okino Kaiun KK** - *Komatsushima, Tokushima* *Japan* MMSI: 431501743 Official number: 137025	*3,789* Class: NK - 4,998	**2002-11 K.K. Miura Zosensho — Saiki** Yd No: 1258 Loa 104.45 Br ex - Dght 6.264 Lbp 99.20 Br md 16.00 Dpth 8.10 Welded, 1 dk	**(A13B2TP) Products Tanker** Double Hull (13F) Liq: 6,400; Liq (Oil): 6,400	**1 oil engine** driving 1 FP propeller Total Power: 2,942kW (4,000hp) 13.5kn Hanshin LH46L 1 x 4 Stroke 6 Cy. 460 x 880 2942kW (4000bhp) The Hanshin Diesel Works Ltd-Japan Fuel: 330.0
9709283 **YUYO MARU** *JD3669* - **Yoshida Kaiun KK** - *Imabari, Ehime* *Japan* MMSI: 431005234 Official number: 142152	*746* Class: NK - 1,312	**2014-03 Asakawa Zosen K.K. — Imabari** Yd No: 591 Loa 69.32 Br ex - Dght 4.310 Lbp 65.00 Br md 11.20 Dpth 4.65 Welded, 1 dk	**(A13C2LA) Asphalt/Bitumen Tanker**	**1 oil engine** reduction geared to sc. shaft driving 1 Propeller Total Power: 1,082kW (1,471hp) Akasaka AX33BR 1 x 4 Stroke 6 Cy. 330 x 620 1082kW (1471bhp) Akasaka Tekkosho KK (Akasaka DieselLtd)-Japan AuxGen: 3 x 580kW a.c
9124067 **YUYO MARU** *JG5415* - **Nichiyo Kaiun YK** - *Tokyo* *Japan* Official number: 135197	*499* - 1,156	**1995-06 Kyoei Zosen KK — Mihara HS** Yd No: 268 Loa 75.60 (BB) Br ex - Dght 3.892 Lbp 62.00 Br md 10.00 Dpth 4.50 Welded, 1 dk	**(A12A2TC) Chemical Tanker** Liq: 1,200 Compartments: 8 Wing Ta, ER 2 Cargo Pump (s): 2x300m³/hr	**1 oil engine** driving 1 FP propeller Total Power: 736kW (1,001hp) 10.7kn Hanshin LH28G 1 x 4 Stroke 6 Cy. 280 x 460 736kW (1001bhp) The Hanshin Diesel Works Ltd-Japan AuxGen: 2 x 120kW a.c Thrusters: 1 Thwart. FP thruster (f) Fuel: 32.0 (d.f.) 3.4pd
9079561 **YUYO MARU** *JL6230* - **YK Tomita Kaiun** - *Sukumo, Kochi* *Japan* Official number: 133962	*199* - 340	**1994-07 Imura Zosen K.K. — Komatsushima** Yd No: 270 Loa 48.40 Br ex - Dght - Lbp - Br md 8.00 Dpth 3.40 Welded, 1 dk	**(A13B2TP) Products Tanker** Liq: 650; Liq (Oil): 650 1 Cargo Pump (s): 1x500m³/hr	**1 oil engine** driving 1 FP propeller Total Power: 736kW (1,001hp) 10.0kn Hanshin LH26G 1 x 4 Stroke 6 Cy. 260 x 440 736kW (1001bhp) The Hanshin Diesel Works Ltd-Japan
8410756 **YUYO MARU** *V4ZL* - **Yuyo Maru Co** MFH (Maritime Fleet Handling) *Basseterre* *St Kitts & Nevis* MMSI: 341667000 Official number: SKN 1001667	**676** Class: IS (NK) 172 296	**1984-09 Sanyo Zosen K.K. — Onomichi** Yd No: 883 Loa 36.94 Br ex - Dght 3.820 Lbp 35.13 Br md 10.00 Dpth 4.63 Welded, 1 dk	**(B32B2SP) Pusher Tug**	**2 oil engines** driving 2 CP propellers Total Power: 2,942kW (4,000hp) 12.8kn Akasaka DM38AK 2 x 4 Stroke 6 Cy. 380 x 600 each-1471kW (2000bhp) Akasaka Tekkosho KK (Akasaka DieselLtd)-Japan AuxGen: 3 x 136kW a.c
8808343 **YUYO MARU No. 8** *JK4873* - **Fujino Kaiun YK** - *Hiroshima, Hiroshima* *Japan* Official number: 130946	*499* - 1,051	**1988-06 Hitachi Zosen Mukaishima Marine Co Ltd — Onomichi HS** Yd No: 8 Loa 54.70 (BB) Br ex 12.08 Dght 3.901 Lbp 50.00 Br md 12.00 Dpth 4.25 Welded, 1 dk	**(B33A2DG) Grab Dredger** Grain: 783; Bale: 700 Compartments: 1 Ho, ER 1 Ha: ER	**1 oil engine** with clutches & reverse reduction geared to sc. shaft driving 1 FP propeller Total Power: 736kW (1,001hp) Hanshin 6LU32G 1 x 4 Stroke 6 Cy. 320 x 510 736kW (1001bhp) Hanshin Nainenki Kogyo-Japan Thrusters: 1 Thwart. FP thruster (f)
9395501 **YUYO SPIRITS** *3FNF4* - **Gas Spirits Shipping SA** A P Moller - Maersk A/S SatCom: Inmarsat C 435711710 *Panama* *Panama* MMSI: 357117000 Official number: 4067209	**45,966** Class: NK 13,790 49,999 T/cm 70.3	**2009-08 Mitsubishi Heavy Industries Ltd. — Nagasaki** Yd No: 2240 Loa 230.00 (BB) Br ex 36.63 Dght 10.795 Lbp 219.00 Br md 36.60 Dpth 20.80 Welded, 1 dk	**(A11B2TG) LPG Tanker** Double Bottom Entire Compartment Length Liq (Gas): 77,324 5 x Gas Tank (s); 4 independent pri horizontal, ER 8 Cargo Pump (s): 8x550m³/hr Manifold: Bow/CM: 113.9m	**1 oil engine** driving 1 FP propeller Total Power: 14,315kW (19,463hp) 16.7kn Mitsubishi 7UEC60LSII 1 x 2 Stroke 7 Cy. 600 x 2300 14315kW (19463bhp) Mitsubishi Heavy Industries Ltd-Japan AuxGen: 3 x 900kW a.c Fuel: 357.0 (d.f.) 2500.0 (r.f.)
9414553 **YUZAN MARU** *JD2427* - **Nippo Shosen YK** - *Imabari, Ehime* *Japan* MMSI: 431000189 Official number: 140552	*749* - 2,630	**2007-05 Yamanaka Zosen K.K. — Imabari** Yd No: 737 Loa 74.64 Br ex - Dght 5.290 Lbp 70.00 Br md 13.40 Dpth 8.78 Welded, 1 dk	**(A24E2BL) Limestone Carrier** Grain: 2,762; Bale: 2,762 1 Ha: ER (36.0 x 9.5)	**1 oil engine** driving 1 FP propeller Total Power: 1,471kW (2,000hp) Hanshin LH36LAG 1 x 4 Stroke 6 Cy. 360 x 670 1471kW (2000bhp) The Hanshin Diesel Works Ltd-Japan
9135212 **YUZAN MARU** *JHHL* - - - *Tokyo* *Japan* MMSI: 431836000 Official number: 135813	*499* - 619	**1996-03 Miho Zosensho K.K. — Shimizu** Yd No: 1455 Loa 65.00 (BB) Br ex - Dght - Lbp 58.00 Br md 9.00 Dpth 4.00 Welded, 1 dk	**(B12D2FP) Fishery Patrol Vessel**	**1 oil engine** with flexible couplings & sr gearedto sc. shaft driving 1 FP propeller Total Power: 1,839kW (2,500hp) Yanmar 6N280-EN 1 x 4 Stroke 6 Cy. 280 x 380 1839kW (2500bhp) Yanmar Diesel Engine Co Ltd-Japan
9204180 **YUZAN MARU No. 5** *JM6647* - **Taishin Kaiun KK** - *Kamiamakusa, Kumamoto* *Japan* Official number: 136393	*498* - -	**1998-04 Amakusa Zosen K.K. — Amakusa** Yd No: 123 Loa 70.13 Br ex - Dght - Lbp 64.00 Br md 13.20 Dpth 7.20 Welded, 1 dk	**(A31A2GX) General Cargo Ship**	**1 oil engine** driving 1 FP propeller Total Power: 2,060kW (2,801hp) 13.0kn Niigata 6M38GT 1 x 4 Stroke 6 Cy. 380 x 720 2060kW (2801bhp) Niigata Engineering Co Ltd-Japan
8724482 **YUZHMORGEOLOGIYA** *UBSZ* - **SSC FSUGE Yuzhmorgeologiya** - SatCom: Inmarsat A 1400633 *Novorossiysk* *Russia* MMSI: 273422600 Official number: 841099	**4,430** Class: RS 1,329 1,959	**1985-10 GP Chernomorskiy Sudostroitelnyy Zavod — Nikolayev** Yd No: 803 Loa 104.50 Br ex 16.03 Dght 5.900 Lbp 96.40 Br md 16.00 Dpth 10.20 Welded, 2 dks	**(B31A2SR) Research Survey Vessel** Ice Capable	**2 oil engines** reduction geared to sc. shaft driving 1 CP propeller Total Power: 5,148kW (7,000hp) 14.7kn Russkiy 6CHN40/46 2 x 4 Stroke 6 Cy. 400 x 460 each-2574kW (3500bhp) Mashinostroitelnyy Zavod"Russkiy-Dizel"-Leningrad AuxGen: 2 x 1600kW 220/380V 50Hz a.c, 3 x 200kW 220/380V 50Hz a.c Fuel: 1596.0 (d.f.)

8897320 **YUZHNAYA** 175 Class: (RS)
UAHZ 52
- **Kamkorn & Co (OOO 'Kamkorn i Ko')** 59
-
Petropavlovsk-Kamchatskiy *Russia*
Official number: 865958

1986-01 in Japan
Loa 35.20 Br ex 7.70 Dght 2.200
Lbp 30.20 Br md - Dpth 2.60
Welded, 1 dk

(B11A2FS) Stern Trawler

1 oil engine driving 1 FP propeller
Total Power: 331kW (450hp) 10.0kr
Pervomaysk 6CHN25/34
1 x 4 Stroke 6 Cy. 250 x 340 331kW (450bhp)
Pervomaydizelmash (PDM)-Pervomaysk
AuxGen: 1 x 75kW a.c, 1 x 50kW a.c
Fuel: 72.0 (d.f.)

8957302 **YUZHNOYE PRIMORYE** 115
- *ex* Liao Da Gan Yu 8716 *-2000* 39
- - 97
-
Vladivostok *Russia*
Official number: 990185

1999-05 Rongcheng Shipbuilding Industry Co Ltd — Rongcheng SD Yd No: Y040199525
Loa 34.00 Br ex - Dght 2.100
Lbp 29.62 Br md 6.00 Dpth 2.70
Welded, 1 dk

(B11B2FV) Fishing Vessel

1 oil engine geared to sc. shaft driving 1 FP propeller
Total Power: 220kW (299hp)
Chinese Std. Type Z6170ZL
1 x 4 Stroke 6 Cy. 170 x 200 220kW (299bhp)
Zibo Diesel Engine Factory-China

8226997 **YUZHNYY** 1,896 Class: UA (RS)
EMSB *ex* Manganary *-1997* 989
- **State Enterprise 'Marine Administration of Sevastopol Sea Fishing Port'** 3,412
Star Light Cargo SA
Sevastopol *Ukraine*
MMSI: 272021000

1984-02 Shipbuilding & Shiprepairing Yard 'Ivan Dimitrov' — Rousse Yd No: 431
Converted From: Bunkering Vessel-2003
Loa 77.53 Br ex 14.34 Dght 5.360
Lbp 73.24 Br md 14.02 Dpth 6.51
Welded, 1 dk

(A12D2LV) Vegetable Oil Tanker
Grain: 64; Liq: 3,224; Liq (Oil): 3,224
Compartments: 1 Ho, 8 Ta, ER
Ice Capable

1 oil engine driving 1 FP propeller
Total Power: 883kW (1,201hp) 10.0kn
S.K.L. 8NVD48A-2U
1 x 4 Stroke 8 Cy. 320 x 480 883kW (1201bhp) (made 1982)
VEB Schwermaschinenbau "KarlLiebknecht" (SKL)-Magdeburg
AuxGen: 2 x 150kW
Fuel: 160.0 (d.f.)

8227329 **YUZHNYY** 789 Class: (RS)
UGFM *ex* Leonidovo *-1996* 236
- **OOO 'Bereg Nadezhdy'** 332
-
Nevelsk *Russia*
MMSI: 273432500

1984 Volgogradskiy Sudostroitelnyy Zavod — Volgograd Yd No: 215
Loa 53.75 (BB) Br ex 10.72 Dght 4.239
Lbp 47.92 Br md 10.50 Dpth 6.74
Welded, 1 dk

(B11A2FS) Stern Trawler
Ins: 218
Compartments: 1 Ho, ER
1 Ha: (1.6 x 1.6)
Derricks: 2x1.5t
Ice Capable

1 oil engine driving 1 CP propeller
Total Power: 971kW (1,320hp) 12.7kn
S.K.L. 8NVD48A-2U
1 x 4 Stroke 8 Cy. 320 x 480 971kW (1320bhp)
VEB Schwermaschinenbau "KarlLiebknecht" (SKL)-Magdeburg
AuxGen: 1 x 300kW, 3 x 160kW, 2 x 135kW
Fuel: 182.0 (d.f.)

7914767 **YUZUKI** *123*
JG3778 -
- **Government of Japan (Ministry of Land, Infrastructure & Transport) (The Coastguard)** 76
-
Tokyo *Japan*
Official number: 121710

1979-03 Mitsubishi Heavy Industries Ltd. — Shimonoseki Yd No: 804
Loa 26.00 Br ex 6.30 Dght 1.130
Lbp 24.50 Br md 6.29 Dpth 3.04
Welded, 1 dk

(B34H2SQ) Patrol Vessel
Hull Material: Aluminium Alloy

3 oil engines driving 3 FP propellers
Total Power: 2,208kW (3,003hp) 22.0kn
Mitsubishi 12DM20TK
3 x Vee 4 Stroke 12 Cy. 160 x 200 each-736kW (1001bhp)
Mitsubishi Heavy Industries Ltd-Japan

9270232 **YVAN BARRETTO** *3,360* Class: BV (NV)
PPPR 1,008
- **Bourbon Offshore Maritima SA** 2,240
-
Rio de Janeiro *Brazil*
MMSI: 710050000
Official number: 3810511781

2004-07 FELS Setal SA — Angra dos Reis Yd No: 102
Loa 75.60 Br ex - Dght 6.600
Lbp 64.40 Br md 18.00 Dpth 8.00
Welded

(B21B20A) Anchor Handling Tug Supply
Passengers: 12

2 oil engines geared to sc. shafts driving 2 CP propellers
Total Power: 9,000kW (12,236hp) 10.0kn
Bergens B32: 40L9P
2 x 4 Stroke 9 Cy. 320 x 400 each-4500kW (6118bhp)
Rolls Royce Marine AS-Norway
AuxGen: 2 x 350kW 440/220V 60Hz a.c, 2 x 2240kW 440/220V 60Hz a.c
Thrusters: 2 Thwart. CP thruster (f); 1 Thwart. CP thruster (a); 1 Retract. directional thruster (f)
Fuel: 840.0 (d.f.) 13.0pd

9179622 **YVES JACOB** **40,705** Class: AB
A8VX6 *ex* Los Roques *-2009* 21,529
- **Schiffahrtsgesellschaft 'Los Roques' mbH & Co KG** 71,562
Ernst Jacob GmbH & Co KG T/cm
Monrovia *Liberia* 67.9
MMSI: 636092052
Official number: 92052

2000-09 '3 Maj' Brodogradiliste dd — Rijeka Yd No: 673
Loa 228.58 (BB) Br ex 32.24 Dght 14.120
Lbp 220.00 Br md 32.20 Dpth 20.10
Welded, 1 dk

(A13A2TW) Crude/Oil Products Tanker
Double Hull (13F)
Liq: 80,012; Liq (Oil): 78,136
Compartments: 10 Wing Ta, 2 Wing Slop Ta, ER
10 Cargo Pump (s): 10x900m³/hr
Manifold: Bow/CM: 111m

1 oil engine driving 1 FP propeller
Total Power: 12,000kW (16,315hp) 15.0kn
Sulzer 6RTA62U
1 x 2 Stroke 6 Cy. 620 x 2150 12000kW (16315bhp)
'3 Maj' Motori i Dizalice dd-Croatia
AuxGen: 3 x 960kW 220/440V 60Hz a.c
Fuel: 265.0 (d.f.) 2520.0 (r.f.) 43.0pd

9360013 **YVONNE** **31,532** Class: NK
A8NE8 18,767
- **Laurus Enterprises Corp** 56,557
Byzantine Maritime Corp T/cm
Monrovia *Liberia* 56.9
MMSI: 636013469
Official number: 13469

2008-08 IHI Marine United Inc — Yokohama KN Yd No: 3242
Loa 190.00 (BB) Br ex - Dght 12.735
Lbp 185.00 Br md 32.26 Dpth 18.10
Welded, 1 dk

(A21A2BC) Bulk Carrier
Grain: 72,111; Bale: 67,110
Compartments: 5 Ho, ER
5 Ha: 4 (20.9 x 18.6)ER (14.6 x 18.6)
Cranes: 4x35t

1 oil engine driving 1 FP propeller
Total Power: 8,892kW (12,090hp) 14.5kn
Wartsila 6RT-flex50
1 x 2 Stroke 6 Cy. 500 x 2050 8892kW (12090bhp)
Diesel United Ltd.-Aioi
AuxGen: 3 x 430kW a.c
Fuel: 2170.0

9423671 **YVONNE** **2,528** Class: BV (LR)
V2EB5 1,053 ✠ Classed LR until 9/2/10
- **Reederei ms Yvonne GmbH & Co KG** 3,500
Reederei Andre Wieczorek GmbH & Co KG
Saint John's *Antigua & Barbuda*
MMSI: 305376000

2008-12 Leda doo — Korcula (Hull)
2008-12 Scheepswerf Peters B.V. — Kampen Yd No: 1211
Loa 89.99 (BB) Br ex 12.58 Dght 5.250
Lbp 84.95 Br md 12.50 Dpth 8.00
Welded, 1 dk

(A31A2GX) General Cargo Ship
Grain: 4,927
TEU 157 C Ho 105 TEU C Dk 52 TEU
Compartments: 1 Ho, ER
1 Ha: ER
Ice Capable

1 oil engine with clutches, flexible couplings & sr geared to sc. shaft driving 1 CP propeller
Total Power: 1,800kW (2,447hp) 13.0kn
Wartsila 9L20
1 x 4 Stroke 9 Cy. 200 x 280 1800kW (2447bhp)
Wartsila Finland Oy-Finland
AuxGen: 1 x 168kW 400V 50Hz a.c, 1 x 250kW 400V 50Hz a.c
Thrusters: 1 Thwart. FP thruster (f)

9195638 **YVONNE K.** **2,545** Class: BV (LR) (GL)
PBLX *ex* HC Freya *-2007* *ex* Oosterbrug *-2004* 1,460 ✠ Classed LR until 10/12/04
- **Rufinia Beheer BV** 3,783
Flagship Management Co BV
Delfzijl *Netherlands*
MMSI: 244948000
Official number: 40340

2002-01 Daewoo-Mangalia Heavy Industries S.A. — Mangalia (Hull) Yd No: 1038
2002-01 B.V. Scheepswerf Damen Bergum — Bergum Yd No: 9333
Loa 88.60 Br ex 12.52 Dght 5.420
Lbp 84.99 Br md 12.50 Dpth 7.00
Welded, 1 dk

(A31A2GX) General Cargo Ship
Double Bottom Entire Compartment Length
Grain: 5,248
TEU 193 C Ho 113 TEU C Dk 80 TEU.
Compartments: 1 Ho, ER
1 Ha: (61.7 x 10.1)ER

1 oil engine with clutches, flexible couplings & sr reverse geared to sc. shaft driving 1 FP propeller
Total Power: 1,520kW (2,067hp) 10.5kn
MaK 8M20
1 x 4 Stroke 8 Cy. 200 x 300 1520kW (2067bhp)
Caterpillar Motoren GmbH & Co. KG-Germany
AuxGen: 1 x 264kW 400V 50Hz a.c, 1 x 96kW 400V 50Hz a.c
Thrusters: 1 Thwart. FP thruster (f)
Fuel: 79.4 (d.f.) 1874.4 (r.f.)

7933945 **YVONNE MICHELLE** *167*
WDE5578 121
- **Trawler Yvonne Michele Inc** -
-
Cape May, NJ *United States of America*
MMSI: 366235720
Official number: 607685

1979-08 Master Marine, Inc. — Bayou La Batre, Al
L reg 24.75 Br ex 6.79 Dght -
Lbp - Br md - Dpth 3.36
Welded, 1 dk

(B11B2FV) Fishing Vessel

1 oil engine driving 1 FP propeller
Total Power: 493kW (670hp)
G.M. (Detroit Diesel) 12V-149
1 x Vee 2 Stroke 12 Cy. 146 x 146 493kW (670bhp)
General Motors Detroit DieselAllison Divn-USA

9631498 **YVONNE W** **254** Class: BV
PCMG 76
- **Stemat BV** -
Bhagwan Marine Pty Ltd
Rotterdam *Netherlands*
MMSI: 246690000
Official number: 54558

2011-08 Neptune Shipyards BV — Aalst (Nl) Yd No: 396
Loa 31.90 Br ex - Dght 2.630
Lbp - Br md 11.00 Dpth 3.50
Welded, 1 dk

(B34L2QU) Utility Vessel
Cranes: 1x15t

2 oil engines reduction geared to sc. shafts driving 2 FP propellers
Total Power: 1,940kW (2,638hp) 10.0kn
Caterpillar C32 ACERT
2 x Vee 4 Stroke 12 Cy. 145 x 162 each-970kW (1319bhp)
Caterpillar Inc-USA
Thrusters: 1 Directional thruster
Fuel: 106.0 (d.f.)

8662440 **YX 668** **2,813** Class: IZ
T3ML2 *ex* Yong Xing 668 *-2014* 1,575
- **PT Pusaka Armada Sakti** 4,755
-
Tarawa *Kiribati*
Official number: K-17041484

2004-08 Zhejiang Yueqing Qiligang Ship Industry Co Ltd — Yueqing ZJ
Loa 95.90 Br ex - Dght 6.100
Lbp 89.00 Br md 13.80 Dpth 7.40
Welded, 1 dk

(A31A2GX) General Cargo Ship

1 oil engine driving 1 Propeller
Total Power: 1,470kW (1,999hp)
Chinese Std. Type
1 x 1470kW (1999bhp)
Wuxi Antai Power Machinery Co Ltd-China

8804440 **YXLAN** **449**
SBLO *ex* Elektra *-1994* *ex* Farja 61/329 *-1988* 164
- **Government of The Kingdom of Sweden (Vagverket Farjerederiet)** 800
Government of The Kingdom of Sweden (Farjerederiet Produktion Ost)
SatCom: Inmarsat C 426549010
Vaxholm *Sweden*
MMSI: 265546920

1988-10 Scheepswerf K Damen BV — Hardinxveld Yd No: 664
Loa 76.71 Br ex - Dght 3.400
Lbp 62.82 Br md 12.41 Dpth -
Welded

(A36A2PR) Passenger/Ro-Ro Ship (Vehicles)

4 oil engines with clutches, flexible couplings & sr geared to sc. shafts driving 2 Directional propellers 1 fwd and 1 aft
Total Power: 1,472kW (2,000hp)
Scania DSI1440M
4 x Vee 4 Stroke 8 Cy. 127 x 140 each-368kW (500bhp)
Saab Scania AB-Sweden

613956	**YYR MAX** *ex* Graciela *ex* Fukuei Maru No. 7 *-2003* *ex* Fukutoku Maru No. 7 *-2003* - - SatCom: Inmarsat Mini-M 765052633 *Mexico*	**542** 164 -		**1986-10 KK Kanasashi Zosen — Shizuoka SZ** Yd No: 3105 Loa 53.52 (BB) Br ex 8.74 Dght 3.401 Lbp 46.89 Br md 8.70 Dpth 3.76 Welded	**(B11B2FV) Fishing Vessel**	**1 oil engine** with clutches,flexible couplings & sr reverse geared to sc. shaft driving 1 FP propeller Total Power: 736kW (1,001hp) 10.5kn Niigata 6M28AFTE 1 x 4 Stroke 6 Cy. 280 x 480 736kW (1001bhp) Niigata Engineering Co Ltd-Japan
103377 *CTH3*	**Z. CANSU** *ex* Cansu *-2009* *ex* Corn Dolly *-2002* *ex* Humbergracht *-2001* *ex* Carpaper *-1989* **Yildirim Dis Ticaret ve Pazarlama AS** Yilmar Denizcilik Nakliyat ve Ticaret Ltd Sti (Yilmar Shipping & Trading Ltd) *Istanbul* *Turkey* MMSI: 271002700 Official number: 1661	**4,281** 2,846 7,435	Class: LR ✠ **100A1** SS 04/2011 Ice Class 1A at a draught not exceeding 5.937m ✠ **LMC** Eq.Ltr: U; Cable: 467.5/46.0 U2 (a)	**1982-01 Miho Zosensho K.K. — Shimizu** Yd No: 1199 Loa 95.38 (BB) Br ex 16.11 Dght 5.906 Lbp 89.79 Br md 16.01 Dpth 10.52 Welded, 2 dks	**(A31A2GX) General Cargo Ship** Grain: 9,282; Bale: 9,111 TEU 320 C. 320/20' Compartments: 1 Ho, ER, 1 Tw Dk 2 Ha: (20.5 x 12.8) (24.7 x 12.8)ER Cranes: 2x10t Ice Capable	**1 oil engine** driving 1 CP propeller Total Power: 2,243kW (3,050hp) 11.0kn Hanshin 6LUS40 1 x 4 Stroke 6 Cy. 400 x 640 2243kW (3050bhp) The Hanshin Diesel Works Ltd-Japan AuxGen: 3 x 200kW 445V 60Hz a.c, 1 x 132kW 445V 60Hz a.c Fuel: 58.5 (d.f.) 453.0 (r.f.)
194177 *WDE7721*	**Z-FIVE** **Tugz International LLC** Harley Marine Services Inc *Wilmington, DE* *United States of America* MMSI: 366763440 Official number: 1072785	**256** 76 -	Class: AB	**1999-02 MARCO Shipyard, Inc. — Seattle, Wa** Yd No: 481 Loa 28.70 Br ex - Dght 3.510 Lbp 27.43 Br md 9.75 Dpth 4.27 Welded, 1 dk	**(B32A2ST) Tug**	**2 oil engines** gearing integral to driving 2 Z propellers Total Power: 2,942kW (4,000hp) Caterpillar 3516B 2 x Vee 4 Stroke 16 Cy. 170 x 190 each-1471kW (2000bhp) Caterpillar Inc-USA AuxGen: 1 x 105kW 60Hz a.c, 1 x 99kW 60Hz a.c
194165 *WDE7715*	**Z-FOUR** **Tugz International LLC** Harley Marine Services Inc *Wilmington, DE* *United States of America* Official number: 1072783	**256** 76 -	Class: AB	**1999-02 MARCO Shipyard, Inc. — Seattle, Wa** Yd No: 480 Loa 28.70 Br ex - Dght 3.510 Lbp 27.43 Br md 9.75 Dpth 4.27 Welded, 1 dk	**(B32A2ST) Tug** Ice Capable	**2 oil engines** gearing integral to driving 2 Z propellers Total Power: 3,282kW (4,462hp) Caterpillar 3516B 2 x Vee 4 Stroke 16 Cy. 170 x 190 each-1641kW (2231bhp) Caterpillar Inc-USA AuxGen: 1 x 105kW 60Hz a.c, 1 x 99kW 9/9V 60Hz a.c
649163 *7YX9*	**Z-ONE** **Balmont Overseas Corp** - *Jaluit* *Marshall Islands* MMSI: 538070867 Official number: 70867	**260** 78 160	Class: RP (Class contemplated)	**2009 Azimut-Benetti SpA — Viareggio** Yd No: 116/35 Loa 35.50 Br ex 7.40 Dght 2.100 Lbp 28.54 Br md 7.32 Dpth 3.68 Bonded, 1 dk	**(X11A2YP) Yacht** Hull Material: Reinforced Plastic	**2 oil engines** geared to sc. shaft driving 2 Propellers Total Power: 3,580kW (4,868hp) 30.0kn M.T.U. 16V2000M93 2 x Vee 4 Stroke 16 Cy. 135 x 156 each-1790kW (2434bhp) MTU Friedrichshafen GmbH-Friedrichshafen
159696 *WCW9643*	**Z-ONE** *ex* Matthew Mcallister *-2009* *ex* Z-One *-2005* **Tugz International LLC** The Great Lakes Towing Co (Great Lakes Group) *Wilmington, DE* *United States of America* MMSI: 367044030 Official number: 1042196	**256** 76 -	Class: AB	**1996-11 Halter Marine, Inc. — Lockport, La** Yd No: 1528 Loa 29.10 Br ex - Dght 3.540 Lbp 28.62 Br md 9.75 Dpth 4.80 Welded, 1 dk	**(B32A2ST) Tug** Ice Capable	**2 oil engines** gearing integral to driving 2 Z propellers Total Power: 3,236kW (4,400hp) 14.0kn Caterpillar 3516TA 2 x Vee 4 Stroke 16 Cy. 170 x 190 each-1618kW (2200bhp) Caterpillar Inc-USA
194153 *WDE7712*	**Z-THREE** **General Electric Credit Corp of Tennessee (GECC Tennessee)** Harley Marine Services Inc *Wilmington, DE* *United States of America* Official number: 1072784	**256** 76 -	Class: AB	**1999-02 MARCO Shipyard, Inc. — Seattle, Wa** Yd No: 479 Loa 28.70 Br ex - Dght 3.510 Lbp 27.43 Br md 9.75 Dpth 4.27 Welded, 1 dk	**(B32A2ST) Tug**	**2 oil engines** gearing integral to driving 2 Z propellers Total Power: 2,942kW (4,000hp) Caterpillar 3516B 2 x Vee 4 Stroke 16 Cy. 170 x 190 each-1471kW (2000bhp) Caterpillar Inc-USA AuxGen: 1 x 105kW 60Hz a.c, 1 x 99kW 60Hz a.c
609072	**Z-TWO** *ex* Deletovci *-2010* *ex* Ina Deletovci *-2002* *ex* Shohu Maru *-1998* **Sierra Fishing Co** -	**724** 344 1,312	Class: IS (CS)	**1986-06 Sasaki Shipbuilding Co Ltd — Osakikamijima HS** Yd No: 501 Loa 64.22 Br ex 10.01 Dght 4.202 Lbp 60.03 Br md 10.00 Dpth 4.53 Welded, 1 dk	**(A12A2TC) Chemical Tanker** Double Bottom Entire Compartment Length Liq: 1,276 Compartments: 8 Ta, ER	**1 oil engine** with clutches, flexible couplings & reverse reduction geared to sc. shaft driving 1 FP propeller Total Power: 956kW (1,300hp) 10.0kn Niigata 6M28AFTE 1 x 4 Stroke 6 Cy. 280 x 480 956kW (1300bhp) Niigata Engineering Co Ltd-Japan AuxGen: 3 x 75kW a.c
642429	**ZA RODINU** - -	*649* 211 404	Class: (RS)	**1974 Zavod "Leninskaya Kuznitsa" — Kiyev** Yd No: 1388 Loa 54.82 Br ex 9.94 Dght 4.109 Lbp - Br md - Dpth 5.01 Welded, 1 dk	**(B11A2FS) Stern Trawler** Ins: 400 Compartments: 2 Ho, ER 3 Ha: 3 (1.4 x 1.6) Derricks: 2x1.3t; Winches: 2 Ice Capable	**1 oil engine** driving 1 CP propeller Total Power: 736kW (1,001hp) 12.0kn S.K.L. 8NVD48A-2U 1 x 4 Stroke 8 Cy. 320 x 480 736kW (1001bhp) VEB Schwermaschinenbau "KarlLiebknecht" (SKL)-Magdeburg
898738 *HMYO7*	**ZA RYOK 2** **Yusong Shipping Co** *Nampho* *North Korea* MMSI: 445020000 Official number: 2901064	*1,329* 398 1,370		**1979-10 Ryongampa Shipyard — North Korea** Yd No: 1207 Loa 65.00 Br ex 14.50 Dght 3.300 Lbp 50.50 Br md - Dpth 5.20 Welded, 1 dk	**(A31A2GX) General Cargo Ship**	**1 oil engine** driving 1 FP propeller Total Power: 735kW (999hp)
058957 *FJZ3*	**ZAABEEL** *ex* Cheong Yong *-2003* **FAL Shipping Co Ltd** - *Panama* *Panama* MMSI: 373450000 Official number: 43356PEXT	**6,402** 3,683 10,898	Class: (BV) (KR) (NK)	**1993-04 Tsuneishi Shipbuilding Co Ltd — Fukuyama HS** Yd No: 1022 Loa 130.60 (BB) Br ex 20.03 Dght 7.517 Lbp 122.50 Br md 20.00 Dpth 10.00 Welded, 1 dk	**(A13B2TP) Products Tanker** Double Bottom Entire Compartment Length Liq: 12,811; Liq (Oil): 12,811 Cargo Heating Coils Compartments: 10 Ta, ER 2 Cargo Pump (s): 1x1000m³/hr, 1x500m³/hr	**1 oil engine** driving 1 FP propeller Total Power: 3,530kW (4,799hp) 12.2kn B&W 6L35MC 1 x 2 Stroke 6 Cy. 350 x 1050 3530kW (4799bhp) Makita Corp-Japan AuxGen: 3 x 280kW 450V 60Hz a.c Thrusters: 1 Thwart. FP thruster (f) Fuel: 95.1 (d.f.) (Heating Coils) 482.4 (r.f.) 10.1pd
336282 *4GD2*	**ZAAN TRADER** *ex* SITC Fortune *-2008* *ex* Medadriatica *-2007* **Zaan Trader Beheer BV** GB Shipping & Chartering GmbH *Limassol* *Cyprus* MMSI: 209075000 Official number: 9336282	**6,701** 3,557 8,200 T/cm 20.7	Class: GL (BV)	**2005-11 Yangfan Group Co Ltd — Zhoushan ZJ** Yd No: 2031 Loa 132.60 (BB) Br ex - Dght 7.210 Lbp 123.40 Br md 19.20 Dpth 9.20 Welded, 1 dk	**(A33A2CC) Container Ship (Fully Cellular)** TEU 672 C Ho 188 TEU C Dk 484 TEU incl 116 ref C.	**1 oil engine** reduction geared to sc. shaft driving 1 CP propeller Total Power: 6,300kW (8,565hp) 17.0kn MaK 7M43 1 x 4 Stroke 7 Cy. 430 x 610 6300kW (8565bhp) Caterpillar Motoren GmbH & Co. KG-Germany AuxGen: 3 x 360kW a.c Thrusters: 1 Tunnel thruster (f)
156527 *PDAN*	**ZAANDAM** **HAL Antillen NV** Holland America Line NV SatCom: Inmarsat C 424644210 *Rotterdam* *Netherlands* MMSI: 246442000 Official number: 38326	**61,396** 31,457 6,150	Class: LR (RI) ✠ **100A1** CS 04/2010 passenger ship *IWS LI ✠ **LMC** Eq.Ltr: R†; Cable: 687.5/84.0 U3 (a)	**2000-04 Fincantieri-Cant. Nav. Italiani S.p.A. (Breda) — Venezia** Yd No: 6036 Loa 237.00 (BB) Br ex 32.28 Dght 8.100 Lbp 202.75 Br md 32.25 Dpth 11.00 Welded, 5 dks plus 7 superstructure dks.	**(A37A2PC) Passenger/Cruise** Passengers: cabins: 719; berths: 1440	**5 diesel electric oil engines** driving 5 gen. each 8400kW 6600V a.c Connecting to 2 elec. motors each (13000kW) driving 2 CP propellers Total Power: 43,200kW (58,735hp) 22.0kn Sulzer 12ZAV40S 5 x Vee 4 Stroke 12 Cy. 400 x 560 each-8640kW (11747bhp) Wartsila Italia SpA-Italy Boilers: 5 e (ex.g.) 10.7kgf/cm² (10.5bar), 2 AuxB (o.f.) 10.1kgf/cm² (9.9bar) Thrusters: 2 Thwart. CP thruster (f); 2 Thwart. CP thruster (a) Fuel: 144.0 (d.f.) 2796.0 (r.f.)
801860 *XTZ*	**ZAANDAM** *ex* Atlantic Toni *-1980* **Potensol SA** - *Montevideo* *Uruguay* MMSI: 770576064 Official number: 7897	*623* 295 300	Class: (LR) ✠ Classed LR until 27/8/76	**1968-03 Geo T Davie & Sons Ltd — Levis QC** Yd No: 107 Loa 46.41 Br ex 9.68 Dght 3.849 Lbp 40.01 Br md 9.30 Dpth 6.66 Welded, 2 dks	**(B11A2FS) Stern Trawler** Ins: 340 Compartments: 2 Ho, ER 3 Ha: 3 (2.2 x 1.1)ER Ice Capable	**1 oil engine** driving 1 CP propeller Total Power: 1,103kW (1,500hp) 13.5kn De Industrie 6D8HD 1 x 4 Stroke 6 Cy. 400 x 600 1103kW (1500bhp) NV Motorenfabriek 'De Industrie'-Netherlands AuxGen: 1 x 84kW 440V 60Hz a.c, 1 x 80kW 440V 60Hz a.c Fuel: 116.0 (d.f.)
020379	**ZAANDAM** **Bernie Markey** - *Cairns, Qld* *Australia* Official number: 386086	*138* 84 -		**1980-12 Australian Shipbuilding Industries (WA) Pty Ltd — Fremantle WA** Yd No: 191 Loa 22.59 Br ex - Dght 2.941 Lbp 21.37 Br md 6.27 Dpth 3.79 Welded, 1 dk	**(B11A2FT) Trawler**	**1 oil engine** driving 1 FP propeller Total Power: 268kW (364hp) Caterpillar 3408TA 1 x Vee 4 Stroke 8 Cy. 137 x 152 268kW (364bhp) Caterpillar Tractor Co-USA

IMO / Call sign	Name / Owner	Tonnage	Class	Builder / Dimensions	Type	Machinery
9593373 *7TFE* -	**ZABANA AHMED I** **Entreprise Portuaire d'Oran (EPO)** *Oran* *Algeria* MMSI: 605106431	**369** 111 285	Class: BV	**2011-07 Astilleros Armon SA — Navia** Yd No: 702 Loa 30.00 Br ex - Dght 4.450 Lbp 26.83 Br md 9.85 Dpth 5.40 Welded, 1 dk	**(B32A2ST) Tug**	**2 oil engines** reduction geared to sc. shafts driving 2 Directional propellers Total Power: 2,800kW (3,806hp) A.B.C. 6DZ 2 x 4 Stroke 6 Cy. 256 x 310 each-1400kW (1903bhp) Anglo Belgian Corp NV (ABC)-Belgium AuxGen: 2 x 92kW 50Hz a.c Fuel: 140.0 (d.f.)
9593385 *7TFF* -	**ZABANA AHMED II** **Entreprise Portuaire d'Oran (EPO)** *Oran* *Algeria* MMSI: 605106432	**369** 111 285	Class: BV	**2011-09 Astilleros Armon SA — Navia** Yd No: 703 Loa 30.00 Br ex - Dght 4.450 Lbp 26.83 Br md 9.85 Dpth 5.40 Welded, 1 dk	**(B32A2ST) Tug**	**2 oil engines** reduction geared to sc. shafts driving 2 Directional propellers Total Power: 2,400kW (3,264hp) A.B.C. 6DZ 2 x 4 Stroke 6 Cy. 256 x 310 each-1200kW (1632bhp) Anglo Belgian Corp NV (ABC)-Belgium AuxGen: 2 x 92kW 50Hz a.c Fuel: 130.0 (d.f.)
9671840 - -	**ZABAVA** **Yar-yachting Ltd** *St Petersburg* *Russia* Official number: ST24M2/305	**123** 71 -	Class: RR (Class contemplated)	**2012-10 AO Yaroslavskiy Sudostroitelnyy Zavod — Yaroslavl** Yd No: 305 Loa 24.44 Br ex 7.97 Dght 1.270 Lbp 21.83 Br md 7.87 Dpth 2.33 Welded, 1 dk	**(X11A2YP) Yacht** Hull Material: Aluminium Alloy	**2 oil engines** reduction geared to sc. shafts driving 2 Propellers Total Power: 204kW (278hp)
7001443 *D6FE6* -	**ZABEEL** *ex* Mahra *-2010* *ex* Anwar *-2009* *ex* Sigiri *-2006* *ex* Salvor *-1997* *ex* Pacific Salvor *-1996* *ex* Wongara *-1991* **Farkaad Aljader** - *Moroni* *Union of Comoros* MMSI: 616817000 Official number: 1200948	**402** 120 -	Class: (LR) ✠ Classed LR until 11/7/01	**1970-01 Adelaide Ship Construction Pty Ltd — Port Adelaide SA** Yd No: 62 Loa 38.59 Br ex 10.47 Dght 5.087 Lbp 35.16 Br md 10.14 Dpth 5.47 Welded, 1 dk	**(B32A2ST) Tug**	**1 oil engine** driving 1 CP propeller Total Power: 1,765kW (2,400hp) 13.5k Ruston 16RK 1 x Vee 4 Stroke 16 Cy. 254 x 305 1765kW (2400bhp) English Electric Diesels Ltd.-Glasgow AuxGen: 2 x 98kW 415V 50Hz a.c Fuel: 245.0 (d.f.)
8007456 - -	**ZABEEL-4** *ex* Belgio *-1992* **Dubai Drydocks** *Dubai* *United Arab Emirates* Official number: 4274	**246** 73 191	Class: LR (RI) **100A1** SS 08/2010 tug **LMC** Eq.Ltr: G; Cable: 302.5/20.0 U2	**1982-03 Cantieri Navali Campanella SpA — Savona** Yd No: 89 Loa 29.93 Br ex 8.44 Dght 3.840 Lbp 29.18 Br md 8.40 Dpth 4.40 Welded, 1 dk	**(B32A2ST) Tug**	**1 oil engine** with clutches, flexible couplings & sr geared to sc. shaft driving 1 CP propeller Total Power: 2,282kW (3,103hp) 11.0k Nohab F312 1 x Vee 4 Stroke 12 Cy. 250 x 300 2282kW (3103bhp) Nohab Diesel AB-Sweden AuxGen: 2 x 52kW 380V 50Hz a.c Thrusters: 2 Thwart. FP thruster (f) Fuel: 114.0 (d.f.) 7.0pd
8660595 *XCUX5* -	**ZACATAL** *ex* Robin T *-2013* *ex* Robin Bordelon *-2012* *ex* Redeemer *-2012* **Unifin Financiera SAPI de CV SOFOM ENR** Marinsa de Mexico SA de CV *Ciudad del Carmen* *Mexico* MMSI: 345070402 Official number: 04013644275	**150** 45 -	Class: RI	**1981 Breaux Bay Craft, Inc. — Loreauville, La** Yd No: 1504 Loa 33.53 Br ex 7.32 Dght - Lbp - Br md 7.31 Dpth 1.83 Welded, 1 dk	**(B34J2SD) Crew Boat**	**4 oil engines** reduction geared to sc. shafts driving 4 Propellers 20.0k G.M. (Detroit Diesel) 12V-7 4 x Vee 2 Stroke 12 Cy. 108 x 127 Detroit Diesel Corporation-Detroit, Mi
5397501 - -	**ZACATECAS** *launched as* Mexico II *-1962* **Government of Mexico** *Veracruz* *Mexico*	*476* - -	Class: (LR) Classed LR until 3/64	**1962-03 Astilleros de Ulua — Veracruz** Loa 53.70 Br ex 8.34 Dght 3.074 Lbp 48.01 Br md 8.28 Dpth 4.02 Welded, 1 dk	**(A31A2GX) General Cargo Ship** Compartments: 1 Dp Ta in Hold, 1 Ho, ER 1 Ha: (7.7 x 4.2)	**1 oil engine** driving 1 FP propeller Total Power: 412kW (560hp) MaK MSU42 1 x 4 Stroke 6 Cy. 290 x 420 412kW (560bhp) Maschinenbau Kiel AG (MaK)-Kiel
9105621 - -	**ZACHARY** *ex* Taishin Maru *-2012* **Avega Bros Marine Carriers Inc**	*467* - 1,207		**1994-05 Yamakawa Zosen Tekko K.K. — Kagoshima** Yd No: 723 Loa 72.09 Br ex - Dght - Lbp 66.70 Br md 11.00 Dpth 6.30 Welded, 1 dk	**(A31A2GX) General Cargo Ship**	**1 oil engine** reverse geared to sc. shaft driving 1 FP propeller Total Power: 736kW (1,001hp) 11.5k Akasaka A31 1 x 4 Stroke 6 Cy. 310 x 600 736kW (1001bhp) Akasaka Tekkosho KK (Akasaka DieselLtd)-Japan
8982589 *WDF4780* -	**ZACHARY TAYLOR** *ex* Samuel P. *-2013* **R & R Boats Inc** - *New Orleans, LA* *United States of America* MMSI: 367455780 Official number: 1033999	**219** 65 -		**1995 Breaux Bay Craft, Inc. — Loreauville, La** Yd No: 1652 L reg 35.50 Br ex - Dght - Lbp - Br md 7.98 Dpth 3.35 Welded, 1 dk	**(B21A20C) Crew/Supply Vessel** Hull Material: Aluminium Alloy	**1 oil engine** driving 1 Propeller
7203302 *WCU4692* -	**ZACHERY REINAUER** *ex* Tioga *-1993* *ex* Mobil 1 *-1991* **Reinauer Transportation Companies LLC** - *New York, NY* *United States of America* MMSI: 366695940 Official number: 533403	*271* 184 -	Class: (AB)	**1971 Matton Shipyard Co., Inc. — Cohoes, NY** Yd No: 339 Loa - Br ex - Dght 3.785 Lbp 30.48 Br md 8.54 Dpth 4.55 Welded, 1 dk	**(B32A2ST) Tug**	**2 oil engines** reverse reduction geared to sc. shafts driving 2 FP propellers Total Power: 2,206kW (3,000hp) EMD (Electro-Motive) 12-645-E 2 x Vee 2 Stroke 12 Cy. 230 x 254 each-1103kW (1500bhp) General Motors Corp-USA AuxGen: 2 x 75kW Fuel: 173.5
9109079 *3FFX2* -	**ZAD ELKHIR** *ex* Gudrun *-2012* *ex* City of Oporto *-2004* *ex* Pelayo *-2001* *ex* City of Oporto *-1998* *ex* Jane *-1998* *ex* Gudrun *-1995* **Tarek Mustfa Aboamod** Al Anam General Trading SatCom: Inmarsat C 437390510 *Panama* *Panama* MMSI: 373905000 Official number: 43764PEXT1	**4,628** 2,447 5,660 T/cm 15.9	Class: BV (Class contemplated) GL	**1995-04 Detlef Hegemann Rolandwerft GmbH & Co. KG — Berne** Yd No: 173 Loa 113.28 (BB) Br ex - Dght 6.056 Lbp 104.92 Br md 16.40 Dpth 7.85 Welded, 1 dk	**(A33A2CC) Container Ship (Fully Cellular)** Grain: 7,504 TEU 510 C Ho 160 TEU C Dk 350 TEU incl 60 ref C. Compartments: 3 Cell Ho, ER 3 Ha: ER	**1 oil engine** with flexible couplings & sr geared to sc. shaft driving 1 CP propeller Total Power: 3,825kW (5,200hp) 16.0k MWM TBD645L 1 x 4 Stroke 9 Cy. 330 x 450 3825kW (5200bhp) Motoren Werke Mannheim AG (MWM)-Mannheim AuxGen: 1 x 600kW 400V 50Hz a.c, 2 x 248kW 400V 50Hz a.c Thrusters: 1 Thwart. FP thruster (f) Fuel: 125.0 (d.f.) 370.0 (r.f.) 18.5pd
9021485 *9A9766* -	**ZADAR** *ex* Isla de La Gomera *-2004* *ex* Ciudad de Tanger *-2003* *ex* Ibn Battouta 2 *-1998* **Jadrolinija** - *Rijeka* *Croatia* MMSI: 238201000 Official number: 2T-787	**9,487** 2,846 2,152	Class: BV CS	**1993-03 Hijos de J. Barreras S.A. — Vigo** Yd No: 1543 Loa 116.00 (BB) Br ex 18.92 Dght 5.150 Lbp 103.00 Br md 18.90 Dpth 7.15 Welded, 2 dks	**(A36A2PR) Passenger/Ro-Ro Ship (Vehicles)** Passengers: unberthed: 1300 Bow door/ramp Len: 13.00 Wid: 5.50 Swl: - Stern door/ramp Len: 10.50 Wid: 8.60 Swl: - Lane-Len: 450 Lane-clr ht: 4.70 Lorries: 29, Cars: 283	**2 oil engines** with flexible couplings & sr geared to sc. shafts driving 2 CP propellers Total Power: 7,002kW (9,520hp) 17.5k MAN 8L40/54 2 x 4 Stroke 8 Cy. 400 x 540 each-3501kW (4760bhp) EN Bazan de Construcciones NavalesMilitares SA-Spain Thrusters: 1 Thwart. CP thruster (f)
6723915 *5B7088* -	**ZAFER** *ex* Athina Sky I *-2002* *ex* Lady Linda I *-2001* *ex* Marianna II *-2001* *ex* Anna *-1998* *ex* Rigel K *-1997* *ex* Cenk II *-1997* *ex* Dursun Reis *-1993* *ex* Lisa B *-1990* *ex* Zejtun *-1982* *ex* Taos *-1974* *ex* Wasa *-1973* - - *Turkey*	**2,243** 673 1,377	Class: (HR) (BV) (GL)	**1967-09 J.J. Sietas Schiffswerft — Hamburg** Yd No: 606 Loa 78.80 Br ex - Dght 4.280 Lbp 74.40 Br md 13.85 Dpth 9.00 Welded, 2 dks	**(A35A2RR) Ro-Ro Cargo Ship** Stern ramp Lane-clr ht: 4.00 Lorries: 12, Cars: 250 Grain: 4,898; Bale: 4,530 TEU 86 C.Ho.58/20' (40') C.Dk.28/20' (40') Compartments: 1 Ho, ER 2 Ha: 2 (14.4 x 10.2)ER Derricks: 2x10.5t Ice Capable	**1 oil engine** driving 1 FP propeller Total Power: 1,618kW (2,200hp) 11.5k MaK 9ZU451A 1 x 4 Stroke 9 Cy. 320 x 450 1618kW (2200bhp) Atlas MaK Maschinenbau GmbH-Kiel AuxGen: 2 x 232kW 380V d.c, 1 x 175kW 380V d.c Fuel: 50.0 (d.f.) (Heating Coils) 90.0 (r.f.) 4.5pd
9655365 *9V9765* -	**ZAFER** **New Maritime Tankers Pte Ltd** New Maritime Pte Ltd *Singapore* *Singapore* MMSI: 566475000 Official number: 397562	**2,608** 1,139 3,941	Class: CC	**2012-06 Ningbo Dongsheng Shiprepair & Building Co Ltd — Xiangshan County ZJ** Yd No: BDS-02-1102A Loa 94.80 (BB) Br ex - Dght 5.400 Lbp 87.80 Br md 14.20 Dpth 6.90 Welded, 1 dk	**(A13B2TP) Products Tanker** Double Hull (13F) Compartments: 5 Wing Ta, 5 Wing Ta, 1 Wing Slop Ta, 1 Wing Slop Ta, ER Ice Capable	**1 oil engine** reduction geared to sc. shaft driving 1 FP propeller Total Power: 1,618kW (2,200hp) 12.0k Daihatsu 6DKM-2 1 x 4 Stroke 6 Cy. 260 x 380 1618kW (2200bhp) Anqing Marine Diesel Engine Works-China AuxGen: 3 x 250kW 400V a.c

IMO / Call sign	Name / Owner	Tonnage	Class	Builder / Dimensions	Type / Capacity	Machinery
9579315 *9HA2609*	**ZAFER** **Zafer Maritime Ltd** Ciner Gemi Acente Isletmeleri Sanayi ve Ticaret AS (Ciner Ship Management) SatCom: Inmarsat C 421502510 *Valletta* *Malta* MMSI: 215025000 Official number: 9579315	**23,204** 11,900 35,186	Class: AB	**2011-01 Samho Shipbuilding Co Ltd — Tongyeong** Yd No: 1233 Loa 180.47 (BB) Br ex - Dght 9.500 Lbp 172.00 Br md 30.00 Dpth 14.70 Welded, 1 dk	**(A21A2BC) Bulk Carrier** Grain: 48,148; Bale: 46,704 Compartments: 5 Ho, ER 5 Ha: ER Cranes: 4x35t	**1 oil engine** driving 1 FP propeller Total Power: 5,832kW (7,929hp) 14.2kn MAN-B&W 6S42MC 1 x 2 Stroke 6 Cy. 420 x 1764 5832kW (7929bhp) Hyundai Heavy Industries Co Ltd-South Korea AuxGen: 3 x 600kW a.c Fuel: 190.0 (d.f.) 1600.0 (r.f.)
7021390 -	**ZAFER-F** *ex* Lady Nadin *-2008* *ex* Lady Katerina *-2007* *ex* Timber Trader *-2006* *ex* Houssam *-2005* *ex* Nado Mar *-2005* *ex* Saturn *-2004* *ex* Fjordhav *-1988* *ex* Anders Kjonno *-1984* *ex* Grethe Steen *-1975* *ex* Gulf Navigator *-1972* *ex* Grethe Steen *-1971* - -	**782** 330 864	Class: (BV) (KC)	**1970-07 Orskovs Staalskibsvaerft A/S — Frederikshavn** Yd No: 59 Loa 55.33 Br ex 10.52 Dght 3.328 Lbp 49.69 Br md 10.51 Dpth 5.67 Welded, 2 dks	**(A31A2GX) General Cargo Ship** Grain: 1,800; Bale: 1,600 Compartments: 1 Ho, ER 1 Ha: (25.3 x 6.1)ER Derricks: 1x10t,1x5t; Winches: 2 Ice Capable	**1 oil engine** driving 1 CP propeller Total Power: 647kW (880hp) 11.0kn Alpha 408-26VO 1 x 2 Stroke 8 Cy. 260 x 400 647kW (880bhp) (new engine 1989) MAN B&W Diesel A/S-Denmark AuxGen: 2 x 64kW 380V a.c, 1 x 21kW 380V a.c Fuel: 67.0 (d.f.)
8518156 *T3YS* -	**ZAFER N** *ex* Dorothy Trader *-2004* *ex* Claudia *-1997* *ex* Lys Clipper *-1991* *ex* Neidenburg *-1990* **Act Star Inc** ACT Deniz Tasimaciligi Sanayi Ve Ticaret Ltd Sti *Tarawa* *Kiribati* MMSI: 529379000	**1,680** 708 2,632	Class: (RS) (GL)	**1986-04 Martin Jansen GmbH & Co. KG Schiffsw. u. Masch. — Leer** Yd No: 202 Loa 82.50 (BB) Br ex 10.83 Dght 4.152 Lbp 78.21 Br md 10.81 Dpth 6.02 Welded, 1 dk	**(A31A2GX) General Cargo Ship** Grain: 3,016; Bale: 2,953 TEU 72 C.Ho 48/20' (40') C.Dk 24/20' (40') Compartments: 1 Ho, ER 1 Ha: (49.2 x 8.5)ER Ice Capable	**1 oil engine** with clutches, flexible couplings & sr reverse geared to sc. shaft driving 1 FP propeller Total Power: 677kW (920hp) 10.5kn MWM TBD444-6 1 x 4 Stroke 6 Cy. 230 x 320 677kW (920bhp) Motoren Werke Mannheim AG (MWM)-West Germany Thrusters: 1 Thwart. FP thruster (f)
9016387 *9MIC6* -	**ZAFIRAH** *ex* Konpira Maru No. 2 *-2008* **EA Marine Services Sdn Bhd** - SatCom: Inmarsat C 453301117 *Port Klang* *Malaysia* MMSI: 533870000 Official number: 333907	*496* 330 1,125	Class: BV	**1991-03 Maebata Zosen Tekko K.K. — Sasebo** Yd No: 189 Converted From: Chemical Tanker-2008 Loa 65.50 Br ex - Dght 4.000 Lbp 59.00 Br md 10.00 Dpth 4.50 Welded, 1 dk	**(A13B2TP) Products Tanker**	**1 oil engine** driving 1 FP propeller Total Power: 736kW (1,001hp) 11.0kn Niigata 6M28BGT 1 x 4 Stroke 6 Cy. 280 x 480 736kW (1001bhp) Niigata Engineering Co Ltd-Japan
7311989 *D5FP* -	**ZAFIRO PRODUCER** *ex* Swift *-1995* *ex* Mobil Swift *-1992* *ex* Takakurasan Maru *-1978* **Mobil Equitorial Guinea Inc** - SatCom: Inmarsat A 1240606 *Monrovia* *Liberia* MMSI: 636006269 Official number: 6269	**133,118** 87,865 272,494 T/cm 164.7	Class: AB (NK)	**1973-05 Mitsui Eng. & SB. Co. Ltd., Chiba Works — Ichihara** Yd No: 961 Converted From: Crude Oil Tanker-1996 Loa 331.53 Br ex 56.06 Dght 20.581 Lbp 317.91 Br md 56.01 Dpth 26.42 Welded, 1 dk	**(B22E20F) FPSO, Oil** Single Hull Liq: 326,364; Liq (Oil): 326,364 Compartments: 16 Ta, ER 4 Cargo Pump (s) Manifold: Bow/CM: 195m	**1 oil engine** driving 1 FP propeller Total Power: 27,951kW (38,002hp) 15.0kn B&W 10K98FF 1 x 2 Stroke 10 Cy. 980 x 2000 27951kW (38002bhp) Mitsui Shipbuilding & Engineering CLtd-Japan AuxGen: 1 x 1120kW 450V 60Hz a.c, 2 x 760kW 450V 60Hz a.c Fuel: 433.5 (d.f.) 7419.5 (r.f.) 127.0pd
8816778 *CNGG* -	**ZAG** **Union Maroc Emirats Arabes Unis de Peche UMEP** - SatCom: Inmarsat C 424246810 *Casablanca* *Morocco*	**328** 124 325	Class: LR ✠ **100A1** SS 10/2009 stern trawler ✠ **LMC** Cable: 500.0/24.0 U2	**1989-10 Naval Gijon S.A. (NAGISA) — Gijon** Yd No: 495 Loa 39.45 Br ex 9.08 Dght 4.309 Lbp 33.02 Br md 9.01 Dpth 6.23 Welded, 2 dks	**(B11A2FS) Stern Trawler** Ins: 348	**1 oil engine** with clutches, flexible couplings & sr reverse geared to sc. shaft driving 1 FP propeller Total Power: 927kW (1,260hp) 11.8kn Deutz SBA6M628 1 x 4 Stroke 6 Cy. 240 x 280 927kW (1260bhp) Kloeckner Humboldt Deutz AG-West Germany AuxGen: 2 x 160kW 380V 50Hz a.c, 1 x 40kW 380V 50Hz a.c
9231171 *IBBQ* -	**ZAGARA** **Motia Compagnia di Navigazone SpA** - SatCom: Inmarsat B 324799280 *Palermo* *Italy* MMSI: 247060900	**25,651** 9,111 37,320 T/cm 50.8	Class: AB RI	**2002-04 STX Shipbuilding Co Ltd — Changwon (Jinhae Shipyard)** Yd No: 1072 Loa 180.00 (BB) Br ex 32.03 Dght 10.016 Lbp 171.20 Br md 32.00 Dpth 16.20 Welded, 1 dk	**(A12B2TR) Chemical/Products Tanker** Double Hull (13F) Liq: 43,381; Liq (Oil): 43,381 Compartments: 12 Wing Ta, 2 Wing Slop Ta, ER 12 Cargo Pump (s): 12x450m³/hr Manifold: Bow/CM: 88.9m	**1 oil engine** driving 1 FP propeller Total Power: 9,601kW (13,054hp) 14.6kn MAN-B&W 6S50MC 1 x 2 Stroke 6 Cy. 500 x 1910 9601kW (13054bhp) Doosan Engine Co Ltd-South Korea AuxGen: 3 x 615kW a.c Thrusters: 1 Tunnel thruster (f) Fuel: 114.8 (d.f.) 1442.2 (r.f.)
9235878 *SYXW* -	**ZAGORA** *ex* Hedwig Oldendorff *-2004* **Sea Powerful II Special Maritime Enterprise (ENE)** Goulandris Brothers (Hellas) Ltd *Andros* *Greece* MMSI: 240236000 Official number: 597	**38,391** 24,724 73,435 T/cm 65.4	Class: LR (AB) (NK) **100A1** SS 07/2011 bulk carrier, strengthened for heavy cargoes, Nos. 2, 4 & 6 holds may be empty ESN ESP LI **LMC** **UMS** Eq.Ltr: O†; Cable: 660.0/78.0 U3 (a)	**2001-07 Sumitomo Heavy Industries Ltd. — Yokosuka Shipyard, Yokosuka** Yd No: 1281 Loa 225.00 (BB) Br ex - Dght 13.850 Lbp 216.00 Br md 32.26 Dpth 19.20 Welded, 1 dk	**(A21A2BC) Bulk Carrier** Grain: 87,298 Compartments: 7 Ho, ER 7 Ha: ER	**1 oil engine** driving 1 FP propeller Total Power: 9,520kW (12,943hp) 14.5kn Sulzer 7RTA48T 1 x 2 Stroke 7 Cy. 480 x 2000 9520kW (12943bhp) Diesel United Ltd.-Aioi AuxGen: 3 x 475kW 450V 60Hz a.c Boilers: AuxB (Comp) 7.0kgf/cm² (6.9bar)
9111486 *9HA2662*	**ZAGORA** *ex* CMA CGM Belem *-2004* *ex* Hasselwerder *-2002* *ex* CMBT Oceania *-2000* *ex* Hasselwerder *-1996* **Idris Shipping Co** Costamare Shipping Co SA *Valletta* *Malta* MMSI: 215163000 Official number: 9111486	**10,795** 5,478 14,100 T/cm 29.3	Class: LR (GL) **100A1** SS 08/2010 container ship **LMC** **UMS** Eq.Ltr: E†; Cable: 577.5/56.0 U3 (a)	**1995-07 Stocznia Szczecinska SA — Szczecin** Yd No: B183/2/26 Loa 162.80 (BB) Br ex - Dght 8.100 Lbp 153.40 Br md 22.30 Dpth 11.10 Welded, 1 dk	**(A33A2CC) Container Ship (Fully Cellular)** TEU 1162 C Ho 390 TEU C Dk 782 TEU incl 102 ref C. Compartments: 4 Cell Ho, ER 8 Ha: (12.5 x 10.4)7 (12.5 x 18.0)ER Cranes: 3x40t	**1 oil engine** driving 1 CP propeller Total Power: 6,930kW (9,422hp) 17.7kn B&W 6L50MC 1 x 2 Stroke 6 Cy. 500 x 1620 6930kW (9422bhp) H Cegielski Poznan SA-Poland AuxGen: 1 x 1000kW 440/220V 60Hz a.c, 3 x 610kW 440/220V 60Hz a.c Boilers: e (ex.g.) 7.1kgf/cm² (7.0bar), AuxB (o.f.) 9.2kgf/cm² (9.0bar) Thrusters: 1 Thwart. FP thruster (f) Fuel: 1333.0
7384558 - -	**ZAGORSKIY** - -	**2,027** 608 823	Class: (RS)	**1975-04 Stocznia Polnocna im Bohaterow Westerplatte — Gdansk** Yd No: B422/113 Loa 72.83 Br ex 13.01 Dght 4.852 Lbp 65.00 Br md - Dpth 7.90 Welded, 2 dks	**(B11A2FS) Stern Trawler** Grain: 119; Ins: 775; Liq: 117 Compartments: 3 Ho, ER 2 Ha: Derricks: 2x5t,4x1.5t; Winches: 4 Ice Capable	**3 diesel electric oil engines** driving 3 gen. each 750kW Connecting to 1 elec. Motor driving 1 CP propeller Total Power: 2,298kW (3,123hp) 13.0kn Sulzer 6ASL25/30 3 x 4 Stroke 6 Cy. 250 x 300 each-766kW (1041bhp) Zaklady Przemyslu Metalowego 'HCegielski' SA-Poznan AuxGen: 1 x 320kW 400V 50Hz a.c, 1 x 72kW 400V 50Hz a.c
9384502 *9AA5910*	**ZAGREB** **Atlant Tramp Corp** Atlantska Plovidba dd *Dubrovnik* *Croatia* MMSI: 238249000 Official number: 7T-479	**43,717** 26,399 80,300 T/cm 71.9	Class: CS LR ✠ **100A1** SS 10/2013 bulk carrier BC-A strengthened for heavy cargoes, Nos. 2, 4 & 6 holds may be empty, ESP **ShipRight** (SDA, FDA, CM) ESN *IWS LI Ice Class 1D at draught of 14.934m Max/min draughts fwd 14.745/4.714m ✠ **LMC** **UMS** Eq.Ltr: Q†; Cable: 677.0/81.0 U3 (a)	**2008-10 Jiangsu Eastern Heavy Industry Co Ltd — Jingjiang JS** Yd No: 05C-061 Loa 229.00 (BB) Br ex 32.30 Dght 14.580 Lbp 222.00 Br md 32.26 Dpth 20.25 Welded, 1 dk	**(A21A2BC) Bulk Carrier** Double Hull Grain: 97,000; Bale: 90,784 Compartments: 7 Ho, ER 7 Ha: 5 (18.3 x 15.0) (15.7 x 15.1)ER (13.1 x 13.2) Ice Capable	**1 oil engine** driving 1 FP propeller Total Power: 11,620kW (15,799hp) 14.0kn Wartsila 7RT-Flex50 1 x 2 Stroke 7 Cy. 500 x 2050 11620kW (15799bhp) Yichang Marine Diesel Engine Co Ltd-China AuxGen: 3 x 700kW 450V 60Hz a.c Boilers: AuxB (Comp) 8.8kgf/cm² (8.6bar) Fuel: 163.0 (d.f.) 2572.0 (r.f.)
7336616 - -	**ZAHARA DE LOS ATUNES** - -	*238* 81 203	Class: (BV)	**1974-01 Sociedad Metalurgica Duro Felguera — Gijon** Yd No: 104 Loa 37.34 Br ex 7.47 Dght 3.849 Lbp 32.01 Br md 7.40 Dpth 4.02 Welded, 1 dk	**(B11A2FT) Trawler** Grain: 380 Compartments: 2 Ho, ER	**1 oil engine** driving 1 FP propeller Total Power: 736kW (1,001hp) 11.5kn Krupps 1 x 4 Stroke 8 Cy. 295 x 420 736kW (1001bhp) La Maquinista Terrestre y Mar (MTM)-Spain Fuel: 125.0 (d.f.)

Ship	Tonnage	Class	Builder / Dimensions	Type	Machinery
9292333 **ZAHARA DOS** *ECGS* 3-CA-37-03 **Albacora SA (GRUPO ALBACORA)** - *Cadiz* *Spain* MMSI: 224307000 Official number: 3-7/2003	**193** - -		**2004-09 Astilleros Ria de Aviles SL — Nieva** Yd No: 90 Loa 35.20 Br ex - Dght - Lbp - Br md 7.50 Dpth 3.60 Welded, 1 dk	**(B11B2FV) Fishing Vessel**	**1 oil engine** geared to sc. shaft driving 1 Propeller Total Power: 478kW (650hp) GUASCOR F360TB-SP 1 x Vee 4 Stroke 12 Cy. 152 x 165 478kW (650bhp) Gutierrez Ascunce Corp (GUASCOR)-Spain
9292735 **ZAHARA TRES** *ECHG* 3-CA-38-03 **Albacora SA (GRUPO ALBACORA)** - *Cadiz* *Spain* MMSI: 224303000 Official number: 3-8/2003	**193** - -		**2004-11 Astilleros Ria de Aviles SL — Nieva** Yd No: 91 Loa 35.20 Br ex - Dght - Lbp - Br md 7.50 Dpth 3.60 Welded, 1 dk	**(B11B2FV) Fishing Vessel**	**1 oil engine** geared to sc. shaft driving 1 Propeller Total Power: 478kW (650hp) GUASCOR F360TB-SP 1 x Vee 4 Stroke 12 Cy. 152 x 165 478kW (650bhp) Gutierrez Ascunce Corp (GUASCOR)-Spain
9292321 **ZAHARA UNO** *ECFS* 3-CA-36-03 **Albacora SA (GRUPO ALBACORA)** - *Cadiz* *Spain* MMSI: 224276000 Official number: 3-6/2003	**193** - -		**2004-07 Astilleros Ria de Aviles SL — Nieva** Yd No: 89 Loa 35.20 Br ex - Dght - Lbp - Br md 7.50 Dpth 3.60 Welded, 1 dk	**(B11B2FV) Fishing Vessel**	**1 oil engine** geared to sc. shaft driving 1 Propeller Total Power: 588kW (799hp) GUASCOR F360TB-SP 1 x Vee 4 Stroke 12 Cy. 152 x 165 588kW (799bhp) Gutierrez Ascunce Corp (GUASCOR)-Spain
8423143 **ZAHARAH** *9MAB4* - **Perkhidmatan Perkapalan Chembee (Malaysia) Sdn Bhd** - *Penang* *Malaysia* Official number: 325398	*133* 38 -		**1984 Hong Leong-Lurssen Shipyard Bhd — Butterworth** Loa 21.75 Br ex 8.01 Dght - Lbp - Br md - Dpth 3.00 Welded, 1 dk	**(A37B2PS) Passenger Ship**	**2 oil engines** driving 2 FP propellers Total Power: 650kW (884hp) MAN D2542MTE 2 x Vee 4 Stroke 12 Cy. 125 x 142 each-325kW (442bhp) Maschinenbau Augsburg Nuernberg (MAN)-Augsburg
7931985 **ZAHER 1** *ODVS* *ex* Med Vision *-2011* *ex* Aylmer *-2010* *ex* Assil *-2006* *ex* Scan Nordic *-2005* *ex* Nordic *-2003* *ex* Nordic Link *-2003* **Bissar Sleiman & Karim Sleiman** Tamara Shipping *Beirut* *Lebanon* MMSI: 450548000 Official number: B-4347	**12,630** 5,542 6,805	Class: BV (LR) (RS) (BR) ✠ Classed LR until 18/2/09	**1981-06 AB Finnboda Varf — Stockholm** Yd No: 414 Converted From: Ro-Ro Cargo Ship-2012 Loa 120.20 Br ex 21.04 Dght 6.768 Lbp 111.21 Br md 21.01 Dpth 14.51 Welded, 8 dks	**(A38A2GL) Livestock Carrier** Ice Capable	**1 oil engine** sr geared to sc. shaft driving 1 CP propeller Total Power: 4,720kW (6,417hp) 14.5kn Pielstick 12PC2-3V-400 1 x Vee 4 Stroke 12 Cy. 400 x 460 4720kW (6417bhp) Lindholmen Motor AB-Sweden AuxGen: 1 x 600kW 450V 60Hz a.c, 3 x 800kW 450V 60Hz a.c Thrusters: 1 Thwart. FP thruster (f)
7104972 **ZAHER III** *ODQV* - *ex* Bismillah *-1995* *ex* Oruda *-1994* *ex* Bismillah *-1984* **Zoha Ali Assaf** Tamara Shipping SatCom: Inmarsat B 3307100978 *Beirut* *Lebanon* MMSI: 450421000 Official number: B-4259	**3,181** 1,107 2,794	Class: BV (HR) (NV) (CS) (JR)	**1971-10 Molde Verft AS — Hjelset** Yd No: (60) **1971-10 Ulstein Mek. Verksted AS — Ulsteinvik** Yd No: 60 Converted From: General Cargo Ship (with Ro-Ro Facility)-1998 Loa 87.03 (BB) Br ex 15.04 Dght 6.154 Lbp 77.35 Br md 15.02 Dpth 10.85 Welded, 3 dks	**(A38A2GL) Livestock Carrier** Side doors (s) Ice Capable	**1 oil engine** geared to sc. shaft driving 1 CP propeller Total Power: 3,236kW (4,400hp) 14.8kn Werkspoor 8TM410 1 x 4 Stroke 8 Cy. 410 x 470 3236kW (4400bhp) Stork Werkspoor Diesel BV-Netherlands AuxGen: 3 x 160kW 450V 60Hz a.c Thrusters: 1 Thwart. FP thruster (f) Fuel: 23.5 (d.f.) 219.0 (r.f.) 19.0pd
6703343 **ZAHER V** *ODTX* - *ex* Afroditi *-1995* *ex* Fastock *-1987* *ex* Livestock *-1984* *ex* Purcell Livestock *-1982* *ex* Somerset *-1981* **Christina D Moratides** Tamara Shipping *Beirut* *Lebanon* MMSI: 450501000 Official number: B-4315	**6,542** 1,963 2,045	Class: CS (PR) (HR) (BV)	**1966-03 Helsingor Skibsvaerft og Maskinbyggeri A/S — Helsingor** Yd No: 380 Converted From: Ro-Ro Cargo Ship-1981 Lengthened-1973 Loa 124.19 Br ex 17.02 Dght 5.411 Lbp 108.59 Br md 17.00 Dpth 5.92 Welded, 2 dks	**(A38A2GL) Livestock Carrier** Ice Capable	**4 oil engines** geared to sc. shafts driving 2 FP propellers Total Power: 4,856kW (6,604hp) 20.0kn B&W 10-26MTBF-40V 4 x Vee 4 Stroke 10 Cy. 260 x 400 each-1214kW (1651bhp) Holeby Dieselmotor Fabrik A/S-Denmark Thrusters: 1 Thwart. FP thruster (f) Fuel: 236.5 (d.f.) 20.5pd
7723534 **ZAHRA** - - - - *Khorramshahr* *Iran*	*241* 22 219	Class: (AB)	**1977-12 Promet Pte Ltd — Singapore** Yd No: 136 Loa 36.58 Br ex - Dght 3.010 Lbp 33.15 Br md 8.54 Dpth 3.66 Welded, 1 dk	**(B34L2QU) Utility Vessel**	**2 oil engines** geared to sc. shafts driving 2 FP propellers Total Power: 832kW (1,132hp) Caterpillar D379SCAC 2 x Vee 4 Stroke 8 Cy. 159 x 203 each-416kW (566bhp) Caterpillar Tractor Co-USA
8201208 **ZAHRA** - - **West Coast Fisheries Ltd** - *Lagos* *Nigeria*	*130* - -		**1981 Marine Mart, Inc. — Port Isabel, Tx** Loa 25.33 Br ex - Dght - Lbp - Br md - Dpth - Welded, 1 dk	**(B11A2FT) Trawler**	**1 oil engine** driving 1 FP propeller Total Power: 382kW (519hp) Caterpillar 3412TA 1 x Vee 4 Stroke 12 Cy. 137 x 152 382kW (519bhp) Caterpillar Tractor Co-USA
9581473 **ZAHRAT AL BEHAR** *A4D09* - **Khimji's Sparkle Marine Services Co LLC** - *Port Sultan Qaboos* *Oman* MMSI: 461000096 Official number: 94	**346** 103 218	Class: AB	**2010-11 Hin Lee (Zhuhai) Shipyard Co Ltd — Zhuhai GD (Hull)** Yd No: 222 **2010-11 Cheoy Lee Shipyards Ltd — Hong Kong** Yd No: 5013 Loa 30.50 Br ex - Dght 4.000 Lbp 26.66 Br md 9.80 Dpth 4.88 Welded, 1 dk	**(B32A2ST) Tug**	**2 oil engines** reduction geared to sc. shafts driving 2 Z propellers Total Power: 2,942kW (4,000hp) Niigata 6L26HLX 2 x 4 Stroke 6 Cy. 260 x 350 each-1471kW (2000bhp) Niigata Engineering Co Ltd-Japan AuxGen: 2 x 108kW a.c
5306875 **ZAHRATHALLAH** *HZNS* - *ex* Rana *-1981* *ex* Wyegarth *-1980* *ex* St. Woolos *-1977* **Oriental Commercial & Shipping Co Ltd** - *Jeddah* *Saudi Arabia*	*152* 55 -	Class: (LR) (BV) ✠ Classed LR until 11/61	**1960-01 P K Harris & Sons Ltd — Bideford** Yd No: 118 Loa 28.35 Br ex 8.18 Dght 3.048 Lbp 26.12 Br md 7.83 Dpth 3.59 Welded, 1 dk	**(B32A2ST) Tug**	**2 oil engines** geared to sc. shafts driving 2 FP propellers Total Power: 882kW (1,200hp) 11.0kn Blackstone ERS8M 2 x 4 Stroke 8 Cy. 222 x 292 each-441kW (600bhp) Lister Blackstone Marine Ltd.-Dursley AuxGen: 2 x 50kW 110V d.c
8303769 **ZAIN** *A6E2284* - *ex* Arab Leo *-2005* *ex* Union Leo *-1989* **Gulf Glory Marine Services (LLC)** Whitesea Shipping & Supply (LLC) SatCom: Inmarsat C 447047410 *Dubai* *United Arab Emirates* MMSI: 470474000 Official number: 777	**614** 185 671	Class: GL (NK)	**1983-07 Kanagawa Zosen — Kobe** Yd No: 252 Loa 49.92 Br ex - Dght 3.852 Lbp 46.28 Br md 11.02 Dpth 4.53 Welded, 1 dk	**(B21B20T) Offshore Tug/Supply Ship** Cranes: 1x5t	**2 oil engines** sr geared to sc. shafts driving 2 CP propellers Total Power: 2,648kW (3,600hp) 12.5kn Pielstick 6PA5 2 x 4 Stroke 6 Cy. 255 x 270 each-1324kW (1800bhp) Niigata Engineering Co Ltd-Japan AuxGen: 2 x 175kW 445V 60Hz a.c Thrusters: 1 Thwart. CP thruster (f)
6907327 **ZAINAB** *HO2874* - *ex* Noora 1 *-2007* *ex* Blue Jade *-2005* *ex* Stella *-1989* *ex* Pelti *-1989* *ex* Gabrielle *-1980* *ex* Rodon *-1979* *ex* Jodonna *-1976* **Jassim K Addulhasan Al-Lami** Allami Shipping Services LLC *Panama* *Panama* MMSI: 372782000 Official number: 35673PEXT	**1,276** 784 2,136	Class: (GL)	**1968 Angyalfold Shipyard, Hungarian Ship & Crane Works — Budapest** Yd No: 2131 Loa 71.46 Br ex 11.54 Dght 5.309 Lbp 65.21 Br md 11.21 Dpth 6.28 Welded, 2 dks	**(A31A2GX) General Cargo Ship** Grain: 2,832; Bale: 2,492 Compartments: 2 Ho, ER 2 Ha: (16.7 x 7.0) (17.3 x 7.0) Derricks: 1x10t,3x5t Ice Capable	**1 oil engine** driving 1 FP propeller Total Power: 1,103kW (1,500hp) 11.5kn Sulzer 6TAD36 1 x 2 Stroke 6 Cy. 360 x 600 1103kW (1500bhp) Tvornica Dizel Motora 'Jugoturbina'-Yugoslavia
8134766 **ZAINALREZA II** - - **Haji Abdullah Alireza & Co Ltd** - *Dhahran* *Saudi Arabia*	*173* - -	Class: (BV)	**1976 B.V. Scheepswerf Damen Hardinxveld — Hardinxveld-Giessendam** Loa - Br ex - Dght - Lbp 15.70 Br md 4.81 Dpth 2.32 Welded, 1 dk	**(B34L2QU) Utility Vessel**	**1 oil engine** driving 1 FP propeller Total Power: 171kW (232hp) 8.8kn Caterpillar 3306TA 1 x 4 Stroke 6 Cy. 121 x 152 171kW (232bhp) Caterpillar Tractor Co-USA
7821491 **ZAIZOOM** *V4LB2* - *ex* Sara Folk *-2012* *ex* Agios Nikolaos *-2009* *ex* Samudra Ayu *-2003* *ex* Agios Nikolaos *-2003* *ex* Samudra Ayu *-2003* *ex* Hope No. 1 *-1990* *ex* Jeddah Hope *-1989* *ex* Tatsumiya Maru No. 8 *-1983* **Byar Ali Petroleum Trading Inc** Soqya Commercial Broker LLC *Basseterre* *St Kitts & Nevis* MMSI: 341138000 Official number: SKN 1002292	**3,082** 1,280 4,350	Class: (NK) (KI)	**1979-03 Imabari Shipbuilding Co Ltd — Imabari EH (Imabari Shipyard)** Yd No: 383 Loa 97.69 Br ex 16.51 Dght 5.572 Lbp 92.00 Br md 16.50 Dpth 6.50 Welded, 1 dk	**(A13B2TP) Products Tanker** Double Hull (13F) Liq: 4,473; Liq (Oil): 4,474 1 Cargo Pump (s): 1x1500m³/hr Manifold: Bow/CM: 46.9m	**1 oil engine** driving 1 CP propeller Total Power: 2,354kW (3,200hp) 12.0kn Hanshin 6LU50A 1 x 4 Stroke 6 Cy. 500 x 800 2354kW (3200bhp) (made 1979) The Hanshin Diesel Works Ltd-Japan AuxGen: 3 x 560kW 445V 60Hz a.c Fuel: 32.0 (d.f.) 190.0 (r.f.) 11.5pd

385564 **ZAKAIA**
*BBJ
ex Ponmudi *-2010* *ex* Blair *-2007*
ex Zakareia *-2006* *ex* Samawada *-2003*
ex Zebulun *-2001* *ex* Metro *-1997*
ex Mustansir *-1996* *ex* Extramar Sur *-1993*
GH Bakhtiyari
-
Bandar Imam Khomeini *Iran*
MMSI: 422575000
Official number: 772

1,255 799 1,927
Class: AS IS (LR) (HR)
✠ Classed LR until 12/9/96

1976-05 Ast. y Talleres Celaya S.A. — Bilbao
Yd No: 153
Loa 77.02 (BB) Br ex 11.84 Dght 4.525
Lbp 69.02 Br md 11.76 Dpth 5.26
Welded, 1 dk

(A31A2GX) General Cargo Ship
Grain: 2,964; Bale: 2,617
TEU 76 C.Ho 40/20' (40') C.Dk 36/20' (40')
Compartments: 1 Ho, ER
1 Ha: (43.9 x 7.7)ER

1 oil engine driving 1 FP propeller
Total Power: 1,177kW (1,600hp) 12.5kn
MaK 8M451AK
1 x 4 Stroke 8 Cy. 320 x 450 1177kW (1600bhp)
MaK Maschinenbau GmbH-Kiel
AuxGen: 2 x 72kW 380V 50Hz a.c, 1 x 28kW 380V 50Hz a.c
Fuel: 135.0 (d.f.) 5.0pd

951413 **ZAKAMSK**
*6BJ2
ex Akvamarin *-2003* *ex* Volgo-Balt 27 *-1999*
Private Enterprise 'Valship'
-
SatCom: Inmarsat C 461681910
Moroni *Union of Comoros*
MMSI: 616819000

2,406 1,030 3,328
Class: UA (RS) (RR)

1966-11 Astrakhanskaya Sudoverf im. "Kirova" — Astrakhan Yd No: 2721
Loa 114.15 Br ex 13.22 Dght 3.660
Lbp 107.08 Br md 13.00 Dpth 5.50
Welded, 1 dk

(A31A2GX) General Cargo Ship
Grain: 4,500
Compartments: 4 Ho, ER
4 Ha: ER

2 oil engines driving 2 FP propellers
Total Power: 970kW (1,318hp) 10.0kn
S.K.L. 6NVD48A-U
2 x 4 Stroke 6 Cy. 320 x 480 each-485kW (659bhp)
VEB Schwermaschinenbau "KarlLiebknecht" (SKL)-Magdeburg
AuxGen: 3 x 50kW a.c
Fuel: 97.0 (d.f.)

005962 **ZAKARIA 3**
*OPY
ex Tokuyo Maru No. 25 *-2012*
-
-
Indonesia
MMSI: 525010165

699 - 946
Class: (NK)

1990-10 Shitanoe Shipbuilding Co Ltd — Usuki OT
Yd No: 1112
Loa 64.83 (BB) Br ex 12.02 Dght 4.031
Lbp 60.00 Br md 12.00 Dpth 4.90
Welded, 1 dk

(A11B2TG) LPG Tanker
Liq (Gas): 1,507
3 x Gas Tank (s);

1 oil engine reverse reduction geared to sc. shaft driving 1 FP propeller
Total Power: 736kW (1,001hp) 10.0kn
Akasaka K31SFD
1 x 4 Stroke 6 Cy. 310 x 530 736kW (1001bhp)
Akasaka Tekkosho KK (Akasaka DieselLtd)-Japan
AuxGen: 4 x 146kW a.c
Fuel: 130.0 (d.f.)

921535 **ZAKARIA 5**
ZAU
ex Platinum 1 *-2013* *ex* Hoju Maru *-2005*
ex Takasago Maru No. 3 *-1999*
PT Tri Ariesta Dinamika
-
Indonesia

1,069 325 951
Class: (NK)

1990-10 Shirahama Zosen K.K. — Honai
Yd No: 147
Loa 65.00 (BB) Br ex - Dght 4.050
Lbp 60.00 Br md 11.00 Dpth 5.10
Welded, 1 dk

(A11B2TG) LPG Tanker
Double Bottom Entire Compartment Length
Liq (Gas): 1,247
2 x Gas Tank (s);
2 Cargo Pump (s): 2x300m³/hr

1 oil engine driving 1 FP propeller
Total Power: 1,324kW (1,800hp) 12.8kn
Akasaka A31R
1 x 4 Stroke 6 Cy. 310 x 600 1324kW (1800bhp)
Akasaka Tekkosho KK (Akasaka DieselLtd)-Japan
AuxGen: 3 x 150kW a.c

740709 **ZAKARIA I**

PT Tri Ariesta Dinamika
-
Samarinda *Indonesia*

485 146 -
Class: KI

2009-05 C.V. Karya Lestari Industri — Samarinda
Loa 54.35 Br ex - Dght -
Lbp 50.10 Br md 10.50 Dpth 3.20
Welded, 1 dk

(A35D2RL) Landing Craft

2 oil engines driving 2 Propellers
Total Power: 1,000kW (1,360hp)
Yanmar 6AYM-ETE
2 x 4 Stroke 6 Cy. 155 x 180 each-500kW (680bhp)
Yanmar Diesel Engine Co Ltd-Japan

607256 **ZAKHAR SOROKIN**
*DYG
1-0006
Taurus CJSC
Murmansk Trawl Fleet Co (OAO 'Murmanskiy Tralovyy Flot')
SatCom: Inmarsat A 1400770
Murmansk *Russia*
MMSI: 273522400
Official number: 891420

7,765 2,329 3,372
Class: RS

1989-08 VEB Volkswerft Stralsund — Stralsund
Yd No: 816
Loa 120.48 Br ex - Dght 6.632
Lbp 108.13 Br md 19.02 Dpth 12.25
Welded, 1 dk

(B11A2FG) Factory Stern Trawler
Ins: 3,900

2 oil engines with clutches, flexible couplings & reduction geared to sc. shaft driving 1 CP propeller
Total Power: 5,298kW (7,204hp) 14.9kn
S.K.L. 6VDS48/42AL-2
2 x 4 Stroke 6 Cy. 420 x 480 each-2649kW (3602bhp)
VEB Schwermaschinenbau "KarlLiebknecht" (SKL)-Magdeburg
AuxGen: 2 x 1500kW a.c, 2 x 760kW a.c

434280 **ZAKHER ADMIRAL**
8B3790
Zakher Marine International Inc
-
Kingstown *St Vincent & The Grenadines*
MMSI: 377128000
Official number: 10263

890 267 -
Class: BV

2007-11 Tuong Aik Shipyard Sdn Bhd — Sibu
Yd No: 2613
Loa 47.00 Br ex - Dght 4.000
Lbp 41.40 Br md 12.80 Dpth 4.85
Welded, 1 dk

(B21B20A) Anchor Handling Tug Supply
Cranes: 1x5t

2 oil engines reduction geared to sc. shafts driving 2 FP propellers
Total Power: 2,574kW (3,500hp) 12.0kn
Caterpillar 3512B-HD
2 x Vee 4 Stroke 12 Cy. 170 x 215 each-1287kW (1750bhp)
Caterpillar Inc-USA
AuxGen: 2 x 245kW 415V 50Hz a.c
Thrusters: 1 Tunnel thruster (f)

640865 **ZAKHER ALPHA**
8B4723
ex Jaya Aster *-2012*
Zakher Marine International Inc
-
SatCom: Inmarsat C 437606810
Kingstown *St Vincent & The Grenadines*
MMSI: 376068000
Official number: 11196

1,575 472 1,350
Class: BV

2012-06 Guangzhou Hangtong Shipbuilding & Shipping Co Ltd — Jiangmen GD
Yd No: HT102103
Loa 60.50 Br ex - Dght 4.750
Lbp 55.00 Br md 14.60 Dpth 5.50
Welded, 1 dk

(B21B20A) Anchor Handling Tug Supply

2 oil engines reduction geared to sc. shafts driving 2 CP propellers
Total Power: 3,282kW (4,462hp) 13.5kn
Caterpillar 3516B
2 x Vee 4 Stroke 16 Cy. 170 x 190 each-1641kW (2231bhp)
Caterpillar Inc-USA
AuxGen: 2 x 1012kW 50Hz a.c, 2 x 450kW 50Hz a.c
Fuel: 510.0

582219 **ZAKHER AMAZON**
8B4757
ex Jaya Amazon *-2012*
Zakher Marine International Inc
-
Kingstown *St Vincent & The Grenadines*
MMSI: 375217000
Official number: 11230

1,458 437 1,351
Class: AB

2011-01 Guangzhou Hangtong Shipbuilding & Shipping Co Ltd — Jiangmen GD
Yd No: 072010
Loa 58.70 Br ex - Dght 4.762
Lbp 53.20 Br md 14.60 Dpth 5.50
Welded, 1 dk

(B21B20A) Anchor Handling Tug Supply

2 oil engines reduction geared to sc. shafts driving 2 CP propellers
Total Power: 3,240kW (4,406hp) 10.0kn
Wartsila 9L20
2 x 4 Stroke 9 Cy. 200 x 280 each-1620kW (2203bhp)
Wartsila Finland Oy-Finland
AuxGen: 3 x 430kW a.c
Thrusters: 2 Tunnel thruster (f)
Fuel: 480.0 (d.f.)

309825 **ZAKHER AWAL**
9D2813
ex Pac-Union *-2004*
Awal Marine Services Establishment WLL
Zakher Marine International Inc
Bahrain *Bahrain*
MMSI: 408765000
Official number: BN 3073

252 75 132
Class: AB

2003-12 Jiangsu Wuxi Shipyard Co Ltd — Wuxi JS (Hull) Yd No: (1148)
2003-12 Pacific Ocean Engineering & Trading Pte Ltd (POET) — Singapore Yd No: 1148
Loa 29.00 Br ex - Dght 3.500
Lbp 27.00 Br md 9.00 Dpth 4.20
Welded, 1 dk

(B32A2ST) Tug

2 oil engines reduction geared to sc. shafts driving 2 FP propellers
Total Power: 2,060kW (2,800hp)
Yanmar 8N21A-UN
2 x 4 Stroke 8 Cy. 210 x 290 each-1030kW (1400bhp)
Yanmar Diesel Engine Co Ltd-Japan
AuxGen: 2 x 160kW 415V 50Hz a.c
Thrusters: 1 Tunnel thruster (f)

131345 **ZAKHER BRAVO**
8TA7
ex Nordic Bravo *-2005* *ex* Bravo *-2000*
ex PM 204 *-1997*
Zakher Marine International Inc
-
Kingstown *St Vincent & The Grenadines*
MMSI: 376111000
Official number: 7413

245 73 335
Class: AB

1996-12 President Marine Pte Ltd — Singapore
Yd No: 204
Loa 29.00 Br ex - Dght 3.720
Lbp 27.07 Br md 8.60 Dpth 4.08
Welded, 1 dk

(B32A2ST) Tug

2 oil engines geared to sc. shafts driving 2 FP propellers
Total Power: 1,766kW (2,402hp) 10.0kn
Yanmar M220-EN
2 x 4 Stroke 6 Cy. 220 x 300 each-883kW (1201bhp)
Yanmar Diesel Engine Co Ltd-Japan
AuxGen: 2 x 60kW a.c
Thrusters: 1 Tunnel thruster (f)

535890 **ZAKHER COMMANDER**
6ET3

Zakher Marine International Inc
-
Moroni *Union of Comoros*
MMSI: 616728000
Official number: 1200852

1,973 592 1,850
Class: AB

2009-12 Berjaya Dockyard Sdn Bhd — Miri
Yd No: 59
Loa 61.20 Br ex - Dght 5.090
Lbp 59.30 Br md 16.00 Dpth 6.00
Welded, 1 dk

(B21B20A) Anchor Handling Tug Supply

2 oil engines reduction geared to sc. shafts driving 2 CP propellers
Total Power: 3,840kW (5,220hp) 12.0kn
Caterpillar 3516B-HD
2 x Vee 4 Stroke 16 Cy. 170 x 215 each-1920kW (2610bhp)
Caterpillar Inc-USA
AuxGen: 2 x 405kW 415V 50Hz a.c, 2 x a.c
Thrusters: 1 Thwart. CP thruster (f); 1 Thwart. CP thruster (a)
Fuel: 470.0 (d.f.)

545194 **ZAKHER CREST**
8B4229
Zakher Marine International Inc
-
Kingstown *St Vincent & The Grenadines*
MMSI: 376347000
Official number: 10702

1,405 421 1,500
Class: BV

2009-10 Tuong Aik Shipyard Sdn Bhd — Sibu
Yd No: 2801
Loa 60.00 Br ex - Dght 4.500
Lbp 54.40 Br md 13.80 Dpth 5.50
Welded, 1 dk

(B21B20A) Anchor Handling Tug Supply

2 oil engines reduction geared to sc. shafts driving 2 FP propellers
Total Power: 4,414kW (6,002hp) 10.0kn
Mitsubishi S12U-MPTK
2 x Vee 4 Stroke 12 Cy. 240 x 260 each-2207kW (3001bhp)
Mitsubishi Heavy Industries Ltd-Japan
AuxGen: 3 x 245kW 415V 50Hz a.c
Thrusters: 1 Directional thruster (f)

309318 **ZAKHER DELMON**
9GS
ex Tongbao Hope *-2005*
Awal Marine Services Establishment WLL
Zakher Marine International Inc
Bahrain *Bahrain*
MMSI: 408774000

1,159 347 998
T/cm 6.6
Class: BV (CC)

2005-01 Hangzhou Dongfeng Shipbuilding Co Ltd — Hangzhou ZJ Yd No: 2001-28
Loa 59.90 Br ex - Dght 4.500
Lbp 55.00 Br md 12.40 Dpth 5.80
Welded, 1 dk

(B21B20A) Anchor Handling Tug Supply

2 oil engines reduction geared to sc. shafts driving 2 CP propellers
Total Power: 2,880kW (3,916hp) 10.0kn
Wartsila 8L20
2 x 4 Stroke 8 Cy. 200 x 280 each-1440kW (1958bhp)
Wartsila Finland Oy-Finland
AuxGen: 3 x 250kW 440/220V 50Hz a.c
Thrusters: 1 Tunnel thruster (f)
Fuel: 678.0 (d.f.)

9387475 *J8B3400* -
ZAKHER DOLPHIN
Zakher Marine International Inc
Kingstown *St Vincent & The Grenadines*
MMSI: 375355000
Official number: 9872
575 172 489 Class: AB
2006-07 Jiangsu Wuxi Shipyard Co Ltd — Wuxi JS (Hull) Yd No: (1198)
2006-07 Pacific Ocean Engineering & Trading Pte Ltd (POET) — Singapore Yd No: 1198
Loa 42.90 Br ex - Dght 3.600
Lbp 38.50 Br md 10.00 Dpth 4.20
Welded, 1 dk
(B22A20V) Diving Support Vessel
2 oil engines reduction geared to sc. shafts driving 2 CP propellers
Total Power: 2,648kW (3,600hp)
Yanmar 8N21A-E
2 x 4 Stroke 8 Cy. 210 x 290 each-1324kW (1800bhp)
Yanmar Diesel Engine Co Ltd-Japan
AuxGen: 3 x 145kW a.c
Thrusters: 1 Tunnel thruster (f)

9545235 *A9IO* -
ZAKHER DUTY
Awal Marine Services Establishment WLL
Zakher Marine International Inc
SatCom: Inmarsat C 440834910
Bahrain *Bahrain*
MMSI: 408349000
1,405 421 1,500 Class: BV
2009-06 Tuong Aik Shipyard Sdn Bhd — Sibu Yd No: 2705
Loa 60.00 Br ex - Dght 4.500
Lbp 54.40 Br md 13.80 Dpth 5.50
Welded, 1 dk
(B21B20A) Anchor Handling Tug Supply
2 oil engines geared to sc. shafts driving 2 FP propellers
Total Power: 3,676kW (4,998hp) 10.0k
Niigata 6MG28H
2 x 4 Stroke 6 Cy. 280 x 370 each-1838kW (2499bhp)
Niigata Engineering Co Ltd-Japan
AuxGen: 3 x 245kW 415V 50Hz
Thrusters: 1 Tunnel thruster (f)

9488463 *D6EL2* -
ZAKHER EAGLE
Zakher Marine International Inc
Moroni *Union of Comoros*
MMSI: 616663000
Official number: 1200772
1,092 327 1,222 Class: AB
2008-05 Berjaya Dockyard Sdn Bhd — Miri Yd No: 50
Loa 55.00 Br ex 13.80 Dght 4.300
Lbp 48.00 Br md 13.80 Dpth 5.50
Welded, 1 dk
(B21A20S) Platform Supply Ship
Cranes: 1x2t
2 oil engines reduction geared to sc. shafts driving 2 FP propellers
Total Power: 2,942kW (4,000hp)
Niigata 6MG26HL
2 x 4 Stroke 6 Cy. 260 x 350 each-1471kW (2000bhp)
Niigata Engineering Co Ltd-Japan
AuxGen: 2 x 245kW 415V 50Hz a.c
Thrusters: 1 Tunnel thruster (f)
Fuel: 340.0 (d.f.)

9535888 *J8B5000* -
ZAKHER EMPEROR
Zakher Marine International Inc
-
Kingstown *St Vincent & The Grenadines*
MMSI: 375044000
Official number: 11473
1,973 592 1,785 Class: AB
2009-08 Berjaya Dockyard Sdn Bhd — Miri Yd No: 56
Loa 61.20 Br ex - Dght 5.090
Lbp 59.30 Br md 16.00 Dpth 6.00
Welded, 1 dk
(B21B20A) Anchor Handling Tug Supply
2 oil engines reduction geared to sc. shafts driving 2 CP propellers
Total Power: 3,840kW (5,220hp) 12.5k
Caterpillar 3516B-H
2 x Vee 4 Stroke 16 Cy. 170 x 215 each-1920kW (2610bhp
Caterpillar Inc-USA
AuxGen: 2 x 405kW a.c, 2 x a.c
Thrusters: 1 Tunnel thruster (f); 1 Tunnel thruster (a)
Fuel: 430.0 (r.f.)

9545895 *J8B4170* -
ZAKHER FALCON
Zakher Marine International Inc
-
Kingstown *St Vincent & The Grenadines*
MMSI: 377742000
Official number: 10643
828 248 851 Class: BV
2009-12 Nanjing East Star Shipbuilding Co Ltd — Nanjing JS (Hull) Yd No: 07ESS-T4702
2009-12 Tuong Aik Shipyard Sdn Bhd — Sibu Yd No: 07ESS-T4702)
Loa 47.00 Br ex - Dght 4.200
Lbp 41.40 Br md 12.80 Dpth 4.85
Welded, 1 dk
(B21B20A) Anchor Handling Tug Supply
2 oil engines reduction geared to sc. shafts driving 2 FP propellers
Total Power: 2,942kW (4,000hp)
Mitsubishi S8U-MPT
2 x 4 Stroke 8 Cy. 240 x 260 each-1471kW (2000bhp)
Mitsubishi Heavy Industries Ltd-Japan
AuxGen: 3 x 245kW 415V 50Hz a.c
Thrusters: 1 Thwart. FP thruster (f)
Fuel: 533.0 (r.f.)

9549889 *J8B4395* -
ZAKHER FORCE
Zakher Marine International Inc
-
SatCom: Inmarsat C 437550610
Kingstown *St Vincent & The Grenadines*
MMSI: 375506000
Official number: 10868
1,092 327 841 Class: BV
2011-01 Nanjing East Star Shipbuilding Co Ltd — Nanjing JS Yd No: 08ESS-T5002
Loa 50.00 Br ex - Dght 4.500
Lbp 44.20 Br md 13.20 Dpth 5.20
Welded, 1 dk
(B21B20A) Anchor Handling Tug Supply
Cranes: 1x2t
2 oil engines reduction geared to sc. shafts driving 2 FP propellers
Total Power: 3,840kW (5,220hp) 12.5k
Caterpillar 3516B-H
2 x Vee 4 Stroke 16 Cy. 170 x 215 each-1920kW (2610bhp
Caterpillar Inc-USA
AuxGen: 3 x 245kW 415V 50Hz a.c
Thrusters: 1 Tunnel thruster (f)
Fuel: 636.0 (d.f.)

9200873 *J8B2995* -
ZAKHER FUGRO
ex Ryan T -2004
Zakher Marine International Inc
-
Kingstown *St Vincent & The Grenadines*
MMSI: 377696000
Official number: 9467
604 181 390 Class: AB
1998-09 Service Marine Industries Inc — Amelia LA Yd No: 187
Loa 44.20 Br ex - Dght 2.890
Lbp 40.77 Br md 10.97 Dpth 3.51
Welded, 1 dk
(B21A20S) Platform Supply Ship
Cranes: 1x5t
2 oil engines reverse reduction geared to sc. shafts driving 2 FP propellers
Total Power: 1,038kW (1,412hp) 12.0k
Caterpillar 3508T
2 x Vee 4 Stroke 8 Cy. 170 x 190 each-519kW (706bhp)
Caterpillar Inc-USA
AuxGen: 2 x 105kW 480V a.c
Thrusters: 1 Thwart. FP thruster (f)

9443346 *D6EC4* -
ZAKHER GLORY
Zakher Marine International Inc
-
Moroni *Union of Comoros*
MMSI: 616603000
Official number: 1200696
252 75 122 Class: AB
2007-05 Bengbu Shenzhou Machinery Co Ltd — Bengbu AH Yd No: 1236
Loa 29.50 Br ex - Dght 3.900
Lbp 27.00 Br md 9.00 Dpth 4.16
Welded, 1 dk
(B32A2ST) Tug
Passengers: cabins: 6
2 oil engines reduction geared to sc. shafts driving 2 FP propellers
Total Power: 2,354kW (3,200hp)
Yanmar 8N21A-S
2 x 4 Stroke 8 Cy. 210 x 290 each-1177kW (1600bhp)
Yanmar Diesel Engine Co Ltd-Japan
AuxGen: 2 x 130kW 415V 50Hz a.c
Thrusters: 1 Tunnel thruster (f)
Fuel: 162.7 (r.f.)

9398852 *J8B3545* -
ZAKHER HOPE
Zakher Marine International Inc
-
Kingstown *St Vincent & The Grenadines*
MMSI: 375616000
Official number: 10018
433 130 281 Class: AB (GL)
2006-10 Sterling Bay Shipbuilding Sdn Bhd — Sibu Yd No: 010
Loa 37.00 Br ex 10.62 Dght 4.000
Lbp 34.08 Br md 10.60 Dpth 4.95
Welded, 1 dk
(B21B20A) Anchor Handling Tug Supply
2 oil engines reduction geared to sc. shafts driving 2 FP propellers
Total Power: 2,316kW (3,148hp)
Caterpillar 3512
2 x Vee 4 Stroke 12 Cy. 170 x 190 each-1158kW (1574bhp
Caterpillar Inc-USA
AuxGen: 2 x 245kW 415V 50Hz a.c
Thrusters: 1 Tunnel thruster (f)

9314698 *J8B2948* -
ZAKHER KING
Zakher Marine International Inc
-
Kingstown *St Vincent & The Grenadines*
MMSI: 377633000
Official number: 9420
475 143 317 Class: AB (NK)
2004-04 Piasau Slipways Sdn Bhd — Miri Yd No: 125
Loa 37.00 Br ex - Dght 4.062
Lbp 34.69 Br md 11.40 Dpth 4.95
Welded, 1 dk
(B21B20A) Anchor Handling Tug Supply
2 oil engines reduction geared to sc. shafts driving 2 FP propellers
Total Power: 2,350kW (3,196hp) 12.5k
Caterpillar 3512
2 x Vee 4 Stroke 12 Cy. 170 x 190 each-1175kW (1598bhp
Caterpillar Inc-USA
AuxGen: 3 x 150kW a.c
Thrusters: 1 Tunnel thruster (f)

9385180 *A9HP* -
ZAKHER OCEAN
launched as Coastal 35167US -2006
Awal Marine Services Establishment WLL
Zakher Marine International Inc
Bahrain *Bahrain*
MMSI: 408809000
674 202 - Class: BV
2006-12 Guangzhou Panyu Lingshan Shipyard Ltd — Guangzhou GD Yd No: 137
Loa 48.00 Br ex - Dght 3.800
Lbp 42.40 Br md 11.80 Dpth 4.60
Welded, 1 dk
(B21B20A) Anchor Handling Tug Supply
2 oil engines reduction geared to sc. shafts driving 2 FP propellers
Total Power: 2,574kW (3,500hp)
Caterpillar 3512
2 x Vee 4 Stroke 12 Cy. 170 x 190 each-1287kW (1750bhp
Caterpillar Inc-USA
AuxGen: 3 x 215kW 415V 50Hz a.c
Thrusters: 1 Tunnel thruster (f)
Fuel: 513.0 (d.f.)

9544956 *J8B4069* -
ZAKHER PELICAN
Zakher Marine International Inc
-
SatCom: Inmarsat C 437764610
Kingstown *St Vincent & The Grenadines*
MMSI: 377646000
Official number: 10542
1,456 436 1,110 Class: AB
2009-05 Jingjiang Nanyang Shipbuilding Co Ltd — Jingjiang JS (Hull) Yd No: (1270)
2009-05 Pacific Ocean Engineering & Trading Pte Ltd (POET) — Singapore Yd No: 1270
Loa 55.00 Br ex - Dght 3.650
Lbp 53.20 Br md 15.80 Dpth 5.50
Welded, 1 dk
(B34L2QU) Utility Vessel
Cranes: 1
2 oil engines reduction geared to sc. shafts driving 2 Z propellers
Total Power: 2,644kW (3,594hp) 11.0k
Niigata 6L25H
2 x 4 Stroke 6 Cy. 250 x 350 each-1322kW (1797bhp)
Niigata Engineering Co Ltd-Japan
AuxGen: 4 x 475kW
Thrusters: 2 Tunnel thruster (f)
Fuel: 430.0

9544968 *J8B4070* -
ZAKHER PIONEER
Zakher Marine International Inc
-
SatCom: Inmarsat C 437767410
Kingstown *St Vincent & The Grenadines*
MMSI: 377674000
Official number: 10543
1,456 436 1,104 Class: AB
2009-08 Jingjiang Nanyang Shipbuilding Co Ltd — Jingjiang JS (Hull) Yd No: (1271)
2009-08 Pacific Ocean Engineering & Trading Pte Ltd (POET) — Singapore Yd No: 1271
Loa 55.00 Br ex - Dght 3.650
Lbp 53.20 Br md 15.80 Dpth 5.50
Welded, 1 dk
(B34L2QU) Utility Vessel
Cranes: 1
2 oil engines geared to sc. shafts driving 2 Z propellers
Total Power: 2,644kW (3,594hp) 11.0k
Niigata 6L25H
2 x 4 Stroke 6 Cy. 250 x 350 each-1322kW (1797bhp)
Niigata Engineering Co Ltd-Japan
AuxGen: 4 x 475kW
Thrusters: 2 Tunnel thruster (f)
Fuel: 580.0

IMO / Call sign	Name / Owner / Registry	Tonnage	Class	Builder / Dimensions	Type	Machinery
9583275 J8B4380	**ZAKHER POWER** **Zakher Marine International Inc** SatCom: Inmarsat C 437674813 *Kingstown* *St Vincent & The Grenadines* MMSI: 376748000 Official number: 10853	**1,416** 425 1,500	Class: BV	**2010-11 Tuong Aik Shipyard Sdn Bhd — Sibu** Yd No: 2901 Loa 60.00 Br ex - Dght 4.500 Lbp 57.50 Br md 13.80 Dpth 5.50 Welded, 1 dk	**(B21B20A) Anchor Handling Tug Supply**	**2 oil engines** reduction geared to sc. shafts driving 2 FP propellers Total Power: 4,414kW (6,002hp) 10.0kn Mitsubishi S12U-MPTK 2 x Vee 4 Stroke 12 Cy. 240 x 260 each-2207kW (3001bhp) Mitsubishi Heavy Industries Ltd-Japan AuxGen: 3 x 245kW 415V 50Hz a.c Thrusters: 1 Tunnel thruster (f)
9274719 J8B2716 -	**ZAKHER PRINCE** **Zakher Marine International Inc** - *Kingstown* *St Vincent & The Grenadines* MMSI: 377352000 Official number: 9188	**475** 143 322	Class: AB (NK)	**2002-06 Piasau Slipways Sdn Bhd — Miri** Yd No: 122 Loa 37.00 Br ex - Dght 4.062 Lbp 34.92 Br md 11.40 Dpth 4.95 Welded, 1 dk	**(B21B20A) Anchor Handling Tug Supply**	**2 oil engines** reduction geared to sc. shafts driving 2 FP propellers Total Power: 1,910kW (2,596hp) Caterpillar 3512 2 x Vee 4 Stroke 12 Cy. 170 x 190 each-955kW (1298bhp) Caterpillar Inc-USA AuxGen: 2 x 150kW a.c Thrusters: 1 Tunnel thruster (f)
9614414 J8B4648 -	**ZAKHER PROVIDER** **Zakher Marine International Inc** - *Kingstown* *St Vincent & The Grenadines* MMSI: 376156000 Official number: 11121	**1,976** 592 1,683	Class: AB	**2012-03 Berjaya Dockyard Sdn Bhd — Miri** Yd No: 64 Loa 61.25 Br ex - Dght 4.500 Lbp 53.90 Br md 16.00 Dpth 6.00 Welded, 1 dk	**(B21B20A) Anchor Handling Tug Supply**	**2 oil engines** reduction geared to sc. shafts driving 2 CP propellers Total Power: 3,676kW (4,998hp) 12.5kn Niigata 6MG28HX 2 x 4 Stroke 6 Cy. 280 x 370 each-1838kW (2499bhp) Niigata Engineering Co Ltd-Japan AuxGen: 2 x 1000kW 415V 50Hz a.c, 2 x 400kW 415V 50Hz a.c Thrusters: 1 Tunnel thruster (f); 1 Tunnel thruster (a) Fuel: 550.0 (d.f.)
9337535 J8B3091 -	**ZAKHER QUEEN** **Zakher Marine International Inc** - *Kingstown* *St Vincent & The Grenadines* MMSI: 376002200 Official number: 9563	**499** 149 494	Class: BV	**2005-05 Tuong Aik Shipyard Sdn Bhd — Sibu** Yd No: 2315 Loa 45.00 Br ex - Dght 3.200 Lbp 40.00 Br md 11.00 Dpth 4.00 Welded, 1 dk	**(B32A2ST) Tug**	**2 oil engines** reduction geared to sc. shafts driving 2 CP propellers Total Power: 3,000kW (4,078hp) Caterpillar 3512B-HD 2 x Vee 4 Stroke 12 Cy. 170 x 215 each-1500kW (2039bhp) Caterpillar Inc-USA AuxGen: 3 x 245kW a.c Thrusters: 1 Tunnel thruster (f)
9193654 D6BY7 -	**ZAKHER SERVICE** *ex* Mugzy T *-2003* *ex* Ethel B. *-2001* **Zakher Marine International Inc** - *Moroni* *Union of Comoros* MMSI: 616194000 Official number: 1200237	**525** 157 -	Class: BV (AB)	**1998-06 Service Marine Industries Inc — Amelia LA** Yd No: 186 Loa 44.20 Br ex - Dght 2.890 Lbp 40.77 Br md 10.97 Dpth 3.51 Welded, 1 dk	**(B21A20S) Platform Supply Ship** Cranes: 1x20t	**2 oil engines** reverse reduction geared to sc. shafts driving 2 FP propellers Total Power: 1,110kW (1,510hp) 12.0kn Caterpillar 3508TA 2 x Vee 4 Stroke 8 Cy. 170 x 190 each-555kW (755bhp) Caterpillar Inc-USA AuxGen: 2 x 100kW 480V a.c Thrusters: 1 Thwart. FP thruster (f) Fuel: 95.5 (d.f.)
9549877 J8B4394 -	**ZAKHER SPIRIT** **Zakher Marine International Inc** - SatCom: Inmarsat C 437689611 *Kingstown* *St Vincent & The Grenadines* MMSI: 376896000 Official number: 10867	**1,092** 327 841	Class: BV	**2010-12 Nanjing East Star Shipbuilding Co Ltd — Nanjing JS** Yd No: 08ESS-T5001 Loa 50.00 Br ex - Dght 4.500 Lbp 44.20 Br md 13.20 Dpth 5.20 Welded, 1 dk	**(B21B20A) Anchor Handling Tug Supply** Cranes: 1x2t	**2 oil engines** reduction geared to sc. shafts driving 2 FP propellers Total Power: 3,840kW (5,220hp) 12.5kn Caterpillar 3516B-HD 2 x Vee 4 Stroke 16 Cy. 170 x 215 each-1920kW (2610bhp) Caterpillar Inc-USA AuxGen: 3 x 245kW 415V 50Hz a.c Thrusters: 1 Tunnel thruster (f) Fuel: 636.0 (d.f.)
9583287 J8B4556 -	**ZAKHER STAR** **Zakher Marine International Inc** - *Kingstown* *St Vincent & The Grenadines* MMSI: 376039000 Official number: 11029	**1,416** 425 1,500	Class: BV	**2011-09 Tuong Aik Shipyard Sdn Bhd — Sibu** Yd No: 2902 Loa 60.00 Br ex - Dght 4.500 Lbp 57.50 Br md 13.80 Dpth 5.50 Welded, 1 dk	**(B21B20A) Anchor Handling Tug Supply**	**2 oil engines** reduction geared to sc. shafts driving 2 FP propellers Total Power: 4,414kW (6,002hp) 10.0kn Mitsubishi S12U-MPTK 2 x Vee 4 Stroke 12 Cy. 240 x 260 each-2207kW (3001bhp) Mitsubishi Heavy Industries Ltd-Japan AuxGen: 3 x 245kW 415V 50Hz a.c Thrusters: 1 Tunnel thruster (f)
9545247 A9IU -	**ZAKHER SUPPLIER** **Awal Marine Services Establishment WLL** Zakher Marine International Inc *Bahrain* *Bahrain* MMSI: 408354000	**1,405** 421 1,500	Class: BV	**2009-09 Tuong Aik Shipyard Sdn Bhd — Sibu** Yd No: 2706 Loa 60.00 Br ex - Dght 4.500 Lbp 54.50 Br md 13.80 Dpth 5.50 Welded, 1 dk	**(B21B20A) Anchor Handling Tug Supply**	**2 oil engines** reduction geared to sc. shafts driving 2 FP propellers Total Power: 3,676kW (4,998hp) 10.0kn Niigata 6MG28HX 1 x 4 Stroke 6 Cy. 280 x 370 1838kW (2499bhp) Niigata Engineering Co Ltd-Japan AuxGen: 2 x 245kW 415/50V a.c Thrusters: 1 Tunnel thruster (f) Fuel: 821.0 (d.f.)
9314399 A9GN -	**ZAKHER VICTORY** *ex* Vicky II *-2005* **Awal Marine Services Establishment WLL** Zakher Marine International Inc *Bahrain* *Bahrain* MMSI: 408766000 Official number: BN 3075	**914** 274 1,192	Class: AB	**2004-03 Guangzhou Hangtong Shipbuilding & Shipping Co Ltd — Jiangmen GD** Yd No: 022005 Loa 53.80 Br ex 14.00 Dght 3.500 Lbp 48.60 Br md 13.80 Dpth 4.50 Welded, 1 dk	**(B21A20S) Platform Supply Ship** TEU 25 Cranes: 1x9.3t	**2 oil engines** reduction geared to sc. shafts driving 2 FP propellers Total Power: 1,766kW (2,402hp) 9.0kn Yanmar M220-EN 2 x 4 Stroke 6 Cy. 220 x 300 each-883kW (1201bhp) Yanmar Diesel Engine Co Ltd-Japan AuxGen: 2 x 140kW 415V 50Hz a.c Thrusters: 1 Thwart. FP thruster (f) Fuel: 757.0 (d.f.)
7638844 - -	**ZAKI YOUNIS** - **Suez Canal Authority** - *Port Said* *Egypt*	*1,052* 401 -	Class: AB	**1977-12 Mitsubishi Heavy Industries Ltd. — Hiroshima** Yd No: 289 Loa 45.32 Br ex 20.30 Dght 2.210 Lbp 44.99 Br md 19.99 Dpth 3.76 Welded, 1 dk	**(B34B2SC) Crane Vessel** Cranes: 1x100t	**2 diesel electric oil engines** Connecting to 2 elec. motors driving 2 CP propellers Total Power: 562kW (764hp) 5.0kn Deutz SBA6M528 2 x 4 Stroke 6 Cy. 220 x 280 each-281kW (382bhp) Kloeckner Humboldt Deutz AG-West Germany AuxGen: 2 x 400kW a.c, 1 x 75kW a.c
7320291 SW6516 -	**ZAKINTHOS I** *ex* Ville de Corte *-1989* **Anonymos Naftiliaki Eteria Zakinthou (ANEZ)** Kefalonian Lines 1 Maritime Co *Piraeus* *Greece* MMSI: 237011800 Official number: 9684	**2,157** 1,648 1,274	Class: RI (HR) (BV)	**1973-07 Schulte & Bruns Schiffswerft — Emden** Yd No: 272 Loa 101.40 Br ex - Dght 3.600 Lbp 81.34 Br md 16.00 Dpth 4.70 Welded, 2 dks	**(A36A2PR) Passenger/Ro-Ro Ship (Vehicles)** Stern door & ramp Side door (p) Side door (s) Lane-Len: 350 Lane-Wid: 6.00 Lane-clr ht: 4.50 Cars: 30, Trailers: 30 Grain: 5,305; Bale: 4,368; Liq: 97	**2 oil engines** reverse reduction geared to sc. shafts driving 2 CP propellers Total Power: 3,236kW (4,400hp) 16.0kn Crepelle 12PSN 2 x Vee 4 Stroke 12 Cy. 260 x 280 each-1618kW (2200bhp) Crepelle et Cie-France AuxGen: 3 x 152kW 380V 50Hz a.c Thrusters: 1 Thwart. FP thruster (f) Fuel: 183.0 (d.f.)
7712030 EROP -	**ZAKMAR** *ex* Furkan *-2013* *ex* Dr. Ahmad *-2004* *ex* Alsyta *-2003* *ex* Alsydon *-1998* *ex* Alsyta Smits *-1993* **Zakmar Shipping & Trading Ltd** IMS Hellenic Co *Giurgiulesti* *Moldova* MMSI: 214181516	**3,708** 2,231 6,110	Class: BR (LR) (TL) ✠ Classed LR until 18/8/04	**1979-02 Scheepswerf en Machinefabriek de Groot & van Vliet B.V. — Bolnes** Yd No: 398 Loa 83.70 (BB) Br ex 17.10 Dght 8.395 Lbp 74.81 Br md 17.00 Dpth 10.14 Welded, 2 dks	**(A31A2GX) General Cargo Ship** Grain: 7,020; Bale: 6,811 Compartments: 1 Ho, ER 1 Ha: (45.4 x 12.8)ER	**1 oil engine** with flexible couplings & sr gearedto sc. shaft driving 1 FP propeller Total Power: 2,940kW (3,997hp) 11.0kn MaK 8M453AK 1 x 4 Stroke 8 Cy. 320 x 420 2940kW (3997bhp) MaK Maschinenbau GmbH-Kiel AuxGen: 3 x 144kW 380V 50Hz a.c Fuel: 409.5 10.0pd
7012375 ERRH -	**ZAKYNTHOS** *ex* Dimitris *-2012* *ex* Kapitan Aristov *-1997* *ex* El Goajiro *-1990* *ex* Neptun *-1986* **Ocean Soul Trade Co** Tech Project LLC *Moldova* MMSI: 214181808	**620** 183 -	Class: BV (Class contemplated) (RS) (NV)	**1970-05 Molde Verft AS — Hjelset** (Hull) Yd No: (61) **1970-05 Ulstein Mek. Verksted AS — Ulsteinvik** Yd No: 61 Loa 45.03 Br ex 10.85 Dght 5.701 Lbp 38.49 Br md 10.80 Dpth 6.58 Welded, 2 dks	**(B32A2ST) Tug** Ice Capable	**2 oil engines** dr geared to sc. shaft driving 1 CP propeller Total Power: 4,120kW (5,602hp) 15.0kn Polar SF116VS-F 2 x Vee 4 Stroke 16 Cy. 250 x 300 each-2060kW (2801bhp) AB NOHAB-Sweden AuxGen: 1 x 225kW 440V 60Hz a.c, 2 x 156kW 440V 60Hz a.c Thrusters: 1 Thwart. FP thruster (f) Fuel: 345.5 (d.f.) 4.5pd

IMO / Call sign	Name / Owner	Tonnage	Class	Build / Dimensions	Type / Capacities	Machinery
9417529 *ZDJW8* -	**ZAKYNTHOS** - **Zakynthos Marine SA** Aegean Bunkering Services Inc SatCom: Inmarsat C 423657510 *Gibraltar* *Gibraltar (British)* MMSI: 236575000	**4,580** 1,967 6,303	Class: NV	**2010-01 Qingdao Hyundai Shipbuilding Co Ltd — Jiaonan SD** Yd No: 215 Loa 102.50 Br ex 17.82 Dght 6.600 Lbp 95.20 Br md 17.80 Dpth 8.80 Welded, 1 dk	**(A13B2TP) Products Tanker** Double Hull (13F) Liq: 6,642; Liq (Oil): 6,642 Cargo Heating Coils 3 Cargo Pump (s): 2x750m³/hr, 1x300m³/hr	**1 oil engine** reduction geared to sc. shaft driving 1 FP propeller Total Power: 2,610kW (3,549hp) 14.0kn Hyundai Himsen 9H25/33 1 x 4 Stroke 9 Cy. 250 x 330 2610kW (3549bhp) Hyundai Heavy Industries Co Ltd-South Korea AuxGen: 3 x 400kW a.c Thrusters: 1 Tunnel thruster (f)
9095266 *ECLH* 3-SS-12-06	**ZALA** - **Pesqueras Orratz SA** - *Pasaia* *Spain* MMSI: 224002820 Official number: 3-2/2006	**278** 84 -		**2007-01 Astilleros Armon SA — Navia** Yd No: 639 Loa 31.40 Br ex - Dght - Lbp 25.70 Br md 8.50 Dpth 3.50 Welded, 1 dk	**(B11A2FS) Stern Trawler**	**1 oil engine** geared to sc. shaft driving 1 Propeller Total Power: 301kW (409hp) Yanmar 6N18A-UN 1 x 4 Stroke 6 Cy. 180 x 280 301kW (409bhp) Yanmar Diesel Engine Co Ltd-Japan
7302782 - -	**ZALBIDEA J** *ex Blue Tuna -2011* *ex Christophe Colomb -2004* **Larrabide Inversiones SL** - *Ecuador*	**1,127** 338 -	Class: (BV)	**1973-10 Soc Industrielle et Commerciale de Consts Navales (SICCNa) — St-Malo** Yd No: 125 Loa 62.74 Br ex 11.54 Dght 5.589 Lbp 56.16 Br md 11.50 Dpth 7.80 Welded, 2 dks	**(B11B2FV) Fishing Vessel** Ins: 1,012	**1 oil engine** reduction geared to sc. shaft driving 1 FP propeller Total Power: 2,685kW (3,651hp) 16.4kn EMD (Electro-Motive) 20-645-E7B 1 x Vee 2 Stroke 20 Cy. 230 x 254 2685kW (3651bhp) General Motors Corp.Electro-Motive Div.-La Grange AuxGen: 3 x 260kW 220/380V Fuel: 243.5 (d.f.)
8317019 *YBLS* -	**ZALEHA FITRAT** *ex Darya Chand -2007 ex Soarer Cupid -1991* **PT Perpel Gurita Lintas Samudera** PT Gurita Lintas Samudera *Jakarta* *Indonesia* MMSI: 525016135 Official number: 4492/L	**26,014** 13,673 43,594 T/cm 50.4	Class: (LR) (NK) Classed LR until 15/1/11	**1986-02 Hashihama Shipbuilding Co Ltd — Tadotsu KG** Yd No: 836 Loa 185.83 (BB) Br ex 30.43 Dght 11.319 Lbp 176.99 Br md 30.41 Dpth 16.21 Welded, 1 dk	**(A21A2BC) Bulk Carrier** Grain: 53,594; Bale: 52,280 TEU 1082 Compartments: 5 Ho, ER 5 Ha: (19.2 x 15.3)4 (20.8 x 15.3)ER Cranes: 4x25t	**1 oil engine** driving 1 FP propeller Total Power: 7,115kW (9,674hp) 14.0kn B&W 6L60MCE 1 x 2 Stroke 6 Cy. 600 x 1944 7115kW (9674bhp) Mitsui Engineering & Shipbuilding CLtd-Japan AuxGen: 2 x 460kW 450V 60Hz a.c Boilers: e (ex.g.) 7.0kgf/cm² (6.9bar), AuxB (o.f.) 7.0kgf/cm² (6.9bar) Fuel: 269.0 (d.f.) 1450.0 (r.f.) 27.0pd
7828786 *UBZS* -	**ZALESYE** - **Vlak JSC (A/O 'Vlak')** - *Kaliningrad* *Russia* Official number: 791701	**193** 58 80	Class: RS	**1979 Sudostroitelnyy Zavod "Avangard" — Petrozavodsk** Yd No: 328 Loa 31.63 Br ex 7.32 Dght 2.900 Lbp 29.15 Br md 7.20 Dpth 3.51 Welded, 1 dk	**(B11B2FV) Fishing Vessel** Ins: 100 Compartments: 1 Ho, ER 1 Ha: (1.5 x 1.2) Derricks: 1x1.5t Ice Capable	**1 oil engine** driving 1 FP propeller Total Power: 221kW (300hp) 9.5kn S.K.L. 8NVD36-1U 1 x 4 Stroke 8 Cy. 240 x 360 221kW (300bhp) VEB Schwermaschinenbau "KarlLiebknecht" (SKL)-Magdeburg Fuel: 36.0 (d.f.)
8857239 - -	**ZALIV** - **GPO 'Balkanbalyk'** - *Turkmenbashy* *Turkmenistan* Official number: 860244	**191** 85 323	Class: (RS)	**1986 Svetlovskiy Sudoremontnyy Zavod — Svetlyy** Yd No: 30 Loa 29.45 Br ex 8.15 Dght 3.120 Lbp 28.50 Br md - Dpth 3.60 Welded, 1 dk	**(B34G2SE) Pollution Control Vessel** Liq: 332; Liq (Oil): 332 Compartments: 8 Ta Ice Capable	**1 oil engine** geared to sc. shaft driving 1 FP propeller Total Power: 166kW (226hp) 7.5kn Daldizel 6CHNSP18/22 1 x 4 Stroke 6 Cy. 180 x 220 166kW (226bhp) Daldizel-Khabarovsk AuxGen: 1 x 50kW, 1 x 25kW Fuel: 13.0 (d.f.)
8714592 *UBWH9* -	**ZALIV AMERIKA** *ex Ning Hua 407 -2011 ex D. Y. Knight -1996* *ex Ingrid Terkol -1995* **Nayada Co Ltd** - SatCom: Inmarsat C 427305169 *Nakhodka* *Russia* MMSI: 273355440	**1,952** 972 3,302 T/cm 9.6	Class: CC RS (LR) ✠ Classed LR until 7/2/96	**1989-12 A/S Nordsovaerftet — Ringkobing** Yd No: 198 Loa 90.65 (BB) Br ex 13.53 Dght 5.570 Lbp 85.48 Br md 13.50 Dpth 6.61 Welded, 1 dk	**(A12A2TC) Chemical Tanker** Liq: 3,113 Cargo Heating Coils Compartments: 12 Wing Ta, 2 Wing Slop Ta, ER 12 Cargo Pump (s): 12x80m³/hr Ice Capable	**1 oil engine** with clutches, flexible couplings & sr geared to sc. shaft driving 1 CP propeller Total Power: 1,342kW (1,825hp) 10.5kn MaK 6MU452AK 1 x 4 Stroke 6 Cy. 320 x 450 1342kW (1825bhp) Krupp MaK Maschinenbau GmbH-Kiel AuxGen: 1 x 680kW 380V 50Hz a.c, 2 x 216kW 380V 50Hz a.c Thrusters: 1 Thwart. FP thruster (f)
9354301 *C4ZR2* -	**ZALIV AMERIKA** - **Boussol Shipping Ltd** Prisco (Singapore) Pte Ltd SatCom: Inmarsat Mini-M 764828451 *Limassol* *Cyprus* MMSI: 210435000	**60,178** 31,496 104,535 T/cm 92.0	Class: NV	**2008-01 Hyundai Heavy Industries Co Ltd — Ulsan** Yd No: 1854 Loa 243.88 (BB) Br ex 42.04 Dght 14.920 Lbp 234.00 Br md 42.00 Dpth 22.00 Welded, 1 dk	**(A13A2TV) Crude Oil Tanker** Double Hull (13F) Liq: 121,797; Liq (Oil): 121,797 Cargo Heating Coils Compartments: 12 Wing Ta, 2 Wing Slop Ta, ER 3 Cargo Pump (s): 3x2750m³/hr Manifold: Bow/CM: 121.6m Ice Capable	**1 oil engine** driving 1 FP propeller Total Power: 15,820kW (21,509hp) 15.0kn MAN-B&W 7S60MC-C 1 x 2 Stroke 7 Cy. 600 x 2400 15820kW (21509bhp) Hyundai Heavy Industries Co Ltd-South Korea AuxGen: 3 x 1130kW a.c Fuel: 223.0 (d.f.) (Heating Coils) 2810.0 (r.f.) 56.5pd
9354313 *5BEV2* -	**ZALIV AMURSKIY** - **Malthus Navigation Ltd** Prisco (Singapore) Pte Ltd SatCom: Inmarsat Mini-M 764863233 *Limassol* *Cyprus* MMSI: 210493000	**60,178** 31,496 104,542 T/cm 92.0	Class: NV	**2008-07 Hyundai Heavy Industries Co Ltd — Ulsan** Yd No: 1855 Loa 243.88 (BB) Br ex - Dght 14.920 Lbp 234.00 Br md 42.00 Dpth 22.00 Welded, 1 dk	**(A13A2TV) Crude Oil Tanker** Double Hull (13F) Liq: 121,797; Liq (Oil): 104,000 Cargo Heating Coils Compartments: 12 Wing Ta, 2 Wing Slop Ta, ER 3 Cargo Pump (s): 3x2750m³/hr Manifold: Bow/CM: 121.6m Ice Capable	**1 oil engine** driving 1 FP propeller Total Power: 15,820kW (21,509hp) 15.0kn MAN-B&W 7S60MC-C 1 x 2 Stroke 7 Cy. 600 x 2400 15820kW (21509bhp) Hyundai Heavy Industries Co Ltd-South Korea AuxGen: 3 x 1130kW a.c Fuel: 223.0 (d.f.) 2809.0 (r.f.)
9418494 *5BRM2* -	**ZALIV ANIVA** - **Kandita Shipmanagement Ltd** SCF Unicom Singapore Pte Ltd SatCom: Inmarsat C 421272110 *Limassol* *Cyprus* MMSI: 212721000 Official number: 9418494	**60,325** 31,496 102,946 T/cm 92.0	Class: NV	**2009-06 Hyundai Heavy Industries Co Ltd — Ulsan** Yd No: 2026 Loa 245.38 (BB) Br ex 42.04 Dght 14.920 Lbp 234.00 Br md 42.00 Dpth 22.00 Welded, 1 dk	**(A13A2TV) Crude Oil Tanker** Double Hull (13F) Liq: 121,797; Liq (Oil): 103,000 Cargo Heating Coils Compartments: 12 Wing Ta, 2 Wing Slop Ta, ER 3 Cargo Pump (s): 3x2750m³/hr Manifold: Bow/CM: 123.1m Ice Capable	**1 oil engine** driving 1 FP propeller Total Power: 15,820kW (21,509hp) 14.8kn MAN-B&W 7S60MC-C 1 x 2 Stroke 7 Cy. 600 x 2400 15820kW (21509bhp) Hyundai Heavy Industries Co Ltd-South Korea AuxGen: 3 x 1130kW a.c Fuel: 160.0 (d.f.) 2400.0 (r.f.) 56.5pd
8802806 *UBBI2* -	**ZALIV ANIVA** *ex Ning Hua 408 -2011 ex D. Y. Spirit -1996* *ex Grete Terkol -1995* **Nayada Co Ltd** - SatCom: Inmarsat C 427305240 *Nakhodka* *Russia* MMSI: 273355740	**1,952** 972 3,302 T/cm 9.6	Class: RS (LR) (CC) ✠ Classed LR until 7/2/96	**1990-07 A/S Nordsovaerftet — Ringkobing** Yd No: 201 Lengthened-2005 Loa 90.65 (BB) Br ex 19.72 Dght 5.180 Lbp 85.48 Br md 13.50 Dpth 6.60 Welded, 1 dk	**(A12A2TC) Chemical Tanker** Double Hull Liq: 3,113 Compartments: 12 Wing Ta, 2 Wing Slop Ta, ER 12 Cargo Pump (s): 12x80m³/hr Ice Capable	**1 oil engine** with clutches, flexible couplings & sr geared to sc. shaft driving 1 CP propeller Total Power: 1,100kW (1,496hp) 10.5kn MaK 6M452AK 1 x 4 Stroke 6 Cy. 320 x 450 1100kW (1496bhp) Krupp MaK Maschinenbau GmbH-Kiel AuxGen: 1 x 680kW 380V 50Hz a.c, 2 x 216kW 380V 50Hz a.c Thrusters: 1 Thwart. FP thruster (f)
8899732 - -	**ZALIV AVACHINSKIY** - **OOO Rybokolkhoz 'Zaliv Avachinskiy'** -	**745** 223 335	Class: (RS)	**1994-03 AO Yaroslavskiy Sudostroitelnyy Zavod — Yaroslavl** Yd No: 389 Loa 54.82 Br ex 10.15 Dght 4.140 Lbp 50.30 Br md - Dpth 5.00 Welded, 1 dk	**(B11A2FS) Stern Trawler** Ins: 254 Ice Capable	**1 oil engine** driving 1 CP propeller Total Power: 970kW (1,319hp) 12.6kn S.K.L. 8NVD48A-2U 1 x 4 Stroke 8 Cy. 320 x 480 970kW (1319bhp) SKL Motoren u. Systemtechnik AG-Magdeburg AuxGen: 1 x 300kW a.c, 3 x 150kW a.c Fuel: 192.0 (d.f.)
9360128 *A8RM5* -	**ZALIV BAIKAL** - **Baikal Shipping Ltd** Prisco (Singapore) Pte Ltd SatCom: Inmarsat C 463703631 *Monrovia* *Liberia* MMSI: 636014126 Official number: 14126	**60,178** 31,496 104,532 T/cm 92.0	Class: NV	**2009-01 Hyundai Heavy Industries Co Ltd — Ulsan** Yd No: 1873 Loa 243.88 (BB) Br ex 42.02 Dght 14.920 Lbp 234.00 Br md 42.00 Dpth 22.00 Welded, 1 dk	**(A13A2TW) Crude/Oil Products Tanker** Double Hull (13F) Liq: 121,797; Liq (Oil): 104,000 Cargo Heating Coils Compartments: 12 Wing Ta, 2 Wing Slop Ta, ER 3 Cargo Pump (s): 3x2750m³/hr Manifold: Bow/CM: 121.6m Ice Capable	**1 oil engine** driving 1 FP propeller Total Power: 15,820kW (21,509hp) 15.0kn MAN-B&W 7S60MC-C 1 x 2 Stroke 7 Cy. 600 x 2400 15820kW (21509bhp) Hyundai Heavy Industries Co Ltd-South Korea AuxGen: 3 x 1130kW 450V 60Hz a.c Fuel: 223.0 (d.f.) 2810.0 (r.f.)
9509073 *9HA2790*	**ZALIV III** - **Percival Shipping Co Ltd** - *Valletta* *Malta* MMSI: 256100000 Official number: 13294	**498** 149 -	Class: AB	**2011-06 Mondo Marine SpA — Savona** Yd No: 22/2 Loa 49.36 Br ex - Dght 2.300 Lbp 48.77 Br md 9.00 Dpth 4.40 Welded, 1 dk	**(X11A2YP) Yacht** Hull Material: Aluminium Alloy	**2 oil engines** reduction geared to sc. shafts driving 2 Propellers Total Power: 5,440kW (7,396hp) 18.0kn M.T.U. 16V4000M90 2 x Vee 4 Stroke 16 Cy. 165 x 190 each-2720kW (3698bhp) MTU Friedrichshafen GmbH-Friedrichshafen AuxGen: 3 x 115kW a.c Fuel: 80.0 (d.f.)

IMO / Call sign	Name / Owner	Tonnage	Class	Builder / Dimensions	Type / Cargo	Machinery
130834 *CEP*	**ZALIV NAKHODKA** **Oplot Mira JSC (A/O 'Oplot Mira')** - *Nevelsk* Russia MMSI: 273812100	**767** 230 414	Class: RS	**1995-07 ATVT Zavod "Leninska Kuznya" — Kyyiv** Yd No: 1687 Loa 54.82 Br ex 10.15 Dght 4.140 Lbp 50.30 Br md 9.80 Dpth 5.00 Welded, 1 dk	**(B11A2FS) Stern Trawler**	**1 oil engine** driving 1 CP propeller Total Power: 852kW (1,158hp) 12.0kn S.K.L. 8NVD48A-2U 1 x 4 Stroke 8 Cy. 320 x 480 852kW (1158bhp) SKL Motoren u. Systemtechnik AG-Magdeburg AuxGen: 4 x 160kW a.c Fuel: 155.0 (d.f.) 3.5pd
880286 *BPN*	**ZALIV OLGI** **JSC Dalryba (A/O 'Dalryba')** - SatCom: Inmarsat C 427321067 *Vladivostok* Russia MMSI: 273816200 Official number: 930517	**754** 226 400	Class: RS	**1994-06 ATVT Zavod "Leninska Kuznya" — Kyyiv** Yd No: 1676 Loa 54.82 Br ex 10.15 Dght 4.140 Lbp 50.30 Br md 9.80 Dpth 5.00 Welded, 1 dk	**(B11A2FS) Stern Trawler** Ice Capable	**1 oil engine** driving 1 CP propeller Total Power: 852kW (1,158hp) 12.0kn S.K.L. 8NVD48A-2U 1 x 4 Stroke 8 Cy. 320 x 480 852kW (1158bhp) SKL Motoren u. Systemtechnik AG-Magdeburg AuxGen: 4 x 160kW a.c Fuel: 155.0 (d.f.)
130822 *CDT*	**ZALIV PETRA** **ZAO 'Sevrybflot'** - SatCom: Inmarsat C 427320817 *Magadan* Russia MMSI: 273819000	**748** 224 414	Class: RS	**1995 ATVT Zavod "Leninska Kuznya" — Kyyiv** Yd No: 1685 Loa 54.82 Br ex 10.15 Dght 4.140 Lbp 50.30 Br md 9.80 Dpth 5.00 Welded, 1 dk	**(B11A2FS) Stern Trawler**	**1 oil engine** driving 1 CP propeller Total Power: 852kW (1,158hp) 12.0kn S.K.L. 8NVD48A-2U 1 x 4 Stroke 8 Cy. 320 x 480 852kW (1158bhp) SKL Motoren u. Systemtechnik AG-Magdeburg AuxGen: 4 x 160kW a.c Fuel: 155.0 (d.f.)
216904 *BDF6*	**ZALIV RADUGA** *ex* Kai Yun *-2008* *ex* Yan An Ba Hao *-2005* *ex* Toshin Maru *-1992* **STK Co Ltd (Kompaniy STK)** - *Nevelsk* Russia MMSI: 273339110	**1,431** 479 1,343	Class: RS (CC) (NK)	**1983-05 Honda Zosen — Saiki** Yd No: 711 Loa 75.77 Br ex 11.82 Dght 4.172 Lbp 70.01 Br md 11.80 Dpth 7.17 Welded, 2 dks	**(A34A2GR) Refrigerated Cargo Ship** Ins: 1,787 Compartments: 2 Ho, ER 2 Ha: 2 (4.5 x 3.9)ER Derricks: 4x3t; Winches: 4	**1 oil engine** driving 1 FP propeller Total Power: 1,324kW (1,800hp) 12.3kn Makita GSLH633 1 x 4 Stroke 6 Cy. 330 x 530 1324kW (1800bhp) Makita Diesel Co Ltd-Japan AuxGen: 2 x 240kW Fuel: 504.0 (r.f.) 4.5pd
857007 *EFW*	**ZALIV VOSTOK** **JSC Yuzhmorrybflot** - *Nakhodka* Russia MMSI: 273825700 Official number: 902926	**8,289** 2,486 2,886	Class: RS	**1992-07 OAO Sudostroitelnyy Zavod 'Okean' — Nikolayev** Yd No: 604 Loa 126.30 Br ex - Dght 5.710 Lbp 118.00 Br md 18.20 Dpth 7.30 Welded, 1 dk	**(B12A2FF) Fish Factory Ship** Ice Capable	**1 oil engine** driving 1 FP propeller Total Power: 2,649kW (3,602hp) 12.8kn S.K.L. 6VDS48/42AL-2 1 x 4 Stroke 6 Cy. 420 x 480 2649kW (3602bhp) SKL Motoren u. Systemtechnik AG-Magdeburg AuxGen: 3 x 800kW Fuel: 1320.0 (d.f.)
835005	**ZALIV VOSTOK** **Trading House Mortrans Co Ltd** Mortrans Co Ltd SatCom: Inmarsat C 427302739 *Vladivostok* Russia MMSI: 273440870	*370* 113 96	Class: RS	**1970-12 Kanonerskiy Sudoremontnyy Zavod — Leningrad** Yd No: 6 Loa 39.80 Br ex 10.20 Dght 2.800 Lbp 36.00 Br md 9.70 Dpth 4.20 Welded, 1 dk	**(A36A2PR) Passenger/Ro-Ro Ship (Vehicles)** Passengers: unberthed: 300 Ice Capable	**3 diesel electric oil engines** driving 3 gen. each 221kW Connecting to 2 elec. motors each (312kW) driving 2 FP propellers Total Power: 663kW (900hp) 9.0kn Pervomaysk 6CH25/34-2 3 x 4 Stroke 6 Cy. 250 x 340 each-221kW (300bhp) Pervomaydizelmash (PDM)-Pervomaysk AuxGen: 3 x 30kW Fuel: 30.0 (d.f.)
360130 *3RM6*	**ZALIV VOSTOK** **Vostok Navigation Ltd** Prisco (Singapore) Pte Ltd 773151001 *Monrovia* Liberia MMSI: 636014127 Official number: 14127	**60,178** 31,496 104,527 T/cm 92.0	Class: NV	**2009-01 Hyundai Heavy Industries Co Ltd — Ulsan** Yd No: 1874 Loa 243.88 (BB) Br ex 42.02 Dght 14.900 Lbp 234.00 Br md 42.00 Dpth 22.00 Welded, 1 dk	**(A13A2TW) Crude/Oil Products Tanker** Double Hull (13F) Liq: 121,797; Liq (Oil): 104,000 Cargo Heating Coils Compartments: 12 Wing Ta, 2 Wing Slop Ta, ER 3 Cargo Pump (s): 3x2750m³/hr Manifold: Bow/CM: 121.6m Ice Capable	**1 oil engine** driving 1 FP propeller Total Power: 15,820kW (21,509hp) 15.0kn MAN-B&W 7S60MC-C 1 x 2 Stroke 7 Cy. 600 x 2400 15820kW (21509bhp) Hyundai Heavy Industries Co Ltd-South Korea AuxGen: 3 x 1130kW a.c Fuel: 223.0 (d.f.) 2810.0 (r.f.) 56.5pd
237711 *3PK3*	**ZALIV VOSTOK** *ex* Vingatank *-2013* **Nayada Co Ltd** - *Nakhodka* Russia MMSI: 273333980	**2,878** 1,282 4,298	Class: BV	**2002-06 Celiktekne Sanayii ve Ticaret A.S. — Tuzla, Istanbul** Yd No: 35 Loa 96.30 (BB) Br ex 14.20 Dght 6.200 Lbp 88.85 Br md 14.20 Dpth 7.65 Welded, 1 dk	**(A12B2TR) Chemical/Products Tanker** Double Hull (13F) Liq: 4,633; Liq (Oil): 4,633 Cargo Heating Coils Compartments: 12 Wing Ta, Wing ER 3 Cargo Pump (s): 2x300m³/hr, 1x700m³/hr Manifold: Bow/CM: 52.5m Ice Capable	**1 oil engine** geared to sc. shaft driving 1 FP propeller Total Power: 2,040kW (2,774hp) 11.5kn MAN-B&W 6L27/38 1 x 4 Stroke 6 Cy. 270 x 380 2040kW (2774bhp) MAN B&W Diesel A/S-Denmark AuxGen: 3 x 270kW 380/220V 50Hz a.c, 1 x 400kW a.c Thrusters: 1 Water jet (f) Fuel: 75.0 (d.f.) (Heating Coils) 200.0 (r.f.)
376410 *EAJ*	**ZALIV ZABIYAKA** *ex* Oyang *-2004* *ex* O Yang *-2003* *ex* Heung Yang *-1982* **JSC Tralkom (ZAO 'Tralkom')** - *Magadan* Russia MMSI: 273440840	**4,986** 1,670 4,969	Class: RS (KR) (NK)	**1974-07 Hayashikane Shipbuilding & Engineering Co Ltd — Nagasaki NS** Yd No: 839 Loa 112.10 Br ex 17.02 Dght 7.250 Lbp 104.15 Br md 17.00 Dpth 11.21 Welded, 2 dks	**(B11A2FS) Stern Trawler** Ins: 3,526 2 Ha: 2 (3.2 x 3.2) Derricks: 4x5t	**1 oil engine** driving 1 FP propeller Total Power: 4,266kW (5,800hp) 15.8kn Mitsubishi 8UET45/80D 1 x 2 Stroke 8 Cy. 450 x 800 4266kW (5800bhp) Kobe Hatsudoki KK-Japan AuxGen: 3 x 800kW 450V a.c Fuel: 2041.0 (d.f.) 19.0pd
205067 *9GG*	**ZALLAQ** **Arab Maritime Petroleum Transport Co (AMPTC)** - SatCom: Inmarsat C 440870710 *Manama* Bahrain MMSI: 408707000 Official number: BN3026	**79,812** 48,822 153,019 T/cm 109.0	Class: NV	**2001-01 Hyundai Heavy Industries Co Ltd — Ulsan** Yd No: 1236 Loa 269.18 (BB) Br ex 46.04 Dght 17.521 Lbp 258.00 Br md 46.00 Dpth 24.40 Welded, 1 dk	**(A13A2TV) Crude Oil Tanker** Double Hull (13F) Liq: 166,384; Liq (Oil): 166,384 Cargo Heating Coils Compartments: 12 Wing Ta, 2 Wing Slop Ta, ER 3 Cargo Pump (s): 3x4000m³/hr Manifold: Bow/CM: 135m	**1 oil engine** driving 1 FP propeller Total Power: 15,372kW (20,900hp) 15.3kn B&W 6S70MC 1 x 2 Stroke 6 Cy. 700 x 2674 15372kW (20900bhp) Hyundai Heavy Industries Co Ltd-South Korea AuxGen: 3 x 700kW 450V 60Hz a.c Fuel: 3728.0 (r.f.) (Heating Coils) 60.0pd
023172 *LLU2*	**ZAMAN AVCI II** **Zaman Su Urunleri Ticaret AS** Mem Ltd *Georgia* MMSI: 213944000 Official number: C-00489	**650** 195 -	Class: MG	**2003-09 Basaran Gemi Sanayi — Trabzon** Yd No: 58 Loa 49.50 (BB) Br ex - Dght - Lbp 46.90 Br md 15.20 Dpth 3.80 Welded, 1 dk	**(B11B2FV) Fishing Vessel**	**3 oil engines** reduction geared to sc. shafts driving 3 FP propellers Total Power: 2,210kW (3,004hp) 15.4kn Caterpillar 1 x 4 Stroke 562kW (764bhp) Caterpillar Inc-USA Cummins 2 x 4 Stroke each-471kW (640bhp) Cummins Engine Co Inc-USA
370563 *EJI7*	**ZAMBALES** **Leyte Navigation SA** Toko Kaiun Kaisha Ltd *Panama* Panama MMSI: 372534000 Official number: 3246807	**10,409** 3,123 5,164	Class: NK	**2007-03 Kegoya Dock K.K. — Kure** Yd No: 1097 Loa 119.50 (BB) Br ex - Dght 6.114 Lbp 112.00 Br md 20.50 Dpth 14.85 Welded	**(A35B2RV) Vehicles Carrier** Quarter stern door/ramp (s. a.) Len: 25.00 Wid: 5.00 Swl: 50 Vehicles: 615	**1 oil engine** driving 1 FP propeller Total Power: 4,507kW (6,128hp) 13.9kn MAN-B&W 6L35MC 1 x 2 Stroke 6 Cy. 350 x 1050 4507kW (6128bhp) The Hanshin Diesel Works Ltd-Japan AuxGen: 3 x 380kW a.c Thrusters: 1 Tunnel thruster (f) Fuel: 113.0 (d.f.) 552.0 (r.f.)
208631 *WDN5*	**ZAMBATEK 33** *ex* YSK Satu *-2004* **Focus Fleet Sdn Bhd** - *Kuching* Malaysia Official number: 329210	**150** 45 165	Class: NK	**1999-03 Sealink Shipyard Sdn Bhd — Miri** Yd No: 103 Loa 25.30 Br ex - Dght 2.862 Lbp 23.55 Br md 7.30 Dpth 3.50 Welded, 1 dk	**(B32A2ST) Tug**	**2 oil engines** reduction geared to sc. shafts driving 2 FP propellers Total Power: 988kW (1,344hp) 12.0kn Caterpillar 3412TA 2 x Vee 4 Stroke 12 Cy. 137 x 152 each-494kW (672bhp) Caterpillar Inc-USA Fuel: 117.0 (d.f.)
612246 *QLZ*	**ZAMBESI** **ms 'Zambesi' Schiffahrtsgesellschaft mbH & co kg** John T Essberger GmbH & Co KG *Madeira* Portugal (MAR) MMSI: 255805460	**24,341** 11,521 34,205 T/cm 49.6	Class: GL	**2013-05 Yangfan Group Co Ltd — Zhoushan ZJ** Yd No: 2183 Loa 179.97 Br ex - Dght 10.100 Lbp 176.75 Br md 30.00 Dpth 14.70 Welded, 1 dk	**(A21A2BC) Bulk Carrier** Double Hull Grain: 46,700; Bale: 46,545 Compartments: 5 Ho, ER 5 Ha: 4 (19.2 x 20.3)ER (16.0 x 18.7) Cranes: 4x35t	**1 oil engine** driving 1 FP propeller Total Power: 6,900kW (9,381hp) 14.2kn Wartsila 5RT-flex50 1 x 2 Stroke 5 Cy. 500 x 2050 6900kW (9381bhp) AuxGen: 3 x 570kW 450V a.c Fuel: 160.0 (d.f.) 1400.0 (r.f.)

IMO / Call sign	Name / Owner / Port	Tonnage	Class	Builder / Dimensions	Type	Machinery
7325722 *V5ZZ* -	**ZAMBEZI** - - *Walvis Bay* *Namibia*	*582* 375 -	Class: (NV)	**1973**-10 **Salthammer Baatbyggeri AS — Vestnes** (Hull) Yd No: 109 **1973**-10 **Sterkoder Mek. Verksted AS — Kristiansund** Yd No: 33 Loa 45.12 Br ex - Dght 4.268 Lbp 40.24 Br md 9.00 Dpth 6.43 Welded, 2 dks	**(B11A2FS) Stern Trawler** Ice Capable	**1 oil engine** driving 1 FP propeller Total Power: 1,103kW (1,500hp) Normo LDM- 1 x 4 Stroke 9 Cy. 250 x 300 1103kW (1500bhp) AS Bergens Mek Verksteder-Norway
9412000 *2CKK9* -	**ZAMBEZI STAR** **Rigel Reederei GmbH & Co KG mt 'Zambezi Star'** Rigel Schiffahrts GmbH & Co KG *Douglas* *Isle of Man (British)* MMSI: 235073548 Official number: DR0168	**23,312** 9,972 37,874 T/cm 45.2	Class: LR ✠ **100A1** SS 02/2010 Double Hull oil and chemical tanker, Ship Type 3 CSR ESP *IWS LI ✠ **LMC** **UMS IGS** Eq.Ltr: J†; Cable: 605.0/66.0 U3 (a)	**2010**-02 **Hyundai Mipo Dockyard Co Ltd — Ulsan** Yd No: 2097 Loa 184.00 (BB) Br ex 27.40 Dght 11.515 Lbp 176.00 Br md 27.40 Dpth 17.20 Welded, 1 dk	**(A12B2TR) Chemical/Products Tanker** Double Hull (13F) Liq: 40,758; Liq (Oil): 42,630 Compartments: 12 Wing Ta, 2 Wing Slop Ta, ER 12 Cargo Pump (s): 10x500m³/hr, 2x300m³/hr Manifold: Bow/CM: 92.2m	**1 oil engine** driving 1 FP propeller Total Power: 7,860kW (10,686hp) 14.5k MAN-B&W 6S46MC-C 1 x 2 Stroke 6 Cy. 460 x 1932 7860kW (10686bhp) Hyundai Heavy Industries Co Ltd-South Korea AuxGen: 3 x 730kW a.c Boilers: e (ex.g.) 9.1kgf/cm² (8.9bar), WTAuxB (o.f.) 9.0kgf/cm² (8.8bar) Fuel: 155.0 (d.f.) 950.0 (r.f.)
7312165 *V5ZA* L805	**ZAMBIA** **ETALE Fishing Co (Pty) Ltd** - *Walvis Bay* *Namibia* Official number: 95WB003	*650* 375 -	Class: (NV)	**1973**-05 **Salthammer Baatbyggeri AS — Vestnes** (Hull) Yd No: 108 **1973**-05 **Sterkoder Mek. Verksted AS — Kristiansund** Yd No: 32 Loa 47.00 Br ex 9.05 Dght 4.268 Lbp 40.16 Br md 9.00 Dpth 6.43 Welded, 2 dks	**(B11A2FS) Stern Trawler**	**1 oil engine** driving 1 FP propeller Total Power: 1,103kW (1,500hp) Normo LDM-9 1 x 4 Stroke 9 Cy. 250 x 300 1103kW (1500bhp) AS Bergens Mek Verksteder-Norway AuxGen: 2 x 112kW 440V 60Hz a.c
9168324 *A8VP3* -	**ZAMBIA** *ex* MSC Zambia *-2012* *ex* NYK Sirius *-2010* **Strachur Shipping Ltd** Zodiac Maritime Agencies Ltd SatCom: Inmarsat C 463707428 *Monrovia* *Liberia* MMSI: 636014643 Official number: 14643	**76,847** 30,006 82,171	Class: NK	**1998**-04 **Mitsui Eng. & SB. Co. Ltd., Chiba Works — Ichihara** Yd No: 1445 Loa 299.90 (BB) Br ex - Dght 14.032 Lbp 287.00 Br md 40.00 Dpth 23.90 Welded, 1 dk	**(A33A2CC) Container Ship (Fully Cellular)** TEU 6208 C Ho 3156 TEU C Dk 3052 TEU incl 500 ref C. Compartments: ER, 8 Cell Ho 18 Ha: ER	**1 oil engine** driving 1 FP propeller Total Power: 52,960kW (72,004hp) 23.0kn B&W 12K90MC 1 x 2 Stroke 12 Cy. 900 x 2550 52960kW (72004bhp) Mitsui Engineering & Shipbuilding CLtd-Japan AuxGen: 1 x 1500kW a.c, 4 x 2100kW a.c Thrusters: 2 Thwart. FP thruster (f) Fuel: 8950.0 (r.f.) 183.0pd
7377660 *DUH2142* -	**ZAMBOANGA FERRY** *ex* Tanegashima No. 2 *-1993* *ex* Tanegashima Maru No. 2 *-1992* **George & Peter Lines Inc** *Cebu* *Philippines* Official number: CEB1001134	*851* 408 100		**1974**-03 **Honda Zosen — Saiki** Yd No: 618 Loa - Br ex 12.22 Dght 3.480 Lbp 68.99 Br md 12.20 Dpth 3.61 Welded, 1 dk	**(A36A2PR) Passenger/Ro-Ro Ship (Vehicles)** Passengers: 704	**1 oil engine** driving 1 FP propeller Total Power: 1,692kW (2,300hp) Hanshin 6LU38 1 x 4 Stroke 6 Cy. 380 x 580 1692kW (2300bhp) Hanshin Nainenki Kogyo-Japan
9139799 *A9D2713* -	**ZAMIL 1** **Zamil Offshore Services Co Ltd** *Bahrain* *Bahrain* MMSI: 408732000 Official number: BN 3015	**1,282** 385 1,337	Class: AB (NK)	**1996**-07 **Southern Ocean Shipbuilding Co Pte Ltd — Singapore** Yd No: 205 Loa 61.00 Br ex - Dght 4.566 Lbp 56.54 Br md 14.00 Dpth 5.30 Welded, 1 dk	**(B21B20A) Anchor Handling Tug Supply**	**2 oil engines** reduction geared to sc. shafts driving 2 CP propellers Total Power: 3,602kW (4,898hp) 12.0kn Stork-Werkspoor 6SW280 2 x 4 Stroke 6 Cy. 280 x 300 each-1801kW (2449bhp) Stork Wartsila Diesel BV-Netherlands AuxGen: 3 x 270kW 440V 60Hz a.c Thrusters: 1 Thwart. CP thruster (f) Fuel: 335.8 (d.f.) 16.0pd
9139804 *A9D2714* -	**ZAMIL 2** **Zamil Offshore Services Co Ltd** *Bahrain* *Bahrain* MMSI: 408733000 Official number: BN 3014	**1,282** 385 1,312	Class: AB (NK)	**1996**-08 **Southern Ocean Shipbuilding Co Pte Ltd — Singapore** Yd No: 206 Loa 61.00 Br ex - Dght 4.566 Lbp 56.54 Br md 14.00 Dpth 5.30 Welded, 1 dk	**(B21B20A) Anchor Handling Tug Supply**	**2 oil engines** reduction geared to sc. shafts driving 2 CP propellers Total Power: 3,602kW (4,898hp) 12.0kn Stork-Werkspoor 6SW280 2 x 4 Stroke 6 Cy. 280 x 300 each-1801kW (2449bhp) Stork Wartsila Diesel BV-Netherlands AuxGen: 3 x 270kW 440V 60Hz a.c Thrusters: 1 Thwart. CP thruster (f) Fuel: 335.8 (d.f.) 16.0pd
9139816 *A9D2715* -	**ZAMIL 3** **Zamil Offshore Services Co Ltd** *Bahrain* *Bahrain* MMSI: 408734000 Official number: BN 3017	**1,282** 385 1,312	Class: AB (NK)	**1997**-03 **Southern Ocean Shipbuilding Co Pte Ltd — Singapore** Yd No: 207 Loa 61.00 Br ex - Dght 4.550 Lbp 56.54 Br md 14.00 Dpth 5.30 Welded, 1 dk	**(B21B20A) Anchor Handling Tug Supply**	**2 oil engines** reduction geared to sc. shafts driving 2 CP propellers Total Power: 3,602kW (4,898hp) 13.1kn Stork-Werkspoor 6SW280 2 x 4 Stroke 6 Cy. 280 x 300 each-1801kW (2449bhp) Stork Wartsila Diesel BV-Netherlands AuxGen: 3 x 270kW 440V 60Hz a.c Thrusters: 1 Thwart. CP thruster (f) Fuel: 335.8 (d.f.) 16.0pd
9193604 *A9D2716* -	**ZAMIL 4** **Zamil Offshore Services Co Ltd** *Bahrain* *Bahrain* MMSI: 408735000 Official number: BN 3018	**1,161** 349 1,173	Class: AB (NK)	**1998**-08 **Kanmon Zosen K.K. — Shimonoseki** Yd No: 601 Loa 60.85 Br ex - Dght 4.650 Lbp 56.25 Br md 13.15 Dpth 5.50 Welded, 1 dk	**(B21B20A) Anchor Handling Tug Supply**	**2 oil engines** reverse reduction geared to sc. shafts driving 2 CP propellers Total Power: 3,236kW (4,400hp) 12.0kn Daihatsu 6DKM-26 2 x 4 Stroke 6 Cy. 260 x 380 each-1618kW (2200bhp) Daihatsu Diesel Manufacturing Co Lt-Japan AuxGen: 3 x 243kW 440V 60Hz a.c Thrusters: 1 Thwart. CP thruster (f) Fuel: 295.7 (d.f.) 15.0pd
9193616 *A9D2717* -	**ZAMIL 5** **Zamil Offshore Services Co Ltd** *Bahrain* *Bahrain* MMSI: 408736000 Official number: BN 3019	**1,161** 349 1,173	Class: AB (NK)	**1998**-10 **Kanmon Zosen K.K. — Shimonoseki** Yd No: 602 Loa 60.85 Br ex - Dght 4.650 Lbp 54.20 Br md 13.15 Dpth 5.50 Welded, 1 dk	**(B21B20A) Anchor Handling Tug Supply**	**2 oil engines** reduction geared to sc. shafts driving 2 CP propellers Total Power: 3,236kW (4,400hp) 12.0kn Daihatsu 6DKM-26 2 x 4 Stroke 6 Cy. 260 x 380 each-1618kW (2200bhp) Daihatsu Diesel Manufacturing Co Lt-Japan AuxGen: 3 x 243kW 440V 60Hz a.c Thrusters: 1 Thwart. CP thruster (f) Fuel: 295.7 (d.f.) 15.0pd
9188893 *A9D2718* -	**ZAMIL 6** **Zamil Offshore Services Co Ltd** *Bahrain* *Bahrain* MMSI: 408737000 Official number: BN 3020	**1,267** 380 1,369	Class: AB	**1998**-12 **Pan-United Shipyard Pte Ltd — Singapore** Yd No: 123 Loa 61.00 Br ex - Dght 4.540 Lbp 55.00 Br md 14.00 Dpth 5.30 Welded, 1 dk	**(B21B20A) Anchor Handling Tug Supply**	**2 oil engines** with clutches & reduction geared to sc. shafts driving 2 CP propellers Total Power: 3,900kW (5,302hp) 13.0kn Stork-Wartsila 6SW28 2 x 4 Stroke 6 Cy. 280 x 300 each-1950kW (2651bhp) Wartsila NSD Nederland BV-Netherlands AuxGen: 3 x 210kW 220/440V 60Hz a.c Thrusters: 1 Thwart. FP thruster (f) Fuel: 286.3 (d.f.) 12.0pd
9198343 *A9D2719* -	**ZAMIL 7** **Zamil Offshore Services Co Ltd** *Bahrain* *Bahrain* MMSI: 408738000 Official number: BN 3021	**1,267** 380 1,360	Class: AB	**1999**-08 **Pan-United Shipyard Pte Ltd — Singapore** Yd No: 125 Loa 61.09 Br ex - Dght 4.540 Lbp 55.00 Br md 14.00 Dpth 5.30 Welded, 1 dk	**(B21B20A) Anchor Handling Tug Supply**	**2 oil engines** reduction geared to sc. shafts driving 2 CP propellers Total Power: 3,900kW (5,302hp) 13.0kn Wartsila 6L26 2 x 4 Stroke 6 Cy. 260 x 320 each-1950kW (2651bhp) Wartsila NSD Nederland BV-Netherlands AuxGen: 3 x 210kW a.c
8215699 *HP5711* -	**ZAMIL 9** *ex* Parrot Fish *-2002* *ex* Red Castor *-1990* *ex* Trans Castor *-1987* **Delta Offshore International FZE** Tek Management Corp *Panama* *Panama* MMSI: 373677000 Official number: 44903PEXT	**1,151** 345 1,135	Class: (AB) (BV) (GL)	**1983**-04 **Neue Jadewerft GmbH — Wilhelmshaven** Yd No: 163 Loa 60.61 (BB) Br ex 13.06 Dght 4.252 Lbp 57.10 Br md 13.01 Dpth 4.91 Welded, 1 dk	**(B21B20A) Anchor Handling Tug Supply**	**2 oil engines** with flexible couplings & sr gearedto sc. shafts driving 2 CP propellers Total Power: 3,236kW (4,400hp) 12.0kn MaK 6M453AK 2 x 4 Stroke 6 Cy. 320 x 420 each-1618kW (2200bhp) Krupp MaK Maschinenbau GmbH-Kiel AuxGen: 2 x 350kW 220/380V 50Hz a.c, 2 x 200kW 220/380V 50Hz a.c Thrusters: 1 Thwart. CP thruster (f)

No. / Call sign	Name / Owner / Flag	Tonnage	Class	Build / Dimensions	Type	Machinery
358797 *9HC*	**ZAMIL 10** **Zamil Offshore Services Co Ltd** - *Bahrain* *Bahrain* MMSI: 408786000 Official number: BN 4022	**1,621** 486 1,239	Class: AB	**2005-10 Zamil Operations & Maintenance Co Ltd (ZOMCO) — al-Khubar** Yd No: 106 Loa 64.00 Br ex - Dght 4.700 Lbp 57.00 Br md 14.80 Dpth 6.20 Welded, 1 dk	**(B21B20A) Anchor Handling Tug Supply**	**4 diesel electric oil engines** driving 4 gen. each 1820kW a.c Connecting to 2 elec. motors each (1950kW) driving 2 Z propellers Total Power: 7,368kW (10,016hp) 11.0kn Yanmar 6N280L-XV 4 x 4 Stroke 6 Cy. 280 x 380 each-1842kW (2504bhp) Yanmar Diesel Engine Co Ltd-Japan Thrusters: 2 Tunnel thruster (f)
362281 *9HE*	**ZAMIL 11** **Zamil Offshore Services Co Ltd** - *Bahrain* *Bahrain* MMSI: 408787000 Official number: BN 4027	**1,621** 486 1,232	Class: AB	**2005-10 Zamil Operations & Maintenance Co Ltd (ZOMCO) — al-Khubar** Yd No: 107 Loa 64.00 Br ex - Dght 4.700 Lbp 57.00 Br md 14.80 Dpth 6.20 Welded, 1 dk	**(B21B20A) Anchor Handling Tug Supply**	**4 diesel electric oil engines** driving 4 gen. Connecting to 2 elec. motors each (1950kW) driving 2 Z propellers Total Power: 7,280kW (9,896hp) 11.0kn Yanmar 6N280L-XV 4 x 4 Stroke 6 Cy. 280 x 380 each-1820kW (2474bhp) Yanmar Diesel Engine Co Ltd-Japan Thrusters: 2 Tunnel thruster (f)
367085 *9HJ*	**ZAMIL 12** **Zamil Offshore Services Co Ltd** - *Bahrain* *Bahrain* MMSI: 408793000 Official number: BN 4033	**1,621** 486 1,239	Class: AB	**2006-01 Zamil Operations & Maintenance Co Ltd (ZOMCO) — al-Khubar** Yd No: 108 Loa 64.00 Br ex - Dght 4.700 Lbp 57.00 Br md 14.80 Dpth 6.20 Welded, 1 dk	**(B21B20A) Anchor Handling Tug Supply**	**4 diesel electric oil engines** driving 4 gen. each 1820kW a.c Connecting to 2 elec. motors each (1950kW) driving 2 Z propellers Total Power: 7,280kW (9,896hp) 11.0kn Yanmar 6N280L-XV 4 x 4 Stroke 6 Cy. 280 x 380 each-1820kW (2474bhp) Yanmar Diesel Engine Co Ltd-Japan Thrusters: 2 Tunnel thruster (f)
367097 *9HL*	**ZAMIL 13** **Zamil Offshore Services Co Ltd** - *Bahrain* *Bahrain* MMSI: 408796000 Official number: BN 4038	**1,621** 486 1,239	Class: AB	**2006-04 Zamil Operations & Maintenance Co Ltd (ZOMCO) — al-Khubar** Yd No: 109 Loa 64.00 Br ex - Dght 4.600 Lbp 57.00 Br md 14.80 Dpth 6.20 Welded, 1 dk	**(B21B20A) Anchor Handling Tug Supply**	**4 diesel electric oil engines** driving 4 gen. each 1820kW a.c Connecting to 2 elec. motors each (1950kW) driving 2 Z propellers Total Power: 7,280kW (9,896hp) 11.0kn Yanmar 6N280L-XV 4 x 4 Stroke 6 Cy. 280 x 380 each-1820kW (2474bhp) Yanmar Diesel Engine Co Ltd-Japan Thrusters: 2 Tunnel thruster (f) Fuel: 565.0 (r.f.)
371488 *9D2861*	**ZAMIL 14** **Zamil Offshore Services Co Ltd** - *Bahrain* *Bahrain* MMSI: 408803000 Official number: BN 4049	**1,705** 511 1,849	Class: AB	**2006-08 Keppel Singmarine Pte Ltd — Singapore** Yd No: 302 Loa 60.00 Br ex 16.02 Dght 4.200 Lbp 58.70 Br md 15.97 Dpth 5.90 Welded, 1 dk	**(B21B20A) Anchor Handling Tug Supply**	**2 oil engines** reduction geared to sc. shafts driving 2 CP propellers Total Power: 3,000kW (4,078hp) Wartsila 6L26 2 x 4 Stroke 6 Cy. 260 x 320 each-1500kW (2039bhp) Wartsila Italia SpA-Italy AuxGen: 2 x 400kW a.c, 1 x 600kW a.c
371476 *9D2862*	**ZAMIL 15** **Zamil Offshore Services Co Ltd** - *Bahrain* *Bahrain* MMSI: 408804000 Official number: BN 4050	**1,705** 511 2,301	Class: AB	**2006-09 Keppel Singmarine Pte Ltd — Singapore** Yd No: 301 Loa 60.00 Br ex 16.02 Dght 4.200 Lbp 54.00 Br md 16.00 Dpth 6.00 Welded, 1 dk	**(B21B20A) Anchor Handling Tug Supply**	**2 oil engines** reduction geared to sc. shafts driving 2 CP propellers Total Power: 3,000kW (4,078hp) Wartsila 6L26 2 x 4 Stroke 6 Cy. 260 x 320 each-1500kW (2039bhp) Wartsila Italia SpA-Italy AuxGen: 2 x 400kW a.c, 1 x 600kW a.c
387891 *9D2888*	**ZAMIL 16** **Zamil Offshore Services Co Ltd** - *Bahrain* *Bahrain* MMSI: 408810000 Official number: BN 4066	**1,641** 492 1,239	Class: AB	**2007-05 Zamil Operations & Maintenance Co Ltd (ZOMCO) — al-Khubar** Yd No: 110 Loa 64.00 Br ex - Dght 4.700 Lbp 57.00 Br md 14.80 Dpth 6.20 Welded, 1 dk	**(B21B20A) Anchor Handling Tug Supply**	**4 diesel electric oil engines** driving 4 gen. each 1820kW a.c Connecting to 2 elec. motors each (1950kW) driving 2 Z propellers Total Power: 7,280kW (9,896hp) 11.0kn Yanmar 6N280L-XV 4 x 4 Stroke 6 Cy. 280 x 380 each-1820kW (2474bhp) Yanmar Diesel Engine Co Ltd-Japan
387906 *9D2901*	**ZAMIL 17** **Zamil Offshore Services Co Ltd** - *Bahrain* *Bahrain* MMSI: 408812000 Official number: BN 4084	**1,641** 492 1,239	Class: AB	**2007-05 Zamil Operations & Maintenance Co Ltd (ZOMCO) — al-Khubar** Yd No: 111 Loa 64.00 Br ex - Dght 4.700 Lbp 57.00 Br md 14.80 Dpth 6.20 Welded, 1 dk	**(B21B20A) Anchor Handling Tug Supply**	**4 diesel electric oil engines** driving 4 gen. each 1820kW a.c Connecting to 2 elec. motors each (1950kW) driving 2 Z propellers Total Power: 7,280kW (9,896hp) 11.0kn Yanmar 6N280L-XV 4 x 4 Stroke 6 Cy. 280 x 380 each-1820kW (2474bhp) Yanmar Diesel Engine Co Ltd-Japan Fuel: 519.4 (r.f.)
437012 *9D2915*	**ZAMIL 18** **Zamil Offshore Services Co Ltd** - *Bahrain* *Bahrain* MMSI: 408818000 Official number: BN4095	**1,641** 492 1,239	Class: AB	**2007-05 Zamil Operations & Maintenance Co Ltd (ZOMCO) — al-Khubar** Yd No: 112 Loa 64.00 Br ex - Dght 4.600 Lbp 57.00 Br md 14.80 Dpth 6.20 Welded, 1 dk	**(B21B20A) Anchor Handling Tug Supply**	**4 diesel electric oil engines** driving 4 gen. each 1820kW a.c Connecting to 2 elec. motors each (1950kW) driving 2 Z propellers Total Power: 7,280kW (9,896hp) 13.0kn Yanmar 6N280L-XV 4 x 4 Stroke 6 Cy. 280 x 380 each-1820kW (2474bhp) Yanmar Diesel Engine Co Ltd-Japan Fuel: 519.4 (r.f.)
439187 *9D2926*	**ZAMIL 19** **Zamil Offshore Services Co Ltd** - *Bahrain* *Bahrain* MMSI: 408322000 Official number: BN 4099	**1,641** 492 1,239	Class: AB	**2007-07 Zamil Operations & Maintenance Co Ltd (ZOMCO) — al-Khubar** Yd No: 113 Loa 64.00 Br ex - Dght 4.700 Lbp 57.00 Br md 14.80 Dpth 6.20 Welded, 1 dk	**(B21B20A) Anchor Handling Tug Supply**	**4 diesel electric oil engines** driving 4 gen. each 1820kW a.c Connecting to 2 elec. motors each (1950kW) driving 2 Azimuth electric drive units Total Power: 7,280kW (9,896hp) 13.0kn Yanmar 6N280L-XV 4 x 4 Stroke 6 Cy. 280 x 380 each-1820kW (2474bhp) Yanmar Diesel Engine Co Ltd-Japan Fuel: 519.4 (r.f.)
269439 *9D2794*	**ZAMIL 21** **Zamil Offshore Services Co Ltd** - *Bahrain* *Bahrain* MMSI: 408756000 Official number: BN 3059	**691** 207 536	Class: AB	**2003-04 ABG Shipyard Ltd — Surat** Yd No: 196 Loa 49.50 Br ex 11.62 Dght 3.000 Lbp 45.26 Br md 11.60 Dpth 4.30 Welded, 1 dk	**(B21A20C) Crew/Supply Vessel**	**2 oil engines** geared to sc. shafts driving 2 CP propellers Total Power: 2,162kW (2,940hp) Wartsila 6L20 2 x 4 Stroke 6 Cy. 200 x 280 each-1081kW (1470bhp) Wartsila Finland Oy-Finland
269441 *9D2795*	**ZAMIL 22** **Zamil Offshore Services Co Ltd** - *Bahrain* *Bahrain* MMSI: 408757000 Official number: BN 3060	**701** 210 536	Class: AB	**2003-05 ABG Shipyard Ltd — Surat** Yd No: 198 Loa 49.50 Br ex 11.62 Dght 3.000 Lbp 45.00 Br md 11.60 Dpth 4.30 Welded, 1 dk	**(B21A20C) Crew/Supply Vessel**	**2 oil engines** geared to sc. shafts driving 2 CP propellers Total Power: 2,162kW (2,940hp) Wartsila 6L20 2 x 4 Stroke 6 Cy. 200 x 280 each-1081kW (1470bhp) Wartsila Finland Oy-Finland
269453 *9D2796*	**ZAMIL 23** **Zamil Offshore Services Co Ltd** - *Bahrain* *Bahrain* MMSI: 408758000 Official number: BN 3061	**701** 210 536	Class: AB	**2003-09 ABG Shipyard Ltd — Surat** Yd No: 199 Loa 49.50 Br ex 11.62 Dght 3.500 Lbp 45.26 Br md 11.60 Dpth 4.30 Welded, 1 dk	**(B21A20C) Crew/Supply Vessel**	**2 oil engines** geared to sc. shafts driving 2 CP propellers Total Power: 2,128kW (2,894hp) Wartsila 6L20 2 x 4 Stroke 6 Cy. 200 x 280 each-1064kW (1447bhp) Wartsila Finland Oy-Finland
269465 *9D2797*	**ZAMIL 24** **Zamil Offshore Services Co Ltd** - *Bahrain* *Bahrain* MMSI: 408759000 Official number: BN 3062	**701** 210 536	Class: AB	**2003-11 ABG Shipyard Ltd — Surat** Yd No: 200 Loa 49.50 Br ex 11.62 Dght 3.050 Lbp 45.26 Br md 11.60 Dpth 4.30 Welded, 1 dk	**(B21A20C) Crew/Supply Vessel**	**2 oil engines** geared to sc. shafts driving 2 CP propellers Total Power: 2,128kW (2,894hp) Wartsila 6L20 2 x 4 Stroke 6 Cy. 200 x 280 each-1064kW (1447bhp) Wartsila Finland Oy-Finland
287572 *ZG5728*	**ZAMIL 25** **Zamil Offshore Services Co Ltd** - *Dammam* *Saudi Arabia* MMSI: 403709110 Official number: 911	**701** 210 475	Class: AB	**2003-05 Zamil Operations & Maintenance Co Ltd (ZOMCO) — al-Khubar** Yd No: 100 Loa 49.50 Br ex - Dght 3.050 Lbp 45.26 Br md 11.60 Dpth 4.30 Welded, 1 dk	**(B21A20C) Crew/Supply Vessel**	**2 oil engines** geared to sc. shafts driving 2 CP propellers Total Power: 2,160kW (2,936hp) Wartsila 6L20 2 x 4 Stroke 6 Cy. 200 x 280 each-1080kW (1468bhp) Wartsila Finland Oy-Finland AuxGen: 3 x 93kW a.c

Ship	Tonnage	Class	Builder / Dimensions	Type	Machinery
9299006 *HZG5024* - **ZAMIL 26** **Zamil Offshore Services Co Ltd** - *Dammam* *Saudi Arabia* MMSI: 403706710 Official number: 939	**701** 210 468	Class: AB	**2003-12 Zamil Operations & Maintenance Co Ltd (ZOMCO) — al-Khubar** Yd No: 101 Loa 49.23 Br ex - Dght 3.050 Lbp 45.26 Br md 11.60 Dpth 4.30 Welded, 1 dk	**(B21A20C) Crew/Supply Vessel**	**2 oil engines** reduction geared to sc. shafts driving 2 CP propellers Total Power: 1,912kW (2,600hp) Yanmar 6N21A-E 2 x 4 Stroke 6 Cy. 210 x 290 each-956kW (1300bhp) Yanmar Diesel Engine Co Ltd-Japan AuxGen: 2 x 150kW a.c
9467110 *A9JP* - **ZAMIL 31** *ex* ASL Harmony *-2011* **Zamil Offshore Services Co Ltd** - *Bahrain* *Bahrain* MMSI: 408835000 Official number: BN 6039	**1,092** 327 1,267	Class: AB	**2008-06 Berjaya Dockyard Sdn Bhd — Miri** Yd No: 49 Loa 55.00 Br ex - Dght 4.300 Lbp 48.10 Br md 13.80 Dpth 5.50 Welded, 1 dk	**(B21A20S) Platform Supply Ship**	**2 oil engines** reverse reduction geared to sc. shafts driving 2 Propellers Total Power: 2,942kW (4,000hp) Niigata 6MG26HL 2 x 4 Stroke 6 Cy. 260 x 350 each-1471kW (2000bhp) Niigata Engineering Co Ltd-Japan AuxGen: 2 x 245kW a.c
8827351 *A9GY* - **ZAMIL 32** *ex* Malaviya Eleven *-2005* *ex* SKBB Kemajuan 301 *-1998* **Zamil Offshore Services Co Ltd** - *Bahrain* *Bahrain* MMSI: 408780000 Official number: BN 3098	**877** 263 885	Class: AB (IR) (BV)	**1989 Greenbay Marine Pte Ltd — Singapore** Yd No: 70 Loa 59.00 Br ex - Dght 2.510 Lbp 51.30 Br md 12.00 Dpth 3.80 Welded, 1 dk	**(B21A20S) Platform Supply Ship**	**2 oil engines** driving 2 FP propellers Total Power: 1,908kW (2,594hp) 12.5kn Caterpillar 3512TA 2 x Vee 4 Stroke 12 Cy. 170 x 190 each-954kW (1297bhp) Caterpillar Inc-USA AuxGen: 3 x 655kW 220V 50Hz a.c Fuel: 151.9 (d.f.)
9332274 *A9HB* - **ZAMIL 33** *completed as* Atlantic 8 *-2005* **Zamil Offshore Services Co Ltd** - *Bahrain* *Bahrain* MMSI: 408784000 Official number: BN 4014	**1,095** 328 1,039	Class: AB	**2005-04 Hin Lee (Zhuhai) Shipyard Co Ltd — Zhuhai GD** (Hull) Yd No: 076 **2005-04 Cheoy Lee Shipyards Ltd — Hong Kong** Yd No: 4846 Loa 53.80 Br ex 13.83 Dght 3.600 Lbp 48.50 Br md 13.80 Dpth 4.50 Welded, 1 dk	**(B21A20S) Platform Supply Ship**	**2 oil engines** reverse reduction geared to sc. shafts driving 2 FP propellers Total Power: 2,316kW (3,148hp) 11.0kn Caterpillar 3512B 2 x Vee 4 Stroke 12 Cy. 170 x 190 each-1158kW (1574bhp) Caterpillar Inc-USA AuxGen: 3 x 99kW 440V 60Hz a.c Thrusters: 1 Tunnel thruster (f)
9369801 *A9HM* - **ZAMIL 34** **Zamil Offshore Services Co Ltd** - *Bahrain* *Bahrain* MMSI: 408799000 Official number: BN 4051	**1,163** 349 955	Class: AB	**2006-06 Hin Lee (Zhuhai) Shipyard Co Ltd — Zhuhai GD** (Hull) Yd No: 103 **2006-06 Cheoy Lee Shipyards Ltd — Hong Kong** Yd No: 4881 Loa 53.80 Br ex - Dght 3.600 Lbp 48.80 Br md 13.80 Dpth 4.50 Welded, 1 dk	**(B22A20R) Offshore Support Vessel** Cranes: 1	**2 oil engines** reverse reduction geared to sc. shafts driving 2 FP propellers Total Power: 2,316kW (3,148hp) 11.0kn Caterpillar 3512B 2 x Vee 4 Stroke 12 Cy. 170 x 190 each-1158kW (1574bhp) Caterpillar Inc-USA AuxGen: 3 x 260kW a.c Thrusters: 1 Tunnel thruster (f)
9570735 *A9JJ* - **ZAMIL 35** *ex* Hims 10 *-2009* **Zamil Offshore Services Co Ltd** - *Bahrain* *Bahrain* MMSI: 408800000 Official number: BN 6029	**1,211** 363 1,138	Class: AB	**2009-12 Zhongshan Jinhui Shipbuilding & Repair Yard Co Ltd — Zhongshan GD** Yd No: JH2005 Loa 53.80 Br ex - Dght 3.990 Lbp 48.66 Br md 13.80 Dpth 5.00 Welded, 1 dk	**(B21A20S) Platform Supply Ship**	**2 oil engines** reverse reduction geared to sc. shaft driving 2 FP propellers Total Power: 2,386kW (3,244hp) Cummins KTA-50-M2 2 x Vee 4 Stroke 16 Cy. 159 x 159 each-1193kW (1622bhp) Cummins Engine Co Inc-USA AuxGen: 3 x 240kW a.c
9550400 *A9JK* - **ZAMIL 36** **Zamil Offshore Services Co Ltd** - *Bahrain* *Bahrain* MMSI: 408397000 Official number: BN 6030	**1,060** 318 960	Class: AB (BV)	**2010-01 Guangzhou Panyu Lingshan Shipyard Ltd — Guangzhou GD** Yd No: 216 Loa 53.80 Br ex - Dght 3.000 Lbp 49.50 Br md 13.80 Dpth 4.50 Welded, 1 dk	**(B21A20S) Platform Supply Ship**	**2 oil engines** reduction geared to sc. shafts driving 2 FP propellers Total Power: 1,940kW (2,638hp) 12.0kn Caterpillar 3512B 2 x Vee 4 Stroke 12 Cy. 170 x 190 each-970kW (1319bhp) Caterpillar Inc-USA Thrusters: 1 Tunnel thruster (f)
9634048 *A9JT* - **ZAMIL 37** **Zamil Offshore Services Co Ltd** - *Bahrain* *Bahrain* MMSI: 408429000 Official number: BN 6040	**1,214** 364 -	Class: AB (BV)	**2011-12 Guangzhou Panyu Lingshan Shipyard Ltd — Guangzhou GD** Yd No: 217 Loa 56.00 Br ex - Dght 4.000 Lbp 51.30 Br md 13.80 Dpth 5.00 Welded, 1 dk	**(B21A20S) Platform Supply Ship**	**2 oil engines** reduction geared to sc. shafts driving 2 FP propellers Total Power: 2,548kW (3,464hp) 12.0kn Caterpillar 3512B 2 x Vee 4 Stroke 12 Cy. 170 x 190 each-1274kW (1732bhp) Caterpillar Inc-USA AuxGen: 3 x 245kW 50Hz a.c Thrusters: 1 Tunnel thruster (f) Fuel: 480.0
9335769 *A9HF* - **ZAMIL 41** **Zamil Offshore Services Co Ltd** - *Bahrain* *Bahrain* MMSI: 408788000 Official number: BN 4029	**188** 56 84	Class: AB	**2005-08 Colombo Dockyard Ltd. — Colombo** Yd No: 185 Loa 33.50 Br ex 6.95 Dght 2.300 Lbp 29.17 Br md 6.80 Dpth 3.70 Welded, 1 dk	**(B21A20C) Crew/Supply Vessel** Hull Material: Aluminium Alloy Passengers: unberthed: 30; berths: 8	**2 oil engines** reduction geared to sc. shafts driving 2 FP propellers Total Power: 2,850kW (3,874hp) Caterpillar 3512B 2 x Vee 4 Stroke 12 Cy. 170 x 190 each-1425kW (1937bhp) Caterpillar Inc-USA AuxGen: 2 x 175kW a.c
9335771 *A9HG* - **ZAMIL 42** **Zamil Offshore Services Co Ltd** - *Bahrain* *Bahrain* MMSI: 408789000 Official number: BN 4030	**188** 56 84	Class: AB	**2005-08 Colombo Dockyard Ltd. — Colombo** Yd No: 186 Loa 33.50 Br ex 6.95 Dght 2.300 Lbp 29.17 Br md 6.80 Dpth 3.70 Welded, 1 dk	**(B21A20C) Crew/Supply Vessel** Hull Material: Aluminium Alloy Passengers: unberthed: 30; berths: 8	**2 oil engines** reduction geared to sc. shafts driving 2 FP propellers Total Power: 2,850kW (3,874hp) Caterpillar 3512B 2 x Vee 4 Stroke 12 Cy. 170 x 190 each-1425kW (1937bhp) Caterpillar Inc-USA AuxGen: 2 x 175kW a.c
9452892 *A9D2951* - **ZAMIL 50** **Zamil Offshore Services Co Ltd** - *Bahrain* *Bahrain* MMSI: 408823000 Official number: BN5020	**1,641** 492 1,239	Class: AB	**2007-12 Zamil Operations & Maintenance Co Ltd (ZOMCO) — al-Khubar** Yd No: 114 Loa 64.00 Br ex - Dght 4.600 Lbp 57.00 Br md 14.80 Dpth 6.20 Welded, 1 dk	**(B21B20A) Anchor Handling Tug Supply**	**4 diesel electric oil engines** driving 4 gen. each 1820kW a.c Connecting to 2 elec. motors each (1950kW) driving 2 Azimuth electric drive units Total Power: 7,280kW (9,896hp) 13.0kn Yanmar 6N280L-XV 4 x 4 Stroke 6 Cy. 280 x 380 each-1820kW (2474bhp) Yanmar Diesel Engine Co Ltd-Japan Thrusters: 2 Tunnel thruster (f)
9487512 *A9HV* - **ZAMIL 51** **Zamil Offshore Services Co Ltd** - *Bahrain* *Bahrain* MMSI: 408825000 Official number: BN 5037	**1,737** 521 1,239	Class: AB	**2008-07 Zamil Offshore Services Co Ltd — al-Khubar** Yd No: 115 Loa 64.00 Br ex - Dght 4.800 Lbp 57.00 Br md 14.80 Dpth 6.20 Welded, 1 dk	**(B21B20A) Anchor Handling Tug Supply**	**4 diesel electric oil engines** driving 4 gen. each 1820kW a.c Connecting to 2 elec. motors each (1950kW) driving 2 Azimuth electric drive units Total Power: 7,280kW (9,896hp) 13.0kn Yanmar 6N280L-XV 4 x 4 Stroke 6 Cy. 280 x 380 each-1820kW (2474bhp) Yanmar Diesel Engine Co Ltd-Japan Fuel: 467.0
9515890 *A9IB* - **ZAMIL 52** **Zamil Offshore Services Co Ltd** - *Bahrain* *Bahrain* MMSI: 408314000 Official number: BN5054	**1,574** 513 1,600	Class: AB	**2008-12 Zamil Offshore Services Co Ltd — al-Khubar** Yd No: 116 Loa 65.45 (BB) Br ex - Dght 5.100 Lbp 57.90 Br md 14.50 Dpth 6.00 Welded, 1 dk	**(B21B20A) Anchor Handling Tug Supply**	**2 oil engines** reduction geared to sc. shafts driving 2 Directional propellers Total Power: 5,220kW (7,098hp) 14.5kn Bergens C25: 33L9P 2 x 4 Stroke 9 Cy. 250 x 330 each-2610kW (3549bhp) Rolls Royce Marine AS-Norway AuxGen: 2 x 272kW 440V 60Hz a.c, 2 x 1400kW 440V 60Hz a.c Thrusters: 1 Tunnel thruster (f) Fuel: 637.0 (d.f.)
9530723 *A9IJ* - **ZAMIL 53** **Zamil Offshore Services Co Ltd** - *Bahrain* *Bahrain* MMSI: 408336000 Official number: BN5068	**1,574** 513 1,600	Class: AB	**2009-04 Zamil Offshore Services Co Ltd — al-Khubar** Yd No: 117 Loa 63.70 Br ex - Dght 4.500 Lbp 56.55 Br md 14.50 Dpth 6.00 Welded, 1 dk	**(B21B20A) Anchor Handling Tug Supply**	**2 oil engines** Connecting to 2 elec. motors each (1950kW) geared to sc. shafts driving 2 Directional propellers Total Power: 5,220kW (7,098hp) Bergens C25: 33L9P 2 x 4 Stroke 9 Cy. 250 x 330 each-2610kW (3549bhp) Rolls Royce Marine AS-Norway AuxGen: 2 x 272kW 440V 60Hz a.c, 2 x 1400kW 440V 60Hz a.c Thrusters: 1 Tunnel thruster (f) Fuel: 637.0 (d.f.)

IMO / Call sign	Name / Owner	Tonnage	Class	Build / Dimensions	Type	Machinery
541473 9IN	**ZAMIL 54** **Zamil Offshore Services Co Ltd** - SatCom: Inmarsat C 440834410 *Bahrain* Bahrain MMSI: 408344000 Official number: BN5091	**1,574** 513 1,855	Class: AB	**2009-06 Zamil Offshore Services Co Ltd — al-Khubar** Yd No: 118 Loa 65.45 (BB) Br ex - Dght 4.500 Lbp 57.90 Br md 14.50 Dpth 6.00 Welded, 1 dk	**(B21B20A) Anchor Handling Tug Supply**	**2 oil engines** reduction geared to sc. shafts driving 2 Propellers Total Power: 5,400kW (7,342hp) Bergens C25: 33L9P 2 x 4 Stroke 9 Cy. 250 x 330 each-2700kW (3671bhp) Rolls Royce Marine AS-Norway Thrusters: 2 Tunnel thruster (f); 1 Tunnel thruster (a)
541485 A9IS	**ZAMIL 55** **Zamil Offshore Services Co Ltd** - *Bahrain* Bahrain MMSI: 408347000 Official number: BN5092	**1,574** 513 1,853	Class: AB	**2009-08 Zamil Offshore Services Co Ltd — al-Khubar** Yd No: 119 Loa 63.70 (BB) Br ex - Dght 4.500 Lbp 56.55 Br md 14.50 Dpth 6.00 Welded, 1 dk	**(B21B20A) Anchor Handling Tug Supply**	**2 oil engines** reduction geared to sc. shafts driving 2 Propellers Total Power: 5,400kW (7,342hp) Bergens C25: 33L9P 2 x 4 Stroke 9 Cy. 250 x 330 each-2700kW (3671bhp) Rolls Royce Marine AS-Norway AuxGen: 2 x 1400kW 440V 60Hz a.c, 2 x 272kW 440V 60Hz a.c
9541497 A9IV	**ZAMIL 56** **Zamil Operation & Maintenance Co Ltd (ZOMCO)** - *Bahrain* Bahrain MMSI: 408351000 Official number: BN 6001	**1,574** 513 1,600	Class: AB	**2010-01 Zamil Offshore Services Co Ltd — al-Khubar** Yd No: 120 Loa 65.45 (BB) Br ex - Dght 4.500 Lbp 60.00 Br md 14.50 Dpth 6.00 Welded, 1 dk	**(B21B20A) Anchor Handling Tug Supply**	**2 oil engines** geareding integral to driving 2 Directional propellers Total Power: 5,220kW (7,098hp) Bergens C25: 33L9P 2 x 4 Stroke 9 Cy. 250 x 330 each-2610kW (3549bhp) Rolls Royce Marine AS-Norway AuxGen: 2 x 1400kW a.c, 2 x 305kW a.c
9541980 A9JC -	**ZAMIL 57** **Zamil Offshore Services Co Ltd** - *Bahrain* Bahrain MMSI: 408371000 Official number: BN6017	**1,514** 454 1,600	Class: AB	**2010-06 Zamil Offshore Services Co Ltd — al-Khubar** Yd No: 122 Loa 63.70 (BB) Br ex - Dght 5.100 Lbp 56.55 Br md 14.50 Dpth 6.00 Welded, 1 dk	**(B21B20A) Anchor Handling Tug Supply**	**2 oil engines** reduction geared to sc. shafts driving 2 Directional propellers Total Power: 5,220kW (7,098hp) Bergens C25: 33L9P 2 x 4 Stroke 9 Cy. 250 x 330 each-2610kW (3549bhp) Rolls Royce Marine AS-Norway AuxGen: 2 x 1400kW a.c, 2 x 272kW a.c
9541992 A9JD -	**ZAMIL 58** **Zamil Offshore Services Co Ltd** - *Bahrain* Bahrain MMSI: 408372000 Official number: BN6018	**1,514** 454 1,600	Class: AB	**2010-07 Zamil Offshore Services Co Ltd — al-Khubar** Yd No: 123 Loa 63.70 (BB) Br ex - Dght 5.100 Lbp 55.55 Br md 14.50 Dpth 6.00 Welded, 1 dk	**(B21B20A) Anchor Handling Tug Supply**	**2 oil engines** reduction geared to sc. shafts driving 2 FP propellers Total Power: 5,220kW (7,098hp) Bergens C25: 33L9P 2 x 4 Stroke 9 Cy. 250 x 330 each-2610kW (3549bhp) Rolls Royce Marine AS-Norway AuxGen: 2 x 1400kW a.c, 2 x 305kW a.c
9540493 A9IH -	**ZAMIL 59** **Zamil Offshore Services Co Ltd** - *Bahrain* Bahrain MMSI: 408337000 Official number: BN 5079	**1,330** 400 1,393	Class: AB	**2009-04 Hin Lee (Zhuhai) Shipyard Co Ltd — Zhuhai GD** (Hull) Yd No: 156 **2009-04 Cheoy Lee Shipyards Ltd — Hong Kong** Yd No: 4938 Loa 58.00 Br ex - Dght 4.750 Lbp 56.50 Br md 13.80 Dpth 5.50 Welded, 1 dk	**(B21B20A) Anchor Handling Tug Supply**	**2 oil engines** reduction geared to sc. shafts driving 2 Directional propellers Total Power: 3,676kW (4,998hp) 12.0kn Niigata 6L28HX 2 x 4 Stroke 6 Cy. 280 x 370 each-1838kW (2499bhp) Niigata Engineering Co Ltd-Japan AuxGen: 3 x 320kW a.c Thrusters: 1 Tunnel thruster (f) Fuel: 400.0
9540508 A9IP -	**ZAMIL 60** **Zamil Offshore Services Co Ltd** - SatCom: Inmarsat C 440834810 *Bahrain* Bahrain MMSI: 408348000 Official number: BN5093	**1,330** 399 1,393	Class: AB	**2009-07 Hin Lee (Zhuhai) Shipyard Co Ltd — Zhuhai GD** (Hull) Yd No: 157 **2009-07 Cheoy Lee Shipyards Ltd — Hong Kong** Yd No: 4939 Loa 58.00 Br ex - Dght 4.750 Lbp 56.50 Br md 13.80 Dpth 5.50 Welded, 1 dk	**(B21B20A) Anchor Handling Tug Supply**	**2 oil engines** reduction geared to sc. shafts driving 2 Directional propellers Total Power: 3,676kW (4,998hp) 12.0kn Niigata 6L28HX 2 x 4 Stroke 6 Cy. 280 x 370 each-1838kW (2499bhp) Niigata Engineering Co Ltd-Japan AuxGen: 3 x 320kW a.c
9540510 A9IW -	**ZAMIL 61** **Zamil Offshore Services Co Ltd** - *Bahrain* Bahrain MMSI: 408352000 Official number: BN 6002	**1,330** 399 1,361	Class: AB	**2009-11 Hin Lee (Zhuhai) Shipyard Co Ltd — Zhuhai GD** (Hull) Yd No: 158 **2009-11 Cheoy Lee Shipyards Ltd — Hong Kong** Yd No: 4940 Loa 58.00 Br ex - Dght 4.750 Lbp 56.50 Br md 13.80 Dpth 5.50 Welded, 1 dk	**(B21B20A) Anchor Handling Tug Supply**	**2 oil engines** geared to sc. shafts driving 2 Directional propellers Total Power: 3,676kW (4,998hp) 12.0kn Niigata 6L28HX 2 x 4 Stroke 6 Cy. 280 x 370 each-1838kW (2499bhp) Niigata Engineering Co Ltd-Japan AuxGen: 3 x 320kW a.c Thrusters: 1 Tunnel thruster (f) Fuel: 446.0
9540522 A9JB -	**ZAMIL 62** **Zamil Operation & Maintenance Co Ltd (ZOMCO)** Zamil Offshore Services Co Ltd *Bahrain* Bahrain MMSI: 408367000 Official number: BN6015	**1,330** 399 1,393	Class: AB	**2010-04 Hin Lee (Zhuhai) Shipyard Co Ltd — Zhuhai GD** (Hull) Yd No: 159 **2010-04 Cheoy Lee Shipyards Ltd — Hong Kong** Yd No: 4941 Loa 58.00 Br ex - Dght 4.750 Lbp 51.70 Br md 13.80 Dpth 5.50 Welded, 1 dk	**(B21B20A) Anchor Handling Tug Supply**	**2 oil engines** reduction geared to sc. shafts driving 2 Directional propellers Total Power: 3,676kW (4,998hp) 12.0kn Niigata 6L28HX 2 x 4 Stroke 6 Cy. 280 x 370 each-1838kW (2499bhp) Niigata Engineering Co Ltd-Japan AuxGen: 3 x 320kW a.c Thrusters: 1 Tunnel thruster (f)
9497012 A9JL -	**ZAMIL 63** **Zamil Offshore Services Co Ltd** - *Bahrain* Bahrain MMSI: 408398000 Official number: BN 6028	**2,383** 714 1,531	Class: AB	**2011-09 Zamil Offshore Services Co Ltd — al-Khubar** Yd No: 130 Loa 65.50 (BB) Br ex - Dght 4.800 Lbp 58.90 Br md 14.80 Dpth 6.50 Welded, 1 dk	**(B21B20A) Anchor Handling Tug Supply** Cranes: 1x20t	**2 oil engines** gearing integral to driving 2 Z propellers Total Power: 5,200kW (7,070hp) Wartsila 8L26 2 x 4 Stroke 8 Cy. 260 x 320 each-2600kW (3535bhp) Wartsila Finland Oy-Finland AuxGen: 4 x 650kW a.c Thrusters: 2 Tunnel thruster (f)
9497024 A9JQ -	**ZAMIL 64** **Zamil Offshore Services Co Ltd** - *Bahrain* Bahrain MMSI: 408399000 Official number: BN 6033	**2,383** 714 1,538	Class: AB	**2012-01 Zamil Offshore Services Co Ltd — al-Khubar** Yd No: 131 Loa 65.50 (BB) Br ex - Dght 5.190 Lbp 63.12 Br md 14.80 Dpth 6.50 Welded, 1 dk	**(B21B20A) Anchor Handling Tug Supply**	**2 oil engines** gearing integral to driving 2 Z propellers Total Power: 5,200kW (7,070hp) Wartsila 8L26 2 x 4 Stroke 8 Cy. 260 x 320 each-2600kW (3535bhp) Wartsila Italia SpA-Italy AuxGen: 4 x 650kW a.c Thrusters: 2 Tunnel thruster (f)
9660487 A9D3173 -	**ZAMIL 101** **Zamil Offshore Services Co Ltd** - *Bahrain* Bahrain MMSI: 408486000 Official number: BN6067	**173** 52 67	Class: AB (Class contemplated) (BV)	**2012-11 Grandweld — Dubai** Yd No: H100/11 Loa 34.30 Br ex 6.85 Dght 1.800 Lbp 31.15 Br md 6.70 Dpth 3.50 Welded, 1 dk	**(B21A20C) Crew/Supply Vessel** Hull Material: Aluminium Alloy	**3 oil engines** reduction geared to sc. shafts driving 3 FP propellers Total Power: 3,198kW (4,347hp) 22.0kn Caterpillar 3 x 4 Stroke each-1066kW (1449bhp) Caterpillar Inc-USA
9660499 A9D3174 -	**ZAMIL 102** **Zamil Offshore Services Co Ltd** - *Bahrain* Bahrain MMSI: 408487000 Official number: BN6068	**173** 52 72	Class: AB (BV)	**2012-12 Grandweld — Dubai** Yd No: H101/11 Loa 34.30 Br ex 6.85 Dght 1.800 Lbp 31.15 Br md 6.70 Dpth 3.50 Welded, 1 dk	**(B21A20C) Crew/Supply Vessel** Hull Material: Aluminium Alloy	**3 oil engines** reduction geared to sc. shafts driving 3 FP propellers Total Power: 3,198kW (4,347hp) 24.0kn Caterpillar 3 x 4 Stroke each-1066kW (1449bhp) Caterpillar Inc-USA
9660504 A9D3175 -	**ZAMIL 103** **Zamil Offshore Services Co Ltd** - *Bahrain* Bahrain MMSI: 408488000 Official number: BN 6069	**173** 52 69	Class: AB (BV)	**2013-01 Grandweld — Dubai** Yd No: H102/11 Loa 34.30 Br ex 6.85 Dght 1.800 Lbp 31.15 Br md 6.70 Dpth 3.50 Welded, 1 dk	**(B21A20C) Crew/Supply Vessel** Hull Material: Aluminium Alloy	**3 oil engines** reduction geared to sc. shafts driving 3 FP propellers Total Power: 3,132kW (4,257hp) 22.0kn Caterpillar C32 3 x Vee 4 Stroke 12 Cy. 145 x 162 each-1044kW (1419bhp) Caterpillar Inc-USA AuxGen: 2 x 58kW a.c Fuel: 50.0 (d.f.)

IMO / Call sign	Name / Owner / Flag	Tonnage	Class	Builder / Dimensions	Type	Machinery
9657727 *A9KG* -	**ZAMIL 301** *ex* Swissco Ruby *-2012* *ex* Tavana 5 *-2012* **Zamil Offshore Services Co Ltd** - *Bahrain* *Bahrain* MMSI: 408849000 Official number: BN 6077	**1,182** 354 1,172	Class: AB (BV)	**2012-08 Guangzhou Panyu Lingshan Shipyard Ltd — Guangzhou GD** Yd No: 206 Loa 56.20 Br ex 13.86 Dght 4.300 Lbp 49.18 Br md 13.80 Dpth 5.50 Welded, 1 dk	**(B21B20A) Anchor Handling Tug Supply**	**2 oil engines** reduction geared to sc. shafts driving 2 FP propellers Total Power: 3,090kW (4,202hp) 12.0kn Caterpillar 3516B-HD 2 x Vee 4 Stroke 16 Cy. 170 x 215 each-1545kW (2101bhp) Caterpillar Inc-USA AuxGen: 3 x 245kW 415V 50Hz a.c Thrusters: 1 Tunnel thruster (f) Fuel: 610.0
9653630 *A9D3152* -	**ZAMIL 401** **Zamil Offshore Services Co Ltd** - *Bahrain* *Bahrain* MMSI: 408441000 Official number: BN6046	**1,241** 372 1,013	Class: AB	**2012-07 Zhongshan Jinhui Shipbuilding & Repair Yard Co Ltd — Zhongshan GD** Yd No: JH2011 Loa 53.80 Br ex - Dght 4.000 Lbp 48.60 Br md 13.80 Dpth 5.00 Welded, 1 dk	**(B34T2QR) Work/Repair Vessel**	**2 oil engines** reduction geared to sc. shafts driving 2 Propellers Total Power: 2,316kW (3,148hp) Caterpillar 2 x 4 Stroke each-1158kW (1574bhp) Caterpillar Inc-USA
9653642 *A9KB* -	**ZAMIL 402** **Zamil Offshore Services Co Ltd** - *Bahrain* *Bahrain* MMSI: 408844000 Official number: BN6047	**1,241** 372 1,014	Class: AB	**2012-12 Zhongshan Jinhui Shipbuilding & Repair Yard Co Ltd — Zhongshan GD** Yd No: JH2012 Loa 53.80 Br ex - Dght 4.000 Lbp 48.60 Br md 13.80 Dpth 5.00 Welded, 1 dk	**(B34T2QR) Work/Repair Vessel**	**2 oil engines** reduction geared to sc. shafts driving 2 Propellers Total Power: 2,350kW (3,196hp) Caterpillar 3512C 2 x Vee 4 Stroke 12 Cy. 170 x 215 each-1175kW (1598bhp) Caterpillar Inc-USA AuxGen: 3 x 170kW a.c Fuel: 800.0
9653654 *A9JV* -	**ZAMIL 403** **Zamil Offshore Services Co Ltd** - *Bahrain* *Bahrain* MMSI: 408837000 Official number: BN 6050	**1,284** 385 -	Class: AB (BV)	**2012-09 Guangzhou Panyu Lingshan Shipyard Ltd — Guangzhou GD** Yd No: 229 Loa 57.20 Br ex - Dght 3.680 Lbp 54.90 Br md 13.80 Dpth 5.00 Welded, 1 dk	**(B21A20S) Platform Supply Ship**	**2 oil engines** reduction geared to sc. shafts driving 2 FP propellers Total Power: 2,682kW (3,646hp) 12.0kn Caterpillar 3512C 2 x Vee 4 Stroke 12 Cy. 170 x 215 each-1341kW (1823bhp) Caterpillar Inc-USA Fuel: 560.0
9653666 *A9JW* -	**ZAMIL 404** **Zamil Offshore Services Co Ltd** - *Bahrain* *Bahrain* MMSI: 408838000 Official number: BN 6051	**1,284** 385 -	Class: AB (BV)	**2012-09 Guangzhou Panyu Lingshan Shipyard Ltd — Guangzhou GD** Yd No: 230 Loa 57.20 Br ex - Dght 3.680 Lbp 54.90 Br md 13.80 Dpth 5.00 Welded, 1 dk	**(B21A20S) Platform Supply Ship**	**2 oil engines** reduction geared to sc. shafts driving 2 FP propellers Total Power: 3,530kW (4,800hp) 12.0kn Caterpillar 3512C 2 x Vee 4 Stroke 12 Cy. 170 x 215 each-1765kW (2400bhp) Caterpillar Inc-USA AuxGen: 3 x 250kW 60Hz a.c Fuel: 560.0
9663946 *A9D3192* -	**ZAMIL 405** *ex* Zamil 501 *-2013* **Zamil Offshore Services Co Ltd** - *Bahrain* *Bahrain* MMSI: 408851000 Official number: BN6080	**1,394** 418 751	Class: AB	**2012-12 Zamil Offshore Services Co Ltd — al-Khubar** Yd No: 141 Loa 54.20 Br ex 14.80 Dght 3.600 Lbp 49.80 Br md 13.80 Dpth 5.00 Welded, 1 dk	**(B34T2QR) Work/Repair Vessel** Cranes: 1x60t	**2 oil engines** reduction geared to sc. shafts driving 2 FP propellers Total Power: 3,240kW (4,406hp) Yanmar 6EY26 2 x 4 Stroke 6 Cy. 260 x 385 each-1620kW (2203bhp) Yanmar Diesel Engine Co Ltd-Japan AuxGen: 3 x 270kW a.c Fuel: 470.0 (d.f.)
9663958 *A9D3194* -	**ZAMIL 406** **Zamil Offshore Services Co Ltd** - *Bahrain* *Bahrain* MMSI: 408852000 Official number: BN6081	**1,394** 418 751	Class: AB	**2013-01 Zamil Offshore Services Co Ltd — al-Khubar** Yd No: 142 Loa 54.20 Br ex 14.80 Dght 3.600 Lbp 49.80 Br md 13.80 Dpth 5.00 Welded, 1 dk	**(B34T2QR) Work/Repair Vessel** Cranes: 1	**2 oil engines** reduction geared to sc. shafts driving 2 FP propellers Total Power: 3,240kW (4,406hp) Yanmar 6EY26 2 x 4 Stroke 6 Cy. 260 x 385 each-1620kW (2203bhp) Yanmar Diesel Engine Co Ltd-Japan AuxGen: 3 x 270kW a.c Fuel: 460.0 (d.f.)
9663960 *A9D3195* -	**ZAMIL 407** **Zamil Offshore Services Co Ltd** - *Bahrain* *Bahrain* MMSI: 408853000 Official number: BN6082	**1,462** 438 1,053	Class: AB	**2013-03 Zamil Offshore Services Co Ltd — al-Khubar** Yd No: 143 Loa 59.60 Br ex 14.80 Dght 3.600 Lbp 55.20 Br md 13.80 Dpth 5.00 Welded, 1 dk	**(B34T2QR) Work/Repair Vessel**	**2 oil engines** reduction geared to sc. shafts driving 2 Propellers Yanmar Yanmar Diesel Engine Co Ltd-Japan
9660140 *A9JX* -	**ZAMIL 501** **Zamil Offshore Services Co Ltd** - *Bahrain* *Bahrain* MMSI: 408839000 Official number: BN 6055	**1,438** 404 1,513	Class: AB (BV)	**2012-11 Guangzhou Panyu Lingshan Shipyard Ltd — Guangzhou GD** Yd No: 221 Loa 58.60 Br ex 14.24 Dght 4.750 Lbp 51.00 Br md 14.20 Dpth 5.50 Welded, 1 dk	**(B21B20A) Anchor Handling Tug Supply**	**2 oil engines** reduction geared to sc. shafts driving 2 CP propellers Total Power: 3,840kW (5,220hp) 12.5kn Caterpillar 3516B 2 x Vee 4 Stroke 16 Cy. 170 x 190 each-1920kW (2610bhp) Caterpillar Inc-USA AuxGen: 3 x 350kW 50Hz a.c Thrusters: 2 Tunnel thruster (f) Fuel: 570.0
9684914 *A9D3231* -	**ZAMIL 502** **Zamil Offshore Services Co Ltd** - *Bahrain* *Bahrain* MMSI: 408545000	**1,405** 421 1,321	Class: BV	**2013-10 Guangzhou Panyu Lingshan Shipyard Ltd — Guangzhou GD** Yd No: 212 Loa 58.60 Br ex 14.24 Dght 4.750 Lbp 51.20 Br md 14.20 Dpth 5.50 Welded, 1 dk	**(B21B20A) Anchor Handling Tug Supply**	**2 oil engines** reduction geared to sc. shafts driving 2 CP propellers Total Power: 3,282kW (4,462hp) 13.0kn Caterpillar 3516B 1 x Vee 4 Stroke 16 Cy. 170 x 190 1641kW (2231bhp) Caterpillar Inc-USA AuxGen: 2 x 1000kW 50Hz a.c, 3 x 350kW a.c Fuel: 550.0
9660231 *A9D3232* -	**ZAMIL 503** **Zamil Offshore Services Co Ltd** - *Bahrain* *Bahrain* MMSI: 408546000 Official number: BN6098	**1,933** 580 1,456	Class: AB	**2013-09 Guangxin Shipbuilding & Heavy Industry Co Ltd — Zhongshan GD** Yd No: GS11131 Loa 60.50 Br ex - Dght 5.200 Lbp 54.30 Br md 15.80 Dpth 6.50 Welded, 1 dk	**(B21B20A) Anchor Handling Tug Supply** Cranes: 1x3t	**2 oil engines** reduction geared to sc. shafts driving 2 CP propellers Total Power: 4,706kW (6,398hp) 12.5kn Niigata 8MG28HX 2 x 4 Stroke 8 Cy. 280 x 370 each-2353kW (3199bhp) Niigata Engineering Co Ltd-Japan AuxGen: 2 x 1000kW a.c, 3 x 400kW a.c Fuel: 590.0
9660243 *A9D3233* -	**ZAMIL 504** **Zamil Offshore Services Co Ltd** - *Bahrain* *Bahrain* MMSI: 408547000 Official number: BN6099	**1,933** 580 1,455	Class: AB	**2013-11 Guangxin Shipbuilding & Heavy Industry Co Ltd — Zhongshan GD** Yd No: GS11132 Loa 60.50 Br ex - Dght 5.000 Lbp 54.30 Br md 15.80 Dpth 6.50 Welded, 1 dk	**(B21B20A) Anchor Handling Tug Supply** Cranes: 1x3t	**2 oil engines** reduction geared to sc. shafts driving 2 CP propellers Total Power: 4,706kW (6,398hp) 12.5kn Niigata 8MG28HX 2 x 4 Stroke 8 Cy. 280 x 370 each-2353kW (3199bhp) Niigata Engineering Co Ltd-Japan AuxGen: 2 x 1000kW a.c, 3 x 400kW a.c Fuel: 590.0
9639799 *A9KN* -	**ZAMIL - L.B. 1** *ex* Hai Heng 1 *-2012* **Zamil Group Holding Co** - *Bahrain* *Bahrain* MMSI: 408544000 Official number: BN7004	**3,836** 1,150 1,534	Class: AB	**2012-07 China Merchants Heavy Industry (Shenzhen) Co Ltd — Shenzhen GD** Yd No: CMHI-108 Loa 49.20 Br ex - Dght 3.820 Lbp 46.80 Br md 42.67 Dpth 6.80 Welded, 1 dk	**(B22A2ZM) Offshore Construction Vessel, jack up** Cranes: 2x190t	**2 oil engines** reduction geared to sc. shafts driving 2 FP propellers Total Power: 2,740kW (3,726hp) 6.0kn Deutz TBD620V12 2 x Vee 4 Stroke 12 Cy. 170 x 195 each-1370kW (1863bhp) Henan Diesel Engine Industry Co Ltd-China AuxGen: 4 x 1200kW a.c Fuel: 400.0
9174385 *HCZA* -	**ZAMORA** **Empresa Publica Flota Petrolera Ecuatoriana (EP FLOPEC)** - *Guayaquil* *Ecuador* MMSI: 735057550 Official number: TN-00-00002	**27,607** 11,947 45,268 T/cm 50.6	Class: AB	**1999-09 Hyundai Heavy Industries Co Ltd — Ulsan** Yd No: 1131 Loa 183.07 (BB) Br ex - Dght 12.020 Lbp 174.00 Br md 32.20 Dpth 18.00 Welded, 1 dk	**(A13B2TP) Products Tanker** Double Hull (13F) Liq: 48,402; Liq (Oil): 48,402 Cargo Heating Coils Compartments: 12 Wing Ta, ER, 2 Wing Slop Ta 3 Cargo Pump (s): 3x1500m³/hr Manifold: Bow/CM: 91m	**1 oil engine** driving 1 FP propeller Total Power: 8,562kW (11,641hp) 14.5kn B&W 6S50MC 1 x 2 Stroke 6 Cy. 500 x 1910 8562kW (11641bhp) Hyundai Heavy Industries Co Ltd-South Korea Fuel: 192.1 (d.f.) (Heating Coils) 1292.0 (r.f.)

	Name / Owner	Tonnage	Class	Builder / Dimensions	Type	Machinery
312232 5ZM 323	**ZAMORA** **Consortium Evisa Fisheries (Pty) Ltd** - *Walvis Bay* *Namibia* MMSI: 659008000 Official number: 95WB009	*650* 375 -	Class: (NV)	**1973-03 Kystvaagen Slip & Baatbyggeri — Kristiansund** (Hull) Yd No: 31 **1973-03 Sterkoder Mek. Verksted AS — Kristiansund** Yd No: 31 Loa 47.00 Br ex 9.05 Dght 4.268 Lbp 40.16 Br md 9.00 Dpth 6.43 Welded, 2 dks	**(B11A2FS) Stern Trawler** Ice Capable	**1 oil engine** driving 1 FP propeller Total Power: 1,103kW (1,500hp) 13.0kn Normo LDM-9 1 x 4 Stroke 9 Cy. 250 x 300 1103kW (1500bhp) AS Bergens Mek Verksteder-Norway AuxGen: 2 x 112kW 440V a.c
077587 HP05	**ZAMOSKVORECHYE** *launched as* Kapitan Ryntsyn *-1997* **Shipline Five Ltd** Joint Stock Northern Shipping Co (A/O 'Severnoye Morskoye Parokhodstvo') (NSC ARKHANGELSK) SatCom: Inmarsat B 324803612 *Valletta* *Malta* MMSI: 248036000 Official number: 5770	**4,998** 1,654 4,678	Class: RS	**1997-10 OAO Kvaerner-Vyborg Verf — Vyborg** Yd No: 204 Loa 98.18 Br ex 17.60 Dght 6.700 Lbp 89.33 Br md - Dpth 7.80 Welded, 1 dk	**(A31A2GX) General Cargo Ship** Grain: 5,654; Bale: 5,539 TEU 130 C.Ho 96/20' C.Dk 34/20' Compartments: 3 Ho, ER 3 Ha: (10.4 x 12.8) (18.8 x 12.8) (12.8 x 12.8)ER Cranes: 2x8t Ice Capable	**1 oil engine** driving 1 CP propeller Total Power: 3,356kW (4,563hp) 13.3kn B&W 6L35MC 1 x 2 Stroke 6 Cy. 350 x 1050 3356kW (4563bhp) AO Bryanskiy MashinostroitelnyyZavod (BMZ)-Bryansk AuxGen: 1 x 500kW 400V 50Hz a.c, 3 x 320kW 400V 50Hz a.c Thrusters: 1 Tunnel thruster (f) Fuel: 54.0 (d.f.) 313.0 (r.f.) 13.2pd
721129 DHY	**ZAMOSKVORECHYE** *ex* Leningradskaya Pravda *-1996* **Westrybflot JSC (ZAO 'Westrybflot')** Sovrybflot JSC (A/O 'Sovrybflot') *Kaliningrad* *Russia* MMSI: 273259100 Official number: 862131	**4,407** 1,322 1,810	Class: RS	**1987-11 GP Chernomorskiy Sudostroitelnyy Zavod — Nikolayev** Yd No: 564 Loa 104.50 Br ex 16.03 Dght 5.900 Lbp 96.40 Br md 16.00 Dpth 10.20 Welded, 2 dks	**(B11A2FG) Factory Stern Trawler** Ice Capable	**2 oil engines** geared to sc. shaft driving 1 CP propeller Total Power: 5,152kW (7,004hp) 16.1kn Pielstick 6PC2-5L-400 2 x 4 Stroke 6 Cy. 400 x 460 each-2576kW (3502bhp) Mashinostroitelnyy Zavod"Russkiy-Dizel"-Leningrad AuxGen: 2 x 1600kW a.c, 3 x 200kW a.c
19558 NNN	**ZAMOURA** *ex* El Hafid *-2007* **Action Shipping** - *Casablanca* *Morocco* MMSI: 242923000	*248* - -	Class: BV	**1982-02 Scheepswerf "De Waal" B.V. — Zaltbommel** Yd No: 718 Loa 32.64 Br ex 9.33 Dght 4.101 Lbp 29.01 Br md 8.81 Dpth 4.32 Welded, 1 dk	**(B32A2ST) Tug**	**1 oil engine** with flexible couplings & sr gearedto sc. shaft driving 1 FP propeller Total Power: 2,059kW (2,799hp) 12.0kn Deutz SBV12M628 1 x Vee 4 Stroke 12 Cy. 240 x 280 2059kW (2799bhp) Kloeckner Humboldt Deutz AG-West Germany
54163 YS6	**ZAMPA BLUE** **Trinity Bulk SA** Meiji Shipping Group *Panama* *Panama* MMSI: 372549000 Official number: 4271311	**92,249** 57,461 178,459	Class: NK	**2011-05 Mitsui Eng. & SB. Co. Ltd., Chiba Works — Ichihara** Yd No: 1728 Loa 292.00 (BB) Br ex - Dght 17.985 Lbp 282.00 Br md 44.98 Dpth 24.70 Welded, 1 dk	**(A21A2BC) Bulk Carrier** Double Hull Grain: 197,392 Compartments: 9 Ho, ER 9 Ha: ER	**1 oil engine** driving 1 FP propeller Total Power: 18,660kW (25,370hp) 14.5kn MAN-B&W 6S70MC-C 1 x 2 Stroke 6 Cy. 700 x 2800 18660kW (25370bhp) Mitsui Engineering & Shipbuilding CLtd-Japan Fuel: 5920.0
10299 BV4	**ZAMZAM** *ex* Argo *-2012* *ex* Arno *-2006* *ex* Jonas *-2004* *ex* Pegwell Bay *-1998* *ex* Altair *-1995* **Zamzam Marine Ltd** BIA Shipping Co *Lome* *Togo* MMSI: 671317000 Official number: TG-00381L	**2,729** 1,102 3,851	Class: DR (RS) (GL)	**1985-09 Martin Jansen GmbH & Co. KG Schiffsw. u. Masch. — Leer** Yd No: 190 Loa 98.41 (BB) Br ex 13.52 Dght 5.310 Lbp 92.41 Br md 13.50 Dpth 7.01 Welded, 2 dks	**(A31A2GX) General Cargo Ship** Grain: 5,380; Bale: 5,210 TEU 157 C.Ho 117/20' (40') C.Dk 40/20' (40') incl. 20 ref C. Compartments: 1 Ho, ER 1 Ha: (61.5 x 10.5)ER Cranes: 2x25t Ice Capable	**1 oil engine** with flexible couplings & sr reverse geared to sc. shaft driving 1 FP propeller Total Power: 1,100kW (1,496hp) 11.5kn Deutz SBV9M628 1 x 4 Stroke 9 Cy. 240 x 280 1100kW (1496bhp) Kloeckner Humboldt Deutz AG-West Germany AuxGen: 2 x 185kW 220/380V 50Hz a.c, 1 x 120kW 220/380V 50Hz a.c Thrusters: 1 Thwart. FP thruster (f) Fuel: 43.0 (d.f.) 162.0 (r.f.) 5.0pd
728869	**ZAMZAM** **Alexandria Port Authority** - *Egypt*	*199* - 128	Class: (LR) ✠ Classed LR until 13/3/81	**1979-01 Towa Zosen K.K. — Shimonoseki** Yd No: 513 Loa - Br ex - Dght 2.915 Lbp 30.03 Br md 8.41 Dpth 3.61 Welded, 1 dk	**(B32A2ST) Tug**	**2 oil engines** reverse reduction geared to sc. shafts driving 2 FP propellers Total Power: 1,176kW (1,598hp) 12.0kn Yanmar 6GL-DT 2 x 4 Stroke 6 Cy. 240 x 290 each-588kW (799bhp) Yanmar Diesel Engine Co Ltd-Japan AuxGen: 2 x 52kW 380/220V 50Hz a.c
497666	**ZAMZAM** - -	*280* 104 544		**1961 F Schichau GmbH — Bremerhaven** Yd No: 1714 Loa 41.31 Br ex 7.55 Dght - Lbp 36.96 Br md 7.50 Dpth 2.80 Welded, 1 dk	**(A13B2TU) Tanker (unspecified)**	**1 oil engine** driving 1 FP propeller Deutz RV6M536 1 x 4 Stroke 6 Cy. 270 x 360 Kloeckner Humboldt Deutz AG-West Germany
649034 63695 000002284	**ZAN FA NO. 3** **Lu Chun-Te** - *Kaohsiung* *Chinese Taipei* MMSI: 416235700 Official number: 015076	**185** 58 -		**2010-08 Shing Sheng Fa Boat Building Co — Kaohsiung** Yd No: 648375 Loa - Br ex - Dght - Lbp - Br md - Dpth - Welded, 1 dk	**(B11A2FT) Trawler**	**1 oil engine** reduction geared to sc. shaft driving 1 Propeller Mitsubishi 1 x 4 Stroke 6 Cy. Mitsubishi Heavy Industries Ltd-Japan
45169	**ZANA** *ex* SV-1 *-1992* **MVK Co Ltd** -	*204* 76 326	Class: (RS)	**1975 Bakinskiy Sudostroitelnyy Zavod im Vano Sturua — Baku** Yd No: 302 Loa 29.17 Br ex 8.01 Dght 3.160 Lbp 28.50 Br md - Dpth 3.60 Welded, 1 dk	**(B34G2SE) Pollution Control Vessel** Liq: 336; Liq (Oil): 336 Compartments: 8 Ta Ice Capable	**1 oil engine** geared to sc. shaft driving 1 FP propeller Total Power: 165kW (224hp) 7.5kn Daldizel 6CHNSP18/22 1 x 4 Stroke 6 Cy. 180 x 220 165kW (224bhp) Daldizel-Khabarovsk AuxGen: 1 x 50kW a.c, 1 x 30kW a.c Fuel: 12.0 (d.f.)
06597	**ZANA** **Sindicato Pesquero del Peru SA (SIPESA)** - *Huacho* *Peru* Official number: HO-006173-PM	*274* 124 266		**1991-03 Factoria Naval S.A. — Callao** Yd No: 09 Loa 33.55 Br ex 7.85 Dght - Lbp - Br md 7.70 Dpth 4.00 Welded	**(B11B2FV) Fishing Vessel**	**1 oil engine** with clutches, flexible couplings & dr reverse geared to sc. shaft driving 1 FP propeller Total Power: 420kW (571hp) Caterpillar 3508TA 1 x Vee 4 Stroke 8 Cy. 170 x 190 420kW (571bhp) Caterpillar Inc-USA
728995 /8019	**ZANADU** *ex* Sergey Yesenin *-2009* **Zanadu Shipping Co** *Piraeus* *Greece* MMSI: 239144900 Official number: 11584	**206** 69 31	Class: RS (HR)	**1989-06 Ilyichyovskiy Sudoremontnyy Zavod im. "50-letiya SSSR" — Ilyichyovsk** Yd No: 18 Loa 37.60 Br ex 7.21 Dght 1.690 Lbp 33.97 Br md 6.90 Dpth 2.90 Welded, 1 dk	**(A37B2PS) Passenger Ship** Passengers: unberthed: 250	**3 oil engines** reduction geared to sc. shafts driving 3 FP propellers Total Power: 960kW (1,306hp) 16.5kn Barnaultransmash 3D6C 2 x 4 Stroke 6 Cy. 150 x 180 each-110kW (150bhp) Barnaultransmash-Barnaul Zvezda M412 1 x Vee 4 Stroke 12 Cy. 180 x 200 740kW (1006bhp) "Zvezda"-Leningrad AuxGen: 2 x 16kW Fuel: 5.0 (d.f.)
27970 JM	**ZANATANY** *ex* Boanamary *-2008* *ex* General Pau *-1999* **Fidahoussen Hounein** - *Mahajanga* *Madagascar* Official number: MJ 92009	*265* 120 300	Class: (BV)	**1915-09 Montrose SB. Co. — Montrose** Yd No: 68 Loa 40.01 Br ex 7.62 Dght 2.134 Lbp - Br md 7.57 Dpth - Riveted, 1 dk	**(A31A2GX) General Cargo Ship** Grain: 334 Compartments: 1 Ho, ER 2 Ha: (6.1 x 2.4) (5.5 x 2.4)ER Derricks: 1x3.5t,1x2.5t; Winches: 2	**1 oil engine** driving 1 FP propeller Total Power: 221kW (300hp) 9.0kn MAN G6V285/42 1 x 4 Stroke 6 Cy. 285 x 420 221kW (300bhp) (new engine 1949) Soc. Gen. de Const. Mec. (S.G.C.M.)-La Courneuve
48495 BF	**ZANCLE** **Caronte & Tourist SpA** - *Reggio Calabria* *Italy* MMSI: 247054400 Official number: 280	*1,901* 1,048 1,428	Class: RI	**1993-01 Cantiere Navale Visentini Srl — Porto Viro** Yd No: 166 Lengthened-2011 Loa 114.98 (BB) Br ex 17.00 Dght 3.800 Lbp 106.82 Br md 16.51 Dpth 4.90 Welded, 1 dk	**(A36A2PR) Passenger/Ro-Ro Ship (Vehicles)** Bow ramp (f) Stern ramp (a)	**2 oil engines** gearing integral to driving 2 Voith-Schneider propellers 1 fwd and 1 aft Total Power: 3,580kW (4,868hp) 16.0kn Nohab 12V25 2 x Vee 4 Stroke 12 Cy. 250 x 300 each-1790kW (2434bhp) Wartsila Diesel AB-Sweden
712767 ET3	**ZANDER** *ex* Brennholm *-2007* *ex* Brennholmen *-2006* *ex* Skipsholmen *-2006* *ex* Mogsterbas *-2001* *ex* Veabas *-1999* *ex* Kings Cross *-1994* *launched as* Disko *-1978* **Nordicfish Ltd** Zandic AB *Belize City* *Belize* MMSI: 312506000 Official number: 350820060	**939** 454 700	Class: NV	**1978-12 Hjorungavaag Verksted AS — Hjorungavaag** Yd No: 30 Lengthened-1983 Loa 58.96 (BB) Br ex 10.24 Dght 6.025 Lbp 52.63 Br md 10.22 Dpth 7.32 Welded, 2 dks	**(B11A2FS) Stern Trawler** Compartments: 1 Ho, ER, 6 Ta Ice Capable	**1 oil engine** geared to sc. shaft driving 1 CP propeller Total Power: 1,942kW (2,640hp) 13.0kn Nohab F212V 1 x Vee 4 Stroke 12 Cy. 250 x 300 1942kW (2640bhp) AB Bofors NOHAB-Sweden AuxGen: 2 x 178kW 380V 50Hz a.c, 1 x 100kW 380V 50Hz a.c Thrusters: 1 Tunnel thruster (f); 1 Tunnel thruster (a)

8926042 *YL2016* -
ZANE
ex MRTK-1049 *-1978*
Al & Co Ltd (SIA 'Al un Ko')
-
Riga *Latvia*
MMSI: 275138000
Official number: 0518
119 35 30
Class: (RS)
1978 Sosnovskiy Sudostroitelnyy Zavod — Sosnovka Yd No: 3269
Loa 25.50 Br ex 7.00 Dght 2.390
Lbp 22.00 Br md - Dpth 3.30
Welded, 1 dk
(B11A2FS) Stern Trawler
Bale: 64
Ice Capable
1 oil engine driving 1 FP propeller
Total Power: 221kW (300hp) 9.6k
S.K.L. 6NVD26A-
1 x 4 Stroke 6 Cy. 180 x 260 221kW (300bhp) (new engine 1985)
VEB Schwermaschinenbau "KarlLiebknecht" (SKL)-Magdeburg
AuxGen: 2 x 12kW a.c
Fuel: 15.0 (d.f.)

7024897 *UDSV* -
ZANGAN-3
ex Orinoko *-2008* *ex* Aleksandr Vermishev *-1996*
Volga Shipping Ltd
-
SatCom: Inmarsat C 427310539
Astrakhan *Russia*
MMSI: 273424140
2,478 917 3,135
Class: RS
1969 Sudostroitelnyy Zavod im Volodarskogo — Rybinsk Yd No: 58
Loa 114.20 Br ex 13.21 Dght 3.760
Lbp 108.01 Br md - Dpth 5.52
Welded, 1 dk
(A31A2GX) General Cargo Ship
Bale: 4,297
Compartments: 4 Ho, ER
4 Ha: (17.6 x 9.3)3 (18.1 x 9.3)ER
Ice Capable
2 oil engines driving 2 FP propellers
Total Power: 970kW (1,318hp) 10.5k
S.K.L. 6NVD48A-
2 x 4 Stroke 6 Cy. 320 x 480 each-485kW (659bhp)
VEB Schwermaschinenbau "KarlLiebknecht" (SKL)-Magdeburg
AuxGen: 3 x 50kW
Fuel: 134.0 (d.f.)

8824579 *DUE2472* -
ZANIAH
ex Izumi Maru *-2010*
Harbor Star Shipping Services Inc
-
Batangas *Philippines*
Official number: 04-0001345
198 92 86
1989-05 Hatayama Zosen KK — Yura WK
Loa 31.82 Br ex - Dght 2.650
Lbp 26.50 Br md 8.60 Dpth 3.50
Welded, 1 dk
(B32A2ST) Tug
2 oil engines geared to sc. shafts driving 2 FP propellers
Total Power: 1,912kW (2,600hp)
Yanmar T260L-S
2 x 4 Stroke 6 Cy. 260 x 330 each-956kW (1300bhp)
Yanmar Diesel Engine Co Ltd-Japan

9261451 *A8UY9* -
ZANTE
ex Kota Singa *-2012* *ex* Zante *-2010*
ex Shanghai Bridge *-2010*
Zante Shipping Co
International Maritime Enterprises SAM
SatCom: Inmarsat C 463707326
Monrovia *Liberia*
MMSI: 636014574
Official number: 14574
66,332 25,129 67,164
Class: NK
2002-07 Koyo Dockyard Co Ltd — Mihara HS Yd No: 2136
Loa 278.94 (BB) Br ex - Dght 14.021
Lbp 262.00 Br md 40.00 Dpth 24.00
Welded, 1 dk
(A33A2CC) Container Ship (Fully Cellular)
TEU 5576 incl 480 ref C.
17 Ha: (3.2 x 14.4) (3.2 x 25.8) (2.2 x 25.8)2 (6.5 x 36.2)9 (6.3 x 36.2) (9.6 x 36.2)2 (6.3 x 10.3)ER
1 oil engine driving 1 FP propeller
Total Power: 60,389kW (82,105hp) 25.0k
Sulzer 11RTA96
1 x 2 Stroke 11 Cy. 960 x 2500 60389kW (82105bhp)
Diesel United Ltd.-Aioi
AuxGen: 4 x a.c
Thrusters: 1 Tunnel thruster (f)
Fuel: 9916.0 (r.f.)

8221179 *8KPB* -
ZAO
Government of Japan (Ministry of Land, Infrastructure & Transport) (The Coastguard)
SatCom: Inmarsat B 343138310
Tokyo *Japan*
MMSI: 431383000
Official number: 125966
3,245 - -
1982-03 Mitsubishi Heavy Industries Ltd. — Nagasaki Yd No: 1888
Loa 105.40 Br ex 14.64 Dght 5.080
Lbp 96.85 Br md 14.60 Dpth 8.00
Welded, 1 dk
(B34H2SQ) Patrol Vessel
2 oil engines driving 1 FP propeller
Total Power: 11,474kW (15,600hp) 21.5k
Pielstick 12PC2-5V-40
2 x Vee 4 Stroke 12 Cy. 400 x 460 each-5737kW (7800bhp)
Ishikawajima Harima Heavy IndustrieCo Ltd (IHI)-Japan
AuxGen: 1 x 416kW 450V 60Hz a.c, 1 x 96kW 450V 60Hz a.c
Fuel: 724.0 (d.f.)

9566150 *V7YK9* -
ZAO GALAXY
Argent Navigation SA
Unix Line Pte Ltd
SatCom: Inmarsat C 453837819
Majuro *Marshall Islands*
MMSI: 538004682
Official number: 4682
16,408 7,612 26,198 T/cm 37.0
Class: NK
2012-06 Shin Kurushima Dockyard Co. Ltd. — Akitsu Yd No: 5717
Loa 159.03 (BB) Br ex 27.13 Dght 10.013
Lbp 151.50 Br md 27.10 Dpth 14.20
Welded, 1 dk
(A12B2TR) Chemical/Products Tanker
Double Hull (13F)
Liq: 27,915; Liq (Oil): 29,000
Compartments: 9 Wing Ta, 9 Wing Ta, 2 Wing Slop Ta, ER
18 Cargo Pump (s): 18x300m³/hr
Manifold: Bow/CM: 77.8m
1 oil engine driving 1 FP propeller
Total Power: 7,470kW (10,156hp) 15.5k
Mitsubishi 6UEC45LS
1 x 2 Stroke 6 Cy. 450 x 1840 7470kW (10156bhp)
Kobe Hatsudoki KK-Japan
AuxGen: 3 x 500kW 450V 60Hz a.c
Thrusters: 1 Tunnel thruster (f)
Fuel: 129.2 (d.f.) 1211.1 (r.f.)

9167540 *JE3143* -
ZAO MARU
Miyagi Marine Service KK
-
Shiogama, Miyagi *Japan*
Official number: 133363
208 - -
1997-03 Kanagawa Zosen — Kobe Yd No: 443
Loa 34.10 Br ex - Dght -
Lbp 29.50 Br md 9.40 Dpth 4.17
Welded, 1 dk
(B32A2ST) Tug
2 oil engines Geared Integral to driving 2 Z propellers
Total Power: 2,648kW (3,600hp) 14.2k
Niigata 6L28H
2 x 4 Stroke 6 Cy. 280 x 370 each-1324kW (1800bhp)
Niigata Engineering Co Ltd-Japan

9151321 *JE3142* -
ZAO MARU
Corporation for Advanced Transport & Technology & Kowa Kaiun KK
Kowa Kaiun KK (Kowa Shipping Co Ltd)
Shiogama, Miyagi *Japan*
MMSI: 431700103
Official number: 133362
4,125 - 6,682
Class: NK
1996-10 Kanda Zosensho K.K. — Kawajiri Yd No: 381
Loa 113.02 (BB) Br ex - Dght 7.049
Lbp 104.00 Br md 16.00 Dpth 8.50
Welded, 1 dk
(A24A2BT) Cement Carrier
Grain: 5,536
Compartments: 4 Ho, ER
1 oil engine driving 1 FP propeller
Total Power: 3,163kW (4,300hp) 12.9k
Akasaka A45
1 x 4 Stroke 6 Cy. 450 x 880 3163kW (4300bhp)
Akasaka Tekkosho KK (Akasaka DieselLtd)-Japan
AuxGen: 2 x 600kW 450V a.c
Fuel: 168.0 (d.f.) 14.4pd

8845688 *UGIX* -
ZAPADNAYA LITSA
ex Donskaya Zemlya *-2002*
OOO Rybolovnaya Kompaniya 'Vostochnaya Ekspeditsiya' (Eastern Expedition Fishing Co Ltd)
-
SatCom: Inmarsat C 427320781
Petropavlovsk-Kamchatskiy *Russia*
MMSI: 273421860
Official number: 903562
770 235 414
Class: (RS)
1991-08 Zavod "Leninskaya Kuznitsa" — Kiyev Yd No: 1640
Loa 54.82 Br ex 10.15 Dght 4.140
Lbp 50.30 Br md - Dpth 5.00
Welded, 1 dk
(B11A2FS) Stern Trawler
Ins: 412
1 oil engine driving 1 CP propeller
Total Power: 852kW (1,158hp) 12.0k
S.K.L. 8NVD48A-2
1 x 4 Stroke 8 Cy. 320 x 480 852kW (1158bhp)
SKL Motoren u. Systemtechnik AG-Magdeburg
AuxGen: 4 x 160kW a.c

8957314 - -
ZAPADNOYE PRIMORYE
ex Liao Da Gan Yu 8717 *-2000*
-
-
Vladivostok *Russia*
Official number: 990190
115 39 97
1999-05 Rongcheng Shipbuilding Industry Co Ltd — Rongcheng SD Yd No: Y040199526
Loa 34.00 Br ex - Dght 2.100
Lbp 29.62 Br md 6.00 Dpth 2.70
Welded, 1 dk
(B11B2FV) Fishing Vessel
1 oil engine geared to sc. shaft driving 1 FP propeller
Total Power: 220kW (299hp)
Chinese Std. Type Z6170Z
1 x 4 Stroke 6 Cy. 170 x 200 220kW (299bhp)
Zibo Diesel Engine Factory-China

8711837 *V3MT6* -
ZAPADNYY
Excel Sea Legend SA
JSC 'Yugreftransflot'
Belize City *Belize*
MMSI: 312786000
Official number: 500820013
1,896 990 3,297
Class: RS
1988-12 Shipbuilding & Shiprepairing Yard 'Ivan Dimitrov' — Rousse Yd No: 467
Converted From: Products Tanker-2008
Loa 77.53 Br ex 14.34 Dght 5.340
Lbp 73.20 Br md 14.00 Dpth 6.50
Welded, 1 dk
(A14F2LM) Molasses Tanker
Single Hull
Liq: 3,424; Liq (Oil): 3,514
Compartments: 8 Wing Ta, ER
Ice Capable
1 oil engine driving 1 FP propeller
Total Power: 885kW (1,203hp) 10.2k
S.K.L. 8NVD48A-2
1 x 4 Stroke 8 Cy. 320 x 480 885kW (1203bhp)
VEB Schwermaschinenbau "KarlLiebknecht" (SKL)-Magdeburg
AuxGen: 2 x 150kW a.c
Thrusters: 1 Thwart. CP thruster (f)
Fuel: 123.0 (d.f.)

8509662 *YYV2157* -
ZAPARA
PDV Marina SA
-
Maracaibo *Venezuela*
Official number: AJZL-13931
224 67 -
Class: (LR)
✠ Classed LR until 6/4/05
1987-12 Diques y Ast. Nac. C.A. (DIANCA) — Puerto Cabello Yd No: 168
Loa 32.95 Br ex 9.81 Dght 4.401
Lbp 28.86 Br md 9.52 Dpth 4.91
Welded, 1 dk
(B32A2ST) Tug
2 oil engines with clutches, flexible couplings & sr geared to sc. shafts driving 2 CP propellers
Total Power: 3,088kW (4,198hp) 12.0k
Kromhout 9FHD24
2 x 4 Stroke 9 Cy. 240 x 260 each-1544kW (2099bhp)
Stork Werkspoor Diesel BV-Netherlands
AuxGen: 2 x 90kW 440V 60Hz a.c
Fuel: 182.0 (d.f.)

8033077 *UCUM* MG-1350
ZAPOLARYE
ex Mishukov *-2005*
Andeg Fishing Collective (Rybolovetskiy Kolkhoz 'Andeg')
-
SatCom: Inmarsat Mini-M 761322987
Murmansk *Russia*
MMSI: 273525900
Official number: 810940
1,400 420 493
Class: RS
1981-07 Sudostroitelnyy Zavod "Baltiya" — Klaypeda Yd No: 350
Loa 59.03 (BB) Br ex 13.01 Dght 4.873
Lbp 55.00 Br md 13.00 Dpth 8.89
Welded, 2 dks
(B11A2FS) Stern Trawler
Grain: 95; Ins: 500
Compartments: 2 Ho, 1 Ta, ER
3 Ha: (1.2 x 1.3) (0.7 x 0.7) (1.9 x 1.9)
Ice Capable
1 oil engine driving 1 CP propeller
Total Power: 1,618kW (2,200hp) 13.0k
Skoda 6L525IIP
1 x 4 Stroke 6 Cy. 525 x 720 1618kW (2200bhp)
CKD Praha-Praha
Fuel: 300.0 (d.f.)

404027 *GWF*	**ZAPOLYARNYY** **JSC Mining & Metallurgical Company 'Norilsk Nickel'** Murmansk Transport Branch of JSC Mining & Metallurgical Company 'Norilsk Nickel' *Murmansk* *Russia* MMSI: 273349820	**16,994** 5,257 18,339	Class: RS	**2008-11 Wadan Yards MTW GmbH — Wismar** (Aft & pt cargo sections) Yd No: 158 **2008-11 Wadan Yards Warnow GmbH — Rostock** (Fwd & pt cargo sections) Loa 169.04 Br ex 26.45 Dght 10.000 Lbp 157.74 Br md 23.10 Dpth 14.20 Welded, 2 dks	**(A31A2GX) General Cargo Ship** TEU 648 C Ho 389 TEU C Dk 259 TEU incl 21 ref C Compartments: 4 Ho, ER 4 Ha: (19.2 x 18.1)2 (25.6 x 18.1)ER (10.4 x 11.8) Ice Capable	**3 diesel electric oil engines** driving 3 gen. each 5820kW a.c Connecting to 1 elec. Motor of (13000kW) driving 1 Azimuth electric drive unit Total Power: 18,000kW (24,474hp) 15.5kn Wartsila 12V32 3 x Vee 4 Stroke 12 Cy. 320 x 400 each-6000kW (8158bhp) Wartsila Finland Oy-Finland AuxGen: 1 x 800kW Thrusters: 1 Thwart. CP thruster (f) Fuel: 2500.0 (r.f.)
524205 *BEF5*	**ZAPOLYARYE** *ex* Perseverance *-2008* **Murmansk Shipping Co (MSC)** - *Murmansk* *Russia* MMSI: 273338310	**15,868** 7,206 23,645	Class: RS	**2008-08 Chengxi Shipyard Co Ltd — Jiangyin JS** Yd No: CX4227 Loa 180.50 Br ex 22.90 Dght 9.910 Lbp 173.28 Br md 22.86 Dpth 13.50 Welded, 1 dk	**(A21A2BC) Bulk Carrier** Grain: 25,298 TEU 520 Compartments: 7 Ho, ER 7 Ha: 6 (12.8 x 13.5)ER (12.8 x 10.8) Ice Capable	**1 oil engine** driving 1 FP propeller Total Power: 9,480kW (12,889hp) 13.0kn MAN-B&W 6S50MC-C 1 x 2 Stroke 6 Cy. 500 x 2000 9480kW (12889bhp) AO Bryanskiy MashinostroitelnyyZavod (BMZ)-Bryansk AuxGen: 3 x 680kW 60Hz a.c Fuel: 1220.0 (r.f.)
553505 *CMU9*	**ZAPOTITLAN** *ex* Bourbon Liberty 114 *-2009* **Navegacion Costa Fuera SA de CV** - *Tampico* *Mexico* MMSI: 345010061 Official number: 2804483122-4	**1,517** 455 1,517	Class: AB	**2009-08 Yangzhou Dayang Shipbuilding Co Ltd — Yangzhou JS** Yd No: DY814 Loa 57.90 Br ex - Dght 4.900 Lbp 54.90 Br md 14.00 Dpth 5.50 Welded, 1 dk	**(B21A20S) Platform Supply Ship**	**3 diesel electric oil engines** driving 2 gen. each 1235kW 480V a.c 1 gen. of 435kW 480V a.c Connecting to 3 elec. motors each (843kW) driving 3 Z propellers fixed unit Total Power: 3,364kW (4,575hp) 10.5kn Cummins KT-19-M 1 x 4 Stroke 6 Cy. 159 x 159 380kW (517bhp) Cummins Engine Co Inc-USA Cummins KTA-50-M2 2 x Vee 4 Stroke 16 Cy. 159 x 159 each-1492kW (2029bhp) Cummins Engine Co Inc-USA Thrusters: 2 Tunnel thruster (f) Fuel: 447.0 (d.f.)
391957 *HA2214*	**ZAPPHIRE** **Sapphire Marine Co Ltd** SOCOMAR Srl SatCom: Inmarsat C 424815910 *Valletta* *Malta* MMSI: 248159000 Official number: 9391957	**27,015** 13,622 47,329 T/cm 50.4	Class: LR (BV) **100A1** SS 01/2010 Double Hull oil tanker ESP *IWS LI **LMC** **UMS IGS**	**2010-01 Onomichi Dockyard Co Ltd — Onomichi HS** Yd No: 547 Loa 182.50 (BB) Br ex 32.23 Dght 12.617 Lbp 172.00 Br md 32.20 Dpth 18.10 Welded, 1 dk	**(A13B2TP) Products Tanker** Double Hull (13F) Liq: 50,537; Liq (Oil): 50,560 Cargo Heating Coils Compartments: 12 Wing Ta, 2 Wing Slop Ta, ER 4 Cargo Pump (s): 4x1000m³/hr Manifold: Bow/CM: 91.8m	**1 oil engine** driving 1 FP propeller Total Power: 8,580kW (11,665hp) 14.0kn MAN-B&W 6S50MC 1 x 2 Stroke 6 Cy. 500 x 1910 8580kW (11665bhp) Mitsui Engineering & Shipbuilding CLtd-Japan AuxGen: 3 x a.c Fuel: 110.0 (d.f.) 1450.0 (r.f.)
830718	**ZAPRAVSHCHIK-01** **Techinvest Plus Co Ltd (OOO 'Tekhinvest Plyus')** - *Vladivostok* *Russia* Official number: 780209	*189* 73 252	Class: RS	**1979 Sudoremontnyy Zavod "Yakor" — Sovetskaya Gavan** Yd No: 674 Loa 36.01 Br ex 7.65 Dght 2.500 Lbp 33.50 Br md 7.37 Dpth 3.10 Welded, 1 dk	**(B35E2TF) Bunkering Tanker** Liq: 253; Liq (Oil): 253 Compartments: 6 Ta Ice Capable	**1 oil engine** geared to sc. shaft driving 1 FP propeller Total Power: 165kW (224hp) 7.9kn Daldizel 6CHNSP18/22 1 x 4 Stroke 6 Cy. 180 x 220 165kW (224bhp) Daldizel-Khabarovsk AuxGen: 1 x 30kW a.c Fuel: 7.0 (d.f.)
830720	**ZAPRAVSHCHIK-02** **Nakhodka-Portbunker Co Ltd** - *Nakhodka* *Russia* MMSI: 273438180 Official number: 792723	*189* 72 264	Class: RS	**1980 Sudoremontnyy Zavod "Yakor" — Sovetskaya Gavan** Yd No: 2 Loa 36.01 Br ex 7.65 Dght 2.500 Lbp 33.50 Br md 7.44 Dpth 3.10 Welded, 1 dk	**(B35E2TF) Bunkering Tanker** Liq: 253; Liq (Oil): 253 Compartments: 6 Ta Ice Capable	**1 oil engine** geared to sc. shaft driving 1 FP propeller Total Power: 165kW (224hp) 7.0kn Daldizel 6CHNSP18/22 1 x 4 Stroke 6 Cy. 180 x 220 165kW (224bhp) Daldizel-Khabarovsk AuxGen: 1 x 30kW a.c Fuel: 6.0 (d.f.)
830732	**ZAPRAVSHCHIK-03** **Nikolayevsk-na-Amure Port Authority (Nikolayevskiy-na-Amure Morskoy Torgovyy Port)** - *Nikolayevsk-na-Amure* *Russia* Official number: 801458	*189* 72 264	Class: (RS)	**1980 Sudoremontnyy Zavod "Yakor" — Sovetskaya Gavan** Yd No: 3 Loa 36.01 Br ex 7.65 Dght 2.500 Lbp 33.50 Br md - Dpth 3.10 Welded, 1 dk	**(B35E2TF) Bunkering Tanker** Liq: 253; Liq (Oil): 253 Compartments: 6 Ta Ice Capable	**1 oil engine** geared to sc. shaft driving 1 FP propeller Total Power: 165kW (224hp) 7.0kn Daldizel 6CHNSP18/22 1 x 4 Stroke 6 Cy. 180 x 220 165kW (224bhp) Daldizel-Khabarovsk AuxGen: 1 x 30kW a.c Fuel: 7.0 (d.f.)
830744 *HJ*	**ZAPRAVSHCHIK-05** **Nakhodka-Portbunker Co Ltd** - SatCom: Inmarsat C 427303274 *Nakhodka* *Russia* MMSI: 273439180 Official number: 812537	*189* 73 264 T/cm 2.0	Class: RS	**1982 Sudoremontnyy Zavod "Yakor" — Sovetskaya Gavan** Yd No: 5 Loa 36.01 Br ex 7.44 Dght 2.500 Lbp 34.71 Br md 7.00 Dpth 3.10 Welded, 1 dk	**(B35E2TF) Bunkering Tanker** Double Bottom Entire Compartment Length Liq: 256; Liq (Oil): 253 Compartments: 6 Ta 3 Cargo Pump (s): 3x25m³/hr Manifold: Bow/CM: 21m Ice Capable	**1 oil engine** geared to sc. shaft driving 1 FP propeller Total Power: 165kW (224hp) 7.0kn Daldizel 6CHNSP18/22 1 x 4 Stroke 6 Cy. 180 x 220 165kW (224bhp) Daldizel-Khabarovsk AuxGen: 1 x 30kW a.c Fuel: 6.0 (d.f.)
831704	**ZAPRAVSHCHIK-07** **Rosmortrans Ltd** - *Temryuk* *Russia* Official number: 831010	**205** 72 264	Class: RS	**1984 Sudoremontnyy Zavod "Yakor" — Sovetskaya Gavan** Yd No: 759 Loa 36.01 Br ex 7.65 Dght 2.500 Lbp 35.50 Br md - Dpth 3.10 Welded, 1 dk	**(B35E2TF) Bunkering Tanker** Liq: 253; Liq (Oil): 253 Compartments: 6 Ta, ER Ice Capable	**1 oil engine** geared to sc. shaft driving 1 FP propeller Total Power: 166kW (226hp) 7.0kn Daldizel 6CHNSP18/22 1 x 4 Stroke 6 Cy. 180 x 220 166kW (226bhp) Daldizel-Khabarovsk AuxGen: 1 x 30kW a.c Fuel: 7.0 (d.f.)
826436	**ZAPRAVSHCHIK-12** **New Time Co Ltd (OOO 'Novoye Vremya')** - *Vostochnyy* *Russia*	**204** 83 264	Class: RS	**1989-12 Sudoremontnyy Zavod "Yakor" — Sovetskaya Gavan** Yd No: 856 Loa 36.01 Br ex 7.65 Dght 2.500 Lbp 34.71 Br md 7.44 Dpth 3.10 Welded, 1 dk	**(B35E2TF) Bunkering Tanker** Liq: 253; Liq (Oil): 253 Compartments: 6 Ta, ER Ice Capable	**1 oil engine** geared to sc. shaft driving 1 FP propeller Total Power: 165kW (224hp) 7.0kn Daldizel 6CHNSP18/22 1 x 4 Stroke 6 Cy. 180 x 220 165kW (224bhp) Daldizel-Khabarovsk AuxGen: 1 x 30kW a.c Fuel: 7.0 (d.f.)
896430	**ZARA** - - -	**228** 69 -		**2002-01 in Thailand** Yd No: 202 Loa 27.00 Br ex - Dght - Lbp - Br md 8.00 Dpth 3.40 Welded, 1 dk	**(B32A2ST) Tug**	**2 oil engines** geared to sc. shafts driving 2 Propellers Total Power: 1,324kW (1,800hp) Yanmar 2 x 4 Stroke each-662kW (900bhp) Yanmar Diesel Engine Co Ltd-Japan
206284 *JGL5*	**ZARA** *ex* Plori *-2009* *ex* Liski *-2007* *ex* Lux Conqueror *-1989* *ex* Vinuesa *-1988* **A T Mar Ltd SA** Buzzard Marine SA *Phnom Penh* *Cambodia* MMSI: 515301000 Official number: 1383173	**5,869** 2,974 8,556	Class: (BV) (CS)	**1983-12 Hijos de J. Barreras S.A. — Vigo** Yd No: 1474 Loa 119.51 Br ex - Dght 7.445 Lbp 110.01 Br md 18.51 Dpth 9.53 Welded, 1 dk	**(A31A2GX) General Cargo Ship** Grain: 10,675; Bale: 10,404 TEU 160 C. 160/20' (40') Compartments: 2 Ho, ER 2 Ha: 2 (25.9 x 10.7)ER Derricks: 4x25t; Winches: 4	**1 oil engine** with flexible couplings & sr gearedto sc. shaft driving 1 FP propeller Total Power: 2,942kW (4,000hp) 11.5kn Deutz SBV8M540 1 x 4 Stroke 8 Cy. 370 x 400 2942kW (4000bhp) Hijos de J Barreras SA-Spain AuxGen: 3 x 260kW 380V 50Hz a.c
801477 *JA2280*	**ZARA** *ex* Fortuna P *-2011* *ex* Mark Philip 10 *-1999* *ex* Shoshin Maru No. 30 *-1988* **Mega Fishing Corp** - *Manila* *Philippines* Official number: MNLD001654	*149* 89 119		**1978-03 Niigata Engineering Co Ltd — Niigata NI** Yd No: 1587 L reg 30.95 (BB) Br ex 7.70 Dght 2.401 Lbp 30.82 Br md 7.01 Dpth 2.77 Welded, 1 dk	**(B11B2FV) Fishing Vessel**	**1 oil engine** geared to sc. shaft driving 1 FP propeller Total Power: 809kW (1,100hp) Niigata 6L28BX 1 x 4 Stroke 6 Cy. 280 x 320 809kW (1100bhp) Niigata Engineering Co Ltd-Japan
866151 *5E2766*	**ZARARAH** *ex* Zarara *-2012* **Services Holding Company LLA** Marine Capabilities (MARCAP) LLC *Abu Dhabi* *United Arab Emirates* MMSI: 470573000	**621** 186 722	Class: RS (LR) Classed LR until 22/3/00	**1993-01 Abu Dhabi Defence Shipyard — Abu Dhabi** Yd No: 003 Loa 60.00 Br ex 12.24 Dght 2.160 Lbp 54.80 Br md 12.00 Dpth 3.00 Welded, 1 dk	**(A35D2RL) Landing Craft** Bow door/ramp	**2 oil engines** reverse geared to sc. shafts driving 2 FP propellers Total Power: 1,324kW (1,800hp) 12.0kn Caterpillar 3508TA 2 x Vee 4 Stroke 8 Cy. 170 x 190 each-662kW (900bhp) Caterpillar Inc-USA AuxGen: 2 x 125kW 415V 50Hz a.c Fuel: 30.0 (d.f.)

Ship / Owner	Tonnage	Class	Builder / Dimensions	Type / Cargo	Machinery
9349679 **ZARDIS** *EPBR4* *ex* Ramona *-2012* *ex* Decretive *-2011* - *ex* Sixth Ocean *-2008* **Oghiaanous Khoroushan Shipping Lines Co of Kish** Rahbaran Omid Darya Ship Management Co *Qeshm Island* *Iran* MMSI: 422031700	**75,395** 42,788 81,021	Class: (LR) (BV) ✠ Classed LR until 9/2/12	**2008-06 Hyundai Heavy Industries Co Ltd — Ulsan** Yd No: 1823 Loa 304.00 (BB) Br ex 40.10 Dght 14.000 Lbp 292.00 Br md 40.00 Dpth 24.50 Welded, 1 dk	**(A33A2CC) Container Ship (Fully Cellular)** TEU 6415 C Ho 3125 TEU C Dk 3290 TEU incl 480 ref C Compartments: 8 Cell Ho, ER 8 Ha: ER	**1 oil engine** driving 1 FP propeller Total Power: 60,200kW (81,848hp) 25.8k MAN-B&W 10K98MC- 1 x 2 Stroke 10 Cy. 980 x 2400 60200kW (81848bhp) Hyundai Heavy Industries Co Ltd-South Korea AuxGen: 4 x 2200kW 450V 60Hz a.c Boilers: e (ex.g.) 11.2kgf/cm² (11.0bar), AuxB (o.f.) 8.2kgf/cm² (8.0bar) Thrusters: 1 Thwart. CP thruster (f)
9459395 **ZARECHENSK** *ONGC* - **SBM-4 Inc** Sobelmar Antwerp NV SatCom: Inmarsat C 420556110 *Antwerpen* *Belgium* MMSI: 205561000 Official number: 02 00021 2009	**20,748** 11,689 31,800	Class: BV	**2009-12 Nanjing Dongze Shipyard Co Ltd — Nanjing JS** Yd No: 06H-06 Loa 179.90 (BB) Br ex - Dght 10.150 Lbp 172.43 Br md 28.40 Dpth 14.10 Welded, 1 dk	**(A21A2BC) Bulk Carrier** Grain: 43,127 Compartments: 5 Ho, ER 5 Ha: ER Cranes: 4x30t	**1 oil engine** driving 1 FP propeller Total Power: 6,480kW (8,810hp) 13.7k MAN-B&W 6S42M 1 x 2 Stroke 6 Cy. 420 x 1764 6480kW (8810bhp) Yichang Marine Diesel Engine Co Ltd-China AuxGen: 3 x 465kW 60Hz a.c Fuel: 1810.0
9431214 **ZARGA** *V7QF2* - **Nakilat SHI 1752 Inc** Qatar Gas Transport Co Ltd (Nakilat) SatCom: Inmarsat C 453835051 *Majuro* *Marshall Islands* MMSI: 538003346 Official number: 3346	**163,922** 51,596 130,211 T/cm 163.3	Class: AB	**2010-03 Samsung Heavy Industries Co Ltd — Geoje** Yd No: 1752 Loa 345.33 (BB) Br ex 53.83 Dght 12.200 Lbp 332.00 Br md 53.80 Dpth 27.00 Welded, 1 dk	**(A11A2TN) LNG Tanker** Double Hull Liq (Gas): 261,104 6 x Gas Tank (s); 5 membrane (s.stl) pri horizontal, ER 10 Cargo Pump (s): 10x1400m³/hr Manifold: Bow/CM: 170.4m	**2 oil engines** driving 2 FP propellers Total Power: 43,540kW (59,196hp) 19.0k MAN-B&W 7S70ME- 2 x 2 Stroke 7 Cy. 700 x 2800 each-21770kW (29598bhp) Doosan Engine Co Ltd-South Korea AuxGen: 4 x 4300kW 6600V 60Hz a.c Fuel: 674.0 (d.f.) 8611.0 (r.f.)
9233181 **ZARGANA** *TCA2240* - **Marin Tug & Pilot (Marin Romorkor ve Kilavuzluk AS)** *Istanbul* *Turkey* MMSI: 271010375 Official number: 633	**168** 97 -	Class: BV (AB)	**2004-02 Yardimci Tersanesi A.S. — Tuzla** Yd No: 23 Loa 20.50 Br ex - Dght 2.400 Lbp 18.90 Br md 7.80 Dpth 3.30 Welded, 1 dk	**(B32A2ST) Tug**	**2 oil engines** driving 2 FP propellers Total Power: 1,766kW (2,402hp) Cummins KTA-19-M 2 x 4 Stroke 6 Cy. 159 x 159 each-883kW (1201bhp) Cummins Engine Co Inc-USA AuxGen: 2 x 45kW 380/220V a.c
9565247 **ZARIA** *5NUX* - **Nigerian Ports Authority (NPA)** - *Lagos* *Nigeria* MMSI: 657804000	**176** 52 382	Class: LR ✠ **100A1** SS 07/2012 Tug **LMC** Eq.Ltr: B; Cable: 247.5/17.5 U2	**2012-07 Stocznia Tczew Sp z oo — Tczew** (Hull) Yd No: (509840) **2012-07 B.V. Scheepswerf Damen — Gorinchem** Yd No: 509840 Loa 27.09 Br ex 8.50 Dght 3.390 Lbp 25.52 Br md 7.94 Dpth 4.05 Welded, 1 dk	**(B32A2ST) Tug**	**2 oil engines** with clutches, flexible couplings & sr reverse geared to sc. shafts driving 2 FP propellers Total Power: 2,236kW (3,040hp) Caterpillar 3512 2 x Vee 4 Stroke 12 Cy. 170 x 190 each-1118kW (1520bhp Caterpillar Inc-USA AuxGen: 2 x 86kW 400V 50Hz a.c Thrusters: 1 Tunnel thruster (f)
9234642 **ZARIFA ALIYEVA** *9HFT7* *ex* Discovery *-2007* - **Ocean Navigation 2 Co Ltd** Palmali Gemicilik ve Acentelik AS (Palmali Shipping & Agency) SatCom: Inmarsat C 421533910 *Valletta* *Malta* MMSI: 215339000 Official number: 7647	**84,598** 53,710 164,533 T/cm 123.0	Class: AB	**2003-01 Hyundai Heavy Industries Co Ltd — Ulsan** Yd No: 1391 Loa 274.18 (BB) Br ex 50.04 Dght 17.010 Lbp 264.00 Br md 50.00 Dpth 23.10 Welded, 1 dk	**(A13A2TV) Crude Oil Tanker** Double Hull (13F) Liq: 173,751; Liq (Oil): 181,829 Cargo Heating Coils Compartments: 12 Wing Ta, 2 Wing Slop Ta, ER 3 Cargo Pump (s): 3x4000m³/hr Manifold: Bow/CM: 135.8m	**1 oil engine** driving 1 FP propeller Total Power: 18,623kW (25,320hp) 15.5k B&W 6S70MC- 1 x 2 Stroke 6 Cy. 700 x 2800 18623kW (25320bhp) Hyundai Heavy Industries Co Ltd-South Korea AuxGen: 3 x 950kW a.c Fuel: 130.0 (d.f.) 4100.0 (r.f.)
8741789 **ZARKOH** *A6E2707* - **Jumaa Ahmed Al Bawardi Al Falasi** - *Abu Dhabi* *United Arab Emirates* MMSI: 470594000 Official number: 7352	**746** 223 1,439	Class: BV	**2003 Abu Dhabi Ship Building PJSC — Abu Dhabi** Yd No: 023 Converted From: Infantry Landing Craft-2009 Loa 64.00 Br ex - Dght 2.500 Lbp 54.34 Br md 12.00 Dpth 3.50 Welded, 1 dk	**(A35D2RL) Landing Craft** Bow ramp (centre)	**2 oil engines** reduction geared to sc. shafts driving 2 FP propellers Total Power: 1,332kW (1,810hp) 12.0k Caterpillar 350 2 x Vee 4 Stroke 8 Cy. 170 x 190 each-666kW (905bhp) Caterpillar Inc-USA
9422392 **ZARUMA** *3FDY8* - **Pisces Oil Shipping Inc** Empresa Publica Flota Petrolera Ecuatoriana (EP FLOPEC) SatCom: Inmarsat C 435120610 *Panama* *Panama* MMSI: 351206000 Official number: 4175410	**57,258** 32,926 105,073	Class: LR ✠ **100A1** SS 11/2009 Double Hull oil tanker CSR ESP **ShipRight** (CM) *IWS LI SPM ✠ **LMC** **UMS IGS** Eq.Ltr: T†; Cable: 715.0/87.0 U3 (a)	**2009-11 Hyundai Heavy Industries Co Ltd — Ulsan** Yd No: 2027 Loa 238.00 (BB) Br ex 42.04 Dght 15.000 Lbp 234.00 Br md 42.00 Dpth 21.00 Welded, 1 dk	**(A13A2TW) Crude/Oil Products Tanker** Double Hull (13F) Liq: 105,000; Liq (Oil): 105,000 Compartments: 12 Wing Ta, 2 Wing Slop Ta, ER 3 Cargo Pump (s): 3x3000m³/hr Manifold: Bow/CM: 118.4m	**1 oil engine** driving 1 FP propeller Total Power: 13,560kW (18,436hp) 15.4k MAN-B&W 6S60MC- 1 x 2 Stroke 6 Cy. 600 x 2400 13560kW (18436bhp) Hyundai Heavy Industries Co Ltd-South Korea AuxGen: 3 x 710kW 440V 60Hz a.c Boilers: e (ex.g.) 21.4kgf/cm² (21.0bar), WTAuxB (o.f.) 18.4kgf/cm² (18.0bar)
9012214 **ZARYA** *UFCR* *ex* Kosei Maru *-2003* - **Marine Alliance Co Ltd** - *Korsakov* *Russia* MMSI: 273442580 Official number: 906005	**959** 287 701	Class: RS (NK)	**1991-02 K.K. Mukai Zosensho — Nagasaki** Yd No: 628 Loa 71.10 Br ex - Dght 3.557 Lbp 65.00 Br md 10.20 Dpth 3.60 Welded	**(A34A2GR) Refrigerated Cargo Ship** Ins: 1,015 Compartments: 2 Ho, ER 2 Ha: 2 (6.0 x 4.6)ER Cranes: 1x2t	**1 oil engine** driving 1 FP propeller Total Power: 1,471kW (2,000hp) 15.0k Akasaka DM38A 1 x 4 Stroke 6 Cy. 380 x 600 1471kW (2000bhp) Akasaka Tekkosho KK (Akasaka DieselLtd)-Japan AuxGen: 3 x 122kW a.c
8228191 **ZARYA** - - **SK Portovyy Flot Ltd** - *Nakhodka* *Russia* Official number: 820266	**228** 68 86	Class: RS	**1984 Brodogradiliste 'Tito' — Belgrade** Yd No: 1094 Loa 35.84 Br ex 9.10 Dght 3.150 Lbp 30.00 Br md 9.01 Dpth 4.50 Welded, 1 dk	**(B32A2ST) Tug** Ice Capable	**2 oil engines** geared to sc. shafts driving 2 FP propellers Total Power: 1,854kW (2,520hp) 11.5k Sulzer 6ASL25/3 2 x 4 Stroke 6 Cy. 250 x 300 each-927kW (1260bhp) Tvornica Dizel Motora 'Jugoturbina'-Yugoslavia Fuel: 61.0 (r.f.)
7921772 **ZARZA** *3EIL* *ex* Zarzaitine *-2006* *ex* Shoun Maru No. 6 *-1986* - **Rochdale Shipping Corp** - *Panama* *Panama* MMSI: 372272000 Official number: 35137PEXT	**3,529** 1,869 6,007 T/cm 13.4	Class: (LR) (NK) Classed LR until 7/2/07	**1980-02 K.K. Taihei Kogyo — Akitsu** Yd No: 1355 Loa 101.00 Br ex 16.03 Dght 6.865 Lbp 94.01 Br md 16.01 Dpth 8.21 Welded, 1 dk	**(A12B2TR) Chemical/Products Tanker** Double Bottom Entire Compartment Length Liq: 6,287; Liq (Oil): 6,287 Cargo Heating Coils Compartments: 10 Wing Ta, ER, 2 Wing Slop Ta 4 Cargo Pump (s): 4x400m³/hr Manifold: Bow/CM: 48m	**1 oil engine** driving 1 FP propeller Total Power: 2,648kW (3,600hp) 12.7k Hanshin 6LU50 1 x 4 Stroke 6 Cy. 500 x 800 2648kW (3600bhp) The Hanshin Diesel Works Ltd-Japan AuxGen: 2 x 180kW 450V 60Hz a.c Boilers: AuxB (o.f.) 9.9kgf/cm² (9.7bar), AuxB (ex.g.) rcv 10.1kgf/cm² (9.9bar)rcv 9,9kgf/cm (9,8bar) Fuel: 61.0 (d.f.) 479.0 (r.f.)
8134754 **ZARZOUNA** - - **Government of The Republic of Tunisia (Ministere de l'Equipment)** - *Bizerte* *Tunisia*	*304* 207 150	Class: (BV)	**1970 Fr Schweers Schiffs- und Bootswerft GmbH & Co KG — Berne** Loa 49.00 Br ex - Dght 1.601 Lbp 32.01 Br md 15.00 Dpth 2.42 Welded, 1 dk	**(A37B2PS) Passenger Ship**	**4 oil engines** driving 4 FP propellers Total Power: 440kW (600hp) 7.5k Daimler OM34 4 x 4 Stroke 6 Cy. 128 x 140 each-110kW (150bhp) Daimler Benz AG-West Germany
8729626 **ZASHCHITNYY** *UBFJ* - **Aleksandrovskiy Rybozavod Co Ltd** - *Nevelsk* *Russia* MMSI: 273844010	**723** 216 414	Class: RS	**1989-04 Zavod "Leninskaya Kuznitsa" — Kiyev** Yd No: 1607 Loa 54.84 Br ex 10.15 Dght 4.141 Lbp 49.40 Br md 9.80 Dpth 5.01 Welded, 1 dk	**(B11A2FS) Stern Trawler**	**1 oil engine** with hydraulic couplings & geared to sc. shaft driving 1 CP propeller Total Power: 852kW (1,158hp) 12.0k S.K.L. 8NVD48A-2 1 x 4 Stroke 8 Cy. 320 x 480 852kW (1158bhp) VEB Schwermaschinenbau "KarlLiebknecht" (SKL)-Magdeburg AuxGen: 3 x 150kW 400V 50Hz a.c, 1 x 220kW a.c Fuel: 155.0 (d.f.) 4.8pd
7533941 **ZASLAVL** - *ex* RS-300 No. 74 *-1986* - **Revkhvylya Fishing Collective (Rybkolkhoz Revkhvylya)**	*164* 39 89	Class: (RS)	**1975 Astrakhanskaya Sudoverf im. "Kirova" — Astrakhan** Yd No: 74 Loa 34.02 Br ex 7.12 Dght 2.890 Lbp 30.00 Br md - Dpth 3.69 Welded, 1 dk	**(B11B2FV) Fishing Vessel** Bale: 95 Compartments: 1 Ho, ER 1 Ha: (1.6 x 1.9) Derricks: 2x2t; Winches: 2 Ice Capable	**1 oil engine** driving 1 FP propeller Total Power: 224kW (305hp) 9.5k S.K.L. 8NVD36-1 1 x 4 Stroke 8 Cy. 240 x 360 224kW (305bhp) VEB Schwermaschinenbau "KarlLiebknecht" (SKL)-Magdeburg AuxGen: 1 x 75kW, 1 x 50kW Fuel: 20.0 (d.f.)

897927	**ZAT UL SAWARI** *launched as* Lattaquie *-1957* **Lattakia General Port Co** - *Syria*	*174* 102 -	Class: (LR) ✠ Classed LR until 11/72	**1957-02 Obuda Shipyard, Hungarian Ship & Crane Works — Budapest** Loa 28.48 Br ex 6.89 Dght - Lbp 26.01 Br md 6.51 Dpth 3.26 Welded, 1 dk	**(B32A2ST) Tug**	**1 oil engine** driving 1 CP propeller Total Power: 485kW (659hp) Lang 8LD315RF 1 x 4 Stroke 8 Cy. 315 x 450 485kW (659bhp) Lang Gepgyar-Budapest AuxGen: 2 x 120kW 220V d.c, 1 x 115kW 220V d.c
018600 *A2415*	**ZATON** *ex* Anna-Luise *-1968* **Dario Karlic Shipping & Dredging Co (Brodoprijevoznicki obrt i Vadjenje Pijeska Dario Karlic)** - *Zadar* *Croatia* Official number: 3T-214	*292* 190 460	Class: (CS) (JR)	**1957 Gustav Adolf Klahn Werft — West Berlin** Yd No: 143 Loa 47.40 Br ex 8.13 Dght 2.540 Lbp 43.52 Br md 8.08 Dpth 2.90 Welded, 1 dk	**(A31A2GX) General Cargo Ship** Grain: 623; Bale: 566 Compartments: 1 Ho, ER 1 Ha: (23.0 x 5.4)ER Cranes: 1	**1 oil engine** driving 1 FP propeller Total Power: 221kW (300hp) 8.5kn MAN G6V235/330ATL 1 x 4 Stroke 6 Cy. 235 x 330 221kW (300bhp) Maschinenbau Augsburg Nuernberg (MAN)-Augsburg AuxGen: 2 x 2kW 24V a.c
924497 *3FH8*	**ZAURAK STAR** **Vela International Marine Ltd** Vela International Marine Ltd *Monrovia* *Liberia* MMSI: 636012413 Official number: 12413	**32,083** 12,794 49,000 T/cm 57.4	Class: LR ✠ **100A1** SS 11/2011 Double Hull oil tanker ESP **ShipRight** (SDA, FDA, CM) *IWS LI SPM ✠ **LMC** **UMS IGS** Eq.Ltr: 0†; Cable: 660.0/78.0 U3 (a)	**2006-11 Daewoo Shipbuilding & Marine Engineering Co Ltd — Geoje** Yd No: 5285 Loa 200.00 (BB) Br ex 32.25 Dght 11.800 Lbp 191.00 Br md 32.20 Dpth 18.00 Welded, 1 dk	**(A13A2TW) Crude/Oil Products Tanker** Double Hull (13F) Liq: 54,390; Liq (Oil): 54,390 Cargo Heating Coils Compartments: 12 Wing Ta, 2 Wing Slop Ta, ER 12 Cargo Pump (s): 12x600m³/hr Manifold: Bow/CM: 98.5m	**1 oil engine** driving 1 FP propeller Total Power: 8,561kW (11,640hp) 14.4kn MAN-B&W 6S50MC 1 x 2 Stroke 6 Cy. 500 x 1910 8561kW (11640bhp) Doosan Engine Co Ltd-South Korea AuxGen: 3 x 970kW 450V 60Hz a.c Boilers: AuxB (Comp) 9.2kgf/cm² (9.0bar), WTAuxB (o.f.) 9.2kgf/cm² (9.0bar) Fuel: 183.0 (d.f.) 1685.0 (r.f.)
21918	**ZAVITINSK** **Fishing Collective Farm 'Ogni Vostoka' (Rybolovetskiy Kolkhoz 'Ogni Vostoka')** -	**617** 105 318	Class: (RS)	**1971-09 Khabarovskiy Sudostroitelnyy Zavod im Kirova — Khabarovsk** Yd No: 209 Loa 54.23 Br ex 9.38 Dght 3.810 Lbp 48.80 Br md - Dpth 4.69 Welded, 1 dk	**(B11A2FT) Trawler** Ins: 284 Compartments: 2 Ho, ER 2 Ha: 2 (1.5 x 1.6) Derricks: 1x2.5t; Winches: 1	**1 oil engine** driving 1 FP propeller Total Power: 588kW (799hp) 11.8kn S.K.L. 8NVD48AU 1 x 4 Stroke 8 Cy. 320 x 480 588kW (799bhp) VEB Schwermaschinenbau "KarlLiebknecht" (SKL)-Magdeburg AuxGen: 3 x 100kW Fuel: 110.0 (d.f.)
837629	**ZAVNURA** *ex* Daya Makmur *-2011* *ex* Nila Samudera II *-2001* **PT Bayumas Jaya Mandiri Lines** - *Surabaya* *Indonesia*	*720* 358 -	Class: KI	**1989-08 P.T. Nila Kandi — Palembang** Loa 59.60 Br ex - Dght 3.750 Lbp 54.00 Br md 8.50 Dpth 4.50 Welded, 1 dk	**(A31A2GX) General Cargo Ship**	**1 oil engine** geared to sc. shaft driving 1 FP propeller Total Power: 360kW (489hp) 12.0kn Chinese Std. Type 6300ZC 1 x 4 Stroke 6 Cy. 300 x 380 360kW (489bhp) Wuxi Antai Power Machinery Co Ltd-China AuxGen: 1 x 50kW 220/380V a.c
705034 *AVU* -0033	**ZAVOLZHSK** **JSC Arkhangelsk Trawl Fleet (A/O 'Arkhangelskiy Tralflot')** - *Murmansk* *Russia* MMSI: 273297500	**3,816** 1,144 1,727	Class: RS	**1988-12 Stocznia Gdanska im Lenina — Gdansk** Yd No: B408/33 Loa 94.00 Br ex 15.92 Dght 5.670 Lbp 85.00 Br md 15.90 Dpth 10.01 Welded, 2 dks	**(B11A2FG) Factory Stern Trawler**	**1 oil engine** geared to sc. shaft driving 1 CP propeller Total Power: 3,824kW (5,199hp) 15.8kn Sulzer 8ZL40/48 1 x 4 Stroke 8 Cy. 400 x 480 3824kW (5199bhp) Zaklady Urzadzen Technicznych'Zgoda' SA-Poland AuxGen: 1 x 1200kW a.c, 2 x 800kW a.c
82313	**ZAWIA FIVE** - -	*100* - -		**1990 B.V. Scheepswerf Damen — Gorinchem** Loa - Br ex - Dght - Lbp - Br md - Dpth - Welded, 1 dk	**(B32A2ST) Tug**	**1 oil engine** driving 1 FP propeller
806258 *TCB*	**ZAYD** **SOMASCIR Groupe MAOA Peche** ARPECO SA *Nouadhibou* *Mauritania*	*391* 117 -	Class: BV	**1988-02 Bodewes' Scheepswerven B.V. — Hoogezand** (Hull) **1988-02 B.V. Scheepswerf Damen — Gorinchem** Yd No: 3624 Loa 36.02 Br ex - Dght 3.600 Lbp - Br md 9.01 Dpth - Welded, 1 dk	**(B11A2FS) Stern Trawler** Ins: 300	**1 oil engine** with clutches, flexible couplings & sr reverse geared to sc. shaft driving 1 FP propeller Total Power: 875kW (1,190hp) Caterpillar 3512TA 1 x Vee 4 Stroke 12 Cy. 170 x 190 875kW (1190bhp) Caterpillar Inc-USA
718715 *PCM6*	**ZAYTON 1** **Farzanegan Mandegar Co** Shenavaran Ziba Shipbuilding Co *Bandar Imam Khomeini* *Iran* MMSI: 422050700 Official number: 1/0163	**864** 509 1,200	Class: AS (Class contemplated)	**2013-10 Shenavaran Ziba Shipbuilding Co — Khorramshahr** Yd No: B-003-86600 Loa 50.00 Br ex - Dght 4.300 Lbp 48.50 Br md 12.30 Dpth 5.30 Welded, 1 dk	**(A31A2GX) General Cargo Ship** Compartments: 1 Ho, ER 1 Ha: ER	**2 oil engines** reduction geared to sc. shafts driving 2 Propellers Total Power: 970kW (1,318hp) Yanmar 6AYM-STE 2 x 4 Stroke 6 Cy. 155 x 180 each-485kW (659bhp) Yanmar Diesel Engine Co Ltd-Japan
29049	**ZBIK** - -	*184* - -	Class: (PR)	**1975 "Petrozavod" — Leningrad** Yd No: 849 Loa 29.29 Br ex 8.31 Dght 3.080 Lbp 25.43 Br md - Dpth 3.79 Welded, 1 dk	**(B32A2ST) Tug** Ice Capable	**2 oil engines** driving 2 CP propellers Total Power: 882kW (1,200hp) 10.5kn Russkiy 6DR30/50-4-2 2 x 2 Stroke 6 Cy. 300 x 500 each-441kW (600bhp) Mashinostroitelnyy Zavod"Russkiy-Dizel"-Leningrad AuxGen: 2 x 20kW 380V a.c
901378 *BBY*	**ZE KUN** *ex* Yan Chang *-2013* *ex* Da Yang He *-2007* **Weifang Great Shipping Agency Co Ltd** Weihai Weitong Marine Shipping Co Ltd *Weifang, Shandong* *China* MMSI: 413322230	**1,999** 1,113 2,847	Class: CC	**2003-10 Tianjin Xinhe Shipyard — Tianjin** Yd No: 204 Loa 79.99 Br ex - Dght 5.200 Lbp 74.00 Br md 13.60 Dpth 7.00 Welded, 1 dk	**(A31A2GX) General Cargo Ship** Compartments: 1 Ho, ER 1 Ha: ER (38.4 x 10.0)	**1 oil engine** geared to sc. shaft driving 1 FP propeller Total Power: 1,080kW (1,468hp) MAN-B&W 8L23/30 1 x 4 Stroke 8 Cy. 225 x 300 1080kW (1468bhp) Zhenjiang Marine Diesel Works-China
20513 *Z4247*	**ZEAL** *ex* Gulf Gallant *-1978* **Steinar Fishing Co Ltd** - *Vancouver, BC* *Canada* MMSI: 316001025 Official number: 322138	*183* 61 78	Class: (LR) ✠ Classed LR until 6/69	**1965-06 Bathurst Marine Ltd — Bathurst NB** Yd No: 10 Loa 28.66 Br ex 6.74 Dght - Lbp 24.39 Br md 6.71 Dpth 3.66 Welded	**(B11A2FS) Stern Trawler** Compartments: 1 Ho, ER 2 Ha: (2.4 x 1.2) (0.6 x 0.4) Derricks: 1x3t	**1 oil engine** driving 1 CP propeller Total Power: 364kW (495hp) Normo RTG-7 1 x 4 Stroke 7 Cy. 250 x 360 364kW (495bhp) AS Bergens Mek Verksteder-Norway AuxGen: 1 x 30kW 110/208V 60Hz a.c, 1 x 20kW 110/208V 60Hz a.c
86744 *PA4155*	**ZEAL 01** **PT Marunda Graha Mineral** - *Jakarta* *Indonesia*	**127** 39 101	Class: KI NK	**2006-04 Tuong Aik Shipyard Sdn Bhd — Sibu** Yd No: 2520 Loa 23.17 Br ex - Dght 2.412 Lbp 21.79 Br md 7.00 Dpth 3.00 Welded, 1 dk	**(B32A2ST) Tug**	**2 oil engines** reduction geared to sc. shafts driving 2 Propellers Total Power: 940kW (1,278hp) Yanmar 6LAH-STE3 2 x 4 Stroke 6 Cy. 150 x 165 each-470kW (639bhp) Yanmar Diesel Engine Co Ltd-Japan Fuel: 65.0 (d.f.)
86756 *PA4156*	**ZEAL 02** **PT Marunda Graha Mineral** - *Jakarta* *Indonesia*	**127** 39 101	Class: KI NK	**2006-04 Tuong Aik Shipyard Sdn Bhd — Sibu** Yd No: 2522 Loa 23.17 Br ex - Dght 2.412 Lbp 21.79 Br md 7.00 Dpth 3.00 Welded, 1 dk	**(B32A2ST) Tug**	**2 oil engines** reduction geared to sc. shafts driving 2 Propellers Total Power: 942kW (1,280hp) Yanmar 6LAH-STE3 2 x 4 Stroke 6 Cy. 150 x 165 each-471kW (640bhp) Yanmar Diesel Engine Co Ltd-Japan Fuel: 65.0 (d.f.)
98187 *PA4157*	**ZEAL 03** **PT Marunda Graha Mineral** - *Jakarta* *Indonesia* Official number: 2006 PST. NO.4122/L	**127** 39 101	Class: KI NK	**2006-06 Tuong Aik Shipyard Sdn Bhd — Sibu** Yd No: 2521 Loa 23.17 Br ex - Dght 2.412 Lbp 21.79 Br md 7.00 Dpth 3.00 Welded, 1 dk	**(B32A2ST) Tug**	**2 oil engines** reduction geared to sc. shafts driving 2 Propellers Total Power: 942kW (1,280hp) Yanmar 6LAH-STE3 2 x 4 Stroke 6 Cy. 150 x 165 each-471kW (640bhp) Yanmar Diesel Engine Co Ltd-Japan Fuel: 81.0 (d.f.)
73195 *CRH*	**ZEALAND ALMERE** **Zealand Almere BV** Q-Shipping BV *Amsterdam* *Netherlands* MMSI: 246889000 Official number: 55411	**33,312** 18,893 57,195 T/cm 57.3	Class: GL RI (LR) ✠ Classed LR until 12/9/12	**2012-09 STX Offshore & Shipbuilding Co Ltd — Changwon (Jinhae Shipyard)** Yd No: 4007 Loa 190.00 (BB) Br ex 32.29 Dght 13.000 Lbp 183.00 Br md 32.26 Dpth 18.50 Welded, 1 dk	**(A21A2BC) Bulk Carrier** Grain: 71,850 Compartments: 5 Ho, ER 5 Ha: ER Cranes: 4x30t	**1 oil engine** driving 1 FP propeller Total Power: 9,480kW (12,889hp) 14.5kn MAN-B&W 6S50MC-C8 1 x 2 Stroke 6 Cy. 500 x 2000 9480kW (12889bhp) STX Engine Co Ltd-South Korea AuxGen: 3 x 620kW 450V 60Hz a.c Boilers: AuxB (Comp) 9.2kgf/cm² (9.0bar)

IMO / Call sign	Name / Owner / Manager	Tonnage	Class	Builder / Dimensions	Type / Cargo	Machinery
9674921 *PCPN* -	**ZEALAND AMALIA** **Zealand Amalia BV** Q-Shipping BV *Amsterdam* *Netherlands* MMSI: 244710882 Official number: 55744	**18,036** 8,400 26,052	Class: RI	**2013-07 Sefine Shipyard Co Inc — Altinova** Yd No: 10 Loa 173.76 (BB) Br ex - Dght 8.500 Lbp 166.00 Br md 27.23 Dpth 12.60 Welded, 1 dk	**(A31A2GX) General Cargo Ship** Grain: 34,000; Bale: 34,000 Compartments: 4 Ho, ER 4 Ha: ER Cranes: 3 Ice Capable	**1 oil engine** reduction geared to sc. shaft driving 1 CP propeller Total Power: 6,300kW (8,565hp) 13.6k MAN-B&W 6L48/60 1 x 4 Stroke 6 Cy. 480 x 600 6300kW (8565bhp) MAN B&W Diesel AG-Augsburg AuxGen: 3 x 360kW 440/220V 50Hz a.c
9610884 *PBIF* -	**ZEALAND AMSTERDAM** **Zealand Amsterdam BV** Navig8 Bulk Asia Pte Ltd *Amsterdam* *Netherlands* MMSI: 244785000	**33,312** 18,893 57,111 T/cm 57.3	Class: GL (LR) ✠ Classed LR until 24/8/12	**2012-08 STX Offshore & Shipbuilding Co Ltd — Changwon (Jinhae Shipyard)** Yd No: 4017 Loa 190.00 (BB) Br ex 32.30 Dght 13.000 Lbp 183.30 Br md 32.26 Dpth 18.50 Welded, 1 dk	**(A21A2BC) Bulk Carrier** Grain: 71,850 Compartments: 5 Ho, ER 5 Ha: ER Cranes: 4x30t	**1 oil engine** driving 1 FP propeller Total Power: 9,480kW (12,889hp) 14.5k MAN-B&W 6S50MC-C 1 x 2 Stroke 6 Cy. 500 x 2000 9480kW (12889bhp) STX Engine Co Ltd-South Korea AuxGen: 3 x 620kW 450V 60Hz a.c Boilers: AuxB (Comp) 9.2kgf/cm² (9.0bar)
9507087 *PCKH* -	**ZEALAND BEATRIX** *ex* Beatrix *-2011* **Zealand Beatrix BV** Q-Shipping BV *Amsterdam* *Netherlands* MMSI: 246789000 Official number: 54248	**9,514** 4,316 13,089	Class: RI	**2010-06 Sefine Shipyard Co Inc — Altinova** Yd No: 001 Loa 134.71 (BB) Br ex 20.72 Dght 8.150 Lbp 126.94 Br md 20.50 Dpth 11.00 Welded, 1 dk	**(A31A2GX) General Cargo Ship** Grain: 15,557; Bale: 15,350 Compartments: 3 Ho, ER 3 Ha: ER Cranes: 2	**1 oil engine** driving 1 CP propeller Total Power: 4,440kW (6,037hp) 13.0k MAN-B&W 6S35MC 1 x 2 Stroke 6 Cy. 350 x 1400 4440kW (6037bhp) STX Engine Co Ltd-South Korea AuxGen: 3 x 440kW 440V 60Hz a.c Thrusters: 1 Tunnel thruster (f)
9507075 *PBZI* -	**ZEALAND DELILAH** **Zealand Delilah BV** Q-Shipping BV SatCom: Inmarsat C 424593511 *Amsterdam* *Netherlands* MMSI: 245935000 Official number: 54354	**9,514** 4,316 13,089	Class: RI (GL)	**2011-04 Sefine Shipyard Co Inc — Altinova** Yd No: 002 Loa 134.71 (BB) Br ex 20.72 Dght 8.160 Lbp 126.94 Br md 20.50 Dpth 11.00 Welded, 1 dk	**(A31A2GX) General Cargo Ship** Grain: 15,557; Bale: 15,350 Compartments: 3 Ho, ER 3 Ha: 2 (26.6 x 17.5)ER (25.9 x 15.0) Cranes: 2x30t	**1 oil engine** driving 1 CP propeller Total Power: 4,440kW (6,037hp) 13.0k MAN-B&W 6S35M 1 x 2 Stroke 6 Cy. 350 x 1400 4440kW (6037bhp) STX Engine Co Ltd-South Korea Thrusters: 1 Tunnel thruster (f)
9655951 *PCQP* -	**ZEALAND JULIANA** **Zealand Juliana BV** Q-Shipping BV *Amsterdam* *Netherlands* MMSI: 246882000	**11,953** 5,712 16,736	Class: GL RI (BV)	**2012-09 Sefine Shipyard Co Inc — Altinova** Yd No: 16 Loa 152.50 (BB) Br ex - Dght 7.750 Lbp 146.00 Br md 22.50 Dpth 10.80 Welded, 1 dk	**(A31A2GX) General Cargo Ship** Grain: 21,760; Bale: 21,760 Compartments: 4 Ho, ER 4 Ha: ER Cranes: 3x30t Ice Capable	**1 oil engine** driving 1 CP propeller Total Power: 4,440kW (6,037hp) 12.0k MAN-B&W 6S35MC 1 x 2 Stroke 6 Cy. 350 x 1400 4440kW (6037bhp) STX Engine Co Ltd-South Korea Fuel: 151.0 (d.f.) 700.0 (r.f.)
9674933 *PCYC* -	**ZEALAND MAXIMA** **Zealand Maxima BV** Q-Shipping BV *Amsterdam* *Netherlands* MMSI: 244810600 Official number: 56119	**18,036** 8,400 24,000	Class: RI	**2014-03 Sefine Shipyard Co Inc — Altinova** Yd No: 11 Loa 173.45 (BB) Br ex - Dght 8.500 Lbp 166.00 Br md 27.20 Dpth 12.60 Welded, 1 dk	**(A31A2GX) General Cargo Ship** Grain: 34,000; Bale: 34,000	**1 oil engine** reduction geared to sc. shaft driving 1 FP propeller Total Power: 7,200kW (9,789hp) 15.0k MAN-B&W 6L48/60 1 x 4 Stroke 6 Cy. 480 x 600 7200kW (9789bhp)
9477440 *PCRF* -	**ZEALAND ROTTERDAM** **Zealand Rotterdam BV** Q-Shipping BV *Amsterdam* *Netherlands* MMSI: 246888000 Official number: 55413	**33,312** 18,893 57,157 T/cm 57.3	Class: GL RI (LR) ✠ Classed LR until 27/8/12	**2012-07 STX Offshore & Shipbuilding Co Ltd — Changwon (Jinhae Shipyard)** Yd No: 4009 Loa 190.00 (BB) Br ex 32.29 Dght 13.000 Lbp 183.30 Br md 32.26 Dpth 18.50 Welded, 1 dk	**(A21A2BC) Bulk Carrier** Grain: 71,850 Compartments: 5 Ho, ER 5 Ha: ER Cranes: 4x30t	**1 oil engine** driving 1 FP propeller Total Power: 9,480kW (12,889hp) 14.4k MAN-B&W 6S50MC-C 1 x 2 Stroke 6 Cy. 500 x 2000 9480kW (12889bhp) STX Engine Co Ltd-South Korea AuxGen: 3 x 620kW 450V 60Hz a.c Boilers: AuxB (Comp) 9.2kgf/cm² (9.0bar)
9486269 *9HA2378* -	**ZEALAND ZARIA** *ex* Sider Tino *-2013* **Brook Shipping Ltd** Navigest Trust Services & Ship Management SA *Valletta* *Malta* MMSI: 248472000 Official number: 9486269	**15,545** 8,149 25,011	Class: BV (RI)	**2010-07 Ningbo Xinle Shipbuilding Co Ltd — Ningbo ZJ** Yd No: XL-120 Loa 157.00 (BB) Br ex 24.83 Dght 9.800 Lbp 149.80 Br md 24.80 Dpth 13.70 Welded, 1 dk	**(A21A2BC) Bulk Carrier** Grain: 30,800; Bale: 30,297 Compartments: 4 Ho, ER 4 Ha: 3 (19.2 x 17.2)ER (17.6 x 14.0) Cranes: 3x30t	**1 oil engine** driving 1 FP propeller Total Power: 4,900kW (6,662hp) 13.0k MAN-B&W 7S35MC 1 x 2 Stroke 7 Cy. 350 x 1400 4900kW (6662bhp) STX Engine Co Ltd-South Korea
5013258 - -	**ZEBONITA** *ex* Zebron *-1990* *ex* Alvtank *-1979* *ex* Tanker *-1951* *ex* Felita *-1948* *ex* Sir William *-1948* **Rozete Marine Services Ltd** Panafric Maritime Ltd *Nigeria* Official number: 377682	**216** 129 360 T/cm 0.9		**1914 Abdela & Mitchell Ltd. — Deeside** Yd No: 355 Lengthened-1957 Loa 39.22 Br ex 6.43 Dght 3.201 Lbp - Br md 6.38 Dpth - Riveted, 1 dk	**(A13B2TP) Products Tanker** Liq: 475; Liq (Oil): 475 Compartments: 8 Ta, ER 1 Cargo Pump (s): 1x225m³/hr Manifold: Bow/CM: 5m	**1 oil engine** driving 1 FP propeller Total Power: 331kW (450hp) 9.0k Polar SF14R 1 x 4 Stroke 4 Cy. 250 x 300 331kW (450bhp) (new engine 1962) Nydqvist & Holm AB-Sweden Fuel: 10.0 (d.f.) 1.0pd
9401855 *3FCZ4* -	**ZEBRA WIND** **Eastern Cross Shipping SA** Toyo Kaiun Co Ltd SatCom: Inmarsat C 437200711 *Panama* *Panama* MMSI: 372007000 Official number: 38985TJ	**29,105** 15,527 50,820	Class: NK	**2009-05 Oshima Shipbuilding Co Ltd — Saikai NS** Yd No: 10517 Loa 182.98 (BB) Br ex - Dght 12.149 Lbp 179.30 Br md 32.26 Dpth 17.15 Welded, 1 dk	**(A21A2BC) Bulk Carrier** Double Hull Grain: 59,117; Bale: 58,700 Compartments: 5 Ho, ER 5 Ha: 4 (20.5 x 25.8)ER (14.8 x 19.8) Cranes: 4x30t	**1 oil engine** driving 1 FP propeller Total Power: 7,760kW (10,550hp) 14.5k MAN-B&W 6S50MC-C 1 x 2 Stroke 6 Cy. 500 x 2000 7760kW (10550bhp) Mitsui Engineering & Shipbuilding CLtd-Japan AuxGen: 3 x 420kW 60Hz a.c Fuel: 2350.0
6806236 - -	**ZEBRON** *ex* Norsk Polar *-1990* *ex* Rodshell *-1988* *ex* Sannoil *-1986* - - *Lome* *Togo* MMSI: 671414000	**391** 180 526	Class: (NV)	**1968-07 Elsflether Werft AG — Elsfleth** Yd No: 357 Loa 45.88 Br ex 8.54 Dght 3.468 Lbp 40.04 Br md 8.51 Dpth 3.54 Welded, 1 dk	**(A13B2TP) Products Tanker** Liq: 702; Liq (Oil): 702 Cargo Heating Coils Compartments: 8 Ta, ER 3 Cargo Pump (s): 3x90m³/hr Manifold: Bow/CM: 29m	**1 oil engine** driving 1 FP propeller Total Power: 405kW (551hp) 10.0k Caterpillar D379T 1 x Vee 4 Stroke 8 Cy. 159 x 203 405kW (551bhp) Caterpillar Tractor Co-USA AuxGen: 2 x 36kW 220V 50Hz a.c, 1 x 16kW 220V 50Hz a.c Fuel: 31.0 (d.f.) (Heating Coils) 2.0pd
5426974 - -	**ZEBU** *ex* Enid Sharon *-1978* **Royal Seafoods Inc** - *St John's, NL* *Canada* Official number: 320744	*127* 63 -	Class: (LR) ✠ Classed LR until 5/71	**1963-11 Les Chantiers Maritimes de Paspebiac Inc — Paspebiac QC** Yd No: 9 Loa 24.69 Br ex 6.89 Dght - Lbp 22.46 Br md 6.56 Dpth 3.36 Welded	**(B11A2FT) Trawler**	**1 oil engine** with hydraulic coupling driving 1 CP propeller Total Power: 250kW (340hp) 10.0k Alpha 404-24VO 1 x 2 Stroke 4 Cy. 240 x 400 250kW (340bhp) Alpha Diesel A/S-Denmark
9117923 *SWLD* -	**ZED** *ex* Kronos *-2013* *ex* Latona *-2004* *ex* Atalanta *-2001* *ex* Anaisai *-1998* **Medusa Marine Special Maritime Enterprise (ENE)** Niovis Shipping Co SA *Andros* *Greece* MMSI: 240187000 Official number: 594	**38,639** 24,551 73,301 T/cm 65.7	Class: GL (LR) (KR) ✠ Classed LR until 27/11/98	**1996-04 Samsung Heavy Industries Co Ltd — Geoje** Yd No: 1150 Loa 224.95 (BB) Br ex 32.28 Dght 13.913 Lbp 216.00 Br md 32.24 Dpth 19.10 Welded, 1 dk	**(A21A2BC) Bulk Carrier** Grain: 85,551 Compartments: 7 Ho, ER 7 Ha: (16.6 x 11.0)6 (16.6 x 14.1)ER	**1 oil engine** driving 1 FP propeller Total Power: 8,679kW (11,800hp) 14.5k B&W 6S60MC 1 x 2 Stroke 6 Cy. 600 x 2292 8679kW (11800bhp) Hyundai Heavy Industries Co Ltd-South Korea AuxGen: 3 x 550kW 450V 60Hz a.c
7909748 *V5ZD* -	**ZEE-AREND** **Benguella Sea Products (Pty) Ltd** - *Walvis Bay* *Namibia*	**236** 71 -		**1980-11 Scheepswerf Vooruit B.V. — Zaandam** (Hull) Yd No: 361 **1980-11 B.V. Scheepswerf Maaskant — Stellendam** Yd No: 385 Loa 33.86 Br ex - Dght 2.850 Lbp - Br md 7.56 Dpth 4.58 Welded, 1 dk	**(B11A2FT) Trawler**	**1 oil engine** reverse reduction geared to sc. shaft driving 1 FP propeller Total Power: 1,030kW (1,400hp) Deutz SBV8M628 1 x 4 Stroke 8 Cy. 240 x 280 1030kW (1400bhp) Kloeckner Humboldt Deutz AG-West Germany
9226853 *PBDP* -	**ZEEAREND** **Government of The Kingdom of The Netherlands (Rijkswaterstaat Directie Noordzee)** - *Rijswijk, Zuid Holland* *Netherlands* MMSI: 245888000 Official number: 38384	**245** 73 -	Class: LR ✠ **100A1** SS 05/2012 SSC patrol mono HSC G4, service from an EC port ✠ **LMC** **UMS** Cable: 137.5/16.0 U2 (a)	**2002-05 Scheepswerf Made B.V. — Made** (Hull) Yd No: 00029 **2002-05 B.V. Scheepswerf Damen — Gorinchem** Yd No: 549851 Loa 42.80 Br ex - Dght 2.000 Lbp 38.30 Br md 6.80 Dpth 3.77 Welded, 1 dk	**(B34H2SQ) Patrol Vessel**	**2 oil engines** with clutches, flexible couplings & sr reverse geared to sc. shafts driving 2 FP propellers Total Power: 4,176kW (5,678hp) 22.5k Caterpillar 3516B 2 x Vee 4 Stroke 16 Cy. 170 x 190 each-2088kW (2839bhp) Caterpillar Inc-USA AuxGen: 2 x 85kW 415V 50Hz a.c Thrusters: 1 Tunnel thruster (f)

IMO / Call sign	Name / Owner / Manager / Port / Flag	Tonnage	Class	Builder / Dimensions	Type / Cargo	Machinery
712987 6GQ4	**ZEEBONY** *ex* Bergon *-2003* *ex* Mini Star *-1983* **Zeebony Shipping & Trading Inc** Kirazoglu Denizcilik ve Ticaret Ltd (Kirazoglu Shipping & Trade Ltd) *Moroni* *Union of Comoros* MMSI: 616000125	**3,700** 2,118 5,514	Class: (GL) (NV)	**1978-11 Ulstein Hatlo AS — Ulsteinvik** Yd No: 160 Loa 100.83 (BB) Br ex 16.43 Dght 6.200 Lbp 93.60 Br md - Dpth 8.00 Welded, 2 dks	**(A31A2GX) General Cargo Ship** Grain: 7,803; Bale: 7,280 TEU 220 C. 220/20' Compartments: 2 Ho, ER 2 Ha: 2 (30.5 x 12.5)ER Ice Capable	**1 oil engine** reduction geared to sc. shaft driving 1 CP propeller Total Power: 2,501kW (3,400hp) 13.5kn MaK 9M453AK 1 x 4 Stroke 9 Cy. 320 x 420 2501kW (3400bhp) MaK Maschinenbau GmbH-Kiel AuxGen: 2 x 172kW 380V 50Hz a.c, 1 x 44kW 380V 50Hz a.c Fuel: 359.0 13.0pd
915483 RLZ	**ZEEBRUGGE** - **URS Belgie NV** Unie van Redding - en Sleepdienst NV (Union de Remorquage et de Sauvetage SA) (Towage & Salvage Union Ltd) *Zeebrugge* *Belgium* MMSI: 205071000 Official number: 01 00322 1996	*249* 74 196	Class: BV	**1992-03 N.V. Scheepswerf van Rupelmonde — Rupelmonde** Yd No: 466 Loa 30.50 Br ex 9.05 Dght 3.600 Lbp 25.00 Br md 8.70 Dpth 4.64 Welded, 1 dk	**(B32A2ST) Tug**	**2 oil engines** sr geared to sc. shafts driving 2 Z propellers Total Power: 2,000kW (2,720hp) 13.0kn A.B.C. 6MDZC 2 x 4 Stroke 6 Cy. 256 x 310 each-1000kW (1360bhp) Anglo Belgian Corp NV (ABC)-Belgium AuxGen: 2 x 108kW 400V 50Hz a.c Fuel: 65.0 (d.f.)
804883 8B3871	**ZEEBRUGGE I** - **Baggerwerken Decloedt en Zoon NV** - *Kingstown* *St Vincent & The Grenadines* MMSI: 377327000 Official number: 10344	**282** 84 375	Class: BV	**1978-02 B.V. Scheepswerf Damen — Gorinchem** Yd No: 920 Loa 34.02 Br ex 10.04 Dght 2.301 Lbp 32.01 Br md 10.00 Dpth 3.00 Welded, 1 dk	**(A13B2TU) Tanker (unspecified)**	**2 oil engines** geared to sc. shafts driving 2 FP propellers Total Power: 368kW (500hp) Caterpillar 3406T 2 x 4 Stroke 6 Cy. 137 x 165 each-184kW (250bhp) Caterpillar Tractor Co-USA
607290	**ZEELA** - - -	*162* 48 66	Class: (LR) ✠ Classed LR until 5/7/06	**1966-04 Atlas Werke AG — Bremen** Yd No: 436 Loa 28.68 Br ex 7.83 Dght 3.449 Lbp 24.52 Br md 7.60 Dpth 3.92 Welded, 1 dk	**(B32A2ST) Tug**	**2 oil engines** sr reverse geared to sc. shaft driving 1 FP propeller Total Power: 736kW (1,000hp) 10.5kn Deutz SBA6M528 2 x 4 Stroke 6 Cy. 220 x 280 each-368kW (500bhp) Kloeckner Humboldt Deutz AG-West Germany AuxGen: 2 x 88kW 400V 50Hz a.c Fuel: 32.5 (d.f.)
508178	**ZEELAND** *ex* Niels-Iris *-1993* *ex* Cattleya *-1984* *ex* Gitte Henning *-1981* - -	*259* - -		**1974-12 A/S Bogense Skibsvaerft — Bogense** Yd No: 217 Loa 32.39 Br ex 7.22 Dght - Lbp - Br md 7.19 Dpth 2.95 Welded	**(B11B2FV) Fishing Vessel**	**1 oil engine** driving 1 CP propeller Total Power: 441kW (600hp) Alpha 406-26VO 1 x 2 Stroke 6 Cy. 260 x 400 441kW (600bhp) Alpha Diesel A/S-Denmark
117483 PIWQ	**ZEELAND** - **Wijsmuller Harbour & Coastal Tugs BV** Svitzer Europe Holding BV *IJmuiden* *Netherlands* MMSI: 244190000 Official number: 467	**252** 75 192	Class: BV	**1982-04 Tille Scheepsbouw B.V. — Kootstertille** Yd No: 228 Loa 28.70 Br ex 9.33 Dght 4.050 Lbp 26.19 Br md 9.02 Dpth 4.68 Welded, 1 dk	**(B32A2ST) Tug**	**2 oil engines** geared to sc. shafts driving 2 FP propellers Total Power: 1,766kW (2,402hp) 11.8kn Bolnes 8DNL150/600 2 x 2 Stroke 8 Cy. 190 x 350 each-883kW (1201bhp) 'Bolnes' Motorenfabriek BV-Netherlands
901913 PIWT SCH 123	**ZEELAND** - **Jaczon Visserij Maatschappij Zeeland BV** Jaczon BV SatCom: Inmarsat C 424458310 *Scheveningen* *Netherlands* MMSI: 244583000 Official number: 5562	**6,128** 2,495 5,162	Class: LR ✠ **100A1** SS 08/2012 stern trawler ✠ **LMC** **UMS +Lloyd's RMC** Eq.Ltr: W; Cable: 495.0/50.0 U2	**1989-12 YVC Ysselwerf B.V. — Capelle a/d IJssel** Yd No: 233 Loa 113.97 (BB) Br ex 17.25 Dght 6.850 Lbp 106.68 Br md 17.00 Dpth 10.20 Welded, 1 dk, 2nd & 3rd dks in way of cargohold	**(B11A2FS) Stern Trawler**	**1 oil engine** with flexible couplings & sr gearedto sc. shaft driving 1 CP propeller Total Power: 6,600kW (8,973hp) 16.0kn MaK 6M601AK 1 x 4 Stroke 6 Cy. 580 x 600 6600kW (8973bhp) Krupp MaK Maschinenbau GmbH-Kiel AuxGen: 1 x 2500kW 440V 60Hz a.c, 2 x 2000kW 440V 60Hz a.c Boilers: 2 TOH (ex.g.) 10.2kgf/cm² (10.0bar), TOH (o.f.) 10.2kgf/cm² (10.0bar) Thrusters: 1 Thwart. FP thruster (f)
9411771 PBYI -	**ZEELAND** - **M Verkooijen** Wagenborg Shipping BV *Goes* *Netherlands* MMSI: 244847000 Official number: 50519	**2,281** 1,170 3,245	Class: BV	**2010-01 Lodenice Nova Melnik — Melnik** (Hull) Yd No: (766) **2010-01 Bijlsma Shipyard BV — Lemmer** Yd No: 766 Loa 88.97 Br ex - Dght 5.050 Lbp 78.90 Br md 11.80 Dpth 6.70 Welded, 1 dk	**(A31A2GX) General Cargo Ship** Grain: 4,502 TEU 104 Compartments: 1 Ho, ER 1 Ha: ER (63.0 x 9.6)	**1 oil engine** reduction geared to sc. shaft driving 1 CP propeller Total Power: 1,440kW (1,958hp) 11.0kn Wartsila 8L20 1 x 4 Stroke 8 Cy. 200 x 280 1440kW (1958bhp) Wartsila Finland Oy-Finland AuxGen: 1 x 312kW 400V a.c, 1 x 140kW 400V a.c Fuel: 250.0
9314363 HBEI -	**ZEELANDIA** *ex* Nirint Zeelandia *-2012* *ex* Scl Basilea *-2011* *ex* Safmarine Basilea *-2010* **SCL Basilea AG** Enzian Ship Management AG *Basel* *Switzerland* MMSI: 269076000 Official number: 172	**9,990** 4,483 12,500	Class: GL (LR) ✠ Classed LR until 25/9/13	**2005-07 Kyokuyo Shipyard Corp — Shimonoseki YC** Yd No: 457 Loa 139.95 (BB) Br ex 21.53 Dght 8.420 Lbp 133.50 Br md 21.50 Dpth 11.65 Welded, 1 dk	**(A31A2GX) General Cargo Ship** Grain: 17,010; Bale: 17,010 TEU 766 C Ho 306 TEU C Dk 460 TEU incl 120 ref C. Compartments: 3 Ho, ER 3 Ha: ER Cranes: 2x80t	**1 oil engine** driving 1 FP propeller Total Power: 8,208kW (11,160hp) 17.0kn MAN-B&W 8S42MC 1 x 2 Stroke 8 Cy. 420 x 1764 8208kW (11160bhp) Hitachi Zosen Corp-Japan AuxGen: 3 x 680kW 450V 60Hz a.c Boilers: AuxB New (Comp) 0.7kgf/cm² (0.7bar) Thrusters: 1 Thwart. CP thruster (f) Fuel: 83.0 (d.f.) 1034.0 (r.f.)
8664319 PDIE	**ZEELEEUW** *ex* Candy *-2001* **Kapitein Maritiem** - *Urk* *Netherlands* MMSI: 246245000 Official number: 26322	**110** 33 -	Class: BV	**1993-12 Scheepswerf Ravestein BV — Deest** Yd No: 47 Loa 18.65 Br ex - Dght 1.530 Lbp 17.52 Br md 9.30 Dpth 2.41 Welded, 1 dk	**(B34L2QU) Utility Vessel**	**2 oil engines** reduction geared to sc. shafts driving 2 Directional propellers Total Power: 980kW (1,332hp) 6.0kn Mitsubishi S6A3-MPTK 2 x 4 Stroke 6 Cy. 150 x 175 each-490kW (666bhp) (new engine 2004) Mitsubishi Heavy Industries Ltd-Japan
9641596 ORBT	**ZEESCHELDE** - **DAB Vloot** - *Antwerpen* *Belgium* MMSI: 205639000	**309** 92 -	Class: BV	**2012-11 Euro-Industry Sp z oo Stocznia Ustka — Ustka** (Hull) Yd No: (571671) **2012-11 B.V. Scheepswerf Damen Hardinxveld — Hardinxveld-Giessendam** Yd No: 571671 Loa 30.08 Br ex 9.32 Dght 3.300 Lbp 29.38 Br md 9.10 Dpth 4.40 Welded, 1 dk	**(B32A2ST) Tug**	**2 oil engines** reduction geared to sc. shaft (s) driving 2 FP propellers Total Power: 2,460kW (3,344hp) Caterpillar 3512B 2 x Vee 4 Stroke 12 Cy. 170 x 190 each-1230kW (1672bhp) Caterpillar Inc-USA AuxGen: 2 x 84kW 50Hz a.c Thrusters: 1 Tunnel thruster (f)
9581526 ORBO	**ZEETIJGER** - **DAB Vloot** - *Antwerpen* *Belgium* MMSI: 205595000 Official number: 16985P	**309** 92 -	Class: BV	**2010-11 MKJ Stocznia Ustka Sp z oo — Ustka** (Hull) **2010-11 B.V. Scheepswerf Damen Hardinxveld — Hardinxveld-Giessendam** Yd No: 571629 Loa 30.08 Br ex 9.30 Dght 3.200 Lbp 27.99 Br md 9.10 Dpth 4.40 Welded, 1 dk	**(B32A2ST) Tug**	**2 oil engines** reduction geared to sc. shafts driving 2 FP propellers Total Power: 2,460kW (3,344hp) Caterpillar 3512B-TA 2 x Vee 4 Stroke 12 Cy. 170 x 190 each-1230kW (1672bhp) Caterpillar Inc-USA AuxGen: 2 x 84kW 50Hz a.c Thrusters: 1 Tunnel thruster (f)
8302739 PIWR	**ZEEZAND EXPRESS** *ex* Seelowe *-1996* **Noordzeezand BV** Spaansen Zand & Grind BV *Harlingen* *Netherlands* MMSI: 246384000 Official number: 26258	**994** 298 1,500	Class: GL (DS)	**1982-08 'Ilya Boyadzhiev' Shipyard — Bourgas** Yd No: 555 Converted From: Hopper-1996 Lengthened-1997 Loa 76.50 Br ex 9.53 Dght 4.132 Lbp 73.01 Br md 9.15 Dpth 4.44 Welded, 1 dk	**(B33B2DT) Trailing Suction Hopper Dredger** Hopper: 842 Compartments: 1 Ho, ER 1 Ha: ER Ice Capable	**2 oil engines** reduction geared to sc. shafts driving 2 FP propellers Total Power: 678kW (922hp) 8.0kn Caterpillar 3408TA 2 x Vee 4 Stroke 8 Cy. 137 x 152 each-339kW (461bhp) (new engine 1995) Caterpillar Inc-USA AuxGen: 1 x 122kW 380/220V a.c Thrusters: 1 Thwart. FP thruster (f)
8004088 D2P019 -	**ZEFERINO LOPES** *ex* Barmouth *-2005* *ex* Per *-1986* **Transfal Comercio Geral Transportes e Pescas Lda** - *Luanda* *Angola* MMSI: 603900500 Official number: 003/2004	**1,144** 613 1,774 T/cm 6.6	Class: (LR) (BV) (NK) Classed LR until 26/10/06	**1980-08 Fukuoka Shipbuilding Co Ltd — Fukuoka FO** Yd No: 1080 Loa 69.52 Br ex 11.82 Dght 4.313 Lbp 64.01 Br md 11.80 Dpth 5.15 Welded, 1 dk	**(A13B2TP) Products Tanker** Single Hull Liq: 2,075; Liq (Oil): 2,075 Compartments: 8 Wing Ta, ER, 2 Wing Slop Ta 3 Cargo Pump (s): 3x660m³/hr	**1 oil engine** with clutches & dr reverse geared to sc. shaft driving 1 FP propeller Total Power: 1,030kW (1,400hp) 10.5kn Yanmar 6ZL-DT 1 x 4 Stroke 6 Cy. 280 x 340 1030kW (1400bhp) Yanmar Diesel Engine Co Ltd-Japan AuxGen: 2 x 320kW 440V 60Hz a.c, 1 x 96kW 440V 60Hz a.c Fuel: 95.0 (d.f.) 5.0pd

1011094 *9HA2459* -	**ZEFIRA** **AUXIFIP SA** - *Valletta* *Malta* MMSI: 248663000	**363** 108 -	Class: LR ✠**100A1** SS 07/2010 SSC Yacht, mono, G6 Cable: 320.0/19.0 U2 (a)	**2010-07 Fitzroy Yachts Ltd — New Plymouth** Yd No: 14 Loa 49.69 Br ex - Dght - Lbp 44.56 Br md 9.95 Dpth 4.90 Welded, 1 dk	**(X11A2YS) Yacht (Sailing)** Hull Material: Aluminium Alloy	**1 oil engine** with clutches & sr reverse geared to sc. shaft driving 1 CP propeller Total Power: 1,045kW (1,421hp) 14.0 Caterpillar C 1 x Vee 4 Stroke 12 Cy. 145 x 162 1045kW (1421bhp) Caterpillar Inc-USA AuxGen: 2 x 89kW 400V 50Hz a.c Thrusters: 1 Thwart. FP thruster (f); 1 Thwart. FP thruster (a)
9607643 *ICSM* -	**ZEFIREA** **Carichi Liquidi Societa Armatoriale SpA (CALISA)** - *Genoa* *Italy* MMSI: 247322500	**25,923** 10,400 40,023 T/cm 52.5	Class: GL RI	**2012-11 Santierul Naval Constanta S.A. — Constanta** Yd No: 588 Loa 179.83 (BB) Br ex 32.23 Dght 10.940 Lbp 172.00 Br md 32.20 Dpth 16.50 Welded, 1 dk	**(A12B2TR) Chemical/Products Tanker** Double Hull (13F) Liq: 47,776; Liq (Oil): 47,776 Ice Capable	**1 oil engine** driving 1 FP propeller Total Power: 9,480kW (12,889hp) 14.0 Wartsila 6RT-flex 1 x 2 Stroke 6 Cy. 500 x 2050 9480kW (12889bhp) '3 Maj' Motori i Dizalice dd-Croatia
8327557 *SV7665* -	**ZEFS D** *ex* Oinoussai II *-2011* *ex* Aetos *-2011* **Kontogouris Naftiki Eteria** - *Thessaloniki* *Greece* MMSI: 237033800 Official number: 247	*138* 107 -	Class: (HR)	**1978 Homatas Brothers Shipyard — Thessaloniki** Loa 29.70 Br ex 6.51 Dght - Lbp 26.60 Br md - Dpth 3.00 Welded, 1 dk	**(A37B2PS) Passenger Ship**	**2 oil engines** driving 1 FP propeller Total Power: 926kW (1,258hp) Maybach MB820D 2 x Vee 4 Stroke 12 Cy. 175 x 205 each-463kW (629bhp) Daimler Benz AG-West Germany
8916748 *YJQK7* -	**ZEFYROS** *ex* Southern Harvest *-2010* *ex* Serene Harvest *-2000* **Olympus Marine Ltd** Lavinia Corp *Port Vila* *Vanuatu* MMSI: 576689000 Official number: 1965	**8,483** 3,619 8,946	Class: BV (NV) (NK)	**1990-11 Sasebo Heavy Industries Co. Ltd. — Sasebo Yard, Sasebo** Yd No: 378 Loa 141.00 (BB) Br ex 22.60 Dght 8.140 Lbp 133.00 Br md 20.60 Dpth 13.00 Welded	**(A34A2GR) Refrigerated Cargo Ship** Bale: 12,449; Ins: 12,457 TEU 30 incl 20 ref C Compartments: 4 Ho, ER 4 Ha: ER Derricks: 8x5t	**1 oil engine** driving 1 FP propeller Total Power: 7,760kW (10,550hp) 19.0 Mitsubishi 6UEC52 1 x 2 Stroke 6 Cy. 520 x 1850 7760kW (10550bhp) Akasaka Tekkosho KK (Akasaka DieselLtd)-Japan AuxGen: 4 x 462kW a.c Fuel: 240.4 (d.f.) 27.3pd
9515917 *3FFL3* -	**ZEFYROS** **Zefyros Trading SA** Benetech Surveys SA *Panama* *Panama* MMSI: 354949000 Official number: 4507313	**29,924** 13,429 50,155 T/cm 51.9	Class: BV (AB)	**2013-06 SPP Shipbuilding Co Ltd — Sacheon** Yd No: S5042 Loa 183.00 (BB) Br ex 32.24 Dght 13.076 Lbp 174.00 Br md 32.20 Dpth 19.10 Welded, 1 dk	**(A12B2TR) Chemical/Products Tanker** Double Hull (13F) Liq: 52,126; Liq (Oil): 52,100 Cargo Heating Coils Compartments: 12 Wing Ta, 2 Wing Slop Ta, ER 12 Cargo Pump (s): 12x600m³/hr Manifold: Bow/CM: 92.7m	**1 oil engine** driving 1 FP propeller Total Power: 9,480kW (12,889hp) 15.0 MAN-B&W 6S50MC 1 x 2 Stroke 6 Cy. 500 x 2000 9480kW (12889bhp) Doosan Engine Co Ltd-South Korea AuxGen: 3 x 900kW 60Hz a.c Fuel: 134.0 (d.f.) 1187.0 (r.f.)
9324382 *SZHX* -	**ZEFYROS** **Derris Finance Inc** Elin Shipping Co *Piraeus* *Greece* MMSI: 240485000 Official number: 11515	**1,723** 542 1,999	Class: LR ✠**100A1** SS 08/2011 Double Hull oil tanker ESP LI roll on-roll off upper deck aft EP (B,G,N,R,S,O) ✠**LMC** **UMS** Eq.Ltr: A†; Cable: 442.3/32.0 U3 (a)	**2006-08 Brodosplit - Brodogradiliste doo — Split** Yd No: 453 Loa 76.95 (BB) Br ex 13.01 Dght 4.500 Lbp 72.32 Br md 12.99 Dpth 6.30 Welded, 1 dk	**(A13B2TP) Products Tanker** Double Hull (13F) Stern door/ramp (centre) Len: 9.50 Wid: 6.00 Swl: 35 Compartments: 12 Wing Ta, 1 Slop Ta, ER	**2 oil engines** with clutches, flexible couplings & sr geared to sc. shafts driving 1 CP propeller Total Power: 2,040kW (2,774hp) 12.4 MaK 6M2 2 x 4 Stroke 6 Cy. 200 x 300 each-1020kW (1387bhp) Caterpillar Motoren GmbH & Co. KG-Germany AuxGen: 3 x 320kW 400V 50Hz a.c Thrusters: 1 Thwart. FP thruster (f); 2 Thwart. FP thruster (a)
8987591 *TCA2313* -	**ZEHRA JALE** **Fatih Jale-Jale Turizm ve Seyahat Acentesi** - *Canakkale* *Turkey* MMSI: 271010054 Official number: 268	**375** 113 -		**2004 Engin Jale — Ayvalik** Yd No: 709 Loa 38.40 Br ex 10.50 Dght 2.300 Lbp 35.10 Br md 10.00 Dpth 3.40 Welded, 1 dk	**(A37B2PS) Passenger Ship**	**3 oil engines** driving 3 Propellers Total Power: 1,215kW (1,653hp) Volvo Penta 3 x 4 Stroke each-405kW (551bhp) AB Volvo Penta-Sweden
9444687 *YKNR* -	**ZEIN** **Tartous General Port Co** - *Tartous* *Syria*	**176** 52 -	Class: (LR) ✠ Classed LR until 17/7/09	**2008-04 Stocznia Tczew Sp z oo — Tczew** (Hull) Yd No: (509820) **2008-04 B.V. Scheepswerf Damen — Gorinchem** Yd No: 509820 Loa 26.16 Br ex 8.54 Dght 3.980 Lbp 23.96 Br md 7.94 Dpth 4.05 Welded, 1 dk	**(B32A2ST) Tug**	**2 oil engines** with clutches, flexible couplings & sr reverse geared to sc.shafts driving 2 FP propellers Total Power: 3,000kW (4,078hp) Caterpillar 3512B-H 2 x Vee 4 Stroke 12 Cy. 170 x 215 each-1500kW (2039bhp) Caterpillar Inc-USA AuxGen: 2 x 51kW 400V 50Hz a.c Thrusters: 1 Tunnel thruster (f) Fuel: 72.0 (r.f.)
7622041 *3EPC6* -	**ZEIN I** *ex* Albert I *-2008* *ex* Northern Ice *-2003* *ex* Tropical Reefer *-2001* *ex* Orion Reefer *-1996* *ex* Golfo de Guacanayabo *-1994* **Albert Compania Naviera SA** Arab Ship Management Ltd (ASM) *Panama* *Panama* MMSI: 371446000 Official number: 3495810	**15,608** 6,090 10,554	Class: IS (LR) (RC) ✠ Classed LR until 30/3/08	**1978-03 Kanda Zosensho K.K. — Kure** Yd No: 218 Converted From: Refrigerated Cargo Ship-2008 Loa 163.02 (BB) Br ex 22.66 Dght 9.224 Lbp 152.03 Br md 22.61 Dpth 13.52 Welded, 3 dks, 4th dk in Nos. 2 & 3 holds	**(A38A2GL) Livestock Carrier** Side doors (p) Side doors (s) Compartments: ER, 4 Ho 4 Ha: (7.6 x 6.2)ER 3 (8.2 x 6.2) Derricks: 4x5t Ice Capable	**1 oil engine** driving 1 FP propeller Total Power: 11,400kW (15,499hp) 23.3 B&W 6K84E 1 x 2 Stroke 6 Cy. 840 x 1800 11400kW (15499bhp) Hitachi Zosen Corp-Japan AuxGen: 3 x 1000kW 450V 60Hz a.c Boilers: e (ex.g.) 10.0kgf/cm² (9.8bar), AuxB (o.f.) 8.0kgf/cm² (7.8bar) Fuel: 479.0 (d.f.) 2249.5 (r.f.)
7333846 *XUAW7* -	**ZEINA. J** *ex* Aures *-2003* **Jendico Shipping SA** Global Management & Trading Co Ltd SatCom: Inmarsat C 451546010 *Phnom Penh* *Cambodia* MMSI: 515460000 Official number: 0373084	**4,932** 3,056 7,385	Class: IS PR (GL)	**1973-12 Schlichting-Werft GmbH — Luebeck** Yd No: 1363 Loa 116.69 (BB) Br ex 17.25 Dght 7.519 Lbp 107.96 Br md 17.20 Dpth 9.89 Welded, 2 dks	**(A31A2GX) General Cargo Ship** Grain: 10,660; Bale: 10,012 TEU 216 Compartments: 3 Ho, ER 3 Ha: (13.0 x 7.7)2 (19.5 x 10.5)ER Derricks: 1x60t,10x10t,1x1t; Winches: 10 Ice Capable	**1 oil engine** sr geared to sc. shaft driving 1 FP propeller Total Power: 2,942kW (4,000hp) 15.5 MaK 8M551A 1 x 4 Stroke 8 Cy. 450 x 550 2942kW (4000bhp) MaK Maschinenbau GmbH-Kiel AuxGen: 2 x 256kW 220/380V 50Hz a.c, 1 x 136kW 220/380V 50Hz a.c Fuel: 69.0 (d.f.) 293.5 (r.f.)
8132603 *TCQX* -	**ZEKAI ONEL** *ex* Denizsan 1 *-2007* *ex* Salih Kaptan *-1987* **Ada Denizcilik Fikri Akin ve Ortaklari Adi Ortakligi** Arel Denizcilik Ticaret ve Sanayi AS *Istanbul* *Turkey* MMSI: 271000414 Official number: 4838	**2,547** 1,551 4,147	Class: (BV) (TL)	**1980-07 Gelibolu Gemi Insa Kizaklari Koll Sti — Gelibolu** Loa 84.60 Br ex - Dght 5.960 Lbp 77.10 Br md 13.72 Dpth 7.44 Welded, 1 dk	**(A31A2GX) General Cargo Ship** Grain: 3,758; Bale: 3,625 Compartments: 2 Ho, ER 2 Ha: ER Derricks: 4x1t	**1 oil engine** driving 1 FP propeller Total Power: 1,692kW (2,300hp) 12.0 De Industrie 8D8H 1 x 4 Stroke 8 Cy. 400 x 600 1692kW (2300bhp) B.V. Motorenfabriek "De Industrie"-Alphen a/d Rijn
9132818 *JMUT* -	**ZEKREET** **Mitsui OSK Lines Ltd, Nippon Yusen Kaisha, Kawasaki Kisen Kaisha Ltd & Iino Kaiun Kaisha Ltd** Kawasaki Kisen Kaisha Ltd (Kawasaki Kisen KK) ('K' Line) SatCom: Inmarsat B 343132510 *Kobe, Hyogo* *Japan* MMSI: 431325000 Official number: 134266	**111,124** 33,337 72,316 T/cm 108.8	Class: NK	**1998-12 Mitsui Eng. & SB. Co. Ltd., Chiba Works — Ichihara** Yd No: 1432 Loa 297.50 (BB) Br ex 45.84 Dght 11.250 Lbp 283.00 Br md 45.75 Dpth 25.50 Welded, 1 dk	**(A11A2TN) LNG Tanker** Double Hull Liq (Gas): 134,733 5 x Gas Tank (s); 5 independent (alu) sph 10 Cargo Pump (s): 10x1200m³/hr Manifold: Bow/CM: 119.8m	**1 Steam Turb** with flexible couplings & dr gearedto sc. shaft driving 1 FP propeller Total Power: 26,804kW (36,443hp) 19.5 Mitsubishi MS40- 1 x steam Turb 26804kW (36443shp) Mitsubishi Heavy Industries Ltd-Japan AuxGen: 3 x 2000kW a.c, 1 x 2000kW a.c Fuel: 290.2 (d.f.) 5000.0 (r.f.)
6930661 *A7D4003* -	**ZEKRIT** *ex* Dodo Creek *-1975* *ex* Dodo River *-1971* **Qatar Petroleum** - *Doha* *Qatar* Official number: 096/87	*121* 37 120	Class: (LR) ✠ Classed LR until 18/2/07	**1969-08 Holland Launch N.V. — Zaandam** Yd No: 436 Loa 26.01 Br ex 6.79 Dght 2.007 Lbp 23.93 Br md 6.51 Dpth 3.15 Welded, 1 dk	**(B35X2XX) Vessel (function unknown)**	**2 oil engines** reverse reduction geared to sc. shafts driving 2 FP propellers Total Power: 956kW (1,300hp) 12.0 Cummins KTA-19-M 2 x 4 Stroke 6 Cy. 159 x 159 each-478kW (650bhp) (new engine 2004) Cummins Engine Co Inc-USA AuxGen: 2 x 62kW 440V 50Hz a.c

	Ship / Owner	Tonnage	Class	Build / Dimensions	Type / Cargo	Machinery
402081 *PVV*	**ZELADA DESGAGNES** *launched as* Beluga Freedom *-2009* **Transport Desgagnes Inc** - *Bridgetown* *Barbados* MMSI: 314295000	9,611 4,260 12,692	Class: GL	**2009**-01 **Qingshan Shipyard — Wuhan HB** Yd No: 20060303 Loa 138.98 (BB) Br ex - Dght 8.000 Lbp 130.00 Br md 21.00 Dpth 11.00 Welded, 2 dks	**(A31A2GX) General Cargo Ship** Double Bottom Entire Compartment Length Grain: 15,950 TEU 665 C Ho 334 TEU C Dk 331 TEU Compartments: 3 Ho, 3 Tw Dk, ER 3 Ha: (42.3 x 18.0) (26.0 x 18.0)ER (19.3 x 15.4) Cranes: 2x180t Ice Capable	**1 oil engine** reduction geared to sc. shaft driving 1 CP propeller Total Power: 5,400kW (7,342hp) 14.0kn MaK 6M43C 1 x 4 Stroke 6 Cy. 430 x 610 5400kW (7342bhp) Caterpillar Motoren GmbH & Co. KG-Germany AuxGen: 3 x 395kW 400/230V 50Hz a.c, 1 x 700kW 400/230V 50Hz a.c Thrusters: 1 Tunnel thruster (f) Fuel: 130.0 (d.f.) 818.0 (r.f.)
98599	**ZELAN Z1** *ex* Tropical Regal *-2008* *ex* Regal 5 *-2001* **Zelan Holdings (M) Sdn Bhd** -	213 64 234	Class: (BV) (AB)	**1998**-08 **Zhenjiang Sumec Shipbuilding & Engineering Co — Zhenjiang JS** Yd No: KM94/1701 Loa 27.00 Br ex - Dght 3.550 Lbp 25.70 Br md 8.20 Dpth 4.00 Welded, 1 dk	**(B32A2ST) Tug**	**2 oil engines** with clutches, flexible couplings & sr reverse geared to sc. shafts driving 2 FP propellers Total Power: 1,176kW (1,598hp) 10.0kn Yanmar 6N165-EN 2 x 4 Stroke 6 Cy. 165 x 232 each-588kW (799bhp) Yanmar Diesel Engine Co Ltd-Japan AuxGen: 2 x 40kW 380V 50Hz a.c Fuel: 112.0 (d.f.) 5.5pd
33250	**ZELAN Z8** *ex* LM Eagle *-2008* **Zelan Holdings (M) Sdn Bhd** -	195 59 -	Class: (BV) (NK)	**2008**-02 **in Indonesia** Yd No: 180 Loa - Br ex - Dght 3.000 Lbp 24.35 Br md 8.00 Dpth 3.65 Welded, 1 dk	**(B32A2ST) Tug**	**2 oil engines** reduction geared to sc. shafts driving 2 FP propellers Total Power: 2,440kW (3,318hp) Yanmar 2 x 4 Stroke each-1220kW (1659bhp) Yanmar Diesel Engine Co Ltd-Japan
19998 *XX*) 6	**ZELDEN RUST** **Vof Visserijbedrijf P Sperling en Zonen** - *Ouddorp* *Netherlands* MMSI: 245794000 Official number: 2302	291 106 -		**1987**-10 **Constructie en Scheepsbouw van Santen B.V. — Sliedrecht** Yd No: 122 Loa 37.99 Br ex - Dght 3.001 Lbp 33.75 Br md 7.51 Dpth 3.92 Welded, 1 dk	**(B11B2FV) Fishing Vessel**	**1 oil engine** with flexible couplings & sr gearedto sc. shaft driving 1 FP propeller Total Power: 1,214kW (1,651hp) Kromhout 8FDHD240 1 x 4 Stroke 8 Cy. 240 x 260 1214kW (1651bhp) Stork Werkspoor Diesel BV-Netherlands
79117 *TL4*	**ZELEK STAR** *ex* Bao Tai *-2005* **Kuru Shipping Inc** Fuden Denizcilik Ticaret ve Sanayi AS *Port Vila* *Vanuatu* MMSI: 577180000 Official number: 2243	2,833 1,318 4,500	Class: BR	**2005**-03 **Taizhou Yongtai Shipbuilding Co Ltd — Taixing JS** Yd No: 25 Loa 90.69 Br ex 14.20 Dght 5.520 Lbp 85.00 Br md 14.16 Dpth 7.20 Welded, 1 dk	**(A31A2GX) General Cargo Ship**	**1 oil engine** driving 1 FP propeller Total Power: 1,323kW (1,799hp) Chinese Std. Type G6300ZC 1 x 4 Stroke 6 Cy. 300 x 380 1323kW (1799bhp) Ningbo CSI Power & Machinery GroupCo Ltd-China
23741	**ZELENETS** **Bunkering Co (ZAO 'Bunkernaya Kompaniya')** - *Arkhangelsk* *Russia* Official number: 733161	889 491 1,634	Class: RR (RS)	**1974**-04 **Shipbuilding & Shiprepairing Yard 'Ivan Dimitrov' — Rousse** Yd No: 100 Loa 60.55 Br ex 11.00 Dght 4.780 Lbp 56.67 Br md - Dpth 5.50 Welded, 1 dk	**(B35E2TF) Bunkering Tanker** Single Hull Liq: 1,701; Liq (Oil): 1,701 Cargo Heating Coils Compartments: 13 Ta, ER 2 Cargo Pump (s): 2x150m³/hr Ice Capable	**2 oil engines** driving 2 FP propellers Total Power: 448kW (610hp) 8.7kn S.K.L. 8NVD36-1U 2 x 4 Stroke 8 Cy. 240 x 360 each-224kW (305bhp) VEB Schwermaschinenbau "KarlLiebknecht" (SKL)-Magdeburg AuxGen: 1 x 34kW a.c, 2 x 25kW a.c
62856 *RP*	**ZELENGA** **JSC Volga Shipping (OAO Sudokhodnaya Kompaniya 'Volzhskoye Parokhodstvo')** - SatCom: Inmarsat C 427304160 *St Petersburg* *Russia* MMSI: 273446660 Official number: 784131	1,522 804 1,810	Class: RS	**1978**-07 **VEB Elbewerften Boizenburg/Rosslau — Rosslau** Yd No: 3421 Loa 82.00 Br ex 11.60 Dght 2.750 Lbp 78.00 Br md - Dpth 4.00 Welded, 1 dk	**(A31A2GX) General Cargo Ship**	**2 oil engines** driving 2 FP propellers Total Power: 882kW (1,200hp) 10.0kn S.K.L. 8VD36/24A-1U 2 x 4 Stroke 8 Cy. 240 x 360 each-441kW (600bhp) VEB Schwermaschinenbau "KarlLiebknecht" (SKL)-Magdeburg AuxGen: 2 x 100kW a.c Fuel: 87.0 (d.f.)
43564 *A3111*	**ZELLA OLDENDORFF** *ex* Violet *-2012* **Oldendorff Carriers GmbH & Co KG** - *Valletta* *Malta* MMSI: 229154000 Official number: 9243564	27,989 17,077 50,326 T/cm 53.5	Class: GL (Class contemplated) NK	**2001**-10 **Kawasaki Heavy Industries Ltd — Kobe HG** Yd No: 1517 Loa 189.80 (BB) Br ex - Dght 11.925 Lbp 181.00 Br md 32.26 Dpth 16.90 Welded, 1 dk	**(A21A2BC) Bulk Carrier** Double Bottom Entire Compartment Length Grain: 63,198; Bale: 60,713 Compartments: 5 Ho, ER 5 Ha: (17.6 x 18.0)4 (20.2 x 18.0)ER Cranes: 4x30.5t	**1 oil engine** driving 1 FP propeller Total Power: 8,090kW (10,999hp) 14.0kn B&W 6S50MC-C 1 x 2 Stroke 6 Cy. 500 x 2000 8090kW (10999bhp) Kawasaki Heavy Industries Ltd-Japan Fuel: 97.0 (d.f.) (Heating Coils) 1500.0 (r.f.) 31.0pd
42821	**ZELTEN** **Government of Libya (Socialist Ports Co)** - *Tripoli* *Libya*	*303* 136 450	Class: (BV)	**1976**-01 **Societe Provencale des Ateliers Terrin (SPAT) — Marseilles** Loa 41.31 Br ex 7.80 Dght 2.502 Lbp 40.01 Br md 7.50 Dpth 3.00 Welded, 1 dk	**(A13B2TU) Tanker (unspecified)**	**2 oil engines** reverse reduction geared to sc. shafts driving 2 FP propellers Total Power: 442kW (600hp) Duvant W6LSR 2 x 4 Stroke 6 Cy. 180 x 220 each-221kW (300bhp) Moteurs Duvant-France
34999 *LE*	**ZELZATE** *ex* Nathalie Letzer *-2000* **URS Belgie NV** Unie van Redding - en Sleepdienst NV (Union de Remorquage et de Sauvetage SA) (Towage & Salvage Union Ltd) *Antwerpen* *Belgium* MMSI: 205074000 Official number: 01 00307 1996	249 74 184	Class: LR ✠ **100A1** SS 11/2012 tug Belgian coastal service ✠ **LMC** Eq.Ltr: (D) ; Cable: 275.0/19.0 U2	**1993**-04 **N.V. Scheepswerf van Rupelmonde — Rupelmonde** Yd No: 471 Loa 31.99 Br ex 9.05 Dght 3.950 Lbp 27.28 Br md 8.70 Dpth 4.67 Welded, 1 dk	**(B32A2ST) Tug**	**1 oil engine** with clutches, flexible couplings & sr reverse geared to sc. shaft driving 1 FP propeller Total Power: 1,470kW (1,999hp) 13.0kn A.B.C. 8MDZC 1 x 4 Stroke 8 Cy. 256 x 310 1470kW (1999bhp) Anglo Belgian Corp NV (ABC)-Belgium AuxGen: 2 x 120kW 400V 50Hz a.c Thrusters: 1 Retract. directional thruster (f) Fuel: 61.3 (d.f.)
59518 *QU*	**ZEMELLO II** **Impresa Boscolo Stelio & C SnC** - *Chioggia* *Italy* Official number: 3228	*153* 100 -	Class: (RI)	**1991 Carpenteria Metallica Veneta Srl (CMV) — Contarina** L reg 40.00 Br ex - Dght - Lbp - Br md 9.22 Dpth 2.60 Welded, 1 dk	**(A31C2GD) Deck Cargo Ship**	**2 oil engines** driving 2 FP propellers Total Power: 412kW (560hp) Fiat 8281M32 2 x Vee 4 Stroke 8 Cy. 145 x 130 each-206kW (280bhp) IVECO AIFO S.p.A.-Pregnana Milanese AuxGen: 1 x 35kW 380V 50Hz a.c
23394	**ZEMES** **Oil Terminal SA** - *Constanta* *Romania* Official number: 153	689 392 1,243	Class: (RN)	**1972**-03 **Santierul Naval Giurgiu — Giurgiu** Yd No: 4363 Loa 54.26 Br ex - Dght 3.620 Lbp 52.35 Br md 9.99 Dpth 4.95 Welded, 1 dk	**(B35E2TF) Bunkering Tanker** Liq: 1,358; Liq (Oil): 1,358 Compartments: 8 Ta, ER	**2 oil engines** geared to sc. shafts driving 2 FP propellers Total Power: 410kW (558hp) 6.5kn Maybach MB836BB 2 x 4 Stroke 8 Cy. 175 x 205 each-205kW (279bhp) Uzina 23 August Bucuresti-Bucuresti AuxGen: 2 x 100kW 400V 50Hz a.c Fuel: 17.5 (d.f.)
82562 *WR2*	**ZEMGALE** **Imula Shipping Corp** Latvian Shipping Co (Latvijas Kugnieciba) SatCom: Inmarsat C 427516110 *Majuro* *Marshall Islands* MMSI: 538004371 Official number: 4371	29,694 14,113 51,406 T/cm 52.3	Class: LR ✠ **100A1** SS 07/2011 Double Hull oil and chemical tanker, Ship Type 3 CSR ESP **ShipRight** (ACS (B)) *IWS LI SPM Ice Class 1B FS at draught of 13.461m Max/min draughts fwd 14.141/6.165m Max/min draughts aft 13.131/6.535m Power required 9480kw, power installed 9480kw ✠ **LMC** **UMS IGS** Eq.Ltr: M†; Cable: 632.5/73.0 U3 (a)	**2011**-07 **Hyundai Mipo Dockyard Co Ltd — Ulsan** Yd No: 2220 Loa 183.00 (BB) Br ex 32.23 Dght 13.300 Lbp 174.00 Br md 32.20 Dpth 19.10 Welded, 1 dk	**(A12B2TR) Chemical/Products Tanker** Double Hull (13F) Liq: 53,033; Liq (Oil): 53,033 Cargo Heating Coils Compartments: 12 Wing Ta, 2 Wing Slop Ta, 1 Slop Ta, ER 12 Cargo Pump (s): 12x600m³/hr Manifold: Bow/CM: 90m Ice Capable	**1 oil engine** driving 1 FP propeller Total Power: 9,480kW (12,889hp) 15.2kn MAN-B&W 6S50MC-C 1 x 2 Stroke 6 Cy. 500 x 2000 9480kW (12889bhp) Hyundai Heavy Industries Co Ltd-South Korea AuxGen: 3 x 730kW 450V 60Hz a.c Boilers: e (ex.g.) 12.2kgf/cm² (12.0bar), WTAuxB (o.f.) 9.2kgf/cm² (9.0bar) Fuel: 280.0 (d.f.) 1400.0 (r.f.)

9397767 **ZEMIRA** **2,532** Class: NK
VKV7077 1,251
\- **Hong Lam Marine Pte Ltd** 3,876
ASP Ship Management Pty Ltd
Melbourne, Vic *Australia*
MMSI: 503542000
Official number: 858506

2007-02 Guangzhou Hangtong Shipbuilding & Shipping Co Ltd — Jiangmen GD
Yd No: 042011
Loa 74.50 (BB) Br ex 16.82 Dght 6.016
Lbp 70.91 Br md 16.80 Dpth 8.25
Welded, 1 dk

(A13B2TP) Products Tanker
Double Hull (13F)
Liq: 4,519; Liq (Oil): 4,519
3 Cargo Pump (s): 3x500m³/hr

2 oil engines reduction geared to sc. shafts driving 2 FP propellers
Total Power: 1,912kW (2,600hp)
Daihatsu 6DKM-2
2 x 4 Stroke 6 Cy. 200 x 300 each-956kW (1300bhp)
Anqing Marine Diesel Engine Works-China
AuxGen: 3 x a.c
Thrusters: 1 Tunnel thruster (f)
Fuel: 135.0

8704066 **ZEMMOUR 3** **222** Class: (BV)
\- *ex* Zemour 1 *-2009* *ex* Es Smara 1 *-1989* 70
\- *ex* In Pec I *-1988* 138
Societe Palaymon SA
SatCom: Inmarsat C 424241810
Agadir *Morocco*

1987-05 Astilleros Armon SA — Navia Yd No: 165
Loa 29.52 Br ex Dght 3.152
Lbp 25.56 Br md 7.76 Dpth 4.22
Welded, 1 dk

(B11B2FV) Fishing Vessel
Ins: 187

1 oil engine with clutches, flexible couplings & reverse reduction geared to sc. shaft driving 1 FP propeller
Total Power: 570kW (775hp) 11.1k
Caterpillar 3508
1 x Vee 4 Stroke 8 Cy. 170 x 190 570kW (775bhp)
Caterpillar Inc-USA
AuxGen: 2 x 80kW 380V a.c

8704078 **ZEMOUR 2** **222** Class: (BV)
CNYJ *ex* Es Smara 2 *-1989* *ex* Terwen *-1988* 70
\- **Benis Peche** 138
\-
Casablanca *Morocco*

1987-06 Astilleros Armon SA — Navia Yd No: 166
Loa 29.52 Br ex Dght 3.152
Lbp 25.56 Br md 7.76 Dpth 4.22
Welded, 1 dk

(B11B2FV) Fishing Vessel
Ins: 187

1 oil engine with clutches, flexible couplings & reduction geared to sc. shaft driving 1 FP propeller
Total Power: 570kW (775hp) 11.0k
Caterpillar 3508
1 x Vee 4 Stroke 8 Cy. 170 x 190 570kW (775bhp)
Caterpillar Inc-USA
AuxGen: 2 x 160kW 380V a.c

8720589 **ZEN MARU No. 7** *468*
9LY2610 -
\- **PT Armada Contener Nusantara** 1,037
\-
Freetown *Sierra Leone*
MMSI: 667003413
Official number: SL103413

1988-04 Azumi Zosen Kensetsu K.K. — Himeji
Loa 60.50 Br ex 12.02 Dght 4.070
Lbp 56.00 Br md 12.00 Dpth 6.00
Welded, 1 dk

(A31A2GX) General Cargo Ship

1 oil engine driving 1 FP propeller
Total Power: 736kW (1,001hp) 11.0k
Makita LN31
1 x 4 Stroke 6 Cy. 310 x 600 736kW (1001bhp)
Makita Diesel Co Ltd-Japan

8925098 **ZEN MARU No. 16** *497*
JJ3834 -
\- **Kemjo Kaiun Kensetsu KK** 1,369
\-
Ieshima, Hyogo *Japan*
Official number: 134179

1996-08 Azumi Zosen Kensetsu K.K. — Himeji
Yd No: 116
Loa 70.50 Br ex - Dght 4.070
Lbp 63.00 Br md 13.00 Dpth 7.00
Welded, 1 dk

(A24D2BA) Aggregates Carrier

1 oil engine driving 1 FP propeller
Total Power: 1,618kW (2,200hp) 11.0k
Hanshin LH34L
1 x 4 Stroke 6 Cy. 340 x 640 1618kW (2200bhp)
The Hanshin Diesel Works Ltd-Japan

9714410 **ZEN MARU NO. 17** *499*
JD3496 -
\- **Kemjo Kaiun Kensetsu KK** 1,800
\-
Himeji, Hyogo *Japan*
MMSI: 431004359
Official number: 141888

2013-03 Yamanaka Zosen K.K. — Imabari
Loa 74.81 (BB) Br ex - Dght -
Lbp 69.00 Br md 12.00 Dpth 7.12
Welded, 1 dk

(A31A2GX) General Cargo Ship

1 oil engine driving 1 Propeller
Total Power: 735kW (999hp)
Hanshin LA3
1 x 4 Stroke 6 Cy. 320 x 680 735kW (999bhp)
The Hanshin Diesel Works Ltd-Japan

9691266 **ZEN MARU NO. 17** *499*
\- -
\- **Kenyo Kaiun Kensetsu KK** 1,730
\-
Japan

2013-05 K.K. Watanabe Zosensho — Nagasaki
Yd No: 201
Loa 74.81 (BB) Br ex - Dght 7.120
Lbp - Br md 12.00 Dpth -
Welded, 1 dk

(A31A2GX) General Cargo Ship

1 oil engine reduction geared to sc. shaft driving 1 Propeller
Total Power: 1,618kW (2,200hp)
Hanshin LA32
1 x 4 Stroke 6 Cy. 320 x 680 1618kW (2200bhp)
The Hanshin Diesel Works Ltd-Japan

9461233 **ZEN-NOH GRAIN MAGNOLIA** **43,012** Class: NK
3EYV2 27,239
\- **KTM Corp & Kawana Kaiun KK** 82,165
Kawana Kaiun Co Ltd T/cm
SatCom: Inmarsat C 435798610 70.2
Panama *Panama*
MMSI: 357986000
Official number: 4324611

2011-10 Tsuneishi Shipbuilding Co Ltd — Fukuyama HS Yd No: 1449
Loa 228.99 Br ex - Dght 14.429
Lbp 222.00 Br md 32.26 Dpth 20.05
Welded, 1 dk

(A21A2BC) Bulk Carrier
Grain: 97,294
Compartments: 7 Ho, ER
7 Ha: ER

1 oil engine driving 1 FP propeller
Total Power: 9,710kW (13,202hp) 14.5
MAN-B&W 6S60MC-
1 x 2 Stroke 6 Cy. 600 x 2400 9710kW (13202bhp)
Mitsui Engineering & Shipbuilding CLtd-Japan
Fuel: 3180.0

9402017 **ZEN-NOH GRAIN PEGASUS** **30,619** Class: NK
3FBC9 18,206
\- **TS Central Shipping Co Ltd** 54,958
Tamai Steamship Co Ltd
Panama *Panama*
MMSI: 353320000
Official number: 4162710

2010-05 Oshima Shipbuilding Co Ltd — Saikai NS
Yd No: 10567
Loa 189.99 (BB) Br ex - Dght 12.449
Lbp 185.79 Br md 32.26 Dpth 17.62
Welded, 1 dk

(A21A2BC) Bulk Carrier
Grain: 69,339; Bale: 68,274
Compartments: 5 Ho, ER
5 Ha: ER
Cranes: 4x30t

1 oil engine driving 1 FP propeller
Total Power: 8,208kW (11,160hp) 14.5k
MAN-B&W 6S50MC
1 x 2 Stroke 6 Cy. 500 x 2000 8208kW (11160bhp)
Kawasaki Heavy Industries Ltd-Japan
Fuel: 1810.0 (r.f.)

5016626 **ZENA** *299* Class: (BV)
\- *ex* Zeina *-1993* *ex* Hiam D *-1992* 157
\- *ex* Salta *-1992* *ex* Christa *-1980* 457
ex Andreas Boye *-1976*
Abdelkader Abu Bakr
\-

1962 A/S Nordsovaerftet — Ringkobing Yd No: 8
Converted From: General Cargo Ship
Loa 43.92 Br ex 7.68 Dght 2.950
Lbp 38.99 Br md 7.60 Dpth 3.20
Welded, 1 dk

(A38A2GL) Livestock Carrier

1 oil engine driving 1 FP propeller
Total Power: 313kW (426hp) 10.0k
Alpha 405-24V
1 x 2 Stroke 5 Cy. 240 x 400 313kW (426bhp)
Alpha Diesel A/S-Denmark
AuxGen: 3 x 10kW 220V d.c
Fuel: 18.5 (d.f.)

9087221 **ZENA A** **25,503** Class: KR (NV)
3FJN4 *ex* Nena A *-2012* *ex* Pacific King *-2002* 14,222
\- **Atlasnavios - Navegacao Lda** 42,975
SeaFlag Srl T/cm
SatCom: Inmarsat C 435371810 50.8
Panama *Panama*
MMSI: 353718000
Official number: 23430PEXT2

1994-09 Hyundai Heavy Industries Co Ltd — Ulsan Yd No: 887
Loa 185.06 (BB) Br ex 30.03 Dght 11.216
Lbp 175.09 Br md 30.00 Dpth 16.00
Welded, 1 dk

(A21A2BC) Bulk Carrier
Grain: 54,232; Bale: 52,442
Compartments: 5 Ho, ER
5 Ha: (14.4 x 15.3)4 (19.2 x 15.3)ER
Cranes: 4x25t

1 oil engine driving 1 FP propeller
Total Power: 7,779kW (10,576hp) 14.5
B&W 6S50M
1 x 2 Stroke 6 Cy. 500 x 1910 7779kW (10576bhp)
Hyundai Heavy Industries Co Ltd-South Korea
AuxGen: 3 x 600kW 450V a.c
Fuel: 1690.0 (r.f.)

9087233 **ZENA C** **25,503** Class: KR (NV)
3FLA4 *ex* Nena C *-2012* *ex* Pacific Prince *-2002* 14,222
\- **Atlasnavios - Navegacao Lda** 43,188
SeaFlag Srl T/cm
SatCom: Inmarsat C 435380210 50.8
Panama *Panama*
MMSI: 353802000
Official number: 3172994D

1994-10 Hyundai Heavy Industries Co Ltd — Ulsan Yd No: 888
Loa 185.06 (BB) Br ex - Dght 11.216
Lbp 175.09 Br md 30.50 Dpth 16.00
Welded, 1 dk

(A21A2BC) Bulk Carrier
Grain: 54,232; Bale: 52,442
Compartments: 5 Ho, ER
5 Ha: (14.4 x 15.3)4 (19.2 x 15.3)ER
Cranes: 4x25t

1 oil engine driving 1 FP propeller
Total Power: 7,779kW (10,576hp) 14.5k
B&W 6S50M
1 x 2 Stroke 6 Cy. 500 x 1910 7779kW (10576bhp)
Hyundai Heavy Industries Co Ltd-South Korea
AuxGen: 3 x 600kW 450V a.c
Fuel: 1690.0 (r.f.)

9152076 **ZENEI MARU** *499*
JL6499 -
\- **Odomari Kaiun YK** 1,600
\-
Anan, Tokushima *Japan*
Official number: 135122

1996-11 Honda Zosen — Saiki Yd No: 1001
Loa - Br ex - Dght 4.200
Lbp 70.00 Br md 12.00 Dpth 7.15
Welded, 1 dk

(A31A2GX) General Cargo Ship

1 oil engine driving 1 FP propeller
Total Power: 736kW (1,001hp)
Niigata 6M34AG
1 x 4 Stroke 6 Cy. 340 x 620 736kW (1001bhp)
Niigata Engineering Co Ltd-Japan

6289309 **ZENEI MARU No. 103** *103*
\- *ex* Raicho Maru *-1985* -
\- -
\-
South Korea

1962 Ando Tekkosho — Tokyo Yd No: 138
Loa 23.63 Br ex 6.79 Dght 2.201
Lbp 21.34 Br md 6.48 Dpth 2.85
Welded, 1 dk

(B32A2ST) Tug

2 oil engines driving 2 CP propellers
Total Power: 574kW (780hp) 10.0k
Fuji 6SD27B
2 x 4 Stroke 6 Cy. 270 x 400 each-287kW (390bhp)
Fuji Diesel Co Ltd-Japan

9140920 **ZENG CHENG YI HAO** **464** Class: (CC)
BXCC 151
\- **Zengcheng Xintang Passenger Transportation Co Ltd** 33
\-
Guangzhou, Guangdong *China*

1996-06 Austal Ships Pty Ltd — Fremantle WA
Yd No: 119
Loa 40.10 (BB) Br ex 10.30 Dght 1.184
Lbp 35.00 Br md 10.00 Dpth 3.80
Welded, 1 dk

(A37B2PS) Passenger Ship
Hull Material: Aluminium Alloy
Passengers: unberthed: 268

2 oil engines with clutches, flexible couplings & sr geared to sc. shafts driving 2 Water jets
Total Power: 3,960kW (5,384hp) 33.7k
M.T.U. 16V396TE74
2 x Vee 4 Stroke 16 Cy. 165 x 185 each-1980kW (2692bhp)
MTU Friedrichshafen GmbH-Friedrichshafen

9498171 **ZENGEZUR** **7,834** Class: RS
4JNP 3,356
\- **Azerbaijan State Caspian Shipping Co (ASCSS)** 13,470
\- T/cm
Baku *Azerbaijan* 25.0
MMSI: 423306100
Official number: DGR-0532

2008-10 Sudostroitelnyy Zavod "Krasnoye Sormovo" — Nizhniy Novgorod
Yd No: 19619/10
Loa 150.15 (BB) Br ex - Dght 7.140
Lbp 143.11 Br md 17.30 Dpth 10.50
Welded, 1 dk

(A13B2TP) Products Tanker
Double Hull (13F)
Liq: 14,770; Liq (Oil): 14,770
Cargo Heating Coils
Compartments: 12 Wing Ta, ER, 2 Wing Slop Ta
6 Cargo Pump (s): 6x250m³/hr
Ice Capable

2 oil engines reduction geared to sc. shafts driving 2 FP propellers
Total Power: 3,240kW (4,406hp) 10.0k
Wartsila 9L2
2 x 4 Stroke 9 Cy. 200 x 280 each-1620kW (2203bhp)
Wartsila France SA-France
AuxGen: 3 x 384kW a.c
Thrusters: 1 Thwart. FP thruster (f)
Fuel: 73.0 (d.f.) 273.0 (r.f.) 7.0pd

IMO / Call sign	Name, owner, manager, port	Tonnage	Class	Builder & dimensions	Type & capacity	Machinery
724834 *IDI*	**ZENGILAN** *ex* Zangelan *-2003* *ex* Grigoriy Kalustov *-2003* **Azerbaijan State Caspian Shipping Co (ASCSS)** Meridian Shipping & Management LLC *Baku* *Azerbaijan* MMSI: 423067100 Official number: DGR-0074	**4,134** 1,240 5,353 T/cm 19.1	Class: RS	**1988-11 Volgogradskiy Sudostroitelnyy Zavod — Volgograd** Yd No: 36 Loa 125.06 (BB) Br ex 16.63 Dght 4.150 Lbp 121.12 Br md 16.60 Dpth 6.90 Welded, 1dk	**(A13B2TP) Products Tanker** Liq: 5,903; Liq (Oil): 5,903 Cargo Heating Coils Compartments: 6 Ta, ER 2 Cargo Pump (s): 2x400m³/hr Ice Capable	**2 oil engines** driving 2 FP propellers Total Power: 2,296kW (3,122hp) 11.3kn Dvigatel Revolyutsii 6CHRNP36/45 2 x 4 Stroke 6 Cy. 360 x 450 each-1148kW (1561bhp) Zavod "Dvigatel Revolyutsii"-Gorkiy AuxGen: 4 x 160kW a.c Fuel: 79.0 (d.f.) 190.0 (r.f.)
009783 *MGE4*	**ZENGO II** *ex* Tuah Kuantan *-2010* *ex* Meiho Maru No. 8 *-2004* *ex* Meiho Maru *-2001* **Platinum Sector Sdn Bhd** Victory Supply Sdn Bhd *Port Klang* *Malaysia* MMSI: 533000088 Official number: 330372	**310** 106 449		**1989-07 Mukaishima Zoki Co. Ltd. — Onomichi** Yd No: 257 Loa 43.20 Br ex 7.82 Dght 2.931 Lbp 40.00 Br md 7.80 Dpth 3.40 Welded, 1 dk	**(A13B2TP) Products Tanker** Liq: 416; Liq (Oil): 416 Compartments: 6 Ta, ER	**1 oil engine** with clutches & sr reverse geared to sc. shaft driving 1 FP propeller Total Power: 368kW (500hp) Niigata 6MG18CX 1 x 4 Stroke 6 Cy. 180 x 240 368kW (500bhp) Niigata Engineering Co Ltd-Japan
711235	**ZENGYOREN MARU No. 8** *ex* Sumiho Maru No. 68 *-1990* *ex* Tomiei Maru No. 51 *-1985* *ex* Shinyo Maru No. 21 *-1982* *ex* Ryoei Maru No. 11 *-1982* **Grand Link Shipping S de RL** - *Honduras*	*286* - -		**1966 KK Kanasashi Zosen — Shizuoka SZ** Yd No: 753 Loa 46.31 Br ex 7.75 Dght 2.998 Lbp 41.46 Br md 7.73 Dpth 3.46 Welded, 1 dk	**(B11B2FV) Fishing Vessel**	**1 oil engine** driving 1 FP propeller Total Power: 588kW (799hp) Hanshin V6 1 x 4 Stroke 6 Cy. 320 x 450 588kW (799bhp) Hanshin Nainenki Kogyo-Japan
382811 *5ZE* 304	**ZENICA** **ETALE Fishing Co (Pty) Ltd** - *Walvis Bay* *Namibia* Official number: 95WB004	*671* 393 -	Class: (NV)	**1974 Sterkoder Mek. Verksted AS — Kristiansund** Yd No: 44 Loa 45.09 Br ex 9.30 Dght 4.268 Lbp 40.31 Br md 9.00 Dpth 6.43 Welded, 2 dks	**(B11A2FS) Stern Trawler**	**1 oil engine** driving 1 FP propeller Total Power: 1,103kW (1,500hp) 13.0kn Normo LDM-9 1 x 4 Stroke 9 Cy. 250 x 300 1103kW (1500bhp) AS Bergens Mek Verksteder-Norway
330607	**ZENIT** *ex* SCHS-7041 *-1995* **Lingvest JSC** -	**104** 31 61	Class: (RS)	**1983 Azovskaya Sudoverf — Azov** Yd No: 7041 Loa 26.50 Br ex 6.58 Dght 2.340 Lbp 22.90 Br md - Dpth 3.05 Welded, 1 dk	**(B11B2FV) Fishing Vessel**	**1 oil engine** geared to sc. shaft driving 1 FP propeller Total Power: 165kW (224hp) 9.3kn Daldizel 6CHNSP18/22 1 x 4 Stroke 6 Cy. 180 x 220 165kW (224bhp) Daldizel-Khabarovsk AuxGen: 2 x 30kW a.c Fuel: 10.0 (d.f.)
700228 *3OL5*	**ZENIT** *ex* Amer Choapa *-2008* *ex* Choapa *-1996* **Destiny Int Inc** Ost-West-Handel und Schiffahrt GmbH *Monrovia* *Liberia* MMSI: 636013650 Official number: 13650	**13,312** 4,796 12,848 T/cm 26.9	Class: RS (LR) ✠ Classed LR until 12/11/10	**1987-11 Shin Kurushima Dockyard Co. Ltd. — Onishi** Yd No: 2525 Loa 152.00 (BB) Br ex 23.53 Dght 9.002 Lbp 144.00 Br md 23.50 Dpth 15.70 Welded, 1 dk	**(A34A2GR) Refrigerated Cargo Ship** Side doors (p) Side doors (s) Ins: 19,093 TEU 306 C Ho 138 TEU C Dk 168 TEU incl 54 ref C Compartments: 4 Ho, ER 4 Ha: (12.7 x 8.0)3 (12.7 x 10.4)ER Cranes: 2x30t,2x12.5t	**1 oil engine** driving 1 FP propeller Total Power: 7,134kW (9,699hp) 18.5kn B&W 6S50MC 1 x 2 Stroke 6 Cy. 500 x 1910 7134kW (9699bhp) Mitsui Engineering & Shipbuilding CLtd-Japan AuxGen: 3 x 750kW 450V 60Hz a.c, 1 x 450kW 450V 60Hz a.c Boilers: e 9.9kgf/cm² (9.7bar), AuxB (o.f.) 6.9kgf/cm² (6.8bar) Fuel: 170.0 (d.f.) 1291.5 (r.f.)
127813 *7KP8*	**ZENIT** *ex* MOL Universe *-2012* *ex* Safmarine Amazon *-2008* *ex* Maersk Wellington *-2001* *ex* Zenit *-1998* **Alpha Ship GmbH & Co KG ms 'Zenit'** Alpha Shipmanagement GmbH & Co KG *Majuro* *Marshall Islands* MMSI: 538090252 Official number: 90252	**21,199** 8,574 25,057 T/cm 40.5	Class: GL	**1998-08 Stocznia Gdynia SA — Gdynia** Yd No: 8138/4 Loa 178.05 (BB) Br ex 28.24 Dght 11.520 Lbp 164.20 Br md 28.20 Dpth 16.75 Welded, 1 dk	**(A33A2CC) Container Ship (Fully Cellular)** TEU 1617 C Ho 676 TEU C Dk 941 TEU incl 353 ref C. Compartments: 4 Cell Ho, ER 8 Ha: (12.8 x 18.5)Tappered 7 (12.8 x 23.6)ER Cranes: 3x45t	**1 oil engine** driving 1 FP propeller Total Power: 17,200kW (23,385hp) 21.0kn B&W 6L70MC 1 x 2 Stroke 6 Cy. 700 x 2268 17200kW (23385bhp) H Cegielski Poznan SA-Poland AuxGen: 2 x 1180kW 440/220V 60Hz a.c, 1 x 880kW 440/220V 60Hz a.c Thrusters: 1 Thwart. FP thruster (f) Fuel: 228.0 (d.f.) (Heating Coils) 2066.0 (r.f.) 72.0pd
313187 *3HX*	**ZENIT** **Government of The Federal Republic of Germany (Wasser- und Schiffahrtsamt Bremerhaven)** - *Bremerhaven* *Germany* MMSI: 211411980	**148** 44 115	Class: GL	**2004-02 Fr Fassmer GmbH & Co KG — Berne** Yd No: 03/1/1960 Loa 30.00 Br ex 6.50 Dght 2.000 Lbp 27.59 Br md 6.25 Dpth 3.50 Welded, 1 dk	**(B31A2SR) Research Survey Vessel**	**1 oil engine** geared to sc. shaft driving 1 FP propeller Total Power: 447kW (608hp) 12.5kn Cummins KTA-19-M3 1 x 4 Stroke 6 Cy. 159 x 159 447kW (608bhp) Cummins Engine Co Inc-USA
001098 *JPQ*	**ZENITE** *ex* Praia da Barra *-1986* **Sociedade de Pesca do Miradouro Lda** - *Aveiro* *Portugal* MMSI: 263441000	*152* 45 -	Class: (LR) ✠ Classed LR until 8/3/93	**1984-08 Estaleiros Sao Jacinto S.A. — Aveiro** Yd No: 140 Loa 31.20 Br ex 8.36 Dght 3.201 Lbp 25.00 Br md 8.01 Dpth 3.81 Welded, 1 dk	**(B11A2FS) Stern Trawler** Ins: 130	**1 oil engine** sr geared to sc. shaft driving 1 CP propeller Total Power: 699kW (950hp) MaK 6M282AK 1 x 4 Stroke 6 Cy. 240 x 280 699kW (950bhp) (new engine ,made 1973, fitted 1984) MaK Maschinenbau GmbH-Kiel AuxGen: 2 x 80kW 380V 50Hz a.c Fuel: 67.5 (d.f.)
133097 *DF4625*	**ZENITH** **Washington State (Seattle Maritime Academy)** - SatCom: Inmarsat C 436638410 *Seattle, WA* *United States of America* MMSI: 367453980 Official number: 628313	**382** 114 -		**1980-01 Steiner Shipyard, Inc. — Bayou La Batre, Al** Yd No: 104 L reg 24.72 Br ex 7.24 Dght - Lbp - Br md - Dpth 3.66 Welded, 1 dk	**(B11B2FV) Fishing Vessel**	**1 oil engine** driving 1 FP propeller Total Power: 416kW (566hp) Caterpillar D379SCAC 1 x Vee 4 Stroke 8 Cy. 159 x 203 416kW (566bhp) Caterpillar Tractor Co-USA
306395 *4XP*	**ZENITH** *ex* Maxim *-2008* *ex* Michelle Trader *-2004* *ex* Paola *-1995* *ex* Paul Brinkman *-1988* **Maxim Shipping & Trading Inc** Sargem Denizcilik Gem Acenteligi Ticaret Ltd Sti *Basseterre* *St Kitts & Nevis* MMSI: 341612000	**994** 509 1,591	Class: IS (LR) (RS) ✠ Classed LR until 17/9/03	**1983-10 E.J. Smit & Zoon's Scheepswerven B.V. — Westerbroek** Yd No: 827 Loa 63.66 Br ex 11.84 Dght 3.901 Lbp 59.52 Br md 11.70 Dpth 4.70 Welded, 1 dk	**(A31A2GX) General Cargo Ship** Grain: 1,898; Bale: 1,858 Compartments: 1 Ho, ER 1 Ha: (33.0 x 8.2)ER	**1 oil engine** with clutches, flexible couplings & sr reverse geared to sc. shaft driving 1 FP propeller Total Power: 625kW (850hp) 10.0kn Bolnes 5DNL170/600 1 x 2 Stroke 5 Cy. 190 x 350 625kW (850bhp) 'Bolnes' Motorenfabriek BV-Netherlands AuxGen: 1 x 65kW 260V d.c, 3 x 52kW 220/380V 50Hz a.c Fuel: 147.5 (d.f.)
011458 *GBR4*	**ZENITH** **Star 7 Holdings LLC** - *George Town* *Cayman Islands (British)* MMSI: 319036500 Official number: 743577	**461** 138 46	Class: LR ✠ **100A1** SS 05/2012 SSC Yacht, catamaran G6 **LMC** Cable: 275.0/17.5 U2 (a)	**2012-05 Sabre Catamarans Pty Ltd — Fremantle WA** Yd No: 154 Loa 40.50 Br ex 10.70 Dght 1.800 Lbp 35.70 Br md 10.30 Dpth 3.60 Welded, 1 dk	**(X11A2YP) Yacht** Hull Material: Aluminium Alloy	**2 oil engines** with clutches, flexible couplings & sr reverse geared to sc. shafts driving 2 FP propellers Total Power: 3,700kW (5,030hp) M.T.U. 12V4000M71 2 x Vee 4 Stroke 12 Cy. 165 x 190 each-1850kW (2515bhp) MTU Friedrichshafen GmbH-Friedrichshafen AuxGen: 2 x 99kW 208V 60Hz a.c Thrusters: 1 Thwart. FP thruster (f)
205887 *WFS*	**ZENITH** *ex* Prosperity *-1988* *ex* Lemberg *-1988* **GIE Armement** - *Dakar* *Senegal*	**271** 65 -	Class: HR (LR) ✠ Classed LR until 7/5/97	**1961-11 J. S. Doig (Grimsby) Ltd. — Grimsby** Yd No: 72 L reg 35.10 Br ex 7.50 Dght - Lbp 35.03 Br md 7.40 Dpth 3.97 Riveted\Welded	**(B11A2FT) Trawler**	**1 oil engine** driving 1 FP propeller Total Power: 552kW (750hp) Mirrlees KSSDM-6 1 x 4 Stroke 6 Cy. 381 x 457 552kW (750bhp) Mirrlees, Bickerton & Day-Stockport
568004 *DNP8*	**ZENITH** **Zenith Holdings Ltd** - *Gibraltar* *Gibraltar (British)* MMSI: 236111999 Official number: 745316	**155** 46 -	Class: RN (Class contemplated)	**2013-09 Ada Turizm Mumessillik Yatcilik ve Ticaret AS — Bodrum** Yd No: 05 Loa 40.88 Br ex - Dght - Lbp - Br md 8.14 Dpth 3.45 Welded, 1 dk	**(X11A2YS) Yacht (Sailing)**	**1 oil engine** driving 1 Propeller Total Power: 368kW (500hp) Yanmar 6HYM-ETE 1 x 4 Stroke 6 Cy. 133 x 165 368kW (500bhp) Yanmar Diesel Engine Co Ltd-Japan

IMO / Call sign	Name / Owner / Manager / Flag	Tonnage	Class	Builder / Dimensions	Type / Cargo	Machinery
8918136 *9HXM8* -	**ZENITH** **Pullmantur Cruises Zenith Ltd** Pullmantur Cruises Ship Management Ltd SatCom: Inmarsat C 425656110 *Valletta* *Malta* MMSI: 256561000 Official number: 8918136	**47,413** 25,488 4,915 T/cm 45.5	Class: GL (LR) ✠ Classed LR until 14/3/10	**1992**-03 **Jos L Meyer GmbH & Co — Papenburg** Yd No: 620 Loa 208.00 (BB) Br ex 29.33 Dght 7.700 Lbp 175.03 Br md 29.00 Dpth 24.10 Welded, 6 dks and 2 pt dks	**(A37A2PC) Passenger/Cruise** Passengers: cabins: 720; berths: 1828	**4 oil engines** with clutches, flexible couplings & sr tandem geared to sc. shafts driving 2 CP propellers Total Power: 19,960kW (27,138hp) 21.4 MAN 6L40/5 2 x 4 Stroke 6 Cy. 400 x 540 each-3990kW (5425bhp) MAN B&W Diesel AG-Augsburg MAN 9L40/5 2 x 4 Stroke 9 Cy. 400 x 540 each-5990kW (8144bhp) MAN B&W Diesel AG-Augsburg AuxGen: 5 x 3000kW 660V 60Hz a.c Boilers: 5 e (ex.g.) 9.2kgf/cm² (9.0bar), 2 AuxB (o.f.) 9.2kgf/cm² (9.0bar) Thrusters: 2 Thwart. CP thruster (f); 1 Tunnel thruster (a) Fuel: 89.2 (d.f.) 1697.8 (r.f.)
9524217 *DSQG6* -	**ZENITH BUSAN** **Han Kook Capital Co Ltd** Kumjin Shipping Co Ltd SatCom: Inmarsat C 444057110 *Jeju* *South Korea* MMSI: 441571000 Official number: JJR-092219	**4,713** 2,165 7,232	Class: KR	**2009**-05 **Yangzhou Longchuan Shipbuilding Co Ltd — Jiangdu JS** Yd No: 721 Loa 107.40 Br ex - Dght 7.019 Lbp 102.20 Br md 17.00 Dpth 9.00 Welded, 1 dk	**(A31A2GX) General Cargo Ship** Compartments: 2 Ho, ER 2 Ha: ER 2 (25.2 x 12.6) Cranes: 2x30t	**1 oil engine** driving 1 Propeller Total Power: 2,648kW (3,600hp) 12.5 Hanshin LH41L 1 x 4 Stroke 6 Cy. 410 x 800 2648kW (3600bhp) The Hanshin Diesel Works Ltd-Japan AuxGen: 4 x 280kW 450V a.c
8106410 - -	**ZENITH CROWN** *ex* Kum Jin No. 7 *-2002* *ex* Zenith Post *-1999* *ex* Yaekawa Maru *-1996* **DaeHo Shipping Co Ltd** Kumjin Shipping Co Ltd *Busan* *South Korea* MMSI: 440134360 Official number: BSR-090961	**1,524** 851 3,073	Class: (BV) (NK)	**1981**-09 **Sanyo Zosen K.K. — Onomichi** Yd No: 822 Loa 75.39 Br ex - Dght 4.423 Lbp 70.01 Br md 14.01 Dpth 7.20 Welded, 1 dk	**(A31A2GX) General Cargo Ship** Grain: 4,568; Bale: 3,938 Compartments: 1 Ho, ER 1 Ha: (39.6 x 10.8)ER Derricks: 2x4t	**1 oil engine** driving 1 FP propeller Total Power: 1,471kW (2,000hp) 11.5 Hanshin 6EL3 1 x 4 Stroke 6 Cy. 320 x 640 1471kW (2000bhp) The Hanshin Diesel Works Ltd-Japan AuxGen: 2 x 96kW
9464534 *3ESI* -	**ZENITH EXPLORER** **Zenith Explorer Corp** Sincere Industrial Corp *Panama* *Panama* MMSI: 370307000 Official number: 3424208A	**17,018** 10,109 28,343 T/cm 39.7	Class: NK	**2008**-08 **Imabari Shipbuilding Co Ltd — Marugame KG (Marugame Shipyard)** Yd No: 1513 Loa 169.37 (BB) Br ex - Dght 9.819 Lbp 160.40 Br md 27.20 Dpth 13.60 Welded, 1 dk	**(A21A2BC) Bulk Carrier** Grain: 37,320; Bale: 35,742 Compartments: 5 Ho, ER 5 Ha: 4 (19.2 x 17.6)ER (13.6 x 16.0) Cranes: 4x30.5t	**1 oil engine** driving 1 FP propeller Total Power: 5,850kW (7,954hp) 14.0 MAN-B&W 6S42M 1 x 2 Stroke 6 Cy. 420 x 1764 5850kW (7954bhp) Makita Corp-Japan AuxGen: 3 x 440kW 60Hz a.c Fuel: 1232.0
9599339 *3EWJ4* -	**ZENITH GOLD** **Golden Phoenix Maritime SA** DaeHo Shipping Co Ltd SatCom: Inmarsat C 437064510 *Panama* *Panama* MMSI: 370645000 Official number: 4237111A	**2,081** 778 3,612	Class: KR	**2010**-12 **Yangzhou Nakanishi Shipbuilding Co Ltd — Yizheng JS** Yd No: 201 Loa 84.90 Br ex - Dght 5.269 Lbp 79.31 Br md 13.00 Dpth 7.50 Welded, 1 dk	**(A31A2GX) General Cargo Ship** Compartments: 1 Ho, ER 1 Ha: ER (45.0 x 10.0)	**1 oil engine** driving 1 Propeller Total Power: 1,618kW (2,200hp) 12.0 Niigata 6M34BG 1 x 4 Stroke 6 Cy. 340 x 620 1618kW (2200bhp) Niigata Engineering Co Ltd-Japan
8971293 - -	**ZENITH JUMP** *ex* Shoshin Maru *-2004* **Kumjin Shipping Co Ltd** - *Busan* *South Korea* MMSI: 440152450 Official number: BSR-120028	**396** 149 -	Class: (BV)	**2001**-11 **Hongawara Zosen K.K. — Fukuyama** Yd No: 536 Loa 32.65 Br ex - Dght 4.160 Lbp - Br md 9.80 Dpth 6.20 Welded, 1 dk	**(B32B2SA) Articulated Pusher Tug**	**2 oil engines** driving 2 FP propellers Total Power: 2,942kW (4,000hp) 12.0 Niigata 6M34BLG 2 x 4 Stroke 6 Cy. 340 x 680 each-1471kW (2000bhp) Niigata Engineering Co Ltd-Japan
9384942 *2ACU6* -	**ZENITH LEADER** **RBSSAF (25) Ltd** Zodiac Maritime Agencies Ltd SatCom: Inmarsat C 423590630 *London* *United Kingdom* MMSI: 235058697 Official number: 913640	**62,080** 18,624 22,602 T/cm 55.6	Class: NK	**2007**-10 **Imabari Shipbuilding Co Ltd — Marugame KG (Marugame Shipyard)** Yd No: 1490 Loa 199.94 (BB) Br ex - Dght 10.016 Lbp 190.00 Br md 32.26 Dpth 34.80 Welded, 12 dks	**(A35B2RV) Vehicles Carrier** Side door/ramp (s) Len: 20.00 Wid: 4.20 Swl: 15 Quarter stern door/ramp (s. a.) Len: 35.00 Wid: 8.00 Swl: 80 Cars: 5,415	**1 oil engine** driving 1 FP propeller Total Power: 15,540kW (21,128hp) 20.1 Mitsubishi 8UEC60LS 1 x 2 Stroke 8 Cy. 600 x 2300 15540kW (21128bhp) Kobe Hatsudoki KK-Japan AuxGen: 3 x a.c Thrusters: 1 Tunnel thruster (f) Fuel: 3301.0
8419570 *DSFM8* -	**ZENITH MINE** *ex* Shin Ryuko Maru *-1997* **DaeHo Shipping Co Ltd** - *Busan* *South Korea* MMSI: 441055000 Official number: BSR-010030	**1,323** 757 2,266	Class: KR (BV) (NK)	**1984**-06 **Yamanaka Zosen K.K. — Imabari** Yd No: 283 Loa 72.93 Br ex - Dght 3.714 Lbp 68.03 Br md 11.51 Dpth 6.91 Welded, 1 dk	**(A31A2GX) General Cargo Ship** Grain: 2,251 Compartments: 1 Ho, ER 1 Ha: (38.4 x 8.8)ER	**1 oil engine** driving 1 FP propeller Total Power: 956kW (1,300hp) 11.3 Akasaka A2 1 x 4 Stroke 6 Cy. 280 x 550 956kW (1300bhp) Akasaka Tekkosho KK (Akasaka DieselLtd)-Japan Fuel: 31.5 (d.f.) 77.0 (r.f.) 4.0pd
8921339 *DSOZ6* -	**ZENITH ORION** *ex* Nichiryo Maru *-2003* **Han Kook Capital Co Ltd** DaeHo Shipping Co Ltd *Jeju* *South Korea* MMSI: 440676000 Official number: JJR-078835	**3,678** 1,717 6,329	Class: KR (BV) (NK)	**1990**-04 **Murakami Hide Zosen K.K. — Imabari** Yd No: 313 Converted From: Bulk Limestone Carrier-2003 Lengthened & Deepened-2006 Loa 100.43 Br ex - Dght 6.780 Lbp - Br md 15.50 Dpth 8.60 Welded, 1 dk	**(A31A2GX) General Cargo Ship**	**1 oil engine** driving 1 FP propeller Total Power: 2,427kW (3,300hp) 13.2 Akasaka A4 1 x 4 Stroke 6 Cy. 410 x 800 2427kW (3300bhp) Akasaka Tekkosho KK (Akasaka DieselLtd)-Japan
9191644 *DSPY9* -	**ZENITH ROYAL** *ex* Maritime Queen *-2010* *ex* Woody Heart *-2008* **Han Kook Capital Co Ltd** DaeHo Shipping Co Ltd *Jeju* *South Korea* MMSI: 441497000 Official number: JJR-089585	**6,448** 3,584 8,746	Class: KR (NK)	**1998**-06 **Higaki Zosen K.K. — Imabari** Yd No: 495 Loa 100.33 Br ex - Dght 8.264 Lbp 93.50 Br md 19.60 Dpth 13.00 Welded	**(A31A2GX) General Cargo Ship** Grain: 14,755; Bale: 13,389 Compartments: 2 Ho, ER 2 Ha: (29.4 x 14.0) (19.6 x 14.0)ER Cranes: 3x25t	**1 oil engine** driving 1 FP propeller Total Power: 3,884kW (5,281hp) 13.0 B&W 6L35M 1 x 2 Stroke 6 Cy. 350 x 1050 3884kW (5281bhp) The Hanshin Diesel Works Ltd-Japan
8514473 *DSFG9* -	**ZENITH SHINE** *ex* Nakagawa Maru *-1997* **DaeHo Shipping Co Ltd** - *Busan* *South Korea* MMSI: 440084000 Official number: BSR-000386	**1,354** 720 2,485	Class: KR (BV)	**1985**-09 **Yamanaka Zosen K.K. — Imabari** Yd No: 315 Loa 72.93 (BB) Br ex - Dght 5.520 Lbp 68.00 Br md 11.51 Dpth 6.91 Welded, 2 dks	**(A31A2GX) General Cargo Ship** Grain: 2,591; Bale: 2,534 Compartments: 1 Ho, ER 1 Ha: (37.2 x 8.5)ER	**1 oil engine** with clutches, flexible couplings & sr reverse geared to sc. shaft driving 1 FP propeller Total Power: 1,030kW (1,400hp) 10.5 Hanshin 6LUN28A 1 x 4 Stroke 6 Cy. 280 x 480 1030kW (1400bhp) The Hanshin Diesel Works Ltd-Japan
9404845 *C6WZ7* -	**ZENITH SPIRIT** **Zenith Spirit LLC** Teekay Marine (Singapore) Pte Ltd SatCom: Inmarsat C 430832911 *Nassau* *Bahamas* MMSI: 308329000 Official number: 9000266	**81,732** 51,287 160,510 T/cm 119.7	Class: LR ✠ **100A1** SS 01/2014 Double Hull oil tanker ESP **ShipRight** (SDA, FDA, CM) *IWS LI ✠ **LMC** **UMS IGS** Eq.Ltr: Yt; Cable: 742.5/97.0 U3 (a)	**2009**-01 **Samsung Heavy Industries Co Ltd — Geoje** Yd No: 1718 Loa 274.39 (BB) Br ex 48.04 Dght 17.022 Lbp 264.00 Br md 48.00 Dpth 23.20 Welded, 1 dk	**(A13A2TV) Crude Oil Tanker** Double Hull (13F) Liq: 167,456; Liq (Oil): 167,456 Cargo Heating Coils Compartments: 12 Wing Ta, 2 Wing Slop Ta, ER 3 Cargo Pump (s): 3x3800m³/hr Manifold: Bow/CM: 137.6m	**1 oil engine** driving 1 FP propeller Total Power: 18,660kW (25,370hp) 15.5 MAN-B&W 6S70ME- 1 x 2 Stroke 6 Cy. 700 x 2800 18660kW (25370bhp) Doosan Engine Co Ltd-South Korea AuxGen: 3 x 950kW 450V 60Hz a.c Boilers: e (ex.g.) 18.4kgf/cm² (18.0bar), AuxB (o.f.) 18.4kgf/cm² (18.0bar) Fuel: 190.0 (d.f.) 3800.0 (r.f.)
8405438 *3FGL*	**ZENITH STAR** *ex* Fair Swan *-2013* *ex* Chem Adriatic *-2007* *ex* Kilchem Adriatic *-2000* *ex* Andreas Z *-1990* *ex* Shoun Jupiter *-1989* **Zenith Fuel & Energy Ltd** Aurum Ship Management FZE *Panama* *Panama* MMSI: 357946000 Official number: 45048PEXT	**4,509** 2,140 5,218 T/cm 16.8	Class: RI (LR) (NK) Classed LR until 7/5/09	**1984**-09 **K.K. Taihei Kogyo — Akitsu** Yd No: 1696 Converted From: Chemical/Products Tanker-2009 Conv to DH-2009 Loa 113.34 (BB) Br ex 18.03 Dght 5.350 Lbp 104.00 Br md 18.00 Dpth 8.00 Welded, 1 dk	**(A13B2TP) Products Tanker** Double Hull Liq: 4,198; Liq (Oil): 7,254 Cargo Heating Coils Compartments: 5 Ta, ER 2 Cargo Pump (s): 2x400m³/hr Manifold: Bow/CM: 54m	**1 oil engine** driving 1 FP propeller Total Power: 2,992kW (4,068hp) 13.2 B&W 6L35M 1 x 2 Stroke 6 Cy. 350 x 1050 2992kW (4068bhp) Hitachi Zosen Corp-Japan AuxGen: 2 x 240kW 450V 60Hz a.c Boilers: e (ex.g.) 13.0kgf/cm² (12.7bar), AuxB (o.f.) 10.0kgf/cm² (9.8bar) Fuel: 139.5 (d.f.) 583.0 (r.f.) 13.5pd

36394 *XH2*	**ZENJI** *ex* Katana *-2008* *ex* Santa Maria *-2008* **Zenji Chartering Ltd** Dohle Private Clients Ltd *George Town* *Cayman Islands (British)* MMSI: 319013100 Official number: 737137	**499** 149 573	Class: AB	**2004-05 Perini Navi SpA (Divisione Picchiotti) — Viareggio** Yd No: 2053 Loa 56.00 Br ex - Dght 3.530 Lbp 49.70 Br md 11.51 Dpth 5.55 Welded, 1 dk	**(X11A2YS) Yacht (Sailing)** Hull Material: Aluminium Alloy	**2 oil engines** reduction geared to sc. shafts driving 2 Propellers Total Power: 1,848kW (2,512hp) 13.0kn Deutz TBD616V12 2 x Vee 4 Stroke 12 Cy. 132 x 160 each-424kW (1256bhp) Deutz AG-Koeln AuxGen: 2 x 125kW a.c
54109 *5556*	**ZENKEN MARU** - **Corporation for Advanced Transport & Technology & KK Yokohama Zenken** KK Yokohama Zenken *Yokohama, Kanagawa* *Japan* MMSI: 431100955 Official number: 136952	*2,720* - 6,553	Class: NK	**2001-06 IHI Amtec Co Ltd — Aioi HG** Yd No: 5016 Loa 98.00 Br ex - Dght 7.683 Lbp 88.03 Br md 17.50 Dpth 11.60 Welded, 1 dk	**(B34E2SW) Waste Disposal Vessel** Grain: 5,055; Bale: 5,055 Compartments: 2 Ho, ER 2 Ha: (19.5 x 13.0) (20.2 x 13.0)ER Cranes: 1x19.4t	**1 oil engine** driving 1 FP propeller Total Power: 2,942kW (4,000hp) 13.0kn Hanshin LH46L 1 x 4 Stroke 6 Cy. 460 x 880 2942kW (4000bhp) The Hanshin Diesel Works Ltd-Japan AuxGen: 3 x 400kW a.c Fuel: 180.0
72915	**ZENKO MARU No. 5** - **Handong Shipbuilding Co Ltd** - *South Korea*	*159* - 550		**1993-07 Suzuki Shipyard Co. Ltd. — Yokkaichi** Yd No: 611 Loa 47.09 Br ex - Dght 3.000 Lbp 45.00 Br md 8.00 Dpth 3.20 Welded, 1 dk	**(A13B2TP) Products Tanker**	**1 oil engine** driving 1 FP propeller Total Power: 405kW (551hp) 10.3kn Yanmar S165L-ST 1 x 4 Stroke 6 Cy. 165 x 210 405kW (551bhp) Yanmar Diesel Engine Co Ltd-Japan
63875 *IBCK*	**ZENNA III** - **SLOK Nigeria Ltd** - *Lagos* *Nigeria* Official number: 377258	**345** 103 -	Class: AB	**2003-04 Horizon Shipbuilding, Inc. — Bayou La Batre, Al** Yd No: 42 Loa 46.63 Br ex - Dght 2.438 Lbp 43.28 Br md 9.44 Dpth 3.66 Welded, 1 dk	**(B21A2OC) Crew/Supply Vessel** Hull Material: Aluminium Alloy	**5 oil engines** geared to sc. shafts driving 5 FP propellers Total Power: 3,035kW (4,125hp) Caterpillar 3412C-TA 5 x Vee 4 Stroke 12 Cy. 137 x 152 each-607kW (825bhp) Caterpillar Inc-USA
07483 *CJ6*	**ZENOBIA** - **Zenobia (2011) Ltd** - *George Town* *Cayman Islands (British)* MMSI: 319805000 Official number: 735617	**1,092** 327 187	Class: LR ✠ **100A1** SS 12/2012 SSC Yacht, mono G6 ✠ **LMC** Cable: 360.0/28.0 U2 (a)	**2002-12 AO Pribaltiyskiy Sudostroitelnyy Zavod "Yantar" — Kaliningrad** (Hull) **2002-12 Schiffs- u. Yachtwerft Abeking & Rasmussen GmbH & Co. — Lemwerder** Yd No: 6463 Loa 57.30 Br ex 11.00 Dght 3.500 Lbp 48.75 Br md 10.70 Dpth 6.15 Welded, 1 dk	**(X11A2YP) Yacht**	**2 oil engines** with clutches, flexible couplings & sr reverse geared to sc. shafts driving 2 FP propellers Total Power: 2,796kW (3,802hp) 16.0kn Caterpillar 3516TA 2 x Vee 4 Stroke 16 Cy. 170 x 190 each-1398kW (1901bhp) Caterpillar Inc-USA AuxGen: 2 x 260kW 400V 50Hz a.c Thrusters: 1 Thwart. FP thruster (f)
47037 *SOV5*	**ZENOVIA** *ex* Orient River II *-2002* **KEB Capital Inc** NH Shipmanagement Co Ltd *Jeju* *South Korea* MMSI: 440420000 Official number: JJR-069626	**25,899** 13,673 43,595 T/cm 49.0	Class: KR (NK)	**1992-07 Tsuneishi Shipbuilding Co Ltd — Fukuyama HS** Yd No: 1007 Loa 185.84 (BB) Br ex 30.44 Dght 11.319 Lbp 177.00 Br md 30.40 Dpth 16.20 Welded, 1 dk	**(A21A2BC) Bulk Carrier** Grain: 53,594; Bale: 52,280 Compartments: 5 Ho, ER 5 Ha: (19.2 x 15.3)4 (20.8 x 15.3)ER Cranes: 4x30t	**1 oil engine** driving 1 FP propeller Total Power: 7,120kW (9,680hp) 14.0kn B&W 6L60MCE 1 x 2 Stroke 6 Cy. 600 x 1944 7120kW (9680bhp) Mitsui Engineering & Shipbuilding CLtd-Japan AuxGen: 3 x 330kW 440V 60Hz a.c Fuel: 276.0 (d.f.) 1574.0 (r.f.) 27.0pd
89277 *TJ4*	**ZENOVIA LADY** - **Elfland Corp** Western Shipping Pte Ltd SatCom: Inmarsat C 463705458 *Monrovia* *Liberia* MMSI: 636014368 Official number: 14368	**62,201** 34,325 112,085 T/cm 98.4	Class: LR ✠ **100A1** SS 08/2009 Double Hull oil tanker CSR ESP **ShipRight** (CM) *IWS LI SPM ✠ **LMC** **UMS IGS** Eq.Ltr: Vt; Cable: 715.0/92.0 U3 (a)	**2009-08 Sungdong Shipbuilding & Marine Engineering Co Ltd — Tongyeong** Yd No: 3037 Loa 247.90 (BB) Br ex 44.04 Dght 14.820 Lbp 237.00 Br md 44.00 Dpth 21.00 Welded, 1 dk	**(A13B2TP) Products Tanker** Double Hull (13F) Liq: 122,833; Liq (Oil): 122,833 Cargo Heating Coils Compartments: 12 Wing Ta, 2 Wing Slop Ta, ER 3 Cargo Pump (s): 3x3000m³/hr Manifold: Bow/CM: 128.6m	**1 oil engine** driving 1 FP propeller Total Power: 14,280kW (19,415hp) 14.7kn MAN-B&W 7S60MC-C 1 x 2 Stroke 7 Cy. 600 x 2400 14280kW (19415bhp) (made 2009) Hyundai Heavy Industries Co Ltd-South Korea AuxGen: 3 x 800kW 450V 60Hz a.c Boilers: e (ex.g.) 22.9kgf/cm² (22.5bar), WTAuxB (o.f.) 18.4kgf/cm² (18.0bar) Fuel: 173.0 (d.f.) 2657.0 (r.f.)
56410 *3511*	**ZENPO MARU No. 8** *ex* Kurenai Maru *-1994* **Omi Kaiji Kogyo KK** - *Oma, Aomori* *Japan* Official number: 113124	*189* - -		**1972-12 Honda Zosen — Saiki** Yd No: 608 Loa 26.50 Br ex - Dght - Lbp 23.00 Br md 8.00 Dpth 3.80 Welded, 1 dk	**(B32B2SP) Pusher Tug**	**2 oil engines** driving 2 FP propellers Total Power: 1,176kW (1,598hp) 12.0kn Yanmar 2 x 4 Stroke each-588kW (799bhp) Yanmar Diesel Engine Co Ltd-Japan
11296 *2681* 1-1183	**ZENRYO MARU No. 21** - **Kanetame Suisan KK** - *Wakkanai, Hokkaido* *Japan* Official number: 128598	*160* - -		**1990-09 Narasaki Zosen KK — Muroran HK** Yd No: 1117 Loa 38.12 (BB) Br ex 7.42 Dght 3.336 Lbp 31.50 Br md 7.40 Dpth 4.61 Welded	**(B11A2FS) Stern Trawler**	**1 oil engine** with clutches, flexible couplings & sr geared to sc. shaft driving 1 FP propeller Total Power: 1,030kW (1,400hp) Niigata 6MG28BXF 1 x 4 Stroke 6 Cy. 280 x 350 1030kW (1400bhp) Niigata Engineering Co Ltd-Japan
41625 *3347*	**ZENRYU MARU NO. 68** - **Toyama-ken Keison Gyogyo Kyodo Kumiai (Toyama Salmon & Trout Fishery Cooperative)** - *Uozu, Toyama* *Japan* Official number: 141655	*199* - -		**2012-07 Kidoura Shipyard Co Ltd — Kesennuma MG** Yd No: 626 Loa 46.36 Br ex - Dght 2.920 Lbp - Br md 7.50 Dpth - Welded, 1 dk	**(B11B2FV) Fishing Vessel**	**1 oil engine** reduction geared to sc. shafts driving 1 Propeller Total Power: 1,838kW (2,499hp) Niigata 6MG28HX 1 x 4 Stroke 6 Cy. 280 x 370 1838kW (2499bhp) Niigata Engineering Co Ltd-Japan
21573 *4766*	**ZENTOKU MARU No. 33** - **Marutoku Gyogyo KK** - *Kita-Ibaraki, Ibaraki* *Japan* Official number: 128906	*330* - 550		**1990-02 K.K. Watanabe Zosensho — Nagasaki** Yd No: 1158 Loa 61.75 (BB) Br ex - Dght 4.000 Lbp 53.00 Br md 9.00 Dpth 4.50 Welded, 1 dk	**(B11B2FV) Fishing Vessel** Ins: 662	**1 oil engine** driving 1 FP propeller Total Power: 1,155kW (1,570hp) Niigata 8MG28HX 1 x 4 Stroke 8 Cy. 280 x 370 1155kW (1570bhp) Niigata Engineering Co Ltd-Japan Thrusters: 1 Thwart. FP thruster (f)
12791	**ZENYO MARU** - **Acushla Corp** -	*199* - 449		**1975-09 Oka Zosen Tekko K.K. — Ushimado** Yd No: 232 Loa 44.71 Br ex 7.83 Dght 3.302 Lbp 40.01 Br md 7.80 Dpth 3.38 Riveted\Welded, 1 dk	**(A13B2TU) Tanker (unspecified)**	**1 oil engine** driving 1 FP propeller Total Power: 552kW (750hp) Matsui 6M26KGHS 1 x 4 Stroke 6 Cy. 260 x 400 552kW (750bhp) Matsui Iron Works Co Ltd-Japan
61365 *DA2321*	**ZEPHYR** - **Zephyr Fisheries LLC** - *San Francisco, CA* *United States of America* MMSI: 338290000 Official number: 1101877	**141** 42 -		**2000 La Force Shipyard Inc — Coden AL** Yd No: 105 L reg 23.98 Br ex - Dght - Lbp - Br md 7.31 Dpth 3.65 Welded, 1 dk	**(B11B2FV) Fishing Vessel**	**1 oil engine** driving 1 FP propeller
92845 *DA6249*	**ZEPHYR** *ex* San Francisco *-1973* **Monterey Bay Aquarium Research Institute** - *San Francisco, CA* *United States of America* MMSI: 366830310 Official number: 545818	*119* 35 -		**1973-01 Colberg Boat Works — Stockton, Ca** Yd No: 372-18 Loa 25.90 Br ex - Dght 2.440 Lbp - Br md 7.16 Dpth - Welded, 1 dk	**(B31A2SR) Research Survey Vessel**	**2 oil engines** reduction geared to sc. shaft (s) driving 1 Propeller Total Power: 618kW (840hp) 10.0kn Caterpillar D343 2 x 4 Stroke 6 Cy. 137 x 165 each-309kW (420bhp) Caterpillar Tractor Co-USA AuxGen: 2 x 40kW a.c
47162 *WAW6* 394	**ZEPHYR** - **Zephyr Fishing Co Ltd** LHD Ltd SatCom: Inmarsat B 323434110 *Lerwick* *United Kingdom* MMSI: 234341000 Official number: B14874	**2,060** 668 580	Class: NV	**1996-11 Flekkefjord Slipp & Maskinfabrikk AS AS — Flekkefjord** Yd No: 164 Lengthened-2009 Loa 72.80 (BB) Br ex - Dght 5.800 Lbp 65.78 Br md 13.00 Dpth 8.30 Welded, 1 dk	**(B11A2FS) Stern Trawler** Ins: 1,100	**1 oil engine** reduction geared to sc. shaft driving 1 CP propeller Total Power: 4,920kW (6,689hp) 17.8kn Wartsila 12V32D 1 x Vee 4 Stroke 12 Cy. 320 x 350 4920kW (6689bhp) Wartsila Propulsion AS-Norway AuxGen: 1 x 1520kW 220/480V 60Hz a.c, 2 x 560kW 220/480V 60Hz a.c Thrusters: 1 Thwart. FP thruster (f); 1 Thwart. FP thruster (a)

IMO / Call sign	Name / Owner	Tonnage	Class	Builder / Dimensions	Type	Machinery
9283045 *WDB3983* -	**ZEPHYR** **NYWT Zephyr LLC** - *New York, NY* *United States of America* MMSI: 366893420 Official number: 1139023	**590** 226 70		**2003-08 Austal USA LLC — Mobile AL** Yd No: 611 Loa 43.50 Br ex - Dght 1.400 Lbp 37.40 Br md 11.50 Dpth 3.50 Welded, 1 dk	**(A37B2PS) Passenger Ship** Hull Material: Aluminium Alloy Passengers: unberthed: 600	**4 oil engines** geared to sc. shafts driving 4 Water jets Total Power: 3,580kW (4,868hp) 29.0 Cummins KTA-38-M 4 x Vee 4 Stroke 12 Cy. 159 x 159 each-895kW (1217bhp) Cummins Engine Co Inc-USA AuxGen: 4 x 173kW 60Hz a.c
8408997 *3FXN4* -	**ZEPHYR I** *ex* CGG Zephyr *-1995* *ex* Akademik Gubkin *-1991* **JSC Dalmorneftegeophysica (DMNG)** SatCom: Inmarsat A 1335212 *Panama* *Panama* MMSI: 354915000 Official number: 2644099CH	**2,833** 850 1,328	Class: NV (BV) (RS)	**1987-10 Stocznia Szczecinska im A Warskiego — Szczecin** Yd No: B93/05 Loa 81.85 Br ex 14.83 Dght 5.001 Lbp 73.50 Br md 14.81 Dpth 7.50 Welded	**(B31A2SR) Research Survey Vessel** Ice Capable	**1 oil engine** reduction geared to sc. shaft driving 1 CP propeller Total Power: 3,200kW (4,351hp) 14.2 Sulzer 6ZL40/4 1 x 4 Stroke 6 Cy. 400 x 480 3200kW (4351bhp) Zaklady Urzadzen Technicznych'Zgoda' SA-Poland AuxGen: 1 x 1200kW 220/380V 50Hz a.c, 2 x 504kW 220/380V 50Hz a.c
8302272 *9HHJ5* -	**ZERAN** **Levant Chartering Ltd** POL-Levant Shipping Lines Ltd (POL-Levant Linie Zeglugowe Sp z oo) SatCom: Inmarsat A 1257705 *Valletta* *Malta* MMSI: 249846000 Official number: 5374	**15,685** 4,624 8,044	Class: PR	**1987-08 Stocznia im Komuny Paryskiej — Gdynia** Yd No: B488/01 Loa 147.45 (BB) Br ex - Dght 7.050 Lbp 130.41 Br md 23.51 Dpth 14.91 Welded, 3 dks	**(A35A2RR) Ro-Ro Cargo Ship** Passengers: cabins: 4; berths: 6 Stern door/ramp (a) Len: 16.00 Wid: 12.00 Swl: 200 Lane-Len: 1366 Lane-Wid: 7.30 Lane-clr ht: 6.50 TEU 505 incl 50 ref C.	**2 oil engines** with flexible couplings & dr geared to sc. shaft driving 2 CP propellers Total Power: 4,800kW (6,526hp) 14.5 Sulzer 6ZL40/4 2 x 4 Stroke 6 Cy. 400 x 480 each-2400kW (3263bhp) Zaklady Urzadzen Technicznych'Zgoda' SA-Poland AuxGen: 2 x 1200kW 400V 50Hz a.c, 2 x 842kW 400V 50Hz a.c Thrusters: 1 Thwart. CP thruster (f) Fuel: 194.0 (d.f.) 1481.0 (r.f.) 24.0pd
5398579 *EPNK* -	**ZERANG** **National Iranian Oil Co (NIOC)** Oil Service Co of Iran (Private Co) *Khorramshahr* *Iran*	*357* 45 -	Class: (LR) ✠ Classed LR until 21/5/86	**1959-03 Scott & Sons — Bowling** Yd No: 419 Loa 39.88 Br ex 10.11 Dght 3.849 Lbp 36.76 Br md 9.61 Dpth 4.35 Riveted\Welded, 1 dk	**(B32A2ST) Tug**	**1 oil engine** with flexible couplings & dr reverse geared to sc. shaft driving 1 FP propeller Total Power: 1,103kW (1,500hp) Crossley CR 1 x 2 Stroke 8 Cy. 368 x 483 1103kW (1500bhp) Crossley Bros. Ltd.-Manchester AuxGen: 2 x 67kW 220V d.c
7944102 - -	**ZERIMAR III** *ex* Mar de Cortez IV *-1991* **Pesquera Nicomar SA de CV** - *Mazatlan* *Mexico*	*104* 54 -	Class: (AB)	**1977-11 Astilleros Monarca S.A. — Guaymas** Yd No: 610 Loa - Br ex - Dght - Lbp 20.93 Br md 6.05 Dpth 3.10 Welded, 1 dk	**(B11A2FT) Trawler** Compartments: 1 Ho, ER 1 Ha: (7.0 x 4.6)	**1 oil engine** driving 1 FP propeller Total Power: 246kW (334hp) 9.0 Caterpillar 340 1 x 4 Stroke 6 Cy. 137 x 165 246kW (334bhp) Caterpillar Tractor Co-USA AuxGen: 1 x 3kW d.c, 1 x 2kW d.c
8112885 - -	**ZEROI** **Sierra Fishing Co** -	**891** 350 1,350	Class: IS (BV)	**1983-03 Astilleros de Santander SA (ASTANDER) — El Astillero** Yd No: 157 Loa 60.41 (BB) Br ex 10.42 Dght 4.760 Lbp 54.01 Br md 10.41 Dpth 5.62 Welded, 1 dk	**(B12B2FC) Fish Carrier** Ins: 1,076 Compartments: 3 Ho, ER 3 Ha: ER	**1 oil engine** driving 1 FP propeller Total Power: 956kW (1,300hp) MaK 6M452A 1 x 4 Stroke 6 Cy. 320 x 450 956kW (1300bhp) Krupp MaK Maschinenbau GmbH-Kiel
6517586 - -	**ZETA** - -	*168* -		**1965 Fabricaciones Metallicas E.P.S. (FABRIMET) — Callao** L reg 22.50 Br ex 6.74 Dght - Lbp - Br md - Dpth 3.51 Welded, 1 dk	**(B11B2FV) Fishing Vessel**	**1 oil engine** driving 1 FP propeller Total Power: 386kW (525hp) G.M. (Detroit Diesel) 12V-71 1 x Vee 2 Stroke 12 Cy. 108 x 127 386kW (525bhp) General Motors Corp-USA
8706167 *A8QN5* -	**ZETA** *ex* Sea Queen *-2013* *ex* Corinth *-2008* *ex* Canton *-2001* *ex* Akebono *-2000* *ex* Akebono Maru *-1995* **Sea Spirit International Shipping Inc** FAL Shipping Co Ltd *Monrovia* *Liberia* MMSI: 636013970 Official number: 13970	**25,966** 12,580 45,550 T/cm 46.9	Class: RI (NK)	**1988-03 Tsuneishi Shipbuilding Co Ltd — Fukuyama HS** Yd No: 601 Loa 181.00 (BB) Br ex - Dght 12.522 Lbp 172.00 Br md 30.00 Dpth 18.20 Welded, 1 dk	**(A13A2TW) Crude/Oil Products Tanker** Double Hull Liq: 47,260; Liq (Oil): 47,260 Cargo Heating Coils Compartments: 7 Ta, 2 Wing Slop Ta, ER 4 Cargo Pump (s): 4x1250m³/hr Manifold: Bow/CM: 88.5m	**1 oil engine** driving 1 FP propeller Total Power: 6,546kW (8,900hp) 14.0 B&W 6L60M 1 x 2 Stroke 6 Cy. 600 x 1944 6546kW (8900bhp) Mitsui Engineering & Shipbuilding CLtd-Japan AuxGen: 3 x 440kW 440V 60Hz a.c Fuel: 187.5 (d.f.) 1476.0 (r.f.) 24.5pd
9539676 *3FOD3* -	**ZETA I** **Transportes Maritimos de Venezuela SA** Maritima Avila SM CA SatCom: Inmarsat C 435106212 *Panama* *Panama* MMSI: 351062000 Official number: 4159110	**4,048** 1,940 6,450 T/cm 14.8	Class: BV	**2009-07 Linhai Chengzhou Shipbuilding Industry Co Ltd — Linhai ZJ** Yd No: HCB07-043 Loa 103.00 (BB) Br ex 16.00 Dght 6.500 Lbp 96.52 Br md 16.00 Dpth 8.71 Welded, 1 dk	**(A12B2TR) Chemical/Products Tanker** Double Hull (13F) Liq: 6,720; Liq (Oil): 6,720 Compartments: 12 Wing Ta, 2 Wing Slop Ta, ER 6 Cargo Pump (s): 3x300m³/hr, 3x500m³/hr Manifold: Bow/CM: 54m Ice Capable	**1 oil engine** reduction geared to sc. shaft. driving 1 FP propeller Total Power: 2,574kW (3,500hp) 12.5 Yanmar 6N330-E 1 x 4 Stroke 6 Cy. 330 x 440 2574kW (3500bhp) Qingdao Zichai Boyang Diesel EngineCo Ltd-China AuxGen: 3 x 250kW 60Hz a.c Thrusters: 1 Tunnel thruster (f) Fuel: 95.0 (d.f.) 315.0 (r.f.)
9623984 *V2FT8* -	**ZETAGAS** **mt 'Zetagas' Schifffahrtsgesellschaft mbH & Co KG** Sloman Neptun Schiffahrts-Aktiengesellschaft *Saint John's* *Antigua & Barbuda* MMSI: 305794000 Official number: 4928	**8,009** 2,403 8,641 T/cm 19.5	Class: NV	**2013-03 STX Offshore & Shipbuilding Co Ltd — Busan** Yd No: 5062 Loa 113.00 (BB) Br ex - Dght 8.450 Lbp 106.00 Br md 19.20 Dpth 10.60 Welded, 1 dk	**(A11B2TG) LPG Tanker** Double Hull (13F) Liq (Gas): 6,694 2 x Gas Tank (s); 2 independent cyl horizontal 3 Cargo Pump (s): 3x325m³/hr Manifold: Bow/CM: 53.7m Ice Capable	**1 oil engine** driving 1 FP propeller Total Power: 5,220kW (7,097hp) 14.9 MAN-B&W 6S35ME-B 1 x 2 Stroke 6 Cy. 350 x 1550 5220kW (7097bhp) MAN Diesel A/S-Denmark AuxGen: 3 x a.c Thrusters: 1 Tunnel thruster (f) Fuel: 140.0 (d.f.) 631.0 (r.f.)
9259111 *TCCO9* -	**ZEUGMAN** **Kam Denizcilik ve Ticaret AS (Kam Maritime & Trading Co)** Ares Ship Management (Ares Gemi Isletmeciligi AS) *Istanbul* *Turkey* MMSI: 271000725 Official number: 623	**3,547** 1,612 5,508 T/cm 15.0	Class: BV	**2003-08 Celiktekne Sanayii ve Ticaret A.S. — Tuzla, Istanbul** Yd No: 43 Loa 109.10 (BB) Br ex 16.03 Dght 5.750 Lbp 99.80 Br md 16.00 Dpth 7.25 Welded, 1 dk	**(A12B2TR) Chemical/Products Tanker** Double Hull (13F) Liq: 5,686; Liq (Oil): 5,779 Cargo Heating Coils Compartments: ER, 11 Wing Ta, 1 Slop Ta, 1 Ta 12 Cargo Pump (s): 8x200m³/hr, 4x150m³/hr Manifold: Bow/CM: 61.7m Ice Capable	**1 oil engine** reduction geared to sc. shaft driving 1 CP propeller Total Power: 2,720kW (3,698hp) 13.0 MAN-B&W 8L27/3 1 x 4 Stroke 8 Cy. 270 x 380 2720kW (3698bhp) MAN B&W Diesel A/S-Denmark AuxGen: 3 x 400kW 400/230V 50Hz a.c, 1 x 600kW 400V a.c Thrusters: 1 Tunnel thruster (f) Fuel: 64.0 (d.f.) 233.0 (r.f.)
7364912 - -	**ZEUILA** *ex* Mesogios *-1978* *ex* Panormitis Junior II *-1976* **National Fishing & Marketing Co (NAFIMCO)** - *Benghazi* *Libya*	*144* 62 -	Class: (LR) (BV) Classed LR until 29/1/97	**1975 Salamis Shipyards S.A. — Salamis** Loa 30.25 Br ex 7.00 Dght 2.950 Lbp 26.33 Br md 6.69 Dpth 3.86 Welded, 1 dk	**(B11B2FV) Fishing Vessel**	**1 oil engine** driving 1 CP propeller Total Power: 441kW (600hp) 12.0 Alpha 406-26 1 x 2 Stroke 6 Cy. 260 x 400 441kW (600bhp) Alpha Diesel A/S-Denmark AuxGen: 2 x 72kW 380V 50Hz a.c
6605503 *SQLH* -	**ZEUS** **Otto Wulf GmbH & Co KG** - *Szczecin* *Poland* MMSI: 261205000 Official number: ROS/S/418	**186** 55 76	Class: PR	**1966 A/S Svendborg Skibsvaerft — Svendborg** Yd No: 113 Loa 28.43 Br ex 8.41 Dght 3.250 Lbp 26.01 Br md 8.01 Dpth 3.99 Welded, 1 dk	**(B32A2ST) Tug** Ice Capable	**2 oil engines** geared to sc. shaft driving 1 FP propeller Total Power: 1,214kW (1,650hp) 11.5 B&W 5-26MTBF-4 2 x 4 Stroke 5 Cy. 260 x 400 each-607kW (825bhp) Holeby Dieselmotor Fabrik A/S-Denmark AuxGen: 3 x 50kW 380V a.c, 1 x 12kW 380V a.c
7926643 *WDC5330* -	**ZEUS** *ex* Shady Lady *-1990* *ex* Spirit *-1990* *ex* General E. Lee *-1980* **Stephanie Fishing Corp** - *New Bedford, MA* *United States of America* MMSI: 368486000 Official number: 613082	*162* 110 -		**1979 Quality Marine, Inc. — Bayou La Batre, Al** Loa 27.44 Br ex - Dght - Lbp - Br md 7.32 Dpth 3.97 Welded, 1 dk	**(B11A2FT) Trawler**	**1 oil engine** geared to sc. shaft driving 1 FP propeller Total Power: 533kW (725hp) 11.5 Caterpillar D348SCA 1 x Vee 4 Stroke 12 Cy. 137 x 165 533kW (725bhp) Caterpillar Tractor Co-USA AuxGen: 1 x 30kW
8741454 - -	**ZEUS** **Chokwang Shipping Co Ltd** - *Ulsan* *South Korea* Official number: USR-078294	**198** - -	Class: KR	**2007-12 Namyang Shipbuilding Co Ltd — Yeosu** Yd No: 1084 Loa 33.00 Br ex - Dght - Lbp 29.71 Br md 9.20 Dpth 3.90 Welded, 1 dk	**(B32A2ST) Tug**	**2 oil engines** reduction geared to sc. shafts driving 2 Propellers Total Power: 1,946kW (2,646hp) Niigata 6L25H 2 x 4 Stroke 6 Cy. 250 x 350 each-973kW (1323bhp) Niigata Engineering Co Ltd-Japan

IMO / Call sign	Name, owner, flag	Tonnage	Class	Builder, dimensions	Type	Machinery
33110 MZX	**ZEUS** *ex* Baiduri 33293 *-2008* **PT Pelayaran Isna Agung Permata** Rocktree Logistics Pte Ltd *Jakarta* *Indonesia* MMSI: 525005792	**6,278** 2,099 500	Class: KI RI (AB)	**2008-02 Jinsheng Shipbuilding (Taixing) Co Ltd — Taixing JS** Yd No: JSB-09 Converted From: Unknown Function-2008 Loa 100.58 Br ex - Dght - Lbp 30.48 Br md 30.48 Dpth 6.10 Welded, 1 dk	**(B34B2SC) Crane Vessel** Cranes: 2x35.5t	**3 diesel electric oil engines** driving 3 gen. Connecting to 2 elec. motors driving 2 Directional propellers Total Power: 4,476kW (6,087hp) 8.0kn Cummins KTA-50-M 3 x Vee 4 Stroke 16 Cy. 159 x 159 each-1492kW (2029bhp) (made 2008) Cummins Engine Co Inc-USA
952950 WZ	**ZEUS** *ex* Nicos P *-2008* **Traghetti delle Isole SpA Compagnia di Navigazione** - *Trapani* *Italy* MMSI: 247072100 Official number: 167	*452* 284 -	Class: RI	**1980 D. C. Anastassiades & A. Ch. Tsortanides — Perama** Loa 52.85 Br ex 10.02 Dght 1.780 Lbp 45.50 Br md 10.00 Dpth 2.43 Welded, 1 dk	**(A36A2PR) Passenger/Ro-Ro Ship (Vehicles)**	**3 oil engines** reduction geared to sc. shafts driving 3 FP propellers Total Power: 639kW (870hp) Caterpillar 3406T 2 x 4 Stroke 6 Cy. 137 x 165 each-202kW (275bhp) Caterpillar Tractor Co-USA Mercedes Benz 0M403 1 x Vee 4 Stroke 10 Cy. 125 x 130 235kW (320bhp) Daimler Benz AG-West Germany
881589	**ZEUS** **Government of The Republic of Greece (Hellenic Navy)** - SatCom: Inmarsat M 623941910 *Greece*	**866** 512 -	Class: (HR)	**1988-02 Hellenic Shipyards — Skaramanga** Yd No: 1317 Loa 67.00 Br ex - Dght 4.200 Lbp 60.35 Br md 10.00 Dpth 4.65 Welded, 1 dk	**(A13B2TU) Tanker (unspecified)**	**1 oil engine** geared to sc. shaft driving 1 FP propeller Total Power: 1,184kW (1,610hp) 12.0kn MAN 12V20/27 1 x Vee 4 Stroke 12 Cy. 200 x 270 1184kW (1610bhp) MAN B&W Diesel GmbH-Augsburg AuxGen: 2 x 292kW 380V 50Hz a.c
190212 CIK	**ZEUS** **Flinter Bareboat BV** Flinter Shipping BV *Delfzijl* *Netherlands* MMSI: 246432000 Official number: 36401	**6,142** 3,491 9,100 T/cm 19.0	Class: BV (LR) ✠ Classed LR until 7/10/09	**2000-04 Scheepswerf Ferus Smit BV — Westerbroek** Yd No: 323 Loa 130.65 (BB) Br ex 15.94 Dght 7.460 Lbp 122.19 Br md 15.87 Dpth 10.20 Welded, 1 dk	**(A31A2GX) General Cargo Ship** Grain: 11,978 TEU 503 C Ho 254 TEU C Dk 249 TEU incl 30 ref C. Compartments: 2 Ho, ER 2 Ha: (60.6 x 13.2) (24.9 x 13.2)ER Ice Capable	**1 oil engine** with flexible couplings & sr gearedto sc. shaft driving 1 FP propeller Total Power: 3,960kW (5,384hp) 14.0kn Stork-Wartsila 6SW38 1 x 4 Stroke 6 Cy. 380 x 475 3960kW (5384bhp) Wartsila NSD Nederland BV-Netherlands AuxGen: 1 x 560kW 400V 50Hz a.c, 2 x 180kW 400V 50Hz a.c Boilers: TOH (o.f.) 10.2kgf/cm² (10.0bar), TOH (ex.g.) 10.2kgf/cm² (10.0bar) Thrusters: 1 Thwart. FP thruster (f) Fuel: 58.7 (d.f.) 423.2 (r.f.) 18.0pd
9184146 7LUO	**ZEUS** **Iino Gas Transport Co Ltd** - SatCom: Inmarsat B 343116910 *Kobe, Hyogo* *Japan* MMSI: 431169000 Official number: 135336	**2,595** 778 2,645	Class: NK	**1998-02 K.K. Miura Zosensho — Saiki** Yd No: 1208 Loa 91.30 Br ex - Dght 5.314 Lbp 84.80 Br md 14.50 Dpth 6.40 Welded, 1 dk	**(A11B2TG) LPG Tanker** Liq (Gas): 2,523 2 x Gas Tank (s); independent	**1 oil engine** driving 1 FP propeller Total Power: 2,574kW (3,500hp) 13.0kn Hanshin LH41LA 1 x 4 Stroke 6 Cy. 410 x 800 2574kW (3500bhp) The Hanshin Diesel Works Ltd-Japan Fuel: 460.0
9130729 OJHB	**ZEUS** **Alfons Hakans Oy AB** - SatCom: Inmarsat C 423033911 *Turku* *Finland* MMSI: 230339000 Official number: 11835	**1,102** 331 545	Class: NV	**1995-12 SIMEK AS — Flekkefjord** Yd No: 90 Loa 45.10 Br ex - Dght 6.720 Lbp 39.30 Br md 14.60 Dpth 8.20 Welded, 1 dk	**(B32A2ST) Tug** Ice Capable	**2 oil engines** reduction geared to sc. shafts driving 2 CP propellers Total Power: 5,416kW (7,364hp) 15.3kn Caterpillar 3608TA 2 x 4 Stroke 8 Cy. 280 x 300 each-2708kW (3682bhp) Caterpillar Inc-USA AuxGen: 1 x 1500kW 220/400V 50Hz a.c, 2 x 400kW 220/400V 50Hz a.c Thrusters: 1 Thwart. FP thruster (f); 1 Tunnel thruster (a)
9038828 3FAU3 -	**ZEUS** *launched as* Catatumbo *-1992* **Venfleet Ltd** Bernhard Schulte Shipmanagement (Cyprus) Ltd SatCom: Inmarsat C 435218910 *Panama* *Panama* MMSI: 352189000 Official number: 2060393H	**54,827** 29,295 99,450 T/cm 100.0	Class: BV (AB)	**1992-11 Hyundai Heavy Industries Co Ltd — Ulsan** Yd No: 790 Loa 243.97 (BB) Br ex 45.68 Dght 12.950 Lbp 235.00 Br md 45.64 Dpth 18.40 Welded, 1 dk	**(A13A2TW) Crude/Oil Products Tanker** Double Hull (13F) Liq: 106,200; Liq (Oil): 106,200 Cargo Heating Coils Compartments: 8 Ta, ER 3 Cargo Pump (s): 3x2500m³/hr Manifold: Bow/CM: 122m	**1 oil engine** driving 1 FP propeller Total Power: 15,420kW (20,965hp) 16.1kn B&W 6S70MC 1 x 2 Stroke 6 Cy. 700 x 2674 15420kW (20965bhp) Hyundai Heavy Industries Co Ltd-South Korea AuxGen: 3 x 750kW 440V 60Hz a.c Fuel: 485.7 (d.f.) (Heating Coils) 3081.6 (r.f.) 58.0pd
9199684 V2OR -	**ZEUS** **Reederei M Lauterjung GmbH & Co KG Sunship Eurocoaster** Sunship Schiffahrtskontor KG *Saint John's* *Antigua & Barbuda* MMSI: 304011025 Official number: 2886	**1,846** 1,081 2,500	Class: BV	**2000-04 SC Santierul Naval Tulcea SA — Tulcea** Yd No: 304 Loa 89.71 Br ex - Dght 4.450 Lbp 84.60 Br md 11.65 Dpth 5.80 Welded, 1 dk	**(A31A2GX) General Cargo Ship** Grain: 3,761; Bale: 3,671 TEU 124 C.Ho 52/20' C.Dk 72/20' incl. 16 ref C Compartments: 1 Ho, ER 1 Ha: (57.8 x 9.3)ER Ice Capable	**1 oil engine** reduction geared to sc. shaft driving 1 FP propeller Total Power: 1,500kW (2,039hp) 12.5kn Deutz SBV8M628 1 x 4 Stroke 8 Cy. 240 x 280 1500kW (2039bhp) Motoren Werke Mannheim AG (MWM)-Mannheim AuxGen: 2 x 134kW 220/380V 50Hz a.c Thrusters: 1 Thwart. FP thruster (f) Fuel: 126.9 (d.f.) 6.8pd
9395513 S5EK9 -	**ZEUS** *ex* Fairplay 28 *-2008* *ex* Zeus *-2007* **Adria Tow doo** - SatCom: Inmarsat C 427830110 *Koper* *Slovenia* MMSI: 278301000 Official number: 140	**498** 149 -	Class: RI (BV)	**2006-12 Astilleros Armon SA — Navia** Yd No: 631 Loa 34.50 Br ex - Dght 3.900 Lbp 32.85 Br md 11.60 Dpth 4.70 Welded, 1 dk	**(B32A2ST) Tug**	**2 oil engines** reduction geared to sc. shafts driving 2 Voith-Schneider propellers Total Power: 5,276kW (7,174hp) 13.5kn MaK 8M25 2 x 4 Stroke 8 Cy. 255 x 400 each-2638kW (3587bhp) Caterpillar Motoren GmbH & Co. KG-Germany
9506071 WAO8101 -	**ZEUS** **Zeus LC** Dann Marine Towing LC *Philadelphia, PA* *United States of America* MMSI: 366081080 Official number: 555761	**276** 82 -		**1974-12 Houma Welders Inc — Houma LA** Yd No: 40 Loa 29.26 (BB) Br ex 8.84 Dght - Lbp - Br md - Dpth 4.15 Welded, 1 dk	**(B32A2ST) Tug**	**2 oil engines** reverse reduction geared to sc. shafts driving 2 Propellers Total Power: 1,654kW (2,248hp) Caterpillar D399 2 x Vee 4 Stroke 16 Cy. 159 x 203 each-827kW (1124bhp) Caterpillar Tractor Co-USA AuxGen: 2 x 60kW a.c
9660968 WDH2353 -	**ZEUS** **Suderman & Young Towing Co LP** G & H Towing Co *Houston, TX* *United States of America* MMSI: 367596750 Official number: 1250505	**332** 99 100	Class: AB	**2014-01 Leevac Shipyards Jennings LLC — Jennings LA** Yd No: 362 Loa 24.60 Br ex - Dght - Lbp 24.38 Br md 11.70 Dpth 4.92 Welded, 1 dk	**(B32A2ST) Tug**	**2 oil engines** reduction geared to sc. shafts driving 2 Z propellers Total Power: 3,650kW (4,962hp) Caterpillar 3516C-HD 2 x Vee 4 Stroke 16 Cy. 170 x 215 each-1825kW (2481bhp) Caterpillar Inc-USA
9255311 9YFU -	**ZEUS 1** *ex* Zeus *-2006* *ex* Zeus I *-2002* **Svitzer Marine Trinidad & Tobago Ltd** Svitzer (Caribbean) Ltd *Port of Spain* *Trinidad & Tobago*	**343** 102 247	Class: LR ✠ **100A1** SS 05/2012 tug *IWS ✠ **LMC** **UMS** Eq.Ltr: G; Cable: 440.0/20.5 U2 (a)	**2002-05 Astilleros Zamakona SA — Santurtzi** Yd No: 574 Loa 30.83 Br ex 10.53 Dght 4.340 Lbp 30.00 Br md 9.50 Dpth 5.10 Welded, 1 dk	**(B32A2ST) Tug**	**2 oil engines** geared to sc. shafts driving 2 Directional propellers Total Power: 2,942kW (4,000hp) 12.2kn Niigata 6L26HLX 2 x 4 Stroke 6 Cy. 260 x 350 each-1471kW (2000bhp) Niigata Engineering Co Ltd-Japan AuxGen: 2 x 236kW 415V 50Hz a.c
9467885 3EUP3 -	**ZEUS I** *ex* Elliot Aconcagua *-2009* **Falcon Shipping Inc** Trident Shipping Ltd *Panama* *Panama* MMSI: 354962000 Official number: 4144810A	**16,833** 9,568 27,000	Class: BV	**2009-06 Zhejiang Zhenghe Shipbuilding Co Ltd — Zhoushan ZJ** Yd No: 1005 Loa 168.80 Br ex - Dght 9.800 Lbp 160.00 Br md 26.00 Dpth 13.70 Welded, 1 dk	**(A21A2BC) Bulk Carrier** Grain: 35,286 Compartments: 5 Ho, ER 5 Ha: 4 (16.0 x 19.2)ER (12.0 x 14.4) Cranes: 4x30t	**1 oil engine** reduction geared to sc. shaft driving 1 FP propeller Total Power: 5,882kW (7,997hp) 13.8kn MAN-B&W 6L42MC 1 x 2 Stroke 6 Cy. 420 x 1360 5882kW (7997bhp) Hudong Heavy Machinery Co Ltd-China AuxGen: 3 x 500kW a.c
9559212 9HA2151 -	**ZEUS I** *ex* Zeus *-2009* **Sea Leasing Ltd** Moores Rowland *Valletta* *Malta* MMSI: 248062000 Official number: 9559212	**488** 146 48	Class: AB	**2009-02 Overmarine SpA — Viareggio** Yd No: 165/03 Loa 49.90 Br ex - Dght 1.600 Lbp 45.70 Br md 9.20 Dpth 5.10 Bonded, 1 dk	**(X11A2YP) Yacht** Hull Material: Reinforced Plastic	**3 oil engines** reduction geared to sc, shaft driving 3 Propellers Total Power: 8,160kW (11,094hp) 38.0kn M.T.U. 16V4000M90 3 x Vee 4 Stroke 16 Cy. 165 x 190 each-2720kW (3698bhp) MTU Friedrichshafen GmbH-Friedrichshafen AuxGen: 2 x 100kW a.c

IMO / Call sign / Flag	Name / Owner	Tonnage	Class	Builder / Dimensions	Type	Machinery
9098115 *YD6892* -	**ZEUS I** - **PT Surya Maritim Shippindo** - *Samarinda* *Indonesia*	**248** 75 -	Class: KI	**2005-01 P.T. Suryanusa Permatabahari — Samarinda** Loa 30.00 Br ex - Dght - Lbp - Br md 9.00 Dpth 4.00 Welded, 1 dk	**(B32A2ST) Tug**	**2 oil engines** reduction geared to sc. shafts driving 2 Propellers Total Power: 1,412kW (1,920hp) 350 Caterpillar 2 x Vee 4 Stroke 8 Cy. 170 x 190 each-706kW (960bhp) Caterpillar Inc-USA AuxGen: 2 x 120kW a.c
8654900 - -	**ZEUS III** - **PT Surya Maritim Shippindo** - *Samarinda* *Indonesia*	**316** 95 -	Class: KI	**2010-06 P.T. Suryanusa Permatabahari — Samarinda** Loa 32.60 Br ex - Dght - Lbp 29.18 Br md 9.00 Dpth 4.00 Welded, 1 dk	**(B32A2ST) Tug**	**2 oil engines** reduction geared to sc. shafts driving 2 FP propellers AuxGen: 2 x 9kW 380/220V a.c
9476733 *7JEX* -	**ZEUS LEADER** - **Ship I Co Ltd, Ship II Co Ltd, Ship III Co Ltd, Ship IV Co Ltd** NYK Container Line Ltd SatCom: Inmarsat C 443271210 *Tokyo* *Japan* MMSI: 432712000 Official number: 140985	**60,212** 19,312 18,697	Class: NK	**2009-07 Mitsubishi Heavy Industries Ltd. — Nagasaki** Yd No: 2254 Loa 199.90 (BB) Br ex - Dght 9.725 Lbp 192.00 Br md 32.26 Dpth 34.52 Welded, 12 dks including 2 liftable dks	**(A35B2RV) Vehicles Carrier** Side door/ramp (s) Len: - Wid: - Swl: 20 Quarter stern door/ramp (s. a.) Len: - Wid: - Swl: 100 Cars: 6,341	**1 oil engine** driving 1 Propeller Total Power: 12,390kW (16,845hp) 20.6 Mitsubishi 7UEC60 1 x 2 Stroke 7 Cy. 600 x 2200 12390kW (16845bhp) Mitsubishi Heavy Industries Ltd-Japan Thrusters: 1 Tunnel thruster (f) Fuel: 2600.0
9208071 *IBVO* -	**ZEUS PALACE** *ex* Eurostar Barcelona *-2009* *ex* Prometheus *-2005* **Atlantica SpA di Navigazione** Grimaldi Group *Palermo* *Italy* MMSI: 247131600	**31,730** 12,166 7,680	Class: RI (GL)	**2001-02 Samsung Heavy Industries Co Ltd — Geoje** Yd No: 1279 Loa 211.94 (BB) Br ex - Dght 6.800 Lbp 198.00 Br md 25.00 Dpth 15.40 Welded	**(A36A2PR) Passenger/Ro-Ro Ship (Vehicles)** Passengers: 1000; cabins: 52; berths: 200 Stern door/ramp (p. a.) Stern door/ramp (s. a.) Lane-Len: 2000 Lorries: 116, Cars: 100	**4 oil engines** reduction geared to sc. shafts driving 2 CP propellers Total Power: 50,424kW (68,556hp) 28.4 Wartsila 12V4 4 x Vee 4 Stroke 12 Cy. 460 x 580 each-12606kW (17139bhp) Wartsila Nederland BV-Netherlands AuxGen: 2 x 2300kW a.c, 2 x 2300kW a.c Thrusters: 2 Thwart. FP thruster (f); 1 Thwart. FP thruster (a) Fuel: 103.6 (d.f.) 828.0 (r.f.)
8658346 - -	**ZEUS V** - **PT Surya Borneo Shippindo** - *Samarinda* *Indonesia*	**309** 93 -	Class: KI	**2011-04 P.T. Suryanusa Permatabahari — Samarinda** Loa 31.00 Br ex - Dght 2.990 Lbp 28.41 Br md 9.00 Dpth 4.00 Welded, 1 dk	**(B32A2ST) Tug**	**2 oil engines** reduction geared to sc. shafts driving 2 FP propellers AuxGen: 2 x 51kW 400V a.c
8607531 - -	**ZEVA** *ex* Unitra *-2008* *ex* Finwhale *-2007* *ex* Gui Hua Xiang *-2005* *ex* Ying Bao *-1998* - -	*3,995* 1,918 5,036	Class: (CC) (RN)	**1991-07 Santierul Naval Galati S.A. — Galati** Yd No: 816 Loa 101.50 Br ex - Dght 6.970 Lbp 94.13 Br md 16.40 Dpth 8.60 Welded, 2 dks	**(A31A2GX) General Cargo Ship** Grain: 6,680; Bale: 6,135 TEU 180 Compartments: 3 Ho, ER 3 Ha: (13.4 x 7.0)2 (13.4 x 12.7)ER Derricks: 6x5t Ice Capable	**1 oil engine** geared to sc. shaft driving 1 FP propeller Total Power: 2,758kW (3,750hp) 14.0 MAN 6L40/5 1 x 4 Stroke 6 Cy. 400 x 540 2758kW (3750bhp) MAN B&W Diesel AG-Augsburg AuxGen: 3 x 264kW 390V a.c, 1 x 120kW 390V a.c
9049372 - -	**ZEVRA** *ex* Diana Jaya I *-2008* *ex* Adetia Pratama *-2005* **Cabochen Marine Inc** - *Georgia*	**23,153** 47 39,244	Class: KI	**1994-06 PT Yasa Wahana Tirta Samudera — Semarang** Loa 29.30 Br ex - Dght 1.410 Lbp 27.90 Br md 6.48 Dpth 1.85 Welded, 1 dk	**(A13B2TU) Tanker (unspecified)**	**2 oil engines** geared to sc. shafts driving 2 Propellers Total Power: 456kW (620hp) 7.0 Mitsubishi 8DC8 2 x Vee 4 Stroke 8 Cy. each-228kW (310bhp) Mitsubishi Heavy Industries Ltd-Japan AuxGen: 1 x 56kW 400/230V a.c, 1 x 11kW 400/230V a.c
8729834 - -	**ZEVS** *ex* PTR-50 No. 58 *-2001* **JSC Nord Fishmen (OOO 'Rybak Severa')** -	**242** 173 68	Class: (RS) (RR)	**1989-04 Astrakhanskaya Sudoverf im. "Kirova" — Astrakhan** Yd No: 58 Loa 31.85 Br ex - Dght 2.101 Lbp 27.80 Br md 6.89 Dpth 3.15 Welded, 1 dk	**(B12B2FC) Fish Carrier** Ins: 100 Compartments: 2 Ho	**1 oil engine** geared to sc. shaft driving 1 FP propeller Total Power: 221kW (300hp) 10.2 Daldizel 6CHNSP18/22-3 1 x 4 Stroke 6 Cy. 180 x 220 221kW (300bhp) Daldizel-Khabarovsk AuxGen: 2 x 25kW Fuel: 14.0 (d.f.)
8304206 *UDYF* -	**ZEVS** *ex* Zavino *-2010* *ex* Akebono I *-1998* *ex* Akebono Maru No. 3 *-1998* **Kamchatka Industrial-Commercial Firm 'Kamline' Co Ltd (Kamchatskaya Proizvodstvenno-Kommercheskaya Firma 'Kamlayn' OOO)** *Petropavlovsk-Kamchatskiy* *Russia* MMSI: 273410310	**1,125** 361 643	Class: RS	**1983-10 Narasaki Zosen KK — Muroran HK** Yd No: 1056 Loa 63.68 Br ex 11.03 Dght 4.110 Lbp 55.50 Br md 11.00 Dpth 6.51 Welded, 1 dk	**(B11A2FS) Stern Trawler** Ins: 630 Compartments: 1 Ho, ER 2 Ha: ER	**1 oil engine** driving 1 CP propeller Total Power: 2,207kW (3,001hp) 14.0 Hanshin 6EL 1 x 4 Stroke 6 Cy. 400 x 800 2207kW (3001bhp) The Hanshin Diesel Works Ltd-Japan AuxGen: 1 x 400kW 445V 60Hz a.c, 1 x 356kW 445V 60Hz a Fuel: 26.5 (d.f.) 309.5 (r.f.) 7.5pd
7942960 *UBLF6* -	**ZEYA** - **Peterburgskiy Otryad Spetsmorprovodki** - SatCom: Inmarsat C 427302293 *St Petersburg* *Russia* MMSI: 273333220	*1,085* 229 404	Class: (RS)	**1981-03 Yaroslavskiy Sudostroitelnyy Zavod — Yaroslavl** Yd No: 216 Loa 58.55 Br ex 12.67 Dght 4.690 Lbp 51.62 Br md - Dpth 5.90 Welded, 1 dk	**(B32A2ST) Tug** Ice Capable	**2 diesel electric oil engines** driving 2 gen. each 1000kW 900V Connecting to 2 elec. motors each (950kW) driving 1 FP propeller Total Power: 2,208kW (3,002hp) 13.2 Kolomna 6CHN30/3 2 x 4 Stroke 6 Cy. 300 x 380 each-1104kW (1501bhp) Kolomenskiy Zavod-Kolomna AuxGen: 2 x 300kW 400V a.c, 2 x 160kW 400V a.c Fuel: 250.0 (d.f.)
9118355 *UHMI* -	**ZEYA** *ex* Ute Johanna *-2009* **Sakhalin Shipping Co (SASCO)** - *Kholmsk* *Russia* MMSI: 273347430	**2,984** 1,311 4,850 T/cm 14.0	Class: RS (GL)	**1995-10 Kroeger Werft GmbH & Co. KG — Schacht-Audorf** Yd No: 1534 Loa 98.43 (BB) Br ex 17.09 Dght 5.860 Lbp 91.45 Br md 16.90 Dpth 7.55 Welded, 1 dk	**(A33A2CC) Container Ship (Fully Cellular)** Grain: 4,450; Bale: 4,160 TEU 366 C Ho 80 TEU C Dk 286 TEU incl 46 ref C. Compartments: 1 Cell Ho, ER 3 Ha: ER Ice Capable	**1 oil engine** with clutches, flexible couplings & sr geared to sc. shaft driving 1 CP propeller Total Power: 2,940kW (3,997hp) 15.0 Alpha 12V28/3 1 x Vee 4 Stroke 12 Cy. 280 x 320 2940kW (3997bhp) MAN B&W Diesel A/S-Denmark AuxGen: 1 x 783kW 440V 60Hz a.c, 2 x 256kW 440V 60Hz a. Thrusters: 1 Thwart. FP thruster (f) Fuel: 40.8 (d.f.) 233.2 (r.f.) 14.0pd
9040663 *TCMG4* -	**ZEYBE** *ex* Bluemarine *-2011* *ex* Nermin N *-2007* *ex* Paradise *-2006* *ex* Marine Jade *-2003* **Zeybe Denizcilik ve Ticaret Ltd Sti (Zeybe Shipping & Trading Co Ltd)** Dogru Denizcilik Brokerlik Ticaret Ltd Sti *Istanbul* *Turkey* MMSI: 271042650	**1,511** 881 2,200	Class: TL (LR) ✠ Classed LR until 11/3/09	**1994-09 Zhejiang Shipyard — Ningbo ZJ** Yd No: 91Z-50 Loa 71.82 Br ex 12.82 Dght 4.800 Lbp 68.20 Br md 12.80 Dpth 6.20 Welded, 1 dk	**(A31A2GX) General Cargo Ship** Compartments: 2 Ho, ER 2 Ha: 2 (13.0 x 7.0)ER Derricks: 4	**1 oil engine** driving 1 FP propeller Total Power: 662kW (900hp) Chinese Std. Type 63 1 x 4 Stroke 6 Cy. 350 x 500 662kW (900bhp) Yichang Marine Diesel Engine Co Ltd-China AuxGen: 2 x 90kW 400V 50Hz a.c
8213732 *E5U2787* -	**ZEYBEK** *ex* Sari Zeybek *-2013* *ex* Corn Pride *-2008* *ex* Klippergracht *-2002* **Med Net Shipping Trading Inc** Aknur Denizcilik ve Dis Ticaret Ltd Sti *Avatiu* *Cook Islands* MMSI: 518840000	**4,921** 3,299 5,022	Class: BV (LR) ✠ Classed LR until 27/4/11	**1984-01 Miho Zosensho K.K. — Shimizu** Yd No: 1227 Loa 106.30 (BB) Br ex 16.62 Dght 5.865 Lbp 99.85 Br md 16.01 Dpth 10.49 Welded, 2 dks	**(A31A2GX) General Cargo Ship** Double Sides Entire Compartment Length Grain: 11,055; Bale: 10,769 TEU 365 C.Ho 224/20' (40') C.Dk 141/20' (40') Compartments: 1 Ho, ER, 1 Tw Dk 3 Ha: (2.6 x 7.3) (36.9 x 12.8) (33.3 x 12.8)ER Cranes: 2x25t Ice Capable	**1 oil engine** driving 1 CP propeller Total Power: 2,464kW (3,350hp) 11.0 Hanshin 6LUS 1 x 4 Stroke 6 Cy. 400 x 640 2464kW (3350bhp) The Hanshin Diesel Works Ltd-Japan AuxGen: 4 x 200kW 445V 60Hz a.c Fuel: 57.8 (d.f.) 440.0 (r.f.) 10.0pd
9564994 *9HA2489* -	**ZEYCAN ANA** *launched as* Garip Baba *-2010* **Zeycan Maritime Ltd** Yilmar Denizcilik Nakliyat ve Ticaret Ltd Sti (Yilmar Shipping & Trading Ltd) *Valletta* *Malta* MMSI: 248737000 Official number: 9564994	**5,857** 2,887 8,500	Class: BV	**2010-08 Marmara Tersanesi — Yarimca** Yd No: 86 Loa 120.00 Br ex - Dght 8.100 Lbp 115.00 Br md 16.40 Dpth 9.90 Welded, 1 dk	**(A31A2GX) General Cargo Ship** Grain: 10,301; Bale: 10,142 Compartments: 3 Ho, ER 3 Ha: ER	**1 oil engine** reduction geared to sc.shaft driving 1 CP propeller Total Power: 2,620kW (3,562hp) 14.0 Hyundai Himsen 9H25/33 1 x 4 Stroke 9 Cy. 250 x 330 2620kW (3562bhp) Hyundai Heavy Industries Co Ltd-South Korea AuxGen: 2 x 300kW 60Hz a.c

667514 **ZEYCAN Y**
CWC5
ex Bogacay *-2013*
Gemport Gemlik Liman ve Depolama Isletmeleri AS (Gemlik Port & Warehousing Administration Co Inc)
-
Istanbul *Turkey*
MMSI: 271043476
Official number: TUGS 2216

291 / 165 / 108 — Class: AB

2013-05 Sanmar Denizcilik Makina ve Ticaret — Istanbul Yd No: 03
Loa 24.40 Br ex - Dght 3.050
Lbp 24.03 Br md 11.25 Dpth 4.38
Welded, 1 dk

(B32A2ST) Tug

2 oil engines reduction geared to sc. shafts driving 2 Z propellers
Total Power: 3,530kW (4,800hp) 12.0kn
Caterpillar 3512C
2 x Vee 4 Stroke 12 Cy. 170 x 215 each-1765kW (2400bhp)
Caterpillar Inc-USA
AuxGen: 2 x 86kW 50Hz a.c
Fuel: 85.0 (d.f.)

356957 **ZEYNALABDIN TAGIYEV**
HLD8
Palmali Voyager Three Shipping Co Ltd
Palmali Gemicilik ve Acentelik AS (Palmali Shipping & Agency)
Valletta *Malta*
MMSI: 256107000
Official number: 9927

5,684 / 3,230 / 6,970 / T/cm 22.0 — Class: RS

2006-05 OAO Volgogradskiy Sudostroitelnyy Zavod — Volgograd Yd No: 225
Loa 139.63 (BB) Br ex 16.70 Dght 4.600
Lbp 134.00 Br md 16.50 Dpth 6.00
Welded, 1 dk

(A31A2GX) General Cargo Ship
Grain: 11,521
TEU 274
4 Ha: (26.0 x 13.2)2 (26.6 x 13.2)ER (13.0 x 13.2)

2 oil engines geared to sc. shafts driving 2 Directional propellers
Total Power: 2,240kW (3,046hp) 10.5kn
Wartsila 6L20
2 x 4 Stroke 6 Cy. 200 x 280 each-1120kW (1523bhp)
Wartsila Finland Oy-Finland
AuxGen: 2 x 212kW a.c
Fuel: 350.0 (d.f.)

13205 **ZEYNAZ**
CBZ5
ex Fatih Saribas *-2003* *ex* Akbay I *-1987*
Zeynaz Denizcilik ve Ticaret Ltd
Aksel Denizcilik ve Ticaret AS
Istanbul *Turkey*
MMSI: 271002116

697 / 434 / 800 — Class: (TL)

1983-10 Akdenizler Gemi Insa Sanayi — Karadeniz Eregli Yd No: 1A
Loa 55.85 Br ex - Dght 3.480
Lbp 53.03 Br md 9.02 Dpth 3.75
Welded, 1 dk

(A31A2GX) General Cargo Ship

1 oil engine driving 1 FP propeller
Total Power: 300kW (408hp) 8.0kn
S.K.L. 6NVD36-1U
1 x 4 Stroke 6 Cy. 240 x 360 300kW (408bhp) (made 1976)
VEB Schwermaschinenbau "KarlLiebknecht" (SKL)-Magdeburg
AuxGen: 2 x 38kW a.c

424223 **ZEYNEP A**
HCU9
Transteck Shipping Ltd
CSM Denizcilik Ltd Sti (Chemfleet)
Valletta *Malta*
MMSI: 256801000
Official number: 9424223

7,244 / 3,643 / 11,276 / T/cm 21.7 — Class: BV

2007-09 Admarin Gemi Yapim Sanayi ve Ticaret AS — Basiskele Yd No: 12
Loa 129.75 (BB) Br ex - Dght 8.000
Lbp 123.20 Br md 19.60 Dpth 10.40
Welded, 1 dk

(A12B2TR) Chemical/Products Tanker
Double Hull (13F)
Liq: 12,379; Liq (Oil): 12,909
Cargo Heating Coils
Compartments: 14 Wing Ta, 2 Wing Slop Ta, ER
14 Cargo Pump (s): 14x300m³/hr
Manifold: Bow/CM: 68.6m
Ice Capable

1 oil engine driving 1 CP propeller
Total Power: 4,440kW (6,037hp) 14.0kn
MAN-B&W 6S35MC
1 x 2 Stroke 6 Cy. 350 x 1400 4440kW (6037bhp)
AuxGen: 3 x 620kW a.c
Thrusters: 1 Tunnel thruster (f)
Fuel: 85.0 (d.f.) 460.0 (r.f.)

516582 **ZEYNEP DUNDAR**
3AV2
ex Burak N *-2013* *ex* Golden Bridge *-2006*
ex Arktis Sky *-2002*
ex P&O Nedlloyd Coral *-1998*
ex P&O Nedlloyd Eritrea *-1997*
ex Arktis Sky *-1997*
Bay International SA
ACT Deniz Tasimaciligi Sanayi Ve Ticaret Ltd Sti
Tarawa *Kiribati*
MMSI: 529454000
Official number: K-14871179

1,829 / 1,123 / 2,671 — Class: BV (LR) (RI) (CC)
✠ Classed LR until 20/3/02

1987-12 A/S Nordsovaerftet — Ringkobing Yd No: 189
Loa 73.94 (BB) Br ex 13.41 Dght 5.180
Lbp 73.67 Br md 13.25 Dpth 6.40
Welded, 2 dks

(A31A2GX) General Cargo Ship
Grain: 3,870; Bale: 3,509
TEU 118 C.Ho 42/20' (40') C.Dk 76/20' (40') incl. 10 ref C.
Compartments: 1 Ho, ER, 1 Tw Dk
2 Ha: 2 (20.0 x 10.2)ER
Derricks: 1x40t,1x32t; Winches: 2
Ice Capable

1 oil engine with flexible couplings & sr gearedto sc. shaft driving 1 CP propeller
Total Power: 749kW (1,018hp) 11.0kn
MaK 6M452AK
1 x 4 Stroke 6 Cy. 320 x 450 749kW (1018bhp)
Krupp MaK Maschinenbau GmbH-Kiel
AuxGen: 1 x 180kW 380V 50Hz a.c, 2 x 165kW 380V 50Hz a.c

483827 **ZEYNEP K**
7TK8
Ace Navigation Ltd
Haci Ismail Kaptanoglu Shipmanagement & Trading Ltd
Majuro *Marshall Islands*
MMSI: 538003822
Official number: 3822

43,834 / 26,694 / 80,370 / T/cm 71.9 — Class: LR
✠ **100A1** SS 04/2010
bulk carrier
CSR
BC-A
GRAB (20)
Nos. 2, 4 & 6 holds may be empty
ESP
ShipRight (ACS (B), CM)
*IWS
LI
EP (B)
✠ **LMC** **UMS**
Eq.Ltr: Qt;
Cable: 687.5/81.0 U3 (a)

2010-04 STX Offshore & Shipbuilding Co Ltd — Changwon (Jinhae Shipyard) Yd No: 4030
Loa 229.00 (BB) Br ex 32.28 Dght 14.450
Lbp 222.00 Br md 32.24 Dpth 20.10
Welded, 1 dk

(A21A2BC) Bulk Carrier
Grain: 95,172
Compartments: 7 Ho, ER
7 Ha: ER 7 (17.2 x -)

1 oil engine driving 1 FP propeller
Total Power: 11,060kW (15,037hp) 14.4kn
MAN-B&W 7S50MC-C
1 x 2 Stroke 7 Cy. 500 x 2000 11060kW (15037bhp)
STX Engine Co Ltd-South Korea
AuxGen: 3 x 620kW 440V 60Hz a.c
Boilers: AuxB (Comp) 9.0kgf/cm² (8.8bar)

015577 **ZEYNEP KIRAN**
CZK
launched as Beclan *-2001*
Kirbulk Uluslararasi Gemi Turizm Tasimacilik
Pasifik Gemi Isletmeciligi ve Ticaret AS
Istanbul *Turkey*
MMSI: 271000642

17,934 / 9,955 / 29,330 — Class: BV

2001-06 Tuzla Gemi Endustrisi A.S. — Tuzla (Hull) Yd No: 001
2001-06 Santierul Naval "2 Mai" Mangalia S.A. — Mangalia Yd No: 865
Loa 181.50 (BB) Br ex - Dght 10.550
Lbp 169.60 Br md 24.80 Dpth 14.10
Welded, 1 dk

(A21A2BC) Bulk Carrier
Double Bottom Entire Compartment Length
Grain: 34,712; Bale: 33,582
Compartments: 5 Ho, ER
5 Ha: (12.6 x 12.0)4 (17.6 x 13.6)ER
Cranes: 4x30.5t
Ice Capable

1 oil engine driving 1 CP propeller
Total Power: 7,860kW (10,686hp) 15.0kn
B&W 6S46MC-C
1 x 2 Stroke 6 Cy. 460 x 1932 7860kW (10686bhp)
AO Bryanskiy MashinostroitelnyyZavod (BMZ)-Bryansk
AuxGen: 3 x 550kW a.c
Fuel: 195.0 (d.f.) 1378.1 (r.f.) 34.0pd

619857 **ZEYTINBURNU**
CBX4
Istanbul Deniz Otobusleri Sanayi ve Ticaret AS (IDO)
-
Istanbul *Turkey*
MMSI: 271002499
Official number: 5776

1,077 / 391 / 376 — Class: TL

1989-08 Marmara Tersanesi — Yarimca Yd No: 36A
Loa 67.26 Br ex - Dght 3.740
Lbp 63.40 Br md 17.70 Dpth 4.10
Welded, 1 dk

(A36A2PR) Passenger/Ro-Ro Ship (Vehicles)
Lorries: 24, Cars: 62

2 oil engines reduction geared to sc. shafts driving 2 CP propellers 1 fwd and 1 aft
Total Power: 1,248kW (1,696hp) 11.0kn
Sulzer 8AL20/24
2 x 4 Stroke 8 Cy. 200 x 240 each-624kW (848bhp)
Turkiye Gemi Sanayii AS-Turkey
AuxGen: 2 x 180kW 380V 50Hz a.c
Fuel: 68.0 (d.f.) 3.6pd

704239 **ZEYTINBURNU**
TCDD Izmir Liman Isletmesi Mudurlugu
-
Turkey

108 / - / -

1985-10 Turkiye Gemi Sanayii A.S. — Alaybey, Izmir Yd No: 46
Loa - Br ex - Dght -
Lbp - Br md - Dpth -
Welded, 1 dk

(B32A2ST) Tug

1 oil engine driving 1 FP propeller
Niigata
1 x 4 Stroke
Niigata Engineering Co Ltd-Japan

297955 **ZF T1**
D4941
ex Poet Maple *-2003*
PT Zulinda Fery Marine
PT Sumber Kencana Patria
Tanjung Priok *Indonesia*

194 / 59 / 204 — Class: KI (NK)

2003-08 Forward Shipbuilding Enterprise Sdn Bhd — Sibu Yd No: 91
Loa 26.00 Br ex - Dght 3.062
Lbp 24.24 Br md 8.00 Dpth 3.65
Welded, 1 dk

(B32A2ST) Tug

2 oil engines geared to sc. shafts driving 2 FP propellers
Total Power: 1,204kW (1,636hp) 10.0kn
Mitsubishi S6R2-MPTK
2 x 4 Stroke 6 Cy. 170 x 220 each-602kW (818bhp)
Mitsubishi Heavy Industries Ltd-Japan

387480 **ZHADEIT**
6EY5
ex Volgo-Don 5026 *-1998*
Kama Six Shipping Co Ltd
Sailtrade Denizcilik ve Ticaret Ltd Sti
Moroni *Union of Comoros*
MMSI: 616769000

3,994 / 1,302 / 5,303 — Class: RR (RS)

1970-07 Santierul Naval Oltenita S.A. — Oltenita Yd No: 456
Loa 138.80 Br ex 16.70 Dght 3.380
Lbp 131.20 Br md 16.50 Dpth 5.50
Welded, 1 dk

(A31A2GX) General Cargo Ship
Grain: 6,270
Compartments: 2 Ho, ER
2 Ha: (45.1 x 13.6)ER (44.1 x 13.6)

2 oil engines driving 2 FP propellers
Total Power: 1,324kW (1,800hp) 10.8kn
Dvigatel Revolyutsii 6CHRNP36/45
2 x 4 Stroke 6 Cy. 360 x 450 each-662kW (900bhp)
Zavod "Dvigatel Revolyutsii"-Gorkiy

353060 **ZHAIK**
Government of The Republic of Kazakhstan
-
Aqtau *Kazakhstan*

196 / 49 / 35 — Class: (RS)

2008-05 OAO Astrakhanskaya Sudoverf — Astrakhan Yd No: 128
Loa 31.85 Br ex - Dght 1.800
Lbp 27.80 Br md 6.90 Dpth 3.15
Welded, 1 dk

(B31A2SR) Research Survey Vessel
Ins: 100
Ice Capable

1 oil engine geared to sc. shaft driving 1 FP propeller
Total Power: 248kW (337hp) 10.4kn
Deutz BF6M1015MC
1 x Vee 4 Stroke 6 Cy. 132 x 145 248kW (337bhp) (made 2007)
Deutz AG-Koeln
AuxGen: 2 x 75kW a.c
Fuel: 19.0 (d.f.)

381659 **ZHAN JIANG**
SPD
ex CO 834 *-1975*
CCCC Guangzhou Dredging Co Ltd
Guangzhou, Guangdong *China*
MMSI: 412052580

1,955 / 677 / 1,769 — Class: CC (BV)

1975-02 Scheepsw. en Mfbk."De Biesbosch-Dordrecht" B.V. — Dordrecht Yd No: 663
Loa 83.85 Br ex 13.11 Dght 4.064
Lbp 78.03 Br md 13.04 Dpth 4.79
Welded, 1 dk

(B33B2DT) Trailing Suction Hopper Dredger
Hopper: 1,500

2 oil engines driving 2 FP propellers
Total Power: 2,472kW (3,360hp) 11.8kn
Smit-Bolnes 307HD
2 x 2 Stroke 7 Cy. 300 x 550 each-1236kW (1680bhp)
Motorenfabriek Smit & Bolnes NV-Netherlands
Thrusters: 1 Thwart. FP thruster (f)
Fuel: 262.0

832007 **ZHAN YOU 4**
China Marine Bunker Supply Co (Zhanjiang Branch)
-
Zhanjiang, Guangdong *China*

398 / 222 / 500

1980 Shantou Shipyard — Shantou GD
Loa 45.40 Br ex - Dght 3.500
Lbp 43.30 Br md 8.80 Dpth 4.20
Welded, 1 dk

(A13B2TU) Tanker (unspecified)

1 oil engine geared to sc. shaft driving 1 FP propeller
Total Power: 441kW (600hp) 10.0kn
Chinese Std. Type 6300
1 x 4 Stroke 6 Cy. 300 x 380 441kW (600bhp)
Guangzhou Diesel Engine Factory CoLtd-China
AuxGen: 2 x 64kW 400V a.c

ID	Ship / Owners	Tonnage	Class	Builder / Dimensions	Type	Machinery	Speed / Engine
8621642 - -	**ZHAN YOU 5** *ex* Nan Hai 603 *-1984* **China Marine Bunker Supply Co (Zhanjiang Branch)** - *Zhanjiang, Guangdong* *China* MMSI: 412058040	*789* 335 1,000		**1979 Guangdong New China Shipyard Co Ltd — Dongguan GD** Loa 67.42 Br ex - Dght 4.000 Lbp 60.00 Br md 10.02 Dpth 4.50 Welded, 1 dk	**(A13B2TU) Tanker (unspecified)**	**1 oil engine** driving 1 FP propeller Total Power: 662kW (900hp) Chinese Std. Type 1 x 4 Stroke 6 Cy. 350 x 500 662kW (900bhp) Shanghai Diesel Engine Co Ltd-China AuxGen: 2 x 90kW 400V a.c	12.0k 635
9152715 *BTQQ* -	**ZHAN YOU 7** **China Marine Bunker Supply Co (Zhanjiang Branch)** - *Zhanjiang, Guangdong* *China* MMSI: 412058050	**998** 506 1,740	Class: (CC)	**1996-10 Hunan Changsha Shipyard — Changsha HN** Yd No: 921001 Loa 74.80 Br ex - Dght - Lbp 69.00 Br md 11.40 Dpth 5.20 Welded, 1 dk	**(B35E2TF) Bunkering Tanker** Liq: 2,000; Liq (Oil): 2,000 2 Cargo Pump (s)	**1 oil engine** geared to sc. shaft driving 1 FP propeller Total Power: 810kW (1,101hp) Alpha 1 x 4 Stroke 6 Cy. 225 x 300 810kW (1101bhp) Zhenjiang Marine Diesel Works-China	6L23/30
8307894 *BNCA* -	**ZHANG HONG NO. 1** *ex* Chc No. 1 *-2012* *ex* Rubin Stein *-1992* *ex* New Lily *-1991* *ex* Sanko Lily *-1986* **Zhang Hong Shipping Co Ltd** Yu Pin Shipping Corp Ltd *Kaohsiung* *Chinese Taipei* MMSI: 416361000 Official number: 014041	**22,009** 12,589 37,715 T/cm 45.8	Class: CR (NK)	**1984-05 Sasebo Heavy Industries Co. Ltd. — Sasebo Yard, Sasebo** Yd No: 329 Loa 188.00 (BB) Br ex 28.05 Dght 10.861 Lbp 180.01 Br md 28.01 Dpth 15.40 Welded, 1 dk	**(A21A2BC) Bulk Carrier** Grain: 47,588; Bale: 45,961 Compartments: 5 Ho, ER 5 Ha: 5 (19.2 x 14.0)ER Cranes: 4x25t	**1 oil engine** driving 1 FP propeller Total Power: 6,002kW (8,160hp) Sulzer 1 x 2 Stroke 6 Cy. 580 x 1700 6002kW (8160bhp) Hitachi Zosen Corp-Japan AuxGen: 3 x 400kW 450V 60Hz a.c Fuel: 122.5 (d.f.) (Heating Coils) 1435.5 (r.f.) 22.5pd	14.0kn 6RTA58
8312617 *3FPP4* -	**ZHANG HONG NO. 2** *ex* Ever Glory Ii *-2013* *ex* Nosco Peace *-2010* *ex* Maritime Peace *-2008* *ex* Maritime Phuket *-2001* *ex* Maritime Associate *-1995* *ex* Tonic Venture *-1987* **Zhang Hong Shipping SA** - *Panama* *Panama* MMSI: 372129000 Official number: 4026209B	**15,850** 9,110 26,384	Class: (NK)	**1983-12 Kurushima Dockyard Co. Ltd. — Onishi** Yd No: 2286 Loa 160.00 (BB) Br ex - Dght 10.372 Lbp 150.32 Br md 25.40 Dpth 14.20 Welded, 1 dk	**(A21A2BC) Bulk Carrier** Grain: 33,139; Bale: 31,879 Compartments: 4 Ho, ER 4 Ha: (17.6 x 11.4) (20.8 x 13.1) (22.4 x 13.1) (21.6 x 13.1)ER Cranes: 4x25t	**1 oil engine** driving 1 FP propeller Total Power: 5,296kW (7,200hp) Mitsubishi 1 x 2 Stroke 6 Cy. 520 x 1250 5296kW (7200bhp) Kobe Hatsudoki KK-Japan AuxGen: 2 x 400kW Fuel: 1310.0 (r.f.)	13.8kn 6UEC52HA
7916569 *BRRV* -	**ZHANG LONG** *ex* Chun Xin No. 9 *-1998* *ex* Propane Maru No. 8 *-1998* **Shenzhen Southern China LPG Shipping Co Ltd** - *Shenzhen, Guangdong* *China* MMSI: 412461950	*998* 629 1,136 T/cm 5.8	Class: (CC) (NK)	**1979-11 Naikai Shipbuilding & Engineering Co Ltd — Onomichi HS (Taguma Shipyard)** Yd No: 451 Loa 65.28 Br ex 11.43 Dght 4.565 Lbp 60.03 Br md 11.41 Dpth 5.16 Welded, 1 dk	**(A11B2TG) LPG Tanker** Liq (Gas): 1,556 2 x Gas Tank (s); 2 independent (C.mn.stl) cyl horizontal 2 Cargo Pump (s): 2x500m³/hr Manifold: Bow/CM: 25m	**1 oil engine** driving 1 FP propeller Total Power: 1,545kW (2,101hp) Akasaka 1 x 4 Stroke 6 Cy. 380 x 600 1545kW (2101bhp) Akasaka Tekkosho KK (Akasaka DieselLtd)-Japan AuxGen: 2 x 580kW Fuel: 17.5 (d.f.) 68.0 (r.f.) 7.0pd	12.3kn DM38AR
7387990 *3ECP5* -	**ZHANG YUAN YU** *ex* Victory *-2009* *ex* Zhang Yuan Yu *-2007* *ex* Chang Hai 1 *-2006* *ex* Rio Najasa *-2001* **Zhang Zi Dao Fishery Co Ltd** - *Panama* *Panama* MMSI: 352849000 Official number: 34593LG	**2,579** 774 3,206	Class: RC (LR) ✠ Classed LR until 4/84	**1977-06 Astilleros Construcciones SA — Vigo** Yd No: 243 Loa 106.86 (BB) Br ex 14.61 Dght 5.627 Lbp 95.20 Br md 14.51 Dpth 8.51 Welded, 2 dks	**(B11A2FG) Factory Stern Trawler** Ins: 3,084 Compartments: 2 Ho, ER 2 Ha: (4.5 x 2.9) (3.8 x 2.9)ER	**1 oil engine** geared to sc. shaft driving 1 CP propeller Total Power: 2,942kW (4,000hp) Deutz 1 x Vee 4 Stroke 12 Cy. 400 x 500 2942kW (4000bhp) Hijos de J Barreras SA-Spain AuxGen: 4 x 400kW 380V 50Hz a.c Fuel: 32.0 (d.f.) 1052.0 (r.f.)	15.0kn RBV12M350
9030321 *UNAL* -	**ZHANNA** *ex* Boss *-2010* *ex* H. O. S. Boss Hoss *-1996* *ex* Ronnie Roussel *-1994* **GAC Marine Kazakhstan LLP** KazGac Marine Services LLP *Aqtau* *Kazakhstan* MMSI: 436000154	**1,124** 337 1,499	Class: AB RS	**1991-11 Halter Marine, Inc. — Lockport, La** Yd No: 1257 Loa 67.06 Br ex - Dght 4.110 Lbp 60.44 Br md 13.41 Dpth 4.88 Welded	**(B21A2OS) Platform Supply Ship**	**2 oil engines** reverse reduction geared to sc. shafts driving 2 FP propellers Total Power: 2,868kW (3,900hp) EMD (Electro-Motive) 2 x Vee 2 Stroke 16 Cy. 230 x 254 each-1434kW (1950bhp) General Motors Detroit DieselAllison Divn-USA AuxGen: 2 x 360kW a.c Thrusters: 1 Tunnel thruster (f) Fuel: 190.0 (d.f.)	9.0kn 16-645-E6
9036569 *XUHH4* -	**ZHAO FENG 1** *ex* Munakata Maru No. 25 *-2014* **Metro Harvest Shipping Ltd** KK DCAM *Cambodia* MMSI: 515956000 Official number: 1491260	**1,357** 407 1,702	Class: (NK)	**1991-12 Imamura Zosen — Kure** Yd No: 356 Loa 72.95 (BB) Br ex - Dght 4.712 Lbp 68.00 Br md 12.00 Dpth 5.60 Welded, 1 dk	**(A12A2LP) Molten Sulphur Tanker** Liq: 788 Compartments: 6 Ta, ER	**1 oil engine** driving 1 CP propeller Total Power: 1,471kW (2,000hp) Hanshin 1 x 4 Stroke 6 Cy. 350 x 700 1471kW (2000bhp) The Hanshin Diesel Works Ltd-Japan AuxGen: 3 x 124kW a.c Fuel: 145.0 (r.f.)	12.4kn 6EL35
9466403 *BJJJ* -	**ZHAO GANG** **Hainan Zhaogang Marine Co Ltd** - *Haikou, Hainan* *China* MMSI: 413520250	**2,014** 604 1,646	Class: CC	**2007-10 Jiangmen Yinxing Shipbuilding Co Ltd — Jiangmen GD** Yd No: YX2-005 Loa 76.80 Br ex - Dght 4.400 Lbp 70.00 Br md 13.60 Dpth 5.80 Welded, 1 dk	**(A11B2TG) LPG Tanker** Liq (Gas): 2,011 2 x Gas Tank (s); independent	**1 oil engine** geared to sc. shaft driving 1 Propeller Total Power: 1,765kW (2,400hp) Chinese Std. Type 1 x 4 Stroke 8 Cy. 300 x 380 1765kW (2400bhp) Ningbo CSI Power & Machinery GroupCo Ltd-China AuxGen: 2 x 200kW 400V a.c	8300ZC
8664668 *BI2453* CT7-0453	**ZHAO HUNG NO. 6** *ex* Hung Fu No. 11 *-2012* *ex* Hui Hsing No. 1 *-2000* **Zhao Hung Fishery Co Ltd** - *Kaohsiung* *Chinese Taipei* Official number: 011929	**712** 272 -		**1990-08 Jong Shyn Shipbuilding Co., Ltd. — Kaohsiung** L reg 48.90 Br ex - Dght - Lbp - Br md 8.90 Dpth 3.85 Welded, 1 dk	**(B11B2FV) Fishing Vessel**	**1 oil engine** reduction geared to sc. shaft driving 1 FP propeller Daihatsu Daihatsu Diesel Manufacturing Co Lt-Japan	
9146687 *3FOD6* -	**ZHAO QING HE** *ex* YM Hochiminh *-2004* *ex* Zhao Qing He *-2002* **Zhaoqinghe Maritime Inc** COSCO Container Lines Co Ltd (COSCON) SatCom: Inmarsat C 435684810 *Panama* *Panama* MMSI: 356848000 Official number: 2327596F	**12,122** 5,598 15,919	Class: AB	**1996-09 KK Kanasashi — Shizuoka SZ** Yd No: 3388 Loa 144.73 (BB) Br ex - Dght 8.617 Lbp 135.50 Br md 25.00 Dpth 12.80 Welded, 1 dk	**(A33A2CC) Container Ship (Fully Cellular)** TEU 836 incl 100 ref C. Compartments: 4 Cell Ho, ER 14 Ha: ER	**1 oil engine** driving 1 FP propeller Total Power: 7,988kW (10,860hp) B&W 1 x 2 Stroke 6 Cy. 500 x 1620 7988kW (10860bhp) Kawasaki Heavy Industries Ltd-Japan AuxGen: 3 x 560kW a.c Thrusters: 1 Thwart. FP thruster (f) Fuel: 1138.0 (r.f.) 31.2pd	17.0kn 6L50MC
7908677 - -	**ZHAO SHANG LIU** *ex* Zhao Gang Er Hao *-2006* *ex* Zhao Gang No. 2 *-2002* *ex* Daiken Maru *-1996* **Shenzhen Southern China LPG Shipping Co Ltd** - *Shenzhen, Guangdong* *China* MMSI: 412468980	**1,566** 469 1,567	Class: (CC) (NK)	**1979-06 Kishigami Zosen K.K. — Akitsu** Yd No: 1318 Loa 69.50 Br ex - Dght 4.513 Lbp 65.03 Br md 13.01 Dpth 6.20 Welded, 1 dk	**(A11B2TG) LPG Tanker** Liq (Gas): 1,558 2 x Gas Tank (s);	**1 oil engine** driving 1 FP propeller Total Power: 1,839kW (2,500hp) Akasaka 1 x 4 Stroke 6 Cy. 380 x 600 1839kW (2500bhp) Akasaka Tekkosho KK (Akasaka DieselLtd)-Japan AuxGen: 2 x 200kW 450V 60Hz a.c Fuel: 36.5 (d.f.) 143.5 (r.f.) 9.0pd	12.0kn AH38A
9233674 *BIJF* -	**ZHAO SHANG YI** **China Merchants Yangtze LPG Transportation Co Ltd** - *Shanghai* *China* MMSI: 412371190	**2,994** 898 1,630	Class: CC	**2001-07 Jiangnan Shipyard (Group) Co Ltd — Shanghai** Yd No: H2259 Loa 94.60 Br ex - Dght 3.600 Lbp 88.00 Br md 15.60 Dpth 5.60 Welded, 1 dk	**(A11B2TG) LPG Tanker** Liq (Gas): 3,042 2 x Gas Tank (s); 2 independent (stl) cyl horizontal 2 Cargo Pump (s): 2x300m³/hr	**2 oil engines** reduction geared to sc. shafts driving 2 FP propellers Total Power: 2,206kW (3,000hp) Yanmar 2 x 4 Stroke 8 Cy. 210 x 290 each-1103kW (1500bhp) Yanmar Diesel Engine Co Ltd-Japan AuxGen: 3 x 210kW 400V a.c Fuel: 36.0 (d.f.) 62.0 (r.f.)	13.0kn 8N21A-EN
7916064 *BJOI* -	**ZHAO SHUN** *ex* Zhong Hua 2 *-2004* *ex* Koyo Maru No. 3 *-1995* **Hainan Zhaogang Marine Co Ltd** - *Haikou, Hainan* *China* MMSI: 412522190	*998* 606 1,206	Class: (CC) (NK)	**1979-10 Higaki Zosen K.K. — Imabari** Yd No: 230 Loa 67.62 Br ex - Dght 4.379 Lbp 62.01 Br md 11.41 Dpth 5.01 Welded, 1 dk	**(A11B2TG) LPG Tanker** Liq (Gas): 1,606 2 x Gas Tank (s);	**1 oil engine** driving 1 FP propeller Total Power: 1,545kW (2,101hp) Daihatsu 1 x 4 Stroke 6 Cy. 320 x 380 1545kW (2101bhp) Daihatsu Diesel Manufacturing Co Lt-Japan AuxGen: 3 x 376kW	12.0kn 6DSM-32
9488736 - -	**ZHAO TONG** - -	**2,997** 1,935 5,000		**2007-10 Yantai Haotong Shipbuilding Co Ltd — Penglai SD** Yd No: 4 Loa 94.50 (BB) Br ex 14.85 Dght 6.500 Lbp 89.40 Br md 14.80 Dpth 8.90 Welded, 1 dk	**(A31A2GX) General Cargo Ship** Grain: 6,760; Bale: 6,440 Compartments: 2 Ho, ER 2 Ha: ER	**1 oil engine** driving 1 Propeller Total Power: 1,471kW (2,000hp) Hanshin 1 x 4 Stroke 6 Cy. 340 x 640 1471kW (2000bhp) The Hanshin Diesel Works Ltd-Japan	10.0kn LH34LG

No. / Call sign	Ship / Owner	Tonnage	Class	Built / Dimensions	Type	Machinery
625308 *JUA*	**ZHAO YANG** **Hainan Zhaogang Marine Co Ltd** - *Haikou, Hainan* *China* MMSI: 412523910	**2,563** 769 2,080	Class: CC	**2011-09 Jiangsu Sunhoo Shipbuilding Co Ltd — Taixing JS** Yd No: SH-012 Loa 88.50 Br ex - Dght 4.400 Lbp 82.20 Br md 14.00 Dpth 6.60 Welded, 1 dk	**(A11B2TG) LPG Tanker** Liq (Gas): 500 Ice Capable	**1 oil engine** driving 1 FP propeller
676791 *RPJ*	**ZHAO YANG FENG** **China Shipping Tanker Co Ltd** - *Shanghai* *China* MMSI: 414706000	**40,913** 25,963 75,396 T/cm 68.2	Class: CC	**2012-04 Jiangnan Shipyard (Group) Co Ltd — Shanghai** Yd No: H2474 Loa 225.00 (BB) Br ex - Dght 14.200 Lbp 217.00 Br md 32.26 Dpth 19.60 Welded, 1 dk	**(A21A2BC) Bulk Carrier** Grain: 90,725 Compartments: 7 Ho, ER 7 Ha: 6 (15.5 x 14.4)ER (15.5 x 13.2)	**1 oil engine** driving 1 FP propeller Total Power: 10,200kW (13,868hp) 14.5kn MAN-B&W 5S60MC 1 x 2 Stroke 5 Cy. 600 x 2292 10200kW (13868bhp) Hudong Heavy Machinery Co Ltd-China
24843	**ZHAR III** *ex* Siac II *-1993* *ex* Dublin III *-1993* *ex* Chuyo Maru No. 21 *-1993* **Inter-Arika SA** - *Nouadhibou* *Mauritania*	*349* 188 -	Class: (RI)	**1971 Yamanishi Shipbuilding Co Ltd — Ishinomaki MG** Yd No: 682 Loa 54.41 Br ex 9.05 Dght 3.353 Lbp 48.44 Br md 9.01 Dpth 5.87 Welded, 2 dks	**(B11B2FV) Fishing Vessel**	**1 oil engine** driving 1 CP propeller Total Power: 1,839kW (2,500hp) Niigata 6M40AX 1 x 4 Stroke 6 Cy. 400 x 600 1839kW (2500bhp) Niigata Engineering Co Ltd-Japan AuxGen: 1 x 352kW 220V 60Hz a.c
28438 *HVH*	**ZHARKIY** **Sakhalin Fishing Collective (Rybolovetskiy Kolkhoz 'Sakhalin')** - *Nevelsk* *Russia*	*448* 134 207	Class: (RS)	**1984-08 Zavod 'Nikolayevsk-na-Amure' — Nikolayevsk-na-Amure** Yd No: 1226 Loa 44.89 Br ex 9.48 Dght 3.771 Lbp 39.37 Br md 9.30 Dpth 5.11 Welded, 1 dk	**(B11B2FV) Fishing Vessel** Ice Capable	**1 oil engine** driving 1 FP propeller Total Power: 588kW (799hp) 11.5kn S.K.L. 6NVD48A-2U 1 x 4 Stroke 6 Cy. 320 x 480 588kW (799bhp) VEB Schwermaschinenbau "KarlLiebknecht" (SKL)-Magdeburg AuxGen: 3 x 150kW Fuel: 109.0 (d.f.)
99779	**ZHAULY** *ex* Ardesen 2 *-2011* *ex* Transpetrol-I *-2007* **Batys Munai Trans LLP** - *Aqtau* *Kazakhstan* MMSI: 436000122	*236* 190 533	Class: RS	**1985-01 Gunsin Gemi Insaat Ve Ticaret Ltd. Sti. — Tuzla** Loa - Br ex - Dght - Lbp - Br md - Dpth - Welded, 1 dk	**(A13B2TU) Tanker (unspecified)**	**1 oil engine** reduction geared to sc. shaft driving 1 Propeller Total Power: 273kW (371hp) Volvo Penta TAMD121C 1 x 4 Stroke 6 Cy. 130 x 150 273kW (371bhp) AB Volvo Penta-Sweden
24827 *VF8*	**ZHE DAI YU 02316** **Chen Fang An** Zhoushan Donghong Seafood Co Ltd *Zhoushan, Zhejiang* *China*	**232** 69 -		**2000-12 Daishan Qiujiamen Shipyard — Daishan County ZJ** Loa 40.00 Br ex - Dght 2.300 Lbp 34.39 Br md 6.40 Dpth 3.05 Welded, 1 dk	**(B12C2FL) Live Fish Carrier (Well Boat)**	**1 oil engine** geared to sc. shaft driving 1 Propeller Total Power: 257kW (349hp) Chinese Std. Type 6180ZLC 1 x 4 Stroke 6 Cy. 180 x 225 257kW (349bhp) Shanghai Diesel Engine Co Ltd-China
24762 *VF4*	**ZHE DAI YU 02605** **Wang Ren Guang** Zhoushan Donghong Seafood Co Ltd *Zhoushan, Zhejiang* *China*	**232** 69 -		**2000-12 Daishan Gaoting Shipyard — Daishan County ZJ** Loa 40.00 Br ex - Dght 2.300 Lbp 34.39 Br md 6.40 Dpth 3.05 Welded, 1 dk	**(B12C2FL) Live Fish Carrier (Well Boat)**	**1 oil engine** geared to sc. shaft driving 1 Propeller Total Power: 258kW (351hp) Chinese Std. Type Z6170ZL 1 x 4 Stroke 6 Cy. 170 x 200 258kW (351bhp) Shanghai Diesel Engine Co Ltd-China
24774 *VF3*	**ZHE DAI YU 03247** **Shen You Chang** Zhoushan Donghong Seafood Co Ltd *Zhoushan, Zhejiang* *China*	**232** 69 -		**2000-12 Daishan Gaoting Shipyard — Daishan County ZJ** Loa 40.00 Br ex - Dght 2.300 Lbp 34.39 Br md 6.40 Dpth 3.05 Welded, 1 dk	**(B12C2FL) Live Fish Carrier (Well Boat)**	**1 oil engine** geared to sc. shaft driving 1 Propeller Total Power: 260kW (353hp) Chinese Std. Type Z6170ZL 1 x 4 Stroke 6 Cy. 170 x 200 260kW (353bhp) Zibo Diesel Engine Factory-China
24786 *VF6*	**ZHE DAI YU 10004** **Yu He Ping** Zhoushan Donghong Seafood Co Ltd *Zhoushan, Zhejiang* *China*	**232** 69 -		**2000-12 Daishan Qiujiamen Shipyard — Daishan County ZJ** Loa 40.00 Br ex - Dght 2.300 Lbp 34.29 Br md 6.40 Dpth 3.05 Welded, 1 dk	**(B12C2FL) Live Fish Carrier (Well Boat)**	**1 oil engine** geared to sc. shaft driving 1 Propeller Total Power: 257kW (349hp) Chinese Std. Type 6180ZLC 1 x 4 Stroke 6 Cy. 180 x 225 257kW (349bhp) Shanghai Diesel Engine Co Ltd-China
24798 *VF5*	**ZHE DAI YU 10209** **Yu He Li** Zhoushan Donghong Seafood Co Ltd *Zhoushan, Zhejiang* *China*	**232** 69 -		**2000-12 Daishan Gaoting Shipyard — Daishan County ZJ** Loa 40.00 Br ex - Dght 2.300 Lbp 34.39 Br md 6.40 Dpth 3.05 Welded, 1 dk	**(B12C2FL) Live Fish Carrier (Well Boat)**	**1 oil engine** geared to sc. shaft driving 1 Propeller Total Power: 257kW (349hp) Chinese Std. Type 6180ZLC 1 x 4 Stroke 6 Cy. 180 x 225 257kW (349bhp) Shanghai Diesel Engine Co Ltd-China
24803 *VF7*	**ZHE DAI YU 10213** **Ren Zong Ding** Zhoushan Donghong Seafood Co Ltd *Zhoushan, Zhejiang* *China*	**232** 69 -		**2000-12 Daishan Gaoting Shipyard — Daishan County ZJ** Loa 40.00 Br ex - Dght 2.300 Lbp 34.39 Br md 6.40 Dpth 3.05 Welded, 1 dk	**(B12C2FL) Live Fish Carrier (Well Boat)**	**1 oil engine** geared to sc. shaft driving 1 Propeller Total Power: 257kW (349hp) Chinese Std. Type 6180ZLC 1 x 4 Stroke 6 Cy. 180 x 225 257kW (349bhp) Shanghai Diesel Engine Co Ltd-China
24815 *VF9*	**ZHE DAI YU 10235** **Wang Hai Bing** Zhoushan Donghong Seafood Co Ltd *Zhoushan, Zhejiang* *China*	**177** 53 -		**2001-01 Zhoushan Putuo Luomen Shiprepair & Building Co Ltd — Zhoushan ZJ** Loa 35.30 Br ex - Dght 2.300 Lbp 30.15 Br md 6.30 Dpth 3.00 Welded, 1 dk	**(B12C2FL) Live Fish Carrier (Well Boat)**	**1 oil engine** reverse reduction geared to sc. shaft driving 1 Propeller Total Power: 258kW (351hp) Weifang X6170ZC 1 x 4 Stroke 6 Cy. 170 x 200 258kW (351bhp) Weifang Diesel Engine Factory-China
24748 *UR9*	**ZHE DAI YU 11413** **Zhoushan Donghong Seafood Co Ltd** - *Zhoushan, Zhejiang* *China*	**182** 54 -		**2000-12 Zhoushan Daishan South Industrial Co Ltd — Daishan County ZJ** Loa 36.40 Br ex - Dght 2.200 Lbp 31.11 Br md 6.40 Dpth 2.95 Welded, 1 dk	**(B12C2FL) Live Fish Carrier (Well Boat)**	**1 oil engine** geared to sc. shaft driving 1 Propeller Total Power: 260kW (353hp) Chinese Std. Type Z6170ZL 1 x 4 Stroke 6 Cy. 170 x 200 260kW (353bhp) Zibo Diesel Engine Factory-China
96002 *US3*	**ZHE DAI YU 11590** **Zhoushan Donghong Seafood Co Ltd** - *Zhoushan, Zhejiang* *China* Official number: 070006000003	**182** 54 -	Class: CC	**2000-12 Daishan Qiujiamen Shipyard — Daishan County ZJ** Yd No: X0987873-3 Loa 36.40 Br ex - Dght 2.200 Lbp 31.33 Br md 6.40 Dpth 2.95 Welded, 1 dk	**(B12C2FL) Live Fish Carrier (Well Boat)**	**1 oil engine** driving 1 Propeller
48127	**ZHE DING GONG 28** *ex* Gan Nan Chang Cai 0110 *-2002* **Yang Liang Jun, Yuan Fu Qiang & Sun Zhou Na** Smart Fortune Shipping Co Ltd	**1,116** 334 449	Class: UB (Class contemplated) (ZC)	**2002-07 Zhejiang Hongguan Ship Industry Co Ltd — Linhai ZJ** Yd No: HG0202 Loa 69.20 Br ex - Dght 2.000 Lbp 63.40 Br md 11.30 Dpth 3.70 Welded, 1 dk	**(B33A2DL) Bucket Wheel Suction Dredger**	**2 oil engines** reduction geared to sc. shafts driving 2 Propellers Total Power: 1,344kW (1,828hp) Cummins 2 x 4 Stroke each-672kW (914bhp) Chongqing Cummins Engine Co Ltd-China
67489 *KS2*	**ZHE HAI 1** *ex* Zhe Hai 701 *-2012* **Sea Xiu Co Ltd** Shanghai CP International Ship Management & Broker Co Ltd *Hong Kong* *Hong Kong* MMSI: 477813500 Official number: HK-3541	**22,295** 12,759 35,056	Class: CC	**2012-06 Zhoushan Wuzhou Ship Repairing & Building Co Ltd — Zhoushan ZJ** Yd No: WZ0702 Loa 179.90 Br ex - Dght 10.800 Lbp 171.50 Br md 28.40 Dpth 15.00 Welded, 1 dk	**(A21A2BC) Bulk Carrier** Grain: 44,295 Compartments: 5 Ho, ER 5 Ha: 3 (20.3 x 19.2) (18.7 x 19.2)ER (14.7 x 17.6) Cranes: 4x30t	**1 oil engine** driving 1 FP propeller Total Power: 6,480kW (8,810hp) 13.7kn MAN-B&W 6S42MC 1 x 2 Stroke 6 Cy. 420 x 1764 6480kW (8810bhp) Imex Co Ltd-Japan AuxGen: 3 x 465kW 450V a.c
67491 *LR3*	**ZHE HAI 2** **Sea 1 Leasing Co Ltd** Zhehai Shipping Co Ltd *Hong Kong* *Hong Kong* MMSI: 477222800 Official number: HK-3745	**22,295** 12,023 35,104	Class: CC	**2012-12 Zhoushan Wuzhou Ship Repairing & Building Co Ltd — Zhoushan ZJ** Yd No: WZ0709 Loa 179.90 (BB) Br ex - Dght 10.800 Lbp 171.50 Br md 28.40 Dpth 15.00 Welded, 1 dk	**(A21A2BC) Bulk Carrier** Grain: 44,295; Bale: 42,270 Compartments: 5 Ho, ER 5 Ha: 3 (20.3 x 19.2) (18.7 x 19.2)ER (14.7 x 17.6) Cranes: 4x30t	**1 oil engine** driving 1 FP propeller Total Power: 6,480kW (8,810hp) 13.7kn MAN-B&W 6S42MC 1 x 2 Stroke 6 Cy. 420 x 1764 6480kW (8810bhp) Imex Co Ltd-Japan AuxGen: 3 x 465kW 450V a.c
03875 *LJ*	**ZHE HAI 101** **ICBC Financial Leasing Co Ltd** Zhejiang Shipping Group Wenzhou Shipping Co Ltd *Wenzhou, Zhejiang* *China* MMSI: 413451140	**30,421** 17,035 49,031	Class: CC	**2013-01 Jinling Shipyard — Nanjing JS** Yd No: JLZ9110405 Loa 199.99 Br ex - Dght 10.900 Lbp - Br md 32.26 Dpth 16.20 Welded, 1 dk	**(A21A2BC) Bulk Carrier** Grain: 57,400 Compartments: 5 Ho, ER 5 Ha: ER	**1 oil engine** driving 1 FP propeller Total Power: 6,450kW (8,769hp) 14.0kn MAN-B&W 6S46MC-C 1 x 2 Stroke 6 Cy. 460 x 1932 6450kW (8769bhp) Yichang Marine Diesel Engine Co Ltd-China

9703887 *BLMZ* -	**ZHE HAI 102** **ICBC Financial Leasing Co Ltd** Zhejiang Shipping Group Wenzhou Shipping Co Ltd *Wenzhou, Zhejiang* *China* MMSI: 414158000	**30,421** 17,035 48,972	Class: CC	**2013-05 Jinling Shipyard — Nanjing JS** Yd No: JLZ9110406 Loa 199.99 Br ex - Dght 10.900 Lbp - Br md 32.26 Dpth 16.20 Welded, 1 dk	**(A21A2BC) Bulk Carrier** Grain: 57,400 Compartments: 5 Ho, ER 5 Ha: ER	**1 oil engine** driving 1 FP propeller Total Power: 6,450kW (8,769hp) MAN-B&W 1 x 2 Stroke 6 Cy. 460 x 1932 6450kW (8769bhp) Yichang Marine Diesel Engine Co Ltd-China	14.0k 6S46MC-
9703899 *BKLC* -	**ZHE HAI 105** **ICBC Financial Leasing Co Ltd** Zhejiang Shipping Group Wenzhou Shipping Co Ltd *Wenzhou, Zhejiang* *China*	**30,421** 17,035 48,972	Class: CC	**2013-10 Jinling Shipyard — Nanjing JS** Yd No: JLZ9110407 Loa 199.99 Br ex - Dght 10.900 Lbp 192.00 Br md 32.26 Dpth 16.20 Welded, 1 dk	**(A21A2BC) Bulk Carrier** Grain: 57,400 Compartments: 5 Ho, ER 5 Ha: ER	**1 oil engine** driving 1 FP propeller Total Power: 6,450kW (8,769hp) MAN-B&W 1 x 2 Stroke 6 Cy. 460 x 1932 6450kW (8769bhp) Yichang Marine Diesel Engine Co Ltd-China	14.0k 6S46MC-
8426963 *BLJQ* -	**ZHE HAI 116** **Zhejiang Shipping Group Wenzhou Shipping Co Ltd** *Wenzhou, Zhejiang* *China* Official number: 070402000209	*2,908* 1,628 3,800		**1983 Wuhu Shipyard — Wuhu AH** Loa 98.25 Br ex - Dght 5.781 Lbp 92.83 Br md 14.03 Dpth 6.87 Welded, 1 dk	**(A31A2GX) General Cargo Ship** Compartments: 3 Ho, ER 3 Ha: (7.8 x 8.0)2 (11.7 x 9.5) Derricks: 6x5t; Winches: 6	**2 oil engines** driving 1 FP propeller Total Power: 1,324kW (1,800hp) Chinese Std. Type 2 x 4 Stroke 6 Cy. 350 x 500 each-662kW (900bhp) Shanghai Diesel Engine Co Ltd-China	6350Z
8507597 *BLKO* -	**ZHE HAI 126** *ex Giorgis -2002 ex Halla Moon -1998* *ex Ocean Cosmos -1994* **Zhejiang Wenzhou Marine Shipping Co** - SatCom: Inmarsat C 441231115 *Wenzhou, Zhejiang* *China* MMSI: 412409160	**14,814** 8,915 25,660 T/cm 36.4	Class: (GL) (KR) (NK)	**1985-06 Imabari Shipbuilding Co Ltd — Imabari EH (Imabari Shipyard)** Yd No: 451 Loa 159.44 (BB) Br ex 26.04 Dght 9.902 Lbp 149.82 Br md 26.01 Dpth 13.62 Welded, 1 dk	**(A21A2BC) Bulk Carrier** Grain: 32,014; Bale: 30,501 Compartments: 4 Ho, ER 4 Ha: (18.5 x 12.8)3 (21.6 x 12.8)ER	**1 oil engine** driving 1 CP propeller Total Power: 4,707kW (6,400hp) B&W 1 x 2 Stroke 5 Cy. 500 x 1620 4707kW (6400bhp) Hitachi Zosen Corp-Japan	14.0k 5L50MC
8400256 *BLJK* -	**ZHE HAI 151** *ex Bonasia -2004 ex Southeast Alaska -2002* *ex Alaska -1995* *launched as Sanko Prosperity -1986* **Zhejiang Wenzhou Marine Shipping Co** - SatCom: Inmarsat C 441282215 *Wenzhou, Zhejiang* *China* MMSI: 412427650	**16,608** 9,208 27,610 T/cm 37.5	Class: CC (NK)	**1986-11 Mitsui Eng. & SB. Co. Ltd. — Tamano** Yd No: 1313 Loa 168.30 (BB) Br ex - Dght 9.765 Lbp 160.00 Br md 26.00 Dpth 13.63 Welded, 1 dk	**(A21A2BC) Bulk Carrier** Grain: 34,665; Bale: 33,417 Compartments: 5 Ho, ER 5 Ha: (9.5 x 13.3)4 (18.9 x 13.3)ER Cranes: 4x25t	**1 oil engine** driving 1 FP propeller Total Power: 5,516kW (7,500hp) B&W 1 x 2 Stroke 6 Cy. 500 x 1620 5516kW (7500bhp) Mitsui Engineering & Shipbuilding CLtd-Japan	14.5k 6L50MC
9569164 *BKKZ* -	**ZHE HAI 156** **Zhejiang Shipping Group Co Ltd** - SatCom: Inmarsat C 441367010 *Wenzhou, Zhejiang* *China* MMSI: 413670000	**14,246** 7,978 23,527	Class: (CC)	**2009-05 Zhejiang Haifeng Shipbuilding Co Ltd — Linhai ZJ** Loa 166.50 Br ex - Dght 9.500 Lbp 158.00 Br md 23.00 Dpth 13.20 Welded, 1 dk	**(A21A2BC) Bulk Carrier** Grain: 28,632; Bale: 28,632 Compartments: 4 Ho, ER 4 Ha: 3 (21.0 x 13.8)ER (16.5 x 13.8) Ice Capable	**1 oil engine** reduction geared to sc. shaft driving 1 FP propeller Total Power: 4,400kW (5,982hp) Pielstick 1 x 4 Stroke 8 Cy. 400 x 460 4400kW (5982bhp) Shaanxi Diesel Heavy Industry Co Lt-China AuxGen: 2 x 320kW 400V a.c	12.6k 8PC2-
9644275 *BLLB* -	**ZHE HAI 158** **Bank of Communications Finance Leasing Co Ltd** Wenzhou Shipping Co Ltd *Wenzhou, Zhejiang* *China*	**17,271** 9,671 27,319	Class: CC	**2012-10 Zhejiang Hongxin Shipbuilding Co Ltd — Taizhou ZJ** Yd No: 2010-07 Loa 169.60 (BB) Br ex - Dght 9.500 Lbp 162.50 Br md 26.00 Dpth 13.80 Welded, 1 dk	**(A21A2BC) Bulk Carrier** Grain: 30,350 Compartments: 4 Ho, ER 4 Ha: ER Cranes: 4x30.5t	**1 oil engine** driving 1 FP propeller Daihatsu 1 x 2 Stroke	14.0k
9424302 *BLMB* -	**ZHE HAI 161** **Zhejiang Wenzhou Marine Shipping Co** - SatCom: Inmarsat C 441300079 *Wenzhou, Zhejiang* *China* MMSI: 413413210 Official number: 0704070001	**19,983** 11,456 33,478	Class: CC	**2007-07 Zhoushan Wuzhou Ship Repairing & Building Co Ltd — Zhoushan ZJ** Yd No: 0502 Loa 178.00 (BB) Br ex - Dght 9.600 Lbp 170.80 Br md 27.60 Dpth 13.90 Welded, 1 dk	**(A21A2BC) Bulk Carrier** Grain: 40,522 Compartments: 5 Ho, ER 5 Ha: 4 (19.2 x 14.4)ER (13.6 x 14.4) Cranes: 4x25t	**1 oil engine** driving 1 FP propeller Total Power: 6,480kW (8,810hp) MAN-B&W 1 x 2 Stroke 6 Cy. 420 x 1764 6480kW (8810bhp) Yichang Marine Diesel Engine Co Ltd-China AuxGen: 3 x 425kW 400V a.c	13.6k 6S42M
9552305 *BKLD* -	**ZHE HAI 162** **Zhejiang Wenzhou Marine Shipping Co** *Wenzhou, Zhejiang* *China* MMSI: 413654000	**19,944** 11,709 33,400	Class: CC	**2009-02 Zhejiang Tianshi Shipbuilding Co Ltd — Wenling ZJ** Yd No: TS023 Loa 178.00 Br ex - Dght 9.600 Lbp 170.80 Br md 27.60 Dpth 13.90 Welded, 1 dk	**(A21A2BC) Bulk Carrier** Grain: 40,210 Compartments: 5 Ho, ER 5 Ha: 4 (19.2 x 14.4)ER (13.6 x 14.4)	**1 oil engine** driving 1 FP propeller Total Power: 6,389kW (8,686hp) MAN-B&W 1 x 2 Stroke 6 Cy. 420 x 1764 6389kW (8686bhp) Yichang Marine Diesel Engine Co Ltd-China AuxGen: 3 x 425kW 400V a.c	13.5k 6S42M
9467093 *BKME* -	**ZHE HAI 167** **Wenzhou Shipping Co Ltd** - SatCom: Inmarsat C 441301498 *Wenzhou, Zhejiang* *China* MMSI: 413439080	**33,147** 19,624 57,014	Class: CC	**2011-04 Zhoushan Wuzhou Ship Repairing & Building Co Ltd — Zhoushan ZJ** Yd No: WZ0608 Loa 189.99 (BB) Br ex - Dght 12.890 Lbp 183.00 Br md 32.26 Dpth 18.00 Welded, 1 dk	**(A21A2BC) Bulk Carrier** Grain: 72,000 Compartments: 5 Ho, ER 5 Ha: 4 (21.3 x 18.3)ER (18.9 x 18.3) Cranes: 4x36t	**1 oil engine** driving 1 FP propeller Total Power: 9,480kW (12,889hp) MAN-B&W 1 x 2 Stroke 6 Cy. 500 x 2000 9480kW (12889bhp) Hudong Heavy Machinery Co Ltd-China AuxGen: 3 x 615kW 450V a.c	14.5k 6S50MC-
9492373 *BIAH8* -	**ZHE HAI 168** **CMB Financial Leasing Co Ltd** Wenzhou Shipping Co Ltd SatCom: Inmarsat C 441301733 *Shanghai* *China* MMSI: 413376320	**33,147** 19,624 57,014	Class: CC	**2011-03 Zhoushan Wuzhou Ship Repairing & Building Co Ltd — Zhoushan ZJ** Yd No: WZ0703 Loa 189.99 (BB) Br ex - Dght 12.890 Lbp 183.80 Br md 32.26 Dpth 18.00 Welded, 1 dk	**(A21A2BC) Bulk Carrier** Grain: 71,633 Compartments: 5 Ho, ER 5 Ha: 4 (21.3 x 18.3)ER (18.9 x 18.3) Cranes: 4x36t	**1 oil engine** driving 1 FP propeller Total Power: 9,960kW (13,542hp) MAN-B&W 1 x 2 Stroke 6 Cy. 500 x 2000 9960kW (13542bhp) Hudong Heavy Machinery Co Ltd-China AuxGen: 3 x 615kW 450V a.c	14.5k 6S50MC
9622784 *BIAN4* -	**ZHE HAI 169** **Bank of Communications Finance Leasing Co Ltd** Zhejiang Shipping Group Wenzhou Shipping Co Ltd *Shanghai* *China* MMSI: 412029000	**32,962** 19,142 57,000 T/cm 58.8	Class: CC	**2011-08 China Shipping Industry (Jiangsu) Co Ltd — Jiangdu JS** Yd No: IS57000/B-06 Loa 189.99 (BB) Br ex 32.30 Dght 12.800 Lbp 185.00 Br md 32.26 Dpth 18.00 Welded, 1 dk	**(A21A2BC) Bulk Carrier** Grain: 71,634; Bale: 68,200 Compartments: 5 Ho, ER 5 Ha: 4 (21.3 x 18.3)ER (18.9 x 18.3) Cranes: 4x30t	**1 oil engine** driving 1 FP propeller Total Power: 9,480kW (12,889hp) MAN-B&W 1 x 2 Stroke 6 Cy. 500 x 2000 9480kW (12889bhp) Yichang Marine Diesel Engine Co Ltd-China AuxGen: 3 x 615kW 450V a.c	14.2k 6S50MC-
9073115 *BLGR* -	**ZHE HAI 302** **Zhejiang Shipping Group Wenzhou Shipping Co Ltd** - SatCom: Inmarsat C 441289212 *Taizhou, Zhejiang* *China* MMSI: 412400390 Official number: 070502000337	*3,421* 1,916 4,652		**1993-11 Wuhu Shipyard — Wuhu AH** Yd No: 4300-8 Loa - Br ex - Dght - Lbp - Br md - Dpth - Welded, 1 dk	**(A31A2GX) General Cargo Ship**	**1 oil engine** driving 1 FP propeller	
8863044 *BLGF* -	**ZHE HAI 307** **Xiangshan County Shipping Co Ltd** - *Ningbo, Zhejiang* *China*	*883* 517 1,186	Class: (CC)	**1982-07 Zhejiang Shipyard — Ningbo ZJ** Loa 64.88 Br ex - Dght 4.200 Lbp 59.23 Br md 10.80 Dpth 5.35 Welded, 1 dk	**(A31A2GX) General Cargo Ship** Grain: 1,617; Bale: 1,509 Compartments: 2 Ho, ER 2 Ha: 2 (9.9 x 4.5)ER	**1 oil engine** driving 1 FP propeller Total Power: 662kW (900hp) Chinese Std. Type 1 x 4 Stroke 6 Cy. 350 x 500 662kW (900bhp) Shanghai Diesel Engine Co Ltd-China AuxGen: 2 x 75kW 400V a.c	11.0k 635
8858269 *BLGJ* -	**ZHE HAI 311** **Government of The People's Republic of China (Zhejiang Province Shipping Co - Haimen Branch)** - *Ningbo, Zhejiang* *China*	*492* 276 950	Class: (CC)	**1979 Zhejiang Shipyard — Ningbo ZJ** Loa 53.56 Br ex - Dght 3.600 Lbp 48.00 Br md 8.80 Dpth 4.20 Welded, 1 dk	**(A31A2GX) General Cargo Ship** Grain: 898; Bale: 809 Compartments: 2 Ho, ER 2 Ha: 2 (8.1 x 4.1)ER	**1 oil engine** geared to sc. shaft driving 1 FP propeller Total Power: 294kW (400hp) Chinese Std. Type 1 x 4 Stroke 6 Cy. 300 x 380 294kW (400bhp) (made 1978) Guangzhou Diesel Engine Factory CoLtd-China AuxGen: 2 x 50kW 400V a.c	10.0k 63

832435 *LGP*	**ZHE HAI 312** **Government of The People's Republic of China (Zhejiang Province Shipping Co - Haimen Branch)** - SatCom: Inmarsat C 441289312 *China* MMSI: 412400470	*3,347* 1,874 4,812		**1989 Wuhu Shipyard — Wuhu AH** Loa 106.55 Br ex - Dght 5.800 Lbp 99.93 Br md 14.00 Dpth 7.80 Welded, 1 dk	**(A21A2BC) Bulk Carrier** Grain: 4,906 Compartments: 2 Ho, ER 2 Ha: 2 (22.1 x 9.5)ER	**2 oil engines** geared to sc. shafts driving 2 FP propellers Total Power: 1,500kW (2,040hp) 12.0kn Chinese Std. Type 6300 2 x 4 Stroke 6 Cy. 300 x 380 each-750kW (1020bhp) Yichang Marine Diesel Engine Co Ltd-China AuxGen: 3 x 90kW 400V a.c
201349 *LGO*	**ZHE HAI 323** *ex* St. Croix *-2002* *ex* General Mojica *-1999* **Taizhou Shipping Co Ltd** - *Taizhou, Zhejiang* *China* MMSI: 412411430 Official number: 412411430	**12,516** 6,143 18,392 T/cm 29.9	Class: (LR) (CC) ✠ Classed LR until 22/11/02	**1985-09 Guangzhou Shipyard — Guangzhou GD** Yd No: 1106 Loa 160.00 (BB) Br ex 22.05 Dght 8.816 Lbp 149.99 Br md 22.00 Dpth 12.50 Welded, 1 dk	**(A21A2BC) Bulk Carrier** Grain: 23,865; Bale: 22,505 Compartments: 5 Ho, ER 5 Ha: (14.0 x 11.2)4 (16.0 x 11.2)ER Cranes: 4x15t	**1 oil engine** driving 1 FP propeller Total Power: 4,928kW (6,700hp) 13.5kn B&W 5L55GA 1 x 2 Stroke 5 Cy. 550 x 1380 4928kW (6700bhp) Hudong Shipyard-China AuxGen: 3 x 376kW 450V 60Hz a.c Boilers: e 11.5kgf/cm² (11.3bar), AuxB (o.f.) 8.0kgf/cm² (7.8bar) Fuel: 143.0 (d.f.) 1115.5 (r.f.)
110564 *LGB*	**ZHE HAI 331** *ex* Ling Quan He *-2009* *ex* Papua *-1985* **Taizhou Jiangnan Shipping Co Ltd** - SatCom: Inmarsat C 441273610 *Taizhou, Jiangsu* *China* MMSI: 413415240	*7,722* 4,237 10,937 T/cm 24.4	Class: (LR) (CC) ✠ Classed LR until 15/3/85	**1983-06 Guangzhou Shipyard — Guangzhou GD** Yd No: 1101 Loa 134.45 (BB) Br ex 20.86 Dght 7.750 Lbp 124.55 Br md 20.80 Dpth 10.50 Welded, 1 dk	**(A31A2GX) General Cargo Ship** Grain: 14,200 TEU 672 C Ho 276 TEU C Dk 396 TEU incl 32 ref C. Compartments: 6 Ho, ER 12 Ha: 12 (12.9 x 8.3)ER	**1 oil engine** driving 1 FP propeller Total Power: 5,180kW (7,043hp) 14.5kn B&W 8L45GB 1 x 2 Stroke 8 Cy. 450 x 1200 5180kW (7043bhp) Mitsui Engineering & Shipbuilding CLtd-Japan AuxGen: 3 x 480kW 450V 60Hz a.c Thrusters: 1 Thwart. CP thruster (f) Fuel: 139.5 (d.f.) 565.0 (r.f.)
560962 *IAB2*	**ZHE HAI 360** *ex* Yuan Xiang 11 *-2010* **Bank of Communications Finance Leasing Co Ltd** Taizhou Shipping Co Ltd *Shanghai* *China* MMSI: 413561000	**19,958** 11,456 33,100	Class: CC	**2010-01 Zhejiang Tianshi Shipbuilding Co Ltd — Wenling ZJ** Yd No: TS025 Loa 178.00 (BB) Br ex - Dght 9.600 Lbp 170.80 Br md 27.60 Dpth 13.90 Welded, 1 dk	**(A21A2BC) Bulk Carrier** Grain: 40,528 Compartments: 5 Ho, ER 5 Ha: 4 (19.2 x 14.4)ER (13.6 x 14.4) Cranes: 4x30t	**1 oil engine** driving 1 FP propeller Total Power: 5,830kW (7,926hp) 13.5kn MAN-B&W 6S42MC 1 x 2 Stroke 6 Cy. 420 x 1764 5830kW (7926bhp) STX Engine Co Ltd-South Korea AuxGen: 3 x 425kW 400V a.c
562477 *IAC9*	**ZHE HAI 362** *ex* Xing Long Zhou 818 *-2010* *ex* HQ1016 *-2010* *ex* Hangguan 818 *-2010* **Bank of Communications Finance Leasing Co Ltd** Taizhou Shipping Co Ltd *Shanghai* *China* MMSI: 412377290	**22,382** 11,772 35,091 T/cm 47.4	Class: CC (BV)	**2010-04 Zhejiang Tenglong Shipyard — Wenling ZJ** Yd No: HQ1016 Loa 179.88 (BB) Br ex - Dght 10.270 Lbp 172.00 Br md 28.80 Dpth 14.60 Welded, 1 dk	**(A21A2BC) Bulk Carrier** Grain: 45,647 Compartments: 5 Ho, ER 5 Ha: 4 (20.0 x 20.0)ER (13.6 x 15.4) Cranes: 4x30.5t	**1 oil engine** reduction geared to sc. shaft driving 1 FP propeller Total Power: 6,480kW (8,810hp) 14.0kn MAN-B&W 6S42MC 1 x 2 Stroke 6 Cy. 420 x 1764 6480kW (8810bhp) STX Engine Co Ltd-South Korea AuxGen: 3 x 465kW 450V a.c
580778 *IAK5*	**ZHE HAI 363** **CMB Financial Leasing Co Ltd** Zhejiang Shipping Group Co Ltd *Shanghai* *China* MMSI: 414016000	**33,147** 19,899 57,525	Class: CC	**2011-03 Zhoushan Wuzhou Ship Repairing & Building Co Ltd — Zhoushan ZJ** Yd No: WZ0609 Loa 189.99 (BB) Br ex - Dght 12.890 Lbp 183.80 Br md 32.26 Dpth 18.00 Welded, 1 dk	**(A21A2BC) Bulk Carrier** Grain: 71,633 Compartments: 5 Ho, ER 5 Ha: 4 (21.3 x 18.3)ER (18.9 x 18.3) Cranes: 4x36t	**1 oil engine** driving 1 FP propeller Total Power: 9,480kW (12,889hp) 14.5kn MAN-B&W 6S50MC-C8 1 x 2 Stroke 6 Cy. 500 x 2000 9480kW (12889bhp) Hudong Heavy Machinery Co Ltd-China AuxGen: 3 x 615kW 450V a.c
449302 *LGZ*	**ZHE HAI 365** *ex* Zhe Hai 358 *-2012* **CMB Financial Leasing Co Ltd** Taizhou Shipping Co Ltd SatCom: Inmarsat C 441300118 *Taizhou, Zhejiang* *China* MMSI: 413415250	**19,983** 11,456 33,348	Class: CC	**2007-10 Zhoushan Wuzhou Ship Repairing & Building Co Ltd — Zhoushan ZJ** Yd No: 0503 Loa 178.00 (BB) Br ex - Dght 9.600 Lbp 170.80 Br md 27.60 Dpth 13.90 Welded, 1 dk	**(A21A2BC) Bulk Carrier** Grain: 40,726; Bale: 40,522 Compartments: 5 Ho, ER 5 Ha: ER 5 (19.2 x 14.4)	**1 oil engine** driving 1 FP propeller Total Power: 5,830kW (7,926hp) 13.5kn MAN-B&W 6S42MC 1 x 2 Stroke 6 Cy. 420 x 1764 5830kW (7926bhp) Yichang Marine Diesel Engine Co Ltd-China AuxGen: 3 x 425kW 400V a.c
567477 *LWN*	**ZHE HAI 505** **Zhejiang Shipping Group Co Ltd** - *Ningbo, Zhejiang* *China* MMSI: 413442980	**22,295** 12,759 35,130	Class: CC	**2011-11 Zhoushan Wuzhou Ship Repairing & Building Co Ltd — Zhoushan ZJ** Yd No: WZ0701 Loa 179.90 (BB) Br ex - Dght 10.800 Lbp 171.50 Br md 28.40 Dpth 15.00 Welded, 1 dk	**(A21A2BC) Bulk Carrier** Grain: 44,295; Bale: 42,270 Compartments: 5 Ho, ER 5 Ha: 3 (20.3 x 19.2) (18.7 x 19.2)ER (14.7 x 17.6) Cranes: 4x30t	**1 oil engine** driving 1 FP propeller Total Power: 6,480kW (8,810hp) 13.7kn MAN-B&W 6S42MC7 1 x 2 Stroke 6 Cy. 420 x 1764 6480kW (8810bhp) STX Engine Co Ltd-South Korea AuxGen: 3 x 465kW 450V a.c
416513 *LWO*	**ZHE HAI 507** **Zhehai Shipping Co Ltd** - *Hangzhou, Zhejiang* *China* MMSI: 413409620	**19,921** 11,456 33,478	Class: CC	**2007-04 Zhoushan Wuzhou Ship Repairing & Building Co Ltd — Zhoushan ZJ** Yd No: 0501 Loa 178.00 (BB) Br ex - Dght 9.600 Lbp 170.80 Br md 27.60 Dpth 13.90 Welded, 1 dk	**(A21A2BC) Bulk Carrier** Grain: 40,522 Compartments: 5 Ho, ER 5 Ha: 4 (19.2 x 14.4)ER (13.6 x 14.4)	**1 oil engine** driving 1 FP propeller Total Power: 6,480kW (8,810hp) 13.5kn MAN-B&W 6S42MC 1 x 2 Stroke 6 Cy. 420 x 1764 6480kW (8810bhp) Yichang Marine Diesel Engine Co Ltd-China AuxGen: 3 x 425kW 400V a.c
670092 *LWS*	**ZHE HAI 511** **Zhejiang Shipping Group Co Ltd** Zhehai Shipping Co Ltd *Ningbo, Zhejiang* *China* MMSI: 414161000	**30,136** 16,296 48,573	Class: CC	**2013-02 Zhoushan Wuzhou Ship Repairing & Building Co Ltd — Zhoushan ZJ** Yd No: WZ1101 Loa 189.99 (BB) Br ex - Dght 11.200 Lbp 185.00 Br md 32.26 Dpth 16.00 Welded, 1 dk	**(A21A2BC) Bulk Carrier** Grain: 62,697; Bale: 58,758 Compartments: 5 Ho, ER 5 Ha: 4 (21.3 x 18.3)ER (18.9 x 18.3) Cranes: 4x36t Ice Capable	**1 oil engine** driving 1 FP propeller Total Power: 7,415kW (10,081hp) 13.7kn MAN-B&W 6S50MC-C8 1 x 2 Stroke 6 Cy. 500 x 2000 7415kW (10081bhp) Hudong Heavy Machinery Co Ltd-China AuxGen: 3 x 778kW 400V a.c
677583 *IBH5*	**ZHE HAI 512** **CMB Financial Leasing Co Ltd** Zhehai Shipping Co Ltd *Shanghai* *China* MMSI: 414170000	**30,136** 16,296 48,662	Class: CC	**2013-06 Zhoushan Wuzhou Ship Repairing & Building Co Ltd — Zhoushan ZJ** Yd No: WZ1102 Loa 189.99 (BB) Br ex - Dght 11.200 Lbp 185.00 Br md 32.26 Dpth 16.00 Welded, 1 dk	**(A21A2BC) Bulk Carrier** Grain: 62,508; Bale: 58,758 Compartments: 5 Ho, ER 5 Ha: 4 (21.3 x 18.3)ER (18.9 x 18.3) Cranes: 4x36t Ice Capable	**1 oil engine** driving 1 FP propeller Total Power: 7,415kW (10,081hp) 13.7kn MAN-B&W 6S50MC-C8 1 x 2 Stroke 6 Cy. 500 x 2000 7415kW (10081bhp) Hudong Heavy Machinery Co Ltd-China AuxGen: 3 x 622kW 400V a.c
679062 *SEH*	**ZHE HAI 515** **ICBC Financial Leasing Co Ltd** Zhehai Shipping Co Ltd *Tianjin* *China* MMSI: 414171000	**30,136** 16,296 48,679	Class: CC	**2013-08 Zhoushan Wuzhou Ship Repairing & Building Co Ltd — Zhoushan ZJ** Yd No: WZ1103 Loa 189.99 (BB) Br ex - Dght 11.200 Lbp 185.00 Br md 32.26 Dpth 16.00 Welded, 1 dk	**(A21A2BC) Bulk Carrier** Grain: 62,509; Bale: 58,758 Compartments: 5 Ho, ER 5 Ha: 4 (21.3 x 18.3)ER (18.9 x 18.3) Cranes: 4x36t Ice Capable	**1 oil engine** driving 1 FP propeller Total Power: 7,415kW (10,081hp) 13.7kn MAN-B&W 6S50MC-C8 1 x 2 Stroke 6 Cy. 500 x 2000 7415kW (10081bhp) Hudong Heavy Machinery Co Ltd-China AuxGen: 3 x 590kW 400V a.c
679074 *SEN*	**ZHE HAI 516** **Zhejiang Shipping Group Co Ltd** - *Tianjin* *China* MMSI: 414169000	**30,171** 16,296 48,558	Class: CC	**2013-11 Zhoushan Wuzhou Ship Repairing & Building Co Ltd — Zhoushan ZJ** Yd No: WZ1104 Loa 189.99 (BB) Br ex - Dght 10.500 Lbp 185.00 Br md 32.26 Dpth 16.00 Welded, 1 dk	**(A21A2BC) Bulk Carrier** Grain: 62,509; Bale: 58,758 Compartments: 5 Ho, ER 5 Ha: 4 (21.3 x 18.3)ER (18.9 x 18.3) Cranes: 4x36t Ice Capable	**1 oil engine** driving 1 FP propeller Total Power: 7,415kW (10,081hp) 13.7kn MAN-B&W 6S50MC-C8 1 x 2 Stroke 6 Cy. 500 x 2000 7415kW (10081bhp) STX Engine Co Ltd-South Korea AuxGen: 3 x 590kW 400V a.c
702998 *IBK3*	**ZHE HAI 517** **CMB Financial Leasing Co Ltd** Zhejiang Shipping Group Co Ltd *Shanghai* *China* MMSI: 414180000	**30,171** 16,296 48,614	Class: CC	**2013-11 Zhoushan Wuzhou Ship Repairing & Building Co Ltd — Zhoushan ZJ** Yd No: WZ1105 Loa 189.99 (BB) Br ex - Dght 10.500 Lbp 185.00 Br md 32.26 Dpth 16.00 Welded, 1 dk	**(A21A2BC) Bulk Carrier** Grain: 62,509; Bale: 58,758 Compartments: 5 Ho, ER 5 Ha: 4 (21.3 x 18.3)ER (18.9 x 18.3) Cranes: 4x36t Ice Capable	**1 oil engine** driving 1 FP propeller Total Power: 7,415kW (10,081hp) 13.7kn MAN-B&W 6S50MC-C8 1 x 2 Stroke 6 Cy. 500 x 2000 7415kW (10081bhp) Hudong Heavy Machinery Co Ltd-China AuxGen: 3 x 590kW 400V a.c
706322 *LWE*	**ZHE HAI 519** **ICBC Financial Leasing Co Ltd** Zhehai Shipping Co Ltd *Ningbo, Zhejiang* *China* MMSI: 413453060	**30,171** 16,296 49,000	Class: CC	**2013-12 Zhoushan Wuzhou Ship Repairing & Building Co Ltd — Zhoushan ZJ** Yd No: WZ1106 Loa 189.99 (BB) Br ex - Dght 11.200 Lbp 185.00 Br md 32.26 Dpth 16.00 Welded, 1 dk	**(A21A2BC) Bulk Carrier** Grain: 62,500; Bale: 58,758 Compartments: 5 Ho, ER 5 Ha: 4 (21.3 x 18.3)ER (18.9 x 18.3) Cranes: 4x36t	**1 oil engine** driving 1 FP propeller Total Power: 9,960kW (13,542hp) 13.7kn MAN-B&W 6S50MC-C8 1 x 2 Stroke 6 Cy. 500 x 2000 9960kW (13542bhp) Hudong Heavy Machinery Co Ltd-China AuxGen: 3 x a.c
467079 *LWP*	**ZHE HAI 521** **Zhehai Shipping Co Ltd** - *Ningbo, Zhejiang* *China* MMSI: 413364000	**31,568** 18,779 54,036	Class: CC	**2008-05 Zhoushan Wuzhou Ship Repairing & Building Co Ltd — Zhoushan ZJ** Yd No: WZ0606 Loa 189.90 (BB) Br ex 32.66 Dght 11.000 Lbp 182.00 Br md 32.26 Dpth 17.60 Welded, 1 dk	**(A21A2BC) Bulk Carrier** Grain: 68,023 Compartments: 5 Ho, ER 5 Ha: 4 (21.3 x 18.3)ER (18.9 x 18.3) Cranes: 4x36t	**1 oil engine** driving 1 FP propeller Total Power: 9,480kW (12,889hp) 14.6kn MAN-B&W 6S50MC-C 1 x 2 Stroke 6 Cy. 500 x 2000 9480kW (12889bhp) Hudong Heavy Machinery Co Ltd-China AuxGen: 3 x 570kW 450V a.c

9467081 **ZHE HAI 522**
BLWQ
-
Zhehai Shipping Co Ltd
SatCom: Inmarsat C 441377610
Ningbo, Zhejiang *China*
MMSI: 413776000

31,561 Class: CC
18,938
54,243

2009-08 Zhoushan Wuzhou Ship Repairing & Building Co Ltd — Zhoushan ZJ
Yd No: WZ0607
Loa 189.90 (BB) Br ex - Dght 12.630
Lbp 182.00 Br md 32.26 Dpth 17.60
Welded, 1 dk

(A21A2BC) Bulk Carrier
Grain: 68,126
Compartments: 5 Ho, ER
5 Ha: 4 (21.3 x 18.3)ER (18.9 x 18.3)
Cranes: 4x36t

1 oil engine driving 1 FP propeller
Total Power: 9,480kW (12,889hp) 14.6k
MAN-B&W 6S50MC-(
1 x 2 Stroke 6 Cy. 500 x 2000 9480kW (12889bhp)
Hudong Heavy Machinery Co Ltd-China
AuxGen: 3 x 570kW 450V a.c
Fuel: 1638.0 (r.f.)

9567518 **ZHE HAI 525**
BLWR
-
Zhehai Shipping Co Ltd
-
Ningbo, Zhejiang *China*
MMSI: 414061000

33,147 Class: CC
19,899
57,283

2011-12 Zhoushan Wuzhou Ship Repairing & Building Co Ltd — Zhoushan ZJ
Yd No: WZ0706
Loa 189.99 (BB) Br ex - Dght 12.890
Lbp 183.80 Br md 32.26 Dpth 18.00
Welded, 1 dk

(A21A2BC) Bulk Carrier
Grain: 72,245
Compartments: 5 Ho, ER
5 Ha: 4 (21.3 x 18.3)ER (18.9 x 18.3)
Cranes: 4x36t

1 oil engine driving 1 FP propeller
Total Power: 9,960kW (13,542hp) 14.5kr
MAN-B&W 6S50MC-C8
1 x 2 Stroke 6 Cy. 500 x 2000 9960kW (13542bhp)
Hudong Heavy Machinery Co Ltd-China
AuxGen: 3 x 615kW 450V a.c

9567532 **ZHE HAI 526**
BIAX7
-
Bank of Communications Finance Leasing Co Ltd
Zhejiang Shipping Group Co Ltd
Shanghai *China*
MMSI: 412537000

33,147 Class: CC
19,899
57,226

2012-06 Zhoushan Wuzhou Ship Repairing & Building Co Ltd — Zhoushan ZJ
Yd No: WZ0708
Loa 189.99 (BB) Br ex - Dght 12.890
Lbp 183.80 Br md 32.26 Dpth 18.00
Welded, 1 dk

(A21A2BC) Bulk Carrier
Grain: 72,245
Compartments: 5 Ho, ER
5 Ha: 4 (21.3 x 18.3)ER (18.9 x 18.3)
Cranes: 4x36t

1 oil engine driving 1 FP propeller
Total Power: 9,960kW (13,542hp) 14.5kn
MAN-B&W 6S50MC-C8
1 x 2 Stroke 6 Cy. 500 x 2000 9960kW (13542bhp)
Hudong Heavy Machinery Co Ltd-China
AuxGen: 3 x 615kW 450V a.c

8884414 **ZHE HAI 702**
BLPJ
-
Zhejiang Zhoushan No 1 Sea Transportation Co
-
Zhoushan, Zhejiang *China*

496 Class: (CC)
222
-

1981-07 Zhoushan No 1 Sea Transportation Corp Shipyard — Zhoushan ZJ
Loa 53.36 Br ex - Dght -
Lbp 48.00 Br md 8.80 Dpth 4.20
Welded, 1 dk

(A31A2GX) General Cargo Ship
Grain: 809
Compartments: 2 Ho, ER
2 Ha: 2 (8.1 x 4.2)ER

1 oil engine geared to sc. shaft driving 1 FP propeller
Total Power: 216kW (294hp) 11.1kn
Chinese Std. Type 6300
1 x 4 Stroke 6 Cy. 300 x 380 216kW (294bhp)
Guangzhou Diesel Engine Factory CoLtd-China
AuxGen: 2 x 50kW 400V a.c

8832370 **ZHE HAI 906**
-
Zhejiang Shipping Group Wenzhou Shipping Co Ltd
-
Wenzhou, Zhejiang *China*

276
154
360

1984-01 Wenzhou Shipyard — Wenzhou ZJ
Loa 38.55 Br ex - Dght 3.000
Lbp 35.00 Br md 7.40 Dpth 3.50
Welded, 1 dk

(A31A2GX) General Cargo Ship
Grain: 421
Compartments: 1 Ho, ER
1 Ha: (14.4 x 3.6)ER

1 oil engine reduction geared to sc. shaft driving 1 FP propeller
Total Power: 136kW (185hp) 9.0kn
Chinese Std. Type 6160A
1 x 4 Stroke 6 Cy. 160 x 225 136kW (185bhp)
Weifang Diesel Engine Factory-China
AuxGen: 1 x 24kW 400V a.c

8832382 **ZHE HAI 907**
-
Zhejiang Shipping Group Wenzhou Shipping Co Ltd
-
Wenzhou, Zhejiang *China*

276
154
360

1984-01 Wenzhou Shipyard — Wenzhou ZJ
Loa 38.55 Br ex - Dght 3.000
Lbp 35.00 Br md 7.40 Dpth 3.50
Welded, 1 dk

(A31A2GX) General Cargo Ship
Grain: 421
Compartments: 1 Ho, ER
1 Ha: (14.4 x 3.6)ER

1 oil engine reduction geared to sc. shaft driving 1 FP propeller
Total Power: 136kW (185hp) 9.0kn
Chinese Std. Type 6160A
1 x 4 Stroke 6 Cy. 160 x 225 136kW (185bhp)
Weifang Diesel Engine Factory-China
AuxGen: 1 x 24kW 400V a.c

9699531 **ZHE JIAO JI 1041**
-
-
SMI Co Ltd

622 Class: IZ ZC (Class contemplated)
348
993

2013-08 Taizhou Donghai Shiprepair & Building Co Ltd — Wenling ZJ Yd No: DH201221
Loa 59.05 Br ex - Dght -
Lbp 55.60 Br md 9.20 Dpth 4.35
Welded, 1 dk

(A13B2TP) Products Tanker
Double Hull (13F)

1 oil engine reduction geared to sc. shaft driving 1 Propeller
Total Power: 956kW (1,300hp)
Daihatsu 6DKM-20
1 x 4 Stroke 6 Cy. 200 x 300 956kW (1300bhp)
Anqing Marine Diesel Engine Works-China

9713258 **ZHE JIAO JI 1044**
T3MN2
-
SMI Co Ltd
-
Tarawa *Kiribati*
Official number: K-17141487

643 Class: IZ ZC (Class contemplated)
360
999

2014-02 Taizhou Donghai Shiprepair & Building Co Ltd — Wenling ZJ Yd No: DH201308
Loa 59.60 Br ex - Dght 3.400
Lbp 56.15 Br md 9.20 Dpth 4.35
Welded, 1 dk

(A13B2TP) Products Tanker
Double Hull (13F)

1 oil engine reduction geared to sc. shaft driving 1 Propeller
Total Power: 956kW (1,300hp)
Daihatsu 6DKM-20
1 x 4 Stroke 6 Cy. 200 x 300 956kW (1300bhp)
Anqing Marine Diesel Engine Works-China

9025649 **ZHE LENG 7**
BKAE5
ex Min Yuan Yu Yun 8 *-2007*
Linguocun Lichengzhuang
Ningbo Merchant Shipping Co Ltd
SatCom: Inmarsat C 441200193
Ningbo, Zhejiang *China*
MMSI: 412672930

473 Class: CC
141
-

1986-08 Fu'an Saiqi Shipyard — Fu'an FJ
Loa 56.80 Br ex - Dght 3.100
Lbp 49.70 Br md 8.40 Dpth 4.00
Welded, 1 dk

(B12C2FL) Live Fish Carrier (Well Boat)

1 oil engine reduction geared to sc. shaft driving 1 Propeller
Total Power: 736kW (1,001hp)
Chinese Std. Type 8300ZC
1 x 4 Stroke 8 Cy. 300 x 380 736kW (1001bhp)
Sichuan Diesel Engine Factory-China

8977053 **ZHE LENG 8**
BLER
-
Xiangshan Haihua Economic & Trading Co Ltd
Ningbo Merchant Shipping Co Ltd
SatCom: Inmarsat C 441263215
Ningbo, Zhejiang *China*
MMSI: 412418270

499 Class: CC
180
645

2001-01 Wenling Shiprepair & Building Co — Wenling ZJ
Converted From: Refrigerated Cargo Ship-2007
Lengthened-2009
Loa 59.39 Br ex - Dght 3.200
Lbp 54.55 Br md 8.25 Dpth 4.10
Welded, 1 dk

(A34A2GR) Refrigerated Cargo Ship
Compartments: 6 Ho/Ta, ER
6 Ha: ER

1 oil engine geared to sc. shaft driving 1 FP propeller
Total Power: 440kW (598hp)
Chinese Std. Type Z6170ZL
1 x 4 Stroke 6 Cy. 170 x 200 440kW (598bhp)
Zibo Diesel Engine Factory-China

9575890 **ZHE LIN GONG 12**
BLGI7
-
Zhejiang Fangyuan Ship Industry Co Ltd
-
Taizhou, Zhejiang *China*
MMSI: 413437940

5,104 Class: CC
1,531
7,863

2010-07 Zhejiang Fangyuan Ship Industry Co Ltd — Linhai ZJ Yd No: FY10
Loa 105.00 Br ex - Dght 4.800
Lbp 95.20 Br md 19.00 Dpth 8.00
Welded, 1 dk

(B33B2DT) Trailing Suction Hopper Dredger
Hopper: 5,500

2 oil engines reduction geared to sc. shafts driving 2 Propellers
Total Power: 5,594kW (7,606hp) 12.0kn
Chinese Std. Type X8320ZC
2 x 4 Stroke 8 Cy. 320 x 440 each-2797kW (3803bhp)
Wuxi Antai Power Machinery Co Ltd-China

8649072 **ZHE LING YU YUN 925**
-
ex Zhe Ling Yu Leng 125 *-2000*
Wenling Shitang Fisheries Management Co Ltd

357
189
-

2000-10 Taizhou Jiaojiang Yuanshan Shbldg & Repair Yard — Taizhou ZJ
Loa 49.86 Br ex - Dght 3.150
Lbp 46.50 Br md 8.00 Dpth 3.80
Welded, 1 dk

(A34A2GR) Refrigerated Cargo Ship

1 oil engine reduction geared to sc. shaft driving 1 Propeller
Total Power: 300kW (408hp)
Chinese Std. Type Z8E160C
1 x 4 Stroke 8 Cy. 160 x 225 300kW (408bhp)
in China

8745826 **ZHE LING YU YUN 933**
-
-
Wenling Shitang Fisheries Management Co Ltd
-
China
Official number: 331000001053

390
210
500

2001-04 Haidong Shipyard — Taizhou ZJ
Loa 53.05 Br ex - Dght 3.400
Lbp 49.60 Br md 8.20 Dpth 4.10
Welded, 1 dk

(A34A2GR) Refrigerated Cargo Ship

1 oil engine reduction geared to sc. shaft driving 1 FP propeller
Total Power: 350kW (476hp)
Chinese Std. Type Z8E160C
1 x 4 Stroke 8 Cy. 160 x 225 350kW (476bhp)
in China

8745814 **ZHE LING YU YUN 988**
-
-
Wenling Shitang Fisheries Management Co Ltd
-
China
Official number: 331000001032

403
221
-

2001-05 Wenling Songzai Shipyard Co Ltd — Wenling ZJ
Loa 55.00 Br ex - Dght 3.600
Lbp 51.00 Br md 8.40 Dpth 4.40
Welded, 1 dk

(A34A2GR) Refrigerated Cargo Ship

1 oil engine reduction geared to sc. shaft driving 1 FP propeller
Total Power: 350kW (476hp)
Chinese Std. Type Z8E160C
1 x 4 Stroke 8 Cy. 160 x 225 350kW (476bhp)
in China

9674634 **ZHE LU GONG 002**
BLFJ5
-
Taizhou Baoxiang Shipping Co Ltd
-
Taizhou, Jiangsu *China*
MMSI: 413450130

5,329 Class: CC
1,598
7,179

2013-07 Zhejiang Hongguan Ship Industry Co Ltd — Linhai ZJ Yd No: 5003
Loa 105.00 Br ex - Dght 4.800
Lbp 95.20 Br md 19.00 Dpth 8.00
Welded, 1 dk

(B33B2DT) Trailing Suction Hopper Dredger
Hopper: 5,586
Compartments: 1 Ho, ER
1 Ha: ER (48.0 x 7.6)

2 oil engines reduction geared to sc. shafts driving 2 Propellers
Total Power: 5,000kW (6,798hp) 11.5kn
Chinese Std. Type GN8320ZC
2 x 4 Stroke 8 Cy. 320 x 380 each-2500kW (3399bhp)
Ningbo CSI Power & Machinery GroupCo Ltd-China
AuxGen: 3 x 450kW 400V a.c

8955213 **ZHE LU YOU**
BLCX
-
Xiangshan County Shipping Co Ltd
-
China

298 Class: (CC)
139
500

1983-01 Zhoushan Shipyard — Zhoushan ZJ
Loa 52.97 Br ex - Dght -
Lbp 48.52 Br md 8.20 Dpth 3.50
Welded, 1 dk

(A13B2TU) Tanker (unspecified)

1 oil engine geared to sc. shaft driving 1 FP propeller
Total Power: 216kW (294hp) 10.0kn
Chinese Std. Type 6300
1 x 4 Stroke 6 Cy. 300 x 380 216kW (294bhp)
Guangzhou Diesel Engine Factory CoLtd-China
AuxGen: 2 x 64kW 400V a.c

8955249 **ZHE LU YOU 2**
BLCP
-
Xiangshan County Shipping Co Ltd
-
Ningbo, Zhejiang *China*
MMSI: 412401750

492 Class: (CC)
231
782

1984-04 Guangzhou Shipyard — Guangzhou GD
Loa 61.20 Br ex - Dght -
Lbp 55.58 Br md 8.20 Dpth 4.10
Welded, 1 dk

(A13C2LA) Asphalt/Bitumen Tanker

1 oil engine geared to sc. shaft driving 1 FP propeller
Total Power: 216kW (294hp) 10.0kn
Chinese Std. Type 6300
1 x 4 Stroke 6 Cy. 300 x 380 216kW (294bhp)
Guangzhou Diesel Engine Factory CoLtd-China
AuxGen: 2 x 75kW 400V a.c

IMO / Call sign	Name, Owner, Port	Tonnage	Class	Builder / Dimensions	Type	Machinery
832461	**ZHE PU 107** **Zhejiang Putuo Sea Transportation Co** - *Shenjiamen, Zhejiang* *China*	*494* 229 510	Class: (CC)	**1983 Jiangxi Jiangzhou Shipyard — Ruichang JX** Loa 53.56 Br ex - Dght 3.400 Lbp 48.49 Br md 8.80 Dpth 4.20 Welded, 1 dk	**(A31A2GX) General Cargo Ship** Grain: 819; Bale: 750 Compartments: 2 Ho, ER 2 Ha: 2 (8.1 x 4.2)ER	**1 oil engine** geared to sc. shaft driving 1 FP propeller Total Power: 294kW (400hp) 10.0kn Chinese Std. Type 6300 1 x 4 Stroke 6 Cy. 300 x 380 294kW (400bhp) Guangzhou Diesel Engine Factory CoLtd-China AuxGen: 2 x 50kW 400V a.c
832473 ZM	**ZHE PU 108** **Zhejiang Putuo Sea Transportation Co** - *Shenjiamen, Zhejiang* *China*	*494* 229 510	Class: (CC)	**1983 Jiangxi Jiangzhou Shipyard — Ruichang JX** Loa 53.56 Br ex - Dght 3.400 Lbp 48.49 Br md 8.80 Dpth 4.20 Welded, 1 dk	**(A31A2GX) General Cargo Ship** Grain: 819; Bale: 750 Compartments: 2 Ho, ER 2 Ha: 2 (8.1 x 4.2)ER	**1 oil engine** geared to sc. shaft driving 1 FP propeller Total Power: 294kW (400hp) 10.0kn Chinese Std. Type 6300 1 x 4 Stroke 6 Cy. 300 x 380 294kW (400bhp) Guangzhou Diesel Engine Factory CoLtd-China AuxGen: 2 x 50kW 400V a.c
55667 Y2530	**ZHE PU 01016** **Chinnavat Logistic Co Ltd** - *Freetown* *Sierra Leone* MMSI: 667003333 Official number: SL103333	**1,818** 1,018 2,500		**2001-09 Zhejiang Yueqing Qiligang Ship Industry Co Ltd — Yueqing ZJ** Loa 81.50 Br ex - Dght - Lbp 74.90 Br md 12.60 Dpth 6.40 Welded, 1 dk	**(A31A2GX) General Cargo Ship**	**1 oil engine** driving 1 Propeller Total Power: 441kW (600hp) Chinese Std. Type 6300ZC 1 x 4 Stroke 6 Cy. 300 x 380 441kW (600bhp) Ningbo CSI Power & Machinery GroupCo Ltd-China
61135	**ZHE PU GONG 72** **Zhejiang Huashun Marine Co Ltd** Sanhe Marine Co Ltd *Zhoushan, Zhejiang* *China* Official number: 07011000288	**485** 145 -	Class: ZC	**1999-01 Linhai Gangzha Shipyard — Linhai ZJ** Yd No: GZ-9904 Loa 58.50 Br ex - Dght 1.550 Lbp 56.20 Br md 8.90 Dpth 2.70 Welded, 1 dk	**(A24D2BA) Aggregates Carrier**	**2 oil engines** reduction geared to sc. shafts driving 2 Propellers Total Power: 368kW (500hp) Chinese Std. Type 2 x each-184kW (250bhp) Weifang Diesel Engine Factory-China
48141 KOR4	**ZHE SHUI JIAN 18** - - *China* MMSI: 413432120	**5,968** 1,790 8,064		**2008-12 Zhoushan Zhaobao Shipbuilding & Repair Co Ltd — Zhoushan ZJ** Yd No: ZB0709 Loa 110.40 Br ex - Dght 6.800 Lbp 100.60 Br md 20.60 Dpth 8.50 Welded, 1 dk	**(B33A2DS) Suction Dredger**	**2 oil engines** reduction geared to sc. shafts driving 2 Propellers 7.0kn
55767 KP06	**ZHE WU 168** **Zhejiang Wugang Shipping Co Ltd** Zhoushan Putuo Jiarun Shipping Management Co Ltd *Zhoushan, Zhejiang* *China* MMSI: 414127000	**29,236** 15,731 47,500	Class: CC	**2012-11 Zhejiang Taitong Shipyard Co Ltd — Zhoushan ZJ** Yd No: T1008 Loa 189.99 (BB) Br ex - Dght 10.500 Lbp 185.00 Br md 32.26 Dpth 15.50 Welded, 1 dk	**(A21A2BC) Bulk Carrier** Double Hull Grain: 60,000 Compartments: 5 Ho, ER 5 Ha: ER	**1 oil engine** driving 1 FP propeller Total Power: 8,280kW (11,257hp) 14.5kn
833623 BW	**ZHE YONG 9** **Ningbo Waihai Navigation Co** - *Ningbo, Zhejiang* *China*	*342* 291 513		**1988 Zhejiang Province Shipping Co — Ningbo ZJ** Loa 45.50 Br ex - Dght 3.200 Lbp - Br md 8.00 Dpth 3.70 Welded, 1 dk	**(A31A2GX) General Cargo Ship** Grain: 661; Bale: 595 Compartments: 1 Ho, ER 2 Ha: 2 (8.3 x 4.0)ER	**1 oil engine** driving 1 FP propeller Total Power: 221kW (300hp) 10.5kn Chinese Std. Type 6250 1 x 4 Stroke 6 Cy. 250 x 300 221kW (300bhp) Hongyan Machinery Factory-China AuxGen: 2 x 24kW 400V a.c
745759	**ZHE YONG TUO 618** *ex* Xian Xing 605 **Ningbo Far-East Underwater Engineers Co Ltd** -	**115** 34 -		**1982-12 in the People's Republic of China** Loa 22.83 Br ex - Dght 2.350 Lbp 21.10 Br md 6.82 Dpth 3.30 Welded, 1 dk	**(B32A2ST) Tug**	**1 oil engine** reduction geared to sc. shaft driving 1 FP propeller Total Power: 441kW (600hp) Yanmar S185-ET 1 x 4 Stroke 6 Cy. 185 x 230 441kW (600bhp) Yanmar Diesel Engine Co Ltd-Japan
609580 BJ	**ZHE YONG YU 7103** **Ningbo Daxie Development Zone Fishery & Foreign Trade Co Ltd** Zhoushan Xingye Products Co Ltd *Ningbo, Zhejiang* *China*	**133** 43 -	Class: CC	**1993-04 Zhoushan General Mechanical Factory — Zhoushan ZJ** Yd No: ZYY7103 Loa 32.70 Br ex - Dght 2.250 Lbp 28.00 Br md 6.30 Dpth 2.85 Welded, 1 dk	**(B12B2FC) Fish Carrier**	**1 oil engine** geared to sc. shaft driving 1 FP propeller Total Power: 198kW (269hp) Chinese Std. Type 6250 1 x 4 Stroke 6 Cy. 250 x 300 198kW (269bhp) Hongyan Machinery Factory-China
609592 XAA2	**ZHE YONG YU 7104** **Ningbo Daxie Development Zone Fishery & Foreign Trade Co Ltd** Zhoushan Xingye Products Co Ltd *Ningbo, Zhejiang* *China*	**133** 43 -	Class: CC	**1993-04 Zhoushan General Mechanical Factory — Zhoushan ZJ** Yd No: ZYY7103 Loa 32.70 Br ex - Dght 2.250 Lbp 28.00 Br md 6.30 Dpth 2.85 Welded, 1 dk	**(B12B2FC) Fish Carrier**	**1 oil engine** geared to sc. shaft driving 1 FP propeller Total Power: 198kW (269hp) Chinese Std. Type 6250 1 x 4 Stroke 6 Cy. 250 x 300 198kW (269bhp) Hongyan Machinery Factory-China
833635	**ZHE YU 5** **Yuhuan Shipping Co** - *Taizhou, Jiangsu* *China*	*373* 208 480		**1989 Xiangyang Machinery Factory — Zongyang County AH** Loa 48.00 Br ex - Dght 3.200 Lbp 43.75 Br md 8.00 Dpth 3.70 Welded, 1 dk	**(A31A2GX) General Cargo Ship** Grain: 674; Bale: 613 Compartments: 2 Ho, ER 2 Ha: 2 (8.8 x 3.9)ER	**1 oil engine** driving 1 FP propeller Total Power: 221kW (300hp) 9.3kn Chinese Std. Type 6250 1 x 4 Stroke 6 Cy. 250 x 300 221kW (300bhp) Hongyan Machinery Factory-China AuxGen: 2 x 24kW 400V a.c
833685 XH	**ZHE YU 601** *ex* Dong Yu 2013 *-1988* **Zhoushan No 2 Ocean Fishing Shipping Co** - *Ningbo, Zhejiang* *China*	*270* 81 -	Class: (CC)	**1987 Ningbo Fishing Vessel Shipyard — Ningbo ZJ** Loa 43.50 Br ex - Dght - Lbp 37.00 Br md 7.60 Dpth 3.80 Welded, 1 dk	**(B11B2FV) Fishing Vessel**	**1 oil engine** geared to sc. shaft driving 1 FP propeller Total Power: 294kW (400hp) 12.0kn Chinese Std. Type 6300 1 x 4 Stroke 6 Cy. 300 x 380 294kW (400bhp) Ningbo Electrical Machinery Factory-China AuxGen: 2 x 64kW 400V a.c
833697	**ZHE YU 602** *ex* Dong Yu 2014 *-1988* **Zhoushan No 2 Ocean Fishing Shipping Co** - *Ningbo, Zhejiang* *China*	*270* 81 -	Class: (CC)	**1987 Ningbo Fishing Vessel Shipyard — Ningbo ZJ** Loa 43.50 Br ex - Dght - Lbp 37.00 Br md 7.60 Dpth 3.80 Welded, 1 dk	**(B11B2FV) Fishing Vessel**	**1 oil engine** geared to sc. shaft driving 1 FP propeller Total Power: 294kW (400hp) 12.0kn Chinese Std. Type 6300 1 x 4 Stroke 6 Cy. 300 x 380 294kW (400bhp) Ningbo Electrical Machinery Factory-China AuxGen: 2 x 64kW 400V a.c
832148 XW	**ZHE YU 603** *ex* Dong Yu 2015 *-1988* **Zhoushan No 2 Ocean Fishing Shipping Co** - *Ningbo, Zhejiang* *China*	*270* 81 -	Class: (CC)	**1987 Dalian Fishing Vessel Co — Dalian LN** Loa 43.50 Br ex - Dght - Lbp 37.00 Br md 7.60 Dpth 3.80 Welded, 1 dk	**(B11B2FV) Fishing Vessel**	**1 oil engine** geared to sc. shaft driving 1 FP propeller Total Power: 441kW (600hp) 12.0kn Chinese Std. Type 8300 1 x 4 Stroke 8 Cy. 300 x 380 441kW (600bhp) Dalian Fishing Vessel Co-China AuxGen: 2 x 90kW 400V a.c
832150	**ZHE YU 604** *ex* Dong Yu 2016 *-1988* **Zhoushan No 2 Ocean Fishing Shipping Co** - *Ningbo, Zhejiang* *China*	*270* 81 -	Class: (CC)	**1987 Dalian Fishing Vessel Co — Dalian LN** Loa 43.50 Br ex - Dght - Lbp 37.00 Br md 7.60 Dpth 3.80 Welded, 1 dk	**(B11B2FV) Fishing Vessel**	**1 oil engine** geared to sc. shaft driving 1 FP propeller Total Power: 441kW (600hp) 12.0kn Chinese Std. Type 8300 1 x 4 Stroke 8 Cy. 300 x 380 441kW (600bhp) Dalian Fishing Vessel Co-China AuxGen: 2 x 90kW 400V a.c
832162 XDH	**ZHE YU 605** *ex* Ning Yu 705 *-1988* **Ningbo Marine Fishery Co** - *Ningbo, Zhejiang* *China*	*270* 81 -	Class: (CC)	**1987 Ningbo Fishing Vessel Shipyard — Ningbo ZJ** Loa 43.50 Br ex - Dght - Lbp 37.00 Br md 7.60 Dpth 3.80 Welded, 1 dk	**(B11B2FV) Fishing Vessel**	**1 oil engine** geared to sc. shaft driving 1 FP propeller Total Power: 294kW (400hp) 12.0kn Chinese Std. Type 6300 1 x 4 Stroke 6 Cy. 300 x 380 294kW (400bhp) Ningbo Electrical Machinery Factory-China AuxGen: 2 x 64kW 400V a.c
832174	**ZHE YU 606** *ex* Ning Yu 706 *-1988* **Ningbo Marine Fishery Co** - *Ningbo, Zhejiang* *China*	*270* 81 -	Class: (CC)	**1987 Ningbo Fishing Vessel Shipyard — Ningbo ZJ** Loa 43.50 Br ex - Dght - Lbp 37.00 Br md 7.60 Dpth 3.80 Welded, 1 dk	**(B11B2FV) Fishing Vessel**	**1 oil engine** geared to sc. shaft driving 1 FP propeller Total Power: 294kW (400hp) 12.0kn Chinese Std. Type 6300 1 x 4 Stroke 6 Cy. 300 x 380 294kW (400bhp) Ningbo Electrical Machinery Factory-China AuxGen: 2 x 64kW 400V a.c
566673 FL3	**ZHE YU BO 189** **Lu Zhengfa** Taizhou Xianglong Shipping Co Ltd *Taizhou, Zhejiang* *China* Official number: 070509000203	**998** 299 -	Class: ZC	**1999-06 Zhejiang Yangfan Ship Group Co Ltd — Zhoushan ZJ** Loa 69.70 Br ex - Dght 3.200 Lbp 66.00 Br md 14.20 Dpth 4.80 Welded, 1 dk	**(A31A2GX) General Cargo Ship**	**2 oil engines** reduction geared to sc. shafts driving 2 Propellers Total Power: 882kW (1,200hp) 12.0kn Chinese Std. Type 6300ZC 2 x 4 Stroke 6 Cy. 300 x 380 each-441kW (600bhp) Guangzhou Diesel Engine Factory CoLtd-China

8514124 XUXN3 -	**ZHE ZHOU 208** *ex* Xing Yun 115 *-2000* *ex* Koai Maru *-1999* **Mingyuan Shipping Co Ltd** Yilong Shipping Co Ltd *Phnom Penh* *Cambodia* MMSI: 514628000 Official number: 1087531	**1,334** 717 1,577		**1986-02 K.K. Matsuura Zosensho — Osakikamijima** Yd No: 327 Loa 70.69 (BB) Br ex 11.54 Dght 4.423 Lbp 66.02 Br md 11.51 Dpth 6.71 Welded, 2 dks	**(A31A2GX) General Cargo Ship** Grain: 2,422; Bale: 2,302 Compartments: 1 Ho, ER 1 Ha: ER	**1 oil engine** with clutches, flexible couplings & sr geared to sc. shaft driving 1 CP propeller Total Power: 883kW (1,201hp) Akasaka DM28AKF 1 x 4 Stroke 6 Cy. 280 x 460 883kW (1201bhp) Akasaka Tekkosho KK (Akasaka DieselLtd)-Japan
9237278 - -	**ZHE ZHOU 272** - **Zhoushan Putuo Shenjiamen Haishang Shipping Co** - *China* MMSI: 412403620	**1,370** 766 2,480		**2000-03 Yueqing Shipyard Co Ltd — Yueqing ZJ** Loa 73.10 Br ex - Dght - Lbp - Br md 12.00 Dpth 6.20 Welded, 1 dk	**(A31A2GX) General Cargo Ship**	**1 oil engine** geared to sc. shaft driving 1 FP propeller Total Power: 735kW (999hp) Daihatsu 8PSTCM-3 1 x 4 Stroke 8 Cy. 300 x 380 735kW (999bhp) Daihatsu Diesel Manufacturing Co Lt-Japan
6927444 UCUA -	**ZHELEZNYAKOV** - **Grant Co Ltd (OOO 'Grant')** - SatCom: Inmarsat C 427303560 *Makhachkala* *Russia* MMSI: 273441660 Official number: 663791	**653** 189 341	Class: (RS)	**1967 Zavod "Leninskaya Kuznitsa" — Kiyev** Yd No: 1267 Loa 54.82 Br ex 9.89 Dght 4.080 Lbp 49.99 Br md - Dpth 5.03 Welded, 1 dk	**(B11A2FT) Trawler** Ins: 382 Compartments: 2 Ho, ER 3 Ha: 3 (1.5 x 1.6) Ice Capable	**1 oil engine** driving 1 CP propeller Total Power: 588kW (799hp) 12.0k S.K.L. 8NVD48A 1 x 4 Stroke 8 Cy. 320 x 480 588kW (799bhp) VEB Schwermaschinenbau "KarlLiebknecht" (SKL)-Magdeburg AuxGen: 3 x 88kW Fuel: 175.0 (d.f.)
8729456 UBGZ -	**ZHEMCHUZHINA** - **FCF Vskhody Kommunizma (Rybolovetskiy Kolkhoz 'Vskhody Kommunizma')** - *Murmansk* *Russia* MMSI: 273559400 Official number: 884107	**735** 220 414	Class: RS	**1989-06 Zavod "Leninskaya Kuznitsa" — Kiyev** Yd No: 1610 Loa 54.84 Br ex 10.15 Dght 4.140 Lbp 50.32 Br md 9.80 Dpth 5.00 Welded, 1 dk	**(B11A2FS) Stern Trawler** Ins: 412	**1 oil engine** driving 1 CP propeller Total Power: 852kW (1,158hp) 12.0k S.K.L. 8NVD48A-2U 1 x 4 Stroke 8 Cy. 320 x 480 852kW (1158bhp) VEB Schwermaschinenbau "KarlLiebknecht" (SKL)-Magdeburg AuxGen: 4 x 160kW a.c
8400749 BPMI -	**ZHEN FEN 9** - **China Shipping Bulk Carrier Co Ltd** - SatCom: Inmarsat C 441240910 *Shanghai* *China* MMSI: 412726000	*12,827* 6,980 20,420	Class: (CC)	**1985-11 Shanghai Shipyard — Shanghai** Yd No: 126 Loa 164.00 Br ex - Dght 9.800 Lbp 154.00 Br md 22.00 Dpth 13.00 Welded, 1 dk	**(A21A2BC) Bulk Carrier** Grain: 25,564 Compartments: 5 Ho, ER 5 Ha: (12.6 x 11.2)4 (14.0 x 12.8)ER Ice Capable	**1 oil engine** driving 1 FP propeller Total Power: 6,620kW (9,001hp) 15.0k Sulzer 6RLB56 1 x 2 Stroke 6 Cy. 560 x 1150 6620kW (9001bhp) Shanghai Diesel Engine Co Ltd-China AuxGen: 3 x 388kW 400V a.c
8407682 BPMJ -	**ZHEN FEN 10** - **China Shipping Bulk Carrier Co Ltd** - *Shanghai* *China* MMSI: 412041560	**12,827** 6,980 20,420	Class: (CC)	**1985-12 Shanghai Shipyard — Shanghai** Yd No: 127 Loa 164.00 Br ex - Dght 9.800 Lbp 154.00 Br md 22.00 Dpth 13.45 Welded, 1 dk	**(A21A2BC) Bulk Carrier** Grain: 25,564 Compartments: 5 Ho, ER 5 Ha: (12.6 x 11.2)4 (14.0 x 12.8)ER Ice Capable	**1 oil engine** driving 1 FP propeller Total Power: 6,620kW (9,001hp) 15.0kn Sulzer 6RLB56 1 x 2 Stroke 6 Cy. 560 x 1150 6620kW (9001bhp) Shanghai Diesel Engine Co Ltd-China AuxGen: 3 x 388kW 400V a.c
9008225 BPMM -	**ZHEN FEN 13** - **Shanghai Youhao Shipping Co Ltd** - SatCom: Inmarsat B 341272710 *Shanghai* *China* MMSI: 412727000	*13,003* 6,873 19,129	Class: ZC (CC)	**1991-12 Tianjin Xingang Shipyard — Tianjin** Yd No: 273 Loa 164.00 Br ex - Dght 9.840 Lbp 154.00 Br md 22.00 Dpth 13.40 Welded, 1 dk	**(A21A2BC) Bulk Carrier** Grain: 24,108 Compartments: 5 Ho, ER 5 Ha: (11.9 x 11.2)4 (13.3 x 12.6)ER Ice Capable	**1 oil engine** driving 1 FP propeller Total Power: 5,119kW (6,960hp) 13.5kn B&W 6L42MC 1 x 2 Stroke 6 Cy. 420 x 1360 5119kW (6960bhp) Hudong Shipyard-China
9008366 BPMN -	**ZHEN FEN 14** - **China Shipping Bulk Carrier Co Ltd** - SatCom: Inmarsat B 341272810 *Shanghai* *China* MMSI: 412728000	*13,003* 6,873 20,328	Class: (CC)	**1992-05 Tianjin Xingang Shipyard — Tianjin** Yd No: 274 Loa 164.00 Br ex - Dght 9.810 Lbp 154.00 Br md 22.00 Dpth 13.40 Welded, 1 dk	**(A21A2BC) Bulk Carrier** Grain: 24,108 Compartments: 5 Ho, ER 5 Ha: (11.9 x 11.2)4 (13.3 x 12.6)ER Ice Capable	**1 oil engine** driving 1 FP propeller Total Power: 5,119kW (6,960hp) 13.5kn B&W 6L42MC 1 x 2 Stroke 6 Cy. 420 x 1360 5119kW (6960bhp) Hudong Shipyard-China
9021540 BPMQ -	**ZHEN FEN 17** *ex* Xiang Li *-2008* *ex* Zhen Fen 17 *-1999* **China Shipping Bulk Carrier Co Ltd** - SatCom: Inmarsat B 341273010 *Shanghai* *China* MMSI: 412730000	**18,996** 9,431 28,828	Class: (CC)	**1992-11 Tianjin Xingang Shipyard — Tianjin** Yd No: 275 Converted From: Container Ship (Fully Cellular)-2008 Converted From: Bulk Carrier-1999 Loa 186.40 (BB) Br ex - Dght 10.000 Lbp 176.00 Br md 25.00 Dpth 14.30 Welded, 1 dk	**(A21A2BC) Bulk Carrier** Compartments: 5 Ho, ER 5 Ha: ER Ice Capable	**1 oil engine** driving 1 FP propeller Total Power: 5,119kW (6,960hp) 13.0kn B&W 6L42MC 1 x 2 Stroke 6 Cy. 420 x 1360 5119kW (6960bhp) Hudong Shipyard-China AuxGen: 3 x 440kW 400V a.c
9021552 BPMR -	**ZHEN FEN 18** *ex* Xiang Zhuang *-2009* *ex* Zhen Fen 18 *-1999* **China Shipping Bulk Carrier Co Ltd** - SatCom: Inmarsat C 441211710 *Shanghai* *China* MMSI: 412501000	**18,996** 9,431 29,186	Class: (CC)	**1993-04 Tianjin Xingang Shipyard — Tianjin** Yd No: 276 Converted From: Container Ship (Fully Cellular)-2009 Converted From: Bulk Carrier-1999 Loa 186.40 (BB) Br ex - Dght 10.000 Lbp 176.00 Br md 25.00 Dpth 14.30 Welded, 1 dk	**(A21A2BC) Bulk Carrier** Compartments: 5 Ho, ER 5 Ha: ER Ice Capable	**1 oil engine** driving 1 FP propeller Total Power: 5,119kW (6,960hp) 13.0kn B&W 6L42MC 1 x 2 Stroke 6 Cy. 420 x 1360 5119kW (6960bhp) Hudong Shipyard-China AuxGen: 3 x 440kW 400V a.c
9118197 BPMS -	**ZHEN FEN 19** *ex* Xiang Mao *-2008* *ex* Zhen Fen 19 *-1999* **China Shipping Bulk Carrier Co Ltd** - SatCom: Inmarsat A 1572464 *Guangzhou, Guangdong* *China* MMSI: 412502000	**18,996** 9,431 26,388	Class: (CC)	**1995-01 Tianjin Xingang Shipyard — Tianjin** Yd No: 283 Converted From: Container Ship (Fully Cellular)-2008 Converted From: Bulk Carrier-1999 Loa 186.40 (BB) Br ex - Dght 9.860 Lbp 176.00 Br md 25.00 Dpth 14.30 Welded, 1 dk	**(A21A2BC) Bulk Carrier** Compartments: 5 Ho, ER 5 Ha: 5 (12.9 x 16.4)ER Ice Capable	**1 oil engine** driving 1 FP propeller Total Power: 5,980kW (8,130hp) 13.5kn B&W 6L42MC 1 x 2 Stroke 6 Cy. 420 x 1360 5980kW (8130bhp) Hudong Shipyard-China AuxGen: 3 x 440kW 400V a.c Fuel: 300.0 (d.f.) 580.0 (r.f.)
9118202 BPMT -	**ZHEN FEN 20** *ex* Xiang Yue *-2008* *ex* Zhen Fen 20 *-2000* **China Shipping Bulk Carrier Co Ltd** - SatCom: Inmarsat C 441215710 *Shanghai* *China* MMSI: 412781000	**18,996** 9,431 29,194	Class: (CC)	**1995-06 Tianjin Xingang Shipyard — Tianjin** Yd No: 284 Converted From: Container Ship (Fully Cellular)-2008 Converted From: Bulk Carrier-1999 Loa 186.40 (BB) Br ex - Dght 10.000 Lbp 176.00 Br md 25.00 Dpth 14.30 Welded, 1 dk	**(A21A2BC) Bulk Carrier** Compartments: 5 Ho, ER 5 Ha: 5 (12.9 x 16.4)ER Ice Capable	**1 oil engine** driving 1 FP propeller Total Power: 5,980kW (8,130hp) 13.5kn B&W 6L42MC 1 x 2 Stroke 6 Cy. 420 x 1360 5980kW (8130bhp) Hudong Shipyard-China AuxGen: 3 x 440kW 400V a.c Fuel: 300.0 (d.f.) 580.0 (r.f.)
9260691 BAWH -	**ZHEN HUA** - **Dalian Zhenhua Marine Products Co Ltd** - SatCom: Inmarsat C 441248915 *Dalian, Liaoning* *China* MMSI: 412023530	**467** 140 540	Class: CC	**2001-11 Huanghai Shipbuilding Co Ltd — Rongcheng SD** Yd No: HC406 Loa 54.35 Br ex - Dght 3.700 Lbp 48.00 Br md 8.80 Dpth 4.30 Welded, 1 dk	**(B12B2FC) Fish Carrier**	**1 oil engine** reduction geared to sc. shaft driving 1 FP propeller Total Power: 882kW (1,199hp) 12.0kn Chinese Std. Type LB6250ZLC 1 x 4 Stroke 6 Cy. 250 x 320 882kW (1199bhp) Zibo Diesel Engine Factory-China AuxGen: 2 x 150kW 400V a.c
9166560 D5FR2 -	**ZHEN HUA 7** *ex* Mako *-2014* *ex* Overseas Takamar *-2011* *ex* Takamar *-2006* *ex* P. Alliance *-2001* **Zhen Hua 7 Shipping Co Ltd** Shanghai Zhenhua Shipping Co Ltd *Monrovia* *Liberia*	**60,504** 29,906 104,000 T/cm 92.1	Class: CC (Class contemplated) (LR) (AB) Classed LR until 10/1/14	**1998-09 Samsung Heavy Industries Co Ltd — Geoje** Yd No: 1215 Loa 243.66 (BB) Br ex - Dght 14.720 Lbp 233.00 Br md 42.00 Dpth 22.10 Welded, 1 dk	**(A13B2TP) Products Tanker** Double Hull (13F) Liq: 118,119; Liq (Oil): 118,119 Compartments: 12 Wing Ta, 2 Wing Slop Ta, ER 3 Cargo Pump (s): 3x2800m³/hr Manifold: Bow/CM: 116m	**1 oil engine** driving 1 FP propeller Total Power: 14,517kW (19,737hp) 15.0kn MAN-B&W 7S60MC 1 x 2 Stroke 7 Cy. 600 x 2292 14517kW (19737bhp) Samsung Heavy Industries Co Ltd-South Korea AuxGen: 3 x 720kW a.c Fuel: 309.0 (d.f.) 3347.0 (r.f.)
7800784 J8B2817 -	**ZHEN HUA 8** *ex* Dolvi *-2004* *ex* Dolviken *-2000* *ex* BT Stream *-2000* *ex* Thorsaga *-1996* *ex* Ambra Beluga *-1993* *ex* Thoraas *-1992* *ex* Akademik Lukyanenko *-1990* *ex* Viking Falcon *-1986* **Zhen Hua 8 Shipping (SVG) Co Ltd** Shanghai Zhenhua Shipping Co Ltd *Kingstown* *St Vincent & The Grenadines* MMSI: 377488000 Official number: 9289	**37,456** 11,237 44,926 T/cm 86.0	Class: CC (AB)	**1980-09 Uddevallavarvet AB — Uddevalla** Yd No: 310 Converted From: Crude Oil Tanker-2004 Loa 228.61 Br ex 42.35 Dght 8.500 Lbp 219.60 Br md 42.31 Dpth 13.50 Welded, 1 dk	**(A38C2GH) Heavy Load Carrier**	**1 oil engine** driving 1 FP propeller Total Power: 11,622kW (15,801hp) 15.4kn B&W 6L80GF 1 x 2 Stroke 6 Cy. 800 x 1950 11622kW (15801bhp) Uddevallavarvet AB-Sweden AuxGen: 2 x 800kW 440V 60Hz a.c, 1 x 700kW 440V 60Hz a.c Fuel: 249.5 (d.f.) 3660.5 (r.f.)

IMO / Call sign	Name, former names, owner, manager, port, flag	Tonnage	Class	Builder, dimensions	Type	Machinery
021971 8B3020	**ZHEN HUA 9** *ex* Elgin *-2005* *ex* Peregrine *-2003* *ex* Anette *-1998* *ex* Wei Shan Hu *-1995* **Zhen Hua 9 Shipping (SVG) Co Ltd** Shanghai Zhenhua Shipping Co Ltd *Kingstown* *St Vincent & The Grenadines* MMSI: 377729000 Official number: 9492	**28,896** 8,669 33,748 T/cm 64.4	Class: CC (LR) Classed LR until 9/3/05	**1982**-11 **Namura Shipbuilding Co Ltd — Imari SG** Yd No: 856 Converted From: Oil Tanker-2005 Loa 224.62 Br ex 40.00 Dght 8.500 Lbp 218.20 Br md 32.20 Dpth 13.50 Welded, 1 dk	**(A38C2GH) Heavy Load Carrier** Cranes: 2x15t	**1 oil engine** driving 1 FP propeller Total Power: 10,001kW (13,597hp) 15.0kn B&W 7L67GFCA 1 x 2 Stroke 7 Cy. 670 x 1700 10001kW (13597bhp) Hitachi Zosen Corp-Japan AuxGen: 3 x 580kW 450V 60Hz a.c Boilers: e (ex.g.) 22.4kgf/cm² (22.0bar), AuxB (o.f.) 18.0kgf/cm² (17.7bar)
917410 8B3026	**ZHEN HUA 10** *ex* Panos G *-2005* *ex* Tomis Liberty *-1995* *ex* Thorstar *-1993* *ex* Jarmona *-1989* *ex* Eva *-1989* **Zhen Hua 10 Shipping (SVG) Co Ltd** Shanghai Zhenhua Shipping Co Ltd *Kingstown* *St Vincent & The Grenadines* MMSI: 377736000 Official number: 9498	**37,658** 11,297 45,323 T/cm 86.5	Class: CC (NV) (AB)	**1981**-12 **Astilleros y Talleres del Noroeste SA (ASTANO) — Fene** Yd No: 257 Converted From: Crude Oil/Products Tanker-2005 Loa 243.82 (BB) Br ex 39.40 Dght 8.500 Lbp 233.03 Br md 39.36 Dpth 13.50 Welded, 1 dk	**(A38C2GH) Heavy Load Carrier** Cranes: 1x30t	**1 oil engine** driving 1 FP propeller Total Power: 12,356kW (16,799hp) 12.0kn Sulzer 7RND76M 1 x 2 Stroke 7 Cy. 760 x 1550 12356kW (16799bhp) Astilleros Espanoles SA (AESA)-Spain AuxGen: 2 x 600kW 450V 60Hz a.c, 1 x 575kW 450V 60Hz a.c Fuel: 315.0 (d.f.) (Heating Coils) 4013.5 (r.f.) 55.0pd
917446 8B3190	**ZHEN HUA 11** *ex* Star 2 *-2005* *ex* Star *-1998* *ex* Caribbean Star *-1995* *ex* Intermar Alliance *-1988* **Zhen Hua 11 Shipping (SVG) Co Ltd** Shanghai Zhenhua Shipping Co Ltd *Kingstown* *St Vincent & The Grenadines* MMSI: 377097000 Official number: 9662	**37,743** 11,323 45,403 T/cm 85.6	Class: CC (BV) (AB)	**1981**-06 **Astilleros y Talleres del Noroeste SA (ASTANO) — Fene** Yd No: 254 Converted From: Crude Oil Tanker-2006 Loa 244.03 (BB) Br ex 39.88 Dght 8.500 Lbp 233.03 Br md 39.36 Dpth 13.50 Welded, 1 dk	**(A38C2GH) Heavy Load Carrier**	**1 oil engine** driving 1 FP propeller Total Power: 12,798kW (17,400hp) 15.3kn B&W 8L67GFCA 1 x 2 Stroke 8 Cy. 670 x 1700 12798kW (17400bhp) Mitsui Engineering & Shipbuilding CLtd-Japan AuxGen: 2 x 600kW 440V 60Hz a.c, 1 x 575kW 440V 60Hz a.c Fuel: 349.9 (d.f.) (Heating Coils) 3697.1 (r.f.) 55.0pd
546136 PQB	**ZHEN HUA 12** **Shanghai Zhenhua Shipping Co Ltd** - *Shanghai* *China* MMSI: 413462000	**11,442** 3,433 14,612	Class: CC	**2008**-09 **Nanjing East Star Shipbuilding Co Ltd — Nanjing JS** Yd No: 06TKS-1381 Loa 137.80 Br ex 40.00 Dght 6.100 Lbp 130.40 Br md 34.00 Dpth 9.50 Welded, 1 dk	**(A38C2GH) Heavy Load Carrier**	**2 oil engines** geared to sc. shafts driving 2 FP propellers Total Power: 4,852kW (6,596hp) 11.0kn Chinese Std. Type G8300ZC 2 x 4 Stroke 8 Cy. 300 x 380 each-2426kW (3298bhp) Wuxi Antai Power Machinery Co Ltd-China
008761 8B3292	**ZHEN HUA 13** *ex* Tamyra *-2005* *ex* Dido *-1993* *ex* Marine Renaissance *-1989* **Zhen Hua 13 Shipping (SVG) Co Ltd** Shanghai Zhenhua Shipping Co Ltd *Kingstown* *St Vincent & The Grenadines* MMSI: 375235000 Official number: 9764	**37,743** 11,323 44,770 T/cm 87.0	Class: CC (AB)	**1983**-11 **Astilleros y Talleres del Noroeste SA (ASTANO) — Fene** Yd No: 260 Converted From: Crude Oil/Products Tanker-2006 Loa 243.82 (BB) Br ex 39.40 Dght 8.500 Lbp 233.03 Br md 39.36 Dpth 13.50 Welded, 1 dk	**(A38C2GH) Heavy Load Carrier** Cranes: 1x15t	**1 oil engine** driving 1 FP propeller Total Power: 12,798kW (17,400hp) 15.3kn B&W 8L67GB 1 x 2 Stroke 8 Cy. 670 x 1700 12798kW (17400bhp) Mitsui Engineering & Shipbuilding CLtd-Japan AuxGen: 2 x 600kW 440V 60Hz a.c, 1 x 575kW 440V 60Hz a.c
901590 8B3443	**ZHEN HUA 14** *ex* Kalymnos *-2006* *ex* Melita *-2000* *ex* Skaubay *-1996* *ex* Skaudrott *-1991* *ex* Kosmos Spirit *-1991* *ex* Atlantic Spirit *-1990* *ex* Atlantic Peace *-1988* *ex* Cys Olympia *-1984* **Zhen Hua 14 Shipping (SVG) Co Ltd** Shanghai Zhenhua Shipping Co Ltd *Kingstown* *St Vincent & The Grenadines* MMSI: 375423000 Official number: 9915	**40,486** 12,145 46,433	Class: AB (LR) ✠ Classed LR until 22/10/96	**1983**-06 **Stocznia im Komuny Paryskiej — Gdynia** Yd No: B555/201 Converted From: Crude Oil Tanker-2006 Loa 248.62 (BB) Br ex 41.64 Dght 8.500 Lbp 236.46 Br md 41.61 Dpth 13.50 Welded, 1 dk	**(A38C2GH) Heavy Load Carrier**	**1 oil engine** driving 1 FP propeller Total Power: 14,033kW (19,079hp) 15.3kn Sulzer 6RND90M 1 x 2 Stroke 6 Cy. 900 x 1550 14033kW (19079bhp) Zaklady Przemyslu Metalowego 'HCegielski' SA-Poznan AuxGen: 3 x 720kW 440V 60Hz a.c Fuel: 489.3 (d.f.) 3917.8 (r.f.)
714970 RFE7	**ZHEN HUA 15** *ex* Cerigo *-2009* *ex* Koyagi Spirit *-2005* **Zhen Hua 15 Shipping (Hong Kong) Co Ltd** Shanghai Zhenhua Shipping Co Ltd *Hong Kong* *Hong Kong* MMSI: 477661900 Official number: HK-2395	**39,771** 11,931 46,671 T/cm 88.6	Class: AB (LR) (NK) Classed LR until 20/7/09	**1989**-04 **Mitsubishi Heavy Industries Ltd. — Nagasaki** Yd No: 2017 Converted From: Crude Oil Tanker-2010 Loa 233.30 (BB) Br ex 42.03 Dght - Lbp 222.20 Br md 42.00 Dpth 13.50 Welded, 1 dk	**(A38C3GH) Heavy Load Carrier, semi submersible**	**1 oil engine** driving 1 FP propeller Total Power: 11,385kW (15,479hp) 15.5kn Sulzer 6RTA62 1 x 2 Stroke 6 Cy. 620 x 2150 11385kW (15479bhp) Mitsubishi Heavy Industries Ltd-Japan AuxGen: 3 x 660kW 440V 60Hz a.c, 2 x 1075kW 440V 60Hz a.c Boilers: AuxB (Comp) 7.0kgf/cm² (6.9bar), AuxB (o.f.) 18.0kgf/cm² (17.7bar) Fuel: 139.8 (d.f.) 2270.1 (r.f.)
014667 8B3445	**ZHEN HUA 16** *ex* Apageon *-2006* *ex* Pernas Duyong *-1997* *ex* Sawako *-1997* *launched as* George Anson *-1982* **Zhen Hua 15 Shipping (SVG) Co Ltd** Shanghai Zhenhua Shipping Co Ltd *Kingstown* *St Vincent & The Grenadines* MMSI: 375427000 Official number: 9917	**38,519** 11,555 45,028 T/cm 86.8	Class: CC (LR) ✠ Classed LR until 25/8/06	**1982**-03 **Nippon Kokan KK (NKK Corp) — Tsu ME** Yd No: 73 Converted From: Crude Oil Tanker-2006 Loa 241.00 (BB) Br ex 42.04 Dght 8.500 Lbp 230.00 Br md 42.00 Dpth 13.50 Welded, 1 dk	**(A38C2GH) Heavy Load Carrier**	**1 oil engine** driving 1 FP propeller Total Power: 12,504kW (17,000hp) 14.8kn Sulzer 5RLA90 1 x 2 Stroke 5 Cy. 900 x 1900 12504kW (17000bhp) Sumitomo Heavy Industries Ltd-Japan AuxGen: 3 x 580kW 450V 60Hz a.c Boilers: 2 WTAuxB 17.5kgf/cm² (17.2bar), e 21.0kgf/cm² (20.6bar) Fuel: 211.5 (d.f.) 2634.5 (r.f.)
301955 TWP	**ZHEN HUA 17** *ex* North Duchess *-2006* **Zhen Hua 16 Shipping (SVG) Co Ltd** Shanghai Zhenhua Shipping Co Ltd *Shanghai* *China* MMSI: 413652000	**27,264** 8,179 30,126 T/cm 62.2	Class: CC (LR) ✠ Classed LR until 5/7/06	**1985**-01 **B&W Skibsvaerft A/S — Copenhagen** Yd No: 914 Converted From: Bulk Carrier-2006 Loa 224.87 (BB) Br ex 32.31 Dght 8.500 Lbp 218.45 Br md 32.25 Dpth 13.50 Welded, 1 dk	**(A38C2GH) Heavy Load Carrier**	**1 oil engine** driving 1 FP propeller Total Power: 7,355kW (10,000hp) 14.5kn B&W 4L80MCE 1 x 2 Stroke 4 Cy. 800 x 2592 7355kW (10000bhp) Hitachi Zosen Corp-Japan AuxGen: 3 x 500kW 450V 60Hz a.c Boilers: AuxB (Comp) 8.1kgf/cm² (7.9bar) Fuel: 323.0 (d.f.) (Heating Coils) 2107.0 (r.f.) 27.5pd
026921 8B3446	**ZHEN HUA 18** *ex* Orient Constellation *-2006* *ex* Grain Union *-2003* **Zhen Hua 17 Shipping (SVG) Co Ltd** Shanghai Zhenhua Shipping Co Ltd *Kingstown* *St Vincent & The Grenadines* MMSI: 375428000 Official number: 9918	**28,436** 8,530 30,651 T/cm 64.4	Class: CC CR (GL) (AB)	**1986**-01 **China Shipbuilding Corp (CSBC) — Kaohsiung** Yd No: 217 Converted From: Bulk Carrier-2006 Loa 229.78 (BB) Br ex - Dght 8.500 Lbp 217.02 Br md 32.21 Dpth 13.50 Welded, 1 dk	**(A38C2GH) Heavy Load Carrier**	**1 oil engine** driving 1 FP propeller Total Power: 6,767kW (9,200hp) 13.0kn Sulzer 6RLB76 1 x 2 Stroke 6 Cy. 760 x 1600 6767kW (9200bhp) Taiwan Machinery ManufacturingCorp.-Kaohsiung AuxGen: 3 x 520kW 440V 60Hz a.c Fuel: 201.0 (d.f.) 3310.0 (r.f.) 48.0pd
026907 8B3447	**ZHEN HUA 19** *ex* New Horizon *-2006* *ex* Panamax Cosmos *-1991* **Zhen Hua 3 Shipping (SVG) Co Ltd** Shanghai Zhenhua Shipping Co Ltd *Kingstown* *St Vincent & The Grenadines* MMSI: 375429000 Official number: 9919	**28,559** 8,567 30,451 T/cm 64.4	Class: CC (BV) (CR)	**1984**-04 **China Shipbuilding Corp (CSBC) — Kaohsiung** Yd No: 215 Converted From: Bulk Carrier-2006 Loa 229.78 (BB) Br ex 32.26 Dght 8.500 Lbp 217.02 Br md 32.21 Dpth 13.50 Welded, 1 dk	**(A38C2GH) Heavy Load Carrier**	**1 oil engine** driving 1 FP propeller Total Power: 9,731kW (13,230hp) 15.0kn Sulzer 6RLB76 1 x 2 Stroke 6 Cy. 760 x 1600 9731kW (13230bhp) Taiwan Machinery ManufacturingCorp.-Kaohsiung AuxGen: 3 x 520kW 440V 60Hz a.c Fuel: 260.0 (d.f.) (Heating Coils) 3840.0 (r.f.) 43.0pd
826180 8B3502	**ZHEN HUA 20** *ex* Sereno 2 *-2006* *ex* Sereno *-1998* *ex* Fina Belgica *-1993* *ex* Eagle *-1983* *launched as* World Eagle *-1983* **Zhen Hua 20 Shipping (SVG) Co Ltd** Shanghai Zhenhua Shipping Co Ltd *Kingstown* *St Vincent & The Grenadines* MMSI: 375541000 Official number: 9974	**39,923** 11,976 47,801	Class: AB (LR) ✠ Classed LR until 8/11/06	**1983**-07 **Stocznia im Komuny Paryskiej — Gdynia** Yd No: B557/01 Converted From: Crude Oil Tanker-2006 Loa 247.20 (BB) Br ex 41.64 Dght 8.500 Lbp 236.02 Br md 41.61 Dpth 13.50 Welded, 1 dk	**(A38C2GH) Heavy Load Carrier**	**1 oil engine** driving 1 FP propeller Total Power: 16,317kW (22,185hp) 15.3kn Sulzer 6RND90M 1 x 2 Stroke 6 Cy. 900 x 1550 16317kW (22185bhp) Zaklady Przemyslu Metalowego 'HCegielski' SA-Poznan AuxGen: 3 x 720kW 440V 60Hz a.c Boilers: 2 WTAuxB (o.f.) 17.8kgf/cm² (17.5bar), AuxB (ex.g.) 8.7kgf/cm² (8.5bar) Fuel: 345.5 (d.f.) 3997.5 (r.f.)
018223 8B3570	**ZHEN HUA 21** *ex* Iokasti *-2007* *ex* Aven *-2003* *ex* Raven *-2003* *ex* Terra Nova *-1998* *ex* Buena Empresa *-1992* **Zhen Hua 21 Shipping (SVG) Co Ltd** Shanghai Zhenhua Shipping Co Ltd *Kingstown* *St Vincent & The Grenadines* MMSI: 376265000 Official number: 10043	**28,902** 8,670 34,588 T/cm 64.3	Class: AB (NK)	**1983**-01 **Oshima Shipbuilding Co Ltd — Saikai NS** Yd No: 10057 Converted From: Crude Oil/Products Tanker-2007 Loa 225.00 (BB) Br ex 32.24 Dght 8.500 Lbp 216.00 Br md 32.20 Dpth 13.50 Welded, 1 dk	**(A38C2GH) Heavy Load Carrier**	**1 oil engine** driving 1 FP propeller Total Power: 10,591kW (14,400hp) 15.0kn Sulzer 6RND76M 1 x 2 Stroke 6 Cy. 760 x 1550 10591kW (14400bhp) Sumitomo Heavy Industries Ltd-Japan AuxGen: 3 x 600kW

8106446 *VRCT6* -	**ZHEN HUA 22** *ex* Priamos *-2007* *ex* Fidelity L *-1995* **Shanghai Zhenhua Port Machinery (Hong Kong) Co Ltd** Shanghai Zhenhua Shipping Co Ltd *Hong Kong* *Hong Kong* MMSI: 477926400 Official number: HK-1891	**29,233** 8,769 32,292 T/cm 64.8	Class: AB	**1983-07 Sasebo Heavy Industries Co. Ltd. — Sasebo Yard, Sasebo** Yd No: 303 Converted From: Crude Oil Tanker-2007 Loa 228.51 (BB) Br ex 32.24 Dght - Lbp 218.00 Br md 32.21 Dpth 13.50 Welded, 1 dk	**(A38C3GH) Heavy Load Carrier, semi submersible**	**1 oil engine** driving 1 FP propeller Total Power: 10,812kW (14,700hp) 16.0k Sulzer 6RLB7 1 x 2 Stroke 6 Cy. 760 x 1600 10812kW (14700bhp) Ishikawajima Harima Heavy IndustrieCo Ltd (IHI)-Japan AuxGen: 3 x 850kW
8414738 *VRDA8* -	**ZHEN HUA 23** *ex* Rich Duchess *-2007* **Shanghai Zhenhua Shipping Co Ltd** - *Hong Kong* *Hong Kong* MMSI: 477007300 Official number: HK-1950	**37,879** 11,363 48,412 T/cm 86.0	Class: AB	**1986-10 Kasado Dockyard Co Ltd — Kudamatsu YC** Yd No: 359 Converted From: Crude Oil/Products Tanker-2007 Loa 243.85 (BB) Br ex 40.04 Dght 8.500 Lbp 234.02 Br md 40.01 Dpth 13.50 Welded, 1 dk	**(A38C2GH) Heavy Load Carrier** Double Sides Entire Compartment Length	**1 oil engine** driving 1 FP propeller Total Power: 10,444kW (14,200hp) 14.3k Sulzer 6RTA7 1 x 2 Stroke 6 Cy. 760 x 2200 10444kW (14200bhp) Mitsubishi Heavy Industries Ltd-Japan AuxGen: 3 x 640kW 450V 60Hz a.c Fuel: 279.0 (d.f.) 2938.0 (r.f.)
8414726 *VRDA9* -	**ZHEN HUA 24** *ex* Regent *-2007* *ex* Rich Duke *-1999* **Shanghai Zhenhua Port Machinery (Hong Kong) Co Ltd** Shanghai Zhenhua Shipping Co Ltd *Hong Kong* *Hong Kong* MMSI: 477044300 Official number: HK-1951	**37,879** 11,363 48,184 T/cm 87.0	Class: AB (NK)	**1986-07 Kasado Dockyard Co Ltd — Kudamatsu YC** Yd No: 358 Converted From: Crude Oil Tanker-2007 Loa 243.85 (BB) Br ex - Dght 8.500 Lbp 234.02 Br md 40.01 Dpth 13.50 Welded, 1 dk	**(A38C2GH) Heavy Load Carrier** Double Sides Entire Compartment Length	**1 oil engine** driving 1 FP propeller Total Power: 10,297kW (14,000hp) 14.5k Sulzer 6RTA7 1 x 2 Stroke 6 Cy. 760 x 2200 10297kW (14000bhp) Mitsubishi Heavy Industries Ltd-Japan AuxGen: 3 x 640kW a.c
8700242 *VRDX3* -	**ZHEN HUA 25** *ex* Yellow Sea *-2008* *ex* Columbia Spirit *-2005* *ex* Bona Skipper *-1999* *ex* Ocean Explorer *-1994* **Shanghai Zhenhua Port Machinery (Hong Kong) Co Ltd** Shanghai Zhenhua Shipping Co Ltd *Hong Kong* *Hong Kong* MMSI: 477141700 Official number: HK-2129	**38,255** 11,476 49,099	Class: AB (LR) (NV) ✠ Classed LR until 30/6/08	**1988-06 Mitsubishi Heavy Industries Ltd. — Nagasaki** Yd No: 2007 Converted From: Crude Oil Tanker-2008 Loa 233.61 (BB) Br ex 44.05 Dght 12.215 Lbp 224.01 Br md 44.01 Dpth 13.50 Welded, 1 dk	**(A38C2GH) Heavy Load Carrier**	**1 oil engine** driving 1 FP propeller Total Power: 11,033kW (15,000hp) 15.1k Sulzer 6RTA6 1 x 2 Stroke 6 Cy. 680 x 2000 11033kW (15000bhp) Mitsubishi Heavy Industries Ltd-Japan AuxGen: 3 x 800kW 450V 60Hz a.c Boilers: AuxB (ex.g.) 11.9kgf/cm² (11.7bar), WTAuxB (o.f.) 17.9kgf/cm² (17.6bar) Fuel: 116.9 (d.f.) 2124.3 (r.f.)
8700254 *VREG4* -	**ZHEN HUA 26** *ex* China Sea *-2008* *ex* Hudson Spirit *-2005* *ex* Bona Spinner *-2000* *ex* Ocean Navigator *-1994* **Zhen Hua 26 Shipping (Hong Kong) Co Ltd** Shanghai Zhenhua Shipping Co Ltd *Hong Kong* *Hong Kong* MMSI: 477177900 Official number: HK-2202	**38,255** 11,476 49,060	Class: AB (LR) (NV) ✠ Classed LR until 29/11/08	**1988-11 Mitsubishi Heavy Industries Ltd. — Nagasaki** Yd No: 2008 Converted From: Crude Oil Tanker-2008 Loa 233.60 (BB) Br ex 44.05 Dght 12.215 Lbp 224.01 Br md 44.01 Dpth 13.50 Welded, 1 dk	**(A38C2GH) Heavy Load Carrier**	**1 oil engine** driving 1 FP propeller Total Power: 11,033kW (15,000hp) 15.1k Sulzer 6RTA6 1 x 2 Stroke 6 Cy. 680 x 2000 11033kW (15000bhp) Mitsubishi Heavy Industries Ltd-Japan AuxGen: 3 x 800kW 450V 60Hz a.c Boilers: AuxB (ex.g.) 11.9kgf/cm² (11.7bar), WTAuxB (o.f.) 17.9kgf/cm² (17.6bar) Fuel: 183.0 (d.f.) 2304.0 (r.f.)
8710182 *VREG5* -	**ZHEN HUA 27** *ex* Red Sea *-2009* *ex* Sabine Spirit *-2005* *ex* Bona Shimmer *-1999* *ex* Ocean Leader *-1994* **Zhen Hua 27 Shipping (Hong Kong) Co Ltd** Shanghai Zhenhua Shipping Co Ltd *Hong Kong* *Hong Kong* MMSI: 477201900 Official number: HK-2203	**38,255** 11,476 49,060	Class: AB (LR) (NV) ✠ Classed LR until 19/3/09	**1989-08 Mitsubishi Heavy Industries Ltd. — Nagasaki** Yd No: 2009 Converted From: Crude Oil Tanker-2009 Loa 233.60 (BB) Br ex 44.05 Dght 8.500 Lbp 224.01 Br md 44.01 Dpth 13.05 Welded, 1 dk	**(A38C2GH) Heavy Load Carrier**	**1 oil engine** driving 1 FP propeller Total Power: 11,033kW (15,000hp) 15.1k Sulzer 6RTA6 1 x 2 Stroke 6 Cy. 680 x 2000 11033kW (15000bhp) Mitsubishi Heavy Industries Ltd-Japan AuxGen: 3 x 800kW 450V 60Hz a.c Boilers: AuxB (ex.g.) 11.9kgf/cm² (11.7bar), WTAuxB (o.f.) 17.9kgf/cm² (17.6bar) Fuel: 183.1 (d.f.) 2124.3 (r.f.)
8700266 *VREF4* -	**ZHEN HUA 28** *ex* Meandros *-2008* *ex* Wenatchi *-2001* *ex* American Pegasus *-1999* *ex* Neptune Pegasus *-1994* *ex* Caribbean First *-1992* **Zhen Hua 28 Shipping (Hong Kong) Co Ltd** Shanghai Zhenhua Shipping Co Ltd *Hong Kong* *Hong Kong* MMSI: 477399500 Official number: HK-2194	**40,015** 12,004 47,107	Class: AB (NV) (NK)	**1988-06 Sumitomo Heavy Industries Ltd. — Oppama Shipyard, Yokosuka** Yd No: 1152 Converted From: Crude Oil/Products Tanker-2009 Loa 232.04 (BB) Br ex 42.04 Dght 8.500 Lbp 222.00 Br md 42.00 Dpth 20.30 Welded, 1 dk	**(A38C3GH) Heavy Load Carrier, semi submersible** Double Hull	**1 oil engine** driving 1 FP propeller Total Power: 10,445kW (14,201hp) 14.0k Sulzer 6RTA6 1 x 2 Stroke 6 Cy. 620 x 2150 10445kW (14201bhp) Sumitomo Heavy Industries Ltd-Japan AuxGen: 4 x 460kW a.c Fuel: 181.4 (d.f.) 1994.2 (r.f.)
8700498 *VRFE8* -	**ZHEN HUA 29** *ex* Merbabu *-2009* *ex* Cook Spirit *-2003* *ex* Blue Sky River *-1999* **Zhen Hua 29 Shipping (Hong Kong) Co Ltd** Shanghai Zhenhua Shipping Co Ltd *Hong Kong* *Hong Kong* MMSI: 477622600 Official number: HK-2396	**41,580** 12,474 51,500	Class: AB (NK)	**1987-08 Hashihama Shipbuilding Co Ltd — Tadotsu KG** Yd No: 856 Converted From: Crude Oil Tanker-2010 Loa 243.80 (BB) Br ex 42.35 Dght - Lbp 235.00 Br md 42.02 Dpth 19.11 Welded, 1 dk	**(A38C3GH) Heavy Load Carrier, semi submersible**	**1 oil engine** driving 1 FP propeller Total Power: 9,709kW (13,200hp) 14.0k B&W 6S60M 1 x 2 Stroke 6 Cy. 600 x 2292 9709kW (13200bhp) Kawasaki Heavy Industries Ltd-Japan AuxGen: 4 x 440kW a.c Fuel: 3000.0 (r.f.)
9107021 *VRFO5* -	**ZHEN HUA 30** *ex* El Junior *-2009* *ex* Tohzan *-2003* **Zhen Hua 30 Shipping (Hong Kong) Co Ltd** Shanghai Zhenhua Shipping Co Ltd *Hong Kong* *Hong Kong* Official number: HK-2472	**149,896** 81,511 260,870	Class: KR NK	**1995-07 Hitachi Zosen Corp — Nagasu KM** Yd No: 4890 Loa 335.00 (BB) Br ex 58.42 Dght 19.351 Lbp 322.00 Br md 58.00 Dpth 28.80 Welded, 1 dk	**(A13A2TV) Crude Oil Tanker**	**1 oil engine** driving 1 FP propeller Total Power: 21,125kW (28,722hp) 15.5k B&W 7S80M 1 x 2 Stroke 7 Cy. 800 x 3056 21125kW (28722bhp) Hitachi Zosen Corp-Japan AuxGen: 2 x 1040kW 440V 60Hz a.c, 1 x 860kW 440V 60Hz a.c Fuel: 532.0 (d.f.) (Heating Coils) 5070.0 (r.f.) 81.0pd
7804211 - -	**ZHEN HUA TUO 18** *ex* Chang Feng Ii *-2014* *ex* Bao Feng *-2009* *ex* Zhao Bao Shan *-2006* *ex* Mana *-2004* *ex* Drossini *-2000* *ex* Topaz XL *-1999* *ex* Maraki *-1998* *ex* Hyundai No. 9 *-1993* *ex* Hai Jung *-1988* **Dalian Chain Star Ship Management Co Ltd** - *China* MMSI: 412375910	**14,458** 8,621 24,586	Class: IB (LR) (BV) (KR) ✠ Classed LR until 20/12/85	**1979-11 Hyundai Heavy Industries Co Ltd — Ulsan** Yd No: 2597 Loa 153.19 Br ex 27.59 Dght 10.310 Lbp 143.50 Br md 27.55 Dpth 14.18 Welded, 1 dk	**(A21A2BC) Bulk Carrier** Grain: 30,011; Bale: 28,290 Compartments: 4 Ho, ER 4 Ha: (12.4 x 13.7)3 (17.5 x 13.7)ER Derricks: 4x25t; Winches: 4	**1 oil engine** driving 1 FP propeller Total Power: 6,900kW (9,381hp) 12.0k B&W 7L55G 1 x 2 Stroke 7 Cy. 550 x 1380 6900kW (9381bhp) Hyundai Engine & Machinery Co Ltd-South Korea AuxGen: 2 x 449kW 440V 60Hz a.c Fuel: 148.5 (d.f.) 1357.5 (r.f.)
9028158 *BKOU3* -	**ZHEN WEI 2** - - *China* MMSI: 412435190	**1,806** 1,023 2,650		**2005-09 Zhoushan Longtai Shipbuilding Co Ltd — Zhoushan ZJ** Loa 78.50 Br ex - Dght 5.290 Lbp 71.75 Br md 12.00 Dpth 6.50 Welded, 1 dk	**(A31A2GX) General Cargo Ship**	**1 oil engine** reduction geared to sc. shaft driving 1 Propeller Total Power: 735kW (999hp) 8.0k Chinese Std. Type G6300ZC 1 x 4 Stroke 6 Cy. 300 x 380 735kW (999bhp) Zibo Diesel Engine Factory-China
8605428 - -	**ZHEN XING** *ex* Shun He *-2005* *ex* Yoshinogawa Maru *-2001* - - *Indonesia*	**1,369** 495 1,584		**1986-04 Yamanaka Zosen K.K. — Imabari** Yd No: 323 Loa 72.83 (BB) Br ex - Dght 4.393 Lbp 68.03 Br md 11.51 Dpth 6.91 Welded, 2dks	**(A31A2GX) General Cargo Ship**	**1 oil engine** with clutches, flexible couplings & sr reverse geared to sc. shaft driving 1 FP propeller Total Power: 1,030kW (1,400hp) 10.5k Hanshin 6LUN28AR 1 x 4 Stroke 6 Cy. 280 x 480 1030kW (1400bhp) The Hanshin Diesel Works Ltd-Japan
8989446 - -	**ZHEN XING 1** - **Zhenfa Shipping Co Ltd** Yuan Da Shipping Co Ltd	**1,405** 495 1,250		**1998-02 Guangzhou Fishing Vessel Shipyard — Guangzhou GD** Loa - Br ex - Dght - Lbp 63.80 Br md 11.40 Dpth 6.40 Welded, 1 dk	**(A34A2GR) Refrigerated Cargo Ship**	**1 oil engine** driving 1 Propeller Total Power: 1,213kW (1,649hp)
9056014 *BOHC* -	**ZHEN XING HAI** - **COSCO Bulk Carrier Co Ltd (COSCO BULK)** - SatCom: Inmarsat A 1572525 *Tianjin* *China* MMSI: 412201000	**38,603** 24,351 66,133	Class: CC	**1995-03 Jiangnan Shipyard — Shanghai** Yd No: 2207 Loa 225.00 Br ex - Dght 13.620 Lbp 215.00 Br md 32.20 Dpth 18.70 Welded, 1 dk	**(A21A2BC) Bulk Carrier** Grain: 84,019; Bale: 81,365 Compartments: 7 Ho, ER 7 Ha: 6 (14.6 x 15.0)ER (14.6 x 13.2)	**1 oil engine** driving 1 FP propeller Total Power: 8,459kW (11,501hp) 14.0k B&W 6S60M 1 x 2 Stroke 6 Cy. 600 x 2292 8459kW (11501bhp) Dalian Marine Diesel Works-China AuxGen: 3 x 610kW 450V a.c

65479 *RLR7*	**ZHEN YANG 29** **Zhe Jiang Zhen Yang Shipping Co Ltd** - *Hong Kong* *Hong Kong* MMSI: 477250200 Official number: HK-3749	**8,548** 4,051 12,629	Class: CC	**2010-07 Linhai Hongsheng Shipbuilding Co Ltd — Linhai ZJ** Yd No: 2006-12 Loa 134.85 Br ex 22.03 Dght 7.800 Lbp 126.00 Br md 22.00 Dpth 10.60 Welded, 1 dk	**(A12B2TR) Chemical/Products Tanker** Double Hull (13F) Liq: 13,839; Liq (Oil): 13,839 Compartments: 10 Wing Ta, 2 Wing Slop Ta, ER Ice Capable	**1 oil engine** driving 1 FP propeller Total Power: 4,400kW (5,982hp) 13.5kn MAN-B&W 6S35MC 1 x 2 Stroke 6 Cy. 350 x 1400 4400kW (5982bhp) Yichang Marine Diesel Engine Co Ltd-China AuxGen: 3 x 420kW 400V a.c
05240	**ZHEN YUAN** *ex* Zheling Yuleng 198 *-2004* *ex* Kazuei *-2004* *ex* Kazuei Maru *-1998* - - *China* MMSI: 412301260	**498** 276 916		**1980-06 Nakatani Shipyard Co. Ltd. — Etajima** Yd No: 461 Loa 52.81 Br ex - Dght 4.100 Lbp 48.52 Br md 8.81 Dpth 5.00 Welded, 1 dk	**(A31A2GX) General Cargo Ship**	**1 oil engine** driving 1 FP propeller Total Power: 552kW (750hp) 12.0kn Yanmar MF24-UT 1 x 4 Stroke 6 Cy. 240 x 420 552kW (750bhp) Yanmar Diesel Engine Co Ltd-Japan
00066	**ZHEN ZHU MEI** **Guangzhou Maritime Transport (Group) Co Ltd** - *Guangzhou, Guangdong* *China*	*7,669* 3,847 3,019		**1984-11 Hudong Shipyard — Shanghai** Yd No: 1138 Loa 138.00 Br ex - Dght 6.001 Lbp 124.00 Br md 17.60 Dpth 8.40 Welded, 2 dks	**(A32A2GF) General Cargo/Passenger Ship**	**1 oil engine** driving 1 FP propeller Total Power: 6,620kW (9,001hp) Hudong 9ESDZ43/82B 1 x 2 Stroke 9 Cy. 430 x 820 6620kW (9001bhp) Hudong Shipyard-China
63628 *BNK*	**ZHEN ZHU QUAN** *ex* Hu Po Quan *-2007* *ex* Ma Nao Quan *-2003* **Qingdao Friend Shipping Co Ltd** Qingdao Shunhe Ship Management Co Ltd SatCom: Inmarsat C 441202010 *Qingdao, Shandong* *China* MMSI: 412320680	*2,238* 1,344 3,402	Class: CC	**1992-10 Qingdao Shipyard — Qingdao SD** Loa 81.15 Br ex - Dght 5.200 Lbp 76.00 Br md 15.00 Dpth 6.80 Welded, 1 dk	**(A31A2GX) General Cargo Ship** Grain: 4,690; Bale: 4,311 TEU 44 C.Ho 24/20' C.Dk 20/20' Compartments: 2 Ho, ER 2 Ha: 2 (14.9 x 7.8)ER Derricks: 2x5t	**1 oil engine** geared to sc. shaft driving 1 FP propeller Total Power: 971kW (1,320hp) 11.1kn Chinese Std. Type 6320ZC 1 x 4 Stroke 6 Cy. 320 x 440 971kW (1320bhp) Guangzhou Diesel Engine Factory CoLtd-China AuxGen: 3 x 120kW 400V a.c
06855 *QCY*	**ZHEN ZHU WAN** **COSCO Southern Asphalt Shipping Co Ltd** - SatCom: Inmarsat C 441336811 *Haikou, Hainan* *China* MMSI: 413368000	**5,569** 1,671 6,315 T/cm 16.6	Class: CC	**2008-07 Guangzhou Huangpu Shipbuilding Co Ltd — Guangzhou GD** Yd No: 2263 Loa 106.84 (BB) Br ex 17.62 Dght 6.600 Lbp 101.50 Br md 17.60 Dpth 10.10 Welded, 1 dk	**(A13C2LA) Asphalt/Bitumen Tanker** Double Hull (13F) Cargo Heating Coils Compartments: 8 Wing Ta, ER 2 Cargo Pump (s): 2x400m³/hr Manifold: Bow/CM: 50.3m	**1 oil engine** reduction geared to sc. shaft driving 1 CP propeller Total Power: 4,000kW (5,438hp) 13.6kn Wartsila 8L32 1 x 4 Stroke 8 Cy. 320 x 400 4000kW (5438bhp) Wartsila Finland Oy-Finland AuxGen: 3 x 360kW a.c Fuel: 93.0 (d.f.) 486.0 (r.f.)
086057 *FR08*	**ZHENG BANG** *ex* Pride Of Indore *-2013* *ex* Hainan *-2008* *ex* Luigi d'Amato *-2003* **Zheng Bang Shipping Group Ltd** Fujian Ocean Shipping Co Ltd (FOSCO) *Panama* *Panama* MMSI: 354548000 Official number: 45313PEXT	**39,385** 24,519 75,473 T/cm 67.8	Class: RI (LR) (GL) Classed LR until 12/12/13	**1996-01 Fincantieri-Cant. Nav. Italiani S.p.A. (Breda) — Venezia** Yd No: 5947 Loa 225.00 Br ex 32.26 Dght 14.312 Lbp 221.00 Br md 32.24 Dpth 19.70 Welded, 1 dk	**(A21A2BC) Bulk Carrier** Grain: 85,158 Compartments: 7 Ho, ER 7 Ha: (16.2 x 11.6)Tappered 6 (16.2 x 14.6)ER	**1 oil engine** driving 1 FP propeller Total Power: 10,800kW (14,684hp) 14.0kn Sulzer 5RTA62 1 x 2 Stroke 5 Cy. 620 x 2150 10800kW (14684bhp) Fincantieri Cantieri Navalitaliani SpA-Italy AuxGen: 1 x 650kW 440V 60Hz a.c, 2 x 650kW 440V 60Hz a.c Fuel: 230.0 (d.f.) (Heating Coils) 2160.0 (r.f.) 32.0pd
03856	**ZHENG BANG 8** *ex* Baosha 022 *-2012* *ex* Jin Yang 8 *-2012* *ex* Qing You 8 *-2012* **Ningbo Yongsen Fuel Co Ltd** -	**2,699** 1,060 3,000	Class: (CC)	**1984-10 Murakami Hide Zosen K.K. — Imabari** Yd No: 222 Loa 95.60 Br ex - Dght 5.710 Lbp 88.60 Br md 14.00 Dpth 7.00 Welded, 1 dk	**(A13B2TP) Products Tanker** Liq: 3,720; Liq (Oil): 3,720 Compartments: 12 Ta, ER	**1 oil engine** driving 1 FP propeller Total Power: 2,060kW (2,801hp) Hanshin 6EL38 1 x 4 Stroke 6 Cy. 380 x 760 2060kW (2801bhp) The Hanshin Diesel Works Ltd-Japan AuxGen: 3 x 275kW 390V a.c, 1 x 80kW 390V a.c Thrusters: 1 Thwart. FP thruster (f)
58656	**ZHENG GANG** *ex* Yi Li *-2005* *ex* Xing Wen 6 *-2005* *completed as* Xin Da 86 *-2005* **Jin Yi Shipping Co Ltd** -	**491** 274 1,191		**2005-05 Fu'an Saiqi Shipyard — Fu'an FJ** Loa 52.80 Br ex - Dght 3.400 Lbp 48.00 Br md 8.80 Dpth 4.10 Welded, 1 dk	**(A31A2GX) General Cargo Ship**	**1 oil engine** driving 1 FP propeller Total Power: 218kW (296hp) Chinese Std. Type 1 x 4 Stroke 218kW (296bhp) Zibo Diesel Engine Factory-China
48982 *KNG*	**ZHENG HE** **Zheng SA** Vasco SA *Luxembourg* *Luxembourg* MMSI: 253261000	**8,015** 2,404 2,680	Class: BV	**2010-10 'Uljanik' Brodogradiliste dd — Pula** Yd No: 481 Loa 138.50 Br ex - Dght 5.500 Lbp 110.50 Br md 26.00 Dpth 8.80 Welded, 1 dk	**(B33A2DC) Cutter Suction Dredger**	**3 diesel electric oil engines** driving 3 gen. each 6300kW a.c Connecting to 2 elec. motors each (3500kW) driving 2 FP propellers Total Power: 21,600kW (29,367hp) 13.0kn MAN-B&W 6L48/60B 3 x 4 Stroke 6 Cy. 480 x 600 each-7200kW (9789bhp) MAN B&W Diesel AG-Augsburg
593799 *EZG2*	**ZHENG HENG** **Zheng Hong Shipping Group Ltd** Fujian Ocean Shipping Co Ltd (FOSCO) *Panama* *Panama* MMSI: 373299000 Official number: 4432612	**43,951** 27,690 81,948 T/cm 71.6	Class: LR ✠ **100A1** SS 09/2012 bulk carrier CSR BC-A GRAB (20) Nos. 2, 4 & 6 holds may be empty ESP **ShipRight** (CM,ACS (B)) *IWS LI ✠ **LMC** **UMS** Cable: 687.5/81.0 U3 (a)	**2012-09 Wuhu Xinlian Shipbuilding Co Ltd — Wuhu AH** Yd No: W1012 Loa 229.03 (BB) Br ex 32.28 Dght 14.500 Lbp 225.51 Br md 32.24 Dpth 20.06 Welded, 1 dk	**(A21A2BC) Bulk Carrier** Grain: 95,700 Compartments: 7 Ho, ER 7 Ha: ER	**1 oil engine** driving 1 FP propeller Total Power: 11,900kW (16,179hp) 14.5kn MAN-B&W 5S60ME-C 1 x 2 Stroke 5 Cy. 600 x 2400 11900kW (16179bhp) Hefei Rong'an Power Machinery Co Lt-China AuxGen: 3 x 550kW 450V 60Hz a.c Boilers: AuxB (Comp) 9.2kgf/cm² (9.0bar)
596105 *FNH*	**ZHENG HUI** **Zheng Hui Shipping Group Ltd** Fujian Ocean Shipping Co Ltd (FOSCO) *Panama* *Panama* MMSI: 370550000 Official number: 45437PEXT	**43,951** 27,684 82,500 T/cm 71.6	Class: LR ✠ **100A1** SS 01/2014 bulk carrier CSR BC-A GRAB (20) Nos. 2, 4 & 6 holds may be empty ESP **ShipRight** (CM, ACS (B)) *IWS LI ✠ **LMC** **UMS** Cable: 687.5/81.0 U3 (a)	**2014-01 Wuhu Xinlian Shipbuilding Co Ltd — Wuhu AH** Yd No: W1017 Loa 229.02 (BB) Br ex 32.30 Dght 14.500 Lbp 225.52 Br md 32.26 Dpth 20.05 Welded, 1 dk	**(A21A2BC) Bulk Carrier** Grain: 95,700 Compartments: 7 Ho, ER 7 Ha: ER	**1 oil engine** driving 1 FP propeller Total Power: 11,900kW (16,179hp) 14.2kn MAN-B&W 5S60ME-C 1 x 2 Stroke 5 Cy. 600 x 2400 11900kW (16179bhp) Dalian Marine Diesel Co Ltd-China AuxGen: 3 x 550kW 450V 60Hz a.c Boilers: AuxB (Comp) 9.1kgf/cm² (8.9bar)
593804 *FNM2*	**ZHENG JUN** **Zheng Jun Shipping Group Ltd** Fujian Ocean Shipping Co Ltd (FOSCO) *Panama* *Panama* MMSI: 355124000 Official number: 4467813	**43,951** 27,684 81,810 T/cm 71.6	Class: LR ✠ **100A1** SS 03/2013 bulk carrier CSR BC-A GRAB (20) Nos. 2, 4 & 6 holds may be empty ESP **ShipRight** (CM, ACS (B)) *IWS LI ✠ **LMC** **UMS** Cable: 687.5/81.0 U3 (a)	**2013-03 Wuhu Xinlian Shipbuilding Co Ltd — Wuhu AH** Yd No: W1013 Loa 229.00 (BB) Br ex 32.28 Dght 14.500 Lbp 225.50 Br md 32.24 Dpth 20.06 Welded, 1 dk	**(A21A2BC) Bulk Carrier** Grain: 95,700 Compartments: 7 Ho, ER 7 Ha: ER	**1 oil engine** driving 1 FP propeller Total Power: 11,900kW (16,179hp) 14.2kn MAN-B&W 5S60ME-C 1 x 2 Stroke 5 Cy. 600 x 2400 11900kW (16179bhp) Hefei Rong'an Power Machinery Co Lt-China AuxGen: 3 x 550kW 450V 60Hz a.c Boilers: AuxB (Comp) 9.2kgf/cm² (9.0bar)

9593787 *3FGV* -	**ZHENG KAI** **Zheng Kai Shipping Group Ltd** Fujian Ocean Shipping Co Ltd (FOSCO) *Panama* *Panama* MMSI: 373515000 Official number: 42865PEXT	**43,951** 27,684 81,877 T/cm 71.6	Class: LR ✠**100A1** SS 08/2012 bulk carrier CSR BC-A Nos. 2, 4 & 6 holds may be empty **ShipRight** (CM,ACS (B)) GRAB (20) ESP LI *IWS ✠**LMC** **UMS** Cable: 687.5/81.0 U3 (a)	**2012-08 Wuhu Xinlian Shipbuilding Co Ltd — Wuhu AH** Yd No: W1011 Loa 228.97 (BB) Br ex 32.30 Dght 14.450 Lbp 225.50 Br md 32.26 Dpth 20.06 Welded, 1 dk	**(A21A2BC) Bulk Carrier** Grain: 95,700 Compartments: 7 Ho, ER 7 Ha: ER	**1 oil engine** driving 1 FP propeller Total Power: 11,900kW (16,179hp) MAN-B&W 1 x 2 Stroke 5 Cy. 600 x 2400 11900kW (16179bhp) Hefei Rong'an Power Machinery Co Lt-China AuxGen: 3 x 550kW 450V 60Hz a.c Boilers: AuxB (Comp) 9.2kgf/cm^2 (9.0bar)	14.5k 5S60ME-
9593828 *HP2834* -	**ZHENG RONG** **Zheng Rong Shipping Group Ltd** Fujian Ocean Shipping Co Ltd (FOSCO) *Panama* *Panama* MMSI: 371397000 Official number: 4508713	**43,951** 27,684 81,793 T/cm 71.6	Class: LR ✠**100A1** SS 07/2013 bulk carrier CSR BC-A GRAB (20) Nos. 2, 4 & 6 holds may be empty ESP **ShipRight** (CM, ACS (B)) *IWS LI ✠**LMC** **UMS** Cable: 687.5/81.0 U3 (a)	**2013-07 Wuhu Xinlian Shipbuilding Co Ltd — Wuhu AH** Yd No: W1015 Loa 229.00 (BB) Br ex 32.30 Dght 14.500 Lbp 225.48 Br md 32.26 Dpth 20.06 Welded, 1 dk	**(A21A2BC) Bulk Carrier** Grain: 95,700 Compartments: 7 Ho, ER 7 Ha: ER	**1 oil engine** driving 1 FP propeller Total Power: 11,900kW (16,179hp) MAN-B&W 1 x 2 Stroke 5 Cy. 600 x 2400 11900kW (16179bhp) Hefei Rong'an Power Machinery Co Lt-China AuxGen: 3 x 550kW 450V 60Hz a.c Boilers: AuxB (Comp) 9.0kgf/cm^2 (8.8bar)	14.2k 5S60ME-C
9593816 *3FFV2* -	**ZHENG RUN** **Zheng Run Shipping Group Ltd** Fujian Ocean Shipping Co Ltd (FOSCO) *Panama* *Panama* MMSI: 356680000 Official number: 44233PEXT	**43,951** 27,684 81,810 T/cm 71.6	Class: LR ✠**100A1** SS 05/2013 bulk carrier CSR BC-A GRAB (20) Nos. 2, 4 & 6 holds may be empty ESP **ShipRight** (CM, ACS (B)) *IWS LI ✠**LMC** **UMS** Cable: 687.5/81.0 U3 (a)	**2013-05 Wuhu Xinlian Shipbuilding Co Ltd — Wuhu AH** Yd No: W1014 Loa 229.00 (BB) Br ex 32.31 Dght 14.450 Lbp 225.54 Br md 32.27 Dpth 20.06 Welded, 1 dk	**(A21A2BC) Bulk Carrier** Grain: 98,091 Compartments: 7 Ho, ER 7 Ha: 6 (17.3 x 15.0)ER (14.7 x 12.8)	**1 oil engine** driving 1 FP propeller Total Power: 11,900kW (16,179hp) MAN-B&W 1 x 2 Stroke 5 Cy. 600 x 2400 11900kW (16179bhp) Hefei Rong'an Power Machinery Co Lt-China AuxGen: 3 x 550kW 450V 60Hz a.c Boilers: AuxB (Comp) 9.2kgf/cm^2 (9.0bar)	14.2kn 5S60ME-C8
9118666 *3EJL2* -	**ZHENG TAI** *ex* Global Triumph *-2014* *ex* Maratha Mighty *-2002* **Zheng Tong Shipping Group Ltd** - *Panama* *Panama* MMSI: 370760000 Official number: 45584PEXT	**38,852** 24,176 72,870 T/cm 66.4	Class: BV RI (IR)	**1996-11 China Shipbuilding Corp — Keelung** Yd No: 616 Loa 224.80 (BB) Br ex 32.20 Dght 13.750 Lbp 214.37 Br md 32.00 Dpth 19.00 Welded, 1 dk	**(A21A2BC) Bulk Carrier** Double Bottom Entire Compartment Length Grain: 87,021 Compartments: 7 Ho, ER 7 Ha: (16.7 x 13.2)6 (17.5 x 14.9)ER	**1 oil engine** driving 1 FP propeller Total Power: 9,709kW (13,200hp) Sulzer 1 x 2 Stroke 5 Cy. 620 x 2150 9709kW (13200bhp) Hitachi Zosen Corp-Japan AuxGen: 3 x 588kW 450V 60Hz a.c Fuel: 117.0 (d.f.) (Heating Coils) 2240.0 (r.f.) 34.0pd	14.5kn 5RTA62U
8732702 - -	**ZHENG XING 1** *ex* Jin An 16 *-2008* **Dalian Zhengteng Shipping Co Ltd** - *Dalian, Liaoning* *China* MMSI: 413320380 Official number: 030008000079	**493** 276 -		**1994-10 Qingdao Shipyard — Qingdao SD** L reg 55.54 Br ex - Dght - Lbp - Br md 9.20 Dpth 4.65 Welded, 1 dk	**(A31A2GX) General Cargo Ship**	**1 oil engine** driving 1 Propeller Total Power: 294kW (400hp)	
8918253 *H9UH* -	**ZHENG YANG** *ex* Tasman Pathfinder *-2012* *ex* La Esperanza *-2002* **Zhong Qiang Shipping SA** Eastern Rain International Ship Management Co Ltd *Panama* *Panama* MMSI: 354103000 Official number: 30117PEXT1	**17,331** 8,142 22,551 T/cm 38.7	Class: NK	**1991-06 Naikai Shipbuilding & Engineering Co Ltd — Onomichi HS (Setoda Shipyard)** Yd No: 557 Loa 176.68 (BB) Br ex 27.03 Dght 10.023 Lbp 164.00 Br md 27.00 Dpth 14.60 Welded, 2 dks	**(A31A2GX) General Cargo Ship** Grain: 30,834; Bale: 29,511 TEU 950 incl 100 ref C. Compartments: 5 Ho, ER 9 Ha: (13.3 x 8.0) (20.3 x 8.0)5 (20.3 x 10.2)2 (13.3 x 10.2)ER Cranes: 1x35t,4x25t	**1 oil engine** driving 1 FP propeller Total Power: 11,401kW (15,501hp) B&W 1 x 2 Stroke 6 Cy. 600 x 2292 11401kW (15501bhp) Hitachi Zosen Corp-Japan AuxGen: 4 x 510kW a.c, 4 x 424kW a.c, 1 x 80kW a.c Fuel: 2900.0 (r.f.)	18.0kn 7S60MC
7944308 *BOYC* -	**ZHENG YANG** **Guangdong Sun Font Shipping Co** - *Guangzhou, Guangdong* *China* MMSI: 412065170	**10,234** 6,174 14,270	Class: (GL) (CC)	**1980-07 Guangzhou Shipyard — Guangzhou GD** Loa 161.25 Br ex - Dght 9.530 Lbp 147.00 Br md 20.40 Dpth 12.40 Welded, 2 dks	**(A31A2GX) General Cargo Ship** Grain: 19,943; Bale: 17,886 Compartments: ER, 5 Ho 5 Ha: (7.7 x 6.0) (15.0 x 8.0)2 (12.7 x 8.0)ER (9.0 x 8.0) Derricks: 1x60t,6x10t,10x5t; Winches: 17	**1 oil engine** driving 1 FP propeller Total Power: 8,826kW (12,000hp) Sulzer 1 x 2 Stroke 6 Cy. 760 x 1550 8826kW (12000bhp) Zaklady Przemyslu Metalowego 'HCegielski' SA-Poznan AuxGen: 3 x 400kW 400V 50Hz a.c	17.5kn 6RND76
7651157 - -	**ZHENG YANG** *ex* Dragon 2 *-1995* *ex* Dragon I *-1992* *ex* Golden Dragon II *-1991* *ex* Tenryu Maru No. 15 *-1983* - -	*489* 331 1,092	Class: (NK)	**1970 K.K. Uno Zosensho — Imabari** Yd No: 23 Loa 53.90 Br ex - Dght 4.112 Lbp 49.51 Br md 9.61 Dpth 4.40 Welded, 1 dk	**(A13B2TU) Tanker (unspecified)** Liq: 1,291; Liq (Oil): 1,291 Compartments: 4 Ta, ER	**1 oil engine** driving 1 FP propeller Total Power: 883kW (1,201hp) Niigata 1 x 4 Stroke 6 Cy. 280 x 440 883kW (1201bhp) Niigata Engineering Co Ltd-Japan AuxGen: 2 x 36kW a.c	10.0kn 6M28X
8000159 *BROJ* -	**ZHENG YANG 3** *ex* Hun Jiang *-2007* **COSCO Shipping Co Ltd (COSCOL)** - SatCom: Inmarsat A 1571773 *Guangzhou, Guangdong* *China* MMSI: 412046000	**9,182** 6,152 15,265	Class: (LR) (CC) ✠ Classed LR until 22/10/82	**1981-02 Austin & Pickersgill Ltd. — Southwick, Sunderland** Yd No: 1403 Loa 144.75 Br ex 20.45 Dght 8.867 Lbp 137.50 Br md 20.42 Dpth 11.75 Welded, 1 dk, 2nd dk except in No. 5 hold	**(A31A2GX) General Cargo Ship** Grain: 21,379; Bale: 19,536 TEU 40 Compartments: ER, 5 Ho, 3 Tw Dk 5 Ha: (11.6 x 6.7) (13.7 x 8.5)2 (12.9 x 8.5)ER (11.4 x 6.7) Derricks: 6x10t,4x5t; Winches: 10	**1 oil engine** driving 1 FP propeller Total Power: 5,600kW (7,614hp) Sulzer 1 x 2 Stroke 4 Cy. 680 x 1250 5600kW (7614bhp) Clark Hawthorn Ltd.-Newcastle AuxGen: 3 x 350kW 440V 60Hz a.c Fuel: 130.0 (d.f.) 1126.5 (r.f.) 26.0pd	13.8kn 4RND68M
9601883 *HPAN* -	**ZHENG YAO** **Zheng Yao Shipping Group Ltd** Fujian Ocean Shipping Co Ltd (FOSCO) *Panama* *Panama* MMSI: 352211000 Official number: 45438PEXT	**43,951** 27,679 82,500 T/cm 71.6	Class: LR ✠**100A1** SS 01/2014 bulk carrier CSR BC-A GRAB (20) Nos. 2, 4 & 6 holds may be empty ESP **ShipRight** (CM,ACS (B)) *IWS LI ✠**LMC** **UMS** Cable: 687.5/81.0 U3 (a)	**2014-01 Wuhu Xinlian Shipbuilding Co Ltd — Wuhu AH** Yd No: W1018 Loa 229.00 (BB) Br ex 32.30 Dght 14.500 Lbp 225.52 Br md 32.26 Dpth 20.05 Welded, 1 dk	**(A21A2BC) Bulk Carrier** Grain: 95,700 Compartments: 7 Ho, ER 7 Ha: ER	**1 oil engine** driving 1 FP propeller Total Power: 11,900kW (16,179hp) MAN-B&W 1 x 2 Stroke 5 Cy. 600 x 2400 11900kW (16179bhp) Hefei Rong'an Power Machinery Co Lt-China AuxGen: 3 x 550kW 450V 60Hz a.c Boilers: AuxB (Comp) 9.1kgf/cm^2 (8.9bar)	14.2kn 5S60ME-C
8830487 *BBKK* -	**ZHENG YUE** *ex* Shun Quan *-1992* **Shandong Rongcheng Marine Shipping Co** - *Qingdao, Shandong* *China*	**481** 268 671	Class: CC	**1981 Nanjing Shipyard — Nanjing JS** Loa 53.56 Br ex - Dght 3.600 Lbp 48.00 Br md 8.80 Dpth 4.20 Welded, 1 dk	**(A31A2GX) General Cargo Ship** Compartments: 2 Ho, ER 2 Ha: 2 (8.1 x 4.2)ER	**1 oil engine** geared to sc. shaft driving 1 FP propeller Total Power: 294kW (400hp) Chinese Std. Type 1 x 4 Stroke 6 Cy. 300 x 380 294kW (400bhp) Guangzhou Diesel Engine Factory CoLtd-China AuxGen: 2 x 50kW 400V a.c	10.0kn 6300

IMO / Call sign	Name / Owner / Manager / Flag	Tonnage	Class	Builder / Dimensions	Type	Machinery
596090 8BP	**ZHENG ZHI** **Zheng Zhi Shipping Group Ltd** Fujian Ocean Shipping Co Ltd (FOSCO) *Panama* *Panama* MMSI: 371089000 Official number: 4522313	**43,951** 27,701 81,804 T/cm 71.6	Class: LR ✠ **100A1** SS 08/2013 bulk carrier CSR BC-A GRAB (20) Nos. 2, 4 & 6 holds may be empty ESP **ShipRight** (CM,ACS (B)) *IWS LI ✠ **LMC** **UMS** Cable: 687.5/81.0 U3 (a)	**2013-08 Wuhu Xinlian Shipbuilding Co Ltd — Wuhu AH** Yd No: W1016 Loa 229.02 (BB) Br ex 32.30 Dght 14.500 Lbp 225.48 Br md 32.26 Dpth 20.05 Welded, 1 dk	**(A21A2BC) Bulk Carrier** Grain: 95,700 Compartments: 7 Ho, ER 7 Ha: ER	**1 oil engine** driving 1 FP propeller Total Power: 11,900kW (16,179hp) 15.0kn MAN-B&W 5S60ME-C8 1 x 2 Stroke 5 Cy. 600 x 2400 11900kW (16179bhp) Hefei Rong'an Power Machinery Co Lt-China AuxGen: 3 x 550kW 450V 60Hz a.c Boilers: AuxB (Comp) 9.2kgf/cm² (9.0bar)
451161 NK	**ZHENIS** *ex Jenis -2008* **RSE Aktau International Commercial Sea Port** - *Aqtau* *Kazakhstan*	**100** 30 46	Class: RS (LR) ✠ Classed LR until 10/7/08	**2008-07 Safe Co Ltd Sp z oo — Gdynia** (Hull) **2008-07 B.V. Scheepswerf Damen — Gorinchem** Yd No: 503413 Loa 19.54 Br ex 7.32 Dght 2.570 Lbp 17.44 Br md 7.30 Dpth 3.39 Welded, 1 dk	**(B32A2ST) Tug** Ice Capable	**2 oil engines** with clutches, flexible couplings & sr geared to sc. shafts driving 2 FP propellers Total Power: 1,268kW (1,724hp) 10.6kn Caterpillar C32 ACERT 2 x Vee 4 Stroke 12 Cy. 145 x 162 each-634kW (862bhp) Caterpillar Inc-USA AuxGen: 2 x 36kW 400V 50Hz a.c Fuel: 21.0 (d.f.)
453200	**ZHENNA-2** **Alberto Neptali Luque Navarro** - *Peru*	**200** - -		**2008-04 SIMA Serv. Ind. de la Marina Chimbote (SIMACH) — Chimbote** Yd No: 511 Loa - (BB) Br ex - Dght - Lbp 36.50 Br md 7.80 Dpth 3.80 Welded, 1 dk	**(B11B2FV) Fishing Vessel** Ins: 184	**1 oil engine** reduction geared to sc. shaft driving 1 Propeller Total Power: 416kW (566hp) Caterpillar D379 1 x Vee 4 Stroke 8 Cy. 159 x 203 416kW (566bhp) Caterpillar Inc-USA
655274	**ZHEXING 191** **Wenzhou Zhen'ou Shipping Co Ltd** - *Taizhou, Zhejiang* *China*	**7,023** 3,932 11,000	Class: CC (Class contemplated)	**2013-02 Linhai Hongsheng Shipbuilding Co Ltd — Linhai ZJ** Yd No: 2011-36 Loa - Br ex - Dght - Lbp - Br md - Dpth - Welded, 1 dk	**(A12B2TR) Chemical/Products Tanker** Double Hull (13F)	**1 oil engine** driving 1 Propeller 13.0kn
070785 JKV	**ZHI CHENG** *ex Lake Globe -2009 ex Lake Ranger -2006* *ex Bunga Orkid Dua -2005* **Grand China Shipping Development Co Ltd** Grand China Shipping Development Co Ltd SatCom: Inmarsat C 441392910 *Shanghai* *China* MMSI: 413929000	**25,498** 14,071 43,246 T/cm 50.8	Class: CC (BV) (NV)	**1994-06 Hyundai Heavy Industries Co Ltd — Ulsan** Yd No: 857 Loa 185.06 (BB) Br ex 30.03 Dght 11.220 Lbp 176.80 Br md 30.00 Dpth 16.00 Welded, 1 dk	**(A21A2BC) Bulk Carrier** Grain: 54,232; Bale: 52,442 Compartments: 5 Ho, ER 5 Ha: (14.4 x 15.3)4 (19.2 x 15.3)ER Cranes: 4x25t	**1 oil engine** driving 1 FP propeller Total Power: 7,981kW (10,851hp) 15.0kn B&W 6S50MC 1 x 2 Stroke 6 Cy. 500 x 1910 7981kW (10851bhp) Hyundai Heavy Industries Co Ltd-South Korea
474034 RJX2	**ZHI DA** **Zhida Shipping SA** China Shipping Development Co Ltd Tramp Co *Hong Kong* *Hong Kong* MMSI: 477739200 Official number: HK-3372	**116,396** 46,519 228,749 T/cm 156.4	Class: CC	**2012-01 Guangzhou Longxue Shipbuilding Co Ltd — Guangzhou GD** Yd No: L0016 Loa 324.99 (BB) Br ex - Dght 18.100 Lbp 314.60 Br md 52.50 Dpth 24.30 Welded, 1 dk	**(A21B2BO) Ore Carrier** Grain: 153,315 Compartments: 5 Ho, ER 9 Ha: 8 (16.7 x 16.5)ER (16.7 x 13.6)	**1 oil engine** driving 1 FP propeller Total Power: 22,500kW (30,591hp) 15.0kn MAN-B&W 6S80MC-C 1 x 2 Stroke 6 Cy. 800 x 3200 22500kW (30591bhp) CSSC MES Diesel Co Ltd-China AuxGen: 3 x 960kW 450V a.c
567180 LTG8	**ZHI HE** **China Huarong Financial Leasing Co Ltd** Grand China Shipping Development Co Ltd SatCom: Inmarsat C 441410410 *Jiaxing, Zhejiang* *China* MMSI: 414104000	**43,349** 27,334 79,496 T/cm 71.9	Class: CC	**2012-06 Jinhai Heavy Industry Co Ltd — Daishan County ZJ** Yd No: J0080 Loa 229.00 (BB) Br ex - Dght 14.580 Lbp 222.00 Br md 32.26 Dpth 20.25 Welded, 1 dk	**(A21A2BC) Bulk Carrier** Grain: 97,886; Bale: 90,784 Compartments: 7 Ho, ER 7 Ha: 5 (15.6 x 15.0) (13.1 x 15.0)ER (13.1 x 13.2)	**1 oil engine** driving 1 FP propeller Total Power: 11,900kW (16,179hp) 14.5kn MAN-B&W 5S60MC-C8 1 x 2 Stroke 5 Cy. 600 x 2400 11900kW (16179bhp) Hitachi Zosen Corp-Japan AuxGen: 3 x 700kW 450V a.c
850580	**ZHI JIANG 01** **Wenzhou Marine Fishery Corp** - *Wenzhou, Zhejiang* *China*	*125* 60 -	Class: (CC)	**1990 Ningbo Fishing Vessel Shipyard — Ningbo ZJ** Loa 43.50 Br ex - Dght - Lbp 37.00 Br md 7.60 Dpth 3.80 Welded, 1 dk	**(B11B2FV) Fishing Vessel**	**1 oil engine** geared to sc. shaft driving 1 FP propeller Total Power: 294kW (400hp) Chinese Std. Type 6300 1 x 4 Stroke 6 Cy. 300 x 380 294kW (400bhp) Ningbo Engine Factory-China AuxGen: 2 x 64kW 400V a.c
850592	**ZHI JIANG 02** **Wenzhou Marine Fishery Corp** - *Wenzhou, Zhejiang* *China*	*125* 60 -	Class: (CC)	**1991 Ningbo Fishing Vessel Shipyard — Ningbo ZJ** Loa 43.50 Br ex - Dght - Lbp 37.00 Br md 7.60 Dpth 3.80 Welded, 1 dk	**(B11B2FV) Fishing Vessel**	**1 oil engine** geared to sc. shaft driving 1 FP propeller Total Power: 294kW (400hp) Chinese Std. Type 6300 1 x 4 Stroke 6 Cy. 300 x 380 294kW (400bhp) Ningbo Engine Factory-China AuxGen: 2 x 64kW 400V a.c
863862 KJV	**ZHI JIANG 03** **Zhejiang International Fisheries Corp** - *Wenzhou, Zhejiang* *China*	*299* 90 -	Class: (CC)	**1992 Guangzhou Fishing Vessel Shipyard — Guangzhou GD** Loa 44.86 Br ex - Dght 3.000 Lbp 38.00 Br md 7.60 Dpth 4.00 Welded, 1 dk	**(B11B2FV) Fishing Vessel** Ins: 224	**1 oil engine** geared to sc. shaft driving 1 FP propeller Total Power: 541kW (736hp) 12.0kn Chinese Std. Type 8300 1 x 4 Stroke 8 Cy. 300 x 380 541kW (736bhp) Zibo Diesel Engine Factory-China AuxGen: 2 x 115kW 400V a.c
863874 KJU	**ZHI JIANG 04** **Zhejiang International Fisheries Corp** - *Wenzhou, Zhejiang* *China*	*299* 90 -	Class: (CC)	**1992 Guangzhou Fishing Vessel Shipyard — Guangzhou GD** Loa 44.86 Br ex - Dght 3.000 Lbp 38.00 Br md 7.60 Dpth 4.00 Welded, 1 dk	**(B11B2FV) Fishing Vessel** Ins: 224	**1 oil engine** geared to sc. shaft driving 1 FP propeller Total Power: 541kW (736hp) 12.0kn Chinese Std. Type 8300 1 x 4 Stroke 8 Cy. 300 x 380 541kW (736bhp) Zibo Diesel Engine Factory-China AuxGen: 2 x 75kW 400V a.c
884397 KZA	**ZHI JIANG 05** **Zhejiang International Fisheries Corp** - *Wenzhou, Zhejiang* *China*	**342** 102 160	Class: (CC)	**1993-07 Guangzhou Fishing Vessel Shipyard — Guangzhou GD** Loa 44.86 Br ex - Dght 2.880 Lbp 38.00 Br md 8.00 Dpth 4.00 Welded, 1 dk	**(B11B2FV) Fishing Vessel**	**1 oil engine** geared to sc. shaft driving 1 FP propeller Total Power: 595kW (809hp) 12.5kn Chinese Std. Type 8300 1 x 4 Stroke 8 Cy. 300 x 380 595kW (809bhp) Zibo Diesel Engine Factory-China AuxGen: 2 x 120kW 400V a.c
058361 KZB	**ZHI JIANG 06** **Zhejiang International Fisheries Corp** - *Wenzhou, Zhejiang* *China*	*342* 102 487	Class: (CC)	**1993 Guangzhou Fishing Vessel Shipyard — Guangzhou GD** Loa 44.86 Br ex - Dght - Lbp 38.00 Br md 8.00 Dpth 4.00 Welded	**(B11B2FV) Fishing Vessel**	**1 oil engine** geared to sc. shaft driving 1 FP propeller Total Power: 735kW (999hp) Chinese Std. Type 8300 1 x 4 Stroke 8 Cy. 300 x 380 735kW (999bhp) Zibo Diesel Engine Factory-China
453561 IAD4	**ZHI JING** *ex Xin Dong Guan 6 -2010* *launched as Zhe Hai 509 -2008* **Anji Leasing Co Ltd** Grand China Shipping Development Co Ltd *Dongguan, Guangdong* *China* MMSI: 413334000	**19,983** 11,456 33,076	Class: CC	**2008-01 Zhoushan Wuzhou Ship Repairing & Building Co Ltd — Zhoushan ZJ** Yd No: WZ0601 Loa 178.00 (BB) Br ex - Dght 9.600 Lbp 170.80 Br md 27.60 Dpth 13.90 Welded, 1 dk	**(A21A2BC) Bulk Carrier** Grain: 40,522 Compartments: 5 Ho, ER 5 Ha: 4 (19.2 x 14.4)ER (13.6 x 14.4) Cranes: 4x25t	**1 oil engine** driving 1 FP propeller Total Power: 5,800kW (7,886hp) 13.5kn Wartsila 8L38 1 x 4 Stroke 8 Cy. 380 x 475 5800kW (7886bhp) Wartsila Italia SpA-Italy AuxGen: 3 x 450kW 400V a.c
664149 LY2663	**ZHI KUN 1** *ex Hong Zhou 1 -2013* **Wang Chang Bin** Sanying International Trade (HK) Co Ltd *Kingstown* *Sierra Leone* MMSI: 667075000 Official number: SL103466	**2,978** 1,667 -	Class: SL (Class contemplated)	**2005-11 Yuhuan Damaiyu Harbour Shiprepair & Building Yard — Yuhuan County ZJ** Loa 99.50 Br ex - Dght 5.950 Lbp - Br md 14.60 Dpth 7.40 Welded, 1 dk	**(A31A2GX) General Cargo Ship**	**1 oil engine** reduction geared to sc. shafts driving 1 FP propeller Total Power: 1,765kW (2,400hp) Chinese Std. Type G8300ZC18B 1 x 4 Stroke 8 Cy. 300 x 380 1765kW (2400bhp) Ningbo CSI Power & Machinery GroupCo Ltd-China
144483 RVP8	**ZHI QIANG** **Fullbest Shipping Ltd** COSCO (HK) Shipping Co Ltd SatCom: Inmarsat B 347759710 *Hong Kong* *Hong Kong* MMSI: 477597000 Official number: HK-0392	**26,062** 14,872 45,704 T/cm 49.8	Class: NK	**1998-04 Tsuneishi Shipbuilding Co Ltd — Fukuyama HS** Yd No: 1120 Loa 186.00 (BB) Br ex - Dght 11.620 Lbp 177.00 Br md 30.40 Dpth 16.50 Welded, 1 dk	**(A21A2BC) Bulk Carrier** Grain: 57,208; Bale: 55,564 Compartments: 5 Ho, ER 5 Ha: (20.0 x 15.3)4 (20.8 x 15.3)ER Cranes: 4x25t	**1 oil engine** driving 1 FP propeller Total Power: 7,172kW (9,751hp) 14.0kn B&W 6S50MC 1 x 2 Stroke 6 Cy. 500 x 1910 7172kW (9751bhp) Mitsui Engineering & Shipbuilding CLtd-Japan Fuel: 1535.0 (r.f.)

IMO / Call sign	Name / Owner	Tonnage / Class	Builder / Dimensions	Type	Machinery
8863460 *BIAH2* -	**ZHI SHUN** *ex* Da Xin Hua Zhi Shun *-2011* *ex* Bai Long Quan *-2008* **Grand China Shipping Development Co Ltd** - *Shanghai* *China* MMSI: 413376450	**2,542** Class: (CC) 1,013 3,328	**1992 Shandong Weihai Shipyard — Weihai SD** Loa 84.57 Br ex - Dght 5.300 Lbp 79.00 Br md 15.00 Dpth 7.30 Welded, 1 dk	**(A31A2GX) General Cargo Ship** Grain: 3,129 TEU 170 C.Ho 88/20' C.Dk 82/20' Compartments: 2 Ho, ER 4 Ha: 4 (12.6 x 10.4)ER Ice Capable	**1 oil engine** geared to sc. shaft driving 1 FP propeller Total Power: 811kW (1,103hp) 11.3k Chinese Std. Type 6320ZC 1 x 4 Stroke 6 Cy. 320 x 440 811kW (1103bhp) Guangzhou Diesel Engine Factory CoLtd-China AuxGen: 3 x 120kW 400V a.c
9591246 *BIHL* -	**ZHI XIAN 2** **Shanghai Zhixian Transportation Shipping Co Ltd** - *Shanghai* *China* MMSI: 412377210	**5,986** Class: CC 1,795 9,301	**2010-07 Huajie Shipbuilding Co Ltd — Linhai ZJ** Yd No: 0803-C Loa 118.00 (BB) Br ex 26.03 Dght 5.400 Lbp 109.30 Br md 26.00 Dpth 7.38 Welded, 1 dk	**(A38B2GB) Barge Carrier** Ice Capable	**2 oil engines** reduction geared to sc. shaft (s) driving 2 Propellers Total Power: 4,000kW (5,438hp) 10.0k Chinese Std. Type G8300Z 2 x 4 Stroke 8 Cy. 300 x 380 each-2000kW (2719bhp) Ningbo CSI Power & Machinery GroupCo Ltd-China AuxGen: 2 x 300kW 400V a.c
9395381 - -	**ZHI XIAN 38** - -	**2,220** 1,243 3,306	**2006-03 Zhejiang Tenglong Shipyard — Wenling ZJ** Yd No: 0516 Loa 86.00 Br ex - Dght 3.600 Lbp 81.10 Br md 18.00 Dpth 5.20 Welded, 1 dk	**(A31A2GX) General Cargo Ship**	**2 oil engines** reverse reduction geared to sc. shafts driving 2 FP propellers Total Power: 1,854kW (2,520hp) Chinese Std. Type CW8200Z 2 x 4 Stroke 8 Cy. 200 x 270 each-927kW (1260bhp) Weifang Diesel Engine Factory-China
9567192 *BLTG7* -	**ZHI XIANG** **China Huarong Financial Leasing Co Ltd** Shanghai Zhi Jing International Ship Management Co SatCom: Inmarsat C 441410310 *Jiaxing, Zhejiang* *China* MMSI: 414103000	**43,349** Class: CC 27,334 79,463 T/cm 71.9	**2012-05 Jinhai Heavy Industry Co Ltd — Daishan County ZJ** Yd No: J0081 Loa 229.00 (BB) Br ex - Dght 14.620 Lbp 222.00 Br md 32.26 Dpth 20.25 Welded, 1 dk	**(A21A2BC) Bulk Carrier** Grain: 97,886; Bale: 90,784 Compartments: 7 Ho, ER 7 Ha: 5 (15.6 x 15.0) (13.1 x 15.0)ER (13.1 x 13.2)	**1 oil engine** driving 1 FP propeller Total Power: 11,900kW (16,179hp) 14.5k MAN-B&W 5S60MC-C 1 x 2 Stroke 5 Cy. 600 x 2400 11900kW (16179bhp) Hitachi Zosen Corp-Japan AuxGen: 3 x 700kW 450V a.c
8731485 - -	**ZHI XING** **Shenzhen Qinglong High-Speed Passenger Shipping Co Ltd** - *Shenzhen, Guangdong* *China* Official number: 140008000029	**124** Class: (CC) 37 12	**2007-09 Dongguan Xingyang Shipbuilding Co Ltd — Dongguan GD** Loa 27.00 Br ex - Dght 1.000 Lbp 21.00 Br md 7.40 Dpth 2.50 Bonded, 1 dk	**(A37B2PS) Passenger Ship** Hull Material: Reinforced Plastic	**2 oil engines** geared to sc. shafts driving 2 Propellers Total Power: 720kW (978hp) 26.0k MWM TBD604BL6 2 x 4 Stroke 6 Cy. 170 x 195 each-360kW (489bhp) Henan Diesel Engine Industry Co Ltd-China AuxGen: 2 x 20kW 400V a.c
8990378 *DUA2745* -	**ZHIA** **ABL Shipping Corp** *Lucena* *Philippines* Official number: 04-0001757	**497** 297 1,200	**1997 Mauban Shipyard — Mauban** Loa 67.00 Br ex - Dght - Lbp - Br md 12.19 Dpth 3.35 Welded, 1 dk	**(A35D2RL) Landing Craft** Bow ramp (f)	**2 oil engines** driving 2 Propellers Total Power: 736kW (1,000hp) Cummins 2 x 4 Stroke 6 Cy. each-368kW (500bhp) Cummins Engine Co Inc-USA
7630608 - -	**ZHIZDRA** **Gemma Enterprise (M/P 'Gemma')** -	*1,122* Class: (RS) 347 556	**1976 Sudostroitelnyy Zavod "Baltiya" — Klaypeda** Yd No: 310 Loa 59.01 (BB) Br ex 13.01 Dght 4.871 Lbp 52.00 Br md - Dpth 8.89 Welded	**(B11A2FS) Stern Trawler** Bale: 95; Ins: 500 Compartments: 3 Ho, 1 Ta, ER 3 Ha: (1.2 x 1.3) (0.7 x 0.7) (1.9 x 1.9) Derricks: 2x1.5t; Winches: 2 Ice Capable	**1 oil engine** driving 1 FP propeller Total Power: 1,618kW (2,200hp) 13.3k Skoda 6L525IIPS 1 x 4 Stroke 6 Cy. 525 x 720 1618kW (2200bhp) CKD Praha-Praha
8826448 *UGXU* -	**ZHIZHGIN** **Arkhangelsk Sea Commercial Port (Arkhangelskiy Morskoy Torgovyy Port)** - *Arkhangelsk* *Russia* MMSI: 273132800	**278** Class: RS 81 89	**1989-10 Brodogradiliste 'Tito' — Belgrade** Yd No: 1127 Loa 35.78 Br ex 9.49 Dght 3.280 Lbp 30.23 Br md 9.00 Dpth 4.50 Welded, 1 dk	**(B32A2ST) Tug**	**2 oil engines** driving 1 CP propeller Total Power: 1,854kW (2,520hp) 13.5k Sulzer 6ASL25D 2 x 4 Stroke 6 Cy. 250 x 300 each-927kW (1260bhp) Tvornica Dizel Motora 'Jugoturbina'-Yugoslavia AuxGen: 1 x 150kW a.c
9044425 *3EEQ9* -	**ZHONG BANG 1** *ex* Tpc Auckland *-2013* *ex* Avon *-2004* *ex* Captain Corelli *-2000* *ex* Golden Bell *-2000* *ex* Ocean Great *-1997* **Zhong Bang 1 Shipping Co Ltd** IMU Ship Management Pte Ltd *Panama* *Panama* MMSI: 356483000 Official number: 3375908B	**16,722** Class: KR (NK) 10,435 28,451 T/cm 39.5	**1991-09 Imabari Shipbuilding Co Ltd — Imabari EH (Imabari Shipyard)** Yd No: 486 Loa 169.03 (BB) Br ex - Dght 9.745 Lbp 160.40 Br md 27.20 Dpth 13.60 Welded, 1 dk	**(A21A2BC) Bulk Carrier** Grain: 37,550; Bale: 35,789 Compartments: 5 Ho, ER 5 Ha: (13.3 x 16.0)4 (19.2 x 17.6)ER Cranes: 4x30.5t	**1 oil engine** driving 1 FP propeller Total Power: 5,737kW (7,800hp) 13.7kn B&W 5S50MC 1 x 2 Stroke 5 Cy. 500 x 1910 5737kW (7800bhp) Hitachi Zosen Corp-Japan AuxGen: 2 x 440kW 450V 60Hz a.c, 1 x 300kW 450V 60Hz a.c Fuel: 1301.7 (r.f.) 20.7pd
8511718 *BLHR* -	**ZHONG CHANG 58** *ex* Maltigua *-2012* *ex* Millenium Dawn *-2001* *ex* Golden Alpha *-1999* *ex* Maersk Cedar *-1992* *ex* Melanie *-1990* *ex* Marimo *-1987* **Shengsi Zhongchang Shipping Co Ltd** - *Zhoushan, Zhejiang* *China* MMSI: 412412410	**15,832** Class: ZC (NK) 8,866 26,563 T/cm 37.6	**1985-09 The Hakodate Dock Co Ltd — Hakodate HK** (Hull) Yd No: 728 **1985-09 Kurushima Dockyard Co. Ltd. — Onishi** Yd No: 2432 Loa 167.20 (BB) Br ex 26.29 Dght 9.543 Lbp 160.00 Br md 26.00 Dpth 13.30 Welded, 1 dk	**(A21A2BC) Bulk Carrier** Grain: 33,917; Bale: 32,681 Compartments: 5 Ho, ER 5 Ha: (13.1 x 13.8)4 (13.1 x 19.2)ER Cranes: 4x30t	**1 oil engine** driving 1 FP propeller Total Power: 5,075kW (6,900hp) 14.0kn B&W 6L50MCE 1 x 2 Stroke 6 Cy. 500 x 1620 5075kW (6900bhp) Mitsui Engineering & Shipbuilding CLtd-Japan AuxGen: 3 x 360kW 450V 60Hz a.c
8120703 *BSAD* -	**ZHONG CHANG 68** *ex* Regina Oldendorff *-2004* *launched as* St. Croix *-1986* **Zhoushan Zhongchang Shipping Co Ltd** - *Zhoushan, Zhejiang* *China* MMSI: 413038000	**18,121** Class: (LR) (CC) 10,713 ✠ Classed LR until 21/8/04 28,031 T/cm 38.6	**1986-05 Dalian Shipyard Co Ltd — Dalian LN** Yd No: B270/8 Loa 195.00 (BB) Br ex 23.12 Dght 10.240 Lbp 183.01 Br md 23.00 Dpth 14.30 Welded, 1 dk	**(A21A2BC) Bulk Carrier** Grain: 39,399; Bale: 33,137 Compartments: 5 Ho, ER 5 Ha: (17.5 x 11.0) (13.2 x 11.0)2 (21.5 x 11.0) (17.4 x 11.0)ER Cranes: 4x25t	**1 oil engine** driving 1 FP propeller Total Power: 7,870kW (10,700hp) 14.5kn B&W 8L55GFCA 1 x 2 Stroke 8 Cy. 550 x 1380 7870kW (10700bhp) Dalian Marine Diesel Works-China AuxGen: 3 x 440kW 450V 60Hz a.c Boilers: e 9.1kgf/cm² (8.9bar), AuxB (o.f.) 7.9kgf/cm² (7.7bar) Fuel: 174.0 (d.f.) 1644.0 (r.f.)
8401303 *BKPM3* -	**ZHONG CHANG 88** *ex* Sea Blessing *-2005* *ex* Irene *-2003* *ex* Trans Effort *-1993* *launched as* Okeanis *-1987* **Zhoushan Zhongchang Shipping Co Ltd** - *Zhoushan, Zhejiang* *China* MMSI: 412435460	**24,536** Class: (LR) (HR) 13,815 ✠ Classed LR until 1/3/06 42,637 T/cm 48.8	**1987-12 Mitsui Eng. & SB. Co. Ltd. — Tamano** Yd No: 1319 Loa 182.81 (BB) Br ex 30.54 Dght 11.215 Lbp 174.02 Br md 30.51 Dpth 15.78 Welded, 1 dk	**(A21A2BC) Bulk Carrier** Grain: 51,026; Bale: 50,026 Compartments: 5 Ho, ER 5 Ha: (16.7 x 15.6)3 (19.2 x 15.6) (18.4 x 15.6)ER Cranes: 4x25t	**1 oil engine** driving 1 FP propeller Total Power: 6,193kW (8,420hp) 14.5kn B&W 6L60MCE 1 x 2 Stroke 6 Cy. 600 x 1944 6193kW (8420bhp) Mitsui Engineering & Shipbuilding CLtd-Japan AuxGen: 3 x 480kW 450V 60Hz a.c Boilers: AuxB (Comp) 6.0kgf/cm² (5.9bar) Fuel: 165.0 (d.f.) 1641.0 (r.f.)
8913552 *BYCL* -	**ZHONG CHANG 118** *ex* Great Ocean *-2007* **Zhoushan Zhongchang Shipping Co Ltd** - *Yangjiang, Guangdong* *China* MMSI: 413839000	**25,905** Class: (NV) 13,656 43,473 T/cm 49.6	**1991-07 Hashihama Shipbuilding Co Ltd — Tadotsu KG** (Hull) Yd No: 877 **1991-07 Tsuneishi Shipbuilding Co Ltd — Fukuyama HS** Yd No: 650 Loa 185.90 (BB) Br ex - Dght 11.323 Lbp 177.00 Br md 30.40 Dpth 16.20 Welded, 1 dk	**(A21A2BC) Bulk Carrier** Grain: 53,594; Bale: 52,280 TEU 1082 C Ho 516 TEU C Dk 566 TEU Compartments: 5 Ho, ER 5 Ha: (19.2 x 15.3)4 (20.8 x 15.3)ER Cranes: 4x30t Ice Capable	**1 oil engine** driving 1 FP propeller Total Power: 7,832kW (10,648hp) 14.0kn B&W 6L60MCE 1 x 2 Stroke 6 Cy. 600 x 1944 7832kW (10648bhp) Mitsui Engineering & Shipbuilding CLtd-Japan AuxGen: 3 x 440kW 450V 60Hz a.c Fuel: 169.0 (d.f.) (Heating Coils) 1665.0 (r.f.) 26.8pd
9449027 *BKOS4* -	**ZHONG CHANG 128** **China Huarong Financial Leasing Co Ltd** Zhoushan Zhongchang Shipping Co Ltd *Hangzhou, Zhejiang* *China* MMSI: 413415440	**13,389** Class: CC 7,898 21,207	**2007-08 Ningbo Beilun Lantian Shipbuilding Co Ltd — Ningbo ZJ** Yd No: ZY1 Loa 159.29 Br ex - Dght 9.500 Lbp 149.60 Br md 23.20 Dpth 13.00 Welded, 1 dk	**(A21A2BC) Bulk Carrier** Grain: 25,385 Compartments: 4 Ho, ER 4 Ha: 3 (21.0 x 13.8)ER (22.5 x 11.0) Cranes: 3x25t	**1 oil engine** driving 1 FP propeller Total Power: 4,440kW (6,037hp) 12.0kn MAN-B&W 6S35MC 1 x 2 Stroke 6 Cy. 350 x 1400 4440kW (6037bhp) Yichang Marine Diesel Engine Co Ltd-China AuxGen: 3 x 250kW 400V a.c
9082764 *BFAB7* -	**ZHONG CHANG 168** *ex* London Bridge *-2009* *ex* Obc Anna *-2007* *ex* Lucasta *-2006* *ex* Bulk Orion *-2004* **Minsheng Financial Leasing Co Ltd** Shengsi Zhongchang Shipping Co Ltd SatCom: Inmarsat C 441389210 *Tianjin* *China* MMSI: 413892000	**26,059** Class: (CC) (IR) (NK) 14,880 45,708 T/cm 49.8	**1994-12 Tsuneishi Shipbuilding Co Ltd — Fukuyama HS** Yd No: 1044 Loa 185.74 (BB) Br ex 30.43 Dght 11.600 Lbp 177.00 Br md 30.40 Dpth 16.50 Welded, 1 dk	**(A21A2BC) Bulk Carrier** Grain: 57,175; Bale: 55,560 Compartments: 5 Ho, ER 5 Ha: (20.0 x 15.3)4 (20.8 x 15.3)ER Cranes: 4x25t	**1 oil engine** driving 1 FP propeller Total Power: 7,172kW (9,751hp) 14.0kn B&W 6S50MC 1 x 2 Stroke 6 Cy. 500 x 1910 7172kW (9751bhp) Mitsui Engineering & Shipbuilding CLtd-Japan AuxGen: 3 x 440kW a.c Fuel: 1469.0 (r.f.) 25.0pd

	Name / Owner	Tonnage	Class	Built	Type / Capacity	Machinery
510470 KTR5	**ZHONG CHANG 228** **Minsheng Financial Leasing Co Ltd** Zhoushan Zhongchang Shipping Co Ltd SatCom: Inmarsat C 441402410 *Tianjin* *China* MMSI: 414024000	**32,888** 19,142 57,146 T/cm 58.8	Class: CC	**2011-05 Qingshan Shipyard — Wuhan HB** Yd No: 20100305 Loa 189.99 (BB) Br ex - Dght 12.800 Lbp 185.00 Br md 32.26 Dpth 18.00 Welded, 1 dk	**(A21A2BC) Bulk Carrier** Grain: 71,634; Bale: 68,200 Compartments: 5 Ho, ER 5 Ha: 4 (21.3 x 18.3)ER (18.9 x 18.3)	**1 oil engine** driving 1 FP propeller Total Power: 9,480kW (12,889hp) 14.5kn MAN-B&W 6S50MC-C 1 x 2 Stroke 6 Cy. 500 x 2000 9480kW (12889bhp) Yichang Marine Diesel Engine Co Ltd-China AuxGen: 3 x 600kW 450V a.c
510482 IAO3	**ZHONG CHANG 258** **Minsheng Financial Leasing Co Ltd** Zhongchang Marine (Shanghai) Co Ltd SatCom: Inmarsat C 441404810 *Tianjin* *China* MMSI: 414048000	**32,888** 19,142 57,122 T/cm 58.8	Class: CC	**2011-10 Qingshan Shipyard — Wuhan HB** Yd No: 20100306 Loa 189.99 (BB) Br ex 32.66 Dght 12.800 Lbp 185.00 Br md 32.26 Dpth 18.00 Welded, 1 dk	**(A21A2BC) Bulk Carrier** Grain: 71,634; Bale: 68,200 Compartments: 5 Ho, ER 5 Ha: 4 (21.3 x 18.3)ER (18.9 x 18.3)	**1 oil engine** driving 1 FP propeller Total Power: 9,480kW (12,889hp) 14.2kn MAN-B&W 6S50MC-C 1 x 2 Stroke 6 Cy. 500 x 2000 9480kW (12889bhp) Yichang Marine Diesel Engine Co Ltd-China AuxGen: 3 x 600kW 450V a.c
557173 IAR6	**ZHONG CHANG JUN 16** *ex* Xia Zhi Yuan 9 *-2011* **Zhejiang Share-Ever Business Co Ltd** - SatCom: Inmarsat C 441301621 *Hangzhou, Zhejiang* *China* MMSI: 413440180	**13,511** 4,180 21,617	Class: CC	**2010-12 Zhoushan Haitian Shipyard Co Ltd — Daishan County ZJ** Yd No: HT0803 Loa 151.71 (BB) Br ex 26.84 Dght 7.500 Lbp 135.20 Br md 26.80 Dpth 11.00 Welded, 1 dk	**(B33A2DS) Suction Dredger**	**2 oil engines** reduction geared to sc. shafts driving 2 Propellers Total Power: 8,824kW (11,998hp) 12.5kn Chinese Std. Type G16V300ZC 2 x Vee 4 Stroke 16 Cy. 300 x 380 each-4412kW (5999bhp) Wuxi Antai Power Machinery Co Ltd-China Thrusters: 1 Tunnel thruster (f)
317150 FYC	**ZHONG CHENG 1** *ex* Free Envoy *-2011* *ex* Apostolos *-2004* *ex* Halla Star *-1998* *ex* Sammi Spirit *-1994* **Zhong Cheng 1 Shipping Co Ltd** IMU Ship Management Pte Ltd *Panama* *Panama* MMSI: 354921000 Official number: 4285711	**15,715** 9,110 26,318	Class: PD RI (Class contemplated) (KR) (NK)	**1984-01 Kurushima Dockyard Co. Ltd. — Onishi** Yd No: 2287 Loa 160.00 (BB) Br ex 25.43 Dght 10.372 Lbp 149.99 Br md 25.40 Dpth 14.20 Welded, 1 dk	**(A21A2BC) Bulk Carrier** Grain: 33,139; Bale: 31,879 Compartments: 4 Ho, ER 4 Ha: (17.6 x 11.4) (20.8 x 13.1) (22.4 x 13.1) (21.6 x 13.1)ER Cranes: 4x25t	**1 oil engine** driving 1 FP propeller Total Power: 5,296kW (7,200hp) 13.8kn Mitsubishi 6UEC52HA 1 x 2 Stroke 6 Cy. 520 x 1250 5296kW (7200bhp) Kobe Hatsudoki KK-Japan AuxGen: 2 x 400kW
342097 RFA6	**ZHONG CHI** **Zhong Chi Shipping SA** China Shipping Tanker Co Ltd *Hong Kong* *Hong Kong* MMSI: 477201800 Official number: HK-2363	**26,992** 11,381 41,968 T/cm 51.4	Class: CC	**2009-03 Guangzhou Shipyard International Co Ltd — Guangzhou GD** Yd No: 06130009 Loa 187.80 (BB) Br ex 31.53 Dght 10.500 Lbp 178.00 Br md 31.50 Dpth 16.80 Welded, 1 dk	**(A13B2TP) Products Tanker** Double Hull (13F) Liq: 44,646; Liq (Oil): 44,646 Cargo Heating Coils Compartments: 12 Wing Ta, 2 Wing Slop Ta, ER 3 Cargo Pump (s): 3x1200m³/hr Manifold: Bow/CM: 64.6m Ice Capable	**1 oil engine** driving 1 FP propeller Total Power: 8,580kW (11,665hp) 14.5kn MAN-B&W 6S50MC 1 x 2 Stroke 6 Cy. 500 x 1910 8580kW (11665bhp) Dalian Marine Diesel Co Ltd-China AuxGen: 3 x 664kW 450V a.c Fuel: 82.1 (d.f.) 1340.0 (r.f.)
748957 DYA	**ZHONG DA 2** **Zhongda Co Ltd** - *Suva* *Fiji* Official number: 000394	**136** 40 -		**2003-03 Huanghai Shipbuilding Co Ltd — Rongcheng SD** Loa 30.00 Br ex - Dght 2.000 Lbp - Br md 6.00 Dpth 2.00 Welded, 1 dk	**(B11B2FV) Fishing Vessel**	**1 oil engine** reduction geared to sc. shaft driving 1 Propeller Total Power: 217kW (295hp)
748969 DOP	**ZHONG DA 3** **Zhongda Co Ltd** - *Suva* *Fiji* Official number: 000544	**173** 63 -		**2006-09 Huanghai Shipbuilding Co Ltd — Rongcheng SD** Loa 36.00 Br ex - Dght 2.350 Lbp - Br md 6.40 Dpth 3.05 Welded, 1 dk	**(B11B2FV) Fishing Vessel**	**1 oil engine** driving 1 Propeller Total Power: 325kW (442hp)
099767 VMB2	**ZHONG DA 9 HAO** *ex* Yuan Xian 358 *-2005* **Fuzhou Sinostar Shipping Co Ltd** - *Fuzhou, Fujian* *China* MMSI: 412457130 Official number: 08000500010	**1,256** 703 1,996		**1993-05 in the People's Republic of China** Loa 73.87 Br ex 12.60 Dght 4.350 Lbp 70.49 Br md 12.60 Dpth 5.20 Welded, 1 dk	**(A31A2GX) General Cargo Ship**	**1 oil engine** reduction geared to sc. shaft driving 1 FP propeller Total Power: 808kW (1,099hp) Chinese Std. Type 8300ZC 1 x 4 Stroke 8 Cy. 300 x 380 808kW (1099bhp) Yichang Marine Diesel Engine Co Ltd-China
639086 DNS	**ZHONG DA NO. 5** **Zhong Da Co Ltd** - *Suva* *Fiji* Official number: 000981	**264** 79 -		**2011-06 Huanghai Shipbuilding Co Ltd — Rongcheng SD** Loa 39.60 Br ex - Dght - Lbp - Br md 6.90 Dpth 3.60 Welded, 1 dk	**(B11B2FV) Fishing Vessel** Ins: 140	**1 oil engine** driving 1 Propeller Total Power: 480kW (653hp) 12.0kn
639098 DNT	**ZHONG DA NO. 6** **Zhong Da Co Ltd** - *Suva* *Fiji* Official number: 000982	**264** 79 -		**2011-06 Huanghai Shipbuilding Co Ltd — Rongcheng SD** Loa 39.60 Br ex - Dght - Lbp - Br md 6.90 Dpth 3.60 Welded, 1 dk	**(B11B2FV) Fishing Vessel** Ins: 140	**1 oil engine** driving 1 Propeller Total Power: 480kW (653hp) 12.0kn
646467 KVQ5	**ZHONG DA YOU 16** **Zhoushan Zhongda Freight Services Co Ltd** - *Zhoushan, Zhejiang* *China* MMSI: 413443620	**4,132** 1,941 6,864	Class: CC	**2012-05 Zhoushan Zhaobao Shipbuilding & Repair Co Ltd — Zhoushan ZJ** Yd No: ZB1010 Loa 105.20 Br ex 16.02 Dght 6.900 Lbp 98.60 Br md 16.00 Dpth 8.70 Welded, 1 dk	**(A13B2TP) Products Tanker** Double Hull (13F) Liq: 3,336; Liq (Oil): 3,336 Compartments: 5 Wing Ta, 5 Wing Ta, ER Ice Capable	**1 oil engine** reduction geared to sc. shaft driving 1 FP propeller Total Power: 2,206kW (2,999hp) 11.5kn Guangzhou 8320ZC 1 x 4 Stroke 8 Cy. 320 x 440 2206kW (2999bhp) Guangzhou Diesel Engine Factory CoLtd-China AuxGen: 2 x 250kW 400V a.c
682063 KKD	**ZHONG DA YOU 56** *ex* Hua Chen 88 *-2011* **Zhoushan Zhongda Marine Co Ltd** - *Zhoushan, Zhejiang* *China* MMSI: 413437510	**7,041** 3,418 11,094	Class: CC	**2010-06 Wenzhou Xinwanyu Ship Industry Co Ltd — Yueqing ZJ** Yd No: XWY11000-5 Loa 132.00 Br ex - Dght 7.600 Lbp 124.00 Br md 19.80 Dpth 10.00 Welded, 1 dk	**(A12B2TR) Chemical/Products Tanker** Double Hull (13F) Liq: 11,566; Liq (Oil): 11,566 Compartments: 10 Wing Ta, 2 Wing Slop Ta, ER Ice Capable	**1 oil engine** reduction geared to sc. shaft driving 1 FP propeller Total Power: 3,310kW (4,500hp) 12.8kn Yanmar 8N330-EN 1 x 4 Stroke 8 Cy. 330 x 440 3310kW (4500bhp) Qingdao Zichai Boyang Diesel EngineCo Ltd-China AuxGen: 3 x 330kW 400V a.c
715493 ESM7	**ZHONG DE 1** *ex* Feggites *-2012* *ex* Neelam *-2011* *ex* Unity T *-2007* *ex* Mui Kim *-2000* **Zhong de 1 Shipping Co Ltd** IMU Ship Management Pte Ltd SatCom: Inmarsat A 1333142 *Panama* *Panama* MMSI: 355652000 Official number: 1877590F	**37,086** 22,646 68,774 T/cm 67.1	Class: PR (LR) (BV) ✠ Classed LR until 7/11/09	**1989-11 Hyundai Heavy Industries Co Ltd — Ulsan** Yd No: 627 Loa 224.36 (BB) Br ex 32.24 Dght 13.201 Lbp 215.00 Br md 32.20 Dpth 18.30 Welded, 1 dk	**(A21A2BC) Bulk Carrier** Grain: 80,428; Bale: 76,407 Compartments: 7 Ho, ER 7 Ha: (14.4 x 12.0)6 (14.4 x 15.0)ER Cranes: 4	**1 oil engine** driving 1 FP propeller Total Power: 7,497kW (10,193hp) 14.0kn B&W 5S60MCE 1 x 2 Stroke 5 Cy. 600 x 2292 7497kW (10193bhp) Hyundai Heavy Industries Co Ltd-South Korea AuxGen: 3 x 460kW 450V 60Hz a.c Boilers: e 11.9kgf/cm² (11.7bar), AuxB (o.f.) 6.9kgf/cm² (6.8bar)
624536	**ZHONG FU BO 6** **Ningde Zhongfu Shipping Co Ltd** - *Ningde, Fujian* *China* Official number: 440011000013	**1,509** 453 -		**2011-01 in the People's Republic of China** Yd No: HG-1023 Loa 76.00 Br ex 16.20 Dght 3.150 Lbp 71.40 Br md 16.00 Dpth 4.30 Welded, 1 dk	**(A31A2GA) General Cargo Ship (with Ro-Ro facility)** Bow door/ramp (centre)	**2 oil engines** reduction geared to sc. shafts driving 2 Propellers 10.0kn Cummins 2 x 4 Stroke Chongqing Cummins Engine Co Ltd-China
741583 SRZ	**ZHONG GANG TUO 1** **CCCC Tianjin Dredging Co Ltd** - SatCom: Inmarsat C 441215725 *Tianjin* *China* MMSI: 413017010	**1,498** 449 889	Class: CC	**2007-01 China Harbour Group Tianjin Shbldg & Eng Co Ltd — Qinhuangdao HE** Loa 64.00 Br ex - Dght 4.300 Lbp 57.00 Br md 12.65 Dpth 5.80 Welded, 1 dk	**(B32A2ST) Tug**	**2 oil engines** reduction geared to sc. shafts driving 2 Propellers Total Power: 2,942kW (4,000hp) Chinese Std. Type G8300ZC 2 x 4 Stroke 8 Cy. 300 x 380 each-1471kW (2000bhp) Ningbo CSI Power & Machinery GroupCo Ltd-China
592355 FAK6	**ZHONG GANG TUO 702** **Tianjin China Port Well Yield Logistics Co Ltd** - *Tianjin* *China* MMSI: 413592420	**2,686** 805 -	Class: CC	**2010-07 Fujian Huahai Shipbuilding Co Ltd — Fu'an FJ** Yd No: 009 Loa 70.60 Br ex - Dght 5.800 Lbp 62.20 Br md 16.80 Dpth 7.50 Welded, 1 dk	**(B21B20T) Offshore Tug/Supply Ship** Ice Capable	**4 oil engines** reduction geared to sc. shafts driving 2 Propellers Total Power: 5,296kW (7,200hp) 13.5kn Chinese Std. Type LB8250ZLC 4 x 4 Stroke 8 Cy. 250 x 320 each-1324kW (1800bhp) Zibo Diesel Engine Factory-China AuxGen: 2 x 400kW 400V a.c, 2 x 980kW 400V a.c

IMO / Call sign	Name / Owner / Port	Tonnage	Class	Builder / Dimensions	Type	Machinery
8908181 *BIBK9* -	**ZHONG GU TAI SHAN** *ex* Da Xin Hua Quan Zhou *-2013* *ex* Conti Jork *-2010* *ex* Kota Permas *-2000* *ex* Conti Jork *-1999* *ex* Contship Jork *-1997* **Jiangsu Financial Leasing Co Ltd** - *Shanghai* *China* MMSI: 413377840	**16,236** 9,475 23,596 T/cm 36.0	Class: CC (GL)	**1990-12 Schichau Seebeckwerft AG — Bremerhaven** (Hull) **Yd No:** 1086 **1990-12 Bremer Vulkan AG Schiffbau u. Maschinenfabrik — Bremen Yd No:** 86 Loa 163.33 (BB) Br ex 27.80 Dght 10.660 Lbp 153.73 Br md 27.51 Dpth 14.30 Welded, 1 dk	**(A33A2CC) Container Ship (Fully Cellular)** Grain: 32,650; Bale: 32,025 TEU 1599 C Ho 618 TEU C Dk 981 TEU incl 70 ref C. Compartments: 3 Cell Ho, ER 8 Ha: 2 (12.4 x 20.5)6 (12.4 x 23.0)ER Cranes: 3x40t Ice Capable	**1 oil engine** driving 1 FP propeller Vane wheel Total Power: 10,440kW (14,194hp) 17.7k B&W 6L60M 1 x 2 Stroke 6 Cy. 600 x 1944 10440kW (14194bhp) Bremer Vulkan AG Schiffbau u.Maschinenfabrik-Bremen AuxGen: 1 x 992kW 220/440V 60Hz a.c, 2 x 785kW 220/440V 60Hz a.c Thrusters: 1 Thwart. FP thruster (f) Fuel: 186.5 (d.f.) 1900.0 (r.f.) 45.0pd
9365063 *BNPS* -	**ZHONG GUO HAI JIAN 15** **Government of The People's Republic of China (North Sea Branch of State Oceanic Administration)** - SatCom: Inmarsat C 441301383 *Qingdao, Shandong* *China* MMSI: 413325050	**1,819** 545 370	Class: CC	**2010-11 Wuchang Shipbuilding Industry Co Ltd — Wuhan HB Yd No:** A197L Loa 88.00 Br ex - Dght 3.580 Lbp 79.00 Br md 12.00 Dpth 5.60 Welded, 1 dk	**(B31A2SR) Research Survey Vessel** Ice Capable	**2 oil engines** reduction geared to sc. shafts driving 2 CP propellers Total Power: 3,420kW (4,650hp) 14.0k MaK 9M20 2 x 4 Stroke 9 Cy. 200 x 300 each-1710kW (2325bhp) Caterpillar Motoren GmbH & Co. KG-Germany AuxGen: 2 x 280kW 400V a.c, 1 x 500kW 400V a.c
9352717 *BNPO* -	**ZHONG GUO HAI JIAN 17** **Government of The People's Republic of China (North Sea Branch of State Oceanic Administration)** - SatCom: Inmarsat C 441322010 *Qingdao, Shandong* *China* MMSI: 413220000	**1,111** 333 897	Class: CC	**2005-05 Wuchang Shipyard — Wuhan HB Yd No:** A105L Loa 73.90 Br ex - Dght 4.600 Lbp 69.50 Br md 10.20 Dpth 4.60 Welded, 1 dk	**(B34H2SQ) Patrol Vessel** Ice Capable	**1 oil engine** reduction geared to sc. shaft driving 1 FP propeller Total Power: 1,710kW (2,325hp) MaK 9M2 1 x 4 Stroke 9 Cy. 200 x 300 1710kW (2325bhp) Caterpillar Motoren GmbH & Co. KG-Germany AuxGen: 2 x 250kW 400V a.c, 1 x 400kW 400V a.c
9147344 *BNPM* -	**ZHONG GUO HAI JIAN 18** **Government of The People's Republic of China (North Sea Branch of State Oceanic Administration)** - SatCom: Inmarsat C 441231910 *Qingdao, Shandong* *China* MMSI: 412948000	**912** 273 340	Class: CC	**1996-03 Wuchang Shipyard — Wuhan HB** Loa 71.40 Br ex - Dght 3.370 Lbp 65.00 Br md 10.20 Dpth 4.50 Welded, 1 dk	**(B31A2SR) Research Survey Vessel**	**1 oil engine** geared to sc. shaft driving 1 FP propeller Total Power: 974kW (1,324hp) Alpha 6L28/3 1 x 4 Stroke 6 Cy. 280 x 320 974kW (1324bhp) Zhenjiang Marine Diesel Works-China
9596519 *BNPT* -	**ZHONG GUO HAI JIAN 23** **Government of The People's Republic of China (The North China Sea Sub-Bureau of The National Oceanology Bureau)** - SatCom: Inmarsat C 441301584 *Qingdao, Shandong* *China* MMSI: 413325370	**1,149** 344 282	Class: CC	**2010-12 Guangzhou Huangpu Shipbuilding Co Ltd — Guangzhou GD Yd No:** 2306 Loa 77.70 Br ex 10.40 Dght 4.000 Lbp 70.40 Br md 10.20 Dpth 4.70 Welded, 1 dk	**(B31A2SR) Research Survey Vessel** Ice Capable	**2 oil engines** reduction geared to sc. shafts driving 1 Propelle Total Power: 4,760kW (6,472hp) 20.0k MAN-B&W 7L27/3 2 x 4 Stroke 7 Cy. 270 x 380 each-2380kW (3236bhp) MAN B&W Diesel AG-Augsburg AuxGen: 2 x 250kW 400V a.c, 1 x 430kW 400V a.c
9607497 *BNPU* -	**ZHONG GUO HAI JIAN 26** **Government of The People's Republic of China (The North China Sea Sub-Bureau of The National Oceanology Bureau)** - SatCom: Inmarsat C 441219587 *Qingdao, Shandong* *China* MMSI: 412330560	**1,149** 344 299	Class: CC	**2011-03 Guangzhou Huangpu Shipbuilding Co Ltd — Guangzhou GD Yd No:** 2308 Loa 77.70 (BB) Br ex 10.40 Dght 4.000 Lbp 70.40 Br md 10.20 Dpth 4.70 Welded, 1 dk	**(B31A2SR) Research Survey Vessel** Ice Capable	**2 oil engines** reduction geared to sc. shafts driving 2 Propellers Total Power: 4,760kW (6,472hp) 20.0k MAN-B&W 7L27/3 2 x 4 Stroke 7 Cy. 270 x 380 each-2380kW (3236bhp) MAN B&W Diesel AG-Augsburg Thrusters: 1 Tunnel thruster (f)
9341811 *BNPN* -	**ZHONG GUO HAI JIAN 27** **Government of The People's Republic of China (North Sea Branch of State Oceanic Administration)** - *Qingdao, Shandong* *China* MMSI: 413045000	**1,124** 337 322	Class: CC	**2004-12 Guangzhou Huangpu Shipyard — Guangzhou GD** Loa 75.80 Br ex - Dght 4.000 Lbp 70.40 Br md 10.20 Dpth 4.70 Welded, 1 dk	**(B34H2SQ) Patrol Vessel** Ice Capable	**2 oil engines** reduction geared to sc. shafts driving 2 Propellers Total Power: 4,760kW (6,472hp) MAN-B&W 7L27/3 2 x 4 Stroke 7 Cy. 270 x 380 each-2380kW (3236bhp) MAN B&W Diesel A/S-Denmark
9351878 *BNRP* -	**ZHONG GUO HAI JIAN 46** **Government of The People's Republic of China (East Sea Branch of the State Oceanic Administration)** - SatCom: Inmarsat C 441321010 *Ningbo, Zhejiang* *China* MMSI: 413210000	**1,111** 333 253	Class: CC	**2005-05 Wuchang Shipyard — Wuhan HB Yd No:** A104L Loa 73.90 Br ex - Dght 3.400 Lbp 69.50 Br md 10.20 Dpth 4.60 Welded, 1 dk	**(B34H2SQ) Patrol Vessel** Ice Capable	**1 oil engine** reduction geared to sc. shaft driving 1 FP propeller Total Power: 1,710kW (2,325hp) MaK 9M2 1 x 4 Stroke 9 Cy. 200 x 300 1710kW (2325bhp) Caterpillar Motoren GmbH & Co. KG-Germany
9150949 *BNRN* -	**ZHONG GUO HAI JIAN 49** **Government of The People's Republic of China (East Sea Branch of the State Oceanic Administration)** - SatCom: Inmarsat C 441242915 *Ningbo, Zhejiang* *China* MMSI: 412969536	**912** 273 345	Class: CC	**1995-06 Wuchang Shipyard — Wuhan HB** Loa 71.40 Br ex - Dght 3.340 Lbp 65.00 Br md 10.20 Dpth 4.50 Welded, 1 dk	**(B31A2SR) Research Survey Vessel** Ice Capable	**1 oil engine** reduction geared to sc. shaft driving 1 FP propeller Total Power: 1,324kW (1,800hp) 15.5k Alpha 6L28/3 1 x 4 Stroke 6 Cy. 280 x 320 1324kW (1800bhp) Zhenjiang Marine Diesel Works-China AuxGen: 1 x 280kW 400V a.c, 2 x 200kW 400V a.c
9625279 *BNRS* -	**ZHONG GUO HAI JIAN 50** **Government of The People's Republic of China (East Sea Branch of the State Oceanic Administration)** - *Shanghai* *China* MMSI: 413376370	**3,216** 965 3,336	Class: CC	**2011-07 Wuchang Shipbuilding Industry Co Ltd — Wuhan HB Yd No:** A199L Loa 98.00 Br ex - Dght 5.000 Lbp 86.00 Br md 15.20 Dpth 7.80 Welded, 1 dk	**(B31A2SR) Research Survey Vessel**	**2 oil engines** reduction geared to sc. shafts driving 2 Propellers Total Power: 3,870kW (5,262hp) MAN-B&W 9L21/3 2 x 4 Stroke 9 Cy. 210 x 310 each-1935kW (2631bhp) MAN B&W Diesel AG-Augsburg
9361316 *BNRQ* -	**ZHONG GUO HAI JIAN 51** **Government of The People's Republic of China (East Sea Branch of the State Oceanic Administration)** - *Shanghai* *China* MMSI: 413213000 Official number: 05S3008	**1,937** 581 374	Class: CC	**2005-11 Wuchang Shipyard — Wuhan HB Yd No:** A107L Loa 88.00 Br ex - Dght - Lbp 79.00 Br md 12.00 Dpth 5.60 Welded, 1 dk	**(B34H2SQ) Patrol Vessel** Ice Capable	**2 oil engines** reduction geared to sc. shafts driving 2 Propellers Total Power: 3,420kW (4,650hp) MaK 9M2 2 x 4 Stroke 9 Cy. 200 x 300 each-1710kW (2325bhp) Caterpillar Motoren GmbH & Co. KG-Germany AuxGen: 2 x 280kW 400V a.c
8326723 *BNRC* -	**ZHONG GUO HAI JIAN 52** *ex* Shi Jian *-2000* **Government of The People's Republic of China (East Sea Branch of the State Oceanic Administration)** - *Shanghai* *China* MMSI: 412920000	**2,421** 726 436	Class: CC	**1969 Hudong Shipyard — Shanghai** Loa 94.73 Br ex - Dght 5.001 Lbp 83.00 Br md 14.00 Dpth 7.80 Welded, 2 dks	**(B31A2SR) Research Survey Vessel** Derricks: 2x5t; Winches: 4	**2 oil engines** driving 2 FP propellers Total Power: 2,942kW (4,000hp) 16.0k Hudong 6ESDZ43/82 2 x 2 Stroke 6 Cy. 430 x 820 each-1471kW (2000bhp) Hudong Shipyard-China AuxGen: 4 x 250kW 230V d.c
8952223 *BNRO* -	**ZHONG GUO HAI JIAN 53** *ex* You Dian 1 *-2005* **Government of The People's Republic of China (East Sea Branch of the State Oceanic Administration)** - SatCom: Inmarsat C 441273715 *Shanghai* *China* MMSI: 412372330	**949** 284 618	Class: CC	**1976-04 Zhonghua Shipyard — Shanghai** Loa 71.40 Br ex - Dght 3.600 Lbp 63.00 Br md 10.50 Dpth 5.20 Welded, 1 dk	**(B34D2SL) Cable Layer**	**2 oil engines** reduction geared to sc. shafts driving 2 FP propellers Total Power: 1,100kW (1,496hp) 14.0k Chinese Std. Type 8300Z 2 x 4 Stroke 8 Cy. 300 x 380 each-550kW (748bhp) Hongwei Machinery Factory-China

IMO / Call sign	Name / Owner / Manager	Tonnage	Class	Builder / Dimensions	Type	Machinery
603312 *NRT*	**ZHONG GUO HAI JIAN 66** **Government of The People's Republic of China (East Sea Branch of the State Oceanic Administration)** - SatCom: Inmarsat C 441301678 *Xiamen, Fujian* *China* MMSI: 413695960	**1,149** 344 289	Class: CC	**2011-01 Guangzhou Huangpu Shipbuilding Co Ltd — Guangzhou GD** Yd No: 2307 Loa 77.70 Br ex 10.40 Dght 4.000 Lbp 70.40 Br md 10.20 Dpth 4.70 Welded, 1 dk	**(B31A2SR) Research Survey Vessel** Ice Capable	**2 oil engines** reduction geared to sc. shafts driving 1 Propeller Total Power: 4,760kW (6,472hp) 20.0kn MAN-B&W 7L27/38 2 x 4 Stroke 7 Cy. 270 x 380 each-2380kW (3236bhp) MAN B&W Diesel AG-Augsburg
355678 *VTF*	**ZHONG GUO HAI JIAN 71** **Government of The People's Republic of China (South Sea Branch of the State Oceanic Administration)** - *Guangzhou, Guangdong* *China* MMSI: 413211000	**1,111** 333 253	Class: CC	**2005-08 Wuchang Shipyard — Wuhan HB** Yd No: A106L Loa 73.90 Br ex - Dght - Lbp 67.92 Br md 10.20 Dpth 4.60 Welded, 1 dk	**(B34H2SQ) Patrol Vessel** Ice Capable	**1 oil engine** reduction geared to sc. shafts driving 1 Propeller Total Power: 1,710kW (2,325hp) MaK 9M20 1 x 4 Stroke 9 Cy. 200 x 300 1710kW (2325bhp) Caterpillar Motoren GmbH & Co. KG-Germany AuxGen: 2 x 250kW 400V a.c, 1 x 400kW 400V a.c
333582 *VTG*	**ZHONG GUO HAI JIAN 72** **Government of The People's Republic of China (South Sea Branch of the State Oceanic Administration)** - SatCom: Inmarsat C 441292211 *Guangzhou, Guangdong* *China* MMSI: 412922000	*881* 246 205	Class: CC	**1989 Wuchang Shipyard — Wuhan HB** Loa 70.00 Br ex - Dght - Lbp 63.00 Br md 9.40 Dpth 4.50 Welded, 1 dk	**(B31A2SR) Research Survey Vessel**	**2 oil engines** geared to sc. shaft driving 1 FP propeller Total Power: 2,648kW (3,600hp) 18.8kn Alpha 6L28/32 2 x 4 Stroke 6 Cy. 280 x 320 each-1324kW (1800bhp) Zhenjiang Marine Diesel Works-China AuxGen: 2 x 280kW 400V a.c, 1 x 64kW 400V a.c
53680 *VTL*	**ZHONG GUO HAI JIAN 74** **Government of The People's Republic of China (South Sea Branch of the State Oceanic Administration)** - SatCom: Inmarsat C 441273811 *Guangzhou, Guangdong* *China* MMSI: 412852000	**912** 273 360	Class: CC	**1996-05 Wuchang Shipyard — Wuhan HB** Yd No: A960 Loa 71.40 Br ex - Dght 3.350 Lbp 65.00 Br md 10.20 Dpth 4.50 Welded, 1 dk	**(B31A2SR) Research Survey Vessel** Ice Capable	**1 oil engine** reduction geared to sc. shaft driving 1 FP propeller Total Power: 1,324kW (1,800hp) 15.5kn Alpha 6L28/32 1 x 4 Stroke 6 Cy. 280 x 320 1324kW (1800bhp) Zhenjiang Marine Diesel Works-China AuxGen: 2 x 200kW 400V a.c
333609 *VTH*	**ZHONG GUO HAI JIAN 75** **Government of The People's Republic of China (South Sea Branch of the State Oceanic Administration)** - *Guangzhou, Guangdong* *China*	*163* 49 -		**1966 Qiuxin Shipyard — Shanghai** Loa 36.18 Br ex - Dght 2.620 Lbp 31.00 Br md 6.60 Dpth 3.90 Welded, 1 dk	**(B31A2SR) Research Survey Vessel**	**1 oil engine** geared to sc. shaft driving 1 FP propeller Total Power: 294kW (400hp) Chinese Std. Type 6300 1 x 4 Stroke 6 Cy. 300 x 380 294kW (400bhp) Qiuxin Shipyard-China AuxGen: 2 x 19kW 115V d.c
591791 *VDX*	**ZHONG GUO HAI JIAN 75** **Government of The People's Republic of China (South Sea Branch of the State Oceanic Administration)** - *Guangzhou, Guangdong* *China* MMSI: 412473820	**1,149** 344 1,000	Class: CC	**2010-10 Guangzhou Huangpu Shipbuilding Co Ltd — Guangzhou GD** Yd No: 2305 Loa 77.70 Br ex 10.40 Dght 4.000 Lbp 70.40 Br md 10.20 Dpth 4.70 Welded, 1 dk	**(B31A2SR) Research Survey Vessel**	**2 oil engines** reduction geared to sc. shafts driving 1 Propeller Total Power: 4,760kW (6,472hp) MAN-B&W 7L27/38 2 x 4 Stroke 7 Cy. 270 x 380 each-2380kW (3236bhp) MAN B&W Diesel AG-Augsburg
333611 *VWD*	**ZHONG GUO HAI JIAN 76** **Government of The People's Republic of China (South Sea Branch of the State Oceanic Administration)** - *Guangzhou, Guangdong* *China*	*176* 53 -		**1966 Qiuxin Shipyard — Shanghai** Loa 36.18 Br ex - Dght 3.200 Lbp 31.00 Br md 6.60 Dpth 3.90 Welded, 1 dk	**(B31A2SR) Research Survey Vessel**	**1 oil engine** geared to sc. shaft driving 1 FP propeller Total Power: 294kW (400hp) Chinese Std. Type 6300 1 x 4 Stroke 6 Cy. 300 x 380 294kW (400bhp) Qiuxin Shipyard-China AuxGen: 2 x 19kW 115V d.c
364679 *VTA*	**ZHONG GUO HAI JIAN 83** **Government of The People's Republic of China (South Sea Branch of the State Oceanic Administration)** - SatCom: Inmarsat C 441311210 *Guangzhou, Guangdong* *China* MMSI: 413112000	**3,276** 982 1,021	Class: CC	**2005-08 Jiangnan Shipyard (Group) Co Ltd — Shanghai** Yd No: H2292 Loa 98.00 (BB) Br ex - Dght 5.500 Lbp 86.00 Br md 15.20 Dpth 7.80 Welded, 1 dk	**(B34H2SQ) Patrol Vessel** Ice Capable	**3 oil engines** reduction geared to sc. shafts driving 3 Propellers Total Power: 3,972kW (5,400hp) AuxGen: 3 x 1800kW 690V a.c, 1 x 600kW 690V a.c Thrusters: 1 Tunnel thruster (f)
599107 *YDZ*	**ZHONG GUO HAI JIAN 84** **Government of The People's Republic of China (South China Sea Geological Investigation Headquarters)** - *Guangzhou, Guangdong* *China* MMSI: 412473810	**1,819** 545 370	Class: CC	**2011-04 Wuchang Shipbuilding Industry Co Ltd — Wuhan HB** Yd No: A198L Loa 88.00 Br ex - Dght 3.580 Lbp 79.00 Br md 12.00 Dpth 5.60 Welded, 1 dk	**(B31A2SR) Research Survey Vessel** Ice Capable	**2 oil engines** reduction geared to sc. shafts driving 2 CP propellers Total Power: 3,420kW (4,650hp) 14.0kn MaK 9M20C 2 x 4 Stroke 9 Cy. 200 x 300 each-1710kW (2325bhp) Caterpillar Motoren GmbH & Co. KG-Germany AuxGen: 2 x 280kW 400V a.c, 1 x 500kW 400V a.c
718598 *BEA3*	**ZHONG GUO YU ZHENG 404** **Government of The People's Republic of China (Shandong Provincial Bureau of Aquatic Products)** - *China*	*141* 42 24		**1988-03 K.K. Odo Zosen Tekko — Shimonoseki** Yd No: 336 Loa 33.00 Br ex 5.97 Dght 1.201 Lbp 30.00 Br md 5.81 Dpth 3.00 Welded, 1 dk	**(B34H2SQ) Patrol Vessel**	**2 oil engines** with clutches & sr geared to sc. shafts driving 2 FP propellers Total Power: 1,472kW (2,002hp) Yanmar 12LAAK-UT1 2 x Vee 4 Stroke 12 Cy. 148 x 165 each-736kW (1001bhp) Yanmar Diesel Engine Co Ltd-Japan
117715 *FXG5*	**ZHONG HAI** **Zhonghai Shipping Inc** COSCO Bulk Carrier Co Ltd (COSCO BULK) SatCom: Inmarsat B 335601310 *Panama* *Panama* MMSI: 356013000 Official number: 2276096CH	**26,123** 14,853 45,189 T/cm 51.0	Class: CC (NV)	**1996-02 KK Kanasashi — Toyohashi AI** Yd No: 3407 Loa 188.33 (BB) Br ex - Dght 11.373 Lbp 179.50 Br md 31.00 Dpth 16.30 Welded, 1 dk	**(A21A2BC) Bulk Carrier** Grain: 58,148; Bale: 56,250 Compartments: 5 Ho, ER 5 Ha: (16.8 x 16.0)4 (20.0 x 16.0)ER Cranes: 4x25t	**1 oil engine** driving 1 FP propeller Total Power: 7,061kW (9,600hp) 14.2kn B&W 6S50MC 1 x 2 Stroke 6 Cy. 500 x 1910 7061kW (9600bhp) Kawasaki Heavy Industries Ltd-Japan AuxGen: 3 x 400kW 220/450V 60Hz a.c Fuel: 102.8 (d.f.) (Heating Coils) 25.5pd
469417 *PQS*	**ZHONG HAI CHANG YUN 1** **China Shipping Industry Co Ltd (CIC)** Wuhu Shipping Co Ltd SatCom: Inmarsat C 441357910 *Shanghai* *China* MMSI: 413579000	**33,511** 18,766 57,000	Class: ZC	**2009-01 China Shipping Industry (Jiangsu) Co Ltd — Jiangdu JS** Loa 199.99 (BB) Br ex - Dght 12.500 Lbp 192.00 Br md 32.26 Dpth 18.00 Welded, 1 dk	**(A21A2BC) Bulk Carrier** Grain: 71,634 Compartments: 5 Ho, ER 5 Ha: ER	**1 oil engine** driving 1 FP propeller Total Power: 9,960kW (13,542hp) 14.2kn MAN-B&W 6S50MC-C 1 x 2 Stroke 6 Cy. 500 x 2000 9960kW (13542bhp)
469431 *PQT*	**ZHONG HAI CHANG YUN 2** **China Shipping Tanker Co Ltd** - SatCom: Inmarsat C 441369210 *China* MMSI: 413692000	**30,000** 19,142 57,000		**2009-03 China Shipping Industry (Jiangsu) Co Ltd — Jiangdu JS** Loa 199.99 (BB) Br ex - Dght 12.500 Lbp 192.00 Br md 32.26 Dpth 18.00 Welded, 1 dk	**(A21A2BC) Bulk Carrier** Grain: 71,634 Compartments: 5 Ho, ER 5 Ha: ER	**1 oil engine** driving 1 FP propeller Total Power: 9,960kW (13,542hp) 14.2kn MAN-B&W 6S50MC-C 1 x 2 Stroke 6 Cy. 500 x 2000 9960kW (13542bhp)
493391 *PQV*	**ZHONG HAI CHANG YUN 3** **China Shipping Bulk Carrier Co Ltd** - *China* MMSI: 413837000	**30,000** 19,142 57,000		**2009-05 China Shipping Industry (Jiangsu) Co Ltd — Jiangdu JS** Loa 199.99 (BB) Br ex - Dght 12.500 Lbp 192.00 Br md 32.26 Dpth 18.00 Welded, 1 dk	**(A21A2BC) Bulk Carrier** Grain: 71,634 Compartments: 5 Ho, ER 5 Ha: ER	**1 oil engine** driving 1 FP propeller Total Power: 9,960kW (13,542hp) 14.2kn MAN-B&W 6S50MC-C 1 x 2 Stroke 6 Cy. 500 x 2000 9960kW (13542bhp)

IMO / Call sign / Flag	Name / History / Owner / Manager	Tonnage	Class	Builder / Dimensions	Type / Capacity	Machinery
9617179 *BPQF* -	**ZHONG HAI CHANG YUN 6** *launched as* Tian Ying *-2012* **China Shipping Industry Co Ltd (CIC)** Wuhu Shipping Co Ltd SatCom: Inmarsat C 441471210 *Shanghai* *China* MMSI: 414712000	**32,962** 19,142 56,639 T/cm 58.8	Class: CC	**2012-05 China Shipping Industry (Jiangsu) Co Ltd — Jiangdu JS** Yd No: IS57000/E-03 Loa 189.99 (BB) Br ex 32.30 Dght 12.800 Lbp 185.00 Br md 32.26 Dpth 18.00 Welded, 1 dk	**(A21A2BC) Bulk Carrier** Grain: 71,634; Bale: 68,200 Compartments: 5 Ho, ER 5 Ha: 4 (21.3 x 18.3)ER (18.9 x 18.3) Cranes: 4x30t	**1 oil engine** driving 1 FP propeller Total Power: 9,480kW (12,889hp) 14.2 MAN-B&W 6S50MC 1 x 2 Stroke 6 Cy. 500 x 2000 9480kW (12889bhp) Yichang Marine Diesel Engine Co Ltd-China AuxGen: 3 x 600kW 450V a.c
8413227 *BPAX* -	**ZHONG HAI GAO SU** *ex* Emerald Highway *-2005* **China Shipping Car Carrier Co Ltd** *Dalian, Liaoning* *China* MMSI: 413126000	**33,131** 9,939 11,889	Class: CC (NK)	**1985-05 Mitsubishi Heavy Industries Ltd. — Kobe** Yd No: 1163 Loa 173.01 (BB) Br ex - Dght 8.202 Lbp 163.00 Br md 28.01 Dpth 24.49 Welded	**(A35B2RV) Vehicles Carrier** Side door/ramp (p) Len: 15.00 Wid: 4.00 Swl: 5 Side door/ramp (s) Len: 15.00 Wid: 4.00 Swl: 5 Quarter stern door/ramp (s. a.) Len: 24.50 Wid: 6.00 Swl: 50 Lane-Len: 2400 Lane-clr ht: 2.79 Cars: 3,300	**1 oil engine** sr geared to sc. shaft driving 1 FP propeller Total Power: 7,870kW (10,700hp) 18.0 MAN 10V52/55 1 x Vee 4 Stroke 10 Cy. 520 x 550 7870kW (10700bhp) Mitsubishi Heavy Industries Ltd-Japan AuxGen: 3 x 500kW 450V 60Hz a.c Fuel: 187.0 (d.f.) 1460.0 (r.f.) 29.0pd
8108913 *BRTE* -	**ZHONG HAI TONG 19** *ex* Jing Bo Hu *-2011* *ex* Crystal *-2003* *ex* Seaqueen *-1995* *ex* Jing Bo Hu *-1992* **Shenzhen Sinocean Marine Co Ltd** - *Shenzhen, Guangdong* *China* MMSI: 413006000	**12,474** 6,985 19,989	Class: ZC (CC)	**1982-10 Hayashikane Shipbuilding & Engineering Co Ltd — Shimonoseki YC** Yd No: 1254 Converted From: Products Tanker-2008 Loa 158.00 (BB) Br ex 22.08 Dght 9.200 Lbp 149.00 Br md 22.00 Dpth 12.20 Welded, 1 dk	**(A21A2BC) Bulk Carrier** Grain: 23,500	**1 oil engine** driving 1 FP propeller Total Power: 5,582kW (7,589hp) 14.0 Sulzer 6RLA 1 x 2 Stroke 6 Cy. 560 x 1150 5582kW (7589bhp) Ishikawajima Harima Heavy IndustrieCo Ltd (IHI)-Japan AuxGen: 3 x 500kW 450V 60Hz a.c
9723772 - -	**ZHONG HAI TONG 66** - - *China*	**2,600** - 3,800		**2013-12 Fujian Changxing Shipbuilding Co Ltd — Fu'an FJ** Loa 94.89 Br ex - Dght 5.400 Lbp - Br md 14.20 Dpth 6.90 Welded, 1 dk	**(A12B2TR) Chemical/Products Tanker**	**1 oil engine** driving 1 Propeller 11.5
9060235 *3EQQ3* -	**ZHONG HE 2** *ex* Sea Napier *-2013* *ex* Tpc Napier *-2012* *ex* Galini S *-2005* *ex* Red Stag *-2003* *ex* Sea Ace *-1996* **Zhong He 2 Shipping Co Ltd** IMU Ship Management Pte Ltd *Panama* *Panama* MMSI: 353656000 Official number: 3377008B	**17,429** 9,829 28,500 T/cm 39.3	Class: KR (NK)	**1993-10 Kanda Zosensho K.K. — Kawajiri** Yd No: 349 Loa 170.00 (BB) Br ex 27.04 Dght 9.700 Lbp 162.00 Br md 27.00 Dpth 13.80 Welded, 1 dk	**(A21A2BC) Bulk Carrier** Grain: 37,500; Bale: 35,600 Compartments: 5 Ho, ER 5 Ha: (14.1 x 15.0)4 (19.2 x 18.0)ER Cranes: 4x30t	**1 oil engine** driving 1 FP propeller Total Power: 5,884kW (8,000hp) 14.0 Mitsubishi 5UEC52L 1 x 2 Stroke 5 Cy. 520 x 1600 5884kW (8000bhp) Akasaka Tekkosho KK (Akasaka DieselLtd)-Japan AuxGen: 3 x 293kW a.c
8401200 *T8XO* -	**ZHONG HE 3** *ex* Notori Dake *-2013* *ex* New Vigor *-2004* *ex* Early Bird *-1997* *ex* Atlantic Focus *-1993* **Zhong He 3 Shipping Co Ltd** IMU Ship Management Pte Ltd *Malakal Harbour* *Palau* MMSI: 511011033 Official number: 013-000-044	**17,999** 10,120 29,105 T/cm 40.1	Class: NK	**1985-02 Imabari Shipbuilding Co Ltd — Marugame KG (Marugame Shipyard)** Yd No: 1128 Loa 174.93 (BB) Br ex - Dght 10.121 Lbp 164.80 Br md 27.01 Dpth 14.03 Welded, 1 dk	**(A21A2BC) Bulk Carrier** Grain: 37,335; Bale: 35,706 TEU 182 Compartments: 4 Ho, ER 4 Ha: (19.2 x 14.4)3 (25.6 x 14.4)ER Cranes: 4x25t	**1 oil engine** driving 1 FP propeller Total Power: 6,252kW (8,500hp) 14.0 Sulzer 6RTA 1 x 2 Stroke 6 Cy. 580 x 1700 6252kW (8500bhp) Mitsubishi Heavy Industries Ltd-Japan Fuel: 1250.0 (r.f.)
8840652 - -	**ZHONG HONG** *ex* Showa *-2004* *ex* Showa Maru *-2004* **Zhong Hong Shipping Co Ltd** Dalian Yanping Shipping Agency Co Ltd	**2,582** - 1,500		**1989 Y.K. Matsubara Koki Zosen — Onomichi** Loa 49.20 Br ex - Dght 2.400 Lbp 45.00 Br md 12.00 Dpth 2.90 Welded, 1 dk	**(A31A2GX) General Cargo Ship**	**1 oil engine** driving 1 FP propeller
9706578 *BVHZ8* -	**ZHONG HONG 28** **Xiamen Zhonghong Shipping Co Ltd** - *Xiamen, Fujian* *China* MMSI: 412704110	**11,856** 6,639 17,848	Class: CC	**2013-04 Fujian Changxing Shipbuilding Co Ltd — Fu'an FJ** Loa 158.43 (BB) Br ex - Dght 8.100 Lbp 149.50 Br md 22.60 Dpth 11.30 Welded, 1 dk	**(A31A2GX) General Cargo Ship** TEU 1080	**1 oil engine** driving 1 Propeller Total Power: 4,265kW (5,799hp) 12.0
9706451 *BVHF8* -	**ZHONG HONG 29** **Xiamen Zhonghong Shipping Co Ltd** - *Xiamen, Fujian* *China* MMSI: 413697910	**12,199** 6,831 16,500	Class: CC	**2012-10 Fujian Changxing Shipbuilding Co Ltd — Fu'an FJ** Loa 160.86 (BB) Br ex - Dght 7.930 Lbp 149.80 Br md 22.90 Dpth 10.90 Welded, 1 dk	**(A33A2CC) Container Ship (Fully Cellular)** TEU 1100	**1 oil engine** driving 1 Propeller Total Power: 4,265kW (5,799hp) 12.0
9003574 *BJRJ* -	**ZHONG HUA 6** *ex* Howa *-2001* **Sinochem Shipping Co Ltd (Hainan)** Aoxing Ship Management (Shanghai) Ltd *Haikou, Hainan* *China* MMSI: 412522050 Official number: 110002000116	**4,801** 2,430 7,974 T/cm 16.8	Class: CC (NK)	**1991-03 Asakawa Zosen K.K. — Imabari** Yd No: 355 Loa 111.30 (BB) Br ex 18.22 Dght 7.300 Lbp 103.00 Br md 18.20 Dpth 8.95 Welded, 1 dk	**(A12B2TR) Chemical/Products Tanker** Double Bottom Entire Compartment Length Liq: 8,493; Liq (Oil): 8,493 Cargo Heating Coils Compartments: 9 Ta, 12 Wing Ta, ER, 2 Wing Slop Ta 21 Cargo Pump (s): 9x200m³/hr, 12x150m³/hr Manifold: Bow/CM: 63.3m	**1 oil engine** driving 1 FP propeller Total Power: 3,089kW (4,200hp) 12.5 Mitsubishi 6UEC37L 1 x 2 Stroke 6 Cy. 370 x 880 3089kW (4200bhp) Akasaka Tekkosho KK (Akasaka DieselLtd)-Japan AuxGen: 3 x 214kW 320V a.c Fuel: 123.0 (d.f.) 818.0 (r.f.) 12.3pd
7720788 *BJMU* -	**ZHONG HUA 8** *ex* Jin Lian 1 *-2004* *ex* Jin Lian *-1994* *ex* Global Express No. 5 *-1991* *ex* Novmarina *-1990* *ex* Nuvamarina *-1989* **Hainan Nan Jin Shipping Co** - *Haikou, Hainan* *China* MMSI: 412522490	**5,443** 3,104 8,142	Class: (LR) (CC) (BV) ✠ Classed LR until 2/89	**1979-11 Hijos de J. Barreras S.A. — Vigo** Yd No: 1452 Loa 118.65 (BB) Br ex 18.24 Dght 7.527 Lbp 110.22 Br md 18.20 Dpth 9.91 Welded, 2 dks	**(A31A2GX) General Cargo Ship** Grain: 11,169 Compartments: 3 Ho, ER, 3 Tw Dk 3 Ha: (13.1 x 7.7) (19.6 x 10.5) (19.5 x 10.5)ER Derricks: 1x60t,5x10t	**1 oil engine** sr geared to sc. shaft driving 1 FP propeller Total Power: 3,236kW (4,400hp) 14.0 Deutz RBV8M54 1 x 4 Stroke 8 Cy. 370 x 400 3236kW (4400bhp) Hijos de J Barreras SA-Spain AuxGen: 3 x 240kW 380V 50Hz a.c Fuel: 125.0 (d.f.) 445.0 (r.f.)
9147904 *BJNJ* -	**ZHONG HUA 10** *ex* Sinochem 10 *-2005* *ex* Sunny Chemi *-2004* **Sinochem Shipping Co Ltd (Hainan)** Aoxing Ship Management (Shanghai) Ltd *Haikou, Hainan* *China* MMSI: 412522890	**1,999** 1,087 3,398 T/cm 9.8	Class: CC (KR)	**1996-04 Banguhjin Engineering & Shipbuilding Co Ltd — Ulsan** Yd No: 99 Loa 85.60 (BB) Br ex 14.00 Dght 5.636 Lbp 78.00 Br md 14.00 Dpth 6.60 Welded, 1 dk	**(A12B2TR) Chemical/Products Tanker** Double Bottom Entire Compartment Length Liq: 3,763; Liq (Oil): 3,763 Cargo Heating Coils Compartments: 10 Ta, ER 2 Cargo Pump (s): 2x400m³/hr Manifold: Bow/CM: 47m	**1 oil engine** with clutches, flexible couplings & sr geared to sc. shaft driving 1 FP propeller Total Power: 1,851kW (2,517hp) 12.0 Caterpillar 3606 1 x 4 Stroke 6 Cy. 280 x 300 1851kW (2517bhp) Caterpillar Inc-USA AuxGen: 3 x 250kW 440V 60Hz a.c Fuel: 55.0 (d.f.) 142.0 (r.f.)
9186170 *VRCM8* -	**ZHONG HUA 11** *ex* Zhong Hua 12 *-2006* *ex* Guardian *-2004* *ex* Royal Phoenix *-2002* **Lucky Harvest Shipping Co Ltd** Aoxing Ship Management (Shanghai) Ltd SatCom: Inmarsat Mini-M 763684015 *Hong Kong* *Hong Kong* MMSI: 477656300 Official number: HK-1837	**1,914** 748 2,772 T/cm 8.6	Class: CC (KR) (NK)	**1998-02 Kyoei Zosen KK — Mihara HS** Yd No: 286 Loa 79.84 Br ex - Dght 5.612 Lbp 74.00 Br md 13.00 Dpth 6.50 Welded, 1 dk	**(A12B2TR) Chemical/Products Tanker** Double Hull (13F) Liq: 2,642; Liq (Oil): 2,736 Cargo Heating Coils Compartments: 8 Wing Ta, 2 Wing Slop Ta, ER 8 Cargo Pump (s): 8x150m³/hr Manifold: Bow/CM: 39.7m	**1 oil engine** driving 1 FP propeller Total Power: 2,405kW (3,270hp) 12.8 B&W 6S26M 1 x 2 Stroke 6 Cy. 260 x 980 2405kW (3270bhp) The Hanshin Diesel Works Ltd-Japan AuxGen: 2 x 240kW 445V a.c Fuel: 58.0 (d.f.) 209.0 (r.f.)
8863850 *BFBC* -	**ZHONG HUAN** **Northsea Oils & Grains Industries (Tianjin) Co Ltd** - *Tianjin* *China* MMSI: 412300390	**723** 306 1,087	Class: (CC)	**1979 Nippon Kokan KK (NKK Corp) — Shizuoka SZ** Loa 64.45 Br ex - Dght - Lbp 59.00 Br md 9.50 Dpth 4.75 Welded, 1 dk	**(A13B2TU) Tanker (unspecified)**	**1 oil engine** driving 1 FP propeller Total Power: 883kW (1,201hp) Akasaka DM28A 1 x 4 Stroke 6 Cy. 280 x 460 883kW (1201bhp) Akasaka Tekkosho KK (Akasaka DieselLtd)-Japan AuxGen: 1 x 90kW 225V a.c, 1 x 55kW 225V a.c, 1 x 50kW 230V a.c
9575369 *3FGK6* -	**ZHONG HUI** **Shanghai Zhonghui Shipping Co Ltd** Shanghai Huihai Ship Technology Co Ltd *Panama* *Panama* MMSI: 372661000 Official number: 40095PEXTF1	**2,962** 1,996 5,500	Class: OM PD	**2009-12 Yizheng Hongjiang Shipbuilding Co Ltd — Yizheng JS** Yd No: 09 Loa 96.50 Br ex - Dght - Lbp 90.90 Br md 15.80 Dpth 7.40 Welded, 1 dk	**(A33A2CC) Container Ship (Fully Cellular)** TEU 370	**1 oil engine** reduction geared to sc. shaft driving 1 Propeller Total Power: 1,765kW (2,400hp) 11.6 Chinese Std. Type G8300Z 1 x 4 Stroke 8 Cy. 300 x 380 1765kW (2400bhp) Wuxi Antai Power Machinery Co Ltd-China

24172 FER5	**ZHONG JIAN** *ex* Glory Xiamen *-2013* *ex* Rubin Camellia *-2010* **Sino Construction Shipping (HK) Ltd** Five Ocean Maritime Services Co Ltd *Panama* *Panama* MMSI: 357545000 Official number: 2220295E	**38,367** 24,093 71,024 T/cm 42.2 Class: NK	**1995-07 Namura Shipbuilding Co Ltd — Imari SG** Yd No: 941 Loa 224.95 (BB) Br ex - Dght 13.652 Lbp 217.00 Br md 32.20 Dpth 18.80 Welded, 1 dk	**(A21A2BC) Bulk Carrier** Grain: 85,011 Compartments: 7 Ho, ER 7 Ha: (16.6 x 13.2)6 (16.6 x 14.9)ER	**1 oil engine** driving 1 FP propeller Total Power: 8,018kW (10,901hp) 14.3kn Sulzer 6RTA62 1 x 2 Stroke 6 Cy. 620 x 2150 8018kW (10901bhp) Mitsubishi Heavy Industries Ltd-Japan AuxGen: 3 x 480kW 450V 60Hz a.c Fuel: 134.0 (d.f.) (Heating Coils) 2364.0 (r.f.) 27.8pd
324048 LY2516	**ZHONG LIAN 3** *ex* Ocean Pearl *-2012* *ex* Ocean Pearl 2 *-2011* *ex* Xun Yang *-2011* *ex* Nisshin Maru *-1985* **Zhang Junsheng** Aoyang International Co Ltd *Freetown* *Sierra Leone* MMSI: 667003319 Official number: SL103319	**2,818** 1,631 4,460 Class: UV (CC) (NK)	**1984-04 Miyoshi Shipbuilding Co Ltd — Uwajima EH** Yd No: 196 Loa 87.33 Br ex - Dght 8.500 Lbp 83.27 Br md 14.80 Dpth 8.85 Welded, 2 dks	**(A31A2GX) General Cargo Ship** Grain: 6,588; Bale: 6,060 Compartments: 2 Ho, ER 2 Ha: ER	**1 oil engine** driving 1 FP propeller Total Power: 1,471kW (2,000hp) 11.5kn Makita LS38L 1 x 4 Stroke 6 Cy. 380 x 740 1471kW (2000bhp) Makita Diesel Co Ltd-Japan AuxGen: 2 x 144kW 445V 60Hz a.c
739396	**ZHONG LIAN 9** *ex* Liao Yuan 12 *-2013* *ex* Tian Rui 2 *-2009* **Leting Zhonglian Coal Trading Co Ltd** East Grand Shipping Co Ltd *China*	**2,888** 1,617 5,010 Class: UB	**2005-06 Yueqing Donggang Shipbuilding Co Ltd — Yueqing ZJ** Yd No: 010 Loa 98.00 Br ex - Dght 6.100 Lbp - Br md 16.00 Dpth - Welded, 1 dk	**(A31A2GX) General Cargo Ship**	**1 oil engine** driving 1 Propeller 11.0kn
719898 LGT9	**ZHONG LIANG BEI HAI** - **Maple Leaf Shipping Co Ltd** - *Taizhou, Jiangsu* *China*	**9,449** 5,291 13,596 Class: CC (Class contemplated)	**2013-12 Taizhou Maple Leaf Shipbuilding Co Ltd — Linhai ZJ** Yd No: ML822TEU-01 Loa 146.24 (BB) Br ex - Dght 7.900 Lbp 136.50 Br md 20.80 Dpth 10.80 Welded, 1 dk	**(A33A2CC) Container Ship (Fully Cellular)** TEU 882 Ice Capable	**1 oil engine** reduction geared to sc. shaft driving 1 FP propeller Total Power: 2,574kW (3,500hp) 18.0kn Yanmar 6N330-EW 1 x 4 Stroke 6 Cy. 330 x 440 2574kW (3500bhp) Yanmar Diesel Engine Co Ltd-Japan
374938 GQW	**ZHONG LU 701** - **Nduman Fisheries Co Ltd** - SatCom: Inmarsat C 462781710 *Takoradi* *Ghana* MMSI: 627817000 Official number: 316817	*278* - -	**1993 Qingdao Marine Fishery Co Fishing Vessel Shipyard — Qingdao SD** Loa 43.50 Br ex 7.60 Dght - Lbp - Br md - Dpth 3.82 Welded, 1 dk	**(B11A2FT) Trawler**	**1 oil engine** driving 1 FP propeller Total Power: 433kW (589hp) 10.0kn Chinese Std. Type 6250 1 x 4 Stroke 6 Cy. 250 x 300 433kW (589bhp) Zibo Diesel Engine Factory-China
374940 GQS	**ZHONG LU 702** - **Komal Ltd** - *Takoradi* *Ghana* Official number: 316815	*278* - -	**1993 Qingdao Marine Fishery Co Fishing Vessel Shipyard — Qingdao SD** Loa 43.50 Br ex 7.60 Dght - Lbp - Br md - Dpth 3.82 Welded, 1 dk	**(B11A2FT) Trawler**	**1 oil engine** driving 1 FP propeller Total Power: 433kW (589hp) 10.0kn Chinese Std. Type 6250 1 x 4 Stroke 6 Cy. 250 x 300 433kW (589bhp) Zibo Diesel Engine Factory-China
374952 GQT	**ZHONG LU 703** - **Komal Ltd** - *Takoradi* *Ghana* MMSI: 627816000 Official number: 316816	*299* - -	**1992 Shanghai Fishing Vessel Shipyard — Shanghai** Loa 40.14 Br ex 7.80 Dght - Lbp - Br md - Dpth 3.85 Welded, 1 dk	**(B11A2FT) Trawler**	**1 oil engine** geared to sc. shaft driving 1 FP propeller Total Power: 405kW (551hp) 10.0kn Chinese Std. Type 6300 1 x 4 Stroke 6 Cy. 300 x 380 405kW (551bhp) Zibo Diesel Engine Factory-China
374976 GQX	**ZHONG LU 705** - **Obourwe & Co Ltd** - SatCom: Inmarsat C 462781910 *Takoradi* *Ghana* Official number: 316819	*299* - -	**1992 Shanghai Fishing Vessel Shipyard — Shanghai** Loa 40.14 Br ex 7.80 Dght - Lbp - Br md - Dpth 3.85 Welded, 1 dk	**(B11A2FT) Trawler**	**1 oil engine** geared to sc. shaft driving 1 FP propeller Total Power: 552kW (750hp) 10.0kn Chinese Std. Type 6300 1 x 4 Stroke 6 Cy. 300 x 380 552kW (750bhp) Zibo Diesel Engine Factory-China
374964 GQZ	**ZHONG LU 708** *ex* Zhong Lu 704 *-1998* **Obourwe & Co Ltd** - SatCom: Inmarsat C 462782010 *Takoradi* *Ghana* MMSI: 627818000 Official number: 316818	*299* - -	**1992 Shanghai Fishing Vessel Shipyard — Shanghai** Loa 40.12 Br ex 7.80 Dght - Lbp - Br md - Dpth 3.85 Welded, 1 dk	**(B11A2FT) Trawler**	**1 oil engine** geared to sc. shaft driving 1 FP propeller Total Power: 552kW (750hp) 10.0kn Chinese Std. Type 6300 1 x 4 Stroke 6 Cy. 300 x 380 552kW (750bhp) Zibo Diesel Engine Factory-China
258296	**ZHONG LU YU 1001** - **Shandong Zhonglu Oceanic Fisheries Co Ltd** - *Qingdao, Shandong* *China* Official number: Y040J01032	**311** 93 -	**2001-08 Qingdao Zhenyuan Shipbuilding & Repair Co Ltd — Qingdao SD** Yd No: 2001-1 Loa 44.98 Br ex - Dght 3.000 Lbp 38.60 Br md 7.80 Dpth 3.92 Welded, 1 dk	**(B11B2FV) Fishing Vessel**	**1 oil engine** driving 1 FP propeller Total Power: 735kW (999hp) 12.0kn Chinese Std. Type 8300ZLC 1 x 4 Stroke 8 Cy. 300 x 380 735kW (999bhp) Zibo Diesel Engine Factory-China
258301	**ZHONG LU YU 1002** - **Shandong Zhonglu Oceanic Fisheries Co Ltd** - *Qingdao, Shandong* *China* Official number: Y040J01033	**311** 93 -	**2001-08 Qingdao Zhenyuan Shipbuilding & Repair Co Ltd — Qingdao SD** Yd No: 2001-2 Loa 44.98 Br ex - Dght 3.000 Lbp 38.60 Br md 7.80 Dpth 3.92 Welded, 1 dk	**(B11B2FV) Fishing Vessel**	**1 oil engine** driving 1 FP propeller Total Power: 735kW (999hp) 12.0kn Chinese Std. Type 8300ZLC 1 x 4 Stroke 8 Cy. 300 x 380 735kW (999bhp) Zibo Diesel Engine Factory-China
099705	**ZHONG LU YU 1003** - **Yaw Addo Fisheries Co Ltd** - *Takoradi* *Ghana* Official number: GSR 0060	**311** 93 -	**2002-01 Qingdao Zhenyuan Shipbuilding & Repair Co Ltd — Qingdao SD** Loa 44.98 Br ex - Dght 3.000 Lbp 38.60 Br md 7.80 Dpth 3.92 Welded, 1 dk	**(B11B2FV) Fishing Vessel**	**1 oil engine** reduction geared to sc. shaft driving 1 Propeller Total Power: 735kW (999hp) 12.0kn Chinese Std. Type 8300 1 x 4 Stroke 8 Cy. 300 x 380 735kW (999bhp) Zibo Diesel Engine Factory-China
099717	**ZHONG LU YU 1004** - **Yaw Addo Fisheries Co Ltd** - *Takoradi* *Ghana* Official number: GSR 0061	**311** 93 -	**2002-01 Qingdao Zhenyuan Shipbuilding & Repair Co Ltd — Qingdao SD** Loa 44.98 Br ex - Dght 3.000 Lbp 38.60 Br md 7.80 Dpth 3.92 Welded, 1 dk	**(B11B2FV) Fishing Vessel**	**1 oil engine** reduction geared to sc. shaft driving 1 Propeller Total Power: 735kW (999hp) 12.0kn Chinese Std. Type 8300 1 x 4 Stroke 8 Cy. 300 x 380 735kW (999bhp) Zibo Diesel Engine Factory-China
420124 9VM5	**ZHONG MAY** - **Zhong May Maritime LLC** Foremost Maritime Corp SatCom: Inmarsat C 463709160 *Monrovia* *Liberia* MMSI: 636014629 Official number: 14629	**91,412** 57,770 176,403 T/cm 120.6 Class: BV	**2011-01 Shanghai Waigaoqiao Shipbuilding Co Ltd — Shanghai** Yd No: 1120 Loa 292.00 (BB) Br ex 45.05 Dght 18.300 Lbp 282.00 Br md 45.00 Dpth 24.80 Welded, 1 dk	**(A21A2BC) Bulk Carrier** Grain: 194,179; Bale: 183,425 Compartments: 9 Ho, ER 9 Ha: ER	**1 oil engine** driving 1 FP propeller Total Power: 16,860kW (22,923hp) 14.0kn MAN-B&W 6S70MC 1 x 2 Stroke 6 Cy. 700 x 2674 16860kW (22923bhp) Hudong Heavy Machinery Co Ltd-China AuxGen: 3 x 900kW 60Hz a.c
657466 KEW	**ZHONG NING HAI** - **Ningbo Jinbai Shipping Co Ltd** - *Ningbo, Zhejiang* *China*	**17,449** 9,771 28,213 Class: CC	**2012-03 Nantong Dongxin Heavy Industry Co Ltd — Nantong JS** Loa 174.65 (BB) Br ex - Dght 9.900 Lbp 166.00 Br md 24.80 Dpth 14.10 Welded, 1 dk	**(A21A2BC) Bulk Carrier** Grain: 36,500 Compartments: 5 Ho, ER 5 Ha: ER Cranes: 4x30t Ice Capable	**1 oil engine** driving 1 FP propeller Total Power: 4,440kW (6,037hp) 12.0kn MAN-B&W 6S35MC 1 x 2 Stroke 6 Cy. 350 x 1400 4440kW (6037bhp)
377121 OGY	**ZHONG RAN 21** - **China Marine Bunker Supply Co (Guangzhou Branch)** - *Guangzhou, Guangdong* *China* MMSI: 413117000	**2,216** 763 4,800 Class: CC	**2005-12 Jiujiang Xinxing Shipbuilding Co Ltd — Hukou County JX** Yd No: 2300-1 Loa 82.00 Br ex - Dght - Lbp 76.00 Br md 14.80 Dpth 6.00 Welded, 1 dk	**(A13B2TP) Products Tanker** Double Hull (13F) Liq: 2,583; Liq (Oil): 2,583 Compartments: 8 Wing Ta, 2 Wing Slop Ta, ER	**1 oil engine** reduction geared to sc. shaft driving 1 FP propeller Total Power: 1,470kW (1,999hp) 12.6kn MAN-B&W 6L28/32A 1 x 4 Stroke 6 Cy. 280 x 320 1470kW (1999bhp) Zhenjiang Marine Diesel Works-China AuxGen: 2 x 420kW 400V a.c

IMO / Call sign	Name / Owner / Port	Tonnage	Class	Build / Dimensions	Type	Machinery
9376414 *BOGZ* -	**ZHONG RAN 22** **China Marine Bunker Supply Co (Guangzhou Branch)** - *Guangzhou, Guangdong* *China* MMSI: 413256000	**2,216** 763 2,383	Class: CC	**2007-02 Tongfang Jiangxin Shipbuilding Co Ltd — Hukou County JX** Yd No: 2300-2 Loa 82.00 Br ex - Dght 4.500 Lbp 76.00 Br md 14.80 Dpth 6.00 Welded, 1 dk	**(A13B2TP) Products Tanker** Double Hull (13F) Liq: 2,583; Liq (Oil): 2,583 Compartments: 8 Wing Ta, 2 Wing Slop Ta, ER	**1 oil engine** reduction geared to sc. shaft driving 1 FP propeller Total Power: 1,470kW (1,999hp) 12.6k MAN-B&W 6L28/32 1 x 4 Stroke 6 Cy. 280 x 320 1470kW (1999bhp) Zhenjiang Marine Diesel Works-China AuxGen: 2 x 420kW 400V a.c
9674696 *BYGR* -	**ZHONG RAN 37** **China Marine Bunker Supply Co (Guangzhou Branch)** - *Guangzhou, Guangdong* *China* MMSI: 413470920 Official number: 1570513	**2,537** 1,420 3,546	Class: CC (Class contemplated)	**2012-07 CNPC Liaohe Petroleum Equipment Co (CPLEC) — Panjin LN** Yd No: LH502-3 Loa 87.70 Br ex - Dght 5.600 Lbp 84.00 Br md 15.00 Dpth 7.10 Welded, 1 dk	**(A13B2TP) Products Tanker** Double Hull (13F)	**2 oil engines** reduction geared to sc. shafts driving 2 FP propellers Guangzhou Guangzhou Diesel Engine Factory CoLtd-China
8889567 *BOGW* -	**ZHONG RAN 51** *ex Yuan Shen -2005* **Chimbusco Shipping Co Ltd** - *Dalian, Liaoning* *China* MMSI: 413096000	**3,785** 1,598 5,587	Class: CC	**1994-03 Jinling Shipyard — Nanjing JS** Yd No: 92-7011 Loa 104.65 Br ex - Dght 6.700 Lbp 98.00 Br md 16.40 Dpth 8.15 Welded, 1 dk	**(A13B2TP) Products Tanker** Double Hull Liq: 9,120; Liq (Oil): 9,120 Compartments: 8 Wing Ta, 2 Wing Slop Ta, ER Ice Capable	**1 oil engine** driving 1 FP propeller Total Power: 2,206kW (2,999hp) 12.8k Hudong 6E34/82SDZ 1 x 2 Stroke 6 Cy. 340 x 820 2206kW (2999bhp) Hudong Shipyard-China AuxGen: 2 x 312kW 400V a.c
8879885 *BAID* -	**ZHONG RAN 53** *ex Pu You 10 Hao -2008* **Chimbusco Shipping Co Ltd** - *Dalian, Liaoning* *China* MMSI: 412055520 Official number: 050100290	**3,785** 1,598 5,595	Class: CC	**1993 Jinling Shipyard — Nanjing JS** Yd No: 90-7015 Loa 104.56 Br ex - Dght 6.700 Lbp 98.00 Br md 16.40 Dpth 8.15 Welded, 1 dk	**(A13B2TP) Products Tanker** Double Hull (13F) Liq: 6,426; Liq (Oil): 6,426 Cargo Heating Coils Compartments: 10 Ta, ER	**1 oil engine** driving 1 FP propeller Total Power: 2,207kW (3,001hp) 12.8k Hudong 6E34/82SDZ 1 x 2 Stroke 6 Cy. 340 x 820 2207kW (3001bhp) Hudong Shipyard-China AuxGen: 2 x 312kW 400V a.c
9238129 *BIAJ3* -	**ZHONG RAN ZHI XING** *ex Bougainville -2011 ex Salisbury -2005* **Shanghai Huachen Shipping Co Ltd** - *Shanghai* *China* MMSI: 413376420	**4,229** 1,374 4,867 T/cm 13.8	Class: CC (NK)	**2001-05 Murakami Hide Zosen K.K. — Imabari** Yd No: 516 Loa 99.98 (BB) Br ex 17.53 Dght 6.163 Lbp 93.50 Br md 17.50 Dpth 7.80 Welded, 1 dk	**(A11B2TG) LPG Tanker** Double Bottom Entire Compartment Length Liq (Gas): 4,931 2 x Gas Tank (s); 2 independent (stl) cyl horizontal 2 Cargo Pump (s): 2x300m³/hr Manifold: Bow/CM: 46.8m	**1 oil engine** driving 1 FP propeller Total Power: 3,089kW (4,200hp) 14.3k Mitsubishi 6UEC37LA 1 x 2 Stroke 6 Cy. 370 x 880 3089kW (4200bhp) Akasaka Tekkosho KK (Akasaka DieselLtd)-Japan AuxGen: 2 x 350kW a.c Thrusters: 1 Thwart. FP thruster (f) Fuel: 117.6 (d.f.) 458.9 (r.f.)
8749107 *BBFB3* -	**ZHONG RONG 13** **Rongcheng Ocean Fishery Co Ltd** - *Shidao, Shandong* *China* Official number: G0201090455	**219** 81 -		**2009-12 Rongcheng Yandunjiao Shipbuilding Aquatic Co Ltd — Rongcheng SD** Loa 35.16 Br ex - Dght - Lbp - Br md 6.70 Dpth 3.35 Welded, 1 dk	**(B11B2FV) Fishing Vessel**	**1 oil engine** reduction geared to sc. shaft driving 1 FP propeller
8749119 *BBFB4* -	**ZHONG RONG 15** **Rongcheng Ocean Fishery Co Ltd** - *Shidao, Shandong* *China* Official number: G0201090456	**219** 81 -		**2009-12 Rongcheng Yandunjiao Shipbuilding Aquatic Co Ltd — Rongcheng SD** Loa 35.16 Br ex - Dght 3.350 Lbp - Br md 6.70 Dpth 3.35 Welded, 1 dk	**(B11B2FV) Fishing Vessel**	**1 oil engine** reduction geared to sc. shaft driving 1 FP propeller
9635509 *BLGG2* -	**ZHONG RONG CHU YUN 001** *completed as Xing Hai Chu Yun 702 -2012* **Zhongrong Logistics Co Ltd** - *Taizhou, Jiangsu* *China*	**5,028** 2,816 8,200	Class: CC	**2012-06 Ningbo Dongfang Shipyard Co Ltd — Ningbo ZJ** Yd No: DFC10-111 Loa 119.95 Br ex - Dght 7.300 Lbp 112.00 Br md 16.70 Dpth 8.80 Welded, 1 dk	**(A13B2TP) Products Tanker** Double Hull (13F) Ice Capable	**1 oil engine** reduction geared to sc. shaft driving 1 FP propeller Total Power: 2,206kW (2,999hp) 14.0kn Chinese Std. Type 8320ZC 1 x 4 Stroke 8 Cy. 320 x 440 2206kW (2999bhp) Guangzhou Diesel Engine Factory CoLtd-China
8649096 *BBEU1* -	**ZHONG RONG NO. 5** **Rongcheng Ocean Fishery Co Ltd** - *Shidao, Shandong* *China* Official number: GQ0201070322	**157** 63 -		**2007-07 Rongcheng Haida Shipbuilding Co Ltd — Rongcheng SD** Loa 31.93 Br ex 6.30 Dght - Lbp - Br md - Dpth 2.90 Welded, 1 dk	**(B11B2FV) Fishing Vessel**	**1 oil engine** reduction geared to sc. shaft driving 1 Propeller Chinese Std. Type 1 x 4 Stroke Henan Diesel Engine Industry Co Ltd-China
8649101 *BBIR8* -	**ZHONG RONG NO. 6** **Rongcheng Ocean Fishery Co Ltd** - *Shidao, Shandong* *China* Official number: GQ0201070323	**157** 63 -		**2007-07 Rongcheng Haida Shipbuilding Co Ltd — Rongcheng SD** Loa 31.93 Br ex 6.30 Dght - Lbp - Br md - Dpth 2.90 Welded, 1 dk	**(B11B2FV) Fishing Vessel**	**1 oil engine** reduction geared to sc. shaft driving 1 Propeller Total Power: 330kW (449hp) Chinese Std. Type 1 x 4 Stroke 330kW (449bhp) Henan Diesel Engine Industry Co Ltd-China
9678343 *BBCH1* -	**ZHONG RONG NO. 32** **Rongcheng Ocean Fishery Co Ltd** - *Shidao, Shandong* *China* MMSI: 412326882 Official number: 3700002012030004	**255** 103 -		**2012-03 Rongcheng Yandunjiao Shipbuilding Aquatic Co Ltd — Rongcheng SD** L reg 35.16 Br ex - Dght - Lbp - Br md 7.00 Dpth 3.70 Welded, 1 dk	**(B11B2FV) Fishing Vessel**	**1 oil engine** reduction geared to sc. shaft driving 1 Propeller Total Power: 480kW (653hp) Chinese Std. Type CW6200ZC 1 x 4 Stroke 6 Cy. 200 x 270 480kW (653bhp) in China
9678355 *BBCH2* -	**ZHONG RONG NO. 33** **Rongcheng Ocean Fishery Co Ltd** - *Shidao, Shandong* *China* MMSI: 412326881 Official number: 3700002012030005	**255** 103 -		**2012-03 Rongcheng Yandunjiao Shipbuilding Aquatic Co Ltd — Rongcheng SD** L reg 35.16 Br ex - Dght - Lbp - Br md 7.00 Dpth 3.70 Welded, 1 dk	**(B11B2FV) Fishing Vessel**	**1 oil engine** reduction geared to sc. shaft driving 1 Propeller Total Power: 480kW (653hp) Chinese Std. Type CW6200ZC 1 x 4 Stroke 6 Cy. 200 x 270 480kW (653bhp) in China
9108879 *BXBD* -	**ZHONG SHAN** **Zhongshan Hong Kong Passenger Shipping Co-op Co Ltd** - *Zhongshan, Guangdong* *China* MMSI: 412461640	**484** 168 48	Class: CC	**1994-12 Austal Ships Pty Ltd — Fremantle WA** Yd No: 115 Loa 40.10 (BB) Br ex 11.81 Dght 1.250 Lbp 38.00 Br md 11.50 Dpth 3.80 Welded, 1 dk	**(A37B2PS) Passenger Ship** Hull Material: Aluminium Alloy Passengers: unberthed: 355	**2 oil engines** reduction geared to sc. shafts driving 2 Water jets Total Power: 4,000kW (5,438hp) 40.2kn M.T.U. 16V396TE74L 2 x Vee 4 Stroke 16 Cy. 165 x 185 each-2000kW (2719bhp) (new engine 2003) MTU Friedrichshafen GmbH-Friedrichshafen AuxGen: 2 x 108kW 380V a.c
8665882 - -	**ZHONG SHAN HONG HONG 122** **CCCC Fourth Harbor Engineering Co Ltd** - *China* Official number: 2006v5100176	**1,037** 581 -		**2006-01 Zhongshan Honghong Shiprepair & Building Co Ltd — Zhongshan GD** Yd No: NSH512 Loa 60.69 Br ex - Dght 1.400 Lbp 57.00 Br md 13.00 Dpth 4.50 Welded, 1 dk	**(B34A2SH) Hopper, Motor**	**2 oil engines** reduction geared to sc. shafts driving 2 Propellers Total Power: 900kW (1,224hp) Chinese Std. Type Z6170ZLC 2 x 4 Stroke 6 Cy. 170 x 200 each-450kW (612bhp) Zibo Diesel Engine Factory-China
8843824 *BXDM* -	**ZHONG SHAN HU** **Damaiyu Wharf High Speed Passenger Ship Co Ltd** - *Taizhou, Zhejiang* *China*	*306* 92 28	Class: (CC)	**1990 Italthai Marine Co., Ltd. — Samut Prakan** Yd No: 78 Loa 32.50 Br ex - Dght 1.290 Lbp 27.70 Br md 9.60 Dpth 3.70 Welded, 1 dk	**(A37B2PS) Passenger Ship** Hull Material: Aluminium Alloy	**2 oil engines** driving 2 FP propellers Total Power: 1,854kW (2,520hp) 28.0kn MWM TBD604BV12 2 x Vee 4 Stroke 12 Cy. 170 x 195 each-927kW (1260bhp) Motoren Werke Mannheim AG (MWM)-West Germany AuxGen: 2 x 80kW 380V a.c

124943 *8B2673*	**ZHONG SHAN MEN** *ex* Catharina Oldendorff *-2003* *ex* Cape Conway *-2002* *ex* Catharina Oldendorff *-2000* *ex* Cape Keppel *-2000* *ex* Catharina Oldendorff *-1998* *ex* Luangwa Bridge *-1992* *ex* Catharina Oldendorff *-1991* *ex* Captain Cook *-1990* *ex* Hyundai Con Seven *-1989* **YCM Shipping Co Ltd** Nanjing Ocean Shipping Co Ltd (NASCO) *Kingstown* *St Vincent & The Grenadines* MMSI: 377309000 Official number: 9145	**15,194** 9,108 23,503	Class: LR (KR) ✠ **100A1** SS 08/2009 strengthened for heavy cargoes ✠ **LMC** Eq.Ltr: G†; Cable: U3 (a)	**1982-12 Hyundai Heavy Industries Co Ltd — Ulsan** Yd No: 217 Loa 157.94 (BB) Br ex 26.04 Dght 10.017 Lbp 149.99 Br md 26.01 Dpth 14.03 Welded, 1 dk	**(A31A2GX) General Cargo Ship** Grain: 33,542; Bale: 31,866 TEU 598 C Ho 394 TEU C Dk 204 TEU Compartments: 4 Ho, ER, 4 Tw Dk 4 Ha: 4 (19.2 x 15.3)ER Cranes: 4x25t	**1 oil engine** driving 1 FP propeller Total Power: 8,018kW (10,901hp) 15.4kn B&W 5L67GFCA 1 x 2 Stroke 5 Cy. 670 x 1700 8018kW (10901bhp) Hyundai Engine & Machinery Co Ltd-South Korea AuxGen: 2 x 460kW 450V 60Hz a.c Fuel: 243.5 (d.f.) 1341.0 (r.f.)
604677 *FAT5*	**ZHONG SHENG 8** **Minsheng Financial Leasing Co Ltd** Quanzhou Ansheng Shipping Co Ltd *Tianjin* *China* MMSI: 414120000	**29,108** 15,731 47,523	Class: CC	**2012-09 Jiangsu Eastern Heavy Industry Co Ltd — Jingjiang JS** Yd No: JEHIC10-806 Loa 189.99 (BB) Br ex - Dght 10.500 Lbp 185.00 Br md 32.26 Dpth 15.50 Welded, 1 dk	**(A21A2BC) Bulk Carrier** Grain: 60,276 Compartments: 5 Ho, ER 5 Ha: 4 (21.3 x 18.3)ER (18.9 x 18.3) Cranes: 3x30t Ice Capable	**1 oil engine** driving 1 FP propeller Total Power: 8,280kW (11,257hp) 14.2kn MAN-B&W 6S46MC-C 1 x 2 Stroke 6 Cy. 460 x 1932 8280kW (11257bhp) Doosan Engine Co Ltd-South Korea AuxGen: 3 x 535kW 400V a.c
831924	**ZHONG SHI 94** **China National Cereals, Oils & Foodstuffs Import & Export Corp** - *Guangzhou, Guangdong* *China*	*175* 52 200	Class: (CC)	**1985 Wang Tak Engineering & Shipbuilding Co Ltd — Hong Kong** Loa 40.15 Br ex - Dght 2.690 Lbp 37.00 Br md 7.50 Dpth 3.20 Welded, 1 dk	**(B12B2FC) Fish Carrier** Ins: 324 Compartments: 2 Ho, ER 2 Ha: 2 (5.8 x 3.2)ER	**2 oil engines** geared to sc. shafts driving 2 FP propellers Total Power: 422kW (574hp) 10.5kn Chinese Std. Type 6160A 2 x 4 Stroke 6 Cy. 160 x 225 each-211kW (287bhp) Weifang Diesel Engine Factory-China AuxGen: 2 x 120kW 400V a.c
832306	**ZHONG SHI 95** **China National Cereals, Oils & Foodstuffs Import & Export Corp** - *Guangzhou, Guangdong* *China*	*175* 52 185	Class: (CC)	**1985 Wang Tak Engineering & Shipbuilding Co Ltd — Hong Kong** Loa 40.15 Br ex - Dght 2.690 Lbp 37.00 Br md 7.50 Dpth 3.20 Welded, 1 dk	**(B12B2FC) Fish Carrier**	**2 oil engines** geared to sc. shafts driving 2 FP propellers Total Power: 424kW (576hp) 10.5kn Chinese Std. Type 6160A 2 x 4 Stroke 6 Cy. 160 x 225 each-212kW (288bhp) Weifang Diesel Engine Factory-China AuxGen: 2 x 120kW 400V a.c
832318	**ZHONG SHI 99** **China National Cereals, Oils & Foodstuffs Import & Export Corp** - *Ronggui, Guangdong* *China*	*229* 68 196	Class: (CC)	**1987 Wang Tak Engineering & Shipbuilding Co Ltd — Hong Kong** Loa 40.34 Br ex - Dght 2.650 Lbp 37.00 Br md 7.50 Dpth 3.20 Welded, 1 dk	**(B12B2FC) Fish Carrier**	**2 oil engines** geared to sc. shafts driving 2 FP propellers Total Power: 332kW (452hp) 10.5kn Chinese Std. Type 6160A 2 x 4 Stroke 6 Cy. 160 x 225 each-166kW (226bhp) Weifang Diesel Engine Factory-China AuxGen: 2 x 90kW 400V a.c, 1 x 24kW 400V a.c
832320	**ZHONG SHI 100** **China National Cereals, Oils & Foodstuffs Import & Export Corp** - *Zhongshan, Guangdong* *China*	*229* 68 195	Class: (CC)	**1987 Wang Tak Engineering & Shipbuilding Co Ltd — Hong Kong** Loa 40.34 Br ex - Dght 2.650 Lbp 37.00 Br md 7.50 Dpth 3.20 Welded, 1 dk	**(B12B2FC) Fish Carrier**	**4 oil engines** geared to sc. shafts driving 2 FP propellers Total Power: 848kW (1,152hp) 10.5kn Chinese Std. Type 6160A 4 x 4 Stroke 6 Cy. 160 x 225 each-212kW (288bhp) Weifang Diesel Engine Factory-China AuxGen: 2 x 90kW 400V a.c, 1 x 24kW 400V a.c
832332	**ZHONG SHI 101** **China National Cereals, Oils & Foodstuffs Import & Export Corp** - *Foshan, Guangdong* *China*	*229* 68 195	Class: (CC)	**1987 Wang Tak Engineering & Shipbuilding Co Ltd — Hong Kong** Loa 40.34 Br ex - Dght 2.650 Lbp 37.00 Br md 7.50 Dpth 3.20 Welded, 1 dk	**(B12B2FC) Fish Carrier**	**2 oil engines** geared to sc. shafts driving 2 FP propellers Total Power: 424kW (576hp) 10.5kn Chinese Std. Type 6160A 2 x 4 Stroke 6 Cy. 160 x 225 each-212kW (288bhp) Weifang Diesel Engine Factory-China AuxGen: 2 x 90kW 400V a.c, 1 x 24kW 400V a.c
650069 *YLQ6*	**ZHONG SHUI 601** **CNFC Overseas Fishery Co Ltd** - *Zhanjiang, Guangdong* *China*	**119** 42 34		**1997-03 Guangxi Fishing Vessel Shipyard — Beihai GX** Loa 26.26 Br ex - Dght 2.600 Lbp 22.85 Br md 6.40 Dpth 3.40 Welded, 1 dk	**(B11B2FV) Fishing Vessel**	**1 oil engine** yes, unknown arrgmt driving 1 Propeller Total Power: 235kW (320hp) Hanshin 1 x 4 Stroke 235kW (320bhp) Nantong Diesel Engine Co Ltd-China
650071 *YLQ5*	**ZHONG SHUI 602** **CNFC Overseas Fishery Co Ltd** - *Zhanjiang, Guangdong* *China*	**119** 42 34		**1997-03 Guangxi Fishing Vessel Shipyard — Beihai GX** Loa 26.26 Br ex - Dght 2.600 Lbp 22.85 Br md 6.40 Dpth 3.40 Welded, 1 dk	**(B11B2FV) Fishing Vessel**	**1 oil engine** yes, unknown arrgmt driving 1 Propeller Total Power: 235kW (320hp) Hanshin 1 x 4 Stroke 235kW (320bhp) Nantong Diesel Engine Co Ltd-China
650083 *YLQ7*	**ZHONG SHUI 603** **CNFC Overseas Fishery Co Ltd** - *Zhanjiang, Guangdong* *China*	**119** 42 34		**1997-03 Guangxi Fishing Vessel Shipyard — Beihai GX** Loa 26.26 Br ex - Dght 2.600 Lbp 22.85 Br md 6.40 Dpth 3.40 Welded, 1 dk	**(B11B2FV) Fishing Vessel**	**1 oil engine** yes, unknown arrgmt driving 1 Propeller Total Power: 235kW (320hp) Hanshin 1 x 4 Stroke 235kW (320bhp) Nantong Diesel Engine Co Ltd-China
650095 *YLQ8*	**ZHONG SHUI 604** **CNFC Overseas Fishery Co Ltd** - *Zhanjiang, Guangdong* *China*	**119** 42 34		**1997-03 Guangxi Fishing Vessel Shipyard — Beihai GX** Loa 26.26 Br ex - Dght 2.600 Lbp 22.85 Br md 6.40 Dpth 3.40 Welded, 1 dk	**(B11B2FV) Fishing Vessel**	**1 oil engine** yes, unknown arrgmt driving 1 Propeller Total Power: 235kW (320hp) Hanshin 1 x 4 Stroke 235kW (320bhp) Nantong Diesel Engine Co Ltd-China
628860 *YLQ9*	**ZHONG SHUI 605** **CNFC Overseas Fishery Co Ltd** - *Zhanjiang, Guangdong* *China* Official number: YD 000028	**119** 42 33		**1997-03 Qidong Fishing Vessel Shipyard — Qidong JS** Loa 26.26 Br ex - Dght 2.600 Lbp 22.85 Br md 6.40 Dpth 3.40 Welded, 1 dk	**(B11B2FV) Fishing Vessel**	**1 oil engine** reduction geared to sc. shaft driving 1 Propeller Total Power: 235kW (320hp) Chinese Std. Type 1 x 4 Stroke 235kW (320bhp) Nantong Diesel Engine Co Ltd-China
628872 *YM02*	**ZHONG SHUI 606** **CNFC Overseas Fishery Co Ltd** - *Zhanjiang, Guangdong* *China* Official number: YD000029	**119** 42 33		**1997-03 Qidong Fishing Vessel Shipyard — Qidong JS** Loa 26.26 Br ex - Dght 2.600 Lbp 22.85 Br md 6.40 Dpth 3.40 Welded, 1 dk	**(B11B2FV) Fishing Vessel**	**1 oil engine** driving 1 Propeller Total Power: 235kW (320hp) Chinese Std. Type 1 x 4 Stroke 235kW (320bhp) Nantong Diesel Engine Co Ltd-China
628884 *YM03*	**ZHONG SHUI 607** **CNFC Overseas Fishery Co Ltd** - *Zhanjiang, Guangdong* *China* Official number: YD000030	**119** 42 33		**1997-03 Qidong Fishing Vessel Shipyard — Qidong JS** Loa 26.26 Br ex - Dght 2.600 Lbp 22.85 Br md 6.40 Dpth 3.40 Welded, 1 dk	**(B11B2FV) Fishing Vessel**	**1 oil engine** GEARED YES, UNKNOWN ARRGMT: driving 1 Propeller Total Power: 235kW (320hp) Chinese Std. Type 1 x 4 Stroke 235kW (320bhp) Nantong Diesel Engine Co Ltd-China
628896 *YM04*	**ZHONG SHUI 608** **CNFC Overseas Fishery Co Ltd** - *Zhanjiang, Guangdong* *China* Official number: YD000031	**119** 42 33		**1997-03 Qidong Fishing Vessel Shipyard — Qidong JS** Loa 26.26 Br ex - Dght 2.600 Lbp 22.85 Br md 6.40 Dpth 3.40 Welded, 1 dk	**(B11B2FV) Fishing Vessel**	**1 oil engine** GEARED YES, UNKNOWN ARRGMT: driving 1 Propeller Total Power: 235kW (320hp) Chinese Std. Type 1 x 4 Stroke 235kW (320bhp) Nantong Diesel Engine Co Ltd-China
650100 *YWB4*	**ZHONG SHUI 618** *ex* Zhong Yuan Yu 802 *-2000* **CNFC Overseas Fishery Co Ltd** - *Zhanjiang, Guangdong* *China*	**115** 40 32		**1991-06 Guangxi Fishing Vessel Shipyard — Beihai GX** Loa 25.50 Br ex - Dght 2.800 Lbp 20.70 Br md 6.40 Dpth 3.40 Welded, 1 dk	**(B11B2FV) Fishing Vessel**	**1 oil engine** driving 1 Propeller Total Power: 236kW (321hp) Cummins 1 x 4 Stroke 236kW (321bhp) Chongqing Cummins Engine Co Ltd-China
650112 *YWB5*	**ZHONG SHUI 619** *ex* Zhong Yuan Yu 806 *-1993* **CNFC Overseas Fishery Co Ltd** - *Zhanjiang, Guangdong* *China*	**115** 40 32		**1993-04 Guangxi Fishing Vessel Shipyard — Beihai GX** Loa 25.50 Br ex - Dght 2.800 Lbp 20.70 Br md 6.40 Dpth 3.40 Welded, 1 dk	**(B11B2FV) Fishing Vessel**	**1 oil engine** unknown arrgmt driving 1 Propeller Total Power: 237kW (322hp) Cummins 1 x 4 Stroke 237kW (322bhp) Cummins Engine Co Ltd-United Kingdom
628901 *ZZZ5*	**ZHONG SHUI 701** **CNFC Overseas Fishery Co Ltd** - *Yantai, Shandong* *China* Official number: YG0200080051	**191** 74 59		**2008-05 Shandong Baibuting Shipbuilding Co Ltd — Rongcheng SD** Loa 36.60 Br ex - Dght 2.600 Lbp 32.70 Br md 6.60 Dpth 3.60 Welded, 1 dk	**(B11B2FV) Fishing Vessel**	**1 oil engine** GEARED YES, UNKNOWN ARRGMT: driving 1 Propeller Total Power: 330kW (449hp) Chinese Std. Type 1 x 4 Stroke 330kW (449bhp) Zibo Diesel Engine Factory-China

IMO / Call sign / MMSI	Name / Owner / Port / Flag	Tonnage	Built / Builder / Dimensions	Type	Machinery
8628913 *BZZZ6* -	**ZHONG SHUI 702** - **CNFC Overseas Fishery Co Ltd** - *Zhanjiang, Guangdong* *China* Official number: YG0200080052	**191** 74 59	**2008-05 Shandong Baibuting Shipbuilding Co Ltd — Rongcheng SD** Loa 36.60 Br ex - Dght 2.600 Lbp 32.70 Br md 6.60 Dpth 3.60 Welded, 1 dk	**(B11B2FV) Fishing Vessel**	**1 oil engine** GEARED YES, UNKNOWN ARRGMT driving 1 Propeller Total Power: 330kW (449hp) Chinese Std. Type 1 x 4 Stroke 330kW (449bhp) Zibo Diesel Engine Factory-China
8628925 *BZZZ7* -	**ZHONG SHUI 703** - **CNFC Overseas Fishery Co Ltd** - *Yantai, Shandong* *China* Official number: TG020080059	**191** 74 59	**2008-07 Shandong Baibuting Shipbuilding Co Ltd — Rongcheng SD** Loa 36.60 Br ex - Dght 2.600 Lbp 32.70 Br md 6.60 Dpth 3.30 Welded, 1 dk	**(B11B2FV) Fishing Vessel**	**1 oil engine** GEARED YES, UNKNOWN ARRGMT: driving 1 Propeller Total Power: 330kW (449hp) Chinese Std. Type 1 x 4 Stroke 330kW (449bhp) Zibo Diesel Engine Factory-China
8628949 *BZZZ8* -	**ZHONG SHUI 704** - **CNFC Overseas Fishery Co Ltd** - *Yantai, Shandong* *China* Official number: YG0200080060	**191** 74 59	**2008-07 Shandong Baibuting Shipbuilding Co Ltd — Rongcheng SD** Loa 36.60 Br ex - Dght 2.600 Lbp 32.70 Br md 6.60 Dpth 3.30 Welded, 1 dk	**(B11B2FV) Fishing Vessel**	**1 oil engine** GEARED YES, UNKNOWN ARRGMT driving 1 Propeller Total Power: 330kW (449hp) Chinese Std. Type 1 x 4 Stroke 330kW (449bhp) Zibo Diesel Engine Factory-China
8628951 *BZZZ9* -	**ZHONG SHUI 705** - **CNFC Overseas Fishery Co Ltd** - *Yantai, Shandong* *China* Official number: YG0200080061	**191** 74 59	**2008-07 Shandong Baibuting Shipbuilding Co Ltd — Rongcheng SD** Loa 36.60 Br ex - Dght 2.600 Lbp 32.70 Br md 6.60 Dpth 3.30 Welded, 1 dk	**(B11B2FV) Fishing Vessel**	**1 oil engine** GEARED YES, UNKNOWN ARRGMT driving 1 Propeller Total Power: 330kW (449hp) Chinese Std. Type 1 x 4 Stroke 330kW (449bhp) Zibo Diesel Engine Factory-China
8628963 *BZZY3* -	**ZHONG SHUI 706** - **CNFC Overseas Fishery Co Ltd** - *Yantai, Shandong* *China* Official number: YG0200080063	**191** 74 59	**2008-07 Shandong Baibuting Shipbuilding Co Ltd — Rongcheng SD** Loa 36.60 Br ex - Dght 2.600 Lbp 32.70 Br md 6.60 Dpth 3.30 Welded, 1 dk	**(B11B2FV) Fishing Vessel**	**1 oil engine** GEARED YES, UNKNOWN ARRGMT driving 1 Propeller Total Power: 330kW (449hp) Chinese Std. Type 1 x 4 Stroke 330kW (449bhp) Zibo Diesel Engine Factory-China
8628937 *BZZR6* 35929	**ZHONG SHUI 707** - **CNFC Overseas Fishery Co Ltd** - *Yantai, Shandong* *China* Official number: YG0200080062	**199** 80 64	**2009-09 Huanghai Shipbuilding Co Ltd — Rongcheng SD** Loa 37.60 Br ex - Dght 2.700 Lbp 33.76 Br md 6.60 Dpth 3.30 Welded, 1 dk	**(B11B2FV) Fishing Vessel**	**1 oil engine** GEARED YES, UNKNOWN ARRGMT driving 1 Propeller Total Power: 330kW (449hp) Chinese Std. Type 1 x 4 Stroke 330kW (449bhp) Zibo Diesel Engine Factory-China
8628975 *BZZR7* -	**ZHONG SHUI 708** - **CNFC Overseas Fishery Co Ltd** - *Yantai, Shandong* *China* Official number: YG0200080063	**199** 80 64	**2009-09 Huanghai Shipbuilding Co Ltd — Rongcheng SD** Loa 37.60 Br ex - Dght 2.700 Lbp 33.76 Br md 6.60 Dpth 3.30 Welded, 1 dk	**(B11B2FV) Fishing Vessel**	**1 oil engine** GEARED YES, UNKNOWN ARRGMT driving 1 Propeller Total Power: 330kW (449hp) Chinese Std. Type 1 x 4 Stroke 330kW (449bhp) Zibo Diesel Engine Factory-China
8628987 *BZZR8* 35934	**ZHONG SHUI 709** - **CNFC Overseas Fishery Co Ltd** - *Yantai, Shandong* *China* Official number: YQ0200090064	**199** 80 64	**2009-09 Huanghai Shipbuilding Co Ltd — Rongcheng SD** Loa 37.60 Br ex - Dght 2.700 Lbp 33.00 Br md 6.60 Dpth 3.30 Welded, 1 dk	**(B11B2FV) Fishing Vessel**	**1 oil engine** GEARED YES, UNKNOWN ARRGMT driving 1 Propeller Total Power: 330kW (449hp) Chinese Std. Type 1 x 4 Stroke 330kW (449bhp) Zibo Diesel Engine Factory-China
8628999 *BZZR9* 35932	**ZHONG SHUI 710** - **CNFC Overseas Fishery Co Ltd** - *Yantai, Shandong* *China* Official number: YG0200080065	**199** 80 64	**2009-09 Huanghai Shipbuilding Co Ltd — Rongcheng SD** Loa 37.60 Br ex - Dght 2.700 Lbp 33.76 Br md 6.60 Dpth 3.30 Welded, 1 dk	**(B11B2FV) Fishing Vessel**	**1 oil engine** GEARED YES, UNKNOWN ARRGMT: driving 1 Propeller Chinese Std. Type 1 x 4 Stroke Zibo Diesel Engine Factory-China
8653592 *BZSI6* -	**ZHONG SHUI 711** - **CNFC Overseas Fishery Co Ltd** - *Yantai, Shandong* *China*	**255** 126 255	**2011-09 Huanghai Shipbuilding Co Ltd — Rongcheng SD** Loa 39.60 Br ex - Dght 2.800 Lbp 35.50 Br md 6.80 Dpth 3.60 Welded, 1 dk	**(B11B2FV) Fishing Vessel**	**1 oil engine** reduction geared to sc. shaft driving 1 Propeller Total Power: 447kW (608hp) Cummins KTA-19-M3 1 x 4 Stroke 6 Cy. 159 x 159 447kW (608bhp) Chongqing Cummins Engine Co Ltd-China
8653607 *BZSI7* -	**ZHONG SHUI 712** - **CNFC Overseas Fishery Co Ltd** - *Yantai, Shandong* *China*	**255** 126 255	**2011-09 Huanghai Shipbuilding Co Ltd — Rongcheng SD** Loa 39.60 Br ex - Dght 2.800 Lbp 35.50 Br md 6.80 Dpth 3.60 Welded, 1 dk	**(B11B2FV) Fishing Vessel**	**1 oil engine** reduction geared to sc. shaft driving 1 Propeller Total Power: 447kW (608hp) Cummins KTA-19-M3 1 x 4 Stroke 6 Cy. 159 x 159 447kW (608bhp) Chongqing Cummins Engine Co Ltd-China
9686089 *BZTK2* -	**ZHONG SHUI 717** - **CNFC Overseas Fishery Co Ltd** - *Yantai, Shandong* *China*	**270** 108 -	**2012-10 Huanghai Shipbuilding Co Ltd — Rongcheng SD** Loa 36.52 Br ex - Dght 2.800 Lbp - Br md 7.00 Dpth 3.60 Welded, 1 dk	**(B11B2FV) Fishing Vessel**	**1 oil engine** reduction geared to sc. shaft driving 1 FP propeller Total Power: 748kW (1,017hp) Chinese Std. Type 6210ZLC 1 x 4 Stroke 6 Cy. 210 x 290 748kW (1017bhp)
9686091 *BZTK3* -	**ZHONG SHUI 727** - **CNFC Overseas Fishery Co Ltd** - *Yantai, Shandong* *China*	**270** 108 -	**2012-10 Huanghai Shipbuilding Co Ltd — Rongcheng SD** Loa 36.52 Br ex - Dght 2.800 Lbp - Br md 7.00 Dpth 3.60 Welded, 1 dk	**(B11B2FV) Fishing Vessel**	**1 oil engine** reduction geared to sc. shaft driving 1 FP propeller Total Power: 748kW (1,017hp) Chinese Std. Type 6210ZLC 1 x 4 Stroke 6 Cy. 210 x 290 748kW (1017bhp)
9686106 *BZTK4* -	**ZHONG SHUI 737** - **CNFC Overseas Fishery Co Ltd** - *Yantai, Shandong* *China*	**270** 108 -	**2012-10 Huanghai Shipbuilding Co Ltd — Rongcheng SD** Loa 36.52 Br ex - Dght 2.800 Lbp - Br md 7.00 Dpth 3.60 Welded, 1 dk	**(B11B2FV) Fishing Vessel**	**1 oil engine** reduction geared to sc. shaft driving 1 FP propeller Total Power: 748kW (1,017hp) Chinese Std. Type 6210ZLC 1 x 4 Stroke 6 Cy. 210 x 290 748kW (1017bhp)
9686118 *BZTK5* -	**ZHONG SHUI 747** - **CNFC Overseas Fishery Co Ltd** - *Yantai, Shandong* *China*	**270** 108 -	**2012-10 Huanghai Shipbuilding Co Ltd — Rongcheng SD** Loa 36.52 Br ex - Dght 2.800 Lbp - Br md 7.00 Dpth 3.60 Welded, 1 dk	**(B11B2FV) Fishing Vessel**	**1 oil engine** reduction geared to sc. shaft driving 1 FP propeller Total Power: 748kW (1,017hp) Chinese Std. Type 6210ZLC 1 x 4 Stroke 6 Cy. 210 x 290 748kW (1017bhp)
9686120 *BZTK6* -	**ZHONG SHUI 757** - **CNFC Overseas Fishery Co Ltd** - *Yantai, Shandong* *China*	**270** 108 -	**2012-10 Huanghai Shipbuilding Co Ltd — Rongcheng SD** Loa 36.52 Br ex - Dght 2.800 Lbp - Br md 7.00 Dpth 3.60 Welded, 1 dk	**(B11B2FV) Fishing Vessel**	**1 oil engine** reduction geared to sc. shaft driving 1 FP propeller Total Power: 748kW (1,017hp) Chinese Std. Type 6210ZLC 1 x 4 Stroke 6 Cy. 210 x 290 748kW (1017bhp)
9686132 *BZTK7* -	**ZHONG SHUI 767** - **CNFC Overseas Fishery Co Ltd** - *Yantai, Shandong* *China*	**270** 108 -	**2012-10 Huanghai Shipbuilding Co Ltd — Rongcheng SD** Loa 36.52 Br ex - Dght 2.800 Lbp - Br md 7.00 Dpth 3.60 Welded, 1 dk	**(B11B2FV) Fishing Vessel**	**1 oil engine** reduction geared to sc. shaft driving 1 FP propeller Total Power: 748kW (1,017hp) Chinese Std. Type 6210ZLC 1 x 4 Stroke 6 Cy. 210 x 290 748kW (1017bhp)
8629060 *BZZZ* -	**ZHONG SHUI 801** - **CNFC Overseas Fishery Co Ltd** - *Yantai, Shandong* *China* Official number: YG0200020044	**128** 47 37	**2002-06 Dalian Fishing Vessel Co — Dalian LN** Loa 34.80 Br ex - Dght 2.550 Lbp 32.40 Br md 6.40 Dpth 3.10 Welded, 1 dk	**(B11B2FV) Fishing Vessel**	**1 oil engine** GEARED YES, UNKNOWN ARRGMT driving 1 Propeller Total Power: 407kW (553hp) Cummins 1 x 4 Stroke 407kW (553bhp) Chongqing Cummins Engine Co Ltd-China
8629072 *BZZZ2* -	**ZHONG SHUI 802** - **CNFC Overseas Fishery Co Ltd** - *Yantai, Shandong* *China* Official number: YG0200020045	**128** 47 37	**2002-06 Dalian Fishing Vessel Co — Dalian LN** Loa 34.80 Br ex - Dght 2.550 Lbp 32.40 Br md 6.40 Dpth 3.10 Welded, 1 dk	**(B11B2FV) Fishing Vessel**	**1 oil engine** GEARED YES, UNKNOWN ARRGMT: driving 1 Propeller Total Power: 407kW (553hp) Cummins 1 x 4 Stroke 407kW (553bhp) Chongqing Cummins Engine Co Ltd-China

IMO / Call sign	Name / Owner / Port	Tonnage	Class	Build / Dimensions	Type	Machinery
629084 *ZZZ3*	**ZHONG SHUI 803** **CNFC Overseas Fishery Co Ltd** - *Yantai, Shandong* *China* Official number: YG0200020046	**128** 47 37		**2002-06 Dalian Fishing Vessel Co — Dalian LN** Loa 34.80 Br ex - Dght 2.550 Lbp 32.40 Br md 6.40 Dpth 3.10 Welded, 1 dk	**(B11B2FV) Fishing Vessel**	**1 oil engine** GEARED YES, UNKNOWN ARRGMT: driving 1 Propeller Total Power: 407kW (553hp) Cummins 1 x 4 Stroke 407kW (553bhp) Chongqing Cummins Engine Co Ltd-China
629096 *ZZZ4*	**ZHONG SHUI 804** **CNFC Overseas Fishery Co Ltd** - *Yantai, Shandong* *China* Official number: YG0200020047	**128** 47 37		**2002-06 Dalian Fishing Vessel Co — Dalian LN** Loa 34.80 Br ex - Dght 2.550 Lbp 32.40 Br md 6.40 Dpth 3.10 Welded, 1 dk	**(B11B2FV) Fishing Vessel**	**1 oil engine** GEARED YES, UNKNOWN ARRGMT: driving 1 Propeller Total Power: 407kW (553hp) Chinese Std. Type 1 x 4 Stroke 407kW (553bhp) Zibo Diesel Engine Factory-China
629008 *ZYJ2*	**ZHONG SHUI 805** **CNFC Overseas Fishery Co Ltd** - *Yantai, Shandong* *China* Official number: YG0200100123	**223** 92 73		**2010-08 Huanghai Shipbuilding Co Ltd — Rongcheng SD** Loa 37.60 Br ex - Dght 3.000 Lbp 33.74 Br md 6.80 Dpth 3.50 Welded, 1 dk	**(B11B2FV) Fishing Vessel**	**1 oil engine** GEARED YES, UNKNOWN ARRGMT: driving 1 Propeller Total Power: 447kW (608hp) Cummins 1 x 4 Stroke 447kW (608bhp) Chongqing Cummins Engine Co Ltd-China
629010 *ZYJ3*	**ZHONG SHUI 806** **CNFC Overseas Fishery Co Ltd** - *Yantai, Shandong* *China* Official number: YG0200100124	**223** 92 73		**2010-08 Huanghai Shipbuilding Co Ltd — Rongcheng SD** Loa 37.60 Br ex - Dght 3.000 Lbp 33.74 Br md 6.80 Dpth 3.50 Welded, 1 dk	**(B11B2FV) Fishing Vessel**	**1 oil engine** GEARED YES, UNKNOWN ARRGMT driving 1 Propeller Total Power: 447kW (608hp) Cummins 1 x 4 Stroke 447kW (608bhp) Chongqing Cummins Engine Co Ltd-China
629022 *ZYJ4*	**ZHONG SHUI 807** **CNFC Overseas Fishery Co Ltd** - *Yantai, Shandong* *China* Official number: YG0200100141	**223** 92 73		**2010-09 Huanghai Shipbuilding Co Ltd — Rongcheng SD** Loa 37.60 Br ex - Dght 3.000 Lbp 33.74 Br md 6.80 Dpth 3.50 Welded, 1 dk	**(B11B2FV) Fishing Vessel**	**1 oil engine** GEARED YES, UNKNOWN ARRGMT driving 1 Propeller Total Power: 447kW (608hp) Cummins 1 x 4 Stroke 447kW (608bhp) Chongqing Cummins Engine Co Ltd-China
629034 *ZYJ5*	**ZHONG SHUI 808** **CNFC Overseas Fishery Co Ltd** - *Yantai, Shandong* *China* Official number: YG0200100142	**223** 92 73		**2010-09 Huanghai Shipbuilding Co Ltd — Rongcheng SD** Loa 37.60 Br ex - Dght 3.000 Lbp 33.74 Br md 6.80 Dpth 3.50 Welded, 1 dk	**(B11B2FV) Fishing Vessel**	**1 oil engine** GEARED YES, UNKNOWN ARRGMT driving 1 Propeller Total Power: 447kW (608hp) Cummins 1 x 4 Stroke 447kW (608bhp) Chongqing Cummins Engine Co Ltd-China
629046 *ZYJ6*	**ZHONG SHUI 809** **CNFC Overseas Fishery Co Ltd** - *Yantai, Shandong* *China* Official number: YG0200100143	**223** 92 73		**2010-09 Huanghai Shipbuilding Co Ltd — Rongcheng SD** Loa 37.60 Br ex - Dght 3.000 Lbp 33.74 Br md 6.80 Dpth 3.50 Welded, 1 dk	**(B11B2FV) Fishing Vessel**	**1 oil engine** GEARED YES, UNKNOWN ARRGMT driving 1 Propeller Total Power: 447kW (608hp) Cummins 1 x 4 Stroke 447kW (608bhp) Chongqing Cummins Engine Co Ltd-China
629058 *ZYJ7*	**ZHONG SHUI 810** **CNFC Overseas Fishery Co Ltd** - *Yantai, Shandong* *China* Official number: YG0200100144	**223** 92 73		**2010-09 Huanghai Shipbuilding Co Ltd — Rongcheng SD** Loa 37.60 Br ex - Dght 3.000 Lbp 33.74 Br md 6.80 Dpth 3.50 Welded, 1 dk	**(B11B2FV) Fishing Vessel**	**1 oil engine** GEARED YES, UNKNOWN ARRGMT driving 1 Propeller Total Power: 447kW (608hp) Cummins 1 x 4 Stroke Chongqing Cummins Engine Co Ltd-China
653619 *ZSI8*	**ZHONG SHUI 811** **CNFC Overseas Fishery Co Ltd** - *Yantai, Shandong* *China*	**255** 126 255		**2011-09 Huanghai Shipbuilding Co Ltd — Rongcheng SD** Loa 39.60 Br ex - Dght 2.800 Lbp 35.50 Br md 6.80 Dpth 3.60 Welded, 1 dk	**(B11B2FV) Fishing Vessel**	**1 oil engine** reduction geared to sc. shaft driving 1 Propeller Total Power: 447kW (608hp) Cummins KTA-19-M3 1 x 4 Stroke 6 Cy. 159 x 159 447kW (608bhp) Chongqing Cummins Engine Co Ltd-China
653621 *ZSI9*	**ZHONG SHUI 812** **CNFC Overseas Fishery Co Ltd** - *Yantai, Shandong* *China*	**255** 126 255		**2011-09 Huanghai Shipbuilding Co Ltd — Rongcheng SD** Loa 39.60 Br ex - Dght 2.800 Lbp 35.50 Br md 6.80 Dpth 3.60 Welded, 1 dk	**(B11B2FV) Fishing Vessel**	**1 oil engine** reduction geared to sc. shaft driving 1 Propeller Total Power: 447kW (608hp) Cummins KTA-19-M3 1 x 4 Stroke 6 Cy. 159 x 159 447kW (608bhp) Chongqing Cummins Engine Co Ltd-China
863903 *XAH6*	**ZHONG SHUI 9201** **China National Fisheries Corp** - *Guangzhou, Guangdong* *China*	*295* 88 150	Class: CC	**1992 Guangzhou Fishing Vessel Shipyard — Guangzhou GD** Loa 44.86 Br ex - Dght 3.030 Lbp 38.00 Br md 7.60 Dpth 4.00 Welded, 1 dk	**(B11B2FV) Fishing Vessel** Ins: 213	**1 oil engine** driving 1 FP propeller Total Power: 552kW (750hp) 12.0kn Chinese Std. Type 6250 1 x 4 Stroke 6 Cy. 250 x 300 552kW (750bhp) (made 1991) Zibo Diesel Engine Factory-China AuxGen: 2 x 90kW 400V a.c
863915 *XAH7*	**ZHONG SHUI 9202** **China National Fisheries Corp** - *Guangzhou, Guangdong* *China*	**196** 69 150	Class: CC	**1992 Guangzhou Fishing Vessel Shipyard — Guangzhou GD** Loa 44.86 Br ex - Dght 3.030 Lbp 38.00 Br md 7.60 Dpth 4.00 Welded, 1 dk	**(B11B2FV) Fishing Vessel** Ins: 213	**1 oil engine** driving 1 FP propeller Total Power: 552kW (750hp) 12.0kn Chinese Std. Type 6250 1 x 4 Stroke 6 Cy. 250 x 300 552kW (750bhp) (made 1991) Zibo Diesel Engine Factory-China AuxGen: 2 x 90kW 400V a.c
863927	**ZHONG SHUI 9203** **China National Fisheries Corp** - *Shanghai* *China*	*295* 88 150	Class: CC	**1992 Guangzhou Fishing Vessel Shipyard — Guangzhou GD** Loa 44.86 Br ex - Dght 3.030 Lbp 38.00 Br md 7.60 Dpth 4.00 Welded, 1 dk	**(B11B2FV) Fishing Vessel** Ins: 213	**1 oil engine** driving 1 FP propeller Total Power: 552kW (750hp) 12.0kn Chinese Std. Type 6250 1 x 4 Stroke 6 Cy. 250 x 300 552kW (750bhp) Zibo Diesel Engine Factory-China
863939	**ZHONG SHUI 9204** **China National Fisheries Corp** - *Guangzhou, Guangdong* *China*	**299** 90 140	Class: CC	**1992 Guangzhou Fishing Vessel Shipyard — Guangzhou GD** Loa 44.86 Br ex - Dght 3.030 Lbp 38.00 Br md 7.60 Dpth 4.00 Welded, 1 dk	**(B11B2FV) Fishing Vessel** Ins: 224	**1 oil engine** geared to sc. shaft driving 1 FP propeller Total Power: 541kW (736hp) 12.0kn Chinese Std. Type 8300 1 x 4 Stroke 8 Cy. 300 x 380 541kW (736bhp) Zibo Diesel Engine Factory-China AuxGen: 2 x 90kW 400V a.c
883070	**ZHONG SHUI 9401** **China National Fisheries Corp** - *Yantai, Shandong* *China*	**313** 94 130	Class: (CC)	**1994-07 Dalian Fishing Vessel Co — Dalian LN** Loa 43.24 Br ex - Dght 2.950 Lbp 37.00 Br md 7.60 Dpth 3.85 Welded, 1 dk	**(B11B2FV) Fishing Vessel** Ins: 246	**1 oil engine** geared to sc. shaft driving 1 FP propeller Total Power: 433kW (589hp) 12.0kn Chinese Std. Type 6300 1 x 4 Stroke 6 Cy. 300 x 380 433kW (589bhp) Dalian Fishing Vessel Co-China AuxGen: 1 x 90kW 400V a.c
883068 *BHC*	**ZHONG SHUI 9402** **China National Fisheries Corp** - *Yantai, Shandong* *China*	**313** 94 130	Class: (CC)	**1994-07 Dalian Fishing Vessel Co — Dalian LN** Loa 43.24 Br ex - Dght 2.950 Lbp 37.00 Br md 7.60 Dpth 3.85 Welded, 1 dk	**(B11B2FV) Fishing Vessel** Ins: 246	**1 oil engine** geared to sc. shaft driving 1 FP propeller Total Power: 433kW (589hp) 12.0kn Chinese Std. Type 6300 1 x 4 Stroke 6 Cy. 300 x 380 433kW (589bhp) Dalian Fishing Vessel Co-China AuxGen: 1 x 90kW 400V a.c
883056	**ZHONG SHUI 9403** **China National Fisheries Corp** - *Yantai, Shandong* *China*	**313** 94 130	Class: (CC)	**1994-07 Dalian Fishing Vessel Co — Dalian LN** Loa 43.25 Br ex - Dght 2.950 Lbp 37.00 Br md 7.60 Dpth 3.85 Welded, 1 dk	**(B11B2FV) Fishing Vessel** Ins: 246	**1 oil engine** geared to sc. shaft driving 1 FP propeller Total Power: 433kW (589hp) 12.0kn Chinese Std. Type 6300 1 x 4 Stroke 6 Cy. 300 x 380 433kW (589bhp) Dalian Fishing Vessel Co-China AuxGen: 1 x 90kW 400V a.c
883082	**ZHONG SHUI 9405** **China National Fisheries Corp** - *Zhoushan, Zhejiang* *China*	**290** 87 135	Class: (CC)	**1994 Dalian Fishing Vessel Co — Dalian LN** Loa 44.38 Br ex - Dght 2.850 Lbp 38.00 Br md 7.60 Dpth 3.75 Welded, 1 dk	**(B11B2FV) Fishing Vessel** Ins: 232	**1 oil engine** geared to sc. shaft driving 1 FP propeller Total Power: 541kW (736hp) 11.5kn Chinese Std. Type 8300 1 x 4 Stroke 8 Cy. 300 x 380 541kW (736bhp) Dalian Fishing Vessel Co-China AuxGen: 2 x 120kW 400V a.c
883094 *KUB3*	**ZHONG SHUI 9406** **China National Fisheries Corp** - *Zhoushan, Zhejiang* *China*	**290** 87 135	Class: (CC)	**1994 Dalian Fishing Vessel Co — Dalian LN** Loa 44.38 Br ex - Dght 2.850 Lbp 38.00 Br md 7.60 Dpth 3.75 Welded, 1 dk	**(B11B2FV) Fishing Vessel** Ins: 232	**1 oil engine** geared to sc. shaft driving 1 FP propeller Total Power: 541kW (736hp) 11.5kn Chinese Std. Type 8300 1 x 4 Stroke 8 Cy. 300 x 380 541kW (736bhp) Dalian Fishing Vessel Co-China AuxGen: 2 x 120kW 400V a.c

IMO / Call sign	Name / Owner	Tonnage	Class	Builder / Dimensions	Type	Machinery	Speed
8883109 *BKUC3* -	**ZHONG SHUI 9407** **China National Fisheries Corp** - *Zhoushan, Zhejiang* *China*	**290** 87 135	Class: (CC)	**1994 Dalian Fishing Vessel Co — Dalian LN** Loa 44.38 Br ex - Dght 2.850 Lbp 38.00 Br md 7.60 Dpth 3.75 Welded, 1 dk	**(B11B2FV) Fishing Vessel** Ins: 232	**1 oil engine** geared to sc. shaft driving 1 FP propeller Total Power: 541kW (736hp) Chinese Std. Type 1 x 4 Stroke 8 Cy. 300 x 380 541kW (736bhp) Dalian Fishing Vessel Co-China AuxGen: 2 x 120kW 400V a.c	11.5k 830
8883111 *BKUD3* -	**ZHONG SHUI 9408** **China National Fisheries Corp** - *Zhoushan, Zhejiang* *China*	**290** 87 135	Class: (CC)	**1994 Dalian Fishing Vessel Co — Dalian LN** Loa 44.38 Br ex - Dght 2.850 Lbp 38.00 Br md 7.60 Dpth 3.75 Welded, 1 dk	**(B11B2FV) Fishing Vessel** Ins: 232	**1 oil engine** geared to sc. shaft driving 1 FP propeller Total Power: 541kW (736hp) Chinese Std. Type 1 x 4 Stroke 8 Cy. 300 x 380 541kW (736bhp) Dalian Fishing Vessel Co-China AuxGen: 2 x 120kW 400V a.c	11.5k 830
8883147 *BYSH2* -	**ZHONG SHUI 9411** **China National Fisheries Corp** - *Zhanjiang, Guangdong* *China*	**299** 90 -	Class: (CC)	**1994 Guangzhou Fishing Vessel Shipyard — Guangzhou GD** Loa 44.86 Br ex - Dght 3.000 Lbp 38.00 Br md 7.60 Dpth 4.00 Welded, 1 dk	**(B11B2FV) Fishing Vessel** Ins: 224	**1 oil engine** geared to sc. shaft driving 1 FP propeller Total Power: 541kW (736hp) Chinese Std. Type 1 x 4 Stroke 8 Cy. 300 x 380 541kW (736bhp) Dalian Fishing Vessel Co-China AuxGen: 2 x 90kW 400V a.c	12.0k 830
8883159 *BYSB4* -	**ZHONG SHUI 9412** **China National Fisheries Corp** - *Zhanjiang, Guangdong* *China*	**299** 90 -	Class: (CC)	**1994-07 Guangzhou Fishing Vessel Shipyard — Guangzhou GD** Loa 44.86 Br ex - Dght 3.000 Lbp 38.00 Br md 7.60 Dpth 4.00 Welded, 1 dk	**(B11B2FV) Fishing Vessel** Ins: 224	**1 oil engine** geared to sc. shaft driving 1 FP propeller Total Power: 541kW (736hp) Chinese Std. Type 1 x 4 Stroke 8 Cy. 300 x 380 541kW (736bhp) Dalian Fishing Vessel Co-China AuxGen: 2 x 90kW 400V a.c	12.0k 830
8883161 *BYSB3* -	**ZHONG SHUI 9414** **China National Fisheries Corp** - *Zhanjiang, Guangdong* *China*	**299** 90 -	Class: (CC)	**1994 Guangzhou Fishing Vessel Shipyard — Guangzhou GD** Loa 44.86 Br ex - Dght 3.000 Lbp 38.00 Br md 7.60 Dpth 4.00 Welded, 1 dk	**(B11B2FV) Fishing Vessel** Ins: 224	**1 oil engine** geared to sc. shaft driving 1 FP propeller Total Power: 541kW (736hp) Chinese Std. Type 1 x 4 Stroke 8 Cy. 300 x 380 541kW (736bhp) Dalian Fishing Vessel Co-China AuxGen: 2 x 90kW 400V a.c	12.0kn 8300
8883173 *BYSB5* -	**ZHONG SHUI 9415** **China National Fisheries Corp** - *Zhanjiang, Guangdong* *China*	**299** 90 -	Class: (CC)	**1994-07 Guangzhou Fishing Vessel Shipyard — Guangzhou GD** Loa 44.86 Br ex - Dght 3.000 Lbp 38.00 Br md 7.60 Dpth 4.00 Welded, 1 dk	**(B11B2FV) Fishing Vessel** Ins: 224	**1 oil engine** geared to sc. shaft driving 1 FP propeller Total Power: 541kW (736hp) Chinese Std. Type 1 x 4 Stroke 8 Cy. 300 x 380 541kW (736bhp) Dalian Fishing Vessel Co-China AuxGen: 2 x 90kW 400V a.c	12.0kn 8300
8883185 - -	**ZHONG SHUI 9416** **China National Fisheries Corp** - *Yantai, Shandong* *China*	**290** 87 135	Class: (CC)	**1994 Dalian Fishing Vessel Co — Dalian LN** Loa 44.38 Br ex - Dght 2.850 Lbp 38.00 Br md 7.60 Dpth 3.75 Welded, 1 dk	**(B11B2FV) Fishing Vessel** Ins: 232	**1 oil engine** geared to sc. shaft driving 1 FP propeller Total Power: 541kW (736hp) Chinese Std. Type 1 x 4 Stroke 8 Cy. 300 x 380 541kW (736bhp) Dalian Fishing Vessel Co-China AuxGen: 2 x 120kW 400V a.c	11.5kn 8300
8883197 - -	**ZHONG SHUI 9417** **China National Fisheries Corp** - *Yantai, Shandong* *China*	**290** 87 135	Class: (CC)	**1994 Dalian Fishing Vessel Co — Dalian LN** Loa 44.38 Br ex - Dght 2.850 Lbp 38.00 Br md 7.60 Dpth 3.75 Welded, 1 dk	**(B11B2FV) Fishing Vessel** Ins: 232	**1 oil engine** geared to sc. shaft driving 1 FP propeller Total Power: 541kW (736hp) Chinese Std. Type 1 x 4 Stroke 8 Cy. 300 x 380 541kW (736bhp) Dalian Fishing Vessel Co-China AuxGen: 2 x 120kW 400V a.c	11.5kn 8300
8884373 *BBRG* -	**ZHONG SHUI 9418** **China National Fisheries Corp** - SatCom: Inmarsat A 1572735 *Yantai, Shandong* *China*	**290** 87 135	Class: (CC)	**1994 Dalian Fishing Vessel Co — Dalian LN** Loa 44.38 Br ex - Dght 2.850 Lbp 38.00 Br md 7.60 Dpth 3.75 Welded, 1 dk	**(B11B2FV) Fishing Vessel**	**1 oil engine** geared to sc. shaft driving 1 FP propeller Total Power: 541kW (736hp) Chinese Std. Type 1 x 4 Stroke 8 Cy. 300 x 380 541kW (736bhp) Dalian Fishing Vessel Co-China AuxGen: 2 x 120kW 400V a.c	11.5kn 8300
8884385 - -	**ZHONG SHUI 9419** **China National Fisheries Corp** - *Yantai, Shandong* *China*	**290** 87 135	Class: (CC)	**1994 Dalian Fishing Vessel Co — Dalian LN** Loa 44.38 Br ex - Dght 2.850 Lbp 38.00 Br md 7.60 Dpth 3.75 Welded, 1 dk	**(B11B2FV) Fishing Vessel**	**1 oil engine** geared to sc. shaft driving 1 FP propeller Total Power: 541kW (736hp) Chinese Std. Type 1 x 4 Stroke 8 Cy. 300 x 380 541kW (736bhp) Dalian Fishing Vessel Co-China AuxGen: 2 x 120kW 400V a.c	11.5kn 8300
9419060 *BKWQ3* -	**ZHONG TAI 8** **Zhoushan Putuo Edible Oils Transportation & Trade Co Ltd** - *Zhoushan, Zhejiang* *China* MMSI: 413405430	**8,564** 4,374 11,806	Class: CC	**2007-06 Zhoushan Longtai Shipbuilding Co Ltd — Zhoushan ZJ** Yd No: 0601 Loa 139.36 (BB) Br ex - Dght 7.650 Lbp 130.50 Br md 19.80 Dpth 10.50 Welded, 1 dk	**(A33A2CC) Container Ship (Fully Cellular)** Bale: 15,630 TEU 642 C Ho 298 TEU C Dk 344 TEU. Compartments: 4 Cell Ho, ER 4 Ha: 3 (15.4 x 25.5)ER (6.8 x 9.9) Ice Capable	**1 oil engine** reduction geared to sc. shaft driving 1 FP propeller Total Power: 4,409kW (5,994hp) Pielstick 1 x 4 Stroke 6 Cy. 400 x 460 4409kW (5994bhp) Shaanxi Diesel Heavy Industry Co Lt-China AuxGen: 3 x 440kW 400V a.c	14.8kn 6PC2-6
8995457 - -	**ZHONG TAI NO. 1** *ex Ching Feng No. 867 -2004* **Profit Peak Inc** Kando Maritime Co Ltd *Chinese Taipei*	**1,087** 375 -		**1991-01 Lien Ho Shipbuilding Co, Ltd — Kaohsiung** L reg 58.70 Br ex - Dght - Lbp - Br md 11.80 Dpth 4.55 Welded, 1 dk	**(B11B2FV) Fishing Vessel**	**1 oil engine** reduction geared to sc. shaft driving 1 Propeller Total Power: 2,205kW (2,998hp) Niigata 1 x 4 Stroke 6 Cy. 320 x 420 2205kW (2998bhp) Niigata Engineering Co Ltd-Japan	14.0kn 6MG32CLX
8919477 *BZZW9* -	**ZHONG TAI NO. 2** *ex Castel Braz -2004 ex Aristotel -1996* **China National Fisheries Corp** - SatCom: Inmarsat C 441329811 *Qinhuangdao, Hebei* *China* MMSI: 413298000	**2,109** 633 1,650	Class: (BV)	**1992-07 Ast. de Huelva S.A. — Huelva** Yd No: 468 Loa 79.80 Br ex - Dght 6.500 Lbp 69.20 Br md 13.50 Dpth 8.90 Welded, 2 dks	**(B11B2FV) Fishing Vessel** Ins: 1,840	**1 oil engine** with clutches & sr reverse geared to sc. shaft driving 1 FP propeller Total Power: 3,641kW (4,950hp) Wartsila 1 x 4 Stroke 9 Cy. 320 x 350 3641kW (4950bhp) Construcciones Echevarria SA-Spain Thrusters: 1 Thwart. CP thruster (f); 1 Tunnel thruster (a)	15.0kn 9R32E
9558074 *BQAV* -	**ZHONG TENG HAI** **COSCO Bulk Carrier Co Ltd (COSCO BULK)** - SatCom: Inmarsat C 441301243 *Tianjin* *China* MMSI: 413827000	**91,205** 59,001 178,242 T/cm 120.6	Class: CC	**2009-07 Shanghai Waigaoqiao Shipbuilding Co Ltd — Shanghai** Yd No: 1097 Loa 291.95 (BB) Br ex - Dght 18.300 Lbp 282.00 Br md 45.00 Dpth 24.80 Welded, 1 dk	**(A21A2BC) Bulk Carrier** Grain: 194,179; Bale: 183,425 Compartments: 9 Ho, ER 9 Ha: 7 (15.5 x 20.0)ER 2 (15.5 x 16.5)	**1 oil engine** driving 1 FP propeller Total Power: 16,860kW (22,923hp) MAN-B&W 1 x 2 Stroke 6 Cy. 700 x 2674 16860kW (22923bhp) Hudong Heavy Machinery Co Ltd-China AuxGen: 3 x 900kW 450V a.c	14.0kn 6S70MC
9383390 *BBHE* -	**ZHONG TIE BO HAI 1 HAO** **Sinorail Bohai Train Ferry Co Ltd (Zhongtie Bohai Railway Ferry Co Ltd)** - SatCom: Inmarsat Mini-M 763674830 *Yantai, Shandong* *China* MMSI: 412328490	**24,975** 12,987 7,200	Class: CC	**2006-10 Tianjin Xingang Shipyard — Tianjin** Yd No: 346-1 Loa 182.60 (BB) Br ex - Dght 6.000 Lbp 164.60 Br md 24.80 Dpth 9.00 Welded, 2 dks	**(A36A2PT) Passenger/Ro-Ro Ship (Vehicles/Rail)** Passengers: 480; cabins: 138 Stern door/ramp (centre) Rail Wagons: 50 Ice Capable	**4 diesel electric oil engines** driving 4 gen. each 2880kW 6600V a.c Connecting to 2 elec. motors each (4000kW) driving 2 Azimuth electric drive units Total Power: 11,520kW (15,664hp) MaK 4 x 4 Stroke 9 Cy. 255 x 400 each-2880kW (3916bhp) Caterpillar Motoren (Guangdong) CoLtd-China Thrusters: 2 Tunnel thruster (f) Fuel: 280.0 (r.f.)	18.0kn 9M25
9383405 *BBHF* -	**ZHONG TIE BO HAI 2 HAO** **Sinorail Bohai Train Ferry Co Ltd (Zhongtie Bohai Railway Ferry Co Ltd)** - SatCom: Inmarsat Mini-M 763675796 *Yantai, Shandong* *China* MMSI: 412328510	**24,975** 12,987 7,200	Class: CC	**2007-01 Tianjin Xingang Shipyard — Tianjin** Yd No: 346-2 Loa 182.60 (BB) Br ex - Dght 6.000 Lbp 164.60 Br md 24.80 Dpth 9.00 Welded, 2 dks	**(A36A2PT) Passenger/Ro-Ro Ship (Vehicles/Rail)** Passengers: 480; cabins: 138 Stern door/ramp (centre) Rail Wagons: 50 Bale: 25,137 Ice Capable	**4 diesel electric oil engines** driving 4 gen. each 2880kW 6600V a.c Connecting to 2 elec. motors each (4000kW) driving 2 Azimuth electric drive units Total Power: 12,200kW (16,588hp) MaK 1 x 4 Stroke 9 Cy. 255 x 400 3050kW (4147bhp) Caterpillar Motoren (Guangdong) CoLtd-China MaK 3 x 4 Stroke 9 Cy. 255 x 400 each-3050kW (4147bhp) Caterpillar Motoren (Guangdong) CoLtd-China Thrusters: 2 Tunnel thruster (f) Fuel: 280.0 (r.f.)	18.0kn 9M25C 9M25C

399375 *BCX*	**ZHONG TIE BO HAI 3 HAO** **Sinorail Bohai Train Ferry Co Ltd (Zhongtie Bohai Railway Ferry Co Ltd)** - *Yantai, Shandong* *China* MMSI: 413321000	**25,040** 13,521 8,776	Class: CC	**2008-07 Tianjin Xingang Shipbuilding Industry Co Ltd — Tianjin** Yd No: 346-3 Loa 182.60 (BB) Br ex - Dght 5.800 Lbp 164.60 Br md 24.80 Dpth 9.00 Welded, 1 dk	**(A36A2PT) Passenger/Ro-Ro Ship (Vehicles/Rail)** Passengers: 480 Stern door/ramp (centre) Rail Wagons: 50 Ice Capable	**4 diesel electric oil engines** driving 4 gen. each 2880kW 6600V a.c driving 4 Azimuth electric drive units Total Power: 11,880kW (16,152hp) 18.0kn MaK 9M25 4 x 4 Stroke 9 Cy. 255 x 400 each-2970kW (4038bhp) Caterpillar Motoren (Guangdong) CoLtd-China Thrusters: 2 Tunnel thruster (f)
600542 *HZZ*	**ZHONG WAI YUN CHANG JIANG 001** **China National Foreign Trade Transportation Corp (SINOTRANS)** - *China* MMSI: 413359190	**4,272** 2,392 4,987	Class: CC (Class contemplated)	**2011-08 Zijinshan Shipyard of Nanjing Tanker Corp — Yizheng JS** Loa 108.00 Br ex - Dght 4.800 Lbp - Br md 17.00 Dpth 8.00 Welded, 1 dk	**(A33A2CC) Container Ship (Fully Cellular)**	**1 oil engine** driving 1 Propeller
600554 *HZZ2*	**ZHONG WAI YUN CHANG JIANG 002** **China National Foreign Trade Transportation Corp (SINOTRANS)** - *Nanjing, Jiangsu* *China*	**4,272** 2,392 4,690	Class: CC (Class contemplated)	**2011-10 Zijinshan Shipyard of Nanjing Tanker Corp — Yizheng JS** Loa 108.00 Br ex - Dght 4.800 Lbp 102.50 Br md 17.00 Dpth 8.00 Welded, 1 dk	**(A33A2CC) Container Ship (Fully Cellular)**	**1 oil engine** driving 1 Propeller
600566 *HZZ3*	**ZHONG WAI YUN CHANG JIANG 003** **China National Foreign Trade Transportation Corp (SINOTRANS)** - *Nanjing, Jiangsu* *China*	**4,272** 2,392 4,705	Class: CC (Class contemplated)	**2012-01 Zijinshan Shipyard of Nanjing Tanker Corp — Yizheng JS** Loa 108.00 Br ex - Dght 4.800 Lbp 102.50 Br md 17.00 Dpth 8.00 Welded, 1 dk	**(A33A2CC) Container Ship (Fully Cellular)**	**1 oil engine** driving 1 Propeller
064841 *BA9*	**ZHONG WAI YUN HU MEN** *ex* Northern Trust *-2012* *ex* Cosco Bremerhaven *-2008* *ex* Cosco Norfolk *-2006* *ex* Choyang Phoenix *-2001* *ex* Ville de Lyra *-1997* **Sinotrans Sunnyexpress Co Ltd** - *Shanghai* *China* MMSI: 414141000	**35,944** 20,871 43,025	Class: CC (GL) (BV)	**1993-12 Hyundai Heavy Industries Co Ltd — Ulsan** Yd No: 844 Loa 240.45 (BB) Br ex 32.07 Dght 11.719 Lbp 225.20 Br md 32.00 Dpth 19.00 Welded, 1 dk	**(A33A2CC) Container Ship (Fully Cellular)** TEU 3538 C Ho 1466 TEU C Dk 2072 TEU incl 150 ref C. Compartments: ER, 7 Cell Ho 13 Ha: ER	**1 oil engine** driving 1 FP propeller Total Power: 22,479kW (30,562hp) 21.8kn B&W 8S70MC 1 x 2 Stroke 8 Cy. 700 x 2674 22479kW (30562bhp) Hyundai Heavy Industries Co Ltd-South Korea AuxGen: 3 x 900kW 440/220V 60Hz a.c Thrusters: 1 Thwart. CP thruster (f) Fuel: 3531.0 (r.f.)
642057 *BG9*	**ZHONG WAI YUN NAN JING** *ex* Sinotrans Nanjing *-2013* **Sinotrans Sunnyexpress Co Ltd** - *Shanghai* *China* MMSI: 413377710	**19,500** 10,800 27,000	Class: CC	**2013-07 Qingshan Shipyard — Wuhan HB** Yd No: QS1800-1 Loa 179.70 (BB) Br ex - Dght 10.200 Lbp 170.00 Br md 27.60 Dpth 14.20 Welded, 1 dk	**(A33A2CC) Container Ship (Fully Cellular)** TEU 1800 Ice Capable	**1 oil engine** driving 1 FP propeller Total Power: 6,480kW (8,810hp) 15.0kn MAN-B&W 6S46MC-C 1 x 2 Stroke 6 Cy. 460 x 1932 6480kW (8810bhp)
009176 *AC3*	**ZHONG WAI YUN QUAN ZHOU** *ex* STX Asia *-2010* *ex* ACX Marigold *-2005* *ex* ACX Violet *-2003* **Sinotrans Sunnyexpress Co Ltd** - SatCom: Inmarsat C 441276910 *Shanghai* *China* MMSI: 412769000	**18,487** 9,141 24,502	Class: CC (KR) (NK)	**1991-10 KK Kanasashi — Toyohashi AI** Yd No: 3255 Loa 192.99 (BB) Br ex - Dght 9.529 Lbp 181.00 Br md 28.00 Dpth 14.00 Welded, 1 dk	**(A33A2CC) Container Ship (Fully Cellular)** TEU 1461 C Ho 600 TEU C Dk 861 TEU incl 200 ref C. Compartments: 6 Cell Ho, ER 19 Ha: (12.8 x 8.0)2 (12.8 x 8.5)16 (12.8 x 11.0)ER	**1 oil engine** driving 1 FP propeller Total Power: 12,380kW (16,832hp) 20.0kn Mitsubishi 8UEC60LS 1 x 2 Stroke 8 Cy. 600 x 2200 12380kW (16832bhp) Kobe Hatsudoki KK-Japan AuxGen: 3 x 680kW 450V 60Hz a.c Thrusters: 1 Thwart. CP thruster (f) Fuel: 121.9 (d.f.) 1870.4 (r.f.)
908524 *AI7*	**ZHONG WAI YUN TAI CANG** *ex* Mildburg *-2011* *ex* Tiger Sky *-2009* *ex* Mildburg *-2002* *ex* Direct Condor *-1999* *ex* Mildburg *-1996* *ex* Contship Australia *-1995* **Sinotrans Sunnyexpress Co Ltd** - *Shanghai* *China* MMSI: 412462000	**16,236** 9,475 23,596 T/cm 36.0	Class: CC (GL)	**1991-03 Schichau Seebeckwerft AG — Bremerhaven** Yd No: 1072 Loa 164.06 (BB) Br ex - Dght 10.660 Lbp 153.70 Br md 27.50 Dpth 14.30 Welded, 1 dk	**(A33A2CC) Container Ship (Fully Cellular)** Grain: 32,650; Bale: 32,025 TEU 1599 C Ho 618 TEU C Dk 981 TEU incl 70 ref C. Compartments: 3 Cell Ho, ER 8 Ha: 2 (12.4 x 20.5)6 (12.4 x 23.0)ER Ice Capable	**1 oil engine** driving 1 FP propeller Vane wheel Total Power: 10,440kW (14,194hp) 17.0kn B&W 6L60MC 1 x 2 Stroke 6 Cy. 600 x 1944 10440kW (14194bhp) Bremer Vulkan AG Schiffbau u.Maschinenfabrik-Bremen AuxGen: 1 x 992kW 220/440V a.c, 2 x 785kW 220/440V a.c Thrusters: 1 Thwart. FP thruster (f) Fuel: 186.5 (d.f.) 1900.0 (r.f.) 45.0pd
155092 *BG2*	**ZHONG WAI YUN XIN GANG** *ex* Northern Victory *-2013* *ex* MSC Salvador *-2006* *ex* Safmarine Everest *-2002* *ex* CMBT Everest *-2001* *launched as* Northern Victory *-1997* **Sinotrans Sunnyexpress Co Ltd** - *Shanghai* *China* MMSI: 413377680	**29,115** 17,030 40,100 T/cm 52.8	Class: CC (GL)	**1997-08 Hyundai Heavy Industries Co Ltd — Ulsan** Yd No: 1045 Loa 195.72 (BB) Br ex - Dght 12.500 Lbp 184.00 Br md 32.25 Dpth 18.80 Welded, 1 dk	**(A33A2CC) Container Ship (Fully Cellular)** TEU 2808 C Ho 1174 TEU C Dk 1634 TEU incl 400 ref C Compartments: 6 Ho	**1 oil engine** driving 1 FP propeller Total Power: 23,942kW (32,552hp) 22.0kn Sulzer 8RTA72U 1 x 2 Stroke 8 Cy. 720 x 2500 23942kW (32552bhp) Hyundai Heavy Industries Co Ltd-South Korea AuxGen: 3 x 1479kW 440V 60Hz a.c Thrusters: 1 Thwart. FP thruster (f) Fuel: 199.0 (d.f.) 3773.0 (r.f.)
302167 *AC4*	**ZHONG WAI YUN YING KOU** *ex* Northern Fortune *-2010* *ex* Canmar Trader *-2003* *ex* Northern Fortune *-2002* *ex* Zim Ashdod I *-2001* *ex* OOCL Dragon *-2000* *ex* CMA Kawasaki *-2000* *ex* Northern Fortune *-1998* *ex* Zim Ravenna *-1998* *ex* Northern Fortune *-1997* *ex* Zim Brisbane *-1997* *ex* Valencia Senator *-1995* *ex* Northern Fortune *-1994* *ex* A. Abraham *-1994* **Sinotrans Sunnyexpress Co Ltd** - SatCom: Inmarsat C 441277210 *Shanghai* *China* MMSI: 412772000	**30,509** 12,885 30,685	Class: CC (GL) (PR)	**1991-09 Stocznia Gdanska SA — Gdansk** Yd No: B355/03 Loa 202.40 (BB) Br ex - Dght 10.550 Lbp 195.46 Br md 31.00 Dpth 15.50 Welded, 1 dk	**(A33A2CC) Container Ship (Fully Cellular)** TEU 1939 C Ho 917 TEU C Dk 1022 TEU incl 370 ref C. Compartments: ER, 9 Cell Ho 9 Ha: ER Ice Capable	**1 oil engine** driving 1 FP propeller Total Power: 16,260kW (22,107hp) 19.2kn Sulzer 6RTA76 1 x 2 Stroke 6 Cy. 760 x 2200 16260kW (22107bhp) Zaklady Przemyslu Metalowego 'HCegielski' SA-Poznan AuxGen: 3 x 1000kW 380V a.c Thrusters: 1 Thwart. FP thruster (f); 1 Tunnel thruster (a)
686780 *RVY*	**ZHONG WEI 6** **Maoming Zhong Wei Shipping Co Ltd** - *Maoming, Guangdong* *China* MMSI: 412476930 Official number: 091613000004	**2,512** 1,406 3,900	Class: CC (Class contemplated)	**2013-01 Taizhou Maple Leaf Shipbuilding Co Ltd — Linhai ZJ** Yd No: LPT3900-009. Loa 95.63 (BB) Br ex - Dght - Lbp 89.60 Br md 14.00 Dpth 6.50 Welded, 1 dk	**(A13B2TP) Products Tanker** Double Hull (13F)	**1 oil engine** reduction geared to sc. shaft driving 1 Propeller Total Power: 1,136kW (1,545hp) Chinese Std. Type 1 x 1136kW (1545bhp)
714920 *7BM6*	**ZHONG XIANG** *ex* Tasman Independence *-2010* *ex* New Independence *-2003* *ex* Abidjan Star 1 *-2001* *ex* New Independence *-2000* *ex* Cornelie Oldendorff *-2000* *ex* New Independence *-1999* *ex* Sunshine La Plata *-1998* **Zhong Xiang Shipping SA** Eastern Rain International Ship Management Co Ltd SatCom: Inmarsat A 1554456 *Majuro* *Marshall Islands* MMSI: 538001305 Official number: 1305	**18,936** 7,808 23,853 T/cm 37.5	Class: BV (NV) (NK)	**1989-02 Ishikawajima-Harima Heavy Industries Co Ltd (IHI) — Kure** Yd No: 2977 Loa 173.95 (BB) Br ex 27.64 Dght 10.027 Lbp 165.00 Br md 27.60 Dpth 15.40 Welded, 1 dk, 2nd dk in 1, 2, 4 & 6 holds only	**(A31A2GX) General Cargo Ship** Grain: 33,332; Bale: 31,870 TEU 957 C Ho 528 TEU C Dk 429 TEU incl 100 ref C. Compartments: 6 Ho, ER, 4 Tw Dk 6 Ha: ER Cranes: 1x25t; Gantry cranes: 2x40t	**1 oil engine** driving 1 FP propeller Total Power: 11,386kW (15,480hp) 17.5kn Sulzer 6RTA62 1 x 2 Stroke 6 Cy. 620 x 2150 11386kW (15480bhp) Ishikawajima Harima Heavy IndustrieCo Ltd (IHI)-Japan AuxGen: 3 x 800kW 450V 60Hz a.c Fuel: 203.0 (d.f.) 1782.0 (r.f.)
654107	**ZHONG XIN 5** - -	**904** 227 -		**2002 Guangzhou Xintang Shipping Co Shipyard — Zengcheng GD** Loa 57.23 Br ex - Dght - Lbp - Br md 13.00 Dpth 3.30 Welded, 1 dk	**(A24D2BA) Aggregates Carrier**	**1 oil engine** driving 1 Propeller 7.0kn

8735314 - - -	**ZHONG XIN 6** *ex* Pu Ji 383 *-2009* - -	**1,544** 445 -		**2005-09 Zhongshan Jinhui Shipbuilding & Repair Yard Co Ltd — Zhongshan GD** Yd No: 200502 Loa 66.83 Br ex - Dght - Lbp - Br md 15.00 Dpth 5.00 Welded, 1 dk	**(A24D2BA) Aggregates Carrier**	**2 oil engines** geared to sc. shafts driving 2 FP propellers Total Power: 800kW (1,088hp) 8.0 Chinese Std. Type 6190ZL 2 x 4 Stroke 6 Cy. 190 x 210 each-400kW (544bhp) Jinan Diesel Engine Co Ltd-China
8735326 - - -	**ZHONG XIN 7** *ex* Shun Li 86 *-2009* - -	**1,572** 254 -		**2006-06 Qingyuan Qingcheng Yongli Shipyard — Qingyuan GD** Yd No: 200601 Loa 72.80 Br ex - Dght - Lbp - Br md 15.20 Dpth 4.50 Welded, 1 dk	**(A24D2BA) Aggregates Carrier**	**2 oil engines** geared to sc. shafts driving 2 FP propellers Total Power: 814kW (1,106hp) 8.0 Cummins KTA-19-M6 2 x 4 Stroke 6 Cy. 159 x 159 each-407kW (553bhp) Chongqing Cummins Engine Co Ltd-China
9497074 - - -	**ZHONG XIN 8** - - -	**1,375** 770 -		**2007 in the People's Republic of China** Loa 66.00 Br ex - Dght - Lbp - Br md 14.50 Dpth 4.20 Welded, 1 dk	**(A24D2BA) Aggregates Carrier**	**1 oil engine** driving 1 Propeller 7.0
8740917 - - -	**ZHONG XIN 9** *ex* Shun Li 81 *-2009* *ex* Shun Yang 16 *-2008* - -	**1,540** 454 -		**2005-04 Guangzhou Panyu Shilou Xiuxiang Ship Repair & Building Yard — Guangzhou** Yd No: 200502 Loa 72.81 Br ex - Dght - Lbp - Br md 15.20 Dpth 4.50 Welded, 1 dk	**(A24D2BA) Aggregates Carrier**	**2 oil engines** reduction geared to sc. shafts driving 2 Propellers Total Power: 900kW (1,224hp) 8.0 Chinese Std. Type 6190ZL 2 x 4 Stroke 6 Cy. 190 x 210 each-450kW (612bhp) Jinan Diesel Engine Co Ltd-China
9017642 *9MLF5* -	**ZHONG XIN 18** *ex* Hakko Maru *-2009* *ex* Seisho Maru *-2005* **Alam Armada Corp Sdn Bhd** Alamgala Resources Sdn Bhd *Port Klang* *Malaysia* MMSI: 533041300 Official number: 334162	*498* - 1,198		**1991-06 Mukaishima Zoki Co. Ltd. — Onomichi** Yd No: 270 Loa 64.33 Br ex 10.02 Dght 4.174 Lbp 60.00 Br md 10.00 Dpth 4.50 Welded, 1 dk	**(A12A2TC) Chemical Tanker** Liq: 1,299 Compartments: 8 Ta, ER	**1 oil engine** with clutches & sr reverse geared to sc. shaft driving 1 FP propeller Total Power: 1,030kW (1,400hp) 11.7 Hanshin LH28 1 x 4 Stroke 6 Cy. 280 x 460 1030kW (1400bhp) The Hanshin Diesel Works Ltd-Japan AuxGen: 2 x 150kW 225V a.c
9684134 *VRMC3* -	**ZHONG XIN PEARL** *ex* Dinghai *-2013* **Zhong Xin Marine Co Ltd** - *Hong Kong* *Hong Kong* MMSI: 477519800 Official number: HK-3833	**40,946** 25,611 75,321	Class: CC	**2013-09 Guangzhou Huangpu Shipbuilding Co Ltd — Guangzhou GD** Yd No: H3040 Loa 225.00 (BB) Br ex - Dght 14.200 Lbp 217.00 Br md 32.26 Dpth 19.60 Welded, 1 dk	**(A21A2BC) Bulk Carrier** Grain: 90,097; Bale: 90,066 Compartments: 7 Ho, ER 7 Ha: 6 (15.5 x 14.4)ER (14.6 x 13.2)	**1 oil engine** driving 1 FP propeller Total Power: 8,833kW (12,009hp) 14.5 MAN-B&W 5S60ME 1 x 2 Stroke 5 Cy. 600 x 2400 8833kW (12009bhp) Hudong Heavy Machinery Co Ltd-China AuxGen: 3 x 560kW 450V a.c
9516507 *3FXV2* -	**ZHONG XING HAI** - **Zhongxinghai Shipping Inc** COSCO Bulk Carrier Co Ltd (COSCO BULK) *Panama* *Panama* MMSI: 370138000 Official number: 4272211	**105,936** 67,880 207,978 T/cm 140.5	Class: CC (AB)	**2011-05 Nantong COSCO KHI Ship Engineering Co Ltd (NACKS) — Nantong JS** Yd No: 090 Loa 300.00 Br ex 50.06 Dght 18.225 Lbp 295.00 Br md 50.00 Dpth 24.70 Welded, 1 dk	**(A21A2BC) Bulk Carrier** Double Hull Grain: 224,873 Compartments: 9 Ho, ER 9 Ha: ER	**1 oil engine** driving 1 FP propeller Total Power: 17,950kW (24,405hp) 14.8 MAN-B&W 6S70MC 1 x 2 Stroke 6 Cy. 700 x 2800 17950kW (24405bhp) CSSC MES Diesel Co Ltd-China AuxGen: 3 x 700kW a.c Fuel: 460.0 (d.f.) 5900.0 (r.f.)
9671747 *BZXD72* -	**ZHONG YANG 16** - **Shenzhen Shuiwan Pelagic Fisheries Co Ltd** - *Shekou, Guangdong* *China* MMSI: 412763490 Official number: 440301104683799	**317** 158 -		**2012-05 Huanghai Shipbuilding Co Ltd — Rongcheng SD** Loa 49.00 Br ex 7.00 Dght - Lbp - Br md - Dpth 3.80 Welded, 1 dk	**(B11B2FV) Fishing Vessel**	**1 oil engine** reduction geared to sc. shaft driving 1 Propeller Total Power: 720kW (979hp) Chinese Std. Type XCW6200Z 1 x 4 Stroke 6 Cy. 200 x 270 720kW (979bhp)
9671759 *BZXD73* -	**ZHONG YANG 18** - **Shenzhen Shuiwan Pelagic Fisheries Co Ltd** - *Shidao, Shandong* *China* MMSI: 413441090 Official number: 440301104683799	**317** 158 -		**2012-05 Huanghai Shipbuilding Co Ltd — Rongcheng SD** Loa 49.00 Br ex 7.00 Dght - Lbp - Br md - Dpth 3.80 Welded, 1 dk	**(B11B2FV) Fishing Vessel**	**1 oil engine** driving 1 Propeller Total Power: 720kW (979hp) Chinese Std. Type XCW6200Z 1 x 4 Stroke 6 Cy. 200 x 270 720kW (979bhp)
9671761 *BZXD74* -	**ZHONG YANG 19** - **Shenzhen Shuiwan Pelagic Fisheries Co Ltd** - *Shidao, Shandong* *China* Official number: 440301104683799	**317** 158 -		**2012-05 Huanghai Shipbuilding Co Ltd — Rongcheng SD** Loa 49.00 Br ex 7.00 Dght - Lbp - Br md - Dpth 3.80 Welded, 1 dk	**(B11B2FV) Fishing Vessel**	**1 oil engine** reduction geared to sc. shaft driving 1 Propeller
9671785 *BZXD76* -	**ZHONG YANG 28** - **Shenzhen Shuiwan Pelagic Fisheries Co Ltd** - *Shidao, Shandong* *China* MMSI: 412764850 Official number: 440301104683799	**317** 158 -		**2012-05 Huanghai Shipbuilding Co Ltd — Rongcheng SD** Loa 49.00 Br ex 7.00 Dght - Lbp - Br md - Dpth 3.80 Welded, 1 dk	**(B11B2FV) Fishing Vessel**	**1 oil engine** reduction geared to sc. shaft driving 1 Propeller Total Power: 720kW (979hp) Chinese Std. Type XCW6200Z 1 x 4 Stroke 6 Cy. 200 x 270 720kW (979bhp)
9671797 *BZXD77* -	**ZHONG YANG 29** - **Shenzhen Shuiwan Pelagic Fisheries Co Ltd** - *Shidao, Shandong* *China* Official number: 440301104683799	**317** 158 -		**2012-05 Huanghai Shipbuilding Co Ltd — Rongcheng SD** Loa 49.00 Br ex 7.00 Dght - Lbp - Br md - Dpth 3.80 Welded, 1 dk	**(B11B2FV) Fishing Vessel**	**1 oil engine** reduction geared to sc. shaft driving 1 Propeller Total Power: 720kW (979hp) Chinese Std. Type XCW6200Z 1 x 4 Stroke 6 Cy. 200 x 270 720kW (979bhp)
8665909 *BZXD82* -	**ZHONG YANG 61** - **Shenzhen Shuiwan Pelagic Fisheries Co Ltd** - *Shekou, Guangdong* *China* Official number: 440301104683799	**159** 47 -		**2013-01 Daishan Zhakou Shipyard — Daishan County ZJ** Loa 27.60 Br ex - Dght - Lbp - Br md 6.30 Dpth 3.10 Welded, 1 dk	**(B11B2FV) Fishing Vessel**	**1 oil engine** reduction geared to sc. shaft driving 1 Propeller Total Power: 720kW (979hp) Chinese Std. Type XCW6200Z 1 x 4 Stroke 6 Cy. 200 x 270 720kW (979bhp) Weichai Power Co Ltd-China
8667452 *BZXD83* -	**ZHONG YANG 62** - **Shenzhen Shuiwan Pelagic Fisheries Co Ltd** - *Shekou, Guangdong* *China* MMSI: 412460068 Official number: 440301104683899	**159** 47 -		**2013-01 Daishan Zhakou Shipyard — Daishan County ZJ** Loa 27.60 Br ex - Dght - Lbp - Br md 6.30 Dpth 3.10 Welded, 1 dk	**(B11B2FV) Fishing Vessel**	**1 oil engine** reduction geared to sc. shaft driving 1 Propeller Total Power: 720kW (979hp) Chinese Std. Type XCW6200Z 1 x 4 Stroke 6 Cy. 200 x 270 720kW (979bhp) Weichai Power Co Ltd-China
8667464 *BZXD84* -	**ZHONG YANG 66** - **Shenzhen Shuiwan Pelagic Fisheries Co Ltd** - *Shekou, Guangdong* *China* MMSI: 412460069 Official number: 440301104683899	**159** 47 -		**2013-01 Daishan Zhakou Shipyard — Daishan County ZJ** Loa 27.60 Br ex - Dght - Lbp - Br md 6.30 Dpth 3.10 Welded, 1 dk	**(B11B2FV) Fishing Vessel**	**1 oil engine** reduction geared to sc. shaft driving 1 Propeller Total Power: 720kW (979hp) Chinese Std. Type XCW6200Z 1 x 4 Stroke 6 Cy. 200 x 270 720kW (979bhp) Weichai Power Co Ltd-China
8667476 *BZXD85* -	**ZHONG YANG 68** - **Shenzhen Shuiwan Pelagic Fisheries Co Ltd** - *Shekou, Guangdong* *China* MMSI: 412460071 Official number: 440301104683899	**159** 47 -		**2013-01 Daishan Zhakou Shipyard — Daishan County ZJ** Loa 27.60 Br ex - Dght - Lbp - Br md 6.30 Dpth 3.10 Welded, 1 dk	**(B11B2FV) Fishing Vessel**	**1 oil engine** reduction geared to sc. shaft driving 1 Propeller Total Power: 720kW (979hp) Chinese Std. Type XCW6200Z 1 x 4 Stroke 6 Cy. 200 x 270 720kW (979bhp) Weichai Power Co Ltd-China
8667488 *BZXD86* -	**ZHONG YANG 69** - **Shenzhen Shuiwan Pelagic Fisheries Co Ltd** - *Shekou, Guangdong* *China* MMSI: 412460072 Official number: 440301104683899	**159** 47 -		**2013-01 Daishan Zhakou Shipyard — Daishan County ZJ** Loa 27.60 Br ex - Dght - Lbp - Br md 6.30 Dpth 3.10 Welded, 1 dk	**(B11B2FV) Fishing Vessel**	**1 oil engine** reduction geared to sc. shaft driving 1 Propeller Total Power: 720kW (979hp) Chinese Std. Type XCW6200Z 1 x 4 Stroke 6 Cy. 200 x 270 720kW (979bhp) Weichai Power Co Ltd-China

IMO / Call sign	Name / Owner / Flag	Tonnage	Class	Builder / Dimensions	Type / Capacity	Machinery
400232 EPT3	**ZHONG YE 1** *ex* Royal Ruby *-2012* *ex* Gold Carrier *-2008* *ex* Kavo Platanos *-2004* *ex* Nordic Bulker *-2000* *ex* Pactrader *-1993* *ex* Hellespont Defiant *-1988* *ex* Sanko Defiant *-1985* **Zhong Ye 1 Shipping Co Ltd** IMU Ship Management Pte Ltd SatCom: Inmarsat C 435236610 *Panama* Panama MMSI: 352366000 Official number: 3377908B	**16,605** 9,208 27,601 T/cm 37.5	Class: KR (LR) (GL) (NK) (AB) (NV) Classed BC until 8/8/02	**1985-04 Mitsui Eng. & SB. Co. Ltd. — Tamano** Yd No: 1311 Loa 168.31 (BB) Br ex - Dght 9.765 Lbp 160.70 Br md 26.01 Dpth 13.64 Welded, 1 dk	**(A21A2BC) Bulk Carrier** Grain: 34,665; Bale: 33,417 Compartments: 5 Ho, ER 5 Ha: (9.5 x 13.3)4 (18.9 x 13.3)ER Cranes: 4x25t	**1 oil engine** driving 1 FP propeller Total Power: 5,520kW (7,505hp) 14.4kn B&W 6L50MCE 1 x 2 Stroke 6 Cy. 500 x 1620 5520kW (7505bhp) (made 1984) Mitsui Engineering & Shipbuilding CLtd-Japan AuxGen: 3 x 400kW 450V 60Hz a.c Boilers: AuxB (Comp) 6.0kgf/cm² (5.9bar) Fuel: 102.0 (d.f.) (Heating Coils) 1360.0 (r.f.) 21.5pd
495789 BINY	**ZHONG YE 5** **Shanghai Wanrong Shipping Co Ltd** - *Shanghai* China MMSI: 413370690 Official number: 010006000339	**4,877** 2,731 7,146	Class: ZC	**2006-12 Zhejiang Fanshun Shipbuilding Industry Co Ltd — Yueqing ZJ** Yd No: 2005001 Loa 118.00 (BB) Br ex - Dght 6.600 Lbp 110.00 Br md 17.60 Dpth 9.00 Welded, 1 dk	**(A13B2TP) Products Tanker** Double Hull (13F) Liq: 8,199; Liq (Oil): 8,199 Compartments: 10 Wing Ta, 2 Wing Slop Ta, ER	**1 oil engine** reduction geared to sc. shaft driving 1 FP propeller Total Power: 2,060kW (2,801hp) 12.0kn Chinese Std. Type 8320ZC 1 x 4 Stroke 8 Cy. 320 x 440 2060kW (2801bhp) Guangzhou Diesel Engine Factory CoLtd-China
533218 BINZ	**ZHONG YE 6** **Shanghai Wanrong Shipping Co Ltd** - *Shanghai* China MMSI: 413370710 Official number: 010006000343	**4,753** 2,530 7,056	Class: ZC	**2007-01 Zhejiang Antai Shipyard Co Ltd — Dongtou County ZJ** Loa 117.40 (BB) Br ex - Dght 6.900 Lbp 109.00 Br md 16.50 Dpth 8.30 Welded, 1 dk	**(A13B2TP) Products Tanker** Double Hull (13F) Liq: 8,586; Liq (Oil): 8,586 Compartments: 10 Wing Ta, 2 Wing Slop Ta, ER	**1 oil engine** reduction geared to sc. shaft driving 1 FP propeller Total Power: 2,426kW (3,298hp) 12.0kn Chinese Std. Type G8300ZC 1 x 4 Stroke 8 Cy. 300 x 380 2426kW (3298bhp) Wuxi Antai Power Machinery Co Ltd-China
417232 BFFK -	**ZHONG YOU HAI 251** **CNPC Offshore Engineering Co Ltd** - *Tianjin* China MMSI: 412302150	**1,295** 388 2,180	Class: CC	**2007-03 Wuchang Shipyard — Wuhan HB** Yd No: A157L Loa 67.20 Br ex - Dght 4.000 Lbp 60.00 Br md 13.00 Dpth 5.20 Welded, 1 dk	**(B21B20A) Anchor Handling Tug Supply** Ice Capable	**2 oil engines** reduction geared to sc. shafts driving 2 CP propellers Total Power: 4,082kW (5,550hp) 14.0kn MAN-B&W 6L27/38 2 x 4 Stroke 6 Cy. 270 x 380 each-2041kW (2775bhp) MAN Diesel A/S-Denmark AuxGen: 2 x 550kW 400V 50Hz a.c, 2 x 240kW 400V a.c
417282 BFFL -	**ZHONG YOU HAI 252** **CNPC Offshore Engineering Co Ltd** - *Tianjin* China MMSI: 412302160	**1,295** 388 738	Class: CC	**2007-06 Wuchang Shipyard — Wuhan HB** Yd No: A158L Loa 67.20 Br ex - Dght 4.000 Lbp 60.00 Br md 13.00 Dpth 5.20 Welded, 1 dk	**(B21B20A) Anchor Handling Tug Supply** Ice Capable	**2 oil engines** Reduction geared to sc. shafts driving 2 CP propellers Total Power: 4,082kW (5,550hp) 14.0kn MAN-B&W 6L27/38 2 x 4 Stroke 6 Cy. 270 x 380 each-2041kW (2775bhp) MAN Diesel A/S-Denmark AuxGen: 2 x 550kW 400V 50Hz a.c, 2 x 240kW 400V a.c
9508184 BFEW -	**ZHONG YOU HAI 261** **CNPC Offshore Engineering Co Ltd** - *Tianjin* China MMSI: 413316000	**1,822** 546 1,800	Class: CC	**2008-07 Guangzhou Huangpu Shipbuilding Co Ltd — Guangzhou GD** Yd No: 0633004 Loa 70.40 Br ex 14.50 Dght 4.800 Lbp 60.00 Br md 14.20 Dpth 6.90 Welded, 1 dk	**(B21B20T) Offshore Tug/Supply Ship** Ice Capable	**2 oil engines** reduction geared to sc. shafts driving 2 Propellers Total Power: 5,100kW (6,934hp) 15.0kn MAN-B&W 7L27/38 2 x 4 Stroke 7 Cy. 270 x 380 each-2550kW (3467bhp) MAN B&W Diesel AG-Augsburg AuxGen: 4 x 400kW 400V a.c, 2 x 750kW 400V a.c Thrusters: 1 Tunnel thruster (f)
9510917 BFEX -	**ZHONG YOU HAI 262** **CNPC Offshore Engineering Co Ltd** - *Tianjin* China MMSI: 413317000	**1,822** 546 1,800	Class: CC	**2008-10 Guangzhou Huangpu Shipbuilding Co Ltd — Guangzhou GD** Yd No: 0633005 Loa 70.40 Br ex 14.50 Dght 4.800 Lbp 60.00 Br md 14.20 Dpth 6.90 Welded, 1 dk	**(B21B20T) Offshore Tug/Supply Ship** Ice Capable	**2 oil engines** reduction geared to sc. shafts driving 2 Propellers Total Power: 4,760kW (6,472hp) 15.0kn MAN-B&W 7L27/38 2 x 4 Stroke 7 Cy. 270 x 380 each-2380kW (3236bhp) MAN B&W Diesel AG-Augsburg AuxGen: 2 x 399kW 400V a.c, 2 x 750kW 400V a.c
9589700 BFAK3 -	**ZHONG YOU HAI 263** **CNPC Offshore Engineering Co Ltd** - *Tianjin* China MMSI: 413302110	**1,804** 541 1,800	Class: CC	**2010-09 Guangzhou Huangpu Shipbuilding Co Ltd — Guangzhou GD** Yd No: 2315 Loa 70.40 Br ex - Dght 4.800 Lbp 60.00 Br md 14.20 Dpth 6.90 Welded, 1 dk	**(B21B20T) Offshore Tug/Supply Ship** Ice Capable	**2 oil engines** reduction geared to sc. shafts driving 2 Propellers Total Power: 4,760kW (6,472hp) 15.0kn MAN-B&W 7L27/38 2 x 4 Stroke 7 Cy. 270 x 380 each-2380kW (3236bhp) MAN B&W Diesel AG-Augsburg AuxGen: 2 x 398kW 400V a.c, 2 x 750kW 400V a.c
9598531 BFAK4 -	**ZHONG YOU HAI 264** **CNPC Offshore Engineering Co Ltd** - SatCom: Inmarsat C 441301549 *Tianjin* China MMSI: 413302120	**1,822** 546 1,800	Class: CC	**2010-12 Guangzhou Huangpu Shipbuilding Co Ltd — Guangzhou GD** Yd No: 2316 Loa 70.40 Br ex - Dght 4.800 Lbp 60.00 Br md 14.20 Dpth 6.90 Welded, 1 dk	**(B21B20T) Offshore Tug/Supply Ship**	**2 oil engines** reduction geared to sc. shafts driving 2 Propellers Total Power: 4,760kW (6,472hp) MAN-B&W 7L27/38 2 x 4 Stroke 7 Cy. 270 x 380 each-2380kW (3236bhp) MAN B&W Diesel AG-Augsburg
9488255 BFEY -	**ZHONG YOU HAI 281** **CNPC Offshore Engineering Co Ltd** - *Tianjin* China MMSI: 413318000	**2,095** 628 1,691	Class: CC	**2008-04 Guangzhou Huangpu Shipbuilding Co Ltd — Guangzhou GD** Yd No: 2259 Loa 72.50 Br ex - Dght 4.800 Lbp 63.80 Br md 15.00 Dpth 7.00 Welded, 1 dk	**(B21B20T) Offshore Tug/Supply Ship** Ice Capable	**2 oil engines** reduction geared to sc. shafts driving 2 Propellers Total Power: 6,120kW (8,320hp) 15.0kn MAN-B&W 9L27/38 2 x 4 Stroke 9 Cy. 270 x 380 each-3060kW (4160bhp) MAN B&W Diesel AG-Augsburg AuxGen: 2 x 399kW 400V a.c, 2 x 1100kW 400V a.c
9500027 BFEZ -	**ZHONG YOU HAI 282** **CNPC Offshore Engineering Co Ltd** - *Tianjin* China MMSI: 413319000	**2,095** 628 1,691	Class: CC	**2008-10 Guangzhou Huangpu Shipbuilding Co Ltd — Guangzhou GD** Yd No: 2260 Loa 72.50 Br ex - Dght 4.800 Lbp 63.80 Br md 15.00 Dpth 7.00 Welded, 1 dk	**(B21B20T) Offshore Tug/Supply Ship** Ice Capable	**2 oil engines** reduction geared to sc. shafts driving 2 Propellers Total Power: 6,120kW (8,320hp) 15.0kn MAN-B&W 9L27/38 2 x 4 Stroke 9 Cy. 270 x 380 each-3060kW (4160bhp) MAN B&W Diesel AG-Augsburg AuxGen: 2 x 399kW 400V a.c, 2 x 1100kW 400V a.c
9364057 BFFG -	**ZHONG YOU HAI 511** **China National Petroleum Corp (CNPC)** - *Tianjin* China MMSI: 412302170	**1,990** 1,114 1,357	Class: CC	**2006-11 AVIC Weihai Shipyard Co Ltd — Weihai SD** Loa 86.60 Br ex - Dght 2.500 Lbp 81.80 Br md 16.00 Dpth 4.20 Welded, 1 dk	**(A13B2TP) Products Tanker** Double Hull (13F) Liq: 1,650; Liq (Oil): 1,650	**2 oil engines** reduction geared to sc. shafts driving 2 Propellers 11.0kn
9364069 BFFH -	**ZHONG YOU HAI 512** **China National Petroleum Corp (CNPC)** - *Tianjin* China MMSI: 412302180	**1,990** 1,114 1,357	Class: CC	**2006-12 AVIC Weihai Shipyard Co Ltd — Weihai SD** Loa 86.60 Br ex - Dght 2.500 Lbp 81.80 Br md 16.00 Dpth 4.20 Welded, 1 dk	**(A13B2TP) Products Tanker** Double Hull (13F) Liq: 1,650; Liq (Oil): 1,650	**2 oil engines** reduction geared to sc. shafts driving 2 Propellers 11.0kn
9656711 BLFH4 -	**ZHONG YU 18** **Zhongyu Ocean Shipping Co Ltd (ZYOCO)** - *Taizhou, Zhejiang* China MMSI: 413446170 Official number: 20086305911	**5,920** 2,803 8,572	Class: CC	**2012-06 Taizhou Yongqing Shipbuilding Co Ltd — Taizhou JS** Yd No: YQ08001 Loa 111.85 Br ex 18.63 Dght 7.200 Lbp 106.00 Br md 18.60 Dpth 9.50 Welded, 1 dk	**(A31A2GX) General Cargo Ship** Grain: 9,716 Compartments: 2 Ho, ER 2 Ha: ER 2 (27.3 x 10.8) Cranes: 2x25t Ice Capable	**1 oil engine** reduction geared to sc. shaft driving 1 FP propeller Total Power: 3,163kW (4,300hp) 12.5kn Yanmar 8N330-SN 1 x 4 Stroke 8 Cy. 330 x 440 3163kW (4300bhp) Qingdao Zichai Boyang Diesel EngineCo Ltd-China AuxGen: 3 x 250kW 400V a.c
9604201 BLGR6 -	**ZHONG YU 28** *ex* Zhong Tuo 89 *-2013* *completed as* Huanqiu No. 8 *-2012* **Zhongyu Ocean Shipping Co Ltd (ZYOCO)** - SatCom: Inmarsat C 441369287 *Taizhou, Zhejiang* China MMSI: 413446930	**15,592** 8,201 24,347	Class: CC	**2012-06 Taizhou Yuehang Shipbuilding Industry Co Ltd — Linhai ZJ** Yd No: YH-03 Loa 159.99 (BB) Br ex - Dght 10.360 Lbp 149.80 Br md 24.40 Dpth 14.20 Welded, 1 dk	**(A21A2BC) Bulk Carrier** Double Sides Entire Compartment Length Grain: 29,039 Compartments: 4 Ho, ER 4 Ha: ER 4 (19.5 x 16.0)	**1 oil engine** driving 1 FP propeller Total Power: 4,440kW (6,037hp) 12.0kn MAN-B&W 6S35MC 1 x 2 Stroke 6 Cy. 350 x 1400 4440kW (6037bhp) STX Engine Co Ltd-South Korea AuxGen: 3 x 448kW 450V a.c

9661273 *BLGG8* -	**ZHONG YU 68** *ex* Ping An Da 67 *-2013* **Zhongyu Ocean Shipping Co Ltd (ZYOCO)** - SatCom: Inmarsat C 441369262 *Taizhou, Zhejiang* *China* MMSI: 413446470	**23,670** 13,049 38,268	Class: CC	**2012-06 Jiangsu Mingyang Shipbuilding Co Ltd — Guannan County JS** Yd No: HXCC1002 Loa 183.50 (BB) Br ex 28.64 Dght 11.300 Lbp 175.00 Br md 28.60 Dpth 15.80 Welded, 1 dk	**(A21A2BC) Bulk Carrier** Double Sides Entire Compartment Length Grain: 46,144 Compartments: 5 Ho, ER 5 Ha: 4 (20.0 x 16.0)ER (13.6 x 16.0) Cranes: 4x30t Ice Capable	**1 oil engine** driving 1 FP propeller Total Power: 7,860kW (10,686hp) 12.5 MAN-B&W 6S46MC- 1 x 2 Stroke 6 Cy. 460 x 1932 7860kW (10686bhp) Yichang Marine Diesel Engine Co Ltd-China AuxGen: 3 x 420kW 400V a.c
9650729 *BLGD2* -	**ZHONG YU 88** *ex* Ping An Da 96 *-2013* **Zhongyu Ocean Shipping Co Ltd (ZYOCO)** - SatCom: Inmarsat C 441408910 *Taizhou, Zhejiang* *China* MMSI: 414089000	**37,730** 21,204 65,311	Class: CC	**2012-06 Zhejiang Hexing Shipyard — Wenling ZJ** Yd No: HXCC1005 Loa 199.90 (BB) Br ex - Dght 12.500 Lbp 194.00 Br md 36.00 Dpth 17.80 Welded, 1 dk	**(A21A2BC) Bulk Carrier** Double Sides Entire Compartment Length Grain: 78,578 Compartments: 5 Ho, ER 5 Ha: 4 (23.0 x 17.6)ER (16.4 x 16.0)	**1 oil engine** driving 1 FP propeller Total Power: 9,960kW (13,542hp) 14.0 MAN-B&W 6S50MC- 1 x 2 Stroke 6 Cy. 500 x 2000 9960kW (13542bhp) STX (Dalian) Engine Co Ltd-China AuxGen: 3 x 500kW 400V a.c
9643752 *BLGS3* -	**ZHONG YU I** **Zhongyu Ocean Shipping Co Ltd (ZYOCO)** - *Taizhou, Zhejiang* *China* MMSI: 413444580	**2,231** 1,233 3,157	Class: CC	**2012-01 Zhejiang Hexing Shipyard — Wenling ZJ** Yd No: HXCC1008 Loa 70.20 Br ex - Dght 5.800 Lbp 64.98 Br md 13.00 Dpth 8.20 Welded, 1 dk	**(A21A2BC) Bulk Carrier** Grain: 4,286 Compartments: 1 Ho, ER 1 Ha: ER (36.0 x 8.8) Ice Capable	**1 oil engine** reduction geared to sc. shaft driving 1 Propeller Total Power: 1,324kW (1,800hp) 11.9 Chinese Std. Type 6320 1 x 4 Stroke 6 Cy. 320 x 440 1324kW (1800bhp) Guangzhou Diesel Engine Factory CoLtd-China AuxGen: 2 x 120kW 400V a.c
9642411 *BKSN6* -	**ZHONG YUN 57** *ex* Hua Heng 6 *-2013* **Zhoushan Zhong Yun Shipping Co Ltd** Zhoushan Chao Yang Shipping Co Ltd *Zhoushan, Zhejiang* *China* MMSI: 413445490	**2,991** 1,366 4,732	Class: CC	**2012-06 Ningbo Zhenhe Shipbuilding Co Ltd — Xiangshan County ZJ** Yd No: ZHCCS1002 Loa 96.43 (BB) Br ex 15.83 Dght 5.600 Lbp 89.80 Br md 15.80 Dpth 7.15 Welded, 1 dk	**(A13B2TP) Products Tanker** Double Hull (13F) Liq: 4,584; Liq (Oil): 4,584 Compartments: 4 Wing Ta, 4 Wing Ta, 1 Wing Slop Ta, 1 Wing Slop Ta, ER Ice Capable	**1 oil engine** reduction geared to sc. shaft driving 1 Propeller Total Power: 735kW (999hp) 11.0 Chinese Std. Type GN6320 1 x 4 Stroke 6 Cy. 320 x 380 735kW (999bhp) Ningbo CSI Power & Machinery GroupCo Ltd-China AuxGen: 2 x 200kW 400V a.c, 1 x 150kW 400V a.c
8601824 *3EHO* -	**ZHONG ZHAN** *ex* Baltic Ace *-2009* *ex* Pacific Ace *-2006* *ex* Cannanore *-2004* *ex* Tomis West *-2000* *ex* Cimpina *-1991* **Zhong Zhan Shipping Co Ltd** IMU Ship Management Pte Ltd *Panama* *Panama* MMSI: 372189000 Official number: 35060PEXT1	**24,248** 12,317 39,350 T/cm 46.7	Class: (NV) (CC) (RN)	**1990-09 Santierul Naval Galati S.A. — Galati** Yd No: 798 Loa 190.00 Br ex 28.01 Dght 12.004 Lbp 180.00 Br md 28.00 Dpth 16.79 Welded, 1 dk	**(A13A2TW) Crude/Oil Products Tanker** Double Bottom Entire Compartment Length Liq: 42,834; Liq (Oil): 42,834 Compartments: 7 Ta, 10 Wing Ta, ER 4 Cargo Pump (s): 4x700m³/hr Manifold: Bow/CM: 97m	**1 oil engine** driving 1 FP propeller Total Power: 8,422kW (11,451hp) 15.0 MAN K6SZ70/15 1 x 2 Stroke 6 Cy. 700 x 1500 8422kW (11451bhp) U.C.M. Resita S.A.-Resita AuxGen: 4 x 640kW 440V 50Hz a.c
9044358 *V3KS3* -	**ZHONG ZHOU 1** *ex* Monterrey *-2011* *ex* Kapitan Churilov *-2004* **Zhoushan Huaxi Pelagic Fishery Ltd** - *Belize City* *Belize* MMSI: 312621000 Official number: 471330026	**12,413** 4,903 9,952 T/cm 23.4	Class: BV (NV) (RS)	**1991-04 Mathias-Thesen-Werft GmbH — Wismar** Yd No: 264 Converted From: Fish Carrier-2009 Loa 152.87 (BB) Br ex 22.23 Dght 8.020 Lbp 141.99 Br md 22.20 Dpth 9.40 Welded, 1 dk, 2nd & 3rd dk in holds only	**(A34A2GR) Refrigerated Cargo Ship** Ins: 4,744 Compartments: 4 Ho, ER, 8 Tw Dk 4 Ha: 4 (6.0 x 3.9)ER Derricks: 9x5t; Winches: 9 Ice Capable	**1 oil engine** driving 1 FP propeller Total Power: 7,600kW (10,333hp) 13.0 MAN K5SZ70/125E 1 x 2 Stroke 5 Cy. 700 x 1250 7600kW (10333bhp) Dieselmotorenwerk Rostock GmbH-Rostock AuxGen: 5 x 512kW 380/220V 50Hz a.c Fuel: 334.0 (d.f.) 3540.0 (r.f.) 30.0pd
8883044 - -	**ZHONG ZHUI 9404** **China National Fisheries Corp** - *Yantai, Shandong* *China*	**313** 94 130	Class: (CC)	**1994 Dalian Fishing Vessel Co — Dalian LN** Loa 43.25 Br ex - Dght 2.950 Lbp 37.00 Br md 7.60 Dpth 3.85 Welded, 1 dk	**(B11B2FV) Fishing Vessel** Ins: 246	**1 oil engine** geared to sc. shaft driving 1 FP propeller Total Power: 433kW (589hp) 12.0 Chinese Std. Type 630 1 x 4 Stroke 6 Cy. 300 x 380 433kW (589bhp) Dalian Fishing Vessel Co-China AuxGen: 1 x 90kW 400V a.c
9454137 *BKWT3* -	**ZHONGDAYOU7** *ex* ZD Giant *-2010* *ex* Zhong Da You 7 *-2006* **Zhoushan Zhongda Marine Co Ltd** - *Zhoushan, Zhejiang* *China* MMSI: 413405750 Official number: 070307000094	**1,993** 1,116 3,150	Class: ZC	**2006-10 Yueqing Jiangnan Ship Co Ltd — Yueqing ZJ** Loa 88.02 Br ex - Dght 5.200 Lbp - Br md 13.50 Dpth 6.00 Welded, 1 dk	**(A12B2TR) Chemical/Products Tanker** Double Hull (13F)	**1 oil engine** reduction geared to sc. shaft driving 1 Propeller Total Power: 735kW (999hp) 8.0 Chinese Std. Type G6300ZC 1 x 4 Stroke 6 Cy. 300 x 380 735kW (999bhp) Zibo Diesel Engine Factory-China
8662529 *BHVV3* -	**ZHONGGANG HUA YUN 6** *ex* Hua Hai 318 *-2013* **Nanjing Zhonggang Shipping Co Ltd** - *Nantong, Jiangsu* *China* MMSI: 413357830 Official number: 2010G0000823	**2,636** 1,476 3,700	Class: (BV)	**2010-12 Zhejiang Zhuangji Shipping Co Ltd — Yueqing ZJ** Yd No: ZJ1002 Loa 95.68 Br ex - Dght 5.400 Lbp 90.00 Br md 15.00 Dpth 6.90 Welded, 1 dk	**(A12B2TR) Chemical/Products Tanker** Double Hull (13F)	**1 oil engine** driving 1 Propeller Total Power: 2,574kW (3,500hp) Yanmar 6N330-E 1 x 4 Stroke 6 Cy. 330 x 440 2574kW (3500bhp) Qingdao Zichai Boyang Diesel EngineCo Ltd-China
9672870 *BPXO* -	**ZHONGHAIHUARUN 1** **Tianjin CS & CR Shipping Co Ltd** - *Tianjin* *China* MMSI: 414755000	**40,913** 25,963 75,397 T/cm 68.2	Class: CC	**2013-09 Jiangnan Shipyard (Group) Co Ltd — Shanghai** Yd No: H2521 Loa 225.00 (BB) Br ex - Dght 14.200 Lbp 217.00 Br md 32.26 Dpth 19.60 Welded, 1 dk	**(A21A2BC) Bulk Carrier** Grain: 90,016 Compartments: 7 Ho, ER 7 Ha: 6 (15.5 x 14.4)ER (15.5 x 13.2)	**1 oil engine** driving 1 FP propeller Total Power: 8,833kW (12,009hp) 14.5 MAN-B&W 5S60ME- 1 x 2 Stroke 5 Cy. 600 x 2400 8833kW (12009bhp) Hudong Heavy Machinery Co Ltd-China AuxGen: 3 x 560kW 450V a.c
9379818 *VRDI4* -	**ZHONGJI NO. 1** **Zhong Ji International Shipping Co Ltd** Navig8 Shipmanagement Pte Ltd *Hong Kong* *Hong Kong* MMSI: 477049100 Official number: HK-2010	**29,578** 12,471 45,719 T/cm 53.4	Class: NV (CC)	**2008-04 Bohai Shipbuilding Heavy Industry Co Ltd — Huludao LN** Yd No: 510-11 Loa 184.95 (BB) Br ex 32.26 Dght 12.000 Lbp 176.00 Br md 32.20 Dpth 18.20 Welded, 1 dk	**(A12B2TR) Chemical/Products Tanker** Double Hull (13F) Liq: 51,068; Liq (Oil): 52,100 Compartments: 12 Wing Ta, ER, 2 Wing Slop Ta 6 Cargo Pump (s): 6x600m³/hr Manifold: Bow/CM: 92m Ice Capable	**1 oil engine** driving 1 FP propeller Total Power: 9,600kW (13,052hp) 14.0 Wartsila 6RTA52 1 x 2 Stroke 6 Cy. 520 x 1800 9600kW (13052bhp) Wartsila Switzerland Ltd-Switzerland AuxGen: 3 x 750kW 450V a.c Fuel: 327.0 (d.f.) 1292.0 (r.f.)
9401025 *VRDI5* -	**ZHONGJI NO. 2** **Zhong Ji International Shipping Co Ltd** Navig8 Shipmanagement Pte Ltd SatCom: Inmarsat Mini-M 764903762 *Hong Kong* *Hong Kong* MMSI: 477049200 Official number: HK-2011	**29,597** 12,471 45,697 T/cm 53.4	Class: NV (CC)	**2008-06 Bohai Shipbuilding Heavy Industry Co Ltd — Huludao LN** Yd No: 510-12 Loa 184.95 (BB) Br ex 32.26 Dght 12.000 Lbp 176.00 Br md 32.20 Dpth 18.20 Welded, 1 dk	**(A12B2TR) Chemical/Products Tanker** Double Hull (13F) Liq: 51,068; Liq (Oil): 52,101 Compartments: 12 Wing Ta, 2 Wing Slop Ta, ER 6 Cargo Pump (s): 6x600m³/hr Manifold: Bow/CM: 92m Ice Capable	**1 oil engine** driving 1 FP propeller Total Power: 9,600kW (13,052hp) 14.0 Wartsila 6RTA52 1 x 2 Stroke 6 Cy. 520 x 1800 9600kW (13052bhp) Wartsila Switzerland Ltd-Switzerland AuxGen: 3 x 750kW 450V a.c Fuel: 325.0 (d.f.) 1280.0 (r.f.)
9346653 - -	**ZHONGLIAN NO. 6** **Government of The People's Republic of China (Ningbo Port Administration Bureau - Ministry of Communications)** - *China*	**400** - -	Class: (CC)	**2006-10 Jiangsu Zhenjiang Shipyard Co Ltd — Zhenjiang JS** Loa 32.00 Br ex - Dght 4.990 Lbp - Br md 11.60 Dpth 5.36 Welded, 1 dk	**(B32A2ST) Tug**	**2 oil engines** geared to sc. shafts driving 2 Z propellers Total Power: 3,530kW (4,800hp) Niigata 6L28H 2 x 4 Stroke 6 Cy. 280 x 370 each-1765kW (2400bhp) Niigata Engineering Co Ltd-Japan AuxGen: 2 x 100kW a.c
9350549 - -	**ZHONGLIAN NO. 7** **Government of The People's Republic of China (Ningbo Port Administration Bureau - Ministry of Communications)** - *China*	**400** - -		**2006-10 Jiangsu Zhenjiang Shipyard Co Ltd — Zhenjiang JS** Loa 32.00 Br ex Dght 4.990 Lbp - Br md 11.60 Dpth 5.36 Welded, 1 dk	**(B32A2ST) Tug**	**2 oil engines** geared to sc. shafts driving 2 Z propellers Total Power: 3,530kW (4,800hp) Niigata 6L28H 2 x 4 Stroke 6 Cy. 280 x 370 each-1765kW (2400bhp) Niigata Engineering Co Ltd-Japan AuxGen: 2 x 100kW a.c
8747800 *8ROD* -	**ZHONGMU 1** **China Timber Maritime Ltd** - *Georgetown* *Guyana* MMSI: 750000030 Official number: 0000507	**1,416** 503 1,839		**2009-08 Surinaamse Dok en Scheepsbouw Mij — Paramaribo** Loa 63.00 Br ex - Dght 3.500 Lbp 57.80 Br md 13.50 Dpth 5.50 Welded, 1 dk	**(A31A2GX) General Cargo Ship**	**2 oil engines** reduction geared to sc. shafts driving 2 FP propellers Total Power: 760kW (1,034hp) Cummins KT-19- 2 x 4 Stroke 6 Cy. 159 x 159 each-380kW (517bhp) Cummins Engine Co Inc-USA
9623776 *8RPE* -	**ZHONGMU 2** **Bondwell International Group Ltd** - *Georgetown* *Guyana* MMSI: 750000033 Official number: 0000555	**1,674** 563 2,400		**2010-12 Surinaamse Dok en Scheepsbouw Mij — Paramaribo** Loa 69.80 Br ex - Dght 3.500 Lbp 65.80 Br md 13.50 Dpth 5.50 Welded, 1 dk	**(A31A2GX) General Cargo Ship** Compartments: 2 Ho, ER 2 Ha: ER Cranes: 1	**2 oil engines** reduction geared to sc. shafts driving 2 FP propellers Total Power: 760kW (1,034hp) Cummins KT-19- 2 x 4 Stroke 6 Cy. 159 x 159 each-380kW (517bhp) Cummins Engine Co Inc-USA

359976 ZHONKIYER — **608** / 186 / 310 — Class: RS
EPF
Promflot Co Ltd (OOO 'Promflot')
-
Nevelsk — *Russia*
MMSI: 273891700

1991-11 **Zavod 'Nikolayevsk-na-Amure' — Nikolayevsk-na-Amure** Yd No: 1284
Lengthened-2002
Loa 49.98 Br ex 9.47 Dght 3.830
Lbp 44.54 Br md 9.30 Dpth 5.13
Welded, 1 dk

(B11A2FS) Stern Trawler
Ice Capable

1 oil engine driving 1 FP propeller
Total Power: 588kW (799hp) 11.5kn
S.K.L. 6NVD48A-2U
1 x 4 Stroke 6 Cy. 320 x 480 588kW (799bhp)
SKL Motoren u. Systemtechnik AG-Magdeburg

592111 ZHOU DIAN 7 — **2,106** / 631 / 1,520 — Class: CC
KRB5
Zhoushan Electric Power Co
-
SatCom: Inmarsat C 441219481
Hangzhou, Zhejiang — *China*
MMSI: 412763680

2010-12 **in the People's Republic of China** Yd No: 48007
Loa 73.75 Br ex - Dght 3.500
Lbp 70.70 Br md 15.00 Dpth 5.50
Welded, 1 dk

(B34D2SL) Cable Layer
Compartments: 1 Ho, ER
1 Ha: ER (22.1 x 10.0)
Ice Capable

2 oil engines reduction geared to sc. shafts driving 2 Propellers
Total Power: 2,724kW (3,704hp) 11.0kn
Chinese Std. Type CW8200ZC
2 x 4 Stroke 8 Cy. 200 x 270 each-1362kW (1852bhp)
Weichai Power Co Ltd-China
AuxGen: 3 x 500kW 400V a.c

622435 ZHOU GANG HAI 7 — **29,103** / 16,297 / 45,000 — Class: ZC
BKWJ5
Zhoushan Port Xing Gang Shipping Co Ltd
-
Zhoushan, Zhejiang — *China*
MMSI: 413444760

2012-03 **Zhejiang Zengzhou Shipyard Co Ltd — Zhoushan ZJ** Yd No: 007
Loa 200.00 (BB) Br ex - Dght 11.000
Lbp - Br md 32.00 Dpth 15.40
Welded, 1 dk

(A21A2BC) Bulk Carrier
Grain: 55,500
Compartments: 5 Ho, ER
5 Ha: ER

1 oil engine driving 1 FP propeller 14.5kn

622447 ZHOU GANG HAI 8 — **29,103** / 16,297 / 45,000 — Class: ZC (Class contemplated)
BKWK5
Zhoushan Port Xing Gang Shipping Co Ltd
-
Zhoushan, Zhejiang — *China*
MMSI: 413444770

2012-05 **Zhejiang Zengzhou Shipyard Co Ltd — Zhoushan ZJ** Yd No: 008
Loa 200.00 (BB) Br ex - Dght 11.000
Lbp - Br md 32.00 Dpth 15.40
Welded, 1 dk

(A21A2BC) Bulk Carrier
Grain: 55,500
Compartments: 5 Ho, ER
5 Ha: ER

1 oil engine driving 1 FP propeller 14.5kn

569566 ZHOU GANG YUN 1 — **1,967** / 1,183 / - — Class: IB
BKTA6
ex Hao Xiang 66 *-2013*
ex Zhou Gang Yun 1 *-2009*
-
-
China
MMSI: 413434540

2009-06 **Ningbo Beilun Kangda Shipbuilding & Repair Co — Ningbo ZJ** Yd No: KD0803
Loa 81.00 Br ex - Dght 5.300
Lbp 74.80 Br md 12.60 Dpth 6.50
Welded, 1 dk

(A31A2GX) General Cargo Ship

1 oil engine reduction geared to sc. shaft driving 1 Propeller
Total Power: 735kW (999hp) 11.0kn
Chinese Std. Type G6300ZCA
1 x 4 Stroke 6 Cy. 300 x 380 735kW (999bhp)
Ningbo CSI Power & Machinery GroupCo Ltd-China

831950 ZHOU HAI 110 — *380* / 213 / 515
-
Zhoushan Shipping Co
-
Zhoushan, Zhejiang — *China*

1987 Jianbi Shipyard — Zhenjiang JS
Loa 47.58 Br ex - Dght 3.100
Lbp 42.00 Br md 8.40 Dpth 3.70
Welded, 1 dk

(A31A2GX) General Cargo Ship
Grain: 630; Bale: 563
Compartments: 2 Ho, ER
2 Ha: (7.7 x 4.0) (9.9 x 4.0)ER

1 oil engine geared to sc. shaft driving 1 FP propeller
Total Power: 184kW (250hp) 9.9kn
Chinese Std. Type 6160A
1 x 4 Stroke 6 Cy. 160 x 225 184kW (250bhp)
Weifang Diesel Engine Factory-China
AuxGen: 2 x 24kW 400V a.c

9646479 ZHOU HAI YOU 78 — **7,544** / 3,852 / 12,476 — Class: CC
BKNM6
-
Zhoushan Haiguang Shipping Transportation Co
-
Zhoushan, Zhejiang — *China*
MMSI: 413445560

2012-05 **Zhoushan Zhaobao Shipbuilding & Repair Co Ltd — Zhoushan ZJ** Yd No: ZB1011
Loa 126.08 Br ex - Dght 8.200
Lbp 118.00 Br md 19.80 Dpth 11.00
Welded, 1 dk

(A13B2TP) Products Tanker
Double Hull (13F)
Liq: 6,368; Liq (Oil): 6,368
Compartments: 5 Ta, 1 Slop Ta, ER
Ice Capable

1 oil engine reduction geared to sc. shaft driving 1 FP propeller
Total Power: 2,970kW (4,038hp) 13.5kn
Chinese Std. Type GN8320ZC
1 x 4 Stroke 8 Cy. 320 x 380 2970kW (4038bhp)
Ningbo CSI Power & Machinery GroupCo Ltd-China
AuxGen: 3 x 250kW 400V a.c

9640372 ZHOU HANG 2 — **4,675** / 2,486 / 6,653 — Class: CC
BKNG6
-
Jiang Shi Yuan
Zhejiang Huale Ocean Shipping Co Ltd
SatCom: Inmarsat C 441369259
Zhoushan, Zhejiang — *China*
MMSI: 413446380
Official number: CN20118966596

2012-06 **Ningbo Jintao Shipbuilding Co Ltd — Ningbo ZJ** Yd No: JT1002
Loa 112.11 Br ex 16.43 Dght 6.350
Lbp 105.00 Br md 16.40 Dpth 8.40
Welded, 1 dk

(A21A2BC) Bulk Carrier
Grain: 8,353
Compartments: 2 Ho, ER
2 Ha: ER 2 (30.7 x 9.8)
Ice Capable

1 oil engine reduction geared to sc. shaft driving 1 FP propeller
Total Power: 2,206kW (2,999hp) 11.8kn
Chinese Std. Type 8320ZC
1 x 4 Stroke 8 Cy. 320 x 440 2206kW (2999bhp)
Guangzhou Diesel Engine Factory CoLtd-China
AuxGen: 2 x 150kW 400V a.c

8981315 ZHOU HANG JI NO. 6 — **986** / 654 / -
-
-
Jiangyan Zhoucheng Shipping Co Ltd
Shanghai Puhai Shipping Co Ltd
Taizhou, Jiangsu — *China*
Official number: 271203001869

2003-08 **Huaxin Shipyard — Taizhou JS**
Loa 71.60 Br ex 13.25 Dght 3.650
Lbp 66.50 Br md 13.20 Dpth 4.60
Welded, 1 dk

(A31A2GX) General Cargo Ship

2 oil engines driving 1 Propeller
Total Power: 428kW (582hp)
Chinese Std. Type 6E160C
2 x 4 Stroke 6 Cy. 160 x 225 each-214kW (291bhp)
Nantong Diesel Engine Co Ltd-China

8981327 ZHOU HANG NO. 8 — **966** / 630 / -
-
-
Jiangyan Zhoucheng Shipping Co Ltd
Shanghai Puhai Shipping Co Ltd
Taizhou, Jiangsu — *China*
Official number: 271203000978

2000-07 **Shuguang Shipyard — Taizhou JS**
Loa 68.00 Br ex 13.30 Dght 4.200
Lbp 66.00 Br md 13.10 Dpth 4.95
Welded, 1 dk

(A31A2GX) General Cargo Ship

2 oil engines driving 1 Propeller
Total Power: 428kW (582hp)
Chinese Std. Type 6E160C
2 x 4 Stroke 6 Cy. 160 x 225 each-214kW (291bhp)
Nantong Diesel Engine Co Ltd-China

8850073 ZHOU HE No. 1 — **221** / 126 / -
-
ex Kiku Maru No. 23 *-1997*
-
-
-

1974 Hachinohekou Zosen KK — Hachinohe AO
L reg 29.40 Br ex - Dght -
Lbp - Br md 6.20 Dpth 2.50
Welded, 1 dk

(B11B2FV) Fishing Vessel

1 oil engine driving 1 FP propeller
Total Power: 250kW (340hp)
Niigata
1 x 4 Stroke 250kW (340bhp)
Niigata Engineering Co Ltd-Japan

9295919 ZHOU QIAO 2 — **3,267** / 1,698 / - — Class: CC
BLXC
-
Shengsi Orient Marine Shipping Co Ltd
-
Zhoushan, Zhejiang — *China*
MMSI: 412413440

2003-06 **Ningbo Xinle Shipbuilding Co Ltd — Ningbo ZJ** Yd No: 2002-2
Loa 74.50 Br ex - Dght 3.200
Lbp 69.70 Br md 15.00 Dpth 5.00
Welded, 1 dk

(A36A2PR) Passenger/Ro-Ro Ship (Vehicles)

2 oil engines driving 2 gen. each 250kW 400V geared to sc. shafts driving 2 Propellers
Total Power: 2,206kW (3,000hp) 8.0kn
Chinese Std. Type G6300ZC
2 x 4 Stroke 6 Cy. 300 x 380 each-1103kW (1500bhp)
Ningbo CSI Power & Machinery GroupCo Ltd-China

8843991 ZHOU SHAN 17 — **1,097** / 372 / 772 — Class: (CC)
BKPW2
ex Jing Leng 1 *-1996*
Zhoushan Putuo Marine Fishery (Holding) Co
-
Ningbo, Zhejiang — *China*
MMSI: 412400940

1978-07 **Bohai Shipyard — Huludao LN**
Loa 66.80 Br ex - Dght 3.750
Lbp 60.00 Br md 11.50 Dpth 6.00
Welded, 2 dks

(A34A2GR) Refrigerated Cargo Ship
Ins: 1,266
Compartments: 3 Ho, ER
3 Ha: ER
Cranes: 2x2t

1 oil engine driving 1 FP propeller
Total Power: 971kW (1,320hp) 11.5kn
S.K.L. 8NVD48A-2U
1 x 4 Stroke 8 Cy. 320 x 480 971kW (1320bhp)
VEB Schwermaschinenbau "KarlLiebknecht" (SKL)-Magdeburg
AuxGen: 3 x 150kW 400V a.c

9446180 ZHOU SHAN HAI — **33,044** / 19,231 / 57,000 / T/cm 58.8
3EUZ7
-
Zhoushanhai Shipping Inc
COSCO Bulk Carrier Co Ltd (COSCO BULK)
SatCom: Inmarsat C 435632910
Panama — *Panama*
MMSI: 356329000
Official number: 4118810B

Class: LR (BV)
100A1 SS 10/2009
bulk carrier
CSR
BC-A
GRAB (20)
Nos. 2 & 4 holds may be empty
ESP
*IWS
LI
LMC **UMS**

2009-10 **COSCO (Zhoushan) Shipyard Co Ltd — Zhoushan ZJ** Yd No: ZS07003
Loa 189.99 (BB) Br ex 32.30 Dght 12.800
Lbp 185.00 Br md 32.26 Dpth 18.00
Welded, 1 dk

(A21A2BC) Bulk Carrier
Grain: 71,634; Bale: 68,200
Compartments: 5 Ho, ER
5 Ha: ER
Cranes: 4x30t

1 oil engine reduction geared to sc. shafts driving 1 FP propeller
Total Power: 9,473kW (12,879hp) 14.2kn
MAN-B&W 6S50MC-C
1 x 2 Stroke 6 Cy. 500 x 2000 9473kW (12879bhp)
STX Engine Co Ltd-South Korea
AuxGen: 3 x 600kW 60Hz a.c
Fuel: 2189.0

8996566 ZHOU SHUN — **841** / 471 / -
-
-
ex Huang He 18 *-2005*
Edong Shipping Co Ltd
-
Wuhan, Hubei — *China*

1993-12 **Chongqing Shipyard — Chongqing**
Loa 67.00 Br ex - Dght 4.200
Lbp 62.20 Br md 10.00 Dpth 5.00
Welded, 1 dk

(A31A2GX) General Cargo Ship

1 oil engine driving 1 Propeller
Total Power: 441kW (600hp)
Chinese Std. Type
1 x 4 Stroke 441kW (600bhp)
Guangzhou Diesel Engine Factory CoLtd-China

8982890 ZHOU YU 623 — **195** / 58 / -
-
-
Chen Cailong
-

1979 Yantai Fishing Vessel Shipyard — Yantai SD
Loa - Br ex - Dght -
Lbp 36.40 Br md 7.20 Dpth 3.70
Welded, 1 dk

(B11B2FV) Fishing Vessel

1 oil engine driving 1 Propeller
Total Power: 441kW (600hp)
Chinese Std. Type 8300
1 x 4 Stroke 8 Cy. 300 x 380 441kW (600bhp)
Zibo Diesel Engine Factory-China

8982905 ZHOU YU 624 — **195** / 58 / -
-
-
Chen Cailong
-

1979 Yantai Fishing Vessel Shipyard — Yantai SD
Loa - Br ex - Dght -
Lbp 36.40 Br md 7.20 Dpth 3.70
Welded, 1 dk

(B11B2FV) Fishing Vessel

1 oil engine driving 1 Propeller
Total Power: 441kW (600hp)
Chinese Std. Type 8300
1 x 4 Stroke 8 Cy. 300 x 380 441kW (600bhp)
Zibo Diesel Engine Factory-China

8982917 - -	**ZHOU YU 625** - **Chen Cailong** -	**195** 58 -		**1982 Ningbo Fishing Vessel Shipyard — Ningbo ZJ** Loa - Br ex - Dght - Lbp 36.40 Br md 7.20 Dpth 3.70 Welded, 1 dk	**(B11B2FV) Fishing Vessel**	**1 oil engine** driving 1 Propeller Total Power: 441kW (600hp) Chinese Std. Type 1 x 4 Stroke 8 Cy. 300 x 380 441kW (600bhp) Zibo Diesel Engine Factory-China	 830
8982929 - -	**ZHOU YU 626** - **Chen Cailong** -	**195** 58 -		**1980 Ningbo Fishing Vessel Shipyard — Ningbo ZJ** Loa - Br ex - Dght - Lbp 36.40 Br md 7.20 Dpth 3.70 Welded, 1 dk	**(B11B2FV) Fishing Vessel**	**1 oil engine** driving 1 Propeller Total Power: 441kW (600hp) Chinese Std. Type 1 x 4 Stroke 8 Cy. 300 x 380 441kW (600bhp) Zibo Diesel Engine Factory-China	 830
8982931 - -	**ZHOU YU 627** - **Chen Cailong** -	**195** 58 -		**1980 Ningbo Fishing Vessel Shipyard — Ningbo ZJ** Loa - Br ex - Dght - Lbp 36.40 Br md 7.20 Dpth 3.70 Welded, 1 dk	**(B11B2FV) Fishing Vessel**	**1 oil engine** driving 1 Propeller Total Power: 441kW (600hp) Chinese Std. Type 1 x 4 Stroke 8 Cy. 300 x 380 441kW (600bhp) Zibo Diesel Engine Factory-China	 830
8982943 - -	**ZHOU YU 628** - **Chen Cailong** -	**195** 58 -		**1980 Ningbo Fishing Vessel Shipyard — Ningbo ZJ** Loa - Br ex - Dght - Lbp 36.40 Br md 7.20 Dpth 3.70 Welded, 1 dk	**(B11B2FV) Fishing Vessel**	**1 oil engine** driving 1 Propeller Total Power: 441kW (600hp) Chinese Std. Type 1 x 4 Stroke 8 Cy. 300 x 380 441kW (600bhp) Zibo Diesel Engine Factory-China	 830
8831936 - -	**ZHOU YU 629** - **Zhoushan Marine Fisheries Co** - *Shenjiamen, Zhejiang* China	*199* 59 -	Class: (CC)	**1981 Ningbo Fishing Vessel Shipyard — Ningbo ZJ** Loa 41.00 Br ex - Dght - Lbp 36.00 Br md 7.20 Dpth 3.70 Welded, 1 dk	**(B11B2FV) Fishing Vessel**	**1 oil engine** geared to sc. shaft driving 1 FP propeller Total Power: 441kW (600hp) Chinese Std. Type 1 x 4 Stroke 8 Cy. 300 x 380 441kW (600bhp) Zibo Diesel Engine Factory-China AuxGen: 2 x 19kW 230V a.c	 12.0k 830
8982955 - -	**ZHOU YU 632** - **Chen Cailong** -	**195** 58 -		**1981 Ningbo Fishing Vessel Shipyard — Ningbo ZJ** Loa - Br ex - Dght - Lbp 36.40 Br md 7.20 Dpth 3.70 Welded, 1 dk	**(B11B2FV) Fishing Vessel**	**1 oil engine** driving 1 Propeller Total Power: 441kW (600hp) Chinese Std. Type 1 x 4 Stroke 8 Cy. 300 x 380 441kW (600bhp) Zibo Diesel Engine Factory-China	 830
8833647 - -	**ZHOU YU 634** - **Zhoushan Marine Fisheries Co** - *Shenjiamen, Zhejiang* China	*217* 65 -	Class: (CC)	**1983 Yantai Fishing Vessel Shipyard — Yantai SD** Loa 41.00 Br ex - Dght - Lbp 36.00 Br md 7.20 Dpth 3.70 Welded	**(B11B2FV) Fishing Vessel**	**1 oil engine** geared to sc. shaft driving 1 FP propeller Total Power: 441kW (600hp) Chinese Std. Type 1 x 4 Stroke 8 Cy. 300 x 380 441kW (600bhp) Zibo Diesel Engine Factory-China AuxGen: 2 x 19kW 230V a.c	 12.0k 830
8833659 - -	**ZHOU YU 641** - **Chen Cailong** -	*195* 58 103	Class: (CC)	**1983 Yantai Fishing Vessel Shipyard — Yantai SD** Loa 41.00 Br ex - Dght 2.800 Lbp 36.00 Br md 7.20 Dpth 3.70 Welded, 1 dk	**(B11B2FV) Fishing Vessel** Ins: 375	**1 oil engine** geared to sc. shaft driving 1 FP propeller Total Power: 294kW (400hp) Chinese Std. Type 1 x 4 Stroke 6 Cy. 300 x 380 294kW (400bhp) Zibo Diesel Engine Factory-China AuxGen: 2 x 64kW 400V a.c	 12.2k 630
8833661 - -	**ZHOU YU 642** - **Chen Cailong** -	*195* 58 103	Class: (CC)	**1983 Yantai Fishing Vessel Shipyard — Yantai SD** Loa 41.00 Br ex - Dght 2.800 Lbp 36.00 Br md 7.20 Dpth 3.70 Welded, 1 dk	**(B11B2FV) Fishing Vessel** Ins: 375	**1 oil engine** geared to sc. shaft driving 1 FP propeller Total Power: 294kW (400hp) Chinese Std. Type 1 x 4 Stroke 6 Cy. 300 x 380 294kW (400bhp) Zibo Diesel Engine Factory-China AuxGen: 2 x 64kW 400V a.c	 12.2k 630
8850607 - -	**ZHOU YU 665** - **Zhoushan Marine Fisheries Co** - *Ningbo, Zhejiang* China	*258* 77 -		**1989 Ningbo Fishing Vessel Shipyard — Ningbo ZJ** Loa 39.50 Br ex - Dght 2.900 Lbp 33.00 Br md 7.40 Dpth 3.70 Welded, 1 dk	**(B11B2FV) Fishing Vessel** Ins: 205	**1 oil engine** geared to sc. shaft driving 1 FP propeller Total Power: 324kW (441hp) Chinese Std. Type 1 x 4 Stroke 6 Cy. 300 x 380 324kW (441bhp) Zibo Diesel Engine Factory-China AuxGen: 3 x 40kW 400V a.c	 11.0k 630
8850619 - -	**ZHOU YU 666** - **Zhoushan Marine Fisheries Co** - *Ningbo, Zhejiang* China	*258* 77 -		**1989 Ningbo Fishing Vessel Shipyard — Ningbo ZJ** Loa 39.50 Br ex - Dght 2.900 Lbp 33.00 Br md 7.40 Dpth 3.70 Welded, 1 dk	**(B11B2FV) Fishing Vessel**	**1 oil engine** geared to sc. shaft driving 1 FP propeller Total Power: 324kW (441hp) Chinese Std. Type 1 x 4 Stroke 6 Cy. 300 x 380 324kW (441bhp) Zibo Diesel Engine Factory-China AuxGen: 3 x 40kW 400V a.c	 11.0k 630
8831986 *BKWF* -	**ZHOU YU LENG 3** - **Zhoushan Haibao Transport Co** - SatCom: Inmarsat C 441215212 *Ningbo, Zhejiang* China MMSI: 412400810	**826** 248 431	Class: CC	**1987 Guangzhou Fishing Vessel Shipyard — Guangzhou GD** Loa 60.80 Br ex - Dght 3.410 Lbp 54.00 Br md 9.90 Dpth 5.70 Welded, 2 dks	**(B12B2FC) Fish Carrier** Ins: 1,037 Compartments: 2 Ho, ER 2 Ha: 2 (2.5 x 4.6)ER	**1 oil engine** geared to sc. shaft driving 1 FP propeller Total Power: 809kW (1,100hp) Chinese Std. Type 1 x 4 Stroke 8 Cy. 300 x 380 809kW (1100bhp) Dalian Fishing Vessel Co-China AuxGen: 3 x 90kW 400V a.c	 11.5k 830
8887985 *BKWE* -	**ZHOU YU LENG 7** - **Zhoushan Haibao Transport Co** - *Ningbo, Zhejiang* China MMSI: 412400790	**943** 282 776	Class: (CC)	**1995-07 Guangzhou Fishing Vessel Shipyard — Guangzhou GD** Loa 65.80 Br ex - Dght 3.500 Lbp 59.00 Br md 10.10 Dpth 8.80 Welded, 1 dk	**(A34A2GR) Refrigerated Cargo Ship** Ins: 1,285 Compartments: 4 Ho, ER 4 Ha: ER	**1 oil engine** reduction geared to sc. shaft driving 1 FP propeller Total Power: 692kW (941hp) Chinese Std. Type 1 x 4 Stroke 6 Cy. 135 x 140 692kW (941bhp) Zibo Diesel Engine Factory-China	 613
8887997 *BKWD* -	**ZHOU YU LENG 8** - **Zhoushan Haibao Transport Co** - *Ningbo, Zhejiang* China MMSI: 412400780	**943** 282 776	Class: (CC)	**1995-07 Guangzhou Fishing Vessel Shipyard — Guangzhou GD** Loa 65.80 Br ex - Dght 3.500 Lbp 59.00 Br md 10.10 Dpth 8.80 Welded, 2 dks	**(A34A2GR) Refrigerated Cargo Ship** Grain: 1,285; Ins: 5,140 Compartments: 4 Ho, ER 4 Ha: 4 (4.6 x 2.5)ER	**1 oil engine** reduction geared to sc. shaft driving 1 FP propeller Total Power: 692kW (941hp) Chinese Std. Type 1 x 4 Stroke 6 Cy. 135 x 140 692kW (941bhp) Zibo Diesel Engine Factory-China AuxGen: 2 x 124kW 380V a.c	 11.5k 613
8708294 - -	**ZHOU YU NO. 5** *ex* Tenyu Maru No. 88 *-2002* **China National Fisheries Corp** - China	**1,096** 337 -		**1987-11 Sanuki Shipbuilding & Iron Works Co Ltd — Mitoyo KG** Yd No: 1178 Loa 69.30 (BB) Br ex - Dght 4.152 Lbp 63.02 Br md 10.61 Dpth 6.96 Welded, 2 dks	**(B11B2FV) Fishing Vessel**	**1 oil engine** geared to sc. shaft driving 1 FP propeller Total Power: 1,324kW (1,800hp) Akasaka 1 x 4 Stroke 6 Cy. 310 x 530 1324kW (1800bhp) Akasaka Tekkosho KK (Akasaka DieselLtd)-Japan	 K31F
8911047 - -	**ZHOU YU NO. 6** *ex* Tenyu Maru No. 28 *-2002* **China National Fisheries Corp** - China	**980** 359 -		**1989-11 Sanuki Shipbuilding & Iron Works Co Ltd — Mitoyo KG** Yd No: 1208 Loa 67.10 (BB) Br ex - Dght 3.952 Lbp 60.47 Br md 10.20 Dpth 6.60 Welded, 2 dks	**(B11B2FV) Fishing Vessel** Ins: 847	**1 oil engine** geared to sc. shaft driving 1 FP propeller Total Power: 1,324kW (1,800hp) Akasaka 1 x 4 Stroke 6 Cy. 310 x 530 1324kW (1800bhp) Akasaka Tekkosho KK (Akasaka DieselLtd)-Japan	 K31F
9614610 *3FGH8* -	**ZHOU YUN** - **Anji Leasing Co Ltd** Zhouyun International Shipping Management Ltd SatCom: Inmarsat C 435683111 *Panama* Panama MMSI: 356831000 Official number: 41870PEXTF2	**8,646** 5,637 13,500	Class: PD	**2010-11 Zhejiang Mingfa Shipbuilding Co Ltd — Taizhou ZJ** Yd No: MFJ-2008-05 Loa 140.70 Br ex - Dght 7.900 Lbp 134.90 Br md 20.00 Dpth 10.80 Welded, 1 dk	**(A31A2GX) General Cargo Ship** Grain: 18,998	**1 oil engine** reduction geared to sc. shaft driving 1 FP propeller Total Power: 2,574kW (3,500hp) Yanmar 1 x 4 Stroke 6 Cy. 330 x 440 2574kW (3500bhp) Qingdao Zichai Boyang Diesel EngineCo Ltd-China	 12.7k 6N330-E
9610729 *VRLY2* -	**ZHOUSHAN ISLAND** - **Zhoushan Shipping Ltd** Pacific Basin Shipping Ltd *Hong Kong* Hong Kong MMSI: 477243200 Official number: HK-3800	**32,356** 19,458 58,044 T/cm 57.4	Class: NK	**2013-03 Tsuneishi Group (Zhoushan) Shipbuilding Inc — Daishan County ZJ** Yd No: SS-125 Loa 190.00 (BB) Br ex - Dght 12.826 Lbp 185.60 Br md 32.26 Dpth 18.00 Welded, 1 dk	**(A21A2BC) Bulk Carrier** Grain: 72,689; Bale: 70,122 Compartments: 5 Ho, ER 5 Ha: ER Cranes: 4x30t	**1 oil engine** driving 1 FP propeller Total Power: 8,400kW (11,421hp) MAN-B&W 1 x 2 Stroke 6 Cy. 500 x 2000 8400kW (11421bhp) Mitsui Engineering & Shipbuilding CLtd-Japan Fuel: 2380.0	 14.5k 6S50MC-

429792 - -	**ZHU CHUAN 2001** - **Guangdong Zhu Chuan Navigation Co Ltd** - *Guangzhou, Guangdong* China	1,000 - 1,500		**2006-07 Guangzhou Panyu Shenghai Shipyard Co Ltd — Guangzhou GD** Loa 49.98 Br ex - Dght - Lbp 48.85 Br md 15.60 Dpth - Welded, 1 dk	**(A31A2GX) General Cargo Ship** TEU 118	**2 oil engines** reduction geared to sc. shafts driving 2 FP propellers Total Power: 746kW (1,014hp) Cummins KTA-19-M2 2 x 4 Stroke 6 Cy. 159 x 159 each-373kW (507bhp) Chongqing Cummins Engine Co Ltd-China AuxGen: 2 x 58kW a.c
429845 - -	**ZHU CHUAN 2002** - **Guangdong Zhu Chuan Navigation Co Ltd** - *Guangzhou, Guangdong* China	1,000 - 1,500		**2006-07 Guangzhou Panyu Shenghai Shipyard Co Ltd — Guangzhou GD** Loa 49.98 Br ex - Dght - Lbp 48.85 Br md 15.60 Dpth - Welded, 1 dk	**(A31A2GX) General Cargo Ship** TEU 118	**2 oil engines** reduction geared to sc. shafts driving 2 FP propellers Total Power: 746kW (1,014hp) Cummins KTA-19-M2 2 x 4 Stroke 6 Cy. 159 x 159 each-373kW (507bhp) Chongqing Cummins Engine Co Ltd-China AuxGen: 2 x 58kW a.c
069073 - -	**ZHU DIAN JUN 1** - **Guangdong Zhuhai Power Station Co Ltd** - *Zhuhai, Guangdong* China MMSI: 412468910	1,210 373 1,894	Class: CC	**2000-05 Guangzhou Huangpu Shipyard — Guangzhou GD** Loa 63.88 Br ex - Dght 4.600 Lbp 59.80 Br md 12.00 Dpth 5.40 Welded, 1 dk	**(B33A2DS) Suction Dredger** 1 Ha: (24.0 x 7.2)	**2 oil engines** geared to sc. shafts driving 2 Propellers 8.0kn Chinese Std. Type 6300ZC 2 x 4 Stroke 6 Cy. 300 x 380 Guangzhou Diesel Engine Factory CoLtd-China
365570 3ILP -	**ZHU HAI** - **Shanghai Changhang Shipping Co Ltd** - *Shanghai* China MMSI: 412372830	1,997 1,483 3,300	Class: CC	**2005-12 Chongqing Dongfeng Ship Industry Co — Chongqing** Yd No: K04-1012 Loa 80.60 Br ex - Dght 5.500 Lbp 76.00 Br md 13.60 Dpth 6.90 Welded, 1 dk	**(A31A2GX) General Cargo Ship** Bale: 4,563 Compartments: 2 Ho, ER 2 Ha: (19.8 x 10.0)ER (18.6 x 10.0) Ice Capable	**1 oil engine** driving 1 FP propeller Total Power: 1,280kW (1,740hp) 11.3kn Sulzer 8ATL25R 1 x 4 Stroke 8 Cy. 250 x 300 1280kW (1740bhp) (made 1993, fitted 2005) H Cegielski Poznan SA-Poland AuxGen: 2 x 150kW 400V a.c
831948 BRZI -	**ZHU HAI CHUN** - **Shenzhen Pengxing Shipping Co Ltd** - *Shenzhen, Guangdong* China MMSI: 412462520	*134* 70 20	Class: (CC)	**1987 Afai Engineers & Shiprepairers Ltd — Hong Kong** Loa 21.99 Br ex - Dght 1.660 Lbp 19.28 Br md 8.71 Dpth 2.72 Welded, 1 dk	**(A37B2PS) Passenger Ship**	**2 oil engines** driving 2 FP propellers Total Power: 1,294kW (1,760hp) 25.0kn Isotta Fraschini ID36SS8V 2 x Vee 4 Stroke 8 Cy. 170 x 170 each-647kW (880bhp) Isotta Fraschini SpA-Italy AuxGen: 2 x 50kW 400V a.c
9428865 9VHR2 -	**ZHU JIANG** - **Nan Chuan Maritime Pte Ltd** Ocean Tankers (Pte) Ltd SatCom: Inmarsat Mini-M 764884177 *Singapore* Singapore MMSI: 564281000 Official number: 393461	30,964 14,816 50,192 T/cm 52.2	Class: AB	**2009-04 SLS Shipbuilding Co Ltd — Tongyeong** Yd No: 458A Loa 189.00 (BB) Br ex - Dght 13.515 Lbp 181.49 Br md 32.20 Dpth 20.20 Welded, 1 dk	**(A13B2TP) Products Tanker** Double Hull (13F) Liq: 60,450; Liq (Oil): 60,450 Cargo Heating Coils Compartments: 1 Ta, 10 Wing Ta, 2 Wing Slop Ta, ER 3 Cargo Pump (s): 3x1700m³/hr Manifold: Bow/CM: 95.8m	**1 oil engine** driving 1 FP propeller Total Power: 9,480kW (12,889hp) 15.0kn MAN-B&W 6S50MC-C 1 x 2 Stroke 6 Cy. 500 x 2000 9480kW (12889bhp) Hyundai Heavy Industries Co Ltd-South Korea AuxGen: 3 x 680kW a.c Fuel: 85.0 (d.f.) 1700.0 (r.f.)
9157519 3FBL7 -	**ZHU MIN VICTORIA** *ex Spring Ursa -2011* **Great Lakes Shipping Maritime Inc** Ocean Tankers Corp SatCom: Inmarsat C 435693310 *Panama* Panama MMSI: 356933000 Official number: 2382097G	9,549 4,830 16,026 T/cm 25.3	Class: NK (AB)	**1997-03 Shin Kurushima Dockyard Co. Ltd. — Akitsu** Yd No: 2935 Loa 138.62 (BB) Br ex 22.10 Dght 9.072 Lbp 130.60 Br md 21.80 Dpth 12.10 Welded, 1 dk	**(A12A2TC) Chemical Tanker** Double Hull (13F) Liq: 15,984 Compartments: 20 Wing Ta (s.stl), ER, 2 Wing Slop Ta 20 Cargo Pump (s): 6x300m³/hr, 10x200m³/hr, 4x150m³/hr Manifold: Bow/CM: 72m	**1 oil engine** driving 1 FP propeller Total Power: 4,891kW (6,650hp) 14.2kn B&W 7S35MC 1 x 2 Stroke 7 Cy. 350 x 1400 4891kW (6650bhp) Makita Corp-Japan AuxGen: 3 x 320kW Fuel: 62.3 (d.f.) 950.1 (r.f.)
8835310 - -	**ZHU SHI 8** - **Government of The People's Republic of China** - China	*293* 164 -		**1980 in the People's Republic of China** Loa - Br ex - Dght - Lbp - Br md - Dpth - Welded, 1 dk	**(A13B2TU) Tanker (unspecified)**	**1 oil engine** driving 1 FP propeller
7929190 - -	**ZHU WAN** *ex Marusumi Maru No. 7 -1999* - -	*198* 123 550		**1979-12 Higaki Zosen K.K. — Imabari** Yd No: 233 Loa 51.19 Br ex - Dght 3.106 Lbp 50.02 Br md 10.00 Dpth 4.81 Welded, 2 dks	**(A31A2GX) General Cargo Ship**	**1 oil engine** driving 1 FP propeller Total Power: 883kW (1,201hp) Hanshin 6LU28 1 x 4 Stroke 6 Cy. 280 x 440 883kW (1201bhp) Hanshin Nainenki Kogyo-Japan
9287596 BXCS -	**ZHU XIAO LING YI** - **Fire Protection Bureau of Zhuhai** - *Zhuhai, Guangdong* China Official number: 03J1012	266 80 50	Class: CC	**2003-02 Guangzhou Wenchong Shipyard Co Ltd — Guangzhou GD** Yd No: 303 Loa 38.50 Br ex - Dght 2.100 Lbp 36.00 Br md 7.80 Dpth 3.40 Welded, 1 dk	**(B34F2SF) Fire Fighting Vessel**	**2 oil engines** geared to sc. shafts driving 2 Propellers
9014779 BOFO -	**ZHU YUAN** *ex Lady Pauline -1996* **Shenzhen COSCO LPG Shipping Co Ltd** - SatCom: Inmarsat C 441221310 *Shenzhen, Guangdong* China MMSI: 412470660	3,376 1,013 3,422 T/cm 12.5	Class: CC (BV)	**1991-12 Kanrei Zosen K.K. — Naruto** Yd No: 352 Loa 99.60 (BB) Br ex - Dght 5.750 Lbp 92.00 Br md 15.80 Dpth 7.30 Welded, 1 dk	**(A11B2TG) LPG Tanker** Liq (Gas): 3,311 2 x Gas Tank (s); 2 independent (C.mn.stl) cyl horizontal 21 Cargo Pump (s)	**1 oil engine** driving 1 FP propeller Total Power: 2,427kW (3,300hp) 12.7kn Mitsubishi 6UEC37LA 1 x 2 Stroke 6 Cy. 370 x 880 2427kW (3300bhp) Akasaka Tekkosho KK (Akasaka DieselLtd)-Japan AuxGen: 3 x 163kW 100/440V 60Hz a.c Fuel: 84.6 (d.f.) 449.0 (r.f.) 7.0pd
9650339 VRKU4 -	**ZHUANG YUAN AO** - **Xin De Yuan (Hong Kong) Shipping Ltd** COSCO Southern Asphalt Shipping Co Ltd *Hong Kong* Hong Kong MMSI: 477938700 Official number: HK-3559	9,963 3,197 12,000	Class: BV	**2012-07 COSCO (Dalian) Shipyard Co Ltd — Dalian LN** Yd No: N409 Loa 146.00 Br ex - Dght 7.800 Lbp 137.20 Br md 22.00 Dpth 10.80 Welded, 1 dk	**(A13C2LA) Asphalt/Bitumen Tanker** Double Hull (13F) Liq: 11,490; Liq (Oil): 11,490 Compartments: 4 Wing Ta, 4 Wing Ta, ER	**1 oil engine** driving 1 FP propeller Total Power: 4,440kW (6,037hp) 13.5kn MAN-B&W 6S35MC 1 x 2 Stroke 6 Cy. 350 x 1400 4440kW (6037bhp) Yichang Marine Diesel Engine Co Ltd-China AuxGen: 3 x 560kW 50Hz a.c Fuel: 917.3
9617351 3EXD -	**ZHUSHUI 3** - **Seroja-Zhushui 3 Shipping Ltd** Seroja-Zhushui Shipping Ltd SatCom: Inmarsat C 437384610 *Panama* Panama MMSI: 373846000 Official number: 42878PEXT	43,472 27,687 79,501 T/cm 71.9	Class: LR ✠ **100A1** SS 01/2012 bulk carrier CSR BC-A GRAB (20) Nos. 2, 4 & 6 holds may be empty ESP **ShipRight** CM *IWS LI ✠ **LMC** UMS Eq.Ltr: Q†; Cable: 687.5/81.0 U3 (a)	**2012-01 Jinhai Heavy Industry Co Ltd — Daishan County ZJ** Yd No: J0033 Loa 229.00 (BB) Br ex - Dght 14.600 Lbp 222.00 Br md 32.26 Dpth 20.25 Welded, 1 dk	**(A21A2BC) Bulk Carrier** Grain: 98,378; Bale: 90,784 Compartments: 7 Ho, ER 7 Ha: ER	**1 oil engine** driving 1 FP propeller Total Power: 11,900kW (16,179hp) 14.0kn MAN-B&W 5S60MC-C 1 x 2 Stroke 5 Cy. 600 x 2400 11900kW (16179bhp) Hitachi Zosen Corp-Japan AuxGen: 3 x 700kW 450V 60Hz a.c Boilers: AuxB (Comp) 8.9kgf/cm² (8.7bar)
9617430 3FBZ5 -	**ZHUSHUI 5** - **Seroja-Zhushui 5 Shipping Ltd** Seroja-Zhushui Shipping Ltd SatCom: Inmarsat C 437309910 *Panama* Panama MMSI: 373099000 Official number: 42879PEXT	43,472 27,703 79,501 T/cm 71.9	Class: LR ✠ **100A1** SS 01/2012 bulk carrier CSR BC-A GRAB (20) Nos. 2, 4 & 6 holds may be empty ESP **ShipRight** CM *IWS LI ✠ **LMC** UMS Eq.Ltr: Q†; Cable: 687.5/81.0 U3 (a)	**2012-01 Jinhai Heavy Industry Co Ltd — Daishan County ZJ** Yd No: J0034 Loa 229.00 (BB) Br ex 32.30 Dght 14.600 Lbp 222.00 Br md 32.26 Dpth 20.25 Welded, 1 dk	**(A21A2BC) Bulk Carrier** Grain: 98,378; Bale: 90,784 Compartments: 7 Ho, ER 7 Ha: ER	**1 oil engine** driving 1 FP propeller Total Power: 11,900kW (16,179hp) 14.0kn MAN-B&W 5S60MC-C 1 x 2 Stroke 5 Cy. 600 x 2400 11900kW (16179bhp) Hitachi Zosen Corp-Japan AuxGen: 3 x 700kW 450V 60Hz a.c Boilers: AuxB (Comp) 9.0kgf/cm² (8.8bar)

IMO / Call sign / Flag	Ship / Former names / Owner / Registry	Tonnage	Class	Build / Dimensions	Type / Cargo	Machinery	Speed / Model
8401389 *BVAI8*	**ZI BAO SHI** *ex* Tai Yang Hai *-2006* *ex* Sun Sea *-2003* *ex* Konkar Theodora *-2002* *ex* Flavia *-1997* *ex* Anafi *-1993* **Fujian Xiamen Shipping Co Ltd** - SatCom: Inmarsat C 441201517 *Xiamen, Fujian* *China* MMSI: 412701470	**34,626** 21,233 65,282 T/cm 64.0	Class: (CC) (AB) (NV)	**1985-09 Nippon Kokan KK (NKK Corp) — Yokohama KN (Tsurumi Shipyard)** Yd No: 1025 Loa 222.00 (BB) Br ex 32.29 Dght 12.902 Lbp 212.02 Br md 32.25 Dpth 17.81 Welded, 1 dk	**(A21A2BC) Bulk Carrier** Grain: 74,938; Bale: 71,442 Compartments: 7 Ho, ER 7 Ha: (13.5 x 11.2)6 (14.7 x 14.4)ER	**1 oil engine** driving 1 FP propeller Total Power: 8,018kW (10,901hp) Sulzer 1 x 2 Stroke 7 Cy. 580 x 1700 8018kW (10901bhp) Sumitomo Heavy Industries Ltd-Japan AuxGen: 3 x 500kW 440V 60Hz a.c Fuel: 157.0 (d.f.) 1896.0 (r.f.) 31.0pd	14.0k 7RTA5
8996334 - -	**ZI DA YE** - **Sun Big Fishery Co Ltd** -	**980** - -		**2004-01 Jong Shyn Shipbuilding Co., Ltd. — Kaohsiung** Yd No: 131 Loa - Br ex - Dght - Lbp - Br md - Dpth - Welded, 1 dk	**(B11B2FV) Fishing Vessel**	**1 oil engine** driving 1 Propeller	
9534535 *BJRK* -	**ZI DING XIANG** **Sinochem Shipping Co Ltd (Hainan)** Shanghai Sinochem-Stolt Shipping Ltd *Haikou, Hainan* *China* MMSI: 412523660	**2,442** 1,143 3,820 T/cm 12.2	Class: CC	**2009-08 Shenjia Shipyard — Shanghai** Yd No: 44002 Loa 93.80 (BB) Br ex - Dght 5.400 Lbp 89.00 Br md 15.00 Dpth 6.70 Welded, 1 dk	**(A12B2TR) Chemical/Products Tanker** Double Hull (13F) Liq: 4,154; Liq (Oil): 4,068 Cargo Heating Coils Compartments: 4 Wing Ta, 4 Ta, ER 15 Cargo Pump (s): 15x100m^3/hr Manifold: Bow/CM: 51.8m	**1 oil engine** reduction geared to sc. shaft driving 1 Directional propeller Total Power: 2,380kW (3,236hp) MAN-B&W 1 x 4 Stroke 7 Cy. 270 x 380 2380kW (3236bhp) Zhenjiang Marine Diesel Works-China Fuel: 36.0 (d.f.) 139.0 (r.f.)	12.5k 7L27/38
9054743 *HO3968* -	**ZI HONG** *ex* Shiko Maru *-2002* **V-Sky Shipping Ltd** - *Panama* *Panama* MMSI: 371141000 Official number: 3083205	**1,407** 642 1,184		**1992-06 K.K. Miura Zosensho — Saiki** Yd No: 1038 L reg 59.60 Br ex - Dght - Lbp - Br md 13.20 Dpth 6.30 Welded	**(A31A2GX) General Cargo Ship**	**1 oil engine** geared to sc. shaft driving 1 FP propeller Total Power: 736kW (1,001hp) Hanshin 1 x 4 Stroke 6 Cy. 350 x 550 736kW (1001bhp) The Hanshin Diesel Works Ltd-Japan	6LU35G
7525384 *BORS* -	**ZI JIN SHAN** *ex* Aegis Pilot *-1980* - - SatCom: Inmarsat C 441207710 *Tianjin* *China*	**9,513** 6,402 15,751 T/cm 25.0	Class: (CC) (AB)	**1978-03 Astilleros Espanoles SA (AESA) — Bilbao** Yd No: 302 Loa 144.00 Br ex 21.44 Dght 8.902 Lbp 134.00 Br md 21.35 Dpth 12.20 Welded, 2 dks	**(A31A2GX) General Cargo Ship** Grain: 22,011; Bale: 20,290 Compartments: 4 Ho, ER 4 Ha: (13.4 x 8.0) (7.4 x 12.6)2 (20.2 x 12.6)ER Derricks: 8x10t	**1 oil engine** driving 1 FP propeller Total Power: 4,523kW (6,149hp) B&W 1 x 2 Stroke 7 Cy. 450 x 900 4523kW (6149bhp) Astilleros Espanoles SA (AESA)-Spain AuxGen: 3 x 252kW 450V 60Hz a.c	14.0kn 7K45GF
9274771 - -	**ZI JING HUA** - **Guangdong Zhanjiang Navigation Co** - *Zhanjiang, Guangdong* *China* MMSI: 412465220	**4,757** 2,473 1,098	Class: (CC)	**2002-05 Wuchang Shipyard — Wuhan HB** Yd No: A065/1L Loa 89.90 Br ex - Dght 3.400 Lbp 83.00 Br md 18.00 Dpth 5.40 Welded, 1 dk	**(A36A2PR) Passenger/Ro-Ro Ship (Vehicles)** Passengers: 498 Trailers: 30	**2 oil engines** reduction geared to sc. shafts driving 2 FP propellers Total Power: 2,648kW (3,600hp) Chinese Std. Type 2 x 4 Stroke 8 Cy. 250 x 320 each-1324kW (1800bhp) Zibo Diesel Engine Factory-China AuxGen: 2 x 280kW 400V a.c	14.6kn LB8250ZLC
9663647 - -	**ZI JING SHI YI HAO** - **Guangdong Xuwen Port & Shipping Holdings Co Ltd** - *Zhanjiang, Guangdong* *China*	**8,869** 4,789 2,122	Class: CC	**2012-08 Taizhou Kouan Shipbuilding Co Ltd — Taizhou JS** Yd No: TK0409 Loa 120.80 Br ex - Dght 4.250 Lbp 113.30 Br md 20.60 Dpth 6.30 Welded, 1 dk	**(A36A2PR) Passenger/Ro-Ro Ship (Vehicles)** Passengers: unberthed: 900 Vehicles: 45	**2 oil engines** reduction geared to sc. shafts driving 2 CP propellers Total Power: 4,120kW (5,602hp) Chinese Std. Type 2 x 4 Stroke 8 Cy. 320 x 440 each-2060kW (2801bhp)	14.7kn 8320ZC
9608910 *VRKK7* -	**ZI JING SONG** **COSCOL (HK) Investment & Development Co Ltd** COSCO Shipping Co Ltd (COSCOL) *Hong Kong* *Hong Kong* MMSI: 477001800 Official number: HK-3482	**20,692** 11,468 27,000	Class: CC	**2012-11 Taizhou Kouan Shipbuilding Co Ltd — Taizhou JS** Yd No: TK0506 Loa 179.50 (BB) Br ex 27.24 Dght 10.200 Lbp 169.50 Br md 27.20 Dpth 14.50 Welded, 1 dk	**(A31A2GX) General Cargo Ship** Grain: 40,419; Bale: 38,088 TEU 1391 C ho 606 TEU C Dk 785 TEU Compartments: 5 Ho, ER 5 Ha: ER Cranes: 1x90t,2x45t,1x40t Ice Capable	**1 oil engine** driving 1 FP propeller Total Power: 8,250kW (11,217hp) MAN-B&W 1 x 2 Stroke 6 Cy. 500 x 2000 8250kW (11217bhp)	15.1kn 6S50ME-C8
8506866 - -	**ZI LANG** - **Nantong Hi-Speed Passenger Ship Co** - *Nantong, Jiangsu* *China*	*378* 140 100	Class: (CC) (NV)	**1986-09 Westamarin AS — Mandal** Yd No: 89 Loa 36.30 Br ex - Dght 1.700 Lbp 32.26 Br md 9.77 Dpth 3.81 Welded, 1 dk	**(A37B2PS) Passenger Ship** Passengers: unberthed: 354	**2 oil engines** driving 2 FP propellers Total Power: 2,938kW (3,994hp) M.T.U. 2 x Vee 4 Stroke 16 Cy. 165 x 185 each-1469kW (1997bhp) (made 1986) MTU Friedrichshafen GmbH-Friedrichshafen AuxGen: 2 x 56kW 220V 50Hz a.c	16V396TB83
9098048 *BHWX* -	**ZI LANG SHAN** *ex* Zhe Jiao 51 *-2008* **Nantong Kanghai Shipping Co Ltd** - *Nantong, Jiangsu* *China* Official number: 060302000016	**2,751** 1,540 4,000		**1980-01 in the People's Republic of China** Loa 93.15 Br ex - Dght 6.800 Lbp 86.05 Br md 13.60 Dpth 8.60 Welded, 1 dk	**(A31A2GX) General Cargo Ship**	**1 oil engine** driving 1 Propeller Total Power: 1,470kW (1,999hp) Chinese Std. Type 1 x 4 Stroke 6 Cy. 390 x 450 1470kW (1999bhp) Shanghai Diesel Engine Co Ltd-China	6E390
8996322 - -	**ZI LI FA** - - -	**968** 443 -		**2004-01 Jong Shyn Shipbuilding Co., Ltd. — Kaohsiung** Yd No: 130 Loa - Br ex - Dght - Lbp - Br md - Dpth - Welded, 1 dk	**(B11B2FV) Fishing Vessel**	**1 oil engine** driving 1 Propeller	
9426178 *BIJL* -	**ZI LUO LAN** **Shanghai Sinochem-Stolt Shipping Ltd** - SatCom: Inmarsat Mini-M 76124290 *Shanghai* *China* MMSI: 413374860	**2,442** 1,143 3,866 T/cm 12.2	Class: CC	**2007-11 Shenjia Shipyard — Shanghai** Yd No: 44001 Loa 93.80 (BB) Br ex - Dght 5.400 Lbp 89.00 Br md 15.00 Dpth 6.70 Welded, 1 dk	**(A12B2TR) Chemical/Products Tanker** Double Hull (13F) Liq: 4,063; Liq (Oil): 4,062 Cargo Heating Coils Compartments: 4 Wing Ta (s.stl), 4 Ta (s.stl), ER (s.stl) 8 Cargo Pump (s): 8x100m^3/hr Manifold: Bow/CM: 51.8m	**1 oil engine** reduction geared to sc. shafts driving 1 Directional propeller Total Power: 2,380kW (3,236hp) MAN-B&W 1 x 4 Stroke 7 Cy. 270 x 380 2380kW (3236bhp) Zhenjiang Marine Diesel Works-China AuxGen: 3 x 240kW 400V a.c Fuel: 36.0 (d.f.) 139.0 (r.f.)	12.5kn 7L27/38
9469261 *BIQL* -	**ZI TONG** **Shanghai Sinochem-Stolt Shipping Ltd** - SatCom: Inmarsat Mini-M 764637655 *Shanghai* *China* MMSI: 413373780	**2,646** 1,105 3,784 T/cm 11.9	Class: CC	**2007-12 Ningbo Xinle Shipbuilding Co Ltd — Ningbo ZJ** Yd No: 3600-04-04 Loa 95.68 (BB) Br ex 15.24 Dght 5.400 Lbp 90.00 Br md 15.00 Dpth 6.90 Welded, 1 dk	**(A12B2TR) Chemical/Products Tanker** Double Hull (13F) Liq: 3,981; Liq (Oil): 3,981 Cargo Heating Coils Compartments: 4 Wing Ta, 4 Ta, ER 8 Cargo Pump (s): 2x150m^3/hr, 6x120m^3/hr Manifold: Bow/CM: 49m	**1 oil engine** reduction geared to sc. shaft driving 1 FP propeller Total Power: 2,500kW (3,399hp) Daihatsu 1 x 4 Stroke 6 Cy. 280 x 390 2500kW (3399bhp) Shaanxi Diesel Heavy Industry Co Lt-China AuxGen: 3 x 240kW 400V a.c Fuel: 40.0 (d.f.) 147.0 (r.f.)	15.0kn 8DKM-28
9086899 *BPGN* -	**ZI YU LAN** **Shanghai Marine (Group) Co** - SatCom: Inmarsat C 441216310 *Shanghai* *China* MMSI: 412786000 Official number: 90445	**16,071** 5,295 6,512	Class: CC (GL)	**1995-08 MTW Schiffswerft GmbH — Wismar** Yd No: 161 Loa 150.45 (BB) Br ex - Dght 6.850 Lbp 137.50 Br md 24.00 Dpth 13.20 Welded, 1 dk	**(A33B2CP) Passenger/Container Ship** Passengers: cabins: 122; berths: 392 TEU 293 incl 30 ref C. Compartments: 3 Cell Ho, ER 3 Ha: ER Cranes: 1x36t	**2 oil engines** with clutches & sr geared to sc. shafts driving 1 CP propeller Total Power: 15,000kW (20,394hp) MaK 2 x 4 Stroke 6 Cy. 580 x 600 each-7500kW (10197bhp) Krupp MaK Maschinenbau GmbH-Kiel AuxGen: 1 x 2000kW 230/400V 50Hz a.c, 3 x 1020kW 230/400V 50Hz a.c Thrusters: 1 Thwart. CP thruster (f) Fuel: 855.0 (r.f.)	20.0kn 6M601C
9127447 *BHW* -	**ZI YUN FENG** *ex* Bando Korea *-1998* **Nanjing Zhonggang Shipping Co Ltd** - *Nanjing, Jiangsu* *China* MMSI: 412351000	**1,640** 735 2,584 T/cm 8.1	Class: CC (KR)	**1995-06 Shinyoung Shipbuilding Industry Co Ltd — Yeosu** Yd No: 178 Loa 81.50 (BB) Br ex - Dght 5.270 Lbp 75.00 Br md 12.50 Dpth 6.30 Welded, 1 dk	**(A12A2TC) Chemical Tanker** Double Hull (13F) Liq: 2,720 Part Cargo Heating Coils Compartments: 8 Wing Ta, 2 Wing Slop Ta, ER 10 Cargo Pump (s) Manifold: Bow/CM: 41.1m	**1 oil engine** reduction geared to sc. shaft driving 1 FP propeller Total Power: 1,320kW (1,795hp) Alpha 1 x 4 Stroke 6 Cy. 280 x 320 1320kW (1795bhp) Ssangyong Heavy Industries Co Ltd-South Korea	12.0kn 6L28/32

522667 RQD
ZI YUN SHAN
ex Seamerit *-1990* *ex* Belo Mundo *-1987*
ex Bless River *-1981* *launched as* Lelaps *-1978*
China Shipping International Intermodal Co Ltd
-
SatCom: Inmarsat C 441223510
Guangzhou, Guangdong *China*
MMSI: 412578000
19,674 11,035 33,663 T/cm 41.3
Class: (CC) (AB)
1978-05 KK Kanasashi Zosen — Toyohashi AI Yd No: 020
Loa 182.18 (BB) Br ex 27.03 Dght 10.940
Lbp 170.01 Br md 27.01 Dpth 15.22
Welded, 1 dk
(A21A2BC) Bulk Carrier
Grain: 46,225; Bale: 39,141
Compartments: 5 Ho, ER
5 Ha: (12.5 x 11.9) (12.8 x 11.9)3 (16.8 x 11.9)ER
Derricks: 5x15t
1 oil engine driving 1 FP propeller
Total Power: 8,532kW (11,600hp) 13.0kn
B&W 6K74EF
1 x 2 Stroke 6 Cy. 740 x 1600 8532kW (11600bhp)
Mitsui Engineering & Shipbuilding CLtd-Japan
AuxGen: 3 x 400kW 440V 60Hz a.c
Fuel: 170.0 (d.f.) (Part Heating Coils) 1996.5 (r.f.) 39.0pd

5418381 5VAQ5
ZIA
ex Lolia *-2011* *ex* Flisvos *-2010*
ex Agios Stefanos *-2004* *ex* Georgios D. *-2002*
ex Chrisopigi *-2002* *ex* Mark X *-1985*
ex Southern Venture *-1979*
ex Vitta Theresa *-1976*
Aransas Marine Co
-
Lome *Togo*
MMSI: 671127000
480 306 1,030
Class: (LR) (HR) ✠ Classed LR until 6/79
1963-09 Kroegerwerft GmbH & Co. KG — Schacht-Audorf Yd No: 1190
Loa 62.41 Br ex 9.66 Dght 3.760
Lbp 56.22 Br md 9.45 Dpth 4.09
Welded, 1 dk
(A13B2TU) Tanker (unspecified)
Compartments: 8 Ta, ER
Ice Capable
1 oil engine driving 1 FP propeller
Total Power: 552kW (750hp) 10.0kn
Alpha 496R
1 x 2 Stroke 6 Cy. 310 x 490 552kW (750bhp)
Alpha Diesel A/S-Denmark
Fuel: 53.0 (d.f.) 3.0pd

9426685 IR8840
-
ZIACANAIA
UniCredit Leasing SpA
-
SatCom: Inmarsat M 600261446
Rimini *Italy*
MMSI: 247101500
183 54 20
Class: RI
2008-05 C.R.N. Cant. Nav. Ancona S.r.l. — Ancona Yd No: 33/01
Loa 32.60 Br ex - Dght -
Lbp 27.10 Br md 7.00 Dpth 2.90
Bonded, 1 dk
(X11A2YP) Yacht
Hull Material: Reinforced Plastic
2 oil engines reduction geared to sc. shaft (s) driving 2 FP propellers
Total Power: 1,618kW (2,200hp)
MAN D2842LE
2 x Vee 4 Stroke 12 Cy. 128 x 142 each-809kW (1100bhp)
MAN Nutzfahrzeuge AG-Nuernberg

7901693 ERGA
-
ZIAD JUNIOR
ex Mingo *-2009* *ex* Sota Begona *-1987*
Glorious Maritime Co SA
Raouf Maritime Co
Giurgiulesti *Moldova*
MMSI: 214180701
Official number: MDM09377
2,693 1,330 3,550
Class: DR (NV) (BV)
1980-11 S.A. Balenciaga — Zumaya Yd No: 294
Loa 89.00 (BB) Br ex 14.41 Dght 6.180
Lbp 80.77 Br md 14.22 Dpth 8.39
Welded, 1 dk
(A31A2GX) General Cargo Ship
Grain: 4,773; Bale: 4,510
TEU 168 C.ho 82/20' C.dk 86/20'
Compartments: 1 Ho, ER
1 Ha: (51.6 x 10.4)ER
1 oil engine reduction geared to sc. shaft driving 1 FP propeller
Total Power: 1,471kW (2,000hp) 13.5kn
Deutz RBV6M358
1 x 4 Stroke 6 Cy. 400 x 580 1471kW (2000bhp)
Hijos de J Barreras SA-Spain

5410872 VC8993
-
ZIBET
ex Doreen Elaine *-1978*
Royal Seafoods Inc
-
St John's, NL *Canada*
Official number: 310509
128 64 -
Class: (LR) ✠ Classed LR until 5/71
1963-05 Marine Industries Ltee (MIL) — Sorel QC Yd No: 295
Loa 24.95 Br ex 6.89 Dght -
Lbp 22.48 Br md 6.56 Dpth 3.36
Welded, 1 dk
(B11A2FT) Trawler
1 oil engine with hydraulic coupling driving 1 CP propeller
Total Power: 250kW (340hp) 10.0kn
Alpha 404-24VO
1 x 2 Stroke 4 Cy. 240 x 400 250kW (340bhp)
Alpha Diesel A/S-Denmark

5398828 WTQ2472
-
ZIBET
-
Sea Roy Enterprises
-
New Bedford, MA *United States of America*
Official number: 501627
158 107 -
1947-01 Electric Boat Co. — Groton, Ct Yd No: 129
Loa 27.44 Br ex 6.53 Dght 3.658
Lbp - Br md - Dpth -
Welded, 1 dk
(B11B2FV) Fishing Vessel
1 oil engine driving 1 FP propeller
Total Power: 294kW (400hp)
Enterprise DMG6
1 x 4 Stroke 6 Cy. 305 x 381 294kW (400bhp)
Enterprise Engine & Foundry Co-USA

8969898 WDD9800
-
ZIBET
ex Lucky Andy II *-2007*
Zibet Inc
-
New Bedford, MA *United States of America*
MMSI: 367316510
Official number: 1109998
204 61 -
2001 La Force Shipyard Inc — Coden AL Yd No: 109
L reg 26.18 Br ex - Dght -
Lbp - Br md 7.62 Dpth 3.71
Welded, 1 dk
(B11A2FT) Trawler
2 oil engines geared to sc. shafts driving 2 Propellers
Total Power: 794kW (1,080hp)
Caterpillar 3412
2 x Vee 4 Stroke 12 Cy. 137 x 152 each-397kW (540bhp)
Caterpillar Inc-USA

8418758 A8DP2
-
ZIEMIA CIESZYNSKA
ex Lake Carling *-2003*
ex Ziemia Cieszynska *-1993*
Ziemia Three Ltd
Polska Zegluga Morska PP (POLSTEAM)
Monrovia *Liberia*
MMSI: 636012131
Official number: 12131
17,464 9,395 26,264 T/cm 36.7
Class: NV (PR)
1992-09 Turkiye Gemi Sanayii A.S. — Pendik Yd No: 016
Loa 180.16 (BB) Br ex - Dght 9.850
Lbp 171.80 Br md 23.10 Dpth 13.90
Welded, 1 dk
(A21A2BC) Bulk Carrier
Grain: 34,920; Bale: 34,022
Compartments: 5 Ho, ER
5 Ha: 2 (26.4 x 12.9)3 (14.4 x 12.9)ER
Ice Capable
1 oil engine driving 1 FP propeller
Total Power: 6,680kW (9,082hp) 14.0kn
Sulzer 4RTA58
1 x 2 Stroke 4 Cy. 580 x 1700 6680kW (9082bhp)
H Cegielski Poznan SA-Poland
AuxGen: 3 x 504kW 380V 50Hz a.c
Fuel: 130.0 (d.f.) (Heating Coils) 1044.0 (r.f.) 24.5pd

8418746 A8DQ4
-
ZIEMIA LODZKA
ex Lake Champlain *-2003*
ex Ziemia Lodzka *-1992*
Ziemia One Ltd
Polska Zegluga Morska PP (POLSTEAM)
SatCom: Inmarsat A 1554152
Monrovia *Liberia*
MMSI: 636012139
Official number: 12139
17,458 9,406 26,264 T/cm 36.7
Class: NV (PR)
1992-04 Turkiye Gemi Sanayii A.S. — Pendik Yd No: 015
Loa 179.97 (BB) Br ex - Dght 9.850
Lbp 171.20 Br md 23.10 Dpth 13.90
Welded, 1 dk
(A21A2BC) Bulk Carrier
Grain: 34,929; Bale: 34,022
Compartments: 5 Ho, ER
5 Ha: 2 (26.4 x 12.9)3 (14.4 x 12.9)ER
Ice Capable
1 oil engine driving 1 FP propeller
Total Power: 6,680kW (9,082hp) 14.0kn
Sulzer 4RTA58
1 x 2 Stroke 4 Cy. 580 x 1700 6680kW (9082bhp)
H Cegielski Poznan SA-Poland
AuxGen: 3 x 504kW 380V 50Hz a.c
Fuel: 130.0 (d.f.) (Heating Coils) 1044.0 (r.f.) 24.5pd

8858489 9A2190
-
ZIGLJEN
ex Olof Tratalja *-1992* *ex* Dobeln *-1990*
ex Farja 62/287 *-1979*
Viadukt doo
Jadrolinija
Rijeka *Croatia*
Official number: 2T-537
250 79 -
Class: CS
1971-08 AB Asi-Verken — Amal Yd No: 97
Loa 54.02 Br ex 9.02 Dght 2.800
Lbp - Br md - Dpth -
Welded, 1 dk
(A36A2PR) Passenger/Ro-Ro Ship (Vehicles)
Passengers: unberthed: 200
Cars: 44
2 oil engines driving 2 FP propellers , 1 aft
Total Power: 714kW (970hp)
Polar SF13RS-F
2 x 4 Stroke 3 Cy. 250 x 300 each-357kW (485bhp)
AB NOHAB-Sweden

8921274
-
-
ZIKRON DEFENDER
ex Shoryu *-2010*
C & I Leasing Plc
-
Lagos *Nigeria*
100 - 19
Class: (BV) (NK)
1990-06 Mitsubishi Heavy Industries Ltd. — Nagasaki Yd No: 2040
Loa 35.00 Br ex - Dght 1.301
Lbp 32.10 Br md 6.10 Dpth 3.12
Welded, 1 dk
(B34H2SQ) Patrol Vessel
2 oil engines with clutches & sr reverse geared to sc. shafts driving 2 FP propellers
Total Power: 2,000kW (2,720hp) 20.0kn
Mitsubishi S16N-TK
2 x Vee 4 Stroke 16 Cy. 160 x 180 each-1000kW (1360bhp)
Mitsubishi Heavy Industries Ltd-Japan
Fuel: 8.0 (d.f.)

8918734 PBFB
-
ZILLERTAL
Rufinia Beheer BV
Flagship Management Co BV
Delfzijl *Netherlands*
MMSI: 246230000
Official number: 40517
5,602 2,363 7,177
Class: GL
1996-12 OAO Sudostroitelnyy Zavod "Severnaya Verf" — St.-Peterburg (Hull launched by) Yd No: 435
1996-12 Barthels & Lueders — Hamburg (Hull completed by)
Loa 109.70 Br ex - Dght 7.217
Lbp 100.00 Br md 17.80 Dpth 9.00
Welded
(A31A2GX) General Cargo Ship
Double Hull
Grain: 7,760
TEU 342 incl 20 ref C
Compartments: 3 Ho, ER
3 Ha: (24.5 x 12.5) (25.0 x 12.5)ER (12.5 x 12.5)
Ice Capable
1 oil engine driving 1 FP propeller
Total Power: 3,360kW (4,568hp) 12.0kn
B&W 6DKRN35/105
1 x 2 Stroke 6 Cy. 350 x 1050 3360kW (4568bhp)
AO Bryanskiy MashinostroitelnyyZavod (BMZ)-Bryansk
AuxGen: 3 x 320kW 380/220V a.c
Thrusters: 1 Tunnel thruster (f)

9199206 HPIG
-
ZILOS
ex Los Vilos *-2013*
Seaside Maritime Inc
Karlog Shipping Co Ltd
Panama *Panama*
MMSI: 370205000
Official number: 45218PEXT
25,543 15,898 46,541 T/cm 49.8
Class: NK
2000-07 Oshima Shipbuilding Co Ltd — Saikai NS Yd No: 10269
Loa 183.00 (BB) Br ex - Dght 11.808
Lbp 174.30 Br md 30.95 Dpth 16.40
Welded, 1 dk
(A21A2BC) Bulk Carrier
Grain: 58,209; Bale: 57,083
Compartments: 5 Ho, ER
5 Ha: 3 (19.8 x 15.6)2 (17.1 x 15.6)ER
Cranes: 4x30t
1 oil engine driving 1 FP propeller
Total Power: 7,488kW (10,181hp) 14.3kn
Sulzer 6RTA48T
1 x 2 Stroke 6 Cy. 480 x 2000 7488kW (10181bhp)
Diesel United Ltd.-Aioi
Fuel: 1920.0

8878142
-
-
ZILVERMEEUW
-
-
193 57 -
1981 Troost Staal en Service B.V. — Vlissingen Yd No: 07021
Loa 37.58 Br ex - Dght 1.380
Lbp - Br md 9.01 Dpth -
Welded, 1 dk
(B11B2FV) Fishing Vessel
2 oil engines reduction geared to sc. shafts driving 2 FP propellers
Total Power: 590kW (802hp)
Volvo Penta TAMD122A
2 x 4 Stroke 6 Cy. 130 x 150 each-295kW (401bhp)
AB Volvo Penta-Sweden

7907594
-
-
ZILVERMEEUW
ex Peter *-2000* *ex* Grietje Hendrikje *-1989*
-
-
349 104
1980-03 Tille Scheepsbouw B.V. — Kootstertille (Hull) Yd No: 213
1980-03 B.V. Scheepswerf Maaskant — Stellendam Yd No: 383
Loa 39.86 Br ex - Dght -
Lbp 35.62 Br md 8.01 Dpth 4.58
Welded, 1 dk
(B11A2FT) Trawler
1 oil engine reverse reduction geared to sc. shaft driving 1 FP propeller
Total Power: 1,177kW (1,600hp)
Deutz SBV8M628
1 x 4 Stroke 8 Cy. 240 x 280 1177kW (1600bhp)
Kloeckner Humboldt Deutz AG-West Germany
Thrusters: 1 Thwart. FP thruster (f)

7936777 *OPA0* 0 15
ZILVERMEEUW
ex Stephanie -1997 ex De Kottens -1988
Zeearend BVBA
-
Ostend *Belgium*
Official number: 01 00180 1996
236 70 -
1975 **Scheepswerven West-Vlaamse N.V. — Oostkamp**
Loa 34.80 Br ex - Dght -
Lbp - Br md 7.68 Dpth -
Welded, 1 dk
(B11B2FV) Fishing Vessel
1 oil engine driving 1 FP propeller
Total Power: 883kW (1,201hp)
A.B.C.
1 x 4 Stroke 883kW (1201bhp) (new engine 1985)
Anglo Belgian Corp NV (ABC)-Belgium

9471226 *V7VD5* -
ZIM ALABAMA
Marown Navigation Ltd
Polaris Shipmanagement Co Ltd
SatCom: Inmarsat C 453835869
Majuro *Marshall Islands*
MMSI: 538004094
Official number: 4094
40,542 23,747 50,157
Class: GL
2010-12 **Jiangsu Newyangzi Shipbuilding Co Ltd — Jingjiang JS** Yd No: YZJ2007-789C
Loa 261.08 (BB) Br ex - Dght 12.600
Lbp 247.09 Br md 32.25 Dpth 19.30
Welded, 1 dk
(A33A2CC) Container Ship (Fully Cellular)
TEU 4250 incl 400 ref C.
1 oil engine driving 1 FP propeller
Total Power: 36,540kW (49,680hp) 24.5k
MAN-B&W 8K90MC-
1 x 2 Stroke 8 Cy. 900 x 2300 36540kW (49680bhp)
STX Engine Co Ltd-South Korea
AuxGen: 4 x 1700kW 450V a.c
Thrusters: 1 Tunnel thruster (f)

9398448 *A8SI6* -
ZIM ANTWERP
Pelican Maritime (S346) Co Ltd
Zim Integrated Shipping Services Ltd
SatCom: Inmarsat C 463705646
Monrovia *Liberia*
MMSI: 636014220
Official number: 14220
114,044 58,784 116,294
Class: LR
✠ **100A1** SS 12/2009
container ship
ShipRight (SDA, FDA, CM)
*IWS
LI
EP (B)
✠ **LMC** **UMS**
Eq.Ltr: D*;
Cable: 770.0/114.0 U3 (a)
2009-12 **Hyundai Samho Heavy Industries Co Ltd — Samho** Yd No: S346
Loa 349.00 (BB) Br ex 45.73 Dght 15.000
Lbp 334.00 Br md 45.60 Dpth 27.30
Welded, 1 dk
(A33A2CC) Container Ship (Fully Cellular)
TEU 10062 C Ho 4878 TEU C Dk 5184 TEU incl 800 ref C
Compartments: 10 Cell Ho, ER
10 Ha: ER
1 oil engine driving 1 FP propeller
Total Power: 68,640kW (93,323hp) 24.8k
MAN-B&W 12K98M
1 x 2 Stroke 12 Cy. 980 x 2660 68640kW (93323bhp)
Hyundai Heavy Industries Co Ltd-South Korea
AuxGen: 3 x 2195kW 6600V 60Hz a.c, 2 x 2800kW 6600V 60Hz a.c
Boilers: e (ex.g.) 10.6kgf/cm² (10.4bar), WTAuxB (o.f.) 8.3kgf/cm² (8.1bar)
Thrusters: 1 Thwart. CP thruster (f)

9113654 *A8OZ2* -
ZIM ASIA
Zim Asia Maritime Co Sarl
Zim Integrated Shipping Services Ltd
Monrovia *Liberia*
MMSI: 636091516
Official number: 91516
41,507 16,353 45,850 T/cm 69.8
Class: LR
✠ **100A1** SS 06/2011
container ship
*IWS
LI
✠ **LMC** **UMS**
Eq.Ltr: R†; Cable: 687.5/84.0 U3
1996-06 **Howaldtswerke-Deutsche Werft AG (HDW) — Kiel** Yd No: 322
Loa 253.70 (BB) Br ex 32.29 Dght 11.780
Lbp 241.50 Br md 32.20 Dpth 19.20
Welded, 1 dk
(A33A2CC) Container Ship (Fully Cellular)
TEU 3429 C Ho 1560 TEU C Dk 1869 TEU incl 165 ref C.
Compartments: ER, 7 Cell Ho
14 Ha: ER
1 oil engine driving 1 FP propeller
Total Power: 28,350kW (38,545hp) 21.7kn
Sulzer 7RTA84C
1 x 2 Stroke 7 Cy. 840 x 2400 28350kW (38545bhp)
Dieselmotorenwerk Vulkan GmbH-Rostock
AuxGen: 1 x 1650kW 450V 60Hz a.c, 3 x 1240kW 450V 60Hz a.c
Boilers: AuxB (Comp) 10.2kgf/cm² (10.0bar)
Thrusters: 1 Thwart. FP thruster (f)
Fuel: 617.0 (d.f.) 5617.0 (r.f.) 90.0pd

9113678 *A8OY8* -
ZIM ATLANTIC
Zim Atlantic Maritime Co Sarl
Zim Integrated Shipping Services Ltd
Monrovia *Liberia*
MMSI: 636091514
Official number: 91514
41,507 16,353 45,850 T/cm 69.8
Class: LR
✠ **100A1** SS 12/2011
container ship
*IWS
✠ **LMC** **UMS**
Eq.Ltr: R†; Cable: 687.5/84.0 U3
1996-12 **Howaldtswerke-Deutsche Werft AG (HDW) — Kiel** Yd No: 324
Loa 253.70 (BB) Br ex 32.29 Dght 11.780
Lbp 241.50 Br md 32.20 Dpth 19.20
Welded, 1 dk
(A33A2CC) Container Ship (Fully Cellular)
TEU 3429 C Ho 1560 TEU C Dk 1869 TEU incl 165 ref C.
Compartments: ER, 7 Cell Ho
14 Ha: ER
1 oil engine driving 1 FP propeller
Total Power: 28,350kW (38,545hp) 21.0kn
Sulzer 7RTA84C
1 x 2 Stroke 7 Cy. 840 x 2400 28350kW (38545bhp)
Dieselmotorenwerk Vulkan GmbH-Rostock
AuxGen: 1 x 1650kW 450V 60Hz a.c, 3 x 1240kW 450V 60Hz a.c
Boilers: AuxB (Comp) 10.2kgf/cm² (10.0bar)
Thrusters: 1 Thwart. FP thruster (f)
Fuel: 617.0 (d.f.) 5617.0 (r.f.) 90.0pd

9280835 *4XIS* -
ZIM BARCELONA
Zim Barcelona Maritime Co Sarl
Zim Integrated Shipping Services Ltd
Haifa *Israel*
MMSI: 428010000
53,453 33,604 62,740 T/cm 82.5
Class: LR
✠ **100A1** SS 04/2009
container ship
*IWS
LI
ShipRight (SDA, FDA, CM)
✠ **LMC** **UMS**
Eq.Ltr: T†;
Cable: 715.0/87.0 U3 (a)
2004-04 **Hyundai Heavy Industries Co Ltd — Ulsan** Yd No: 1526
Loa 294.10 (BB) Br ex 32.25 Dght 13.500
Lbp 283.20 Br md 32.20 Dpth 21.80
Welded, 1 dk
(A33A2CC) Container Ship (Fully Cellular)
TEU 4814 C Ho 2301 TEU C Dk 2513 TEU incl 330 ref C.
Compartments: ER, 6 Cell Ho
17 Ha: (12.6 x 12.9) (12.6 x 23.0)ER 14 (12.6 x 20.2) (12.6 x 10.0)
1 oil engine driving 1 FP propeller
Total Power: 41,079kW (55,851hp) 24.0kn
B&W 9K90MC-C
1 x 2 Stroke 9 Cy. 900 x 2300 41079kW (55851bhp)
Hyundai Heavy Industries Co Ltd-South Korea
AuxGen: 3 x 1990kW 450V 60Hz a.c
Boilers: e (ex.g.) 9.7kgf/cm² (9.5bar), AuxB (o.f.) 8.0kgf/cm² (7.8bar)
Thrusters: 1 Thwart. FP thruster (f)
Fuel: 330.5 (d.f.) 6366.4 (r.f.)

9289544 *A8FU7* -
ZIM BEIJING
completed as E. R. Beijing -2005
ms 'ER Beijing' Schiffahrts GmbH & Co KG
ER Schiffahrt GmbH & Cie KG
Monrovia *Liberia*
MMSI: 636090807
Official number: 90807
54,626 34,983 66,939
Class: GL
2005-01 **Hyundai Samho Heavy Industries Co Ltd — Samho** Yd No: S220
Loa 294.15 (BB) Br ex - Dght 13.650
Lbp 283.20 Br md 32.20 Dpth 22.10
Welded, 1 dk
(A33A2CC) Container Ship (Fully Cellular)
TEU 5075 C Ho 2295 TEU C Dk 2780 TEU incl 450 ref C.
1 oil engine driving 1 FP propeller
Total Power: 45,780kW (62,242hp) 24.5kn
Sulzer 8RTA96C
1 x 2 Stroke 8 Cy. 960 x 2500 45780kW (62242bhp)
Hyundai Heavy Industries Co Ltd-South Korea
AuxGen: 4 x 1800kW 440/220V 60Hz a.c
Thrusters: 1 Thwart. CP thruster (f)

9231793 *D5BC6* -
ZIM CALIFORNIA
Halton Maritime SA
XT Management Ltd
Monrovia *Liberia*
MMSI: 636015497
Official number: 15497
53,453 33,604 66,686 T/cm 82.5
Class: AB
2002-07 **Hyundai Heavy Industries Co Ltd — Ulsan** Yd No: 1387
Loa 294.00 (BB) Br ex - Dght 13.500
Lbp - Br md 32.20 Dpth 21.80
Welded, 1 dk
(A33A2CC) Container Ship (Fully Cellular)
TEU 4839 C Ho 2301 TEU C Dk 2538 TEU incl 350 ref C.
1 oil engine driving 1 FP propeller
Total Power: 41,040kW (55,798hp) 24.0kn
B&W 9K90MC-C
1 x 2 Stroke 9 Cy. 900 x 2300 41040kW (55798bhp)
Hyundai Heavy Industries Co Ltd-South Korea
AuxGen: 3 x 1990kW a.c
Thrusters: 1 Thwart. FP thruster (f)

9398424 *A8SI9* -
ZIM CHICAGO
Flamingo Navigation (S352) Co Ltd
Zim Integrated Shipping Services Ltd
SatCom: Inmarsat C 463706748
Monrovia *Liberia*
MMSI: 636014223
Official number: 14223
91,158 60,300 108,574
Class: LR
✠ **100A1** SS 07/2010
container ship
ShipRight (SDA, FDA, CM)
*IWS
LI
EP (B)
✠ **LMC** **UMS**
Eq.Ltr: B*;
Cable: 742.5/107.0 U3 (a)
2010-07 **Hyundai Samho Heavy Industries Co Ltd — Samho** Yd No: S352
Loa 334.00 (BB) Br ex 42.92 Dght 14.500
Lbp 319.00 Br md 42.80 Dpth 24.80
Welded, 1 dk
(A33A2CC) Container Ship (Fully Cellular)
TEU 8200 C Ho 3835 TEU C Dk 4365 TEU incl 700 ref C
Compartments: 9 Cell Ho, ER
1 oil engine driving 1 FP propeller
Total Power: 68,640kW (93,323hp) 25.6kn
MAN-B&W 12K98MC
1 x 2 Stroke 12 Cy. 980 x 2660 68640kW (93323bhp)
Hyundai Heavy Industries Co Ltd-South Korea
AuxGen: 4 x 2800kW 6600V 60Hz a.c
Boilers: e (ex.g.) 10.5kgf/cm² (10.3bar), WTAuxB (o.f.) 8.1kgf/cm² (7.9bar)
Thrusters: 1 Thwart. CP thruster (f)

9139921 *A8OZ3* -
ZIM CHINA
Zim China Maritime Co Sarl
Zim Integrated Shipping Services Ltd
Monrovia *Liberia*
MMSI: 636091517
Official number: 91517
41,507 16,353 45,850 T/cm 69.8
Class: LR
✠ **100A1** SS 11/2012
container ship
*IWS
LI
✠ **LMC** **UMS**
Eq.Ltr: R†; Cable: 687.5/84.0 U3
1997-11 **Howaldtswerke-Deutsche Werft AG (HDW) — Kiel** Yd No: 331
Loa 253.70 (BB) Br ex 32.29 Dght 11.780
Lbp 241.50 Br md 32.20 Dpth 19.20
Welded, 1 dk
(A33A2CC) Container Ship (Fully Cellular)
TEU 3429 C Ho 1560 TEU C Dk 1869 TEU incl 175 ref C.
Compartments: ER, 7 Cell Ho
14 Ha: ER
1 oil engine driving 1 FP propeller
Total Power: 28,350kW (38,545hp) 21.7kn
Sulzer 7RTA84C
1 x 2 Stroke 7 Cy. 840 x 2400 28350kW (38545bhp)
Dieselmotorenwerk Vulkan GmbH-Rostock
AuxGen: 1 x 1650kW 450V 60Hz a.c, 3 x 1240kW 450V 60Hz a.c
Boilers: AuxB (Comp) 10.2kgf/cm² (10.0bar)
Thrusters: 1 Thwart. FP thruster (f)

9456977 *A8UC5* -
ZIM COLOMBO
launched as Atlas J -2009
Schifffahrtsgesellschaft 'Merkur Archipelago' mbH & Co KG
Jungerhans Maritime Services GmbH & Co KG
Monrovia *Liberia*
MMSI: 636091883
Official number: 91883
41,331 23,882 51,534
Class: GL
2009-11 **Hyundai Samho Heavy Industries Co Ltd — Samho** Yd No: S415
Loa 262.07 (BB) Br ex 32.25 Dght 12.500
Lbp 248.00 Br md 32.20 Dpth 19.50
Welded, 1 dk
(A33A2CC) Container Ship (Fully Cellular)
TEU 4255 incl 600 ref C
1 oil engine driving 1 FP propeller
Total Power: 36,160kW (49,163hp) 24.4kn
Wartsila 8RTA82C
1 x 2 Stroke 8 Cy. 820 x 2646 36160kW (49163bhp)
Hyundai Heavy Industries Co Ltd-South Korea
AuxGen: 2 x 2405kW 450V a.c, 2 x 1803kW 450V a.c
Thrusters: 1 Tunnel thruster (f)

9471202 *4XFB* -
ZIM CONSTANZA
Tacton Shipping Inc
XT Management Ltd
Haifa *Israel*
MMSI: 428042000
Official number: 14785
40,542 23,747 50,106
Class: GL
2010-08 **Jiangsu Newyangzi Shipbuilding Co Ltd — Jingjiang JS** Yd No: YZJ2007-787C
Loa 261.09 (BB) Br ex - Dght 12.600
Lbp 247.09 Br md 32.25 Dpth 19.30
Welded, 1 dk
(A33A2CC) Container Ship (Fully Cellular)
TEU 4250 incl 400 ref C.
1 oil engine driving 1 FP propeller
Total Power: 36,540kW (49,680hp) 24.5kn
MAN-B&W 8K90MC-C
1 x 2 Stroke 8 Cy. 900 x 2300 36540kW (49680bhp)
STX Engine Co Ltd-South Korea
AuxGen: 4 x 1700kW 450V a.c
Thrusters: 1 Tunnel thruster (f)

9398436 *A8SI4* -
ZIM DJIBOUTI
Pelican Maritime (S345) Co Ltd
Zim Integrated Shipping Services Ltd
SatCom: Inmarsat C 463705162
Monrovia *Liberia*
MMSI: 636014218
Official number: 14218
114,044 58,784 116,440
Class: LR
✠ **100A1** SS 07/2009
container ship
ShipRight (SDA, FDA, CM)
*IWS
LI
EP (B)
✠ **LMC** **UMS**
Eq.Ltr: D*;
Cable: 770.0/114.0 U3 (a)
2009-07 **Hyundai Samho Heavy Industries Co Ltd — Samho** Yd No: S345
Loa 349.00 (BB) Br ex 45.73 Dght 15.000
Lbp 334.00 Br md 45.60 Dpth 27.30
Welded, 1 dk
(A33A2CC) Container Ship (Fully Cellular)
TEU 10062 C Ho 4878 TEU C Dk 5184 TEU incl 800 ref C
Compartments: 10 Cell Ho, ER
10 Ha: ER
1 oil engine driving 1 FP propeller
Total Power: 68,640kW (93,323hp) 24.8kn
MAN-B&W 12K98MC
1 x 2 Stroke 12 Cy. 980 x 2660 68640kW (93323bhp)
Hyundai Heavy Industries Co Ltd-South Korea
AuxGen: 3 x 2195kW 6600V 60Hz a.c, 2 x 2800kW 6600V 60Hz a.c
Boilers: e (ex.g.) 10.6kgf/cm² (10.4bar), WTAuxB (o.f.) 8.2kgf/cm² (8.0bar)
Thrusters: 1 Thwart. CP thruster (f)

113692 8OY6	**ZIM EUROPA** **Zim Europa Maritime Co Sarl** Zim Integrated Shipping Services Ltd *Monrovia* *Liberia* MMSI: 636091512 Official number: 91512	**41,507** 16,353 45,850 T/cm 69.8	Class: LR ✠ **100A1** SS 04/2012 container ship *IWS LI ✠ **LMC** **UMS** Eq.Ltr: R†; Cable: 687.5/84.0 U3	**1997-04 Howaldtswerke-Deutsche Werft AG (HDW) — Kiel** Yd No: 326 Loa 253.70 (BB) Br ex 32.29 Dght 11.780 Lbp 241.50 Br md 32.20 Dpth 19.20 Welded, 1 dk	**(A33A2CC) Container Ship (Fully Cellular)** TEU 3429 C Ho 1560 TEU C Dk 1869 TEU incl 165 ref C. Compartments: ER, 7 Cell Ho 14 Ha: ER	**1 oil engine** driving 1 FP propeller Total Power: 28,350kW (38,545hp) 21.7kn Sulzer 7RTA84C 1 x 2 Stroke 7 Cy. 840 x 2400 28350kW (38545bhp) Dieselmotorenwerk Vulkan GmbH-Rostock AuxGen: 1 x 1650kW 450V 60Hz a.c, 3 x 1240kW 450V 60Hz a.c Boilers: AuxB (Comp) 10.2kgf/cm² (10.0bar) Thrusters: 1 Thwart. FP thruster (f)
318187 8KW9	**ZIM GENOVA** **Derone Maritime Ltd** XT Management Ltd *Monrovia* *Liberia* MMSI: 636013143 Official number: 13143	**39,906** 24,504 50,532	Class: LR ✠ **100A1** SS 04/2012 container ship **ShipRight** (SDA, FDA, CM) *IWS LI ✠ **LMC** **UMS** Eq.Ltr: S†; Cable: 695.5/87.0 U3 (a)	**2007-04 Dalian Shipbuilding Industry Co Ltd — Dalian LN (No 2 Yard)** Yd No: C4250-11 Loa 260.56 (BB) Br ex 32.31 Dght 12.600 Lbp 245.98 Br md 32.26 Dpth 19.30 Welded, 1 dk	**(A33A2CC) Container Ship (Fully Cellular)** TEU 3853 C Ho 1514 TEU C Dk 2339 TEU incl 400 ref C. Compartments: 7 Cell Ho, ER	**1 oil engine** driving 1 FP propeller Total Power: 36,560kW (49,707hp) 24.5kn MAN-B&W 8K90MC-C 1 x 2 Stroke 8 Cy. 900 x 2300 36560kW (49707bhp) Doosan Engine Co Ltd-South Korea AuxGen: 4 x 1700kW 450V 60Hz a.c Boilers: AuxB (Comp) 11.2kgf/cm² (11.0bar) Thrusters: 1 Thwart. CP thruster (f)
288904 XIM	**ZIM HAIFA** **Zim Haifa Maritime Co Sarl** Zim Integrated Shipping Services Ltd SatCom: Inmarsat C 442801110 *Haifa* *Israel* MMSI: 428011000	**54,626** 34,983 66,938	Class: AB (GL)	**2004-09 Hyundai Samho Heavy Industries Co Ltd — Samho** Yd No: S202 Loa 294.10 (BB) Br ex - Dght 13.500 Lbp 283.20 Br md 32.20 Dpth 22.10 Welded, 1 dk	**(A33A2CC) Container Ship (Fully Cellular)** TEU 5040 C Ho 2288 TEU C Dk 2752 TEU incl 450 ref C.	**1 oil engine** driving 1 FP propeller Total Power: 43,920kW (59,714hp) 24.5kn Sulzer 8RTA96C 1 x 2 Stroke 8 Cy. 960 x 2500 43920kW (59714bhp) Hyundai Heavy Industries Co Ltd-South Korea AuxGen: 4 x 1800kW 440/220V 60Hz a.c Thrusters: 1 Thwart. CP thruster (f)
139919 8OY9	**ZIM IBERIA** **Zim Iberia Maritime Co Sarl** Zim Integrated Shipping Services Ltd *Monrovia* *Liberia* MMSI: 636091515 Official number: 91515	**41,507** 16,353 46,850 T/cm 69.8	Class: LR ✠ **100A1** SS 09/2012 container ship *IWS LI ✠ **LMC** **UMS** Eq.Ltr: R†; Cable: 687.5/84.0 U3	**1997-09 Howaldtswerke-Deutsche Werft AG (HDW) — Kiel** Yd No: 330 Loa 253.70 (BB) Br ex 32.29 Dght 11.780 Lbp 241.50 Br md 32.20 Dpth 19.20 Welded, 1 dk	**(A33A2CC) Container Ship (Fully Cellular)** TEU 3429 C Ho 1560 TEU C Dk 1869 TEU incl 165 ref C. Compartments: ER, 7 Cell Ho 14 Ha: ER	**1 oil engine** driving 1 FP propeller Total Power: 28,350kW (38,545hp) 21.7kn Sulzer 7RTA84C 1 x 2 Stroke 7 Cy. 840 x 2400 28350kW (38545bhp) Dieselmotorenwerk Vulkan GmbH-Rostock AuxGen: 1 x 1650kW 450V 60Hz a.c, 3 x 1240kW 450V 60Hz a.c Boilers: AuxB (Comp) 10.2kgf/cm² (10.0bar) Thrusters: 1 Thwart. FP thruster (f)
322358 5EZ5	**ZIM INDIA** **Lombard Corporate Finance (December 3) Ltd** Eastern Pacific Shipping (UK) Ltd *Monrovia* *Liberia* MMSI: 636016203 Official number: 16203	**39,912** 24,504 50,608	Class: LR ✠ **100A1** SS 10/2007 container ship **ShipRight** (SDA, FDA, CM) *IWS LI ✠ **LMC** **UMS** Eq.Ltr: s†; Cable: 695.5/87.0 U3 (a)	**2007-10 Dalian Shipbuilding Industry Co Ltd — Dalian LN (No 1 Yard)** Yd No: C4250-17 Loa 260.64 (BB) Br ex 32.29 Dght 12.600 Lbp 246.07 Br md 32.24 Dpth 19.30 Welded, 1 dk	**(A33A2CC) Container Ship (Fully Cellular)** TEU 4250 C Ho 1586 TEU C Dk 2664 TEU incl 400 ref C. Compartments: ER, 7 Cell Ho 7 Ha: ER	**1 oil engine** driving 1 FP propeller Total Power: 36,560kW (49,707hp) 24.5kn MAN-B&W 8K90MC-C 1 x 2 Stroke 8 Cy. 900 x 2300 36560kW (49707bhp) Doosan Engine Co Ltd-South Korea AuxGen: 4 x 1700kW 450V 60Hz a.c Boilers: AuxB (Comp) 11.2kgf/cm² (11.0bar) Thrusters: 1 Thwart. FP thruster (f)
113680 8OY7	**ZIM JAMAICA** **Zim Jamaica Maritime Co Sarl** Zim Integrated Shipping Services Ltd *Monrovia* *Liberia* MMSI: 636091513 Official number: 91513	**41,507** 16,353 45,850 T/cm 69.8	Class: LR ✠ **100A1** SS 02/2012 container ship *IWS ✠ **LMC** **UMS** Eq.Ltr: R†; Cable: 687.5/84.0 U3	**1997-02 Howaldtswerke-Deutsche Werft AG (HDW) — Kiel** Yd No: 325 Loa 253.70 (BB) Br ex 32.29 Dght 11.780 Lbp 241.50 Br md 32.20 Dpth 19.20 Welded, 1 dk	**(A33A2CC) Container Ship (Fully Cellular)** TEU 3429 C Ho 1560 TEU C Dk 1869 TEU incl 165 ref C. Compartments: ER, 7 Cell Ho 14 Ha: ER	**1 oil engine** driving 1 FP propeller Total Power: 28,350kW (38,545hp) 21.7kn Sulzer 7RTA84C 1 x 2 Stroke 7 Cy. 840 x 2400 28350kW (38545bhp) Dieselmotorenwerk Vulkan GmbH-Rostock AuxGen: 1 x 1650kW 450V 60Hz a.c, 3 x 1240kW 450V 60Hz a.c Boilers: AuxB (Comp) 10.2kgf/cm² (10.0bar) Thrusters: 1 Thwart. FP thruster (f) Fuel: 617.0 (d.f.) 5617.0 (r.f.) 90.0pd
318175 8JX3	**ZIM LIVORNO** **Jakoby Maritime SA** XT Management Ltd *Monrovia* *Liberia* MMSI: 636013001 Official number: 13001	**39,906** 24,504 50,689	Class: LR ✠ **100A1** SS 11/2011 container ship **ShipRight** (SDA, FDA, CM) *IWS LI ✠ **LMC** **UMS** Eq.Ltr: s†; Cable: 695.5/87.0 U3 (a)	**2006-11 Dalian Shipbuilding Industry Co Ltd — Dalian LN (No 2 Yard)** Yd No: C4250-10 Loa 260.68 (BB) Br ex 32.30 Dght 12.980 Lbp 246.03 Br md 32.25 Dpth 19.30 Welded, 1 dk	**(A33A2CC) Container Ship (Fully Cellular)** TEU 3853 C Ho 1514 TEU C Dk 2339 TEU incl 400 ref C. Compartments: 7 Cell Ho, ER 7 Ha: ER	**1 oil engine** driving 1 FP propeller Total Power: 36,560kW (49,707hp) 24.5kn MAN-B&W 8K90MC-C 1 x 2 Stroke 8 Cy. 900 x 2300 36560kW (49707bhp) Doosan Engine Co Ltd-South Korea AuxGen: 4 x 1700kW 450V 60Hz a.c Boilers: AuxB (Comp) 11.2kgf/cm² (11.0bar) Thrusters: 1 Thwart. CP thruster (f)
332846 ANQ9	**ZIM LONDON** *ex APL London -2013* **Lombard Corporate Finance (December 3) Ltd** Zodiac Maritime Agencies Ltd SatCom: Inmarsat C 423590872 *London* *United Kingdom* MMSI: 235061354 Official number: 914211	**71,786** 26,914 72,982 T/cm 95.3	Class: NK	**2008-03 Koyo Dockyard Co Ltd — Mihara HS** Yd No: 2240 Loa 293.20 (BB) Br ex 40.10 Dght 14.021 Lbp 276.00 Br md 40.00 Dpth 24.30 Welded, 1 dk	**(A33A2CC) Container Ship (Fully Cellular)** TEU 6350 C Ho 2912 TEU C Dk 3438 TEU incl 500 ref C Compartments: ER, 8 Cell Ho 8 Ha: (12.8 x 30.5)ER 6 (12.8 x 35.6) (13.8 x 25.4)	**1 oil engine** driving 1 FP propeller Total Power: 62,920kW (85,546hp) 25.0kn MAN-B&W 11K98MC 1 x 2 Stroke 11 Cy. 980 x 2660 62920kW (85546bhp) Mitsui Engineering & Shipbuilding CLtd-Japan AuxGen: 5 x 2024kW a.c Thrusters: 1 Tunnel thruster (f) Fuel: 9210.0
398395 8SI3	**ZIM LOS ANGELES** **Flamingo Navigation (S349) Co Ltd** Zim Integrated Shipping Services Ltd SatCom: Inmarsat C 463705077 *Monrovia* *Liberia* MMSI: 636014217 Official number: 14217	**91,158** 60,300 108,574	Class: LR ✠ **100A1** SS 07/2009 container ship **ShipRight** (SDA, FDA, CM) *IWS LI EP (B) ✠ **LMC** **UMS** Eq.Ltr: B†; Cable: 742.5/107.0 U3 (a)	**2009-07 Hyundai Samho Heavy Industries Co Ltd — Samho** Yd No: S349 Loa 334.00 (BB) Br ex 42.92 Dght 14.500 Lbp 319.00 Br md 42.80 Dpth 24.80 Welded, 1 dk	**(A33A2CC) Container Ship (Fully Cellular)** TEU 8200 C Ho 3835 TEU C Dk 4365 TEU incl 700 ref C Compartments: 9 Cell Ho, ER 9 Ha: ER	**1 oil engine** driving 1 FP propeller Total Power: 68,640kW (93,323hp) 25.6kn MAN-B&W 12K98MC 1 x 2 Stroke 12 Cy. 980 x 2660 68640kW (93323bhp) Hyundai Heavy Industries Co Ltd-South Korea AuxGen: 4 x 2800kW 6600V 60Hz a.c Boilers: e (ex.g.) 10.7kgf/cm² (10.5bar), WTAuxB (o.f.) 8.2kgf/cm² (8.0bar) Thrusters: 1 Thwart. CP thruster (f)
403229 HA2029	**ZIM LUANDA** **Blacksea Marine Inc** Danaos Shipping Co Ltd SatCom: Inmarsat C 424983010 *Valletta* *Malta* MMSI: 249830000 Official number: 9403229	**40,030** 24,450 50,550 T/cm 70.4	Class: NV	**2009-06 Samsung Heavy Industries Co Ltd — Geoje** Yd No: 1699 Loa 260.03 (BB) Br ex 32.26 Dght 12.600 Lbp 244.77 Br md 32.25 Dpth 19.30 Welded, 1 dk	**(A33A2CC) Container Ship (Fully Cellular)** TEU 4253 incl 400 ref C	**1 oil engine** driving 1 FP propeller Total Power: 36,560kW (49,707hp) 23.3kn MAN-B&W 8K90MC-C 1 x 2 Stroke 8 Cy. 900 x 2300 36560kW (49707bhp) Doosan Engine Co Ltd-South Korea AuxGen: 4 x 1700kW a.c Thrusters: 1 Tunnel thruster (f)
231779 5BC5	**ZIM MEDITERRANEAN** **Liss Maritime Inc** XT Management Ltd *Monrovia* *Liberia* MMSI: 636015496 Official number: 15496	**53,453** 33,604 66,686 T/cm 82.5	Class: AB	**2002-02 Hyundai Heavy Industries Co Ltd — Ulsan** Yd No: 1385 Loa 294.10 (BB) Br ex - Dght 13.500 Lbp 283.20 Br md 32.20 Dpth 21.80 Welded, 1 dk	**(A33A2CC) Container Ship (Fully Cellular)** TEU 4839 C Ho 2301 TEU C Dk 2538 TEU incl 350 ref C.	**1 oil engine** driving 1 FP propeller Total Power: 41,110kW (55,893hp) 24.0kn B&W 9K90MC-C 1 x 2 Stroke 9 Cy. 900 x 2300 41110kW (55893bhp) Hyundai Heavy Industries Co Ltd-South Korea AuxGen: 3 x 1990kW a.c Thrusters: 1 Thwart. FP thruster (f)
389708 HTY9	**ZIM MONACO** **Continent Marine Inc** Danaos Shipping Co Ltd *Valletta* *Malta* MMSI: 249509000 Official number: 9389708	**40,030** 24,450 50,829 T/cm 70.4	Class: NV	**2009-01 Samsung Heavy Industries Co Ltd — Geoje** Yd No: 1673 Loa 260.01 (BB) Br ex 32.30 Dght 12.600 Lbp 244.78 Br md 32.26 Dpth 19.30 Welded, 1 dk	**(A33A2CC) Container Ship (Fully Cellular)** TEU 4253 incl 400 ref C. Compartments: 7 Cell Ho, ER	**1 oil engine** driving 1 FP propeller Total Power: 36,560kW (49,707hp) 23.3kn MAN-B&W 8K90MC-C 1 x 2 Stroke 8 Cy. 900 x 2300 36560kW (49707bhp) Doosan Engine Co Ltd-South Korea AuxGen: 4 x 1700kW a.c Thrusters: 1 Tunnel thruster (f)
401776 8TR3	**ZIM MOSKVA** **ms 'Benito' Schifffahrtsgesellschaft mbH & Co KG** Zim Integrated Shipping Services Ltd *Monrovia* *Liberia* MMSI: 636091850 Official number: 91850	**40,741** 24,178 52,315 T/cm 70.5	Class: GL	**2009-10 HHIC-Phil Inc — Subic** Yd No: 011 Loa 258.91 (BB) Br ex - Dght 12.600 Lbp 246.69 Br md 32.20 Dpth 19.30 Welded, 1 dk	**(A33A2CC) Container Ship (Fully Cellular)** TEU 4330 C Ho 1606 TEU C Dk 2724 TEU incl 326 ref C Compartments: 7 Cell Ho, ER 7 Ha: ER	**1 oil engine** driving 1 FP propeller Total Power: 36,560kW (49,707hp) 24.8kn MAN-B&W 8K90MC-C 1 x 2 Stroke 8 Cy. 900 x 2300 36560kW (49707bhp) Hyundai Heavy Industries Co Ltd-South Korea AuxGen: 3 x 1950kW 450V a.c Thrusters: 1 Tunnel thruster (f) Fuel: 252.0 (d.f.) 7877.0 (r.f.)

IMO / Call sign	Name / Owner / Manager	Tonnage	Class	Builder / Dimensions	Type / Capacity	Machinery	
9231810 *VRGA7* -	**ZIM NEW YORK** *ex* China Sea *-2006* *ex* Zim New York *-2004* **Angistri Corp** Shanghai Costamare Ship Management Co Ltd *Hong Kong* *Hong Kong* MMSI: 477634700 Official number: HK-2571	**53,453** 33,604 66,686 T/cm 82.5	Class: AB	**2002-09 Hyundai Heavy Industries Co Ltd — Ulsan** Yd No: 1389 Loa 294.00 (BB) Br ex - Dght 13.500 Lbp - Br md 32.20 Dpth 21.80 Welded, 1 dk	**(A33A2CC) Container Ship (Fully Cellular)** TEU 4992 C Ho 2301 TEU C Dk 2691 TEU incl 330 ref C.	**1 oil engine** driving 1 FP propeller Total Power: 41,107kW (55,889hp) B&W 1 x 2 Stroke 9 Cy. 900 x 2300 41107kW (55889bhp) Hyundai Heavy Industries Co Ltd-South Korea AuxGen: 3 x 1990kW 440/220V 60Hz a.c Thrusters: 1 Thwart. CP thruster (f)	24.0k 9K90MC-
9398400 *A8SI5* -	**ZIM NINGBO** **Flamingo Navigation (S350) Co Ltd** Zim Integrated Shipping Services Ltd SatCom: Inmarsat C 463704640 *Monrovia* *Liberia* MMSI: 636014219 Official number: 14219	**91,158** 60,300 108,427	Class: LR **✠100A1** SS 12/2009 container ship **ShipRight** (SDA, FDA, CM) *IWS LI EP (B) **✠LMC** **UMS** Eq.Ltr: B*; Cable: 742.5/107.0 U3 (a)	**2009-12 Hyundai Samho Heavy Industries Co Ltd — Samho** Yd No: S350 Loa 334.00 (BB) Br ex 42.92 Dght 14.500 Lbp 319.00 Br md 42.80 Dpth 24.80 Welded, 1 dk	**(A33A2CC) Container Ship (Fully Cellular)** TEU 8200 C Ho 3835 TEU C Dk 4365 TEU incl 700 ref C Compartments: 9 Cell Ho, ER 9 Ha: ER	**1 oil engine** driving 1 FP propeller Total Power: 68,640kW (93,323hp) MAN-B&W 1 x 2 Stroke 12 Cy. 980 x 2660 68640kW (93323bhp) Hyundai Heavy Industries Co Ltd-South Korea AuxGen: 4 x 2800kW 6600V 60Hz a.c Boilers: e (ex.g.) 10.5kgf/cm² (10.3bar), WTAuxB (o.f.) 8.1kgf/cm² (7.9bar) Thrusters: 1 Thwart. CP thruster (f)	25.6k 12K98M
9400136 *DFZB2* -	**ZIM ONTARIO** *launched as* Conti Ontario *-2009* **Conti 160 Container Schiffahrts GmbH & Co KG Nr 1** NSB Niederelbe Schiffahrtsgesellschaft mbH & Co KG *Hamburg* *Germany* MMSI: 218186000 Official number: 22127	**50,963** 30,224 63,350	Class: GL	**2009-04 Daewoo Shipbuilding & Marine Engineering Co Ltd — Geoje** Yd No: 4213 Loa 274.98 (BB) Br ex - Dght 13.500 Lbp 262.00 Br md 32.20 Dpth 21.50 Welded, 1 dk	**(A33A2CC) Container Ship (Fully Cellular)** TEU 4860 incl 500 ref C.	**1 oil engine** driving 1 FP propeller Total Power: 39,970kW (54,343hp) MAN-B&W 1 x 2 Stroke 7 Cy. 980 x 2400 39970kW (54343bhp) Doosan Engine Co Ltd-South Korea AuxGen: 4 x 1950kW 450V a.c Thrusters: 1 Tunnel thruster (f)	24.0k 7K98MC-
9113666 *A8OZ4* -	**ZIM PACIFIC** **Zim Pacific Maritime Co Sarl** Zim Integrated Shipping Services Ltd *Monrovia* *Liberia* MMSI: 636091518 Official number: 91519	**41,507** 16,353 45,850 T/cm 69.8	Class: LR **✠100A1** SS 08/2011 container ship *IWS LI **✠LMC** **UMS** Eq.Ltr: R†; Cable: 687.5/84.0 U3	**1996-08 Howaldtswerke-Deutsche Werft AG (HDW) — Kiel** Yd No: 323 Loa 253.70 (BB) Br ex 32.29 Dght 11.780 Lbp 241.50 Br md 32.20 Dpth 19.20 Welded, 1 dk	**(A33A2CC) Container Ship (Fully Cellular)** TEU 3429 C Ho 1560 TEU C Dk 1869 TEU incl 165 ref C. Compartments: ER, 7 Cell Ho 14 Ha: ER	**1 oil engine** driving 1 FP propeller Total Power: 28,350kW (38,545hp) Sulzer 1 x 2 Stroke 7 Cy. 840 x 2400 28350kW (38545bhp) Dieselmotorenwerk Vulkan GmbH-Rostock AuxGen: 1 x 1650kW 450V 60Hz a.c, 3 x 1240kW 450V 60Hz a.c Boilers: AuxB (Comp) 10.2kgf/cm² (10.0bar) Thrusters: 1 Thwart. FP thruster (f) Fuel: 617.0 (d.f.) 5617.0 (r.f.) 90.0pd	21.7k 7RTA84
9231781 *VSWW5* -	**ZIM PANAMA** **Assetfinance December (W) Ltd** Zodiac Maritime Agencies Ltd *London* *United Kingdom* MMSI: 235474000 Official number: 905552	**53,453** 33,604 66,686 T/cm 82.5	Class: LR (AB) **100A1** SS 04/2012 container ship *IWS LI **LMC** **UMS** Eq.Ltr: U; Cable: 715.0/87.0	**2002-04 Hyundai Heavy Industries Co Ltd — Ulsan** Yd No: 1386 Loa 294.12 (BB) Br ex - Dght 13.500 Lbp 283.20 Br md 32.20 Dpth 21.80 Welded, 1 dk	**(A33A2CC) Container Ship (Fully Cellular)** TEU 4992 C Ho 2301 TEU C Dk 2691 TEU incl 350 ref C. Compartments: ER, 6 Cell Ho 6 Ha: ER	**1 oil engine** driving 1 FP propeller Total Power: 41,040kW (55,798hp) B&W 1 x 2 Stroke 9 Cy. 900 x 2300 41040kW (55798bhp) Hyundai Heavy Industries Co Ltd-South Korea AuxGen: 3 x 1990kW 440/220V 60Hz a.c Thrusters: 1 Thwart. CP thruster (f)	24.0k 9K90MC-
9280847 *VRGA5* -	**ZIM PIRAEUS** *ex* Yangtze Star *-2006* *ex* Zim Piraeus *-2005* **Alexia Transport Corp** Shanghai Costamare Ship Management Co Ltd *Hong Kong* *Hong Kong* MMSI: 477634800 Official number: HK-2569	**53,453** 33,604 62,740 T/cm 82.5	Class: LR **✠100A1** SS 05/2009 container ship *IWS LI **ShipRight** (SDA, FDA, CM) **✠LMC** **UMS** Eq.Ltr: T†; Cable: 715.0/87.0 U3 (a)	**2004-05 Hyundai Heavy Industries Co Ltd — Ulsan** Yd No: 1527 Loa 294.10 (BB) Br ex 32.25 Dght 13.500 Lbp 283.20 Br md 32.20 Dpth 21.80 Welded, 1 dk	**(A33A2CC) Container Ship (Fully Cellular)** TEU 4814 C Ho 2301 TEU C Dk 2513 TEU incl 330 ref C Compartments: ER, 6 Cell Ho	**1 oil engine** driving 1 FP propeller Total Power: 41,079kW (55,851hp) B&W 1 x 2 Stroke 9 Cy. 900 x 2300 41079kW (55851bhp) Hyundai Heavy Industries Co Ltd-South Korea AuxGen: 3 x 1990kW 450V 60Hz a.c Boilers: e (ex.g.) 9.3kgf/cm² (9.1bar), AuxB (o.f.) 8.0kgf/cm² (7.8bar) Thrusters: 1 Thwart. CP thruster (f)	24.0k 9K90MC-
9280861 *D5EZ6* -	**ZIM PUSAN** **Lombard Corporate Finance (December 3) Ltd** Eastern Pacific Shipping (UK) Ltd *Monrovia* *Liberia* MMSI: 636016204 Official number: 16204	**53,453** 33,604 62,740 T/cm 82.5	Class: LR **✠100A1** SS 07/2009 container ship *IWS LI **ShipRight** (SDA, FDA, CM) **✠LMC** **UMS** Eq.Ltr: T†; Cable: 715.0/87.0 U3 (a)	**2004-07 Hyundai Heavy Industries Co Ltd — Ulsan** Yd No: 1529 Loa 294.10 (BB) Br ex 32.25 Dght 13.500 Lbp 283.20 Br md 32.20 Dpth 21.80 Welded, 1 dk	**(A33A2CC) Container Ship (Fully Cellular)** TEU 4992 C Ho 2301 TEU C Dk 2691 TEU incl 330 ref C. Compartments: ER, 7 Cell Ho 7 Ha: ER	**1 oil engine** driving 1 FP propeller Total Power: 41,079kW (55,851hp) B&W 1 x 2 Stroke 9 Cy. 900 x 2300 41079kW (55851bhp) Hyundai Heavy Industries Co Ltd-South Korea AuxGen: 3 x 1990kW 450V 60Hz a.c Boilers: e (ex.g.) 10.1kgf/cm² (9.9bar), AuxB (o.f.) 8.1kgf/cm² (7.9bar) Thrusters: 1 Thwart. CP thruster (f)	24.0k 9K90MC-
9318163 *A8IZ2* -	**ZIM QINGDAO** **Konza Shipping Ltd** Zim Integrated Shipping Services Ltd *Monrovia* *Liberia* MMSI: 636012904 Official number: 12904	**39,906** 24,504 50,689	Class: LR **✠100A1** SS 08/2011 container ship *IWS LI **ShipRight** (SDA, FDA, CM) **✠LMC** **UMS** Eq.Ltr: S†; Cable: 695.5/87.0 U3 (a)	**2006-08 Dalian Shipbuilding Industry Co Ltd — Dalian LN (No 2 Yard)** Yd No: C4250-9 Loa 260.62 (BB) Br ex 32.29 Dght 12.626 Lbp 246.84 Br md 32.24 Dpth 19.30 Welded, 1 dk	**(A33A2CC) Container Ship (Fully Cellular)** TEU 3853 C Ho 1514 TEU C Dk 2339 TEU incl 400 ref C. Compartments: 7 Cell Ho, ER 7 Ha: ER	**1 oil engine** driving 1 FP propeller Total Power: 36,560kW (49,707hp) MAN-B&W 1 x 2 Stroke 8 Cy. 900 x 2300 36560kW (49707bhp) Doosan Engine Co Ltd-South Korea AuxGen: 4 x 1700kW 450V 60Hz a.c Boilers: AuxB (Comp) 11.2kgf/cm² (11.0bar) Thrusters: 1 Thwart. FP thruster (f)	24.5k 8K90MC-
9363376 *9HNV9* -	**ZIM RIO GRANDE** **Bayview Shipping Inc** Danaos Shipping Co Ltd *Valletta* *Malta* MMSI: 249253000 Official number: 9363376	**40,030** 24,450 50,842 T/cm 70.4	Class: NV	**2008-07 Samsung Heavy Industries Co Ltd — Geoje** Yd No: 1670 Loa 260.06 (BB) Br ex - Dght 12.600 Lbp 244.80 Br md 32.25 Dpth 19.30 Welded, 1 dk	**(A33A2CC) Container Ship (Fully Cellular)** TEU 4253 TEU incl 400 ref C. Compartments: ER, 7 Cell Ho 7 Ha: ER	**1 oil engine** driving 1 FP propeller Total Power: 36,560kW (49,707hp) MAN-B&W 1 x 2 Stroke 8 Cy. 900 x 2300 36560kW (49707bhp) Doosan Engine Co Ltd-South Korea AuxGen: 4 x 1700kW a.c Thrusters: 1 Tunnel thruster (f)	23.3k 8K90MC-
9398450 *A8SI8* -	**ZIM ROTTERDAM** **Pelican Maritime (S347) Co Ltd** Zim Integrated Shipping Services Ltd SatCom: Inmarsat C 463706139 *Monrovia* *Liberia* MMSI: 636014222 Official number: 14222	**114,044** 58,784 116,499	Class: LR **✠100A1** SS 03/2010 container ship **ShipRight** (SDA, FDA, CM) *IWS LI EP (B) **✠LMC** **UMS** Eq.Ltr: D*; Cable: 770.0/114.0 U3 (a)	**2010-03 Hyundai Samho Heavy Industries Co Ltd — Samho** Yd No: S347 Loa 349.00 (BB) Br ex 45.73 Dght 15.000 Lbp 334.00 Br md 45.60 Dpth 27.30 Welded, 1 dk	**(A33A2CC) Container Ship (Fully Cellular)** TEU 10062 C Ho 4878 TEU C Dk 5184 TEU incl 800 ref C Compartments: 10 Cell Ho, ER	**1 oil engine** driving 1 FP propeller Total Power: 68,640kW (93,323hp) MAN-B&W 1 x 2 Stroke 12 Cy. 980 x 2660 68640kW (93323bhp) Hyundai Heavy Industries Co Ltd-South Korea AuxGen: 2 x 2800kW 6600V 60Hz a.c, 3 x 2195kW 6600V 60Hz a.c Boilers: e (ex.g.) 10.7kgf/cm² (10.5bar), WTAuxB (o.f.) 8.3kgf/cm² (8.1bar) Thrusters: 1 Thwart. CP thruster (f)	24.8k 12K98M
9398412 *A8SI7* -	**ZIM SAN DIEGO** **Flamingo Navigation (S351) Co Ltd** Zim Integrated Shipping Services Ltd SatCom: Inmarsat C 463706144 *Monrovia* *Liberia* MMSI: 636014221 Official number: 14221	**91,158** 60,300 108,464	Class: LR **✠100A1** SS 01/2010 container ship **ShipRight** (SDA, FDA, CM) *IWS LI EP (B) **✠LMC** **UMS** Eq.Ltr: B*; Cable: 742.5/107.0 U3 (a)	**2010-01 Hyundai Samho Heavy Industries Co Ltd — Samho** Yd No: S351 Loa 334.00 (BB) Br ex 42.92 Dght 14.500 Lbp 319.00 Br md 42.80 Dpth 24.80 Welded, 1 dk	**(A33A2CC) Container Ship (Fully Cellular)** TEU 8200 C Ho 3835 TEU C Dk 4365 TEU incl 700 ref C Compartments: 9 Cell Ho, ER	**1 oil engine** driving 1 FP propeller Total Power: 68,640kW (93,323hp) MAN-B&W 1 x 2 Stroke 12 Cy. 980 x 2660 68640kW (93323bhp) Hyundai Heavy Industries Co Ltd-South Korea AuxGen: 4 x 2800kW 6600V 60Hz a.c Boilers: e (ex.g.) 10.7kgf/cm² (10.5bar), WTAuxB (o.f.) 8.2kgf/cm² (8.0bar) Thrusters: 1 Thwart. CP thruster (f)	25.6k 12K98M
9400112 *DFZA2* -	**ZIM SAN FRANCISCO** *launched as* Conti San Francisco *-2009* **Conti 159 Container Schiffahrts-GmbH & Co KG ms 'Conti San Francisco'** NSB Niederelbe Schiffahrtsgesellschaft mbH & Co KG SatCom: Inmarsat C 421816110 *Hamburg* *Germany* MMSI: 218161000 Official number: 22126	**50,963** 30,224 63,355	Class: GL	**2009-02 Daewoo Shipbuilding & Marine Engineering Co Ltd — Geoje** Yd No: 4212 Loa 274.98 (BB) Br ex - Dght 13.500 Lbp 262.00 Br md 32.20 Dpth 21.50 Welded, 1 dk	**(A33A2CC) Container Ship (Fully Cellular)** TEU 4860 incl 350 ref C.	**1 oil engine** driving 1 FP propeller Total Power: 39,970kW (54,343hp) MAN-B&W 1 x 2 Stroke 7 Cy. 980 x 2400 39970kW (54343bhp) Doosan Engine Co Ltd-South Korea AuxGen: 4 x 1950kW 450V a.c Thrusters: 1 Tunnel thruster (f)	24.0k 7K98MC-
9389681 *9HRL9* -	**ZIM SAO PAOLO** *launched as* Sao Paolo *-2008* **Channelview Marine Inc** Danaos Shipping Co Ltd *Valletta* *Malta* MMSI: 249414000 Official number: 9389681	**40,030** 24,450 50,818 T/cm 70.4	Class: NV	**2008-09 Samsung Heavy Industries Co Ltd — Geoje** Yd No: 1671 Loa 260.03 (BB) Br ex 32.30 Dght 12.600 Lbp 244.80 Br md 32.25 Dpth 19.30 Welded, 1 dk	**(A33A2CC) Container Ship (Fully Cellular)** TEU 4253 incl 400 ref C. Compartments: 7 Cell Ho, ER	**1 oil engine** driving 1 FP propeller Total Power: 36,560kW (49,707hp) MAN-B&W 1 x 2 Stroke 8 Cy. 900 x 2300 36560kW (49707bhp) Doosan Engine Co Ltd-South Korea AuxGen: 4 x 1700kW a.c Thrusters: 1 Tunnel thruster (f)	23.3k 8K90MC-

IMO / Call sign	Name / Owner / Manager	Tonnage	Class	Builder / Dimensions	Type / Cargo	Machinery
282974 8ER9	**ZIM SAVANNAH** *launched as* E. R. Savannah *-2004* **ms 'ER Savannah' Schiffahrts GmbH & Co KG** ER Schiffahrt GmbH & Cie KG *Monrovia* *Liberia* MMSI: 636090752 Official number: 90752	**54,626** 34,983 66,937	Class: GL	**2004**-08 **Hyundai Samho Heavy Industries Co Ltd — Samho** Yd No: S201 Loa 294.10 (BB) Br ex - Dght 13.650 Lbp 283.20 Br md 32.20 Dpth 22.10 Welded, 1 dk	**(A33A2CC) Container Ship (Fully Cellular)** TEU 5075 C Ho 2295 TEU C Dk 2780 TEU incl 450 ref C.	**1 oil engine** driving 1 FP propeller Total Power: 45,764kW (62,221hp) 24.5kn Sulzer 8RTA96C 1 x 2 Stroke 8 Cy. 960 x 2500 45764kW (62221bhp) Hyundai Heavy Industries Co Ltd-South Korea AuxGen: 4 x 1800kW 440/220V 60Hz a.c Thrusters: 1 Thwart. CP thruster (f)
9231822 VRGA6	**ZIM SHANGHAI** **Fastsailing Maritime Co** Shanghai Costamare Ship Management Co Ltd *Hong Kong* *Hong Kong* MMSI: 477634600 Official number: HK-2570	**53,453** 33,604 66,597 T/cm 82.5	Class: AB	**2002**-10 **Hyundai Heavy Industries Co Ltd — Ulsan** Yd No: 1390 Loa 294.12 (BB) Br ex - Dght 13.520 Lbp 283.20 Br md 32.20 Dpth 21.80 Welded, 1 dk	**(A33A2CC) Container Ship (Fully Cellular)** TEU 4992 C Ho 2301 TEU C Dk 2691 TEU incl 330 ref C.	**1 oil engine** driving 1 FP propeller Total Power: 41,107kW (55,889hp) 24.0kn B&W 9K90MC-C 1 x 2 Stroke 9 Cy. 900 x 2300 41107kW (55889bhp) Hyundai Heavy Industries Co Ltd-South Korea AuxGen: 3 x 1990kW 440/220V 60Hz a.c Thrusters: 1 Thwart. CP thruster (f)
9322322 A8KX2	**ZIM SHEKOU** **Lympic Maritime Ltd** XT Management Ltd SatCom: Inmarsat C 463700430 *Monrovia* *Liberia* MMSI: 636013144 Official number: 13144	**39,906** 24,504 50,629	Class: NK (LR) ✠ Classed LR until 7/9/09	**2007**-05 **Dalian Shipbuilding Industry Co Ltd — Dalian LN (No 1 Yard)** Yd No: C4250-14 Loa 260.01 (BB) Br ex 32.29 Dght 12.600 Lbp 246.02 Br md 32.24 Dpth 19.30 Welded, 1 dk	**(A33A2CC) Container Ship (Fully Cellular)** TEU 4250 C Ho 1586 TEU C Dk 2664 TEU incl 400 ref C. Compartments: 7 Cell Ho, ER	**1 oil engine** driving 1 FP propeller Total Power: 36,560kW (49,707hp) 24.5kn MAN-B&W 8K90MC-C 1 x 2 Stroke 8 Cy. 900 x 2300 36560kW (49707bhp) Doosan Engine Co Ltd-South Korea AuxGen: 4 x 1700kW 450V 60Hz a.c Boilers: AuxB (Comp) 11.2kgf/cm² (11.0bar) Thrusters: 1 Thwart. CP thruster (f) Fuel: 5930.0
9280859 VQUQ4 -	**ZIM SHENZHEN** **Lombard Corporate Finance (December 3) Ltd** Zodiac Maritime Agencies Ltd *London* *United Kingdom* MMSI: 235007500 Official number: 908826	**53,453** 33,604 62,740 T/cm 82.5	Class: LR ✠ **100A1** SS 06/2009 container ship *IWS LI **ShipRight** (SDA, FDA, CM) ✠ **LMC** **UMS** Eq.Ltr: T†; Cable: 715.0/87.0 U3 (a)	**2004**-06 **Hyundai Heavy Industries Co Ltd — Ulsan** Yd No: 1528 Loa 294.12 (BB) Br ex 32.25 Dght 13.500 Lbp 283.20 Br md 32.20 Dpth 21.80 Welded, 1 dk	**(A33A2CC) Container Ship (Fully Cellular)** TEU 4992 C Ho 2301 TEU C Dk 2691 TEU incl 330 ref C. Compartments: ER, 7 Cell Ho 7 Ha: ER	**1 oil engine** driving 1 FP propeller Total Power: 41,079kW (55,851hp) 24.0kn B&W 9K90MC-C 1 x 2 Stroke 9 Cy. 900 x 2300 41079kW (55851bhp) Hyundai Heavy Industries Co Ltd-South Korea AuxGen: 3 x 1990kW 450V 60Hz a.c Boilers: e (ex.g.) 10.1kgf/cm² (9.9bar), AuxB (o.f.) 8.0kgf/cm² (7.8bar) Thrusters: 1 Thwart. CP thruster (f)
9471214 4XFA -	**ZIM TARRAGONA** **Jazton Shipping Inc** XT Management Ltd *Haifa* *Israel* MMSI: 428041000	**40,542** 23,747 50,088	Class: GL	**2010**-08 **Jiangsu Newyangzi Shipbuilding Co Ltd — Jingjiang JS** Yd No: YZJ2007-788C Loa 261.06 (BB) Br ex - Dght 12.600 Lbp 247.09 Br md 32.25 Dpth 19.30 Welded, 1 dk	**(A33A2CC) Container Ship (Fully Cellular)** TEU 4250 incl 400 ref C.	**1 oil engine** driving 1 FP propeller Total Power: 36,540kW (49,680hp) 24.5kn MAN-B&W 8K90MC-C 1 x 2 Stroke 8 Cy. 900 x 2300 36540kW (49680bhp) STX Engine Co Ltd-South Korea AuxGen: 4 x 1700kW 450V a.c Thrusters: 1 Tunnel thruster (f)
9471238 V7VE3 -	**ZIM TEXAS** **Tynwald Navigation Ltd** Polaris Shipmanagement Co Ltd SatCom: Inmarsat C 453835871 *Majuro* *Marshall Islands* MMSI: 538004099 Official number: 4099	**40,542** 23,747 50,134	Class: GL	**2011**-01 **Jiangsu Newyangzi Shipbuilding Co Ltd — Jingjiang JS** Yd No: YZJ2007-790C Loa 261.03 (BB) Br ex - Dght 12.600 Lbp 247.09 Br md 32.25 Dpth 19.30 Welded, 1 dk	**(A33A2CC) Container Ship (Fully Cellular)** TEU 4250 incl 400 ref C.	**1 oil engine** driving 1 FP propeller Total Power: 36,560kW (49,707hp) 24.5kn MAN-B&W 8K90MC-C 1 x 2 Stroke 8 Cy. 900 x 2300 36560kW (49707bhp) STX Engine Co Ltd-South Korea AuxGen: 4 x 1700kW 450V a.c Thrusters: 1 Tunnel thruster (f)
9139907 A8WN9 -	**ZIM U.S.A.** **Yellow Sea Shipping Inc** Zim Integrated Shipping Services Ltd *Monrovia* *Liberia* MMSI: 636014790 Official number: 14790	**41,507** 16,353 46,350 T/cm 69.8	Class: LR ✠ **100A1** SS 07/2012 container ship *IWS LI ✠ **LMC** **UMS** Eq.Ltr: R†; Cable: 687.5/84.0 U3	**1997**-07 **Howaldtswerke-Deutsche Werft AG (HDW) — Kiel** Yd No: 329 Loa 253.70 (BB) Br ex 32.29 Dght 11.780 Lbp 241.50 Br md 32.20 Dpth 19.20 Welded, 1 dk	**(A33A2CC) Container Ship (Fully Cellular)** TEU 3429 C Ho 1560 TEU C Dk 1869 TEU incl 165 ref C. Compartments: ER, 7 Cell Ho 14 Ha: ER	**1 oil engine** driving 1 FP propeller Total Power: 28,350kW (38,545hp) 21.7kn Sulzer 7RTA84C 1 x 2 Stroke 7 Cy. 840 x 2400 28350kW (38545bhp) Dieselmotorenwerk Vulkan GmbH-Rostock AuxGen: 1 x 1650kW 450V 60Hz a.c, 3 x 1240kW 450V 60Hz a.c Boilers: AuxB (Comp) 10.2kgf/cm² (10.0bar) Thrusters: 1 Thwart. FP thruster (f)
9403396 A8TR4 -	**ZIM UKRAYINA** **ms 'Bahia' Schifffahrtsgesellschaft mbH & Co KG** Zim Integrated Shipping Services Ltd *Monrovia* *Liberia* MMSI: 636091851 Official number: 91851	**40,741** 24,178 52,316 T/cm 70.5	Class: GL	**2009**-11 **HHIC-Phil Inc — Subic** Yd No: 012 Loa 258.91 (BB) Br ex 32.26 Dght 12.600 Lbp 246.69 Br md 32.20 Dpth 19.30 Welded, 1 dk	**(A33A2CC) Container Ship (Fully Cellular)** TEU 4330 C Ho 1606 TEU C Dk 2724 TEU incl 326 ref C Compartments: 7 Cell Ho, ER 7 Ha: ER	**1 oil engine** driving 1 FP propeller Total Power: 36,560kW (49,707hp) 24.8kn MAN-B&W 8K90MC-C 1 x 2 Stroke 8 Cy. 900 x 2300 36560kW (49707bhp) Hyundai Heavy Industries Co Ltd-South Korea AuxGen: 3 x 2053kW a.c Thrusters: 1 Tunnel thruster (f) Fuel: 225.0 (d.f.) 7800.0 (r.f.)
9322334 A8LK5 -	**ZIM VANCOUVER** *ex* Pearl River I *-2012* *ex* Zim Vancouver *-2007* **Kateland Navigation SA Liberia** XT Management Ltd *Monrovia* *Liberia* MMSI: 636013214 Official number: 13214	**39,906** 24,504 50,532	Class: NK (LR) ✠ Classed LR until 14/9/09	**2007**-08 **Dalian Shipbuilding Industry Co Ltd — Dalian LN (No 2 Yard)** Yd No: C4250-15 Loa 260.62 (BB) Br ex 32.30 Dght 12.630 Lbp 246.04 Br md 32.25 Dpth 19.30 Welded, 1 dk	**(A33A2CC) Container Ship (Fully Cellular)** TEU 4250 C Ho 1586 TEU C Dk 2664 TEU incl 400 ref C. Compartments: 7 Cell Ho, ER	**1 oil engine** driving 1 FP propeller Total Power: 36,560kW (49,707hp) 24.5kn MAN-B&W 8K90MC-C 1 x 2 Stroke 8 Cy. 900 x 2300 36560kW (49707bhp) Doosan Engine Co Ltd-South Korea AuxGen: 4 x 1700kW 450V 60Hz a.c Boilers: AuxB (Comp) 11.2kgf/cm² (11.0bar) Thrusters: 1 Thwart. CP thruster (f) Fuel: 5930.0
9231808 4XFV -	**ZIM VIRGINIA** **Ymir International Ltd** Zim Integrated Shipping Services Ltd *Haifa* *Israel* MMSI: 428002000 Official number: MS.370	**53,453** 33,604 66,686 T/cm 82.5	Class: AB	**2002**-08 **Hyundai Heavy Industries Co Ltd — Ulsan** Yd No: 1388 Loa 294.00 (BB) Br ex - Dght 13.500 Lbp - Br md 32.20 Dpth 21.80 Welded, 1 dk	**(A33A2CC) Container Ship (Fully Cellular)** TEU 4839 C Ho 2301 TEU C Dk 2538 TEU incl 350 ref C.	**1 oil engine** driving 1 FP propeller Total Power: 41,040kW (55,798hp) 24.0kn B&W 9K90MC-C 1 x 2 Stroke 9 Cy. 900 x 2300 41040kW (55798bhp) Hyundai Heavy Industries Co Ltd-South Korea AuxGen: 3 x 1990kW a.c Thrusters: 1 Thwart. CP thruster (f)
9318151 MLCA2	**ZIM XIAMEN** **Lombard Corporate Finance (December 3) Ltd** Zodiac Maritime Agencies Ltd *London* *United Kingdom* MMSI: 235010440 Official number: 911605	**39,906** 24,504 50,689	Class: LR ✠ **100A1** SS 06/2011 container ship *IWS LI **ShipRight** (SDA, FDA, CM) ✠ **LMC** **UMS** Eq.Ltr: A†; Cable: 695.0/87.0 U3 (a)	**2006**-06 **Dalian Shipbuilding Industry Co Ltd — Dalian LN (No 2 Yard)** Yd No: C4250-8 Loa 260.57 (BB) Br ex 32.30 Dght 12.985 Lbp 246.24 Br md 32.25 Dpth 19.30 Welded, 1 dk	**(A33A2CC) Container Ship (Fully Cellular)** TEU 4253 C Ho 1514 TEU C Dk 2339 TEU incl 400 ref C. Compartments: ER, 7 Cell Ho 7 Ha: ER 6 (12.6 x 28.1) (6.6 x 15.8)	**1 oil engine** driving 1 FP propeller Total Power: 36,560kW (49,707hp) 24.5kn MAN-B&W 8K90MC-C 1 x 2 Stroke 8 Cy. 900 x 2300 36560kW (49707bhp) Doosan Engine Co Ltd-South Korea AuxGen: 4 x 1700kW 450V 60Hz a.c Boilers: AuxB (Comp) 11.2kgf/cm² (11.0bar) Thrusters: 1 Thwart. CP thruster (f) Fuel: 265.5 (d.f.) 6217.2 (r.f.)
9322346 A8MY4 -	**ZIM YOKOHAMA** *ex* Yokohama *-2012* *ex* Zim Yokohama *-2009* **Darsal Shipping Inc** Zim Integrated Shipping Services Ltd *Monrovia* *Liberia* MMSI: 636013436 Official number: 13436	**39,906** 24,504 50,532	Class: LR ✠ **100A1** SS 08/2012 container ship **ShipRight** (SDA, FDA, CM) *IWS LI ✠ **LMC** **UMS** Eq.Ltr: s†; Cable: 695.5/87.0 U3 (a)	**2007**-08 **Dalian Shipbuilding Industry Co Ltd — Dalian LN (No 2 Yard)** Yd No: C4250-16 Loa 261.00 (BB) Br ex 32.30 Dght 12.600 Lbp 246.07 Br md 32.25 Dpth 19.30 Welded, 1 dk	**(A33A2CC) Container Ship (Fully Cellular)** TEU 4250 C Ho 1586 TEU C Dk 2664 TEU incl 400 ref C. Compartments: 7 Cell Ho, ER	**1 oil engine** driving 1 FP propeller Total Power: 36,560kW (49,707hp) 24.5kn MAN-B&W 8K90MC-C 1 x 2 Stroke 8 Cy. 900 x 2300 36560kW (49707bhp) Doosan Engine Co Ltd-South Korea AuxGen: 4 x 1700kW 450V 60Hz a.c Boilers: AuxB (Comp) 11.2kgf/cm² (11.0bar) Thrusters: 1 Thwart. CP thruster (f)
8861230 YQWK -	**ZIMBRU 4** *ex* Zimbrul 4 *-2009* **SC Compania de Remorcare Maritima SA (Maritime Towage Company) COREMAR SA** - *Constanta* *Romania* MMSI: 264900044 Official number: 7074	**464** - -	Class: (RN)	**1986**-01 **Santierul Naval Galati S.A. — Galati** Yd No: 716 Loa 34.55 Br ex - Dght 4.600 Lbp 33.40 Br md 10.80 Dpth 5.75 Welded, 1 dk	**(B32A2ST) Tug** Ice Capable	**2 oil engines** driving 2 FP propellers Total Power: 3,630kW (4,936hp) 11.0kn Alco 12V251F 2 x Vee 4 Stroke 12 Cy. 229 x 267 each-1815kW (2468bhp) U.C.M. Resita S.A.-Resita AuxGen: 2 x 140kW 400V 50Hz a.c

7641968 **ZIMBRUL** — 858 / 229 / 386 — Class: (RN)
1975 in the U.S.S.R. Loa 38.42 Br ex - Dght 2.020; Lbp - Br md 20.00 Dpth 3.40; Welded, 1 dk
(B34B2SC) Crane Vessel Ice Capable
2 diesel electric oil engines driving 2 gen. each 320kW 400V a.c Connecting to 2 elec. motors driving 2 Directional propellers
Pervomaysk 10.0k 6CHN25/34
2 x 4 Stroke 6 Cy. 250 x 340
Pervomaydizelmash (PDM)-Pervomaysk
AuxGen: 1 x 50kW 380V 50Hz a.c
Fuel: 101.5 (d.f.)

8523369 *YQFV* **ZIMBRUL 2** — 481 / 145 / - — Class: (RN)
SC Canal Services Srl
Constanta *Romania*
MMSI: 264900249
Official number: 135
1984-10 Santierul Naval Galati S.A. — Galati Yd No: 714
Loa 34.55 Br ex - Dght 4.601; Lbp 33.40 Br md 10.48 Dpth 5.75; Welded, 1 dk
(B32A2ST) Tug
2 oil engines driving 2 FP propellers
Total Power: 3,530kW (4,800hp) 11.0kn
Alco 12V251
2 x Vee 4 Stroke 12 Cy. 229 x 267 each-1765kW (2400bhp)
U.C.M. Resita S.A.-Resita
AuxGen: 2 x 140kW 400V 50Hz a.c

8861228 *YQWB* **ZIMBRUL 3** — 464 / - / - — Class: (RN)
SC Compania de Remorcare Maritima SA (Maritime Towage Company) COREMAR SA
Constanta *Romania*
MMSI: 264900043
Official number: 89
1986-04 Santierul Naval Galati S.A. — Galati Yd No: 715
Loa 34.54 Br ex - Dght 4.600; Lbp 33.35 Br md 10.80 Dpth 5.75; Welded, 1 dk
(B32A2ST) Tug Ice Capable
2 oil engines driving 2 FP propellers
Total Power: 3,630kW (4,936hp) 11.0kn
Alco 12V251
2 x Vee 4 Stroke 12 Cy. 229 x 267 each-1815kW (2468bhp)
U.C.M. Resita S.A.-Resita
AuxGen: 2 x 140kW 400V 50Hz a.c

9486465 *9HA2910* **ZINA** — 23,322 / 11,202 / 33,861 — Class: AB
MB Zina Shipping Ltd
Transship Bulk
SatCom: Inmarsat C 425671310
Valletta *Malta*
MMSI: 256713000
Official number: 9486465
2012-05 21st Century Shipbuilding Co Ltd — Tongyeong Yd No: 1013
Loa 181.10 (BB) Br ex - Dght 9.930; Lbp 172.00 Br md 30.00 Dpth 14.80; Welded, 1 dk
(A21A2BC) Bulk Carrier Grain: 47,558; Bale: 45,180; Compartments: 5 Ho, ER; 5 Ha: ER; Cranes: 4x30t
1 oil engine driving 1 FP propeller
Total Power: 6,480kW (8,810hp) 14.5kn
MAN-B&W 6S42MC
1 x 2 Stroke 6 Cy. 420 x 1764 6480kW (8810bhp)
Hyundai Heavy Industries Co Ltd-South Korea
AuxGen: 3 x 570kW a.c

6805684 **ZINDER** — *651* / 314 / 391 — Class: (LR) ✠ Classed LR until 6/69
Wealth International Network Pty Ltd (WIN)
1968-04 Marine Industries Ltee (MIL) — Sorel QC Yd No: 378
Loa 50.78 Br ex 9.25 Dght 4.395; Lbp 42.98 Br md 9.22 Dpth 6.76; Welded, 2 dks
(B11A2FS) Stern Trawler
1 oil engine sr geared to sc. shaft driving 1 CP propeller
Total Power: 1,125kW (1,530hp)
Deutz RBV8M545
1 x 4 Stroke 8 Cy. 320 x 450 1125kW (1530bhp)
Kloeckner Humboldt Deutz AG-West Germany
AuxGen: 2 x 68kW 230V 60Hz a.c

8137225 **ZINDER-1** — 188 / 56 / - — Class: (GL)
ex Dalal *-2001* *ex* Katja *-2000*
ex Anneliese *-2000*
1976 Planaco S.A. — Aegina Yd No: 8012
Loa 26.75 Br ex 7.24 Dght -; Lbp 22.66 Br md 6.68 Dpth 4.70; Bonded, 1 dk
(B11B2FV) Fishing Vessel Hull Material: Reinforced Plastic
1 oil engine sr geared to sc. shaft driving 1 FP propeller
Total Power: 421kW (572hp) 10.3kn
Caterpillar D398T
1 x Vee 4 Stroke 12 Cy. 159 x 203 421kW (572bhp) (made 1974, fitted 1976)
Caterpillar Tractor Co-USA
AuxGen: 1 x 25kW 380V a.c, 1 x 32kW 380V a.c

7329091 *CNTR* **ZINEB** — *270* / 124 / - — Class: (BV)
ex Aquiles *-1979*
Sisnipeche SA
Casablanca *Morocco*
1974-09 Ast. Neptuno — Valencia Yd No: 51
Loa 37.39 Br ex - Dght 3.471; Lbp 31.50 Br md 7.31 Dpth 3.92; Welded, 1 dk
(B11A2FT) Trawler
1 oil engine driving 1 CP propeller
Total Power: 588kW (799hp) 10.8kn
Alpha 408-26V
1 x 2 Stroke 8 Cy. 260 x 400 588kW (799bhp)
Construcciones Echevarria SA-Spain

9124562 *DQKX* **ZINGST** — 976 / 293 / 1,781 — Class: GL (BV)
Detlef Hegemann Dredging GmbH
Wolgast *Germany*
MMSI: 211228710
Official number: 3375
1995-05 Peene-Werft GmbH — Wolgast Yd No: 454
Loa 65.07 Br ex - Dght 3.163; Lbp 61.59 Br md 12.00 Dpth 4.00; Welded, 1 dk
(B33B2DT) Trailing Suction Hopper Dredger Hopper: 1,000
2 oil engines reduction geared to sc. shafts driving 2 FP propellers
Total Power: 1,090kW (1,482hp) 8.0kn
Deutz TBD616V12
2 x Vee 4 Stroke 12 Cy. 132 x 160 each-545kW (741bhp)
Motoren Werke Mannheim AG (MWM)-Mannheim

9153501 *3FKE8* **ZINI** — 17,542 / 10,264 / 28,412 / T/cm 40.1 — Class: NK (KR)
ex Global Escort *-2009*
Eastmed Co SA
Elmar Shipping Co SA
SatCom: Inmarsat B 335586810
Panama *Panama*
MMSI: 355868000
Official number: 2568898D
1998-05 The Hakodate Dock Co Ltd — Hakodate HK Yd No: 770
Loa 177.46 (BB) Br ex - Dght 9.672; Lbp 170.01 Br md 26.00 Dpth 13.60; Welded, 1 dk
(A21A2BC) Bulk Carrier Grain: 38,000; Bale: 36,500; Compartments: 5 Ho, ER; 5 Ha: (16.2 x 13.1)4 (20.0 x 18.0)ER; Cranes: 4x30.5t
1 oil engine driving 1 FP propeller
Total Power: 6,157kW (8,371hp) 14.1kn
B&W 6S42MC
1 x 2 Stroke 6 Cy. 420 x 1764 6157kW (8371bhp)
Mitsui Engineering & Shipbuilding CLtd-Japan
Fuel: 1140.0

9381940 *TCSW5* **ZINNET CAVUSOGLU** — 3,034 / 1,700 / 4,962 — Class: TL (RI)
ex A. P. Sunshine *-2007*
completed as Hymoon *-2006*
Cavusoglu Kara ve Deniz Nakliyat Ticaret Ltd Sti
CVS Denizcilik Sanayi Ticaret Ltd Sti
Istanbul *Turkey*
MMSI: 271001001
2006-04 Wenling Xingyuan Shipbuilding & Repair Co Ltd — Wenling ZJ Yd No: 0411
Loa 99.80 Br ex - Dght 5.350; Lbp 92.89 Br md 15.80 Dpth 7.10; Welded, 1 dk
(A31A2GX) General Cargo Ship
1 oil engine driving 1 FP propeller
Total Power: 1,765kW (2,400hp)
Chinese Std. Type G8300ZC
1 x 4 Stroke 8 Cy. 300 x 380 1765kW (2400bhp)
Wuxi Antai Power Machinery Co Ltd-China
AuxGen: 2 x 129kW 450V 50Hz a.c

8913320 *TCGH* **ZINNET METE** — 8,220 / 4,608 / 12,231 — Class: TL (AB)
ex Mehmet Kalkavan *-2003*
Irem Denizcilik AS
Akarlar Tasimacilik ve Ticaret AS
SatCom: Inmarsat A 1740410
Istanbul *Turkey*
MMSI: 271000261
Official number: 72
1993-09 Torgem Gemi Insaat Sanayii ve Ticaret a.s. — Tuzla, Istanbul Yd No: 49
Loa 139.00 (BB) Br ex - Dght 7.900; Lbp 128.33 Br md 19.70 Dpth 10.40; Welded, 1 dk
(A33A2CC) Container Ship (Fully Cellular) Grain: 15,129; Bale: 14,719; TEU 598 incl 60 ref C.; Compartments: 3 Ho, ER; 3 Ha: 3 (24.8 x 15.3)ER; Cranes: 2x24.7t,2x14.8t
1 oil engine driving 1 FP propeller
Total Power: 4,472kW (6,080hp) 14.0kn
B&W 8L35MC
1 x 2 Stroke 8 Cy. 350 x 1050 4472kW (6080bhp)
MAN B&W Diesel A/S-Denmark
AuxGen: 2 x 520kW a.c, 1 x 200kW a.c

9411460 *YDA4223* **ZINNIA** — 251 / 76 / 191 — Class: KI (NK)
PT Gurita Lintas Samudera
Jakarta *Indonesia*
Official number: 1396/PPM
2006-10 PT Palma Progress Shipyard — Batam Yd No: 266
Loa 28.05 Br ex 8.60 Dght 3.312; Lbp 25.06 Br md 8.60 Dpth 4.30; Welded, 1 dk
(B32A2ST) Tug
2 oil engines reduction geared to sc. shafts driving 2 FP propellers
Total Power: 1,516kW (2,062hp)
Mitsubishi S6R2-MPTK3
2 x 4 Stroke 6 Cy. 170 x 220 each-758kW (1031bhp)
Mitsubishi Heavy Industries Ltd-Japan
AuxGen: 2 x 75kW 380V a.c
Fuel: 227.0 (r.f.)

6913819 *DZNA* **ZINNIA 2** — *491* / 329 / 1,000
ex Bird of Paradise *-1990*
ex Sayuri Maru No. 11 *-1980*
ex Tokuyoshi Maru No. 5 *-1980*
Frabelle Fishing Corp
SatCom: Inmarsat C 454899021
Manila *Philippines*
Official number: MNLD000257
1968 Sasaki Shipbuilding Co Ltd — Osakikamijima HS Yd No: 127
Converted From: Water Tanker
Loa 54.39 Br ex 9.02 Dght 4.242; Lbp 49.00 Br md 9.00 Dpth 4.50; Welded, 1 dk
(B11B2FV) Fishing Vessel Compartments: ER
1 oil engine driving 1 FP propeller
Total Power: 736kW (1,001hp) 11.0kn
Daihatsu 8PSHTCM-26D
1 x 4 Stroke 8 Cy. 260 x 320 736kW (1001bhp)
Daihatsu Kogyo-Japan
AuxGen: 1 x 25kW 220V a.c, 1 x 20kW 220V a.c

7434274 *DUA2427* **ZINNIA 5** — *497* / 282 / 1,279
ex Shinei Maru No. 7 *-1989*
ex Fukuju Maru *-1987* *ex* Taiho Maru *-1978*
Frabelle Fishing Corp
SatCom: Inmarsat C 454899032
Manila *Philippines*
Official number: 00-0002165
1974-12 K.K. Matsuura Zosensho — Osakikamijima Yd No: 225
Converted From: Oil Tanker
Loa 58.60 Br ex 10.52 Dght 4.192; Lbp 53.98 Br md 10.49 Dpth 4.50; Welded, 1 dk
(B11B2FV) Fishing Vessel Compartments: ER
1 oil engine driving 1 FP propeller
Total Power: 956kW (1,300hp) 11.8kn
Hanshin 6LU32
1 x 4 Stroke 6 Cy. 320 x 510 956kW (1300bhp)
Hanshin Nainenki Kogyo-Japan

9675341 *JD3489* **ZINSHIN MARU** — *498* / - / 1,298
Tatsumi Unyu KK
Osaka, Osaka *Japan*
Official number: 141881
2013-03 Koa Sangyo KK — Marugame KG Yd No: 657
Loa 66.01 (BB) Br ex - Dght 4.190; Lbp - Br md 10.20 Dpth -; Welded, 1 dk
(A12A2TC) Chemical Tanker Double Hull (13F); Liq: 715
1 oil engine reduction geared to sc. shaft driving 1 Propeller
Total Power: 1,370kW (1,863hp)
Yanmar 6EY22
1 x 4 Stroke 6 Cy. 220 x 320 1370kW (1863bhp)
Yanmar Diesel Engine Co Ltd-Japan

502878	**ZION** *ex* Papur *-2012* *ex* Oruc Reis *-2010* **Bukrot Investment Business Ltd** -	**496** 317 950	Class: (TL) (AB)	**1964 Denizcilik Anonim Sirketi Beykoz Tersanesi — Beykoz** Yd No: 7 Loa 60.30 Br ex 9.20 Dght 3.520 Lbp 54.50 Br md 9.11 Dpth 4.02 Welded, 1 dk	**(A13B2TU) Tanker (unspecified)** Compartments: 8 Ta, ER	**1 oil engine** driving 1 FP propeller Total Power: 552kW (750hp) 10.0kn Deutz RBV6M545 1 x 4 Stroke 6 Cy. 320 x 450 552kW (750bhp) Kloeckner Humboldt Deutz AG-West Germany AuxGen: 2 x 15kW Fuel: 40.5
7906837 WDD6582	**ZION FALGOUT** *ex* OSG Freedom *-2013* *ex* Freedom *-2006* **Zion Falgout LLC** Global Towing Service LLC *Larose, LA United States of America* MMSI: 367174870 Official number: 615200	**675** 202 179	Class: AB	**1979-12 Main Iron Works, Inc. — Houma, La** Yd No: 345 Loa 41.61 Br ex - Dght 5.709 Lbp 38.28 Br md 11.29 Dpth 6.10 Welded, 1 dk	**(B32B2SP) Pusher Tug**	**2 oil engines** reverse reduction geared to sc. shafts driving 2 FP propellers Total Power: 4,192kW (5,700hp) 12.0kn EMD (Electro-Motive) 16-645-E7 2 x Vee 2 Stroke 16 Cy. 230 x 254 each-2096kW (2850bhp) General Motors Corp.Electro-Motive Div.-La Grange AuxGen: 2 x 98kW
003996 IQFG5	**ZION II** *ex* Koei Maru No. 7 *-1991* *ex* R. O. C. No. 1 *-1979* *ex* Kaiyo Maru No. 8 *-1978* **Sociedad Mercantil Yoido Trading S de RL** - *San Lorenzo Honduras* Official number: L-1923087	*224* 89 -		**1969 Niigata Engineering Co Ltd — Niigata NI** Yd No: 837 Loa 44.53 Br ex 7.62 Dght 2.953 Lbp 38.99 Br md 7.60 Dpth 3.31 Welded, 1 dk	**(B11B2FV) Fishing Vessel**	**1 oil engine** driving 1 FP propeller Total Power: 699kW (950hp) Niigata 1 x 4 Stroke 6 Cy. 280 x 440 699kW (950bhp) Niigata Engineering Co Ltd-Japan
6824238 IGPZ	**ZION No. 1** *ex* Halleluya No. 1 *-1989* *ex* Pais del Este No. 75 *-1986* *ex* Kintoku Maru No. 8 *-1978* **Enyo Fishing Enterprise** - *Takoradi Ghana* Official number: 316735	*349* 151 428	Class: (KR)	**1968 Niigata Engineering Co Ltd — Niigata NI** Yd No: 771 Loa 53.01 Br ex 8.82 Dght 3.429 Lbp 47.20 Br md 8.79 Dpth 3.79 Welded, 1 dk	**(B11A2FS) Stern Trawler** Ins: 199 4 Ha: (1.0 x 2.0) (1.6 x 2.0) (1.7 x 2.9) (1.2 x 1.4)ER	**1 oil engine** driving 1 FP propeller Total Power: 1,346kW (1,830hp) 11.2kn Niigata 8MG31X 1 x 4 Stroke 8 Cy. 310 x 380 1346kW (1830bhp) Niigata Engineering Co Ltd-Japan AuxGen: 2 x 64kW 225V a.c
879457	**ZIQI NO. 2** *ex* Kashima *-2013* *ex* Toba Maru *-2010* - - *Tarawa Kiribati*	*198* - -		**1994-10 Hatayama Zosen KK — Yura WK** Yd No: 216 Loa 32.82 Br ex - Dght 3.160 Lbp 26.50 Br md 9.50 Dpth 4.29 Welded, 1 dk	**(B32A2ST) Tug**	**2 oil engines** geared integral to driving 2 Z propellers Total Power: 2,648kW (3,600hp) 9.5kn Yanmar 6Z280-EN 2 x 4 Stroke 6 Cy. 280 x 360 each-1324kW (1800bhp) Yanmar Diesel Engine Co Ltd-Japan
113812	**ZIQI NO. 3** *ex* Dairyu Maru *-2013* *ex* Tokyo Maru *-2005* **Zhangjiagang Gangxin Shipping Co Ltd** -	*198* - -	Class: IZ	**1994-10 Kanagawa Zosen — Kobe** Yd No: 412 Loa 33.90 Br ex - Dght 3.100 Lbp 29.50 Br md 9.20 Dpth 4.00 Welded, 1 dk	**(B32A2ST) Tug**	**2 oil engines** Geared Integral to driving 2 Z propellers Total Power: 2,910kW (3,956hp) 14.1kn Niigata 6L28HX 2 x 4 Stroke 6 Cy. 280 x 370 each-1455kW (1978bhp) Niigata Engineering Co Ltd-Japan AuxGen: 2 x 80kW 225V 60Hz a.c Fuel: 44.0 (d.f.) 13.0pd
279343	**ZIQI NO. 5** *ex* Musashi Maru *-2013* **Yangjiang Port Yechang Tugboat Co Ltd** -	*175* - -		**2002-08 Kanagawa Zosen — Kobe** Yd No: 510 Loa 33.20 Br ex - Dght - Lbp 29.00 Br md 8.80 Dpth 3.78 Welded, 1 Dk.	**(B32A2ST) Tug**	**2 oil engines** geared integral to driving 1 Propeller , 1 Z propeller Total Power: 2,280kW (3,100hp) 12.5kn Niigata 6L25HX 2 x 4 Stroke 6 Cy. 250 x 350 each-1140kW (1550bhp) Niigata Engineering Co Ltd-Japan
726820	**ZIRA** *ex* SCHS-1022 *-2002* **TOO 'Zire Ltd'** - *Aqtau Kazakhstan* Official number: 870049	**104** 31 58	Class: (RS)	**1987-11 Azovskaya Sudoverf — Azov** Yd No: 1022 Loa 26.50 Br ex 6.59 Dght 2.360 Lbp 22.40 Br md - Dpth 3.05 Welded, 1 dk	**(B11A2FS) Stern Trawler**	**1 oil engine** geared to sc. shaft driving 1 FP propeller Total Power: 165kW (224hp) 9.3kn Daldizel 6CHNSP18/22 1 x 4 Stroke 6 Cy. 180 x 220 165kW (224bhp) Daldizel-Khabarovsk AuxGen: 2 x 30kW a.c Fuel: 9.0 (d.f.)
300245 WEZ8	**ZIRCON** - **Marineco Ltd** Chuan Hup Agencies Pte Ltd *Port Klang Malaysia* MMSI: 533000142 Official number: 330080	**1,592** 477 1,609	Class: AB	**2004-11 Keppel Singmarine Pte Ltd — Singapore** Yd No: 267 Loa 60.00 Br ex - Dght 4.200 Lbp 53.90 Br md 16.00 Dpth 5.50 Welded, 1 dk	**(B21B20A) Anchor Handling Tug Supply**	**2 oil engines** geared to sc. shafts driving 2 CP propellers Total Power: 3,792kW (5,156hp) 12.8kn MaK 6M25 2 x 4 Stroke 6 Cy. 255 x 400 each-1896kW (2578bhp) Caterpillar Motoren GmbH & Co. KG-Germany AuxGen: 2 x 270kW 440V 60Hz a.c, 2 x 1000kW 440V 60Hz a.c Thrusters: 1 Tunnel thruster (f) Fuel: 487.8 (r.f.)
010929 CSZ	**ZIRCONE** - **Finbeta SpA** - SatCom: Inmarsat Mini-M 762318535 *Savona Italy* MMSI: 247278000 Official number: 02	**5,045** 2,469 8,000 T/cm 17.0	Class: RI (LR) (BV) ✠ Classed LR until 1/10/99	**1993-02 Fincantieri-Cant. Nav. Italiani S.p.A. — La Spezia** (Hull) Yd No: 5933 **1993-03 Nuovi Cantieri Apuania SpA — Carrara** Yd No: 1158 Loa 124.86 (BB) Br ex 17.37 Dght 7.119 Lbp 114.35 Br md 17.22 Dpth 9.00 Welded, 1 dk	**(A12B2TR) Chemical/Products Tanker** Double Hull (13F) Liq: 8,639; Liq (Oil): 8,639 Cargo Heating Coils Compartments: 18 Wing Ta (s.stl), ER 20 Cargo Pump (s): 14x175m³/hr, 4x100m³/hr, 2x30m³/hr Manifold: Bow/CM: 66m Ice Capable	**1 oil engine** with clutches, flexible couplings & sr geared to sc. shaft driving 1 CP propeller Total Power: 4,080kW (5,547hp) 14.0kn Wartsila 12V32 1 x Vee 4 Stroke 12 Cy. 320 x 350 4080kW (5547bhp) Wartsila Diesel Oy-Finland AuxGen: 1 x 1000kW 440/220V 60Hz a.c, 1 x 840kW 440/220V 60Hz a.c, 1 x 860kW 440/220V 60Hz a.c Thrusters: 1 Thwart. FP thruster (f) Fuel: 56.0 (d.f.) 411.0 (r.f.) 15.0pd
046497 PBZV	**ZIRFAEA** - **Government of The Kingdom of The Netherlands (Rijkswaterstaat Directie Noordzee)** - SatCom: Inmarsat C 424609610 *Rijswijk, Zuid Holland Netherlands* MMSI: 246096000 Official number: 22164	**1,261** 378 1,000	Class: BV	**1993-05 Bodewes Scheepswerf "Volharding" Foxhol B.V. — Foxhol** Yd No: 313 Loa 63.00 Br ex - Dght 3.850 Lbp 58.14 Br md 11.50 Dpth 6.00 Welded, 1 dk	**(B31A2SR) Research Survey Vessel** Liq: 200; Liq (Oil): 200 A-frames: 1x5t; Cranes: 1x12t,1x3t	**4 diesel electric oil engines** driving 4 gen. each 468kW 660V a.c Connecting to 2 elec. motors each (650kW) driving 2 Directional propellers Total Power: 1,960kW (2,664hp) 12.0kn Mitsubishi S6R-MPTA 4 x 4 Stroke 6 Cy. 170 x 180 each-490kW (666bhp) Mitsubishi Heavy Industries Ltd-Japan Thrusters: 2 Thwart. FP thruster (f) Fuel: 113.1 (d.f.)
8707692 JVFK	**ZIRKA DNIPRA** *ex* Marshal Rybalko *-2004* *ex* Cruising Dream *-2004* *ex* Marshal Rybalko *-1992* - - *Kherson Ukraine* MMSI: 272020700 Official number: 01737	*5,475* 1,928 480	Class: UA	**1988-03 VEB Elbewerften Boizenburg/Rosslau — Boizenburg** Yd No: 392 Loa 129.15 Br ex - Dght 2.900 Lbp 122.43 Br md 16.00 Dpth 4.50 Welded, 1 dk	**(A37A2PC) Passenger/Cruise** Passengers: cabins: 144; berths: 350	**3 oil engines** driving 3 FP propellers Total Power: 2,208kW (3,003hp) Dvigatel Revolyutsii 6CHRN36/45 3 x 4 Stroke 6 Cy. 360 x 450 each-736kW (1001bhp) Zavod "Dvigatel Revolyutsii"-Gorkiy
7345681	**ZIRKU** - **HH Sheikh Khalifa bin Zayed Al Nahyan** - *Sharjah United Arab Emirates*	*207* 97 -		**1973 Singapore Shipbuilding & Engineering Pte Ltd — Singapore** Loa 35.06 Br ex 8.84 Dght 1.220 Lbp 33.84 Br md 8.54 Dpth 1.83 Welded, 1 dk	**(A35D2RL) Landing Craft** Bow door/ramp	**2 oil engines** driving 2 FP propellers Caterpillar 2 x 4 Stroke 6 Cy. Caterpillar Tractor Co-USA
9237802 A6E2922	**ZIRKU** - **Arab Maritime Petroleum Transport Co (AMPTC)** - *Abu Dhabi United Arab Emirates* MMSI: 470729000 Official number: 4876	**57,190** 32,775 105,846 T/cm 91.9	Class: AB	**2003-04 Hyundai Heavy Industries Co Ltd — Ulsan** Yd No: 1420 Loa 243.97 (BB) Br ex 42.03 Dght 14.900 Lbp 234.00 Br md 42.00 Dpth 21.00 Welded, 1 dk	**(A13A2TV) Crude Oil Tanker** Double Hull (13F) Liq: 118,055; Liq (Oil): 118,055 Cargo Heating Coils Compartments: 12 Wing Ta, 2 Wing Slop Ta, ER 3 Cargo Pump (s): 3x3000m³/hr Manifold: Bow/CM: 122m	**1 oil engine** driving 1 FP propeller Total Power: 11,484kW (15,614hp) 14.5kn B&W 6S60MC 1 x 2 Stroke 6 Cy. 600 x 2292 11484kW (15614bhp) Hyundai Heavy Industries Co Ltd-South Korea AuxGen: 3 x 730kW a.c Fuel: 230.0 (d.f.) (Heating Coils) 2839.0 (r.f.)

1008437 *ZCOW7* -	**ZITA** *ex* Larisa *-2012* *ex* Romanza *-2008* **Zita Shipping Ltd** YCO SAM *George Town* *Cayman Islands (British)* MMSI: 319943000 Official number: 738538	**444** 133 -	Class: LR ✠ **100A1** SS 05/2011 SSC Yacht, mono, G6 **LMC** Cable: 330.0/19.0 U2 (a)	**2006-05 Azimut-Benetti SpA — Viareggio** Yd No: BV006 Loa 44.20 Br ex 9.26 Dght 2.750 Lbp 36.20 Br md 8.96 Dpth 4.60 Welded, 1 dk	**(X11A2YP) Yacht**	**2 oil engines** with clutches, flexible couplings & sr reverse geared to sc. shafts driving 2 FP propellers Total Power: 1,940kW (2,638hp) Caterpillar 3508T 2 x Vee 4 Stroke 8 Cy. 170 x 190 each-970kW (1319bhp) Caterpillar Inc-USA AuxGen: 2 x 104kW 380V 50Hz a.c Thrusters: 1 Thwart. FP thruster (f)
9169732 *V2GJ5* -	**ZITA** *ex* Alserbach *-2013* *ex* Claudia-Isabell *-2000* **Abrams Schiffahrts GmbH & Co KG ms 'Heinrich Abrams'** Abrams Schiffahrtskontor GmbH & Co KG *Saint John's* *Antigua & Barbuda* MMSI: 305962000 Official number: 5040	**2,905** 1,534 4,490	Class: GL	**1997-12 OAO Sudostroitelnyy Zavod 'Slip' — Rybinsk** (Hull launched by) Yd No: 61604 **1997-12 Schiffs. Hugo Peters Wewelsfleth Peters & Co. GmbH — Wewelsfleth** (Hull completed by) Yd No: 667 Loa 88.20 Br ex 13.66 Dght 6.106 Lbp 84.90 Br md 13.60 Dpth 7.70 Welded, 1 dk	**(A31A2GX) General Cargo Ship** Double Hull Grain: 5,661 TEU 198 C Ho 105 TEU C Dk 93 TEU. Compartments: 1 Ho, ER 1 Ha: ER Ice Capable	**1 oil engine** with flexible couplings & sr geared to sc. shaft driving 1 CP propeller Total Power: 1,800kW (2,447hp) 12.5k MaK 6M2 1 x 4 Stroke 6 Cy. 255 x 400 1800kW (2447bhp) MaK Motoren GmbH & Co. KG-Kiel AuxGen: 1 x 520kW a.c, 1 x 232kW a.c Thrusters: 1 Thwart. FP thruster (f) Fuel: 160.0 (d.f.)
8857904 *TCAW4* -	**ZIYA KOC** *ex* Koclar IV *-1997* **Koclar Insaat Malzeme Sanayi Ticaret Ltd Sti** - *Istanbul* *Turkey* MMSI: 271002010 Official number: 5593	**955** 710 2,103	Class: (TL) (BV)	**1987-07 Yildirim Gemi Insaat Sanayii A.S. — Tuzla** Loa 60.70 Br ex - Dght 4.200 Lbp 58.25 Br md 10.02 Dpth 4.22 Welded, 1 dk	**(A31A2GX) General Cargo Ship**	**1 oil engine** driving 1 FP propeller Total Power: 720kW (979hp) Skoda 6L350IIP 1 x 4 Stroke 6 Cy. 350 x 500 720kW (979bhp) Skoda-Praha
9122629 *3FFA6* -	**ZIYAHE** **Ziyahe Shipping Inc** COSCO Container Lines Co Ltd (COSCON) SatCom: Inmarsat C 435639910 *Panama* *Panama* MMSI: 356399000 Official number: 2311096CH	**9,471** 5,188 12,714 T/cm 25.4	Class: NK	**1996-06 Kyokuyo Shipyard Corp — Shimonoseki YC** Yd No: 401 Loa 144.83 (BB) Br ex 22.47 Dght 8.215 Lbp 134.00 Br md 22.40 Dpth 11.00 Welded, 1 dk	**(A33A2CC) Container Ship (Fully Cellular)** TEU 764 C Ho 318 TEU C Dk 446 TEU incl 60 ref C. Compartments: 7 Cell Ho, ER 7 Ha: ER	**1 oil engine** driving 1 FP propeller Total Power: 7,988kW (10,860hp) 17.0k B&W 6L50M 1 x 2 Stroke 6 Cy. 500 x 1620 7988kW (10860bhp) Kawasaki Heavy Industries Ltd-Japan Fuel: 1070.0 (r.f.)
8215132 *9A8811* -	**ZLATKO** *ex* Krajan Dva *-2009* *ex* Delamaris II *-2003* **Hypo - Leasing Steiermark doo** Krajani doo *Rijeka* *Croatia* Official number: 7R-46	**124** 37 90	Class: CS	**1982-03 Brodogradiliste Greben — Vela Luka** Yd No: 814 Loa 23.19 Br ex 7.19 Dght 3.271 Lbp 19.89 Br md 6.86 Dpth 3.71 Bonded, 1 dk	**(B11A2FS) Stern Trawler** Hull Material: Reinforced Plastic Ins: 85 Compartments: 1 Ho, ER 1 Ha:	**1 oil engine** sr geared to sc. shaft driving 1 CP propeller Total Power: 367kW (499hp) 10.0k Iveco Aifo C13 ENT M5 1 x 4 Stroke 6 Cy. 135 x 150 367kW (499bhp) (new engine ,made 1982) IVECO AIFO S.p.A.-Pregnana Milanese
8138592 *UFVJ* -	**ZLATOUSTOVSK** **Fleet Marine Co Ltd (OOO 'Flot Marin')** *Nevelsk* *Russia* MMSI: 273894010	**752** 226 414	Class: RS	**1983-06 Zavod "Leninskaya Kuznitsa" — Kiyev** Yd No: 1520 Loa 54.84 Br ex 9.96 Dght 4.111 Lbp 50.29 Br md 9.80 Dpth 5.01 Welded, 1 dk	**(B11A2FS) Stern Trawler** Ins: 412 Compartments: 2 Ho, ER Ice Capable	**1 oil engine** driving 1 CP propeller Total Power: 852kW (1,158hp) 12.0k S.K.L. 8NVD48A-2 1 x 4 Stroke 8 Cy. 320 x 480 852kW (1158bhp) VEB Schwermaschinenbau "KarlLiebknecht" (SKL)-Magdeburg AuxGen: 4 x 160kW a.c Fuel: 180.0 (d.f.)
9655377 *9V9764* -	**ZMAGA** **NM Tankers Pte Ltd** New Maritime Pte Ltd *Singapore* *Singapore* MMSI: 566474000 Official number: 397561	**2,608** 1,139 3,941	Class: CC	**2012-06 Ningbo Dongsheng Shiprepair & Building Co Ltd — Xiangshan County ZJ** Yd No: BDS-02-1102B Loa 94.80 (BB) Br ex - Dght 5.400 Lbp 87.80 Br md 14.20 Dpth 6.90 Welded, 1 dk	**(A13B2TP) Products Tanker** Double Hull (13F) Compartments: 5 Wing Ta, 5 Wing Ta, 2 Wing Slop Ta, ER Ice Capable	**1 oil engine** reduction geared to sc. shaft driving 1 FP propeller Total Power: 1,618kW (2,200hp) 11.8k Daihatsu 6DKM-2 1 x 4 Stroke 6 Cy. 260 x 380 1618kW (2200bhp) Anqing Marine Diesel Engine Works-China AuxGen: 3 x 250kW 400V a.c
8125363 - -	**ZO KWANG** *ex* Arco No. 2 *-2000* *ex* Mana *-1996* *ex* Yuki Maru *-1995* **Korea Zoming Shipping Co** -	**1,292** 794 1,634	Class: KC (CC)	**1981 K.K. Murakami Zosensho — Naruto** Yd No: 127 Loa 70.63 Br ex - Dght 4.294 Lbp 66.71 Br md 11.70 Dpth 6.20 Welded, 1 dk	**(A31A2GX) General Cargo Ship** Bale: 1,550 Compartments: 1 Ho, ER 1 Ha: ER	**1 oil engine** driving 1 FP propeller Total Power: 1,177kW (1,600hp) Makita KSLH63 1 x 4 Stroke 6 Cy. 300 x 480 1177kW (1600bhp) Makita Diesel Co Ltd-Japan
8965036 - -	**ZOAL ALBRECHT** **Lionstore Energy & Marine Services Ltd** Meridien Maritime & Offshore Services *Nigeria* Official number: SR759	*212* 73 -		**1981 Sun Contractors, Inc. — Harvey, La** L reg 22.56 Br ex - Dght - Lbp - Br md 11.58 Dpth 2.13 Welded, 1 dk	**(B22A2ZM) Offshore Construction Vessel, jack up**	**2 oil engines** reduction geared to sc. shafts driving 2 FP propellers Total Power: 500kW (680hp) 10.0k G.M. (Detroit Diesel) 12V-71- 2 x Vee 2 Stroke 12 Cy. 108 x 127 each-250kW (340bhp) General Motors Corp-USA
8935160 - -	**ZODIAC** *ex* Vlakosta *-2001* **Ekspromt JSC (TOO 'Ekspromt')** -	**252** 76 165	Class: (RS)	**1957 Baltiyskiy Zavod — Leningrad** Yd No: 748 Loa 39.15 Br ex 7.36 Dght 2.700 Lbp 35.40 Br md - Dpth 3.49 Welded, 1 dk	**(A31A2GX) General Cargo Ship** Grain: 248 Compartments: 2 Ho 2 Ha:	**1 oil engine** driving 1 FP propeller Total Power: 294kW (400hp) 7.0k S.K.L. 6NVD4 1 x 4 Stroke 6 Cy. 320 x 480 294kW (400bhp) (new engine 1969) VEB Schwermaschinenbau "KarlLiebknecht" (SKL)-Magdeburg AuxGen: 1 x 57kW, 1 x 54kW Fuel: 50.0 (d.f.)
8037542 - -	**ZODIAC II** - -	*103* 70 -		**1980 Marine Mart, Inc. — Port Isabel, Tx** L reg 19.69 Br ex 6.13 Dght - Lbp - Br md - Dpth 3.43 Welded, 1 dk	**(B11A2FS) Stern Trawler**	**1 oil engine** geared to sc. shaft driving 1 FP propeller Total Power: 268kW (364hp) Cummins KT-1150-M 1 x 4 Stroke 6 Cy. 159 x 159 268kW (364bhp) Cummins Engine Co Inc-USA
9057343 *CUUX* A-3336-C	**ZODIACO** **Testa y Cunhas SA** SatCom: Inmarsat C 426344010 *Aveiro* *Portugal* Official number: A-3336-C	**248** 74 -	Class: (BV)	**1992-11 Astilleros Armon SA — Navia** Yd No: 259 Loa 28.00 Br ex - Dght 3.000 Lbp 25.00 Br md 8.00 Dpth 5.70 Welded	**(B11A2FS) Stern Trawler**	**1 oil engine** reduction geared to sc. shaft driving 1 FP propeller Total Power: 588kW (799hp) 10.5k Yanmar M200-SI 1 x 4 Stroke 6 Cy. 200 x 260 588kW (799bhp) Yanmar Diesel Engine Co Ltd-Japan
9183556 *UIDP* -	**ZODIAK** **Magadan Fishing Industry Co (A/O 'Magadanskaya Rybopromyshlennaya Komp')** - *Magadan* *Russia* Official number: 960071	**455** 138 148	Class: RS	**1997-08 AO Zavod 'Nikolayevsk-na-Amure' — Nikolayevsk-na-Amure** Yd No: 1307 Loa 44.88 Br ex - Dght 3.770 Lbp 39.37 Br md 9.47 Dpth 5.13 Welded, 1 dk	**(B11A2FS) Stern Trawler** Ins: 139 Compartments: 1 Ho Ice Capable	**1 oil engine** reduction geared to sc. shaft driving 1 FP propeller Total Power: 589kW (801hp) 11.4k S.K.L. 6NVD48A-2 1 x 4 Stroke 6 Cy. 320 x 480 589kW (801bhp) SKL Motoren u. Systemtechnik AG-Magdeburg AuxGen: 3 x 150kW a.c Fuel: 88.0 (d.f.)
8712300 *UBFG9* -	**ZODIAK** *ex* Zodiac *-2010* *ex* Onekotan-106 *-2008* *ex* Tetsushin No. 7 *-1997* *ex* Tetsushin Maru No. 7 *-1991* **STK Co Ltd (Kompaniy STK)** - *Nevelsk* *Russia* MMSI: 273349630	**933** 332 887	Class: RS (BV) (NK)	**1987-12 Kambara Marine Development & Shipbuilding Co Ltd — Fukuyama HS** Yd No: OE-153 Loa 63.25 (BB) Br ex - Dght 3.801 Lbp 57.96 Br md 10.60 Dpth 6.35 Welded, 1 dk	**(A34A2GR) Refrigerated Cargo Ship** Ins: 1,384 Compartments: 2 Ho, ER 4 Ha: ER	**1 oil engine** driving 1 FP propeller Total Power: 736kW (1,001hp) 11.5k Akasaka A245 1 x 4 Stroke 6 Cy. 245 x 450 736kW (1001bhp) Akasaka Tekkosho KK (Akasaka DieselLtd)-Japan AuxGen: 2 x 200kW 450V 60Hz a.c Fuel: 161.0 (d.f.)
8725137 - -	**ZODIAK** *ex* PTR-50 No. 40 *-2004* **AN Bychkova**	**187** 56 77	Class: (RS)	**1988-04 Astrakhanskaya Sudoverf im. "Kirova" — Astrakhan** Yd No: 40 Loa 31.85 Br ex 7.08 Dght 2.100 Lbp 27.80 Br md 6.90 Dpth 3.15 Welded, 1 dk	**(B12B2FC) Fish Carrier** Ins: 100 Compartments: 2 Ho	**1 oil engine** reduction geared to sc. shaft driving 1 FP propeller Total Power: 221kW (300hp) 10.2kn Daldizel 6CHNSP18/22-300 1 x 4 Stroke 6 Cy. 180 x 220 221kW (300bhp) Daldizel-Khabarovsk AuxGen: 2 x 25kW Fuel: 14.0 (d.f.)

IMO / Call sign	Name / Owner	Tonnage	Class	Builder / Dimensions	Type / Capacity	Machinery
030908 *QLX*	**ZODIAK** **Urzad Morski w Gdyni (Gdynia Marine Board)** - *Gdynia* *Poland* MMSI: 261194000	*751* 215 243	Class: PR	**1982-03 Stocznia Polnocna im Bohaterow Westerplatte — Gdansk** Yd No: B91/01 Loa 61.33 Br ex - Dght 3.271 Lbp 57.39 Br md 10.84 Dpth 4.53 Welded, 1 dk	**(B34Q2QB) Buoy Tender** Ice Capable	**2 oil engines** geared to sc. shafts driving 2 FP propellers Total Power: 1,412kW (1,920hp) Sulzer 6AL25/30 2 x 4 Stroke 6 Cy. 250 x 300 each-706kW (960bhp) Zaklady Przemyslu Metalowego 'HCegielski' SA-Poznan AuxGen: 3 x 192kW 400V a.c, 1 x 48kW 400V a.c
102798 *ACN* I-0586	**ZODIAK** *ex* Samfrost *-1997* *ex* Elshout *-1972* **Vega JSC** - *Murmansk* *Russia* MMSI: 273213600 Official number: 611867	**984** 375 783	Class: (LR) (RS) ✠ Classed LR until 13/6/97	**1961-07 N.V. v/h Scheepswerven Gebr. van Diepen — Waterhuizen** Yd No: 967 Converted From: General Cargo Ship-1973 Loa 68.64 Br ex 10.22 Dght 3.960 Lbp 62.26 Br md 10.20 Dpth 6.15 Riveted\Welded, 2 dks	**(B12B2FC) Fish Carrier** Ins: 1,083 Compartments: 1 Ho, ER 2 Ha: (14.3 x 5.6) (8.7 x 5.6)ER Derricks: 2x5t,2x3t; Winches: 4 Ice Capable	**1 oil engine** driving 1 FP propeller Total Power: 735kW (999hp) 11.0kn Russkiy G74 1 x 4 Stroke 6 Cy. 360 x 450 735kW (999bhp) Zavod "Dvigatel Revolyutsii"-Nizhniy Novgorod AuxGen: 1 x 148kW 230V 50Hz a.c, 1 x 176kW 50Hz a.c Fuel: 100.0 (d.f.)
822483 *Y5381*	**ZOE** *ex* Samin Trader *-2004* *ex* Sea Mosel *-1994* *ex* Huberna *-1989* **Zoe P Shipping Co** Artemis P Shipping Co *Piraeus* *Greece* MMSI: 240246000 Official number: 11342	**1,456** 489 1,703	Class: (GL)	**1979-12 Martin Jansen GmbH & Co. KG Schiffsw. u. Masch. — Leer** Yd No: 158 Loa 81.90 Br ex 10.04 Dght 3.571 Lbp 77.02 Br md 10.01 Dpth 5.67 Welded, 2 dks	**(A31A2GX) General Cargo Ship** Grain: 2,358; Bale: 2,346 Compartments: 1 Ho, ER 1 Ha: (46.7 x 7.6)ER Ice Capable	**1 oil engine** reverse reduction geared to sc. shaft driving 1 FP propeller Total Power: 441kW (600hp) 10.0kn MWM TBD440-8 1 x 4 Stroke 8 Cy. 230 x 270 441kW (600bhp) Motoren Werke Mannheim AG (MWM)-West Germany
662447 *BXE3*	**ZOE** **Glovertwo Shipping Corp** Safety Management Overseas SA *Limassol* *Cyprus* MMSI: 209870000 Official number: 9662447	**40,334** 24,948 75,005 T/cm 67.3	Class: AB	**2013-07 Sasebo Heavy Industries Co. Ltd. — Sasebo Yard, Sasebo** Yd No: 814 Loa 225.00 (BB) Br ex 32.25 Dght 14.110 Lbp 218.00 Br md 32.20 Dpth 19.80 Welded, 1 dk	**(A21A2BC) Bulk Carrier** Double Hull Grain: 90,771; Bale: 88,950 Compartments: 7 Ho, ER 7 Ha: 6 (17.0 x 14.4)ER (15.3 x 12.9)	**1 oil engine** driving 1 FP propeller Total Power: 8,700kW (11,829hp) 14.5kn MAN-B&W 7S50MC-C8 1 x 2 Stroke 7 Cy. 500 x 2000 8700kW (11829bhp) Mitsui Engineering & Shipbuilding CLtd-Japan AuxGen: 3 x 560kW a.c Fuel: 328.0 (d.f.) 2412.0 (r.f.)
124851	**ZOE II** *ex* Frank *-1989* *ex* G. M. Daneker *-1972* **Multilog SA** Shipmarc (EPZ) Ltd *Gabon*	*286* 136 -	Class: (GL)	**1955 Schulte & Bruns Schiffswerft — Emden** Yd No: 174 Loa 41.86 Br ex 7.73 Dght 2.807 Lbp 38.41 Br md - Dpth 3.41 Welded, 1 dk	**(B11B2FV) Fishing Vessel** Compartments: 2 Ho, ER Ice Capable	**1 oil engine** driving 1 FP propeller Total Power: 441kW (600hp) 9.0kn MWM TRH348SU 1 x 4 Stroke 6 Cy. 320 x 480 441kW (600bhp) Motoren Werke Mannheim AG (MWM)-West Germany AuxGen: 1 x 80kW 380V 50Hz a.c, 1 x 24kW 380V 50Hz a.c, 1 x 10kW 380V 50Hz a.c
912927 *OBZ*	**ZOE III** *ex* Ozora *-1991* **Cobelfret SA** Sabre Shipping Corp *Jakarta* *Indonesia*	**363** 109 -	Class: (BV)	**1979-09 Kanagawa Zosen — Kobe** Yd No: 202 Loa - Br ex - Dght 3.840 Lbp 30.51 Br md 9.61 Dpth 4.53 Welded, 1 dk	**(B32A2ST) Tug**	**2 oil engines** driving 2 FP propellers Total Power: 2,354kW (3,200hp) 13.5kn Niigata 8L25CX 2 x 4 Stroke 8 Cy. 250 x 320 each-1177kW (1600bhp) Niigata Engineering Co Ltd-Japan
008093 *HA2393*	**ZOEY** *ex* Silvana *-2010* *ex* Socofl Stream *-2003* **Gomina Shipping Ltd** Namar Denizcilik ve Tasimacilik Sanayi ve Ticaret Ltd Sti SatCom: Inmarsat C 424850910 *Valletta* *Malta* MMSI: 248509000 Official number: 9008093	**4,885** 2,221 6,311 T/cm 17.8	Class: BV (LR) (RI) ✠ Classed LR until 16/1/04	**1992-10 Kyokuyo Shipyard Corp — Shimonoseki YC** Yd No: 376 Loa 111.60 (BB) Br ex 18.05 Dght 5.813 Lbp 105.00 Br md 18.00 Dpth 7.60 Welded, 1 dk	**(A31A2GX) General Cargo Ship** Double Hull Grain: 7,935; Bale: 7,835 TEU 248 C.Ho 135/20' C.Dk 123/20' Compartments: 2 Ho, ER 2 Ha: 2 (31.5 x 13.5)ER Cranes: 2x25t	**1 oil engine** driving 1 FP propeller Total Power: 2,575kW (3,501hp) 11.7kn Hanshin 6LF46 1 x 4 Stroke 6 Cy. 460 x 740 2575kW (3501bhp) The Hanshin Diesel Works Ltd-Japan AuxGen: 3 x 270kW 450V 60Hz a.c Boilers: TOH (ex.g.) 8.6kgf/cm² (8.4bar), TOH (o.f.) 8.6kgf/cm² (8.4bar) Fuel: 102.0 (d.f.) 317.0 (r.f.) 10.8pd
624548 *FUK2*	**ZOEY** **New Eagle Shipping SA** Koyo Kaiun Asia Pte Ltd SatCom: Inmarsat C 435613112 *Panama* *Panama* MMSI: 356131000 Official number: 42251TJ	**7,271** 3,740 12,124 T/cm 21.2	Class: NK	**2011-09 Asakawa Zosen K.K. — Imabari** Yd No: 582 Loa 123.52 (BB) Br ex 20.22 Dght 8.464 Lbp 116.00 Br md 20.20 Dpth 10.85 Welded, 1 dk	**(A12B2TR) Chemical/Products Tanker** Double Hull (13F) Liq: 12,161; Liq (Oil): 12,950 Cargo Heating Coils Compartments: 18 Wing Ta, 2 Wing Slop Ta, ER 18 Cargo Pump (s): 12x200m³/hr, 6x300m³/hr Manifold: Bow/CM: 68.8m	**1 oil engine** driving 1 FP propeller Total Power: 4,440kW (6,037hp) 14.1kn MAN-B&W 6S35MC 1 x 2 Stroke 6 Cy. 350 x 1400 4440kW (6037bhp) Makita Corp-Japan AuxGen: 4 x 400kW a.c Thrusters: 1 Tunnel thruster (f) Fuel: 118.0 (r.f.) 631.0 (d.f.)
405857 *5ZG* 760	**ZOGI** **Consortium Evisa Fisheries (Pty) Ltd** - *Walvis Bay* *Namibia* Official number: 94WB007	*671* 394 -	Class: (NV)	**1974-06 Sterkoder Mek. Verksted AS — Kristiansund** Yd No: 38 Loa 46.92 Br ex 9.33 Dght 4.268 Lbp 40.21 Br md 9.25 Dpth 6.41 Welded, 2 dks	**(B11A2FS) Stern Trawler** Ins: 360 Ice Capable	**1 oil engine** driving 1 FP propeller Total Power: 1,103kW (1,500hp) 13.0kn Normo LDM-9 1 x 4 Stroke 9 Cy. 250 x 300 1103kW (1500bhp) AS Bergens Mek Verksteder-Norway
914697 *FOP6*	**ZOGRAFIA I** *ex* Zografia *-2013* *ex* Pacific Hope *-2009* **Venezia Enterprises Co** Vulcanus Technical Maritime Enterprises SA *Panama* *Panama* MMSI: 372888000 Official number: 4538013	**22,147** 12,665 38,855 T/cm 47.2	Class: NK	**1991-01 Ishikawajima-Harima Heavy Industries Co Ltd (IHI) — Tokyo** Yd No: 3003 Loa 180.80 (BB) Br ex 30.54 Dght 10.931 Lbp 171.00 Br md 30.50 Dpth 15.30 Welded, 1 dk	**(A21A2BC) Bulk Carrier** Grain: 46,112; Bale: 44,492 Compartments: 5 Ho, ER 5 Ha: (15.2 x 12.8)4 (19.2 x 15.2)ER Cranes: 4x25t	**1 oil engine** driving 1 FP propeller Total Power: 5,811kW (7,901hp) 14.6kn Sulzer 6RTA52 1 x 2 Stroke 6 Cy. 520 x 1800 5811kW (7901bhp) Diesel United Ltd.-Aioi AuxGen: 3 x 450kW 450V a.c Fuel: 1650.0 (r.f.)
611884 *8B4771*	**ZOGREO** *ex* Count Turk *-2009* *ex* Count Turf *-2007* *ex* H. O. S. Count Turf *-1996* *ex* Juan J. Orgeron *-1994* **Selig Services Ltd** Guardian Maritime Ltd *Kingstown* *St Vincent & The Grenadines* MMSI: 376961000 Official number: 11244	**559** 167 -	Class: (AB)	**1976-08 Halter Marine, Inc. — Pierre Part, La** Yd No: 547 Loa 49.20 Br ex 11.89 Dght 3.372 Lbp 47.33 Br md 11.59 Dpth 3.97 Welded, 1 dk	**(B21A20S) Platform Supply Ship**	**2 oil engines** reverse reduction geared to sc. shafts driving 2 FP propellers Total Power: 1,648kW (2,240hp) 12.0kn G.M. (Detroit Diesel) 16V-149-TI 2 x Vee 2 Stroke 16 Cy. 146 x 146 each-824kW (1120bhp) General Motors Detroit DieselAllison Divn-USA AuxGen: 2 x 75kW Thrusters: 1 Thwart. FP thruster (f) Fuel: 135.0 (d.f.)
727616 *JGM*	**ZOHRAB VELIYEV** *ex* Charait *-1993* **Southern Oil Fleet Administration (Yuzhnoye Upravleniye Neftyanogo Morskogo Flota)** - *Baku* *Azerbaijan* MMSI: 423122100 Official number: DGR-0131	**775** 232 313	Class: RS	**1985 Yaroslavskiy Sudostroitelnyy Zavod — Yaroslavl** Yd No: 604 Loa 53.74 Br ex 10.71 Dght 4.380 Lbp 47.25 Br md 10.50 Dpth 6.00 Welded, 1 dk	**(B31A2SR) Research Survey Vessel** Ice Capable	**1 oil engine** driving 1 CP propeller Total Power: 971kW (1,320hp) 12.4kn S.K.L. 8NVD48A-2U 1 x 4 Stroke 8 Cy. 320 x 480 971kW (1320bhp) VEB Schwermaschinenbau "KarlLiebknecht" (SKL)-Magdeburg AuxGen: 1 x 300kW a.c, 3 x 150kW a.c
720729 *EPBN9*	**ZOHREH** **Ahmad Poursameri** - *Bandar Abbas* *Iran* MMSI: 422028700 Official number: 16789	*125* 14 -	Class: (LR) ✠ Classed LR until 20/5/77	**1967-08 Ando Tekkosho — Tokyo** Yd No: 191 Loa 26.01 Br ex 6.86 Dght - Lbp 23.50 Br md 6.51 Dpth 3.00 Welded, 1 dk	**(B32A2ST) Tug**	**1 oil engine** reverse geared to sc. shaft driving 1 FP propeller Total Power: 883kW (1,201hp) Caterpillar 1 x 4 Stroke 883kW (1201bhp) (new engine 2011) Caterpillar Inc-USA AuxGen: 2 x 20kW 110V d.c
8814158 *9LH2039*	**ZOJA I** *ex* Don *-1989* **Ship & Shore Services Ltd** - *Freetown* *Sierra Leone*	**18,625** 8,626 28,610 T/cm 39.6	Class: (NV) **100A1** SS 09/2008 Double Hull oil tanker ESP LI **LMC** **IGS**	**1988-10 Khersonskiy Sudostroitelnyy Zavod — Kherson** Yd No: 1411 Loa 178.96 (BB) Br ex - Dght 11.020 Lbp 165.00 Br md 25.30 Dpth 15.02 Welded, 1 dk	**(A13A2TW) Crude/Oil Products Tanker** Double Hull Liq: 30,555; Liq (Oil): 30,555 Cargo Heating Coils Compartments: 14 Ta, ER 4 Cargo Pump (s): 4x700m³/hr Manifold: Bow/CM: 90m	**1 oil engine** driving 1 FP propeller Total Power: 9,600kW (13,052hp) 14.8kn B&W 6L67GFCA 1 x 2 Stroke 6 Cy. 670 x 1700 9600kW (13052bhp) Bryanskiy Mashinostroitelnyy Zavod (BMZ)-Bryansk AuxGen: 3 x 560kW 380V 50Hz a.c, 1 x 160kW 380V 50Hz a.c Fuel: 250.1 (d.f.) 1600.3 (r.f.) 32.0pd
8819108 *9LH2040*	**ZOJA II** *ex* Kmir *-1990* **Sarco Petroleum & Gas Ltd** Ship & Shore Services Ltd *Freetown* *Sierra Leone*	**18,625** 8,626 28,557 T/cm 39.6	Class: LR (NV) (RS) **100A1** SS 12/2008 Double Hull oil tanker ESP LI **LMC** **IGS**	**1989-01 Khersonskiy Sudostroitelnyy Zavod — Kherson** Yd No: 1413 Loa 178.96 Br ex - Dght 11.020 Lbp 164.71 Br md 25.32 Dpth 15.02 Welded, 1 dk	**(A12B2TR) Chemical/Products Tanker** Double Hull Liq: 30,565; Liq (Oil): 30,565 Cargo Heating Coils Compartments: 14 Wing Ta, 2 Wing Slop Ta, ER 4 Cargo Pump (s): 4x700m³/hr Manifold: Bow/CM: 89m Ice Capable	**1 oil engine** driving 1 FP propeller Total Power: 8,694kW (11,820hp) 14.0kn B&W 6DKRN67/170 1 x 2 Stroke 6 Cy. 670 x 1700 8694kW (11820bhp) Bryanskiy Mashinostroitelnyy Zavod (BMZ)-Bryansk AuxGen: 3 x 560kW 440V 50Hz a.c, 1 x 160kW 440V 50Hz a.c Fuel: 224.0 (d.f.) 1710.0 (r.f.) 33.0pd

9093634 *9BDX* -	**ZOLFAGHAR 3** - - *Bandar Imam Khomeini* *Iran* MMSI: 422421000 Official number: 20424	**375** 221 700	Class: AS	**1974-01 in Iran** Loa 44.87 Br ex - Dght 3.200 Lbp - Br md 8.16 Dpth 3.60 Welded, 1 dk	**(A31A2GX) General Cargo Ship**	**1 oil engine** driving 1 Propeller Total Power: 309kW (420hp) Kelvin TASC 1 x 4 Stroke 8 Cy. 165 x 184 309kW (420bhp) Kelvin Diesels Ltd.-Glasgow
7906966 *UEZK* -	**ZOLOTAYA KOLYMA** *ex* Necat A *-2002* *ex* Bronson *-1991* *ex* Federal Elbe *-1989* **North Eastern Shipping Co Ltd (NESCO Ltd) (OOO 'Severo-Vostochnoye Morskoye Parokhodstvo')** - SatCom: Inmarsat C 427322469 *Magadan* *Russia* MMSI: 273443400	**18,237** 10,900 28,645 T/cm 27.6	Class: RS (NV) (BV)	**1981-03 VEB Mathias-Thesen-Werft — Wismar** Yd No: 125 Lengthened-1981 Loa 199.80 (BB) Br ex 22.91 Dght 8.551 Lbp 192.31 Br md 22.86 Dpth 14.00 Welded, 1 dk	**(A21A2BC) Bulk Carrier** Grain: 35,777; Bale: 35,112 TEU 828 C Ho 474 TEU C Dk 354 TEU Compartments: 6 Ho, ER 6 Ha: ER Cranes: 4x25t Ice Capable	**1 oil engine** driving 1 CP propeller Total Power: 8,238kW (11,200hp) 17.9k MAN K8Z70/120 1 x 2 Stroke 8 Cy. 700 x 1200 8238kW (11200bhp) VEB Dieselmotorenwerk Rostock-Rostock AuxGen: 3 x 640kW 440V 60Hz a.c Thrusters: 1 Thwart. CP thruster (f) Fuel: 355.0 (d.f.) (Heating Coils) 1196.0 (r.f.) 33.5pd
8724432 *UDTP* -	**ZOLOTISTYY** *ex* Seaprimfico-01 *-1989* *ex* Zolotistyy *-1990* **OOO 'Yunichek'** - SatCom: Inmarsat C 427320845 *Sovetskaya Gavan* *Russia* MMSI: 273814410 Official number: 852873	**677** 233 492	Class: (RS) (VR)	**1986-08 Khabarovskiy Sudostroitelnyy Zavod im Kirova — Khabarovsk** Yd No: 858 Loa 55.01 Br ex 9.52 Dght 4.340 Lbp 50.04 Br md 9.30 Dpth 5.16 Welded, 1 dk	**(B12B2FC) Fish Carrier** Ins: 632 Ice Capable	**1 oil engine** driving 1 FP propeller Total Power: 589kW (801hp) 11.3k S.K.L. 6NVD48A-2 1 x 4 Stroke 6 Cy. 320 x 480 589kW (801bhp) VEB Schwermaschinenbau "KarlLiebknecht" (SKL)-Magdeburg AuxGen: 3 x 150kW a.c Fuel: 114.0 (d.f.)
8212099 *UDYI* -	**ZOLOTO KOLYMY** *ex* Utviken *-2012* *ex* C. Blanco *-1995* *ex* Bijelo Polje *-1992* **North Eastern Shipping Co Ltd (NESCO Ltd) (OOO 'Severo-Vostochnoye Morskoye Parokhodstvo')** - *Nakhodka* *Russia* MMSI: 273350680	**17,191** 11,303 30,052 T/cm 37.6	Class: RS (AB) (NV) (BV) (JR)	**1987-05 Astilleros Espanoles SA (AESA) — Bilbao** Yd No: 356 Loa 189.41 (BB) Br ex 22.89 Dght 10.680 Lbp 178.01 Br md 22.81 Dpth 14.61 Welded, 1 dk	**(A21A2BC) Bulk Carrier** Grain: 36,848; Bale: 34,536 TEU 468 Compartments: 7 Ho, ER 7 Ha: 7 (12.8 x 11.0)ER Cranes: 4x16t Ice Capable	**1 oil engine** driving 1 FP propeller Total Power: 7,999kW (10,875hp) 16.0k B&W 5L67GFC 1 x 2 Stroke 5 Cy. 670 x 1700 7999kW (10875bhp) (made 1983, fitted 1987) Astilleros Espanoles SA (AESA)-Spain AuxGen: 3 x 440kW 440V 60Hz a.c Fuel: 180.0 (d.f.) 1564.0 (r.f.) 30.5pd
8124204 *WDG8480* -	**ZOLOTOI** *ex* Norcrown *-1993* *ex* Margaret G *-1990* *ex* Alaska Invader *-1990* **AAUR LLC** - *Seattle, WA* *United States of America* MMSI: 367577950 Official number: 625095	*199* 147 -		**1980-08 Bender Shipbuilding & Repair Co Inc — Mobile AL** Yd No: 136 Converted From: Stern Trawler-2013 Lengthened & Widened-1998 Loa 30.90 Br ex - Dght - Lbp - Br md 10.97 Dpth 4.19 Welded, 1 dk	**(B31A2SR) Research Survey Vessel**	**1 oil engine** driving 1 FP propeller Total Power: 496kW (674hp) G.M. (Detroit Diesel) 12V-14 1 x Vee 2 Stroke 12 Cy. 146 x 146 496kW (674bhp) General Motors Detroit DieselAllison Divn-USA
8899926 *UCGJ* -	**ZOLOTOY** **Vanino Marine Trading Port JSC (Vaninskiy Morskoy Torgovyy Port OAO)** - *Vanino* *Russia* Official number: 831171	**279** 83 86	Class: RS	**1985-05 Brodogradiliste 'Tito' — Belgrade** Yd No: 1100 Loa 35.23 Br ex 9.01 Dght 3.160 Lbp 30.00 Br md 9.00 Dpth 4.50 Welded, 1 dk	**(B32A2ST) Tug** Ice Capable	**2 oil engines** geared to sc. shaft driving 1 CP propeller Total Power: 1,854kW (2,520hp) 11.5k Sulzer 6ASL25/3 2 x 4 Stroke 6 Cy. 250 x 300 each-927kW (1260bhp) Tvornica Dizel Motora 'Jugoturbina'-Yugoslavia AuxGen: 2 x 100kW a.c Fuel: 61.0 (d.f.)
7353444 *ERTN* -	**ZOMOROD** *ex* Permina Supply No. 3 *-1998* **Star Petroleum Group Co** Star Petroleum Co FZC *Giurgiulesti* *Moldova* MMSI: 214182014	**712** 214 934	Class: GL (KI) (AB)	**1974-01 Shikoku Dockyard Co. Ltd. — Takamatsu** Yd No: 767 Loa 49.99 (BB) Br ex 11.66 Dght 4.201 Lbp 45.47 Br md 11.59 Dpth 4.88 Welded, 1 dk	**(B21B20A) Anchor Handling Tug Supply** Cranes: 1x7t	**2 oil engines** reverse reduction geared to sc. shafts driving 2 FP propellers Total Power: 2,206kW (3,000hp) 10.0k Niigata 8MG25B 2 x 4 Stroke 8 Cy. 250 x 320 each-1103kW (1500bhp) Niigata Engineering Co Ltd-Japan AuxGen: 2 x 160kW 450V 60Hz a.c Thrusters: 1 Thwart. FP thruster (f) Fuel: 340.5
9138044 *EQVC* -	**ZOMOROUD** **Valfajre Eight Shipping Co** Valfajre Shipping Co *Bandar Abbas* *Iran* MMSI: 422022000 Official number: 681	**673** 202 80	Class: (NV)	**1996-12 WaveMaster International Pty Ltd — Fremantle WA** Yd No: 134 Loa 44.90 Br ex 12.75 Dght 2.450 Lbp 37.60 Br md 12.00 Dpth 4.00 Welded, 1 dk	**(A36A2PR) Passenger/Ro-Ro Ship (Vehicles)** Hull Material: Aluminium Alloy Passengers: unberthed: 236 Side ramp (p. a.) Len: 2.80 Wid: 2.50 Swl: - Lane-Len: 19 Cars: 10	**2 oil engines** with clutches, flexible couplings & sr geared to sc. shafts driving 2 Water jets Total Power: 3,920kW (5,330hp) 28.5k M.T.U. 16V396TE74 2 x Vee 4 Stroke 16 Cy. 165 x 185 each-1960kW (2665bhp) MTU Friedrichshafen GmbH-Friedrichshafen AuxGen: 2 x 160kW 220/380V 50Hz a.c Fuel: 15.0 (d.f.) 7.0pd
9139359 *9MAM6* -	**ZON 1** **Langkawi Ferry Services Sdn Bhd** *Penang* *Malaysia* MMSI: 533531000 Official number: 325497	**152** 59 20	Class: (NV)	**1996-07 NQEA Australia Pty Ltd — Cairns QLD** Yd No: 197 Loa 25.40 Br ex 8.64 Dght 1.340 Lbp 22.11 Br md 8.40 Dpth 2.65 Welded, 1 dk	**(A37B2PS) Passenger Ship** Hull Material: Aluminium Alloy Passengers: unberthed: 166	**2 oil engines** with clutches, flexible couplings & sr reverse geared to sc. shafts driving 2 FP propellers Total Power: 1,250kW (1,700hp) 24.0k MAN D2842L 2 x Vee 4 Stroke 12 Cy. 128 x 142 each-625kW (850bhp) MAN Nutzfahrzeuge AG-Nuernberg AuxGen: 2 x 38kW 415V 50Hz a.c Fuel: 4.3 (d.f.) 7.6pd
9139361 *9MAM7* -	**ZON 2** **Langkawi Saga Travel & Tours Sdn Bhd** *Penang* *Malaysia* MMSI: 533617000 Official number: 325498	**152** 59 20	Class: (NV)	**1996-07 NQEA Australia Pty Ltd — Cairns QLD** Yd No: 198 Loa 25.40 Br ex 8.64 Dght 1.340 Lbp 22.11 Br md 8.40 Dpth 2.65 Welded, 1 dk	**(A37B2PS) Passenger Ship** Hull Material: Aluminium Alloy Passengers: unberthed: 166	**2 oil engines** with clutches, flexible couplings & sr reverse geared to sc. shafts driving 2 FP propellers Total Power: 1,250kW (1,700hp) 24.0k MAN D2842L 2 x Vee 4 Stroke 12 Cy. 128 x 142 each-625kW (850bhp) MAN Nutzfahrzeuge AG-Nuernberg AuxGen: 2 x 38kW 415V 50Hz a.c Fuel: 4.3 (d.f.) 7.6pd
7329962 - -	**ZONACE I** *ex* Of. Union *-1998* *ex* Oceanic Moon *-1989* - -	*607* 146 -	Class: (AB) (BV)	**1973 Bludworth Shipyard Inc. — Houston, Tx** Yd No: 7600 Converted From: Offshore Supply Ship-1989 Loa 53.03 Br ex 11.89 Dght 3.677 Lbp 51.83 Br md 11.59 Dpth 4.27 Welded, 1 dk	**(B11B2FV) Fishing Vessel**	**2 oil engines** reverse reduction geared to sc. shafts driving 2 FP propellers Total Power: 1,654kW (2,248hp) 13.0k Caterpillar D399SCA 2 x Vee 4 Stroke 16 Cy. 159 x 203 each-827kW (1124bhp) Caterpillar Tractor Co-USA AuxGen: 2 x 90kW Thrusters: 1 Thwart. FP thruster (f) Fuel: 235.0 (d.f.)
8881010 *UHFS* -	**ZOND** **Kaliningradgeofizika (A/O Kaliningradgeofizika)** - *Kaliningrad* *Russia* MMSI: 273530210	**747** 224 354	Class: (RS)	**1987-07 Khabarovskiy Sudostroitelnyy Zavod im Kirova — Khabarovsk** Yd No: 612 Loa 55.76 Br ex 9.51 Dght 4.220 Lbp 49.87 Br md 9.30 Dpth 5.17 Welded, 1 dk	**(B31A2SR) Research Survey Vessel** Ice Capable	**1 oil engine** driving 1 CP propeller Total Power: 736kW (1,001hp) 12.2k S.K.L. 6NVD48A-2 1 x 4 Stroke 6 Cy. 320 x 480 736kW (1001bhp) VEB Schwermaschinenbau "KarlLiebknecht" (SKL)-Magdeburg
7503439 *LW4496* -	**ZONDA** **Rio Lujan Navegacion SA de Transportes Fluviales y Remolques (Rio Lujan Navegacion SA Towage & Salvage)** - *Argentina* MMSI: 701000963 Official number: 02348	*245* 115 -	Class: (AB)	**1977-10 Astilleros Principe, Menghi y Penco S.A. — Avellaneda** Yd No: 87 Loa 31.70 Br ex - Dght 3.302 Lbp 28.68 Br md 8.60 Dpth 4.20 Welded, 1 dk	**(B32A2ST) Tug**	**1 oil engine** sr geared to sc. shaft driving 1 CP propeller Total Power: 993kW (1,350hp) 12.0k GMT A300.6 1 x 4 Stroke 6 Cy. 300 x 450 993kW (1350bhp) Grandes Motores Diesel SAIC (FIAT Concord)-Argentina AuxGen: 2 x 60kW
8852239 *WAW7811* -	**ZONE FIVE** **Heuker Bros Inc** - *Warrendale, OR* *United States of America* MMSI: 368217000 Official number: 974423	*193* 131 -		**1991 Long's Marine Enterprises — Toledo, Or** Yd No: 18 Loa - Br ex - Dght - Lbp - Br md - Dpth - Welded, 1 dk	**(B11B2FV) Fishing Vessel**	**2 oil engines** reduction geared to sc. shafts driving 2 FP propellers Total Power: 592kW (804hp) Caterpillar 3408T 2 x Vee 4 Stroke 8 Cy. 137 x 152 each-296kW (402bhp) Caterpillar Inc-USA

IMO / Call sign	Name, owner, port	Tonnage	Class	Builder / Dimensions	Type / Cargo	Machinery
424449 - -	**ZONGWE** **Government of The Democratic Republic of Congo (Office Congolais des Chemins de Fer des Grand Lacs)** - *Kalemie* *Congo (Democratic Republic)*	*200* - -		**1975 Schiffswerft Germersheim GmbH — Germersheim** Yd No: 698 Loa 30.00 Br ex 8.51 Dght 2.515 Lbp 27.51 Br md 8.49 Dpth 3.71 Welded, 1 dk	**(B32A2ST) Tug**	**2 oil engines** driving 2 FP propellers Total Power: 762kW (1,036hp) MWM TD440-6 2 x 4 Stroke 6 Cy. 230 x 270 each-381kW (518bhp) Motoren Werke Mannheim AG (MWM)-West Germany
350587 *COC3* -	**ZOOM ZOOM ZOOM** **Winora Finance Corp** - *George Town* *Cayman Islands (British)* MMSI: 319395000 Official number: 737666	**465** 139 157	Class: AB	**2005-08 Trinity Yachts LLC — New Orleans LA** Yd No: 030 Loa 47.80 Br ex 8.84 Dght 2.360 Lbp 40.50 Br md 8.53 Dpth 4.17 Welded, 1 dk	**(X11A2YP) Yacht** Hull Material: Aluminium Alloy	**2 oil engines** reduction geared to sc. shafts driving 2 Propellers Total Power: 2,795kW (3,800hp) Caterpillar 3516B-HD 2 x Vee 4 Stroke 16 Cy. 170 x 215 each-1397kW (1899bhp) Caterpillar Inc-USA
907714 5NHT -	**ZOR** *ex* Al-Hodaibia *-2002* *ex* Misfah 6 *-2001* *ex* J. O. R. C. 6 *-1983* **Ship & Shore Services Ltd** - *Lagos* *Nigeria* MMSI: 657155000 Official number: 377473	*381* 114 -	Class: LR ✠ **100A1** SS 07/2009 tug ✠ **LMC** Eq.Ltr: (G) E; Cable: 275.0/22.0 U2	**1980-06 Martin Jansen GmbH & Co. KG Schiffsw. u. Masch. — Leer** Yd No: 156 Loa 36.50 Br ex 11.00 Dght 4.312 Lbp 34.14 Br md 10.60 Dpth 5.19 Welded, 1 dk	**(B32A2ST) Tug**	**2 oil engines** reverse reduction geared to sc. shafts driving 2 FP propellers Total Power: 2,060kW (2,800hp) 13.5kn MWM TBD440-8K 2 x 4 Stroke 8 Cy. 230 x 270 each-1030kW (1400bhp) Motoren Werke Mannheim AG (MWM)-West Germany AuxGen: 3 x 50kW 400V 50Hz a.c
7415644 - -	**ZORA** *ex* Maria del Mar Franco *-1999* **Emafish Sarl** - *Nouadhibou* *Mauritania*	*248* 86 -	Class: (RI) (BV)	**1976-03 Ast. Ojeda y Aniceto S.A. — Aviles** Yd No: 20 Loa 36.86 Br ex 7.88 Dght 3.676 Lbp 32.01 Br md 7.82 Dpth 3.87 Welded, 1 dk	**(B11A2FT) Trawler**	**1 oil engine** driving 1 FP propeller Total Power: 924kW (1,256hp) 10.8kn A.B.C. 8MDXC 1 x 4 Stroke 8 Cy. 242 x 320 924kW (1256bhp) Anglo Belgian Co NV (ABC)-Belgium Fuel: 134.0 (d.f.)
7739155 - -	**ZORA** **Raymond Laurence Clarke** - *Port Adelaide, SA* *Australia*	*229* 187 -		**1978 Kali Boat Building Pty Ltd — Port Adelaide SA** Loa - Br ex - Dght - Lbp 24.41 Br md 7.90 Dpth 2.49 Welded, 1 dk	**(B11B2FV) Fishing Vessel**	**1 oil engine** driving 1 FP propeller Total Power: 852kW (1,158hp) 11.5kn G.M. (Detroit Diesel) 16V-149-TI 1 x Vee 2 Stroke 16 Cy. 146 x 146 852kW (1158bhp) General Motors Detroit DieselAllison Divn-USA
6406892 *9A2545* -	**ZORA** **Milos Zelika Cimera** - *Zadar* *Croatia* Official number: 225	*194* 98 320	Class: CS (JR)	**1942 Jadranska Brodogradilista — Kraljevica** Loa 31.91 Br ex 7.24 Dght 2.693 Lbp 30.08 Br md 7.19 Dpth 3.13 Welded, 1 dk	**(A31A2GX) General Cargo Ship** Grain: 250 2 Ha: 2 (4.6 x 2.9)	**1 oil engine** driving 1 FP propeller Total Power: 265kW (360hp) 6.0kn Sulzer 6BAH22 1 x 4 Stroke 6 Cy. 220 x 320 265kW (360bhp) (new engine 1960) Tvornica Dizel Motora 'Jugoturbina'-Yugoslavia AuxGen: 2 x 2kW 24V a.c
8302399 *TCBC6* -	**ZORER KARDESLER** **Haci Saban Zorer Deniz Nakliyat ve Ticaret Ltd Sti** Alka Deniz Tasimacilik Insaat Madencilik ve Orman Urunleri Pazarlama Sanayi ve Ticaret Ltd Sti *Istanbul* *Turkey* MMSI: 271002128 Official number: 5277	**978** 598 1,922	Class: TL (AB)	**1984-10 Dearsan Gemi Insaat ve Sanayii Koll. Sti. — Tuzla** Yd No: 3 Loa 67.21 Br ex - Dght 5.701 Lbp 61.18 Br md 10.41 Dpth 6.20 Welded, 1 dk	**(A31A2GX) General Cargo Ship** Grain: 2,237; Bale: 2,095 Compartments: 2 Ho, ER 2 Ha: ER Derricks: 3x3t	**1 oil engine** driving 1 FP propeller Total Power: 736kW (1,001hp) 11.0kn S.K.L. 6NVD48A-2U 1 x 4 Stroke 6 Cy. 320 x 480 736kW (1001bhp) VEB Schwermaschinenbau "KarlLiebknecht" (SKL)-Magdeburg AuxGen: 2 x 80kW a.c, 1 x 41kW a.c
9599391 *3EUU6* -	**ZORINA** **Zorina Navigation Corp** - SatCom: Inmarsat C 437365110 *Panama* *Panama* MMSI: 373651000 Official number: 4370012	**32,987** 19,208 57,000 T/cm 58.8	Class: LR ✠ **100A1** SS 12/2011 bulk carrier CSR BC-A GRAB (20) Nos. 2 & 4 holds may be empty ESP **ShipRight** (ACS (B,D),CM) *IWS LI ✠ **LMC** **UMS** Eq.Ltr: M†; Cable: 634.2/73.0 U3 (a)	**2011-12 Zhejiang Zengzhou Shipyard Co Ltd — Zhoushan ZJ** Yd No: 002 Loa 189.99 (BB) Br ex 32.30 Dght 12.800 Lbp 185.00 Br md 32.26 Dpth 18.01 Welded, 1 dk	**(A21A2BC) Bulk Carrier** Grain: 71,634; Bale: 68,200 Compartments: 5 Ho, ER 5 Ha: ER Cranes: 4x30t	**1 oil engine** driving 1 FP propeller Total Power: 9,480kW (12,889hp) 14.2kn MAN-B&W 6S50MC-C 1 x 2 Stroke 6 Cy. 500 x 2000 9480kW (12889bhp) STX Engine Co Ltd-South Korea AuxGen: 3 x 600kW 450V 60Hz a.c Boilers: AuxB (Comp) 8.8kgf/cm² (8.6bar)
7945261 *9AA2216* -	**ZORNIK** *ex* Katria Prima *-1999* *ex* Plutone *-1999* *ex* M. S. C. Merlin *-1999* **Marituna dd** - *Zadar* *Croatia* Official number: 3T-732	**137** 41 -	Class: CS (RI)	**1940-04 Henry Robb Ltd. — Leith** Yd No: 295 Loa 28.20 Br ex 7.07 Dght 2.930 Lbp 26.24 Br md 7.01 Dpth 3.66 Welded, 1 dk	**(B32A2ST) Tug**	**2 oil engines** geared to sc. shaft driving 1 FP propeller Total Power: 882kW (1,200hp) Deutz SBF12M716 2 x Vee 4 Stroke 12 Cy. 135 x 160 each-441kW (600bhp) Kloeckner Humboldt Deutz AG-Germany
8623937 *OBPP*	**ZORRITOS** *ex* Grigoriy Nesterenko *-2007* **BBVA Banco Continental** Servicio Naviero de la Marina de Guerra del Peru *Callao* *Peru* MMSI: 760114000	**18,641** 8,641 28,750 T/cm 39.1	Class: LR (RS) **100A1** SS 11/2011 Double Hull oil tanker MARPOL 13G (1) (c) ESP LI Ice Class 1C **LMC UMS IGS** Cable: 304.0/72.0	**1986-08 Khersonskiy Sudostroitelnyy Zavod — Kherson** Yd No: 1406 Loa 178.96 (BB) Br ex 25.33 Dght 11.000 Lbp 165.00 Br md 25.30 Dpth 15.00 Welded, 1 dk	**(A13B2TP) Products Tanker** Double Hull (13F) Liq: 31,168; Liq (Oil): 31,168 Cargo Heating Coils Compartments: 14 Wing Ta, ER 4 Cargo Pump (s): 4x660m³/hr Manifold: Bow/CM: 89.5m Ice Capable	**1 oil engine** driving 1 FP propeller Total Power: 9,600kW (13,052hp) 14.8kn B&W 6L67GFCA 1 x 2 Stroke 6 Cy. 670 x 1700 9600kW (13052bhp) Bryanskiy Mashinostroitelnyy Zavod (BMZ)-Bryansk AuxGen: 1 x 600kW a.c, 3 x 500kW a.c Boilers: 2 WTAuxB (o.f.) 17.0kgf/cm² (16.7bar), AuxB (ex.g.) 10.0kgf/cm² (9.8bar) Fuel: 300.0 (d.f.) 1774.0 (r.f.) 29.0pd
7008166 - -	**ZORRITOS 2** *ex* Dali *-1977* **Pesquera Marbella SA** - *Chimbote* *Peru* Official number: CE-004083-PM	*225* 106 -	Class: (GL)	**1969 Ast. Picsa S.A. — Callao** Yd No: 260 L reg 30.70 Br ex 7.40 Dght - Lbp - Br md - Dpth 3.46 Welded, 1 dk	**(B11B2FV) Fishing Vessel**	**1 oil engine** reverse reduction geared to sc. shaft driving 1 FP propeller Total Power: 375kW (510hp) 10.8kn Caterpillar D379B 1 x Vee 4 Stroke 8 Cy. 159 x 203 375kW (510bhp) Caterpillar Tractor Co-USA
6915647 - -	**ZORRITOS 3** *ex* Velasquez *-1975* **Empresa Del Mar Pacifico** - *Chimbote* *Peru* Official number: SE-004020-PM	*225* 105 -	Class: (GL)	**1968 Ast. Picsa S.A. — Callao** Yd No: 252 Loa - Br ex 7.37 Dght - Lbp 27.08 Br md 7.35 Dpth 3.46 Welded, 1 dk	**(B11B2FV) Fishing Vessel**	**1 oil engine** driving 1 FP propeller Total Power: 375kW (510hp) 10.8kn Caterpillar D379B 1 x Vee 4 Stroke 8 Cy. 159 x 203 375kW (510bhp) Caterpillar Tractor Co-USA
6930922 - -	**ZORRITOS 4** *ex* Santa Elena XIV *-1976* - -	*200* - -	Class: (LR) ✠ Classed LR until 28/7/82	**1969-10 Fabricaciones Metallicas E.P.S. (FABRIMET) — Callao** Yd No: 390 Loa 30.18 Br ex 7.80 Dght 3.696 Lbp 26.45 Br md 7.68 Dpth 3.69 Welded	**(B11B2FV) Fishing Vessel**	**1 oil engine** sr reverse geared to sc. shaft driving 1 FP propeller Total Power: 439kW (597hp) MAN R8V16/18TL 1 x 4 Stroke 8 Cy. 160 x 180 439kW (597bhp) Maschinenbau Augsburg Nuernberg (MAN)-Augsburg
7002069 - -	**ZORRITOS 5** *ex* Santa Elena XV *-1975* - -	*200* - -	Class: (LR) ✠ Classed LR until 28/7/82	**1969-11 Fabricaciones Metallicas E.P.S. (FABRIMET) — Callao** Yd No: 391 Loa 30.18 Br ex 7.80 Dght 3.696 Lbp 26.45 Br md 7.68 Dpth 3.69 Welded	**(B11B2FV) Fishing Vessel**	**1 oil engine** sr reverse geared to sc. shaft driving 1 FP propeller Total Power: 439kW (597hp) MAN R8V16/18TL 1 x 4 Stroke 8 Cy. 160 x 180 439kW (597bhp) Maschinenbau Augsburg Nuernberg (MAN)-Augsburg
6915752 - PS7789	**ZORRITOS 7** *ex* PA 10 *-1975* **Pesquera Dona Lita SCRL** - *Chimbote* *Peru* Official number: CE-002959-PM	**260** - -	Class: (GL)	**1968 Ast. Picsa S.A. — Callao** Yd No: 253 L reg 30.70 Br ex 7.37 Dght - Lbp - Br md 7.35 Dpth 3.46 Welded, 1 dk	**(B11B2FV) Fishing Vessel**	**1 oil engine** driving 1 FP propeller Total Power: 375kW (510hp) 10.8kn Caterpillar D379B 1 x Vee 4 Stroke 8 Cy. 159 x 203 375kW (510bhp) Caterpillar Tractor Co-USA

6916811 - -	**ZORRITOS 10** *ex* PA 11 *-1976* - -	*225* 106 -	Class: (GL)	**1969 Ast. Picsa S.A. — Callao** Yd No: 258 Loa - Br ex 7.37 Dght - Lbp 27.77 Br md 7.35 Dpth 3.46 Welded, 1 dk	**(B11B2FV) Fishing Vessel**	**1 oil engine** driving 1 FP propeller Total Power: 375kW (510hp) Caterpillar 1 x Vee 4 Stroke 8 Cy. 159 x 203 375kW (510bhp) Caterpillar Tractor Co-USA	10.8k D379
8881682 *5VBE4* -	**ZORTURK** *ex* Aspet *-2011* *ex* Inia *-2004* *ex* Maria-K *-2002* *ex* Maria-K 1 *-1998* *ex* Maria K *-1998* *ex* Nevskiy-21 *-1998* **Durmusoglu Holding SA** Ozturk Denizcilik Insaat ve Dis Ticaret Ltd Sti SatCom: Inmarsat C 467100030 *Lome* *Togo* MMSI: 671204000	**2,976** 1,915 2,965	Class: IC KC (RS)	**1983 Nevskiy Sudostroitelnyy i Sudoremontnyy Zavod — Petrokrepost** Yd No: 21 Loa 110.70 Br ex - Dght 2.520 Lbp 104.83 Br md 14.80 Dpth 4.30 Welded, 1 dk	**(A31A2GX) General Cargo Ship** Grain: 1,733 Compartments: 1 Ho, ER 1 Ha: (58.0 x 7.5)ER	**2 oil engines** driving 2 FP propellers Total Power: 1,134kW (1,542hp) S.K.L. 2 x 4 Stroke 6 Cy. 320 x 480 each-567kW (771bhp) VEB Schwermaschinenbau "KarlLiebknecht" (SKL)-Magdeburg AuxGen: 4 x 50kW a.c Fuel: 633.0 (d.f.)	10.0k 6NVD48A-2
9582831 *3EEA9* -	**ZOSCO DALIAN** **ZOSCO Dalian Shipping Corp** Zhejiang Fuchuen Shipping & Enterprises Co Ltd SatCom: Inmarsat C 435142410 *Panama* *Panama* MMSI: 351424000 Official number: 4206010	**94,710** 59,527 180,371 T/cm 124.3	Class: CC	**2010-09 Dalian Shipbuilding Industry Co Ltd — Dalian LN (No 2 Yard)** Yd No: BC1800-5 Loa 295.00 (BB) Br ex - Dght 18.100 Lbp 285.00 Br md 46.00 Dpth 24.80 Welded, 1 dk	**(A21A2BC) Bulk Carrier** Grain: 201,953 Compartments: 9 Ho, ER 9 Ha: 7 (15.5 x 20.0)ER 2 (15.5 x 16.5)	**1 oil engine** driving 1 FP propeller Total Power: 18,660kW (25,370hp) MAN-B&W 1 x 2 Stroke 6 Cy. 700 x 2800 18660kW (25370bhp) Dalian Marine Diesel Co Ltd-China AuxGen: 3 x 900kW 450V a.c	14.5k 6S70MC-
9436513 *3FGJ4* -	**ZOSCO HONGKONG** **ZOSCO Hongkong Shipping Corp** Zhejiang Fuchuen Shipping & Enterprises Co Ltd SatCom: Inmarsat C 435252010 *Panama* *Panama* MMSI: 352520000 Official number: 4231411	**94,710** 59,527 180,154 T/cm 124.3	Class: CC	**2010-10 Dalian Shipbuilding Industry Co Ltd — Dalian LN (No 2 Yard)** Yd No: BC1800-6 Loa 295.00 (BB) Br ex - Dght 18.120 Lbp 285.00 Br md 46.00 Dpth 24.80 Welded, 1 dk	**(A21A2BC) Bulk Carrier** Grain: 201,953 Compartments: 9 Ho, ER 9 Ha: 7 (15.5 x 20.0)ER 2 (15.5 x 16.5)	**1 oil engine** driving 1 FP propeller Total Power: 18,397kW (25,013hp) MAN-B&W 1 x 2 Stroke 6 Cy. 700 x 2800 18397kW (25013bhp) Dalian Marine Diesel Co Ltd-China AuxGen: 3 x 900kW 450V a.c	14.5k 6S70MC-
9467677 *3EWU2* -	**ZOSCO HUZHOU** **ZOSCO Huzhou Shipping Corp** Zhejiang Fuchuen Shipping & Enterprises Co Ltd SatCom: Inmarsat C 437125110 *Panama* *Panama* MMSI: 371251000 Official number: 4173610	**91,971** 59,546 175,949 T/cm 120.8	Class: AB	**2010-06 Jinhai Heavy Industry Co Ltd — Daishan County ZJ** Yd No: J0038 Loa 291.80 (BB) Br ex - Dght 18.250 Lbp 282.20 Br md 45.00 Dpth 24.75 Welded, 1 dk	**(A21A2BC) Bulk Carrier** Grain: 198,243 Compartments: 9 Ho, ER 9 Ha: ER	**1 oil engine** driving 1 FP propeller Total Power: 16,860kW (22,923hp) MAN-B&W 1 x 2 Stroke 6 Cy. 700 x 2674 16860kW (22923bhp) Hyundai Heavy Industries Co Ltd-South Korea AuxGen: 3 x 900kW a.c Fuel: 340.0 (d.f.) 4400.0 (r.f.)	14.5k 6S70M
9557874 *3FX03* -	**ZOSCO JIAXING** **Bright Zhejiang Shipping Corp** Zhejiang Fuchuen Shipping & Enterprises Co Ltd SatCom: Inmarsat C 437243110 *Panama* *Panama* MMSI: 372431000 Official number: 4102210	**91,971** 59,546 175,886 T/cm 120.8	Class: BV (AB)	**2009-10 Jinhai Heavy Industry Co Ltd — Daishan County ZJ** Yd No: J0011 Loa 291.80 (BB) Br ex - Dght 18.250 Lbp 282.20 Br md 45.00 Dpth 24.75 Welded, 1 dk	**(A21A2BC) Bulk Carrier** Grain: 198,476 Compartments: 9 Ho, ER 9 Ha: ER	**1 oil engine** driving 1 FP propeller Total Power: 16,860kW (22,923hp) MAN-B&W 1 x 2 Stroke 6 Cy. 700 x 2674 16860kW (22923bhp) Doosan Engine Co Ltd-South Korea AuxGen: 3 x 900kW 60Hz a.c	14.5k 6S70M
9493626 *3EWI2* -	**ZOSCO JINHUA** **ZOSCO Jinhua Shipping Corp** Zhejiang Fuchuen Shipping & Enterprises Co Ltd *Panama* *Panama* MMSI: 355336000 Official number: 4320111	**91,971** 59,546 175,931 T/cm 120.8	Class: AB	**2011-09 Jinhai Heavy Industry Co Ltd — Daishan County ZJ** Yd No: J0022 Loa 291.80 (BB) Br ex - Dght 18.250 Lbp 282.20 Br md 45.00 Dpth 24.75 Welded, 1 dk	**(A21A2BC) Bulk Carrier** Grain: 197,374 Compartments: 9 Ho, ER 9 Ha: ER	**1 oil engine** driving 1 FP propeller Total Power: 16,860kW (22,923hp) MAN-B&W 1 x 2 Stroke 6 Cy. 700 x 2674 16860kW (22923bhp) Hitachi Zosen Corp-Japan AuxGen: 3 x 900kW 440/220V a.c	14.5k 6S70M
9493614 *3FPV5* -	**ZOSCO LISHUI** **ZOSCO Lishui Shipping Corp** Zhejiang Fuchuen Shipping & Enterprises Co Ltd *Panama* *Panama* MMSI: 370815000 Official number: 4292311	**91,971** 59,546 175,911 T/cm 120.8	Class: CC (AB)	**2011-07 Jinhai Heavy Industry Co Ltd — Daishan County ZJ** Yd No: J0019 Loa 291.80 (BB) Br ex - Dght 18.250 Lbp 282.20 Br md 45.00 Dpth 24.75 Welded, 1 dk	**(A21A2BC) Bulk Carrier** Grain: 198,252 Compartments: 9 Ho, ER 9 Ha: 7 (15.6 x 20.0)ER 2 (15.6 x 16.5)	**1 oil engine** driving 1 FP propeller Total Power: 16,860kW (22,923hp) MAN-B&W 1 x 2 Stroke 6 Cy. 700 x 2674 16860kW (22923bhp) Hitachi Zosen Corp-Japan AuxGen: 3 x 900kW a.c	14.9k 6S70M
9454577 *3FJG2* -	**ZOSCO QINGDAO** **ZOSCO Qingdao Shipping Corp** Zhejiang Fuchuen Shipping & Enterprises Co Ltd *Panama* *Panama* MMSI: 354257000 Official number: 4294711	**94,710** 59,527 180,389 T/cm 124.3	Class: CC	**2011-07 Dalian Shipbuilding Industry Co Ltd — Dalian LN (No 2 Yard)** Yd No: BC1800-12 Loa 295.00 (BB) Br ex 46.12 Dght 18.100 Lbp 285.00 Br md 46.00 Dpth 24.80 Welded, 1 dk	**(A21A2BC) Bulk Carrier** Grain: 201,953 Compartments: 9 Ho, ER 9 Ha: 7 (15.5 x 20.0)ER 2 (15.5 x 16.5)	**1 oil engine** driving 1 FP propeller Total Power: 18,660kW (25,370hp) MAN-B&W 1 x 2 Stroke 6 Cy. 700 x 2800 18660kW (25370bhp) Dalian Marine Diesel Co Ltd-China AuxGen: 3 x 900kW 450V a.c	14.5k 6S70MC-
9579884 *3FEU5* -	**ZOSCO QUZHOU** **ZOSCO Quzhou Shipping Corp** Zhejiang Fuchuen Shipping & Enterprises Co Ltd SatCom: Inmarsat C 447702873 *Panama* *Panama* MMSI: 354658000 Official number: 4216811	**91,971** 59,546 175,886 T/cm 120.8	Class: CC (AB)	**2010-09 Jinhai Heavy Industry Co Ltd — Daishan County ZJ** Yd No: J0039 Loa 291.80 (BB) Br ex - Dght 18.250 Lbp 282.20 Br md 45.00 Dpth 24.75 Welded, 1 dk	**(A21A2BC) Bulk Carrier** Grain: 198,243 Compartments: 9 Ho, ER 9 Ha: ER	**1 oil engine** driving 1 FP propeller Total Power: 16,860kW (22,923hp) MAN-B&W 1 x 2 Stroke 6 Cy. 700 x 2674 16860kW (22923bhp) Hyundai Heavy Industries Co Ltd-South Korea AuxGen: 3 x 900kW a.c Fuel: 354.0 (d.f.) 4735.0 (r.f.)	14.5k 6S70M
9454565 *3EWZ5* -	**ZOSCO SHANGHAI** **ZOSCO Shanghai Shipping Corp** Zhejiang Fuchuen Shipping & Enterprises Co Ltd SatCom: Inmarsat C 435505610 *Panama* *Panama* MMSI: 355056000 Official number: 4263211	**94,710** 59,527 180,145 T/cm 124.3	Class: CC	**2011-01 Dalian Shipbuilding Industry Co Ltd — Dalian LN (No 2 Yard)** Yd No: BC1800-11 Loa 295.00 (BB) Br ex 46.12 Dght 18.100 Lbp 284.81 Br md 46.00 Dpth 24.80 Welded, 1 dk	**(A21A2BC) Bulk Carrier** Grain: 201,953 Compartments: 9 Ho, ER 9 Ha: 7 (15.5 x 20.0)ER 2 (15.5 x 16.5)	**1 oil engine** driving 1 FP propeller Total Power: 18,660kW (25,370hp) MAN-B&W 1 x 2 Stroke 6 Cy. 700 x 2800 18660kW (25370bhp) Dalian Marine Diesel Co Ltd-China AuxGen: 3 x 900kW 440/220V a.c	14.5k 6S70MC-
9467665 *3EZH8* -	**ZOSCO SHAOXING** **Bright Zhejiang Shipping Corp** Zhejiang Fuchuen Shipping & Enterprises Co Ltd SatCom: Inmarsat C 437208310 *Panama* *Panama* MMSI: 372083000 Official number: 4111510	**91,971** 59,546 175,879 T/cm 120.8	Class: BV (AB)	**2009-11 Jinhai Heavy Industry Co Ltd — Daishan County ZJ** Yd No: J0012 Loa 291.80 (BB) Br ex - Dght 18.250 Lbp 282.20 Br md 45.00 Dpth 24.75 Welded, 1 dk	**(A21A2BC) Bulk Carrier** Grain: 198,252 Compartments: 9 Ho, ER 9 Ha: ER	**1 oil engine** driving 1 FP propeller Total Power: 16,860kW (22,923hp) MAN-B&W 1 x 2 Stroke 6 Cy. 700 x 2674 16860kW (22923bhp) Doosan Engine Co Ltd-South Korea AuxGen: 2 x 1125kW 60Hz a.c, 1 x 900kW 60Hz a.c Fuel: 340.0 (d.f.) 4819.0 (r.f.)	14.5k 6S70M
9572666 *H07535* -	**ZOSCO TAIZHOU** **ZOSCO Taizhou Shipping Corp** Zhejiang Fuchuen Shipping & Enterprises Co Ltd SatCom: Inmarsat C 437276110 *Panama* *Panama* MMSI: 372761000 Official number: 4169610	**91,971** 59,546 175,885 T/cm 120.8	Class: AB	**2010-05 Jinhai Heavy Industry Co Ltd — Daishan County ZJ** Yd No: J0037 Loa 291.80 (BB) Br ex - Dght 18.250 Lbp 282.20 Br md 45.00 Dpth 24.75 Welded, 1 dk	**(A21A2BC) Bulk Carrier** Grain: 198,243 Compartments: 9 Ho, ER 9 Ha: ER	**1 oil engine** driving 1 FP propeller Total Power: 16,860kW (22,923hp) MAN-B&W 1 x 2 Stroke 6 Cy. 700 x 2674 16860kW (22923bhp) Hyundai Heavy Industries Co Ltd-South Korea AuxGen: 3 x 900kW a.c Thrusters: 1 Tunnel thruster (f) Fuel: 340.0 (d.f.) 4397.0 (r.f.)	14.5k 6S70M
9075656 *3EHN3* -	**ZOSCO ZHOUSHAN** *ex* Goldstar *-2006* *ex* Cape Iris *-2006* **ZOSCO Zhoushan Shipping Corp** Zhejiang Ocean Shipping Co Ltd (ZOSCO) SatCom: Inmarsat C 437217510 *Panama* *Panama* MMSI: 372175000 Official number: 3235507A	**75,871** 48,666 149,309 T/cm 105.4	Class: NK	**1994-09 Hyundai Heavy Industries Co Ltd — Ulsan** Yd No: 873 Loa 269.88 (BB) Br ex 43.30 Dght 17.417 Lbp 259.00 Br md 43.00 Dpth 23.80 Welded, 1 dk	**(A21A2BC) Bulk Carrier** Grain: 165,614; Bale: 157,778 Compartments: 9 Ho, ER 9 Ha: 2 (14.0 x 17.0)7 (14.0 x 20.0)ER	**1 oil engine** driving 1 FP propeller Total Power: 14,049kW (19,101hp) B&W 1 x 2 Stroke 5 Cy. 700 x 2674 14049kW (19101bhp) Hyundai Heavy Industries Co Ltd-South Korea AuxGen: 4 x a.c Fuel: 4570.0 (r.f.)	14.2k 5S70M

412775 **ZOUZOU**
FGI7
Doran Navigation Inc
Opera SA
Panama — Panama
MMSI: 354102000
Official number: 44731PEXT

30,075 / 13,325 / 50,651 / T/cm 52.0

Class: LR
✠ **100A1** SS 01/2010
Double Hull oil and chemical tanker, Ship Type 3
ESP
ShipRight (SDA, FDA, CM)
*IWS
LI
SPM
EP
✠ **LMC** **UMS IGS**
Eq.Ltr: M†;
Cable: 632.5/73.0 U3 (a)

2010-01 SPP Plant & Shipbuilding Co Ltd — Sacheon Yd No: S1028
Loa 183.00 (BB) Br ex 33.08 Dght 13.000
Lbp 174.00 Br md 32.20 Dpth 19.10
Welded, 1 dk

(A12B2TR) Chemical/Products Tanker
Double Hull (13F)
Liq: 52,145; Liq (Oil): 52,145
Cargo Heating Coils
Compartments: 12 Wing Ta, 2 Wing Slop Ta, ER
12 Cargo Pump (s): 12x600m³/hr
Manifold: Bow/CM: 92m

1 oil engine driving 1 FP propeller
Total Power: 9,480kW (12,889hp) 14.9kn
MAN-B&W 6S50MC-C
1 x 2 Stroke 6 Cy. 500 x 2000 9480kW (12889bhp)
Doosan Engine Co Ltd-South Korea
AuxGen: 3 x 900kW 450V 60Hz a.c
Boilers: e (ex.g.) 11.7kgf/cm² (11.5bar), WTAuxB (o.f.) 9.0kgf/cm² (8.8bar)

410222 **ZOUZOU N.**
A8SM6
Finaco Trade & Investment SA
Dynacom Tankers Management Ltd
SatCom: Inmarsat C 463705985
Monrovia — Liberia
MMSI: 636014251
Official number: 14251

85,362 / 47,365 / 149,991 / T/cm 122.3

Class: AB

2010-01 New Times Shipbuilding Co Ltd — Jingjiang JS Yd No: 0316303
Loa 274.20 (BB) Br ex 50.04 Dght 16.000
Lbp 264.00 Br md 50.00 Dpth 23.20
Welded, 1 dk

(A13A2TV) Crude Oil Tanker
Double Hull (13F)
Liq: 177,392; Liq (Oil): 182,178
Cargo Heating Coils
Compartments: 12 Wing Ta, ER, 2 Wing Slop Ta
3 Cargo Pump (s): 3x4000m³/hr
Manifold: Bow/CM: 139.6m

1 oil engine driving 1 FP propeller
Total Power: 18,660kW (25,370hp) 15.3kn
MAN-B&W 6S70MC-C
1 x 2 Stroke 6 Cy. 700 x 2800 18660kW (25370bhp)
Hyundai Heavy Industries Co Ltd-South Korea
AuxGen: 3 x 950kW a.c
Fuel: 385.0 (d.f.) 4250.0 (r.f.)

7724265 **ZOYA**
V3MA4
-
ex Merchant Brilliant *-2008*
ex Jolly Bruno *-1993*
ex Norwegian Challenger *-1982*
Williston Impex Corp
Subsidiary Company 'Almar' of 'Almar Shipping Corp'
Belize City — Belize
MMSI: 312717000
Official number: 370830043

9,368 / 6,971 / 5,300

Class: RS (NV) (BV) (RI)

1979-07 Vaagen Verft AS — Kyrksaeterora Yd No: 43
Loa 133.05 Br ex 21.65 Dght 5.031
Lbp 122.71 Br md 21.01 Dpth 12.22
Welded, 1 dk & S dk

(A35A2RR) Ro-Ro Cargo Ship
Passengers: driver berths: 6
Stern door/ramp (centre)
Len: 11.00 Wid: 12.00 Swl: -
Lane-Len: 1272
Cars: 56, Trailers: 106
TEU 524 C RoRo Dk 201 TEU C Dk 323 TEU incl 10 ref C.
Compartments: 2 Ho, ER
Ice Capable

2 oil engines sr geared to sc. shafts driving 2 CP propellers
Total Power: 6,616kW (8,996hp) 17.0kn
MaK 12M453AK
2 x Vee 4 Stroke 12 Cy. 320 x 420 each-3308kW (4498bhp)
MaK Maschinenbau GmbH-Kiel
AuxGen: 1 x 504kW 440V 60Hz a.c, 3 x 220kW 440V 60Hz a.c
Thrusters: 2 Thwart. CP thruster (f)
Fuel: 1013.0 (r.f.) 30.5pd

7423495 **ZOYA**
AVDE
-
ex Seabulk Toota *-2009* *ex* GMMOS Toota *-1997*
ex Toota *-1995* *ex* Gulf Fleet No. 12 *-1989*
Prince Marine Transport Services Pvt Ltd
Amba Shipping & Logistics Pvt Ltd
Mumbai — India
MMSI: 419093900
Official number: 3651

775 / 232 / 1,084

Class: IR (BV) (AB)

1975-07 Quality Equipment Inc — Houma LA Yd No: 127
Loa 56.37 Br ex 12.20 Dght 4.185
Lbp 50.86 Br md 12.15 Dpth 4.88
Welded, 1 dk

(B21B20T) Offshore Tug/Supply Ship

2 oil engines reverse reduction geared to sc. shafts driving 2 FP propellers
Total Power: 2,868kW (3,900hp) 10.0kn
EMD (Electro-Motive) 16-645-E6
2 x Vee 2 Stroke 16 Cy. 230 x 254 each-1434kW (1950bhp) (Reconditioned , Reconditioned & fitted 1975)
General Motors Corp.Electro-Motive Div.-La Grange
AuxGen: 2 x 99kW 440/225V 60Hz a.c
Thrusters: 1 Thwart. FP thruster (f)
Fuel: 328.0 (d.f.)

9597355 **ZP BOXER**
9HA3213
-
ZP Boxer Ltd
Kotug International BV
Valletta — Malta
MMSI: 229295000
Official number: 11127

205 / 89 / 99

Class: GL (LR)
✠ Classed LR until 13/11/12

2012-11 Song Thu Co. — Da Nang (Hull)
Yd No: (545003)
2012-11 B.V. Scheepswerf Damen — Gorinchem
Yd No: 545003
Loa 24.47 Br ex 12.60 Dght 3.230
Lbp 23.14 Br md 12.00 Dpth 4.60
Welded, 1 dk

(B32A2ST) Tug

2 oil engines gearing integral to driving 2 Z propellers
Total Power: 4,200kW (5,710hp)
Caterpillar 3516B
2 x Vee 4 Stroke 16 Cy. 170 x 190 each-2100kW (2855bhp)
Caterpillar Inc-USA
AuxGen: 2 x 69kW 400V 50Hz a.c

9597367 **ZP BULLDOG**
9HA3212
-
ZP Bulldog Ltd
Kotug International BV
Valletta — Malta
MMSI: 229294000
Official number: 11128

205 / 89 / 150

Class: GL (LR)
✠ Classed LR until 13/11/12

2012-11 Song Thu Co. — Da Nang (Hull)
Yd No: (545004)
2012-11 B.V. Scheepswerf Damen — Gorinchem
Yd No: 545004
Loa 24.85 Br ex 12.60 Dght 3.230
Lbp 23.14 Br md 12.00 Dpth 4.60
Welded, 1 dk

(B32A2ST) Tug

2 oil engines gearing integral to driving 2 Z propellers
Total Power: 4,200kW (5,710hp)
Caterpillar 3516B
2 x Vee 4 Stroke 16 Cy. 170 x 190 each-2100kW (2855bhp)
Caterpillar Inc-USA
AuxGen: 2 x 69kW 400V 50Hz a.c

8103078 **ZP CHALONE**
PH2109
-
Kotug Twee BV
Kotug Europe BV
Rotterdam — Netherlands
Official number: 18970BR1989

194 / 132 / 337

Class: AB

1982-02 Valley Shipbuilding, Inc. — Brownsville, Tx Yd No: 113
Loa 28.50 Br ex - Dght 5.060
Lbp 26.93 Br md 10.37 Dpth 3.81
Welded, 1 dk

(B32A2ST) Tug

2 oil engines sr geared to sc. shafts driving 2 Directional propellers
Total Power: 2,206kW (3,000hp) 8.0kn
EMD (Electro-Motive) 12-645-E6
2 x Vee 2 Stroke 12 Cy. 230 x 254 each-1103kW (1500bhp)
General Motors Corp.Electro-Motive Div.-La Grange
AuxGen: 2 x 99kW 440V 60Hz a.c

8103066 **ZP CONDON**
PH2411
-
Kotug Een BV
Kotug Europe BV
Rotterdam — Netherlands
Official number: 18969BR1989

194 / 132 / 337

Class: AB

1981-09 Valley Shipbuilding, Inc. — Brownsville, Tx Yd No: 112
Loa 28.50 Br ex - Dght 5.060
Lbp 26.93 Br md 10.37 Dpth 3.81
Welded, 1 dk

(B32A2ST) Tug

2 oil engines reverse reduction geared to sc. shafts driving 2 Directional propellers
Total Power: 2,206kW (3,000hp) 8.0kn
EMD (Electro-Motive) 12-645-E6
2 x Vee 2 Stroke 12 Cy. 230 x 254 each-1103kW (1500bhp)
General Motors Corp.Electro-Motive Div.-La Grange
AuxGen: 2 x 99kW 440V 60Hz a.c

6729933 **ZRMANJA**
9A2267
-
ex Bristva *-1987* *ex* Hornisse *-1982*
Mediteran 2000 doo

Zadar — Croatia
Official number: 3T-208

424 / 200 / 942 / T/cm 2.7

Class: CS (JR) (GL)

1967-07 Schiffswerft u. Maschinenfabrik Max Sieghold — Bremerhaven Yd No: 142
Loa 55.71 Br ex 9.30 Dght 3.577
Lbp 50.02 Br md - Dpth 4.20
Welded, 1 dk

(A13B2TU) Tanker (unspecified)
Liq: 1,070; Liq (Oil): 1,070
Cargo Heating Coils
Compartments: 6 Wing Ta, ER
1 Cargo Pump (s): 1x250m³/hr
Manifold: Bow/CM: 33m
Ice Capable

1 oil engine driving 1 FP propeller
Total Power: 405kW (551hp) 10.0kn
MWM D4846U
1 x 4 Stroke 6 Cy. 320 x 480 405kW (551bhp)
Motoren Werke Mannheim AG (MWM)-West Germany
AuxGen: 2 x 100kW 380V 50Hz a.c

5239058 **ZU**
-
-
ex Molipesca *-1993*
-
-

201 / 60 / -

Class: (BV)

1961 Hijos de J. Barreras S.A. — Vigo Yd No: 1120
Loa 35.13 Br ex 6.89 Dght 3.550
Lbp 29.77 Br md 6.80 Dpth 3.97
Welded, 1 dk

(B11A2FT) Trawler
2 Ha:

1 oil engine driving 1 FP propeller
Total Power: 316kW (430hp) 10.5kn
Werkspoor 6TM270
1 x 4 Stroke 6 Cy. 270 x 500 316kW (430bhp)
Hijos de J Barreras SA-Spain

5399262 **ZUBAIDY**
-
-
-
-

141 / 69 / -

Class: (LR)
✠ Classed LR until 7/54

1950-03 J. Morris & Co. (Gosport) Ltd. — Fareham Yd No: 552
Loa 27.44 Br ex 6.28 Dght 2.248
Lbp - Br md 6.23 Dpth -
Riveted\Welded

(B11A2FT) Trawler
Compartments: 1 Ho, ER
1 Ha: (3.0 x 3.0)

1 oil engine driving 1 FP propeller
7.0kn
Widdop
1 x 2 Stroke 6 Cy. 215 x 305
H. Widdop & Co. Ltd.-Keighley
Fuel: 4.0

9551234 **ZUBAIR**
-
-
Government of The Republic of Iraq (Ministry of Oil) (South Oil Co - SOC)
Jawar Al Khaleej Shipping (LLC)

168 / 50 / 74

Class: (BV)

2009-05 in the Netherlands (Hull) Yd No: (544811)
2009-05 B.V. Scheepswerf Damen — Gorinchem
Yd No: 544811
Loa 33.25 Br ex - Dght 1.930
Lbp 32.99 Br md 6.34 Dpth 3.30
Welded, 1 dk

(B21A20C) Crew/Supply Vessel
Hull Material: Aluminium Alloy
Passengers: unberthed: 80

3 oil engines reduction geared to sc. shafts driving 3 FP propellers
Total Power: 2,460kW (3,345hp) 25.0kn
Caterpillar C32
3 x Vee 4 Stroke 12 Cy. 145 x 162 each-820kW (1115bhp)
Caterpillar Inc-USA
AuxGen: 2 x 69kW 400/230V 60Hz a.c

8038302 **ZUBAN**
UIYE
-
Dvina-M Ltd

Petropavlovsk-Kamchatskiy — Russia

173 / 51 / 88

Class: (RS)

1982-09 Astrakhanskaya Sudoverf im. "Kirova" — Astrakhan Yd No: 155
Loa 34.01 Br ex 7.09 Dght 2.890
Lbp 29.98 Br md - Dpth 3.69
Welded, 1 dk

(B11B2FV) Fishing Vessel
Ins: 115
Compartments: 1 Ho, ER
1 Ha: (1.6 x 1.3)
Derricks: 2x2t; Winches: 2
Ice Capable

1 oil engine driving 1 CP propeller
Total Power: 224kW (305hp) 9.0kn
S.K.L. 8NVD36-1U
1 x 4 Stroke 8 Cy. 240 x 360 224kW (305bhp)
VEB Schwermaschinenbau "KarlLiebknecht" (SKL)-Magdeburg
Fuel: 17.0 (d.f.)

6926373 **ZUBEIDI 1**
-
-
ex Hamoor I *-1982* *ex* Kindam 2 *-1978*
ex Hamoor I *-1971*
United Fisheries of Kuwait KSC

Kuwait — Kuwait
Official number: KT105/F

131 / 64 / -

Class: (AB) (BV)

1969 Ateliers & Chantiers de La Rochelle-Pallice — La Rochelle Yd No: 5170-6/2
Loa 25.20 Br ex 6.81 Dght 2.490
Lbp 22.59 Br md 6.71 Dpth 3.51
Welded, 1 dk

(B11A2FT) Trawler
Ins: 148

1 oil engine reverse reduction geared to sc. shaft driving 1 FP propeller
Total Power: 291kW (396hp) 10.0kn
Caterpillar D353SCAC
1 x 4 Stroke 6 Cy. 159 x 203 291kW (396bhp)
Caterpillar Tractor Co-USA
AuxGen: 2 x 10kW
Fuel: 56.0 (d.f.)

IMO / Call sign / Official no.	Name / Former names / Owner / Port / Flag	Tonnage	Class	Builder / Dimensions	Type	Machinery	Speed / Model
7104312 - -	**ZUBEIDI 2** **United Fisheries of Kuwait KSC** - *Kuwait* *Kuwait*	*131* 63 -	Class: (AB) (BV)	**1971 Ch. Normands Reunis — Courseulles-sur-Mer** Yd No: 24 Loa 25.20 Br ex 6.81 Dght 2.302 Lbp 22.56 Br md 6.71 Dpth 3.51 Welded, 1 dk	**(B11A2FT) Trawler** Ins: 140 Compartments: 1 Ho, ER 1 Ha: (1.0 x 1.4)	**1 oil engine** driving 1 FP propeller Total Power: 279kW (379hp) Caterpillar 1 x 4 Stroke 6 Cy. 159 x 203 279kW (379bhp) Caterpillar Tractor Co-USA AuxGen: 2 x 10kW	9.5k D353SCA
6928814 - -	**ZUBEIDI 4** *ex* Hamoor IV *-1982* **United Fisheries of Kuwait KSC** - *Kuwait* *Kuwait*	*131* 65 -	Class: (AB) (BV)	**1969 Ch. Normands Reunis — Courseulles-sur-Mer** Yd No: 9 Loa 25.20 Br ex 6.81 Dght 2.490 Lbp 22.59 Br md 6.71 Dpth 3.51 Welded, 1 dk	**(B11A2FT) Trawler** Ins: 142 Compartments: 1 Ho, ER 1 Ha: (1.1 x 1.6)	**1 oil engine** reverse reduction geared to sc. shaft driving 1 FP propeller Total Power: 291kW (396hp) Caterpillar 1 x 4 Stroke 6 Cy. 159 x 203 291kW (396bhp) Caterpillar Tractor Co-USA AuxGen: 2 x 10kW Fuel: 56.0 (d.f.)	10.0k D353SCA
8874237 *FGON* GV 724521	**ZUBERNOA** **Furic Maree Armement Sarl** *Guilvinec* *France* MMSI: 228150000 Official number: 724521	*145* - -		**1990 Chantiers Barde Aquitaine — Hendaye** Loa 23.80 Br ex - Dght - Lbp - Br md - Dpth - Welded, 1 dk	**(B11B2FV) Fishing Vessel**	**1 oil engine** driving 1 FP propeller	
8906456 *EGW* BI-22876	**ZUBEROA** *ex* Agur Zuberoa *-1996* **Atuneros Congeladores y Transportes Frigorificos SA (ATUNSA)** - SatCom: Inmarsat C 422458710 *Bermeo* *Spain* MMSI: 224587000 Official number: 3-2876/	**2,172** 651 1,743	Class: BV	**1991-04 Hijos de J. Barreras S.A. — Vigo** Yd No: 1540 Loa 92.40 (BB) Br ex - Dght 6.350 Lbp 68.44 Br md 13.60 Dpth 6.65 Welded, 2 dks	**(B11A2FT) Trawler** Ins: 1,885	**1 oil engine** with flexible couplings & sr geared to sc. shaft driving 1 FP propeller Total Power: 3,450kW (4,691hp) MaK 1 x 4 Stroke 6 Cy. 450 x 550 3450kW (4691bhp) Krupp MaK Maschinenbau GmbH-Kiel AuxGen: 4 x 516kW 220/380V 50Hz a.c Thrusters: 1 Thwart. FP thruster (f); 1 Thwart. FP thruster (a)	15.3kn 6M551AK
9275414 *TCCJ6* -	**ZUBEYDE ANA** *ex* TDI Zubeyde Ana *-2010* **Government of The Republic of Turkey (Kiyi Emniyeti ve Gemicilik Kurtarma Isletmesi Genel Mudurlugu Gemicilik Kur Dairesi Bsk)** - *Istanbul* *Turkey* MMSI: 271000671 Official number: 7975	**489** 147 840	Class: TL (AB)	**2002-05 Yardimci Tersanesi A.S. — Tuzla** Yd No: 22 Loa 34.00 Br ex 12.20 Dght 3.800 Lbp 32.08 Br md 11.60 Dpth 5.40 Welded, 1 dk	**(B32A2ST) Tug**	**2 oil engines** geared to sc. shafts driving 2 Directional propellers Total Power: 4,046kW (5,500hp) Deutz 2 x 4 Stroke 9 Cy. 240 x 280 each-2023kW (2750bhp) Deutz AG-Koeln AuxGen: 2 x 160kW a.c	SBV9M628
8611348 *TC5908* -	**ZUBEYDE HANIM** *ex* Rumelikavagi *-2009* **Government of The Republic of Turkey (Kiyi Emniyeti ve Gemicilik Kurtarma Isletmesi Genel Mudurlugu Gemicilik Kur Dairesi Bsk)** - *Istanbul* *Turkey* Official number: 5603	*307* 76 100	Class: TL	**1987-11 Turkiye Gemi Sanayii A.S. — Halic, Istanbul** Yd No: 270 Loa 49.13 Br ex - Dght - Lbp 44.62 Br md 8.95 Dpth 3.15 Welded, 1 dk	**(A37B2PS) Passenger Ship**	**2 oil engines** driving 2 FP propellers Total Power: 936kW (1,272hp) Sulzer 2 x 4 Stroke 6 Cy. 200 x 240 each-468kW (636bhp)	6AL20/24
8227135 - -	**ZUBR** *ex* Prangli *-2013* **MTA Logistika Ltd** - *St Petersburg* *Russia*	**228** 68 86	Class: RS	**1983 Brodogradiliste 'Tito' — Belgrade** Yd No: 1093 Loa 35.83 Br ex 9.10 Dght 3.180 Lbp 30.00 Br md 9.01 Dpth 4.50 Welded, 1 dk	**(B32A2ST) Tug** Ice Capable	**2 oil engines** geared to sc. shafts driving 2 FP propellers Total Power: 1,854kW (2,520hp) Sulzer 2 x 4 Stroke 6 Cy. 250 x 300 each-927kW (1260bhp) Tvornica Dizel Motora 'Jugoturbina'-Yugoslavia Fuel: 61.0 (r.f.)	11.5kn 6ASL25/30
8929965 - -	**ZUBR** **JSC Russian Port** Pionerskiy Ocean Fishing Marine Center (Pionerskaya Baza Okeanicheskogo Rybolovnogo Flota (BORF)) *Kaliningrad* *Russia* Official number: 742264	*187* - 46	Class: (RS)	**1974 "Petrozavod" — Leningrad** Yd No: 847 Loa 29.30 Br ex 8.49 Dght 3.090 Lbp 27.00 Br md - Dpth 4.34 Welded, 1 dk	**(B32A2ST) Tug** Ice Capable	**2 oil engines** driving 2 CP propellers Total Power: 882kW (1,200hp) Russkiy 2 x 2 Stroke 6 Cy. 300 x 500 each-441kW (600bhp) Mashinostroitelnyy Zavod"Russkiy-Dizel"-Leningrad AuxGen: 2 x 25kW a.c Fuel: 36.0 (d.f.)	11.4kn 6D30/50-4-2
7014206 - -	**ZUDAR** - -	**636** 190 1,107	Class: (DS)	**1970 VEB Elbewerft — Boizenburg** Yd No: 280 Loa 60.00 Br ex 10.32 Dght 2.899 Lbp 57.00 Br md 10.01 Dpth 3.51 Welded, 1 dk	**(B34A2SH) Hopper, Motor** Grain: 550 Ice Capable	**2 oil engines** driving 2 FP propellers Total Power: 470kW (640hp) S.K.L. 2 x 4 Stroke 6 Cy. 240 x 360 each-235kW (320bhp) VEB Schwermaschinenbau "KarlLiebknecht" (SKL)-Magdeburg AuxGen: 2 x 40kW 390V a.c	8.0kn 6NVD36A-1U
7006649 *EANL* -	**ZUDAR PRIMERO** *ex* Omafe Cuarto *-2000* *ex* Jasmund *-1999* **Ayora Puertos y Obras SL** - *La Coruna* *Spain* MMSI: 224353000 Official number: 1-2/1996	**615** 185 1,107	Class: (DS) (GL)	**1969-06 VEB Elbewerft — Boizenburg** Yd No: 276 Loa 60.00 Br ex 10.32 Dght 2.896 Lbp 57.00 Br md 10.05 Dpth 3.49 Welded, 1 dk	**(B34A2SH) Hopper, Motor** Hopper: 550 Ice Capable	**2 oil engines** driving 2 FP propellers Total Power: 470kW (640hp) S.K.L. 2 x 4 Stroke 6 Cy. 240 x 360 each-235kW (320bhp) VEB Schwermaschinenbau "KarlLiebknecht" (SKL)-Magdeburg AuxGen: 2 x 40kW 220/380V 50Hz a.c	8.0kn 6NVD36A-1U
9405784 *TCTT5* -	**ZUGA** *ex* Golden Freesia *-2011* *ex* Elena *-2008* **Ak Gemi Tasimaciligi Sanayi ve Ticaret AS** - *Istanbul* *Turkey* MMSI: 271043004	**4,598** 1,668 6,436 T/cm 16.1	Class: BV (AB)	**2008-03 Zhenjiang Sopo Shiprepair & Building Co Ltd — Zhenjiang JS** Yd No: SP0505 Loa 100.12 (BB) Br ex - Dght 6.513 Lbp 94.00 Br md 18.00 Dpth 9.60 Welded, 1 dk	**(A12B2TR) Chemical/Products Tanker** Double Hull (13F) Liq: 6,988; Liq (Oil): 7,300 Part Cargo Heating Coils Compartments: 12 Wing Ta, 2 Wing Slop Ta, ER 12 Cargo Pump (s): 12x300m³/hr	**1 oil engine** reduction geared to sc. shaft driving 1 CP propeller Total Power: 2,970kW (4,038hp) MaK 1 x 4 Stroke 9 Cy. 255 x 400 2970kW (4038bhp) Caterpillar Motoren GmbH & Co. KG-Germany AuxGen: 3 x 450kW a.c Thrusters: 1 Tunnel thruster (f) Fuel: 113.0 (d.f.) 257.0 (r.f.)	12.0kn 9M25
9023718 *9MEH5* -	**ZUHAIRI** *ex* Whitsunday Experience *-2000* **Citra Line Sdn Bhd** - *Port Klang* *Malaysia* MMSI: 533000215 Official number: 328412	**119** 56 -		**1992-09 Cougar Catamarans — Gold Coast QLD** Loa 23.40 Br ex 9.30 Dght 1.200 Lbp 22.20 Br md 8.38 Dpth 2.85 Welded, 1 dk	**(A37B2PS) Passenger Ship**	**2 oil engines** geared to sc. shafts driving 2 Propellers Caterpillar 2 x 4 Stroke Caterpillar Inc-USA	
8718641 *JVMP4* -	**ZUHAL** *ex* Rawu Ii *-2011* *ex* Leo *-2011* *ex* Shinyo *-2008* *ex* Eisho Maru *-2006* **Saturn Marine & Trading Pte Ltd** - *Ulaanbaatar* *Mongolia* MMSI: 457425000 Official number: 29131188	**496** 167 750		**1988-02 Taiyo Shipbuilding Co Ltd — Sanyoonoda YC** Yd No: 206 Loa 54.32 Br ex - Dght 3.501 Lbp 50.22 Br md 8.51 Dpth 3.81 Welded, 1 dk	**(A12B2TR) Chemical/Products Tanker**	**1 oil engine** reverse geared to sc. shaft driving 1 FP propeller Total Power: 746kW (1,014hp) Akasaka 1 x 4 Stroke 6 Cy. 260 x 440 746kW (1014bhp) Akasaka Tekkosho KK (Akasaka DieselLtd)-Japan	T26SR
8106317 - -	**ZUID** *ex* Eishin *-2007* *ex* Seiko *-2007* *ex* Rest No. 23 *-2006* *ex* Pharos *-2006* *ex* Shosei Maru No. 1 *-2003* *ex* Kissho Maru No. 88 *-2003* *ex* Ryotei Maru No. 18 *-1999* *ex* Keisho Maru No. 101 *-1987* **Federal State Unitary Enterprise Rosmorport** -	**257** 77 122		**1981-06 Niigata Engineering Co Ltd — Niigata NI** Yd No: 1721 Loa 36.50 Br ex - Dght 2.782 Lbp 30.82 Br md 7.41 Dpth 4.65 Welded, 1 dk	**(B11A2FS) Stern Trawler**	**1 oil engine** reduction geared to sc. shaft driving 1 FP propeller Total Power: 754kW (1,025hp) Niigata 1 x 4 Stroke 6 Cy. 280 x 320 754kW (1025bhp) Niigata Engineering Co Ltd-Japan	6MG28BX

IMO / Call sign	Name / Owner	Tonnage	Class	Builder / Dimensions	Type	Machinery
221279 *BIG*	**ZUIDERDAM** **HAL Antillen NV** Holland America Line NV SatCom: Inmarsat C 424530411 *Rotterdam* *Netherlands* MMSI: 245304000 Official number: 41220	**82,305** 48,129 10,965 T/cm 74.9	Class: LR (RI) ✠ **100A1** CS 11/2012 passenger ship *IWS LI ✠ **LMC** Eq.Ltr: U†; Cable: 725.5/90.0 U3 (a)	**2002**-11 **Fincantieri-Cant. Nav. Italiani S.p.A. (Breda) — Venezia** Yd No: 6075 Loa 285.42 (BB) Br ex 32.28 Dght 8.016 Lbp 254.07 Br md 32.25 Dpth 36.98 Welded	**(A37A2PC) Passenger/Cruise** Passengers: cabins: 924; berths: 2388	**5 diesel electric oil engines & 1 turbo electric Gas Turb** driving 3 gen. each 11200kW 11000V a.c 2 gen. each 8400kW 11000V a.c 1 gen. of 14000kW 11000V a.c Connecting to 2 elec. motors each (17600kW) driving 2 Azimuth electric drive units Total Power: 75,140kW (102,162hp) 22.0kn Sulzer 12ZAV40S 2 x Vee 4 Stroke 12 Cy. 400 x 560 each-8640kW (11747bhp) Wartsila Italia SpA-Italy Sulzer 16ZAV40S 3 x Vee 4 Stroke 16 Cy. 400 x 560 each-11520kW (15663bhp) Wartsila Italia SpA-Italy GE Marine LM2500 1 x Gas Turb 23300kW (31679shp) General Electric Co.-Lynn, Ma Boilers: e (ex.g.) 11.0kgf/cm² (10.8bar), e (ex.g.) 11.2kgf/cm² (11.0bar), e (ex.g.) 11.1kgf/cm² (10.9bar), WTAuxB (o.f.) 9.6kgf/cm² (9.4bar) Thrusters: 3 Thwart. FP thruster (f) Fuel: 588.0 (d.f.) 2315.0 (r.f.)
9056167 *PCAR* HD 27	**ZUIDERHAAKS** *ex* Aaltje Jan *-2008* **Rederij Jac Bakker en Zonen BV** - SatCom: Inmarsat C 424622210 *Den Helder* *Netherlands* MMSI: 246222000 Official number: 25270	**489** 146 -		**1993 Stocznia Gdynia SA — Gdynia** (Hull) Yd No: B682/02 **1993 B.V. Scheepswerf Maaskant — Stellendam** Yd No: 507 Loa 41.99 Br ex - Dght 3.750 Lbp 37.21 Br md 8.50 Dpth 5.00 Welded	**(B11A2FT) Trawler**	**1 oil engine** geared to sc. shaft driving 1 FP propeller Total Power: 1,470kW (1,999hp) Caterpillar 3606TA 1 x 4 Stroke 6 Cy. 280 x 300 1470kW (1999bhp) Caterpillar Inc-USA
6923838 *PBAK* UK 24	**ZUIDERKRUIS** *ex* Leni *-2001* *ex* Elisabeth *-1986* *ex* Nooit Verwacht *-1983* *ex* Willem *-1978* **Adriaantje Holding BV** - SatCom: Inmarsat M 623922110 *Urk* *Netherlands* MMSI: 244987000 Official number: 28823	**188** 56 -		**1969 van Goor's Scheepswerf en Mfbk N.V. — Monnickendam** Yd No: 639 Loa 29.21 Br ex - Dght - Lbp - Br md 6.63 Dpth 3.08 Welded, 1 dk	**(B11B2FV) Fishing Vessel**	**1 oil engine** driving 1 FP propeller Total Power: 706kW (960hp) 10.0kn Bolnes 8DNL190/600 1 x 2 Stroke 8 Cy. 190 x 350 706kW (960bhp) (new engine 1971) NV Machinefabriek 'Bolnes' v/h JHvan Cappellen-Netherlands
7365605 - -	**ZUIDERKRUIS** *ex* Wybrigje *-1984* *ex* De Enige Zoon *-1977* - -	*198* 79 -		**1974**-06 **Scheepswerf Haak N.V. — Zaandam** Yd No: 924 Loa 33.99 Br ex 7.50 Dght - Lbp 30.00 Br md 7.41 Dpth 4.02 Welded, 1 dk	**(B11A2FT) Trawler**	**1 oil engine** driving 1 FP propeller Deutz 1 x 4 Stroke Kloeckner Humboldt Deutz AG-West Germany
6701278 *CB2348* -	**ZUIDERSTER 2** *ex* L. A. Sjong *-1970* **Pesquera San Jose SA** - *Valparaiso* *Chile* Official number: 2330	*301* 128 -	Class: (NV)	**1966 Bolsones Verft AS — Molde** Yd No: 212 Loa 39.63 Br ex 8.11 Dght 4.001 Lbp 35.74 Br md - Dpth - Welded, 1 dk	**(B11B2FV) Fishing Vessel** Compartments: 6 Ho, ER 6 Ha: ER Cranes: 3x10t; Derricks: 1; Winches: 1	**1 oil engine** driving 1 FP propeller Total Power: 662kW (900hp) 11.5kn Wichmann 6ACA 1 x 2 Stroke 6 Cy. 280 x 420 662kW (900bhp) Wichmann Motorfabrikk AS-Norway AuxGen: 2 x 50kW 220V 50Hz a.c
6603749 - -	**ZUIDERSTER 3** *ex* Linda *-1970* *ex* Odel *-1969* - -	*279* 137 -	Class: (NV)	**1966 Kleven Mek Verksted AS — Ulsteinvik** Yd No: 12 Loa 38.54 Br ex 7.65 Dght - Lbp 33.36 Br md 7.62 Dpth - Welded, 1 dk	**(B11B2FV) Fishing Vessel**	**1 oil engine** driving 1 FP propeller Total Power: 500kW (680hp) 10.0kn Caterpillar D398SCAC 1 x Vee 4 Stroke 12 Cy. 159 x 203 500kW (680bhp) Caterpillar Tractor Co-USA
5330723 - -	**ZUIDERSTER 6** *ex* Sjovarden *-1974* - -	*279* 87 -	Class: (NV)	**1956**-12 **Aukra Bruk AS — Aukra** Yd No: 4 Lengthened-1964 Loa 37.65 Br ex 7.04 Dght 3.499 Lbp 33.02 Br md 7.01 Dpth 3.71 Welded, 1 dk	**(B11B2FV) Fishing Vessel** Compartments: 1 Ho, ER 3 Ha: (1.4 x 0.9) (3.5 x 2.2) (2.5 x 1.9) Derricks: 1x3t; Winches: 1	**1 oil engine** sr geared to sc. shaft driving 1 FP propeller Total Power: 625kW (850hp) Caterpillar D398SCAC 1 x Vee 4 Stroke 12 Cy. 159 x 203 625kW (850bhp) (new engine 1976) Caterpillar Tractor Co-USA AuxGen: 1 x 34kW 220V 50Hz a.c, 1 x 32kW 220V 50Hz a.c
6922365 - -	**ZUIDERSTER 7** *ex* Sverdrupson *-1975* - -	*236* 92 -	Class: (NV)	**1969 Leirvik Sveis AS — Stord** Yd No: 35 Loa 35.06 Br ex 7.50 Dght - Lbp 30.99 Br md 7.47 Dpth 3.97 Welded, 1 dk	**(B11B2FV) Fishing Vessel**	**1 oil engine** driving 1 FP propeller Total Power: 662kW (900hp) Wichmann 6ACA 1 x 2 Stroke 6 Cy. 280 x 420 662kW (900bhp) Wichmann Motorfabrikk AS-Norway AuxGen: 2 x 50kW 220V 50Hz a.c
6704713 - -	**ZUIDERSTER 8** *ex* Asgeir *-1978* - -	*299* 137 -	Class: (NV)	**1966 N.V. Scheepswerf Gebr. van der Werf — Deest** Yd No: 322 Lengthened-1973 Loa 41.69 Br ex 7.62 Dght 3.772 Lbp 33.69 Br md 7.60 Dpth 3.97 Welded, 1 dk	**(B11A2FT) Trawler** Compartments: 2 Ho, ER 2 Ha: 2 (2.5 x 1.6)ER Derricks: 1x3t; Winches: 1 Ice Capable	**1 oil engine** geared to sc. shaft driving 1 CP propeller Total Power: 588kW (799hp) Blackstone ESS8 1 x 4 Stroke 8 Cy. 222 x 292 588kW (799bhp) Lister Blackstone Marine Ltd.-Dursley AuxGen: 2 x 40kW 220V 50Hz a.c
7367859 *ZR2934* PEA 115	**ZUIDERZEE** **Eyethu Fishing Pty Ltd** - *Cape Town* *South Africa* Official number: 19103	*221* 66 -		**1974**-01 **Scheepswerf Vooruit B.V. — Zaandam** Yd No: 345 Converted From: Trawler-1991 Loa 29.37 Br ex 7.19 Dght - Lbp - Br md - Dpth 3.81 Welded, 1 dk	**(B11A2FS) Stern Trawler**	**1 oil engine** geared to sc. shaft driving 1 FP propeller Total Power: 827kW (1,124hp) Blackstone ESL8MK2 1 x 4 Stroke 8 Cy. 222 x 292 827kW (1124bhp) (new engine 1979) Mirrlees Blackstone (Stamford)Ltd.-Stamford
8333568 *OPBM* Z 39	**ZUIDERZEE** **Vita Nova BVBA** - *Zeebrugge* *Belgium* MMSI: 205149000 Official number: 01 00271 1996	**251** 75 -		**1982 Scheepswerven West-Vlaamse N.V. — Oostkamp** Loa 32.50 Br ex - Dght - Lbp - Br md 8.08 Dpth - Welded, 1 dk	**(B11A2FT) Trawler**	**1 oil engine** driving 1 FP propeller Total Power: 772kW (1,050hp) Bolnes 1 x 2 Stroke 772kW (1050bhp) 'Bolnes' Motorenfabriek BV-Netherlands
9097264 *PIYX*	**ZUIDERZEE** *ex* Genius *-1986* *ex* Unity *-1965* *ex* Klaus Hinrich Karstens *-1933* *ex* Pirat *-1927* *ex* Holtenau *-1925* *ex* Hans *-1916* *ex* Ernst Wilhelm *-1914* **Schoener BV** Stormvogel BV *Enkhuizen* *Netherlands* MMSI: 246084000 Official number: 5354	**131** 67 -		**1910 N.V. Scheepswerf J.J. Pattje & Zonen — Waterhuizen** Yd No: 23 Converted From: Passenger Ship-1992 Converted From: General Cargo Ship-1978 Lengthened-1950 Loa 40.00 Br ex 7.00 Dght 1.880 Lbp 27.50 Br md 6.80 Dpth 2.92 Riveted, 1 dk	**(A37A2PC) Passenger/Cruise** Passengers: cabins: 8; berths: 22	**1 oil engine** reduction geared to sc. shaft driving 1 Propeller Total Power: 191kW (260hp) G.M. (Detroit Diesel) 8V-71 1 x Vee 2 Stroke 8 Cy. 108 x 127 191kW (260bhp) (new engine ,made 1986) General Motors Corp-USA
9204611	**ZUIDERZEE** **Government of The Kingdom of The Netherlands (Rijkswaterstaat Directie Noordzee)** - *Lelystad* *Netherlands*	**181** - -	Class: (LR) ✠ Classed LR until 29/10/03	**1999**-10 **Werf "De Hoop" (Schiedam) B.V. — Schiedam** Yd No: 195 Loa 34.75 Br ex 7.00 Dght 1.500 Lbp 32.05 Br md 6.80 Dpth 2.80 Welded, 1 dk	**(B31A2SR) Research Survey Vessel**	**2 oil engines** with clutches, flexible couplings & sr reverse geared to sc. shafts driving 2 FP propellers Total Power: 522kW (710hp) 18.0kn Cummins NTA-855-M 2 x 4 Stroke 6 Cy. 140 x 152 each-261kW (355bhp) Cummins Engine Co Ltd-United Kingdom AuxGen: 1 x 78kW 380V 50Hz a.c, 1 x 37kW 380V 50Hz a.c Thrusters: 1 Thwart. FP thruster (f)
9629809 *PBZE*	**ZUIDVLIET** **Beheermaatschappij ms Zuidvliet BV** Hudig & Veder Chartering BV *Rotterdam* *Netherlands* MMSI: 244650317	**2,597** 1,460 3,850	Class: LR (Class contemplated) **100A1** 01/2014 Class contemplated	**2014**-01 **DAHK Chernomorskyi Sudnobudivnyi Zavod — Mykolayiv** (Hull) Yd No: (9408) **2014**-01 **B.V. Scheepswerf Damen Bergum — Bergum** Yd No: 9408 Loa 88.60 Br ex - Dght - Lbp - Br md 12.50 Dpth 7.00 Welded, 1 dk	**(A31A2GX) General Cargo Ship** TEU 188 C Ho 108 TEU C Dk 80 TEU	**1 oil engine** with clutches, flex coup & sr rev geared to sc. shaft driving 1 CP propeller Total Power: 1,520kW (2,067hp) 11.5kn MaK 8M20 1 x 4 Stroke 8 Cy. 200 x 300 1520kW (2067bhp) Caterpillar Motoren GmbH & Co. KG-Germany AuxGen: 1 x 140kW 400V 50Hz a.c, 1 x 259kW 400V 50Hz a.c Thrusters: 1 Tunnel thruster (f)

IMO / Call sign / Flag	Name / Owner / Port	Tonnage	Class	Builder / Dimensions	Type	Machinery	
9580168 *JD3075* -	**ZUIHO MARU** **Nitto Tugboat KK** *Kurashiki, Okayama* Japan Official number: 141260	*195* - -		**2010-06 Kanagawa Zosen — Kobe** Yd No: 610 Loa 38.20 Br ex - Dght - Lbp 33.45 Br md 9.00 Dpth 3.89 Welded, 1 dk	**(B32A2ST) Tug**	**2 oil engines** reduction geared to sc. shafts driving 2 Propellers Total Power: 3,680kW (5,004hp) Yanmar 2 x 4 Stroke 6 Cy. 260 x 385 each-1840kW (2502bhp) Yanmar Diesel Engine Co Ltd-Japan	6EY2
9691333 *7JQW* -	**ZUIHO MARU** *ex* Shitanoe 1326 *-2014* **Iino Gas Transport Co Ltd** *Kobe, Hyogo* Japan MMSI: 432970000 Official number: 142109	*997* - 1,447	Class: NK	**2014-03 Shitanoe Shipbuilding Co Ltd — Usuki OT** Yd No: 1326 Loa 71.50 Br ex - Dght 4.500 Lbp - Br md 12.50 Dpth 5.55 Welded, 1 dk	**(A11B2TG) LPG Tanker** Single Hull Liq (Gas): 1,820	**1 oil engine** reduction geared to sc. shaft driving 1 Propeller Total Power: 1,618kW (2,200hp) Akasaka 1 x 4 Stroke 6 Cy. 330 x 620 1618kW (2200bhp) Akasaka Tekkosho KK (Akasaka DieselLtd)-Japan	AX33
8889490 *JJ3900* -	**ZUIHO MARU** **Taiho Kaiun YK** *Amagasaki, Hyogo* Japan Official number: 132434	*499* - 1,550		**1995-02 Yamanaka Zosen K.K. — Imabari** Yd No: 570 Loa 74.90 Br ex - Dght 4.080 Lbp 70.00 Br md 12.00 Dpth 7.00 Welded, 1 dk	**(A31A2GX) General Cargo Ship** Bale: 2,476 Compartments: 1 Ho, ER 1 Ha: (40.0 x 9.5)ER	**1 oil engine** driving 1 FP propeller Total Power: 1,324kW (1,800hp) Hanshin 1 x 4 Stroke 6 Cy. 300 x 600 1324kW (1800bhp) The Hanshin Diesel Works Ltd-Japan	11.0k LH30L
9067013 - -	**ZUIHO MARU No. 5** -	**619** 248 487		**1993-04 Miho Zosensho K.K. — Shimizu** Yd No: 1421 Loa 57.00 (BB) Br ex - Dght 3.490 Lbp 50.50 Br md 9.00 Dpth 3.90 Welded, 1 dk	**(B11B2FV) Fishing Vessel** Ins: 545	**1 oil engine** with flexible couplings & sr geared to sc. shaft driving 1 FP propeller Total Power: 1,177kW (1,600hp) Akasaka 1 x 4 Stroke 6 Cy. 310 x 530 1177kW (1600bhp) Akasaka Tekkosho KK (Akasaka DieselLtd)-Japan AuxGen: 2 x 320kW 225V a.c Fuel: 310.0 (d.f.) 3.0pd	14.5k K31F
9016404 *JL5937* -	**ZUIHO MARU No. 5** **Chuo Kaiun KK** - *Anan, Tokushima* Japan Official number: 131506	*499* - 1,577		**1991-02 K.K. Miura Zosensho — Saiki** Yd No: 1010 Loa - Br ex - Dght 4.101 Lbp 70.01 Br md 12.51 Dpth 7.01 Welded	**(A31A2GX) General Cargo Ship**	**1 oil engine** geared to sc. shaft driving 1 FP propeller Total Power: 736kW (1,001hp) Hanshin 1 x 4 Stroke 6 Cy. 310 x 530 736kW (1001bhp) The Hanshin Diesel Works Ltd-Japan	LH31
6725975 - -	**ZUIHO MARU No. 8** - -	*495* 171 762		**1967 Narasaki Zosen KK — Muroran HK** Yd No: 602 Loa 52.48 Br ex 9.50 Dght 3.963 Lbp 47.50 Br md 9.48 Dpth 4.09 Welded, 1 dk	**(B11A2FT) Trawler**	**1 oil engine** driving 1 FP propeller Total Power: 1,214kW (1,651hp) Niigata 1 x 4 Stroke 6 Cy. 430 x 620 1214kW (1651bhp) Niigata Engineering Co Ltd-Japan	M6F43CH
9053634 - -	**ZUIHO MARU NO. 18** *ex* Eishin Maru No. 88 *-2009* - -	*409* - -		**1992-07 Niigata Engineering Co Ltd — Niigata NI** Yd No: 2236 Loa 57.39 (BB) Br ex - Dght 3.530 Lbp 49.70 Br md 9.00 Dpth 3.90 Welded, 1 dk	**(B11B2FV) Fishing Vessel** Ins: 502	**1 oil engine** with clutches, flexible couplings & sr reverse geared to sc. shaft driving 1 FP propeller Total Power: 699kW (950hp) Niigata 1 x 4 Stroke 6 Cy. 280 x 480 699kW (950bhp) Niigata Engineering Co Ltd-Japan	6M28HF
8743232 *JD2870* -	**ZUIKEI MARU** **Itsuki Kaiun KK** *Imabari, Ehime* Japan Official number: 140934	*498* - 1,800		**2009-01 Namikata Shipbuilding Co Ltd — Imabari EH** Yd No: 228 Loa 72.99 Br ex - Dght 4.330 Lbp 68.00 Br md 12.00 Dpth 7.35 Welded, 1 dk	**(A31A2GX) General Cargo Ship** 1 Ha: ER (40.0 x 9.5)	**1 oil engine** driving 1 FP propeller Total Power: 1,618kW (2,200hp) Hanshin 1 x 4 Stroke 6 Cy. 340 x 640 1618kW (2200bhp) The Hanshin Diesel Works Ltd-Japan	11.0k LH34L
9061526 *JL6191* -	**ZUIKO** **Ishizaki Kisen KK** *Matsuyama, Ehime* Japan MMSI: 431500513 Official number: 132939	*189* - 22		**1993-11 Hitachi Zosen Corp — Kawasaki KN** Yd No: 117309 Loa 31.00 Br ex - Dght 1.960 Lbp 27.00 Br md 9.00 Dpth 3.00 Welded, 1 dk	**(A37B2PS) Passenger Ship** Hull Material: Aluminium Alloy Passengers: unberthed: 160	**2 oil engines** with clutches, flexible couplings & sr reverse geared to sc. shafts driving 2 Water jets Total Power: 3,678kW (5,000hp) Niigata 2 x Vee 4 Stroke 16 Cy. 165 x 185 each-1839kW (2500bhp) Niigata Engineering Co Ltd-Japan AuxGen: 2 x 60kW 225V 60Hz a.c	34.0k 16V16F
9078189 *JL6145* -	**ZUIKO MARU** **Hatayama Marine Co Ltd** *Komatsushima, Tokushima* Japan MMSI: 431500104 Official number: 133900	*1,591* - 3,251	Class: NK	**1993-07 Higaki Zosen K.K. — Imabari** Yd No: 432 Loa 85.16 (BB) Br ex 13.02 Dght 6.104 Lbp 79.50 Br md 13.00 Dpth 6.85 Welded, 1 dk	**(A13B2TP) Products Tanker** Liq: 3,300; Liq (Oil): 3,300 Compartments: 10 Ta, ER	**1 oil engine** reverse geared to sc. shaft driving 1 FP propeller Total Power: 2,060kW (2,801hp) Hanshin 1 x 4 Stroke 6 Cy. 380 x 760 2060kW (2801bhp) The Hanshin Diesel Works Ltd-Japan Thrusters: 1 Thwart. CP thruster (f) Fuel: 165.0 (r.f.)	12.4k 6EL38
9266217 *JJ4038* -	**ZUIKO MARU** **Iino Gas Transport Co Ltd** *Kobe, Hyogo* Japan MMSI: 431301612 Official number: 135984	*749* - 1,184	Class: NK	**2002-04 K.K. Miura Zosensho — Saiki** Yd No: 1255 Loa 61.95 (BB) Br ex 12.80 Dght 4.239 Lbp 58.00 Br md 12.00 Dpth 4.89 Welded, 1 dk	**(A11B2TG) LPG Tanker** Double Sides Entire Compartment Length Liq (Gas): 1,460 2 x Gas Tank (s); 2 independent cyl horizontal 2 Cargo Pump (s): 2x350m³/hr Manifold: Bow/CM: 28m	**1 oil engine** driving 1 CP propeller Total Power: 1,471kW (2,000hp) Akasaka 1 x 4 Stroke 6 Cy. 340 x 620 1471kW (2000bhp) Akasaka Tekkosho KK (Akasaka DieselLtd)-Japan AuxGen: 2 x 240kW 450V 60Hz a.c Thrusters: 1 Thwart. FP thruster (f) Fuel: 180.0 (r.f.)	12.5k A34
9459515 *JD2536* -	**ZUIRYU** **Isewan Bosai KK** *Toba, Mie* Japan Official number: 140667	*112* - 25	Class: NK	**2007-12 Kanagawa Zosen — Kobe** Yd No: 574 Loa 36.20 Br ex - Dght - Lbp 33.20 Br md 6.20 Dpth 3.34 Welded, 1 dk	**(B34H2SQ) Patrol Vessel**	**2 oil engines** reduction geared to sc. shafts driving 2 Propellers Total Power: 3,088kW (4,198hp) Niigata 2 x Vee 4 Stroke 12 Cy. 165 x 185 each-1544kW (2099bhp) Niigata Engineering Co Ltd-Japan AuxGen: 2 x 80kW a.c Fuel: 8.5 (d.f.)	12V16F
9712993 *JD3668* -	**ZUISEN MARU** **Japan Railway Construction, Transport & Technology Agency, Shinpo Kaiun KK & Asahi Tanker Co Ltd** Shinpo Kaiun KK *Matsuyama, Ehime* Japan MMSI: 431005238 Official number: 142151	*997* - 2,309	Class: NK	**2014-03 Yamanaka Zosen K.K. — Imabari** Yd No: 1005 Loa 79.90 Br ex - Dght 5.062 Lbp 76.00 Br md 12.00 Dpth 5.75 Welded, 1 dk	**(A13B2TP) Products Tanker** Double Hull (13F)	**1 oil engine** reduction geared to sc. shafts driving 1 Propeller Total Power: 1,618kW (2,200hp) Hanshin 1 x 4 Stroke 6 Cy. 320 x 680 1618kW (2200bhp) The Hanshin Diesel Works Ltd-Japan	LA32
9016351 - -	**ZUISHO** *ex* Zuisho Maru *-2012* **PT Indo Shipping Operator** -	*199* - 525		**1990-12 Koa Sangyo KK — Takamatsu KG** Yd No: 558 Loa 49.59 Br ex - Dght 3.125 Lbp 45.00 Br md 7.80 Dpth 3.30 Welded, 1 dk	**(A12A2TC) Chemical Tanker** Liq: 393 Compartments: 6 Ta, ER	**1 oil engine** reverse geared to sc. shaft driving 1 FP propeller Total Power: 588kW (799hp) Yanmar 1 x 4 Stroke 6 Cy. 240 x 420 588kW (799bhp) Yanmar Diesel Engine Co Ltd-Japan	MF24-U
8869892 - -	**ZUISHO MARU** *ex* Taiseizan Maru *-2008* **Union Venture Marine** -	*191* - 479	Class: IZ	**1993-02 Tokuoka Zosen K.K. — Naruto** Loa 52.75 Br ex - Dght 3.320 Lbp 47.00 Br md 8.50 Dpth 5.10 Welded, 1 dk	**(A31A2GX) General Cargo Ship**	**1 oil engine** driving 1 FP propeller Total Power: 625kW (850hp) Niigata 1 x 4 Stroke 6 Cy. 260 x 460 625kW (850bhp) Niigata Engineering Co Ltd-Japan	10.0k 6M26BG
8125325 - -	**ZUISHO MARU No. 5** - - -	*184* - 484		**1981 Ishida Zosen Kogyo YK — Onomichi HS** Yd No: 143 Loa 42.79 Br ex - Dght 3.100 Lbp 41.00 Br md 8.00 Dpth 4.80 Welded, 1 dk	**(A31A2GX) General Cargo Ship** Compartments: 1 Ho, ER 1 Ha: ER	**1 oil engine** driving 1 FP propeller Total Power: 441kW (600hp) Matsui 1 x 4 Stroke 6 Cy. 260 x 400 441kW (600bhp) Matsui Iron Works Co Ltd-Japan	6M26KGH
9548067 *JD2878* -	**ZUISHOU** **Koyo Kisen YK** *Hofu, Yamaguchi* Japan Official number: 140945	*198* - 499		**2009-03 Hongawara Zosen K.K. — Fukuyama** Yd No: 622 Loa 49.71 Br ex 7.82 Dght 3.100 Lbp 45.00 Br md 7.79 Dpth 3.30 Welded, 1 dk	**(A12A2TC) Chemical Tanker** Double Hull (13F) 1 Cargo Pump (s): 1x200m³/hr	**1 oil engine** driving 1 Propeller Total Power: 736kW (1,001hp) Yanmar 1 x 4 Stroke 6 Cy. 180 x 280 736kW (1001bhp) Yanmar Diesel Engine Co Ltd-Japan	6N18A-E

IMO / Call sign	Name / Owner / Port	Tonnage	Class	Builder / Dimensions	Type / Cargo	Machinery
364995 *K5189*	**ZUIUN MARU** **Zuiun Kisen YK** - *Kure, Hiroshima* *Japan* Official number: 133043	*163* - 350		**1992-07 Hongawara Zosen K.K. — Fukuyama** L reg 39.00 Br ex - Dght 2.500 Lbp - Br md 7.20 Dpth 3.00 Welded, 1 dk	**(A13B2TU) Tanker (unspecified)**	**1 oil engine** driving 1 FP propeller Total Power: 405kW (551hp) Matsui 6M26KGHS 1 x 4 Stroke 6 Cy. 260 x 400 405kW (551bhp) Matsui Iron Works Co Ltd-Japan
136711 *M6393*	**ZUIYO MARU** **Kowa Kogyo KK** - *Nagasaki, Nagasaki* *Japan* Official number: 134492	*179* - -		**1995-09 Mitsubishi Heavy Industries Ltd. — Nagasaki** Yd No: 2111 Loa 31.00 Br ex - Dght 2.800 Lbp 26.00 Br md 8.80 Dpth 3.85 Welded, 1 dk	**(B32A2ST) Tug**	**2 oil engines** Geared Integral to driving 2 Z propellers Total Power: 2,648kW (3,600hp) 12.6kn Niigata 6L26HLX 2 x 4 Stroke 6 Cy. 260 x 350 each-1324kW (1800bhp) Niigata Engineering Co Ltd-Japan
152313 *G5475*	**ZUIYO MARU** **Iino Gas Transport Co Ltd** - *Kobe, Hyogo* *Japan* MMSI: 431306000 Official number: 135837	**1,357** 486 1,446	Class: NK	**1996-08 K.K. Miura Zosensho — Saiki** Yd No: 1166 Loa 69.95 Br ex - Dght 4.650 Lbp 65.50 Br md 12.50 Dpth 5.50 Welded, 1 dk	**(A11B2TG) LPG Tanker** Liq (Gas): 1,839 2 x Gas Tank (s); independent	**1 oil engine** driving 1 FP propeller Total Power: 1,765kW (2,400hp) 12.8kn Hanshin LH36L 1 x 4 Stroke 6 Cy. 360 x 670 1765kW (2400bhp) The Hanshin Diesel Works Ltd-Japan Fuel: 220.0 (d.f.)
385875	**ZUKA-ZUKA** *ex* Monte Xoxote *-1997* **Peche Maritime Congolaise SA (Pemaco SA)** Pesqueras Loyola SRC *Pointe Noire* *Congo*	*413* 145 329	Class: RP (BV)	**1974-12 Astilleros Luzuriaga SA — Pasaia** Yd No: 175 Loa 44.51 Br ex 9.66 Dght 4.014 Lbp 36.50 Br md 9.64 Dpth 4.50 Welded, 2 dks	**(B11A2FS) Stern Trawler**	**1 oil engine** driving 1 FP propeller Total Power: 1,177kW (1,600hp) 11.0kn MaK 8M451AK 1 x 4 Stroke 8 Cy. 320 x 450 1177kW (1600bhp) MaK Maschinenbau GmbH-Kiel AuxGen: 3 x 204kW 380V 50Hz a.c Fuel: 237.0 (d.f.)
763000 *NUQ2*	**ZUKUS ADVANTAGE** *ex* Superior Advantage *-2011* *ex* Power II *-2005* *ex* Dickson II *-2000* *ex* Power II *-2000* **Zukus Industries Ltd** - *Warri* *Nigeria* MMSI: 657685000 Official number: SR.1674	**369** 110 -		**1984 Crown Point Industries — Marrero, La** Yd No: 10687 Loa 24.40 Br ex 12.19 Dght 1.830 Lbp - Br md - Dpth 2.43 Welded, 1 dk	**(B22A2ZM) Offshore Construction Vessel, jack up**	**2 oil engines** geared to sc. shafts driving 2 Propellers Total Power: 736kW (1,000hp) G.M. (Detroit Diesel) 12V-71 2 x Vee 2 Stroke 12 Cy. 108 x 127 each-368kW (500bhp) Detroit Diesel Corporation-Detroit, Mi
767393 *NUQ*	**ZUKUS FREEDOM** *ex* Superior Freedom *-2013* *ex* C.A. Babin *-2013* *ex* Blue Streak 10 *-2013* **Zukus Industries Ltd** - *Nigeria* MMSI: 657684000 Official number: SR1673	**185** 128 -		**1981 Blue Streak Industries, Inc. — Chalmette, La** Yd No: BLU JB 54 L reg 24.07 Br ex - Dght - Lbp - Br md 11.58 Dpth 2.43 Welded, 1 dk	**(B22A2ZM) Offshore Construction Vessel, jack up**	**2 oil engines** reduction geared to sc. shafts driving 2 Propellers G.M. (Detroit Diesel) 12V-71 General Motors Corp-USA
763103 *NUQ3*	**ZUKUS VALOR** *ex* Superior Valor *-2013* *ex* Gulf Island VIII *-2013* *ex* Vermilion *-1992* *ex* Titan *-1992* **Zukus Industries Ltd** - *Nigeria* MMSI: 657686000 Official number: SR1672	**428** 128 -		**1985-01 Gulf Coast Fabrication, Inc. — Bay Saint Louis, Ms** Yd No: 144 Loa 27.40 Br ex 12.19 Dght 2.430 Lbp - Br md - Dpth 3.05 Welded, 1 dk	**(B22A2ZM) Offshore Construction Vessel, jack up** Cranes: 1x60t,1x15t	**2 oil engines** geared to sc. shafts driving 2 Propellers Total Power: 662kW (900hp) G.M. (Detroit Diesel) 12V-71 2 x Vee 2 Stroke 12 Cy. 108 x 127 each-331kW (450bhp) Detroit Diesel Corporation-Detroit, Mi
309139 *M550*	**ZULAL** *ex* Zulal N *-2012* *ex* Abeer *-2010* *ex* DD Trader *-2006* *ex* Lady P *-2004* *ex* Ocean Atlas *-1999* *ex* Polillo Sampaguita *-1994* *ex* Diamond Cyclamen *-1989* *ex* Sanko Cyclamen *-1987* **Zahranos Shipping Co SA** Zahra Maritime Services Co *Zanzibar* *Tanzania (Zanzibar)* MMSI: 677045000 Official number: 300292	**11,147** 7,373 23,911 T/cm 32.1	Class: NK	**1984-08 Minaminippon Shipbuilding Co Ltd — Usuki OT** Yd No: 567 Loa 160.00 (BB) Br ex 24.44 Dght 9.928 Lbp 150.00 Br md 24.40 Dpth 13.62 Welded, 1 dk	**(A21A2BC) Bulk Carrier** Grain: 30,546; Bale: 29,211 Compartments: 4 Ho, ER 4 Ha: (18.6 x 11.2)3 (19.2 x 12.8)ER Cranes: 3x25t	**1 oil engine** driving 1 FP propeller Total Power: 4,759kW (6,470hp) 14.0kn Mitsubishi 6UE52LA 1 x 2 Stroke 6 Cy. 520 x 1600 4759kW (6470bhp) Kobe Hatsudoki KK-Japan AuxGen: 3 x 360kW 445V 60Hz a.c Fuel: 89.0 (d.f.) (Heating Coils) 898.0 (r.f.) 19.0pd
310463 *OBY*	**ZULEIKA** *ex* Kinsen Maru No. 7 *-1991* *ex* Andhika Persada *-1989* **Strategic Operations Ltd** Sabre Shipping Corp *Jakarta* *Indonesia*	**400** 120 -	Class: (BV) (NK) (KI)	**1983-05 K.K. Odo Zosen Tekko — Shimonoseki** Yd No: 302 Loa 35.50 Br ex - Dght 3.601 Lbp 31.00 Br md 9.80 Dpth 4.56 Welded, 1 dk	**(B32A2ST) Tug**	**2 oil engines** with clutches, flexible couplings & dr geared to sc. shafts driving 2 Z propellers Total Power: 2,354kW (3,200hp) 11.5kn Niigata 6L28BXE 2 x 4 Stroke 6 Cy. 280 x 320 each-1177kW (1600bhp) Niigata Engineering Co Ltd-Japan AuxGen: 4 x 112kW a.c
912161 *JCF*	**ZULFI HAJIYEV** *ex* Kapitan Dolgopolov *-1992* *launched as* Shirvan *-1982* **Specialized Sea Oil Fleet Organisation, Caspian Sea Oil Fleet, State Oil Co of the Republic of Azerbaijan** - *Baku* *Azerbaijan* MMSI: 423118100 Official number: DGR-0218	*2,700* 943 1,392	Class: RS	**1982-05 Brodogradiliste 'Titovo' — Kraljevica** Yd No: 432 Loa 98.98 Br ex 17.43 Dght 3.201 Lbp 92.47 Br md 17.01 Dpth 6.71 Welded, 1 dk	**(B34B2SC) Crane Vessel** Cranes: 1x100t	**2 oil engines** sr geared to sc. shafts driving 2 FP propellers Total Power: 3,178kW (4,320hp) Sulzer 8ASL25/30 2 x 4 Stroke 8 Cy. 250 x 300 each-1589kW (2160bhp) Tvornica Dizel Motora 'Jugoturbina'-Yugoslavia Thrusters: 1 Thwart. FP thruster (f) Fuel: 4.0 (d.f.)
724837 *YV2009*	**ZULIANO IX** *ex* Shoei Maru No. 32 *-1980* **Zulia Towing & Barge Co** - *Maracaibo* *Venezuela* Official number: AJZL-10334	*479* 215 286	Class: (LR) (NK) Classed LR until 20/11/02	**1979 Matsuura Tekko Zosen K.K. — Osakikamijima** Yd No: 268 Loa 34.50 Br ex 9.22 Dght 3.950 Lbp 30.00 Br md 9.01 Dpth 4.20 Welded, 1 dk	**(B32A2ST) Tug**	**2 oil engines** sr geared to sc. shafts driving 2 FP propellers Total Power: 2,354kW (3,200hp) 13.3kn Fuji 6L27.5G 2 x 4 Stroke 6 Cy. 275 x 320 each-1177kW (1600bhp) Fuji Diesel Co Ltd-Japan AuxGen: 2 x 80kW 445V 60Hz a.c
915797 *YV2578*	**ZULIANO XV** *ex* Sea Leopard *-1997* **Zulia Towing & Barge Co** - *Maracaibo* *Venezuela* Official number: AJZL-22679	*237* 182 148	Class: (LR) ✠ Classed LR until 20/11/02	**1980-10 Singapore Slipway & Engineering Co. Pte Ltd — Singapore** Yd No: 144 Loa 27.51 Br ex 9.89 Dght 3.401 Lbp 24.52 Br md 9.50 Dpth 3.97 Welded, 1 dk	**(B32A2ST) Tug**	**2 oil engines** dr geared to sc. shafts driving 2 Directional propellers Total Power: 1,986kW (2,700hp) Hedemora V12A/12 2 x Vee 4 Stroke 12 Cy. 185 x 210 each-993kW (1350bhp) Hedemora Diesel AB-Sweden AuxGen: 2 x 80kW 440V 60Hz a.c
911442 *YV2579*	**ZULIANO XVI** *ex* Sea Cheetah *-1998* **Zulia Towing & Barge Co** - *Maracaibo* *Venezuela* Official number: AJZL - 22.680	**237** 182 173	Class: (AB)	**1979-12 Singapore Slipway & Engineering Co. Pte Ltd — Singapore** Yd No: 140 Loa 27.51 Br ex 9.68 Dght 3.704 Lbp 24.52 Br md 9.52 Dpth 3.97 Welded, 1 dk	**(B32A2ST) Tug**	**2 oil engines** driving 2 FP propellers Total Power: 1,986kW (2,700hp) Hedemora V12A/12 2 x Vee 4 Stroke 12 Cy. 185 x 210 each-993kW (1350bhp) Hedemora Diesel AB-Sweden
660856 *CYR5*	**ZULU** *ex* Beyond *-2013* **Zulu Yachting Ltd** Edmiston & Co SAM *George Town* *Cayman Islands (British)* Official number: 741480	**229** 68 -		**2009-09 Industria Naval do Ceara S.A. (INACE) — Fortaleza** Yd No: 569 Loa 30.48 Br ex - Dght 2.980 Lbp 28.00 Br md 7.15 Dpth 3.51 Welded, 1 dk	**(X11A2YP) Yacht**	**2 oil engines** reduction geared to sc. shafts driving 2 Propellers Total Power: 1,066kW (1,450hp) Caterpillar C18 2 x 4 Stroke 6 Cy. 145 x 183 each-533kW (725bhp) Caterpillar Inc-USA
308821 *ZOM*	**ZUMA** *ex* Corcovado *-2006* **Oceanus Owning Co Ltd** Heidmar Inc *Piraeus* *Greece* MMSI: 240601000 Official number: 11558	**58,418** 31,369 105,188 T/cm 92.1	Class: AB	**2005-06 Shanghai Waigaoqiao Shipbuilding Co Ltd — Shanghai** Yd No: 1017 Loa 243.80 (BB) Br ex 42.03 Dght 14.800 Lbp 233.00 Br md 42.00 Dpth 21.40 Welded, 1 dk	**(A13A2TV) Crude Oil Tanker** Double Hull (13F) Liq: 118,078; Liq (Oil): 118,078 Cargo Heating Coils Compartments: 12 Wing Ta, 2 Wing Slop Ta, ER 3 Cargo Pump (s): 3x2500m³/hr Manifold: Bow/CM: 118m	**1 oil engine** driving 1 FP propeller Total Power: 13,548kW (18,420hp) 15.0kn MAN-B&W 6S60MC-C 1 x 2 Stroke 6 Cy. 600 x 2400 13548kW (18420bhp) Hudong Heavy Machinery Co Ltd-China AuxGen: 3 x 740kW a.c Fuel: 180.0 (d.f.) 3000.0 (r.f.)

7408861 H3SO -
ZUMA ROCK
ex Taurogas I *-2011* *ex* Zuma Rock *-2007*
ex Taurogas I *-2007* *ex* Balina *-2000*
ex Tarquin Ranger *-1992* *ex* Deltagas *-1986*
Petrobulk Shipping Co Ltd
-
Panama *Panama*
MMSI: 352701000
Official number: 31618PEXT4
4,226 Class: (GL)
1,497
6,153
1975-07 Jos L Meyer — Papenburg Yd No: 572
Loa 106.61 (BB) Br ex 15.80 Dght 7.541
Lbp 98.61 Br md 15.41 Dpth 9.96
Welded, 1 dk
(A11B2TG) LPG Tanker
Liq (Gas): 5,495
3 x Gas Tank (s); 3 independent (C.mn.stl) cyl horizontal
6 Cargo Pump (s): 6x85m³/hr
Manifold: Bow/CM: 50m
Ice Capable
1 oil engine reduction geared to sc. shaft driving 1 FP propeller
Total Power: 3,972kW (5,400hp) 16.5k
Deutz RBV12M54
1 x Vee 4 Stroke 12 Cy. 370 x 400 3972kW (5400bhp)
Kloeckner Humboldt Deutz AG-West Germany
AuxGen: 4 x 256kW 400V 50Hz a.c
Fuel: 113.0 (d.f.) 578.5 (r.f.) 20.5pd

8112653 3EWP3 -
ZUMAQUE TRACER
ex Oil Tracer *-2012* *ex* Lowland Prowler *-1995*
ex British Viking *-1986* *ex* Balder Grip *-1984*
Neptuno Shipping Ltd
Cross Caribbean Services Ltd Corp
Panama *Panama*
Official number: 43226PEXT
2,594 Class: AB (GL) (NV)
926
3,325
1982-10 Sterkoder Mek. Verksted AS — Kristiansund Yd No: 96
Lengthened-1997
Loa 85.95 Br ex - Dght 5.008
Lbp 75.95 Br md 17.51 Dpth 7.32
Welded, 2 dks
(B21A20P) Pipe Carrier
2 oil engines sr geared to sc. shafts driving 2 CP propellers
Total Power: 3,972kW (5,400hp) 14.0k
MaK 6M453A
2 x 4 Stroke 6 Cy. 320 x 420 each-1986kW (2700bhp)
Krupp MaK Maschinenbau GmbH-Kiel
AuxGen: 2 x 1225kW 220/440V 60Hz a.c, 2 x 245kW 220/440V 60Hz a.c
Thrusters: 2 Thwart. CP thruster (f); 2 Tunnel thruster (a)
Fuel: 1110.0 (d.f.)

7739416 HP6857 -
ZUMAX I
ex Mitch Zampikos *-1992*
Redsear Ltd
-
Panama *Panama*
Official number: 21819PEXT
137
93
-
1978 Sun Contractors, Inc. — Harvey, La
L reg 18.75 Br ex 9.76 Dght -
Lbp - Br md - Dpth 2.04
Welded, 1 dk
(B21A20S) Platform Supply Ship
1 oil engine driving 1 FP propeller
Total Power: 338kW (460hp)

9306603 ECBF 3-VI-735-0
ZUMAYA DOUS
Pesqueras Zumaya SL
-
La Guardia *Spain*
MMSI: 224132000
Official number: 3-35/2002
148
78
-
2003-11 Astilleros Armon Vigo SA — Vigo Yd No: 25
Loa 30.00 (BB) Br ex - Dght -
Lbp 23.50 Br md 7.20 Dpth 3.35
Welded, 2 dks
(B11B2FV) Fishing Vessel
1 oil engine reduction geared to sc. shaft driving 1 FP propeller
Total Power: 511kW (695hp)
GUASCOR F360-SF
1 x Vee 4 Stroke 12 Cy. 152 x 165 511kW (695bhp)
Gutierrez Ascunce Corp (GUASCOR)-Spain

9453810 PPNM -
ZUMBI DOS PALMARES
Petrobras Transporte SA (TRANSPETRO) - Fronape
-
Rio de Janeiro *Brazil*
MMSI: 710239000
81,429 Class: AB
50,978
157,055
2013-04 Estaleiro Atlantico Sul SA (EAS) — Ipojuca Yd No: EAS-C-002
Loa 274.20 (BB) Br ex 48.04 Dght 17.000
Lbp 264.00 Br md 48.00 Dpth 23.20
Welded, 1 dk
(A13A2TV) Crude Oil Tanker
Double Hull (13F)
Liq: 170,996; Liq (Oil): 171,000
Compartments: 12 Wing Ta, 2 Wing Slop Ta, ER
3 Cargo Pump (s)
1 oil engine driving 1 FP propeller
Total Power: 16,890kW (22,964hp) 15.0kn
MAN-B&W 6S70ME-C
1 x 2 Stroke 6 Cy. 700 x 2800 16890kW (22964bhp)
Doosan Engine Co Ltd-South Korea
AuxGen: 3 x 1040kW a.c
Fuel: 270.0 (d.f.) 4250.0 (r.f.)

8122945 A9D2144 -
ZUMURRUD
ex Gabbari *-1982*
Bahrain Petroleum Co Ltd (BAPCO)
-
Bahrain *Bahrain*
Official number: A1861
272 Class: (AB)
116
203
1982-06 Sanyo Zosen K.K. — Onomichi Yd No: 832
Loa 34.35 Br ex - Dght 3.417
Lbp 29.11 Br md 9.61 Dpth 4.30
Welded, 1 dk
(B32A2ST) Tug
2 oil engines reverse reduction geared to sc. shafts driving 2 Z propellers
Total Power: 2,942kW (4,000hp) 12.5kn
Niigata 8L27.5X
2 x 4 Stroke 8 Cy. 275 x 320 each-1471kW (2000bhp)
Niigata Engineering Co Ltd-Japan
AuxGen: 2 x 176kW

9055644 - -
ZUN FEN
Government of The People's Republic of China (Hainan Development Co of Guangzhou Waterway Bureau)
-
Guangzhou, Guangdong *China*
1,000 Class: (CC)
-
-
1993-01 Tianjin Xinhe Shipyard — Tianjin Yd No: 100/003
Loa 40.60 Br ex - Dght 2.050
Lbp - Br md 15.00 Dpth 3.00
Welded, 1 dk
(B33A2DU) Dredger (unspecified)
1 oil engine reduction geared to sc. shaft driving 1 FP propeller
Total Power: 140kW (190hp)
Caterpillar
1 x 4 Stroke 140kW (190bhp)
Caterpillar Inc-USA

9344930 BPFW -
ZUN YI TAN
China Shipping Tanker Co Ltd
-
Shanghai *China*
MMSI: 413162000
31,004 Class: CC
15,326
53,687
T/cm
54.2
2007-09 Guangzhou Shipyard International Co Ltd — Guangzhou GD Yd No: 04130020
Loa 184.00 (BB) Br ex 32.60 Dght 13.300
Lbp 175.00 Br md 32.26 Dpth 18.90
Welded, 1 dk
(A13A2TW) Crude/Oil Products Tanker
Double Hull (13F)
Liq: 53,656; Liq (Oil): 58,500
Cargo Heating Coils
Compartments: 12 Wing Ta, 2 Wing Slop Ta, ER
3 Cargo Pump (s): 3x1300m³/hr
Manifold: Bow/CM: 94m
Ice Capable
1 oil engine driving 1 FP propeller
Total Power: 9,720kW (13,215hp) 14.6kn
Wartsila 6RT-flex50
1 x 2 Stroke 6 Cy. 500 x 2050 9720kW (13215bhp)
Dalian Marine Diesel Works-China
AuxGen: 3 x 975kW 450V a.c
Thrusters: 1 Thwart. FP thruster (f); 1 Tunnel thruster (a)
Fuel: 177.0 (d.f.) 1512.3 (r.f.)

9706724 - -
ZUNGARO LAUT
ex Lun Feng Tuo 3 *-2013*
PT Sumber Mahtera Kenkana
-
211
63
41
2013-06 Fujian Fu'an Shunjiang Shipyard Co Ltd — Fu'an FJ
Loa 28.50 Br ex - Dght 2.500
Lbp 25.50 Br md 7.80 Dpth 3.60
Welded, 1 dk
(B32A2ST) Tug
2 oil engines reduction geared to sc. shafts driving 2 Propellers
Total Power: 1,200kW (1,632hp)
Chinese Std. Type CW6200ZC
2 x 4 Stroke 6 Cy. 200 x 270 each-600kW (816bhp)
Weichai Power Co Ltd-China

8410847 - -
ZUNXIA NG
ex Sunbright *-2010* *ex* Little Lady *-2005*
ex Pacific Spirit *-2004* *ex* Blankvann *-1992*
ex Brage Trader *-1990*
-
-
4,839 Class: (LR) (NV) (NK)
2,200 Classed LR until 1/90
7,303
T/cm
16.9
1985-01 Towa Zosen K.K. — Shimonoseki Yd No: 559
Loa 114.51 (BB) Br ex 18.22 Dght 6.728
Lbp 105.01 Br md 18.20 Dpth 8.31
Welded, 1 dk
(A13B2TP) Products Tanker
Double Bottom Entire Compartment Length
Liq: 7,439; Liq (Oil): 7,439
Cargo Heating Coils
Compartments: 10 Wing Ta, ER
4 Cargo Pump (s): 2x500m³/hr, 2x250m³/hr
Manifold: Bow/CM: 48m
1 oil engine sr geared to sc. shaft driving 1 FP propeller
Total Power: 2,940kW (3,997hp) 11.8kn
MaK 8M453AK
1 x 4 Stroke 8 Cy. 320 x 420 2940kW (3997bhp)
Ube Industries Ltd-Japan
AuxGen: 2 x 360kW 440V 60Hz a.c, 1 x 250kW 440V 60Hz a.c
Thrusters: 1 Thwart. FP thruster (f)

9181091 ECLK -
ZURBARAN
ex Northern Merchant *-2006*
Cia Trasmediterranea SA (Acciona Trasmediterranea)
-
SatCom: Inmarsat C 422488210
Santa Cruz de Tenerife *Spain (CSR)*
MMSI: 224882000
Official number: 11/2006
22,152 Class: LR
6,645 ✠ **100A1** SS 02/2010
7,396 roll on - roll off cargo and passenger ship
✠ **LMC** **UMS**
2000-02 Astilleros de Sevilla SRL — Seville Yd No: 289
Loa 179.93 (BB) Br ex 25.00 Dght 6.600
Lbp 168.70 Br md 24.30 Dpth 8.71
Welded, 2 dks plus 4 superstructure dks
(A36A2PR) Passenger/Ro-Ro Ship (Vehicles)
Passengers: unberthed: 134; cabins: 55; berths: 118
Bow door/ramp (centre)
Len: 15.00 Wid: 4.50 Swl: 45
Stern door/ramp (centre)
Len: 13.00 Wid: 17.00 Swl: 90
Lane-Len: 2130
Lane-Wid: 3.00
Lane-clr ht: 5.20
Trailers: 146
4 oil engines with clutches, flexible couplings & sr geared to sc. shafts driving 2 CP propellers
Total Power: 23,760kW (32,304hp) 22.5kn
Wartsila 9L38
4 x 4 Stroke 9 Cy. 380 x 475 each-5940kW (8076bhp)
Wartsila NSD Nederland BV-Netherlands
AuxGen: 2 x 1400kW 450V 60Hz a.c, 2 x 640kW 450V 60Hz a.c, 2 x 880kW 450V 60Hz a.c
Boilers: 2 AuxB (ex.g.) 6.8kgf/cm² (6.7bar), AuxB (o.f.) 6.8kgf/cm² (6.7bar)
Thrusters: 2 Thwart. FP thruster (f)
Fuel: 13.0 (d.f.) (Heating Coils) 938.0 (r.f.) 105.0pd

6704749 CXTF -
ZURITA
ex Atlantic Ellen *-1982*
Leyla SA
-
Montevideo *Uruguay*
MMSI: 770576063
Official number: 7898
624 Class: (LR)
317 ✠ Classed LR until 6/8/76
300
1967-05 Geo T Davie & Sons Ltd — Levis QC Yd No: 104
Loa 46.46 Br ex 9.66 Dght 3.849
Lbp 40.01 Br md 9.30 Dpth 6.66
Welded, 2 dks
(B11A2FS) Stern Trawler
Ins: 340
Compartments: 2 Ho, ER
2 Ha: 2 (2.2 x 1.1)ER
Winches: 1
Ice Capable
1 oil engine driving 1 CP propeller
Total Power: 1,103kW (1,500hp) 13.5kn
De Industrie 6D8HD
1 x 4 Stroke 6 Cy. 400 x 600 1103kW (1500bhp)
NV Motorenfabriek 'De Industrie'-Netherlands
AuxGen: 1 x 84kW 440V 60Hz a.c, 1 x 80kW 440V 60Hz a.c
Fuel: 116.0 (d.f.)

6601715 EPNI
ZURMAND
National Iranian Oil Co (NIOC)
Oil Service Co of Iran (Private Co)
Khorramshahr *Iran*
Official number: 193
367 Class: (LR)
44 ✠ Classed LR until 21/5/86
-
1966-04 Appledore Shipbuilders Ltd — Bideford Yd No: A.S. 13
Loa 39.96 Br ex 10.11 Dght 3.779
Lbp 36.58 Br md 9.61 Dpth 4.35
Welded, 1 dk
(B32A2ST) Tug
1 oil engine with flexible couplings & dr reverse geared to sc. shaft driving 1 FP propeller
Total Power: 1,214kW (1,651hp) 12.5kn
Crossley CGL8
1 x 2 Stroke 8 Cy. 368 x 483 1214kW (1651bhp)
Crossley Bros. Ltd.-Manchester
AuxGen: 2 x 75kW 220V d.c
Fuel: 86.5 (d.f.)

8228206 UAYE -
ZUYKOVO
Evening Star Kam Co Ltd
-
SatCom: Inmarsat M 627323010
Petropavlovsk-Kamchatskiy *Russia*
MMSI: 273840100
828 Class: RS
248
397
1984 Volgogradskiy Sudostroitelnyy Zavod — Volgograd Yd No: 218
Converted From: Stern Trawler-1996
Loa 53.75 (BB) Br ex 10.72 Dght 4.500
Lbp 47.92 Br md - Dpth 6.02
Welded, 1 dk
(B11B2FV) Fishing Vessel
1 oil engine driving 1 CP propeller
Total Power: 971kW (1,320hp) 12.7kn
S.K.L. 8NVD48A-2U
1 x 4 Stroke 8 Cy. 320 x 480 971kW (1320bhp)
VEB Schwermaschinenbau "KarlLiebknecht" (SKL)-Magdeburg
AuxGen: 1 x 300kW, 3 x 160kW, 2 x 135kW
Fuel: 182.0 (d.f.)

03555 *5U2677*	**ZUZANNA** *ex* Beaver *-2006* *ex* RMS Lagune *-2002* *ex* RMS Normandia *-1993* *ex* Lagune *-1993* **Zuzanna AS** - *Avatiu* *Cook Islands* Official number: 1766	**1,059** 317 1,130	Class: PR (GL)	**1982-12 C. Luehring Schiffswerft GmbH & Co. KG — Brake** Yd No: 8203 Loa 74.17 Br ex 9.86 Dght 2.920 Lbp 70.21 Br md 9.81 Dpth 5.41 Welded, 2 dks	**(A31A2GX) General Cargo Ship** Grain: 1,699 TEU 60 C. 60/20' (40') Compartments: 1 Ho, ER 1 Ha: (46.7 x 7.5)ER	**1 oil engine** with flexible couplings & sr reverse geared to sc. shaft driving 1 FP propeller Total Power: 440kW (598hp) 10.0kn Deutz SBA6M528 1 x 4 Stroke 6 Cy. 220 x 280 440kW (598bhp) Kloeckner Humboldt Deutz AG-West Germany AuxGen: 2 x 40kW 380V 50Hz a.c Thrusters: 1 Thwart. CP thruster (f)
01261	**ZVEREVO** *ex* Lastochka *-2005* *ex* Gizhiga *-1998* *ex* Azimut-4 *-1993* - -	**446** 133 207	Class: (RS)	**1993-11 AO Zavod 'Nikolayevsk-na-Amure' — Nikolayevsk-na-Amure** Yd No: 1297 Loa 44.88 Br ex 9.47 Dght 3.770 Lbp 39.37 Br md - Dpth 5.13 Welded, 1 dk	**(B11A2FS) Stern Trawler** Ins: 210 Compartments: 1 Ho 1 Ha: (2.1 x 2.1) Derricks: 4x3t Ice Capable	**1 oil engine** driving 1 FP propeller Total Power: 589kW (801hp) 11.5kn S.K.L. 6NVD48A-2U 1 x 4 Stroke 6 Cy. 320 x 480 589kW (801bhp) SKL Motoren u. Systemtechnik AG-Magdeburg
22850 *CIZ*	**ZVEYNIEKS** *ex* Zvejnieks *-1996* *ex* Zveynieks *-1992* **Bios-Shelf JSC (A/O 'Bios-Shelf')** - SatCom: Inmarsat C 427300842 *Murmansk* *Russia* MMSI: 273426300 Official number: 873066	*742* 221 332	Class: RS	**1988-07 Zavod "Leninskaya Kuznitsa" — Kiyev** Yd No: 268 Loa 53.74 Br ex - Dght 4.360 Lbp 47.92 Br md 10.71 Dpth 6.00 Welded, 1 dk	**(B11A2FS) Stern Trawler** Ice Capable	**1 oil engine** driving 1 CP propeller Total Power: 971kW (1,320hp) 12.6kn S.K.L. 8NVD48A-2U 1 x 4 Stroke 8 Cy. 320 x 480 971kW (1320bhp) VEB Schwermaschinenbau "KarlLiebknecht" (SKL)-Magdeburg AuxGen: 1 x 300kW a.c, 3 x 160kW a.c
42807	**ZVEZDA BALTIKI** *ex* Baltijas Zvaigzne *-1994* *ex* Zvezda Baltiki *-1992* **Bionet II JSC (A/O 'Bionet II')** - *Russia* MMSI: 273315940	**738** 221 382	Class: (RS)	**1976 Zavod "Leninskaya Kuznitsa" — Kiyev** Yd No: 1430 Loa 54.82 Br ex 9.96 Dght 4.140 Lbp 50.29 Br md - Dpth 5.03 Welded, 1 dk	**(B11A2FS) Stern Trawler** Ins: 405 Compartments: 2 Ho, ER 3 Ha: 3 (1.5 x 1.6) Derricks: 2x1.5t; Winches: 2 Ice Capable	**1 oil engine** driving 1 CP propeller Total Power: 736kW (1,001hp) 12.0kn S.K.L. 8NVD48AU 1 x 4 Stroke 8 Cy. 320 x 480 736kW (1001bhp) VEB Schwermaschinenbau "KarlLiebknecht" (SKL)-Magdeburg AuxGen: 2 x 160kW, 2 x 100kW Fuel: 155.0 (d.f.)
32179 *EDV*	**ZVEZDA MURMANA** *ex* Kappin *-2011* *ex* Olympic Prawn *-2001* *ex* Pero *-1995* *ex* Ny-Pero *-1983* *ex* Arab *-1983* *ex* Ranger Cadmus *-1973* **Murmanrybflot-2 JSC (ZAO 'Murmanrybflot-2')** - *Murmansk* *Russia* MMSI: 273352230	**1,499** 458 793	Class: RS (LR) (NV) ✠ Classed LR until 2/83	**1971-09 Brooke Marine Ltd. — Lowestoft** Yd No: 372 Converted From: Diving Support Vessel-1984 Converted From: Stern Trawler-1983 Loa 66.07 Br ex 12.25 Dght 5.855 Lbp 58.70 Br md 12.20 Dpth 7.77 Welded, 2 dks	**(B11A2FS) Stern Trawler** Ins: 1,010 Ice Capable	**1 oil engine** geared to sc. shaft driving 1 FP propeller Total Power: 1,912kW (2,600hp) 12.0kn Wartsila 8R32 1 x 4 Stroke 8 Cy. 320 x 350 1912kW (2600bhp) (new engine 1987) Wartsila Diesel Oy-Finland AuxGen: 2 x 480kW 380V 50Hz a.c, 1 x 300kW 380V 50Hz a.c Thrusters: 1 Thwart. FP thruster (f)
11323 *OWB*	**ZVEZDA RYBAKA** - **JSC 'Rosagrolizing'** Vozneseniye Co Ltd *Murmansk* *Russia* MMSI: 273445060 Official number: 020184	**147** 44 49	Class: (RS)	**2004-06 OAO Astrakhanskaya Sudoverf — Astrakhan** Yd No: 801 Loa 26.70 Br ex - Dght 2.450 Lbp 23.30 Br md 7.00 Dpth 3.45 Welded, 1 dk	**(B11A2FS) Stern Trawler** Ice Capable	**1 oil engine** geared to sc. shaft driving 1 CP propeller Total Power: 562kW (764hp) Wartsila UD25V12M5D 1 x Vee 4 Stroke 12 Cy. 150 x 180 562kW (764bhp) Wartsila France SA-France
11335 *ORL*	**ZVEZDA UDACHI** - **JSC 'Rosagrolizing'** Vozneseniye Co Ltd *Astrakhan* *Russia* MMSI: 273444060 Official number: 020199	**147** 44 49	Class: (RS)	**2004-06 OAO Astrakhanskaya Sudoverf — Astrakhan** Yd No: 802 Loa 26.70 Br ex - Dght 2.450 Lbp 23.30 Br md 7.00 Dpth 3.45 Welded, 1 dk	**(B11A2FS) Stern Trawler** Ice Capable	**1 oil engine** geared to sc. shaft driving 1 CP propeller Total Power: 562kW (764hp) 11.5kn Wartsila UD25V12M5D 1 x Vee 4 Stroke 12 Cy. 150 x 180 562kW (764bhp) Wartsila France SA-France Fuel: 26.0 (d.f.)
42571 *HGN*	**ZVEZDNIY** *ex* Diomid *-2013* **Dilmas Co Ltd** - *Vladivostok* *Russia* MMSI: 273437070	**271** 81 89	Class: RS	**1990-11 Brodogradiliste 'Tito' — Belgrade** Yd No: 1131 Loa 35.78 Br ex 9.49 Dght 3.310 Lbp 30.23 Br md 9.00 Dpth 4.50 Welded, 1 dk	**(B32A2ST) Tug** Ice Capable	**2 oil engines** geared to sc. shaft driving 1 CP propeller Total Power: 1,854kW (2,520hp) 13.5kn Sulzer 6ASL25D 2 x 4 Stroke 6 Cy. 250 x 300 each-927kW (1260bhp) in Yugoslavia AuxGen: 1 x 150kW a.c
28503	**ZVEZDNYY** - **Bangladesh Fisheries Development Corp** - *Bangladesh*	*699* 262 329	Class: (RS)	**1967 Khabarovskiy Sudostroitelnyy Zavod im Kirova — Khabarovsk** Yd No: 149 Loa 54.21 Br ex 9.38 Dght 3.683 Lbp 49.99 Br md 9.30 Dpth 4.86 Welded, 1 dk	**(B11A2FT) Trawler** Ins: 361 Compartments: 2 Ho, ER 2 Ha: 2 (1.5 x 1.6) Derricks: 1x2t,1x1.5t; Winches: 2 Ice Capable	**1 oil engine** driving 1 CP propeller Total Power: 588kW (799hp) 12.0kn S.K.L. 8NVD48AU 1 x 4 Stroke 8 Cy. 320 x 480 588kW (799bhp) VEB Schwermaschinenbau "KarlLiebknecht" (SKL)-Magdeburg AuxGen: 3 x 88kW
99885	**ZVONKIY** - - -	**270** 81 89	Class: (RS)	**1988 Brodogradiliste 'Tito' — Belgrade** Yd No: 1122 Loa 35.78 Br ex 9.49 Dght 3.280 Lbp 30.23 Br md - Dpth 4.50 Welded, 1 dk	**(B32A2ST) Tug** Ice Capable	**2 oil engines** geared to sc. shaft driving 1 CP propeller Total Power: 1,854kW (2,520hp) 13.5kn Sulzer 6ASL25D 2 x 4 Stroke 6 Cy. 250 x 300 each-927kW (1260bhp) in Yugoslavia AuxGen: 1 x 150kW a.c, 1 x 70kW a.c Fuel: 51.0 (d.f.)
51599 *43829*	**ZVONKO** *ex* Sarom VI *-2001* *ex* Siog 1 *-1996* **Sub Mar doo** - *Rijeka* *Croatia* Official number: 2T-594	*133* - -	Class: CS	**1974-10 Cooperativa Metallurgica Ing G Tommasi Srl — Ancona** Yd No: 21 Loa 28.34 Br ex - Dght 1.400 Lbp 25.72 Br md 8.00 Dpth 2.40 Welded, 1 dk	**(B34B2SC) Crane Vessel** Cranes: 1x30t,2x5t	**2 oil engines** driving 2 Propellers Total Power: 410kW (558hp) Deutz SBF6M716 2 x 4 Stroke 6 Cy. 135 x 160 each-205kW (279bhp) Kloeckner Humboldt Deutz AG-West Germany
29991 *VE* E 69	**ZWALUW** - **D van der Bosch & Zn** - *Yerseke* *Netherlands* MMSI: 246378000 Official number: 31576	**236** 70 -		**1996 Gebr. Kooiman B.V. Scheepswerf en Machinefabriek — Zwijndrecht** Yd No: 153 Loa 40.14 Br ex - Dght 1.830 Lbp 37.62 Br md 9.00 Dpth 2.44 Welded, 1 dk	**(B11A2FT) Trawler**	**1 oil engine** reduction geared to sc. shaft driving 1 FP propeller Total Power: 634kW (862hp) Cummins KT-19-M 1 x 4 Stroke 6 Cy. 159 x 159 634kW (862bhp) Cummins Engine Co Inc-USA
29011	**ZWARA** - - - *Mauritania*	*156* 61 -	Class: (RI)	**1980-09 Soc. Esercizio Cant. S.p.A. — Viareggio** Yd No: 656 Loa 30.31 Br ex 7.22 Dght 2.794 Lbp 23.91 Br md 7.21 Dpth 3.28 Welded, 1 dk	**(B11A2FS) Stern Trawler** Ins: 83	**1 oil engine** reverse reduction geared to sc. shaft driving 1 FP propeller Total Power: 1,200kW (1,632hp) MaK 6M282AK 1 x 4 Stroke 6 Cy. 240 x 280 1200kW (1632bhp) Krupp MaK Maschinenbau GmbH-Kiel
19436	**ZWARA** - **Government of Libya (Socialist Ports Co)** - *Benghazi* *Libya*	*1,453* 521 200	Class: (LR) (GL) Classed LR until 11/9/96	**1980-06 Osterreichische Schiffswerften AG Linz-Korneuburg — Linz** Yd No: 1267 Loa 50.25 Br ex 24.16 Dght 2.510 Lbp 49.74 Br md 23.64 Dpth 3.99 Welded, 1 dk	**(B34B2SC) Crane Vessel**	**2 oil engines** gearing integral to driving 2 Voith-Schneider propellers Total Power: 1,590kW (2,162hp) 6.0kn MWM TBD440-8 2 x 4 Stroke 8 Cy. 230 x 270 each-795kW (1081bhp) Motoren Werke Mannheim AG (MWM)-West Germany AuxGen: 1 x 300kW 400V 50Hz a.c, 1 x 250kW 400V 50Hz a.c, 1 x 72kW 400V 50Hz a.c
423425 *HJQ*	**ZWERVER I** - **HvS Dredging Support BV** - *Harlingen* *Netherlands* MMSI: 244473000 Official number: 48350	**297** 89 244	Class: BV	**2007-02 Gebr. Kooiman B.V. Scheepswerf en Machinefabriek — Zwijndrecht** Yd No: 173 Loa 28.50 Br ex 13.20 Dght 2.600 Lbp 25.90 Br md 12.50 Dpth 3.65 Welded, 1 dk	**(B32B2SP) Pusher Tug** Cranes: 2x20.1t	**3 oil engines** reduction geared to sc. shafts driving 3 FP propellers Total Power: 1,413kW (1,920hp) 10.5kn Cummins KTA-19-M3 3 x 4 Stroke 6 Cy. 159 x 159 each-471kW (640bhp) Cummins Engine Co Inc-USA AuxGen: 2 x 64kW 220/380V 50Hz a.c Thrusters: 1 Retract. directional thruster (f) Fuel: 13.0

9614878 PCLQ -
ZWERVER III
HvS Dredging Support BV
-
Harlingen *Netherlands*
MMSI: 246024000
Official number: 54225
499 149 840
Class: BV
2011-12 Gebr. Kooiman B.V. Scheepswerf en Machinefabriek — Zwijndrecht Yd No: 192
Loa 35.10 Br ex 15.06 Dght 3.000
Lbp 31.50 Br md 15.00 Dpth 4.07
Welded, 1 dk
(B32A2ST) Tug
Cranes: 2x10t
Ice Capable
3 oil engines reduction geared to sc. shafts driving 3 FP propellers
Total Power: 2,820kW (3,834hp)
Mitsubishi S12R-MP
3 x Vee 4 Stroke 12 Cy. 170 x 180 each-940kW (1278bhp)
Mitsubishi Heavy Industries Ltd-Japan
AuxGen: 2 x 96kW 400/230V 50Hz a.c
Thrusters: 2 Tunnel thruster 1 (p) 1 (s)
Fuel: 280.0 (d.f.)

9593622 VRIG2 -
ZY HI SHENG
ex GCL Melody *-2011* *ex* Hua Yun *-2010*
Zhuoyuan Shipping (HK) Co Ltd
-
Hong Kong *Hong Kong*
MMSI: 477861700
Official number: HK-3034
18,084 9,341 27,000
Class: BV
2010-07 Ningbo Dongfang Shipyard Co Ltd — Ningbo ZJ Yd No: DFC07-055
Loa 169.40 (BB) Br ex - Dght 10.200
Lbp 159.80 Br md 25.00 Dpth 14.30
Welded, 1 dk
(A21A2BC) Bulk Carrier
Grain: 35,489
Compartments: 4 Ho, ER
4 Ha: 2 (22.5 x 15.0) (23.2 x 15.0)ER (21.0 x 15.0)
Cranes: 3x25t
Ice Capable
1 oil engine driving 1 FP propeller
Total Power: 5,220kW (7,097hp) 13.5
MAN-B&W 6S35ME-
1 x 2 Stroke 6 Cy. 350 x 1550 5220kW (7097bhp)
Yichang Marine Diesel Engine Co Ltd-China
AuxGen: 1 x 120kW 380V 60Hz a.c, 2 x 440kW 380V 60Hz a
Fuel: 2900.0

7941289 - -
ZYUYD
Sevastopol Port Authority
-
Sevastopol *Ukraine*
Official number: 802499
149 101 20
Class: (RS)
1980 Ilyichyovskiy Sudoremontnyy Zavod im. "50-letiya SSSR" — Ilyichyovsk Yd No: 5
Loa 28.70 Br ex 6.35 Dght 1.480
Lbp 27.00 Br md - Dpth 2.50
Welded, 1 dk
(A37B2PS) Passenger Ship
Passengers: unberthed: 250
2 oil engines driving 2 FP propellers
Total Power: 220kW (300hp) 10.4
Barnaultransmash 3D
2 x 4 Stroke 6 Cy. 150 x 180 each-110kW (150bhp)
Barnaultransmash-Barnaul
AuxGen: 2 x 1kW
Fuel: 2.0 (d.f.)

8929941 UEYQ -
ZYUYD
Marine Gaz Design LLC Co
LLC 'MorSpecFlot'
St Petersburg *Russia*
Official number: 720617
180 54 46
Class: RS
1972-12 Gorokhovetskiy Sudostroitelnyy Zavod — Gorokhovets Yd No: 306
Loa 29.30 Br ex 8.49 Dght 3.090
Lbp 27.00 Br md - Dpth 4.35
Welded, 1 dk
(B32A2ST) Tug
Ice Capable
2 oil engines driving 2 CP propellers
Total Power: 882kW (1,200hp) 11.4
Russkiy 6D30/50-4
2 x 2 Stroke 6 Cy. 300 x 500 each-441kW (600bhp)
Mashinostroitelnyy Zavod"Russkiy-Dizel"-Leningrad
AuxGen: 2 x 25kW a.c
Fuel: 43.0 (d.f.)

8929953 - -
ZYUYD
Nikolayev Commercial Sea Port
Nikolayev *Ukraine*
Official number: 780088
187 - 46
Class: (RS)
1979 Gorokhovetskiy Sudostroitelnyy Zavod — Gorokhovets Yd No: 374
Loa 29.30 Br ex 8.49 Dght 3.090
Lbp 27.00 Br md - Dpth 4.30
Welded, 1 dk
(B32A2ST) Tug
Ice Capable
2 oil engines driving 2 CP propellers
Total Power: 884kW (1,202hp) 11.4
Russkiy 6D30/50-4
2 x 2 Stroke 6 Cy. 300 x 500 each-442kW (601bhp)
Mashinostroitelnyy Zavod"Russkiy-Dizel"-Leningrad
AuxGen: 2 x 30kW a.c
Fuel: 36.0 (d.f.)

8736186 - -
2 B
ex Grand Beige *-2009*
Atlantic Explorator Co SA
Non Plus Ultra SA
SatCom: Inmarsat M 600968465
Luxembourg *Luxembourg*
Official number: 9-30
226 67 -
Class: (BV)
2008-11 Jade Yachts Inc — Kaohsiung Yd No: 106
Loa 27.90 Br ex - Dght 2.200
Lbp 23.75 Br md 7.50 Dpth 3.80
Welded, 1 dk
(X11A2YP) Yacht
2 oil engines geared to sc. shafts driving 2 Propellers
Total Power: 1,618kW (2,200hp)
MAN D2842
2 x Vee 4 Stroke 12 Cy. 128 x 142 each-809kW (1100bhp)
MAN Nutzfahrzeuge AG-Nuernberg

1011927 9HA2974 -
2 LADIES
Belaz Ocean Services Ltd
Ocean Management GmbH
Valletta *Malta*
MMSI: 256969000
499 150 70
Class: LR
✠ **100A1** SS 07/2012
SSC
Yacht, mono, G6
LMC **UMS**
Cable: 330.0/22.0 U3 (a)
2012-07 Fratelli Rossi Cantiere Navale Srl — Viareggio Yd No: FR 025
Loa 46.35 Br ex 9.00 Dght 3.200
Lbp 38.67 Br md 8.65 Dpth 5.34
Welded, 1 dk
(X11A2YP) Yacht
Passengers: unberthed: 12
2 oil engines with clutches, flexible couplings & sr reverse geared to sc. shafts driving 2 FP propellers
Total Power: 1,938kW (2,634hp) 10.0
Caterpillar C
2 x Vee 4 Stroke 12 Cy. 145 x 162 each-969kW (1317bhp)
Caterpillar Inc-USA
AuxGen: 2 x 114kW 400V 50Hz a.c

5391571 3XAL -
3 AVRIL
ex Kaloum *-1985* *ex* Solvar *-1982*
ex Willy *-1965*
Nouvelle Soguipeche
Government of The People's Revolutionary Republic of Guinea (Ministere de l'Elevage la Peche)
Conakry *Guinea*
318 140 -
Class: (BV) (NV)
1951-09 N.V. Scheepsbouw. "De Dageraad" v/h Wed. J. Boot — Woubrugge Yd No: 468
Lengthened-1972
Loa 43.44 Br ex 7.04 Dght 3.353
Lbp 38.64 Br md 7.01 Dpth 3.76
Welded, 1 dk
(B11B2FV) Fishing Vessel
1 oil engine driving 1 FP propeller
Total Power: 662kW (900hp)
Wichmann 6A
1 x 2 Stroke 6 Cy. 280 x 420 662kW (900bhp) (new engine 1967)
Wichmann Motorfabrikk AS-Norway
AuxGen: 2 x 66kW 220V 50Hz a.c
Thrusters: 1 Thwart. FP thruster (f); 1 Tunnel thruster (a)
Fuel: 45.5 (d.f.) 4.0pd

9360972 9HA3214 -
3 OAK
ex Euro Solid *-2012*
Oak 3 Shipping Inc
Woodstreet Inc
Valletta *Malta*
MMSI: 229296000
Official number: 9360972
7,112 3,095 8,800
Class: GL
2006-09 Peters Schiffbau GmbH — Wewelsfleth Yd No: 683
Loa 125.85 (BB) Br ex - Dght 7.820
Lbp 117.20 Br md 21.70 Dpth 9.15
Welded, 1 dk
(A33A2CC) Container Ship (Fully Cellular)
Double Bottom Entire Compartment Length
TEU 801 incl 200 ref C
Ice Capable
1 oil engine geared to sc. shaft driving 1 CP propeller
Total Power: 8,400kW (11,421hp) 17.9
MaK 9M43
1 x 4 Stroke 9 Cy. 430 x 610 8400kW (11421bhp)
Caterpillar Motoren GmbH & Co. KG-Germany
AuxGen: 1 x 1920kW 400V a.c, 2 x 266kW 400V a.c
Thrusters: 1 Tunnel thruster (f)

8521658 H03497 -
4-WINDS
ex Maria Helena II *-2006* *ex* Maria Helena *-2004*
Rederij Groen BV
-
Panama *Panama*
MMSI: 354498000
Official number: 3322907A
499 150 -
Class: UV
1986-08 Scheepswerf Metz B.V. — Urk Yd No: 75
Converted From: Trawler-2006
Loa 45.57 Br ex - Dght 3.831
Lbp 40.61 Br md 9.00 Dpth 5.10
Welded, 1 dk
(B22G20Y) Standby Safety Vessel
1 oil engine with clutches, flexible couplings & sr reverse geared to sc. shaft driving 1 FP propeller
Total Power: 705kW (959hp) 14.0
Mitsubishi S12R-MP
1 x Vee 4 Stroke 12 Cy. 170 x 180 705kW (959bhp) (new engine 1986)
AuxGen: 2 x 120kW a.c, 2 x 116kW a.c
Thrusters: 1 Thwart. FP thruster (f)
Fuel: 345.0

9564413 2CYB8 -
4 YOU
Gildo Finance Corp
Moran Yacht Management Inc
George Town *Cayman Islands (British)*
MMSI: 319012100
Official number: 741355
493 148 -
Class: AB
2009-11 Heesen Shipyards B.V. — Oss Yd No: 14647
Loa 47.00 Br ex 8.89 Dght 1.875
Lbp 34.00 Br md 8.50 Dpth 3.92
Welded, 1 dk
(X11A2YP) Yacht
Hull Material: Aluminium Alloy
2 oil engines reverse reduction geared to sc. shaft (s) driving 2 Propellers
Total Power: 5,440kW (7,396hp) 14.0
M.T.U. 16V4000M9
2 x Vee 4 Stroke 16 Cy. 165 x 190 each-2720kW (3698bhp)
MTU Friedrichshafen GmbH-Friedrichshafen
AuxGen: 2 x 99kW 50Hz a.c
Thrusters: 1 Tunnel thruster
Fuel: 60.0 (d.f.)

9496575 2AAZ6 -
4H
4 H Ltd
-
Douglas *Isle of Man (British)*
MMSI: 235058335
Official number: 739337
317 95 300
Class: AB
2008-01 Cant. Nav. San Lorenzo SpA — Viareggio Yd No: 101/38
Loa 38.50 Br ex - Dght 1.500
Lbp 32.56 Br md 7.60 Dpth 3.90
Welded, 1 dk
(X11A2YP) Yacht
Hull Material: Aluminium Alloy
2 oil engines geared to sc. shafts driving 2 Propellers
Total Power: 4,080kW (5,548hp) 27.0
M.T.U. 12V4000M9
2 x Vee 4 Stroke 12 Cy. 165 x 190 each-2040kW (2774bhp)
MTU Friedrichshafen GmbH-Friedrichshafen

1011111 ZGCH -
4YOU
Galaxias Oceanic Ltd
Ocean Management GmbH
The Creek *Cayman Islands (British)*
MMSI: 319009700
672 201 -
Class: LR
✠ **100A1** SS 06/2012
SSC
Yacht, mono, G6
LMC **UMS**
Cable: 330.0/22.0 U2 (a)
2012-06 Damen Shipyards Gdynia SA — Gdynia (Hull) Yd No: (461)
2012-06 Amels BV — Vlissingen Yd No: 461
Loa 52.30 Br ex 9.47 Dght 3.150
Lbp 45.00 Br md 9.00 Dpth 4.90
Welded, 1 dk
(X11A2YP) Yacht
2 oil engines with clutches, flexible couplings & sr reverse geared to sc. shafts driving 2 FP propellers
Total Power: 2,100kW (2,856hp)
M.T.U. 16V2000M7
2 x Vee 4 Stroke 16 Cy. 130 x 150 each-1050kW (1428bhp)
MTU Friedrichshafen GmbH-Friedrichshafen
AuxGen: 2 x 155kW 400V 50Hz a.c
Thrusters: 1 Thwart. FP thruster (f)

9506033 H05045 -
5 DE NOVIEMBRE
Panama Canal Authority
-
Panama *Panama*
Official number: 020601789HK
386 115 -
Class: BV
2008-04 Hin Lee (Zhuhai) Shipyard Co Ltd — Zhuhai GD (Hull) Yd No: 173
2008-04 Cheoy Lee Shipyards Ltd — Hong Kong Yd No: 4928
Loa 42.00 Br ex - Dght 2.200
Lbp 40.32 Br md 14.00 Dpth 2.60
Welded, 1 dk
(A36A2PR) Passenger/Ro-Ro Ship (Vehicles)
2 oil engines reduction geared to sc. shafts driving 2 FP propellers
Total Power: 1,192kW (1,620hp) 8.0
Caterpillar 3406
2 x 4 Stroke 6 Cy. 137 x 165 each-596kW (810bhp) (new engine 2008)
Caterpillar Inc-USA

8953796 - -
5 DE SEPTIEMBRE
Empresa de Navegacion Caribe
-
177 53 -
1972 "Petrozavod" — Leningrad
Loa 29.29 Br ex 8.30 Dght 3.070
Lbp 25.40 Br md 7.95 Dpth 4.35
Welded, 1 dk
(B32A2ST) Tug
2 oil engines driving 2 FP propellers
Total Power: 882kW (1,200hp) 10.0
Russkiy 6D30/50-4
2 x 2 Stroke 6 Cy. 300 x 500 each-441kW (600bhp)
Mashinostroitelnyy Zavod"Russkiy-Dizel"-Leningrad

409264	**5 FISHES** *ex* Lady Anna Of Fife *-2007* *ex* Ocean Trilogy *-1997* *ex* Trilogy *-1989* **Petronom Ltd** -	**235** 71 50	Class: NV	**1986-02 SBF Shipbuilders (1977) Pty Ltd — Fremantle WA** Yd No: P98 Loa 35.22 Br ex - Dght 2.440 Lbp 29.80 Br md 8.03 Dpth 3.84 Welded, 1 dk	**(X11A2YP) Yacht** Hull Material: Aluminium Alloy	**2 oil engines** sr geared to sc. shafts driving 2 FP propellers Total Power: 910kW (1,238hp) MWM TBD604-6 2 x 4 Stroke 6 Cy. 160 x 185 each-455kW (619bhp) Motoren Werke Mannheim AG (MWM)-West Germany AuxGen: 2 x 53kW 415V 50Hz a.c Thrusters: 1 Thwart. FP thruster (f)
477036 *GBS*	**5G** *ex* CRN Ancona 128/06 *-2011* - - *George Town* *Cayman Islands (British)* MMSI: 319328000	**328** 98 33	Class: RI	**2011-07 C.R.N. Cant. Nav. Ancona S.r.l. — Ancona** Yd No: 128/06 Loa 39.60 Br ex - Dght 1.654 Lbp 33.91 Br md 7.70 Dpth 3.75 Bonded, 1 dk	**(X11A2YP) Yacht** Hull Material: Reinforced Plastic Passengers: 10; cabins: 5	**2 oil engines** reduction geared to sc. shafts driving 2 FP propellers Total Power: 4,080kW (5,548hp) 19.0kn M.T.U. 12V4000M90 2 x Vee 4 Stroke 12 Cy. 165 x 190 each-2040kW (2774bhp) MTU Friedrichshafen GmbH-Friedrichshafen
052199 *2WD*	**6-231** *ex* Brisha *-1975* **Bangladesh Inland Water Transport Corp** - *Chittagong* *Bangladesh* Official number: 185846	*352* 81 -	Class: (LR) ✠ Classed LR until 4/7/80	**1952-03 Garden Reach Workshops Ltd. — Kolkata** (Assembled by) **1952-03 Wm. Denny & Bros. Ltd. — Dumbarton** (Parts for assembly by) Yd No: 1451 Loa 41.15 Br ex 8.26 Dght 2.210 Lbp 39.76 Br md 8.23 Dpth 2.75 Welded, 1 dk	**(B32A2ST) Tug**	**2 Steam Recips** driving 2 FP propellers 2 x Steam Recip. Wm. Denny & Bros. Ltd.-Dumbarton
801389	**6-232** *ex* Labonna *-1975* *ex* Balaka *-1968* **Bangladesh Inland Water Transport Corp** - *Chittagong* *Bangladesh*	*120* 31 -	Class: (LR) ✠ Classed LR until 4/11/77	**1967-08 Geibi Zosen Kogyo — Kure** Yd No: 191 Loa 26.22 Br ex 6.74 Dght - Lbp 23.86 Br md 6.41 Dpth 2.60 Welded, 1 dk	**(B32A2ST) Tug**	**2 oil engines** sr reverse geared to sc. shafts driving 2 FP propellers Total Power: 470kW (640hp) Kelvin TAS8 2 x 4 Stroke 8 Cy. 165 x 184 each-235kW (320bhp) Bergius Kelvin Co. Ltd.-Glasgow AuxGen: 1 x 7kW 225V d.c, 1 x 5kW 225V d.c
801511	**6-233** *ex* Sadaf *-1975* *ex* Shaheen *-1968* **Bangladesh Inland Water Transport Corp** - *Chittagong* *Bangladesh*	*120* 31 -	Class: (LR) ✠ Classed LR until 15/8/84	**1967-08 Geibi Zosen Kogyo — Kure** Yd No: 192 Loa 26.22 Br ex 6.74 Dght - Lbp 23.86 Br md 6.41 Dpth 2.60 Welded, 1 dk	**(B32A2ST) Tug**	**2 oil engines** sr reverse geared to sc. shafts driving 2 FP propellers Total Power: 470kW (640hp) Kelvin TAS8 2 x 4 Stroke 8 Cy. 165 x 184 each-235kW (320bhp) Bergius Kelvin Co. Ltd.-Glasgow AuxGen: 1 x 7kW 225V d.c, 1 x 5kW 225V d.c
045637	**6-234** *ex* Surja *-1975* **Bangladesh Inland Water Transport Corp** - *Chittagong* *Bangladesh* Official number: 184744	*352* 81 -	Class: (LR) ✠ Classed LR until 24/7/81	**1952-05 Garden Reach Workshops Ltd. — Kolkata** (Assembled by) **1952-05 Wm. Denny & Bros. Ltd. — Dumbarton** (Parts for assembly by) Yd No: 1450 Loa 41.15 Br ex 8.56 Dght 2.198 Lbp 39.63 Br md 8.23 Dpth 2.75 Welded, 1 dk	**(B32A2ST) Tug**	**2 Steam Recips** driving 2 FP propellers Lobnitz & Co. Ltd.-Renfrew
409073 *2ZK*	**6-235** *launched as* B. T. 1079 *-1975* **Bangladesh Inland Water Transport Corp** - *Chittagong* *Bangladesh* Official number: 356477	*241* 57 117	Class: (LR) ✠ Classed LR until 19/1/00	**1975-01 Hongawara Zosen K.K. — Fukuyama** Yd No: 111 Loa 31.63 Br ex 7.85 Dght 2.337 Lbp 28.50 Br md 7.60 Dpth 2.75 Welded, 1 dk	**(B32A2ST) Tug**	**2 oil engines** reverse reduction geared to sc. shafts driving 2 FP propellers Total Power: 706kW (960hp) 10.0kn Cummins VT-28-M 2 x Vee 4 Stroke 12 Cy. 140 x 152 each-353kW (480bhp) Cummins Engine Co Inc-USA AuxGen: 2 x 24kW 225V 60Hz a.c
409085 *2ZM*	**6-237** *launched as* B. T. 1081 *-1975* **Bangladesh Inland Water Transport Corp** - *Chittagong* *Bangladesh* Official number: 356495	*241* 57 115	Class: (LR) ✠ Classed LR until 2/8/00	**1975-05 Hongawara Zosen K.K. — Fukuyama** Yd No: 114 Loa 31.63 Br ex 7.85 Dght 2.337 Lbp 28.50 Br md 7.60 Dpth 2.75 Welded, 1 dk	**(B32A2ST) Tug**	**2 oil engines** reverse reduction geared to sc. shafts driving 2 FP propellers Total Power: 706kW (960hp) 10.0kn Cummins VT-28-M 2 x Vee 4 Stroke 12 Cy. 140 x 152 each-353kW (480bhp) Cummins Engine Co Inc-USA AuxGen: 2 x 24kW 225V 60Hz a.c
425950 *2ZN*	**6-238** *ex* B.T. 1082 *-1975* **Bangladesh Inland Water Transport Corp** - *Chittagong* *Bangladesh* Official number: 356616	*241* 57 115	Class: (LR) ✠ Classed LR until 26/4/89	**1975-05 Ito Iron Works & SB. Co. Ltd. — Sasebo** Yd No: 115 Loa 31.63 Br ex 7.83 Dght 2.337 Lbp 28.50 Br md 7.60 Dpth 2.75 Welded, 1 dk	**(B32A2ST) Tug**	**2 oil engines** reverse reduction geared to sc. shafts driving 2 FP propellers Total Power: 706kW (960hp) 10.0kn Cummins VT12-700-M 2 x Vee 4 Stroke 12 Cy. 140 x 152 each-353kW (480bhp) Cummins Engine Co Inc-USA AuxGen: 2 x 24kW 225V 60Hz a.c
500334 *2ZO*	**6-239** *launched as* B. T. 1083 *-1975* **Bangladesh Inland Water Transport Corp** - *Chittagong* *Bangladesh* Official number: 356617	*241* 57 115	Class: (LR) ✠ Classed LR until 19/4/00	**1975-05 Shin Nikko Zosen K.K. — Onomichi** Yd No: 116 Loa 31.63 Br ex 7.85 Dght 2.337 Lbp 28.50 Br md 7.60 Dpth 2.75 Welded, 1 dk	**(B32A2ST) Tug**	**2 oil engines** reverse reduction geared to sc. shafts driving 2 FP propellers Total Power: 706kW (960hp) 10.0kn Cummins VT-28-M 2 x Vee 4 Stroke 12 Cy. 140 x 152 each-353kW (480bhp) Cummins Engine Co Inc-USA AuxGen: 2 x 24kW 225V 60Hz a.c
301544 *WYZ7019*	**6 VC** **Torch Inc** - *New Orleans, LA* *United States of America* Official number: 538545	*117* 89 -		**1972 Halter Marine Services, Inc. — New Orleans, La** L reg 22.41 Br ex 7.93 Dght - Lbp - Br md 7.88 Dpth 1.73 Welded, 1 dk	**(B21A2OC) Crew/Supply Vessel**	**1 oil engine** driving 1 FP propeller Total Power: 350kW (476hp)
898831 *MYO3*	**7-28** **Yusong Shipping Co** - *Nampho* *North Korea* Official number: 3805755	**1,548** 465 1,289		**1989-09 Nampo Shipyard — Nampo** Converted From: General Cargo Ship-1989 Loa 74.30 Br ex 12.00 Dght 4.300 Lbp 68.00 Br md - Dpth 6.50 Welded, 1 dk	**(B22B20D) Drilling Ship**	**1 oil engine** driving 1 FP propeller Total Power: 1,655kW (2,250hp)
701985 *W6735*	**7 DE DICIEMBRE** **7 de Diciembre SA-Pesquera Emilian** - *Mar del Plata* *Argentina* MMSI: 701000719 Official number: 0607	**117** 83 114	Class: (AB)	**1987-08 SANYM S.A. — Buenos Aires** Yd No: 82 Loa 25.51 Br ex - Dght 2.901 Lbp 25.46 Br md 6.51 Dpth 3.31 Welded, 1 dk	**(B11A2FT) Trawler** Ins: 140	**1 oil engine** sr reverse geared to sc. shaft driving 1 FP propeller Total Power: 397kW (540hp) 10.0kn Caterpillar 3412TA 1 x Vee 4 Stroke 12 Cy. 137 x 152 397kW (540bhp) Caterpillar Inc-USA AuxGen: 2 x 24kW a.c
210118 *HP9264*	**7-SEAS** *ex* Pacific Rapier *-2002* **Rederij Groen BV** - SatCom: Inmarsat C 435678611 *Panama* *Panama* MMSI: 356786000 Official number: 2559098CH	**855** 341 1,260	Class: NV (BV) (AB)	**1982-09 Imamura Zosen — Kure** Yd No: 289 Loa 57.71 Br ex 12.22 Dght 3.990 Lbp 52.51 Br md 12.21 Dpth 4.50 Welded, 1 dk	**(B21A2OS) Platform Supply Ship** Passengers: berths: 32 Cranes: 1x10t	**2 oil engines** reverse reduction geared to sc. shafts driving 2 FP propellers Total Power: 2,060kW (2,800hp) 12.0kn Yanmar T260-ST 2 x 4 Stroke 6 Cy. 260 x 330 each-1030kW (1400bhp) Yanmar Diesel Engine Co Ltd-Japan AuxGen: 3 x 160kW 440V 60Hz a.c Thrusters: 1 Thwart. CP thruster (f) Fuel: 448.8 (d.f.) 7.2pd
301556 *WYZ7014*	**7 VC** **Waterfront Construction Inc** - *New Orleans, LA* *United States of America* Official number: 537135	*117* 89 -		**1972 Halter Marine Services, Inc. — New Orleans, La** L reg 22.41 Br ex 7.93 Dght - Lbp - Br md 7.88 Dpth 1.73 Welded, 1 dk	**(B21A2OC) Crew/Supply Vessel**	**1 oil engine** driving 1 FP propeller Total Power: 390kW (530hp)
705420	**8 NOVEMBRE** **Government of The People's Revolutionary Republic of Guinea** - *Conakry* *Guinea*	*119* - -	Class: (GL)	**1967 Yacht- u. Bootswerft Abeking & Rasmussen — Lemwerder** Yd No: 6287 Loa 26.14 Br ex 7.12 Dght 2.667 Lbp 24.01 Br md 6.71 Dpth 3.46 Welded, 1 dk	**(B32A2ST) Tug**	**1 oil engine** driving 1 FP propeller Deutz RV8M536 1 x 4 Stroke 8 Cy. 270 x 360 Kloeckner Humboldt Deutz AG-West Germany

Ship	Tonnage	Classification	Builder / Dimensions	Type / Cargo	Machinery
7230719 *WYZ7013* - **8 VC** **Empire Barges Inc** - *New Orleans, LA* *United States of America* Official number: 536740	*117* 89 -		**1971 Halter Marine Services, Inc. — New Orleans, La** L reg 22.41 Br ex 7.93 Dght - Lbp - Br md 7.88 Dpth 1.73 Welded, 1 dk	**(B21A2OC) Crew/Supply Vessel**	**1 oil engine** driving 1 FP propeller Total Power: 390kW (530hp)
8500379 - - **9 SEA STARS 1** *ex* 9 Sea Stars *ex* Man Boon *-2000* **Sea Starcruise Co Ltd** - *Thailand* Official number: 421000734	*1,489* 447 500		**1984 Taiwan Machinery Manufacturing Corp. — Kaohsiung** Yd No: 6376 Loa 64.01 Br ex 13.85 Dght 3.301 Lbp 56.75 Br md 13.42 Dpth 4.45 Welded	**(A36A2PR) Passenger/Ro-Ro Ship (Vehicles)** Lane-Len: 400 Lane-Wid: 2.80 Lane-clr ht: 4.02 Lorries: 34, Cars: 30	**1 oil engine** driving 1 FP propeller Total Power: 1,000kW (1,360hp) M.T.U. 1 x 4 Stroke 1000kW (1360bhp) MTU Friedrichshafen GmbH-Friedrichshafen
9211705 *ONK7732* - **10** **Port of Antwerp Authority (Havenbedrijf Antwerpen)** - *Antwerpen* *Belgium* Official number: 65.03502	**350** - 548		**1999-02 Chantier Naval de Nameche — Nameche** (Hull) **1999-02 Scheepvaart en Konstruktie Bedrijf (SKB) — Antwerpen** Yd No: 98002 Loa 29.50 Br ex 11.03 Dght - Lbp 28.00 Br md 11.00 Dpth 2.87 Welded, 1 dk	**(B32A2ST) Tug**	**2 oil engines** gearing integral to driving 2 Voith-Schneider propellers Total Power: 3,536kW (4,808hp) 12.3k A.B.C. 8DZ 2 x 4 Stroke 8 Cy. 256 x 310 each-1768kW (2404bhp) Anglo Belgian Corp NV (ABC)-Belgium
7814230 - - **10 DE DEZEMBRO** **Cabotagem Nacional Angolana (Cabotang UEE)** - *Luanda* *Angola*	*500* 163 575	Class: (BV)	**1979-04 Scheepswerf Ton Bodewes B.V. — Franeker** Yd No: F70 Loa 53.01 Br ex 11.59 Dght 2.121 Lbp 44.73 Br md 11.51 Dpth 2.82 Welded, 1 dk	**(A14A2LO) Water Tanker** Liq: 440 Compartments: 4 Ta, ER 1 Cargo Pump (s): 1x100m³/hr	**2 oil engines** driving 2 FP propellers Total Power: 536kW (728hp) 10.5k Caterpillar 3408PCT 2 x Vee 4 Stroke 8 Cy. 137 x 152 each-268kW (364bhp) Caterpillar Tractor Co-USA Fuel: 35.5 (d.f.)
9071301 *LW9227* - **10 DE NOVIEMBRE** *ex* Raquel *-2010* **PIEA SA** - *Mar del Plata* *Argentina* MMSI: 701000788 Official number: 01074	*110* 101 111		**1993-08 SANYM S.A. — Buenos Aires** Yd No: 96 Loa 26.50 Br ex - Dght 2.920 Lbp 23.90 Br md 6.50 Dpth 3.30 Welded, 1 dk	**(B11A2FS) Stern Trawler** Ins: 165	**1 oil engine** with clutches, flexible couplings & reverse reduction geared to sc. shaft driving 1 FP propeller Total Power: 459kW (624hp) 10.0kr Caterpillar 3412TA 1 x Vee 4 Stroke 12 Cy. 137 x 152 459kW (624bhp) Caterpillar Inc-USA
9211717 *ONK7733* - **11** **Port of Antwerp Authority (Havenbedrijf Antwerpen)** - *Antwerpen* *Belgium* Official number: 65.03503	**350** - 548		**1999-07 Chantier Naval de Nameche — Nameche** (Hull) **1999-07 Scheepvaart en Konstruktie Bedrijf (SKB) — Antwerpen** Yd No: 98003 Loa 30.98 Br ex 11.40 Dght - Lbp 28.00 Br md 11.00 Dpth 2.87 Welded, 1 dk	**(B32A2ST) Tug**	**2 oil engines** gearing integral to driving 2 Voith-Schneider propellers Total Power: 3,536kW (4,808hp) 12.3kn A.B.C. 8DZC 2 x 4 Stroke 8 Cy. 256 x 310 each-1768kW (2404bhp) Anglo Belgian Corp NV (ABC)-Belgium
7814242 *D3V2109* - **11 DE NOVEMBRO** **Cabotagem Nacional Angolana (Cabotang UEE)** - *Luanda* *Angola*	*500* 163 575	Class: (BV)	**1979-10 Scheepswerf Ton Bodewes B.V. — Franeker** Yd No: F71 Loa 53.01 Br ex 11.59 Dght 2.112 Lbp 46.74 Br md 11.51 Dpth 2.82 Welded, 1 dk	**(A14A2LO) Water Tanker** Liq: 440 Compartments: 4 Ta, ER 1 Cargo Pump (s): 1x100m³/hr	**2 oil engines** geared to sc. shafts driving 2 FP propellers Total Power: 536kW (728hp) 10.5kn Caterpillar 3408PCTA 2 x Vee 4 Stroke 8 Cy. 137 x 152 each-268kW (364bhp) Caterpillar Tractor Co-USA Fuel: 35.5 (d.f.)
8323771 *EQOO* - **12 FARVARDIN** *ex* Davazdah Farvardin *-2010* **NIOC Tug Boat Services** - *Bushehr* *Iran* MMSI: 422194000 Official number: 2.4566	**578** 173 414	Class: AS (LR) ✠ Classed LR until 1/5/96	**1984-04 Matsuura Tekko Zosen K.K. — Osakikamijima** Yd No: 305 Loa 40.01 Br ex 11.33 Dght 4.342 Lbp 35.01 Br md 11.00 Dpth 5.01 Welded, 1 dk	**(B32A2ST) Tug**	**2 oil engines** with clutches, flexible couplings & dr geared to sc. shafts driving 2 CP propellers Total Power: 3,458kW (4,702hp) Fuji 8L27.5G 2 x 4 Stroke 8 Cy. 275 x 320 each-1729kW (2351bhp) Fuji Diesel Co Ltd-Japan AuxGen: 3 x 200kW 445V 50Hz a.c Thrusters: 1 Thwart. CP thruster (f) Fuel: 195.0 (d.f.)
9072977 *D4DF* - **13 DE JANEIRO** **Companhia Nacional de Navegacao 'Arca Verde'** - *Sao Vicente* *Cape Verde* Official number: 082	**486** 211 634	Class: (NK)	**1993-08 Wakamatsu Zosen K.K. — Kitakyushu** Yd No: 505 Loa 48.50 Br ex 9.02 Dght 3.581 Lbp 44.60 Br md 9.00 Dpth 4.00 Welded, 1 dk	**(A31A2GX) General Cargo Ship** Bale: 700 TEU 4 C. 4/20' Compartments: 1 Ho, ER 1 Ha: (17.6 x 6.4)ER Derricks: 2x3.5t	**1 oil engine** with clutches, flexible couplings & sr geared to sc. shaft driving 1 CP propeller Total Power: 736kW (1,001hp) 10.8kn Yanmar M220-UN 1 x 4 Stroke 6 Cy. 220 x 300 736kW (1001bhp) Yanmar Diesel Engine Co Ltd-Japan
6826652 - - **14TH OCTOBER** **The Yemen Ports & Shipping Corp** - *Aden* *Yemen* Official number: 008	*208* - -	Class: (LR) ✠ Classed LR until 18/10/95	**1969-01 Scott & Sons (Bowling) Ltd. — Bowling** Yd No: 438 Loa 32.29 Br ex 8.67 Dght 3.741 Lbp 29.27 Br md 8.23 Dpth 3.97 Welded, 1 dk	**(B32A2ST) Tug**	**2 oil engines** sr reverse reduction geared to sc. shaft driving 1 FP propeller Total Power: 1,154kW (1,568hp) Ruston 6VEBCZM 2 x 4 Stroke 6 Cy. 260 x 368 each-577kW (784bhp) Ruston & Hornsby Ltd.-Lincoln AuxGen: 2 x 42kW 110V d.c
8323795 *EQOQ* - **15 KHORDAD** *ex* Panzdah Khordad *-2010* **NIOC Tug Boat Services** - *Bushehr* *Iran* MMSI: 422195000 Official number: 2.4896	**578** 173 414	Class: AS (LR) ✠ Classed LR until 15/6/94	**1984-07 Matsuura Tekko Zosen K.K. — Osakikamijima** Yd No: 307 Loa 41.41 Br ex 11.33 Dght 4.342 Lbp 35.01 Br md 11.00 Dpth 5.01 Welded, 1 dk	**(B32A2ST) Tug**	**2 oil engines** with clutches, flexible couplings & dr geared to sc. shafts driving 2 CP propellers Total Power: 3,458kW (4,702hp) Fuji 8L27.5G 2 x 4 Stroke 8 Cy. 275 x 320 each-1729kW (2351bhp) Fuji Diesel Co Ltd-Japan AuxGen: 3 x 200kW 445V 50Hz a.c Thrusters: 1 Thwart. CP thruster (f) Fuel: 195.0 (d.f.)
9380893 *5AWO* - **17 FEBRUARY** *ex* Aisha *-2011* *ex* Apex Spirit *-2008* **17 February Shipping Co Ltd** International Tanker Management Holding Ltd (ITM Holding) SatCom: Inmarsat C 464200050 *Tripoli* *Libya* MMSI: 642122012	**81,732** 51,287 160,391 T/cm 119.6	Class: LR ✠ **100A1** SS 05/2013 Double Hull oil tanker ESP **ShipRight** (SDA, FDA, CM) *IWS LI ✠ **LMC** **UMS IGS** Eq.Ltr: Y†; Cable: 742.5/97.0 U3 (a)	**2008-05 Samsung Heavy Industries Co Ltd — Geoje** Yd No: 1680 Loa 274.39 (BB) Br ex 48.04 Dght 17.050 Lbp 264.00 Br md 48.00 Dpth 23.20 Welded, 1 dk	**(A13A2TV) Crude Oil Tanker** Double Hull (13F) Liq: 167,456; Liq (Oil): 167,000 Cargo Heating Coils Compartments: 12 Wing Ta, 2 Wing Slop Ta, ER 3 Cargo Pump (s): 3x3800m³/hr Manifold: Bow/CM: 132.4m	**1 oil engine** driving 1 CP propeller Total Power: 18,660kW (25,370hp) 15.7kn MAN-B&W 6S70ME-C 1 x 2 Stroke 6 Cy. 700 x 2800 18660kW (25370bhp) Doosan Engine Co Ltd-South Korea AuxGen: 3 x 950kW 450V 60Hz a.c Boilers: e (ex.g.) 22.4kgf/cm² (22.0bar), AuxB (o.f.) 18.4kgf/cm² (18.0bar) Fuel: 176.0 (d.f.) 3371.0 (r.f.)
8109840 *3CAZ* - **18HEAVEN** *ex* Smooth Sea 7 *-2010* *ex* Dutaryo Stk *-2005* *ex* Alpha 2 *-2003* *ex* Bunga Kiambang *-1996* **Azer Enterprises Ltd** - *Malabo* *Equatorial Guinea* MMSI: 631837000	**2,621** 1,644 4,434 T/cm 11.6	Class: (AB)	**1982-02 Hayashikane Shipbuilding & Engineering Co Ltd — Nagasaki NS** Yd No: 907 Loa 90.10 Br ex 14.64 Dght 6.114 Lbp 84.03 Br md 14.61 Dpth 7.42 Welded, 1 dk	**(A13B2TP) Products Tanker** Liq: 5,902; Liq (Oil): 5,902 Compartments: 8 Ta, ER 2 Cargo Pump (s): 2x600m³/hr Manifold: Bow/CM: 39m	**1 oil engine** driving 1 FP propeller Total Power: 1,471kW (2,000hp) 10.0kn Hanshin 6EL32 1 x 4 Stroke 6 Cy. 320 x 640 1471kW (2000bhp) The Hanshin Diesel Works Ltd-Japan AuxGen: 1 x 240kW 445V 60Hz a.c, 2 x 150kW 445V 60Hz a.c Fuel: 36.5 (d.f.) (Heating Coils) 160.5 (r.f.) 6.5pd
8019605 - - **20 DE OCTUBRE** **Empresa Portuaria Nacional** - *Guatemala* MMSI: 332999994	*100* - -	Class: (AB)	**1980-11 Depend-A-Craft — Pierre Part, La** Yd No: 111 Loa 23.17 Br ex 7.95 Dght - Lbp 22.33 Br md 7.93 Dpth 3.05 Welded, 1 dk	**(B32A2ST) Tug**	**2 oil engines** reduction geared to sc. shafts driving 2 FP propellers Total Power: 1,030kW (1,400hp) 12.0kn G.M. (Detroit Diesel) 12V-149 2 x Vee 2 Stroke 12 Cy. 146 x 146 each-515kW (700bhp) General Motors Corp-USA AuxGen: 2 x 40kW
5329449 - - **20TH JUNE** *ex* Al Aidrus *-1969* *ex* Sir Charles Johnston *-1968* **The Yemen Ports & Shipping Corp** - *Aden* *Yemen* Official number: 004	*197* - 104	Class: (LR) ✠ Classed LR until 28/2/86	**1963-07 W. J. Yarwood & Sons Ltd. — Northwich** Yd No: 939 Loa 31.86 Br ex 8.56 Dght - Lbp 29.27 Br md 8.23 Dpth 3.97 Riveted\Welded, 1 dk	**(B32A2ST) Tug**	**2 oil engines** with hydraulic couplings & sr reverse geared to sc. shaft, 2 ahead speeds driving 1 FP propeller Total Power: 956kW (1,300hp) Ruston 6VEBXM 2 x 4 Stroke 6 Cy. 260 x 368 each-478kW (650bhp) Ruston & Hornsby Ltd.-Lincoln AuxGen: 1 x 42kW 110V d.c, 1 x 10kW 110V d.c

14676 IK	**22 BAHMAN** *ex* Seetrans 8 *-1983* *ex* Mania Express *-1982* **Khark Municipality** Siri Maritime Services *Bushehr* *Iran* MMSI: 422200000 Official number: 2.4562	*247* 74 40	Class: AS (LR) ✠ Classed LR until 24/7/96	**1976-06 Boghammar Marin AB — Lidingo** Yd No: 1062 Loa 36.56 Br ex 7.01 Dght 1.401 Lbp 31.86 Br md 6.99 Dpth 2.77 Welded, 1 dk	**(A37B2PS) Passenger Ship** Hull Material: Aluminium Alloy Passengers: unberthed: 334	**2 oil engines** reverse reduction geared to sc. shafts driving 2 FP propellers Total Power: 1,802kW (2,450hp) M.T.U. 12V331TC51 2 x Vee 4 Stroke 12 Cy. 165 x 155 each-901kW (1225bhp) MTU Friedrichshafen GmbH-Friedrichshafen AuxGen: 2 x 30kW 380V 50Hz a.c
05963	**22 MAY** **Hodeidah Port Authority** - *Hodeidah* *Yemen*	**208** 62 -	Class: (LR) ✠ Classed LR until 22/6/05	**1991-12 Tczewska Stocznia Rzeczna — Tczew** (Hull) Yd No: HP2600L1 **1991-12 B.V. Scheepswerf Damen — Gorinchem** Yd No: 3166 Loa 30.02 Br ex 8.07 Dght 3.430 Lbp 27.06 Br md 7.80 Dpth 4.05 Welded, 1 dk	**(B32A2ST) Tug**	**2 oil engines** reverse reduction geared to sc. shafts driving 2 FP propellers Total Power: 2,550kW (3,466hp) Caterpillar 3516TA 2 x Vee 4 Stroke 16 Cy. 170 x 190 each-1275kW (1733bhp) Caterpillar Inc-USA AuxGen: 2 x 50kW 380V 50Hz a.c
03868	**24TH OCTOBER** **Suez Stevedoring Co** - *Suez* *Egypt*	*200* - -	Class: (GL)	**1990-09 Port Said Engineering Works — Port Said** Yd No: 205 Loa 23.00 Br ex - Dght 2.500 Lbp - Br md 3.40 Dpth - Welded, 1 dk	**(B32A2ST) Tug**	**1 oil engine** geared to sc. shaft driving 1 FP propeller Total Power: 460kW (625hp) G.M. (Detroit Diesel) 16V-92 1 x Vee 2 Stroke 16 Cy. 123 x 127 460kW (625bhp) General Motors Corp-USA
38478 CF6	**26 AGUSTOS** *ex* Pinar K *-2008* *ex* Yasa Kaptan Erbil *-2006* **Nemtas Nemrut Liman Isletmeleri AS** - SatCom: Inmarsat B 327100251 *Izmir* *Turkey* MMSI: 271000666 Official number: 172	**30,303** 17,734 52,455 T/cm 55.5	Class: NK	**2002-03 Tsuneishi Heavy Industries (Cebu) Inc — Balamban** Yd No: SC-028 Loa 189.99 (BB) Br ex - Dght 12.024 Lbp 182.00 Br md 32.26 Dpth 17.00 Welded, 1 dk	**(A21A2BC) Bulk Carrier** Grain: 67,756; Bale: 65,601 Compartments: 5 Ho, ER 5 Ha: (20.4 x 18.4)4 (21.3 x 18.4)ER Cranes: 4x30t	**1 oil engine** driving 1 FP propeller Total Power: 8,562kW (11,641hp) 14.3kn B&W 6S50MC 1 x 2 Stroke 6 Cy. 500 x 1910 8562kW (11641bhp) Mitsui Engineering & Shipbuilding CLtd-Japan Fuel: 2140.0
20996	**26TH SEPTEMBER** **The Yemen Ports & Shipping Corp** - *Aden* *Yemen* Official number: 049	*232* 75 203	Class: (LR) ✠ Classed LR until 16/9/92	**1978-10 B.V. Scheepswerven v/h H.H. Bodewes — Millingen a/d Rijn** Yd No: 743 Loa 30.13 Br ex 9.35 Dght 4.553 Lbp 28.50 Br md 9.01 Dpth 3.48 Welded, 1 dk	**(B32A2ST) Tug**	**2 oil engines** dr geared to sc. shafts driving 2 Directional propellers Total Power: 1,472kW (2,002hp) 11.8kn Deutz SBA8M528 2 x 4 Stroke 8 Cy. 220 x 280 each-736kW (1001bhp) Kloeckner Humboldt Deutz AG-West Germany AuxGen: 2 x 52kW 380/220V 50Hz a.c, 1 x 20kW 380/220V 50Hz a.c
84029 T5017	**30** **Port of Antwerp Towage (Havenbedrijf Antwerpen Sleepdienst)** - *Antwerpen* *Belgium* MMSI: 205501790 Official number: 06105141	**312** - -	Class: (BV)	**2011-02 Barkmet SRO — Lovosice** (Hull) Yd No: VST0706 **2011-02 Scheepvaart en Konstruktie Bedrijf (SKB) — Antwerpen** Yd No: 409 Loa 29.50 Br ex - Dght 2.850 Lbp - Br md 11.00 Dpth 4.00 Welded, 1 dk	**(B32A2ST) Tug**	**2 oil engines** reduction geared to sc. shafts driving 2 Voith-Schneider propellers Total Power: 3,890kW (5,288hp) A.B.C. 8MDZC 2 x 4 Stroke 8 Cy. 256 x 310 each-1945kW (2644bhp) Anglo Belgian Corp NV (ABC)-Belgium AuxGen: 2 x 199kW 50Hz a.c Fuel: 40.0 (d.f.)
39803	**30 DE JUNIO** **Empresa Portuaria Nacional** *Guatemala* MMSI: 332999995 Official number: CCPST-497-R-2004	**130** 110 -		**1982-01 Slowing Construcciones Navales — Amatitlan** Yd No: 2208 Loa 23.75 Br ex - Dght - Lbp - Br md 7.81 Dpth - Welded, 1 dk	**(B32A2ST) Tug**	**1 oil engine** reduction geared to sc. shaft driving 1 Propeller Total Power: 1,103kW (1,500hp)
56188	**30 LET POBEDY** **VF Cargo Transportation Ltd** JSC Volga Shipping (OAO Sudokhodnaya Kompaniya 'Volzhskoye Parokhodstvo') SatCom: Inmarsat C 427330449 *Nizhniy Novgorod* *Russia* MMSI: 273345210 Official number: V-05-875	*3,904* 1,663 5,150	Class: RR	**1975 Navashinskiy Sudostroitelnyy Zavod 'Oka' — Navashino** Yd No: 1107 Loa 138.30 Br ex 16.70 Dght 3.430 Lbp 135.00 Br md 16.50 Dpth 5.50 Welded, 1 dk	**(A31A2GX) General Cargo Ship** Grain: 6,270 Compartments: 2 Ho, ER 2 Ha: 2 (44.4 x 13.1)ER	**2 oil engines** driving 2 FP propellers Total Power: 1,324kW (1,800hp) 10.0kn Dvigatel Revolyutsii 6CHRN36/45 2 x 4 Stroke 6 Cy. 360 x 450 each-662kW (900bhp) Zavod "Dvigatel Revolyutsii"-Gorkiy AuxGen: 2 x 110kW Fuel: 122.0 (d.f.)
20984	**30TH NOVEMBER** **The Yemen Ports & Shipping Corp** - *Aden* *Yemen* Official number: 045	*232* 75 199	Class: (LR) ✠ Classed LR until 21/1/98	**1978-09 B.V. Scheepswerven v/h H.H. Bodewes — Millingen a/d Rijn** Yd No: 742 Loa 30.13 Br ex 9.35 Dght 4.547 Lbp 28.50 Br md 9.01 Dpth 3.48 Welded, 1 dk	**(B32A2ST) Tug**	**2 oil engines** dr geared to sc. shafts driving 2 Directional propellers Total Power: 1,472kW (2,002hp) 11.8kn Deutz SBA8M528 2 x 4 Stroke 8 Cy. 220 x 280 each-736kW (1001bhp) Kloeckner Humboldt Deutz AG-West Germany AuxGen: 2 x 52kW 380/220V 50Hz a.c, 1 x 20kW 380/220V 50Hz a.c
84031 T5041	**31** **Port of Antwerp Towage (Havenbedrijf Antwerpen Sleepdienst)** - *Antwerpen* *Belgium* MMSI: 205504190 Official number: 06105142	**312** - -	Class: (BV)	**2011-05 Barkmet SRO — Lovosice** (Hull) Yd No: VST0707 **2011-05 Scheepvaart en Konstruktie Bedrijf (SKB) — Antwerpen** Yd No: 410 Loa 29.50 Br ex - Dght 2.850 Lbp - Br md 11.00 Dpth 4.00 Welded, 1 dk	**(B32A2ST) Tug**	**2 oil engines** reduction geared to sc. shafts driving 2 Voith-Schneider propellers Total Power: 3,890kW (5,288hp) A.B.C. 8MDZC 2 x 4 Stroke 8 Cy. 256 x 310 each-1945kW (2644bhp) Anglo Belgian Corp NV (ABC)-Belgium AuxGen: 2 x 199kW 50Hz a.c Fuel: 40.0 (d.f.)
84043 T5063	**32** **Port of Antwerp Towage (Havenbedrijf Antwerpen Sleepdienst)** - *Antwerpen* *Belgium* MMSI: 205506390 Official number: 06105143	**312** - -	Class: (BV)	**2011-07 Barkmet SRO — Lovosice** (Hull) Yd No: VST0708 **2011-07 Scheepvaart en Konstruktie Bedrijf (SKB) — Antwerpen** Yd No: 411 Loa 29.50 Br ex - Dght 2.850 Lbp - Br md 11.00 Dpth 4.00 Welded, 1 dk	**(B32A2ST) Tug**	**2 oil engines** reduction geared to sc. shafts driving 2 Voith-Schneider propellers Total Power: 3,890kW (5,288hp) A.B.C. 8MDZC 2 x 4 Stroke 8 Cy. 256 x 310 each-1945kW (2644bhp) Anglo Belgian Corp NV (ABC)-Belgium AuxGen: 2 x 199kW 50Hz a.c Fuel: 40.0 (d.f.)
10127	**40** **Domenico Palumbo Snc di Agostino Palumbo e C** - *Cayman Islands (British)*	**395** 118 220	Class: RI	**2013-11 Palumbo Spa — Napoli** Yd No: 003 Loa 40.00 Br ex - Dght - Lbp 38.37 Br md 8.20 Dpth 4.20 Welded, 1 dk	**(X11A2YP) Yacht** Hull Material: Aluminium Alloy	**2 oil engines** reduction geared to sc. shafts driving 2 Propellers Total Power: 2,942kW (4,000hp) M.T.U. 2 x each-1471kW (2000bhp) MTU Friedrichshafen GmbH-Friedrichshafen
02095 RQK	**40** **Port of Antwerp Towage (Havenbedrijf Antwerpen Sleepdienst)** - *Antwerpen* *Belgium* MMSI: 205625000 Official number: 01 00797 2012	**430** 129 200	Class: BV	**2012-06 Union Naval Valencia SA (UNV) — Valencia** Yd No: 488 Loa 29.50 Br ex - Dght 4.540 Lbp 27.50 Br md 12.50 Dpth - Welded, 1 dk	**(B32A2ST) Tug**	**2 oil engines** driving 2 Voith-Schneider propellers Total Power: 5,280kW (7,178hp) A.B.C. 12VDZC 2 x Vee 4 Stroke 12 Cy. 256 x 310 each-2640kW (3589bhp) Anglo Belgian Corp NV (ABC)-Belgium Fuel: 140.0 (d.f.)
725656 3MZ5	**40 LET POBEDY** **Ivory Bay Ltd** AzimutTrans Ltd *Belize City* *Belize* MMSI: 312368000 Official number: 370920052	**2,466** 988 3,135	Class: RS	**1985-12 Sudostroitelnyy Zavod "Krasnoye Sormovo" — Gorkiy** Yd No: 83 Loa 114.02 Br ex 13.22 Dght 3.670 Lbp 110.76 Br md 13.00 Dpth 5.50 Welded, 1 dk	**(A31A2GX) General Cargo Ship** Grain: 3,397	**2 oil engines** driving 2 FP propellers Total Power: 970kW (1,318hp) 10.7kn S.K.L. 6NVD48A-2U 2 x 4 Stroke 6 Cy. 320 x 480 each-485kW (659bhp) VEB Schwermaschinenbau "KarlLiebknecht" (SKL)-Magdeburg Fuel: 100.0 (r.f.)
27680	**40 LET POBEDY** **Zaliv Fishing Cooperative (Rybolovetskoye Artel 'Zaliv')** -	**104** 31 61	Class: (RS)	**1985-06 Azovskaya Sudoverf — Azov** Yd No: 7051 Loa 26.50 Br ex 6.59 Dght 2.340 Lbp 22.90 Br md 6.50 Dpth 3.05 Welded, 1 dk	**(B11B2FV) Fishing Vessel**	**1 oil engine** geared to sc. shaft driving 1 FP propeller Total Power: 165kW (224hp) 9.3kn Daldizel 6CHNSP18/22 1 x 4 Stroke 6 Cy. 180 x 220 165kW (224bhp) Daldizel-Khabarovsk AuxGen: 2 x 30kW Fuel: 10.0 (d.f.)

IMO / Call sign	Name / Owner / Port	Tonnage	Class	Builder / Dimensions	Type	Machinery
7045968 *UCRN* -	**40 LET TAYMYRU** *ex* MB-7029 **Fishing Artel Co Ltd (OOO 'Rybolovetskaya Artel')** - *Petropavlovsk-Kamchatskiy* *Russia*	**201** 60 107	Class: (RS)	**1970-06 VEB Schiffswerft "Edgar Andre" — Magdeburg** Yd No: 7029 Loa 34.60 Br ex 8.22 Dght 2.969 Lbp 31.85 Br md - Dpth 3.70 Welded, 1 dk	**(B32A2ST) Tug** Ice Capable	**1 oil engine** driving 1 CP propeller Total Power: 552kW (750hp) 10.0 S.K.L. 6NVD48A- 1 x 4 Stroke 6 Cy. 320 x 480 552kW (750bhp) VEB Schwermaschinenbau "KarlLiebknecht" (SKL)-Magdeburg
9602100 *ORQL* -	**41** **Port of Antwerp Towage (Havenbedrijf Antwerpen Sleepdienst)** - *Antwerpen* *Belgium* MMSI: 205626000	**430** 130 200	Class: BV	**2012-09 Union Naval Valencia SA (UNV) — Valencia** Yd No: 489 Loa 29.50 Br ex - Dght 4.540 Lbp 27.50 Br md 12.50 Dpth - Welded, 1 dk	**(B32A2ST) Tug**	**2 oil engines** reduction geared to sc. shafts driving 2 Voith-Schneider propellers Total Power: 5,280kW (7,178hp) A.B.C. 12VD 2 x Vee 4 Stroke 12 Cy. 256 x 310 each-2640kW (3589bh Anglo Belgian Corp NV (ABC)-Belgium AuxGen: 2 x 199kW 50Hz a.c
9602112 *ORQM* -	**42** **Port of Antwerp Towage (Havenbedrijf Antwerpen Sleepdienst)** - *Antwerpen* *Belgium* MMSI: 205627000	**430** 129 200	Class: BV	**2012-11 Union Naval Valencia SA (UNV) — Valencia** Yd No: 490 Loa 29.50 Br ex - Dght 4.500 Lbp 27.50 Br md 12.50 Dpth - Welded, 1 dk	**(B32A2ST) Tug**	**2 oil engines** driving 2 Voith-Schneider propellers Total Power: 5,280kW (7,178hp) A.B.C. 12VD 2 x Vee 4 Stroke 12 Cy. 256 x 310 each-2640kW (3589bh Anglo Belgian Corp NV (ABC)-Belgium AuxGen: 2 x 199kW 50Hz a.c Fuel: 140.0 (d.f.)
9602124 *ORQN* -	**43** **Port of Antwerp Towage (Havenbedrijf Antwerpen Sleepdienst)** - *Antwerpen* *Belgium* MMSI: 205628000	**430** 129 200	Class: BV	**2012-12 Union Naval Valencia SA (UNV) — Valencia** Yd No: 491 Loa 29.50 Br ex - Dght 4.540 Lbp 27.50 Br md 12.50 Dpth - Welded, 1 dk	**(B32A2ST) Tug**	**2 oil engines** driving 2 Voith-Schneider propellers Total Power: 5,280kW (7,178hp) A.B.C. 12VD 2 x Vee 4 Stroke 12 Cy. 256 x 310 each-2640kW (3589bh Anglo Belgian Corp NV (ABC)-Belgium Fuel: 140.0 (d.f.)
9152959 *UGYU* -	**50 LET POBEDY** **Government of The Russian Federation** Federal State Unitary Enterprise 'Atomflot' SatCom: Inmarsat C 427351996 *Murmansk* *Russia* MMSI: 273316240 Official number: 55152	**23,439** 7,032 3,505	Class: RS	**2007-03 AO Baltiyskiy Zavod — Sankt-Peterburg** Yd No: 01705 Loa 159.63 Br ex 30.03 Dght 11.000 Lbp 139.80 Br md 28.00 Dpth 17.22 Welded, 1 dk	**(B34C2SI) Icebreaker** Passengers: 128; berths: 180 Ice Capable	**2 turbo electric Steam Turbs** driving 2 gen. each 200kW a. 1 gen. of 1000kW a.c Connecting to 3 elec. motors each (17600kW) driving 3 FP propellers Total Power: 55,200kW (75,050hp) 21.0 Russkiy TGG-27.50 2 x steam Turb each-27600kW (37525shp) AO Kirovskiy Zavod-Sankt-Peterburg
8868745 - -	**51 11 31** **Transport Department of Logistics General Departments (Cuc Van Tai Tong Cuc Hau Can)** *Haiphong* *Vietnam*	**380** 180 400	Class: (VR)	**1992 Hanoi Shipyard — Hanoi** Loa 48.50 Br ex - Dght 3.200 Lbp - Br md 8.20 Dpth 4.10 Welded, 1 dk	**(A31A2GX) General Cargo Ship** Grain: 644 Compartments: 2 Ho, ER 2 Ha: 2 (8.0 x 4.1)ER	**1 oil engine** driving 1 FP propeller Total Power: 300kW (408hp) 10.0 S.K.L. 8NVD36- 1 x 4 Stroke 8 Cy. 240 x 360 300kW (408bhp) (made 1989 VEB Schwermaschinenbau "KarlLiebknecht" (SKL)-Magdeburg AuxGen: 2 x 30kW a.c
9722601 - -	**51-31-06** - - *Vietnam*	**155** 46 82	Class: VR	**2013-08 Yard N.51 — Vietnam** Yd No: L166 Loa 25.02 Br ex 7.50 Dght 2.800 Lbp 21.73 Br md 7.26 Dpth 3.75 Welded, 1 dk	**(B32A2ST) Tug**	**2 oil engines** reduction geared to sc. shafts driving 2 FP propellers Total Power: 1,066kW (1,450hp) Caterpillar C 2 x 4 Stroke 6 Cy. 145 x 183 each-533kW (725bhp) Caterpillar Inc-USA AuxGen: 2 x 56kW 400V a.c
7521534 - -	**80** **Port of Antwerp Towage (Havenbedrijf Antwerpen Sleepdienst)** *Antwerpen* *Belgium*	*110* - -		**1976-09 N.V. Scheepswerf van Rupelmonde — Rupelmonde** Yd No: 432 Loa 28.45 Br ex 9.12 Dght 4.217 Lbp 26.98 Br md 8.86 Dpth 3.20 Welded, 1 dk	**(B32A2ST) Tug**	**2 oil engines** geared to sc. shafts driving 2 Directional propellers Total Power: 1,618kW (2,200hp) 11.0 Kromhout 6FDHD2 2 x 4 Stroke 6 Cy. 240 x 260 each-809kW (1100bhp) Stork Werkspoor Diesel BV-Netherlands
7505140 - -	**81** **Port of Antwerp Towage (Havenbedrijf Antwerpen Sleepdienst)** *Antwerpen* *Belgium*	*110* - -		**1976-12 Scheepswerven St. Pieter N.V. — Hemiksem** Yd No: 267 Loa 28.45 Br ex 9.12 Dght 3.201 Lbp 27.01 Br md 8.86 Dpth 4.22 Welded, 1 dk	**(B32A2ST) Tug**	**2 oil engines** geared to sc. shafts driving 2 Directional propellers Total Power: 1,618kW (2,200hp) 11.0 Kromhout 6FDHD2 2 x 4 Stroke 6 Cy. 240 x 260 each-809kW (1100bhp) Stork Werkspoor Diesel BV-Netherlands
7521546 -	**82** **Port of Antwerp Towage (Havenbedrijf Antwerpen Sleepdienst)** - *Antwerpen* *Belgium*	*110* - -		**1976-11 N.V. Scheepswerf van Rupelmonde — Rupelmonde** Yd No: 433 Loa 28.45 Br ex 9.12 Dght 3.201 Lbp 27.01 Br md 8.86 Dpth 4.22 Welded, 1 dk	**(B32A2ST) Tug**	**2 oil engines** geared to sc. shafts driving 2 Directional propellers Total Power: 1,618kW (2,200hp) 11.0 Kromhout 6FDHD2 2 x 4 Stroke 6 Cy. 240 x 260 each-809kW (1100bhp) Stork Werkspoor Diesel BV-Netherlands
8843082 - -	**84** - -	**190** 57 70	Class: (RS)	**1991-01 Astrakhanskaya Sudoverf im. "Kirova" — Astrakhan** Yd No: 84 Loa 31.85 Br ex 7.08 Dght 2.100 Lbp 27.80 Br md - Dpth 3.15 Welded, 1 dk	**(B12B2FC) Fish Carrier** Ins: 100	**1 oil engine** geared to sc. shaft driving 1 FP propeller Total Power: 232kW (315hp) 10.2 Daldizel 6CHSPN2A18-3 1 x 4 Stroke 6 Cy. 180 x 220 232kW (315bhp) Daldizel-Khabarovsk AuxGen: 2 x 25kW a.c Fuel: 14.0 (d.f.)
8952170 - -	**88 KOPAS** *ex* Jin Yang 823 *-1999* **Island Oil Exploration** - *Sao Tome* *Sao Tome & Principe*	**167** 59 -		**1984 Hyangdo Shipbuilding Co Ltd — Pohang** L reg 30.86 Br ex - Dght - Lbp 29.55 Br md 6.00 Dpth 2.85 Welded, 1 dk	**(B11B2FV) Fishing Vessel**	**1 oil engine** driving 1 FP propeller Total Power: 331kW (450hp) 9.0 Caterpillar 1 x 4 Stroke 331kW (450bhp) Caterpillar Tractor Co-USA
8331560 *LYAK* -	**100** *ex* 0100 *-2012* *ex* Aiste *-1997* *ex* Saturn *-1995* *ex* Kapitan Moskalenko *-1992* **JSC 'Banginis' (UAB 'Banginis')** - *Klaipeda* *Lithuania* MMSI: 277194000 Official number: 149	**104** 31 61	Class: PR (RS)	**1985-01 Azovskaya Sudoverf — Azov** Yd No: 7050 Loa 26.50 Br ex 6.59 Dght 2.290 Lbp 22.90 Br md 6.50 Dpth 3.05 Welded, 1 dk	**(B11B2FV) Fishing Vessel**	**1 oil engine** geared to sc. shaft driving 1 FP propeller Total Power: 165kW (224hp) 9.3 Daldizel 6CHNSP18/2 1 x 4 Stroke 6 Cy. 180 x 220 165kW (224bhp) Daldizel-Khabarovsk AuxGen: 2 x 30kW a.c Fuel: 11.0 (d.f.)
7606114 *XYBF* -	**0101** **Government of The Union of Myanmar (People's Pearl & Fishery Board)** - *Yangon* *Myanmar*	*170* 55 -	Class: (LR) ✠ Classed LR until 1/12/78	**1977-08 Daedong Shipbuilding Co Ltd — Busan** Yd No: 175 Loa 28.58 Br ex 7.27 Dght 2.752 Lbp 24.62 Br md 7.21 Dpth 3.61 Welded, 1 dk	**(B11A2FS) Stern Trawler**	**1 oil engine** reverse reduction geared to sc. shaft driving 1 F propeller Total Power: 346kW (470hp) 11.0 Yanmar 6ML- 1 x 4 Stroke 6 Cy. 200 x 240 346kW (470bhp) Yanmar Diesel Engine Co Ltd-Japan AuxGen: 2 x 88kW 445V 50Hz a.c
8827882 *6KCB9* -	**101 HAERANG** *ex* Chang Bo Go I *-2013* *ex* Sam Kyung No. 71 *-1993* *ex* Oriental Star No. 1 *-1989* *ex* Jeong Chang No. 2 *-1989* - - *South Korea* MMSI: 441879000	*397* 126 643	Class: (KR)	**1987-12 Hyangdo Shipbuilding Co Ltd — Pohang** Yd No: 56 Loa 57.70 Br ex - Dght 3.660 Lbp 49.50 Br md 9.00 Dpth 3.80 Welded, 1 dk	**(B11B2FV) Fishing Vessel** Ins: 635	**1 oil engine** geared to sc. shaft driving 1 FP propeller Total Power: 919kW (1,249hp) 12.3 Cummins KTA-50- 1 x Vee 4 Stroke 16 Cy. 159 x 159 919kW (1249bhp) Ssangyong Heavy Industries Co Ltd-South Korea AuxGen: 2 x 560kW 225V a.c
9186467 *DSNA8* -	**101 HYODONG CHEMI** *ex* Myung Jin No. 3 *-2012* **Hyo Dong Marine Service Co Ltd** - *Busan* *South Korea* MMSI: 441277000 Official number: BSR-021568	**2,204** 1,050 3,566 T/cm 10.7	Class: KR	**1998-02 Ilheung Shipbuilding & Engineering Co Ltd — Mokpo** Yd No: 96-73 Loa 90.62 (BB) Br ex 14.43 Dght 5.712 Lbp 82.50 Br md 14.40 Dpth 6.92 Welded, 1 dk	**(A12B2TR) Chemical/Products Tanker** Double Hull (13F) Liq: 3,429; Liq (Oil): 4,000 Cargo Heating Coils Compartments: 12 Wing Ta, 2 Wing Slop Ta, ER 10 Cargo Pump (s): 10x165m³/hr Manifold: Bow/CM: 39.8m	**1 oil engine** driving 1 FP propeller Total Power: 2,405kW (3,270hp) 14.7 B&W 6S26M 1 x 2 Stroke 6 Cy. 260 x 980 2405kW (3270bhp) Ssangyong Heavy Industries Co Ltd-South Korea AuxGen: 3 x 320kW 445V 60Hz a.c Fuel: 92.0 (d.f.) 311.0 (r.f.)

IMO / Call sign	Name / Owner	Tonnage / Class	Builder / Dimensions	Type	Machinery
01967	**0101 MARINE** *ex* Lucky Star IV *-1997* *ex* Ain Chanech *-1997* *ex* Daishin Maru No. 18 *-1981* *ex* Oshika Maru No. 2 *-1977* **Sunfish Marine Co SA** -	*999* Class: (BV) (NK) 451 -	**1966 Niigata Engineering Co Ltd — Niigata NI** Yd No: 662 Loa 66.65 Br ex 11.43 Dght 4.801 Lbp 61.83 Br md 11.41 Dpth 5.11 Welded, 2 dks	**(B11A2FS) Stern Trawler**	**1 oil engine** driving 1 FP propeller Total Power: 1,618kW (2,200hp) 12.5kn Niigata M8F43CHS 1 x 4 Stroke 8 Cy. 430 x 620 1618kW (2200bhp) Niigata Engineering Co Ltd-Japan AuxGen: 3 x 184kW Fuel: 323.0
606126 *YBG*	**0103** **Government of The Union of Myanmar (People's Pearl & Fishery Board)** - *Yangon* *Myanmar*	*170* Class: (LR) 55 ✠ Classed LR until 1/12/78 -	**1977-10 Daedong Shipbuilding Co Ltd — Busan** Yd No: 176 Loa 28.58 Br ex 7.27 Dght 2.752 Lbp 24.62 Br md 7.21 Dpth 3.61 Welded, 1 dk	**(B11A2FS) Stern Trawler**	**1 oil engine** reverse reduction geared to sc. shaft driving 1 FP propeller Total Power: 346kW (470hp) 11.0kn Yanmar 6ML-DT 1 x 4 Stroke 6 Cy. 200 x 240 346kW (470bhp) Yanmar Diesel Engine Co Ltd-Japan AuxGen: 2 x 88kW 445V 50Hz a.c
606138 *YBH*	**0105** **Government of The Union of Myanmar (People's Pearl & Fishery Board)** - *Yangon* *Myanmar*	*170* Class: (LR) 55 ✠ Classed LR until 1/12/78 -	**1977-10 Daedong Shipbuilding Co Ltd — Busan** Yd No: 177 Loa 28.58 Br ex 7.24 Dght 2.752 Lbp 24.62 Br md 7.21 Dpth 3.61 Welded, 1 dk	**(B11A2FS) Stern Trawler**	**1 oil engine** reverse reduction geared to sc. shaft driving 1 FP propeller Total Power: 346kW (470hp) 11.0kn Yanmar 6ML-DT 1 x 4 Stroke 6 Cy. 200 x 240 346kW (470bhp) Yanmar Diesel Engine Co Ltd-Japan AuxGen: 2 x 88kW 445V 50Hz a.c
606140 *XYBI*	**0107** **Government of The Union of Myanmar (People's Pearl & Fishery Board)** - *Yangon* *Myanmar*	*170* Class: (LR) 55 ✠ Classed LR until 1/12/78 -	**1977-10 Daedong Shipbuilding Co Ltd — Busan** Yd No: 178 Loa 28.58 Br ex 7.27 Dght 2.752 Lbp 24.62 Br md 7.21 Dpth 3.61 Welded, 1 dk	**(B11A2FS) Stern Trawler**	**1 oil engine** reverse reduction geared to sc. shaft driving 1 FP propeller Total Power: 346kW (470hp) 11.0kn Yanmar 6ML-DT 1 x 4 Stroke 6 Cy. 200 x 240 346kW (470bhp) Yanmar Diesel Engine Co Ltd-Japan AuxGen: 2 x 88kW 445V 50Hz a.c
606152 *XYBJ*	**0109** **Government of The Union of Myanmar (People's Pearl & Fishery Board)** - *Yangon* *Myanmar*	*170* Class: (LR) 55 ✠ Classed LR until 1/12/78 -	**1977-11 Daedong Shipbuilding Co Ltd — Busan** Yd No: 179 Loa 28.58 Br ex 7.27 Dght 2.752 Lbp 24.62 Br md 7.21 Dpth 3.61 Welded, 1 dk	**(B11A2FS) Stern Trawler**	**1 oil engine** reverse reduction geared to sc. shaft driving 1 FP propeller Total Power: 346kW (470hp) 11.0kn Yanmar 6ML-DT 1 x 4 Stroke 6 Cy. 200 x 240 346kW (470bhp) Yanmar Diesel Engine Co Ltd-Japan AuxGen: 2 x 88kW 445V 50Hz a.c
7606164 *XYBK*	**0111** **Government of The Union of Myanmar (People's Pearl & Fishery Board)** - *Yangon* *Myanmar*	*170* Class: (LR) 55 ✠ Classed LR until 1/12/78 -	**1977-10 Daedong Shipbuilding Co Ltd — Busan** Yd No: 180 Loa 28.58 Br ex 7.27 Dght 2.752 Lbp 24.62 Br md 7.21 Dpth 3.61 Welded, 1 dk	**(B11A2FS) Stern Trawler**	**1 oil engine** reverse reduction geared to sc. shaft driving 1 FP propeller Total Power: 346kW (470hp) 11.0kn Yanmar 6ML-DT 1 x 4 Stroke 6 Cy. 200 x 240 346kW (470bhp) Yanmar Diesel Engine Co Ltd-Japan AuxGen: 2 x 88kW 445V 50Hz a.c
7606176 *XYBL* -	**0113** **Government of The Union of Myanmar (People's Pearl & Fishery Board)** - *Yangon* *Myanmar*	*170* Class: (LR) 55 ✠ Classed LR until 1/12/78 -	**1977-11 Daedong Shipbuilding Co Ltd — Busan** Yd No: 181 Loa 28.58 Br ex 7.27 Dght 2.752 Lbp 24.62 Br md 7.21 Dpth 3.61 Welded, 1 dk	**(B11A2FS) Stern Trawler**	**1 oil engine** reverse reduction geared to sc. shaft driving 1 FP propeller Total Power: 346kW (470hp) 11.0kn Yanmar 6ML-DT 1 x 4 Stroke 6 Cy. 200 x 240 346kW (470bhp) Yanmar Diesel Engine Co Ltd-Japan AuxGen: 2 x 88kW 445V 50Hz a.c
7606188 *XYBM* -	**0115** **Government of The Union of Myanmar (People's Pearl & Fishery Board)** - *Yangon* *Myanmar*	*170* Class: (LR) 55 ✠ Classed LR until 1/12/78 -	**1977-11 Daedong Shipbuilding Co Ltd — Busan** Yd No: 182 Loa 28.58 Br ex 7.27 Dght 2.752 Lbp 24.62 Br md 7.21 Dpth 3.61 Welded, 1 dk	**(B11A2FS) Stern Trawler**	**1 oil engine** reverse reduction geared to sc. shaft driving 1 FP propeller Total Power: 346kW (470hp) 11.0kn Yanmar 6ML-DT 1 x 4 Stroke 6 Cy. 200 x 240 346kW (470bhp) Yanmar Diesel Engine Co Ltd-Japan AuxGen: 2 x 88kW 445V 50Hz a.c
7606190 *XYBN* -	**0117** **Government of The Union of Myanmar (People's Pearl & Fishery Board)** - *Yangon* *Myanmar*	*170* Class: (LR) 55 ✠ Classed LR until 1/12/78 -	**1977-12 Daedong Shipbuilding Co Ltd — Busan** Yd No: 183 Loa 28.58 Br ex 7.27 Dght 2.752 Lbp 24.62 Br md 7.21 Dpth 3.61 Welded, 1 dk	**(B11A2FS) Stern Trawler**	**1 oil engine** reverse reduction geared to sc. shaft driving 1 FP propeller Total Power: 346kW (470hp) 11.0kn Yanmar 6ML-DT 1 x 4 Stroke 6 Cy. 200 x 240 346kW (470bhp) Yanmar Diesel Engine Co Ltd-Japan AuxGen: 2 x 88kW 445V 50Hz a.c
7606205 *XYBO* -	**0119** **Government of The Union of Myanmar (People's Pearl & Fishery Board)** - *Yangon* *Myanmar*	*170* Class: (LR) 55 ✠ Classed LR until 1/12/78 -	**1977-12 Daedong Shipbuilding Co Ltd — Busan** Yd No: 184 Loa 28.58 Br ex 7.27 Dght 2.752 Lbp 24.62 Br md 7.21 Dpth 3.61 Welded, 1 dk	**(B11A2FS) Stern Trawler**	**1 oil engine** reverse reduction geared to sc. shaft driving 1 FP propeller Total Power: 346kW (470hp) 11.0kn Yanmar 6ML-DT 1 x 4 Stroke 6 Cy. 200 x 240 346kW (470bhp) Yanmar Diesel Engine Co Ltd-Japan AuxGen: 2 x 88kW 445V 50Hz a.c
9495090 *CNEL* -	**130** **Government of The Kingdom of Morocco (Royal Navy of Morocco)** - *Casablanca* *Morocco*	**110** Class: (LR) - ✠ Classed LR until 28/4/10 75	**2008-06 Rodman Polyships S.A. — Vigo** Yd No: 101043 Loa 30.00 Br ex 6.01 Dght 1.100 Lbp 25.30 Br md 6.00 Dpth 3.48 Welded, 1 dk	**(B34H2SQ) Patrol Vessel**	**2 oil engines** with clutches, flexible couplings & reverse reduction geared to sc. shafts driving 2 Water jets Total Power: 2,100kW (2,856hp) M.T.U. 16V2000M70 2 x Vee 4 Stroke 16 Cy. 130 x 150 each-1050kW (1428bhp) MTU Friedrichshafen GmbH-Friedrichshafen AuxGen: 2 x 64kW 400V 50Hz a.c
9495105 - -	**131** **Government of The Kingdom of Morocco (Royal Navy of Morocco)** - *Casablanca* *Morocco*	**110** Class: (LR) - ✠ Classed LR until 11/11/09 75	**2008-08 Rodman Polyships S.A. — Vigo** Yd No: 101044 Loa 30.00 Br ex 6.00 Dght 1.100 Lbp 25.30 Br md 6.00 Dpth 3.48 Welded, 1 dk	**(B34H2SQ) Patrol Vessel**	**2 oil engines** with clutches, flexible couplings & reverse reduction geared to sc.shafts driving 2 Water jets Total Power: 2,100kW (2,856hp) M.T.U. 16V2000M70 2 x Vee 4 Stroke 16 Cy. 130 x 150 each-1050kW (1428bhp) MTU Friedrichshafen GmbH-Friedrichshafen AuxGen: 2 x 64kW 400V 50Hz a.c
9495117 - -	**132** **Government of The Kingdom of Morocco (Royal Navy of Morocco)** - *Casablanca* *Morocco*	**110** Class: (LR) - ✠ Classed LR until 19/5/10 75	**2008-11 Rodman Polyships S.A. — Vigo** Yd No: 101045 Loa 30.00 Br ex 6.00 Dght 1.100 Lbp 25.30 Br md 6.00 Dpth 3.48 Welded, 1 dk	**(B34H2SQ) Patrol Vessel**	**2 oil engines** with clutches, flexible couplings & reverse reduction geared to sc. shafts driving 2 Water jets Total Power: 2,100kW (2,856hp) M.T.U. 16V2000M70 2 x Vee 4 Stroke 16 Cy. 130 x 150 each-1050kW (1428bhp) MTU Friedrichshafen GmbH-Friedrichshafen AuxGen: 2 x 64kW 400V 50Hz a.c
8925517 *LYNQ* -	**169** *ex* KM-1069 *-2004* *ex* MRTK-1069 *-1996* **JSC 'Stekutis'** - SatCom: Inmarsat C 427721510 *Klaipeda* *Lithuania* MMSI: 277215000 Official number: 247	**120** Class: RS 36 33	**1982-06 Sosnovskiy Sudostroitelnyy Zavod — Sosnovka** Yd No: 627 Loa 25.50 Br ex 7.00 Dght 2.390 Lbp 22.00 Br md 6.80 Dpth 3.30 Welded, 1 dk	**(B11A2FS) Stern Trawler**	**1 oil engine** driving 1 FP propeller Total Power: 221kW (300hp) 9.5kn S.K.L. 6NVD26A-2 1 x 4 Stroke 6 Cy. 180 x 260 221kW (300bhp) VEB Schwermaschinenbau "KarlLiebknecht" (SKL)-Magdeburg AuxGen: 2 x 16kW a.c Fuel: 15.0 (d.f.)
7048740 *WX8868* -	**0190 FATHOMS** **International Oceanographic** - *Galveston, TX* *United States of America* Official number: 508253	*114* 77 -	**1967 M & F Seacraft, Inc. — Palacios, Tx** L reg 20.67 Br ex 6.66 Dght - Lbp - Br md - Dpth 3.54 Welded	**(B12D2FR) Fishery Research Vessel**	**1 oil engine** geared to sc. shaft driving 1 FP propeller Total Power: 243kW (330hp)
6708666 *YGLQ* -	**250** *ex* Delta I *-2000* *ex* Sai Hong *-1990* *ex* Belier *-1987* **PT Indoliziz Marine** - *Jakarta* *Indonesia*	**383** Class: (KI) (BV) 115 310	**1967-04 Ateliers & Chantiers de La Rochelle-Pallice — La Rochelle** Yd No: 5154 Loa 39.68 Br ex 9.81 Dght 4.598 Lbp 35.69 Br md 9.10 Dpth 4.65 Welded, 1 dk	**(B32A2ST) Tug**	**1 oil engine** driving 1 FP propeller Total Power: 1,802kW (2,450hp) 13.5kn Deutz RBV8M358 1 x 4 Stroke 8 Cy. 400 x 580 1802kW (2450bhp) Kloeckner Humboldt Deutz AG-West Germany AuxGen: 2 x 75kW 440V 60Hz a.c Fuel: 193.0 (d.f.)

IMO / Call sign	Name / Owner	Tonnage	Class	Builder / Dimensions	Type	Machinery
7366647 - -	**277 PARK** **Compania Pesquera Vikingos de Colombia SA** - *Cartagena de Indias* *Colombia* Official number: MC-05-397	*142* 97 60	Class: (BV)	**1973 Diesel Shipbuilding Co. — Jacksonville, Fl** Yd No: 195 L reg 22.80 Br ex 6.71 Dght - Lbp - Br md 6.66 Dpth 3.74 Welded, 1 dk	**(B11A2FT) Trawler** Compartments: 1 Ho, ER 1 Ha: (1.8 x 1.5) Derricks: 1x2t	**1 oil engine** driving 1 FP propeller Total Power: 313kW (426hp) 10.0 Caterpillar D353SC 1 x 4 Stroke 6 Cy. 159 x 203 313kW (426bhp) Caterpillar Tractor Co-USA Fuel: 82.0 (d.f.)
7721718 - -	**0280-B TEHUELCHE** **Government of The Argentine Republic (Secretaria de Estado de Obras Publicas)** -	*120* 29 59	Class: (LR) ✠ Classed LR until 30/10/81	**1979-06 Maritima de Axpe S.A. — Bilbao** Yd No: 112 Loa 22.51 Br ex 7.07 Dght 2.401 Lbp 20.50 Br md 6.71 Dpth 3.46 Welded, 1 dk	**(B32B2SP) Pusher Tug**	**1 oil engine** reverse reduction geared to sc. shaft driving 1 F propeller Total Power: 640kW (870hp) Deutz SBA6M52 1 x 4 Stroke 6 Cy. 220 x 280 640kW (870bhp) Hijos de J Barreras SA-Spain AuxGen: 2 x 51kW 380V 50Hz a.c
6906567 *XYAR* -	**0301 BARANI** **Government of The Union of Myanmar (People's Pearl & Fishery Board)** - *Yangon* *Myanmar*	*184* 63 -	Class: (LR) ✠ Classed LR until 12/71	**1969-03 N.V. Scheepswerf en Machinefabriek "Vahali" — Gendt** Yd No: 421 Loa 30.10 Br ex 7.57 Dght 3.150 Lbp 25.76 Br md 7.50 Dpth 3.99 Welded	**(B11A2FS) Stern Trawler**	**1 oil engine** sr geared to sc. shaft driving 1 CP propeller Total Power: 368kW (500hp) Dorman 12QT 1 x Vee 4 Stroke 12 Cy. 159 x 165 368kW (500bhp) W. H. Dorman & Co. Ltd.-Stafford AuxGen: 2 x 23kW 380V 50Hz a.c
7432721 *DSOW8* -	**301 CHOYANGHO** *ex* Nam Chang 2007 *-2011* *ex* Il Sung T-1 *-2007* *ex* Sekyung No. 5 *-2006* *ex* Uzushio Maru *-2005* **Choyang Shipping Co Ltd** - *Busan* *South Korea* MMSI: 440560000 Official number: BSR-012663	*216* 64 77	Class: KR (NK)	**1975-11 Kochi Jyuko K.K. — Kochi** Yd No: 883 Loa 29.19 Br ex - Dght - Lbp 26.47 Br md 8.62 Dpth 3.79 Riveted\Welded, 1 dk	**(B32A2ST) Tug**	**2 oil engines** driving 2 FP propellers Total Power: 2,060kW (2,800hp) 12.8 Hanshin 6LU3 2 x 4 Stroke 6 Cy. 320 x 510 each-1030kW (1400bhp) Hanshin Nainenki Kogyo-Japan
6906579 *XYAT* -	**0303 YAWHANI** **Government of The Union of Myanmar (People's Pearl & Fishery Board)** - *Yangon* *Myanmar*	*184* 63 -	Class: (LR) ✠ Classed LR until 12/71	**1969-04 N.V. Scheepswerf v/h Fa. J. Hendriks — Dodewaard** Yd No: 506 Loa 30.10 Br ex 7.57 Dght 3.150 Lbp 25.76 Br md 7.50 Dpth 3.99 Welded	**(B11A2FS) Stern Trawler**	**1 oil engine** sr geared to sc. shaft driving 1 CP propeller Total Power: 368kW (500hp) Dorman 12QT 1 x Vee 4 Stroke 12 Cy. 159 x 165 368kW (500bhp) W. H. Dorman & Co. Ltd.-Stafford AuxGen: 2 x 23kW 380V 50Hz a.c
6917633 *XYAS* -	**0305 MIGATHI** **Government of The Union of Myanmar (People's Pearl & Fishery Board)** - *Yangon* *Myanmar*	*184* 63 -	Class: (LR) ✠ Classed LR until 12/71	**1969-03 van Goor's Scheepswerf en Mfbk N.V. — Monnickendam** Yd No: 635 Loa 30.10 Br ex 7.57 Dght 3.150 Lbp 25.58 Br md 7.50 Dpth 3.99 Welded	**(B11A2FS) Stern Trawler**	**1 oil engine** sr geared to sc. shaft driving 1 CP propeller Total Power: 368kW (500hp) Dorman 12QT 1 x Vee 4 Stroke 12 Cy. 159 x 165 368kW (500bhp) W. H. Dorman & Co. Ltd.-Stafford AuxGen: 2 x 23kW 380V 50Hz a.c
7405376 *DTBW5* -	**307CHANGJIN** *ex* Sam Young No. 701 *-2005* *ex* MS No. 12 *-2005* *ex* Dae Wang No. 12 *-2005* - - *South Korea* MMSI: 440618000	**670** 263 510	Class: (KR)	**1974-08 Mie Shipyard Co. Ltd. — Yokkaichi** Yd No: 125 Loa 55.63 Br ex - Dght 3.745 Lbp 48.98 Br md 9.00 Dpth 3.99 Welded, 1 dk	**(B11B2FV) Fishing Vessel** Ins: 567 3 Ha: 2 (1.3 x 1.0) (1.6 x 1.6)	**1 oil engine** driving 1 FP propeller Total Power: 1,103kW (1,500hp) 12.5 Akasaka AH3 1 x 4 Stroke 6 Cy. 300 x 480 1103kW (1500bhp) Akasaka Tekkosho KK (Akasaka DieselLtd)-Japan AuxGen: 2 x 200kW 225V a.c
7822237 - -	**0330-752** **Government of The People's Republic of China** *Shanghai* *China*	*1,732* 495 332	Class: (NK)	**1979-11 Nippon Kokan KK (NKK Corp) — Tsu ME** Yd No: SP.2 Loa 74.10 Br ex - Dght 3.168 Lbp 69.91 Br md 14.00 Dpth 5.11 Welded, 1 dk	**(B33A2DB) Bucket Ladder Dredger**	**1 diesel electric oil engine** driving 1 gen. of 700kW d.c Connecting to 1 elec. Motor driving 1 FP propeller Total Power: 1,250kW (1,700hp) 8.5 Niigata 8MG31E 1 x 4 Stroke 8 Cy. 310 x 380 1250kW (1700bhp) Niigata Engineering Co Ltd-Japan AuxGen: 2 x 275kW
1007897 *ZCIW9*	**360** *ex* Sonka *-2010* *ex* April Fool II *-2007* *ex* April Fool *-2006* **Al Njaeb Pty Ltd** Pierre Makdessi *George Town* *Cayman Islands (British)* MMSI: 319928000 Official number: 736854	**498** 149 80	Class: LR RI ✠ **100A1** SS 06/2013 SSC Yacht, mono, G6 ✠ **LMC** Cable: 151.2/19.0 U2 (a)	**2003-09 ISA Produzione Srl — Ancona** Yd No: 470.1 Loa 47.50 Br ex 8.90 Dght 2.510 Lbp 40.60 Br md 8.60 Dpth 4.50 Welded, 1 dk	**(X11A2YP) Yacht**	**2 oil engines** with clutches, flexible coulpings & sr reverse geared to sc. shafts driving 2 FP propellers Total Power: 3,480kW (4,732hp) 17.0 M.T.U. 12V4000M7 2 x Vee 4 Stroke 12 Cy. 165 x 190 each-1740kW (2366bhp) MTU Friedrichshafen GmbH-Friedrichshafen AuxGen: 2 x 125kW 380V 50Hz a.c Thrusters: 1 Thwart. FP thruster (f)
7644427 - -	**0380-B** **Government of The Argentine Republic (Direccion Nacional de Construcciones Portuarias y Vias Navegables)**	**584** 526 1,000	Class: (AB)	**1977-01 Astilleros Principe, Menghi y Penco S.A. — Avellaneda** Yd No: 91 Loa 65.18 Br ex - Dght 2.750 Lbp 63.15 Br md 12.51 Dpth 3.51 Welded, 1 dk	**(B34E2SW) Waste Disposal Vessel**	**2 oil engines** reverse reduction geared to sc. shafts driving 2 FP propellers Total Power: 742kW (1,008hp) 7.8 MAN R6B16/18T 2 x 4 Stroke 6 Cy. 160 x 180 each-371kW (504bhp) Industrias Argentinas MAN SAIC-Argentina AuxGen: 2 x 26kW Fuel: 44.5 (d.f.)
7733993 - -	**0381-B** **Government of The Argentine Republic (Direccion Nacional de Construcciones Portuarias y Vias Navegables)** -	**584** 526 1,000	Class: (AB)	**1977-04 Astilleros Principe, Menghi y Penco S.A. — Avellaneda** Yd No: 92 Loa 65.18 Br ex - Dght 2.750 Lbp 63.15 Br md 12.51 Dpth 3.51 Welded, 1 dk	**(B34E2SW) Waste Disposal Vessel**	**2 oil engines** geared to sc. shafts driving 2 FP propellers Total Power: 742kW (1,008hp) 7.8 MAN R6B16/18T 2 x 4 Stroke 6 Cy. 160 x 180 each-371kW (504bhp) Industrias Argentinas MAN SAIC-Argentina AuxGen: 2 x 26kW
7734002 - -	**0382-B** **Government of The Argentine Republic (Direccion Nacional de Construcciones Portuarias y Vias Navegables)** -	*570* - 1,000	Class: (AB)	**1977-08 Astilleros Principe, Menghi y Penco S.A. — Avellaneda** Yd No: 93 Loa 65.18 Br ex - Dght 2.750 Lbp 63.15 Br md 12.51 Dpth 3.51 Welded, 1 dk	**(B34E2SW) Waste Disposal Vessel**	**2 oil engines** geared to sc. shafts driving 2 FP propellers Total Power: 742kW (1,008hp) 7.8 MAN R6B16/18T 2 x 4 Stroke 6 Cy. 160 x 180 each-371kW (504bhp) Industrias Argentinas MAN SAIC-Argentina AuxGen: 2 x 26kW
7734014 - -	**0383-B** **Government of The Argentine Republic (Direccion Nacional de Construcciones Portuarias y Vias Navegables)** -	*570* - 1,000	Class: (AB)	**1977-11 Astilleros Principe, Menghi y Penco S.A. — Avellaneda** Yd No: 94 Loa 65.18 Br ex - Dght 2.750 Lbp 63.15 Br md 12.51 Dpth 3.51 Welded, 1 dk	**(B34E2SW) Waste Disposal Vessel**	**1 oil engine** geared to sc. shaft driving 1 FP propeller Total Power: 743kW (1,010hp) 7.8 MAN R6B16/18T 1 x 4 Stroke 6 Cy. 160 x 180 743kW (1010bhp) Industrias Argentinas MAN SAIC-Argentina AuxGen: 2 x 26kW
7820318 - -	**0385-B** **Government of The Argentine Republic (Direccion Nacional de Construcciones Portuarias y Vias Navegables)** -	*570* - 1,000	Class: (AB)	**1978-03 Astilleros Principe, Menghi y Penco S.A. — Avellaneda** Yd No: 96 Loa 65.18 Br ex - Dght 2.750 Lbp 63.15 Br md 12.51 Dpth 3.51 Welded, 1 dk	**(B34E2SW) Waste Disposal Vessel**	**2 oil engines** geared to sc. shafts driving 2 FP propellers Total Power: 742kW (1,008hp) 7.8 MAN R6B16/18T 2 x 4 Stroke 6 Cy. 160 x 180 each-371kW (504bhp) Industrias Argentinas MAN SAIC-Argentina AuxGen: 2 x 26kW
7820320 - -	**0386-B** **Government of The Argentine Republic (Direccion Nacional de Construcciones Portuarias y Vias Navegables)** -	*570* - 1,000	Class: (AB)	**1978-03 Astilleros Principe, Menghi y Penco S.A. — Avellaneda** Yd No: 97 Loa 65.18 Br ex - Dght 2.750 Lbp 63.15 Br md 12.51 Dpth 3.51 Welded, 1 dk	**(B34E2SW) Waste Disposal Vessel**	**2 oil engines** geared to sc. shafts driving 2 FP propellers Total Power: 742kW (1,008hp) 7.8 MAN R6B16/18T 2 x 4 Stroke 6 Cy. 160 x 180 each-371kW (504bhp) Industrias Argentinas MAN SAIC-Argentina AuxGen: 2 x 26kW
7820332 - -	**0387-B** **Government of The Argentine Republic (Direccion Nacional de Construcciones Portuarias y Vias Navegables)** -	*570* - 1,000	Class: (AB)	**1978-07 Astilleros Principe, Menghi y Penco S.A. — Avellaneda** Yd No: 98 Loa 65.18 Br ex - Dght 2.750 Lbp 63.15 Br md 12.51 Dpth 3.51 Welded, 1 dk	**(B34E2SW) Waste Disposal Vessel**	**2 oil engines** geared to sc. shafts driving 2 FP propellers Total Power: 742kW (1,008hp) 7.8 MAN R6B16/18T 2 x 4 Stroke 6 Cy. 160 x 180 each-371kW (504bhp) Industrias Argentinas MAN SAIC-Argentina AuxGen: 2 x 26kW
7820344 - -	**0388-B** **Government of The Argentine Republic (Direccion Nacional de Construcciones Portuarias y Vias Navegables)** -	**584** 526 1,000	Class: (AB)	**1978-08 Astilleros Principe, Menghi y Penco S.A. — Avellaneda** Yd No: 99 Loa 65.18 Br ex - Dght 2.750 Lbp 63.15 Br md 12.51 Dpth 3.51 Welded, 1 dk	**(B34E2SW) Waste Disposal Vessel**	**2 oil engines** geared to sc. shafts driving 2 FP propellers Total Power: 742kW (1,008hp) 7.8 MAN R6B16/18T 2 x 4 Stroke 6 Cy. 160 x 180 each-371kW (504bhp) Industrias Argentinas MAN SAIC-Argentina AuxGen: 2 x 26kW

No.	Name / Owner	Tonnage	Class	Builder / Dimensions	Type	Machinery
20356	**0389-B** **Government of The Argentine Republic (Direccion Nacional de Construcciones Portuarias y Vias Navegables)** -	**584** 526 1,000	Class: (AB)	**1978-10 Astilleros Principe, Menghi y Penco S.A. — Avellaneda** Yd No: 100 Loa 65.18 Br ex - Dght 2.750 Lbp 63.15 Br md 12.51 Dpth 3.51 Welded, 1 dk	**(B34E2SW) Waste Disposal Vessel**	**2 oil engines** geared to sc. shafts driving 2 FP propellers Total Power: 742kW (1,008hp) 7.8kn MAN R6B16/18TL 2 x 4 Stroke 6 Cy. 160 x 180 each-371kW (504bhp) Industrias Argentinas MAN SAIC-Argentina AuxGen: 2 x 26kW
20368	**0390-B** **Government of The Argentine Republic (Direccion Nacional de Construcciones Portuarias y Vias Navegables)** -	*570* - 1,000	Class: (AB)	**1978-10 Astilleros Principe, Menghi y Penco S.A. — Avellaneda** Yd No: 101 Loa 65.18 Br ex - Dght 2.750 Lbp 63.15 Br md 12.51 Dpth 3.51 Welded, 1 dk	**(B34E2SW) Waste Disposal Vessel**	**2 oil engines** geared to sc. shafts driving 2 FP propellers Total Power: 742kW (1,008hp) 7.8kn MAN R6B16/18TL 2 x 4 Stroke 6 Cy. 160 x 180 each-371kW (504bhp) Industrias Argentinas MAN SAIC-Argentina AuxGen: 2 x 26kW
20370	**0391-B** **Government of The Argentine Republic (Direccion Nacional de Construcciones Portuarias y Vias Navegables)** -	*570* - 1,000	Class: (AB)	**1978-11 Astilleros Principe, Menghi y Penco S.A. — Avellaneda** Yd No: 102 Loa 65.18 Br ex - Dght 2.750 Lbp 63.15 Br md 12.51 Dpth 3.51 Welded, 1 dk	**(B34E2SW) Waste Disposal Vessel**	**2 oil engines** geared to sc. shafts driving 2 FP propellers Total Power: 742kW (1,008hp) 7.8kn MAN R6B16/18TL 2 x 4 Stroke 6 Cy. 160 x 180 each-371kW (504bhp) Industrias Argentinas MAN SAIC-Argentina AuxGen: 2 x 26kW
20382	**0392-B** **Government of The Argentine Republic (Direccion Nacional de Construcciones Portuarias y Vias Navegables)** -	*570* - 1,000	Class: (AB)	**1978-12 Astilleros Principe, Menghi y Penco S.A. — Avellaneda** Yd No: 103 Loa 65.18 Br ex - Dght 2.750 Lbp 63.15 Br md 12.51 Dpth 3.51 Welded, 1 dk	**(B34E2SW) Waste Disposal Vessel**	**2 oil engines** geared to sc. shafts driving 2 FP propellers Total Power: 742kW (1,008hp) 7.8kn MAN R6B16/18TL 2 x 4 Stroke 6 Cy. 160 x 180 each-371kW (504bhp) Industrias Argentinas MAN SAIC-Argentina AuxGen: 2 x 26kW
17621 *4Q*	**0401 YEWADI** **Government of The Union of Myanmar (People's Pearl & Fishery Board)** - *Yangon* *Myanmar*	*162* 58 -	Class: (LR) ✠ Classed LR until 12/71	**1969-06 N.V. Scheepswerven "Nicolaas Witsen en Vis" — Alkmaar** Loa 28.50 Br ex 7.70 Dght - Lbp 24.46 Br md 7.50 Dpth 3.99 Welded	**(B11B2FV) Fishing Vessel** Ins: 96	**1 oil engine** reverse reduction geared to sc. shaft driving 1 FP propeller Total Power: 368kW (500hp) 10.5kn Dorman 12QTM 1 x Vee 4 Stroke 12 Cy. 159 x 165 368kW (500bhp) W. H. Dorman & Co. Ltd.-Stafford AuxGen: 2 x 44kW 380V 50Hz a.c
20273	**0465** **Government of The Union of Myanmar (People's Pearl & Fishery Board)** - *Yangon* *Myanmar*	*113* 35 84	Class: (LR) ✠	**1980-12 Carl B Hoffmanns Maskinfabrik A/S — Esbjerg** (Hull) Yd No: 34 **1980-10 Aalborg Vaerft A/S — Aalborg** Yd No: 230 Loa 24.52 Br ex 6.86 Dght 2.891 Lbp 20.50 Br md 6.81 Dpth 3.20 Welded, 1 dk	**(B11A2FS) Stern Trawler**	**1 oil engine** with hydraulic couplings & reverse reduction geared to sc. shaft driving 1 CP propeller Total Power: 324kW (441hp) Alpha 404-26VO 1 x 2 Stroke 4 Cy. 260 x 400 324kW (441bhp) B&W Alpha Diesel A/S-Denmark AuxGen: 2 x 32kW 380V 50Hz a.c
20285	**0467** **Government of The Union of Myanmar (People's Pearl & Fishery Board)** *Yangon* *Myanmar*	*113* 35 84	Class: (LR) ✠	**1980-10 Carl B Hoffmanns Maskinfabrik A/S — Esbjerg** (Hull) Yd No: 35 **1980-10 Aalborg Vaerft A/S — Aalborg** Yd No: 231 Loa 24.52 Br ex 6.86 Dght 2.891 Lbp 20.50 Br md 6.81 Dpth 3.20 Welded, 1 dk	**(B11A2FS) Stern Trawler**	**1 oil engine** with hydraulic couplings & reverse reduction geared to sc. shaft driving 1 CP propeller Total Power: 324kW (441hp) Alpha 404-26VO 1 x 2 Stroke 4 Cy. 260 x 400 324kW (441bhp) B&W Alpha Diesel A/S-Denmark AuxGen: 2 x 32kW 380V 50Hz a.c
20297	**0469** **Government of The Union of Myanmar (People's Pearl & Fishery Board)** - *Yangon* *Myanmar*	*113* 35 84	Class: (LR) ✠	**1980-10 Soby Motorfabrik og Staalskibsvaerft A/S — Soby** (Hull) Yd No: 60 **1980-10 Aalborg Vaerft A/S — Aalborg** Yd No: 232 Loa 24.52 Br ex 6.86 Dght 2.891 Lbp 20.50 Br md 6.81 Dpth 3.20 Welded, 1 dk	**(B11A2FS) Stern Trawler**	**1 oil engine** with hydraulic couplings & reverse reduction geared to sc. shaft driving 1 CP propeller Total Power: 324kW (441hp) Alpha 404-26VO 1 x 2 Stroke 4 Cy. 260 x 400 324kW (441bhp) B&W Alpha Diesel A/S-Denmark AuxGen: 2 x 32kW 380V 50Hz a.c
20302	**0471** **Government of The Union of Myanmar (People's Pearl & Fishery Board)** - *Yangon* *Myanmar*	*113* 35 84	Class: (LR) ✠	**1980-10 Soby Motorfabrik og Staalskibsvaerft A/S — Soby** (Hull) Yd No: 61 **1980-10 Aalborg Vaerft A/S — Aalborg** Yd No: 233 Loa 24.52 Br ex 6.86 Dght 2.891 Lbp 20.50 Br md 6.81 Dpth 3.20 Welded, 1 dk	**(B11A2FS) Stern Trawler**	**1 oil engine** with hydraulic couplings & reverse reduction geared to sc. shaft driving 1 CP propeller Total Power: 324kW (441hp) Alpha 404-26VO 1 x 2 Stroke 4 Cy. 260 x 400 324kW (441bhp) B&W Alpha Diesel A/S-Denmark AuxGen: 2 x 32kW 380V 50Hz a.c
06085 *3C*	**0519** **Government of The Union of Myanmar (People's Pearl & Fishery Board)** - *Yangon* *Myanmar* Official number: 1570	*250* 115 243	Class: (LR) ✠ Classed LR until 1/12/78	**1977-01 Daedong Shipbuilding Co Ltd — Busan** Yd No: 172 Loa 40.26 Br ex 8.21 Dght 3.201 Lbp 34.83 Br md 8.01 Dpth 3.74 Welded, 1 dk	**(B11A2FS) Stern Trawler**	**1 oil engine** driving 1 CP propeller Total Power: 736kW (1,001hp) 13.0kn Makita KNLH625 1 x 4 Stroke 6 Cy. 250 x 420 736kW (1001bhp) Makita Diesel Co Ltd-Japan AuxGen: 2 x 112kW 445V 50Hz a.c, 1 x 80kW 445V 50Hz a.c
06097 *BD*	**0521** **Government of The Union of Myanmar (People's Pearl & Fishery Board)** - *Myanmar* Official number: 1571	*298* 115 243	Class: (LR) ✠ Classed LR until 1/12/78	**1977-01 Daedong Shipbuilding Co Ltd — Busan** Yd No: 173 Loa 40.44 Br ex 8.21 Dght 3.201 Lbp 34.19 Br md 7.99 Dpth 3.71 Welded, 1 dk	**(B11A2FS) Stern Trawler**	**1 oil engine** driving 1 CP propeller Total Power: 736kW (1,001hp) 13.0kn Makita KNLH625 1 x 4 Stroke 6 Cy. 250 x 420 736kW (1001bhp) Makita Diesel Co Ltd-Japan AuxGen: 2 x 112kW 445V 50Hz a.c, 1 x 80kW 445V 50Hz a.c
06102 *BE*	**0523** **Government of The Union of Myanmar (People's Pearl & Fishery Board)** - *Yangon* *Myanmar* Official number: 1572	*298* 115 243	Class: (LR) ✠ Classed LR until 1/12/78	**1977-01 Daedong Shipbuilding Co Ltd — Busan** Yd No: 174 Loa 40.26 Br ex 8.21 Dght 3.201 Lbp 34.04 Br md 7.99 Dpth 3.71 Welded, 1 dk	**(B11A2FS) Stern Trawler**	**1 oil engine** driving 1 CP propeller Total Power: 736kW (1,001hp) 13.0kn Makita KNLH625 1 x 4 Stroke 6 Cy. 250 x 420 736kW (1001bhp) Makita Diesel Co Ltd-Japan AuxGen: 2 x 112kW 445V 50Hz a.c, 1 x 80kW 445V 50Hz a.c
10167 *PS*	**0527** **Government of The Union of Myanmar (People's Pearl & Fishery Board)** - *Yangon* *Myanmar*	*350* 147 269	Class: (NV)	**1979-11 Hasund Mek. Verksted AS — Ulsteinvik** (Hull) Yd No: 24 **1979-11 A.M. Liaaen AS — Aalesund** Yd No: 135 Loa 40.42 Br ex 9.53 Dght 3.422 Lbp 36.50 Br md 9.50 Dpth 4.37 Welded, 1 dk	**(B11A2FS) Stern Trawler**	**1 oil engine** reduction geared to sc. shaft driving 1 CP propeller Total Power: 1,103kW (1,500hp) Normo LDMB-8 1 x 4 Stroke 8 Cy. 250 x 300 1103kW (1500bhp) AS Bergens Mek Verksteder-Norway
09951 *QF*	**0533** **Government of The Union of Myanmar (People's Pearl & Fishery Board)** - *Yangon* *Myanmar* Official number: 533	*331* 145 -	Class: (LR) ✠ Classed LR until 31/1/86	**1983-08 Fujishin Zosen K.K. — Kamo** Yd No: 377 Loa 40.64 Br ex 8.74 Dght 3.425 Lbp 34.52 Br md 8.51 Dpth 3.71 Welded, 1 dk	**(B11A2FS) Stern Trawler**	**1 oil engine** with clutches, flexible couplings & dr geared to sc. shaft driving 1 CP propeller Total Power: 883kW (1,201hp) Yanmar 6GAL-ET 1 x 4 Stroke 6 Cy. 240 x 290 883kW (1201bhp) Yanmar Diesel Engine Co Ltd-Japan AuxGen: 2 x 160kW 405V 50Hz a.c, 1 x 96kW 405V 50Hz a.c Fuel: 75.0 (d.f.)
09963 *QG*	**0535** **Government of The Union of Myanmar (People's Pearl & Fishery Board)** - *Yangon* *Myanmar* Official number: 535	*331* 145 -	Class: (LR) ✠ Classed LR until 31/1/86	**1983-08 Fujishin Zosen K.K. — Kamo** Yd No: 378 Loa 40.64 Br ex 8.74 Dght 3.425 Lbp 34.52 Br md 8.51 Dpth 3.71 Welded, 1 dk	**(B11A2FS) Stern Trawler**	**1 oil engine** with clutches, flexible couplings & dr geared to sc. shaft driving 1 CP propeller Total Power: 883kW (1,201hp) Yanmar 6GAL-ET 1 x 4 Stroke 6 Cy. 240 x 290 883kW (1201bhp) Yanmar Diesel Engine Co Ltd-Japan AuxGen: 2 x 160kW 405V 50Hz a.c, 1 x 96kW 405V 50Hz a.c Fuel: 75.0 (d.f.)
15703	**0573-B** **Government of The Argentine Republic (Direccion Nacional de Construcciones Portuarias y Vias Navegables)** Hidrovia SA	*388* 175 235	Class: BV	**1980-02 Astilleros Mestrina S.A. — Tigre** Yd No: 45 Loa 48.52 Br ex 9.00 Dght 3.350 Lbp 48.49 Br md 8.98 Dpth 3.89 Welded, 1 dk	**(B34Q2QB) Buoy Tender**	**2 oil engines** reduction geared to sc. shafts driving 2 FP propellers Total Power: 1,016kW (1,382hp) 13.5kn Stork 6DRO210K 2 x 4 Stroke 6 Cy. 210 x 300 each-508kW (691bhp) Motores Stork Werkspoor-Argentina

7815715 - -	**0574-B** **Government of The Argentine Republic (Direccion Nacional de Construcciones Portuarias y Vias Navegables)** Hidrovia SA	*388* 175 235	Class: BV	**1980-06 Astilleros Mestrina S.A. — Tigre** Yd No: 46 Loa 53.12 Br ex - Dght 3.350 Lbp 48.52 Br md 9.01 Dpth 3.92 Welded	**(B34Q2QB) Buoy Tender**	**2 oil engines** driving 2 FP propellers Total Power: 882kW (1,200hp) Stork 6DRO21 2 x 4 Stroke 6 Cy. 210 x 300 each-441kW (600bhp) Motores Stork Werkspoor-Argentina
6856437 - -	**0632** *ex* MB-0632 *-1992* *ex* MB-6033 *-1992* -	*129* 3 52	Class: (RS)	**1956 VEB Schiffswerft "Edgar Andre" — Magdeburg** Yd No: 6033 Loa 28.75 Br ex 6.76 Dght 2.490 Lbp - Br md - Dpth 3.03 Welded, 1 dk	**(B32A2ST) Tug**	**1 oil engine** driving 1 FP propeller Total Power: 294kW (400hp)
6856487 - -	**0634** *ex* MB-0634 *-1992* *ex* MB-6039 *-1992* -	**131** 33 42	Class: (RS)	**1957 VEB Schiffswerft "Edgar Andre" — Magdeburg** Yd No: 6039 Loa 28.73 Br ex 6.52 Dght 2.490 Lbp 25.62 Br md - Dpth 3.03 Welded, 1 dk	**(B32A2ST) Tug** Ice Capable	**1 oil engine** driving 1 FP propeller Total Power: 294kW (400hp)
8138982 *LYLM* -	**652** *ex* MRTK-0652 *-1997* **JSC Trading House Aistra (UAB Prekybos Namai Aistra)** - *Klaipeda* *Lithuania* MMSI: 277217000 Official number: 366	**117** 35 30	Class: RS	**1983 Sosnovskiy Sudostroitelnyy Zavod — Sosnovka** Yd No: 652 Loa 25.51 Br ex 7.01 Dght 2.390 Lbp 22.00 Br md - Dpth 3.31 Welded, 1 dk	**(B11B2FV) Fishing Vessel** Ice Capable	**1 oil engine** driving 1 FP propeller Total Power: 221kW (300hp) 9.5 Fuel: 15.0 (d.f.)
8722496 *LYJB* -	**694** *ex* MRTK-0694 *-1992* **JSC 'Spika'** - *Klaipeda* *Lithuania* MMSI: 277189000 Official number: 377	**117** 35 30	Class: RS	**1986-05 Sosnovskiy Sudostroitelnyy Zavod — Sosnovka** Yd No: 694 Loa 25.50 Br ex 7.00 Dght 2.390 Lbp 22.00 Br md 6.80 Dpth 3.30 Welded, 1 dk	**(B11A2FS) Stern Trawler** Grain: 64 Compartments: 1 Ho 1 Ha: (1.4 x 1.5) Ice Capable	**1 oil engine** driving 1 FP propeller Total Power: 221kW (300hp) 9.5 S.K.L. 6NVD26A 1 x 4 Stroke 6 Cy. 180 x 260 221kW (300bhp) VEB Schwermaschinenbau "KarlLiebknecht" (SKL)-Magdeburg AuxGen: 2 x 14kW a.c Fuel: 15.0 (d.f.)
8623353 - -	**0702** - -	*117* - -		**1986 Sosnovskiy Sudostroitelnyy Zavod — Sosnovka** Yd No: 702 Loa 25.68 Br ex 7.01 Dght - Lbp - Br md - Dpth - Welded, 1 dk	**(B11B2FV) Fishing Vessel**	**1 oil engine** driving 1 FP propeller Total Power: 220kW (299hp) S.K.L. 6NVD26A 1 x 4 Stroke 6 Cy. 180 x 260 220kW (299bhp) VEB Schwermaschinenbau "KarlLiebknecht" (SKL)-Magdeburg
8006892 *XYPU* -	**0705** **Government of The Union of Myanmar (People's Pearl & Fishery Board)** - *Yangon* *Myanmar* Official number: 1766	*541* 265 468	Class: (LR) ✠ Classed LR until 8/6/84	**1981-09 Richards (Shipbuilders) Ltd — Great Yarmouth** Yd No: 552 Loa 44.00 Br ex 9.43 Dght 3.612 Lbp 38.99 Br md 9.40 Dpth 5.87 Welded, 1 dk	**(A34A2GR) Refrigerated Cargo Ship** Ins: 702 Compartments: 2 Ho, ER 2 Ha: 2 (2.9 x 2.5)ER Derricks: 2x3t	**1 oil engine** with clutches, flexible couplings & sr reverse geared to sc. shaft driving 1 FP propeller Total Power: 516kW (702hp) Blackstone ESL6M 1 x 4 Stroke 6 Cy. 222 x 292 516kW (702bhp) Mirrlees Blackstone (Stamford)Ltd.-Stamford AuxGen: 3 x 72kW 400V 50Hz a.c, 1 x 15kW 400V 50Hz a.c
8729585 *LYOH* -	**756** *ex* MRTK-0756 *-1992* **JSC 'Starkis'** - *Klaipeda* *Lithuania* MMSI: 277233000 Official number: 577	**117** 35 30	Class: RS	**1989-05 Sosnovskiy Sudostroitelnyy Zavod — Sosnovka** Yd No: 756 Loa 25.51 Br ex - Dght 2.391 Lbp 22.03 Br md 7.01 Dpth 3.31 Welded, 1 dk	**(B11A2FS) Stern Trawler** Grain: 64 Compartments: 1 Ho 1 Ha: (1.4 x 1.5)	**1 oil engine** driving 1 FP propeller Total Power: 220kW (299hp) 9.5 S.K.L. 6NVD26A 1 x 4 Stroke 6 Cy. 180 x 260 220kW (299bhp) VEB Schwermaschinenbau "KarlLiebknecht" (SKL)-Magdeburg AuxGen: 2 x 14kW a.c Fuel: 15.0 (d.f.)
7922219 - -	**0801** **Government of The Union of Myanmar (People's Pearl & Fishery Board)** - *Yangon* *Myanmar*	*487* - 800	Class: (NV)	**1980-07 Hjorungavaag Verksted AS — Hjorungavaag** Yd No: 36 Loa 54.01 Br ex - Dght 3.501 Lbp 50.02 Br md 11.00 Dpth 4.09 Welded, 1 dk	**(A13B2TU) Tanker (unspecified)**	**1 oil engine** driving 1 FP propeller Total Power: 783kW (1,065hp) Normo LDM 1 x 4 Stroke 6 Cy. 250 x 300 783kW (1065bhp) AS Bergens Mek Verksteder-Norway AuxGen: 2 x 60kW 440V 60Hz a.c
6908242 - -	**0901 KOJE** *ex* Seishu Maru No. 27 *-1992* *ex* Seishu Maru No. 26 *-1989* *ex* Daitei Maru No. 32 *-1980* *ex* Sasano Maru No. 21 *-1978* **Geoje Engineering & Trading Pte Ltd** - *San Lorenzo* *Honduras* Official number: L-1923340	*314* 157 -		**1969 Miho Zosensho K.K. — Shimizu** Yd No: 683 Loa 51.41 Br ex 8.03 Dght 2.998 Lbp 45.62 Br md 8.01 Dpth 3.61 Welded, 1 dk	**(B11B2FV) Fishing Vessel**	**1 oil engine** driving 1 FP propeller Total Power: 736kW (1,001hp) Akasaka SR6 1 x 4 Stroke 6 Cy. 350 x 500 736kW (1001bhp) Akasaka Tekkosho KK (Akasaka DieselLtd)-Japan
5215856 - -	**0940** *ex* M. O. P. 940 *-1974* **Ruel Business Corp**	**865** 477 1,219		**1948 Ingalls SB. Corp. — Pascagoula, Ms** Yd No: 517 L reg 70.84 Br ex 13.06 Dght - Lbp - Br md 12.94 Dpth 4.72 Welded, 1 dk	**(A31A2GX) General Cargo Ship**	**2 oil engines** driving 2 FP propellers Enterprise DM 2 x 4 Stroke 6 Cy. 305 x 381 Enterprise Engine & Foundry Co-USA
8722238 *LYNL* -	**1095** *ex* LBB-1095 *-2002* *ex* MRTK-1095 Aryogala *-2002* **Jurij Niznikovskij** - *Klaipeda* *Lithuania* MMSI: 277210000 Official number: 664	**117** 35 30	Class: RS	**1985-05 Sosnovskiy Sudostroitelnyy Zavod — Sosnovka** Yd No: 673 Loa 25.50 Br ex 7.00 Dght 2.390 Lbp 22.00 Br md 6.80 Dpth 3.30 Welded, 1 dk	**(B11A2FS) Stern Trawler** Ice Capable	**1 oil engine** driving 1 FP propeller Total Power: 221kW (300hp) 9.5 S.K.L. 6NVD26A 1 x 4 Stroke 6 Cy. 180 x 260 221kW (300bhp) VEB Schwermaschinenbau "KarlLiebknecht" (SKL)-Magdeburg AuxGen: 2 x 12kW a.c Fuel: 15.0 (d.f.)
5241063 *CG2227* -	**1999-01** *ex* Montmagny *-1999* **Verreault Navigation Inc** - *Ottawa, ON* *Canada* Official number: 318536	*497* 195 108	Class: (LR) ✠ Classed LR until 23/6/78	**1963-06 Russel Brothers Ltd — Owen Sound ON** Yd No: 1200 Loa 44.99 Br ex 9.12 Dght 2.604 Lbp 40.98 Br md 8.84 Dpth 3.51 Welded, 1 dk	**(B34Q2QB) Buoy Tender** Compartments: 1 Ho, ER 2 Ha: 2 (3.7 x 4.1)ER Cranes: 1x7t; Derricks: 1x4t Ice Capable	**2 oil engines** with hydraulic couplings driving 2 FP propeller Total Power: 772kW (1,050hp) 12.0 Werkspoor 2 x 4 Stroke 8 Cy. 270 x 500 each-386kW (525bhp) NV Werkspoor-Netherlands AuxGen: 3 x 75kW 230V d.c Fuel: 48.0 (d.f.)
8702783 - -	**2001** *ex* Tassie Devil 2001 *-1988* **Ross Andrew Courtenay & Wade Sprowles** - *Hobart, Tas* *Australia* Official number: 852712	*183* 71 50	Class: (NV)	**1987-01 International Catamarans Pty Ltd — Hobart TAS** Yd No: 017 Loa 30.46 Br ex - Dght - Lbp - Br md 13.01 Dpth 2.01 Welded, 1 dk	**(A37B2PS) Passenger Ship** Hull Material: Aluminium Alloy	**2 oil engines** with clutches, flexible couplings & sr reverse reduction geared to sc. shafts driving 2 FP propellers Total Power: 1,508kW (2,050hp) MWM TBD234V 2 x Vee 4 Stroke 16 Cy. 128 x 140 each-754kW (1025bhp Motoren Werke Mannheim AG (MWM)-West Germany AuxGen: 2 x 24kW 415V 50Hz a.c
8803288 - -	**2002-02** *ex* R. B. Young *-2002* - -	*305* 76 108		**1990-03 Allied Shipbuilders Ltd — North Vancouver BC** Yd No: 250 Loa 32.20 Br ex - Dght 2.300 Lbp 29.70 Br md 7.92 Dpth 3.04 Welded	**(B31A2SR) Research Survey Vessel**	**2 oil engines** with clutches, flexible couplings & sr geared to sc. shafts driving 2 CP propellers Total Power: 552kW (750hp) 11.6 Caterpillar 340 2 x 4 Stroke 6 Cy. 137 x 165 each-276kW (375bhp) Caterpillar Inc-USA Thrusters: 1 Thwart. FP thruster (f)
5328603 *CGSQ* -	**2007-01** *ex* Simcoe *-2008* **Government of Canada (Ministry of Fisheries & Oceans)** - *Ottawa, ON* *Canada* MMSI: 316001862 Official number: 318532	*961* 361 457	Class: (LR) ✠ Classed LR until 23/6/78	**1962-11 Canadian Vickers Ltd — Montreal QC** Yd No: 279 Loa 54.72 Br ex 11.64 Dght 4.014 Lbp 50.35 Br md 11.59 Dpth 4.73 Welded, 1 dk	**(B34Q2QB) Buoy Tender** Compartments: 1 Ho, ER 1 Ha: (4.3 x 3.1)ER Derricks: 1x10t Ice Capable	**2 diesel electric oil engines** driving 4 gen. each 410kW 600 d.c Connecting to 2 elec. motors driving 2 FP propellers Total Power: 2,206kW (3,000hp) 13.0 Paxman 12YLC 2 x Vee 4 Stroke 12 Cy. 248 x 267 each-1103kW (1500bh Davey, Paxman & Co. Ltd.-Colchester AuxGen: 2 x 230kW 115/230V d.c Fuel: 156.0 (d.f.)

06766	**2011-02** *ex* Provo Wallis *-2013* **Jason Beaulieu** - *Ottawa, ON* *Canada* Official number: 328104	*1,462* 581 515	Class: (LR) ✠ Classed LR until 23/6/78	**1969**-10 **Marine Industries Ltee (MIL) — Sorel QC** Yd No: 387 Loa 57.74 Br ex 13.09 Dght 3.823 Lbp 51.72 Br md 12.96 Dpth 5.06 Welded, 1 dk	**(B34Q2QB) Buoy Tender** Ice Capable	**2 oil engines** driving 2 CP propellers Total Power: 1,544kW (2,100hp) 11.0kn Mirrlees KLSSDM-6 2 x 4 Stroke 6 Cy. 381 x 508 each-772kW (1050bhp) Mirrlees Blackstone (Stockport)Ltd.-Stockport AuxGen: 3 x 180kW 460V 60Hz a.c Fuel: 195.0 (d.f.)
406631	**2011-03** *ex* Nahidik *-2013* **Northern Transportation Co Ltd** - *Ottawa, ON* *Canada* Official number: 347496	*856* 392 562		**1974**-08 **Allied Shipbuilders Ltd — North Vancouver BC** Yd No: 186 Loa 53.52 Br ex 15.42 Dght 1.829 Lbp 52.89 Br md 15.24 Dpth 3.20 Welded, 1 dk	**(B34Q2QB) Buoy Tender**	**2 oil engines** geared to sc. shafts driving 2 FP propellers Total Power: 1,176kW (1,598hp) 14.0kn EMD (Electro-Motive) 12-645-E5 2 x Vee 2 Stroke 12 Cy. 230 x 254 each-588kW (799bhp) General Motors Detroit DieselAllison Divn-USA Fuel: 231.0 (d.f.)
422643	**2012-01** *ex* Tembah *-2013* **Government of Canada (Ministry of Fisheries & Oceans)** - *Ottawa, ON* *Canada* Official number: 320934	*189* 58 -	Class: (LR) ✠ Classed LR until 1/71	**1963**-10 **Allied Shipbuilders Ltd — North Vancouver BC** Yd No: 135 Loa 39.37 Br ex 8.06 Dght 0.910 Lbp 36.58 Br md 7.93 Dpth 1.53 Welded, 1 dk	**(B34Q2QB) Buoy Tender** Compartments: 1 Ho, ER 1 Ha: (1.2 x 2.2) Cranes: 1x5t	**2 oil engines** sr reverse geared to sc. shafts driving 2 FP propellers Total Power: 500kW (680hp) 13.0kn Cummins V12-500-M 2 x Vee 4 Stroke 12 Cy. 140 x 152 each-250kW (340bhp) Cummins Engine Co Inc-USA AuxGen: 1 x 47kW 440V 60Hz a.c, 1 x 38kW 440V 60Hz a.c Fuel: 21.0 (d.f.)
815108	**2012-03** *ex* E. P. Le Quebecois *-2013* **Government of Canada (Ministry of Fisheries & Oceans)** - *Ottawa, ON* *Canada* Official number: 328387	*201* 60 -	Class: (LR) ✠ Classed LR until 6/72	**1968**-05 **Les Chantiers Maritimes de Paspebiac Inc — Paspebiac QC** Yd No: 374 Loa 28.35 Br ex 7.27 Dght 3.175 Lbp 24.77 Br md 7.01 Dpth 3.74 Welded, 1 dk	**(B34H2SQ) Patrol Vessel**	**1 oil engine** driving 1 CP propeller Total Power: 372kW (506hp) Caterpillar D379TA 1 x Vee 4 Stroke 8 Cy. 159 x 203 372kW (506bhp) (new engine ,made 1965, fitted 1968) Caterpillar Tractor Co-USA AuxGen: 2 x 75kW 230V 60Hz a.c
393573	**2013-02** *ex* Shamook *-2013* **Government of Canada (Ministry of Fisheries & Oceans)** - *Ottawa, ON* *Canada* Official number: 347507	*117* 35 -	Class: (LR) ✠ Classed LR until 14/9/79	**1975**-06 **Georgetown Shipyard Inc — Georgetown PE** Yd No: 33 Loa 23.07 Br ex 6.66 Dght 2.718 Lbp 20.12 Br md 6.56 Dpth 3.20 Welded, 1 dk	**(B12D2FR) Fishery Research Vessel**	**1 oil engine** sr geared to sc. shaft driving 1 CP propeller Total Power: 496kW (674hp) 10.0kn Caterpillar D379SCAC 1 x Vee 4 Stroke 8 Cy. 159 x 203 496kW (674bhp) (new engine 1977) Caterpillar Tractor Co-USA AuxGen: 1 x 40kW 220/120V 60Hz a.c, 1 x 15kW 220/120V 60Hz a.c Fuel: 21.5
7702011 - -	**2013-03** *ex* Louisbourg *-2013* **Government of Canada (Ministry of Fisheries & Oceans)** - *Ottawa, ON* *Canada* Official number: 371740	*295* 65 -		**1977**-09 **Breton Industrial & Marine Ltd — Point Tupper NS** Yd No: 6 Loa 38.10 Br ex 8.31 Dght 2.517 Lbp 37.17 Br md 8.25 Dpth 3.51 Welded, 1 dk	**(B12D2FP) Fishery Patrol Vessel** Hull Material: Aluminium Alloy	**2 oil engines** geared to sc. shafts driving 2 FP propellers Total Power: 3,310kW (4,500hp) 20.0kn M.T.U. 12V538TB91 2 x Vee 4 Stroke 12 Cy. 185 x 200 each-1655kW (2250bhp) MTU Friedrichshafen GmbH-Friedrichshafen
9650028 *V7CR4* -	**6711** **Alliance Vista Assets Ltd** Imperial Yachts SARL *Bikini* *Marshall Islands* MMSI: 538070967 Official number: 70967	**1,143** 342 388	Class: LR (Class contemplated) **100A1** 03/2014 Class contemplated	**2014**-03 **Song Cam Shipyard — Haiphong** (Hull) Yd No: (547602) **2014**-03 **B.V. Scheepswerf Damen — Gorinchem** Yd No: 547602 Loa 67.15 Br ex 11.48 Dght 4.000 Lbp 64.24 Br md 11.00 Dpth 5.40 Welded, 1 dk	**(B34R2QY) Supply Tender**	**4 oil engines** driving 2 Propellers Total Power: 8,960kW (12,184hp) 19.0kn M.T.U. 16V4000M63L 4 x Vee 4 Stroke 16 Cy. 170 x 210 each-2240kW (3046bhp) Thrusters: 1 Tunnel thruster (f); 1 Tunnel thruster (a)
6816970 *4DEE2* -	**7107 ISLANDS CRUISE** *ex* Coco Explorer 2 *-2009* *ex* Caribic Star *-2005* *ex* Arcadia *-2002* *ex* Angelina Lauro *-1991* *ex* Arcadia *-1990* *ex* Vicente Puchol *-1987* **7107 Islands Cruise Corp** - *Manila* *Philippines* MMSI: 548334100 Official number: MNLD011181	**5,113** 1,992 1,871	Class: (HR) (BV)	**1968**-12 **Union Naval de Levante SA (UNL) — Valencia** Yd No: 101 Converted From: General Cargo/Passenger Ship-1990 Loa 106.91 Br ex 16.31 Dght 4.979 Lbp 98.00 Br md 16.26 Dpth 7.19 Welded, 4 dks	**(A37A2PC) Passenger/Cruise** Passengers: cabins: 137; berths: 342 Compartments: ER	**2 oil engines** driving 2 CP propellers Total Power: 4,590kW (6,240hp) 17.5kn B&W 10-35VBF-62 2 x 2 Stroke 10 Cy. 350 x 620 each-2295kW (3120bhp) La Maquinista Terrestre y Mar (MTM)-Spain
9612090 - -	**8001** **Cuc Canh Sat Bien Viet Nam (Vietnam Marine Police)** - *Vietnam* MMSI: 574001870	**3,091** 927 -	Class: LR ✠ **100A1** SS 10/2013 ✠ **LMC** **UMS** Eq.Ltr: R; Cable: 440.0/36.0 U3 (a)	**2013**-10 **189 Company — Haiphong** (Hull) Yd No: DN 2000 **2013**-10 **B.V. Scheepswerf Damen — Gorinchem** Yd No: 556058 Loa 90.00 (BB) Br ex 14.00 Dght 3.750 Lbp 83.94 Br md 14.00 Dpth 7.00 Welded, 1 dk	**(B34H2SQ) Patrol Vessel**	**4 oil engines** with clutches, flexible couplings & dr reverse geared to sc. shafts driving 2 CP propellers Total Power: 8,960kW (12,184hp) Caterpillar 3516C HD TA 4 x Vee 4 Stroke 16 Cy. 170 x 215 each-2240kW (3046bhp) Caterpillar Inc-USA AuxGen: 2 x 460kW 400V 50Hz a.c Thrusters: 1 Tunnel thruster (f)